THE DIRECTORY OF BUSINESS INFORMATION RESOURCES

2017

24th Edition

The

Directory

of

Business Information Resources

Grey House Publishing

PUBLISHER: Leslie Mackenzie
EDITOR: Richard Gottlieb
EDITORIAL DIRECTOR: Laura Mars

PRODUCTION MANAGER & COMPOSITION: Kristen Hayes
PRODUCTION ASSISTANTS: Daniella D'souza, Geoff Graves, Charlotte Smith
MARKETING DIRECTOR: Jessica Moody

Grey House Publishing, Inc.
4919 Route 22
Amenia, NY 12501
518.789.8700
FAX 518.789.0545
www.greyhouse.com
e-mail: books@greyhouse.com

First edition published 1992
Twenty-fourth edition published 2017
Printed in Canada
The directory of business information resources. – 1992-2017

v. ; 27.5 cm.
Annual
Other title: Business information resources

1. Business information services – United States – Directories. 2. Reference books – Business – Bibliography – Periodicals. 3. Association, institutions, etc. – United States – Directories. 4. Business – Databases – Directories. 5. Trade shows – Directories. I. Title: Business information resources.

HF54.52.U5 D56
016.65
ISBN: 978-1-61925-900-3 softcover
ISSN: 1549-7224

Table of Contents

Indexes

Introduction

This twenty-fourth edition of *The Directory of Business Information Resources* has been the premier reference book for business researchers since 1992. With comprehensive coverage of 102 industries, it provides ways to find new customers, increase loyalty among existing customers, and improve the bottom line. As America's economy continues to improve, current, comprehensive business information is more valuable than ever.

This reference work offers an unequaled collection of valuable, industry-specific resources. Reach out to new customers through industry **Associations, Directories, Databases,** and **Trade Shows**. Find new ways to cut costs and improve efficiency through **Magazines, Journals** and **Newsletters**. Learn what your competitors are up to by visiting the latest, most important **Web Sites**.

New & Revised Content

The 102 industry chapters include the new **National Security & International Affairs**. Plus, we've freshened up the focus of several other chapters, including changing Automotive to **Motor Vehicles**, Liquor to **Brewing & Distilling**, and Shoes to **Footwear**. In addition, you'll find over 100 new records and thousands of updates across all chapters.

With 24,207 listings, this twenty-fourth edition is the most comprehensive guide to business information on the market today. All listings include name, address, phone, fax, web site, email, key contacts and a brief description, making your research focused and productive. When available, we have indicated an association's presence on Facebook, Twitter and LinkedIn.

Online-only information, however, is often confusing, unreliable, and outdated. The value of the focused, comprehensive data in *The Directory of Business Information Resources*, compiled with the business researcher in mind, cannot be overstated. This edition provides immediate assistance with your business: attend industry Trade Shows to **promote your product and find new customers**; subscribe to Publications to **stay competitive and ahead of the curve**; join Associations for **business support and educational opportunities**.

2017 Features

Content Summary of Chapter Listings: Lists more than 1,600 specific businesses under each chapter name. For example, *Accounting* lists auditors, bookkeepers, payroll and taxes; *Engineering* includes cost engineers, geologists, and robotics; *Restaurants* covers bakers, cookware and caterers.

NAICS and SIC Reference Tables: Enable users to approach their topic based on the North American Industry Classification System (NAICS), or the Department of Labor's Standard Industrial Classification System (SIC).

User Guide: Defines fields for entry type. In addition to name, address, phone, fax, web site, e-mail, and description, *Associations* include number of members, dues and founding year. *Publications* include cost and frequency. *Trade shows* include location, number of exhibitors and attendees.

Two Indexes

- *Entry Index*—Alphabetical list of all entries
- *Publisher Index*—Alphabetical list of publishers of industry literature, or sponsors of trade shows, etc. The entry number listed identifies the title of the published material/trade show listed in this directory. Note that publishers often offer additional material not included here.

The Directory of Business Information Resources answers the need for well-organized, accessible business information for market researchers, advertising agencies, job placement and career planning offices, public relations personnel, and business schools and colleges—a need well-documented by one of the identified high-growth sectors: Information.

Numbers are up in all categories for 2017: 6,452 Associations, 2,929 Newsletters, 4,964 Magazines and Journals, 3,736 Trade Shows, 2,451 Directories and Databases, 252 International Resources. Plus, 58,312 contact names, 18,548 fax numbers, 19,125 web sites, and 14,072 e-mail addresses.

Praise for previous editions:

"...convenient, efficient vehicle for locating sources of information on U.S. businesses... recommended for academic libraries... ideal for collection development."

American Reference Books Annual

"...continues to be an essential reference source..."

Choice

"...a worthy addition to academic and large public libraries serving business researchers..."

Booklist

"...substantial reference, recommended for marketing and industry research collections..."

Library Journal

The Directory of Business Information Resources is available for subscription online at http://gold.greyhouse.com for even faster, easier access to this vast array of information. With a subscription, users can search by keyword, geographic area, organization type, key contact name and so much more. Visit the site or call 800-562-2139 to set up a free trial of the Online Database.

User Guide

Descriptive listings in *The Directory of Business Information Resources* are organized into 98 industry chapters. You will find the following types of listings throughout the book: Associations; Newsletters; Magazines & Journals; Trade Shows; Directories & Databases; and Web Sites.

Below is a sample listing illustrating the kind of information that is or might be included in an Association entry, with additional fields that apply to publication and trade show listings. Each numbered item of information is described in the paragraphs on the following page.

---

(1) **12345**

(2) **National Association of Big Band Musicians**

(3) 2061 Ryders Avenue
Westerville, OH 43081

(4) 002-208-0843

(5) 800-208-0845

(6) 002-208-0844

(7) info@bigb.com

(8) www.bigb.com

(9) Linda Whare, Executive Director
Keith Fallon, Secretary
Bill Jenkins, Editor

(10) A national organization that supports those musicians and instructors whose main interest is big band music. Committed to furthering the art of big bands through teaching, performance, compositions and scholarly research. Also promotes the growth and establishment of big band literature and libraries, and offers musicians and teachers guidance in instrument maintenance and performing venues.

(11) 1M *Members*

(12) *Founded*: 1984

(13) Bi Monthly

(14) $59.00

(15) 110,000

(16) **Special Issues:**
Top 100 Music Dealers
January

(17) 3,000 Attendees

(18) April

Resources User Key

1 **Record Number**: Entries are listed alphabetically within each category and numbered sequentially. Entry numbers, rather than page number, are used in the indexes to refer to listings.

2 **Title**: Formal name of company or organization. Where organization names are completely capitalized, the listing will appear at the beginning of the alphabetized section.

3 **Address**: Location or permanent address of the association.

4 **Phone Number**: The listed phone number is usually for the main office, but may also be for the sales, marketing, or public relations office as provided.

5 **Toll-Free Number:** This is listed when provided by the association.

6 **Fax Number**: This is listed when provided by the association.

7 **E-Mail**: This is listed when provided, and is generally the main office e-mail.

8 **Web Site**: This is listed when provided, and is also referred to as an URL address. These web sites are accessed through the Internet by typing http:// before the URL address.

9 **Key Executives:** Lists key contacts of the association, publication or sponsoring organization.

10 **Description:** This paragraph contains a brief description of the association and their purpose and services.

11 **Members:** Total number of association members.

12 **Founded:** Year association was founded, or publication began.

13 **Frequency**, if listing is a publication.

14 **Subscription price**, if listing is a publication.

15 **Circulation**, if listing is a publication.

16 **Scheduled special issues**, if listing is a magazine.

17 **Attendees**, if listing is a trade show.

18 **Month**, if listing is a trade show.

Content Summary of Chapter Listings

Chapters in this directory often include a wide range of topics. The following list of keywords from the Association listings shows the subjects covered in each chapter.

Accounting
Accounting Historians
Accounting Standards
Accreditation
Auditors
Black Accountants
Bookkeepers
Broadcast Cable Financial Management
Budget & Program Analysis
Computerized Accounting
Construction Financial Management
Cost Estimating
Government Accountability
Government Financial Officers
Healthcare Financial Management
Hospitality Financial Management
Insolvency
Insurance
Latino Accountants
Military Comptrollers
Newspapers Financial Management
Payroll
Public Accountants
Taxes
Trucking Financial Management
Valuation
Women Accountants

Advertising
Advertising Agencies
Advertising Research
Cable TV Advertising
Children's Advertising
Commercials
Communications
E Marketing
Educational Advertising
Exhibition Management
Newspaper Advertising
Outdoor Advertising
Photographers
Point of Purchase
Public Opinion
Railroad Advertising
Signs
Transportation Advertising
Women in Advertising

Agriculture
4-H
Agricultural Aviation
Agricultural Communications
Agricultural Consultants
Agricultural County Agents
Agricultural Economics
Agricultural Education
Agricultural Engineers
Agricultural Fairs
Agricultural History
Agricultural Law
Agricultural Management
Agricultural Manufacturers
Agricultural Marketing
Agricultural Research
Agricultural Retail
Agricultural Teachers
Agronomy
Alfalfa
Angus
Animal Health
Animal Hides
Animal Science
Aquatics
Arid Lands
Bedding Plants
Bee Keeping
Beef
Bio-Dynamic Farming
Biomolecular Study
Blacksmiths
Blueberries
Brahman Beef
Canola
Cereal
Christmas Trees
Conservation
Corn
Cotton
Cottonseed
Cranberries
Crops
Dairy
Ecological Farming
Eggs
Enology
Entomology
Family Farming
Feed
Fertilizer
Fisheries
Florals
Foresters
Gardening
Grain
Grapes
Grasslands
Guernsey
Hay
Herbs
Hereford
Holstein
Horticulture
Irrigation
Jersey Cattle
Livestock
Maple Syrup
Millers
Oil Seed
Onions
Organic
Pesticides
Phytopathology
Pork
Potato
Poultry
Produce
Santa Gertrudis
Seeds
Sheep
Soil
Soybean
Sugar
Sunflowers
Veal
Walnuts
Weeds
Wheat

Alternative Energy
Biodiesel
Biogas
Biomass
Clean Energy
Energy Recovery
Ethanol
Geothermal Energy
Hydrogen
Lignite Energy
Low Impact Hydropower
Ocean Renewable Energy
Renewable Energy
Solar Energy
Sustainable Energy
Thermal Energy
Wind Energy

Amusement & Entertainment
Amusement Equipment Manufacturers
Amusement Equipment Rentals
Amusement Industry Marketing
Amusement Parks
Amusement Safety
Aquariums
Caves
Circus
Coin Operated
Concessions
Gambling
Game Developers
Go-Karts
Haunted Attractions
Jugglers
Kiddie Rides
Laser Attractions
Motor Sports
Roller Coasters
Spectator Sports
Theaters
Themed Amusements
Ticketing
Water Parks
Zoos

Apparel & Accessories
Cashmere & Camel Hair Manufacturers
Clothing Contractors
Clothing Manufacturers
Costume Designers
Cotton
Cotton Shippers
Fashion Designers
Footwear
Fur Manufacturers
Fur Merchants
Headwear
Home Sewing/Crafts
Hosiery
Infant & Children Wear
Intimate Apparel
Knitting
Leather
Millners, Dressmakers & Tailors
Neckwear
Needlework
Sportswear
Sunglasses
Uniform Manufacturers
Union Manufacturers & Distributors
Western & English Tack Apparel

Appliances
Manufacturers
Parts Suppliers
Repair
Retail Dealers
Service

Architecture
Accessibility for the Disabled
Architectural Historians
Building Officials
Cast Stone
Code Administrators
Concrete
Conservation
Design Drafting
Education
Environmental Design
Impact Assessment
Insulated Cable Engineers
Intelligent Buildings
Landscape Architects
Livable Communities
Marine Engineers
Naval Architects
Precasts
Preservation
Schools of Architecture
Sustainable Buildings
Urban Design

Art & Antiques
Aesthetics
American History
Animal Artists
Antique Dealers
Appraisal
Art Dealers
Art Education
Art Libraries
Art Materials
Art Museums
Art Placement
Art Research
Art Therapy
Auctioneers
Blacksmiths
College Art
Collectors
Conservation
Fine Arts
Fine Print Dealers
Illustrators
Library Art
Limited Edition Dealers
Photography
Picture Framers
Preservation Technology
School Programs
State Art Agencies

Automotive
Aftermarkets
Air Conditioning
Antique Trucks
Auto Auctions

Content Summary of Chapter Listings

Autobody Work
Automatic Transmission Rebuilders
Battery Manufacturers
Bearing Specialists
Body Engineers
Body Parts
Brake Manufacturers
Buses
Chemical Products
Collision Repair
Dealers
Diesel
Driving School
Emission Controls
Engine Rebuilders
Engineering
Filter Manufacturers
Fleet Administrators
Gasoline Marketers
Glass
Highway Users
Law Enforcement
Lifts
Maintenance
Mobile Air Conditioning
Motor & Equipment Manufacturers
Motoring & Leisure Travel
Motor Sports
Original Equipment
Overseas Market
Parking
Parts & Suppliers
Public Relations
Public Transit
Radiators
Recreation Vehicle Dealers
Recreational Vehicle Aftermarket
Recycling
Remanufacturing
Repair
Replacement Parts
Rubber
Safety
Service
Show Cars
Specialty Equipment Market
Stock Car Auto Racing
Teachers
Technicians
Theft Investigators
Tires & Rims
Tire Retread
Trucks
Used Cars
Warehouse Distributors
Wheels & Rims

Aviation & Aerospace
Aerospace Workers
Air Cargo
Air Medical Services
Air Traffic Controllers
Air Transportation
Aircraft Owners & Pilots Historical Airlines
Airport Executives
Army Aviation
Astronautics
Beech Aircraft
Bonanza Aircraft
Buoyant Flight
Careers
Cessna Aircraft
Commercial Airports
Commercial Pilots
Consultants
Distributors
Electrical Equipment
Electronic Instrumentation
Flight Attendants
Flight Engineers
Flight Instructors
Flight Safety
Flight Test Engineers
Food
Gliding & Soaring
Helicopters
Insurance
Light Aircraft Manufacturers
Machinists
Maintenance
Management
Manufacturers
Medical Care
Medical Transport
Naval Aircraft
Noise
Nonflying Pilots
Owners & Pilots
Parachutes
Piper Aircraft
Public Airport Facilities
Safety
Seaplane Pilots
Small Satellites
Space Science
Survival & Flight Equipment
Technical Education
Test Pilots
Traffic Control
Transportation Communication
Ultralight
Vintage Aircraft
Women Pilots

Banking
ABA Endorsement
Affordable Housing Lenders
Bank Directors
Bankers Insurance
Bankruptcy
Certified Bankers
Certified Professionals
Community Bankers
Consumer Banks
Credit Unions
Education & Training
Electronic Payments
Federal Credit Unions
Finance & Trade
Financial Management
Government Lenders
Independent Bankers
Interbank Marketing
Investment Management
Marine Bankers
Marketing
Military Banks
Minority & Women Banking
Mortgage Bankers
Mortgage Lenders
Risk Management
Safe Deposit
State Savings
Women in Finance

Barbers & Beauty Shops
Aesthetics
Barber Styling
Barber Supply
Cosmetology
Electrology
Nail Technicians

Biotechnology
Biomaterials
Biomolecular Screening
Chemical
Chronobiology
Electrophoresis
Magnetic Resonance
Molecular Biology
Protein
Reproductive Medicine
Soil & Plant Analysis
Women in Science

Boating
Antique & Classic Boats
Boat Builders
Boat Owners
Canoes
Industrial Fabrics
Marine Operators
Marine Accessories
Marine Bankers
Marine Distributors
Marine Manufacturers
Marine Retailers
Marine Safety
Marine Trade
Merchant Marines
Personal Watercraft
Power Boats
Power Squadrons
Propellers
Sailing
State Boating Laws
Tides
Traditional Small Craft
Yacht Brokers
Yachting

Broadcasting
Antenna Television
Auto Racing Writers
Broadcast Designers
Broadcast Education
Broadcast Engineers
Broadcasting History
Cable & Telecommunications Marketing
Cable Television
College Radio/TV
Commercial Producers
Community Media
Correspondents
Country Radio
Educational Broadcasting
Electronic News Professionals
Emmy Awards
Families & TV
Farm Broadcasters
Geospatial Information & Technology
Industrial Radio
International Television
Local Cable Programmers
Local Television
Media Communications
Monitors
News Analysts
News Monitoring
Press Broadcasters
Private Radio
Public Service Radio
Public Television
Radio Communications
Radio Advertising
Radio Frequency Advisory
Religious Broadcasting
Reporters
Satellite Communications
Signal Theft
Speakers
Sportscasters
Sportswriters
Television Engineers
Television Producers
Television & Radio Artists
Television Arts & Sciences
Television Program Executives
Women In Radio & Television

Building & Construction
Acoustical Consultants
Apartment Management
Asbestos
Asphalt Manufacturers
Asphalt Pavement
Brick
Bridge Grid Flooring Manufacturers
Building Codes & Standards
Building Materials
Building Stone
Ceramic Tile & Dimensional Stones
Code Administrators
Concrete
Concrete Pipe
Concrete Pumping
Construction Estimators
Deep Foundations
Demolition Contractors
Distribution & Retail
Ducts, Pipes & Fittings
Education
Electrical Contractors
Elevator Contractors
Estimators
Facing Tile
Factory Built Housing
Fences
Floor Covering
Foundation Drilling
Garage Doors
Granite
Granite Quarriers
Hollow Metal Doors
Housing Endowment
Independent Contractors
Insulation Manufacturers
Interlocking Concrete
Laminating Materials
Lath & Plaster
Log & Dome Homes
Manufactured Housing
Masonry
Membrane Roofing
Metal Architecture
Metal Contractors
Metal Framing Manufacturers
Modular Building
Painting & Decorating Contractors
Panelized Systems
Perlite
Pile Driving
Pipe Fabrication
Pipe Fittings
Plasterers
Portable Sanitation
Power Equipment
Precast Prestressed Concrete
Public Works
Quartz Producers
Railroad Construction
Resilient Floors

Retail Lumber
Roof Coatings
Roof Tile
Rubber Pavements
Safety Glazing
Scaffolds
Screen Manufacturers
Senior Housing
Slag
Slurry Surfacing
Steel Joists
Steel Windows
Stone, Sand & Gravel
Structural Insulated Panel
Stucco Manufacturers
Subcontractors
Tech Home
Terrazzo & Mosaic
Tile Contractors
Tilt-Up Concrete
Timber Framers
Tools & Fasteners
Truck Mixer
Underground Construction
Unions
Utility Contractors
Wall & Ceiling Industries
Western Building Material
Women In Construction
Woodwork

Chemicals
Acrylonitrile
Adhesion
Aerosol
Agricultural Chemicals
Alkyl Amines
Analytical & Life Science Systems
Analytical Chemists
Analytical Communities
Bioanalysts
Biochemistry & Molecular Biology
Brewing Chemists
Cadmium
Catalysis
Chemical Engineers
Chemical Heritage
Chemical Manufacturers
Chemical Marketing Research
Chemical Recyclers
Chemical Strategies
Chlorine
Chlorine Chemistry
Chlorine Free
Chlorobenzene Producers
Clinical Chemistry
Coatings Technology
Coke & Coal Chemicals
Colorists
Consumer Specialty Chemicals
Cosmetic Chemists
Crystal Growth
Drug, Chemical & Allied Trades
Electrochemical
Embalming Chemical
Manufacturers
Fiber Manufacturers
Hydrogen
Leather Chemists
Liquid Terminals
Lubricant Manufacturers
Mass Spectrometry
Materials Technology
Methanol
Oil Chemists
Oxygenated Fuels
Ozone
Pest Management
Pesticide Applicators
Phosphate Chemicals
Pine Chemicals
Polyisocyanurate Insulation
Polyurethane Foam
Powder Coating
Process Equipment Manufacturers
Spectroscopy
Synthetic Organic Chemicals
Textile Chemists
Toxicology

Cleaners & Laundries
Building Service Contractors
Diaper Services
Drycleaners
Environmental Management
Fabricare
Halogenated Solvents
Kitchen Exhaust
Linens
Power Washers
Uniform & Textile Service

Communications & Media
Abstracting & Information Services
Freedom Information Center
Information & Image Management
Information Systems
Information Technology
Medical Illustrators
Newspapers
Personal Achievement
Postal Commerce
Regional Magazines
Speakers
Technology in Education
Telecommunications Industry
Toastmasters
Translators
Writers

Computers & Data Processing
Alpha Micro Users
Artificial Intelligence
Audiovisual Catalogers
Automated Reasoning
Data Interchange Standards
Digital Dealers
Educational Communications &
Technology
Electronic Engineers
Event Marketing
Identification Manufacturers
Imaging Science
Image Management
Information Display
Information Networking
Information Processing
Information Science
Information Systems Management
Intelligence
Interactive Multimedia
Knowledge Engineers
Language Instruction
Managing Human Resource
Information
Medical Imaging
Medical Information
Open Applications
Optical Engineering
Precision Engineering
Recognition Technologies
Regional Sciences
Reprographic
Science Association
Security
Serial Storage Architecture
Software Users
Systems Management Technology
Technology in Education

Cosmetics, Perfumes & Personal Care
Aesthetics Manufacturers &
Distributors
Aloe Science
Aromatics
Color
Consumer Healthcare
Manufacturers
Cosmetology
Drug, Chemical & Allied Trades
Fragrance Research
Fragrances
Nail & Beauty
Nail Manufacturers
Tanning Manufacturers

Credit & Lending Services
Bankruptcy
Business Producers Credit
Commercial Collectors
Commercial Finance
Consumer Data
Consumer Debt Counseling
Credit Union Research &
Consulting
Electronic Transactions
Financial Services
Fraud & Theft
Mortgage Brokers
Recovery Association
Risk Management

Cyber Security
Cyber Crime
Cyber Forensics
Automated Teller Machines
Intelligence Communities
Homeland Security
Defense Security
Microcomputers
Professional Certifications
Information Technology
Security Research
Firewalls
Intrusion Prevention
Advanced Technology Crimes
Information Security
Assurance
Risk Management
Governance
Federal Bureau of Investigation
National Security
Corporate Security
Cyber Crime Threats
Forensics
Cyber Watch

Direct Marketing
Art Directors
Digital Concepts
E-Marketing
Hispanic Marketing
Mail Marketing
Mobile Telecommunications
Publication Designers
Teleservices
Third Party Mailing
Writers

Drugs & Pharmaceuticals
Clinical
Clinical Laboratory
Distribution
Education
Efficient Operation
Ethical Pharmacies
Excipients
Generic
Health System
History of Pharmacy
Hospitals
Managed Care
Oil Chemists
Outsourcing Research
Parenteral & Enteral Nutrition
Pharmacy Law
Pharmaceutical Alliance
Pharmacy Cooperative
Senior Care
Standardization
Wholesale Druggists

E-Commerce & Internet
Advertising
Computing in Education
eMarketing
Hispanic Chamber
Public Technology
Security
Software Alliance
Uniform Council
Women in ECommerce

Electrical
Apparatus Service
Bioelectrmagnetics
Contractors
Electrical Instruments
Electrochemical
Electronic Assembly
Electronic Measuring Instruments
Engineers
Generating Systems
Insulated Cable
Intercommunications Applications
Laser and Electro-Optic
Magnetic
Microelectronics
Microwave
Overstress/Electrostatic
Public Owned Utilities
Relay Electronics
Research
Rural Electric Cooperative
Safety
Sound Systems
Technical Certifications
Testing
Variable Resistive Products

Electronics
Agricultural
Aircraft
Armed Forces
Assembly
Certified Technicians
Commercialization Research
Consumer Electronics
Environmental
Instrumentation & Measurement
Interactive Services
Marine Electronics
Metals
Microchip Industry
Microelectronics
Minerals

Content Summary of Chapter Listings

Content Summary of Chapter Listings

The North American Industry Classification System (NAICS, pronounced Nakes) was developed as the standard for use by Federal statistical agencies in classifying business establishments for the collection, analysis, and publication of statistical data related to the business economy of the U.S. NAICS was developed under the auspices of the Office of Management and Budget (OMB), and adopted in 1997 to replace the old Standard Industrial Classification (SIC) system (see page xxiii). Below are all relevant NAICS codes and descriptions. For a more detailed explanation of the NAICS, visit www.naics.com.

11	**Agriculture, Forestry, Fishing and Hunting**
11141	Food Crops Grown Under Cover
11191	Tobacco Farming
114	Fishing, Hunting and Trapping
115	Support Activities for Agriculture and Forestry
21	**Mining**
211111	Crude Petroleum and Natural Gas Extraction
212	Mining (except Oil and Gas)
22	**Utilities**
22131	Water Supply and Irrigation Systems
23	**Construction**
236	Construction of Buildings
237	Heavy and Civil Engineering Construction
23815	Glass and Glazing Contractors
23821	Electrical Contractors
23822	Plumbing, Heating, and Air-Conditioning Contractors
2383	Building Finishing Contractors
31-33	**Manufacturing**
311	Food Manufacturing
3111	Animal Food Manufacturing
31121	Flour Milling and Malt Manufacturing
3113	Sugar and Confectionery Product Manufacturing
3114	Fruit and Vegetable Preserving and Specialty Food Manufacturing
3115	Dairy Product Manufacturing
3117	Seafood Product Preparation and Packaging
3118	Bakeries and Tortilla Manufacturing
31191	Snack Food Manufacturing
31192	Coffee and Tea Manufacturing
31193	Flavoring Syrup and Concentrate Manufacturing
31194	Seasoning and Dressing Manufacturing
312	Beverage and Tobacco Product Manufacturing
3141	Textile Furnishings Mills
315	Apparel Manufacturing
315211	Men's and Boys' Cut and Sew Apparel Contractors
315212	Women's, Girls', and Infants' Cut and Sew Apparel Contractors
315292	Fur and Leather Apparel Manufacturing
3159	Apparel Accessories and Other Apparel Manufacturing
316	Leather and Allied Product Manufacturing
3162	Footwear Manufacturing
321	Wood Product Manufacturing
322	Paper Manufacturing
323	Printing and Related Support Activities
324	Petroleum and Coal Products Manufacturing
325	Chemical Manufacturing
3252	Resin, Synthetic Rubber, and Artificial Synthetic Fibers and Filaments Manufacturing
3253	Pesticide, Fertilizer, and Other Agricultural Chemical Manufacturing
3254	Pharmaceutical and Medicine Manufacturing
3255	Paint, Coating, and Adhesive Manufacturing
3256	Soap, Cleaning Compound, and Toilet Preparation Manufacturing
32591	Printing Ink Manufacturing
32592	Explosives Manufacturing
325992	Photographic Film, Paper, Plate, and Chemical Manufacturing
326	Plastics and Rubber Products Manufacturing
3262	Rubber Product Manufacturing
32621	Tire Manufacturing
32622	Rubber and Plastics Hoses and Belting Manufacturing
32629	Other Rubber Product Manufacturing
327	Nonmetallic Mineral Product Manufacturing
32711	Pottery, Ceramics, and Plumbing Fixture Manufacturing
32712	Clay Building Material and Refractories Manufacturing
3272	Glass and Glass Product Manufacturing
3273	Cement and Concrete Product Manufacturing
3274	Lime and Gypsum Product Manufacturing
32791	Abrasive Product Manufacturing
331	Primary Metal Manufacturing
332	Fabricated Metal Product Manufacturing
3325	Hardware Manufacturing
333	Machinery Manufacturing
3331	Agriculture, Construction, and Mining Machinery Manufacturing
3333	Commercial and Service Industry Machinery Manufacturing
3334	Ventilation, Heating, Air-Conditioning, and Commercial Refrigeration Equipment Manufacturing
3335	Metalworking Machinery Manufacturing
3336	Engine, Turbine, and Power Transmission Equipment Manufacturing
334	Computer and Electronic Product Manufacturing
3342	Communications Equipment Manufacturing
33422	Radio and Television Broadcasting and Wireless Communications Equipment Manufacturing
3343	Audio and Video Equipment Manufacturing
3344	Semiconductor and Other Electronic Component Manufacturing
3345	Navigational, Measuring, Electromedical, and Control Instruments Manufacturing
334518	Watch, Clock, and Part Manufacturing
3346	Manufacturing and Reproducing Magnetic and Optical Media
335	Electrical Equipment, Appliance, and Component Manufacturing
3353	Electrical Equipment Manufacturing
336	Transportation Equipment Manufacturing
3361	Motor Vehicle Manufacturing
3363	Motor Vehicle Parts Manufacturing
3364	Aerospace Product and Parts Manufacturing
3365	Railroad Rolling Stock Manufacturing
3366	Ship and Boat Building
336991	Motorcycle, Bicycle, and Parts Manufacturing
336992	Military Armored Vehicle, Tank, and Tank Component Manufacturing
337	Furniture and Related Product Manufacturing
3372	Office Furniture (including Fixtures) Manufacturing
3391	Medical Equipment and Supplies Manufacturing
33991	Jewelry and Silverware Manufacturing
33992	Sporting and Athletic Goods Manufacturing
33993	Doll, Toy, and Game Manufacturing
33994	Office Supplies (except Paper) Manufacturing
33995	Sign Manufacturing
42	**Wholesale Trade**
423	Merchant Wholesalers, Durable Goods
424	Merchant Wholesalers, Nondurable Goods
425	Wholesale Electronic Markets and Agents and Brokers
44-45	**Retail Trade**
441	Motor Vehicle and Parts Dealers
442	Furniture and Home Furnishings Stores
443	Electronics and Appliance Stores
444	Building Material and Garden Equipment and Supplies Dealers
445	Food and Beverage Stores
446	Health and Personal Care Stores
451	Sporting Goods, Hobby, Book, and Music Stores
453	Miscellaneous Store Retailers
454	Nonstore Retailers
48-49	**Transportation and Warehousing**
481	Air Transportation
482	Rail Transportation
483	Water Transportation
484	Truck Transportation

485	Transit and Ground Passenger Transportation
486	Pipeline Transportation
487	Scenic and Sightseeing Transportation
4885	Freight Transportation Arrangement
493	Warehousing and Storage
51	**Information**
511	Publishing Industries (except Internet)
5111	Newspaper, Periodical, Book, and Directory Publishers
5121	Motion Picture and Video Industries
51223	Music Publishers
515	Broadcasting (except Internet)
516	Internet Publishing and Broadcasting
517	Telecommunications
518	Data Processing, Hosting and Related Services
51912	Libraries and Archives
51913	Internet Publishing and Broadcasting and Web Search Portals
52	**Finance and Insurance**
522	Credit Intermediation and Related Activities
52211	Commercial Banking
522292	Real Estate Credit
522293	International Trade Financing
52311	Investment Banking and Securities Dealing
52392	Portfolio Management
52399	All Other Financial Investment Activities
524	Insurance Carriers and Related Activities
525	Funds, Trusts, and Other Financial Vehicles
5251	Insurance and Employee Benefit Funds
52593	Real Estate Investment Trusts
53	**Real Estate and Rental and Leasing**
531	Real Estate
5321	Automotive Equipment Rental and Leasing
53212	Truck, Utility Trailer, and RV (Recreational Vehicle) Rental and Leasing
53221	Consumer Electronics and Appliances Rental
53223	Video Tape and Disc Rental
5324	Commercial and Industrial Machinery and Equipment Rental and Leasing
533	Lessors of Nonfinancial Intangible Assets (except Copyrighted Works)
54	**Professional, Scientific, and Technical Services**
5411	Legal Services
5412	Accounting, Tax Preparation, Bookkeeping, and Payroll Services
5413	Architectural, Engineering, and Related Services
54135	Building Inspection Services
54141	Interior Design Services
54143	Graphic Design Services
541613	Marketing Consulting Services
54162	Environmental Consulting Services
5418	Advertising and Related Services
54182	Public Relations Agencies
54183	Media Buying Agencies
541921	Photography Studios, Portrait
56	**Administrative and Support and Waste Management and Remediation Services**
561422	Telemarketing Bureaus
56145	Credit Bureaus
5615	Travel Arrangement and Reservation Services
5616	Investigation and Security Services
5617	Services to Buildings and Dwellings
56191	Packaging and Labeling Services
562	Waste Management and Remediation Services
61	**Educational Services**
6114	Business Schools and Computer and Management Training
71	**Arts, Entertainment, and Recreation**
711	Performing Arts, Spectator Sports, and Related Industries
713	Amusement, Gambling, and Recreation Industries
71321	Casinos (except Casino Hotels)
71394	Fitness and Recreational Sports Centers
72	**Accommodation and Food Services**
7211	Traveler Accommodation
72111	Hotels (except Casino Hotels) and Motels
72112	Casino Hotels
7212	RV (Recreational Vehicle) Parks and Recreational Camps
722	Food Services and Drinking Places
7221	Full-Service Restaurants
81	**Other Services (except Public Administration)**
8111	Automotive Repair and Maintenance
811211	Consumer Electronics Repair and Maintenance
8113	Commercial and Industrial Machinery and Equipment (except Automotive and Electronic) Repair and Maintenance
81141	Home and Garden Equipment and Appliance Repair and Maintenance
8121	Personal Care Services
81231	Coin-Operated Laundries and Drycleaners
813211	Grantmaking Foundations
813312	Environment, Conservation and Wildlife Organizations
92	**Public Administration**
921	Executive, Legislative, and Other General Government Support
922	Justice, Public Order, and Safety Activities
924	Administration of Environmental Quality Programs
92612	Regulation and Administration of Transportation Programs
92613	Regulation and Administration of Communications, Electric, Gas, and Other Utilities
92614	Regulation of Agricultural Marketing and Commodities
928	National Security and International Affairs

The Standard Industrial Classification (SIC) is a United States government system for classifying industries by a four-digit code. Established in 1937, it has been supplanted by the six-digit North American Industry Classification System (NAICS) (see page ixx), which was released in 1997; however certain government departments and agencies, such as the U.S. Securities and Exchange Commission (SEC), still use SIC codes. Below are all major SIC codes and descriptions. For a more detailed explanation of the SIC system, visit http://www.census.gov/epcd/www/sic.html.

01 Agricultural Production - Crops

07 Agricultural Services

09 Fishing, Hunting and Trapping

10 Metal Mining

12 Coal Mining

13 Oil and Gas Extraction

14 Mining and Quarrying of Nonmetallic Minerals, Except Fuels

15 Building Construction - General Contractors & Operative Builders

16 Heavy Construction, Except Building Construction - Contractors

17 Construction - Special Trade Contractors

20 Food and Kindred Products

21 Tobacco Products

22 Textile Mill Products

23 Apparel and Other Finished Products Made From Fabrics and Similar Materials

24 Lumber and Wood Products, Except Furniture

25 Furniture and Fixtures

26 Paper and Allied Products

27 Printing, Publishing, and Allied Industries

28 Chemicals and Allied Products

29 Petroleum Refining and Related Industries

30 Rubber and Miscellaneous Plastics Products

31 Leather and Leather Products

32 Stone, Clay, Glass, and Concrete Products

33 Primary Metal Industries

34 Fabricated Metal Products, Except Machinery and Transportation Equipment

35 Industrial and Commercial Machinery and Computer Equipment

36 Electronic and Other Electrical Equipment and Components, Except Computer Equipment

37 Transportation Equipment

38 Measuring, Analyzing, and Controlling Instruments; Photographic, Medical and Optical Goods; Watches

39 Miscellaneous Manufacturing Industries

41 Local and Suburban Transit and Interurban Highway Passenger Transportation

42 Motor Freight Transportation and Warehousing

44 Water Transportation

45 Transportation By Air

47 Pipelines, Except Natural Gas

47 Transportation Services

48 Communications

49 Electric, Gas and Sanitary Services

50 Wholesale Trade-Durable Goods

51 Wholesale Trade-Non-Durable Goods

60 Depository Institutions

61 Non-Depository Credit Institutions

63 Insurance Carriers

65 Real Estate

73 Business Services

75 Automotive Repair, Services, and Parking

76 Miscellaneous Repair Services

78 Motion Pictures

79 Amusement and Recreation Services

80 Health Services

81 Legal Services

82 Educational Services

84 Museums, Art Galleries, and Botanical and Zoological Gardens

87 Engineering, Accounting, Research, Management, and Related Services

92 Justice, Public Order, and Safety

94 Administration of Human Resource Programs

95 Administration of Environmental Quality and Housing Programs

96 Administration of Economic Programs

97 National Security and International Affairs

Associations

1 **AGN International - North America**
2851 S Parker Rd
Suite 850
Aurora, CO 80014-2744

303-743-7880
800-782-2272; *Fax:* 303-743-7660
rhood@agn.org; www.agn.org
Social Media: Facebook, LinkedIn

Rita J. Hood, Executive Director
Patsy Bowen, Director, Member Info Services
Mark Pigg, Director, Internal Info Systems
Nathalie Champagne, Director/Member Programs
Courtney Mino, Director, Meetings/Staff Dev.

Worldwide association of separate and independent accounting and consulting firms. Composed of CPA consulting firms who share information and resources via the association programs. AGN-NA operates under the premise that by sharing information and resources, members' growth and quality goals can be achieved more quickly.
53 Members
Founded in: 1978

2 **ARMA International**
11880 College Blvd
Suite 450
Overland Park, KS 66210

913-341-3808
800-422-2762; *Fax:* 913-341-3742
headquarters@armaintl.org; www.arma.org
Social Media: Facebook, Twitter, LinkedIn

Peter Kurilecz, IGP, CRM, CA, President
Tera Ladner, J.D., IGP, CRM, President-Elect
Brenda Prowse, CRM, Treasurer
Fred Pulzello, IGP, CRM, Immediate Past President
Candace Daniels, Product Marketing Manager

ARMA International is a not-for-profit association and a source for authoritative education, the latest legislative updates, standards & best practices. The association was established in 1955. Its approximately 10,000 members include records managers, archivists, corporate librarians, imaging specialists, legal professionals, IT managers, consultants, and educators, all of whom work in a wide variety of industries.
27000 Members
Founded in: 1955

3 **Academy of Accounting Historians**
Case Western Reserve University
10900 Euclid Avenue
Cleveland, OH 44106

216-368-2058; *Fax:* 205-368-6244
acchistory@case.edu; www.aahhq.org
Social Media: Facebook, Twitter, LinkedIn, YouTube

Massimo Sargiacomo, President
Robert Colson, President Elect
Gary Spraakman, VP, Partnerships
Yvette Lazdowski, VP,Communications
Stephanie Moussalli, Secretary

Subjects include modern prespectives of accounting history.
600 Members
Founded in: 1973

4 **Accounting & Financial Women's Alliance**
2365 Harrodsburg Road, A325
Lexington, KY 40504

859-219-3532
800-326-2163; *Fax:* 859-219-3532
afwa@afwa.org; www.afwa.org
Social Media: Facebook, Twitter, LinkedIn

Dianna M. Patton, CPA, CFP, President
Linda Harris, CPA, President Elect
Mary E. Duff, CPA, VP, Chapter Initiatives
Karyn Hartke, CPA, Vice President - Membership
Ericka Harney, Executive Director

To enable women in all accounting and related fields to achieve their full personal, professional and economic potential and to contribute to the future development of their profession.
Founded in: 1938

5 **Accreditation Council for Accountancy and Taxation**
1330 Braddock Place
Suite 540
Alexandria, VA 22314

888-289-7763; *Fax:* 703-549-2984;
www.acatcredentials.org

Michael P. Salazar, CPA, EA, ABA, President
Virginia Bruns, Vice President
Christine Giovetti, Secretary/Treasurer
Carla Rich, Education Director
Peter M. Berkery, Jr., JD, CFP, Public Director

To identify professionals in independent practice who specialize in providing financial, accounting and taxation services to individuals and small to mid-size businesses.
Founded in: 1973

6 **Advancing Government Accountability**
2208 Mount Vernon Avenue
Alexandria, VA 22301-1314

703-684-6931
800-AGA-7211; *Fax:* 703-548-9367
agamembers@agacgfm.org; www.agacgfm.org
Social Media: Facebook, Twitter, LinkedIn, Twitter, GovLoop

John E. Homan, 2015-2016 AGA National President
Ann M. Ebberts, MS, PMP, Chief Executive Officer
Maryann Malesardi, Director of Com/Journal Editor
Cristina Barbudo, MS, CPA, Director of Finance & Admin
Jerome Bruce, Director, Meetings & Expositions

AGA supports the careers and professional development of government finance professionals working in federal, state and local governments as well as the private sector and academia. Through education, research, publications, certification and conferences, AGA reaches thousands of professionals and offers more than 100,000 continuing professional education (CPE) hours annually.
15000 Members
Founded in: 1950
Mailing list available for rent: 18,000 names

7 **Affordable Housing Association of Certified Public Accountants**
459 N 300 W
Suite 11
Kaysville, UT 84037

801-547-0809
800-532-0809; *Fax:* 801-547-5070
info@ahacpa.org; www.ahacpa.org

Les Sparks, President
Kathy Christensen, Contact
Mike Olsen, Contact
Susan Harris, Contact

AHACPA is a national association of CPAs and financial professionals providing financial services, support and education for the affordable housing and HUD-approved lender communities, informing members of financial requirements and provide specific guidance on how to efficiently implement those requirements.
500 Members
Founded in: 1998
Mailing list available for rent

8 **American Accounting Association**
5717 Bessie Drive
Sarasota, FL 34233-2399

941-921-7747; *Fax:* 941-923-4093
info@aaahq.org; www.aaahq.org
Social Media: Facebook, Twitter

Tracey Sutherland, Executive Director
Julie Smith David, Chief Innovation Officer
Dave Frazier, Finance Director
Diane Hazard, Publications Director
Stephanie Austin, Publications Assistant

The American Accounting Association promotes worldwide excellence in accounting education, research and practice. The Association is a voluntary organization of persons interested in accounting education and research.
9000 Members
Founded in: 1916

9 **American Association for Budget and Program Analysis**
PO Box 1157
Falls Church, VA 22041

703-828-4333; *Fax:* 703-941-1535
aabpa@aabpa.org; www.aabpa.org
Social Media: Facebook, Twitter, LinkedIn, GovLoop

Melissa Neuman, President
Ben Wilson, Vice President for Membership
Sandra Beattie, Vice President for Programs
Justin Ryan Riordan, Vice President for Communications
Darreisha Bates, Treasurer/Secretary

Helps federal, state, and local government managers and analysts, corporate executives and academic specialists meet the unique challenges of their careers. By helping members keep up with the latest developments in their fields, establish and maintain contacts with colleagues, represent their interests and share opportunities, AABPA serves the key difference between simply having a job and being part of a highly respected and well trained profession.
400 Members
Founded in: 1976

10 **American Association of Attorney-Certified Public Accountants**
PO Box 706
Warrendale, PA 15095

703-352-8064
888-288-9272; *Fax:* 703-352-8073
info@attorney-cpa.com;
www.attorney-cpa.com
Social Media: Facebook, Twitter, LinkedIn

John W. Pramberg, President
David M. Berger, President Elect/ Vice President
Jo Ann M. Koontz, Secretary
Melissa R. Benowitz, CMP, Director of Meetings
Kimmy Livingston, Director, Membership

The AAA-CPA is the only association in the nation whose members are comprised of professionals dually qualified as both attorneys and certified public accountants. Today, the AAA-CPA offers an array of products and services to help members succeed in their practice such as; networking and referral
1370 Members
Founded in: 1964

11 **American Association of Finance & Accounting**
1702 E. Highland Ave
Suite 200
Phoenix, AZ 85016

602-277-3700; *Fax:* 602-926-2629
mnolan@afpersonnel.com; www.aafa.com

An alliance of executive search firms specializing in the recruiting of finance and accounting professionals.
Founded in: 1978

12 **American Association of Managing General Agents**
610 Freedom Business Center
Suite 110
King of Prussia, PA 19406

610-992-0022; *Fax:* 610-992-0021
mark@aamga.org; www.aamga.org
Social Media: Facebook, Twitter, LinkedIn

Bernd G. Heinze, Esq, Executive Director
Roger Ware, Jr., ARM, President
Marty Bair, CFO
Caitlin Skelton, Director of Meetings and Projects
Jeff Henry, Director of Education

Trade association to international wholesale insurance professionals and leader in representing the interests of its members before federal, state,and local governments and regulatory agencies
Founded in: 1926

13 **American College of Trust and Estate Counsel**
901 15th Street, NW
Suite 525
Washington, DC 20005

202-684-8460; *Fax:* 202-684-8459;
www.actec.org
Social Media: Facebook, Twitter, LinkedIn

Bruce Stone, President
Cynda C. Ottaway, President Elect
Susan T. House, Vice President
Charles D. Fox, IV, Treasurer
John A. Terrill, II, Secretary

Nonprofit association of lawyers that advises clients on planning for tax efficient transfer of wealth during life and after death, preparing real estate planning documents, administering trusts, guardianships, planning for employee benefits, etc.
2700+ Members
Founded in: 1949

14 **American Council of Life Insurers**
101 Constitution Avenue
Suite 700
Washington, DC 20001-2133

202-624-2000
877-674-4659
contact@acli.com; www.acli.com
Social Media: Facebook, Twitter, YouTube, RSS

Deanna Mulligan, Chairman
Pete Schaefer, Chairman-Elect
Dirk Kempthorne, President & Chief Executive Officer
Brian Waidmann, Chief of Staff
Larry Burton, Chief Operating Officer

Trade association advocating federal, state, and international forums for public policy that supports the industry marketplace. ACLI members offer life insurance, annuities, retirement plans, long-term care, disability income insurance, and reinsurance.
300 Members

15 **American Institute of Certified Public Accountants**
1211 Avenue of the Americas
New York, NY 10036-8775

212-596-6200
888-777-7077; *Fax:* 212-596-6213
service@aicpa.org; www.aicpa.org
Social Media: Facebook, Twitter, LinkedIn, RSS

Tim L. Christen, CPA, CGMA, Chairman
Barry C Melancon, CPA, CGMA, President & Chief Executive Officer
Susan Coffey, CPA, CGMA, Senior Vice President
Mark Peterson, Senior Vice President
Anthony Pugliese, Senior Vice President

The American Institute of Certified Public Accountants is the national, professional organization for all Certified Public Accountants. Its mission is to provide members with the resources, information, and leadership that enable them to provide valuable services in the highest professional manner to benefit the public as well as employers and clients.
41200 Members
Founded in: 1887

16 **American Institute of Professional Bookkeepers**
6001 Montrose Road
Suite 500
Rockville, MD 20852

800-622-0121; *Fax:* 800-541-0066
info@aipb.org; www.aipb.org

Stanley Hartman, Executive Director
Stephen Sahlein, Director of Publishing
Carol Watson, Director
Robin Merrill, Assistant Manager
Kenia Salgado, Manager

Achieve recognition of bookkeepers as accounting professionals, keep bookkeepers up to date on changes in bookkeeping, accounting and tax, answer questions on bookkeeping and accounting, and certify bookkeepers.
30000 Members
Founded in: 1987

17 **American Payroll Association**
660 North Main Avenue
Suite 100
San Antonio, TX 78205-1217

210-226-4600; *Fax:* 210-226-4027
apa@americanpayroll.org;
www.americanpayroll.org
Social Media: Facebook, Twitter, LinkedIn

The American Payroll Association is the leading advocate for the advancement of payroll professionals and a catalyst for connecting the payroll industry with employers and government. Our vision is to create opportunities and forge a community by providing the education, skills, and resources necessary for payroll professionals to become successful leaders and strategic partners within their organizations.
20000 Members
Founded in: 1982

18 **American Property Tax Counsel**
1970 East Grand Ave.
Suite 330
El Segundo, CA 90245

310-364-0193
844-227-0407; www.aptcnet.com
Social Media: LinkedIn

Provides property tax services locally and nationally.

19 **American Society of Military Comptrollers**
415 N Alfred St
Alexandria, VA 22314-2269

703-549-0360
800-462-5637; *Fax:* 703-549-3181;
www.asmconline.org
Social Media: Facebook, Twitter, LinkedIn

Craig Bennett, President
Gretchen Anderson, Vice President
Al Runnels, Executive Director
Riitta Silverman, Associate Director for Finance
Phara G. Rodrigue, Associate Director

ASMC is the non-profit educational and professional organization for persons, military and civilian, involved in the overall field of military comptrollership. ASMC promotes the education and training of its members, and supports the development and advancement of the profession of military comptrollership. The society sponsors research, provides professional programs to keep members abreast of current issues and encourages the exchange of techniques and approaches.
20000 Members
Founded in: 1948

20 **American Woman's Society of Certified Public Accountants**
136 South Keowee Street
Dayton, OH 45402

713-893-5685
800-297-2721; *Fax:* 937-222-5794
info@awscpa.org; www.awscpa.org
Social Media: Facebook, Twitter, LinkedIn

Cynthia Cox, President
Christina Flynn, VP, Programs
Krista D. Saul, Secretary
Belicia Cespedes, Treasurer
Wendy Lewis, VP/Marketing

The American Woman's Society of Certified Public Accountants (AWSCPA) began in 1933 as a group of nine women CPAs united in facing the challenges affecting women in the profession at that time. Over the years, the organization has grown. Membership increased dramatically in 1982 when the membership amended the Society's bylaws to allow affiliated local groups. Today, AWSCPA has 25 affiliates located throughout the country with a membership of approximately 2,000.
1500 Members
Founded in: 1933

21 **Appraisers Association of America**
212 West 35th Street
11th Floor South
New York, NY 10001

212-889-5404; *Fax:* 212-889-5503
referrals@appraisersassociation.org;
www.appraisersassociation.org
Social Media: Facebook, Twitter, LinkedIn

Deborah G. Spanierman, AAA, President
Cynthia D. Herbert, AAA, First Vice President
Edward Yee, AAA, Second Vice President
Linda Selvin, Executive Director
Sharon Chrust, AAA, Recording Secretary

Develop and promote skills in the profession of appraising through education and professional practice.
Founded in: 1949

22 **Association for Accounting Administration**
136 S Keowee Street
Dayton, OH 45402

937-222-0030; *Fax:* 937-222-5794
info@cpafma.org; www.cpafma.org
Social Media: Facebook, Twitter, LinkedIn

Kim Fantaci, President
Jim Fahey, AAAPM, Chair

Robert E. Biddle, Jr., AAAPM, Vice Chair
Sharon Trabbic, AAAPM, Director of Education
Larry Sheftel, PHR, Director of Membership & Growth

The Association of Accounting Administrators enables accounting firm administrators to communicate with one another and provide each other with the benefits of everyone's experiences in what was a new and emerging profession.
900 Members
Founded in: 1984

23 Association for Accounting Marketing

9 Newport Drive
Suite 200
Forest Hill, MD 21050

443-640-1061; *Fax:* 856-439-0525
info@accountingmarketing.org;
www.accountingmarketing.org
Social Media: Facebook, Twitter, LinkedIn

Jack Kolmansberger, President
Laura Snyder, Vice President
Lauren Clemmer, Executive Director
Amy Chetelat, Financial Director
Jessica Bialczak, Association Coordinator

The Association for Accounting Marketing (AAM) is a national organization and is the only trade association of its kind that provides resources, education, seminars, workshops, support and a global network to the accounting marketing industry. Our membership includes accounting firm marketers from Big Four and other national, regional, local and sole proprietor firms. Others include sales and business development professionals, accounting partners, firm administrators, and students.
843 Members
Founded in: 1989

24 Association for Management Information in Financial Services

14247 Saffron Circle
Carmel, IN 46032

317-815-5857
ami2@amifs.org; www.amifs.org
Social Media: Facebook, Twitter, LinkedIn

Kevin Link, Executive Director
Robert McDonald, President
Meg Foster, Executive Vice President
Krissa Hatfield, Asst. Executive Director

A nonprofit professional association dedicated to developing and advancing the profession of management information for the financial services industry.
Founded in: 1980

25 Association of Accounting Administrators

136 South Keowee Street
Dayton, OH 45402

937-222-0030
info@cpafma.org; www.cpafma.org
Social Media: Facebook, Twitter, LinkedIn

Kim Fantaci, President
Jim Fahey, AAAPM, Chair
Ginny Fedrich, AAAPM, Secretary
Jane Johnson, AAAPM, Treasurer
Sharon Trabbic, AAAPM, Director of Education
Founded in: 1984

26 Association of Certified Fraud Examiners

716 West Ave
Austin, TX 78701-2727

512-478-9000
800-245-3321; *Fax:* 512-478-9297
memberservices@acfe.com; www.acfe.com
Social Media: Facebook, Twitter, LinkedIn

Joseph T Wells, Chairman
James D Ratley, President/CEO
John D Gill, VP/Education
John Warren, VP/General Counsel
Jeanette LeVie, VP/Administration

The ACFE is reducing business fraud world-wide and inspiring public confidence in the integrity and objectivity within the profession.
75000 Members
Founded in: 1988

27 Association of Chartered Accountants in the United States

3887 Punahele Road
Princeville, HI 96722

508-395-0224
admin@acaus.org; www.acaus.org
Social Media: Facebook, LinkedIn

David Powell FCA (ICAEW), President
Sasha Carlson, Executive Director
Natasha Holbeck, Vice President
Timothy Clackett, Secretary
Robert McDonald, Treasurer

ACAUS is a nonprofit professional and educational organization representing interests of U.S. based chartered accountants from the institutes of Chartered Accountants across the globe.
6000 Members
Founded in: 1980

28 Association of College & University Auditors

PO Box 14306
Lenexa, KS 66285-4306

913-895-4620; *Fax:* 913-895-4652;
www.acua.org
Social Media: Facebook, Twitter, LinkedIn, YouTube

Vijay Patel, President
Sandy Jansen, Immediate Past President
Stephanie Newman, Executive Director
Raven Hardin, Association Manager
Dede Gish Panjada, Education Director

The Association of College & University Auditors (ACUA) is a professional organization comprised of audit professionals from all over the globe. We strive to continually improve the internal operations and processes of the individual institutions we serve, through continued professional development and the dissemination of individual internal audit experiences in an open forum with friends and colleagues.
Founded in: 1958

29 Association of Credit Union Internal Auditors

1727 King Street
Suite 300
Alexandria, VA 22314

703-688-2284; *Fax:* 703-348-7602
acuia@acuia.org; www.acuia.org
Social Media: Facebook, Twitter, LinkedIn

John Gallagher, Chairman
Kara Giano, CIA, CIDA, CRMA, Vice Chair
Margaret Chamberlain, CUERME, Secretary
Barry Lucas, Treasurer
Linda Goff, CUCE, Director

ACUIA is committed to being a quality provider of credit union internal audit resources. ACUIA is an international professional organization dedicated to the practice of internal auditing in credit unions. ACUIA's objectives are: to unify and encourage cooperative relationships among credit union internal auditors to facilitate the exchange of information and ideas; to provide educational opportunities for developing and enhancing audit and leadership skills; promote the IA profession.
600 Members
Founded in: 1991

30 Association of Government Accountants

2208 Mount Vernon Ave
Alexandria, VA 22301-1314

703-684-6931
800-AGA-7211; *Fax:* 703-548-9367
communications@agacgfm.org;
www.agacgfm.org
Social Media: LinkedIn

John E. Homan, National President
Susan Fritzlen, Chief Operating Officer
Cristina Barbudo, Director of Finance/Administration
Maryann Malesardi, Director of Comm/Journal Editor
Ann M. Ebberts, MS, PMP, Chief Executive Officer

AGA supports the careers and professional development of government finance professionals working in federal, state and local governments as well as the private sector and academia. Through education, research, publications, certification and conferences, AGA reaches thousands of professionals and offers more than 100,000 continuing professional education (CPE) hours annually.
Founded in: 1950

31 Association of Healthcare Internal Auditors

10200 W 44th Avenue
Suite 304
Wheat Ridge, CO 80003

303-327-7546
888-ASK-AHIA; *Fax:* 720-881-6101
info@ahia.org; www.ahia.org
Social Media: LinkedIn, YouTube

Cavell Alexander, Chairman
David Richstone, Vice Chair
David Stumph, Executive Director
Michelle Cunningham, Account Executive
Bryon Neaman, CPA, CIA, Secretary/Treasurer

The Association of Internal Auditors (AHIA) is a network of experienced healthcare internal auditing professionals who come together to share tools, knowledge and insight on how to assess and evaluate risk within a complex and dynamic healthcare environment. AHIA is an advocate for the profession, continuing to elevate and champion the strategic importance of healthcare internal auditors with executive management and the Board.
885 Members
Founded in: 1981

32 Association of Independent Accounting Professionals

E-Mail: staff@aiaponline.com;
www.aiaponline.com

An online resource designed for today's independent accountant—provides practice expansion opportunities, information, and resources.

33 Association of Insolvency Advisors and Restructuring Advisors

221 Stewart Avenue
Suite 207
Medford, OR 97501-3647

541-858-1665; *Fax:* 541-858-9187
aira@aira.org; www.aira.org
Social Media: Twitter, LinkedIn

Matthew Schwartz, CIRA, Chairman
Thomas Morrow, CIRA, President
David Payne, CIRA, CDBV, Vice President - Conferences
Teri Stratton, CIRA, Vice President - CIRA, CDBV
Joel Waite, Vice President - Development

AIRA is a nonprofit professional association serving the bankruptcy, restructuring and turn-

around practice area. AIRA's membership consists of accountants, financial advisors, investment bankers, attorneys, workout consultants, trustees, and others in the field of business turnaround, restructuring and bankruptcy. AIRA members are among the most trusted and sought-after professionals in matters dealing with limited capital resources and deteriorating operating performance.
2000+ Members
Founded in: 1982

34 **Association of Insolvency and Reconstruction**
221 W. Stewart Avenue
Suite 207
Medford, OR 97501

541-858-1665; *Fax:* 541-858-9187
aira@aira.org; www.aira.org
Matthew Schwartz, CIRA, Chairman
Thomas Morrow, CIRA, President
David Payne, CIRA, CDBV, Vice President - Conferences
Teri Stratton, CIRA, Vice President - CIRA, CDBV
Grant Newton, Executive Director
Founded in: 1982

35 **Association of Latino Professionals in Finance and Accounting**
801 South Grand Avenue
Suite 400
Los Angeles, CA 90017

714-757-6133
carlos.perez@national.alpfa.org; www.alpfa.org
Social Media: Facebook, Twitter, LinkedIn, YouTube, Instagram

Yvonne Garcia, Chair
Charles P. Garcia, Chief Executive Officer
Selene Benavides, Chief Financial Officer
Julio Carbonell, Chief Information Officer
Migdalia Diaz, Chief Operating Officer
ALPFA is the leading professsional association dedicated to enhancing opportunities for Latinos in the accounting, finance and related professions. ALPFA is a nonprofit entity registered with the IRS.
72000 Members
Founded in: 1972

36 **Association of Local Government Auditors**
859-276-0686
kyoung@nasact.org
algaonline.org
Social Media: Twitter, LinkedIn, RSS

Kymber Waltmunson, President
David Givans, President Elect
Corrie Stokes, Past President
Kristine Adams Wannberg, Treasurer
Tina Adams, Secretary
A professional organization committed to supporting and improving local government auditing through advocacy, collaboration, education, and training.
Founded in: 1985

37 **Association of Public Pension Fund Auditors**
PO Box 16064
Columbus, OH 43216-6064

E-Mail: webmaster@appfa.org; www.appfa.org
Ryan Babin, President
Greg Beck, Vice President
Amy L. Barett, Secretary
Mary Kay Howard, Treasurer
Dave McKnight, Board Member
A professional association consisting of internal auditors dedicated to providing comprehensive professional development and networking opportunities for its members.
100+ Members
Founded in: 1991

38 **BCCA**
550 W. Frontage Road
Suite 3600
Northfield, IL 60093

847-881-8757; *Fax:* 847-784-8059
info@bccacredit.com; www.bccacredit.com
Social Media: Twitter, LinkedIn

Mary Collin, President & CEO
Jamie Smith, Director of Operations
Arcelia Pimentel, Sales/Membership
Susan Graves, Credit Investigator
Tracey Harris, Credit Investigator
BCCA is the media industry's credit association that functions as a central clearing house for credit information on advertisers, agencies and buying services, both locally and nationally. Also provides an Electronic Media Credit Application (EMCAPP.com) to members that helps streamline the application process. One app in one location!
545 Members
Founded in: 1972

39 **Beta Alpha Psi**
220 Leigh Farm Road
Durham, NC 27707
919-402-4044
bap@bap.org; www.bap.org
Social Media: Facebook, Twitter, LinkedIn

Shawn Harter, President
Margaret Fiorentino, Executive Director
Samantha Simunyu, Associate Manager - Marketing
George Gamble, Director of Administration
Lisa Wicker, Manager - Chapter Services
BETA ALPHA PSI is an honorary organization for Financial Information students and professionals. The primary objective of Beta Alpha Psi is to encourage and give recognition to scholastic and professional excellence in the business information field. This includes promoting the study and practice of accounting, finance and information systems; providing opportunities for self-development, service and association among members and practicing professionals.
300K Members
Founded in: 1919

40 **Broadcast Cable Credit Association**
550 W Frontage Rd
Suite 3600
Northfield, IL 60093-1243

847-881-8757; *Fax:* 847-784-8059
info@bccacredit.com; www.bccacredit.com
Social Media: Facebook, Twitter, LinkedIn

Mary Collin, President/CEO
Jamie Smith, Director/Operations
Arcelia Pimentel, BCCA Sales/Membership
Susan Graves, Credit Investigator
Tracey Harris, Credit Investigator
BCCA, a subsidiary of Media Financial Management Association, represents credit and collection professionals from TV, radio, cable, system operators, newspaper, and magazine organizations in the U.S. and Canada. BCCA functions as a central clearinghouse for credit information on advertisers, agencies and buying services, both locally and nationally.
600 Members
Founded in: 1972

41 **CPA Associates International**
Meadows Office Complex
301 Route 17 North
Rutherford, NJ 07070-2599

201-804-8686; *Fax:* 201-804-9222
homeoffice@cpaai.com; www.cpaai.com

Hans van den Besselaar, Chairman
James F. Flynn, President
Ted A. Carnevale, Treasurer
Claudio Cifali, Secretary
CPA Associates International was established as a global group of high-quality independent CPA and chartered accounting firms; it is market exclusive, with members in major cities throughout the world. The organized association provides members with the capabilities of the largest firm, yet allows each to maintain its local practice while avoiding costly overhead and unnecessary controls.
148 Members
Founded in: 1960

42 **CPAsNET.com**
PO Box 7648
Princeton, NJ 8543

609-890-0800; *Fax:* 609-689-9720
solutions@cpasnet.com; www.cpasnet.com

An association of accounting and business consulting firms who havepooled their resources to provide their clients with the local, national, and international perspective needed to prosper.
500 Members

43 **Construction Financial Management Association**
100 Village Blvd
Suite 200
Princeton, NJ 08540-5783

609-452-8000
888-421-9996; *Fax:* 609-452-0474
info@cfma.org; www.cfma.org
Social Media: Facebook, Twitter, LinkedIn, YouTube

Stuart Binstock, President/CEO
Brian Summers, VP, Content Strategy & Education
Robert Rubin, CPA, VP, Finance & Administration
Michael Verbanic, Director/Member Experience
Stacy Williams, Admin Assistant, Membership
CFMA is the only organization dedicated to bringing together construction financial professionals and those partners serving their unique needs. CFMA has 89 chapters located throughout the US and Canada.
7000 Members
Founded in: 1981

44 **Construction Industry CPA/Consultants Association**
15011 East Twilight View Drive
Fountain Hills, AZ 85268

480-836-0300
800-864-0491; *Fax:* 480-836-0400
info@cicpac.com; www.cicpac.com
Social Media: Facebook, LinkedIn

Chris Iannuzzi, President
Jacquelyn Daenen, Vice President
Kathleen Baldwin, Secretary/ Treasurer
Ken Gardiner, President Elect
John J. Corcoran, CPA, Executive Director
The Construction Industry CPAs/Consultants Association (CICPAC) is a national association of CPA firms recognized in their respective markets for providing high quality financial and consulting services. Each firm is the exclusive member in its area and must demonstrate profi-

ciency in construction industry services and a reputation for high-quality work and integrity.
7500 Members
Founded in: 1989

45 **Construction Industry CPAs/Consultants Association**
15011 East Twilight View Drive
Fountain Hills, AZ 85268

480-836-0300; *Fax:* 480-836-0400
info@cicpac.com; www.cicpac.com
Social Media: Facebook, LinkedIn

Chris Iannuzzi, President
Ken Gardiner, President Elect
Jacquelyn Daenen, Vice President
Kathleen Baldwin, Secretary/Treasurer
John J. Corcoran, CPA, Executive Director
Founded in: 1989

46 **Federal Accounting Standards Advisory Board**
441 G St. NW
Mailstop 6H19
Washington, DC 20548

202-512-7350; *Fax:* 202-512-7366
fasab@fasab.gov; www.fasab.gov
Social Media: Twitter, LinkedIn

Tom Allen, Chairman
Wendy Payne, Executive Director
Robin Gillam, Assistant Director
Melissa Batchelor, Assistant Director
Domenic Savini, Assistant Director

Establishes accounting standards for financial reporting entities of the United States Government.
Founded in: 1990

47 **Federation of Schools of Accountancy**
220 Leigh Farm Road
Durham, NC 27707-8110

919-402-4825
mtarasi@aicpa.org; www.thefsa.org

Michael Roberts, President
Rebecca Shortridge, Vice President/ President Elect
Michael Akers, Secretary
Parveen Gupta, Treasurer
Robert Ricketts, Past President

Promotes and supports high-quality graduate accounting programs andachieves public trust in the accounting profession through leadership in supporting and shaping high quality accounting education.
169 Members
Founded in: 1978

48 **Federation of Tax Administrators**
444 N. Capitol Street NW
Suite 348
Washington, DC 20001

202-624-5890; *Fax:* 202-624-7888;
www.taxadmin.org

Linda Tanton, Chief Counsel
Verenda Smith, Deputy Director
Darrell Reeves, Office Manager
Gale Garriott, Executive Director
John Feldmann, Senior Manager of Compliance

A nonprofit corporation designed to improve the quality of state tax administration by providing services to state tax authorities and administrators. These services include research and information exchange, training, and intergovernmental and interstate coordination.
Founded in: 1937

49 **Financial Accounting Standards Board**
401 Merritt Boulevard
PO Box 5116
Norwalk, CT 06856-5116

203-847-0700; *Fax:* 203-849-9714
director@fasb.org; www.fasb.org
Social Media: Facebook, LinkedIn, RSS, YouTube

Russell G. Golden, Chairman
Jeffrey D. Mechanick, Assistant Director
Susan M Cosper, Technical Director
Suzanne Q. Bielstein, Director-Planning and Support
Matthew Esposito, Assistant Director

The mission of the FASB is to establish and improve standards of financial accounting and reporting that foster financial reporting by nongovernmental entities that provides decision-useful information to investors and other users of financial reports. That mission is accomplished through a comprehensive and independent process that encourages broad participation, objectively considers all stakeholder views, and is subject to oversight by the Financial Accounting Foundation's Board of Trustees.
Founded in: 1973

50 **Financial Executives International**
1250 Headquarters Plaza
West Tower, 7th Floor
Morristown, NJ 07960

973-765-1000; *Fax:* 973-765-1018
membership@financialexecutives.org;
www.financialexecutives.org
Social Media: Facebook, Twitter, LinkedIn, YouTube, Google+

Mitch Danaher, Chairman
Andrej Suskavcevic, President/CEO
Lili DeVita, VP & Chief Operating Officer
Paul Chase, VP and CFO
Jamie Cherkas, Executive Assistant to the CEO

FEI strives to be recognized globally as the leading organization for senior-level financial executives. Connects members through: interaction: providing local and international forums for connecting with peers, information: providing insight to assist with informed business decisions, influence: providing authoritative representation for members' interests, and integrity: providing the tools to advance the profession through ethical leadership.
15M Members
Founded in: 1931

51 **Financial Management Association International**
University of South Florida
4202 E Fowler Ave
BSN 3331
Tampa, FL 33620-5500

813-974-2084; *Fax:* 813-974-3318
fma@coba.usf.edu; www.fma.org
Social Media: Facebook, Twitter

Jay R. Ritter, President
David Denis, President Elect
Brad Barber, VP Program
Ronald Masulis, VP Global Services
Andrea J. Heuson, Secretary/Treasurer

Serving the global finance community by: Promoting the development of high-quality research that extends the frontier of financial knowledge; Promoting the understanding of basic and applied research and of sound financial practices; Enhancing the quality and relevance of education in finance; Providing opportunities for professional interaction between and among academics, practitioners, and students.
Founded in: 1970

52 **Financial Managers Society**
1 North LaSalle Street
Suite 3100
Chicago, IL 60602-4003

312-578-1300
800-275-4367; *Fax:* 312-578-1308
info@fmsinc.org; www.fmsinc.org
Social Media: Facebook, Twitter, LinkedIn

Sydney K. Garmong, CPA, Chairman
John Westwood, Vice Chairman
Dick Yingst, President
Tom King, Director, Professional Dev
Mark Loehrke, Editor/Writer

Provides service to financial personnel such as savings and loan financial officers, and to community commercial banks and credit unions.
Founded in: 1948

53 **Government Finance Officers Association**
203 N. LaSalle Street
Suite 2700
Chicago, IL 60601-1210

312-977-9700; *Fax:* 312-977-4806;
www.gfoa.org
Social Media: Facebook, Twitter, LinkedIn, YouTube

Heather A. Johnston, President
Marc Gonzales, President Elect
Jeffrey Esser, Executive Director/CEO
John Jurkash, Chief Financial Officer
Tami Garrett, Secretary

Represents public finance officials throughout the United States and Canada and promotes the professional management of governmental financial resources by indentifying, developing, and advancing fiscal strategies, policies, and practices for the public benefit.
Founded in: 1906

54 **Government Officers Finance Association**
203 North Lasalle Street
Suite 2700
Chicago, IL 60601-1210

312-977-9700; *Fax:* 312-977-4806;
www.gfoa.org
Social Media: Facebook, Twitter, LinkedIn, YouTube

Heather A. Johnston, President
Marc Gonzales, President-Elect
Jeffrey L. Esser, Executive Director CEO
John Jurkash, Chief Financial Officer
Tami Garrett, Secretary

The purpose of the Government Finance Officers Association is to enhance and promote the professional management of governments for the public benefit by identifying and developing financial policies and best practices and promoting their use through education, training, facilitation of member networking, and leadership.
16000 Members
Founded in: 1906

55 **Healthcare Financial Management Association**
3 Westbrook Corporate Center
Suite 7600
Westchester, IL 60154-5723

708-531-9600
800-252-4362; *Fax:* 708-531-0032
jfifer@hfma.org; www.hfma.org
Social Media: Facebook, Twitter, LinkedIn, YouTube

Joseph J. Fifer, FHFMA, CPA, President & Chief Executive Officer
Edwin P. Czopek, Executive Vice President & CFO
Susan Brenkus, VP, HR & Chapter Relations
Richard L. Gundling, VP, Healthcare Financial

Practices
Todd Nelson, VP, Education & Org Solutions

HFMA is the nation's leading membership organization for healthcare financial management executives and leaders. HFMA's vision is to be the indispensable resource for healthcare finance.
40000 Members
Founded in: 1950

56 Hospitality Financial and Technology Professionals
11709 Boulder Lane
Suite 110
Austin, TX 78726

512-249-5333
800-646-4387; *Fax:* 512-249-1533
Membership@hftp.org; www.hftp.org
Social Media: Facebook, Twitter, LinkedIn

Daniel N. Conti, Jr., CHAE, CAM, President
Arlene Ramirez, Vice President
Frank I Wolfe, Ex Officio
Lyle Worthington, CHTP, Treasurer
Jerry M. Trieber, Immediate Past President

HFTP is an international, professional association providing a global network, continuing education and resources to the hospitality, finance and technology communities.
4600 Members
Founded in: 1952

57 INPACT Americas
PO Box 495
Frederick, MD 21705-0495

301-694-8580; *Fax:* 301-694-5804
Mara@inpactam.org; www.inpactam.org

Reynold P. Cicalese, President
Mara Ambrose, Executive Director
Kevin R. Hessler, Treasurer / President-Elect
Loraine Koepenick, Coordinator of Member Services
James A. Ruzon, Immediate Past President

A nonprofit association focused on contributing to the profitability and success of North America's accounting and consulting firms through management and marketing programs and resources.

58 Information Resources Management Association
701 E Chocolate Ave
Suite 200
Hershey, PA 17033-1240

717-533-8845; *Fax:* 717-533-8661
member@irma-international.org;
www.irma-international.org

Jan Travers, Executive Director
Sherif Kamel, Communications Director
Lech Janczewski PhD, IRMA World Representative Director
Gerald Grant, IRMA Doctoral Symposium Director
Paul Chalekian, IRMA United States Representative

An international professional organization dedicated to advancing the concepts and practices of information resources management in modern organizations. The primary objective of IRMA is to assist organizations and professionals in enhancing the overall knowledge and understanding of effective information resource management in the early 21st century and beyond.

59 Information Systems Audit & Control Association (ISACA)
3701 Algonquin Rd
Suite 1010
Rolling Meadows, IL 60008-3124

847-253-1545; *Fax:* 847-253-1443
news@isaca.org; www.isaca.org
Social Media: Facebook, Twitter, LinkedIn, Google+

Tony Hayes, International President
Allan Boardman, International Vice President
Juan Luis Carselle, International Vice President
Rams,s Gallego, International Vice President
Theresa Grafenstine, International Vice President

With members in more than 160 countries, ISACA is a recognized worldwide leader in IT governance, control, security and assurance. Sponsors international conferences, publishes the thw ISACA Journal and develops international information systems auditing and control standards.
14000 Members
Founded in: 1969

60 Institute for Professionals in Taxation
600 Northpark Town Center
1200 Abernathy Rd., Suite L-2
Atlanta, GA 30328-1040

404-240-2300; *Fax:* 404-240-2315
website@ipt.org; www.ipt.org

Margaret C. Wilson, CMI, Esq., President
Chris G. Muntifering, CMI, First Vice President
Kellianne N. Nagy, CMI, CAE, Second Vice President
Margaret Dickson, Chief Financial Officer
Cass D. Vickers, Executive Director

A nonprofit educational association that provides educational programs, certifies, and establishes strict codes of conduct for state and local income, property, and sales.
4100+ Members
Founded in: 1976

61 Institute of Internal Auditors
247 Maitland Ave
Altamonte Springs, FL 32701-4201

407-937-1111; *Fax:* 407-937-1101
CustomerRelations@theiia.org
na.theiia.org
Social Media: Facebook, Twitter, LinkedIn, Auditchannel.tv

Lawrence J. Harrington, Chairman
Angela Witzany, Senior Vice Chairman of the Board
Frank M. O'Brien, CIA, QIAL, Vice Chairman - Research
Harold C. Silverman, Vice Chairman
Naohiro Mouri, CIA, Vice Chairman

Independent, objective assurance and consulting activity designed to add value to an organization's operations. It helps an organization accomplish its objectives by bringing a systematic, disciplined approach to evaluate and improve the effectiveness of risk management, control and governance processes. Representation from more than 100 countries.
18000 Members
Founded in: 1941

62 Institute of Management Accountants
10 Paragon Dr
Suite 1
Montvale, NJ 07645-1760

201-573-9000
800-638-4427; *Fax:* 201-474-1600
ima@imanet.org; www.imanet.org
Social Media: Facebook, Twitter, LinkedIn, YouTube

Benjamin R. Mulling, Chair
Jeffrey C. Thomson, President and CEO
Marc P. Palker, CMA, Chair-Elect
Joseph A. Vincent, CMA, Chair-Emeritus

Professional organization devoted exclusively to management accounting and financial management. Goals are to help members develop both personally and professionally, by means of education, certification and association with other business professionals.
70,00 Members
Founded in: 1919

63 Institute of Management and Administration
3 Bethesda Metro Center
Suite 250
Bethesda, MD 20814-5377

800-372-1033
703-341-3500; *Fax:* 800-253-0332
blawhelp@bna.com; www.bna.com
Social Media: Facebook, Twitter, LinkedIn, YouTube

Gregory C. McCaffery, CEO & President
Sue Martin, Chief Operating Officer
Paul Albergo, Bureau Chief
Joe Breda, EVP, Product
Daniel M. Fine, EVP, Strategy

An independent source of exclusive business management information for experienced senior and middle management proessionals.

64 Insurance Accounting & Systems Association, Inc.
3511 Shannon Road
Suite 160
Durham, NC 27707

919-489-0991; *Fax:* 919-489-1994
info@iasa.org; www.iasa.org
Social Media: Facebook, Twitter, LinkedIn, YouTube

Forrest Mills, Jr., Chairman
Tim Morgan, President
Joe Pomilia, Executive Director
Tom Ewbank, CFO
Carlos A Correa, CIO

A nonprofit, education association that strives to enhance the knowledge of insurance professionals and participants from similar organizations closely allied with the insurance industry by facilitating the exchange of ideas and information.

65 International Cost Estimating and Analysis Association
8221 Old Courthouse Rd
Suite 106
Vienna, VA 22182

703-938-5090; *Fax:* 703-938-5091
iceaa@iceaaonline.org; www.iceaaonline.org
Social Media: Facebook, Twitter

Paul R. Marston, President
Michael J. Thompson, Executive Vice President
Peter Braxton, VP, Professional Development
Greg Kiviat, Secretary
Bob Hunt, Treasurer

A non-profit organization dedicated to improving cost estimating and analysis in government and industry by enhancing the competence and achievements of its professional members
2015 Members
Founded in: 2012

66 International Federation of Accountants
529 Fifth Avenue
6th Floor
New York, NY 10017

212-286-9344; *Fax:* 212-286-9570
communications@ifac.org; www.ifac.org
Social Media: Facebook, Twitter, LinkedIn, YouTube

Olivia Kirtley, President
Rachel Grimes, Deputy President
Fayezul Choudhury, CEO
Russell Guthrie, Executive Director
Alta Prinsloo, Executive Director

IFAC is the global organization for the accountancy profession. It works with members and as-

sociates in 123 countries and jurisdictions to protect the public interest by encouraging high quality practices by the world's accountants.
173 Members
Founded in: 1977

67 **National Academy of Public Administration**
1600 K Street NW
Suite 400
Washington, DC 20006

202-347-3190; *Fax:* 202-223-0823
feedback@napawash.org; www.napawash.org
Social Media: Facebook, Twitter, LinkedIn, Vimeo

Robert J. Shea, Chair
Nancy R. Kingsbury, Vice Chair
Dan G Blair, President and CEO
B.J Reed, Secretary
Sallyanne Harper, Treasurer

An independent, nonprofit, and non-partisan organization that helpsthe Federal government address its critical management challenges through in-depth studies and analyses, advisory services and technical assistance, Congressional testimony, forums and conferences, and online stakeholder engagement.
800 Members
Founded in: 1967

68 **National Association of Black Accountants**
7474 Greenway Center Drive
Suite 1120
Greenbelt, MD 20770

301-474-6222
888-571-2939; *Fax:* 301-474-3114
customerservice@nabainc.org;
www.nabainc.org
Social Media: Facebook, Twitter, LinkedIn, YouTube

Jina Etienne, CPA, CGMA, President/CEO
Lauren Yost, SPHR, Chief Operating Officer
Kenneth E. Cooke, CPA, Chairman
Rhonda Johnson Adams, Controller
Stephen Schultz, Director of Conferences

Nationwide professional association with the primary purpose of developing, encouraging and serving as a resource for greater participation by African-Americans and other minorities in the accounting and finance professions.
Founded in: 1969

69 **National Association of Certified Valuators and Analysts (NACVA)**
5217 South State Street
Suite 400
Salt Lake City, UT 84107

801-486-0600
800-677-2009; *Fax:* 801-486-7500
nacva1@nacva.com; www.nacva.com
Social Media: Facebook, Twitter, YouTube

Terry A. Isom, WA, Chairman
Brien K. Jones, COO/EVP
Melissa Cardwell, Director of Project Management
Parnell Black, CEO
Pam Bailey, Executive Director

Global, professional association that supports the business valuation and litigation consulting disciplines within the CPA and professional communities. Along with its training and certification progams, NACVA offers a range of support services, reference materials, software, and customized databases to enahnce the professional capabilities and capacities of its members.
6500 Members
Founded in: 1990

70 **National Association of Computerized Tax Processors**
H&R Block
4400 Main Street
Kansas City, MO 64111

816-328-8485; *Fax:* 800-996-3526;
www.nactp.org
Social Media: Facebook

Rebecca McCaulley, President
Zeke Gikas, Vice President
Mary Zuroske, Treasurer
Vicki Massey, Secretary
Angela Camp, Webmaster

Nonprofit association that represents tax processing software and hardware developers, electronic filing processors, tax form publishers and tax processing service bureaus. The association promotes standards in tax processing and works closely with the Internal Revenue Service and state governments to promote efficient and effective tax filing.
14100 Members
Founded in: 1969

71 **National Association of Construction Auditors**
7305 Hancock Village Drive
Suite 519
Chesterfield, VA 23832

804-608-8703; *Fax:* 888-702-1059
info@thenaca.org; www.thenaca.org
Social Media: Facebook, Twitter, LinkedIn

Brian D. Felix, Chairman/Founder
Carl E. Hansen, Vice Chairman
Larry G. Baker, Secretary/Treasurer

Provides resources, information, and leadership for NACA members, their clients, and the public to ensure the highest standard of construction control environments possible.

72 **National Association of Enrolled Agents**
1730 Rhode Island Avenue, NW
Suite 400
Washington, DC 20036-3953

202-822-6232
855-880-6232; *Fax:* 202-822-6270
info@naea.org; www.naea.org
Social Media: Facebook, Twitter, LinkedIn, YouTube

Terry Durkin, EA, MBA, President
John L. Fiegel, CAE, Interim Executive Vice President
Katrina Holland, Director of Membership
Gloriel Rodriguez, Membership Coordinator
Maya English, Senior Program Coordinator

Members are individuals who are enrolled to represent taxpayers before the Internal Revenue Service. We advise, represent and prepare tax returns for individuals, partnerships, corporations, estates, trusts and any entities with tax reporting requirements.
11000 Members
Founded in: 1972

73 **National Association of Insurance and Financial Advisors**
2901 Telestar Court
Falls Church, VA 22042-1205

877-866-2432; www.naifa.org
Social Media: Facebook, Twitter, LinkedIn, YouTube

Jules O. Gaudreau, Jr., President
Paul R. Dougherty, President Elect
Keith M. Gillies, Secretary
Matthew S. Tassey, Treasurer
Kevin M. Mayeux, CAE, Chief Executive Officer

Serves and represents insurance and financial advisors, advocates for a positive legislative and regulatory environment, enhances business and professional skills, and promotes the ethical conduct of its members.
Founded in: 1890

74 **National Association of Mutual Insurance Companies**
3601 Vincennes Road
Indianapolis, IN 46268

317-875-5250; *Fax:* 317-879-8408;
www.namic.org
Social Media: Facebook, Twitter, LinkedIn, YouTube, RSS

Paul G. Stueven, PFMM, Chairman
Steve Linkous, Chairman Elect
Paul A. Ehlert, J.D., Vice Chairman
Charles Chamness, President/CEO
Christopher P. Taft, CIC, CPA, Secretary/Treasurer

The largest property/casualty insurance trade association that has educational and advocacy programs to promote public policy solutions that benefit policyholders and the NAMIC member companies that exist to serve them.
Founded in: 1920

75 **National Association of Personal Financial Advisors**
8700 W. Bryn Mawr Avenue
Suite 700N
Chicago, IL 60631

847-483-5400
888-333-6659; *Fax:* 847-483-5415
info@napfa.org; www.napfa.org
Social Media: Facebook, Twitter, LinkedIn, YouTube

Frank Moore, Chair
Tim Kober, Vice Chair
J. David Lewis, Treasurer
Geoffrey Brown, CEO
Chris Hale, Managing Editor

Professional association of Fee-Only financial advisors who advocate for client-focused financial planning with a Fee-Only compensation.
Founded in: 1983

76 **National Association of State Auditors, Comptrollers and Treasurers**
449 Lewis Hargett Circle
Suite 290
Lexington, KY 40503-3590

859-276-1147; *Fax:* 859-278-0507;
www.nasact.org

Calvin McKelvogue, President
Richard K. Ellis, First Vice President
Debbie Davenport, Second Vice President
R. Kinney Poynter, CPA, Executive Director
D. Clark Partridge, Secretary

Serves as the premier organization working to bring together state auditors, state comptrollers and state treasurers to cooperatively address government financial management issues.

77 **National Association of State Boards of Accountancy**
150 Fourth Ave. North
Ste. 700
Nashville, TN 37219-2417

615-880-4200; *Fax:* 615-880-4290
cpe@nasba.org
nasba.org
Social Media: Facebook, Twitter, LinkedIn, YouTube, RSS

Walter C. Davenport, Chairman
Donald H. Burkett, Vice Chairman
Ken L. Bishop, President/CEO
Laurie J. Tish, Secretary
E. Kent Smoll, Treasurer

Enhances the effectiveness and advances the common interests of theBoards of Accountancy by creating a forum for accounting regulators and practitioners to address issues relevant to the viability of the accounting profession.
Founded in: 1908

78 **National Association of State Budget Officers**
444 North Capitol Street NW
Suite 642
Washington, DC 20001
202-624-5382; *Fax:* 202-624-7745
nasbo-direct@nasbo.org; www.nasbo.org
Social Media: Facebook, Twitter, LinkedIn, Google+
Tom Mullaney, President
Margaret Kelly, President Elect
Scott D. Pattison, Executive Director
Stacey Mazer, Senior Staff Associate
Brian Sigritz, Director of State Fiscal Studies
Provides a range of publications, services, and knowledge-sharing opportunities for its members and others interested in state finance issues.

79 **National Association of Tax Professionals**
PO Box 8002
Appleton, WI 54912-8002
800-558-3402; *Fax:* 800-747-0001
natp@natptax.com; www.natptax.com
Social Media: Facebook, Twitter, LinkedIn, MySpace, YouTube
Jean Millerchip, EA, CFP, President
Kelly A. Nokleby, EA, Vice President
Gerard F. Cannito, CPA, CFP, Interim CEO
Matt Bone, CPA, Director of Finance/ Administration
Nancy Kasten, Director, Marketing & BD
NATP members have access to a wide range of the most reliable industry resources, which ultimately save time and money. Members enjoy the support and knowledge that comes from joining the only professional organization that is 100% devoted to tax expertise.
Founded in: 1979

80 **National CPA Health Care Advisors Association**
1801 West End Avenue
Suite 800
Nashville, TN 37203
615-373-9880
800-231-2524; *Fax:* 615-377-7092
info@hcaa.com; www.hcaa.com
Social Media: Twitter
Hal (Buzz) Coons, III, President
James White, Vice President
Brian Bourke, Secretary
William Rooney, Treasurer
Greg Papineau, Past President
HCAA is an association of CPA firms that provide services to health care providers beyond traditional compliance work. Members are admitted on a territorial exclusive basis, one member in each territory.

81 **National Conference of CPA Practitioners**
22 Jericho Turnpike
Suite 110
Mineola, NY 11501
516-333-8282
888-488-5400; *Fax:* 516-333-4099
go.nccpap.org/
Social Media: Facebook, Twitter, LinkedIn, Flickr, YouTube
NCCAP is a group of CPA professionals that allows small CPA firms and the sole practitioner to have a greater community impact and presence. This organization also gives back through its local chapters and at the national level.

82 **National Society of Accountants**
1330 Braddock Place
Suite 540
Alexandria, VA 22314-1574
703-549-6400
800-966-6679; *Fax:* 703-549-2984
members@nsacct.org; www.nsacct.org
Social Media: Facebook, Twitter, LinkedIn
Kathy R. Hettick, President
Alfred Giovetti, First Vice President
Brian Thompson, Second Vice President
John G. Ams, Executive Vice President
Jodi Goldberg, Vice President
Professional society of practicing accountants and tax practitioners that sponsors the Accreditation Council for Accountancy and Taxation and supports the National Society of Public Accountants Political Action Committee and NSPA Scholarship Foundation.
30000 Members
Founded in: 1945

83 **National Society of Accountants for Cooperatives**
136 South Keowee Street
Dayton, OH 45402
937-222-6707; *Fax:* 937-222-5794
info@nsacoop.org; www.nsacoop.org
Social Media: Facebook
Kim Fantaci, Executive Director
Carrie Parrish, President
Stanley Mitchell, CFO, Vice President
Jeff Roberts, Association Executive
Krista Saul, Client Accounting Manager
A professional society involved with the financial management and planning of cooperative business. It also provides educational programming, networking opportunities, and a directory of other professionals.
2000 Members
Founded in: 1936

84 **National Tax Association**
725 15th St. NW
Ste. 600
Washington, DC 20005-2109
202-737-3325; *Fax:* 202-737-7308
natltax@aol.com; www.ntanet.org
Alan Auerbach, President
Peter Brady, Vice President
Victoria Perry, Vice President
Charmaine J. Wright, Secretary
Eric Toder, Treasurer
A nonpartisan, nonpolitical educational association of tax professionals dedicatd to advancing understanding of the theory and practice of public finance.
Founded in: 1907

85 **PKF North America**
1745 N. Brown Road
Suite 350
Lawrenceville, GA 30043
770-279-4560; *Fax:* 770-279-4566
tsnyder@pkfna.com; www.pkfna.com
Social Media: Facebook, Twitter, LinkedIn, YouTube
Terry Snyder, President
Debbie Kuhl, Vice President
An association of legally independently-owned accounting and consulting firms with offices in North America and throughout the world through its affiliation with PKF International.
402 Members

86 **PrimeGlobal**
3235 Satellite Bvld Bldg. 400
Suite 300
Duluth, GA 30096
678-417-7730; *Fax:* 678-999-3959
kmead@primeglobal.net; www.primeglobal.net
Social Media: Facebook, Twitter, LinkedIn, YouTube
Michelle Arnold, Chief Regional Officer
Kevin Mead, President/CEO
Anne Hampson, CFO
Stacey Sanchez, Director, Global Events
Kathy Sautters, Communications Director
PrimeGlobal is an international affiliation of independent accounting and consulting firms.
200 Members
Founded in: 1978

87 **Society of Actuaries**
475 N Martingale Rd
Suite 600
Schaumburg, IL 60173-2252
847-706-3500
888-697-3900; *Fax:* 847-706-3599
customerservice@soa.org; www.soa.org
Social Media: Twitter, LinkedIn, YouTube
Greg Heidrich, Executive Director
Stacy Lin, Deputy Executive Director/CFO
Tiffany Berger, Director of Finance & Facilities
Richard Veys, General Counsel
Michael Boot, Managing Director of Sections
An educational, research and professional organization dedicated to serving the public and society members. The vision is for actuaries to be recognized as the leading professional in the modeling and management of risk.
17000 Members
Founded in: 1889
Mailing list available for rent: 17000 names at $300 per M

88 **Society of Financial Examiners**
12100 Sunset Hills Rd
Suite 130
Reston, VA 20190-3221
703-234-4140
800-787-7633; *Fax:* 888-436-8686
sofe@sofe.org; www.sofe.org
Social Media: Facebook, LinkedIn
Annette Knief, CFE, President
Joanne Campanelli, CFE, Vice President
Susan Bernard, CFE, AES, Vice President
Mark Murphy, CFE, Secretary
Colette Hogan Sawyer, CFE, Vice President
The Society of Financial Examiners is a professional society for examiners of insurance companies, banks, savings and loans, and credit unions.
1700+ Members
Founded in: 1973

89 **Society of Financial Service Professionals**
3803 West Chester Pike
Suite 225
Newtown Square, PA 19073-3239
610-526-2500
800-392-6900; *Fax:* 610-359-8115
info@societyoffsp.org; www.financialpro.org
Social Media: Facebook, Twitter, LinkedIn, YouTube, Flickr, RSS
Joseph E. Frack, Chief Executive Officer
Anthony R. Bartlett, President
James S. Aussem, President Elect
Elvin D. Turner, Secretary
Provides financial products and planning services in order to help individuals, families, and businesses achieve financial security.
9000 Members
Founded in: 1928
Mailing list available for rent

90 **The American Society of IRS Problem Solvers**
170 South River Road
Bedford, NH 3110

800-322-0933; www.irsproblemsolvers.com

A select group of licensed tax professionals located in communities across the United States to help taxpayers end individual and business IRS problems.

91 **The Professional Accounting Society of America**
www.thepasa.org

A professional organization designed specifically for entry-level and mid-level associates working at accounting firms across America.
Founded in: 2005

Newsletters

92 **AAA Report**
Association for Accounting Administration
136 S Keowee Street
Dayton, OH 45402

937-222-0030; *Fax:* 937-222-5794
aaainfo@cpaadmin.org; www.cpaadmin.org

Dennis Lemieux, President
Norman Saale, Vice President
Janine Zirrith, Secretary
Jim Fahey, Treasurer
Jane Johnson, Director of Education

Qarterly newsletter for the professional manager.
12 Pages
Frequency: Four/Year
Founded in: 1984
Printed in 4 colors

93 **AGA Today**
Association of Government Accountants
2208 Mount Vernon Ave
Alexandria, VA 22301-1314

703-562-0900
800-242-7211; *Fax:* 703-548-9367
agacgfm@agacgfm.org; www.agacgfm.org

Relmond Van Daniker, Executive Director
Evelyn Brown, National President

This publication acts as a clearinghouse for current government financial management information.
Frequency: Bi-Weekly
Circulation: 12,000

94 **ARCH**
Society of Actuaries
475 N Martingale Rd
Suite 600
Schaumburg, IL 60173-2252

847-706-3500; *Fax:* 847-706-3599
webmaster@soa.org; www.soa.org

Greg Heidrich, Executive Director
Stacy Lin, Deputy Executive Director/CFO
Tiffany Berger, Director of Finance
Richard Veys, General Counsel

ARCH is an informal communication providing current actuarial research to friends and members of the actuarial community. Its primary goal is the speedy dissemination of current thinking and aids to research.

95 **ASMC Connections**
415 N Alfred St
Alexandria, VA 22314-2269

703-549-0360
800-462-5637; *Fax:* 703-549-3181;
www.asmconline.org
Social Media: Facebook, Twitter, LinkedIn

Marilyn Thomas, President
Art Hagler, VP
Kathy Watern, VP
Nancy Phillips, Treasurer

Provides insight into defense financial news, chapter spot lights, and other society news.
19m+ Members
Founded in: 1948

96 **AWSCPA News**
American Woman's Society of CPAs
136 South Keowee Street
Dayton, OH 45402
937-222-1872
800-297-2721; *Fax:* 937-222-5794
info@awscpa.org; www.awscpa.org

Amy Knowles-Jones, President
Kelly Welter, President Elect
Alexandria Miller, Secretary/Treasurer
Cynthia Cox, VP - Member Services

Available electronically.
Frequency: Quarterly
Circulation: 1500
Founded in: 1933
Printed in 4 colors

97 **AcSEC Update**
American Institute of Certified Public Accountants
1211 Avenue of the Americas
Suite 6
New York, NY 10036-8701
212-596-6200; *Fax:* 212-596-6213
service@aicpa.org; www.aicpa.org
Social Media: Facebook, Twitter, LinkedIn

Barry C Melancon, CEO
Susan Coffey, Senior Vice President
Lawson Carmichael, SVP - Strategy, People, Innovation
Arleen Thomas, SVP - Mgmt Accounting

Provides information about recently issued AcSEC pronouncments and current AcSEC projects.
Frequency: 4 Times/Year
Founded in: 1887

98 **Accounting Alerts**
Grant Thornton
175 W Jackson Blvd
20th Floor
Chicago, IL 60604-2687

312-856-0001; *Fax:* 312-602-8099;
www.grantthornton.com
Social Media: Twitter

Stephen Chipman, CEO
Lou Grabowsky, COO
Russ Wieman, Chief Financial Officer

Periodic newsletter that highlights important accounting developments.
Founded in: 1924

99 **Accounting Education News**
American Accounting Association
5717 Bessie Dr
Sarasota, FL 34233-2399

941-921-7747; *Fax:* 941-923-4093
info@aaahq.org
aaahq.org

Tracey Sutherland, Executive Director
Deirdre Harris, Publication Contact
Diane Hazard, Publications Director

Information on industry development and associations, the newsletter is only available to members.
8600 Members
Frequency: Quarterly
Circulation: 8500
Founded in: 1916
Printed in 3 colors on matte stock

100 **Accounting Historians Notebook**
Academy of Accounting Historians
10900 Euclid Avenue
Cleveland, OH 44106-7235

216-368-2058; *Fax:* 216-368-6244
acchistory@case.edu; www.aahhq.org

Joanne Cross, President
Robert Colson, President Elect
Yvette Lazdowski, VP, Communications
Robert Colson, VP Communications
Stephanie Moussalli, Secretary

Published by the Academy of Accounting Historians, the Notebook provides information about the Academy, its members, conference, and publications. Subscription to the semi-annual publication is included in membership to the Academy.
600 Members
8 Pages
Frequency: Semi-Annual
Founded in: 1973
Printed in one color

101 **Accounting Office Management & Administration Report**
Institute of Management and Administration
3 Bethesda Metro Center
Suite 250
Bethesda, MD 20814-5377

800-372-1033
703-341-3500; *Fax:* 800-253-0332
customercare@bna.com; www.ioma.com

Designed for use by anyone responsible for the day-to-day management of a CPA firm. Provides actionable information that readers can use to manage their firms efficiently and profitably.
Cost: $469.00
Frequency: Monthly
Founded in: 1984

102 **Accounting and Auditing Update Service**
Thomson Reuters
2395 Midway Rd
Carrollton, TX 75006
817-332-3709
800-431-9025; *Fax:* 888-216-1929
trta.lei-support@thomsonreuters.com;
www.ria.thomsonreuters.com

Elaine Yadlon, Plant Manager
Thomas H Glocer, CEO & Director
Robert D Daleo, Chief Financial Officer
Kelli Crane, Senior Vice President & CIO

Analyzes FASB and AICPA pronouncements.
Cost: $465.00
Frequency: Bi-Weekly
Founded in: 1935

103 **Attorney/CPA Newsletter**
American Association of Attorney-CPAs
8647 Richmond Highway
Suite 639
Alexandria, VA 22309

703-352-8064
888-288-9272; *Fax:* 703-352-8073
info@attorney-cpa.com;
www.attorney-cpa.com

Robert Driegert, President
Domenick Lioce, President Elect
Joseph Cordell, Treasurer
John Pramberg, Secretary

To promote the study and understanding of law and accounting and those related professions.
Frequency: Quarterly
Founded in: 1964

104 **Behavioral Research in Accounting**
American Accounting Association

5717 Bessie Dr
Sarasota, FL 34233

941-921-7747; *Fax:* 941-923-4093
info@aaahq.org; www.aaahq.org

Tracey Sutherland, Executive Director
Julie Smith David, CIO
Diane Ledger, Director of Finance

To promote the wide dissemination of the results of systematic scholarly inquiries into the broad field of accounting.
Cost: $20.00
Frequency: Twice per Year
Circulation: 1400

105 **BusIndNews**
American Institute of Certified Public Accountants
1211 Avenue of the Americas
Suite 6
New York, NY 10036-8701

212-596-6200; *Fax:* 212-596-6213
service@aicpa.org; www.aicpa.org
Social Media: Facebook, Twitter, LinkedIn

Barry C Melancon, CEO
Susan Coffey, Senior Vice President
Lawson Carmichael, SVP - Strategy
Arleen Thomas, SVP - Mgmt Accounting

The AICPA e-newsletter for members in business and industry, contains timely information on current issues and developments in areas related to business and industry.
Frequency: Monthly
Founded in: 1887

106 **Business Valuation Monitor**
Grant Thornton
175 W Jackson Blvd
20th Floor
Chicago, IL 60604-2687

312-856-0001; *Fax:* 312-602-8099;
www.grantthornton.com
Social Media: Twitter, LinkedIn

Stephen Chipman, CEO
Lou Grabowsky, COO
Russ Wieman, CFO

Newsletter covering value creation perspectives for corporate executives and the investment community in the areas of financial reporting, transaction support, damage calculations in disputes, intellectual property, bankruptcy proceedings and corporate tax planning.
Founded in: 1924

107 **CAE Bulletin**
Institute of Internal Auditors
247 Maitland Ave
Altamonte Spgs, FL 32701-4201

407-830-7600; *Fax:* 407-937-1101
custserv@theiia.org; www.theiia.org

J. Michael Pepper, Chairman
Carolyn Saint, Senior Vice President
John Wxzelaki, Vice Chairman - Finance/Security

Newsletter that alerts members to news, guidance and information that helps professionals become as effective as possible in their jobs.
Frequency: Twice Monthly

108 **CPA Insider**
American Institute of Certified Public Accountants
1211 Avenue of the Americas
Suite 6
New York, NY 10036-8701
212-596-6200; *Fax:* 212-596-6213
service@aicpa.org; www.aicpa.org
Social Media: Facebook, Twitter, LinkedIn

Barry C Melancon, CEO
Susan Coffey, Senior Vice President
Lawson Carmichael, SVP - Strategy
Arleen Thomas, SVP - Mgmt Accounting

Delivers need-to-know news of the profession, hard-hitting commentary, recommended products and professional development resources.
Frequency: Weekly
Founded in: 1887

109 **Chapter Weekly**
National Association of Tax Professionals
PO Box 8002
Appleton, WI 54912-8002

800-558-3402; *Fax:* 800-747-0001
natp@natptax.com; www.natptax.com
Social Media: Facebook, Twitter, MySpace

Jo Ann Schoen, President
Jean Millerchip, Vice President
Gerard Cannito, Treasurer
Patricia M. McNeer, Secretary

E-Newsletter features Chapter events and updates.
Frequency: Weekly

110 **Client Information Bulletin**
WPI Communications
55 Morris Ave
Springfield, NJ 07081-1422

973-467-8700
800-323-4995; *Fax:* 973-467-0368
info@wpicommunications.com;
www.wpicomm.com

Steve Klinghoffer, Owner
Lori Klinghoffer, Executive Vice President
Marilyn Lang, Circulation Manager
Sandy McMurray, Sales Manager
Anna Cooley, Managing Editor

This monthly newsletter covers important new tax developments, general business principles, financial planning, estate planning and other related topics.
4 Pages
Frequency: Monthly
Founded in: 1952
Printed in 2 colors

111 **Controller's Report**
Institute of Management and Administration
3 Bethesda Metro Center
Suite 250
Bethesda, MD 20814-5377

800-372-1033
7033413500; *Fax:* 800-253-0332
customercare@bna.com; www.ioma.com

Aimed at corporate controllers in companies of all sizes.
Cost: $437.00
20 Pages
Frequency: Monthly
Founded in: 1984
Printed in 2 colors

112 **Controller's Tax Letter**
Institute of Management and Administration
3 Bethesda Metro Center
Suite 250
Bethesda, MD 20814-5377

800-372-1033
7033413500; *Fax:* 800-253-0332
customercare@bna.com; www.ioma.com

Focuses on the tax implications of business decisions and provides readers in corporate finance/accounting details on recently settled cases from US Tax Court, with full citations for those who want to know more. CTL also shows controllers, accounting managers and tax managers the effects of business decisions as they relate to a company's strategic planning for new sales efforts, expanding their overseas or foreign presence, and exemptions and deductions available where laws have changed.
Cost: $259.00
Frequency: Monthly
Founded in: 1984

113 **Controllers Update**
Institute of Certified Management Accountants
10 Paragon Drive
Suite 1
Montvale, NJ 07645-1718

800-638-4427; *Fax:* 201-474-1600
ima@imanet.org; www.imanet.org
Social Media: Facebook, Twitter, LinkedIn

Jeffrey C. Thomson, President and CEO
Brian L. McGuire, Chair
John C. Macaulay, Chair-Elect
Sandra B. Richtermeyer, Chair-Emeritus

Monthly newsletter with useful information for chief financial officers, plant controllers and financial management personnel.
Frequency: Monthly
Circulation: 2,200

114 **Corporate Finance Insider**
American Institute of Certified Public Accountants
1211 Avenue of the Americas
Suite 6
New York, NY 10036-8701

212-596-6200; *Fax:* 212-596-6213
service@aicpa.org; www.aicpa.org
Social Media: Facebook, Twitter, LinkedIn

Barry C Melancon, CEO
Susan Coffey, Senior Vice President
Lawson Carmichael, SVP - Strategy
Arleen Thomas, SVP - Mgmt Accounting

Covers financial management and corporate compliance issues, nationwide job opportunities, plus career advancement strategies from the experts, self assessment tools, compensation research and hiring trends for those who recruit, train and manage CPAs and other financial professionals.
Frequency: Monthly
Founded in: 1887

115 **Corporate Taxation Insider**
American Institute of Certified Public Accountants
1211 Avenue of the Americas
Suite 6
New York, NY 10036-8701

212-596-6200; *Fax:* 212-596-6213
service@aicpa.org; www.aicpa.org
Social Media: Facebook, Twitter, LinkedIn

Barry C Melancon, CEO
Susan Coffey, Senior Vice President
Lawson Carmichael, SVP - Strategy
Arleen Thomas, SVP - Mgmt Accounting

Delivers need-to-know news of the profession, hard-hitting commentary, recommended products and professional development resources to its subscribers.
Frequency: Monthly
Founded in: 1887

116 **Currency**
Grant Thornton
175 W Jackson Blvd
20th Floor
Chicago, IL 60604-2687

312-856-0001; *Fax:* 312-602-8099;
www.grantthornton.com
Social Media: Twitter, LinkedIn

Stephen Chipman, CEO
Lou Grabowsky, COO
Russ Wieman, Chief Financial Officer

Electronic newsletter for bank executives that covers issues and trends in the financial institutions industry.
Founded in: 1924

117 E@lert
National Association of Enrolled Agents
1120 Connecticut Avenue NW
Suite 460
Washington, DC 20036-3922
202-822-6232; *Fax:* 202-822-6270
info@naea.org; www.naea.org
Social Media: Facebook, Twitter, LinkedIn
Frank I Degen, President
Betsey Buckingham, president-elect
Robert Reedy, Treasurer/Secretary
Newsletter that provides brief updates on the latest tax news affecting clients and practices.
11000 Members

118 FSA Times
Institute of Internal Auditors
247 Maitland Ave
Altamonte Spgs, FL 32701-4201
407-937-1100; *Fax:* 407-937-1101
custserv@theiia.org; www.theiia.org
J. Michael Pepper, Chairman
Carolyn Saint, Senior Vice President
John Wxzelaki, Vice Chairman - Finance/Security
Quarterly publication provided to members of the Institute of Internal Auditors' Financial Services Auditor Group to support knowledge development for financial services auditors.
Frequency: Quarterly

119 Financial Bulletin
Grant Thornton
175 W Jackson Blvd
20th Floor
Chicago, IL 60604-2687
312-856-0001; *Fax:* 312-602-8099;
www.grantthornton.com
Social Media: Twitter, LinkedIn
Stephen Chipman, CEO
Lou Grabowsky, COO
Russ Wieman, Chief Financial Officer
Electronic publication that covers regulations and developments affecting financial services industry.
Founded in: 1924

120 Focus on Forensics
Grant Thornton
175 W Jackson Blvd
20th Floor
Chicago, IL 60604-2687
312-856-0001; *Fax:* 312-602-8099;
www.grantthornton.com
Social Media: Twitter, LinkedIn
Stephen Chipman, CEO
Lou Grabowsky, COO
Russ Wieman, Chief Financial Officer
Periodic newsletter providing valuable forensic accounting insights into some of the most complex and critical challenges that businesses and legal counsel face today.
Founded in: 1924

121 General Ledger
American Institute of Professional Bookkeepers
6001 Montrose Rd
Suite 500
Rockville, MD 20852-4873
800-622-0121; *Fax:* 800-541-0066
info@aipb.org; www.aipb.org
Stan Hartman, Owner
The latest bookkeeping, accounting and tax news, keep current on bookkeeping and reporting techniques, time and money-saving charts, practical tips, sharpen skills with a Bookkeeper's Quiz in every issue, and monthly and annual rates and numbers are included.
Frequency: Monthly
Circulation: 30000
Founded in: 1987
Mailing list available for rent

122 Government Accounting and Auditing Update
Thomson Reuters
2395 Midway Rd
Carrollton, TX 75006
817-332-3709
800-431-9025; *Fax:* 888-216-1929
trta.lei-support@thomsonreuters.com;
www.ria.thomsonreuters.com
Elaine Yadlon, Plant Manager
Thomas H Glocer, CEO & Director
Robert D Daleo, Chief Financial Officer
Kelli Crane, Senior Vice President & CIO
Includes changes taking place in government accounting and financial reporting, analysis of the latest developments, explanations of how they affect work and practical guidance on adapting to these changes.
Cost: $370.00
8 Pages
Frequency: Monthly
Founded in: 1935
Mailing list available for rent: 5000 names
Printed in 2 colors on glossy stock

123 Government Financial Management TOPICS
2208 Mount Vernon Avenue
Alexandria, VA 22301
703-684-6931
800-AGA-7211; *Fax:* 703-548-9367
agacgfm@agacgfm.org; www.agacgfm.org
Social Media: Facebook, Twitter, LinkedIn, GovLoop
Evelyn A. Brown, President
Relmond P Van Daniker, Executive Director
An AGA member service, designed to give national exposure to chapter events, community service projects and member accomplishments while offering the most up-to-date Association news.
15000 Members
Frequency: Bi-Weekly
Founded in: 1950
Mailing list available for rent: 18,000 names

124 Governmental Accounting Standards Board Action Report
Governmental Accounting Standards Board
401 Merritt 7
PO Box 5116
Norwalk, CT 06856-5116
203-847-0700; *Fax:* 203-849-9714
webmaster@gasb.org; www.gasb.org
Social Media: Twitter, LinkedIn
David A. Vaudt, Chairman
David Bean, Director Research/Technical Active
Action Report newsletter that includes developments in the standards-setting process and the status of technical projects.
Cost: $155.00
Frequency: Monthly

125 IIA Insight
Institute of Internal Auditors
247 Maitland Ave
Altamonte Spgs, FL 32701-4201
407-937-1100; *Fax:* 407-937-1101
custserv@theiia.org; www.theiia.org
Social Media: Facebook, Twitter, LinkedIn
J. Michael Pepper, Chairman
Carolyn Saint, Senior Vice President
John Wxzelaki, Vice Chairman - Finance/Security
Member newsletter designed to instruct members on using IIA services, products, and training opportunities.
Frequency: Monthly

126 IIA Today
Institute of Internal Auditors
247 Maitland Ave
Altamonte Spgs, FL 32701-4201
407-830-7600; *Fax:* 407-937-1101
custserv@theiia.org; www.theiia.org
J. Michael Pepper, Chairman
Carolyn Saint, Senior Vice President
John Wxzelaki, Vice Chairman - Finance/Security
Provides relevent and timely information on internal audit news. In print and electronic formats available.
Frequency: Twice Monthly

127 IMA Educational Case Journal
Institute of Management Accountants
10 Paragon Dr
Suite 1
Montvale, NJ 07645-1760
800-638-4427; *Fax:* 201-474-1600
ima@imanet.org; www.imanet.org
Social Media: Facebook, Twitter, LinkedIn
Jeffrey C. Thomson, President and CEO
Brian L. McGuire, Chair
John C. Macaulay, Chair-Elect
Sandra B. Richtermeyer, Chair-Emeritus
The journal publishes teaching cases and research related to case writing or teaching with cases in management accounting and related fields.
Cost: $250.00
60000 Members
Frequency: Quarterly

128 IOMA's Report on Salary Surveys
Institute of Management and Administration
3 Bethesda Metro Center
Suite 250
Bethesda, MD 20814-5377
800-372-1033
7033413500; *Fax:* 800-253-0332
customercare@bna.com; www.ioma.com
Analyzes data from major salary surveys released during the year by the biggest compensation survey companies, WorldatWork, SHRM, state HR societies, and the Big Four accounting firms, to give readers an overview of those expensive, hard-to-manage services.
Cost: $445.00
Founded in: 1984

129 Infoline
Hospitality Financial & Technology Professionals
11709 Boulder Lane
Suite 110
Austin, TX 78726-1832
512-249-5333
800-646-4387; *Fax:* 512-249-1533
membership@hftp.org; www.hftp.org
Frank I Wolfe, Executive VP/CEO
Lucinda Hart, COO
Thomas Atzenhofer, CFO
Eliza Selig, Director of Communications
Provides information regarding chapter and officer activities.
Frequency: Monthly
Founded in: 1952

130 Information Management Newsletter
Information Resources Management Association

701 E Chocolate Ave
Suite 200
Hershey, PA 17033-1240

717-533-8845; *Fax:* 717-533-8861
member@irma-international.org;
www.irma-international.org

Jan Travers, Executive Director
Sherif Kamel, Communications Director
Lech Janczewski PhD, IRMA World Representative Director
Gerald Grant, IRMA Doctoral Symposium Director
Paul Chalekian, IRMA United States Representative

This practical, informative newsletter is a leading publication of information technology resources management. Short, concise articles give objective, professional views of newly emerging technologies and trends.
Cost: $60.00
Frequency: Semi-Annually
ISSN: 1080-286X

131 **Internal Auditing Report**
Thomson Reuters
2395 Midway Rd
Carrollton, TX 75006

817-332-3709
800-431-9025; *Fax:* 888-216-1929
trta.lei-support@thomsonreuters.com;
www.ria.thomsonreuters.com

Elaine Yadlon, Plant Manager
Thomas H Glocer, CEO & Director
Robert D Daleo, Chief Financial Officer
Kelli Crane, Senior Vice President & CIO

Perfect for keeping up to date on new auditing standards and developments. Offers guidance on managing internal auditing departments, covers new audit technology, offers new audit techniques used by successful audit management practices, and provides practitioner level feedback on current Institute of Internal Auditors standards.
Cost: $320.00
12 Pages
Frequency: Six Times/Year
Circulation: 5000
Founded in: 1935
Mailing list available for rent: 5000 names
Printed in 2 colors on glossy stock

132 **Jacobs Report**
Offshore Press
PO Box 8137
Prairie Village, KS 66208-2824

913-362-9667
888-516-3177; *Fax:* 913-432-7174
jacobs@offshorepress.com;
www.offshorepress.com

Vernon K Jacobs, President

Contains International tax news.
Frequency: Daily
Founded in: 1981

133 **Letter Ruling Review**
Tax Analysts
400 S Maple Ave
Suite 400
Falls Church, VA 22046-4245

703-533-4400
800-955-2444; *Fax:* 703-533-4444
cservice@tax.org; www.taxanalysts.com

Chris Bergin, CEO
Martin Lobel, Chairman of the Board

Publication analyzes significant private letter rulings issued by the Internal Revenue Service during the month.
4 Pages
Frequency: Monthly
Founded in: 1970
Printed in one color on matte stock

134 **Management & Administration Report (ADMAR)**
Institute of Management and Administration
3 Bethesda Metro Center
Suite 250
Bethesda, MD 20814-5377

800-372-1033
7033413500; *Fax:* 800-253-0332
customercare@bna.com; www.ioma.com

How to manage corporate accounting departments more effectively, boost staff productivity, reduce operation costs and adopt new systems and technology, and take charge of your dealings with auditors and lenders.
Founded in: 1984

135 **Managing Accounts Payable**
Institute of Management and Administration
3 Bethesda Metro Center
Suite 250
Bethesda, MD 20814-5377

800-372-1033
7033413500; *Fax:* 800-253-0332
customercare@bna.com; www.ioma.com

The source of information for accounts payable and those responsible for the function. Each issue contains 5-7 articles, 6-10 short news clips, a manager's forum on the back page and calendar of upcoming seminars and conferences.
Cost: $419.00
Frequency: Monthly
Founded in: 1984

136 **Managing the General Ledger**
Institute of Management and Administration
3 Bethesda Metro Center
Suite 250
Bethesda, MD 20814-5377

800-372-1033
7033413500; *Fax:* 800-253-0332
customercare@bna.com; www.ioma.com

Aimed at controllers and corporate accounting managers and shows the most current techniques for efficient monthly closings and AICPA approved methods for general ledger entries.
Cost: $308.14
Frequency: Monthly
Founded in: 1984

137 **NSPA Washington Reporter**
National Society of Public Accountants
1010 N Fairfax St
Alexandria, VA 22314-1574

703-549-6400
800-966-6679; *Fax:* 703-549-2984
members@nsacct.org; www.nsacct.org
Social Media: Facebook, Twitter, LinkedIn

Harlan Rose, President
Steven Hanson, First Vice President
Marilyn Niwao, Second Vice President
Brian Thompson, Secretary-Treasurer

Coverage of NSPA activity with the government, and news on members in various states.
Frequency: Monthly
Founded in: 1955

138 **National Estimator**
Society of Cost Estimating and Analysis
8221 Old Courthouse Rd
Suite 106
Vienna, VA 22182

703-938-5090; *Fax:* 703-938-5091
scea@sceaonline.org; www.sceaonline.org

Erin Whittaker, Executive Director
Sharon Burger, Certification Program Admin
Brittany Walker, Membership Coordinator
Debra Lehman, Treasurer

Information on cost estimating and analysis, earned value management, budget and financial analysis, and program control.
Cost: $55.00
2015 Members
Frequency: Biannual
Founded in: 1990

139 **National Newsletter**
415 N Alfred St
Alexandria, VA 22314-2269

703-549-0360
800-462-5637; *Fax:* 703-549-3181;
www.asmconline.org
Social Media: Facebook, Twitter, LinkedIn

Marilyn Thomas, President
Art Hagler, VP
Kathy Watern, VP
Nancy Phillips, Treasurer

Focuses on society information such as training, events, and other issues related to supporting the membership of ASMC.
19m+ Members
Frequency: Monthly
Founded in: 1948

140 **New Developments Summary**
Grant Thornton
175 W Jackson Blvd
20th Floor
Chicago, IL 60604-2687

312-856-0001; *Fax:* 312-602-8099;
www.grantthornton.com
Social Media: Twitter, LinkedIn

Stephen Chipman, CEO
Lou Grabowsky, COO
Russ Wieman, Chief Financial Officer

Periodic bulletin providing a detailed summary of a recent technical development or accounting pronouncement.
Founded in: 1924

141 **News Plus**
National Association of Black Accountants
7474 Greenway Center Dr
Suite 1120
Greenbelt, MD 20770-3504

301-474-6222
888-571-2939; *Fax:* 301-474-3114
newsplus@nabainc.org; www.nabainc.org
Social Media: Facebook, Twitter, LinkedIn, YouTube

Calvin Harris Jr., President/CEO
Guillermo Hysaw, Executive Director and COO
Veda Stanley, Executive Vice President
Sheila Taylor-Clark, CPA
Ronald Walker, Chairman, Division of Firms

Updates on accounting proposals and regulations.
Cost: $20.00
Frequency: Quarterly
Founded in: 1969

142 **Nonprofit Report: Accounting, Taxation Management**
Thomson Reuters
2395 Midway Rd
Carrollton, TX 75006

817-332-3709
800-431-9025; *Fax:* 888-216-1929
trta.lei-support@thomsonreuters.com;
www.ria.thomsonreuters.com

Elaine Yadlon, Plant Manager
Thomas H Glocer, CEO & Director
Robert D Daleo, Chief Financial Officer
Kelli Crane, Senior Vice President & CIO

Offers CPAs with nonprofit clients, and professionals working in the nonprofit sector. A practical, timely look at today's key nonprofit issues, including IRS rulings and pronouncements, AICPA changes and legislation governing the financial management of most nonprofit organiza-

tions.
Cost: $250.00
Frequency: Monthly
Founded in: 1935
Mailing list available for rent
Printed in 2 colors on glossy stock

143 **On the Horizon**
Grant Thornton
175 W Jackson Blvd
20th Floor
Chicago, IL 60604-2687
312-856-0001; *Fax:* 312-602-8099;
www.grantthornton.com
Social Media: Twitter, LinkedIn
Stephen Chipman, CEO
Lou Grabowsky, COO
Russ Wieman, Chief Financial Officer
Updates on announcements, meetings and proposals from the accounting standards-setting bodies and industry regulators.
Frequency: Weekly
Founded in: 1924

144 **Partner's Report for Law Firm Owners**
Institute of Management and Administration
3 Bethesda Metro Center
Suite 250
Bethesda, MD 20814-5377
800-372-1033
703-341-3500; *Fax:* 800-253-0332
customercare@bna.com; www.ioma.com
Keeps partners up-to-date on salary guidelines and benefits, as well as provides the reader with tips on increasing profit margins and exercising leadership skills.
Cost: $464.00
Frequency: Monthly
Founded in: 1984

145 **PayState Update**
American Payroll Association
660 North Main Avenue
Suite 100
San Antonio, TX 78205-1710
210-226-4600; *Fax:* 210-226-4027
apa@americanpayroll.org;
www.americanpayroll.org
Social Media: Facebook, Twitter, LinkedIn
association e-newsletter offering members news on updates in state and local payroll compliance.

146 **Payroll Currently**
American Payroll Association
660 N Main Ave
Suite 100
San Antonio, TX 78205-1217
210-226-4600; *Fax:* 210-226-4027
apamail@mindspring.com; www.payroll.org
Social Media: Facebook, Twitter, LinkedIn
Daniel Maddux, President
Member newsletter containing breaking payroll compliance news and updates.
Frequency: Bi-Weekly

147 **Payroll Manager's Report**
Institute of Management and Administration
3 Bethesda Metro Center
Suite 250
Bethesda, MD 20814-5377
800-372-1033
703-341-3500; *Fax:* 800-253-0332;
www.ioma.com
Written for payroll practitioners working with small and large employers. Provides how-to information on managing a payroll department cost effectively and service-efficiently.
Cost: $399.00
Frequency: Monthly
Founded in: 1984

148 **Payroll Practitioner's Monthly**
Institute of Management and Administration
3 Bethesda Metro Center
Suite 250
Bethesda, MD 20814-5377
800-372-1033
703-341-3500; *Fax:* 800-253-0332
customercare@bna.com; www.ioma.com
Shows payroll professionals what they need to do and how to do it when it comes to the many rules, regulations and laws they must follow to prepare and distribute a corporate payroll.
Cost: $399.00
16 Pages
Frequency: Monthly
Founded in: 1984

149 **Payroll Tax Alert**
Institute of Management and Administration
3 Bethesda Metro Center
Suite 250
Bethesda, MD 20814-5377
800-372-1033
703-341-3500; *Fax:* 800-253-0332
customercare@bna.com; www.ioma.com
Used by payroll managers and professionals in accounting or human resources. Provides quick, hard hitting updates on changes to federal and state payroll policy (wage-hour rules, industrial orders, new posting requirements and tax issues) from every agency that has a hand in corporate payroll & benefits administration.
Cost: $240.00
Frequency: Monthly
Circulation: 2000
Founded in: 1984

150 **Pocket MBA**
Practising Law Institute
810 Seventh Avenue
21st Floor
New York, NY 10019-5818
212-824-5700
800-260-4754; *Fax:* 212-581-4670
info@pli.edu; www.pli.edu
Social Media: Facebook, Twitter
Victor J Rubino, President
Nickola Francis, Subscription Manager
Provides information every lawyer needs to know about business and finance.
Cost: $1295.00
Frequency: Weekly
Founded in: 1933

151 **Polaris International Newsletter**
Polaris International
9200 South Dadeland Boulevard
Suite 510
Miami, FL 33156
305-670-0580; *Fax:* 305-670-3818;
www.accountants.org
Social Media: Facebook, Twitter, LinkedIn, Youtube
Kevin Mead, President
Lydie Jubin, Chief Regional Officer
Anne Hampson, CFO
Pedro Figueroa, Administrative Manager
Newsletter containing information regarding events, activities and recent news for accounting and consulting firms.
Frequency: Quarterly
Founded in: 1978

152 **Practicing CPA**
American Institute of Certified Public Accountants
1211 Avenue of the Americas
Suite 6
New York, NY 10036-8701
212-596-6200; *Fax:* 212-596-6213
service@aicpa.org; www.aicpa.org
Social Media: Facebook, Twitter, LinkedIn
Barry C Melancon, CEO
Susan Coffey, Senior Vice President
Lawson Carmichael, SVP - Strategy
Arleen Thomas, SVP - Mgmt Accounting
Articles on development and management of firms.
Frequency: Monthly
Founded in: 1887

153 **Public Accounting Desk Book**
Strafford Publications
590 Dutch Valley Road
PO Box 13729
Atlanta, GA 30324-0729
404-881-1141
800-926-7926; *Fax:* 404-881-0074
customerservice@straffordpub.com;
www.straffordpub.com
Social Media: Twitter
Richard Ossoff, President
Jon McKenna, Executive Editor
Provides public accounting firms with authoritative news and analysis of developments in the accounting profession today and emerging trends for the future. Also reports SEC auditor changes, mergers, acquisitions, personnel changes and related events.
Cost: $39.00
Frequency: Annual
ISSN: 0161-309X
Founded in: 1984

154 **Public Accounting Report**
CCH
2700 Lake Cook Rd
Riverwoods, IL 60015-3867
847-940-4600
800-835-5224; *Fax:* 773-866-3095;
www.cch.com
Mike Sabbatis, President
Douglas M Winterrose, Vice President & CFO
Jim Bryant, EVP Software Products
Written for public accounting firm partners and professionals, it is renowned for its straight reporting and analysis of the news, developments, and trends that have influenced the profession for more than 20 years.
Cost: $449.00
8 Pages
Frequency: Bi-Weekly

155 **SEC Accounting Report**
Thomson Reuters
2395 Midway Rd
Carrollton, TX 75006
817-332-3709
800-431-9025; *Fax:* 888-216-1929
trta.lei-support@thomsonreuters.com;
www.ria.thomsonreuters.com
Elaine Yadlon, Plant Manager
Thomas H Glocer, CEO & Director
Robert D Daleo, Chief Financial Officer
Kelli Crane, Senior Vice President & CIO
For senior executives needing monthly news and insights on emerging SEC issues. The SEC Accounting Report can help you to understand SEC changes and their subsequent compliance requirements.
Cost: $365.00
8 Pages
Frequency: Monthly
Circulation: 5000
Founded in: 1935
Mailing list available for rent: 5000 names
Printed in 2 colors on glossy stock

156 Strategic TechNotes
Institute of Management Accountants
10 Paragon Dr
Suite 1
Montvale, NJ 07645-1774

201-573-9000
800-638-4427; *Fax:* 201-474-1600
ima@imanet.org; www.imanet.org
Social Media: Facebook, Twitter, LinkedIn

Jeffrey C. Thomson, President and CEO
Brian L. McGuire, Chair
John C. Macaulay, Chair-Elect
Sandra B. Richtermeyer, Chair-Emeritus

Award-winning technology e-newsletter designed for IMA members and others who want a look into the world of today's and tomorrow's technological trends and tools.
60000 Members
Frequency: 2 Times/Month

157 TAXPRO Monthly
National Association of Tax Professionals
PO Box 8002
Appleton, WI 54912-8002

800-558-3402; *Fax:* 800-747-0001
natp@natptax.com; www.natptax.com
Social Media: Facebook, Twitter, MySpace

Jo Ann Schoen, President
Jean Millerchip, Vice President
Gerard Cannito, Treasurer
Patricia M. McNeer, Secretary
Kathy Stanek, CEO

Covers the latest news in detail and explores critical new developments in federal tax laws while providing practical applications of tax laws and procedures.
Frequency: Monthly

158 TAXPRO Weekly
National Association of Tax Professionals
PO Box 8002
Appleton, WI 54912-8002

800-558-3402; *Fax:* 800-747-0001
natp@natptax.com; www.natptax.com
Social Media: Facebook, Twitter, MySpace

Jo Ann Schoen, President
Jean Millerchip, Vice President
Gerard Cannito, Treasurer
Patricia M. McNeer, Secretary
Kathy Stanek, CEO

Members receive e-Newsletter featuring tax alerts and news briefs hot off the press.
Frequency: Weekly

159 TOPICS Newsletter
Association of Government Accountants
2208 Mount Vernon Ave
Alexandria, VA 22301-1314

703-684-6931
800-AGA-7211; *Fax:* 703-548-9367
agacgfm@agacgfm.org; www.agacgfm.org

Relmond Van Daniker, Executive Director
Evelyn Brown, National President

Designed to give national exposure to chapter events, community service projects and member accomplishments while offering the most up-to-date Association news, released every other Monday morning by e-mail to members.
Frequency: 2x/Month

160 Tax Hot Topics
Grant Thornton
175 W Jackson Blvd
20th Floor
Chicago, IL 60604-2687

312-856-0001; *Fax:* 312-602-8099;
www.grantthornton.com
Social Media: Twitter, LinkedIn

Stephen Chipman, CEO
Lou Grabowsky, COO
Russ Wieman, Chief Financial Officer

Electronic newsletter addressing a wide range of tax issues, including Internal Revenue Service rulings, tax-related litigation, and state, local and international tax developments
Frequency: Biweekly
Founded in: 1924

161 Tax Incentives Alert
Strafford Publications
590 Dutch Valley Road NE
PO Box 13729
Atlanta, GA 30324-0729

404-881-1141
800-926-7926; *Fax:* 404-881-0074
customerservice@straffordpub.com;
www.straffordpub.com

Richard Ossoff, President
Jon McKenna, Executive Editor

Reports on the new and ever-evolving array of federal and state tax credits, exemptions, deductions, abatements and other incentives.
Cost: $467.00
Frequency: Monthly
ISSN: 0161-309X
Founded in: 1984

162 Tax Insider
American Institute of Certified Public Accountants
1211 Avenue of the Americas
Suite 6
New York, NY 10036-8701

212-596-6200; *Fax:* 212-596-6213
service@aicpa.org; www.aicpa.org
Social Media: Facebook, Twitter, LinkedIn

Barry C Melancon, CEO
Susan Coffey, Senior Vice President
Lawson Carmichael, SVP - Strategy
Arleen Thomas, SVP - Mgmt Accounting

Delivers need-to-know news of the profession, hard-hitting commentary, recommended products and professional development resources to tax and financial planning professionals.
Frequency: 2x/Month
Founded in: 1887

163 Tax Letter and Social Security Report
Scott Peyron & Associates
209 Main Street
Suite 200
Boise, ID 83702-7356

208-388-3800; *Fax:* 208-388-8898;
www.peyron.com

Scott Peyron, Owner

Covers taxes, social security tax, benefit tips and information for middle income individuals and professionals.
Cost: $56.00
4 Pages
Frequency: Monthly
Circulation: 2000
Printed in one color on matte stock

164 The CPA Letter
American Institute of Certified Public Accountants
1211 Avenue of the Americas
Suite 6
New York, NY 10036-8701

212-596-6200; *Fax:* 212-596-6213
service@aicpa.org; www.aicpa.org
Social Media: Facebook, Twitter, LinkedIn

Barry C Melancon, CEO
Susan Coffey, Senior Vice President
Lawson Carmichael, SVP - Strategy
Arleen Thomas, SVP - Mgmt Accounting

A news source for certified public accountants.
Frequency: Monthly
Founded in: 1887

165 The Gaming Auditorium
Institute of Internal Auditors
247 Maitland Ave
Altamonte Spgs, FL 32701-4201

707-937-1100; *Fax:* 407-937-1101
custserv@theiia.org; www.theiia.org

J. Michael Pepper, Chairman
Carolyn Saint, Senior Vice President
John Wxzelaki, Vice Chairman - Finance/security

Quarterly publication provided to members of the Institute of Internal Auditors's Gaming Audit Group to support knowledge development for gaming audit professionals.
Frequency: Quarterly

166 Tone at the Top
Institute of Internal Auditors
247 Maitland Ave
Altamonte Spgs, FL 32701-4201

407-937-1100; *Fax:* 407-937-1101
custserv@theiia.org; www.theiia.org

J. Michael Pepper, Chairman
Carolyn Saint, Senior Vice President
John Wxzelaki, Vice Chairman - Finance/security

Newsletter that provides executive management, boards of directors, and audit committees with concise, leading-edge information in issues such as risk, internal control, governance, ethics, and the changing role of internal auditing.
Frequency: Quarterly

167 Wealth Management Insider
American Institute of Certified Public Accountants
1211 Avenue of the Americas
Suite 6
New York, NY 10036-8701
212-596-6200; *Fax:* 212-596-6213
service@aicpa.org; www.aicpa.org
Social Media: Facebook, Twitter, LinkedIn

Barry C Melancon, CEO
Susan Coffey, Senior Vice President
Lawson Carmichael, SVP - Strategy
Arleen Thomas, SVP - Mgmt Accounting

Delivers need-to-know news of the profession, hard-hitting commentary, recommended products and professional development resources to CPAs who currently provide financial planning services or are looking to expand their practice.
Frequency: 2x/Month
Founded in: 1887

Magazines & Journals

168 **AIRA Journal**
Association of Insolvency & Restructuring Advisors
221 W Stewart Ave
Suite 207
Medford, OR 97501-3647

541-858-1665; *Fax:* 541-858-9187
aira@aira.org; www.airacira.org

Anthony Sasso, President
Thomas Morrow, Vice President
Mathew Schwartz, Treasurer
Joel Waite, VP

Publication provides accurate and authoritative information in regard to current issues and developments relevant to the insolvency and restructuring practice, as well as to inform members of upcoming Association events.
Frequency: Bi-Monthly

169 **Accountants SEC Practice Manual**
CCH
2700 Lake Cook Rd
Riverwoods, IL 60015-3867

847-940-4600
800-835-5224; *Fax:* 773-866-3095;
www.cch.com

Mike Sabbatis, President
Douglas M Winterrose, Vice President & CFO
Jim Bryant, EVP Software Products

Offers guidance for preparing and filing financial statements with the SEC, including regulations, forms and helpful summaries and checklists.
Cost: $819.00
Frequency: Annual
Founded in: 1913

170 **Accounting Historians Journal**
Academy of Accounting Historians
10900 Euclid Avenue
Cleveland, OH 44106-7235

216-368-2058; *Fax:* 216-368-6244
acchistory@case.edu; www.aahhq.org

Joanne Cross, President
Robert Colson, President Elect
Yvette Lazdowski, VP, Communications
Robert Colson, VP Communications
Stephanie Moussalli, Secretary

Published by the Academy of Accounting Historians, the Journal provides research on the evolution of accounting thought and accounting practice. Subscription to the semi-annual publication is included in membership to the Academy.
600 Members
200 Pages
Frequency: Semi-Annual
Founded in: 1973
Printed in one color

171 **Accounting Horizons**
American Accounting Association
5717 Bessie Dr
Sarasota, FL 34233-2399

941-921-7747; *Fax:* 941-923-4093
info@aaahq.org
aaahq.org
Social Media: Facebook

Tracey Sutherland, Executive Director
Deirdre Harris, Publications Contact

Accounting and business information.
Cost: $100.00
8600 Members
Frequency: Quarterly
Circulation: 6000
Founded in: 1916
Printed in 3 colors on matte stock

172 **Accounting Today**
Accountants Media Group & SourceMedia, Inc.
1 State Street Plaza
25th Floor
New York, NY 10004

212-258-8445
800-221-1809; *Fax:* 212-292-5216;
www.accountingtoday.com
Social Media: Facebook, Twitter, LinkedIn

Michael Cohn, Editor-in-Chief
Tamika Cody, Managing Editor
Daniel Hood, Editor in Chief
Seth Fineberg, Technology Editor

Covers accounting and auditing standards, taxation and practice management.
Cost: $99.00
48 Pages
Circulation: 34991
ISSN: 1044-5714
Founded in: 1987
Printed in 4 colors on glossy stock

173 **Accounting and Tax Highlights**
Thomson Reuters
2395 Midway Rd
Carrollton, TX 75006

817-332-3709
800-431-9025; *Fax:* 888-216-1929
trta.lei-support@thomsonreuters.com;
www.ria.thomsonreuters.com

Elaine Yadlon, Plant Manager
Thomas H Glocer, CEO & Director
Robert D Daleo, Chief Financial Officer
Kelli Crane, Senior Vice President & CIO

Covers current news and developments in the field. Audiocassette program for CPAs for continuing professional education. Accepts advertising.
Cost: $112.00
28 Pages
Frequency: Monthly
Founded in: 1935

174 **Accounting and the Public Interest**
American Accounting Association
5717 Bessie Dr
Sarasota, FL 34233-2399

941-921-7747; *Fax:* 941-923-4093
deirdre@aaahq.org
aaahq.org

Tracey Sutherland, Executive Director
Deirdre Harris, Publications Contact

An academic journal taking the view that accounting is a social activity with far-ranging consequences for every citizen, welcoming innovation and eclecticism, alternative theories and methodologies, as well as the more traditional ones. The common element in this diversity is the requirement that the study and its findings be linked to the public interest by situating them within a historical, social, and political context, and ultimately providing guidance.
8600 Members
Frequency: Periodically
Circulation: 400
Founded in: 1916

175 **Achieve**
National Association of Black Accountants
7474 Greenway Center Dr
Suite 1120
Greenbelt, MD 20770-3504

301-474-6222
888-571-2939; *Fax:* 301-474-3114
customerservice@nabainc.org;
www.nabainc.org
Social Media: Facebook, Twitter, LinkedIn, YouTube

Calvin Harris Jr., President/CEO
Guillermo Hysaw, Executive Director and COO
Veda Stanley, Executive Vice President
Sheila Taylor-Clark, CPA
Ronald Walker, Chairman, Division of Firms

Magazine for NABA student members. Discussed are issues relevant to student academic, career, and personal aspirations.
Frequency: 2 Times/Year
Founded in: 1969

176 **Actuary Magazine**
Society of Actuaries
475 N Martingale Rd
Suite 600
Schaumburg, IL 60173-2252

847-706-3500; *Fax:* 847-706-3599
webmaster@soa.org; www.soa.org

Greg Heidrich, Executive Director
Stacy Lin, Deputy Executive Director/CFO

Provides informative feature articles that focus on a variety of actuarial topics, plus career information, SOA education initiatives and trends in international business.
Frequency: Bimonthly
Printed in 4 colors on glossy stock

177 **Armed Forces Comptroller**
415 N Alfred St
Alexandria, VA 22314-2269

703-549-0360
800-462-5637; *Fax:* 703-549-3181;
www.asmconline.org
Social Media: Facebook, Twitter, LinkedIn

Robert Hale, Executive Director
John Bunnell, Associate Director of Certification
Jennifer Sizemore, Chapter Management
Don W Fox, General Counsel

Leading industry journal, is one of the Society's means of sharing professional information. Articles are received from a variety of sources, such as academia, the government, and our members.
18000 Members
Founded in: 1948

178 **Audit Report**
Association of Credit Union Internal Auditors
PO Box 150908
Alexandria, VA 22315

703-688-2284
866-254-8128; *Fax:* 703-683-0295
acuia@acuia.org; www.acuia.org
Social Media: Facebook, Twitter, LinkedIn

Samuel Capuano, Chairman of the Board
Jill Chase, Vice Chair

Articles of interest to those in the auditing profession.
800 Members
Frequency: Quarterly
Founded in: 1989
Printed in 4 colors

179 **Auditing: A Journal of Practice & Theory**
American Accounting Association
5717 Bessie Dr
Sarasota, FL 34233-2399

941-921-7747; *Fax:* 941-923-4093
deirdre@aaahq.org
aaahq.org

Tracey Sutherland, Executive Director
Deirdre Harris, Publications Contact

The journal is distributed to members of the Auditing section of the Association, as well as libraries.
8600 Members
Frequency: Twice/Year

Circulation: 2000
Founded in: 1916

180 **CFMA Building Profits**
Construction Financial Management Association
100 Village Blvd
Suite 200
Princeton, NJ 08540-5783

609-452-8000
888-421-9996; *Fax:* 609-452-0474
info@cfma.org; www.cfma.org
Social Media: Facebook, Twitter, LinkedIn, YouTube

Stuart Binstock, President and CEO
Brian Summers, COO
Robert Rubin, CPA

Information for financial managers and CPAs concerned with financial management.
7000 Members
Frequency: Bi-Monthly
Circulation: 7,000
Founded in: 1981

181 **CPA Practice Management Forum**
CCH
2700 Lake Cook Rd
Riverwoods, IL 60015-3867

847-940-4600
800-835-5224; *Fax:* 773-866-3095;
www.cch.com

Mike Sabbatis, President
Douglas M Winterrose, Vice President & CFO
Jim Bryant, EVP Software Products

Mini-journal that includes articles featuring best practices, tips and advice from the nation's leading practice management experts.
Cost: $529.00
24 Pages
Frequency: Monthly

182 **CPA Technology Advisor**
Cygnus Publishing
1233 Janesville Avenue
Fort Atkinson, WI 53538-0803

800-547-7377
shari.dodgen@cygnuspub.com;
www.cygnusb2b.com

John French, CEO
Paul Bonaiuto, CFO
Ed Wood, VP
Kris Flitcroft, EVP

The magazine is a resource for accountants and managers that features a Buyer's Guide that lists hundreds of businesses, manufacturers and professionals that can assist public accounting firms in delivering a variety of services to their clients in various industries.
Cost: $48.00
Circulation: 50,000+
Founded in: 1991
Printed in 4 colors on glossy stock

183 **CPA Wealth Provider**
Accountants Media Group & SourceMedia, Inc.
One State Street Plaza
25th Floor
New York, NY 10004

212-258-8445
800-221-1809; *Fax:* 212-292-5216;
www.accountingtoday.com
Social Media: Facebook

Michael Cohn, President and CEO
Joseph Wells, Chairman
John Gill, VP of Education
John Warren, VP and General Counsel

Offers financial planning strategies, product information and practivve-building advice in an environment that recognizes the special needs of accountants.
Frequency: Quarterly
Circulation: 37000
Founded in: 1968
Printed in 4 colors on glossy stock

184 **Computers in Accounting**
Thomson Reuters
2395 Midway Rd
Carrollton, TX 75006

817-332-3709
800-431-9025; *Fax:* 888-216-1929
trta.lei-support@thomsonreuters.com;
www.ria.thomsonreuters.com

Elaine Yadlon, Plant Manager
Thomas H Glocer, CEO & Director
Robert D Daleo, Chief Financial Officer
Kelli Crane, Senior Vice President & CIO

Contains the latest information on accounting, tax and business software, electronic spreadsheets, and available hardware.
Cost: $58.00
40 Pages
Founded in: 1935

185 **Controller's Cost & Profit Report**
Thomson Reuters
2395 Midway Rd
Carrollton, TX 75006

817-332-3709
800-431-9025; *Fax:* 888-216-1929
trta.lei-support@thomsonreuters.com;
www.ria.thomsonreuters.com

Elaine Yadlon, Plant Manager
Thomas H Glocer, CEO & Director
Robert D Daleo, Chief Financial Officer
Kelli Crane, Senior Vice President & CIO

Targets cash flow issues, risk/reward decisions, personnel trends, ways to increase productivity while reducing overhead costs, and technology updates for the new millennium.
Cost: $195.50
Frequency: SemiMonthly
Founded in: 1935

186 **Current Issues in Auditing**
American Accounting Association
5717 Bessie Dr
Sarasota, FL 34233-2399

941-921-7747; *Fax:* 941-923-4093
info@aaahq.org; www.aaahq.org

Tracey Sutherland, Executive Director
Julie Smith David, CIO
Diane Ledger, Director of Finance

This open-access journal offers free access to AAA members, non-members, and libraries.
Frequency: Periodically

187 **EA Journal**
National Association of Enrolled Agents
1120 Connecticut Avenue NW
Suite 460
Washington, DC 20036-3922

202-822-6232; *Fax:* 202-822-6270
info@naea.org; www.naea.org
Social Media: Facebook, Twitter, LinkedIn

Frank I Degen, President
Betsey Buckingham, President-elect
Robert Reedy, Treasurer/Secretary
Gigi Jarvis, Sr. Dir. Marketing/Communication
William Grutzkuhn, Director Finance/Administration

EA Journal brings information that helps set professionals apart from other tax practitioners.
12000 Members
Frequency: Every Other Month
Founded in: 1972

188 **Financial Executive**
Financial Executives International
1250 Headquarters Plaza
West Tower, 7th Floor
Morristown, NJ 07960

973-765-1000; *Fax:* 973-765-1018
membership@financialexecutives.org;
www.financialexecutives.org
Social Media: Facebook, Twitter, LinkedIn, YouTube

Marie N Hollein, President & CEO
Marsha Hunt, VP
Mitch Danaher

Addresses accounting and treasury subjects, as well as overall strategies in corporate financial management.
Cost: $69.00
72 Pages
Frequency: 10x/yr
Circulation: 17000
ISSN: 0895-4186
Founded in: 1931
Printed in 4 colors on glossy stock

189 **Financial Executive Magazine**
200 Campus Drive
PO Box 674
Florham Park, NJ 07932

973-360-0177; *Fax:* 973-898-4649;
www.financialexecutives.org

Marie N Hollein, President & CEO
Marsha Hunt, VP
Mitch Danaher
Paul Chase, VP/Chief Financial Officer
Christopher Allen, VP/Chief Marketing Officer

Award-winning flagship publication of FEI, providing senior-level financial executives with financial, business and management news, trends and strategies to help them work better, faster and smarter. Covers professional, strategic and technological practices and developments that affect financial executives' day-to-day and longer-term issues, reflecting the financial executive's increasing involvement in the general management of their companies.
15M Members
Frequency: 10x/ Year
Founded in: 1931

190 **Financial Management**
Financial Management Association International
College of Business Administration
4202 East Fowler Avenue BSN 3331
Tampa, FL 33620-5500

813-974-2084; *Fax:* 813-974-3318
fma@coba.usf.edu; www.fma.org

William G Christie, Executive Editor

Financial Management serves the profession by publishing significant new scholarly research in finance that is of the highest quality. The principal criteria for publishability are originality, rigor, timeliness, practical relevance and clarity.
Frequency: Quarterly

191 **ISACA Journal**
Information Systems Audit & Control Association
3701 Algonquin Rd
Suite 1010
Rolling Meadows, IL 60008-3124

847-253-1545; *Fax:* 847-253-1443
news@isaca.org; www.isaca.org
Social Media: Facebook, Twitter, LinkedIn

Susan Caldwell, CEO
Kristen Kessinger, Manager Of Media Relations

Provides professional development information to those spearheading IT governance and those involved with information systems audit, control and security.
Cost: $75.00
10000 Members
Frequency: Bimonthly

Circulation: 86000
Founded in: 1969

192 **Information Management**
ARMA International
11880 College Blvd
Suite 450
Overland Park, KS 66215
913-341-3808
800-422-2762; *Fax:* 913-341-3742
hq@arma.org; www.arma.org
Social Media: Facebook, Twitter, LinkedIn

Komal Gulich, President
Julie Colgan, President-elect
Brenda Prowse, Treasurer

ARMA International is a not-for-profit association and a source for authoritative education, the latest legislative updates, standards & best practices.
11000 Members
Founded in: 1955

193 **Information Management Magazine**
ARMA International
11880 College Blvd
Suite 450
Overland Park, KS 66215
913-341-3808
800-422-2762; *Fax:* 913-341-3742
hq@arma.org; www.arma.org
Social Media: Facebook, Twitter, LinkedIn

Komal Gulich, President
Julie Colgan, President-elect
Brenda Prowse, Treasurer

The leading source of information on topics and issues central to the management of records and information worldwide. Each issue features insightful articles written by experts in the management of records and information.
Cost: $115.00
Frequency: Bi-monthly
Circulation: 11000
ISSN: 1535-2897
Mailing list available for rent: 9000 names
Printed in 4 colors on glossy stock

194 **Insight**
Illinois CPA Society
550 W Jackson Blvd
Suite 900
Chicago, IL 60661-5742
312-993-0407
800-993-0407; *Fax:* 312-993-9954;
www.icpas.org
Social Media: Facebook, Twitter, LinkedIn, YouTube

Elaine Weiss, President & CEO
Todd Shapiro, CFO & VP Finance & Administration
Judy Giannetto, INSIGHT Director

Editorial content focuses on practical issues affecting professional development.
Frequency: Monthly
Circulation: 23000
Founded in: 1980

195 **Internal Auditing**
Thomson Reuters
2395 Midway Rd
Carrollton, TX 75006
817-332-3709
800-431-9025; *Fax:* 888-216-1929
trta.lei-support@thomsonreuters.com;
www.ria.thomsonreuters.com

Elaine Yadlon, Plant Manager
Thomas H Glocer, CEO & Director
Robert D Daleo, Chief Financial Officer
Kelli Crane, Senior Vice President & CIO

Provides solutions to internal auditing problems. Only professional resource written exclusively by leading practitioners.
Cost: $275.00
Frequency: Annual+
Founded in: 1935

196 **Internal Auditor Magazine**
Institute of Internal Auditors
247 Maitland Ave
Altamonte Spgs, FL 32701-4201
407-937-1100; *Fax:* 407-937-1101
iia@theiia.org; www.theiia.org
Social Media: Facebook, Twitter, LinkedIn

J. Michael Pepper, Chairman
Carolyn Saint, Senior Vice President
John Wxzelaki, Vice Chairman - Finance/security

World's leading publication covering the internal audit profession. Shares timely, helpful- indispensable -information for professionals who want to keep pace with the diverse, dynamic field of internal auditing.
160M Members
Founded in: 1941

197 **International Journal of Business Data Communications and Networking**
Information Resources Management Association
701 E Chocolate Ave
Suite 200
Hershey, PA 17033-1240
717-533-8845; *Fax:* 717-533-8661
member@irma-international.org;
www.irma-international.org

Jan Travers, Executive Director
Sherif Kamel, Communications Director
Lech Janczewski PhD, IRMA World Representative Director
Gerald Grant, IRMA Doctoral Symposium Director
Paul Chalekian, IRMA United States Representative

This journal examines the impact of data communications and networking technologies, policies, and management on business organizatios, capturing their effect on IT-enabled management practices.
Cost: $545.00
Frequency: Quarterly
ISSN: 1548-0631

198 **Interpreter Magazine**
Insurance Accounting Systems Association
PO Box 51340
Durham, NC 27717-1340
919-489-0991; *Fax:* 919-489-1994
info@iasa.org; www.iasa.org
Social Media: Facebook, Twitter

Ruth Estrich, President
Elizabeth Mercier, CIO
Ernie Pearson, Board Chair
Joseph Pomilia, Executive Director

This magazine includes reports on actions by the NAIC, interviews with business leaders, reports on industry trends and news about IASA activities.
Cost: $45.00
12 Pages
Frequency: Quarterly
Founded in: 1940

199 **Issues in Accounting Education**
American Accounting Association
5717 Bessie Dr
Sarasota, FL 34233-2399
941-921-7747; *Fax:* 941-923-4093
deirdre@aaahq.org
aaahq.org

Tracey Sutherland, Executive Director
Deirdre Harris, Publications Contact

Provides a forum for exchange of education-related ideas and techniques among accounting professors. A widley cited resource for academic members of the Association.
8600 Members
Frequency: Quarterly
Circulation: 5500
Founded in: 1983

200 **Journal of Accountancy**
American Institute of Certified Public Accountants
1211 Avenue of the Americas
New York, NY 10036-8701
212-596-6200; *Fax:* 212-596-6213
service@aicpa.org; www.aicpa.org
Social Media: Facebook, Twitter, LinkedIn, RSS

Barry C Melancon, CEO
Susan Coffey, Senior Vice President
Lawson Carmichael, SVP - Strategy
Arleen Thomas, SVP - Mgmt Accounting and Global

AICPA publication that focuses on the latest news and developments related to the field of accounting
Frequency: Monthly
Founded in: 1887

201 **Journal of Accounting Research**
University of Chicago Booth School of Business
5807 S Woodlawn Ave
Chicago, IL 60637-1656
773-702-7743; *Fax:* 773-702-2225
jar@chicagobooth.edu; www.chicagobooth.edu
Social Media: Facebook, Twitter, LinkedIn, YouTube

Ted Snyder, Manager
Nicholas Dopuch, Consulting Editor

Publishes original research using analytical, empirical, experimental, and field study methods in accounting research.
Cost: $49.00
Frequency: 5 Times/Year
Circulation: 2800
Founded in: 1963

202 **Journal of Accounting and Public Policy**
Elsevier
3251 Riverport Lane
Maryland Heights, MO 63043
314-447-8878
877-839-7126; *Fax:* 314-447-8077
journalcustomerservice-usa@elsevier.com;
www.elsevier.com

Ron Mobed, CEO
David Lomas, CFO
Gavin Howe, EVP, Human Resources

Publishes research papers that focus on the intersection between accounting and public policy. It offers articles on accounting including public administration, political science and the law.
Cost: $126.00
Frequency: 6x Yearly
ISSN: 0278-4254
Founded in: 1997

203 **Journal of Applied Finance**
Financial Management Association International
College of Business Administration
4202 East Fowler Avenue BSN 3331
Tampa, FL 33620-5500
813-974-2084; *Fax:* 813-974-3318
fma@coba.usf.edu; www.fma.org

Betty J Simkins, Editor
Ramesh P Rao, Editor
Charles W Smithson, Editor

The Journal of Applied Finance's goal is to be the leading bridging journal between practitioners and academics. The mission is to publish well-crafted papers of interest to practitioners and of use to academics in stimulating research and in their teaching function.
Frequency: 2 Times/Year

204 Journal of Construction Accounting & Taxation
Thomson Reuters
2395 Midway Rd
Carrollton, TX 75006

817-332-3709
800-431-9025; *Fax:* 888-216-1929
trta.lei-support@thomsonreuters.com; www.ria.thomsonreuters.com

Elaine Yadlon, Plant Manager
Thomas H Glocer, CEO & Director
Robert D Daleo, Chief Financial Officer
Kelli Crane, Senior Vice President & CIO

Authoritative, targeted articles and experience-based columns cover several areas, including job-costing, risk assessment, dispute resolution, financial reporting, and benchmarking contractor performance.
Cost: $270.00
Frequency: 6 Times/Year
Circulation: 3400
Founded in: 1935

205 Journal of Cost Analysis and Parametrics
Society of Cost Estimating and Analysis
8221 Old Courthouse Rd
Suite 106
Vienna, VA 22182

703-938-5090; *Fax:* 703-938-5091
scea@sceaonline.org; www.sceaonline.org

Erin Whittaker, Executive Director
Sharon Burger, Certification Program Admin
Brittany Walker, Membership Coordinator

The Journal of Cost Analysis and Parametrics is a joint publication with the International Society of Parametric Analysts. It is dedicated to promoting excellence in cost estimating, cost analysis, and cost management.
Cost: $ 55.00
2015 Members
Frequency: Twice/Year
Founded in: 1990

206 Journal of Cost Management
Thomson Reuters
2395 Midway Rd
Carrollton, TX 75006

817-332-3709
800-431-9025; *Fax:* 888-216-1929
trta.lei-support@thomsonreuters.com; www.ria.thomsonreuters.com

Elaine Yadlon, Plant Manager
Thomas H Glocer, CEO & Director
Robert D Daleo, Chief Financial Officer
Kelli Crane, Senior Vice President & CIO

Journal of modern cost management (including cost and managerial accounting topics), especially activity-based costing, activity-based management, performance measurement, target costing and investment justification. Accepts advertising.
Cost: $275.00
64 Pages
Founded in: 1935

207 Journal of Emerging Technologies in Accounting
American Accounting Association
5717 Bessie Dr
Sarasota, FL 34233-2399

941-921-7747; *Fax:* 941-923-4093
info@aaahq.org
aaahq.org
Social Media: Facebook, Twitter

Tracey Sutherland, Executive Director
Deirdre Harris, Publications Contact

This journal is distributed to members of the AI/Emerging Technologies section of the Association, as well as libraries.
8600 Members
Frequency: Annually
Circulation: 300
Founded in: 1916

208 Journal of Government Financial Management
Association of Government Accountants
2208 Mount Vernon Ave
Alexandria, VA 22301-1314

703-684-6931
800-242-7211; *Fax:* 703-548-9367
agacgfm@agacgfm.org; www.agacgfm.org

Relmond Van Daniker, Executive Director
Evelyn Brown, National President

Provides valuable information for governmental decision makers. Examines budgeting, accounting, auditing and data process developments.
Cost: $60.00
Frequency: Quarterly
Circulation: 14,769
Mailing list available for rent: 18,000 names

209 Journal of Information Systems
American Accounting Association
5717 Bessie Dr
Sarasota, FL 34233-2399

941-921-7747; *Fax:* 941-923-4093
deirdre@aaahq.org
aaahq.org

Tracey Sutherland, Executive Director
Deirdre Harris, Publications Contact

Covers developments relating to information systems in use in the accounting industry.
Cost: $35.00
8600 Members
Frequency: Twice/Year
Founded in: 1916

210 Journal of International Accounting Research
American Accounting Association
5717 Bessie Dr
Sarasota, FL 34233-2399

941-921-7747; *Fax:* 941-923-4093
deirdre@aaahq.org
aaahq.org

Tracey Sutherland, Executive Director
Deirdre Harris, Publications Contact

Has a diverse readership and is interested in articles in auditing, financial accounting, managerial accounting, systems, tax, and other specialties within the field of accounting.
8600 Members
Frequency: Twice/Year
Circulation: 1300
Founded in: 1916

211 Journal of Legal Tax Research
American Accounting Association
5717 Bessie Dr
Sarasota, FL 34233-2399

941-921-7747; *Fax:* 941-923-4093
deirdre@aaahq.org
aaahq.org

Tracey Sutherland, Executive Director
Deirdre Harris, Publications Contact

Publishes creative and innovative studies employing legal research methodologies that logically and clearly identify, decribe and illuminate important current tax issues, propose improvements in tax systems and unique solutions to problems, and critically analyze proposed or recent tax rule changes from both technical and policy perspectives.
8600 Members
Frequency: Twice/Year
Circulation: 900
Founded in: 1916

212 Journal of Management Accounting Research
American Accounting Association
5717 Bessie Dr
Sarasota, FL 34233-2399

941-921-7747; *Fax:* 941-923-4093
deirdre@aaahq.org
aaahq.org

Tracey Sutherland, Executive Director
Deirdre Harris, Publications Contact

Devoted exclusively to management accounting research. Contributingto the expansion of knowledge related to the theory and practice of management accounting. Covers all areas of management accounting including, budgeting, internal reporting, incentives, performance evaluation, and the interface between internal and external reporting.
8600 Members
Frequency: Annually, December
Circulation: 2000
Founded in: 1916

213 Journal of Organizational and End User Computing
Information Resources Management Association
701 E Chocolate Ave
Suite 200
Hershey, PA 17033-1240

717-533-8845; *Fax:* 717-533-8661;
www.irma-international.org

Jan Travers, Executive Director
Sherif Kamel, Communications Director
Lech Janczewski PhD, IRMA World Representative Director
Gerald Grant, IRMA Doctoral Symposium Director
Paul Chalekian, IRMA United States Representative

The Journal of Organizational and End User Computing (JOEUC) provides a forum to information technology educators, researchers, and practitioners to advance the practice and understanding of organizational and end user computing. The journal features a major emphasis on how to increase organizational and end user productivity and performance, and how to achieve organizational, strategic and competitive advantage.
Cost: $125.00
Frequency: Quarterly
ISSN: 1546-2234

214 Journal of the American Taxation Association
American Accounting Association
5717 Bessie Dr
Sarasota, FL 34233-2399

941-921-7747; *Fax:* 941-923-4093
info@aaahq.org
aaahq.org

Tracey Sutherland, Executive Director
Deirdre Harris, Publications Contact

Dedicated to disseminating a wide variety of tax knowledge and publishes research that employs quantitative, analytical, experimental, and descriptive methods to address tax topics of interest to its readership.
8600 Members
Frequency: Twice/Year
Circulation: 1100
Founded in: 1916

215 **National Public Accountant**
National Society of Accountants
1010 N Fairfax St
Alexandria, VA 22314-1574

703-549-6400
800-966-6679; *Fax:* 703-549-2984
members@nsacct.org; www.nsacct.org
Social Media: Facebook, Twitter, LinkedIn

Harlan Rose, President
Steven Hanson, First Vice President
Marilyn Niwao, Second Vice President
Brian Thompson, Secretary-Treasurer

News for practicing accountants and tax practitioners.
48 Pages
Circulation: 20000
ISSN: 0027-9978
Founded in: 1945

216 **New Accountant**
REN Publishing
3550 W Peterson Avenue
Suite 403
Chicago, IL 60659

773-866-9900; *Fax:* 773-866-9881
inquiries@RenPublishing.com;
www.renpublishing.com/

Steven N Polydoris, President/Publisher/Editor

A professional publication for accounting students and the accounting profession. Each issue includes articles to introduce students to the many and diverse career opportunities available to accounting majors and to prepare college accounting students and recent graduates to sit for the CPA exam. Also available in an online format.
Cost: $85.00
17 Pages
Frequency: Monthly
Circulation: 68000
Founded in: 1883

217 **Newspaper Financial Executive Journal**
Interactive & Newsmedia Financial Executives
550 W. Frontage Road
Suite 3500
Northfield, IL 50093

847-715-7000; *Fax:* 847-715-7004;
www.infe.org
Social Media: Facebook, Twitter, LinkedIn

Trade publication for financial management of newspapers. More than 800 members.
Frequency: Weekly
Circulation: 1000
Founded in: 1947

218 **North American Actuarial Journal**
Society of Actuaries
475 N Martingale Rd
Suite 600
Schaumburg, IL 60173-2252

847-706-3500; *Fax:* 847-706-3599
webmaster@soa.org; www.soa.org

Greg Heidrich, Executive Director
Stacy Lin, Deputy Executive Director/CFO
Harry H Panjer, Editor

Scientically addresses domestic and international problems, interests and concerns of actuaries, their customers, and public policy decision makers.
Frequency: Quarterly
Circulation: 22800
ISSN: 1092-0277
Founded in: 1997
Mailing list available for rent: **17000 names at $105 per M**

219 **PayState Update**
American Payroll Association
660 N Main Ave
Suite 100
San Antonio, TX 78205-1217

210-226-4600; *Fax:* 210-226-4027;
www.payroll.org
Social Media: Facebook, Twitter, LinkedIn

Daniel Maddux, President

Newsletter dedicated exclusively to state and local payroll compliance news and issues.
Cost: $289.00
Frequency: Bi-Weekly

220 **Payroll Administration Guide**
Bureau of National Affairs
3 Bethesda Metro Center
Suite 250
Bethesda, MD 20814

800-372-1033; *Fax:* 800-253-0332
customercare@bna.com; www.bna.com

Gregory McCaffery, President and CEO
John Camp, VP and CTO
Lisa Fitzpatrick, VP and CMO

A notification and reference service for payroll professionals. Covers federal and state employment tax, wage-hour and wage-payment laws.
Cost: $896.00
Frequency: Bi-Weekly
Founded in: 1929

221 **Paytech**
American Payroll Association
660 N Main Ave
Suite 100
San Antonio, TX 78205-1217

210-226-4600; *Fax:* 210-226-4027
apa@americanpayroll.org; www.payroll.org
Social Media: Facebook, Twitter, LinkedIn

Daniel Maddux, President

Member magazine that includes case studies, topical articles, themed issues and comprehensive Buyer's Guides.
Cost: $200.00
Frequency: Monthly
Circulation: 40000
Founded in: 1982

222 **Practical Tax Strategies**
Thomson Reuters
2395 Midway Rd
Carrollton, TX 75006

817-332-3709
800-431-9025; *Fax:* 888-216-1929
trta.lei-support@thomsonreuters.com;
www.ria.thomsonreuters.com

Elaine Yadlon, Plant Manager
Thomas H Glocer, CEO & Director
Robert D Daleo, Chief Financial Officer
Kelli Crane, Senior Vice President & CIO

Features offer in-depth articles and technical notes on taxation.
Cost: $185.00
64 Pages
Frequency: Monthly
Circulation: 12000
Founded in: 1935

223 **Public Budgeting and Finance**
American Association for Budget and Program
PO Box 1157
Falls Church, VA 22041

703-941-4300; *Fax:* 703-941-1535
aabpa@aol.com; www.aabpa.org
Social Media: Facebook, Twitter, LinkedIn, GovLoop

Judy Thomas, President
Melissa Neuman, President Elect
Anthony Rainey, VP
Patrick Vallely, Treasurer

Budget and program analysis professionals.
Frequency: Quarterly

224 **Real Estate Taxation**
Thomson Reuters
2395 Midway Rd
Carrollton, TX 75006

817-332-3709
800-431-9025; *Fax:* 888-216-1929
trta.lei-support@thomsonreuters.com;
www.ria.thomsonreuters.com

Elaine Yadlon, Plant Manager
Thomas H Glocer, CEO & Director
Robert D Daleo, Chief Financial Officer
Kelli Crane, Senior Vice President & CIO

Timely source of new ideas, trends and legal developments in real estate taxation. This journal gives you complete, ongoing coverage of all aspects of real estate tax planning.
Cost: $350.00
Frequency: Quarterly
Founded in: 1935

225 **Review of Taxation of Individuals**
Thomson Reuters
2395 Midway Rd
Carrollton, TX 75006

817-332-3709
800-431-9025; *Fax:* 888-216-1929
trta.lei-support@thomsonreuters.com;
www.ria.thomsonreuters.com

Elaine Yadlon, Plant Manager
Thomas H Glocer, CEO & Director
Robert D Daleo, Chief Financial Officer
Kelli Crane, Senior Vice President & CIO

Offers information on the taxation of individuals, legislation, etc.
Cost: $58.00
Frequency: Monthly
Founded in: 1935

226 **Sales & Use Tax Monitor**
Strafford Publications
590 Dutch Valley Road NE
PO Box 13729
Atlanta, GA 30324-0729

404-881-1141
800-926-7926; *Fax:* 404-881-0074
customerservice@straffordpub.com;
www.straffordpub.com
Social Media: Twitter

Richard Ossoff, President
Jon McKenna, Executive Editor

Provides updates on compliance requirements and tax avoidance opportunities in every state.
Cost: $487.00
Frequency: 2 Times/Month
ISSN: 0161-309X
Founded in: 1984

227 **Spectrum Magazine**
National Association Of Black Accountants
7474 Greenway Center Dr
Suite 1120
Greenbelt, MD 20770-3504

301-474-6222
888-571-2939; *Fax:* 301-474-3114;
www.nabainc.org
Social Media: Facebook, Twitter, LinkedIn, YouTube

Calvin Harris Jr., President/CEO
Guillermo Hysaw, Executive Director and COO
Veda Stanley, Executive Vice President
Sheila Taylor-Clark, CPA
Ronald Walker, Chairman, Division of Firms

Provides a communication mechanism whereby readers are kept abreast of key topics of interest

within the accounting, finance, and business professions.
Frequency: Annual

228 **State Income Tax Monitor**
Strafford Publications
590 Dutch Valley Road NE
PO Box 13729
Atlanta, GA 30324-0729

404-881-1141
800-926-7926; *Fax:* 404-881-0074
customerservice@straffordpub.com;
www.straffordpub.com

Richard Ossoff, President
Jon McKenna, Executive Editor

This journal is a comprehensive briefing on the latest revenue rulings, tax codes, regulations, court decisions and more in every state.
Cost: $467.00
Frequency: 2 Times/Month
ISSN: 0161-309X
Founded in: 1984

229 **Strategic Finance**
Institute of Management Accountants
10 Paragon Dr
Suite 1
Montvale, NJ 07645-1774

201-573-9000
800-638-4427; *Fax:* 201-474-1600
ima@imanet.org; www.imanet.org
Social Media: Facebook, Twitter, LinkedIn

Jeffrey C. Thomson, President and CEO
Brian L. McGuire, Chair
John C. Macaulay, Chair-Elect
Sandra B. Richtermeyer, Chair-Emeritus

IMA's award winning magazine that provides the latest information about practices and trends in finance, accounting, and information management that will impact members and their jobs.
Cost: $195.00
Frequency: Monthly
Printed in 4 colors on glossy stock

230 **TAXPRO Journal**
National Association of Tax Professionals
PO Box 8002
Appleton, WI 54912-8002

800-558-3402; *Fax:* 800-747-0001
natp@natptax.com; www.natptax.com
Social Media: Facebook, Twitter, MySpace

Jo Ann Schoen, President
Jean Millerchip, Vice President
Gerard Cannito, Treasurer
Patricia M. McNeer, Secretary
Kathy Stanek, CEO

In-depth tax information and timely feature articles on such issues as new tax acts, practical tax applications, and solutions to the day-to-day challenges of running a tax practice.
Frequency: Quarterly

231 **Tax Management Estates, Gifts and Trusts Journal**
Bureau of National Affairs
3 Bethesda Metro Center
Suite 250
Bethesda, MD 20814

800-372-1033; *Fax:* 301-294-6760;
www.bna.com

Gregory McCaffery, President and CEO
John Camp, VP and CTO
Lisa Fitzpatrick, VP and CMO

Provides articles by leading tax practitioners and proven techniques for estate planning and planning opportunities. It also features reviews of legislative, administrative and judicial developments.
Frequency: Bimonthly

232 **Tax and Business Advisor**
Grant Thornton
175 W Jackson Blvd
Suite 20
Chicago, IL 60604-2687

312-856-0001; *Fax:* 312-602-8099;
www.grantthornton.com
Social Media: Twitter, LinkedIn

Stephen Chipman, CEO
Lou Grabowsky, COO
Russ Wieman, Chief Financial Officer

Current tax and general business issues.
Founded in: 1924

233 **The Accounting Review**
American Accounting Association
5717 Bessie Dr
Sarasota, FL 34233-2399

941-921-7747; *Fax:* 941-923-4093
info@aaahq.org
aaahq.org
Social Media: Facebook, Twitter

Tracey Sutherland, Executive Director
Deirdre Harris, Publications Contact

A respected journal covering accounting theory and research, business problems and the teaching of business and accounting subjects. Read by businessmen, teachers, and students of accounting, as well as practicing accountants throughout the world.
Cost: $275.00
8600 Members
Frequency: 6/Year
Circulation: 8000
Founded in: 1916

234 **The Bottom Line**
PO Box 1157
Falls Church, VA 22041

703-941-4300; *Fax:* 703-941-1535
aabpa@aabpa.org; www.aabpa.org
Social Media: Facebook, Twitter, LinkedIn, GovLoop

Judy Thomas, President
Melissa Neuman, President Elect
Anthony Rainey, VP
Patrick Vallely, Treasurer

Helps federal, state, and local government managers and analysts, corporate executives and academic specialists meet the unique challenges of their careers. By helping members keep up with the latest developments in their fields, establish and maintain contacts with colleagues, represent their interests and share opportunities, AABPA serves the key difference between simply having a job and being part of a highly respected and well trained profession.
400 Members
Frequency: Monthly
Founded in: 1976

235 **The Bottomline**
Hospitality Financial & Technology Professionals
11709 Boulder Lane
Suite 110
Austin, TX 78726-1832

512-249-5333
800-646-4387; *Fax:* 512-249-1533
membership@hftp.org; www.hftp.org

Frank I Wolfe, Executive VP/CEO
Lucinda Hart, COO
Thomas Atzenhofer, CFO
Eliza Selig, Director of Communications

The Bottomline chronicles the most important industry news with focuses on both finance, technology and general management in hospitality.
4800 Members
Frequency: 10x/Year
Founded in: 1952

236 **The Compass**
American Society of Women Accountants
1760 Old Meadow Road
Suite 500
McLean, VA 22102

703-506-3265
800-326-2163; *Fax:* 703-506-3266
aswa@aswa.org; www.aswa.org
Social Media: Facebook, Twitter, LinkedIn

Cheryl E Heitz, President
Catherine Mulder, President-elect
Berranthia Brown, VP

Each e-magazine includes content in the areas of accounting & auditing, controllership, leadership, and tax and quick and easy links to the popular sections of the American Society of Women Accountants web site.
Frequency: Monthly
Founded in: 1938

237 **The Tax Adviser**
American Institute of Certified Public Accountants
1211 Avenue of the Americas
New York, NY 10036-8701

212-596-6200; *Fax:* 212-596-6213
service@aicpa.org; www.aicpa.org
Social Media: Facebook, Twitter, LinkedIn

Barry C Melancon, CEO
Susan Coffey, Senior Vice President
Lawson Carmichael, SVP - Strategy
Arleen Thomas, SVP - Mgmt Accounting

Monthly tax journal for CPAs and other tax professionals. It includes tax-planning techniques and tax-saving methods which make it a premier source of cutting-edge tax strategies.
Frequency: Monthly
Founded in: 1887

238 **Today's CPA**
Texas Society of CPAs
14651 Dallas Pkwy
Suite 700
Dallas, TX 75254-7408

972-687-8500
800-428-0272; *Fax:* 972-687-8646;
www.tscpa.org
Social Media: Facebook, Twitter, LinkedIn

Fred Timmons, Chairman
William Hornberger, Chairman/Elect
Stephen W Parker, Treasurer
Roxie Samaniego, Secretary

Includes articles, news and professional tips.
Cost: $28.00
27000 Members
Frequency: Bimonthly

Trade Shows

239 **AAA Annual Meeting**
American Accounting Association
5717 Bessie Dr
Sarasota, FL 34233-2399

941-921-7747; *Fax:* 941-923-4093
info@aaahq.org
aaahq.org

Tracey Sutherland, Executive Director
Karen Pincus, President
Deirdre Harris, Publications Contact

Highlighting the difference made when members are actively engaged in the profession. Striving for thought leadership through research, teaching, involvement in practice, and standard setting. 70 booths of accounting equipment, supplie and services. Accounting and business educa-

tion, research and practice textbooks, publishers, software, etc.
8600 Members
Frequency: Annual/Summer
Founded in: 1916

240 AAH Research Conference
Academy of Accounting Historians
10900 Euclid Avenue
Cleveland, OH 44106-7235
216-368-2058; *Fax:* 216-368-6244
acchistory@case.edu; www.aahhq.org
Joanne Cross, President
Robert Colson, President Elect
Yvette Lazdowski, VP, Communications
Robert Colson, VP Communications
Stephanie Moussalli, Secretary
Subjects include modern perspectives of accounting history.
600 Members
Founded in: 1973

241 ACUA Annual Conference
Association of College and University Auditors
PO Box 14306
Lenexa, KS 66285-4306
913-895-4620; *Fax:* 913-895-4652
acua-info@goamp.com; www.acua.org
M Kevin Robinson, President
J Richard Dawson, Vice President
Karen R Hinen, Executive Director
Annual conference for professionals in the auditing profession.
Frequency: Annual

242 ACUA Midyear Conference
Association of College and University Auditors
PO Box 14306
Lenexa, KS 66285-4306
913-895-4620; *Fax:* 913-895-4652
acua-info@goamp.com; www.acua.org
Social Media: Facebook, Twitter, LinkedIn
M Kevin Robinson, President
J Richard Dawson, Vice President
Karen R Hinen, Executive Director
The Midyear Conference was designed to offer a more intense type of training with two-and-a-half days spent on a particular subject matter.
273 Attendees
Frequency: Annual

243 ACUIA Annual Conference & One-Day Seminar
Association of Credit Union Internal Auditors
PO Box 150908
Alexandria, VA 22315
703-688-2284
866-254-8128; *Fax:* 703-683-0295
acuia@acuia.org; www.acuia.org
Social Media: Facebook, Twitter, LinkedIn
Brad Feldman, Executive Director
Barry Lucas, Director
This four-day event covers the latest developments and features some of the industry's most popular speakers.

244 AGA's Professional Development Conference & Exposition
Association of Government Accountants
2208 Mount Vernon Avenue
Alexandria, VA 22301
703-684-6931
800-242-7211; *Fax:* 703-548-9367
agacgfm@agacgfm.org; www.agacgfm.org
Relmond Van Daniker, Executive Director
Evelyn Brown, National President
Worth 24 CPE hours, the conferenc covers the latest research and information about the American Recovery Act, the constantly changing rules and standards, new management techniques, technological advances and practical tips for bringing greater efficiency to government operations. $800 for members, $1000 for nonmembers
Frequency: Annual

245 AHIA Annual Conference
The Association of Healthcare Internal Auditors
10200 W 44th Avenue
Suite 304
Wheat Ridge, CO 80033
888-275-2442; *Fax:* 303-422-8894
ahia@ahia.org; www.ahia.org
Mark Eddy, Director
Pat Bogusz, Executive Director
Exhibits concerning cost containment and increased productivity in health care institutions through internal auditing.
1000 Attendees
Founded in: 1981

246 AM&AA Summer Conference
Alliance of Merger and Acquisition Advisors
200 E. Randolph Street
24th Floor
Chicago, IL 60601
312-856-9590
877-844-2535; *Fax:* 312-729-9800
info@amaaonline.org; www.amaaonline.com
Matthew C Hawkins, Conference Chairman
Hosts many of the world's leading mid-market M&A executives, top tier speakers, as well as an invaluable networking opportunity.
Frequency: Semi-Annual

247 AM&AA Winter Conference
Alliance of Merger and Acquisition Advisors
200 E. Randolph Street
24th Floor
Chicago, IL 60601
312-856-9590
877-844-2535; *Fax:* 312-729-9800
info@amaaonline.com; www.amaaonline.com
Matthew C Hawkins, Conference Chairman
The conference covers a wide range of current topics of interest to members, such as new accounting and tax regulations, value-added intermediary services, financing, licensure, marketing and business development services and networking opportunities.
Frequency: Semi-Annual

248 ARMA International Conference & Expo
ARMA International
11880 College Blvd.
Suite 450
Overland Park, KS 66210
913-341-3808
800-422-2762; *Fax:* 913-341-3742
hq@arma.org; www.arma.org/conference
Social Media: Facebook, Twitter, LinkedIn
Carol Jorgenson, Meetings/Education Coordinator
Wanda Wilson, Senior Manager, Conferences
Elizabeth Zlitni, Exposition Manager
Conference, seminar, workshop, banquet, award ceremony and 175 exhibits of micrographics, optical disk, automated document storage and retrieval systems and more technology of interest to information professionals.
3500 Attendees
Frequency: Annual
Founded in: 1956

249 ASWA/AWSCPA Joint Annual Conference
American Woman's Society of CPAs
136 S Keowee Street
Dayton, OH 45402
937-222-1872
800-297-2721; *Fax:* 937-222-5794
info@awscpa.org; www.awscpa.org
Social Media: Facebook, Twitter, LinkedIn
Amy Knowles-Jones, President
Kelly Welter, President Elect
Alexandra Miller, Secretary/Treasurer
Cynthia Cox, VP - Member Services
The conference presents an opportunity to learn from leading experts on ways to develop a variety of your skills, leadership development, networking, education and fun.
Frequency: Annual/September
Founded in: 2001

250 ASWA/AWSCPA Joint National Conference
American Society of Women Accountants
1760 Old Meadow Road
Suite 500
McLean, VA 22102
703-506-3265
800-326-2163; *Fax:* 703-506-3266
aswa@aswa.org; www.aswa.org
Social Media: Facebook, Twitter, LinkedIn
Julia Merrill, Annual Conference Contact
Banquet, luncheon, tours and exhibits of accounting, business and employment opportunities. In conjunction with American Women's Society of CPAs
400 Attendees
Frequency: Annual

251 Academy of Accounting Historians Annual Research Conference
Academy of Accounting Historians
10900 Euclid Avenue
Cleveland, OH 44106-7235
216-368-2058; *Fax:* 216-368-6244
acchistory@case.edu; www.aahhq.org
Joanne Cross, President
Robert Colson, President Elect
Yvette Lazdowski, VP, Communications
Robert Colson, VP Communications
Stephanie Moussalli, Secretary
Encourages research, publication, teaching and personal interchanges in all phases of accounting history and its inter-relation with business and economic history. Members are individuals and institutional affiliates with business and economic history.
600 Members
Frequency: Annual
Founded in: 1973

252 Accounting Technology New York Show & Conference
Flagg Management
353 Lexington Avenue
New York, NY 10016
212-286-0333; *Fax:* 212-286-0086
flaggmgmnt@msn.com; www.flaggmgmt.com
Russell Flagg, President
The free Show focuses on new computer-savvy systems for accounting practices and client operations. See new products offered for the first time. The Conference offers CPE sessions with more than 100 exhibitors and nationally recognized speakers.
Frequency: Annual

253 All Star Conference
Institute of Internal Auditors

247 Maitland Avenue
Altamonte Springs, FL 32701-4201

407-371-1100; *Fax:* 407-937-1101
iia@theiia.org; www.theiia.org

J. Michael Pepper, Chairman
Carolyn Saint, Senior Vice President
John Wxzelaki, Vice Chairman - Finance/security

Event features concurrent sessions in tracks focusing on strategies for excellence, risk management, emerging issues, organization best practices, and preventing fraud.
400 Members
Frequency: October/Annual

254 Alliance of Merger & Acquisition Advisors Semi-Annual Conference

200 E Randolph St
24th Floor
Chicago, IL 60601-6435

312-856-9590
877-844-2535; *Fax:* 312-729-9800
info@amaaonline.org; www.amaaonline.com

Michael Nall, Owner

AM&AA is the premier International Organization serving the educational and resource needs of the middle market M&A profession. Conferences cover a wide range of current topics of interest to our members, such as new accounting and tax regulations, value-added intermediary services, financing, licensure, marketing and business development services and networking.
Frequency: Semi-Annual
Founded in: 1998

255 American Association of Attorney-Certified Public Accountants Convention

American Association of Attorney-CPAs
8647 Richmond Highway
Suite 639
Alexandria, VA 22309

703-352-8064
888-288-9272; *Fax:* 703-352-8073
info@attorney-cpa.com;
www.attorney-cpa.com

Robert Driegert, President
Domenick Lioce, President Elect
Joseph Cordell, Treasurer
John Pramberg, Secretary

Exhibits for persons licensed both as attorneys and CPAs.
Frequency: July/Annual
Founded in: 1964

256 American Payroll Association Annual Congress

American Payroll Association
660 North Main Avenue
Suite 100
San Antonio, TX 78205

210-226-4600; *Fax:* 210-224-6038
apa@americanpayroll.org;
www.americanpayroll.org
Social Media: Facebook, Twitter, LinkedIn, YouTube

The Annual Congress is the premier payroll event of the year. With over 190 workshops and special programs and entertainment, Congress is an excellent opportunity for payroll and other financial professionals to learn and network.
1500 Attendees
Frequency: Annual
Founded in: 1982

257 American Payroll Association Fall Forum

American Payroll Association
660 North Main Avenue
Suite 100
San Antonio, TX 78205

210-226-4600; *Fax:* 210-224-6038
apa@americanpayroll.org;
www.americanpayroll.org
Social Media: Facebook, Twitter, LinkedIn, YouTube

Dave Maddux, Executive Director

APA's Fall Forum is conducted under the auspices of APA's Strategic Payroll Leadership Task Force. This conference includes APA's Payroll Best Practices Survey and the presentation of APA's Prism Award winners.
1500 Attendees
Frequency: Annual
Founded in: 1982

258 Annual ACFE Fraud Conference and Exhibition

716 West Ave
Austin, TX 78701-2727

512-478-9070
800-245-3321; *Fax:* 512-478-9297
accounting@acfe.com; www.acfe.com
Social Media: Facebook, Twitter, LinkedIn

James D Ratley, President and CEO
Scott Grossfeld, Chief Executive Officer

The ACFE is the world's largest anti-fraud organization and premier provider of anti-fraud training and education.
50000 Members

259 Annual Conference for Women in Accounting

1760 Old Meadow Road
Suite 500
McLean, VA 22102

703-506-3265
800-326-2163; *Fax:* 703-506-3266
aswa@aswa.org; www.aswa.org
Social Media: Facebook, Twitter, LinkedIn, ASWA Presidents Blog

Barbara W Cornington, President
Monika P Miles CPA, VP of Membership
Tracy L Johnson CPA, VP of Chapter Partnering
Vivian L Moller CPA, VP of Communications

Provides a program that offers a myriad of opportunities to help you meet your continuing education goals, whether technical or soft-skills focused, as well as an opportunity to network with other women of similar backgrounds.
4000 Members
Founded in: 1938

260 BCCA Media Credit Seminar

550 W Frontage Rd
Suite 3600
Northfield, IL 60093-1243

847-881-8757; *Fax:* 847-784-8059
info@bccacredit.com; www.bccacredit.com
Social Media: Facebook, Twitter

Cherryl Ingram, Chairman
Chad Richardson, Vice Chairman
Dalton Lee, Secretary
Ralph Bender, Treasurer

Subsidiary of the Media Financial Management Association. BCCA provides credit information, education, and networking opportunities which enables members to efficiently manage credit risk and increase profitability.
600 Members
Founded in: 1972

261 CPAAI Regional Meetings

301 State Rt 17
Rutherford, NJ 07070-2599

201-804-8686; *Fax:* 201-804-9222
homeoffice@cpaai.com; www.cpaai.com

James F Flynn, President
Glenda Nixon, Chairman
Ted Carnevale, Secretary

CPA Associates International was established as a global group of high-quality independent CPA and chartered accounting firms; it is market exclusive, with members in major cities throughout the world. The organized association provides members with the capabilities of the largest firm, yet allows each to maintain its local practice while avoiding costly overhead and unnecessary controls.
2050 Members
Founded in: 1960

262 Capital Summit

American Payroll Association
660 North Main Avenue
Suite 100
San Antonio, TX 78205

210-226-4600; *Fax:* 210-226-4027
apa@americanpayroll.org;
www.americanpayroll.org
Social Media: Facebook, Twitter, LinkedIn, YouTube

Dave Maddux, Executive Director

APA hosts the Capital Summit in Washington, D.C. This conference offers attendees the opportunity to meet with government officials and learn about the latest compliance initiatives.
Frequency: Annual
Founded in: 1982

263 Club and Hotel Controllers Conference

11709 Boulder Lane
Suite 110
Austin, TX 78726

512-249-5333
800-646-4387; *Fax:* 512-249-1533;
www.hftp.org
Social Media: Facebook, Twitter, LinkedIn

Frank I Wolfe, Executive VP/CEO
Lucinda Hart, COO
Thomas Atzenhofer, CFO
Eliza Selig, Director of Communications

The program offers a range of sessions that reflect diverse responsibilities, from technology to taxes, human resource management to personal inspiration.
4600 Members
Founded in: 1952

264 Current Financial Reporting Issues Conference

200 Campus Drive
PO Box 674
Florham Park, NJ 07932

973-360-0177; *Fax:* 973-898-4649;
www.financialexecutives.org

Marie N Hollein, President & CEO
Marsha Hunt, VP
Mitch Danaher
Paul Chase, VP/Chief Financial Officer
Christopher Allen, VP/Chief Marketing Officer

Get updated in all the areas of financial reporting critical to the sustainability of your company. FASB/IASB technical accounting, revenue recognition, accounting for leases by lessors and lessees, financial instruments-recognition, measurement, hedging and expected loss model, Washington tax update, and the latest SEC happenings.
15M Members
Founded in: 1931

265 **Detecting & Deterring Financial Reporting Fraud**
200 Campus Drive
PO Box 674
Florham Park, NJ 07932
973-360-0177; *Fax:* 973-898-4649;
www.financialexecutives.org
Marie N Hollein, President & CEO
Marsha Hunt, VP
Mitch Danaher
Paul Chase, VP/Chief Financial Officer
Christopher Allen, VP/Chief Marketing Officer
Executive workshop for exploring strategies for building an ethical philosophy that deters fraud, employs skepticism-an enemy of fraud- in management's attitude and developing a culture of collaboration and knowledge sharing to deter and detect fraud.
15M Members
Frequency: 10x/Year
Founded in: 1931

266 **Distance Learning Seminar**
550 W Frontage Rd
Suite 3600
Northfield, IL 60093-1243
847-881-8757; *Fax:* 847-784-8059
info@bccacredit.com; www.bccacredit.com
Social Media: Facebook, Twitter
Cherryl Ingram, Chairman
Chad Richardson, Vice Chairman
Dalton Lee, Secretary
Ralph Bender, Treasurer
Credit & Collections 101 for the New Credit Professional
600 Members
Founded in: 1972

267 **Educational Institutions Payroll Conference**
American Payroll Association
660 North Main Avenue
Suite 100
San Antonio, TX 78205
210-226-4600; *Fax:* 210-226-4027
apa@americanpayroll.org;
www.americanpayroll.org
Social Media: Facebook, Twitter, LinkedIn, YouTube
Dave Maddux, Executive Director
This conference focuses on compliance issues impacting payroll professionals working in the higher education community.
Frequency: Annual
Founded in: 1982

268 **FMA Annual Meeting**
University of South Florida
4202 E Fowler Ave
BSN 3331
Tampa, FL 33620-9951
813-974-2084; *Fax:* 813-974-3318
fma@coba.usf.edu; www.fma.org
Jack S Rader, Executive Director
Douglas R Emery, President Elect
Franklin Allen, VP Program
Alexander J Triantis, VP Global Services
Ajay Patel, Secretary/Treasurer
The Financial Management Association International (FMA) is the global leader in developing and disseminating knowledge about financial decision making. FMA's members include adademicians and practitioners worldwide.
Founded in: 1970

269 **Financial Leadership Forum**
200 Campus Drive
PO Box 674
Florham Park, NJ 07932
973-360-0177; *Fax:* 973-898-4649;
www.financialexecutives.org
Marie N Hollein, President & CEO
Marsha Hunt, VP
Mitch Danaher
Paul Chase, VP/Chief Financial Officer
Christopher Allen, VP/Chief Marketing Officer
Forum to help advance the success of senior-level financial executives.
15M Members
Frequency: 10x/Year
Founded in: 1931

270 **Gaming Conference**
Institute of Internal Auditors
247 Maitland Avenue
Altamonte Springs, FL 32701-4201
407-371-1100; *Fax:* 407-937-1101
iia@theiia.org; www.theiia.org
J. Michael Pepper, Chairman
Carolyn Saint, Senior Vice President
John Wxzelaki, Vice Chairman - Finance/security
A must attend event for knowledge-seeking auditors, compliance officers, regulators, and professionals from gaming sectors.
300 Members
Frequency: April/Annual

271 **General Audit Management Conference**
Institute of Internal Auditors
247 Maitland Avenue
Altamonte Springs, FL 32701-4201
407-371-1100; *Fax:* 407-937-1101
iia@theiia.org; www.theiia.org
J. Michael Pepper, Chairman
Carolyn Saint, Senior Vice President
John Wxzelaki, Vice Chairman - Finance/security
The premiere opportunity for chief audit executives (CAEs), audit directors, and audit leaders to network with peers, benchmark against best practices, and tap into the knowledge of the profession's highest-level practitioners.
800 Members
Frequency: March/Annual

272 **Governance, Risk and Control Conference**
Institute of Internal Auditors
247 Maitland Avenue
Altamonte Springs, FL 32701-4201
407-371-1100; *Fax:* 407-937-1101
iia@theiia.org; www.theiia.org
J. Michael Pepper, Chairman
Carolyn Saint, Senior Vice President
John Wxzelaki, Vice Chairman - Finance/security
Develop and enhance your auditing skills.
400 Members
Frequency: August/Annual

273 **HITEC**
11709 Boulder Lane
Suite 110
Austin, TX 78726
512-249-5333
800-646-4387; *Fax:* 512-249-1533;
www.hftp.org
Social Media: Facebook, Twitter, LinkedIn
Frank I Wolfe, Executive VP/CEO
Lucinda Hart, COO
Thomas Atzenhofer, CFO
Eliza Selig, Director of Communications
Attend HITEC and network with the industry's innovators, gain knowledge from an expert-led education program and find technology products and services to take your organization to the next level.
4600 Members
Founded in: 1952

274 **Hall of Fame Gala**
200 Campus Drive
PO Box 674
Florham Park, NJ 07932
973-360-0177; *Fax:* 973-898-4649;
www.financialexecutives.org
Marie N Hollein, President & CEO
Marsha Hunt, VP
Mitch Danaher
Paul Chase, VP/Chief Financial Officer
Christopher Allen, VP/Chief Marketing Officer
Providing recognition to senior-level financial executives who have epitomized the performance, leadership and integrity of the most exemplary financial professionals throughout their careers and in doing so, have made significant contributions to the betterment of their respective organizations and to the profession as a whole.
15M Members
Founded in: 1931

275 **IASA Annual Conference**
Insurance, Accounting & Systems Association
PO Box 51340
Durham, NC 27717-1340
919-489-0991; *Fax:* 919-489-1994
info@iasa.org; www.iasa.org
Social Media: Facebook, Twitter
Ruth Estrich, President
Joseph Pomilia, Executive Director
Ernie Pearson, Board Chair
H. Louise Ziemann, president-elect
Tom Ewbank, CFO
Provides comprehensive education programs targeted for financial and technology professionals in the industry.
1800 Attendees
Frequency: Annual

276 **IFRS Boot Camp**
200 Campus Drive
PO Box 674
Florham Park, NJ 07932
973-360-0177; *Fax:* 973-898-4649;
www.financialexecutives.org
Marie N Hollein, President & CEO
Marsha Hunt, VP
Mitch Danaher
Paul Chase, VP/Chief Financial Officer
Christopher Allen, VP/Chief Marketing Officer
Provides an update on various recent convergence and regulatory/ statutory matters impacting U.S. GAAP and IFRS reporting companies. Provides financial executives with practical information for addressing global accounting convergence in their organizations, including potential operational considerations rellated to topics such as leases and revenue recognition.
15M Members
Frequency: 10x/Year
Founded in: 1931

277 **IMA's Annual Conference & Exposition**
10 Paragon Dr
Suite 1
Montvale, NJ 07645-1774
201-573-9000
800-638-4427; *Fax:* 201-474-1600

ima@imanet.org; www.imanet.org
Social Media: Facebook, Twitter, LinkedIn

Jeffrey C. Thomson, President and CEO
Brian L. McGuire, Chair
John C. Macaulay, Chair-Elect
Sandra B. Richtermeyer, Chair-Emeritus

Offers three days of knowledge building, education, networking, optional pre-conference workshops, and opportunities to earn NASBA-approved credits.
67000 Members
Founded in: 1919

278 IMA's Student Leadership Conference
10 Paragon Dr
Suite 1
Montvale, NJ 07645-1774
201-573-9000
800-638-4427; *Fax:* 201-474-1600
ima@imanet.org; www.imanet.org
Social Media: Facebook, Twitter, LinkedIn

Jeffrey C. Thomson, President and CEO
Brian L. McGuire, Chair
John C. Macaulay, Chair-Elect
Sandra B. Richtermeyer, Chair-Emeritus

Offers three days of learning and career networking opportunities for college students and educators. Accounting, finance, and business students will learn from veteran practitioners about the critical role of accountants and financial professionals within business.
67000 Members
Founded in: 1919

279 Information Resources Management Association Conferences
Information Resources Management Association
701 E Chocolate Avenue
Suite 200
Hershey, PA 17033
717-533-8845; *Fax:* 717-533-8861
member@irma-international.org;
www.irma-international.org

Jan Travers, Executive Director
Sherif Kamel, Communications Director
Lech Janczewski PhD, IRMA World Representative Director
Gerald Grant, IRMA Doctoral Symposium Director
Paul Chalekian, IRMA United States Representative

Provides forums for researchers and practitioners to share leading-edge knowledge in the global information resource management area. Various seminars, conventions, conferences and other training programs are offered by IRMA throughout the year.

280 Joint ISPA/SCEA Conference & Workshop
Society of Cost Estimating & Analysis
8221 Old Courthouse Rd
Suite 106
Vienna, VA 22182
703-938-5090; *Fax:* 703-938-5091
scea@sceaonline.org; www.sceaonline.net

Erin Whittaker, Executive Director
Sharon Burger, Certification Program Admin
Brittany Walker, Membership Coordinator
Debra Lehman, Treasurer

Speakers and panel sessions, integrated training tracks, informative workshops and vendor exhibits. Three of every four years, the annual conference is a joint conference with the International Society of Parametric Analysts (ISPA). Certification exams are offered at the conference for a separate fee.
2015 Members
400 Attendees
Frequency: Annual/June
Founded in: 1990

281 NATP National Conference and Expo
National Association of Tax Professionals
PO Box 8002
Appleton, WI 54912-8002

800-558-3402; *Fax:* 800-747-0001
natp@natptax.com; www.natptax.com
Social Media: Facebook, Twitter, MySpace

Jo Ann Schoen, President
Jean Millerchip, Vice President
Gerard Cannito, Treasurer
Patricia M. McNeer, Secretary
Kathy Stanek, CEO

Four days filled with top-notch tax education, fun social events, networking, and much more.
Frequency: Annual

282 National Leadership Conference
Association of Government Accountants
2208 Mount Vernon Avenue
Alexandria, VA 22301

703-684-6931
800-242-7211; *Fax:* 703-548-9367
agacgfm@agacgfm.org; www.agacgfm.org

Relmond Van Daniker, Executive Director
Evelyn Brown, National President

Presents new tools, and innovations, insights from financial management and accountability leaders, their strategies, mistakes, new management techniques, and the most current standards and regulations updates.
Frequency: Annual/February

283 Performance Management Conference (PMC)
Association of Government Accountants
2208 Mount Vernon Avenue
Alexandria, VA 22301

703-684-6931
800-242-7211; *Fax:* 703-548-9367
agacgfm@agacgfm.org; www.agacgfm.org

Relmond Van Daniker, Executive Director
Evelyn Brown, National President

Leaders in performance reporting from all levels of goverment, the private sector and academia share how-tos, lessons learned and cooperative initiatives among governments. Registration begins at $395 for Members, $450 for nonmembers.
Frequency: Annual/November

284 Practice Management Conference
Association for Accounting Administration
136 S Keowee Street
Dayton, OH 45402

937-222-0030; *Fax:* 937-222-5794
aaainfo@cpaadmin.org; www.cpaadmin.org
Social Media: Twitter, LinkedIn

Dennis Lemieux, President
Norman Saale, Vice President
Janine Zirrith, Secretary
Jim Fahey, Treasurer
Jane Johnson, Director of Education

Information and displays of accounting administration equipment and products.
200 Attendees
Frequency: Annual/June

285 SCEA/ISPA Joint Annual Conference & Training Workshop
Society of Cost Estimating and Analysis
8221 Old Courthouse Rd
Suite 106
Vienna, VA 22182
703-938-5090; *Fax:* 703-938-5091
scea@sceaonline.org; www.sceaonline.org

Erin Whittaker, Executive Director
Sharon Burger, Certification Program Admin
Brittany Walker, Membership Coordinator

Features training sessions to help attendees enhance their skill set or prepare for the CCEA or CPP exams, study sessions, Professional Papers give attendees the chance to hear about best practices, lessons learned and the latest developments in the field.
2015 Members
500+ Attendees
Frequency: Annual
Founded in: 1990

286 Society of Actuaries Annual Meeting & Exhibit
Society of Actuaries
475 N Martingale Road
Suite 600
Schaumburg, IL 60173
847-697-3900
customerservice@soa.org; www.soa.org

Greg Heidrich, Executive Director
Stacy Lin, Deputy Executive Director/CFO

Sessions and keynote presentations about cutting edge research, and discussions, networking opportunities, the latest and greatest technologies, sponsorship opportunities; sometimes held in conjunction with the Academy Luncheon. Registration fees begin at $55 for the luncheon and go to $995 for full meeting attendance.
1,700 Attendees
Frequency: Annual/November

287 SourceMedia Conferences & Events
SourceMedia
One State Street Plaza
27th floor
New York, NY 10004

212-803-6093
800-803-3424; *Fax:* 212-803-8515
abconferences@sourcemedia.com;
www.sourcemedia.com/

James M Malkin, Chairman & CEO
William Johnson, CFO
Steve Andreazza, VP, Sales & Customer Service
Celie Baussan, SVP, Operations
Anne O'Brien, EVP Marketing & Strategic Planning

SourceMedia Conferences & Events attract over 20,000 attendees worldwide. The content embraces a variety of formats, including: conferences, executive roundtables, expositions, Web seminars, custom events and pod casts. With over 70 events annually, participants are provided with premier content as well as access to the industry's top solution providers. Markets served include: accounting; banking; capital markets; financial services; information technology; insurance; and real estate.

288 Technology and Office Productivity (TOP) Conference
National Association of Tax Professionals
PO Box 8002
Appleton, WI 54912-8002

800-558-3402; *Fax:* 800-747-0001
natp@natptax.com; www.natptax.com
Social Media: Facebook, Twitter, MySpace

Jo Ann Schoen, President
Jean Millerchip, Vice President
Gerard Cannito, Treasurer
Patricia M. McNeer, Secretary
Kathy Stanek, CEO

Two days filled with valuable education on what it takes to run a small business, fun social events, networking, and more.
Frequency: Annual

289 **The IIA's International Conference**
The Institute of Internal Auditors
247 Maitland Avenue
Altamonte Springs, FL 32701-4201
407-937-1100; *Fax:* 407-937-1101
iia@theiia.org; www.theiia.org
William J Mulcahy, Conference Chairman
Richard Chambers, President & CEO
Annual conference that features and unprecedented number of concurrent sessions on today's top issues, industry best practices, and unique challenges to help you add value to your organization.
84000 Attendees
Frequency: Annual
Founded in: 1941

290 **The World Congress Annual Leadership Summit on Mergers & Acquisitions**
200 E Randolph St
24th Floor
Chicago, IL 60601-6435
312-856-9590
877-844-2535; *Fax:* 312-729-9800
info@amaaonline.org; www.amaaonline.com
Michael Nall, Owner
AM&AA is the premier International Organization serving the educational and resource needs of the middle market M&A profession.
Founded in: 1998

291 **Valcon**
Association of Insolvency & Restructuring Advisors
221 Stewart Avenue
Suite 207
Medford, OR 97501
541-858-1665; *Fax:* 541-858-9187
aira@aira.org; www.airacira.org
Anthony Sasso, President
Thomas Morrow, Vice President
Mathew Schwartz, Treasurer
Joel Waite, VP
Matthew Schwartz, Treasurer
Join leading restructuring and valuation experts - attorneys, private equity investors, bankers, financial advisors and workout specialists - to discuss cutting-edge valuation issues and market developments.
Frequency: Annual/February
Founded in: 1984

Directories & Databases

292 **ARMA International's Buyers Guide**
ARMA International
11880 College Blvd
Suite 450
Overland Park, KS 66215
913-341-3808
800-422-2762; *Fax:* 913-341-3742
hq@arma.org; www.arma.org/conference
Social Media: Facebook, Twitter, LinkedIn
75-100 companies listed. Free.

293 **Accountancy: A Professional Reference Guide**
Georgia State University
35 Broad Street
5th Floor
Atlanta, GA 30302-3991
404-413-7200; *Fax:* 404-413-7203
admissions@gsu.edu
robinson.gsu.edu/accountancy/index.html
Carla Hines, Administrative Coordinator
Allison Jacobs, Director of Student Services
Listings of accounting firms, associations, regulatory agencies and schools offering accredited accounting programs.
Cost: $99.95
450 Pages
Frequency: Hardcover

294 **Accounting Research Directory**
Markus Wiener Publishing
231 Nassau St
Princeton, NJ 08542-4601
609-921-1141; *Fax:* 609-921-1140;
www.markuswiener.com
Social Media: Facebook
Markus Wiener, Owner
Lawrence D Brown, Editor
Markus Wiener, President
Quick guide arranged by author's names for key articles. It can enable those interested in quantitative literature analysis to test and verify much of the work in this area by the authors in this book.
Cost: $79.95
Frequency: Hardcover
ISBN: 1-558760-68-7

295 **Accounting, Tax & Banking Collection**
ProQuest Information and Learning
789 E Eisenhower Parkway
PO Box 1346
Ann Arbor, MI 48106-1346
734-761-4700
800-889-3358; *Fax:* 800-864-0019;
www.proquest.com
Social Media: Facebook, Twitter, LinkedIn
Offers comprehensive global scholarly journals and key resources on a range of topics relating to accoutning and finance

296 **American Association of Attorney-Certified Public Accountants Directory**
American Association of Attorney-CPAs
8647 Richmond Highway
Suite 639
Alexandria, VA 22309
703-352-8064
888-288-9272; *Fax:* 703-352-8073
info@attorney-cpa.com;
www.attorney-cpa.com
Robert Driegert, President
Domenick Lioce, President Elect
Joseph Cordell, Treasurer
John Pramberg, Secretary
Driegert, Secretary
Offers names, addresses and biographical data on 1,400 individuals licensed as both attorneys and CPAs.
100 Pages
Frequency: Annual
Founded in: 1964
Printed in one color

297 **Directory of Actuarial Memberships**
Society of Actuaries
475 N Martingale Rd
Suite 600
Schaumburg, IL 60173-2252
847-706-3500; *Fax:* 847-706-3599
webmaster@soa.org; www.soa.org
Social Media: Twitter, LinkedIn
Greg Heidrich, Executive Director
Stacy Lin, Deputy Executive Director/CFO
Tiffany Berger, Director of Finance
Richard Veys, General Counsel
Francis P. Sabatini, Vice President
Lists member names, affiliations and contact information for major US and international actuarial professional associations.
Cost: $150.00
Mailing list available for rent: 17000 names at $300 per M

298 **Federal Tax Coordinator 2D**
Thomson Reuters
2395 Midway Rd
Carrollton, TX 75006
817-332-3709
800-431-9025; *Fax:* 888-216-1929
trta.lei-support@thomsonreuters.com;
www.ria.thomsonreuters.com
Elaine Yadlon, Plant Manager
Thomas H Glocer, CEO & Director
Robert D Daleo, Chief Financial Officer
Kelli Crane, Senior Vice President & CIO
Provides verbatim text of the Internal Revenue Code and IRS Regulations. Information is arranged by subject rather than in Code order. Professional tax preparers are heavy users of this service because of the thorough authoritative analysis it provides.
Cost: $2460.00
Founded in: 1935

299 **Future Actuary**
Society of Actuaries
475 N Martingale Rd
Suite 600
Schaumburg, IL 60173-2252
847-706-3500; *Fax:* 847-706-3599
webmaster@soa.org; www.soa.org
Greg Heidrich, Executive Director
Stacy Lin, Deputy Executive Director/CFO
Full coverage on topics like career development, non-traditional careers, grading systems, study tips, professional conduct and ethics and the structure of actuarial organizations.
Mailing list available for rent: 17000 names at $300 per M

300 **International Guide to Accounting Journals**
Markus Weiner Publishers
231 Nassau St
Princeton, NJ 08542-4601
609-921-1141; *Fax:* 609-921-1140
info@markuswiener.com;
www.markuswiener.com
Markus Wiener, Owner
Surendra Agrawal, Editor
Approximately 300 journals in accounting and related areas, including about 150 published in the US and 150 from 33 other countries that are published in English.
Cost: $49.95
ISBN: 1-558760-67-9

301 **National Society of Public Accountants Yearbook**
National Society of Public Accountants
1010 N Fairfax St
Alexandria, VA 22314-1574
703-549-6400
800-966-6679; *Fax:* 703-549-2984
members@nsacct.org; www.nsacct.org
Social Media: Facebook, Twitter, LinkedIn
Harlan Rose, President
Steven Hanson, First Vice President
Marilyn Niwao, Second Vice President
Brian Thompson, Secretary-Treasurer
Association members and committees, lists of affiliated state organizations and members of governing board.
Frequency: Annual

Industry Web Sites

302 **www.aabpa.org**
American Assoc for Budget and Program Analysis

Social Media: LinkedIn

The American Association for Budget and Program Analysis helps federal, state and local government managers and analysts, corporate executives and academic specialists meet the unique challenges of their careers related to the fields of public budgeting and program analysis.

303 **www.acatcredentials.org**
Accreditation Council for Accountancy and Taxation

Identifies and accredits specialists in accountancy and federal taxation who serve the financial needs of individuals and small to mid-sized business entities. Offers 3 credentials: Accreditation in Accountancy/Accredited Business Accountant, Accredited Tax Preparer and Accredited Tax Advisor.

304 **www.acaus.org**
Association of Chartered Accountants in the U.S.

ACAUS is a nonprofit professional and educational organization representing interests of over 6,000 U.S. based chartered accountants from the institutes of Chartered Accountants across the globe.

305 **www.accountants.org**
IGAF Polaris

Association of over 136 independent accounting firms located throughout the world. We developed this comprehensive search site as a means of helping people locate an accounting or consulting firm anywhere in the world.

306 **www.acfe.com**
Association of Certified Fraud Examiners

The ACFE is the world's largest anti-fraud organization and premier provider of anti-fraud training and education.

307 **www.agacgfm.org**
Advancing Government Accountability

Educational organization dedicated to the enhancement of public financial management.

308 **www.agn.org**
Accountants Global Network International

Composed of CPA consulting firms who share information and resources via the associated programs.

309 **www.ahia.org**
Association of Healthcare Internal Auditors

Promotes cost containment and increased productivity in health care institutions through internal auditing. Serves as a forum for the exchange of experience, ideas, and information among members; provides continuing professional education courses and informs members of developments in health care internal auditing. Offers employment clearinghouse services.

310 **www.aicpa.org**
American Institute of Certified Public Accountants

The American Institute of Certified Public Accountants is the national, professional organization for all Certified Public Accountants. Its mission is to provide members with the resources, information, and leadership that enable them to provide valuable services in the highest professional manner to benefit the public as well as employers and clients.

311 **www.aipb.org**
American Institute of Professional Bookkeepers

Achieve recognition of bookkeepers as accounting professionals, to keep bookkeepers up-to-date on changes in bookkeeping, accounting and tax, to answer bookkeepers everyday bookkeeping and accounting questions, and to certify bookkeepers who meet high national standards.

312 **www.amaaonline.com**
Alliance of Merger & Acquisition Advisors

AM&AA is the premier International Organization serving the educational and resource needs of the middle market M&A profession.

313 **www.americanpayroll.org**
American Payroll Association

American Payroll Association provides numerous opportunities for payroll education and information.

314 **www.aswa.org**
American Society of Women Accountants

Organization for networking and information exchange in pursuit of professional development.

315 **www.attorney-cpa.com**
American Association of Attorney-CPAs

Seeks to safeguard the professional and legal rights of CPA attorneys.

316 **www.awscpa.org**
American Woman's Society of CPAs

Provides supportive environment that promotes equity and provides opportunities for the achievement of career goals in a competitive and rapidly changing profession.

317 **www.bap.org**
Beta Alpha Psi

Beta Alpha Psi is an honorary organization for Financial Information students and professionals. The primary objective is to encourage and give recognition to scholastic and professional excellence in the business information field.

318 **www.bccacredit.com**
Broadcast Cable Credit Association

Information on Credit Inquiry Service, credit and collection seminars yearly, credit personnel directories, surveys and on-line services.

319 **www.bna.com**
Bureau of National Affairs

A national organization that has a broad range of employment topics, designed for the small to medium-sized organization.

320 **www.computercpa.com**
Accountant's Home Page

Provides information on general accounting for manufacturing, contstruction, service, not-for-profit, e-commerce and more.

321 **www.cpa.net**
Mark Dietrich, CPA, PC

Includes information on social security and alternatives, bill presentation and payment.

322 **www.cpaadmin.org**
Association for Accounting Administration

Enables accounting firm administrators to communicate with one another and share experiences in the profession.

323 **www.cpaai.com**
CPA Associates International

CPA Associates International was established as a global group of high-quality independent CPA and chartered accounting firms; it is market exclusive, with members in major cities throughout the world. The organized association provides members with the capabilities of the largest firm, yet allows each to maintain its local practice while avoiding costly overhead and unnecessary controls.

324 **www.cpatechadvisor.com**
The CPA Technology Advisor

Online resource for accountants and managers. The Web site features a Buyer's Guide that lists hundreds of businesses, manufacturers, and professionals that can assist public accounting firms in delivering a variety of services to their clients in various industries.

325 **www.expresscarriers.com**
Express Carriers Association

A member organization of chief financial officers within the American Trucking Association.

326 **www.gasb.org**
Governmental Accounting Standards Board

Establishes and improves standards of state and local governmental accounting and financial reporting that will result in useful information for users of financial reports and guide and educate the public, including issuers, auditors and users of those financial institutions.

327 **www.grantthornton.com**
Grant Thornton LLP

Grant Thornton LLP is the U.S. member firm of Grant Thornton International Ltd., one of the six global audit, tax and advisory organizations.

328 **www.greyhouse.com**
Grey House Publishing

Authoritative reference directories for business information and general reference, including accounting, banking and financial markets. Users can search the online databases with varied search criteria allowing for custom searches by product category, geographic area, sales volume, keyword, subject and more. Full Grey House catalog and online ordering also available.

329 **www.hftp.org**
Hospitality Financial & Technology Professionals

HFTP is the global professional association for financial and technology personnel working in hotels, clubs, and other hospitality-related businesses.

330 **www.iasa.org**
Insurance, Accounting & Systems Association

The Insurance Accounting & Systems Association Web site offers information about membership in the organization, accounting seminars, events, publications and textbooks.

331 **www.ifac.org**
International Federation of Accountants

IFAC is the global organization for the accountancy profession. It works with its 157 members and associates in 123 countries and jurisdictions to protect the public interest by encouraging high quality practices by the world's accountants.

332 **www.igafworldwide.org**
International Group of Accounting Firms

IGAF Worldwide is one of the oldest, largest, and most well-respected accounting associations in the world. It was founded for the purpose of providing member firms with the tools and resources they need to furnish a broad spectrum of efficient, cost-effective accounting, auditing and management services to clients around the globe.

333 **www.imanet.org**
Institute of Management Accountants

Professional organization devoted exclusively to management accounting and financial management. Goals are to help members develop both personally and professionally, by means of education, certification, and association with other business professionals.

334 **www.infe.org**
Interactive & Newsmedia Financial Executives
Controllers, chief accountants, auditors, business managers, treasurers, secretaries and related newspaper executives, educators and public accountants.

335 **www.nabainc.org**
National Association of Black Accountants
Nationwide professional association with the primary purpose of developing, encouraging and serving as a resource for greater participation by African-Americans and other minorities in the accounting and finance professions.

336 **www.nactp.org**
Nat'l Association of Computerized Tax Processors
A nonprofit association that represents tax processing software and hardware developers, electronic filing processors, tax form publishers and tax processing service bureaus. The association promotes standards in tax processing and works closely with the Internal Revenue Service and state governments to promote efficient and effective tax filing.

337 **www.nacva.com**
National Assoc of Certified Valuation Analysts
Global, professional association that supports the business valuation and litigation consulting disciplines within the CPA and professional communities. Along with its training and certification programs, NACVA offers a range of support services, marketing tools, software programs, reference materials and customized databases to enhance the professional capabilities of its members.

338 **www.naea.org**
National Association of Enrolled Agents
Members are enrolled to represent taxpayers before the Internal Revenue Service. We advise, represent and prepare tax returns for individuals, partnerships, corporations, estates, trusts and any entities with tax reporting requirements.

339 **www.nsacct.org**
National Society of Accountants
Professional society of practicing accountants and tax practitioners that sponsors the Acceditation Council for Accountancy and Taxation and supports the National Society of Public Accountants Political Action Committee and NSPA Scholarship Foundation.

340 **www.sceaonline.org**
Society of Cost Estimating and Analysis
Dedicated to improving cost estimating and analysis in government and industry. Offers a unique collection of educational and training materials on cost estimating, cost analysis, earned value management and related disciplines through its professional development program.

341 **www.taxsites.com**
Tax and Accounting Sites Directory
A comprehensive index of internet resources, designed to be a starting point for people who are searching for tax and accounting information and services.

342 **www.theiia.org**
Institute of Internal Auditors
International organization of internal auditors, corporate executives and board members. Contact and current development information.

Associations

343 **Ad Council**
815 Second Avenue
9th Floor
New York, NY 10017-4503

212-922-1500; *Fax:* 212-962-1676
info@adcouncil.org; www.adcouncil.org
Social Media: Facebook, Twitter, LinkedIn, YouTube, Tumblr, Pinterest, In

David Christopher, Chairman
Lisa Sherman, President and CEO
Jon Fish, Executive Vice President/CFO
Priscilla Natkins, EVP, Director of Client Services
Paula Veale, EVP, Corporate Communications

Our mission is to identify a select number of significant public issues and stimulate action on those issues through communications programs that make a measurable difference in our society. To that end, the Ad Council marshals volunteer talent from the advertising and communications industries, the facilities of the media, and the resources of the business and non-profit communities to create awareness, foster understanding and motivate action.
100 Members
Founded in: 1941

344 **Advertising Council Inc**
1707 L Street NW
Suite 600
Washington, DC 20036

202-331-9153; *Fax:* 202-331-9186
kpastre@adcouncil.org; www.adcouncil.org
Social Media: Facebook, Twitter, LinkedIn, YouTube, Tumblr, Pinterest, In

David Christopher, Chairman
Lisa Sherman, President and CEO
Jon Fish, Executive Vice President/CFO
Priscilla Natkins, EVP, Director of Client Services
Paula Veale, EVP, Corporate Communications

The Ad Council marshals volunteer talent from the advertising and communications industries, the facilities of the media, and the resources of the business and non-profit communities to create awareness, foster understanding and motivate action.
Founded in: 1941

345 **Advertising Educational Foundation**
220 E 42nd St
Suite 3300
New York, NY 10017-5806

212-986-8060; *Fax:* 212-986-8061
pa@aef.com; www.aef.com
Social Media: Facebook, Twitter

Gordon McLean, Chairman
Sharon Hudson, VP/Manager
Paula Alex, President/CEO
Janice Spector, EVP, Managing Director
Marcia Solling, VP, Content Manager

The AEF is supported by ad agencies, advertisers and media companies. The AEF acknowledges that advertising is a vital and highly visible force in American society. Thus, a realistic understanding of how advertising is created, how it works and what it contributes to our social and economic life is important for all who play active roles in our complex society.
48 Members
Founded in: 1983

346 **Advertising Media Credit Executives Association**
PO Box 740031
Louisville, KY 40201-7431

502-582-4327; *Fax:* 502-582-4330
myounger@gannett.com; www.amcea.org

Norman TaylorNorman Taylor, President
Kimberly Archibald Russell, Vice President
Newt Collins, Secretary/Treasurer
Vickie Bolinger, Immediate Past President
Sandra Lawson, Director

The objectives of the AMCEA: To improve the professionalism, principles, understanding and techniques of media credit management by encouraging the exchange of ideas, methods and procedures within the membership; To provide additional education and training in the business fundamentals of media credit and credit policies; and in the related areas of finance, accounting, law and economics for the purpose of enhancing the career development of the members.
Founded in: 1953

347 **Advertising Photographers of America**
2221-D Peachtree Rd, NE
Suite 553
Atlanta, GA 30309

800-272-6264
888-889-7190; *Fax:* 888-889-7190
info@apaatlanta.com; www.apaatlanta.com

Harold Daniels, Chairman
Juliette Wolf-Robin, National Executive Director
David Fine, Treasurer
Jason Fobart, Board Member
Nate Dorn, Board Member

APA's mission is Successful Professional Photographers. Our goal is to establish, endorse, and promote professional practices, standards, and ethics in the photographic and advertising community. We seek to mentor, motivate, educate, and inspire in the pursuit of excellence. Our aim is to champion and speak as one common voice for advertising photographers and image makers to the advertising industry in the United States and the World.
Founded in: 1981

348 **Advertising Research Foundation**
432 Park Ave South
6th Floor
New York, NY 10016-8013

212-751-5656; *Fax:* 212-319-5265
info@thearf.org; www.thearf.org
Social Media: Facebook, Twitter, LinkedIn, YouTube, Flickr

David Poltrack, Chairman
Gayle Fuguitt, CEO & President
Rachael Feigenbaum, SVP, Events Program Producer
Michael Heitner, EVP, Member Needs & Value
Navarrow Wright, Chief Technology Officer

The Advertising Research Foundation (ARF) is an open forum where the best and brightest from every avenue of advertising gather to exchange ideas and research strategies. Together, we challenge conventional maxims, take on the latest issues, and discover new insights that benefit us all. This collaboration yields something invaluable: knowledge. Knowledge that is meaningful, actionable, and indispensable. Knowledge that empowers our members to have a true impact on their marketing programs.
Founded in: 1936

349 **Advertising Self-Regulatory Council**
112 Madison Avenue
3rd Floor
New York, NY 10016

212-705-0104
lbean@asrc.bbb.org; www.asrcreviews.org
Social Media: Facebook, Twitter, RSS

C. Lee Peeler, President & CEO
Linda Bean, Director of Communication
Reshma Persaud, Marketing Manager
Sarah Agler, Administrative Coordinator
Camille Sasena, Office Coordinator

Establishes the policies and procedures for advertising industry self-regulation. The self-regulatory system is administered by the Council of Better Business Bureaus.

350 **Advertising Specialty Institute**
4800 Street Rd
Trevose, PA 19053

215-953-4000
800-546-1350; *Fax:* 215-953-3045
customerservice@asicentral.com; www.asicentral.com
Social Media: Facebook, Twitter, LinkedIn, YouTube, Instagram, Pinterest

Norman Unger Cohn, Chairman
Timothy Andrews, President/CEO
Steve Bright, EVP/General Counsel
Rob Watson, SVP, Marketing
Vince Bucolo, Chief Operating Officer

The Advertising Specialty Institute, or ASI, has been providing award-winning products and services to the advertising specialty and promotional products industry for over 50 years. ASI publishes print and online business magazines, product catalogs, Web sites and informational directories. ASI's mission, then, is to bring together these participants by providing catalogs, information directories, newsletters, magazines, Web sites and databases, and offering interactive e-commerce, and marketing
26000 Members
Founded in: 1950

351 **Advertising Women of New York**
28 West 44th Street
Suite 912
New York, NY 10036-4910

212-221-7969; *Fax:* 212-221-8296
lynn.branigan@awny.org; www.awny.org
Social Media: Facebook, Twitter, LinkedIn, YouTube, Bloggr

Amy Wilkins, President
Sheila Buckley, First Vice President
Nadine McHugh, Second Vice President
Lynn Branigan, Executive Director
Suzanne Hogan, Associate Director, Events

AWNY was founded as the first women's association in the communications industry. It's active affiliate of the American Advertising Federation. Provides a forum for personal and professional growth; to serve as a catalyst for the advancement of women in the communications field.
1700 Members
Founded in: 1912

352 **Alliance for Audited Media**
48 W. Seegers Road
Arlington Heights, IL 60005-3913

224-366-6939; *Fax:* 224-366-6949
auditedmedia.com
Social Media: Facebook, Twitter, LinkedIn, YouTube, Instagram

Christina Meringolo, Chairwoman
Scott Kruse, Vice Chair
Evan Ray, Vice Chair
Chris Daly, Secretary
Liberta Abbondante, Treasurer

A nonprofit, member-based organization that works with media companies, advertising technology providers, ad agencies, and advertisers to provide them with independently verified data and information critical to evaluating and purchasing media.
Founded in: 1914

353 **American Academy of Advertising**
24710 Shaker Blvd.
Beachwood, OH 44122
786-393-3333
director@aaasite.org;
www.aaoa.wildapricot.org
Social Media: Facebook, Twitter

Karen M. Lancendorfer, President
Michelle Renee Nelson, Vice President
Patricia B. Rose, Executive Director
Jami Fullerton, Secretary
Gayle Kerr, Treasurer

The American Academy of Advertising (AAA) is an organization of advertising scholars and professionals with an interest in advertising and advertising education. The Academy fosters research that is relevant to the field and provides a forum for the exchange of ideas among its academic and professional members.
600 Members
Founded in: 1957

354 **American Advertising Federation**
1101 Vermont Ave NW
Suite 500
Washington, DC 20005-6306
202-898-0089
800-999-2231; *Fax:* 202-898-0159
aaf@aaf.org; www.aaf.org
Social Media: Facebook, Twitter, YouTube, RSS

Jim Norton, Chairman
James Edmund Datri, President & CEO
Joanne Schecter, EVP/Club Services
Karen Cohn, SVP, Conference & Meeting Logistics
Lisa Rubin, EVP, Special Events & Corp Services

The AAF is the oldest national advertising trade association, and protects and promotes the well-being of advertising. The AAF accomplishes this through a unique, nationally coordinated grassroots network of advertisers, agencies, media companies, local advertising clubs and college chapters.
40000 Members
Founded in: 1967

355 **American Association for Public Opinion Research**
One Parkview Plaza
Suite 800
Oakbrook Terrace, IL 60181
847-686-2230; *Fax:* 847-686-2251
athocher@aapor.org; www.aapor.org
Social Media: Facebook, Twitter, LinkedIn, YouTube

Mollyann Brodie, President
Roger Tourangeau, Vice President
Adam Thocher, Executive Director
Heidi Diederich, Administrative Director
Crystal Stone, Administrator

The AAPOR community includes producers and users of survey data from a variety of disciplines. Our members span a range of interests including election polling, market research, statistics, research methodology, health related data collection and education.
1700 Members
Founded in: 1947
Mailing list available for rent: 1000 names at $400 per M

356 **American Association of Advertising Agencies**
1065 Avenue of the Americas
16th Floor
New York, NY 10018
212-682-2500; *Fax:* 212-682-8391
nhill@aaaa.org; www.aaaa.org
Social Media: Facebook, Twitter, LinkedIn, YouTube, Google+

Nancy Hill, President/CEO
Michael D Donahue, Executive VP
Laura J. Bartlett, CFO & COO
Tom Finneran, EVP, Agency Management Services
Mike Donahue, EVP, Strategic Partnerships

The national trade association reprsenting the advertising volume placed by agencies nationwide.
600 Members
Founded in: 1917

357 **American Marketing Association**
311 S Wacker Dr
Suite 5800
Chicago, IL 60606-6629
312-542-9000
800-262-1150; *Fax:* 312-542-9001;
www.ama.org
Social Media: Facebook, Twitter, LinkedIn, Youtube, Pinterest, Google+

Rob Malcolm, Chairperson
Valarie Zeithaml?, Chairman-Elect
Mary Garrett, VP/Finance/Secretary
Russ Klein?, Chief Executive Officer
Beth Taylor, Chief Operations Officer

The AMA is a professional association for individuals and organizations leading the practice, teaching and development of marketing knowledge worldwide. Our principle role is to serve as a forum to connect like-minded individuals and foster knowledge sharing, provide resources, tools and training and support marketing practice and thought leadership around the globe.
40000 Members
Founded in: 1953

358 **Asian American Advertising Federation**
6230 Wilshire Blvd
Suite 1216
Los Angeles, CA 90048
E-Mail: ghomfranzen@3af.org; www.3af.org
Social Media: Facebook, Twitter

Edward Chang, President
Jay Kim, Vice President
Iris Yim, Secretary
Sandra Lee, Treasurer
Genny Hom-Franzen, Executive Director

Consists of Asian American advertising agency principals, media, advertisers and strategic partners that seek to grow the Asian American advertising and marketing industry, raise public awareness of the Asian community, and increase professionalism within the industry.

359 **Association of Canadian Advertisers**
95 St Clair Avenue West
Suite 1103
Toronto, ON M4V 1N6
416-964-3805
800-565-0109; *Fax:* 416-964-0771
rlund@acaweb.ca; www.acaweb.ca
Social Media: Twitter, LinkedIn

Patrick Dickinson, Chair
Ron Lund, President, CEO
Paul Hetu, Vice President, Montreal
Susan Charles, Vice President, Member Services
Christina Wang, Communications Specialist

The Association of Canadian Advertisers (ACA) is a national, not-for-profit association exclusively dedicated to serving the interests of companies that market and advertise their products and services in Canada. Membership in the ACA is restricted to client marketers only, making it the premier Canadian marketing association. It cuts across all products and service sectors, and speaks on behalf of over 200 companies.
Founded in: 1914

360 **Association of Hispanic Advertising Agencies**
8280 Willow Oaks Corporate Drive
Suite 600
Fairfax, VA 22031
703-745-5531; *Fax:* 703-610-0227
info@ahaa.org; www.ahaa.org
Social Media: Facebook, Twitter, LinkedIn, YouTube, Storify

Aldo Quevedo, Chairman
Horacio Gavilan, Executive Director
Fulvia Lee, Program Manager
Carlos Santiago, Secretary
Gabriela Alcantara-D¡az, Treasurer

Our mission is to grow, strengthen and protect the Hispanic marketing and advertising industry by providing leadership in raising awareness of the value of the Hispanic market opportunities and enhancing the professionalism of the industry.
100 Members
Founded in: 1996

361 **Association of Marketing Service Providers**
1800 Diagonal Road
Suite 320
Alexandria, VA 22314-2862
703-836-9200; *Fax:* 703-548-8204
webmaster@epicomm.org
epicomm.org
Social Media: Facebook, Twitter, LinkedIn, Pinterest, Google+, YouTube

Ken Garner, President/CEO
Leo Raymond, VP-Postal & Member Relations
Tyler T. Keeney, Director of Member Satisfaction
Dean D'Ambrosi, Executive Vice President
Mike Philie, SVP/Managing Director

MFSA is the national trade association for the mailing and fulfillment services industry and works to improve the business environment for mailing and fulfillment companies and to provide opportunities for the learning and professional development of the managers of these companies. MFSA provides: instant postal info; periodicals, surveys, and manuals unique to the industry; networking opportunities; and management education and information.
Founded in: 2014

362 **Association of National Advertisers**
Association of National Advertisers
708 Third Avenue
33 Floor
New York, NY 10017
212-697-5950; *Fax:* 212-687-7310
info@ana.net; www.ana.net
Social Media: Facebook, Twitter, LinkedIn, Instagram

Christine Manna, Chief Operating Officer
Robert D Liodice, President and CEO
Marni Gordon, Senior Vice President
Nick Primola, Senior Vice President
Kristen McDonough, Vice President

The Association of National Advertisers (ANA) is the advertising industry's oldest trade association. Currently, the ANA leads the marketing community by providing its members insights, collaboration, and advocacy. ANA's membership includes 10,000 brands that collectively spend over $250 billion in marketing communications and advertising.
450 Members
Founded in: 1910

363 **Better Business Bureau**
3033 Wilson Blvd
Suite 600
Arlington, VA 22201

703-276-0100; *Fax:* 703-525-8277;
www.bbb.org
Social Media: Facebook, Twitter, LinkedIn, YouTube, Google+, Pinterest, F

Mary E. Power, CAE, President
Beverly Baskin, SVP/Chief Mission Officer
David Diedrich, Chief Operating Officer
Bill Fanelli, CISSP, Chief Security Officer
Bennie F. Johnson, Chief Strategy Officer

The BBB is a leader in public services related to ethical business practices and dispute resolution. It is our passion to promote honesty and integrity in the marketplace. We are committed to and guided by trust, respect and fairness.
Founded in: 1912

364 **Brand Activation Association**
650 First Avenue
Suite 2-SW
New York, NY 10016

212-420-1100; *Fax:* 212-533-7622
bcarlson@pmalink.org; www.baalink.org
Social Media: Facebook, Twitter, LinkedIn, Flickr

Bonnie J. Carlson, President & CEO
Edward M. Kabak, Chief Legal Officer
Lana Mavreshko, Chief Financial Officer
Christine Goonan, Director of Membership
Mike Kaufman, VP, Marketing & Events

Organization that advocates networking, recognition, and provides educational resources to help brand marketers overcome the significant challengesthey face in a rapidly changing marketplace.
Founded in: 1911

365 **Cabletelevision Advertising Bureau**
830 3rd Avenue
2nd Floor
New York, NY 10022

212-508-1200; *Fax:* 212-832-3268
ChuckT@theVAB.com; www.thecab.tv
Social Media: Facebook, Twitter, LinkedIn

Sean Cunningham, President & CEO
Charles (Chuck) Thompson, EVP, Strategic Operations
Danielle DeLauro, SVP, Strategic Sales Insights
Gary Tietjen, VP, Local Sales & Initiatives
Evelyn Skurkovich, Sr. Director

366 **Eight-Sheet Outdoor Advertising Association**
PO Box 582096
Elk Grove, CA 95758

209-251-7622
800-874-3387; *Fax:* 209-251-7658
ddjesoaa@comcast.net;
www.juniorbillboard.org
Social Media: Facebook

Carla Osmus, Chairman
Peter Maloney, President
David Jacobs, Executive Director
Mike Cossota, Vice President
Billboard Guru, Secretary/Treasurer

The Association has helped establish size, structure and location standards, has adopted a code of ethics and standards of business practices. These self-policing efforts have helped stabilize the industry and added the standardization needed for planning
140 Members
Founded in: 1953

367 **Insurance and Financial Communications Association**
515 East Grant Rd Ste 141
Box 250
Tucson, AZ 85705

602-350-0717; *Fax:* 866-402-7336
info@ifcaonline.com; www.ifcaonline.com
Social Media: Facebook, Twitter, LinkedIn, YouTube

Jaimee Niles, President
Ralph Chaump, Vice President
Laurie Swinton, Past President
Katherine Gebhardt, Director, Communications
Tara Haselden, Director, Social Media

IFCA's primary objective is to encourage and promote the exchange of experience and ideas among its members through an extensive program of formal schools, workshops, seminars, Newsletters, research studies, networking, international awards competition and IFCA's showcase event: the three-day annual meeting. The IFCA name reflects the diversity of our members and helps us recruit new members from more companies.
700 Members
Founded in: 1933

368 **Interactive Advertising Bureau**
116 E 27th Street
7th Floor
New York, NY 10016

212-380-4700; www.iab.net
Social Media: Facebook, Twitter, LinkedIn, YouTube, Instagram, Google+

Carl Kalapesi, VP, Industry Initiatives
Randall Rothenberg, President & Chief Executive Officer
Patrick Dolan, EVP/COO
Sherrill Mane, SVP, Research, Analytics
David Doty, EVP/Chief Marketing Officer

The Interactive Advertising Bureau (IAB) is comprised of leading media and technology companies that are responsible for selling 86% of online advertising in the United States. On behalf of its members, the IAB is dedicated to the growth of the interactive advertising marketplace, of interactive's share of total marketing spend, and of its members' share of total marketing spend. The IAB educates marketers, agencies, and media companies about the value of interactive advertising.
500 Members
Founded in: 1996

369 **Intermarket Advertising Network**
5307 S 92nd Street
Hales Corners, WI 53130

414-425-8800; *Fax:* 414-425-0021
camg@greenrubino.com;
www.intermarketnetwork.com
Social Media: LinkedIn

Deborah Pfluger, President
Joe Erwin, Vice President
Tom Wilson, Co-Chairman
Dan Borgmeyer, Co-Chairman

IAN (Intermarket Agency Network) is a forum for leaders of noncompetitive marketing agencies to openly exchange knowledge in a collaborative setting. A nationwide association of carefully selected agencies, its members meet twice annually to freely discuss important issues like new business, financials, HR, creativity, growth and much more. No topic is off limits.
19 Members
Founded in: 1967

370 **International Advertising Association**
747 Third Ave.
2nd Fl.
New York, NY 10017

646-722-2612; *Fax:* 646-722-2501
iaa@iaaglobal.org; www.iaaglobal.org
Social Media: Facebook, Twitter, LinkedIn

Michael Lee, Managing Director
Marie Scotti, Director, Membership Services

International network comprising thousands of members working in all areas of marketing communications.
Founded in: 1938

371 **International Communications Agency Network**
P.O. Box 3417
Nederland, CO 80466

808-965-8240; *Fax:* 303-484-4087
info@icomagencies.com;
www.icomagencies.com
Social Media: Facebook, Twitter, Pinterest

Emma Keenan, Executive Director
Galina Epishkina, Eurasia Regional Director
Patrick Gaulon, Director Finance
Alice Lemoine, Finance Manager
DeAnna Moxley, Manager of Administration

One of the world's largest networks of independent advertising and marketing communications agencies. Our mission is: To provide effective integrated communications resources to clients internationally; To provide a free exchange of ideas, information & support for members.
80+ Members
Founded in: 1950

372 **International Sign Association**
1001 N Fairfax Street
Suite 301
Alexandria, VA 22314

703-836-4012
866-WHY-SIGN; *Fax:* 703-836-8353
info@signs.org; www.signs.org
Social Media: Facebook, Twitter, LinkedIn, YouTube

Lori Anderson, President & CEO
Brandon Hensley, COO
David Hickey, Vice President, Government Relation
Bill Winslow, Vice President, Finance
Alison Kent, Director, Workforce Development

The International Sign Association (ISA) is devoted to supporting, promoting and improving the sign industry through government advocacy, education and training programs, technical resources, stakeholder outreach and industry networking events. Our members are manufacturers, users and suppliers of on-premise signs and other visual communications systems.
2600 Members
Founded in: 1944

373 **Internet Marketing Association**
10 Mar Del Rey San
Clemente, CA 92673

949-443-9300; *Fax:* 949-443-2215
info@imanetwork.org
imanetwork.org
Social Media: Facebook, Twitter, LinkedIn, YouTube, Google+, RSS

Sinan Kanatsiz, Chairman & Founder
Matthew Langie, Vice Chairman
Lei Lani Fera, Chief Creative Officer
Rachel Reenders, Executive Director
Vince Walden, Chief Accountant
Founded in: 2001

374 League of Advertising Agencies
915 Clifton Avenue
Clifton, NJ 07013

973-473-6643; *Fax:* 973-473-0685
info@weinrichadv.com;
www.theweinrichgroup.com

Andy Weinrich, Executive Vice President
Robert Weinrich, Marketing Director

Provides marketing solutions that maximize success.

375 MAGNET: Marketing & Advertising Global Network
1017 Perry Hwy
Suite 5
Pittsburgh, PA 15237-2173

412-366-6850; *Fax:* 412-366-6840
cheri@magnetglobal.org;
www.magnetglobal.org
Social Media: Facebook, Twitter, RSS Feed

Mark Lethbridge, President
Joanne Kim, Vice President
Scott Morgan, Vice President - Membership
Gary Leopold, Vice President
Kevin Flynn, Vice President - Programs

Today, MAGNET is a group of non-competing, independently owned advertising agencies in major markets throughout the world. The network is comprised of leading agencies, with billings ranging from 8 million to 200 million US dollars, sharing a desire to pursue and achieve excellence in this profession we call marketing.
40 Members
Founded in: 1999

376 Newspaper Association of America
4401 Wilson Blvd
Suite 900
Arlington, VA 22203

571-366-1000; *Fax:* 571-366-1009;
www.naa.org
Social Media: Facebook, Twitter, LinkedIn, YouTube, Google+, RSS

Donna Barrett, Chairman
Stephen P. Hills, Vice Chairman
Robert J. Dickey, Past Chairman
Tony W. Hunter, Secretary
Michael J. Klingensmith, Treasurer

377 Outdoor Advertising Association of America
1850 M St NW
Suite 1040
Washington, DC 20036-5821

202-833-5566; *Fax:* 202-833-1522
nfletcher@oaaa.org; www.oaaa.org
Social Media: Facebook, Twitter, LinkedIn, YouTube, Pinterest

William Reagan, Chairman
Nancy J Fletcher, President/CEO
Ken Klein, EVP, Government Affairs
Marci Werlinich, VP, Membership & Admin
Kerry Yoakum, Vice President, Government Affairs
1000 Members
Founded in: 1891

378 Point of Purchase Advertising International
440 N. Wells Street
Suite 740
Chicago, IL 60654

312-863-2900; *Fax:* 312-229-1152
todddittman@retailenvironments.org;
www.popai.com
Social Media: Facebook, Twitter, LinkedIn, Pinterest

Michelle Adams, Chairman
Scott Eisen, Treasurer
Madeline Baumgartner, Market Research Manager
Nancy Carpenter, Director of Member Relations
Chelsea Kidd-Edie, Communications Coordinator

Education, globalization, technology, advocacy and elevating marketing at retail as a measured medium on a par with print, broadcast, and other advertising mediums are the driving strategies behind POPAI's direction. Throughout the years we have focused on strengthening global partnerships, enriching our research and educational programs, and utilizing technology to better serve our members.
1400+ Members
Founded in: 1936

379 Promotional Products Association International
3125 Skyway Circle North
Irving, TX 75038-3526

972-252-0404
888-426-7724; *Fax:* 972-258-3004;
www.ppai.org
Social Media: Facebook, Twitter, YouTube, RSS

Paul Bellantone, President and CEO
Bob McLean, EVP
Lisa Beck, Member Engagement Programs Manager
Sara Besly, Foundation Manager
Sandy Mendoza, Business Analytics Manager

Offers credibility, viability, visibility, community and opportunity to individuals and companies in the promotional products industry. PPAI's Mission: The Promotional Products Association International advocates the power and value of promotional products in the marketing and advertising professions to ensure the success of its members and the global industry.
7500 Members
Founded in: 1904

380 Retail Advertising and Marketing Association
1101 New York Ave NW
Washington, DC 20005

202-783-7971
800-673-4692; *Fax:* 202-737-2849
gattim@nrf.com
nrf.com
Social Media: Facebook, Twitter, LinkedIn, Youtube, Instagram

Kip Tindell, Chairman
Carleen Kohut, EVP/COO
Vicki Cantrell, SVP/ Executive Director
Mallory Duncan, SVP/General Counsel
David French, SVP, Government Relations

Provides visionary leadership that promotes creativity, innovation and excellence within all marketing disciplines that strategically elevates our members and our industry.
1600 Members
Founded in: 1952

381 The Outdoor Advertising Association of America, Inc.
1850 M St. NW
Suite 140
Washington, DC 20036

202-833-5566; *Fax:* 202-833-1522;
www.oaaa.org
Social Media: Facebook, Twitter, LinkedIn, Pinterest, YouTube

William Reagan, Chairman
Nancy Fletcher, President & CEO
Ken Klein, EVP, Govt. Affairs
Stephen Freitas, Chief Marketing Officer

Out-of-home advertising industry association.
Founded in: 1891

382 Traffic Audit Bureau for Media Measurement
271 Madison Ave
Suite 1504
New York, NY 10016-1012

212-972-8075; *Fax:* 212-972-8928
inquiry@tabonline.com; www.tabonline.com

Joseph Philport, President/CEO
Larry Hennessey, VP, Audit Policy & Member Services
Jeff Casper, Senior Vice President
Sean McCarthy, Senior Vice President - Information
Shawn Ballard, Vice President - Finance

The Traffic Audit Bureau for Media Measurement Inc. is a non-profit organization whose historical mission has been to audit the circulation of out of home media in the United States. Recently TAB's role has been expanded to lead and/or support other major out of home industry research initiatives.
450 Members
Founded in: 1933

383 Transworld Advertising Agency Network: TAAN
814 Watertown Street
Newton, MA 02465

617-795-1706; *Fax:* 419-730-1706
info@taan.org; www.taan.org
Social Media: Twitter

Jon Bailey, Chairman
Peter Gerritsen, President
Peter Colee, Governor - International/Europe
Marcy Tessmann, US Governor
John McCallum, Governor - International/Europe

TAAN exists to enhance the intelligence, expertise, reach and personal effectiveness of the owners of its member agencies: Intelligence, through the sharing of best practices, management information, processes and technologies; Expertise, through cooperative utilization of the talents, skills and experience of each member; Reach, through hands-on affiliations with local independent agencies around the world; Personal Effectiveness, through education and close, confidential, trusted relations.
47+ Members
Founded in: 1936

384 eMarketing Association
40 Blue Ridge Dr.
Charlestown, RI 2813

800-496-2950; *Fax:* 408-884-2461
admin@emarketingassociation.com;
www.emarketingassociation.com
Social Media: Facebook, Twitter, LinkedIn

International association of emarketing professionals committed to enriching the marketing community and its members through recognition, research, advocacy, education, and service.
Founded in: 1997

Newsletters

385 A Formula for Fueling Ad Agency New Business Through Social Media
American Association of Advertising Agencies
1065 Avenue of the Americas
16th Floor
New York, NY 10018
212-682-2500; *Fax:* 212-682-8391;
www.aaaa.org
Social Media: Facebook, Twitter, LinkedIn

Nancy Hill, President
Michael D. Donahue, Executive Vice President

Laura J. Bartlett, CFO & COO
Michele Adams, Board Secretary

Designed to focus and kick-start your agency's understanding, participation, credibility and leadership in social media with less expense, time and frustration. Created for C level and senior executives charged with the responsibility of new business development.

386 **AAA Newsletter**
American Academy of Advertising
24710 Shaker Blvd.
Beachwood, OH 44122

786-393-3333
director@aaasite.org; www.aaasite.org
Social Media: Facebook, Twitter

Debbie Treise, President
Kim Sheehan, President Elect
Margie Morrison, Vice President
Nancy Mitchell, Treasurer
Glen Griffin, Secretary

The newsletter is designed to keep members up-to-date on activities of the Academy and to share information between members regarding their activities.
600 Members
Frequency: Quarterly
Founded in: 1957

387 **ACT Newsletter**
Advertising Communications Times
29 Bala Ave
Suite 114
Bala Cynwyd, PA 19004

484-562-0063; *Fax:* 484-562-0068
adcomtimes@aol.com;
www.phillybizmedia.com

Joseph H. Ball, Publisher/Executive Editor
Elena Cruz, Executive Assistant

Business to business newsletter for company owners and executives in Philadelphia, Eastern Pennsylvania, Southern New Jersey & Delaware.
Frequency: Monthly
Circulation: 40000

388 **Associated Spring Newsletter**
Associated Spring
18 Main St
Bristol, CT 06010-6581

860-582-9581
800-528-3795; *Fax:* 860-589-3122
springs@asbg.com; www.asbg.com

Paulo Coit, Manager

Offers news, conferences and seminars.
Frequency: Quarterly

389 **Business Owner**
Mailing & Fulfillment Service Association
1421 Prince Street
Suite 410
Alexandria, VA 22314-2806

703-836-9200; *Fax:* 703-548-8204;
www.mfsanet.org
Social Media: Facebook, Twitter, LinkedIn

Ken Garner, President/CEO
Leo Raymond, Vice President
Karen Loveridge, Executive Assistant

Distributed to the owner or CEO of all member companies as a dues-supported benefit of membership. Developed specifically to communicate with owners and CEOs on issues unique to them.
Frequency: Bi-Monthly

390 **Conexion Newsletter**
Association of Hispanic Advertising Agencies
8400 Westpark Drive
2nd Floor
McLean, VA 22102

703-610-9014; *Fax:* 703-610-0227
info@ahaa.org; www.ahaa.org
Social Media: Facebook, Twitter, LinkedIn, YouTube

Ingrid Otero-Smart, President/CEO
Leo Olper, CEO
Roberto Orci, Chair

AHAA represents the best minds and resources dedicated to Hispanic-specialized marketing.
Frequency: Monthly

391 **DMA Daily Digest**
Direct Marketing Association
1120 Avenue of the Americas
New York, NY 10036-6700

212-768-7277; *Fax:* 212-302-6714
customerservice@the-dma.org;
www.the-dma.org
Social Media: Facebook, Twitter, LinkedIn

Lawrence M Kimmel, CEO

A summary of today's industry news from trade publications and national media. Also available as an e-mail newsletter.

392 **Direct Hit**
Midwest Direct Marketing Association
PO Box 75
Andover, MN 55304

763-607-2943; *Fax:* 763-753-2240
mdma@mdma.org; www.mdma.org

Beth Gervais, President
Vicki Erickson, Secretary/Treasurer

Brings members news of meetings, activities, local and regional events, pertinent articles and changes in legislation and postal requirements that affect the direct marketing industry.
Frequency: Bi-Monthly
Circulation: 600

393 **Display Newsletter**
Eight-Sheet Outdoor Advertising Association
1244 Lake Park Ave
Galt, CA 95632

209-251-7622
800-847-3387; *Fax:* 209-251-7658
ddjesoaa@comcast.net; www.esoaa.com
Social Media: Facebook

David Jacobs, Executive Director
Nick Sr. Keyes, Chairman
Carla Osmus, President
Deb Justus, Vice President
Stuart Rayburn, Secretary/ Treasurer

Includes updates and supplements to the Rates and Allotments book.
Frequency: Monthly
Circulation: 350

394 **Dos and Dont's in Advertising**
Council of Better Business Bureaus
4200 Wilson Blvd
Suite 800
Arlington, VA 22203-1838

703-276-0100; *Fax:* 703-525-8277
webmaster@bbb.org; www.bbb.org

Stephen A Cox, CEO

Provides in-depth coverage of the laws and regulations governing the advertising industry. Helps you to write, place and manage ads that foster consumer trust and confidence, follow federal and state ad rules, regulations and laws. It has helped legal and advertising professionals produce advertising that is ethical and correct for 50 years.
4000 Pages
Frequency: Monthly
Founded in: 1970

395 **Employment Points**
Mailing & Fulfillment Service Association
1421 Prince Street
Suite 410
Alexandria, VA 22314-2806

703-836-9200; *Fax:* 703-548-8204
mfsa-mail@mfsanet.org; www.mfsanet.org

The content is written for business owners and operators who want to stay informed about current employment issues. The editorial is targeted on human resource issues and employment practices in the mailing and fulfillment services industry.
Frequency: 4x/Year
Circulation: 2000

396 **Globe Newsletter**
International Communications Agency Network
1649 Lump Gulch Road
PO Box 490
Rollinsville, CO 80474-0490

303-258-9511; *Fax:* 303-484-4087
info@icomagencies.com;
www.icomagencies.com
Social Media: Facebook, Twitter

Bob Morrison, Director
Joe Phelps, North American Member at Large

A review of industry trends, member agency news and network happenings.
Frequency: Monthly
Circulation: 150

397 **IAB Informer**
Interactive Advertising Bureau
116 E 27th Street
7th Floor
New York, NY 10016

212-380-4700; www.iab.net
Social Media: Facebook, Twitter, LinkedIn

Randall Rothenberg, President/CEO

Features the latest need-to-know information from the IAB as well as research and other highlights from the world of Internet advertising and marketing
Frequency: Monthly

398 **IAB SmartBrief**
Interactive Advertising Bureau
116 E 27th Street
7th Floor
New York, NY 10016

212-380-4700; www.iab.net
Social Media: Facebook, Twitter, LinkedIn

Randall Rothenberg, President/CEO

Designed specifically for advertising, marketing and media executives, providing the latest need-to-know news and industry information that maximizes your time, giving you and edge over your competition.
Frequency: Monthly

399 **ISA SmartBrief**
International Sign Association
1001 N Fairfax Street
Suite 301
Alexandria, VA 22314

703-836-4012
866-WHY-SIGN; *Fax:* 703-836-8353
info@signs.org; www.signs.org

Duane Laska, Chairman
Harry Niese, Vice Chairman
Chad Jones, Secretary/Treasurer

ISA SmartBrief is a weekly e-newsletter, providing industry developments, new technology, and special offers from ISA.
2600 Members
Frequency: Weekly/Online

400 **InsideAPA Newsletter**
Advertising Photographers of America
27 W 20th Street
Suite 601
New York, NY 10011
212-807-0399; *Fax:* 212-727-8120
jocelyn@apany.com; www.apanational.com

Theresa Raffetto, National President
Michael Grecco, VP
George Simian, Treasurer

InsideAPA is a blog style newsletter focused on photographers and the membership of the Advertising Photographers of America, APA.

401 **PPB Newslink**
Promotional Products Association International
3125 Skyway Cir N
Irving, TX 75038-3539
972-252-0404; *Fax:* 972-258-3004
ppb@ppai.org; www.ppai.org
Social Media: Facebook, Twitter, LinkedIn, YouTube

Paul Bellantone, President
Steven Meyer, Chairman of the Board
Marc Simon, Chair-Elect

Electronic newsletter providing news and information about PPAI and the industry with links to articles in the online version of PPB Magazine.
Frequency: Weekly

402 **PostScripts**
Mailing & Fulfillment Service Association
1421 Prince Street
Suite 410
Alexandria, VA 22314-2806
703-836-9200; *Fax:* 703-548-8204
mfsa-mail@mfsanet.org; www.mfsanet.org
Social Media: Facebook, Twitter, LinkedIn

Leo Raymond, Editor

Each issue of PostScripts highlights a theme relevant to mailing or fulfillment operations, such as production management or information technology.
Frequency: 18x/Year
Circulation: 2800

403 **Postal Points**
Mailing & Fulfillment Service Association
1421 Prince Street
Suite 410
Alexandria, VA 22314-2806
703-836-9200; *Fax:* 703-548-8204
mfsa-mail@mfsanet.org; www.mfsanet.org
Social Media: Facebook, Twitter, LinkedIn

Leo Raymond, Editor

Deals exclusively with current and pending postal and delivery issues. Here you will find the facts and analysis of developing postal issues.
Frequency: 18x/Year

404 **STORES First Edition**
Retail Advertising & Marketing International
325 7th St Nw
Suite 1100
Washington, DC 20004-2818
202-661-3052; *Fax:* 202-737-2849;
www.rama-nrf.org
Social Media: Facebook, Twitter

Kevin Brown, RAMA Chairman
Rob Gruen, Vice Chairman
Gwen Morrison, CEO
Julie Gardner, CMO

E-newsletter alerting readers to new stories including web only content as well as STORES and NRF events taking place in the upcoming month.
Frequency: Monthly

405 **STORES Retail Deals**
Retail Advertising & Marketing International
325 7th St Nw
Suite 1100
Washington, DC 20004-2818
202-661-3052; *Fax:* 202-737-2849;
www.rama-nrf.org

Kevin Brown, RAMA Chairman
Rob Gruen, Vice Chairman
Gwen Morrison, CEO
Julie Gardner, CMO

Provides coverage of retail industry product and service provider news.
Frequency: Semi-Monthly

406 **Shopping Center Ad Trends**
National Research Bureau
320 Valley St
Burlington, IA 52601-5513
319-752-5415; *Fax:* 319-752-3421
contactus@supervisionmagazine.com;
www.national-research-bureau.com

Diane M Darnall, President
Nancy Heinzel, Editor

Advertising and marketing information for the clothing and furniture industry.
Frequency: Monthly
Founded in: 1993

407 **Signals**
International Sign Association
1001 N Fairfax Street
Suite 301
Alexandria, VA 22314
703-836-4012
866-WHY-SIGN; *Fax:* 703-836-8353
info@signs.org; www.signs.org

Duane Laska, Chairman
Harry Niese, Vice Chairman
Chad Jones, Secretary/Treasurer

ISA's legislative newsletter.
2600 Members
Frequency: Weekly/Online

408 **Signline**
International Sign Association
1001 N Fairfax Street
Suite 301
Alexandria, VA 22314
703-836-4012
866-WHY-SIGN; *Fax:* 703-836-8353
info@signs.org; www.signs.org

Duane Laska, Chairman
Harry Niese, Vice Chairman
Chad Jones, Secretary/Treasurer

ISA's newsletter developed especially for sign users, sign companies, planners, building and zoning officials, and other government groups connected with the sign industry. Find important legal and planning information on signage, as well as information on traffic safety, amortization, the economic value of on-premise signs, and other related topics.
2600 Members
Frequency: Weekly/Online

409 **Weekly Information Newsletter**
MAGNET: Marketing & Advertising Global Network
1017 Perry Hwy
Suite 5
Pittsburgh, PA 15237-2173
412-366-6850; *Fax:* 412-366-6840
cheri@magnetglobal.org;
www.magnetglobal.org
Social Media: Facebook, Twitter

Jim Nash, President

Keeps members alert to such items as new business activities, personnel information, purchases of new equipment and software, industry trends and projections.
Frequency: Weekly

Magazines & Journals

410 **Advantages**
Advertising Specialty Institute
4800 E Street Rd
Trevose, PA 19053-6698
215-953-4000
800-546-1350; *Fax:* 215-953-3045
info@asicentral.com; www.asicentral.com
Social Media: Facebook, Twitter, LinkedIn

Timothy M. Andrews, President & CEO
Norman Cohn, Chairman
Andy Cohen, Editorial Director

Written especially for the promotional products sales professional, Advantages can help you sell more.
Frequency: 15x/Year

411 **Advertiser**
The Pohly Company
253 Summer Street
Floor 3
Boston, MA 02210
617-451-1700
800-383-0888; *Fax:* 617-338-7767
info@pohlyco.com; www.pohlyco.com
Social Media: Facebook, Twitter, LinkedIn

Diana Pohly, President & CEO
Bill Pryor, Media Sales General Manager
Kevin Miller, Chief Creative Officer
Bill Dugan, VP/General Manager, FuelNet
Matt Thorsen, Director of Operations & Production

Reports on today's most critical marketing issues such as measuring brand equity, using emerging technologies and global marketing. It also contains articles on key benchmarks and industry trends.
Frequency: 6x/Year

412 **Advertising & Society Review**
Advertising Educational Foundation
220 E 42nd St
Suite 3300
New York, NY 10017-5813
212-986-8060; *Fax:* 212-986-8061;
www.aef.com
Social Media: Facebook

John Partilla, Chairman
Paula Alex, CEO

Directed to professors and students in liberal arts colleges, universities and professional schools, Advertising & Society Review is an academic publication that publishes articles, essays and other scholarships about advertising in society, culture, history and the economy.

413 **Advertising Age**
Ad Age Group/Division of Crain Communications
711 3rd Ave
New York, NY 10017-4014
212-210-0785; *Fax:* 212-210-0465
kwheaton@adage.com; www.adage.com
Social Media: Facebook, Twitter, LinkedIn

Norm Feldman, President

Editorial insights, exclusive analysis and proprietary data take readers beyond the day's news, helping our audience understand ongoing and emerging trends.
Frequency: Weekly
Circulation: 56650

414 **Adweek**
Prometheus Global Media
770 Broadway
7th Floor
New York, NY 10003-9595

212-493-4100; *Fax:* 646-654-5368;
www.prometheusgm.com
Social Media: Facebook, Twitter

Richard D. Beckan, CEO
James A. Finkelstein, Chairman
Madeline Krakowsky, Vice President Circulation
Tracy Brater, Executive Director Creative Service

Adweek is the source for advertising and agency news, information and opinion. Covering the industry from an agency perspective, Adweek focuses on the image makers and those who create the strategy and the ads as well as those who buy the media and handle client relations.
Cost: $149.00
Frequency: Weekly
Circulation: 36000
Founded in: 1978

415 **Billboard Magazine**
Prometheus Global Media
770 Broadway
7th Floor
New York, NY 10003-9595

212-493-4100; *Fax:* 646-654-5368;
www.prometheusgm.com
Social Media: Facebook, Twitter, RSS

Richard D. Beckman, CEO
James Finkelstein, Chairman
Madeline Krakowsky, Vice President Circulation
Tracy Brater, Executive Director Creative Service

Packed with in-depth music and entertainment features including the latest in new media and digital music, global coverage, music and money, touring, new artists, radio news and retail reports.
Cost: $149.00
Frequency: Weekly
Founded in: 1894

416 **Brandweek**
Prometheus Global Media
770 Broadway
7th Floor
New York, NY 10003-9595

212-493-4100; *Fax:* 646-654-5368;
www.prometheusgm.com

Richard D. Beckman, CEO
James A. Finkelstein, Chairman
Madeline Krakowsky, Vice President Circulation
Tracy Brater, Executive Director Creative Service

Focuses on marketing strategy and services, brand identity, sponsorships, licensing, media usage and distribution and promotions.
Frequency: Weekly
Circulation: 26000
Founded in: 1991

417 **BtoB Magazine**
Crain Communications, Inc.
1155 Gratiot Ave
Detroit, MI 48207-2732

313-446-6000
info@crain.com; www.crain.com

Keith Crain, Chairman
Rance Crain, President
Mary Kay Crain, Treasurer/Assistant Secretary
Merrilee P. Crain, Secretary/Assistant Treasurer
Robert Felsenthal, Vice President/Publisher

Dedicated to integrated business to business marketing. Every page is packed with substance news, reports, technologies, benchmarks, and best practices served up by the most knowledgeable journalists.
Frequency: Monthly
Circulation: 45000

418 **Corporate Logo Magazine**
Virgo Publishing LLC
3300 N Central Ave
Suite 300
Phoenix, AZ 85012-2532

480-675-9925; *Fax:* 480-990-0819
kkennedy@vpico.com; www.vpico.com

Jenny Bolton, President

Provides promotional products distributors with tools to grow their businesses in a competitive marketplace.
Circulation: 20000
Founded in: 1986
Printed in on glossy stock

419 **Counselor**
Advertising Specialty Institute
4800 E Street Rd
Trevose, PA 19053-6698

215-953-4000
800-546-1350; *Fax:* 215-953-3045
info@asicentral.com; www.asicentral.com
Social Media: Facebook, Twitter, LinkedIn, YouTube, Instagram, Pinterest

Timothy M. Andrews, President & CEO
Norman Cohn, Chairman
Andy Cohen, Editorial Director

Counselor's coverage of marketing trends and new products is a must read for distributor principals.
Frequency: Monthly

420 **Creativity**
Ad Age Group/Division of Crain Communications
1155 Gratiot Ave
Detroit, MI 48207-2732

313-446-6000
info@crain.com; www.crain.com

Norm Feldman, Manager

Information, insight and inspiration in the brand creativity world. Each month we showcase the best work and take readers inside the making of ground breaking brand communications and experiences, while exploring the issues facing those in the idea business.
Frequency: Monthly
Circulation: 33000

421 **Government Relations: How To Guide for Clubs & Federations**
American Advertising Federation
1101 Vermont Ave NW
Suite 500
Washington, DC 20005-6306

202-898-0089
800-999-2231; *Fax:* 202-898-0159
aaf@aaf.org; www.aaf.org
Social Media: Facebook, Twitter, YouTube

James Edmund Datri, President
Constance Cannon Frazier, COO
Joanne Schecter, Executive Vice President

The purpose of this manual is to help reduce the anxiety level that many feel when dealing with lawmakers.

422 **Hispanic Business Magazine**
Hispanic Business Inc
425 Pine Ave
Santa Barbara, CA 93117-3709

805-964-4554; *Fax:* 805-964-5539
info@hispanstar.com; www.hnmagazine.com

Jesus Chavarria, President

Our feature stories highlight significant trends in the US Hispanic market and include profiles of successful entrepreneurs, analysis of economic trends and news and data on such topics as government procurement, workplace diversity, politics, advertising, entertainment and events.
Frequency: Monthly
Circulation: 225000
Founded in: 1979

423 **Hospitality Style**
ST Media Group International
11262 Cornell Park Dr
Cincinnati, OH 45242-1812

513-421-2050
800-421-1321; *Fax:* 513-421-5144
customer@stmediagroup.com;
www.stmediagroup.com

Tedd Swormstedt, CEO
Brian Foos, CFO

Publication for design and architecture of hotels, restaurants, spas, resorts, casinos, complexes or convention centers. Covers hospitality design with the eye of a fashion magazine, identifying trends and showcasing them seasonally in a photo-rich format.
Frequency: Monthly
Circulation: 17000
Founded in: 1906

424 **IQ News Adweek**
Prometheus Global Media
770 Broadway
7th Floor
New York, NY 10003-9595

212-493-4100; *Fax:* 646-654-5368;
www.prometheusgm.com
Social Media: Facebook, Twitter, RSS

Richard D. Beckman, CEO
James A. Finkelstein, Chairman
Madeline Krakowsky, Vice President Circulation
Tracy Brater, Executive Director Creative Service

Adweek IQ Daily goes out every weekday morning with a briefing of the most important news on interactive advertising, the latest moves by major brands and agencies in terms of content creation, media partnerships and distribution strategies in the digital realm.
Frequency: Daily

425 **In-Store Marketer**
In-Store Marketing Institute
7400 Skokie Blvd
Skokie, IL 60077-3339

847-675-7400; *Fax:* 847-675-7494
pdproducts_editor@instoremarketer.org;
www.instoremarketer.org
Social Media: Facebook, Twitter, LinkedIn

Peter Hoyt, President

Members-only e-newsletter highlights new content added to the Institute's website, including research, audio-enabled presentations, image galleries and trends articles.
Frequency: Bi-Monthly
Circulation: 15000
Printed in 4 colors on glossy stock

426 **Industrial + Specialty Printing**
ST Media Group International
11262 Cornell Park Dr
Cincinnati, OH 45242-1812

513-421-2050
800-421-1321; *Fax:* 513-421-5144
customer@stmediagroup.com;
www.stmediagroup.com

Tedd Swormstedt, CEO
Brian Foos, CFO

Covers functional and decorative printing done as part of the manufacturing process, examining

the challenges printers face when setting up and maintaining efficient workflows and provides the solutions to keep production on track in industrial printing operations.
Frequency: Monthly
Circulation: 17000
Founded in: 1906

427 **Insight Briefs**
Association of National Advertisers
708 Third Avenue
33 Floor
New York, NY 10017
212-697-5950; *Fax:* 212-661-8057
info@ana.net; www.ana.net
Social Media: Facebook, Twitter, LinkedIn, YouTube
Bob Liodice, President & CEO
Christine Manna, COO
William Zengel, EVP
Association of National Advertisors collections of their best materials on a given subject. These resources incorporate information gathered from ANA's vast archive of proprietary information, including: best practices, case studies, charts, data, and quotes from client-side marketers. The purpose of the Briefs is to give high-level insights on a range of timely and important marketing topics.
Frequency: Monthly

428 **International Archive Magazine**
Luerzer's Archive Inc
106 West 29th St
New York, NY 10001
212-643-4297; *Fax:* 646-619-4264;
www.luerzersarchive.net
Sandra Lehnst, CEO
Michael Weinzettl, Publisher
Christina Hrdlicka, Managing Editor
Michael Weinzettl, Editor in Chief
Presents new and innovative TV, magazine, poster and newspaper ads from 20 countries. Devoted to presentation of ads. Translations are provided.
Frequency: Bi-Monthly

429 **Journal of Advertising (JA)**
American Academy of Advertising
24710 Shaker Blvd.
Beachwood, OH 44122
512-471-8149; *Fax:* 512-471-7018
jaeditor@austin.utexas.edu;
www.journalofadvertising.org
Social Media: Facebook, Twitter
Herbert J Rotfeld, President
Debbie Treise, President Elect
Steve Edwards, Vice President
Margie Morrison, Treasurer
Wei-Na Lee, Ph.D, Editor
The premier academic publication covering significant intellectual development pertaining to advertising theories and their relationship with practice. The goal is to provide a public forum that reflects the current understanding of advertising as a process of communication, its role in the changing environment, and the relationships between these and other components of the advertising business and practice.
600 Members
Frequency: Quarterly
Founded in: 1957

430 **Journal of Advertising Research**
World Advertising Research Center Ltd
2233 Wisconsin Ave NW
Suite 535
Washington, DC 20007-4144
202-778-4544; *Fax:* 202-778-4546
americas@warc.com; www.noralgroup.com
Social Media: Facebook, Twitter
Eva Kasten, President
The mission of the Journal of Advertising Research is to act as the research and development vehicle for professionals in all areas of marketing including media, research, advertising and communications
Frequency: Quarterly
Circulation: 1850

431 **Journal of Current Issues and Research in Advertising**
CTC Press
PO Box 290159
Columbia, SC 29229-0159
803-754-3112
800-382-8856; *Fax:* 803-754-3013
j-leigh@tamu.edu; www.ctcpress.com
James H Leigh, Co-Editor
Educates advertising students, professionals and all others interested in advertising.

432 **Journal of Euromarketing**
Taylor & Francis Inc
325 Chestnut St
Suite 800
Philadelphia, PA 19106-2614
215-625-8900
800-354-1420; *Fax:* 215-625-2940;
www.taylorandfrancis.com
Kevin Bradley, President
Aims to meet the needs of academicians, practitioners, and public policymakers in the discussion of marketing issues pertaining to Europe. It helps to increase our understanding of the strategic planning aspects of marketing in Europe and the marketing aspects of the trading relationship between European and foreign firms.
Frequency: Quarterly
ISSN: 1049-6483

433 **Journal of Interactive Advertising**
American Academy of Advertising
24710 Shaker Blvd.
Beachwood, OH 44122
786-393-3333
patrose@aaasite.org; www.aaasite.org
Social Media: Facebook, Twitter
Debbie Treise, President
Kim Sheehan, President Elect
Margie Morrison, Vice President
nancy Mitchell, Treasurer
Glen Griffin, Secretary
A refereed online publication designed to promote our understanding of interactive advertising, marketing and communication in a networked world.
600 Members
Frequency: 2x/Year
Founded in: 1957

434 **Media**
Media Index Publishing
PO Box 24365
Seattle, WA 98124-0365
206-382-9220
800-332-1736; *Fax:* 206-382-9437
media@media-inc.com; www.media-inc.com
Katie Sauro, Editor
James Baker, President
Contains the most up-to-date information and issues that are important to you as a member of the marketing, advertising, broadcast, film and video production, multimedia and creative services industries, along with special focus segments and lists each issue, helpful advice from industry leaders and insightful reporting.
Frequency: Bi-Monthly
Circulation: 10,000
Mailing list available for rent: 35M names

435 **Mediaweek**
Prometheus Global Media
770 Broadway
7th Floor
New York, NY 10003-9595
212-493-4100; *Fax:* 646-654-5368;
www.prometheusgm.com
Social Media: Facebook, Twitter, RSS
Richard D. Beckman, CEO
James A. Finkelstein, Chairman
Madeline Krakowsky, Vice President Circulation
Tracy Brater, Executive Director Creative Service
Highly targeted circulation covers media decision makers at the top 350 ad agencies in America, all top buying services and client media departments.
Frequency: Weekly
Circulation: 21000
Founded in: 1991

436 **News & Views**
Advertising Media Credit Executives Association
8840 Columbia 100 Parkway
Columbia, MD 21045-2158
410-992-7609; *Fax:* 410-740-5574
amcea@amcea.org; www.amcea.org
Sheila Wroten, President
Mary Younger, Vice President
Josie Salazar, Secretary/ Treasurer
Vickie Bolinger, Director
Grace Carter, Director
Our magazine reports on current trends and legal issues while offering tips on customer service, time management and collections.
Frequency: Quarterly

437 **Outdoor Advertising Magazine**
Outdoor Advertising Magazine
Rapid City, SD 57702
877-926-5406; www.oam.net
Social Media: Facebook, Twitter, LinkedIn
Randall Williamson, Publisher
A major source for the outdoor and out-of-home advertising industry. Contains the latest information on products, services, supplies, technology, creative ideas, financial and industry news.
Cost: $24.95
Founded in: 1920

438 **PC Today**
Promotional Products Association International
3125 Skyway Cir N
Irving, TX 75038-3539
972-252-0404; *Fax:* 972-258-3004
ppb@ppai.org; www.ppai.org
Social Media: Facebook, Twitter, LinkedIn, YouTube
Paul Bellantone, President
Steven Meyer, Chairman of the Board
Marc Simon, Chair-Elect
Quick-read, daily, electronic newsletter serves the unique educational needs of distributor salespeople.
Frequency: Weekly

439 **POP Design**
In-Store Marketing Institute

7400 Skokie Blvd
Skokie, IL 60077-3339

847-675-7400; *Fax:* 847-675-7494
pdproducts_editor@instoremarketer.org;
www.instoremarketer.org
Social Media: Facebook, Twitter, LinkedIn

Peter Hoyt, President

Serves the news and product information needs of producers and designers of in-store displays, signs and fixtures. Each issue features the latest trends and technologies vital to building and designing successful in-store merchandising.
Frequency: Bi-Monthly
Circulation: 15000
Printed in 4 colors on glossy stock

440 **PPB Magazine**
Promotional Products Association International
3125 Skyway Cir N
Irving, TX 75038-3539

972-252-0404
888-426-7724; *Fax:* 972-258-3004
ppb@ppai.org; www.ppai.org
Social Media: Facebook, Twitter, YouTube

Paul Bellantone, President
Steven Meyer, Chairman of the Board
Marc Simon, Chair-Elect

Coverage concentrates on news activities and events of the promotional products industry.
Cost: $62.00
Frequency: Monthly

441 **Package Design Magazine**
ST Media Group International
11262 Cornell Park Dr
Cincinnati, OH 45242-1812

513-421-2050
800-421-1321; *Fax:* 513-421-5144
customer@stmediagroup.com;
www.stmediagroup.com

Tedd Swormstedt, CEO
Brian Foos, CFO

Full of the news and information professional package designers need to stay abreast of the latest innovations, materials, and technology driving the packaging industry. Presents readers with the useful insights they need to succeed in competitive retail markets.
Frequency: Monthly
Circulation: 17000
Founded in: 1906

442 **Politically Direct**
Direct Marketing Association
1120 Avenue of the Americas
New York, NY 10036-6713

212-768-7277; *Fax:* 212-302-6714
customerservice@the-dma.org;
www.the-dma.org
Social Media: Facebook, Twitter, LinkedIn

Matt Blumberg, Chairman
Glenn Eisen, Vice Chairman
Rick Erwin, Treasurer

Published in both print and digital versions, this newsletter on DMA advocacy efforts keeps DMA members informed and involved in the politics and policies that impact them today and ahead of the curve on developments that will affect them tomorrow.
Frequency: Quarterly

443 **Promotional Consultant Magazine**
Promotional Products Association International
3125 Skyway Cir N
Irving, TX 75038-3539

972-252-0404; *Fax:* 972-258-3004
ppb@ppai.org; www.ppai.org
Social Media: Facebook, Twitter, YouTube

Paul Bellantone, President
Steven Meyer, Chairman of the Board
Marc Simon, Chair-Elect

Featuring short, sales-specific articles, relevant trends, targeted strategies, expert voices and compelling case studies.
Frequency: Bi-Monthly
Circulation: 20000

444 **Public Opinion Journal**
American Association for Public Opinion Research
111 Deer Land Road
Suite 100
Deerfield, IL 60015-4943

913-895-4601; *Fax:* 913-895-4652
aapor-info@goamp.com; www.aapor.org
Social Media: Facebook, Twitter, LinkedIn

Paul Lavrakas, President
Rob Santos, VP/President-Elect
Scott Keeter, Secretary-Treasurer

Offers articles about the science and practice of survey and opinion research to give people a voice in the decisions that affect their daily lives.
Frequency: Quarterly
Founded in: 1948
Mailing list available for rent: 1000 names at $400 per M

445 **Public Relations Unplugged: PR Strategies For AAF Ad Clubs and Members**
American Advertising Federation
1101 Vermont Ave NW
Suite 500
Washington, DC 20005-6306

202-898-0089
800-999-2231; *Fax:* 202-898-0159
aaf@aaf.org; www.aaf.org

James Edmund Datri, President
Constance Cannon Frazier, COO
Joanne Schecter, Executive Vice President

In this text you will find guidance, instructions and examples to help your ad club deflect legislative threats and become a more prominent voice within your community.

446 **Response**
201 Sandpointe Ave
Suite 500
Santa Ana, CA 92707-8700

714-338-6700
800-854-3112; *Fax:* 714-513-8482
thaire@questex.com;
www.responsemagazine.com
Social Media: Facebook, Twitter, LinkedIn, YouTube

Thomas Haire, Editor
Don Rosenberg, VP
Kristina Kronenberg, Marketing Director

Magazine of direct response television reporting. Educates marketers and advertising executives on how to sell products, generate leads and drive store sales through infomercials, short-form commercials, televised shopping and multi-media retailing.
Frequency: Monthly
Circulation: 12000
Founded in: 1987

447 **STORES Magazine**
Retail Advertising & Marketing International
325 7th St NW
Suite 1100
Washington, DC 20004-2818

202-661-3052; *Fax:* 202-737-2849;
www.rama-nrf.org

Kevin Brown, RAMA Chairman
Rob Gruen, Vice Chairman
Gwen Morrison, CEO
Julie Gardner, CMO

A publication devoted to retail news and trends as well as notification of conferences and meetings.
Frequency: Monthly

448 **Screen Printing Magazine**
ST Media Group International
11262 Cornell Park Dr
Cincinnati, OH 45242-1812

513-421-2050
800-421-1321; *Fax:* 513-421-5144
customer@stmediagroup.com;
www.stmediagroup.com

Tedd Swormstedt, CEO
Brian Foos, CFO

Leading publication and trusted source of information for the screen-printing industry. Landmark coverage of the latest techniques and technologies that save time, energy and money.
Frequency: Monthly
Circulation: 17000
Founded in: 1906

449 **Shopper Marketing**
In-Store Marketing Institute
7400 Skokie Blvd
Skokie, IL 60077-3339

847-675-7400; *Fax:* 847-675-7494
pdproducts_editor@instoremarketer.org;
www.instoremarketer.org
Social Media: Facebook, Twitter, LinkedIn

Peter Hoyt, President

The leading information source for news and information surrounding the shopper marketing industry. Each month, more than 18000 marketers, manufacturers, agencies and retailers of consumer products or services who buy and specify in-store marketing solutions turn to Shopper Marketing to learn about the latest insights, data and trends surrounding the industry.
Frequency: Bi-Monthly
Circulation: 15000
Printed in 4 colors on glossy stock

450 **Shopper Marketing Newswire**
In-Store Marketing Institute
7400 Skokie Blvd
Skokie, IL 60077-3339

847-675-7400; *Fax:* 847-675-7494
pdproducts_editor@instoremarketer.org;
www.instoremarketer.org
Social Media: Facebook, Twitter, LinkedIn

Peter Hoyt, President

Delivered to a powerful audience of brands, retailers, agencies and solution providers. Offering personnel updates, company news, research/ data reports, path-to-purchase innovations, co-marketing initiatives across FDM and specialty chains and more.
Frequency: Bi-Monthly
Circulation: 15000
Printed in 4 colors on glossy stock

451 **Sign & Digital Graphics**
National Business Media Inc
2800 W Midway Boulevard
PO Box 1416
Broomfield, CO 80020

303-469-0424
800-669-0424; *Fax:* 303-469-5730

mdixon@nbm.com; www.nbm.com/sb
Social Media: Facebook, Twitter

James Kochevar, Publisher
Ken Mergentime, Executive Editor
Matt Dixon, Managing Editor

A comprehensive monthly trade publication covering the business of visual communications offering a broad range of in-depth reporting for professionals. Topics covered include commercial signage, wide-format commercial printing, electric signs and letters, architectural signage, electronic displays, vehicle wraps and graphics and much more.
Cost: $38.00
120 Pages
Frequency: Monthly
Circulation: 18300
Founded in: 1986
Mailing list available for rent: 1000 names at $225 per M
Printed in 4 colors

452 Sign Builder Illustrated
Simmons-Boardman Publishing Corporation
345 Hudson St
12th Floor
New York, NY 10014-7123

212-620-7200; *Fax:* 212-633-1165;
www.simmonsboardman.com

Arthur J McGinnis Jr, President

How-to magazine featuring the latest products, technology and techniques to enhance the sign maker's craft.
Frequency: Monthly
Circulation: 19055

453 Sign Business
National Business Media Inc
2800 W Midway Boulevard
PO Box 1416
Broomfield, CO 80020

303-469-0424
800-669-0424; *Fax:* 303-469-5730
mdixon@nbm.com; www.nbm.com/sb

James Kochevar, Publisher
Ken Mergentime, Executive Editor
Matt Dixon, Managing Editor

Contains information on electrical illuminated signage, outdoor advertising and commercial sign shops.
Cost: $38.00
120 Pages
Frequency: Monthly
Circulation: 18348
Founded in: 1986
Mailing list available for rent: 1000 names at $225 per M
Printed in 4 colors

454 SignCraft Magazine
SignCraft Publishing Company
PO Box 60031
Fort Myers, FL 33906

239-939-4644
800-204-0204; *Fax:* 239-939-0607
signcraft@signcraft.com; www.signcraft.com

Tom McIltrot, Editor

Each issue includes an inside look at several sign shops, plus articles on techniques, materials, pricing, sales and computer aided sign making and puts hundreds of layout ideas at your fingertips.
Frequency: Monthly
Circulation: 14000
Mailing list available for rent: 25M names

455 Signs of the Times Magazine
ST Media Group International
11262 Cornell Park Dr
Cincinnati, OH 45242-1812

513-421-2050
800-421-1321; *Fax:* 513-421-5144
customer@stmediagroup.com;
www.stmediagroup.com

Tedd Swormstedt, CEO
Brian Foos, CFO

It is our mission to educate and inspire signage and graphics professionals worldwide through award winning editorial perspectives, technology updates, CAS reports, new product reviews, one of a kind Electric, CAS and Commercial State of the Industry reports, graphics techniques and much more.
Frequency: Monthly
Circulation: 17000
Founded in: 1906

456 Supplier Global Resource
Advertising Specialty Institute
4800 E Street Rd
Trevose, PA 19053-6698

215-953-4000
800-546-1350; *Fax:* 215-953-3045
info@asicentral.com; www.asicentral.com
Social Media: Facebook, Twitter, LinkedIn, YouTube, Instagram, Pinterest

Timothy M. Andrews, President & CEO
Norman Cohn, Chairman
Andy Cohen, Editorial Director

The buying power of Supplier Global Resource readers is large-scale and powerful.
Frequency: 6x/Year

457 Survey Practice
American Association for Public Opinion Research
111 Deer Land Road
Suite 100
Deerfield, IL 60015-4943

913-895-4601; *Fax:* 913-895-4652
aapor-info@goamp.com; www.aapor.org
Social Media: Facebook, Twitter, LinkedIn

Paul Lavrakas, President
Rob Santos, VP/President-Elect
Scott Keeter, Secretary-Treasurer

AAPOR's e-journal with public opinion and survey research articles and commentary.
Frequency: Quarterly
Founded in: 1948
Mailing list available for rent: 1000 names at $400 per M

458 TelevisionWeek
Crain Communications
1155 Gratiot Ave
Detroit, MI 48207-2732

313-446-6000
info@crain.com; www.crain.com

Norm Feldman, Manager
Chuck Ross, Managing Director

Covers all aspects of the business programming and production, distribution and talent, broadcast, cable and satellite, advertising and media, government and regulation, finance and emerging technologies.
Founded in: 1982

459 The Advertiser Magazine
Pohly Company
99 Bedford Street
Floor 5
Boston, MA 02111

617-457-3938
bliodice@ana.net; www.ana.net

Kristina Sweet, Assoc Publisher, Director Sales

Reports on today's most critical marketing issues such as measuring brand equity, using emerging technologies and global marketing. It also contains articles on key benchmarks and industry trends. Offers news and events in the advertising industry. Produced by Association of National Adverstisers.
Frequency: 6x/Year
Circulation: 25000

460 The Big Picture
ST Media Group International
11262 Cornell Park Dr
Cincinnati, OH 45242-1812

513-421-2050
800-421-1321; *Fax:* 513-421-5144
customer@stmediagroup.com;
www.stmediagroup.com

Tedd Swormstedt, CEO
Brian Foos, CFO

Provides real-world solutions to today's design and production challenges. This publication reports on digital printing of visual communications with coverage of digital printing from image capture and processing to finishing and display.
Frequency: Monthly
Circulation: 17000
Founded in: 1906

461 VMSD
ST Media Group International
11262 Cornell Park Dr
Cincinnati, OH 45242-1812

513-421-2050
800-421-1321; *Fax:* 513-421-5144
customer@stmediagroup.com;
www.stmediagroup.com

Tedd Swormstedt, CEO
Brian Foos, CFO

Leading magazine for retail designers and store display professionals, showcasing the latest store designs and visual presentations, presents merchandising strategies and new products, and reports on industry news and events.
Frequency: Monthly
Circulation: 17000
Founded in: 1906

462 Wearables
Advertising Specialty Institute
4800 E Street Rd
Trevose, PA 19053-6698

215-953-4000
800-546-1350; *Fax:* 215-953-3045
info@asicentral.com; www.asicentral.com
Social Media: Facebook, Twitter, LinkedIn

Timothy M. Andrews, President & CEO
Norman Cohn, Chairman
Andy Cohen, Editorial Director

Serves the apparel and accessories segment of the advertising specialty industry.
Frequency: 10x/Year

463 Winning at Retail
In-Store Marketing Institute
7400 Skokie Blvd
Skokie, IL 60077-3339

847-675-7400; *Fax:* 847-675-7494
pdproducts_editor@instoremarketer.org;
www.instoremarketer.org
Social Media: Facebook, Twitter, LinkedIn

Peter Hoyt, President

Shares insights, case studies and lessons learned from thousands of studies conducted by Perception Research Services, the leading company in packaging and shopper marketing research.
Frequency: Bi-Monthly
Circulation: 15000
Printed in 4 colors on glossy stock

Trade Shows

464 **AAPOR Annual Conference**
American Association for Public Opinion Research
111 Deer Lake Road
Suite 100
Deerfield, IL 60015

847-205-2651; *Fax:* 847-480-9282
aapor-info@goamp.com; www.aapor.org
Social Media: Facebook, Twitter, LinkedIn

Paul Lavrakas, President
Rob Santos, VP/President-Elect
Scott Keeter, Secretary-Treasurer

Features cutting edge research and informal access to leaders in the fields.
850 Attendees
Frequency: Annual
Mailing list available for rent: 1000 names at $400 per M

465 **ADMERICA!**
American Advertising Federation
1101 Vermont Ave NW
Suite 500
Washington, DC 20005-6306

202-898-0089
800-999-2231; *Fax:* 202-898-0159
aaf@aaf.org; www.aaf.org
Social Media: Facebook, Twitter, YouTube

James Edmund Datri, President
Constance Cannon Frazier, COO
Joanne Schecter, Executive Vice President

Connects all aspects of the advertising industry. Influential agencies, clients, media companies, suppliers, and colleges from across the country will address how to thrive in a recovering economy and how the changing culture of business and consumers is impacting our industry.

466 **AMCEA Conference**
Advertising Media Credit Executives Association
8840 Columbia 100 Parkway
Columbia, MD 21045-2158

410-992-7609; *Fax:* 410-740-5574
amcea@amcea.org; www.amcea.org

J Dee Stevenson, President
Kimberly Riley, VP
Vickie Bolinger, Director

The conference encompasses four days and is a networking extravaganza. Top attorneys discuss bankruptcy and legal issues. We invite advertising agencies to discuss network buying and liability problems.
Frequency: Annual

467 **ANA Advertising Financial Management Conference**
Association of National Advertisers
708 Third Avenue
33 Floor
New York, NY 10017

212-697-5950; *Fax:* 212-661-8057
info@ana.net; www.ana.net
Social Media: Facebook, Twitter, LinkedIn, YouTube

Bob Liodice, President & CEO
Christine Manna, COO
William Zengel, EVP

Brings together top marketing finance and procurement professionals from the client side with agency CFOs and other key industry stakeholders interested in efficiencies, cost savings, return on investment, and delivering greater value to organizations.

468 **ANA Advertising Law & Public Policy Conference**
Association of National Advertisers
708 Third Avenue
33 Floor
New York, NY 10017

212-697-5950; *Fax:* 212-661-8057
info@ana.net; www.ana.net
Social Media: Facebook, Twitter, LinkedIn, YouTube

Bob Liodice, President & CEO
Christine Manna, COO
William Zengel, EVP

Keeping up with the digital revolution is becoming a nearly impossible task. This conference enters the battlefield by putting together a stellar faculty, including leading regulators, top practitioners, and serious critics, capped off by a session that puts it all together led by a leading law professor.

469 **ANA Annual Conference - The Masters of Marketing**
Association of National Advertisers
708 Third Avenue
33 Floor
New York, NY 10017

212-697-5950; *Fax:* 212-661-8057
info@ana.net; www.ana.net
Social Media: Facebook, Twitter, LinkedIn, YouTube

Bob Liodice, President & CEO
Christine Manna, COO
William Zengel, EVP

The conference offers an opportunity to learn from and engage with the leaders of the industry as they build brands, leverage the expanding array of media, make marketing more accountable and improve the quality of their marketing organizations.

470 **ANA Digital & Social Media Conference**
Association of National Advertisers
708 Third Avenue
33 Floor
New York, NY 10017

212-697-5950; *Fax:* 212-661-8057
info@ana.net; www.ana.net
Social Media: Facebook, Twitter, LinkedIn, YouTube

Bob Liodice, President & CEO
Christine Manna, COO
William Zengel, EVP

Discussing how to use social media to impact the consumer decision journey and how to effectively partner with other companies to maximize social media reach and more.

471 **ANA TV & Everything Video Forum Presented by Google**
Association of National Advertisers
708 Third Avenue
33 Floor
New York, NY 10017

212-697-5950; *Fax:* 212-661-8057
info@ana.net; www.ana.net
Social Media: Facebook, Twitter, LinkedIn, YouTube

Bob Liodice, President & CEO
Christine Manna, COO
William Zengel, EVP

The forum recognizes that the role of television in the media mix is being redefined and broadened. In addition to traditional television, the TV & Everything Video Forum will explore the use of video on any type of screen or device: the computer, Internet, mobile, point-of-purchase, gaming, and more. Registration starts at $595.
Frequency: Annual

472 **ANA/WFA Global Marketing Conference**
Association of National Advertisers
708 Third Avenue
33 Floor
New York, NY 10017

212-697-5950; *Fax:* 212-661-8057
info@ana.net; www.ana.net
Social Media: Facebook, Twitter, LinkedIn, YouTube

Bob Liodice, President & CEO
Christine Manna, COO
William Zengel, EVP

Offers tips on marketing on a worldwide scale.

473 **Ad:tech Adweek**
Prometheus Global Media
770 Broadway
7th Floor
New York, NY 10003-9595

212-493-4100; *Fax:* 646-654-5368;
www.prometheusgm.com
Social Media: Facebook, Twitter, RSS

Richard D. Beckman, CEO
James A. Finkelstein, Chairman
Madeline Krakowsky, Vice President Circulation
Tracy Brater, Executive Director Creative Service

An interactive advertising and technology conference and exhibition. Worldwide shows blend keynote speakers, topic driven panels and workshops to provide attendees with the tools and techniques they need to compete in a changing world.

474 **Advertising Financial Management Conference**
Association of National Advertisers
708 Third Avenue
33 Floor
New York, NY 10017

212-697-5950; *Fax:* 212-661-8057
info@ana.net; www.ana.net
Social Media: Facebook, Twitter, LinkedIn, YouTube

Bob Liodice, President & CEO
Christine Manna, COO
William Zengel, EVP

The agenda is developed with input from members of the Advertising Financial Management Committee and topics focus on efficiency, return on investment, cost savings and new ideas to bring greater value to organizations. Registration begins at $1,095.
Frequency: Annual

475 **Advertising Law & Public Policy Conference**
Association of National Advertisers
708 Third Avenue
33 Floor
New York, NY 10017

212-697-5950; *Fax:* 212-661-8057
info@ana.net; www.ana.net
Social Media: Facebook, Twitter, LinkedIn, YouTube

Bob Liodice, President & CEO
Christine Manna, COO
William Zengel, EVP

Discuss new policy initiatives and how they will transform advertising; recent court decisions, regulatory changes reshaping the legal environment for advertising. Hear from FCC, FTC, and FDA experts and representatives. Registration begins at $795.
Frequency: Annual

476 **Advertising Media Credit Executives Association Annual Conference**
Advertising Media Credit Executives Association
PO Box 433
Louisville, KY 40201
502-582-4327; *Fax:* 502-582-4330
amcea@amcea.org; www.amcea.org
Cheryl E Szluzer, President
Sheila Wroten, Vice President
Media credit managers, editors, business managers and other professionals gather for exhibits of advertising media such as newspapers, magazines, radio and television.
400 Attendees
Frequency: Annual
Founded in: 1896

477 **Annual Action Taker Series**
Retail Advertising & Marketing International
325 7th Street NW
Suite 1100
Washington, DC 20004
202-661-3052; *Fax:* 202-737-2849; www.rama-nrf.org
Kevin Brown, RAMA Chairman
Rob Gruen, Vice Chairman
Gwen Morrison, CEO
Julie Gardner, CMO
Come hear real case studies and inspiring concepts from today's retail creative leaders.
400 Attendees
Frequency: Annual

478 **Annual Advertising Conference**
Advertising Women of New York
25 W 45th Street
Suite 403
New York, NY 10036
212-221-7969; *Fax:* 212-221-8296
awny@awny.org; www.awny.org
Social Media: Facebook, Twitter, LinkedIn, You tube
Carol Watson, President
Melissa Goidel, VP
To meet some of the top people in the field of advertising; to discover techniques of career planning that can help you get the job of your choice with greater ease; to network with some of the most influential advertising executives of the time from a variety of disciplines.
600 Attendees

479 **Annual Conference and Mailing & Fulfillment Expo**
Mailing & Fulfillment Service Association
1421 Prince Street
Suite 410
Alexandria, VA 22314-2806
703-836-9200; *Fax:* 703-548-8204
mfsa-mail@mfsanet.org; www.mfsanet.org
Ken Garner, President
Jennifer Root, Director
Bill Stevenson, Director Marketing
Quality educational sessions, industry specific exhibit hall, networking and more.
Frequency: Annual

480 **Annual Global Marketing Summit**
International Advertising Association - NY Chapter
World Serivce Center
275 Madison Avenue Suite 2102
New York, NY 10016
212-338-0222; *Fax:* 212-983-0455
coordinator@iaany.org; www.iaany.org
Social Media: Facebook, Twitter, LinkedIn
Tom Brookbanks, President
Larry Levy, Treasurer
Sean Lough, Secretary
Designed to provide participants with the knowledge, tools and inspiration needed to market global brands. Various registration options. Visit website for details.
1000 Attendees
Frequency: Annual

481 **Annual MAPOR Conference- Public Opinion Frontiers**
American Association for Public Opinion Research
111 Deer Lake Road
Suite 100
Deerfield, IL 60015
847-205-2651; *Fax:* 847-480-9282
aapor-info@goamp.com; www.aapor.org
Social Media: Facebook, Twitter, LinkedIn
Paul Lavrakas, President
Rob Santos, VP/President-Elect
Scott Keeter, Secretary-Treasurer
Focusing on emerging methods in data collection and analysis and research into attitude formation.
850 Attendees
Frequency: Annual
Mailing list available for rent: 1000 names at $400 per M

482 **Annual Proceedings Conference**
American Academy of Advertising
24710 Shaker Blvd.
Beachwood, OH 44122
786-393-3333
patrose@aaasite.org; www.aaasite.org
Social Media: Facebook, Twitter
Debbie Treise, President
Kim Sheehan, President Elect
Margie Morrison, Vice President
nancy Mitchell, Treasurer
Glen Griffin, Secretary
Every year the American Academy of Advertising holds a conference at which advertising research findings and theories are presented, as well as papers concerning methods of teaching advertising.
600 Members
Founded in: 1957

483 **Asian-Pacific Conference**
American Academy of Advertising
24710 Shaker Blvd.
Beachwood, OH 44122
786-393-3333
patrose@aaasite.org; www.aaasite.org
Social Media: Facebook, Twitter
Debbie Treise, President
Kim Sheehan, President Elect
Margie Morrison, Vice President
nancy Mitchell, Treasurer
Glen Griffin, Secretary
Focusing on issues in the Asian-Pacific region, this conference welcomes research on any aspect of advertising as broadly defined in one or more Asian-Pacific countries or in multiple countries involving at least one Asian-Pacific country. This conference is co-sponsored by China Advertising Association of Commerce and Communication University of China.
600 Members
Founded in: 1957

484 **Audience Measurement 7.0**
Advertising Research Foundation
432 Park Avenue S
6th Floor
New York, NY 10016-8013
212-751-5656; *Fax:* 212-319-5265
info@thearf.org; www.thearf.org
Social Media: Facebook, Twitter, LinkedIn, youtube
Colleen Fahey Rush, Chief Research Officer
David Poltrack, Secretary
Bernard Bradpiece, Treasurer
Knowing the latest developments in audience composition and measurement across platforms is critical to ensuring your company's money is spent most effectively. Get up-to-the-minute on the latest evaluation approaches and technology.
400 Members
Founded in: 1936

485 **Cable Advertising Conference**
Cabletelevision Advertising Bureau
830 3rd Avenue
2nd Floor
New York, NY 10022
212-508-1200; *Fax:* 212-832-3268; www.thecab.tv
Sean Cunningham, President
Annual conference and exhibits of advertising-supported cable television networks and services to support local advertising sales.
2000 Attendees
Frequency: Annual/April

486 **Cannes Lion Advertising Festival Screening**
American Association of Advertising Agencies
1065 Avenue of the Americas
16th Floor
New York, NY 10018
212-682-2500; *Fax:* 212-682-8391
kipp@aaaa.org; www.aaaa.org
Social Media: Facebook, Twitter, LinkedIn
Nancy Hill, President
Chris Weil, Chair
Andrew Bennett, Director at Large
Sharon Napier, Secretary/Treasurer
The screening will bring together hundreds of industry professionals to view the winning work of Cannes and celebrate the Philadelphia advertising community.

487 **Channel Partners Conference & Expo**
Virgo Publishing LLC
3300 N Central Ave
Suite 300
Phoenix, AZ 85012-2532
480-675-9925; *Fax:* 480-990-0819
kkennedy@vpico.com; www.vpico.com
John Siefert, CEO
Kelly Ridley, CFO
Jon Benninger, VP
John LyBarger, Director of IT
The communications industry's only event designed exclusively for indirect sales organizations - agents, VARs, systems integrators, interconnects and consultants - focused on transforming their businesses to become converged solutions providers.
Circulation: 20000
Founded in: 1986
Printed in on glossy stock

488 **Co-Creation and the Future of Agencies**
American Association of Advertising Agencies

1065 Avenue of the Americas
16th Floor
New York, NY 10018

212-682-2500; *Fax:* 212-682-8391
kipp@aaaa.org; www.aaaa.org
Social Media: Facebook, Twitter, LinkedIn

Nancy Hill, President
Chris Weil, Chair
Andrew Bennett, Director at Large
Sharon Napier, Secretary/Treasurer

Learn how to be part of the trend toward the disintermediation of agents, marketers are increasing going around agencies to work directly with the media, production companies, and even directly to creative talent via crowdsourcing.

489 **Comprehensive CRM & Database Marketing**
Direct Marketing Association
1120 Avenue of the Americas
New York, NY 10036-6700

212-768-7277; *Fax:* 212-302-6714
customerservice@the-dma.org;
www.the-dma.org
Social Media: Facebook, Twitter, LinkedIn

Lawrence M Kimmel, CEO

In an increasingly digital marketing landscape, metrics and ROI are being scrutinized and recalibrated like never before. Whether interested in classic database statistics or emerging trends in web analytics, the insights gained in our classes will add up to success.

490 **DMA Annual Conference & Exhibition**
Direct Marketing Association
1120 Avenue of Americas
New York, NY 10036-6700

212-768-7277; *Fax:* 212-302-6714
dmaconferences@the-dma.org;
www.the-dma.org
Social Media: Facebook, Twitter, LinkedIn

Lawrence M Kimmel, CEO
Julie A Hogan, SVP Conferences/Education Services

Offers a progressive marketers to help better engage customers and improve bottom line results in all channels, including social, search, monile, video and more.
12000 Attendees
Frequency: Annual/October

491 **Direct Marketing Institute**
Direct Marketing Association
1120 Avenue of the Americas
New York, NY 10036-6700

212-768-7277; *Fax:* 212-302-6714
customerservice@the-dma.org;
www.the-dma.org
Social Media: Facebook, Twitter, LinkedIn

Lawrence M Kimmel, CEO

A three-day intensive direct marketing seminar, the DMI iwll give step-by-step tactics to maximize the ROI of your campaigns.

492 **Effective Email Marketing**
Direct Marketing Association
1120 Avenue of the Americas
New York, NY 10036-6700

212-768-7277; *Fax:* 212-302-6714
customerservice@the-dma.org;
www.the-dma.org
Social Media: Facebook, Twitter, LinkedIn

Lawrence M Kimmel, CEO

The online world presents a myriad of options for establishing and developing customer and community relationships. If you want to segment and target your email database or launch a mobile campaign, we can teach you the best practices and strategies you need to meet and exceed your goals.

493 **Email Evolution Conference**
Direct Marketing Association
1120 Avenue of Americas
New York, NY 10036-6700

212-768-7277; *Fax:* 212-302-6714;
www.dmaconference@the-dma.org;
www.the-dma.org
Social Media: Facebook, Twitter, LinkedIn

Lawrence M Kimmel, CEO
Julie A Hogan, SVP Conferences/Education Services

Focuses on the ever-changing and evolving world of email marketing, providing attendees with the best ways to capitalize on the high ROI this low-cost communication tool can provide both on its own, and integrated with social, search, mobile, video and other email enhancers.
10M Attendees
Frequency: Annual/February

494 **Giving and Receiving Feedback with Grace & Style**
American Association of Advertising Agencies
1065 Avenue of the Americas
16th Floor
New York, NY 10018

212-682-2500; *Fax:* 212-682-8391
kipp@aaaa.org; www.aaaa.org
Social Media: Facebook, Twitter, LinkedIn

Nancy Hill, President
Chris Weil, Chair
Andrew Bennett, Director at Large
Sharon Napier, Secretary/Treasurer

The majority of professionals cringe when it comes time for performance evaluations, self assessments, and even everyday feedback. Participants learn how to speak assertively and deliver constructive criticism while also understanding how to receive feedback openly and grow professionally from the experience.

495 **Global Shop Conference**
Nielsen Business Media
1145 Sanctuary Parkway
Suite 355
Alpharetta, GA 30074

770-569-1540; *Fax:* 770-569-5105;
www.globalshop.org
Social Media: Facebook, Twitter, LinkedIn

David Loechner, President
Michael Alicea, SVP/Human Resources
Denise Bashem, VP/Finance

Retail designers and brand marketers find the most innovative concepts, newest products and services to create unique store design and in-store marketing solutions.
50000 Attendees
Frequency: Annual/March

496 **Government Affairs Conference**
American Advertising Federation
1101 Vermont Avenue NW
Suite 500
Washington, DC 20005

800-999-2231; *Fax:* 202-898-0159
aaf@aaf.org; www.aaf.org

James Edmund Datri, President
Constance Cannon Frazier, COO
Joanne Schecter, Executive Vice President

The conference is held annually in conjunction with the Association of National Advertisers and the American Association of Advertising Agencies.
807 Attendees
Frequency: Annual

497 **Hospitality Match**
ST Media Group International
11262 Cornell Park Dr
Cincinnati, OH 45242-1812

513-421-2050
800-421-1321; *Fax:* 513-421-5144
customer@stmediagroup.com;
www.stmediagroup.com

Tedd Swormstedt, CEO
Brian Foos, CFO

A series of targeted and exclusive invitation-only events that bring key decision makers from top design firms, purchasing companies and hotel groups together with relevan suppliers, face-to-face for a weekend of serious business and exceptional networking events. Suppliers will meet with pre-qualified hospitality buyers through pre-arranged one-on-one meetings.
Frequency: Monthly
Circulation: 17000
Founded in: 1906

498 **IAA World Congress**
International Advertising Association
747 Third Ave.
2nd Fl.
New York, NY 10017

646-722-2612; *Fax:* 646-722-2501
iaa@iaaglobal.org; www.iaaglobal.org

Bi-annual event attracts more than a thousand marketing communications professionals from all over the world.
1200 Attendees
Frequency: Bi-annual

499 **IAB Annual Leadership Meeting**
Interactive Advertising Bureau
116 E 27th Street
7th Floor
New York, NY 10016

212-380-4700; www.iab.net
Social Media: Facebook, Twitter, LinkedIn

Randall Rothenberg, President/CEO

Addresses head-on issues taking place right now in the digital industry.
Frequency: Monthly

500 **ICOM International World Management Conference**
International Communications Agency Network
1649 Lump Gulch Road
PO Box 490
Rollinsville, CO 80474-0490

303-258-9511; *Fax:* 303-484-4087
info@icomagencies.com;
www.icomagencies.com
Social Media: Facebook, Twitter, LinkedIn, YouTube

Bob Morrison, Director
Joe Phelps, North American Member at Large

Members will network and share ideas and success stories. Members will share learned information from the worst global economic crisis since 1929, what they learned about their businesses, their clients and their staffs and what they will do differently going forward.
80 Attendees
Frequency: Annual

501 **IFCA Annual Conference**
Insurance and Financial Communications Association
1037 N 3rd Ave
Tucson, AZ 85705

602-350-0717
info@ifcaonline.com; www.ifcaonline.com

Social Media: Facebook, Twitter, LinkedIn, YouTube

Susan o'Neill, President
Ralph Chaump, VP
Kim Schultz, Secretary

Offers networking among peers, education through platform speeches and practical workshops, display of the best industry communications work being done and volunteer opportunities.

502 ISA International Sign Expo
International Sign Association
1001 N Fairfax Street
Suite 301
Alexandria, VA 22314

703-836-4012
866-WHY-SIGN; *Fax:* 703-836-8353
info@signs.org; www.signs.org

Duane Laska, Chairman
Harry Niese, Vice Chairman
Chad Jones, Secretary/Treasurer

ISA's annual internation sign Expo is a premier platform for the sign industry to conduct business. 500 exhibitors. Admission from $15 to $40.
12800 Attendees

503 ISA Supplier & Distributor Conference
International Sign Association
1001 N Fairfax Street
Suite 301
Alexandria, VA 22314

703-836-4012
866-WHY-SIGN; *Fax:* 703-836-8353
info@signs.org; www.signs.org

Duane Laska, Chairman
Harry Niese, Vice Chairman
Chad Jones, Secretary/Treasurer

The conference featured a slate of experts speaking on a wide range of topics specifically of interest to companies that sell to sign manufacturers.
Frequency: Annual

504 Integrated Marketing Members Only Conference by Microsoft Advertising
Pohly Company
99 Bedford Street
Floor 5
Boston, MA 02111

617-457-3938
ksweet@pohlyco.com; www.ana.net

Kristina Sweet, Assoc Publisher, Director Sales

The development of new communications and the evolution of traditional communications have shifted power from the marketer to the consumer, which created enormous opportunities, providing marketers with the ability to better target their customers. Discover how top marketers develop, execute, and evaluate their overall marketing communications strategy based on consumer insight.
Frequency: 6x/Year
Circulation: 25000

505 International Career Developmemt Conference
DECA Inc
1908 Association Drive
Reston, VA 20191

703-860-5000; *Fax:* 703-860-4013;
www.deca.org

Jacklyn Schiller, President
Jim Brock, President-elect
Lynore Levenhagen

Gathering of members, advisors, businesspersons and alumni who attend. Most of the participants are competitors in one of DECA's competency based competitive events.
15000 Attendees

506 MFSA Midwinter Executive Conference
Mailing & Fulfillment Service Association
1421 Prince Street
Suite 410
Alexandria, VA 22314-2806

703-836-9200; *Fax:* 703-548-8204
mfsa-mail@mfsanet.org; www.mfsanet.org

Ken Garner, President
Jennifer Root, Director
Bill Stevenson, Director Marketing

Addresses financial operations and business valuation, marketing your own company, the changing world of postal regulations, technology in fulfillment, building a sales team, being strong in digital printing and the landscape of employment law.

507 MIXX Conference & Expo
Interactive Advertising Bureau
116 E 27th Street
7th Floor
New York, NY 10016

212-380-4700
lisa@iab.net; www.iab.net

Lisa Milgram, Events Director
Margaret Southwell, Events Coordinator

The preeminet event for marketing and agency professionals-and the publishers and technology firms who help drive their efforts. Brings together the industry's most prominent and influential figures to share insights on the most pressing topics in advertising.
Frequency: Annual

508 Mailer Strategies Conference
Mailing & Fulfillment Service Association
1421 Prince Street
Suite 410
Alexandria, VA 22314-2806

703-836-9200; *Fax:* 703-548-8204
mfsa-mail@mfsanet.org; www.mfsanet.org

Ken Garner, President
Jennifer Root, Director
Bill Stevenson, Director Marketing

This conference will focus solely on postal issues that are important to your operations.

509 Media Conference & Tradeshow
American Association of Advertising Agencies
1065 Avenue of the Americas
16th Floor
New York, NY 10018

212-682-2500; *Fax:* 212-682-8391
kipp@aaaa.org; www.aaaa.org
Social Media: Facebook, Twitter, LinkedIn

Nancy Hill, President
Chris Weil, Chair
Andrew Bennett, Director at Large
Sharon Napier, Secretary/Treasurer

Empowered consumers will be featured center stage in live focus groups during the conference.

510 Media and Account Management Conference
Association of Hispanic Advertising Agencies
8400 Westpark Drive
2nd Floor
McLean, VA 22102

703-610-9014; *Fax:* 703-610-0227
info@ahaa.org; www.ahaa.org
Social Media: Facebook, Twitter

Horacio Gavilan, Executive Director
Melissa Chen, Membership/Directory
Ayanna Wiggins, Marketing

Examines the myriad of changes facing Hispanic agencies in and beyond including shifts in approaches to communications planning, demographics and client needs.

511 Multicultural Council Meeting
Interactive Advertising Bureau
116 E 27th Street
7th Floor
New York, NY 10016
212-380-4700; www.iab.net
Social Media: Facebook, Twitter, LinkedIn

Randall Rothenberg, President/CEO

IAB members contributing information on the interactive advertising marketplace.
Frequency: Monthly

512 NCDM Conference
Direct Marketing Association
1120 Avenue of Americas
New York, NY 10036-6700

212-768-7277; *Fax:* 212-302-6714
dmaconferences@the-dma.org;
www.the-dma.org
Social Media: Facebook, Twitter, LinkedIn

Julie A Hogan, SVP Conferences/Events

Presents industry experts and hard-hitting case studies from a variety of verticles, such as financial services, retail, automotive, publishing, non-profit and many more, who will share the latest strategies and methodologies in gathering, analyzing, leveraging and protecting the most valuable business asset, customer data.
10M Attendees
Frequency: Annual/December

513 NRF Annual Convention & EXPO
Retail Advertising & Marketing International
325 7th Street NW
Suite 1100
Washington, DC 20004

202-661-3052; *Fax:* 202-737-2849;
www.rama-nrf.org

Kevin Brown, RAMA Chairman
Rob Gruen, Vice Chairman
Gwen Morrison, CEO
Julie Gardner, CMO

RAMA is undertaking in important transformation to become an organization that's representative of the changes that are affecting the retail marketing community with a strategic view that includes the integration of mobile, digital and traditional media.
400 Attendees
Frequency: Annual

514 National Conference on Operations & Fulfillment (NCOF)
Direct Marketing Association
1120 Avenue of Americas
New York, NY 10036-6700

212-768-7277; *Fax:* 211-302-6714
dmaconferences@the-dma.org;
www.the-dma.org
Social Media: Facebook, Twitter, LinkedIn

Julie A Hogan, SVP Conference/Events
Lawrence M Kimmel, CEO

Focuses on innovative solutions for the warehouse, distribution, operations, and ecommerce needs in the ever-changing world of operations and fulfillment.
10M Attendees

515 New York Nonprofit Confernce
Direct Marketing Association
1120 Avenue of Americas
New York, NY 10036-6700

212-768-7277; *Fax:* 212-302-6714
dmaconferences@the-dma.org;

www.the-dma.org
Social Media: Facebook, Twitter, LinkedIn

Lawrence M Kimmel, CEO
Julie A Hogan, SVP Conferences/Education Services

Discover which acknowledgement problems work best and why, increase revenue with membership options-as well as traditional fundraising appeals, learn how the internet and e-mail campaigns can improve fundraising, lowering costs and increase advocacy.
10M Attendees

516 **OAAA National Convention**
Outdoor Advertising Association of America
1850 M Street NW
Suite 1040
Washington, DC 20036

202-833-5566; *Fax:* 202-833-1522
nfletcheter@oaaa.org; www.oaaa.org

Nancy Fletcher, President
Willliam reagan, Secretary
Kevin Reily, Treasurer

The national convention program will offer depth of content and a diverse schedule of activities with something important for everyone engaged in the out of home business.
Frequency: Biennial

517 **OAAA\TAB National Convention + Expo**
Outdoor Advertising Association of America
1850 M St. NW
Suite 140
Washington, DC 20036

202-833-5566; *Fax:* 202-833-1522;
www.oaaa.org

Responsibility for the program alternates between the Outdoor Advertising Association of America (OAAA) and Traffic Audit Bureau (TAB).
Frequency: Annual

518 **PPAI Brand**
Promotional Products Association International
3125 Skyway Cir N
Irving, TX 75038-3539

972-252-0404; *Fax:* 972-258-3004
ppb@ppai.org; www.ppai.org
Social Media: Facebook, Twitter, LinkedIn, YouTube

Steve Slagel, President

The industry's most highly regarded incentive products showcase, gives an all-access pass to the $46 billion incentives market.

519 **PPAI Decorate**
Promotional Products Association International
3125 Skyway Cir N
Irving, TX 75038-3539

972-252-0404; *Fax:* 972-258-3004
ppb@ppai.org; www.ppai.org
Social Media: Facebook, Twitter, LinkedIn, YouTube

Paul Bellantone, President
Steven Meyer, Chairman of the Board
Marc Simon, Chair-Elect

The best in screen printing, embroidery and digital technology. Experience demonstrations of the newest products and equipment.

520 **PPAI Expo**
Promotional Products Association International
3125 Skyway Circle N
Irving, TX 75038-3526

972-258-3104; *Fax:* 972-258-3012
ppb@ppai.org; www.ppa.org

Paul Bellantone, President
Steven Meyer, Chairman of the Board
Marc Simon, Chair-Elect

Offering you the tools, opportunities and innovative ideas you need to excel, to grow your business beyond expectation and become the example to be followed.

521 **PPAI MASCAS**
Promotional Products Association International
3125 Skyway Cir N
Irving, TX 75038-3539

972-252-0404; *Fax:* 972-258-3004
ppb@ppai.org; www.ppai.org
Social Media: Facebook, Twitter, LinkedIn, YouTube

Paul Bellantone, President
Steven Meyer, Chairman of the Board
Marc Simon, Chair-Elect

Master Advertising Specialist (MAS) and Certified Advertising Specialist (CAS) are the promotional products industry's professional designations.

522 **Powering Creativity Outside the Creative Department**
American Association of Advertising Agencies
1065 Avenue of the Americas
16th Floor
New York, NY 10018

212-682-2500; *Fax:* 212-682-8391
kipp@aaaa.org; www.aaaa.org
Social Media: Facebook, Twitter, LinkedIn

Nancy Hill, President
Chris Weil, Chair
Andrew Bennett, Director at Large
Sharon Napier, Secretary/Treasurer

The success of any communication, any campaign, any brand, any company or community depends on smarter, more creative, more impactful thinking from everyone involved. Young professionals who work in account management, media, research and production disciplines should look to attend.

523 **RAMA CMO Summit**
Retail Advertising & Marketing International
325 7th Street NW
Suite 1100
Washington, DC 20004

202-661-3052; *Fax:* 202-737-2849;
www.rama-nrf.org

Kevin Brown, RAMA Chairman
Rob Gruen, Vice Chairman
Gwen Morrison, CEO
Julie Gardner, CMO

To provide a networking and discussion forum for senior retail marketing executives.
50 Attendees

524 **RAMACON: Thoughtful Topics, Fearless Ideas Remarkable People**
Retail Advertising & Marketing International
325 7th Street NW
Suite 1100
Washington, DC 20004

202-661-3052; *Fax:* 202-737-2849;
www.rama-nrf.org

Kevin Brown, RAMA Chairman
Rob Gruen, Vice Chairman
Gwen Morrison, CEO
Julie Gardner, CMO

RAMA is undertaking in important transformation to become an organization that's representative of the changes that are affecting the retail marketing community with a strategic view that includes the integration of mobile, digital and traditional media.
400 Attendees
Frequency: Annual

525 **Re:Think The ARF Annual Convention & Expo**
Advertising Research Foundation
432 Park Avenue S
6th Floor
New York, NY 10016-8013

212-751-5656; *Fax:* 212-319-5265
info@thearf.org; www.thearf.org
Social Media: Facebook, Twitter, LinkedIn, YouTube

Colleen Fahey Rush, Chief Research Officer
David Poltrack, Secretary
Bernard Bradpiece, Treasurer

Re:Think is a research forum where the ad industry gathers to dispense, explore and challenge the latest knowledge driving the advertising and marketing industry. Showcases innovative market research services and products, high-level networking, free education, and leading-edge industry resources. Various registration options are available. Visit the ARF website for details.
400 Members
Founded in: 1936

526 **Reinventing Account Management**
American Association of Advertising Agencies
1065 Avenue of the Americas
16th Floor
New York, NY 10018

212-682-2500; *Fax:* 212-682-8391
kipp@aaaa.org; www.aaaa.org
Social Media: Facebook, Twitter, LinkedIn

Nancy Hill, President
Chris Weil, Chair
Andrew Bennett, Director at Large
Sharon Napier, Secretary/Treasurer

Next Practices for Senior Agency Professionals. The traditional account management function at advertising agencies and other marketing communications firms is changing dramatically to meet the needs of a 24/7 digitally connected multichannel marketplace.

527 **Response Expo**
201 Sandpointe Ave
Suite 500
Santa Ana, CA 92707-8700
714-338-6700
800-854-3112; *Fax:* 714-513-8482
thaire@questex.com;
www.responsemagazine.com
Social Media: Facebook, Twitter, LinkedIn, YouTube

Thomas Haire, Editor
Don Rosenberg, VP
Kristina Kronenberg, Marketing Director

Focuses on the evolution of consumers from passive watchers to active and empowered brand evangelists. Technology and social media have enabled and encouraged consumers to engage and interact with content. Learn how to take DR marketing from traditional campaign management to the future of customer engagement.
Frequency: Monthly
Circulation: 12000
Founded in: 1987

528 **Shopper Marketing Expo**
In-Store Marketing Institute

7400 Skokie Blvd
Skokie, IL 60077-3339

847-675-7400; *Fax:* 847-675-7494
pdproducts_editor@instoremarketer.org; www.instoremarketer.org
Social Media: Facebook, Twitter, LinkedIn

Peter Hoyt, President

The premier annual event in the in-store industry filled with symposia, seminars, exhibits and awards dedicated to integrating the wide variety of solutions, tools and expertise needed to influence decision-making along the path to purchase.
Circulation: 15000
Printed in 4 colors on glossy stock

529 **Shopper Marketing Summit**
In-Store Marketing Institute
7400 Skokie Blvd
Skokie, IL 60077-3339

847-675-7400; *Fax:* 847-675-7494
pdproducts_editor@instoremarketer.org; www.instoremarketer.org
Social Media: Facebook, Twitter, LinkedIn

Peter Hoyt, President

A world-class senior level conference offering ideas and solutions to retailers, manufacturers and marketers of consumer products and services, agencies and other solution providers who are looking to achieve new heights at retail.
Printed in 4 colors on glossy stock

530 **Signage and Graphics Summit**
ST Media Group International
11262 Cornell Park Dr
Cincinnati, OH 45242-1812

513-421-2050
800-421-1321; *Fax:* 513-421-5144
customer@stmediagroup.com; www.stmediagroup.com

Tedd Swormstedt, CEO
Brian Foos, CFO

Three days of education and networking for high-volume sign companies, screen printers and digital print shops.
Founded in: 1906

531 **Speak to Be Heard! Influencing Others to Take Action**
American Association of Advertising Agencies
1065 Avenue of the Americas
16th Floor
New York, NY 10018

212-682-2500; *Fax:* 212-682-8391
kipp@aaaa.org; www.aaaa.org
Social Media: Facebook, Twitter, LinkedIn

Nancy Hill, President
Chris Weil, Chair
Andrew Bennett, Director at Large
Sharon Napier, Secretary/Treasurer

Eliminate the static that plagues communicative delivery- to persuade, sell your ideas, motivate, influence or simply effectively communicate face-to-face with a clear message. Account executives, media directors, senior managers should attend.

532 **Stratconn**
In-Store Marketing Institute
7400 Skokie Blvd
Skokie, IL 60077-3339

847-675-7400; *Fax:* 847-675-7494
pdproducts_editor@instoremarketer.org; www.instoremarketer.org
Social Media: Facebook, Twitter, LinkedIn

Peter Hoyt, President

Gathering the leading designers/producers of displays, signs and fixtures together with teams of merchandising experts from leading CPG manufacturers and retailers.
Printed in 4 colors on glossy stock

533 **Strategy for Account Managers**
American Association of Advertising Agencies
1065 Avenue of the Americas
16th Floor
New York, NY 10018

212-682-2500; *Fax:* 212-682-8391
kipp@aaaa.org; www.aaaa.org
Social Media: Facebook, Twitter, LinkedIn

Nancy Hill, President
Chris Weil, Chair
Andrew Bennett, Director at Large
Sharon Napier, Secretary/Treasurer

Workshop is designed for mid-an-higher-level account managers at marketing communication firms of all types who have clients that want them to think more strategically.

534 **SupplySide International Tradeshow and Conference**
Virgo Publishing LLC
3300 N Central Ave
Suite 300
Phoenix, AZ 85012-2532

480-675-9925; *Fax:* 480-990-0819
kkennedy@vpico.com; www.vpico.com

John Siefert, CEO
Kelly Ridley, CFO
Jon Benninger, VP
John LyBarger, Director of IT

The world's largest event for healthy and innovative ingredients. Food, beverage, dietary supplement and cosmeceutical manufacturers, marketers and formulators attend to source cutting edge ingredients and learn from outstanding educational presentations at the largest event of its kind.
Founded in: 1986

535 **Transformation LA**
American Association of Advertising Agencies
1065 Avenue of the Americas
16th Floor
New York, NY 10018

212-682-2500; *Fax:* 212-682-8391
kipp@aaaa.org; www.aaaa.org
Social Media: Facebook, Twitter, LinkedIn

Nancy Hill, President
Chris Weil, Chair
Andrew Bennett, Director at Large
Sharon Napier, Secretary/Treasurer

Talent recruitment and retention; regulatory updates; mobility; social media; and growing your business are a few of the sessions scheduled. Tour some of the entertainment capital's most creative facilities, including innovative 4A's member agencies.

536 **VMSD International Retail Design Conference**
ST Media Group International
11262 Cornell Park Dr
Cincinnati, OH 45242-1812

513-421-2050
800-421-1321; *Fax:* 513-421-5144
customer@stmediagroup.com; www.stmediagroup.com

Tedd Swormstedt, CEO
Brian Foos, CFO

The premier educational event created especially for members of the retail design community.
Circulation: 17000
Founded in: 1906

Directories & Databases

537 **AMCEA Member Handbook & Roster**
Advertising Media Credit Executives Association
8840 Columbia 100 Parkway
Columbia, MD 21045-2158

410-992-7609; *Fax:* 410-740-5574
amcea@amcea.org; www.amcea.org

J Dee Stevenson, President
Kimberly Riley, VP
Vickie Bolinger, Director

Inside you will find direct telephone numbers to every credit manager in our association along with numbers for credit references and fax inquiries. We also include their e-mail addresses and computer hardware and software information.

538 **Advertisers and Agency Red Book Plus**
Canon Communications Pharmaceutical Medial Group
300 American metro Bvld
Newtown, PA 18940

215-944-9800; *Fax:* 215-867-0053
sandra.baker@cancom.com; www.pharmalive.com

Karl Engel, President
Styli Engel, Executive VP/Editor-in-Chief
James Hannan, CEO/Group Publisher
Lisa Aberman, CFO/COO

Advertising information.
Cost: $1788.00
Frequency: Quarterly
Founded in: 1982

539 **Advertising Age: Leading National Advertisers Issue**
Ad Age Group/Crain Communications
711 3rd Ave
New York, NY 10017-4014

212-210-0785; *Fax:* 212-210-0200
subs@crain.com; www.adage.com
Social Media: Facebook, Twitter, LinkedIn

Keith E Crain, Chairman/Publisher
Rance E Crain, President/Editor-In-Chief
David S Klein, VP Publishing/Editorial Director

Featuring comprehensive ad spending estimates on 100 elite, company profiles and sales and earnings reports for our annual 100 Leading National Advertisers Report.
Cost: $5.00
Frequency: Annual
Circulation: 59,000
Founded in: 1930

540 **Advertising Growth Trends**
Schonfeld & Associates Inc
1931 Lynn Circle
Libertyville, IL 60048-1323

847-816-4870
800-205-0030; *Fax:* 847-816-4872
saiinfo@saibooks.com; www.saibooks.com

Carol Greenhut, Publisher

Information on publicly owned corporations that spend on advertising. Measures of profitability and effectiveness of the company's advertising expenditures are shown.
Cost: $395.00
217 Pages
Frequency: Annual
ISBN: 1-932024-84-0

541 **Advertising Ratios & Budgets**
Schonfeld & Associates Inc

1931 Lynn Circle
Libertyville, IL 60048-1323

847-816-4870
800-205-0030; *Fax:* 847-816-4872
saiinfo@saibooks.com; www.saibooks.com

Carol Greenhut, Publisher

The detailed annual report covers over 5,000 companies and 300 industries with information on current advertising budgets, ad-to-sales ratios and ad-to-gross margin ratios, as well as budgets and growth rate forecasts. Use it to track competition, win new ad agency clients, set and justify ad budgets, sell space and time or plan new media ventures and new products. Includes industry and advertiser ad spending rankings.
Cost: $395.00
186 Pages
Frequency: Annual
ISBN: 1-932024-80-8

542 Advertising Red Books

PO Box 1514
Summit, NJ 07902

800-908-5395
info@redbooks.com; www.redbooks.com

Advertising Red Books has been providing competitive intelligence and prospecting data to media companies, advertising agencies, manufacturers, libraries, advertising service and suppliers.
Founded in: 1922

543 Advertising and Marketing Intelligence

New York Times
1719 State Route 10
#A
Parsippany, NJ 07054-4507

E-Mail: hartman-center@duke.edu;
www.library.duke.edu

Contains abstracts of articles from over 75 publications on advertising, marketing and the media.

544 Adweek Directory

Prometheus Global Media
770 Broadway
7th Floor
New York, NY 10003-9595

212-493-4100; *Fax:* 646-654-5368;
www.prometheusgm.com
Social Media: Facebook, Twitter

Richard D. Beckman, CEO
James A. Finkelstein, Chairman
Madeline Krakowsky, Vice President Circulation
Tracy Brater, Executive Director Creative Service

Adweek Directories Online is where you will find searchable databases with comprehensive information on ad agencies, brand marketers and multicultural media.
Frequency: Annual
Circulation: 800
Founded in: 1981

545 Brands and Their Companies

Gale/Cengage Learning
PO Box 09187
Detroit, MI 48209-0187

248-699-4253
800-877-4253; *Fax:* 248-699-8049
galee.galeord@cengage.com; www.gale.com
Social Media: Facebook, Twitter, LinkedIn, YouTube

Patrick C Sommers, President

This source lists manufacturers and distributors from small businesses to large corporations, from both the public and private sectors offering complete coverage of more than 426,000 US consumer brands.
Frequency: Annual
ISBN: 1-414434-26-X

546 Buyers Guide to Outdoor Advertising

DoMedia LLC
247 Marconi Boulevard
Suite 400
Columbus, OH 43215

866-939-3663; www.domedia.com

FC Miller, Publisher
Robert Gainey, Circulation Manager

Offers valuable information on outdoor advertising companies and their markets.

547 Circulation

Standard Rate & Data Services
1700 E Higgins Rd
Des Plaines, IL 60018-5610

847-375-5000
800-851-7737; *Fax:* 847-375-5001
contact@srds.com; www.srds.com

George Carens, Executive Vice President
Trish Delaurier, Publisher

This print service provides complete circulation, penetration and consumer demographic information on your newspaper options so you can make objective comparisons in multi newspaper markets and across markets. You'll be able to analyze circulation, number of households, retail sales, average household income and market rankings to determine what papers deliver your target audience.
Frequency: Annual
Circulation: 1000+

548 Co-op Advertising Programs Sourcebook

National Register Publishing
430 Mountain Ave.
Suite 400
New Providence, NJ 07974

800-473-7020; *Fax:* 908-673-1189
nrpeditorial@marquiswhoswho.com;
www.co-opsourcebook.com

The best source for media companies, wholesalers, retailers and others for finding available advertising dollars to fund co-op programs. Includes 52 product classifications.
Frequency: Semi-Annual

549 Consumer Magazine Advertising Source

Standard Rate & Data Services
1700 E Higgins Rd
Des Plaines, IL 60018-5610

847-375-5000
800-851-7737; *Fax:* 847-375-5001
contact@srds.com; www.srds.com

George Carens, Executive Vice President
Joseph Hayes, Publisher

This service provides complete planning information on US consumer magazines, including standardized ad rates, dates, contact information and links to online media kits, Web sites and audit statements that provide additional facts on readership information and positioning.
Frequency: Semi-Annual
Circulation: 2000+

550 Creative Industry Director

Black Book Inc
740 Broadway
Suite 202
New York, NY 10003-9518

212-979-6700
800-841-1246; *Fax:* 212-673-4321;
www.blackbook.com

Joe Resudek, Janet

Designed to meet the needs of professionals who seek creative services in every aspect of media, advertising, production and the fashion industry.
Frequency: Annual

551 Fashion and Print Directory: Madison Avenue Handbook

Peter Glenn Publications
777 E Atlantic Ave
Suite C2337
Delray Beach, FL 33438

561-404-4209
888-332-6700; *Fax:* 561-892-5786
gjames@pgdirect.com; www.pgdirect.com

Gregory James, Publisher
Todd Heustess, Editor

The most reliable and comprehensive entertainment resource includes over 400 pages of national information including everyone you need to know within the advertising, fashion and print industries.
Frequency: Annual
Founded in: 1956

552 IQ Directory Adweek

Prometheus Global Media
770 Broadway
7th Floor
New York, NY 10003-9595

212-493-4100; *Fax:* 646-654-5368;
www.prometheusgm.com

Richard D. Beckman, CEO
James A. Finkelstein, Chairman
Madeline Krakowsky, Vice President Circulation
Tracy Brater, Executive Director Creative Service

Profile of companies at the leading edge of digital marketing, has the specifics you'll need to investigate, launch and/or expand your digital presence. Profiles over 2,200 interactive agencies, web developers, brand marketers, online media, CD-ROM developers, POP/Kiosk designers and multimedia creative companies
Founded in: 1981

553 IRS Corporate Financial Ratios

Schonfeld & Associates Inc
1931 Lynn Circle
Libertyville, IL 60048-1323

847-816-4870
800-205-0030; *Fax:* 847-816-4872
saiinfo@saibooks.com; www.saibooks.com

Carol Greenhut, Publisher

An ideal reference for CPAs, controllers, bankers, CFOs, tax lawyers, financial analysts, investment advisors and corporate planners, this reference book features 70-plus key financial ratios calculated from the latest income statement and balance sheet data available from the IRS.
Cost: $225.00
293 Pages
Frequency: Annual
ISBN: 1-932024-79-4

554 ISA Membership & Buyer's Guide

International Sign Association
1001 N Fairfax Street
Suite 301
Alexandria, VA 22314

703-836-4012
866-WHY-SIGN; *Fax:* 703-836-8353
info@signs.org; www.signs.org

Duane Laska, Chairman
Harry Niese, Vice Chairman
Chad Jones, Secretary/Treasurer

Discover a new supplier or distributor. Use our database to search members by company, location, products, services or equipment.
2600 Members

555 Illustrated Guide to P.O.P. Exhibits and Promotion
Creative Magazine
31 Merrick Avenue
Merrick, NY 11566

516-378-0800; *Fax:* 516-378-0884
info@creativemag.com; www.creativemag.com

Larry Flasterstein, Publisher

The Illustrated Guide serves over 15,000 P.O.P buyers, sales promotion and event managers in the leading corporations in North America with quick, up to the minute information about the resources in this industry.
Frequency: Annual

556 Infomercial Marketing Sourcebook
Prometheus Global Media
770 Broadway
7th Floor
New York, NY 10003-9595

212-493-4100; *Fax:* 646-654-5368;
www.prometheusgm.com

Richard D. Beckman, CEO
James A. Finkelstein, Chairman
Madeline Krakowsky, Vice President Circulation
Tracy Brater, Executive Director Creative Service

A complete resource guide for everyone involved in the infomercial industry.

557 Internship Directory
American Advertising Federation
1101 Vermont Ave NW
Suite 500
Washington, DC 20005-6306

202-898-0089
800-999-2231; *Fax:* 202-898-0159
aaf@aaf.org; www.aaf.org

James Edmund Datri, President
Constance Cannon Frazier, COO
Joanne Schecter, Executive Vice President

More than 1,500 advertising and marketing internships are listed in this valuable resource.
Circulation: 50000

558 Mediaweek Multimedia Directory
Prometheus Global Media
770 Broadway
7th Floor
New York, NY 10003-9595

212-493-4100; *Fax:* 646-654-5368;
www.prometheusgm.com

Richard D. Beckman, CEO
James A. Finkelstein, Chairman
Madeline Krakowsky, Vice President Circulation
Tracy Brater, Executive Director Creative Service

Focuses on the most powerful segments covering 9,000 media companies from the top 100 media markets for radio, broadcast TV, cable TV and daily newspapers. Also includes the top 300 consumer magazines, the top 150 trade magazines, networks, syndicators, sales representatives, multi-media holding companies, trade associations and rating organizations.
Frequency: Annual
Circulation: 800

559 Medical Marketing and Media
Haymarket Media Inc
114 W 26th St
4th Floor
New York, NY 10001-6812

212-206-0606; *Fax:* 212-638-6117
custserv@haymarketmedia.com;
www.haymarket.com

William Bekover, Chief Executive Officer

Offers a comprehensive editorial resource to leaders, thinkers and executives dedicated to the promotion and commercialization of prescription drugs and other medical products and services in the US.
Frequency: Monthly
Circulation: 15000
Founded in: 1996

560 Navigator
Promotional Products Association International
3125 Skyway Circle N
Irving, TX 75038-3539

972-252-0404; *Fax:* 972-258-3004
ppb@ppai.org; www.ppai.org

Paul Bellantone, President
Steven Meyer, Chairman of the Board
Marc Simon, Chair-Elect

An invaluable resource designed to educate distributors about PPAI supplier and business services members and the products they offer.
Frequency: Annual

561 Online Advertising Playbook
John Wiley & Sons
111 River St
Hoboken, NJ 07030-5790

201-748-6000; *Fax:* 201-748-6088
info@wiley.com; www.wiley.com

Stephen Smith, President & Chief Executive Officer
Vincent Marzano, Vice President

The book focuses on the enduring strategies necessary for marketers to have the knowledge base necessary to execute winning campaigns.

562 Planning for Out of Home Media
Traffic Audit Bureau for Media Measurement
271 Madison Ave
Suite 1504
New York, NY 10016-1012

212-972-8075; *Fax:* 212-972-8928
inquiry@tabonline.com; www.tabonline.com

Joseph Philport, President
Larry Hennessy, Vice President

Reference book contains up-to-date descriptions of O-O-H media and their production specifications, O-O-H local and national case history success stories and creative guidelines, travel trend data, new technologies and a glossary of O-O-H terminology.

563 Print Media Production Source
Standard Rate & Data Services
1700 E Higgins Rd
Des Plaines, IL 60018-5610

847-375-5000
800-851-7737; *Fax:* 847-375-5001
contact@srds.com; www.srds.com

Trish Delaurier, Publisher
George Carens, Executive Vice President

This service provides complete data on all critical ad production specifications for business and consumer magazines and newspapers. Production, traffic and graphic design personnel use this current, accurate resource to confirm essential production information so they can control production deadlines and budgets.
Frequency: Quarterly
Circulation: 800+

564 R&D Ratios & Budgets
Schonfeld & Associates Inc
1931 Lynn Circle
Libertyville, IL 60048-1323

847-816-4870
800-205-0030; *Fax:* 847-816-4872
saiinfo@saibooks.com; www.saibooks.com

Carol Greenhut, Publisher

The comprehensive annual report covers over 4,700 companies and 280 industries with information on current R&D budgets, R&D-to-sales ratios and R&D-to-gross margin ratios. Use it to track competition, set and justify R&D budgets, screen potential acquisitions, sell the laboratory and technology markets or plan new ventures and develop new products. Includes industry and R&D spender rankings.
Cost: $395.00
163 Pages
Frequency: Annual
ISBN: 1-932024-81-6

565 Radio Creative Resources Directory
Radio Advertising Bureau
1320 Greenway Dr
Suite 500
Irving, TX 75038-2547

972-753-6700
800-232-3131; *Fax:* 972-753-6727
jhaley@rab.com; www.rab.com

Erica Farber, President
Van Allen, EVP and CFO
Beverly Fraser, SVP

A list of radio production companies and studios in response to advertisers and agencies who want to find companies that specialize in writing, casting and producing great radio spots. Our current edition contains over 60 companies including many Radio-Mercury Award winners.
Frequency: Annual

566 Research & Development Growth Trends
Schonfeld & Associates Inc
1931 Lynn Circle
Libertyville, IL 60048-1323

847-816-4870
800-205-0030; *Fax:* 847-816-4872
saiinfo@saibooks.com; www.saibooks.com

Carol Greenhut, Publisher

Information on publicly owned corporations that spend on R&D.
Cost: $395.00
273 Pages
Frequency: Annual
ISBN: 1-932024-85-9

567 Standard Industry Directory
Association of Hispanic Advertising Agencies
8400 Westpark Drive
2nd Floor
McLean, VA 22102

703-610-9014; *Fax:* 703-610-0227
info@ahaa.org; www.ahaa.org
Social Media: Facebook, Twitter

Horacio Gavilan, President
Melissa Chen, Membership/Directory
Ayanna Wiggins, Marketing

AHAA represents the best minds and resources that are dedicated to Hispanic-specialized marketing.

568 Suppliers Directory
Eight-Sheet Outdoor Advertising Association
1244 Lake Park Ave
Galt, CA 95632

209-251-7622
800-847-3387; *Fax:* 209-251-7658
ddjesoaa@comcast.net; www.esoaa.com

Rebecca Lambert, Editor

Lists suppliers to the Eight-Sheet outdoor billboard industry; arranged by specialty. Includes definitions of basic industry terms.
Frequency: Annual
Circulation: 800

569 **The Art & Science of Managing a Content Marketing Strategy**
Direct Marketing Association
1120 Avenue of the Americas
New York, NY 10036-6700
212-768-7277; *Fax:* 212-302-6714
customerservice@the-dma.org;
www.the-dma.org
Social Media: Facebook, Twitter, LinkedIn
Lawrence M Kimmel, CEO
Effective Search Engine Optimization and Search Engine Marketing can have a dramatic effect on a website's performance and ROI. From optimization techniques to keyword bidding, our Search course offerings will give the insights and strategies to improve search results and efficiency.

570 **Tie-In Promotion Service**
Association of National Advertisers
708 Third Avenue
33 Floor
New York, NY 10017
212-697-5950; *Fax:* 212-661-8057
info@ana.net; www.ana.net
Social Media: Facebook, Twitter, LinkedIn, YouTube
Bob Liodice, President & CEO
Christine Manna, COO
William Zengel, EVP
Brand names listed by their companies as available for possible tie-in promotions with other companies.
Frequency: Annual/December

571 **U.S. Sourcebook of R&D Spenders**
Schonfeld & Associates Inc
1931 Lynn Circle
Libertyville, IL 60048-1323
847-816-4870
800-205-0030; *Fax:* 847-816-4872
saiinfo@saibooks.com; www.saibooks.com
Carol Greenhut, Publisher
A directory of publicly owned corporations that spend on R&D, published annually. Corporate name, address, telephone number, and website are provided along with the names and titles of three senior executives, R&D budgets, sales, fiscal year closing, and more. Organized by state and ZIP code. The ideal reference for sales people who call on R&D centers and for economic development agencies.
Cost: $395.00
157 Pages
Frequency: Annual
ISBN: 1-932024-83-2

572 **US Source Book of Advertisers**
Schonfeld & Associates Inc
1931 Lynn Circle
Libertyville, IL 60048-1323
847-816-4870
800-205-0030; *Fax:* 847-816-4872
saiinfo@saibooks.com; www.saibooks.com
Carol Greenhut, Publisher
A directory of publicly owned corporations that advertise. Corporate name, address, telephone number and website are provided along with the names and titles of three senior executives, ad budgets, sales, fiscal year closing and more. The ideal reference for media sales, ad agency new business development and selling corporate services.
Cost: $395.00
224 Pages
Frequency: Annual
ISBN: 1-932024-55-7

573 **Who's Who: MASA Buyer's Guide to Blue Ribbon Mailing Services**
Mailing & Fulfillment Service Association
1421 Prince Street
Suite 410
Alexandria, VA 22314-2806
703-836-9200; *Fax:* 703-548-8204
mfsa-mail@mfsanet.org; www.mfsanet.org
Ken Garner, President
Bill Stevenson, Director Marketing
Offers a detailed listing of suppliers of equipment, products and services to the direct mail industry, most containing a description of the specific products they provide.
Frequency: Annual

574 **Workbook**
Scott & Daughters Publishing
6762 Lexington Avenue
Los Angeles, CA 90038-2482
323-856-0008
800-547-2688; *Fax:* 323-856-4368;
www.workbook.com
Social Media: Facebook, Twitter
Alexis Scott, Owner
Susan Haller, Managing Editor
Bill Daniels, Publisher
This directory, offered in four volumes, lists over 25,000 advertising agencies, art directors and freelance illustrators in the United States.
Frequency: Annual
Circulation: 35,000

575 **Workforce Growth Trends**
Schonfeld & Associates Inc
1931 Lynn Circle
Libertyville, IL 60048-1323
847-816-4870
800-205-0030; *Fax:* 847-816-4872
saiinfo@saibooks.com; www.saibooks.com
Carol Greenhut, Publisher
Information on all publicly owned corporations. Study is ordered by U.S. Department of Commerce SIC(Standard Industrial Classification) and alphabetically by company name within each SIC. Each companys historical information, average annual percent change, sales and shares are displayed.
Cost: $495.00
565 Pages
Frequency: Annual
ISBN: 1-932024-87-5

576 **Workforce Ratios & Forecasts**
Schonfeld & Associates Inc
1931 Lynn Circle
Libertyville, IL 60048-1323
847-816-4870
800-205-0030; *Fax:* 847-816-4872
saiinfo@saibooks.com; www.saibooks.com
Carol Greenhut, Publisher
This comprehensive annual study by Schonfeld & Associates covers over 6,600 companies and 420 industries. The information reported includes current number of employees, a forecast of projected employee headcount and growth rates, as well as sales per employee and gross margin per employee. Use it to track competition, set and justify manpower budgets, screen potential acquisitions, plan new ventures and develop new businesses. Includes rankings by size and growth rate.
Cost: $495.00
243 Pages
Frequency: Annual
ISBN: 1-932024-86-7

Industry Web Sites

577 **www.aaaa.org**
American Association of Advertising Agencies
To improve and strengthen the advertising agency business in the United States by counseling members on operations and management.

578 **www.aaasite.org**
American Academy of Advertising
An organization of advertising scholars and professionals with an interest in advertising and advertising education.

579 **www.aaf.org**
American Advertising Federation
The American Advertising Federation protects and promotes the wellbeing of advertising.

580 **www.aapor.org**
American Association for Public Opinion Research
The American Advertising Federation protects and promotes the wellbeing of advertising.

581 **www.adcouncil.org**
Advertising Council
The Ad Council is a private, non-profit organization that marshals volunteer talent from the advertising and communications industries, the facilities of the media, and the resources of the business and non-profit communities to deliver critical messages to the American public.

582 **www.aef.com**
Advertising Educational Foundation
The advertising industry's provider and distributor of educational content to enrich the understanding of advertising and it's role in culture, society and the economy.

583 **www.ahaa.org**
Association of Hispanic Advertising Agencies
Mission to grow, strengthen and protect the Hispanic marketing and advertising industry by providing leadership in raising awareness of the value of the Hispanic market opportunities and enhancing the professionalism of the industry.

584 **www.ana.net**
Association of National Advertisers
Provides indispensable leadership that drives marketing excellence and champions, promotes and defends the interests of the marketing community.

585 **www.apanational.com**
Advertising Photographers of America
Our goal is to establish, endorse and promote professional practices, standards and ethics in the photographic and advertising community.

586 **www.awny.org**
Advertising Women of New York
The organization now consists of influential women and men representing the advertising, marketing, media, promotion and public relations fields.

587 **www.bbb.org**
Better Business Bureau
To be the leader in advancing marketplace trust.

588 **www.biznetis.net**
Biznet Internet Solutions
Biznet Internet Solutions is a full-service Web solutions company that focuses on business and mobile Web sites, provides advertising agency support, and Internet marketing.

589 **www.esoaa.com**
Eight-Sheet Outdoor Advertising Association
To provide leadership, services and standards to promote, protect and advance the eight sheet industry.

590 **www.greyhouse.com**
Grey House Publishing
Authoritative reference directories for business information and general reference including advertising, communications, marketing and media markets. Users can search the online databases with varied search criteria allowing for custom searches by product category, geographic area, sales volume, keyword, subject and more. Full Grey House catalog and online ordering also available.

591 **www.iaany.org**
International Advertising Association
Promoting the value of advertising globally, advocacy of freedom of commercial speech and consumer choice and encouraging industry self regulation.

592 **www.iab.net**
Interactive Advertising Bureau
Dedicated to the growth of the interactive advertising marketplace, of interactive's share of total marketing spend, and of its members' share of total marketing spend

593 **www.icomagencies.com**
International Communications Agency Network
The international organization of museums and museum professionals which is committed to the conservation, continuation and communication to society of the world's natural and cultural heritage, present and future, tangible and intangible.

594 **www.ifcaonline.com**
Insurance and Financial Communicators Association
An international association for insurance and financial communicators offering professional development and networking.

595 **www.magnetglobal.org**
MAGNET: Marketing & Advertising Global Network
Provides a way for member agencies to share their experience, knowledge and ideas with other agencies in other parts of the world.

596 **www.marketingpower.com**
American Marketing Association
It is a professional association for individuals and organizations involved in the practice, teaching and study of marketing and advertising worldwide.

597 **www.mfsanet.org**
Mailing & Fulfillment Service Association
The national trade association for the mailing and fulfillment services industry.

598 **www.oaaa.org**
Outdoor Advertising Association of America
To provide leadership, services and standards to promote, protect and advance the outdoor advertising industry.

599 **www.popai.com**
Point of Purchase Advertising International
Dedicated to promoting Marketing at Retail as a powerful advertising medium being rapidly integrated into the strategic marketing mix as retail programs deliver a critical combination of brand messaging and information at the critical moment of the consumer purchase decision.

600 **www.ppa.org**
Promotional Products Association International
To lead the industry by expanding the market, providing indispensable products and services, and enhancing our members' professionalism and success.

601 **www.rama-nrf.com**
Retail Advertising & Marketing International
Provides visionary leadership that promotes creativity, innovation and excellence within all marketing disciplines that strategically elevates our members and our industry.

602 **www.signs.org**
International Sign Association
Supports, promotes and improves the sign industry, which sustains the nation's retail industry.

603 **www.tabonline.com**
Traffic Audit Bureau for Media Measurement
An independent third party provider of standardized and valid circulation measures for out of home media.

604 **www.thearf.org**
Advertising Research Foundation
An open forum where the best and brightest from every avenue of advertising can gather to exchange ideas and research strategies

605 **www.thecab.tv**
Cabletelevision Advertising Bureau
Dedicated to providing advertisers and agencies with the most current, complete and actionable cable television media insights at the national, DMA and local levels.

606 **www.tradepromo.org**
Trade Promotion Management Association
Provides members with information, education and research on the dynamic world of trade promotion, including co op advertising, market development funds, slotting fees, off invoice deductions, channel promotions and more.

Associations

607 **4-H**
7100 Connecticut Ave.
Chevy Chase, MD 20815

301-961-2800; www.4-h.org
Social Media: Facebook, Twitter, LinkedIn, Instagram, Pinterest, YouTube

Lisa A. Lauxman, Contact

A global network of youth development organizations operating independently in more than 50 countries. The club's slogan is "Learn by doing."
Founded in: 1902

608 **AACC International**
3340 Pilot Knob Road
St. Paul, MN 55121-2055

651-454-7250
800-328-7560; *Fax:* 651-454-0766
aacc@scisoc.org; www.aaccnet.org
Social Media: Facebook, Twitter, LinkedIn, Pinterest

Lydia Tooker Midness, Chair of the Board
Robert L. Cracknell, President
Dave L. Braun, Treasurer
Samuel Millar, Director
Anne M. Birkett, Director

Formerly the American Association of Cereal Chemists, a non-profit organization of members who are specialists in the use of cereal grains in foods.
2000 Members
Founded in: 1915

609 **Agribusiness Council(ABC)**
PO Box 5565
Washington, DC 20016

202-296-4563; *Fax:* 202-887-9178
info@agribusinesscouncil.org;
www.agribusinesscouncil.org

Nicholas E Hollis, President/CEO

The Agribusiness Council (ABC) is a private, nonprofit/tax-exempt, membership organization dedicated to strengthening U.S. agro-industrial competitiveness through programs which highlight international trade and development potentials as well as broad issues which encompass several individual agribusiness sectors and require a food systems approach. Examples of such issues are commercialization of new tech/crops, environmental impacts, human resource development, trade and investment policy.
Founded in: 1967

610 **Agricultural & Applied Economics Association**
555 E Wells Street
Suite 1100
Milwaukee, WI 53202-6600

414-918-3190; *Fax:* 414-276-3349
info@aaea.org; www.aaea.org
Social Media: Facebook, Twitter, LinkedIn, Blogger, Google+

Jill McCluskey, President
Jayson Lusk, President-Elect
Barry Goodwin, Past President
Michael Boland, Director
Ani Katchova, Director

The Agricultural & Applied Economics Association (AAEA) is a not-for-profit association serving the professional interests of members working in agricultural and broadly related fields of applied economics. Members of the AAEA are employed by academic or government institutions, as well as in industry and not-for-profit organizations, and engage in a variety of teaching, research, and extension/outreach activities.
3000 Members
Founded in: 1910

611 **Agricultural Communicators of Tomorrow**
PO Box 110180
Gainesville, FL 32611-0180

352-392-1971; *Fax:* 352-392-9589;
www.ifas.ufl.edu
Social Media: Facebook, Twitter

Dr Jack Payne, Senior Vice President

A national organization of college students professionally interested in communications related to agriculture, food, natural resources and allied fields. The Mission of UF/IFAS is to develop knowledge in agricultural, human and natural resources and to make that knowledge accessible to sustain and enhance the quality of human life.
Founded in: 1853

612 **Agricultural Retailers Association**
1156 15th St NW
Suite 500
Washington, DC 20005-1745

202-457-0825; *Fax:* 202-457-0864
info@aradc.org; www.aradc.org
Social Media: Facebook, Twitter

Dave DuFault, Chairman
Daren Coppock, President & CEO
Richard Gupton, SVP, Public Policy & Counsel
Donnie Taylor, VP, Membership & Corp Relations
Brian Reuwee, Dir., Comm. & Marketing

The Agricultural Retailers Association (ARA) is a nonprofit trade association that serves as the political voice of agricultural retailers and distributors. We're advocates, educators, and champions for the American ag retailer. The Agricultural Retailers Association (ARA) is a nonprofit trade association that serves as the political voice of agricultural retailers and distributors. We're advocates, educators, and champions for the American ag retailer.
Frequency: Annual
Founded in: 1993

613 **Agriculture Council of America**
11020 King St
Suite 205
Overland Park, KS 66210-1201

913-491-1895; *Fax:* 913-491-6502
info@agday.org; www.agday.org
Social Media: Facebook, Twitter, Flickr, YouTube

Curt Blades, Chair
Annette Degnan, Vice Chair
Curt Blades, Secretary/Treasurer
Lynn Henderson, Board Member
Nancy Barcus, Bard Member

The Agriculture Council of America (ACA) is an organization uniquely composed of leaders in the agriculture, food and fiber communities dedicated to increasing the public awareness of agriculture's vital role in our society.
75 Members
Founded in: 1973

614 **Agriculture Federal Credit Union**
1400 Independence Ave SW
Room SM2
Washington, DC 20250

202-479-2270
800-368-3552; *Fax:* 202-479-3877
members@agriculturefcu.org; www.agfed.org
Social Media: Facebook, Twitter

Margie Click, President/CEO
Theodora Ezekwerre, Senior Vice President
Tom Bowles, Senior Vice President
Clifton Jeter, Chair
Stephen J Hawkins, Vice Chair

Agriculture Federal Credit Union meets the highest standards for long term financial soundness. AgFed's workplace environment motivates and empowers employees to provide quality service to our members. AgFed offers a wide range of financial services and products to satisfy the diverse needs of our members throughout their lifetimes. AgFed has state-of-the-art technology designed to meet our members' needs.
23000 Members
Founded in: 1934

615 **American Agricultural Law Association**
P.O. Box 5861
Columbia, SC 29250

803-728-3200; *Fax:* 360-423-2287
ellenberg@aglaw-assn.org;
www.aglaw-assn.org

Jesse J. Richardson, Jr., President
Kristy Thomason Ellenberg, Executive Director
Anne 'Beth' Crocker, President-Elect
Justin Schneider, Director
Amber Miller, Director

The AALA is a membership organization that focuses on the legal needs of the agricultural community.
600 Members
Founded in: 1980

616 **American Agriculture Movement**
AAM National Secretary/Treasurer
11232 Road K
Liberal, KS 67901

620-482-6306
jrice@swko.net; www.aaminc.org

Larry Matlack, President
Arthur Chaney, Executive Vice President
John Willis, Vice President
Lynn Kirkpatrick, Vice President of Marketing
Marc Wetzel, Vice President of Membership

The creation of the AAM has provided a farmer-created, farmer-built organization within which farmers themselves have been the leaders, speakers and organizers; empowering farmers as they had not been in the past, to speak for and advocate for themselves.
Founded in: 1977

617 **American Angus Association**
3201 Frederick Ave
St Joseph, MO 64506-2997

816-383-5100; *Fax:* 816-233-9703
angus@angus.org; www.angus.org
Social Media: Facebook, Twitter, Pinterest, Youtube, Vimeo

Richard Wilson, Iinterim CEO
Jim Sitz, Vice President
Charlie Boyd II, Treasurer
Diane Strahm, Administrative Assistant
Richard Wilson, CFO

The American Angus Association is the nation's largest beef registry association. Our goal is to serve the beef cattle industry, and increase the production of consistent, high quality beef that will better satisfy consumers throughout the world.
36000 Members
Founded in: 1873

618 **American Association of Crop Insurers**
1 Massachusetts Ave NW
Suite 800
Washington, DC 20001-1401

202-789-4100; *Fax:* 202-408-7763
aaci@mwmlaw.com; www.cropinsurers.com

Michael R. McLeod, Executive Director
David Graves, President
Bill O'Conner, Senior Government Relations
Laura Phelps, Senior Government Relations

The American Association of Crop Insurers is a nonprofit industry service organization repre-

senting the interests of insurance companies, agents, and adjusters involved in the Federal crop insurance program. AACI's reinsured company members write more than 80 percent of the crop insurance sold by private companies nationwide. AACI's primary purpose is governmental relations with Congress, the U.S. Department of Agriculture, and other executive agencies whose decisions influence the program.
25 Members
Founded in: 1980

619 **American Beekeeping Federation**
3525 Piedmont Road
Bldg 5 Suite 300
Atlanta, GA 30305-1509

404-760-2875; *Fax:* 404-240-0998
info@abfnet.org; www.abfnet.org

Regina Robuck, Executive Director
Gene Brandi, President
Tim May, Vice President

The ABF is a national organization that continually works in the interest of all beekeepers, large or small, and those associated with the industry to ensure the future of the honey bee. Our members share a common interest to work toward better education and information for all segments of the industry in the hope of increasing our chances for survival in today's competitive world.
4700 Members
Founded in: 1943

620 **American Brahman Breeders Association**
3003 South Loop West
Suite 520
Houston, TX 77054

713-349-0854; *Fax:* 713-349-9795
abba@brahman.org; www.brahman.org
Social Media: Facebook, Twitter, YouTube, Instagram

J. D. Sartwelle, Jr., President
George Kempfer, Vice President
Loren Pratt, Secretary/Treasurer
Chris Shivers, Executive Vice President
Armelinda Ibarra, Recording Secretary / Office Mgr

American Brahman Breeders is a beef crossbreeding organization that plays a big role in the United States and beyond.
Founded in: 1924

621 **American Dairy Science Association**
1800 South Oak Street
Suite 100
Champaign, IL 61820-6974

217-356-5146; *Fax:* 217-398-4119
adsa@assochq.org; www.adsa.org
Social Media: RSS

Susan Duncan, President
Lou Armentano, Vice President
Peter Studney, Executive Director
Matt Lucy, Editor-in-Chief
Vicki Paden, Administrative Assistant

The American Dairy Science Association (ADSA) is an international organization of educators, scientists, and industry representatives who are committed to advancing the dairy industry and keenly aware of the vital role the dairy sciences play in fulfilling the economic, nutritive, and health requirements of the world's population. Together, ADSA members have discovered new methods and technologies that have revolutionized the dairy industry.
3000 Members
Founded in: 1998
Mailing list available for rent

622 **American Farm Bureau Federation**
600 Maryland Ave SW
Suite 1000W
Washington, DC 20024-2555

202-484-3600; *Fax:* 202-484-3604
bstallman@fb.org; www.fb.org
Social Media: Facebook, Twitter, RSS, You Tube, Google+, Pinter

Bob Stallman, President
Don Lipton, Executive Director
Julie Anna Potts, Executive Vice President/Treasurer
Ellen Steen, General Counsel & Secretary
Mace Thornton, Acting Director

Farm Bureau is an independent, non-governmental, voluntary organization governed by and representing farm and ranch families united for the purpose of analyzing their problems and formulating action to achieve educational improvement, economic opportunity and social advancement and, thereby, to promote the national well-being. Farm Bureau is local, county, state, national and international in its scope and influence and is non-partisan, non-sectarian and non-secret in character.
3M Members
Founded in: 1919

623 **American Feed Industry Association**
American Feed Industry Association
2101 Wilson Blvd
Suite 916
Arlington, VA 22201-3047

703-524-0810; *Fax:* 703-524-1921
afia@afia.org; www.afia.org
Social Media: Facebook, Twitter, LinkedIn, YouTube

Rob Sheffer, Chairman
Joel G. Newman, President & Treasurer
Shakera Daley, Accounting and Admin Coordinator
Sarah Novak, VP/Membership
Richard Sellers, AFIA, SVP/Corporate Secretary

AFIA is the world's largest organization devoted exclusively to representing the business, legislative and regulatory interests of the U.S. animal feed industry and its suppliers. AFIA also is the recognized leader on international industry developments. Members include more than 500 domestic and international companies and state, regional and national associations.
690 Members
Founded in: 1909

624 **American Forage and Grassland Council**
PO Box 867
Berea, KY 40403

800-944-2342
tina.bowling@afgc.org; www.afgc.org
Social Media: Facebook, Twitter, YouTube

Tina Bowling, Executive Director
Howard Straub, President
Ray Smith, Senior Vice President
Roger L Staff, Treasurer
Coy Fitch, Director

The American Forage and Grassland Council (AFGC) is an international organization made up of 20 affiliate councils in the United States and Canada. Our primary objective is to promote the profitable production and sustainable utilization of quality forage and grasslands. Mission is to be recognized as the leader and voice of economically and environmentally sound forage agriculture.
2700 Members

625 **American Guernsey Association**
1224 Alton Darby Creeek Road
Suite G
Columbus, OH 43228

614-864-2409; *Fax:* 614-864-5614
info@usguernsey.com; www.usguernsey.com

David Trotter, President
Duane Schuler, 1st Vice President
David Coon, 2nd Vice President
Brian Schnebly, Executive Secretary
Deb Hoffman, Office Manager

The AGA's mission is to provide and promote programs and services to enhance the value and profitability of the Guernsey breed for the members, owners and dairy industry worldwide.
900 Members
Founded in: 1877

626 **American Hereford Association**
PO Box 014059
Kansas City, MO 64101

816-842-3757; *Fax:* 816-842-6931
aha@hereford.org; www.hereford.org
Social Media: Facebook

Craig Huffhines, Executive Vice President
Jack Ward, COO
Angie Stump Denton, Communications Director
Amy Cowen, Youth Activities Director
Joe Rickabaugh, Field Mgmt Director

Association for people in the Hereford cattle industry.
Founded in: 1910

627 **American Jersey Cattle Association**
6486 E Main Street
Reynoldsburg, OH 43068-2362

614-861-3636; *Fax:* 614-861-8040;
www.usjersey.com
Social Media: Facebook, Twitter

Neal Smith, CEO/Executive Secretary
Vickie J. White, Treasurer
Cherie L Bayer, Director
Cari Wolfe, Director/Research
Kristin Paul, Director of Field Service

They improve and promote the Jersey cattle breed.
2178 Members
Founded in: 1868

628 **American Livestock Breeds Convervancy (ALBC)**
PO Box 477
33 Hillsboro St
Pittsboro, NC 27312

919-542-5704; *Fax:* 919-545-0022;
www.livestockconservancy.org
Social Media: Facebook, Twitter, LinkedIn, Blogger, YouTube

Charles Bassett, Executive Director
Terry Wollen, President
Angelique Thompson, Operations Manager
James McConnell, Treasurer
Anneke Jakes, Manager of Breed Registry

The American Livestock Breeds Conservancy is a nonprofit membership organization working to protect over 180 breeds of livestock and poultry from extinction. Included are asses, cattle, goats, horses, sheep, pigs, rabbits, chickens, ducks, geese, and turkeys.
Founded in: 1977

629 **American Meat Science Association**
201 W Springfield Ave
Ste 1202
Champaign, IL 61822-7676

217-356-5370
800-517-AMSA; *Fax:* 888-205-5834; *Fax:* 217-356-5370
information@meatscience.org;
www.meatscience.org

Social Media: Facebook, Twitter, LinkedIn, Vimeo

Bucky Gwartney, Ph.D., President
Thomas Powell, Executive Director
Deidrea Mabry, Director, Scientific Communications
Jen Persons, Membership and Marketing Manager
Rachel Adams, M.S., Youth Programs Coordinator

The American Meat Science Association is a broad-reaching organization of individuals that discovers, develops, and disseminates its collective meat science knowledge to provide leadership, education, and professional development. Our passion is to help meat science professionals achieve previously unimaginable levels of performance and reach even higher goals.
Founded in: 1964

630 American Phytopathological Society

3340 Pilot Knob Road
Saint Paul, MN 55121-2097

651-454-7250
800-328-7560; *Fax:* 651-454-0766
aps@scisoc.org; www.apsnet.org
Social Media: Facebook, Twitter, LinkedIn, YouTube, Pinterest

Michelle Bjerkness, Operations/Membership
Amy Hope, Exeutive Vice President
Kim Davis, Finance
Erik Uner, IT
Betty Ford, Meetings

APS is a diverse global community of scientists that: provides credible and beneficial information related to plant health; advocates and participates in the exchange of knowledge with the public, policy makers, and the larger scientific community; and promotes and provides opportunities for scientific communication, career preparation, and professional development for its members.
4500 Members
Founded in: 1908

631 American Seed Trade Association

1701 Duke Street
Suite 275
Alexandria, VA 22314-3415

703-837-8140; *Fax:* 703-837-9365
info@amseed.com; www.amseed.org
Social Media: Facebook, Twitter, YouTube, Google+

Risa DeMasi, Chairman
Andrew LaVigne, President/CEO
Bernice Slutsky, SVP, Domestic and Intl. Policy
Jane DeMarchi, VP, Gov & Regulatory Affairs
Ric Dunkle, Ph.D., Senior Dir., Seed Health & Trade

ASTA's mission is to be an effective voice of action in all matters concerning the development, marketing and movement of seed, associated products and services throughout the world. ASTA promotes the development of better seed to produce better crops for a better quality of life.
700+ Members
Founded in: 1883

632 American Sheep Industry Association

9785 Maroon Circle
Suite 360
Englewood, CO 80112

303-771-3500; *Fax:* 303-771-8200
eatlamb@wildblue.net; www.sheepusa.org
Social Media: Facebook, Twitter

Burton Pfliger, President
Mike Corn, Vice President
Peter Orwick, Executive Director
Larry Kincaid, Chief Financial Officer
Paul Rodgers, Deputy Director of Policy

ASI is the national organization representing the interests of sheep producers located throughout the United States. From East to West, farm flocks to range operations, ASI works to represent the interests of all producers. ASI is a federation of 45 state sheep associations as well as individual members.
82000 Members
Founded in: 1865

633 American Society for Enology and Viticulture

PO Box 1855
Davis, CA 95617-1855

530-753-3142; *Fax:* 530-753-3318
society@asev.org; www.asev.org
Social Media: Twitter, LinkedIn, Picasa

Mark Greenspan, President
Nichola Hall, 1st Vice President
James Harbertson, 2nd Vice President
Tom Collins, Secretary/Treasurer
Dan Howard, Executive Director

The American Society for Enology and Viticulture (the sciences of winemaking and grape growing) is a 501 (c)(6), tax exempt professional society dedicated to the interests of enologists, viticulturists, and others in the fields of wine and grape research and production throughout the world. Our membership includes professionals from wineries, vineyards, academic institutions and organizations.
2400+ Members
Founded in: 1950

634 American Society for Horticultural Science

1018 Duke Street
Alexandria, VA 22314

703-836-4606; *Fax:* 703-836-2024
webmaster@ashs.org; www.ashs.org
Social Media: Facebook, Twitter, LinkedIn, Pinterest

Curt Rom, Chairman
John Dole, President
Michael W. Neff, Executive Director
Heather Hilko, Member Services

A cornerstone of research and education in horticulture and an agent for active promotion of horticultural science.
1200 Members
Founded in: 1903

635 American Society of Agricultural Consultants

605 Columbus Ave South
New Prague, MN 56071

952-758-5811; *Fax:* 952-758-5813
asac@gandgcomm.com;
www.agconsultants.org
Social Media: Facebook, Twitter, LinkedIn, YouTube

Den Gardner, Executive Vice President
Kristy Mach, Associate
Gary Wagner, VP/Secretary

An association representing the full range of agricultural consultants which serves as an information, resource, and networking base for its members. The specific purpose of ASAC is to foster the science of agricultural consulting in all its varied fields; to promote the profession and maintain high standards under which the members conduct their service to the public; hold meetings for the exchange of ideas and the study of the profession of agricultural consulting;
181 Members
Founded in: 1963

636 American Society of Agricultural and Biological Engineers

2950 Niles Rd
St Joseph, MI 49085-8607

269-429-0300
800-371-2723; *Fax:* 269-429-3852
hq@asabe.org; www.asabe.org
Social Media: Facebook, Twitter, LinkedIn, YouTube

Darrin Drollinger, Executive Director
Joe Walker, Publication Director
Dolores Landeck, Director/Public Affairs
Scott Cedarquist, Dir., Standards & Tech Activities
Mark Crossley, Director/Membership

The American Society of Agricultural and Biological Engineers is an educational and scientific organization dedicated to the advancement of engineering applicable to agricultural, food, and biological systems. With members in more than 100 countries. The Society's Agricultural, Food and Biological Engineers develop efficient and environmentally sensitive methods of producing food, fiber, timber, and renewable energy sources.
8000 Members
Founded in: 1907
Mailing list available for rent: 10000 names at $120 per M

637 American Society of Agronomy

5585 Guilford Road
Madison, WI 53711-5801

608-273-8080; *Fax:* 608-273-2021
membership@agronomy.org;
www.agronomy.org
Social Media: Facebook, Twitter, LinkedIn, RSS

Jean L. Steiner, President
Wes Meixelsperger, Chief Financial Officer
Sara Uttech, Senior Manager - Governance
Wes Meixelsperger, Director of Meetings
Ian Popkewitz, Director of IT and Operations

Promote human welfare through advancing the acquisition and dissemination of scientific knowledge concerning the nature, use improvement and interrelationships of plants, soils, water and environment. The society shall promote effective research, disseminate scientific information, facilitate technology transfer, foster high standards of education, strive to maintain high standards of ethics, promote advancements in this profession and cooperate with other organizations of similar objectives.
11000 Members
Founded in: 1907

638 American Society of Animal Science

PO Box 7410
Champaign, IL 61826-7410

217-356-9050; *Fax:* 217-568-6070
asas@asas.org; www.asas.org
Social Media: Facebook, Twitter, LinkedIn, YouTube

Dr. Michael L. Looper, President
Jacelyn Hemmelgarn, Chief Operations Officer
Meghan Wulster-Radcliffe, Chief Executive Officer
Melissa Burnett, Membership Manager
Samantha Walker, Program Director

The American Society of Animal Science is a membership society that supports the careers of scientists and animal producers in the United States and internationally. The American Society of Animal Science fosters the discovery, sharing and application of scientific knowledge concerning the responsible use of animals to enhance human life and well-being.
ISSN: 0021-8812
Founded in: 1908

639 American Society of Consulting Arborists
9707 Key West Avenue
Suite 100
Rockville, MD 20850-3992

301-947-0483; *Fax:* 301-990-9771
asca@mgmtsol.com; www.asca-consultants.org
Social Media: Twitter, LinkedIn, Pinterest

Chris D. Ahlum, President
Beth W. Palys, Executive Director
Amy Hager, Deputy Director
Shannon Sperati, Senior Member Services Manager
Julie Hill, Marketing Director

The industry's premier professional association focusing solely on arboricultural consulting. Consulting Arborists are authoritative experts on trees, consulting property owners, municipalities, attorneys, insurance professionals and others on tree disease, placement, preservation and dispute resolution in addition to providing consulting and expert testimony in the legal, insurance and environmental arenas.
Founded in: 1967

640 American Society of Farm Managers and Rural Appraisers (ASFMRA)
950 S Cherry St
Suite 508
Denver, CO 80246-2664

303-758-3513; *Fax:* 303-758-0190
info@asfmra.org; www.asfmra.org
Social Media: Facebook, Twitter, LinkedIn, Plaxo

Fred L. Hepler, AFM, AAC, President
Merrill E. Swanson, President-Elect
LeeAnn E. Moss, Academic Vice President
Debe Alvarez, Manager/Education
Cheryl Cooley, Manager/Meetings & IT

The ASFMRA provides members with the resources, information, and leadership that enable them to provide valuable services to the agricultural community. The focus of the ASFMRA is providing education and networking opportunities for a professional group of members providing farm and ranch management, rural and real property appraising, review appraisal, and agricultural consulting services to the private and public sectors and to the governmental and lending communities.
1900 Members
Founded in: 1929
Mailing list available for rent

641 American Soybean Association
12125 Woodcrest Executive
Suite 100
St. Louis, MO 63141-5009

314-576-1770
800-688-7692; *Fax:* 314-576-2786
membership@soy.org; www.soygrowers.com
Social Media: Facebook, Twitter, LinkedIn, YouTube, RSS

Ray Gaesser, Chairman
Wade Cowan, President
Richard Wilkins, 1st Vice President
Steve Censky, CEO
Julie Hawkins, Meeting Planner/Executive Asst.

The American Soybean Association (ASA) is recognized by the majority of U.S. soybean growers and industry for its vital role as their domestic and international policy advocate. ASA is clearly leading an expanding soybean value-chain, with farmers capturing a growing percentage. ASA's development of influential and effective grower leaders is recognized throughout the agriculture industry.
22000 Members
Founded in: 1920

642 Animal Agriculture Alliance
2101 Wilson Blvd
Suite 916-13
Arlington, VA 22201

703-562-5160; *Fax:* 703-524-1921
info@animalagalliance.org;
www.animalagalliance.org
Social Media: Facebook, Twitter

Sherrie Webb, Chairman
Kay Johnson Smith, President and CEO
Hannah Thompson, Communications Director
Casey Whitaker, Communications Coordinator
Morgan Hawley, Project Manager

The Animal Agriculture Alliance, is a broad based coalition of individual farmers, ranchers, producer organizations, suppliers, packer-processors, scientists, veterinarians and retailers. The Alliance with its members are interested in helping consumers better understand the role animal agriculture plays in providing a safe, abundant food supply to a hungry world.
3000 Members
Founded in: 1987

643 Aquatic Plant Management Society
7922 NW 71st Street
Gainesville, FL 32653

Fax: 601-634-5502
webmaster@apms.org; www.apms.org
Social Media: Facebook, Twitter, LinkedIn, Bloggr

Mike Netherland, President
Rob Richardson, Vice-President
Jeff Schardt, Secretary
Jason Ferrell, Editor
Sherry Whitaker, Treasurer

The Aquatic Plant Management Society, Inc. is an international organization of scientists, educators, students, commercial pesticide applicators, administrators, and concerned individuals interested in the management and study of aquatic plants. The Aquatic Plant Management Society (APMS) strives to promote environmental stewardship through scientific innovation and development of technology related to integrated plant management in aquatic and riparian systems.
Founded in: 1961

644 Association for Arid Lands Studies
601 Indiana Avenue
PO Box 45004
Lubbock, TX 79409-5004

806-742-3667; *Fax:* 806-742-1286
gay.riggan@ttu.edu; www.iaff.ttu.edu
Social Media: Facebook

Tibor Nagy, VP
Dr. A C Correa, International Director/ICASALS
Bob Crosier, Director
Dawn Cepica, International Faculty Counselor
Stephanie Cloninger, Special Projects Coordinator

To promote the university's special mission of the interdisciplinary study of arid and semi-arid environments and the human relationship to these environments from an international perspective.
200 Members
Founded in: 1977

645 Association of American Feed Control Officials
1800 South Oak Street
Suite 100
Champaign, IL 61820-6974

217-356-4221; *Fax:* 217-398-4119
aafco@aafco.org; www.aafco.org
Social Media: Facebook

Tim Darden, President
Doug Lueders, President Elect
Ali Kashani, Secretary/Treasurer
Mark LeBlanc, Senior Director
Ken Bowers, Junior Director

The Association of American Feed Control Officials (AAFCO) is a voluntary membership association of local, state and federal agencies charged by law to regulate the sale and distribution of animal feeds and animal drug remedies.Although AAFCO has no regulatory authority, the Association provides a forum for the membership and industry representation to achieve two main goals: Ensure consumer protection and safeguarding the health of animals and humans.
Founded in: 1909

646 Association of American Seed Control Officials
Utah Department of Agriculture
350 N Redwood Road
PO Box 146500
Salt Lake City, UT 84114-6500

801-848-8543; *Fax:* 801-538-7189
walshm@purdue.edu; www.seedcontrol.org

Jim Drews, President
Johnny Zook, First Vice President
Greg Stordahl, Second Vice President
Greg Helmbrecht, Treasurer
John Heaton, Secretary

The Association of American Seed Control Officials is an organization of seed regulatory officials from the United States and Canada. The members meet to discuss mutual concerns of seed law enforcement, to be updated on new developments in the seed industry, and to update the Recommended Uniform State Seed Law which the organization developed and maintains as model law.
Founded in: 1949

647 Association of Equipment
6737 W Washington Street
Suite 2400
Milwaukee, WI 53214-5647

414-272-0943; *Fax:* 414-272-1170
aem@aem.org; www.aem.org
Social Media: Twitter

John Patterson, Chairman
Nick Yaksich, VP, Government & Industry Relations
Megan Tanel, VP, Exhibitions & Events
Anne Forristall Luke, VP, Political & Public Affairs
Al Cervero, VP, Construction, Mining & Utility
850 Members
Founded in: 1946

648 Association of Equipment Manufacturers
6737 W Washington St
Suite 2400
Milwaukee, WI 53214-5647

414-272-0943
866-236-0442; *Fax:* 414-272-1170
aem@aem.org; www.aem.org
Social Media: Facebook, Twitter, LinkedIn, StumbleUpon, Google+

John Patterson, Chairman
Dennis Slater, President
Anne Forristall Luke, Vice President
Renee Peters, Chief Financial Officer
Judy Gaus, VP, HR & Admin Affairs

A trade association that provides services on a global basis for companies that manufacture equipment, products and services used worldwide in the following industries: Agriculture, Construction, Forestry, Mining and Utility. AEM's membership and represents 200+ product lines.
850 Members
Founded in: 1894

649 **Bio-Dynamic Farming and Gardening Association**
1661 North Water Street
Suite 307
Milwaukee, WI 53202
262-649-9212; *Fax:* 262-659-9213; *Fax:* new
info@biodynamics.com;
www.biodynamics.com
Steffen Schneider, President
Janet Gamble, Vice President and Secretary
Greg Georgaklis, Treasurer
Zachary Krebs, Technology
Penny Molina, Business Relationships
The Bio-Dynamic Farming and Gardeing Association (BDA) is an association of individuals and organizations in North America who are committed to the transformation of the whole food system.
Founded in: 1938

650 **Biodynamic Farming and Gardening Association**
1661 N Water Street
Suite 307
Milwaukee, WI 53202
262-649-9212; *Fax:* 262-649-9213
info@biodynamics.com;
www.biodynamics.com
Social Media: Facebook
Steffen Schneider, President
Janet Gamble, Vice President and Secretary
Greg Georgaklis, Treasurer
Zachary Krebs, Technology
Penny Molina, Business Relationships
The Biodynamic Farming and Gardening Association (BDA) is an association of individuals and organizations in North America who are committed to the transformation of the whole food system, from farm to table, and who draw inspiration from the spiritual-scientific insights of Rudolf Steiner. Biodynamics is a worldwide movement for the renewal of agriculture based on an understanding of the spiritual forces at work in nature and in human social life.
Founded in: 1938

651 **Cape Cod Cranberry Growers' Association**
1 Carver Square Boulevard
PO Box 97
Carver, MA 02330
508-866-7878; *Fax:* 508-866-4220
info@cranberries.org; www.cranberries.org
Social Media: Facebook
Brad Morse, President
Gary Garretson, 1st Vice President
Keith Mann, 2nd Vice President
Brian Wick, Executive Director
Henry Gillet, Jr,, Government Affairs Director
Promotes the success of US and Canadian cranberry growers through health, agricultural and environmental stewardship research and education.
Founded in: 1888

652 **Committee on Organic and Sustainable Agriculture**
5585 Guilford Road
Madison, WI 53711-5801
608-273-8080; *Fax:* 608-273-2021
queries@dl.sciencesocieties.org
dl.sciencesocieties.org
Social Media: Facebook, Twitter, LinkedIn
Ann-Marie Fortuna, Chair
Develops programming for members and divisions interested in sustainable and organic agriculture for the Societies' annual meeting; obtain input and develop recommendations on ways to better serve members interested in sustainable and organic agriculture beyond the activities ata the annual meeting
Founded in: 2003

653 **Communicating for AMERICA**
112 E Lincoln Avenue
PO Box 677
Fergus Falls, MN 56537
218-739-3241
800-432-3276; *Fax:* 218-739-3832
memberbenefits@cainc.org;
www.communicatingforamerica.org
Social Media: Facebook
Milt Smedsrud, Chairman
Patty Strickland, President/ Chief Operations Officer
Stephen Rufer, Vice President/General Counsel
Ben Shierer, Vice President of Government Rel
David Ramey, Owner
Strives to promote health, well-being and advancement of people in agriculture and agribusiness.
40M Members
Founded in: 1972

654 **Community Alliance with Family Farmers**
36355 Russell Boulevard
PO Box 363
Davis, CA 95616
530-756-8518
800-892-3832; *Fax:* 530-756-7857
info@caff.org; www.caff.org
Social Media: Facebook, Twitter, YouTube, Flickr
Rich Collins, Board Chair
David Runsten, Policy Director
Diane Del Signore, Executive Director
Diana Aberella, Chief Operating Officer
Megan Sabato, Director of Communications
Mission is to build a movement of rural and urban people to foster family-scale agriculture that cares for the land, sustains local economies and promotes social justice.
Cost: $47.95
Founded in: 1978

655 **Corn Refiners Association**
1701 Pennsylvania Ave NW
Suite 950
Washington, DC 20006-5806
202-331-1634; *Fax:* 202-331-2054
comments@corn.org; www.corn.org
Social Media: Facebook, Twitter, LinkedIn, StumbleUpon, Google+
Audrae Erickson, President
Thomas D Malkoski, Vice Chairman of the Board
J Patrick Mohan, Treasurer
Supports carbohydrate research programs through grants to colleges, government laboratories and private research centers.
8 Members
Founded in: 1913

656 **Council for Agricultural Science and Technology**
4420 Lincoln Way
Ames, IA 50014-3447
515-292-2125; *Fax:* 515-292-4512
cast@cast-science.org; www.cast-science.org
Social Media: Facebook, Twitter, LinkedIn, YouTube, Blogspot, Schooltube
David Songstad, President
Kent G. Schescke, Executive Vice President
Dan Gogerty, Managing Communications Editor
Carol Gostele, Managing Scientific Editor
Melissa Sly, Director of Council Operations
Assembles, interprets and communicates science based information regionally, nationally and internationally on food, fiber, agriculture, natural resources, and related societal and environmental issues.
2000+ Members
Founded in: 1972

657 **Crop Insurance and Reinsurance Bureau Inc.**
440 First St NW
Suite 500
Washington, DC 20001
202-544-0067; *Fax:* 202-330-5255
mtorrey@cropinsurance.org;
www.cropinsurance.org
Sheri Bane, Chairwoman
Mike Torrey, Executive Vice President
Tara Smith, Federal Affairs Vice President
Sarah Hubbart, Director of Communications
Stephanie Butler, Director of Operations
The Crop Insurance Research Bureau is a national trade association made up of insurance providers and related organizations that provide a variety of insurance products to farmers. CIRB companies are big and small and offer private hail/fire coverage on growing crops, as well as participate in the federal crop insurance program which offers a greater variety of subsidized insurance products from yield based coverages to revenue products.
Founded in: 1964

658 **Crop Science Society of America**
5585 Guilford Road
Madison, WI 53711-1086
608-273-8086; *Fax:* 608-273-2021
membership@agronomy.org;
www.agronomy.org
Social Media: Facebook, Twitter, LinkedIn
Jean L. Steiner, President
Wes Meixelsperger, Chief Financial Officer
Sara Uttech, Senior Manager - Governance
Wes Meixelsperger, Director of Meetings
Luther Smith, Dir, Prof Dev& Buss. Relations
Seeks to advance research, extension, and teaching of all basic and applied phases of the crop sciences.
4700 Members
Founded in: 1955

659 **CropLife America**
1156 15th St NW
Suite 400
Washington, DC 20005-1752
202-296-1585; *Fax:* 202-463-0474
Info@croplifeamerica.org;
www.croplifeamerica.org
Social Media: Facebook, Twitter, LinkedIn, YouTube, RSS Feeds
Jay Vroom, President and CEO
Beau Greenwood, EVP, Gov Relations & Public Affairs
William Kuckuck, EVP/COO
Rachel G. Lattimore, SVP/General Counsel
Douglas T. Nelson, Senior Advisor
A trade association of the manufacturers, formulators, and distributors of agricultural crop protection, pest control, and biotechnology products. Membership is composed of companies that produce, sell and distribute virtually all the active ingredients used in crop protection chemicals.
86 Members
Founded in: 1933

660 **Ecological Farming Association**
2901 Park Ave.
Suite D-2
Soquel, CA 95073
831-763-2111
info@eco-farm.org

eco-farm.org
Social Media: Facebook, Twitter, Instagram

Ken Dickerson, Executive Director
Isabelle Jenniches, Programs & Operations Manager
Deborah Yashar, Communications Manager
Allie Wilson, Conference Production
Emily Summerlin, Communications Coordinator

EcoFarm is a nonprofit educational organization that promotes sustainable agriculture.
Founded in: 1981

661 Equipment Marketing & Distribution Association (EMDA)

PO Box 1347
Iowa City, IA 52244

319-354-5156; *Fax:* 319-354-5157
pat@emda.net; www.emda.net
Social Media: Facebook, Twitter, LinkedIn

Patricia A Collins, Executive VP

EMDA members are devoted to the marketing of specialized eqipment: agricultural, outdoor power, light industrial, forestry, irrigation, turf and grounds maintenance, lawn and garden and parts/components for those segments of industry.
250 Members
Founded in: 1945

662 Farm Equipment Manufacturers Association

1000 Executive Parkway Dr
Suite 100
St Louis, MO 63141-6369

314-878-2304; *Fax:* 314-732-1480
info@farmequip.org; www.farmequip.org

Mike Kloster, President
Richard Kirby, 1st Vice President
Paul Jeffrey, 2nd Vice President
Vernon Schmidt, Executive Vice President
Kristi Ruggles, Publications Editor

An information gathering and distributing organization for farm equipment manufacturers and suppliers. The Farm Equipment Manufacturers Association shall provide industry leadership to enhance business opportunities and profitability to the Membership by providing a forum for marketing shortline equipment through networking, communications, and technology, and a forum for purchasing materials and services required by the Members.
730+ Members
Founded in: 1950

663 Farm Foundation

1301 W 22nd St
Suite 615
Oak Brook, IL 60523-2197

630-571-9393; *Fax:* 630-571-9580
mary@farmfoundation.org;
www.farmfoundation.org
Social Media: Facebook, Twitter, YouTube, RSS Feeds, Blogger

Mark Scholl, Chairman
Neilson C. Conklin, President
Sheldon R. Jones, VP, Finance and Programs
Mary Thompson, VP, Communications and Operations
Tim Brennan, Director of Development

A publicly supported nonprofit organization working to improve the economic health and social well-being of US agriculture, the food system and rural people by helping private and public sector decision makers identify and understand forces that will shape the future.
Founded in: 1993

664 Fertilizer Institute

425 Third Street, SW
Suite 950
Washington, DC 20024

202-962-0490; *Fax:* 202-962-0577
information@tfi.org; www.tfi.org
Social Media: Facebook, Twitter, LinkedIn, YouTube

Chris Jahn, President
Bradley Cheng, Director, Accounting
Monica Conway, Executive Assis to the President
Ener Cunanan, Manager, Office Services
Kathy Mathers, Vice President, Public Affairs

TFI is the leading voice in the fertilizer industry, representing the public policy, communication and statistical needs of producers, manufacturers, retailers and transporters of fertilizer. Issues of interest to TFI members include security, international trade, energy, transportation, the environment, worker health and safety, farm bill and conservation programs to promote the use of enhanced efficiency fertilizer.
325 Members
Founded in: 1883

665 Foundation for Agronomic Research

107 S State St
Suite 300
Monticello, IL 61856-1968

605-692-6280
pfixen@ipni.net; www.farmresearch.com

Harold Reetz, President
Dr Paul Fixen, Senior Vice President

The Foundation for Agronomic Research (FAR) is a non-profit (501(c)(3) research and education foundation, created in 1980 by the Board of Directors of the Potash & Phosphate Institute (PPI), now the International Plant Nutrition Institute (IPNI), to expand its research efforts beyond that possible with PPI's resources and mandate. The mission of FAR is to improve the economic vigor and sustainability of agriculture in N.A. and around the world, while protecting and enhancing the environment.
Founded in: 1980

666 Fresh Produce Association of the Americas

590 East Frontage Road
PO Box 848
Nogales, AZ 85628

520-287-2707; *Fax:* 520-287-2948
info@freshfrommexico.com;
www.freshfrommexico.com

Matt Mandel, Chairman
Lance Jungmeyer, President
Paula Beemer, Communications Coordinator
Georgina Felix, International Affairs Director
Allison Moore, Dir., Legislative & Reg. Affairs

The Fresh Produce Association of the Americas and its members help to ensure North America's uninterrupted access to fresh, high-quality, healthy and delicious Mexican-grown fruits and vegetables. The FPAA is the leading agent of produce trade at the U.S.-Mexico border and across the country.
125+ Members
Founded in: 1944

667 Fresh Produce and Floral Council

2400 E. Katella Ave.
Ste. 330
Anaheim, CA 92806

714-739-0177; *Fax:* 714-739-0226
info@fpfc.org; www.fpfc.org

Brad Martin, Chairman
Carissa Mace, President
Amy Wun, Manager Member Programs
Angela Steier, Events and Maketing Consultant
Connie Stukenberg, Secretary/Treasurer

Promotes through communication and education, fresh fruit, vegetable and floral products. Acts as a trade organization providing an environment for better communication within the industry.
600+ Members
Founded in: 1965

668 Herb Growing and Marketing Network

PO Box 245
Silver Springs, PA 17575-0245

717-393-3295; *Fax:* 717-393-9261
herbworld@aol.com; www.herbworld.com

Maureen Rogers, Director

The Herb Growing & Marketing Network is the largest trade association for the herb industry. We are an information service. We have a library of over 3000 books, subscribe to over 200 periodicals, monitor blogs of all types and search the Web looking for resources and research on the herb industry that we can pass on to our members.
Cost: $48.00
1000 Members
Founded in: 1990

669 Holstein Association USA

1 Holstein Place
PO Box 808
Brattleboro, VT 05302-0808

802-254-4551
800-952-5200; *Fax:* 802-254-8251
info@holstein.com; www.holsteinusa.com
Social Media: Facebook, Twitter, You Tube

John Meyer, CEO
Lisa Perrin, Marketing

Holstein Association USA maintains records on over 22 million Registered Holsteinsr, collecting and analyzing production, type and genetic data to provide useable information that enables dairy producers to improve their businesses by breeding better cows. The Holstein Association works to help dairy producers recognize the full potential of their herds.
30000 Members
Founded in: 1885

670 International Association of Fairs and Expositions

3043 E Cairo Street
PO Box 985
Springfield, MO 65802

417-862-5771
800-516-0313; *Fax:* 417-862-0156
iafe@fairsandexpos.com;
www.fairsandexpos.com
Social Media: Facebook, Twitter, You Tube

Jim Tucker, President/CEO
Steve Siever, Director of Sales
Max Willis, CFO
Missy McCormack, Comm. Design and Prod. Manager
Rebekah Lee, Director of Comm. and Editor

The International Association of Fairs and Expositions (IAFE) is a voluntary, non-profit corporation whose members provide services and products that promote the overall development and improvement of fairs, shows, expositions, and allied fields. Mission is to lead in representing and facilitating the evolving interests of agricultural fairs, exhibitions and show associations.
1300 Members
Founded in: 1885

671 **International Association of Operative Millers**
12351 w. 96th Terrace
Suite 100
Lenexa, KS 66215

913-338-3377; *Fax:* 913-338-3553
info@iaom.info; www.iaom.info
Social Media: Facebook, Twitter, LinkedIn

Roy Loepp, President
Brad Allen, Vice President
Melinda Farris, Executive Vice President
Shannon Henson, Director of Meetings and Exhibits
Annette Peterson, Administrative Assistant

The International Association of Operative Millers (IAOM) is comprised of grain millers and allied trades representatives devoted to the advancement of education and training opportunities in the grain milling industries. Among its members, IAOM promotes a spirit of fellowship and cooperation, enhances their proficiency, and advances their interests in industry activities.
1500 Members
Founded in: 1896

672 **International Fruit Tree Association**
16020 Swingley Ridge Rd.
Suite 300
Chesterfield, MO 63017

636-449-5083; *Fax:* 636-449-5051
dungey@ifruittree.org; www.ifruittree.org
Social Media: Facebook, Twitter

Tim Welsh, President
Rod Farrow, Vice President
Chris Hedges, Treasurer

The association promotes research on, and understanding of, Intensive Orchard Systems.
Founded in: 1958

673 **International Maple Syrup Institute**
5072 Rock St.
RR#4
Spencerville, ON KOE 1XO

860-974-1235; *Fax:* 802-868-5445
agrofor@ripnet.com;
www.internationalmaplesyrupinstitute.com

Dave Chapeskie, Executive Director
Alfred Bolduc, Board Member
Roger Palmer, Board Member
Tim Perkins, Advisor
Steve Childs, Advisor

The International Maple Syrup Institute (IMSI) was founded to promote and protect pure maple syrup and other pure maple products. The organization provides an important international framework for communication, information exchange and cooperation on a variety of issues related to the production, sale and marketing of pure maple syrup. In addition, the Institute has been a strong monitor for adulteration around the world, protecting the integrity of maple products.
15M Members
Founded in: 1975

674 **International Weed Science Society**
University of Arkansas
1366 W. Altheimer Drive
Fayetteville, AR 72704

479-575-3984; *Fax:* 479-575-3975
secretary@iwss.info; www.iwss.info

Dr Albert Fischer, President
Dr Nilda Burgos, Vice President
Dr Frank Dayan, Treasurer
Dr Baruch Rubin, Past President
Dr Bernal Valverde, Ex-Officio

The International Weed Science Society (IWSS) was formed in 1975, by individuals from Europe, North America, South America, and the Asian-Pacific area, to deal with global weed science issues. The IWSS is a worldwide scientific organization, open to all who are interested in weeds and their control. The formation of IWSS was promoted actively by the six existing regional weed science societies. The purpose of IWSS is to supplement and complement their vital role.
Founded in: 1975

675 **Irrigation Association**
8280 Willow Oaks Corporate Drive
Suite 400
Fairfax, VA 22031

703-536-7080; *Fax:* 703-536-7019
info@irrigation.org; www.irrigation.org

Aric J. Olson, President
Gregory R. Hunter, Vice President
Deborah M. Hamlin, CAE, FASAE, Chief Executive Officer
John R. Farner, Jr, Government & PA Director
Rebecca J. Bayless, Finance Director

The Irrigation Association is the leading membership organization for irrigation equipment and system manufacturers, dealers distributors, designers, consultants, contractors and end users.
1600 Members
Founded in: 1949

676 **Livestock Marketing Association**
10510 NW Ambassador Drive
Kansas City, MO 64153-1278

816-891-0502
800-821-2048; *Fax:* 816-891-0552
lmainfo@lmaweb.com; www.lmaweb.com
Social Media: Facebook, Twitter, YouTube, Instagram

Tim Starks, Chairman of the Board
Dan Harris, President
Neal Brosnan, Facilities Manager
Mark Mackey, CEO
Vincent Nowak, CFO

We are committed to the support and protection of the local livestock auction markets. Auctions are a vital part of the livestock industry, serving producers and assuring a fair, competitive price through the auction method of selling.
800 Members
Founded in: 1947

677 **Maryland and Virginia Milk Producers Cooperative**
1985 Isaac Newton Square West
Reston, VA 20190-5094

703-742-6800; *Fax:* 703-742-7459;
www.mdvamilk.com

Richard Mosemann, Second VP
Dwayne Meyers, NC President

Known for being a leader in the dairy industry, the Eastern Milk Producers Cooperative has a reputation for integrity, service and high quality products.
Founded in: 1920

678 **Midwest Equipment Dealers Association**
5330 Wall St
Suite 100
Madison, WI 53718-7929

608-240-4700; *Fax:* 608-240-2069
gmanke@medaassn.com; www.medaassn.com

Gary W. Manke, Executive Vice President, CEO
Antoniewicz Gaugert, Wisconsin & Illinois Legal Counsel
Julie Roisum, Executive Assistant
Jerry Deblaey, Vice President

Our mission is to promote the farm, industrial, outdoor power equipment, dairy and farmstead mechanization industry and to provide services that will assist Association members in becoming more profitable and better equipped to operate in today's business environment.
Founded in: 1991

679 **NCBA CLUSA**
1401 New York Ave NW
Suite 1100
Washington, DC 20005-2160

202-638-6222; *Fax:* 202-638-1374
ncba@ncba.coop; www.ncba.coop
Social Media: Facebook, Twitter, YouTube, Google+

Andrew Jacob, Chair
Michael Beall, President & Chief Executive Officer
Patricia Brownell Sterner, Chief Operating Officer, NCBA
Amy Coughenour Betancourt, Chief Operating Officer
Valeria Roach, Chief Financial Officer

Leading US organization strengthening the cooperative form of business to empower people and improve quality of life worldwide. To make cooperatives a strong, distinct and unified sector, recognized by the American public. Our member co-ops operate in the areas including, agricultural supply and marketing, children, energy, food distribution, healthcare and housing.
1800 Members
Founded in: 1916

680 **National 4-H Council**
7100 Connecticut Ave
Chevy Chase, MD 20815-4934

301-961-2800; *Fax:* 301-961-2894
info@fourhcouncil.edu; www.4-h.org
Social Media: Facebook, Twitter, LinkedIn, Google+, Pinterest, YouTube

Donald Floyd, President/CEO
Jennifer Sirangelo, EVP/COO
Andy Ferrin, Senior Vice President
Paul Koehler, Senior Vice President
Jill Bramble, Senior Vice President

Works to advance the 4-H youth development movement, building a world in which youth and adults learn, grow, and work together as catalysts for positive change. National 4-H Council partners with the Cooperative Extension System and other organizations to provide technical support and training, develop curricula, create model programs and promote positive youth development to fulfill its mission. National 4-H Council also manages the National 4-H Conference.
7M Members
Founded in: 1902

681 **National Agri-Marketing Association**
11020 King St
Suite 205
Overland Park, KS 66210-1201

913-491-6500; *Fax:* 913-491-6502
agrimktg@nama.org; www.nama.org
Social Media: Facebook, Twitter, LinkedIn, Flicker, You Tube

Marvin Kokes, President
Matt Coniglio, First VP/ President Elect
Amy Bradford, Secretary/Treasurer
Amy Bugg, Vice President
Amber Harrison, Vice President

Marketing and communication suppliers, including trade publications, radio and television broadcast sales organizations, premium/incentive manufacturers, printers, marketing research firms, photographers and related professionals.
3500 Members
Founded in: 1957

682 **National Agricultural Aviation Association**
1440 Duke Street
Alexandria, VA 22314

202-546-5722; *Fax:* 202-546-5726
information@agaviation.org;
www.agaviation.org
Social Media: Facebook

Rick Boardman, President
Harley Curless, Vice President
Andrew D. Moore, Executive Director
Jay Calleja, Manager of Communications
Lindsay Barber, Manager of Meetings, Marketing

NAAA supports the interests of small business owners and pilots licensed as professional commercial aerial applicators who use aircraft to enhance food, fiber and bio-fuel production, protect forestry and control health-threatening pests. NAAA provides networking, educational, government relations, public relations, recruiting and informational services to its members.
1900 Members
Founded in: 1966

683 **National Alliance of Independent Crop Consultants**
349 E Nolley Dr
Collierville, TN 38017-3538

901-861-0511; *Fax:* 901-861-0512
AllisonJones@NAICC.org; www.naicc.org

Gary Coukell, P.Ag., President
Debra Keenan, President Elect
Marla Siruta, Secretary
Nathan Goldschmidt, Treasurer
James E. Todd, Past President

The national society of agricultural professionals who provide research and advisory services. Memebers comprise 40 states and several foreign countries, and have expertise in the production of most crops grown around the world.
500+ Members
Founded in: 1978

684 **National Association of Agricultural Educators (NAAE)**
300 Garrigus Building
University of Kentucky
Lexington, KY 40546-0215

859-257-2224
800-509-0204; *Fax:* 859-323-3919
jay_jackman@ffa.org; www.naae.org
Social Media: Facebook, Twitter, YouTube, Pinterest, Flickr

Charlie Sappington, President
Wm. Jay Jackman, Executive Director
Alissa Smith, Associate Executive Director
Katie Wood, Meeting Planner/Program Assistant
Julie Fritsch, Comm. & Marketing Director

Professionals providing agricultural education for the global community through visionary leadership, advocacy and service. NAAE seeks to advance agricultural education and promote the professional interests and growth of agriculture teachers as well as recruit and prepare students who have a desire to teach agriculture.
7800+ Members
Founded in: 1948

685 **National Association of Agricultural Fairs**
Tennessee Department of Agriculture
440 Hogan Road
PO Box 40627
Nashville, TN 37220

615-837-5160
800-342-8206; *Fax:* 615-837-5194
pick.tn@tn.gov; www.picktnproducts.org
Social Media: Facebook, Twitter, Pinterest

Ed Harlan, Agribusiness Coordinator
Dan Strasser, Director of Market Development
Nelson Owen, Livestock Grading/Market News

US and Canadian representatives of state/provincial agencies that are responsible for the support of educational and agricultural fairs.
35 Members
Founded in: 1966

686 **National Association of Animal Breeders**
PO Box 1033
Columbia, MO 65205-1033

573-445-4406; *Fax:* 573-446-2279
naab-css@naab-css.org; www.naab-css.org

Dr Charles Brown II, Chairman
Dr Gordon Doak, Secretary - Treasurer - President
Dr Roger Weigle, Vice Chairman
Jere R Mitchell, Service Director
Dr Roger Weigle, Vice Chairman

The purpose of the National Association of Animal Breeders (NAAB) as defined by its By-Laws is to unite those individuals and organizations engaged in the artificial insemination of cattle and other livestock into an affiliated federation operating under self-imposed standards of performance and to conduct and promote the mutual interest and ideals of its members.
20 Members
Founded in: 1975

687 **National Association of County Agricultural Agents**
6584 W Duroc Road
Maroa, IL 61756

217-794-3700; *Fax:* 217-794-5901
exec-dir@nacaa.com; www.nacaa.com
Social Media: Facebook, Twitter

Cynthia Gregg, President
Mark Nelson, President-Elect
Alan Galloway, Vice President
Matt Herring, Secretary
Alan Galloway, Treasurer

The NACAA strives to: Advance the professional status of Extension agents and specialists with agriculture-related Extension appointments. Encourage, promote, and provide professional improvement for all members. Provide for the exchange of ideas, methods, and techniques. Represent professional interests of members in matters of public policy and affairs. Promote public confidence, esteem, and respect for Cooperative Extension. Recognize excellence in Cooperative Extension nationwide.
3850 Members
Founded in: 1917
Mailing list available for rent: 3500 names at $500 per M

688 **National Association of Extension 4-H Agents**
University of Georgia
3801 Lake Boone Trail
Suite 190
Raleigh, NC 27607

919-232-0112; *Fax:* 919-779-5642
execdir@nae4ha.com; www.nae4ha.org
Social Media: Facebook, Twitter

Kimberly Gressley, President
Shawn Tiede, VP, Finance & Operations
Kori Myers, Vice President for Professional Dev
Casey Mull, VP, Marketing & Outreach
Linda Tripp, VP, Programs

Designed to meet the needs of youth development professionals by maximizing the use of technology, provide progressive levels of professional development, elevate the quality of youth development work through scholarship, research and practice, advocate for the 4-H youth development profession.
3600 Members
Founded in: 1946

689 **National Association of State Departments of Agriculture**
4350 North Fairfax Drive
#910
Arlington, VA 22203

202-296-9680; *Fax:* 703-880-0509
nasda@nasda.org; www.nasda.org
Social Media: Facebook, Twitter

Greg Ibach, President
Michael Strain, Vice President
Steven Reviczky, Second Vice President
DeWitt Ashby, Director, Trade Shows & Grants
Carol Black, Project Manager, Pesticide Workers

Represents the state departments of agriculture in the development, implementation and communication of sound public policy and programs which support and promote the American agricultural industry, while protecting consumers and the environment.
Founded in: 1916

690 **National Association of Wheat Growers**
415 2nd Street NE
Suite 300
Washington, DC 20002-4993

202-547-7800; *Fax:* 202-546-2638
wheatworld@wheatworld.org;
www.wheatworld.org
Social Media: Facebook, Twitter, RSS Feed, Youtube

Brett Blankenship, President
Gordon Stoner, Vice President
David Schemm, Treasurer
Jim Palmer, Chief Executive Officer
Hugh Whaley, Director of Corporate Relations

Nonprofit partnership of US wheat growers, by combining their strengths, voices and ideas are working to ensure a better future for themselves, their industry and the general public. NAWG's mission statement is: NAWG unites U.S. wheat growers to create beneficial policies for wheat growers; effective relationships with industry; and profitable opportunities through research and technology.
Founded in: 1950

691 **National Bison Association**
8690 Wolff Court
Suite 200
Westminster, CO 80031

303-292-2833; *Fax:* 303-845-9081
david@bisoncentral.com;
www.bisoncentral.com
Social Media: Facebook

Bruce Anderson, President
Roy Liedtke, Vice President
Dave Carter, Executive Director
Jim Matheson, Assistant Director
Marilyn Wentz, Bison World Editor

Formed to promote the production, marketing and preservation of bison. The mission of the National Bison Association is to bring together stakeholders to celebrate the heritage of American bison/buffalo, to educate, and to create a sustainable future for our industry.
1100+ Members
Founded in: 1995

692 **National Christmas Tree Association**
16020 Swingley Ridge Rd
Suite 300
Chesterfield, MO 63017-6030
636-449-5070; *Fax:* 636-449-5051
info@realchristmastrees.org;
www.realchristmastrees.org

Social Media: Facebook, Twitter, YouTube, Blogger

Blake Rafeld, President
Paul Schroeder, Vice President
Bob Schaefer, Vice President
Tom Dull, President-Elect
Rick Dungey, Executive Director

The National Christmas Tree Association (NCTA) is the national trade association representing the Christmas tree industry. NCTA represents more than 700 active member farms, 29 state and regional associations, and more than 4,000 affiliated businesses that grow and sell Christmas trees or provide related supplies and services.
700 Members
Founded in: 1955
Mailing list available for rent: 5100 names

693 **National Cotton Council of America**
National Cotton Council of America
PO Box 2995
7193 Goodlett Farms Pkwy
Cordova, TN 38088-2995

901-274-9030; *Fax:* 901-725-0510;
www.cotton.org

Sledge Taylor, Chairman
Gary Adams, President & Chief Executive Officer
Dr. Jody Campiche, VP, Economy and Policy Analysis
Dr Bill M. Norman, VP, Technical Services
Craig Brown, VP Producer Affairs

The National Cotton Council is a unifying force of the U.S. cotton industry, bringing together representatives from the seven industry segments in the 17 cotton-producing states of the Cotton Belt to work out common problems and develop programs of mutual benefit.
35 Members

694 **National Cottonseed Products Association**
866 Willow Tree Circle
Cordova, TN 38018-6376

901-682-0800; *Fax:* 901-682-2856
info@cottonseed.com; www.cottonseed.com

Ben Morgan, BS, MBA, EVP/Secretary
Bobby Crum, Vice President
Sandi Stine, Treasurer

National association of cottonseed products. NCPA is an organization of firms and individuals engaged in the processing of cottonseed and the marketing of cottonseed products, as well as cottonseed. These include oil mills, refiners, product dealers and product brokers.
200 Members
Founded in: 1929

695 **National Council of Agricultural Employers**
525 9th Street, NW
Suite 800
Washington, DC 20004

202-629-9320; *Fax:* 202-728-0303
info@ncaeonline.org; www.ncaeonline.org
Social Media: Facebook

Luawanna Hallstrom, President
Fred Leitz, Eastern Vice President
Ray Prescott, Western Vice President
Joe Young, Treasurer
Bryan Little, Secretary

NCAE represents Agricultural Employer interests before Congress and Regulatory/Administrative bodies such as the Departments of Labor, Homeland Security, Agriculture, the Occupational Safety and Health Administration, and the Environmental Protection Agency.
250 Members
Founded in: 1964

696 **National Crop Insurance Services**
8900 Indian Creek Pkwy
Suite 600
Overland Park, KS 66210-1567

913-685-2767
800-951-6247; *Fax:* 913-685-3080
webmaster@ag-risk.org; www.ag-risk.org
Social Media: Facebook, Twitter

Dr. Thomas P. Zacharias, President and CEO
Linda Kovelan, Director Executive Services
Laurie Langstraat, V.P. Public Relations
Sherri Scharff, V.P. Membership Services
Jim Crist, CFO/COO

NCIS is an association of insurance companies writing insurance for damage by hail, fire and other weather perils to growing crops.
60+ Members
Founded in: 1915

697 **National Dairy Herd Information Association**
PO Box 930399
Verona, WI 53593-0399

608-848-6455; *Fax:* 608-260-7772
jmattison@requestltd.com; www.dhia.org

Kent Buttars, President
Susan Lee, Vice President
Jay Mattison, CEO/Administrator
Leslie Thoman, Accounting/Bookkeeping
Steven Sievert, Quality Certification Services

The objective is to promote accuracy, credibility and uniformity of DHI records. To represent the DHI system on issues involving other National and International organizations
65M Members

698 **National Farmers Organization**
528 Billy Sunday Road
Suite 100, PO Box 2508
Ames, IA 50010-2508

515-292-2000
800-247-2110; *Fax:* 866-629-3976
nfo@nfo.org; www.nfo.org
Social Media: Facebook, Twitter, YouTube

Paul Olson, President, Chairman of the Board
Paul Riniker, Vice President
Perry Gainer, Communications Director

National Farmers defines itself by its sophisticated commodity marketing and ag risk management programs and services. Through National Farmers MaximumMarketing, producers market their commodities in pooled groups, and their bank accounts benefit.
30M Members
Founded in: 1955

699 **National Farmers Union**
20 F Street NW
Suite 300
Washington, DC 20001
202-554-1600
800-347-1961; *Fax:* 202-554-1654
info@nfudc.org; www.nfu.org
Social Media: Facebook, Twitter, YouTube, Instagram

Roger Johnson, President
Donn Teske, Vice President
Jeff Knudson, SVP, Operations
Chandler Goule, Senior Vice President of Programs
Ethan Whitmore, Director of Information Services

Farmers Union helped shape national policy, organized cooperative businesses that thrive today, delivered educational programs designed to build rural leaders, and provided farmers and ranchers with opportunities to be at the table.
25000 Members
Founded in: 1902

700 **National Fisheries Institute**
7918 Jones Branch Dr
Suite 700
Mc Lean, VA 22102-3319

703-752-8880; *Fax:* 703-752-7583
bsb@nfi.org; www.aboutseafood.com
Social Media: Facebook, Twitter, LinkedIn, Pinterest, google+

John Connely, President
Gavin Gibbons, Director, Media Relations

The National Fisheries Institute is a non-profit organization dedicated to education about seafood safety, sustainability, and nutrition. From vessels at sea to your favorite seafood restaurant, our diverse member companies bring delicious fish and shellfish to American families. NFI promotes the US Dietary Guidelines that suggest Americans include fish and shellfish in their diets twice per week for longer, healthier lives.
241 Members
Founded in: 1945

701 **National Future Farmers of America Organization**
6060 FFA Drive
P.O. Box 68960
Indianapolis, IN 46268-0960

317-802-6060
800-772-0939; *Fax:* 317-802-6051
shop@ffa.org; www.ffa.org
Social Media: Facebook, Twitter, LinkedIn, Instagram, YouTube

Steve A. Brown, Board Chair
Andy Paul, President
W. Dwight Armstrong, Ph.D., Chief Executive Officer
Joshua Bledsoe, Chief Operating Officer
David Schapker, Chief Financial Officer

Headquarters of the National FFA Organization, the organization's mission is to prepare students for successful careers and a lifetime of informed choices in the global agriculture, food, fiber and natural resources systems.
507M Members
Founded in: 1928

702 **National Grain and Feed Association**
1250 I St NW
Suite 1003
Washington, DC 20005-3939

202-289-0873; *Fax:* 202-289-5388
ngfa@ngfa.org; www.ngfa.org
Social Media: Facebook, Twitter, LinkedIn, Flickr

Randall C Gordon, President
Todd E. Kemp, Vice President of Marketing
Charles M. Delacruz, VP/General Counsel/Secretary
David A. Fairfield, Vice President of Feed Services
Sarah Gonzalez, Dir. Comm & Digital Media

NGFA is the national trade association of grain elevators, feed and feed ingredient manufacturers, grain and oilseed processors, exporters, livestock and poultry integrators, and firms providing products and services to the industry.
Founded in: 1896

703 **National Grange**
1616 H St NW
Suite 10
Washington, DC 20006-4999
202-628-3507
888-447-2643; *Fax:* 202-347-1091
eluttrell@nationalgrange.org;
www.nationalgrange.org
Social Media: Facebook, Twitter, YouTube, RSS Feeds

Ed Luttrell, President/Master
Stephanie Tiller, Executive Assistant/Event Planner

Burton Eller, Legislative Director
Charlene Shupp Espenshade, Youth and Young Adult Director
Sandor Szima, Building Engineer

Promotes general welfare and agriculture through local organizations. Presides over the advancement and promotion of the farming and agriculture industry.
300K Members
Founded in: 1867

704 **National Hay Association**
Ellington Agricultural Center
432 Hogan Rd.
Nashville, TN 37220

615-837-5560
800-707-0014; *Fax:* 615-523-1385
NHAExecOffice@gmail.com;
www.nationalhay.org
Social Media: Facebook

Bob Eckenberg, President
Terry Button, First Vice President
Amy Freeburg, Second Vice President
Paul Dugger, Executive Director
Carl Blackmer, Director

The National Hay Association is made up of people that are involved in the production, sale and transportation of forage products across the United States and the world. As an organization we work for the good of the hay industry through knowledge among members, to following government legislation. We operate as an independent organization with no commitments or ties to any government groups.
750 Members
Founded in: 1895

705 **National Institute for Animal Agriculture**
13570 Meadowgrass Dr
Suite 201
Colorado Springs, CO 80921-3058

719-538-8843; *Fax:* 719-538-8847
niaa@animalagriculture.org;
www.animalagriculture.org
Social Media: Facebook, Twitter, LinkedIn, YouTube

Glenn K. Fischer, Chairman of the Board
Katie Ambrose, Chief Operating Officer
R. Scott Stuart, Chief Executive Officer
Mona Wolverton, Event Coordinator
Polly Welden, Marketing

NIAA is an organization that satisfies your needs, concerns and interests about the animal agriculture industry. NIAA's purpose is quite simple - to provide a source for individuals, organizations, and the entire animal agriculture industry to obtain information, education and solutions for challenges facing animal agriculture.
250 Members

706 **National Oilseed Processors Association**
1300 L St NW
Suite 1020
Washington, DC 20005-4168

202-842-0463; *Fax:* 202-842-9126
thammer@nopa.org; www.nopa.org

Thomas A. Hammer, President
David J. Hovermale, EVP, Gov. Relations
David C. Ailor, EVP, Regulatory Affairs
Jeanne L. Seibert, Office Administrator
Mark Sandeen, Secretary-Treasurer

NOPA now represents oilseed crushers of soybeans, canola, flaxseed, safflower seed and sunflower seed. NOPA represents twelve (12) regular member firms engaged in the actual processing of oilseeds, and eight (8) associate member firms who are consumers of vegetable oil or oilseed meal, including some refiners.
Founded in: 1989

707 **National Onion Association**
822 7th St
Suite 510
Greeley, CO 80631-3941

970-353-5895; *Fax:* 970-353-5897
kreddin@onions-usa.org; www.onions-usa.org
Social Media: Twitter, LinkedIn, Pinterest, RSS

Shawn Hartley, President
John Rietveld, Vice President
Doug Stanley, 2nd Vice President
Wayne Mininger, Executive VP
Kim Reddin, Director of Public & Industry Rel

The National Onion Association (NOA) is the official organization representing growers, shippers, brokers, and commercial representatives of the U.S. onion industry.
500 Members
Founded in: 1913
Mailing list available for rent: 600 names

708 **National Pork Producers Council**
122 C Street NW
Suite 875
Washington, DC 20001

202-347-3600
800-937-7675; *Fax:* 202-347-5265
news@nppc.org; www.nppc.org
Social Media: Facebook, Twitter, LinkedIn, Pinterest, Flickr, Swinecast

Ron Prestage, DVM, President
Ken Maschhoff, Vice President
Neil Dierks, Chief Executive Officer
Dallas Hockman, VP, Industry Relations
Pete Houska, Regional Dir. Producer Services

The National Pork Producers Council conducts public-policy outreach on behalf of its affiliated state associations, enhancing opportunities for the success of U.S. pork producers and other industry stakeholders by establishing the U.S. pork industry as a consistent and responsible supplier of high-quality pork to the domestic and world markets.
44 Members

709 **National Potato Council**
1300 L St NW
Suite 910
Washington, DC 20005-4107

202-682-9456; *Fax:* 202-682-0333
spudinfo@nationalpotatocouncil.org;
www.nationalpotatocouncil.org
Social Media: Facebook, Twitter, YouTube

Dan Lake, President
Jim Tiede, First Vice President
Larry Alsum, VP, Finance & Office Procedures
John Keeling, EVP/CEO
Hollee Alexander, Senior Director, Programs & Events

The National Potato Council is the advocate for the economic well-being of U.S. potato growers on federal legislative, regulatory, environmental, and trade issues.
45000 Members
Founded in: 1948

710 **National Potato Promotion Board**
4949 S. Syracuse St.
#400
Denver, CO 80237

303-369-7783; *Fax:* 303-369-7718
info@uspotatoes.com; www.uspotatoes.com
Social Media: Facebook, Twitter, YouTube, Pinterest, Instagram

Carl Hoverson, Chairman
Blair Richardson, President & CEO
Diana LeDoux, VP, Finance & IT
David Fraser, VP, Industry Comm. & Policy
John Toaspern, Chief Marketing Officer

Also known as the US Potato Board. Organized to operate a national marketing program to position potatoes as low calorie, nutritious vegetables and to facilitate market expansion into domestic and export sales.
2500+ Members
Founded in: 1971

711 **National Sunflower Association**
2401 46th Avenue SE
Suite 206
Mandan, ND 58554-4829

701-328-5100
888-718-7033; *Fax:* 701-328-5101
larryk@sunflowernsa.com;
www.sunflowernsa.com
Social Media: Facebook, YouTube

John Sandbakken, Executive Director
Tina Mittelsteadt, Business & Office Manager
Lerrene Kroh, Meeting Planner & Advertising Sales

Trade association for the sunflower industry.
20000 Members
Founded in: 1981
Printed in 4 colors on glossy stock

712 **National Turkey Federation**
1225 New York Avenue NW
Suite 400
Washington, DC 20005

202-898-0100; *Fax:* 202-898-0203
info@turkeyfed.org; www.eatturkey.com
Social Media: Facebook, Twitter, YouTube, Pinterest

Jennifer Dansereau, Vice President Of Member Services
Joel Brandenberger, President

(NTF) is the national Advocate for all segments of the $8 billion turkey industry, providing services and conducting activities that increase demand for its members' products. The federation also protects and enhances its members' ability to effectively and profitably provide wholesome, high quality, nutritious turkey products.
264 Members
Founded in: 1947

713 **National Young Farmer Educational Association**
PO Box 20326
Montgomery, AL 36120
334-546-9951
888-332-2668; *Fax:* 334-213-0421
nyfea-main@nyfea.org; www.nyfea.org
Social Media: Facebook, Twitter, Google+

Allen Tyler, President
Tim Kelley, President-Elect
Denise Sanner, Secretary

To promote the personal and professional growth of all people involved in agriculture.

714 **Nebraska Alfalfa Dehydrators Association**
8810 Craig Dr
Overland Park, KS 66212-2916

913-341-0562
800-678-9192; *Fax:* 913-341-0564
wcobbkc@sbcglobal.net; www.nebada.org

Carlton Bert, President
David Rhea, Vice President
Chris Healey, Director

Information for the processors and suppliers in the alfalfa industry.
Founded in: 1941

715 **North American Farm Show Council**
590 Woody Hayes Drive
Columbus, OH 43210
614-292-4278; *Fax:* 614-292-9448
gamble.19@osu.edu;
www.farmshowcouncil.org
Doug Wagner, President
Dennis Alford, First Vice President
Chip Blalock, Second Vice President
Chuck Gamble, Secretary-Treasurer
Members are agriculture trade show sponsors and suppliers of services to these shows. Provides members with education, communication and evaluation. Provides the best possible marketing showcase for exhibitors and related products to the farmer/rancher/producer customer.
37 Members
Founded in: 1972

716 **North American Millers' Association**
600 Maryland Ave SW
Suite 825 W
Washington, DC 20024
202-484-2200; *Fax:* 202-488-7416
generalinfo@namamillers.org;
www.namamillers.org
Social Media: Facebook, Twitter, LinkedIn, Flickr
Dan Dye, Chairman
James A McCarthy, President and CEO
Christopher Clark, CAE, VP, Communications & Administration
Paul B. Green, Export Consultant
Benjamin Boroughs, Dir., Reg. & Technical Affairs
Trade association representing the wheat, corn, oat and rye milling industry. NAMA members operate one hundred and seventy mills in thrirty-eight states and Canada. Their aggregate production of more than one hundred and sixty million pounds per day is approximately ninety-five percent of the industry capacity in the U.S.
45 Members
Founded in: 1902

717 **Northeastern Weed Science Society**
P.O. Box 25
Woodstown, NJ 08098
315-209-7580
northeasternweedscience@hotmail.com;
www.newss.org
Rakesh Chandran, President
Randy Prostak, Vice President
Erin Hitchner, Treasurer
Art Gover, Editor
Todd Mervosh, Public Relations
Serves the Northeastern US by bringing together those who are concerned with the knowledge of weeds and their control, cooperates with other scientific societies to promote research, education and outreach activities and publishes scientific and practical information of value concerning weed sciences and other fields.
Founded in: 1946

718 **Oregon Tilth**
2525 SE 3rd Street
Corvallis, OR 97333
503-378-0690
877-378-0690; *Fax:* 541-753-4924
organic@tilth.org; www.tilth.org
Social Media: Facebook, Twitter, Instagram
Lynn Youngbar, President
Chris Schreiner, Executive Director
Susan Schechter, Secretary
Ryan Wist, Treasurer
Connie Karr, Certification Director
Oregon Tilth is a nonprofit research and education membership organization dedicated to biologicaly sound and socially equitable agriculture. Oregon Tilth offers educational events throughout the state of Oregon, and provides organic certification services to organic growers, processors and handlers internationally.
Founded in: 1974

719 **Organic Crop Improvement Association**
1340 North Cotner Boulevard
Lincoln, NE 68505-1838
402-477-2323; *Fax:* 402-477-4325
info@ocia.org; www.ocia.org
Social Media: Facebook, Twitter
Jack Geiger, President
Susan Linkletter, First Vice-President
Joel Koskan, Second Vice-President
Demetria Stephens, Secretary
Jeff Kienast, Treasurer
OCIA International is a farmer owned international program of certification, which adheres to strict organic standards. It currently certifies thousands of farmers and processors in North, Central and South America and Asia. OCIA International is IFOAM accredited and adheres to the USDA ISO Guide 65, Japan Agriculture Standards and the Quebec Accreditation Council. OCIA has also been accredited from the USDA National Organic Program and Costa Rica Ministry of Agriculture.
3500 Members
Founded in: 1985
Mailing list available for rent: 3500 names at $50 per M

720 **Organic Seed Alliance**
PO Box 772
Port Townsend, WA 98368
360-385-7192; *Fax:* 360-385-7455
info@seedalliance.org; www.seedalliance.org
Social Media: Facebook, Twitter
Sebastian Aguilar, President
Micaela Colley, Executive Director
Atina Diffley, Vice President
Sean Schmidt, Secretary
Zea Sonnabend, Treasurer
Supports the ethical development and stewardship of the genetic resources of agricultural seed.
Founded in: 2003

721 **Produce Marketing Association**
Po Box 6036
Newark, DE 19714-6036
302-738-7100; *Fax:* 302-731-2409
solutionctr@pma.com; www.pma.com
Social Media: Facebook, Twitter, YouTube, Flickr, Pinterest
Bryan Silbermann, CEO
Tony Parassio, Chief Operating Officer
Yvonne Bull, Chief Financial Officer
Robert J Whitaker, Chief Science/Technology Officer
Margi Prueitt, Senior Vice President
The Produce Marketing Association is a not-for-profit trade association serving members who market fresh fruits, vegetables, and floral products worldwide. Its members are involved in the production, distribution, retail, and foodservice sectors of the industry.
2500 Members
Founded in: 1949

722 **Professional Farmers of America**
1818 Market Street 31st Floor
Philadelphia, PA 19103
319-277-1278
800-772-0023
editors@profarmer.com;
www.agweb.com/profarmer
Social Media: Facebook, Twitter, LinkedIn
Chip Flory, Editor/Publisher
Julianne Johnston, Sr. Markets Editor
Meghan Pederson, Pro Farmer Reporter
Brian Grete, Senior Market Analyst
Jim Wiesemeyer, Washington Consultant
Provides farmers with marketing strategies and market-trend data, as well as seminars and home study courses.
25M Members
Founded in: 1973

723 **Santa Gertrudis Breeders International**
PO Box 1257
Kingsville, TX 78364-1257
361-592-9357; *Fax:* 361-592-8572
jford@santagertrudis.com
santagertrudis.com/
Social Media: Facebook
John E Ford, Executive Director
Diana L. Ruiz, Association Services
America's First Beef Breed developed in 1918 at the famous King Ranch in Texas. Recognized in 1940 by the USDA. Famous for raid and efficient growth, solid red color, hardiness and good disposition. They are adaptable to many environments and are present throughout the US and in other countries.

724 **Society of American Foresters**
5400 Grosvenor Ln
Bethesda, MD 20814-2198
301-897-8720
866-897-8720; *Fax:* 301-897-3690
membership@safnet.org; www.safnet.org
Social Media: Facebook, Twitter, LinkedIn
Michael T Goergen Jr, Executive VP/CFO
Louise Murgia, Interim Executive Vice-President
Jorge Esguerra, Chief Financial Officer
Christopher Whited, Senior Director, Marketing
Elaine Cook, Office Manager, Marketing & Members
Provides access to information and networking opportunities to prepare members for the challenges and the changes that face natural resource professionals.
Founded in: 1900

725 **Society of Commercial Seed Technologists**
653 Constitution Avenue NE
Washington, DC 20002
202-870-2412; *Fax:* 607-273-1638
scst@seedtechnology.net;
www.seedtechnology.net
Social Media: Facebook, Twitter
Barbara Cleave, President
David Stimpson, Vice President
Steve Beals, Director-at-Large
DaNell Jamieson RST, RGT, Director-at-Large
Heidi Jo Larson, RST, Director-at-Large
Professionals involved in the testing and analysis of seeds, including research, production and handling based on botanical and agricultural sciences.
250 Members
Founded in: 1922

726 **Soil and Plant Analysis Council**
347 North Shores Circle
Windsor, CO 80550
970-686-5702; *Fax:* 402-476-0302;
www.spcouncil.com
Rao Mylavarapu, President
Robert Mikkelsen, Vice President International Plant
Robert Miller, Secretary/Treasurer
Rigas Karamanos, Past President

Promotes uniform soil test and plant analysis methods, use, interpretation and terminology.
250 Members
Founded in: 1969

727 **Southern Cotton Ginners Association**
874 Cotton Gin Pl
Memphis, TN 38106-2588

901-947-3104; *Fax:* 901-947-3103;
www.southerncottonginners.org
Social Media: Facebook

Riley James, Chairman of Board
Holt Shoaf, President
Henry G. Tri Watkins, Vice President
Timothy L. Price, Executive Vice President
Andrea Steadman, Marketing Communications Specialist

Operates in a five state area as an information center covering safety and governmental regulations. Serves its members by providing safety, training and regulatory representation. Sponsors certification programs and hosts the industry's leading trade show, The Mid-South Farm & Gin Show.
700 Members
Founded in: 1967

728 **Texas Agribusiness Market Research Center**
600 John Kimbrough Blvd.
Suite 371 - 2124 TAMU
College Station, TX 77843

979-845-5911; *Fax:* 979-845-6378
afcerc.tamu.edu
Social Media: Facebook, LinkedIn

Loren Schroeder, Program Manager
Senarath Dharmasena, Assistant Professor
Robin Hanselman, Graphic Design/Data Specialist

Provide a single point to all agricultural resources on the internet. Objective is to promote agribusiness and to enhance agricultural product marketing and research.

729 **The William H. Miner Agricultural Research Institute**
1034 Miner Farm Road
PO Box 90
Chazy, NY 12921

518-846-7121; *Fax:* 518-846-8445;
www.whminer.com
Social Media: Facebook, Google+

Dr Joseph C Burke, Chairman
Richard J. Grant, Ph.D., President
Kirk Beattie, VP/Administration
Catherine S. Ballard, Director of Research
Steve J. Fessette, Director of Physical Plant

Miner Institute conducts integrated, cutting-edge education, research, and demonstration programs that optimize the biological and economic relationships among forage-crop production, dairy and equine management, and environmental stewardship.We envision a vital agricultural community in northern New York and surrounding regions built on effective use of forage crops and management technologies that optimize animal production and well-being while sustaining the natural environment.
Founded in: 1903

730 **USA Dry Pea & Lentil Council**
2780 W. Pullman Road
Moscow, ID 83843

208-882-3023; *Fax:* 208-882-6406
pulse@pea-lentil.com; www.pea-lentil.com

Tim D. McGreevy, CEO
Pete Klaiber, VP, Marketing
Jessie Hunter, Director of Domestic Marketing
Drex Rhoades, Director of Communications
Tayebeh Soltani, Assistant Marketing Manager

The USA Dry Pea & Lentil Council(USADPLC) is a non-profit organization to promote and protect the interests of growers, processors, warehousemen and sellers of dry peas, lentils and chickpeas in the United States.
Founded in: 1965

731 **USA Rice Federation**
USA Rice Federation
2101 Wilson Bvld
Suite 610
Arlington, VA 22201

703-226-2300; *Fax:* 703-236-2301
riceinfo@usarice.com; www.usarice.com
Social Media: Facebook, Twitter, LinkedIn, Pinterest, YouTube, Google+

Johnny Broussard, Director, Legislative Affairs
Lauren Echols, Manager, Government Affairs/PAC
Reece Langley, Vice President, Government Affairs
Steve Hensley, Senior Director, Regulatory Affairs

The global advocate for all segments of the U.S. rice industry with a mission to promote and protect the interests of producers, millers, merchants and allied businesses. USA Rice is made up of the USA Rice Grower's Assoc, USA Rice Millers' Assoc, USA Rice Council, and the USA Rice Merchants' Association.

732 **United Fresh Produce Association**
1901 Pennsylvania Ave NW
Suite 1100
Washington, DC 20006-3412

202-303-3400; *Fax:* 202-303-3433
united@unitedfresh.org; www.unitedfresh.org
Social Media: Facebook, Twitter, LinkedIn, YouTube

Tom Stenzel, President/CEO
Jeff Oberman, Vice President, Trade Relations
Victoria Backer, Executive Vice President
Jessica Mosley, Director, Education
Lorelei DiSogra, Ed.D., R.D., Vice President Nutrition & Health

Equipment, supplies, cartons, packaging machinery, computers, sorting and sizing equipment, harvesting equipment, film wrap manufacturing and commodity organizations.
1000+ Members
Founded in: 1904

733 **United Producers**
8351 N High St
Sute 250
Columbus, OH 43235-1440

614-890-6666
800-456-3276; *Fax:* 614-890-4776
webmaster@uproducers.com;
www.uproducers.com
Social Media: Facebook, LinkedIn

Dennis Bolling, President/CEO
Joe Werstak, CFO

A cooperative marketing organization owned by farmers and ranchers in the United States' corn belt, midwest and southeast.
36000 Members
Frequency: Annual Meetings
Founded in: 1962

734 **United States Animal Health Association**
4221 Mitchell Ave.
St Joseph, MO 64507

816-671-1144; *Fax:* 816-671-1201
usaha@usaha.org; www.usaha.org
Social Media: Facebook, Twitter

Dr. David Meeker, President
Dr. Bruce King, President
Barbara Determan, Second Vice President
Dr. Kristin Haas, Third Vice President
Dr. Annette Jones, Treasurer

Seeks to prevent, control and eliminate livestock diseases.
1400 Members
Founded in: 1897

735 **United States Canola Association**
600 Pennsylvania Ave SE
Suite 320
Washington, DC 20003-6300

202-969-8113; *Fax:* 202-969-7036
info@uscanola.com; www.uscanola.com
Social Media: Facebook, Twitter, YouTube

John Gordley, Executive Director
Dale Thorenson, Assistant Director
Angela Dansby, Communications Director
Mary O'Donohue, Advertising Sales Representative

USCA members are producers and processors of canola and grapeseed.
Founded in: 1989

736 **United States Egg Marketers**
4500 Hugh Howell Road
Suite 270
Tucker, GA 30084

770-360-9220; *Fax:* 770-360-7058
info@unitedegg.org; www.unitedegg.org
Social Media: Facebook, Twitter, RSS Feed

Chad Gregory, President & CEO
David Inall, Senior Vice President
Sherry Shedd, Vice President of Finance
Derreck Nassa, Director of Operations
Oscar Garrison, Director of Food Safety

A producer cooperative established specifically for the purpose of exporting large quantities of U.S. Shell Eggs.

737 **United States Grains Council**
20 F Street NW
Suite 600
Washington, DC 20001

202-789-0789; *Fax:* 202-898-0522
grains@grains.org; www.grains.org
Social Media: Facebook, Twitter, LinkedIn, YouTube, Flickr, Pinterest

Alan Tiemann, Chairman
Thomas Sleight, President and CEO
Debra Keller, Secretary/Treasurer
Chip Councell, Vice Chairman
Mark Seastrand, Barley Sector Director

Motivated by the grain sorghum, barley and corn producer associations and representatives of the agricultural community. Provides commodity export market development.
175 Members
Founded in: 1960

738 **United States Hide, Skin & Leather Association**
1150 Connecticut Ave, NW
12th Floor
Washington, DC 20036

202-587-4250
ssothmann@meatinstitute.org; www.ushsla.org

Jamie Zitnik, Chairman
Stephen Sothmann, President
Henry Bank, Vice Chairman
Chris Mullally, Secretary

Exclusive representative of the hides and skin industry in the United States. Members range in size from small family-owned businesses to large corporations. Participates in two annual trade shows in Asia as a cooperator through the US Department of Agriculture's Foreign Agriculture Service.
35 Members

739 Veal Quality Assurance Program & Veal Issues Management Program
7501 NW Tiffany Springs Parkway
Suite 200
Kansas City, MO 64153

717-823-6995
info@vealfarm.com; www.vealfarm.com

Members include veal producers and processors.
1300 Members
Founded in: 1984

740 Walnut Council
Wright Forestry Center
1007 N 725 W
West Lafayette, IN 47906-9431

765-583-3501; *Fax:* 765-583-3512
walnutcouncil@walnutcouncil.org;
www.walnutcouncil.org

Jerry Van Sambeek, President
Dan Harris, VP
Liz Jackson, Executive Director
Bill Hoover, Treasurer
John Katzke, Quartermaster

A science based organization that encourages research, discussion, and application of knowledge about growing hardwood trees.
1000 Members
Founded in: 1970

741 Weed Science Society of America
810 East 10th St.
Lawrence, KS 66044-7065

785-865-9250
800-627-0326; *Fax:* 785-843-1274
jlancaster@allenpress.com; www.wssa.net
Social Media: Facebook, Twitter, LinkedIn, RSS, YouTube

Joyce Lancaster, Executive Secretary
Beverly Lindeen, Managing Editor
John Madsen, Secretary
Ian Burkel, Treasurer

Promotes research, education and extension outreach activities related to weeds, provides science-based information to the public and policy makers; and fosters awareness of weeds and their impacts on managed and natural ecosystems.
2000 Members
Founded in: 1956

742 Western Fairs Association
1776 Tribute Rd
Suite 210
Sacramento, CA 95815-4495

916-927-3100; *Fax:* 916-927-6397
info@fairsnet.org; www.fairsnet.org
Social Media: Facebook, Twitter, YouTube, Instagram

Troy Bowers, President
Barbara Quaid, VP
Stephen Chambers, Executive Director
Tami Davis Triggs, Accounting Manager
Jessica Boudevin, Communications Manager

A non-profit association with members throughout the Western United States and Canada that strives to promote industry standards. Membership includes access to conventions and trade shows, educational training programs as well as legislative advocacy support.
2000 Members
Founded in: 1922

743 Western United States Agricultural Trade Association
4601 NE 77th Avenue
Suite 240
Vancouver, WA 98662-2697

360-693-3373; *Fax:* 360-693-3464
export@wusata.org; www.wusata.org
Social Media: Facebook, Twitter, LinkedIn

Andy Anderson, Executive Director
Janet Kenefsky, Deputy Director/Intl. Mark. Dir.
Tricia Walker, FundMatch Manager
Terri Curtis, Office Coordinator
Becky Rein, Executive Administrator

The Western United States Agricultural Trade Association (WUSATAr) is a non-profit trade association whose members are the thirteen western state departments of agriculture. WUSATA is administered by the USDA 's Foreign Agricultural Service (FAS) and funded through the Market Access Program (MAP) with a mission to support and assist members and agribusinesses in the thirteen Western States in developing and enhancing international markets for U.S. food and agricultural products.
Founded in: 1980

Newsletters

744 AAM Newsletter
American Agriculture Movement
24800 Sage Creek Road
Scenic, SD 57780

605-993-6201; *Fax:* 605-993-6185
jjobgen@hotmail.com; www.aaminc.org

Larry Matlack, President
Arthur Chaney, Executive Vice President
John Willis, Vice President
Jim Rice, Secretary/Treasurer
John Willis, Vice President

The creation of the AAM has provided a farmer-created, farmer-built organization within which farmers themselves have been the leaders, speakers and organizers; empowering farmers as they had not been in the past, to speak for and advocate for themselves. Updates about events, news, articles and letters to the editor.
Founded in: 1977
Mailing list available for rent

745 ALBC News
American Livestock Breeds Conservancy
PO Box 477
Pittsboro, NC 27312

919-542-5704; *Fax:* 919-545-0022;
www.albc-usa.org
Social Media: Facebook, Blogger

Charles Bassett, Executive Director

Provides in-depth information about current ALBC activities, breed information, member updates, and more.
Frequency: Bi-Monthly

746 ARA Retailer Facts
Agricultural Retailers Association
1156 15th St Nw
Suite 500
Washington, DC 20005-1745

202-457-0825; *Fax:* 202-457-0864
ara@aradc.org; www.aradc.org
Social Media: Facebook, Twitter, RSS Feed

Daren Coppock, President and CEO
Richard Gupton, SVP
Donnie Taylor, VP of Membership
Gary Baise, General Counsel

The Agricultural Retailers Association advocates before Congress and the Executive Branch to ensure a profitable business environment for members.
Frequency: Daily

747 ARClight
National Agri-Marketing Association
11020 King St
Suite 205
Overland Park, KS 66210-1201

913-491-6500; *Fax:* 913-491-6502
agrimktg@nama.org; www.nama.org
Social Media: Facebook, Twitter, LinkedIn, Flicker, You Tube

Jennifer Pickett, CEO
Vicki Henrickson, President
Paul Redhage, Secretary/Treasurer
Matt Coniglio, Vice President

Agricultural Relations Council - a national association with members involved in agricultural public relations. Electronic newsletter of interest to association members.

748 ASA Today
American Soybean Association
12125 Woodcrest Executive
Suite 100
Saint Louis, MO 63141-5009

314-576-1770
800-688-7692; *Fax:* 314-576-2786
bcallanan@soy.org; www.soygrowers.com
Social Media: Facebook, Twitter, RSS Feed

Steve Censky, CEO
Cassandra Schlef, Communications Coordinator

For members only
Frequency: Weekly

749 ASAC News
American Society of Agricultural Consultants
N78W14573 Appleton Ave
#287
Menomonee Falls, WI 53051

262-253-6902; *Fax:* 262-253-6903
cmerry@countryside-marketing.com;
www.agconsultants.org
Social Media: Facebook, LinkedIn

˜the American Society of Agricultural Consultants (ASAC) is a non-profit organization oriented around raising the standards and image of professional agricultural consultants. ASAC is the only association representing the full range of agricultural consultants.
Frequency: Quarterly
Founded in: 1963

750 Agri Times Northwest
PO Box 1626
Pendleton, OR 97801

541-276-6202; *Fax:* 541-278-4778
editor@agritimesnw.com;
www.agritimesnw.com

Sterling Allen, Publisher
Jim Eardley, Editor
Brianna Walker, Graphics

Contains news stories and columns pertaining to rural life and agri-business, designed to keep farmers and ranchers up to date with agriculture in their backyard.
Cost: $20.00
Frequency: Bi-Monthly
Founded in: 1981

751 AgriMarketing Weekly
Henderson Communications LLC

1422 Elbridge Payne Rd
Suite 250
Chesterfield, MO 63017-8544

636-728-1428; *Fax:* 636-777-4178
info@agrimarketing.com;
www.agrimarketing.com

Lynn Henderson, Publisher/Editorial Director
Stephanie Wobbe, Editorial Assistant
Audrey Evans, Customer Service Manager

It includes a recap of the most important news within the industry during the prior week.
Frequency: Weekly
Circulation: 4500

752 **Agricultural Law Update**
American Agricultural Law Association
127 Young Rd
Kelso, WA 98626

360-200-5699; *Fax:* 360-432-2287;
www.aglaw-assn.org

Amy Swanson, President
Robert Achenbach, Jr., Executive Director
David K Waggoner, Director
Ruth A Moore, Director
Beth Crocker, Director

Articles written about environmental and agricultural issues.

753 **Agweek**
Grand Forks Herald
375 2nd Avenue N
Grand Forks, ND 58206-6008

701-780-1100; *Fax:* 701-780-1211;
www.gfherald.com
Social Media: RSS Feed

Matthew C Cory, Managing Editor
Tom Dennis, Editorial/Opinion Page Editor
Mary Jo Hotler, Editor

Features classifieds, weather information, farming, ranch news and opinion for the Upper Midwest
Cost: $32.00
Frequency: Weekly

754 **Alliance Link Newsletter**
Animal Agriculture Alliance
2101 Wilson Blvd
Suite 916-B
Arlington, VA 22201

703-562-5160; *Fax:* 703-524-1921
info@animalagalliance.org;
www.animalagalliance.org
Social Media: Facebook, Twitter

Kay Johnson, Executive VP
Sarah Hubbart, Communications Coordinator

Helps members and industry stakeholders stay informed about the key issues impacting animal agriculture
Frequency: Monthly

755 **American Beekeeping Federation Newsletter**
American Beekeeping Federation
3525 Piedmont Rd NE
Bldg 5 Suite 300
Atlanta, GA 30305-1509

404-760-2875; *Fax:* 404-240-0998
info@abfnet.org; www.abfnet.org

Regina Robuck, Executive Director
Gene Brandi, President
Tim May, Vice President
Susan Reu, Membership Coordinator

Newsletter for members of the American Beekeeping Federation.
Cost: $35.00
24 Pages
Frequency: Bi-Monthly
Circulation: 1750
Founded in: 1943

756 **American Feed Industry Newlsetter**
American Feed Industry Association
2101 Wilson Boulevard
Suite 916
Arlington, VA 22201

703-524-0810; *Fax:* 703-524-1921
afia@afia.org; www.afia.org
Social Media: Facebook, Twitter, LinkedIn

Al Gunderson, Chairman of the Board
Jeff Cannon, Chair/Elect
Joel Newman, President and Treasurer
Richard Sellers, VP and Corporate Security

Newsletter published every two weeks by the American Feed Industry for members only.
Frequency: Bi-Monthly
Circulation: 700
Founded in: 1909

757 **Aquatic Plant News**
Aquatic Plant Management Society
PO Box 821265
Vicksburg, MS 39182-1265

Fax: 601-634-5502
dpetty@ndrsite.com; www.apms.org
Social Media: Facebook, LinkedIn

Terry Goldsby, President
Mike Netherland, President-elect
Sherry Whitaker, Treasurer

Aquatic Plant News is produced 3 times each year, and is distributed primarily by email.
Frequency: 3x Yearly
Founded in: 1961

758 **Association of American Seed Control Officials Bulletin**
Utah Department of Agriculture
350 N Redwood Road
PO Box 146500
Salt Lake City, UT 84114-6500

801-538-7100; *Fax:* 801-538-7126
agriculture@utah.gov; www.ag.utah.gov
Social Media: Facebook, Twitter, YouTube

Stephen T Burningham, Control Officer
Leonard Blachham, Commissioner
Jed Christenson, Marketing

Seed laws in the United States and Canada.
Frequency: Annual+
Circulation: 5000

759 **CSA News**
5585 Guilford Road
Madison, WI 53711-1086

608-273-8080; *Fax:* 608-273-2021
headquarters@agronomy.org;
www.agronomy.org
Social Media: Facebook, Twitter, LinkedIn

Ellen E Bergfeld, Executive VP
Luther Smith, Executive Director
Michela Cobb, Director Financial Services
Audrey Jankowski, Analyst/Programmer
Ian Popkewitz, Director IT/Operations

The official magazine for members of the American Society of Agronomy, Crop Science Society of America, and Soil Science Society of America.
11000 Members
Founded in: 1907

760 **Chaff Newsletter**
American Association of Grain Inspection
PO Box 26426
Kansas City, MO 64196

816-569-4020; *Fax:* 816-221-8189
info@aagiwa.org; www.aagiwa.org

Larry Kitchen, President
Mark Fulmer, VP

Welcomes member information about new products, business changes, personnel changes and other items that may be of interest to AAGIWA members.
Frequency: Monthly

761 **Council for Agricultural Science and Technology Newsletter**
Council For Agricultural Science and Technology
4420 Lincoln Way
Ames, IA 50014-3447

515-292-2125; *Fax:* 515-292-4512
info@cast-science.org; www.cast-science.org
Social Media: Facebook, Twitter, LinkedIn, YouTube

Phillip Stahlman, President
Lowell Midla, President-elect
Turner Sutton, Treasurer

Identifies food, fiber, environmental and other agricultural issues for all stake holders, including legislators, policy makers and the public.
Founded in: 1972

762 **Country Folks**
Lee Publications
6113 State Highway 5
PO Box 121
Palatine Bridge, NY 13428

518-673-3237
800-836-2888; *Fax:* 518-673-3245
info@leepub.com; www.leepub.com
Social Media: Facebook, Twitter

Frederick Lee, Publisher
Scott Duffy, Sales Manager

Agricultural news from national, state and local levels. Some features on farm and agricultural industry, rural interest, etc.
75 Pages
Frequency: Weekly
Circulation: 27000
Founded in: 1973

763 **Country World Newspaper**
Echo Publishing Company
401 Church St
Sulphur Springs, TX 75482-2681

903-885-0861
800-245-2149; *Fax:* 903-885-8768
scott@ssecho.com;
www.countryworldnews.com

Scott Key, President
Kari Arnold, Editor

A newspaper offering agricultural information to farmers, ranchers, dairyfarmers, and agribusinesses.
Frequency: Weekly
Founded in: 1981

764 **Dair-e-news**
American Dairy Science Association
1800 S. Oak Street
Suite 100
Champaign, IL 61820-6974

217-356-5146; *Fax:* 217-398-4119
adsa@assochq.org; www.adsa.org
Social Media: Facebook

Peter Studney, Executive Director
Cara Tharp, Executive Assistant

Timely topics and important announcements, industry calendar of events, and news of the Association.

765 **DairyProfit Weekly**
6437 Collamer Road
East Syracuse, NY 13057-1031

315-703-7979
800-334-1904; *Fax:* 315-703-7988
dgarno@dairybusiness.com;

www.dairybusiness.com
Social Media: Facebook, Twitter, YouTube

Keeps readers up to date with a quick, timely summary of news, markets and trends that impact your business.
Frequency: Weekly
Founded in: 1904

766 **Decision Support Systems for Agrotechnology Transfer**
ICASA
2440 Campus Road
PO Box 527
Honolulu, HI 96822

808-956-2713; *Fax:* 808-956-2711;
www.dssat.net

Jeffrey White, Co-Chair
Martin Ittersum, Co-Chair
Gordon Tsuji, Secretariat

Systems analysis and crop simulation models for agrotechnology transfers and risk assessment. Reference guides and models for maize, wheat, rice, sorghum, millet, barley, soybean, peanut and potato are included. Linked to GIS software.

767 **Doane's Agricultural Report**
Doane Agricultural Services
77 Westport Plz
Suite 250
St Louis, MO 63146-3121

314-569-2700
866-647-0918; *Fax:* 314-569-1083;
www.doane.com

Rich Pottorff, Chief Economist
Marty Foreman, Senior Economist
Sam Funk, Senior Economist

Provides information to US farmers and agricultural professionals. Doane keeps you up to date on factors affecting your farm program benefits and production costs too.
Frequency: Weekly

768 **Farm Managers & Rural Appraisers News**
Amer. Society of Farm Managers & Rural Appraisers
950 S Cherry St
Suite 508
Denver, CO 80246-2664

303-758-3513; *Fax:* 303-758-0190
asfmra@asfmra.org; www.asfmra.org
Social Media: Facebook, Twitter, LinkedIn, Plaxo

Paul Joerger, President
Jim Rickert, President-elect
Fred Hepler, First Vice President

Provides members and other agricultural professionals with current information relative to the industry and educational offerings.
Frequency: Bi-Monthly
Founded in: 1929

769 **Farm and Ranch Guide**
2401 46th Avenue SE
Mandan, ND 58554

701-255-4905; *Fax:* 701-255-2312
office@farmandranchguide.com;
www.farmandranchguide.com
Social Media: Facebook, Twitter, RSS Feed

Brian Kroshus, Group Publisher
Mark Conlon, Editor
Patrick Sitter, General Manager
Andrea Johnson, Assistant Editor

Inform and entertain while serving as a conduit between our valued advertising customers and our loyal readers
Cost: $32.95
Frequency: Bi-Monthly
Circulation: 38,000

770 **Farmer's Friend**
116 Main Street
Towanda, PA 18846

570-265-2151
800-253-3662; *Fax:* 570-265-6130
kandrus@thedailyreview.com;
www.farmers-friend.com

Ronald W Hosie, Editor
Kelly Andrus, Managing Editor
Debbie Bump, Circulation

Farming news.
Frequency: Weekly
Founded in: 1977

771 **Feedstuffs**
The Miller Publishing Company
5810 W. 78th St
Suite 200
Bloomington, MN 55339

952-931-0211; *Fax:* 952-938-1832
smuirhead@feedstuffs.com;
www.feedstuffs.com

Sarah Muirhead, Publisher/Editor
Rod Smith, Staff Editor/Livestock & Poultry
Tim Lundeen, Staff Editor/Nutrition & Health
Jacqui Fatka, Staff Editor/Policy
Kristin Bakker, Editorial Production Manager

A newspaper for agribusiness, each week of the month focuses on a different animal species. Topics include nutrition, health, marketing issues and the popular Bottom Line of Nutrition section.
Cost: $144.00
24 Pages
Frequency: Weekly
Circulation: 16600
Founded in: 1895

772 **Fencepost**
The Fencepost
423 Main Street
Windsor, CO 80550-5129

970-686-5691; *Fax:* 970-686-5694;
www.thefencepost.com
Gary Loftus, Publisher
Amiella Diaz, Editor
Robyn Scherer, Staff Reporter

Farming news and reports.
Cost: $39.00
Frequency: Weekly
Founded in: 1980

773 **Forestry Source**
Society of American Foresters
5400 Grosvenor Ln
Bethesda, MD 20814-2198

301-897-8720
866-897-8720; *Fax:* 301-897-3690
safweb@podi.com; www.safnet.org
Social Media: Facebook, Twitter, LinkedIn

Joe Smith, Editor
Michael T Goergen, Jr., Executive Vice President
Patricia Adadevoh, Leadership Services Manager

Offers the latest information on national forestry trends, the latest developments in forestry policy at the federal, state, and local levels, the newest advances in forestry-related research and technology, and up-to-date information about SAF programs and activities
Cost: $35.00
Frequency: Monthly
Founded in: 1990

774 **Friday Notes**
Council For Agricultural Science and Technology
4420 West Lincoln Way
Ames, IA 50014-3447

515-292-2125; *Fax:* 515-292-4512
cast@cast-science.org; www.cast-science.org

John Bonner, Executive VP/CEO
Phillip Stahlman, President
Turner Sutton, Treasurer

E-Newsletter featuring lead articles on current topics being discussed in agriculture, congressional updates, announcements of upcoming CAST publications and activities, and information about CAST's scientific society, company, and nonprofit members.
Frequency: Quarterly
Circulation: 4000
Founded in: 1972

775 **Global Dairy Update**
DairyBusiness Communications
6437 Collamer Road
East Syracuse, NY 13057-1031

315-703-7979
800-334-1904; *Fax:* 315-703-7988
dgarno@dairybusiness.com;
www.dairybusiness.com
Social Media: Facebook, Twitter, YouTube

Dave Natzke, Editor
Scott Smith, Chairman/Co-CEO
John Montandon, President/Co-CEO
Joel Hastings, President, Dairy Business

Focuses on dairy developments throughout the world.
Founded in: 1904

776 **Goats on the Move**
Meat & Livestock Australia
1401 K Street NW
Suite 602
Washington, DC 20005

202-521-2551; *Fax:* 202-521-2699
info@mla.com.au; www.mla.com.au
Social Media: Facebook, Twitter, YouTube

Don Heatley, Chairman
David Palmer, Managing Director
Bernie Bindon, Director
Chris Hudson, Director

eNewsletter providing information on the latest developments in MLA's goat program and the broader Australian goatmeat industry.
Frequency: Quarterly
Founded in: 1998

777 **Greenhouse Product News**
Scranton Gillette Communications
3030 W Salt Creek Lance
Suite 201
Arlington Heights, IL 60005-5025

847-391-1000; *Fax:* 847-390-0408
bbellew@sgcmail.com; www.gpnmag.com

Bob Bellew, VP/Group Publisher
Tim Hodson, Editorial Director
Jasmina Radjevic, Managing Editor

Features the industry's leading Buyer's Guide directory, the PGR table and the bookstore are just a few reasons the industry's buyers keep coming back to GPN.
Frequency: Monthly
Mailing list available for rent: 19,000 names

778 **Hay Market News**
US Department of Agriculture
1400 Independence Ave., S.W.
Washington, DC 20250-0506

202-690-7650; *Fax:* 509-457-7132
shessman2@kda.state.ks.us; www.usda.gov

Tom Vilsack, Secretary
Chris Smith, Chief Information Officer
Matt Paul, Director of Communications
Ramona Romero, General Counsel

Federal newsletter offering information and updates on crops and farming.
Cost: $40.00
8 Pages
Circulation: 180
Founded in: 1862

779 **Holstein Association News**
Holstein Association
1 Holstein Place
PO Box 808
Brattleboro, VT 05302-0808

802-254-4551
800-952-5200; *Fax:* 802-254-8251
info@holstein.com; www.holsteinusa.com

John Meyer, CEO/Executive Secretary
Chuck Worden, President
Glenn E Brown, Vice President
Barbara Casna, CFO/Treasurer

Bimonthly newsletter provides active customers with information on the association programs and services and how to integrate them into their dairy operations.
Founded in: 1885

780 **Holstein Pulse**
Holstein Association USA Inc
1 Holstein Place
PO Box 808
Brattleboro, VT 05302-0808

802-254-4551
800-052-5200; *Fax:* 802-254-8251
info@holstein.com; www.holsteinusa.com

Chuck Worden, President
Glenn E Brown, Vice President
Barbara Casna, Treasurer

Includes information relevant to our members, new developments in the industry, as well as updates from the CEO and President.
Cost: $2.00
Frequency: Quarterly
Founded in: 1885

781 **Irrigation Association E-Newsletter**
Irrigation Association
6540 Arlington Blvd
Falls Church, VA 22042-6638

703-536-7080; *Fax:* 703-536-7019
info@irrigation.org; www.irrigation.org

Deborah Hamlin, Executive Director
Noreen Rich, Foundation Manager
Kathleen Markey, Marketing Director

Published on a quarterly basis, this e-newsletter provides updates on Foundation activities and accomplishments.
Frequency: Monthly
Founded in: 1949

782 **Irrigation Association IA Times**
Irrigation Association
6540 Arlington Blvd
Falls Church, VA 22042-6638

703-536-7080; *Fax:* 703-536-7019
info@irrigation.org; www.irrigation.org

Deborah Hamlin, Executive Director
Kathleen Markey, Marketing Director

Reports on federal and state policies and legislation that affect the irrigation industry. Status updates on industry initiatives, and information on the latest association events, programs, services and awards.
1600 Members
Frequency: Monthly
Founded in: 1949

783 **Kiplinger Agricultural Letter**
Kiplinger Washington Editors
1100 13th St. NW
Washington, DC 20005

202-887-6400
800-544-0155; *Fax:* 202-778-8976
sub.services@kiplinger.com;
www.kiplinger.com
Social Media: Facebook, Twitter, RSS

Knight A Kiplinger, President, Editor-in-Chief
Ed Maixner, Editor

Forecasts and judgments on wages, income, food packaging, processing and marketing techniques.
Cost: $137.00
Frequency: Biweekly
Founded in: 1929

784 **NAMA Newsletter**
North American Millers' Association
600 Maryland Ave SW
Suite 825 W
Washington, DC 20024

202-484-2200; *Fax:* 202-488-7416
generalinfo@namamillers.org;
www.namamillers.org

Mary Waters, President
James Bair, Vice President
Paul B Green, Export Consultant
Sherri Lehman, Director of Government Relations
Mary Waters, President

Trade association representing the wheat, corn, oat and rye milling industry. NAMA members operate one hundred and seventy mills in thrirty-eight states and Canada. Their aggregate production of more than one hundred and sixty million pounds per day is approximately ninety-five percent of the industry capacity in the U.S.
Frequency: Monthly
Circulation: 250

785 **NASDA News**
1156 15th St NW
Suite 1020
Washington, DC 20005-1711

202-296-9680; *Fax:* 202-296-9686
nasda@nasda.org; www.nasda.org
Social Media: Facebook, Twitter

Stephen Haterius, CEO
Steve Troxler, President
Chuck Ross, Vice President

Represents the state departments of agriculture in the development, implementation and communication of sound public policy and programs which support and promote the American agricultural industry, while protecting consumers and the environment.
Founded in: 1915

786 **NBA Weekly Update**
National Bison Association
8690 Wolff Ct
200
Westminster, CO 80031

303-292-2833; *Fax:* 303-845-9081
marilyn@bisoncentral.com;
www.bisoncentral.com

Dave Carter, Executive Director
Jim Matheson, Assistant Director
Marilyn Wentz, Bison World Editor

Mailed exclusively to all Life, Active and Allied Industry members. Contains the most up to date information available on the bison industry.
Frequency: Weekly

787 **NCPA Newsletter**
National Cottonseed Products Association
866 Willow Tree Cir
Cordova, TN 38018-6376

901-682-0800; *Fax:* 901-682-2856
info@cottonseed.com; www.cottonseed.com

Ben Morgan, Executive VP & Secretary
Sandi Stine, Treasurer

Providing members with information on legislation, administrative rulings, federal regulations and court decisions affecting their business.
Founded in: 1897

788 **National Honey Report**
Federal Market News Service
1400 Independence Avenue SW
STOP 0238
Washington, DC 20250

202-720-2175; *Fax:* 202-720-0547;
www.ams.usda.gov/mnreports/fvmhoney.pdf

Billy Cox, Director
Becky Unkenholz, Deputy Director
Joan Shaffer, Senior Public Affairs Specialist

Current honey market information and colony conditions in the United States and other countries.
16 Pages
Frequency: Monthly
Founded in: 1915

789 **National Onion Association Newsletter**
National Onion Association
822 7th St
Suite 510
Greeley, CO 80631-3941

970-353-5895; *Fax:* 970-353-5897
wmininger@onions-usa.org;
www.onions-usa.org
Social Media: Twitter

Mike Meyer, President
Gary Mayfield, Vice President
Kim Reddin, Director of Public & Industry

Newsletter published by and only for the National Onion Association.
Frequency: Monthly
Circulation: 600
Founded in: 1913
Mailing list available for rent: 600 names

790 **Nebraska Alfalfa Dehydrators Bulletin**
Nebraska Alfalfa Dehydrators Association
8810 Craig Dr
Overland Park, KS 66212-2916

913-648-6800; *Fax:* 913-648-2648
wcobbkc@sbcglobal.net; www.nebada.org

Jon Montgomery, President
David Rhea, Vice President
Dallas Buck, Director
Wanda Cobb, Executive Director/Secretary

Information for the processors and suppliers in the alfalfa industry.
Frequency: Weekly
Founded in: 1941

791 **New England Farm Bulletin and Garden**
Jacob's Meadow Inc.
PO Box 67
Townton, MA 02780

E-Mail: kimberlee@jacobsmeadow.org;
www.jacobsmeadow.org

Articles explore relevant topics; extensive farm clasifieds, doings around New England, book reviews and discount prices.

792 **News of the Association of Official Seed Analysts**
Association of Official Seed Analysts (AOSA)

101 East State Street
#214
Ithaca, NY 14850

607-256-3313; *Fax:* 607-273-1638
aosa.office@twcny.rr.com; www.aosaseed.com

Dan Curry, President
Michael Stahr, Vice President
Janine Maruschak, Secretary/Treasurer

News items, technical reports, rules changes for testing seeds, surveys, identification and tax news, legislative updates and updates on the Association and publications in progress.

793 **No-Till Farmer**
Lessiter Media
16655 West Wisconsin Avenue
P.O. Box 624
Brookfield, WI 53005-5738

262-782-4480
800-645-8455; *Fax:* 262-782-1252
info@no-tillfarmer.com;
www.no-tillfarmer.com
Social Media: Facebook, Twitter, LinkedIn, YouTube

Frank Lessiter, Executive Editor
Mike Lessiter, President
Laura Barrera, Managing Editor

Management information for farmers interested in conservation tillage.

794 **North American Millers' Association Newsletter**
600 Maryland Ave SW
Suite 825 W
Washington, DC 20024

202-484-2200; *Fax:* 202-488-7416
generalinfo@namamillers.org;
www.namamillers.org

Mary Waters, President
James Bair, VP

Trade association representing the wheat, corn, oat and rye milling industry. NAMA members operate one hundred and seventy mills in thrirty-eight states and Canada. Their aggregate production of more than one hundred and sixty million pounds per day is approximately ninety-five percent of the industry capacity in the U.S.
45 Members
Founded in: 1902

795 **Northeastern Weed Science Society Newsletter**
PO Box 307
Fredericksburg, PA 17026

814-574-4067
northeasternweedscience@hotmail.com;
www.newss.org

Antonio DiTommaso, President
Greg Armel, Vice President
Melissa Bravo, Secretary/Treasurer
Darren Lycan, Editor
Javier Vargas, Public Relations

Serves the Northeastern US by bringing together those who are concerned with the knowledge of weeds and their control, cooperates with other scientific societies to promote research, education and outreach activities and publishes scientific and practical information of value concerning weed sciences and other fields.
Founded in: 1946

796 **OCIA Communicator Newletter**
1340 North Cotner Boulevard
Lincoln, NE 68505-1838

402-477-2323; *Fax:* 402-477-4325
info@ocia.org; www.ocia.org

Kevin Koester, President/ First Vice President
Jack Geiger, Second Vice President
Demetria Stephens, Secretary
Terrence Sheehan, Treasurer
Amy Krasne, Secretary

A quarterly newsletter published by the Organic Crop Improvement Association International (OCIA).
Cost: $50.00
Frequency: Quarterly
Circulation: 300
Mailing list available for rent: 3500 names at $50 per M

797 **Organic Report**
Organic Trade Association
28 Vernon Street
Suite 413
Brattleboro, VT 05301

802-275-3800; *Fax:* 802-275-3801
info@ota.com; www.ota.com
Social Media: Facebook, Twitter, LinkedIn

Matthew McLean, President
Sarah Bird, Vice President
Tony Bedard, Treasurer
Kelly Shea, Secretary

Targets an audience of manufacturers, growers, retailers, importers, distributors, and consultants in the organic food and fiber industry.
Frequency: Monthly
Circulation: 2500
Founded in: 1985

798 **Peterson Patriot**
Peterson Patriot Printers-Publishers
202 Main Street
PO Box 126
Peterson, IA 51047-0126
712-295-7711
patriot@iowatelecom.net

Roger Stoner, Publisher
Jane Stoner, Editor/Circulation Manager

Agricultural news.
Cost: $18.00
12 Pages
Frequency: Weekly
Circulation: 549

799 **Pro Farmer**
Farm Journal Media
1550 N Northwest HW
Suite 403
Park Ridge, IL 60068

215-578-8900
800-320-7992; *Fax:* 215-568-6782;
www.farmjournalmedia.com
Andy Weber, Chief Executive Officer
Steve Custer, Executive Vice President/Publishing
Jeff Pence, Division President
Chuck Roth, Senior Vice President
Mitch Rouda, President, eMedia

Farm market news, analysis and management advice.
8 Pages
Frequency: Weekly
Founded in: 1973

800 **SHORTLINER**
Farm Equipment Manufacturers Association
1000 Executive Parkway Dr
Suite 100
St Louis, MO 63141-6369

314-878-2304; *Fax:* 314-732-1480
info@farmequip.org; www.farmequip.org
Social Media: Twitter

Andrew Cummings, President
Bob Atkinson, Treasurer
Marc McConnell, 1st Vice President
Mike Kloster, 2nd Vice President
Richard Kirby, Secretary

A review of news stories, press reports, and government actions affecting the industry.
Frequency: Bi-Monthly

801 **Salt & Trace Mineral Newsletter**
Salt Institute
700 N Fairfax Street
Suite 600
Alexandria, VA 22314-2040

703-549-4648; *Fax:* 703-548-2194
info@saltinstitute.org; www.saltinstitute.org

Lori Roman, President
Morton Satin, VP/Science & Research

Information on animal nutrition.
Frequency: Quarterly
Founded in: 1914

802 **Seed News**
PO Box 772
Port Townsend, WA 98368

360-385-7192; *Fax:* 360-385-7455
info@seedalliance.org; www.seedalliance.org
Social Media: Facebook, Twitter

Sebastian Aguilar, President
Atina Diffley, Vice President
Zea Sonnabend, Treasurer

Information covering events, seminars and meetings.
Cost: $8.00
8 Pages

803 **Seed Technologist Newsletter**
Association of Official Seed Analysts (AOSA)
101 East State Street
#214
Ithaca, NY 14850

607-256-3313; *Fax:* 607-273-1638
aosa.office@twcny.rr.com; www.aosaseed.com

Dan Curry, President
Michael Stahr, Vice President
Janine Maruschak, Secretary/Treasurer

News items, technical reports, rules changes for testing seeds, surveys, identification and tax news, legislative updates and updates on the Association and publications in progress.
Cost: $20.00
Frequency: TriAnnual
Circulation: 500

804 **Signals Newsletter**
Association for Communication Excellence
ACE Headquarters
59 College Road, Taylor Hall
Durham, NH 03824

603-862-1564; *Fax:* 603-862-1585
ace.info@unh.edu; www.aceweb.org

Faith Peppers, President
Joanne Littlefield, Vice President
Elaine Edwards, Treasurer
Emily Eubanks, Professional Development Director
Jason Ellis, Research Director

The newsletter includes articles with a professional development focus; updates from special interest groups, states and regions; announcements about upcoming workshops and conferences; and write-ups about members' awards and accomplishments, job changes and more.
Cost: $75.00
Frequency: Bimonthly

805 **Smart Choices Newsletter**
Communicating for America

112 E Lincoln Avenue
Fergus Falls, MN 56537

218-739-3241
80- 43- 327; *Fax:* 218-739-3832
info@cabenefits.org; www.cabenefits.org

Milt Smedsrud, CEO
Wayne Nelson, President

Filled with updates on legislative accomplishments and advocacy, articles about healthy living and first-hand accounts from those participating in CA Education Programs.
40M Members
Founded in: 1972

806 Society for Laboratory Automation and Screening
100 Illinois Street
Suite 242
St. Charles, IL 60174

630-256-7527
877-990-7557; *Fax:* 630-741-7527
slas@slas.org; www.slas.org
Social Media: Facebook, Twitter, LinkedIn, YouTube

Greg Dummer, CEO
Mary Geismann, Manager
Carol Brady, Coordinator

Provides forums for education and information exchange to encourage the study of and advance science and technology for the drug discovery, agrochemical, biotechnology, chemical, clinical diagnostic, consumer product, energy, forensic, pharmaceutical, security and other industries.
Frequency: Bi-Monthly

807 Southern Cotton Ginners Association Newsletter
874 Cotton Gin Pl
Memphis, TN 38106-2588

901-947-3104; *Fax:* 901-947-3103
carmen.griffin@southerncottonginners.org; www.southerncottonginners.org
Social Media: Facebook

George LaCour, President
Robert Royal, Vice President
Sledge Taylor, Treasurer
Timothy Price, Secretary

Operates in a five state area as an information center covering safety and governmental regulations. Serves its members by providing safety, training and regulatory representation. Sponsors certification programs and hosts the industry's leading trade show, The Mid-South Farm & Gin Show.
Founded in: 1950

808 The Agrarian Advocate
36355 Russell Boulevard
P.O. Box 363
Davis, CA 95617

530-756-8518
800-892-3832; *Fax:* 530-756-7857
judith@fullbellyfarm.com; www.caff.org
Social Media: Facebook, Twitter, YouTube

Carol Presley, Board Chair
Pete Price, Vice President
Judith Redmond, Secretary
Vicki Williams, Treasurer

Provides timely reporting on the food and farming issues
Cost: $47.95
Frequency: 3x/Year
Founded in: 1978

809 The Alliance Link
Animal Agriculture Alliance
2101 Wilson Blvd
Suite 916-B
Arlington, VA 22201

703-562-5160
info@animalagalliance.org; www.animalagalliance.org
Social Media: Facebook, Twitter

Kay Johnson, President and CEO
Emily Meredith, Communications Director

Provides information about specific animal rights organizations and their campaigns, referenced quotes by the activists themselves, as well as information to help with security at your facilities.
Frequency: Monthly

810 The Exchange
American Agricultural Economics Association
555 E Wells Street
Suite 1100
Milwaukee, WI 53202-6600

414-918-3190; *Fax:* 414-276-3349
info@aaea.org; www.aaea.org
Social Media: Facebook

Richard Sexton, President
Julie Caswell, President-elect

Electronic newsletter for members of AAEA. Includes association announcements, membership news, and updates from the profession.
Frequency: Bi-Monthly
Founded in: 1910

811 USA Rice Daily
USA Rice Federation
2101 Wilson Blvd
Suite 610
Arlington, VA 22201

703-226-2300; *Fax:* 703-236-2301
riceinfo@usarice.com; www.usarice.com
Social Media: Facebook, Twitter, RSS, You Tube

Betsy Ward, President/CEO
Ann Banville, Vice President Domestic Promotion
Patricia Alderson, Vice President Member Services
Jim Guinn, Vice President International
Bob Cummings, Chief Operating Officer

The latest news on issues and activities for the U.S. rice industry.

812 Update
6060 FFA Drive
PO Box 68960
Indianapolis, IN 46268-0960

317-802-6060
888-332-2668; www.ffa.org

Important news, information and program updates.
12 Pages
Frequency: Monthly
Circulation: 45,000
Founded in: 1928

813 Vegetarian Journal
Vegetarian Resource Group
PO Box 1463
Baltimore, MD 21203

410-366-8343; *Fax:* 410-366-8804
vrg@vrg.org; www.vrg.org
Social Media: Facebook, Twitter, RSS

Charles Stahler, President
Jeannie McStay, Catalog Manager
Debra Wasserman, Treasurer
Keryl Cryer, Senior Editor
Sonja Helman, Coordinator

Informative articles, recipes, book reviews, notices about vegetarian events, product evaluations, where to find vegetarian products and services. All nutrition information based on scientific studies.
Frequency: Quarterly
Circulation: 15000

814 WSSA Newsletter
P.O.Box 7065
Lawrence, KS 66044-7065

785-429-9622
800-627-0629; *Fax:* 785-843-1274
wssa@allenpress.com; www.wssa.net

Rod Lym, President
Joe DiTomaso, Vice President
John Madsen, Secretary
Ian Burke, Treasurer
James Anderson, Director Publications

Promotes research, education and extension outreach activities related to weeds, provides science-based information to the public and policy makers; and fosters awarenes of weeds and their impacts on managed and natural ecosystems.
Founded in: 1956

815 Webster Agricultural Letter
Webster Communications Corporation
3835 9th St N
Suite 401W
Arlington, VA 22203-5812

703-525-4512; *Fax:* 703-852-3534
editor@agletter.com; www.agletter.com

James C Webster, President
Marilyn Webster, Vice President

Agricultural politics and policy issues.
Cost: $397.00
6 Pages
Frequency: 2x Monthly
ISSN: 1073-4813
Founded in: 1980
Printed in one color on matte stock

816 Weekly Livestock Reporter
PO Box 7655
Fort Worth, TX 76111-0655

817-831-3147; *Fax:* 817-831-3117
service@weeklylivestock.com; www.weeklylivestock.com

Ted Gouldy, Publisher
Phil Stoll, CEO/President
Mickey Schwarz, Circulation Manager

Offers comprehensive weekly information for cattle farmers and livestock agricultural professionals.
Cost: $18.00
Frequency: Weekly
Circulation: 10000
Founded in: 1897

817 Weekly Weather and Crop Bulletin
NOAA/USDA Joint Agricultural Weather Facility
1400 Independence Ave SW
Washington, DC 20250

202-720-2791; www.usda.gov

Douglas LeComte, Publisher
Annette Holmes, Secretary

Provides a vital source of information on weather, climate and agricultural developments worldwide, along with detailed charts and tables of agrometeorological information that are appropriate for the season.
Cost: $60.00
Frequency: Weekly
Circulation: 1,500
Founded in: 1862

Magazines & Journals

818 AFIA Journal
American Feed Industry Association

2101 Wilson Boulevard
Suite 916
Arlington, VA 22201

703-524-0810; *Fax:* 703-524-1921
afia@afia.org; www.afia.org
Social Media: Facebook, Twitter, LinkedIn

Joel Newman, President
Richard Sellers, VP and Corporate Secretary
Keith Epperson, Vice President
Sarah Novak, Vice President

Variety of topics about the animal feed industry and its suppliers.
Frequency: Quarterly
Founded in: 1909

819 Acreage Magazine
Heartland Communications Group
1003 Central Avenue
Fort Dodge, IA 50501

515-955-1600
800-247-2000; www.acreagelife.com
Social Media: Facebook

Francis McLean, Publisher

Cultural news and features edited for rural farm producers magazine.
Cost: $5.00
40 Pages
Frequency: Monthly
Founded in: 1985

820 Acres USA
5321 Industrial Oaks Boulevard
Suite 128
Austin, TX 78735

51- 8-2 44
800-355-5315; *Fax:* 512-892-4448
info@acresusa.com; www.acresusa.com
Social Media: Facebook, Twitter, LinkedIn

Fred C Walters, CEO/President

Commercial-scale organic/ sustainable farming news.
Cost: $27.00
Frequency: Monthly
Circulation: 19000
ISSN: 1076-4968
Founded in: 1970

821 Agri Marketing Magazine
Henderson Communications LLC
1422 Elbridge Payne Rd
Suite 250
Chesterfield, MO 63017-8544

636-728-1428; *Fax:* 636-777-4178
info@agrimarketing.com;
www.agrimarketing.com

Lynn Henderson, Editorial Director
Audrey Evans, Customer Service Manager
Stephanie Wobbe, Editorial Assistant
Judy Henderson, Artist

Covers the unique interests of corporate agribusiness executives, their marketing communications agencies, the agricultural media, ag trade associations and other ag-related professionals.
Circulation: 8000
Founded in: 1962

822 AgriSelling Principles and Practices
Henderson Communications LLC
1422 Elbridge Payne Rd
Suite 250
Chesterfield, MO 63017-8544

636-728-1428; *Fax:* 636-777-4178
info@agrimarketing.com;
www.agrimarketing.com

Lynn Henderson, Editorial Director
Audrey Evans, Customer Service Manager
Stephanie Wobbe, Editorial Assistant
Judy Henderson, Artist

This 448-page book is utilized by many major agribusiness corporations and academic institutions for training its sales and marketing staff and or students.
Founded in: 1962

823 Agribusiness Fieldman
Western Agricultural Publishing Company
4969 E Clinton Way
Suite 104
Fresno, CA 93727-1549

559-252-7000
westag@psnw.com; www.westagpubco.com

For the professional agricultural consultant, featuring the latest information on chemical regulation, pest control techniques and feature stories on PCA and PCO community.

824 Agrichemical Age
Farm Progress Publishers
191 S Gary Ave
Carol Stream, IL 60188-2024

630-690-5600
800-441-1410; *Fax:* 630-462-2869;
www.farmprogress.com

Jeffry M Lapin, President
John Vogel, Editor
Willie Vogt, Corporate Editorial Director
John Otte, Economics Editor
Dan Crummett, Executive Editor

Information for fertilizer/pesticide dealers, distributors, commercial applicators and crop consultants.

825 Agricultural Aviation
National Agricultural Aviation Association
1440 Duke Street
Alexandria, VA 22314

202-546-5722; *Fax:* 202-546-5726
information@agaviation.org;
www.agaviation.org

Dana Ness, President
Rick Boardman, Vice President
Doug Davidson, Secretary
Brenda Watts, Treasurer

Official publication for legislative updates, industry trends, new products and more.
Frequency: 6x Yearly
Founded in: 1978

826 Agricultural History
The Sheridan Press
MSU History Department
PO Box H
Mississippi State, MS 39762

662-268-2247
aimarcus@history.msstate.edu;
www.aghistorysociety.org

Claire Strom, Editor
James C Giesen, Executive Secretary
Alan I Marcus, Treasurer

Traces historical lineage of agriculture in the US.
Cost: $47.00
Frequency: Quarterly
Circulation: 900
Founded in: 1924

827 Agriculture Research Magazine
Agricultural Research Service
George Washington Carver Center
5601 Sunnyside Avenue
Beltsville, MD 20705-5130

301-504-1651; *Fax:* 301-504-1641
info@ars.usda.gov; www.ars.usda.gov/ar

Robert Sowers, Editor/Circulation Manager
William Johnson, Art Director
Edward Knipling, CEO
Carol Durflinger, Secretary
Cost: $50.00
27 Pages
Frequency: Monthly
Circulation: 45000
Founded in: 1954

828 Agronomy Journal
5585 Guilford Road
Madison, WI 53711-1086

608-273-8080; *Fax:* 608-273-2021
headquarters@agronomy.org;
www.agronomy.org
Social Media: Facebook, Twitter, LinkedIn

Ellen E Bergfeld, Executive VP
Luther Smith, Executive Director
Michela Cobb, Director Financial Services
Audrey Jankowski, Analyst/Programmer
Ian Popkewitz, Director IT/Operations

Journal of agriculture and natural resource sciences. Articles convey original research in soil science, crop science, agroclimatology, agronomic modeling, production agriculture, instrumentation, and more.
Founded in: 1907

829 Agweek
Grand Forks Herald
375 2nd Avenue N
Grand Forks, ND 58203

701-780-1100
800-477-6572; *Fax:* 701-780-1123
onlineteam@gfherald.com; www.agweek.com
Social Media: RSS

Michael Jacobs, Publisher/Editor
Tom Dennis, Editorial/Opinion Page Editor
Dawn Zimney, Circulation Director
Cory Matt, Managing Editor

Agweek features classified, weather information, farming, ranch news and opinions for the Upper Midwest.
Cost: $32.00
80 Pages
Frequency: Weekly
Circulation: 25,000
Founded in: 1879
Printed in 4 colors

830 Alimentos Balanceados Para Animales
WATT Publishing Company
303 N Main Street
Rockford, IL 61101

815-966-5400; *Fax:* 815-966-6416
gill@wattmm.com; www.wattnet.com

Jim Watt, Chairman/CEO
Clayton Gill, Editorial Director
Christina Karmer, Human Resources Consultant

For feed industry professionals in Latin America.
Founded in: 1994

831 American Agriculturist
Farm Progress Companies
5227 B Baltimore Park
Littlestown, PA 17340

717-359-0150
800-441-1410; *Fax:* 717-359-0250
jvogel@farmprogress.com;
www.farmprogress.com

John Vogel, Editor
Willie Vogt, Corporate Editorial Director
Dan Crummett, Executive Editor

Serves Northeast producers with information to help them maximize their productivity and profitability. Each issue is packed with information, ideas, news and analysis.
Cost: $26.95
Frequency: Monthly
Founded in: 1842

832 **American Bee Journal**
Dadant and Sons
51 S 2nd St
Hamilton, IL 62341-1397

217-847-3324
888-922-1293; *Fax:* 217-847-3660
editor@americanbeejournal.com;
www.americanbeejournal.com
Social Media: Facebook, Twitter

Tim C Dadant, President
Marta Menn, Advertising
Dianne Behnke, Publisher
Joe Graham, Editor

Read by commercial and hobby beekeepers and entomologists.
Cost: $22.95
80 Pages
Frequency: Monthly
Circulation: 11000
ISSN: 0002-7626
Founded in: 1861
Printed in 4 colors on glossy stock

833 **American Christmas Tree Journal**
National Christmas Tree Association
16020 Swingley Ridge Rd
Suite 300
Chesterfield, MO 63017-6030

636-449-5070; *Fax:* 636-449-5051
info@realchristmastrees.org;
www.realchristmastrees.org

Cline Church Ciocci, President
DeLaine Bender, Executive Director
Becky Rasmussen, Assistant Director
Rick Dungey, PR/Marketing Director
Lauren Mangnall, Project Coordinator

Covers production and research topics, marketing advice, feature stories, legislative updates, tax and business management info, NCTA news and more
Cost: $57.00
Frequency: Quarterly
Circulation: 1500
ISSN: 0569-3845

834 **American Feed Industry Association Journal**
2101 Wilson Blvd
Suite 916
Arlington, VA 22201-3047

703-524-0810; *Fax:* 703-524-1921
afia@afia.org; www.afia.org
Social Media: Facebook, Twitter, LinkedIn

Joel Newman, President
Richard Sellers, VP/Feed Regulation & Nutrition
Keith Epperson, VP/Manufacturing & Training
Sarah Novak, VP/Membership & Public Relations
Leanna Nail, Director of Administration

Includes a variety of topics about the animal feed industry and its suppliers.
Founded in: 1909

835 **American Fruit Grower**
Meister Media Worldwide
37733 Euclid Ave
Willoughby, OH 44094-5992

440-942-2000
800-572-7740; *Fax:* 440-975-3447
info@meistermedia.com;
www.meistermedia.com

Gary Fitzgerald, Chairman and CEO
Michael Deluca, President
Donald Hohmeier, VP and CFO

Specialized production and marketing information and industry-wide support for fruit growers.
Cost: $19.95
66 Pages
Frequency: Monthly
Circulation: 14000
Founded in: 1880

836 **American Journal of Agricultural Economics (AJAE)**
American Agricultural Economics Association
555 E Wells Street
Suite 1100
Milwaukee, WI 53202-6600

414-918-3190; *Fax:* 414-276-3349
info@aaea.org; www.aaea.org
Social Media: Facebook

Richard Sexton, President
Julie Caswell, President-elect

The leading journal for agricultural economics.
3000 Members
Frequency: 5x Yearly
Founded in: 1910

837 **American Journal of Enology and Viticulture**
1784 Picasso Avenue, Suite D
PO Box 1855
Davis, CA 95617-1855

530-753-3142; *Fax:* 530-753-3318
society@asev.org; www.asev.org
Social Media: Twitter, LinkedIn

Lyndie Boulton, Executive Director
Dan Howard, Assistant Executive Director
Leticia Chacon-Rodriguez, President
James Kennedy, First Vice President

The official journal of the American Society for Enology and Viticulture and is the premier journal dedicated to scientific research on winemaking and grapegrowing.
Frequency: Quarterly
Founded in: 1950

838 **American Small Farm Magazine**
Back 40 Group
P.O. Box 8
Hartshorn, MO 65479

573-858-3244
866-284-9844; *Fax:* 573-858-3245
Publisher@SmallFarm.com;
www.smallfarm.com

Paul Berg, Editor
Herman Beck-Chenoweth, Publisher

Published for the owner/operator of farms from 5 to 300 acres. Focuses on production agriculture including alternative and sustainable farming ideas and technology, case studies, small farm lifestyle and tradition.
Cost: $18.00
Frequency: Monthly
Circulation: 62,444
ISSN: 1064-7473
Founded in: 1992

839 **American Vegetable Grower**
Meister Media Worldwide
37733 Euclid Ave
Willoughby, OH 44094-5992

440-942-2000
800-572-7740; *Fax:* 440-975-3447;
www.growingproduce.com/americanvegetablegrower/

Gary Fitzgerald, President
Rosemary Gordon, Editor
Jo Monahan, Publisher
Brian Sparks, Group Editor
Paul Rusnak, Managing Editor

American Vegetable Grower magazine provides insight on field, greenhouse and organic production, marketing, and new varieties and products.
Cost: $19.95
Frequency: Monthly
Circulation: 26000
Founded in: 1908

840 **Animal & Dairy News**
American Dairy Science Association
2441 Village Green Pl
Champaign, IL 61822-7676

217-356-5146; *Fax:* 217-398-4119
adsa@assochq.org; www.adsa.org

Donald C Beitz, President
Philld C Tongz, VP
Peter Studney, Executive Director
William R Aimutis, Treasurer

A Publication of ADSA
Founded in: 1898
Mailing list available for rent

841 **Applied Economic Perspectives and Policy (AEPP)**
American Agricultural Economics Association
555 E Wells Street
Suite 1100
Milwaukee, WI 53202-6600

414-918-3190; *Fax:* 414-276-3349
info@aaea.org; www.aaea.org
Social Media: Facebook

Richard Sexton, President
Julie Caswell, President-elect

Formerly the Review of Agricultural Economics, each issue includes both featured and submitted articles.
3000 Members
Frequency: Quarterly
Founded in: 1910

842 **Beef Today**
Farm Journal Media
1818 Market Street
31st Floor
Philadelphia, PA 19103-3654

215-578-8900
800-331-9310; *Fax:* 215-568-6782
jstruyk@farmjournal.com;
www.agweb.com/livestock/beef
Social Media: Facebook, Twitter, YouTube

Andy Weber, Chief Executive Officer
Steve Custer, Executive Vice President
Jeff Pence, President, Electronic Media
Chuck Roth, Senior Vice President
Boyce Thompson, Editorial Director

This is the only nationwide publication that currently serves beef producers of all sizes-large and small. It delivers the tools cattlemen need to make sustainable and profitable choices to transition their herd to the next generation. Topics include genetics, animal health, business planning, pasture management, wildlife management and market analysis.
Frequency: Weekly
Founded in: 1973

843 **Belt Pulley**
Belt Pulley Pub Company
PO Box 58
Jefferson, WI 53549-1341

920-674-9732; www.beltpulley.com

Katie Elmore, Publisher
Jane Aumann, Managing Editor

Covers antique tractors and farm machinery of all makes and models.
Cost: $20.00
Frequency: Monthly
Circulation: 3500
Founded in: 1987

844 **Better Crops International Magazine**
Potash and Phosphate Institute

3500 Parkway Lane
Suite 550
Norcross, GA 30092-2844

770-447-0335; *Fax:* 770-448-0439
info@ipni.net
http://www.ipni.net/wave

Terry Roberts, President
Steve Couch, VP Administration
Gavin Sulewski, Editor

Researchers report on nutrient-related topics for corn, wheat, groundnut, oil palm, sugarcane, rice, crop rotations, and fish ponds. The issue concludes with a back cover commentary explaining why support of agricultural development is the right thing to do.

845 **Biodynamics Journal**
PO Box 944
East Troy, WI 53120-0944

26- 6-9 92
888-516-7797; *Fax:* 26- 6-9 92
info@biodynamics.com;
www.biodynamics.com
Social Media: Facebook

Jean-Paul Courtens, President
Janet Gamble, Secretary
Steffen Schneider, Treasurer
Robert Karp, Executive Director

Provides a thoughtful collection of original articles centered on a theme of interest to the biodynamic community. Recent themes have included urban agriculture, biodynamic community, earth healing, raw milk, and the biodynamic preparations.

846 **Capital Press**
Press Publishing Company
1400 Broadway NE
PO Box 2048
Salem, OR 97308-2048

503-364-4431
800-882-6789; *Fax:* 503-370-4383
bnipp@capitalpress.com;
www.capitalpress.com
Social Media: Facebook, Twitter, LinkedIn, MySpace, Stumble Upon

Mike Forrester, President
John Perry, COO
Michael O'Brien, Publisher
Joe Beach, Editor

For the agricultural and forest community of the Pacific Northwest.
Cost: $44.00
60 Pages
Frequency: Weekly
Circulation: 37000
Founded in: 1928
Printed in 4 colors

847 **Carrot Country**
Columbia Publishing
8405 Ahtanum Rd
Yakima, WA 98903-9432

509-248-2452
800-900-2452; *Fax:* 509-248-4056
dbrent@columbiapublications.com;
www.carrotcountry.com

Brent Clement, Editor/Publisher
Mike Stoker, Publisher

Includes information on carrot production, grower and shipper feature stories, carrot research, new varieties, market reports, spot reports on overseas production and marketing and other key issues and trends of interest to US and Canadian carrot growers.
Cost: $10.00
Frequency: Quarterly
Circulation: 2500
ISSN: 1071-6653
Founded in: 1993
Printed in 4 colors on glossy stock

848 **Cattle Guard**
Colorado Cattlemen's Agricultrual Land Trust
8833 Ralston Road
Arvada, CO 80002-2239

303-431-6422; *Fax:* 303-431-6446;
www.coloradocattle.org

T Wright Dickinson, President
Frank Daley, First VP
Tim Canterbury, Treasurer
Terry Frankhauser, Executive VP
Heidi Brown, Membership and Operations Manager

A full overview of information is given through this magazine for cattle farmers and breeders.
Founded in: 1867

849 **Cattleman**
Texas & Southwestern Cattle Raisers Association
1301 W 7th St
Suite 201
Fort Worth, TX 76102-2665

817-332-7064
800-242-7820; *Fax:* 817-332-8523
tscra@tscra.org; www.texascattleraisers.org
Social Media: Facebook, Twitter

Joe Parker, President
Eldon White, Executive VP and CEO
Clay Birdwell, First VP
Pete Bonds, Second VP
Matt Brockman, Manager

Full overview of information for the cattle producer in Texas and Oklahoma.
Cost: $25.00
130 Pages
Frequency: Monthly
Circulation: 16000
Founded in: 1877
Printed in 4 colors on glossy stock

850 **Cereal Foods World**
AACC International
3340 Pilot Knob Rd
St. Paul, MN 55121-2055

651-454-7250; *Fax:* 651-454-0766
akohn@scisoc.org; www.aaccnet.org

Robert L. Cracknell, President
Lydia Tooker Midness, Chair of Board
Dave L. Braun, Treasurer

Articles on scientific studies that focus on advances in grain based food science.
Founded in: 1915

851 **Choices**
Agricultural & Applied Economics Association
1709 Darien Club Drive
Darien, IL 60561

630-271-1679; *Fax:* 630-908-3384
Walt@farmfoundation.org;
www.choicesmagazine.org

Walter J Armbruster, Editor
James Novak, Associate Editor

Provides current coverage regarding economic implications of food, farm, resource, or rural community issues directed toward a broad audience. Publishes thematic groupings of papers and individual papers.
Frequency: Quarterly
ISSN: 0886-5558
Founded in: 1910
Printed in 4 colors on glossy stock

852 **Choices Magazine**
American Agricultural Economics Association
555 E Wells Street
Suite 1100
Milwaukee, WI 53202-6600

414-918-3190; *Fax:* 414-276-3349
info@aaea.org; www.aaea.org
Social Media: Facebook

Richard Sexton, President
Julie Caswell, President-elect

Designed to provide current coverage regarding economic implications of food, farm, resource, or rural community issues directed toward a broad audience. Online only.
3000 Members
Frequency: Quarterly
Founded in: 1910

853 **Christmas Tree Lookout**
Pacific Northwest Christmas Tree Association
4093 12th Street SE
PO Box 3366
Salem, OR 97302

503-364-2942; *Fax:* 503-581-6819
info@christmas-tree.com; www.nwtrees.com

Bruce Wiseman, President
John Tillman, VP- Washington
Jan Hupp, Secretary/Treasurer
Mike Ramsby, V.P. Oregon
Bryan Ostlund, Executive Director

Marketing research and industry information for Christmas tree growers. Mailing list available.
Cost: $25.00
80 Pages
Frequency: Quarterly
Circulation: 1500
Founded in: 1955
Printed in 4 colors on glossy stock

854 **Christmas Trees**
Tree Publishers
PO Box 107
Lecompton, KS 66050-0107

785-887-6324
ctreesmag@gmail.com;
www.christmastreesmagazine.com
Social Media: Facebook, Twitter

Catherine Howard, Publisher/Editor/Advertising

Magazine of plantation management for Christmas tree growers, shearing, shaping and marketing. Accepts advertising.
Cost: $16.00
44 Pages
Frequency: Quarterly
Circulation: 3200
ISSN: 0149-0217
Founded in: 1973
Printed in 4 colors on glossy stock

855 **Citrus & Vegetable Magazine**
Vance Publishing
400 Knightsbridge Pkwy
Lincolnshire, IL 60069

847-634-2600; *Fax:* 847-634-4379
info@vancepublishing.com;
www.vancepublishing.com

Shawn Etheridge, VP and Publishing Director
Matthew Morgan, Director
Greg Johnson, Editorial Director
Vicky Boyd, Editor

Devlivers profitable production and management strategies to commercial citrus and vegetable growers in Florida.
Cost: $45.00
Frequency: Monthly
Circulation: 12000
Founded in: 1937
Printed in 4 colors on glossy stock

856 **Citrus Industry**
Southeast AgNet Publications

5053 NW Hwy 225-A
Ocala, FL 34482

352-671-1909; *Fax:* 888-943-2224;
www.citrusindustry.net

William Cooper, President
Robin Loftin, Vice President
Ernie Neff, Editor

News, facts and data of interest to citrus growers, processors and shippers.
Cost: $24.00
64 Pages
Frequency: 6 issues per year
Circulation: 9900
Founded in: 1920
Printed in 4 colors on glossy stock

857 **Cotton Farming**
One Grower Publishing, LLC
Collierville, TN 38117-5710

901-853-5067; *Fax:* 901-853-2197
lguthrie@onegrower.com;
www.cottonfarming.com
Social Media: Twitter, RSS, Flickr

Mike Rolfs, President
Lia Guthrie, Publisher
Tommy Horton, Editor
Carroll Smith, Senior Writer
Debbie Gibbs, Sales Manager

For commercial cotton growers across the United States Cotton Belt.
52 Pages
Frequency: Monthly
Circulation: 36300
Founded in: 1993
Printed in 4 colors on glossy stock

858 **Country Living**
Arens Publications
395 S High Street
Covington, OH 45318-0069

937-473-2028; *Fax:* 937-473-2500;
www.arenspub.com

Gary Godfrey, Owner
Connie Didier, Manager
Don Selanders, Sales Manager

Current news and features devoted to the agricultural industry.
Cost: $13.95
Frequency: Monthly
Circulation: 17000
Founded in: 1954

859 **Country Woman**
Reiman Publications
5400 S 60th St
Greendale, WI 53129-1404

414-423-0100
888-861-1264; *Fax:* 414-423-1143;
www.reimanpub.com
Social Media: Facebook, Twitter

Barbara Newton, President
Marylin Kruse, Editor
Lisa Karpinski, Director/Marketing
Reese Ludewig, Marketing Manager

Offers recipes, stories, profiles and articles pertaining to the country woman.
Cost: $14.98
68 Pages
Frequency: 6 issues in a year
Circulation: 50,000 +
Founded in: 1970

860 **Countryside and Small Stock Journal**
Countryside Publications
145 Industrial Dr
Medford, WI 54451-1711

715-785-7979
800-551-5691; *Fax:* 715-785-7414
customerservice@countrysidemag.com;
www.countrysidemag.com

Mike Campbell, Publisher
Anne-Marie Belanger, Managing Editor
Elen Grunseth, Circulation & Fulfillment

Offers information for homesteaders seeking a self-reliant lifestyle.
Cost: $18.00
132 Pages
Circulation: 115000
ISSN: 8750-7595
Founded in: 1917
Printed in on newsprint stock

861 **County Agents**
National Association of County Agricultural Agents
6584 W Duroc Road
Maroa, IL 61756

217-794-3700; *Fax:* 217-794-5901
exec-dir@nacaa.com; www.nacaa.com
Social Media: Facebook, Twitter

Paul Craig, President
Henry Dorough, President-elect
Mike Hogan, Vice President
Richard Fetcher, Secretary
Parman Green, Treasurer

Members receive professional improvement, news of association activities, shared education efforts from other states and reports from NACAA leadership and member states.
Cost: $10.00
Frequency: Quarterly
Circulation: 5000
Founded in: 1916
Mailing list available for rent: 3850 names at $125 per M
Printed in 4 colors on matte stock

862 **Cranberries Magazine**
Cranberries Magazine
PO Box 190
Rochester, MA 02770

508-763-8080; *Fax:* 508-763-4141
cranberries@comcast.net

Carolyn Gilmore, Editor/Publisher

Containing up-to-date news, technical articles, new product information, grower profiles, economic data and other related features regarding the cranberry industry. Accepts advertising.
Cost: $25.00
28 Pages
Frequency: Monthly
Circulation: 850
Founded in: 1936

863 **Crop Insurance Today**
National Crop Insurance Services
8900 Indian Creek Pkwy
Suite 600
Overland Park, KS 66210-1567

913-685-2767; *Fax:* 913-685-3080
webmaster@ag-risk.org; www.ag-risk.org

Thomas Zacharias, President

A quarterly magazine published by the National Crop Insurance Services. Includes current rate information, tips and advice, industry news, forecasts, and resources.
Cost: $13.00
Frequency: Quarterly
Circulation: 18000
Founded in: 1915
Printed in 4 colors on glossy stock

864 **Crop Science**
Crop Science Society of America
5585 Guilford Road
Madison, WI 53711-5801

608-273-8080; *Fax:* 608-273-2021
headquarters@crops.org; www.crops.org
Social Media: Facebook, Twitter, LinkedIn

Ellen Bergfeld, CEO
Wes Meixelsperger, CFO

Publishes original research in crop breeding and genetics, crop physiology and metabolism, crop ecology, production and management, and much more.
Founded in: 1955

865 **DVM Magazine**
Advanstar Communications
8033 Flint St
Lenexa, KS 66214-3335

913-492-4300
800-225-6864; *Fax:* 913-871-3808
dverdon@advanstar.com; www.dvm360.com
Social Media: Facebook, Twitter

Margaret Rampey, Editor
Marnette Falley, Principal
Sabrina Wilcox, COO
Dot Theisen, Sales Manager
Mindy Valcarcel, Senior Editor

The leading news in veterinary medicine covering news, features, practice management and new products and services.
Cost: $48.00
Frequency: Monthly
Circulation: 20000+
ISSN: 0012-7337
Founded in: 1992

866 **Dairy Herd Management**
Vance Publishing
400 Knightsbridge Parkway
Lincolnshire, IL 60069

847-634-2600; *Fax:* 847-634-4379
info@vancepublishing.com;
www.vancepublishing.com

Tom Quaife, Editor/Associate Publisher
Matthew Morgan, Director

Helps top dairy producers prepare for and adapt to the different management skills needed in this increasingly evolving industry
Cost: $60.00
Frequency: Monthly
Circulation: 61638

867 **Dairy Today**
Farm Journal
30 S 15th Street
Suite 900
Philadelphia, PA 19102-4803

215-578-8900
800-320-7992; www.farmjournal.com
Social Media: Facebook, Twitter, RSS, You Tube

Charlene Finck, Editor
Katie Humphreys, Managing Editor
Beth Snyder, Art Director
Sara Schafer, Business & Crops Online Editor

Award-winning editorial covers the broad spectrum of production, nutrition and marketing information. It serves dairy producers who milk 40+ cows or are members of the Dairy Herd Improvement Association.
Frequency: Monthly
Circulation: 125000
Founded in: 1989

868 **Dealer & Applicator**
Vance Publishing

400 Knightsbridge Pkwy
Lincolnshire, IL 60069-3628

847-634-2600; *Fax:* 847-634-4379;
www.vancepublishing.com

Peggy Walker, President
Dean Horowitz, VP eMedia & Marketing
Steve Reiss, VP Salon & Woodworking
William C. Vance, CEO
Shawn Etheridge, VP Produce & Raw Crop

Serves as the reader's business partner to provide full-service dealers and custom applicators with management and business strategies to increase profitability.
Founded in: 1937

869 **Drovers**
Vance Publishing
400 Knightsbridge Parkway
Lincolnshire, IL 60069

847-634-2600; *Fax:* 847-634-4379
info@vancepublishing.com;
www.vancepublishing.com

William C Vance, Chairman
Peggy Walker, President

Recognized as the beef industry leader for more than 130 years, valued for its management, production and marketing information.
Cost: $60.00
Frequency: Monthly
Circulation: 92000
Founded in: 1873

870 **Eastern DairyBusiness**
DairyBusiness Communications
6437 Collamer Road
East Syracuse, NY 13057-1031

315-703-7979
800-334-1904; *Fax:* 315-703-7988
kjentz@dairybusiness.com;
www.dairybusiness.com
Social Media: Facebook, Twitter, YouTube

Joel P Hastings, President
John Montandon, President & Co-CEO
Scott A Smith, Chairman / Co-CEO

Reports on milk production and prices, quotes on hay and feed markets, animal health and nutrition, and the newest innovations in dairying technology, specifically tailored to the Eastern parts of the United States
Cost: $49.95
67 Pages
Frequency: Monthly
Circulation: 14000
ISSN: 1528-4360
Founded in: 1904
Printed in 4 colors on glossy stock

871 **Egg Industry**
WATT Publishing Company
303 N Main Street
Suite 500
Rockford, IL 61101

815-966-5400; *Fax:* 815-966-6416
tokeefe@wattnet.net; www.wattnet.com

James Watt, Chairman
Greg Watt, President/CEO
Terrance O'Keefe, Content Director

Regarded as the standard for information on current issues, trends, production practices, processing, personalities and emerging technology. A pivotal source of news, data and information for decision-makers in the buying centers of companies producing eggs and further-processed products.
Cost: $36.00
Frequency: Monthly
Circulation: 2500

872 **Executive Guide to World Poultry Trends**
WATT Publishing Company
303 N Main Street
Suite 500
Rockford, IL 61101

815-966-5400; *Fax:* 815-966-6416;
www.wattnet.com

James Watt, Chairman/CEO
Greg Watt, President/COO
Jeff Swanson, Publishing Director

Offers detailed analysis on a country-by-country and market-by-market basis.

873 **FFA New Horizons**
National FFA Organization
6060 FFA Drive
P.O. Box 68960
Indianapolis, IN 46268

317-802-6060
800-772-0939; *Fax:* 317-802-6051
newhorizons@ffa.org;
www.ffanewhorizons.org
Social Media: Facebook, Twitter

Jessy Yancey, Association Editor
Christina Carden, Associate Production Director
Julie Woodard, FFA Publications Manager

The official member magazine of the FFA contains information about agricultural education, career possibilities, chapter and individual accomplishments and news on FFA. Now available online.
100 Pages
Frequency: Bi-Monthly
Circulation: 525000
ISSN: 1069-806x
Founded in: 1928
Printed in 4 colors

874 **FRONTIER**
Meat & Livestock Australia
1401 K Street NW
Suite 602
Washington, DC 20005

202-521-2551; *Fax:* 202-521-2699
info@mla.com.au; www.mla.com.au
Social Media: Facebook, Twitter, YouTube

Don Heatley, Chairman
David Palmer, Managing Director
Bernie Bindon, Director
Chris Hudson, Director

Offers northern beef producers practical information on how to best manage their cattle enterprise and improve on-property profits and sustainability.
30000 Members
Frequency: Quarterly
Founded in: 1998

875 **Farm Chemicals International**
Meister Media Worldwide
65 Germantown Ct.
Suite 202
Cordova, TN 38018

901-756-8822
800-572-7740;
www.farmchemicalsinternational.com
Social Media: Facebook, Twitter, RSS

William Miller II, President
Rosemary Gordon, Editor
Robert White, COO
Roger Hercl, CFO
Richard Meister, Director

Information on production, marketing and application of crop protection chemicals and fertilizers.
Circulation: 8000
Founded in: 1986

876 **Farm Equipment**
Cygnus Publishing
1233 Janesville Avenue
PO Box 803
Fort Atkinson, WI 53538-0803

920-000-1111
800-547-7377; *Fax:* 920-563-1699
editor@cpasn.com; www.cygnus.com

John French, Chief Executive Officer
Paul Bonaiuto, Chief Financial Officer
Kathy Scott, Director of Public Relations
Ed Wood, Vice President, Human Resources
Kris Flitcroft, Executive Vice President

An industry-wide information and product news curriculum for farm equipment dealers that enhances their knowledge of business management principles.
Cost: $48.00
Frequency: Monthly
Circulation: 10000
Founded in: 1937
Printed in 4 colors on glossy stock

877 **Farm Equipment Guide**
Heartland Communications
1003 Central Avenue
PO Box 1115
Fort Dodge, IA 50501-1115

515-955-1600
800-247-2000; *Fax:* 515-574-2182
dustin@agdeal.com; www.farmershotline.com
Social Media: Facebook, Twitter

Sandra J Simonson, Group Publisher
Tracy Roper, Production Manager
Tammy Sweeney, Operational Manager
Dustin Hector, Sales Manager
Chet Frahm, Advertising Sales Associate

A subscription that includes an annual blue book of specifications, serial numbers and average pricing on farm machinery with monthly updates that list thousands of pieces for sale and thousands of actual auction values.
120 Pages
Frequency: Monthly
Circulation: 20,000
ISSN: 1047-725X
Founded in: 1981
Printed in 4 colors on glossy stock

878 **Farm Impact**
314 E Church Street
Mascoutah, IL 62258-2100

618-566-8282; *Fax:* 618-566-8283

Greg Hoskins, Publisher
Michael King, Advertising Manager

Offers information to farmers.
Frequency: Monthly

879 **Farm Journal**
30 S 15th Street
Suite 900
Philadelphia, PA 19102-4803

215-557-8900
800-523-1538; *Fax:* 215-568-4436
scuster@farmjournal.com;
www.farmjournalmedia.com

Andrew J Weber Jr, CEO/President
Crain Freiberg, Editor
Steve Custer, President/Publishing
Chuck Roth, Senior Vice President/Project Dev

Published for operators and owners of commercial farms and ranches. Provides timely, useful marketing and management information to help them produce more efficiently, buy more wisely, sell their products at the highest possible prices, and retain as much of their income as possible.
Cost: $24.75
182 Pages
Frequency: Monthly
Circulation: 440,000
Founded in: 1878

880 Farm Reporter
Meridian Star
814 22nd Avenue
PO Box 1591
Meridian, MS 39302
601-693-1551; *Fax:* 601-485-1210;
www.meridianstar.com
Social Media: Facebook, Twitter
Michael Stewart, Executive Editor
Steve Gillespie, Assistant Editor
Ida Brown, Staff Writer
Briand Livingston, Staff Writer
Otha Barham, Outdoors Page
Reports on every phase of farming including timber, cattle, poultry and all growing crops.
Cost: $2.00
Frequency: Monthly

881 Farm Review
Lewis Publishing Company
PO Box 153
Lynden, WA 98264-0153
360-354-4444; *Fax:* 360-354-4445;
www.lyndentribune.com
Michael D Lewis, Publisher
Calvin Bratt, Editor
Diane Partlow, Circulation Manager
Offers a review of farming techniques and trends nationwide.
Cost: $30.00
Frequency: Quarterly
Circulation: 7000
Founded in: 1888

882 Farm Show Magazine
Farm Show Publishing
Johnson Building
PO Box 1029
Lakeville, MN 55044-1029
952-469-5572
800-834-9665; *Fax:* 952-469-5579;
www.farmshow.com/
Social Media: Facebook
Mark Newhall, Editor/Publisher
Bill Gergen, Associate Editor
Focuses on latest agricultural products, and product evaluation. Contains no advertising.
Cost: $17.95
Founded in: 1977

883 Farm Talk
Farm Talk
1801 S Highway 59
PO Box 601
Parsons, KS 67357-4900
620-421-9450
800-356-8255; *Fax:* 620-421-9473
farmtalk@terraworld.net;
www.farmtalknewspaper.com
Mark Parker, Publisher
Ted Gum, Manager
Agriculture for Eastern Kansas, Western Missouri, Northeast Oklahoma and Northwest Arkansas.
Cost: $30.00
60 Pages
Frequency: Weekly
Circulation: 10000
Founded in: 1974

884 Farm World (Farm Week)
Mayhill Publications
27 N Jefferson Street
PO Box 90
Knightstown, IN 46148-1242
317-326-2235
800-876-5133; *Fax:* 765-345-3398;
www.mayhill-publications.com/
Dave Blower Jr, Editor
Richard Lewis, Publisher
Diana Scott, Marketing Manager
Agriculture, farming, and related areas in Indiana, Ohio and Kentucky. Accepts advertising.
Cost: $28.50
84 Pages
Frequency: Monthly

885 Farm and Dairy
Lyle Printing and Publishing Company
185 E State Street
PO Box 38
Salem, OH 44460
330-337-3419
800-837-3419; *Fax:* 330-337-9550
farmanddairy@aol.com;
www.farmanddairy.com
Scot Darling, Chief Executive Officer, Publisher
Susan Crowell, Editor
Billy Sekely, Advertising Manager
Howard Marsh, Circulation Manager
Briefs of research reports from experiment stations in agriculture, success stories concerning farmers of Ohio, Pennsylvania and West Virginia, sale and livestock market reports, auctions and more. Accepts advertising.
Cost: $ 28.00
132 Pages
Circulation: 33500
ISSN: 0014-7826
Founded in: 1914
Printed in 4 colors on n stock

886 Farm and Ranch Living
Reiman Publications
5400 S 60th St
Greendale, WI 53129-1404
414-423-0100
888-858-5417; *Fax:* 414-423-1143
editors@farmandranchliving.com;
www.reimanpub.com
Barbara Newton, President
Catherine Cassidy, SVP/Editor-in-Chief
Ann Kaiser, Editor
Lisa Karpinski, Marketing & Circulation Manager
Gretchen Trautman, Membership Director
Includes stories written by working farm families, antique tractor events and rural photo contests.
Cost: $3.99
68 Pages
Frequency: Bimonthly
Founded in: 1978

887 FarmWorld
DMG World Media
27 N Jefferson Street
PO Box 90
Knightstown, IN 46148-1242
765-345-5133
800-876-5133; *Fax:* 765-345-5133
webmaster@farmworldonline.com;
www.farmworldonline.com
Tony Gregory, Publisher
David Blower Jr, Editor
Meggie Foster, Assistant Editor
Toni Hodson, Advertising Manager
Agriculture, farming, and related areas in Indiana, Ohio and Kentucky. Accepts advertising.
Cost: $38.95
84 Pages
Frequency: Weekly
Founded in: 1955
Printed in 4 colors on newsprint stock

888 Farmers Digest
Heartland Communications
1003 Central Avenue
PO Box 1115
Fort Dodge, IA 50501-1115
515-955-1600
800-247-2000; *Fax:* 515-574-2182;
www.agdeal.com
Sandra J Simonsoa, Group Publisher
Melanie Filloon, Subscription Coordinator
Straightforwarded, commonsense articles on every aspect of farming and ranching edited with one goal in mind - to make you a better farmer or rancher.
Founded in: 1941

889 Farmers Hot Line
Heartland Communications
1003 Central Avenue
Fort Dodge, IA 50501-1052
515-955-1600
800-247-2000; *Fax:* 515-955-1668
dustin@agdeal.com; www.agdeal.com
Social Media: Facebook, Twitter
Gale W McKinney II, President/CFO
Mary Gonnerman, Vice President
Sandy Simonson, Publisher
Dustin Hector, Sales Manager
Chet Frahm, Advertising Sales Associate
Distributed to manufacturers, farmers, auctioneers and service companies nationwide. Designed to help buyers and sellers of new and used farm machinery, auctions, farm real estate, services and supplies.
Cost: $9.95
Circulation: 50000
Founded in: 1988

890 Farmers' Advance
Camden Publications
331 E Bell Street
PO Box 130
Camden, MI 49232
517-368-0365
800-222-6336; *Fax:* 517-368-5131;
www.farmersadvance.com/
Social Media: Facebook
Don Lee, Circulation Manager
Richard Aginian, President
Ken Ungar, Senior Vice President
Kyle Hupfer, Director
Farming technology magazine.
Cost: $25.00
Frequency: Weekly
Circulation: 20000
Founded in: 1898

891 Farmers' Exchange
Exchange
PO Box 490
Fayetteville, TN 37334
931-433-9737; *Fax:* 931-433-0053
exchange@vallnet.com; www.fexonline.com
William Thomas, Publisher/Editor/CEO
Jim Bowers, Sales/Marketing Manager
Magazine offers a forum for the exchange of farming ideas and information country-wide.
56 Pages
Frequency: Monthly
Circulation: 30000
Founded in: 1987

892 Farmshine
Dieter Krieg

State and Main Streets
PO Box 219
Brownstown, PA 17508

717-656-8050
866-724-6455; *Fax:* 717-656-8188;
www.farmshine.com

Dieter Krieg, Publisher/Editor
Tammy Krieg, Ad Sales

Information pertaining to the farming community.
Cost: $12.00
Frequency: Weekly
ISSN: 0745-7553
Founded in: 1979
Printed in on newsprint stock

893 **Fastline Catalog**
Fastline Publications
4900 Fox Run Road
P.O. Box 248
Buckner, KY 40010

502-222-0146
800-626-6409; *Fax:* 502-222-0615;
www.fastline.com
Social Media: Facebook, Twitter, YouTube, Flickr

William G Howard, President/Editor
Susan Arterburn, Marketing Director
Pat Higgins, Vice President, Sales

Nationwide and regional picture buying guides for the farming industry.
Frequency: Monthly
Founded in: 1978

894 **Feed & Grain**
Cygnus Business Media
1233 Janesville Ave
Fort Atkinson, WI 53538

631-845-2700
800-547-7377
info@cygnus.com; www.cygnusb2b.com

John French, CEO
Paul Bonaiuto, CFO
Edward Wood, Vice President, HR & Communications

Provides techniques and solutions on ways yo increase productivity and profitability for the commercial feed, grain and allied processing industry.
Frequency: Bi-Monthly
Circulation: 16,500

895 **Feed Additive Compendium**
The Miller Publishing Company
5810 W 78th St
Suite 200
Bloomington, MN 55439

952-931-0211; *Fax:* 952-938-1832
smuirhead@feedstuffs.com;
www.feedstuffs.com

Sarah Muirhead, Publisher
Rod Smith, Staff Editor/Livestock & Poultry
Sally Schuff, Staff Editor/Washington Bureau
Jacqui Fatka, Staff Editor/Grains & Ingredients
Kristin Baker, Editorial Production Manager

This magazine takes a closer look at the food additives and agriculture industries.
Cost: $260.00
Frequency: Weekly
Founded in: 1935

896 **Feed International**
WATT Publishing Company
303 N Main Street
Suite 500
Rockford, IL 61101

815-966-5400; *Fax:* 815-966-6416
kjennison@wattnet.net; www.wattnet.com

James Watt, Chairman/CEO
Greg Watt, President/COO
Ken Jennison, Editor

Provides feed formulators and manufacturers outside North America with the latest feed and grain market developments, management strategies, and information on nutrition and regulations to efficiently and safely formulate, process and market animal feeds and become more competitive in the world market.
Cost: $48.00
Frequency: Monthly
Circulation: 19191
ISSN: 9274-5771
Founded in: 1980
Mailing list available for rent: 19,191 names at $225 per M
Printed in 4 colors

897 **Feed Management**
WATT Publishing Company
303 N Main Street
Suite 500
Rockford, IL 61101
815-966-5400; *Fax:* 815-966-6416;
www.wattnet.com

Jim Watt, Chairman/CEO
Greg Watt, President/COO
Ken Jennison, Editor

Covers the latest news in feed production, nutritional developments and trends, food safety and regulatory developments, grain markets, management strategies and new products.
Cost: $48.00
Circulation: 20,250
ISSN: 0014-956X
Founded in: 1950
Mailing list available for rent: 20,249 names at $155 per M
Printed in 4 colors on glossy stock

898 **Flue Cured Tobacco Farmer**
Tabacco Farmer.Com
3101 Poplarwood Court
Suite 115
Raleigh, NC 27604

91- 8-2 47; *Fax:* 919-876-6531
publisher@tobaccofarmer.com;
www.tobaccofarmer.com

Dayton Matlick, Chairman
Taco Tuinstra, Editor in Chief
Noel Morris, Publisher

Business of farming publication for commercial tobacco producers. Feature articles deal with the research-backed production, harvesting and marketing aspects of the flue cured tobacco.
Cost: $25.00
Circulation: 14000
ISSN: 0015-4512
Founded in: 1964
Printed in 4 colors on glossy stock

899 **Food Aid Needs Assessment**
US Department of Agriculture
1400 Independence Avenue SW
Washington, DC 20250

202-690-7650
800-999-6779; *Fax:* 202-720-2030;
www.usda.gov
Social Media: Facebook, Twitter, LinkedIn, YouTube, Flickr

Gene Mathia, Branch Chief

This annual report assesses the food situation in 60 developing countries. Most of the data are presented by region; crisis countries are covered individually.
Cost: $30.00
Founded in: 1862

900 **Forest Science**
5400 Grosvenor Ln
Bethesda, MD 20814-2198

301-897-8720
866-897-8720; *Fax:* 301-897-3690
safweb@podi.com; www.safnet.org
Social Media: Facebook, Twitter, LinkedIn

Michael T Goergen Jr, Executive VP/CFO
Brittany Brumby, Assistant to the CEO/Council
Amy Ziadi, Information Technology Manager
Larry D Burner CPA, Sr. Director Finance

Provides access to information and networking opportunities to prepare members for the challenges and the changes that face natural resource professionals.
Founded in: 1900

901 **Fresh Cut Magazine**
Great American Publishing
75 Applewood Drive, Suite A
PO Box 128
Sparta, MI 49345

616-887-9008; *Fax:* 616-887-2666
fcedit@freshcut.com; www.freshcut.com

Matt McCallum, Publisher
Kimberly Baker, Director of Media Services
Beecky Bosserd, Circulation Manager
Lee Dean, Editorial Director

Covers all sectors of the international value-added produce industry. Features industry profiles, research reports, governmental legislation coverage, industry columnists, news reports, new equipment showcases and much more.
Cost: $15.00
40 Pages
Frequency: Monthly
ISSN: 1072-2831
Founded in: 1993
Printed in 4 colors on glossy stock

902 **Fresh Digest**
Fresh Produce & Floral Council
16700 Valley View Ave
Suite 130
La Mirada, CA 90638-5844

714-739-0177; *Fax:* 714-739-0226
info@fpfc.org; www.fpfc.org

Carissa Mace, President
Pauleen Yoshikane, Director of Operations

Addresses issues concerning the Western US, with heavy emphasis on the important California market, read by thousands of professionals in the produce and floral industries.
600+ Members
Founded in: 1965

903 **Fruit Country**
Clintron Publishing
PO Box 547
Yakima, WA 98907-0547

509-248-2452
800-869-7923; *Fax:* 509-248-4056

Clintke Withers, Publisher
John M Dahlin, Editor

Written for and about growers, their operations and their needs. Stories on growers and shippers, developments and trends in the fruit industry, human interest stories and politics, new products, chemicals and supplies, avant garde management techniques, cultural practices and tips on profitability. Advertising equipment and services to the fruit industry and distribution system.
Cost: $12.00
Frequency: Monthly
Circulation: 11,500

904 **Futures Magazine**
Futures Magazine
111 W Jackson Blvd
7th Floor
Chicago, IL 60604-4139

312-977-0999; *Fax:* 312-846-4638;
www.aip.com

Steve Lown, Manager
James T Holter, Editor

Agriculture commodities charted by various technical studies, plus analysis.
Cost: $39.00
24 Pages
Frequency: Monthly
Founded in: 1972

905 **Game Bird Breeders, Agiculturists, Zoologists and Conservationists**
Game Bird Breeders
1155 W 4700 S
Salt Lake City, UT 84123
George Allen, Editor

Articles on how to keep and breed all types of game birds.
Cost: $18.00
45 Pages
Frequency: Monthly
Founded in: 1974

906 **Glimpsing Kentucky's Forgotten Heroes: Profiles & Lessons from an American**
Agribusiness Council
PO Box 5565
Washington, DC 20016

202-296-4563; *Fax:* 202-887-9178
info@agribusinesscouncil.org;
www.agribusinesscouncil.org
Cost: $10.00

907 **Grape Grower**
Western Agricultural Publishing Company
4969 E Clinton Way
Suite 104
Fresno, CA 93727

559-252-7000; *Fax:* 559-252-7387
westag@psnw.com; www.westagpubco.com

Paul Baltimore, Co Publisher
Jim Baltimore, Co Publisher
Randy Bailey, Editor
Robert Fujimoto, Assistant Editor

The West's most widely read authority on the cultivation of table grapes, raising grapes and wine grapes. All aspects of production are covered with the most current university, government and private research.

908 **Greenhouse Grower**
Meister Media Worldwide
37733 Euclid Ave
Willoughby, OH 44094-5992

440-942-2000
800-572-7740; *Fax:* 440-975-3447;
www.meistermedia.com

Gary Fitzgerald, President
Rick T Melnick, Corporate Editorial Director

Industry-leading voice for the commercial floriculture industry in the United States. Compiles buyers' directories and annual reports on the largest growers in the nation, produces vibrant emedia products and manages industry-leading events and awards programs.
Frequency: Monthly
Circulation: 20000
Founded in: 1932

909 **Grower**
Vance Publishing
400 Knightsbridge Parkway
Lincolnshire, IL 60069

847-634-2600; *Fax:* 847-634-4379
info@vancepublishing.com;
www.vancepublishing.com

William C Vance, Chairman
Peggy Walker, President

Positioned as the key source of profitable production and management strategies to commercial producers who control 90% of the U.S. fruit and vegetable market.
Cost: $45.00
Frequency: Monthly
Circulation: 22,000
Founded in: 1937

910 **Growertalks Magazine**
Ball Publishing
622 Town Road
PO Box 1660
West Chicago, IL 60186

630-231-3675
888-888-0013; *Fax:* 630-231-5254
info@ballpublishing.com;
www.growertalks.com

Chris Beytes, Editor/Publisher
Jennifer Zurko, Managing Editor

Specializes in the publishing of horticulture information, primarily related to floriculture production and marketing.
Frequency: Monthly
Circulation: 12000
Founded in: 1937

911 **Guernsey Breeders' Journal**
Purebred Publishing Inc
1224 Alton Darby Creeek Road
Suite G
Columbus, OH 43228

614-864-2409; *Fax:* 614-864-5614
info@usguernsey.com; www.usguernsey.com

Seth Johnson, Executive Secretary-Treasurer
Brian Schnebly, Programs Coordinator
Katie Hensen, Editor
Ashley Shaffer, Assistant Editor

The journal discusses breeder stories, management trends and events in the Guernsey industry.
Frequency: 10x Yearly

912 **Gulf Coast Cattleman**
EC Larkin
11201 Morning Ct
San Antonio, TX 78213-1300

21- 3-4 77; *Fax:* 210-344-4258
info@gulfcoastcattleman.com;
www.gulfcoastcattleman.com

E C Larkin Jr, President
Joan Dover, Circulation
M'Lys Lloyd, Managing Editor

Services commercial cattlemen along the Gulf Coast states with industry news, management and herd health related articles.
Cost: $15.00
64 Pages
Frequency: Monthly
Circulation: 16000
ISSN: 0017-5552
Founded in: 1935
Printed in 4 colors on glossy stock

913 **Hereford World**
American Hereford Association
PO Box 014059
Kansas City, MO 64101

81- 8-2 37; *Fax:* 816-842-6931
aha@hereford.org; www.hereford.org

Craig Huffhines, Executive VP
Mary Ellen Hummel, Executive Assistant

Trade magazine for breeders of registered Polled Hereford cattle.
Frequency: Monthly
Circulation: 9500
Founded in: 1742

914 **High Country News**
High Country Foundation
119 Grand Avenue
P.O. Box 1090
Paonia, CO 81428

970-527-4898
800-905-1155; *Fax:* 970-527-4897
circulation@hcn.org; www.hcn.org
Social Media: Facebook, Twitter, LinkedIn, YouTube, Instagram, Google+

Paul Larmer, Executive Director/Publisher
Brian Calvert, Managing Editor
Gretchen King, Director, Engagement
Laurie Milford, Director, Development

High Country News is the nation's leading source of reporting on the American West. Its mission is to inform and inspire people - through in-depth jurnalism - to act on behalf of the West's diverse natural and human communities.
32000 Members
Founded in: 1970
Mailing list available for rent: 53,000 names

915 **High Plains Journal/Midwest Ag Journal**
High Plains Publishing Company
1500 E Wyatt Earp Boulevard
PO Box 760
Dodge City, KS 67801

620-227-1834
800-452-7171; *Fax:* 620-227-7173
journal@hpj.com; www.hpj.com

Tom Tayor, Publisher/CEO
Holly Martin, Editor
John Seatvet, Sales Manager
Sarah Farlee, Marketing Director

Farming news for the central states.
Cost: $46.00
Frequency: Weekly
Circulation: 50000
Printed in 4 colors on glossy stock

916 **Hog Producer**
Farm Progress
6200 Aurora Avenue
Suite 609 E
Urbandale, IA 50322-2838

515-278-6693; *Fax:* 515-278-7797
jotte@farmprogress.com;
www.farmprogress.com

Sara Wyant, Publisher
John Otte, Editor

Management publication to help pork producers in the production, housing, genetics, health care and marketing of hogs.

917 **Holstein Pulse**
Holstein Association USA
PO Box 808
Brattleboro, VT 05302-0808

802-254-4551
800-965-5200; *Fax:* 802-254-8251
info@holstein.com; www.holsteinusa.com

John Meyer, CEO
Lisa Perrin, Marketing
Frequency: Quarterly
Circulation: 19000

918 **Holstein World**
Dairy Business Communications

6437 Collamer Road
East Syracuse, NY 13057

315-703-7979
800-334-1904; *Fax:* 315-703-7988;
www.holsteinworld.com

Joel P Hastings, Publisher/Editor
Janice Barrett, Associate Editor

Showcases breeders who own America's genetically superior cattle. Elite group of progressive dairymen who have income, herd size, and milk production considerably above the national averages.
Cost: $38.95
123 Pages
Frequency: Monthly
Circulation: 12000
ISSN: 0199-4239
Founded in: 1904
Printed in 4 colors on glossy stock

919 **HortScience**
American Society for Horticultural Science
1018 Duke Street
Alexandria, VA 22314-2851

703-836-4606; *Fax:* 703-836-2024
webmaster@ashs.org; www.ashs.org

Michael Neff, Executive Director

HortScience is a monthly journal concentrating on significant research, education, extension findings, and methods.
Cost: $85.00
160 Pages
Frequency: Monthly
Circulation: 2500
ISSN: 0018-5345
Founded in: 1903
Mailing list available for rent: 2500 names at $100 per M

920 **IMPACT Magazine**
Agricultural Communicators of Tomorrow
P.O. Box 110180
Gainesville, FL 32611-0180

352-392-1971; *Fax:* 352-392-9589;
www.ifas.ufl.edu
Social Media: Facebook, Twitter

Jack Payne, Senior Vice President

Features news about the statewide teaching, research and extension programs of the University of Florida's Institute of Food and Agricultural Sciences.
Founded in: 1970

921 **Implement & Tractor**
Farm Journal Media
1818 Market Street
31st Floor
Philadelphia, PA 19103-3654

215-578-8900
800-331-9310; *Fax:* 215-568-6782
jstruyk@farmjournal.com;
www.agweb.com/machinery/implement_tractor.aspx

Andy Weber, Chief Executive Officer
Steve Custer, Executive Vice President
Jeff Pence, President, Electronic Media
Chuck Roth, Senior Vice President

Implement & Tractor is a bimonthly publication providing news and insights for dealers, distributors, OEMs, engineers and the associations that make up the more than $40 billion dealer and wholesaler equipment industry.
Frequency: Bimonthly
Founded in: 1885

922 **International Journal of Vegetable Science**
Taylor & Francis Group LLC
325 Chestnut St
Suite 800
Philadelphia, PA 19106-2614

215-625-8900
800-354-1420; *Fax:* 215-625-2940
haworthorders@taylorandfrancis.com;
www.taylorandfrancis.com

Vincent M. Russo, Editor

Features innovative articles on all aspects of vegetable production, including growth regulation, pest management, sustainable production, harvesting, handling, storage, shipping and final consumption.
Frequency: Quarterly

923 **International Poultry Exposition Guide**
WATT Publishing Company
122 S Wesley Ave
Mt Morris, IL 61054-1451

815-734-7937; *Fax:* 815-734-4201
olentine@wattmm.com; www.wattnet.com

Jim Watt, Chairman/CEO
Lisa Thornton, Managing Editor
Clay Schreiber, Publisher

924 **Invasive Plant Science and Management Journal**
P.O.Box 7065
Lawrence, KS 66044-7065

785-429-9622
800-627-0326; *Fax:* 785-843-1274
wssa@allenpress.com; www.wssa.net

Dale Shaner, President
Jeff Derr, VP
Tom Mueller, Secretary
Dave Gealy, Treasurer
Michael Foley, Director Publications

Promotes research, education and extension outreach activities related to weeds, provides science-based information to the public and policy makers; and fosters awarenes of weeds and their impacts on managed and natural ecosystems.
2000 Members
Founded in: 1956

925 **Jojoba Happenings**
John S Turner Public Relations
805 N 4th Avenue
Unit 404
Phoenix, AZ 85003-1304

Fax: 602-252-5722

John Turner, Publisher
Ken Lucas, Editor

Jojoba farming. Accepts advertising.
8 Pages
Frequency: Bi-Monthly

926 **Journal of Agricultural & Food Chemistry**
American Chemical Society
1155 16th St NW
Washington, DC 20036-4892

202-872-4600
800-227-9919; *Fax:* 202-872-4615;
www.pubs.acs.org

Madeleine Jacobs, CEO
John W Finley, Associate Editor
Elizabeth Waters, Associate Editor

Research results in pesticides, fertilizers, agricultural and food processing chemistry.
Cost: $146.00
Frequency: Monthly
Circulation: 159000
Founded in: 1856

927 **Journal of Animal Science (JAS)**
PO Box 7410
Champaign, IL 61826

217-356-9050; *Fax:* 217-398-4119;
www.asas.org
Social Media: Facebook, Twitter, RSS

Meghan Wulster-Radcli, CEO
Jacelyn Hemmelgarn, COO

Premier journal for animal science and serves as the leading source of new knowledge and perspective in this area. JAS consistently ranks as on of the top journals in the category of Agriculture, Dairy, and Animal Sciences.
Frequency: Monthly
ISSN: 0021-8812
Founded in: 1908

928 **Journal of Applied Communications**
Association for Communications Excellence
University of Florida
407 Rolfs Hall
Gainesville, FL 32611-0540

352-273-2094; *Fax:* 352-392-8583
rwtelg@ufl.edu; www.aceweb.org

Holly Young, Interim Executive Director
Faith Peppers, President
Joanne Littlefield, Vice President

A referred journal offering professional development for educational communicators who emphasize agriculture, natural resources, and life and human sciences.
Frequency: Quarterly
ISSN: 1051-0834

929 **Journal of Applied Communications (JAC)**
ACE
448 Agricultural Hall
Stillwater, OK 74078

40- 7-4 04
866-941-3048;
www.journalofappliedcommunications.org

Dwayne Cartmell, Executive Editor
Ricky Telg, Editorial Board Chair

The Journal of Applied Communications is a refereed journal offering professional development for educational communicators who emphasize agriculture, natural resources, and life and human sciences.
Frequency: Quarterly
Founded in: 1970

930 **Journal of Aquatic Plant Management**
PO Box 821265
Vicksburg, MS 39182-1265

Fax: 601-634-5502
webmaster@apms.org; www.apms.org
Social Media: Facebook, LinkedIn

Terry Goldsby, President
Cody Gray, VP
Sherry Whitaker, Treasurer
Jeff Schardt, Secretary
Robert J. Richardson, Editor

A publication of the Aquatic Plant Management Society, Inc.
Founded in: 1961

931 **Journal of Biomolecular Screening**
36 Tamarack Ave
Suite 348
Danbury, CT 06811

203-778-8828; *Fax:* 203-748-7557
email@aol.com; www.sbsonline.org

Jeff Paslay, President
Michelle Palmer, Executive Director
Christine Giordano, Executive Director

The leading peer-reviewed journal focusing on drug-discovery sciences. Delivers the latest ad-

vancements in quantitative biomolecular sciences.
Cost: $175.00
Frequency: 10x/Year

932 **Journal of Dairy Science**
American Dairy Science Association
2441 Village Green Pl
Champaign, IL 61822-7676

217-356-5146; *Fax:* 217-398-4119
adsa@assochq.org; www.adsa.org

Donald C Beitz, President
Philld C Tongz, VP
Peter Studney, Executive Director
William R Aimutis, Treasurer

Official Journal of the American Dairy Science Association
3000 Members
Founded in: 1898
Mailing list available for rent

933 **Journal of Environmental Quality**
5585 Guilford Road
Madison, WI 53711-1086

608-273-8080; *Fax:* 608-273-2021
headquarters@agronomy.org;
www.agronomy.org
Social Media: Facebook, Twitter, LinkedIn

Ken Barbarick, President
Sharon Clay, President Elect
Ellen Bergfeld, CEO

Published by ASA, CSSA, and SSSA. Papers are grouped by subject matter and cover water, soil, and atmospheric research as it relates to agriculture and the environment.
11000 Members
Founded in: 1907

934 **Journal of Forestry**
Society of American Foresters
5400 Grosvenor Ln
Bethesda, MD 20814-2198

301-897-8720
866-897-8720; *Fax:* 301-897-3690
safweb@podi.com; www.safnet.org
Social Media: Facebook, Twitter, LinkedIn

Michael T Goergen Jr, Executive VP/CEO
Matthew Walls, Publications Dir./Managing Editor

To advance the profession of forestry by keeping professionals informed about significant developments and ideas in the many facets of forestry: economics, education and communication, entomology and pathology, fire, forest ecology, geospatial technologies, history, international forestry, measurements, policy, recreation, silviculture, social sciences, soils and hydrology, urband and community forestry, utilization and engineering, and wildlife management.
Cost: $85.00
Frequency: 8x Yearly
ISSN: 0022-1201
Founded in: 1902

935 **Journal of Natural Resources & Life Sciences Education**
5585 Guilford Road
Madison, WI 53711-1086

608-273-8080; *Fax:* 608-273-2021
headquarters@agronomy.org;
www.agronomy.org
Social Media: Facebook, Twitter, LinkedIn

Ellen E Bergfeld, CEO
Wes Meixelsperger, CFO
Alexander Barton, Director of Business Development
Lisa Al-Moodi, Managing Editor

Today's educators look here for the latest teaching ideas in the life sciences, natural resources, and agriculture.
11000 Members
Founded in: 1907

936 **Journal of Plant Registrations**
Crop Science Society of America
5585 Guilford Road
Madison, WI 53711-5801

608-273-8080; *Fax:* 608-273-2021
headquarters@crops.org; www.crops.org
Social Media: Facebook, Twitter, LinkedIn

Maria Gallo, President
Jeffrey Volenec, President-elect

Publishes cultivar, germplasm, parental line, genetic stock, and mapping population registration manuscripts.
4700 Members
Founded in: 1955

937 **Journal of Soil and Water Conservation**
Soil and Water Conservation Society
945 SW Ankeny Rd
Ankeny, IA 50021

515-289-2331
800-843-7645; *Fax:* 515-289-1227
pubs@swcs.org; www.swcs.org

Oksana Gieseman, Editor
Jorge Delgado, Research Editor
Jim Gulliford, Executive Director
Annie Binder, Director Of Publications

The JSWC is a multidisciplinary journal of natural resource conservation research, practice, policy, and perspectives. The journal has two sections: the A Section containing various departments and features and the Research Section containing peer-reviewed research papers.
Cost: $99.00
Frequency: 6x Yearly
Circulation: 2000
ISSN: 0022-4561
Founded in: 1945

938 **Journal of Sustainable Agriculture**
Taylor & Francis Group LLC
325 Chestnut St
Suite 800
Philadelphia, PA 19106-2614

215-625-8900
800-354-1420; *Fax:* 215-625-2940;
www.taylorandfrancis.com

Stephen R. Gliessman, Editor

Focuses on new and unique systems in which resource usage and environmental protection are kept in balance with the needs of productivity, profits, and incentives that are necessary for the agricultural marketplace. It increases professional and public awareness and gains support for these necessary changes in our agricultural industry.
Frequency: 8x Yearly

939 **Journal of Vegetable Science**
Taylor & Francis Group LLC
825 Chestnut Street
Suite 800
Philadelphia, PA 19106

215-625-8900
800-354-1420; *Fax:* 215-625-2940;
www.haworthpress.com

Vincent M Russo PhD, Editor

Features innovative articles on all aspects of vegetable production, including growth regulation, pest management, sustainable production, harvesting, handling, storage, shipping and final consumption.
Frequency: Quarterly
ISSN: 1931-5260

940 **Journal of the American Society of Farm Managers and Rural Appraisers**
950 S Cherry St
Suite 508
Denver, CO 80246-2664

303-758-3513; *Fax:* 303-758-0190
nhardiman@agri-associations.org;
www.asfmra.org
Social Media: Facebook, Twitter, LinkedIn

Nancy Hardiman, Director Education
Brian Stockman, Executive VP
Debe L Alvarez, Manager Education/Faculty

Provides the most up-to-date studies, research, practices, and methodologies proposed by the leading academic, management, appraisal and consulting members of our professions.
2300 Members
Founded in: 1929
Mailing list available for rent

941 **Land**
Free Press Company
418 S 2nd Street
PO Box 3169
Mankato, MN 56001

507-344-6395
800-657-4665; www.the-land.com

Kevin Schulz, Editor
Lynnae Schrader, Assistant Editor
Kim Henrickson, Advertising Manager
Ken Lingen, Manager

Agricultural news
Cost: $20.00
48 Pages
Frequency: Weekly
Circulation: 40000
ISSN: 0279-1633
Founded in: 1976
Printed in 4 colors on newsprint stock

942 **Landscape Management**
Advanstar Communications
7500 Old Oak Blvd
Cleveland, OH 44130-3343

440-243-8100
800-225-4569; *Fax:* 440-891-2740;
www.ubmamericas.com

Ron Hall, Editor-in-Chief
Jason Stahl, Managing Editor

Covers news, market trends, business and operations management, technical information on horticulture and agronomy for professional landscape contractors, lawncare operators and in-house grounds managers.
Cost: $3.83
Circulation: 60014
Founded in: 1962
Printed in 4 colors on glossy stock

943 **Meat Science Journal**
American Meat Science Association
2441 Village Green Pl
Champaign, IL 61822-7676

217-356-5368
800-517-AMSA; *Fax:* 888-205-5834; *Fax:* 217-356-5370
information@meatscience.org;
www.meatscience.org

Thomas Powell, Executive Director

The official journal of AMSA. Peer-reviewed resource is the best way to stay current on the latest research in meat science across all meat products and in all aspects of meat production and processing.

944 **MidAmerican Farmer Grower**
MidAmerica Farm Publications

19 N Main Street
PO Box 323
Perryville, MO 63775

573-547-2244
877-486-6997; *Fax:* 573-547-5663
publisher@mafg.net; www.mafg.net

John M LaRose, CEO/Publisher
Barbara Galeski, Editor
Jack Thompson II, Marketing

Offers farming news for the middle states.
Cost: $19.00
Frequency: Weekly

945 **Midwest DairyBusiness**
DairyBusiness Communications
6437 Collamer Road
East Syracuse, NY 13057-1031

315-703-7979; *Fax:* 315-703-7988;
www.dairybusiness.com/midwest

Dave Natzke, Editorial Director
Joel P Hastings, Publisher
JoDee Sattler, Associate Editor
Tom Vilsack, Secretary

Business resource for successful milk producers. Only business-oriented dairy publication exclusively for the large herd, Midwest milk producer.
Cost: $45.00
43 Pages
Frequency: Monthly
Circulation: 27500
ISSN: 1087-7096
Founded in: 1904
Printed in 4 colors on glossy stock

946 **Milling Journal**
3065 Pershing Court
Decatur, IL 62526

217-877-9660
800-728-7511; *Fax:* 217-877-6647
webmaster@grainnet.com; www.grainnet.com

Mark Avery, Publisher
Arvin Donley, Editor
Jody Sexton, Production Manager

Mailed to all active AOM members in the US, Canada, and internationally, including wheat flour/corn mills and corn/oilseed processors in US and Canada.
Frequency: Quarterly
Circulation: 1224

947 **Mushroom News**
American Mushroom Institute
1284 Gap Newport Pike
Suite 2
Avondale, PA 19311-9503

610-268-7483; *Fax:* 610-268-8015
ami@mwmlaw.com;
www.americanmushroom.org

For growers and scientists in the mushroom production.
Cost: $275.00
Frequency: Monthly
Founded in: 1955

948 **NWAC News: National Warmwater Aquaculture Center**
127 Experiment Station Road
PO Box 197
Stoneville, MS 38776

662-686-3302; *Fax:* 662-686-3568
sharris@drec.msstate.edu;
www.msstate.edu/dept/tcnwac

Jammy Avery, Publisher
J Charles Lee, President
Frequency: Bi-annually
Circulation: 1000
Founded in: 1993
Printed in 3 colors on matte stock

949 **National Farmers Union News**
National Farmers Union
11900 E Cornell Ave
Aurora, CO 80014-6201

303-368-7300
800-347-1961; *Fax:* 303-368-1390;
www.nfu.org

Dave Frederickson, President
Rae Price, Editor

Grass roots structure in which policy positions are initiated locally. The goal is to sustain and strengthen family farm and ranch agriculture.
Cost: $10.00
Frequency: Monthly
Circulation: 250000
Founded in: 1902

950 **National Hog Farmer**
7900 International Dr
Suite 300
Minneapolis, MN 55425-2562

952-851-4710; *Fax:* 952-851-4601;
www.nationalhogfarmer.com

Dale Miller, Manager
Steve May, Publisher
John Frinch, President
Robert Moraczewski, Senior Vice President
Susan Rowland, Marketing Manager

Offers production information for hog farming business managers.
Cost: $35.00
Frequency: Monthly
Circulation: 31000
Founded in: 1956
Mailing list available for rent: 84M names
Printed in 4 colors on glossy stock

951 **National Wheat Growers Journal**
National Association of Wheat Growers
415 2nd St NE
Suite 300
Washington, DC 20002-4993

202-547-7800; *Fax:* 202-546-2638
wheatworld@wheatworld.org;
www.wheatworld.org
Social Media: Facebook, Twitter

David Cleavinger, Publisher
Karl Scronce, Second Vice President
Dana Peterson, Second Vice President
Melissa George Kessler, Director of Communications

Information for wheat growers.
Founded in: 1950

952 **North Africa and Middle East Int'l Agricultural and Trade Report**
US Department of Agriculture
200 Independence Ave SW
Washington, DC 20201-0007

202-690-7650
800-999-6779; *Fax:* 202-512-2250;
www.usda.gov

Michael Kurrzig, Editor
Chris Smith, Chief Information Officer
Matt Paul, Director of Communications
Ramona Romero, General Counsel

Information on current and projected agriculture production and trade in North Africa and the Middle East. Reports include trade and production data, highlights United States and European trade with the region.
Frequency: Annual
Founded in: 1862

953 **North American Deer Farmers Magazine**
North American Deer Farmers Association
4501 Hills and Dales Rd NW
Suite C
Canton, OH 44708

330-454-3944; *Fax:* 330-454-3950
info@nadefa.org; www.nadefa.org

Shawn Schafer, Executive Director
Tim Condict, First VP
Bill Pittenger, Second VP

National association of deer farming and ranching. Membership dues include this quarterly magazine.
Cost: $15.00
32 Pages
Frequency: Quarterly
Circulation: 1000
ISSN: 1084-0583
Founded in: 1983
Printed in 4 colors on glossy stock

954 **Northeast Dairy Business**
DairyBusiness Communications
6437 Collamer Road
East Syracuse, NY 13057-1031

315-703-7979
800-334-1904; *Fax:* 315-703-7988;
www.dairybusiness.com/northeast

Eleanor Jacobs, Editor
Susan Harlow, Managing Editor
Joel Hasting, CEO/Publisher
Tom Vilsack, Secretary
Sue Miller, Circulation Manager

Business resource for successful milk producers. Devoted exclusively to the business and dairy management needs of milk producers in the 12 northeastern states.
Cost: $3.00
51 Pages
Frequency: Monthly
Circulation: 17500
ISSN: 1523-7095
Founded in: 1904
Printed in 4 colors on glossy stock

955 **Nut Grower**
Western Agricultural Publishing Company
4969 E Clinton Way
Suite 119
Fresno, CA 93727-1549

559-252-7000; *Fax:* 559-252-7387
westag@psnw.com; www.westagpubco.com

Paul Baltimore, Co Publisher
Jim Baltimore, Co Publisher
Randy Bailey, Editor
Robert Fujimoto, Assistant Editor

Covers production topics, the latest in research developments, and crop news on almonds, walnuts, pistachios, pecans and chestnuts.

956 **OEM Off-Highway**
1233 Janesville Avenue
Fort Atkinson, WI 53538-2738

920-563-6388
800-547-7377; *Fax:* 920-563-1701
Leslie.Shalabi@cygnuspub.com;
www.cygnusb2b.com

Richard Reiff, President
Leslie Shalabi, Publisher
Chad Elmore, Associate Editor
James S. Rank, VP
Kathy Scott, Director of Public Relations

Offers information on off-road machinery and farm equipment.
Founded in: 1966

957 **Onion World**
Columbia Publishing

8405 Ahtanum Rd
Yakima, WA 98903-9432

509-248-2452
800-900-2452; *Fax:* 509-248-4056;
www.onionworld.net

Brent Clement, Editor
Mike Stoker, Publisher
Includes information on onion production and marketing, grower and shipper feature stories, onion research, from herbicide and pesticide studies to promising new varieties, martket reports, feedback from major onion meetings and conventions, spot reports on overseas production and marketing, and other key issues and trends of interest to US and Canadian onion growers.
Cost: $16.00
32 Pages
Circulation: 6500
Founded in: 1984
Printed in 4 colors on glossy stock

958 **Organic World**
Loft Publishing
3939 Leary Way NW
Seattle, WA 98107-5043

206-632-2767; *Fax:* 206-632-7055

Covers the news of organic gardening.
Cost: $15.00
Frequency: Quarterly

959 **Pacific Farmer-Stockman**
999 W Riverside
PO Box 2160
Spokane, WA 99201

509-595-5385
800-624-6618; *Fax:* 509-459-5102;
www.farmerstockmaninsurance.com

Michael R Craigen, General Manager
Tracy Sikes, Manager
Kathy Bergloff, Manager
Michelle Musgrave, Administrative Assistant

Offers farming news and information for farmers and herdsmen located in the Pacific states.

960 **Peanut Farmer**
Specialized Agricultural Publications
5808 Faringdon Place
Suite 200
Raleigh, NC 27609

919-872-5040; *Fax:* 919-876-6531
publisher@peanutfarmer.com;
www.peanutfarmer.com

Dayton H Matlick, Chairman
Mary Evans, Publisher/Sales Director
Mary Ann Rood, Editor

Offers peanut farmers profitable methods of raising, marketing and promoting peanuts, plus key related issues.
Cost: $15.00
24 Pages
Frequency: Monthly January-July
Circulation: 18,500
Founded in: 1965
Printed in 4 colors on glossy stock

961 **Peanut Grower**
Vance Publishing
10901 W 84th Ter
Suite 200
Lenexa, KS 66214-1631

913-438-5721; *Fax:* 913-438-0697
mweeks@vancepublishing.com;
www.vancepublishing.com

Cliff Becker, VP
William C Vance, CEO

Written for the US peanut farmers. Covers disease, weed and insect control, legislation, farm equipment, marketing and new research.

962 **Pesticide Chemical News Guide**
FCN Publishing
2200 Clarendon Blvd
Suite 1401
Arlington, VA 22201

888-732-7070; www.agra-net.com

Jason Huffman, Editor-in-Chief

Reference tool on pesticides and chemicals.
Frequency: Monthly

963 **Pig International**
WATT Publishing Company
303 N Main Street
Suite 500
Rockford, IL 61101

815-966-5400; *Fax:* 815-966-6416
rabbott@wattnet.net; www.wattnet.com

James Watt, Chairman/CEO
Greg Watt, President/COO
Roger Abbott, Editor

Covers nutrition, animal health issues, feed procurement, and how producers can be profitable in the world pork market.
Frequency: Monthly
Circulation: 17600
ISSN: 0191-8834
Founded in: 1971
Mailing list available for rent
Printed in 4 colors on glossy stock

964 **Plant Disease**
American Phytopathological Society
3340 Pilot Knob Road
St. Paul, MN 55121-2097

651-454-7250
800-328-7560; *Fax:* 651-454-0766
aps@scisoc.org; www.apsnet.org
Social Media: Facebook, Twitter, LinkedIn, YouTube

R. Michael Davis, Editor-in-Chief

Published to stimulate plant disease research and to enable those throughout the world to benefit from the advances made in this environmentally important science.
Frequency: Monthly
Circulation: 1200
ISSN: 0191-2917

965 **Pork**
Vance Publishing
400 Knightsbridge Parkway
Lincolnshire, IL 60069

847-634-2600; *Fax:* 847-634-4379
info@vancepublishing.com;
www.vancepublishing.com

William C Vance, Chairman
Peggy Walker, President

Delivers practical, how-to information on production management, business techniques, industry trends and market analysis to the pork industry.
Cost: $50.00
Frequency: Monthly
Circulation: 16,000
Mailing list available for rent

966 **Pork Report**
PO Box 10383
Clive, IA 50325

515-223-6186; *Fax:* 515-223-2646

Charles Harness, Publisher

Hog farming news and information.

967 **Potato Country**
Columbia Publishing
8405 Ahtanum Rd
Yakima, WA 98903-9432

509-248-2452
800-900-2452; *Fax:* 509-248-4056;
www.potatocountry.com

Brent Clement, Editor/Publisher
Mike Stoker, Publisher

Edited for potato growers and allied industry people throughout the Western fall-production states. Editorial material covers production, seed, disease forecast, equipment, fertilizer, irrigation, pest/weed management, crop reports and annual buyers guide.
Cost: $18.00
32 Pages
Frequency: Daily
Circulation: 7500
ISSN: 0886-4780
Founded in: 1993
Printed in 4 colors on glossy stock

968 **Potato Grower**
Harris Publishing Company
360 B Street
Idaho Falls, ID 83402

208-524-4217; *Fax:* 208-522-5241;
www.potatogrower.com

Jason Harris, Publisher
Gary Rawlings, Editor

Current news on growing potatoes, market trends, technology.
Cost: $20.95
48 Pages
Frequency: Monthly
Founded in: 1971
Printed in on glossy stock

969 **Poultry Digest**
WATT Publishing Company
122 S Wesley Ave
Mt Morris, IL 61054-1451

815-734-7937; *Fax:* 815-734-4201
olentine@wattmm.com; www.wattnet.com

Jim W Watt, Chairman/CEO
Charles G Olentine Jr PhD, VP/Publisher
Clay Schreiber, Publisher
Jim Wessel, Circulation Director

A magazine serving the production side of the entire poultry industry.

970 **Poultry International**
WATT Publishing Company
303 N Main Street
Suite 500
Rockford, IL 61101

815-966-5400; *Fax:* 815-966-6416
mclements@wattnet.net; www.wattnet.com

James Watt, Chairman/CEO
Greg Watt, President/COO
Mark Clements, Editor

Viewed by commercial poultry integrators as the leading international source of news, data and information for their businesses.
68 Pages
Frequency: Monthly
Circulation: 20,000
ISSN: 0032-5767
Founded in: 1962
Printed in 4 colors

971 **Poultry Times**
Poultry & Egg News
345 Green Street NW
PO Box 1338
Gainesville, GA 30503

770-536-2476; *Fax:* 770-532-4894;
www.poultrytimes.net
Social Media: Facebook

Christopher Hill, Publisher/Editor
David Strickland, Editor

Barbara Olejnik, Associate Editor
Dinah Winfree, National Sales Representative
Stacy Louis, National Sales Representative
The only newspaper in the poultry industry. We deliver the most up to date news in teh poultry industry.
Cost: $22.00
Frequency: Twice Monthly
Circulation: 13000
Founded in: 1954

972 **Poultry USA**
WATT Publishing Company
303 N Main Street
Suite 500
Rockford, IL 61101
815-966-5400; *Fax:* 815-966-6416;
www.wattnet.com
James Watt, Chairman/CEO
Greg Watt, President/COO
Jeff Swanson, Publishing Director
The only resource focused on the entire integrated poultry market, delivering relevant and timely information to industry professionals across the entire poultry supply chain - from farm to table.
Frequency: Monthly

973 **Practical Winery & Vineyard**
58 Paul Dr
Suite D
San Rafael, CA 94903-2054
415-479-5819; *Fax:* 415-492-9325
Office@practicalwinery.com;
www.practicalwinery.com
A bi-monthly magazine of wine-growing and winemaking news and reviews.
Cost: $31.00
Circulation: 7500
Founded in: 1985

974 **Prairie Farmer**
Prairie Farm Dairy
300 E Washington St
PO Box 348
Pana, IL 62557-1239
217-562-3956; *Fax:* 217-877-9695
info@prairiefarms.com; www.prairiefarms.com
James R Smith, Manager
Mike Wilson, Editor
Agricultural news.

975 **Progressive Farmer**
2100 Lakeshore Drive
Birmingham, AL 35209-6721
205-445-6000; *Fax:* 205-445-6422
bruce_thomas@timeinc.com;
www.progressivefarmer.com
Bruce Thomas, Publisher
Jack Odle, Editor
Allen Vaughan, Business Manager
Farming news with regional focus on the midwest, midsouth and southwest.
Cost: $18.00
106 Pages
Frequency: 6 issues/Year
Circulation: 610000
ISSN: 0033-0760
Founded in: 1886

976 **RF Design**
RFD News
131 E Main Street
Bellevue, OH 44811-1449
419-483-7410; *Fax:* 419-483-3737
Barry LeCerf, Publisher
Comprehensive source of rural agricultural news and information for farmers and the general public.
Frequency: Weekly

977 **Rice Farming**
Vance Publishing
400 Knightsbridge Pkwy
Lincolnshire, IL 60069-3628
847-634-2600
800-888-9784; *Fax:* 847-634-4379
vlboyd@worldnet.att.net;
www.vancepublishing.com
Peggy Walker, President
William Vance, Chairman
Judy Riggs, Director
Vicky Boyd, Editor
Profitable production strategies for commercial rice growers.
Founded in: 1937

978 **Rice Journal**
Specialized Agricultural Publications
3000 Highwoods Boulevard
Suite 300
Raleigh, NC 27604-1029
919-878-0540; *Fax:* 919-876-6531;
www.ricejournal.com
Dayton H Matlick, President
Mary Evans, Publisher
Offers rice growers profitable methods of producing, marketing and promoting rice, plus key related issues.
Founded in: 1897

979 **RuraLife**
William Johnston
1172 Orangeburg Mall Circle
Orangeburg, SC 29115-3439
803-534-1980
Jaun Maults, Executive Director
Gary Grimmond, Editor
Farm and agricultural news.

980 **Rural Heritage**
Allan Damerow
281 Dean Ridge Ln
Gainesboro, TN 38562-5039
931-268-0655
info@ruralheritage.com;
www.ruralheritage.com
Gail Damerow, Owner
Publication for people who farm and log with horses and other draft animals.
Cost: $26.00
100 Pages
Frequency: Bi-Monthly
Circulation: 8500
ISSN: 0889-2970
Founded in: 1976
Printed in 4 colors on matte stock

981 **Rural Living**
Michigan Farm Bureau
7373 W Saginaw Highway
PO Box 30960
Lansing, MI 48909-8460
517-323-7000; *Fax:* 517-323-6793
mifarmnews@michfb.com;
www.michiganfarmbureau.com
Dennis Rudat, Editor
Paul W Jackson, President
Brigette Leach, Director
Earl Butz, Secretary
Editorial emphasis on consumer food news, travel information and issue analysis.
24 Pages
Frequency: Quarterly
Circulation: 200000

982 **Santa Gertrudis USA**
Caballo Rojo Publishing
PO Box 1257
Kingsville, TX 78364-1257
361-592-9357; *Fax:* 361-592-8572;
www.santagertrudis.com
Ervin Kaatz, Executive Director
Official Journal of the Breed developed in 1918 at the famous King Ranch in Texas. Famous solid red color, hardiness and good disposition. They are adaptable to many environments and are present throughout the US and in other countries.

983 **Seed Industry Journal**
Freiberg Publishing Company
2701 Minnetonka Dr
PO Box 7
Cedar Falls, IA 50613-1531
319-553-0642; *Fax:* 319-277-3783;
www.care4elders.com
Bill Freiberg, Owner
Carol Cutler, Editor
International seed industry news.

984 **Seed Technology Journal**
Society of Commerical Seed Technologists
101 E State Street
Suite 214
Ithaca, NY 14850
607-256-3313; *Fax:* 607-256-3313
scst@twcny.rr.com; www.seedtechnology.net
Brent Reschly, President
Neal Foster, Vice President
Published jointly with the Association of Official Seed Analysts. an international journal containing scientific and technological papers in all areas of seed science and technology. The emphasis is on applied and basic research in seed physiology, pathology and biology that may relate to seed development, maturation, germination, dormancy and deterioration.
Cost: $125.00
Frequency: Members Cost: $75.00
Founded in: 1922

985 **Seed Today**
Grain Journal Publishing Company
3065 Pershing Ct
Decatur, IL 62526-1564
217-877-9660
800-728-7511; *Fax:* 217-877-6647
webmaster@grainnet.com; www.grainnet.com
Mark Avery, Publisher
Joe Funk, Editor
Kay Merryfield, Circulation Administrator
Ayanna Green, Manager
Information for individuals related to seeds.
Frequency: Quarterly
Circulation: 4000
Founded in: 1978

986 **Seed World**
Scranton Gillette Communications
380 E Northwest Highway
Suite 200
Des Plaines, IL 60016-2282
847-298-6622; *Fax:* 847-390-0408;
www.seedworld.com
E S Gillette, Publisher
Angela Dansby, Editor
Seed marketers.
Cost: $30.00
48 Pages
Frequency: Monthly
Circulation: 5000
ISSN: 0037-0797
Founded in: 1915

987 **Seed and Crops Industry**
Freiberg Publishing Company

2701 Minnetonka Dr
Cedar Falls, IA 50613-1531

319-553-0642
800-959-3276; *Fax:* 319-277-3783
informa@cfu.net; www.care4elders.com

Bill Freiberg, Owner

Offers information for farmers related to crop protection.
Frequency: Monthly

988 **Self Employed Country**
Communicating for Agriculture & the Self Employed
112 E Lincoln Ave
Fergus Falls, MN 56537-2217

218-739-3241
800-432-3276; *Fax:* 218-739-3832;
www.selfemployedcountry.org

Milt Smedsrud, Owner
Jerry Barney, Production Manager

For members of Communicating for Agriculture, including legislation relating to CA activities, exchange program activities, rural seniors news, health and insurance material, feature stories and columns.
Cost: $6.00
Frequency: Quarterly
Founded in: 1985

989 **Shorthorn Country**
Durham Management Company
5830 S 142nd St
Siote A
Omaha, NE 68137-2894

402-827-8003; *Fax:* 402-827-8006;
www.durhamstaffingsolutions.com

Machael Durham, President
Tracy Duncan, Editor
Peggy Gilliland, Circulation Manager

Magazine published for cattle producers who breed and sell registered Shorthorn and Polled Shorthorn cattle.
Cost: $24.00
Circulation: 3000
ISSN: 0149-9319
Founded in: 1956

990 **Soil Science**
Lippincott Williams & Wilkins
351 W Camden St
Baltimore, MD 21201-2436

410-949-8000
800-638-6423; *Fax:* 410-528-4414;
www.lww.com

J Arnold Anthony, Operations

Covers investigations in environmental soils.
Cost: $205.00
Frequency: Monthly
Circulation: 2800
ISSN: 0038-075X

991 **Soil Science of America Journal**
Soil Science Society of America
677 S Segoe Rd
Madison, WI 53711-1086

608-273-8095; *Fax:* 608-273-2021
headquarters@soils.org; www.soils.org

Ellen Bergfeld, CEO

For those involved in research, teaching and extension activities in physics, chemistry, mineralogy, microbiology, soil fertility and plant nutrition
Cost: $600.00
Circulation: 4000
Founded in: 1961

992 **Southeast Farm Press**
14920 US Highway 61
Clarksdale, MS 38614

662-624-8503
866-505-7173; *Fax:* 662-627-1977;
www.southeastfarmpress.com

Grey Frey, Publisher
Paul Hollis, Editor

Offers farming news for the southeastern states.
Founded in: 1989

993 **Southeastern Peanut Farmer**
Southern Peanut Farmer's Federation
110 E 4th Street
Po Box 706
Tifton, GA 31794

229-386-3470; *Fax:* 229-386-3501
info@gapeanuts.com; www.gapeanuts.com

Joy Carter, Editor

Offers information to peanut farmers.
Cost: $25.00
20 Pages
Frequency: Monthly
Circulation: 8400
ISSN: 0038-3694
Founded in: 1961
Printed in 4 colors on glossy stock

994 **Southwest Farm Press**
Farm Press Publications
2104 Harvell Circle
Bellevue, NE 68005

402-505-7173
866-505-7173; *Fax:* 402-293-0741
sscs@pbsub.com
southwestfarmpress.com

Greg Frey, Publisher
Ron Smith, Editor
Hembree Brandon, Editorial Director
Forrest Laws, Executive Editor
Darrah Parker, Marketing Manager

Farming news.
Cost: $40.00
Frequency: Fortnightly
Circulation: 33,100
Founded in: 1974

995 **Soybean South**
6263 Poplar Avenue
Suite 540
Memphis, TN 38119-4736

901-385-0595; *Fax:* 901-767-4026

John Sowell, Publisher
Jeff Kehl, Circulation Director

Profitable prediction strategies for soybean farmers.
Frequency: 5 per year
Printed in 4 colors on glossy stock

996 **Speedy Bee**
American Beekeeping Federation
3525 Piedmont Road NE
Bldg 5 Suite 300
Atlanta, GA 30305-1509

404-760-2875; *Fax:* 404-240-0998
info@abfnet.org; www.abfnet.org

Troy Fore, Publisher/Editor

The latest news affecting the beekeeping and honey industry.
Cost: $17.95
16 Pages
Frequency: Monthly
Circulation: 1500
ISSN: 0190-6798
Founded in: 1972
Printed in on newsprint stock

997 **Spudman Magazine**
Great American Publishing
Po Box 128
Suite A
Sparta, MI 49345-0128

616-887-9008; *Fax:* 616-887-2666;
www.spudman.com

Matt McCallum, Owner
Kimberly Warren, Managing Editor
Erica Bernard, Circulation Manager
Marnie Draper, Advertising Manager
Jill Peck, Creative Director

Information for potato farming and marketing.
Circulation: 15500
Printed in on glossy stock

998 **Successful Farming**
Meredith Corporation
1716 Locust St
Des Moines, IA 50309-3023

515-284-3000
800-678-2659; *Fax:* 515-284-3563
shareholderhelp@meredith.com;
www.meredith.com

Stephen M Lacy, CEO
Sandy Williams, Production Manager
William Kerr, CEO
Tom Davis, Publisher

U.S. commerical farmers, ranchers and those employed in those operations or a directly related occupation.
Cost: $15.95
Frequency: Monthly
Circulation: 442000
Founded in: 1902
Mailing list available for rent: 500M names at $75 per M
Printed in 4 colors on glossy stock

999 **Sugar: The Sugar Producer Magazine**
Harris Publishing Company
360 B Street
Idaho Falls, ID 83402

208-524-4217
800-638-0135; *Fax:* 208-522-5241;
www.sugarproducer.com

Jason Harris, Publisher
David FairBourn, Editor
Rob Erickson, Marketing
Eula Endecott, Circulation Manager

Sugar beet industry information.
Cost: $15.95
Frequency: Monthly
Circulation: 16000
Founded in: 1975

1000 **Sugarbeet Grower**
Sugar Publications
503 Broadway
Fargo, ND 58102-4416

701-476-2111; *Fax:* 701-476-2182;
www.sugarpub.com

Provides news and feature articles pertaining to sugarbeet production practices, research, legislation and marketing, along with profiles of industry leaders and outstanding producers. Primary audience is United States and Canadian sugarbeet growers.
Cost: $12.00
Circulation: 11,300
Founded in: 1963

1001 **Sunflower Magazine**
National Sunflower Association
Ste 206
2401 46th Ave SE
Mandan, ND 58554-4829

701-328-5100
888-718-7033; *Fax:* 701-328-5101;
www.sunflowernsa.com

John Sandbakken, Executive Director
Sonia Mullally, Communications Director

Magazine geared to sunflower products.
Cost: $9.00
Circulation: 29300
Founded in: 1981
Printed in 4 colors

1002 **Sunflower and Grain Marketing Magazine**
Sunflower World Publishers
3307 Northland Drive
Suite 130
Austin, TX 78731-4964

512-407-3434; *Fax:* 512-323-5118

Ed R Allen, Editor

Offers news and information on the sunflower and grain industries.
Circulation: 15,000

1003 **Super Hay Today Magazine**
Mt Adams Publishing and Design
14161 Fort Road
White Swan, DC 98552-9786

509-848-2706
800-554-0860; *Fax:* 509-848-3896;
www.hortexponw.com

Vee Graves, Editor
Julie LaForge, Advertising Manager

1004 **Swine Practitioner**
10901 W 84th Terrace
Suite 200
Lenexa, KS 66214-1649

913-438-8700
800-255-5113; *Fax:* 913-438-0695
info@vancepublishing.com;
www.vancepublishing.com

Kristal Arnold, Editor
Kevin Murphy, Sales/Marketing Manager
Bill Newham, Publishing Director
Cliff Becker, Group Publisher
Lori Eppel, Chief Financial Officer

Offers technical information, primarily on swine health and related production areas, to veterinarians and related industry professionals.
Frequency: Monthly
Circulation: 4800
Mailing list available for rent

1005 **The Forestry Source**
5400 Grosvenor Ln
Bethesda, MD 20814-2198

301-897-8720; *Fax:* 301-897-3690
safweb@safnet.org; www.safnet.org
Social Media: Facebook, Twitter, LinkedIn

Michael T Goergen Jr, Executive VP/CFO
Brittany Brumby, Assistant to the CEO/Council
Amy Ziadi, Information Technology Manager
Larry D Burner CPA, Sr Director Finance

Provides access to information and networking opportunities to prepare members for the challenges and the changes that face natural resource professionals.
Founded in: 1900

1006 **The Grower**
Vance Publishing
400 Knightsbridge Parkway
Lincolnshire, IL 60069

847-634-2600; *Fax:* 847-634-4379
info@vancepublishing.com;
www.vancepublishing.com
Social Media: Facebook, Twitter

William C Vance, Chairman
Peggy Walker, President

The key source of profitable production and management strategies to commercial producers who control 90% of the U.S. fruit and vegetable market.
Cost: $45.00
Frequency: Monthly
Circulation: 22,004
Founded in: 1937
Printed in 4 colors on glossy stock

1007 **The Plant Genome**
Crop Science Society of America
5585 Guilford Road
Madison, WI 53711-5801

608-273-8080; *Fax:* 608-273-2021
headquarters@crops.org; www.crops.org
Social Media: Facebook, Twitter, LinkedIn

Maria Gallo, President
Jeffrey Volenec, President-Elect

Electronic journal that provides readership with a short publication of the latest advances and breakthroughs in plant genomics research.
Founded in: 1955

1008 **The Sunflower Magazine**
2401 46th Avenue SE
Suite 206
Mandan, ND 58554-4829

701-328-5100
888-718-7033; *Fax:* 701-663-8652;
www.sunflowernsa.com
Social Media: Facebook, YouTube

Larry Kleingartner, Executive Director
John Sandbakken, Marketing Director

Contains fresh, current and important articles on production strategies, ongoing research and market information.
Founded in: 1981
Printed in 4 colors on glossy stock

1009 **Today's Farmer**
MFA
201 Ray Young Dr
Columbia, MO 65201-3599

573-874-5111; *Fax:* 573-876-5521;
www.mfa-inc.com

William Streeter, CEO
J Brian Griffith, Senior Vice President of Operations

Management and marketing news.
Cost: $12.00
Founded in: 1914

1010 **Tomato Country**
Columbia Publishing
8405 Ahtanum Rd
Yakima, WA 98903-9432

509-248-2452
800-900-2452; *Fax:* 509-248-4056;
www.tomatomagazine.com

Brent Clement, Editor/Publisher
Mike Stoker, Publisher

Includes information on tomato production and marketing, grower and shipper feature stories, tomato research, from herbicide and pesticide studies to new varieties, market reports, feedback from major tomato meetings and conventions, along with other key issues and points of interest for USA and Canada tomato growers.

1011 **Top Producer**
Farm Journal Media
1818 Market Street
31st Floor
Philadelphia, PA 19103-3654

215-578-8900
800-320-7992; *Fax:* 215-568-6782
topproducer@farmjournal.com;
www.agweb.com/topproducer

Andy Weber, Chief Executive Officer
Steve Custer, Executive Vice President
Jeff Pence, President, Electronic Media
Chuck Roth, Senior Vice President

Top Producer is the premier magazine devoted to the business of farming. The focus on industry leaders, entrepreneurs and innovators in agriculture make this magazine the authoritative business resource for commercial farm operators.
Frequency: Weekly
Founded in: 1973

1012 **Tree Farmer Magazine, the Guide to Sustaining America's Family Forests**
American Forest Foundation
1111 19th St NW
Suite 780
Washington, DC 20036

202-463-2700; *Fax:* 202-463-2785
info@forestfoundation.org;
www.forestfoundation.org

Tom Martin, President & CEO
Brigitte Johnson APR, Director Communications, Editor

The official magazine of ATFS, this periodical provides practical, how-to and hands-on information and techniques, and services to help private fore landowners to become better stewards, save money and time, and add to the enjoyment of their land.

1013 **Tree Fruit**
Western Agricultural Publishing Company
4969 E Clinton Way
Suite 104
Fresno, CA 93727-1546

559-252-7000; *Fax:* 559-252-7387
westag@psnw.com; www.westagpubco.com

Paul Baltimore, Co Publisher
Jim Baltimore, Co Publisher
Randy Bailey, Editor
Robert Fujimoto, Assistant Editor

For tree fruit growers in California.

1014 **Valley Potato Grower**
420 Business Highway 2
PO Box 301
East Grand Forks, MN 56721

218-773-7783; *Fax:* 218-773-6227
vpgsales@nppga.org; www.nppga.org

Todd Phelph, CEO
Duane Maatz, Chairman

Information on potato farming.
Circulation: 10600
Founded in: 1946

1015 **Vegetable Growers News**
Great American Publishing
75 Applewood Drive Suite A
PO Box 128
Sparta, MI 49345

616-887-9008; *Fax:* 616-887-2666;
www.vegetablegrowersnews.com

Matt McCallum, Executive Publisher
Brenda Bradford, Advertising
Kimberly Warren, Managing Editor
Erica Bernard, Circulation Department
Jill Peck, Creative Director

Market and marketing news.
Cost: $12.00
Frequency: Monthly

1016 **Vegetables**
Western Agricultural Publishing Company
4969 E Clinton Way
#104
Fresno, CA 93727-1549

559-252-7000; *Fax:* 559-252-7387
westag@psnw.com; www.westagpubco.com

Paul Baltimore, Co Publisher
Jim Baltimore, Co Publisher
Randy Bailey, Editor
Robert Fujimoto, Assistant Editor

The definitive source for information on all aspects of western vegetable production.

1017 Vineyard and Winery Management
PO Box 2358
Winsdor, CA 95492

707-366-6820
800-535-5670; *Fax:* 607-535-2998
rmerletti@vwm-online.com;
www.vwm-online.com

Robert Merletti, Publisher
Tom Loid, General Manager
Dennis Black, General Manager
Suzanne Webb, Marketing Director

To be the bottom line resource for growers and vintners; to keep our readers tuned and primed for profit.
Cost: $37.00
100 Pages
Circulation: 6000
ISSN: 1047-4951
Founded in: 1975
Printed in 4 colors on glossy stock

1018 Wallaces Farmer
Farm Progress Companies
255 38th Avenue
Suite P
St Charles, IL 60174-5410

630-462-2224
800-441-1410
rswoboda@farmprogress.com;
www.farmprogress.com

Rod Swoboda, Editor
Willie Vogt, Corporate Editorial Director
Frank Holdmeyer, Executive Editor

Serves Iowa farmers and ranchers with information to help them maximize their productivity and profitability. Each issue is packed with information, ideas, news and analysis.
Cost: $26.95
ISSN: 0043-0129
Founded in: 1855

1019 Weed Science Journal
P.O.Box 7065
Lawrence, KS 66044-7065

785-429-9622
800-627-0629; *Fax:* 785-843-1274
wssa@allenpress.com; www.wssa.net

Dale Shaner, President
Jeff Derr, VP
Tom Mueller, Secretary
Dave Gealy, Treasurer
Michael Foley, Director Publications

Promotes research, education and extension outreach activities related to weeds, provides science-based information to the public and policy makers; and fosters awarenes of weeds and their impacts on managed and natural ecosystems.
2000 Members
Founded in: 1956

1020 Weed Technology Journal
P.O.Box 7065
Lawrence, KS 66044-7065

785-429-9622
800-627-0629; *Fax:* 785-843-1274
wssa@allenpress.com; www.wssa.net

Dale Shaner, President
Jeff Derr, VP
Tom Mueller, Secretary
Dave Gealy, Treasurer
Michael Foley, Director Publications

Promotes research, education and extension outreach activities related to weeds, provides science-based information to the public and policy makers; and fosters awarenes of weeds and their impacts on managed and natural ecosystems.
Founded in: 1956

1021 Western DairyBusiness
DairyBusiness Communications
6437 Collamer Road
East Syracuse, NY 13057-1031

315-703-7979
800-334-1904; *Fax:* 315-703-7988
bbaker@dairyline.com;
www.dairybusiness.com

Joel P Hastings, Editor
John Montandon, President & Co-CEO
Debbie Morneau, Marketing Coordinator

Business resource for successful milk producers. Covers 13 Western states. Provides information and news that is helpful in the daily operations of dairymen.
Cost: $49.95
67 Pages
Frequency: Monthly
Circulation: 14000
ISSN: 1528-4360
Founded in: 1904
Printed in 4 colors on glossy stock

1022 Western Farm Press
Penton Media
249 W 17th Street
New York, NY 10011

212-204-4200
hbrandon@farmpress.com
westernfarmpress.com

Greg Frey, VP
Hembree Brandon, Editorial Director
Harry Cline, Editor

Provides growers and agribusiness with in-depth coverage of the region's major crops plus the legislative, environmental and regulatory issues that affect their businesses.

1023 Western Fruit Grower
Meister Media Worldwide
37733 Euclid Ave
Willoughby, OH 44094-5992

440-942-2000
800-572-7740; *Fax:* 440-975-3447
rljones@meistermedia.com;
www.meisternet.com

Gary Fitzgerald, President
John Monahan, Publisher
Richard Jones, Editor

Edited for commercial growers of deciduous crops, citrus fruit and nut grape crops in the Western US.
Cost: $19.95
66 Pages
Frequency: Monthly
Circulation: 36000
Founded in: 1933

1024 Western Livestock Journal
Crow Publications
7355 E Orchard Road
Suite 300
Greenwood Village, CO 80111

303-722-7600
800-850-2769; *Fax:* 303-722-0155
editorial@wlj.net; www.wlj.net

Pete Crow, Publisher

Offers its readers the best coverage of timely, necessary news and information that affects the livestock industry, particularly cattle.
Cost: $45.00
Frequency: Weekly
Circulation: 30000+
Founded in: 1922

Trade Shows

1025 AACC International Annual Meeting
3340 Pilot Knob Road
St. Paul, MN 55121-2055

651-454-7250
800-328-7560; *Fax:* 651-454-0766
aacc@scisoc.org; www.aaccnet.org
Social Media: Facebook, Twitter, LinkedIn

Robert L. Cracknell, President
Lydia Tooker Midness, Chairman
Dave L. Braun, Treasurer

Formerly the American Association of Cereal Chemists, the AACC meeting offers a chance to come together, network with peers, discuss critical issues in the science and discover the methods of others.
Frequency: Annual/October
Founded in: 1915

1026 AAEA Annual Meeting
Agricultural & Applied Economics Association
415 S Duff Avenue
Suite C
Ames, IA 50010-6600

515-233-3202; *Fax:* 515-233-3101;
www.aaea.org

Per Pinstrup-Anderson, President
Yvonne C Bennett, Executive Director
Nancy Knight, Manager Meetings
Joan Greiner, Events Coordinator

Annual meeting and trade show of 25 exhibitors.
1700 Attendees
Frequency: Annual/August
Founded in: 1985

1027 AAEA Symposia
555 E Wells Street
Suite 1100
Milwaukee, WI 53202-6600

414-918-3190; *Fax:* 414-276-3349
info@aaea.org; www.aaea.org

Otto C Doering III, President
Yvonne C Bennett, Executive Director

Providing a platform for research on the economics related to the role of consumers' food environments on their choices and health outcomes. The conference is aimed at providing insights into the influence of the food environment on the quality, price, and availability of food, associatec health or environmental impacts, and to uncover the impact of policies aimed at influencing the food production and choice.
3000 Members
Frequency: Annual
Founded in: 1910
Mailing list available for rent

1028 AAFCO Meeting
Association of American Feed Control Officers
PO Box 478
Oxford, IN 47971

765-385-1029; *Fax:* 765-385-1032;
www.aafco.org

Sharon Krebs, Assistant Secretary/Treasurer
Frequency: Annual/July/August

1029 AAW Annual Convention
American Agri-Women

2103 Zeandale Road
Manhattan, KS 66502

785-537-6171; *Fax:* 785-537-9727;
www.americanagriwomen.org
Social Media: Facebook, Twitter

Karen Yost, President
Jody Elrod, Secretary
Peggy Clark, Treasurer

Tradeshow consisting of products of interest to women in agribusiness, farms and ranches.
350 Attendees
Frequency: Annual/November
Founded in: 1974

1030 AEM Annual Conference

Association of Equipment Manufacturers
6737 W Washington St
Suite 2400
Milwaukee, WI 53214-5650

414-272-0943
866-236-0442; *Fax:* 414-272-1170
info@aem.org; www.aem.org

Dennis Slater, President
Frequency: Annual/November

1031 AFIA Pet Food Conference

American Feed Industry Association
2101 Wilson Blvd
Suite 916
Arlington, VA 22201-3047

703-524-0810; *Fax:* 703-524-1921
afia@afia.org; www.afia.org
Social Media: Facebook, Twitter, LinkedIn

Joel Newman, President
Richard Sellers, VP
Donald E Orr, Chairman
Anne Keller, Communications Director

Organization devoted to representing companies in the animal feed industry and its suppliers.
690 Members
Founded in: 1909

1032 ALBC Conference

American Livestock Breeds Conservancy
PO Box 477
Pittsboro, NC 27312

919-542-5704; *Fax:* 919-545-0022;
www.albc-usa.org
Social Media: Facebook

Charles Bassett, Executive Director

An educational opportunity where members can share their knowledge with other members by sharing posters at the annual conference, subtting articles to the newsletter and more.
Frequency: Annual

1033 AMSA Reciprocal Meat Conference

American Meat Science Association
2441 Village Green Place
Champaign, IL 61822

217-356-5370
800-517-AMSA; *Fax:* 888-205-5834; *Fax:* 217-356-5370
information@meatscience.org;
www.meatscience.org\rmc

William Mikel, President
Scott J. Eilert, President-Elect
Casey B. Frye, Treasurer

RMC is the annual meeting for AMSA, featuring an interactive program tailored to bring attendees the very best and inspiring educational experience. Attendees are professionals in academia, government and industry, as well as students in the meat, food and animal science fields.

1034 AOSA/SCST Annual Meeting-Association of Official Seed Analysts

PMB #411
101 East State Street
Suite 214
Ithaca, NY 14850

607-256-3313; *Fax:* 607-273-1638;
www.aosaseed.com

Ellen Chirco, President
Wayne Guerke, VP
Dan Curry, Secretary/Treasurer
Aaron Palmer, Certificate/Analysis
Larry Nees, Membership

Seed testing and laboratory equipment, supplies and services; workshops and discussions.
Frequency: Annual/June

1035 ARA Conference & Expo

1156 15th St NW
Suite 500
Washington, DC 20005-1745

202-457-0825; *Fax:* 202-457-0864
info@aradc.org; www.aradc.org

Jack Eberstacher, CEO
Jon Nienas, Secretary/Treasurer
Stacy Mayuga, Marketing Director

Advocates in the ag retail and distribution industry.
Frequency: Annual
Founded in: 1993

1036 ARBA National Convention

American Rabbit Breeders Association
8 Westport Court
Bloomington, IL 61704

309-664-7500; *Fax:* 309-664-0941;
www.arba.net

Mike Avesing, President
Erik Bengtson, Vice-President
Eric Stewart, Executive Director
David Freeman, Treasurer

Seminar, banquet, luncheon and 1500 rabbit breeders exhibits.
3000 Attendees
Frequency: Annual/April
Founded in: 1910

1037 ASA-CSSA-SSSA International Annual Meeting

American Society of Agronomy
5585 Guilford Road
Madison, WI 53711-5801

608-273-8080; *Fax:* 608-273-2021
pscullion@agronomy.org; www.agronomy.org
Social Media: Facebook, Twitter, LinkedIn

Newell Kitchen, President
Kenneth Barbarick, President-Elect

Society members are dedicated to the conservation and wise use of natural resources to produce food, feed and fiber crops while maintaining and improving the environment. Annual meeting and exhibits of agricultural equipment, supplies and services.
Frequency: Annual/Fall

1038 ASABE Annual International Meeting

American Society of Agricultural & Bio-Engineers
2950 Niles Road
St. Joseph, MI 49085-9659

269-429-0300
800-371-2723; *Fax:* 269-429-3852;
www.asabe.org
Social Media: Facebook, Twitter, YouTube

Melissa Moore, Exec VP/Meetings & Conference Dir
Donna Hull, Publication Director

A forum to expand awareness of industry trends, promote and acknowledge innovations in design and technology, and provide opportunities for professional development. Networking, trade show, technical workshops and presentations, specialty sessions, and career fair.
Frequency: Annual/June
Founded in: 1907

1039 ASAS-ADSA Annual Meeting

American Society of Animal Science
1800 S. Oak Street
Suite 100
Champaign, IL 61820-6974

217-356-9050; *Fax:* 217-398-4119;
www.asas.org
Social Media: Facebook, Twitter

Dr. Margaret E. Benson, President
Dr. James L. Sartin, President-Elect
Dr. Meghan Wulster-Radcliffe, CEO
Jacelyn Friedrich, COO

Professional organization for animal scientists designed to help members provide effective leadership through research, extension, teaching and service for the dynamic and rapidly changing livestock and meat industries. Containing 45 booths. Always a joint meeting with ADSA, and usually with one or more of these organizations: CSAS, AMPA, WSASAS, and PSA.
2000 Attendees
Frequency: Annual/July
Founded in: 1908

1040 ASCA Annual Conference

American Society of Consulting Arborists
9707 Key West Avenue
Suite 100
Rockville, MD 20850-3992

301-947-0483; *Fax:* 301-990-9771
asca@mgmtsol.com; www.asca-consultants.org
Social Media: Twitter, LinkedIn

Beth Palys, Executive Director
Amy Hager, Deputy Director
Chris D. Ahlum, President
Jonathan E. Butcher, Vice President

Recognized as a high quality, in depth conference with cutting edge speakers. Combining the best forum for discussion of current and relevant arboricultural issues, as well as consulting practice management issues and key consulting topics such as the role of the expert witness, risk assessment and tree appraisal
300 Attendees
Frequency: Annual
Founded in: 1967

1041 ASEV National Conference

American Society for Enology and Vinticulture
PO Box 1855
Davis, CA 95617-1855

530-753-3142; *Fax:* 530-753-3318
society@asev.org; www.asev.org
Social Media: LinkedIn

Dr. Sara Spayd, President
Leticia Chacon-Rodriguez, 1st Vice President
Dr. James Kennedy, 2nd Vice President
Dr. James Harbertson, Secretary/Treasurer

Provides a forum for the presentation of research in the fields of enology and viticulture or related sciences.
Frequency: Annual/June
Founded in: 1950

1042 ASFMRA Annual Meeting

American Socitey of Farm Mgrs & Rural Appraisers

950 S Cherry Street
Suite 508
Denver, CO 80246-2664

303-758-3513; *Fax:* 303-758-0190
meetings@asfmra.org; www.asfmra.org
Social Media: Facebook, Twitter, LinkedIn

Jeffrey Berg, President
Paul Joerger, President-Elect
Jim Rickert, 1st Vice President

Twenty-five exhibits of agricultural equipment, supplies and services; educational seminars and program sessions.
375 Attendees
Frequency: Annual/November

1043 ASHS Annual Conference
American Society for Horticultural Science
1018 Duke Street
Alexandria, VA 22314-2851

703-836-4606; *Fax:* 703-836-2024
webmaster@ashs.org; www.ashs.org
Social Media: Facebook, Twitter, LinkedIn

Curt Rom, Chair
John Dole, President
Michael W. Neff, Executive Director
Negar Mahdavian, Conference Manager

Facilitating the mutual exchange of ideas and information concerning horticultural research, extension, education, and industry.
Cost: $560.00
Frequency: Annual

1044 ATA Annual Conference
Animal Transportation Association
12100 Sunset Hills Road
Suite 130
Reston, VA 20190

703-437-4377; *Fax:* 703-435-4390
info@animaltransportationassociation.org;
www.animaltransportationassociation.org

Robin Turner, Association Director
Lisa Schoppa, AATA President
Erik Liebegott, President-Elect
Chris Santarelli, Secretary/Treasurer

The latest information and technology relating to the transportation of animals. Subtopics include welfare, stress, meat quality, environmental control, biosecurity guidelines, training programs, and new transport designed crates and trailers.
150 Attendees
Frequency: Annual

1045 AVMA Annual Convention
American Veterinary Medical Association
1931 N Meacham Road
Suite 100
Schaumburg, IL 60173

800-248-2862; *Fax:* 847-925-1329
avmaininfo@avma.org; www.avma.org
Social Media: Facebook, Twitter, Flickr, YouTube

Rene Carlson, President
Douglas Aspros, President-Elect
Jan Strother, Vice President
Barbara Schmidt, Treasurer
W. Ron DeHaven, Executive Vice President

Seminar and more than 300 exhibits of products, materials, equipment, data, and services for veterinary medicine. Education and hands-on labs, exhibit hall, charitable events and networking.
10000 Attendees
Frequency: Annual/July

1046 Acres USA Conference
5321 Industrial Oaks Boulevard
Suite 128
Austin, TX 78735

512-892-4446
800-355-5315; *Fax:* 512-892-4448
info@acresusa.com; www.acresusa.com
Social Media: Facebook, Twitter, LinkedIn

Fred C Walters, Publisher/Editor
1300 Attendees
Founded in: 1970
Printed in on newsprint stock

1047 Ag Progress Days
College of Agricultural Sciences
Penn State University
420 Agricultural Admin Building
University Park, PA 16802

814-865-2081; *Fax:* 814-865-1677
agprogressdays@psu.edu; www.apd.psu.edu

Bob Oberheim, Manager

Agricultural trade show focusing on the innovations and progress made in the agricultural industry. More than 400 commercial exhibitors, interactive educational exhibits, guided tours and workshops, machinery and field demonstrations, live animals and equine seminars and demonstrations.
50M Attendees
Frequency: Annual/August
Founded in: 1976

1048 Agri News Farm Show
Agri News
18 1st Avenue SE
Rochester, MN 55904-6118

507-857-7707
800-533-1727; *Fax:* 507-281-7436;
www.agrinew.com

John Losness, Publisher
Rosie Allen, Advertsising Manager
Mychal Wilmes, Managing Editor

Annual show of 123 exhibitors of farming equipment, supplies and services.
7,500 Attendees
Frequency: Annual/March

1049 Agricultural Retailers Association Convention and Expo
Agricultural Retailers Association
1156 15th Street
Suite 302
Washington, DC 20005

202-570-0825
800-535-6272; *Fax:* 314-567-6808
kelly@aradc.org; www.aradc.org
Social Media: Facebook, Twitter

Daren Coppock, President/CEO
Richard Gupton, Sr, VP, Public Policy
Michelle Hummel, VP
Marketing/Communications

Annual show of 120 manufacturers, suppliers and distributors of agricultural chemicals and fertilizers. Seminar, conference and banquet.
1200 Attendees
Frequency: Annual/December
Founded in: 1993

1050 Allied Social Sciences Association Annual Meeting
555 E Wells Street
Suite 1100
Milwaukee, WI 53202-6600

414-918-3190; *Fax:* 414-276-3349
info@aaea.org; www.aaea.org

Otto C Doering III, President
Yvonne C Bennett, Executive Director

The professional association for agricultural economists and related fields.
3000 Members
Frequency: Annual
Founded in: 1910
Mailing list available for rent

1051 America Trades Produce Conference
590 East Frontage Road
PO Box 848
Nogales, AZ 85628

520-287-2707; *Fax:* 520-287-2948
info@freshfrommexico.com; www.fpaota.org

Lee Frank, President
Alicia Bon Martin, Vice Chair
Allison Moore, Communications Director
Jose Luis Obregon, Deputy Director
Martha Rascon, Public Affairs Director

Represents companies involved in growing, harvesting, marketing and importing of Mexican produce entering the US.
125+ Members
Founded in: 1944

1052 American Farriers Association Annual Convention Marketplace
American Farriers Association
4059 Iron Works Parkway
Suite 1
Lexington, KY 40511

859-233-7411; *Fax:* 859-231-7862
info@americanfarriers.org;
www.americanfarriers.org
Social Media: Facebook

Buck McClendon, President
Thomas Trosin, President Elect
John Blombach, Vice President
Alan Larson, Treasurer
Jason Knight, Secretary

One-hundred and seventy exhibits of equipment and supplies for farriers, seminar, banquet, luncheon and tours.
1500 Attendees
Frequency: Annual/February
Founded in: 1971

1053 American Livestock Breeds Convervancy ALBC Conference
PO Box 477
Pittsboro, NC 27312

919-542-5704; *Fax:* 919-545-0022;
www.albc-usa.org
Social Media: Facebook, Blogger

Charles Bassett, Executive Director

Ensuring the future of agriculture through genetic conservation and the promotion of endangered breeds of livestock and poultry. A nonprofit membership organization working to protect over 180 breeds of livestock and poultry from extinction.

1054 American Seed Trade Association Annual Conference
1701 Duke Street
Suite 275
Alexandria, VA 22314-2878

703-837-8140; *Fax:* 703-837-9365;
www.amseed.com

Andy Lavigna, CEO

Producers of seeds for planting purposes. Consists of companies involved in seed production and distribution, plant breeding and related industries in North America.
850 Members
Founded in: 1883

1055 Americas Food & Beverage Show
4601 NE 77th Avenue
Suite 200
Vancouver, WA 98662-2697

360-693-3373; *Fax:* 360-693-3464;
www.wusata.org

Andy Anderson, Executive Director
Eliza Lane, Outreach Coordinator

A nonprofit organization that promotes the export of food and agricultural products from the

Western region of the US Comprised of 13 state funded agricultural promotion agencies.

1056 **Annual Agricultural Law Symposium**
127 Young Rd.
Kelso, WA 98626

360-200-5699; *Fax:* 360-423-2287
roberta@aglaw-assn.org; www.aglaw-assn.org

Patricia A. Jensen, President
Amy Swanson, President-Elect
Robert P. Achenbach Jr., Executive Director

Bringing opportunities and ideas.
Frequency: Annual/October
Founded in: 1980

1057 **Annual Board of Delegates Meeting**
1400 K St NW
Suite 1200
Washington, DC 20005-2449

202-789-0789; *Fax:* 202-898-0522
grains@grains.org; www.grains.org

Kenneth Hobbie, President
Michael T Callahan, Director International Operations
Cheri Johnson, Manager Communications
Valerie Smiley, Manager Membership
Andrew Pepito, Director Finance/Administration

Motivated by the grain sorghum, barley and corn producer associations and representatives of the agricultural community. Provides commodity export market development.
Founded in: 1960

1058 **Annual Convention of the American Assoc. of Bovine Practitioners**
American Association of Bovine Practicioners
PO Box 3610
Auburn, AL 36831-3610

334-821-0442; *Fax:* 334-821-9532
aabphq@aabp.org; www.aabp.org

Brian J. Gerloff, President
Nigel B. Cook, President-Elect
Daniel L. Grooms, Vice President
Brian K. Reed, Treasurer
Charles W. Hatcher, Exhibits Chairman

130 exhibits of pharmaceutical and biological manufacturers, equipment and agricultural companies, computer programs and supplies.
1905 Attendees
Frequency: Annual/September
Founded in: 1967

1059 **Annual Meeting and Professional Improvement Conferences (AM/PIC)**
6584 W Duroc Road
Maroa, IL 61756

217-794-3700; *Fax:* 217-794-5901
exec-dir@nacaa.com; www.nacaa.com
Social Media: Facebook, Twitter

Rick Gibson, President

Hundreds of NACAA members from all over the country, every one relates to the same challenges faced every day on the job. Networking with other professional organizations.
Founded in: 1917
Mailing list available for rent: 3500 names at $500 per M

1060 **Aquatic Plant Management Society Annual Meeting**
Aquatic Plant Management Society
PO Box 821265
Vicksburg, MS 39182-1265

Fax: 601-634-5502
dpetty@ndrsite.com; www.apms.org
Social Media: Facebook, LinkedIn

Tyler Koschnick, President
Mike Netherland, VP
Sherry Whitaker, Treasurer
Jeff Schardt, Secretary
Craig Aguillard, Director

An international organization of educators, scientists, commercial pesticide applicators, administrators and individuals interested in aquatic plant species and plant management.
Founded in: 1961

1061 **Argi-Marketing Conference**
11020 King St
Suite 205
Overland Park, KS 66210-1201

913-491-6500; *Fax:* 913-491-6502
agrimktg@nama.org; www.nama.org
Social Media: Facebook, Twitter, LinkedIn, YouTube, Flickr

Jennifer Pickett, CEO
Vicki Henrickson, Vice President

Marketing and communication suppliers, including trade publications, radio and television broadcast sales organizations, premium/incentive manufacturers, printers, marketing research firms, photographers and related professionals.
Founded in: 1957

1062 **Asia Pacific Leather Fair**
1150 Connecticut Ave, NW
12th Floor
Washington, DC 20036

202-587-4250
jreddington@meatami.com; www.ushsla.org

John Reddington, President
Susan Hogan, Manager
John Hochstein, Chairman

Exclusive representative of the hides and skin industry in the United States. Members range in size from small family-owned businesses to large corporations. Participates in two annual trade shows in Asia as a cooperator through the US Department of Agriculture's Foreign Agriculture Service.

1063 **Beltwide Cotton Conference**
National Cotton Council of America
7193 Goodlett Farms Parkway
Cordova, TN 38016

901-274-9030; *Fax:* 901-725-0510;
www.cotton.org

Dr. Mark D. Lange, President & CEO
A. John Maguire, Sr. Vice President
Charles H. Parker, Chairman
Chuck Coley, Vice Chairman
Meredith B. Allen, Vice President

Offers a forum for agricultural professionals.
Frequency: Annual/January

1064 **Big Iron Farm Show and Exhibition**
Red River Valley Fair Association
1201 West Main Avenue
PO Box 797
West Fargo, ND 58078-0797

701-282-2200
800-456-6408; *Fax:* 701-282-6909
info@redrivervalleyfair.com;
www.bigironfarmshow.com
Social Media: Facebook

Bryan Schulz, General Manager

Annual show of 750 manufacturers of agricultural machinery and related products with over 1,000 exhibit spaces.
70M Attendees
Frequency: Annual/September

1065 **Breeders of the Carolinas Field Day**
PO Box 1257
Kingsville, TX 78364-1257

361-592-9357; *Fax:* 361-592-8572;
www.santagertrudis.com

Ervin Kaatz, Executive Director

Devoted to the interests and the needs of the breed developed in 1918 at the famous King Ranch in Texas. Recognized in 1940 by the USDA, and famou for efficient growth, solid red color, hardiness and good disposition. They areadaptable to many environments and are present throughout the US and in other countries.

1066 **COSA Annual Meeting**
Committee on Organic and Sustainable Agriculture
5585 Guilford Road
Madison, WI 53711-5801

608-273-8080; *Fax:* 608-273-2021;
www.cosagroup.org

Ann-Marie Fortuna, Chair

COSA is a committee of the Tri-Societies for agronomy. The annual committee meeting is held in conjunction with the ASA-CSSA-SSSA Annual Meeting.
Frequency: Annual/Fall

1067 **CPMA Convention**
590 East Frontage Road
PO Box 848
Nogales, AZ 85628

520-287-2707; *Fax:* 520-287-2948
info@freshfrommexico.com; www.fpaota.org

Lee Frank, President
Alicia Bon Martin, Vice Chair
Allison Moore, Communications Director
Jose Luis Obregon, Deputy Director
Martha Rascon, Public Affairs Director

Represents more than 125 member companies involved in growing, harvesting, marketing and importing of mexican produce entering the US at Nogales, Arizona.
125+ Members
Founded in: 1944

1068 **Citrus Expo**
Southeast AgNet Publications/Citrus Industry Mag
5053 NW Hwy 225-A
Ocala, FL 34482

352-671-1909; *Fax:* 888-943-2224;
www.citrusexpo.net

Maryann Holland, Show Manager

Citrus Trade Show with seminars, containing 150 exhibits. Complimentary attendance and lunch are provided to bona-fide grove owners & managers, citrus production managers, professional crop advisors, association execs & board members, government & legislative officials and the citrus research community.
1500 Attendees
Frequency: Annual/August
Founded in: 1992

1069 **Commodity Classic**
Commodity Classic: ASA, NWGA, NCGA, NSP
632 Cepi Drive
Chesterfield, MO 63005-6397

636-733-9004; *Fax:* 636-733-9005
corninfo@ncga.com;
www.commodityclassic.com

Dave Burmeister, Registration Information
Kristi Burmeister, Exhibitor Information
Susan Powers, Media/Press Information
Beth Musgrove, General Information
Peggy Findley, Sponsorship Information

550 booths of equipment, seed and chemicals. Lecture series, classes, entertainment, awards, annual meetings of several agri-organziations/associations, and the trade show.
4000 Attendees
Frequency: February

1070 Contractor Summit
6540 Arlington Blvd
Falls Church, VA 22042-6638

703-536-7080; *Fax:* 703-536-7019
info@irrigation.org; www.irrigation.org

Deborah Hamlin, Executive Director
Denise Stone, Meetings Director

Promotes education and use of irrigation in many areas of agriculture.
1600 Members
Founded in: 1949

1071 Country Elevator Conference & Trade Shows
1250 I St NW
Suite 1003
Washington, DC 20005-3939

202-289-0873; *Fax:* 202-289-5388
ngfa@ngfa.org; www.ngfa.org

Kendell Keith, President
Ronald D Olson, Chairman
Tom Coyle, Second Vice Chair
Randall Gordon, Vice President

NGFA is the national trade association of grain elevators, feed and feed ingredient manufacturers, grain and oilseed processors, exporters, livestock and poultry integrators, and firms providing products and services to the industry.
Founded in: 1896

1072 EMDA Industry Showcase
Equipment Marketing & Distribution Association
PO Box 1347
Iowa City, IA 52244

319-354-5156; *Fax:* 319-354-5157
pat@edma.net; www.edma.net

Patricia A Collins, Executive VP

Annual convention and 130 exhibits of equipment, supplies and services for wholesaler-distributors and independent manufacturer's representatives of shortline and specialty farm equipment, light industrial, lawn and garden, turf care equipment, estate and park maintenance equipment.
600 Attendees
Frequency: November

1073 Eastern Milk Producers Cooperative Annual Meeting
1985 Isaac Newton Square West
Reston, VA 20190-5094

703-742-6800; *Fax:* 703-742-7459;
www.mdvamilk.com

Known for being a leader in the dairy industry, the Eastern Milk Producers Cooperative has an 85-plus year reputation for integrity, service and high quality products.
ISSN: west-

1074 EcoFarm Conference
Ecological Farming Association
2901 Park Ave.
Suite D-2
Soquel, CA 95073

831-763-2111
info@eco-farm.org
eco-farm.org

Allie Wilson, Conference Production

The largest sustainable agriculture conference in the western US, with a technical focus.
Frequency: Annual
Founded in: 1980

1075 El Foro
WATT Publishing Company
122 S Wesley Avenue
Mount Morris, IL 61054

815-734-4171; *Fax:* 815-734-4201
olentine@wattmm.com; www.wattnet.com

Jim Watt, Chairman/CEO

A trade show and technical symposium for the Latin American poultry, pig and feed industries. Containing 50 booths and 150 exhibits.
275 Attendees
Frequency: July

1076 Equipment Manufacturers Conference
American Feed Industry Association
2101 Wilson Blvd
Suite 916
Arlington, VA 22201-3047

703-524-0810; *Fax:* 703-524-1921
afia@afia.org; www.afia.org
Social Media: Facebook, Twitter, LinkedIn

Joel Newman, President
Richard Sellers, VP
Donald E Orr, Chairman
Anne Keller, Communications Director

Organization devoted to representing companies in the animal feed industry and its suppliers.
690 Members
Founded in: 1909

1077 European Seafood Exposition
4601 NE 77th Avenue
Suite 200
Vancouver, WA 98662-2697

360-693-3373; *Fax:* 360-693-3464;
www.wusata.org

Andy Anderson, Executive Director
Eliza Lane, Outreach Coordinator

A nonprofit organization that promotes the export of food and agricultural products from the Western region of the US Comprised of 13 state funded agricultural promotion agencies.

1078 FFA National Agricultural Career Show
National FFA Organization
PO Box 68960
6060 FFA Drive
Indianapolis, IN 46268-0960

888-332-2589; *Fax:* 800-366-6556
careershow@ffa.org; www.ffa.org

850 booths encouraging high school youth to select careers in the agricultural industry. Held during the National FFA Convention.
45M Attendees
Frequency: Fall, Annually

1079 FPAA Convention & Golf Tournament
590 East Frontage Road
PO Box 848
Nogales, AZ 85628

520-287-2707; *Fax:* 520-287-2948
info@freshfrommexico.com; www.fpaota.org

Lee Frank, President
Alicia Bon Martin, Vice Chair
Allison Moore, Communications Director
Jose Luis Obregon, Deputy Director
Martha Rascon, Public Affairs Director

Represents companies involved in growing, harvesting, marketing and importing of Mexican produce entering the US.
125+ Members
Founded in: 1944

1080 Farm Bureau Showcase
American Farm Bureau Federation
1850 Howard Avenue
Suite C
Elk Grove, IL 60007

224-656-6600; *Fax:* 847-685-8696
webmaster@fb.org; www.fb.org

Bob Stallman, President

Two-hundred plus booths featuring exhibits of agricultural equipment, supplies and services.
6-8M Attendees
Frequency: January

1081 Farm Equipment Manufacturers Association Spring Management Clinic
1000 Executive Parkway
Suite 100
St Louis, MO 63141-6369

314-878-2304; *Fax:* 314-732-1480
info@farmequip.org; www.farmequip.org

Robert K Schnell, Executive VP
James Bearden, First VP
Richard W Heiniger, Second VP

An information gathering and distributing organization for farm equipment manufacturers and suppliers.
Founded in: 1950

1082 Farm Progress Show
Farm Progress Companies
255 38th Avenue
Suite P
St Charles, IL 60174-5410

630-462-2224
800-441-1410
mjungmann@farmprogress.com;
www.farmprogressshow.com

Matt Jungman, National Shows Manager

Annual farm show of 400 exhibitors representing various types of agricultural products and services for farmers and agribusiness, including small operations to top producers.
Frequency: August/September

1083 Farm Science Review
Ohio State University
590 Woody Hayes Drive
232 Ag Engineering Building
Columbus, OH 43210-1057

614-926-6691
800-644-6377; *Fax:* 614-292-9448
gamble.18@osu.edu
fsr.osu.edu

Chuck Gamble, Manager
Mattk Sullivan, Assistant Manager
Suzanne Steel, Media Coordinator

Annual show of 600 exhibitors of agricultural equipment, supplies and services.
140M Attendees
Frequency: Annual/September

1084 Farm/Ranch Expo
Bacon Hedland Management
475 S Frontage Road
Suite 101
Burr Ridge, IL 60527
630-323-6880; *Fax:* 630-898-3550

Gene Bacon, Show Manager
160 booths
7M Attendees
Frequency: January

1085 Farmfest
Farm Fairs
Highway 60 West
PO Box 731
Lake Crystal, MN 56055

507-726-6863; *Fax:* 507-726-6750

Annual show of 450 manufacturers, suppliers and distributors of farm equipment and machinery, computers and software products, chemicals, seeds and crops, and techniques of planting, tillage and harvesting.
50M Attendees

1086 Fertilizer Outlook and Technology Conference
425 Third Street SW
Suite 950
Washington, DC 20002-8037

202-962-0490; *Fax:* 202-962-0577
information@tfi.org; www.tfi.org

Ford West, President
Ener Cunanan, Office Manager
Harry L Vroomen PhD, VP
Kathy Mathers, VP
Pamela D Guffain, Director/Government Relations
Gain perspective on the outlook for agriculture and major fertilizer materials and inputs from industry experts.
Founded in: 1970

1087 Fresh Summit International Convention & Expo
1500 Casho Mill Road
PO Box 6036
Newark, DE 19714-6036

302-738-7100; *Fax:* 302-731-2409
pma@pma.com; www.pma.com
Social Media: Facebook, Twitter, Flickr, YouTube, Xchange

Bryan Silbermann, President
Lorna Christie, VP/Industry Products & Services
Julie Stewart, Director Communications
Nancy Tucker, VP Global Business Development
Rayne Yori, VP Finance
PMA brings together leaders from around the world and from every segment of the supply chain. Participants throughout the global fresh produce and floral supply chains come together as a community to learn, network, build relationships, and do business.
Founded in: 1949

1088 GEAPS Operations, Management, & Technology Seminar
Grain Elevator & Processing Society
4248 Park Glen Road
Minneapolis, MN 55416

952-928-4640; *Fax:* 952-929-1318
info@geaps.com; www.geaps.com

David Krejci, Executive VP/Secretary
Darren Grahsl, Manager/Member & Chapter Services
Chuck House, Manager/Comm & Professional Dev
Amy McGarrigle, Manager/Member Ser & Information
Jason Stones, Manager/Member Ser & Publications
Offered in collaboration with the National Grain and Feed Association, boasted a faculty of industry experts covering topics including contamination, purity and salvage; handling, storage and incident response; theft protection and inventory management beset practices; and natural disaster response and preparedness
2,000 Attendees
Frequency: March
Founded in: 1937

1089 GIE+EXPO - Green Industry & Equipment Expo
Professional Lawncare Network, Inc
222 Pearl Street
Suite 300
New Albany, IN 47150

812-949-9200
800-558-8767; *Fax:* 812-949-9600
info@gie-expo.com; www.gie-expo.com
Social Media: Facebook, Twitter

Annual show of 400 manufacturers, suppliers and distributors of lawn care equipment, supplies and services, including fertilizers, weed control materials, insurance information and power equipment, plus education sessions and presentations and demos.

1090 Government Affairs Conference
USA Rice Federation
4301 N Fairfax Drive
Suite 425
Arlington, VA 22203

703-226-2300; *Fax:* 703-236-2301
riceinfo@usarice.com; www.usarice.com

Jamie Warshaw, Chairman
Discuss issues and activities for the U.S. rice industry, legislation, training, and seminars.
Frequency: Annual

1091 Grain Feed Association Trade Show
National Grain and Feed Association
1250 I Street NW
Suite 1003
Washington, DC 20005-3922

202-289-0873; *Fax:* 202-289-5388
ngfa@ngfa.org; www.ngfa.org

Randall Gordon, President
Dave Hoogmoed, Chairman
One hundred and thirty booths exhibiting agribusiness products, supplies and services.
1.3M Attendees
Frequency: March

1092 Grange Growth Summit
1616 H St NW
Suite 10
Washington, DC 20006-4999

202-628-3507
888-447-2643; *Fax:* 202-347-1091;
www.nationalgrange.org

Ed Luttrell, President
Jennifer Dugent, Communications Manager
Leroy Watson, Legislative Director
Cindy Greer, Director Youth\Young Adult
DoriAnn Gedris, Marketing Director
Promotes general welfare and agriculture through local organizations. Presides over the advancement and promotion of the farming and agriculture industry.
300k Members
Founded in: 1960

1093 Grape Grower Magazine Farm Show
Western Agricultural Publishing Company
4974 E Clinton Way
Suite 123
Fresno, CA 93727-1520

559-261-0396; *Fax:* 559-252-7387;
www.westagpubco.com

Phill Rhoads, Manager
Seminars, exhibits and prizes for grape growers. Contianing 80 booths and exhibits.

1094 Green Industry Conference - GIC
Professional Lawncare Network, Inc (PLANET)
950 Herndon Parkway
Suite 450
Herndon, VA 20170
703-736-9666
800-395-2522; *Fax:* 703-736-9668;
www.landscapeprofessionals.org

Held in conjunction with the GIE+EXPO, the conference offers leadership series, workshops, educational opportunities, events, and new member orientation.
Frequency: Annual

1095 GrowerExpo
Ball Publishing
335 N River Street
PO Box 9
Batavia, IL 60510-0009

630-208-9080
800-456-5380; *Fax:* 630-208-9350
info@ballpublishing.com

Diane Blazek, President
A trade show devoted to horticulture and floriculture production and marketing. 200 booths.
2M Attendees
Frequency: January

1096 Hawkeye Farm Show
Midwest Shows
PO Box 737
Austin, MN 55912

507-437-7969; *Fax:* 507-437-7752
salesfsu@farmshowsusa.com;
www.farmshowsusa.com

Penny Swank, Show Manager
18000 Attendees
Frequency: March

1097 Holstein Association USA Regional Meeting
1 Holstein Place
PO Box 808
Brattleboro, VT 05302-0808

802-254-4551
800-965-5200; *Fax:* 802-254-8251
info@holstein.com; www.holsteinusa.com

John Meyer, CEO
Lisa Perrin, Marketing
Dairy cattle breed association with a membership base of people with strong interests in breeding, raising and milking Holstein cattle.
Founded in: 1885

1098 IAOM Conferences and Expos
International Association of Operative Millers
10100 West 87th Street
Suite 306
Overland Park, KS 66212

913-338-3377; *Fax:* 913-338-3553
info@iaom.info; www.iaom.info
Social Media: Facebook, LinkedIn

Joe Woodard, President
Aaron Black, Vice President
Joel Hoffa, Treasurer
Melinda Farris, Executive Vice President
Premier educational events for grain milling and seed processing professionals. The annual events gather milling and allied trade professionals from around the world for several days of education, networking and fellowship.
Frequency: Annual/May
Founded in: 1896

1099 IFTA Annual Conference
International Fruit Tree Association

16020 Swingley Ridge Rd.
Suite 300
Chesterfield, MO 63017

636-449-5083; *Fax:* 636-449-5051
dungey@ifruittree.org; www.ifruittree.org

Tim Welsh, President
Rod Farrow, Vice President
Chris Hedges, Treasurer

Distinguished speakers, workshops and a regional orchard tour are highlights of the association's annual conference.
Frequency: Annual
Founded in: 1958

1100 International Feed Expo
American Feed Industry Association
2101 Wilson Blvd
Suite 916
Arlington, VA 22201-3047

703-524-0810; *Fax:* 703-524-1921
afia@afia.org; www.afia.org
Social Media: Facebook, Twitter, LinkedIn

Joel Newman, President
Richard Sellers, VP
Donald E Orr, Chairman
Anne Keller, Communications Director

Organization devoted to representing companies in the animal feed industry and its suppliers.
Founded in: 1909

1101 International Hoof-Care Summit
American Farriers Journal
223 Regency Court, PO Box 624
Suite 200
Brookfield, WI 53008-0624

262-782-4480
800-645-8455; *Fax:* 262-782-1252
info@lesspub.com; www.americanfarriers.com

Alice Musser, Conference Manager

Conference held for America's leading most innovative hoof-care professionals.
800 Attendees
Frequency: January

1102 International Marketing Conference & Annual Membership Meeting
1400 K St NW
Suite 1200
Washington, DC 20005-2449

202-789-0789; *Fax:* 202-898-0522
grains@grains.org; www.grains.org

Kenneth Hobbie, President
Michael T Callahan, Director International Operations
Cheri Johnson, Manager Communications
Valerie Smiley, Manager Membership
Andrew Pepito, Director Finance/Administration

Motivated by the grain sorghum, barley and corn producer associations and representatives of the agricultural community. Provides commodity export market development.
Founded in: 1960

1103 International Off-Highway and Power Plant Meeting and Exposition
Society of Automotive Engineers
400 Commonwealth Drive
Warrendale, PA 15096-0001

724-776-4841; *Fax:* 724-776-4026;
www.sae.org

Diane Rogne, Show Manager
Sam Barill, Treasurer
Andrew Brown, Treasurer

Annual show of 270 suppliers of parts, components, materials and systems utilized in farm and industrial machinery and off-road and recreational vehicles.
5000 Attendees
Circulation: 84,000

1104 International Sweets & Biscuits Fair (ISM)
4601 NE 77th Avenue
Suite 200
Vancouver, WA 98662-2697

360-693-3373; *Fax:* 360-693-3464;
www.wusata.org

Andy Anderson, Executive Director
Eliza Lane, Outreach Coordinator

A nonprofit organization that promotes the export of food and agricultural products from the Western region of the US Comprised of 13 state funded agricultural promotion agencies.

1105 Irrigation Show
Irrigation Association
6540 Arlington Blvd
Falls Church, VA 22042-6638

703-536-7080; *Fax:* 703-536-7019
info@irrigation.org; www.irrigation.org

Phil A. Burkart, President
Robert D. Dobson, President-Elect
Warren C. Thoma, Vice President
John E. Vikupitz, Treasurer

The Irrigation Show is the industry's one-stop event. Discover innovations on the show floor and in technical sessions, make connections with industry experts, business partners, and peers and build expertise with targeted education and certification.
3.5M Attendees
Frequency: Annual/November

1106 KFYR Radio Agri International Stock & Trade Show
KFYR Radio
3500 East Rosser Avenue
PO Box 1658
Bismarck, ND 58501

701-580-0550
800-472-2170; *Fax:* 701-255-8155
mwall@clearchannel.com; www.kfyr.com

Syd Stewart, General Manager
Neil Cary, Manager
Jim Lowe, Manager

Annual show of 400 exhibitors of agricultural equipment, livestock and services.
15M Attendees
Frequency: February

1107 Kentucky Grazing Conference
151 Treasure Island Cswy. #2
St. Petersburg, FL 33706-4734
727-367-9702
800-707-0014; *Fax:* 727-367-9608
darthay@yahoo.com; www.nationalhay.org

Ron Bradtmueller, President
Gary Smith, First VP
Richard Larsen, Second VP
Rollie Bernth, Director
Don Kieffer, Executive Director

NHA is the trade group that represents the interests of the hay industry throughout the United States and internationally.
Founded in: 1895

1108 Kosherfest
4601 NE 77th Avenue
Suite 200
Vancouver, WA 98662-2697

360-693-3373; *Fax:* 360-693-3464;
www.wusata.org

Andy Anderson, Executive Director
Eliza Lane, Outreach Coordinator

A nonprofit organization that promotes the export of food and agricultural products from the Western region of the US Comprised of 13 state funded agricultural promotion agencies.

1109 Legislative Action Conference National Pork Producers Council
122 C Street NW
Suite 875
Washington, DC 20001

202-347-3600
800-937-7675; *Fax:* 202-347-5265
warnerd@nppc.org; www.nppc.org
Social Media: Facebook, Twitter

Don Butler, President
Sam Carney, President-Elect
Doug Wolf, Vice President
Neil Dierks, CEO

National Pork Producers Council hosts a legislative action conference twice a year for pork producers from around the nation to learn about, discuss and lobby on agriculture legislation important to the U.S. pork industry.

1110 Legislative Conference
6540 Arlington Blvd
Falls Church, VA 22042-6638

703-536-7080; *Fax:* 703-536-7019
info@irrigation.org; www.irrigation.org

Deborah Hamlin, Executive Director
Denise Stone, Meetings Director

Promotes education and use of irrigation in many areas of agriculture.
Founded in: 1949

1111 Liquid Feed Symposium
American Feed Industry Association
2101 Wilson Blvd
Suite 916
Arlington, VA 22201-3047

703-524-0810; *Fax:* 703-524-1921
afia@afia.org; www.afia.org
Social Media: Facebook, Twitter, LinkedIn

Joel Newman, President
Richard Sellers, VP
Donald E Orr, Chairman
Anne Keller, Communications Director

Organization devoted to representing companies in the animal feed industry and its suppliers.
Founded in: 1909

1112 Mid South Farm Gin Supply Exhibit
Southern Cotton Ginners Association
874 Cotton Gin Place
Memphis, TN 38106

901-947-3104; *Fax:* 901-947-3103;
www.southerncottonginners.org

Chris Clegg, Chairman
Will Wade, President/Tennessee
Tim Price, Executive VP
Richard Kelly, VP/Tennessee
Allen Espey, Vice President/Tenessee

Exhibits new technology and practices for those in the cotton industry.
Frequency: Annual/February

1113 Mid-America Farm Show
Salina Area Chamber of Commerce
120 W Ash St.
PO Box 586
Salina, KS 67401

785-827-9301; *Fax:* 785-827-9758;
www.salinakansas.org

Don Weiser, Show Manager

Annual show of 325 exhibitors of agricultural equipment, supplies and services, including irrigation equipment, fertilizer, farm implements, hybrid seed, agricultural chemicals, tractors,

feed, farrowing crates and equipment, silos and bins, storage equipment and farm buildings.
13M Attendees
Frequency: Annual/March
Founded in: 1911

1114 **Mid-America Horticulture Trade Show**
Mid Am Trade Show
401 N. Michigan Ave.
Suite 2200
Chicago, IL 60611

312-321-5130
800-300-6103; *Fax:* 312-673-6882
mail@midam.org; www.midam.org
Social Media: Facebook, Twitter, LinkedIn, YouTube

Barbara Rosborough, President
Bill Vogel, Vice President
Jim Melka, Secretary
Dave Story, Treasurer

Mid-Am is a green-industry event featuring more than 650 leading suppliers offering countless products, equipment, and services for the horticulture industry. Mid-Am also offers a variety of educational seminars featuring the best and the brightest in the horticultural and business communities to help keep you informed of the latest trends.
Frequency: Annual/January

1115 **Midwest Ag Expo: OH**
590 Woody Hayes Drive
Room 232
Columbus, OH 43210

614-292-4278; *Fax:* 614-292-9448
gamble.19@osu.edu; www.worldagexpo.com

Doug Wagner, President
Dennis Alford, 1st Vice President
Chip Blalock, 2nd Vice President
Chuck Gamble, Secretary-Treasurer

Members are agriculture trade show sponsors and suppliers of services to these shows. Provides members with education, communication and evaluation. Provides the best possible marketing showcase for exhibitors and related products to the farmer/rancher/producer customer.
Founded in: 1972

1116 **Midwest Expo: IL**
Illinois Fertilizer & Chemical Association
130 W Dixie Highway
PO Box 186
Saint Anne, IL 60964-0186

815-939-1566
800-892-7122; *Fax:* 815-427-6573

Jean Trobec, President

Annual show of 130 manufacturers, suppliers and distributors of agricultural chemical and fertilizer application equipment, supplies and services.
2500 Attendees
Frequency: August, Danville

1117 **Midwest Farm Show**
North Country Enterprises
5330 Wall St
Suite 100
Madison, WI 53718

608-240-4700; *Fax:* 608-240-2069
medaassn.com

Bill Henry, President
Massey Ferguson, Vice-President
Julie Roisum, Executive Assistant

250 booths. Top farm show exhibiting dairy and Wisconsin's tillage equipment, feed and seed.
175 Members
11M+ Attendees
Frequency: January

1118 **NCTA Convention & Trade Show**
National Christmas Tree Association
16020 Swingley Ridge Rd
Suite 300
Chesterfield, MO 63017-6030

636-449-5070; *Fax:* 636-449-5051
info@realchristmastrees.org; www.realchristmastrees.org

Steve Drake, CEO
Pam Helmsing, Executive Director
Becky Rasmussen, Assistant Director
Rick Dungey, PR/Marketing Director

Draws christmas tree growers, retailers and suppliers from around the world for education, contests, networking and the trade show.
500 Attendees
Frequency: Annual/August

1119 **NDHIA Annual Meeting**
National Dairy Herd Improvement Association
421 S Nine Mound Round
PO Box 930399
Verona, WI 53593-0399

608-848-6455; *Fax:* 608-848-7675
info@dhia.org; www.dhia.org

Jay Mattison, CEO
Dan Sheldon, President
Lee Maassen, VP
250 Attendees

1120 **NHA Annual Convention**
National Hay Association
151 Treasure Island Cswy
#2
St. Petersburg, FL 33706

727-367-9702
800-707-0014; *Fax:* 727-367-9608
darthay@yahoo.com; www.nationalhay.org

Information and technology affecting the Hay industry.
Frequency: Annual/September

1121 **National 4-H Conference**
4-H
National 4-H Conference Center
7100 Connecticut Ave.
Chevy Chase, MD 20815
www.4-h.org/4-h-conference

Annual leadership and personal development event for 4-H members, 15 to 19 years old.
Frequency: Annual
Founded in: 1927

1122 **National Agri-Marketing Association Conference**
National Agri-Marketing Association
11020 King Street
Suite 205
Overland Park, KS 66210

913-491-6500; *Fax:* 913-491-6502
agrimktg@nama.org; www.nama.org

Paul Redhage, President
Kenna Rathai, Ist Vice President

Annual show of 60 exhibitors of marketing and communication suppliers, including trade publications, radio and television broadcast sales organizations, premium/incentive manufacturers, printers, marketing research firms and photographers.
1400 Attendees
Frequency: April

1123 **National Agricultural Plastics Congress**
American Society for Plasticulture
526 Brittany Drive
State College, PA 16803

814-238-7045; *Fax:* 814-238-7051
contact@plasticulture.org; www.plasticulture.org

William Tietjen, President
Jodi Fleck-Arnold, VP
Edward Cary, Secretary/Treasurer
Patricia Heuser, Executive Director

Congress of research presentations, with exhibit area of equipment, supplies and services relating to greenhouse production and mulch film production of agricultural and horticultural crops.
225 Attendees
Frequency: March

1124 **National Alliance of Independent Crop Consultants Annual Meeting**
349 E Nolley Dr
Collierville, TN 38017-3538

901-861-0511; *Fax:* 901-861-0512
jonesnaicc@aol.com; www.naicc.org

Allison Jones, Executive VP
Shannon Gomes, Secretary

Represents individual crop consultants and contract researchers.
500+ Members
Founded in: 1978

1125 **National Association Extension 4-H Agents Convention**
University of Georgia
Hoke Smith Annex
Athens, GA 30602

706-542-8804
freemand@vt.edu

Bo Ryles, State 4-H Leader
Heather Schultz, Live Stock Coordinator

50 booths for young people, youth staff and volunteers involved in 4-H.
1.2M Attendees
Frequency: November

1126 **National Association of Agricultural Educators (NAAE) Convention**
300 Garrigus Building
University of Kentucky
Lexington, KY 40545

859-257-2224
800-509-0204; *Fax:* 859-323-3919
jay_jackman@ffa.org; www.naae.org

Greg Curlin, President
Ken Couture, President-elect
Jay Jackman PhD, CAE, Executive Director
Alissa Smith, Associate Executive Director
Julie Fritsch, Com. and Marketing Coordinator

A federation of 50 affiliated state vocational agricultural teacher associations.
7600 Members
Founded in: 1948

1127 **National Association of County Agricultural Agents Conference**
National Association of County Agricultural Agents
6584 W Duroc Road
Maroa, IL 61756

217-794-3700; *Fax:* 217-794-5901
exec-dir@nacaa.com; www.nacaa.com
Social Media: Facebook, Twitter

Paul Wigley, President
Paul Craig, President-Elect
Henry Dorough, Vice President
Richard Fechter, Secretary
Parman Green, Treasurer

Annual conference and exhibits for county agricultural agents and extension workers.
Frequency: Annual

1128 **National Association of Wheat Growers Convention**
National Association of Wheat Growers
415 2nd St NE
Suite 300
Washington, DC 20002-4993
202-547-7800; *Fax:* 202-546-2638
wheatworld@wheatworld.org; www.wheatworld.org
Social Media: Facebook, Twitter

Brett Blankenship, President
Jim Palmer, Chief Executive Officer

Convention and trade show for the wheat, corn, soybean and sorghum industries.
Frequency: Annual/February
Founded in: 1950

1129 **National Cotton Council Annual Meeting**
7193 Goodlett Farms Parkway
Cordova, TN 38016
901-274-9030; *Fax:* 901-725-0510;
www.cotton.org

Mark Lange, President/CEO
A. John Maguire, Senior Vice President

Membership consists of approximately 300 delegates named by cotton interests in the cotton-producing states.
35 Members

1130 **National Custom Applicator Exposition**
Agribusiness Association of Iowa
900 Des Moines Street
Suite 150
Des Moines, IA 50309-5549
515-262-8323; *Fax:* 515-262-8960
info@agribiz.org; www.agribiz.org

Ed Beaman, President/CEO

Annual show of 70 manufacturers, suppliers and distributors of agrichemicals, fertilizers, spray equipment, tanks, agriplanes and agricomputer and flotation equipment.
2500 Attendees
Frequency: August

1131 **National Farm Machinery Show & Tractor Pull**
590 Woody Hayes Drive
Room 232
Columbus, OH 43210
614-292-4278; *Fax:* 614-292-9448
gamble.19@osu.edu; www.worldagexpo.com

Doug Wagner, President
Dennis Alford, 1st Vice President
Chip Blalock, 2nd Vice President
Chuck Gamble, Secretary-Treasurer

Members are agriculture trade show sponsors and suppliers of services to these shows. Provides members with education, communication and evaluation. Provides the best possible marketing showcase for exhibitors and related products to the farmer/rancher/producer customer.
37 Members
Founded in: 1972

1132 **National Farm Machinery Show and Championship Tractor Pull**
Kentucky Fair and Exposition Center
937 Phillips Lane
PO Box 37130
Louisville, KY 40233-7130
502-367-5000; *Fax:* 502-367-5299;
www.farmmachineryshow.org

Harold Workman, President/CEO

Annual show of 800 plus exhibitors of agricultural products, equipment, supplies and services.
293M Attendees
Frequency: February

1133 **National Farmers Union Convention**
20 F Street NW
Suite 300
Washington, DC 20001
202-554-1600
800-347-1961; *Fax:* 202-554-1654;
www.nfu.org
Social Media: Facebook, Twitter, YouTube

Roger Johnson, President
Claudia Svarstad, Vice President
Jeff Knudson, VP of Operations
Chandler Goule, VP of Government Relations

Promotes educational, cooperative and legislative activities of farm families in 26 states.
25000 Members
Founded in: 1902

1134 **National Grain Feed Association Annual Convention**
National Grain Feed Association
1250 I Street NW
Suite 1003
Washington, DC 20005
202-289-0873; *Fax:* 202-289-5388
ngfa@ngfa.org; www.ngfa.org

Kendall Keith, NGFA President
Todd Kemp, Director Marketing/Treasurer
Rachel Lyon, Meetings Manager
Marion Wimbush, Pressman

Committee meetings addressing issues essential to the business; Ag Village exhibitors and speakers.
1.3M Attendees
Frequency: March/April
Founded in: 1896

1135 **National Grange Convention**
1616 H St NW
Suite 10
Washington, DC 20006-4999
202-628-3507
888-447-2643; *Fax:* 503-622-0343;
www.nationalgrange.org

Ed Luttrell, President
Jennifer Dugent, Communications Manager
Leroy Watson, Legislative Director
Cindy Greer, Director Youth\Young Adult
DoriAnn Gedris, Marketing Director

Promotes general welfare and agriculture through local organizations. Presides over the advancement and promotion of the farming and agriculture industry.
300k Members
Founded in: 1960

1136 **National No-Tillage Conference**
No-Till Farmer
16655 West Wisconsin Avenue
Brookfield, WI 53005-5738
262-782-4480
800-645-8455; *Fax:* 262-782-1252
info@no-tillfarmer.com;
www.no-tillfarmer.com
Social Media: Facebook, Twitter, LinkedIn

Mike Lessiter, President
Bree Greenawalt, Conference Manager

Conference held for America's leading most innovative no-till farmers.
Frequency: January

1137 **National Orange Show Fair**
National Orange Show
689 South E Street
San Bernardino, CA 92408
909-888-6788; *Fax:* 909-889-7666
http://nationalorageshow.com
Social Media: Facebook

Five days of entertainment, art, exhibits, music, food and rides celebrating and educating the community on the California orange.
80000 Attendees
Frequency: Annual/May
Founded in: 1889

1138 **National Potato Council Annual Meeting**
1300 L St NW
Suite 910
Washington, DC 20005-4107
202-682-9456; *Fax:* 202-682-0333
spudinfo@nationalpotatocouncil.org;
www.nationalpotatocouncil.org
Social Media: Twitter

John Keeling, Executive VP/CEO
Hollee Stubblebine, Director Industry Communications
Keith Masser, President
Jim Wysocki, VP Finance
Dan Elmore, VP Grower/Public Relations

Connect with other grower leaders from across the country on shaping national public policy impacting potato production and distribution. Such issues as keeping potatoes in schools, finalizing free trade agreements, and gearing up for the next Farm Bill will be reviewed and strategies will be developed.
45000 Members
Founded in: 1948

1139 **National Potato Council's Annual Meeting**
National Potato Council
1300 L Street
Suite 910
Washington, DC 20005
202-682-9456
spudinfo@nationalpotatocouncil.org;
www.nationalpotatocouncil.org

John Keeling, CEO
Holly Stubblebine, Director of Public Relations
Mark Szymanski, Director of Public Relations

Annual meeting and exhibits of potato growing equipment, supplies and services.

1140 **New England Grows**
New England Grows
8-D Pleasant Street South
Natick, MA 01760
508-653-3009; *Fax:* 508-653-4112
info@newenglandgrows.org;
www.negrows.org

M. Virginia Wood, Executive Director
Jennifer A. Barich, Event Manager
Diane A. Zinck, Exhibit Sales & Marketing Manager
Owen J. Regan, Director of Operations
Elaine A. Kiesewetter, Conference Assistant

One of the largest and most visited horticulture and green industry events in North America, this event is known for its progressive educational conference and world-class trade show.
13000 Attendees
Frequency: Annual/February

1141 **North American Beekeeping Conference & Tradeshow**
American Beekeeping Federation

3525 Piedmont Road
Bldg 5 Suite 300
Atlanta, GA 30305-1509

404-760-2875; *Fax:* 404-240-0998
info@abfnet.org; www.abfnet.org

Regina Robuck, Executive Director
Gene Brandi, President
Tim May, Vice President

Expert talks and discussions about beekeeping hot topics; exhibits and introduction of new products; and workshops.
Frequency: Annual/January
Founded in: 1943

1142 **North American Deer Farmers Association Annual Conference & Exhibit**
North American Deer Farmers Association
104 S Lakeshore Drive
Lake City, MN 55041-1266

651-345-5600; *Fax:* 651-345-5603
info@nadefa.org; www.nadefa.org

Carolyn Laughlin, President
Dave McQuaig, First VP
Glenn Dice Jr, Second VP

Annual show of 30+ exhibitors of deer farming equipment, supplies and services.
300 Attendees
Frequency: February
Founded in: 1983

1143 **North American Farm and Power Show**
Tradexpos
811 W Oakland Avenue
PO Box 1067
Austin, MN 55912

507-437-4697
800-949-3976; *Fax:* 507-437-8917
steve@tradexpos.com; www.tradexpos.com

Steve Guenthner, Show Director

Agri-business farm show for the 5-state region. Free admission and parking.
28M Attendees
Frequency: March

1144 **North American Fertilizer Transportation Conference**
425 Third Street SW
Suite 950
Washington, DC 20002-8037

202-962-0490; *Fax:* 202-962-0577
information@tfi.org; www.tfi.org

Ford West, President
Ener Cunanan, Office Manager
Harry L Vroomen PhD, VP
Kathy Mathers, VP
Pamela D Guffain, Director/Government Relations

Co-hosted by The Fertilizer Institute and the Canadian Fertilizer Institute. Provides and opportunity for shippers and carriers to discuss issues of concern and work to reach mutually-beneficial solutions to logistical problems.
325 Members
Founded in: 1970

1145 **North American International Livestock Exposition**
Kentucky Fair and Exposition Center
937 Phillips Lane
PO Box 37130
Louisville, KY 40209-7130

502-367-5000; *Fax:* 502-367-5139;
www.livestockexpo.org

Debbie Burda, Booking/Events
Ellen Anderson, Event Contact

Purebred livestock show with more than 20,000 entries in eight major divisions: dairy cattle, dairy goats, llamas, quarter horses, draft horses, market swine, beef cattle, sheep. Held at Kentucky Fair and Exposition Center in Louisville, Kentucky.
Frequency: November

1146 **Northwest Agricultural Congress**
4991 Drift Creek Rd SE
Sublimity, OR 97385-9764

503-769-8940; *Fax:* 503-769-8946;
www.nwagshow.com

Jim Heater, Show Manager

Second largest agricultural show on the west coast. Show is produced by the Northwest Horticultural Congress which is a partnership between Oregon Horticultural Society, the Oregon Association of Nurseries and Northwest Nut Growers Association. Show held in conjunction with annual meetings and seminars by all three of the horticultural groups.
21000 Members

1147 **Nut Grower Magazine Farm Show**
Western Agricultural Publishing Company
4974 E Clinton Way
Suite 123
Fresno, CA 93727-1520

559-252-7000; *Fax:* 559-252-7387

Phill Rhoads, Manager

Productions seminars, guest speakers, prizes and exhibits for nut growers. Containing 80 booths and exhibits.

1148 **Organic Seed Growers Conference**
PO Box 772
Port Townsend, WA 98368

360-385-7192; *Fax:* 360-385-7455
info@seedalliance.org; www.seedalliance.org
Social Media: Facebook, Twitter

Dan Hobbs, Executive Director
Matthew Dillon, Executive Director

Supports the ethical development and stewardship of the genetic resources of agricultural seed.
Founded in: 1975

1149 **Ozark Fall Farmfest**
Ozark Empire Fair
3001 North Grant Street
PO Box 630
Springfield, MO 65308

417-833-2660; *Fax:* 417-833-3769;
www.ozarkempirefair.com

Pat Lloyd, Manager

Annual show of 700 exhibitors with about 600 booths of agricultural products and services, including livestock.
40M Attendees
Frequency: October

1150 **PMA Convention & Exposition**
Produce Marketing Association
1500 Casho Mill Road
Newark, DE 19711-3547

302-738-7100; *Fax:* 302-731-2409
pma@pma.com; www.pma.com
Social Media: Twitter, Flickr, YouTube

Bryan Silbermann, President & CEO
Lorna D. Christie, Vice President & COO
Yvonne Bull, CFO

A trade association of companies engaged in the marketing of fresh and safe produce and floral products. Show will inlcude 600 exhibitors with 1,600 booths.
16000 Attendees
Frequency: Annual/October
Founded in: 1949

1151 **PMA Fresh Summit**
590 East Frontage Road
PO Box 848
Nogales, AZ 85628

520-287-2707; *Fax:* 520-287-2948
info@freshfrommexico.com; www.fpaota.org

Lee Frank, President
Alicia Bon Martin, Vice Chair
Allison Moore, Communications Director
Jose Luis Obregon, Deputy Director
Martha Rascon, Public Affairs Director

Represents more than 125 member companies involved in growing, harvesting, marketing and importing of mexican produce entering the US at Nogales, Arizona.
125+ Members
Founded in: 1944

1152 **Pest World**
National Pest Management Association
9300 Lee Highway
Suite 301
Fairfax, VA 22031

703-738-8330; *Fax:* 703-352-3031;
www.pestworld.org

Robert Lederer, Executive VP
Dominique Broyles, Director Conventions/Meetings

240 booths.
4000 Attendees
Frequency: October

1153 **Potato Expo**
1300 L St NW
Suite 910
Washington, DC 20005-4107

202-682-9456; *Fax:* 202-682-0333
spudinfo@nationalpotatocouncil.org;
www.nationalpotatocouncil.org
Social Media: Twitter

John Keeling, Executive VP/CEO
Hollee Stubblebine, Director Industry Communications
Keith Masser, President
Jim Wysocki, VP Finance
Dan Elmore, VP Grower/Public Relations

Largest conference and tradeshow for the potato industry held in North America. Offers educational programming covering the top issues facing the potato industry, provides networking opportunities with key decision makers and showcases the latest products and services for potato production and distribution.
45000 Members
Founded in: 1948

1154 **Power Show**
590 Woody Hayes Drive
Room 232
Columbus, OH 43210

614-292-4278; *Fax:* 614-292-9448
gamble.19@osu.edu; www.worldagexpo.com

Doug Wagner, President
Dennis Alford, 1st Vice President
Chip Blalock, 2nd Vice President
Chuck Gamble, Secretary-Treasurer

Members are agriculture trade show sponsors and suppliers of services to these shows. Provides members with education, communication and evaluation. Provides the best possible marketing showcase for exhibitors and related products to the farmer/rancher/producer customer.
37 Members
Founded in: 1972

1155 **Prairie Farmer Farm Progress Show**
Farm Progress Publishers

1301 E Mound Road
Decatur, IL 62526-9394

217-877-9070; *Fax:* 217-877-9695

Sherry Stout, Editor
Jeffrey Smith, Advertising

One of the largest farm shows in the country.

1156 Pro Farmer Midwest Crop Tour
1818 Market Street 31st Floor
Philadelphia, PA 19103

800-772-0023
editors@profarmer.com; www.profarmer.com
Social Media: Twitter

Sue King, Contact

Join the Pro Farmer editors at these seminars to discuss commodity markets, world economy, farm policy, land prices and more.
25M Members
Founded in: 1973

1157 Produce Executive Development Program
1901 Pennsylvania Ave NW
Suite 1100
Washington, DC 20006-3412

202-303-3400; *Fax:* 202-303-3433
united@unitedfresh.org; www.uffva.org
Social Media: Facebook, Twitter, YouTube

Thomas E Stenzel, CEO
Nicholas J Tompkins, Chair
Robert A Grimm, Executive Committee
Daniel G Vache, Secretary/Treasurer

Equipment, supplies, cartons, packaging machinery, computers, sorting and sizing equipment, harvesting equipment, film wrap manufacturing and commodity organizations.
1000+ Members
Founded in: 1904

1158 Produce Inspection Training Program
1901 Pennsylvania Ave NW
Suite 1100
Washington, DC 20006-3412

202-303-3400; *Fax:* 202-303-3433
united@unitedfresh.org; www.uffva.org
Social Media: Facebook, Twitter, YouTube

Thomas E Stenzel, CEO
Nicholas J Tompkins, Chair
Robert A Grimm, Executive Committee
Daniel G Vache, Secretary/Treasurer

Equipment, supplies, cartons, packaging machinery, computers, sorting and sizing equipment, harvesting equipment, film wrap manufacturing and commodity organizations.
1000+ Members
Founded in: 1904

1159 Produce for Better Health Annual Meeting
590 East Frontage Road
PO Box 848
Nogales, AZ 85628

520-287-2707; *Fax:* 520-287-2948
info@freshfrommexico.com; www.fpaota.org

Lee Frank, President
Alicia Bon Martin, Vice Chair
Allison Moore, Communications Director
Jose Luis Obregon, Deputy Director
Martha Rascon, Public Affairs Director

Represents companies involved in growing, harvesting, marketing and importing of Mexican produce entering the US.
125+ Members
Founded in: 1944

1160 Profit Briefing Professional Farmers of America
1818 Market Street 31st Floor
Philadelphia, PA 19103

800-772-0023
editors@profarmer.com; www.profarmer.com
Social Media: Twitter

Sue King, Contact

Join the Pro Farmer editors at these seminars to discuss commodity markets, world economy, farm policy, land prices and more.
25M Members
Founded in: 1973

1161 Purchasing & Ingredient Suppliers Conference
American Feed Industry Association
2101 Wilson Blvd
Suite 916
Arlington, VA 22201-3047

703-524-0810; *Fax:* 703-524-1921
afia@afia.org; www.afia.org
Social Media: Facebook, Twitter, LinkedIn

Joel Newman, President
Richard Sellers, VP
Donald E Orr, Chairman
Anne Keller, Communications Director

Organization devoted to representing companies in the animal feed industry and its suppliers.
690 Members
Founded in: 1909

1162 SAF National Convention
5400 Grosvenor Ln
Bethesda, MD 20814-2198
301-897-8720; *Fax:* 301-897-3690
safweb@safnet.org; www.safnet.org

Michael T Goergen Jr, Executive VP/CFO
Brittany Brumby, Assistant to the CEO/Council
Amy Ziadi, Information Technology Manager
Larry D Burner CPA, Sr Director Finance

Provides access to information and networking opportunities to prepare members for the challenges and the changes that face natural resource professionals.
Founded in: 1900

1163 SBS Conference & Exhibition
Society for Biomolecular Sciences
100 Illinois Street
Suite 242
St. Charles, IL 60174

630-256-7527
877-990-7527; *Fax:* 630-741-7527
slas@slas.org; www.slas.org
Social Media: Facebook, Twitter, LinkedIn

Michelle Palmer, Ph.D, President
David Dorsett, Vice President
Erick Rubin, Ph.D, Treasurer
Andy Zaayenga, Secretary

Scientists, innovators, researchers and industry analysts from around the world will converge to learn about the latest trends and basic and applied research that are transforming the way new pharmaceuticals are developed.
2000 Attendees
Frequency: Annual

1164 Santa Gertrudis Breeders International Annual Meeting
PO Box 1257
Kingsville, TX 78364-1257

361-592-9357; *Fax:* 361-592-8572;
www.santagertrudis.com

Ervin Kaatz, Executive Director

Information and issues regarding America's First Beef Breed developed in 1918 at the famous King Ranch in Texas. Recognized in 1940 by the USDA. Famous for rapid and efficient growth, solid red color, hardiness and good disposition. They are adaptable to many environments and are present throughout the US and in other countries.

1165 Society for Biomolecular Screening
Society for Biomolecular Screening
36 Tamarack Avenue
Suite 348
Danbury, CT 06810

203-788-8828; *Fax:* 203-748-7557;
www.sbsonline.org

Al Kolbh, President
Christine Giordano, Executive Director
Larry Walker, Editor-in-Chief
Marietta Manono, Manager Meetings/Exhibitions

Technical sessions, exhibits, exhibitor tutorials, short courses, discussion groups related to discovery in the pharmaceutical and agrochemical industry and 181 exhibits.

1166 Soil and Water Conservation Society Annual International Conference
Soil and Water Conservation Society
945 SW Ankeny Road
Ankeny, IA 50021-9764

515-289-2331
800-843-7645; *Fax:* 515-289-1227
swcs@swcs.org; www.swcs.org

Bill Boyer, President
Dan Towery, Vice-President
Clark Gantzer, Secretary
Jerry Pearce, Treasurer

Explores ways to improve the linkages among conservation science, policy and application at local, national, and international scales. The conference will provide participants an opportunity to teach skills, learn techniques, compare successes, and improve understanding.
1200 Attendees
Frequency: Annual

1167 Southern Farm Show
590 Woody Hayes Drive
Room 232
Columbus, OH 43210

614-292-4278; *Fax:* 614-292-9448
gamble.19@osu.edu; www.worldexpo.com

Doug Wagner, President
Dennis Alford, 1st Vice President
Chip Blalock, 2nd Vice President
Chuck Gamble, Secretary-Treasurer

Members are agriculture trade show sponsors and suppliers of services to these shows. Provides members with education, communication and evaluation. Provides the best possible marketing showcase for exhibitors and related products to the farmer/rancher/producer customer.
37 Members
Founded in: 1972

1168 St. Louis All Equipment Expo
SouthWestern Association
P.O. Box 419264
Kansas City, MO 64141

816-762-5616
800-561-5323; *Fax:* 816-561-1249
oholcombe@swassn.com; www.swassn.com

Jeffrey Flora, CEO
Cory Hayes, Director of Education

Manufacturers, suppliers and distributors of farm equipment, outdoor power equipment, supplies and agriculture products. Containing 350 booths.
15M Attendees
Frequency: December

1169 **State Masters Conference**
1616 H St NW
Suite 10
Washington, DC 20006-4999

202-628-3507
888-447-2643; *Fax:* 202-347-1091;
www.nationalgrange.org

Ed Luttrell, President
Jennifer Dugent, Communications Manager
Leroy Watson, Legislative Director
Cindy Greer, Director Youth\Young Adult
DoriAnn Gedris, Marketing Director

Promotes general welfare and agriculture through local organizations. Presides over the advancement and promotion of the farming and agriculture industry.
300k Members
Founded in: 1960

1170 **Sunbelt Agricultural Exposition**
Sunbelt Ag Expo
290-G Harper Boulevard
Moultrie, GA 31788-2157

229-985-1968; *Fax:* 229-890-8518
info@sunbeltexpo.com; www.sunbeltexpo.com
Social Media: Facebook

Over 1,200 exhibitors showing the latest agricultural technology in products and equipment plus harvesting and tillage demonstrations in the field. Largest farm show in North America's premier farm show.
200M Attendees
Frequency: Annual/October

1171 **Sustainable Foods Summit**
1340 North Cotner Blvd
Lincoln, NE 68505

402-477-2323; *Fax:* 402-477-4325
info@ocia.org; www.ocia.org

Jeff See, Executive Director

OCIA International is a farmer owned international program of certification, which adheres to strict organic standards. It currently certifies thousands of farmers and processors in North, Central and South America and Asia. OCIA International is IFOAM accredited and adheres to the USDA ISO Guide 65, Japan Agriculture Standards and the Quebec Accreditation Council. OCIA has also been accredited from the USDA National Organic Program and Costa Rica Ministry of Agriculture.
3500 Members
Founded in: 1985
Mailing list available for rent: 3500 names at $50 per M

1172 **Sweetener Symposium**
2111 Wilson Blvd
Suite 600
Arlington, VA 22201-3051

703-351-5055; *Fax:* 703-351-6698
info@sugaralliance.org;
www.sugaralliance.org

James Johnson, President
Jack Roney, Director Economics/Policy Analysis
Luther Markwart, Executive Vice President
Carolyn Cheney, Vice President

Covering a broad range of timely issues affecting the industry.
Founded in: 1983

1173 **TFI Fertilizer Marketing & Business Meeting**
425 Third Street SW
Suite 950
Washington, DC 20002-8037

202-962-0490; *Fax:* 202-962-0577
information@tfi.org; www.tfi.org

Ford West, President
Ener Cunanan, Office Manager
Harry L Vroomen PhD, VP
Kathy Mathers, VP
Pamela D Guffain, Director/Government Relations

Brings together members from each sector of the fertilizer industry for two days of networking and conducting business leading up to the spring planting season.
325 Members
Founded in: 1970

1174 **TFI World Fertilizer Conference**
425 Third Street SW
Suite 950
Washington, DC 20002-8037

202-962-0490; *Fax:* 202-962-0577
information@tfi.org; www.tfi.org

Ford West, President
Ener Cunanan, Office Manager
Harry L Vroomen PhD, VP
Kathy Mathers, VP
Pamela D Guffain, Director/Government Relations

Provides two days of networking and conducting business with industry leaders from as many as 60 different countries that represent all sectors of the fertilizer industry.
325 Members
Founded in: 1970

1175 **Tree Fruit Expo**
Western Agricultural Publishing Company
4974 E Clinton Way
Suite 123
Fresno, CA 93727-1520

559-252-7000; *Fax:* 559-252-7387

Phill Rhoads, Manager

Productions seminars, dessert contest, guest speakers, prizes and exhibits for tree fruit growers. Containing 80 booths and exhibits.

1176 **USA Rice Outlook Conference**
USA Rice Federation
4301 N Fairfax Drive
Suite 425
Arlington, VA 22203

703-226-2300; *Fax:* 703-236-2301
riceinfo@usarice.com; www.usarice.com

Jamie Warshaw, Chairman
Jeannette Davis, Conference Contact

Discuss issues and activities for the U.S. rice industry, legislation, training, and seminars.
Frequency: Annual

1177 **USHSLA Annual Convention**
United States Hide, Skin & Leather Association
1150 Connecticut Avenue, NW
12th Floor
Washington, DC 20036

202-587-4250; www.ushsla.org

John Hochstein, Chairman
John Reddington, President

Represents the hide, skin and leather industries. Members range from small family-owned businesses to large corporations.
Frequency: Annual

1178 **United Fresh Convention**
590 East Frontage Road
PO Box 848
Nogales, AZ 85628

520-287-2707; *Fax:* 520-287-2948
info@freshfrommexico.com; www.fpaota.org

Lee Frank, President
Alicia Bon Martin, Vice Chair
Allison Moore, Communications Director
Jose Luis Obregon, Deputy Director
Martha Rascon, Public Affairs Director

Represents companies involved in growing, harvesting, marketing and importing of Mexican produce entering the US.
125+ Members
Founded in: 1944

1179 **United Fresh Fruit and Vegetable Association Annual Convention**
United Fresh Fruit & Vegetable Association
1901 Pennsylvania Avenue NW
Suite 1100
Washington, DC 20006

202-624-4989; *Fax:* 202-303-3433
united@uffva.org; www.uffva.org

Thomas Stenzel, CEO
Mark Overbay, Manager Communications
30000 Attendees

1180 **United States Animal Health Association Annual Meeting**
4221 Mitchell Ave.
St Joseph, MO 64508

816-671-1144; *Fax:* 816-671-1201
usaha@usaha.org; www.usaha.org

Benjamin Richey, Executive Director
Kelly Janicek, Executive Assistant

Seeks to prevent, control and eliminate livestock diseases.
1400 Members
Founded in: 1897

1181 **United States Hide, Skin & Leather Assoc. - Asia Pacific Leather Fair**
1150 Connecticut Ave, NW
12th Floor
Washington, DC 20036

202-587-4250
jreddington@meatami.com; www.ushsla.org

John Reddington, President
Susan Hogan, Manager
John Hochstein, Chairman
Stephen Sothmann, Director/International Affairs
Stephen Sothmann, Event Coordinator

Buyers will see the complete spectrum of the leather sector featuring the latest technology and products for leather making and footwear, as well as the widest range of leathers from around the globe displayed under one roof.
35 Members

1182 **Virginia Farm Show**
Lee Publications
6113 State Highway 5
PO Box 121
Palatine Bridge, NY 13428-0121

518-673-2269
800-218-5586; *Fax:* 518-673-3245
kmaring@leepub.com; www.leepub.com

Ken Maring, Trade Show Manager

This show caters to the full-time farmer, with exhibits of all the major lines of equipment and services, and seminars presented by industry experts in dairy, beef and crop production.
Frequency: January
Founded in: 1982

1183 **Walnut Council Annual Meeting**
1011 N 725 W
West Lafayette, IN 47906-9431
765-583-3501; *Fax:* 765-583-3512
walnutcouncil@walnutcouncil.org;
www.walnutcouncil.org
Liz Jackson, Executive Director
Larry R Frye, VP
William Hoover, Treasurer
Inviting scientists with the latest research on hardwood forestry, black walnut in particular, to present.
1000 Members
Founded in: 1970

1184 **Washington Public Policy Conference**
United Fresh Produce Association
1901 Pennsylvania Ave NW
Suite 1100
Washington, DC 20006-3412
202-303-3400; *Fax:* 202-303-3433
united@unitedfresh.org; www.uffva.org
Social Media: Facebook, Twitter, YouTube
Thomas E Stenzel, CEO
Nicholas J Tompkins, Chair
Robert A Grimm, Executive Committee
Daniel G Vache, Secretary/Treasurer
Equipment, supplies, cartons, packaging machinery, computers, sorting and sizing equipment, harvesting equipment, film wrap manufacturing and commodity organizations.
1000+ Members
Founded in: 1904

1185 **Water Conference**
6540 Arlington Blvd
Falls Church, VA 22042-6638
703-536-7080; *Fax:* 703-536-7019
info@irrigation.org; www.irrigation.org
Deborah Hamlin, Executive Director
Denise Stone, Meetings Director
Promotes education and use of irrigation in many areas of agriculture.
1600 Members
Founded in: 1949

1186 **Western Fairs Association Convention & Trade Show**
1776 Tribute Rd
Suite 210
Sacramento, CA 95815-4495
916-927-3100; *Fax:* 916-927-6397
stephenc@fairsnet.org; www.fairsnet.org
Stephen J Chambers, Executive Director
Jon Baker, VP
A non-profit association with members throughout the Western United States and Canada that strives to promote industry standards. Membership includes access to conventions and trade shows, educational training programs as well as legislative advocacy support.
2000 Members
Founded in: 1922

1187 **Western Farm Show**
Investment Recovery Association
638 W 39th Street
Kansas City, MO 64111
816-561-5323
800-728-2272; *Fax:* 816-561-1991
Annual show of 700 manufacturers, suppliers and distributors of equipment, supplies and services relating to the agricultural industry.
35M Attendees
Frequency: February
Founded in: 1962

1188 **Wheat Industry Conference**
415 2nd Street NE
Washington, DC 20002-4993
202-547-7800; *Fax:* 202-546-2638
wheatworld@wheatworld.org;
www.wheatworld.org
Social Media: Facebook, Twitter, YouTube
David Cleavinger, First Vice President
Karl Scronce, Second Vice President
Dana Peterson, CEO
Melissa George Kessler, Director of Communications
Nonprofit partnership of US wheat growers, by combining their strengths, voices and ideas are working to ensure a better future for themselves, their industry and the general public.
Founded in: 1950

1189 **Winter Fancy Food Show**
4601 NE 77th Avenue
Suite 200
Vancouver, WA 98662-2697
360-693-3373; *Fax:* 360-693-3464;
www.wusata.org
Andy Anderson, Executive Director
Eliza Lane, Outreach Coordinator
A nonprofit organization that promotes the export of food and agricultural products from the Western region of the US Comprised of 13 state funded agricultural promotion agencies.

1190 **World Dairy Expo**
151 Treasure Island Cswy. #2
St. Petersburg, FL 33706-4734
727-367-9702
800-707-0014; *Fax:* 727-367-9608
darthay@yahoo.com; www.nationalhay.org
Ron Bradtmueller, President
Gary Smith, First VP
Richard Larsen, Second VP
Rollie Bernth, Director
Don Kieffer, Executive Director
NHA is the trade group that represents the interests of the hay industry throughout the United States and internationally.
750 Members
Founded in: 1895

1191 **World Pork Expo**
122 C Street NW
Suite 875
Washington, DC 20001
202-347-3600
800-937-7675; *Fax:* 202-347-5265
warnerd@nppc.org; www.nppc.org
Social Media: Facebook, Twitter
Don Butler, President
Sam Carney, President-Elect
Doug Wolf, Vice President
Neil Dierks, CEO
The world's largest pork-specific trade show featuring business seminars, hundreds of exhibitors, breed shows and sales, and plenty of food and entertainment for everyone.
44 Members

Directories & Databases

1192 **AGRICOLA**
US National Agricultural Library
10301 Baltimore Ave
Beltsville, MD 20705-2351
301-504-5755; *Fax:* 301-504-5675;
www.agricola.nal.usda.gov/
Simon Y Liu, Director
Chris Cole, Acting Deputy Director
A database containing more than 3.3 million citations to journal literature, government reports, proceedings, books, periodicals, theses, patents, audiovisuals, electronic information, and other materials related to agriculture and its allied sciences.
Founded in: 1962

1193 **ARI Network**
Ari Network Services
10850 W Park Pl
Suite 1200
Milwaukee, WI 53224-3636
414-973-4300
800-558-9044; *Fax:* 414-973-4619;
www.arinet.com
Social Media: Facebook, Twitter, LinkedIn, YouTube
Roy W. Olivier, President & CEO
Darin R. Janecek, CFO
Brian E. Dearing, Chairman
Offers current information on agricultural business, financial and weather information as well as statistical information for farmers.

1194 **Ag Ed Network**
ARI Network Services
10850 W Park Pl
Suite 900
Milwaukee, WI 53224-3636
414-973-4300
800-558-9044; *Fax:* 414-973-4619
info@arinet.com; www.arinet.com
Roy W Olivier, Chief Executive Officer
John C Bray, New Market Development
Offers access to more than 1500 educational agriculture lessons covering farm business management and farm production.
Frequency: Full-text

1195 **AgriMarketing Services Guide**
Henderson Communications LLC
1422 Elbridge Payne Rd
Suite 250
Chesterfield, MO 63017-8544
636-728-1428; *Fax:* 636-777-4178
info@agrimarketing.com;
www.agrimarketing.com
Richard A Herrett, Executive Director
AgriMarketing Services Guide is published each December and is commonly referred to as the Who's Who in the North American ag industry sector.
Frequency: Annual/December

1196 **Agricultural Research Institute: Membership Directory**
Agricultural Research Institute
9650 Rockville Pike
Bethesda, MD 20814-3998
301-530-7122; *Fax:* 301-571-1816
Richard A Herrett, Executive Director
125 member institutions; also lists study panels and committees interested in environmental issues, pest control, agricultural meteorology, biotechnology, food irradiation, agricultural policy, research and development, food safety, technology transfer and remote sensing.
Cost: $50.00
Frequency: Annual

1197 **American Feed Industry Association: Software Directory**
American Feed Industry Association

2101 Wilson Blvd
Suite 916
Arlington, VA 22201-3047

703-524-0810; *Fax:* 703-524-1921
afia@afia.org; www.afia.org

Joel Newman, President/CEO
Richard Sellers, Vice President
Anne Keller, Communications Director
Donald E Orr, Chairman

Companies that design software programs applicable to the feed industry.
Cost: $25.00

1198 **American Fruit Grower: Source Book Issue**
Meister Media Worldwide
37733 Euclid Ave
Willoughby, OH 44094-5992

440-942-2000
800-572-7740; *Fax:* 440-975-3447
joe_monahan@meistermedia.com;
www.meistermedia.com

Richard T Meister, Chairman
Gary T Fitzgerald, President
Joe Monahan, Group Publisher

Offers a list of manufacturers and distributors of equipment and supplies for the commercial fruit growing industry.
Cost: $19.95
66 Pages
Circulation: 35,143

1199 **American Meat Science Association Directory of Members**
American Meat Science Association
2441 Village Green Place
Champaign, IL 61822

217-356-5370
800-517-AMSA; *Fax:* 888-205-5834; *Fax:* 217-356-5370
information@meatscience.org;
www.meatscience.org

William Mikel, President
Scott J. Eilert, President Elect
Casey B. Frye, Treasurer

Directory for American Meat Science members only.
Cost: $20.00
230 Pages
Frequency: Biennial

1200 **American Society of Consulting Arborists: Membership Directory**
American Society of Consulting Arborists
9707 Key West Ave
Suite 100
Rockville, MD 20850-3992

301-947-0483; *Fax:* 301-990-9771
asca@mgmtsol.com; www.asca-consultants.org

Beth W. Palys, Executive Director
Chris D. Ahlum, President
Amy Hager, Deputy Director
Shannon Sperati, Senior Member Services Manager

About 270 persons specializing in the growth and care of urban shade and ornamental trees; includes expert witnesses and monetary appraisals.
Frequency: Annual

1201 **Biological & Agricultural Index**
HW Wilson Company
950 Dr Martin Luther King Jr Blvd
Bronx, NY 10452-4297

718-588-8405
800-367-6770; *Fax:* 718-590-1617;
www.hwwilson.com

Harold Regan, President & CEO
Ann Case, Vice President, Editorial
Phillip Taylor, Customer Service Director
Amy Rosenbaum, Senior Manager
Kathleen McEvoy, Director of Public Relations

Provides fast access to core literature. In addition to citations to research and feature articles, users finding indexing of reports of symposia and conferences, and citations to current book reviews. Available on Web and disc.
359 Pages
Founded in: 1898

1202 **Citrus & Vegetable Magazine: Farm Equipment Directory Issue**
Vance Publishing
10901 W 84th Ter
Suite 200
Lenexa, KS 66214-1631

913-438-5721; *Fax:* 913-438-0697
cvmscott@compuserve.com;
www.vancepublishing.com

Michael H Ross, President, Chief Operating Officer
William C Vance, Chairman, Chief Executive Officer
Judy Riggs, Director/Research Marketing

Offers information on a list of manufacturers of produce and citrus growing, handling, picking and packaging equipment.
Cost: $25.00
48 Pages
Frequency: Annual
Circulation: 12,000
ISSN: 0009-7586
Founded in: 1938

1203 **Complete Guide to Gardening and Landscaping by Mail**
Mailorder Gardening Association
5836 Rockburn Woods Way
Elkridge, MD 21075-7302

410-540-9830; *Fax:* 410-540-9827;
www.mailordergardening.com

Bruce Frasier, President
Jim Bryant, First Vice President
Roberta Simpson, Second Vice President
Jean Vivlamore Norton, Treasurer
Camille Cimino, Executive Director

Member catalogers who sell gardening and nursery stock and supplies to consumers.
Cost: $2.00
Frequency: Annual
Founded in: 1934

1204 **Contemporary World Issues: Agricultural Crisis in America**
ABC-CLIO
130 Cremona Drive
PO Box 1911
Santa Barbara, CA 93117-1911

805-681-1911
800-422-2546; *Fax:* 805-685-9685
CustomerService@abc-clio.com;
www.abc-clio.com

Ron Boehm, President/CEO

List of agencies and organizations in the US concerned with agricultural issues.
Cost: $50.00
Founded in: 1953

1205 **Crop Protection Reference**
Vance Communications Corporation
315 W 106th St
Suite 504
New York, NY 10025-3473

212-932-1727
800-839-2420; *Fax:* 646-733-6010
GreenbookCustomerService@Greenbook.net;
www.greenbook.net

Hilda Vazquez, Director Marketing, Sales

A single comprehensive source of up-to-date label information of crop protection products marketed in the United States by basic manufacturers and formulators. Extensive product indexing helps to locate products by: brand name, manufacturer crop site, mode of action, disease, insect, week, product category, common name, tank mix.
Cost: $50.00
Frequency: Annual

1206 **Directory for Small-Scale Agriculture**
US Department of Agriculture
Secretary oF Agriculture
Whitten Building/Room 200A
Washington, DC 20250-0001

202-012-2000

Offers information on persons involved with projects and activities relating to small-scale agriculture.
Cost: $5.50
119 Pages

1207 **Directory of American Agriculture**
Agricultural Resources & Communications
P.O.Box 283
Wamego, KS 66547-0283

785-456-9705
800-404-7940; *Fax:* 785-456-1654
chris@agresources.com; www.agresources.com

Christina Wilson, President

This directory lists over 7,000 state and national associations involved in providing products and services related to food and fiber industries, in 27 categories. There are categorical indexes as well. Includes guide to Washington, D.C. offices, USDA listings, and guide to ag commodity commissions. Available on CD for $99.
Cost: $64.95
350 Pages
ISSN: 0897-1919
Founded in: 1988
Printed in on matte stock

1208 **EMDA Membership Directory**
Equipment Marketing & Distribution Association
PO Box 1347
Iowa City, IA 52244-1347

319-354-5156; *Fax:* 319-354-5157
pat@edma.net; www.emda.net

Patricia A Collins, Executive VP

Annual directory of FEWA-AIMRA members, includes address, phone, fax, web, e-mail, territory covered (with map) product descriptions, key personneland descriptive paragraph.
Cost: $50.00

1209 **Electronic Pesticide Reference: EPR II**
Vance Communications Corporation
315 W 106th St
Suite 504
New York, NY 10025-3473

212-932-1727; *Fax:* 646-733-6020
GreenbookCustomerService@Greenbook.net;
www.greenbook.net

Hilda Vazquez, Director Marketing, Sales

Complete electronic reference to our 1,500 crop protection products; a full range of product information: full text labels and supplemental labels, full text MSDS's, product summaries, list of labeled tank mixes, worker protection information, DOT shipping information, SARA Title III reporting information. Search by brand name, manufacturer, common name crop, plant, site, weed, disease, insect plus much more. All versions of EPR II are provided on CD-ROM for windows.

1210 **Food & Beverage Marketplace**
Grey House Publishing

4919 Route 22
PO Box 56
Amenia, NY 12501

518-789-8700
800-562-2139; *Fax:* 845-373-6390
books@greyhouse.com; www.greyhouse.com
Social Media: Facebook, Twitter

Richard Gottlieb, President
Leslie Mackenzie, Publisher

The most comprehensive resource in the food and beverage industry. Available in a three-volume printed directory, a subscription-based Online Database, as well as mailing list and database formats.
Cost: $595.00
2000 Pages
ISBN: 1-592373-61-5
Founded in: 1981

1211 **Food & Beverage Marketplace: Online Database**
Grey House Publishing
4919 Route 22
PO Box 56
Amenia, NY 12501

518-789-8700
800-562-2139; *Fax:* 845-373-6390
gold@greyhouse.com;
www.gold.greyhouse.com
Social Media: Facebook, Twitter

Richard Gottlieb, President
Leslie Mackenzie, Publisher

This complete updated Food & Beverage Market Place: Online Database is the go-to source for the food and beverage industry. Anyone involved in the food and beverage industry needs this 'industry bible' and the important contacts to develop critical research data that can make for successful business growth.
Frequency: Annual
Founded in: 1981

1212 **Food and Agricultural Export Directory**
National Technical Information Service
5285 Port Royal Rd
Springfield, VA 22161-0001

703-605-6000
800-553-6847; *Fax:* 703-605-6900
info@ntis.gov; www.ntis.gov

Linda Davis, Vice President
Patrik Ekstr"m, Business Development Manager
Reuel Avila, Managing Director

Includes up to date listings of federal and state agencies, trade associations and a host of other organizations that can help you penetrate foreign markets. Includes phone and fax numbers.
100 Pages
Frequency: Annual

1213 **Food, Hunger, Agribusiness: A Directory of Resources**
Center For Third World Organizing
1218 E 21st St
Oakland, CA 94606-3132

510-533-7583; *Fax:* 510-533-0923;
www.ctwo.org

Lian Cheun, MAAP Director
Dan Ringer-Barwick, Operations Director

Offers information on organizations and publishers of books and other materials on food, hunger and agribusiness overseas.
Cost: $12.95
160 Pages

1214 **Grain & Milling Annual**
Sosland Publishing Company
4801 Main St
Suite 100
Kansas City, MO 64112-2513

816-756-1000; *Fax:* 816-756-0494;
www.sosland.com

Offers a list of milling companies, mills, grain companies and cooperatives.
Cost: $100.00
Frequency: Annual
Circulation: 6,000
ISSN: 1098-4615

1215 **Guernsey Breeders' Journal: Convention Directory Issue**
Purebred Publishing Inc
7616 Slate Ridge Blvd
Reynoldsburg, OH 43068-3126

614-575-4620; *Fax:* 614-864-5614
sjohnson@usguernsey.com;
www.usguernsey.com

Seth Johnson, Manager
Dale Jensen, President
Tom Ripley, VP

A convention directory offering a list of officers and national members of the American Guernsey Cattle Association.
Cost: $20.00
Frequency: 10x Yearly

1216 **Hort Expo Northwest**
Mt Adams Publishing and Design
14161 Fort Road
White Swan, WA 98952-9786

509-848-2706
800-554-0860; *Fax:* 509-848-3896;
www.hortexponw.com

Vee Graves, Editor
Julie LaForge, Advertising Manager

The directory is mailed to subscribers and is also available complimentary at horticulture shows in the Northwest.
32 Pages
Frequency: Annually
Circulation: 8,700
Founded in: 1989
Printed in 4 colors on glossy stock

1217 **Industrial Economic Information**
Global Insight
800 Baldwin Tower
Eddystone, PA 19022

610-490-4000
800-933-3374; *Fax:* 610-490-2557
info@globalinsight.com;
www.globalinsight.com

Joseph E Kasputys, Chair/President/CEO
Pricella Trumbull, Chief Operations Officer
Vicki Van Mater, VP
Kenneth J McGill, Product Management

Global Insight's unique perspective provides the most comprehensive economic and financial coverage of countries, regions and industries from any source.

1218 **International Green Front Report**
Friends of the Trees Society
PO Bo 253
Twisp, WA 98856

509-997-9200; *Fax:* 509-997-4812;
www.friendsofthetrees.net

Michael Pilarski, Director

Organizations and periodicals concerned with sustainable forestry and agriculture and related fields.
Cost: $7.00
192 Pages
Frequency: Irregular
Circulation: 8,000
Founded in: 1978

1219 **International Soil Tillage Research Organization**
International Soil Tillage Research
1680 Madison Avenue
Wooster, OH 44691-4114

330-263-3700; *Fax:* 330-263-3658

A Franzluebbers, Editor-in-Chief

More than 750 individuals and institutions in 72 countries involved in the research or application of soil tilage and related subjects.
Cost: $100.00
Frequency: 10 per year

1220 **Journal of the American Society of Farm Managers and Rural Appraisers**
ASFMRA
950 S Cherry St
Suite 508
Denver, CO 80246-2664

303-758-3513; *Fax:* 303-758-0190
asfmra@agri-associations.org;
www.asfmra.org

Cheryl L Cooley, Manager Communications/PR
Frequency: Annually
Mailing list available for rent: 2500 names at $1M per M

1221 **Landscape & Irrigation: Product Source Guide**
Adams Business Media
11 Hanover Square
Suite 501
New York, NY 10005

212-566-7600; *Fax:* 212-566-7877
lenadams@acgresources.com;
www.acgresources.com

Len Adams, CEO

Offers information on suppliers, distributors and manufacturers serving the professional agriculture and landscaping community.
Circulation: 37,000

1222 **Material Safety Data Sheet Reference**
Vance Communications Corporation
315 W 106th St
Suite 504
New York, NY 10025-3473

212-932-1727; *Fax:* 646-733-6020
GreenbookCustomerService@Greenbook.net;
www.greenbook.net

Susan J Vannucci, Manager

Regulatory and product safety requirements. Contains full text MSDS's for products listed in the 1999 15th Edition Crop Protection Reference plus additional safety information such as DOT shipping information, SARA Title III regulations, Hazardous Chemical inventory reporting information plus much more.

1223 **Meat and Poultry Inspection Directory**
US Department of Agriculture
Administration Building
Room 344
Washington, DC 20250-0001

202-690-7650; *Fax:* 202-512-2250;
www.access.gpo.gov

Offers valuable information on all meat and poultry plants that ship meat interstate and therefore come under the US Department of Agriculture inspection.
Cost: $16.00
600 Pages
Frequency: SemiAnnual

1224 **NASDA Directory**
National Association of State Dept of Agriculture

1156 15th St NW
Suite 1020
Washington, DC 20005-1711

202-296-9680; *Fax:* 202-296-9686
nasda@nasda.org; www.nasda.org

Stephen Haterius, Executive Director
Richard Kirchoff, Executive VP/CEO

Top agricultural officials in 50 states and four territories.
Cost: $100.00
Frequency: Annual

1225 National Agri-Marketing Association Directory
11020 King St
Suite 205
Overland Park, KS 66210-1201

913-491-6500; *Fax:* 913-491-6502
agrimktg@nama.org; www.nama.org
Social Media: Facebook, Twitter, LinkedIn, Flickr, YouTube

Vicki Henrickson, President
Beth Burgy, 1st VP/ President-Elect
Paul Redhage, Secretary/Treasurer

Orginated as the Chicago Area Agricultural Advertising Association with 39 charter members. In 1963 the name was changed to the National Agricultural Advertising and Marketing Association and the present name was assumed in 1973.
Cost: $150.00
2500 Pages
Frequency: Annual
Founded in: 1956

1226 National Organic Directory
Community Alliance with Family Farmers
36355 Russell Boulevard
PO Box 363
Davis, CA 95617-0363

530-756-8518
800-892-3832; *Fax:* 530-756-7857
info@caff.org; www.caff.org

Judith Redmond, President
George Davis, VP
Pete Price, Secretary
Poppy Davis, Treasurer
Leland Swendon, Executive Director

Wriiten for all sectors of the booming organic food and fiber industry. Offers international listing with full contact information and extensive, cross-referenced index. Also provides regulatory updates, essays by industry leaders and other ressources.
Cost: $47.95
400 Pages
Frequency: Annual
Circulation: 2,500
ISBN: 1-891894-04-8
Founded in: 1983

1227 Organic Pages Online North American Resource Directory
Organic Trade Association
28 Vernon St.
Suite 413
Brattleboro, VT 05301

802-275-3800; *Fax:* 802-275-3801
info@ota.com; www.ota.com
Social Media: Facebook, Twitter, LinkedIn

Matt McLean, President
Sarah Bird, Vice President
Todd Linsky, Secretary
Kristen Holt, Treasurer

Provides over 1,300 listings by company name, brand name, business type, supply chain, product and service.

1228 Produce Marketing Association Membership Directory and Buyer's Guide
Produce Marketing Association
PO Box 6036
Newark, DE 19714-6036

302-738-7100; *Fax:* 302-731-2409
pma@pma.com; www.pma.com

Bryan Silbermann, President
Julie Koch, Production Manager

A list of over 2,000 members that are involved in retail grocery and foodservice marketing businesses, including international companies.
Cost: $70.00
280 Pages
Frequency: Annual

1229 Professional Workers in State Agricultural Experiment Stations
US Department of Agriculture
200 Independence Ave SW
Whitten Bldg/Room 200A
Washington, DC 20201-0007

202-690-7650; *Fax:* 202-512-2250;
www.access.gpo.gov

Mike Johanns, Secretary of Agriculture

This directory offers information on academic and research personnel in all agricultural, forestry, aquaculture and home economics industries.
Cost: $15.00
289 Pages
Frequency: Annual
Founded in: 1963

1230 Turf & Ornamental Reference
Vance Communications Corporation
315 W 106th St
Suite 504
New York, NY 10025-3473

212-932-1727; *Fax:* 646-733-6020
GreenbookCustomerService@Greenbook.net;
www.greenbook.net

Susan J Vannucci, Manager

Professional guide to plant protection problems. Provides the turf and ornamental industry with a single comprehensive source of up to date label and MSDS information of plant protection products marketed in the United States by basic manufacturers and formulators. Extensive product indexing helps to locate products by: brand name; manufacturer; plant site; mode of action; disease, insect, weed; product category; common name; tank mix.
Cost: $159.00

1231 USAHA Report of the Annual Meeting
United States Animal Health Association
4221 Mitchelle Ave.
St Joseph, MO 64507

816-671-1144; *Fax:* 816-671-1201
usaha@usaha.org; www.usaha.org

Benjamin Richey, Executive Director
Kelly Janicek, Executive Assistant

Held in conjunction with the American Association of Veterinary Laboratory Diagnosticians. (AAVLD)
Founded in: 1897

1232 Warehouses Licensed Under US Warehouse Act
Farm Service Agency-US Dept. of Agriculture
1400 Independence Avenue SW
Stop Code 0506
Washington, DC 20013-2415

202-720-7809; *Fax:* 202-690-0014

Eric Parsons, Chief Public Affairs

Agricultural warehouses voluntarily licensed under the US Warehouse Act governing public storage facilities.
Frequency: Annual

1233 Who's Who International
WATT Publishing Company
303 N Main Street
Suite 500
Rockford, IL 61101

815-966-5400; *Fax:* 815-966-6416;
www.wattnet.com

James Watt, Chairman/CEO
Greg Watt, President/COO
Jeff Swanson, Publishing Director

Contains a detailed statistical section of key contacts in the industry. Includes industry phone book, genetic hatcheries and products, company directories, poultry marketers by city and state, refrigerated warehouses and federal agencies and associations.
310 Pages

1234 Who's Who in the Egg & Poultry Industry in the US and Canada
WATT Publishing Company
303 N Main Street
Suite 500
Rockford, IL 61101

815-966-5400; *Fax:* 815-966-6416;
www.wattnet.com

James Watt, Chairman/CEO
Greg Watt, President/CEO
Jeff Swanson, Publishing Director

Contains a detailed statistical section of key contacts in the industry. Includes industry phone book, genetic hatcheries and products, company directories, poultry marketers by city and state, refrigerated warehouses and federal agencies and associations.
Cost: $105.00
Frequency: Annual
ISSN: 0510-4130

1235 World Databases in Agriculture
National Register Publishing
430 Mountain Ave.
Suite 400
New Providence, NJ 07974

800-473-7020; *Fax:* 908-673-1189
nrpeditorial@marquiswhoswho.com;
www.nationalregisterpub.com

Agricultural information on databases, including CD-ROM, magnetic tape, diskette, online, fax or databroadcast worldwide.

Industry Web Sites

1236 http://gold.greyhouse.com
G.O.L.D Grey House OnLine Databases

Grey House Publishing's online database platform, GOLD, includes Quick Search, Keyword Search and Expert Search for most business sectors including agriculture and food markets. The GOLD platform makes finding the information you need quick and easy. All of Grey House's directory products are available for subscription on the GOLD platform.

1237 www.aaccnet.org
AACC International

A non-profit organization of members who are specialists in the use of cereal grains in foods.

1238 www.aaea.org
Agricultural & Applied Economics Association

A not-for-profit association serving the professional interests of members working in agricultural and boradly related fields of applied economics.

1239 **www.aafco.org**
Association of American Feed Control Officials
Provides a mechanism for develping and implementing uniform and equitab;e laws, regulations, standrads and enforcement policies for regulating the manufacture, distribution and sale of animal feeds; resulting in safe, effective, and useful feeds.

1240 **www.aagiwa.org**
American Assoc of Grain Inspection & Weighing
The national association representing grain inspection and weighing agencies. These agencies provide official inspection services to measure the quantity of grain being bough and sold in the United States.

1241 **www.aaminc.org**
American Agriculture Movement
An umbrella organization composed of state organizations representing family farm producers.

1242 **www.aapausa.org**
AFIA Alfalfa Processors Council
Information for the processors and suppliers in the alfalfa industry.

1243 **www.abfnet.org**
American Beekeeping Federation
A national organiation with about 1,000 members that continually works in the interest of all beekeepers, large or small, and those associated with the industry to ensure the future of the honeybee.

1244 **www.aceweb.org**
Agricultural Communicators in Education
An international association of communicators and information technologists. Develops professional skills of its members to extend knowledge about agriculture, natural resources and life and human sciences to people worldwide.

1245 **www.adsa.org**
American Dairy Science Association
Provides leadership in scientific and technical support to sustain and grow the global dairy through generation, dissemination, and exchange of information and services.

1246 **www.aem.org**
Association of Equipment Manufacturers
A trade association that provides services on a global basis for companies that manufacture equipment, products and services used worldwide in the following industries: Agriculture, Construction, Forestry, Mining and Utility. AEM's membership is made up of more than 750 companies and represents 200+ product lines.

1247 **www.afgc.org**
American Forage and Grassland Council
Dedicated to advancing the use of forage as a prime feed resource. Members present the academic community, producers, private industry, institutes and foundations.

1248 **www.afia.org**
American Feed Industry Association
Represents the total feed industry, as a key segment of the food chain, and member copmanies' interests, with one industry leadership voice on matters involving federal/state legislation and regulation

1249 **www.ag.ohio-state.edu/~farmshow**
North American Farm Show Council/Ohio State Univ
Strives to improve the value of its member shows through education, communication and evaluation. Provides the best possible marketing showcase for exhibitors of agricultural equipment and related products to the farmer/rancher/producer customer.

1250 **www.agconsultants.org**
American Society of Agricultural Consultants
A non-profit organization oriented around raising the standards and image of professional agricultural consultants.

1251 **www.agday.org**
Agriculture Council of America
A nonprofit organization composed of leaders in the agricultural, food and fiber community, dedicating its efforts to increasing the public's awareness of agriculture's role in modern society.

1252 **www.agnic.org**
Agriculture Network Information Center
A voluntary alliance of members based on the concept of centers of excellence. The member institutions are dedicated to enhancing collective information and services among the members and their partners for all those seeking agriculture information over the Internet.

1253 **www.agribusiness.com**
National Agri-Marketing Association
The nation's largest professional association for professionals in marketing and agribusiness

1254 **www.amseed.com**
American Seed Trade Association
Promotes the development of better seed to produce better crops for a better quality of life.

1255 **www.angus.org**
American Angus Association
The nation's largest beef registry association with over 30,000 adult and junior members. The goal is to serve the beef cattle industry, and increase the production of consistent, high quality beef that will better satisfy consumers throughout the world.

1256 **www.animalalliance.org**
Animal Agricultural Alliance
A non-profit organization that is dedicated to the protection of wildlife, the alleviation of animal suffering and the preservation of our environment.

1257 **www.aomillers.org**
International Association of Operative Millers
An international organization, comprised of flour millers, cereal grain and seed processors and allied trades representatives and companies devoted to the advancement of technology in the flour milling and cereal grain processing industries.

1258 **www.apms.org**
Aquatic Plant Management Society
An international organization of scientists, educators, students, commercial pedticide applicators, administrators, and concerned individuals interested in the management and study of aquatic plants.

1259 **www.asabe.org**
American Society of Agricultural & Biological Eng
An educational and scientific organization dedicated to the advancement of engineering applicable to agriculture, food, and biological systems.

1260 **www.asas.org**
American Society of Animal Science
Discover, disseminate and apply knowledge for sustainable use of animals for food and other human needs.

1261 **www.asca-consultants.org**
American Society of Consulting Arborists
The industry's premier professional association focusing solely on arboricultural consulting. Consulting Arborists are authoritative experts on trees, consulting property owners, municipalities, attorneys, insurance professionals and others on tree disease, placement, preservation and dispute resolution in addition to providing consulting and expert testimony in the legal, insurance and environmental arenas.

1262 **www.asev.org**
American Society for Enology and Viticulture
A tax exempt professional society dedicated to the interests of enologists, viticulturists, and others in the fields of wine and grape research and production throughout the world.

1263 **www.biodynamics.com**
Biodynamic Farming and Gardening Association
A non-profit, membership organization that fosters tknowledge of the practices and principles of the biodynamic method of agriculture, horticulture, and forestry in the North American continent

1264 **www.cast-science.org**
Council for Agricultural Science and Technology
A nonprofit organization composed of scientific societies an many individual, student, copmany, nonprofit, and associate society members.

1265 **www.christmastree.org**
National Christmas Tree Association
Strives to be one voice representing Christmas Tree Professionals and promoting the use of Real Christmas Trees

1266 **www.corn.org**
Corn Refiners Association
The national trade association representing the corn refining (wet milling) industry of the United States.

1267 **www.cottonseed.com**
National Cottonseed Products Association
An organization of firms and individuals engaged in the processing of cottonseed and the marketing of cottonseed products, as well as cottonseed. These include oil mills, refiners, product dealers and product brokers.

1268 **www.cropinsurance.org**
Crop Insurance Research Bureau
Working to improve crop insurance through unity and leadership

1269 **www.croplifeamerica.org**
CropLife America
Represents the developers manufacturers, formulators and distributors of plant science solutions for agriculture and pest management in the United States.

1270 **www.crops.org**
Crop Science Society of America
Seeks to advance research, extension, and teaching of all basic and applied phases of the crop sciences.

1271 **www.dhia.org**
National Dairy Herd Improvement Association
Promote accuracy, credibility, and uniformity of DHI records; represent the DHIA system on is-

sues involving other National and International organizations; organize industry activities that benefit members of National DHIA

1272 **www.eap.mcgill.ca/cfbmc.htm**
Canadian Farm Business Management Council
To share and co-ordinate informatio non farm business management in order to help prevent duplication, encourage cost-sharing and build partnerships; to act as a forum for dialogue on farm business management issues of concern nationally or in more than on province of the country; to develop, adapt and distribute information products in farm business management to help increase the competitiveness of Canadian Agriculture.

1273 **www.fairsandexpos.com**
International Association of Fairs & Expositions
A voluntary, non-profit corporation, organizing state, provincial, regional, and county agricultural fairs, shows, exhibitions and expositions.

1274 **www.farmers-friend.com**
Farmers Friend
Farming news.

1275 **www.fb.org**
American Farm Bureau Federation
The unified national voice of agriculture, working through our grassroots organization to enhance and strengthen the lives of rural American and to build strong, prosperous agricultural communities

1276 **www.fewa-aimra.org**
FEWA-AIMRA Marketing & Distribution Association
Merged with AIMRA to form the leading association devoted to the marketing of specialized equipment.

1277 **www.fourhcouncil.edu**
National 4-H Council
Empowers youth to reach their full potential, working and learning in partnership with caring adults.

1278 **www.fpaota.org**
Fresh Produce Association of the Americas
A non-profit trade group of more than 100 members who are involved in the growth, harvest, import and distribution of the finest produce from Mexico.

1279 **www.fpfc.org**
Fresh Produce and Floral Council
Stimulates the promotion and sale of fresh fruit, vegetables and floral products; improves communications between all segments of the fresh produce and floral industries; and to exchange ideas on better and more economical handling of fresh fruit, vegetables and floral products from the farm to table.

1280 **www.freshcut.com**
Great American Publishing
Information on carrot production, growers and shippers.

1281 **www.grains.org**
US Grains Council
Develops export markets for U.S. barley corn, grain sorghum and related products. A private, non-profit corporation with nine international offices and programs in more than 50 countries.

1282 **www.greyhouse.com**
Grey House Publishing
Authoritative reference directories for business information and general reference, including agriculture and food markets. Users can search the online databases with varied search criteria allowing for custom searches by product category, geographic area, sales volume, keyword, subject and more. Full Grey House catalog and online ordering also available.

1283 **www.hereford.org**
American Hereford Association
For the raising and breeding of stock in the hereford cattle industry.

1284 **www.holsteinusa.com**
Holstein Association USA
The largest breed organization in the world, comprised of members who have a strong interest in breeding, raising and milking Holstein cattle.

1285 **www.iaff.ttu.edu/aals**
Association for Arid Land Studies

1286 **www.iaom.info**
International Association of Operative Millers
An international organization, comprised of flour millers, cereal grain and seed processors and allied trades representatives and companies devoted to the advancement of technology in the flour milling and cereal grain processing industries.

1287 **www.ifas.ufl.edu**
Institute of Food & Agriculture/Univ of Florida
For college students professionally interested in communications related to agriculture, food, natural resources and allied fields.

1288 **www.ipaa.net**
International Pesticide Applicators Association
Provides education and information for the professional horticultural applicator. Legislative work involves the states of Washington, Oregon, Idaho in the area of laws and regulations.

1289 **www.irrigation.org**
Irrigation Association
Membership organization for irrigation equipment and system manufacturers, dealers, distributors, designers, consultants, contractors and end users.

1290 **www.mailordergardening.com**
Mailorder Gardening Association
nonprofit organization serving the needs of companies involved in marketing gardening products to consumers

1291 **www.meatami.org**
American Meat Institute
Dedicated to increasing the efficiency, profitability and safety of meat and poultry worldwide.

1292 **www.naab-css.org**
National Association of Animal Breeders
To unite thos individuals and organizations engaged in the artificial insemination of cattle and other livestock into an affiliated federation operating under self-imposed standards of performance and to conduct and promote the mutual interest and ideals of its members.

1293 **www.nacaa.com**
National Association County Agricultural Agents
For agents focusing on educational programs for the youth of the community.

1294 **www.naicc.org**
National Alliance of Independent Crop Consultants
A professional society that represents the nation's crop porduction and research consultants.

1295 **www.nama.org**
National Agri-Marketing Association
Professional association for professionals in marketing and agribusiness.

1296 **www.nationalgrange.org**
Nat'l Grange of the Order of Patrons of Husbandry
Provides opportunities for individuals and families to develop to their highest potential in order to build stronger communities and states, as well as a stronger nation.

1297 **www.nationalplantboard.org**
National Plant Board
A non-profit organization of the plant pest regulatory agencies opf each of the staes and Commonwealth of Puerto Rico.

1298 **www.nationalpotatocouncil.Org**
National Potato Council
The advocate for the economic well-being of U.S. potato growers on federal legislative, regulatory, environmental and trade issues.

1299 **www.nfu.org**
National Farmers Union
Protects and enhances the economic well-being and quality of life for family farmers and ranchers and their rural communities

1300 **www.nppc.org**
National Pork Producers Council
Conducts public-policy outreach on behalf of its 43 affiliated state associations, enhancing opportunities for the success of U.S. pork producers and other industry stakeholders by establishing the U.S. pork industry as a consistent and responsible supplier of high-quality pork to the domestic and world markets.

1301 **www.ocia.org**
Organic Crop Improvement Association International
Dedicated to providing the highest quality organic certification serices and access to global organic markets

1302 **www.onions-usa.org**
National Onion Association
The official organization representing growers, shippers, brokers, and commerical representatives of the U.S. onion industry.

1303 **www.ota.com**
Organic Trade Association
A membership-based business association that focuses on the organic business community in North America. Promotes and protects the growth of organic trade to benefit the environment, farmers, the public and the economy.

1304 **www.pma.com**
Produce Marketing Association
Global trade association serving the entire produce and floral supply chains by enhancing the marketing of produce, floral, and related products and services worldwide.

1305 **www.profarmer.com**
Professional Farmers of America
Gives customers a competitive edge in marketing and financial management through timely delivery and accurate analysis of market-sensitive news and views.

1306 **www.sbsonline.org**
Society for Biomolecular Sciences
Non-profit scientific society dedicated to drug discovery and its related disciplines. Provides a

forum for global educationand information exchange among professionals in the chemical, pharmaceutical, biotech and agrochemical industries.

1307 **www.seedtechnology.net**
Society Commercial Seed Technologists
An organization comprised of commercial, independent and government seed technologists.

1308 **www.sheepusa.org**
American Sheep Industry Association
The national organization representing the interests of sheep producers located throughout the United States.

1309 **www.southerncottonginners.org**
Southern Cotton Ginners Association
Serves its members by providing safety, training, and regulatory representation.

1310 **www.southwesternassn.com**
SouthWestern Association
Established by a progressive group of independent hardware and farm implement/mercantile dealers to help increase their profitability and solve common problems.

1311 **www.soygrowers.com**
American Soybean Association
Represents U.S. soybean farmers through policy advocacy and international market development.

1312 **www.sugaralliance.org**
American Sugar Alliance
A natinoal coalition of sugarcane and sugarbeet farmers, processoris, refiners, suppliers, workers and others dedicated to preserving a strong domestic sugar industry.

1313 **www.sunflowernsa.com**
National Sunflower Association
A non-profit commodity organization working on problems and opportunities for the improvement of all members.

1314 **www.tfi.org**
Fertilizer Institute
The leading voice in the fertilizer industry, representing the public policy, communication and statistical needs of producers, manufacturers, retailers and transporters of fertilizer.

1315 **www.turfweeds.net**
Turfgrass Weed Science/Virginia Polytech Institute
Provides weed management information and research reports to turfgrass managers.

1316 **www.unitedfresh.org**
United Fresh Produce Association
Commited to driving the growth and success of produce companies and their partners. Represents the interests of member companies throughout the global, fresh produce supply chain, including family-owned, private and publicly traded businesses as well as regional, national and international companies.

1317 **www.usguernsey.com**
American Guernsey Association
Register and deliver guernsey cattle throughout the United States.

1318 **www.uspotatoes.com**
United States Potato Board
The central organizing force in implementing programs that will increase demand for potatoes.

1319 **www.vealfarm.com**
Veal Quality Association Program
For veal producers and processors.

1320 **www.wawgg.org**
Washington Association of Wine Grape Growers
Advocates for the Washington wine growing industry by educating, promotin, representing, and unifying the industry and fostering a positive business environment for continued growth and production of world-class, Washington-grown wines.

1321 **www.wildblueberries.com**
Wild Blueberry Association of North America
For processors and growers of wild blueberries in Eastern Canada and Maine.

Associations

1322 **Advanced BioFuels USA**
507 North Bentz Street
Frederick, MD 21701

301-644-1395
advancedbiofuelsusa.info

Joanne M. Ivancic, President/Executive Director
Robert E. Kozak, Treasurer
Dr. Craig Laufer, Secretary

A nonprofit organization that advocates for the adoption of advanced biofuels as an energy security, military flexibility, economic development andclimate change mitigation/pollution control solution though its promotion of public understanding, acceptance, and research.

1323 **Advanced Biofuels Association**
800 17th Street, NW
Suite 1100
Washington, DC 20006

www.advancedbiofuelsassociation.com
Social Media: Facebook, Twitter, LinkedIn, YouTube

Wayne Simmons, Chairman
Chris Ryan, Vice Chairman
Michael McAdams, President
Andrew Rojeski, Secretary
Christopher Higby, Treasurer

Organization that seeks to help America transform to a low carbon economy by supporting and advocating for public policies that are technology neutral, use sustainable feedstocks, and offering financial support to its member companies to bring products to market that are competitive and compatible with petroleum-based fuels and byproducts.
40 Members

1324 **Alliance for Affordable Energy**
P.O. Box 751133
New Orleans, LA 70175

504-208-9761
all4energy.org
Social Media: Facebook, Twitter, LinkedIn, YouTube, Instagram, Flickr

Casey DeMoss, Chief Executive Officer
Logan Atkinson Burke, Manager, Admin & Reg. Affairs
John Williams, Treasurer
Logan Atkinson, Office Development Manager
Logan Williams, Volunteer & Intern Manager

An environmental advocacy organization that promotes fair, affordable, environmentally responsible energy.
Founded in: 1985

1325 **Alliance to Save Energy**
1850 M Street, NW
Suite 610
Washington, DC 20036

202-857-0666; www.ase.org
Social Media: Facebook, Twitter, LinkedIn, YouTube, Google+, Flickr

Sen Mark Warner, Chairman
Jane Palmieri, Co-Chairman
Kateri Callahan, President
William Von Hoene, 1st Vice Chair
Frank Murray, Secretary

Organization that leads worldwide energy efficiency initiatives in policy advocacy, research, education and technology deployment.

1326 **Alternative Energy Association**
1061 East Indiantown Road
Suite 400
Jupiter, FL 33477

561-776-8600
alternativeenergyassn@gmail.com;
www.alternativeenergyassn.com

Organization that uses marketing campaigns, seminars, and eduactional activities to promote awareness of clean, renewable sources of power generation as alternatives to the use of fossil fuels for energy production.

1327 **Alternative Energy Resources Organization**
432 N. Last Chance Gulch
Helena, MT 59601

406-443-7272; *Fax:* 406-442-9120
aero@aeromt.org; www.aeromt.org
Social Media: Facebook, Twitter, Myspace, Pinterest, Google+

Jennifer Hill-Hart, Executive Director
Corrie Williamson, Comm. & Membership Director
Rosie Goldich, Abundant Montana Intern

A grassroots nonprofit organization dedicated to solutions that promote resource conservation and local economic vitality. By bringing people together, AERO offers a vehicle for collective action and a sense of common purpose for citizens within their communities to shape a more sustainable future.
Founded in: 1974

1328 **American Biogas Council**
1211 Connecticut Ave NW
Suite 600
Washington, DC 20036-2701

202-640-6595
info@americanbiogascouncil.org;
www.americanbiogascouncil.org
Social Media: Twitter, LinkedIn, YouTube, Flickr

Bernie Sheff, PE, Chairman
Paul Greene, Vice-Chair
Melissa VanOrnum, Treasurer
Mark Stoermann, Vice-Chair
Patrick Serfass, Executive Director (ex-officio)

Mission is to create jobs, environmental sustainability and energy independence by growing the American biogas industry.
Mailing list available for rent

1329 **American Coalition for Ethanol**
5000 South Broadband Lane
Suite 224
Sioux Falls, SD 57108

605-334-3381
cbeck@ethanol.org
ethanol.org
Social Media: Facebook, Twitter

Ron Alverson, President
Duane Kristensen, Vice President
Brian Jennings, Executive Vice President
Ron Lamberty, Senior Vice President
Chuck Beck, Director of Communications

Environmental advocacy organization that promotes the use of ethanol as the most successful renewable energy platform in the world.
Founded in: 1987

1330 **American Council for an Energy-Efficient Economy**
529 14th Street N.W
Suite 600
Washington, DC 20045-1000

202-507-4000; *Fax:* 202-429-2248;
www.aceee.org
Social Media: Facebook, Twitter, RSS

Alison Silverstein, President
Timothy M Stout, Treasurer
Peter A. Molinaro, Secretary
Roland J. Risser, Special Advisor
Jim Barrett, Chief Economist

A nonprofit organization that seeks to advance energy efficiency policies, programs, technologies, investments, and behaviors.

1331 **American Council on Renewable Energy**
1600 K Street NW
Suite 650
Washington, DC 20006

202-393-0001
weirich@acore.org; www.acore.org
Social Media: Facebook, Twitter, LinkedIn, YouTube

Michael R. Brower, Interim President and CEO
Todd Foley, Senior VP of Policy and Government
Dawn Butcher, Director of Event Planning
Cindi Ec, Director, Leadership Programs
Kevin Haley, Strategic Communications Manager

Works to bring all forms of renewable energy into the mainstream of America's economy and lifestyle. Members include every aspect and sector of the renewable energy industries and their trade associations, including wind, solar, geothermal, biomass and biofuels, hydropower tidal/current energy and waste energy.
Founded in: 2001

1332 **American Hydrogen Association**
P.O. Box 4205
Mesa, AZ 85201

480-234-5070
help@clean-air.org;
www.americanhydrogenassociation.org
Social Media: Facebook, YouTtube

Roy McAlister, President
Ben Ferguson, Vice President
Douglas Hawley, Secretary/Treasurer

Providing information on the use of hydrogen as a fuel.

1333 **American Solar Energy Society**
2525 Arapahoe Ave
Ste E4-253
Boulder, CO 80302

303-443-3130; *Fax:* 303-443-3212
info@ases.org; www.ases.org
Social Media: Facebook, Twitter, LinkedIn, Digg

David Panich, Chair
Tiffiny Harrower, Finance & Accounting Manager
Carly Rixham, Executive Director
Richard Behlmann, Secretary
Lauren Harrower, Membership Manager/Data Analyst

The nation's leading association of solar professionals & advocates. Mission is to inspire an era of energy innovation and speed the transition to a sustainable energy economy. Advancing education, research and policy.
13M Members
Founded in: 1954

1334 **American Water Works Association**
6666 W. Quincy Ave.
Denver, CO 80235-3098

303-794-7711
800-926-7337; *Fax:* 303-347-0804;
www.awwa.org
Social Media: Facebook, Twitter, LinkedIn, YouTube

Gene C. Koontz, President
Jeanne M. Bennett-Bailey, President Elect
John J. Donahue, Immediate Past President
David E. Rager, Treasurer
Jon Eaton, VP/Minnesota Section Director

The largest nonprofit, scientific and educational association dedicated to managing and treating water.
Founded in: 1881

1335 **American Wind Energy Association**
1501 M Street NW
Suite 1000
Washington, DC 20005

202-383-2500; *Fax:* 202-383-2505
windmail@awea.org; www.awea.org
Social Media: Facebook, Twitter, LinkedIn, YouTube, Flickr

Mike Garland, Chair
Pam Poisson, SVP Operations/CFO
Matthew Fuller, Director, Finance
Chi Wei, Director, Information Technology
Tom Kiernan, Chief Executive Officer

Promotes wind energy as a clean source of electricity for consumers around the world. Representing wind power project developers, equipment suppliers, services providers, parts manufacturers, utilities, researchers, and others involved in the wind industry - one of the world's fastest growing energy industries.
2500+ Members

1336 **Association of Energy Engineers**
3168 Mercer University Drive
Atlanta, GA 30341

770-447-5083
al@aeecenter.org; www.aeecenter.org
Social Media: Facebook, Twitter, LinkedIn, YouTube

Dr. Scott Dunning, President
Asit Patel, President Elect
Randy Haines, Past President
Ian Boylan, Secretary
Paul Goodman, Treasurer
17500 Members
Founded in: 1977

1337 **Association of Energy Engineers (AEE)**
3168 Mercer University Drive
Atlanta, GA 30341

770-447-5083; *Fax:* 770-446-3969
al@aeecenter.org; www.aeecenter.org
Social Media: Facebook, Twitter, YouTube

Dr. Scott Dunning, President
Albert Thumann, Executive Director
Kate Feltgen, Information Services Director
Lauren Lake, Event and Marketing Director
Patricia Ardavin, Membership Director

Information and networking in the dynamic fields of energy engineering and energy management, renewable and alternative energy, power generation, energy services, sustainability, and all related areas.
17500 Members
Founded in: 1977

1338 **Biomass Energy Research Association**
901 D Street, S.W
Suite 100
Washington, DC 20024

410-953-6202; *Fax:* 410-290-0377
bera@beraonline.org
beraonline.org

Joan Pellegrino, President/Treasurer
Phillip C. Badger, Secretary/Director
Mark A. Paisley, Director
Janis L. Tabor, Director
Dr. Evan Hughes, Director

An association of bioenergy researchers, companies, and advocates that promotes education and research on renewable biomass energy and waste-to-energy systems.

1339 **Biomass Power Association**
100 Middle St.
PO Box 9729
Portland, ME 04104-9729

202-494-2493
carrie@usabiomass.org; www.usabiomass.org

Bob Cleaves, President & CEO
Carrie Annand, VP of External Affairs
Nicholas Mazuroski, Director of Operations and Research
Katherine A. Pe¤a, Web Director

The nation's leading organization working to expand and advance the use of clean, renewable biomass power. Educates policymakers at the state and federal level about the benefits of biomass and provides regular briefings and research to keep members fully informed about public policy impacting the biomass industry. Members include local owners and operators of existing biomass facilities, suppliers, plant developers and others.
80 Members

1340 **Biomass Thermal Energy Council**
1211 Connecticut Avenue NW
Suite 600
Washington, DC 20036-2701

202-596-3974; *Fax:* 202-223-5537
info@biomassthermal.org;
www.biomassthermal.org
Social Media: Facebook, Twitter, LinkedIn, SlideShare, Vimeo

Dan Wilson, Chairman
Joel Stronberg, Executive Director
Dayanita Ramesh, Project Assistant
Emanuel Wagner, Programs Director
Ben Bell Walker, Technical Affairs

An association of biomass fuel producers, appliance manufacturers and distributors, supply chain companies and non-profit organizations that view biomass thermal energy as a renewable, responsible, clean and energy-efficient pathway to meeting America's energy needs. BTEC engages in research, education, and public advocacy for the fast growing biomass thermal energy industry.
Founded in: 2009

1341 **Business Council for Sustainable Energy**
805 15th Street, NW
Suite 708
Washington, DC 20005

202-785-0507; *Fax:* 202-785-0514
bcse@bcse.org; www.bcse.org
Social Media: Facebook, Twitter, LinkedIn

Mark Wagner, Chair
Rob Gramlich, Vice Chair
Scott Crider, Vice Chair
Lisa Jacobson, President
Ruth McCormick, Director, Federal and State Affairs

A coalition of companies and trade associations from the energy efficiency, natural gas and renewable energy sectors, and includes independent electric power producers, investor-owned utilities, public power, commercial end-users and project developers and service providers for environmental markets.

1342 **Canadian Renewable Fuels Association(CRFA)**
350 Sparks Street
Suite 605
Ottawa, ON K1R 7S8

613-594-5528; *Fax:* 613-594-3076
a.kent@greenfuels.org; www.greenfuels.org
Social Media: Facebook, Twitter, LinkedIn, Instagram

Andrea Kent, President
Deborah Elson, VP, Public Affairs & Membership
Tyler Bjornson, Executive Director
William Meyer, Manager, Communication
Jim Grey, Chair

Promotes and advances the use of renewable fuels for transporation- to protect our environment by reducing harmful emissions and to grow our economy by creating the good, green-energy jobs of the future.
Founded in: 1984

1343 **Center for Energy Efficiency and Renewable Technologies**
1100 11th Street
Suite 311
Sacramento, CA

916-442-7785
info@ceert.org
ceert.org
Social Media: Facebook, Twitter, LinkedIn

Jonathan M. Weisgall, Chairman
Ralph Cavanagh, Vice Chair
V. John White, Executive Director
John Shahabian, Director of Operations
Kevin Lynch, Secretary/Treasurer

A partnership of major environmental groups and private-sector clean energy companies that advocate for policies that promote global warming solutions and increased reliance on clean, renewable energy sources for California andthe West.
Founded in: 1990

1344 **Clean Energy Group**
50 State St.
Suite 1
Montpelier, VT 05602

802-223-2554; *Fax:* 802-223-4967;
www.cleanegroup.org
Social Media: Facebook, Twitter

Lewis Milford, President & Founder
Warren Leon, Executive Director, Clean Energy
Robert Sanders, Senior Finance Director
Valerie Stori, Project Director
Anthony Vargo, Chief Financial Officer

A leading nonprofit advocacy organization working in the US and internationally on innovative clean energy technology, finance, and policy programs. Supported by major foundations, as well as state, federal and international energy agencies.
Founded in: 1998

1345 **Distributed Wind Energy Association**
1065 Main Ave
Suite 209
Durango, CO 81301

928-380-6012
jjenkins@distributedwind.org

distributedwind.org
Social Media: Facebook, Twitter, LinkedIn

Mike Bergey, President
Chris Diaz, Vice President
Roger Dixon, Acting Secretary
Kevin Schulte, Acting Treasurer
Jennifer Jenkins, Executive Director

A collaborative group comprised of manufacturers, distributors, project developers, dealers, installers, and advocates, whose primary mission is to promote and foster all aspects of the American distributed wind energy industry.

1346 **Ducks Unlimited**
One Waterfowl Way
Memphis, TN 38120

901-758-3825
800-45D-UCKS; www.ducks.org
Social Media: Facebook, Twitter, YouTube, Instagram

George Dunklin, Jr., Chairman
Paul R. Bonderson, Jr., President
Dale Hall, Chief Executive Officer
Rogers Hoyt, Jr., First Vice President
Wendell Weakley, Treasurer

Conserves, restores, and manages wetlands and associated habitats for North America's waterfowl.
Founded in: 1937

1347 **Efficient Windows Collaborative**
21629 Zodiac Street NE
Wyoming, MN 55092

E-Mail: efficientwindowscollaborative@gmail.com; www.efficientwindows.org
Social Media: Facebook, Twitter, LinkedIn

A nonprofit organization that partners with window, door, skylight,and component manufacturers, research organizations, federal, state and local government agencies, and others interested in expanding the market for high-efficiency fenestration products.

1348 **Energy Recovery Council**
2200 Wilson Boulevard
Suite 310
Arlington, VA 22201

202-467-6240
tmichaels@energyrecoverycouncil.org;
www.energyrecoverycouncil.org

Ted Michaels, President

Represents the waste-to-energy industry and communities that own waste-to-energy facilities. Current ERC members own and operate modern waste-to-energy facilities that operate nationwide, safely disposing of municipal solid waste, while at the same time generating renewable electricity using modern combustion technology equipped with state-of-the-art emission control systems.

1349 **Environmental and Energy Study Institute**
1112 16th Street, NW
Suite 300
Washington, DC 20036-4819

202-628-1400; *Fax:* 202-204-5244
info@eesi.org; www.eesi.org
Social Media: Facebook, Twitter, LinkedIn, Vimeo

Jared Blum, Chairman
Carol Werner, Executive Director
David Robison, Director of Finance & Admin
Susan Williams, Director of Development
Alison Alford, Programs & Administrative Assistant

A nonprofit organization that advances innovative policy solutions that set us on a cleaner, more secure and sustainable energy path.
Founded in: 1984

1350 **Export Council for Energy Efficiency**
www.ecee.org

Laura Gubisch, Executive Director

A nonprofit association that promotes the export of energy efficient products, services, and technologies worldwide.
Founded in: 1994

1351 **Florida Solar Energy Center**
1679 Clearlake Rd.
Cocoa, FL 32922-5703

321-638-1000; *Fax:* 321-638-1010;
www.fsec.ucf.edu
Social Media: Facebook

James Fenton, Director

Created by the State of Florida in 1975, FSEC is the largest publicly-supported alternative energy research institute in the United States.
Founded in: 1975

1352 **Fuel Cell and Hydrogen Energy Association**
1211 Connecticut Avenue Northwest
#600
Washington, DC 20036

202-261-1337
info@fchea.org; www.fchea.org
Social Media: Facebook, Twitter, LinkedIn, Google+

Morry B. Markowitz, President
Bud DeFlaviis, Director of Government Affairs
Jennifer Gangi, Director of Comm. & Outreach
Sandra Curtin, Research & Comm. Manager
Connor Dolan, Director Of External Affairs

A trade association for the fuel cell and hydrogen energy industry,and is dedicated to the commercialization of fuel cells and hydrogen energy technologies.
Founded in: 2010

1353 **Geothermal Energy Association**
209 Pennsylvania Avenue SE
Washington, DC 20003

202-454-5261; *Fax:* 202-454-5265
jgreco@terra-genpower.com;
www.geo-energy.org
Social Media: Facebook, Twitter, LinkedIn, YouTube, Wordpress

Karl Gawell, Executive Director
Leslie Blodgett, Geothermal News Specialist
Kathy Kent, Sr. Director of Marketing
Mihaela-Daniela Lobontiu, Business Manager
Yoram Bronicki, President

Advocates for public policies that will promote the development and utilization of geothermal resources, provides a forum for the industry to discuss issues and problems, encourages research and development to improve geothermal technologies, presents industry views to governmental organizations, and conducts education and outreach projects.

1354 **Geothermal Exchange Organization**
312 S. Fourth St
Suite 100
Springfield, IL 62701

888-255-4436; www.geoexchange.org
Social Media: Facebook, Twitter, LinkedIn, Google+

Douglas Dougherty, President & CEO
Ted Clutter, Manager of Outreach

A nonprofit trade association that promotes the manufacture, designand installation of GeoExchange systems—an energy efficient and environmentallyfriendly heating and cooling technology.

1355 **Geothermal Resources Council**
630 Pe□a Dr.
Ste. 400
Davis, CA 95618-5476

530-758-2360; *Fax:* 530-758-2839
grc@geothermal.org; www.geothermal.org
Social Media: Facebook, Twitter, LinkedIn, YouTube, Flickr, Pinterest, Bl

Steve Ponder, Executive Director
Ian Crawford, Director of Communications, Editor
Estela M. Smith, GRC Office Manager
Anh Lay, Office Associate
Chi-Meng Moua, Graphic Designer

Nonprofit, educational association actively seeking to expand its role as a primary professional educational association for the international geothermal community.
1300+ Members
Founded in: 1970

1356 **Intergovernmental Renewable Energy Organization**
884 2nd Avenue, UN Centre
No. 20050
New York, NY 10017

917-862-6444; *Fax:* 212-202-4100;
www.ireoigo.org
Social Media: Facebook, Twitter

Dr. Anthony James Watson, Chairman
Heidi Walters, Chief Protocol Officer
Diane Mello, Executive Director Operations
John Hill, Secretary-General
Michael Rubin, Under Secretary

Promotes the urgent transition to renewable energy sources and sustainable development through collaborative effort and the implementation of projects that improve the lives of people while preserving the environment and our resources for future generations of humans.
Founded in: 2008

1357 **International Association for Energy Economics**
28790 Chagrin Blvd
Suite 350
Cleveland, OH 44122-4642

216-464-5365; *Fax:* 216-464-2737
iaee@iaee.org; www.iaee.org
Social Media: Facebook, LinkedIn

David Newbery, President
Jacques Percebois, Vice President for Publications
Christophe Bonnery, Vice President for Business & Govt.
G□rkan Kumbaroglu, Vice President for Conferences
Ricardo B. Raineri, Vice President for Academic Affairs

Association for those involved in energy economics including publications, consultants, energy database software.
3400 Members
Founded in: 1977
Mailing list available for rent

1358 **International Association for Hydrogen Energy**
5794 SW 40 St.
#303
Miami, FL 33155

E-Mail: info@iahe.org; www.iahe.org

Dr. T. Nejat Veziroglu, President
John W. Sheffield, Vice President
Juan Carlos Bolcich, Vice President for South America

Ibrahim Dinçer, Vice President for Strategy
Bruno Pollet, Vice President for South Africa

An association that stimulates the exchange of information in the Hydrogen Energy field through its publications and sponsorship of international workshops, short courses and conferences and endeavors to inform the general public of the important role of Hydrogen Energy in the planning of an inexhaustible and clean energy system.

1359 International District Energy Association
24 Lyman Street
Suite 230
Westborough, MA 1581

508-366-9339; *Fax:* 508-366-0019
idea@districtenergy.org;
www.districtenergy.org
Social Media: Facebook, Twitter, YouTube, Flickr, RSS

Bruce Ander, Chair
Tim Griffin, Vice Chair
Chris Lyons, Second Vice Chair
James Adams, Secretary/Treasurer
Ken Smith, Past Chair

An organization that actively works to foster the success of its members as leaders in providing reliable, economical, efficient and environmentally sound district heating, district cooling and cogeneration (combined heat and power) services.
Founded in: 1909

1360 International Ground Source Heat Pump Association
1201 S. Innovation Way Dr.
Suite 400
Stillwater, OK 74074

405-744-5175
800-626-4747; *Fax:* 405-744-5283
igshpa@okstate.edu; www.igshpa.okstate.edu
Social Media: Facebook, Twitter, Youtube, Google+

John Turley, President
Gail Ezepek, Conference and Membership Assistant
Janet Reeder, Technical Writer
Ben Champlin, Graphic Designer
Roshan Revankar, Manager

Member-driven organization established to advance ground source heat pump technology on local, state, national and international levels. IGSHPA utilizes state-of-the-art facilities for conducting GSHP system installation training and geothermal research. Mission is to promote the use of ground source heat pump technology worldwide through education and communication.
Founded in: 1987

1361 Interstate Renewable Energy Council
PO Box 1156
Latham, NY 12110-1156

518-458-6059
info@irecusa.org; www.irecusa.org
Social Media: Facebook, Twitter, LinkedIn, Pinterest, YouTube

Larry Shirley, Chair
Jane Weissman, President and CEO
Larry Sherwood, Vice President, COO
Maryteresa Colello, Administrative Coordinator
Louise Urgo, Administration

Works with industry, government, educators and other stakeholders to ensure that the broader use of renewable energies is possible, safe, affordable and practical, particularly for the individual consumer.
Founded in: 1982

1362 Lignite Energy Council
1016 E. Owens Avenue
PO Box 2277
Bismarck, ND 58502-2277

701-258-7117
800-932-7117; *Fax:* 701-258-2755
lec@lignite.com; www.lignite.com
Social Media: Facebook, Twitter, YouTube, RSS Feeds

Jason Bohrer, President/CEO
Marie Hoerner, Dir., Finance & Benefit Resources
Mike Jones, Ph. D., VP, Research and Development
Steve Van Dyke, Vice President of Communications
Kay LaCoe, Director of Membership Marketing

Regional Trade Association - promotes policies and activities that maintain a viable lignite industry and enhance development of our regions' lignite resources.
355 Members
Founded in: 1974

1363 Low Impact Hydropower Institute
PO Box 194
Harrington Park, NJ 07640

201-906-2189; *Fax:* 206-984-3086
mjsale@lowimpacthydro.org;
www.lowimpacthydro.org
Social Media: Facebook, Twitter, Google+ Pinterest

Julie Keil, Chair
John Seebach, Vice-Chair
Michael J. Sale, PhD, Executive Director
Dana Hall, Deputy Director
Jacob Palmer, Treasurer

Dedicated to reducing the impacts of hydropower generation through the certification of hydropower projects that have avoided or reduced their environmental impacts pursuant to the Low Impact Hydropower Institute's criteria. Mission is to reduce the impacts of hydropower dams through market incentives.

1364 NABCEP
56 Clifton Country Rd.
Suite 202
Clifton Park, NY 12065

800-654-0021; *Fax:* 518-899-1092
info@nabcep.org; www.nabcep.org
Social Media: Facebook

Don Warfield, Chair
Richard Lawrence, Executive Director
Kathryn Casey, Program Manager
Sue Pratt, Business Manager
Melissa Bell, Program Assistant

Mission is to support, and work with, the renewable energy and energy efficiency industries, professionals, and stakeholders. Goal is to develop voluntary national certification programs that will; promote renewable energy, provide value to practitioners, promote worker safety and skill, and promote consumer confidence.
Founded in: 2002

1365 National Association of Energy Service Companies
1615 M Street, NW
Suite 800
Washington, DC 20036

202-822-0950; *Fax:* 202-822-0955
info@naesco.org; www.naesco.org
Social Media: Facebook, LinkedIn

David Weiss, Chairman
Mike Kearney, Vice Chair
Terry E. Singe, Executive Director
Donald Gilligan, President
Scott Ririe, Secretary

An organization that promotes energy efficiency at state, federal, and international facilities; ensures the key role of ESCOs in delivering energyefficiency resources; and builds new market opportunities while growing existingmarkets.

1366 National Association of State Energy Officials
2107 Wilson Boulevard
Suite 850
Arlington, VA 22201

703-299-8800; *Fax:* 703-299-6208
energy@naseo.org; www.naseo.org
Social Media: Facebook, Twitter, LinkedIn, YouTube, Flickr

Janet Streff, Chair
Robert Jackson, Vice Chair
David Terry, Executive Director
Jeffrey C. Genzer, General Counsel
Marion Gold, Treasurer

A national nonprofit association that facilitates peer learning among state energy officials, serves as a resource for and about state energy offices, and advocates the interests of the state energy offices to Congress and federal agencies.
Founded in: 1986

1367 National Biodiesel Board
605 Clark Avenue
PO Box 104898
Jefferson City, MO 65110-4898

573-635-3893
800-929-3437; *Fax:* 573-635-7913
info@biodiesel.org; www.biodiesel.org
Social Media: Facebook, Twitter, YouTube, RSS Feeds, Google+

Kent Engelbrecht, Chairman
Mark Cunnningham, Vice-Chair
Greg Anderson, Treasurer
Chad Stone, Secretary

Mission is to advance the interests of its members by creating sustainable biodiesel industry growth. NBB serves as the industry's central coordinating entity and will be the single voice for its diverse membership base.

1368 National Fenestration Rating Council
6305 Ivy Lane
Suite 140
Greenbelt, MD 20770

301-589-1776; *Fax:* 301-589-3884
info@nfrc.org; www.nfrc.org
Social Media: Facebook, Twitter, LinkedIn, YouTube

James C. Benney, Chief Executing Officer
Deborah Callahan, Chief Operating Officer
Jessica Finn, Membership Coordinator
Cheryl Gendron, Meeting Manager
Scott Hanlon, Program Director

A nonprofit organization that administers an independent rating andlabeling system for the energy performance of windows, doors, skylights, and attachment products.
Founded in: 1989

1369 National Hydropower Association
601 New Jersey Ave NW
Suite 660
Washington, DC 20001

202-750-8402; *Fax:* 202-682-9478
help@hydro.org; www.hydro.org
Social Media: Facebook, Twitter

Linda Church Ciocci, Executive Director
Steve Wenke, Vice President
John McCormick, President
Debbie Mursch, Treasurer
John Suloway, Secretary

Dedicated to promoting the growth of clean, affordable US hydropower. Seeks to secure hydropower's place as a climate-friendly, renewable and reliable energy source that serves national environmental, energy, and economic policy objectives. Members are involved in projects throughout the US hydropower industry, including both federal and non-federal hydroelectric facilities.

1370 **National Renewable Energy Association**
629 North Main Street
Hattiesburg, MS 39401

601-582-3330; *Fax:* 601-582-3354
nrea@megagate.com;
www.nationalrenewableenergyassociation.org

A nonprofit organization dedicated to helping Americans use less energy and to use more renewable energy in the future.
Founded in: 2007

1371 **National Renewable Energy Laboratory**
15013 Denver West Parkway
Golden, CO 80401

303-275-3000; www.nrel.gov
Social Media: Facebook, Twitter, LinkedIn, YouTube

Dr. Dan Arvizu, President
Dr. Dana Christensen, Deputy Laboratory Director
Bobi Garrett, Deputy Laboratory Director
David Post, Acting Deputy Lab Director/COO
Howard Branz, Research Fellow

Develops renewable energy and energy efficiency technologies and practices, advances related science and engineering, and transfers knowledge and innovations to address the nation's energy and environmental goals.

1372 **National Wind Coordinating Collaborative**
1110 Vermont Ave NW
Suite 950
Washington, DC 20005

202-656-3303
info@awwi.org
nationalwind.org

Lauren Flinn, Facilitator
Abby Arnold, Senior Mediator

Provides a neutral forum for various stakeholders to pursue the shared objective of developing environmentally, economically, and politically sustainable commercial markets for wind power in the United States.
Founded in: 1994

1373 **Natural Resources Defense Council**
40 West 20th Street
New York, NW 10011

212-727-2700; *Fax:* 212-727-1773
webmaster@nrdc.org; www.nrdc.org
Social Media: Facebook, Twitter, YouTube, Tumblr, RSS

Daniel R. Tishman, Chairman
Frederick A.O. Schwarz, Chair Emeritus
Patricia Bauman, Vice Chair
Mary Moran, Treasurer
Alan F. Horn, Vice Chair

A nonprofit environmental action group that works to restore the natural elements, defend endangered species, and strives to safeguard the Earth: its people, its plants and animals and the natural systems on which all life depends.
14000 Members

1374 **North American Board of Certified Energy Practitioners**
56 Clifton Country Rd
Suite 202
Clifton Park, NY 12065

800-654-0021; *Fax:* 518-899-1092
info@nabcep.org; www.nabcep.org
Social Media: Facebook

Don Warfield, Chair
Richard Lawrence, Executive Director
Kathryn Casey, Program Manager
Sue Pratt, Business Manager
Melissa Bell, Program Assistant

Offers entry level knowledge assessment, professional certification, and company accreditation programs to renewable energy professionals throughout North America.
Founded in: 2002

1375 **Northeast Sustainable Energy Association**
50 Miles Street
Greenfield, MA 01301-3255

413-774-6051; *Fax:* 413-774-6053
nesea@nesea.org; www.nesea.org
Social Media: Facebook, Twitter, LinkedIn, YouTube

Jennifer Marrapese, Executive Director
Miriam Aylward, Director of Program Development
Mary Biddle, Deputy Executive Director
Gina Sieber, Business manager
Jenny Goldberg, Outreach & Event Coordinator

The nation's leading regional membership organization focused on promoting the understanding, development and adoption of energy conservation and non-polluting, renewable energy technologies.
1802 Members
Founded in: 1974

1376 **Ocean Renewable Energy Coalition**
12909 Scarlet Oak Drive
Darnestown, MD 20878

301-869-3790; *Fax:* 301-869-5637
info@oceanrenewable.com;
www.oceanrenewable.typepad.com
Social Media: Facebook, Twitter, RSS

Sean O'Neill, President
Carolyn Elefant, General and Regulatory Counsel

Exclusively dedicated to promoting marine and hydrokinetic energy technologies from clean, renewable ocean resources. Organization embraces a wide range of renewable technologies; including wave, tidal, current, offshore wind, ocean thermal, marine biomass and all other technologies that utilize renewable resources from oceans, tidal areas and other unimpounded water bodies to produce electricity, desalinized water, hydrogen, mariculture and other by products.
40+ Members
Founded in: 2005

1377 **Office of Energy Efficiency & Renewable Energy**
Forrestal Building
1000 Independence Avenue, SW
Washington, DC 20585

202-586-8302
energy.gov/eere/office-energy-efficiency-renewable-energy
Social Media: Facebook, Twitter, LinkedIn

David Danielson, Assistant Secretary
David Friedman, Principal Deputy Assis Secretary
Michael Budney, Director of Business Operations
John Lushetsky, Strategic Programs Director
Kathleen Hogan, Deputy Assistant Secretary

Leads the U.S. Department of Energy's efforts to develop and deliver market-driven solutions for energy-saving homes, buildings, and manufacturing;sustainable transportation; and renewable electricity generation.

1378 **One Sky**
One Sky
1635 Grandview Road
Gibsons, BC V0N 1V5

604-886-0508; www.onesky.ca

Michael S. Smithers, Executive Director
Lisa Gibson, Nigeria Integral Leadership Coord.
Gail Hochachka, Integral Program Coordinator

Explores and promotes practical solutions and appropriate technologies for our environmental. social and economic challenges in a global setting.
Founded in: 2000

1379 **Pellet Fuels Institute**
1901 North Moore St
Suite 600
Arlington, VA 22209

703-522-6778; *Fax:* 703-522-0548
hedrick@pelletheat.org; www.pelletheat.org
Social Media: Facebook, Twitter, LinkedIn

Stephen Faehner, Chairman
Jennifer Hedrick, Executive Director
Andrew Estep, Association Executive
John Crouch, Director of Public Affairs
Chris Amey, Vice Chairman

Promotes energy independence through the effiecient use of clean, renewable, densified biomass fuel.
Founded in: 1985

1380 **Portable Rechargeable Battery Association**
1776 K Street
4th Floor
Washington, DC 20006

202-719-4978; www.prba.org

Charlie Monahan, Chairman
Stephen P. Victor, President & COO
Chris Carlson, Vice President of Logistics
Andrew J. Sirjord, Vice President
Mark HickoK, Director

A nonprofit trade association that develops plans for workable battery recycling programs to be used industry wide and that serves as the voice of the Rechargeable Power Industry, representing its members on legislative, regulatory and standards issues at the state, federal and international level.
Founded in: 1991

1381 **Renewable Energy Markets Association (REMA)**
1211 Connecticut Ave NW
Suite 650
Washington, DC 20036-2701

202-640-6597; *Fax:* 202-223-5537
info@renewablemarketers.org;
www.renewablemarketers.org
Social Media: Facebook, Twitter

Richard Anderson, President
Ian McGowan, Vice President
Patrick Serfass, General Manager
Joel Stronberg, Director - Policy and Gov. Affairs
Kevin Maddaford, Treasurer

A nonprofit association dedicated to maintaining and growing strong markets for renewable energy in the United States. Representing organizations that sell, purchase, or promote renewable energy products.

1382 **Renewable Energy and Efficiency Business Association, Inc.**
185 Asylum Street
CityPlace I
Hartford, CT 06103-3469

E-Mail: pmichaud@murthalaw.com;
www.reeba.org

Jim Daylor, Chairman/Treasurer
John Michael Callahan, Vice Chairman
Christopher F. Haplin, President
Paul Michaud, Executive Director/Founder
Jackie Rowe, Director of Operations & Membership

An active business organization that promotes the sustainable deployment of renewable energy, DSM and energy efficiency advocacy, collaboration, networking, and information sharing.
Founded in: 2010

1383 **Renewable Fuels Association (RFA)**
425 Third Street SW
Suite 1150
Washington, DC 20024

202-289-3835; *Fax:* 202-289-7519;
www.ethanolrfa.org
Social Media: Facebook, Twitter, LinkedIn, YouTube, Google+, Instagram

Randall Doyal, RFA Chairman
Bob Dinneen, President & CEO
Kelly Davis, Director of Regulatory Affairs
Samantha Slater, Vice President, Government Affairs
Tony Jackson, Communications Director

The national trade association for the US ethanol industry promoting policies, regulations and research and development initiatives that will lead to the increased production and use of fuel ethanol. Membership includes a broad cross-section of businesses, individuals and organizations dedicated to the expansion of the US fuel ethanol industry.
181 Members
Founded in: 1981

1384 **Rocky Mountain Institute**
1820 Folsom Street
Boulder, CO 80302

303-245-1003
bet@rmi.org; www.rmi.org
Social Media: Facebook, Twitter, YouTube

Amory B. Lovins, Chief Scientist/Chair Emeritus
Marty Pickett, JD, Managing Director
Jules Kortenhorst, Chief Executive Officer
Robert Hutchinson, Senior Fellow
Kathy Wight, Executive Assistant

Emphasizes integrative design, advanced technologies working with the private sector as well as civil society and government to drive the transition from coal and oil to efficiency and renewables.
Founded in: 1982

1385 **Solar Electric Light Fund**
1612 K Street NW
Suite 300
Washington, DC 20006

202-234-7265
info@self.org
self.org
Social Media: Facebook, Twitter, YouTube

Robert A. Freling, Executive Director
Jeff Lahl, Project Director
John Alejandro, Communications Director
Darren Anderson, Project Manager
Lisa Esler, Finance Director

Designs and implements solar energy solutions to assist people living in energy poverty with their economic, educational, health care, and agricultural development.
Founded in: 1990

1386 **Solar Electric Power Association**
1220 19th Street, NW,
Suite 800
Washington, DC 20036-2405

202-857-0898; www.solarelectricpower.org
Social Media: Facebook, Twitter, LinkedIn, YouTube

Steve Malnight, Chair
Joseph Forline, Chair Elect
Julia Hamm, President & CEO
John Hewa, Secretary
Ervan Hancock, Treasurer

An educational nonprofit association dedicated to advancing utilityintegration of solar through collaborative solutions, objective information and shared benefits to the utility, its customers, and the public good.
Founded in: 1992

1387 **Solar Energy Industries Association**
600 14th Street, NW
Suite 400
Washington, DC 20005

202-682-0556
info@seia.org; www.seia.org
Social Media: Facebook, Twitter, LinkedIn, YouTube, Pinterest

Nat Kreamer, Chair
Tom Starrs, Vice Chair
Rhone Resch, President & CEO
Laura Stern, Treasurer
Scott Hennessey, Secretary

Works with its member companies to make solar a mainstream and significant energy source by expanding markets, removing market barriers, strenghtening the industry and educating the public on the benefits of solar energy.
1000 Members

1388 **Solar Energy International**
39845 Mathews Lane
Paonia, CO 81428

970-527-7657; www.solarenergy.org
Social Media: Facebook, Twitter, LinkedIn, YouTube

Ed Marston, Chairperson
Sarah Bishop, President

A nonprofit educational organization that provides industry-leadingtechnical training and expertise in renewable energy to empower people, communities, and businesses worldwide.
Founded in: 1991

1389 **Solar Living Institute**
PO Box 836
13771 S. Hwy 101
Hopland, CA 95449

707-472-2450; *Fax:* 707-472-2498
sli@solarliving.org
solarliving.org
Social Media: Facebook, Twitter, LinkedIn, YouTube

John Schaeffer, Founder/Board President
Karen Kallen, Managing Director
Miranda Mott, Programs Coordinator
Caleb Gordon, Farm & Garden Manager
Everardo Dominguez, Landscaper

A nonprofit solar training and sustainability organization. Mission is to promote sustainable living through inspirational environmental education.
Founded in: 1998

1390 **The Sustainable Biodiesel Alliance**
P.O. Box 1677
Kahului, HI 96732

512-410-7841; *Fax:* 512-410-7841
infoadmin@fuelresponsibly.org
test.sustainablebiodieselalliance.com/SBA/
Social Media: Facebook, Twitter

Kelly King, Chair
Annie Nelson, Vice-Chair
Mike Nasi, Treasurer
Ed Zwick, Secretary

An organization founded to support and encourage sustainable production and use of the renewable fuel biodiesel. Its primary mission is the completion of an independent sustainability certification system for U.S. Biodiesel Feedstock.
Founded in: 2006

1391 **UNEP SEF Alliance**
Clean Energy Group
50 State St.
Suite 1
Montpelier, VT 05602

802-223-2554; *Fax:* 802-223-4967
RTyler@cleanegroup.org;
www.unepsefalliance.org

The only convening body in the international system for public finance agencies in the clean energy sector. Members are visionary organizations from various countries pushing the forefront of how to do public finance for clean energy.

1392 **US Renewable Energy Association, LLC.**
PO Box 0550
Lexington, MI 48450

810-359-2250
sales@usrea.org; www.usrea.org
Social Media: Facebook, Twitter, LinkedIn, Google+, Pinterest, YouTube

Gerald Zack, Founder/ President / CEO

A volunteer renewable energy advocacy group working to educate and promote advanced technologies in the R.E. industry.

1393 **United States Clean Heat & Power Association**
1875 Connecticut Ave. NW
10th Floor
Washington, DC 20009

202-888-0708
information@chpassociation.org;
www.chpassociation.org
Social Media: Facebook, Twitter, Rss Feeds

Chrissy Borskey, Chair
Dale Louda, Executive Director
Debbie Chance, Vice Chair
Jim Kerrigan, Secretary
Paul Lemar, Treasurer

Providing superior advocacy, networking, education and market information to companies in the business of clean, local energy generation. Documents the benefits of clean heat and power to the public and to decision-makers. Also participates in federal agency programs to promote clean distributed energy.
Founded in: 1999

1394 **United States Energy Association**
1300 Pennsylvania Avenue, NW
Suite 550
Washington, DC 20004-3022

202-312-1230; *Fax:* 202-682-1682
reply@usea.org; www.usea.in
Social Media: Facebook, Twitter, LinkedIn

Vickey A. Bailey, Chairman
Will Polen, Senior Director
Sheila Slocum Hollis, Treasurer

Barry K. Worthington, Executive Director
Brian Kerans, Chief Financial Officer

An association of public and private energy-related organizations, corporations, and government agencies that represent the broad interests of the U.S. energy sector by increasing the understanding of energy issues, both domestically and internationally.

1395 **Wind Energy Foundation**
1501 M Street, NW
Suite 900
Washington, DC 20005

202-580-6440
info@windenergyfoundation.org;
www.windenergyfoundation.org
Social Media: Facebook, Twitter, YouTube

Steven Dayney, Chair
Edward Zaelke, Vice-Chair
Jayshree Desai, Treasurer
Tom Kiernan, Secretary
John Kostyack, Executive Director

A nonprofit organization dedicated to raising public awareness of wind as a clean, domestic energy source through communication, research, and education.
Founded in: 1970

1396 **Women's Council on Energy and the Environment**
816 Connecticut Ave NW
Suite 200
Washington, DC 20006

202-997-4512; *Fax:* 202-478-2098;
www.wcee.org
Social Media: Facebook, Twitter, LinkedIn

Robin Cantor, President
Mary Brosnan-Sell, Vice President
Joyce Chandran, Executive Director
Barbara Tyran, Treasurer
Alice Grabowski, Secretary

Supports women involved in the environmental community with education, research, new trend information and several publications.

1397 **World Resources Institute(WRI)**
10 G Street NE
Suite 800
Washington, DC 20002

202-729-7600; *Fax:* 202-729-7686
cpotochny@gmail.com; www.wri.org
Social Media: Facebook, Twitter, LinkedIn, YouTube, RSS

James A. Harmon, Chair
Andrew Steer, President & CEO
Steve Barker, CFO/Chief Administrative Officer
Manish Bapna, EVP/Managing Director
Lawrence MacDonald, VP, Communications

WRI takes research and puts ideas into action, working globally with governments, business and civil society to build transformative solutions that protect the earth and improve people's lives.
Founded in: 1982

Newsletters

1398 **BTEC Newsletter**
Biomass Thermal Energy Council
1211 Connecticut Avenue NW
Suite 600
Washington, DC 20036-2701

202-596-3974; *Fax:* 202-223-5537
info@biomassthermal.org;
www.biomassthermal.org
Social Media: Facebook, Twitter

Joseph Seymour, Executive Director
Charlie Niebling, Chairman
T.J. Morice, Vice-Chairman
Jon Strimling, Secretary
Bob Sourek, Treasurer

Provides member news, industry updates, upcoming events, and breaking BTEC news.
Frequency: Monthly
Founded in: 2009

1399 **Biogas News**
American Biogas Council
1211 Connecticut Ave NW
Suite 600
Washington, DC 20036-2701

202-596-3974; *Fax:* 202-223-5537
info@americanbiogascouncil.org;
www.americanbiogascouncil.org

Paul Greene, Chairman
Norma McDonald, Vice-Chair
Melissa VanOrnum, Treasurer
Nora Goldstein, Secretary

Members only publication includes everything from legislative updates to industry news and funding opportunities.
Frequency: Bi-Weekly

1400 **Clean Energy Direct**
IHS, Inc.

855-417-4155
energy@omeda.com; www.theenergydaily.com
Social Media: RSS

George Lobsenz, Executive Editor
Sabrina Ousmaal, Associate Publisher
Eric Lindeman, Contributing Editor

Get analysis of regulation, technology and industry news of renewables, top news in the clean energy industry as well as access to clean energy articles and archives.
Cost: $695.00
Frequency: Weekly

1401 **Climate Change News**
Environmental and Energy Study Institute
1112 16th Street, NW
Suite 300
Washington, DC 20036-4819

202-628-1400; *Fax:* 202-204-5244
cwerner@eesi.org; www.eesi.org
Social Media: Facebook, Twitter, YouTube

Carol Werner, Executive Director
Jared Blum, Chair
Shelley Fidler, Treasurer
Richard L. Ottinger, Chair Emeritus

Recounts the top climate science, business, and politics stories of the week and includes a list of upcoming events and pending federal legislation.
Frequency: Weekly
Founded in: 1984

1402 **Coal Outlook**
Pasha Publications
1600 Wilson Boulevard
Suite 600
Arlington, VA 22209-2509

703-528-1244
800-424-2908; *Fax:* 703-528-1253

Harry Baisden, Group Publisher
Michael Hopps, Editor
Kathy Thorne, Circulation Manager

Primary strategic information source that keeps coal marketing executives and utilities up-to-date on who's getting coal contracts and at what price.
Cost: $795.00
Frequency: Weekly

1403 **Coal Week International**
McGraw Hill
2 Penn Plz
Suite 25
New York, NY 10121-0101

212-904-2000
800-752-8878; *Fax:* 720-548-5701
support@platts.com; www.mcgraw-hill.com

Peter C Davis, President
David Stellfox, Editor
Harry Sachinis, CEO
Larry Barth, Marketing Manager

A market management intelligence service for executives concerned with world trade metallurgical and steam coal.
Cost: $987.00
8 Pages
Frequency: Weekly
Founded in: 1888

1404 **Coal and Synfuels Technology**
Pasha Publications
1600 Wilson Boulevard
Suite 600
Arlington, VA 22209-2510

703-528-1244
800-424-2908; *Fax:* 703-528-1253

Harry Baisden, Group Publisher
Michael Hopps, Editor

Reports on the US and international advances in clean coal technologies, synthetic fuels and clean air issues.
Cost: $790.00
Frequency: Weekly
Founded in: 1985

1405 **Connecting to the Grid**
Interstate Renewable Energy Council
PO Box 1156
Latham, NY 12110-1156

518-458-6059
info@irecusa.org; www.irecusa.org

Laurel Varnado, Editor
Ken Jurman, Chair
David Warner, Vice Chair
Jane Pulaski, Secretary
Jennifer Szaro, Treasurer

Focusing on the latest news on interconnection and net metering in the US.
Frequency: Monthly

1406 **Council on Women in Energy and Environmental Leadership Newsletter**
Association of Energy Engineers
4025 Pleasantdale Rd
Suite 420
Atlanta, GA 30340-4264

770-447-5083; *Fax:* 770-446-3969
info@aeecenter.org; www.aeecenter.org
Social Media: Facebook, Twitter, LinkedIn, YouTube

Eric A. Woodroof, President
Gary Hogsett, President Elect
Bill Younger, Secretary
Paul Goodman, C.P.A., Treasurer

Addressing the high cost of energy, present and future sources of energy, and the impact of energy on the environment.
8.2M Members
Founded in: 1977

1407 **EESI Update**
Environmental and Energy Study Institute
1112 16th Street, NW
Suite 300
Washington, DC 20036-4819

202-628-1400; *Fax:* 202-204-5244
cwerner@eesi.org; www.eesi.org
Social Media: Facebook, Twitter, YouTube

Carol Werner, Executive Director
Jared Blum, Chair

Shelley Fidler, Treasurer
Richard L. Ottinger, Chair Emeritus

Updating supporters about the current work of EESI.
Frequency: 3x Yearly
Founded in: 1984

1408 Energy Insight
Association of Energy Engineers (AEE)
4025 Pleasantdale Rd.
Suite 420
Atlanta, GA 30340

770-447-5083; *Fax:* 770-446-3969
al@aeecenter.org; www.aeecenter.org
Social Media: Facebook, Twitter, YouTube

Albert Thumann, Executive Director

Written by, about and for the AEE member. Electronic publication includes information on AEE news, officers, award programs, nominations, certification, chapter news, operations report, presidents' message, study missions, upcoming events, and more.
15M Members
Frequency: Tri-Annually
Founded in: 1977
Mailing list available for rent

1409 GRC Bulletin
Geothermal Resources Council
20001 Second Street
Suite 5
Davis, CA 95618-5476

530-758-2360; *Fax:* 530-758-2839
grc@geothermal.org; www.geothermal.org
Social Media: Facebook, Twitter, LinkedIn, YouTube, Flickr

Curt Robinson, Ph.D, Executive Director

Features articles on technical topics and geothermal development issues, as well as commentaries and news briefs.
Frequency: 6x Yearly
Founded in: 1970

1410 Geothermal Energy Weekly
Geothermal Energy Association
209 Pennsylvania Avenue SE
Washington, DC 20003

202-454-5241
jgreco@terra-genpower.com;
www.geo-energy.org

Karl Gawell, Executive Director
Leslie Blodgett, Editor-in-Chief
Paul Thomsen, President
Jonathan M. Weisgall, Chairman

Electronic newsletter providing updates on the national, state, and international levels, and includes news from GEA member companies. Upcoming events, job opportunities, and Requests for Proposals are also found here.
Frequency: Weekly

1411 NABCEP News
56 Clifton Country Rd.
Suite 202
Clifton Park, NY 12065

800-654-0021; *Fax:* 518-899-1092
info@nabcep.org; www.nabcep.org

Ezra Auerbach, Executive Director
Don Warfield, Chair
Jane Weissman, Vice Chair
Les Nelson, Treasurer
Jeff Spies, Secretary

Newsletter from the North American Board of Certified Energy Practitioners featuring news, updates, technical issues and accomplishments of their certificants. Available electronically only.
Frequency: Bi-Monthly
Founded in: 2000

1412 NHA Today
National Hydropower Association
25 Massachusetts Ave, NW
Suite 450
Washington, DC 20001

202-682-1700; *Fax:* 202-682-9478
help@hydro.org; www.hydro.org
Social Media: Facebook, Twitter

Linda Church Ciocci, Executive Director
David Moller, President
James Crew, Treasurer
John Ragonese, Vice President
Tim Oakes, Secretary

Offers the latest information on regulatory and legislative policy, regional concerns, and issues on the horizon. Available electronically to members of NHA only.
Frequency: Bi-Weekly

1413 OREC Newsletter
Ocean Renewable Energy Coalition

301-869-3790
info@oceanrenewable.com;
www.oceanrenewable.typepad.com

Sean O'Neill, President
Carolyn Elefant, General Counsel

Striving to keep members, legislators, regulators, the media and the public at large up to date with OREC's activities as well as ongoing developments in this emerging industry.
40+ Members
Frequency: Weekly
Founded in: 2005

1414 Pellet Fuels Institute
Pellet Fuels Institute.
1901 North Moore Street
Suite 600
Arlington, VA 22209

703-522-6778; *Fax:* 703-522-0548
pfimail@pelletheat.org; www.pelletheat.org

Jennifer Hedrick, Executive Director
Jason Berthiaume, Membership/Gov't Affairs
John Crouch, Director of Public Affairs

Newsletter with industry news, updates published quarterly

1415 Renewable Energy in the 50 States
American Council on Renewable Energy(ACORE)
1660 K Street NW
Suite 650
Washington, DC 20006

202-393-0001; www.acore.org

Dennis V. McGinn, President/CEO
Tom Weirich, VP of Corporate Relations
Dawn Butcher, Director of Event Planning/Mktg.

Executive summary on the status of renewable energy implementation at the state-level. A two-page overview on key developments including installed and planned projects.
Founded in: 2001

1416 Small Wind Energy
Interstate Renewable Energy Council
PO Box 1156
Latham, NY 12110-1156

518-458-6059
info@irecusa.org; www.irecusa.org

Larry Sherwood, Editor
Ken Jurman, Chair
David Warner, Vice Chair
Jane Pulaski, Secretary
Jennifer Szaro, Treasurer

Featuring updates and news about small wind energy issues.
Frequency: Quarterly

1417 Solar@Work
American Solar Energy Society
4760 Walnut Street
Suite 106
Boulder, CO 80301

303-443-3130; *Fax:* 303-443-3212
ases@ases.org; www.ases.org
Social Media: Facebook, Twitter, LinkedIn

Susan Greene, President
David G. Hill, Chair
Bill Poulin, Treasurer
Jason Keyes, Secretary

Get the latest business and market analysis, technology breakthroughs and career advice from ASES professionals.
13M Members
Frequency: Bi-Monthly
Founded in: 1954

1418 Sun Times
Alternative Energy Resources Organization
432 N. Last Chance Gulch
Helena, MT 59601

406-443-7272; *Fax:* 406-442-9120
aero@aeromt.org; www.aeromt.org
Social Media: Facebook, Twitter, Myspace

Bryan von Lossberg, Executive Director

Stay up to date on AERO news and events.
Frequency: Monthly
Founded in: 1974

1419 Sustainable Bioenergy, Farms, and Forests
Environmental and Energy Study Institute
1112 16th Street, NW
Suite 300
Washington, DC 20036-4819

202-628-1400; *Fax:* 202-204-5244
cwerner@eesi.org; www.eesi.org
Social Media: Facebook, Twitter, YouTube

Carol Werner, Executive Director
Jared Blum, Chair
Shelley Fidler, Treasurer
Richard L. Ottinger, Chair Emeritus

A look at sustainable bioenergy, farm, and forest policy issues.
Frequency: Weekly
Founded in: 1984

1420 The Biodiesel Bulletin
National Biodiesel Board
605 Clark Ave
PO Box 104898
Jefferson City, MO 65110-4898

573-635-3893; *Fax:* 573-635-7913
info@biodiesel.org; www.biodiesel.org
Social Media: Facebook, Twitter, YouTube

Kent Engelbrecht, Chairman
Mark Cunningham, Vice-Chair
Greg Anderson, Treasurer
Chad Stone, Secretary

Electronic publication keeping members up to date on the biodiesel industry and technology.
Frequency: Monthly
Mailing list available for rent

1421 The Energy Daily
IHS, Inc.

855-417-4155
energy@omeda.com; www.theenergydaily.com

George Lobsenz, Executive Editor
Sabrinal Ousmaal, Associate Publisher
Erica Lengermann, Manager, Sales

Keeping readers at the forefront of all major developments in the energy industry. Through in-depth analysis of issues, cutting-edge reporting and unbiased journalism, The Energy Daily continues to deliver the news readers need for

business success.
Cost: $2497.00
Frequency: Daily

1422 **The Energy Roundup**
IHS, Inc.

855-417-4155
energy@omeda.com; www.theenergydaily.com

George Lobsenz, Executive Editor
Sabrinal Ousmaal, Associate Publisher
Erica Lengermann, Manager, Sales

The most important developing stories delivered weekly.
Frequency: Weekly

1423 **The IREC Report**
Interstate Renewable Energy Council
PO Box 1156
Latham, NY 12110-1156

518-458-6059
info@irecusa.org; www.irecusa.org

Jane Pulaski, Editor
Ken Jurman, Chair
David Warner, Vice Chair
Jane Pulaski, Secretary
Jennifer Szaro, Treasurer

A monthly recap of the latest news about IREC's programs, policies and best practices in renewable energy.
Frequency: Monthly

1424 **The ISPQ Insider**
Interstate Renewable Energy Council
PO Box 1156
Latham, NY 12110-1156

518-458-6059
info@irecusa.org; www.irecusa.org

Jane Pulaski, Editor
Ken Jurman, Chair
David Warner, Vice Chair
Jane Pulaski, Secretary
Jennifer Szaro, Treasurer

A monthly recap of the latest news, policies and best practices from the ISPQ credentialing program for renewable energy, weatherization and the energy retrofit sector.
Frequency: Monthly

1425 **The SITN Quarterly**
Interstate Renewable Energy Council
PO Box 1156
Latham, NY 12110-1156

518-458-6059
info@irecusa.org; www.irecusa.org

Jane Pulaski, Editor
Ken Jurman, Chair
David Warner, Vice Chair
Jane Pulaski, Secretary
Jennifer Szaro, Treasurer

Summary of the latest news, policies and best practices from the Solar Instructor Training Network.
Frequency: Quarterly

1426 **Utility Reporter: Fuels, Energy and Power**
InfoTeam
PO Box 15640
Plantation, FL 33318-5640

954-473-9560; *Fax:* 954-473-0544
infoteamma@aol.com

Randy M Allen CPA, Editor

Focuses on activities involving: power generation, combustion, delivery and transmission; alternative energy devices and systems; heat transfer, storage and utilization; and myriad of related topics.
Cost: $289.00
20 Pages
Frequency: Monthly
ISBN: 0-890298-4 -
Printed in one color on matte stock

1427 **Wind Energy SmartBrief**
American Wind Energy Association
1501 M Street NW
Suite 1000
Washington, DC 20005

202-383-2500; *Fax:* 202-383-2505
windmail@awea.org; www.awea.org
Social Media: Facebook, Twitter, YouTube, Flickr

Ned Hall, Chair
Thomas Carnahan, Chair-Elect
Gabriel Alonso, Secretary
Don Furman, Treasurer
Denise Bode, CEO

Delivers quickly digestible summaries of the day's wind energy-related stories from across the media, as well as links to those stories. SmartBrief not only keeps readers informed about the industry, it allows them to stay on top of what's being said about it.
2500+ Members
Frequency: Daily

1428 **Wind Energy Weekly**
American Wind Energy Association
1501 M Street NW
Suite 1000
Washington, DC 20005

202-383-2500; *Fax:* 202-383-2505
windmail@awea.org; www.awea.org
Social Media: Facebook, Twitter, YouTube, Flickr

Ned Hall, Chair
Thomas Carnahan, Chair-Elect
Gabriel Alonso, Secretary
Don Furman, Treasurer
Denise Bode, CEO

Packed with detailed and up-to-date information on the world of wind energy that simply can't be obtained elsewhere. Readers have a professional interest in wind energy, need to keep up with wind energy development news or late-breaking legislative, economic, and environmental developments.
2500+ Members
Frequency: Weekly

Magazines & Journals

1429 **Biodiesel Magazine**
BBI International
308 2nd Avenue North
Suite 304
Grand Forks, ND 58203

866-746-8385; *Fax:* 701-746-5367
service@bbiinternational.com;
www.biodieselmagazine.com
Social Media: Twitter, YouTube

Trade journal dedicated to objective, independent coverage of biodiesel news, events and information relevant to the global industry. With editorial focus on US and international methyl ester manufacturing, trade, distribution and markets, Biodiesel Magazine also provides valuable insight into feedstock and market share competition from the non-ester renewable diesel sector.
Frequency: Monthly

1430 **Biomass Power & Thermal**
Biomass Thermal Energy Council
1211 Connecticut Avenue NW
Suite 600
Washington, DC 20036-2701

202-596-3974; *Fax:* 202-223-5537
info@biomassthermal.org;
www.biomassthermal.org
Social Media: Facebook, Twitter

Joseph Seymour, Executive Director
Charlie Niebling, Chairman
T.J. Morice, Vice-Chairman
Jon Strimling, Secretary
Bob Sourek, Treasurer

Tailored for industry professionals engaged in utilizing biomass for the generation of electricity, thermal energy, or both (CHP). Maintains a core editorial focus on biomass logistics; generating, cultivating, collecting, transporting, processing, marketing, procuring and utilizing sustainable biomass for power and heat.
Frequency: Monthly
Founded in: 2009

1431 **Distributed Generation & Alternative Energy Journal**
Association of Energy Engineers (AEE)
4025 Pleasantdale Rd.
Suite 420
Atlanta, GA 30340

770-447-5083; *Fax:* 770-446-3969
al@aeecenter.org; www.aeecenter.org
Social Media: Facebook, Twitter, YouTube

Albert Thumann, Executive Director
Jorge B. Wong, Ph.D, Editor-in-Chief

An authoritative publication which provides readers with detailed information on the latest innovations and developments in the distributed generation and related alternative energy fields.
15M Members
Frequency: Quarterly

1432 **Energy Engineering**
Association of Energy Engineers (AEE)
4025 Pleasantdale Rd.
Suite 420
Atlanta, GA 30340

770-447-5083; *Fax:* 770-446-3969
al@aeecenter.org; www.aeecenter.org
Social Media: Facebook, Twitter, YouTube

Albert Thumann, Executive Director
Jorge B. Wong, Ph.D, Editor-in-Chief

The oldest journal exclusively written for engineers, energy managers, facility managers, utility professionals, VP's of operations, governmental energy managers and plant engineers involved in the design and application of energy management and facility improvement technologies.
15M Members
Frequency: Monthly
Founded in: 1904

1433 **Energy Law Journal**
Federal Energy Bar Association
1990 M St Nw
Suite 350
Washington, DC 20036-3429

202-223-5625; *Fax:* 202-833-5596
admin@eba-net.org; www.eba-net.org

Lorna Wilson, Administrator
Clinton A. Vince, Editor-in-Chief

Lawyers and consultants engaged in energy and public utility law.
Cost: $35.00
Frequency: Monthly
Circulation: 2600
ISSN: 0270-9163
Founded in: 1946
Printed in 2 colors on matte stock

1434 **Geo Outlook**
International Ground Source Heat Pump Association

1201 S Innovation Way
Suite 400
Stillwater, OK 74074

405-744-5175
800-626-4747; *Fax:* 405-744-5283
igshpa@okstate.edu; www.igshpa.okstate.edu

Jim Bose, Ph.D, Executive Director
Shelly Fitzpatrick, Conference & Membership Coordinator
John Turley, Chairman
Jack Henrich, Vice Chairman

The official publication of the geoexchange industry.
Frequency: Quarterly
Circulation: 50000

1435 Home Power Magazine
312 N. Main Street
Phoenix, OR 97535

541-512-0201
800-707-6585; www.homepower.com
Social Media: Facebook, Twitter

Claire Anderson, Associate Editor

For renewable energy and sustainable living enthusiasts- homeowners and industry professionals alike. Specializing in hands-on, practical information about RE technologies, and presenting technical material in an easy-to-use format.
Frequency: Bi-Monthly

1436 IEEE Power and Energy Magazine
IEEE Power Electronics Society
445 Hoes Lane
Piscataway, NJ 08854

732-981-0061; *Fax:* 732-981-9667
pels-staff@ieee.org; www.ieee-pels.org

Mel Olken, Editor
Susan Schneiderman, Business Development

Dedicated to disseminating information on all matters of interest to electric power engineers and other professionals involved in the electric power industry. Feature articles focus on advanced concepts, technologies, and practices associated with all aspects of electric power from a technical perspective in synergy with nontechnical areas such as business, environmental, and social concerns.
Cost: $260.00
82 Pages
Frequency: Monthly
Circulation: 23000
ISSN: 1540-7977
Founded in: 2003
Mailing list available for rent
Printed in on glossy stock

1437 Renewables Global Status Report
REN21
REN21 Secretariat c/o UNEP
15, Rue de Milan 75441
Paris, France CEDEX 09

+33 1 44 3714 5090
secretariat@ren21.net; www.ren21.net

Mohamed EI-Ashry, Chair-UN Foundation
Michael Eckhart, VP- Citygroup
Kevin Nassiep, VP
Christine Lins, Executive Secretary

The Global Status Report(GSR) is the collaborative effort of over 400 authors, contributors and reviewers and is today the most frequently referenced report on renewable energy market, industry and policy trends. it provides testimony of the undeterred growth of electricity. heat and fuel production capacities from renewable energy sources including solar PV, wind power, solar hot water/heating, biofuels. hydropower and geothermal.

1438 SOLAR TODAY
American Solar Energy Society
4760 Walnut Street
Suite 106
Boulder, CO 80301

303-443-3130; *Fax:* 303-443-3212
ases@ases.org; www.ases.org
Social Media: Facebook, Twitter, LinkedIn

Susan Greene, President
David G. Hill, Chair
Bill Poulin, Treasurer
Jason Keyes, Secretary

With the renewable energy industry changing at an unprecedented pace, SOLAR TODAY helps readers understand the changes, where the industry is headed, and how it's affecting the country.
13M Members
Frequency: 9x Yearly
Founded in: 1954

1439 Solar Energy
Elsevier Science
655 Avenue of the Americas
PO Box 945
New York, NY 10010-5107

212-633-3800; *Fax:* 212-633-3850;
www.elsevier.com

Young Suk Chi, Manager

Devoted exclusively to the science and technology of solar energy applications. Presents information not previously published in journals on any aspect of solar energy research, development, application, measurement or policy.
Frequency: Monthly
Circulation: 6400

1440 Strategic Planning for Energy and the Environment
Association of Energy Engineers (AEE)
4025 Pleasantdale Rd.
Suite 420
Atlanta, GA 30340

770-447-5083; *Fax:* 770-446-3969
al@aeecenter.org; www.aeecenter.org
Social Media: Facebook, Twitter, YouTube

Albert Thumann, Executive Director
Dr. Wayne C. Turner, Editor

Concentrates on the background, new developments and policy issues which impact corporate planning for energy savings, operational efficiency, and environmental concerns.
15M Members
Frequency: Quarterly

1441 The Ally
BlueGreen Alliance
1020 19th Street NW
Suite 600
Washington, DC 20036

202-706-6910; www.bluegreenalliance.org
Social Media: Facebook, Twitter, flickr, YouTube

David Foster, Executive Director

A biweekly update providing reports, letters, press releases and other publications along with clean energy industry news.

1442 The Energy Journal
International Association for Energy Economics
28790 Chagrin Blvd
Suite 350
Cleveland, OH 44122-4642

216-464-5365; *Fax:* 216-464-2737
iaee@iaee.org; www.iaee.org
Social Media: Facebook, LinkedIn

Mine Yucel, President
Lars Bergman, President-Elect
David L. Williams, Executive Director

Promotes the advancement and dissemination of new knowledge concerning energy and related topics. Publishing a blend of theoretical, empirical and policy related papers in energy economics.
3400 Members
Founded in: 1977

Trade Shows

1443 AERO Annual Meeting
Alternative Energy Resources Organization
432 N. Last Chance Gulch
Helena, MT 59601

406-443-7272; *Fax:* 406-442-9120
aero@aeromt.org; www.aeromt.org
Social Media: Facebook, Twitter, Myspace

Bryan von Lossberg, Executive Director

Sustainability Begins at Home.
Frequency: Annual/ October
Founded in: 1974

1444 AWEA Offshore Windpower Conference & Exhibition
American Wind Energy Association
1501 M Street NW
Suite 1000
Washington, DC 20005

202-383-2500; *Fax:* 202-383-2505
windmail@awea.org; www.awea.org
Social Media: Facebook, Twitter, YouTube, Flickr

Ned Hall, Chair
Thomas Carnahan, Chair-Elect
Gabriel Alonso, Secretary
Don Furman, Treasurer
Denise Bode, CEO

Brings together exhibitors and attendees from all over the world who are interested in becoming players in this new and highly promising market.
2500+ Members
1700 Attendees
Frequency: Annual/October

1445 AWEA Windpower Conference & Exhibition
American Wind Energy Association
1501 M Street NW
Suite 1000
Washington, DC 20005

202-383-2500; *Fax:* 202-383-2505
windmail@awea.org; www.awea.org
Social Media: Facebook, Twitter, YouTube, Flickr

Ned Hall, Chair
Thomas Carnahan, Chair-Elect
Gabriel Alonso, Secretary
Don Furman, Treasurer
Denise Bode, CEO

Recognized as one of the world's premier wind energy trade shows, bringing together attendees and exhibitors from every aspect of the industry. Exhibitors display the latest industry products and services from manufacturing leaders, component suppliers, and other wind energy organizations. This conference combines education, exhibition, and networking creating a perfect venue for business development.
2500+ Members
16000 Attendees
Frequency: Annual/June

1446 Annual Algae Biomass Summit
Biomass Power Association

100 Middle St.
PO Box 9729
Portland, ME 04104-9729

703-889-8504
info@biomasspowerassociation.com;
www.usabiomass.org

Bob Cleaves, President & CEO
Gary Melow, State Projects Coordinator

This dynamic event unites industry professionals from all sectors of the world's algae utilization industries including, but not limited to; financing, algal ecology, genetic systems, carbon partitioning, engineering & analysis, biofuels, animal feeds, fertilizers, bioplastics, supplements and foods.
80 Members
Frequency: Annual/October

1447 **Annual National Ethanol Conference**
Renewable Fuels Association
425 Third Street SW
Suite 1150
Washington, DC 20024

202-289-3835; *Fax:* 202-289-7519
necregistration@bbiinternational.com;
www.ethanolrfa.org
Social Media: Facebook, Twitter, YouTube, Flickr

Bob Dinneen, President & CEO
Christina Martin, Executive Vice President
Alex Obuchowski, CFO

Recognized as the preeminent conference for delivering accurate, timely information on marketing, legislative and regulatory issues facing the ethanol industry. Meet and interact with key stakeholders and take part in shaping the future of the ethanol industry.
1250+ Attendees
Frequency: Annual/February
Founded in: 1981

1448 **Annual North American Waste-to-Energy Conference**
Solid Waste Association of North America - SWANA

800-GOS-WANA; *Fax:* 301-589-7068;
www.nawtec.org

Co-sponsored by ERC, ASME and SWANA, in partnership with WTERT, the conference and trade show focuses on municipal waste-to-energy operational issues and policy, technology and research initiatives.

1449 **Annual Renewable Energy Technology Conference & Exhibition (RETECH)**
American Council on Renewable Energy
1600 K Street NW
Suite 700
Washington, DC 20006
202-393-0001
vay@acore.org; www.refindirectory.com
Social Media: Facebook, Twitter, LinkedIn, YouTube

Dennis V. McGinn, President

Conference sessions deliver unparalleled educational content including business development opportunities, topical professional development, current trends, the newest technologies and important up-to-date information on the changing legislative and regulatory landscapes. Exhibition offers the best opportunity to meet, network and connect with companies and organizations in the renewable energy industry.
3000+ Attendees
Frequency: Annual/October
Founded in: 2001

1450 **Bioenergy Fuels & Products Conference & Expo**
Biomass Thermal Energy Council
1211 Connecticut Avenue NW
Suite 600
Washington, DC 20036-2701

202-596-3974; *Fax:* 202-223-5537
info@biomassthermal.org;
www.biomassthermal.org
Social Media: Facebook, Twitter

Joseph Seymour, Executive Director
Charlie Niebling, Chairman
T.J. Morice, Vice-Chairman
Jon Strimling, Secretary
Bob Sourek, Treasurer

Speakers and moderators who will address a range of topics including raw material, product and market developments and bio-process technologies.
Frequency: Annual/March
Founded in: 2009

1451 **Biomass Thermal DC Summit**
Biomass Thermal Energy Council
1211 Connecticut Avenue NW
Suite 600
Washington, DC 20036-2701

202-596-3974; *Fax:* 202-223-5537
info@biomassthermal.org;
www.biomassthermal.org
Social Media: Facebook, Twitter

Joseph Seymour, Executive Director
Charlie Niebling, Chairman
T.J. Morice, Vice-Chairman
Jon Strimling, Secretary
Bob Sourek, Treasurer

Summit participants engage policy makers and renewable energy - related groups on the substantial benefits of biomass thermal energy use; increased rural economic activity, energy independence, healthier forests, and effective tax policy.
Frequency: Annual/November
Founded in: 2009

1452 **Building Energy**
Northeast Sustainable Energy Association
50 Miles St
Greenfield, MA 01301-3255

413-774-6051; *Fax:* 413-774-6053
nesea@nesea.org; www.nesea.org
Social Media: Facebook, Twitter, LinkedIn

David Barclay, Executive Director
Sonia Hamel, Vice Chair
Daniel Sagan, Secretary
Michael Skelly, Treasurer

Oldest and largest regional renewable energy event in the country, known for showcasing next-generation thinkers and game-changing ideas.
1802 Members
Founded in: 1974
Mailing list available for rent

1453 **Geothermal Energy Expo**
Geothermal Energy Association
209 Pennsylvania Avenue SE
Washington, DC 20003

202-454-5261; *Fax:* 202-454-5265
jgreco@terra-genpower.com;
www.geo-energy.org

Karl Gawell, Executive Director
Leslie Blodgett, Editor-in-Chief
Paul Thomsen, President
Jonathan M. Weisgall, Chairman
Kathy Kent, Director of Events

The world's largest gathering of vendors providing support for geothermal resource exploration, characterization, development, production and management. Provides a unique opportunity for exhibitors to showcase their projects, equipment, services and state of the art technology to the geothermal community.
Frequency: Annual/October

1454 **GlobalCon Conference & Expo**
Biomass Thermal Energy Council
1211 Connecticut Avenue NW
Suite 600
Washington, DC 20036-2701

202-596-3974; *Fax:* 202-223-5537
info@biomassthermal.org;
www.biomassthermal.org
Social Media: Facebook, Twitter

Joseph Seymour, Executive Director
Charlie Niebling, Chairman
Dan Arnett, Vice-Chairman
John Ackerly, Secretary
Mike Jostrom, Treasurer

Designed specifically to facilitate those seeking to expand their knowledge of fast-moving developments in the energy field, explore promising new technologies, compare energy supply options, and learn about innovative and cost-conscious project implementation strategies.
Frequency: Annual/March
Founded in: 2009

1455 **IGSHPA Conference & Expo**
International Ground Source Heat Pump Association
1201 S Innovation Way
Suite 400
Stillwater, OK 74074

405-744-5175
800-626-4747; *Fax:* 405-744-5283
igshpa@okstate.edu; www.igshpa.okstate.edu

Jim Bose, Ph.D, Executive Director
Shelly Fitzpatrick, Conference & Membership Coordinator
Jack Henrich, Chairman
Greg Wells, Vice Chairman
Jim Bose, Executive Director

The largest technical conference in the US dedicated solely to geothermal. Conference features technical classes, which attract many industry newcomers each year.
Frequency: Annual/October

1456 **International Bioenergy and Bioproducts Conference (IBBC)**
Technical Association of the Pulp & Paper Industry
15 Technology Parkway S
Norcross, GA 30092

770-446-1400
800-322-8686; *Fax:* 770-446-6947
webmaster@tappi.org; www.tappi.org

Norman F. Marsolan, Chair
Thomas J. Garland, Vice Chair
Larry N. Montague, President & CEO

Focusing on technical advancements and commercialization of bioconversion technologies that leverage the forest products manufacturing infrastructure and will include technical presentations, expert panels, case studies, and reports from projects that address feedstock and harvesting improvements to increase yield and quality of biomass, and much more.
500 Attendees
Frequency: Annual/October

1457 **International Biomass Conference & Expo**
Biomass Thermal Energy Council
1211 Connecticut Avenue NW
Suite 600
Washington, DC 20036-2701

202-596-3974; *Fax:* 202-223-5537
info@biomassthermal.org;

www.biomassthermal.org
Social Media: Facebook, Twitter

Joseph Seymour, Executive Director
Charlie Niebling, Chairman
Dan Arnett, Vice-Chairman
John Ackerly, Secretary
Mike Jostrom, Treasurer

This dynamic event unites industry professionals from all sectors of the world's interconnected biomass utilization industries - biobased power, thermal energy, fuels and chemicals. Where future and existing producers of biobased power, fuels and thermal energy products go to network with waste generators and other industry suppliers and technology providers.
Frequency: Annual/April
Founded in: 2009

1458 **International Topical Meeting on Advances in Reactor Physics**
555 N Kensington Ave
La Grange Park, IL 60526-5592

708-352-6611
800-323-3044; *Fax:* 708-352-0499
advertising@ans.org; www.ans.org
Social Media: Facebook, Twitter, LinkedIn

Jack Tuohy, Executive Director
James S Tulenko, VP
William F Naughton, Treasurer

Advances in reactor physics being the main topic of discussion. Promoting the awareness and understanding of the application of nuclear science and technology.
10500 Members
Founded in: 1954

1459 **NABCEP Continuing Education Conference**
NABCEP
56 Clifton Country Rd.
Suite 202
Clifton Park, NY 12065

800-654-0021; *Fax:* 518-899-1092
CEconference@nabcep.org; www.nabcep.org

Ezra Auerbach, Executive Director
Don Warfield, Chair
Jane Weissman, Vice Chair
Les Nelson, Treasurer
Jeff Spies, Secretary

The objective of this conference is to offer NABCEP certified installers and technical sales professionals an opportunity that allows them to fulfill the majority of their CE requirements at a single event. In combination with manufacturer's training sessions, conference registrants will be able to attend workshops on the NEC, financial analysis, safety, and emerging fire codes.
Frequency: Annual/March
Founded in: 2000

1460 **National Biodiesel Conference & Expo**
National Biodiesel Board
605 Clark Avenue
PO Box 104898
Jefferson City, MO 65110-4898
573-635-3893; *Fax:* 573-635-7913
info@biodiesel.org;
www.biodieselconference.org
Social Media: Facebook, Twitter, YouTube

Kent Engelbrecht, Chairman
Mark Cunningham, Vice-Chair
Greg Anderson, Treasurer
Chad Stone, Secretary

The only event that gathers biodiesel decision-makers from across the United States, and the world. Opportunities abound for attendees and exhibitors to network connect and learn. Event explores the topics of governmental policy, technical issues and marketing trends in the biodiesel industry.
Frequency: Annual/February

1461 **National Hydropower Association Annual Conference**
National Hydropower Association
25 Massachusetts Ave, NW
Suite 450
Washington, DC 20001

202-682-1700; *Fax:* 202-682-9478
help@hydro.org; www.hydro.org
Social Media: Facebook, Twitter

Linda Church Ciocci, Executive Director
David Moller, President
Eric Van Deuren, Treasurer
Cherise Oram, Vice President
Suzanne Grassell, Secretary

Program will provide a unique opportunity to hear first-hand from the Administration, Congress, federal regulators and resource agencies on the issues and policies that directly affect individual businesses and projects.
Frequency: Annual/April

1462 **Pellet Fuels Institute Annual Conference**
1901 North Moore Street
Suite 600
Arlington, VA 22209

703-522-6778; *Fax:* 703-522-0548
pfimail@pelletheat.org; www.pelletheat.org

Jennifer Hedrick, Executive Director
Jason Berthiaume, Membership/ Gov't Affairs Associate
John Crouch, Director of Public Affairs

Conference educates industry members on the latest information including new program development and what to expect in upcoming months. Speakers, roundtable panels, annual golf tournament and a beach bash.

1463 **Renewable Energy Finance Forum (REFF) -Wall Street**
American Council on Renewable Energy
1600 K Street NW
Suite 700
Washington, DC 20006
202-393-0001
vay@acore.org; www.refindirectory.com
Social Media: Facebook, Twitter, LinkedIn, YouTube

Dennis V. McGinn, President
Estelle Lloyd, Managing Editor & Co-Founder
Tom, Naylor, Ronan
Murphy Managing Editor

Bringing together the top leaders of the USA's renewable energy industry, drawing attendees from the entire value chain, including financiers, manufacturers and developers.
700 Attendees
Frequency: Annual/June
Founded in: 2001

1464 **Renewable Energy Markets Conference**
Renewable Energy Markets Association
1211 Connecticut Ave NW
Suite 600
Washington, DC 20036-2701

202-640-6597; *Fax:* 202-223-5537;
www.renewablemarketers.org
Social Media: Facebook, Twitter

Richard Anderson, President
Ian McGowan, Vice President
Kevin Maddaford, Treasurer
Sarah Smith, Secretary
Josh Lieberman, General Manager

Bridging the interests of renewable energy generators, sellers, and utilities with those of purchasers, policymakers, and the communities that benefit from clean energy, this is the nation's premier forum for the energy community to gather, learn from each other, and recognize best practices for promoting renewable energy.
400 Attendees
Frequency: Annual/November

1465 **Solar Thermal**
Interstate Renewable Energy Council
PO Box 1156
Latham, NY 12110-1156

518-458-6059
info@irecusa.org; www.irecusa.org

Jane Weissman, Executive Director
Lary Sherwood, Vice Chaie
David Warner, Chair
Jane Pulaski, Secretary
Jennifer Szaro, Treasurer

A two-day conference and networking event for industry professionals including; installers, manufacturers, distributors, engineers, designers, policy makers, code officials, and trainers. A national solar heating and cooling conference.
Frequency: Annual/December

1466 **U.S. Clean Heat & Power Association's Annual Spring CHP Forum**
U.S. Clean Heat & Power Association
105 North Virginia Avenue
Suite 204
Falls Church, VA 22046

703-436-2257
info@uschpa.org; www.uschpa.org
Social Media: Twitter

Jessica Bridges, Executive Director
Joe Allen, Chair
Warren Ferguson, Vice Chair
John Rathbun, Secretary
Paul Lemar, Treasurer

Showcasing a series of knowledgeable speakers sharing their expertise on policies and best practices that have facilitated CHP deployment in overseas markets and offering advice on how to break down barriers to CHP deployment and replicate those successes stateside. Listen to national and international trade and policy authorities, US government officials, and CHP business leaders discuss CHP challenges, success stories, and market expansion opportunities.
Frequency: Annual/May
Founded in: 1999

1467 **UNEP SEF Alliance Annual Meeting**
Clean Energy Group/ UNEP SEF Alliance
50 State St.
Suite 1
Montpelier, VT 05602

802-223-2554; *Fax:* 802-223-4967;
www.unepsefalliance.org

Members engage in candid discussion with peer agencies about current challenges faced, latest programme developments, and plans for future programme design. Experts speak about specialized topics, and proposals for new areas of collaboration are presented and discussed.
Frequency: Annual/September

1468 **World Renewable Energy Forum**
American Solar Energy Society
4760 Walnut Street
Suite 106
Boulder, CO 80301

303-443-3130; *Fax:* 303-443-3212
ases@ases.org; www.ases.org
Social Media: Facebook, Twitter, LinkedIn

Susan Greene, President
David G. Hill, Chair
Bill Poulin, Treasurer
Jason Keyes, Secretary

American Solar Energy Society annual conference and the bi-annual World Renewable Energy Congress have combined, providing a unique opportunity for renewable energy enthusiasts from around the world to share experiences.
13M Members
Frequency: Annual/May
Founded in: 1954

1469 World Shale Gas Conference & Exhibition
Institute of Gas Technology
1700 S Mount Prospect Rd
Des Plaines, IL 60018-1804

847-768-0664; *Fax:* 847-768-0669;
www.gastechnology.org
Social Media: Facebook, Twitter, LinkedIn, YouTube

David Carroll, President & CEO
Ronald Snedic, Vice President/ Corporate Devel.
Paul Chromek, General Counsel & Secretary
Unique platform to uncover the real impact of shale on the global gas market. Provides a valuable opportunity to develop business, explore future prospects and unlock the potential of shale gas globally. Share knowledge and experience among industry professionals, government operators and solution providers.

Directories & Databases

1470 American Solar Energy Society Membership Directory
4760 Walnut Street
Suite 106
Boulder, CO 80301-2843

303-443-3130; *Fax:* 303-443-3212
ases@ases.org; www.ases.org

Susan Greene, President
David G. Hill, Chair
Bill Poulin, Treasurer
Jason Keyes, Secretary
Offers information on over 2,000 manufacturers, professors, architects, engineers and others in the solar energy field.

1471 Association of Energy Service Companies Directory
Association of Energy Service Companies
6060 N Central Expy
Dallas, TX 75206-5209

214-692-0771
800-692-0771; *Fax:* 214-692-0162;
www.aesc.net

Patty Jordan, Publisher
About 750 energy service companies and industry suppliers.
Frequency: Bi-Monthly
Circulation: 10,000

1472 Database of State Incentives for Renewables & Efficiency (DSIRE)
North Carolina State University
Campus Box 7504
Raleigh, NC 27695-7504

919-515-3470; *Fax:* 919-515-2556
DSIREinfo@ncsu.edu; www.dsireusa.org
Social Media: Facebook, Twitter

Amanda Vanega, Program Manager
Funded by the US Department of Energy's Office of Energy Efficiency and Renewable Energy. A comprehensive source of information on state, local, utility and federal incentives and policies that promote renewable energy and energy efficiency.
Founded in: 1995

1473 Energy
WEFA Group
800 Baldwin Tower Boulevard
Eddystone, PA 19022-1368

610-490-4000; *Fax:* 610-490-2770
info@wefa.com; www.wefa.com

Peter McNabb
This database covers energy supply and demand, including weekly rig count and gasoline prices by states; reserves, stocks, production, consumption and trade of petroleum products.

1474 Energy Science and Technology
US Department of Energy
PO Box 62
Oak Ridge, TN 37831-0062

865-574-1000; *Fax:* 865-576-2865;
www.osti.gov

This large database offers over 3 million citations, with abstracts, to literature pertaining to all fields of energy.

1475 Handbook: Solar Energy System Design
American Society of Plumbing Engineers
2980 S River Rd
Des Plaines, IL 60018-4203

847-296-0002; *Fax:* 847-296-2963
info@aspe.org; www.aspe.org

Tom Govedarica, Executive Publisher
Richard Albrecht, Publication Coordinator
Gretchen Pienta, Managing Editor
This manual provides the know-how on solar hot-water systems, collectors, thermal storage and much more.
Cost: $20.00

1476 Membership Roster and Registry of Geothermal Services & Equipment
Geothermal Resources Council
20001 Second Street
Suite 5
Davis, CA 95618-5476

530-758-2360; *Fax:* 530-758-2839
grc@geothermal.org; www.geothermal.org
Social Media: Facebook, Twitter, LinkedIn, YouTube, Flickr

Curt Robinson, Ph.D, Executive Director
Steve Ponder, Interim Executive Director
Estela M. Smith, Office Manager
Ian Crawford, Managing Editor
Chi-Meng Moua, Library Associate
A unique publication that provides business, consulting and research contacts throughout the international geothermal community.
Frequency: Annual
Founded in: 1970

1477 REFIN Directory
American Council on Renewable Energy
1600 K Street NW
Suite 700
Washington, DC 20006

202-393-0001
vay@acore.org; www.refindirectory.com
Social Media: Facebook, Twitter, LinkedIn, YouTube

Dennis V. McGinn, President
Douglas Llyod, CEO and Co-Founder
Estelle Llyod, Managing Editor
Connects suppliers of capital and expertise with industry participants engaged in the scale-up of renewable energy.
Frequency: Annually
Founded in: 2001

1478 The Source for Renewable Energy
Momentum Technologies, LLC
PO Box 460813
Glendale, CO 80246

303-229-4841; *Fax:* 408-705-2031
energy@mtt.com
energy.sourceguides.com

A comprehensive buyer's guide and business directory to more than 18,000 renewable energy businesses and organizations worldwide.

1479 Wind Energy Conversion Systems
South Dakota Renewable Energy Association
PO Box 491
Pierre, SD 57501-0491

605-224-8641

Offers valuable information for electrical-output wind machine manufacturers.
Cost: $2.00
45 Pages
Frequency: Annual

Industry Web Sites

1480 energy.sourceguides.com
Momentum Technologies, LLC
A comprehensive buyer's guide and business directory to more than 18,000 renewable energy businesses and organizations worldwide.

1481 http://gold.greyhouse.com
G.O.L.D Grey House OnLine Databases
Grey House Publishing's online database platform, GOLD, offers Quick Search, Keyword Search and Expert Search for most business sectors including mining, petroleum and alternative energy markets. The GOLD platform makes finding the information you need quick and easy. All of Grey House's directory products are available for subscription on the GOLD platform.

1482 www.acore.org
American Council on Renewable Energy
Works to bring all forms of renewable energy into the mainstream of America's economy and lifestyle. Members include every aspect and sector of the renewable energy industries and their trade associations, including wind, solar, geothermal, biomass and biofuels, hydropower tidal/current energy and waste energy.

1483 www.aeecenter.org
Association of Energy Engineers (AEE)
Information and networking in the dynamic fields of energy engineering and energy management, renewable and alternative energy, power generation, energy services, sustainability, and all related areas.

1484 www.aeromt.org
Alternative Energy Resources Organization
A grassroots nonprofit organization dedicated to solutions that promote resource conservation and local economic vitality. By bringing people together, AERO offers a vehicle for collective action and a sense of common purpose for citizens within their communities to shape a more sustainable future.

1485 www.americanbiogascouncil.org
American Biogas Council
Mission is to create jobs, environmental sustainability and energy independence by growing the American biogas industry.

1486 americanhydrogenassociation.org
American Hydrogen Association
Providing information on the use of hydrogen as a fuel.

1487 **www.ases.org**
American Solar Energy Society
The nation's leading association of solar professionals & advocates. Mission is to inspire an era of energy innovation and speed the transition to a sustainable energy economy. Advancing education, research and policy.

1488 **www.awea.org**
American Wind Energy Association
Promotes wind energy as a clean source of electricity for consumers around the world. Representing wind power project developers, equipment suppliers, services providers, parts manufacturers, utilities, researchers, and others involved in the wind industry - one of the world's fastest growing energy industries.

1489 **www.biodiesel.org**
National Biodiesel Board
Mission is to advance the interests of its members by creating sustainable biodiesel industry growth. NBB serves as the industry's central coordinating entity and will be the single voice for its diverse membership base.

1490 **www.biogaspower.org**
Bio-Gas Power Association
Dedicated to providing the industry with the knowledge needed to operate and maintain these facilities by providing a common ground to learn from each others' experiences. Developed as a way for owners, operators, technicians, and dealerships alike to come together and share ideas, experience, opinions, and tackle the tough issues that come with owning and operating Bio-Gas to Energy Facilities.

1491 **www.biomassthermal.org**
Biomass Thermal Energy Council
An association of biomass fuel producers, appliance manufacturers and distributors, supply chain companies and non-profit organizations that view biomass thermal energy as a renewable, responsible, clean and energy-efficient pathway to meeting America's energy needs. BTEC engages in research, education, and public advocacy for the fast growing biomass thermal energy industry.

1492 **www.cleanegroup.org**
Clean Energy Group
A leading nonprofit advocacy organization working in the US and internationally on innovative clean energy technology, finance, and policy programs. Supported by major foundations, as well as state, federal and international energy agencies.

1493 **www.dsireusa.org**
DSIRE Database
Funded by the US Department of Energy's Office of Energy Efficiency and Renewable Energy. A comprehensive source of information on state, local, utility and federal incentives and policies that promote renewable energy and energy efficiency.

1494 **www.eesi.org**
Environmental and Energy Study Institute
A nonprofit organization that advances innovative policy solutions that set us on a cleaner, more secure and sustainable energy path.

1495 **www.energyrecoverycouncil.org**
Energy Recovery Council
Represents the waste-to-energy industry and communities that own waste-to-energy facilities. Current ERC members own and operate modern waste-to-energy facilities that operate nationwide, safely disposing of municipal solid waste, while at the same time generating renewable electricity using modern combustion technology equipped with state-of-the-art emission control systems.

1496 **www.ethanolrfa.org**
Renewable Fuels Association
The national trade association for the US ethanol industry promoting policies, regulations and research and development initiatives that will lead to the increased production and use of fuel ethanol. Membership includes a broad cross-section of businesses, individuals and organizations dedicated to the expansion of the US fuel ethanol industry.

1497 **www.geo-energy.org**
Geothermal Energy Association
Advocates for public policies that will promote the development and utilization of geothermal resources, provides a forum for the industry to discuss issues and problems, encourages research and development to improve geothermal technologies, presents industry views to governmental organizations, and conducts education and outreach projects.

1498 **www.geothermal.org**
Geothermal Resources Council
Nonprofit, educational association actively seeking to expand its role as a primary professional educational association for the international geothermal community.

1499 **www.greyhouse.com**
Grey House Publishing
Authoritative reference directories for business information and general reference, including alternative energy, mining and petroleum markets. Users can search the online databases with varied search criteria allowing for custom searches by product category, geographic area, sales volume, keyword, subject and more. Full Grey House catalog and online ordering also available.

1500 **www.hydro.org**
National Hydropower Association
Dedicated to promoting the growth of clean, affordable US hydropower. Seeks to secure hydropower's place as a climate-friendly, renewable and reliable energy source that serves national environmental, energy, and economic policy objectives. Members are involved in projects throughout the US hydropower industry, including both federal and non-federal hydroelectric facilities.

1501 **www.iaee.org**
International Association for Energy Economics
Association for those involved in energy economics including publications, consultants, energy database software.

1502 **www.igshpa.okstate.edu**
International Ground Source Heat Pump Association
Member-driven organization established to advance ground source heat pump technology on local, state, national and international levels. IGSHPA utilizes state-of-the-art facilities for conducting GSHP system installation training and geothermal research. Mission is to promote the use of ground source heat pump technology worldwide through education and communication.

1503 **www.irecusa.org**
Interstate Renewable Energy Council
Works with industry, government, educators and other stakeholders to ensure that the broader use of renewable energies is possible, safe, affordable and practical, particularly for the individual consumer.

1504 **www.ireoigo.org**
Intergovernmental Renewable Energy Organization
Promotes the urgent transition to renewable energy sources and sustainable development through collaborative effort and the implementation of projects that improve the lives of people while preserving the environment and our resources for future generations of humans.

1505 **www.lignite.com**
Lignite Energy Council
Regional Trade Association - promotes policies and activities that maintain a viable lignite industry and enhance development of our regions' lignite resources.

1506 **www.nabcep.org**
N. American Board of Cert. Energy Practitioners
Mission is to support, and work with, the renewable energy and energy efficiency industries, professionals, and stakeholders. Goal is to develop voluntary national certification programs that will; promote renewable energy, provide value to practitioners, promote worker safety and skill, and promote consumer confidence.

1507 **www.nationalrenewableenergyassociation.org**
National Renewable Energy Association
A nonprofit organization dedicated to helping Americans use less energy and to use more renewable energy in the future.

1508 **www.nesea.org**
Northeast Sustainable Energy Association
The nation's leading regional membership organization focused on promoting the understanding, development and adoption of energy conservation and non-polluting, renewable energy technologies.

1509 **www.oceanrenewable.com**
Ocean Renewable Energy Coalition
Striving to keep members, legislators, regulators, the media and the public at large up to date with OREC's activities as well as ongoing developments in this emerging industry.

1510 **www.renewablemarketers.org**
Renewable Energy Markets Association
A nonprofit association dedicated to maintaining and growing strong markets for renewable energy in the United States. Representing organizations that sell, purchase, or promote renewable energy products.

1511 **www.seia.org**
Solar Energy Industries Association
Works with its member companies to make solar a mainstream and significant energy source by expanding markets, removing market barriers, strenghtening the industry and educating the public on the benefits of solar energy.

1512 **www.solarliving.org**
Solar Living Institute
A nonprofit solar training and sustainability organization. Mission is to promote sustainable living through inspirational environmental education.

1513 **www.unepsefalliance.org**
UNEP SEF Alliance
The only convening body in the international system for public finance agencies in the clean energy sector. Members are visionary organizations from various countries pushing the forefront of how to do public finance for clean energy.

1514 **www.usabiomass.org**
Biomass Power Association

The nation's leading organization working to expand and advance the use of clean, renewable biomass power. Educates policymakers at the state and federal level about the benefits of biomass and provides regular briefings and research to keep members fully informed about public policy impacting the biomass industry. Members include local owners and operators of existing biomass facilities, suppliers, plant developers and others.

1515 **www.uschpa.org**
US Clean Heat & Power Association

Providing superior advocacy, networking, education and market information to companies in the business of clean, local energy generation. Documents the benefits of clean heat and power to the public and to decision-makers. Also participates in federal agency programs to promote clean distributed energy.

1516 **www.wcee.org**
Women's Council on Energy and the Environment

Supports women involved in the environmental community with education, research, new trend information and several publications.

Associations

1517 **Academy of Science Fiction Fantasy and Horror Films**
334 W 54th St
Los Angeles, CA 90037-3806
323-752-5811; *Fax:* 323-752-5811
saturn.awards@ca.rr.com;
www.saturnawards.org
Social Media: Facebook, Twitter
Robert Holguin, CEO & President
David Bilbrey, Executive Administrator
Michael Laster, Director of Operations
Jeff Rector, Official Spokesperson
Kurt Reichenbach, Art Designer
Honors, recognizes and promotes genre films. Annually presents the prestigious Saturn Awards. In recent years, have added television and home entertainment categories to the media mix. Widened the scope of our awards by celebrating achievement in additional genres including action, adventure, and thrillers as well as international cinema.
Founded in: 1972

1518 **American Alliance for Health, Physical Education, Recreation and Dance**
1900 Association Drive
Reston, VA 20191-1598
703-476-3400
800-213-7193; *Fax:* 703-476-9527
info@aahperd.org; www.shapeamerica.org
Social Media: Facebook, Twitter, Instagram
Steve Jefferies, President
E. Paul Roetert, Chief Executive Officer
Dolly D. Lambdin, President-Elect
Frances Cleland, Member-at-Large
Neil Dougherty, Member-at-Large
Organization that provides educational programs, resources and support for professionals within the fields of health, physical education, recreation and dance. AAHPERD's mission is to promote and support leadership, research, education, and best practices in the professions that support creative, healthy, and active lifestyles.
25000 Members
Founded in: 1885

1519 **American Amusement Machine Association**
450 E Higgins Rd
Suite 201
Elk Grove Vlg, IL 60007-1417
847-290-9088
866-372-5190; *Fax:* 847-290-9121
information@coin-op.org; www.coin-op.org
Social Media: Facebook, Twitter, LinkedIn
Chris Felix, President
Tina Schwartz, Business & Finance Manager
Holly Hampton, Vice President
Frank Consentino, Secretary
Rich Babich, Treasurer
Non profit trade association representing the manufacturers, distributors and part suppliers to the coin-operated and out of home amusement industry.
Founded in: 1981

1520 **American Association of Cheerleading Coaches and Administration**
6745 Lenox Center Court
Suite 318
Memphis, TN 38115
800-533-6583; *Fax:* 901-251-5851
jimlord@aacca.org; www.aacca.org
Social Media: Facebook, Twitter
Jim Lord, Executive Director
Mike Nordengran, Administration
Sheila Noone, Media Relations
AACCA,is a non-profit educational association for cheerleading coaches across the United States. Members of the association include: youth, junior high school, high school, all star, and college or university coaches/advisors, as well as leading national cheerleading instructional companies dedicated to the safe and responsible practice of student cheerleading.
70000 Members
Founded in: 1987

1521 **American Coaster Enthusiasts**
P.O. Box 540261
Grand Prairie, TX 75054-0261
469-278-6223; *Fax:* 740-452-2552
info@aceonline.org; www.aceonline.org
Social Media: Facebook, Twitter, RSS
Jerry Willard, President
David Lipnicky, Vice President
Lee Ann Draud, Public Relations Director
ACE is the world's largest ride enthusiast organization, and its members are the most educated, dedicated, and passionate amusement park guests. ACE's activities include publications, action-packed events, and preservation efforts. ACE is highly visible in the mainstream media. Local television stations and newspapers often consider ACE events in their area to be major news items.
6000 Members
Founded in: 1978

1522 **American Disc Jockey Association**
20118 N 67th Avenue
Suite 300-605
Glendale, CA 85308
888-723-5776; *Fax:* 866-310-4676
office@adja.org; www.adja.org
Social Media: Facebook, Twitter, YouTube
Rob Snyder, Director
An association of professional mobile entertainers. Encourages success for its members through continuous education, camaraderie, and networking. The primary goal is to educate Disc Jockeys so that each member acts ethically and responsibly.

1523 **Amusement Industry Manufacturers & Suppliers International**
P.O. Box 92366
Nashville, TN 37209
714-425-5747; *Fax:* 714-276-9666
info@aimsintl.org; www.aimsintl.org
Social Media: Facebook
Brian D King, President
The Amusement Industry Manufacturers and Suppliers (AIMS) Trade Association evolved from the American Recreational Equipment Association. The Associations purpose is to establish communications and foster working relations using the highest degree of professionalism with other Amusement Industry Trade Associations, Local, State, and Federal Government entities in order to promote and preserve the prosperity of the Amusement Industry.
Founded in: 1994

1524 **Amusement and Music Operators Association**
600 Spring Hill Ring Road
Suite 111
West Dundee, IL 60118
847-428-7699
800-937-2662; *Fax:* 847-428-7719;
www.amoa.com
Social Media: Facebook
Jerry Johnston, President
Gaines C. Butler, 1st Vice President
Jack Kelleher, Executive Vice President
Lori Schneider, Deputy Director
Claudia Kaczmarek, Office Manager
AMOA was created when 68 jukebox owners from around the country banded together to fight the repeal of the jukebox royalty exemption. The modest beginning, created by a common cause, revealed a fierce passion-shared by many-about their business. Harnessing the collective strength, energy, knowledge and entrepreneurial spirit of a growing number of volunteer members, AMOA quickly established itself as a major force.
Founded in: 1948

1525 **Association of College Unions International**
120 W Seventh Street
One City Centre, Suite 200
Bloomington, IN 47404
812-245-2284; *Fax:* 812-245-6710
acui@acui.org; www.acui.org
Social Media: Facebook, Twitter, YouTube
Sarah Aikman, President
John Taylor, Chief Executive Officer
Elizabeth Beltramini, Content Curation Director
Jake Dawes, Events and Operations Coordinator
Jason Cline, Strategic Initiatives Executive
The association is a non-profit organization and has member institutions in a number of countries. ACUI members work at and attend urban and rural campuses at both the two and four year levels and are dedicated to building community on campus through programs, services and publications with the common goal of unifying the union and activities fields.
1000 Members
Founded in: 1914

1526 **Association of Zoos and Aquariums**
8403 Colesville Rd
Suite 710
Silver Spring, MD 20910-3314
301-562-0777; *Fax:* 301-562-0888
membership@aza.org; www.aza.org
Social Media: Facebook, Twitter, Pinterest, Instagram, YouTube
Kris Vehrs, J.D., Executive Director
Jim Maddy, President & CEO
Jill Nicoll, Chief Operating Officer
Phil Wagner, Senior Vice President, Finance
Ana Maria Sanchez, Controller
A nonprofit organization dedicated to the advancement of accredited zoos and aquariums in the areas of animal care, wildlife conservation, education and science.
200 Members
Founded in: 1924

1527 **Circus Fans Association of America**
2704 Marshall Avenue
Lorain, OH 44052-4315
360-452-1919
circusvern@aol.com; www.circusfans.org
Gary C. Payne, President
Cheryl Deptula, Executive Secretary-Treasurer
Peter Wagner, President Elect
Connie Thomas, Central Vice President
Mort Gamble, Public Relations Director

Established to enjoy and preserve the circus as an institution. CFA offers you an opportunity interact with fellow circus enthusiasts in many ways. Local geographic groups (called TENTS) provide a chance for folks who live in the same geographic area to attend shows together and to meet to discuss the circus scene. State organizations (called TOPS) organize larger gatherings and special events.
Founded in: 1926

1528 **Circus Historical Society**
3100 Parkside Lane
Williamsburg, VA 23185

757-259-0412
CircusHistoricalSociety@gmail.com;
www.circushistory.org
Social Media: Facebook, Twitter

Deborah Walk, President
Don Covington, Vice President
Robert Cline, Secretary/Treasurer
Chris Berry, Trustee
Maureen Brunsdale, Trustee

The Circus Historical Society, Inc. (CHS) is a tax-exempt, not-for-profit educational organization dedicated to recording the history of the American circus from the first one in Philadelphia during 1793 to today. Membership includes historians, scholars, circus personnel, memorabilia collectors, Americana specialists who share both a love of the circus and a desire to preserve and disseminate its great heritage.
1000 Members
Founded in: 1939

1529 **Clowns of America International**
PO Box 112
Eustis, FL 32727

352-357-1676
877-816-6941
coaioffice@aol.com; www.coai.org

Glenn Kohlberger, President
Michael B. Cox, Vice-President
Dan Fitzwilly' Langwell, Secretary
Paddee Embrey, Treasurer
Sandra Winstead, Sergeant-at-Arms

The purpose of Clowns of America International Website is to share, educate, and act as a gathering place for serious minded amateurs, semiprofessionals, and professional clowns. COAI provides its membership with necessary resources that allow them to further define and improve their individual clown character. Visitors who are interested in the clown arts will find a variety of resources that will stimulate their interest, foster their curiosity and offer pathways to valuable information.

1530 **Council for Amusement & Recreational Equipment Safety**
PO Box 8236
Des Moines, IO 50301-8236

617-727-3200
217-558-7194
doug.rathbun@illinois.gov;
www.caresofficials.org

Rob Gavel, President
Mike Triplett, 1st Vice President
Dean McKernon, 2nd Vice President
Chad Halsey, Secretary/Treasurer
Mike Triplett, ASTM Liaison

CARES is a voluntary organization of chief government officials who are responsible for the enforcement of amusement ride and recreational equipment regulations within their jurisdiction. Fosters cooperation among regulatory officials and amusement equipment industries to promote public safety. CARES membership has grown to more than two dozen regulatory agencies in the United States and Canada, and includes the informal participation of the U.S. Consumer Product Safety.

1531 **Game Manufacturers Association**
240 North Fifth Street
Suite 340
Columbus, OH 43215

614-255-4500; *Fax:* 614-255-4499
ed@gama.org; www.gama.org
Social Media: Facebook

Travis Severance, Retail Chair
Bob Maher, Distributor Chair
Justin Ziran, President
Jamie Chambers, Vice President
John Ward, Executive Director

The Game Manufacturers Association (GAMA) is the non-profit trade organization dedicated to serving the tabletop game industry. Strengthens and supports industry professionals by advancing their interests, providing educational programs and opportunities, and promoting their form of quality social entertainment. Led by publishers and manufacturers, GAMA promotes the interests of all persons involved in the commerce of games and game-related products.
450 Members
Founded in: 1977

1532 **International Amusement & Leisure Defense Association**
PO Box 4563
Louisville, KY 40204

502-473-0956; *Fax:* 502-473-7352
info@ialda.org; www.ialda.org
Social Media: LinkedIn

Kurt A. Anselmi, Esq., Board Member/Emeritus
David M. Bennett, Esq., Vice-President
Gaylee W. Gillim, Esq., Secretary
Sean P. Hannon, Esq., Treasurer
Thomas Sheehan, Esq., Board Member/Emeritus

The International Amusement & Leisure Defense Association, Inc. is a non-profit association of lawyers and other professionals who are actively engaged in representing the interests of the amusement and leisure industries. IALDA members work closely with those in the amusement and water park industries as well as those involved in the bowling, roller skating, and other leisure industries.

1533 **International Association of Amusement Parks and Attractions (IAAPA)**
1448 Duke St
Alexandria, VA 22314-3403

703-836-4800; *Fax:* 703-836-4801
iaapa@iaapa.org; www.iaapa.org
Social Media: Facebook, Twitter, LinkedIn

Gerardo Arteaga Cerda, Chairman
Paul Noland, President and CEO
Susan Mosedale, Executive Vice President
June Ko, Vice President
David Mandt, SVP, Marketing and Communications

A non-profit organization with a membership consisting of fixed-site enteraimment and attractions facilities and suppliers. The association is dedicated to the preservation and prosperity of the amusement industry worldwide.
4100 Members
Founded in: 1918

1534 **International Association of Fairs Expositions**
3043 East Cairo St.
PO Box 985
Springfield, MO 65802

417-862-5771
800-516-0313; *Fax:* 417-862-0156
iafe@fairsandexpos.com;
www.fairsandexpos.com
Social Media: Facebook, Twitter, You Tube

Jim Tucker, President/CEO
Max Willis, CFO
Steve Siever, Director of Sales
Missy McCormack, Comm. Design and Prod. Manager
Rebekah Lee, Director of Comm. and Editor

The International Association of Fairs and Expositions (IAFE) is a voluntary, non-profit corporation, serving state, provincial, regional, and county agricultural fairs, shows, exhibitions, and expositions. Its associate members include state and provincial associations of fairs, non-agricultural expositions and festivals, associations, corporations, and individuals engaged in providing products and services to its members, all of whom are interested in the improvement of fairs, and expositions.
1300 Members
Founded in: 1885

1535 **International Association of Haunted Attractions**
1001 Greenbay Road
Winnetka, IL 60093

888-320-8494; *Fax:* 609-799-7032
admin@iahaweb.com; www.iahaweb.com
Social Media: Facebook

Patrick Konopelski, President
Gene Schopf, Vice President
John Eslich, Treasurer
Brett Bertolino, Secretary
Lore Callahan, Board Member

The Haunted Attraction Association assists and advances the thriving haunt industry through communication, education, and information. Our worldwide network of members exchange ideas, information, experiences and concerns via our conferences, exclusive networking events, message boards, newsletters, magazines and more. HAA members have been featured on national television shows such as Good Morning America, the Today Show, and our attractions have been featured in national publications.
400 Members
Founded in: 1998

1536 **International Brotherhood of Magicians**
13 Point West Blvd
St Charles, MO 63301-4431

636-724-2400; *Fax:* 636-724-8566
info@magician.org; www.magician.org
Social Media: Facebook, Twitter, YouTube

Joe M. Turner, International President
Becki Wells, International Vice President
Donald E. Wiberg, International Secretary
Charles Arkin, International Treasurer
Oscar Munoz, International President-Elect

The International Brotherhood of Magicians is the world's largest organization dedicated to the art of magic, with members in 88 countries. Our official publication, The Linking Ring, has linked magicians throughout the world. Local branches of the I.B.M., known as Rings, meet each month in hundreds of locations. Our Annual Convention features top professional magicians in our spectacular evening shows.
12000 Members
Founded in: 1922

1537 **International Festivals and Events Association (IFEA)**
2603 W. Eastover Terrace
Boise, ID 83706-2800

208-433-0950; *Fax:* 208-433-9812
nia@ifea.com; www.ifea.com

Social Media: Facebook, Twitter, LinkedIn, YouTube

Cindy Lerick, Chair
Steven Wood Schmader, CFEE, President & CEO
Nia Forster Hovde, CFEE, VP/Dir. of Marketing & Comm.
Beth Peterson, Director of Membership Services
Craig Sarton, Creative & Publications Director

The IFEA exists to serve the needs of our entire industry, who produce and support quality celebrations for the benefit of their respective 'communities' and all those who share our core values of excellence & quality; the sharing of experience, knowledge, creativity and best practices; and the importance of 'community' building both locally and globally. Our success lies in the success of those we serve through professional education, programming, products and resources, and networking.
2000 Members
Founded in: 1956
Mailing list available for rent

1538 International Game Developers Association

19 Mantua Road
Mt Royal, NJ 08061

856-423-2990; *Fax:* 856-423-3420
contact@igda.org; www.igda.org
Social Media: Facebook, Twitter, LinkedIn, YouTube, Flickr, Kickstarter,

Jon Grande, Chair
Kate Edwards, Executive Director
Tristin Hightower, Director of Operations
Jillian Mood, Partner & Member Relations Manager
Dr. Farhad Javidi, Secretary

The International Game Developers Association is the largest non-profit membership organization serving individuals who create video games. We bring together developers at conferences, in local chapters and in special interest groups to improve their lives and craft. The IGDA is dedicated to improving developers' careers and lives through: Community, Professional Development, and Advocacy.
Founded in: 1994

1539 International Jugglers' Association

PO Box 7307
Austin, TX 78713-7307

702-798-0099; *Fax:* 702-248-2550
webmaster@juggle.org; www.juggle.org
Social Media: Facebook, YouTube

Nathan Wakefield, Chair
Art Jennings, Chairman Emeritus
Martin Frost, Communications Director
Kyle Johnson, Marketing Director
Marilyn Sullivan, Membership Director

An organization of individuals dedicated to promoting juggling.
Founded in: 1947

1540 International Laser Display Association

7062 Edgeworth Drive
Orlando, FL 32819-2700

407-797-7654; *Fax:* 503-344-3770
mail@laserist.org; www.laserist.org

Christine Jenkin, President
Patrick Murphy, ILDA Executive Director
Olga Eser, Vice President
Dan Goldsmith, Secretary
Alex Henning, Treasurer

The International Laser Display Association (ILDA) is the world's leading organization dedicated to advancing the use of laser displays in the fields of art, entertainment and education. Promotes the use of laser displays in the international marketplace through awards programs, publications, technology standards and a code of ethics. ILDA also represents the industry on safety issues and provides forums for members to exchange ideas, forge partnerships and explore.
Founded in: 1986

1541 International Laser Tag Association: ILTA

5351 E Thompson Road
Suite 236
Indianapolis, IN 46237

317-786-9755; *Fax:* 317-786-9757
info@lasertag.org; www.lasertag.org

Ryan McQuillen, Executive Director
Eric Gaizat, Membership Director

The International Laser Tag Association (ILTA) is the non-profit developer and operator association for the laser tag industry. Help members become better informed through our research, services, and communications with all levels of the industry. Since the creation of the ILTA, no other source has been more reliable for information about our industry. Assist members by providing them with the most accurate infor available to date.
350 Members
Founded in: 1996

1542 International Magicians Society

581 Ellison Avenue
Westbury, NY 11590

516-333-2377; *Fax:* 516-333-0018
info@imsmagic.com; www.magicims.com

Tony Hassini, Chairman/CEO
Anthony Emin, World President
Remington Scott, Creative Director
William H. Mellhany, Magic Historian
John M. Caluwaert, Legal Counsel

Promotes and preserves the art of magic. IMS helps create new magicians in order to pass the torch to the next generation of magicians.
37000 Members
Founded in: 1968

1543 International Ticketing Association

5868 East 71st Street
Suite E 367
Indianapolis, IN 46220

212-629-4036; *Fax:* 212-628-8532
info@intix.org; www.intix.org
Social Media: Facebook, Twitter, LinkedIn, YouTube

Jena L Hoffman, President/CEO
Tiffany Kelham, Membership Associate
Jane, Pelletier, Meeting Manager
Dorothea Heck, Sales & Service Manager
Mary Leaton, Accounting Associate

The International Ticketing Association is a nonprofit membership organization committed to leading the forum for the entertainment ticketing industry. INTIX represents ticketing, sales, technology, finance, and marketing professionals who work in arts, sports, and entertainment as well as a full range of public venues and institutions. Members represent organizations from across the United States, Canada and 20 countries from around the globe.
1000 Members
Founded in: 1980

1544 National Association of Amusement Ride Safety Officials

PO Box 638
Brandon, FL 33509-0638

813-661-2779
800-669-9053; *Fax:* 813-685-5117
naarsoinfo@aol.com; www.naarso.com

Jack S. Silar, Chairman and Membership Chairman
Jonathan R. Brooks, President
Rick Smith, Vice President
Leonard Cavalier, Executive Director
Tony Rossi, Treasurer

NAARSO is dedicated to the advancement of amusement ride and device safety through the doctrine of Safety Through Communication. NAARSO is a non-profit organization that provides resources for amusement industry professionals dedicated to the safety of the industry and its patrons.
800 Members
Founded in: 1987

1545 National Association of Teachers of Singing

9957 Moorings Drive
Suite 401
Jacksonville, FL 32257-2416

904-992-9101; *Fax:* 904-262-2587
info@nats.org; www.nats.org
Social Media: Facebook, Twitter, LinkedIn, YouTube, Flickr, Pinterest

Linda Snyder, President
Diana Allen, Vice-President (Auditions)
Dan Johnson-Wilmot, Vice President (Membership)
Kristine Hurst-Wajszczuk, Vice President (Workshops)

Encourages the highest standards of the vocal art and of ethical principals in the teaching of singing; and promote vocal education and research at all levels, both for the enrichment of the general public and for the professional advancement of the talented.
7000 Members
Founded in: 1944

1546 National Caves Association

PO Box 625
Cobleskill, NY 12043

270-492-2228; *Fax:* 931-688-3988
info@cavern.com; www.cavern.com
Social Media: Facebook, Twitter

Susan Berdeaux, Executive Director

Nonprofit organization of publicly and privately owned show caves and caverns - caves developed for public visitation.
Founded in: 1965

1547 National Independent Concessionaires Association, Inc.

1043 E. Brandon Blvd.
Brandon, FL 33511

813-438-8926; *Fax:* 813-438-8928
nica@nicainc.org; www.nicainc.org
Social Media: Facebook, RSS Feeds

Joe Potillo, Jr., President
Paulette Keene, 2nd Vice President
Yachika Smith, Office Manager
Rey O'Day, Interim Executive Manager
Stacia Markowitz, Treasurer

Striving towards better communication between fairs, festivals and independent concessionaires nationwide.
1200 Members
Founded in: 1993

1548 National Recreation and Park Association

22377 Belmont Ridge Road
Ashburn, VA 20148-4501

703-858-0784
800-626-6772; *Fax:* 703-858-0794
customerservice@nrpa.org; www.nrpa.org
Social Media: Facebook, Twitter, LinkedIn, YouTube, Pinterest

Robert F. Ashcraft, Chairman/Executive Director
Barbara Tulipane, President/CEO
Ted Mattingly, Director, Facilities

Kevin Conley, Director Information Technology
David Wenner, Administrator

NRPA is the leading advocacy organization dedicated to the advancement of public parks and recreation opportunities. Advances parks, recreation and environmental conservation efforts that enhance the quality of life.
Founded in: 1965

1549 New England Association of Amusement Parks and Attractions
774 Portland Road
PO Box 85
Saco, ME 04072

877-999-8740; *Fax:* 207-283-4716
secretary@neaapa.com; www.neaapa.com
Social Media: Facebook, Twitter, LinkedIn, YouTube

Ryan DeMaria, President
Dorothy Lewis, 1st VP
Eric Anderson, Second Vice President
Charlene Conway, Treasurer

NEAAPA is the premier regional association representing amusement parks, attractions, and their suppliers. NEAAPA works with its members on education opportunities, legislative and policy issues, as well as promotion of the Association's members.
Founded in: 1912

1550 Outdoor Amusement Business Association
1035 S Semoran Blvd
Suite 1045A
Winter Park, FL 32792-5512

407-681-9444
800-517-6222; *Fax:* 407-681-9445
oaba@oaba.org; www.oaba.org
Social Media: Facebook, Twitter, YouTube, Instagram

Michael Wood, Chairman
Robert W Johnson, President
Dee Dee Alford, Vice President
Al DeRusha, Senior Vice President
Brenda Ruiz, Manager of Programs and Services

The OABA manages and influences concerns for its members. OABA believes that all business owners and members of the trade association should continue to raise the level of safety and quality in the mobile amusement industry.
4000 Members
Founded in: 1964

1551 PLASA
630 Ninth Avenue
Suite 609
New York, NY 10036

212-244-1505; *Fax:* 212-244-1502
info@plasa.org; www.plasa.org
Social Media: Facebook, Twitter

Christopher Toulmin, Director of Events
Matthew Griffiths, Chief Executive Officer
Shane McGreevy, Chief Finance Officer
Lori Rubenstein, Director of Membership
Jackie Tien, Group Publisher

PLASA is the lead international membership body for those who supply technologies and services to the event, entertainment and installation industries. As the worldwide voice for those who supply and service the entertainment, event and installation markets, PLASA will develop, promote, support and grow our industry.
1200+ Members

1552 Roller Skating Association International
6905 Corporate Dr
Indianapolis, IN 46278-1927

317-347-2626; *Fax:* 317-347-2636
rsa@rollerskating.com; www.rollerskating.org
Social Media: Facebook, Twitter, LinkedIn, YouTube, Pinterest, Google+

Robert Bentley, President
Michael Jacques, Vice President
Jim McMaho, Executive Director
Tina Robertson, Director of Conventions
Lynette Rowland, Director of Comm./Editor/Publisher

The Roller Skating Association (RSA) is a trade association that serves commercial (for-profit) skating center owner/operators. It also serves those involved in various facets of the roller related industry such as teachers, coaches, manufacturers, distributors and other elements of the family entertainment industry. Promotes the success of members through education and advancing the roller skating business.
1000 Members
Founded in: 1937

1553 Showmen's League of America
1023 W. Fulton Market
Chicago, IL 60607

312-733-9533
800-350-9906; *Fax:* 312-733-9534
office@showmensleague.org;
www.showmensleague.org
Social Media: Facebook, Twitter

Paul Kasin, President
Ron Porter, 1st Vice President
Debbie Powers, 2nd Vice President
Guy Leavitt, 3rd Vice President
Cindy Henning, Executive Secretary

It seeks to promote the success of our members through education and advancing the roller skating business.elp those in need through one of its many programs.
Founded in: 1913

1554 Society of Broadcast Engineers
9102 N Meridian St
Suite 150
Indianapolis, IN 46260-1896

317-846-9000; *Fax:* 317-846-9120;
www.sbe.org
Social Media: Facebook, Twitter, LinkedIn, YouTube

Jerry Massey, President
James E. Leifer, Vice President
John L Poray CAE, Executive Director
Megan Clappe, Certification Director
Debbie Hennessey, Sustaining Member Manager

Committed to serving broadcast engineers. From the studio operator to the maintenance engineer and the chief engineer to the vice president of engineering, SBE members come from commercial and non-commercial radio and television stations and cable facilities. A growing segment of members are engaging the industry on their own as consultants and contractors, field and sales engineers.
5100+ Members
Founded in: 1964
Mailing list available for rent: 5700 names at $170 per M

1555 Society of Camera Operators
PO Box 2006
Toluca Lake, CA 91610

818-563-9110
818-382-7070; *Fax:* 818-563-9117
socoffice@soc.org; www.soc.org
Social Media: Facebook, Twitter

Mark August, President
Michael Scott, First Vice President
Mitch Dubin, Second Vice President
Lisa Stacilauskas, Third Vice President
Bill McClelland, Treasurer

Advances the art and creative contribution of the operating cameraman in the Motion Picture and Television Industries. The Society serves the purpose of bringing into the closest confederation Industry leaders in their fields.
Founded in: 1979

1556 Tennessee Department of Agriculture, Market Development Division
Tennessee Department of Agriculture
440 Hogan Road
PO Box 40627
Nashville, TN 37204

615-837-5160
800-342-8206; *Fax:* 615-837-5194
pick.tn@tn.gov; www.picktnproducts.org
Social Media: Facebook, Twitter, Pinterest

Ed Harlan, Assistant Commissioner
Debbie Ball, Director of Marketing
Nelson Owen, Livestock Grading/Market News
Erica Alexander, TAEP Producer Diversification Coor
Art Colebank, Digital Media Specialist

US and Canadian representatives of state/provincial agencies that are responsible for the support of educational and agricultural fairs.
35 Members
Founded in: 1966

1557 Themed Entertainment Association
150 East Olive Avenue
Suite 306
Burbank, CA 91502-1850

818-843-8497; *Fax:* 818-843-8477
info@teaconnect.org; www.teaconnect.org
Social Media: Facebook, Twitter, LinkedIn, YouTube

Steve Birket PE, President
Melissa Townsend, Vice President
Michael Mercadante, Treasurer
Jennie Nevin, Chief Operating Officer
Marie Brennan, Intern

The Themed Entertainment Association (TEA) is an international non-profit association representing the world's leading creators, developers, designers and producers of compelling places and experiences.
Founded in: 1991

1558 Western Fairs Association
1776 Tribute Rd
Suite 210
Sacramento, CA 95815-4495

916-927-3100; *Fax:* 916-927-6397
info@fairsnet.org; www.fairsnet.org
Social Media: Facebook, Twitter, YouTube, Instagram

Troy Bowers, President
Barbara Quaid, Vice President
Stephen J Chambers, Executive Director
Tami Davis Triggs, Accounting Manager
Jessica Boudevin, Communications Manager

Western Fairs Association (WFA) serves the fair industry throughout the Western United States and Canada. Assists in maintaining the highest professional standards within the fair industry through a voluntary network of individuals and organizations. Promotes the prosperity of fairs through education and training programs.
2000 Members
Founded in: 1922

1559 World Waterpark Association
8826 Santa Fe Drive
Suite 310
Overland Park, KS 66212-3676

913-599-0300; *Fax:* 913-599-0520
wwamemberinfo@waterparks.org;
www.waterparks.org
Social Media: Facebook, Twitter, LinkedIn, YouTube, Instagram

Mark Moore, Chair
Rick Root, President
Kelly Harris, Dir. of Ops & Member Services

Aleatha Ezra, Director of Park Member Development
Patty Miller, Dir. of Trade Show & Advertising
Provides forum for exchange of ideas related to the water amusement park industry.
1200 Members
Founded in: 1982

Newsletters

1560 **ACE News**
American Coaster Enthusiasts
P.O. Box 540261
Grand Prairie, TX 75054-0261
469-278-6223; *Fax:* 740-452-2552
info@aceonline.org; www.aceonline.org
Lee Ann Draud, Publications Director
Jerry Willard, President
Tim Baldwin, Communications Director
Up-to-date information about ACE, the events, roller coasters, and amusement parks.
Frequency: Bi-Monthly

1561 **Adams Gaming Report**
Casino City Press
95 Wells Ave
Newton, MA 02459-3299
617-332-2850
800-490-1715; *Fax:* 617-964-2280
customerservice@casinocitypress.com;
www.casinopromote.com
Michael A Corfman, CEO
Focuses on the gaming industry with nationwide coverage.
Cost: $149.00
Frequency: Monthly

1562 **Affialiate Connection**
International Festivals and Events Association
2603 W Eastover Ter
Boise, ID 83706-2800
208-433-0950; *Fax:* 208-433-9812
craig@ifea.com; www.ifea.com
Steven Schmader, President
Nia Hovde, VP/Marketing
Craig Sarton, Creative &Publications Director
Bette Monteith, Director Of Finance
The IFEA newsletter provides information and news 24 hours a day, 7 days a week, keeping members, suppliers and affialiates up-to-date and current.
2000 Members
Circulation: 2,700
Founded in: 1956
Mailing list available for rent: 20000 names at $235 per M

1563 **Celebrity Bulletin**
Celebrity Service
252 West 37th St
Suite 1204
New York, NY 10017-3632
212-757-7979; *Fax:* 212-582-7701
mark@celebrityservice.com;
www.celebrityservice.com
Mark Kerrigan, Manager
Nicole Bagley, COO
Nancy R. Bagley, President
Soroush Shehabi, CEO
A daily guide on the whereabouts and vital information of the famous. Includes celebrity contacts including agents, business managers, publicists, and record companies. Gives advanced notice of who's coming to town, what projects they're working on and how to get in touch with them. Features an International Page noting arrivals in cities worldwide.
Cost: $2245.00
4 Pages
Frequency: Daily
Founded in: 1939

1564 **Connector**
Society of Broadcast Engineers
9102 N Meridian St
Suite 150
Indianapolis, IN 46260-1896
317-846-9000; *Fax:* 317-846-9120;
www.sbe.org
John L Poray CAE, Executive Director
Ralph Hogan, President
Joseph Snelson, Vice President
James Leifer, Secretary
Jerry Massey, Treasurer
To youth members and high schools across the country that have radio or television stations. Provides students with information on careers in broadcast engineering, post-secondary education, high school student stations, scholarships and technical information.
Frequency: 3x/Year
Circulation: 300

1565 **Entertainment Marketing Letter**
EPM Communications
19 W.21st St, # 303
New York, NY 10012-3208
212-941-0099
888-852-9467; *Fax:* 212-941-1622
info@epmcom.com; www.epmcom.com
Ira Mayer, Owner
Michele Khan, Marketing
Terence Keegan, Editor
Covers marketing techniques used in the entertainment industry, and by others who link their goods and services marketing through entertainment properties.
Cost: $449.00
Frequency: 24x Year
ISSN: 1048-5112
Printed in on matte stock

1566 **INTIX e-Newsletter**
330 W 38th Street
Suite 605
New York, NY 10018
212-629-4036; *Fax:* 212-629-8532
info@intix.org; www.intix.org
Jena L Hoffman, President/CEO
Kathleen O'Donnell, Deputy Director
Kevin McDonnell, Sales Manager
Mary Leaton, Accounting Associate
Tiffany Kelham, Membership Associate
E-mail bulletin which includes news from the association, promotions, replacements, clips from industry news sources; vendor updates, conferences and exhibitions, the latest job postings, and listings of members searching for a job.
Frequency: Monthly

1567 **SBE-News**
Society of Broadcast Engineers
9102 N Meridian St
Suite 150
Indianapolis, IN 46260-1896
317-846-9000; *Fax:* 317-846-9120;
www.sbe.org
John L Poray CAE, Executive Director
Ralph Hogan, President
Joseph Snelson, Vice President
James Leifer, Secretary
Jerry Massey, Treasurer
Email subscription of timely news and updates sent from the National Office.
Frequency: Semimonthly
Circulation: 4,000

1568 **Signal**
Society of Broadcast Engineers
9102 N Meridian St
Suite 150
Indianapolis, IN 46260-1896
317-846-9000; *Fax:* 317-846-9120;
www.sbe.org
John L Poray CAE, Executive Director
Ralph Hogan, President
Joseph Snelson, Vice President
James Leifer, Secretary
Jerry Massey, Treasurer
Provides members with timely articles on various broadcast-related topics, information on upcoming events, recognition of members' activities and achievements and details of SBE services.
Frequency: Bimonthly
Circulation: 5,500

1569 **Theme and Museum Index Report**
Themed Entertainment Association/AECOM
150 E. Olive Ave.
Suite 306
Burbank, CA 91502-1850
818-843-8497; *Fax:* 818-843-8477
judy@teaconnect.org;
www.aecom.com/What+We+Do/Economics/Theme+Index+Report
Judith Rubin, TEA Publications, PR & Social Media
Jennie Nevin, TEA COO
Annual attendance figures for the global attractions industry.
Frequency: Annual

Magazines & Journals

1570 **Amusement Business**
VNU Business Media
49 Music Sq W
Suite 300
Nashville, TN 37203-3213
615-321-4251
888-900-3782; *Fax:* 615-327-1575
mshear@amusementbusiness.com;
www.amusementbusiness.com
Michael Marchesano, President/CEO
Karen Oertley, Publisher
James Zoltak, Editor
Lisa Krugel, Classified Ad Manager
Serves the management of more than 10,000 mass entertainment and amusement facilities.
Cost: $129.00
Frequency: Monthly
Founded in: 1894

1571 **Amusement Today**
Amusement Today
2012 E Randol Mill Rd
Suite 203
Arlington, TX 76011-8222
817-460-7220; *Fax:* 817-265-6397
gslade@amusementtoday.com;
www.amusementtoday.com
Gary Slade, Publisher
Bill Rea, Director
Sammy Piccola, Accounting/Circulation
Sue Nicholas, Advertising
Keeps decision makers in the amusement industry up-to-date with current events, business, international developments and new attractions at amusement parks and waterparks.
Cost: $50.00
Frequency: Monthly
Circulation: 36000
Mailing list available for rent: 3000 names

1572 **Balloons and Parties**
PartiLife Publications
65 Sussex Street
Hackensack, NJ 07601

201-441-4224; *Fax:* 201-342-8118
info@balloonsandparties.com;
www.balloonsandparties.com
Social Media: Facebook, Twitter

Andrea P Zettler, Editor
Janet Slowik, Director

A decorating resource offering tips and suggestions for parties, special occasions, holidays, banquets and events. Targeted, informative and practical ideas for the event decorating industry. Motivates readers to produce professional, innovative party services.
Cost: $9.95
2 Members
Frequency: 4x/Year
Circulation: 7000
Founded in: 1986
Printed in 4 colors on glossy stock

1573 **Bandwagon**
Circus Historical Society
3100 Parkside Lane
Williamsburg, VA 23185

757-259-0412
rfsabia@widomaker.com;
www.circushistory.org

Judith L. Griffin, President
Neil C. Cockerline, Vice President
Robert Cline, Secretary/Treasurer

Publishes articles relating to circus history.
Cost: $5.00
Frequency: Bimonthly
Founded in: 1939

1574 **Baseline**
Ziff Davis Media
28 E 28th St
Suite 1
New York, NY 10016-7914

212-503-3500; *Fax:* 212-503-5696;
www.ziffdavis.com

Jason Young, CEO
Eileen Feretic, Editor
Stephanie McCarthy, Marketing

Publication that offers practical information and guidance on the management of information technology.
Cost: $205.00
Frequency: Monthly
Circulation: 125100

1575 **Billboard Magazine**
Prometheus Global Media
770 Broadwaye Blvd.
New York, NY 10003-9595

212-493-4100; *Fax:* 646-654-5368;
www.prometheusgm.com
Social Media: Facebook, Twitter

Richard D. Beckman, CEO
James A. Finkelstein, Chairman
Madeline Krakowsky, Vice President Circulation
Tracy Brater, Executive Director Creative Service

Packed with in-depth music and entertainment features including the latest in new media and digital music, global coverage, music and money, touring, new artists, radio news and retail reports.
Cost: $149.00
Frequency: Weekly
Founded in: 1894

1576 **BoxOffice Magazine**
BoxOffice Media
9107 Wilshire Blvd.
Suite 450
Beverly Hills, CA 90210-4241

310-876-9090; www.boxoffice.com

Peter Crane, Publisher
Kenneth James Bacon, Creative Director
Phil Contrino, Editor
Amy Nicholson, Editor

The premier trade magazine covering the latest developments in the movie industry, from films in production to digital cinema and everything in between.
Founded in: 1948

1577 **Camera Operator**
Society of Camera Operators
PO Box 2006
Toluca Lake, CA 91610

818-382-7070; *Fax:* 323-856-9155;
www.soc.org

Chris Tufty, President
Steve Fracol, Vice President
Dan Turrett, Treasurer
Dan Gold, Recording Secretary

Features articles written by and about SOC members, presented from the camera operator's point of view. Encompassing the latest technological trends while reviewing historical productions, the Camera Operator seeks to enlighten and educate readers on the motion picture, television and commerical industries.
Cost: $20.00
Frequency: Semi-Annual
Printed in 4 colors

1578 **Carnival Magazine**
PO Box 4138
Salisbury, NC 28145-4138

704-638-0878; *Fax:* 704-636-1051;
www.carnivalmag.com

Charles Dabbs, Publisher
Kevin Freese, Editor

Chronicles contemporary outdoor amusement history providing readers with information and news on carnivals, events, people, trade shows, manufacturers, suppliers and more.
Cost: $40.00
Frequency: Monthly

1579 **Carousel News and Trader**
11001 Peoria Street
Sun Valley, CA 91352

818-332-7944; *Fax:* 818-332-7944
roland@carouselnews.com;
www.carouselnews.com

Dan Horenberger, Publisher
Roland Hopkins, Editor
Ted McDonald, Webmaster

Articles devoted to the collecting, restoration and selling of carousel art.
Cost: $35.00
48 Pages
Frequency: Monthly
Founded in: 1985

1580 **Casino Journal**
BNP Media
2401 W Big Beaver Rd
Suite 700
Troy, MI 48084-3333

248-362-3700; *Fax:* 248-332-0317;
www.bnp.com

Taggert Henderson, CEO
Marian Green, Editor
Lynn Davidson, Marketing

A primary information source for the key decision makers in the worldwide casino, lottery, parimutuel, bingo and emerging internet wagering markets.
Frequency: Monthly
Circulation: 13034
Founded in: 1995

1581 **Connect Magazine**
8403 Colesville Rd
Suite 710
Silver Spring, MD 20910-6331

301-562-0777; *Fax:* 301-562-0888
membership@aza.org; www.aza.org
Social Media: Facebook, Twitter

Jim Maddy, President & CEO
Kris Vehrs JD, Executive Director
Jill Nicoll, SVP, Marketing & Corp Strategies
Laura Benson, SVP, Finance & Administration

Your window to the professional zoo and aquarium world. Each month, the magazine features fascinating stories that explore trends, educational initiatives, member achievements and conservation efforts.
200 Members
Founded in: 1924

1582 **Daily Variety**
5900 Wilshire Blvd
Suite 3100
Los Angeles, CA 90036-7209

323-617-9100; *Fax:* 323-965-5375;
www.variety.com

Jay Penske, President
Abe Burns, Marketing
Millie Chiavelli, Managing Director
Steve Gaydos, Executive Editor
Paula Taylor, Creative Director

Focuses on film, television, video, cable, music and theater. Includes coverage of financial, regulatory and legal matters pertaining to the entertainment industry.
Cost: $329.00
Frequency: Daily
Circulation: 38248

1583 **Entertainment, Publishing and the Arts Handbook**
Thomson West Publishing
610 Opperman Dr
St Paul, MN 55123-1340

651-687-7000
800-344-5008; *Fax:* 651-687-5581;
www.west.thomson.com

Charles B Cater, Executive VP
Laurie Zenner, VP

Provides information on the latest development in the expanding legal field of entertainment, publishing, and the arts. The articles focus on such issues as books, copyrights, right-of-publicity and more.
Cost: $538.00
Frequency: Annual

1584 **Fair Dealer**
Western Fairs Association
1776 Tribute Rd
Suite 210
Sacramento, CA 95815-4495

916-927-3100; *Fax:* 916-927-6397
stephenc@fairsnet.org; www.fairsnet.org

Stephen J Chambers, Executive Director
Jon Baker, VP
Nichole Farley, Marketing

Offers information for fairground owners, managers and workers, fair related businesses.
Cost: $35.00
2000 Members
Frequency: Quarterly
Circulation: 1500
Founded in: 1922
Printed in on glossy stock

1585 **Fairs & Expos**
International Association of Fairs & Expositions
3043 E Cairo
PO Box 985
Springfield, MO 65802
417-862-5771
800-516-0313; *Fax:* 417-862-0156
iafe@fairsandexpos.com;
www.fairsandexpos.com
Jim Tucker, President
Steve Siever, Director
Max Willis, CFO
Marla Calico, Director Of Education
Rachel Mundhenke, Director Of technology
The source for information on fair trends, innovative ideas, and association activities.
Circulation: 3250
Founded in: 1885
Printed in 4 colors on glossy stock

1586 **Graphic Impressions**
Pioneer Communications
218 6th Ave
Fleming Building, Suite 610
Des Moines, IA 50309-4009
515-246-0402; *Fax:* 515-282-0125;
www.pioncomm.net
Rick Thomas, President
Provides providing industry news and information including in-depth coverage of PIM, and PIAMS association news and events. Features cover technology, legal, environmental, niche printing, education, new products, marketing, distribution, finance and insurance.
Cost: $20.00
32 Pages
Frequency: 10 per year
Circulation: 7,000
Founded in: 1995
Printed in 4 colors on glossy stock

1587 **Hollywood Reporter**
Prometheus Global Media
770 Broadway
New York, NY 10003-9595
212-493-4100; *Fax:* 646-654-5368;
www.prometheusgm.com
Social Media: Facebook, Twitter, YouTube
Richard D. Beckman, CEO
James A. Finkelstein, Chairman
Madeline Krakowsky, Vice President Circulation
Tracy Brater, Executive Director Creative Service
Gives fresh ideas for film and TV. Covers the full spectrum of craft and commerce in the entertainment industry.
Cost: $199.00
Frequency: Weekly
Circulation: 34770

1588 **Inside Arts**
Association of Performing Arts Presenters
1211 Connecticut Ave NW
Suite 200
Washington, DC 20036-2716
202-833-2787
888-820-2787; *Fax:* 202-833-1543
editor@artspresenters.org;
www.artspresenters.org
Mario Durham, President
Sean Handerhan, Marketing
Alicia Anstead, Editor
Margaret Stevens, Director
Laura Benson, Programme Manager
This publication explores issues critical to the performing arts, presenting and touring field.
Cost: $42.00
1900 Members
Frequency: Bi-Monthly
Founded in: 1957
Printed in 4 colors

1589 **International Gaming and Wagering Business**
BNP Media
PO Box 1080
Skokie, IL 60076-9785
847-763-9534; *Fax:* 847-763-9538
igwb@halldata.com;
www.spectrumgaming.com
James Rutherford, Editor
Lynn Davidson, Marketing
Tammie Gizicki, Director
Focuses on business strategy, legislative information, food service and promotional concerns.
Frequency: Monthly
Circulation: 25000

1590 **JUGGLE**
International Jugglers' Association
3315 E Russell Road
Suite 203
Las Vegas, NV 89120
702-798-0099; *Fax:* 709-248-2550;
www.juggle.org
Alan Howard, Editor
Scott Krause, Treasurer
Marilyn Sullivan, Membership Director
Martin Frost, Store Manager
Dave Pawson, Chair
Offers readers a variety of colorful articles and features on the art of juggling including interviews, a listing of jugggling clubs, upcoming events and more.
Cost: $30.00
Frequency: Quarterly
Founded in: 1947

1591 **Journal of Leisure Research**
22377 Belmont Ridge Road
Ashburn, VA 20148
703-858-0784
800-626-6772; *Fax:* 703-858-0794
customerservice@nrpa.org; www.nrpa.org
Social Media: Facebook, Twitter, LinkedIn, YouTube
Jodie H Adams, President
Jessica Lytle, Director
John Crosby, Marketing
Advancing parks, recreation and environmental conservation efforts that enhance the quality of life for all people.
Founded in: 1965

1592 **Journal of Physical Education, Recreation & Dance (JOPERD)**
1900 Association Dr
Reston, VA 20191-1502
703-476-3400
800-213-7193; *Fax:* 703-476-9527
info@aahperd.org; www.aahperd.org
Social Media: Facebook, Twitter, YouTube
Monica Mize, President
Judith C Young, VP
Paula Kun, Marketing
Provides a variety of information on health, physical education, recreation, and dance issues than any other publication in the field.
25000 Members
Founded in: 1885

1593 **Journal of Singing**
National Association of Teachers of Singing
9957 Moorings Drive
Suite 401
Jacksonville, FL 32257-2416
904-992-9101; *Fax:* 904-262-2587
info@nats.org; www.nats.org
Social Media: Facebook, Twitter, LinkedIn
Richard Dale Sjoerdsma, Editor-in-Chief
Kenneth Bozeman, Chair
Paul Witkowski, Marketing & Communications
The official journal of NATS, offering a wealth of research and insight from scholars and experts on teaching singing, with topics ranging from history and voice science to voice pedagogy.
Frequency: 5x times/year
Founded in: 1944

1594 **Laserist**
International Laser Display Association
7062 Edgeworth Drive
Orlando, FL 32819
407-797-7654; *Fax:* 503-344-3770
president@laserist.org; www.laserist.org
Christine Jenkin, President
Patrick Murphy, Executive Director
Providing the latest news about the art and technology of laser displays.
Frequency: Quarterly
Founded in: 1986
Printed in 4 colors

1595 **Linking Ring Magazine**
International Brotherhood of Magicians
11155 S Towne Square
Suite C
St Louis, MO 63123
314-845-9200; *Fax:* 314-845-9220
info@magician.org; www.magician.org
Joan Pye, President
Shawn Farquhar, VP
Don Wiberg, Secretary
Roger Miller, Treasurer
Keeps IBM members informed about what's happening in the world of magic.
13000 Members
Frequency: Monthly
Founded in: 1922

1596 **Magic-Unity-Might: MUM Magazine**
Society of American Magicians
7566 John Avenue
PO Box 510260
Saint Louis, MO 63129
314-846-5659; *Fax:* 314-846-5659
webmaster@magicsam.com;
www.magicsam.com
John Apperson, President
David Goodsell, National Secretary
Marlene Clark, National Secretary
You will find articles dealing with the business of magic, publicity, showmanship and the history of magic and the lives of famous magicians. Many of the creative minds in the business are regular contributors.
60 Pages
Frequency: Monthly
Circulation: 30,000
Founded in: 1902

1597 **NRPA Express**
22377 Belmont Ridge Road
Ashburn, VA 20148
703-858-0784
800-626-6772; *Fax:* 703-858-0794
customerservice@nrpa.org; www.nrpa.org
Social Media: Facebook, Twitter, LinkedIn, YouTube
Jodie H Adams, President
Jessica Lytle, Director
John Crosby, Marketing

Membership publication delivering the latest news and information about upcoming events, research projects, educational opportunities, grants, and initiatives about NRPA and the parks and recreation community.
Founded in: 1965

1598 **New Calliope**
Clowns of America International
PO Box C
Richeyville, PA 15358-0532

724-938-8765
888-522-5696; *Fax:* 724-938-8765;
www.coai.org

Tom King, President
Pamela Bacher, VP

Contains informative articles regarding the art of clowning, such as make-up, costuming, props, skit development, etc. News of regional and local clown alley activities; resources for your clowning needs; information on the annual international conventions; information on the various regional conventions through the year.
Frequency: Bi-Monthly

1599 **Park & Rec Trades**
Trades Publishing Company
20 Our Way Dr
Crossville, TN 38555-5790

931-484-8819; *Fax:* 931-484-8825
subscribe@thetrades.com;
www.parktrades.com

Tim Wilson, Owner
Kristie Irvin, Marketing

Event calendar and buying guides for amusement and recreation park professionals.
Frequency: Monthly
Circulation: 32000
Printed in 4 colors on newsprint stock

1600 **Parks and Recreation Magazine**
National Recreation and Park Association
22377 Belmont Ridge Road
Ashburn, VA 20148

703-858-0784; *Fax:* 703-858-0794
info@nrpa.org; www.nrpa.org

Douglas Vaira, Editor
Jessica Lytle, Director
John Crosby, Marketing
Barbara Tulipane, President
Michele White, Executive Assistant

NRPA's magazine keeps members informed about parks, recreation and envrionmental conservation efforts.
Circulation: Monthly
Founded in: 1965

1601 **Play Meter**
Skybird Publishing Company
PO Box 337
Metairie, LA 70004-0337

504-488-7003
888-473-2376; *Fax:* 504-488-7083
news@playmeter.com; www.playmeter.com

Bonnie Theard, Editor

Trade publication that provides members with information on the coin-operated entertainment industry, including upcoming trade shows, new products, ongoing trends and more.
Cost: $60.00
Frequency: Monthly
Circulation: 60000
Founded in: 1974

1602 **Pollstar: Concert Hotwire**
4697 W Jacquelyn Ave
Fresno, CA 93722-6443

559-271-7900; *Fax:* 559-271-7979
info@pollstar.com; www.pollstar.com

Gary Smith, COO
Shari Rice, VP
Gary Bongiovanni, CEO

Trade publication for the concert industry offering global coverage and information including concert tour schedules, ticket sales information and more.
Cost: $449.00
Frequency: Weekly
Circulation: 20000
Printed in 4 colors

1603 **Protocol**
Entertainment Services and Technology Association
630 Nonth Avenue
Suite 609
New York, NY 10036

212-244-1505; *Fax:* 212-244-1502
info@esta.org; www.esta.org

Beverly Inglesby, Editor
Lori Rubinstein, Executive Director
Jules Lauve, President

Featuring columns and articles of interest to professionals in the entertainment technology industry on business and technical topics, current standards issues, certification developments, and trade shows.
550 Members
Frequency: Quarterly
Printed in 4 colors

1604 **RePlay Magazine**
PO Box 572829
Tarzana, CA 91357-7004

818-776-2880; *Fax:* 818-776-2888
editor@replaymag.com; www.replaymag.com

Edward Adlum, Owner
Barry Zweben, Marketing

A trade publication for those within the coin-operated amusement machine industry, primarily distributors, manufacturers and operators of jukeboxes and games.
Cost: $65.00
Frequency: Monthly
Circulation: 36000
ISSN: 1534-2328
Founded in: 1975
Printed in 4 colors on glossy stock

1605 **Research Quarterly for Exercise and Sport (RQES)**
1900 Association Dr
Reston, VA 20191-1502

703-476-3400
800-213-7193; *Fax:* 703-476-9527
info@aahperd.org; www.aahperd.org
Social Media: Facebook, Twitter, YouTube

Monica Mize, President
Judith C Young, VP
Paula Kun, Marketing

Publishes research in the art and science of human movement that contributes to the knowledge and development of theory either as new information, reviews, substantiation or contradiction of previous findings, or as application of new or improved techniques.
25000 Members
Founded in: 1885

1606 **Rollercoaster!**
American Coaster Enthusiasts
P.O. Box 540261
Grand Prairie, TX 75054-0261

469-278-6223
info@aceonline.org; www.aceonline.org

Jerry Willard, President
David Lipnicky, Vice President
Tammy Baldwin, Editor

Magazine featuring in-depth articles of parks and coasters of the past along with profiles of today's coaster, parks, people, and places.
6000 Members
Frequency: Quarterly
Founded in: 1978

1607 **Souvenirs, Gifts & Novelties Magazine**
10 E Athens Avenue
Suite 208
Ardmore, PA 19003

610-645-6940; *Fax:* 610-645-6943
sgnmag@kanec.com; www.sgnmag.com

Scott C Borowsky, President
Tony DeMasi, Editor

Trade magazine for the resort-gift, souvenir industry. Articles cover merchandising trends, profile successful operations, new products, trade show calendar, plus buyer's guide issue.
Cost: $40.00
Circulation: 42,362
Printed in 4 colors on glossy stock

1608 **Strategies: A Journal for Physical and Sport Educators**
1900 Association Dr
Reston, VA 20191-1502

703-476-3400
800-213-7193; *Fax:* 703-476-9527
info@aahperd.org; www.aahperd.org
Social Media: Facebook, Twitter, YouTube

Monica Mize, President
Judith C Young, VP
Paula Kun, Marketing

Delivers practical ideas, how-to information, and tips for sport and physical educators.
25000 Members
Founded in: 1885

1609 **The Bulletin**
120 W Seventh Street
One City Centre, Suite 200
Bloomington, IN 47404

812-245-2284; *Fax:* 812-245-6710
acui@acui.org; www.acui.org
Social Media: Facebook, Twitter, YouTube

Rich Steele, President
Marsha Herman-Betzen, Executive Director
Andrea Langeveld, Marketing

Features everything from research analyses to best practices to practical reports about trends in the field.
1000 Members
Founded in: 1914

1610 **The New Calliope**
PO Box 1171
Englewood, FL 34295-1171

941-474-4351
877-816-6941; www.coai.org

Pamela Bacher, President
Michael B. Cox, Vice-President
Catherine Hardebeck, Secretary
Candyce Will, Treasurer

Contains informative articles regarding the art of clowning such as; makeup, costuming, props, skit development, etc. News of regional and local clown alley activities, resources for your clowning needs, information on the annual international convention, and information on various regional conventions through the year.

1611 **Therapeutic Recreation Journal**
22377 Belmont Ridge Road
Ashburn, VA 20148
703-858-0784
800-626-6772; *Fax:* 703-858-0794
customerservice@nrpa.org; www.nrpa.org
Social Media: Facebook, Twitter, LinkedIn, YouTube
Jodie H Adams, President
Jessica Lytle, Director
John Crosby, Marketing
Advancing parks, recreation and environmental conservation efforts that enhance the quality of life for all people.
Founded in: 1965

1612 **Tourist Attractions & Parks**
10 E Athens Avenue
Suite 208
Ardmore, PA 19003
610-645-6940; *Fax:* 610-645-6943
tapmag@kanec.com; www.tapmag.com
Social Media: Facebook, Twitter
Scott C Borosky, President/Ex Editor
Caroline Burns, Managing Editor
Larry White, Publisher
Kittey White, Account Executive
Laurie O'Malley, Account Executive
Trade magazine for amusement, national & waterparks, zoos, and aquariums, bowling, skating + family entertainment centers, forest festivals.
Cost: $49.00
28124 Members
Circulation: 31,388
Founded in: 1972

1613 **Vending Times**
Vending Times
55 Maple Avenue
Suite 102
Rockville Centre, NY 11570
212-302-4700; *Fax:* 212-221-3311;
www.vendingtimes.com
Alicia Lavay, President/Publisher
Nick Montano, VP/Executive Editor
Tim Sanford, Editor-in-Chief
Maria Ackies, Production Manager
Addresses the business, legal, legislative and regulatory concerns of companies providing industrial, institutional and public vending, refreshment, feeding and recreational services
Cost: $40.00
Frequency: Monthly
Circulation: 16,000
Founded in: 1962

1614 **White Tops**
Circus Fans Association of America
1515 S Butler Street
Port Angeles, WA 98363
360-452-1919
feedback@circusfan.org; www.circusfans.org
Vern Mendonca, President
Articles about the illustrious history of circus, including the greatest performers, famous acts and feats, logistical facts and figures, management and marketing, and the shows of yesteryear.
Circulation: 2000
Founded in: 1926

Trade Shows

1615 **ACUI Conference**
Association of College Unions International
120 W 7th Street
One City Centre, Suite 200
Bloomington, IN 47404-3925
812-245-ACUI; *Fax:* 812-245-6710
acui@acui.org; www.acui.org
Michelle Smith, Director, Educational Prgms & Svcs
Marsha Herman, Executive Director
Tim Arth, Event and Corporate Sales Manager
Karen Keith, Financial Service Manager
Julie Sylvester, Office Administrator
Tours and outings, peer learning network, leadership meetings, orientation for new members, education sessions, seminars, networking fair, keynote speakers.
Frequency: Annual
Founded in: 1914

1616 **AIMS International Safety Seminar**
Amusement Industry Manufacturers & Suppliers Intl
3026 S Orange
Santa Ana, CA 92707
714-425-5747; *Fax:* 714-276-9666
info@aimsintl.org; www.aimsintl.org
Brian D King, President
This AIMS event is a comprehensive week of hands-on instruction taught by today's top industry professionals, for individuals responsible for the care and safety of the amusement industry's guests. Certification testing also available.
Frequency: January

1617 **APAP Conference**
Association of Performing Arts Presenters
1211 Connecticut Avenue NW
Suite 200
Washington, DC 20036
202-833-2787
888-717-APAP; *Fax:* 202-833-1543
info@apapconference.org;
www.apapconference.org
Sandra Gibson, President
Sean Handerhan, Marketing
Leah Yoon, Director
Judy Moore, Conference Manager
Providing valuable networking resources and opportunities for performing arts presenters, artists and artist managers throughout the world. Hundreds of exhibitors and performances: see who is doing what in the world of performing arts. Educational tracks are offered; special events; special interests; and clinics.
1900 Members
4000 Attendees
Frequency: January
Founded in: 1957

1618 **Amusement Expo**
American Amusement Machine Association
450 E. Higgins Road
Suite 201
Elk Grove Village, IL 60007-1417
847-290-9088
866-372-5190; *Fax:* 847-290-9121
information@coin-op.org; www.coin-op.org
Social Media: Facebook, Twitter, LinkedIn
John Schultz, President
Tina Schwartz, Business and Finance Manager
John Margold, Chairman
Frank Consentino, Secretary
Rich Babich, Treasurer
Featuring the latest in video games, digital-jukeboxes, dartboards, redemption games, plush toys, smart cards and more, as well as educational programs and seminars.

1619 **Amusement Industry Expo**
I-X Center
One I-X Center Drive
Cleveland, OH 44135
216-676-6000
800-897-3942; *Fax:* 216-265-2621
info@ixamusementpark.com;
www.ixcenter.com
John O'Brien, Director
Supplies and products for the amusement industry.
4100 Attendees
Frequency: March/April

1620 **Amusement Showcase International: ASI**
William T Glasgow Inc
10729 W 163rd Place
Orland Park, IL 60467
708-226-1300; *Fax:* 708-226-1310;
www.asi-show.com
William T Glasgow, Executive Director
Features exhibits and seminars for the coin-operated amusement industry.
4000 Attendees
Frequency: Annual/March

1621 **Amusement and Music Operators Association International Expo**
William T Glasgow Inc
10729 W 163rd Place
Orland Park, IL 60467
708-226-1300; *Fax:* 708-226-1310
info@amoashow.com; www.amoashow.com
William T Glasgow, Executive Director
The AMOA International Expo is designed for professionals from the amusement, music and vending industries.
8000 Attendees
Frequency: Annual/September
Founded in: 1948

1622 **BPAA Convention**
PO Box 4563
Louisville, KY 40204
502-473-0956; *Fax:* 502-473-7352
info@ialda.org; www.ialda.org
Lambert J. Hassinger, Jr., President
Bryan T. Pope, Vice-President
Nonprofit association of lawyers and other professionals who are actively engaged in representing the interests of the amusement and leisure industries.

1623 **Broadcast Engineering Conference (BEC)**
Society of Broadcast Engineers
9102 N Meridian Street
Suite 150
Indianapolis, IN 46260
317-846-9000; *Fax:* 317-846-9120;
www.sbe.org
John L Poray CAE, Executive Director
Vincent A Lopez CEV, CBNT, President
Held in conjunction with the National Association of Broadcasters, features SBE Ennes Workshop followed by sessions covering the latest in broadcast technology.
500 Attendees
Frequency: Annual/Spring
Mailing list available for rent: 4700 names

1624 **COAI Annual Spring International Convention**
Clowns of America International

PO Box C
Richeyville, PA 15358-0532

724-938-8765
888-522-5696; *Fax:* 724-938-8765;
www.coai.org

Glenn Kohlberger, President
Michael Cox, VP
Catherine Hardebeck, Secretary
Padee Embrey, Treasurer

The purpose of these conventions is to provide educational seminars, competitions for individuals and group skits, make up and costume competitions, as well as competitions in balloons and parade ability.
Frequency: Annual/Spring

1625 **COAI Convention**
PO Box 1171
Englewood, FL 34295-1171

941-474-4351
877-816-6941; www.coai.org

Pamela Bacher, President
Michael B. Cox, Vice-President
Catherine Hardebeck, Secretary
Candyce Will, Treasurer

Offering classes, shows and competitions, theme party and banquet.

1626 **CinemaCon**
National Association of Theatre Owners
750 1st St NE
Suite 1130
Washington, DC 20002-4241

202-962-0054; *Fax:* 202-962-0370;
www.cinemacon.com
Social Media: Facebook

Mitch Neuhauser, Managing Director

A gathering of cinema owners and operators.
4000 Members
3500 Attendees
Frequency: Annual/March/ Las Vegas
Founded in: 2010

1627 **Digital Out-of-Home Interactive Entertainment Conference (DNA)**
450 E Higgins Rd
Suite 201
Elk Grove Vlg, IL 60007-1417

847-290-9088
866-372-5190; *Fax:* 847-290-9121
information@coin-op.org; www.coin-op.org
Social Media: Facebook, Twitter, LinkedIn

John Schultz, President
Tina Schwartz, Business & Finance Manager
David Cohen, Chairman
Frank Consentino, Secretary
John Margold, Treasurer

Six dedicated sessions that speak directly to the industry and new opportunities, with a leading selection of speakers with direct experience in the sector and its future.
Founded in: 1981

1628 **Fun Expo**
William T Glasgow
10729 W 163rd Place
Orland Park, IL 60467

708-226-1300; *Fax:* 708-226-1310
info@funexpo.com; www.funexpo.com

William T Glasgow, Executive Director

Devoted to the family and location based entertainment industry and the trends that drive it. A focused and efficient event bringing buyers and sellers together in an atmosphere that allows industry professionals to conduct business.
Frequency: Annual/March

1629 **GAMA Trade Show**
Game Manufacturers Association
240 N.Fifth St
Suite 340
Columbus, OH 43215

614-255-4500; *Fax:* 614-255-4499
ops@gama.org; www.gama.org

John Ward, Executive Director
John Kaufeld, Marketing/Sales
Rick Loomis, President
Jamie Chambers, Vice President
Aaron Witten, Treasurer

For retailers, manufacturers, and industry professionals to network, see the newest products, and learn from others about ways to make their stores and businesses successful.
15000 Attendees

1630 **IAAPA Attractions Expo**
1035 S Semoran Blvd
Suite 1045A
Winter Park, FL 32792-5512

407-681-9444
800-517-6222; *Fax:* 407-681-9445
oaba@aol.com; www.oaba.org
Social Media: Facebook, Twitter, YouTube

Robert W Johnson, President
Al DeRusha, VP
Anita Rockett, Director

The OABA manages and influences concerns for its members. OABA believes that all business owners and members of the trade association should continue to raise the level of safety and quality in the mobile amusement industry.
4000 Members
Founded in: 1964

1631 **IAFE Annual Convention**
3043 East Cairo St.
PO Box 985
Springfield, MO 65802

417-862-5771
800-516-0313; *Fax:* 417-862-0156
iafe@fairsandexpos.com;
www.fairsandexpos.com
Social Media: Facebook, Twitter

Jim Tucker, President
Steve Siever, Director

The International Association of Fairs and Expositions (IAFE) is a voluntary, non-profit corporation whose members provide services and products that promote the overall development and improvement of fairs, shows, expositions, and allied fields.
1300 Members
Founded in: 1885

1632 **IFEA Annual Convention & Expo**
International Festivals and Events Association
2603 W Eastover Terrace
Boise, ID 83706

208-433-0950; *Fax:* 208-433-9812
schmader@ifea.com; www.ifea.com

Steven Wood Schmader, President
Nia Forster, VP/Marketing
Shauna Spencer, Director
Bette Monteith, Director Of Finance
Beth Petersen, Director Of Membership Services

Unites the world's leading festivals and events, suppliers, media, sponsors and related industry professionals to share information on every aspect of event production through in depth workshops, round table discussions and networking.
2000 Members
Frequency: Annual/Sept
Founded in: 1956
Mailing list available for rent: 20000 names at $235 per M

1633 **IISF Trade Show**
1035 S Semoran Blvd
Suite 1045A
Winter Park, FL 32792-5512

407-681-9444
800-517-6222; *Fax:* 407-681-9445
oaba@aol.com; www.oaba.org
Social Media: Facebook, Twitter, YouTube

Robert W Johnson, President
Al DeRusha, VP
Anita Rockett, Director

The OABA manages and influences concerns for its members. OABA believes that all business owners and members of the trade association should continue to raise the level of safety and quality in the mobile amusement industry.
4000 Members
Founded in: 1964

1634 **ILDA Conference**
International Laser Display Association
7062 Edgeworth Drive
Orlando, FL 32819

407-797-7654; *Fax:* 503-344-3770
president@laserist.org; www.laserist.org

Christine Jenkin, President
Patrick Murphy, Executive Director

One of the world's largest exhibitions of entertainment technology. Features international exhibitors from the fields of lighting, lasers, audio, video and staging.
70000 Attendees
Founded in: 1986

1635 **INTIX Annual Conference & Exhibition**
INTIX
330 W 38th Street
Suite 605
New York, NY 10018

212-629-4036; *Fax:* 212-629-8532
info@intix.org; www.intix.org

Jena L Hoffman, President
Kathleen O'Donnell, Deputy Director
Kevin McMacdonnell, Sales Manager

Combines educational workshops, committee and business meetings, networking and social events. Every major supplier serving he entertainment ticketing industry is represented at the exhibition. Launch new products and conduct user meetings for existing clients
Frequency: January

1636 **International Association of Amusement Parks and Attractions Expo**
Int'l Association of Amusement Parks & Attractions
1448 Duke Street
Alexandria, VA 22314

703-836-4800; *Fax:* 703-836-4801;
www.iaapa.org

Chip Cleary, President/CEO
Susan Mosedale, Executive VP
Jan MacCool, Executive Assistant

Features diverese entertainment exhibitions from high tech, to games, rides, food and beverage and much more. IAAPA showcases products and services for amusement parks, water parks, family entertainment centers, zoos, aquariums, museums — any company in the business of entertainment.
30M Attendees
Frequency: Annual/Nov
Founded in: 1918

1637 **International Association of Fairs and Expositions Annual Convention**
International Association of Fairs & Expositions

3043 E Cairo
PO Box 985
Springfield, MO 65802

417-862-5771
800-516-0313; *Fax:* 417-862-0156
iafe@fairsandexpos.com;
www.fairsandexpos.com

Jim Tucker, President
Steve Siever, Director
Max Willis, CFO
Marla Calico, Director Of Education
Rachel Mundhenke, Director Of Technology

Largest event serving fairs and expositions. Convention attendees are able to network and learn from each other during the intensive four days of workshops, special seminars, and round table discussions. Companies showcase themselves while serving as a one-stop shop for all of a fair's booking, product, and service needs.
5000 Attendees
Frequency: Nov

1638 **International Brotherhood of Magicians Annual Convention**
International Brotherhood of Magicians
11155 S Towne Square
Suite C
St Louis, MO 63123

314-845-9200; *Fax:* 314-845-9220
info@magician.org; www.magician.org

John Pye, President
Shawn Farquhar, VP
Jack White, Marketing
Don Wiberg, Secretary
Roger Miller, Treasurer

A place where members can meet and network with others sharing an interest in the art of magic.
13000 Members
Frequency: July
Founded in: 1922

1639 **International Ticketing Association Annual Conference & Exhibition**
330 W 38th Street
Suite 605
New York, NY 10018

212-629-4036; *Fax:* 212-628-8532
info@intix.org; www.intix.org
Social Media: Facebook, Twitter, LinkedIn, YouTube

Jena L Hoffman, President/CEO
Kathleen O'Donnell, Deputy Director

Non-profit association committed to the improvement, progress and advancement of ticket management. Provides educational programs, trade shows, conducts surveys, conference proceedings, and its valuable membership directory.
1000 Members
Founded in: 1979

1640 **Laser Tag Convention**
International Laser Tag Association
5351 E Thompson Road
Suite 236
Indianapolis, IN 46237

317-786-9755; *Fax:* 317-786-9757;
www.lasertag.org

Shane Zimmerman, Executive Director

The source for all things laser tag. Co-located with the Roller Skating Trade Show, this provides an opportunity to meet suppliers and manufacturers of laser tag equipment, video games, kitchen equipment and more.
Frequency: May

1641 **Laughter Works**
Laughter Works Seminars
PO Box 1220
Folsom, CA 95763-1220

916-985-6570
info@laughterworks.com;
www.laughterworks.com

Jim Pelley, President

Seminars and keynote speeches on humor, create positive team environment, unleash creativity and enhance productivity in the workplace.

1642 **NATS National Conference**
National Association of Teachers of Singing
9957 Moorings Drive
Suite 401
Jacksonville, FL 32257-2416

904-992-9101; *Fax:* 904-262-2587
info@nats.org; www.nats.org
Social Media: Facebook, Twitter, LinkedIn

Allen Henderson, Executive Director
Deborah Guess, Director, Operations
Paul Witkowski, Marketing & Communication
Amanda Wood, Membership & Program Coordinator

Gathers professionals, scholars, and experts worldwide to share ideas and participate in lectures, workshops, and demonstrations aimed at promoting vocal arts and the teaching of singing.
Frequency: June/July
Founded in: 1944

1643 **National Recreation and Park Association's Congress and Exposition**
National Recreation and Park Association
22377 Belmont Ridge Road
Ashburn, VA 20148

703-858-0784; *Fax:* 703-858-0794
info@nrpa.org; www.nrpa.org

Britt Esen, Director
Jodie H Adams, President
John Crosby, Marketing

Education and training opportunity plus a tradeshow for the park and recreation industry.
4000 Attendees
Frequency: October
Founded in: 1965

1644 **OABA Annual Meeting & Chairman's Reception**
Outdoor Amusement Business Association
1035 S Semoran Blvd
Suite 1045A
Winter Park, FL 32792-5512

407-681-9444
800-517-6222; *Fax:* 407-681-9445
oaba@oaba.org; www.oaba.org
Social Media: Facebook, Twitter, YouTube

Bill Johnson, Chairman
Jeanne McDonagh, 1st Vice Chair
Rober Johnson, President

The OABA manages and influences concerns for its members. OABA believes that all business owners and members of the trade association should continue to raise the level of safety and quality in the mobile amusement industry.
4000 Members
Founded in: 1965

1645 **Origins Game Fair**
280 N High Street
Suite 230
Columbus, OH 43215

614-255-4500; *Fax:* 614-255-4499
ops@gama.org; www.gama.org
Social Media: Facebook

John Ward, Executive Director
John Kaufeld, Marketing/Sales
Rick Loomis, President

A non-profit trade association dedicated to the advancement of the tabletop game industry
450 Members
Founded in: 1977

1646 **Pinball Expo**
Pinball Expo
3869 Niles Road SE
Warren, OH 44484

330-369-1192
800-323-3547; *Fax:* 330-369-6279
brkpinball@aol.com; www.pinballexpo.org

Robert Berk, Expo Chairman
Mike Pacak, Co-Expo Chairman

Annual show of manufacturers and related suppliers of pinball machines and supplies; tournaments and tours with over 50 exhibitors.
1,000 Attendees
Frequency: October

1647 **RSA Convention and Trade Show**
Roller Skating Association International
6905 Corporate Drive
Indianapolis, IN 46278

317-347-2626; *Fax:* 317-347-2636
rsa@rollerskating.com; www.rollerskating.org

Bobby Braun, President
Ron Liette, VP
John Purcell, Executive Director

Helping roller skating industry professionals discover ways to build strong foundations for their businesses.
1000 Members
Frequency: Annual/August
Founded in: 1937

1648 **SLA Annual Meeting & Convention**
Showmen's League of America
1023 W Fulton Market
Chicago, IL 60607

312-733-9533
800-350-9906; *Fax:* 312-733-9534
joeb@showmensleague.org;
www.showmensleague.org
Social Media: Twitter

Sam Johnston, President
Chris Atkins, 1st Vice President
Ron Porter, 2nd Vice President
Joe Burum, Executive Secretary
John Hanschen, Treasurer

Promotes friendship and fellowship between its members and the outdoor amusement industry, and pledges to help those in need through one of its many programs.
Founded in: 1913

1649 **World Waterpark Association Annual Tradeshow**
World Waterpark Association
8826 Santa Fe Drive
Suite 310
Overland Park, KS 66212

913-599-0300; *Fax:* 913-599-0520
aezra@waterparks.org; www.waterparks.org

Rick Root, President
Patty Miller, Director
Aleatha Ezra, Marketing

Exhibits include waterpark attractions, water quality equipment and apparel, with more than 300 booths.
1000 Members
2600 Attendees
Frequency: October
Founded in: 1981

Directories & Databases

1650 American Casino Guide
Casino Vacations
PO Box 703
Dania, FL 33004-0703
954-989-2766
800-741-1596; *Fax:* 954-966-7048;
www.americancasinoguide.com
Steve Bourie, Author
A guide to every casino/resort, riverboat and Indian casino in the United States.
Cost: $16.95
448 Pages
Frequency: Annually
ISBN: 1-883768-11-X
Founded in: 1992
Printed in one color

1651 Association of Performing Arts Presenters Membership Directory
1211 Connecticut Ave NW
Suite 200
Washington, DC 20036-2716
202-833-2787
888-820-2787; *Fax:* 202-833-1543
info@artspresenters.org;
www.artspresenters.org
Sandra Gibson, President
Sean Handerhan, Marketing
An invaluable resource for members to keep in touch with colleagues. Puts more than 1,450 presenters, service organizations, artists, management consultants, and vendors at your fingertips. An excellent networking tool for everyone on your staff.
1900 Members
Frequency: Annual
Founded in: 1957

1652 Celebrity Access Directory
Celebrity Access
2430 Broadway St
Suite 200
Boulder, CO 80304-4118
303-350-1700; *Fax:* 303-339-6877
sales@celebrityaccess.com;
www.celebrityaccess.com
Peter Denholtz, President
Marc Gentilella, Editor
Keri Mullin, Marketing
Database directory of more than 35,000 performers that includes contact information for agents as well as links to websites, record companies, touring schedules, box office info and more.
Cost: $899.00
Frequency: Annual
Founded in: 1998

1653 Data List & Membership Directory
Western Fairs Association
1776 Tribute Rd
Suite 210
Sacramento, CA 95815-4495
916-927-3100; *Fax:* 916-927-6397
stephenc@fairsnet.org; www.fairsnet.org
Stephen J Chambers, Executive Director
Jon Baker, Vice President
Nichole Farley, Marketing
A premier source of fair industry information for the Western United States and Canada. Referred to as the Bible of the fair industry, this directory contains a complete listing of every member fair, festival, special event, fair-related business, fair association, and agriculture-related organization.
2000 Members
Frequency: Annual
Founded in: 1922
Printed in on glossy stock

1654 Dinner Theatre: A Survey and Directory
Greenwood Publishing Group
88 Post Road W
PO Box 5007
Westport, CT 06881-5007
203-226-3571
800-225-5800; *Fax:* 203-222-1502
customer-service@greenwood.com;
www.greenwood.com
Debra Adams, Editor
Listings of dinner theaters, including in-depth profiles are offered in this comprehensive directory.
Cost: $82.95
160 Pages
Frequency: Hardcover
ISBN: 0-313284-42-3

1655 Directory of Historic American Theatres
Greenwood Publishing Group
88 Post Road W
PO Box 5007
Westport, CT 06881-5007
203-226-3571
800-225-5800; *Fax:* 203-222-1502
customer-service@greenwood.com;
www.greenwood.com
Debra Adams, Editor
Directory of theaters built before 1915.
Cost: $86.95
367 Pages
Frequency: Hardcover
ISBN: 0-313248-68-0

1656 EPM Entertainment Marketing Sourcebook
EPM Communications
19 W.21st St,# 303
3rd Floor
New York, NY 10012-3208
212-941-0099
888-852-9467; *Fax:* 212-941-1622
info@epmcom.com; www.epmcom.com
Ira Mayer, Owner
Michele Khan, Marketing
Over 4,000 media companies, sponsors and retailers that provide products and services to entertainment marketers.
Cost: $95.00
278 Pages
Frequency: Annual
Printed in on matte stock

1657 Grey House Performing Arts Directory
Grey House Publishing
4919 Route 22
PO Box 56
Amenia, NY 12501
518-789-8700
800-562-2139; *Fax:* 845-373-6390
books@greyhouse.com; www.greyhouse.com
Social Media: Facebook, Twitter
Leslie Mackenzie, Publisher
Richard Gottlieb, Editor
The most comprehensive resource covering the Performing Arts. This directory provides current information on over 8,500 dance companies, instrumental music programs, opera companies, choral groups, theater companies, performing arts series and performing arts facilities.
Cost: $185.00
1200 Pages
Frequency: Annual
ISBN: 1-592373-76-3
Founded in: 1981

1658 Grey House Performing Arts Directory - Online Database
Grey House Publishing
4919 Route 22
PO Box 56
Amenia, NY 12501
518-789-8700
800-562-2139; *Fax:* 845-373-6390
gold@greyhouse.com;
www.gold.greyhouse.com
Social Media: Facebook, Twitter
Leslie Mackenzie, Publisher
Richard Gottlieb, President
The Grey House Performing Arts Directory - Online Database provides immediate access to dance companies, orchestras, opera companies, choral groups, theater companies, series, festivals and perfoming arts facilities across the country, or in their region, state, or in your own backyard. It offers unequaled coverage of the Performing Arts - over 8,500 listings - of the major performance organization, facilities, and information resources.
Frequency: Annual
Founded in: 1981

1659 IAAPA Directory & Buyers Guide
Int'l Association of Amusement Parks & Attractions
1448 Duke St
Alexandria, VA 22314-3403
703-836-3677; *Fax:* 703-836-2824
iaapa@iaapa.org; www.iaapa.org
Will Morey, Chairman
Marion Mamon, Vice Chair
Directory of amusement parks, the attraction industry and related topics.
Founded in: 1918

1660 SBE Membership Directory & Buyer's Guide
Society of Broadcast Engineers
9102 N Meridian St
Suite 150
Indianapolis, IN 46260-1896
317-846-9000; *Fax:* 317-846-9120;
www.sbe.org
Ralph Hogan, President
Joseph Snelson, VP
Provides a quick reference to all members and Sustaining Members' services. Offers a yellow-page guide section that contains categorical listings of all SBE Substaining Members and advertisements from leading equipment and service suppliers.
Frequency: Annually
Circulation: 5,500

1661 Travel and Entertaiment Policies and Procedures Guide
Institute of Management & Administration
1 Washington Park
Suite 1300
Newark, NJ 07102
973-718-4700; *Fax:* 973-622-0595;
www.ioma.com
Joe Bremner, President
Perry Patterson, VP
Andy Dzamba, Editor
James Bell, Marketing
The report offers tips and suggestions to improve T&E operations, information on reimbursement policies and benchmark data, current trends, and

more.
Cost: $329.00
Frequency: Annual
Circulation: 185,000

1662 **Who's Who in Festivals and Events Membership Directory & Buyers Guide**
International Festivals and Events Association
2603 W Eastover Terrace
Boise, ID 83706-2800

208-433-0950; *Fax:* 208-433-9812
craig@ifea.com; www.ifea.com

Steven Schmader, President
Nia Forster, VP/Marketing
Craig Sarton, Director

Membership directory list hundreds of festivals and vendor members.
2000 Members
2000 Pages
Founded in: 1956
Mailing list available for rent: 2000 names at $235 per M

Industry Web Sites

1663 **http://gold.greyhouse.com**
G.O.L.D Grey House OnLine Databases
Grey House Publishing's online database platform, GOLD, provides Quick Search, Keyword Search and Expert Search for most business sectors, including amusement, entertainment and recreation markets. The GOLD platform makes finding the information you need quick and easy. All of Grey House's directory products are available for subscription on the GOLD platform.

1664 **www.aceonline.org**
American Coaster Enthusiasts
ACE is a non-profit organization with members across the United States that promotes the roller coaster industry through a variety of events and publications.
7000 Members
Founded in: 1978

1665 **www.acui.org**
Association of College Unions International
Nonprofit educational organization. Dedicated to building community on campus through programs, services and publications with the common goal of unifying the union and activities fields.

1666 **www.amoa.com**
Amusement and Music Operators Association
Providing leadership for the amusement, music, entertainment and vending industry. AMOA works vigorously to protect and promote industry interests. Members include operators, manufacturers, suppliers, distributors, and consultants.

1667 **www.cavern.com**
National Caves Association
Nonprofit organization of publicly and privately owned show caves and caverns developed for public visitation. Provides access to a directory of caves for those seeking out adventure, fun and education.

1668 **www.circushistory.org**
Circus Historical Society
The Circus Historical Society is a not-for-profit educational organization whose mission is to record the history of the American circus. Members have the opportunity to meet and network at circus conventions where there are presentations, films and more.

1669 **www.coin-op.org**
American Amusement Machine Association
Non-profit trade association representing the manufacturers, distributors and part suppliers to the coin-operated and out of home amusement industry.

1670 **www.fairsnet.org**
Western Fairs Association
A non-profit association with members throughout the Western United States and Canada that strives to promote industry standards. Membership includes access to conventions and trade shows, educational training programs, as well as legislative advocacy support.

1671 **www.greyhouse.com**
Grey House Publishing
Reference directories for most business sectors, including amusement, entertainment and recreation markets. Users can search the online databases with varied search criteria allowing for custom searches by product category, geographic area, sales volume, keyword, subject and more. Full Grey House catalog and online ordering also available.

1672 **www.iaapa.org**
International Association of Amusement Parks &
Attractions
An international trade association that seeks to improve and support professional industry standards at permanently situated amustement facilities worldwide.
4,500 Members

1673 **www.ifea.com**
International Festivals and Events Association
A voluntary association of events, event producers, event suppliers and related professionals and organizations whose common purpose is the production and presentation of festivals, events, and civic and private celebrations.

1674 **www.intix.org**
International Ticket Association
Not-for-profit association representing 22 countries worldwide. Committed to the improvement, progress and advancement of ticket management through educational programs, trade shows, conducts surveys, conference proceedings, and produces a membership directory.
1,200 Members

1675 **www.laserist.org**
International Laser Display Association
Dedicated to advancing the use of laser displays, in art, entertainment and education. ILDA supports high industry standards, promotes safety and provides the opportunity for members to meet and network at trade shows and conventions.

1676 **www.lastertag.org**
International Laser Tag Association: ILTA
The ILTA helps individuals and companies start or add a lasertag facility.

1677 **www.magicsam.com**
Society of American Magicians
Promote and maintain harmonious fellowship among those interested in magic as an art, improve ethics of the magical profession, and foster, promote and improve the advancement of magical arts in the field of amusement and entertainment. Membership includes professional and amateur magicians, manufacturers of magical apparatus and collectors.

1678 **www.merchandisegroup.com**
Nielsen Business Media's Merchandise Group ASD/AMD
Leading producer of trade shows and publications in the variety and general merchandise industry.

1679 **www.music-rights.com**
Ad Producer.com
Provides music rights providers with the highest quality platform to leverage the Web to market your services around the world around the clock.

1680 **www.natoonline.org**
National Association of Theatre Owners
Exhibition trade organization, representing more than 30,000 movie screens in all 50 states, and additional cinemas in 50 countries worldwide.

1681 **www.nats.org**
National Association of Teachers of Singing
Promotes and encourages the highest standards of vocal education and research at all levels, both for the enrichment of the general public and for the professional advancement of the talented.

1682 **www.oaba.org**
Outdoor Amusement Business Association
Promotes interest of the outdoor amusement industry. Provides members with public relations and safety services as well as it's monthly Show Time magazine and annual publication The Midway Marquee.
4,000 Members

1683 **www.rollerskating.org**
Roller Skating Association International
A trade association representing skating center owners, operators; teachers, coaches and judges of roller skating; and manufacturers and suppliers of roller skating equipment.

1684 **www.sbe.org**
Society of Broadcast Engineers
Professional organization of television and radio engineers and those in the related fields. SBE has members in 114 chapters across the United States and Hong Kong.

1685 **www.toyassociation.org**
Toy Industry Association
National organization for U.S. producers and importers of toys, games and children's entertainment products. Represents more than 500 member companies including designers, safety consultants, testing laboratories, licensors, communication professionals and inventors.

1686 **www.waterparks.com**
World Waterpark Association
Official Web site for the waterpark and water-leisure industries provides a comprehensive listing of waterparks around the world. It was developed and is maintained by the World Waterpark Association, the international organization created to further safety and business effectiveness in the waterpark industry.

Associations

1687 **American Apparel & Footwear Association (AAFA)**
American Apparel & Footwear Association
1601 N Kent Street
Suite 1200
Arlington, VA 22209

703-524-1864
800-520-2262; *Fax:* 847-522-6741
mrhowell@apparelandfootwear.org;
www.wewear.org
Social Media: Facebook, Twitter, LinkedIn, YouTube, Instagram

Rick Helfenbein, Chairman
Juanita Duggan, President/CEO
Stephen E Lamar, Executive Vice President
Ashley Stewart Bailey, Chief of Staff
Susan Lapetine, VP/Industry Relations

The American Apparel & Footwear Association (AAFA) is the national trade association representing apparel, footwear and other sewn products companies, and their suppliers which compete in the global market. AAFA's mission is to promote and enhance its members' competitiveness, productivity and profitability in the global market by minimizing regulatory, legal, commercial, political, and trade restraints.
Founded in: 2000

1688 **American Cotton Shippers Association**
88 Union Ave
Suite 1204
Memphis, TN 38103-5150

901-525-2272; *Fax:* 901-527-8303
bmay@acsa-cotton.org; www.acsa-cotton.org
Social Media: RSS Feeds

Bobby Walton, Chairman
William E May, President
Vaniece C. Boone, Vice President/Memphis Operations
Linda Colston, Administrative Assistant/Accounting
Laura Skillern, Bookkeeper

ACSA members are engaged in a great enterprise, the purchasing, storing, tansporting and merchandising of America's most valuable cash crop and it's most abundant natural fiber.
Founded in: 1924

1689 **American Flock Association**
PO Box 1090
Cherryville, NC 28021

617-303-6288; *Fax:* 704-671-2366
info@flocking.org; www.flocking.org
Social Media: LinkedIn, Pinterest, YouTube

Steve Rosenthal, Managing Director

AFA members include manufacturers of roll-to-roll coated textiles, papers, and films as well as coaters of three dimensional objects and printers of apparel decoration and graphics art products. Industry suppliers are a key sector of the membership. The AFA is affiliated with the National Textile Association, a non-profit trade organization representing over 150 textile manufacturers and industry suppliers with operations in the U.S., and Canada.
Founded in: 1984

1690 **American Sewing Guild**
9660 Hillcroft St
Suite 510
Houston, TX 77096-3866

713-729-3000; *Fax:* 713-721-9230
margo@asg.org; www.asg.org
Social Media: Facebook, Twitter, YouTube

Betty Brees, Chairman
Jeanette Swanson, Secretary
Jodell Larkin, Treasurer
Margo Martin, Executive Director

ASG is a membership organization that welcomes sewing enthusiasts of all skill levels. Chapters are located in cities all across the country and members meet monthly to learn new sewing skills, network with others who share an interest in sewing and participate in community service sewing projects.
20000 Members
Founded in: 1993

1691 **Cashmere and Camel Hair Manufacturers Institute**
3 Post Office Square
8th Floor
Boston, MA 02110

617-542-7481; *Fax:* 617-542-2199
info@cashmere.org; www.cashmere.org

Karl Spilhaus, President

The Cashmere & Camel Hair Manufacturers Institute (CCMI) is an international trade association representing the interests of producers and manufacturers of camel hair and cashmere fiber, yarn, fabric and garments throughout the world.
25 Members
Founded in: 1984

1692 **Chemical Fabrics and Film Association**
1300 Sumner Avenue
Cleveland, OH 44115-2851

216-241-7333; *Fax:* 216-241-0105
cffa@chemicalfabricsandfilm.com;
www.chemicalfabricsandfilm.com

Susan Young, Executive Secretary

International trade association representing manufacturers of polymer-based fabric and film products, used in the building and construction, automotive, fashion and many other industries.
40 Members
Founded in: 1927

1693 **Color Association of the United States**
33 Whitehall Street
Suite M3
New York, NY 10004

212-947-7774; *Fax:* 212-594-6987
info@colorassociation.com;
www.colorassociation.com
Social Media: Facebook, Twitter, LinkedIn, YouTube, Pinterest, Instagram

Sherrie Donghia, Chairman
Marcella Echavarria, Interior/Forecast
Linda De Franco, Fashion/Forecast
Kelly Kovak, Beauty/Forecast
Sal Cesarani, Men's Fashion/Forecast

The Color Association of The United States creates and delivers global color intelligence across industries. The Color Association serves as premier forecast agent, specialized educator, and trusted advisor to color professionals whose responsibility is to ensure marketplace success for their color decisions in the realm of brands, product and service, and spatial environments.
Founded in: 1915

1694 **Costume Designers Guild**
11969 Ventura Boulevard
First Floor
Studio City, CA 91604-3570

818-752-2400; *Fax:* 818-752-2402
cdgia@cdgia.com;
www.costumedesignersguild.com
Social Media: Facebook, Twitter

Ivy Thaide, Secretary
Nanrose Buchman, Treasurer
Salvador Perez, President
Cate Adair, Vice President
Rachael M. Stanley, Executive Director

The Costume Designers Guild (CDG) is Local 892 of the International Alliance of Theatrical and Stage Employees (I.A.T.S.E.). The Guild represents Costume Designers, Assistant Costume Designers and Costume Illustrators working at the highest levels of skill and expertise in motion pictures, television and commercials. The CDG promotes and protects the economic status of its members while improving working conditions and raising standards for our craft.
810 Members
Founded in: 1953

1695 **Cotton Incorporated**
6399 Weston Pkwy
Cary, NC 27513

919-678-2220; *Fax:* 919-678-2230;
www.cottoninc.com
Social Media: Facebook, Twitter, Youtube, RSS Feeds

J. Berrye AnkenyWorsham, President and CEO
Michael Watson, VP of Fiber Competition
Kater D. Hake, Ph.D., Vice President Agriculture
Edward M. Barnes, Senior Director of Agriculture
Linda De Franco, Director of Product Trend Analysis

To ensure that cotton remains the first choice among consumers in apparel and home products, Cotton Incorporated helps companies manufacture, market, and sell cotton products more efficiently and more profitably.
Founded in: 1970

1696 **Council of Fashion Designers of America**
65 Bleecker St
11th Floor
New York, NY 10012

212-302-1821; *Fax:* 212-768-0515
info@cfda.com; www.cfda.com
Social Media: Facebook, Twitter, Youtube, Google+, Pinterest, T

Diane von Furstenberg, Chairman
Steven Kolb, President/CEO
Lisa Smilor, Executive Vice President
CaSandra Diggs, Deputy Director
Marc Karimzadeh, Editorial & Comm. Director

The CFDA's goals are: to further the position of fashion design as a recognized branch of American art and culture, advance its artistic and professional standards, establish and maintain a code of ethics and practices of mutual benefit in professional, public, and trade relations, and promote and improve public understanding and appreciation of the fashion arts through leadership in quality and taste.
250 Members
Founded in: 1962

1697 **Custom Tailors and Designers Association of America**
229 Forest Hills Road
Rochester, NY 14625

888-248-2832; *Fax:* 866-661-1240
info@ctda.com; www.ctda.com
Social Media: Facebook, Twitter, LinkedIn

Peter Roberti, President
Mitch Gambert, 1st Vice President
Craig Wertheim, 2nd Vice President
Jeff Landis, Treasurer
Gordon Goldstein, Secretary

Established as a venue through which ideas and techniques for design, pattern making, fitting, cutting and tailoring could be shared and exchanged.
300 Members
Founded in: 1880

1698 **Fashion Footwear Association of New York**
274 Madison Avenue
Suite 1701
New York, NY 10016

212-751-6422; *Fax:* 212-751-6404
info@ffany.org; www.ffany.org
Social Media: Facebook, Twitter, Instagram, Pinterest

Jim Issler, Chairman
Ronald A. Fromm, President/CEO
Phyllis Rein, Executive Vice President
Liz Carroll, Executive Assistant
Shelley Berquist, SVP, Operations & Marketing

FFANY's mission is to promote and assist the common business interests of its members. FFANY is committed to supporting New York City as the recognized national center of fashion trade and commerce and aims to ensure the city continues to be the best venue for both national and international footwear industry events.
300 Members
Founded in: 1980

1699 **Fashion Scholarship Fund**
1501 Broadway
Suite 1810
New York, NY 10036

212-278-0008; *Fax:* 212-279-6241;
www.ymafsf.org
Social Media: Facebook, Twitter, Instagram, Pinterest, Vimeo

Debra Malbin, Co-Chairman
Paul Rosengard, Co-Chairman
Peter Sachse, President
Michael Setola, Treasurer
Doug Evans, Secretary

The YMA Fashion Scholarship Fund(FSF) is a national association dedicated to promoting education of the fashion arts and business by granting scholarships to talented students and facilitating internships, mentorships and career programs.
800+ Members
Founded in: 1937

1700 **International Glove Association**
PO Box 146
Brookville, PA 15825

814-328-5208; *Fax:* 814-328-2308;
www.iga-online.com

Kim O'Leary, President
Brent Fidler, Vice President
Bill Trainer, Past President
Matt Reid, Member
Larry Garner, Member

Our mission is to further build an association that improves manufacturing and distribution of hand protection. Studying, clarifying, and recommending government action to help promote proper glove selection and use, and the interests of glove manufacturers and distributors, will help association members achieve success with customers and maintain a financially sound organization.
Founded in: 2003

1701 **Leather Apparel Association**
19 W 21st Street
Suite 403
New York, NY 10010

212-727-1210; *Fax:* 212-727-1218;
www.leatherassociation.com

Morris Goldfarb, President
Richard Harrow, Executive Director
Fran Harrow, Marketing

Represents the nation's leading leather retailers, manufacturers, cleaners and other businesses in promoting leather apparel in the US.
Founded in: 1990

1702 **National Luggage Dealers Association**
1817 Elmdale Avenue
Glenview, IL 60026

847-998-6869; *Fax:* 847-998-6884
inquiry@nlda.com; www.nlda.com

Alex Shapiro, President
George Morri, CEO
Felicia Libbin, Marketing Director

The National Luggage Dealers Association (NLDA) improves the buying power of the many stores it represents, giving the individual store owners the ability to compete with larger companies and department stores. Many of the founding members continue to be represented today by successive generations of family members.
130+ Members
Founded in: 1925

1703 **National NeedleArts Association**
1100-H Brandywine Boulevard
Zanesville, OH 43701-7303
740-455-6773
800-889-8662; *Fax:* 740-452-2552
info@tnna.org; www.tnna.org
Social Media: Facebook, Twitter, LinkedIn, Pinterest, Instagram

Ewe Count, Chair & Board Representative
Dave VanStralen, Board President
Don Lynch, Board Vice President
Barbara Bergstan, Director
Claudia Dutcher, Director

TNNA is an international trade organization representing retailers, manufacturers, distributors, designers, manufacturers' representatives, publishers, teachers and wholesalers of products and supplies for the specialty needlearts market. These businesses create and market hand painted needlepoint canvases, hand-dyed and specialty crochet and knitting yarns, embroidery, needlepoint and cross-stitch materials, kits, tools and more.
2650 Members
Founded in: 1975

1704 **North American Association of Uniform Manufacturers & Distributors**
6800 Jericho Turnpike
Suite 120W
Syosset, NY 11791

516-393-5838; *Fax:* 516-393-5878
rjlerman@naumd.com; www.naumd.com

Aviva Tavel, Chairman
Richard J Lerman, President & CEO
Jackie Rosselli, Director of Communications
Lee Galperin, Vice Chair
Brian Garry, Treasurer

The North-American Association of Uniform Manufacturers & Distributors (NAUMD) is a trade association representing the interests of all parties in the uniform & image apparel industry.
450+ Members
Founded in: 1933

1705 **Private Label Manufacturers Association**
630 Third Avenue
New York, NY 10017-6506

212-972-3131; *Fax:* 212-983-1382
info@plma.com; www.plma.com

John Shields, Former Chairman & CEO
Myra Rosen, VP

PLMA has steadily grown in size, reflecting the increasing importance of store brands to retailers and consumers. As you will see, PLMA member services have mirrored store brands new role in the marketplace, too.
3200+ Members
Founded in: 1979

1706 **The Fashion Group International, Inc.**
8 W. 40th St.
7th Fl.
New York, NY 10018

212-302-5511; *Fax:* 212-302-5533
pmaffei@fgi.org; www.fgi.org
Social Media: Facebook, Twitter, LinkedIn, YouTube

Margaret Hayes, President
Patricia Maffei, Managing/Membership Director

Global, nonprofit organization supporting the professional development of its members in the fashion and lifestyle industries.
5000 Members
Founded in: 1930

1707 **The Knitting Guild Association (TKGA)**
1100-H Brandywine Boulevard
Zanesville, OH 43701-7303

740-452-4541; *Fax:* 740-452-2552
tkga@tkga.com; www.tkga.com
Social Media: Facebook, Twitter, Pinterest

Penny Sitler, Executive Director

Membership organization for knitters with focus on knitting education and enhancing knitters skills. TKGA seeks to advance creativity, knowledge and the quality of workmanship in knitting through education and communication.
11000 Members
Founded in: 1984

1708 **The Vision Council of America**
Sunglass and Reader Division
225 Reinekers Lane
Suite 700
Alexandria, VA 22314-2846

703-548-4560
866-826-0290; *Fax:* 703-548-4580
info@thevisioncouncil.org;
www.thevisioncouncil.org
Social Media: Facebook, Twitter, LinkedIn, YouTube

Mike Daley, Chief Executive Officer
Maureen Beddis, Vice President of Marketing
Deborah Malakoff-Castor, Vice President of Shows
Greg Chavez, Vice President of Member Services
Brian Carroll, Chief Operating Officer

Serving as the global voice for vision care products and services, The Vision Council represents the manufacturers and suppliers of the optical industry. We position our members to be successful in a competitive marketplace through education, advocacy, consumer outreach, strategic relationship building and industry forums.
263 Members
Founded in: 1999

1709 **Tri-State Linen Supply Association**
1800 Diagonal Rd
Suite 200
Alexandria, VA 22314-2842

703-519-0029
877-770-9274; *Fax:* 703-519-0026
trsa@trsa.org; www.trsa.org
Social Media: Facebook, Twitter, LinkedIn, YouTube, RSS Feeds

Roger Cocivera, President/CEO
George Ferencz, VP

Provides hygienic sustainable laundering services that offer cost-effective, energy-efficient solutions while protecting the environment and employing hundreds of thousands of individuals in highly safety-conscious workplaces nationwide.
1400 Members
Founded in: 1913

1710 **Uniform Code Council**
Princeton Pike Corporate Center
1009 Lenox Drive Suite 202
Lawrenceville, NJ 08648

609-620-0200; *Fax:* 609-620-1200;
www.gs1us.org
Social Media: Facebook, Twitter, LinkedIn

W. Rodney McMullen, Chairman
Bob Carpenter, President and CEO
Laura DiSciullo, Senior Vice President, Solutions
Bernie Hogan, Senior Vice President
Yegneswaran Kumar, Senior Vice President

Barcodes, eCommerce and data synchronization, to EPC/RFID and business process automation standards.
Frequency: Members 280,000
Founded in: 1974

1711 **Unite Here International Union**
275 Seventh Avenue
New York, NY 10001-6708

212-265-7000; *Fax:* 212-265-3415
ccarrera@unitehere.org; www.unitehere.org
Social Media: Facebook, Twitter, Google+, RSS Feeds

D. Taylor, President
Tho Thi Do, General VP, Immigration
Sherri Chiesa, Secretary/Treasurer
Peter Ward, Recording Secretary

UNITE HERE represents workers throughout the U.S. and Canada who work in the hotel, gaming, food service, manufacturing, textile, distribution, laundry, and airport industries.
850k Members
Founded in: 2004

1712 **United States Fashion Industry Association**
1140 Connecticut Ave.
Suite 950
Washington, DC 20036

202-419-0444; *Fax:* 202-783-0727
info@usfashionindustry.com;
www.usfashionindustry.com
Social Media: Facebook, Twitter, LinkedIn, Google+

Julia K. Hughes, President
Samantha Sault, VP, Communications

Representing brands, retailers, importers and wholesalers, the association works to eliminate tariffs, quotas and other impediments to the free movement of textiles and apparel globally.
Founded in: 1989

1713 **Western and English Sales Association**
451 E 58th Avenue
Suite 4128
Denver, CO 80216

303-295-1040
800-295-1041; *Fax:* 303-295-0941
info@denver-wesa.com;
www.denver-wesa.com
Social Media: Facebook

Gene House, Chairman
Mark Broughton, President
Scott Piper, Vice President
Gerald Adame, Treasurer
Jay Phillips, Secretary

WESA began under the corporate name Men's Apparel Club of Colorado. The goal was to create a forum where retailers, manufacturers, and sales representatives could conduct business in an atmosphere of fair trade and fellowship.
1200 Members
Founded in: 1921

Newsletters

1714 **AAFA Newsletter**
American Apparel & Footwear Association
1601 N Kent Street
Suite 1200
Arlington, VA 22209

703-524-1864
800-520-2262; *Fax:* 847-522-6741;
www.apparelandfootwear.org

Kevin M Burke, President
Stephen E Lamar, VP
Scott Elmore, Marketing

The nationwide trade association representing apparel, footwear and other sewn products companies and their suppliers which compete in the global market.
Founded in: 2000

1715 **Barbara's View/Shopping Guides**
Barbara's View
PO Box 531006
Miami, FL 33153-1006

305-757-7638; *Fax:* 305-756-5353
barbara@barbarasview.com;
www.barbarasview.com

Barbara Wexner Levy, President

Shopping guides for fashion cities around the world.
Cost: $18.00
Frequency: Monthly
Founded in: 1976

1716 **Clothing Manufacturers Association of the USA**
Clothing Manufacturers Association of the USA
770 Broadway
10th Floor
New York, NY 10003-9559

646-654-5000; *Fax:* 646-654-5001

David L Calhoun, CEO

Statistical report on profit sales, production and marketing trends for the men's and boy's tailored clothing industry.
Cost: $30.00
Frequency: Annual
Circulation: 300
Founded in: 1933
Mailing list available for rent: 100 names at $200 per M

1717 **DNR-Daily News Record**
Fairchild Publications
7 W 34th St
New York, NY 10001-8100

212-630-3880
800-360-1700; *Fax:* 212-630-3868;
www.dnronline.com

Samuel Farrel, President/CEO
John Birmingham, Editor-in-Chief
Jim Rossi, Marketing
Don Miller, Circulation Manager
Tom Beebe, Creative Director

Supplies retail fashion, product merchandising and marketing news for men's and boys' fashion.
Cost: $85.00
Frequency: Weekly
Circulation: 15755

1718 **International Association of Clothing Designers & Executives Newsletter**
475 Park Avenue South
Floor 9 No. 9
New York, NY 10016-6901

212-685-6602
newyorkiacde@cox.net; www.iacde.com

Joachim Hensch, President
Mina Henry, Director

1719 **The Vision Voice**
The Vision Council Of America
225 Reinekers Lane
Suite 700
Alexandria, VA 22314

703-548-4560
866-826-0290; *Fax:* 703-548-4580
info@thevisioncouncil.org;
www.thevisioncouncil.org
Social Media: Facebook, Twitter

Ed Greene, CEO
Brian Carroll, CFO
Maureen Beddis, VP of Marketing & Communications
Greg Chavez, VP of Member Services

Newsletter for the membership of The Vision Council of America. A nonprofit association of manufacturers and distributors of sunglasses and sunglass parts.
12 Pages
Founded in: 1940

1720 **Uniformer**
Professional Apparel Association
994 Old Eagle School Road
Suite 1019
Wayne, PA 19087-1802

610-971-4850; *Fax:* 610-971-4859

Sharon Tannahill, Executive Director

Seeks to enhance the growth of the professional apparel industry by educating uniform retailers.
1200+ Members
16 Pages
Frequency: Quarterly
Circulation: 500

1721 **UpFront Newsletter**
Embroidery Trade Association
P O Box 794534
Dallas, TX 75379-4534

888-628-2545; *Fax:* 972-755-2561
info@embroiderytrade.org;
www.mesadist.com/trade_associations

John Swinburn, Executive Director
Dolores Cheek, Manager Of Member Services

A newsletter with advice and information on topics such as marketing, business operations and problem solving
1200 Members
Frequency: Weekly
Founded in: 1990

Magazines & Journals

1722 **Accessories**
Business Journals
50 Day Street
Norwalk, CT 06854

203-853-6015; *Fax:* 203-852-8175;
www.busjour.com

Britton Jones, President/CEO
Stuart Nifoussi, VP
Mac Brighton, Chairman & COO
Christone Sullivan, Controller

This magazine profiles the national fashion trade for women's accessories.
Cost: $35.00
Frequency: Monthly
Circulation: 100000
Founded in: 1931

1723 **Apparel Magazine**
Susan S. Nichols
801 Gervais St.
Suite 101
Columbia, SC 29201

803-771-7500
800-845-8820; *Fax:* 803-799-1461
cdeberry@apparelmag.com;
www.apparel.edgl.com

Susan S. Nichols, Publisher
Jordan Speer, Editor in Chief
Cindy DeBerry, Sales Manager

Trade publication for apparel/sewn products, manufacturing executives. Accepts advertising. Covers topics ranging from new products and technology to production management, sourcing, fabrics and financial news.
Cost: $48.00
180 Pages
Frequency: Monthly
Circulation: 18752
Printed in 4 colors on matte stock

1724 **California Apparel News**
MnM Publishing Corp
110 E 9th Street
Suite A-777
Los Angeles, CA 90079-1777

213-627-3737
info@apparelnews.net; www.apparelnews.net

Alison A Nieder, Executive Editor
N Jayne Seward, Fashion Editor
Deborah Belgum, Senior Editor

News and analysis on the largest manufacturing center in the country, special supplements on denim, lingerie, trade shows, textiles and more. Contains the only comprehensive coverage of Los Angeles Fashion Week.
Cost: $89.00
450 Pages
Frequency: Weekly
Founded in: 1945

1725 **Children's Business**
Fairchild Publications
Po Box 5121
New York, NY 10087-5121

212-630-3880
800-932-4724; *Fax:* 212-630-3868;
www.fairchildbooks.com

Debra Goldberg, Publisher
Tracy R Mitchell, Executive Editor
Ralph Erardy, Senior VP

Infants' and toddlers' wear, juvenile merchandise, footwear and toys.
Cost: $5.00
45 Pages
Frequency: Monthly
Circulation: 30458
ISSN: 0884-2280
Founded in: 1985

1726 **Clothing & Textile Research Journal**
International Textile & Apparel Association
PO Box 70687
Knoxville, TN 37938-0687

865-992-1535; *Fax:* 916-722-8149
info@itaaonline.org; www.itaaonline.org
Social Media: Facebook

Jana Hawley, President
Laurel E Wilsonn, VP
Nancy Rutherford,Ph.D, Executive Director

Offers the latest information on all areas of clothing and textiles.
Cost: $85.00
64 Pages
Frequency: Quarterly
Circulation: 1300
ISSN: 0887-3020
Founded in: 1944
Printed in one color on matte stock

1727 **Costume! Business**
Gift Basket Review
815 Haines Street
Jacksonville, FL 32206-6025

904-634-1902
800-729-6338; *Fax:* 904-633-8764;
www.festivities-pub.com

Debra Paulk, Publisher
Kathy Horak, Editor

News and current issues in the costume retailing business.
Cost: $29.95
Frequency: Quarterly
Circulation: 8,000

1728 **Dress**
Costume Society of America
390 Amwell Road
Suite 402
Hillsborough, NJ 08844

908-359-1471
800-272-9447; *Fax:* 908-450-1118;
www.costumesocietyamerica.com/
Social Media: Facebook, Twitter

Sally Halverston, Associate Editor
Rosalyn M Lester, President
Linda Welters, Editor-in-Chief
Margaret Ordonez, Managing Editor

Journal of the Costume Society of America. The Costume Society of America advances the global understanding of all aspects of dress and appearance.
ISSN: 0361-2112
Founded in: 1973
Printed in on matte stock

1729 **Fashion Accessories Magazine**
SCM Publications
10 DeGraaf Court
PO Box 859
Mahwah, NJ 07430

201-684-9222; *Fax:* 201-684-9228;
www.accessoriesmagazine.com

Lorrie Frost, Publisher
Lauren Parker, Editor

Offers information on the latest in fashion, jewelry and accessories.
Founded in: 1951

1730 **Fashion Market Magazine**
Fashion Market Magazine Group
617 West 46th Street
New York, NY 10036

212-541-9350; *Fax:* 212-541-9340;
www.fmmg.com
Social Media: Facebook, Twitter

Victoria Monjo, Editor
Nicole Phillip, Fashion Editor

News for the apparel industry in New York, with original pictures and news in fashion, technology, finance and real estate.
Cost: $84.74
64 Pages
Frequency: Monthly
Circulation: 80000
Founded in: 1985

1731 **Footwear Plus**
Symphony Publishing
36 Cooper Square
4th Floor
New York, NY 10003

646-278-1550; *Fax:* 646-278-1553;
www.footwearplusmagazine.com
Social Media: Facebook, Twitter

Greg Dutter, Editor-in-Chief
Pauline Lee, Associate Editor

Focuses on fashion, merchandising, trends and ideas in the retail footwear industry.
Cost: $50.58
Founded in: 1989
Printed in on glossy stock

1732 **Hosiery News**
Home Sewing Association
105 Mall Boulevard
Po Box 369
Monroeville, PA 15146

412-372-5950; *Fax:* 412-372-5953;
www.sewing.org

Dotty Grexa, President
Dale Sutherland, Treasurer
Jenna Sheldon, Director Trade Show/Meetings
Jenny Prevatte, Director Information Services

It covers all THA activities, industry news, personnel changes, statistics, legislative and regulatory concerns, marketing, technology, financial reports and new product information.

1733 **Impressions Magazine**
1145 Sanctuary Parkway
Suite 355
Alpharetta, GA 30009-4772

800-241-9034
impressions@bill.com;
www.impressionsmag.com

Chris Casey, Publisher
Marcia Derryberry, Editor-in-Chief
Jamar Laster, Senior Editor

Offers news and information on the development or imprintable and imprinted sportswear and textiles.
Cost: $69.00
Circulation: 30000

1734 **Industrial Fabric Products Review**
U.S. Industrial Fabrics Association International
1801 County Road BW
Roseville, MN 55113-4061

651-222-2508
800-225-4324; *Fax:* 651-631-9334
generalinfo@ifai.com; www.ifai.com

Stephen M Warner, President
JoAnne Ferris, Director Of Marketing

Keeps individuals up to date on the information needed to keep their business growing.
Cost: $69.00
Frequency: Monthly
Founded in: 1915

1735 **Juvenile Merchandising**
EW Williams Publications Company
2125 Center Ave
Suite 305
Fort Lee, NJ 07024-5898

201-592-7007; *Fax:* 201-592-7171
philpl@ewwpi.com;
www.williamspublications.com

Andrew Williams, President
Phillip Russo, Publisher
Peter Berlinski, Editor-in-Chief

Offers news on the juvenile clothing, accessories and furniture industry.
Cost: $85.00
Circulation: 8000
Founded in: 1938

1736 Knit Ovations Magazine
Woolknit Associates
267 5th Avenue
Suite 806-807
New York, NY 10016

212-683-7785; *Fax:* 212-683-2682

Eleanor Kairalla, Publisher

Fashions in knitwear for men and women trends in market; fashion color forecasts; guest features on knitwear by retail executives.

1737 Made to Measure
Halper Publishing Company
633 Skokie Blvd
Suite 490
Northbrook, IL 60062

224-406-8850; *Fax:* 224-406-8850
news@uniformmarket.com;
www.madetomeasuremag.com
Social Media: Facebook, Twitter

Rick Levine, President

Serves the uniform and career apparel industry.
Frequency: Bi-annually
Circulation: 25000
Founded in: 1930
Printed in 4 colors on glossy stock

1738 Market Maker
Advanstar Communications
6200 Canoga Avenue
2nd Floor
Woodland Hills, CA 91367

818-593-5000; *Fax:* 818-593-5020
info@advanstar.com; www.advanstar.com

Chirs DeMoulin, VP
Susannah George, Marketing Director
Joseph Loggia, President

Industry fashions
Cost: $2.00
Circulation: 14900
Founded in: 1987

1739 Menswear Retailing Magazine
Business Journals Inc
1384 Broadway
Suite 11
New York, NY 10018-6111

212-686-4412; *Fax:* 212-686-6821
karena@mrketplace.com;
www.mrketplace.com

Bethany Raborn, Manager
Stuart Nifoussi, VP
Karen Alberg, Editor

Includes accurate information on the menswear retailing business, insightful analysis, bold ideas and real world fashion.
Circulation: monthly

1740 Needle's Eye
Union Special Corporation
1 Union Special Plz
Huntley, IL 60142-7007

847-669-5101; *Fax:* 847-669-4535
dkanies@unionspecial.com;
www.unionspecial.com

Terence A Hitpas, President

Industry events, developments in machine-sewed products, informs about improved manufacturing methods, and promotes interest in Union Special machinery.
Frequency: Monthly
Circulation: 28595
Founded in: 1881

1741 Notions
American Sewing Guild
9660 Hillcroft St
Suite 510
Houston, TX 77096-3866

713-729-3000; *Fax:* 713-729-9230;
www.asg.org

Margo Martin, Executive Director

Contains articles written exclusively for us by the world's leading sewing experts, messages from the ASG Board of Directors and ASG National Headquarters, information about the latest sewing products and books.
Frequency: Quarterly

1742 Outerwear
Creative Marketing Plus
213-37 39th Avenue
Suite 228
Bayside, NY 11361

718-606-0767; *Fax:* 718-606-6345
rharrow@creativemarketingplus.com;
www.creativemarketingplus.com

Richard Harrow, Presidetn/CEO
Duke Wollsoncoft, Creative Director

Focuses on outerwear buyers' needs, fashion trends, as well as leading buying offices and promotional plans.
Cost: $62.00
30 Pages
Frequency: Monthly
Circulation: 16000
Founded in: 1983
Printed in 4 colors on glossy stock

1743 Printwear Magazine
National Business Media Inc
PO Box 1416
Broomfield, CO 80038-1416

303-469-0424
800-669-0424; *Fax:* 303-465-3424
pweditor@nbm.com; www.nbm.com

Bob Wieber, President
Mark Buchanan, Editor

Screen printing and embroidery equipment and technique, apparel styles and trends, heat-applied graphics, special effects printing and embroidery, business management and sales/marketing skills, digital transfers and sublimation, promotional products, embroidery digitizing, new products and the latest industry literature.
Frequency: Monthly
Circulation: 25000

1744 Promotional Sportswear
520 W Foothill Pkwy
Corona, CA 92882-6305

951-279-9327; *Fax:* 909-279-9327
customerservice@promowear.com;
www.promowear.com

Ted Taylor, Owner

Commercial direct screen printing, embroidery and complete art services on the highest quality sportswear available.

1745 Promowear
National Bussines Media Inc
P.O Box 1416
Broomfield, CO 80038

303-469-0424
800-669-0424; *Fax:* 303-469-5730
pweditor@nbm.com; www.nbm.com/pr
Social Media: Facebook, Twitter

Bob Wieber, President
Mark Buchanan, Editor

The latest style trends, detailed product and sourcing information, sales and marketing tips, industry news.
Frequency: 6 Issues/Year
Founded in: 1990

1746 Stitches
4800 Street Road
Trevose, PA 19053

800-546-1350
800-546-1350; *Fax:* 215-953-3107;
www.asipublications.com/stitches
Social Media: Facebook, Twitter

Nicole Rollender, Editor
Ed Koehler, Advertising Director

Information and the latest technology for embroidery professionals.
Circulation: 17233
Founded in: 1987

1747 Tack N' Togs Merchandising
The Miller Publishing Company
12400 Whitewater Dr
Suite 160
Minnetonka, MN 55343-4590

952-931-0211; *Fax:* 952-938-1832;
www.tackntogs.com
Social Media: Facebook, Twitter

Sarah Muirhead, Publisher
Julie Golson-Richards, Associate Editor
Cindy Miller-Johnson, Adverting Sales Manager
Michelle Adaway, Advertising Account Excutive

Providing the latest news and information on equine retailing.
Frequency: Monthly
Circulation: 20424
Founded in: 1970

1748 Textile Rental Magazine
Textile Rental Services Association
1800 Diagonal Rd
Suite 200
Alexandria, VA 22314-2842

703-519-0029
877-770-9274; *Fax:* 703-519-0026
trsa@trsa.org; www.trsa.org

Roger Cocivera, President/CEO
Jack Morgan, Editor

Packed with valuable tips and ideas.
Frequency: Monthly

1749 Uniformer
Professional Apparel Association
994 Old Eagle School Road
Suite 1019
Wayne, PA 19087-1866

610-971-4850; *Fax:* 771-261-4859

Hope Silverman, Executive Director
Frequency: Quarterly

1750 Vows Magazine
Peter Grimes
24 Daisy St
Ladera Ranch, CA 92694-0709

949-388-4848; *Fax:* 949-388-8448
info@vowsmagazine.com;
www.vowsmagazine.com

Kori Grimes, Owner
Karlnon Nazarro, Director

Bridal retail, including how to survive as an independent retailer, how to merchandise and promote your business, how to effectively sell and train a sales staff, as well as identifying fashion and consumer shopping trends and preferences.
Founded in: 1990

1751 Women's Wear Daily
Fairchild Publications
750 3rd Ave
New York, NY 10017-2703

212-630-3500
800-289-0273; *Fax:* 212-630-3566;

www.wwd.com
Social Media: Twitter

Mary G Berner, CEO
Christine Guilfoyle, Publisher
Edward Nardoza, Editor in Chief

Serves as the voice of authority, international newswire and agent of change for the fashion, beauty and retail industries
Cost: $195.00
Frequency: Daily
Circulation: 43618
Founded in: 1892

Trade Shows

1752 **ASD/AMD Las Vegas Trade Show**
ASD/AMD Group
6255 W. Sunset Blvd
19th Floor
Los Angeles, CA 90028

323-817-2200
800-421-4511; *Fax:* 310-481-1900;
www.asdonline.com

Greg Farrar, President
Mark Hosbein, Marketing

Provides a portfolio of innovative face to face, print and online products for the wholesale industry.
10000 Attendees
Frequency: BiAnnual/August/March

1753 **ASG Conference**
American Sewing Guild
9660 Hillcroft
Suite 510
Houston, TX 77096

713-729-3000; *Fax:* 713-729-9230;
www.asg.org

Martha Ramey, President

Gives all Guild members the opportunity to meet sewing professionals, industry representatives, and other sewing enthusiasts from around the country, and to participate in sewing seminars and sewing related special events and tours.
20000 Attendees
Frequency: Annual/July

1754 **AccessoriesTheShow**
Accessories Magazine
50 Day Street
Norwalk, CT 06854

203-853-6015
800-358-6678; *Fax:* 203-852-8175
sharon@busjour.com;
www.accessoriestheshow.com

Britton Jonese, President
Sharon Enright, VP

All accessories trade event in the fashion capital of the US attracts thousands of fine specialty buyers
22k + Attendees

1755 **Action Sports Retailer Trade Exposition**
Miller Freeman Publications
PO Box 1899
Laguna Beach, CA 92652

847-296-6742; *Fax:* 847-391-9827
info@nsga.org; www.nsga.org

Matt Carlson, President & Ceo

Manufacturers, suppliers, retailers, buyers, guides, outfitters, distributors, importers, exporters, press and industry influencers have converged at Fly-Fishing Retailer to chart the future of their business.

1756 **American Flock Association Annual Meeting**
American Flock Association
6 Beacon Street
Suite 1125
Boston, MA 02108

617-303-6288; *Fax:* 704-671-2366
info@flocking.org; www.flocking.org

Karl Spilhaus, President
Steve Rosenthal, Managing Director

Provides positive leadership to foster a strong flock industry in North America.
60 Members
Founded in: 1984

1757 **Apparel Importers Trade and Transportation Conference**
United States Fashion Industry Association (USFIA)
1140 Connecticut Ave.
Suite 950
Washington, DC 20036

202-419-0444; *Fax:* 202-783-0727;
www.importersapparelconference.com
Social Media: Facebook, Twitter, LinkedIn, Google+

Julia K. Hughes, President

Hot topics from the apparel products supply chain.
Frequency: Annual
Founded in: 1989

1758 **Apparel Show of the Americas**
Bobbin Publishing/Miller Freeman
PO Box 279
Euless, TX 76039

817-215-1600
800-693-1363; *Fax:* 817-215-1666
bobbin.expoinfo@mfi.com; www.mfi.com

Betty Webb, Trade Show Director

Conference, seminar and 329 exhibits of equipment, fabrics, accessories and services for sewn products and apparel.
Founded in: 1992

1759 **Arnold Sports Festival**
Arnold Sports Festival
1215 Worthington Woods Blvd.
Worthington, OH 43805

614-431-2600; *Fax:* 516-625-1023
lpinney@arnoldexpo.com;
www.arnoldsportsfestival.com
Social Media: Facebook, Twitter

Lucy Pinneyr, Event Chair
Brent LaLonda, Media Contact

Five days of fitness equipment, sports entertainment, supplements, apparel and athletic stars, with more than 17,000 competitive athletes in 40 sporting events. Over 500 exhibitors.
150M+ Attendees
Frequency: March
Founded in: 1976

1760 **Bead and Button Show**
Kalmbach Publishing Company
21027 Crossroads Circle
PO Box 1612
Waukesha, WI 53187-1612

262-796-8776
800-533-6644; *Fax:* 262-796-1615;
www.beadandbuttonshow.com
Social Media: Facebook

Gerald Boettcher, President

The biggest bead show in the country.
3500 Attendees
Frequency: Annual/May
Founded in: 1985

1761 **Big and Tall Men's Apparel Needs Show**
Specialty Trade Show
3939 Hardie Road
Coconut Grove, FL 33133-6437

305-663-6635; *Fax:* 305-661-8118
info@spectrade.com; www.spectrade.com

A gathering of buyers and vendors of apparel and accessories for tall and plus sized men. 200 Exhibitors.
1,500 Attendees
Frequency: February/August

1762 **Chicago Men's Collective: Winter**
Merchandise Mart Properties Inc
222 Merchandise Mart Plaza
Suite 470
Chicago, IL 60654

312-527-7635
800-677-6278
bschedler@mmart.com; www.mmart.com

Bruce Schedler, VP

Approximately 300 exhibitors and over 1,000 lines of product featuring men's fashion business attire.
5000 Attendees
Frequency: August

1763 **Convergence**
Handweavers Guild of America
1255 Buford Highway
Suite 211
Suwanee, GA 30024-1701

678-730-0010; *Fax:* 678-730-0836
hga@weavespindye.org;
www.weavespindye.org

Nancy Peck, President
Mary Ann Sanborn, VP
Elaine Bradley, Marketing
Sandra Bowles, Executive Director

Conference for everyone who loves and works in fiber.
3000 Attendees
Frequency: June, Biennial

1764 **E-Sports & Business Services Show at the Super Show**
Communications & Show Management
1450 NE 123rd Street
North Miami, FL 33161

305-893-8771; *Fax:* 305-893-8783;
www.bizbash.com
Social Media: Facebook, Twitter

Tom Cove, President

Retailers, distributors, wholesalers, importers/exporters and other buyers of sports related products come for 10,000 exhibits of sports apparel, footwear, accessories and e-commerce products and services.
100k Attendees
Frequency: Annual/January

1765 **EGA National Seminar**
Embroiderers' Guild of America
1355 Bardstown Road
Suite 157
Louisville, KY 40204

502-589-6956; *Fax:* 502-584-7900
sem2010@egausa.org; www.egausa.org

Lorie Welker, President
Barbara Harrison, VP

Lectures, workshops and networking.
20000 Attendees

1766 **Eastern Men's Market/Collective**
AmericasMart Atlanta

240 Peachtree Street NW
Suite 2200
Atlanta, GA 30303-1327

404-220-3000
800-285-6278; *Fax:* 404-220-3030
webmaster@americasmart.com;
www.americasmart.com
Social Media: Facebook, Twitter

Jeff Portman, President/COO
Hank Almquist, VP

An outlet for the latest trends and designs in products and services.
500 Attendees

1767 **Embroidery Trade Association Convention**
Embroidery Trade Association
PO Box 794534
Dallas, TX 75379-4534

972-247-0415
888-628-2545; *Fax:* 972-755-2561
info@embroiderytrade.org;
www.mesadrist.com/trade_associations

John Swinburn, Executive Director

An organization with the objective to continually strengthen the commercial embroidery business.
1200 Members
Founded in: 1990

1768 **FFANY Collections**
Fashion Footwear Association of New York
274 Madison Avenue
Suite 1701
New York, NY 10016

212-751-6422; *Fax:* 212-751-6404
info@ffany.org; www.ffany.org
Social Media: Facebook, Twitter

Joseph C Moore, President/CEO
Phyllis Rein, Senior VP

The essential venue for fashion footwear. Held at FFANY participating show rooms.
300 Attendees
Frequency: August
Founded in: 1980

1769 **Fabric Exhibition**
Advanstar Communications
2501 Colorado Avenue
Suite 280
Santa Monica, CA 90404

310-857-7500; *Fax:* 310-857-7500
info@advanstar.com; www.advanstar.com

Joseph Loggia, President
Chris DeMoulin, VP
Susannah George, Marketing Director

Conference and exhibition of interest to those in the fabric and garment industry.
7000 Attendees

1770 **Fitness Show at the Super Show**
Communications & Show Management
1450 NE 123rd Street
North Miami, FL 33161

305-893-8771; *Fax:* 305-893-8783;
www.bizbash.com

Tom Cove, President

Retailers, distributors, wholesalers, importers/exporters and other buyers of sports related products come for 10,000 exhibits of sports apparel, footwear, accessories and e-commerce products and services.
100k Attendees
Frequency: Annual/January

1771 **Gatlinburg Apparel & Jewelry Market**
Norton Shows
PO Box 265
Gatlinburg, TN 37738

865-436-6151; *Fax:* 865-436-6152;
www.nortonshows.com

Tom Norton, Show Manager/Owner
Linda Norton, Owner

Trade show that has wholesale, cash-and-carry, ladies, men's, and children's apparel, fashion jewelry, accessories, fine jewelry and gifts from around the world. There are 500-700 booths.
20000 Attendees
Frequency: March/June/Sept/Nov
Founded in: 1987
Mailing list available for rent: 70,000 names

1772 **Global Leather**
American Apparel & Footwear Association
1601 N Kent Street
Suite 1200
Arlington, VA 22205

703-524-1864
800-520-2262; *Fax:* 847-522-6741
info@globalleathers.com
globalleathers.com

Kevin M Burke, President
Stephen E Lamar, VP
Dawn Van Dyke, Marketing

Showcases the best in new leather materials and components for footwear leather, needle and allied trades of North America. Brings together hundreds of exhibitors from the major sourcing cities around the world, showcasing thousands of products.
1500 Attendees
Frequency: February/August
Founded in: 1981

1773 **Holiday Sample Sale**
San Francisco Design Center
635 8th Street
San Francisco, CA 94103

415-490-5800; *Fax:* 415-490-5885;
www.sfdesigncenter.com

Dianne Travalini, Show Director
Aruex Dalmacio, Show Manager

Open to the public and offers jewelry, accessories and leather items, gift items, home accessories, housewares, toys and apparel.
11000 Attendees
Frequency: November

1774 **Hospitality Design Expo**
American Flock Association
6 Beacon Street
Suite 1125
Boston, MA 02108

617-303-6288; *Fax:* 617-542-2199
info@flocking.org; www.flocking.org

Steve Rosenthal, Director

Provides positive leadership to foster a strong flock industry in North America.
Frequency: May

1775 **IACDE Convention**
Internatl Assoc of Clothing Designers & Executives
835 NW 36th Terrace
Oklahoma City, OK 73118

405-602-8037; *Fax:* 405-602-8038;
www.iacde.com

Joachim Hensch, President
Mina Henry, Director

Focus is on the retail link in the apparel supply chain. The students and faculty of the Fashion Institute of Technology are involved in the planning and presentation of many of the convention programs.
Frequency: Annual
Founded in: 1910

1776 **ISAM: International Swimwear and Activewear Market**
California Market Center
110 E 9th Street
Los Angeles, CA 90079

213-303-3688
800-225-6278; *Fax:* 213-630-3708
info@californiamarketcenter.com

Barbara Brady, Director

Serves the swimwear and resortwear industry.
Frequency: August/September
Founded in: 1978

1777 **Imprinted Sportswear Shows (ISS)**
Imprinted Sportswear Shows (ISS)
Nielson Business Media
1145 Sanctuary Parkway, Ste 355
Alpharetta, GA 30004-4756

800-933-8735; *Fax:* 770-777-8700
issshows@xpressreg.net; www.issshows.com

David Loechner, President
Michael Alicea, Senior VP

Shows in: Long Beach, Orlando, Atlantic City, Atlanta and Fort Worth. Showcases the newest products, apparel, and equipment featuring new technology, sublimation, and techniques with hands-on demos. There are new conferences at every show providing learning and networking opportunities. Discuss business opportunities, best practices, artistic trends, and techniques.
Founded in: 1981

1778 **International Fashion Boutique Show**
Advanstar Communications
757 3rd Ave
New York, NY 10017-2013

212-951-6600; *Fax:* 212-951-6793
info@advanstar.com; www.advanstar.com

Offers a variety of fashion trade shows throughout each year at the Javitz Convention Center in New York.
25000 Attendees

1779 **International Fashion Fabric Exhibition**
Advanstar Communications
641 Lexington Avenue
8th Floor
New York, NY 10022

212-951-6600; *Fax:* 212-951-6793
info@advanstar.com; www.advanstar.com

Joseph Loggia, CEO
Tony Calanca, Executive Vice President
Steven Sturm, Executive Vice President

Conference and exhibits of interest to those in the fabric and garment industries.
15000 Attendees

1780 **International Hosiery Exposition**
Home Sewing Association
105 Mall Boulevard
PO Box 369
Monroeville, PA 15146

412-372-5950; *Fax:* 412-372-5953;
www.sewing.org

Dotty Grexa, President
Jenna Sheldon, Director Trade Show/Meetings
Jenny Prevatte, Director Information Services

Specialize in the latest hosiery and sewn products industries' supplies and services. 250 Exhibitors.
10000 Attendees

1781 **International Intimate Apparel Lingerie Show**
Specialty Trade Show

3939 Hardle Road
Coconut Grove, FL 33133-6437

305-663-6635; *Fax:* 305-661-8118;
www.lingerieshow.cc

Jeff Yunis, President

Specializing in lingerie and adult products.
2,000 Attendees
Frequency: October

1782 International Kids Fashion Show
Advanstar Communications
641 Lexington Avenue
8th Floor
New York, NY 10022

212-951-6600; *Fax:* 212-951-6793
info@advanstar.com; www.advanstar.com

Joseph Loggia, CEO
Thomas Ehardt, Executive Vice President

Children's fashions, accessories, gift items, and footwear.
3500 Attendees
Frequency: Jan/March/August/October

1783 International Show at the Super Show
Communications & Show Management
1450 NE 123rd Street
North Miami, FL 33161

305-808-3531; *Fax:* 305-893-8783;
www.bizbash.com

Richard Aaron, President
David Adler, CEO, Founder
Ann Keusch, COO

Retailers, distributors, wholesalers, importers/exporters and other buyers of sports related products come for 10,000 exhibits of sports apparel, footwear, accessories and e-commerce products and services.
100k Attendees
Frequency: January

1784 International Vision Expo
The Vision Council of America
225 Reinekers Lane
Suite 700
Alexandria, VA 22314

703-548-4560
866-826-0290; *Fax:* 703-548-4580
info@thevisioncouncil.org;
www.thevisioncouncil.org

Ed Greene, President
Brian Carroll, VP
Maureen Beddis, Marketing Director

Learn about new market information, statistics, training and industry trends.
Frequency: Biennial
Founded in: 1999

1785 International Western Apparel and Accessories Market
Dallas Market Center
2100 Stemmons Freeway
Dallas, TX 75207

214-655-6100
800-325-6587; *Fax:* 800-637-6833;
www.dallasmarketcenter.com

Bill Winsor, President/CEO
Pat Zajac, Contact Home Expo

Offers array of services geared toward helping retailers expand business and increase profits.
200M Attendees
Frequency: March/August
Founded in: 1957

1786 Licensed Sports Show at the Super Show
Communications & Show Management
1450 NE 123rd Street
North Miami, FL 33161

305-808-3531; *Fax:* 305-893-8783;
www.bizbash.com

Richard Aaron, President
David Adler, CEO, Founder
Ann Keusch, COO

Retailers, distributors, wholesalers, importers/exporters and other buyers of sports related products come for 10,000 exhibits of sports apparel, footwear, accessories and e-commerce products and services.
100k Attendees
Frequency: January

1787 MAGIC International Show
MAGIC International
2501 Colorado Avenue
Suite 280
Santa Monica, CA 90404

310-857-7500; *Fax:* 310-593-5020
cs@MAGIConline.com;
www.magiconline.com

Joe Loggia, President/CEO
Francine Rich, Womens Sales Contact
Christopher Giffin, Vice President Sales
Pam Thompson, Attendee Relations

Fashion trade show in Las Vegas. 3,000 exhibitors.
75000 Attendees
Frequency: February/August
Founded in: 1933

1788 Management Conference & Team Dealer Summit
National Sporting Goods Association
1601 Feehanville Drive
Suite 300
Mount Prospect, IL 60056

847-296-6742
800-815-5422; *Fax:* 847-391-9827
info@nsga.org; www.nsga.org

Bob Dickman, Chairman of the Board
Matt Carlson, President/CEO
Dustin Dobrin, Research and Information Director

The goal is to stimulate fresh, agile thinking. How you and your company can create a culture that encourages and stimulates action, focus on the solution and fresh thinking.

1789 Manufacturers Wholesalers Outerwear Sportswear Show
I. Spiewak & Sons
463 7th Avenue
10th Floor
New York, NY 10018-6505

212-695-1620
800-223-6850; *Fax:* 212-629-4803
jerry@spiewak.com; www.spiewak.com

Gerald Spiewak, Executive Director
Roy Spiewak, President

180 booths for manufacturers and importers of outerwear and rainwear.
3M Attendees
Frequency: January

1790 Material World
Urban Expositions
1395 S Marietta Parkway
Building 400, Suite 210
Marietta, GA 30067

770-180-0972
800-318-2238; *Fax:* 678-285-7469;
www.material-world.com

Doug Miller, President
Tim von Gal, Executive VP
Suzanne Pruitt, Contact

From design to delivery, Material World is the international full package, sourcing and fashion information event for the fabric related industries.
10600 Attendees
Frequency: May

1791 Men's and Boy's Apparel Show
Miami International Merchandise Mart
777 NW 72nd Avenue
Miami, FL 33126

305-665-5630; *Fax:* 305-261-3659;
www.miamimart.net

Martiza Agudo, President
Glorys Covo, Administrator

This is a three-day show where wholesale buyers will find an extensive display of apparel lines including Calvin Klein, Perruzo, Supreme, just to name a few.
1000 Attendees
Frequency: April/May

1792 National Bridal Market: Fall
Merchandise Mart Properties Inc
222 Merchandise Mart Plaza
Suite 470
Chicago, IL 60654

312-527-4141
800-677-6278; *Fax:* 312-527-7971
mmailand@mmart.com; www.mmart.com

Christopher Kennedy, President
Stephanie Ambuehl, Marketing

Specializing in leading bridal and special occasion resources for department and specialty stores.
3000 Attendees
Frequency: October

1793 National Halloween & Costume & Party Show
Transworld Exhibits
1850 Oak Street
Northfield, IL 60093

847-784-6905
800-323-5462; *Fax:* 847-446-3523;
www.tweshows.com

Joe Thaler, CEO
Paul O'Connor, Executive Director

Attracts people from across the US and over 50 foreign countries to see what over 700 manufacturers and distributors are showcasing as new and exciting for parties, shops and haunted houses. Free educational seminars and workshops.
10000 Attendees
Frequency: February

1794 National Needlework Market
The National NeedleArts Association
1100-H Brandywine Blvd
Zanesville, OH 43701

740-455-6773
800-889-8662; *Fax:* 740-452-2552
info@tnna.org; www.tnna.org

Enabling professionals to come together to share knowledge, products and experiences.
5M Attendees
Frequency: Annual

1795 National Sewing Show
Home Sewing Association
PO Box 369
Monroeville, PA 15146

412-372-5950; *Fax:* 412-372-5953;
www.sewing.org

Dotty Grexa, President

Offers free sewing projects, guidelines and also a chat room where you can share with other about your ideas and collaborate on others.
Frequency: September

1796 **New England Apparel Club**
New England Apparel Club
75 McNeil Way
Suite 207
Dedham, MA 02026
781-326-9223; *Fax:* 781- 32- 689
neacrlg@aol.com; www.neacshow.com
Richard Usherwood, President
Donald Hurowitz, Vice President
Rhonda Goldberg, Executive Director
2500 regional sales reps exhibiting clothing and related equipment, supplies and services.
2000 Attendees
Frequency: October, Boston

1797 **Northstar Fashion Exhibitors**
Northstar Fashion Exhibitors
175 Kellogg Blvd West
St Paul, MN 55102
763-546-8717
800-272-6972; *Fax:* 763-546-9176
northstarfashion.com
Rick Siegel, President
Stanley Kaye, Show Coordinator
Debi Higgins, Manager
Trade show collections for men's, women's, Childrens apparel, accessories and textiles. 250 Booths.
1,260 Attendees
Frequency: 5/Year

1798 **Northwest Shoe Traveler's Buying Shoe Market**
Northwest Shoe Traveler's
12630 12th Street N
Lake Elmo, MN 55042
651-436-2709; *Fax:* 651-436-2028
Teri Tompkins, Show Manager
Trade show collections for men's, women's and Childrens.
250 Attendees
Frequency: January

1799 **Off-Price Specialist Show**
Off Price Specialist Center
16985 W Bluemound Road
Suite 210
Brookfield, WI 53005
262-782-1600; *Fax:* 262-782-1601
info@offpriceshow.com;
www.offpriceshow.com
Social Media: Facebook, Twitter
Stephen Krogulski, President/CEO
David Lapidos, Executive Vice President
Faye Osvatic, Buyers Contact
Kevin Redlich, Product Manager
Premiere show for off-price apparel and accessories.
12000 Attendees
Frequency: May 8-10
Founded in: 1995

1800 **Outdoor Retailer Summer Market**
Nielsen Sports Group
31910 Del Obispo
Suite 200
San Juan Capistrano, CA 92675
949-226-5722; www.outdoorretailer.com
Kenji Haroutunian, Director
Margle Lelvis, Marketing
Krista Dill, Account Executive
Jennifer Holcomb, Marketing Manager
Kenji Haroutunian, Show Director
The leading growth vehicle for brands that are interested in progressing and advancing into multiple channels of the outdoor marketplace.
17000 Attendees
Frequency: August

1801 **Outdoor Retailer Winter Market**
VNU Expositions
PO Box 1899
Laguna Beach, CA 92652
949-226-5722; *Fax:* 949-226-5625;
www.outdoorretailer.com
Marisa Nicholson, National Sales Manager
Paul Dillman, Senior Account Executive
Peter Devin, Group Show Director
David Lockner, Manager
Features the most comprehensive collection of outdoor apparel, gear, equipment, climbing technology, footwear, ski mountaineering, hunting, rescue outerwear and accessory companies from which to buy products.

1802 **PGA Merchandise Show**
Reed Exhibition Companies
383 Main Avenue
Suite 3
Norwalk, CT 06851
203- 84- 562
800-840-5628; *Fax:* 203-840-9628
inquiry@pga.reedexpo.com;
www.pgaexpo.com
Andre Smith, Director Marketing/Special Events
Marc Simon, Group Sales Director
Sherry Major, Media Contact
World's largest golf industry trade event. Open to retail buyers and golf industry professionals. Not open to the public
38500 Attendees
Frequency: January
Founded in: 1954

1803 **Performance & Lifestyle Footwear Show at the Super Show**
Communications & Show Management
1450 NE 123rd Street
North Miami, FL 33161
305-893-8771; *Fax:* 305-893-8783;
www.bizbash.com
Richard Aaron, President
David Adler, CEO/President
Chad Kaydo, Editor in Chief
Dana Price, COO
Retailers, distributors, wholesalers, importers/exporters and other buyers of sports related products come for 10,000 exhibits of sports apparel, footwear, accessories and e-commerce products and services.
100k Attendees
Frequency: January

1804 **Printwear Show**
National Business Media Inc
PO Box 1416
Broomfield, CO 80038
303-469-0424
800-669-0424; *Fax:* 303-465-3424;
www.nbmshows.com
Social Media: Twitter
Bob Wieber, President
The event for buyers involved in screen printing, embroidery, heat applied graphics, digital textile printing, sublimation and apparel.
Frequency: August

1805 **Professional Apparel Association Trade**
Professional Apparel Association
994 Old Eagle School Road
Suite 1019
Wayne, PA 19087-1866
610-971-4850; *Fax:* 610-971-4859
Dr. Sharon Tannahill, Executive Director
Exhibitors display health care and hospitality uniforms, shoes, and accessories, and career apparel. Workshops and seminars for uniform retailers are also available. Biennial.

1806 **Seattle Trend Show**
Pacific Northwest Apparel Association
P.O. Box 3050
Issaquah, WA 98027
206-767-9200; *Fax:* 206-767-0707
pnaa@nwtrendshow.com;
www.nwtrendshow.com
Jane Powell, Director
Gary Morgan, President
Show and exhibits of apparel and related accessories.
2000 Attendees
Frequency: Jan/Apr/Jun/Aug/Oct

1807 **Shoe Market of America**
Miami Merchandise Mart
2335 NW 107 Ave
Suite 2M31 Box 120
Miami, FL 33172
786-331-9000; *Fax:* 786-331-9955
info@smota.com; www.smota.com
Dianne Travalini, Executive Director
Alex Meme, Manager
Features the entire spectrum of footwear companies.
2500 Attendees
Frequency: 3x per year

1808 **Southwestern Shoe Traveler's**
Southwestern Shoe Traveler's Association
1024 Oxfordshire Dr.
Cannollton, TX 75007
972-446-4089; *Fax:* 214-292-9691
southwestshoeexpo@verizon.net
Mona Bennight, Executive Director
Definitive footwear trade site for footwear retailers.
1800 Attendees
Frequency: June

1809 **Syracuse Super Show**
Oncenter Complex
800 So. State Street
Syracuse, NY
315-488-4201
abc43@juno.com;
www.syracusesupershow.com
Carol Sweet, Menswear Contact
Dick Pirozzolo, Footwear Contact
Rhonda Goldberg, Women's & Children's Contact
Largest assortment of fashions in Upstate New York. The show is open to the wholesale trade only - sales representatives, manufacturers and retailers.

1810 **TNNA Trade Shows**
National Needlework Association
1100-H Brandywine Boulevard
Zanesville, OH 43701
740-455-6773
800-889-8662; *Fax:* 740-452-2552
info@tnna.org; www.tnna.org
Social Media: Facebook, Twitter
A market for serious needleart buyers and sellers learn about trends in fashion, color and design. With over 800 booths.
Frequency: 4x per year

1811 **Team Sports Show at the Super Show**
Communications & Show Management

1450 NE 123rd Street
North Miami, FL 33161

305-893-8771; *Fax:* 305-893-8783;
www.bizbash.com

Richard Aaron, President
David Adler, CEO/founder
Chad Kaydo, Editor in Chief
Dana Price, COO

Retailers, distributors, wholesalers, importers/exporters and other buyers of sports related products come for 10,000 exhibits of sports apparel, footwear, accessories and e-commerce products and services.
100k Attendees
Frequency: January

1812 **Tennis & Golf Show at the Super Show**
Communications & Show Management
1450 NE 123rd Street
North Miami, FL 33161

305-893-8771; *Fax:* 305-893-8783;
www.bizbash.com

Richard Aaron, President
David Adler, CEO/Founder
Chad Kaydo, Editor in Chief
Dana Price, COO

Retailers, distributors, wholesalers, importers/exporters and other buyers of sports related products come for 10,000 exhibits of sports apparel, footwear, accessories and e-commerce products and services.
100k Attendees
Frequency: January

1813 **Trimmings, Accessories, Fabrics Expo**
National Knitwear & Sportswear Association
386 Park Avenue S
Suite 5741
New York, NY 10016-8804

212-683-7520; *Fax:* 212-532-0766

Seth Bodner, Executive Director

The only all-inclusive trimmings show in the United States. 160 booths.
6M Attendees
Frequency: November

1814 **WAM: Western Apparel Manufacturers Show**
Dallas Market Center
2300 Stemmons Freeway
Dallas, TX 75207

214-556-6100; *Fax:* 214-638-7221
info@dmcmail.com;
www.dallasmarketcenter.com
Social Media: Facebook, Twitter

Apparel manufacturing equipment. Held to meet the needs of the TOLA retailers who take advantage of the early fall buying opportunities.
3.2M Attendees
Frequency: April

1815 **WSA: Western Shoe Associates**
Western Shoe Associates
20281 SW Birch Street
Newport Beach, CA 92660

949-851-8451; *Fax:* 949-851-8523

Mitch Fisherman, President
Steve Katz, VP
Marie Mussabini, Exhibitor Coordinator
Dave Darling, Treasurer

Trade show held twice a year and featuring footwear.

1816 **WWD Magic**
MAGIC International
2501 Colorado Avenue
Suite 280
Santa Monica, CA 90404

310-857-7500; *Fax:* 310-857-7510
cs@magiconline.com; www.magiconline.com
Social Media: Facebook, Twitter

Joe Loggia, President/CEO
Laura McConnell, VP

WWD Magic, a joint venture with Women's Wear Daily, is the recognized leader in women's apparel and accessories expositions in the world. WWD Magic offers the opportunity to discover new resources, network with industry peers, attend trend seminars and fashion shows, and meet with major manufacturers in an exciting and efficient forum. Containing over 1,000 exhibitors and 2,000 booths.
85000 Attendees
Frequency: August
Founded in: 1933

1817 **Western Shoe Associates International**
Western Shoe Associates
20281 SW Birch Street
Suite 100
Newport Beach, CA 92660

949-851-8451; *Fax:* 949-851-8523

Mitch Fisherman, President
Marie Mussabini, Exhibitor Coordinator

Footwear trade market.

1818 **Western and English Sales Association Trade Show**
Western and English Sales Association
451 E 58th Avenue
Suite 4128
Denver, CO 80216
303-295-1040
800-295-1041; *Fax:* 303-295-0941
info@denver-wesa.com;
www.denver-wesa.com

Toni High, Executive Director
Amy Thomas, Trade Show Director

Trade shows for Equestrian-related products; wholesalers to retailers
10000 Attendees
Frequency: 2x/Year

1819 **Women and Children's Market**
AMC Trade Shows/DMC Expositions
2140 Peachtree Street NW
Suite 2200
Atlanta, GA 30303

404-220-3000
800-285-6278; *Fax:* 404-220-3030

Sarah Adamson, Show Manager

Women and children's apparel.
9000 Attendees

1820 **Women's and Children's Apparel Market**
Dallas Market Center
2100 Stemmons Freeway
Dallas, TX 75207

214-556-6100
800-325-6587
ahood@dmcmail.com;
www.dallasmarketcenter.com
Social Media: Facebook, Twitter

Pat Zajac, Home Expo

Features the most comprehensive variety of apparel and accessories lines.
20000 Attendees
Frequency: October
Founded in: 1957

1821 **Women's and Children's Fall Market**
Merchandise Mart Properties Inc
222 Merchandise Mart Plaza
Suite 470
Chicago, IL 60654

312-527-4141
800-677-6278; *Fax:* 312-527-7782;
www.merchandisemart.com

Christopher Kennedy, President

Hundreds of designers featuring women's and children's clothing and accessories
5000 Attendees
Founded in: 1950

1822 **Women's and Children's Summer/Fall Preview Market**
Merchandise Mart Properties
222 Merchandise Mart Plaza
Suite 470
Chicago, IL 60654

312-527-4141
800-677-6278; *Fax:* 312-527-7782;
www.merchandisemart.com

H Brennen III, Executive VP

Women's and children's apparel.
5000 Attendees
Frequency: June

1823 **Wonderful World of Weddings and Occasions**
Expo Productions
510 Hartbrook Drive
Hartland, WI 53029

262-367-5500
800-367-5520; *Fax:* 262-367-9956
monica@epishows.com;
www.weddingshowepi.com

Monica Seeger, Sales Manager

Wedding and other special occasion products, services, ideas including live and recorded music, still and video photography, cakes and catering, formal wear, gifts and much more.
6000 Attendees
Frequency: January
Founded in: 1967

1824 **X-treme Sports Show at the Super Show**
Communications & Show Management
1450 NE 123rd Street
North Miami, FL 33161

305-893-8771; *Fax:* 305-893-8783;
www.bizbash.com

Richard Aaron, President
David Adler, CEO/Founder
Chad Kaydo, Editor in Chief
Dana Price, COO

Retailers, distributors, wholesalers, importers/exporters and other buyers of sports related products come for 10,000 exhibits of sports apparel, footwear, accessories and e-commerce products and services.
100k Attendees
Frequency: January

Directories & Databases

1825 **Action Sports Retailer Buyer's Guide Issue**
Miller Freeman Publications
2655 Seely Avenue
San Jose, CA 95134

408-943-1234; *Fax:* 408-943-0513

Pat Cochran, Editor

Guide to 1,600 manufacturers and distributors of specialty watersports, beach, skateboarding, snowboarding, volleyball and bicycling equipment and clothing.
Cost: $25.00

1826 **American Apparel Contractors Association Directory - American Made Apparel**
4870 Nome Street
Denver, CO 80239-2728
303-373-2924; *Fax:* 703-522-6741
Sue C Strickland, Executive Director
Sunny Park, Owner
Over 300 listings are offered pertaining to contractors, manufacturers and suppliers to the apparel industry.
30 Members
100 Pages
Frequency: Annual
Founded in: 1981

1827 **Apparel Specialty Stores Directory**
Chain Store Guide
10117 Princess Palm Dr
Tampa, FL 33610
813-627-6700
800-927-9292; *Fax:* 813-627-6888
webmaster@chainstoreguide.com;
www.csgis.com
Mike Jarvis, Publisher
Chris Leedy, Advertising Sales
Shami Choon, Manager
The facts on more than 4,800 companies operating more than 70,700 stores all involved in the sale of women's, men's, family and children's wear. Also included are sporting goods stores that offer apparel and active wear as well as related merchandise. Includes more than 15,000 key buyers and executives.
Cost: $335.00

1828 **Bobbin-Suppliers Sourcing Issue**
Bobbin Blenheim Media Corporation
1110 Shop Road
PO Box 1986
Columbia, SC 29201-4743
800-845-8820; *Fax:* 803-799-1461
Offers information on over 8,000 suppliers to the apparel/sewn products industry.

1829 **College Store Executive: Emblematics Directory Issue**
Executive Business Media
825 Old Country Road
Westbury, NY 11590
516-334-3030; *Fax:* 516-334-3059
ebm-mail@ebmpubs.com; www.ebmpubs.com
Murry Greenwald, President
List of distributors of products with emblems or insignia; coverage includes Canada.
Cost: $5.00
Frequency: Annual, February

1830 **Complete Directory of Apparel**
Sutton Family Communications & Publishing Company
155 Sutton Lane
Fordsville, KY 42343
270-740-0870
jlsutton@apex.net;
www.suttoncompliance.com
Theresa Sutton, Editor
Lee Sutton, General Manager
Print-out from database of wholesalers, manufacturers, distributors, importers and close-out houses. Database is updated daily to guarantee the most current sources available.
Cost: $77.65
100+ Pages

1831 **Complete Directory of Apparel Close-Outs**
Sutton Family Communications & Publishing Company
155 Sutton Lane
Fordsville, KY 42343
270-740-0870
jlsutton@apex.net;
www.suttoncompliance.com
Theresa Sutton, Editor
Lee Sutton, General Manager
Print-out from database of wholesalers, manufacturers, distributors, importers and close-out houses. Database is updated daily to guarantee the most current sources available to the close-out apparel industry.
Cost: $55.20
100+ Pages

1832 **Complete Directory of Baby Goods and Gifts**
Sutton Family Communications & Publishing Company
155 Sutton Lane
Fordsville, KY 42343
270-740-0870
jlsutton@apex.net;
www.suttoncompliance.com
Theresa Sutton, Editor
Lee Sutton, General Manager
Print-out from database of wholesalers, manufacturers, distributors, importers and close-out houses for baby goods and gifts. Database is updated daily to guarantee the most current sources available.
Cost: $57.65
100+ Pages

1833 **Complete Directory of Belts, Buckles & Boots**
Sutton Family Communications & Publishing Company
155 Sutton Lane
Fordsville, KY 42343
270-740-0870
jlsutton@apex.net;
www.suttoncompliance.com
Theresa Sutton, Editor
Lee Sutton, General Manager
Print-out from database of wholesalers, manufacturers, distributors, importers and close-out houses. Database is updated daily to guarantee the most current sources available.
Cost: $55.20
100+ Pages

1834 **Complete Directory of Brand New Surplus Merchandise**
Sutton Family Communications & Publishing Company
155 Sutton Lane
Fordsville, KY 42343
270-740-0870
jlsutton@apex.net;
www.suttoncompliance.com
Theresa Sutton, Editor
Lee Sutton, General Manager
Print-out from database of wholesalers, manufacturers, distributors, importers and close-out houses. Database is updated daily to guarantee the most current sources available.
Cost: $92.70
100+ Pages

1835 **Complete Directory of Caps & Hats**
Sutton Family Communications & Publishing Company
155 Sutton Lane
Fordsville, KY 42343
270-740-0870
jlsutton@apex.net;
www.suttoncompliance.com
Theresa Sutton, Editor
Lee Sutton, General Manager
Print-out from database of wholesalers, manufacturers, distributors, importers and close-out houses. Database is updated daily to guarantee the most current sources available.
Cost: $55.20
100+ Pages

1836 **Complete Directory of Clothing & Uniforms**
Sutton Family Communications & Publishing Company
155 Sutton Lane
Fordsville, KY 42343
270-740-0870
jlsutton@apex.net;
www.suttoncompliance.com
Theresa Sutton, Editor
Lee Sutton, General Manager
Print-out from database of wholesalers, manufacturers, distributors, importers and close-out houses. Database is updated daily to guarantee the most current sources available.
Cost: $55.20
100+ Pages

1837 **Complete Directory of Hat Pins, Feathers and Fads**
Sutton Family Communications & Publishing Company
155 Sutton Lane
Fordsville, KY 42343
270-740-0870
jlsutton@apex.net;
www.suttoncompliance.com
Theresa Sutton, Editor
Lee Sutton, General Manager
Print-out from database of wholesalers, manufacturers, distributors, importers and close-out houses. Database is updated daily to guarantee the most current sources available.
Cost: $67.70
100+ Pages

1838 **Complete Directory of Purses & Handbags**
Sutton Family Communications & Publishing Company
155 Sutton Lane
Fordsville, KY 42343
270-740-0870
jlsutton@apex.net;
www.suttoncomlpiance.com
Theresa Sutton, Editor
Lee Sutton, General Manager
Print-out from database of wholesalers, manufacturers, distributors, importers and close-out houses. Database is updated daily to guarantee the most current sources available.
Cost: $55.20
100+ Pages

1839 **Complete Directory of Sunglasses & Eye Weather**
Sutton Family Communications & Publishing Company
155 Sutton Lane
Fordsville, KY 42343
270-740-0870
jlsutton@apex.net;
www.suttoncompliance.com
Theresa Sutton, Editor
Lee Sutton, General Manager

Print-out from database of wholesalers, manufacturers, distributors, importers and close-out houses. Database is updated daily to guarantee the most current sources available.
Cost: $55.20
100+ Pages

1840 Complete Directory of T-Shirts, Heat Transfers & Supplies
Sutton Family Communications & Publishing Company
155 Sutton Lane
Fordsville, KY 42343
270-740-0870
jlsutton@apex.net; www.suttoncompliance.com
Theresa Sutton, Editor
Lee Sutton, General Manager
Print-out from database of wholesalers, manufacturers, distributors, importers and close-out houses. Database is updated daily to guarantee the most current sources available.
Cost: $55.20
100+ Pages

1841 Complete Directory of Western Wear
Sutton Family Communications & Publishing Company
155 Sutton Lane
Fordsville, KY 42343
270-740-0870
jlsutton@apex.net; www.suttoncompliance.com
Theresa Sutton, Editor
Lee Sutton, General Manager
Print-out from database of wholesalers, manufacturers, distributors, importers and close-out houses. Database is updated daily to guarantee the most current sources available.
Cost: $55.20
100+ Pages

1842 Complete Directory of Women's Accessories
Sutton Family Communications & Publishing Company
155 Sutton Lane
Fordsville, KY 42343
270-740-0870
jlsutton@apex.net; www.suttoncompliance.com
Theresa Sutton, Editor
Lee Sutton, General Manager
Print-out from database of wholesalers, manufacturers, distributors, importers and close-out houses. Database is updated daily to guarantee the most current sources available.
Cost: $55.20
100+ Pages

1843 Directory of Active Sportswear
Sutton Family Communications & Publishing Company
155 Sutton Lane
Fordsville, KY 42343
270-740-0870
jlsutton@apex.net; www.suttoncompliance.com
Theresa Sutton, Editor
Lee Sutton, General Manager
Print-out from database of wholesalers, manufacturers, distributors, importers and close-out houses. Database is updated daily to guarantee the most current sources available. Approximately 740 wholesale sources in a 3-ring binder.
Cost: $67.20
100+ Pages

1844 Directory of Apparel Specialty Stores
AKTRIN Textile Information Center
164 S Main Street
PO Box 898
High Point, NC 27261
336-418-8583; *Fax:* 336-841-5435; www.textile-info.com
Information resource for people seeking in-depth, up-to-date data on the apparel specialty stores marketplace. Fully searchable database, either in form of a CD-ROM or downloadable over the Internet.
Cost: $780.00
Frequency: Annual

1845 Directory of Mail Order Catalogs
Grey House Publishing
4919 Route 22
PO Box 56
Amenia, NY 12501
518-789-8700
800-562-2139; *Fax:* 518-789-0556
books@greyhouse.com; www.greyhouse.com
Social Media: Facebook, Twitter
Leslie Mackenzie, Publisher
Richard Gottlieb, President
The premier source of information on the mail order catalog industry. Covers over 13,000 consumer and business catalog companies with 44 different product chapters including clothing and sportswear.
Cost: $395.00
1900 Pages
Frequency: Annual
ISBN: 1-592373-96-8
Founded in: 1981

1846 Directory of Mail Order Catalogs - Online Database
Grey House Publishing
4919 Route 22
PO Box 56
Amenia, NY 12501
518-789-8700
800-562-2139; *Fax:* 518-789-0556
gold@greyhouse.com
http://gold.greyhouse.com
Social Media: Facebook, Twitter
Leslie Mackenzie, Publisher
Richard Gottlieb, President
Reach over 10,000 consumer catalog companies in one easy-to-use source with The Directory of Mail Order Catalogs - Online Database. Filled with business-building detail, each company profile gives you the information you need to access that organization quickly and easily. Listings provide key contacts, sales volume, employee size, printing information, circulation, list data, product descriptions and much more.
Frequency: Annual
Founded in: 1981

1847 Earnshaw's Buyer's Guide to the New York Market
Earnshaw Publications
36 Cooper Square
4th Floor
New York, NY 10003
646-278-1550; *Fax:* 646- 27- 155; www.earnshaws.com
Noelle Heffernan, Publisher
A children's wear guide offering over 1,200 manufacturers and suppliers of clothing for infants, boys and girls apparel.
200 Pages
Frequency: Annual
Circulation: 10,000

1848 Earnshaw's Infants', Girls', Boys' Wear Review: Children's Wear Directory
Earnshaw Publications
36 Cooper Square
4th Floor
New York, NY 10003
646-278-1550; *Fax:* 646-278-1553; www.earnshaws.com
Noelle Heffernan, Publisher
A directory of over 1,500 children's apparel and accessory firms with offices or showrooms in the United States.
Cost: $10.00
Frequency: Annual
Circulation: 10,000

1849 Financial Performance Profile of Public Apparel Companies
Kurt Salmon Associates
650 Fifth Avenue
New York, NY 10019
212-319-9450; www.kurtsalmon.com
John Karonis, CEO
Information on over 60 publicly held apparel manufacturers are available.
Cost: $400.00
300 Pages
Frequency: Annual
Founded in: 1935

1850 Garment Manufacturers Index
Klevens Publications
411 S Main Street
Suite 209
Los Angeles, CA 90013
213-625-9000; *Fax:* 213-625-5002; www.garmentindex.com
Herbert Schwartz, Editor
A list of over 5,000 manufacturers and suppliers of products and services such as fabrics, trimmings, factory equipment and sewing contractors used in the manufacture of apparel and other sewn products.
Cost: $105.00
264 Pages
Frequency: Annual
Circulation: 29,495
ISSN: 1065-1330
Founded in: 1938
Printed in 4 colors on matte stock

1851 Hosiery and Bodywear: Buyer's Guide to Support and Control Top Pantyhose
Advanstar Communications
641 Lexington Ave
8th Floor
New York, NY 10022-4503
212-951-6600; *Fax:* 212-951-6793
info@advanstar.com; www.advanstar.com
Joseph Loggia, CEO
List of about 50 hosiery manufacturers.
Cost: $3.00
Frequency: Annual September
Circulation: 10,500

1852 Impressions: Directory Issue
Miller Freeman Publications
501 W. President George Bush Hwy. #150
Richardson, TX 75080
813-366-2877
800-697-8859
nimp@omeda.com; www.impressionsmag.com
Marcia Derrberry, Editor in Chief
A list of more than 1,500 suppliers of products, services and equipment used in the imprinted sportswear industry including textile screen print equipment, supplies, embroidery equipment and supplies, and all types of imprintables.
Cost: $18.00
Frequency: Annual
Circulation: 60,000

1853 **International Nonwovens Directory**
1100 Crescent Green Suite 115
PO Box 1288
Cary, NC 27518

919-233-1210; *Fax:* 919-233-1282;
www.inda.org

Rory Holmes, President
Annette Balint, Director Finance
Ian Butler, Director Market Research/Stats

A Who's Who directory of services and supplies to the nonwovens industry.
300 Members
750 Pages
Frequency: Biennial
Circulation: 2,000

1854 **Nationwide Directory of Men's & Boys' Wear Buyers**
Reed Reference Publishing RR Bowker
630 Central Ave
New Providence, NJ 07974-1544

908-286-1090
888-269-5372; *Fax:* 908-464-3553
info@bowker.com; www.bowker.com

A who's who directory of services and supplies to the industry.
Cost: $147.00
700 Pages
Frequency: Annual
Circulation: 1,000

1855 **Outerwear Sourcebook: Directory Issue**
Creative Marketing Plus
213-37 39th Avenue
Suite 228
Bayside, NY 11361

718-606-0767; *Fax:* 718-606-6345
rharrow@creativemarketingplus.com;
www.creativemarketingplus.com

Richard Harrow, President

List of more than 3,500 outerwear manufacturers in the US and Canada; 1,000 companies providing products and services to the outerwear trade.
Cost: $40.00
Frequency: Annual

1856 **WWD Buyers Guide: Womens Apparel and Accessories Manufacturers**
Fairchild Publications
750 3rd Ave
New York, NY 10017-2703

212-630-4000; *Fax:* 212-630-3563

Mary G Berner, Chief Executive Officer
Christine Guilfoyle, Publisher

Over 5,500 apparel and accessory manufacturers.
Founded in: 1892

1857 **WWD Suppliers Guide**
Fairchild Books and Visuals
750 3rd Ave
New York, NY 10017-2700

212-630-4320; *Fax:* 212-630-3566

Mary G Berner, Chief Executive Officer
Christine Guilfoyle, Publisher

Over 5,500 apparel and accessory manufacturers in the US. Supplement to WWD Magazine.
Founded in: 1892

Industry Web Sites

1858 **http://gold.greyhouse.com**
G.O.L.D Grey House OnLine Databases

Grey House Publishing's online database platform, GOLD, offers Quick Search, Keyword Search and Expert Search in most business sectors, including apparel and accessories markets. The GOLD platform makes finding the information you need quick and easy - whether you're a novice searcher or an experienced database user. All of Grey House's directory products are available for subscription on the GOLD platform.

1859 **www.apparelandfootwear.org**
American Apparel & Footwear Association

The national trade association for the apparel and footwear industries. Conducts seminars, compiles statistics and produces industry reports.

1860 **www.cashmere.org**
Cashmere and Camel Hair Manufacturers Institute

For cashmere and camel hair product manufacturers.

1861 **www.chemicalfabricsandfilm.com**
Chemical Fabrics and Film Association

An international trade association representing manufacturers of polymer-based fabric and film products, used in the building and construction, automotive, fashion and many other industries.

1862 **www.colorassociation.com**
Color Association of the US

Information on color/design issues; issues color charts two years in advance of selling seasons in order to profile popular American colors. Forecasts are issued in women's fashions and men's and children's clothing.

1863 **www.costumedesignersguild.com**
Costume Designers Guild

Works to promote employment and to create improved working conditions for costume designers.

1864 **www.ctda.com**
Custom Tailors and Designers Assn of America

Seeks to promote awareness of designers and makers of men's custom tailored clothing.

1865 **www.embroiderytrade.org**
Embroidery Trade Association

An organization with the objective to continually strengthen the commercial embroidery business.

1866 **www.formalwear.org**
International Formalwear Association

For the formal wear industry.

1867 **www.greyhouse.com**
Grey House Publishing

Authoritative reference directories for most industries, including apparel and accessories. Users can search the online databases with varied search criteria allowing for custom searches by product category, geographic area, sales volume, keyword, subject and more. Full Grey House catalog and online ordering also available.

1868 **www.ifai.com**
Industrial Fabrics Association International

For geosynthetics, fabricators, installers, equipment manufacturers, suppliers, testing firms, consultants, and educators, who produce textiles, nets, mats, grids, and other products.

1869 **www.itaaonline.org**
Int'l Textile & Apparel Assn Membership Directory

For college professors of clothing and textile studies.

1870 **www.naumd.com**
North American Assoc. of Uniform Manufacturers

For manufacturers and distributors of uniforms and career wear.

1871 **www.sewing.org**
American Home Sewing and Craft Association

Handicraft and collectibles forum.

1872 **www.uc-council.org**
GS1 US

Members rely on the standards and services of GS1 US for the effective management and control of their supply chains. Everyday we strive to keep a leader's pace in developing, maintaining, supporting and expanding the services we offer to fulfill our mission.

1873 **www.uniteunion.org**
Union of Needletrade Industrial Textile Employees

A union fighting for working people.

1874 **www.vowsmag.com**
Grimes & Associates

Information on the business specifics necessary for today's wedding professional.

Associations

1875 **Air Conditioning Contractors of America**
2800 S Shirlington Rd
Suite 300
Arlington, VA 22206-3607
703-575-4477
info@acca.org; www.acca.org
Social Media: Facebook, Twitter, LinkedIn, YouTube, RSS Feeds, Flickr
Paul T. Stalknecht, President & CEO
Kevin W. Holland, Senior Vice President
Chris Hoelzel, Vice President, Product Fulfillment
Kimya Bailey Cajchun, Vice President of Membership
Craig Gotthardt, Vice President of Information
ACCA is a non-profit association serving the HVACR community, working to promote professional contracting, energy efficiency, and healthy, comfortable indoor environments.
64000 Members
Founded in: 1914

1876 **Air-Conditioning, Heating and Refrigeration Institute**
2111 Wilson Boulevard
Suite 500
Arlington, VA 22201
703-524-8800; *Fax:* 703-562-1942
ahri@ahrinet.org; www.ahrinet.org
Social Media: Facebook, Twitter, RSS Feeds
Stephen Yurek, President and CEO
Stephanie Murphy, Chief Financial Officer
Francis Dietz, Vice President of Public Affairs
Bob Johnston, Director/Accounting
Doug Burkes, Manager/Office Operations
AHRI is one of the largest trade associations in the nation, representing heating, water heating, ventilation, air conditioning and commercial refrigeration manufacturers within the global HVACR industry.
300 Members
Founded in: 1953

1877 **American Boiler Manufacturers Association**
8221 Old Courthouse Rd
Suite 207
Vienna, VA 22182-3839
703-356-7172; *Fax:* 703-356-4543;
www.abma.com
Social Media: Facebook, Twitter, LinkedIn
Robert Stemen, Chairman
W. Randall Rawson, President & CEO
Geoffrey Hailey, Director of Technical Affairs
Hugh K. Webster, General Counsel
Cheryl Jamall, Director of Meetings
The American Boiler Manufacturers Association (ABMA) is the national, nonprofit trade association of commercial, institutional, industrial and electricity-generating boiler system manufacturing companies (400,000 Btuh heat input), dedicated to the advancement and growth of the boiler and combustion equipment industry.
Founded in: 1888

1878 **American Society of Heating, Refrigeration & Air-Conditioning Engineers**
1791 Tullie Cir NE
Atlanta, GA 30329-2398
404-636-8400
800-527-4723; *Fax:* 404-321-5478
ashrae@ashrae.org; www.ashrae.org
Social Media: Facebook, Twitter, LinkedIn, YouTube
William P. Bahnfleth, President
Jeff H Littleton, Executive VP
Darryl K. Boyce, P.Eng., Vice President
Bjarne W. Olesen, Ph.D., Vice President
Daniel C. Pettway, Vice President
An international organization that fulfills its mission of advancing heating, ventilation, air conditioning and refrigeration to serve humanity and promote a sustainable world through research, standards writing, publishing and continuing education.
55000 Members
Founded in: 1894

1879 **American Society of Mechanical Engineers**
Two Park Avenue
New York, NY 10016-5900
973-882-1170
800-843-2763; *Fax:* 202-429-9417
infocentral@asme.org; www.asme.org
Social Media: Facebook, Twitter, LinkedIn
Madiha El Mehelmy Kotb, President
Thomas G. Loughlin, Executive Director
Chitra Sethi, Managing Editor
David Walsh, Editor
John Kosowatz, Senior Editor
ASME is a not-for-profit membership organization that enables collaboration, knowledge sharing, career enrichment, and skills development across all engineering disciplines, toward a goal of helping the global engineering community develop solutions to benefit lives and livelihoods.
12000 Members
Founded in: 1880

1880 **American Vacuum Society (AVS)**
125 Maiden Lane
15th Floor
New York, NY 10038
212-248-0200; *Fax:* 212-248-0245;
www.avs.org
Social Media: Facebook, Twitter, LinkedIn, RSS Feeds
Susan B. Sinnott, President
Jeannette DeGennaro, Exhibition & Sales Manager
Yvonne Towse, Managing Director
Ricky Baldeo, Office Services Coordinator
Angela Klink, Member Services Administrator
As an interdisciplinary, professional Society, AVS supports networking among academic, industrial, government, and consulting professionals involved in a variety of disciplines - chemistry, physics, biology, mathematics, business, sales, etc through common interests related to the basic science, technology development and commercialization of materials, interfaces, and processing areas.
4500 Members
Founded in: 1953

1881 **Association of Home Appliance Manufacturers**
1111 19th Street NW
Suite 402
Washington, DC 20036
202-872-5955; *Fax:* 202-872-9354
info@aham.org; www.aham.org
Paul V. Sikir, Board Chair
Joseph M. McGuire, President
Peter Frank, Vice President, Finance
Nick Baker, Manager, Communications
Jennifer Cleary, Director/Regulatory Affairs
A not-for-profit trade association representing manufacturers of major and portable home appliance, floor care appliances and suppliers to the industry .
Founded in: 1915

1882 **Industrial Heating Equipment Association**
5040 Old Taylor Mill Rd.
PMB 13
Taylor Mill, KY 41015
859-356-1575; *Fax:* 859-356-0908
ihea@ihea.org; www.ihea.org
Social Media: Facebook
Tim Lee, President
Bill Pasley, 1st Vice President
Mike Shay, 2nd Vice President
Jay Cherry, Treasurer
Anne Goyer, Executive Vice President
The Industrial Heating Equipment Association (IHEA) is a voluntary national trade association representing the major segments of the industrial heat processing equipment industry.
Founded in: 1929

1883 **International Housewares Association**
6400 Shafer Ct
Suite 650
Rosemont, IL 60018-4929
847-292-4200; *Fax:* 847-292-4211
pbrandl@housewares.org;
www.housewares.org
Social Media: Facebook, Twitter, LinkedIn, YouTube
Richard L. Boynton, Chairman
Phil J. Brandl, President
Dean Kurtis, Vice President, Finance
Mia Rampersad, Vice President, Trade Show
Perry Reynolds, Vice President, Marketing
A full-service trade association dedicated to promoting the sales and marketing of housewares.
Founded in: 1938

1884 **International Institute of Ammonia Refrigeration**
1001 N. Fairfax Street
Suite 503
Alexandria, VA 22314
703-312-4200; *Fax:* 703-312-0065
info@iiar.org; www.iiar.org
Social Media: Facebook, Twitter, LinkedIn, YouTube, Google+
Robert Port, Jr., Chairman
David L. Rule, President
Bruce Badger, Chief Operating Officer
Marcos Braz, Chair-Elect
Tom Leighty, Vice Chair
IAR is an organization providing advocacy, education, standards, and information for the benefit of the ammonia refrigeration industry worldwide. IIAR's vision is to be recognized as the world's leading advocate for the safe, reliable and efficient use of ammonia and other natural refrigerants for industrial applications.
1200 Members
Founded in: 1971

1885 **International Kitchen Exhaust Cleaning Association**
100 North 20th Street
Suite 400
Philadelphia, PA 19103
215-320-3876; *Fax:* 215-564-2175
information@ikeca.org; www.ikeca.org
Social Media: Facebook, Twitter, LinkedIn, YouTube, Blog
Kathy Slomer, President
Sarah Hagy, Executive Director
Lisa Chester, Associate Director
Hanna Linn, Administrative Director
Gina Marinilli, Standard Development Director
Promotes fire safety in restaurants and professionalism in the kitchen exhaust cleaning industry. This not for profit trade association, has established stringent standards and practices for contractors engaged in kitchen exhaust cleaning,

conducted a variety of educational programs, and worked with influential code setting bodies such as the National Fire Protection Association to improve existing codes and regulations.
Founded in: 1989

1886 **International Microwave Power Institute**
PO Box 1140
PO Box 1140
Mechanicsville, VA 23111-5007

804-559-6667; *Fax:* 804-559-4087
info@impi.org; www.impi.org
Social Media: Facebook, Twitter

Molly Poisant, Executive Director
Ben Wilson, Executive Committee
John Gerling, Executive Committee
Ric Gonzalez, Executive Committee
Bob Schiffman, Executive Committee

The International Microwave Power Institute (IMPI) was founded in 1966 in Canada to serve the information needs of specialists working with microwave and RF heating systems. In 1977, the Institute reorganized to expand its industrial and scientific base to meet the information needs evolving in consumer microwave ovens and related products.
Founded in: 1966

1887 **National Air Duct Cleaners Association**
1120 Route 73
Suite 200
Mt Laurel, NJ 08054

856-380-6810; *Fax:* 856-439-0525
info@nadca.com; www.nadca.com
Social Media: Facebook, Twitter, LinkedIn, YouTube

Michael Vinick, President
Richard Lantz,ASCS, 1st Vice President
Ric MacDonald,ASCS, 2nd Vice President
Mike Dwyer, CAE, Chief Relationship Officer
Jodi Araujo, Executive Director

NADCA: The HVAC Inspection, Maintenance and Restoration Association, otherwise known as the National Air Duct Cleaners Association (NADCA), was formed in 1989 as a non-profit association of companies engaged in the cleaning of HVAC systems. Its mission was to promote source removal as the only acceptable method of cleaning and to establish industry standards for the association.
1000 Members
Founded in: 1989

1888 **National Kitchen and Bath Association**
687 Willow Grove St
Hackettstown, NJ 07840-1731

908-850-1206
800-843-6522; *Fax:* 908-852-1695
feedback@nkba.org; www.nkba.org
Social Media: Facebook, Twitter, LinkedIn, Pinterest

John K. Morgan, President
Carolyn F. Cheetham, CMKBD, Vice President
Bill Darcy, Chief Executive Officer
Stephen Graziano, Senior Director of Finance
Nancy Barnes, Director of Learning

The NKBA enhances the success of its members in the kitchen and bath industry through networking, education, certification, marketing and business tools, leadership opportunities, and the annual Kitchen/Bath Industry Show.
40000 Members
Founded in: 1963

1889 **North American Retail Dealers Association**
222 South Riverside Plaza
Suite 2100
Chicago, IL 60606

312-648-0649
800-621-0298; *Fax:* 312-648-1212
nardasvc@narda.com; www.narda.com
Social Media: Facebook, LinkedIn

Leon Barbachano, Chairman
Timothy W. Seavey, First Vice Chairman
Otto Papasadero, Executive Director
Pam Clark, Administrative Assistant
Bob Goldberg, Legal Counsel

To enhance the ability of independent appliance retailers to build progressive, profitable businesses. NARDA members sell and serve kitchen and laundry appliances, consumer home and mobile electronics, computers and other home and small office products, furniture, sewing machines, vacuum cleaners, room air conditioners, and other consumer home products.
3000 Members
Founded in: 1943

1890 **Professional Service Association**
71 Columbia Street
Cohoes, NY 12047-2939

518-237-7777
888-777-8851; *Fax:* 518-237-0418
psaworld@aol.com; www.psaworld.com

Don Holman, President
Carmine D'Alessandro, Vice President
Linda Knudsen, Administrative Vice President
Randy Carney, Executive Director
Ralph Wolff, Director

PSA is an independent trade association dedicated to the highest standards of quality service. The purpose of PSA is to be the voice of the independent service provider and to assess and identify industry related problems and provide solutions. PSA is dedicated to providing educational training, certification, business management training, support and fairness to the independent service industry. PSA encourages professionalism and honesty identifies those techs who provide that kind of service.
Cost: $150.00
1105 Members
Frequency: Membership Fee
Founded in: 1989

1891 **Refrigeration Service Engineers Society**
1911 Rohlwig Road
Suite A
Rolling Meadows, IL 60008-1397

847-297-6464
800-297-5660; *Fax:* 847-297-5038
general@rses.org; www.rses.org
Social Media: Facebook, Twitter, LinkedIn, RSS Feeds, Pinterest, Tumblr,

Roger M. Hensley, CMS, E&E, Board Chairman
Harlan Krepcik, International President
Michael Thompson, International Vice President
Nick Reggi, CMS, RCT, International Secretary/Treasurer
Roger M. Hensley, CMS, RCT, International Sergeant at Arms

To provide opportunities for enhanced technical competence by offering comprehensive, cutting-edge education and certification to our members and the HVACR industry. To advance the professionalism and proficiency of our industry through alliances with other HVACR associations. To be the definitive industry leader in all segments of the HVACR industry by providing superior educational training.
15231 Members
Founded in: 1933

1892 **Silicon Valley Compucycle**
1096 Pecten Ct
Milpitas, CA 95035

408-432-1239
866-989-2970; *Fax:* 408-432-1249
svcinfo@svc.com; www.svc.com
Social Media: Facebook, Twitter

Vivienne Harwood Mattox, Executive Director
Yvonne Swartz, Executive Manager
Beth Strong, Marketing & Communications Manager

Association dedicated to promote technical excellence by providing a global forum to inform, educate, and engage the members, the technical community, and the public on all aspects of vacuum coating, surface engineering and related technologies.
Founded in: 2001

1893 **United Servicers Association**
3501 N. Southport Ave.
Suite 199
Chicago, IL 60657

800-683-2558; *Fax:* 855-290-5366
administration@unitedservicers.com;
www.unitedservicers.com
Social Media: Facebook, LinkedIn

James Dolbeare, President
Bob Dougherty, Vice President
Jennifer Webert, Secretary
Manny Ortega Jr., Treasurer
Paul MacDonald, Executive Director

Organization provides technical and service process training and education for appliance service professionals.

Newsletters

1894 **ACCA Insider**
Air Conditioning Contractors of America
2800 Shirlington Rd
Suite 300
Arlington, VA 22206-3607

703-575-4477
info@acca.org; www.acca.org
Social Media: Facebook, Twitter, LinkedIn, YouTube

Paul T Stalknecht, President & CEO

Each issue contains association and industry news, boiled down into a brief, easy to read format that will keep you up to date in just five minutes each Monday.
Frequency: Weekly

1895 **AVEM Newsletter**
Association of Vacuum Equipment Manufacturers International
201 Park Washington Court
Falls Church, VA 22046-4527

703-538-3543; *Fax:* 703-241-5603
aveminfo@avem.org; www.avem.org

Dennis S. Pellegrino, President

Association news, member company news and informational articles regarding government programs, standards, economics, international trade and other issues affecting business operations.
49 Members
Frequency: Quarterly
Founded in: 1969
Mailing list available for rent

1896 **Insights**
1791 Tullie Cir NE
Atlanta, GA 30329-2398

404-636-8400
800-527-4723; *Fax:* 404-321-5478

ashrae@ashrae.org; www.ashrae.org
Social Media: Facebook, Twitter

Lee Burgett, President
Jeff H Littleton, Executive VP

ASHRAE Insights is the Society's newsletter with articles of interest to members, including Chapter News, Obituaries, Membership Advancement and other news.
55000 Members
Frequency: 6x/Year
Founded in: 1894

1897 **SVC Bulletin**
Society of Vacuum Coaters
71 Pinon Hill Place NE
Albuquerque, NM 87122

505-856-7188; *Fax:* 505-856-6716;
www.svc.com
Social Media: Facebook, Twitter

Vivienne Harwood Mattox, Executive Director
Yvonne Swartz, Executive Manager
Beth Strong, Marketing & Communications Manager

The SVC bulletin is distributed to professionals working in the vacuum coating community and related sciences and technologies. Each issue contains contributed articles, previews, or reviews of the TechCon; SVC committee activities; technical articles from the Conference Proceedings; book reviews, Corporate Sponsor news and profiles; and Society news.
Frequency: 3x/Year
Circulation: 15000

1898 **The Buzz**
Air Conditioning Contractors of America
2800 Shirlington Rd
Suite 300
Arlington, VA 22206-3607

703-575-4477
info@acca.org; www.acca.org
Social Media: Facebook, Twitter, LinkedIn, YouTube

Paul Stalknecht, President & CEO

Roundup of latest news and interesting links for HVACR professionals.
Frequency: Weekly
Founded in: 1984

1899 **Your Business**
Air Conditioning Contractors of America
2800 Shirlington Rd
Suite 300
Arlington, VA 22206-3607

703-575-4477
info@acca.org; www.acca.org
Social Media: Facebook, Twitter, LinkedIn, YouTube

Paul Stalknecht, President & CEO

Contains management advice for small business owners.
Frequency: Bi-Weekly
Founded in: 1984

1900 **eSociety**
1791 Tullie Cir NE
Atlanta, GA 30329-2398
404-636-8400
800-527-4723; *Fax:* 404-321-5478
ashrae@ashrae.org; www.ashrae.org
Social Media: Facebook, Twitter

Lee Burgett, President
Jeff H Littleton, Executive VP

The official electronic newsletter of ASHRAE. Contains monthly news form the society about its activities and chapters.
55000 Members
Frequency: Monthly
Founded in: 1894

Magazines & Journals

1901 **ACCA Contractor Excellence**
Air Conditioning Contractors of America
2800 Shirlington Rd
Suite 300
Arlington, VA 22206-3607

703-575-4477
info@acca.org; www.acca.org
Social Media: Facebook, Twitter, LinkedIn, YouTube

Paul T Stalknecht, President & CEO

Representing the HVACR contracting industry. We help our members acquire and satisfy customers while upholding the most stringent requirements for professional ethics, and advocating for improvements to the industry overall.
Founded in: 1914

1902 **ACR Standard: Assessment, Cleaning & Restoration of HVAC Systems**
National Air Duct Cleaners Association
1518 K St NW
Suite 503
Washington, DC 20005-1203

202-737-2926; *Fax:* 202-347-8847
info@nadca.com; www.nadca.com

Ken Sufka, Owner

1903 **AHRI Trends Magazine**
Air Conditioning & Refrigeration Institute
2111 Wilson Boulevard
Suite 500
Arlington, VA 22201

703-524-8800; *Fax:* 703-562-1942
ahri@ahri.net; www.ahrinet.org
Social Media: Facebook, Twitter

Stephen Yurek, President & CEO

A resource for HVAC contractors and technicians.
300+ Members

1904 **ASHRAE Journal**
American Society of Heating, Refrigeration & AC
1791 Tullie Cir NE
Atlanta, GA 30329-2398
404-636-8400
800-527-4723; *Fax:* 404-321-5478
ashrae@ashrae.org; www.ashrae.org

Lee Burgett, President
Jeff H Littleton, Executive VP

Explores topical technical issues, such as: indoor air quality, energy management, thermal storage, alternative refrigerants, fire and life safety and more.
Cost: $59.00
Frequency: Monthly

1905 **ASME International Journal**
American Society of Mechanical Engineers
3 Park Ave
Floor 22
New York, NY 10016-5902
212-591-7000
800-843-2763; *Fax:* 212-591-8676
infocentral@asme.org; www.asme.org

David Walsh, Editor
Chitra Sethi, Managing Editor

Provides advanced scientific and technological information for the mechanical engineering industry to facilitate the international exchange and transfer of technology.
Cost: $375.00
Frequency: Monthly

1906 **Appliance**
Dana Chase Publications
1110 Jorie Boulevard
PO Box 90919
Oak Brook, IL 60522-9019

630-990-3484; *Fax:* 630-990-0078;
www.appliancemagazine.com

George Shurtleff, Production Manager
Maria Nigro, Circulation Director
Dana Chase Jr, Chairman

Devoted to serving the appliance industry worldwide, producers of consumer, commercial, business and medical appliances. Editorial material serves product engineering and design, production management and supervision, purchasing, management, marketing, sales and service. Accepts advertising.
Cost: $75.00
90 Pages
Frequency: Monthly
Circulation: 34500
ISSN: 0003-6781
Founded in: 1944

1907 **Appliance Design**
Business News Publishing
2401 W Big Beaver Rd
Suite 700
Troy, MI 48084-3333
248-362-3700
877-747-1625; *Fax:* 248-362-0317
info@asnews.com; www.bnpmedia.com
Social Media: Facebook, Twitter

Mitchell Henderson, CEO
Richard Babyak, Editor-in-Chief
Amy Alef, Production Manager
Mary Lowe, Associate Editor

Devoted to providing solutions for design and engineering teams in the global, commercial, and medical appliance/durable goods industry.
Circulation: 25,000
ISSN: 0003-6803
Founded in: 1955
Printed in 4 colors on glossy stock

1908 **Appliance Service News**
Gamit Enterprises
1917 S Street
PO Box 808
St Charles, IL 60174

630-845-9481
877-747-1625; *Fax:* 630-845-9483
info@asnews.com;
www.applianceservicenews.com

William Wingstedt, Editor/Publisher
Peggy Wingstedt, Sales Representative

Published for owners, managers and technicians of appliance repair dealers. Accepts advertising.
Cost: $59.95
36 Pages
Frequency: Monthly
Circulation: 33000
ISSN: 0003-6803
Founded in: 1950
Printed in 4 colors on glossy stock

1909 **Boiler Systems Engineering Magazine**
American Boiler Manufacturers Association
8221 Old Courthouse Rd
Suite 202
Vienna, VA 22182-3839

703-356-7172; *Fax:* 703-522-2665
randy@abma.com; www.abma.com
Social Media: Facebook, Twitter, LinkedIn

Randell Rawson, President
Diana McClung, Executive Assistant
Cheryl Jamall, Director Of Meetings
Frequency: Monthly
Founded in: 1888

1910 **Contractor Excellence**
Air Conditioning Contractors of America
2800 S Shirlington Rd
Suite 300
Arlington, VA 22206-3607

703-575-4477
info@acca.org; www.acca.org

Paul Stalknecht, President

A quality source of business information for the HVAC industry, available to members.
Frequency: Quarterly
Founded in: 2002

1911 **HPE Magazine**
American Boiler Manufacturers Association
8221 Old Courthouse Rd
Suite 202
Vienna, VA 22182-3839

703-356-7172; *Fax:* 703-522-2665
randy@abma.com; www.abma.com
Social Media: Facebook, Twitter, LinkedIn

Randell Rawson, President
Diana McClung, Executive Assistant
Cheryl Jamall, Director Of Meetings
Founded in: 1888

1912 **HVAC&R Research Journal**
American Society of Heating, Refrigeration & AC
1791 Tullie Circle NE
Atlanta, GA 30329-2398

404-636-8400
800-527-4723; *Fax:* 404-321-5478
ashrae@ashrae.org; www.ashrae.org

Tom Watson, President
Jeff H Littleton, Executive VP

Offers the most comprehensive reporting of archival research in the fields of environmental control for the built environment. Also covers cooling technolgies for a wide range of applications and related processes and concepts, including underlying thermodynamics, fluid dynamics, and heat transfer.
Frequency: Bi-Monthly
ISBN: 1-883413-98-2

1913 **Indoor Comfort News Magazine**
Institute of Heating and Air Conditioning
454 W Broadway
Glendale, CA 91204-1209

818-551-1555; *Fax:* 818-551-1115
ihaci@ihaci.org; www.ihaci.org

Susan Evans, Senior VP

A tool for attaining the trade association's goal of educating and promoting the HVAC/R/SM industry. Readers are top buyers and decision makers. They service and install new construction and replacement/retrofit projects.
Frequency: Monthly
Founded in: 1955

1914 **Journal of Microwave Power and Electromagnetic Energy**
International Microwave Power Institute
7076 Drinkard Way
P O Box 1140
Mechanicsville, VA 23111-5007

804-559-6667; *Fax:* 804-559-4087
info@impi.org; www.impi.org

Molly Poisant, Executive Director

Designed for the information needs of professionals specializing in the research and design of industrial and bio-medical applications, the Journal exemplifies the highest standards of scientific and technical information on the theory and application of electromagnetic power.
Cost: $250.00
Frequency: Quarterly

1915 **RSES Journal**
Refrigeration Service Engineers Society
1911 Rohlwing Road
Suite A
Rolling Meadows, IL 60008-1397

847-297-6464
800-297-5660; *Fax:* 847-297-5038
general@rses.org; www.rses.org
Social Media: Facebook, Twitter, LinkedIn

Mark Lowry, Executive Vice President
Lori A Kasallis, Editor

Providing quality technical content in digital and printed forms that can be applied on the job site.
Frequency: Monthly
Circulation: 15231

1916 **Today's Boiler**
American Boiler Manufacturers Association
8221 Old Courthouse Rd
Suite 202
Vienna, VA 22182-3839

703-356-7172; *Fax:* 703-522-2665;
www.abma.com

W Randy Rawson, President & CEO

Trends, Technologies & Innovations, The Official Magazine of the American Boiler Manufacturers Association.
Founded in: 1888

Trade Shows

1917 **ABMA Annual Meeting**
American Boiler Manufacturers Association
8221 Old Courthouse Road
Suite 207
Vienna, VA 22182-3839

703-356-7172; *Fax:* 703-356-4543;
www.abma.com

Jack Rentz, Chairman
W Randall Rawson, President/CEO
Kevin Hoey, Vice Chairman
Tom Giaier, Secretary

The association's premier membership networking event where members have the opportunity to learn about developments and trends inside and outside the industry, and have the opportunity, through committee and product/market group meetings to focus on issues and concerns of specific relevance to their product and market segments.
Frequency: Bi-Annual

1918 **ABMA Manufacturers Conference**
American Boiler Manufacturers Association
8221 Old Courthouse Road
Suite 207
Vienna, VA 22182-3839
703-356-7172; *Fax:* 703-356-4543;
www.abma.com

Jack Rentz, Chairman
W Randall Rawson, President/CEO
Kevin Hoey, Vice Chairman
Tom Giaier, Secretary

Designed to bring together manufacturing plant, office and others concerned with the design, fabrication, sales and distribution of ABMA products and services to network, discuss trends and developments, and problem solve with others in the industry and with outside experts.
Frequency: Annual/October

1919 **ACCA Conference & Indoor Air Expo**
Air Conditioning Contractors of America
2800 Shirlington Rd
Suite 300
Arlington, VA 22206

703-575-4477
info@acca.org; www.acca.org
Social Media: Facebook, Twitter, LinkedIn, YouTube

Paul Stalknecht, President & CEO
Rosemary Graeme, Executive Assistant
Kevin W. Holland, Senior Vice President

Workshops and learning opportunities for HVAC contractors.
Frequency: Annual/March

1920 **AHAM Annual Meeting**
Association of Home Appliance Manufacturers
1111 19th Street NW
Suite 402
Washington, DC 20036

202-872-5955; *Fax:* 202-872-9354
info@aham.org; www.aham.org

Edward V McAssey III, Chairman
Nick Baker, Manager
Alan M Holaday, Treasurer
Joseph M McGuire, President
Kevin Messner, Vice President

Provides ideas for the solution of problems and concerns of the Cross Functional Design.
Frequency: Annual/April

1921 **AHRI Annual Meeting**
Air-Conditioning, Heating & Refrigeration Inst
2111 Wilson Boulevard
Suite 500
Arlington, VA 22201

703-524-8800; *Fax:* 703-528-3816
ahri@ahrinet.org; www.ahrinet.org

Stephen Yurek, President & CEO
Stephanie Murphy, Chief Financial Officer
Amanda Donahue, Executive Assistant
Monica Snipes, Manager, Office Operations

The premiere networking experience of the heating, ventillation, air conditioning and commercial refrigeration manufacturing industry addresses the topics and issues you want most. Offers opportunities to learn about the top issues facing the industry, network with industry leaders and colleagues, and participate in product section business
300+ Members
480+ Attendees
Frequency: November

1922 **ASME International Mechanical Engineering Congress and Exposition**
American Society of Mechanical Engineers
Three Park Avenue
New York, NY 10016-5990
973-882-1170
800-843-2763
infocentral@asme.org; www.asme.org

Sam Y Zamrik PhD, President
David Walsh, Editor
Chitra Sethi, Managing Editor
John Kosowatz, Senior Editor

Hundreds of sessions, forums, exhibits, tours and social events keep you current on the latest trends in technology and industry, and provide the opportunity to trade tips and share ideas with engineers in different industries and companies around the world.
Frequency: Annual/Fall

1923 **Fall Tech Conference**
15000 Commerce Parkway
Suite C
Mt. Laurel, NJ 08054

856-380-6810; *Fax:* 856-439-0525
info@nadca.com; www.nadca.com

Kenneth M Sufka, Executive Vice President
Jodi Araujo, Executive Director
Leanne Murray, Director Membership

Jess Madden, Director Publications
Claire MacNab, Director Meetings

One-stop shop for training and certification. Designed to help members stand out from the competition. NADCA's trainers are highly experienced and know what it takes to be ultra successful in the HVAC cleaning industry.
1000 Members
Founded in: 1989

1924 **GAMA Annual Meeting**
Gas Appliance Manufacturers Association
2107 Wilson Boulevard
Suite 600
Arlington, VA 22201

703-525-7060; *Fax:* 703-525-6790;
www.gamanet.org

Stacy Heit, Manager of Meetings/Events

National trade association whose members manufacture space and water heating appliances, components and related products.
405 Attendees
Frequency: Annual
Founded in: 1935

1925 **HARDI Annual Fall Conference**
15000 Commerce Parkway
Suite C
Mt. Laurel, NJ 08054

856-380-6810; *Fax:* 856-439-0525
info@nadca.com; www.nadca.com

Kenneth M Sufka, Executive Vice President
Jodi Araujo, Executive Director
Leanne Murray, Director Membership
Jess Madden, Director Publications
Claire MacNab, Director Meetings

Conference offers information on profitability, confidence in navigating the economic waters, and finding the most effective and efficient means to achieve the market and profit objectives.
1000 Members
Founded in: 1989

1926 **IIAR**
1001 N. Fairfax Street
Suite 503
Alexandria, VA 22314

703-312-4200; *Fax:* 703-312-0065
iiar_request@iiar.org; www.iiar.org

David L. Rule, President

IIAR provides advocacy, education, and standards for the benefit of the global community in the safe and sustainable installation and operation of ammonia and other natural refrigerant systems.
2086 Members
Founded in: 1971

1927 **IMPI Annual Symposium**
International Microwave Power Institute
7076 Drinkard Way
P O Box 1140
Mechanicsville, VA 23111

804-596-6667; *Fax:* 804-559-4087
info@impi.org; www.impi.org

Molly Poisant, Executive Director
Neal Cooper, Treasurer

Brings together researchers from across the globe to share the latest findings related to non-communications uses of microwave energy.
Frequency: Annual/June

1928 **International Consumer Electronics Show (CES)**
Consumer Technology Association
1919 South Eads Street
Arlington, VA 22202

703-907-7600
866-858-1555; *Fax:* 703-907-7675
cta@cta.tech; www.cta.tech

Gary Shapiro, President & CEO
David Hagan, Chairman

World's largest consumer technology tradeshow.
Frequency: Annual

1929 **International Home & Housewares Show**
International Housewares Associaton
6400 Shafer Court
Suite 650
Rosemont, IL 60018

847-292-4200; *Fax:* 847-292-4211;
www.housewares.org

Mia Rampersad, VP, Trade Shows
Sharon Janota, Manager, Trade Show Operations
David Reeves, Manager, Information Technology
Dean Kurtis, Finance & Information Technology
Judy Colitz, Manager Special Events

International housewares marketplace, showcasing thousands of new products and designs.
18500 Attendees
Frequency: March

1930 **International Housewares Show**
1111 19th Street NW
Suite 402
Washington, DC 20036

202-872-5955; *Fax:* 202-872-9354
info@aham.org; www.aham.org

Paul Sikir, Chairman
Jennifer Mintman, First Vice Chairperson
Jennifer Mintman, Treasurer
Joseph M McGuire, President

The center of the IHA's yearly activities. One of the top 20 largest trade shows in the U.S. and in the top 10 in Chicago.
Founded in: 1915

1931 **Kitchen & Bath Industry Show**
1111 19th Street NW
Suite 402
Washington, DC 20036

202-872-5955; *Fax:* 202-872-9354
info@aham.org; www.aham.org

Paul Sikir, Chairman
Jennifer Mintman, First Vice Chairperson
Jennifer Mintman, Treasurer
Joseph M McGuire, President

The ultimate Kitchen & Bath destination. The freshest designs, products and technology from 500 leading manufacturers and suppliers. The brightest and best in the industry assemble to spot trends, see and experience product introductions, acquire knowledge and find the practical solutions and valuable connections.
Founded in: 1915

1932 **Kitchen/Bath Industry Show and Conference**
National Kitchen & Bath Association
687 Willow Grove Street
Hackettstown, NJ 07840

800-843-6522; *Fax:* 908-852-1695
feedback@nkba.org; www.nkba.org

Alan Zielinski, CEO& President
Timothy Captain, PR Manager
John A Petrie, Vice President
Carolyn Cheetham, Treasurer
Bill Darcy, CEO

Showcases the latest products and cutting-edge design ideas of the kitchen and bath industry.
40000 Attendees
Frequency: May

1933 **NADCA's Annual Meeting & Exposition**
15000 Commerce Parkway
Suite C
Mt. Laurel, NJ 08054

856-380-6810; *Fax:* 856-439-0525
info@nadca.com; www.nadca.com

Kenneth M Sufka, Executive Vice President
Jodi Araujo, Executive Director
Leanne Murray, Director Membership
Jess Madden, Director Publications
Claire MacNab, Director Meetings

Promises educational sessions, live equipment demonstrations, and opportunities to meet peers.
1000 Members
Founded in: 1989

1934 **NASA Convention & Trade Show**
National Appliance Service Association
3407 Williams Drive
PO Box 2514
Kokomo, IN 46904

765-453-1820; *Fax:* 765-453-1895
nasahq2011@gmail.com; www.nasa1.org

Scott Kopin, President
Gordon Daniels, VP/Treasurer
Carrie Giannakos, Executive Director
Mike Hanika, Director
Don Kehoe, Director

Classes on marketing, advertising, customer service, machine repair by experienced professionals in the industry. Attendees are informed about industry trends and products, and have the opportunity to take advantage of show specials offered by exhibitors.
Frequency: Annual

1935 **NCCA Annual Meeting**
National Coil Coaters Association
1300 Sumner Avenue
Cleveland, OH 44115

216-241-7333; *Fax:* 216-241-0105
ncca@coilcoating.org; www.coilcoating.org

Jeff Alexander, President
Jeff Widenor, Vice President
John Favilla, Treasurer
Frequency: April

1936 **National Appliance Parts Suppliers**
National Appliance Parts Suppliers Association
4015 W MARSHALL AVE
Longview, TX 75604

903- 75- 398
board11@napsaweb.org; www.napsaweb.org
Jim Bossman, President
Sherry Harrell, Secretary, Treasurer
Jason Cunningham, Secretary

For those in the appliance parts replacement business. Containing 62 booths and 60 exhibits.

1937 **RSES Annual Conference and HVAC Technology Expo**
Refrigeration Service Engineers Society
1911 Rohlwing Road
Suite A
Rolling Meadows, IL 60008-1397

847-297-6464
800-297-5660
general@rses.org; www.rses.org
Social Media: Facebook, Twitter, LinkedIn

Mark Lowry, Executive Vice President
Lori Kasallis, Publisher Editor
Jean Birch, Conference & Seminar Manager

80 booths consisting primarily of products and services.

1938 **SMACNA Annual Convention**
15000 Commerce Parkway
Suite C
Mt. Laurel, NJ 08054

856-380-6810; *Fax:* 856-439-0525
info@nadca.com; www.nadca.com

Kenneth M Sufka, Executive Vice President
Jodi Araujo, Executive Director
Leanne Murray, Director Membership
Jess Madden, Director Publications
Claire MacNab, Director Meetings

Business and skill tips for HVAC and Contractor professionals.
1000 Members
Founded in: 1989

1939 **The International Roundtable of Household Appliance Manufacturer Associations**
E-Mail: jnotini@aham.org; www.irhma.org

Jill A. Notini, VP, Communications & Marketing

Informal forum for discussion of issues facing global appliance manufacturer associations.
Founded in: 2014

1940 **VDTA/SDTA International Trade Show**
1111 19th Street NW
Suite 402
Washington, DC 20036

202-872-5955; *Fax:* 202-872-9354
info@aham.org; www.aham.org

Paul Sikir, Chairman
Jennifer Mintman, First Vice Chairperson
Jennifer Mintman, Treasurer
Joseph M McGuire, President

Featuring exhibits, and seminars for the vacuum and sewing business.
Founded in: 1915

1941 **World Educational Congress for Laundering and Drycleaning (Clean Show)**
Riddle & Associates
3098 Piedmont Road NE
Suite 350
Atlanta, GA 30305

404-876-1988; *Fax:* 404-876-5121
info@cleanshow.com; www.cleanshow.com
Social Media: Facebook, Twitter

John Riddle, Manager
Ann Howell, Communications

World's largest exposition for laundry, drycleaning and textile services industry featuring working equipment and educational program. Draws international attendance.
11000 Attendees
Frequency: Biennial, Odd Years
Founded in: 1977

Directories & Databases

1942 **A Portrait of the US Appliance Industry**
UBM Canon
11444 W. Olympic Blvd.
Los Angeles, CA 90064

310-445-4200; *Fax:* 310-445-4299
www.ubm.com; www.appliancemagazine.com

David J Chase, President
Susan Chase Korin, CEO

Appliance companies in the US.
Cost: $45.00
Frequency: Annual
Founded in: 1944

1943 **Complete Directory of Small Appliances**
Sutton Family Communications & Publishing Company
920 State Route 54 East
Elmitch, KY 42343

270-276-9500
jlsutton@apex.net

Theresa Sutton, Publisher
Lee Sutton, Editor

Print-out from database of wholesalers, manufacturers, distributors, importers and close-out houses. Database is updated daily to guarantee the most current and up-to-date sources available.
Cost: $55.20
100 Pages

1944 **Directory of Certified Performance (Online)**
Air Conditioning & Refrigeration Institute
Ste 500
2111 Wilson Blvd
Arlington, VA 22201-3036

703-524-8800; *Fax:* 703-528-3816
ari@ari.org; www.ari.org

Stephen R Yurek, President

The trusted source of performace certified heating, ventilation, air-conditioning, and commercial refrigeration equipment and components.

Industry Web Sites

1945 **http://gold.greyhouse.com**
G.O.L.D Grey House OnLine Databases
Grey House Publishing's online database platform, GOLD, offers Quick Search, Keyword Search and Expert Search for most business sectors including appliances and small electroincs. The GOLD platform makes finding the information you need quick and easy. All of Grey House's directory products are available for subscription on the GOLD platform.

1946 **www.abma.com**
American Boiler Manufacturers Association
Represents companies involved in utility, industrial and commercial steam generation.

1947 **www.acca.org**
Air Conditioning Contractors of America
Representing the HVACR contracting industry. We help our members acquire and satisfy customers while upholding the most stringent requirements for professional ethics, and advocating for improvements to the industry overall.

1948 **www.aga.org**
American Gas Association
Represents local energy utility companies that deliver natural gas to more than 56 million homes, businesses and industries throughout the United States.

1949 **www.aham.org**
Association of Home Appliance Manufacturers
Statistical information and summaries on appliances.

1950 **www.apda.com**
Appliance Parts Distributors Association
Promotes the sale of appliance parts through independent distributors.

1951 **www.appliancemagazine.com**
Dana Chase Publications
Appliance industry information content focused into 20 industry zones for targeted editorial coverage.

1952 **www.ari.org**
Air Conditioning & Refrigeration Institute
Representing manufacturers of central air-conditioning and commercial refrigeration equipment.

1953 **www.ashrae.org**
American Society of Heating, Refrigeration & A/C
Serving the heating, ventilation, air conditioning and refrigeration industries.

1954 **www.asme.org**
American Society of Mechanical Engineers
Focuses on technical, educational and research issues of the engineering and technology community.

1955 **www.bema.org**
Bakery Equipment Manufacturers Association
Serves the baking and snack food industries.

1956 **www.gamanet.org**
Gas Appliance Manufacturers Association
Serves the residential, commercial and industrial gas and oil fired appliance industries.

1957 **www.ge.com**
General Electric
Information on home appliances, lighting, home solutions, corporate trends and customer service.

1958 **www.greyhouse.com**
Grey House Publishing
Authoritative reference directories for most business sectors including appliances and small electronics markets. Users can search the online databases with varied search criteria allowing for custom searches by product category, geographic area, sales volume, keyword, subject and more. Full Grey House catalog and online ordering also available.

1959 **www.housewares.org**
International Housewares Association
Provides information on the international home & housewares industry, with search tools, consumer purchase trend data, and access to global opportunities and discount business services.

1960 **www.ihea.org**
Industrial Heating Equipment Association
A voluntary national trade association representing the major segments of the industrial heat processing equipment industry.

1961 **www.impi.org**
International Microwave Power Institute
A forum for the exchange of information on all aspects of microwave and RF heating technologies.

1962 **www.napsaweb.org**
National Appliance Parts Suppliers Association
Provides distributors of replacement parts for major home appliances with information and services.

1963 **www.narda.com**
North American Retail Dealers Association
Serves the independent retailer industry.

1964 **www.nasa1.org**
National Appliance Service Association
Promotes interests of portable and commercial appliance service repair and sales to industry owners.

1965 **www.nkba.com**
National Kitchen & Bath Association
Protects the interests of members by fostering a better business climate, awarding certification, and conducting training and seminars.

1966 **www.psaworld.com**
Professional Service Association
Information for companies that service and repair electronics and appliances.

1967 **www.repairclinic.com**
RepairClinic
Installation tips and how-to information on all appliances.

1968 **www.reta.com**
Refrigerating Engineers & Technicians Association
Seeks to upgrade the skills and knowledge of experienced members. Offers home-study courses on refrigeration and air conditioning.

1969 **www.rses.org**
Refrigeration Service Engineers Society
The world's leading education, training and certification association for heating, ventilation, air conditioning and refrigeration professionals.

1970 **www.supco.com**
Sealed Unit Parts
Serves the precision electronic test and service instruments, and refrigeration & air conditioning components industries; dedicated to producing high quality, innovative products at affordable prices to a wide range of customers.

Associations

1971 **American Architectural Foundation**
740 15th Street NW
Suite 225
Washington, DC 20005

202-787-1001; *Fax:* 202-787-1002
info@archfoundation.org;
www.archfoundation.org
Social Media: Facebook, Twitter, RSS

G. Sandy Diehl, III, Chair
Ron Bogle, Hon. AIA, President & CEO
John Syvertsen, Vice Chair & Secretary
James R. Tolbert, III, Treasurer

The American Architectural Foundation (AAF) is dedicated to the vibrant social, economic, and environmental future of cities. In the past decade alone, AAF has worked directly with local leaders through more than 500 city engagements. During this time, AAF has served every major metropolitan region and most second-tier cities in the United States.

1972 **American Architectural Manufacturers Association**
1827 Walden Office Square
Suite 550
Schaumburg, IL 60173-4268

847-303-5664; *Fax:* 847-303-5774
customerservice@aamanet.org;
www.aamanet.org
Social Media: Facebook, Twitter, LinkedIn, YouTube, Flickr, RSS

Rich Walker, President and CEO
Dean Lewis, Technical Information Manager
Maureen Knight, Government Affairs
Jannine Klemencic, Executive Assistant
Melissa McCord, Staff Accountant

Advocate for manufacturers and professionals in the fenestration industry with respect to product certification, standards development, education and training, legislative regulations, and building and energy codes.

1973 **American College of Healthcare Architects**
18000 W.105th St.
Olathe, KS 66061-7543

913-895-4604; *Fax:* 913-895-4652;
www.healtharchitects.org
Social Media: Twitter, YouTube

Anthony J. Haas, President
Mark A. Nichols, President-Elect
John W. Rogers, Secretary/Treasurer
Vince G. Avallone, Regent
Ellen Belknap, Regent

Provides certificate holders with networking, educational, and marketplace opportunities and distinguishes healthcare architects through certification, experience, and rigorous standards.

1974 **American Design Drafting Association & American Digital Design Association**
105 East Main Street
Newbern, TN 38059-1526

731-627-0802; *Fax:* 731-627-9321;
www.adda.org
Social Media: Facebook, Twitter, LinkedIn, Google+

Rick Frymyer, Chairman of the Board
Richard Button, Governor - CFO
Danny G. Lewis, Governor
Bruce Nielsen, Governor
H. Duane Moore, Governor

The American Design Drafting Association was conceived by a dedicated and enthusiastic group of oil and gas piping drafters who were involved in various phases of design drafting. This group consisted of highly specialized industry drafters, educational instructors, piping designers, and engineering personnel.
1000+ Members
Founded in: 1948

1975 **American Institute of Architects (AIA)**
1735 New York Ave Nw
Washington, DC 20006-5292

202-626-7300
800-242-3837; *Fax:* 202-626-7547
infocentral@aia.org; www.aia.org
Social Media: Facebook, Twitter, LinkedIn, Youtube, RSS Feeds, Instagram,

Christine McEntee, Executive Vice President

Based in Washington, D.C., the AIA is the leading professional membership association for licensed architects, emerging professionals, and allied partners.
83000 Members
Founded in: 1857

1976 **American Institute of Architects (AIAA)**
1735 New York Ave Nw
Washington, DC 20006-5292

202-626-7300
800-242-3837; *Fax:* 202-626-7547
infocentral@aia.org; www.aia.org
Social Media: Facebook, Twitter, LinkedIn, YouTube, RSS, Instagram, Flick

Christine McEntee, Executive Vice President
83000 Members
Founded in: 1857

1977 **American Institute of Architecture Students**
1735 New York Ave, NW
Suite 300
Washington, DC 20006-5209

202-808-0075; *Fax:* 202-626-7414
mailbox@aias.org; www.aias.org
Social Media: Facebook, Twitter, Instagram, YouTube

Charlie Klecha, President
Obi Okolo, Vice President
Nick Serfass, AIA, CAE, Executive Director

An independent, non-profit, student-run organization dedicated to providing unmatched programs, information, and resources on issues critical to architectural education.
Founded in: 1956

1978 **American Planning Association**
205 N. Michigan Ave.
Suite 1200
Chicago, IL 60601

312-431-9100; *Fax:* 312-786-6700
customerservice@planning.org;
www.planning.org
Social Media: Facebook, Twitter, LinkedIn, YouTube, Flickr, RSS, Google+

William Anderson, President
Carol Rhea, President Elect
Lee Brown, Director
James Drinan, Executive Director
Ann Simms, Chief Operating Officer

An independent, nonprofit educational organization that provides leadership in the development of vital communities.
Founded in: 1978

1979 **American Society for Aesthetics**
1550 Larimer Street
Suite 644
Denver, CO 80202-1602

562-331-4424
asa@aesthetics-online.org;
www.aesthetics-online.org
Social Media: Facebook, Twitter

Cynthia Freeland, President
Kathleen M. Higgins, Vice President

The American Society for Aesthetics promotes study, research, discussion, and publication in aesthetics. Aesthetics, in this connection, is understood to include all studies of the arts and related types of experience from a philosophic, scientific, or other theoretical standpoint, including those of psychology, sociology, anthropology, cultural history, art criticism, and education. The arts include the visual arts, literature, music, and theater arts.
Founded in: 1942

1980 **American Society for Healthcare Engineering**
155 N. Wacker Drive
Suite 400.
Chicago, IL 60606

312-422-3800; *Fax:* 312-422-4571
ashe@aha.org; www.ashe.org
Social Media: Facebook, Twitter, YouTube

Philip C. Stephens, President
David A. Dagenais, President Elect
Dale Woodin, Senior Executive Director
Patrick J. Andrus, Deputy Executive Director
Susan B. McLaughli, Associate Member Director

One of the largest associations devoted to optimizing the health care built environment and is a personal membership organization of the American Hospital Association.

1981 **American Society of Architectural Illustrators**
294 Merrill Hill Road
Hebron, ME 4238

207-966-2062
HQ@asai.org; www.asai.org
Social Media: Facebook

Jon Soules, President
Carlos Cristerna, Vice President
W. Daniel Church, Secretary
Columbus Cook, Treasurer
Tina Bryant, Executive Director

An international, nonprofit organization dedicated to the advancement and recognition of the art, science, and profession of architectural illustration. Through communication, education, and advocacy, this society strives to redefine and emphasize the role of illustration in the practice and appreciation of architecture.
Founded in: 1986

1982 **American Society of Concrete Contractors**
2025 S. Brentwood Blvd.
Suite 105
St. Louis, MO 63144

314-962-0210
866-788-2722; *Fax:* 314-968-4367
questions@ascconline.org;
www.ascconline.org
Social Media: Facebook, LinkedIn, Pinterest

Mike Poppoff, President
Scott M. Anderson, First Vice President
Rocky R. Geans, Vice President
Beverly Garnant, Executive Director
Bruce Suprenant, Technical Director

Provides knowledge on technical production and distribution of concrete construction, educates the industry on constructability, develops business savvy members, and helps them deliver a high quality product.
500 Members

1983 **American Society of Golf Course Architects**
125 N. Executive Drive
Suite 302
Brookfield, WI 53005

262-786-5960; *Fax:* 262-786-5919;
www.asgca.org
Social Media: Facebook, Twitter, LinkedIn, Instagram

Lee Schmidt, President
Steve Smyers, Vice President
Greg Martin, Treasurer
John Sanford, Secretary
Chad Ritterbusch, Executive Director

The leader in advancing the interests of golf course architects andthe profession of golf course architecture for the benefit of ASGCA members and their clients, the golf industry, and the game of golf.
Founded in: 1946

1984 **American Society of Landscape Architects**
636 Eye St NW
Washington, DC 20001-3736

202-898-2444
888-999-2752; *Fax:* 202-898-1185
info@asla.org; www.asla.org
Social Media: Facebook, Twitter, LinkedIn, RSS Feeds, Pinterest, Instagra

K. Richard Zweifel, FASLA, President
Jeffery A. Townsend, ALSA, VP Finance
Hunter L. Beckham, FALSA, VP Professional Practice
Keith P. Wilson, ASLA, VP Membership
Pamela J. Linn, ALSA, VP Communication

Residential and commercial real estate developers, federal and state agencies, city planning commissions and individual property owners are all among the thousands of people and organizations in America and Canada that will retain the services of a landscape architect this year.
15000 Members
Founded in: 1899

1985 **Applied Technology Council**
201 Redwood Shores Parkway
Suite 240
Redwood City, CA 94065

650-595-1542; *Fax:* 650-593-2320;
www.atcouncil.org

James A. Amundson, President
Victoria Arbitrio, Vice President
William Staehlin, Secretary/Treasurer
Roberto Leon, Past President
Chris Rojahn, Executive Director

A nonprofit, tax-exempt corporation that develops and promotes state-of-the-art, user-friendly engineering resources and applications for use in mitigating the effects of natural and other hazards on the built enviroment. ATC also identifies and encourages needed research and develops consensus opinions onstructural engineering issues in a nonproprietary format.

1986 **Architectural League**
594 Broadway
Suite 607
New York, NY 10012

212-753-1722; *Fax:* 212-486-9173
info@archleague.org; www.archleague.org
Social Media: Facebook, Twitter, YouTube, Instagram, Vimeo

Annabelle Selldorf, President
Paul Lewis, Vice President
Leo Villareal, Vice President
Michael Bierut, Vice President
Kate Orff, Vice President
Founded in: 1881

1987 **Architectural Precast Association**
325 John Knox Rd
Ste L103
Tallahassee, FL 32303

850-205-5637; *Fax:* 850-222-3019
info@archprecast.org; www.archprecast.org

Paul Rossi, President
Chris Cox, Vice President
Fred L. McGee, Executive Director
Cari Renfro, Project Manager & Event Planner
Chris Leonhardt, Associate Director

A national trade association organized to advance the interests of architectural precast in North America.
Founded in: 1966

1988 **Architectural Research Centers Consortium**

www.arcc-arch.org
Social Media: Facebook, Twitter, LinkedIn, Google+

Hazem Rashed Ali, President
Chris Jarrett, Vice President
Saif Haq, Treasurer
Leonard Bachman, Secretary

An international association of architectural research centers committed to the expansion of the research culture and a supporting infrastructure in architecture and related design disciplines.
Founded in: 1976

1989 **Association for Computer Aided Design in Architecture**

E-Mail: membership@acadia.org
acadia.org

Michael Fox, President
Aron Temkin, Vice President
Greg Luhan, Secretary
Michael Christenson, Treasurer
Wei Yan, Membership

An international network of digital design researchers and professionals that facilitate critical investigations into the role of computation in architecture, planning, and building science, encouraging innovation in design creativity, sustainability, and education.

1990 **Association for Environment Conscious Building**
PO Box 32
Llandysul, SA

845-456-9773; www.aecb.net
Social Media: Facebook, Twitter

Keith & Sally Hall, Founder
Chris Baines, Honorary President
Andy Simmonds, Chief Executive Officer
Sally Hall, Finance and Administration Officer
Gill Rivers, Business Operations Manager

A network of individuals, students, educational establishments, andcompanies with a common aim of promoting sustainable building. It brings together builders, architects, designers, manufacturers, housing associations, and local authorities to develop, share, and promote best practice in environmentally sustainable building.
Founded in: 1989

1991 **Association for Preservation Technology International**
3085 Stevenson Drive
Suite 200
Springfield, IL 62703

217-529-9039; *Fax:* 888-723-4242
info@apti.org; www.apti.org
Social Media: Facebook, LinkedIn

Gretchen Pfaehler, President
John Diodati, Vice President, Co-chair Conference
Michael Schuller, Vice-President, Co-chair Training
Nathela Chatara, CAEAdministrative Director
Lesley Gilmore, Treasurer

The Association for Preservation Technology (APT) is a cross-disciplinary, membership organization dedicated to promoting the best technology for conserving historic structures and their settings.
Founded in: 1968

1992 **Association for Women in Architecture + Design**
1315 Storm Pkwy.
Torrance, CA 90501

310-534-8466; *Fax:* 310-257-1942
awaplusd.org
Social Media: Facebook, Twitter, LinkedIn, Instagram, Pinterest

Kishani De Silva, President
Christina Monti, Vice President
Anna Harris, Parliamentarian
Linda Daley, Chief Financial Officer
Terri Moore, Secretary

Organization dedicated to the professional development of women working in the fields of architecture and design.
Founded in: 1915

1993 **Association of Architecture Organizations**
224 South Michigan Avenue
Suite 116
Chicago, IL 60604

312-561-2159; *Fax:* 312-922-2607;
www.aaonetwork.org
Social Media: Facebook, Twitter, RSS

Lynn Osmond, Hon. AIA, President & CEO
Margie O'Driscoll, Hon. AIACC, Vice Chair
Nate Eudaly, Treasurer
Linda Sylvan, Secretary
Michael Wood, Executive Director

A member-based network that connects organizations around the worlddedicated to enhancing public dialogue about architecture and design.
Founded in: 2005

1994 **Association of Collegiate Schools of Architecture**
1735 New York Ave NW
3rd Floor
Washington, DC 20006-5209

202-785-2324; *Fax:* 202-628-0448
info@acsa-arch.org; www.acsa-arch.org
Social Media: Facebook, Twitter, LinkedIn, Vimeo

Norman R. Millar, President
Hsin-Ming Fung, Vice President/President-Elect
Michael J Monti, PhD, Executive Director
Eric Wayne Ellis, Director of Operations and Programs
Pascale J. Vonier, Director of Communications

Nonprofit membership association founded to advance the quality of architectural education.
500 Members
Founded in: 1912

1995 **Association of Licensed Architects**
One East Northwest Hwy.
Suite 200
Palatine, IL 60067

847-382-0630; *Fax:* 847-382-8380
ala@alatoday.org; www.alatoday.org
Social Media: Facebook, Twitter, LinkedIn

Jeffrey Budgell, President
James K. Zahn, Esq, Vice President
Patrick C. Harris, Treasurer
Mark V. Spann, Secretary
Joanne Sullivan, Executive Director

An organization open to all architects and professions related to architecture and it represents architects registered or licensed in any state, territory, or possession of the United States or foreign country.

1996 Association of Professional Landscape Designers
2207 Forest Hills Drive
Harrisburg, PA 17112

717-238-9780; *Fax:* 717-238-9985; www.apld.com
Social Media: Facebook, Twitter, LinkedIn, Pinterest

Denise Calabrese, Executive Director
Lisa M. (Frye) Ruggiers, Associate Executive Director
Angela Burkett, Membership Director
Michelle Keyser, Director of Communications
Jennifer Swartz, Bookkeeper

An international organization dedicated to advancing the professionof landscape design and promoting the recognition of landscape designers as qualified and dedicated professionals.
Founded in: 1986

1997 Association of University Architects
17595 S Tamiami Trail
Fort Myers, FL 33908-4570

Fax: 239-590-1010
information@auaweb.net; www.auaweb.net

Evie Asken, Director Campus Planning
Steven Thweatt, President

Purpose is to achieve more effective planning in the field of higher education, improve the design and construction standards of university buildings and to develop common bonds and establish standards which will ensure clarity of communications and render effective the exchange of information.
Founded in: 1955

1998 Business Architecture Guild

E-Mail: info@businessarchitectureguild.org; www.businessarchitectureguild.org
Bob Carlston, Director of Business Management
William Ulrich, President
Mike Rosen, Vice President
Kathy Ulrich, Executive Director

A professional association that offers exclusive content to its members. Additional benefits include a private online community, opportunities to provide feedback and collaborate with them on content, a knowledge repository, newsletters, webinars, and more.

1999 Cast Stone Institute
813 Chestnut Street
PO Box 68
Lebanon, PA 17042-7218

717-272-3744; *Fax:* 717-272-5147
staff@caststone.org; www.caststone.org

Jesse Hawthorne, President
Scott Mathews, Vice President
Jan Boyer, Executive Director
Tim Michael, Director
David Owen, Director

An organization of cast stone manufacturers, associates, professional architects, engineers and concrete technologists formed for the purpose of improving the quality of cast stone and disseminating information regarding its use.
70 Members
Founded in: 1927

2000 Center for Environmental Design Research
University of California at Berkeley
390 Wurster Hall
Suite 1839
Berkeley, CA 94720-1839

510-642-2896; *Fax:* 510-643-5571
earens@berkeley.edu; www.cedr.berkeley.edu
Social Media: Facebook, Twitter, LinkedIn, Flickr, Youtube

Tom J. Buresh, M.Arch., Chair, Department of Architecture
Paul Waddell, M.S., Ph.D, Chair, Department of City
G. Mathias Kondolf, M.S., Ph.D., Chair, Department of Landscaping
Jennifer Wolch, Ph.D., Dean
Gary Brown, M.Arch, Associate Dean for Faculty Affairs

Mission is to foster research in environmental planning and design

2001 Construction Sciences Research Foundation, Inc.
www.csrf.org

Raymond K. Best, President
Kurt T. Preston, VP Finance and Administration
Michael D. Dell'Isola, Vice President
Charles Chief Boyd, Secretary/Treasurer
Julie K Brown, Director

An independent, nonprofit construction industry research organization dedicated to unifying and integrating communication between programs and design/communications processes used in facilities design and construction.

2002 Council on Tall Buildings and Urban Habitat
SR Crown Hall, Illinois Institute of Technology
3360 S State Street
Chicago, IL 60616-3796

312-567-3487; *Fax:* 312-567-3820
info@ctbuh.org; www.ctbuh.org
Social Media: Facebook, Twitter, YouTube

David Malott, Chairman
Antony Wood, Executive Director
Patti Thurmond, Operations
Carissa Devereux, Membership
Steven Henry, Design & Production

Supported by architecture, engineering, planning development and construction professionals, designed to facilitate exchanges among those involved in all aspects of the planning, design, construction and operation of tall buildings.
Founded in: 1969

2003 Environmental Design Research Association
7918 Jones Branch Drive
Suite 300
McLean, VA 22102

703-506-2895; *Fax:* 703-506-3266
headquarters@edra.org; www.edra.org
Social Media: Facebook, Twitter, LinkedIn, YouTube, Flickr, Instagram

Gowri Betrabet Gulwadi, Chair
Lynne Manzo, Chair Elect
Paula Horrigan, Secretary
Shanuna Mallery-Hill, Treasurer
Kate O Donnell, Executive Director

An organization dedicated to advancing and distributing environmental design research, thereby improving understanding of the interrelationships between people, their built and natural surroundings. EDRA's goal is also to facilitate the creation of environments that are responsive to human needs.
Founded in: 1968

2004 Green Building Alliance
33 Terminal Way
Suite 331
Pittsburgh, PA 15219

412-431-0709
info@gbapgh.org; www.go-gba.org
Social Media: Facebook, Twitter, LinkedIn, YouTube

Michael Kuhn, President
Christine Mondor, Vice President
Mike Schiller, CEO
Kevin Clarke, Secretary
Mark Smith, Treasurer

An organization that promotes healthy, high performing places for everyone by inspiring and leading the market, demonstrating and proving value, and equipping the community with knowledge and resources.
1200 Members
Founded in: 1993

2005 Historic New England
Soc for Preservation of New England Antiquities
141 Cambridge St
Boston, MA 02114-2702

617-227-3956; *Fax:* 617-227-9204; www.historicnewengland.org
Social Media: Facebook, Twitter, YouTube, Tumblr, Zazzle

Carl R. Nold, President/CEO
Diane Viera, Executive Vice President/COO
Kimberlea Tracey, Vice President for Advancement
Wendy Gus, Director of Finance
Benjamin Haavik, Team Leader for Property Care

Focuses on buildings, landscapes and objects reflecting New England life from the 17th century to the present. Also publishes a magazine about the organizations objects, architectural holdings and activities.
6000 Members
Founded in: 1910

2006 Institute for Urban Design
17 West 17th Street, 7th Floor
New York, NY 10014-3731

212-366-0780; *Fax:* 212-633-0125
info@ifud.org; www.ifud.org
Social Media: Facebook, Twitter, LinkedIn, RSS Feeds, vimeo

Anne Guiney, Executive Director
Alexandra Sutherland-Brown, Program Coordinator

Responsible for city planning.
1M Members
Founded in: 1979

2007 Insulated Cable Engineers Association
P.O. Box 2694
Alpharetta, GA 30023

www.icea.net

R.O. Bristol, President
Rick Williamson, 1st VP
Kim Nuckles, 2nd VP

A professional organization dedicated to developing cable standardsfor the electric power, control, and telecommunications industries.
Founded in: 1925

2008 Interior Design Educators Council
One Parkview Plaza
Suite 800
Oakbrook Terrace, IL 60181

630-544-5057
info@idec.org; www.idec.org

Social Media: Facebook, Twitter, LinkedIn, YouTube, Flickr, Yahoo, Google

Cynthia Mohr, President
Katherine Ankerson, Past President
Migette Kaup, President Elect
Cindy Martimo, Secretary/Treasurer
Jill Pable, Director

An organization dedicated to the advancement of interior design education, scholarship, and service.
Founded in: 1972

2009 **International Association for Impact Assessment**
1330 23rd Street S
Suite C
Fargo, ND 58103-3705

701-297-7908; *Fax:* 701-297-7917
info@iaia.org; www.iaia.org
Social Media: Facebook, Twitter, YouTube

Rita Hamm, CEO
Jennifer Howell, Publications/Meetings Specialist
Bridget John, Marketing/Financial Specialist
Shelli LaPlante, Member Liaison/Conference Registrar
Loreley Fortuny, Special Project Associate

A forum for advancing innovation, development, and communication of best practice in impact assessment. Exists to improve and better inform the decision-making of today that has environmental consequences for tomorrow.
2500 Members
Founded in: 1980

2010 **International Association of Innovation Professionals**
4422 Castle Wood Street
Suite 200
Sugar Land, TX 77479

925-858-0905
800-276-1180; www.iaoip.org
Social Media: Facebook, Twitter, LinkedIn, Instagram, Vimeo

Brett Trusko, President/ CEO
Lewis Archer, Webmaster
Charisma Aggarwal, Development Manager
Dana J. Landry, VP Certification Programs
Marco D. Mancin, Director

Creates events and provides resources to help professionals learn the latest innovation methodologies, and offer certification testing to help themadvance in their careers.
800 Members

2011 **International Code Council**
500 New Jersey Avenue, NW
6th Floor
Washington, DC 20001

708-799-4981
888-422-7233; *Fax:* 708-799-4981
members@iccsafe.org; www.iccsafe.org
Social Media: Facebook, Twitter, LinkedIn, Youtube

C.P. Ramani, President
Pat Nathan, Vice President
Mark Johnson, Executive VP and Director, Business
Hamid Naderi, Sr. VP, Product Development
Laurence Genest, VP, Sales Marketing

A nonprofit membership association dedicated to preserving the public health, safety and welfare in the built environment through the promulgation of model codes suitable for adoption by governmental entities and assisting code enforcement officials, design professionals, builders, manufacturers and others involved in the design, construction and regulatory processes.
16000 Members
Founded in: 1915

2012 **International Interior Design Association**
222 Mechandise Mart
Suite 567
Chicago, IL 60654

312-467-1950
888-799-4432
312-467-1950
iidahq@iida.org; www.iida.org
Social Media: Facebook, Twitter, LinkedIn, YouTube, Instagram

Julio Braga, President
Scott Hierlinger, President Elect
Viveca Bissonnette, Vice President
Dennis Krause, Senior Vice President
Cheryl Dust, Executive Vice President

Association that provides its members with sources, knowledge, and contacts necessary in the interior design field.

2013 **Marine Engineers' Beneficial Association**
444 N. Capitol Street, NW
Suite 800
Washington, DC 20001

202-638-5355; *Fax:* 202-638-5369;
www.mebaunion.org
Social Media: Facebook, Twitter, YouTube

Marshall Ainley, President
Bill Van Loo, Secretary/ Treasurer
Mark Gallagher, Contracts Rep
Eric C. Pittman, Comptroller

The oldest maritime trade union that represents licensed mariners, deck and engine officers and has a training plan to provide further technical training. It has worked hard in Washington, DC to ensure proper examination and licensing of engineers and the abolition of controversial license fees.
Founded in: 1875

2014 **Marine Technology Society**
1100 H St., NW
Suite LL-100
Washington, DC 20005

202-717-8705; *Fax:* 202-347-4302
membership@mtsociety.org;
www.mtsociety.org

Drew Michel, President
Jerry Boatman, Immediate Past President
Ray Toll, Vice President
Richard lawson, Executive Director
Chris Barett, Director

A growing organization with a membership that includes businesses, institutions, individual professionals, and students who are ocean engineers, technologists, policy makers, and educators. This group works to promote awareness, understanding, advancement, and the application of marine technology.
Founded in: 1963

2015 **National Academy of Environmental Design**

E-Mail: info@naedonline.org;
www.naedonline.org

Daniel Friedman, President
Thomas R. Fisher, Vice President
Frederick Steiner, Immediate Past President
James F. Palmer, Secretary
Claudia Phillips, Treasurer

A nonprofit organization that provides the public with expertise and leadership in the creation of healthier, greener, safer, and more resilient American communitites through environmental design.

2016 **National Architectural Accrediting Board**
1101 Connecticut Avn., NW
Suite 410
Washington, DC 20036

202-783-2007; *Fax:* 202-783-2822
info@naab.org; www.naab.org
Social Media: Facebook, Twitter

Shannon B. Kraus, President
Scott Veazey, President Elect
Patricia Kucker, Treasurer
Brian R. Kelly, Secretary
Andrea S. Rutledge, Executive Director

Develops and maintains a system of accreditation in professional architecture education that is responsive to the needs of society and allows institutions with varying resources and circumstances to evolve according to their individual needs.

2017 **National Association of Home Builders**
1201 15th Street NW
Washington, DC 20005

202-266-8200
800-368-5242; *Fax:* 202-266-8400;
www.nahb.org
Social Media: Facebook, Twitter, LinkedIn, Google+, Pinterest

Kevin Kelly, Chairman
Tom Woods, Chairman-Elect
Ed Brady, Second Vice Chairman
Granger MacDonald, Third Vice Chairman
Gerald M. Howard, Chief Executive Officer

A trade association that helps promote the policies that make housing a national priority.
Founded in: 1940

2018 **National Council of Architectural Registration Boards**
1801 K St NW
Suite 700k
Washington, DC 20006-1320

202-783-6500; *Fax:* 202-783-0290;
www.ncarb.org
Social Media: Facebook, Twitter, LinkedIn, YouTube

Blakely C. Dunn, Vice President
Michael Armstrong, CEO

Committed to protecting the health, safety, and welfare of the public through effective regualtion and exemplary service.
Founded in: 1919

2019 **National Organization of Minority Architects**
1735 New York Avenue
NW #357
Washington, DC 20006

202-586-6682
president@noma.net; www.noma.net
Social Media: Facebook, Twitter, LinkedIn

Kathy Dixon, President
Kevin M. Holland, President Elect
Aminah Wright, Secretary
Walter Wilson, Treasurer
Gianna Pigford, Recording Secretary

A national organization that strives to minimize the effects of racism in the architecture profession and also battles against apathy, bigotry, and abuse of the natural environment.

2020 **Organization of Women Architects and Designers**
PO Box 10078
Berkeley, CA 94709

www.owa-usa.org
Social Media: Facebook

Janet Crane, President
Mui Ho, Secretary
Bill Hocker, Webmaster
Anne Jakiemiec, Health Plan Consultant
Judy L. Rowe, FAIA, Treasurer

A nonprofit organization that is an active support network for women involved in architecture, engineering, planning, landscape architecture, interior and graphic design, and related environmental design fields.
Founded in: 1970

2021 **Partners for Livable Communities**
1429 21st St Nw
Washington, DC 20036-5902

202-887-5990; *Fax:* 202-466-4845
livability@livable.org; www.livable.org
Social Media: RSS

Robert H. McNulty, President
Penny Cuff, Vice President of Programs
Irene Garnett, Vice President of Finance
Faith Koleszar, Executive Assistant
Arianna Koudounas, Program Officer

A non-profit leadership organization working to improve the livability of communities by promoting quality of life, economic development, and social equity.
Founded in: 1977

2022 **Society for Environmental Graphic Design**
1900 L Street NW
Suite 710
Washington, DC 20036

202-638-5555; *Fax:* 202-478-2286
segd@segd.org; www.segd.org
Social Media: Facebook, Twitter, LinkedIn, RSS Feeds

Clive Roux, CEO
Ann Makowski, COO
Pat Matson Knapp, Director of Communications
Justin Molloy, Director of Education
Sara Naegelin, Director of Sponsorship

The global community of people who work at the intersection of communication design and the built environment.
Founded in: 1974

2023 **Society of American Registered Architects**
14 E. 38th Street
New York, NY 10016

888-385-7272; *Fax:* 888-385-7272
cmoscato@sara-national.org;
www.sara-national.org
Social Media: Facebook

Ron Knabb, Jr., FARA, President
Gaetano Ragusa, FARA, President-Elect
John J. Di Benedetto, FARA, Vice-President
Francisco J. Urrutia, FARA, Treasurer
Cathie Moscato, Executive Director

A professional society that includes the participation of all architects, regardless of their roles in the architectural community, the opportunity to share information and ideas.
Founded in: 1956

2024 **Society of Architectural Historians**
1365 N Astor St
Chicago, IL 60610-2144

312-573-1365; *Fax:* 312-573-1141
info@sah.org; www.sah.org
Social Media: Facebook, Twitter, LinkedIn, YouTube, Instagram, RSS

Kenneth Breish, President
Ken Tadashi Oshima, Vice President
Sandy Isenstadt, 2nd Vice President
Pauline Saliga, Executive Director
Michael J. Gibson, Treasurer

A not-for-profit membership organization and learned society that promotes the study and preservation of the built environment worldwide.
2500 Members
Founded in: 1940

2025 **Society of Naval Architects and Marine Engineers**
99 Canal Center Plaza
Suite 310
Alexandria, VA 22314
703-997-6701
800-798-2188; *Fax:* 703-997-6702;
www.sname.org

Edward N. Comstock, President
Erik Seither, Executive Director

Internationally recognized nonprofit technical, professional society of individual members serving the maritime and offshore industries and their suppliers. Dedicated to advancing the industry by recording information, sponsoring research, offering career guidance and supporting education.
10000 Members
Founded in: 1893

2026 **Sustainable Buildings Industry Council**
1090 Vermont Avenue NW
Suite700
Washington, DC 20005

202-289-7800; *Fax:* 202- 28- 109
nibs@nibs.org; www.sbicouncil.org
Social Media: Facebook, Twitter, LinkedIn, Pinterest

Bud DeFlaviis, Executive Director
Kimberly Lowry, Executive Assistant

Mission is to unite and inspire the building industry toward higher performance through education, outreach, advocacy and the mutual exchange of ideas.
Founded in: 1980

2027 **The Architectural League of New York**
594 Broadway
Suite 607
New York, NY 10012

212-753-1722; *Fax:* 212-486-9173
info@archleague.org
archleague.org
Social Media: Facebook, Twitter, YouTube, Instagram, Vimeo

Rosalie Genevro, Executive Director
Anne Rieselbach, Program Director
Nicholas Anderson, Communications Director

The League provides a forum for debate about current issues in architecture, design and urbanism.
Founded in: 1881

2028 **The National Institute of Building Sciences**
1090 Vermont Avenue, NW
Suite 700
Washington, DC 20005-4950
202-289-7800; *Fax:* 202-289-1092
nibs@nibs.org; www.nibs.org
Social Media: RSS

James T. Ryan, Chairman
Stephen Ayers, Vice Chairman
Henry L. Green, President
John G Lloyrd, Vice President
John Marshall Ortiz, AIA, Secretary

A nonprofit, non-governmental organization that brings together representatives of government, the professions, industry, labor and consumer interests, and regulatory agencies to focus on the identification and resolution of problems that hamper the contruction of safe, affordable structures for housing, commerce, and industry throughout the United States.

2029 **U.S. Green Building Council**
2101 L Street, NW
Suite 500
Washington, DC 20037

202-742-3792
800-795-1747
info@usgbc.org; www.usgbc.org
Social Media: Facebook, Twitter, LinkedIn, YouTube, Instagram, Google+

Kunal Gulati, Product Marketing Specialist
Mark de Groh, Director, Philanthropy
Aline Peterson, Media & Communications Specialist
Lee Brown, Account Manager
Alex Hammack, Operations Associate

This organization is made up of tens of thousands of member organizations, chapters, and student and community volunteers that strive to transform the way buildings and communities are operated, enabling an environmentally and socially responsible, healthy, and prosperous environment that improves the quality of life.
Founded in: 1973

2030 **United States Access Board**
Access Board
1331 F St Nw
Suite 1000
Washington, DC 20004-1111

202-272-0080
800-872-2253; *Fax:* 202-272-0081
info@access-board.gov;
www.access-board.gov
Social Media: Facebook, Twitter, Vimeo

Karen L. Braitmayer, FAIA, Chair
David M. Capozzi, Executive Director
Neil Melick, Director
James J. Raggio, General Counsel
Lisa Fairhall, Deputy General Counsel

Independent federal agency devoted to accessibility for people with disabilities. Its key missions include developing and maintaining guidelines for the built environment, transit vehicles, telecommunications equipment and standards for electronic and information technology; providing technical assistance and training on these guidelines and standards and enforcing design standards for federally funded facilities.
Founded in: 1968

2031 **Urban Design Associates**
3 PPG Place
3rd Floor
Pittsburgh, PA 15222

412-263-5200; *Fax:* 844-270-8374;
www.urbandesignassociates.com
Social Media: Facebook, Twitter, Vimeo

Designs resilient neighborhoods, towns, villages, districts, places, and buildings.
Founded in: 1964

Newsletters

2032 **A/E Business Review**
6524 E Rockaway Hills Drive
PO Box 4808
Cave Creek, AZ 85331-7609
480-488-0311; *Fax:* 480-488-0311
Clare Ross, Publisher
The management and marketing newsletter of architects, engineers and planners.
7 Pages
Frequency: Monthly

2033 **AIA Architect**
American Institute of Architects
1735 New York Ave Nw
Washington, DC 20006-5292
202-626-7300
800-242-3837; *Fax:* 202-626-7547
infocentral@aia.org; www.aia.org
Robert Ivy, CEO
Jeff Potter, President
News of America's community of architects
Frequency: Weekly

2034 **Access Currents**
Access Board
1331 F St Nw
Suite 1000
Washington, DC 20004-1135
202-272-0080
800-872-2253; *Fax:* 202-272-0081
info@access-board.gov;
www.access-board.gov
David Capozzi, Executive Director
Frequency: Bi-Monthly

2035 **Certifier**
Nat'l Council of Architectural Registration Boards
1801 K St Nw
Suite 700K
Washington, DC 20006-1320
202-879-0520; *Fax:* 202-783-0290;
www.ncarb.org
Michael Armstrong, CEO
Blakely Dunn, Vice President
State architectural registration boards.
Frequency: Annual
Founded in: 1919

2036 **Design Drafting News**
American Design Drafting Association
105 E Main Street
Newbern, TN 38059-1526
731-627-0802; *Fax:* 731-627-9321
corporate@adda.org; www.adda.org
Ron McDonald, President
Dennis Schwartz, Executive VP
Newsletter for the American Design Drafting Association and American Digital Design Association.
Frequency: Bi-Monthly
Circulation: 1800

2037 **Design Firm Management & Administration Report**
Institute of Management and Administration
3 Bethesda Metro Center
Suite 250
Bethesda, MD 20814-537
703-341-3500
800-372-1033; *Fax:* 800-253-0332;
www.ioma.com
Provides practical, hands-on, timely information to design firm managers and administrators about the marketing and management aspects of operating a firm.
Cost: $429.00
Frequency: Monthly

2038 **Designline**
American Institute of Building Design
529 14th St NW
Suite 750
Washington, DC 20045
202-249-1407
800-366-2423; *Fax:* 866-204-0293
info@aibd.org; www.aibd.org
Dan Sater, President
Alan Kent, Vice President
Focuses on issues, education, and events as they happen in the building design industry.
Frequency: Quarterly

2039 **Direct Connection**
Nat'l Council of Architectural Registration Boards
1801 K St NW
Suite 700K
Washington, DC 20006-1301
202-870-0520; *Fax:* 202-782-0290
customerservice@ncarb.org; www.ncarb.org
Ron McDonald, CEO
Blakely Dunn, Vice President
Offers information and news on licensing, board certification, architectural trends and more for the professional architect and intern architect.
16 Pages
Circulation: 50000
Printed in 2 colors on glossy stock

2040 **Energy Design Update**
Aspen Publishers
76 Ninth Avenue
7th Floor
New York, NY 10011
212-771-0600
800-638-8437; www.aspenlawschoo.com
Mark Dorman, CEO
Gustavo Dobles, VP Operations
For professionals concerned with residential load management and energy efficient design and construction in housing.
Cost: $297.00
16 Pages
Frequency: Monthly

2041 **Guidelines Letter: New Directions and Techniques in the Design Profession**
Guidelines
PO Box 2590
Alameda, CA 94501
510-235-5174
800-634-7779; *Fax:* 510-523-5175
info@sfia.net; www.sfia.net
Fred Stitt, Director/Editor
Chandler Vienneau, Circulation Director
Business and technical information for design professionals including comprehensive survey information regarding fees and client costs. The Guidelines Letter is in its 28th year of publication.
Cost: $70.00
4 Pages
Frequency: Monthly
ISSN: 1089-2141
Founded in: 1992

2042 **Landscape Architectural News Digest**
American Society of Landscape Architects
636 Eye St NW
Washington, DC 20001-3736
202-898-2444
800-787-2752; *Fax:* 202-898-1185
membership@asla.org; www.asla.org
Jonathan Mueller, President
Seck Hardi, Editor
Provides a comprehensive view of the latest developments in regional, residential and corporate architecture.
Cost: $42.00
16 Pages
Frequency: Monthly

2043 **Memo**
American Institute of Architects
1735 New York Ave Nw
Washington, DC 20006-5292
202-626-7300
800-242-3837; *Fax:* 202-626-7547
infocentral@aia.org; www.aia.org
Robert Ivy, CEO
Jeff Potter, President
Norman Koonce, Editor
Scott Frank, Director
Architectural news and information.
Frequency: Monthly
Circulation: 85000

2044 **SARAscope**
Society of American Registered Architects
P.O. Box 280
Newport, TN 37822
888-385-7272
cmoscato@sara-national.org;
www.sara-national.org
Suzette Stoler, President
Cathie Moscato, Executive Director
Listing society conventions, meetings and other activities. Discusses news about the Society of interest to members.
Frequency: BiWeekly
Founded in: 1956

2045 **SBIC Newsletter**
Sustainable Buildings Industry Council
1090 Vermont Avenue NW
Suite 700
Washington, DC 20005
202-289-7800; *Fax:* 202-289-1092
nibs@nibs.org; www.sbicouncil.org
Henry Green, President
John Lloyd, Vice President
Gretchen Hesbacher, Editor
Published to inform the members of the mission to advance the design, affordability, energy performance and environmental soundness of residential, institutional and commercial buildings. Newsletter is free to members.
6-8 Pages
Frequency: 2-3 per year
Circulation: 400
Founded in: 1995
Printed in 2 colors on matte stock

2046 **Society of Architectural Historians Newsletter**
Society of Architectural Historians
1365 N Astor St
Chicago, IL 60610-2144
312-573-1365; *Fax:* 312-573-1141
info@sah.org; www.sah.org
Dr. Abigail Van Slyck, President
Prof. Ken Breisch, Vice President
Keeps readers informed about upcoming SAH events, conferences, tours, awards, publications and exhibitors.
Frequency: Bi-Monthly

2047 **Times**
Council of Tall Buildings and Urban Habitat
Illinois Institute of Technology SR Crown
3360 S State Street
Chicago, IL 60616-3793

312-567-3487; *Fax:* 312-567-3820
info@ctbuh.org; www.ctbuh.org

Patti Thurmond, Operations Manager
Antony Wood, Executive Director
Tansri Muliani, News Editor
Steven Henry, Publications

Newsletter for members of CTBUH.
Cost: $75.00
Frequency: Monthly
Circulation: 1200
ISSN: 1061-5121
Founded in: 1969
Printed in 2 colors on matte stock

Magazines & Journals

2048 **AI Communications**
AIAA
1735 New York Ave NW
Washington, DC 20006-5209

202-626-7300
800-242-3837; *Fax:* 202-626-7547
infocentral@aia.org; www.aia.org

Jeffery Potter, President
Mickey Jacob, Vice President

Student programs and issues dealing with architectural education.
Founded in: 1857

2049 **APT Bulletin: The Journal of Preservation Technology**
Association for Preservation Technology Int'l
3085 Stevenson Drive
Suite 200
Springfield, IL 62705

217-529-9039; *Fax:* 888-723-4242
info@apti.org; www.apti.org

Joan Berkowitz, President
Gretchen Pfaehler, Vice President

Articles showcase cutting-edge preservation techniques, as well as innovative applications of established restoration technologies.

2050 **Adobe Magazine**
Adobe Systems
345 Park Ave
San Jose, CA 95110-2704

408-536-6000; *Fax:* 408-537-6000;
www.adobe.com

Shantanu Narayen, CEO
Mark Garrett, SVP

Devoted to adobe and earthen architecture. Showing both old and new traditions of building the earth.
Cost: $4.00
Circulation: 4,500

2051 **American School & University**
PRIMEDIA Intertec Publication
9800 Metcalf Ave.
Overland Park, KS 66212

913-341-1300; *Fax:* 913-967-1898;
www.penton.com

Nicola Alais, Senior VP
Gregg Herring, Publisher
David KIESELSTEIN, CEO

The industry's definitive educational facilities publication.
Cost: $50.00
508 Pages
Frequency: Monthly
Circulation: 63540
Founded in: 1928
Printed in 4 colors on glossy stock

2052 **Architectural Design**
John Wiley & Sons
111 River St
Hoboken, NJ 07030-5790

201-748-6000; *Fax:* 201-748-6088
info@wiley.com; www.wiley.com

Matthew Kissner, CEO/President
Jean-Lou Chameau, President

Continues to publish a vigorous and wide range treatment of architectural trends of topical importance.
Cost: $145.00
Founded in: 1807

2053 **Architectural Digest**
4 Times Square
Suite 15
New York, NY 10036-6518

212-286-2860; *Fax:* 212-286-6790;
www.architecturaldigest.com

Giulio Capua, Publisher
Margaret Russell, Editor-in-Chief

For the connoisseur of interior design. The purpose is to cultivate an appreciation of excellence in the luxury world of design and furnishing.
Cost: $39.95
Frequency: Monthly
Circulation: 840,995
Founded in: 1999

2054 **Architectural Record**
McGraw Hill
2 Penn Plaza
9th Floor
New York, NY 10121-2298

212-904-2594; *Fax:* 212-904-4256
william_hanley@mcgraw-hill.com
archrecord.construction.com

William Hanley, Web Editor
Cathleen McGuigan, Editor in Chief
Ilan Kapla, Sr. Manager, Web Production
Rama Bandu, Web Producer
Elisabeth Broome, Managing Editor

Provides a compelling editorial mix of design ideas and trends, building science, business and professional strategies, exploration of key issues, news products and computer-aided practice.
Cost: $49.00
Frequency: Monthly

2055 **Architecture Magazine**
American Institute of Architects
One Thomas Circle, NW
Suite 600
Washington, DC 20005

202-452-0800; *Fax:* 202-785-1974
info@architecturemag.com;
www.architecturemag.com

Ned Cramer, Editor-in-Chief
Greig O'Brien, Managing Editor
Katie Gerfen, Senior Editor

Evaluation of new and existing buildings and related news that affects the profession.
Frequency: Monthly
Circulation: 63449

2056 **Ballast Quarterly Review**
Ballast
2022 X Avenue
Dysart, IA 52224-9767

E-Mail: ballast@netins.net

Roy Behrens, Editor

Examines an eclectic assortment of publications with an emphasis on graphic design and architecture.
16 Pages
Frequency: Quarterly

2057 **Building Design & Construction**
Reed Business Information
360 Park Ave S
New York, NY 10010-1737

1 -46 -46 6; *Fax:* 646-756-7583
subsmail@reedbusiness.com;
www.reedbusiness.com

Mark Kelsey, CEO
James Reed, President

Serves the needs of the design and construction professionals of commercial, industrial and institutional buildings that include new and retrofit projects. Geared towards the building team that includes professionals from building firms, owning firms and design firms.
Frequency: Monthly
Founded in: 1946

2058 **CRIT: Journal of the American Institute of Architecture Students**
American Institute of Architecture Students
1735 New York Ave NW
Washington, DC 20006-5292

202-626-7472; *Fax:* 202-626-7414
mailbox@aias.org; www.aias.org

Joshua Caulfield, CEO
Joshua Caulfield, Executive Director
Yurly Napelenok, Programs & Membership
Laura Meader, Editor in Chief

The premier source of and the only international journal of student design work.
Frequency: Bi-Annual
Circulation: 13,000
Founded in: 1976

2059 **CTBUH Review Journal**
Council on Tall Buildings and Urban Habitat
S.R.Crown Hall,
3360 South State Street
Chicago, IL 60616

312-567-3487; *Fax:* 312-567-3820
info@ctbuh.org;
www.ctbuh.org/Publications/Journal/tabid/72/language/en-GB/Defaul

Marshall Ali, Editor
Anthony Wood, Executive Director
Robert Lau, Associate Editor

CTBUH Review is the Professional Journal of the Council on Tall Buildings and Urban Habitat. It includes refereed papers submitted by researchers, scholars, suppliers, and practicing professionals engaged in the planning, design, construction, and operation of tall buildings and the urban environment throughout the world. Membership benefits include monthly e-updates, access to on-line buildings database, discounts on selected publications and registration at Council-sponsored activities.
Cost: $150.00
1400 Pages
Frequency: Quarterly

2060 **Classicist**
Transaction Publishing Rutgers
35 Berrue Circle
Piscataway, NJ 08854-8042

732-445-2280
888-999-6778; *Fax:* 732-445-3138
trans@transactionpub.com;
www.transactionpub.com

Mary Curtis, President
Prof. David Shulman, Editor

Dedicated to the theory and practice of architecture and artistic classicism.
Cost: $39.95
164 Pages

2061 Computer-Aided Engineering
Penton Media
1300 E 9th St
Suite 316
Cleveland, OH 44114-1503

216-696-7000; *Fax:* 216-696-1752
information@penton.com; www.penton.com

David Kieselstein, CEO
Nicola Allais, EVP
Jasmine Alexander, Senior VP & CIO

Database applications in design and manufacturing.
Cost: $50.00
96 Pages
Founded in: 1982

2062 Concrete Masonry Designs
13750 Sunrise Valley Drive
Herndon, VA 20171-4662

703-713-1900; *Fax:* 703-713-1910
ncma@ncma.org; www.ncma.org

Mary Arntson-Terrell, Director of Sales
Robert Thomas, President

Highlights concrete masonry applications, best practice tips, specifications and details. Also showcases concrete masonry landscape products.
Cost: $2.50
Frequency: Monthly
Circulation: 25000
Founded in: 1918
Printed in 4 colors on glossy stock

2063 Contemporary Stone & Tile Design
BNP Media
210 E State Rt 4
Suite 203
Paramus, NJ 07652-5103

201-291-9001; *Fax:* 201-291-9002
info@stoneworld.com; www.stoneworld.com

Alex Bachrach, Publisher
Michael Reis, Editor
Jennifer Adams, Editor

Focuses on stone and ceramic tile use in interior design for architects, interior designers, specifiers and consumrs with the buying influence for stone or stone materials and a variety of architectural and construction products and services.

2064 Design Issues
MIT Press
55 Hayward Street
Cambridge, MA 02142-1315

617-253-5646; *Fax:* 617-258-6779;
www.mitpress.mit.edu

Michael Sims, Managing Editor
Ellen Faran, Director

Provokes inquiry into the cultural and intellectual issues surrounding design. Regular features include theoretical and critical articles by professional and scholarly contributions, extensive book reviews, and illustrations.
110 Pages
Frequency: Quarterly
ISSN: 0747-9360
Founded in: 1984

2065 Design Journal
Journal Communications Group
1720 20th St #201
Santa Monica, CA 90404

310-394-4394; *Fax:* 310-394-0966
customer.services@benjamins.nl
designjournalmag.com

Kees Vaes, Editor
Karin Plijnaar, Marketing Manager

Focuses on the design and architecture marketplace. Includes newsbites and a calendar, as well as designer and lighting resources.
Frequency: Monthly
Circulation: 34000
Founded in: 1982

2066 Design Solutions Magazine
Architectural Woodwork Institute
46179 Westlake Drive
Suite 120
Potomac Falls, VA 20165

571-323-3636; *Fax:* 571-323-3630
adsales@awinet.org; www.awinet.org

Teresa McCain, Director of Operations
Philip Duvic, Executive VP

Featuring beautiful woodwork projects manufactured by members of the Architectural Woodwork Institute (AWI). Many other related publications, including woodworking quality standards used by woodwork manufacturers and design professionals.
Cost: $25.00
Frequency: Quarterly
Circulation: 25000
Founded in: 1953

2067 Design/Build Business
Cygnus Publishing
12735 Morris Road
Bldg. 200
Alpharetta, GA 30152-0803

770-427-5290
800-547-7377; *Fax:* 404-935-9290
kathy.scott@cygnusb2b.com;
www.cygnusb2b.com

John French, CEO
Michael Martin, President

Serves builders, architects and designing and remodeling firms, nationwide. Edited to these professions serving the residential and light commercial marketplaces.
Cost: $24.00
72 Pages
Frequency: Monthly
Circulation: 60424
ISSN: 1068-9433
Founded in: 1935

2068 Dodge Construction News
McGraw Hill
PO Box 182604
Columbus, OH 43272

614-866-5769
877-833-5524; *Fax:* 614-759-3749
customer.service@mcgraw-hill.com;
www.mcgraw-hill.com

Jennifer Hayes, Editor
Harold McGraw III, President/CEO

Consists of program edition and proceedings and recap edition for the National Conventions of the American Institute of Architects and Construction Specifications Institute.
Circulation: 86400
Founded in: 1958

2069 Enquiry: A Journal for Architectural Research
Architectural Research Centers Consortium

www.arcc-arch.org
Hazem Rashed Ali, President
Chris Jarrett, Vice President
Saif Haq, Treasurer
Leonard Bachman, Secretary
Frequency: Annual
ISSN: 2329-9339
Founded in: 1976

2070 Fabrics Architecture
U.S. Industrial Fabrics Association International
1801 County Road NW
Roseville, MN 55113-4061

651-222-2508
800-225-4324; *Fax:* 651-631-9334;
www.usifi.com

Ruth Stephens, Executive Director

Strives to inform architects, designers, landscape architects, engineers and other specifiers about architectural fabric structures, the fibers and fabrics used to make them, their design possibilities, their construction, and issues regarding their applicability and acceptance.
Cost: $39.00
Frequency: Bi-Monthly

2071 Glass Magazine
National Glass Association
1945 Old Gallows Rd
Suite 750
Vienna, VA 22182

703-442-4890
866-342-5642; *Fax:* 703-442-0630
editorialinfo@glass.org; www.glass.org

Phil James, CEO
Nicole Harris, Vice President

Offers readers experienced editorial direction and informative coverage including market segment surveys, resource guides, reader polls, industry profiles, industry states, and industry products.
Frequency: Monthly

2072 Harvard Design Magazine
Harvard University Graduate School of Design
48 Quincy St
Gund Hall
Cambridge, MA 02138-3000

617-495-5453; *Fax:* 617-495-8949
hdm@gsd.harvard.edu; www.gsd.harvard.edu
Social Media: Facebook, Twitter, LinkedIn

Mohsen Mostafavi, Dean

Aims to provide a forum for thoughtful and articulate practitioners, journalists, and academics, primarily from architecture, landscape architecture and urban design and planning.
Frequency: Bi-Annual

2073 Impact Assessment and Project Appraisal (IAPA)
International Association for Impact Assessment
1330 23rd Street S
Suite C
Fargo, ND 58103-3705

701-297-7908; *Fax:* 701-297-7917
info@iaia.org; www.iaia.org

Rita Hamm, CEO
Jennifer Howell, Publications

IAPA is an international refereed journal. It welcomes papers on the environmental, social, health, technology, integrated, sustainability, etc. assessment of projects, programs, plans and policies.
Frequency: Quarterly
Circulation: 1600
ISSN: 1461-5517

2074 Inland Architect
Real Estate News Corporation

3500 West Peterson Avenue
Suite 403
Chicago, IL 60659

773-866-9900
888-641-3169; *Fax:* 773-866-9881
rencorpil@aol.com;
www.inlandarchitectmag.com

Steven Polydoris, Publisher/Editor

Covers distinguished and historical buildings.
Cost: $27.00
120 Pages
Founded in: 1883
Printed in 4 colors on glossy stock

2075 **Journal of Architectural Education**
Blackwell Publishing Inc
350 Main St
Suite 6
Malden, MA 02148-5089
781-388-8598
800-835-6770; *Fax:* 781-388-8210
cs-journals@wiley.com;
www.blackwellpublishing.com

Vincent Marzano, VP
Stephen Smith, CEO

Enhances architectural design education, theory and practice.
Frequency: Quarterly
ISBN: 0-262753-24-3
Founded in: 1947

2076 **Journal of Architectural and Planning Research**
Locke Science Publishing
332 S. Michigan Avenue
Suite 1032 #L221
Chicago, IL 60604

E-Mail: japr@lockescience.com;
www.lockescience.com

Andrew Seidel, Editor-in-Chief
Ajay Garde, Editor

The major international disciplinary resource for professionals and scholars in architecture, design, and planning. Also provides a link between theory and practice for researchers and practicing professionals.

2077 **Journal of Urban Technology**
New York City Technical College
300 Jay St
Brooklyn, NY 11201-1909

718-260-5250; *Fax:* 718-260-5524
connect@citytech.cuny.edu; www.cuny.edu

Russell Hotzler, President
Miguel Cairol, VP

Covers technological developments in the architecture and transporatation fields.
Circulation: 10000
Founded in: 1946

2078 **Journal of the Society of Architectural Historians**
Society of Architectural Historians
1365 N Astor St
Chicago, IL 60610-2144

312-573-1365; *Fax:* 312-573-1141
info@sah.org; www.sah.org

Prof. Ken Breisch, Vice President
Abigail Van Slyck, President

Offers three to four scholarly articles on American and International topics, reviews of recently-published books, reviews of architecture exhibitions, and a variety of editorials designed to place the discipline of architectural history within a larger intellectual context.
Frequency: Quarterly

2079 **Metal Architecture**
Modern Trade Communications
7450 Skokie Blvd
Suite 200
Skokie, IL 60077-3374

847-674-2200; *Fax:* 847-674-3676;
www.moderntrade.com
Social Media: Facebook, Twitter, LinkedIn

Paul Deffenbaugh, Editorial Director
Mark Robins, Senior Editor
John S. Lawrence, CEO
John Paul Lawrence, President

Low-rise construction involving architects, engineers and specifiers.
Frequency: Monthly
Circulation: 33000
Founded in: 1980

2080 **Metropolis Magazine**
Bellerophon Publications
61 W 23rd St
4th Floor
New York, NY 10010-4246

212-627-9977; *Fax:* 212-627-9988
edit@metropolismag.com;
www.metropolismag.com
Social Media: Facebook, Twitter, LinkedIn

Horace Havemeyer, Publisher
Susan Szenasy, Editor-in-Chief

The only magazine that covers all facets of design: architecture, interiors, furniture, preservation, urban design, graphics and crafts.
Cost: $27.95
Circulation: 61000
Founded in: 1980

2081 **Old House Interiors**
Gloucester Publishers Corporation
10 Harbor Rd
Gloucester, MA 01930-3222

978-283-3200
800-356-9313; *Fax:* 978-283-4629
info@oldhouseinteriors.com;
www.oldhouseinteriors.com

Regina Cole, Editor

Covers restoration techniques for the pre-1939 home.
Cost: $26.00
116 Pages
Circulation: 100000
Founded in: 1995
Printed in 4 colors on glossy stock

2082 **Places: A Forum of Environmental Design**
Journal of Environmental Design
100 Higgans Hall
Brooklyn, NY 11205

Fax: 718-399-4332

James F Fulton, Publisher

Covers architecture, landscape architecture, urban design, with a multidisciplinary view of all aspects of public and private places.
Cost: $35.00

2083 **Preservation Magazine**
National Trust for Historic Preservation
1785 Massachusetts Ave NW
Washington, DC 20036-2189

202-588-6000
800-944-6847; *Fax:* 202-588-6038
info@savingplaces.org;
www.preservationnation.org

Stephanie Meeks, CEO
David Brown, EVP

Offers lively writing by the nation's best journalists on controversies, trends, accomplishments, and events of importance to cities, towns, suburbs, and rural communities.

2084 **Professional Builder**
Reed Business Information
360 Park Ave S
New York, NY 10010-1737

646-746-6845; *Fax:* 646-756-7583
corporatecommunications@reedbusiness.com;
www.reedbusiness.com

Mark Kelsey, CEO
James Reed, President

New residential construction magazine with a tradition of providing builders the solutions they need to maximize profits.
Frequency: Monthly
Founded in: 1936

2085 **Reed Bulletin**
Reed Business Informtion
30 Technology Parkway South
Suite 100
Norcross, GA 30092

800-424-3996
talisha.jackson@reedbusiness.com;
www.reedconstructiondata.com

Talisha Jackson, Media Contact

Provides contractors with project news and tools suppliers.

2086 **Residential Architect**
Hanley-Wood
1 Thomas Circle NW
Suite 600
Washington, DC 20005-5811

202-452-0800
888-269-8410; *Fax:* 202-785-1974
cconroy@hanleywood.com;
www.residentialarchitect.com

Claire Conroy, Editorial Director
Jennifer Lash, Managing Editor
Bruce Snider, Senior Editor

It delivers substantive editorial on marketing, presentation, products, technology and business management to architects and designers.
Cost: $39.95
Frequency: 9x Yearly
Circulation: 22000
Founded in: 1976

2087 **Society of Architectural Administrators News Journal**
Society of Architectural Administrators
15 E 7th Street NW
Cincinatti, OH 45202

513-684-3451

Patsy Frost, Publisher

Society news for professionals in the architectural community.

2088 **Urban Omnibus**
The Architectural League of New York
594 Broadway
Suite 607
New York, NY 10012

212-753-1722
info@urbanomnibus.net
urbanomnibus.net
Social Media: Facebook, Twitter, Vimeo, YouTube

Jonathan Tarleton, Senior Editor
Emily Schmidt, Senior Editor

Online publication exploring new ideas and projects for the built environment of New York.
Frequency: Weekly
Founded in: 2009

2089 **World Monuments Fund**
350 Fifth Avenue
Suite 2412
New York, NY 10118

646-424-9594; *Fax:* 646-424-9593
wmf@wmf.org; www.wmf.org

Bonnie Burnham, President
Jonathan Foyle, Chief Executive
Darlene McCloud, VP
Lisa Ackerman, Executive VP, COO

This magazine offers information on the latest architectural trends, specifically landmarks, monuments, antiquities.
Cost: $17.95
16 Pages
Frequency: Quarterly
Founded in: 1965
Printed in 4 colors on glossy stock

Trade Shows

2090 **AIA National Convention and Design Exposition**
American Institute of Architects
1735 New York Avenue NW
Washington, DC 20006-5292

202-626-7300
800-242-3837; *Fax:* 202-626-7547
infocentral@aia.org; www.aia.org

Christine McEntee, CEO

Offers the chance to meet with more than 800 exhibitors and discover new products and technologies that can be used in future projects.
Frequency: Annual/April

2091 **ASLA Annual Meeting & EXPO**
American Society of Landscape Architects
636 Eye Street NW
Washington, DC 20001-3736

202-988-2444
800-787-2752; *Fax:* 202-898-1185
info@asla.org; www.asla.org

Thomas Tavella, President
Mark Hough, VP

Landscape architect educational session and workshop plus 500 exhibits of outdoor lighting, playground and park equipment, landscape maintenance equipment, computer hardware and software and much more.
6000 Attendees

2092 **American Institute of Architects Minn. Convention & Products Exhibition**
American Institute of Architects, Minnesota Chap.
275 Market Street
Suite 54
Minneapolis, MN 55405

612-339-6904; *Fax:* 612-338-7981
infocentral@aia.org; www.aia-mn.org

Christine McEntee, CEO

175 exhibits of windows, concrete, roofing, millwork, tile and more, plus conference, seminar and dinner.
2500 Attendees
Frequency: Annual
Founded in: 1934

2093 **American Institute of Building Design Annual Convention**
American Institute of Building Design
529 14th St NW
Suite750
Washington, DC 20045

800-366-2423; *Fax:* 866-204-0293
info@aibd.org; www.aibd.org

Dan Sater, President
Alan Kent, VP

A four day convention and trade show for residential design professionals
Frequency: Annual/July

2094 **American Society for Aesthetics Annual Conference**
American Society for Aesthetics
1550 Larimer Street
Suite 644
Denver, CO 80202

562-331-4424
asa@aesthetics-online.org;
www.aesthetics-online.org

Cynthia Freeland, President
Kathleen Higgins, Vice President

Seminar, conference, and exhibits related to the study of the arts, all disciplines.
Frequency: Annual
Founded in: 1942

2095 **Annual Technical & Educational Conference**
American Design Drafting Association
105 E Main St
Newbern, TN 38059-1526

731-627-0802; *Fax:* 731-627-9321
corprorate@adda.org; www.adda.org

Ron McDonald, President
Dennis Schwartz, Executive VP

Annual professional educational conference dedicated to serve the professional growth and advancement of the individuals working in the extremely fast paced, professional graphic community.
100 Members
Frequency: Annual/April

2096 **Computers for Contractors and A/E/C Systems Fall**
AEC Systems International/Penton Media
1300 E 9th St
Suite 316
Cleveland, OH 44114

216-696-7000; *Fax:* 216-696-6662
information@penton.com;
www.aecsystemsibt.com

Sharon Rowlands, CEO
Nicola Allais, EVP

Computers for construction is the only tradeshow and conference dedicated exclusively to computer use by contractors. A/E/C SYSTEMS Fall is the regional technology event for the entire design and construction industry.
7000 Attendees
Frequency: Annual/November

2097 **Council on Tall Buildings & Urban Habitat Congress**
Lehigh University
11 East Packer Avenue
Bethlehem, PA 18015

610-583-3000; *Fax:* 610-758-4522
inctbuh@lehigh.edu; www.ctbuh.orh

Antony Wood, Executive Director

Brings the world's leading decision makers together. For additional information visit our website or email us.
600+ Attendees
Frequency: Annual/February
Founded in: 1969
Mailing list available for rent: 4500 names

2098 **EDM/PDM Expo**
AEC Systems International/Penton Media
1300 E 9th St
Suite 316
Cleveland, OH 44114

216-696-7000; *Fax:* 216-696-7000
info@aecsystems.com; www.aecsystems.com

Sharon Rowlands, CEO
Nicola Allais, EVP

Showcases ways to manage technical/engineering documents, product management, and drawing conversion. Over 500 exhibits are shown.
20M Attendees
Frequency: Annual/May

2099 **International Manufacturing & Engineering Technology Congress**
AEC Systems International/Penton Media
1300 E 9th St
Suite 316
Cleveland, OH 44114

216-696-7000; *Fax:* 216-696-6662
info@aecsystems.com; www.aecsystems.com

Sharon Rowlands, CEO
Nicola Allais, EVP

Automotive, aeronautics, and aerospace, electrical and electronics, consumer products, industrial, heavy equipment, and process industries.
1000 exhibits.
15M Attendees
Frequency: Annual/November

2100 **LightFair**
AMC
120 Wall Street
17th Floor
New York, NY 10005

212-248-5000; *Fax:* 212-248-5017
ies@ies.org; www.iesna.org

Chip Israel, President
Daniel Salinas, Vice President

A major lighting trade show in North America featuring architectural lighting products from all spectrons of the industry. Containing 600 booths and 400 exhibits.
17M Attendees
Frequency: Annual/June
Mailing list available for rent: 10M names at $100 per M

2101 **Lightfair International**
Atlanta Market Center
240 Peachtree Street NW
Suite 2200
Atlanta, GA 30303-1327

404-220-3000
800-ATL-MART; *Fax:* 404-220-3030
webmaster@americasmart.com;
www.americasmart.com

John Portman, CEO
Jeffery Portman, COO

The world's largest annual architectural/commercial lighting trade show and conference program. Lightfair International features the latest technology, products, education, information, awards and industry association events. 600 booths.
20M Attendees
Frequency: Annual/May

2102 **M/Tech**
AEC Systems International/Penton Media
1300 E 9th Street
Suite 316
Cleveland, OH 44114

216-696-7000; *Fax:* 216-696-6662
info@aecsystems.com; www.aecsystems.com

Sharon Rowlands, CEO
Nicola Allais, EVP

Focuses on applications to improve every phase of the product development cycle including CAD/CAM/CAE, Internet/intra/extranct, rapid prototyping and tooling, project/financial management, simulation and analysis, EDM/PDM and much more. 300 exhibits.
15M Attendees
Frequency: Annual/November

2103 **M/Tech West**
AEC Systems International/Penton Media
1300 E 9th St
Suite 316
Cleveland, OH 44114
216-696-7000; *Fax:* 216-696-6662;
www.acesystems.com
Sharon Rowlands, CEO
Nicola Allais, EVP
Explores concurrent engineering practices, computer integrated manufacturing, and mechanical engineering applications. 50 exhibits.
20M Attendees
Frequency: Annual/May

2104 **National Council of Architectural Registration Boards Annual Meeting**
Natl. Council of Architectural Registration Boards
1801 K Street NW
Suite 700K
Washington, DC 20006
202-783-6500; *Fax:* 202-783-0290
customerservice@ncarb.org; www.ncarb.org
Ronald Biltch, President
Blakely Dunn, VP
Annual meeting and exhibits of architecture equipment, supplies and services.

2105 **Retail Design & Construction Conference & Expo**
Primedia
3585 Engineering Drive
Suite 100
Norcross, GA 30092
678-421-3000
800-216-1423; *Fax:* 913-967-1898;
www.primedia.com
Charles Stubbs, President
Kim Payne, SVP
Annual show of 145 exhibitors of equipment, supplies and services for retail design, construction, development, operations and maintenance, including signage, building equipment and materials, fixtures, floor coverings, furnishings, lighting, landscaping, store fronts, roofing, HVAC, maintenance materials and contractor services.
1000 Attendees

2106 **SARA National Conference**
Society Of American Registered Architects
P.O. Box 280
Newport, TN 37822
888-385-7272; *Fax:* 888-385-7272
cmoscato@sara-national.org;
www.sara-national.org
Social Media: LinkedIn
Guy Ragusa, Membership Chair
Cathie Moscato, Executive Director
Suzette Stoler, President
Gaetano Ragusa, Vice President
Annual conference holding the National Board Meeting, Architecture & Design Banquet, President's Celebration Banquet & Installation of Officers, and the International & Distinguished Building Award Presentations
503 Members
Founded in: 1956

2107 **TCAA Convention**
Tile Contractors Association of America
10434 Indiana Avenue
Kansas City, MO 64137
816- 86- 930
800-655-8453; *Fax:* 816-767-0194
info@tcaainc.org; www.tcaainc.org
Chris Pattavina, Associate Director
Carole Damon, Executive Director
Architect/designer learning exchange, speakers, business meetings, new products and technology
Founded in: 1903

2108 **Technology for Construction**
Hanley-Wood
6191 N State Hwy 161
Suite 500
Irving, TX 75038
972-366-6300
866-962-7469; *Fax:* 972-536-6301
rmcconnell@hanleywood.com;
www.technologyforconstruction.com
Rick McConnell, President
Tom Cindric, Group Director
Annual forum that showcases the technology, tools and solutions for the design, construction, maintenance and modification of commercial buildings, institutions and other structures. These tools and education are essential for the seamless collaboration and communication between all those involved throughout the asset lifecycle.
72M Attendees
Frequency: Annual
Founded in: 1976

Directories & Databases

2109 **Akron School Design Institute**
American Architectural Foundation
1020 19th Street NW
Suite 525
Washington, DC 20036
202-787-1001; *Fax:* 202-78 -002
info@archfoundation.org;
www.archfoundation.org
Ron Bogie, President/CEO
Scott Lauer, VP of Programs
Frequency: Annual

2110 **Dodge Building Stock**
DRI/McGraw-Hill
148 Princeton Heights Town Road
Height Town, NJ 08520
609- 42- 500
800-393-6343
support@construction.com;
www.dodge.construction.com
Social Media: Facebook, Twitter, LinkedIn
Keith Fox, President
Linda Brennan, VP of Operations
This database contains more than 18,000 historical and forecast quarterly time series on US buildings, including total square footage, number of buildings, and roof area for groups of structures in the categories of commercial, institutionals, manufacturing and residential.

2111 **Pro File/Official Directory of the American Institute of Architects**
American Institute of Architects (AIAA)
1735 New York Avenue NW
Washington, DC 20006-5292
202-783-6500
800-242-3837; *Fax:* 202-626-7364
infocentral@aia.org; www.aia.org
Christine McEntee, CEO
Over 18,000 architectural firms are listed. These listings have one or more principals who is a member of the American Institute of Architects.
Cost: $225.00
1800 Pages
Frequency: Annual

2112 **Progressive Architecture: Information Sources Issue**
Penton Media
1300 E 9th St
Suite 316
Cleveland, OH 44114-1503
216-696-7000; *Fax:* 216-696-1752
information@penton.com; www.penton.com
David Rowlands, CEO
Nicola Allais, EVP
List of trade and professional architecture associations.
Cost: $48.00

2113 **Sweets Directory**
Grey House Publishing/McGraw Hill Construction
1221 Avenue of the Americas
New York, NY 10020-1095
212-512-2000
800-442-2258; *Fax:* 212-512-3840
webmaster@mcgraw-hill.com;
www.mcgraw-hill.com
Social Media: Facebook, Twitter
Harold W McGraw III, CEO
Jack Callahan, Vice President
The leading desktop reference and preliminary research guide, featuring more than 10,000 building product manufacturers and their products.
Cost: $145.00
950 Pages
Frequency: Annual
ISBN: 1-592378-50-1
Founded in: 1906

2114 **ThomasNet**
Thomas Publishing Company, LLC
User Services Department
5 Penn Plaza
New York, NY 10001
212-695-0500
800-699-9822; *Fax:* 212-290-7362
contact@thomaspublishing.com;
www.thomasnet.com
Social Media: Facebook, Twitter, LinkedIn
Carl Holst-Knudsen, President
Robert Anderson, VP, Planning
Mitchell Peipert, VP, Finance
Ivy Molofsky, VP, Human Resources
A way to reach qualified businesses that list their company information on ThomasNet.com. Detailed profiles promote their products, services, capabilities and brands carried. The ThomasNet.com web site is the most up-to-date compilation of 650,000 North American manufacturers, distributors, and service companies in 67,000 industrial categories.
Founded in: 1898

2115 **Visual Merchandising and Store Design**
ST Media Group International
P.O. Box 1060
Skokie, IL 60076
847-763-4938
800-421-1321; *Fax:* 847-763-9030
customer@stmediagroup.com;
www.stmediagroup.com
Steve Duccilli, Group Publisher
Wade Swormstedt, Editor/Publisher
Ted Swormstedt, President/CEO
Visual Merchandising and Store Design showcases the latest store designs and visual presentations, presents merchandising strategies and new

products and reports on industry news and events.
Frequency: Monthly
Circulation: 27000
Founded in: 1922

Industry Web Sites

2116 http://gold.greyhouse.com
G.O.L.D Grey House OnLine Databases
Grey House Publishing's online database platform, GOLD. offers Quick Search, Keyword Search and Expert Search for most business sectors including architecture, building and construction markets. The GOLD platform makes finding the information you need quick and easy. All of Grey House's directory products are available for subscription on the GOLD platform.

2117 www.access-board.gov
Architectural & Transportation Barriers Compliance
Devoted to accessibility for people with disabilities.

2118 www.acsa-arch.org
Association of Collegiate Schools of Architecture
A nonprofit, membership association founded to advance the quality of architectural education.

2119 www.adda.org
American Design Drafting Association
The premier professional organization for drafters, designers, engineers, architects, ilustrators, graphics artist, digital technicians, digitial imaging, visual communications and multimedia

2120 www.aecsystems.com.au
A/E/C Systems International/Penton Media
Focuses on Internet/Intranet for the design, engineering and construction industries.

2121 www.aia.org
American Institute of Architects
A professional membership association for licensed, emerging professionals, and allied partners.

2122 www.apti.org
Association for Preservation Technology Int'l
A cross-disciplinary, membership organization dedicated to promoting the best technology for conserving historic structures and their settings.

2123 www.archprecast.org
Architectural Precast Association
A national trade association organized to advance the interests of architectural precast concrete in North America.

2124 www.asla.org
American Society of Landscape Architects
The national professional association representing landscape architects.

2125 www.builderspace.com
BuilderSpace.com
An online directory for the building industry and resources created to help users find the services and information they need.

2126 www.construction.com
McGraw-Hill Construction
McGraw-Hill Construction (MHC), part of The McGraw-Hill Companies, connects people and projects across the design and construction industry, serving owners, architects, engineers, general contractors, subcontractors, building product manufacturers, suppliers, dealers, distributors and adjacent markets.

2127 www.ctbuh.org
Council on Tall Buildings and Urban Habitat
Studies and reports on all aspects of the planning, design, and construction of tall buildings.

2128 www.greyhouse.com
Grey House Publishing
Authoritative reference directories for most business sectors including architecture, building and construction markets. Users can search the online databases with varied search criteria allowing for custom searches by product category, geographic area, sales volume, keyword, subject and more. Full Grey House catalog and online ordering also available.

2129 www.historicnewengland.org
Soc. for Preservation of New England Antiquities
Focuses on buildings, landscapes and objects reflecting New England life from the 17th century to the present.

2130 www.icea.net
Insulated Cable Engineers Association
Professional organization dedicated to developing cable standards for the electric power, control and telecommunications industries. Ensures safe, economical and efficient cable systems utilizing proven state-of-the-art materials and concepts. ICEA documents are of interest to cable manufacturers, architects and engineers, utility and manufacturing plant personnel, telecommunication engineers, consultants and OEMs.

2131 www.ihs.com
International Code Council
Nonprofit membership association with more than 16,000 members who span the building community, from code enforcement officials to materials manufacturers. Dedicated to preserving the public health, safety and welfare in the built environment through the effective use and enforcement of model codes.

2132 www.ncarb.org
Nat'l Council of Architectural Registration Boards
For state registration boards in the United States regulating the practice of architecture.

2133 www.reedconstructiondata.com
Architects First Source Online
Comprehensive building products information.

2134 www.sah.org
Society of Architectural Historians
Provides an international forum for those who care about architecture and its related arts.

2135 www.sara-national.org
Society of American Registered Architects
Architects helping Architects by sharing ideas and information.

2136 www.sarc.msstate.edu
Small Town Center
To maintain and improve the quality of life in American small towns.

2137 www.sbicouncil.org
Sustainable Buildings Industry Council
Information on the design, affordability, energy performance, and enviromental soundness of residential, institutional and commercial buildings.

2138 www.sname.org
Society of Naval Architects and Marine Engineers
Internationally recognized nonprofit, technical, professional society of individual members serving the maritime and offshore industries and their suppliers. Dedicated to advancing the industry by recording information, sponsoring research, offering career guidance and supporting education.

2139 www.sweets.construction.com
McGraw Hill Construction
In depth product information that lets you find, compare, select, specify and make purchase decisions in the industrial product marketplace.

Associations

2140 American Academy of Equine Art
117 North Water Street
PO Box 1364
Georgetown, KY 40324
502-570-8567; *Fax:* 859-281-6043
fcconner@aaea.net; www.aaea.net
Xochitl Barnes, AAEA Vice President
Frances Clay Conner, Executive Director
The AAEA serves to educate and encourage a broad awareness and appreciation of contemporary equine art as a specific and distinctively worthy segment of fine art in America.
90 Members
Founded in: 1980

2141 American Alliance of Museums
2451 Crystal Dr.
Suite 1005
Arlington, VA 22202
202-289-1818; *Fax:* 202-289-6578
membership@aam-us.org; www.aam-us.org
Social Media: Facebook, Twitter, LinkedIn
Laura L. Lott, President & CEO
Kyle Ange, VP, Finance & Operations
Brent Mundt, VP, Development
Janet Vaughan, VP, Membership & Programs
Elizabeth Merritt, VP, Strategic Foresight
Dedicated to promoting excellence within the museum community. Through advocacy, professional education, information exchange, accreditation and guidance on current professional standards of performance, AAM assists museum staff, boards and volunteers across the country to better serve the public.
16000 Members
Founded in: 1906

2142 American Art Therapy Association
4875 Eisenhower Avenue
Suite 240
Alexandria, VA 22304-3302
703-212-2238
888-290-0878
info@arttherapy.org; www.arttherapy.org
Social Media: Facebook, Twitter, LinkedIn, RSS
Donna Betts, PHD, ATR-BC, President
Susan Corrigan, Executive Director
Michele Basham, Director, Membership Information
Julia Connell, Communications Manager
Barbara Florence, Director, Communication, Education
An organization of professionals dedicated to the belief that the creative process involved in art making is healing and life enhancing. Its mission is to serve its members and the general public by providing standards of professional competence, and developing and promoting knowledge in, and of, the field of art therapy.
4500 Members
Founded in: 1969

2143 American Association of Museums
2451 Crystal Drive
Suite 1005
Arlington, VA 22202
202-289-1818; *Fax:* 202-289-6578
membership@aam-us.org; www.aam-us.org
Social Media: Facebook, Twitter, LinkedIn
Meme Omogbai, Chairman
Ford W. Bell, President
Laura Lott, COO
Canan Abayhan, Senior Director, Information
Carol Constantine, Director, Finance & Administration
16000 Members
Founded in: 1906

2144 American Society for Aesthetics
1550 Larimer Street
Suite 644
Denver, CO 80202-1602
562-331-4424
asa@aesthetics-online.org; www.aesthetics-online.org
Social Media: Facebook, Twitter
Cynthia Freeland, President
Kathleen Higgins, Vice President
Promotes study, research, discussion and publication in aesthetics, which includes all studies of the arts and related experience including philosophic, scientific and theoretical viewpoints.
Founded in: 1942

2145 American Society of Bookplate Collectors & Designers
5802 Bullock Loop
Suite C1 #84404
Laredo, TX 78041-8807
414-228-7831
info@bookplate.org; www.bookplate.org
Social Media: Facebook, Twitter, LinkedIn, YouTube, Flickr, Pinterest, In
For designers, owners and collectors of bookplates.
Founded in: 1977

2146 Antique Appraisal Association of America
1403 Gloria Lane
Boulder City, NV 89005
702-629-4502
888-791-0033
aaaofamerica@att.net; www.antiqueappraisalassn.com
Helen Nolan, Executive Director
Members are well known for their Code of Ethics in their dealing with their customers. Our qualified professional appraisers have expertise in all types of appraisals and appraisal-related services, including insurance damage claims, estate probate, estate liquidation, estate auctions, court testimony, consultants and much more.
Founded in: 1972

2147 Antique Coin Machine Collectors Association
E-Mail: diermanor@gmail.com
Association for collectors and enthusiasts of antique coin-operated devices.
Founded in: 1985

2148 Antiques & Collectibles National Association
PO Box 4389
Davidson, NC 28036
704-895-9088
800-287-7127; *Fax:* 704-895-0230;
www.antiqueandcollectible.com
Angie Becker, President
Mike Becker, Vice President
Association founded in 1991 for the benefit of antique dealers and collectors.
Founded in: 1991

2149 Antiques Council
PO Box 1508
Warren, MA 01083
413-436-7064; *Fax:* 413-436-0448
info@antiquescouncil.com; www.antiquescouncil.com
Marty Shapiro, President
Alan Cunha, VP
John Copenhaver, Education Director
David Bernard, Facilities Director
Joel Fletcher, Communications Director
A nonprofit organization created by professional antique dealers to improve the confidence of the public in antiques and their dealers through education, service and example.
100 Members
Founded in: 1990

2150 Art Dealers Association of America
205 Lexington Avenue
Suite 901
New York, NY 10016
212-488-5550; *Fax:* 646-688-6809
adaa@artdealers.org; www.artdealers.org
Social Media: Facebook, Twitter, Instagram
Dorsey Waxter, President
Mary Sabbatino, Vice President
Adam Sheffer, Vice President
Laurence Shopmaker, Secretary
Mark Brady, Treasurer
Nonprofit organzation that works to improve the stature and standing of the art gallery business. Members deal primarily with paintings, sculpture, prints, drawings and photographs from the Renaissance to the present day. We have more than 160 member galleries in more than 25 US cities.
160 Members
Founded in: 1962

2151 Art Libraries Society of North America
7044 S. 13th St.
Oak Creek, WI 53154
414-768-8000
800-817-0621; *Fax:* 414-768-8001
customercare@arlisna.org; www.arlisna.org
Social Media: Facebook, Twitter, LinkedIn, Pinterest
Kristen Regina, President
Heather Gendron, Vice-President/President Elect
Jamie Lausch Vander Broek, Secretary
Mark Pompelia, Treasurer
Robert J. Kopchinski, Association & Conference Manager
Devoted to fostering excellence in art librarianship, visual resources and curatorship for the advancement of visual arts. See website for available publications.
1000 Members
Founded in: 1972
*Mailing list available for rent*at $200 per M

2152 Art and Antique Dealers League of America
PO Box 2066
Lenox Hill Station
New York, NY 10021
212-879-7558; *Fax:* 212-772-7197
secretary@artantiquedealersleague.com; www.artantiquedealersleague.com
Clinton Howell, President
Robert Simon, VP
David Mayer, Secretary-Executive Director
Susan Kaplan Jacobson, Treasurer
109 Members
Founded in: 1926

2153 Art and Creative Materials Institute/ACMI
99 Derby Street
Suite 200
Hingham, MA 02043
781-556-1044; *Fax:* 781-207-5550
debbieg@acminet.org; www.acminet.org
Michael Storei, President
Joan Lilly, Vice President
Timothy Gomez, Treasurer
Debbie Gustafson, Associate Director
Debbie Munroe, Certification Director

A non-profit association of manufacturers of art, craft and other creative materials, ACMI sponsors a certification program for both children's and adult's art materials and products, certifying that these products are non-toxic and meet voluntary standards of quality and performance. ACMI seeks to create and maintain a positive environment for art, craft and other creative materials usage, promoting safety in the materials and providing information and service resources on such products.
210 Members
Founded in: 1936
Mailing list available for rent: 199 names

2154 **Arts Midwest**
2908 Hennepin Ave.
Suite 200
Minneapolis, MN 55408-1954

612-341-0755; www.artsmidwest.org
Social Media: Facebook, Twitter, YouTube, Flickr

David J. Fraher, President & CEO
Peter Capell, Chair

One of six regional arts organizations established with funding from the National Endowment for the Arts, Arts Midwest provides access to performing, visual and literary arts programs in Illinois, Indiana, Iowa, Michigan, Minnesota, North Dakota, Ohio, South Dakota and Wisconsin.

2155 **Association for Preservation Technology International**
3085 Stevenson Drive
Suite 200
Springfield, IL 62703

217-529-9039; *Fax:* 888-723-4242
info@apti.org; www.apti.org
Social Media: Facebook, LinkedIn

Gretchen Pfaehler, President
John Diodati, Vice President
Dean Koga, Vice President
Lesley Gilmore, Treasurer
Nathela Chatara, CAE, Administrative Director

The Association for Preservation Technology (APT) is a cross-disciplinary, membership organization dedicated to promoting the best technology for conserving historic structures and their settings.
Founded in: 1968

2156 **Association of Historians of American Art**

E-Mail: info@ahaaonline.org; www.ahaaonline.org
Social Media: Facebook, LinkedIn

Ellery Foutch, Chair
Austen Barron Bailly, Co-Chair
Anna Marley, Chair Emerita
Jillian Russo, Secretary
Monica Jovanovich-Kelley, Treasurer

An association for the promotion of scholarship in American art.
Founded in: 1979

2157 **Association of Restorers**
8 Medford Place
New Hartford, NY 13413

315-733-1952
800-260-1829; *Fax:* 315-724-7231;
www.assoc-restorers.com

Andrea Daley, Founder

It is the mission of the AOR, Association of Restorers Inc, to increase the awareness of choice to consere, refurbish or restore historical works of art, household furnishings and architectural constructions
Founded in: 1997

2158 **College Art Association**
TERRA Foundation
50 Broadway
21st Floor
New York, NY 10004

212-691-1051; *Fax:* 212-627-2381
nyoffice@collegeart.org; www.collegeart.org
Social Media: Facebook, Twitter, YouTube

DeWitt Godfrey, President
John Richardson, Vice President for External Affairs
Charles A. Wright, Vice President for Committees
Doralynn Pines, Secretary
John Hyland Jr., Treasurer

Promotes excellence in scholarship and technology in the criticisim of the visual arts and in the creativity and technical skill in the teaching and practices of art.
13000 Members
Founded in: 1911

2159 **Indian Arts & Crafts Association**
4010 Carlisle NE
Suite C
Albuquerque, NM 87107

505-265-9149; *Fax:* 505-265-8251
info@iaca.com; www.iaca.com
Social Media: Facebook, Twitter

Joseph P. Zeller, President
Cliff Fragua, Vice President
Beth Hale, Secretary
Kathi Ouellet, Treasurer

Nonprofit trade association whose mission is to promote, protect and preserve Indian arts.
700 Members
Founded in: 1974

2160 **International Fine Print Dealers Association (IFPDA)**
250 W 26th St
Suite 405
New York, NY 10001-6737

212-674-6095; *Fax:* 212-674-6783
info@ifpda.org; www.ifpda.org
Social Media: Facebook, Twitter

Paula McCarthy Panczenko, President
David Cleaton-Roberts, Vice President
Barbara Krakow, Vice President
Joni Moisant Weyl, Treasurer
Armin Kunz, Secretary

A nonprofit organzation that aspires to create a greater awareness and appreciation of fine prints among collectors and the general public. Povides funding for a variety of print-related educational programs, including pubications, lectures and symposia.
160 Members
Founded in: 1987

2161 **International Foundation for Art Research**
500 5th Avenue
Suite 935
New York, NY 10110

212-391-6234; *Fax:* 212-391-8794
kferg@ifar.org; www.ifar.org

Jack A Josephson, Chairman
Sharon Flescher, Executive Director

Nonprofit educational and research organization working for the interests of art scholarship, law and the public interest.
Founded in: 1969

2162 **Mid Atlantic Arts Foundation**
201 N. Charles St.
Suite 401
Baltimore, MD 21201

410-539-6656; *Fax:* 410-837-5517;
www.midatlanticarts.org
Social Media: Facebook, Twitter, YouTube, Pinterest

Alan W. Cooper, Executive Director
E. Scott Johnson, Chair

One of six regional arts organizations established with funding from the National Endowment for the Arts, Mid Atlantic Arts Foundation promotes access to and participation in the arts in Delaware, the District of Columbia, Maryland, New Jersey, New York, Pennsylvania, the US Virgin Islands, Virginia and West Virginia.
Founded in: 1979

2163 **Mid-America Arts Alliance**
2018 Baltimore Ave.
Kansas City, MO 64108

816-421-1388; www.maaa.org
Social Media: Facebook, Twitter, Flickr

Mary Kennedy, Chief Executive Officer
C. Kendrick Fergeson, Chair

One of six regional arts organizations established with funding from the National Endowment for the Arts, Mid-America Arts Alliance supports artists, cultural organizations and traveling exhibitions in underserved communities in Arkansas, Kansas, Missouri, Nebraska, Oklahoma and Texas.
Founded in: 1972

2164 **National Antique & Collectible Association**
PO Box 4389
Davidson, NC 28036

704-895-9088
800-287-7127; *Fax:* 704-895-0230
info@acna.us; www.acna.us
Social Media: Facebook, Twitter

Angie Becker, President
Mike Becker, Vice President

The largest trade association for antique dealers & private collectors in the country. Our association has members in all 50 states. We offer an array of benefits including our insurance programs, merchant services, quarterly newsletter, educational seminars, travel, supply discounts and many more.
4300 Members
Founded in: 1991

2165 **National Antique Doll Dealers Association (NADDA)**

www.nadda.org
Social Media: Facebook

Lynette Gross, President
Ed Kolibaba, Vice President
Diane Costa, Secretary
Richard K. Saxman, Treasurer

NADDA was formed to promote honesty and integrity in the increasingly popular antique doll trade.
Founded in: 1986

2166 **National Art Education Association**
901 Prince Street
Suite 300
Alexandria, VA 22314

703-860-8000
800-299-8321; *Fax:* 703-860-2960
info@arteducators.org; www.arteducators.org/
Social Media: Facebook, Twitter, LinkedIn

Dennis Inhulson, President
Patricia Franklin, President Elect
Deborah B Reeve, Executive Director

Promote art education through professional development, service, advancment of knowledge and leadership.
22000 Members
Founded in: 1947
Mailing list available for rent: 22,000 names at $95 per M

2167 **National Art Materials Trade Association**
20200 Zion Ave.
Cornelius, NC 28031

704-892-6244
info@namta.org; www.namta.org
Social Media: Facebook, Twitter, LinkedIn

Hayley Prendergast, President
Kevin P Lavin, Executive VP & CFO
Howard Krinsky, Vice President
Reggie Hall, Executive Director
Rick Munisteri, Director of Meetings

International association of manufacturers, importers, wholesalers and retailers of art materials.
2.1M Members

2168 **National Assembly of State Arts Agencies**
1200 18th St NW
Suite 1100
Washington, DC 20036
202-347-6352
202-347-5948; *Fax:* 202-737-0526
nasaa@nasaa-arts.org; www.nasaa-arts.org
Social Media: Facebook

Gary Gibbs, President
Jonathan Katz, Chief Executive Officer
Laura S. Smith, CFRE, Chief Advancement Officer
Kelly J Barsdate, Chief Planning Officer
Sharon Gee, Director of Meetings and Events

NASAA's mission is to advance and promote a meaningful role for the arts in the lives of individuals, families and communities throughout the United States. We empower state art agencies through strategic assistance that fosters leadership, enhances planning and decision making, and increases resources. TDD 202-347-5948.
56 Members
Founded in: 1968

2169 **National Association of Fine Arts**
1155 F Street NW
Suite 1050
Washington, DC 20004
414-332-9306; *Fax:* 888-884-6232;
www.nafa.com
Social Media: Facebook, Twitter, LinkedIn

Kim O'Brien, President & CEO
Chip Anderson, Vice Chair
S Christopher Johnson, Secretary
Nathan Zuidema, Treasurer

Seeks to provide services and networking opportunities to individuals in the arts community.
100 Members
Founded in: 1986

2170 **National Auctioneers Association**
8880 Ballentine St
Overland Park, KS 66214

913-541-8084; *Fax:* 913-894-5281
support@auctioneers.org; www.auctioneers.org
Social Media: Facebook, Twitter, LinkedIn, YouTube

Spanky Assiter, CAI, AARE, President
John S. Nicholls, AARE, VP
James Devin Ford, CAI, CES, Treasurer
Hannes Combest, CEO
Thomas W. Saterly, Past President

NAA promotes the auction method of marketing and enhances the professionalism of its practitioners
6,000 Members
Founded in: 1948

2171 **National Guild of Community Schools of the Arts**
520 8th Avenue
3rd Floor, Suite 302
New York, NY 10018

212-268-3337; *Fax:* 212-268-3995
guildinfo@nationalguild.org;
www.nationalguild.org
Social Media: Facebook, Twitter, LinkedIn, YouTube, Instagram, RSS

Jonathan Herman, Executive Director
Ken Cole, Assosiate Director
Claire Wilmoth, Membership Associate
James Harton, Program Director
Traci Horgen, Business Manager

Arts Management in Community Institutions (AMICI) Summer Institute trains administrators to meet needs of growing and emerging arts schools. Other programs, services, guildnotes newsletter, job opportunities listings, and publications catalog available upon request on online. Mailing list $25 for non-members, free for members.
300 Members
Founded in: 1937

2172 **National Network for Art Placement**
935 W Avenue 37
Los Angeles, CA 90065

323-222-4035
800-354-5348
NNAPnow@aol.com;
www.americansforthearts.org
Social Media: Facebook, Pinterest, RSS

Warren Christensen, Consultant

An organization that helps any artist with start up capital and services for small businesses.

2173 **National Trust for Historic Preservation**
2600 Virginia Avenue
Suite 1000
Washington, DC 20037

202-588-6000
800-944-6847; *Fax:* 202-588-6038
info@savingplaces.org; www.savingplaces.org
Social Media: Facebook, Twitter, Pinterest, Instagram, YouTube

Stephanie K. Meeks, President &CEO
David J. Brown, Vice President & CPO
Paul Edmondson, Chief Legal Officer
Terry Richey, Chief Marketing Officer
Rosemarie Rae, Chief Financial Officer

A private, nonprofit membership organization dedicated to saving historic places and revitlizing America's communities. Also provides leadership, education, advocacy, and resources to save America's diverse historic places and revitalize the communities.
270k Members
Founded in: 1949

2174 **New England Foundation for the Arts**
145 Tremont St.
7th Fl.
Boston, MA 02111

617-951-0010; www.nefa.org

Cathy Edwards, Executive Director
Lawrence J. Simpson, Chair

One of six regional arts organizations established with funding from the National Endowment for the Arts, New England Foundation for the Arts supports artists and their endeavours in Connecticut, Maine, Massachusetts, New Hampshire, Rhode Island and Vermont.
Founded in: 1976

2175 **Professional Picture Framers Association**
2282 Springport Road
Suite F
Jackson, MI 49202

517-788-8100
800-762-9287; *Fax:* 517-788-8371
ppfa@ppfa.com; www.ppfa.com
Social Media: Facebook

John Pruitt, President
Stuart M Altschuler, VP
Jim Esp, Secretary & Executive Director
Robin Gentry, Treasurer

A trade association of manufacturers, wholesalers, print publishers, importers and retailers selling art, framing and related supplies.
3000 Members
Founded in: 1971

2176 **Society of Animal Artists**
5451 Sedona Hills Drive
Berthoud, CO 80513

970-532-3127; *Fax:* 970-532-2537
admin@societyofanimalartists.com;
www.societyofanimalartists.com
Social Media: Facebook

Diane Mason, President
Allen Bragden, VP
Marilyn Newmark, VP
Douglas Allen, VP
Renee Headings-Bemis, Treasurer

Devoted to promoting excellence in the portrayal of the creatures sharing our planet and to the education of the public through informative art seminars, lectures and teaching demonstrations.
360 Members
Founded in: 1960

2177 **Society of Illustrators**
128 E 63rd St
New York, NY 10065

212-838-2560; *Fax:* 212-838-2561
info@societyillustrators.org;
www.societyillustrators.org
Social Media: Facebook, Twitter

Tim O'Brien, President
Karen Green, Vice President
Victor Juhasz, Executive VP
Leslie Cober-Gentry, Secretary
David Ruess, Treasurer

A professional society of illustrators and art directors.
950 Members
Founded in: 1901

2178 **South Arts**
1800 Peachtree St. NW
Suite 808
Atlanta, GA 30309

404-874-7244; *Fax:* 404-873-2148;
www.southarts.org
Social Media: Facebook, Twitter, LinkedIn

Suzette M. Surkamer, Executive Director
Ted Abernathy, Chair

One of six regional arts organizations established with funding from the National Endowment for the Arts, South Arts assists state arts agencies in Alabama, Florida, Georgia, Kentucky, Louisiana, Mississippi, North Carolina, South Carolina and Tennessee with the production, promotion and presentation of southern arts and culture.
Founded in: 1975

2179 The American Institute for Conservation of Historic & Artistic Works
1156 15th Street
Suite 320
Washington, DC 20005-1714
202-452-9545; *Fax:* 202-452-9328
info@conservation-us.org;
www.conservation-us.org
Social Media: Facebook, Twitter, YouTube, Flickr
Eryl P. Wentworth, Executive Director
Ruth Seyler, Membership & Meetings Director
Eric Pourchot, Institutional Advancement Director
Sandy T. Nguyen, Finance Director
Abigail Choudhury, Development and Education
Conservators of artistic and cultural property.
3500 Members
Founded in: 1961

2180 The Art Students League of New York
215 W 57th Street
New York, NY 10019
212-247-4510; *Fax:* 212-541-7024
info@artstudentsleague.org;
www.theartstudentsleague.org
Social Media: Facebook, Twitter, YouTube, Pinterest, Instagram
Salvatore Barbieri, President
Susan Matz, Vice President
Howard A. Friedman, Vice President
Ira Golberg, Executive Director
Ken Park, Director of Communications
Educational organization that provides space, studios and offices to members.
Founded in: 1875

2181 The Art and Antique Dealers League of America, Inc.
PO Box 2066
Lenox Hill Station
New York, NY 10021
212-879-7558; *Fax:* 212-772-7197
secretary@artantiquedealersleague.com;
www.artantiquedealersleague.com
Clinton Howell, President
Robert Simon, Vice President
David Mayer, Secretary-Executive Director
Susan Kaplan Jacobson, Treasurer
Nonprofit organization promotes interests of retailers and wholesalers of antiques and art objects.
110 Members
Founded in: 1926

2182 The Maven Co.
Maven Company
PO Box 937
Plandome, NY 11020-0937
51 -62 -880; *Fax:* 914-248-0800
fasttrack@erols.com;
www.mavencompany.com
N Chittenden, VP
An innovator of new and unique programs to help antique dealers sell their merchandise and to make their shows more successful.
5,000 Attendees
Frequency: January/Annual
Founded in: 1970

2183 The National Antique & Art Dealers Association of America
220 E 57th St
New York, NY 10022
212-826-9707; *Fax:* 212-832-9493;
www.naadaa.org
James R McConnaughy, President
Mark Jacoby, VP
Arlie Sulka, Secretary
Steven J Chait, Treasurer
Works to promote the best interests of the antique art exhibitions and to promote just, honorable and ethical trade practices.
38 Members
Founded in: 1954

2184 Train Collectors Association
PO Box 248
Strasburg, PA 17579-0248
717-687-8623; www.traincollectors.org
Wayne S. Sheriff, President
The worldwide organization for tinplate train collectors and enthusiasts.
30000 Members
Founded in: 1954

2185 Volunteer Committees of Art Museums
5139 Thorncroft Court
Royal Oak, MI 48073
504-488-2631; *Fax:* 504-484-6662
co_presidents@vcam.org; www.vcam.org
Social Media: Facebook, Twitter, LinkedIn, YouTube
Peter Milne, President
Linda McGinty, Co President
Julie George, Secretary
Victoria Cather, Treasurer
An internationally recognized non-profit organization. VCAM is committed to provide a forum for information exchange, mutual education and enhancement of services to its art museum volunteer committee members through international conferences, regional meetings, published comprehensive conference reports, resource files and the VCAM NEWS publication.
19 Members
Founded in: 1952

2186 Western States Arts Federation (WESTAF)
1743 Wazee St.
Suite 300
Denver, CO 80202
303-629-1166; www.westaf.org
Social Media: Facebook, Twitter
Anthony Radich, Executive Director
Virginia Gowski, Chair
One of six regional arts organizations established with funding from the National Endowment for the Arts, WESTAF advances the preservation and development of the arts in Alaska, Arizona, California, Colorado, Hawaii, Idaho, Montana, Nevada, New Mexico, Oregon, Utah, Washington and Wyoming.

Newsletters

2187 ARTnewsletter
ARTnews Associates
48 W 38th Street
New York, NY 10018-6211
212-398-1690
800-284-4625; *Fax:* 212-819-0394;
www.artnewsonline.com
Milton Esterow, Publisher/CEO
Robin Cembalest, Executive Editor
Debra Melson, Marketing
Elizabeth McNamara, Circulation Manager
Business report on the world art market. Targeted to private collectors, dealers, gallery owners, museum directors and curators, tax and estate buyers.
Cost: $279.00
Frequency: Bi-weekly
Circulation: 83375
Founded in: 1902

2188 ASA Newsletter
American Society for Aesthetics
1550 Larimer Street
Suite 644
Denver, CO 80202
562-331-4424
asa@aesthetics-online.org;
www.aesthetics-online.org
Social Media: Facebook, Twitter
Cynthia Freeland, President
Kathleen Higgins, Vice President
Promotes study, research, discussion and publication in aesthetics, which includes all studies of the arts and related experience including philosophic, scientific and theoretical viewpoints.
Founded in: 1942

2189 Antique Appraisal Association of America Newsletter
Antique Appraisal Association of America
1403 Gloria Lane
Boulder City, NV 89005
702-629-4502
888-791-0033
aaaofamerica@att.net;
www.antiqueappraisalassn.com
Marge Swenson, Publisher
Supplies members with additional knowledge of antiques from research.

2190 Art Hazards Newsletter
New York Foundation for the Arts
155 Avenue of the Americas
14th Floor
New York, NY 10013
212-366-6900; *Fax:* 212-366-1778
csa@tmn.com
Theodore Berger, Executive Director
Toni Lewis, Director Administration
Contains information on all hazardous materials; art materials and articles.
Cost: $24.00
Frequency: Quarterly
Founded in: 1977

2191 Art Research News
500 5th Avenue
Suite 935
New York, NY 10110
212-391-6234; *Fax:* 212-391-8794
kferg@ifar.org; www.ifar.org
Sharon Flescher, Executive Director
The latest news on authenticity, ownership, theft, and other artistic, legal and ethical issues concerning art objects.
Founded in: 1969

2192 Arts & Culture Funding Report
Capitol City Publishers
4416 East West Hwy
Suite 400
Bethesda, MD 20814-4568
301-916-1800
800-637-9915; *Fax:* 301-528-2497;
www.capitolcitypublishers.com
A monthly newsletter on federal, state, private and nonprofit sector funding and financial assistance to arts and cultural organizations.
Cost: $198.00
Frequency: Monthly
ISSN: 1047-3297

2193 Arts Management
Radius Group

545 5th Ave
New York, NY 10017-3647

212-972-2929; *Fax:* 212-972-7581
postmaster@trflaw.com; www.trflaw.com

Leonard A Rodes, Partner
David Trachtenberg, Partner
Barry Friedberg, Partner

The national news service for those who finance, manage and communicate the arts.
Cost: $18.00
Frequency: 5 per year

2194 **Artsfocus**
Colorado Springs Fine Arts Center
30 W Dale St
Colorado Spring, CO 80903-3249

719-634-5581; *Fax:* 719-634-0570
info@csfineartscenter.org;
www.csfineartscenter.org

Sam Gappmayer, CEO
Kari Torgerson, COO
Tom Jackson, Director of Development

Museum members publication.
Cost: $5.00
24 Pages
Frequency: Quarterly
Founded in: 1936
Printed in 2 colors on matte stock

2195 **Aviso**
American Association of Museums
1575 Eye Street NW
Suite 400
Washington, DC 20005-1113

202-289-1818; *Fax:* 202-289-6578
membership@aam-us.org; www.aam-us.org

Ford W Bell, President
Douglas Myers, CEO Executive Director

Reports on museums in the news, federal legislation affecting museums, upcoming seminars and workshops, federal grant deadlines and AAM activities and services.
Frequency: Monthly

2196 **Bookplates in the News**
Amer. Society of Bookplate Collectors & Designers
605 N Stoneman Avenue
Suite F
Alhambra, CA 91801-1406

626-579-9147
exlibris@att.net; www.artisanale@hotmail.com

Audrey Spencer Arellanes, Publisher
Victor Amor, Owner

Collectors' news for designers, owners and collectors of bookplates.
Cost: $25.00
200 Pages
Frequency: Quarterly
Circulation: 250

2197 **Communique**
Association for Preservation Technology Int'l.
3085 Stevenson Drive
Suite 200
Springfield, IL 62703

217-529-9039; *Fax:* 888-723-4242
info@apti.org; www.apti.org

Joan Berkwitz, President
Gretchen Pfaehler, Vice President
Kyle Normandin, Treasurer
Nathela Chatara,CAE, Administrative Director

APT's electronic newsletter, enables APT members to exchange preservation information, publicize their news and awards, share project experience with colleagues, post calls for papers, and submit preservation queries to the readership.
Frequency: Quarterly

2198 **Cotton & Quail Antique Gazette**
F+W Media
38 E. 29th Street
New York, NY 10016

212-447-1400; *Fax:* 212-447-5231
contact_us@fwmedia.com;
www.fwpublications.com

Greg Smith, Publisher
Linda Kunkel, Editor
Dave Paul, Marketing

Contains articles about various collecting topics, announcements of upcoming shows, reviews of shows and auctions, a Q & A column on antiques, 'how-to' articles, regular features about collecting and selling, an extensive show and auction calendar.
Cost: $20.00
Frequency: Monthly
Circulation: 25000
Founded in: 1965

2199 **Encouraging Rejection**
Noforehead Press
Box 55
Kearsarge, NH 03847-0130

www.reuben.org

Mark Heath, Editor/Publisher

To inspire and encourage artists in the face of rejection.
Cost: $19.00
Frequency: Bi-Monthly
Founded in: 1994

2200 **Folk Art Finder**
Gallery Press
117 N Main Street
Essex, CT 06426-1302

860-767-0313
folkart.com

Florence Laffal, Editor/Publisher

Contains feature stories, a calendar of events, a readers exchange, news items, book reviews, and classified and display ads relating to 20th century American folk art. Other issues addressed are folk art preservation, laws affecting the arts and funding for the arts.
Cost: $14.00
24 Pages
Frequency: Quarterly
Mailing list available for rent
Printed in one color on matte stock

2201 **IFAR Journal**
International Foundation for Art Research
500 5th Avenue
Suite 935
New York, NY 10110

212-391-6234; *Fax:* 212-391-8794
kferg@ifar.org; www.ifar.org
Social Media: Facebook

Sharon Flescher PhD, CEO
Jack A. Josephson, Chairman

Listings of stolen art and the legal developments of articles on art recovery, art law, cultural property and art authentication.
Cost: $65.00
32 Pages
Frequency: Quarterly
ISSN: 1098-1195
Founded in: 1969

2202 **Indian Arts & Crafts Association Newsletter**
4010 Carlisle NE
Suite C
Albuquerque, NM 87107

505-265-9149; *Fax:* 505-265-8251
info@iaca.com; www.iaca.com

Joseph Zeller, President
Don Standing Bear Forest, VP
Gail Chehak, Executive Director
Susan Pourian, Secretary
Kathi Ouellet, Treasurer

2203 **International Association of Auctioneers Newsletter**
Butterfield & Butterfield Auctioneers
220 San Bruno Ave
San Francisco, CA 94103-5018

415-861-7500
800-222-2854; *Fax:* 415-861-8951
appraisals.us@bonhams.com;
www.butterfields.com

Melcolm Barbar, CEO

A news bulletin with descriptions of upcoming auctions around the world.
8 Pages
Frequency: Quarterly
Circulation: 6500
Founded in: 1865

2204 **Kovels on Antiques and Collectibles**
Antiques
2135 N Milwaukee Ave
Chicago, IL 44122

773-360-8162; *Fax:* 216-752-3115;
www.kovels.com
Social Media: Facebook, Twitter

Terry Kovel, Co-Publisher
Ralph Kovel, Co-Publisher

Newsletter for dealers, investors and collectors.
Cost: $27.00
12 Pages
Frequency: Monthly
Founded in: 1995
Printed in 4 colors on matte stock

2205 **National Association of Antiques Bulletin**
National Association of Dealers in Antiques
PO Box 421
Barrington, IL 60011-0421

847-381-3101; *Fax:* 815-877-4282

Shirley Kowing, Publisher

Educational and association news.

2206 **Professional Picture Framers Association Newsletter**
4305 Sarellen Road
Richmond, VA 23231-4311

804-226-0430; *Fax:* 804-222-2175

Rex P Boynton, Executive Director

Trade association news for manufacturers, wholesalers, print publishers, importers and retailers selling art, framing and related supplies.

2207 **Stolen Art Alert**
500 5th Avenue
Suite 935
New York, NY 10110

212-391-6234; *Fax:* 212-391-8794
kferg@ifar.org; www.ifar.org

Sharon Flescher, Executive Director

Reports on art thefts and recoveries and also covered major art forgery cases.
Founded in: 1969

2208 **VCAM NEWS**
Volunteer Communities of Art Museums

New Orleans Museum of Art
PO Box 19123
New Orleans, LA 70179

504-488-2631; *Fax:* 504-484-6662
president@vcam.org; www.vcam.org

Peter Milne, President
Susan Colangelo, Secretary
Victoria Cather, Treasurer

Informs and invigorates the volunteers.
19 Members
Founded in: 1952

2209 World Fine Art
Art Baron Management Corporation
1356 Cherry Bottom Road
Colombos, OH 43230-6771

614-476-9708

Jeffrey Coffin, Publisher
Steve Shipp, Editor
John Blackburn, Manager

Art history, values and projections regarding artists and movements.
Cost: $95.00
10 Pages
Frequency: 9 per year
Printed in one color

Magazines & Journals

2210 A History of Art Therapy
American Art History
4875 Eisenhower Avenew
Suite 240
Alexandria, VA 22304-3302

703-212-2238
888-290-0878
info@arttherapy.org; www.arttherapy.org

Mercedes ter Maat, President
Charlotte Boston,MA,ATR, Secretary
Joseph Jaworek ATR-BC, Treasurer
Frequency: Yearly

2211 AIC Guide to Digital Photography and Conservation Documentation
American Institute for Conservation
1156 15th St NW
Suite 320
Washington, DC 20005-1714

202-452-9545; *Fax:* 202-452-9328;
www.aic-faic.org

Eryl Wentworth, Executive Director
Adam Allen, Meetings Associate
Steve Charles, Membership Assistant

2212 Advocacy and Lobbying: Speaking up for the Arts
National Assembly of State Arts Agencies
1029 Vermont Ave NW
2nd Floor
Washington, DC 20005-3517

202-347-6352; *Fax:* 202-737-0526
nasaa@nasaa-arts.org; www.nasaa-arts.org

Dennis Dewey, Manager
Arlynn Fishbaugh, President
Pam Breaux, VP
Bobby Kadis, Treasurer
John Bracey, Secretary

2213 Airbrush Action
3209 Atlantic Avenue
PO Box 438
Allenwood, NJ 08720

732-223-7878
800-876-2472; *Fax:* 732-223-2855
customerservice@airbrushaction.com;
www.airbrushaction.com

Clifford S Stieglitz, President/Publisher

Offers information on the art and graphic design community. Airbrush Action's editorial includes features/coverage on: automotive customizing, hobby applications, illustration, signs, t-shirts, body art, home decorative and more.
Cost: $26.95
Circulation: 35000
Printed in 4 colors on glossy stock

2214 Airbrush Art and Action
Paisano Publishers
28210 Dorothy Drive
PO Box 3000
Agoura Hills, CA 91301

818-889-8740
800-247-6246; *Fax:* 818-889-1252;
www.paisanopub.com/

Joseph Teresi, Publisher

A look at new products, step by step instruction features, profiles of professionals in the airbrushing field, and examples of airbrushed artworks.
Frequency: Bi-annually
Circulation: 68500

2215 American Artist
Billboard
770 Broadway
New York, NY 10003-9589

646-654-4400
800-562-2706; *Fax:* 646-654-5514;
www.billboard.com

Jessica Letkemann, Managing Editor
Lisa Ryan Howard, Publisher

A magazine devoted to the best of the best in the art industry.
Cost: $43.45
Frequency: Monthly
Circulation: 71,435
Founded in: 1894

2216 Antique Trader
F+W Media
38 E. 29th Street
New York, NY 10016

212-447-1400; *Fax:* 212-447-5231
contact_us@fwmedia.com;
www.fwpublications.com

Jim Ogle, CFO
Sara Domville, President
Chad Phelps, Chief Digital Officer
David Nussbaum, CEO

For the antiques and collectibles hobby industry. Accepts advertising.
Cost: $38.00
100 Pages
Frequency: Weekly
Circulation: 27363
Founded in: 1957

2217 Antique Week
Mayhill Publications
27 N Jefferson Street
PO Box 90
Knightstown, IN 46148

765-345-5133
800-876-5133; *Fax:* 800-695-8153
tony@antiqueweek.com;
www.antiqueweek.com

Gary Thoe, President
David Blower, Senior Editor

Antique dealers.
Cost: $38.95
Frequency: Weekly
Circulation: 65000
Founded in: 1968

2218 Aristos
Aristos Foundation
PO Box 20845
Park West Station
New York, NY 10025

212-678-8550
aristos@aristos.org; www.aristos.org

Louis Torres, Editor
Michelle Marder Kamhi, Editor

Independent online journal advocating objective standards in arts scholarship and criticism. Our aim is to present well-reasoned commentary on the arts and on the philosophy of art, for a broad audience of general readers and scholars.
Cost: $25.00
Frequency: Monthly
Founded in: 1982

2219 Art & Antiques
Art & Antiques Worldwide Media LLC
1319-cc Military Cutoff Road #192
Wilmington, NC 28405

910-679-4402
888-350-0951; *Fax:* 919-869-1864
info@artandantiquesmag.com;
www.artandantiquesmag.com

Jon Dorfman, Senior Editor

Magazine for collectors of the fine and decorative arts.
Frequency: Monthly

2220 Art & Auction
Art & Auction
601 West 26th Street
Suite 410
New York, NY 10001

212-447-9555
800-777-8718; *Fax:* 212-447-5221
info@artandauction.com; www.artinfo.com

Louise T Blouin, President/Owner
Benjamin Genocchio, Editor-in-Chief

Editorial covers the art market from antiquities to contemporary art, monthly calendar of gallery exhibitions and auction sales.
Cost: $80.00
Frequency: Monthly
Circulation: 38500
Founded in: 1996

2221 Art Business News
Advanstar Communications
600 Unicorn Park Drive
Suite 400
Woburn, MA 01801

339-298-4200
800-552-4346; *Fax:* 781-939-2490
info@advanstar.com; www.advanstar.com/

Julie MacDonald, Editor
Joseph Loggia, CEO

Publication addressing the business aspect of art and framing. Editorial covers everything from trends and sales to new colors and the latest tax changes.
Cost: $43.00
Frequency: Monthly
ISSN: 0273-5652
Founded in: 1992

2222 Art Materials Retailer
Fahy-Williams Publishing
171 Reed Street
PO Box 1080
Geneva, NY 14456-2137

315-789-0458
800-344-0559; *Fax:* 315-789-4263
kfahy@fwpi.com; www.fwpi.com

J Kevin Fahy, Publisher
Tina Manzer, Editorial Director
Bradley G. Gordner, Senior Editor
Frequency: Quarterly
Circulation: 12000
Printed in 4 colors on glossy stock

2223 **Art in America**
Brant Publications
575 Broadway
5th Floor
New York, NY 10012-3227

212-941-2900; *Fax:* 212-941-2885
interview_ad@brantpub.com;
www.interviewmagazine.com

Sandra Brant, Publisher
Elizabeth Baker, Editor

Includes show reviews, event schedules, profiles of artists and genres and updates on literature and materials.
Cost: $24.95
Frequency: Monthly
Circulation: 64,182
Founded in: 1984

2224 **Arts and Activities**
Publishers' Development Corporation
12345 World Trade Dr
San Diego, CA 92128-3743

858-605-0200; *Fax:* 858-605-0247
promo@artsandactivities.com;
www.gunsmagazine.com

Tom Von Rosen, Owner
Maryellen Bridge, Editor

Offers information and news on the latest in the visual arts.
Cost: $24.95
Frequency: Monthly
Founded in: 1932

2225 **Artweek**
PO Box 485
Hilo, HI 96721-0485

800-733-2916
800-733-2916; *Fax:* 262-495-8703
info@artweek.com; www.artweek.com

Debra Koppman, Editor
Laura Richar Janku, Editor

Critical reviews of contemporary West Coast art as well as news, features, articles, interviews, special sections and opinion pieces.
Cost: $34.00
Frequency: Monthly
Founded in: 1968

2226 **Breakthrough Magazine**
Breakthrough Magazine
2271 Old Baton Rouge Highway
PO Box 2945
Hammond, LA 70404-2945

985-345-7266
800-783-7266; *Fax:* 985-542-1831
info@breakthroughmagazine.com;
www.breakthroughmagazine.com

Larry Blomquist, Publisher

Artist profiles, tips, previews, and a calendar of events. Incorporates similar techniques related to wildlife carvings, sculpture and photography,
Cost: $32.00
Frequency: Quarterly
Circulation: 8932

2227 **CNA**
F+W Media
38 E. 29th Street
New York, NY 10016

212-447-1400; *Fax:* 212-447-5231
contact_us@fwmedia.com;
www.fwpublications.com

Jim Ogle, CFO
Sara Domville, President
Chad Phelps, Chief Digital Officer
David Nussbaum, CEO

A craft industry trade magazine reaching retailers and industry leaders. Readers turn to CNA each month in search of trends, innovative products, partnerships, corporate accomplishments, and retail strategies that positively impact their businesses. Regular editorial includes timely product showcases and special sections that target arts, crafts, scrapbooking, children's activities, sewing and needlework products. The editorial team has much experience in the industry.
Cost: $30.00
112 Pages
Circulation: 21777
Founded in: 1945

2228 **Christie's International Magazine**
Christies Publications
20 Rockefeller Plaza
New York, NY 10020

212-636-2000
800-395-6300; *Fax:* 212-636-2399
info@christies.com; www.christies.com

Mark Wrey, Publisher
Victoria Tremlett, Editor
John L Vogelstein, Chairman

Devoted to the promotion of Christie's fine art auctions worldwide.
Cost: $70.00
Circulation: 60000
Founded in: 1766

2229 **Craft and Needlework Age**
F+W Media
38 E. 29th Street
New York, NY 10016

212-447-1400; *Fax:* 212-447-5231
contact_us@fwmedia.com;
www.fwpublications.com

Jim Ogle, CFO
Sara Domville, President
Chad Phelps, Chief Digital Officer
David Nussbaum, CEO

Trade magazine serving the crafts and needlework industry. Accepts advertising.
Cost: $20.00
Frequency: Monthly
Founded in: 1952

2230 **Decorative Artist's Workbook**
F+W Media
38 E. 29th Street
New York, NY 10016

212-447-1400; *Fax:* 212-447-5231
contact_us@fwmedia.com;
www.fwpublications.com

Jim Ogle, CFO
Sara Domville, President
Chad Phelps, Chief Digital Officer
David Nussbaum, CEO

The leading how-to magazine for decorative painters, because it offers detailed step-by-step instruction and illustrations for fabulous projects, plus problem-solving tips, and articles on new techniques, products and books. Readers find a full range of decorative painting subjects and styles painted in a whole range of skill levels and mediums and on a variety of surfaces...and all designed by the most well known artists and instructors in decorative painting!
Cost: $27.00
72 Pages
Frequency: Quarterly
Circulation: 111573
Founded in: 1987

2231 **Folk Art**
American Folk Art Museum
2 Lincoln Square
Columbus Avenue at 66th Street
New York, NY 10023

212-595-9533; *Fax:* 212-265-2350
info@folkartmuseum.org;
www.folkartmuseum.org

Irene Kreney, Manager
Linda Dune, Acting Director
Edward Blanchard, President, Treasurer

An award winning publication. The editorial content is geared toward collectors, scholars, and the museum community interested in traditional and contemporary American folk and decorative arts. A benefit of membership, and is delivered to a targeted national and international readership.

2232 **HOW Magazine**
F&W Publications
10151 Carver Road
Blue Ash, OH 45242

513-531-2690; *Fax:* 513-531-1843
contact_us@fwmedia.com;
www.fwpublications.com
Social Media: Facebook, Twitter, LinkedIn

David Nussbaum, CEO
Jim Ogle, COO/CFO
Sara Domville, President

The industry's leading creativity, business and technology magazine for graphic design professionals. Each issue provides a mix of essential business information, up-to-date technology tips, the creative whys and hows behind noteworthy projects, and profiles of professionals who are influencing design.
Cost: $27.73
140 Pages
Frequency: Monthly
Circulation: 44883
Founded in: 1985

2233 **Hammer's Blow**
Artist-Blacksmith's Association of North America
259 Muddy Fork Road
Jonesborough, TN 37659

423-913-1022; *Fax:* 423-913-1023
hbeditor@abana.org; www.abana.org
Social Media: Facebook, Twitter

Eddie Rainey, President
Tina Chisena, First VP
John Fee, Second VP
Herb Upham, Secretary
Dan Nauman, Editor

Journal of the Artist-Blacksmiths' Association of North America
4500 Members
24 Pages
Frequency: Quarterly
Founded in: 1973

2234 **I.D. Magazine**
F+W Media
38 E. 29th Street
New York, NY 10016

212-447-1400; *Fax:* 212-447-5231
contact_us@fwmedia.com;
www.fwpublications.com

Jim Ogle, CFO
Sara Domville, President
Chad Phelps, Chief Digital Officer
David Nussbaum, CEO
Andr,a Pellegrino, Advertising Director

The international design magazine, showcases innovative products and technologies for sophisticated readers who are at the forefront of shaping the world through design. The multi-disciplinary coverage embraces design trends, theories, experiments and innovators.
Cost: $59.96
96 Pages
Frequency: 1 Year 8 Issues

Circulation: 31,424
Founded in: 1954

2235 IFAR Journal
500 5th Avenue
Suite 935
New York, NY 10110

212-391-6234; *Fax:* 212-391-8794
kferg@ifar.org; www.ifar.org

Sharon Flescher, Executive Director
Jack Josephson, Chairman

Emphasizes education and research regarding the ethical, legal and scholarly issues concerning art objects. In addition to news stories and book reviews, the Journal contains feature articles on art authenticity and attribution; forgery and fraud; art law and ethics; World War II-era art restitution issues; conserving, restoring and caring for art; and art theft.
Founded in: 1969

2236 Journal of Aesthetics and Art Criticism
American Society for Aesthetics
1550 Larimer Street
Suite 644
Denver, CO 80202

562-331-4424
asa@aesthetics-online.org;
www.aesthetics-online.org

Robert Stecker, Editor
Theodore Gracyk, Editor
Cynthia Freeland, President
Kathleen M. Higgins, Vice President

Promotes study, research, discussion and publication in aesthetics, which includes all studies of the arts and related experience including philosophic, scientific and theoretical viewpoints.
Founded in: 1942

2237 Journal of the American Institute for Conservation (JAIC)
1156 15th Street
Suite 320
Washington, DC 20005-1714

202-452-9545; *Fax:* 202-452-9328
info@conservation-us.org;
www.conservation-us.org

Eryl Wentworth, Executive Director
Meg Loew Craft, President
Pamela Hatchfield, VP

Publication of peer-reviewed technical studies, research papers, treatment case studies and ethics and standards discussions relating to the broad field of conservation and preservation of historic and cultural works.
3500 Members
Founded in: 1961

2238 Magazine Antiques
Brant Publications
575 Broadway
5th Floor
New York, NY 10012-3227

212-941-2900; *Fax:* 212-941-2885
interview_ad@brantpub.com;
www.interviewmagazine.com

Sandra Brant, Publisher
Allison Ledes, Editor
Donald Liebling, Circulation Manager
Jennifer Norton, Marketing Executive

Articles on American and European decorative and fine arts, architecture, historic preservation, and collecting.
Cost: $24.95
Frequency: Monthly
Circulation: 64402
Founded in: 1969

2239 Memory Makers
F+W Media
38 E. 29th Street
New York, NY 10016

212-447-1400; *Fax:* 212-447-5231
contact_us@fwmedia.com;
www.fwpublications.com

Jim Ogle, CFO
Sara Domville, President
Chad Phelps, Chief Digital Officer
David Nussbaum, CEO
Buddy Redling, Editor in Chief

Entertains, informs, and inspires the burgeoning number of scrapbook enthusiasts. Features the ideas and stories of its readers - people who believe in keeping scrapbooks and the tradition of the family photo historian alive. Two special newsstand-only issues are dedicated to specific areas of interest including holidays, heritage albums, and more.
Cost: $45.00
144 Pages
Frequency: Bi-annually
Circulation: 203287
Founded in: 1996

2240 Michaels Create!
F+W Media
38 E. 29th Streett
New York, NY 10016

212-447-1400; *Fax:* 212-447-5231
contact_us@fwmedia.com;
www.fwpublications.com

Jim Ogle, CFO
Sara Domville, President
Chad Phelps, Chief Digital Officer
David Nussbaum, CEO

Features contemporary designs reflecting the latest trends with clear instructions. The home decorating, fashion, and gift ideas will inspire experienced crafters as well as seasonal crafters to explore new possibilities. Step-by-step instructions, tips, and techniques will engage crafters of all ages - including kids - with the creative skills of crafting to be enjoyed as a year-round activity.
Cost: $21.97
116 Pages
Frequency: Monthly
Circulation: 24991
Founded in: 1975

2241 Military Trader
F+W Media
38 E. 29th Street
New York, NY 10016

212-447-1400; *Fax:* 212-447-5231
contact_us@fwmedia.com;
www.fwpublications.com
Social Media: Facebook, Twitter, LinkedIn

David Nussbaum, CEO
Jim Ogle, CFO/COO
Sara Domville, President

Monthly publication for collectors of military memorabilia.
Cost: $19.00
Frequency: Monthly
Founded in: 1952

2242 Museum
American Association of Museums
1575 Eye Street NW
Suite 400
Washington, DC 20005-1113

202-289-1818; *Fax:* 202-289-6578
membership@aam-us.org; www.aam-us.org

John Strand, Publisher
Susan Breitkopf, Editor In Chief
Ford Bell, President
Frequency: Bi-Monthly

2243 Panorama
Association of Historians of American Art

journalpanorama.org

Ross Barrett, Executive Editor
Sarah Burns, Executive Editor
Jennifer Jane Marshall, Executive Editor

The online journal of the Association of Historians of American Art.
Frequency: Biannual

2244 Pastel Journal
F+W Media
38 E. 29th Street
New York, NY 10016

212-447-1400; *Fax:* 212-447-5231
contact_us@fwmedia.com;
www.fwpublications.com

Jim Ogle, CFO
Sara Domville, President
Chad Phelps, Chief Digital Officer
David Nussbaum, CEO

Written by pastel artists for pastel artists. Content is geared toward artists, amateur & professional alike, who already work in pastels and who want to further develop their skills through in-depth information on pastel painting processes and thought-provoking ideas from successful pastel artists. Also included is information on workshops and exhibitions, as well as articles providing details on the business aspects of art - creating prints, creating Web sites, framing prints, and shipping.
Cost: $27.00
84 Pages
Circulation: 19167
Founded in: 1999

2245 Picture Framing Magazine
Hobby Publications
83 South Street
Unit 307
Freehold, NJ 07728

732-536-5160
800-969-7176; *Fax:* 732-536-5761;
www.pictureframingmagazine.com

David Gherman, President
Patrick Sarver, Editor
Bruce Gherman, Executive Publisher

News and trends in the picture framing trade, marketing strategies, and economic developments.
Cost: $20.00
Frequency: Monthly
Circulation: 25000
ISSN: 1052-9977
Founded in: 1955

2246 Postcard Collector
F+W Media
38 E. 29th Street
New York, NY 10016

212-447-1400; *Fax:* 212-447-5231
contact_us@fwmedia.com;
www.fwpublications.com

Jim Ogle, CFO
Sara Domville, President
Chad Phelps, Chief Digital Officer
David Nussbaum, CEO

Monthly publication for postcard collectors.
Cost: $29.98
Frequency: Monthly
Founded in: 1982

2247 SchoolArts
Davis Publications
50 Portland Street
Worcester, MA 01618

508-754-7201
800-533-2847; *Fax:* 508-753-3834;

www.davisart.com
Social Media: Facebook, Twitter, LinkedIn

Wyatt Wade, Owner
John Carr, Marketing

For art educators.
Cost: $23.95
60 Pages
Frequency: Monthly
Circulation: 23717
Founded in: 1901
Printed in 4 colors on matte stock

2248 Sotheby's Preview Magazine
Sotheby's
1334 York Ave
New York, NY 10021-4806

212-606-7000
541-312-5682; *Fax:* 212-606-7107
preview@sothebys.com; www.sothebys.com

William F Ruprecht, CEO
Bruno Vinciguerra, Chief Operating Officer

Auction schedule listings, exhibition dates and catalogue pricing.
Cost: $75.00
48 Pages
Circulation: 80,000
Founded in: 1976
Printed in 4 colors on newsprint stock

2249 Style: 1900
199 George Street
Lambertville, NJ 08530

609-397-4104; *Fax:* 609-397-4409;
www.style1900.com
Social Media: Facebook, Twitter, LinkedIn

Fred Albert, Editor
Jennifer Strauss, Director Advertising
David Rago, Publisher

The only publication devoted solely to the works and thoughts of the arts and crafts movement.
Cost: $6.95
88 Pages
Frequency: Quarterly
Circulation: 20000
ISSN: 1080-451X
Founded in: 1987
Mailing list available for rent: 7,000 names at $250 per M
Printed in 4 colors on glossy stock

2250 The Anvil's Ring
259 Muddy Fork Road
Jonesborough, TN 37659

423-913-1022; *Fax:* 423-913-1023
centraloffice@abana.org; www.abana.org

Eddie Rainey, President
Tina Chisena, First VP
John Fee, Second VP
Herb Upham, Secretary

The most comprehensive overview on what's happening in the artist- blacksmithing world or the inspiration to get you out to the forge.
4500 Members
Frequency: Quarterly
Circulation: 2 Mag.
Founded in: 1973

2251 The Chronicle of the Horse
American Academy of Equine Art
117 North Water Street
PO Box 1364
Georgetown, KY 40324

859-281-6031; *Fax:* 859-281-6043;
www.aaea.net

Frances Clay Conner, Executive Director
Xochitl Barnes, AAEA President

The official magazine of the American Academy of Equine Art.
90 Members
Founded in: 1980

2252 Visual Anthropology Review
American Anthropoligical Association
2200 Wilson Blvd
Suite 600
Arlington, VA 22201-3357

703-528-1902; *Fax:* 703-528-3546;
www.aaanet.org

Bill Davis, Executive Director
Oona Schmid, Director of Publishing
Leith Mullings, President

Directed toward the study of visual aspects of human behavior including anthropology of art and museology and the use of media in anthropological research, representation, and teaching.
Cost: $25.00
Circulation: 1000
ISSN: 1053-7147
Founded in: 1902
Mailing list available for rent
Printed in one color on glossy stock

2253 Watercolor Magic
F+W Media
38 E. 29th Street
New York, NY 10016

212-447-1400; *Fax:* 212-447-5231
contact_us@fwmedia.com;
www.fwpublications.com

Jim Ogle, CFO
Sara Domville, President
Chad Phelps, Chief Digital Officer
David Nussbaum, CEO

Offers valuable how-to instruction and creative inspiration for artists who work in water-based media. From page after page of inspirational ideas, to illustrations of the best techniques, to must-have painting tools and materials, watercolorists will find everything they need to know to help them create art from the inside out. Plus, each issue includes special reports and tons of tips from the foremost experts in the field. The definitive source of creative inspiration and technical info.
Cost: $27.00
72 Pages
Frequency: Monthly
Circulation: 94636
Founded in: 1993

Trade Shows

2254 AAM Annual Meeting & MuseumExpo
American Alliance of Museums
2451 Crystal Dr.
Suite 1005
Arlington, VA 22202

202-289-1818; *Fax:* 202-289-6578
membership@aam-us.org; www.aam-us.org

Andrea Street, Director, Meetings & Events

The largest gathering of museum professionals in the world.
Frequency: Annual/May

2255 ABANA International Conferences
Artist-Blacksmith's Association of North America
259 Muddy Fork Road
Jonesborough, TN 37659

423-913-1022; *Fax:* 423-913-1023
conference@abana.org; www.abana.org
Social Media: Facebook, Twitter

Eddie Rainey, President
Tina Chisena, First VP
John Fee, Second VP
Herb Upham, Secretary

Held biennially in the United States for members. Demonstrations, panel discussions and lectures by experts in the field from around the globe. Share knowledge of technical, aesthetic and business areas of the craft for beginners to established professionals.
1000 Attendees
Frequency: Biennial
Founded in: 1975

2256 AHAA Symposium
Association of Historians of American Art

E-Mail: info@ahaaonline.org;
www.ahaaonline.org/?page=Symposium
Social Media: Facebook, Twitter, LinkedIn

Ellery Foutch, Chair
Austen Barron Bailly, Co-Chair
Sarah Kelly Oehler, Symposium Liaison

Biennial syposium (even-numbered years) of the Association of Historians of American Art.
Frequency: Biennial
Founded in: 2010

2257 AIGA Design Conference
American Institute of Graphic Arts (AIGA)
233 Broadway
17th Fl.
New York, NY 10279

212-807-1990
Social Media: Facebook, Twitter, Instagram

Stefan Bucher, Chair
Roman Mars, Conference Committee
Debbie Millman, Conference Committee
Nathan Shedroff, Conference Committee

Speakers, exhibitions, roundtables, professional development and a live, head-to-head design competition for up-and-comers.
Frequency: Annual

2258 American Art Therapy Association Conference
American Art Therapy Association
4875 Eisenhower Avenue
Sute 240
Alexandria, VA 22304

703-548-5860
888-290-0878; *Fax:* 703-783-8468
info@arttherapy.org; www.arttherapy.org

Mercedes ter Maat, President
Susan Corrigan, Executive Director

Over 20 exhibitors of art supplies, books, therapeutic materials and schools.
800 Attendees
Frequency: Annual
Founded in: 1969

2259 American Institute for Conservation Annual Meeting
Amer Institute for Conservation of Historic Works
1156 15th Street NW
Suite 320
Washington, DC 20005

202-452-9545; *Fax:* 202-452-9328
info@conservation-us.org; www.aic-faic.org

Eryl P Wentworth, Executive Director
Adam Allen, Meeting Manager
Meg Loew Craft, President

Annual meeting of conservators of artistic and cultural property, which includes seminars and workshops with over 1,000 members attending yearly. 50 booths.
1000 Attendees
Frequency: June
Founded in: 1971

2260 American Society for Aesthetics Annual Conference
American Society for Aesthetics

1550 Larimer Street
Suite 644
Denver, CO 80202

562-331-4424
asa@aesthetics-online.org;
www.aesthetics-online.org
Social Media: Facebook, Twitter

Cynthia Freeland, President
Kathleen M. Higgins, Vice President

Seminar, conference, and exhibits related to the study of the arts, all disciplines.
500 Attendees
Frequency: Annual
Founded in: 1942

2261 Antique Arms Show
Beinfeld Productions
72 Sunrise Drive
Rancho Mirage, CA 92270

760-202-4489; *Fax:* 760-202-4793;
www.antiquearmsshow.com

Wallace Beinfeld, Show Manager

Public show with 1000 booths of antiques and collectibles.
5M/6M Attendees
Frequency: January

2262 Art Expo New York
Advanstar Communications
641 Lexington Avenue
8th Floor
New York, NY 10022

212-951-6600; *Fax:* 212-951-6793
info@advanstar.com; www.advanstar.com

Joseph Loggia, CEO
Thomas Ehardt, Vice President
Tom Florio, CFO

Five hundred and eighty exhibitors of artwork including: paintings, sculpture, prints and graphics.
15000 Attendees
Frequency: Annual
Founded in: 1985

2263 Art Libraries Society of North America Annual Conference
Art Libraries Society of North America
7044 S. 13th St.
Oak Creek, WI 53154

414-768-8000
800-817-0621; *Fax:* 414-768-8001
arlisna@mercury.interpath.com;
www.arlisna.org

Deborah Kempe, President
Gregory Most, VP

Annual conference and show of publishers, book dealers, library suppliers and visual resources suppliers.
500 Attendees
Frequency: April
Founded in: 1977

2264 Art Miami: International Art Fair
Advanstar Communications
641 Lexinton Avenue
8th Floor
New York, NY 10022

212-951-6600; *Fax:* 212-951-6793
info@advanstar.com; www.advanstar.com

Joseph Loggia, CEO
Thomas Ehardt, Vice President
Tom Florio, CFO

99 exhibits of fine arts, attended by professionals.
44500 Attendees

2265 Art Supply Expo
Marketing Association Services
1516 Pontius Avenue
Floor 2
Los Angeles, CA 90025-3306

310-478-0074

Randy Bauler, Executive Director

Exhibits consist of art and drafting equipment and computer graphics supplies.
10M Attendees
Frequency: October

2266 Art and Creative Materials Institute/ACMI Annual Meeting
99 Derby St.
Suite 200
Hingham, MA 02043

781- 55- 104; *Fax:* 781- 20- 555
debbief@acminet.org; www.acminet.org

Van Foster, President
Deborah S Gustafson, Associate Director
Debbie Munroe, Certification Director
Carol Rourke, Program Director

A non-profit association of manufacturers of art, craft and other creative materials, ACMI sponsors a certification program for both children's and adult's art materials and products, certifying that these products are non-toxic and meet voluntary standards of quality and performance. ACMI seeks to create and maintain a positive environment for art, craft and other creative materials usage, promoting safety in the materials and providing information and service resources on such products.
210 Members
Founded in: 1940
Mailing list available for rent: 199 names

2267 Conference of the Volunteer Committees of Art Museums of Canada and the US
Volunteer Committees of Art Museums
Philbrook Museum
2727 S Rockford
Tulsa, OK 74114

Fax: 918-743-4230

Grace Robin, VCAM President

Triennial conference and exhibits of art museum equipment, supplies and services.
Founded in: 1952

2268 Consumer Show
Maven Company
PO Box 937
Plandome, NY 11030-0937

51- 62- 880
fasttrack@erols.com;
www.mavencompany.com

N Chittenden, VP

Specialty show, doll, toy and teddy bear.
5,000 Attendees
Frequency: Semi-Annual
Founded in: 1970

2269 Craftsmen's Christmas Classic Arts and Crafts Festival
Gilmore Enterprises
3514-A Drawbridge Pkwy
Greensboro, NC 27410-8584

336-282-5550; *Fax:* 336-274-1084
Contact@GilmoreShows.com;
www.gilmoreshows.com

Jennifer Palmer, Show Manager
Clyde Gilmore, Executive Director

Features work from over 305 talented artists and craftspeople. All juried exhibitors work has been hand made by the exhibitors and must be original design and creation. Visit Christmas Tree Village to view the uniquely decorated Christmas Trees by some of our exhibitors. Something from every taste and budget with items from the most contemporary to the most traditional.
Founded in: 1982

2270 Craftsmen's Classic Arts and Crafts Festival
Gilmore Enterprises
3514-A Drawbridge Pkwy
Greensboro, NC 27410-8584

336-282-5550; *Fax:* 336-274-1084
Contact@GilmoreShows.com;
www.gilmoreshows.com

Jennifer Palmer, Show Manager
Clyde Gilmore, Executive Director

Features work from over 305 talented artists and craftspeople. All work has been hand made by the juried exhibitors and must be original design and creation. See the creative process in action with several exhibitors demonstrating their craft in their booths. Something from every style, taste and budget with items from the most contemporary to the most traditional.
15000 Attendees
Frequency: March/April/Aug/Sept/Oct.
Founded in: 1982

2271 Decor Expo
Pfingsten Publishing
6000 Lombardo Center Drive
Suite 420
Seven Hills, OH 44131

216-328-8926
888-772-8926; *Fax:* 216-328-9452;
www.decor-expo.com

Hugh T Tobin, Group Show Director
Rob Spademan, Marketing Director

Five hundred booths exhibiting fine art, limited edition prints, graphics, oil paintings and reproductions. Three shows a year in Orlando (January), New York City (March), and Atlanta (September).
4M Attendees
Frequency: September

2272 Gilmore Shows
Craftsmen's Classic Art & Craft Festivals
3514-A Drawbridge Pkwy
Greensboro, NC 27410-8584

336-282-5550; *Fax:* 336-274-1084
contact@gilmoreshows.com;
www.gilmoreshows.com
Social Media: Facebook

Jennifer Palmer, Show Manager
Clyde Gilmore, Executive Director
Jan Donovon, Marketing Manager

10 shows annually in North Carolina, South Carolina and Virginia. Each show features work from 250-450 talented artists and craftspeople from across the nationa. All juried exhibitors work has been hand made by the exhibitors and must be original design and creation. There is something from every taste and budget with items from traditional to contemporary, functional to whimsical, decorative to fun & funky. Visit Christmas Tree Village to view the trees decorated by some or our exhibitors.
20000 Attendees
Frequency: October/November
Founded in: 1973

2273 IACA Markets
Indian Arts & Crafts Association
4010 Carlisle NE
Suite C
Albuquerque, NM 87107

505-265-9149; *Fax:* 505-265-8251
info@iaca.com; www.iaca.com

Joseph Zeller, President
Don Standing Bear Forest, VP
Susan Pourian, Secretary
Kathy Ouellet, Treasurer

Wholesale and retail markets of authentic, handmade Indian arts & crafts.
300 Attendees
Frequency: Semi-Annually

2274 IFPDA Print Fair
International Fine Print Dealers Association
250 W 26th St
Suite 405
New York, NY 10001-6737
212-674-6095; *Fax:* 212-674-6783
info@ifpda.org; www.ifpda.org
Michele Senecal, Executive Director
Laura Beth Gencarella, PR/Marketing Manager
Tara Reddi, President
Elizabeth Fodde-Reguer, Executive Assistant
The largest and most celebrated art fair dedicated to fine prints.

2275 Morristown Antiques Show
Wendy Management
PO Box 222
Harrison, NY 10528
914-316-4700; *Fax:* 914-698-6273;
www.wendyantiquesshows.com
Meg Wendy, President
Perry Grosser, Marketing and Finance
Three day show of 85 important dealers from the Northeast. Covers the key periods of antiques for budget minded collectors.
Frequency: November/Annual
Founded in: 1930

2276 NAMTA's World of Art Materials
National Art Materials Trade Association
20200 Zion Ave.
Cornelius, NC 28031
704-926-6244; *Fax:* 702-892-6247
info@namta.org; www.namta.org
Reggie Hall, Executive Director
Richard Goodban, President
Seven hundred and fifty booths including educational programs to advance the welfare of the art materials and framing industry.
5M Attendees
Frequency: May

2277 National Art Education Association Convention
National Art Education Association
1806 Robert Fulton Drive
Suite 300
Reston, VA 20191-1590
703-860-8000
800-299-8321; *Fax:* 703-860-2960
info@arteducators.org; www.naea-reston.org
Kathy Duse, Show Manager
Dr. Deborah Reeve, Executive Director
Dr. Robert Sabol, President
Annual show of 140-200 exhibitor booths displaying manufacturers, suppliers, distributors, publishing companies and universities latest art textbooks and high-tech software. Show draws approximately 4,000 or more attendees.
Frequency: April

2278 National Guild of Community Schools of the Arts Conference
National Guild of Community Schools of the Arts
520 Eighth Avenue, 3rd Floor
Suite 302
New York, NY 10018-8018
212-268-3337; *Fax:* 212-268-3995;
www.nationalguild.org
Jonathan Herman, Executive Director
Kenneth Cole, Director
Exhibits of equipment, supplies and services for the advancement of education in the performing and visual arts. Arts Management in Community Institutions (AMICI) Summer Institute trains administrators to meet needs of growing and emerging arts schools. Other programs, services, guildnotes newsletter, job opportunities listings, and publications catalog available upon request on online.
350 Attendees
Frequency: Annual

2279 New York Antiques Show
Wendy Management
PO Box 222
Harrison, NY 10528
914-316-4700; *Fax:* 914-698-6273;
www.wendyantiquesshows.com
Meg Wendy, President
Perry Grosser, Marketing and Finance
This unique, sophisticated show is an important convenient source for trend setting decorators. There are quality antiques for new, young, collectors as well as seasoned pros. This show is filled with 17th, 18th, and 19th Century American, English, French, Oriental and Continental furniture and decorative accessories, including rare books, clocks, silver, brass, paintings, prints, maps, porcelain, rugs, glass, lighting devices, sconces, candlesticks, garden urns, and so much more. 80/90 Dealers
Frequency: September
Founded in: 1930

2280 Professional Picture Framers Association Show
Professional Picture Framers Association
4305 Sarellen Road
Richmond, VA 23231
517-788-8100; *Fax:* 517-788-8100
ppfa@ppfa.com; www.ppfa.com
Mark Klostermeyer, President
Source for manufacturers, wholesalers, print publishers, importers and retailers selling art, framing and related supplies.
Frequency: Annual
Founded in: 1971

2281 Surtex
George Little Management
1133 Westchester Avenue
White Plains, NY 10606-3547
914-421-3200
800-272-7469; *Fax:* 914-948-6180;
www.surtex.com
George(Jeff) Little II, President/COO
Penny Sikalis, VP, Show Manager
Rita Malek, Show Manager
In addition to providing the art and design component of this market we also include important home products.
5000 Attendees
Frequency: May/October

2282 The AADLA Spring Show
PO Box 2066
Lenox Hill Station
New York, NY 10021
212-879-7558; *Fax:* 212-772-7197
secretary@artantiquedealersleague.com;
www.artantiquedealersleague.com
Clinton Howell, President
Robert Simon, VP
Susan Caplan Jacobson, Treasurer
David Mayer, Secretary/Executive Director
Ira Spanierman, Vice Chairperson
The best choice of the very best in fine art. Unique chances to view and buy paintings as well as objects reflecting excellence in the applied arts.
109 Members
Frequency: November/50 Attendees
Founded in: 1926

Directories & Databases

2283 AADA Membership Directory
Art Dealers Association of America
205 Lexington Avenue
Suite 901
New York, NY 10016
212-488-5550; *Fax:* 64- 68- 680;
www.artdealers.org
Lucy Mitchell-Innes, President
Michael Findlay, Vice President
Jeffery Fraenkel, Secretary
An annual directory listing the AADA members. Published by the Art Dealers Association of America.
77 Pages
Founded in: 1962

2284 ARTWEEK Gallery Calendar Section
Spaulding Publishing
PO Box 52100
Palo Alto, CA 94303-0751
800-733-2916; *Fax:* 262-495-8703
info@artweek.com; www.artweek.com
Richard J O'Brien, Chairman
John T Bourger, Vice Chairman
A screened list of galleries on the West coast and other Western states are profiled.
Cost: $34.00
Circulation: 14,500

2285 American Art Directory
National Register Publishing
430 Mountain Ave.
Suite 400
New Providence, NJ 07974
800-473-7020; *Fax:* 908-673-1189
nrpeditorial@marquiswhoswho.com;
www.nationalregisterpub.com
Provides important information on museums, art organizations, art schools, libraries, art editors and critics, scholarships, fellowships, exhibitions and state art countils as well as funding sources and booking agencies.

2286 Art Index
HW Wilson Company
10 Estes Street
Ipswich, MA 01938
800-653-2726; *Fax:* 978-356-6565
information@ebscohost.com;
www.hwwilson.com
Tim Collins, President
Michael Gorrell, EVP of Technology, CIO
Offers more than 500,000 citations to articles and book reviews in over 300 periodicals, yearbooks and museum bulletins.
Founded in: 1929

2287 Art Museums of the World
Greenwood Publishing Group
88 Post Road W
PO Box 5007
Westport, CT 06881-5007
203-226-3571
800-225-5800; *Fax:* 203-222-1502
customer-service@greenwood.com;
www.greenwood.com
Debra Adams, Editor
National and international art museum list.
Cost: $259.00
1696 Pages
ISBN: 0-313213-22-4

2288 **Art in America: Guide to Galleries, Museums, and Artists**
Brant Publications
575 Broadway
New York, NY 10012-3227
212-941-2900; *Fax:* 212-941-2885
interview_ad@brantpub.com;
www.interviewmagazine.com
David Nussman, CEO
A list of over 4,000 museums, galleries and other display areas.
Cost: $15.00
Frequency: Annual
Circulation: 70,000
Founded in: 1969

2289 **Arts and Humanities Search**
Institute for Scientific Information
1500 Spring Garden St
Philadelphia, PA 19130-4067
215-386-0100
800-386-4474; *Fax:* 215-386-2911
Offers data from more than 1100 arts and humanities journals.

2290 **Directory of MA and PhD Programs in Art and Art History**
College Art Association
50 Broadway
21 Floor
New York, NY 10004
212-691-1051; *Fax:* 212-627-2381
nyoffice@collegeart.org; www.collegeart.org
Social Media: Facebook, Twitter, LinkedIn
Linda Downs, Executive Director
Alan Gilbert, Editor
Anne Collins Goodyear, President
Institutions are profiled that offer M.A. and Ph.D. programs in art and art history.
Cost: $12.50
152 Pages
Founded in: 1911

2291 **Films and Videos on Photography**
Program for Art on Film
200 Willoughby Avenue
Brooklyn, NY 11205
718-399-4506; *Fax:* 718-399-4507
info@artfilm.org; www.artfilm.org
Nadine Covert, Executive Director
An annotated directory of over 500 films and videos on photography, photographers, and photographic techniques.
Cost: $15.00
132 Pages
ISBN: 0-870995-75-1
Founded in: 1990

2292 **IACA Directory**
Indian Arts & Crafts Association
4010 Carlisle NE
Suite C
Albuquerque, NM 87107
505-265-9149; *Fax:* 505-265-8251
info@iaca.com; www.iaca.com
Joseph Zeller, President
Don Standing Bear Forest, VP
Susan Pourian, Secretary
Kathy Ouellet, Treasurer
Directory of all IACA members (wholesalers, retailers, artists/craftspeople, collectors, museums and ancillary organizations)
Cost: $15.00

2293 **Illustrators Annual**
Society of Illustrators
128 E 63rd St
New York, NY 10065-7392
212-838-2560; *Fax:* 212-838-2561
info@societyillustrators.org;
www.societyillustrators.org
Denis Dittrich, President
Tim O'Brien, Executive Vice President
Victor Juhasz, Vice President
David Reuss, Treasurer
Published by the Society of Illustrators
Cost: $49.95
320 Pages
Circulation: 7000
Founded in: 1959
Mailing list available for rent: 1000 names at $600 per M
Printed in 4 colors

2294 **Key Guide to Electronic Resources: Art and Art History**
Information Today
143 Old Marlton Pike
Medford, NJ 08055-8750
609-654-6266
800-300-9868; *Fax:* 609-654-4309
custserv@infotoday.com; www.infotoday.com
Thomas H Hogan, President
Roger R Bilboul, Chairman of the Board
An evaluative directory of electronic reference in the fields of art and art history.
Cost: $39.50
120 Pages
ISBN: 1-573870-22-6

2295 **NAMTA International Convention & Trade Show Directory**
National Art Materials Trade Association
20200 Zion Ave.
Cornelius, NC 28031
704-892-6244; *Fax:* 704-892-6247
info@namta.org; www.namta.org
Social Media: Facebook, Twitter, LinkedIn
Richard Fjordbotten, President
Reggie Hall, Executive Director
National Art Materials Trade Association directory.

2296 **Official Museum Directory**
National Register Publishing
430 Mountain Ave.
Suite 400
New Providence, NJ 07974
800-473-7020; *Fax:* 908-673-1189
nrpeditorial@marquiswhoswho.com;
www.nationalregisterpub.com
Comprehensive reference for those seeking information on the country's museums. Features profiles and statistics on more than 7,700 museums in the US.

2297 **The Artful Home: Furniture, Sculpture and Objects**
Kraus Sikes
931 E Main Street
Suite 106
Madison, WI 53703-2955
608-572-2590
877-223-4600; *Fax:* 608-257-2690
info@artfulhome.com; www.guild.com
Lisa Bayne, CEO
Bill Lathrop, Vice President
A wealth of information on craft artists working in furniture, wall decor and accessories are listed.
Cost: $29.95
256 Pages
Frequency: Annual
Circulation: 15,000

2298 **What Museum Guides Need To Know:Access For Blind & Visually Impaired Visitors**
American Foundation for the Blind
2 Penn Plaza
Suite 1102
New York, NY 10121
212-502-7600
800-232-5463; *Fax:* 888- 54- 833
afbinfo@afb.net; www.afb.org
Carl R Augusto, President/CEO
Paul Schroeder, Vice President, Programs
Provides practical, easy-to-use guidelines on how to greet blind and visually impaired museum goers. This handbook also covers aesthetics and visual impairment and a training outline for museum requirements for accessibility.
Cost: $16.95
64 Pages

2299 **Who's Who in Art Materials**
National Art Materials Trade Association
20200 Zion Ave.
Cornelius, NC 28031
704-892-6244; *Fax:* 704-892-6247
info@namta.org; www.namta.org
Social Media: Facebook, Twitter, LinkedIn
Richard Fjordbotten, President
Reggie Hall, Executive Director
Membership directory of the National Art Materials Trade Association.

Industry Web Sites

2300 **http://gold.greyhouse.com**
G.O.L.D Grey House OnLine Databases
Grey House Publishing's online database platform, GOLD, offers Quick Search, Keyword Search and Expert Search for most business sectors including art, antique and renovation markets. The GOLD platform makes finding the information you need quick and easy - whether you're a novice searcher or an experienced database user. All of Grey House's directory products are available for subscription on the GOLD platform.

2301 **www.aam-us.org**
American Association of Museums
For the museum community, enhances the ability of museums to serve the public interest, works on behalf of museums in educating federal legislators, assists museums in improving technical standards.

2302 **www.acminet.org**
Art and Creative Materials Institute
For art and craft product makers who encourage safe use of materials and proper labeling through certification.

2303 **www.albemarle-nc.com/camden**
Watermark Association of Artisans
Provides marketing assistance to craft producers.

2304 **www.aristos.org/aristos2.htm**
Aristos Foundation
The Foundation's purpose is to deepen public understanding of the nature of art as well as to foster the understanding and appreciation of humanistic values in the arts. Publishes an online journal.

2305 **www.artantiquedealersleague.com**
Art and Antique Dealers League of America
Nonprofit organization promotes interests of retailers and wholesalers of antiques and art objects.

2306 **www.artdealers.org**
Art Dealers Association of America
Works to improve the stature and standing of the art gallery business. Members deal primarily in paintings, sculpture, prints, drawings and photographs from the Renaissance to the present day. We have over 160 member galleries in more than 25 US cities.

2307 **www.artnet.com**
Art Net United States
The place to buy, sell and research fine art online.

2308 **www.collegeart.org**
College Art Association
Association for institutions that offer MA and PhD programs in art and art history.

2309 **www.greyhouse.com**
Grey House Publishing
Authoritative reference directories for most business sectors, including art, antique and restoration markets. Users can search the online databases with varied search criteria allowing for custom searches by product category, geographic area, sales volume, keyword, subject and more. Full Grey House catalog and online ordering also available.

2310 **www.iaca.com**
Indian Arts & Crafts Association
Not for profit trade association. Our mission is to promote, protect and preserve Indian arts.

2311 **www.naadaaa.org**
National Association of Dealers in Antiques
Nonprofit trade association of America's leading dealers mutually pledged to safeguard the interests of those who buy, sell or collect antiques and works of art.

2312 **www.naao.net**
National Association of Artist's Organizations
For artists within nonprofit organizations. Dedicated to the presentation of alternative visual arts, media, literature, new music and performing arts.

2313 **www.naea-reston.org**
National Art Education Association
Manufacturers, suppliers, distributors, publishing companies and universities.

2314 **www.naled.com**
National Association of Limited Edition Dealers
For dealers, vendors and publishers involved with collectibles and gifts.

2315 **www.namta.org**
National Art Materials Trade Association
For manufacturers, importers, wholesalers and retailers of art materials.

2316 **www.nasaa-arts.org**
National Assembly of State Arts Agencies
For those in the arts agency field in the US.

2317 **www.societyillustrators.com**
Society of Illustrators
For professional illustrators and art directors.

2318 **www.sothebys.com**
Sotheby's
Auction schedule listings, exhibition dates and catalogue pricing.

Associations

2319 **1394 Trade Association**
23117 39th Ave SE
Bothell, WA 98021
425-870-6574; *Fax:* 425-320-3897
info@1394ta.com; www.1394ta.org
Richard Mourn, Chair
Morten Lave, Vice Chairman
Dave Thompson, Secretary/Editor
Richard Davies, Financial Officer
A trade association devoted to IEEE 1394 communications product furtherance.

2320 **Adult Video Association**
8033 Sunset Boulevard
PMB 851
Los Angeles, CA 90046-5323
323-436-0060; *Fax:* 818-501-7502
bmargold@aol.com
William Margold, Director
Trade association primarily concerned with opposing legislative initiatives to restrict the sale of sexually explicit film and video.
400 Members
Founded in: 1987

2321 **American Rhetoric**
www.americanrhetoric.com
An association dedicated to rhetoric and public communication in the US.

2322 **Association for Recorded Sound Collections**
c/o Nathan Georgitis
Knoght Library, 1299 University of Eugene, OR 97403-1299
E-Mail: execdir@arsc-audio.org; www.arsc-audio.org
Social Media: Facebook, Twitter, YouTube
Nathan Georgitis, Executive Director
A nonprofit organization dedicated to the preservation and study of sound recordings in all genres.
Founded in: 1966

2323 **Association of Visual Communicators**
8130 La Mesa Boulevard
#406
La Mesa, CA 91941-6437
619-427-7524; www.ivca.org
Social Media: Facebook, Twitter, LinkedIn, You Tube
Marco Forgione, CEO
David Cambridge, Head, Finance & Administration
Janet Cambridge, Administration
Dave Comley, Commercial Director
Sponsors seminars and competitions. Presents CINDY awards annually for 16mm films, videotapes, 35mm filmstrips, and video disc production.
500 Members
Founded in: 1957

2324 **Audio Engineering Society**
551 Fifth Ave.
Suite 1225
New York, NY 10176
212-661-8528; *Fax:* 212-682-0477; www.aes.org
Social Media: Facebook, Twitter, LinkedIn, YouTube, RSS, Google+
Andre Mayo, President
David W. Scheirman, Vice President, Western Region
Michael Fleming, Vice President, Central Region
Ron Streicher, Secretary
Garry Margolis, Treasurer
Worldwide professional association for professionals and students involved in the audio industry.
14000 Members
Founded in: 1948

2325 **Audio Publishers Association**
100 North 20th Street, Suite 400
Philadelphia, PA 19103
215-564-2729
info@otrpr.com; www.audiopub.org
Linda Lee, President
Anthony Goff, Vice President
Beth Anderson, Director
Janet Benson, Secretary
Sean McManus, Treasurer
Association for audio publishers.
Founded in: 1987

2326 **BICSI**
Building Industry Consulting Service International
8610 Hidden River Pkwy
Tampa, FL 33637-1000
813-979-1991
800-242-7405; *Fax:* 813-971-4311
bicsi@bicsi.org; www.bicsi.org
Social Media: Facebook, Twitter, LinkedIn, Youtube
Michael Collins, President
Brian Ensign, President Elect
Robert Erickson, Secretary
Mel Lesperance, RCDD, Treasurer
John D. Clark Jr., CAE, Executive Director/CEO
BICSI members include cabling contractors, manufacturers, systems integrators and other telecom professionals.
Founded in: 1977

2327 **Bay Area Video Coalition**
2727 Mariposa St
2nd Floor
San Francisco, CA 94110-1468
415-861-3282; *Fax:* 415-861-4316
edu@bavc.org; www.bavc.org
Social Media: Facebook, Twitter, LinkedIn, YouTube, Flickr, Instagram
Angela Jones, President
Dawn Valadez, VP
Andy Wasklewicz, Treasurer
Carol Varney, Executive Director
Mindy Aronoff, Director of Training
A national organization for independent video producers and artists. Advanced, noncommercial, media arts center dedicated to providing access to media, education and technology.
Founded in: 1976

2328 **Central Station Alarm Association**
8150 Leesburg Pike
Suite 700
Vienna, VA 22182-2721
703-242-4670; *Fax:* 703-242-4675
techadmin@csaaintl.org; www.csaaul.org
Social Media: Facebook, Twitter, LinkedIn, RSS
Jay Hauhn, Executive Director
Madeline Fullerton McMahon, SVP, Finance & Admin
Pamela Petrow, President
John McDonald, VP, Meetings and Conventions
Becky Lane, VP, Membership and Programs
Trade association representing companies offering security/alarm monitoring systems through a central station.
Founded in: 1950

2329 **Church Music Association of America**
12421 New Point Drive
Richmond, VA 23233
505-263-6298
contact@musicasacra.com
musicasacra.com/music/recordings
Social Media: Facebook, Twitter, Google+
William P. Mahrt, President
Horst Buchholz, Vice President
Jeffrey Tucker, Director of Publications
Mary Jane Ballou, Secretary
Adam Wright, Treasurer
A nonprofit association for Catholic church musicians.
Founded in: 1964

2330 **Cinema Audio Society**
827 Hollywood Way #632
Burbank, CA 91505
818-752-8624; *Fax:* 818-752-8624
CASAwards@CinemaAudioSociety.org
cinemaaudiosociety.org
Social Media: Facebook, Twitter, YouTube
Mark Ulano, CAS, President
Phillip Palmer, CAS, Vice President
Deb Adair, Director
David J. Bondelevitch, CAS, Secretary
Peter R. Damski, CAS, Treasurer
An association celebrating the scores of movies and films.
Founded in: 1964

2331 **CompTIA**
3500 Lacey Road
Suite 100
Downers Grove, IL 60515
630-678-8300
866-835- 80; *Fax:* 630-678-8384
techvoice@comptia.org; www.comptia.org
Social Media: Facebook, Twitter, LinkedIn, YouTube, Google+, Pinterest
MJ Shoer, Chairman
Mont Phelps, Vice Chair
Todd Thibodeaux, President/CEO
Nancy Hammervik, SVP, Industry Relations
Brian Laffey, Chief Financial Officer
CompTIA is a trade association representing the international technology community. Its goal is to provide a unified voice, global advocacy, and leadership, and to advance industry growth through standards professional competence, education, and business solutions.

2332 **Consumer Technology Association (CTA)**
1919 South Eads Street
Arlington, VA 22202
703-907-7600
866-858-1555; *Fax:* 703-907-7675
cta@cta.tech; www.cta.tech
Social Media: Facebook, Twitter, LinkedIn, Google+
Gary Shapiro, President & CEO
David Hagan, Chairman
Mike Fasulo, Vice Chairman
Glenda MacMullin, Treasurer
Jacqueline Black, Secretary
Formerly the Consumer Electronics Association (CEA), this organization provides valuable and innovative member-only resources including: exclusive information and unparalleled market research, networking opportunities with business advocates and leaders, up-to-date educational programs and technical training, exposure in extensive promotional programs, and representation from the voice of the industry.

2333 Entertainment Merchants Association
16530 Ventura Blvd, Suite 400
Encino, CA 91436-4551

818-385-1500; *Fax:* 818-933-0911
info@entmerch.org; www.entmerch.org
Social Media: Facebook, Twitter

Marty Graham Rentrak, Chairman
Jonathan Zepp, Vice Chairman
Mark Fisher, President & CEO
Sean Bersell, SVP, Public Affairs
Carla Immordino, VP, Finance & Administration

A nonprofit international trade association dedicated to advancing the interests of the home entertainment industry.
45,00 Members
Founded in: 2006

2334 Entertainment Software Association
601 Massachusetts Ave. NW
Suite 300
Washington, DC 20001

E-Mail: esa@theesa.com; www.theesa.com
Social Media: Facebook, Twitter

Michael D. Gallagher, President and CEO

The trade association of the video game industry.
Founded in: 2000

2335 IFPI-Representing the Recording Industry Worldwide
3470 NW 82nd Avenue
Suite 680
Doral, FL 33122

305-567-0861; *Fax:* 305-567-0871;
www.ifpi.org
Social Media: Twitter

Frances Moore, Chief Executive Officer
Lauri Rechardt, Legal
Ang Kwee Tiang, Regional Director, Asia
Javier Asensio, Regional Director, Latin America
Jeremy Banks, Director, Anti-Piracy

Promoting the value of recorded music, safeguarding record producers' rights and expanding the commercial uses of recoded music in all markets.
1300 Members

2336 International Society of Videographers
8499 S. Tamiami Trail
Suite 208
Sarasota, FL 34238

941-923-5334; *Fax:* 941-921-3836
info@weva.com; www.weva.com
Social Media: Facebook, Twitter, LinkedIn, You Tube

Exchanges information on technologies, techniques, and equipment, sponsors Hall of Fame and an international convention.
Founded in: 1981

2337 National Association of Record Industry Professionals
P.O. Box 2446
Los Angeles, CA 91610-2446

818-769-7007; www.narip.com
Social Media: Facebook, Twitter, YouTube, Vimeo

Association for all professionals in the music business.
130,0 Members
Founded in: 1998

2338 Production Equipment Rental Association
14661 Tustin St.
PO Box 55515
Sherman Oaks, CA 91413-0515

407-629-4122
877-629-4122; *Fax:* 407-629-8884;
www.productionhub.com
Social Media: Facebook, Twitter, LinkedIn, YouTube, Google+, Pinterest, V

Pat Patin, President
Mark Beasley, VP/Marketing
John Johnston, Executive Director

A worldwide trade organization that supplies production equipment to the entertainment industry. PERA promotes the commercial advancement of new technologies available from member companies to meet the ever-changing requirements of their client's artistic challenges.
180 Members
Founded in: 1998

2339 Professional Audio-Video Retailers Association
10 E 22nd Street
Suite 301
Lombard, IL 60148-6191

630-268-1500
800-621-0298; *Fax:* 630-953-8957
webmaster@paralink.org; www.paralink.org

Rosemary Wenstrom

An organization formed to assist the owners and operators of independently owned, high-end audio/video stores to work toward the mutually compatible goal of providing services to members which would be unattainable by retailers working separately.
204 Members

2340 Professional Lighting and Sound Assoiciation
630 Ninth Avenue, Suite 609
New York, NY 10036

212-244-1505; *Fax:* 212-244-1502
info@plasa.org; www.plasa.org
Social Media: Facebook, Twitter

Matthew Griffiths, Chief Executive Officer
Shane McGreevy, Chief Finance Officer
Lori Rubinstein, Director of International Programs
Jackie Tien, Group Publisher
Christopher Toulmin, Director of Events

A trade association for the lighting and sounds of the entertainment industry.
1200+ Members

2341 Recording Industry Association of America
1025 F ST N.W., 10th Floor
Washington, DC 20004
202-775-0101; www.riaa.com

Cary Sherman, Chairman & CEO
Mitch Glazier, Senior Executive Vice President
Steven M. Marks, Chief/ General Counsel, Director
Bill Hearn, Director

A trade group that represents the U.S. recording industry whose mission is to foster a business and legal climate that supports and promotes our members' creative and financial vitality.

2342 Special Interests
590 Knox Run Road
PO Box 193
Lanse, PA 16849-0193

814-345-6845
800-735-6997; *Fax:* 814-345-5566
verasi@verizon.net

Vera A Lockey, Owner

Health and safety sales DVD and videos.
Founded in: 1997

2343 University Film and Video Association

E-Mail: ufvahome@gmail.com; www.ufva.org
Social Media: Facebook, Twitter, LinkedIn, Vimeo, Instagram, YouTube

Francisco Menendez, President
Jennifer Machiorlatti, Executive Vice President
Heather Addison, Conference Vice President
Joseph Brown, Editorial Vice President
Tom Sanny, Treasurer

Association for videography and film making at universities.

2344 Video Software Dealers Association
16530 Ventura Blvd
Suite 400
Encino, CA 91436-4554

818-385-0567
800-955-8732; *Fax:* 818-385-0567
servicecenter@vsda.org; www.vsda.org

Crossan Andersen, President
Carrie Dieterich, VP Marketing
Mark Fisher, VP Membership/Strategic Initiatives
Sean Bersell, VP Public Affairs
Nancy Gordon, iDEA Manager Ops & Special Projects

Nonprofit international trade association with a membership exceeding 4,500 member companies, representing more than 25,000 locations. Members include retailers, as well as manufacturers, distributors and related businesses that constitute the home video industry. Acts as a spokesperson for home video industry both internally and legislatively.
4.5M Members
Founded in: 1981

2345 Wedding and Event Videographers Association International
8499 S. Tamiami Trail, #208
Sarasota, FL 34238

941-923-5334; *Fax:* 941-921-3836
info@weva.com, admin@weva.com;
www.weva.com

International association for wedding and event videographers.

Newsletters

2346 Consumer Multimedia Report
Warren Publishing
2115 Ward Ct Nw
Washington, DC 20037-1209

202-872-9200
800-771-9202; *Fax:* 202-318-8350
info@warren-news.com;
www.warren-news.com

Brig Easley, Manager
Daniel Warren, President/Editor
Paul Warren, Chair/Publisher

Emphasizes on emerging technologies, marketing strategies, and industry events and news.
Cost: $462.00
Frequency: BiWeekly

2347 DVD: Laser Disc Newsletter
PO Box 420
East Rockaway, NY 11518-420
516-594-9304; *Fax:* 516-594-9307
doug@dvdlaser.com; www.dvdlaser.com

Douglas Pratt, Publisher

A consumer guide to DVD's with news, reviews, ads and more.
Cost: $47.50
24 Pages
Frequency: Monthly
Circulation: 5000
ISSN: 0749-5250
Founded in: 1984
Mailing list available for rent: 5000 names at $100 per M

2348 **PRC News**
Corbell Publishing Company
201 S Alvarado St
Suite 410
Los Angeles, CA 90057-2353

213-483-4559; *Fax:* 310-258-8096
info@corbell.com; www.corbell.com

Gabriel Carabello, President
Joseph Daneshrad, Circulation Manager

A weekly newsletter for the home video industry. Covers pre-recorded video statistics, people, calendar, etc.
Cost: $577.00
8 Pages
Frequency: Monthly
Circulation: 2000
ISSN: 0898-302X
Founded in: 1988
Mailing list available for rent: 7000 names at $75 per M
Printed in on newsprint stock

2349 **Production Equipment Rental Association**
1806 Hammerlin Ave
Winter Park, FL 32789

407-629-4122
877-629-4122; *Fax:* 407-629-8884
info@peraonline.org; www.productionhub.com
Social Media: Facebook, Twitter, LinkedIn, You Tube

Pat Patin, President
Mark Beasley, VP/Marketing
John Johnston, Executive Director

A worldwide trade organization that supplies production equipment to the entertainment industry. PERA promotes the commercial advancement of new technologies available from member companies to meet the ever-changing requirements of their client's artistic challenges.
180 Members

2350 **Video Business**
Reed Business Information
2000 Clearwater Dr
Oak Brook, IL 60523-8809

630-574-0825; *Fax:* 630-288-8781
kevin.davis@reedbusiness.com;
www.reedbusiness.com

Jeff Greisch, President
Paul Sweeting, Editor-at-Large
Charles Tanner, Circulation Manager

Publication includes the retail marketplace, probes business trends and issues, reviews new and upcoming video titles, and contains information and advice for running a successful retail business, and charts top video titles.
Cost: $70.00
Frequency: Weekly
Circulation: 47807
Founded in: 1983

2351 **Video Investor**
Kagan Research
1 Lower Ragsdale Dr
Building One Suite 130
Monterey, CA 93940-5749

831-624-1536
800-307-2529; *Fax:* 831-625-3225
info@kagan.com; www.kagan.com
Social Media: Facebook, Twitter, LinkedIn

Tim Baskerville, President
Tom Johnson, Marketing Manager

Authoritative look inside the business of renting and selling video cassettes. Exclusive estimates of retail and wholesale transactions and inventories. Tracking movies into the home. Three month trial is available.
Cost: $ 795.00
Frequency: Monthly

Magazines & Journals

2352 **AudioVideo International**
Dempa Publications
275 Madison Avenue
New York, NY 10016-1101

212-682-3755; *Fax:* 212-682-2730;
www.dempa.net/

Harry Iguchi, General Manager

Articles cover systems of home entertainment.
Cost: $48.00
100 Pages
Frequency: Quarterly
Founded in: 1950

2353 **CE Pro**
EH Publishing
PO Box 989
Framingham, MA 01701-0989

508-820-1515; *Fax:* 508-663-1599
ehpubinc@ionet.net;
www.electronichouse.com

Kenneth D. Moyes, President
Jason Knott, Editor

Provides timely, top quality business, industry and product information, technical how-to articles, product comparisons, dealer profiles and marketing and management tips.
Frequency: Monthly
Circulation: 30,000

2354 **CVC Report**
Creative Video Consulting
PO Box 5195
Saratoga Springs, NY 12866-8038

212-533-9870; *Fax:* 212-473-3772
cvcreort@aol.com; www.cvc.nic.in

Mitchell Rowen, Publisher

Information for music video programming and production fields, contains charts, reviews, play lists, industry dialogue and news.
Cost: $225.00
Frequency: BiMonthly
Circulation: 800

2355 **Digital Content Producer**
Prism Business Media
9800 Metcalf Avenue
Overland Park, KS 66212-2216

913-341-1300; *Fax:* 913-967-1905
subs@prismb2b.com;
www.digitalcontentproducer.com

Scott Schwadron, Publisher
Cynthia Wisehart, Editoral Director
Kerby Asplund, Marketing
Laury Reeves, Circulation Manager

Features new product listings, updates on state of the art technology applied to new production techniques, and business industry news.
Cost: $70.00
Frequency: Monthly
Circulation: 50000
Founded in: 1975

2356 **Markee**
HJK Publications
1018 Rosetta Dr
Deltona, FL 770-341-08

386-774-8881; *Fax:* 386-774-8908
markee@markeemag.com;
www.markeemag.com/
Social Media: Facebook, Twitter, LinkedIn

Janet Karcher, Publisher
Jonathan T Hutchinson, Editor-In-Chief
Shirley Boone, Circulation
Shirley Boone, Circulation

For the Southeast and Southwest film industry.
Cost: $24.00
Frequency: Monthly
Circulation: 12200
Founded in: 1986

2357 **PRC News**
Corbell Publishing Company
201 S Alvarado St
Suite 410
Los Angeles, CA 90057-2353

213-483-4559; *Fax:* 310-312-4551
info@corbell.com; www.corbell.com
Social Media: Facebook, Twitter, LinkedIn

Gabriel Carabello, President
Eric Jacobson, Senior VP
Maria Arnone, Publisher
Kelly Conlin, CEO
Lori Reeves, Circulation Manager

Contains information on pre-recorded videos, software, hardware and blank cassettes, includes industry news, pricing and distribution updates, and reviews videos soon to be released.
Cost: $577.00
8 Pages
Frequency: Monthly
Circulation: 2000
ISSN: 0898-302X
Founded in: 1988
Printed in one color

2358 **Professional Audio-Video Retailers**
10 E 22nd Street
Suite 301
Lombard, IL 60148-6191

630-268-1500
800-621-0298; *Fax:* 630-953-8957
webmaster@paralink.org; www.paralink.org

Rosemary Wenstrom

An organization formed to assist the owners and operators of independently owned, high-end audio/video stores to work toward the mutually compatible goal of providing services to members which would be unattainable by retailers working separately.
204 Members

2359 **Prosound News**
United Entertainment Media
28 East 28th Street
27th Fl
New York, NY 10016

212-378-0400; *Fax:* 212-378-2170
sedorusa@optonline.net;
www.governmentvideo.com
Social Media: Facebook, Twitter, LinkedIn

Gary Rhodes, International Ssales Manager
Frequency: Monthly
Circulation: 25500
Founded in: 1978

2360 **Sound & Video Contractor**
Primedia
PO Box 12901
Shawnee Mission, KS 66282-2901

913-341-1300
866-505-7173; *Fax:* 913-514-6895

svcs@primedia.com; www.primedia.com
Social Media: Facebook, Twitter, LinkedIn

Eric Jacobson, Senior VP
Maria Arnone, Publisher
Kelly Conlin, CEO
Lori Reeves, Circulation Manager
Kiby Asplund, Marketing Manager

Contains information on sound systems, video display, security, CCTV, home theater, and automation. Delivers in depth instruction and examples of successful installations, fundamental acoustical and video theory and news on new technologies affecting the systems contracting business.
Cost: $35.00
Frequency: Monthly
Circulation: 21000
Founded in: 1895
Mailing list available for rent: 20,500 names at $110 per M

2361 **Television Broadcast**
Miller Freeman Publications
28 East 28th Street
Suite 4
New York, NY 10016

212-636-2700; *Fax:* 212-378-2170
sedorusa2optonline.net;
www.governmentvideo.com
Social Media: Facebook, Twitter, LinkedIn

Gary Rhodes, International Sales Manager

Television Broadcast primarily serves TV stations including commercial, public, educational, religious military TV stations or networks; teleproduction facilities including production, post-production, tape duplication, effects, audio production or independent program producer.
Frequency: Monthly
Circulation: 30,374
Founded in: 1978
Printed in 4 colors on glossy stock

2362 **Video & Entertainment**
Fairchild Publications
2407 Timberloch Place
Suite B
New York, NY 77380

281-419-5725
877-652-5295; *Fax:* 281-419-5712;
www.supermarketnews.com

Dan Bagan, President
David Orgal, Editor

2363 **Video Age International**
Video Age International
216 E 75th St
Suite PW
New York, NY 10021-2921

212-288-3933; *Fax:* 212-734-9033
sales@videoageinternational.com;
www.videoageinternational.com
Social Media: Facebook, Twitter, LinkedIn

Dom Serafini, Publisher

Offers information on program sales and distribution of videocassettes, discs and allied media.
Cost: $30.00
Frequency: 7x/Year
Circulation: 12000

2364 **Video Librarian**
Video Librarian
3435 NE Nine Boulder Dr
Poulsbo
Seabeck, WA 98370

360-626-1259
800-692-2270; *Fax:* 360-830-9346
vidlib@videolibrarian.com;
www.videolibrarian.com

Randy Pitman, President
Anne Williams, Marketing Director
Jazza Williams, Associate Editor

Offers video reviews and news for public, school, academic and special libraries.
Cost: $64.00
56 Pages
Circulation: 2000
ISSN: 0887-6851
Founded in: 1986

2365 **Video Store Magazine**
201 Sandpointe Ave
Suite 600
Santa Ana, CA 92707-8700

714-338-6700
800-854-3112; *Fax:* 714-513-8402
selliott@advanstar.com;
www.homemediaretailing.com

Thomas Arnold, Editor
Don Rosenberg, Publisher
Susan Elliott, Publications Coordinator
Steven J. Apple, Director, Business Development
Renee Rosado, Online Manager

Offers market research and buying information for industry people.
Cost: $48.00
Frequency: Weekly
Circulation: 44257

2366 **Videomaker Magazine**
Videomaker
1350 East 9th Street
PO Box 4591
Chico, CA 95927-4591

530-891-8410; *Fax:* 530-891-8443;
www.videomaker.com

Stephen Muratore, Editor-in-Chief
Jennifer O'Rourke, Managing Editor

Information about the world of camcorders, computers, tools and techniques for making video in a way that is timely, applicable, pertinent, engaging and understandable. Each month we teach production techniques, explain technology and include no less than two informative buyer's guides of products central to video. In addition, we are committed to objective analysis of videomaking products so our audience can rely on us for unbiased reporting.
Cost: $3.99
Frequency: Monthly
Circulation: 90,000
ISSN: 0889-4973
Printed in 4 colors on glossy stock

Trade Shows

2367 **International Consumer Electronics Show (CES)**
Consumer Technology Association
1919 South Eads Street
3000 S. Paradise
Arlington, VA 22202

703-907-7600
866-858-1555; *Fax:* 703-907-7675
cta@cta.tech; www.cta.tech
Social Media: Facebook, Twitter, LinkedIn

Gary Shapiro, President & CEO
David Hagan, Chairman

The CES reaches across global markets, connects the industry and enables consumer electronics to grow and thrive. International CES is owned and prroduced by the Consumer Electronics Association (CEA).
Frequency: Annual

2368 **International Society of Videographers**
PO Box 296
Sparkill, NY 10976-0296

859-624-5429; *Fax:* 845-359-8527

Steve Jambeck, Executive Director

Exchanges information on technologies, techniques, and equipment, sponsors Hall of Fame and an international convention.
Founded in: 1981

Directories & Databases

2369 **AV Market Place**
Information Today
143 Old Marlton Pike
Medford, NJ 08055-8750

609-654-6266
800-300-9868; *Fax:* 609-654-4309
custserv@infotoday.com; www.infotoday.com

Thomas H Hogan, President
Roger R Bilboul, Chairman Of The Board

The complete business directory of audio, audio visual, computer systems, film, video, and programming with industry yellow pages. The only guide needed to find more than 7,500 companies that create, apply or distribute AV equipment and services for business, education, science, and government.
Cost: $199.95
1700 Pages
Frequency: February
ISBN: 1-573871-87-7

2370 **Orion Blue Book: Computer**
Orion Research Corporation
14555 N Scottsdale Rd
Suite 330
Scottsdale, AZ 85254-3487

480-951-1114; *Fax:* 480-951-1117

Roger Rohrs, Owner

A list of manufacturers of data processing hardware and products for the computer industry.
Cost: $200.00
Frequency: Annual

2371 **Orion Blue Book: Video and Television**
Orion Research Corporation
14555 N Scottsdale Rd
Suite 330
Scottsdale, AZ 85254-3487

480-951-1114
800-844-0759; *Fax:* 480-951-1117;
www.bluebook.com

Roger Rohrs, Owner

List of more than 450 manufacturers of video and television products such as cameras, recorders, disc players, projectors, extenders, microphones, mixers, processors and color monitors.
Cost: $144.00
Frequency: Annual January

2372 **Video Networks**
Bay Area Video Coalition
1111 17th Street
San Francisco, CA 94107-2406

415-613-3282; *Fax:* 415-861-4316;
www.bavc.com

List of over 100 film festivals for independent video producers and artists.
Cost: $3.00
Frequency: Annual

2373 **Video Source Book**
Gale/Cengage Learning

Po Box 09187
Detroit, MI 48209-0187

248-699-4253
800-877-4253; *Fax:* 248-699-8049
gale.galeord@cengage.com; www.gale.com
Social Media: Facebook, Twitter, LinkedIn, You Tube

Patrick C Sommers, President

The Video Source Book continues its comprehensive coverage of the wide universe of video offerings with listing for more than 130,000 complete program listings, encompassing over 160,000 videos.
Frequency: Annual
ISBN: 1-414435-09-6
Mailing list available for rent

Industry Web Sites

2374 **http://gold.greyhouse.com**
G.O.L.D Grey House OnLine Databases

Grey House Publishing's online database platform, GOLD, offers Quick Search, Keyword Search and Expert Search for most business sectors including video and audio markets. The GOLD platform makes finding the information you need quick and easy - whether you're a novice searcher or an experienced database user. All of Grey House's directory products are available for subscription on the GOLD platform.

2375 **www.1394ta.org**
1394 Trade Association

2376 **www.asid.org**
American Society of Interior Designers (ASID)

2377 **www.avreps.org**
Independent Professional Representatives Org

2378 **www.bavc.org**
Bay Area Video Collection

2379 **www.bicsi.org**
BICSI

2380 **www.caba.org**
Continental Automated Buildings Association (CABA)

2381 **www.cedia.org**
Custom Electronic Design & Installation Associatio

2382 **www.comptia.org**
CompTIA

2383 **www.copper.org**
Copper Development Association (CDA)

2384 **www.csaaul.org**
Central Station Alarm Association

2385 **www.fla-alarms.org**
Alarm Association of Florida

2386 **www.greyhouse.com**
Grey House Publishing

Authoritative reference directories for most business sectors including audio and video markets. Users can search the online databases with varied search criteria allowing for custom searches by product category, geographic area, sales volume, keyword, subject and more. Full Grey House catalog and online ordering also available.

2387 **www.nsca.org**
National Systems Contractors Association (NSCA)

2388 **www.paralink.org**
Professional Audio-Video Retailers Association

2389 **www.riaa.org**
Recording Industry Association of America

2390 **www.siaonline.org**
Security Industry Association

2391 **www.soc.org**
Society of Camera Operators

2392 **www.tiaonline.org**
Telecommunications Industry Association (TIA)

2393 **www.vsda.org**
Video Software Dealers Association

Associations

2394 Aeronautical Radio & Research Incorporated
400 Collins Road N.E.
Cedar Rapids, IA 52498
319-295-1000
800-633-6882; *Fax:* 410-266-2020
corpcomm@arinc.com; www.arinc.com
Social Media: Facebook, Twitter, LinkedIn, YouTube, Google+, Instagram

John M Belcher, Chairman & CEO
Stephen L Waechter, VP & CFO

Provider of communications, engineering and integration solutions, we help our customers in the defense, commercial and government industries mitigate risk, improve operational and systems performance and meet program requirements.
Founded in: 1929

2395 Aeronautical Repair Station Association
121 N Henry St
Alexandria, VA 22314-2903
703-739-9543; *Fax:* 703-299-0254
arsa@arsa.org; www.arsa.org
Social Media: Facebook, Twitter, LinkedIn, RSS, Google+

Gary Hudnall, President
Warner Calvo, Vice President
Basil Barimo, Executive VP
Marshall S Filler, General Counsel/Managing Director
Sarah MacLeod, Executive Director

Helps develop guidance, policy and interpretations that are clear, concise and consistent, and applied uniformly to all similarly situated companies and individuals.
700 Members
Founded in: 1984

2396 Aerospace Industries Association
2310 E El Segundo Blvd
El Segundo, CA 90245-4609
310-336-5000; *Fax:* 310-336-7055
membership@aia-aerospace.org; www.aero.org
Social Media: Facebook, Twitter, Youtube, Google+

W M Austin, President & CEO
R Clinton, Senior VP/General Counsel/Secretary
H J Mitchell, Vice President
M H Goodman, Principal Director

The Aerospace Industries Association shapes public policy that ensures the US aerospace, defense and homeland security industry remains preeminent and that its members are successful and profitable in a changing global market.
283 Members
Founded in: 1919

2397 Aerospace Medical Association
320 S Henry St
Alexandria, VA 22314-3579
703-739-2240; *Fax:* 703-739-9652
jsventek@asma.org; www.asma.org
Social Media: Facebook, Twitter, LinkedIn

Jeffery C. Sventek,MS,CASp, Executive Director
Gisselle Vargas, Operations manager
Gloria Carter, Director

Our mission is to apply and advance scientific knowledge to promote and enhance the health, safety and performance of those involved in aerospace and related activities.
3200 Members
Founded in: 1929
Mailing list available for rent

2398 Air Force Association
1501 Lee Hwy
Suite 400
Arlington, VA 22209-1198
703-247-5800
800-727-3337; *Fax:* 703-247-5853
membership@afa.org; www.afa.org
Social Media: Facebook, Twitter, LinkedIn, Youtube, Blogger

George Muellner, Chairman
Jerry E White, Vice Chairman
Craig R McKinley, President
Len Vernamonti, Treasurer
Marvin L Tooman, Secretary

Independent nonprofit, civilian organization promoting public understanding of aerospace power and the pivotal role it plays in the security of the nation.
1400 Members
Founded in: 1946

2399 Air Taxi Association
300 Galleria Parkway
Atlanta, GA 30339
770-563-7400; wwww.travelport.com
Social Media: Twitter, LinkedIn, Youtube

Gordon Wilson, President & CEO
Eric Bock, Executive VP/CLO/CAO
Philip Emery, Executive VP/CFO
Mark Ryan, Executive VP/CIO
Bryan Conway, Chief Marketing Officer

Backed by leading air taxi companies, ATXA's mission is to speed the adoption of the air taxi model so that more business, individuals, and communities can enjoy the benefits of direct, personal flights.
Founded in: 2006

2400 Air Traffic Control Association
1101 King St
Suite 300
Alexandria, VA 22314
703-299-2430; *Fax:* 703-299-2437
info@atca.org; www.atca.org
Social Media: Facebook, Twitter, LinkedIn, RSS,YouTube

Neil Planzer, Chairman
Charles Keegan Planzer, Chair Elect
Peter F Dumont, President & CEO
Rachel Jackson, Treasurer
Rachel Jackson, Secretary

Works to establish and maintain a safe and efficient air traffic control system.
2400+ Members
Founded in: 1956

2401 Air Transport Association of America
1301 Pennsylvania Ave NW
Suite 1100
Washington, DC 20004-1738
202-626-4000
800-497-3326; *Fax:* 202-626-4166
a4a@airlines.org; www.airlines.org
Social Media: Facebook, Twitter, LinkedIn, YouTube, Instagram

Nicholas E. Calio, President/CEO
Paul R Archambeault, Senior VP/CFO/COO
David A Berg, SVP/General Counsel/Secretary
Christine M. Burgeson, SVP, Global Government Affairs
Sean D. Kennedy, SVP, Global Government Affairs

Supports and assists its members by promoting the air transport industry and the safety, cost effectiveness, and technical advancement of its operators; advocating common industry positions before state and local governments; conducting designated industry-wide programs; and assuring governmental and public understanding of all aspects of air transport.
25 Members
Founded in: 1936

2402 Aircraft Electronics Association
3570 NE Ralph Powell Rd
Lees Summit, MO 64064
816-347-8400; *Fax:* 816-347-8405
info@aea.net; www.aea.net
Social Media: Facebook, Twitter, LinkedIn, Youtube, Flickr

David Loso, Chairman
Michael Kus, Vice Chair
Paula Derks, President
Debra McFarland, Executive Vice President
Kim Stephenson, Secretary

Persons interested in aviation and avionics.
1200 Members

2403 Aircraft Owners & Pilots Association
421 Aviation Way
Frederick, MD 21701-4756
301-695-2000
800-872-2672; *Fax:* 301-695-2375
phil.boyer@aopa.org; www.aopa.org
Social Media: Facebook, Twitter, LinkedIn, Google+, Instagram

Mark Baker, President & CEO
George Perry, CDR USN (Ret), SVP
Bruce Landsberg, Senior Safety Advisor

AOPA has achieved its prominent position through effective advocacy, enlightened leadership, technical competence, and hard work. Providing member services that range from representation at the federal, state, and local levels to legal services, advice, and other assistance, we have built a service organization that far exceeds any other in the aviation community. AOPA ePilot and AOPA ePilot Flight Training Edition unique e-mail newsletters issued every Friday morning only to AOPA members.
405k Members
Founded in: 1939

2404 Airline Pilots Association International
1625 Massachusetts Ave NW
Suite 800
Washington, DC 20036
703-689-2270; *Fax:* 202-797-4052;
www.alpa.org
Social Media: Facebook, Twitter, LinkedIn, YouTube, Instagram, Flickr

Lee Moak, President
Sean Cassidy, First VP
Bill Couette, VP Administration
Randolph Helling, VP Finance

Promotes airplane use and co-operates with government agencies and private and public flying organizations to increase general safety.
64000 Members
Founded in: 1931

2405 Airport Consultants Council
908 King St
Suite 100
Alexandria, VA 22314
703-683-5900; *Fax:* 703-683-2564
info@acconline.org; www.acconline.org
Social Media: Facebook, Twitter, LinkedIn, Google+

Paula P Hochstetler, President
T.J. Schulz, Executive VP
John B Reynolds, Manager of Communicatons
Colleen Flood, Manager, Marketing & Membership
Chris Spaulding, Assistant

Represents the majority of airport consulting firms in the United States.
200+ Members
Founded in: 1978

2406 **Airports Association Council International**
1615 L Street NW
Suite 300
Washington, DC 20036
202-293-8500
888-424-7767; *Fax:* 202-331-1362;
www.aci.aero
Social Media: Facebook, Twitter, LinkedIn, Youtube
Deborah McElroy, Interim President
Nancy Zimini, Senior VP
Kent George, Chairman
Ian A Redhead, VP Airport Services
Patricia Hahn, EVP Operations/General Counsel
Members are boards, commissions, local governmental entities operating public airport facilities and more.
240 Members
Founded in: 1947

2407 **Allied Pilots Association**
14600 Trinity Blvd
Suite 500
Fort Worth, TX 76155-2512
817-302-2272; *Fax:* 817-302-2119
public-comment@alliedpilots.org;
www.alliedpilots.org
Social Media: Facebook, Twitter, Youtube
Dave Ahles, Executive Director
Captian Dave Bates, President
Officer Anthony Chapman, Vice President
Provides all the traditional union representation services for its members. This includes the lobbying of airline pilots views to Congress and government agencies. In addition, it devotes more than 20 percent of its dues income to support aviation safety.
11500 Members
Founded in: 1963

2408 **American Astronautical Society**
6352 Rolling Mill Place
Suite 102
Springfield, VA 22152-2370
703-866-0020; *Fax:* 703-866-3526
aas@astronautical.org; www.astronautical.org
Social Media: Facebook, Twitter, Youtube
Jim Kirkpatrick, Executive Director
Carol S. Lane, President
Alan DeLuna, Executive Vice President
Tracy Lamm, Vice President, Membership
Independent scientific and technical group in the United States exclusively dedicated to the advancement of space science and exploration.
1400 Members
Founded in: 1954

2409 **American Bonanza Society**
Mid-Continent Airport
PO Box 12888
Wichita, KS 67277
316-945-1700; *Fax:* 316-945-1710
bonanza2@bonanza.org; www.bonanza.org
Social Media: Facebook, Twitter, LinkedIn
Nancy Johnson, Executive Director
Tom Turner, Technical Manager
We are nearly 10,000 owners and pilots of Bonanza, Baron and Travel Air type aircraft who have banded together to share information and experiences involving the operation and maintenance of the Beech produced aircraft. Together, we offer an underwriter recognized flight proficiency program, and service clinics scheduled throughout the year at various locations. These clinics provide members the opportunity to have their aircraft evaluated by highly experienced ABS technical personnel.
10K Members
Founded in: 1967

2410 **American Helicopter Society**
2701 Prosperity Avenue
Suite 210
Fairfax, VA 22031
703-684-6777
855-247-4685; *Fax:* 703-739-9279
staff@vtol.org; www.vtol.org
Social Media: Facebook, Twitter, LinkedIn
Mike Hirschberg, Executive Director
Kay Yosua Brackins, Deputy Director
Randy Johnson, Director Of Information Resource
David Renzi, Director Of Meetings & Advertising
Holly Cafferelli, Director Of Administration
Promotes the interests of designers, engineers and manufacturers of the vertical flight industry. Serving as a clearinghouse for technical information, the society publishes several periodicals, organizes the largest vertical flight technology display in the world, and maintains a comprehensive library.
6000 Members
Founded in: 1944

2411 **American Institute of Aeronautics and Astronautics**
1801 Alexander Bell Dr
Suite 500
Reston, VA 20191-4344
703-264-7500
800-639-2422; *Fax:* 703-264-7551
custserv@aiaa.org; www.aiaa.org
Social Media: Facebook, Twitter, LinkedIn, YouTube, Flickr, Instagram
Jim Albaugh, President
Mark J Lewis, President-Elect
Laura McGill, VP Finance
Steven E. Gorrell, VP Education
Annalisa Weigel, VP Member Services
Advancing the arts, sciences and technology of aeronautics and astronautics and promotes the professionalism of those engaged in these pursuits.
31,00 Members
Founded in: 1930

2412 **Army Aviation Association of America**
593 Main Street
Monroe, CT 06468-2830
203-268-2450; *Fax:* 203-268-5870
aaaa@quad-a.org; www.quad-a.org
Social Media: Facebook, Twitter, LinkedIn, Youtube
Bill Harris, Executive Director
Barbara McCann, Executive Assistant
Mark Albertson, Historian
Jennifer Chittem, Marketing Communications
Janis Arena, Manager
A professional force that holds the aviation community, both military and industry together.

2413 **Association of Air Medical Services**
909 N Washington Street
Suite 410
Alexandria, VA 22314
703-836-8732; *Fax:* 703-836-8920
jfiegel@aams.org; www.aams.org
John Fiegel, Executive Director/CEO
Rick Sherlock, President &CEO
Kristin Discher, Office Manager
Voluntary nonprofit organization, encourages and supports its members in maintaining a standard of performance reflecting safe operations and efficient, high quality patient care. Built on the idea that representation from a variety of medical transport services and businesses can be brought together to share information, collectively resolve problems and provide leadership in the medical transport community. We provide a e-mail newsletter called Capitol Watch for AAMS Members.
581 Members
Founded in: 1980

2414 **Association of Flight Attendants-CWA**
501 3rd St NW
Suite 1
Washington, DC 20001
202-434-1300
800-424-2401; *Fax:* 202-434-1411
info@afacwa.org; www.afacwa.org
Social Media: Facebook, Twitter, Youtube
Sara Sara, International President
Debora Sutor, International VP
Kevin Creighan, International Secretary/Treasurer
Represents over 50,000 flight attendants at 26 airlines, serving as a voice for flight attendants at their workplace, in the industry, the media and on Capitol Hill.
55M Members
Founded in: 1930

2415 **Association of Naval Aviation**
6551 Loisdale Road
Suite 222
Springfield, VA 22150
703-960-6806; *Fax:* 703-960-6807
anahqtr@aol.com; www.anahq.org
Social Media: Facebook, Twitter, LinkedIn
James L Holloway, Chairman
David L Philman, President
Michael E Field, Secretary/Treasurer
Linda Bubien, Advertising Director
R M Rausa, Editor
Professional, nonprofit, educational and fraternal society of Naval Aviation, whose main purpose is to educate the public and our national leaders on the vital roles of the Navy, Marine Corp and Coast Guard Aviation as key elements of our national defense posture. ANA continuously seeks to elucidate the key current issues impacting Naval Aviation through published writing, symposia, speeches and discussions with various interest groups.

2416 **Aviation Development Council**
141-07 20th Ave
Suite 404
Whitestone, NY 11357
718-746-0212; *Fax:* 718-746-1006
root@aviationdevelopmentcouncil.org;
www.adcnynj.org
William Huisman, Executive Director
Addresses noise problems from air carriers in the New York - New Jersey region.
Founded in: 1962

2417 **Aviation Distributors and Manufacturers**
Fernley & Fernley Inc
100 North 20th Street
Suite 400
Philadelphia, PA 19103-1462
215-320-3872; *Fax:* 215-564-2175
adma@fernley.com; www.adma.org
Social Media: Facebook
Steve Langston, President
Lise Pearson, VP
Craig Lockerbie, VP
Trudie Bruner, Management Liaison
Kristen Olszewski, Executive Director

Promotes interests of wholesalers and manufacturers of general aviation aircraft parts and supplies.
Founded in: 1943

2418 **Aviation Insurance Association**
7200 W 75th Street
Overland Park, KS 66204
913-627-9632; *Fax:* 913-381-2515
mandie@aiaweb.org; www.aiaweb.org
Social Media: Facebook, Blog
David Sales, President
Paul Herbers, Vice President
Herbers Gardner, Secretary
Christopher R. Zanette, Treasurer
Mandie Bannwarth, Executive Director
A not-for-profit association dedicated to expanding the knowledge of and promoting the general welfare of the aviation insurance industry through numerous educational programs and events.
900 Members
Founded in: 1976

2419 **Aviation Suppliers Association**
2233 Wisconsin Ave. NW
Suite 503
Washington, DC 20007
202-347-6899; *Fax:* 202-347-6894;
www.aviationsuppliers.org
Social Media: Facebook, Twitter, LinkedIn
Michele Dickstein, President
Tony Brigham, Coordinator, Programs & Services
The voice of the aviation parts supply industry on regulatory and legal matters.
570+ Members
Founded in: 1993

2420 **Aviation Technician Education Council**
117 North Henry Street
Alexandria, VA 22314-2903
703-548-2030
atec@atec-amt.org; www.atec-amt.org
Goertzen Ryan, President
Kienast Amy, Vice President
Hoyle Gary, Treasurer
Organization of Federal Aviation Administration approved Aviation Maintenance Technician schools and supporting industries.
Founded in: 1961

2421 **Cessna Owner Organization**
N7528 Aanstad Road
PO Box 5000
Iola, WI 54945
715-445-5000
888-692-3776; *Fax:* 715-445-4053
help@cessnaowner.org; www.cessnaowner.org
Social Media: Facebook
Tery Foerster, Executive Director
Joe Jones, Publisher
Ryan Jones, Executive Publisher
Dennis Piotrowski, Editor/Associate Publisher
Kara Grundman, Graphic Designer
Membership support organization for Cessna aircraft owners.
5000 Members
Founded in: 1975

2422 **Civil Aviation Medical Association**
PO Box 2382
Peachtree City, GA 30269-2382
770-487-0100; *Fax:* 770-487-0080
civilavmed@yahoo.com; www.civilavmed.org
Mark Eidson, President
Clawton T Cowl, President-Elect
Gordon L Ritter, Secretary/Treasurer
David P Millet, Executive VP
James Carpenter, VP Communications & Representation
Aviation medical equipment, supplies and services. Working on behalf of physicians engaged in the practice of aviation medicine and dedicated to civil aviation safety.
Cost: $5.00
800+ Members
Founded in: 1948

2423 **Experimental Aircraft Association**
3000 Poberezny Road
3000 Poberezny road
Oshkosh, WI 54902
920-426-4800
800-564-6322; *Fax:* 920-426-6761
webmaster@eaa.org; www.eaa.org
Social Media: Facebook, Twitter
Tom Poberezny, President
David Berkley, Communications Director
Adam Smith, VP Member Services
Works to keep aviation history alive. Members are active restorers and enthusiasts working to keep vintage aircraft in the air and flying for the pleasure and education of themselves and the public at large. EAA's weekly electronic newsletter e-Hot Line.
170M Members
Founded in: 1953

2424 **Flight Safety Foundation**
801 N Fairfax Street
Suite 400
Alexandria, VA 22314-1774
703-739-6700; *Fax:* 703-739-6708
wahdan@flightsafety.org;
www.flightsafety.org
Social Media: Facebook, Twitter, LinkedIn
David McMillan, Chairman
Kevin L Hiatt, President & CEO
Kenneth P Quinn, Secretary/General Counsel
David Barger, Treasurer
Supported by airlines, aerospace manufacturers, aviation professionals, corporate flight departments and others interested in flight safety.
900 Members
Founded in: 1947

2425 **Forecast International**
Forecast International
22 Commerce Rd
Newtown, CT 06470
203-426-0800
800-451-4975; *Fax:* 203-426-0223
info@forecast1.com;
www.forecastinternational.com
Social Media: Facebook, Twitter, LinkedIn, Google+
Ray Peterson, VP, Research & Editorial Svcs.
Raymond Jaworowski, Senior Aerospace Analyst
Richard Pettibone, Senior Government Analyst
Rebecca Barnett Edwards, Latin America & Caribbean Analyst
Nicole Loeser, Middle East & Africa Analyst
Premier provider of market intelligence, forecasting, proprietary research and consulting services.
Cost: $495.00
24 Pages
Frequency: Weekly
Founded in: 1973
Printed in 4 colors on matte stock

2426 **Future Aviation Professionals of America (FAPA)**
4959 Massachusetts Boulevard
Atlanta, GA 30337
404-997-8097; *Fax:* 770-997-8111;
www.fapa.info/
Linda Nelson, Chairman
Provides career information for those seeking careers in aviation, publications, newsletter, interview briefings and Aviation Job Bank. Also provides personal financial planning for airline pilots.
15M Members
Founded in: 1974

2427 **General Aviation Manufacturers Association**
1400 K St NW
Suite 801
Washington, DC 20005-2485
202-393-1500; *Fax:* 202-842-4063
bforan@GAMA.aero; www.gama.aero
Pete Bunce, President & CEO
Mary Lynn J Rynkiewicz, Director of Communications
Jens Hennig, VP Operations
Paul H Feldman, VP Government Affairs
bree J Foran, Meeting/Office Coordinator
Manufacturers of general aviation aircraft and related equipment. Members also operate fleets of aircraft, fixed based operations and pilot training facilities.
50 Members
Founded in: 1970

2428 **Helicopter Association International**
1920 Ballanger Ave
Alexandria, VA 22314-2898
703-683-4646
800-435-4976; *Fax:* 703-683-4745
rotor@rotor.org; www.rotor.com
Social Media: Facebook, Twitter, LinkedIn
Anthony W Burson, Chairman
Gale Wilson, Vice Chairman
Matthew S Zuccaro, President
Max Lyons, Treasurer
Edward F DiCampli, Executive VP/Secretary
Nonprofit organization provides members with services that directly benefit their operations and advances the civil helicopter industry by providing programs to enhance safety, encourage professionalism and promote the unique societal contributions made by the rotary flight industry.
2500 Members
Founded in: 1948

2429 **Helicopter Safety Advisory Conference**
Marathon Oil Company
PO Box 60136
Houston, TX 77205
281-892-4088
mark.fontenot@bp.com; www.hsac.org
Mark Fontenot, Chairman
Joseph Gross, Treasurer
Ron Domonique, Secretary
Robert Hall, Vice Chair
Promotes safety and seeks to improve operations through establishment of standards of practice.
115 Members
Founded in: 1978

2430 **International Association of Machinists and Aerospace Workers**
9000 Machinists Place
Upper Marlboro, MD 20772-2687
301-967-4500
websteward@iamaw.org; www.goiam.org
Social Media: Facebook, Twitter
R Thomas Buffenbarger, International President
Richard Michalski, VP
Dave Ritchie, General VP
Bill Trbovitch, Director Communications
Warren L Mart, General Secretary/Treasurer
Has an annual budget of approximately $101.3 million.
700K Members

2431 **International Coordinating Council of Aerospace Industries Associations**
1000 Wilson Blvd.
Suite 1700
Arlington, VA 22209-3928

703-358-1064; www.iccaia.org
Social Media: LinkedIn

David F. Melcher, Chairman
Jim Quick, Vice-Chairman

The voice of the world's aerospace manufacturers in matters concerning international standards and regulations for air transport safety and security.
Founded in: 1972

2432 **International Council of Aircraft Owner and Pilot Associations**
421 Aviation Way
Frederick, MD 21701

301-695-2220; *Fax:* 301-695-2375
iaopa@aopa.org; www.iaopa.org

Mark Baker, President
Craig Spence, Secretary General
Jeremy DeLaTorre, Administrator

Nonprofit federation of 53 autonomous, nongovernmental, national general aviation organizations. Facilitates the movement of general aviation aircraft.
40000 Members
Founded in: 1962

2433 **International Flight Services Association**
1100 Johnson Ferry Road
Suite 300
Atlanta, GA 30342

404-252-3663; *Fax:* 404-252-0774
ifsanet@gmail.com; www.ifsanet.org
Social Media: Facebook, Twitter, Youtube

Vicky Stennes, President
Kenneth Samara, Chairman
Pam Chumley, Executive Administrator
Ellen Hoy, Membership Manager
Michelle Moore, Meetings Manager

The International Flight Services Association is a global professional association created to serve the needs and interests of airline and railway personnel, in-flight and rail caterers and suppliers responsible for providing passenger foodservice on regularly scheduled travel routes.
Founded in: 1966

2434 **International Society of Women Airline Pilots**
ISA + 21
723 S. Casino Center Blvd.
2nd Floor
Las Vegas, NV 89101-6716

E-Mail: chairwoman@iswap.org;
www.iswap.org

Liz Jennings Clark, Chair
Maria Haddad, Human Performance
Liana B Hart, Treasurer
Eva Marie Brock, Secretary
Kathy A McCullough, Communications Director

Fosters cooperation and exchange among women airline pilots employed as flight crew members (Captain, First Officer or Second Officer) and holding seniority numbers with an air carrier which operates at least one aircraft with a gross weight of 90,000 pounds or more.
4000 Members
Founded in: 1978

2435 **Light Aircraft Manufacturers Association**
2001 Steamboat Ridge Ct
Daytona Beach, FL 32128-6918

651-592-7565
301-693-2223; *Fax:* 651-226-1825
info@lama.bz; www.lama.bz

Dan Johnson, Chairman/President

Promotes interests of kit-built light aircraft. Membership dues are $125 for voting members and $25 for non-voting members.
50 Members
Founded in: 1984

2436 **Lighter Than Air Society**
Lighter Than Air Society
526 S. MAIN ST
Suite 406
Akron, OH 44311-3311

330-535-5827
suggest@blimpinfo.com; www.blimpinfo.com

Joseph Huber, President
Ron Browning, Director Business Development

Nonprofit organization whose members are devoted to the study of the history, science and techniques of all forms of buoyant flight.
1000 Members
Founded in: 1952

2437 **Mount Diablo Pilots Association**
PO Box 6632
Concord, CA 94524

925-370-0828
president@mdpa.org; www.mdpa.org
Social Media: Facebook, Twitter

Stewart Bowers, President
Natasha Lantsor, VP, Activities
Madeleine Ferguson, VP Communications
Steve Mink, VP Programs
Elaine Yeary, Treasurer

To promote good public relations between general aviation enthusiasts and the local community; to encourage participation in fly-ins and other aviation activities; to promote safety and educational activities for pilots; to provide mutual resources of information on flying for members; to furnish information and support to the Contra Costa Airport Advisory Committee and other governmental agencies concerned with aviation; to be a proxy on aviation matters of community concern for its membership

2438 **National Aeronautic Association**
1 Reagan National Airport
Hangar 7, Suite 202
Washington, DC 20001-6015

703-416-4888
800-644-9777; *Fax:* 703-416-4877
naa@naa.aero; www.naa.aero

Jonathan Gaffney, President
Natasha Clark, Director, Administration
Art Greenfield, Contest & Records Director

A non-profit association that is dedicated to the advancement of the art, sport and science of aviation in the United States.
3000 Members
Founded in: 1905

2439 **National Agricultural Aviation Association**
1440 Duke Street
Alexandria, VA 22314

202-546-5722; *Fax:* 202-546-5726
information@agaviation.org;
www.agaviation.org
Social Media: Facebook

Brian Rau, President
Leif Isaacson, Vice President
Mark Hartz, Secretary
Harley Curless, Treasurer

Voice of the aerial application industry, we work to preserve aerial application's place in the protection and production of America's food and fiber supply. Aerial application is one of the safest, fastest, most efficient and economical ways to apply pesticides. It is also the most environmentally friendly tool of modern agriculture.
1,300 Members
Founded in: 1966

2440 **National Air Traffic Controllers Association**
1325 Massachusetts Ave Nw
Washington, DC 20005-4171

202-628-5451
800-266-0895; *Fax:* 202-628-5767
web_staff@list.natca.net; www.natca.org
Social Media: Facebook, Twitter, LinkedIn, Youtube, Instagram

Paul Rinaldi, President
Trish Gilbert, Executive VP
Clint Lancaster, Alaskan Regional Vice President
Kevin Peterson, Central Regional Vice President
Dean Iacopelli, Eastern Regional Vice President

Founded to ensure safety and longevity of air traffic controller positions around the nation. Represents over 15,000 air traffic controllers throughout the US, Puerto Rico and Guam, along with 2,508 other bargaining unit members that span all areas from engineers and architects to nurses and health care professionals to members of the accounting community.
15000 Members
Founded in: 1987

2441 **National Air Transportation Association**
818 Connecticut Avenue
NW Suite 900
Washington, DC 20006

202-774-1535
800-808-6282; *Fax:* 202-452-0837;
www.nata.aero
Social Media: Facebook, Twitter, LinkedIn, RSS

Andy Priester, Chairman
Priester Hiller, Vice Chair
Priester Aviation, President & CEO
Diane Gleason, Director, Meetings and Conferences

Aggressively promotes safety and the success of aviation service businesses through its advocacy efforts before government, the media and the public as well as by providing valuable programs and forums to further its members' prosperity.
Founded in: 1940

2442 **National Association of Flight Instructors**
EAA Aviation Center
3101 E Milham Ave
Portage, MI 49002

866-806-6156; *Fax:* 920-426-6865
nafi@nafinet.org; www.nafinet.org
Social Media: Facebook, Twitter, LinkedIn, Google+

Robert Meder, Chairman
John Niehas, Program Coordinator
David Hipschman, Mentor Editor
Phil Poynor, VP, Government & Industry Relations
John Gibson, Director Of Sponsorship

Dedicated exclusively to raising and maintaining the professional standing of the flight instructor in the aviation community. Maintains a benefits package available for everyone from the independent instructor to those teaching at flight schools. Every other week we'll send NAFI

members with access to e-mail and electronic eMentor.
Founded in: 1967

2443 **National Business Aviation Association**
1200 G Street NW
Suite 1100
Washington, DC 20005

202-783-9000; *Fax:* 202-331-8364
info@nbaa.org; www.nbaa.org
Social Media: Facebook, Twitter, LinkedIn, instagram,youtube,itunes

Paul Anderson, Chairman
Lloyd "Fig" Newton, ViceChair
Edward M. Bolen, President & CEO
Dan Hubbard, Senior VP, Communications
Steve Brown, Chief Operating Officer

An organization for companies that rely on general aviation aircraft to help make their businesses more efficient, productive and successful.
8000 Members
Founded in: 1947

2444 **National EMS Pilots Association**
PO Box 2128
Layton, UT 84041-9128

801-436-7505
877-668-0430; *Fax:* 866-906-6023
contactus@nemspa.org; www.nemspa.org
Social Media: Facebook, Twitter

Kurt Williams, President
Stuart Buckingham, Treasurer

A professional organization dedicated to serving pilots involved in the air-medical transport industry, and to improving the quality and safety of those services
Founded in: 1984

2445 **Ninety-Nines**
4300 Amelia Earhart Drive
Suite A
Oklahoma City, OK 73159

405-685-7969
800-994-1929; *Fax:* 405-685-7985
99s@ninety-nines.org; www.ninety-nines.org
Social Media: Facebook, Twitter, Google+, Skype

Martha Phillips, President
Jan McKenzie, Vice President
Cynthia Madsen, Secretary
Leslie Ingham, Treasurer
Lin Caywood, Director

International organization of licensed women pilots from 35 countries. We are a nonprofit, charitable membership corporation holding 501(c)(3) US tax status. Members are professional pilots for airlines, industry and government; we are pilots who teach and pilots who fly for pleasure; we are pilots who are technicians and mechanics. First and foremost, we are women who love to fly.
5500 Members
Founded in: 1929

2446 **Piper Owners Society**
N7528 Aanstad Rd
Iola, WI 54945

715-445-5000
866-697-4737; *Fax:* 715-445-4053
help@piperowner.org; www.piperowner.org
Social Media: Facebook

Dan Weiler, Executive Director
Joe Jones, Publisher
Ryan Jones, Executive Publisher
Dennis Piotrowski, Editor
Kara Grundman, Graphic Designer

To support private owners of all models of Piper light aircraft. Members receive a full color monthly magazine which includes flying experiences, aircraft parts explained and historical features.
Founded in: 1987

2447 **Popular Rotorcraft Association**
PO Box 68
Mentone, IN 46539

574-353-7227; *Fax:* 574-353-7021
praofficemgr@gmail.com; www.pra.org
Social Media: Facebook, Youtube

Scott Lewis, President
Douglas Barker, Vice President
Stan Foster, Secretary
Robert Rymer, Treasurer

A nonprofit organization dedicated to the advancement of knowledge, public education and safety among Rotorcraft enthusiasts worldwide.
2000 Members
Founded in: 1962

2448 **Professional Aeromedical Transport**
PO Box 7519
Alexandria, VA 22307

800-541-7517

Purpose is to standardize and upgrade services of aeromedical transport operations. Membership is open to companies and individuals active in the industry.
170 Members
Founded in: 1986

2449 **Professional Aviation Maintenance Association**
400 North Washington Street
Suite 300
Alexandria, VA 22314

87- 90- 541
800-356-1671; *Fax:* 616-527-1327
info@pama.org; www.pama.org
Social Media: Facebook, Twitter, LinkedIn, Google+

Roger Sickler, Chairman
Jeff Gruber, Vice Chairman
Clark Gordon, Secretary

Enhances professionalism and recognition of the Aviation Maintenance Technician through communication, education, representation and support for continuous improvement in aviation safety.
3300 Members
Founded in: 1972

2450 **Regional Airline Association**
2025 M St NW
Suite 800
Washington, DC 20036-3309
202-367-1170; *Fax:* 202-367-2170
raa@raa.org; www.raa.org
Social Media: Facebook, Twitter, YouTube

Roger Cohen, President
Scott Foose, Vice President
Faye Malarkey Black, Senior VP, Legislative Affairs
Liam Connolly, Senior Director
Kelly Murphy, Media Relations

Membership consists of more than 70 airlines, plus 350 Associate members provide goods and services.
510 Members
Founded in: 1975

2451 **Reliability Engineering & Management Institute**
University Of Arizona
1130 N Mountian Avenue
Building 119 Room N 517
Tucson, AZ 85721

520-621-6120; *Fax:* 520-621-8191
dimitri@u.arizona.edu;
www.u.arizona.edu/~dimitri/

Dr Dimitri Kececioglu PE, Prof Aerospace/Mech Engineering

An institute to help provide a working knowledge in reliability engineering.
Frequency: November
Founded in: 1971

2452 **Seaplane Pilots Association**
3859 Laird Blvd
Lakeland, FL 33811

863-701-7979
888-772-8923; *Fax:* 863-701-7588
spa@seaplanes.org; www.seaplanes.org
Social Media: Facebook, Twitter, YouTube

Walter Windus, Chairman
Stephen Williams, President
Lyle Panepinto, VP
Gordon Richardson, Treasurer
John Touchett, Secretary

Represents members in dozens of seaplane access issues annually and provides numerous exclusive benefits. Members who have provided SPA with a valid email address receive Water Flying Update, a bimonthly e-newsletter that provides recent news, advocacy updates, technical tips, upcoming events, and a tip for using SPA's web site.
375 Members
Founded in: 1971

2453 **Soaring Society of America**
PO Box 2100
Hobbs, NM 88241-2100

505-392-1177; *Fax:* 505-392-8154
membership@ssa.org; www.ssa.org
Social Media: Facebook, Twitter

Dennis Layton, Chief Operating Officer
Eric Bick, Editor
Kathey Pope, Accounting Manager
Misty Dodson, Merchandise/Membership Services
Melinda Hughes, Magazine Adv./Membership Services

Fosters and promote all phases of gliding and soaring, nationally and internationally.
16K Members
Founded in: 1932

2454 **Society of Experimental Test Pilots**
44814 N Elm Avenue
Lancaster, CA 93534

661-942-9574; *Fax:* 661-940-0398
setp@setp.org; www.setp.org

Timothy R. Morey, President
Todd Ericson, President Elect
Art Tomassetti, Vice President
John Tougas, Secretary
Dan Wells, Treasurer

International organization that seek to promote air safety and contributes to aeronautical advancement by promoting sound aeronautical design and development; interchanging ideas, thoughts and suggestions of the members, assisting in the professional development of experimental pilots, and providing scholarships and aid to members and the families of deceased members.
2000 Members
Founded in: 1955

2455 Society of Flight Test Engineers
44814 N Elm Avenue
Lancaster, CA 93534

661-949-2095; *Fax:* 661-949-2096
sfte@sfte.org; www.sfte.org
Social Media: Facebook, LinkedIn, RSS

Peter Scheidler, President
Douglas Bell, Vice President

Members are engineers whose principal professional interest is the flight testing of aircraft. Purpose is to improve communications in the fields of flight test operations, analysis, instrumentation and data systems. We offer an online newsletter called SFTE Flight Test News.
900 Members
Founded in: 1968

2456 Space Enterprise Council
3500 Lacey Rd.
Suite 100
Downers Grove, IL 60515

630-678-8300
866-835-8020
Social Media: Facebook, Twitter, LinkedIn, Google+, YouTube, Pinterest

Earl Madison, Chair
Rosanna Sattler, Vice Chair
Joe Cassady, Executive Director

Represents interests of commercial, military and civil sectors of space industry to policymakers.
Founded in: 2000

2457 Space Foundation
4425 Arrowswest Drive
Colorado Spring, CO 80907

719-576-8000
800-691-4000; *Fax:* 719-576-8801
web@spacefoundation.org;
www.spacefoundation.org
Social Media: Facebook, Twitter, LinkedIn, Instagram, Google+, RSS, Pinte

Elliot H. Pulham, CEO
Holly Roberts, CFO
Kevin C Cook, VP, Marketing & Communications
Steve Eisenhart, Senior VP, Strategy
Art Rakewitcz, VP, Operations

To advance space-related endeavors to inspire, enable, and propel humanity.
- Members
Founded in: 1983

2458 Tailhook Association
9696 Businesspark Ave
San Diego, CA 921313-164

858-689-9223
800-322-4665
jrdavis@tailhook.net; www.tailhook.org
Social Media: Facebook, LinkedIn, Google+

Gregory Keithley, President
Capt. J R Davis, Executive Director
Capt. Dennis Irelan, Editor
CDR Mike Dechemedy, Managing Editor

An independent, fraternal, nonprofit organization internationally recognized as the premier supporter of the aircraft carrier and other sea-based aviation.

2459 The Aerospace States Association

202-257-4872
huettner@aerostates.org; www.aerostates.org
Social Media: Facebook, Twitter

Lt. Gov. Kay Ivey (AL), Chair
Lt. Gov. Mark Hutchison (NV), Vice Chair

Represents perspective of states with aerospace industries to the federal government as it defines national aerospace policy.
Founded in: 1991

2460 Transportation-Communications International Union
3 Research Place
Rockville, MD 20850

301-948-4910
websteward@tcunion.org; www.tcunion.org
Social Media: Facebook, Twitter

Robert A Scardelletti, President
Russell C Oathout, National General Counsel

Members come from diverse transportation industries. In addition to bargaining and representation of its members, provides mortgage and bankcard programs and other services to its members.
Founded in: 1899

2461 Tripoli Rocketry Association
PO Box 87
Bellevue, NE 68005

402-884-9530; *Fax:* 402-884-9531
info@tripoli.org; www.tripoli.org
Social Media: Facebook, Twitter, LinkedIn, YouTube, Google+

Stu Barrett, President
Bob Brown, VP
Bruce Lee, Treasurer
David Wilkins, Secretary

This is a non-profit organization dedicated to the advancement and operation of non-professional high power rocketry.
Founded in: 1964

2462 United States Parachute Association
5401 Southpoint Centre Boulevard
Fredricksburg, VA 22407

540-604-9740; *Fax:* 540-604-9741
uspa@uspa.org; www.uspa.org
Social Media: Facebook, Twitter, LinkedIn, YouTube, Google+

Sherry Butcher, President
Randy Allison, Vice President
Ray Lallo, Secretary
Albert Berchtold, Treasurer

The USPA is a voluntary membership organization of individuals who enjoy and support the sport of skydiving. The purpose of USPA is three-fold: to promote safe skydiving through training, licensing, and instructor qualification programs; to ensure skydiving's rightful place on airports and in the airspace system; and to promote competition and record-setting programs.
33000 Members

2463 United States Pilots Association
1652 Indian Point Road
Branson, MO 65616

417-338-2225
jan@uspilots.org; www.uspilots.org

Arnold Zimmerman, Owner
Jan Hoynacki, Executive Director

Works to promote aviation safety and pilot education and also acts as a forum for exchange of ideas.
5000 Members

2464 United States Ultralight Association
16192 Coastal Highway
Lewes, DE 19958

717-339-0200; *Fax:* 717-339-0063
usua@usua.org; www.usua.org

Dale Hooper, Executive VP
Reginald E DeLoach, President

Annual meeting and exhibits of ultralight and microlight aviation equipment, supplies and services. There will be 20 booths.
3000 Members
Founded in: 1985

2465 University Aviation Association
2415 Moore's Mill Road
Suite 265-216
Auburn, AL 36830

901-563-0505
uaamail@uaa.aero; www.uaa.aero
Social Media: Facebook, Twitter, LinkedIn, Youtube

Dawn Vinson, Executive Director
David McAlister, Publications and Member Services
Mary Reece, Accounts Manager
Dr. C. Daniel Prather, President

The voice of collegiate aviation education to its members, the industry, government and the general public. Through the collective expertise of its members, this nonprofit organization plays a pivotal role in the advancement of degree-granting aviation programs that represent all segments of the aviation industry.
625+ Members
Founded in: 1947

2466 Vintage Aircraft Association
P.O. Box 3086
Oshkosh, WI 54903-3086

920-426-6110; *Fax:* 920-426-6579
membership@eaa.org; www.vintageaircraft.org
Social Media: Facebook, Twitter, LinkedIn, Instagram, Google+, Tumblr, Vi

Geoff L Robison, President
Dave Clark, Vice President
Steve Nesse, Secretary
Jerry Brown, Treasurer
Ron Alexander, Director

Brings together people from around the world who share an interest in the aircraft of yesterday.
8000 Members
Founded in: 1971

2467 World Airline Historical Society
P.O. Box 489
Ocoee, FL 34761

904-221-1446; *Fax:* 407-522-9352
Information@WAHSOnline.com;
www.wahsonline.com
Social Media: Facebook, Twitter, LinkedIn, Youtube, RSS

Chris Slimmer, President
Don Levine, VP
William Demarest, Treasurer
Bill Demarest, Secretary/Editor

Open to all persons and groups interested in collecting airline memorabilia and the study of the airline industry, past and current.
500 Members
Founded in: 1977

Newsletters

2468 AIA Update
Aerospace Industries Association
15049 Conference Center Drive
Suite 600
Chantilly, VA 20151-3824

571-307-0000; *Fax:* 571-307-1001
membership@aia-aerospace.org; www.aero.org

Wanda Austin, President
Peter B. Teets, Chairman
Thomas S. Moorman, Vice chairman
Barbara M. Barrett, Ambasador
Frequency: 9x/Year

2469 ATCA Bulletin
Air Traffic Control Association

1101 King St
Suite 300
Alexandria, VA 22314-2963

703-299-2430; *Fax:* 703-299-2437
info@atca.org; www.atca.org
Social Media: Facebook, Twitter, LinkedIn

Peter F Dumont, President
Monte Belger, Chairman
William Cotton, Director South Central
Jeff Greffith, Secretary

Provides information on activities of the association, important developments in the air traffic control industry.
Frequency: Monthly
ISSN: 0400-1915
Founded in: 1956
Printed in on matte stock

2470 ATXA Newsletter
Air Taxi Association
400 Galleria Parkway
Suite 1500
Atlanta, GA 30339

678-390-0001; www.travelport.com

Offers information and association news for professionals in the aviation industry.
Frequency: Bimonthly, E-Newsletter

2471 Accident Prevention
Flight Safety Foundation
801 N Fairfax Street
Suite 400
Alexandria, VA 22314-1774

703-739-6700; *Fax:* 703-739-6708
apparao@flightsafety.org;
www.flightsafety.org

J.A. Donoghue, Director Publications
Mark Lacagnina, Senior Editor
Wayne Rosenkrans, Senior Editor
Linda Werfelman, Senior Editor
Rick Darby, Associate Editor

Focuses on the flight deck, including in-depth reviews of accident reports. Authors offer tips and descriptions on pilot incapacitation, outlines techniques to prevent runway overrun and addresses a wide variety of other subjects aimed at the experienced cockpit crew. Subscription included with FSF membership. Others will be $280.00/year.
4-16 Pages
Frequency: Monthly
Circulation: 3,000
Founded in: 1948
Printed in 2 colors

2472 Aerospace Daily
AviationNow
1200 G St Nw
Suite 900
Washington, DC 20005-3821

202-383-2378
800-525-5003; *Fax:* 202-383-2438
aviationdaily@aviationnow.com;
www.aviationweek.com

Lee Ewing, Editor-in-Chief
Brett Davis, Managing Editor
Mark Lipowicz, Publisher
George Hamilton, President

Daily intelligence on the defense and space industries. If you're a prime or subcontractor, an aviation, defense or space official, a consultant or analyst, or an engineering or research and development manager, you'll benefit from our news on policy and programs.
8 Pages
Frequency: Daily
Founded in: 1963

2473 Air Safety Week
Phillips Publishing
7811 Montrose Road
Potomac, MD 20854

703-522-8502; www.phillips.com

Dan Cook, Publisher

Weekly newsletter dealing with aviation safety, security, recreation, certification and accident investigation.
Cost: $695.00
10 Pages
Frequency: Monthly

2474 Airport Consultants Council News
Airport Consultants Council
908 King St
Suite 100
Alexandria, VA 22314-3067

703-683-5900; *Fax:* 703-683-2564
info@acconline.org; www.acconline.org

Paula Hochstetler, President
Anthony Mavrogiannis, Editor
Sharon Brown, Operations Manager
Cassandra Lamar, Marketing Manager

Council newsletter offering information on important and relevant issues for the aviation consulting community.
Frequency: Quarterly
Circulation: 300
Founded in: 1978

2475 Airport Operations
Flight Safety Foundation
801 N Fairfax Street
Suite 400
Alexandria, VA 22314-1774

703-396-6700; *Fax:* 703-739-6708
apparao@flightsafety.org;
www.flightsafety.org

J.A. Donoghue, Director Publications
Mark Lacagnina, Senior Editor
Wayne Rosenkrans, Senior Editor
Linda Werfelman, Senior Editor
Rick Darby, Associate Editor

Directs attention to ground operations that involve aircraft and other equipment, airport personnel and services, air traffic control and passengers. Subscription included with FSF membership. Others will be $280.00/year.
4-8 Pages
Frequency: Bi-Monthly
Founded in: 1974
Printed in 2 colors on glossy stock

2476 Annual Conference Proceedings
Air Traffic Control Association
1101 King St
Suite 300
Alexandria, VA 22314-2963

703-299-2430; *Fax:* 703-299-2437
info@atca.org; www.atca.org
Social Media: Facebook, Twitter, LinkedIn

Peter F Dumont, President
Monte Belger, Chairman
William Cotton, Director South Central
Jeff Greffith, Secretary

A compendium of fifty or more air traffic control technical papers, covering the entire range of ATC subjects, authored by ATC experts from the full spectrum of public and private organizations engaged in advancement of the science of air traffic control.

2477 Antique Airplane Association Newsletter
Antique Airplance Association
22001 Bluegrass Rd
Ottumwa, IA 52501-8569

641-938-2773; *Fax:* 641-938-2093
antiqueairfield@sirisonline.com;
www.antiqueairfield.com

Robert L Taylor, CEO
Lucinda Reis, Editor

Air museums, US and abroad historical aviation societies, for AAA chapters, flying aircraft company histories, etc. - For AAA Digest: antique and classic aircraft restorations, mystery aircraft, etc.
Founded in: 1953
Printed in 4 colors on glossy stock

2478 Aviation Accident Law & Practice
LexisNexis Matthew Bender & Company
PO Box 933
Dayton, OH 45401-0933

212-448-2000
800-253-5624; *Fax:* 518-487-3584

R Kaye Esq., Publisher
Domestic and international laws.

2479 Aviation Consumer
Belvoir Publishers
PO Box 2626
Greenwich, CT 06836-2626

203-422-7300; *Fax:* 203-661-4802

Robert Englander, Publisher
Richard Weeghman, Editor

Offers valuable information to the consumer regarding airports, airlines, safety and values.

2480 Aviation Daily
Aviation Week
1200 G Street NW
Suite 922
Washington, DC 20005

202-383-2374
800-525-5003; *Fax:* 888-385-1428
aviationdaily@aviationnow.com;
www.aviationweek.com

Anthony Velocci, Editor-in-Chief
James Asker, Executive Editor
Gregory Hamilton, President
Guy Norris, Senior Editor

Daily intelligence information on the commercial aviation and air transportation industry worldwide.
Cost: $1985.00
10 Pages
Frequency: Daily
Founded in: 1939
Printed in on n stock

2481 Aviation Education News Bulletin
Aviation Distributors & Manufacturers Association
100 North 20th Street
4th-Floor
Philadelphia, PA 19103-1443

215-320-3872; *Fax:* 215-564-2175
adma@fernley.com; www.adma.org

F. Charles Elkins, President
Michael Shaw, VP
Kristen Olszewski, Executive Director
Meg Taft, Meeting Manager

Association news pertaining to suppliers, distributors and manufacturers of aviation materials.
Frequency: Monthly
Founded in: 1943

2482 Aviation Law Reports
CCH

2700 Lake Cook Rd
Riverwoods, IL 60015-3867

847-940-4600
800-835-5224; *Fax:* 773-866-3095;
www.cch.com

Mike Sabbatis, President
Douglas M Winterrose, Vice President & CFO
Jim Bryant, EVP Software Products

News covering aviation law and regulations.
Cost: $2495.00
Frequency: Weekly
Founded in: 1913

2483 Aviation Maintenance
Professional Aviation Maintenance Association
972 E Tuttle Road
Building 204
Ionia, MI 48846

724-772-4092
800-356-1671; *Fax:* 616-527-1327
hq@pama.org; www.pama.org

Dale Forton, President
Roger Sickler, Chairman
Jeff Gruber, Vice Chairman
John Wicht, Secretary
Richard Wellman, Treasurer

The source for information on the worldwide aviation aftermarket. Covers the latest new business trends, regulatory developments, technical advancements, and new products and services

2484 Aviation Mechanics Bulletin
Flight Safety Foundation
801 N Fairfax Street
Suite 400
Alexandria, VA 22314-1774

703-739-6700; *Fax:* 703-739-6708
apparao@flightsafety.org;
www.flightsafety.org

William Voss, President/CEO
Roger Rozelle, Publisher
Jerry Lederer, Founder

Directed to the aviation maintenance technician, with an emphasis on airline and corporate operations. Other regular sections include maintenance safety alerts, mechanical-incident reports and reviews of new products of interest to maintenance technicians.
Cost: $24.00
16 Pages
Frequency: Bi-Monthly
Founded in: 1953

2485 Aviation Medical Bulletin
Aviation Insurance Agency
475 N Central Avenue
PO Box 20787
Atlanta, GA 30320

404-767-7501
800-241-6103; *Fax:* 404-761-8326
Pilot@harveywatt.com; www.harveywatt.com

Pat Hiebel, President
Sean Daigre, Claims Director

Health education for the professional airline pilot.
Cost: $13.95
Frequency: Monthly
Founded in: 1951

2486 Aviators Hot Line
Heartland Communications
PO Box 1052
Fort Dodge, IA 50501-1052
515-955-1600
800-247-2000; *Fax:* 515-955-1668;
www.hlipublishing.com

Gale W McKinney Ii, CEO
Joseph W Peed, Chairman
Mary Gonnerman, VP

Airline Trade Magazine.
Cost: $24.95
Frequency: Monthly
Founded in: 1968

2487 Buoyant Flight
Lighter Than Air Society
526 S Main Street
Suite 232
Akron, OH 44311

www.blimpinfo.com

Articles on the history, science and techniques of buoyant flight.
Founded in: 1954

2488 Cabin Crew Safety
Flight Safety Foundation
801 N Fairfax Street
Suite 400
Alexandria, VA 22314-1774

703-739-6700; *Fax:* 703-739-6708
ostrega@flightsafety.org; www.flightsafety.org

William Voss, President
Roger Rozelle, Publisher
Rick Derby, Editor
Patzy Sepezy, Circulation Manager

Focuses attention on the cabin crew, especially in airline operations, but the special requirements of corporate operations are also presented. Explanations on how to deal with hijackers, advocates of child restraints, emergency action plans and tips to reduce stress. Subscription included with FSF membership. Others will be $280.00/year.
Cost: $240.00
4 Pages
Printed in 2 colors

2489 Captain's LOG
World Airline Historical Society
P.O. Box 489
Ocoee, FL 34761

904-221-1446; *Fax:* 407-522-9352
president@wahsonline.com;
www.wahsonline.com

Duane Young, President
Craig Morris, Vice President
Jay Prall, Treasurer
Bill Demarest, Secretary/Editor
Frequency: Quarterly

2490 Command, Control, Communications and Intelligence
American Defense Preparedness Association
22 Commerce Road
Newtown, CT 22201-3062

203-426-0800
800-451-4975; *Fax:* 203-426-1964
info@forecast1.com; www.forecast1.com

Ray Peterson, Vice President
Andrew Briney, Editor

Programs and funding information.
Cost: $1640.00
Founded in: 1973

2491 Federal Air Surgeons Medical Bulletin
US Federal Aviation Administration
800 Independence Avenue SW
Washington, DC 20591

866-835-5322; www.faa.gov

Michael Huerta, Acting Administrator
David Grizzle, Chief Operating Officer
David Weingart, Chief of Staff
Victoria B. Wessmer, Assistant Administrator Of Finance

Published for aviation medical examiners and others interested in aviation safety and aviation medicine.
Frequency: Quarterly
Circulation: 8000
Founded in: 1967

2492 Flight Safety Foundation NEWS
Flight Safety Foundation
801 N Fairfax Street
Suite 400
Alexandria, VA 22314-1774

703-396-6700; *Fax:* 703-739-6708
apparao@flightsafety.org;
www.flightsafety.org

William Voss, President/CEO
Roger Rozelle, Publisher
Allen Smith, Marketing Manager

A primary tool for communicating the Foundation's activities through seminars, workshops, special projects, committee actions, awards to its members.
Cost: $480.00
Frequency: Monthly

2493 Flight Test News
Society of Flight Test Engineers
44814 N Elm Avenue
PO Box 4037
Lancaster, CA 93539-4037

661-949-2095; *Fax:* 661-949-2096
sfte@sfte.org; www.sfte.org

Peter Donath, President
Michael Barrlett, Vice President
Mark Mondt, Secretary
Steve Martin, Treasurer
Barbara A. Wood, Director

Offers specific information for flight test engineers.

2494 Flightlog
Association of Flight Attendants
501 3rd St NW
Washington, DC 20001

202-434-1300; *Fax:* 202-712-9792
info@afacwa.org; www.afanet.org
Social Media: Facebook, Twitter, YouTube

Elliott Kindred, Manager
Veda Shook, International President
Sara Nelson, International President

Offers updated information and news for flight attendants.
Frequency: Monthly

2495 Helicopter News
Phillips Business Information
1201 Seven Locks Road
Potomac, MD 20854

301-354-1400; *Fax:* 301-309-3847

Thomas Phillips, Publisher
Holly Yeager, Editor

Information on the rapidly changing helicopter industry.
Cost: $797.00
Frequency: 25 Issues

2496 Helicopter Safety
Flight Safety Foundation
801 N Fairfax Street
Suite 400
Alexandria, VA 22314-1774

703-396-6700; *Fax:* 703-739-6708
apparao@flightsafety.org;
www.flightsafety.org

J.A. Donaghue, Director Publications
Mark Lacagnina, Senior Editor
Wayne Rosenkrans, Senior Editor
Linda Werfelman, Senior Editor
Rick Darby, Associate Editor

Highlights the broad spectrum of real-world helicopter operations. Subscription included with FSF membership. Others will be $280.00/year.
4-8 Pages
Frequency: Bi-Monthly
Founded in: 1974
Printed in 2 colors

2497 Hotline
Aeronautical Repair Station Association
121 N Henry St
Alexandria, VA 22314-2903

703-739-9543; *Fax:* 703-739-9488
arsa@arsa.org; www.arsa.org
Social Media: Facebook, Twitter, LinkedIn, YouTube

Gary M. Fortner, President
Gary Jordan, VP
Jim Perdue, Treasurer
Devoted to regulatory compliance in aircraft design, production and maintenance.
Frequency: Monthly

2498 Human Factors & Aviation Medicine
Flight Safety Foundation
801 N Fairfax Street
Suite 400
Alexandria, VA 22314-1774

703-396-6700; *Fax:* 703-739-6708
apparao@flightsafety.org;
www.flightsafety.org

J.A. Donaghue, Director Publications
Mark Lacagnina, Senior Editor
Wayne Rosenkrans, Senior Editor
Linda Werfelman, Senior Editor
Rick Darby, Associate Editor

Presents information important to the training and performance of all aviation professionals. Subscription included with FSF membership. Others will be $280.00/year.
4-8 Pages
Frequency: Bi-Monthly
Founded in: 1953
Printed in 2 colors

2499 IE News: Aerospace and Defense
Institute of Industrial Engineers
3577 Parkway Lane
Suite 200
Norcross, GA 30092

770-449-0460
800-494-0460; *Fax:* 770-441-3295
boyeyemi@iienet.org; www.iienet.org

Jane Gaboury, Editorial Director
Don Greene, Vice President
Michael Hughes, Editor

Offers information and updates for industrial engineers.

2500 Inside the Air Force
Inside Washington Publishers
PO Box 7167
Washington, DC 20044-7167

703-685-5009
800-424-9068; *Fax:* 703-416-8543

Donna Haseley, Editor

An executive weekly report on Air Force programs, procurement and policymaking.
Cost: $980.00
Frequency: Weekly
Printed in one color on matte stock

2501 Jet Fuel Intelligence
Energy Intelligence Group
5 E 37th St
Suite 5
New York, NY 10016-2807

212-532-1112; *Fax:* 212-532-4479
info@energyintel.com; www.energyintel.com

Ivan Sandrea, President
Thomas Wallin, Executive Vice President and Editor
Raja W Sidawi, Chairman
Peter Kemp, Editor
Sarah Miller, Editor-at-Large

Offers the latest information on jets, fuel, cargo, safety and legislation.
Cost: $2595.00
Frequency: Weekly
Founded in: 1951

2502 Light Aircraft Manufacturers Association Newsletter
Light Aircraft Manufacturers Association
2001 Steamboat Ridge Ct
Dayton Beach, FL 32128-6918

651-592-7565; *Fax:* 65- 22- 182
info@lama.bz; www.lama.bz

Larry Burke, President
Dave Martin, Editor

Manufacturers, distributors and suppliers receive the latest information and news pertaining to light aircraft, including updated news from Washington, DC.
Frequency: Quarterly
Circulation: 66
Founded in: 1984
Printed in 2 colors on glossy stock

2503 Light Plane Maintenance
Belvoir Publishers
PO Box 5656
Norwalk, CT 06856-5656

203-422-7300
800-829-9085; *Fax:* 203-661-4802;
www.lightplane-maintenance.com

John Likakis, Publisher

Articles of interest for light aircraft owners.
Cost: $19.97
24 Pages

2504 Mx Newsletter
Professional Aviation Maintenance Association
972 E Tuttle Road
Building 204
Ionia, MI 48846

724-772-4095
800-356-1671; *Fax:* 724-772-4064
hq@pama.org; www.pama.org
Social Media: Facebook, Twitter, LinkedIn

Roger Sickler, Chairman
Jeff Gruber, Vice Chairman
John Wicht, Secretary

Features news for and about members, relevant articles and hot legislative information.
Frequency: Six/Year
Printed in one color

2505 NAA Record
National Aeronautic Association
1 Reagan National Airport
Hangar 7
Washington, DC 20001-6015

703-416-4888; *Fax:* 703-416-4877
naa@naa.aero; www.naa.aero

Jonathan Gaffney, President
Nancy Sack, Administration Director
Arthur W Greenfield, Contest & Records Director
Frequency: Monthly
Circulation: 3000

2506 NBAA Management Guide
National Business Aviation Association
1200 G Street NW
Suite 1100
Washington, DC 20005

202-783-9000; *Fax:* 202-331-8364
info@nbaa.org; www.nbaa.org
Social Media: Facebook, Twitter, LinkedIn

Edward Bolen, President/CEO
Paul Anderson, Chair
Dan Hubbard, SVP, Communications
Founded in: 1947

2507 NBAA Update
National Business Aviation Association
1200 G Street NW
Suite 1100
Washington, DC 20005

202-783-9000; *Fax:* 202-331-8364
info@nbaa.org; www.nbaa.org
Social Media: Facebook, Twitter, LinkedIn

Edward Bolen, President
Steven Brown, SVP Operations/Administration
Dan Hubbard, SVP, Communications

Offers weekly updates on the latest in NBAA news as well as business aviation industry news.
Frequency: Weekly
Circulation: 26000
Founded in: 1947

2508 National Aeronautics
National Aeronautic Association
1737 King Street
Suite 220
Alexandria, VA 22314

703-527-0226
800-644-9777; *Fax:* 703-416-4877;
www.nasa.gov

Shannon Chambers, Editor
David L Ivey, Publisher
Nancy Sack, Office Manager

Information on industry events for the aviation community, also opinion articles, records and awards, technology developments, education, and future events.
8 Pages
Circulation: 3500
Founded in: 1905
Printed in 2 colors on glossy stock

2509 National Transportation Safety Board Digest Service
Hawkins Publishing Company
103 River Rd
Edgewater, MD 21037-3824

410-798-1098; *Fax:* 410-798-1098;
www.ntsb.gov

Mark V Rosenker, Chairman

Loose-leafed indexed-digested-analysis of the decisions of the National Transportation Safety Board and its predecessor (the CAB), dealing with Aviation Safety Enforcement matters.
Cost: $390.00
Frequency: Monthly

2510 News & Views
Association of Air Medical Services
909 N Washington Street
Suite 410
Alexandria, VA 22314

703-836-8732; *Fax:* 703-836-8920
information@aams.org; www.aams.org

John Fiegel, Executive Director
David J Dries, Editor
Gloria Dow, Editor

This faxed/e-mailed newsletter contains information on association activity updates, community and member news, crew fitness and survival,

member survey data, member profiles, editorials, and classifieds.
Frequency: Monthly

2511 Ninety-Nines News
Ninety-Nines
4300 Amelia Earhart Dr
Suite A
Oklahoma City, OK 73159-1106
405-685-7969
800-994-1929; *Fax:* 405-685-7985
99s@ninety-nines.org; www.ninety-nines.org
Laura Ohrenberg, Manager
Susan Larson, President
Pat Prentiss, VP
Donna Moore, Secretary
Liz Lundin, Headquarters Manager
News and events for licensed women pilots.
Founded in: 1929

2512 Operations Update
Helicopter Association International
1635 Prince St
Alexandria, VA 22314-2898
703-683-4646; *Fax:* 703-683-4745;
www.rotor.com
Matthew Zuccaro, President
Provides useful information to helicopter owners and operators regarding issues, events and new technologies that may effect or enhance the operator's ability to conduct business with helicopters.
Frequency: Monthly

2513 Parachutist
United States Parachute Association
5401 Southpoint Centre Boulevard
Fredricksburg, VA 22407
540-604-9740; *Fax:* 540-604-9740
uspa@uspa.org; www.uspa.org
Social Media: Facebook, Twitter, LinkedIn, YouTube, RSS
Elijah Florio, Editor in Chief
Laura Sharp, Managing Editor
Guilherme Cunha, Advertising Manager, Web Developer
David Cherry, Graphic Designer
The official newsletter of the USPA.
33000 Members
Founded in: 1946

2514 Preliminary Accident Reports
Helicopter Association International
1635 Prince St
Alexandria, VA 22314-2898
703-683-4646; *Fax:* 703-683-4745;
www.rotor.com
Matthew Zuccaro, President
PARs summarize civil helicopter accident reports as received from the National Transportation Safety Board and the Transportation Safety Board of Canada. One subscription included upon request in Regular and Associate member dues.
Frequency: Quarterly

2515 Rotor Breeze
Bell Helicopter Textron
600 E Hurst Boulevard
PO Box 482
Hurst, TX 76053
817-280-2011; *Fax:* 817-280-2321;
www.bellhelicopter.com
Mike Redenbaugh, Chairman/CEO
Brandon Battles, Editor
Newsletter on Bell Helicopter products and customer support.
Frequency: Quarterly
Founded in: 1935

2516 Space Calendar
Space Age Publishing Company
65-1230 Mamalahoa Hwy
Suite D-20
Kamuela, HI 96743-7301
808-885-3473; *Fax:* 808-885-3475
news@spaceagepub.com;
www.spaceagepub.com
Steve Durst, Owner
Publication for the space industry.
Cost: $59.00
Frequency: Weekly

2517 Space Fax Daily
Space Age Publishing Company
65-1230 Mamalahoa Hwy
Suite D-20
Kamuela, HI 96743-7301
808-885-3473; *Fax:* 808-885-3475
news@spaceagepub.com;
www.spaceagepub.com
Steve Durst, Owner
Charles Bohannan, Associate Editor
Michelle Gonella, Marketing Manager
Information covering the space industry.
Cost: $59.00
Frequency: Weekly
Founded in: 1988

2518 Space Letter
Callahan Publications
6220 Nelway Drive
PO Box 1173
Mclean, VA 22101
703-356-1925
Vincent F Callahan Jr, Editor
Information from Washington on the US multi-billion dollar National Space Program. Legislation, budgets, marketing trends and contracting.
Cost: $190.00
8 Pages
Frequency: 24/Yr
Printed in one color

2519 Space Station News
Phillips Publishing
7811 Montrose Road
Potomac, MD 20854-3363
301-208-6787; *Fax:* 301-340-0877
Tom Phillips, President/CEO/Publisher
Information pertaining to the space station program.
Founded in: 1974

2520 Speednews
Speednews
17383 W. Sunset Boulevard
Suite A 220
Pacific Palisades, CA 90272
310-203-9603; *Fax:* 310-203-9352
admin@speednews.com; www.speednews.com
William Freeman III, Publisher
Stephen Costley, Editor
Joanna Speed, VP, Circulation
Stephen A. Costley, VP, Managing Editor
Pamela Leven, Subscription Sales
Market intelligence newsletter for the aviation industry.
Cost: $687.00
Frequency: Weekly
Circulation: 50000
ISSN: 0271-2598
Founded in: 1979

2521 The NAA Record
1 Reagan National Airport
Hangar 7
Washington, DC 20001-6015
703-416-4888
800-644-9777; *Fax:* 703-416-4877
naa@naa.aero; www.naa.aero
Jonathan Gaffney, President
Nancy Sack, Administration Director
Arthur W Greenfield, Contest & Records Director
A non-profit association that is dedicated to the advancement of the art, sport and science of aviation in the United States.
3000 Members
Frequency: Monthly
Circulation: 3000
Founded in: 1905

2522 World Airline News
Phillips Publishing
7811 Montrose Road
Potomac, MD 20854
301-354-1400; *Fax:* 301-340-0877;
www.phillips.com
Tom Phillips, President/CEO/Publisher
Provides airline executives with news and analysis on route developments, codesharing agreements, and traffic statistics as well as aviation entertainment.
Cost: $697.00
Frequency: Weekly/Newsletter
Circulation: 1,850
Founded in: 1974

2523 World Airport Week
Phillips Publishing
7811 Montrose Road
Potomac, MD 20854
301-354-1400; *Fax:* 301-340-0877;
www.phillips.com
Tom Phillips, CEO
Focuses on commercialization and privatization of airports around the world.
Cost: $597.00
Frequency: Weekly
Circulation: 1800

Magazines & Journals

2524 ABS Magazine
American Bonanza Society
PO Box 12888
Wichita, KS 67277
316-945-1700; *Fax:* 316-945-1710
ABSMail@bonanza.org; www.bonanza.org
Nancy Johnson, Executive Director
Peggy L Fuksa, Events Coordinator
Offers a treasury of practical information on such topics as maintenance, piloting techniques, aircraft restoration, aircraft insurance and ot her important subjects especially chosen for those with a specific interest in Bonanza, Baron, and Travel Air models of aircraft. This colorful magazine also features aircraft owned by an ABS members on its cover every month, as well as schedules of the numerous member activities which are conducted all around the nation.
Frequency: Monthly

2525 AIAA Technical Reports
American Institute of Aeronautics and Astronautics

1801 Alexander Bell Dr
Suite 500
Reston, VA 20191-4344

703-264-7500
800-639-2422; *Fax:* 703-264-7551
tammym@aiaa.org; www.aiaa.org

Cort Durocher, President
Kathy Watkins, Maketing Manager
Dr David S Dolling, VP Publications

Each year AIAA sponsors approximately 25 national meetings where professionals present technical papers on subjects such as guidance and control Computers in Aerospace, etc.
Cost: $3.00
Circulation: 1925
Founded in: 1963

2526 AOPA Flight Training Magazine
Aircraft Owners & Pilots Association
421 Aviation Way
Frederick, MD 21701-4756

301-695-2000
800-872-2672; *Fax:* 301-695-2375;
www.aopa.org

Craig Fuller, President

Provides up-to-date aviation news and safety tips for student pilots and CFIs.

2527 AOPA Pilot Magazine
Aircraft Owners & Pilots Association
421 Aviation Way
Frederick, MD 21701-4756

301-695-2000
800-872-2672; *Fax:* 301-695-2375;
www.aopa.org

Craig Fuller, President
Phil Boyer, President

Will keep you up to date on all the hottest issues in general aviation from the newest technologies in avionics to the latest safety and techniques to enhance your flying. Available only to AOPA members. Membership costs only $39.00/annually.
Frequency: Monthly
Circulation: 34,000

2528 AUSA News
Association of the United States Army
2425 Wilson Boulevard
Arlington, VA 22201-3326

703-841-4300
800-336-4570; *Fax:* 703-525-9039
ausa-info@ausa.org; www.ausa.org

Peter Murphy, Editor
Gordon R Sullivan, President

AUSA represents every American soldier by: being the voice for all components of America's army; fostering public support of the Army's role in national security; providing professional education and information programs.
Frequency: Monthly
Circulation: 10000
Founded in: 1950

2529 Aerospace Engineering
400 Commonwealth Drive
Warrendale, PA 15096-1

724-776-4841
877-606-7323; *Fax:* 724-776-0790
magazines@sae.org; www.sae.org

Richard Klien, President
Mircea Gradu, Executive VP

Serves the international aerospace design and manufacturing field which consists of producers of airliners, helicopters, spacecraft, missiles; their powerplants, propulsion systems, avionics, electronic/electrical systems, parts and components.
Cost: $75.00
Frequency: 10 issues
Circulation: 28440
Founded in: 1905

2530 Agricultural Aviation
National Agricultural Aviation Association
1005 E St SE
Washington, DC 20003-2847

202-546-5722; *Fax:* 202-546-5726
information@agaviation.org;
www.agaviation.org

Andrew Moore, Executive Director
Peggy Knizer, Assistant Executive Director

Official publication of the National Agricultural Aviation Association. Typical subject matter includes information on agricultural aviation business, agricultural aircraft, legislative issues, pesticides, new products and services, safety, maintenance, people profiles.
Cost: $30.00
Circulation: 5200
Founded in: 1921

2531 Air Classics
Challenge Publications
9509 Vassar Ave
Unit A
Chatsworth, CA 91311-0883

818-700-6868
800-562-9182; *Fax:* 818-700-6282
customerservice@challengeweb.com;
www.challengeweb.com

Edwin Schnepf, Owner

Magazine of military aviations.
Cost: $36.95
76 Pages
Frequency: Monthly
Founded in: 1963

2532 Air Force Magazine
Air Force Association
1501 Lee Hwy
Suite 400
Arlington, VA 22209-1198

703-247-5800
800-727-3337; *Fax:* 703-247-5853
letters@afa.org; www.afa.org

Michael Dunn, President
Robert S. Dudney, Editor in Chief
Stephen P. Condon, National President
Suzann Chapman, Editor
John A. Tirpak, Executive Editor

Analysis of all aspects of aerospace power, from military and scientific advances to political ramifications. Includes reports on new technology and studies missile management.
Cost: $36.00
Frequency: Monthly
Circulation: 202718
Founded in: 1946

2533 Air Line Pilot
Air Lines Pilot Association International
1625 Massachusetts Ave NW
Suite 800
Washington, DC 20036-2204

703-689-2270; *Fax:* 202-797-4052;
www.alpa.org

Captain Lee Moak, President
Mary Jo McPherson, Associate Editor
Captain Sean Cassidy, Vice President

Emphasizes advances in air safety, flight technology, industry developments and aviation history.
Cost: $32.00
56 Pages
Frequency: Monthly
Circulation: 86,656
Founded in: 1931

2534 Air Line Pilot Magazine
Airline Pilots Association International
1625 Massachusetts Ave NW
Suite 800
Washington, DC 20036-2204

703-689-2270; *Fax:* 202-797-4052;
www.alpa.org

Captain Lee Moak, President
Captain Sean Cassidy, Vice President
Frequency: Monthly

2535 Air Medical Journal
Elsevier, Health Sciences Division
3251 Riverport Lane
Maryland Heights, MO 63043

314-447-8000
800-401-9962; *Fax:* 314-447-8033
elspcs@elsevier.com; www.elsevier.com

Ron Mobed, CEO
David J Dries, Editor
Adriaan Roosen, Executive Vice President

Is the industry's combined trade and research journal. Each issue contains research articles, abstracts and book reviews designed to keep you up-to-date on the latest discoveries. Membership benefits includes a complimentary subscription.
Cost: $82.00
Founded in: 1986

2536 Air Progress
Challenge Publications
9509 Vassar Ave
Unit A
Chatsworth, CA 91311-0883

818-700-6868; *Fax:* 818-700-6282
customerservice@challengeweb.com;
www.challengeweb.com

Edwin Schnepf, Owner
Taccy Kruger, Editor

Covers all phases of aviation.
Cost: $36.95
84 Pages
Frequency: Monthly
Founded in: 1963

2537 Air Progress - Warbirds International
Challenge Publications
9509 Vassar Ave
Unit A
Chatsworth, CA 91311-0883

818-700-6868
800-562-9182; *Fax:* 818-700-6282
customerservice@challengeweb.com;
www.challengeweb.com

Edwin Schnepf, Owner
Michael O'Leary, Editor
Tim Baudler, Associate Publisher

The magazine of veteran and vintage military aircraft.
Cost: $22.00
80 Pages
Frequency: Quarterly
Circulation: 3836
Founded in: 1963

2538 Air Transport World
Penton Media
8380 Colesville Rd
Suite 700
Silver Spring, MD 20910

301-755-0200; *Fax:* 913-514-3909;
www.atwonline.com

JA Donoghue, Editorial Director
William A Freeman III, Publisher

Lists nationwide and international information on airports, airlines and the latest technology in the aviation industry.
Cost: $65.00
85 Pages
Frequency: Monthly

Circulation: 40000
Founded in: 1964
Printed in 4 colors on glossy stock

2539 Air and Space/Smithsonian
National Air and Space Museum
Smithsonian Institution
PO Box 37012 ,Victor Bldg 7100 MRC
Washington, DC 20013-7012

202-633-6070
800-513-3081; *Fax:* 202-275-1886;
www.airspacemag.com/

Joseph Bonsignore, Publisher
George C Larson, Editor

Smithsonian magazine offering information on the latest developments, technology, and historical news of the aviation industry.
Cost: $24.00
124 Pages
Founded in: 1986

2540 Aircraft Maintenance Technology
Cygnus Business Media
1233 Janesville Avenue
Fort Atkinson, WI 53538

800-547-7377; *Fax:* 920-563-1699
jjezo@amtonline.com; www.cygnusb2b.com

Jon Jezo, Publisher
Ronald Donner, Editor

Provides in depth coverage of the critical technical and professional issues facing today's technicians.
Cost: $90.00
98 Pages
Frequency: Monthly
Circulation: 39000
ISSN: 1072-3145
Founded in: 1989
Mailing list available for rent: 41M names
Printed in 4 colors on glossy stock

2541 Airline Pilot Careers
Aviation Information Resources
1029 Peachtree Parkway N
Suite 352
Peachtree City, GA 30269

404-592-6500
87- 33- 293; *Fax:* 770-487-6617
KitDarby@gmail.com; www.jet-jobs.com

Kit Darby, President/Publisher

Information to assist pilots in their career development as a airline pilot. Includes feature airline news, personnel announcements, aviation medical information, classifieds and calendar events.
Cost: $29.95
40 Pages
Frequency: Monthly
ISSN: 1095-4317
Founded in: 1989

2542 Airport Business
Cygnus Business Media
1233 Janesville Avenue
Fort Atkinson, WI 53538

800-547-7377
john.infanger@cygnuspub.com;
www.cygnusb2b.com

John Infanger, Editorial Director

Targets professionals who manage aitports, airport-based businesses, and corporate flight facilities in North America. Helps managers more effectively operate their operations by sharing case studies of what others are doing successfully, combined with expert analysis, industry news, and product information.
Cost: $60.00
44 Pages
Frequency: Monthly
Circulation: 14100
ISSN: 1072-1797
Founded in: 1986

2543 Airport Equipment & Technology
8380 Colesville Rd
Suite 700
Silver Spring, MD 20910-6257

301-755-0200; *Fax:* 913-514-3909;
www.atwonline.com

William A Freeman III, Publisher
Geoffrey Thomas, Editor-in-Chief

Related to airport and airport operations.
Cost: $65.00
Frequency: Quarterly
Circulation: 40000
Founded in: 1965

2544 Airport Journal
Airport Journal
551 Revere Avenue
PO Box 66001
Westmont, IL 60559

630-986-8132; *Fax:* 630-986-5010;
www.airportjournal.com

John Andrews, Editor

This journal offers news, information, statistics and reviews pertaining to airports across the globe.
Cost: $13.00
Frequency: Monthly

2545 Airports
Aviation Week
1200 G St NW
Suite 900
Washington, DC 20005-3821

202-383-2378
800-525-5003; *Fax:* 202-383-2438
aw_intelligence@aviationnow.com;
www.aviationweek.com

Christopher Fotos, Editor
Kimberley Johnson, Associate Editor
Mark Lipowicz, Publisher

Airports, the weekly for airport managers, users and suppliers, gives you exclusive insider intelligence to meet business challenges with your eyes open.
Cost: $98.00
Frequency: Weekly
Founded in: 1920

2546 Airpower
Sentry Books
Republic Press
PO Box 881526
San Diego, CA 92168

818-368-2012
support@airwingmedia.com;
www.wingsairpower.com

Joseph Mizrahi, Publisher
Mike Machat, Editor/Publisher

Military and commercial aviation history, contains photos, drawings and interviews.
Cost: $44.00
56 Pages
Frequency: Monthly
Circulation: 45000
ISSN: 1067-1048
Founded in: 1971

2547 Airways
Airways International
120 McGhee Road
PO Box 1109
Sandpoint, ID 83864

360-457-6485
800-440-5166; *Fax:* 208-263-5906
airways@airwaysmag.com;
www.airwaysmag.com

John Wegg, Editor-in-Chief
Seija Wegg, VP Marketing

Written for airline and air travel professionals, and the consumer. Focuses on the current air transport industry: the airliner, manufacturers, the people, technologies, the airports and the airways. Plus takes a nostalgic look at the past.
Cost: $39.95
80 Pages
Frequency: Monthly
Circulation: 43000
ISSN: 1074-4320
Founded in: 1994

2548 America's Flyways
United States Pilots Association
1652 Indian Point Road
Brandson, MO 65616

417-338-2225; *Fax:* 309-215-6323
jan@hoynacki.com; www.uspilots.org

Arnold Zimmerman, Owner
Jan Hoynacki, Executive VP
Frequency: Monthly

2549 Army Aviation
Army Aviation Publications
755 Main St
Suite 4D
Monroe, CT 06468-2830

203-268-2450; *Fax:* 203-268-5870
aaaa@quad-a.org; www.quad-a.org

William R Harris, Publisher
Maryann Stirling, Circulation Manager
Daniel Petrosky, President

Is a professional military publication reporting on news and developments pertinent to the field of U.S. Army Aviation and is the official publication of the Army Aviation Association of America. Each issue offers in-depth coverage of a specific development or program within U.S. Army Aviation along with dynamic, easy-to-read feature articles from key offices, agencies, and operational units worldwide.
Cost: $30.00
Frequency: Monthly
Founded in: 1957
Printed in 4 colors on glossy stock

2550 Aviation Business Journal
National Air Transportation Association
4226 King St
Alexandria, VA 22302-1507

703-845-9000
800-808-6282; *Fax:* 703-845-8176
rmulholland@NATA.aero; www.nata.aero
Social Media: Facebook, Twitter, LinkedIn

James K Coyne, President
Tim Heck, VP/CFO
Eric R Byer, Gov't & Industry Affairs

Authored by experienced aviation journalists and industry experts
Frequency: Quarterly

2551 Aviation Digest Associates
P.O. Box 2231
Danbury, CT 06810

203-264-3727

Robert Dorr, Publisher
Sharon Simmons, Associate Publisher

Newsmagazine/shopper distributed to owners of general aviation (private and corporate) aircraft.
Cost: $20.00
Frequency: Monthly
Circulation: 12,000

2552 Aviation Equipment Maintenance
Phillips Business Information

7811 Montrose Road
Potomac, MD 20854

301-354-1400; *Fax:* 301-309-3847;
www.phillips.com

Richard Koulbanis, Publisher
Clif Stroud, Editor
John J. Coyle, President

Produced monthly and is the leading publication for airline and general aviation maintenance managers. AEM provides information on maintenance techniques, management procedures, new products and ground support equipment.
Frequency: Monthly
Founded in: 1974

2553 **Aviation International News**
Convention News Company
81 Kenosia Avenue
Danbury, CT 06810

203-798-2400; *Fax:* 203-798-2104
jhartford@ainonline.com; www.ainonline.com

Anthony Ramodo, Publisher
Charles Alcock, Editor
Jeff Hartford, Circulation Manager
Wilson Leach, Executive Director

Update on business aviation, equipment and services, and business aviation news and events.
Cost: $74.98
116 Pages
Frequency: Monthly
Circulation: 39,000
ISSN: 0887-9877
Founded in: 1972
Printed in 4 colors on glossy stock

2554 **Aviation Safety**
Belvoir Publishers
800 Connecticut Avenue
PO Box 5656
Norwalk, CT 06856

203-857-3100; *Fax:* 203-857-3103
customer_service@belvoir.com;
www.belvoir.com

Ken Ibold, Editor-in-Chief
Robert Englander, CEO
Tom Canfield, VP

Journal on risk management and accident prevention, includes interviews with officials of the FFA.
Cost: $65.00
Frequency: Monthly
Founded in: 1972

2555 **Aviation Week & Space Technology**
Aviation Week
1200 G St NW
Suite 900
Washington, DC 20005-3821

202-383-2378
800-525-5003; *Fax:* 202-383-2438;
www.aviationweek.com

Anthony L Velocci Jr, Editor-in-Chief
James R Asker, Manager Editor
Jim Mathews, Publisher

Articles and features on the aviation/aerospace industry, including aircraft rockets, missiles, space vehicles, powerplants, avionics and related components and equipment.
Cost: $5.00
Frequency: Weekly
Circulation: 140000
Founded in: 1884

2556 **Aviation, Space and Environmental Medicine**
Aerospace Medical Association
320 S Henry St
Alexandria, VA 22314-3579

703-739-2240; *Fax:* 703-739-9652
inquiries@asma.org; www.asma.org

Gisselle Vargas, Manager

Provides contact with physicians, life scientists, bioengineers and medical specialists working in both basic medical research and in its clinical applications.
Frequency: Monthly

2557 **Avionics News**
Aircraft Electronics Association
3570 Ne Ralph Powell Rd
Lees Summit, MO 64064-2360

816-347-8400; *Fax:* 816-347-8405
info@aea.net; www.aea.net
Social Media: Facebook, Twitter, LinkedIn

Gregory Vall, President/Publisher
Gary Harp, Chairman
Jenneie Flattery, Treasurer

A magazine devoted exclusively to persons interested in aviation and avionics. Complimentary within North America.
Cost: $132.00
Frequency: Monthly
Circulation: 8500
Founded in: 1975

2558 **Avionics: The Journal of Global Airspace**
PBI Media
1201 Seven Locks Road
Potomac, MD 20854

301-354-1400
847-559-7314; *Fax:* 301-340-0542;
www.avionicsmagazine.com

Daniel E Comiskey, Publisher
Stuart Bonner, Circulation Manager
Don Pazour, CEO
David Jensen, Editor-In-Chief

Covers electronics carried aboard aircraft, ground navigational and systems for air traffic control.
Cost: $89.00
Frequency: Monthly
Founded in: 1999
Printed in 4 colors on glossy stock

2559 **Business & Commercial Aviation**
McGraw Hill
4 International Drive
Suite 260
Rye Brook, NY 10573

914-939-0300
800-257-9402; *Fax:* 914-939-1184
p02cs@mcgraw-hill.com;
www.aviationweek.com

William Garvey, Editor-in-Chief
Mark Lipowicz, Publisher
Richard Aarons, Safety Editor

Information for the management and executive levels of aircraft companies on improvements in operations and news of today's general aviation industry.
Cost: $60.00
Frequency: Monthly
Circulation: 52329

2560 **Captain's Log**
World Airline Historical Society
PO Box 489
Ocoee, FL 34761

904-221-1446; *Fax:* 407-522-9352
president@WAHSOnline.com;
www.wahsonline.com
Social Media: Facebook, Twitter

Duane Young, President
Craig Morris, VP

The premiere magazine for collectors of airline memorabilia.
Frequency: Quarterly
Circulation: 500

2561 **Cessna Owner Magazine**
Cessna Owner Organization
N7450 Aanstad Rd
Iola, WI 54945-5000

715-445-5000
888-692-3776; *Fax:* 715-445-4053
help@cessnaowner.org; www.cessnaowner.org

Dan Weller, Executive Director
Joe Jones, Publisher

The official publication of the Cessna Owner Organization, it includes pilot tips, owner/aircraft articles, alerts, maintenance tips, new product information, SDR summaries, AD's, insurance updates, and much more.
Cost: $9.95
Frequency: Monthly
Circulation: 5000

2562 **Controller**
Sandhills Publishing
PO Box 82545
Lincoln, NE 68501-5310

402-479-2181
800-331-1978; *Fax:* 402-479-2195
human-resources@sandhills.com;
www.sandhills.com

Tom Peed, Publisher

A magazine designed and edited to provide a means of communication between buyer and seller in today's general aviation marketplace.
Cost: $52.00
60 Pages
Frequency: Weekly
Circulation: 20,000 +
Founded in: 1978

2563 **EAA Sport Aviation**
Experimental Aircraft Association
3000 Poberezny Road
PO Box 3086
Oshkosh, WI 54902

920-426-4800
800-564-6322; *Fax:* 920-426-6761
webmaster@eaa.org; www.eaa.org

Tom Poberezny, President
David Berkley, Communications Director
Adam Smith, VP Member Services

For pilots, designers, and enthusiasts of sport and homebuilt aircraft.
Cost: $40.00
100 Pages
Frequency: Monthly
Circulation: 165000
ISSN: 0038-7835
Founded in: 1953
Printed in 4 colors on glossy stock

2564 **EAA Sport Pilot Magazine**
Experimental Aircraft Association
3000 Poberezny Road
PO Box 3086
Oshkosh, WI 54902

920-426-4800
800-564-6322; *Fax:* 920-426-6761
webmaster@eaa.org; www.eaa.org

Tom Poberezny, President
David Berkley, Communications Director
Adam Smith, VP Member Services

Dedicated to those to fly, buy, build/assemble, maintain, and have fun with light-sport aircraft, sport pilot eligible aircraft, and ultralights, as well as the full spectrum of member activities that give people the opportunity to participate in recreational aviation.

2565 **EAA Vintage Aircraft Association**
Experimental Aircraft Association
PO Box 3086
Oshkosh, WI 54903-3086
920-426-4825
800-564-6322; *Fax:* 920-426-6579
vintageaircraft@eaa.org;
www.vintageaircraft.org
Geoff Robison, President
Devoted to all aspects of antique, classic and contemporary aircraft. (All aircraft cinstructed by the original manufacturer, or its licensee on or before 12/31/1970).
Cost: $36.00
6000+ Members
32 Pages
Frequency: Monthly
Circulation: 10,000
Founded in: 1971

2566 **FAA Aviation News**
Government Printing Office
AFS-805 Room 832
800 Independence Avenue, S.W.
Washington, DC 20591
202-512-0000
866-835-5322
webmasteravnews@faa.gov; www.faa.gov/
Phyllis Duncan, Editor
Michael Huerta, Administrator
David Weingart, Chief of Staff
Daniel J. Mehan, Chief Information Officer
Contains regulations and approved operational techniques, also in depth accident and incident reports.
Cost: $21.00
Frequency: Bi-monthly
Circulation: 50,000
Founded in: 1966

2567 **Flight Physician**
Civil Aviation Medical Association
P.O. Box 2382
Peachtree City, GA 30269-2382
770-487-0100; *Fax:* 770-487-0080
david.millett@yahoo.com;
www.civilavmed.org
David Millett MD, Executive VP
James Heins MD, President
Gordon L Ritter, Secretary/Treasurer
Cost: $5.00
Frequency: Bi-Monthly

2568 **Flight Safety Digest**
Flight Safety Foundation
801 N Fairfax Street
Suite 400
Alexandria, VA 22314-1774
703-247-0700; *Fax:* 703-739-6708
Marshall@flightsafety.org;
www.flightsafety.org
William Voss, President/CEO
Roger Rozelle, Publisher
Mark Lacagnina, Senior Editor
Analyzes controversial industry issues; and authors have shared observations of important, but sometimes subtle influences that affect the airline industry. Authors have described the latest innovations in training, technology and management. Monthly sections present analyses of aviation statistics, brief accident reports and abstracts of information received at FSF Jerry Lederer Aviation Safety Library. Subscription included with FSF membership. Others will be $520.00.
Cost: $520.00
Frequency: Monthly
Circulation: 1000
Founded in: 1982
Printed in one color

2569 **Flight Training**
Aircraft Owners & Pilots Association
421 Aviation Way
Frederick, MD 21701-4756
301-695-2000
800-872-2672; *Fax:* 301-695-2375
flighttraining@aopa.org; www.aopa.org
Craig Fuller, President
Thomas B Haines, Editor-in-Chief
Offers information to new pilots and their instructors as well as flight school managers and owners.
Cost: $21.00
Frequency: Monthly
Circulation: 40000+
Founded in: 1939

2570 **Flightline Magazine**
Allied Pilots Association
14600 Trinity Blvd
Suite 500
Fort Worth, TX 76155-2559
817-302-2272; *Fax:* 817-302-2119
public-comment@alliedpilots.org;
www.alliedpilots.org
Dave Ahles, Executive Director
Captain Dave Bates, President
James Eaton, Secretary/Treasurer

2571 **Flyer**
Flyer Media
5611 76th Street W
PO Box 39099
Lakewood, WA 98439
253-471-9888
800-426-8538; *Fax:* 253-471-9911
comments@generalaviationnews.com;
www.generalaviationnews.com
Janice Wood, Editor
Ben Sclair, Publisher
Roy McGhee, Production Manager
Ron Boydston, Circulation Manager
For general and business aviation.
Cost: $35.00
72 Pages
Frequency: Monthly
Circulation: 50000
ISSN: 1052-9136
Founded in: 1949
Printed in 4 colors on newsprint stock

2572 **Flying**
460 N Orlando Avenue
Suite 20
Winter Park, FL 32789
407-628-4802; *Fax:* 407-628-7061
flying@neodata.com; www.flyingmag.com
J Mac McClellan, Editor-in-Chief
Wayne Lincourt, Associate Publisher
Rachel Goldstein, Sales Development Manager
Dedicated to general aviation and includes industry news, products, reports on every aircraft category, the latest new products, technology and photography.
Cost: $54.00
116 Pages
Frequency: Monthly
Circulation: 310321
Founded in: 1918
Printed in 4 colors

2573 **Flying Magazine**
National Association of Flight Instructors
EAA Aviation Center
730 Grand Street
Allegan, MI 49010
920-426-6801
866-806-6156; *Fax:* 920-426-6865
nafi@eaa.org; www.nafinet.org
Sean Elliot, President
Jason Blair, Executive Director
Provided to all NAFI members, this highly respected general aviation magazine is a great source of information. NAFI and Flying have entered into a partnership that directly benefits you - the NAFI member! Flying is the perfect compliment to the technical flight instruction how-to's contained in NAFI Mentor.

2574 **GPS World**
Advanstar Communications
201 Sandpointe Ave
Suite 500
Santa Ana, CA 92707-8700
714-513-8400; *Fax:* 714-513-8680
info@gpsworld.com; www.gpsworld.com
Mike Weldon, Plant Manager
Alan Cameron, Editor in Chief
Tracy Cozzen, Managing Editor
Covers current news and developments in the area of GPS (global positioning system) technology.
Cost: $54.00
Frequency: Monthly
Circulation: 35010
Founded in: 1987

2575 **Helicopter Association International Magazine**
1635 Prince St
Alexandria, VA 22314-2898
703-683-4646
800-435-4976; *Fax:* 703-683-4745
marty.lenehan@rotor.com; www.rotor.com
Matthew Zuccaro, President
Edward DiCampli, Executive Vice President
Dedicated exclusively to the civil helicopter industry. It covers pertinent helicopter operational safety and regulatory issues, including FAA question and answer column, legislative and lobbying issues, and HAI committee and member activities. Accepts advertising.
Cost: $15.00
48 Pages
Frequency: Quarterly
ISSN: 0897-831X
Founded in: 1988
Printed in 4 colors on matte stock

2576 **Hook Magazine**
Tailhook Association
9696 Businesspark Ave
San Diego, CA 92131
858-689-9223
800-322-4665
thookassn@aol.com; www.tailhook.org
Dennis Trelan, Editor
Jan Jacobs, Managing Editor
Dedicated to telling the story of US Navy carrier aviation, both past and person. Contains a selection of carrier and squadron histories balanced with departments containing the latest news of current units and aerospace industry developments affecting carrier aviation.
Frequency: Quarterly

2577 **IAM Journal**
International Association of Machinists and

9000 Machinists Pl
Upper Marlboro, MD 20772-2675

301-967-4500; *Fax:* 301-967-4588;
www.goiam.org
Social Media: Facebook, Twitter

R Thomas Buffenbarger, CEO

This advocacy magazine addresses the trends and forces that affect us all. It covers stories provide an indepth analysis of today's hot issues and are meant to spark discussion among IAM members. Its feature stories provide a glimpse of the men and women who belong to the IAM. IAM represents works primarily in the air transport, aerospace, metalworking, machinery, manufacturing and automotive industries.

2578 Journal of Aerospace Engineering
American Society of Civil Engineers
9000 Machinists Pl
Upper Marlboro, MD 20772-2675

301-967-4500
800-548-2723; *Fax:* 703-295-6222
marketing@asce.org; www.goiam.org

R Thomas Buffenbarger, President
Bill Henry, Publisher
Richard Michalski, General Vice President

Covers lunar soil mechanics, aerospace structures, and materials, extraterrestrial construction, robotics, remote sensing, applications, and real time data collection systems. Defines the role of civil engineering in space and emphasizes the practical applications of civil engineering in space and on earth.
Cost: $140.00
Frequency: Quarterly
Founded in: 1852

2579 Journal of Air Traffic Control
Air Traffic Control Association
1101 King St
Suite 300
Alexandria, VA 22314-2963

703-299-2430; *Fax:* 703-299-2437
info@atca.org; www.atca.org

Peter F Dumont, President
Brian Courter, Meetings and Program Coordinator
Michele Townes, Communications Director

Devoted to developments in air traffic control. It contains articles on current issues involving ATC operations, innovative concepts and applications of technology to ATC, public policy debates impacting ATC, commentary by noted aviation experts and policy makers, ATC historical material, and reviews of books and videos of interest to the aviation community.
Frequency: Quarterly
Founded in: 1956

2580 Journal of Astronautical Sciences
American Astronautical Society
6352 Rolling Mill Place
Suite 102
Springfield, VA 22152-2370

703-866-0020; *Fax:* 703-866-3526
aas@astronautical.org; www.astronautical.org
Social Media: Facebook, Twitter

Carol S. Lane, President
James Kirkpatrick, Executive Director
David B. Spencer, Vice President, Publications
Dr. Kathleen C. Howell, Editor-in-Chief

An archival publication devoted to the sciences and technology of astronautics.
Cost: $170.00
Frequency: Quarterly
ISSN: 0021-9142

2581 Journal of Guidance, Control & Dynamics
American Institute of Aeronautics and Astronautics
1801 Alexander Bell Dr
Suite 500
Reston, VA 20191-4344

703-264-7500
800-639-2422; *Fax:* 703-264-7551
custserv@aiaa.org; www.aiaa.org

Dr. Brian Dailey, President
George T Schmidt, Editor-in-Chief

Offers information on guidance control, navigation, electronics and more related to astronautical and aeronautical systems.
Cost: $675.00
Frequency: Fortnightly
Circulation: 3000
Founded in: 1930

2582 Journal of Propulsion & Power
American Institute of Aeronautics and Astronautics
1801 Alexander Bell Dr
Suite 500
Reston, VA 20191-4344

703-264-7500
800-639-2422; *Fax:* 703-264-7551
custserv@aiaa.org; www.aiaa.org

Dr. Brian Dailey, President
Vigor Yang MD, Editor

Offers information on new advances and technology in airbreathing, propulsion systems, fuels, power generation and more.
Cost: $730.00
Frequency: Fortnightly
Circulation: 1900
Founded in: 1930

2583 Journal of Rocket Motor and Propellant Developers
California Rocketry Publishing
PO Box 1242
Claremont, CA 91711-1242

626-974-9417; *Fax:* 626-974-9407
01rocket@gte.net; www.v-serv.com/dpt

Jerry Irvine, Publisher

Technical journal covering propellant formulations, motor design, performance results and methods. Back issues available.
Cost: $499.00
16 Pages
Frequency: Annual
Circulation: 500
Founded in: 1994
Printed in on matte stock

2584 Journal of the American Helicopter Society
American Helicopter Society International
217 N Washington St
Alexandria, VA 22314-2538

703-684-6777
855-247-4685; *Fax:* 703-739-9279
webmaster@vtol.org; www.vtol.org

Mike Hirschberg, Executive Director
Ashis Bagai, Associate Editor

The scope of the Journal covers the full range of research, analysis, design, manufacturing, test, operations, and support. A constantly growing list of specialty areas is included within that scope. Is distributed to the AHS membership for $20.00 and is also available for subscription.
Cost: $95.00
Frequency: Quarterly

2585 KITPLANES
Light Aircraft Manufacturers Association
2001 Steamboat Ridge Ct
Daytona Beach, FL 94588-8233

65- 59- 756; *Fax:* 925-426-0771
info@lama.bz; www.lama.bz

Dan Johnson, President

Experimental-category homebuilt aircraft.
Frequency: Monthly

2586 Maintenance Update
Helicopter Association International
1635 Prince St
Alexandria, VA 22314-2898

703-683-4646; *Fax:* 703-683-4745;
www.rotor.com

Matthew Zuccaro, President
Edward DiCampli, Executive Vice President

Provides a forum for mechanics and technicians to exchange information. It includes regulatory issues, airworthiness directives, aircraft alerts and items of special interest.
Cost: $50.00
Frequency: Quarterly

2587 Midwest Flyer Magazine
Flyer Publications
PO Box 199
Oregon, WI 53575-199

608-835-7063; *Fax:* 608-835-7063
info@midwestflyer.com;
www.midwestflyer.com

Dave Weinman, Publisher/Editor

Reaches all aircraft owners in the Upper Midwest. Articles include flying travel destinations, fly-in restaurants and the issues affecting general aviation in the Midwest and nationwide.
Cost: $15.00
32 Pages
Founded in: 1978

2588 NAFI Magazine
National Association of Flight Instructors
730 Grand Street
Allegan, MI 49010

920-426-6801
866-806-6156; *Fax:* 920-426-6865
nafi@nafinet.org; www.nafinet.org

Jason Blair, Executive Director

A monthly magazine published by the National Association of Flight Instructors.
Cost: $39.00
18 Pages
Frequency: Monthly
Circulation: 5400
Founded in: 1967

2589 NAFI Mentor
National Association of Flight Instructors
730 Grand Street
Allegan, MI 49010

920-426-6801
866-806-6156; *Fax:* 920-426-6865
nafi@nafinet.org; www.nafinet.org

Jason Blair, Executive Director
Rusty Sachs, Executive Director
Robert Meder, Board Chairman
Rick Rodd, President
John Niehaus, Program Director

Membership includes this magazine created exclusively for flight instructors.
20 Pages
Frequency: Monthly

2590 NASA Tech Briefs
Associated Business Publications International
261 5th Avenue
Suite 1901
New York, NY 10016

212-490-3999; *Fax:* 212-986-7864
linda@techbriefs.com; www.techbriefs.com

Dominic Mucchetti, CEO
Linda Bell, Editor
Marie Claussell, Circulation Manager
Domenic Mucchetti, CEO
Zoe Wai, Manager

Features exclusive reports of innovations developed by NASA and its partners that can be applied to develop new and improved products and solve engineering or manufacturing problems.
Cost: $49.00
Frequency: Monthly
Circulation: 30000
Founded in: 1985

2591 **Naval Aviation News**
Naval History and Heritage Command
805 Kidder Breese Street SE
Washington Navy Yard
Washington, DC 20374-5060

202-433-4882; *Fax:* 202-433-8200
navymuseum@navy.mil;
www.history.navy.mil
Social Media: Facebook, Twitter

Samuel Cox, Director
Jim Bruns, Director
Edward Furgol, Managing Director

Professional magazine of naval aviation.
ISSN: 0028-1417
Founded in: 1917

2592 **Ninety-Nines News**
Ninety-Nines
4300 Amelia Earhart Dr
Suite A
Oklahoma City, OK 73159-1106

405-685-7969
800-994-1929; *Fax:* 405-685-7985;
www.ninety-nines.org

Laura Ohrenberg, Manager
Susan Larson, President
Boby Row, Editor
Pat Theberge, Vice President

A bi-monthly magazine published by Ninety-Nines.
Cost: $20.00
Circulation: 6500
Founded in: 1929

2593 **Northwest Airlifter**
PO Box 98801
Tacoma, WA 98498

253-584-1212
800-293-1216; *Fax:* 253-581-5962

Tom Swarner, CEO

Features news, mission stories and entertainment for military personnel and families of McChord AFB.
Frequency: Weekly

2594 **Overhaul & Maintenance**
McGraw Hill
1221 Avenue of the Americas
New York, NY 10020-1095

212-512-2000
800-525-5003; *Fax:* 212-512-3840
p18cs@mcgraw-hill.com;
www.mcgraw-hill.com

Harold W McGraw III, CEO

Information for people in airlines, flight departments, maintenance operations, maintenance bases, military logistics, issues on safety, quality, and compliance in the aviation aftermarket.
Cost: $54.00
Frequency: Monthly
Circulation: 35000
ISSN: 0031-1588

2595 **PRA Rotorcraft E-Zine**
Popular Rotorcraft Association
PO Box 68
Mentone, IN 46539

574-353-7227; *Fax:* 574-353-7021
prahq@medt.com; www.pra.org

Igor Bensen, Founder
Douglas Barker, President
Tim O'Connor, VP
Cost: $42.00
Frequency: Monthly
Circulation: 1500

2596 **Parachutist Magazine**
United States Parachute Association
5401 Southpoint Centre Blvd
Fredericksburg, VA 22407-2612

540-604-9740; *Fax:* 540-604-9741
uspa@uspa.org; www.uspa.org
Social Media: Facebook, Twitter

Jay Stokes, President
Ed Scott, Executive Director

Supporting safe skydiving and those who enjoy it.
Cost: $4.50
112 Pages
Frequency: Monthly
Circulation: 35000
Founded in: 1946

2597 **Pipers**
Pipers Owner Society
N7450 Aanstad Rd
Iola, WI 54945

715-445-5000
866-697-4737; *Fax:* 715-445-4053
help@piperowner.org; www.piperowner.org

Keith Mathiowetz, Editor
Daniel Weiler, Executive Director
Joe Jones, Publisher

The official magazine of the Piper Owners Society.
Cost: $9.95
55 Pages
Frequency: Monthly
Circulation: 8400
Mailing list available for rent: 2750 names
Printed in 4 colors

2598 **Plane and Pilot**
Werner Publishing
12121 Wilshire Blvd
12th Floor
Los Angeles, CA 90025-1168

310-820-1500; *Fax:* 310-826-5008
editors@planeandpilotmag.com;
www.wernerpublishing.com

Steve Werner, Owner

Articles on general aviation from light single-engine planes to medium weight twins and related products.
Cost: $11.97
Frequency: Monthly
Founded in: 1965

2599 **Powered Sport Flying Mangazine**
Popular Rotorcraft Association
PO Box 68
Mentone, IN 46539

574-353-7227; *Fax:* 574-353-7021
prahq@medt.com; www.pra.org

Igor Bensen, Founder
B Scott Lewis, President
Tim O'Connor, VP

Devoted exclusively to homebuilt rotorcraft. Also has information, technical articles, photos of autogyros and helicopters, safety tips and news of new products for rotorcraft builders and pilots.
2000 Attendees
Frequency: August

2600 **Professional Pilot**
Queensmith Communications
30 S Quaker Ln
Suite 300
Alexandria, VA 22314-4596

703-370-0606; *Fax:* 703-370-7082
editorial@propilotmag.com;
www.propilotmag.com

Murray Smith, Owner
Anthony Herrera, General Manager
Phil Rose, Managing Editor
Ivor Tafro, Communications Manager

Offers information for career pilots.
Cost: $50.00
Frequency: Monthly
Circulation: 35000
ISSN: 0191-6238
Founded in: 1966
Printed in 4 colors on glossy stock

2601 **ROTOR Magazine**
Helicopter Association International
1635 Prince St
Alexandria, VA 22314-2898

703-683-4646; *Fax:* 703-683-4745;
www.rotor.com

Matthew Zuccaro, President

Dedicated to exclusively to the civil helicopter industry. It covers pertinent helicopter operations, safety and regulatory issues including an FAA question and answer column, legislative and lobbying issues, and HAI committee and member activities. Advertising space is available is this publication. Subscription included with membership.
Cost: $15.00
Frequency: Quarterly

2602 **Rotor & Wing**
Access Intelligence
4 Choke Cherry Rd
2nd Fl
Rockville, MD 20850-4024

301-354-2000; *Fax:* 301-340-0542;
www.aviationtoday.com
Social Media: Facebook, Twitter, LinkedIn

Don Pazour, CEO
Julian Clover, Managing Editor
Jim McKenna, Manager

Semitechnical information for helicopter industry, both civil and military. Includes pilot reports, features, news and product section.
Cost: $90.99
88 Pages
Frequency: Monthly
Circulation: 33,400
Founded in: 1977

2603 **Rotorcraft Magazine**
Popular Rotorcraft Association
PO Box 68
Mentone, IN 46539

574-353-7227; *Fax:* 574-353-7021
prahq@medt.com; www.pra.org

B Scott Lewis, President
Tim O'Connor, VP

Devoted exclusively to homebuilt rotorcraft. Free to members.
Cost: $26.00
60 Pages
Founded in: 1963

2604 **Russian Aeronautics**
Allerton Press
250 W 57th St
New York, NY 10107-2099

212-459-0535; *Fax:* 646-424-9695
journals@allertonpress.com;
www.allertonpress.com

W Shalof, Publisher
Vyacheslav A Firsov, Editor-in-Chief

The sole scientific-technical journal in Russia publishing articles on fundamental research, application, and developments in the field of aeronautical, space, rocket science and engineering that are carried out at institutes of higher education, research institutes, design bureaus, and branch enterprises.Published in English and Russian.
Cost: $1945.00
Frequency: Quarterly
ISSN: 1068-7998
Founded in: 1971

2605 Soaring Magazine
Soaring Society of America
5425 W Jack Gomez Boulevard
PO Box 2100
Hobbs, NM 88241-2100

505-392-1177; *Fax:* 505-392-8154
dlayton@ssa.org; www.ssa.org

Susan Dew, Staff Writer
Amaris Bradford, Editorial Assistant
Denise Layton, Managing Editor
Dennis Wright, Executive Director

Each issue brings you the latest developments on safety issues, delightful accounts of individual soaring accomplishments, a sharing of ideas and experiences, tips from the great soaring pilots of our times, and much more.
Cost: $26.00
60 Pages
Frequency: Monthly
Founded in: 1932

2606 Space News
Army Times Publishing Company
6883 Commercial Dr
Springfield, VA 22151-4202

703-750-7400
800-368-5718; *Fax:* 703-750-8622
cust-svc@gannettgov.com;
www.armytimes.com

Elaine Howard, CEO
Tobias Naegele, Editor-in-Chief
Alex Neill, Managing Editor
Judy McCoy, Publisher

For top level executives in government and industry worldwide. Devoted exclusively to issues for military government and commercial space.
Cost: $55.00
Frequency: Weekly
Circulation: 360000
Founded in: 1990

2607 Space Times
American Astronautical Society
6352 Rolling Mill Place
Suite 102
Springfield, VA 22152-2370

703-866-0020; *Fax:* 703-866-3526
aas@astronautical.org; www.astronautical.org

Carol S. Lane, President
James Kirkpatrick, Executive Director
Diane Thompson, Editor & Production Manager

The voice of the AAS, presenting thought provoking ideas and opinions, features articles on salient issues in space policy and future exploration, and reviews and notes of interest to both the professional and popular community of space flight advocates.
Cost: $85.00
Frequency: Bi-Monthly
Circulation: 1300
ISSN: 1933-2793

2608 The Airline Handbook
Air Transport Association of America
1301 Pennsylvania Ave NW
Suite 1100
Washington, DC 20004-1738

202-626-4000
800-497-3326; *Fax:* 202-626-4166
a4a@airlines.org; www.airlines.org
Social Media: Twitter, LinkedIn

Nicholas Calio, President
Steve Lott, VP Communications

2609 Trade-A-Plane
TAP Publishing Company
174 4th St
Crossville, TN 38555-4303

931-484-5137
800-337-5263; *Fax:* 931-484-2532
info@trade-a-plane.com;
www.trade-a-plane.com

Cosby A Stone, CEO
L Stone, Circulation Manager

World's largest advertising periodical for general aviation.
Cost: $14.95
Frequency: Monthly
Circulation: 118000
Founded in: 1937

2610 Ultralight Flying
Glider Rider
1085 Bailey Avenue
Chattanooga, TN 37404

423-629-5375; *Fax:* 423-629-5379;
www.ultralightflying.com

Tracy Knauss, Publisher
Sharon Hill, Editor

Conventional and motorized ultralight flying.
Cost: $36.95
48 Pages
Frequency: Monthly
Circulation: 50000+
Founded in: 1973
Printed in on newsprint stock

2611 Vertiflite
American Helicopter Society International
217 N Washington St
Alexandria, VA 22314-2538

703-684-6777
855-247-4685; *Fax:* 703-739-9279
staff@vtol.org; www.vtol.org

Michael Hirschberg, Executive Director
Kim Smith, Editor
Mike Hirschberg, Managing Editor

Magazine published for the vertical flight industry, pursuing excellence within the business, stimulating research, debate and expert opinion.
Cost: $80.00
72 Pages
Frequency: Monthly
Circulation: 12000
ISSN: 0042-4455
Founded in: 1943
Printed in 4 colors on glossy stock

2612 Water Flying
Seaplane Pilots Association
3859 Laird Blvd
Lakeland, FL 33811

863-701-7979
888-772-8923; *Fax:* 863-701-7588
spa@seaplanes.org; www.seaplanes.org

Steve McCaughey, Executive Director
Randy Juen, Vice President
J.J. Frey, President

Features articles covering everything from pilot technique and safety to destinations and personalities. Each issue includes industry news and an update on regulatory issues across the country. The March/April issue is our Directory Special, with flight school and float directories.
Cost: $45.00
32 Pages
Circulation: 7500
ISSN: 0733-1754
Founded in: 1972
Mailing list available for rent
Printed in on glossy stock

2613 Western Flyer
Northwest Flyer
PO Box 98786
Tacoma, WA 98498-0786

253-968-3422; *Fax:* 253-588-4005

Dave Sinclair, Publisher
Kirk Gormley, Editor

Covering general aviation, including all aspects of business and sport aviation.
Cost: $24.00
84 Pages
Frequency: BiWeekly
Circulation: 38,000

2614 Wings
Sentry Books
P.O. Box 881526
San Diego, CA 92168

818-368-2012
support@airwingmedia.com;
www.wingsairpower.com

Mike Machat, Publisher/Editor

Historic aviation, heavy on photos, artwork, drawings, interviews with aviation designers, pilots, engineers.
Cost: $44.00
56 Pages
Frequency: Monthly
Circulation: 30000
ISSN: 1067-0637
Founded in: 1971

2615 Wings West
Wiesner Publishing
6160 South Syracuse
Suite 300
Greenwood Village, CO 80111

303-662-5200; *Fax:* 303-397-7619;
www.wiesnerpublishing.com

Babette Andre, Editor
Becky Stairs, Advertising Executive
Dan Wiesner, CEO

Information for the mountain aviation community on various facets of western flying, including travel and safety for active pilots.
Cost: $17.97
72 Pages
Frequency: Bi-Monthly

2616 Wings of Gold Magazine
Association of Naval Aviation
2550 Huntington Avenue
Suite 201
Alexandria, VA 22303-1400

703-960-6806; *Fax:* 703-960-6807
anahqtr@aol.com; www.anahq.org

R M Rausa, Editor
Linda Bubien, Advertising Director
Walter Massenburg, President
Jacqueline M Hayes, Editorial Assistant

Articles and commentary designed to inform the public of the value of a strong maritime air posture to US national policy. Also, articles on subjects related to Navy, Marine Corps and Coast Guard aviation, such as personnel technology, history, readiness, aircraft and weapon systems and budgetary issues within DOD and before the Congress.
Cost: $25.00

2617 World Airshow News
Flyer Publications

PO Box 975
East Troy, WI 53120-0975

262-642-2450; *Fax:* 262-642-4374
jeffparnau@gmail.com; www.airshowmag.com
Social Media: Facebook, Twitter, LinkedIn

Jim Froneberger, Editor
Sandra Ruka, Advertising Sales
Jim Froneberger, Editor
Cost: $24.95
Frequency: Nine Times a Year
Circulation: 6000

Trade Shows

2618 **AAC Annual Conference & Exposition**
Airport Consultants Council
908 King Street
Suite 100
Alexandria, VA 22314-3121

703-683-5900; *Fax:* 703-583-2564
info@acconline.org; www.acconline.org
Social Media: Facebook, Twitter, LinkedIn

Paula P Hochstetler, President
Emily VanderBush, Marketing & Membership Coordinator
John B Reynolds, Coordinator of Communications
Sharon Brown, Director, Programs & Finance

Enhanced networking programs; workshops; keynote speakers; exhibitors.
Frequency: July

2619 **AAC/AAAE Airport Planning, Design & Construction Symposium**
Airport Consultants Council
908 King Street
Suite 100
Alexandria, VA 22314-3121

703-683-5900; *Fax:* 703-683-2564
info@acconline.org; www.acconline.org
Social Media: Facebook, Twitter, LinkedIn

Paula P Hochstetler, President
Emily VanderBush, Marketing & Membership Coordinator
John B Reynolds, Coordinator of Communications
Sharon Brown, Director, Programs & Finance

Planning and development, land side/terminal facilities development, airside/airfield facility development, program and construction management, and information technology are the focus of the symposium.
600 Attendees
Frequency: Spring

2620 **ADMA International Fall Conference**
Aviation Distributors & Manufacturers Association
100 North 20th Street
Suite 400
Philadelphia, PA 19103-1442

215-320-3872; *Fax:* 215-564-2175
adma@fernley.com; www.adma.org

Michael Shaw, President
F Charles Elkins, Past President
Kristen Olszewski, Executive Director
Meg Taft, Meeting Manager

Educational and informational presentations, group activities, and planned networking functions, including Private Conference Sessions.
Frequency: May, November

2621 **AEA International Convention & Trade Show**
Aircraft Electronic Association
3570 NE Ralph Powell Road
Lee's Summit, MO 64064

816-347-8400; *Fax:* 816-347-8405
info@aea.net; www.aea.net
Social Media: Facebook, Twitter, LinkedIn, Youtube

Paula Derks, President
Debra McFarland, Executive Vice President
Aaron Ward, Information Services Director
Mike Adamson, VP, Member Training & Education

Workshops, training sessions, keynote speakers, and hundreds of exhibitors in the field of aviation electronics.
Frequency: April

2622 **AHS International Annual Forum & Tech Display**
American Helicopter Society
217 N Washington Street
Alexandria, VA 22314

703-684-6777; *Fax:* 703-739-9279
staff@vtol.org; www.vtol.org
Social Media: Facebook, Twitter, LinkedIn, RSS, YouTube

Michael Hirschberg, Executive Director
Kay Brackins, Deputy Director/Production Mgr
David Renzi, Director of Meetings & Marketing

Exhibits for technical professionals in aircraft design, engineering, government, operators and industry executives. Over 200 presentations on aerodynamics, acoustics, dynamics, operations, product support, propulsion, testing and evaluation, and other areas. Technology display is concurrent with the Forum and is presented by leading manufacturers, service providers, defense contractors, universities and r&d organizations.
Founded in: 1943

2623 **AIAA New Horizons Forum & Expo at the Aerospace Science Meeting**
American Institute of Aeronautics & Astronautics
1801 Alexander Bell Drive
Suite 500
Reston, VA 20191-4344

703-264-7500
800-639-2422; *Fax:* 703-264-7551
tammym@aiaa.org; www.aiaa.org
Social Media: Facebook, Twitter, LinkedIn, Youtube

Cort Durocher, President
Tammy Marko, Director
Lawrence Garrett, Editor

A forum for scientists and engineers from industry, government and academia to share and disseminate knowledge and research. New Horizons will feature speakers sharing about new technology, challenges, opportunities, and trends, as well as panel discussions. The Aerospace Expo will showcase exhibits from industry, government and small businesses with hardware and software demos, discussions, and opportunities for side meetings.
Frequency: Annual
Founded in: 1930

2624 **ASA Annual Conference**
Aviation Suppliers Association
2233 Wisconsin Ave. NW
Suite 503
Washington, DC 20007

202-347-6899; *Fax:* 202-347-6894;
www.aviationsuppliers.org/Annual-Conference
Social Media: Facebook, Twitter

Michele Dickstein, President
Tony Brigham, Coordinator, Programs & Services

Annual event for the aviation distribution industry featuring workshops, networking opportunities and a vendor showcase.
Frequency: Annual

2625 **Aerofast SAE Aerospace Automated Fastening Conference & Exposition**
Society of Automotive Engineers
400 Commonwealth Drive
Warrendale, PA 15096-0001

72- 77- 484
877-606-7323; *Fax:* 724-776-0790;
www.sae.org

Diane Applegate, Meetings/Exhibits
David Shutt, CEO

Annual show of 45 manufacturers or suppliers of fasteners, assembly systems, CNC's, tooling and fixtures, fully automated systems.
400 Attendees
Frequency: September
Founded in: 1990

2626 **Aerospace Atlantic**
Society of Automotive Engineers
400 Commonwealth Drive
Warrendale, PA 15096-0001

724-776-4841
877-606-7323; *Fax:* 724-776-0790;
www.sae.org

David Shutt, President

Annual show of 30 exhibitors of aircraft systems and components, engineering services, electronics, power systems and computer services.
700 Attendees
Frequency: 84,000 Members

2627 **Aerospace Medical Association Meeting**
Aerospace Medical Association
320 S Henry Street
Alexandria, VA 22314-3579

703-739-2240; *Fax:* 703-739-9652
inquiries@asma.org; www.asma.org

Jeffrey Sventek, Executive Director
Gisselle Vargas, Operations Manager

Provides a multi-faceted forum for all aerospace medical disciplines and concurrently provides continuing education credits for those attending the meeting. Lectures, seminars, panels, poster presentations, workshops, film reports, and technical and scientific exhibits present data on the latest results of clinical and research studies.
Frequency: Annual

2628 **Aerospace Testing Expo**
Society of Flight Test Engineers
44814 N Elm Avenue
Lancaster, CA 93534

661-949-2095; *Fax:* 661-949-2096
sfte@sfte.org; www.sfte.org
Social Media: Facebook, Twitter, LinkedIn, Youtube

Peter Donath, President
Michael Barrlett, Vice President
Frequency: April

2629 **Aerotech: Society of Automotive Engineers Aerospace Technology Congress**
Society of Automotive Engineers
400 Commonwealth Drive
Warrendale, PA 15096-0001

724-776-4841
877-606-7323; *Fax:* 724-776-0790
advertising@sae.org; www.sae.org

David Shutt, President

Annual show of 80 suppliers to aerospace engineers and designers.
2500 Attendees
Frequency: October

2630 Agricultural Aviation Convention
National Agricultural Aviation Association
1440 Duke Street
Alexandria, VA 22314

202-546-5722; *Fax:* 202-546-5726
information@agaviation.org;
www.agaviation.org

Andrew Moore, Executive Director
Jay Calleja, Manager,Programs, & Events

Information on agricultural aviation business, agricultural aircraft, legislative issues, pesticides, new products and services, safety, maintenance, people, state and regional association news. 135 booths.
1300 Attendees

2631 Air Cargo Forum and Exposition
The International Air Cargo Association
PO Box 661510
Miami, FL 33266-1510

786-265-7011; *Fax:* 786-265-7012;
www.tiaca.org

Tom Davis, Deputy Director, Exhibits
Michael Steen, Chairman
Oliver Evans, Vice Chairman

This is the premier show for the Air Cargo Industry.
3000 Attendees
Frequency: September

2632 Air Medical Transport Conference
Association of Air Medical Services
909 N Washington Street
Suite 410
Alexandria, VA 22314

703-836-8732; *Fax:* 703-836-8920
information@aams.org; www.aams.org

John Fiegel, Executive Director/CEO
Blair Marie Beggan, Communications/Marketing Director
Natasha Ross, Education/Meetings Manager
Elena Sierra, Membership Manager

Attendees are emergency medical and critical care professionals from both hospital and independent providers of air and ground medical transport services. CEO's, program directors, medical directors, physicians, nurses, respiratory therapists, paramedics, pilots, communication specialists and mechanics.
1800 Attendees
Frequency: Annual/Fall
Founded in: 1980
Mailing list available for rent: 1600 names

2633 Air Medical Transport Conference (AMTC)
Association of Air Medical Services
909 N Washington Street
Suite 410
Alexandria, VA 22314

703-836-8732; *Fax:* 703-836-8920
information@aams.org; www.aams.org

Rick Sherlock, President
Natasha Ross, Education & Meeetings Manager
Elena Sierra, Membership Manager
Blair Marie Beggan, Communication & Marketing Manager

Provides up-to-date information on the latest techniques and innovative approaches to air medical practice from community experts, and continuing education credits opportunities; keynote speakers and educational offerings, plus technology demos and networking opportunities; and the largest trade show of the industry with exhibits from hundreds of providers.
Frequency: March

2634 Air Show Trade Expo International
Dayton International Airport
3800 Wright Drive
Suite A
Vandalia, OH 45377

937-898-5901
877-359-3291; *Fax:* 937-898-5121
info@daytonairshow.com;
www.daytonairshow.com

Terry Greivous, Executive Director
Brenda Kerfoot, General Manager

One hundred and thirty three booths that encompass all aspects of the global aerospace industry. Commercial and military aircraft and equipment, plus major suppliers' products and services display.
12M Attendees
Frequency: July

2635 Air Traffic Control Association Convention
Air Traffic Control Association
1101 King St
Suite 300
Alexandria, VA 22314

703-299-2430; *Fax:* 703-299-2437
info@atca.org; www.atca.org

Peter Dumont, President
Kenneth Carlisle, Director of Meetings & Expositions

Containing over 325 booths and exhibits of air traffic control products and services.
4,500 Attendees
Frequency: 3 times per year

2636 Aircraft Electronics Association Annual Convention & Trade Show
Aircraft Electronics Association
3570 NE Ralph Powell Road
Lee's Summit, MO 64064

816-347-8400; *Fax:* 816-347-8405
info@aea.net; www.aea.net

Paula Derks, President
Debra McFarland, VP

Annual show of 131 exhibitors of industry related equipment and supplies.
1500 Attendees
Frequency: March/April Annual
Founded in: 1980

2637 Aircraft Owners & Pilots Association Expo
Aircraft Owners & Pilots Association
421 Aviation Way
Frederick, MD 21701

301-695-2000
800-872-2672; *Fax:* 301-695-2375
aopahq@aopa.org; www.aopa.org

Craig Fuller, President
Robert Moran, COO

From the latest technology, to tools and flight gear, you'll find today's best products. 500 Exhibit Booths.
Frequency: June

2638 Aircraft Owners Pilots Association Expo
Aircraft Owners & Pilots Association
421 Aviation Way
Frederick, MD 21701

301-695-2000
888-462-3976; *Fax:* 301-695-2375;
www.aopa.org

Craig Fuller, President
Robert Moran, COO

Annual exhibits of single-engine and multi-engine aircraft, avionics, financing information and related equipment, supplies and services. Expo offers 75 seminar hours covering the latest safety, medical, proficiency, ownership, and technology issues. Over 500 booths.
Frequency: November

2639 Airliners International
World Airline Historical Society
PO Box 489
Ocoee, FL 34761

904-221-1446; *Fax:* 407-522-9352
president@WAHSOnline.com;
www.wahsonline.com
Social Media: Facebook, Twitter

Duane Young, President
Craig Morris, VP
1000 Attendees
Frequency: Annual/August
Founded in: 1977

2640 Airlines Electronic Engineering Committee Conference
Airlines Electronic Engineering Committee
2551 Riva Road
Annapolis, MD 21401-7435

410-266-4000; *Fax:* 410-266-2047;
www.arinc.com

Daniel A Martinec, Chairman
Roger S Goldberg, Show Contact

Annual show and exhibit of air transport avionics equipment and systems.
Frequency: October

2641 Airport Systems Action Planning Meeting
ARINC
2551 Riva Road
Annapolis, MD 21401

410-664-4000
80 -63 -688; *Fax:* 410-266-2329
flightops@arinc.com; www.arinc.com
Social Media: Facebook, Twitter, LinkedIn

Lee Suarez, Staff VP
John M Belcher, Chairman/CEO
Stephen Waechter, VP Business Operations/CFO
Linda Hartwig, Sr Dir Corporate Communications

The meeting format will include organizational, technical, and project updates from the ARINC management team.
Frequency: September
Founded in: 1920

2642 Airports Council International - North America Annual Conference & Expo
Airports Council International
1775 K Street NW
Suite 500
Washington, DC 20006

202-293-8500; *Fax:* 202-331-1362;
www.aci.aero
Social Media: Facebook, Twitter, LinkedIn, Youtube

Gregory Principato, President
Deborah McElroy, VP
Nancy Zimini, SVP Administration and Operations

Representatives from more than 100 airports around the world attend this exhibition and conference; seminars, discussions and speakers about air travel and the industry, developing legal affairs, challenges and best practices; hundreds of exhibitors.
Frequency: September
Founded in: 1948

2643 Airports Council International: North America Convention
Airports Council International-North America

1775 K Street NW
Suite 500
Washington, DC 20006

202-293-8500; *Fax:* 202-331-1362;
www.aci.aero

Deborah McElroy, Vice President
Nancy Zimini, SVP Administration & Operations
Juliet Wright, Senior Director Public Relations
Gregory Principato, President

Annual show and exhibit of air transportation equipment, supplies and services.
Frequency: Annual

2644 **American Bonanza Society Convention**
Midcontinent Airport
PO Box 12888
Wichita, KS 67277

316-945-1700; *Fax:* 316-945-1710
ABSMail@bonanza.org; www.bonanza.org

Nancy Johnson, Executive Director
Peggy L Fuksa, Events Coordinator

Annual convention featuring educational seminars and 75-100 exhibits of equipment, supplies and services for the aviation industry, including aftermarket products, safety items and computer weather services.
1200 Attendees
Frequency: September
Founded in: 1967

2645 **Annual Repair Symposium**
Aeronautical Repair Station Association
121 N Henry Street
Alexandria, VA 22314-2903

703-739-9543; *Fax:* 703-739-9488
arsa@arsa.org; www.arsa.org
Social Media: Facebook, Twitter, LinkedIn, Youtube

Craig Fabian, VP
Daniel Fisher, VP

The Symposium will include a variety of sessions on topical subjects. Legislative Day will inform you about the issues that affect your business, and includes the opportunity for you to arrange Capitol Hill meetings with your representatives, senators and congressional staff.
Frequency: Annual/March

2646 **Annual Scientific Meeting**
Aerospace Medical Association
320 S Henry Street
Alexandria, VA 22314-3579

703-739-2240; *Fax:* 703-739-9652
rrayman@asma.org; www.asma.org

Jeffrey Sventek, Executive Director
Gisselle Vargas, Operations Manager
Russell Rayman MD, Executive Director

Provides a multi-faceted forum for all aerospace medical disciplines and concurrently provides continuing education credits for those attending the meeting.
3000 Attendees
Frequency: Annual/May
Founded in: 1929
Mailing list available for rent

2647 **Army Aviation Association of America Convention**
Army Aviation Association of America
755 Main Street
Suite 4D
Monroe, CT 06468-2830

203-268-2450; *Fax:* 203-268-5870
aaaa@quad-a.org; www.quad-a.org
Social Media: Facebook, Twitter, Youtube

Daniel J Petrosky, President
Howard Yellen, Senior Vice President
E.J. Sinclair, Secretary

A show of 275 or more exhibitors both military and industry displaying technology and material pertinent to the army aviation community.
6000 Attendees
Frequency: Annual/May
Founded in: 1978

2648 **Arnic Aviation Customer Meeting**
British Telecommunications
2551 Riva Road
Annapolis, MD 21401

410-266-4000
800-633-6882; *Fax:* 410-266-2329
flightops@arinc.com; www.arinc.com
Social Media: Facebook, Twitter, LinkedIn, Youtube

Lee Suarez, Staff VP
John M Belcher, Chairman/CEO
Stephen Waechter, VP Business Operations/CFO
Linda Hartwig, Sr Dir Corporate Communications

Up to date information on the current and future products and services of Arnic and its strategic partners in Asia.
Frequency: May
Founded in: 1920

2649 **Arnic Global Communications Workshop**
British Telecommunications
2551 Riva Road
Annapolis, MD 21401

410-266-4000
800-633-6882; *Fax:* 410-266-2329
flightops@arinc.com; www.arinc.com
Social Media: Facebook, Twitter, LinkedIn, Youtube

Lee Suarez, Staff VP
John M Belcher, Chairman/CEO
Stephen Waechter, VP Business Operations/CFO
Linda Hartwig, Sr Dir Corporate Communications

Concentrates on the communications needs of the airlines serving the Latin America/Caribbean region, and provides information on the benefits of implementing a data link program and associated applications.
Frequency: May
Founded in: 1920

2650 **Aviation Insurance Association Conference**
Aviation Insurance Association
400 Admiral Blvd
Kansas City, MO 64106

816-221-8488; *Fax:* 816-472-7765
mandie@aiaweb.org; www.aiaweb.org
Social Media: Facebook

Trevor Light, President
Paul Herbers, Vice President
Meredith Carr, Director, Marketing & Membership

Provides a forum for the biggest names and best minds in the aviation insurance industry. Offers top-notch speakers, continuing education classes, time with vendors and opportunities to network and develop relationships that last a lifetime.
Frequency: Annual
Founded in: 1976

2651 **Aviation Services and Suppliers Supershow**
National Air Transportation Association
4226 King Street
Alexandria, VA 22302

703-845-9000
800-808-6282; *Fax:* 703-845-8176;
www.nata.aero

James K Coyne, President
Eric Byer, VP
Diane Gleason, Manager Meetings/Conventions
Eric R Byer, Dir Government/Industry Affairs

Workshop, conference, seminar and 700 exhibits of aviation products & services for fixed base and air charter operators.
5000 Attendees
Frequency: May/Annual

2652 **Aviation Show South America**
American Aerospace & Defense Industries
212 Carnegie Center
Suite 203
Princeton, NJ 08540

609-987-9050; *Fax:* 609-987-0277;
www.aadi.net

Marianne Ferrandi, Show Contact

One hundred and seven exhibitors of areospace information.
90000 Attendees
Frequency: July

2653 **Aviation Technician Education Council Conference**
Aviation Technician Education Council
2090 Wexford Court
Harrisburg, PA 17112-1579

717-540-7121; *Fax:* 717-540-7121;
www.atec-amt.org

Vince Jones, President
Richard Dumaresq, Executive Director

Annual conference and exhibits of aviation maintenance equipment, supplies and services.
150 Attendees
Frequency: April

2654 **Business Information Technology Conference**
Airports Council International - North America
1775 K Street NW
Suite 500
Washington, DC 20036-2463

202-293-8500; *Fax:* 202-331-1362
meetings@aci-na.org; www.aci.aero

Gregory Principato, President
Diedre Clemmons, Director, Conferences
Cassandra Jackson, Manager, Conferences

Hear from industry experts and peers on the latest way to deal with IT challenges, maximize the value of your IT infrastructure and anticipate new technologies.
Frequency: Annual

2655 **Civil Air Patrol Annual Conference**
Civil Air Patrol
105 S Hansell Street
Building 714
Maxwell AFB, AL 36112-6332

334-834-2236
877-227-9142; *Fax:* 334-953-4262;
www.capmembers.com

Brig Gen Amy Courter, Interim National Commander
1.2M Attendees
Frequency: August
Founded in: 1930

2656 Civil Aviation Medical Association Conference
Civil Aviation Medical Association
PO Box 2382
Peachtree City, GA 30269-2382

77- 48- 010; *Fax:* 77- 48- 008
david.millett@yahoo.com;
www.civilavmed.org

James Heins MD, President
David Millet MD, Executive VP
Gordon Ritter, Secretary/Treasurer

Annual conference and exhibits of aviation medical equipment, supplies and services. Containing 15 booths.
250 Attendees
Frequency: October
Founded in: 1948

2657 Defense & Security Symposium
International Society for Optical Engineering
PO Box 10
Bellingham, WA 98227-0010

360-676-3290
888-504-8171; *Fax:* 360-647-1445
CustomerService@SPIE.org; www.spie.org

Dr John C Carrano, Contact Person
Dr Larry B Stotts, Contact Person
Dr. Katarina Svanberg, President
William Arnold, Vice President

A large, unclassified international symposium related to sensors and sensor networks.
5700 Attendees
Frequency: March

2658 Economic Specialty Conference
Airports Association Council International
1775 K Street NW
Suite 500
Washington, DC 20006

202-293-8500; *Fax:* 202-331-1362;
www.aci.aero

Gregory Principato, President
Nancy Zimini, VP
Christopher Oswald, SVP Technical Affairs
Ian A Redhead, VP Airport Services
Patricia Hahn, EVP Operations/General Counsel

Provided with information on the latest economic trends for airports and the airport industry. Attendees include executive directors and CFOs from airports throughout North America, plys representatives from insurance companies and airport concessionaires.
Frequency: May

2659 Experimental Aircraft Association AirVenture
Experimental Aircraft Association
3000 Poberezny Road
PO Box 3086
Oshkosh, WI 54902

920-426-4800
800-236-4800; *Fax:* 920-232-7772
webmaster@eaa.org; www.airventure.org

Tom Poberezny, President
David Berkley, Communications Dirctor
Adam Smith, VP Member Services

Recreational aviation event, with more than 765,000 people and 10,000 airplanes attending. Containing 900 booths and 730 exhibits.
765M Attendees
Founded in: 1953

2660 Fall Education Conference
University Aviation Association
2415 Moore's Mill Road
Suite 265-216
Auburn, AL 36830-6444

901-563-0505
uaamail@uaa.aero; www.uaa.aero
Social Media: Facebook, Twitter, LinkedIn

Dawn Vinson, Executive Director
David McAlister, Publications & Member Services
Mary Reece, Accounts Manager
Dr. C. Daniel Prather, President
Founded in: 1947

2661 GTO Annual Convention & Fly In
Pipers Owner Society & Cessna Owner Organization
PO Box 5000
Iola, WI 54945

715-445-5000
888-692-3776; *Fax:* 715-445-4053
help@piperowner.org;
www.gto.aircraftownersgroup.com

Dan Weiler, Executive Director
Joe Jones, Publisher

Annual fly in prior to the EAA AirVenture.
150 Attendees
Frequency: Annual

2662 Gate Way to Oshkosh
Cessna Owner Organization
N7450 Aanstad Rd
Iola, WI 54945

715-445-5000
888-692-3776; *Fax:* 715-445-4053
help@cessnaowner.org; www.cessnaowner.org

Dan Weiler, Executive Director
Joe Jones, Publisher
150 Members
Frequency: Annual

2663 Goddard Memorial Symposium
American Astronautical Society
6352 Rolling Mill Place
Suite 102
Springfield, VA 22152-2370

703-866-0020; *Fax:* 703-866-3526
aas@astronautical.org; www.astronautical.org
Social Media: Facebook, Twitter

Carol Lane, President
James Kirkpatrick, Executive Director

Leaders in aerospace come together to discuss the future of the space program.
350 Attendees
Frequency: Annual/ November

2664 Heli-Expo
Helicopter Association International
1635 Prince Street
Alexandria, VA 22314-2818

703-683-4646; *Fax:* 703-683-4745
heliexpo@rotor.com; www.rotor.com

Matthew Zuccaro, President
Edward DiCampli, Executive Vice President
Elaine Little, Administrative Services Manager

The world's largest tradeshow dedicated to the international helicopter community. Attend for new ideas, business solutions, products and services, and networking. Over 550 exhibiting companies offering engines, avionics, instruments, modifications, helicopters for every mission, finance, insurance, software, uniforms and safety gear, mechanic and pilot training, parts, and accessories.
16000 Attendees
Frequency: February

2665 IFSA Annual Conference & Exhibition
Inflight Food Service Association
304 W Liberty Street
Suite 201
Louisville, KY 40202-3011

502-583-3783; *Fax:* 502-589-3602;
www.ifsanet.com

Pam Chumley, Executive Administrator
Jim Fowler, Executive Director
Jacqueline Petty, Manager of Communications
Caitlin Ellery, Membership Manager

An opportunity to experience excellent educational speakers, panel discussions, culinary demos, and general sessions focused on important issues in the in-flight and onboard foodservice industry. An exhibition is held in conjunction with the conference to exhibit the latest innovations while providing network opportunities with key leaders and decision makers in in-flight and railway catering.
Frequency: Annual

2666 International Air Cargo Forum & Exposition
International Air Cargo Association
5600 NW 36th Street
Suite 620
Miami, FL 33266-1510

786-265-7011; *Fax:* 786-265-7012
secgen@tiaca.org; www.tiaca.org

Michael Steen, Chairman
George F Johnson, Treasurer
Daniel F Fernandez, Secretary General

Biennial trade show of the air cargo industry featuring services and products from aircraft manufacturers, airlines, airports, freight forwarders trade publications logistics consultants.
4,000 Attendees
Frequency: September
Founded in: 1960

2667 Joint Airports Environmental/Technical Committee Meeting
Airports Association Council International
1615 L Street
Suite 300
Washington, DC 20006

202-293-8500
888-424-7767; *Fax:* 202-331-1362
memberservices@aci-na.org; www.aci.aero
Social Media: Facebook, Twitter, LinkedIn

Gregory Principato, President
Nancy Zimini, VP
Christopher Oswald, SVP Technical Affairs
Frequency: May
Founded in: 1948

2668 NATA FBO Leadership Conference
National Air Transportation Association
4226 King Street
Alexandria, VA 22302

703-845-9000
800-808-6282; *Fax:* 703-845-8176
info@nata-online.org; www.nata.aero
Social Media: Facebook, Twitter, LinkedIn

James Sweeney, Chairperson
Thomas Hendricks, President

An opportunity for business leaders to meet with their customers and learn about the latest challenges and opportunities facing their industry. d seminars. The Conference will focus on the changing climate of the industry and the developing environment. Opportunities to learn service and marketing techniques, network and exchange best practices.
Frequency: Annual

2669 NBAA Annual Meeting & Convention
National Business Aviation Association

1200 G Street NW
Suite 1100
Washington, DC 20005

202-783-9000; *Fax:* 202-331-8364
info@nbaa.org; www.nbaa.org

Edward M. Bolen, President & CEO
Chris Strong, SVP, Conventions & Membership
Cheryl Padilla, VP, Conventions & Forums Admin
Linda Peters, VP, Exhibits

Learning sessions, networking opportunities, 1,000 exhibitors, demonstrations and displays.
32000 Attendees
Frequency: Annual/September

2670 **National Space Symposium**
Space Foundation
4425 Arrowswest Drive
Colorado Springs, CO 80907

719-768-8000
800-691-4000; *Fax:* 719-576-8801
web@spacefoundation.org;
www.spacefoundation.org
Social Media: Facebook, Twitter, LinkedIn

Martin Faga, Chairman
Elliot G Pulham, President/CEO

The National Space Symposium is the premier U.S. policy and program forum, providing an opportunity for information and interaction on all sectors of space - civil, commercial, and national security. The conference is attended by industry leaders, military and government officials and general space enthusiasts, and covered locally and nationally by broadcast, print and industry trade media.
Frequency: Annually/April

2671 **Ninety Nines International Conference**
International Organization of Women Pilots
4300 Amelia Earhart Road
Oklahoma City, OK 73159-1140

405-685-7969
800-994-1929; *Fax:* 405-685-7985
99s@ninety-nines.org; www.ninety-nines.org

Susan Larson, President
Pat Theberge, VP
Corbi Bulluck, Director
Laura Ohrenberg, Headquarters Manager
Frances Luckhart, Secretary
Frequency: August

2672 **PAMA Aviation Maintenance & Management Symposium**
Professional Aviation Maintenance Association
972 E Tuttle Road
Building 204
Ionia, MI 48846

724-772-4092
800-356-1671; *Fax:* 616-527-1327
hq@pama.org; www.pama.org
Social Media: Facebook, Twitter, LinkedIn

Roger Sickler, Chairman
Jeff Gruber, Vice Chairman
John Wicht, Secretary
Frequency: March
Founded in: 1972

2673 **PRA International Conference**
Popular Rotorcraft Association
PO Box 68
Mentone, IN 46539

574-353-7227; *Fax:* 574-353-7021
prahq@medt.com; www.pra.org

B Scott Lewis, President
Tim O'Connor, VP

Exhibits, flight demonstrations, contests, commercial exhibits, great food, forums on rotorcraft topics, and unlimited fun! There are also many other events sanctioned by PRA and its local chapters.
2000 Attendees
Frequency: August

2674 **PRA International Convention Fly-In**
Popular Rotorcraft Association
PO Box 68
Mentone, IN 46539

574-353-7227; *Fax:* 574-353-7021;
www.pra.org

Igor Bensen, Founder
Scott Lewis, President
Tim O'Connor, VP

The largest gathering of homebuilt rotorcraft in the world. It has exhibits, flight demonstrations, contests, commercial exhibits, great food, forums on rotorcraft topics, and unlimited fun.
3500 Attendees
Frequency: Annual/Summer

2675 **Professional Aviation Maintenance Symposium and Trade Show**
Professional Aviation Maintenance Association
972 E Tuttle Road
Building 204
Ionia, MI 48846

202-300-0258
800-356-1671; *Fax:* 616-527-1327
hq@pama.org; www.pama.org

Dale Forton, President

Annual show of 200 exhibitors of aviation and aerospace products for the aviation maintenance industry.
2000 Attendees
Frequency: March

2676 **Regional Airline Association Convention**
Regional Airline Association
2025 M Street NW
Suite 800
Washington, DC 20036

202-367-1170; *Fax:* 202-367-2170
raa@raa.org; www.raa.org
Social Media: Facebook, Twitter

Roger Cohen, President
Scott Foose, Vice President

A forum for airport and airline professionals held twice a year in the spring and fall.
Frequency: May/October

2677 **Regional Airline Association Spring Meeting**
Regional Airline Association
2025 M Street NW
Suite 800
Washington, DC 20036

202-367-1170; *Fax:* 202-367-2170
raa@raa.org; www.raa.org
Social Media: Facebook, Twitter

Roger Cohen, President
Scott Foose, Vice President

Forum for airport and airline professionals.
1.6M Attendees
Frequency: May

2678 **Reliability Engineering and Management Institute Conference**
Univ of Arizona, Aerospace & Mechanical Engin Dept
1130 N Mountain Avenue
Building 119 Room N 517
Tucson, AZ 85721

520-621-6120; *Fax:* 520-621-8191
dimitri@u.arizona.edu;
www.u.arizona.edu/~dimitri/

Dr Dimitri B Kececioglu, Manager

Provides all engineers, and particularly Reliability Managers and Engineers, and Products Assurance Managers and Engineers in government and Industry, with a working knowledge of Reliability Engineering Theory and Practice; Mechanical Reliability Prediction; Reliability Testing and Demonstration; Failure Analysis (FAMECA); Complete Industry Product Assurance strategies; Maintainability Engineering; Reliability and Quality Management; Manufacturing Techniques, and more.
Frequency: Nov Arizona

2679 **Reliability Testing Institute**
University Of Arizona
1130 N Mountain Avenue
Tucson, AZ 85721

520-621-6120; *Fax:* 520-621-8191
dimitri@u.arizona.edu;
www.u.arizona.edu/~dimitri/

Dr Dimitri Kececioglu PE, Prof Aerospace/Mech Engineering

An institute to help provide a working knowledge in reliability engineering.
Frequency: May

2680 **SAE AeroTech Congress & Exhibition**
Society of Automotive Engineers
400 Commonwealth Drive
Warrendale, PA 15086-7511

724-776-4841
877-606-7323; *Fax:* 724-776-0790
jhudson@sae.org; www.sae.org
Social Media: Facebook, Twitter, LinkedIn, Youtube

David Shutt, President

Provides a forum for the aerospace community to meet and discuss current and future challenges, opportunities and requirements of next-generation R&D, products, and systems, and to develop professional relationships among the worldwide community. Technical sessions, panel discussions, keynote speakers, presentations and demonstrations.
3M Attendees
Frequency: Annual

2681 **SAE Government/Industry Event**
Society of Automotive Engineers
400 Commonwealth Drive
Warrendale, PA 15086-7511

724-776-4841
877-606-7323; *Fax:* 724-776-0790
mjena@sae.org; www.sae.org
Social Media: Facebook, Twitter, LinkedIn, Youtube

David Shutt, President

Awards and presentations, technical sessions, network receptions, and exhibits.
Frequency: Annual

2682 **SAE World Congress**
Society of Automotive Engineers
400 Commonwealth Drive
Warrendale, PA 15096-0001

724-776-4841
877-606-7323; *Fax:* 724-776-0790
agrech@sae.org; www.sae.org
Social Media: Facebook, Twitter, LinkedIn, Youtube

David Shutt, President

Reinvented in 2010, the World Conference provides a highly relevant and engaging technical program, expanded and improved opportunities for networking and information exchange, and innovative exhibits.
3.5M Attendees
Frequency: Annual

2683 **SAFE Symposium**
SAFE Association

PO Box 130
Creswell, OR 97426

541-895-3012; *Fax:* 541-895-3014
safe@peak.org; www.safeassociation.com
Social Media: Facebook

Robert Billings, President
Marcia Baldwin, President-Elect

The Symposium provides an internationally attended marketplace for the exchange of technical information, product and service exhibitions, and the showcasing of industry capabilities for meeting challenges in vehicular occupant protection and personnel worn safety equipment.
Frequency: October

2684 SAMPE Fall Technical Conference
Society for the Advancement of Material & Process
1161 Park View Drive
Suite 200
Covina, CA 91724

626-331-0616
800-562-7360; *Fax:* 626-332-8929
sampeibo@sampe.org; www.sampe.org
Social Media: Facebook, LinkedIn

Priscilla Heredia, Conference & General Information
Karen Chapman, Exhibit Information

The Society for the Advancement of Material and Process Engineering's Fall event showcases the latest technology, applications and materials for the advanced manufacturing marketplace; educational sessions, and exhibits.
Frequency: Annual/Fall

2685 SAMPE Spring Conference & Exhibition
Society for the Advancement of Material & Process
1161 Park View Drive
Suite 200
Covina, CA 91724

626-331-0616
800-562-7360; *Fax:* 626-332-8929
sampeibo@sampe.org; www.sampe.org
Social Media: Facebook, LinkedIn

Priscilla Heredia, Conference & General Information
Karen Chapman, Exhibit Information

The Society for the Advancement of Material and Process Engineering's Spring event showcases the latest technology, applications and materials for the advanced manufacturing marketplace; educational sessions, and exhibits.
Frequency: Annual/Spring

2686 Sea-Air-Space
Navy League of the United States
11208 Waples Mill Road
Suite 112
Fairfax, VA 22030

703-631-6200
800-564-4220; *Fax:* 703-818-9177;
www.jspargo.com

Paul doCarmo, Assistant Director/Exhibit Sales
Connie Shaw, Exhibit Sales Account Manager

Annual event to help promote and develop a technologically advanced naval force.
6000 Attendees
Frequency: April

2687 Seaplane Pilots Association Conference
Seaplane Pilots Association
3859 Laird Blvd
Lakeland, FL 33811

863-701-7979
888-772-8923; *Fax:* 863-701-7588
spa@seaplanes.org; www.seaplanes.org

Steve McCaughey, Executive Director
Randy Juen, Vice President

Thirty booths and conference.
1.5M Attendees
Frequency: September

2688 Soaring Society of America Annual Convention
Soaring Society of America
5425 W Jack Gomez Boulevard
PO Box 2100
Hobbs, NM 88241-2100

505-392-1177; *Fax:* 505-392-8154
merchandise@ssa.org; www.ssa.org

Meetings, exhibits, and displays.
Frequency: Annual

2689 Society of Automotive Engineers: Aerotech Expo
Society of Automotive Engineers
400 Commonwealth Drive
Warrendale, PA 15096-0001

772- 77- 484
877-606-7323; *Fax:* 248-273-2494
advertising@sae.org; www.sae.org
David Shutt, President

Exhibits of commercial, military, business and general aviation.

2690 Society of Experimental Test Pilots
Society of Experimental Test Pilots
44814 Elm Avenue
Lancaster, CA 93534

661-942-9574; *Fax:* 661-940-0398
setp@setp.org; www.setp.org

Steve Rainey, President
Paula Smith, Executive Director

These conferences provide major forums for the discussion of aspects of tax, accounting, administration, statute and case law, which are of general concern to practitioners, as well as providing advance knowledge of developments affecting trusts, estates and subjects of allied subjects. Twenty Booths.
1.5M Attendees
Frequency: September

2691 Strategic Space and Defense
Space Foundation
4425 Arrowswest Drive
Colorado Springs, CO 80907

719-576-8000; *Fax:* 719-576-8801;
www.spacefoundation.org

Elliot G Pullman, President/CEO
Chuck Zimkas, Chief Operating Officer
Holly Roberts, CFO

The definitive global security conference where the senior leadership of U.S. Strategic Command, component and supported commands, and the executive leadership of the national security industrial base gather to gain insight on the Command's mission, global activities and relationships.
Frequency: October

2692 United States Pilots Association Meeting
United States Pilots Association
1652 Indian Point Road
Branson, MO 65616

417-338-2225
jan@hoynacki.com; www.uspilots.org

Paul Hough, Chairman
Jan Hoynacki, Executive Director

Holds two meetings a year — in the spring and fall.
Frequency: June/Septemter

2693 United States Ultralight Association
United States Ultralight Association
PO Box 3501
Gettysburg, PA 17325-1810

717-339-0200; *Fax:* 717-339-0063
usua@usua.com; www.usua.org

Steve McCaughey, Executive Director
Dale Hooper, Executive VP

Annual meeting and exhibits of ultralight and microlight aviation equipment, supplies and services. There will be 20 booths.
3000 Attendees
Frequency: February
Founded in: 1998

2694 Werner Von Braun Memorial Symposium
American Astronautical Society
6352 Rolling Mill Place
Suite 102
Springfield, VA 22152-2370
703-866-0020; *Fax:* 703-866-3526
aas@astronautical.org; www.astronautical.org
Social Media: Facebook, Twitter

Carol Lane, President
James Kirkpatrick, Executive Director

Features panel discussions and guess speakers from academia, government, business, and international aerospace experts.
Frequency: Annual/October

2695 World Airline Historical Society Convention
World Airline Historical Society
PO Box 489
Ocoee, FL 34761

904-221-1446; *Fax:* 407-522-9352
Information@WAHSOnline.com;
www.wahsonline.com

Duane Young, President
Craig Morris, Vice President

Convention and exhibits of airline memorabilia, including airplane models, airline schedules, postcards, posters, photos and publications from airlines.
500 Members
Frequency: Annual
Founded in: 1977

Directories & Databases

2696 AAMS Resource Guide
Association of Air Medical Services
909 N Washington Street
Suite 410
Alexandria, VA 22314

703-836-8732; *Fax:* 703-836-8920
information@aams.org; www.aams.org

John Fiegel, Executive Director
Blair Marie Beggan, Communications & Marketing
Gloria Dow, Editor

The directory contains information on the association and its products and services; pertinent details on members, including demographic and historical information; and special crew listings that help community members perform their jobs better through enhanced networking opportunities. It also provides decision makers with a buyer's guide of community vendors and suppliers and the services they supply.

2697 ABD: Aviation Buyer's Directory
Air Service Directory
116 Radio Circle
Suite #302
Mt Kisco, NY 10549
914-242-8700; *Fax:* 914-242-5422
abd@abdonline.com
abdonline.com/
Manufacturers and dealers of aviation equipment and aircraft are the focus of this directory.
Cost: $25.00
400 Pages
Frequency: Quarterly
Circulation: 17,000

2698 AOPA's Airport Directory
Aircraft Owners & Pilots Association
421 Aviation Way
Frederick, MD 21701-4756
301-695-2000
800-872-2672; *Fax:* 301-695-2375;
www.aopa.org
Craig Fuller, President
Includes information on over 7,400 airports, seaplane bases and heliports. Also covers more than 2,200 private use airports. In addition to basic airport information such as runways, lighting, approaches, frequencies, identifiers and lat/long, you'll also find listings of nearby hotels, transportation, restaurants, etc. Paperback.
Cost: $29.95
680 Pages
Frequency: Annual
Circulation: 300,000
Founded in: 1962
Printed in one color on glossy stock

2699 Address List for Regional Airports Divisions and Airport Districts
US Federal Aviation Administration
800 Independence Avenue SW
Washington, DC 20591-0001
202-366-4000
866-835-5322; *Fax:* 202-493-5032;
www.faa.gov
David Grizzle, COO
David Weingart, Chief of Staff
Offers district offices and airports.
20 Pages

2700 Aerospace Database
Cambridge Scientific Abstracts
Aerospace Access
59 John Street, 7th Floor
New York, NY 10038
212-349-1120; *Fax:* 212-349-1283
Tony Lenti, Managing Editor
Earl Spencer, Owner
Provides bibliographic coverage of basic and applied research in aeronautics, astronautics, and space sciences. The database also covers technology development and applications in complementary and supporting fields such as chemistry, geosciences, physics, communications, and electronics. In addition to periodic literature, the database also includes coverage of reports issued by NASA, other US government agencies, international institutions, universities, and private firms.

2701 Airline Handbook
Air Transport Association
1301 Pennsylvania Ave NW
Suite 1100
Washington, DC 20004
202-626-4000
800-497-3326; *Fax:* 301-206-9789
a4a@airlines.org; www.airlines.org
Nicholas Calio, President/CEO
Overview of the history, structure, economics and operations of the airline industry. Includes a glossary of commonly used airline terminology.
Cost: $10.00
Frequency: Hardcover
Founded in: 2001

2702 Airport Operators Council International
1775 K St NW
Suite 500
Washington, DC 20006-1529
202-293-8500; *Fax:* 202-331-1362
webmaster@aci-na.org; www.aci.aero
Gregory Principato, President
Deborah McElroy, Executive VP External Affairs
Nancy Zimini, Senior Vice President
Contains an annual time series of aviation and airport data for more than 580 airports from the Worldwide Airport Traffic Report.
Founded in: 1948

2703 Airports
CTB/McGraw Hill
20 Ryan Ranch Rd
Monterey, CA 93940-5770
831-393-0700; *Fax:* 831-393-6528
Ellen Haley, President
Offers information on airport management issues, including funding. Congressional and regulatory activities, legal matters, noise and capacity problems are offered as well.
Frequency: Full-text

2704 Aviation Businesses and the Service they Provide
National Air Transportation Association
4226 King St
Alexandria, VA 22302-1507
703-845-9000
800-808-6282; *Fax:* 703-845-8176
csipes@nata-online.org; www.nata.aero
Social Media: Facebook, Twitter, LinkedIn
Thomas Hendricks, President
Timothy Heck, Financial Officer, VP
Shannon Chambers, Director Mktg/Communications
A detailed fact book, complete with statistical data, on the aviation services industry.

2705 Aviation Telephone Directory
Aviation Telephone Directory
6619 Tumbleweed Ridge Lane
Suite 102
Henderson, NV 89015
800-437-2962; *Fax:* 702-943-8982;
www.aviationfinder.com
Is the leading source for General Aviation information with more than 14,000 Companies and 10,000 airports. Yellow pages, White pages, and Blue pages(by airport). Thousands of phone numbers.
Cost: $19.95
790 Pages
Frequency: BiAnnually
Circulation: 20000
ISSN: 1075-1378
Founded in: 1949
Printed in 4 colors on newsprint stock

2706 Collegiate Aviation Guide
University Aviation Association
2415 Moore's Mill Road
Suite 265-216
Auburn, AL 36830-6444
901-563-0505
uaamail@uaa.aero; www.uaa.aero
Dawn Vinson, Executive Director
David McAlister, Publications & Member Services
A comprehensive guide of regionally accredited colleges and universities with aviation offerings ranging from academic completion certificates and associate degrees to doctoral programs. Contains listings of institutions throughout the United States, with some located in Canada.
Founded in: 1947

2707 Commuter Flight Statistics and Online Origin & Destination Data
US Department of Transportation
Kendall Square
Cambridge, MA 02142-1093
617-494-5906
Robin A Caldwell, Director
Covers all areas of the commuter airline flight industry, including statistical information on flights by commuter airlines.
Frequency: Statistical

2708 Flying Annual and Buyers Guide
Hachette Filipacchi Magazines
1633 Broadway
42nd Floor
New York, NY 10019-6708
212-767-6000; *Fax:* 212-767-5600;
www.hfmnewsstand.com/index
Alain Lemarchand, CEO
Richard Collins, Editor at Large
This substantial guide lists manufacturers, dealers, suppliers and professionals in the aviation industry.
Cost: $18.00

2709 General Aviation Statistical DataBook
General Aviation Manufacturers Association
1400 K St NW
Suite 801
Washington, DC 20005-2402
202-393-1500; *Fax:* 202-842-4063
bforan@gama.aero; www.gama.aero
Pete Bunce, President, Chief Executive Officer
Statistics on US general aviation shipments, aircraft fleet, international trade, safety and the most current data on airport statistics and pilot population.
Cost: $10.00
Frequency: Annual

2710 Guide to Selecting Airport Consultants and Membership Directory
Airport Consultants Council
908 King Street
Suite 100
Alexandria, VA 22314-3067
703-683-5900; *Fax:* 703-683-2564
info@acconline.org; www.acconline.org
Paula Hochstetler, President
T.J. Shultz, Executive VP
A full nationwide listing of airport consultants and association news.
Frequency: Annual

2711 Helicopter Annual
Helicopter Association International

1635 Prince St
Alexandria, VA 22314-2898

703-683-4646; *Fax:* 703-683-4745;
www.rotor.com

Matthew Zuccaro, President

A comprehensive reference guide for th civil helicopter industry. Includes specifications, industry statistics, HAI membership directories by class and geographic matrix, listings of international civil aviation contacts, key FAA personnel, association committees, and more. First copy included free with membership.
Cost: $50.00
360 Pages
Frequency: Annual
Circulation: 25,000

2712 International Aerospace Abstracts
American Institute of Aeronautics and Astronautics
1801 Alexander Bell Dr
Suite 500
Reston, VA 20191-4344

703-264-7500
800-639-2422; *Fax:* 703-264-7551
tammym@aiaa.org; www.aiaa.org

Dr. Brian Dailey, President

This database contains more than 2 million references and abstracts of journal and monograph literature relating to aerospace science and technology.
Frequency: Monthly

2713 Light Aircraft Manufacturers Association Directory
2001 Steamboat Ridge Ct
Daytona Beach, FL 94588

651-592-7565; *Fax:* 925-426-0771
info@lama.bz; www.lama.bz

Don Johnson, President
Jan Fridrich, Secretary General

A list of over 400 member manufacturers of light and ultralight aircraft and suppliers of related products and services.

2714 Living with Your Plane
Flyer Media
5611 76th Street W
PO Box 39099
Lakewood, WA 98499-0099

253-471-9888
800-426-8538; *Fax:* 253-471-9911;
www.flyer-online.com/airparks

Dave Sclair, Editor
Janice Wood, Editorial Coordinator

Offers a large amount of information including 400 residential airports with phones, addresses and contact names.
Cost: $20.00
Frequency: Annual
Circulation: 1,000

2715 NBAA Directory of Member Companies, Aircraft & Personnel
National Business Aviation Association
1200 G Street NW; Suite 1100
Washington, DC 20005

202-783-9000; *Fax:* 202-331-8364
info@nbaa.org; www.nbaa.org

Edward Bolen, President & CEO
Paul Anderson, Chair

Furnished to members only and contains a comprehensive listing of NBAA Member companies with their aircraft and flight department personnel.

2716 Space Law
Oceana Publications
198 Madison Avenue
New York, NY 10016

800-334-4249; *Fax:* 212-726-6476
custserv.us@oup.com; www.oceanalaw.com

Paul Stephen Dempsey, Editor

Provides in-depth expert coverage by today's preeminent export of the most pressing issues currently being faced by international regulators in this dynamic and growing area of the law.
Cost: $625.00
40 Pages; *Frequency:* 5 Volume Set
Circulation: 2,000; *ISBN:* 0-379012-92-8
Printed in 4 colors

2717 United States Civil Aircraft Registry
Insured Aircraft Title Service
PO Box 19527
Oklahoma City, OK 73144-0527

405-681-6663
800-654-4882; *Fax:* 405-681-9299
iats@earthlink.net; www.insuredaircraft.com

Matthew Kelly, Owner

This directory covers owners of over 275,000 aircraft.
Cost: $600.00
190 Pages
Frequency: Monthly
Founded in: 1963

2718 Water Landing Directory
Seaplane Pilots Association
3859 Laird Blvd
Lakeland, FL 33811

863-701-7979
888-772-8923; *Fax:* 863-701-7588
spa@seaplanes.org; www.seaplanes.org

Steve McCaughey, Executive Director

Is the only publication that combines federal, state, provincial and special agency regulations affecting seaplane operators. The directory includes waterway closures and restrictions, seaplane bases listed by state and city, informative seaplane base diagrams, customs information, flight planning charts and other miscellaneous quick reference materials.

2719 World Aviation Directory and Aerospace Database
McGraw Hill
1200 G St NW; Suite 922
Washington, DC 20005-3821

202-343-2300; *Fax:* 202-383-2347;
www.mcgraw-hillhomelandsecurity.com

John McNicholas, Marketing Director

Aviation and the aerospace industry are covered in this global directory offering information on manufacturers, subcontractors, support services and associations.
2500 Pages

Industry Web Sites

2720 http://gold.greyhouse.com
G.O.L.D Grey House OnLine Databases

Grey House Publishing's online database platform, GOLD, offers Quick Search, Keyword Search and Expert Search for most business sectors including aviation and aerospace markets. The GOLD platform makes finding the information you need quick and easy - whether you're a novice searcher or an experienced database user. All of Grey House's directory products are available for subscription on the GOLD platform.

2721 www.aams.org
Association of Air Medical Services

Air medical transport equipment, supplies and services.

2722 www.aci-na.org
Airports Council International-North America

Represents local, regional and state governing bodies that own and operate commercial airports throughout the United States and Canada.

2723 www.aeronet.com
Aeronet Worldwide

Specializes in urgent shipping solutions. From computer and technical supplies, to medical equipment, to odd size, one of a kind machine parts, we have always been there for our clients, one shipment at a time.

2724 www.afa.org
Air Force Association

Independent nonprofit, civilian organization promoting public understanding of aerospace power and the pivotal role it plays in the security of the nation.

2725 www.afanet.org
Association of Flight Attendants

Represents over 50,000 flight attendants at 26 airlines, serving as a voice for flight attendants at their workplace, in the industry, the media and on Capitol Hill.

2726 www.agaviation.org
National Agricultural Aviation Association

Voice of the aerial application industry, we work to preserve aerial application's place in the protection and production of America's food and fiber supply. Aerial application is one of the safest, fastest, most efficient and economical ways to apply pesticides. It is also the most environmentally friendly tool of modern agriculture.

2727 www.aia-aerospace.org
Aerospace Industries Association

The Aerospace Industries Association shapes public policy that ensures the US aerospace, defense and homeland security industry remains preeminent and that its members are successful and profitable in a changing global market.

2728 www.aiaa.org
American Institute of Aeronautics and Astronautics

Advances the arts, sciences, and technology of aeronautics and astronautics and promotes the professionalism of those engaged in these pursuits.

2729 www.airlines.org
Air Transport Association

Supports and assits its members by promoting the air transport industry and the safety, cost effectiveness, and technical advancement of its operators; advocating common industry positions before state and local governments; conducting designated industry-wide programs; and assuring governmental and public understanding of all aspects of air transport.

2730 www.airship-association.org
Airship Association

Circulates information on all matters affecting airships.

2731 www.anahq.org
Association of Naval Aviation

Professional, nonprofit, educational and fraternaL society of Naval Aviation, whose main purpose is to educte the public and our national leaders on the vital roles of the Navy, Marine Corp and Coast Guard Aviation as key elements of our national defense posture. ANA continously seeks to elucidate the key current issues impacting Naval Aviation through published writing, symposia, speeches and discussions with various interest groups.

2732 **www.aopa.org**
Aircraft Owners & Pilots Association
Works to make flying safer, more economical and enjoyable for private aircraft owners.

2733 **www.arinc.com**
Aeronautical Radio
Aeronautical Radio provides transportation communications and systems engineering solution for five major industries: aviation, airports, defense, government, and transportation

2734 **www.arsa.org**
Aeronautical Repair Station Association
Helps develop guidance, policy and interpretations that are clear, concise and consistent, and applied uniformly to all similarly situated companies and individuals.

2735 **www.asma.org**
Aerospace Medical Association
Our mission is to apply and advance scientific knowledge to promote and enhance the health, safety and performance of those involved in aerospace and related activities.

2736 **www.astronautical.org**
American Astronautical Society
Independent scientific and technical group in the United States exclusively dedicated to the advancement of space science and exploration.

2737 **www.atec-amt.org**
Aviation Technician Education Council
Organization of Federal Aviation Administration approved Aviation Maintenance Technician schools and supporting industries.

2738 **www.blimpinfo.com**
Lighter Than Air Society
Nonprofit organization whose members are devoted to the study of the history, science and techniques of all forms of buoyant flight.

2739 **www.bonanza.org**
American Bonanza Society
ABS is a group of members who own, fly or have a sincere interest in Bonanza, Baron, and Travel air type aircraft. Because of this common interest we share information and experiences involving the operation and maintenance of the Beech produced aircraft.

2740 **www.cessnaowner.org**
Cessna Owner Organization
Membership support organization for Cessna aircraft owners.

2741 **www.civilavmed.com**
Civil Aviation Medical Association
Aviation medical equipment, supplies and services. Working on behalf of physicians engaged in the practice of aviation medicine, dedicated to civil aviation safety.

2742 **www.eaa.org**
Experimental Aircraft Association
Equipment, supplies and services for sport and recreational flying.

2743 **www.generalaviation.org**
General Aviation Manufacturers Association
Manufacturers of general aviation aircraft, and related equipment.

2744 **www.greyhouse.com**
Grey House Publishing
Authoritative reference directories for most business sectors including aviation and aerospace markets. Users can search the online databases with varied search criteria allowing for custom searches by product category, geographic area, sales volume, keyword, subject and more. Full Grey House catalog and online ordering also available.

2745 **www.iaopa.org**
Int'l Council of Aircraft Owner & Pilot Assns.
Nonprofit federation of 53 autonomous, nongovernmental, national general aviation organizations. Facilitates the movement of general aviation aircraft.

2746 **www.ifsanet.com**
International Inflight Food Service Association
For airline and railway personnel, caterers and suppliers responsible for providing passenger food service.

2747 **www.iswap.org**
International Society of Women Airline Pilots
Organization for all women pilots who are employed as flight crew members (Captain, First Officer, or Second Officer) and hold senority numbers with an airline carrier that operates at least one aircraft with a gross wieght of 90,000 pounds or more.

2748 **www.naa.usa.org**
National Aeronautic Association
For aerospace corporations, aero clubs, affiliates and major national sporting aviation organizations.

2749 **www.nafinet.org**
National Association of Flight Instructors
Dedicated to raising and maintaining the professional standing of the flight instructor in the aviation community. Maintains a benefits package available for everyone from the independent instructor to those teaching at flight schools.

2750 **www.nata.aero**
National Air Transportation Association
National association of aviation business service providers.

2751 **www.natca.org**
National Air Traffic Controllers Association
Founded to ensure the safety and longetivity of air traffic controller positions around the nation. Represents over 15,000 air traffic controllers throughout the US, Puerto Rico and Guam, along with 2,508 other bargaining unit members that span the areas of engineers and architects to nurses and health care professionals to members of the accounting community.

2752 **www.nbaa.org**
National Business Aviation Association
Not-for-profit, nonpartisan corporation dedicated to the success of the business aviation community.

2753 **www.ninety-nines.org**
Ninety-Nines
International organization of licensed women pilots from 35 countries. We are a nonprofit, charitable membership corporation holding 501(c)(3) US tax status. Members are professional pilots for airlines, industry, government; we are pilots who teach and pilots who fly for pleasure; we are pilots who are technicians and mechanics. First and foremost, we are women who love to fly.

2754 **www.ofainc.com.**
Organization of Flying Adjusters
Dedicated to the highest standard of professional ethics in handling aviation insurance claims, investigating causes of aircraft accidents objectively and promoting every aspect of air safety.

2755 **www.piperowner.org**
Pipers Owner Society
Independent group of Piper owners, pilots, and enthusiasts, the POS is committed to the goal of safe, fun, and affordable flying. Membership benefits include: pre-buy referral service; free STC summaries, free parts locating and a referral service. Pipers magazine is exclusively for POS members.

2756 **www.pra.org**
Popular Rotorcraft Association
A nonprofit organization dedicated to the advancement of knowledge, public education and safety among Rotorcraft enthusiasts worldwide.

2757 **www.quad-a.org**
Army Aviation Association of America
Aerospace products, helicopters, rotor blades, engines, tires, helmets and related aviation equipment. Representing membership interests to the Army and the Legislative Branch.

2758 **www.rotor.com**
Helicopter Association International
Receives and disseminates information concerning the use, operation, hiring, contracting and leasing of helicopters.

2759 **www.safeassociation.com**
SAFE Association
Website of the nonprofit organization dedicated to the preservation of human life. It provides a common meeting ground for the sharing of problems, ideas and information.

2760 **www.seaplanes.org**
Seaplane Pilots Association
Represents our members in dozens of seaplane access issues annually and provides numerous exclusive benefits.

2761 **www.ssa.org**
Soaring Society of America
Fosters and promote all phases of gliding and soaring, nationally and internationally.

2762 **www.tcunion.org**
Transportation-Communications International Union
Members come from diverse transportation industries. In addition to bargaining and representation of its members, provides mortgage and bankcard programs and other services to its members.

2763 **www.tiaca.org**
International Air Cargo Association
For air cargo industry services and products from aircraft manufacturers, airlines, airports, freight forwarders trade publications logistics consultants, etc.

2764 **www.ussf.org**
Space Foundation
Nonprofit organization advancing the exploration, development and use of space and space education for the benefit of humankind.

2765 **www.vtol.org**
AHS International
For designers, engineers and manufacturers of the vertical flight industry.

2766 **www.wahsonline.com**
World Airline Historical Society
Open to all persons and groups interested in collecting airline memorabilia and the study of the airline industry, past and current.

Associations

2767 ARMA International
11880 College Blvd
Suite 450
Overland Park, KS 66210

913-341-3808
800-422-2762; *Fax:* 913-341-3742
headquarters@armaintl.org; www.arma.org
Social Media: Facebook, Twitter, LinkedIn

Peter Kurilecz, President
Tera Ladner, President Elect
Brenda Prowse, Treasurer
Fred Pulzello, IGP, CRM, Immediate Past President

A not-for-profit professional association and the authority on managing records and information.
11000 Members
Founded in: 1955

2768 Advancing Financial Crime Professionals Worldwide
80 Southwest 8th Street
Suite 2350
Miami, FL 33130

305-373-0020
866-459-CAMS; *Fax:* 305-373-5229
info@acams.org; www.acams.org
Social Media: Facebook, Twitter, LinkedIn

Ted Weissberg, Chief Executive Officer
John Byrne, Executive Vice President
Ari House, Chief Financial Officer
Ms. Hue Dang, Head of Asia
Geoffrey Fone, Director of Sales

The largest international membership organization dedicated to enhancing the knowledge and expertise of financial crime detection and prevention professionals from a wide range of industries in both public and private sectors.

2769 American Association of Bank Directors
1250 24th Street, NW
Suite 700
Washington, DC 20037

202-463-4888; *Fax:* 202-349-8080
info@aabd.org
aabd.org
Social Media: Twitter, LinkedIn

David Baris, President
Richard M. Whiting, Executive Director
Charles J. Thayer, Chairman Emeritus
Andrew Baris, VP and Director of Marketing
Betty Pelton, Membership Director

Devoted to serving the information, education and advocacy needs of individual bank and savings institution directors. This nonprofit organization has members nationwide.
Founded in: 1989

2770 American Association of Residential Mortgage Regulators
1025 Thomas Jefferson Street, NW
Suite 500 East
Washington, DC 20007

202-521-3999; *Fax:* 202-833-3636
efreundel@aarmr.org; www.aarmr.org

Rod Carnes, President
Tony Florence, Vice President
Robert Niemi, Treasurer
Stacey Valerio, Secretary
David Saunders, Executive Director

Promotes the exchange of information and education concerning the licensing, supervision, and regulation of the residential mortgage industry.

2771 American Bankers Association
1120 Connecticut Avenue NW
Washington, DC 20036

202-663-5000
800-226-5377; *Fax:* 202-828-4540
custserv@aba.com; www.aba.com
Social Media: Facebook, Twitter, LinkedIn, Google+, YouTube, Instagram

John A Ikard, Chairman
R. Daniel Blanton, Chair Elect
Dorothy A. Savarese, Vice Chair
Frank Keating, President & CEO
G. William Beale, Treasurer

Brings together all categories of banking institutions to best represent the interests of this rapidly changing industry. Its membership includes community, regional and money center banks and holding companies, as well as savings associations, trust companies and savings banks.
Founded in: 1875

2772 American Bankers Insurance Association
American Bankers Association
1120 Connecticut Avenue NW
Washington, DC 20036

202-663-5163
800-226-5377; *Fax:* 202-828-4546
vbarton@aba.com; www.theabia.com
Social Media: Facebook, Twitter, LinkedIn

Paul Petrylak, President/Chairman
Neal Aton, Vice President
David Cissell, Secretary
Val Teagarden, Treasurer

The American Bankers Insurance Association (ABIA) is the insurance subsidiary of the American Bankers Association (ABA). The ABIA's mission is to develop policy and provide advocacy for banks in insurance and to support bank insurance operations through research, education, compliance assistance, and peer group networking opportunities.
300 Members
Founded in: 2001

2773 American Bankruptcy Institute
66 Canal Center Plaza
Suite 600
Alexandria, VA 22314

703-739-0800; *Fax:* 703-739-1060
support@abiworld.org; www.abiworld.org
Social Media: Facebook, Twitter, LinkedIn, Google+, Flickr

Patrica A Redmond, Chairman
James Patrick Shea, President
Jeffery N Pomerantz, President Elect
John Tittle Jr., Treasurer
Hon. Dennis R. Dow, Secretary

Multidisciplinary, non-partisan organization dedicated to research and education on matters related to insolvency. Engaged in numerous educational and research activities as well as the production of a number of publications both for the insolvency practitioner and the public.
12000 Members
Founded in: 1982

2774 American Payroll Association
660 North Main Avenue
Suite 100
San Antonio, TX 78205-1217

210-226-4600; *Fax:* 210-226-4027
APA@americanpayroll.org;
www.americanpayroll.org
Social Media: Facebook, Twitter, LinkedIn

Conducts payroll training conferences and seminars across the country and publishes a complete library of resource texts and newsletters.
21000 Members
Founded in: 1982

2775 Arab Bankers Association of North America
150 West 28th Street
Suite 801
New York, NY 10001

212-599-3030; *Fax:* 212-599-3131
info@arabbankers.org; www.arabbankers.org

Mona Aboelnaga Kanaan, President
Susan Peters, Executive Director/COO
Ryah Aqel, Communications Coordinator
Zainab Al Dabbagh, Development Associate
Gabby Elhilow, Administrative Associate

Provides news, job listings, and resources for financial institutions in the U.S. and the Middle East.
Founded in: 1983

2776 Association For Financial Professionals
4520 East West Highway
Suite 750
Bethesda, MD 20814

301-907-2862; *Fax:* 301-907-2864
afp@afponline.org; www.afponline.org
Social Media: Facebook, Twitter, LinkedIn, Youtube, RSS

Anthony Scaglione, Chairman
Roberta Eiseman, Vice Chairman
Jeff Johnson, Vice Chairman
Ann Anthony, Director
Terry Crawford, Director

The Association for Financial Professionals (AFP) serves a network of more than 16,000 treasury and finance professionals. Headquartered in Bethesda, MD, AFP provides members with breaking news, economic research and data on the evolving world of treasury and finance, as well as world-class treasury certification programs, networking events, financial analytical tools, training, and public policy representation to legislators and regulators.

2777 Association for Financial Technology
10813 Pleasant Valley Road
Frazeysburg, OH 43822

614-895-1208; *Fax:* 614-895-3466
aft@aftweb.com; www.aftweb.com
Social Media: Facebook, Twitter, LinkedIn

Wade Arnold, President
Xan Kasprzak, Vice President & Program Chair
Andrew Grinstead, Treasurer
James R Bannister, Executive Director
Susan Hurley, Managing Director

Association founded to promote high standards of professionalism in the planning, development, implementation and application of technology to the financial services industry.
Founded in: 1972

2778 Association for Management Information in Financial Services
14247 Saffron Circle
Carmel, IN 46032-7769

317-815-5857; *Fax:* 317-815-5877
ami2@amifs.org; www.amifs.org
Social Media: Facebook, Twitter, LinkedIn

Kevin Link, Executive Director
Robert McDonald, President
Meg Foster, Executive Vice President
Krissa Hatfield, Asst. Executive Director

The Association for Management Information in Financial Services is the preeminent organization for management information professionals in the financial services industry, and counts among its members individuals who set the policies and advance the concepts of management information at major financial institutions worldwide.
300 Members
Founded in: 1980

2779 Association of Independent Trust Companies
2213 North Broadway
Ada, OK 74820
405-680-7869; *Fax:* 580-332-4714
ato@trustorgs.com; www.trustorgs.com
Social Media: Facebook, Twitter
Bond Payne, President
Tony Guthrie, Treasurer
Thomas Blank, General Counsel/Secretary
Somerlyn Cothran, Executive Director
Jamie Whitefield, Administration
To provide a forum of leaders, owners and operators of trust companies and wealth management providers.
150 Members
Founded in: 1989

2780 Association of Military Banks of America (AMBA)
PO Box 3335
Warrenton, VA 20188
540-347-3305; *Fax:* 540-347-5995
info@ambahq.org; www.ambahq.org
Social Media: Facebook, Twitter
Terry Tuggle, Chairman
Raleigh A Trovillion, Vice Chairman
Steven Lepper, President/CEO
James A Cerrone, Chairman Elect
Steven Lepper, President and CEO
AMBA is a not-for-profit association of banks operating on military installations, banks not located on military installations but serving military customers, and military banking facilities designated by the US Treasury.
130 Members
Founded in: 1959

2781 Association of Residential Mortgage Compliance Professionals
167 West Hudson Street
Suite 200
Long Beach, NY 11561
516-442-3456
armcp.org
Social Media: LinkedIn
The first and only national organization in the Unites States devoted exclusively to residential mortgage compliance professionals offering discussion groups, educational forums, panels, lectures, and other venues for residential mortgage compliance professionals.
Founded in: 2010

2782 Bank Administration Institute
115 S LaSalle St
Suite 3300
Chicago, IL 60603-3801
312-683-2464
888-224-0037; *Fax:* 312-683-2373
info@bai.org; www.bai.org
Social Media: Facebook, Twitter, LinkedIn, YouTube
Scott M Peters, Chairman
Christopher J McComish, Vice Chair
Deborah L Bianucci, President & CEO
Charles G Kim, Secretary
Rilla S Delorier, Treasurer
The financial services industry's partner for breakthrough information and intelligence needed to innovate and stay relevant in an evolving marketplace. Serves a wide segment of the financial services industry, from the largest multinational banks to community-based institutions.

2783 Bank Insurance and Securities Association
2025 M Street NW
Suite 800
Washington, DC 20036
202-367-1111; *Fax:* 202-367-2111
bisa@BISAnet.org; www.bisanet.org
Social Media: Facebook, Twitter, StumbleUpon
Daniel J. McCormack, President
Frank A. Consalo, Vice President
Bruce Hagemann, Secretary/Treasurer
Jeff Hartney, Executive Director
Anna Hildreth, Director, Operations
Dedicated to serving the needs of those responsible for marketing securities, insurance and other investment and risk management products through commercial banks, trust companies, savings institutions, and credit unions.
Founded in: 2002

2784 Bankers' Association for Finance & Trade
1120 Connecticut Avenue NW
Washington, DC 20036
202-663-7575; *Fax:* 202-663-5538
info@baft-ifsa.com; www.baft.org
Social Media: Facebook, Twitter
John Ahearn, Chairman
Michael Quinn, Vice Chairman
Tod R Burwell, CEO
Daniel J Scanlan, Treasurer/Secretary
Rita Gonzalez, Managing Director
A financial services trade association headquartered in Washington, DC, whose membership primarily represents a broad range of financial institutions and service members that provide services throughout the global financial community.
180 Members
Founded in: 1921

2785 Community Development Bankers Association
1444 Eye Street NW
Suite 201
Washington, DC 20005
202-689-8935
info@cdbanks.org; www.cdbanks.org
Social Media: Facebook, Twitter, LinkedIn
Brian Argrett, Chairman
Robert Jones III, Vice-Chair
Huey Townsend, Treasurer
Robert Patrick Cooper, Secretary
Robert McGill, Emeritus Director
The national trade association of the community development bank sector.

2786 Conference of State Bank Supervisors
1129 20th Street, N.W.
9th Floor
Washington, DC 20036
202-296-2840; *Fax:* 202-296-1928
drodgers@csbs.org; www.csbs.org
Melanie G Hall, Chairman
Katherine E Hoyle, Administrative Assistant
Mick Thompson, Vice Chairman
John Ryan, Secretary
Charles J Dolezal, Treasurer
The nationwide organization of banking regulators from all 50 states, the District of Columbia, Guam, Puerto Rico, and the U.S. Virgin Islands.
Founded in: 1902

2787 Consumer Bankers Association
1225 Eye St., NW
Suite 550
Washington, DC 20005
202-552-6382
rhunt@cbanet.org; www.cbanet.org
Social Media: Facebook, Twitter, LinkedIn
Richard Hunt, President/ Chief Executive Officer
Janet Pike, Executive Assistant
Steven I. Zeisel, General Counsel/ EVP
Tiffany Haas, VP, Congressional Affairs
Kristen Fallon, VP, Congressional Affairs
The recognized voice on retail banking issues in the nation's capital.

2788 Council for Electronic Billing and Payment
13450 Sunrise Valley Drive
Suite 100
Herndon, VA 20171
703-561-1100
runger@nacha.org
cebp.nacha.org
Social Media: LinkedIn
Robert Unger, Senior Director
Liz Millard, Assistant Director
Promotes electronic consumer and business-to-business billing and payment programs and services across any delivery channel. It also provides an open forum for education, resource development, solution innovation, research and the exchange of information about the electronic billing and the electronic payment industries.
416 Members
Founded in: 2008

2789 Credit Union National Association
5710 Mineral Point Rd
Madison, WI 53705
800-356-8010
800-356-9655; *Fax:* 608-231-4333
ccsorders@cuna.coop; www.cuna.org
Social Media: Facebook, Twitter, LinkedIn, YouTube
Susan Streifel, Chairman
Rodney Staatz, Vice Chairman
Patrick Jury, Secretary
Maurice Smith, Treasurer
Jim Nussle, President Ex Officio
A national trade association for both state and federally charteredcredit unions located in the United States.

2790 Electronic Funds Transfer Association
4000 Legato Road
Suite 1100
Fairfax, VA 22033
571-318-5556; *Fax:* 571-318-5557;
www.efta.org
Social Media: Twitter
Kurt Helwig, President & CEO
Pat O'Donnell, Chairman
Melanie Renner, Meeting Coordinator
Lynne Barr, Secretary
Keith Harrison, Treasurer
The Electronic Funds Transfer Association (EFTA) is the nation's leading inter-industry professional association promoting the adoption of electronic payment systems and commerce.
Founded in: 1977

2791 Electronic Payments Association NACHA
2550 Wasser Terrace
Suite 400
Herndon, VA 20171
703-561-1100; *Fax:* 703-787-0996
info@nacha.org; www.nacha.org

Social Media: Facebook, Twitter, LinkedIn, YouTube

Donna Schwartze, Media Contact
Joshua Maze, Sponsorship
Janet O Estep, President & CEO

NACHA manages the development, administration, and governance of the ACH Network, the backbone for the electronic movement of money and data. The ACH Network provides a safe, secure, and reliable network for direct account-to-account consumer, business, and government payments. Annually, it facilitates billions of Direct Deposit via ACH and Direct Payment via ACH transactions. Used by all types of financial institutions, the ACH Network is governed by the fair and equitable NACHA Operating Rules
Founded in: 1974

2792 Electronic Transactions Association
1101 16th STREET NW #402
WASHINGTON, DC 20036

202-828-2635
800-695-5509; www.electran.org
Social Media: Facebook, LinkedIn, YouTube, Flickr

Debra Rossi, President
Greg Cohen, President-Elect
Jeff Rosenblatt, Treasurer
Jeff Sloan, Secretary
Kim Fitzsimmons, Immediate Past-President

A trade organization representing independent sales organizations, merchant service providers and those help them serve their merchant clients.
Founded in: 1990

2793 Environmental Bankers Association
1827 Powers Ferry Rd, Building 14
Suite 100
Atlanta, GA 30339

678-619-5045; *Fax:* 678-229-2777
eba@envirobank.org; www.envirobank.org
Social Media: Facebook, Twitter, LinkedIn, YouTube

Sharon Valverde, President
Geogina Dannatt, Vice President
Richard Belyea, Secretary & Communication
David Lambert, Treasurer
Dan Richardson, General Counsel

EBA voting members are banks, trust companies, credit unions, savings and loan associations, and other financial services organizations with an interest in environmental risk management and related issues. Active participants are bankers from Trust or Credit offices with responsibility for environmental liability, and financial services officers with environmental interests. Affiliate members are from law firms, consulting and insurance organizations.
Founded in: 1994

2794 Financial Managers Society
1 North LaSalle Street
Suite 3100
Chicago, IL 60602-4003

312-578-1300
800-275-4367; *Fax:* 312-578-1308
info@fmsinc.org; www.fmsinc.org
Social Media: Facebook, Twitter, LinkedIn, Instagram

Dick Yingst, President/ CEO
Sydney K Garmong, Chairman
John Westwood, Vice Chairman
Darrell E Blocker, Director-at-Large
Diane DelLella, Director-at-Large

A nonprofit professional society serving the financial services industry.
Founded in: 1948

2795 Financial Services Roundtable
600 13th Street, NW
Suite 400
Washington, DC 20005

202-289-4322
info@fsroundtable.org; www.fsround.org
Social Media: Twitter, LinkedIn, YouTube

Frederick H. Waddell, Chairman
Ajaypal S Banga, Chairman-Elect
Larry Zimpleman, Immediate-Past Chairman
Kessel Stelling, Treasurer
Richard K. Davis, Director

The leading advocacy organization for America's financial services industry. Its members include banking, insurance, asset management, finance, andcredit card companies.

2796 Financial Women International
1027 W Roselawn Avenue
Roseville, MN 55113

651-487-7632
866-807-6081; *Fax:* 651-489-1322
info@fwi.org; www.fwi.org

Melissa Curzon, President
Cindy Hass, VP
Carleen DeSisto, Secretary

FWI is dedicated to developing leaders, accelerating careers, and generating results for professionals in the banking and financial services industry.
1000 Members
Founded in: 1921

2797 Financial Women's Association
215 Park Avenue South
Suite 1712
New York, NY 10003

212-533-2141
FWAoffice@FWA.org
fwa.org
Social Media: Facebook, Twitter, LinkedIn

Katrin Dambrot, President
Ria Davis, President-Elect
Maureen Adolf, Pat President
Amy Geffen, Executive Director
Ilene Moskowitz, Secretary

A nonprofit organization established by a group of Wall Street Women to support the role and development of women in the financial services industry.
Founded in: 1956

2798 Global Association of Risk Professionals
111 Town Square Place
14th Floor
Jersey City, NJ 07310

201-719-7210; *Fax:* 201-222-5022
info@garp.com; www.garp.com
Social Media: Facebook, Twitter, LinkedIn, YouTube, Google+

Richard Apostolik, President & CEO
Ken Abbott, Chief Risk Officer
William Martin, Chief Risk Officer
Ben Golub, Chief Risk Officer
Laura Dottori, Senior Executive VP & CRO

To be the leading professional association for risk managers, managed by and for its members dedicated to the advancement of the risk profession through education, training and the promotion of best practices globally. Members come from over 100 countries.
52330 Members
Founded in: 1996

2799 Impact Mortgage Management Advocacy & Advisory Group
2740 S. Newland Street
Lakewood, CO 80227

303-674-1200; *Fax:* 303-674-1664
bill@immaag.com; www.immaag.com

Provides thousands of state licensed mortgage loan originators the information and advocacy support necessary for the industry to deal with absorbing the results of the financial crisis being dealt with by the nation.

2800 Independent Community Bankers of America
1615 L St NW
Suite 900
Washington, DC 20036

202-659-8111
866-843-4222; *Fax:* 202-659-9216
info@icba.org; www.icba.org
Social Media: Facebook, Twitter, LinkedIn, YouTube, Pinterest, Tumblr

Jack A Hartings, Chairman
Rebeca Romero Rainey, Chairman Elect
R. Scott Heitkamp, Vice Chair
Mike Ellenburg, Secretary
Preston Kennedy, Treasurer

Trade association for the nations community banks.
5000 Members

2801 Institute of Certified Bankers
American Bankers Association
1120 Connecticut Avenue NW
Washington, DC 20036

202-663-5092
800-226-5377; *Fax:* 202-828-4540
icb@aba.com; www.aba.com/ICB/default.htm
Social Media: Facebook, Twitter, LinkedIn

Rob Nichols, President & CEO

A national association of certified professionals in the financial services industry whose mission is to provide financial services professionals with confidence, credibility and recognition through its certifications.
Founded in: 1990

2802 Institute of International Bankers
299 Park Avenue
17th Floor
New York, NY 10171

212-421-1611; *Fax:* 212-421-1119
iib@iib.org; www.iib.org
Social Media: Facebook, Twitter, LinkedIn

Roger Blissett, Chairman
Sarah Miller, CEO
Angelo R Aldana, Vice Chair
John Geremia, Secretary
Joseph Cervelli, Treasurer

To help resolve the many special legislative, regulatory and tax issues confronting internationally headquartered financial institutions that engage in banking, securities and/or insurance activities in the United States.
Founded in: 1966

2803 International Financial Services Association
9 Sylvan Way
Suite 130
Parsippany, NJ 07054-3817

973-656-1900; *Fax:* 973-656-1915;
www.ifsaonline.org

Tod Burwell, Vice President
Colleen Kennedy, Manager, Programs & Events

Represents the international operations areas of financial services providers, their customers, suppliers and partners. Dedicates itself to meeting the specific needs of those who provide, use,

and support trade and payments with particular focus on documentary credits, funds transfer, treasury operations, compliance, and regulatory reporting.
Founded in: 1924

2804 Investment Bankers Association
E-Mail:
info2@investmentbankersassociation.org;
www.investmentbankersassociation.org

A national organization for businesses that want to go public and raise capital to meet small regional and independent brokerage firms, investment bankers, capital sources and other capital market service providers.

2805 MasterCard Worldwide
2000 Purchase St
Purchase, NY 10577-2405
914-249-2000; *Fax:* 914-249-4135;
www.mastercardinternational.com
Social Media: Facebook, Twitter, LinkedIn

Robert W Selander, CEO
Sharon Gamsin, VP
Chris Harral, Director
Chris A McWilton, Chief Financial Offcier
Lawrence Flanagan, Chief Marketing Officer

Administers the MasterCard credit and other MasterCard products fo member financial institutions around the world.
25000 Members
Founded in: 1940

2806 Mortgage Bankers Association
1919 M Street NW
5th Floor
Washington, DC 20036
202-557-2700
800-793-6222; *Fax:* 202-721-0248
membership@mba.org;
www.mortgagebankers.org
Social Media: Facebook, Twitter, LinkedIn, Youtube

Bill Emerson, Chairman
Rodrigo Lopez, Chair Elect
J David Motley, Vice Chair
David H. Stevens, President & CEO
Jeffrey M Schummer, VP Education/Business Development

Seeks to improve methods of originating, servicing and marketing loans.
2900 Members
Founded in: 1914

2807 Mortgage Bankers Association of America
1919 M Street NW
5th Floor
Washington, DC 20036
202-557-2700
800-793-6222; www.mbaa.org

Bill Cosgrove, CMB, Chairman
Bill Emerson, Chairman-Elect
Rodrigo Lopez, CMB, Vice Chairman
David H. Stevens, President/ CEO
Marcia Davies, Chief Operating Officer

A national association representing the entire real estate finance industry. This association develops innovative business tools and provides education and training for industry professionals.

2808 NACHA: Electronic Payments Association
2550 Wasser Terrace
Suite 400
Herndon, VA 20171
703-561-1100; *Fax:* 703-787-0996
info@nacha.org; www.nacha.org
Social Media: Facebook, Twitter, LinkedIn, YouTube

Robert Garinger, President/CEO
Janet C Boyst, Executive VP
Deb Evans-Doyle, Senior Director Conference Mktg
Julie Hedlund, Senior Director Electronic Commerce
Michael Herd, Director Public Relations

To promote the development of electronic solutions that improve the payments for the benefit of its members and their customers.
11000 Members
Founded in: 1974

2809 National Association of Affordable Housing Lenders
1667 K Street NW
Suite 210
Washington, DC 20006
202-293-9850; *Fax:* 202-293-9852
naahl@naahl.org; www.naahl.org
Social Media: Twitter, YouTube

Buzz Roberts, President/CEO
Paul Haaland, COO
Sara Olson, Administrator

Represents America's leaders in moving private capital to those in need. Encompasses 200 organizations committed to increasing private lending and investing in low and moderate-income communities.
Founded in: 1990

2810 National Association of Bankruptcy Trustees
One Windsor Cove
Suite 305
Columbia, SC 29223
803-252-5646
800-445-8629; *Fax:* 803-765-0860
info@nabt.com; www.nabt.com

Richard D Nelson, President
Dwayne Murray, President-Elect
Ronald R Peterson, Vice President
Brian L.Budsberg, Treasurer
Raymond J Obuchowski, Secretary

A non profit association formed to address the needs of bankruptcy trustees throughout the country and to promote the effectiveness of the bankruptcy system as a whole.
Founded in: 1982

2811 National Association of Chapter 13 Trustees
1 Windsor Cove
Suite 305
Columbia, SC 29223
803-252-5646
800-445-8629; *Fax:* 803-765-0860
Info@NACTT.com; www.nactt.com

Mary Ida Townson, President
D Sims Crawford, President Elect
Joyce Bradley Babin, VP
David G Peake, Secretary
O. Byron Meredith, Treasurer

Provides a forum within which Chapter 13 Trustees will act as an information and communication resource to advance education, leadership, and continuous improvement in the administration of bankruptcy. We will provide the means to establish and implement professional standards and participate in the national legislative and administrative processes while promoting the highest ethical principles.
1000 Members
Founded in: 1965

2812 National Association of Credit Union Supervisory & Auditing Committees
PO Box 160
Del Mar, CA 92014
800-287-5949; *Fax:* 858-792-3884
nacusac@nacusac.org; www.nacusac.org

Celeste Shelton, Executive Director
Lauren Clark, Associate Director
Bob Spinder, Associate Director
Michael MacFeeters, Chairman
Cecil Short, Vice Chairman

A unique organization of, by and for credit union supervisory committee members. Provides leadership, support and education to enhance the capability of credit union supervisory and auditing committee members to fulfill their responsibilities.
Founded in: 1985

2813 National Association of Federal Credit Unions
3138 10th St N
Arlington, VA 22201-2149
703-522-4770
800-336-4644; *Fax:* 703-524-1082
msc@nafcu.org; www.nafcu.org
Social Media: Facebook, Twitter, LinkedIn, YouTube

Ed Templeton, Chairman
Richard L Harris, Vice Chairman
Jeanne Kuckey, Treasurer
Debra Schwartz, Secretary
B Dan Berger, President & CEO

A respected and influential trade association that exclusively represents the interests of federal credit unions before the federal government and the public.
Founded in: 1967

2814 National Association of Government Guaranteed Lenders
215 East 9th Avenue
Stillwater, OK 74074
405-377-4022; *Fax:* 405-377-3931
info@naggl.org; www.naggl.org
Social Media: Facebook, Twitter, LinkedIn, YouTube

Anthony Wilkinson, President/CEO
Jane Butler, EVP
Jennifer Shaklee, Assistant VP Marketing
Jennifer Sterret-O'Neill, COO
Larry Conley, Chairman

Promotes professional and governmental affairs interests of financial institutions and small businesses who participate in Small Business Administration guaranteed lending and secondary market programs.
600 Members
Founded in: 1984

2815 National Association of Independent Housing Professionals
601 Pennsylvania Ave. NW
South Building, Suite 900
Washington, DC 20004
202-587-9300; *Fax:* 304-267-9046;
www.naihp.org

Marc Savitt, CRMS, President
Peter Gallo, Vice President
Kate Crawford, Secretary/Treasurer
Brian Benjamin, Legislative Chair
William Howe, Director

A legislative and regulatory organization comprised of all housing industry professionals.

2816 **National Association of Professional Mortgage Women**
705 North Mountain Business Center
Suite E-104
Newington, CT 06111

800-827-3034; *Fax:* 469-524-5121
napmw1@napmw.org; www.napmw.org
Social Media: Facebook, LinkedIn, Google+, RSS

Kelly Hendricks, President
Nikki Bell, President Elect
Windee Falla, Secretary
Judy Alderson, Treasurer
Laurel Knight, Vice President

Serves all mortgage professionals and employers who want to excel. Provides business, personal, and leadership development opportunities advancing women in mortgage-related professions.
4500 Members
Founded in: 1964

2817 **National Association of State Credit Union Supervisors**
1655 Fort Myer Dr
Suite 650
Arlington, VA 22209

703-528-8351
800-728-7927; *Fax:* 703-528-3248
offices@nascus.org; www.nascus.org
Social Media: Facebook, Twitter, LinkedIn

Steve Pleger, Chairman
Mary Ellen O'Neil, Chair Elect
Jay Bienvenu, Secretary/Treasurer
John Fields, Director
Linda K Jekel, Past President

State chartered credit unions and state credit union supervisors.
900 Members
Founded in: 1965

2818 **National Bankers Association**
1513 P St NW
Washington, DC 20005

202-588-5432; *Fax:* 202-588-5443
mgrant@nationalbankers.org;
www.nationalbankers.org
Social Media: Facebook, Twitter

Michael Grant, President
Preston Pinkett III, Chairman
Neill S Wright, Treasurer
Cynthia Day, Secretary
B Doyle Mitchell Jr, Past President

Members are minority and women's banking institutions, minority individuals employed by majority banks and institutions.
16000 Members
Founded in: 1927

2819 **National Credit Union Administration**
1775 Duke St
Suite 4206
Alexandria, VA 22314-6115

703-518-6300
800-755-1030; *Fax:* 703-518-6539
pacamsil@ncua.gov; www.ncua.gov
Social Media: Facebook, Twitter, LinkedIn

Deborah Matz, Chairman
David Marquis, Executive Director

Governed by a three member board appointed by the President and confirmed by the US Senate, this independent federal agency charters and supervises federal credit unions. NCUA, with the backing of the full faith and credit of the US government, operates the National Credit Union Share Insurance Fund, insuring the savings of 80 million account holders in all federal credit unions and many state chartered credit unions.
700 Members
Founded in: 1909

2820 **National Investment Banking Association**
422 Chesterfield Road
Bogart, GA 30622

706-208-9620; *Fax:* 706-993-3342
emily@nibanet.org; www.nibanet.org
Social Media: Facebook, Twitter, LinkedIn, Youtube, RSS

James E Hock, Chairman
Carlo Corzine, Chairman
William Jordan, Treasurer
Gerald A Adler, Chairman , Govt & Legal Committee
Lynne Bolduc, Secretary

A national trade association of regional and independent brokerages, investment banking firms, and related capital market service providers.
Founded in: 1932

2821 **National Marine Bankers Association**
231 South LaSalle Street
Suite 2050
Chicago, IL 60604

312-946-6260
info@marinebankers.org;
www.marinebankers.org

Micheal Bryant, President
Peggy Bodenreider, VP
Willaim B Otto, Treasurer
Jayme B Yates, Secretary
Jackie Forese, Director

Created to educate current and prospective lenders in marine financing procedures and to promote the extension of credit to consumer and trade borrowers.
70 Members
Founded in: 1980

2822 **National Mitigation Banking Association**
107 S. West Street # 573
Alexandria, VA 22314

202-457-8409
info@mitigationbanking.org;
www.mitigationbanking.org

Michael Sprague, President
Donald H Ross, Vice President
Donna Collier, Secretary
Randy Vogel, Treasurer
Wayne White, Immediate Past-President

Promotes federal legislation and regulatory policy that encourages mitigation banking and conservation banking as a means of compensating for adverse impacts to America's wetlands and other natural resources.

2823 **National Reverse Mortgage Lenders Association**
1400 16th St., NW
Suite 420
Washington, DC 20036

202-939-1760; *Fax:* 202-265-4435
dhicks@dworbell.com; www.nrmlaonline.org
Social Media: Facebook, Twitter, LinkedIn

Joe DeMarkey, Co-Chairman
Reza Jahangiri, Co-Chairman
Sherry Apanay, Vice-Chairwoman
Mark Browning, Vice-Chairman
Steve McClellan, Secretary

Trade association that serves as an educational resource, policy advocate and public affairs center for reverse mortgage lenders and related professionals.
Founded in: 1997

2824 **Nonprofit Risk Management Center**
204 South King Street
Leesburg, VA 20175

703-777-3504; *Fax:* 202-785-3891;
www.nonprofitrisk.org
Social Media: Twitter

Peter Andrew, President
Lisa Prinz, Treasurer
Carolyn Hayes-Gulston, Secretary
Melanie L Herman, Executive Director
Erin Gloeckner, Project Manager

Provides risk management assistance and resources for community-serving nonprofit organizations.

2825 **Public Risk Management Association**
700 S. Washington St.
Suite 218
Alexandria, VA 22314

703-528-7701; *Fax:* 703-739-0200
info@primacentral.org; www.primacentral.org

Dean Coughenour, President
Regan Rychetsky, Past-President
Terri Evans, President-Elect
Scott Kramer, Director
Lori J Gray, Director

Member based organization which is dedicated to providing practicaleducation, training, and information for public sector risk management practitioners.

2826 **Risk Management Association**
1801 Market Street
Suite 300
Philadelphia, PA 19103-1628

215-446-4000
800-677-7621; *Fax:* 215-446-4101
customers@rmahq.org; www.rmahq.org
Social Media: Facebook, Twitter, LinkedIn, WordPress

J Tol Broome Jr, Chairman
Helga Houston, Vice Chair
William F Githens, CEO
H Lynn Harton, Director
C Matthew Lusco, Director

A not-for-profit, member driven professional association whose sole purpose is to advance the use of sound risk principles in the financial services industry.
3000 Members
Founded in: 1914

2827 **Securities Industry and Financial Markets Association (SIFMA)**
1101 New York Ave Nw
Suite 800
Washington, DC 20005-4279

202-962-7300; *Fax:* 202-962-7305;
www.fisma.org
Social Media: Facebook, Twitter, LinkedIn

T Timothy Ryan Jr, President/CEO
Randy Snook, Senior Managing Director/EVP
Donald D Kittell, CFO

SIFMA's mission is to champion policies and practices that benefit investors and issuers, expand and perfect global capital markets, and foster the development of new products and services. SIFMA provides an enhanced member network of access and forward-looking services, as well as premiere educational resources for the professionals within the industry and the investors whom they serve.

2828 **Society of Financial Examiners**
12100 Sunset Hills Rd
Suite 130
Reston, VA 20190-3221
703-234-4140
800-787-7633; *Fax:* 888-436-8686
sofe@sofe.org; www.sofe.org
L. Brackett, Executive Director
Judy Estus, Administrator
William Latza, General Counsel
Annette Knief, President
James Kattman, Treasurer
Professional society for examiners of insurance companies, banks, savings and loans, and credit unions.
Founded in: 1973

2829 **Society of Risk Management Consultants**
621 North Sherman Avenue
Madison, WI 53704
www.srmcsociety.org
Michael E Norek, President
David L Stegall, President-Elect
Benjamin C Few III, Treasurer
Christopher J Franki, Secretary
Marie E Piccininni, Director
An international organization of professionals engaged in risk management, insurance and employee benefits consulting.
Founded in: 1984

2830 **The Association of Executives in Finance, Credit, & International Business**
8840 Columbia 100 Parkway
Columbia, MD 21045-2158
410-423-1840
888-256-3242; *Fax:* 410-740-5574
fcib_global@fcibglobal.com;
www.fcibglobal.com
Social Media: Twitter, LinkedIn, RSS
Marta Chacon, Director, The Americas
Ron Shepherd, Director, Business Dev.
Noelin Hawkins, Director, Europe, Middle East
Barry Norton, Advisory Board Chairman
Tim Bastian, Board Member
The premier Association for Finance, Credit and International business professionals. The leading resource for global credit information, professional development and education.
1000+ Members
Founded in: 1919

2831 **The Bankers Association for Finance and Trade**
1120 Connecticut Avenue, NW
Washington, DC 20036
202-663-7575; *Fax:* 202-663-5538
info@baft.org; www.baft.org
Social Media: Facebook, Twitter
Rita Gonzalez, Managing Director
Michael Quinn, Vice chair
Tod R. Burwell, CEO
Daniel J Scanlan, Secretary-Treasurer
Ian Stewart, Director

2832 **The Fiduciary and Investment Risk Management**
Post Office Box 507
Stockbridge, GE 30281
678-565-6211; *Fax:* 678-565-8788
info@thefirma.org; www.thefirma.org
Social Media: Facebook, Twitter, LinkedIn, RSS
Bruce K. Goldberg, President
Jennifer De Vries, Vice President
David Jonke, Secretary
Bradley F. Beshea, SVP, Fiduciary Compliance Officer
John L Clark, Director
Provider of current and relevant fiduciary and investment risk management education and networking opportunities to risk management professionals.

2833 **The First**
7054 Jefferson Highway
Baton Rouge, LA 70806
225-228-7275; *Fax:* 225-228-7276;
www.thefirstbank.com
Social Media: Facebook, Twitter
Personal and commercial banking. Offers information about services,products, and locations.

2834 **University Risk Management and Insurance Association**
PO Box 1027
Bloomington, IN 47402
812-855-6683; *Fax:* 812-856-3149
urmia@urmia.org; www.urmia.org
Social Media: Facebook, Twitter, LinkedIn, Flickr. YouTube
Donna McMahon, President
Kathy E Hargis, President-Elect
Cheryl Lloyd, Secretary
Tish Gade-Jones, Treasurer
Sally Alexander, Director
Advances the discipline of risk management in higer education.

2835 **Urban Financial Services Coalition**
1200 G St NW
Suite 800
Washington, DC 20005
202-289-8335
800-996-8335; *Fax:* 202-434-8707
ufsc@ufscnet.org; www.ufscnet.org
Social Media: Facebook, Twitter, LinkedIn, Youtube
Roderick Hayes, President
Dorothy Reed, Vice President
Ola Truelove, Treasurer
Delores Blake, Secretary
Walter Brown, Immediate Past President
Formerly known as the National Association of Urban Bankers is an organization of minority professionals in the financial services industry and related fields.
Founded in: 1974

2836 **Western Independent Bankers**
555 Montgomery Street
Suite 750
San Francisco, CA 94111
415-352-2323; *Fax:* 415-352-2314
info@wib.org; www.wib.org
Social Media: Facebook, Twitter, LinkedIn, YouTube
Russell A. Colombo, Chair
Bryan Luke, Chair-elect
J David Joves, Secretary
Richard T Beard, Immediate Past Chair
Bruce Lowry, Treasurer
A trade association that informs, educates, and connects community banks with the resources and services to achieve the highest standards of personal and organizational performance.
Founded in: 1937

2837 **Women's World Banking**
122 East 42nd Street
42nd Floor
New York, NY 10168
212-768-8513; *Fax:* 212-768-8519;
www.womensworldbanking.org
Social Media: Facebook, Twitter, LinkedIn, YouTube, Google +, Flickr
Jennifer Riria, Chair
Mary Houghton, Vice Chair
Connie Collingsworth, Secretary
Mary Ellen Iskenderian, President and CEO
J. Thomas Jones, Chief Operating Officer
A global nonprofit organization devoted to giving more low-income women access to the financial tools and resources they require to build security and prosperity.

Newsletters

2838 **ABA Bank Directors Briefing**
American Bankers Association
1120 Connecticut Avenue NW
Washington, DC 20036
202-663-5000
800-226-5377; *Fax:* 202-828-4548;
www.aba.com
Social Media: Facebook, Twitter, LinkedIn
Frank Keating, President/CEO
Stephen Crowe, Treasurer
Published by the editors of ABA Banking Journal in cooperation with the American Bankers Association. Focuses on keeping bank directors informed about legislative and regulatory developments, summarizing important banking industry trends, updating all directors on the latest thinking in corporate governance, educating new directors in the basics of community bank directorship
Frequency: Monthly

2839 **ABA Bankers News**
American Bankers Association
1120 Connecticut Avenue NW
Washington, DC 20036-3902
202-635-5000
800-226-5377; *Fax:* 202-663-7543
custserv@aba.com; www.aba.com
Social Media: Facebook, Twitter, LinkedIn
Frank Keating, President/CEO
Stephen Crowe, Treasurer
For everyone in the banking industry especially CEOs and compliance officers. Learn to use the internet effectively, retain your best customers, reduce risk, nurture a sales culture and more.
Cost: $450.00
Frequency: Bi-Weekly
Founded in: 1875

2840 **ABIA Insurance News**
American Bankers Association
1120 Connecticut Avenue NW
Washington, DC 20036
202-663-5163
800-226-5377; *Fax:* 202-828-4546
vbarton@aba.com; www.theabia.com
Paul Petrylak, President/Chairman
Neal Aton, Vice President
David Cissell, Secretary
Val Teagarden, Treasurer
The American Bankers Insurance Association (ABIA) is the insurance subsidiary of the American Bankers Association (ABA). The ABIA's mission is to develop policy and provide advocacy for banks in insurance and to support bank insurance operations through research, education, compliance assistance, and peer group networking opportunities.
300 Members
Frequency: Bi-Weekly
Founded in: 2001

2841 **AITCO Advisor**
Association of Independent Trust Companies

8 S Michigan Ave
Suite 802
Chicago, IL 60603-3452

312-223-1611; *Fax:* 312-580-0165;
www.trustorgs.com

Marcia Williams, Treasurer
Doug Nunn, President
Tom Blank, General Counsel/Secretary

Features professionally written articles on marketing and legislative issues as well as association updates.
Frequency: Quarterly

2842 AMI Bulletin
Assn for Management Information in Financial Svcs
14247 Saffron Circle
Carmel, IN 46032

317-518-5857; *Fax:* 317-518-5877
ami2@amifs.org; www.amifs.org

Robert McDonald, President
Kevin Link, Executive Director

News, calendars, events, and industry articles.
Frequency: Quarterly

2843 Access
American Safe Deposit Association
5433 S 200 E
Franklin, IN 46131-8982

317-738-4432; *Fax:* 317-738-5267
jmclin@aol.com; www.tasda.com

Bill Lee, Publisher
Thomas Cullinan, President
J Wayne Merrill, First VP
Winnifred Howard-Hommack, Second Vice President
Kevin Fanning, Treasurer

A newsletter full of timely articles on safe deposit procedures, policies, problems and solutions.
Cost: $10.00

2844 Advocacy Bulletins
CFA Institute
Po Box 3668
Charlottesville, VA 22903-0668

434-951-5499
800-247-8132; *Fax:* 434-951-5262
info@amir.org; www.cfainstitute.org

Alan Meder, Chair
John Rogers, President

To communicate time-sensitive information to interested AIMR/CFA Member Societies and members.
Frequency: Periodically

2845 Allied News
Allied Finance Adjusters Conference
P.O.Box 41368
Raleigh, NC 27629

800-621-3016
800-843-1232; *Fax:* 888-949-8520
alliedfinanceadjusters@gmail.com;
www.alliedfinanceadjusters.com
Social Media: Facebook, Twitter, LinkedIn

George Badeen, President

Trade Association of recovery specialists.
Cost: $200.00
Founded in: 1936

2846 American Banker
SourceMedia
1 State Street Plaza
27th floor
New York, NY 10004-1561

212-803-8200
800-803-3424; *Fax:* 212-843-9608
custserv@sourcemedia.com;
www.sourcemedia.com

Douglas Manoni, CEO
Richard Antoneck, CFO
Cost: $99.00
Frequency: Monthly
Founded in: 2005

2847 BNA's Banking Report
Bureau of National Affairs
3 Bethesda Metro Center
Suite 250
Bethesda, MD 20814

800-372-1033; *Fax:* 800-253-0332
customercare@bna.com; www.bna.com

Donna Ives, VP Operations
Gregory McCaffery, President

Legal and regulatory developments in the financial services industry.
Cost: $1780.00
Frequency: Weekly
ISSN: 1522-5984
Founded in: 1929

2848 Bank Alerts
Consumer Bankers Association
1000 Wilson Blvd
Suite 2500
Arlington, VA 22209-3912

703-276-1750; *Fax:* 703-528-1290
research@cbanet.org; www.cbanet.org
Social Media: Facebook, Twitter, LinkedIn

Richard Hunt, President
Janet Pike, Executive Assistant

Federal legislative developments.
Frequency: Monthly
Circulation: 10,000
Founded in: 1919
Printed in on newsprint stock

2849 Bank Directors Briefing
American Bankers Association
1120 Connecticut Avenue NW
Washington, DC 20036-3902

202-635-5000
800-226-5377; *Fax:* 202-663-7597;
www.aba.com

Matthew Williams, Chair
John Ikard, Vice Chairman

Newsletter reporting on legislative developments and management issues affecting community banks and their boards of directors.
Frequency: Monthly
Circulation: 33130

2850 Bank Rate Monitor
Bank Rate
11760 US Highway 1
Suite 500
North Palm Beach, FL 33408-8888

561-630-2400; *Fax:* 561-625-4540;
www.bankrate.com

Don Munsell, Production Director

Independent national source for the financial industry.
Cost: $499.00
4 Pages
Frequency: Weekly
Mailing list available for rent: 750 names
Printed in 3 colors

2851 Bank Technology News
SourceMedia
1 State Street Plaza
27th floor
New York, NY 10004-1561

212-803-8200
800-803-3424; *Fax:* 212-843-9608
custserv@sourcemedia.com;
www.sourcemedia.com

Douglas Manoni, CEO
Richard Antoneck, CFO
Cost: $99.00
Frequency: Monthly
Founded in: 2005

2852 Bank Tellers Report
Sheshunoff Information Services
4120 Freidrich Lane
Suite 100
Austin, TX 78744

512-305-6500
800-456-2340; *Fax:* 512-305-6575
customercare.sis@sheshunoff.com;
www.sheshunoff.com

Bob Mate, CEO
Marge Simmons, Author

General interest publication for bank tellers.
Cost: $449.00
Frequency: Monthly
Founded in: 1975

2853 Bank and S&L Quarterly Rating Service
Sheshunoff Information Services
4120 Freidrich Lane
Suite 100
Austin, TX 78744

512-305-6500
800-456-2340; *Fax:* 512-305-6575
customercare.sis@sheshunoff.com;
www.sheshunoff.com

Bob Mate, CEO

Statistical reports and research on savings and loan institutions.
Cost: $580.00
Frequency: Quarterly
Circulation: 5000
Mailing list available for rent: 5000 names

2854 Banks in Insurance Report
John Wiley & Sons
111 River St
Hoboken, NJ 07030-5790

201-748-6000
800-225-5945; *Fax:* 201-748-6088
info@wiley.com; www.wiley.com

Mari Baker, CEO
Jean-Lou Chameau, President
Linda Katehi, Chancellor

Highlights the steps necessary for expansion into insurance products and services through articles that report on legislative activities, regulatory concerns, business and strategies.
Cost: $745.00
16 Pages
Frequency: Monthly
ISSN: 8756-6079
Founded in: 1807
Printed in one color on matte stock

2855 Cheklist
BKB Publications
98 Greenwich Avenue
1st Floor
New York, NY 10011-7743

212-807-7933; *Fax:* 212-807-1821
bkbpub1@ix.netcom.com

Brian Burkart, Publisher
Charlene Komar Storey, Editor

Features general news, feature articles, legislative updates, reports on trends, legal advice, marketing ideas, product information and news of state and national association activities.
Cost: $35.00
Frequency: Quarterly
Circulation: 16,000
ISSN: 1066-3029

2856 Client Quarterly
WPI Communications
55 Morris Ave
Suite 300
Springfield, NJ 07081-1422
973-467-8700
800-323-4995; *Fax:* 973-467-0368
info@wpicommunications.com;
www.wpicomm.com
Steve Klinghoffer, Owner/Publisher
Lori Klinghoffer, Executive Vice President
Information and advice on financial, business and tax matters.
Frequency: Quarterly
Founded in: 1952

2857 Community Bank President
Siefer Consultants
525 Cayuga Street
PO Box 1384
Storm Lake, IA 50588-1384
712-660-1026; *Fax:* 866-680-5866
info@siefer.com; www.siefer.com
Dan Siefer, Publisher
Profit making opportunities for financial institutions.
Cost: $297.00
8 Pages
Frequency: Monthly

2858 Compliance & Management Bulletin
American Bankers Association
1120 Connecticut Avenue NW
Washington, DC 20036-3902
202-663-5000
800-226-5377; *Fax:* 202-828-4540
custserv@aba.com; www.aba.com
Frank Keating, President/CEO
Albert Kelly, Chair
Includes the information you need to keep up with and respond to the latest in new and revised laws and regulations affecting your institution's management and operations.
Cost: $375.00
Frequency: Published, As Needed
Circulation: 2000
Founded in: 1992

2859 Consumer Bankers Association
Consumer Bankers Association
1000 Wilson Blvd
Suite 2500
Arlington, VA 22209-3912
703-276-1750; *Fax:* 703-528-1290
webmaster@cbanet.org; www.cbanet.org
Richard Hunt, President
Janet Pike, Executive Assistant
Legislative newsletter on retail banking for association members.
Founded in: 1919

2860 Credit Card Management
Thomson Financial Publishing
1 State St
27th Floor
New York, NY 10004-1481
212-825-8445
800-328-9378; *Fax:* 212-292-5216
general.info@thomson.com;
www.sourcemedia.com
Douglas Manoni, CEO
Richard Antoneck, CFO
Information on the major developments in the credit card industry.
Cost: $98.00
74 Pages
Frequency: Monthly
Circulation: 19000
Printed in 4 colors on glossy stock

2861 Credit Union Journal
SourceMedia
1 State St
27th Floor
New York, NY 10004-1561
212-803-8200
800-803-3424; *Fax:* 212-843-9608
custserv@sourcemedia.com;
www.sourcemedia.com
Douglas Manoni, CEO
Richard Antoneck, CFO
Cost: $99.00
Frequency: Monthly
Founded in: 2005

2862 DTCC Newsletter
Depository Trust Company
55 Water St
New York, NY 10041-0024
212-855-1000; *Fax:* 212-855-2350
info@dtcc.com; www.dtcc.com
Robert Druskin, Chairman
Michael Bodson, President
Information for the banking and securities industry.
Frequency: Monthly
Circulation: 7000
Founded in: 1999

2863 Daily Treasury Statement
Financial Management Service
3700 E West Highway
Room 502A
Hysttaville, MD 20782
202-874-9790
800-826-9434; *Fax:* 202-874-8447
dts.Questions@fms.treas.gov;
www.fms.treas.gov
Richard L Gregg, Commissioner
Melanie Rigney, Editor
This report offers the latest news of the Treasury Department.
Frequency: Daily
Founded in: 1974

2864 Digest for Corporate & Securities Lawyers
Bowne & Company
55 Water Street
New York, NY 10041
212-924-500
212-229-3400; www.bowne.com
Bruce Brumberg, Editor-in-Chief
Johanna McKenzie, Editor
Susan Koffman, Editor
Karen Axelrod, Managing Editor
David Shea, Chairman/CEO
Summaries of articles on corporate finance, mergers acquisitions, initial public offerings (ipos) and restructuring. Selects articles from hundreds of publications focusing on articles trends, strategies and advice on deal structuring.
2700 Members
Frequency: Monthly
Founded in: 1775

2865 Direct Deposit Authorization Forms
NACHA: Electronic Payments Association
13450 Sunrise Valley Drive
Suite 100
Herndon, VA 20171
703-561-1100; *Fax:* 703-787-0996
info@nacha.org; www.nacha.org
Janet O Estep, CEO
Maurice Haitema, Chairperson
These authorizations are for companies looking for generic authorization forms that market ACH benefits to consumers.
Cost: $30.00
Frequency: Monthly

2866 Directors & Trustees Digest
American Bankers Association
1120 Connecticut Avenue NW
Washington, DC 20036-3902
202-663-5000; *Fax:* 202-828-4540
custserv@aba.com; www.aba.com
Frank Keating, President/CEO
Albert Kelly, Chairman
Steven Crowe, Treasurer
Monique Hanis, Marketing/Business Development
Provides corporate governance guidance, outlines board legal and fiduciary responsibilities and offers resourceful information on board management relations.
Frequency: Monthly

2867 Examiner
Conference of State Bank Supervisors
1129 20th Street, N.W.
9th Floor
Washington, DC 20036-4327
202-296-2840; *Fax:* 202-296-1928;
www.csbs.org
Neal Milner, CEO
Thomas Harlow, CFO
Cecelia Smith, Senior Manager, Administration
John Gorman, General Counsel
Provides news, analysis and commentary on the important events affecting the state banking system.
Frequency: Weekly

2868 FSPA Newsletter
Financial & Security Products Association
Plaza Ladera, 5300 Sequoia NW
Suite 205
Albuquerque, NM 87120
505-839-7958
800-843-6082; *Fax:* 505-839-0017
info@fspa1.com; www.fspa1.com
Mark Thatcher, Chairman
Bill Mercer, President
John M Vrabec, Executive Director
Offers timely ideas and techniques to help you compete and run your business more effectively. Also provides low-cost opportunities for members to advertise their products and/or services within the body of the newsletter, or in an insert included with the newsletter mailing.
Frequency: Monthly

2869 Federal Reserve Bulletin
Board of Governors of the Federal Reserve System
20th St & Constitution Ave N
Washington, DC 20551-0001
202-452-3284; *Fax:* 202-452-3101;
www.federalreserve.gov
Social Media: Facebook, Twitter, LinkedIn
Ben S Bernanke, Chairman
Janet Yellen, Vice Chairman
Reports on analysis on economic developments, regulatory issues and new data. The quarterly version will no longer be published, however the Board will print an annual compendium.
Frequency: Annual
Founded in: 1913

2870 Federal Reserve Regulatory Service
Federal Reserve Board Publishers
20th St & Constitution Ave N
Washington, DC 20551-0001
202-452-3000; *Fax:* 202-452-3819
publication-bog@frbog.frb.gov;

www.federalreserve.gov
Social Media: Facebook, Twitter, LinkedIn

Ben S Bernanke, Chairman
Janet Yellen, Vice Chairman

Consumer and community affairs.
Cost: $200.00
Frequency: Monthly

2871 Financial Services Daily
SNL Securities
One SNL Plaza
PO Box 2124
Charlottesvle, VA 22902

434-977-1600; *Fax:* 434-977-4466
CustomerService@snl.com; www.snl.com

Mike Chinn, President/CEO
Nick Cafferillo, COO

Comprehensive daily coverage of the financial services and technology sectors.
Cost: $795.00
40 Pages
Frequency: Monthly
Founded in: 1987

2872 Funds Transfer Report
Bankers Research
PO Box 431
Westport, CT 06881-0431
Ted Volckhausen Sr, Publisher/Co-Editor
Ted Volckhausen Jr, Editor

Offers banking and financial information to professionals and consumers.
Cost: $324.00
Frequency: Monthly

2873 Global Investment Technology
Global Investment Technology
909 Third Avenue
27th Floor
New York, NY 10022

212-370-3700; *Fax:* 212-370-4606
info@globalinv.com; www.globalinv.com

Micheal Horton, Publisher
Paven Saeghel, Editor-in-Chief

Focuses exclusively on strategic business trends, operations, and automation issues facing US and non-US investment institutions and banks.
Cost: $695.00
Frequency: Bi-Weekly
Circulation: 1800
Founded in: 1991

2874 Global Survey of Regulatory & Market Developments in Banking
Institute of International Bankers
299 Park Ave
17th Floor
New York, NY 10171-3896

212-421-1611; *Fax:* 212-421-1119
iib@iib.org; www.iib.org
Social Media: Facebook, Twitter, LinkedIn

Sarah ""sally"" Miller, CEO
Richard Coffman, General Counsel
William Goodwin, Communications Director

The study documents the economic contributions that international banks make to the United States, and also addresses the benefits that other countries enjoy from the extensive activities of United States and other non-domestic banks in their markets.
Frequency: Annual

2875 IBES Monthly Comments
Lynch, Jones and Ryan
1633 Broadway
48th Floor
New York, NY 10019

212-310-9500
800-992-7526; *Fax:* 646-223-9081;
www.ljr.com

Stanley Chamberlin, Publisher
Todd W Burns, President

Monitors changes in global earning estimates database.
Founded in: 1966

2876 ICBA Washington Report
Independent Community Bankers of American
1615 L Street NW
Suite 900
Washington, DC 20036

202-659-8111
info@icba.org; www.icba.org

Camden R Fine, President/CEO
Rachael Solomon, Advertising Contact

Provides detailed coverage of important federal legislative and regulatory developments specifically for community bankers.
Cost: $60.00
Frequency: Monthly

2877 IFSA Newsletter
International Financial Services Association
1120 Connecticut Avenue, NW
Washington, DC 20036

20 -66 -757; *Fax:* 202-663-5538
info@baft-ifsa.com; www.ifsaonline.org
Social Media: Facebook, Twitter, LinkedIn

Tod Burwell, Vice President
250 Pages
Frequency: Quarterly
Founded in: 1924

2878 In Focus
National Assn of Government Guaranteed Lenders
215 East 9th Avenue
Stillwater, OK 74074

405-377-4022; *Fax:* 405-377-3931
bfortune@naggl.com; www.naggl.org

Tony Wilkinson, President/CEO
Jennifer Sterrett O'Neill, EVP/COO
Jenifer Brake, Assistant VP Marketing
Jennifer Sterrett-O'Neill, Assistant VP Communications

Practical tips that will help you build the little efficiencies that make a big difference.
Frequency: Monthly

2879 Inside Mortgage Compliance
Inside Mortgage Finance Publishers
7910 Woodmont Ave
Suite 1000
Bethesda, MD 20814-7019

301-951-1240; *Fax:* 301-656-1709;
www.imfpubs.com

Guy Cecala, Owner/Publisher

Keeps executives on top of crucial and evolving legal and regulatory issues. Covers fair housing, predatory lending, consumer protection, RESPA, TILA, lawsuits. Features monthly CRA ratings.
Cost: $571.00
14 Pages
Frequency: Monthly
ISSN: 1093-605X
Founded in: 1990
Mailing list available for rent: 750 names
Printed in 2 colors on matte stock

2880 Inside Strategy
Strategy Research Corporation
100 NW 37th Avenue
Miami, FL 33125

305-649-5400; *Fax:* 305-643-5584
strategy@canect.net;
www.strategyresearch.com

Johanna Strouss, Editor
Richard Tobin, President

Inside Strategy is a newsletter that covers trends and developments in Latin America and the US Hispanic market mostly obtained from SRC, studies, products services and reports.
38511 Pages
Frequency: Monthly
Founded in: 1998

2881 Inside The GSEs
Inside Mortgage Finance Publishers
7910 Woodmont Ave
Suite 1000
Bethesda, MD 20814-7019

301-951-1240; *Fax:* 301-656-1709
service@imfpubs.com; www.imfpubs.com

Guy Cecala, Owner
Greg Johnson, Editor
John Bancroft, Managing Editor
Mary L Probka, Director Marketing/Circulation

Subscribers know the latest on GSE finance, products, political contributions, their critics and supporters, and news on potential reform, controversies and regulatory activities.
Cost: $763.00
14 Pages
Frequency: Bi-Weekly
ISSN: 1093-605X
Founded in: 1985
Mailing list available for rent: 400 names
Printed in 2 colors on matte stock

2882 MSRB Manual
Municipal Securities Rulemaking Board
1900 Duke St
Suite 600
Alexandria, VA 22314-3461

703-797-6600; *Fax:* 703-797-6700
MSRBsupport@msrb.org; www.msrb.org

Lynnette Hotkis, Executive Director
Marcelo Vieira, Director Research

Rules of the Municipal Rule-Making Board.
Cost: $7.00
Founded in: 1975

2883 NACHA: Electronic Payments Association Newsletter
NACHA: The Electronic Payments Association
13450 Sunrise Valley Drive
Suite 100
Herndon, VA 20171

703-561-1100; *Fax:* 703-787-0996
info@nacha.org; www.nacha.org

Marcie Haitema, Chairperson
Janet O Estep, CEO

Articles on industry self regulatory organizations for automated clearing house payment systems and other electronic payments.
Cost: $120.00
Printed in 2 colors on matte stock

2884 NAGGL News Flash
National Assn of Government Guaranteed Lenders
215 East 9th Avenue
Stillwater, OK 74074

405-377-4022; *Fax:* 404-377-3931
bfortune@naggl.com; www.naggl.org

Tony Wilkinson, President/CEO
Jennifer Sterrett O'Neill, EVP/COO
Jenifer Brake, Assistant VP Marketing
Jennifer Sterrett-O'Neill, Assistant VP Communications

This email is an at-a-glance review of recent industry news.
Frequency: Bi-Monthly

2885 Nilson Report
HSN Consultants
1110 Eugenia Place
Suite 100
Carpinteria, CA 930113-992
805-684-8800; *Fax:* 805-684-8825
info@nilsonreport.com; www.nilsonreport.com
H Spencer Nilson, Publisher
Credit card newsletter.
Cost: $945.00
12 Pages
Frequency: BiWeekly

2886 Opportunities for Banks in Life Insurance
American Association of Bank Directors
1250 24th Street, NW
Suite 700
Washington, DC 20037
20 -46 -488; *Fax:* 202-349-8080
info@aabd.org; www.aabd.org
David Baris, Executive Director
The guide reviews best insurance sales practices, distribution strategies, selling through investment brokers, using licensed branch bankers, referrals from investment specialists, referrals from licensed branch bankers, stand alone life specialists, direct sales and more.
Cost: $12.50

2887 Origination News
Thomson Financial
One State Street Plaza
27th floor
New York, NY 10004
212-803-8760; *Fax:* 212-292-5216;
www.originationnews.com
Elaine Yadlon, Plant Manager
Richard J Harrington, President/CEO
Information for mortgage industry executives on mortgage brokers, mortgage bankers and mortgage executives in commercial banks, savings banks, savings and loan associations and credit unions.
Cost: $78.00
Frequency: Monthly

2888 Payments System Report
National Automated Clearing House Association
13450 Sunrise Valley Drive
Suite 100
Herndon, VA 20171-4607
703-561-1100
800-487-9180; *Fax:* 703-787-0996
info@nacha.org; www.nacha.org
Social Media: Facebook, Twitter, LinkedIn
Janet O Estep, CEO
Official source for Automated Clearing House (ACH) news and information. Contains reports on rule changes, legislative and regulatory developments, policy issues, market research, product developments and marketing solutions.
Frequency: Monthly

2889 Peer News
American Bankers Association
1120 Connecticut Avenue NW
Washington, DC 20036
202-635-5000
800-226-5377; *Fax:* 202-828-4540
icb@aba.com; www.aba.com/icbcertifications
Frank Keating, President/CEO
Albert Kelly, Chairman
Steven Crowe, Treasurer
Monique Hanis, Marketing/Business Development
Mark DeBaugh, Marketing/Communications Manager
ICB members receive a newsletter that shares program developments, member career notes, insights from ICB leadership, the latest continuing education opportunities, and more.
Frequency: Quarterly

2890 Pratt's Bank Security Report
AS Pratt & Sons
805 15th St. NW
Third Floor
Washington, DC 20005-2207
800-572-2797
customercare.sis@sheshunoff.com;
www.aspratt.com
Peter Knopp, Editor
Security officers and consultants can keep up with the latest developments affecting bank security by subscribing to Pratt's Bank Security Report.
Cost: $455.00
Frequency: Monthly
Founded in: 1867

2891 RTC Suits Against Savings Institution Directors and Officers
American Association of Bank Directors
1250 24th Street, NW
Suite 700
Washington, DC 20037
20 -46 -488; *Fax:* 202-349-8080
info@aabd.org; www.aabd.org
David Baris, Executive Director
This study reviews all 90 of the cases in the RTC's public files that were filed by the RTC against directors and officers.
Cost: $85.00

2892 Regional Mortgage Market Report
Mortgage Bankers Association
1717 Rhode Island Avenue, NW
Suite 400
Washington, DC 20036
202-557-2700
membership@mortgagebankers.org;
www.mortgagebankers.org
Social Media: Facebook, Twitter, LinkedIn
The Regional Mortgage Market Report for MSAs and/or states has been designed to provide mortgage professionals with a primary source of information to help identify mortgage lending opportunities and manage the risks associated with mortgage servicing.
Cost: $395.00
Frequency: Quarterly
Founded in: 1914

2893 Report of Task Force on Asset Freezes of Bank Directors and Officers
American Association of Bank Directors
1250 24th Street, NW
Suite 700
Washington, DC 20037
20 -46 -488; *Fax:* 202-349-8080
info@aabd.org; www.aabd.org
David Baris, Executive Director
Cost: $25.00

2894 SCOR Report
Stewart Gordon Associates
PO Box 781992
Dallas, TX 75378-1992
972-620-2489; *Fax:* 972-406-0213;
www.scor-report.com
Tom Stewart Gordon, Publisher
C Delton Simmons, Circulation Manager
Anne D Hall, Production Manager
Capital information alternatives for small business. Target audience: small business, their lawyers and accountants.
Cost: $280.00
Founded in: 1994

2895 SNL Bank & Thrift Daily
SNL Securities
212 7th Street NE
Charlottesville, VA 22902-2124
434-977-1600; *Fax:* 434-977-4466
subscriptions@snl.com; www.snl.com
Social Media: Twitter, Youtube
Michael Chinn, President/CEO
Nick Cafferillo, COO
Summary of previous week's acquisition announcements, branch sales, merger conversions, FDIC transactions and deal updates and perspectives.
Cost: $1700.00
Frequency: Weekly
Founded in: 1987

2896 SNL REIT Weekly
SNL Securities
212 7th Street NE
Charlottesville, VA 22902
434-977-1600; *Fax:* 434-977-4466
subscriptions@snl.com; www.snl.com
Social Media: Twitter, Youtube
Michael Chinn, President/CEO
Nick Cafferillo, COO
Fax: newsletter that summarizes the previous week's activity involving REITs. Includes comprehensive articles on current industry trends, condensed news stories, recent capital offerings and the latest market information.
Cost: $496.00
15 Pages
Frequency: Weekly
Founded in: 1987

2897 Secondary Mortgage Markets
Federal Home Loan Mortgage Corporation
8200 Jones Branch Drive
McLean, VA 22102-3110
703-903-2000
800-424-5401; *Fax:* 703-903-4045;
www.freddiemac.com
Charles E. Haldeman, CEO
Ralph Boyd, Executive VP Community Relations
Covers buying and selling residential and commercial mortgage-backed and asset-backed loans, marketing, and risk management.
Frequency: Monthly
Circulation: 15000
Founded in: 1970

2898 Securities & Investments M&A
SNL Securities
212 7th Street NE
Charlottesvle, VA 22902
434-977-1600; *Fax:* 434-977-4466
CustomerService@snl.com; www.snl.com
Social Media: Twitter, Youtube
Michael Chinn, President/CEO
Nick Cafferillo, COO
Fully devoted to M&A in the securities and asset management sectors.
Cost: $795.00
40 Pages
Frequency: Monthly
Founded in: 1987

2899 Specialty Finance M&A
SNL Securities

212 7th Street NE
Charlottesvle, VA 22902

434-977-1600; *Fax:* 434-977-4466
CustomerService@snl.com; www.snl.com
Social Media: Twitter, Youtube

Michael Chinn, President/CEO
Nick Cafferillo, COO

A unique source dedicated exclusively to specialty finance M&A.
Cost: $795.00
40 Pages
Frequency: Monthly
Founded in: 1987

2900 Study of Leading Banks in Insurance
American Bankers Insurance Association
1120 Connecticut Avenue NW
Washington, DC 20036

202-663-5163
800-226-5377; *Fax:* 202-828-4546
vbarton@aba.com; www.aba.com

Frank Keating, President/Chairman
Albert Kelly, Chairman
David Cissell, Secretary
Neal Aton, Treasurer

Presents the findings from the eighth research of the current and planned insurance activities of U.S. banks. Designed as a management tool for executives who need to understand how the bank-insurance industry is developing.
300 Members
Frequency: Annual
Founded in: 2001

2901 U.S. Banker
SourceMedia
1 State St
27th Floor
New York, NY 10004-1561

212-803-8200
800-803-3424; *Fax:* 212-843-9608
custserv@sourcemedia.com;
www.sourcemedia.com

Douglas Manoni, CEO
Richard Antoneck, CFO
Cost: $99.00
Frequency: Monthly
Founded in: 2005

2902 World Bank News
World Bank
1818 H St Nw
Room U11-147
Washington, DC 20433-0002

202-473-1000; *Fax:* 202-477-6391;
www.mehr.org

Graeme Wheeler, CEO
Paul Wolfowitz, President
Cynthia Delgadillo, Production Manager

For journalists and the developing community
Frequency: Fortnightly
Circulation: 9000
Founded in: 1980

Magazines & Journals

2903 A Guide to Implementing Direct Payment
NACHA: Electronic Payments Association
13450 Sunrise Valley Drive
Suite 100
Herndon, VA 20171

703-561-1100; *Fax:* 703-787-0996
info@nacha.org; www.nacha.org
Social Media: Facebook, Twitter, LinkedIn

Janet O Estep, CEO

A complete overview of these popular ACH applications. Also discussed are benefits, costs, operational/implementation concerns and promotional efforts. Included are sample promotional materials and implementation checklists.

2904 A Profile of State Chartered Banking
1129 20th Street, N.W.
9th Floor
Washington, DC 20036-4327

202-296-2840
800-886-2727; *Fax:* 202-296-1928
rstromberg@csbs.org; www.csbs.org

John Ryan, President/CEO
Cecelia Smith, Senior Manager, Administration
54 Pages
Frequency: Monthly
Founded in: 1902

2905 ABA Bank Compliance
American Bankers Association
1120 Connecticut Avenue NW
Washington, DC 20036-3971

202-635-5000
800-226-5377; *Fax:* 202-663-7543
custserv@aba.com; www.aba.com

Frank Keating, President
Albert Kelly, Chairman

The source for timely, authoritative analysis of the ever-changing regulatory environment. Covers all the current regulatory issues, such as Privacy and E-Commerce, and perennial Compliance focus areas, such as lending, the Community Reinvestment Act, risk management, training and technology.
Cost: $450.00
Frequency: Bi-Monthly
Founded in: 1875

2906 ABA Bank Marketing
American Bankers Association
1120 Connecticut Avenue NW
Washington, DC 20036-3971

202-635-5000
800-226-5377; *Fax:* 202-828-4540
custserv@aba.com; www.aba.com

Frank Keating, President
Albert Kelly, Chairman

A designed package of marketing intelligence, featuring essential industry news, in-depth articles, award-winning columnists and opinions, useful case studies and time-saving advice.
Cost: $120.00
Frequency: Monthly
Founded in: 1875

2907 ABA Bank Marketing Survey Report
ABA Marketing Network
1120 Connecticut Avenue NW
Washington, DC 20036-3971

202-663-5000
800-226-5377; *Fax:* 202-828-4540
marketingnetwork@aba.com;
www.aba.com/marketingnetwork/

Frank Keating, President
Albert Kelly, Chairman

The ABA Bank Marketing Survey Report provides comprehensive detailed benchmarks of bank marketing in such areas as marketing expenditures, marketing functions, market segmentation strategies, cross-selling/sales incentives, direct marketing, Internet marketing and advertising agency use.

2908 ABA Banking Journal
Simmons-Boardman Publishing Corporation
345 Hudson St
12th Floor
New York, NY 10014-7123

212-620-7200; *Fax:* 212-633-1165;
www.simmonsboardman.com

Arthur J McGinnis Jr, President

The official journal of the American Bank Association, reporting on the banking industry.
Frequency: Monthly
Circulation: 32867
Founded in: 1908
Mailing list available for rent

2909 ABA Consumer Banking Digest
American Bankers Association
1120 Connecticut Avenue NW
Washington, DC 20036-3902

202-635-5000
800-226-5377; *Fax:* 202-828-4547
drhodes@aba.com; www.aba.com

Frank Keating, President
Albert Kelly, Chairman

Provides perspectives on the latest developments, shifts and changes in the e-commerce sector. The goal is to provide a comprehensive, yet concise, description of current events shaping the rapidly emerging world of e-commerce and banking.
Cost: $450.00
Frequency: Bi-Monthly
Founded in: 1875

2910 ABA Reference Guide for Regulatory Compliance
American Bankers Association
1120 Connecticut Avenue NW
Washington, DC 20036-3200

202-635-5000
800-226-5377; *Fax:* 202-663-7597;
www.aba.com

Frank Keating, President
Albert Kelly, Chairman

Ideal source for Compliance Managers, Department Managers and Staff, Product Managers, and Retail/Branch Managers and those preparing for the Certified Regulatory Compliance Manager Exam.
Cost: $350.00
Frequency: Annual

2911 ABA Trust & Investments
American Bankers Association
1120 Connecticut Avenue NW
Washington, DC 20036

202-635-5000
800-226-5377; *Fax:* 202-828-4540
custserv@aba.com; www.aba.com

Frank Keating, President
Albert Kelly, Chairman

Brings current, authoritative, wide-ranging coverage and updates on all aspects of the trust and investments industry
Cost: $120.00
15 Pages
Frequency: Bi-Monthly

2912 ACH Marketing Handbook: A Guide for Financial Institutions & Companies
NACHA: The Electronic Payments Association
13450 Sunrise Valley Drive
Suite 100
Herndon, VA 20171

703-561-1100; *Fax:* 703-787-0996
info@nacha.org; www.nacha.org

Marcie Haitema, Chairperson
Janet O Estep, CEO

Designed for financial institutions and companies to assist them in understanding ACH products and services-their benefits, risk management considerations, and consumer perspectives.
Cost: $70.00
Frequency: Annual+

2913 **ACH Operating Rules & Guidelines**
NACHA: Electronic Payments Association
13450 Sunrise Valley Drive
Suite 100
Herndon, VA 20171

703-561-1100; *Fax:* 703-787-0996
info@nacha.org; www.nacha.org

Janet O Estep, CEO
Marcie Haitema, Chairperson

Reflects the results of the Rules Simplifications initiative.
Cost: $78.00

2914 **ACH Operating Rules, Corporate Edition**
NACHA: Electronic Payments Association
13450 Sunrise Valley Drive
Suite 100
Herndon, VA 20171

703-561-1100; *Fax:* 703-787-0996
info@nacha.org; www.nacha.org

Janet O Estep, CEO
Marcie Haitema, Chairperson

Reflects the results of the Rules Simplification initiative. Previously organized around major topics, the simplified Rules framework is structured around the rights and responsibilities of participants in the ACH Network.
Cost: $46.00

2915 **ACH Settlement Guide**
NACHA: Electronic Payments Association
13450 Sunrise Valley Drive
Suite 100
Herndon, VA 20171

703-561-1100; *Fax:* 703-787-0996
info@nacha.org; www.nacha.org
Social Media: Facebook, Twitter, LinkedIn

Janet O Estep, CEO

Designed to provide a thorough working knowledge of how money flows through the ACH Network and to equip financial institutions with the necessary tools to reconcile the daily ACH. Included in this publication are examples of statements, ACH advices and a sample balancing worksheet that financial institutions can use as a model for daily reconciling. This document was written as a direct result of financial institutions losing money due to the mismanagement of the ACH settlement function.

2916 **AFP Exchange**
Association for Financial Professionals
4520 East West Hwy
Suite 750
Bethesda, MD 20814-3319

301-907-2862; *Fax:* 301-907-2864;
www.afponline.org

Michael Connolly, Chairman of the Board
Susan Glass, Vice Chairman
James Kaitz, President & CEO

AFP Exchange is published for financial professionals. Editorial highlights include case studies and practical business information. Regular departments include outlook, new products and services, calendar and book reviews.
Cost: $90.00
80 Pages
Frequency: Bi-Monthly
Circulation: 12000
Founded in: 1979
Printed in 4 colors on glossy stock

2917 **AITCO Membership Directory**
Association of Independent Trust Companies
8 S Michigan Ave
Suite 1000
Chicago, IL 60603-3452

312-223-1611; *Fax:* 312-580-0165
aitco@gss.net; www.aitco.net

Douglas Nunn, President
Marcia Williams, Treasurer
Tom Blank, General Counsel/Secretary

Provides members with contact information on peers as well as industry vendors. This reference tool also include a listing of key officers as well as detailed descriptions of the company's product line and specialty areas.
50+ Pages

2918 **American Banker**
American Banker/SourceMedia
1 State St
27th Floor
New York, NY 10004-1561

212-803-8450
800-221-1809; *Fax:* 212-843-9600;
www.sourcemedia.com

Douglas Manoni, CEO
Richard Antoneck, CFO

Focuses on the continuing changes in banking, including lending, money market shifts, developments in operations and technology, marketing, mortgages and mergers.
Cost: $945.00
Circulation: 18754
Founded in: 1835

2919 **BAI Banking Strategies**
Bank Administration Institute
115 S. LaSalle Street
Suite 3300
Chicago, IL 60603-3801

312-683-2464
888-284-4078; *Fax:* 312-683-2373
info@bai.org; www.bai.org
Social Media: Facebook, Twitter, LinkedIn, Youtube

Lewis Fischer, Chairman of the Board
Scott Peters, Vice Chairman

Offers insightful editorial perspective in-depth unbiased coverage of important strategic issues and industry best practices.
Frequency: Monthly

2920 **BISA Magazine**
Bank Insurance and Securities Association
2025 M Street NW
Suite 800
Washington, DC 20036

202-367-1111; *Fax:* 202-367-2111
bisa@BISAnet.org; www.bisanet.org

Jeff Hartney, Executive Director
Daniel J. McCormack, President
Andrew W. Singer, Editor-iN-Chief
Jason Meyers, Managing Editor

The official publication of the Bank Insurance & Securities Association, sets the standard for in-depth industry reporting. Offers readers expert advice, exemplary editorials, in-depth articles and timely news updates.
Founded in: 2002

2921 **Bank Director News**
American Association of Bank Directors
1250 24th Street, NW
Suite 700
Washington, DC 20037

202-463-4888; *Fax:* 202-349-8080
info@aabd.org; www.aabd.org

David Baris, Executive Director
Frequency: quarterly

2922 **Bank News**
Bank News Publications
PO Box 29156
Shawnee Mission, KS 66205-9156

913-261-7000
800-336-1120; *Fax:* 913-261-7010
info@banknews.com; www.banknews.com

Janet Holman, President & Publisher
Joel Holman, CEO & Publisher

News and features for banks and bankers.
Cost: $79.00
64 Pages
Frequency: Monthly
Circulation: 7000
Founded in: 1901
Printed in 4 colors on glossy stock

2923 **Bank Notes**
510 King Street
Suite 410
Alexandria, VA 22314

703-549-0977
800-966-7475; *Fax:* 703-548-5945
eba@envirobank.org; www.envirobank.org

Rick Ferguson, President
Scott Beckerman, Treasurer
76 Pages
Frequency: Bi-Monthly
Founded in: 1994

2924 **Bank Systems & Technology**
CMP Media
240 West 35th Street
New York, NY 10001

212-928-8400; *Fax:* 212-600-3080;
www.cmp.com

David Leven, CEO
Dame Helen Alexander, Chairman

In-depth look into the new age of banking where total integration of technology is the driving force of new product business growth. Features deliver critical information on the strategic use of technology for increased profitability and productivity, in turn providing bankers with the tools to gain the competitive advantage on today's changing financial services landscape.
Cost: $52.00
Frequency: Monthly
Circulation: 23753
Founded in: 1918

2925 **Bank Technology News**
Thomson Media
1 State St
27th Floor
New York, NY 10004-1481

212-803-8200; *Fax:* 212-843-9600
custserv@sourcemedia.com;
www.banktechnews.com
Social Media: Facebook, Twitter

Penny Crosman, Editor in Chief
Douglas J. Manoni, CEO

The leading source for financial services technology coverage, written for those individuals who are responsible for the front, middle and back office technology needs of their financial institutes.
52 Pages
Frequency: Monthly
Founded in: 1987
Mailing list available for rent

2926 **Bankers Digest**
P.O. Box 743006
Dallas, TX 75374-3006

214-221-4544; *Fax:* 214-221-4546
bankersdigest@bankersdigest.com;
www.bankersdigest.com

Bonnie J Blackman, Owner
R Blackman Jr, Managing Editor

A weekly news magazine devoted to the southwest banking news. Accepts advertising.
Cost: $29.00
16 Pages
Frequency: Weekly
Circulation: 3100
ISSN: 0140-1800
Founded in: 1942
Printed in 2 colors on glossy stock

2927 **Bankers' Magazine**
Thomson Reuters
195 Broadway
Suite 4
New York, NY 10007-3124

646-822-2000
800-231-1860; *Fax:* 646-822-2800
trta.lei-support@thomsonreuters.com;
www.ria.thomsonreuters.com

Elaine Yadlon, Plant Manager
Thomas H Glocer, CEO & Director
Robert D Daleo, Chief Financial Officer
Kelli Crane, Senior Vice President & CIO

Written by bank professionals who offer urgent information about the banking industry to the banking community.
Cost: $115.00
Frequency: Bi-Monthly
Founded in: 1935

2928 **Banking Strategies**
Bank Administration Institute
115 S. LaSalle Street
Suite 3300
Chicago, IL 60603

312-683-2464
800-224-9889; *Fax:* 312-683-2373
info@bai.org; www.bai.org
Social Media: Facebook, Twitter, LinkedIn, Youtube

Lewis Fischer, Chairman of the Board
Scott Peters, Vice Chairman

Includes information on finance, economics, planning, operations, regulations, retail, technology and human resources management.
Cost: $66.50
66 Pages
Circulation: 42175
ISSN: 1091-6385

2929 **Banking Strategies Magazine**
Bank Administration Institute
115 S LaSalle St
Suite 3300
Chicago, IL 60603

312-683-2464
888-284-4078; *Fax:* 312-683-2373
info@bai.org; www.bai.org
Social Media: Facebook, Twitter, LinkedIn, Youtube

Lewis Fischer, Chairman of the Board
Scott Peters, Vice Chairman

To present the latest in best practices and thought leadership through high-quality, in-depth, unbiased editorial coverage of strategic and managerial issues in today's complex and dynamic financial services business.
Frequency: Annual

2930 **Broker Magazine**
Thomson Media
1 State St
27th floor
New York, NY 10004-1481

212-825-8445
888-501-8850; *Fax:* 212-292-5216;
www.brokerworldmag.com

Mark Fogarty, Editorial Director
Brad Finkelstein, Editor
Timothy Murphy, Group Publisher

Features on training, motivation, technology, legislation and marketing
Cost: $60.00
Frequency: Bi-Monthly

2931 **Business Credit**
Assn of Executives in Finance, Credit & In'tl Bus
8840 Columbia 100 Parkway
Columbia, MD 21045-2158

410-423-1840
888-256-3242; *Fax:* 410-740-5574
fcib_info@fcibglobal.com;
www.fcibglobal.com
Social Media: Twitter, LinkedIn

Kelly Bates, Chairperson
Robin Schauseil, President
Tom Demovic, Director

For professionals responsible for extending credit and collecting receivables. Topics include business law, lien law, technology, credit management, collections, deductions, fraud, credit risk, credit scoring, outsourcing, information services, trade finance and more.
Cost: $54.00
72 Pages
Frequency: 10x/Year
Circulation: 32000
Founded in: 1896
Printed in 4 colors on matte stock

2932 **Business Credit Magazine**
8840 Columbia 100 Parkway
Columbia, MD 21045-2158

410-423-1840
888-256-3242; *Fax:* 410-740-5574;
www.fcibglobal.com
Social Media: LinkedIn

Marta Chacon, Director, The Americas
Ron Shepherd, Director, Business Dev.
Noelin Hawkins, Director, Europe, Middle East

Business Credit
1000+ Members
Frequency: Monthly
Circulation: 38000
Founded in: 1919

2933 **CFA Digest**
CFA Institute
PO Box 3668
Charlottesville, VA 22903-0668

434-951-5499
800-247-8132; *Fax:* 434-951-5262
info@cfainstitute.org; www.cfainstitute.org
Social Media: Facebook, Twitter, LinkedIn

John Rogers, CEO
Daniel J Larocco, Co-Editor

Distills selected current industry research into short, easy-to-read summaries.
Frequency: Quarterly
Founded in: 1971

2934 **CFA Magazine**
CFA Insitute
Po Box 3668
Charlottesville, VA 22903-0668

434-951-5499
800-247-8132; *Fax:* 434-951-5262
info@cfainstitute.org; www.cfainstitute.org
Social Media: Facebook, Twitter, LinkedIn

John Rogers, CEO
Roger Mitchell, Associate Editor

A practice-based, professional member magazine. Created on the feedback from a series of worldwide focus groups and a member survey.
Frequency: Bi-Monthly
Founded in: 2003

2935 **CMBS World**
30 Broad Street
28th Floor
New York, NY 10004

212-509-1844; *Fax:* 212-509-1895
info@crefc.org; www.cmbs.org
Social Media: Facebook, Twitter, LinkedIn

Stephen Renna, CEO
Ed DeAngelo, VP

To inform, educate and stimulate meaningful discussions and exchanges among CMBS members on the risks and benefits of commercial mortgage-backed securities.
309 Pages
Frequency: Quarterly
Founded in: 1994

2936 **Community Bank President**
Siefer Consultants
PO Box 1384
Storm Lake, IA 50588-1384

712-732-7340; *Fax:* 712-732-7906

Dan Siefer, Publisher

Analysis of trends, new ideas and implementation strategies, regulatory compliance, and bank profitability. Provides a glimpse at the latest deposit and loan statistics, marketing and new technology updates and bank management issues.
Frequency: Monthly
Circulation: 1800

2937 **Community Banking Advisor**
624 Grassmere Park Drive
Suite 15
Nasvhille, TN 37211

615-377-3392
800-231-2524; *Fax:* 615-377-7092
info@bankingcpas.com;
www.bankingcpas.com

Brian Blaha, President

A publication for banking professionals that features articles on management, tax, operational, and other issues confronting community banks.
24 Pages
Frequency: Quarterly
Founded in: 1995

2938 **Compliance Manual**
NACHA: The Electronic Payments Association
13450 Sunrise Valley Drive
Suite 100
Herndon, VA 20171

703-561-1100; *Fax:* 703-787-0996
info@nacha.org; www.nacha.org

Janet O Estep, CEO
Marcie Haitema, Chairperson

Covers authorizations, disclosures, processing, funds availability, settlement, error resolution, returns, reversals, retention, audit, all Standard Entry Class Codes and much, much more.
Cost: $90.00

2939 **Credit Union Journal**
Thomson Media
1 State St
27th Floor
New York, NY 10004-1481

212-803-8200
800-221-1809; *Fax:* 800-843-9600

Richard.Scalise@sourcemedia.com; www.cujournal.com

Frank J Diekmann, Editor/Co-Publisher
Lisa Freeman, Managing Publisher

A surging economy, combined with competitive pricing policies and regulatory changes allowing credit unions to expand their field of membership.
Cost: $119.00
Frequency: Weekly

2940 Credit Union Management Magazine
Credit Union Executives Society
5510 Research Park Drive
PO Box 14167
Madison, WI 53708-167

608-271-2664
800-252-2664; *Fax:* 608-271-2303
cues@cues.org; www.cues.org
Social Media: Facebook, Twitter, LinkedIn

Fred Johnson, President/CEO
Mary Arnold, VP Publications
George Hofheimer, VP Professional Development
Barbara Kachelski, CAE, SVP/CIP

Published for credit union CEOs and senior management, the magazine focuses each month on general management, operations, marketing and human resource functions. Includes in-depth coverage of technology, facilities, finance, lending, staffing and card services, among other topics.
Cost: $129.00
11067 Members
Frequency: Monthly
Circulation: 8000
Founded in: 1962

2941 Documentary Credit World
International Financial Services Association
1120 Connecticut Avenue NW
Washington, DC 20036

20 -66 -757; *Fax:* 202-663-5538
info@baft-ifsa.com; www.ifsaonline.org

Frank Keating, President
Albert Kelly, Chairman

Published jointly by the Institute of International Banking Law and Practice and the IFSA. DCW is your source for information on LCs.
Cost: $595.00
Frequency: 10x/Year

2942 Electronic Payments Journal
NACHA: Electronic Payments Association
13665 Dulles Technology Dr
Suite 300
Herndon, VA 20171-4607

703-561-1100; *Fax:* 703-787-0996
info@nacha.org; www.nacha.org

Janet O Estep, CEO

Helps industry professionals to track the latest developments in electronic payments and provides in-depth coverage of a broad array of payment issues.
Founded in: 1978

2943 Electronic Payments Review and Buyer's Guide
NACHA: Electronic Payments Association
13450 Sunrise Valley Drive
Suite 100
Herndon, VA 20171

703-561-1100; *Fax:* 703-787-0996
info@nacha.org; www.nacha.org

Janet O Estep, CEO
Marcie Haitema, Chairperson

A directory of payment services with listings for ACH Services, Authentication & Security Solutions, B2B Invoicing & Presentment Services, Card Services, Check/Electronic Check Services, Consultants & Industry Associations, Consumer-Based Bill Payment & Presentment, Electronic Government Services, Electronic Consumer Services, International Payment Resources, Payment & Processing Software & Hardware, Thrid-Party Service Providers, and Wireless Payment & Commerce
Cost: $3.50
Frequency: Annual

2944 Federal Credit Union Magazine
National Association of Federal Credit Unions
3138 10th St N
Suite 3
Arlington, VA 22201-2160

703-522-4770
800-336-4644; *Fax:* 703-524-1082
tfcu@nafcunet.org; www.nafcu.org

Fred Becker, President

Written for CEOs, senior staff and volunteers of Federal Credit Unions. Offers legislative and regulatory news, as well as technology and operational issues.
Cost: $99.00
80 Pages
Frequency: Bi-Monthly
Circulation: 11136
ISSN: 1043-7789
Founded in: 1967
Printed in 4 colors on glossy stock

2945 Finance and Development
International Monetary Fund
700 19th St NW
Washington, DC 20431-0002

202-623-7000; *Fax:* 202-623-6220
publicaffairs@imf.org; www.imf.org

David Lipton, First Deputy Managing Director
Christine Lagarde, Managing Director

Analysis of financial and economic developments and explanation of the policies and work of the International Monetary Fund and the World Bank.
Cost: $10.00
Frequency: Quarterly
Circulation: 130000
Founded in: 1945
Mailing list available for rent: 120M names
Printed in 4 colors

2946 Financial Analyst
CFA Institute
PO Box 3668
Charlottesville, VA 22903-0668

434-951-5499
800-247-8132; *Fax:* 434-951-5262
info@cfainstitute.org; www.cfainstitute.org

John Rogers, CEO
Rodney N Sullivan, Associate Editor

Is to advance the knowledge and understanding of the practice of investment management through the publication of high-quality, practitioner-relevant research.

2947 Financial Review
Blackwell Publishing
350 Main St
Commerce Place
Malden, MA 02148-5089

781-388-8200; *Fax:* 781-388-8210;
www.blackwellpublishing.com

Steven Smith, President/CEO
Vincent Marzano, Vice President, Treasurer

Publishes original empirical, theoretical and methodological research providing new insights into issues of importance in financial economics.
Frequency: Quarterly
ISSN: 0732-8516

2948 Financial Women Today Magazine
Financial Women International
1027 W Roselawn Avenue
Roseville, MN 55113

651-487-7632
866-807-6081; *Fax:* 651-489-1322
info@fwi.org; www.fwi.org

Melissa Curzon, President
Cindy Hass, VP
Carleen DeSisto, Secretary

Serves nearly 10,000 female financial service professionals, helping them to attain their economic, professional and personal goals.
Cost: $24.00
Frequency: Quarterly
Circulation: 19000
ISSN: 1059-3950
Founded in: 1921
Mailing list available for rent
Printed in 4 colors on matte stock

2949 Global Custodian
Asset International
1055 Washington Blvd
Stamford, CT 06901

203-295-5015
888-374-3722; *Fax:* 203-595-3201
education@globalcustodian.com;
www.globalcustodian.com

Dominic Hobson, Editor-in-Chief
Charles Ruffel, Founder/CEO
Maredith Hughes, VP

Written for international institutional investors. Stories cover engineering markets, cross border investing, securities lending and more.
Cost: $185.00
Frequency: 5x/Year
Circulation: 20000
Founded in: 1989

2950 Government Affairs Bulletin
Financial Services Roundtable
1001 Pennsylvania Ave NW
Suite 500 S
Washington, DC 20004-2508

202-289-4322; *Fax:* 202-289-1903
info@fsround.org; www.fsround.org
Social Media: Facebook, Twitter

Tim Pawlenty, CEO
Richard Whiting, Executive Director

This bulletin keeps the members of the Roundtable informed on issues in the financial services industry and how the Roundtable views them.
100 Pages
Frequency: Weekly
Founded in: 1993

2951 ICBA Independent Banker Magazine
Independent Community Bankers of America
518 Lincoln Road
PO Box 267
Sauk Centre, MN 56378

320-526-6546
800-422-7285; *Fax:* 320-352-5766
info@icba.org; www.icba.org

Camden R Fine, President/CEO
Rachael Solomon, Advertising Contact

ICBA members rely on for community banking news.
Cost: $60.00
Frequency: Monthly

2952 Independent Banker
Inside Mortgage Finance Publishers

7910 Woodmont Ave
Suite 1000
Bethesda, MD 20814-7019

301-951-1240
800-422-8439; *Fax:* 301-656-1709
service@imfpubs.com; www.imfpubs.com
Social Media: Twitter, LinkedIn, Youtube

John Bancroft, VP
George Brooks, Editor

Features strategies for high-performance community banks. Also includes profiles of success stories in community banks and assesses developments in legislation and regulation.
Frequency: Monthly
Circulation: 9,800
Mailing list available for rent

2953 Information Management Magazine
ARMA International
11880 College Blvd
Suite 450
Overland Park, KS 66215

913-341-3808
800-422-2762; *Fax:* 913-341-3742
hq@arma.org; www.arma.org

Komal Gulch, President
Brenda Prowse, Treasurer

The leading source of information on topics and issues central to the management of records and information worldwide. Each issue features insightful articles written by experts in the management of records and information.
Cost: $115.00
Frequency: Bi-monthly
Circulation: 11000
ISSN: 1535-2897
Mailing list available for rent: 9000 names
Printed in 4 colors on glossy stock

2954 International Banking Focus
Institue of International Bankers
299 Park Ave
17th Floor
New York, NY 10171-3896

212-421-1611; *Fax:* 212-421-1119
iib@iib.org; www.iib.org

Sarah ""sally"" Miller, Chief Executive Officer
Richard Coffman, General Counsel
Robin Wilks, Chief Administrative Officer

The Focus describes the latest legislative, regulatory and tax developments in Washington and various states, along with the Institute's efforts to address particular problems that affect international banks.
Frequency: Bi-Monthly
Founded in: 1966

2955 Journal of Performance Management
Assn for Management Information in Financial Svcs
14247 Saffron Circle
Carmel, IN 46032

317-815-5857; *Fax:* 317-815-5877
ami2@amifs.org; www.amifs.org

Robert McDonald, President
Kevin Link, Executive Director
Cost: $200.00
Frequency: 3x/Year
Circulation: 350

2956 Mortgage Banking
Mortgage Bankers Association
1717 Rhode Island Avenue, NW
Suite400
Washington, DC 20036

202-557-2700
membership@mortgagebankers.org;
www.mortgagebankers.org

Janet Reilley Hewett, Editor-in-Chief
Michael Young, Chairman

Provides in-depth coverage of the real estate finance industry. Intelligent analysis of news and the most important issues and trends affecting the industry. Association discount available.
Cost: $60.00
120 Pages
Frequency: 14x/Year
Circulation: 6000
ISSN: 0730-0212
Founded in: 1914
Mailing list available for rent: 2800 names at $100 per M
Printed in 4 colors on glossy stock

2957 Mortgage Servicing News
Thomson Media
1 State Street Plaza
27th Floor
New York, NY 10004-1481

212-825-8445
800-221-1809; *Fax:* 212-292-5216
custserv@thomsonmedia.com;
www.mortgageservicingnews.com/

Mark Fogarty, Editor
Timothy Murphy, Group Publisher
Timothy Reifschneider, Marketing Manager
Virginia Wiese, Custom Publishing

Information on cross serving techniques, legislative decisions, management strategies, and professional profiles.
Cost: $98.00
Frequency: Monthly
Circulation: 20,000

2958 NABTalk It
National Association of Bankruptcy Trustees
One Windsor Cove
Suite 305
Columbia, SC 29223

803-252-5646
800-445-8629; *Fax:* 803-765-0860
info@nabt.com; www.nabt.com

Nancy H Cooper, Staff Editor
Neil Gordon, President
Frequency: Quarterly

2959 NACTT Quarterly
National Association of Chapter 13 Trustees
1 Windsor Cove
Suite 305
Columbia, SC 29223

803-252-5646
800-445-8629; *Fax:* 803-765-0860
info@nactt.com; www.nactt.com

Debra Miller, President
Margaret Burks, VP

The Quarterly emphasizes current local and national developments in Chapter 13. Each Quarterly provides a summary of the most recent Chapter 13 Bankruptcy court decisions.

2960 NACUSAC News
NACUSAC
PO Box 160
Del Mar, CA 92014

800-287-5949; *Fax:* 858-792-3884
nacusac@nacusac.org; www.nacusac.org

Gerald Dunning, Chairman
Robert Butler, Director

Official magazing of the National Association of Credit Union Supervisory & Auditing Committees that keeps you up to date on the latest developments and events affecting supervisory/auditing committee members.
Frequency: Quarterly

2961 National Mortgage Broker Magazine
Banat Communications
23425 N 39th Drive
104-193
Glendale, AZ 85310

623-516-2723; *Fax:* 623-516-7738;
www.nationalmortgagebroker.com

Mike Anderson, VP
Donald Frommeyer, President
Debbie Maxwell, Production Manager
Cost: $59.95
Frequency: Monthly
Founded in: 1984

2962 New England Economic Indicators
Federal Reserve Bank of Boston
600 Atlantic Avenue
Suite 100
Boston, MA 02210-2204

617-973-3000; *Fax:* 617-973-5918
boston.library@bos.frb.org; www.bos.frb.org

Eric S Rosengren, President/CEO
Kenneth Montgomery, VP COO

Contains current and historical economic data for the states of CT, ME, MA, NH, RI, and VT, as well as the US data include employment, unemployment, prices and construction activity.
80 Pages
Frequency: Monthly
Circulation: 7000
Founded in: 1914

2963 North Western Financial Review
NFR Communications
7400 Metro Blvd
Suite 217
Minnieapolis, MN 55439

952-835-2275; *Fax:* 612-831-1464
info@northwesternfinancialreview.com;
www.northwesternfinancialreview.com

Tom Bengston, Publisher

Provides useful information and useful data regarding developments without trade association bias.
Frequency: Annual+
Circulation: 9,000
Founded in: 1989

2964 RMA Journal
Risk Management Association
1801 Market Street
Suite 300
Philadelphia, PA 19103-1628

215-446-4000
800-677-7621; *Fax:* 215-446-4101
customers@rmahq.org; www.rmahq.org
Social Media: Facebook, Twitter, LinkedIn

William Githens, President/CEO
Linda O'Loughlin, Director Marketing
Dwight Overturf, CFO

Expanded both format and content to address an array of risk management issues while respecting and preserving essentials of commercial lending
Cost: $95.00
Frequency: Monthly
Founded in: 1914
Printed in 4 colors on glossy stock

2965 Regional Review
Federal Reserve Bank of Boston
600 Atlantic Ave
Boston, MA 02210-2204

617-973-3000
800-409-1333; *Fax:* 617-973-4292
bostonlibrary@bos.frb.org; www.bos.frb.org

Erin Rosengren, President/CEO

Magazine on economics, banking, business topics, designed for the busy professional.
Frequency: Quarterly
Circulation: 15000
ISSN: 1062-1865

Founded in: 1913
Printed in 5 colors on glossy stock

2966 **SNL Quarterly Bank & Thrift Digest**
SNL Securities
212 7th Street NE
Charlottesvle, VA 22902

434-977-1600; *Fax:* 434-977-4466
customerservice@snl.com; www.snl.com
Social Media: Facebook, Twitter, LinkedIn, Youtube

Mike Chinn, President & CEO

Contains all relevant information on every publicly traded bank and thrift providing insight into each individual institution and allowing quick and accurate comparisons with both peer institutions and industry benchmarks.
Cost: $799.00
600 Pages
Frequency: Quarterly
Founded in: 1987
Mailing list available for rent

2967 **SNL Real Estate Securities Quarterly**
SNL Securities
212 7th Street NE
Charlottesville, VA 22902

434-977-1600; *Fax:* 434-977-4466
subscriptions@snl.com; www.snl.com
Social Media: Facebook, Twitter, LinkedIn, Youtube

Mike Chinn, President & CEO

This data digest provides comprehensive corporate, market, and financial information and portfolio level property data on more than 240 publicly traded and privately held real estate companies. SNL Real Estate Securities Quarterly is the industry's most comprehensive publication for evaluating real estate company performance at both a property and financial level.
Cost: $696.00
Frequency: Quarterly
Founded in: 1987
Mailing list available for rent

2968 **Secondary Marketing Executive Magazine**
Zackin Publications
100 Willenbrock Road
Oxford, CT 06478

203-262-4670
800-325-6745; *Fax:* 203-262-4680
info@secondarymarketingexec.com;
www.secondarymarketingexec.com
Social Media: Facebook, Twitter

Michael Bates, Publisher
Patrick Barnard, Editor
Vanessa Williams, Business Development

Offers how-to information for buyers and sellers of mortgage loans.
Cost: $48.00
Frequency: Monthly
ISSN: 0891-2947
Founded in: 1986

2969 **Servicing Management**
LDJ Corporation
100 Willenbrock Road
Oxford, CT 06478

203-755-0158
800-325-6745; *Fax:* 203-262-4680
info@servicemgmt.com;
www.servicingmgmt.com

Paul Zackin, Publisher
John Clapp, Editor
June Han, Marketing

Includes updates on industry and regulatory trends, and advise on operating their departments more profitably and efficiently.
Cost: $48.00
Frequency: Monthly
Circulation: 22500
Founded in: 1989

2970 **US Banker**
Thomson Media
1 State St
27th Floor
New York, NY 10004-1481

212-803-8200
800-221-1809; *Fax:* 212-843-9600;
www.americanbanker.com

Neil Weinberg, Editor-in-Chief
John Ceasar, Group Publisher
James Malkin, Chairman/CEO

Features on news and technological developments in the banking industry. Includes reports on companies, personalities and industry trends.
Cost: $109.00
Frequency: Monthly
Circulation: 80000
Founded in: 1955

Trade Shows

2971 **ABA National Conference for Community Bankers**
American Bankers Association
1120 Connecticut Avenue NW
Washington, DC 20036

800-226-5377
800-226-5377
custserv@aba.com; www.aba.com

Frank Keating, President
Albert Kelly, Chairman

Features educational sessions, exceptional speakers, networking opportunities and world class exhibit hall.
2 mil Members
1500 Attendees
Frequency: Annual, February
Founded in: 1875

2972 **ABA Sales Management Workshop**
American Bankers Association
1120 Connecticut Avenue NW
Washington, DC 20036

202-635-5000
800-226-5377
custserv@aba.com;
www.salesmanagementworkshop.com

Frank Keating, President
Albert Kelly, Chairman

Workshop on creating and keeping customers, over 13 exhibitors, visited by community bank executives, managers, sales and marketing staff.
Frequency: Annual, September

2973 **ABA Wealth Management & Trust Conference**
American Bankers Association
1120 Connecticut Avenue NW
Washington, DC 20036

800-226-5377
custserv@aba.com; www.aba.com

Frank Keating, President
Albert Kelly, Chairman

Delivers practical, inventive ideas for wealth management and trust professionals.
Frequency: Annual, May

2974 **AMIFS Annual Profitability, Performance & Risk Conference**
Assn for Management Information in Financial Svcs
14247 Saffron Circle
Carmel, IN 46032

317-815-5857; *Fax:* 317-815-5877
ami2@amifs.org; www.amifs.org

Robert McDonald, President
Kevin Link, Executive Director
Krissa Hatfield, Assistant Executive Director

3-day conference consisting of one day of workshops, and two days of educational sessions. 10 exhibitors.
Frequency: Annual/April

2975 **ARMA International Conference & Expo**
ARMA International
11880 College Blvd
Suite 450
Overland Park, KS 66215

913-341-3808
800-422-2762; *Fax:* 913-341-3742
Conference@armaintl.org;
www.arma.org/conference

Carol Jorgenson, Meetings/Education Coordinator
Wanda Wilson, Senior Manager, Conferences
Elizabeth Zlitni, Exposition Manager

Conference, seminar, workshop, banquet, award ceremony and 175 exhibits of micrographics, optical disk, automated document storage and retrieval systems and more technology of interest to information professionals.
3500 Attendees
Frequency: Annual
Founded in: 1956

2976 **American Bankers Insurance Association Annual Conference**
American Bankers Insurance Association
1120 Connecticut Avenue NW
Washington, DC 20036

202-663-5163
800-226-5377; *Fax:* 202-828-4546
vbarton@aba.com; www.aba.com

Paul Petrylak, President/Chairman
Thomas Anderson, VP
David Cissell, Secretary
Neal Aton, Treasurer

The Conference highlights Best Practices Panel presentations as well as numerous break-out sessions with case studies by bankers and providers of insurance products and services.
300 Members
Frequency: September
Founded in: 2001

2977 **American Safe Deposit Association Conference**
American Safe Deposit Association
PO Box 519
Franklin, IN 46131-0519

317-738-4432; *Fax:* 317-738-5267;
www.tasda.com

Thomas Cullinan, President
J Wayne Merrill, First VP
Winnifred Howard-Hammack, Second VP
Joyce A McLin, Executive Director
Kevin Fanning, Treasurer

Offers jam-packed sessions full of information and ideas that can be implemented immediately after conference.
200 Attendees
Frequency: June

2978 **Association for Financial Professionals Annual Conference**
Association for Financial Professionals

4520 East West Highway
Suite 750
Bethesda, MD 20814

301-907-2862; *Fax:* 301-907-2864
AFP@AFPonline.org; www.AFPonline.org
Social Media: Facebook, Twitter, LinkedIn, Youtube

Susan Glass, Chairman
Anita Patterson, Vice Chairman

Workshop and 642 exhibits of lockboxes, check processing systems, computers, investments, pensions, foreign exchange, consulting, mergers, acquisitions and more information of interest to financial professionals.
6000 Attendees
Frequency: October
Founded in: 1979

2979 Association of Independent Trust Companies Conference
Association of Independent Trust Companies
8 South Michigan Avenue
Suite802
Chicago, IL 60603

312-223-1611; *Fax:* 312-580-0615;
www.aitco.net

Douglas Nunn, President
Marcia Williams, Treasurer
Tom Blank, General Counsel/Secretary

Typically attracts more than 50 financial executive to an information-packed program which addresses the practical issues and challenges of doing business within the trust and financial advisory industry.
Frequency: Annual

2980 Association of Military Banks of America Conference
Association of Military Banks of America(AMBA)
PO Box 3335
Warrenton, VA 20188

540-347-3305; *Fax:* 540-347-5995
christiane.jacobs@ambahq.org;
www.ambahq.org

Andrew Egeland, President
John Mitchell, Chairman
Terry Tuggle, Vice Chairman
Frequency: September

2981 Bank Insurance and Securities Association Annual Conference
Bank Insurance and Securities Association
2025 M Street, NW
Suite 800
Washington, DC 20036

202-367-1111; *Fax:* 20 -36 -211
bisa@BISAnet.org; www.bisanet.org

Jim McNeil, Executive Director
Marc A Vosen, President

Focus on the internal administration of the supervisory and compliance functions of the bank broker-dealer and its related activities.
Frequency: June
Founded in: 2002

2982 Bankers' Association for Finance & Trade Annual Conference
Bankers' Association for Finance & Trade
1120 Connecticut Avenue NW
6th Floor
Washington, DC 20036-3902

202-663-7575; *Fax:* 202-663-5538
info@baft-ifsa.com; www.baft.org

Tom Burwell, Vice President
Colleen Kennedy, Manager,Programs, & Events
Donna K Alexander, President

Focused on the global environment and the impact of economic developments in specifications and markets including consecutive breakouts on compliance, risk mitigation and key issues.
Frequency: April

2983 Boot Camp for BSA Professionals
Conference of State Bank Supervisors
1129 20th Street, N.W.
9th Floor
Washington, DC 20036

202-296-2840; *Fax:* 202-296-1928
rstromberg@csbs.org; www.csbs.org

Greg Gonzales, Chairman
Candace Franks, Vice Chairman
David Cotney, Secretary

Will provide BSA Compliance knowledge and value to your regulatory agency, financial institution or money service business.
Frequency: May

2984 CPSA Annual Meeting
Check Payment Systems Association
2025 M Street NW
Suite 800
Washington, DC 20036-2422

202-671-1144; *Fax:* 202-367-2144
info@cpsa-checks.org; www.cpsa-checks.org

Steven Antolick, Executive Director
Renee Lurker, Senior Associate

In addition to the business meeting, there are presentations from top industry performers and innovators.
Frequency: May

2985 CSBS Annual Meeting & Conference
Conference of State Bank Supervisors
1129 20th Street NW
9th Floor
Washington, DC 20036
202-296-2840; *Fax:* 202-296-1928
mbquist@csbs.org; www.csbs.org

Mary Beth Quist, Meetings/Conference Contact
Neil Milner, President

The largest gathering of State 7 Federal banking regulators, state bank CEOs, industry policy makers and representatives of companies who support the banking industry.
Frequency: May

2986 Combating Payments & Check Fraud Conference
Bank Administration Institute
115 S LaSalle St
Suite 3300
Chicago, IL 60603-3801

312-683-2464
888-224-0037; *Fax:* 312-683-2373
info@bai.org; www.bai.org
Social Media: Facebook, Twitter, LinkedIn, Youtube

Lewis Fischer, Chairman of the Board
Scott Peters, Vice Chairman
Frequency: September

2987 Commercial Mortgage Securities Association Conference
Commercial Mortgage Securities Association
900 7th Street, NW
Suite 820
New York, NY 10004-2304

212-509-1844; *Fax:* 212-509-1895
info@crefc.org; www.cmbs.org
Social Media: Facebook, Twitter, LinkedIn

Steven Renna, CEO

Intensive educational offerings and presentations on the CMBS industry's biggest challenges.
Frequency: June

2988 Commerical Real Estate Finance/Multifamily Housing Convention & Expo
Mortgage Bankers Association
1717 Rhode Island Avenue NW
Suite 400
Washington, DC 20036

202-557-2700
meetiings@mortgagebankers.org;
www.mortgagebankers.org

David H Stevens, President/CEO
Elaine Howard, VP Meetings/Conferences

Thousands of commerical real estate industry professionals gathered from across the country to do business with and learn the latest in industry trends, regulatory develoments and strategies to succeed in today's dynamic marketplace.
Frequency: Annual/February

2989 Community & Regional Bank Forum
Bank Insurance and Securities Association
2025 M Street, NW
Suite 800
Washington, DC 20036

202-367-1111; *Fax:* 202-367-2111
bisa@BISAnet.org; www.bisanet.org

Jim McNeil, Executive Director
Marc A Vosen, President
Frequency: September
Founded in: 2002

2990 Community Bank Director's Conference
American Association of Bank Directors
1250 24th Street, NW
Suite 700
Washington, DC 20037

202-463-4888; *Fax:* 20 -34 -808
info@aabd.org; www.aabd.org

Keith Dalrymple, President/CEO
David Baris, Executive Director

Sponsored by the AABD and Bank CEO Network, designed to provide information community bank directors need
Frequency: Annual

2991 Community Banking Advisory Network Super Conference
HCAA
624 Grassmere Park Drive
Suite 15
Nasvhille, TN 37211

615-377-3392
800-231-2524; *Fax:* 615-377-7092
info@hcaa.com; www.hcaa.com

Keith Kamperschroer, President

2992 Credit Congress
8840 Columbia 100 Parkway
Columbia, MD 21045-2158

410-423-1840
888-256-3242; *Fax:* 410-740-5574;
www.fcibglobal.com
Social Media: LinkedIn

Marta Chacon, Director, The Americas
Ron Shepherd, Director, Business Dev.
Noelin Hawkins, Director, Europe, Middle East

Business Credit
1000+ Members
1500 Attendees
Founded in: 1919

2993 Eastern Finance Association Meeting
Eastern Finance Association

220 Holman Hall
PO Box 1848
University, MS 38677

404-498-8937; *Fax:* 404-498-8956
admin@easternfinance.org;
www.easternfinance.org

Mark Lion, President
Jacqueline Garner, VP Local Arrangements

Annual meeting and exhibits relating to any aspect of finance, including financial management, investments and banking.
Frequency: April

2994 **Environmental Bankers Association Membership Meeting**
Environmental Bankers Association
510 King Street
Suite 410
Alexandria, VA 22314

703-549-0977
800-966-7475; *Fax:* 703-548-5945
eba@envirobank.org; www.envirobank.org

Rick Ferguson, President
Scott Beckerman, Treasurer
Frequency: January/June
Founded in: 1994

2995 **Federal Reserve Board Conference**
Federal Reserve Board Publishers
20th Street & Constitution Avenue NW
Washington, DC 20551

202-452-3000; *Fax:* 202-728-5886;
www.federalreserve.gov

Lucrezia Reichlin, Conference Organizer
Dale Henderson, Conference Organizer
Deborah Lagomarsino, Media Contact

Organized by the International Research Forum on Monetary Policy. Its purpose is to encourage research on monetary policy issues that are relevant for monetary policy making in interdependent economies.
Frequency: December

2996 **Financial & Security Products Association Annual Conference**
Financial & Security Products Association
Plaza Ladera, 5300 Sequoia NW
Suite 205
Albuquerque, NM 87120

505-839-7958
800-843-6082; *Fax:* 919-648-0670
info@fspa1.com; www.fspa1.com

Mark Thatcher, Chairman
Bill Mercer, President
John M Vrabec, Executive Director
Frequency: June
Founded in: 1973

2997 **Financial Women International Annual Conference**
Financial Women International
1027 W Roselawn Avenue
Roseville, MN 55113

651-487-7632
866-807-6081; *Fax:* 651-489-1322
info@fwi.org; www.fwi.org

Melissa Curzon, President
Cindy Hass, VP
Carleen DeSisto, Secretary
Frequency: September

2998 **GARP Annual Risk Management Convention & Exhibit**
Global Association of Risk Professionals
111 Town Square Place
Suite 1215
Jersey City, NJ 07310

201-719-7210; *Fax:* 201-222-5022
rich.apostolik@garp.com; www.garp.com
Social Media: Facebook, Twitter, LinkedIn

Richard Apostolik, President/CEO
Kenneth Abbott, Managing Director
Mark Wallace, Chief Operating Officer
Thomas Daula, Chief Risk Officer
Frequency: February
Founded in: 1996

2999 **Global Association of Risk Professionals Annual Exhibition**
111 Town Square Place
Suite 1215
Jersey City, NJ 07310

201-719-7210; *Fax:* 201-222-5022
rich.apostolik@garp.com; www.garp.com
Social Media: Facebook, Twitter, LinkedIn

Richard Apostolik, President/CEO
Kenneth Abbott, Managing Director
Mark Wallace, Chief Operating Officer
Thomas Daula, Chief Risk Officer

GARP's flagship event for Asia, with Keynote presentations, multi-track forum and separate workshops.
Frequency: Annual
Founded in: 1996

3000 **Independent Community Bankers of America National Convention and Techworld**
Independent Community Bankers of America
518 Lincoln Road
PO Box 267
Sauk Centre, MN 56378

320-526-6546
800-422-7285; *Fax:* 320-352-5766
mark_traeger@icba.org; www.icba.org

Jan Meyer, Director Conferences
Mark Traeger, Associate Dir Conferences/Exhibits
Sandy Zehrer, Supervisor Conference/Exhibits
Greg Martinson, Executive Director

Only national trade show exclusively representing America's independent/community banks. Containing 200+ booths and 175+exhibitors.
3000 Attendees
Frequency: March

3001 **Institute of International Bankers Annual Washington Conference**
Institute of International Bankers
299 Park Avenue
17th Floor
New York, NY 10171

212-421-1611; *Fax:* 212-421-1119
iib@iib.org; www.iib.org

Sarah Miller, CEO
Maura Christ, Executive Assistant
William Harris, Controller
Andy Lebron, Membership Associate

A two-day conference featuring senior U.S. and international government policy makers and financial industry leaders. As part of the conference, which is widely attended by general manager and other senior officers of Institute member banks, there is an evening reception for the Washington community, including Administration officials, Members of Congress, banking regulators and senior staff.
Frequency: March
Founded in: 1966

3002 **International Financial Services Association Annual Conference**
International Financial Services Association
1120 Connecticut Avenue NW
Washington, DC 20036

202- 66-757; *Fax:* 202-663-5538;
www.ifsaonline.org

Renee Wigfall, Manager, Meetings/Events
Todd Burwell, Vice President
Frequency: September

3003 **Legal Issues and Regulatory Compliance Conference**
Mortgage Bankers Association
1717 Rhode Island Avenue NW
Suite 400
Washington, DC 20036
202-557-2700
meetings@mortgagebankers.org;
www.mortgagebankers.org

David H Stevens, President/CEO
Elaine Howard, VP Meetings/Conferences

Learn about all the legal and regulatory developments facing the industry.
Frequency: Annual/May

3004 **Microbanker**
Microbanker
PO Box 708
Lake George, NY 12061
518-745-7071; *Fax:* 518-745-7071;
www.microbanker.com

Annual show and exhibits of microcomputer software, hardware and services for banking, savings and loans, and credit unions.
200 Attendees

3005 **Mid-Year Technical Conference**
National Assn of Government Guaranteed Lenders
424 South Squires Street
Stillwater, OK 74074

405-377-4022; *Fax:* 405-377-3931;
www.naggl.com

Tony Wilkinson, President/CEO
Karen High, EVP/COO
Jenifer Brake, Assistant VP Marketing
Jennifer Sterrett-O'Neill, Assistant VP Communications
Cheryl Stone, VP Conferences
Frequency: May

3006 **NACUSAC Annual Conference & Exposition**
NACUSAC
PO Box 160
Del Mar, CA 92014

800-287-5949; *Fax:* 858-792-3884
nacusac@nacusac.org; www.nacusac.org

Celeste Shelton, Executive Director
Laura Clark, Associate Director
Bob Spindler, Associate Director

These events sponsored by the National Association of Credit Union Supervisory & Auditing Committees offer second-to-none networking and educational opportunities for supervisory and auditing committees.
Frequency: June

3007 **National Association of Bankruptcy Trustees Annual Convention**
National Association of Bankruptcy Trustees
One Windsor Cove
Suite 305
Columbia, SC 29223

803-252-5646
800-445-8629; *Fax:* 803-765-0860
info@nabt.com; www.nabt.com

Christina Hicks, President
Kelly Hagen, VP
Frequency: September

3008 **National Association of Chapter 13 Trustees Annual Seminar**
National Association of Chapter 13 Trustees
1 Windsor Cove
Suite 305
Columbia, SC 29223

803-252-5646
800-445-8629; *Fax:* 803-765-0860
info@nactt.com; www.nactt.com

Debra Miller, President
Margaret Burks, VP

This seminar is NAACO's educational highlight. National experts discuss complex issues and recent developments in the Chapter 13 areas.

3009 **National Association of Federal Credit Unions Conference**
National Association of Federal Credit Unions
3138 10th Street N
Suite 300
Arlington, VA 22201-2149

703-522-4770
800-336-4644; *Fax:* 703-524-1082
fbecker@nafcu.org; www.nafcu.org

Fred Becker, President/CEO
Patrick Morris, Executive Vice President/COO

Stands as a national forum for the federal credit union community where new ideas, issues, concerns and trends can be identified, discussed and resolved.
Frequency: July

3010 **National Association of Professional Mortgage Women Annual Conference**
National Assn of Professional Mortgage Women
PO Box 451718
Garland, TX 75045

425-778-6162
800-827-3034; *Fax:* 425-771-9588
napmw1@napmw.org; www.napmw.org

Laurie Abshier, President
Candice Smith, President-Elect
Liz Roberts, Senior Vice President
Patricia Hull, Executive Director
Frequency: May

3011 **National Fraud Issues Conference**
Mortgage Bankers Association
1717 Rhode Island Avenue NW
Suite 400
Washington, DC 20036

202-557-2700
meetings@mortgagebankers.org;
www.mortgagebankers.org

David H Stevens, President/CEO
Elaine Howard, VP Meetings/Conferences

Where industry professionals can learn about the issues related to the growing incidence and complexity of mortgage fraud.
Frequency: Annual/March

3012 **National Investment Banking Association Annual Conference**
National Investment Banking Association
PO Box 6625
Athens, GA 30604

706-208-9620; *Fax:* 706-993-3342
emily@nibanet.org; www.nibanet.org

James Hock, Co Chair
Gerald Alder, Director
Emily Foshee, Executive Director
D Scott Foshee, Chief Technology Officer
Vicki Barone, Treasurer/Secretary

Provides member firms with regularly scheduled forums where they are able to exchange ideas and information, evaluate presentations made by companies being underwritten or sponsored by member firms, collectively voice their positions on issues impacting their livelihood, and enhance their knowledge and expertise through ongoing educational programs designed to enable them to remain competitive.
Frequency: May

3013 **National Marine Bankers Association Annual Conference**
National Marine Bankers Association
231 South LaSalle Street
Suite 2050
Chicago, IL 60604

312-946-6260
bmcardle@nmma.org; www.marinebankers.org

Bernice McArdle, Associate Manager

A three-day member conference where the latest trends issues relating to the marine industry are discussed in detail.
Frequency: September

3014 **National Mortgage Servicing Conference & Expo**
Mortgage Bankers Association
1717 Rhode Island Avenue NW
Suite 400
Washington, DC 20036

202-557-2700
meetings@mortgagebankers.org;
www.mortgagebankers.org

David H Stevens, President/CEO
Elaine Howard, VP Meetings/Conferences

Gives companies the opportunity to reach key servicing executives from residential mortgage companies. Showcase the product offerings, network with key decision makers, and obtain qualified leads.
Frequency: Annual/February

3015 **National Policy Conference**
Mortgage Bankers Association
1717 Rhode Island Avenue NW
Suite 400
Washington, DC 20036

202-557-2700
meetings@mortgagebankers.org;
www.mortgagebankers.org

David H Stevens, President/CEO
Elaine Howard, VP Meetings/Conferences

Brings togethers key officials, cabinet members and special guest speakers to address issues of what is happening in the community as well as the practical effect proposed changes may have on the business and industry
Frequency: Annual/March

3016 **National Technology in Mortgage Banking Conference**
Mortgage Bankers Association
1717 Rhode Island Avenue NW
Suite 400
Washington, DC 20036

202-557-2700
meetings@mortgagebankers.org;
www.mortgagebankers.org

David H Stevens, President/CEO
Elaine Howard, VP Meetings/Conferences

Forum to learn about the newest industry solutions and how they can increase the company's competitive edge. Focuses on relevant topics, including legal/regulatory updates, eMortgages, investor reporting changes adn technology advances such as mobile computing.
Frequency: Annual/March

3017 **Payments**
NACHA: Electronic Payments Association
13450 Sunrise Valley Drive
Suite 100
Herndon, AV 20171

703-561-1100; *Fax:* 703-787-0996
info@nacha.org; www.nacha.org

Marcie Haitema, Chairperson
Janet O Estep, CEO

The premier source for payments professionals from across industries and around the globe to get the most vital and actionable information needed to help address the myriad of issues and opportunities in today's rapidly changing environment.
Frequency: Annual/April-May

3018 **RMA Annual Conference of Lending & Credit Risk Management**
Risk Management Association
1801 Market Street
Suite 300
Philadelphia, PA 19103-1628

215-446-4000
800-677-7621; *Fax:* 215-446-4100
customers@rmahq.org; www.rmahq.org

William Githens, President/CEO
Sonny B Lyles, Vice Chair

Containing 31 booths and 28 exhibits.
600 Attendees
Frequency: October

3019 **Retail Delivery Conference & Expo**
Bank Administration Institute
115 S. LaSalle Street
Suite 3300
Chicago, IL 60603-3801

312-683-2464
888-284-4078; *Fax:* 312-683-2373
info@bai.org; www.bai.org
Social Media: Facebook, Twitter, LinkedIn, Youtube

Lewis Fischer, Chairman of the Board
Scott Peters, Vice Chairman
2M Attendees
Frequency: November

3020 **Sales Management Workshop**
Bank Insurance and Securities Association
2025 M Street NW
Suite 800
Washington, DC 20036

202-367-1111; *Fax:* 20 -36 -211
bisa@BISAnet.org; www.bisanet.org

Jim McNeil, Executive Director
Marc A Vosen, President
Frequency: May/October/December
Founded in: 2002

3021 **Securities Industry and Financial Markets Association (SIFMA) Annual Meeting**
SIFMA
1101 New York Avenue NW
8th Floor
Washington, DC 20005

202-962-7300; *Fax:* 202-962-7305;
www.sifma.org/

Timothy Ryan, President/CEO
Cheryl Crispen, Executive Vice President

The Securities Industry and Financial Markets Association/SIFMA Annual Meeting and Conference program addresses a variety of topics that may include competitiveness of the U.S. capital markets, global exchange consolidation, regulatory and legal initiatives, and trends in the fixed-income and capital markets.

3022 **TransPay Conference & Expo**
Bank Administration Institute

115 S LaSalle St
Suite 3300
Chicago, IL 60603

312-683-2464
800-375-5543; *Fax:* 312-683-2373
info@bai.org; www.bai.org
Social Media: Facebook, Twitter, LinkedIn, Youtube

Lewis Fischer, Chairman of the Board
Scott Peters, Vice Chairman

Offers top solutions providers, innovators and your peers at BAY TransPay - focused on your financial institution profitability in payments.
Frequency: May

3023 **Treasury & Risk Management Conference**
Bank Administration Institute
115 S LaSalle St
Suite 3300
Chicago, IL 60603

312-683-2464
800-375-5443; *Fax:* 312-683-2373
info@bai.org; www.bai.org
Social Media: Facebook, Twitter, LinkedIn, Youtube

Lewis Fischer, Chairman of the Board
Scott Peters, Vice Chairman
Frequency: May

3024 **Urban Financial Services Coalition Annual Conference**
Urban Financial Services Coalition
1200 G Street NW
Suite 800
Washington, DC 20005

202-289-8335
800-996-8335; *Fax:* 202-434-8707
ufsc@ufscnet.org; www.ufscnet.org

Diane Evans, President
Brenda Joseph, Vice President
Linda Smith, Treasurer
Audrey Williams, Secretary
Frequency: June

Directories & Databases

3025 **ABA Directory of Trust Banking**
4709 Golf Road
Skokie, IL 60076

847-676-9600
800-321-3373; *Fax:* 847-933-8101
custserv@accuitysolutions.com;
www.accuitysolutions.com

Hugh Jones, President
Kerry Hewson, VP

An official publication of the American Bankers Association. Listings include information such as national and state rankings, collective investment funds and corporate trusts.
Cost: $403.00
Circulation: 2800
ISBN: 1-563103-53-2

3026 **ABA Financial Institutions Directory**
4709 Golf Road
Skokie, IL 60076

847-676-9600
800-321-3373; *Fax:* 847-933-8101
custserv@accuitysolutions.com;
www.accuitysolutions.com

Hugh Jones, President
Kerry Hewson, VP

This two-volume Executive Desktop Edition includes a special ABA Resource Guide with a Quick Reference Guide to Banking Regulations.
Cost: $500.00
Frequency: January/July
Circulation: 31850

3027 **ABA Key to Routing Numbers**
4709 Golf Road
Skokie, IL 60076

847-676-9600
800-321-3373; *Fax:* 847-933-8101
custserv@accuitysolutions.com;
www.accuitysolutions.com

Hugh Jones, President
Kerry Hewson, VP
Cost: $184.00
Frequency: January/July
Circulation: 83300
Founded in: 1911

3028 **ACH Participant Directory**
4709 Golf Road
Skokie, IL 60076

847-676-9600
800-321-3373; *Fax:* 847-933-8101
custserv@accuitysolutions.com;
www.accuitysolutions.com

Hugh Jones, President
Kerry Hewson, VP
Cost: $207.00
Frequency: February/August
Circulation: 54600

3029 **American Financial Directory**
4709 Golf Road
Skokie, IL 60076

847-676-9600
800-321-3373; *Fax:* 847-933-8101
custserv@accuitysolutions.com;
www.accuitysolutions.com

Hugh Jones, President
Kerry Hewson, VP
Cost: $558.00
Frequency: January/July
Circulation: 41300
ISBN: 1-563103-47-8
Founded in: 1836

3030 **Annual Membership Directory & Buyers' Guide**
Financial & Security Products Association
Plaza Ladera, 5300 Sequoia NW
Suite 205
Albuquerque, NM 87120

505-839-7958
800-843-6082; *Fax:* 505-839-0017
info@fspa1.com; www.fspa1.com

Mark Thatcher, Chairman
Bill Mercer, President

Who's Who of independent firms serving financial institutions hleps readers locate new dealers, products/service suppliers and strategic business partners.

3031 **Annual Report of the Board of Governors of the Federal Reserve System**
Board of Governors
20th St & Constitution Ave N
Washington, DC 20551-0001

202-452-3284; *Fax:* 202-452-3101;
www.federalreserve.gov

Rick McKinney, Manager
Janet Yellen, Vice Chair

Listing of directors, advisory councils and officers of banks and branches involved in mergers and acquisitions.
Frequency: Annual

3032 **Annual Software Guide**
Financial & Security Products Association
Plaza Ladera, 5300 Sequoia NW
Suite 205
Albuquerque, NM 87120

505-839-7958
800-843-6082; *Fax:* 505-839-0017
info@fspa1.com; www.fspa1.com

Mark Thatcher, Chairman
Bill Mercer, President
John Vrabec, Executive Director

This detailed evaluation of the latest software to enhance business performance is provided by Brown Smith Wallace (BSW) only to members of participating associations, including FSPA.

3033 **BankNews Montain States Bank Directory**
BankNews Publications
PO Box 29156
Shawnee Mission, KS 66201-9156

913-261-7000
800-336-1120; *Fax:* 913-261-7010;
www.banknews.com

Janet Holman, President & Publisher
Joel Holman, CEO & Publisher

Over 600 commercial banks, savings and loans, and holding companies are listed in this directory, state banking and regulatory agencies are also studied in the areas of Colorado, Wyoming, New Mexico, Montana and Utah.
Cost: $ 35.00
350 Pages
Frequency: Annual
Circulation: 3,500

3034 **BankRoll II**
US Federal Reserve System, Board of Governors
20th Street & Constitution Avenue NW
Washington, DC 20551-0001

www.federalreserve.gov/
Social Media: Twitter, LinkedIn

This database contains descriptive information and financial information from the Financial Report Bank Holding Companies (Y9) submitted to the Federal Reserve Board.

3035 **Bankcard Barometer**
RAM Research Corporation
1230 Avenue of the Americas
7th Floor, Rockefeller Center
New York, MD 21702-0700

301-954-4660; *Fax:* 301-695-0160;
www.ramresearch.com

Robert B McKinley, Publisher/Editor

Database of nation's capital largest bank credit card issuers.
Cost: $1295.00
600 Pages
Frequency: Monthly
Founded in: 1986
Printed in one color on matte stock

3036 **Branches of Your State: Banks, Savings & Loans, Credit Unions & Savings**
Sheshunoff Information Services
901 South Mopac
Suite 140
Austin, TX 78746-7970

512-472-4000
800-477-1772; *Fax:* 512-305-6575
sales@smslp.com; www.smslp.com
Social Media: Facebook, Twitter, LinkedIn

Gabrielle Sheshunoff, CEO

State editions list banks, savings and loan branches and credit unions. Individual banks are listed for states without branch banking.
Cost: $345.00
Frequency: Annual

3037 **Data Book**
FDIC Public Information Center
550 17th St Nw
Washington, DC 20429-0001

202-898-3631
877-275-3342; *Fax:* 202-898-3984
publicinfo@fdic.gov; www.fdic.gov
Social Media: Facebook, Twitter, LinkedIn

Martin Gruenberg, Chairman
Thomas Hoenig, Vice Chairman
Jeremiah Norton, Director

Offers information on bank names, locations, bank numbers and branches for each banking office, in seven volumes, divided geographically and aggregate bank deposits also known as Summary of Deposits.
Frequency: Quarterly

3038 **Directory of Minority and Women-Owned Investment Bankers**
San Francisco Redevelopment Agency
1 S Van Ness Avenue
Suite 5
San Francisco, CA 94103-5416

415-749-2400; *Fax:* 415-749-2565;
www.sanfranciscofcu.org

Marcia Rosen, Executive Director
Erwin Tanjuaquio, Director Public Affairs

Lists 18 minority-owned investment banking firms.
Frequency: Biennial

3039 **Directory of Venture Capital & Private Equity Firms - Online Database**
Grey House Publishing
4919 Route 22
PO Box 56
Amenia, NY 12501

518-789-8700
800-562-2139; *Fax:* 518-789-0556
gold@greyhouse.com;
www.gold.greyhouse.com
Social Media: Facebook, Twitter

Leslie Mackenzie, Publisher
Richard Gottlieb, Editor

Packed with need-to-know information, this database offers immediate access to 2,300 VC firms, over 10,000 managing partners, and over 11,500 VC investments.
Frequency: Annual

3040 **Directory of Venture Capital and Private Equity Firms**
Grey House Publishing
4919 Route 22
PO Box 56
Amenia, NY 12501

518-789-8700
800-562-2139; *Fax:* 845-373-6390
books@greyhouse.com; www.greyhouse.com
Social Media: Facebook, Twitter

Leslie Mackenzie, Publisher
Richard Gottlieb, Editor

Offers access to over 2,300 domestic and international venture capital and private equity firms, including detailed contact information and extensive data on investments and funds.
Cost: $685.00
1,200 Pages
Frequency: Annual
ISBN: 1-592372-72-4

3041 **Financial Institutions Directory of New England**
4709 Golf Road
Skokie, IL 60076

847-676-9600
800-321-3373; *Fax:* 847-933-8101
custserv@accuitysolutions.com;
www.accuitysolutions.com

Hugh Jones, President
Kerry Hewson, VP
Cost: $114.00
Frequency: January/July

3042 **Financial Management**
University of South Florida COBA
3821 Holly Drive
Tampa, FL 33620-7360

813-974-4133; *Fax:* 813-974-5130
caminfo@arts.usf.edu; www.ira.usf.edu

Margaret Miller, Director
Alexa Favata, Associate Director

Financial management of individual firm, governmental unit or nonprofit institution, as opposed to financial structure of whole economy for practitioners and professors of financial management.
Cost: $20.00
Circulation: 11,500
Founded in: 1970

3043 **National Credit Union Administration Directory**
National Credit Union Administration
1775 Duke St
Alexandria, VA 22314-6115

703-518-6300
800-755-1030; *Fax:* 703-518-6539
consumerassistance@ncua.gov; www.ncua.gov

J Leonard Skiles, Executive Director
Robert Fenner, Director/General Counsel
Jane Walters, Deputy Executive Director

Directory of credit unions governed by a three member board appointed by the President and confirmed by the US Senate, by the independent federal agency that charters and supervises federal credit unions. NCUA, with the backing of the full faith and credit of the US government, operates the National Credit Union Share Insurance Fund, insuring the savings of 80 million account holders in all federal credit unions and many state chartered credit unions.

3044 **North American Financial Institutions Directory**
4709 Golf Road
Skokie, IL 60076

847-676-9600
800-321-3373; *Fax:* 847-933-8101
custserv@accuitysolutions.com;
www.accuitysolutions.com

Hugh Jones, President/CEO
Cost: $495.00
Frequency: January/July
Circulation: 31850
Founded in: 1895

3045 **Ranking the Banks**
American Banker
1 State St
27th Floor
New York, NY 10004-1561

212-803-8450; *Fax:* 212-843-9600;
www.sourcemedia.com

Douglas Manoni, President/CEO
David Longobardi, Editor-in-Chief
Richard Melville, Managing Editor
Timothy Reifschneider, Advertising Director

A comprehensive database of banking and financial services rankings, league tables, and vital statistics. Includes all tables published in the print edition of American Banker, and more. Organized by category with historical data.
Cost: $945.00
128 Pages

3046 **State and Local MBA Directory**
Mortgage Bankers Association of America
1717 Rhode Island Avenue, NW
Suite 400
Washington, DC 20036

202-557-2700
membership@mortgagebankers.org;
www.mortgagebankers.org

Michael Young, Chairman

All state and local MBA officers and a calendar of significant meeting dates.
Cost: $50.00
Frequency: SemiAnnual

3047 **Thomson Bank Directory**
4709 Golf Road
Skokie, IL 60076

847-676-9600
800-321-3373; *Fax:* 847-933-8101
custserv@accuitysolutions.com;
www.accuitysolutions.com

Hugh Jones, President
Kerry Hewson, VP
Cost: $684.00
Frequency: June/December
Circulation: 35000
ISBN: 1-563103-45-1

3048 **Thomson Credit Union Directory**
4709 Golf Road
Skokie, IL 60076-1231

847-676-9600
800-321-3373; *Fax:* 847-933-8101
custserv@accuitysolutions.com;
www.accuitysolutions.com

Hugh Jones, President
Kerry Hewson, VP

Semi-annual directory that includes valuable industry statistics, a quick telephone lookup index of all credit unions and a resource guide featuring vendors within the credit union marketplace. Includes over 12,500 major credit unions and 5,500 branches, with asset rankings, membership totals and more. Published in partnership with the Credit Union National Association.
Cost: $247.00
Frequency: January/July
ISBN: 1-563103-24-9

3049 **Thomson Regulation CC Directory**
4709 Golf Road
Skokie, IL 60076

847-676-9600
800-321-3373; *Fax:* 847-933-8101
custserv@accuitysolutions.com;
www.accuitysolutions.com

Hugh Jones, President
Kerry Hewson, VP
Cost: $144.00
Frequency: January/July
Circulation: 30100

3050 **Thomson Savings Directory**
4709 Golf Road
Skokie, IL 60076-1231

847-676-9600
800-321-3373; *Fax:* 847-933-8101
custserv@accuitysolutions.com;
www.accuitysolutions.com

Hugh Jones, President
Kerry Hewson, VP

Semi-annual directory dedicated to the thrift industry. Listings include primary correspondent information, national industry statistics and breakdowns of mortgage portfolios.
Cost: $316.00
Frequency: January/July

3051 **World Bank Directory**
4709 Golf Road
Skokie, IL 60076-1231
847-676-9600
800-321-3373; *Fax:* 847-933-8101
custserv@accuitysolutions.com;
www.accuitysolutions.com
Hugh Jones, President
Kerry Hewson, VP
Contains detailed listings for 10,000 international banks and their branches worldwide plus the top 1,000 US banks. The information in this annual directory includes world and country rankings, international and correspondent contact information, principal correspondent institutions an standard settlement instructions.
Cost: $495.00
Frequency: September
Founded in: 1895

3052 **Worldwide Correspondents & Resource Guide**
4709 Golf Road
Skokie, IL 60076-1231
847-676-9600
800-321-3373; *Fax:* 847-933-8101
custserv@accuitysolutions.com;
www.accuitysolutions.com
Hugh Jones, President
Kerry Hewson, VP
A convenient one-volume directory listing the principal correspondent relationships for banks worldwide.
Cost: $184.00
Frequency: June/December

3053 **Y-9 Report Analyzer**
Sheshunoff Information Services
901 South Mopac
Suite 140
Austin, TX 78746-7970
512-472-4000
800-477-1772; *Fax:* 512-305-6575
sales@smslp.com; www.smslp.com
Social Media: Facebook, Twitter, LinkedIn
Gabrielle Sheshunoff, CEO
Sheshunoff Information Services provides bank holding companies (BHC) a tool to prepare and electronically file the following government forms: Y-9C, Y9-LP, Y11Q, and Y11I. Built in edit checks ensure the BHC's file the most accurate report possible.
Cost: $495.00
Frequency: Annual w/Quarterly Update

Industry Web Sites

3054 **http://gold.greyhouse.com**
G.O.L.D Grey House OnLine Databases
Grey House Publishing's online database platform, GOLD, offers Quick Search, Keyword Search and Expert Search, for most business sectors including banking and financial markets. The GOLD platform makes finding the information you need quick and easy - whether you're a novice searcher or an experienced database user. All of Grey House's directory products are available for subscription on the GOLD platform.

3055 **www.aabd.org**
American Association of Bank Directors
Devoted to serving the information, education and advocacy needs of individual bank and savings institution directors. This non-profit organization has members nationwide.

3056 **www.aba.com**
American Bankers Association
Brings together all categories of banking institutions to best represent the interests of this rapidly changing industry. It's membership — which includes community, regional and money center banks and holding companies, as well as savings associations, trust companies and savings banks makes ABA one of the largest banking trade associations in the country.

3057 **www.aba.com/ICB/default.htm**
Institute Of Certified Bankers
A national association of certified professionals in the financial services industry whose mission is to provide financial services professionals with confidence, credibility and recognition through its certifications.

3058 **www.abiworld.org**
American Bankruptcy Institute
Dedicated to research and education on matters related to insolvency.

3059 **www.aftweb.com**
Association for Financial Technology
Association founded in 1972 to promote high standards of professionalism in the planning, development, inplemtation and application of technology to the financial services industry.

3060 **www.aitco.net**
Association of Independent Trust Companies
Dedicated to provide a forum of leaders, owners and operators of trust companies and wealth management providers.

3061 **www.ambahq.org**
Association of Military Banks of America (AMBA)
Non-profit association of banks operating on military installments serving military customers and military banking facilities designated by the U.S. Treasury.

3062 **www.baft.org**
Bankers' Association for Finance & Trade
Financial trade association whose membership represents a broad range of internationally active financial institutions and companies that provide important services to the global financial community. BAFT serves as a forum for analysis, discussion and action among international financial professionals on a wide range of topics affecting international trade and finace, including legislative/regulatory issues.

3063 **www.bai.org**
Bank Administration Institute
The financial services industry's partner for breakthrough information and intelligence needed to innovate and stay relevant in an evolving marketplace. Serves a wide segment of the financial services industry, from the largest multinational banks to community-based institutions.

3064 **www.bisanet.org**
Bank Insurance and Securities Association
Dedicated to serving the needs of those responsible for marketing securities, insurance and other investment and risk management products.

3065 **www.bmaatlanta.com**
Business Marketing Association: Atlanta
BMA offers an information-packed website, online skills-building, marketing, certification programs and industry surveys and papers.

3066 **www.cbanet.org**
Consumer Bankers Association
Recognized voice on retail banking issues in the nation's capital. Member institutions are the leaders in consumer financial services, including auto finance, home equity lending, card products, education loans, small business services, community development, investments, deposits, and delivery.

3067 **www.cfainstitute.org**
CFA Institute
The CFA Institute is the global, non-profit professional association that administers the Chartered Financial Analyst curriculum and examination program.

3068 **www.envirobank.org**
Environmental Bankers Association
Dedicated to providing services for individuals with an interest in environmental risk management and related issues.

3069 **www.freddiemac.com**
Freddie Mac
Freddie Mac is a stockholder-owned corporation chartered by Congress to create a continuous flow of funds to mortgage lenders in support of homeownership and rental housing.

3070 **www.fwi.org**
Financial Women International
Formerly the National Association of Bank Women, the Association was founded in 1921 - one year after women won the right to vote, by a group of New York City women bankers. FWI serves women in the financial services industry that seeks to expand their personal and professional capabilities through self-directed growth in a supportive environment.

3071 **www.garp.org**
Global Association of Risk Management
This association is dedicated to being the leading professional association for risk managers, managed by and for its members.

3072 **www.greyhouse.com**
Grey House Publishing
Authoritative reference directories for most business sectors including banking and financial markets. Users can search the online databases with varied search criteria allowing for custom searches by product category, geographic area, sales volume, keyword, subject and more. Full Grey House catalog and online ordering also available.

3073 **www.icba.org**
Independent Community Bankers of America
Dedicated exclusively to enhancing the franchise value of the nation's community banks for the benefit of their customers and the communities they serve.

3074 **www.ifsaonline.org**
International Financial Services Association
Represents the international operations areas of financial services provider, their customers, suppliers and partners.

3075 **www.iib.org**
Institute of International Bankers
Created to help resolve the many special legislative, regulatory and tax issues confronting internationally headquartered financial institutions.

3076 **www.jpmorganchase.com**
JPMorgan Chase
A leading global financial services firm with assets of $1.3 trillion and operations in more than 50 countries.

3077 **www.marinebankers.org**
National Marine Bankers Association
Formed in 1980 in response to a request by the National Marine Manufacturers Association -

NMMA - for additional sources of financing for it's members products. The purpose of the NMBA is to educate prospective lenders in marine finacing procedures, create new lenders to help finance the sales of the manufacturers products, and to create an information exchange for its members.

3078 **www.mastercardinternational.com**
MasterCard Worldwide
Administers the MasterCard credit card and other products for 25,000 member institutions around the world.

3079 **www.mbaa.org**
Mortgage Bankers Association of America
Representing the real estate finance industry, MBA serves its membership by representing their legislative and regulatory interests before the US Congress and federal agencies; by meeting their educational needs through programs and a range of periodicals and publications; and by supporting their business interests with a variety of research initiatives and other products and services.

3080 **www.mortgagebankers.org**
Mortgage Bankers Association
Seeks to improve methods of originating, servicing and marketing loans.

3081 **www.naahl.org**
National Association of Affordable Housing Lenders
For financial institutions and others with an interest in affordable housing and development lending.

3082 **www.nabt.com**
National Association of Bankruptcy Trustees
Nonprofit association formed in 1982 to address the needs of the bankruptcy trustees thoughout the country and to promote the effectiveness of the bankruptcy system as a whole. While the majority of trustees who are members of the NABT are Chapter 7 trustees who primarily liquidate nonexempt assets for the benefit of creditors, many Chapter 7 trustees also serve as Chapter 11 trustees, who operate and reorganize companies. Some of our members are also Chapter 12 or Chapter 13 trustees.

3083 **www.nacha.org**
NACHA: Electronic Payments Association
Organization developing electronic solutions to improve the payments system. Representing more than 12,000 financial institutions through direct memberships and a network of regional payments associations, and 650 organizations through its industry councils, NACHA develops operating rules and business practices for the Automated Clearing House network and for electronic payments in the areas of internet commerce, electronic bill and invoice presentment and payment and other electronic payments.

3084 **www.nactt.com**
National Association of Chapter 13 Trustees
Provides a forum within which Chapteer 13 trustees will act as an information and communication resource to advance education, leadership, and continuous imporvement in the administration of bankruptcy.

3085 **www.nacusac.org**
Nat'l Assoc. of Credit Union Super. & Audit. Comm.
A unique organization of, by and for credit union supervisory committee members.

3086 **www.nafcu.org**
National Association Of Federal Credit Unions
A respected and influential trade association that exclusively represents the interests of federal credit unions before the federal government and the public.

3087 **www.naggl.com**
Nat'l Assoc. of Government Guaranteed Lenders
Promotes professional and governmental affairs interests of financial institutions and small businesses who participate in the Small Business Administration guaranteed lending and secondary market programs.

3088 **www.namb.org**
National Association of Mortgage Brokers
Mortgage brokers who seek to increase professionalism and to foster business relationships among members.

3089 **www.napmw.org**
Nat'l Association of Professional Mortgage Women
Serves all mortgage professionals and employers who want to excel.

3090 **www.nascus.org**
Nat'l Assoc. of State Credit Union Supervisors
State chartered credit unions and state credit union supervisors.

3091 **www.nationalbankers.org**
National Bankers Association
Members are minority and women's banking institutions, minority individuals employed by majority banks and institutions.

3092 **www.ncua.gov**
National Credit Union Administration
Charters and supervises federal credit unions.

3093 **www.nibanet.org**
National Investment Banking Association
A national trade association of regional and independent brokerages, investment banking firms, and related capital market service providers.

3094 **www.rmahq.org**
Risk Management Association
Topics relating to all aspects of commercial lending, financial statement analysis and credit information exchange and managerial aspects of consumer lending.

3095 **www.sifma.org/**
Securities Industry and Financial Markets Assoc.
SIFMA's mission is to champion policies and practices that benefit investors and issuers, expand and perfect global capital markets, and foster the development of new products and services.

3096 **www.snl.com**
SNL Securities
News articles on banks and thrifts, insurance and other financial services. Also features vital company information.

3097 **www.sourcemedia.com**
SourceMedia
Provides market information, including news, analysis, and insight to the financial services and related industries.

3098 **www.ufscnet.org**
Urban Financial Services Coalition
An organization of minority professionals in the financial services industry and related fields.

3099 **www.wiley.com**
John Wiley & Sons
Wiley is a global publisher of print and electronic products, specializing in science, technical, and material books and journals, professional and consumer books and subscription services, textbooks and other educational materials for undergraduate and graduate students as well as lifelong learners. Wiley has approximately 22,700 active titles and about 400 journals, and publishes about 2000 new titles in a variety of print and electronic formats each year.

Associations

3100 **Aesthetics' International Association**
310 E. Interstate 30
Suite B107
Garland, TX 75043

972-203-8530
877-968-7539; *Fax:* 972-226-2339;
www.aestheticsassociation.com/

Patricia Strunk, President
Michelle D'Allaird, Vice President
Melissa Lawrence, Membership Director

International professional organization for aestheticians that represents every facet of the aesthetics industry. We offer something for the student, aesthetician, make-up artist, reflexologist, aromatherapist, massage therapist, nutritionist, nurse, holistic practitioner and physician to the day spa and salon owner.
Founded in: 1972

3101 **American Association of Cosmetology Schools**
9927 East Bell Road
Suite 110
Scottsdale, AZ 85260

480-281-0431
800-831-1086; *Fax:* 480-905-0993
jim@beautyschools.org;
www.beautyschools.org
Social Media: Facebook, Twitter

Jim Cox, CEO
Lisa Zarda, General Manager
Geoff Gerard, Controller
Ashley Morris, Communications Manager
Linda Williams, Membership Manager

National non-profit association open to all privately owned schools of Cosmetology Arts and Sciences. AACS specializes in updating our members with information about new teaching methods, current industry events, and Washington, DC updates.
1100 Members
Founded in: 1924

3102 **American Beauty Association**
15825 N 71st St
Suite 100
Scottsdale, AZ 85254-1521

480-281-0431
Social Media: Facebook, Twitter, LinkedIn

James Cox, Executive Director
Bruce Selan, VP
George Schaeffer, Secretary/Treasurer

ABA members are manufacturers, manufacturer reps and consultants in the professional beauty industry. Associate members are made up of trade publications, distributors and salons. The ABA's mission is to expand, serve and protect the interests of the professional beauty industry.
250 Members
Founded in: 1985

3103 **American Electrology Association**
4711 Midlothian Tpk
Suite 13
Crestwood, IL 60445

708-293-1400; *Fax:* 708-293-1405
infoaea@electrology.com;
www.electrology.com
Social Media: Facebook

Pearl Warner, CPE, President
Mary Kaye Johnson, CPE, 1st Vice President
Deborah Cassin, CPE, Treasurer
Randa Thurman, Membership

The American Electrology Association (AEA), is the largest international nonprofit membership organization for permanent hair removal professionals. Promotes the highest standards in Electrology education, practice and ethics and champions state licensing and regulation of the profession to protect the public interest.
1500 Members
Founded in: 1958

3104 **American Hair Loss Council**
30 South Main
Shenandoah, PA 17976

412-765-3666; *Fax:* 412-765-3669;
www.ahlc.org
Social Media: Facebook, Twitter, LinkedIn

Susan Kettering, Executive Director
Peggy Thornhill, President
Marsha Scott, Vice President
Joseph Ellis, Board Member
Betty Ann Bugden, Treasurer

A not-for-profit agency, dedicated to sorting through this information, discovering what works and what doesn't, and presenting findings to the consumer.

3105 **American Society of Hair Restoration Surgery**
225 W. Wacker Drive
Suite 650
Chicago, IL 60606

312-981-6760; *Fax:* 312-981-6787
info@cosmeticsurgery.org;
www.cosmeticsurgery.org
Social Media: Facebook, Twitter, LinkedIn

Michael J Will, President
Robert A Shumway, President-Elect
Robert H Burke, Treasurer
Joe Niamtu, Secretary
Jane Petro, Immediate Past President
1600 Members

3106 **Associated Bodywork & Massage Professionals**
25188 Genesee Trail Rd.
Suite 200
Golden, CO 80401

303-674-8478
800-458-2267; *Fax:* 800-667-8260
expectmore@abmp.com; www.abmp.com
Social Media: Facebook, Twitter, LinkedIn

Leslie Young, VP, Communication

Practice support and liability insurance for massage/bodywork professionals.
80000 Members
Founded in: 1987

3107 **Association of Cosmetologists and Hairdressers**
15825 N. 71st Street
Suite 100
Scottsdale, AZ 85254-1521

480-281-0424
800-468-2274; *Fax:* 480-905-0708
info@probeauty.org; www.ncacares.org
Social Media: Facebook, Twitter, Google+

Scott Buchanan, Chariman
Reuben Carranza, Vice Chair
Steve Sleeper, Executive Director

Association of Cosmetologists membership includes salon owners, hairdressers, nail technicians, estheticians, educators, and students, and is the world's largest association of salon professionals.
3910 Members
Founded in: 1985

3108 **Association of Cosmetology Salon Professionals**
PO Box 207
Chapin, SC 29036

803-345-2909
contact@mycosmetology.org;
www.mycosmetology.org

Linda Green, President
Sandra Mullins, Vice-President
Terry Frick, Secretary

Association for the promotion of professional standards in the cosmetology, esthetics and nail industries.

3109 **Cosmetologists Chicago**
440 S LaSalle Street
Suite 2325
Chicago, IL

312-321-6809
800-883-7808; *Fax:* 312-673-6612
info@americasbeautyshow.com;
www.americasbeautyshow.com
Social Media: Facebook, Twitter, Youtube, Pinterest, WordPress

Denise Provenzano, President
Larry Silvestri, First VP
Robert Passage, 2nd VP
Lorrene Conino, Treasurer
Karen Gordon, Secretary

Voice of the salon industry, a beauty authority and presenter of the Chicago Midwest Beauty Show, stylists, estheticians, color technicians, salon owners, educators and nail technicians.
35000 Members

3110 **Cosmoprof North America (CPNA)**
15825 N 71st Street
Suite 100
Scottsdale, AZ 85254

480-281-0424
800-468-2274; *Fax:* 480-905-0708
info@cosmoprofnorthamerica.com;
www.cosmoprofnorthamerica.com
Social Media: Facebook, Twitter, LinkedIn, Pinterest, YouTube

Max Wexler, Chariman
Scott Buchanan, Vice Chair
Bruce Selan, Treasurer

Supports all those involved with industry related equipment, supplies and services.
Frequency: Annual
Founded in: 1892

3111 **Intercoiffure of America**
1645 Downtown West Blvd
Suite 18
Knoxville, TN 37919

614-457-7712
800-442-3007; *Fax:* 614-457-7794
info@intercoiffure.com;
www.intercoiffure.com
Social Media: Facebook, Twitter, Google+

Frank Gambuzza, President
Sheila Zaricor-Wilson, VP
Andreas Zafiriadis, 2nd VP
Inge Handing, Secretary
Darlene Gage, Treasurer

Sponsors semiannual hair fashion shows in New York City.
260 Members
Founded in: 1933

3112 **International Guild of Hair Removal Specialists**
1918 Bethel Road
Columbus, OH 43220

800-830-3247; www.ighrs.org

Formerly known as the International Guild of Professional Electrologists. A non-profit organi-

zation dedicated to providing the latest information about permanent and long-term hair removal to the consumer.
2000 Members
Founded in: 1979

3113 International Nail Technicians Association
330 N Wabash Ave
Chicago, IL 60611

312-321-6809
800-883-7808; *Fax:* 312-245-1080
info@americasbeautyshow.com;
www.isnow.com
Social Media: Facebook, Twitter, Youtube, Pinterest, WordPress

Joseph Cartagena, President
Denise Provenzano, First VP
Larry Silvestri, 2nd VP
Karen Gordon, Treasurer
Robert Passage, Secretary

An international organization for nail professionals. In 2001 it was acquired by Cosmetologists Chicago with the purpose of providing an association 'home' to nail care professionals that is dedicated to the needs of technicians and the industry

3114 International Salon Spa Business Network
207 E Ohio Street
#361
Chicago, IL 60611

440-846-6022
866-444-4272; *Fax:* 866-444-5139
margie@salonspanetwork.org;
www.salonspanetwork.org
Social Media: Facebook, Twitter

Jason Volk, President
Paul Brown, Vice President
Scott Colabuono, Vice President
Larry Walt, Treasurer
Philip Gould, Secretary

Dedicated to helping its members grow their business, effect positive change politically, provide a forum for members to share their views and ideas and interface with the professional beauty industry on behalf of the chain salons and spas.
70 Members
Founded in: 1973

3115 National Association of Barber Boards of America

870-230-0777
samdabarberman@yahoo.com

Sam Barcelona, President

Association for the promotion of professional standards in the barbering industry.
110 Members
Founded in: 1926

3116 National Beauty Culturists' League
25 Logan Circle NW
Washington, DC 20005-3725

202-332-2695; *Fax:* 202-332-0940
nbcl@bellsouth.net; www.nbcl.org

Katie B Catalon, President

Established as the National Hair System Culture League, members are black beauticians and cosmetologists who embrace diversity.
3000 Members
Founded in: 1919

3117 National Cosmetology Association
15825 N. 71st Street
Suite 100
Scottsdale, AZ 85254

480-281-0424
800-468-2274; *Fax:* 480-905-0708
info@probeauty.org; www.ncacares.org

Max Wexler, Chariman
Scott Buchanan, Vice Chair
Bruce Selan, Treasurer

Membership includes salon owners, hairdressers, nail technicians, estheticians, educators, and students. Members live and work in all 50 states, and also have the option to participate in the state and local affiliate, along with national activities.
25000 Members
Founded in: 1921

3118 Professional Beauty Association
15825 N 71st Street
Suite 100
Scottsdale, AZ 85254-1521

480-281-0424
800-468-2274; *Fax:* 480-905-0708
info@probeauty.org; www.probeauty.org
Social Media: Facebook, Twitter, LinkedIn, YouTube, Pinterest, Instagram

Reuben Carranza, Chariman
Beth Hickey, Vice Chair
Steve Sleeper, Executive Director
Rachel Molepske, Manager, Leadership Operations
Toni Davis, Director

The Professional Beauty Association (PBA) is a non-profit trade association that represents the interests of the professional beauty industry from manufacturers and distributors to salons and spas. PBA serves the industry through five core competencies: education, government advocacy, commerce opportunities, research/statistics and public relations/image building.
1400 Members
Founded in: 1904

3119 Society of Clinical and Medical Hair Removal
2424 American Lane
Madison, WI 53704-3102

608-443-2470; *Fax:* 608-443-2474
homeoffice@scmhr.org; www.scmhr.org
Social Media: Facebook, Twitter, Google+

William A Moore, President
Fadia Hoyek, Exectuive VP
Sandra Ysassi, Treasurer
Sarikhi Chaffin, Secretary
Ruth G Bayer, Vice President

An international non profit organization with members in the United States, Canada, Australia, Japan and beyond. Supports all methods of hair removal and is dedicated to the research of new technology that will keep its members at the pinnacle of their profession, offering safe, effective hair removal to their clients.
600 Members
Founded in: 1985

Newsletters

3120 ISNOW Cosmetologists Chicago
401 N Michigan Avenue
Chicago, IL 60611-4255

312-321-6809
800-883-7808; *Fax:* 312-245-1080
info@americasbeautyshow.com;
www.isnow.com

Frank Gironda, President
Joseph Cartagena, First VP
Denise Provenzano, Secretary
Larry Silvestri, Treasurer

Represents the industries various constituencies and salon owners.
Cost: $18.95
Frequency: Monthly
Circulation: 5000
Founded in: 2004

3121 National Beauty News
10405 E 55th Place
Suite B
Tulsa, OK 74146-6502

918-627-8000; *Fax:* 918-627-8660

Douglas Von Allmen, Owner

Offers news of shows, seminars, product information and columns for the professional beauty industry.
Cost: $12.00
Frequency: Monthly
Circulation: 35,500

3122 Pink Sheet
685 Route 202/206
Bridgewater, NJ 08807

800-332-2181
908-547-2159; *Fax:* 908-547-2200
custcare@elsevier.com; www.elsevierbi.com
Social Media: RSS

Mike Squires, President
Cathy Kelly, Executive Editor
Brooke McManus, Managing Editor
Jim Chicca, Executive Director
Melissa Carlson, Editorial Operations Manager

Chronicles regulatory and legal news, major scientific developments and testing methodologies, and their effect on these industries. Product marketing news, new product launches, and promotions and advertising at the retail level, are also included.
Cost: $1050.00
Frequency: Weekly
Founded in: 1939

Magazines & Journals

3123 AEA Journal of Electrology
American Electrology Association
4711 Midlothian Tpk
Suite 13
Crestwood, IL 60445

708-293-1400; *Fax:* 708-293-1405
infoaea@electrology.com;
www.electrology.com

Pearl Warner, CPE, President
Karen Portnoff, Marketing

The Journal of Electrology is a membership news publication, published twice per year and is designed to inform and educate the professional electrologist by offering articles of interest and value by reputable authors who are well qualified in the topic area.
Cost: $42.00
1500 Members
Frequency: Semi-Annual
Circulation: 1200
Founded in: 1958

3124 Beauty Store Business
Creative Age Publications
7628 Densmore Ave
Van Nuys, CA 91406-2042

818-782-7328
800-442-5667; *Fax:* 818-782-7450
webmaster@creativeage.com;
www.creativeage.com

Deborah Carver, President/CEO
Mindy Rosiejka, Vice President/COO
Karie Frost, Executive Director

Industry trends and valuable tips concerning real estate, banking, insurance, product liability, advertising, merchandising, and more.
Frequency: Monthly
Circulation: 15000
ISSN: 1098-0660
Founded in: 1971

3125 **BeautyLink**
American Association of Cosmetology Schools
9927 E. Bell Road
Suite 110
Scottsdale, AZ 85260

480-281-0431
800-831-1086; *Fax:* 480-905-0993
jim@beautyschools.org; www.beautyschools.org

Jim Cox, Executive Director
Lisa Zarda, General Manager

Quarterly magazine of the AACS, with cosmetology industry updates and features on new trends and best practices.
Frequency: Quarterly
Circulation: 7000

3126 **Cosmetic World**
Ledes Group
16 East 40th Street
Suite 700
New York, NY 10016

212-840-8800; *Fax:* 212-840-7246; www.cosmeticworld.com

Debra Davis, Advertising Director
Brittany Burhop, Executive Editor
Debbie Ward, Managing Editor

Current industry events, legislation, management changes and corporate activities, as well as marketing developments and financial analysis.
Cost: $175.00
Circulation: 5397
Printed in on glossy stock

3127 **DaySpa Magazine**
Creative Age Publications
7628 Densmore Ave
Van Nuys, CA 91406-2042

818-782-7328; *Fax:* 818-782-7450
sverba@creativeage.com; www.creativeage.com

Deborah Carver, President/CEO
Mindy Rosiejka, Vice President/COO
Karie Frost, Executive Director

DaySpa is dedicated to helping premium salon and spa owners better serve their client enhance their bottom line. Presents the most accurate, up-to-date information available on trends, products, equipment, services, and management and management tools in easy-to-read, entertaining articles.
Cost: $17.50
Frequency: Annual+
Circulation: 24,000+
Founded in: 1972

3128 **Dermascope Magazine**
Aesthetics International Association
310 East I-30,
SuiteB107
Garland, TX 75043

469-429-9300
800-961-3777; *Fax:* 469-429-9301
press@dermascope.com; www.dermascope.com

William Strunk, Publisher
Amy McKay, Editor
Wes Wynne, Marketing Director

Provides education for skin care professionals. One of the oldest magazines in the industry.
Cost: $45.00
148 Pages
Frequency: Monthly
Circulation: 16000
ISSN: 1075-055X
Founded in: 1972

3129 **Looking Fit Magazine**
Virgo Publishing LLC
3300 N Central Ave
Suite 300
Phoenix, AZ 85012-2532

48 - 9 - 11; *Fax:* 480-990-0819
swhitley@vpico.com; www.vpico.com

John Siefert, CEO
Kelly Ridley, Executive VP/ CFO

Educational resource for professionals in the indoor tanning industry.
Cost: $70.00
300 Pages
Frequency: Monthly
Founded in: 1986

3130 **Modern Salon**
Vance Publishing
400 Knightsbridge Pkwy
Lincolnshire, IL 60069

847-634-2600; *Fax:* 847-634-4379
info@vancepublishing.com; www.vancepublishing.com

William C Vance, Chairman
Peggy Walker, President

The constant leader and voice of the professional salon industry. Delivers step-by-step education for the stylist and paid circulation for the advertiser.
Frequency: Monthly
Circulation: 117000
Founded in: 1924
Printed in 4 colors on glossy stock

3131 **NW Stylist and Salon**
Porter Publishing
1750 Sw Skyline Blvd
Suite 8
Portland, OR 97221-2543

503-296-4889
888-297-7010; *Fax:* 503-296-4893; www.portlandpsinc.com

James Pettigrove, President
Lisa Kind, Managing Editor
Joel Holland, VP
Marcy Avenson, Advertising Director

Business trade journal mailed free to every salon school and practitioner in Oregon. Accepts advertising.
Cost: $20.00
36 Pages
Frequency: Monthly
Circulation: 22000
Founded in: 1983

3132 **NailPro**
Creative Age Publications
7628 Densmore Ave
Van Nuys, CA 91406-2042

818-782-7328
800-442-5667; *Fax:* 818-782-7450
webmaster@creativeage.com; www.creativeage.com

Deborah Carver, President/CEO
Mindy Rosiejka, Vice President/COO
Karie Frost, Executive Director

Nail care how-to's, business related articles, information on nail anatomy and pathology, as well as new products, trends, profiles and a calendar of events.
Cost: $21.95
Frequency: Monthly
Circulation: 50713
Founded in: 1971

3133 **Nails Magazine**
Bobit Publishing Company
3520 Challenger St
Torrance, CA 90503-1640

310-533-2400; *Fax:* 310-533-2500
Hannah.Lee@bobit.com; www.bobit.com

Edward J Bobit, CEO
Hannah Lee, Executive Editor
Uyonna Beckham, Sales Assistant
Sarah Paredes, Senior Production Manager
Ty Bobit, CEO

Offers business information on products and application techniques for professional manicurists and salon owners.
Cost: $20.00
Frequency: Monthly
Circulation: 62274
Founded in: 1961

3134 **Salon News**
Fairchild Publications
750 3rd Ave
New York, NY 10017-2703

212-630-4000; *Fax:* 212-630-3563; www.fairchildpub.com

Mary G Berner, CEO

Profitability and stability, salon services and resale, and on motivation and education.
Frequency: Monthly
Circulation: 77,603

3135 **Salon Today**
Vance Publishing
400 Knightsbridge Pkwy
Lincolnshire, IL 60069

847-634-2600; *Fax:* 847-634-4379
info@vancepublishing.com; www.vancepublishing.com

William C Vance, Chairman
Peggy Walker, President

Content is modeled as a monthly exchange of ideas on how to grow salon business. Special issues include annual Salon Today 200, Salon of the Year, Technology and Spa Business.
Frequency: Monthly
Circulation: 25000

3136 **Skin Magazine**
Allured Publishing Corporation
PO Box 50
Congers, NY 10920
845-267-3008
866-616-3008; *Fax:* 845-267-3478
skininc@cambeywest.com; www.skininc.com

Janet Ludwig, President
Lin Getner, Controller

The business magazine preferred by owners and managers of salons and spas and the official publication of the American Aestheticians Education Association. Recently awarded a Gold award for editorial from the American Business Publication editors association.
Cost: $49.00
120 Pages
Frequency: Monthly
Circulation: 16000
Founded in: 1988

3137 **WWD Beauty Biz**
Fairchild Publications

7 W 34th St
New York, NY 10001-8100

212-630-3880; *Fax:* 212-630-3868;
www.fairchildpub.com

Mary Berner, President/CEO
Patrick McCarthy, Chairman/Editorial Director
Jenny B. Fine, Editor-in-Chief
Sarah Murphy, Publisher

The premier guide to the beauty industry. Provides in-depth coverage and analysis on all aspects of the industry, including trends, brands, retailers, and personalities driving both the general consumer and insider sides of the business.
Cost: $60.00
Frequency: Monthly
Circulation: 40,056
Founded in: 1892

Trade Shows

3138 AACS Annual Convention & Expo

American Association of Cosmetology Schools
9927 E. Bell Road
Suite 110
Scottsdale, AZ 85260

480-281-0431
800-831-1086; *Fax:* 480-905-0993
jim@beautyschools.org;
www.beautyschools.org

Jim Cox, Executive Director
Lisa Zarda, General Manager

An opportunity to bring your professional team together to lead your school into the future. Education tracks, classes, social events, and the expo hall complete the experience.
800 Attendees
Frequency: November

3139 ACSP Annual Meeting

Association of Cosmetology Salon Professionals
PO Box 207
Chapin, SC 29036

803-345-2909
contact@mycosmetology.org;
www.mycosmetology.org

Linda Green, President
Sandra Mullins, Vice-President
Terry Frick, Secretary

Competitions, continuing education and annual meeting.
Frequency: Annual

3140 Aesthetics' World Expositions

Aesthetics' International Association
2611 N Belt Line Road
Suite 140
Sunnyvale, TX 75182-9357

972-203-8530
877-968-7539; *Fax:* 972-226-2339;
www.beautyworks.com/aia

150-250 exhibits of skin care, body therapy products make up and equipment. Salon owners, body massage therapists, and dermatologists attend.
3000 Attendees
Frequency: Biennial
Founded in: 1979

3141 American Electrology Association Annual Convention

American Electrology Association
4711 Midlothian Tpk
Suite 13
Crestwood, IL 60445

708-293-1400; *Fax:* 708-293-1405
infoaea@electrology.com;
www.electrology.com

Pearl G. Warner, President
Mary Kaye Johnson, 1st Vice President
Deborah Cassin, CPE, Treasurer
Donna F. Crump, Convention Committee

AEA is the largest international nonprofit membership organization for permanent hair removal. The convention features the largest number of exhibitors with the latest state of the art equipment.
1500 Members
300 Attendees
Frequency: Annual
Founded in: 1958

3142 Big Show Expo

Big Show Expo
1841 Broadway
Room 812
New York, NY 10023-7603

212-580-1407; *Fax:* 212-757-3611

Bernice Calvin, President
Maggie Smallwood, Conference Coordinator

Largest group of ethnic beauty shows. 200 booths updating the skills and expertise of hairdressers with ethnic clientele and spotlighting new trends in hair fashions, with all new styles for today's fashion looks.
15M Attendees
Frequency: August, September

3143 COSMOPROF North America

COSMOPROF North America
15825 North 71st Street
Suite 100
Scottsdale, AZ 85254

480-281-0424
800-468-2274; *Fax:* 480-905-0708
cpnainfo@probeauty.org;
www.cosmoprofnorthamerica.com

Eric Horn, Show Director
Ebony King, Show Manager
Wendy Forakis, Business Relations Manager

The most comprehensive and international professional beauty industry show on the continent. Attendees include manufacturers to distributors , salon owners to spa professionals, importers to retail buyers with hundreds of exhibitors.
25000 Attendees
Frequency: July
Mailing list available for rent

3144 Hairworld

National Cosmetology Association
15825 North 71st Street
Suite 100
Scottsdale, AZ 85254

480-281-0424
800-468-2274; *Fax:* 480-905-0708
info@probeauty.org; www.ncacares.org

Max Wexler, Chairman
Scott Buchanan, Vice Chair
Bruce Selan, Treasurer

Annual show of 125 exhibitors of hair products, cosmetics and jewelry.
3000 Attendees
Frequency: July
Circulation: 30,000

3145 International Congress of Esthetics

Aesthetics' International Association
310 East I-30
Suite B107
Garland, TX 75043

469-429-9300
800-961-3777; *Fax:* 469-429-9301
press@dermascope.com;
www.dermascope.com

Will Strunk, Publisher
Amy McKay, Editor

Biennial show of skin care, makeup and body therapy products and equipment.
3000 Attendees
Frequency: February
Founded in: 1977

3146 NABBA Annual Conference

National Association of Barber Boards of America

870-230-0777
samdabarberman@yahoo.com

Sam Barcelona, President
Frequency: Annual

Directories & Databases

3147 AEA Online Directory

American Electrology Association
4711 Midlothian Tpk
Suite 13
Crestwood, IL 60445

708-293-1400; *Fax:* 708-293-1405
infoaea@electrology.com;
www.electrology.com

Pearl Warner, President
Randa Thurman, Referral Directory

Online directory of electrologists across the country.Available on the AEA Web site.
1500 Members
Founded in: 1958

3148 Drug Store and HBC Chains Database

Chain Store Guide
3922 Coconut Palm Dr
Tampa, FL 33619-1389

813-627-6700
800-927-9292; *Fax:* 813-627-6888
webmaster@chainstoreguide.com;
www.csgis.com

Mike Jarvis, Publisher
Arthur Sciarrotta, Senior VP

Tap into the lucrative drug industry with profiles on more than 1,700 US and Canadian companies operating two or more retail drug stores, deep discount stores, health and beauty care (HBC) stores, cosmetic stores or vitamin stores that have industry sales of at least $250,000. This powerful database empowers you to sell and market your products successfully by reaching more than 8,300 key decision-makers.
Cost: $335.00
Circulation: 8,300

3149 Hayes Chain Drug Store Directory

Hayes Directories
PO Box 3436
Mission Viejo, CA 92690

949-583-0537; *Fax:* 949-583-7419
enhayes@pacbell.net; www.hayesdir.com

James Edward Hayes, Editor

Comes in two volumes and contains information for 34,773 chain pharmacies in the United States, 8 stores or more. First volume lists the chain headquarters, and includes the total count of stores with pharmacies. The second volume groups the individual chain stores alphabetically by chain name followed by the name and address information for the headquarters of the parent

company.
Cost: $250.00
Frequency: Annual,November

3150 **Hayes Drug Store Directory**
Hayes Directories
PO Box 3436
Mission Viejo, CA 92690

949-583-0537; *Fax:* 949-583-7419
enhayes@pacbell.net; www.hayesdir.com

James Edward Hayes, Editor

Contains information for the 53,821 retail drug stores in the United States.
Cost: $335.00
Frequency: Annual,November

3151 **Hayes Independent Drug Store Directory**
Hayes Directories
PO Box 3436
Mission Viejo, CA 92690

949-583-0537; *Fax:* 949-583-7419
enhayes@pacbell.net; www.hayesdir.com

James Edward Hayes, Editor

Published annually and contains information for 19,048 independent retail pharmacies in the United States. Independent stores are 7 stores or less.
Cost: $300.00
Frequency: Annual,November

Industry Web Sites

3152 **http://gold.greyhouse.com**
G.O.L.D Grey House OnLine Databases

Grey House Publishing's online database platform, GOLD, offers Quick Search, Keyword Search and Expert Search for most business sectors including beauty and cosmetics markets. The GOLD platform makes finding the information you need quick and easy - whether you're a novice searcher or an experienced database user. All of Grey House's directory products are available for subscription on the GOLD platform.

3153 **www.bbsi.org**
Beauty and Barber Supply Institute

Our members are wholesaler-distributors, manufacturers and manufacturers' representatives from around the world. Our mission is to maximize the potential of the professional salon industry.

3154 **www.beautyschools.org**
American Association of Cosmetology Schools

Serves privately owned schools of Cosmetology Arts & Sciences.

3155 **www.dermascope.com**
Aesthetics' International Association

International professional organization for aestheticians representing every facet of the aesthetics industry. From the student, aesthetician, make-up artist, reflexologist, aromatherapist, massage therapist, nutritionist, nurse, holistic practitioner and physician to the day spa/salon owner.

3156 **www.electrology.com**
American Electrology Association

Organization of professional hair removal practitioners promoting the highest standards of electrology education through our annual and state conventions with seminars following a prescribed learning standard.

3157 **www.greyhouse.com**
Grey House Publishing

Authoritative reference directories for most business sectors including beauty and cosmetics markets. Users can search the online databases with varied search criteria allowing for custom searches by product category, geographic area, sales volume, keyword, subject and more. Full Grey House catalog and online ordering also available.

3158 **www.isnow.com**
Cosmetologists Chicago

Voice of the salon industry. Presenter of the Chicago Midwest Beauty Show, we are stylists, estheticians, color technicians, salon owners, educators and nail technicians.

3159 **www.oneroof.org**
American Beauty Association

Serves the interests of the professional beauty industry.

3160 **www.salons.org**
The Salon Association

Non-profit organization representing 7,000 employment-based salons and spas across the United States and Canada

Associations

3161 American Association for Medical Chronobiology & Chronotherapeutics

E-Mail: editorial@aamcc.org; www.aamcc.net

Erhard Haus, President
Michael Smolensky, Vice President
Linda Sackett-Lundeen, Secretary-Treasurer
Molly Bray, Director
Martin Young, Director

Provides a forum for the exchange and discussion of new findings, methods, and applications in medical chronobiology and chronotherapeutics.

3162 American Association of Bioanalysts

906 Olive Street
Suite 1200
St Louis, MO 63101

314-241-1445; *Fax:* 314-241-1449
aab@aab.org; www.aab.org

Mark S Birenbaum PhD, Administrator

AAB is committed to the pursuit of excellence in clinical laboratory services by enhancing the professional skills of each of its members; promoting more efficient and productive operations; offering external quality control programs; collaborating with other professional associations and government agencies; promoting safe laboratory practices; and educating legislators, regulators, and the general public about clinical laboratory tests and procedures.
Founded in: 1956

3163 American Association of Immunologists

9650 Rockville Pike
Bethesda, MD 20814

301-634-7178; *Fax:* 301-634-7887
infoaai@aai.org; www.aai.org
Social Media: Facebook

Marc K Jenkins, President
M Michele Hogan, Executive Director
David G Jakson, Director of Finance
Vivian Chin, Senior Accountant
Chhanda Das, Accounting Assistant

AAI is a professional organization founded to advance the knowledge of immunology and related disciplines, foster interchange of ideas and information among scientists, and promote understanding of the field of immunology.
Cost: $50.00
6500 Members
Founded in: 1954

3164 American Geophysical Union

2000 Florida Ave Nw
Washington, DC 20009

202-462-6900
800-966-2481; *Fax:* 202-328-0566
service@agu.org; www.agu.org
Social Media: Facebook, Twitter, LinkedIn, Youtube, RSS

Robin E Bell, President
Eric A Davidson, President Elect
Susan Webb, International Secretary
Christine W McEntee, Executive Director/CEO
Louise Pellerin, General Secretary
52000 Members
Founded in: 1919
Mailing list available for rent

3165 American Institute of Biological Sciences

1800 Alexander Bell Drive
Suite 400
Reston, VA 20191

703-674-2500
800-992-2427; *Fax:* 703-674-2509
rogrady@aibs.org; www.aibs.org
Social Media: Facebook, Twitter, LinkedIn, Youtube, RSS

Joseph Travis, President
John Tobin, Treasurer
Judith Skog, Secretary
Karen Schmaling, Vice President
John Burris, Member

Supports professionals involved with the biological sciences, including research, products, education; sponsors annual conference.
Mailing list available for rent

3166 American Registry of Magnetic Resonance Imaging Technologists

8815 Commonwealth Blvd.
Bellerose, NY 11426

718-347-8690; *Fax:* 718-347-8691
ARMRIT@msn.com
armrit.org

James F. Coffin, President & Executive Director
Thomas K. Schrack, Director
Charles G. Fiore, Senior Director & Legal Counsel
William J. Woodward, Director
Charles W. Kreines, Director

MRI schools, educational resources, certified tech resumes, practice tests, and verification of a tech's certification.
Founded in: 1991

3167 American Society for Biochemistry and Molecular Biology

11200 Rockville Pike
Suite 302
Rockville, MD 20852-3110

240-283-6600; *Fax:* 301-881-2080
asbmb@asbmb.org; www.asbmb.org
Social Media: Facebook, Twitter, LinkedIn, YouTube, Google+

Steven McKnight, President
Karen Allen, Secretary
Toni M Antalis, Treasurer
Natalie Ahn, President-Elect
Barbara A Gordon, Executive Director

A professional and educational association for biochemists and molecular biologists which seeks to extend and utilize the field of biochemistry and molecular biology.
Cost: $18.50
11900 Members
Founded in: 1906
Mailing list available for rent: 11000 names

3168 American Society for Reproductive Medicine

1209 Montgomery Highway
Birmingham, AL 35216-2809

205-978-5000; *Fax:* 205-978-5005
asrm@asrm.org; www.asrm.org
Social Media: Facebook, Twitter, LinkedIn, Tumblr

Rebecca Sokol, President
Owen K. Davis, President Elect
Richard Paulson, Vice President
Linda Giudice, Past President
Richard H. Reindollar, Executive Director

Organization devoted to advancing knowledge and expertise in the study of reproduction and reproductive disorders.
Founded in: 1944

3169 American Society of Plant Biologists

15501 Monona Drive
Rockville, MD 20855-2768

301-251-0560; *Fax:* 301-279-2996
info@aspb.org
my.aspb.org

Crispin Taylor, Executive and Governance
Jotee Pundu, Administrative Staff
Melanie Binder, Member Services
Susan Cato, Member Services
Annette Kessler, Publications

A professional society devoted to the advancement of the plant sciences. It publishes research and organizes conferences that are key to the advancement of plant biology.

3170 American Soybean Association

12125 Woodcrest Executive Drive
Suite 100
St. Louis, MO 63141-5009

314-576-1770
800-688-7692; *Fax:* 314-576-2786
membership@soy.org
soygrowers.com
Social Media: Facebook, Twitter, RSS

Sam Butler, Director
Ted Glaub, Director
Richard Wilkins, Director
Wade Cowan, President
Ray Gaesser, Chairman

Domestic and international policy advocate of increasing market opportunities and value for U.S. soybean farmers.

3171 Association for Women Geoscientists

12000 N. Washington St.
Suite 285
Thornton, CO 80241-3134

303-412-6219; *Fax:* 303-253-9220
office@awg.org; www.awg.org

Blair Schneider, President
Roxy Frary, President Elect
Molly Long, Secretary
Bevin Bailey, Treasurer
Denise Cox, Past President

A professional organization which promotes the professional development of its members, provides geoscience outreach to girls, and encourages womento become geoscientists.
Founded in: 1977

3172 Association of Biomolecular Resource Facilities

9650 Rockville Pike
Bethesda, MD 20814

301-634-7306; *Fax:* 301-634-7455
abrf@abrf.org; www.abrf.org
Social Media: Facebook, LinkedIn, Flickr, YouTube, Google+

Bill Hendrickson, President
Paula Turpen, Secretary/Treasurer
George Grills, Director
Tim Hunter, Director
Anoja Perera, Director

Dedicated to advancing core and research biotechnology laboratoriesthrough research, communication, and education.
700 Members
Founded in: 1988

3173 Association of Women Soil Scientists

9611 S. Riverbend Ave.
Parlier, CA 93648

E-Mail: Suduan.Gao@ars.usda.gov; www.womeninsoils.org

Wendy Greenberg, Chair

A nonprofit organization of women and men in soil science that promotes a better understanding of the role of soil scientists and that provides assistance and encouragement for women in non-traditional fields and for women seeking employment in the field of soil science.

3174 BioSpace
6465 South Greenwood Plaza
Suite 400
Centennial, CO 80111

877-277-7585; *Fax:* 800-595-2929
support@biospace.com; www.biospace.com
Social Media: Facebook, Twitter, LinkedIn

The leading online community for industry news and careers for lifescience professionals.

3175 Biotechnology Industry Organization
1201 Maryland Ave SW
Suite 900
Washington, DC 20024

202-962-9200
info@bio.org; www.bio.org
Social Media: Facebook, Twitter, LinkedIn, Youtube

James C Greenwood, President
Scott Whitaker, COO
Joanne Duncan, CFO/SVP, Finance & Administration
Tom DiLenge, General Counsel/SVP, Legal
Daniel M Junius, Treasurer

Provides support for all those involved in biotechnology from a government, corporate, and trade viewpoint. Also represents biotechnology companies, academic institutions, biotechnology centers and related organizations in all 50 US states and 31 other nations. Researchers expand the boundaries of science to benefit mankind by providing better healthcare, enhanced agriculture, and a cleaner and safer environment.
1100+ Members
Founded in: 1993
Mailing list available for rent

3176 Biotechnology Institute
1201 Maryland Avenue, SW
Suite 900
Washington, DC 20024

202-312-9269; *Fax:* 202-355-6706
info@biotechinstitute.org;
www.biotechinstitute.org
Social Media: Facebook, Twitter, LinkedIn, YouTube

Thomas G. Wiggans, Chairman
Scott W. Morrison, Treasurer
Lawrence Mahan, Ph.D., President
Bianca Blanks, Director of Programs
Quinta Jackson, VP Finance & Administration

An independent nonprofit organization founded to teach the public about the benefits of biotechnology.

3177 Council for Biotechnology Information
1201 Maryland Ave SW
Suite 900
Washington, DC 20024-2149

202-962-9200; *Fax:* 202-589-2547
cbi@whybiotech.com; www.whybiotech.com
Social Media: Facebook, Twitter

James C Greenwood, CEO
Scott Whitaker, COO
Joanne Duncan, CFO/SVP, Finance & Administration
Tom DiLenge, General Counsel/SVP, Legal

A coalition of six of the world's leading biotechnology companies and two trade associations. Its mission is to improve the understanding and acceptance of biotechnology by collecting balanced, science-based information and communicating it through a variety of channels.
Founded in: 2000
Mailing list available for rent

3178 Council of State Bioscience Associations
www.bio.org/council-state-bioscience-associations

Russell Allen, Chair
Nathan Tinker, Vice Chair

The council is comprised of 48 state-based trade organizations. It calls for public policy to support the bioscience industry.

3179 Crop Science Society of America
5585 Guilford Rd.
Madison, WI 53711-5801

608-273-8080; *Fax:* 608-273-2021
membership@crops.org; www.crops.org
Social Media: Facebook, Twitter, LinkedIn

Roch Gaussoin, President
Michael Grusak, President-Elect
Ellen Bergfeld, Member, Ex Officio
Mark Brick, Member, Ex Officio
E Charles Brummer, Member, Ex Officio

An educational and scientific organization comprised of more than 4,700 members dedicated to the advancement of crop science.
Founded in: 1956

3180 CropLife America
1156 15th St. NW
Washington, DC 20005

202-296-1585; *Fax:* 202-463-0474
info@croplifeamerica.org;
www.croplifeamerica.org
Social Media: Facebook, Twitter, YouTube

Jay Vroom, President &CEO
Beau Greenwood, EVP Government Relations
William F. Kuckuck, EVP/ COO
Rachel G. Lattimore, SVP & General Counsel
Priscilla Hammett, CFO

U.S. trade association representing the major manufacturers, formulators, and distributors of crop protection and pest control products.
Founded in: 1933

3181 Electrophoresis Society
1202 Ann Street
Madison, WI 53713

608-258-1565; *Fax:* 608-258-1569
matt-aes@tds.net; www.aesociety.org
Social Media: Facebook, Twitter, LinkedIn

Mark A Hayes, President
Christa Hestekin, VP
Rodrigo Martinez-Duarte, Executive VP
Phil Beckett, Secretary
Lawrence I Grossman, Treasurer

Unique international organization founded to improve and promote technologies necessary for biomolecular separation and detection.
200 Members
Founded in: 1972
Mailing list available for rent

3182 Enzyme Technical Association
1111 Pennsylvania Avenue, NW
Washington, DC 20004-2541

202-739-5613; *Fax:* 202-739-3001
abegley@morganlewis.com;
www.enzymeassociation.org

Ann M Begley, General Counsel and Secretary
Robert Zega, Chairman
Vincent Sewalt, Treasurer
Gary L Yingling, C0-General Counsel
Scott Ravech, Member

Promotes the development, preservation, maintenance and general welfare of the industry to the world of manufacturing and distributing enzyme preparations from any source for direct and indirect addition or application to foods, drugs, and other articles of use by humans or animals.
Founded in: 1970

3183 Federation of American Societies for Experimental Biology
9650 Rockville Pike
Bethesda, MD 20814

301-634-7000; *Fax:* 301-634-7001
info@faseb.org; www.faseb.org
Social Media: Facebook, Twitter, LinkedIn, YouTube

Parker B. Antin, PhD, President
Hudson H. Freeze, PhD, President-Elect
Thomas O Baldwin, Vice President for Science Policy
Mark O. Lively, PhD, Treasurer
Guy Fogleman, PhD, CFA, Federation Secretary

A nonprofit organization that is the principal umbrella organization of U.S. societies in the field of biological and medical research.
Founded in: 1912

3184 International Society for Biomedical Polymeric Biomaterials
42 Broad Street
Rd # 217
Manakin Sabot, VA 23103

804-708-3010; *Fax:* 804-708-0603
info@isbppb.org
isbppb.org
Social Media: Facebook, Twitter, Google +

Mia Galijasevic, Executive Director
Munmaya Mishra, Founding Chairman
Gary L. Bowlin, President

An organization engaged in educating, networking, advocating, and advancing the field of biomedical polymers and polymeric biomaterials internationally.
Founded in: 2011

3185 International Society for Chronobiology
University of Texas-Medical Branch
301 University Boulevard
Galveston, TX 77555

409-611-1011
prf@unife.it; www.chronoint.org

Promotes studies on temporal parameters of biological variables and pursues related scientific and educational purposes. Encourages research centers and the establishment of chronobiology as an academic discipline in its own right.
300 Members
Founded in: 1937
Mailing list available for rent

3186 International Society for Magnetic Resonance in Medicine
2300 Clayton Road
Suite 620
Concord, CA 94520

510-841-1899; *Fax:* 510-841-2340
info@ismrm.org; www.ismrm.org
Social Media: Facebook, Twitter, LinkedIn, RSS

Roberta A Kravitz, Executive Director
Kerry Crockett, Associate Executive Director
Anne-Marie Kahrovic, Director of Meetings
Mariam Barzin, Finance Director
Candace Spradley, Education Director

Nonprofit professional association devoted to furthering the development and application of magnetic resonance techniques in medicine and biology. Also holds annual scientific meeting and sponsors other major educational and scientific workshops.
5000 Members
Founded in: 1994
Mailing list available for rent

3187 International Union of Biochemistry and Molecular Biology
3330 Hospital Drive N.W.
Calgary, AB T2N4N1
403-220-3021; *Fax:* 403-270-2211
walsh@ucalgary.ca; www.iubmb.org
Michael P. Walsh, General Secretary
Joan J Guinovart, President
Andrew H J Wang, President Elect
Francesco Bonomi, Treasurer
Avadhesha Surolia, Member for Publications
An international non-governmental organization concerned with biochemistry and molecular biology.
Founded in: 1955

3188 Massachusetts Biotechnology Council
300 Technology Sq
8th Floor
Cambridge, MA 02139
617-674-5100; *Fax:* 617-674-5101
info@massbio.org; www.massbio.org
Social Media: Facebook, Twitter, LinkedIn, Youtube
Glenn Batchelder, Chairman
Dr. Abbie Celniker, Vice Chair
Michael Ohara, Treasurer
David Lucchino, Clerk
Geoff MacKay, Immediate past Chairman
Not for profit organization that provides services and support for the Massachusetts biotechnology industry. Committed to advancing the development of critical new science technology and medicines that benefit people worldwide.
400+ Members
Founded in: 1985
Mailing list available for rent

3189 National Association of Wheat Growers
415 Second St. NE
Suite 300
Washington, DC 20002
202-547-7800
wheatworld@wheatworld.org;
www.wheatworld.org/issues/biotech
Brett Blankenship, President
Jim Palmer, Chief Executive Officer
The association advocates for the use of biotechnology to increase crop variety and productivity, and meet the growing food requirements of the planet.
Founded in: 1950

3190 National Center for Biotechnology Information
US National Library of Medicine
8600 Rockville Pike
Building 38A
Bethesda, MD 20894
301-496-2475; *Fax:* 301-480-9241
info@ncbi.nlm.nih.gov; www.ncbi.nlm.nih.gov
Social Media: Facebook, Twitter, LinkedIn, YouTube, RSS, Google+
To develop new information technologies to aid in the understanding of fundamental molecular and genetic processes that control health and disease.
Founded in: 1988

3191 National Corn Growers Association
632 Cepi Drive
Chesterfield, MO 63005
636-733-9004; *Fax:* 636-733-9005
corninfo@ncga.com; www.ncga.com
Social Media: Facebook, Twitter, Pinterest. RSS
Chris Novak, Chief Executive Officer
Kathy Baker, Executive Assistant
Susan Claiborne, Receptionist
Martin Barbre, Chairman
Chip Bowling, President
News, facts, and information for growers, media, educators, and anyone else interested in corn.
Founded in: 1957

3192 New York Biotechnology Association
205 East 42nd St
14th Floor
, NY 10017
212-433-2623; *Fax:* 212-433-0779
info@nyba.org; www.newyorkbio.org
Social Media: Facebook, LinkedIn
Robert Easton, Chairman
Nathan Tinker, Executive Director
Joseph Tortorice, VP, Operations
Patricia Wadington, Director, Membership Services
Cynthia Green, Secretary
NYBA has been an active & vocal champion for New York's life science industry. Through the Association's education & advocacy efforts in both Albany and Washington DC, NYBA has focused it's resources on building a powerful innovation force in New York state by working to create an economic atmosphere that rewards entrepreneurism, expands access to capital, invests in the industry's future, and protects patient access to life saving therapies.
250 Members
Founded in: 1990

3193 North Carolina Biotechnology Center
15 TW Alexander Drive
PO Box 13547
Research Triangle Park, NC 27709-3547
919-541-9366; *Fax:* 919-990-9544
info@ncbiotech.org; www.ncbiotech.org
Social Media: Facebook, Twitter, LinkedIn, Youtube
John L Atkins III, Chairman
Doug Edgeton, President & CEO
Judy Orchard, Senior Executive Assistant
Kenneth R Tindall, SVP, Science & Business Dev
Lynne Runyan, VP, Human Resource
To provide long-term economic and societal benefits to North Carolina through support of biotechnology research, business and education.
65 Members
Founded in: 1981

3194 Pan American Marine Biotechnology Association
E-Mail: info@pamba.ca; www.pamba.ca
Heather Manuel, President
Sergio Marshall, Vice President
Brian Dixon, Treasurer
Association for the promotion of sustainable use of marine resources in the Americas.
Founded in: 1999

3195 Pennsylvania Biotechnology Association
650 East Swedesford Road
Suite 190
Wayne, PA 19087
610-947-6800; *Fax:* 610-947-6801
president@pennsylvaniabio.org;
www.pabio.org
Christopher Molineaux, President & CEO
Vin Milano, Treasurer
Robert Bazemore, Chairman
Jeffrey Libson, Secretary
Christian Manders, COO
A catalyst to ensure Pennsylvania is a global leader in the biosciences by developing a cohesive community that unites the region's biotechnology, pharmaceutical research, and financial strategies.

3196 Protein Society
1450 S Rolling Road
Suite 3.007
Baltimore, MD 21227
443-543-5450; *Fax:* 443-543-5453
staff@proteinsociety.org;
www.proteinsociety.org
Social Media: Facebook, Twitter, LinkedIn
Carol B Post, President
Jacquelyn Fetrow, Secretary/Treasurer
James U Bowie, Past President
Charles Brooks III, Councilor
Carlos Bustamante, Councilor
The Protein Society is a not-for-profit scientific and educational membership organization. Our mission is to provide international forums to facilitate communication and collaboration with respect to all aspects of the study of protein molecules, the building blocks of life.
2100 Members
Founded in: 1986
Mailing list available for rent: 3,000 names at $200 per M

3197 Section for Magnetic Resonance Technologists
2300 Clayton Road
Suite 620
Concord, CA 94520
510-841-1899; *Fax:* 510-841-2340
info@ismrm.org; www.ismrm.org
Social Media: Facebook, Twitter, LinkedIn
Roberta A. Kravitz, Executive Director
Kerry Crockett, Associate Executive Director
Mariam Barzin, Director of Finance
Julia White, Accounting Coordinator
Mary Day, Office Manager
A professional organization in the medical imaging community providing education, professional advice and support for magnetic resonance (MR) technologists and radiographers throughout the world.

3198 Sino-American Pharmaceutical Professionals Association
P. O. Box 282
Nanuet, NY 10954
E-Mail: information@sapaweb.org;
www.sapaweb.org
Social Media: Twitter, LinkedIn, YouTube
Dr. Weiguo Dai, President
Dr. Jiwen Chen, Director
Dr. Lei Tang, President-elect
Li Chen, Director
Baoguo Huang, Director
An independent, nonprofit and professional organization with over 4,000 members in the U.S.A., China, Hong Kong, Taiwan, and Japan. It promotes pharmaceutical science and technology.
Founded in: 1993

3199 Society For Freshwater Science
5400 Bosque Blvd.
Suite 680
Waco, TX 76710
254-399-9636; *Fax:* 785-843-1274
webmaster@benthos.org;
www.freshwater-science.org
The Society for Freshwater Science (SFS) is an international scientific organization whose purpose is to promote further understanding of freshwater ecosystems (rivers, streams, lakes, reservoirs, and estuaries) and ecosystems at the interface between aquatic and terrestrial habitats. The society fosters exchange of scientific information among the membership, and with other

professional societies, resource managers, policy makers, educators, and the public.
Founded in: 1953

3200 **Society for Biological Engineering**
120 Wall Street
FL 23
New York, NY 10005-4020
Fax: 203-775-5177
bio@aiche.org; www.aiche.org/sbe
Social Media: Facebook, LinkedIn, YouTube

Georges Belfort, Director
Bill Bentley, Director
Brian Davison, Director
Paula T. Hammond, Director
Pankaj Mohan, Director

A global organization of leading engineers and scientists dedicatedto advancing the integration of biology with engineering.

3201 **Society for Biomaterials**
1120 Route 73
Suite 200
Mt Laurel, NJ 08054
856-439-0826; *Fax:* 856-439-0525
info@biomaterials.org; www.biomaterials.org
Social Media: Facebook, Twitter, LinkedIn

Antonios Mikos, President
Nicholas Ziats, President Elect
David Kohn, Secretary/Treasurer

Promotes advances in all phases of materials, research and development by encouragement of cooperative educational programs, clinical applications, and professional standards in the biomaterials field.
1550 Members
Founded in: 1969

3202 **Society for Biomolecular Screening**
100 Illinois Street
Suite 242
St. Charles, IL 60174
630-256-7527
877-990-7527
slas@slas.org; www.slas.org
Social Media: Facebook, Twitter, LinkedIn, Youtube

Dean Ho, President
Christine Giordano, Executive Director
Richard Eglen, Vice President
Mike Snowden, Treasurer
Michele A Cleary, Secretary

Provides a forum for education and information exchange among professionals within drug discovery and related disciplines.
2000+ Members
Founded in: 1994

3203 **Society for Cardiovascular Magnetic Resonance**
19 Mantua Road
Mt. Royal, NJ 8061
856-423-8955; *Fax:* 856-423-3420
hq@scmr.org; www.scmr.org
Social Media: Facebook, Twitter

Victor A. Ferrari, MD, President
Jeanette Schulz-Menger, Vice-President
Matthias G. Friedrich, MD, Treasurer
Matthias Stuber, Vice Secretary-Treasurer
Orlando Simonetti, Immediate Past President

The leading international society for physicians, scientists, and technologists working in cardiovascular magnetic resonance.

3204 **Society for Freshwater Science, Formerly NABS**
5400 Bosque Blvd
Suite 680
Waco, TX 76710-4446
254-399-9636; *Fax:* 254-776-3767
membership@benthos.org; www.freshwater-science.org

Dave Strayer, President
Michelle Baker, President Assistant
Matt Whiles, President Elect
Sue Norton, Secretary
Mike Swift, Treasurer

International Scientific organization with the purpose to promote better understanding of the biotic communitites of lake and stream bottoms and their role in aquatic ecosystems, by providing media and disseminating new investigation results , new interpretations and other benthological informatoin to aquatic biologists and the scientific community. Also publishes a journal.
Founded in: 1953

3205 **Society for Industrial Microbiology and Biotechnology**
3929 Old Lee Highway
Suite 92A
Fairfax, VA 22030
703-691-3357; *Fax:* 703-691-7991;
www.simbhq.org
Social Media: Facebook, Twitter, LinkedIn, RSS

Christine Lowe, Executive Director
Jennifer Johnson, Director of Member Services
Suzannah Citrenbaum, Web Manager
Espie Montesa, Accountant
Katherine Devins, Publications Coordinator

A nonprofit international association dedicated to the advancement of microbiology sciences, especially as they apply to industrial products, biotechnology, materials, and processes.
Founded in: 1949

3206 **Society for Laboratory Automation and Screening**
100 Illinois Street
Ste. 242
St. Charles, IL 60174
630-256-7527
877-990-7527
slas@slas.org; www.slas.org
Social Media: Facebook, Twitter, LinkedIn, YouTube

Dean Ho, President
Richard Eglen, Vice President
Mike Snowden, Treasurer
Michele A Cleary, Secretary
Alastair Binnie, Director

A global community of more than 18,000 life science research and development professionals.
2000+ Members
Founded in: 1994

3207 **Strategic Information for the Life Sciences**
BioAbility™
PO Box 14569
Research Triangle Park, NC 27709-4569
919-544-5111; *Fax:* 919-544-5401
info@bioability.com; www.bioability.com

Mark D Dibner, President/Founder
Tracey V du Laney, Research Director

BioAbility has provided the knowledge and experience to evaluate any area of the life sciences or biotechnology markets. Partnered with expert life science affiliates to bring a world-class level of expertise to our service offerings.
Founded in: 1994

3208 **The American Society for Cell Biology**
8120 Woodmont Avenue
Suite 750
Bethesda, MD 20814
301-347-9300; *Fax:* 301-347-9310
ascbinfo@ascb.org
ascb.org
Social Media: Facebook, Twitter, LinkedIn

Shirley M Tilghman, President
Jennifer Lippincott-Schwartz, Past President
Peter Walter, President-Elect
Kathleen Green, Secretary
Gary J Gorbsky, Treasurer

A professional society that provides the exchange of scientific knowledge in the area of cell biology.

3209 **Virginia Biotechnology Association**
800 E Leigh St
Suite 14
Richmond, VA 23219-1534
804-643-6360; *Fax:* 804-643-6361
questions@vabio.org; www.vabio.org
Social Media: Facebook, Twitter

Jeffrey M Gallagher, CEO
Sherry Halloran, Director, Membership Services
Susan Moore, Senior Administrative Assistant
Jeff Conroy, Chairman
Crystal Icenhoue, Vice Chairman

Promotes the biotechnology industry in Virginia, to expand the knowledge and expertise of Virginia's businesses concerning biotechnology through seminars, educational publications and other means.
200 Members
Founded in: 1992

3210 **Women in Cognitive Science**
womenincogsci.org
Social Media: Facebook

Laurie Feldman, Officer
Judith Kroll, Officer
Suparna Rajaram, Officer
Debra Titone, Officer
Natasha Tokowicz, Officer

Organization that works to create an environment that encourages young women to join the field of cognitive psychology/science, particularly in cognitive neuroscience and computational modeling areas.

Newsletters

3211 **AAI Newsletter**
American Association of Immunologists
9650 Rockville Pike
Bethesda, MD 20814-3999
301-634-7178; *Fax:* 301-634-7887
infoaai@aai.org; www.aai.org

Leslie Berg, President
Gail Bishop, Vice President
Mitchell Kronenberg, Treasurer/Secretary
Frequency: Bi-Monthly

3212 **BioPeople Magazine**
PO Box 5778
Walnut Creek, CA 94596
925-932-6364; www.biotechmedia.com

Lisa Wagner, Advertising Executive
Charlene Carpentier, Production Manager
Sukaini Virji-Jeganathan, Editor

Provides information and analysis of the international biotechnology industry, including corporate agreements, product status, financial

transactions and new technologies.
Cost: $675.00
Frequency: Quarterly
Circulation: 10,000
Printed in on glossy stock

3213 BioWorld Financial Watch
BioWorld
3525 Piedmont Road
Building 6, Suite 400
Atlanta, GA 30305-4031
404-262-5476
800-688-2421; *Fax:* 404-814-0759
customerservice@bioworld.com;
www.bioworld.com
Donald R Johnston, Publisher
Brady Huggett, Managing Editor
Chris Walker, Marketing Manager
Tracks public financing and portfolio performance offering expert analysis. The weekly source for biotechnology financial news.
Cost: $1197.00
Frequency: Weekly

3214 Biotechnology News
CTB International Publishing
PO Box 218
Maplewood, NJ 07040-218
973-966-0997; *Fax:* 973-966-0242;
www.genengnews.com
F G Racioppi, Marketing Director
A leading biotechnology publication for executives. Provides incisive intelligence on the ever-changing biotechnology industry and includes news on research, product development and corporate doings.
Cost: $634.00
Founded in: 1985
Printed in one color on newsprint stock

3215 Biotechnology Newswatch
McGraw Hill
1221 Avenue of the Americas
Suite C3A
New York, NY 10020-1095
212-512-2000; *Fax:* 212-512-3840
customer.service@mcgraw-hill.com;
www.mcgraw-hill.com
Harold W McGraw III, CEO
Mara Bovsun, Editor
Kenneth M Vittor, VP
Covers the business and technical news affecting companies engaged in serving the biotechnology sciences.
Cost: $737.00
12 Pages
Frequency: Monthly
Founded in: 1910

3216 Genetic Technology News
John Wiley & Sons
111 River St
Hoboken, NJ 07030-5790
201-748-6000; *Fax:* 201-748-6088
info@wiley.com; www.wiley.com
William J Pesce, CEO
Covers technical and business developments in every area of genetic engineering and related techniques, analyzing their applications in the chemical, pharmaceutical and energy industries as well as in agriculture, animal breeding and medicine.
Cost: $585.00
18 Pages
Frequency: Monthly
Founded in: 1807

3217 Industrial Bioprocessing
John Wiley & Sons
111 River St
Hoboken, NJ 07030-5790
201-748-6000; *Fax:* 201-748-6088
info@wiley.com; www.wiley.com
William J Pesce, CEO
Focuses on industrial processes involving biological routes to produce chemicals/energy; the conversion of biomaterials via fermentation, process monitoring and more.
Cost: $545.00
10 Pages
Frequency: Monthly
Founded in: 1807
*Mailing list available for rent*at $180 per M
Printed in one color on matte stock

3218 J Biomolecular Screening
Society for Biomolecular Screening
100 Illinois Street
Suite 242
St.Charles, IL 60174
630-256-7527; *Fax:* 630-741-7527
slas@slas.org; www.sbsonline.org
Michelle Palmer, President
David Dorsett, Vice President
Erik Rubin, Treasurer
Andy Zaayenga, Secretary
Biomolecular industry news and information.
Cost: $478.00
Founded in: 1992

3219 Life Sciences & Biotechnology Update
InfoTeam
PO Box 15640
Plantation, FL 33318-5640
954-473-9560; *Fax:* 954-473-0544
Merton Allen, Editor
Medical and biological technology; health and disease; genetics and genetic engineering; bodily fluids, bones, tissues and organs, cancer, medical diagnoisis and treatment; medical instrumentation and procedures; medical care systems; public health; mental health; child care; medical costs; research; and more.
Frequency: Monthly

3220 Technotrends Newsletter
Burrus Research Associates
PO Box 47
Hartland, WI 53029-2347
262-367-0949
800-827-6770; *Fax:* 262-367-7163
office@burrus.com; www.burrus.com/
Dan Burrus, CEO
Patti A Thomsen, Editor
Jennifer Metcalf, Marketing
This newsletter researches the latest innovations in science and technology. Provides access to information that can give an edge on tomorrow, today and shows how you might benefit from each innovation.
Cost: $39.95
Frequency: Monthly
Circulation: 1000
Founded in: 1984
Printed in 4 colors on matte stock

Magazines & Journals

3221 American Biotechnology Laboratory
International Scientific Communications
PO Box 870
Shelton, CT 06484-0870
203-926-9300; *Fax:* 203-926-9310
webmaster@iscpubs.com; www.iscpubs.com
Brian Howard, Publisher
Robert G Sweeny, Publisher
American Biotechnology Laboratory serves Industry, Universities, Government and others allied to the field with special interest in life science research.
Cost: $173.12
64 Pages
Frequency: Monthly
Circulation: 60058
Mailing list available for rent: 60M names at $170 per M
Printed in 4 colors on glossy stock

3222 Antiretroviral Resistance in Clinical Practice
National Center for Biotechnology Information
8600 Rockville Pike
Bethesda, MD 20894
301-496-2475; *Fax:* 301-480-9241
info@ncbi.nlm.nih.gov; www.ncbi.nlm.nih.gov
Anna Maria Geretti, Editor

3223 Applied Biochemistry and Biotechnology
Humana Press
999 Riverview Drive
Suite 208
Totowa, NJ 07512-1165
973-256-1699; *Fax:* 973-256-8341;
www.humanapress.com
David Watt, Editor
Ashok Mulchandani, Editor-in-Chief
Paul Dolgert, Director
Fran Lipton, Production Manager
Reports on new techniques and original research in biotechnology and biochemistry with a focus on the application of new technologies.
Cost: $1505.00
Frequency: Monthly
Circulation: 373
Founded in: 1977

3224 BioTechniques
52 Vanderbilt Avenue
7th Floor
New York, NY 10017
212-520-2777; *Fax:* 212-520-2705
webmaster@biotechniques.com;
www.biotechniques.com
Nathan Blow, Editor in Chief
Bill Moran, Director of Sales
John C. Yarosh, Production Manager
Serves the biotechnical and pharmaceutical industries.
Cost: $145.00
254 Pages
Frequency: Monthly
Circulation: 85,000
Founded in: 1983
Printed in 4 colors on glossy stock

3225 Biotechnology Progress
American Chemical Society
1155 16th St NW
Suite 600
Washington, DC 20036-4892
202-872-4600
Fax: 202-872-4615
service@acs.org; www.acs.org
Nancy Jackson, President
Information on new technology.
Cost: $924.00
Founded in: 1876

3226 Biotechnology and Bioengineering
John Wiley & Sons

111 River St
Hoboken, NJ 07030-5790

201-748-6000; *Fax:* 201-748-6088
info@wiley.com; www.wiley.com

William J Pesce, CEO
Richard M Hochhauser, CEO

A scientific journal publishing new papers in the field of biotechnology and bioengineering.
Cost: $750.00
Frequency: 1 Year 28 Issue
Founded in: 1807

3227 CleanRooms Magazine
PennWell Publishing Company
98 Spit Brook Rd
Suite L11
Nashua, NH 03062-5737

603-891-0123
80 - 2 - 05; *Fax:* 603-891-9294
mikel@pennwell.com; www.pennwell.com

Christine Shaw, VP
Mark A Desorbo, Associate Editor
James Enos, Publisher

Serves the contamination control and ultrapure materials and process industries. Written for readers in the microelectronics, pharmaceutical, biotech, health care, food processing and other user industries. Provides technology and business news and new product listings.
Frequency: Monthly
Circulation: 35031
Founded in: 1987

3228 Engineering in Medicine and Biology
3 Park Avenue
17th Floor
New York, NY 10016
212-419-7900
800-272-6657; *Fax:* 212-752-4929
jenderle@bme.uconn.edu; www.ieee.org

Dr. John D Enderle, Editor
Desir,e de Myer, Managing Editor
Susan Schneiderman, Advertising Sales Manager

Focuses on up-to-date biomedical engineering applications for engineers who are at the forefront of electrotechnology innovation.
Cost: $300.00
Circulation: 7983
ISSN: 0739-5175
Founded in: 1963

3229 Freshwater Science
Society for Freshwater Science
5400 Bosque Blvd.
Suite 680
Waco, TX 76710-4446

254-399-9636; *Fax:* 254-776-3767;
www.freshwater-science.org

Pamela Silver, Editor
Rosemary J. Mackay, Managing Editor
Irwin Polls, Business Manager

Publishes timely, peer-reviewed scientific research that promotes a better understanding and environmental stewardship of biological communities living on the bottom of streams, rivers, lakes, and wetlands, with an emphasis on freshwater inland habitats. Theoretical discussions, speculative and philosophical articles, and critical appraisals of rapidly developing research fields.
Cost: $65.00
Frequency: Quarterly

3230 Journal For Freshwater Science
The North American Benthological Society
PO Box 7065
Lawrence, KS 66044-7065

254-399-9636; *Fax:* 785-843-1274
info@freshwater-science.org;
www.freshwater-science.org/journal/access-FWS.cfm

Pamela Silver, Managing Editor
Irwin Polls, Business Manager

Articles that will promote further understanding of benthic communities and their role in aquatic ecosystems

3231 Journal of Biological Chemistry
American Society for Biochemistry
11200 Rockville Pike
Suite 302
Rockville, MD 20852-3110

240-283-6620; *Fax:* 301-881-2573
asbmb@asbmb.org; www.asbmb.org

Martha Fedor, Editor-in-Chief
Herbet Tabor, Co-Editor

3232 Journal of Biomolecular Screening
Sage Publications
2455 Teller Rd
Newbury Park, CA 91320-2234

805-499-9774
800-818-7243; *Fax:* 805-499-0871
journals@sagepub.com; www.sagepub.com

Blaise R Simqu, CEO
Mark Beggs, Associate Editor
Stein Roaldset, Advertising Editor
Christine Giordano, Society Updates Editor
Charles Hart, New Products Editor

An official publication of the Society for Biomolecular Sciences. Peer-reviewed publication on drug discovery sciences, with an emphasis on screening methods and technologies; Information on the latest biomolecular sciences, with regular topics including: target identification/validation assay development methods, and technologies, lead generation/optimization, virtual screening/chemo-informatics, data and image analysis, sample management, biomarkers and legal/licensing issues.
Cost: $610.00
Frequency: 10x year/Price Varies
ISSN: 1087-0571
Founded in: 1994

3233 Lab Animal
Nature Publishing Group
1270 Broadway
6th Floor, Suite 807
New York, NY 10001-3224

212-278-8600; *Fax:* 212-564-0217;
www.labanimal.com

Angelo Notaro, Partner
Rachel Burley, Publisher
Richard Charkin, CEO

A peer-reviewed journal for professionals in animal research, emphasizing proper management and care. Offers the latest on animal models, breeds, breeding practices, in vitro and computer models, lab care, nutrition, and improved animal handling techniques. Offers timely and informative material, reaching both the academic research world and applied research industries, including genetic engineering, human therapeutics and pharmaceutical companies.
Cost: $159.00
Founded in: 1869

3234 Molecular Plant: Microbe Interactions
American Phytopathalgical Society
3340 Pilot Knob Road
Saint Paul, MN 55121-2097

651-454-7250
800-328-7560; *Fax:* 651-454-0766
aps@scisoc.org; www.apsnet.org

Steve Nelson, Executive VP
Amy Hope, VP of Operations
Barbara Mock, VP Finance

Molecular biology and molecular genetics of pathological, symbiotic and associative interactions of microbes with plants, including plant response.
Frequency: Monthly
ISSN: 0894-0282
Mailing list available for rent

3235 Nature
Nature Publishing Group
1270 Broadway
Suite 807
New York, NY 10001-3224

212-278-8600
800-221-2123; *Fax:* 212-564-0217
nature@natureny.com; www.nature.com

Angelo Notaro, Partner
Josie Natori, CEO

A reliable source of up-to-date scientific information. Publishes papers from any area of science with great potential impact. Also publishes a broad range of informal material in the form of opinion articles, news stories, briefings and recruitment features, and contributed material.
Frequency: Monthly
Circulation: 60289

3236 Nature Biotechnology
Nature America
345 Park Avenue S
10th Floor
New York, NY 10010-1707

212-726-9200
800-221-2123; *Fax:* 212-696-9635
biotech@natureny.com;
www.biotech.nature.com

Andrew Marshall, Editor
Richard Charkin, CEO
Annette Thomas, Managing Director
Philip Campbell, Editor-in-Chief
Peter Collins, Publishing Director

A monthly magazine of biotechnology news and research.
Cost: $178.00
550 Pages
Frequency: Monthly
Circulation: 18798
ISSN: 1054-0156
Founded in: 1983
Printed in 4 colors on glossy stock

3237 Protein Science
Protein Society
9650 Rockville Pike
Bethesda, MD 20814-3999

301-634-7240
800-992-6466; *Fax:* 301-634-7271
cyablonski@proteinsociety.org;
www.proteinsociety.org

Cynthia A Yablonski, Executive Officer
Arthur G Palmer III, President
Jean Baum, Secretary/Treasurer
2100 Members
Founded in: 1986
Mailing list available for rent: 3,000 names at $200 per M

3238 Science Illustrated
Communications Solutions
8428 Holly Leaf Drive
McLean, VA 22102-2224

703-356-1688; *Fax:* 202-296-1857
http://www.scienceillustrated.com/

Tod Herbers, Editor

Provides physicians with information on research and development in the fields of science related to medicine.
Cost: $18.00
Circulation: 103200
Printed in 4 colors on glossy stock

Trade Shows

3239 **AAB Annual Meeting and Education Conference**
American Association of Bioanalysts
906 Olive Street
Suite 1200
Saint Louis, MO 63101-1448

314-241-1445; *Fax:* 314-241-1449
aab@aab.org; www.aab.org
Social Media: Facebook, Twitter, LinkedIn

Mark S Birenbaum PhD, Administrator

Educational programs, abstract presentations, poster presentations and exhibits
Founded in: 1956

3240 **Biometrics Technology Expo and Consortium Conference**
J Spargo & Associates
11208 Waples Mill Road
Suite 112
Fairfax, VA 22030

703-631-6200
800-564-4220; *Fax:* 703-654-6931;
www.biometricsociety.org

Jeffrey Dunn, Chair
Fernando Podio, Chair

Co-located with the Biometric Consortium Conference, this event offers unparalleled opportunities to reach top buyers, federal and state agencies and leading industry corporations.
2000 Attendees
Frequency: September

3241 **Biophysical Society Annual Meeting**
Biophysical Society
11400 Rockville Pike
Suite 800
Bethesda, MD 20852

240-290-5600; *Fax:* 240-290-5555
society@biophysics.org; www.biophysics.org

Ro Kampman, Executive Officer
Harris Povich, Director of Finance and Operations
Vida Ess, Programs Coordinator

Includes 3,000 poster presentations, 200 exhibits, 20 symposias, workshops, platform sessions, and subgroup meetings. It is also the worlds largest meeting for biophysicists.
6M Attendees
Frequency: February/March
Mailing list available for rent

3242 **Biotechnology Investment Conference**
Massachusetts Biotechnology Council
One Cambridge Center
Cmabridge, MA 02142

617-674-5100; *Fax:* 617-674-5101
inforequest@massbio.org; www.massbio.org
Social Media: Facebook, Twitter, LinkedIn, Youtube

Geoffrey Cox, Chairman
Geoff McKay, Vice Chair
Michael Ohara, Treasurer

New England's largest biotechnology investor forum. Allows more than 70 local public and private companies to showcase their technologies and products in front of portfolio managers, analysts, venture capitalists and other investment professionals.
700 Attendees
Frequency: November

3243 **Int'l Conference on Strategic Business Information in Biotechnology**
Institute for Biotechnology Information
3200 Chapel Hill/Nelson Boulevard Suite 201
PO Box 14569
Research Triangle Park, NC 27709-4569

919-544-5111; *Fax:* 919-544-5401
info@bioability.com; www.biotechinfo.com

For strategists, company managers, information specialists, financial analysts or users of strategic business information in biotechnology.
150 Attendees
Frequency: October

Directories & Databases

3244 **BioWorld Online**
3525 Piedmont Road
Building 6, Suite 400
Atlanta, GA 30305

404-262-5476
800-688-2421; *Fax:* 404-814-0759
customerservice@bioworld.com;
www.bioworld.com

Randy Osborne

This database contains a variety of information on biotechnology companies, products, and services.
Frequency: Full-text

3245 **Biosis/Thomson Scientific**
BIOSIS
1500 Spring Garden St
Fourth Floor
Philadelphia, PA 19130-4067

215-386-0100
800-336-4474; *Fax:* 215-386-2911;
www.biosis.org/support;
scientific.thomson.com
Social Media: Facebook, Twitter, LinkedIn

Vin Caraher, President/CEO
Keith MacGregor, Executive VP
Andrea Degutis, Senior VP/Communications

A bibliographic database covering worldwide research on all biological and biomedical topics. Records contain bibliographic data, indexing information, and abstracts for most references. Biosis joined with the Thomson Corporation in early 2006 to expand its global presence.
Frequency: Updated Weekly

Industry Web Sites

3246 **http://gold.greyhouse.com**
G.O.L.D Grey House OnLine Databases
Grey House Publishing's online database platform, GOLD, offers Quick Search, Keyword Search and Expert Search for most business sectors, including scientific, technical and biotechnical markets. The GOLD platform makes finding the information you need quick and easy - whether you're a novice searcher or an experienced database user. All of Grey House's directory products are available for subscription on the GOLD platform.

3247 **www.aesociety.org**
Electrophoresis Society
International organization founded to improve and promote technologies necessary for biomolecular separation and detection.

3248 **www.asbmb.org**
American Society for Biochemistry and Molecular
Serves members who teach and conduct research at colleges and universities and in various government laboratories, nonprofit research institutions and industry.

3249 **www.asrm.org**
American Society for Reproductive Medicine
Organization devoted to advancing knowledge and expertise in reproductive medicine and biology. Members of this voluntary nonprofit organization must demonstrate the high ethical principals of the medical profession, evince an interest in reproductive medicine and biology, and adhere to the objectives of the Society.

3250 **www.benthos.org**
North American Benthological Society
International scientific organization whose purpose is to promote better understanding of the biotic communities of lake and stream bottoms and their role in aquatic ecosystems, by providing media and disseminating new investigation results, new interpetations, and other benthological information to aquatic biologists and to the scientific community at large.

3251 **www.bio.org**
Biotechnology Industry Organization
For firms involved in the use of recombinant DNA, hybridoma and immulogical technologies in a wide range of applications including human health care, animal husbandry, agriculture and specialty chemical production.

3252 **www.greyhouse.com**
Grey House Publishing
Authoritative reference directories for most business markets including science, technical and biotechnical markets. Users can search the online databases with varied search criteria allowing for custom searches by product category, geographic area, sales volume, keyword, subject and more. Full Grey House catalog and online ordering also available.

3253 **www.ismrm.org**
Int'l Society for Magnetic Resonance in Medicine
For physicians and scientists promoting the applications of magnetic resonance techniques to medicine and biology. The Society holds annual scientific meetings and sponsors other major educational and scientific workshops.

3254 **www.massbio.org**
Massachusetts Biotechnology Council
Organization that provides services and support for the Massachusets biotechnology industry.

3255 **www.proteinsociety.org**
Protein Society
Formed in 1986 to promote international interactions among investigators in order to explore all aspects of the building blocks of life, protien molecules. Members come from universities, foundations, institutes and corporations to provide leadership in this broad field of research. The Society and its members are making a strong impact on the advancements of protien science.

3256 **www.whybiotech.com**
Council for Biotechnology Information
Serves to improve understanding and acceptance of biotechnology by collecting balanced, credible and science based information, then communicating this information through a variety of channels.

Associations

3257 **American Boat Builders and Repairers Association**
1 Washington Street
Newport, RI 02840
401-236-2466; *Fax:* 954-239-2600
info@abbra.org; www.abbra.org
Social Media: Facebook, Twitter, LinkedIn
Graham Wright, President
Kirk Ritter, VP
Peter Sabo, Treasurer
Ron Helbig, Secretary
Cathy Cope, Director
Trade association for marinas, boat builders and repairers. Also offers a monthly newsletter and training seminars.
300 Members
Founded in: 1943

3258 **American Boat and Yacht Council**
613 Third Street
Suite 10
Annapolis, MD 21403
410-990-4460; *Fax:* 410-990-4466
info@abycinc.org; www.abycinc.org
Social Media: Facebook, Twitter, LinkedIn, Youtube
John Adey, President
David Marlow, Chairman
Kenneth Weinbrecht, Vice Chairman
David Slobodien, Treasurer
Jeff Wasil, Secretary
A not-for-profit membership organization that has been developing and updating the safety standards for boat building and repair.
4000+ Members
Founded in: 1954

3259 **American Boatbuilders Association, Inc.**
The Brumby Building, Marietta Stn.
127 Church St., Suite 210
Marietta, GA 30060
770-792-3070; *Fax:* 770-792-3073;
www.ababoats.com
Jay Patton, President
Volume materials purchasing group for independent boat builders.
Founded in: 1992

3260 **American Boating Association**
PO Box 690
New Market, MD 21774
614-497-4088
admin@americanboating.org;
www.americanboating.org
Social Media: Facebook, RSS
Bill Condon, Founder/President
Through their membership in the American Boating Association, boaters and boating enthusiasts from across the nation share a common mission - working together to improve the safety, affordability, environmental cleanliness, growth and fun of our sport.
Cost: $10.00
30000 Members

3261 **American Power Boat Association**
17640 E. Nine Mile Road
Po Box 377
Eastpointe, MI 48021-0377
586-773-9700; *Fax:* 586-773-6490;
www.apba-racing.com
Social Media: Facebook, Twitter, LinkedIn, Youtube, RSS
Dan Wiener, Executive Director
John Flynn, Creative Director
Sabrina Haudek, Membership Coordinator
Mark Wheeler, President
Dutch Squires, Vice President
The nation's authority on power boat racing which sanctions over 200 races each year.
6000 Members
Founded in: 1903

3262 **American Sail Training Association**
221 3rd Street, Building 2, Ste. 101
PO Box 1459
Newport, RI 02840
401-846-1775; *Fax:* 401-849-5400
asta@tallshipsamerica.org;
www.tallships.sailtraining.org
Social Media: Facebook, Twitter, LinkedIn
Mike Rauworth, Chairman
Caleb Pifer, Vice Chair
Eric Shaw, Vice Chair
Dexter Donham, Treasurer
Capt. Christoph Rowsom, Secretary
Supports all those involved with sail training ships and programs, as well as ships under construction or renovation.
300 Members
Founded in: 1973

3263 **American Society of Marine Artists**
P.O.Box 247
Smithfield, VA 23430
757-357-3785
asma1978@verizon.net;
www.americansocietyofmarineartists.com
Social Media: Facebook, Twitter, LinkedIn
Russ Kramer, President
Kim Shaklee, Vice President
Mike Killelea, Secretary
Peter Maytham, Managing Director
Sheri Farabaugh, Treasurer
A non-profit, tax exempt organization, whose objective is to recognize and promote marine art and history, and to encourage cooperation among artists, historians, marine enthusiasts and others in activities related to marine art and maritime history.
500+ Members
Founded in: 1978

3264 **Antique & Classic Boat Society**
422 James St
Clayton, NY 13624
315-686-2628; *Fax:* 315-686-2680
hqs@acbs.org; www.acbs.org
Social Media: Facebook, Twitter, LinkedIn
Jeff Funk, President
John Howard, Senior VP
Rich Lepping, Second VP
Kathy Parker, Secretary
Timothy Bush, Treasurer
Society devoted to disseminating information on building and restoring wooden and antique boats.
12000 Members
Founded in: 1975

3265 **Association of Marina Industries**
50 Water Street
Warren, RI 02885
866-367-6622; *Fax:* 401-247-0074
info@marinaassociation.org;
www.marinaassociation.org
Social Media: Facebook, Twitter, LinkedIn
Jeff Rose, Chairman
Brad Gross, Vice Chairman
Joe Riley, Treasurer
Mick Webber, Secretary
Gary Groenewold, Immediate Past Chairman
The Association of Marina Industries is the international trade marine association for the marina industry.
800+ Members
Founded in: 1986

3266 **Boat Owners Association of the US**
880 South Pickett Street
Alexandria, VA 22304
703-461-2878
800-395-2628; *Fax:* 703-461-2847
mail@baotus.com; www.boatus.com
Social Media: Facebook, Twitter, Youtube
Richard Schwartz, Chairman/Founder
Bill Oakerson, CEO
Margaret Podlich, President
Adam Wheeler, VP & Director of Towing
Heather Lougheed, VP, Membership
Supports all who are involved with legislation, regulations and consumer aspects of the industry.
62500 Members
Founded in: 1966

3267 **Boating Writers International**
108 Ninth Street
Wilmette, IL 60091
847-736-4142
info@bwi.org; www.bwi.org
Social Media: LinkedIn
Alan Wendt, President
Lenny Rudow, 1st VP
Lindsey Johnson, 2nd VP
Alan Jones, Director
Zuzana Prochazka, Director
A non-profit professional organization consisting of writers, broadcasters, editors, photgraphers, public relations specialists and others in the communications profession associated with the boating industry.
Founded in: 1970

3268 **Coastal Yachting Academy**
PO Box 10441
St. Petersburg, FL 33733
727-867-9466
info@yachtdeliveries.com;
www.charternet.com/charters/donharper/index.html
Don Harper, Captain/Owner
To provide the recreational boater reasonably priced training equal to the training of professional mariners.
Founded in: 1970

3269 **Marine Retailers Association of America**
8401 73rd Ave N
Suite 71
Minneapolis, MN 55428
763-315-8043
matt@mraa.com; www.mraa.com
Social Media: Facebook, Twitter, LinkedIn
Randy Wattenbarger, Chairman
Joe Lewis, Vice Chair
Joe Hoffmaster, Secretary/Treasurer
Steve Baum, Immediate Past Chairman
Rob Soucy, Director
Manufacturers and dealers of boats, equipment, supplies and services.
3000 Members
Founded in: 1971

3270 **Marine Safety Foundation**
5050 Industrial Rd
Suite 2
Wall Township, NJ 07727-4044
732-751-0295; *Fax:* 732-751-0508;
www.marinesafety.org
Burt Thompson, Executive Director
Advances the safety of life at sea through research, education and coordination.
131 Members
Founded in: 1993

3271 National Association of Charterboat Operators
PO Box 1070
Hurley, MS 39555

866-981-5136; *Fax:* 877-263-8548
info@nacocharters.org; www.nacocharters.org
Social Media: Facebook

Capt. Robert F Zales II, President
Capt. Tom Baker, Vice President
Capt. Ed O'Brien, Second Vice President
Capt Charlie Phillips, Secretary
Ron Maglio, Treasurer

A national association of charterboat owners and operators that represent thousands of individuals across the United States.
3600+ Members
Founded in: 1991

3272 National Association of Sailing
15 Maritime Drive
Portsmouth, RI 02871

401-683-0800
800-877-2451; *Fax:* 401-683-0840
info@ussailing.org; www.ussailing.org
Social Media: Facebook, Twitter, LinkedIn

Bruce Burton, President
Cory Sertl, Vice President
Martine R Zurinskas, Secretary
Stephen T Freitas, Treasurer
Jack Gierhart, Executive Director

Accredits sailing schools, certifies instructors and provides teaching and management information. Publishes a newsletter and directory of American sailing schools and charter operators. Provides free consulting services for start-ups of new schools.
100 Members
Frequency: Quarterly
Founded in: 1980
Mailing list available for rent

3273 National Association of State Boating Law Administrators
1648 McGrathiana Parkway
Suite 360
Lexington, KY 40511

859-225-9487; *Fax:* 859-231-6403
info@nasbla.org; www.nasbla.org
Social Media: Facebook, Twitter, LinkedIn, Flickr, Foursquare, YouTube

John Johnson, Executive Director & CEO
Tom Hayward, CFO
Ron Sarver, Deputy Director
Darren Rider, VP
Tom Guess, Treasurer

Representing the recreational boating authorities of all 50 States and U.S. territories. To strengthen the ability of the State and territorial boating authorities to reduce death, injury and property damage associated with recreational boating.
56 Members
Founded in: 1960

3274 National Marine Bankers Association
231 South LaSalle St
Suite 2050
Chicago, IL 60604

312-946-6260
info@marinebankers.org;
www.marinebankers.org
Social Media: LinkedIn

Michael Bryant, President
Peggy Bodenreider, VP
William B Otto, Treasurer
Jayme B Yates, Secretary
Jackie Forese, Executive Director

Created for the purpose of educating current and prospective lenders in marine financing procedures, promoting the extension of credit to consumer and trade borrowers.
81 Members
Founded in: 1979

3275 National Marine Distributors Association
37 Pratt St
Suite 3
Essex, CT 06426-1159

860-767-7898; *Fax:* 860-767-7932
executivedirector@nmdaonline.com;
www.nmdaonline.com

Nancy Cueroni, Executive Director
Ryan Barber, President
Laura Leon, Vice President
Mike Connors, Secretary/Treasurer
Rick Chang, Past President

Wholesale distributors of marine accessories and hardware.
200 Members
Mailing list available for rent

3276 National Marine Electronics Association
7 Riggs Ave
Severna Park, MD 21146

410-975-9425
800-808-6632; *Fax:* 410-975-9450
info@nmea.org; www.nmea.org
Social Media: Facebook

David Gratton, Chairman
Johnny Lindstrom, Vice Chairman
Christopher Harley, Secretary
Marilyn S Quarders, Treasurer
Ken Harrison, International Executive Director

Is the unifying force behind the entire marine electronics industry, bringing together all aspects of the industry for the betterment of all in our business.
400 Members
Founded in: 1957

3277 National Marine Manufacturers Association
231 South LaSalle St
Suite 2050
Chicago, IL 60604

312-946-6200; www.nmma.org
Social Media: Twitter, LinkedIn

Thomas Dammrich, President
Ben Wold, EVP
Craig Boskey, VP Finance, CFO
Carl Blackwell, VP, Marketing & Communications
John McKnight, VP, Government Relations

Dedicated to creating, promoting and protecting an environment where members can achieve financial success through excellence in manufacturing, selling and service for their customers.
1400+ Members
Founded in: 1979

3278 National Marine Representative Association
PO Box 360
Gurnee, IL 60031

847-662-3167; *Fax:* 847-336-7126
info@nmraonline.org; www.nmraonline.org

Rob Gueterman, President
Keith LaMarr, VP
Neal Tombley, Treasurer
Clayton Smith, Secretary
Brandon Flack, Past President

A national organization serving marine industry independent sales reps and the marine manufacturers who sell through reps.
300 Members
Founded in: 1960

3279 National Safe Boating Council
9500 Technology
Suite 104
Manassas, VA 20110

703-361-4294; *Fax:* 703-361-5294;
www.safeboatingcouncil.org
Social Media: Facebook, Twitter, LinkedIn, Youtube

Richard Moore, Chairman
Chris Stec, Vice Chairman
Pam Doty, Treasurer
Betsy Woods, Secretary
Rachel Johnson, Executive Director

NSBC has an interest in boating safety and education to reduce accidents and enhance the boating experience.
350 Members
Founded in: 1958
Mailing list available for rent

3280 Northwest Marine Trade Association
1900 N Northlake Way
Suite 233
Seattle, WA 98103

206-634-0911; *Fax:* 206-632-0078
info@nmta.net; www.nmta.net
Social Media: Facebook, Twitter, LinkedIn, Youtube, Pinterest, RSS

Patricia Segulja-Lau, Chairman
Craig Perry, Vice Chair
James Baker, Secretary/Treasurer
Bruce Hedrick, Past Chairman
700+ Members
Founded in: 1947

3281 Offshoreonly
PO Box 10868
St Petersburg, FL 33733

954-463-1101; *Fax:* 727-394-2451
offshoreonly@offshoreonly.com;
www.offshoreonly.com
Social Media: Facebook, Twitter

Kathe Walker, President
Scott Ryerson, VP

OSO is a nonprofit organization catering to fun loving boaters in the Tampa/Clearwater/St. Petersburg areas of Florida.
Mailing list available for rent

3282 Personal Watercraft Industry Association
National Marine Manufacturers Association
231 South Lasalle Street
Suite 2050
Chicago, IL 60604

202-737-9761; *Fax:* 866-861-2931
ddickerson@nmma.org; www.pwia.org

David Dickerson, VP, State Govt Relations
Libby Yranski, Manager, State Govt Relations

Trade association representing manufacturers of personal watercraft.
Founded in: 1987

3283 Propeller Club of the United States
3927 Old Lee Hwy
Suite 101A
Fairfax, VA 22030

703-691-2777; *Fax:* 703-691-4173
shannon@propellerclubhq.com;
www.propellerclubhq.com

Rick Schiappacasse, President
William Van Voorhis, Vice President
Tim Shusta, Secretary
Jack Crockett, Treasurer
Andrew Riester, Executive VP

Dedicated to the enhancement and well-being of all interests of the maritime community on a national and international basis.
10000 Members
Founded in: 1927
Mailing list available for rent

3284 **Recreational Boaters of California**
925 L Street
Suite 260
Sacramento, CA 95814

916-441-4166
rboc@rboc.org; www.rboc.org
Social Media: Facebook, Twitter

Greg Gibeson, President
Otis Brock, Secretary/Treasurer
Jerry Desmond Jr., Director Govt. Relations
Jerry Desmond, EVP
Ralph Longfellow, Vice President

Monitors the proceedings in the State Capitol, reviewing each of the bills that are introduced and/or amended as to whether they would have an impact on boating.
Founded in: 1968

3285 **Sail America**
50 Water St.
Warren, RI 02885

401-289-2540; *Fax:* 401-247-0074;
www.sailamerica.com
Social Media: Facebook, Twitter, Vimeo

Scot West, President
Greg Emerson, VP, Shows
Erin Schanen, VP, Association
Jay Stockmann, VP, Marketing

Trade association for sailing segment of recreational boating industry.
200+ Members
Founded in: 1990

3286 **Shipbuilders Council of America**
20 F Street, NW
Suite 500
Washington, DC 20001

202-737-3234; *Fax:* 202-737-0264
preever@balljanik.com; www.shipbuilders.org
Social Media: Facebook, Twitter

Matt Paxton, President
Courtney Jowers, Director of Operations
Ashley Godwin, Senior Defense Advisor
Stephen Woodring, Government Relations Manager
Joe Carnevale, Senior Defense Advisor

Represents the U.S. shipyard industry. SCA members build, repair and service America's fleet of commercial vessels.
73 Members
Founded in: 1920

3287 **Society of Accredited Marine Surveyors**
7855 Argyle Forest Blvd
Suite 203
Jacksonville, FL 32244

904-384-1494
800-344-9077; *Fax:* 904-388-3958
samshq@marinesurvey.org;
www.marinesurvey.org

Lloyd E Kittredge, President
Rovert V Horvath, Executive Vice President
Bill Trenkle, Secretary/Treasurer
George J Sepel, Vp, Membership
Kenneth Weinbrecht, VP, Education

Dedicated to the advancement of the profession of marine surveying
1000 Members
Founded in: 1986

3288 **Texas Dragon Boat Association**
PO Box 980972
Houston, TX 77098

713-205-7373
webmaster@texasdragonboat.com;
www.houstondragonboat.com
Social Media: Facebook, Twitter

Michael Jhin, Chairman
David Mandell, President/Executive Director
Caroline Long, Secretary
Jim Travlos, Board Chairman

Promotes the tradition and sport of dragon boating; increases the awareness of Asian and Asian-American culture; and enhances cross-cultural understanding.

3289 **Traditional Small Craft Association**
PO Box 350
Mystic, CT 06355

www.tsca.net
Social Media: Facebook

Mary Loken, President
Roger Allen, Vice President
Pete Mathews, Secretary
Bill Meier, Treasurer
John Weiss, Chapter & Membership Coordinator

Nonprofit, tax-exempt educational organization which works to preserve and continue the living traditions, skills, lore and legends surrounding working and pleasure watercraft whose origins predate the marine gasoline engine.

3290 **U.S. Industrial Fabrics Association International**
1801 County Road B W
Roseville, MN 55113-4061

651-222-2508
800-225-4324; *Fax:* 651-631-9334
generalinfo@ifai.com; www.ifai.com
Social Media: Facebook, Twitter, LinkedIn, YouTube

Mary J Hennessy, President & CEO
Steve Schiffman, VP, Media & Sales
Sheila Sumner, Director of Finance/Administration
Pam Egan-Blahna, Director, Human Resource
Andrew M Aho, Vice President of Operations

The mission of the United States Industrial Fabrics Institute (USIFI) is to build a strong coalition of US fiber, fabric, and end product manufacturers and to serve member company interests both domestically and internationally. USIFI is part of the not-for-profit Industrial Fabrics Association International (www.ifai.com), the global association for the specialty fabrics industry.
2000 Members
Founded in: 1912

3291 **United States Power Squadrons**
1504 Blue Ridge Rd
Raleigh, NC 27607

919-821-0281
888-367-8777; *Fax:* 888-304-0813
contactme@HQ.USPS.org; www.usps.org
Social Media: Facebook, Twitter, LinkedIn, Youtube

Mary Catherine Berube, Executive Director
Tammy Brown, Marketing Director
Stephanie Ford, Administrative Assistant
Lena Padro, Manager
Kathy Kesterson, Manager

A non-profit, educational organization dedicated to making boating safer and more enjoyable by teaching classes in seamanship, navigation and related subjects.
45000 Members
Founded in: 1914

3292 **United States Rowing Association**
2 Wall Street
Princeton, NJ 08540

609-751-0700
800-314-4769; *Fax:* 609-924-1578
members@usrowing.org; www.usrowing.org
Social Media: Facebook, Twitter, Flickr, Youtube

Erin O'Connell, President
Jim Dietz, VP
Gary Caldwell, Treasurer
Frances Mennone, Secretary
Daniel Herbert, At-Large Representative

Non-profit membership organization, recognized by the U.S. Olympic Committee as the national governing body for the sport of rowing in the United States.
16000 Members
Founded in: 1982

3293 **United States Sailing Association**
15 Maritime Drive
Portsmouth, RI 02871

401-683-0800
800-877-2451; *Fax:* 401-683-0840
info@ussailing.org; www.ussailing.org
Social Media: Facebook, Twitter, LinkedIn, Youtube, RSS

Bruce J Burton, Us Sailing President
Jack Gierhart, Executive Director
Cory Sertl, Vice President
Martine R Zurinskas, Secretary
Stephen T Freitas, Treasurer

National governing body for the sport of sailing.
100 Members
Founded in: 1897

3294 **Yacht Brokers Association of America**
105 Eastern Avenue
Suite 104
Annapolis, MD 21403

410-940-6345; *Fax:* 410-263-1659
info@ybaa.com; www.ybaa.com
Social Media: Facebook, Twitter, LinkedIn

Hal Slater, President
David Benson, VP
Jean-Pierre Skov, Treasurer
Vincent J Petrella, Executive Director
Joseph Thompson, General Manager

Sets the standards for professional yacht brokers throughout North America
250 Members
Founded in: 1920

3295 **Yachting Club of America**
PO Box 1040
Marco Island, FL 34146

239-642-4448; *Fax:* 239-642-5284
bill@ycaol.com; www.ycaol.com

David Martin, Owner

A membership organization dedicated to the advancement of yachting.
30000 Members
Founded in: 1963

Newsletters

3296 **ASMA News**
American Society of Marine Artists
P.O.Box 247
Smithfield, VA 23430

757-357-3785
asma1978@verizon.net;
www.americansocietyofmarineartists.com

Keeps you up to date with all of the Society's activities, along with providing space where artists like yourself can share ideas, inspirations, tips

and even frustrations. Provides you access to the Society's network of members, local and national marine art news and information about art exhibitions and exhibition opportunities.
Frequency: Quarterly

3297 **American Boat & Yacht Council News**
American Boat and Yacht Council
613 Third Street
Suite 10
Annapolis, MD 21403

410-990-4460; *Fax:* 410-990-4466
info@abycinc.org; www.abycinc.org

David Marlow, Chairman
Kenneth Weinbrecht, Vice Chair
David Slobodien, Treasurer
Jeff Wasil, Secretary

News and technical information of interest to ABYC members.
4000+ Members
8 Pages
Frequency: Quarterly
Founded in: 1954
Mailing list available for rent

3298 **American Boat Builders and Repairers Association Newsletter**
American Boat Builders and Repairers Association
50 Water Street
Warren, RI 02885

401-247-0318
866-367-6622; *Fax:* 401-247-0074;
www.abbra.org

Jonathan Jones Haven, President
Peter Sabo, VP
Mark Amaral, Managing Director
Charles Teran, Treasurer/Secretary

Accepts advertising.
300 Members
4 Pages
Frequency: Monthly
Founded in: 1943

3299 **Anchor Line Newsletter**
National Safe Boating Council
PO Box 509
Bristow, VA 20136

703-361-4294; *Fax:* 703-361-5294;
www.safeboatingcouncil.org
Social Media: Facebook, Twitter

Joyce Shaw, Chairman
Lynda Nutt, Vice Chairman
Virgil Chambers, Executive Officer
Sandy Smith, Chief Financial Officer
350 Members
Founded in: 1958

3300 **Business of Pleasure Boats**
National Marine Bankers Association
231 South LaSalle St
Suite 2050
Chicago, IL 60604

312-946-6260
bmcardle@nmma.org; www.marinebankers.org
Social Media: LinkedIn

Karen Trostle, President
Jackie Forese, Director
Mike Ryan, Vice President
Bernice McArdlen, Manager
81 Members
Frequency: Quarterly
Founded in: 1979

3301 **MRAA Bearings**
Marine Retailers Association of America
P.O.Box 725
Boca Grande, FL 33921-0725

941-964-2534; *Fax:* 941-531-6777
mraa@mraa.com; www.mraa.com

Phil Keeter, President
Marge Eckenroad, Executive Administrator
Larry Innis, Director Government Affairs
Marge Eckenroad, Executive Administrator

A publication encompassing issues that you need to know about, issues such as legislation, environment and compliance, legal, association and industry news, and much more.
3000 Members
Frequency: Monthly
Circulation: 2000
Founded in: 1971

3302 **Mainsheet**
Rhodes 19 Class Association
174 Walnut Street
Reading, MA 01867

781-944-2697
info@rhodes19.org; www.rhodes19.org
Social Media: Facebook

Steve Uhl, President
Mary Kovats, Secretary
Tom Carville, Treasurer
Newsletter concerning the Rhodes 19 design sailboat. Our mission is to promote Rhodes 19 racing by encouraging and supporting local fleet development nationally, and by working to maintain the one-design integrity of the boat.
Founded in: 1965

3303 **Marine Safety and Security Report**
Stamler Publishing Company
178 Thimble Islands Rd
PO Box 3367
Branford, CT 06405-1967

203-488-9808
800-422-4121; *Fax:* 203-488-3129

S Paul Stamler, President/CEO
Business-to-business newsletter providing information on boating and shipping safety and enforcement issues, including federal regulations and Coast Guard Actions, state safety programs, IMO activity, classification studies, vessel recalls, and safety equipment. Accepts no advertising and is solely supported by subscribers worldwide.
Cost: $77.00
4 Pages
Founded in: 1973
Printed in 2 colors on matte stock

3304 **Maritime Reporter and Engineering News**
118 East 25th Street
New York, NY 10010

212-477-6700; *Fax:* 212-254-6271
jomalley@marinelink.com;
www.marinelink.com

John O'Malley, Publisher
Greg Trauthwein, Associate Publisher
Michael Martino, Owner
Lucia M Annunziata, VP
Jennifer Rabulan, Technical Editor

Provides unparalleled coverage of the maritime industry covering the inland, Coastal and Great Lakes region.
95000 Members
Frequency: Monthly
Circulation: 50000
Founded in: 1999

3305 **NACO Newsletter**
National Association of Charterboat Operators
PO Box 2990
Orange Beach, AL 36561

251-981-5136; *Fax:* 251-981-8191
info@nacocharters.org; www.nacocharters.org

Bob Zales II, President
Ed O'Brien, Vice President
Tom Becker, Second Vice President
Gary Krein, Secretary
3600+ Members
Frequency: Quarterly
Circulation: 3500
Founded in: 1991

3306 **Propeller Club Newsletter**
Propeller Club of the United States
3927 Old Lee Hwy
Suite 101A
Fairfax, VA 22030-2422

703-691-2777; *Fax:* 703-691-4173
shannon@propellerclubhq.com;
www.propellerclubhq.com

Thomas Allegretti, President/CEO
Niels Aalund, Sr. Vice President
Shannon Hendrickson-Pluta, Admin Asst
Virgil R Allen, VP Development

Features expanded coverage of Propeller Club activities, including legislative and regulatory reports, feature-length member profiles, regional news and expanded coverage of national maritime issues.
10000 Members
Frequency: Quarterly
Founded in: 1927

3307 **Rudder**
Antique & Classic Boat Society
422 James St
Clayton, NY 13624-1136

315-686-2628; *Fax:* 315-686-2680
hqs@acbs.org; www.acbs.org
Social Media: Facebook, Twitter

Jim Mersman, President
Dunc Hawkins, First VP
Teresa Hoffman, Second VP
Dick Winn, Treasurer
Brian Gagnon, Secretary

Historical news and how-to-restore wooden and antique boats.
12000 Members
Frequency: Quarterly
Founded in: 1975
Printed in 4 colors

3308 **SAMS Newsletter**
Society of Accredited Marine Surveyors
7855 Argyle Forest Blvd
Suite 203
Jacksonville, FL 32244

904-384-1494
800-344-9077; *Fax:* 904-388-3958
samshq@marinesurvey.org;
www.marinesurvey.org

Joseph B Lobley, President
Stuart J. McLea, Executive Vice President
Llyod E. Kittredge, Secretary/Treasurer
For members.
1000 Members
Frequency: 4/Year
Circulation: 1000
Founded in: 1986

3309 **Seamanship Training**
American Boating Association
PO Box 690
New Market, MD 21774

614-497-4088
admin@americanboating.org;
www.americanboating.org
Social Media: Facebook

Bill Condon, Founder/President

Free to all ABA (American Boating Association) members as well as all boaters. Informative content on boating skills and safety issues.
30000 Members
Frequency: Bi-Monthly

3310 **Shipyard Chronicle Newsletter**
Shipbuilders Council of America
655 Fifteenth St NW
Suite 225
Washington, DC 20005
202-347-5462; *Fax:* 202-347-5464
preever@balljanik.com; www.shipbuilders.org
Social Media: Facebook
Matt Paxton, President, Vice Chairman
Allen Walker, President
Irene Ringwood, Manager
The publication is devoted to keeping members up to date on the latest legislative and regulatory developments. It also includes a schedule of upcoming association and industry related government meetings, as well as news regarding SCA member companies.
73 Members
Founded in: 1920

3311 **Soundings Trade Only**
Soundings Publications
10 Bokum Rd
Essex, CT 06426-1536
860-767-3200; *Fax:* 860-767-1048
info@soundingspub.com;
www.soundingsonline.com
Social Media: Facebook
Ian Bowen, Manager
Peter Mitchel, Publisher
Nation's boating business newspaper. Coverage of the recreational boating business; for marine dealers, marine operators, distributors and manufacturers. BPA audited.
Cost: $13.97
15500 Members
33 Pages
Frequency: Monthly
Circulation: 34,000
Founded in: 1965

3312 **Tidings**
National Marine Representatives Association
1333 Delany Road #500
PO Box 360
Gurnee, IL 60031
847-662-3167; *Fax:* 847-336-7126
info@nmraonline.org; www.nmraonline.org
Chris Kelly, President
Kathy Munzinger, VP
Ken Smaga, Treasurer
Brandon Flack, Secretary
Chris Kelly, Secretary
Contains informative articles to help manufacturers develop sound and profitable relationships with independent sales representatives and keep informed about the marine market in general.
300 Members
500+ Pages
Frequency: Quarterly
Founded in: 1960

3313 **Water Life**
Northwest Marine Trade Association
1900 N Northlake Way
Suite 233
Seattle, WA 98103-9087
206-634-0911; *Fax:* 206-632-0078
info@nmta.net; www.nmta.net
Social Media: Facebook, Twitter, LinkedIn
George Harris, President
Laura Snodgrass, Finance Director
John Thorburn, Vice President
Liz Manning, Membership Director
Provides industry information, member benefits, committee activity and new member announcements and anniversaries. Water Life continues to evolve into a valuable tool for Pacific Northwest marine leaders.
700+ Members
Founded in: 1947

3314 **Yacht Broker News**
Yacht Brokers Association of America
105 Eastern Avenue
Suite 104
Annapolis, MD 21403
410-940-6345; *Fax:* 410-263-1659
info@ybaa.com; www.ybaa.com
Vincent J. Petrella, Executive Director
Rod Rowan, President
Amy Luckado, Membership Director
Reports on latest business issues, industry concerns, legislation, regulatory activities and includes a member-to-member section(WayPoints), where members can report on their own company news, personnel updates and business expansion.
250 Members
Frequency: Quarterly
Founded in: 1920

Magazines & Journals

3315 **American Sailor**
US Sailing Association
15 Maritime Drive
PO Box 1260
Portsmouth, RI 02871-0907
401-683-0800
800-877-2451; *Fax:* 401-683-0840
info@ussailing.org; www.ussailing.org
Social Media: Facebook, Twitter, LinkedIn
Tom Hubbell, Us Sailing President
Jack Gierhart, Executive Director
Fred Hagedorn, Secretary
Jack Gierhart, Executive Director
Boating news.
100 Members
Frequency: Monthly
Founded in: 1980

3316 **Ash Breeze**
Traditional Small Craft Association
PO Box 350
Mystic, CT 06355
E-Mail: drathmarine@rockisland.com;
www.tsca.net
Mike Wick, Co-Editor
Ned Asplundh, Co-Editor
Devoted to topics ranging from reports from the chapters to technical details and specific designs with lines and offsets. You may find anecdotal accounts of experiences in traditional boats, and tips on how to spile a plank.
Frequency: Quarterly

3317 **Boat & Motor Dealer**
Preston Publications
6600 W Touhy Ave
PO Box 48312
Niles, IL 60714-4516
847-647-2900; *Fax:* 847-647-1155;
www.prestonpub.com
Tinsley Preston, Owner
Jerome Koncel, Editorial Director
Dedicated to providing businesses in the recreational marine industry with the information, commentary and analysis needed to expand their businesses and improve profitability.
Founded in: 1959
Mailing list available for rent: 30000 names at $100 per M

3318 **BoatUS Magazine**
Boat Owners Association of the US
880 South Pickett Street
Alexandria, VA 22304-4606
703-461-2864; *Fax:* 703-461-2845;
www.boatus.com
Social Media: Facebook, Twitter
Michael Vatalaro, Executive Editor
Richard Schwartz, Chairman/Founder
Chris Landers, Associate Editor
Boating magazine includes legislative, travel, safety, DIY, and consumer news of interest to recreational boat owners.
Cost: $19.00
62500 Members
Frequency: Annual/6
Circulation: 500K+
Founded in: 1966

3319 **Boatbuilder**
Belvoir Publishers
PO Box 5656
Norwalk, CT 06856-5656
203-857-4880; *Fax:* 203-661-4802
customer_service@belvoir.com;
www.belvoir.com
Robert Englander, Owner/CEO
The magazine is for those who build, modify and repair boats.
Founded in: 1972

3320 **Boating Industry**
Ehlert Publishing Group
6420 Sycamore Ln N
Suite 100
Maple Grove, MN 55369-6014
763-383-4400
800-848-6247; *Fax:* 763-383-4499;
www.boatingindustry.com
Social Media: Facebook, Twitter, LinkedIn
Jonathan Sweet, Editor in Chief
Tom Kaiser, Senior Editor
Links together all sectors of the boating market from boat and motor dealers to marinas, boatyards, builders and suppliers. It also provides strategic analysis, in-depth coverage and proprietary research of the most critical issues.
Frequency: 8 Issues/2 Special Issues

3321 **Boating Magazine**
Bonnier Corporation
460 N. Orlando Ave
Suite 200
Winter Park, FL 32789
407-628-4802; *Fax:* 407-628-7061
editor@boatingmag.com;
www.boatingmag.com
Social Media: Facebook, Twitter
John McEver, Publisher
Glenn Hughes, VP
Jonas Bonnier, Chairman
Offers up-to-date information on boats, manufacturers, suppliers, distributors related to the boating industry.
Cost: $17.95
Frequency: Monthly

3322 **Canoe & Kayak Magazine**
Canoe & Kayak
12025 115th Ave. NE
Suite D200
Kirkland, WA 98034
425-827-6363
800-692-2663; *Fax:* 425-827-1893
letters@canoekayak.com;
www.canoekayak.com
Social Media: Facebook, Twitter
Jeff Moag, Editor
Dave Shively, Managing Editor

Published by the Canoe American Associates.
Cost: $17.95
Frequency: 7 Issues
Circulation: 62000
Founded in: 1973
Mailing list available for rent

3323 Dry Stack Marina Handbook
Association of Marina Industries
50 Water Street
Warren, RI 02885

866-367-6622; *Fax:* 401-247-0074
info@marinaassociation.org;
www.marinaassociation.org
Social Media: Twitter, LinkedIn

Jim Frye, CMM, Chairman/President
Gary Groenewold, Vice Chairman
Jeff Rose, Treasurer
Keith Boulais, Secretary

This book covers: Dry stack buildings and racks, Boat handling equipment, Statistics, Site planning, Typical costs, Fire protection problems & solutions, Comparision of dry stack vs. wet slip demand, Marketing, Facility operations, Lease or purchase decision, Loss control considerations.
Cost: $90.00
800+ Members
Frequency: 61 Illustrations
Founded in: 1986

3324 Ensign
United States Power Squadrons
1504 Blue Ridge Rd
Raleigh, NC 27607-3906

919-821-0281
888-367-8777; *Fax:* 888-304-0813;
www.usps.org
Social Media: Facebook, Twitter

Frank A. Dvorak, Executive Officer

Ensign magazine is the official magazine of United States Power Squadrons. The mission is to promote recreational boating safety through education and civic activities while providing fellowship for our members.
Cost: $10.00
45000 Members
48 Pages
Frequency: Monthly
Circulation: 35,000
Founded in: 1914
Printed in 4 colors on glossy stock

3325 Fabric Architecture
U.S. Industrial Fabrics Association International
1801 County Road B W
Roseville, MN 55113-4061

651-222-2508
800-225-4324; *Fax:* 651-631-9334
generalinfo@ifai.com; www.usifi.com

Stephen Warner, CEO
JoAnne Ferris, Marketing Director

Targets architects, designers, specifiers, contractors and developers promoting the architectural advantages of fabric. Educates the industry about designing with fabric and promoting it as an environmentally-responsible choice.
Frequency: Bimonthly
Circulation: 8,000

3326 Fabric Graphics
Industrial Fabrics Association International
1801 County Road B W
Roseville, MN 55113-4061

651-222-2508
800-225-4324; *Fax:* 651-631-9334
generalinfo@ifai.com; www.ifai.com
Social Media: Facebook, Twitter, LinkedIn

Mary J. Hennessy, Executive VP
JoAnne Farris, Marketing Director
Steven C. Rider, CFO, VP

Created to educate and inspire professionals to use fabric to expand their business. Promotes the use of textiles as a printing medium, showcasing the numerous applications for fabric and the technology needed to achieve good results.
Frequency: Bimonthly
Circulation: 8,000
Founded in: 1912

3327 Geosynthetics
Industrial Fabrics Association International
1801 County Road B W
Roseville, MN 55113-4061

651-222-2508
800-225-4324; *Fax:* 651-631-9334
generalinfo@ifai.com; www.ifai.com
Social Media: Facebook, Twitter, LinkedIn

Mary J. Hennessy, Executive VP
JoAnne Farris, Marketing Director
Steven C. Rider, CFO, VP

Targeting those who rely on the publication for the most professional presentation of Geosynthetic products, design, and applications.
Frequency: Bimonthly
Circulation: 14,000
Founded in: 1912

3328 InTents
Industrial Fabrics Association International
1801 County Road B W
Roseville, MN 55113-4061

651-222-2508
800-225-4324; *Fax:* 651-631-9334
generalinfo@ifai.com; www.ifai.com
Social Media: Facebook, Twitter, LinkedIn

Mary J. Hennessy, Executive VP
JoAnne Farris, Marketing Director
Steven C. Rider, CFO, VP

Focuses on tents, fabric structures, and accessories that tent renters need to operate a profitable business. The magazine and its website work together to deliver the total tent experience to readers and visitors.
Frequency: Bimonthly
Circulation: 11,000
Founded in: 1912

3329 Marina/Dock Age
Preston Publications
6600 W Touhy Ave
Niles, IL 60714-4516

847-647-2900; *Fax:* 847-647-1155
atownshend@marinadockage.com;
www.marinadockage.com/
Social Media: Twitter, LinkedIn

Tinsley Preston, Owner
Anna Townshend, Editor

Provide marina/boatyard owners and managers with the information they need to meet ever-changing government regulations, operate more efficiently, expand their business, and improve their profitability.
Cost: $50.00
16500 Members
Frequency: Monthly
Circulation: 24000
Founded in: 1989

3330 Marinas and Small Craft Harbors
Association of Marina Industries
50 Water Street
Warren, RI 02885

866-367-6622; *Fax:* 401-247-0074
info@marinaassociation.org;
www.marinaassociation.org
Social Media: Twitter, LinkedIn

Jim Frye, CMM, Chairman/President
Gary Groenewold, Vice Chairman
Jeff Rose, Treasurer
Keith Boulais, Secretary

The new edition includes updated and redrawn tables, charts, figures and text editing and additions, as well as newly created information on marina design characteristics of megyachts and test data, design loads, and recommendations on design and performance of dock cleats.
Cost: $89.95
800+ Members
Founded in: 1986

3331 Marine Fabricator
Industrial Fabrics Association International
1801 County Road B W
Roseville, MN 55113-4061
651-222-2508
800-225-4324; *Fax:* 651-631-9334
generalinfo@ifai.com; www.ifai.com
Social Media: Facebook, Twitter, LinkedIn

Mary J. Hennessy, Executive VP
JoAnne Farris, Marketing Director
Steven C. Rider, CFO, VP

Educates professionals in the techniques of quality marine craftsmanship and upholstery. Marine shop professionals rely on the magazine to stay informed on the latest techniques, technologies, business management and news.
Cost: $34.00
Frequency: Bi-Monthly
Circulation: 5,000
Founded in: 1912

3332 Marine Log
Simmons-Boardman Publishing Corporation
345 Hudson St
12th Floor, Suite 1201
New York, NY 10014-7123

212-620-7200; *Fax:* 212-633-1165;
www.marinelog.com
Social Media: Facebook, Twitter, LinkedIn

Arthur J McGinnis Jr, President
John Snyder, Publisher/Editor in Chief

For more than 130 years, maritime executives worldwide have turned to Marine Log as the source for news and analysis on issues impacting vessel design, construction and operations.
Frequency: Monthly
Circulation: 29934
Founded in: 1878

3333 Marine News
Maritime Activity Reports
118 East 25th Street
New York, NY 10010

212-477-6700; *Fax:* 212-254-6271
jomalley@marinelink.com;
www.marinelink.com

John O'Malley, Publisher
Greg Trauthwein, Associate Publisher
Michael Martino, Owner
Lucia M Annunziata, VP
Jennifer Rabulan, Technical Editor

Features marine industry news and issues effecting maritime activity. Includes updates on vessel building and acquisitions as well as regular columns on research and devleopment, equipment reports and an events calendar.
95000 Members
Frequency: Monthly
Circulation: 23000
Founded in: 1999

3334 Motor Boating
Time4 Media Marine Group

460 N. Orlando Ave
Suite 200
Winter Park, FL 32789

407-628-4802; *Fax:* 407-628-7061
editor@motorboating.com;
www.motorboating.com
Social Media: Facebook, Twitter

Ed Baker, Associate Publisher
John McEver, Publisher
Glenn Hughes, VP

Helps its readers buy, maintain and get the most out of their powerboats. It focuses on powerboats, people, products, destinations, trends and technological developments in the boating market, as well as cruising, water sports and safety.
Frequency: Monthly
Founded in: 1907
Printed in on glossy stock

3335 National Numbering & Titling
National Association of State Boating Law
1500 Leestown Rd
Suite 330
Lexington, KY 40511-2047

859-225-9487; *Fax:* 859-231-6403
info@nasbla.org; www.nasbla.org
Social Media: Facebook, Twitter, LinkedIn, Flickr, Foursquare

John Johnson, Executive Director
Tom Hayward, Finance & Administration
Ron Sarver, Deputy Director

Facilitate ongoing efforts to evaluate and improve the programs' internal procedures and external interactions in the face of resource constraints and in preparation for implementing the Coast Guard's Vessel Identification System.
Cost: $14.95
56 Members
Founded in: 1960
Mailing list available for rent: 56 names

3336 Paddle Magazine
Paddle Sport Publishing
12025 115th Ave. NE
Suite D200
Kirkland, WA 98034

970-879-1450; *Fax:* 970-870-1404
Eugene@paddlermagazine.com;
www.paddlermagazine.com
Social Media: Facebook, Twitter

Eugene Buchanan, Publisher/Editor
Jeff Moag, Editor
Kevin Thompson, Account Manager

Information to keep the paddle sport equipment dealer up-to-date on issues that will effect their business, industry trends in boats, apparel and accessories, how to articles to assist the reader in selling boats.
Cost: $18.00
Circulation: 5527
Printed in 4 colors on glossy stock

3337 Paddlesports Business
Canoe & Kayak
12025 115th Ave. NE
Suite D200
Kirkland, WA 98034

425-827-6363
800-692-2663; *Fax:* 425-827-1893
letters@canoekayak.com;
www.canoekayak.com
Social Media: Facebook, Twitter

Jeff Moag, Editor
Dave Shively, Managing Editor

Trade publication for the paddlesports industry.
Founded in: 1973
Mailing list available for rent

3338 Professional BoatBuilder
WoodenBoat Publications
41 Wooden Boat La
PO Box 78
Brooklin, ME 04616-0078

207-359-4651
800-877-5284; *Fax:* 207-359-8920
proboat@proboat.com; www.proboat.com
Social Media: Facebook

Paul Lazarus, Sr. Editor
Aaron Porter, Editor
Carl Cramer, Co-Director

Focuses on materials, design, and construction techniques and repair solutions chosen by marine professionals. Regular technical articles provide detailed, real-world examples to improve the efficiency and quality of their work.
Cost: $35.95
76 Pages
Circulation: 27500
ISSN: 1043-2035
Founded in: 1974
Printed in 4 colors on glossy stock

3339 Propeller
American Power Boat Association
17640 E. Nine Mile Road
PO Box 377
Eastpointe, MI 48021-0377

586-773-9700; *Fax:* 586-773-6490
propeller@apba-racing.com;
www.apba-racing.com

Mark Weber, President
Gloria Urbin, Executive Director
Tana Moore, News, Propellor

Propeller magazine is the mouthpiece of the American Power Boat Association, the nation's leading authority on power boat racing which sanctions over 200 races each year.
Cost: $2.50
22 Pages
Frequency: Monthly
ISSN: 0194-6218
Printed in 4 colors on glossy stock

3340 Small Craft Advisory
National Association of State Boating Law Admnstrs
1500 Leestown Rd
Suite 330
Lexington, KY 40511-2047

859-225-9487; *Fax:* 859-231-6403
info@nasbla.org; www.nasbla.org
Social Media: Facebook, Twitter, LinkedIn, Flickr, Foursquare

John Johnson, Executive Director
Tom Hayward, Finance & Administration
Ron Sarver, Deputy Director

Small Craft Advisory, published bimonthly, is for and about the nation's boating law administration professionals. Authoritative articles featuring practices, procedures, and research in recreational boating safety, marine law enforcement, and boating safety education are presented to enhance the efficiency and effectiveness of recreational boating safety. Each issue highlights successful recreational boating safety programs, NASBLA activities, professional news, and legislative updates
Cost: $14.00
56 Members
Frequency: Bi-Monthly
Circulation: 11000
Founded in: 1960
Mailing list available for rent: 56 names

3341 Southern Boating Magazine
330 N Andrews Ave
Suite 200
Fort Lauderdale, FL 33301-1025

954-522-5515
888-882-6284; *Fax:* 954-522-2260
sboating@southernboating.com;
www.southernboating.com
Social Media: Facebook, Twitter

Skip Allen, Owner/Chairman/Publisher/Editor
L.J. Wallace, Executive Editor
Cathryn Allen-Zubi, VP
Rain Hernandez Rouveroy, VP of Finance
Kellie Mackenroth, Circulation Manager

Focus is on boating in the southern US, Bahamas, and Caribbean.
Cost: $22.95
Frequency: Monthly
Circulation: 42000
Founded in: 1972
Printed in 4 colors on matte stock

3342 Specialty Fabrics Review
Industrial Fabrics Association International
1801 County Road B W
Roseville, MN 55113-4061

651-222-2508
800-225-4324; *Fax:* 651-631-9334
generalinfo@ifai.com; www.ifai.com
Social Media: Facebook, Twitter, LinkedIn

Mary J. Hennessy, Executive VP
JoAnne Farris, Marketing Director
Steven C. Rider, CFO, VP

In print since 1915, this international publication targets specialty fabric professionals. Each issue brings timely reporting on industry topics, helpful business articles and a review of global news and market updates.
Frequency: Monthly
Circulation: 13000
Founded in: 1912

3343 The Reference Point
American Boat and Yacht Council
613 Third Street
Suite 10
Annapolis, MD 21403

410-990-4460; *Fax:* 410-990-4466
info@abycinc.org; www.abycinc.org
Social Media: Facebook

David Marlow, Chairman
Kenneth Weinbrecht, Vice Chair
David Slobodien, Treasurer
Jeff Wasil, Secretary

ABYC's technical professional quarterly journal.
4000+ Members
Frequency: Quarterly
Founded in: 1954

3344 US Yacht Racing Union
US Sailing
15 Maritime Drive
PO Box 1260
Portsmouth, RI 02871-0907

401-683-0800
800-877-2451; *Fax:* 401-683-0840
info@ussailing.org; www.ussailing.org
Social Media: Facebook, Twitter, LinkedIn

Gary Jobson, Us Sailing President
Tom Hubbell, Vice President
Fred Hagedorn, Secretary
Jack Gierhart, Executive Director

National news of the Union, the latest in yacht racing, and dealers of yachts are covered.
100 Members
Founded in: 1986

3345 UnderWater Magazine
Naylor, LLC
5950 NW 1st Place
Gainesville, FL 32607

800-369-6220; www.underwater.com

Jamie Williams, Publication Director
Sean Garrity, Editorial
Rebecca Roberts, Marketing Manager

It covers the entire spectrum of underwater contracting, vehicles and technology.
Cost: $50.00
500 Members
Founded in: 1968

3346 **WoodenBoat**
WoodenBoat Publications
41 Wooden Boat La
PO Box 78
Brooklin, ME 04616-0078
207-359-4651
800-877-5284; *Fax:* 207-359-8920;
www.woodenboat.com
Social Media: Facebook
Tom Jackson, Sr. Editor
Carl Cramer, Publisher
Matt Murphy, Editor
Provides readers with a dynamic editorial environment that combines technologies with traditional methods of boat design, construction and repair. The magazine is about craftmanship in wood, and its active boating audience works at all levels of expertise to build, restore, and maintain their boats.
Cost: $29.95
160 Pages
Frequency: Bi-Monthly
Circulation: 98000
Founded in: 1974

3347 **WorkBoat**
Diversified Business Communications
121 Free Street
Portland, ME 04101
207-842-5600; *Fax:* 207-842-5611
info@divcom.com; www.workboat.com
Social Media: Facebook, Twitter
Mike Lodato, VP
Ken Hocke, Senior Editor
David Krapf, Editor In Chief
Jerry Fraser, Publisher
Commercial marine publication serving the North American inland and coastal waterways — the most active sector in the commercial marine market today. Consisting of captains, owners, managers, operators, chief engineers and other industry professionals, the Workboat audience represents important and influential purchasing power in the commercial marine industry.
Cost: $39.00
Frequency: Monthly
Circulation: 25000
ISSN: 0043-8014
Founded in: 1949

3348 **Yachting Magazine**
Time4 Media Marine Group
PO Box 420235
Palm Coast, FL 32142-0235
386-597-4382
800-999-0869
letters@yachtingmagazine.com;
www.yachtingmagazine.com
Social Media: Facebook, Twitter
Ed Baker, Associate Publisher
Rich Rasor, East Coast Sales Director
Covers the finest boats, electronics and equipment, including large yachts and yacht charters. It also covers the passions, adventures and lifestyles of active, affluent boat owners.
Frequency: Monthly
Founded in: 1907

3349 **Young Mariners Guide**
Yachting Club of America
PO Box 1040
Marco Island, FL 34146
239-642-4448; *Fax:* 239-642-5284
ycaol@hotmail.com; www.ycaol.com
David Martin, Owner
Designed to inform and teach young people about boating in simple and handy pocket book to help them on their way to becoming the future of the yachting fraternity in America.
Cost: $5.00
30000 Members
32 Pages
Frequency: Softbound
Founded in: 1963
Mailing list available for rent

Trade Shows

3350 **Annual American and Canadian Sport, Travel and Outdoor Show**
Expositions, Inc.
Edgewater Branch
PO Box 550
Cleveland, OH 44107-0550
216-529-1300; *Fax:* 216-529-0311
showinfo@expoinc.com; www.expoinc.com
Chris Fassnacht, President
Robert Attewell, Vice President
David Rosar, CFO, VP
975 exhibits of hunting and fishing equipment, travel services, boats, recreational vehicles and related equipment, supplies and services.
300k Attendees
Frequency: March
Founded in: 1937

3351 **Annual Boat & Fishing Show at the Lansing Center**
Show Span, Inc
2121 Celebration Drive NE
Grand Rapids, MI 49525
616-447-2860
800-328-6550; *Fax:* 616-447-2861
events@showspan.com; www.showspan.com
John Loeks, President
Henri Boucher, Vice President
Mike Wilbraham, VP, Show Producer
Held in Lansing, Michigan.
Frequency: March
Founded in: 1945

3352 **Annual Boat Show**
General Sports Shows/NMMA
231 S. LaSalle St
Suite 2050
Chicago, IL 60604
312-946-6200
800-777-4766
bmcardle@nmma.org;
www.generalsportshows.com
Jennifer Thompson, Show Manager
Bonnie Schuenemann, Special Events Coordinator
Patty Gibbs, Media Contact
Enjoy 5 days of boating fun, education and one-stop shopping with hundreds of boats and exhibits and special attractions all under one roof.
Frequency: January

3353 **Annual Boat Show & Fishing Exposition**
Greenband Enterprises
3450 South Highland Drive
Suite 105
Salt Lake City, UT 84106
801-485-7399
800-657-3050; *Fax:* 801-485-0687
showinfo@greenband.com;
www.greenband.com
Social Media: Facebook
Jonathan D Greenband, Show Manager
Debra Greenband, Sales Manager
See the latest in Ski Boats, Cruisers, Fishing Boats, everything for boating fun.
45000 Attendees
Frequency: Annual, February
Founded in: 1965

3354 **Annual Boat, Vacation and Outdoor Show**
Showtime Productions, Inc.
PO Box 4372
Rockford, IL 61110
815-877-8043; *Fax:* 815-877-9037
brenda@showtimeproduction.net
showtimeproduction.net
Tom Pellant, President
Brenda Rotoco, Event Coordinator
Boat, travel, outdoor equipment, supplies, and services plus demonstrations.
28000 Attendees
Frequency: February
Founded in: 1970

3355 **Annual Conference & Educational Symposia**
Society of Accredited Marine Surveyors
7855 Argyle Forest Blvd
Suite 203
Jacksonville, FL 32244
904-384-1494
800-344-9077; *Fax:* 904-388-3958
samshq@marinesurvey.org;
www.marinesurvey.org
Joseph B Lobley, President
Stuart J. McLea, Executive Vice President
Llyod E. Kittredge, Secretary/Treasurer
1000 Members
350 Attendees
Frequency: Annual/Fall
Founded in: 1986

3356 **Annual Conference on Sail Training and Tall Ships**
American Sail Training Association
29 Touro Street
PO Box 1459
Newport, RI 02840
401-846-1775; *Fax:* 401-849-5400
asta@sailtraining.org;
www.tallships.sailtraining.org
Social Media: Facebook, Twitter, LinkedIn, Youtube
Mike Rauworth, Chairman
Robert Rogers, Executive Director
Caleb Pifer, Vice Chair
300 Members
Frequency: November
Founded in: 1973

3357 **Annual Iowa Boat and Vacation Show**
Iowa Show Productions
PO Box 2460
Waterloo, IA 50704-2460
319-232-0218; *Fax:* 319-235-8932
info@iowashows.com; www.iowashows.com
John Bunge, Show Manager
Over 25 dealers, 40 brands, 100's of models. Family runabouts, fishing boats, cabin cruisers, cuddies, power boats, waterski boats, personal watercraft, jet boats, bass boats, walleye boats, deck boats, pontoons, fish/ski boats, and marine accessories.
Frequency: January
Founded in: 1975
Mailing list available for rent

3358 **Annual Lido Yacht Expo**
Duncan McIntosh Company

17782 Cowan, Ste A
Irvine, CA 92614

949-757-5959; *Fax:* 949-660-6172
boatshow@goboating.com;
www.lidoyachtexpo.com
Social Media: Facebook

Duncan McIntosh, President
Jeff Fleming, Associate Publisher

An upscale in-the-water show of yachts and big boats. More than 2,000 feet of floating dock.
Frequency: May
Founded in: 1973

3359 Annual National Capital Boat Show
Royal Productions
PO Box 4197
Chester, VA 23831

804-256-6556; *Fax:* 804-288-7132
info@royalshows.com; www.royalshows.com

David Posner, President

Nearly 40 dealers form throughout Maryland and Virginia bring a wide range of boats to the National Capital Boat Show including saltware fishing boats, ski boats, runabouts, motor yachts, jet boats, jon boats, PWC, bass boats, inflatables, deck boats and pontoons.
20000 Attendees
Frequency: March

3360 Annual Spring Boat Show
Southern California Marine Association
1006 East Chapman Ave
Orange, CA 92866

714-633-7581; *Fax:* 714-633-9498;
www.scma.com
Social Media: Facebook, Twitter

Richard Tressler, President
Renee Acencio, Vice President

You'll find a assortment of marine accessory booths featuring the latest and newest products filled with everything that floats, affordable family runabounts, ski boats, fishing boats, cruisers, pontoons, performance sportboats and personal watercraft.
Frequency: June
Founded in: 1956

3361 Annual Spring New Products Show
Pacific Expositions c/o Tihati Productions
3615 Harding Ave
Suite 506
Honolulu, HI 96816

808-732-6037; *Fax:* 808-732-6039
info@pacificexpos.com;
www.pacificexpos.com

Tara Chanel-Thompson, Director/General Manager

The newest and most exciting products on land and sea with 320 exhibits for trade professionals, buyers, and the general public.
17000 Attendees
Frequency: Annual, April
Founded in: 1974

3362 Association of Marina Industries Annual Conference
Association of Marina Industries
50 Water Street
Warren, RI 02885

866-367-6622; *Fax:* 401-247-0074
info@marinaassociation.org;
www.marinaassociation.org
Social Media: Twitter, LinkedIn

Jim Frye, CMM, Chairman/President
Gary Groenewold, Chairman
Brad Gross, Treasurer
Keith Boulais, Secretary
800+ Members
Frequency: May
Founded in: 1986

3363 Atlanta Boat Show
National Marine Manufacturers Association
200 E Randolph Drive
Suite 1500
Chicago, IL 60601

954-441-3228
lberryman@nmma.org;
www.atlantaboatshow.com
Social Media: Facebook, Twitter

Larry Berryman, Show Manager
Scott Cohens, Relationship Manager
Sarah Ryser, PR Manager
Venus Berryman, Show Administrator
Debbie Harewood, Director, Shows Administration

Showcases the latest in boating products and marine technology. 225 exhibitors.
Frequency: January
Founded in: 1961

3364 Atlantic City In-Water Power Boat Show
In-Water Power Boat Show
1650 Market St
36th Floor
Philadelphia, PA 19103

215-732-8001; *Fax:* 215-732-8266
info@acinwaterboatshow.com;
www.acinwaterboatshow.com
Social Media: Facebook, Twitter

Jerry Flaxman, Executive VP

This show provides space for over 700 boats on land and in-water and over 200 booths in the marine marketplace, including 2 tents and walkways along the piers. Showcases the new models for each coming year.
Frequency: September
Founded in: 1983

3365 Atlantic City International Power Boat Show
National Marine Manufacturers Association
37-18 Northern Blvd
Suite 311
Long Islang City, NY 11101

718-707-0719; *Fax:* 888-649-7786
jpritko@nmma.org; www.acboatshow.com
Social Media: Facebook, Twitter

Jon Pritko, Show Manager
Josh Rosales, Operations Manager

Showcases more than 700 all-new models of motor and express yachts, sports fisherman, cruisers and sport boats. Attracts boaters from all of the East Coast.
50000 Attendees
Frequency: February

3366 Boat Show of Grand Rapids
Show Span
2121 Celebration Drive NE
Grand Rapids, MI 49525

616-472-2860
800-328-6550; *Fax:* 616-447-2861
events@showspan.com; www.showspan.com

John Loeks, President
Henri Boucher, Vice President
Mike Wilbraham, VP, Show Producer

Over 400 exhibits of power and sail boats, accessories, clocks, dockominiums and vacation destinations. Held at the Grand Center in Grand Rapids, Michigan.
Frequency: February
Founded in: 1945

3367 Boat Show of New England
North America Expositions Company
33 Rutherford Avenue
Boston, MA 02129-3795

617-472-1442
800-225-1577; *Fax:* 617-242-1817
joneal@nmma.org;
www.newenglandboatshow.com
Social Media: Facebook, Twitter

Joseph B O'Neal, Managing Partner
Bob McAlpine, Operations Manager

Over 600 boats on display, both power and sailboats ranging from dinghies to 45 foot yachts, along with every conceivable accessory for your new or present boat.
215M Attendees
Frequency: February

3368 Brokerage Yacht Show
Yachting Promotions
1115 NE 9th Avenue
Fort Lauderdale, FL 33304-2110

954-764-7642
800-940-7642; *Fax:* 954-462-4140
info@showmanagement.com;
www.showmanagement.com
Social Media: Facebook, Twitter

Steve Sheer, Director Advertising
Kaye Pearson, President

The totally in-water presentation features over 500 new and pre-owned vessels.
Frequency: February
Founded in: 1976
Mailing list available for rent

3369 Education Under Sail Forum
American Sail Training Association
29 Touro Street
PO Box 1459
Newport, RI 02840

401-846-1775; *Fax:* 401-849-5400
asta@sailtraining.org;
www.tallships.sailtraining.org
Social Media: Facebook, Twitter, Youtube

Mike Rauworth, Chairman
Robert Rogers, Executive Director
300 Members
Frequency: Biennial
Founded in: 1973

3370 IBEX Annual Conference
National Marine Manufacturers Association
231 S. LaSalle St
Suite 2050
Chicago, IL 60604

312-946-6200; *Fax:* 312-946-0401;
www.nmma.org

Thomas Dammrich, President
Ben Wold, Executive Vice President
Craig Boskey, VP Finance/CFO

Exhibition features the products and processes now available that will streamline your boatbuilding business. See the advanced technologies ready for the upcoming model-year. Featuring 800 OEMs and suppliers, the exhibit halls offer you an opportunity to source and compare every tool available to boatbuilders.
Frequency: November
Founded in: 1979

3371 IFAI Expo Americas
Internationl Fabrics Association International
1801 County Road B W
Roseville, MN 55113-4061
651-222-2508
800-225-4324; *Fax:* 651-631-9334
generalinfo@ifai.com; www.ifaiexpo.com
Social Media: Facebook, Twitter, LinkedIn

Mary J. Hennessy, Executive VP
JoAnne Farris, Marketing Director
Steven C. Rider, CFO, VP

A trade event in the Americas for the technical textiles and specialty fabrics industry.
Frequency: Annual/October
Founded in: 1912

3372 International Boating and Water Safety Summit
National Safe Boating Council
PO Box 509
Bristow, VA 20136

703-361-4294; *Fax:* 703-361-5294
office@safeboatingcouncil.org;
www.safeboatingcouncil.org
Social Media: Facebook, Twitter, Youtube

Joyce Shaw, Chair
Chris Edmonston, Vice Chair
Veronica Floyd, Past Chair
Frequency: April

3373 International Conference of Professional Yacht Brokers
Yacht Brokers Association of America
105 Eastern Avenue
Suite 104
Annapolis, MD 21403

410-940-6345; *Fax:* 410-263-1659
info@ybaa.com; www.ybaa.com
Social Media: Facebook, Twitter, LinkedIn

Vincent J. Petrella, Executive Director
Rod Rowan, President
250 Members
Frequency: Annual
Founded in: 1920

3374 International Marina & Boatyard Conference
American Boat Builders and Repairers Association
50 Water Street
Warren, RI 02885

401-247-0318
866-367-6622; *Fax:* 401-247-0074
info@marinaassociation.org; www.abbra.org
Social Media: Twitter, LinkedIn

Jim Frye, CMM, Chairman/President
Gary Groenewold, Chairman
Brad Gross, Treasurer
Keith Boulais, Secretary
The conference is designed to meet the growing demand among those delivering the boating experience for an international forum for education and exposition.
800+ Members
Frequency: Annual
Founded in: 1986

3375 International WorkBoat Show
The International WorkBoat Show
121 Fine Street
PO Box 7437
Portland, ME 04101-7437

207-842-5500; *Fax:* 207-842-5503
customerservice@divcom.com;
www.workboatshow.com
Social Media: Facebook, Twitter

Chris Dimmerling, Sales Director
Bob Callahan, Show Director
Denielle Christensen, Marketing Manager
The largest commercial marine tradeshow in North America, serving people in coastal, inland and offshore waters. It features 1000 exhibiting companies and is produced in partnership with WorkBoat magazine.
Frequency: Annual
Founded in: 1978

3376 MEGATEX
Industrial Fabrics Association International
1801 County Road B W
Roseville, MN 55113-4061

651-222-2508
800-225-4324; *Fax:* 651-631-9334
generalinfo@ifai.com; www.ifai.com
Social Media: Facebook, Twitter, LinkedIn

Mary J. Hennessy, Executive VP
JoAnne Farris, Marketing Director
Steven C. Rider, CFO, VP
Jeffrey W Kirk, President
Will be held at the Georgia World Congress Center in Atlanta, Georgia, and is anchored by the IFAI Expo and the ATMW-I shows. Together, the shows are expected to have more than 1,000 exhibitors.
20000 Attendees
Founded in: 1912

3377 Marine Retailers Association of America Annual Convention
Marine Regtailers Association of America
PO Box 1127
Oak Park, IL 60304

708-763-9210; *Fax:* 708-763-9236
mraa@mraa.com; www.mraa.com

Matt Gruhn, President
Liz Walz, Director
Larry Innis, Legislative Affairs
Frequency: November

3378 Mid-America Sail & Power Boat Show
Lake Erie Marine Trade Association
1269 Bassett Road
Cleveland, OH 44145-1116

440-899-5009; *Fax:* 440-899-5013
lemta@aol.com; www.clevelandboatshow.com
Social Media: Facebook

Norm Schultz, President Emeritus
Annual show of 325 manufacturers and suppliers of pleasure boats and related marine equipment, supplies and services.
140M Attendees
Frequency: January

3379 Midwest Boat Show
Lake Erie Marine Trade Association
1269 Bassett Road
Cleveland, OH 44145-1116

440-899-5009; *Fax:* 440-899-5013

Norm Schultz, President
Annual show and exhibits of boats, equipment, supplies and services.
23M Attendees
Frequency: August
Founded in: 1980

3380 NMBA Annual Conference
National Marine Bankers Association
231 South LaSalle Street
Suite 2050
Chicago, IL 60604

312-812-2777
bmcardle@nmma.org; www.marinebankers.org
Social Media: LinkedIn

Michael Bryant, President
Jayme Yates, Secretary
Jackie Forese, Director
NMBA hosts a three day member conference where the latest trends relating to marine industry are discussed in detail.
180 Attendees
Frequency: September

3381 National Association of State Boating Law Administrators Annual Conference
National Association of State Boating Law
1500 Leestown Road
Suite 330
Lexington, KY 40511

859-225-9487; *Fax:* 859-231-6403
info@nasbla.org; www.nasbla.org/

Toby Velasquez, President
Herb Angell, VP
Kevin Bergerson, Treasurer
Conference provides information that focuses on boating education, industry trends, workshops, and programs that discuss the history of recreational boating safety programs including an overview of state-by-state regulatory laws.
Frequency: September

3382 National Capital Boat Show
Royal Productions
PO Box 4197
Chester, VA 23831-8475

804-425-6556; *Fax:* 804-425-6563;
www.royalshows.com

Serving the Washington DC and suburban Virginia/Maryland markets. 40 dealers.
Frequency: March

3383 National Dry Stack Conference
Association of Marina Industries
444 North Capitol Street NW
Suite 645
Washington, DC 20001

202-379-9768; *Fax:* 202-628-8679
info@imimarina.org; www.imimarina.org

Gregg Kenney, Chairman
Alex Laidlaw, Vice Chairman
Maureen Healey, Executive Director
Cris McSparen, Treasurer
Brooke Fishel, Manager Communications
The Dry Stack is a three-day hybrid school which combines an educational program along with networking among leading operations, developers and vendors.
Frequency: October

3384 National Marine Bankers Association Annual Conference
National Marine Bankers Association
231 South LaSalle Street
Suite 2050
Chicago, IL 60604

312-812-2777
bmcardle@nmma.org; www.marinebankers.org
Social Media: LinkedIn

Michael Bryant, President
Jayme Yates, Secretary
Jackie Forese, Director
A three-day member conference where the latest trends issues relating to the marine industry are discussed in detail.
Frequency: September

3385 North American Sail & Power Show
Lake Erie Marine Trade Association
1269 Bassett Road
Cleveland, OH 44145-1116

440-899-5009; *Fax:* 440-899-5013
lemta@aol.com

Norm Schultz, President
Annual show and exhibits of marine equipment, supplies and services.
31M Attendees
Frequency: September

3386 Portland Boat Show
O'Loughlin Trade Shows

3600 SW Multnomah Boulevard
PO Box 80750
Portland, OR 97219-1750

503-246-8291; *Fax:* 503-246-1066
otssport@earthlink.net;
www.oloughlintradeshows.com

Peter O'Loughlin, Show Manager
Robert O'Loughlin Sr, President

Offers hundreds of makes and models, accessories and plenty of expert advice through seminars and hands on demonstrations.
Frequency: January

3387 Professional Boatbuilder: International Boatbuilders Expo and Conference
WoodenBoat Publications
86 Great Cove Drive
PO Box 78
Brooklin, ME 04616

207-359-4651; *Fax:* 207-359-8920;
www.ibexshow.com

Carl Cramer, Publisher
Anne Dunbar, Show Director
Joanne Miller, Registration Manager

Over 450 booths offering products for boat builders, designers, repairers, surveyors, and boatyard/marina operators.
2.5M Attendees
Frequency: November
Founded in: 1989

3388 SCA Spring Safety Seminar
Shipbuilders Council of America
655 Fifteenth St NW
Suite 225
Washington, DC 20005

202-347-5462; *Fax:* 202-347-5464
preever@balljanik.com; www.shipbuilders.org
Social Media: Facebook

Matt Paxton, President

Represents the U.S. shipyard industry. SCA members build, repair and service America's fleet of commercial vessels.
73 Members
Frequency: March
Founded in: 1920

3389 Sail America Industry Conference
Sail America
50 Water St.
Warren, RI 02885

401-289-2540; *Fax:* 401-247-0074;
www.sailamerica.com/events/saic

Scot West, President

A two-day event for sailing industry professionals featuring seminars, workshops and networking events.
Frequency: Annual

3390 Seattle Boat Show
Northwest Marine Trade Association
1900 North Northlake Way
Suite 233
Seattle, WA 98103

206-634-0911; *Fax:* 206-632-0078
info@seattleboatshow.com; www.nmta.net
Social Media: Facebook, Twitter, LinkedIn

George Harris, President
John Thorburn, VP

The ten-day event features more than 1,000 recreational watercraft, seminars and the latest innovations in accessories at Qwest Field Event Center, plus 200 world-class boats in their natural habitat on South Lake Union.
Frequency: January-February
Founded in: 1947

3391 St. Petersburg Boat Show
Show Management
1115 NE 9th Avenue
Fort Lauderdale, FL 33304

954-764-7642
800-940-7642; *Fax:* 954-462-4140
info@showmanagement.com;
www.showmanagement.com
Social Media: Facebook, Twitter

Kaye Pearson, Owner/Promoter
Elise Lipoff, Director Public Relations
Steve Sheer, Director Advertising

More than 600 boats of all types and sizes, electronics, engines and a vast selection of marine accessories will be displayed on land and in water.
10000 Attendees
Frequency: December
Founded in: 1977
Mailing list available for rent

3392 Suncoast Boat Show
Show Management
1115 NE 9th Avenue
Fort Lauderdale, FL 33304

954-764-7642
800-940-7642; *Fax:* 954-462-4140
info@showmanagement.com;
www.showmanagement.com
Social Media: Facebook, Twitter

Kaye Pearson, Owner/Promoter
Elise Lipoff, Director Public Relations
Steve Sheer, Director Advertising
Chuck Bolt, Director Sales

Annual show and exhibits of boats and marine equipment, supplies and services.
30000 Attendees
Frequency: April
Founded in: 1982
Mailing list available for rent

3393 U.S. Rowing Association Annual Convention
United States Rowing Association
2 Wall Street
Princeton, NJ 08540

609-751-0700
800-314-4769; *Fax:* 609-924-1578
members@usrowing.org; www.usrowing.org
Social Media: Facebook, Twitter, Youtube

Elizabeth Webb, Events Manager

Coaching programs and information, referee clinics, speakers, and competitions.
Frequency: December

3394 US Sailboat Show
Annapolis Boatshows
100 Severn Drive
PO Box 4997
Annapolis, MD 21401-4997

410-268-8828; *Fax:* 410-280-3903

Dee Newman, Show Manager
Jim Barthold, General Manager

In-water sailboat show offering over 350 booths.
150M Attendees
Frequency: October

Directories & Databases

3395 American Boat and Yacht Council
American Boat and Yacht Council
613 Third Street
Suite 10
Annapolis, MD 21403
410-990-4466; *Fax:* 410-956-2737
info@abycinc.org; www.abycinc.org

David Marlow, Chair
Kenneth Weinbrecht, Vice Chair
David Slobodien, Treasurer
Jeff Wasil, Secretary

Marine suppliers, engineers and underwriters, as well as architects and designers for the marine industry are listed.
Frequency: Online
Founded in: 1954

3396 Boater's Source Directory
Boat US Foundation
880 S Pickett St
Alexandria, VA 22304-4606

703-461-8952
800-336-2628; *Fax:* 703-461-2855;
www.boatus.com/foundation
Social Media: Facebook, Twitter, LinkedIn, Youtube

Richard Schwartz, President

Pocket guide for boaters containing safety and regulatory information and resources.
Cost: $5.00
Frequency: Paperback, SemiAnnual
Founded in: 1966

3397 Boating Industry: Marine Buyers' Guide Issue
Ehlert Publishing Group
6420 Sycamore Ln N
Suite 100
Maple Grove, MN 55369-6014

763-383-4400
800-848-6247; *Fax:* 763-383-4499;
www.bowhuntingworld.com
Social Media: Facebook, Twitter, Youtube

Steven Hedlund, President
Liz Walz, Senior Editor
Jon Mohrm, Associate Editor
Tammy Galvin, Group Publisher

A who's who directory of services and supplies for the industry.
Cost: $29.95
Frequency: Annual
Circulation: 30,000
Mailing list available for rent

3398 Confined Space Entry Video and Manual
Shipbuilders Council of America
655 Fifteenth St NW
Suite 225
Washington, DC 20004-1166

202-347-5462; *Fax:* 202-347-5464;
www.shipbuilders.org
Social Media: Facebook

Matt Paxton, President

This manual, in combination with the video program, covers some of the more common hazards associated with confined space entry. It also provides you with the information you will need to prevent accidents and injuries.
Cost: $ 50.00
73 Members
Founded in: 1920

3399 Consumer Protection Database
Boat Owners Association of the US
800 South Pickett Street
Alexandria, VA 22304

703-412-2770; *Fax:* 703-461-2847;
www.boatus.com
Social Media: Facebook, Twitter, LinkedIn, Youtube

Richard Schwartz, Chairman/Founder
Jim Ellis, President/CEO

Contains consumer complaints and safety information reported by boat owners, the US Coast Guard, manufacturers, marine surveyors and marine technicians.
Founded in: 1966

3400 ISSPA Sports and Vacation Show Directory and Calendar
International Sport Show Producers Association
PO Box 480084
Denver, CO 80248-0084
303-892-6800
800-457-2434; *Fax:* 303-892-6322
dseymour@iei-expos.com; www.sportshow.org
Dianne Seymour, Executive Secretary
Products of outdoor recreation shows which include boating, travel, RV, hunting, and fishing.
Frequency: Annual

3401 Marine Products Directory
Underwriters Laboratories
12 Laboratory Drive
PO Box 13995
Research Triangle Park, NC 27709-3995
919-549-1400; *Fax:* 919-547-6363
paul.r.ouellette@us.ul.com;
www.ul.com/marine
Social Media: Facebook, Twitter, Youtube
Keith E. Williams, President
Sanjeev Jesudas, President
UL has been testing and certifying products for marine use since 1969. With a UL Marine Mark on your product, you can show consumers, retailers, surveyors, insurers, government agencies, regulatory and ABTC, NFPA and UL Safety Standards.
Cost: $10.00
176 Pages
Frequency: Annual

3402 Membership Directory: Boating Industry Administration
National Association of State Boating Laws
1500 Leestown Road
Suite 300
Lexington, KY 40511-2047
859-225-9487; *Fax:* 859-231-6403
info@nasbla.org; www.nasbla.org
Toby Velasquez, President
Herb Angell, VP
Kevin Bergerson, Treasurer
Published by the National Association of State Boating Law Administration.

3403 NMRA Membership Directory
National Marine Representative Association
1333 Delany Road #500
PO Box 360
Gurnee, IL 60031
847-662-3167; *Fax:* 847-336-7126
info@nmraonline.org; www.nmraonline.org
Norm McLeod, Past President
Tim Luehmann, President
Jeff Gueterman, VP
Rick Silverlake, Treasurer
Chris Kelly, Secretary
Provides a complete listing of all NMRA sales representatives. Includes contact information for their main and associate offices, the territories they cover, the markets they represent, and the list of companies they represent.
Cost: $10.00

3404 National Marine Manufacturers Association Membership List
231 S. LaSalle St
Suite 2050
Chicago, IL 60601-6539
312-946-6200; *Fax:* 312-946-0388;
www.nmma.org
Thomas Dammrich, President
Ben Wold, Executive Vice President
Craig Boskey, VP Finance/CFO
Directory of services and supplies to the industry.
160 Pages
Frequency: Quadrennial

3405 Pacific Boating Almanac
ProStar Publications
3416 Wesley Street
Suite B
Culver City, CA 90232-2901
310-280-1010
800-481-6277; *Fax:* 310-280-1025
editor@prostarpublications.com;
www.prostarpublications.com
Peter Griffes, Owner
Consists of three regional volumes. This information includes the latest Coast Pilot, Tide & Current Tables, First Aid, Electronics, Navigation and Safety, Weather, and Yacht Club Burgees.
Cost: $26.95
Frequency: Annual
Circulation: 20,000
ISBN: 1-577857-05-4
Mailing list available for rent: 19,000 names
Printed in on matte stock

3406 Portbook of Marine Services
Portbook Publications
PO Box 462
Belfast, ME 04915
207-338-1619; *Fax:* 207-338-6025;
www.portbook.net
Sandra Squire, Publisher
Marinas, yacht clubs, boatyards, dealers, marine supply stores, repair facilities, and other services for yachtsmen. For Annapolis, Maryland and Newport/Narragansett Bay, Rhode Island. Distributed free through advertisers, or four dollars by mail.
Cost: $40.00
100 Pages
Frequency: Annual
Circulation: 35M
Founded in: 1982
Printed in on matte stock

3407 Register of American Yacht Clubs
Yachting Club of America
PO Box 1040
Marco Island, FL 34146-1040
239-642-4448; *Fax:* 239-642-5284
info@ycaol.com; www.ycaol.com
A reciprocity guide for yacht and sailing clubs in the United States, Hawaii, Alaska, and the Virgin Islands registered with the Yachting Club of America. 800 yacht clubs registered with the Yachting Club of America.
Cost: $35.00
200 Pages
Frequency: Softbound
Founded in: 1963
Printed in on glossy stock

3408 Sail Tall Ships: Directory of Sail Training and Adventure at Sea
American Sail Training Association
240 Thames Street
PO Box 1459
Newport, RI 02840
401-846-1775; *Fax:* 401-849-5400
asta@sailtraining.org; www.ycaol.com
Lori Aguiar, Editor
Peter A Mello, Executive Director
Offers information on sail training ships, shoreside sail training programs and ships under construction or restoration.
Cost: $50.00
400 Pages
Frequency: Annual
Circulation: 15,000
ISBN: 0-963648-36-5
Founded in: 1963

3409 Seafarers
Admiralty Insurance
6353 Argyle Forest Boulevard
Jacksonville, FL 32244
904-777-0042
800-456-8936; *Fax:* 904-777-0279;
www.seafarers.com
Searchable database of boating associations, yacht clubs, boating clubs and source of nautical information and links.

3410 Ship Agents, Owners, Operators
Maritime Association of the Port of New York
17 Battery Place
Suite 913
New York, NY 10004-1194
212-747-1284; *Fax:* 212-635-9498
themaritimeassoc@erols.com;
www.nymaritime.org
Edward Morgan, President
Brian McAllister, VP
Edward J Kelly, Executive Director
Directory of Atlantic, Gulf and West Coasts listing every steamship, owner, and operator in the major ports with lines that they represent and the countries that they serve.
Cost: $50.00
Frequency: Annual
Circulation: 2,000
Mailing list available for rent

3411 Shipyard Ergonomics Video and Workbook CD
Shipbuilders Council of America
655 Fifteenth St NW
Suite 225
Washington, DC 20004-1166
202-347-5462; *Fax:* 202-347-5464;
www.shipbuilders.org
Social Media: Facebook
Matt Paxton, President
Designed to instruct shipyard employees, supervisors and trainers in identifying ergonomic risks and providing tools to allow the development of creative solutions to reduce the hazards.
Cost: $75.00
73 Members
Founded in: 1920

Industry Web Sites

3412 http://gold.greyhouse.com
G.O.L.D Grey House OnLine Databases
Grey House Publishing's online database platform, GOLD, offers Quick Search, Keyword Search and Expert Search, for most business sectors including boating manufacture and service markets. GOLD is quick and easy - whether you're a novice searcher or an experienced database user. All of Grey House's directory products are available for subscription on the GOLD platform.

3413 www.acbs.org
Antique & Classic Boat Society
Dedicated to the preservation and enjoyment of historic, antique and classic boats. ACBS brings people with this common interest together to share fellowship, information, experiences and ideas.

3414 www.americanboating.org
American Boating Association
ABA's mission is to promote boating safety, affordability, growth, and a clean environment.

It provides exclusive services and benefits for boaters and boating enthusiasts.

3415 **www.apba-racing.com**
American Power Boat Association

The sole authority for UIM approved powerboat racing ine United States.

3416 **www.by-the-sea.com**
By the Sea

Everything for the boat professional and enthusiast alike. News of sales and events, message boards and contact information.

3417 **www.greyhouse.com**
Grey House Publishing

Authoritative reference directories for most business segments incluidng boat manufacturing and service markets. Users can search the online databases with varied search criteria allowing for custom searches by product category, geographic area, sales volume, keyword, subject and more. Full Grey House catalog and online ordering also available.

3418 **www.ifai.com**
Industrial Fabrics Association International

The only trade association in the world representing the entire specialty fabrics/technical textiles industry. Member products range from fiber and fabric suppliers to manufacturers of end products, equipment and hardware.

3419 **www.imimarina.org**
International Marina Institute

International Marina Institute's educational resources include specialized training courses and seminars on fundamental and advanced levels, workshops, conferences the advanced marina management school and the Certified Marina Manager program along with a wide selection of publications.

3420 **www.lemta.com**
Lake Erie Marine Trade Association

E-Mail: info@lemta.com

Trade association of more than 100 recreational boat dealers, marina operators and pleasure boat service companies located across northern Ohio; also plays the key role in looking out for the consumer.

3421 **www.marinebankers.org**
National Marine Bankers Association

The purpose of the NMBA is to educate prospective lenders in marine financing procedures, create new lenders to help finance the sales of the manufacturers products, and to create an information exchange for its members.

3422 **www.mraa.com**
Marine Retailers Association of America

Manufacturers and dealers of boats, equipment, supplies and services.

3423 **www.nauticalworld.com**

Dedicated to bringing all related web sites within easy access to watersports enthusiasts, including advertiser's information. Offers sections on marine electronics and hardware, sailing, boats, dock supplies, fishing accessories, diving accessories, industry news, watersports, weather forecasting and more.

3424 **www.nauticexpo.com**
NauticExpo

This Virtual Boat Show is accessible in five languages and presents all the boats and nautical equipment available on the international market. It offers an accurate and up-to-date source of information to yachtsmen and professionals.

3425 **www.nmdaonline.com**
National Marine Distributors Association

Engages in exclusively nonprofit activities designed to promote the common business interests and improve the business conditions of wholesale distributors of marine accessories and of the marine industry in general.

3426 **www.nmraonline.org**
National Marine Representatives Association

Members are independent boat and marine accessory sales representatives national association.

3427 **www.nmta.net**
Northwest Marine Trade Association

Oldest and largest regional boating trade organization in the nation representing the interests of approximately 800 member companies. Each year it produces the Seattle Boat Show at the Stadium Exhibition Center and the Seattle Boat Show at Shilshole Bay Marina on behalf of its members.

3428 **www.propellerclubhq.com**
Propeller Club of the United States

Grassroots, nonprofit organization, whose membership resides throughout the United States and the world. It is dedicated to the enhancement and well-being of all interests of the maritime community on a national and international basis.

3429 **www.pwia.org**
Personal Watercraft Industry Association

Ensuring that personal watercraft and personal watercraft users are treated fairly when local, state, and federal government officials consider boating regulations. PWIA supports and actively advocates for reasonable regulations, strong enforcement of boating and navigation laws, and mandatory boating safety education for all personal watercraft operators.

3430 **www.rbbi.com**
Polson Enterprises

Offering research tools and papers on new product development and new product development services for boat builders, plus experience in the fields of marine drives, engine, marine vessels, propellar guards, boating safety. Industry and regulation updates are also available on this site.

3431 **www.tsca.com**
Traditional Small Craft Association

Nonprofit, tax-exempt educational organization which works to preserve and continue the living traditions, skills, lore and legends surrounding working and pleasure watercraft including construction and use of boats.

3432 **www.ussailing.org**
United States Sailing Association

Encourages participation and promotes excellence in sailing and racing in the US.

Associations

3433 American Beverage Licensees
5101 River Rd
Suite 108
Bethesda, MD 20816-1560

301-656-1494; *Fax:* 301-656-7539
info@plib.org; www.ablusa.org/
Social Media: Facebook, LinkedIn

John Blodgett, Chairman
Ken Thorlakson, Vice Chairman
Jeff Fantozzi, President
Ben Haynes, Manager
Hannah Petersen, Corporate Secretary

Represents over 15,000 off-premise licensees in the open or license states and on-premise proprietors in markets across the nation. Offers members information on legislation and industry matters.
65 Members
Founded in: 1903

3434 American Craft Spirits Association
PO Box 701414
Louisville, KY 40270

502-299-0238; www.americancraftspirits.org
Social Media: Facebook, Twitter

Tom Mooney, President
Margie A. S. Lehrman, Interim Executive Director

Trade association of U.S. craft spirits industry.

3435 American Society for Enology and Viticulture
1784 Picasso Avenue
Suite D
Davis, CA 95618-0551

530-753-3142; *Fax:* 530-753-3318
pfpa@paforestproducts.org; www.asev.org

Alan Metzler, Chairman
Terry Stockdale, Vice-Chairman
Paul Lyskava, Executive Director
Michelle McManus, Business Manager
Bob Long, Membership Representative

A tax exempt professional society dedicated to the interests of enologists, viticulturists, and others in the fields of wine and grape research and production throughout the world.
Founded in: 1980

3436 American Society of Brewing Chemists
3340 Pilot Knob Rd
St Paul, MN 55121-2055

651-454-7250
800-328-7560; *Fax:* 651-454-0766
ties@rta.org; www.asbcnet.org

Jim Gauntt, Executive Director
Debbie Corallo, Association Administrator
Barbara Stacey, Committee and Website Coordinator
2500 Members
Founded in: 1919

3437 Association of Winery Supplies
21 Tamal Vista Boulevard
Suite 196
Corte Madera, CA 94925-1146

415-924-2640
Social Media: 1983

Warner Executive Director

United States supplier of services and materials used in the winery industry.
John Members
Founded in: 34

3438 Beer Institute
122 C St NW
Suite 350
Washington, DC 20001-2150

202-737-2337
800-379-2739; *Fax:* 202-737-7004
info@calredwood.org; www.beerinstitute.org
Social Media: Youtube

Christopher Grover, President

The national trade association for the brewing industry. Representing both big and small brewers as well as importers and industry suppliers.
Founded in: 1916

3439 Brewers Association
Brewers Association
1327 Spruce Street
Boulder, CO 80302

303-447-0816
888-822-6273; *Fax:* 303-447-2825
membership@safnet.org;
www.brewersassociation.org
Social Media: Facebook, Twitter, LinkedIn

A non-profit educational and trade organization for small and craft brewers. Its mission is to make quality brewing and beer knowledge accessible to all.
Founded in: 1900

3440 Distilled Spirits Council of the United States
1250 Eye St NW
Suite 400
Washington, DC 20005-3998

202-628-3544; *Fax:* 202-682-8844
vicki@swst.org; www.discus.org
Social Media: Facebook

Eric Hansen, President
Bob Smith, Vice-President
Vicki L. Herian, Executive Director
H. Michael Barnes, Editor of Wood and Fiber Science
Barb Hogan, Editorial Assistant

National trade association representing producers and marketers of liquor sold in the US.
450 Members
Founded in: 1958

3441 Distillery, Wine and Allied Workers' International Union
66 Grand Avenue
Englewood, NJ 07631-3506

201-894-8444; *Fax:* 201-569-9216;
www.ufcw.org/

Bryan Smalley, President
Alexis Sivcovich, Member Services Coordinator
Beverly Knight, Accounting Manager
Will Telligman, Government Affairs Manager

Addresses the concerns of wine makers and fellow industry workers.
350 Members
Founded in: 1962

3442 Foundation for Advancing Alcohol Responsibility
2345 Crystal Dr.
Suite 710
Arlington, VA 22202

responsibility.org
Social Media: Facebook, Twitter, YouTube, Pinterest, Instagram

Ralph S. Blackman, President & CEO

Promoting responsible drinking.

3443 Home Wine and Beer Trade Association
PO Box 1373
Valrico, FL 33595

813-685-4261; *Fax:* 813-681-5625;
www.fermentersinternational.org/
Social Media: Facebook, Youtube

Manufacturers, wholesalers, retailers, authors and editors having a commercial interest in the beer and wine trade.
19 Members
Founded in: 1905

3444 Italian Trade Commission
33 East 67th Street
New York, NY 10065

212-980-1500; *Fax:* 212-758-1050
mail@sfpa.org;
www.italtrade.com/countries/americas/usa/new york.htm
Social Media: Twitter, Youtube

Tami Kessler, Executive Director
Richard Wallace, Vice President, Communications
Vernon Barabino, Chief Financial Administrator
Rachel Elton, Admin. Assistant/Program Coor.
Eric Gee, CF, RF, Director

Developments in the Italian wine industry and market, as well as reviews of imported wines from Italy.
265 Members
Founded in: 1915

3445 Italian Wine and Food Institute
Italian Wine and Food Institute
60 East 42nd Street, Suite 2214
Suite 2214
New York, NY 10165

212-867-4111; *Fax:* 212-867-4114
spib@spib.org;
www.italianwineandfoodinstitute.com

T. Furman Brodie, Chairman
Bert H. Jones, Vice Chairman
Steve Singleton, President
Shelly James, Operations & Finance Assistant
Eileen Ehrsam, Accounts Receivable Admin.

Members are producers, distributors and marketers of Italian wines and foods.
Founded in: 1940

3446 National Alcohol Beverage Control Association
4401 Ford Avenue
Suite 700
Alexandria, VA 22302-1433

703-578-4200; *Fax:* 703-820-3551
info@forestinfo.org; www.nabca.org

Robert M Owens, Chairman
Lee F Freeman, President & CEO

Members include control jurisdictions, supplier members and industry trade associations.
Founded in: 1989

3447 National Beer Wholesalers Association
1101 King Street
Suite 600
Alexandria, VA 22314-2944

703-683-4300
800-300-6417; *Fax:* 703-683-8965
tpm@tpmrs.com; www.nbwa.org

Russ Vaagen, Chairman
Tom Shaffer, Vice Chairman
Adam Molenda, President
Chris Chathams, Safety Resource Director
Jolene Skjothaug, Office Manager

NBWA represents the interests of America's 2,850 independent, licensed beer distributors

which service every congressional district and media market in the country.
250 Members
Founded in: 1916

3448 National Wine Distribution Association
2701 E Street
Sacramento, CA 95816-3221
916-979-3051; *Fax:* 916-448-9115
GM Pucilowski, Executive Director
Dedicated to promoting the interests and education of smaller wine wholesalers, importers, wineries, and others who are involved in the wine distribution business.
285 Members
Founded in: 1978

3449 Wine Institute
425 Market St
Suite 1000
San Francisco, CA 94105-2487
415-512-0151; *Fax:* 415-356-7569
tcia@tcia.org; www.wineinstitute.org
Social Media: Facebook, Twitter, LinkedIn, Youtube
Jack W. Guffey, Jr., Chair
Mark Garvin, President
Bob Rouse, Chief Program Officer
Sarah Winslow, Director of Development
Amy Tetreault, Marketing Director
Organization that represents the wine and spirit industry to state and federal lawmaking bodies.
2000 Members
Founded in: 1938

3450 Wine and Spirits Shippers Association
11800 Sunrise Valley Dr
Reston, VA 20191-5302
703-860-2300
800-368-3167; *Fax:* 703-860-2422
info@tpinst.org; www.wssa.com
Michael A Cassidy, Executive Director
Provides members, importers and exporters with efficient and economical ocean transportation and other logistic services.
300 Members
Founded in: 1961
Mailing list available for rent

3451 Wine and Spirits Wholesalers of America
805 15th Street NW
Suite 430
Washington, DC 20005
202-371-9792; *Fax:* 202-789-2405
info@wclib.org; www.wswa.org
John Konecny, President
Rod Lucas, Vice President
Don DeVisser, Exec. Vice Pres.
Kyle Freres, Sec./Treasurer
This association is comprised of wholesale distributors of domestic and imported wine and distilled spirits.
189 Members
Circulation: 1,000
Founded in: 1941

Newsletters

3452 ASBC Newsletter
American Society of Brewing Chemists
3340 Pilot Knob Rd
Eagan, MN 55121-2055
651-454-7250
800-328-7560; *Fax:* 651-454-0766
asbc@scisoc.org; www.asbcnet.org
Steven C Nelson, VP
Jordana Anker, Director of Publications
Karen Cummings, Director Publications
Joan A Raumschuh, Editor
Jody Grider, Director of Operations
Cost: $20.00
Frequency: Quarterly
Founded in: 1934

3453 Alcoholic Beverage Control: From the State Capitals
Wakeman Walworth
PO BOX 7376
Alexandria, VA 22307-7376
703-768-9600; *Fax:* 703-768-9690;
www.statecapitals.com/alcoholbev.html
Keyes Walworth, Publisher
Covers binge drinking laws, internet sales, advertising, taxes, bottle bills, Sunday sales laws, license regulation, drunk driving laws, under-age drinking, mini-bottles and other state laws affecting beer, liquor and wine distribution.
Cost: $245.00
4 Pages
Frequency: Weekly
Printed in one color on matte stock

3454 Beer Marketer's Insights Newsletter
Beer Marketer's Insights
49 E Maple Ave
Suffern, NY 10901-5507
845-624-2337; *Fax:* 845-624-2340;
www.beerinsights.com
Benj Steinman, President
Reports on the competitive battle among brewers for a share of the beer market. Analyzes recent legislation and factors that affect the industry.
Cost: $595.00
Frequency: 23/Year
Founded in: 1975

3455 Beer Statistics News
Beer Marketer's Insights
49 E Maple Ave
Suffern, NY 10901-5507
845-624-2337; *Fax:* 845-624-2340
bmiexpress@aol.com; www.beerinsights.com
Benj Steinman, President
Eric Shephard, Executive Editor
Andy Leinicke, Circulation Manager
Supplies data for major brewers' shipments in 39 reporting states.
Cost: $450.00
Frequency: Monthly
Founded in: 1975

3456 Brewers Bulletin
PO Box 677
Thiensville, WI 53092
262-242-6105; *Fax:* 262-242-5133
bulletindigest@milwpc.com
Tom Volke, President/CEO
Brewing industry newspaper.
Cost: $53.00
Frequency: Monthly
Circulation: 500
Founded in: 1907

3457 Champagne Wines Information Bureau
KCSA
800 2nd Avenue Frnt 5
New York, NY 10017-4709
212-682-6300
800-642-4267; *Fax:* 212-697-0910
info@champagnes.com;
www.champagnes.com
Jean-Louis Carbonnier, Editor
Representative of Comite Interprofessionnel duVinde Champagne, Epernay, France.
4 Pages
Frequency: TriAnnual
Circulation: 10,000
Printed in one color on matte stock

3458 Impact International
M Shanken Communications
387 Park Ave S
Suite 8
New York, NY 10016-8872
212-684-4224
800-848-7113; *Fax:* 212-684-5424;
www.cigaraficionado.com
Marvin Shanken, Publisher
Samantha Shanken, President
Reports on the global alcoholic beverage market.
Cost: $595.00
Frequency: Annual+
Founded in: 1972

3459 Kane's Beverage Week
Whitaker Newsletters
313 S Avenue
#340
Fanwood, NJ 07023-1364
908-889-6339
800-359-6049; *Fax:* 415-027-0608
Whitaker Publisher, Anne
Bittner Editor, Fred
Rossi Editor
News on marketing, economic and regulatory factors affecting the alcohol beverage industry.
Cost: $131.00
Joel Members
6 Pages
Frequency: Monthly
ISSN: 0882-2573

3460 Notiziario
Italian Wine and Food Institute
60 East 42nd Street, Suite 2214
Suite 1341
New York, NY 10165
212-867-4111; *Fax:* 212-867-4114
iwfi@aol.com;
www.italianwineandfoodinstitute.com
Lucio Caputo, President
Vincent Giampaoco, VP
Provides detailed information on the Italian gastronomy and wines. It distributes information materials and give press interviews for the American radio and television. It carries out an intense public relations program, participates in the most important local promotional initiatives and events and maintains contact with the American and Italian authorities in this sector.
Cost: $250.00
Founded in: 1984

3461 On Tap: Newsletter
WBR Publishing
PO Box 71
Clemson, SC 29633
864-654-2300; *Fax:* 864-654-5067
Steve Johnson, Publisher
North America breweries and microbreweries.
Cost: $.95
20 Pages
Frequency: Bi-Monthly
Circulation: 1000
Printed in one color on matte stock

3462 Spirited Living: Dave Steadman's Restaurant Scene
5301 Towne Woods Rd
Coram, NY 11727-2808
631-736-0436; *Fax:* 631-736-0436
Dave Steadman, Editor
Newsletter published Bi-Weekly except January, July, and August.
Cost: $75.00

3463 US Beer Market
Business Trend Analysts/Industry Reports
2171 Jericho Tpke
Suite 200
Commack, NY 11725-2937
631-462-5454
800-866-4648; *Fax:* 631-462-1842;
www.bta-ler.com
Charles J Ritchie, Executive VP
Donna Priani, Marketing Director
Profiles markets for premium, superpremium, popular and light beers.
Cost: $1495.00

3464 Uncorked
California Wine Club
2175 Goodyear Avenue
Suite 102
Ventura, CA 93006-3699
805-650-4330
800-777-4443; *Fax:* 800-700-1599
info@cawineclub.com; www.cawineclub.com
Bruce Boring, Proprietors
Judy Reynolds, Proprietors
Uncorked is an 8 page newsletter that describes the featured winery. It provides an upclose and personal look at a small 'boutique' California Winery.
Frequency: Monthly
Circulation: 10000
Founded in: 1990

3465 Vinotizie Italian Wine Newsletter
Italian Trade Commission
33 E 67th St
New York, NY 10065-5949
212-848-0300; *Fax:* 212-758-1050
newyork@newyork.ice.it; www.italtrade.com
Aniello Musella, President
Giovanni Mafodda, Operations Manager
This newsletter discusses developments in the Italian wine industry and market, as well as reviews of imported wines from Italy.
Frequency: Monthly
Founded in: 1998

3466 Wine Investor Buyers Guide
PGE Publications
1224 N Fairfax Avenue
Apartment 5
Los Angeles, CA 90046-5234
Paul Gillette, Publisher
JD Kronman, Editor
Reviews new releases of wines, recommends the best buys, predicts when wines will be at their peak and surveys markets for pricing trends. Accepts advertising.
Cost: $75.00
10 Pages
Frequency: Monthly

3467 World Beer Review
WBR Publishing
PO Box 71
Clemson, SC 29633-0071
864-654-2300
Steve Johnson, Publisher
Complete coverage of the beer and beermaking industry.

Magazines & Journals

3468 All About Beer
Chautauqua Inc
501 Washington St
Suite H
Durham, NC 27701-2169
919-530-8150
800-977-2337; *Fax:* 919-530-8160
editor@allaboutbeer.com;
www.allaboutbeer.com
Julie Bradford, Publisher
Natalie Abernethy, Circulation Manager
Quality beers, breweries and restaurants.
Cost: $19.99
64 Pages
Founded in: 1981

3469 Atlantic Control States Beverage Journal
Club & Tavern
3 12th Street
Wheeling, WV 26003-3276
304-232-7620; *Fax:* 304-233-1236
Arnold Lazarus, Editor
A magazine for the alcoholic beverage industry. Serving bars, restaurants, clubs and industry personnel with West Virginia, Virginia, and North Carolina state editions. Includes states' liquor price lists.

3470 Bar Business Magazine
Simmons-Boardman Publishing Corporation
345 Hudson St
Suite 1201
New York, NY 10014-7123
212-620-7200; *Fax:* 212-633-1165
cytuarte@sbpub.com;
www.simmonsboardman.com
Arthur J McGinnis Jr, President
The premier How-To publication covering the best business practices and products for owners and managers of nightclubs, bars and lounges across the US.
Frequency: Monthly
Circulation: 8541

3471 Bartender Magazine
Foley Publishing Corporation
PO Box 157
Spring Lake, NJ 07762
732-449-4499; *Fax:* 732-974-8289
barmag@aol.com; www.bartender.com
Social Media: Facebook, Twitter
Raymond Foley, Publisher
Jaclyn Wilson Foley, Editor
Serves all full service drinking establishments. Including individual restaurants, hotels, motels, bars, taverns, lounges, and all other full service on premise licenses. Subscription price is $40 for Canada, and $55 for all other foriegn countries.
Cost: $30.00
72 Pages
Frequency: Monthly
Circulation: 149044
Founded in: 1979
Printed in 4 colors on glossy stock

3472 Beer Perspectives
National Beer Wholesalers Association
1101 King St
Suite 600
Alexandria, VA 22314-2965
703-683-4300; *Fax:* 703-683-8965
info@nbwa.org; www.nbwa.org
Social Media: Facebook, Twitter
Craig A Purser, President & CEO
Michael Johnson, EVP Fed Aff/Chief Advisory Office
Rebecca Spicer, VP Public Affairs/Chief
Paul Pisano, SVP Industry Affairs & Gen. Counsel
Trade association for beer wholesalers. Provides government and public affairs outreach as well as education and training for its wholesaler members.
Founded in: 1938

3473 Beverage Dynamics
The Beverage Information Group
17 High Street
2nd Floor
Norwalk, CT 06851
203-855-8499
lzimmerman@m2media360.com;
www.bevinfogroup.com
Liza Zimmerman, Editor-in-Chief
Jeremy Nedelka, Managing Editor
Devoted to the needs of the off-premise beverage alcohol retailer. Covers wine, beer and spirits categories as well as beset practices for retail decision makers.
Cost: $35.00
Frequency: Bi-Monthly
Founded in: 1934

3474 Beverage Journal
Michigan Licensed Beverage Association
920 N Fairview Ave
Lansing, MI 48912-3238
517-374-9611
800-292-2896; *Fax:* 517-374-1165
info@mlba.org; www.mlba.org
Lou Adado, CEO
Cathy Pavick, Executive Director
Peter Broderick, Director of Communication
Offers information on the alcoholic beverage industry/retail sales
Cost: $52.00
Frequency: Monthly
ISSN: 1050-4427
Founded in: 1939
Printed in on glossy stock

3475 Beverage Network
Beverage Media Group
116 John St
Suite 2305
New York, NY 10038-3419
212-571-3232
800-723-8372; *Fax:* 212-571-4443
info@bevmedia.com; www.bevmedia.com
Jason Glasser, CEO
S Paley, Circulation Manager
Cost: $99.00
Frequency: Monthly
Circulation: 6000
Founded in: 1940

3476 Beverage Retailer Magazine
Oxford Publishing
Ste 1
1903b University Ave
Oxford, MS 38655-4150
662-236-5510
800-247-3881; *Fax:* 662-236-5541;
www.bevindustry.com
Brenda Owen, Editor
Ed Meek, Publisher
Stacy Clark, Production Manager

Jennifer Parsons, Marketing Director
Ruth Ann Wolfe, Circulation Director

A magazine covering the off premise market for retailers in the wine, beer and spirits business.
Cost: $30.00
Circulation: 25000
Founded in: 1985
Printed in 4 colors on glossy stock

3477 **Cheers**
The Beverage Information Group
17 High St
Suite 2
Norwalk, CT 06851

203-855-8499; *Fax:* 203-855-9446
cforman@m2media360.com;
www.bevinfogroup.com

Charlie Forman, SVP/Group Publisher
Liza Zimmerman, Editor-In-Chief
Jeremy Nedelka, Managing Editor

Business magazine for on-premise hospitality professionals. Coverage includes trends and innovations in operations, merchandising, service and training, as well as new developments in beverage product segments.
Cost: $35.00
Frequency: Monthly
Founded in: 1998

3478 **Modern Brewery Age**
Business Journals
50 Day Street
PO Box 5550
Norwalk, CT 06856-5550

203-853-6015; *Fax:* 203-853-8175
FayS@busjour.com; www.breweryage.com

Mac Brighton, Chairman/COO
Britton Jones, President/CEO
Peter V K Reid, Editor/Publisher
Arthur Heilman, Circulation Director
Diane Apicelli, Advertising Director

A magazine for the wholesale and brewing industry.
Cost: $95.00
Founded in: 1933

3479 **Modern Brewery Age: Tabloid Edition**
Business Journals
50 Day Street
PO Box #5550
Norwalk, CT 06856-5550

203-853-6015; *Fax:* 203-853-8175;
www.breweryage.com

Peter VK Reid, Editor
Peter VK Reid, Publisher
Britton Jones, President/CEO
Diane Apicelli, Advertising Director
Mac Brighton, Chairman & COO

Brewery industry tabloid.
Cost: $95.00
Frequency: Weekly
Founded in: 1933

3480 **Nightclub & Bar Magazine**
Oxford Publishing
Ste 1
1903b University Ave
Oxford, MS 38655-4150

662-236-5510
800-247-3881; *Fax:* 662-281-0104;
www.nightclub.com

Ed Meek, Production Manager
Mitchell Diggs, Managing Editor
Laura McCreary, Advertising Director
Jennifer Cummins, Production Manager
Adam Alson, Founder

A monthly publication covering the nightclub and bar hospitality industry.
Frequency: Monthly
Circulation: 30,000
Printed in 4 colors on glossy stock

3481 **Southern Beverage Journal**
Beverage Media Group
14337 Sw 119th Ave
Miami, FL 33186-6006

305-233-7230; *Fax:* 305-252-2580;
www.bevnetwork.com

Sharon Mijares, President
Sharon Mijares, Circulation Manager

A magazine for the alcoholic beverage industry.
Cost: $35.00
Frequency: Monthly
Circulation: 29000
Founded in: 1944

3482 **StateWays**
The Beverage Information Group
17 High Street
2nd Floor
Norwalk, CT 06851

203-855-8499
lzimmerman@m2media360.com;
www.bevinfogroup.com

Liza Zimmerman, Editor-In-Chief
Jeremy Nedelka, Managing Editor

Written for commissioners, board members, headquarters personnel, and retail store managers responsible for buying beverage alcohol in the eighteen control states. Covered editorial includes product knowledge, market trends, store operations, merchandising, warehousing, computerization, administration, training, and other topics.
Cost: $20.00
Frequency: Bi-Monthly
Circulation: 8500

3483 **US Beer Market: Impact Databank Review and Forecast**
M Shanken Communications
387 Park Ave S
Suite 8
New York, NY 10016-8872

212-684-4224; *Fax:* 212-684-5424;
www.cigaraficionado.com

Marvin Shanken, Publisher
Samantha Shanken, Marketing Manager
Cost: $9.10

3484 **US Liquor Industry**
Business Trend Analysts/Industry Reports
2171 Jericho Tpke
Suite 200
Commack, NY 11725-2937

631-462-5454; *Fax:* 631-462-1842
bta@li.net; www.businesstrendanalysts.com

Charles J Ritchie, Executive VP
Donna Priani, Marketing Director
Linda Sherman, Production Manager
Jennifer Wichert, Research Director

A survey summarizing the past, current and future markets and trends in the liquor industry.
Cost: $1195.00
600 Pages
Founded in: 1999

3485 **US Wine Market**
Business Trend Analysts/Industry Reports
2171 Jericho Tpke
Suite 200
Commack, NY 11725-2937

631-462-5454
800- 86- 464; *Fax:* 631-462-1842;
www.businesstrendanalysts.com

Charles J Ritchie, Executive VP
Donna Priani, Marketing Director

An analysis of the wine industry, domestic and imported.
Cost: $1995.00
470 Pages
Circulation: 2004
Founded in: 1978

3486 **Vineyard and Winery Management Magazine**
Vineyard & Winery Management
421 E Street
Santa Rosa, CA 95404

707-577-7700; *Fax:* 707-577-7705;
www.vwm-online.com

Robert Merletti, CEO/Publisher
Dennis Black, General Manager
Tina Caputo, Editor-in-Chief

A leading independent award winning wine trade magazine serving all of North America.
Cost: $37.00
100 Pages
Frequency: Bi-Monthly
Circulation: 6900
ISSN: 1047-4951
Founded in: 1975
Printed in 4 colors on glossy stock

3487 **Wine Advocate**
Robert M Parker Jr
PO Box 311
Monkton, MD 21111

410-329-6477; *Fax:* 410-357-4504
wineadvocate@erobertparker.com;
www.erobertparker.com

Robert M Parker Jr, Publisher/ Editor
Jacques Robinson, President

An independent magazine covering reviews of wine.
Cost: $60.00
64 Pages
Circulation: 40000
Founded in: 1978

3488 **Wine and Spirits**
Winestate Publications
1748 Market Street
San Francisco, CA 94102-4997

415-255-7736; *Fax:* 415-255-9659
mlkinney@wineandspiritsmagazine.com;
www.wineandspiritsmagazine.com/

Joshua Greene, Editor/Publisher
Michael Kinney, Associate Publisher
Ray Isle, Managing Editor
W. Charles Squires, Circulation Director
Gilian Handelman, Marketing Manager

A consumer magazine for wine enthusiasts.
Cost: $26.00
70 Pages
Circulation: 75000
Founded in: 1987
Printed in 4 colors on glossy stock

Trade Shows

3489 **ASBC Annual Meeting**
American Society of Brewing Chemists

3340 Pilot Knob Road
Saint Paul, MN 55121-2055

651-454-7250
800-328-7560; *Fax:* 651-454-0766
bford@scisoc.org; www.meeting.asbcnet.org

Betty Ford, Meetings Director
Sue Casey, Meetings Coordinator
Steven Nelson, VP
300 Attendees
Frequency: June/Non-Members Fee

3490 **American Beverage Licensees Annual Convention & Trade Show**
American Beverage Licensees
5101 River Road
Suite 108
Bethesda, MD 20816-1560

301-656-1494; *Fax:* 301-656-7539;
www.ablusa.org

Harry Wiles, Executive Director
Susan Day Pirieda, Office Manager

Annual show of 75 manufacturers, suppliers and distributors of alcoholic beverages.
700 Attendees
Frequency: March

3491 **American Society for Enology and Viticulture Annual Meeting**
PO Box 1855
Davis, CA 95617-1855

530-753-3142; *Fax:* 530-753-3318
society@asev.org; www.asev.org

Bill Mead, Event/Tradeshow Coordinator

With technical sessions, research forums, symposia and a supplier showcase.
Frequency: June
Founded in: 1950

3492 **American Wine Society National Conference**
American Wine Society
P.O. Box 889
Scranton, PA 18501

888-297-9070; www.americanwinesociety.org
Social Media: Facebook, Twitter, LinkedIn, Instagram

David Falchek, Executive Director
Kristin Casler Kraft, President

Annual event including wine competitions and wine judge certification training.
600 Attendees
Frequency: Annual/November
Founded in: 1967

3493 **Beer, Wine & Spirits Industry Trade Show**
Indiana Association of Beverage
200 S Meridian Street
Suite 350
Indianapolis, IN 46225-3418

317-847-7580; *Fax:* 317-673-4210

Teresa Koch

Annual show of 125 exhibitors of alcohol beverage distillers brewers that are recognized primary sources in the state of Indiana as supplies for retailers.
2500 Attendees

3494 **Craft Brewers Conference and Brew Expo America**
Brewers Association
736 Pearl Street
Boulder, CO 80302

303-447-0816
888-822-6273; *Fax:* 303-447-2825
info@brewersassociation.org;
www.brewersassociation.org
Social Media: Facebook, Twitter, Youtube

Charlie Papazian, President
Bob Pease, VP
Cindy Jones, Sales/Marketing Director
1,200 Attendees
Frequency: April

3495 **Great American Beer Festival**
Brewers Association
736 Pearl Street
Boulder, CO 80302

303-447-0816
888-822-6273; *Fax:* 303-447-2825
info@brewersassociation.org;
www.brewersassociation.org
Social Media: Facebook, Twitter, Youtube

Charlie Papazian, President
Bob Pease, VP
Cindy Jones, Sales/Marketing Director
Frequency: September

3496 **NABR Tasting & Display Event Annual Convention**
American Beverage Licensees
5101 River Road
Suite 108
Bethesda, MD 20816-1560

301-656-1494; *Fax:* 301-656-7539;
www.ablusa.org

Harry Wiles, Executive Director
Shawn Ross, Office Manager

Offers exhibits on spirits, beer and wine industry supplies, equipment, bar accessories and computers. The NABR Annual Convention is a gathering of alcohol beverage retailers and proprietors for networking and educational opportunities. An exclusive trade display and tasting event is held to promote brands and services of use to retailers and proprietors. There are 25-75 booths.
500+ Attendees
Frequency: March

3497 **NBWA Annual Convention**
National Beer Wholesalers Association
1101 King Street
Suite 600
Alexandria, VA 22314-8965

703-683-4300; *Fax:* 703-683-8965
info@nbwa.org; www.nbwa.org
Social Media: Facebook, Twitter

Craig A Purser, President & CEO
Michael Johnson, EVP Fed Aff/Chief Advisory Office
Rebecca Spicer, VP Public Affairs/Chief
Paul Pisano, SVP Industry Affairs & Gen. Counsel

Designed to provide valuable education programs and important networking opportunities for the beer industry. Featuring speakers and seminars on a number of topics of imprtance to beer distributors .
2500 Attendees
Frequency: Fall

3498 **National Beer Wholesalers Association Convention and Trade Show**
Corcoran Expositions
33 N Dearborn Street
Suite 505
Chicago, IL 60602-3103

312-541-0567
800-541-0359; *Fax:* 312-541-0573

Al Natker, Operations Manager

Biennial show of 166 manufacturers, suppliers and distributors of brewery software and hardware, trucking, beer cleaning equipment and related equipment, supplies and services.
3000 Attendees

3499 **Wineries Unlimited**
Vineyard & Winery Services
3883 Airway Drive
Suite 250
Santa Rosea, CA 95403

707-577-7700
800-535-5670; *Fax:* 707-577-7705;
www.wineriesunlimited.com

The largest, most powerful trade show and conference for the eastern wine industry.
2000 Attendees
Frequency: March

Directories & Databases

3500 **Beverage Marketing Directory**
Beverage Marketing Corporation
2670 Commercial Ave
Mingo Junction, OH 43938-1613

740-598-4133
800-332-6222; *Fax:* 740-598-3977;
www.beveragemarketing.com

Andrew Standardi III, Director of Operations
Kathy Smurthwaite, Editor

Publication is available in Print Copy (Price-$1,465), PDF Format (Price-$1,465), CD-ROM Format (For pricing, call number listed for details or visit website), and Online.
1196 Pages

3501 **Brewers Resource Directory**
Brewers Association
736 Pearl Street
Boulder, CO 80302

303-447-0816
888-822-6273; *Fax:* 303-447-2825
info@brewersassociation.org;
www.brewersassociation.org
Social Media: Facebook, Twitter, Youtube

Charlie Papazian, President
Bob Pease, VP
Cindy Jones, Sales/Marketing Director

Various categories of listees are included that have a direct relation to the beer and liquor industry.
Mailing list available for rent

3502 **Contacts**
National Alcohol Beverage Control Association
4401 Ford Avenue, Suite 700
Alexandria, VA 22302-1507

703-578-4200; *Fax:* 703-820-3551;
www.nabca.org
Social Media: Facebook, Twitter

James M Sgueo, Executive Director
Dixie Jamieson, Executive Assistant

Members include control jurisdictions, supplier members and industry trade associations.

3503 **Directory & Products Guide**
Vineyard & Winery Services
PO Box 2358
Windsor, CA 95492

707-836-6820
800-535-5670; *Fax:* 707-836-6825
vwm-online.com

Jennifer Merietti, Sales/Marketing Manager
Dennis Black, General Manager
Suzanne Webb, Marketing Director

A must have reference book that belongs on the desk of every wine professional. Whether it's tracking down a particular vendor, shopping for the best deal on oak barrels or searching for

out-of-state winery contacts, the DPG is a powerhouse of information. Over 2,300 supplier listings and 2,700 winery/vineyard listings, it is a reliable resource that saves time and money.
Cost: $95.00
450+ Pages
Frequency: Annually

3504 **Food & Beverage Market Place**
Grey House Publishing
4919 Route 22
PO Box 56
Amenia, NY 12501
518-789-8700
800-562-2139; *Fax:* 845-373-6390
books@greyhouse.com; www.greyhouse.com
Social Media: Facebook, Twitter
Leslie Mackenzie, Publisher
Richard Gottlieb, Editor
This information-packed 3-volume set is the most powerful buying and marketing guide for the US food and beverage industry. Includes thousands of industry freight and transportation listings.
Cost: $595.00
2000 Pages
Frequency: Annual
ISBN: 1-592373-61-5
Founded in: 1981

3505 **Food & Beverage Marketplace: Online Database**
Grey House Publishing
4919 Route 22
PO Box 56
Amenia, NY 12501
518-789-8700
800-562-2139; *Fax:* 518-789-0556
gold@greyhouse.com
http://gold.greyhouse.com
Social Media: Facebook, Twitter
Richard Gottlieb, President
Leslie Mackenzie, Publisher
This complete updated Food & Beverage Market Place: Online Database is the go-to source for the food and beverage industry. Anyone involved in the food and beverage industry needs this 'industry bible' and the important contacts to develop critical research data that can make for successful business growth.
Frequency: Annual
Founded in: 1981

3506 **Impact International Directory: Leading Spirits, Wine and Beer Companies**
M Shanken Communications
387 Park Ave S
8th Floor
New York, NY 10016-8872
212-684-4224; *Fax:* 212-684-5424;
www.cigaraficionado.com
Marvin Shanken, Publisher
A directory offering information on the major players of the alcoholic beverage industry.
Cost: $295.00

3507 **Impact Yearbook: Directory of the US Wine, Spirits & Beer Industry**
M Shanken Communications
387 Park Ave S
8th Floor
New York, NY 10016-8872
212-684-4224; *Fax:* 212-684-5424;
www.cigaraficionado.com
Marvin Shanken, Publisher
A directory offering information on the top 40 American distributors and profiles of companies.
Cost: $170.00
Frequency: Annual

3508 **US Alcohol Beverage Industry Category CD**
Beverage Marketing Corporation
2670 Commercial Ave
Mingo Junction, OH 43938-1613
740-598-4133
800-332-6222; *Fax:* 740-598-3977;
www.beveragemarketing.com
Andrew Standardi III, Director of Operations
Kathy Smurthwaite, Editor
Contains information on approximately 3,030 companies including breweries, microbreweries, wineries, distilleries, wholesalers and importers.
Cost: $3010.00
Frequency: Annual

3509 **US Beverage Manufacturers and Filling Locations Category CD**
Beverage Marketing Corporation
850 Third Avenue, 18th Floor
New York, NY 10022
212-688-7640
800-332-6222; *Fax:* 212-826-1255;
www.beveragemarketing.com
Andrew Standardi III, Director of Operations
Kathy Smurthwaite, Editor
Contains information on approximately 2,402 companies including breweries, microbreweries, wineries, distilleries, soft drink fillers and franchise companies, bottled water fillers, juice, sports beverages and energy drinks, soy, coffee, tea, and milk manufacturers.
Cost: $2390.00
Frequency: Annual
Mailing list available for rent

3510 **US Wine & Spirits Industry Category CD**
Beverage Marketing Corporation
2670 Commercial Ave
Mingo Junction, OH 43938-1613
740-598-4133
800-332-6222; *Fax:* 740-598-3977;
www.beveragemarketing.com
Andrew Standardi III, Director of Operations
Kathy Smurthwaite, Editor
Contains information on approximately 1,484 companies including wineries, distilleries, wine & spirit wholesalers, and wine & spirit importers.
Cost: $1475.00
Frequency: Annual

3511 **Vineyard & Winery Management Magazine**
Vineyard & Winery Services
421 E Street
Santa Rosa, CA 95404
707-577-7700
800-535-5670; *Fax:* 707-577-7705
vwm-online.com
Jennifer Merletti, Sales/Marketing Manager
Robert Merletti, Chairman/Owner
George Christie, President/CEO
A leading technical trade publication serving the North American Wine Industry and designed for today's serious wine business professional.
Founded in: 1975
Mailing list available for rent

3512 **Who's Who in Beer Wholesaling Directory**
National Beer Wholesalers Association
1101 King Street
Suite 600
Alexandria, VA 22314-8965
703-683-4300; *Fax:* 703-683-8965
info@nbwa.org; www.nbwa.org
Social Media: Facebook, Twitter
Craig A Purser, President & CEO
Michael Johnson, EVP Fed Aff/Chief Advisory Office
Rebecca Spicer, VP Public Affairs/Chief
Paul Pisano, SVP Industry Affairs & Gen. Counsel
A listing of more than 3,000 beer distributors and suppliers in the industry.
Cost: $50.00

3513 **Wholesale Beer Association Executives of America Directory**
Wholesale Beer Association Executives of America
2805 E Washington Avenue
Madison, WI 53704-5165
608-255-6464; *Fax:* 608-255-6466
7 Pages
Frequency: Annual

3514 **Wine & Spirits Industry Marketing**
Jobson Publishing Corporation
100 Avenue of the Americas
9th Floor
New York, NY 10013-1678
212-274-7000; *Fax:* 212-431-0500
Michael J Tansey, CEO
List of about 300 wine and liquor firms including wineries, producers, distillers and importers.
Cost: $150.00
Frequency: Annual April

3515 **Wine on Line**
Wine on Line International
400 E 59th St
Apartment 9F
New York, NY 10022-2342
212-755-4363; *Fax:* 212-755-7365
A database containing information including reviews about wines, production methods, serving advice, and more. Available on the Internet and worldwide web.
Frequency: Daily

3516 **Wines and Vines Directory of the Wine Industry in North America Issue**
Hiaring Company
1800 Lincoln Avenue
San Rafael, CA 94901-1221
415-453-9700; *Fax:* 415-453-2517
info@winesandvines.com;
www.winesandvines.com
Dorthy Kubota-Cordery, Editor
Phil Hiaring, Publisher
Debbie Hennessy, Editor
Renee Skiadas, Circulation Director
Chet Klingensmith, Owner
Annual guide offering listings of wineries and wine industry suppliers in the US, Canada and Mexico.
Cost: $85.00
505 Pages
Frequency: Annual
Circulation: 5000

Industry Web Sites

3517 **http://gold.greyhouse.com**
G.O.L.D Grey House OnLine Databases

Grey House Publishing's online database platform, GOLD, offers Quick Search, Keyword Search and Expert Search for most business sectors including alcoholic beverage markets. The GOLD platform makes finding the information you need quick and easy - whether you're a novice searcher or an experienced database user. All of Grey House's directory products are available for subscription on the GOLD platform.

3518 **www.beerinstitute.org**
Beer Institute
Protects the market environment from unfair burdens imposed by government bodies. Represents members interest before Congress.

3519 **www.beertown.org**
American Homebrewers Association
Devoted to the education of home brewed beer. Publishes the only magazine devoted exclusively to education, art and science of homebrewing. Services include: Beer Judge Certification Program, Sanctioned Competitions, World's Largest Homebrew Competition.

3520 **www.cawineclub.com**
California Wine Club
A wine of the month club that features only California's small boutique wineries. Each month members receive two bottles of award-winning wine.

3521 **www.greyhouse.com**
Grey House Publishing
Authoritative reference directories for most business sectors including alcoholic beverage markets. Users can search the online databases with varied search criteria allowing for custom searches by product category, geographic area, sales volume, keyword, subject and more. Full Grey House catalog and online ordering also available

3522 **www.nbwa.org**
National Beer Wholesalers Association
Research and development, quality control and ingredients.

3523 **www.scisoc.org/asbc**
American Society of Brewing Chemists
Annual scientific meeting for professionals in the brewing industry.

3524 **www.wineinstitute.org**
Wine Institute
Organization that represents the wine and spirit industry to state and federal lawmaking bodies.

3525 **www.wssa.com**
Wine and Spirits Shippers Association
Provides members, importers and exporters with efficient and economical ocean transportation and other logistic services.

Associations

3526 **Academy of Canadian Cinema & Television**
49 Ontario Street
Suite 501
Toronto, ON M5A 2V1
416-366-2227
800-644-5194; *Fax:* 416-366-8454
academie@acct.ca; www.academy.ca
Social Media: Facebook, Twitter, LinkedIn, Flickr, YouTube
Martin Katz, Chair
Robin Mirsky, Vice Chair
Anita McOuat, Treasurer
Julie Bristow, President & CEO
Scott Henderson, Vice President
A national non-profit, professional association dedicated to the promotion, recognition, and celebration of exceptional achievements in Candian film, television, and digital media.
Founded in: 1949

3527 **Academy of Television Arts and Science**
5200 Lankershim Blvd
North Hollywood, CA 91601
818-754-2800; *Fax:* 818-761-2827
lewis.kay@pmkbnc.com; www.emmys.com
Social Media: Facebook, Twitter, YouTube, Instagram, Pinterest
Robert Cook, Chairman
David Eun, Vice Chair
Thomas W Sarnoff, Chair Emeritus
Margaret Loesch, Secretary
Marc Graboff, Treasurer
Nonprofit corporation devoted to the advancement of telecommunications arts and sciences and to fostering creative leadership in the telecommunications industry. In addition to recognizing outstanding programming and individual achivements for Primetime and Los Angeles area programming, ATAS sponsors meetings, conferences and activities for collaboration on a variety of topics involving traditional broadcast interests, new media and emerging digital technology.
12000 Members
Founded in: 1959

3528 **Alaska Broadcasters Association**
700 W 41st Street
Suite 102
Anchorage, AK 99503
907-258-2424; *Fax:* 907-258-2414
akba@gci.net; www.alaskabroadcasters.org
Social Media: Facebook
Matt Wilson, President
Charlie Ellis, VP
Ric Schimdt, Secretary/Treasurer
Dick Olson, VP, Sales Manager
Darlene Simono, Executive Director
To provide assistance, which enables members to serve their communities of license through education, representation and advocacy.
Founded in: 1964

3529 **Alliance for Community Media**
4248 Park Glen Road
Minneapolis, MN 55416
952-928-4643; *Fax:* 202-393-2653
info@allcommunitymedia.org;
www.alliancecm.org
Social Media: Facebook, Twitter, LinkedIn, Youtube, Flickr
Mary Van Sickle, Chair
Jon Funfar, Chair Elect
Alan Bushong, Treasurer
Keri Stokstad, Secretary
Mike Wassenaar, President
Participants include cable access television and community programmers. Individual membership dues are $70.00, organization $350.00.
1000 Members
Founded in: 1976
Mailing list available for rent: 1000 names at $200 per M

3530 **Alliance for Women in Media**
1250 24th St NW
Suite 300
Washington, DC 20037
202-750-3664; *Fax:* 703-506-3266
info@allwomeninmedia.org;
www.allwomeninmedia.org
Social Media: Facebook, Twitter, LinkedIn, Youtube
Kristen Welch, Chair
Sarah Foss, Chair Elect
Keisha Sutton-James, Treasurer
Christine Travaglini, Treasurer Elect
Robin Alston, Director
Leverages the promise, passion, and power of women in all forms of media carrying forth with its mission by educating, advocating, and acting as a resource to its members and the industry at large via inspired thought leadership that illuminates areas of social need.
Founded in: 1951

3531 **Alliance of Motion Picture and Television Producers**
15301 Ventura Blvd
Building E
Sherman Oaks, CA 91403
818-995-3600; *Fax:* 818-382-1793;
www.amptp.org
Nick Counter, President
Trade association with respect to labor issues in the motion picture and television industry. Negotiate industry wide collective bargaining agreements that cover actors, craftspersons, directors, musicians, technicians and writers.
350 Members
Founded in: 1982

3532 **American Auto Racing Writers and Broadcasters Association**
922 North Pass Avenue
Burbank, CA 91505-2703
818-842-7005; *Fax:* 818-842-7020
dusty@aarwba.org; www.aarwba.org
Social Media: Facebook
Norma Brandel, President/Executive Director
Kathy Seymour, VP
Rhonda Williams, Treasurer
Patrick Reynolds, Secretary
Ross R Olney, Past President
The American Auto Racing Writers & Broadcasters Association is the oldest and largest organization devoted to auto racing coverage.
400 Members
Founded in: 1955

3533 **American Center for Children and Media**
5400 North St Louis Avenue
Chicago, IL 60625
703-509-5510; *Fax:* 773-509-5303
https://childrensmediaassociation.wordpress.com
David Kleeman, President
James Fellows, President Emeritus
Mission is to support a vibrant children's media industry by convening key constituencies to develop, implement and promote policies and practices that respect young people's well being, and are sustainable.
Founded in: 1985

3534 **American Disc Jockey Association**
20118 N 67th Avenue
Suite 300-605
Glendale, CA 85308
888-723-5776; *Fax:* 866-310-4676
office@adja.org; www.adja.org
Social Media: Facebook, Twitter, Youtube
Rob Snyder, Director
An association of professional mobile entertainers. Encourages success for its members through continuous education, camaraderie, and networking. The primary goal is to educate Disc Jockeys so that each member acts ethically and responsibly.

3535 **American Private Radio Association (APRA)**
PO Box 4221
Scottsdale, AZ 85261-4221
480-661-5000
Association members are from private radio stations.

3536 **American Public Media**
480 Cedar St.
St. Paul, MN 55101
800-562-8440; www.americanpublicmedia.org
Jon McTaggart, President & CEO
Sylvia Strobel, SVP & General Counsel
David Kansas, SVP & COO
Morris Goodwin, SVP & CFO
Leading producer and distributor of public radio programming in the Upper Midwest, California and Florida, reaching 19 million listeners weekly.
Founded in: 1967

3537 **American Sportscasters Association**
225 Broadway
Suite 2030
New York, NY 10007
212-227-8080; *Fax:* 212-571-0556
lschwa8918@aol.com;
www.americansportscastersonline.com
Louis O Schwartz, President/Founder
Dick Enberg, Chairman
Jim Nantz, Board of Directors
Jon Miller, Board of Directors
Bill Walton, Board of Directors
National Association of Sportscasters, radio, television and cable covering the US, Puerto Rico and Canada. Very active web site. Offers seminars, compiles statistics and operates a placement service, maintains a Hall of Fame and biographical archives and library.
500 Members
Founded in: 1980

3538 **American Sportscasters Association, Inc.**
225 Broadway
Suite 2030
New York, NY 10007-3742
212-227-8080; *Fax:* 212-571-0556
lschwa8918@aol.com;
www.americansportscastersonline.com
Louis O Schwartz, President/Founder
Dick Enberg, Chairman
Jim Nantz, Board of Directors
Jon Miller, Board of Directors
Bill Walton, Board of Directors
National Association of Sportscasters, radio, television and cable covering the US, Puerto Rico and Canada. Very active web site. Offers seminars, compiles statistics and operates a

placement service, maintains a Hall of Fame and biographical archives and library.
500 Members
Founded in: 1980

3539 **Associated Press Broadcasters**
1825 K Street NW
Suite 800
Washington, DC 20006-1202
212-621-1500; *Fax:* 202-736-1107
info@ap.org; www.apexchange.com
Social Media: Facebook, Twitter, LinkedIn, Youtube
Mary E Junck, Chairman
Gary Pruitt, President & CEO
Kathleen Carroll, Senior VP/Executive Editor
Jessica Bruce, VP/Director, Human Resource
Ken Dale, CFO/Senior VP
Seeks to advance journalism through radio and television, and cooperates with the AP to promote accurate and impartial news.
5.9m Members
Founded in: 1846

3540 **Association for Maximum Service Television**
4100 Wisconsin Avenue NW
PO Box 9897
Washington, DC 20036-2224
202-966-1956; *Fax:* 202-966-9617
mstv@mstv.org; www.mstv.org
David Donovan, President
Assures the maintenance of an effective nationwide system of free television and seeks to meet present and future needs of the VHF and UHF system.
400+ Members
Founded in: 1956

3541 **Association of Independent Commercial Producers**
3 W 18th St
5th Floor
New York, NY 10011
212-929-3000; *Fax:* 212-929-3359
mattm@aicp.com; www.aicp.com
Social Media: Facebook, Twitter, LinkedIn, Youtube, Flickr, RSS
Matt Miller, President & CEO
Jerry Solomon, Chairman
Ralph Laucella, Vice Chairman
Mark Androw, Treasurer
Robert L Sacks, Secretary
The national trade association of television commercial producers who account for in excess of 80% of the commercial production done in the United States annually.
500 Members
Founded in: 1972

3542 **Association of Local Television Stations**
1320 19th Street NW
Washington, DC 20036
202-887-1970; www.altv.com

3543 **Association of Public Television Stations**
2100 Crystal Drive
Suite 700
Arlington, VA 22202
202-654-4200; *Fax:* 202-654-4236;
www.apts.org
Social Media: Facebook, Twitter
Patrick Butler, President & CEO
Lonna Thompson, Executive VP/COO & General Counsel
Jennifer Kieley, VP, Government Relations
Stacey Karp, VP, Communications
Emil Mara, VP, Finance & Administration
Nonprofit membership organization that supports the continued growth and development of a strong and financially sound noncommercial television service for the American public. Provides advocacy for public television interests at the national level, as well as consistent leadership and information in marshaling grassroots and congressional support for its members: the nation's public television stations.
153 Members
Founded in: 1979

3544 **Audio Engineering Society**
551 Fifth Avenue
Room 1225
New York, NY 10176
212-661-8528; *Fax:* 212-682-0477
HQ@aes.org; www.aes.org
Social Media: Facebook, Twitter, LinkedIn, Youtube, Google+, RSS
Roger Furness, Executive Director
Andres Mayo, President
Ron Streicher, Secretary
Garry Margolis, Treasurer
John Krivit, Past President
Professional society devoted to audio technology. Membership includes leading engineers, scientists and other authorities in the field. Serves its members, the industry and the public by stimulating and facilitating advances in the constantly changing field of audio.
Founded in: 1948

3545 **Broadcast Designers' Association International**
145 W 45th Street
Room 1100
New York, NY 10036-4008
212-376-6222; *Fax:* 212-376-6202
Association for manufacturers or suppliers of broadcast design equipment, supplies and services.

3546 **Broadcast Education Association**
1771 N St NW
Washington, DC 20036-2891
202-429-5355
888-380-7222; *Fax:* 202-609-9940
help@beaweb.org; www.beaweb.org
Social Media: Facebook, Twitter, LinkedIn
Heather Birks, Executive Director
J D Boyle, Director, Sales & Marketing
Traci Bailey, Manager, Business Operations
John Allen Hendricks, President
Michael Bruce, Secretary/Treasurer
Serves as a higher education association of professors and industry professionals who teach college students worldwide and prepares them to go into the broadcasting and related emerging technologies professions upon graduation from college.
1400 Members
Founded in: 1955
Mailing list available for rent: 1300 names at $100 per M

3547 **Broadcast Pioneers**
7 World Trade Center
250 Greenwich Street
New York, NY 10007-0030
212-220-3000; *Fax:* 212-246-2163;
www.bmi.com
Social Media: Facebook, Twitter, YouTube, Pinterest, Google+
Michael O'Neill, President & CEO
Bruce A Esworthy, Senior Vice President
Phillip R Graham, Senior Vice President
Catherine Brewton, Vice President
Mark Mason, Executive Director
Honors radio or television stations for excellence in art and community service. Maintains library documents on television broadcasting history.
1.4M Members
Founded in: 1942

3548 **Broadcasters Foundation of America**
125 West 55th Street
4th Floor
New York, NY 10019-5366
212-373-8250; *Fax:* 212-373-8254
info@thebfoa.org;
www.broadcastersfoundation.org
George G Beasley, Chairman & CEO
Richard A Foreman, President & CEO
James B Thompson, President
Peter Doyle, VP
Jeff Haley, VP
Provides financial assistance to radio and television broadcasters who are in financial need.

3549 **Cable & Telecommunications Association for Marketing**
120 Waterfront Street
Suite 200
National Harbor, MD 20745
301-485-8900; *Fax:* 301-560-4964
info@ctam.com; www.ctam.com
Social Media: Facebook, Twitter, LinkedIn, Youtube
Matrk Greatrex, Chair
Jamia Bigalow, Vice Chair
Jonathan Hargis, Secretary
Antoinette Allen, Director of Meetings
Dana Fragnoli-Piteo, Director of Marketing
Dedicated to the discipline and development of consumer marketing excellence in cable television, news media and telecommunications services. Members have the advantage of progressive research, insightful publications and forward thinking conferences all designed to help you and your company gain a competitive edge.
5500 Members
Founded in: 1976

3550 **Canadian Association of Broadcast Consultants**
130 Cree Crescent
Winnepeg, MB R3J 3W1
204-889-9202; *Fax:* 204-831-6650
jsadoun@yrh.com; www.cabc-accr.ca
Joseph Sadoun, Ing P Eng, President
Kerry Pelser, Secretary/Treasurer
Prepares technical briefs, coverage studies and frequencies.

3551 **Canadian Association of Broadcasters**
770-45 O'Connor St
Ottawa, ON K1P 1A4
613-233-4035; *Fax:* 613-233-6961;
www.cab-acr.ca
Kevin Goldstein, Chairman
Susan Wheeler, Vice Chair
Sylvie Courtemanche, Secretary
Glenda Spenrath, Treasurer
Paul Cowling, VP, Regulatory Affairs
Serves as the eyes and ears of the private broadcasting community to advocate and lobby on its behalf and to act as a cebtral point on matters of joint interest.

3552 **Canadian Association of Ethnic Broadcasters (Radio)**
622 College Street
Toronto, ON M6G 1B6

416-531-9991; *Fax:* 416-531-5274
info@chinradio.com; www.chinradio.com
Social Media: Facebook, Twitter

Johnny Lombardi, Founder, President

Pioneer in multicultural radio broadcasting and has lead the way for similar briadcast operations to be established.

3553 **Caribbean Broadcasting Union**
Suite 1B, Building 6A
Harbor Industrial Estate
St Michael, BB 11145

246-430-1006; *Fax:* 242-228-9524
patrick.cozier@caribsurf.com; www.discountdominicatravel.com

Patrick Cozier, President

Stimulates the flow of broadcast material among the radio and television systems in the Caribbean region.
Founded in: 1970
Mailing list available for rent

3554 **Coalition Opposing Signal Theft**
25 Massachusetts Ave NW
Suite 100
Washington, DC 20001

202-222-2300
webmaster@ncta.com; www.ncta.com
Social Media: Facebook, Twitter, LinkedIn

Michael Powell, President & CEO
James M Assey, Executive VP
K Dane Snowden, Chief of Staff
Bruce Carnes, Senior VP, Finance & Administration
William Check, Senior VP, Science & Technology

Acts as a clearinghouse of information regarding cable signal theft.

3555 **Community Antenna Television Association**
PO Box 1005
Fairfax, VA 22030-1005

202-775-3550

An association of over 3,000 cable television systems.
3M Members

3556 **Content Delivery & Security Association**
39 N Bayles Ave
Port Washington, NY 11050

516-767-6720; *Fax:* 516-883-5793
info@CDSAonline.org; www.cdsaonline.org

Richard Atkinson, Chairman
Paul W Scott, VP
Tom Moran, Secretary/Treasurer
Joel Bigley, Executive VP

International trade association dealing with every facet of recording, media and related industries. Membership includes raw material providers, manufacturers, replicators, duplicators, packagers, and copyright holders.

3557 **Corporation for Public Broadcasting**
401 9th St NW
Washington, DC 20004-2129

202-879-9600
800-272-2190; *Fax:* 202-879-9700
oigemail@cpb.org; www.cpb.org
Social Media: Facebook, Twitter

Elizabeth Sembler, Chair
Vincent Curren, EVP & COO
William P Tayman Jr., CFO/Treasurer
Westwood Smithers Jr., Senior VP/General Counsel
Michael Levy, Executive VP

Facilitate the development of, and ensure universal access to, non-commercial high-quality programming and telecommunications services. It does this in conjunction with non-commercial educational telecommunications licensees across the country.
Founded in: 1967

3558 **Country Radio Broadcasters**
1009 16th Ave South
Nashville, TN 37212

615-327-4487; *Fax:* 615-329-4492
info@crb.org; www.countryradioseminar.com
Social Media: Facebook, Twitter

Bill Mayne, Executive Director
Chasity Crouch, Business Manager
Carole Bowem, Secretary
R J Curtis, VP
Kristen England, Creative Director

Broadcasting forum.
Founded in: 1969

3559 **Educational Broadcasting Association**
825 Eighth Ave
New York, NY 10019

212-560-1313; *Fax:* 212-560-1314
programming@thirteen.org; www.thirteen.org
Social Media: Facebook, Twitter, Pinterest, YouTube

Neal Shapiro, President & CEO
Claude Johnson, VP Communication
Caroline C Croen, VP, CFO, Treasurer
Robert A Feinberg, VP, General Counsel, Secretary
Carole Wacey, VP, Education

Association members are producers and directors of public educational programming, channel 13, PBS.
500 Members
Mailing list available for rent

3560 **Enterprise Wireless Alliance**
2121 Cooperative Way
Suite 255
Herndon, VA 20171

703-524-1074
800-482-8282
info@EnterpriseWireless.org; www.enterprisewirelessalliance.org

Catherine Leonard, Chairman
Davis Reeves, Vice Chair
Mark E Crosby, President/CEO
Gordon Day, Treasurer
Kenny Adams, Director

Provides a license renewal reminder service. Maintains liaison with major radio manufacturers and mediates problems between licensees.
15 Members
Founded in: 1953

3561 **Geospatial Information and Technology Association**
1360 University Ave W
Suite 455
St. Paul, MN 55104-4086

844-447-4482; *Fax:* 844-223-8218
bsamborski@gita.org; www.gita.org
Social Media: Facebook, Twitter, LinkedIn, YouTube

Mark Limbruner, President
Matthew Thomas, President-Elect
Eric Hoogenraad, Secretary
Elizabeth Bialek, Treasurer
Talbot J Brooks, Past President

Provides unbiased educational programs, forums and publications for professionals involved with geospatial information and technology.
2200 Members
Founded in: 1960

3562 **Hollywood Radio and Television Society**
16530 Ventura Blvd
Suite 411
Encino, CA 91436

818-789-1182; *Fax:* 818-789-1210
info@hrts.org; www.hrts.org
Social Media: Facebook, Twitter, LinkedIn

Bela Bajaria, President
Jennie Nevin, Director of Operations
Ruzzo Martinelli, Events
Meshak Vallesillas, Marketing & Communications
Elvia Gonzalez, Member Services

Sponsors monthly luncheons featuring top industry and government speakers and seminars about broadcasting, maintains film and audio library.
100 Members
Founded in: 1947
Mailing list available for rent

3563 **Intercollegiate Broadcasting Systems**
367 Windsor Highway
New Windsor, NY 12553-7900

845-565-0003; *Fax:* 845-565-7446
ibs@ibsradio.org; www.ibsradio.org
Social Media: Facebook, Twitter

Len Mailloux, Chairman
Norman Prusslin, President/Chair Emeritus
Fritz Kass, CEO
Tom Gibson, Executive VP
Allen Myers, EVP, FCC Licensing

Nonprofit association of student staffed radio stations based at schools and colleges across the country. Some 800 member stations operate all sizes and types of facilities including Internet-Webcasting, closed circuit, AM carrier-current, cable radio and FCC-licensed FM and AM stations.
800 Members
Founded in: 1940

3564 **International Association of Broadcast Monitors**
PO Box 986
Irmo, SC 29063

803-749-9833
800-236-1741; *Fax:* 888-732-9004; www.iabm.com

Mike Ross, Executive Director
Kevin Repka, President
Ron Coucil, VP International
John Croll, Secretary
Holly Wine, Treasurer

Worldwide trade association made up of news retrieval services which monitor television, radio, internet and print news mediums. It acts as a clearinghouse or forum for discussion on topics of collective concerns and acts as a united voice for the news monitoring industry.
Founded in: 1981

3565 **International Council-National Academy**
25 W 52nd Street
New York, NY 10019

212-489-6969; *Fax:* 212-489-6557
iemmys@iemmys.tv; www.iemmys.tv
Social Media: Facebook, Twitter, LinkedIn

Fred Cohen, Chairman
Bruce Paisner, President & CEO
Larry Gershman, VP
Simon Sutton, Secretary
Rainer Siek, Nominating Committee Chairman

Furthers the arts and sciences by bestowing International Emmy Awards, George Movshon Fellowship and the Joan Wilson memorial scholarship.
250+ Members
Founded in: 1969

3566 **International Radio and Television Society Foundation**
1697 Broadway
10th Floor
New York, NY 10019

212-867-6650; *Fax:* 212-867-6653;
www.irts.org

Joyce M. Tudrynff, President & CEO
Jim Cronin, Dir, Member Prgms & Development
Marilyn L. Ellis, Director, Program Administration
Lauren Kruk-Winokur, Dir, Academic Prgms & Communication
Jack Myers, Chairman

The lines between broadcast televison and radio, cable, telephony and the computer industry may be blurring, but one thing remains clear, we all have an affinity for a business that entertains, informs, educates and serves the American public in a meaningful way. The foundation provides a unique common forum for all segments of the communication industry. Members can enjoy sharing insight and ideas with colleagues during the season's numerous events.
750 Members
Founded in: 1939

3567 **International Television Academy**
25 W 52nd Street
New York, NY 10019

212-489-6969; *Fax:* 212-489-6557
iemmys@iemmys.tv; www.iemmys.tv
Social Media: Facebook, Twitter, LinkedIn

Bruce Paisner, President
Fred Cohen, Chairman
Larry Gershman, VP
Simon Sutton, Secretary
Rainer Siek, Nominating Committee Chairman

Organization of global broadcasters, with representatives from over 50 countries based outside of the US, and represents the world's largest production, distribution and broadcast companies.
Founded in: 1969

3568 **Jones/NCTI-National Cable Television Institute**
9697 E Mineral Ave
Centennial, CO 80112

303-792-3111
800-525-7002; *Fax:* 303-797-0829
info@jones.com; www.ncti.com

Glenn R Jones, CEO
Michael Guilfoyle, Director Market Strategy
Jerry Neese, Director Sales
Mary Bliss, Vice President
Stacey Slaughter, CEO/CFO

Workforce performance products, services and education.
30 Members
Founded in: 1969
Mailing list available for rent

3569 **Library of American Broadcasting**
University of Maryland
Mckeldin Library
College Park, MD 20742-7011

301-405-0800; *Fax:* 301-314-2634;
www.lib.umd.edu
Social Media: Facebook, Twitter, YouTube, Flickr

Malachy Wienges, Chair
Barbara Williams Perry, 1st Vice Chair
Alison Gibson, 2nd Vice Chair
Jamie Jensen, Secretary
Terry D Peterson, Treasurer

Holds a wide ranging collection of audio and video recordings, books, pamphlets, periodicals, personal collections, oral histories, photographs, scripts and vertical files devoted exclusively to the history of broadcasting.
Founded in: 1972

3570 **Manufacturers Radio Frequency Advisory Committee**
616 E 34th Street N
Wichita, KS 67219

316-832-9213
800-262-9206
info@mrfac.com; www.mrfac.com

Joe Cramer, President
Danny Hankins, VP
Nate Miler, Secretary
Rich Elersich, Treasurer

Representing the voice of the manufacturing industry and private land mobile radio users before the Federal Communications Commision, the responsibe federal regulatory agency for the nation's industrial communications. The leaders of the manufacturing industry, individually and collectively, have an obligation to influence the policies, plans, and procedures which govern the growth, structure and use of our national radio spectrum and telecommunications systems.
14000 Members
Founded in: 1954

3571 **Media Communications Association International**
P.O.Box 5135
Madison, WI 53705-0135

608-836-0722
800-899-6224; *Fax:* 888-899-6224
loiswei@aol.com; www.mca-i.org
Social Media: Facebook, Twitter, LinkedIn, Google +

Jim Dufek, President
Brian Alberth, President Elect
Art Kirsch, Treasurer
Liz De Nesnera, Secretary
Brian Alberth, Past President

The Media Communications Association-International is a global community that provides professional development seminars and events, opportunities for networking, members-only benefits, forums for education, and information resources for media communications professionals.
Founded in: 1968

3572 **Media Financial Management Association**
550 W Frontage Road
Suite 3600
Northfield, IL 60093

847-716-7000; *Fax:* 847-716-7004
info@mediafinance.org;
www.mediafinance.org
Social Media: Twitter, LinkedIn

Mary M Collins, President/CEO
Ed O'Connor, Director of Operations
Arcelia Pimentel, Membership Manager & Sales
Andy Holdgate, Public Relations Consultant
Ralph Bender, Chairman

Professional society of media's top financial, MIS Credit and HR executives, plus associates in auditing, data processing, software development, law, tax and credit and collections
1300 Members
Founded in: 1961
Mailing list available for rent

3573 **Museum of Broadcast Communications**
360 North State Street
Chicago, IL 60654-5411

312-245-8200; *Fax:* 312-245-8207
info@museum.tv; www.museum.tv
Social Media: Facebook, Twitter

Bruce DuMont, President, CEO
David Plier, VP, Secretary
Jack Weinberg, VP

Collects, preserves, and presents historic and contemporary radio and television content as well as educate, inform , and entertain the public through its archives, public programs, screenings, exhibits, publications, and online access to its resources.

3574 **National Academy of Television Arts and Sciences**
1697 Broadway
Suite 404
New York, NY 10019

212-586-8424; *Fax:* 212-246-8129;
www.emmyonline.tv
Social Media: Facebook, Twitter, LinkedIn, Google +

Brent Stanton, Executive Director
David Winn, Director
Christine Chin, Manager

Dedicated to the advancement of the arts and sciences of television and the promotion of creative leadership for artistic, educational and technical achievements within the television industry. It recognizes excellence in television with the coveted Emmy Award.
12M Members
Founded in: 1957
Printed in on glossy stock

3575 **National Alliance of State Broadcasters Associations**
2333 Wisconsin St. NE
Albuquerque, NM 87110

505-881-4444; www.nasbaonline.net
Social Media: Twitter

Kent Cornish, President
Oscar Rodriguez, President-Elect
Vance Harrison, Vice President
David Donovan, Secretary/Treasurer
Michelle Vetterkind, Past President

The Alliance represents the interests of the 50 state broadcast associations in Washington.

3576 **National Association of Black Owned Broadcasters (NABOB)**
1201 Connecticut Avenue NW
Suite 200
Washington, DC 20036

202-463-8970; *Fax:* 202-429-0657
nabobinfo@nabob.org; www.nabob.org

Micheal L Carter, VP
Karen E Slade, Treasurer
James L Winston, President

Largest trade organization representing the interests of African-American owners of radio and television stations across the country.
Founded in: 2001

3577 **National Association of Broadcasters**
1771 N St Nw
Washington, DC 20036

202-429-5300; *Fax:* 202-429-4199
nab@nab.org; www.nab.org
Social Media: Facebook, Twitter, LinkedIn, YouTube

David K Rehr, CEO
Philip J Lombardo, Chairman
Dean Goodman, COO

Ann Young-Orr, Executive Director
Michelle Duke, Development Director

Full service trade association that represents the interests of free, over-the-air radio and television broadcasters. Offers seminars and workshops to members and holds local meetings that offer support on legal and industry issues. Sponsors the National Association of Broadcasters Educational Foundation, dedicated to serving the public interest via education and training programs, strategies to increase diverse initiatives, community support and philanthropy.
7000 Members
Founded in: 1923

3578 National Association of College Radio/TV Stations
71 George Street
Providence, RI 02912-1824

401-863-2225; *Fax:* 401-863-2221
nacb@aol.com

Members are student radio/TV stations and interested individuals. Has an annual budget of approximately $300,000.
1600 Members
Founded in: 1988

3579 National Association of Farm Broadcasters
1100 Platte Falls Road
PO Box 500
Platte City, MO 64079

816-431-4032; *Fax:* 816-431-4087
info@nafb.com; www.nafb.com
Social Media: Facebook, Twitter

Janet Adkison, President
Susan Littlefield, President Elect
Brian Winnekins, VP

Works to improve quantity and quality of farm programming and serves as a clearinghouse for new ideas in farm broadcasting.
600 Members
Founded in: 1944

3580 National Association of Television Program Executives
5757 Wilshire Blvd
Penthouse 10
Los Angeles, CA 90036

210-857-1601; *Fax:* 310-453-5258
info@natpe.org; www.natpe.org
Social Media: Facebook, Twitter, Youtube

Rod Perth, President/CEO
Olivia Thomas, Executive Assistant to President
Eric Low, Director, Registration
Jordan Ryder, VP, Event Programming
Dann Novak, Programming Producer

A global, non-profit organization dedicated to the creation, development and distribution of televised programming in all forms across all mature and emerging media platforms.
2800 Members
Founded in: 1963
Mailing list available for rent

3581 National Cable & Telecommunications Association
25 Massachusetts Ave. NW
Suite 100
Washington, DC 20001

202-222-2300
webmaster@ncta.com; www.ncta.com
Social Media: Facebook, Twitter, LinkedIn

Michael Powell, President & CEO
Neil Smit, Chairman

Trade association for U.S. cable industry.
200+ Members
Founded in: 1940

3582 National Cable Television Association
25 Massachusetts Ave NW
Suite 100
Washington, DC 20001

202-222-2300; *Fax:* 202-775-3604
webmaster@ncta.com; www.ncta.com
Social Media: Facebook, Twitter, LinkedIn

Michael Powell, President & CEO
Brian Dietz, VP
James E Assey, Executive VP
K Dane Snowden, Chief of Staff
Bruce Carnes, Senior VP, Finance & Administration
200+ Members
Founded in: 1940

3583 National Council for Families & TV
3801 Barham Boulevard
Los Angeles, CA 90068-1000

323-953-7300; *Fax:* 310-208-5984;
www.salonprofessionals.org

Advances and promotes television awareness for family television shows.

3584 National Federation of Community Broadcasting
PO Box 16
1308 Clear Fork Road
Crawford, CO 81415

970-279-3411; *Fax:* 510-451-8208
comments@nfcb.org; www.nfcb.org

Sonya Green, President
Lackisha Freeman, VP
Ann Alquist, Secretary
Ernesto Aguilar, Treasurer
Sally Kane, CEO

A national alliance of stations, producers, and others committed to community radio. NFCB advocates for national public policy, funding, recognition, and resources on behalf of its membership while providing services to empower and strengthen community broadcasters through the core values of localism, diversity, and public service.

3585 National Public Radio Association
1111 North Capitol Street NW
Washington, DC 20002

202-686-0516; *Fax:* 202-513-3329;
www.npr.org
Social Media: Facebook, Twitter

Gary E Knell, President/CEO
Joyce MacDonald, Chief of Staff/Vice President
Jeff Perkins, Chief People Officer
Robert Kempf, General Manager
Deborah Cowan, VP/Chief Financial Officer

Works in partnership with member stations to create a more informed public, one challenged and invigorated by a deeper understanding and appreciation of events, ideas, and cultures.
750 Members
Founded in: 1970

3586 National Religious Broadcasters
9510 Technology Dr
Manassas, VA 20110

703-330-7000; *Fax:* 703-330-7100
info@nrb.org; www.nrb.org
Social Media: Facebook, Twitter, LinkedIn, YouTube, Google+ RSS

Jerry A Johnson, President/CEO
Linda Smith, Executive VP & COO
Craig Parshall, Senior VP/General Counsel
Aaron Mercer, VP of Government Relations
Jennifer Gregorin, President Assistant

Represents evangelical Christian radio and television stations, program producers, multimedia developers and related organizations around the worldMembers are responsible for much of the world's Christian radio and television.
1700 Members
Founded in: 1944
Mailing list available for rent

3587 National Sportscasters and Sportswriters Association
PO Box 1545
Salisbury, NC 28145

704-633-4275; *Fax:* 704-633-2027
nssahalloffame@aol.com;
www.nssahalloffame.com
Social Media: Facebook, Twitter

Dave Goren, Executive Director
Katy Temple, Adminstrative Assistant

Meet annually.
1000 Members
Founded in: 1959
Mailing list available for rent

3588 New England Cable & Telecommunications Associatoin Inc
Ten Forbes Road
Suite 440W
Braintree, MA 02184

781-843-3418; *Fax:* 781-849-6267
ckillian@necta.info; www.necta.info

Paul R Cianelli, President
Mark Reilly, Vice Chair
John Sutich, Treasurer
Jay Allbaugh, Secretary
William D Durand, Executive VP/Chief Counsel

NECTA is a six state regional trade association representing sbtstantially all private cable telecommunications companies in Connecticut, Maine, Massachusetts, New Hampshire, Rhode Island and Vermont.

3589 North American Broadcasters Association (NABA)
205 Wellington Street West
Suite 6C300
Toronto, ON M5V 3G7

416-598-9877; *Fax:* 416-598-9774
contact@nabanet.com; www.nabanet.com

Michael McEwan, Director General
Anh Ngo, Director, Administration
Jason Paris, Senior Coordinator
Jenn Hadfield, Executive Assistant
Vineet Mathur, IT & Web Administrator

A non-profit association of broadcasting organizations in the United States, Mexico, and Canada committed to advancing the interests of broadcasters at home and internationally.

3590 North American Network
3700 Crestwood Pkwy NW
Suite 350
Duluth, GA 30096-7154

770-279-4560; *Fax:* 770-279-4566
rbeilfuss@pkfnan.org; www.pkfnan.org

Terry Snyder, President

Radio broadcasting agency that provides news and programming services to radio stations and organizations. Programming is sponsored by the corporations, government angencies, associations and nonprofit organizations who are indentified in the program notes and scripts.

3591 Public Broadcasting Service (PBS)
2100 Crystal Dr.
Arlington, VA 22202

www.pbs.org
Social Media: Facebook, Twitter, YouTube

Paula Kerger, President & CEO
Barbara Landes, Chief Financial Officer
Jonathan Barzilay, Chief Operating Officer
Mary L. Plantamura, Assoc. General Counsel

Tom Tardivo, SVP, Finance & Business Development

PBS is a private, nonprofit association of public TV stations providing arts content, ecucational programs for children, documentaries and non-commercial news programs to all Americans.
Founded in: 1969

3592 Public Radio in Mid-America (PRIMA)
3651 Olive Street
St Louis, MO 63108

314-516-5968; *Fax:* 307-766-6184;
www.wordpress.prima.org

Tim Eby, General Manager
Terrence Dupuis, Chief Engineer
Shelley Kerley, Director, Development

Trusted source of informationa nd entertainment that opens minds and nourishes the spirit.

3593 Radio Advertising Bureau
1320 Greenway Dr
Suite 500
Irving, TX 75038-2547

972-753-6700
800-232-3131; *Fax:* 972-753-6727
jhaley@rab.com; www.rab.com
Social Media: Facebook, Twitter

Hartley AdkinsII, Chairman
Steve Newberry, Secretary
Ginny Morris, Vice Chair
Susan Larkin, Finance Chairman
Erica Farber, Executive Committee

Our mission is to lead industry initiatives and provide organizational, educational, research and advocacy programs and services that benefit the RAB membership and the Radio industry as a whole.
7000 Members

3594 Radio Television Digital News Assn.
529 14th Street NW
Suite 425
Washington, DC 20045

800-807-8632; *Fax:* 202-223-4007
mikec@rtdna.org; www.rtdna.org
Social Media: Facebook, Twitter, LinkedIn

Mike Cavender, Executive Director
Derrick Hinds, Communications, Marketing & Digital
Katie Switchenko, Programs
Karen Hansen, Membership & Program Manager
Jon Ebinger, International Program Consultant

An association dedicated to setting new standards for newsgathering and reporting.

3595 Radio Television Digital News Association (Canada)
529 14th Street NW
Suite 1240
Washington, DC 20045

800-807-8632; *Fax:* 202-223-4007
mikec@rtdna.org; www.rtdna.org
Social Media: Facebook, Twitter, LinkedIn

Mike Cavender, Executive Director
Derrick Hinds, Communications, Marketing & Digital
Katie Switchenko, Programs
Karen Hansen, Membership & Program Manager
Jon Ebinger, International Program Consultant

An association dedicated to setting new standards for newsgathering and reporting.

3596 Radio Television News Directors Association
529 14th Street NW
Suite 1240
Washington, DC 20045

800-807-8632; *Fax:* 202-223-4007
barbarac@rtnda.org; www.rtnda.org
Social Media: Facebook, Twitter, LinkedIn

Mike Cavender, Executive Director
Derrick Hinds, Communications, Marketing & Digital
Katie Switchenko, Programs
Karen Hansen, Membership & Program Manager
Jon Ebinger, International Program Consultant

Largest professional organization exclusively serving the electronic news profession. Dedicated to setting standards for newsgathering and reporting. Represents electronic journalists in radion, television and all digital media, as well as journalism educators and students.
3000+ Members
Founded in: 1946

3597 Radio Television News Directors Assn. - Canada
439 University Avenue
5th Floor
Toronto, ON M5G 1Y8

437-836-3088
877-257-8632; *Fax:* 416-364-8896
admin@rtndacanada.com;
www.rtdnacanada.com
Social Media: Facebook, Twitter

Ian Koenigsfest, President
Andy LeBlanc, Past President
Michelle McEachern, Secretary/Treasurer
Marissa Nelson, VP, Digital Media
Kym Geddes, International Representative

Progressive organization offering a forum for open discussion and action in the broadcast news industry. Speaks for the leaders of Canada's radio and television news operations on the issues that impact the newsroom.

3598 Radio and Television Research Council
234 5th Ave
#417
New York, NY 10001

212-028-8933; *Fax:* 212-481-3071

Robert M Purcell, Executive Director

Members are professionals actively engaged in radio/television research.
200 Members
Founded in: 1941

3599 Satellite Broadcasting and Communication Association (SBCA)
1100 17th Street NW
Suite 1150
Washington, DC 20036

202-349-3620
800-541-5981; *Fax:* 202-349-3621
info@sbca.org; www.sbca.com
Social Media: Facebook, Twitter, LinkedIn

Jeffrey Blum, Chairman
Andrew Reinsdorf, Vice Chair
Joseph Widoff, Executive Director

National trade organization representing all segments of the satellite consumer services industry. The association is committed to expanding the utilization of satellite technology for the delivery of video, data, voice, interactive and broadband services.
1000 Members
Founded in: 1986

3600 Screen Actors Guild - American Federation of Television and Radio Artists
5757 Wilshire Blvd
7th Floor
Los Angeles, CA 90036

323-954-1600
855-724-2387
sagaftrainfo@sagaftra.org; www.sagaftra.org
Social Media: Facebook, Twitter, Instagram, YouTube, RSS

David White, National Executive Director
Mathis Dunn, Associate Executive Director
Duncan Crabtree-Ireland, Chief Operating Officer
Mary Cavallaro, Chief Broadcast Officer
Pam Greenwalt, Chief Communications & Marketing

Formerly the American Federation of Television and Radio Artists. Represents performers ranging from announcers, dances, journalists, recording artists, stunt performers, to actors, singers, and other media professionals.
Founded in: 1952

3601 Society of Broadcast Engineers
9102 N Meridian St
Suite 150
Indianapolis, IN 46260

317-846-9000; *Fax:* 317-846-9120
mclappe@sbe.org; www.sbe.org
Social Media: Facebook, Twitter, LinkedIn, YouTube

Jerry Massey, President
James E Leifer, VP
Ted Hand, Secretary
Andrea Cummins, Treasurer
Tim Anderson, Director

SBE provides members with the opportunity to network and share ideas and information in keeping current with the ongoing changes within the industry. Members can attend annual conferences and expositions, have access to educational opportunities and obtain professional certification.
5500 Members
Founded in: 1964
Mailing list available for rent: 5700 names at $170 per M

3602 Society of Motion Picture & Television Engineers
3 Barker Ave
5th Floor
White Plains, NY 10601

914-761-1100; *Fax:* 914-761-3115;
www.smpte.org
Social Media: Facebook, Twitter, LinkedIn, YouTube, Flickr

Robert P. Seidel, President
Matthew Goldman, Executive VP
Alan Lambshead, Standards VP
Peter Wharton, Secretary/Treasurer
Paul Michael Stechly, Finance VP

The Society of Motion Picture and Television Engineers (SMPTE), is the leading technical society for the motion imaging industry. SMPTE members are spread throughout 64 countries worldwide. Sustaining (institutional) Members belong to SMPTE, allowing networking and contacts to occur on a larger scale. Touching on every discipline, our members include engineers, technical directors, cameramen, editors, technicians, manufacturers, designers, educators, consultants and field users.
6000 Members
Founded in: 1916

3603 **Statenets National Association of State Radio Networks**
17911 Harwood Avenue
Homewood, IL 60430

708-799-6676
804-364-3075; *Fax:* 708-799-6698
idobrez@statenets.com; www.statenets.com
Social Media: Facebook, Twitter, LinkedIn, RSS

Tom Dobrez, Executive Director
Sharon Kitchell, Deputy Director
Angle Martin, Account Executive
Jason Price, Administrative Coordinator
Carla Litton, Controller

Works with hundreds of regional and national marketers and political campaigns solve marketing challenges.

3604 **Syndicated Network Television Association**
One Penn Plaza
Suite 5310
New York, NY 10119

212-259-3740; *Fax:* 212-259-3770;
www.snta.com

Mitch Burg, President
Jordan Harris, Director, Marketing
Hadassa Gerber, Director. Research

Communicates to advertisers, their agencies and media planners and buyers the benefits of syndication, from the wide range of programming choices to their high ratings and national reach, and the reliability and cost effectiveness of advertising in syndicated programming.

3605 **Television Bureau of Advertising**
120 Wall Street
15th Floor
New York, NY 10005-3908

212-486-1111; *Fax:* 212-935-5631
info@tvb.org; www.tvb.org

Steve Lanzano, President
Abby Auerbach, Executive VP/CMO
Brad Seitter, EVP, Business Development
Jack Poor, VP, Marketing Insights
Scott Roskowski, SVP, Business Development

Not-for-profit trade association of America's broadcast television industry. TVB provides a diverse variety of tools and resources to support its members and to help advertisers make the best use of local television.
600 Members
Founded in: 1954

3606 **Television Bureau of Canada**
160 Bloor Street East
Suite 1005
Toronto, ON M4W 1B9

416-923-8813
800-231-0051; *Fax:* 416-413-3879
tvb@tvb.ca; www.tvb.ca

Catherine MacLeod, President, CEO
Duncan Robertson, Director, Media Insights
Rhonda Lynn Bagnall, Director, Telecaster Services
Alan Dark, Chairman
Perry MacDonald, Vice Chairman

TVB markets the benefits and effectiveness of the TV medium in all its forms to advertisers and agencies. TVB collects, interprets, develops, identifies, and communicates information and data to be used.

3607 **Television Critics Association**
825 East Douglas Avenue
Witchita, KS 67202

316-268-6394; *Fax:* 316-288-6627
info@tvcritics.org; www.tvcritics.org
Social Media: Facebook, Twitter

Amber Dowling, President
Daniel Fienberg, Vice President
Sarah Rodman, Secretary
Melanie MacFarland, Treasurer
Todd VanDerWerff, Director

Represents journalists writing about television for print and online outlets.
220 Members

3608 **Television Operators Caucus**
1176 K Street NW
9th Floor
Washington, DC 20006

202-719-7090; *Fax:* 202-719-7548
info@fundraise.com
Social Media: Facebook, Twitter, Google+

Nate Drouin, Founder/CEO
Kurt Schneider, COO
Kevin Bedell, CTO

Non-profit group of memebers that support television issues and its impacts on the world today.

3609 **The Alliance for Community Media**
4248 Park Glen Road
Minneapolis, MN 55416

952-928-4643; *Fax:* 703-506-3266
info@allcommunitymedia.org;
www.allcommunitymedia.org
Social Media: Facebook, Twitter, RSS, YouTube, Flickr

Keri Stokstad, Chair
Michael Heylin, Vice Chair
Alan Bushong, Treasurer
Mike Wassenaar, President
Melissa Serres, Assistant Director

Promotes civic engagement through community medias.
1000 Members
Founded in: 1976

3610 **The Association for Maximum Service Televi sion**
4100 Wisconsin Avenue NW
PO Box 9897
Washington, DC 20016

202-966-1956; *Fax:* 202-966-9617
lmillory@mstv.org; www.mstv.org
Social Media: Twitter, RSS

Craig Dubow, CEO

MSTV has endeavored to insure that American public receive the highest quality, interference free, over-the-air local television signals. Recognized as the industry leader in broadcasting technology and spectrum policy issues.

3611 **The Broadcasters Hall of Fame**
1240 Ashford Lane, 1A
PO Box 8247
Akron, OH 44320

330-867-3779; *Fax:* 330-867-4907;
www.nab.org

C S (Doc) Williams, Founder, CEO
Henry Dunn, Chairman
Jeannette Camak, Secretary
Dollis Rogers, Assistant Secretary
Melvin L Brown, Trustee

A wealth of memorabilia from the early days of broadcasting, clippings from newspapers and magazines, taped recorded portions of early radio shows and other gems of broadcasting history.
Founded in: 1982

3612 **WGBH Educational Foundation**
One Guest Street
Boston, MA 02135

617-300-5400; www.wgbh.org
Social Media: Facebook, Twitter

Jonathan C Abbott, President/CEO
Benjamin Godley, Executive VP & COO
Vinay Mehra, CFO/VP, Finance & Administration
Susan L Kantrowitz, VP & General Counsel
Stacey Decker, CTO

Make knowledge and the creative life of the arts, sciences, and humanities available to the widest possible public
Founded in: 1836

Newsletters

3613 **American Sportscasters Association Insiders Newsletter**
American Sportscasters Association
225 Broadway
Suite 2030
New York, NY 10007-3742

212-227-8080; *Fax:* 212-571-0556
lschwa8918@aol.com;
www.americansportscastersonline.com
Social Media: Facebook, Twitter

Louis O Schwartz, CEO
Dick Enberg, Chairman Of The Board

Newsletter keeps sportscasters up to date on important issues for the profession.
24 Pages
Frequency: Quarterly
Circulation: 2500
Founded in: 1980

3614 **Bandwidth Investor**
Kagan World Media
126 Clock Tower Place
Carmel, CA 93923-8746

831-624-1536; *Fax:* 831-625-3225;
www.kagan.com

George Niesen, Editor
Harvy Carft, Marketing Manager
Tim Baskerville, CEO/President
Harvy Carft, Circulation Manager
Cost: $945.00
Frequency: Monthly
Founded in: 1969

3615 **Broadband Fixed Wireless**
Kagan World Media
126 Clock Tower Place
Carmel, CA 93923-8746

831-624-1536; *Fax:* 831-625-3225
info@kagan.com; www.kagan.com

George Niesen, Editor
Tom Johnson, Marketing Manager
Cost: $845.00
Frequency: Monthly

3616 **Broadband Systems & Design**
Gordon Publications
301 Gibraltar Drive
#650
Morris Plains, NJ 07950-3400

973-292-5100; *Fax:* 973-539-3476

Terry McCoy Jr, Publisher
Andrea Frucci, Editor

The only product tabloid serving buying influencers, engineers, corporate managers and purchasing professionals in the cable television marketplace.
Circulation: 26,400

3617 **Broadband Technology**
Kagan World Media

126 Clock Tower Place
Carmel, CA 93923-8746

831-624-1536; *Fax:* 831-625-3225
info@kagan.com; www.kagan.com

George Niesen, Editor
Tom Johnson, Marketing Manager
Cost: $1450.00
Frequency: Monthly
Founded in: 1969

3618 Broadcast Banker/Broker
Kagan World Media
126 Clock Tower Place
Carmel, CA 93923-8746

831-624-1536
800-307-2529; *Fax:* 831-625-3225
info@kagan.com; www.kagan.com

George Niesen, Editor
Tom Johnson, Marketing Manager

A readers guide to equity deals and debt financing for radio and TV Station buying and selling analyzed. Key details on station trades with critical yardsticks of value. Three month trial is available.
Cost: $925.00
Frequency: Monthly
Founded in: 1969

3619 Broadcast Investor
Kagan World Media
1 Lower Ragsdale Drive
Building One, Suite 130
Monterey, CA 93940-5749

831-624-1536
800-307-2529; *Fax:* 831-625-3225
info@kagan.com; www.kagan.com/

Tim Baskerville, President
Tom Johnson, Marketing Manager

The newsletter on investments in radio and TV stations and publicly held companies. Comprehensive analysis of cash flow multiples and trends that impact value. Three month trial available.
Cost: $1295.00
Frequency: Monthly
Founded in: 1969

3620 Broadcast Stats
Kagan World Media
126 Clock Tower Place
Carmel, CA 93923-8746

831-624-1536
800-307-2529; *Fax:* 831-624-5882
info@kagan.com; www.kagan.com

George Niesen, Editor
Tom Johnson, Marketing Manager

The numbers behind the broadcast companies. Exclusive data, analysis and projections of radio and TV market billings, revenues, and cash flows, plus complete data on the buy-sell market. The industry's key reference source. Three month trial available.
Cost: $795.00
Frequency: Monthly
Founded in: 1969

3621 Business Radio
Nt'l Association of Business & Educational Radio
500 Montgomery Street
Alexandria, VA 22314

703-548-1500; *Fax:* 703-836-1608

AE Goetz, Publisher

Association news for professionals, owners and consumers regarding radio stations.
Cost: $65.00
Circulation: 3,000

3622 Cable Program Investor
Kagan World Media
1 Lower Ragsdale Dr
Building One, Suite 130
Monterey, CA 93940-5749

831-624-1536
800-307-2529; *Fax:* 831-625-3225
info@kagan.com; www.kagan.com/

Tim Baskerville, President
Tom Johnson, Marketing Manager
Robin Flynn, Senior VP
Sharon Armbrust, Senior Consultant
Derek Baine, Senior Vice President

Covers the economics of basic cable programming networks. Numbers, perspective unavailable from any other source. Programmers applaud its accuracy. Three month trial available.
Cost: $1045.00
Frequency: Monthly
Founded in: 1969

3623 Cable TV Advertising
Kagan World Media
126 Clock Tower Place
Carmel, CA 93923-8746

831-624-1536; *Fax:* 831-624-5882
info@kagan.com; www.kagan.com

George Niesen, Editor
Tom Johnson, Marketing Manager

Analysis of sales of commercial time by cable TV networks, interconnects and local systems. Detailed reports on national and local spot sales. Case studies and projections, all about the industry's upside. Three month trial available.
Cost: $795.00
Frequency: Monthly

3624 Cable TV Finance
Kagan World Media
126 Clock Tower Place
Carmel, CA 93923-8746

831-624-1536
800-307-2529; *Fax:* 831-624-5882
info@kagan.com; www.kagan.com

George Niesen, Editor
Tom Johnson, Marketing Manager
Larry Gerbrandt, CEO/President
Judy Pinney, Circulation Manager
Tim Baskerville, Publisher

Cable's financial bible. Analyzes sources of funding for cable TV. Selling and buying of cable systems. Financing strategies and trends. Exclusive surveys of capital sources. Three month trial available.
Cost: $795.00
Frequency: Monthly
Founded in: 1969

3625 Cable TV Investor
Kagan World Media
1 Lower Ragsdale Dr
Building One, Suite 130
Monterey, CA 93940-5749

831-624-1536
800-307-2529; *Fax:* 831-625-3225
info@kagan.com; www.kagan.com

Tim Baskerville, President
Tom Johnson, Marketing Manager

Readers road map to cable stock trends. Chart service tracking stock price movements of 37 publicly held cable TV companies. Each graph shows two years of stock price activity. Three month trial available.
Cost: $1295.00
Frequency: Monthly
Founded in: 1969

3626 Cable TV Law Reporter
Kagan World Media
1 Lower Ragsdale Dr
Building One, Suite 130
Monterey, CA 93940-5749

831-624-1536
800-307-2529; *Fax:* 831-625-3225
info@kagan.com; www.kagan.com

Tim Baskerville, President
Tom Johnson, Marketing Manager

The quintessential library of cable court cases, arbitrations, legal precedents. Labeled and catalogued for easy reference. Required reading for attorneys, government regulators and top executives. Three month trial available.
Cost: $995.00
Frequency: Monthly
Founded in: 1969

3627 Cable TV Technology
Kagan World Media
1 Lower Ragsdale Dr
Building One, Suite 130
Monterey, CA 93940-5749

831-624-1536
800-307-2529; *Fax:* 831-625-3225
info@kagan.com; www.kagan.com

Tim Baskerville, President
Tom Johnson, Marketing Manager

Incisive, thorough reports on technical advances in cable TV, in terms operating executives can grasp and use to implement strategies. Analyzes growth in addressable converters, high definition TV, fiber optics and other advancements. Three month trial available.
Cost: $925.00
Frequency: Monthly
Founded in: 1969

3628 Community Radio News
National Federation of Community Broadcasting
1970 Broadway
Suite 1000
Oakland, CA 94612

510-451-8200; *Fax:* 510-451-8208
comments@nfcb.org; www.nfcb.org
Social Media: Facebook, Twitter

Ryan Bruce, Publications Manager

Contains calendar of events and information on public broadcasting, job listings, and legislative and regulatory updates. Annual Community Radio Conference and Community Radio Program Awards Competition.
Cost: $75.00
12-16 Pages
Frequency: Monthly
Circulation: 400
Founded in: 1975
Mailing list available for rent: 300 names at $25 per M
Printed in one color on matte stock

3629 Community Television Review
National Federation of Local Cable Programmers
666 11th Street NW
Suite 806
Washington, DC 20001

202-393-2650; *Fax:* 202-393-2653

Andrew Lewis, Publisher

Issues of importance to community programming on cable and other areas of telecommunications.
Cost: $15.00
36 Pages

3630 DBS Report
Kagan World Media

1 Lower Ragsdale Dr
Building One, Suite 130
Monterey, CA 93940-5749

831-624-1536
800-307-2529; *Fax:* 831-625-3225
info@kagan.com; www.kagan.com

Tim Baskerville, President
Tom Johnson, Marketing Manager
Cost: $1045.00
Frequency: Monthly
Founded in: 1969

3631 **Dance on Camera Journal**
Dance Films Association
48 W 21st St
Suite 907
New York, NY 10010-6989

212-727-0764; *Fax:* 212-727-0764
christy@dancefilms.org; www.dancefilms.org

Deidra Towers, Executive Director
Louise Spain, President

The only service organization in the world dedicated to both the dance and the film community.
ISSN: 1098-8084
Founded in: 1956
Printed in on matte stock

3632 **Digital Television**
Kagan World Media
126 Clock Tower Place
Carmel, CA 93923-8746

831-624-1536
800-307-2529; *Fax:* 831-624-5882
info@kagan.com; www.kagan.com

George Niesen, Editor
Tom Johnson, Marketing Manager

News of the Digital Television. Three month trial available.
Cost: $945.00
Frequency: Monthly
Founded in: 1969

3633 **Hearsay**
Association of Radio Reading Services
600 Forbes Ave
Pittsburgh, PA 15219-3002

412-488-3944; *Fax:* 412-488-3953;
www.readingservice.org
Social Media: Facebook, Twitter

Andy Ai, President
Erica Hacker, Vice President

Newsletter for the Radio Reading industry.

3634 **Inside Sports Letter**
American Sportscasters Association
225 Broadway
Suite 2030
New York, NY 10007-3742

212-227-8080; *Fax:* 212-571-0556
lschwa8918@aol.com;
www.americansportscastersonline.com
Social Media: Facebook

Louis O Schwartz, President/Editor
Dick Enberg, Chairman
Elaine Graifer, Associate Editor
Patrick Turturro, Assistant Editor

A quarterly newsletter published by the American Sportscasters Association.
38513 Pages
Frequency: Quarterly
Circulation: 2000
Founded in: 1980

3635 **Interactive Mobile Investor**
Kagan World Media
1 Lower Ragsdale Dr
Building One, Suite 130
Monterey, CA 93940-5749

831-624-1536
800-307-2529; *Fax:* 831-625-3225
info@kagan.com; www.kagan.com

Tim Baskerville, President
Tom Johnson, Marketing Manager
Cost: $945.00
Frequency: Monthly
Founded in: 1969

3636 **Interactive TV Investor**
Kagan World Media
1 Lower Ragsdale Dr
Building One, Suite 130
Monterey, CA 93940-5749

831-624-1536; *Fax:* 831-625-3225
info@kagan.com; www.kagan.com

Tim Baskerville, President
Tom Johnson, Marketing Manager
Cost: $895.00
Frequency: Monthly
Founded in: 1970

3637 **Interactive Television**
Kagan World Media
1 Lower Ragsdale Dr
Building One Suite 130
Monterey, CA 93940-5749

831-624-1536
800-307-2529; *Fax:* 831-625-3225
info@kagan.com; www.kagan.com

Tim Baskerville, President
Tom Johnson, Marketing Manager

News of the Interactive Television. Three month trial available.
Cost: $795.00
Frequency: Monthly
Founded in: 1969

3638 **Internet Media Investor**
Kagan World Media
126 Clock Tower Place
Carmel, CA 93923-8746

831-624-1536; *Fax:* 831-625-3225
info@kagan.com; www.kagan.com

George Niesen, Editor
Tom Johnson, Marketing Manager
Cost: $945.00
Frequency: Monthly
Founded in: 1969

3639 **Interval**
Society of Cable Telecommunications Engineers
140 Philips Road
Exton, PA 19341-1318

610-363-6888
800-542-5040; *Fax:* 610-363-5898
scte@scte.org; www.scte.org

Howard Whitman, Senior Editor
Marci Dodd, President

A monthly member newsletter. Subscription price of $25.00 is for non-members.
Cost: $25.00
Frequency: Monthly
Circulation: 16000
Founded in: 1969

3640 **Kagan Broadband**
Kagan World Media
1 Lower Ragsdale Dr
Building One, Suite 130
Monterey, CA 93940-5749

831-624-1536
800-307-2529; *Fax:* 831-625-3225
info@kagan.com; www.kagan.com

Tim Baskerville, President/CEO
Harvy Craft, Marketing Manager
Robert Nayoor, Circulation Manager
Sandie Borthwick, Executive Director

Daily e-mail or fax.
Cost: $1295.00
Frequency: Monthly
Founded in: 1970

3641 **Kagan Media Money**
Kagan World Media
1 Lower Ragsdale Dr
Building One, Suite 130
Monterey, CA 93940-5749

831-624-1536
800- 30- 252; *Fax:* 831-625-3225
info@kagan.com; www.kagan.com

Tim Baskerville, President
Tom Johnson, Marketing Manager
Sandie Borthwick, Executive Director

Analysts dissect deals, anticipate trends, project revenues, track financings, and value the debt and equity of hundreds of priovately held and publicly traded advertising, broadcasting, cable TV digital TV, home video, Internet media, motion picture, newspaper, pay TV, professional sports and wireless telecommunications companies in the US and abroad.
Cost: $1245.00
Founded in: 1970

3642 **Kagan Music Investor**
Kagan World Media
1 Lower Ragsdale Dr
Building One,Suite 130
Monterey, CA 93940-5749

831-624-1536
800-307-2529; *Fax:* 831-625-3225
info@kagan.com; www.kagan.com

Tim Baskerville, President
Tom Johnson, Marketing Manager
Sandie Borthwick, Executive Director

News and analysis of the music industry for investors.
Cost: $945.00
Frequency: Monthly
Founded in: 1969

3643 **Marketing New Media**
Kagan World Media
1 Lower Ragsdale Dr
Building One, Suite 130
Monterey, CA 93940-5749

831-624-1536
800-307-2529; *Fax:* 831-625-3225
info@kagan.com; www.kagan.com

Tim Baskerville, President
Tom Johnson, Marketing Manager

News of the Marketing New Media. Three month trial available.
Cost: $795.00
Frequency: Monthly
Founded in: 1969

3644 **Media Communications Association News**
Media Communications Association International

P.O.Box 5135
Madison, WI 53705-0135

608-836-0722; *Fax:* 888-899-6224
loiswei@aol.com; www.mca-i.org
Social Media: Facebook, Twitter, LinkedIn

Gary Shifflet, President
Lois Weiland, Executive Director
Mike Brown, Treasurer
Jim Powell, Secretary
John Coleman, Board Member

Coverage of the multimedia industry and association activities.
Frequency: Quarterly
Circulation: 3,000
Founded in: 1968
Printed in on glossy stock

3645 Media Mergers & Acquisitions
Kagan World Media
126 Clock Tower Place
Carmel, CA 93923-8746

831-624-1536; *Fax:* 831-624-5882
info@kagan.com; www.kagan.com

George Niesen, Editor
Tom Johnson, Marketing Manager

Where it all comes together. Exclusive scorecard of deals done by media companies. Dollar amounts, multiples paid, trends captured in succinct summaries of complex transactions. Three month trial available.
Cost: $795.00
Frequency: Monthly

3646 Media Sports Business
Kagan World Media
1 Lower Ragsdale Dr
Building One, Suite 130
Monterey, CA 93940-5749

831-624-1536
800-307-2529; *Fax:* 831-625-3225
info@kagan.com; www.kagan.com

Tim Baskerville, President
Tom Johnson, Marketing Manager
Cost: $945.00
Frequency: Monthly
Founded in: 1969

3647 Monitoring Times
Grove Enterprises
7540 Highway 64 W
Brasstown, NC 28902-8079

828-837-9200
800-438-8155; *Fax:* 828-837-2216
order@grove-ent.com; www.grove-ent.com

Bob Grove, President
Judy Grove, Office Manager
Belinda McDonald, Office Manager

News on radio communication, scanner monitoring, international radio broadcasts and technical advice.
Cost: $28.95
92 Pages
Frequency: Monthly
Circulation: 50000
ISSN: 0889-5341
Founded in: 1970
Printed in 4 colors on glossy stock

3648 Motion Picture Investor
Kagan World Media
1 Lower Ragsdale Dr
Building One Suite 130
Monterey, CA 93940-5749

831-624-1536; *Fax:* 831-625-3225
info@kagan.com; www.kagan.com

Tim Baskerville, President
Tom Johnson, Marketing Manager
Cost: $845.00
Frequency: Monthly
Founded in: 1969

3649 Multichannel News
360 Park Ave S
New York, NY 10010-1710

212-887-8387; *Fax:* 212-463-6703;
www.multichannel.com

Lawrence Oliver, Publisher
Marianne Paskowski, Editorial Director
Kent Gibbons, Editor
Heather Tatrow, Production Manager
Michael Demenchuk, Managing Editor

News of the electronic media industries.
Frequency: Weekly
Circulation: 18,875
Founded in: 1980

3650 NRB Today
National Religious Broadcasters
9510 Technology Dr
Manassas, VA 20110-4149

703-330-7100; *Fax:* 703-330-7100
info@nrb.org; www.nrb.org
Social Media: Facebook

Frank Wright, President/CEO
Linda Smith, EVP/COO
Kenneth Chan, Director of Communications

This weekly newsletter by National Religious Broadcasters covers the latest news from the association and NRB's member organizations. The newsletter also serves as a source for tips, trends, and insights relevant to Christian communicators across the spectrum. Topics include audience building, branding, business strategy, innovation, job hunting, leadership, management, marketing, social media, and web strategy. NRB Today also features occasional columns, movie reviews, and product reviews.
Founded in: 1944

3651 Networks
Geospatial Information & Technology Association
14456 E Evans Ave
Aurora, CO 80014-1409

303-337-0513; *Fax:* 303-337-1001
bsamborski@gita.org; www.gita.org

Bob Samborski, Executive Director
Lisa Connor, Membership Services Manager
Elizabeth Roberts, Marketing

A bi-monthly newsletter published by the Geospatial Information & Technology Association.
Cost: $125.00
28 Pages
Frequency: Monthly
Circulation: 2200
Founded in: 1978

3652 Pay TV Newsletter
Kagan World Media
126 Clock Tower Place
Carmel, CA 93923-8746

831-624-1536; *Fax:* 831-624-5882
info@kagan.com; www.kagan.com

George Niesen, Editor
Tom Johnson, Marketing Manager

The pay TV industry's publication of record since 1973. Exclusive estimates of network subscribers and economics. The pay-per-view business, event-by-event, film-by-film. Three month trial available.
Cost: $795.00
Frequency: Monthly

3653 Public Broadcasting Report
Warren Communications News
2115 Ward Ct Nw
Washington, DC 20037-1209

202-872-9200
800-771-9202; *Fax:* 202-318-8350
info@warren-news.com;
www.warren-news.com

Brig Easley, Manager
Daniel Warren, President/Editor

Industry news, personnel announcements and calendar listings for public broadcasting, digital TV, congress, FCC, and allied friends.
Cost: $575.00
Founded in: 1945
Mailing list available for rent

3654 Radio & Records
Radio & Records
10100 Santa Monica Boulevard
3rd Floor
Los Angeles, CA 90067-4003

310-553-4330; *Fax:* 310-203-8450
radioandrecords@billboard.biz;
www.radioandrecords.com

Erica Farber, Publisher/CEO
Henry Mowry, Director Sales

A music newspaper that covers all aspects of the radio and recording industry.
Cost: $325.00
100 Pages
Frequency: Weekly
Circulation: 8006
Printed in 4 colors on n stock

3655 Radio Business Report
2050 Old Bridge Rd
Suite B-01
Woodbridge, VA 22192-2481

703-492-8191; *Fax:* 703-997-8601;
www.rbr.com

Jim Carnegie, Publisher
Jack Messmer, Executive Editor
Cathy Carnegie, VP Administration
Carl Marcucci, MD/Senior Editor
June Barnes, Sales

Focuses on radio business issues, inside news on people and controversial topics.
Cost: $220.00
Frequency: Daily
Circulation: 5100
Founded in: 1983
Printed in 4 colors on matte stock

3656 Radio Ink
Streamline Publishing
224 Datura St
Suite 1015
West Palm Beach, FL 33401-5638

561-655-8778
800-610-5771; *Fax:* 561-655-6164;
www.radioink.com

Eric Rhoads, Owner
Reed Bunzel, Editor
Marty Sacks, Marketing
Tom Elmo, Circulation

Geared toward radio broadcast management professionals contains information on marketing trends, special reports, sales and programming issues.
Cost: $199.00
Circulation: 5000
Founded in: 1992

3657 Radio World
Industrial Marketing Advisory Services
5827 Columbia Pike
Suite 310
Falls Church, VA 22041-2027

703-998-7600
800-336-3045; *Fax:* 703-998-2966;
www.totse.com

Steve Dana, President/Publisher
Lucia Cobo, Editor

A technical trade newspaper for the broadcast radio industry. Accepts advertising.
48 Pages
Circulation: 18000
Founded in: 1978
Printed in 4 colors on newsprint stock

3658 **Streaming Media Investor**
Kagan World Media
126 Clock Tower Place
Carmel, CA 93923-8746
831-624-1536; *Fax:* 831-624-5882
info@kagan.com; www.kagan.com
George Niesen, Editor
Harvy Craft, Marketing Manager
Tim Baskerville, CEO/President
News of the Streaming Media Investor. Three month trial available.
Cost: $895.00
Frequency: Monthly
Founded in: 1969

3659 **TV Program Investor**
Kagan World Media
1 Lower Ragsdale Dr
Building One, Suite 130
Monterey, CA 93940-5749
831-624-1536
800-307-2529; *Fax:* 831-625-3225
info@kagan.com; www.kagan.com
Tim Baskerville, President
Tom Johnson, Marketing Manager
More than just a newsletter, practically a seminar on how much programs cost and what they are worth. Exclusive spreadsheets with estimates of what goes between the commercials. Three month trial available.
Cost: $895.00
Frequency: Monthly
Founded in: 1969

3660 **Television Digest with Consumer Electronics**
Warren Communications News
2115 Ward Ct Nw
Washington, DC 20037-1209
202-872-9200
800-771-9202; *Fax:* 202-318-8350
info@warren-news.com;
www.warren-news.com
Brig Easley, Manager
Daniel Warren, President/Editor
A weekly newsletter providing continuous coverage of broadcasting, cable, consumer electronics and related industries.
Cost: $943.00
12 Pages
Frequency: Weekly
Mailing list available for rent

3661 **The Signal**
Society of Broadcast Engineers
9102 N Meridian St
Suite 150
Indianapolis, IN 46260-1896
317-846-9000; *Fax:* 317-846-9120
mclappe@sbe.org; www.sbe.org
Social Media: Facebook, Twitter, LinkedIn
John Poray, Executive Director
Vincent A Lopez, President
Provides members with timely articles on various broadcast-related topics, information on upcoming events, recognition of members' activities and achievements and details of SBE services.
Frequency: Bi-Monthly
Circulation: 5500
Mailing list available for rent: 4700 names at $100 per M
Printed in 4 colors on glossy stock

3662 **Video Investor**
Kagan World Media
126 Clock Tower Place
Carmel, CA 93923-8746
831-624-1536; *Fax:* 831-624-5882
info@kagan.com; www.kagan.com
George Niesen, Editor
Harvy Craft, Marketing Manager
Tim Baskerville, CEO/President
Authoritative look inside the business of renting and selling video cassettes. Exclusive estimates of retail and wholesale transactions and inventories. Tracking movies into the home. Three month trial is available.
Cost: $ 795.00
Frequency: Monthly
Founded in: 1969

3663 **Warren Communications News**
Warren
2115 Ward Ct Nw
Washington, DC 20037-1209
202-872-9200
800-771-9202; *Fax:* 202-318-8350
info@warren-news.com;
www.warren-news.com
Social Media: Facebook, Twitter, LinkedIn
Brig Easley, Manager
Daniel Warren, President/Editor
Commercial and noncommercial television stations and networks, including educational, low-power and instructional TV stations, and translators. Lists over 11,000 operating cable systems including subscribers, channel capacities, programming, fees and personnel.
Cost: $6.45
Mailing list available for rent

3664 **Wireless Market Stats**
Kagan World Media
1 Lower Ragsdale Dr
Building One, Suite 130
Monterey, CA 93940-5749
831-624-1536
800-307-2529; *Fax:* 831-625-3225
info@kagan.com; www.kagan.com
Tim Baskerville, President
Tom Johnson, Marketing Manager
News of the Wireless Market Stats. Three month trial available.
Cost: $995.00
Frequency: Monthly
Founded in: 1969

3665 **Wireless Telecom Investor**
Kagan World Media
1 Lower Ragsdale Dr
Building One, Suite 130
Monterey, CA 93940-5749
831-624-1536
800-307-2529; *Fax:* 831-625-3225
info@kagan.com; www.kagan.com
Tim Baskerville, President
Tom Johnson, Marketing Manager
Exclusive analysis of private and public values of wireless telecommunications companies, including cellular telephone, ESMR and PCS. Exclusive databases of subscribers, market penetrations, market potential, industry growth. Catching super-fast growth in a capsule. Three month trial available.
Cost: $895.00
Frequency: Monthly
Founded in: 1969

3666 **Wireless/Private Cable Investor**
Kagan World Media
1 Lower Ragsdale Dr
Building One, Suite 130
Monterey, CA 93940-5749
831-624-1536
800-307-2529; *Fax:* 831-625-3225
info@kagan.com; www.kagan.com/
Tim Baskerville, President
Tom Johnson, Marketing Manager
The original bible of the wireless cable, multipoint distribution pay TV industry. Published continuously since 1972, this newsletter is the window on cable competition. Three month trial available.
Cost: $1095.00
Frequency: Monthly
Founded in: 1969

Magazines & Journals

3667 **ARRL The National Association for Amateur Radio**
American Radio Relay League
225 Main St
Newington, CT 06111-1494
860-594-0200
800-326-3942; *Fax:* 860-594-0259
hq@arrl.org; www.arrl.org
David Sumner, CEO
Kay Craigie, President
Bob Inderbitzen, Marketing Manager
Devoted to amateur radio information.
156M Members
Frequency: Monthly
Circulation: 146000
Founded in: 1914

3668 **Album Network**
110 Spazier
Burbank, CA 91502-1852
818-842-2600; *Fax:* 818-972-2899;
www.musicbiz.com
Steve Smith, Publisher
Editorial emphasis on chart ratings, sales performances, music reviews, and industry news.
Cost: $400.00
Frequency: Weekly
Circulation: 2,500

3669 **Alliance for Community Media**
1100 G St NW
Suite 740
Washington, DC 20005-7415
202-393-2650; *Fax:* 202-393-2653
info@allcommunitymedia.org;
www.alliancecm.org
Hellen Soule, Executive Director
Denise M Woodson, Treasurer
Todd Thayer, Treasurer
Participants include cable access television and community programmers. Individual membership dues are $60.00, organization $305.00.
Cost: $35.00
36 Pages
Frequency: Quarterly
Circulation: 1500
ISSN: 1074-9004
Founded in: 1985

3670 **Almanac**
International Council of NATAS

888 7th Avenue
5th floor
New York, NY 10019-3300

212-489-6969; *Fax:* 212-489-6557;
www.iemmys.tv/

Camille Bide Roizen, Executive Director
Eva Obadia, Marketing Manager
Georges Leclere, Senior VP

An annual publication with highlights of the International Emmy Program, global preference guides, articles on various facets in and around television today.
Founded in: 1969

3671 BE Radio
Primedia
98 Metcalf Avenue
PO Box 12901
Shawnee Mission, KS 66282-2901

913-341-1300
800-441-0294; *Fax:* 913-514-6895
CorporateCustomerService@penton.com;
www.penton.com

Eric Jacobson, Senior VP
Chriss Scherer, Editor
Kirby Asplund, Marketing Director

Provides radio station managers and engineers the information they need to make critical equipment purchase decisions. Presents need-to-know technical information to help readers solve the challenges of technology and the equipment problems they face. BE Radio serves the needs of radio engineers, managers and owners who need to make informed equipment and services buying decisions.
Cost: $30.00
Frequency: Monthly
Circulation: 12000
Founded in: 1959

3672 Broadband Advertising
Kagan World Media
1 Lower Ragsdale Dr
Building One, Suite 130
Monterey, CA 93940-5749

831-624-1536
800-307-2529; *Fax:* 831-625-3225
sgoldberg@snl.com; www.kagan.com

Tim Baskerville, President

Reports and analysis of the sale of commercial time by cable TV networks, interconnects and local spot sales.
Cost: $1095.00
Frequency: Monthly
Founded in: 1969
Printed in 2 colors on n stock

3673 Broadcast Engineering
Primedia
PO Box 12914
Overland Park, KS 66282-2914

913-341-1300
800-441-0294; *Fax:* 913-967-1903
emily.kalmus@penton.com;
www.broadcastengineering.com
Social Media: Facebook, Twitter, LinkedIn

Brad Dick, Editor

Aimed at the market that includes corporate management, engineers/technicians and other management personnel at commercial and public TV stations, post-production and recording studios, broadcast networks, cable, telephone and satellite production centers and networks.
Circulation: 35000
Founded in: 1960

3674 Broadcasting
Reed Business Information
2000 Clearwater Dr
Oak Brook, IL 60523-8809

630-574-0825
800-446-6551; *Fax:* 630-288-8781
webmaster@reedbusiness.com;
www.reedbusiness.com

Jeff Greisch, President
Larry Dunn, Publishing Director
Jim Casella, CEO

Offers comprehensive coverage of television, radio, cable, satellite and the attendant equipment and emerging technologies. Accepts advertising.
Cost: $189.00
Founded in: 1894

3675 CQ Amateur Radio
CQ Communications
25 Newbridge Rd
Suite 405
Hicksville, NY 11801-2887

516-681-2922; *Fax:* 516-681-2926
cq@cq-amateur-radio.com
http://www.cq-amateur-radio.com

Richard Ross, CEO
Rich Moseson, Managing Editor
Gail Sheehan, Managing Editor
Mellisa Gillgan, Circulation

Information for people interested in the developments of in the field radio communications and electronics. Coverage includes reviews of new operating programs, new products and seasonal promotional ideas.
Cost: $32.00
Frequency: Monthly
Circulation: 87000
Founded in: 1950

3676 CTAM Quarterly Marketing Journal
Cable Television Administration & Marketing
201 N Union Street
Suite 440
Alexandria, VA 22314-2642

703-549-4200; *Fax:* 703-684-1167
info@ctam.com; www.ctam.com/

Char Beales, President
Patrick Dougherty, Marketing Manager

A journal offering financial information to persons in the cable television management and executives.
Cost: $295.00
Frequency: Quarterly

3677 Cable Plus/Cable TV Publications
Cable TV Publications/TV Host
PO Box 1665
Harrisburg, PA 17105-1665

800-922-4678; *Fax:* 610-687-2965

Frank Dillahey, Sales Manager
Bob Newell, Marketing Director

Custom cable TV listing guides incorporating exclusive cable programming, editorial, movie reviews and TV listings that are sold to cable subscribers nationally. Circulation of this guide is over 1.75 million.
Cost: $24.00
Frequency: Monthly

3678 Communicator
Radio Television News Directors Association
1025 Thomas Jefferson St
7th Floor, Suite 700E
Washington, DC 20007-5214

202-625-3500
800-807-8632; *Fax:* 202-223-4007
barbarac@rtnda.org; www.rtnda.org
Social Media: Facebook

The latest information on technological breakthroughs, cutting edge newsroom practices, and contemporary management techniques.
Cost: $75.00
Frequency: 11x/yr
Circulation: 4,000

3679 DV Digital Video Magazine
Miller Freeman Publications
PO Box 1212
Skokie, IL 60076

888-776-7002
888-776-7002; *Fax:* 847-763-9614
dv@halldata.com;
www.magazineline.com/digital-video-magazin
e

Dominic Milano, Editorial Director
Armand DerHacobian, Associate Publisher
Jarett Cory, Sales Manager

Video production, animation and audio film, broadcast and new media. Includes discussions on training and communications.
Frequency: Monthly
Circulation: 64382
Founded in: 1993

3680 Digital TV/Television Broadcast
United Entertainment Media
810 7th Avenue
27th Fl
New York, NY 10019

212-378-0400; *Fax:* 212-378-2160
sedorusa@optonline.net;
www.governmentvideo.com
Social Media: Facebook

Gary Rhodes, International Sales Manager

Digital TV/Television Broadcast is an in depth analysis and insider views of the business of television. It discusses the individuals, market trends, technology, products and policies that drive the television industry in the digital age.
Frequency: Monthly
Circulation: 22000
Founded in: 1978
Mailing list available for rent

3681 EQ Magazine
Miller Freeman Publications
810 7th Ave
27th Fl, Suite 4
New York, NY 10019-5818

212-636-2700; *Fax:* 212-636-2750
sedorusa@optonline.net;
www.governmentvideo.com
Social Media: Facebook

Gary Rhodes, International Sales Manager

Articles on recording techniques and tips for musicians, producers, and engineers in the broadcast industry.
Frequency: Monthly
Circulation: 40000
Mailing list available for rent

3682 Emmy Magazine
Academy of Television Arts & Sciences
5200 Lankershim Blvd
North Hollywood, CA 91601-3155

818-754-2800
818-754-2860; *Fax:* 818-761-2827
emmymag@emmys.org; www.emmys.com/

John Shaffner, CEO
Laurel Whitcomb, VP Marketing
Barbara Chase, Director Membership
Juan Morales, Editor
Gail Polevoi, Manager

This magazine tells of association news, EMMY information and awards for the broadcasting and media industries.
Cost: $28.00
Founded in: 1995

3683 FTTX
Information Gatekeepers

1340 Soldiers Field Rd
Suite 302
Brighton, MA 02135-1000

617-782-5033
800-323-1088; *Fax:* 617-782-5735
info@igigroup.com; www.igigroup.com

Paul Polishuk, CEO
Beverly Wilson, Controller
Yesim Taskor, Controller
Brian Mark, Editor

Covers developments, products, competition, technology, and standards for the use of fiber optics and related techniques in the cable TV industry.
Cost: $695.00
Frequency: Monthly
Circulation: 2000
Founded in: 1977

3684 **Financial Manager**
Broadcast Cable Financial Management Association
550 W Frontage Rd
Suite 3600
Northfield, IL 60093-1243

847-716-7000; *Fax:* 847-784-8059
info@bccacredit.com; www.bcfm.com

Mary Collins, President
Jamie Smith, Director of Operations
Rachelle Brooks, BCCA Sales

A bi-monthly magazine published by the Broadcast Cable Financial Management Association.
Cost: $69.00
36 Pages
Frequency: 6 issues per ye
Circulation: 2000
Mailing list available for rent: 1100 names at $495 per M

3685 **Folio**
Pacifica Foundation
1925 Martin Luther King Jr Way
Berkeley, CA 94704-1037

510-849-2590; *Fax:* 510-849-2617
contact@pacifica.org;
www.pacificafoundation.org

Lonnie Hicks, Manager
Dan Coughlin, Executive Director

Listing of programs heard on Pacific Radio Stations.
Cost: $40.00
28 Pages
Frequency: Monthly
Founded in: 1949

3686 **GBH: Member's Magazine**
WGBH Educational Foundation
PO Box 55875
Boston, MA 02205-5875

617-300-5400; *Fax:* 617-300-1026
feedback@wgbh.org; www.wgbh.org

Diane Dion, Editor
Jon Abbott, Owner
Mary Cotton, Owner

Offers information on station programming, personalities and more for members of WGBH, Boston's PBS and NPR station.
Cost: $50.00
Frequency: Monthly
Circulation: 175000
Founded in: 1951

3687 **Hits Magazine**
Color West
3405 Pacific Avenue
Burbank, CA 91505

818-840-8881; *Fax:* 818-840-2753;
www.colorwestprinting.com

Dennis Lavinthal, Publisher
Lynn Jensen, President
Karen Jensen, Controller

Chartmakers and hits in contemporary pop music, industry news and happenings, also includes radio news and playlists.
Cost: $300.00
Frequency: Weekly
Circulation: 10000
Founded in: 1971

3688 **Inside Radio**
Inside Radio
365 Union St
Littleton, NH 03561-5619

603-444-5720
800-248-4242; *Fax:* 603-444-2872
info@insideradio.com; www.insideradio.com

Cathy Devine, Research Director
Kelli Grisez, Operations Manager

Features issues that effect the radio industry and individuals involved in it.
Cost: $455.00
Frequency: Daily
Circulation: 7000

3689 **International Cable**
Phillips Business Information
1201 Seven Locks Road
Potomac, MD 20854-2931

301-354-1400; *Fax:* 301-340-0542;
www.phillips.com

Nancy Umberger-Maynard, Publisher

Articles on technological advances internationally and the businesses that are making it possible.
Cost: $73.75
Frequency: Monthly
Circulation: 11,000

3690 **Journal of Broadcasting and Electronic Media**
Broadcast Education Association
1771 N St NW
Washington, DC 20036-2800

202-429-5355
888-380-7222; *Fax:* 301-869-8608
Don.Godfrey@asu.edu; www.beaweb.org

Heather Birks, Executive Director
Steven D Anderson, President
Donald G Godfrey, Editor
Cost: $50.00
Frequency: Quarterly
ISSN: 0883-8151
Founded in: 1955
Printed in one color on matte stock

3691 **Journal of College Radio**
Intercollegiate Broadcasting System
367 Windsor Highway
New Windsor, NY 12553-7900

845-534-0003; *Fax:* 845-565-7446
IBSHQ@aol.com; www.collegeradio.tv/

Norman Prusslin, President
Jeff Tellis, VP

Magazine of the nonprofit association of student staffed radio stations based at schools and colleges across the country. Accepts advertising.
Cost: $20.00
24 Pages
Frequency: Quarterly
Founded in: 1940

3692 **Journal of Radio & Audio Media**
Broadcast Education Association
1771 N St NW
Washington, DC 20036-2800

202-429-5355; *Fax:* 202-775-2981;
www.beaweb.org

Heather Birks, Executive Director
Traci Bailey, Manager, Business Operations
Phylis Johnson, Editor
Mary Schaffer, President
Cost: $30.00
Frequency: Bi-annually
Founded in: 1955

3693 **Journal of the Audio Engineering Society**
Audio Engineering Society
60 E 42nd Street
Room 2520
New York, NY 10165-2520

212-661-8528; *Fax:* 212-682-0477
hq@aes.org; www.aes.org
Social Media: Facebook, Twitter

Roger Furness, Executive Director
William T McQuaide, Managing Editor

The Journal contains state-of-the-art technical papers and engineering reports; feature articles covering timely topics; ore and post reports of AES conventions and society activities; news from AES sections; Standards and Education Committee work; membership news, patents, new products, and noteworthy developments. Subscriptions available in print, electronic and combination options.
Cost: $280.00
Frequency: 10/Year
Circulation: 12000
ISSN: 0004-7554
Printed in 4 colors on glossy stock

3694 **Ku-Band World Magazine**
Opportunities Publishing
305 Jackson Avenue W
Oxford, MS 38655-2154

Fax: 662-236-5541

Ed Meek, Editor

Business application of developing Ku-band satellite communications systems.
Cost: $25.00
52 Pages
Frequency: Monthly
Founded in: 1985

3695 **Millimeter Magazine**
2104 Harvell Circle
Bellevue, NE 68005

402-505-7100
866-505-7173; *Fax:* 402-293-0741
llcs@pbsub.com; www.millimeter.com

Cynthia Wisehart, Editorial Director
Gayle Grooms, Audience Marketing
Christina Heil, Marketing
Jeff Victor, Associate Editor

Authoritative resource for more than 33,000 qualified professionals in production, postproduction, animation, streaming and visual effects for motion pictures, television and commercials.
Cost: $25.00
150 Pages
Frequency: Monthly

3696 **NRB Magazine**
National Religious Broadcasters
9510 Technology Dr
Manassas, VA 20110-4149

703-330-7100; *Fax:* 703-330-7100
info@nrb.org; www.nrb.org
Social Media: Facebook, Twitter

Frank Wright, President
Linda Smith, President Assistant

Trade publication for Christian communicators, including radio, TV, Internet and international media.
Cost: $24.00
56 Pages
Frequency: Monthly
Circulation: 9000
ISSN: 1521-1754
Founded in: 1969
Printed in 4 colors on glossy stock

3697 **RPM Weekly**
Novasound Productions
PO Box 630071
Irving, TX 75063-71

972-432-8100; *Fax:* 972-432-8102
jv@rapmag.com; www.rapmag.com

Jerry Vigil, Publisher
Shardan Azat, Manager

Information on radio stations and independent production houses, engineering and production directors that manage these studios, industry news and latest technology information.
Cost: $115.00
Frequency: Monthly
Circulation: 7500
Founded in: 1988

3698 **Radio**
1930 Century Park W
Los Angeles, CA 90067-6803

323-263-6991; *Fax:* 310-203-8450

Dwight Case, Editor

A magazine covering all aspects of the radio communications industry.
Cost: $215.00
Frequency: Monthly
Founded in: 1973

3699 **Radio Science**
American Geophysical Union
2000 Florida Ave NW
Washington, DC 20009-1231

202-462-6900
800-966-2481; *Fax:* 202-328-0566
service@agu.org; www.agu.org
Social Media: Facebook, Twitter

Fred Spilhaus, Executive Director

Coverage of radio propagation, communication, and upper atmospheric physics.
Cost: $10.00
Circulation: 1200
Founded in: 1919

3700 **Radio-TV Interview Report**
Bradley Communications
135 E Plumstead Avenue
PO Box 1206
Lansdowne, PA 19050-8206

610-591-1070; *Fax:* 610-284-3704
Circ@rtir.com; www.rtir.com

Bill Harrison, President

A source for finding authors and experts to interview about a wide variety of subjects.
88 Pages
Frequency: Monthly
Circulation: 4000
Founded in: 1986

3701 **SMPTE Motion Imaging Journal**
Society of Motion Picture & Television Engineers
3 Barker Ave
Floor 5
White Plains, NY 10601-1509

914-761-1100; *Fax:* 914-761-3115;
www.smpte.org

Barbara Lange, Executive Director

The gateway to the world of motion imaging featuring industry-leading papers and standards, the Journal keeps its members on the cutting edge of this ever-changing industry.
Cost: $140.00
Frequency: Monthly

3702 **Satellite Retailer**
Triple D Publishing
1300 S Dekalb St
Shelby, NC 28152-7210
704-482-9673; *Fax:* 704-484-6976

Douglas G Brown Sr, President

Edited for the satellite industry.
Cost: $12.00
72 Pages
Frequency: Monthly
Founded in: 1985

3703 **Satvision Magazine**
Satellite Broadcasting/Communications Association
1730 M St NW
Suite 600
Washington, DC 20036-4557

202-349-3620; *Fax:* 202-349-3621
info@sbca.org; www.sbca.com

Joseph Widoff, Executive Director

Offers information for television satellite dealers.
Cost: $35.00
Frequency: Monthly
Circulation: 10000

3704 **Teleguia USA: Novedades USA - Buscando Amor**
Echo Media
900 Circle 75 Pkwy SE
Suite 1600
Atlanta, GA 30339-6014

770-955-3346
salesinfo@echo-media.com;
www.echo-media.com

Michael Puffer, CEO
Kelly Elarbee, Media Director
Frequency: Weekly
Circulation: 100,000
Founded in: 1986
Mailing list available for rent
Printed in 4 colors on newsprint stock

3705 **Via Satellite**
Phillips Business Information
1201 Seven Locks Rd
Suite 300
Potomac, MD 20854

301-541-1400; *Fax:* 301-309-3847;
www.kftv.com/company-30086.html

Scott Chase, Publisher
Richard Summers, Managing Editor

Covers voice, video and data in global commercial communications, including company profiles, market analysis and new products.
Cost: $49.00
Frequency: Monthly
Circulation: 17446

3706 **WNYC Wavelength**
1 Centre St
Suite 2453
New York, NY 10007-1699

212-669-7800; *Fax:* 212-669-3312;
www.wnyc.org

Lori Krushefski, Marketing
Laura Walker, President

Relays broadcasting news. Accepts advertising.
16 Pages
Frequency: Monthly

3707 **Women on the Job: Careers in the Electronic Media**
American Women in Radio and Television
1760 Old Meadow Rd
Suite 800
Mc Lean, VA 22102-4306

703-506-3290; *Fax:* 703-506-3266
info@awrt.org; www.awrt.org

Maria Brennan, President

Association news focusing on women in the workplace, particularly media and communications industries.

3708 **World Screen News**
1123 Broadway
Suite 1201
New York, NY 10010-2007

212-924-7620; *Fax:* 212-924-6940
mdaswani@worldscreen.com;
www.worldscreen.com

Ricardo Duise, Manager
Anna Carugati, Managing Editor
Kristin Brzoznowski, Managing Editor
Rafael Blanco, Executive Editor
Cesar Suero, Advertising Sales Director

Serves the international television cable and satellite industries including advertising agencies within the industry and others allied to the field. Also publishes the following supplements; TV Kids, TV Europe, TV Docs, TV Latina.
Cost: $50.00
Frequency: Monthly
Circulation: 4038
Founded in: 1985

Trade Shows

3709 **AES Convention**
Audio Engineering Society
60 E 42nd Street
Room 2520
New York, NY 10165-2520

212-661-8528; *Fax:* 212-682-0477
HQ@aes.org; www.aes.org

Bob Moses, Executive Director
Roger Furness, Deputy Director
Jan Pederson, President
Frank Wells, President-Elect
Robert Breen, Vice President

An international organization that unites audio engineers, creative artists, scientists and students worldwide by promoting advances in audio and desseminating new knowledge and research.
Frequency: October

3710 **Alaska Broadcasters Association Conference**
Alaska Broadcasters Association
700 W 41st Street
Suite 102
Anchorage, AK 99503

907-258-2424; *Fax:* 907-258-2414
akba@gci.net; www.alaskabroadcaster.org
Social Media: Facebook

Gary Donovan, President
Matt Wilson, Vice President

Provides assistance which enables members to serve their communities of license through educations, representation and advocacy.
225 Attendees
Frequency: Annual

3711 **Annual Community Radio Conference**
National Federation of Community Broadcasters

1970 Broadway
Suite 1000
Oakland, CA 94612
510-451-8200; *Fax:* 510-451-8208;
www.nfcb.org
Carol Pierson, President/CEO
Virginia Z Berson, VP Federation Services
National conference for public community radio stations offering opportunities for staff development, skill building, networking, affinity group, inspiration, new ideas, discussion and exchanges; exhibit area; programming awards. Business meetings for National Federation of Community Broadcasters.
300 Attendees
Frequency: April

3712 **Annual IBS Broadcasting & Webcasting Conference**
Intercollegiate Broadcasting System
367 Windsor Highway
New Windsor, NY 12553-7900
845-565-0003; *Fax:* 845-565-7446
ibshq@aol.com; www.ibsradio.org
Norman Prusslin, President
Fritz Kass, Chief Operating Officer
Over 110 seminars, live music, over 250 top broadcasting professionals, and 1,200 student radio & webcasters from around the world. Live webstream during conference.
1.2M Attendees
Frequency: March

3713 **Audio Engineering Society Meeting**
Audio Engineering Society
60 E 42nd Street
Room 2520
New York, NY 10165-2520
212-661-8528; *Fax:* 212-682-0477;
www.aes.org
Roger K Furness, Executive Director
250 booths, held in the fall and spring of each year.
5M Attendees
Frequency: October

3714 **Broadcast Designers' Association International Conference & Expo**
Broadcast Designers' Association International
145 W 45th Street
Room 1100
New York, NY 10036-4008
212-376-6222; *Fax:* 212-376-6202
Annual show and exhibits of broadcast design equipment, supplies and services.

3715 **Broadcast Engineering Conference (BEC)**
Society of Broadcast Engineers
9102 N Meridian Street
Suite 150
Indianapolis, IN 46260
317-846-9000; *Fax:* 317-846-9120
mclappe@sbe.org; www.sbe.org
John Poray, Executive Director
Vincent A Lopez, President
Offers broadcast engineers the opportunity to attend educational sessions, see the latest equipment and supplies, and meet with peers.
500 Attendees
Frequency: Annual/Spring

3716 **CRS - Country Radio Show**
Country Radion Broadcasters
819 18th Avenue South
Nashville, TN 37203
615-327-4487; *Fax:* 615-329-4492
info@crb.org; www.crb.org
Ed Salamon, Executive Director
Chasity Crouch, Business Manager
Jams, discussions, introduction of new comers, Hall of Fame presentations.
2,000 Attendees
Frequency: March

3717 **Cable Television Trade Show and Convention: East**
Convention Show Management Company
6175 Barfield Road NE
Suite 220
Atlanta, GA 30328-4327
404-252-2454; *Fax:* 404-252-0215
Nancy Horne, Show Manager
Nine hundred booths.
6M Attendees
Frequency: August

3718 **Cable and Satellite: European Broadcasting/Communications Show**
Reed Exhibition Companies
255 Washington Street
Newton, MA 02458-1637
617-584-4900; *Fax:* 617-630-2222
Elizabeth Hitchcock, International Sales
Communications forum for professionals in the broadcasting industry.
7.9M Attendees
Frequency: April

3719 **MFMA/BCCA Annual Conference**
Media Financial Management Association
550 W Frontage Road
Suite 3600
Northfield, IL 60093
847-716-7000; *Fax:* 847-716-7004
info@mediafinance.org; www.bcfm.com
Mary Collins, President/CEO
Jamie Smith, Director of Operations
Offers professional education targeting media financial and business executives; CPE opportunities; exhibitors; roundtables; and networking opportunities.
800 Attendees
Frequency: Annual
Mailing list available for rent: 1,200 names at $495 per M

3720 **MIP-TV: International Television Program Market**
Reed Exhibition Companies
255 Washington Street
Newton, MA 02458-1637
617-584-4900; *Fax:* 617-630-2222
Elizabeth Hitchcock, International Sales
Spring market for the television industry to buy, sell and distribute television programming.
9M Attendees
Frequency: April

3721 **NAB Radio Show**
National Association of Broadcasters
1771 N Street NW
Washington, DC 20036
202-429-5300
888-140-4622
301-682-7962; *Fax:* 202-429-4199
NABSHOW@expressreg.net;
www.nabshow.com
David Wharton, EVP Media Relations
Jennifer Landry-Jackson, Exhibit Sales
Kelly Bryant, Event Operations
A unique networking opportunity for station professionals representing all format and market sizes, with exhibits showcasing technologies, tools and solutions for the industry.
Frequency: Annual

3722 **NAB Show**
National Association of Broadcasters
1771 N Street NW
Washington, DC 20036
202-429-5300
800-342-2460
202-429-3189; *Fax:* 202-429-4199;
www.nabshow.com
David Wharton, EVP Media Relations
Jennifer Landry-Jackson, Exhibit Sales
Kelly Bryant, Event Operations
A global event for boradcasting news, legislation, networking, education and technology. Over 150 countries represented by 85,000+ attendees and exhibitors; conferences, and training sessions, and over 1,500 exhibitors.
85M Attendees
Frequency: April

3723 **NATPE Market & Conference**
National Association of TV Program Executives
5757 Wilshire Boulevard
Penthouse 10
Los Angeles, CA 90036-3681
310-453-4440; *Fax:* 310-453-5258
info@natpe.org; www.natpe.org
Nick Orfanopoulos, Senior VP Exhibitions
Beth Braen, Senior VP Marketing
The National Association of Television Program Executives (NATPE) is a global alliance of business professionals engaged in the creation, development and distribution of content as well as advertising and financial activities. NATPE is the world's largest non-profit association dedicated to facilitating the continued growth and convergence of all content across all distribution platforms.
8000 Attendees
Frequency: Annual
Founded in: 1963

3724 **NATPE: The Alliance of Media Content**
National Association of TV Program Executives
6868 Wilshire Boulevard
Penthouse 10
Los Angeles, CA 90036-3681
310-453-4440
800-NAT-PEGO; *Fax:* 310-453-5258
info@natpe.org; www.natpe.org
Pam Silverman, Exhibition & Advertising
Linda Nichols, Exhibitor Services
Eric Low, Registration & Membership
The National Association of Television Program Executives (NATPE) is a global alliance of business professionals engaged in the creation, development and distribution of content as well as advertising and financial activities. NATPE is the world's largest non-profit association dedicated to facilitating the continued growth and convergence of all content across all distribution platforms.
1000 Attendees
Frequency: January
Founded in: 1963

3725 **NECTA Convention & Exhibition**
New England Cable And Telecommunications Assn

10 Forbes Road
Suite 440W
Braintree, MA 02184-2648

781-843-3418; *Fax:* 781-849-6267
info@necta.info; www.necta.info

Paul Cianelli, President
William Durand, Executive Vice President
Donna Nolan, Office Manager

A six state regional trade association representing substantially all private cable telecommunications companies in Connecticut, Maine, Massachusetts, New Hampshire, Rhode Island, and Vermont.
1.1M Attendees
Frequency: July

3726 **National Public Radio Association**
National Public Radio Association
635 Massachusetts Avenue NW
Washington, DC 20001-3753

202-513-2000; *Fax:* 202-513-3329;
www.npr.org

Vivian Schiller, President & CEO
Howard Stevenson, Chair of the Board of Directors
Mitch Praver, COO

Seventy five booths for public radio professionals and providers of resource materials for public radio.
1.2M Attendees
Frequency: April/May

3727 **National Religious Broadcasters Annual Convention and Exposition**
National Religious Broadcasters
9510 Technology Drive
Manassas, VA 20110

703-330-7000; *Fax:* 703-330-7100
info@nrb.org; www.nrb.org

Dr Frank Wright, President/CEO
Linda Smith, President Assistant
David Keith, VP Operations

Containing 280 exhibits. Broadcast and communications emphasis.
5,700 Attendees
Frequency: February

3728 **OAB Broadcast Engineering Conference**
Society of Broadcast Engineers
9102 N Meridian Street
Suite 150
Indianapolis, IN 46260

317-846-9000; *Fax:* 317-846-9120
mclappe@sbe.org; www.sbe.org

Vincent A Lopez, President
John Poray, Executive Director

Offers broadcast engineers the opportunity to attend educational sessions, see the latest equipment and supplies, and meet with peers.
5500 Members
Frequency: Annual/November
Founded in: 1964
Mailing list available for rent: 5700 names at $170 per M

3729 **RAB2009 Conference**
Radio Advertising Bureau
1320 Greenway Drive
Suite 500
Irving, TX 75038

972-536-6700
800-232-3131; *Fax:* 972-753-6727
jhaley@rab.com; www.rab.com

Erica Ferber, President
Van Allen, CFO

Learn about new media opportunities from new digital platforms and monetizing streams to HD strategies that will empower you to compete at a new level and be an innovator at your station.
1600 Attendees
Frequency: Annual/March

3730 **Recruiting Conference and Expo**
Kennedy Information
1 Phoenix Mill Lane
Floor 3
Peterborough, NH 03458

603-924-1006
800-531-0007
conferences@kennedyinfo.com;
www.recruiting2006.com

Matt Lyons, Director, Recruiting Group

Learn about the winning strategies, best practices, and tools ou will need to succeed in a challenging talent market.
Frequency: Nov New York

3731 **SCTE Cable-Tec EXPO**
Society of Cable Telecommunication Engineers
140 Philips Road
Exton, PA 19341-1318

610-363-6888
800-542-5040; *Fax:* 610-363-5898
scte@scte.org; www.scte.org

Lori Bower, Director
John Clark, CEO

Five hundred booths and, exhibits featuring telecommunications and programming equipment; dozens of workshops, with new technologies showcased.
12M Attendees
Frequency: Annual
Mailing list available for rent

3732 **SMPTE Annual Tech Conference & EXPO**
Society of Motion Picture & Television Engineers
3 Barker Avenue
5th Floor
White Plains, NY 10601

914-761-1100; *Fax:* 914-761-3115
smpte@smpte.org; www.smpte.org
Social Media: Facebook, Twitter, LinkedIn

Barbara Lange, Executive Director
Sally Ann D'Amato, Director, Operations
Roberta Gorman, Manager, Member Relations
Aimee Ricca, Product Marketing Manager

The Technical Conference and Exhibition which is held in the fall. This alternates between the east and west coasts, usually in Pasadena and New York.
Frequency: Annual

3733 **Satellite Broadcasting and Communication Association (SBCA)**
Show Management & Services
900 Jorie Boulevard
Suite 200
Oak Brook, IL 60523-3835

800-654-9276; *Fax:* 630-990-2077

Diana Bubalo, Show Manager

Four hundred fifty booths.
2.5M Attendees

3734 **Television Bureau of Advertising Annual Meeting**
Television Bureau of Advertising
3 E 54th Street
New York, NY 10022

212-486-1111; *Fax:* 212-935-5631
info@tvb.org; www.tvb.org

Steve Lanzano, President
Abby Auerbach, EVP
Gary Bellis, VP/Communications

Annual show of 20-25 exhibitors of services for television stations, including research, sales and management training programs, incentives, collection agencies, advertiser contests and computer software.

3735 **Western Cable Television Conference and Expo**
Trade Associates
11820 Parklawn Drive
Suite 250
Rockville, MD 20852-2505

301-519-1610

Susan Rosenstock, Expo Director

One thousand three hundred booths featuring exhibits of programming, mobile aerial devices, video equipment and products and services for the communications and related industry fields.
10M Attendees
Frequency: November/December

3736 **Western Show**
Trade Associates
11820 Parklawn Drive
Suite 250
Rockville, MD 20852-2505

301-519-1610; *Fax:* 301-468-3662

Susan Rosenstock, Director

One thousand booths featuring exhibits from cable operators and suppliers to the cable industry. The California Cable Television Association and the Arizona Cable Television Association sponsor this annual event.
10M Attendees
Frequency: December

Directories & Databases

3737 **AES E-Library**
Audio Engineering Society
60 E 42nd St
Room 2520
New York, NY 10165

212-661-8528; *Fax:* 212-682-0477
HQ@aes.org; www.aes.org
Social Media: Facebook

Bob Moses, Executive Director
Roger K Furness, Deputy Director

The library contains over 12,000 fully searchable PDF files documenting the progression of audio research from 1953 to the present, and includes every AES paper published at a convention, conference or in the Journal. Available as a subscription or pay per paper download: $135 for members, $245 for non, or $5 per paper for members or $20 for non.
Cost: $5.00
Frequency: Annual or Per-Paper

3738 **Arbitron Radio County Coverage**
Arbitron Company
142 5th Ave
New York, NY 10011-4312

212-887-1300; *Fax:* 212-887-1558;
www.arbitron.com

Stephen Morris, CEO
Marilou Legge, Executive Vice President

This database offers access to audience listening estimates by county.
Frequency: Statistical

3739 **Audio Engineering Society: Directory of Educational Programs**
Audio Engineering Society

60 E 42nd St
Room 2520
New York, NY 10165

212-661-8528; *Fax:* 212-682-0477
HQ@aes.org; www.aes.org
Social Media: Facebook

Bob Moses, Executive Director
Roger K Furness, Deputy Director

Institutions offering postsecondary programs and seminars in audio technology and engineering are searchable by program type or geographic area. Available free online. Educators are asked to confirm the information for their institutions.
Frequency: Free Online

3740 Bacon's Newspaper & Magazine Directories
Cision U.S., Inc.
322 South Michigan Avenue
Suite 900
Chicago, IL 60604

312-263-0070
866-639-5087
info.us@cision.com
us.cision.com

Joe Bernardo, President & CEO
Heidi Sullivan, VP & Publisher
Valerie Lopez, Research Director
Jessica White, Research Director
Rachel Farrell, Research Manager

Two volume set listing all daily and community newspapers, magazines and newsletters, news service and syndicates, syndicated columnists, complete editorial staff listings of each publication provided, covers U.S., Canada, Mexico, and Carribean.
Cost: $350.00
4,700 Pages
Frequency: Annual
ISSN: 1088-9639
Founded in: 1951
Printed in one color on matte stock

3741 Bacon's Radio/TV/Cable Directory
Cision U.S., Inc.
332 South Michigan Avenue
Suite 900
Chicago, IL 60604

312-263-0070
866-639-5087
info.us@cision.com; www.us.cision.com

Joe Bernardo, President & CEO
Heidi Sullivan, VP & Publisher
Valerie Lopez, Research Director
Jessica White, Research Director
Rachel Farrell, Research Manager

Includes comprehensive coverage for contact and programming information for more than 3,500 televsion networks, cable networks, television syndicators, television stations, and cable systems in the United States and Canada.
Cost: $350.00
Frequency: Annual
ISSN: 1088-9639
Printed in one color on matte stock

3742 Broadcast Engineering Equipment Reference Manual
Penton
249 W 17th Street
New York, NY 10011

212-204-4200
corporatecustomerservice@penton.com; www.penton.com

Sharon Rowlands, Chief Executive Officer

Offers a list of more than 1,400 manufacturers and distributors of communications equipment for radio, television and recording applications.
Cost: $20.00
Frequency: Annual
Circulation: 35,500
ISSN: 0007-1994

3743 Burrelle's Media Directory
BurrellesLuce
75 E Northfield Rd
Livingston, NJ 07039-4532

973-992-6600
800-631-1160; *Fax:* 973-992-7675;
www.burrellesluce.com
Social Media: Facebook, Twitter, LinkedIn

Robert C Waggoner, CEO

Offers media outreach, media monitoring and media reporting products.
Cost: $795.00

3744 CPB Public Broadcasting Directory
Corporation for Public Broadcasting
401 9th St NW
Suite 200
Washington, DC 20004-2129

202-879-9600; *Fax:* 202-879-9700
oigemail@cpb.org; www.cpb.org
Social Media: Twitter

Robert T Coonrod, CEO

Offers information on public television stations, national and regional public broadcasting association and networks.
Cost: $15.00
152 Pages
Frequency: Annual
Circulation: 14,000

3745 Cable Online Data Exchange
Prometheus Global Media
770 Broadway
New York, NY 10003-9595

212-493-4100; *Fax:* 646-654-5368;
www.prometheusgm.com

Richard D. Beckman, CEO
James A. Finkelstein, Chairman
Madeline Krakowsky, Vice President Circulation
Tracy Brater, Executive Director Creative Service

This database contains information on more than 10,000 US cable television system franchises.

3746 Complete Television, Radio and Cable Industry Directory
Grey House Publishing
4919 Route 22
PO Box 56
Amenia, NY 12501
518-789-8700
800-562-2139; *Fax:* 845-373-6390; *Fax:* new
books@greyhouse.com; www.greyhouse.com

Richard Gottlieb, President
Leslie Mackenzie, Publisher

The most comprehensive industry data on the US and Canadian Televison, Radio and Cable Industries. Can also subscibe to the database found online.
Cost: $350.00
2000 Pages
ISBN: 9-781619-25-1
Founded in: 1981

3747 Directory of Field Contacts for the Coordination of the Use of Radio
Federal Communications Commission
445 12th Street SW
Washington, DC 20554

202-180-0450; *Fax:* 866-418-0232
fccinfo@fcc.gov; www.fcc.com

Radio frequency coordinating agencies are listed.
170 Pages
Frequency: Annual

3748 Directory of Religious Media
National Religious Broadcasters
9510 Technology Dr
Manassas, VA 20110-4149

703-330-7100; *Fax:* 703-330-7100
info@nrb.org; www.nrb.org

Frank Wright, President
Linda Smith, President Assistant
David Keith, VP Operations

Comprehensive guide to radio, television, music and book publishers.
Frequency: 10 per year

3749 Editors Guild Directory
Motion Picture Editors Guild
7715 Sunset Boulevard
Suite 200
Hollywood, CA 90046

323-876-4770; *Fax:* 323-876-0861
info@editorsguild.com; www.editorsguild.com

Lisa Churgin, Guild President
Dede Allen, VP
Diane Adler, Secretary
Rachel Igel, Treasurer
Tris Carpenter, Manager

An invaluable resource for producers, directors and post production professionals alike. It lists contact, credit, award and classification information for all of the Guild's active members at the time of publication, as well as a list of Oscar and Emmy winners for every year since the awards began. It also include a retirees section.
Cost: $25.00

3750 GMRS National Repeater Guide
Personal Radio Steering Group
PO Box 2851
Ann Arbor, MI 48106-2851

734-662-4533
gmrs.org

Corwin Moore, Administrative Director

Lists the 3,500 GMRS repeaters nationally, along with names and addresses of station licensees.
Frequency: Monthly

3751 Gale Directory of Publications and Broadcast Media
Gale/Cengage Learning
PO Box 09187
Detroit, MI 48209-0187

248-699-4253
800-877-4253; *Fax:* 248-699-8049
gale.galeord@cengage.com; www.gale.com

Patrick C Sommers, President

This media directory contains thousands of listings for radio and television stations and cable companies.
Frequency: Annual
ISBN: 1-414434-71-5
Founded in: 2008

3752 International Motion Picture Almanac Intern Television & Video Almanac
Quigley Publishing Company, Incorporated

64 Wintergreen Lane
Groton, MA 01450

978-448-0272; *Fax:* 978-448-9325
quigleypub@aol.com;
www.quigleypublishing.com

William J Quigley, President/Publisher
Jayme Kulesz, Editor
Michael Quigley, Associate Editor/Ops Manager
Dee Quigley, Associate Editor

Invaluable completely updated information to the most sucscessful people in the business. Are you one of them? With thousands of corporations, 5,000 plus career profiles and the most comprehensive information available on the second largest industry in the US.
Cost: $250.00
780 Pages
Frequency: Annual
ISBN: 0-900610-74-3
ISSN: 0074-7084
Founded in: 1915

3753 **Kagan Media Index**
Kagan World Media
126 Clock Tower Place
Carmel, CA 93923-8746

831-624-1536; *Fax:* 831-625-3225
info@kagan.com; www.kagan.com

George Niesen, Editor
Tom Johnson, Marketing Manager

The most comprehensive collection of media industry databases found anywhere. Current estimates of industry growth for a dozen different media businesses, shown on a 145-line spreadsheet, projected forward and updated monthly. Three month trial available.
Cost: $795.00
Frequency: Monthly

3754 **National Radio Publicity Outlets**
Volt Directory Marketing
1800 Byberry Road
Suite 800
Huntingdon Valley, PA 19006-3520

800-677-3839; *Fax:* 610-832-0878

Offers valuable information on over 7,000 radio stations in all major United States and Canadian markets.
Cost: $188.00
640 Pages
Frequency: SemiAnnual

3755 **Radio & Records**
Radio & Records
10100 Santa Monica Boulevard
5th Floor
Los Angeles, CA 90067-4003

310-553-4330; *Fax:* 310-203-8450;
www.rronline.com

Erica Farber, Publisher/CEO
Sky Daniels, Vice President
Ron Rodriguez, Editor-in-Chief
Page Beaver, Operations Manager
Henry Mowry, Sales Executive

A music newspaper that covers all aspects of the radio and recording industry.
Cost: $299.00
Frequency: BiAnnual
Circulation: 10,000

3756 **Radio Marketing Guide**
Radio Advertising Bureau
1320 Greenway Dr
Suite 500
Irving, TX 75038-2547

972-753-6700
800-232-3131; *Fax:* 972-753-6727
jhaley@rab.com; www.rab.com

Mike Mahone, VP
Leah Kamon, SVP Marketing

A multi dimensional tool for Radio sales management and advertising professionals.
1600 Attendees

3757 **Radio Talk Shows Need Guests**
Pacesetter Publications
PO Box 101330
Denver, CO 80250-1330

303-722-7200; *Fax:* 303-733-2626;
www.joesabah.com

Over 950 radio talk shows that interview guests over the telephone are profiled.
Cost: $198.00
Frequency: SemiAnnual
Founded in: 1992

3758 **SBE Members Directory**
Society of Broadcast Engineers
9102 N Meridian St
Suite 150
Indianapolis, IN 46260-1896

317-846-9000; *Fax:* 317-846-9120
mclappe@sbe.org; www.sbe.org

John Poray, Executive Director
Vincent A Lopez, President

List of all members of SBE, Includes a history, awards earned, leadership, suppliers and other information. Free to members.
108 Pages
Mailing list available for rent: 4700 names at $170 per M

3759 **TV Cable Publicity Guide**
Volt Directory Marketing
1 Sentry Pkwy E
Blue Bell, PA 19422-2310

610-825-7720; *Fax:* 610-941-6874;
www.volt.com

Jerry Di Pippo, CEO
Ronald Kochman, Vice President
Bruce Goodman, General Counsel

Over 5,000 cable and broadcast television stations and systems are profiled.
Cost: $188.00
545 Pages
Frequency: SemiAnnual

3760 **TV Facts**
Cabletelevision Advertising Bureau
830 3rd Ave
2nd Floor
New York, NY 10022-7523

212-508-1200; *Fax:* 212-832-3268;
www.onetvworld.org

Sean Cunningham, President

An essential pocketsized media planning tool that contains 120 pages of essential data, graphs and charts highlighting the extraordinary growth and value of Cable in the changing TV landscape.
Frequency: Annual
Circulation: 20000

3761 **Talk Show Selects**
Broadcast Interview Source
2233 Wisconsin Ave NW
Suite 301
Washington, DC 20007-4132

202-333-5000
800-932-7266; *Fax:* 202-342-5411;
www.expertclick.com

Mitchell Davis, Owner

More than 700 contacts at radio and television talk shows.
Cost: $185.00
240 Pages
Frequency: Annual
ISBN: 0-934333-35-1
Founded in: 1984
Printed in on matte stock

3762 **Television Yearbook**
BIA Research
15120 Enterprise Ct
Suite 100
Chantilly, VA 20151-1275

703-818-8115
800-331-5086; *Fax:* 703-803-3299
pob@bia.com; www.bia.com

Tom Bruno, Owner

US television markets and their inclusive stations, television equipment manufacturers and related service providers and trade associations.
Cost: $64.00
Frequency: Annual

3763 **Television and Cable Factbook**
Warren Communications News
2115 Ward Ct NW
Washington, DC 20037-1209

202-872-9200
800-771-9202; *Fax:* 202-318-8350
info@warren-news.com;
www.warren-news.com

Brig Easley, Manager
Daniel Warren, President/Editor

Commercial and noncommercial television stations and networks are profiled in this comprehensive directory. Educational and instructional stations are also included as one of the many categories of information.
Cost: $595.00
10M Pages
Frequency: 5 Volumes
Founded in: 1932

3764 **Top 200 National TV, News, Talk and Magazine Shows**
Todd Publications
PO Box 635
Nyack, NY 10960-0635

845-358-6213
800-747-1056; *Fax:* 845-358-6213

B Klein, Publisher

The 200 most popular information shows on US television.
Cost: $40.00
Frequency: Annual

3765 **World Broadcast News: International 500 Issue**
Penton
PO Box 12901
Shawnee Mission, KS 66282-2901

913-341-1300; *Fax:* 913-514-6895;
www.penton.com

Eric Jacobson, Senior VP

Directory of services and supplies to the industry.
Cost: $10.00
Frequency: Annual

Industry Web Sites

3766 **http://gold.greyhouse.com**
G.O.L.D Grey House OnLine Databases

Grey House Publishing's online database platform, GOLD, offers Quick Search, Keyword Search and Expert Search for most business sectors including broadcasting, communications and media markets. The GOLD platform makes finding the information you need quick and easy - whether you're a novice searcher or an experienced database user. All of Grey House's directory products are available for subscription on the GOLD platform.

3767 **www.aicp.com**
Association of Independent Commercial Producers

Represents exclusively, the interests of US companies that specialize in producing commercials on various media - film, video, computer- for advertisers and their agencies. AICP members account for 85 percent of all domestic commercials aired nationally, whether produced for traditional broadcast channels or nontraditional use.

3768 **www.alliancecm.org**
Alliance for Community Media
Committed to assuring everyone's access to electronic media, through public education, a progressive legislative and regulatory agenda, coalition building and grassroots organizing. A nonprofit, national membership organization founded in 1976, the Alliance represents over 1,000 Public, Educational and Govermental access organizations and community media centers.

3769 **www.americansportscasters.com**
American Sportscasters Association
Covers the U.S., Puerto Rico, and Canada. Offers seminars, compiles statistics and operates a placement service, maintains a Hall of Fame and biographical archives and library.

3770 **www.amptp.org**
Alliance of Motion Picture & Television Producers
Trade association with respect to labor issues in the motion picture and television industry. We negotiate 80 industry wide collective bargaining agreements and represents over 350 production companies and studios.

3771 **www.apts.org**
Association of Public Televsion Stations
Nonprofit membership organization established in 1980 to support the continued growth and development of a strong and financially sound noncommercial television service for the American public. We provide advocacy for public television interests at the national level, as well as consistent leadership and information in marshalling grassroots and congressional support.

3772 **www.bcfm.com**
Broadcast Cable Financial Management Association
A professional society of over 1,200 of television, radio and cable TV's top financial, MIS and HR executives, plus associates in auditing, data processing, software development, credit and collections.

3773 **www.bdaonline.org**
Broad Designers Association
For broadcast designers. Conferences annually in Asia, Australia, Europe, South and North America.

3774 **www.ctam.com**
Cable Telecommunications Association for Marketing
Dedicated to the discipline and development of consumer marketing excellence in cable television, new media and telecommunication services. Members have the advantage of progressive research, insightful publications and forward thinking conferences.

3775 **www.emmyonline.org**
National Academy of Television Arts & Sciences
Dedicated to the advancement of the arts and sciences of television and the promotion of creative leadership for artistic, educational and technical achievements within the television industry. Bestows the Emmy Award.

3776 **www.genehrts.com**
Hollywood Radio and Television Society
Featuring top industry and government speakers and seminars about broadcasting, maintains film and audio library.

3777 **www.gita.org**
Geospatial Information & Technology Association
A variety of information and useful references for your professional and technical needs, with descriptions of new programs and services, and a stable source of important member contacts, industry news and association related ongoing programs.

3778 **www.greyhouse.com**
Grey House Publishing
Authoritative reference directories for most business sectors including broadcasting, communications and media markets. Users can search the online databases with varied search criteria allowing for custom searches by product category, geographic area, sales volume, keyword, subject and more. Full Grey House catalog and online ordering also available.

3779 **www.halloffame.com**
National Sportscasters & Sportswriters Association

3780 **www.i-newsrelease.com**
Tellmedia Communications
Media research, Internet news, satelite media tours and video news releases.

3781 **www.iabm.com**
International Association of Broadcast Monitors
Website of world wide trade association made up of news retrieval services which monitor television, radio, Internet and print news mediums.

3782 **www.ibsradio.org**
Intercollegiate Broadcasting System
For college and university broadcasting stations.

3783 **www.iemmys.tv**
International Television Academy
Organization of global broadcasters, with representatives from over 50 countries. Sixty percent of the 100-member board of directors come from countries outside the US, and represent the world's largest production, distribution and broadcast companies.

3784 **www.irts.org**
Int'l Radio & Television Society Foundation
For professionals in radio, broadcast and cable televison, corporate video production, collaborative communication, DVD and new media production, marketing and advertising plus related areas, as well as interested laypeople.

3785 **www.kagan.com**
Kagan World Media
For those interested in investments in radio and TV stations and publicly held companies.

3786 **www.lib.umd.edu/LAB**
Library of American Broadcasting
Devoted to television and radio broadcasting materials and archives.

3787 **www.lostremote.com**
Lost Remote
Television industry news, job listings and resources.

3788 **www.mca-i.org**
Media Communications Association International
Website of the global community of professional devoted to the business and art of visual communication.

3789 **www.mediabistro.com**
Media Bistro
News and articles especially for those in broadcasting and publishing.

3790 **www.millimeter.com**
Millimeter Magazine
Authoritative resource for more than 33,000 qualified professionals in production, postproduction, animation, streaming and visual effects for motion pictures, television and commercials.

3791 **www.mrfac.com**
Manufacturer's Radio Frequency Advisory Committee
Representing the voice of the manufacturing industry and private land mobile radio users before the FCC.

3792 **www.nab.org**
National Association of Broadcasters
Full service trade association that represents the interests of free, over-the-air radio and television broadcasters.

3793 **www.naed.org**
National Association of Electrical Distributors
Nonprofit organization dedicated to serving and protecting the electrical distribution channel; provides networking opportunities through approximately 50 meetings and conferences a year, training, industry information and research through TED Magazine, and a marketing campaign for the industry through the NAED Advocacy Initiative.

3794 **www.nafb.org**
National Association of Farm Broadcasters
Works to improve quantity and quality of farm programming and serves as a clearinghouse for new ideas in farm broadcasting.

3795 **www.natpe.org**
Nat'l Association of Television Program Executives
Our mission is a commitment to furthering the quality and quantity of content, offering the wealth of our resources and experience to every content creator, no matter what the medium. Because the industry encompasses so much more today than ever before, NATPE too is expanding to accommodate this change and encourage progress while continuing to keep our members constantly appraised of changes.

3796 **www.ncta.com**
National Cable & Telecommunications Asssociation
National Cable and Telecommunications Association, formerly the National Cable Television Association, is the principal trade association of the cable television industry in the United States. Provides a strong national presence by providing a single, unified voice on issues affecting the cable and telecommunications industry.

3797 **www.ncti.com**
National Cable Television Institute
Independent provider of broadband communications training. Broadband cable system operators, contractors and industry vendors have turned to NCTI to train their employees who construct, operate and maintain broadband systems.

3798 **www.necta.info**
New England Cable & Telecommunications Association
NECTA is a six state regional trade association representing sbtstantially all private cable telecommunications companies in Connecticut,

Maine, Massachusetts, New Hampshire, Rhode Island and Vermont.

3799 **www.nrb.org**
National Religious Broadcasters

For religious broadcasters and religious media. Hosts national convention featuring trade show and educational workshops.

3800 **www.pcia.com**
Personal Communications Industry Association

Represents companies that develop, own, manage and operate towers, commercial rooftops and other facilities for the provision of all types of wireless, broadcasting and telecommunications services. PCIA is dedicated to advancing an understanding of the benefits of wireless services and required infrastructure.

3801 **www.productionhub.com**
Production Hub

Television producers' news, listings, classifieds, casting notices and events.

3802 **www.rab.cpm**
Radio Advertising Bureau

For marketing personnel and raises awareness of radio among advertising and business communities.

3803 **www.radiospace.com**
North American Network

All information contained is provided to radio stations and networks for their free and unrestricted use.

3804 **www.rtndf.org**
Radio Television News Directors Association

Provides training programs, seminars, scholarship support and research in areas of critical concern to electronic news professionals and their audience. Offers professional development opportunities for working and aspiring journalists and journalism educators.

3805 **www.sacredheartprofram.org**
Sacred Heart Hour

Producers and syndicators of Public Service Radio Programs, Contact Radio available in, thirty minute, fifteen minute, five minute versions, Pathways, one minute radio spots.

3806 **www.sbca.com**
Satellite Broadcasting/Communications Association

National trade association representing all segments of the satellite consumer services industry. The association is committed to expanding the utilization of satellite technology for the delivery of video, data, voice, interactive and broadband services.

3807 **www.sbe.org**
Society of Broadcast Engineers

Offers a cooperative educational program intended to assist in the ongoing rollout of digital television.

3808 **www.smpte.org**
Society of Motion Picture & Television Engineers

Serves the needs of film and TV engineers.

3809 **www.thirteen.org**
Educational Broadcasting Association

For producers and directors of public educational programming, channel 13, PBS.

3810 **www.tvspy.com**
TVSpy

Television industry news, articles and links to other sites of interest.

Associations

3811 **ADSC: The International Association of Foundation Drilling**
8445 Freeport Parkway
Suite 325
Irving, TX 75063
469-359-6000; *Fax:* 469-359-6007
adsc@adsc-iafd.com; www.adsc-iafd.com
Social Media: Facebook, Twitter, LinkedIn
Tom Tuozzolo, President
Al Rasband, VP
Martin McDermott, Treasurer
ADSC seeks to advance technology in the foundation of drilling and anchored earth retention industries. Represents drilled shaft, andchored earth retention, micropile contractors, civil engineers and manufacturing firms world wide.
Founded in: 1972

3812 **Adhesive & Sealant Council**
7101 Wisconsin Avenue
Suite 990
Bethesda, MD 20814
301-986-9700; *Fax:* 301-986-9795
data@ascouncil.org; www.ascouncil.org
Social Media: Twitter, LinkedIn, RSS
Bill Allmond, President
Traci Jensen, Chair
Charles R. Williams, Jr., Treasurer
Christine A. Bryant, Director
John P. Carroll, Director
A North American trade association dedicated to representing the adhesive and sealant industry. ASC is bound by the collective efforts of its members, and strives to improve the industry operating environment and strengthen its member companies.
124 Members
Founded in: 1958

3813 **American Architectural Manufacturers Association**
1827 Walden Office Square
Suite 550
Schaumburg, Il 60173-4268
847-303-5664; *Fax:* 847-303-5774
customerservice@aamanet.org;
www.aamanet.org
Social Media: Facebook, Twitter, LinkedIn, YouTube, Flickr, SlideShare
Rich Walker, President, CEO
Dean Lewis, Educational Information Mgr.
Maureen Knight, Govt. Affairs Manager
Jannine Klemencic, Executive Assistant
Karen Allen, Accounting/HR Mgr.
Trade association that advocates for manufacturers and professionals in the fenestration industry and is dedicated to the promotion of quality window, door, curtain wall, storefront and skylight products.
Founded in: 1936

3814 **American Bar Association Forum on Construction Law**
321 N Clark St.
Chicago, IL 60654
www.americanbar.org/groups/construction_industry.html
Social Media: Facebook, Twitter, LinkedIn
Steven B. Lesser, Chair
An association focused on the professional development of construction lawyers and enhancing perception of the role construction lawyers perform in the broader industry.
6000 Members
Founded in: 1976

3815 **American Concrete Pipe Association**
8445 Freeport Parkway
Suite 350
Irving, TX 75063-2595
972-506-7216; *Fax:* 972-506-7682
info@concrete-pipe.org;
www.concrete-pipe.org
Social Media: Facebook, Twitter, LinkedIn, Youtube
Matt Childs, President
Josh Beakley, PE, Technical Services Director
Kim Spahn, PE, Engineering Services Director
The American Concrete Pipe Association (ACPA) is a nonprofit organization, composed primarily of manufacturers of concrete pipe and related conveyance products located throughout the United States, Canada and in over 40 foreign countries. ACPA provides members with research, technical and marketing support to promote and advance the use of concrete pipe for drainage and pollution control applications.
145 Members
Founded in: 1907

3816 **American Concrete Pressure Pipe Association**
4122 E Chapman Avenue
Suite 27
Orange, CA 92869
714-801-0298; *Fax:* 703-273-7230
support@acppa.org; www.acppa.org
Social Media: Facebook, Twitter, LinkedIn
Mark Carpenter, Chairman
Alexander Narcise, Vice Chaiman
David Tantalean, Secretary
Jim Tully, Treasurer
Richard I Mueller, President &Ceo
The American Concrete Pressure Pipe Association (ACPPA) is a nonprofit trade association representing manufacturers of concrete pressure pipe around the world. ACPPA sponsors research projects and conducts educational programs to promote and advance the use of concrete pressure pipe in water and wastewater applications. We also manage an independent audit program to certify compliance with all applicable American Water Works Association (AWWA) standards for the manufacturers.
5 Members
Founded in: 1949

3817 **American Concrete Pumping Association**
606 Enterprise Drive
Lewis Center, OH 43035
614-431-5618; *Fax:* 614-431-6944
acpa@concretepumpers.com;
www.concretepumpers.com
Social Media: Facebook, Twitter, LinkedIn, Youtube, Flickr, RSS
Carl Walker, President
Beth Langhauser, Vice President
Scott Savage, Treasurer
Matt Kaminsky, Secretary
Dennis Andrews, Past President
The American Concrete Pumping Association promotes concrete pumping as the choice method of placing concrete, and to encourage and educate the concrete pumping industry on safe concrete pumping procedures. The ACPA Operator Certification Program is the only industry-recognized certification program for testing concrete pumping practices.
270 Members
Founded in: 1974

3818 **American Congress on Surveying and Mapping**
5119 Pagasus Court
Suite Q
Frederick, MD 21704
240-439-4615; *Fax:* 240-439-4952
curtis.summer@acsm.net; www.acsm.net
Social Media: Facebook, Twitter, Blogger
Curtis W Sumner, Executive Director
Bob Jupin, Accounting Manager
Sara Maggi, CST Program
Trish Milburn, Office Manager/Membership Services
A professional organization representing those who communicate the earth's spatial information using precisely prepared plats, charts, maps, and digital cartographic and related data systems.
7000 Members
Founded in: 1941

3819 **American Council for Construction Education**
1717 N Loop 1604 East
Suite 320
San Antonio, TX 78232-1570
210-495-6161; *Fax:* 210-495-6168
acce@acce-hq.org; www.acce-hq.org
Social Media: LinkedIn
Michael M Holland, President
Allan J Hauck, VP
Michael M Holland, Executive VP
Jim Carr, Treasurer
Dr. Norma Jean Anderson, Secretary
The accrediting agency for postsecondary construction education programs. The mission of ACCE is to be a global advocate for programs of post-secondary construction higher education. To accomplish this mission, ACCE will develop, periodically update, and promulgate comprehensive standards for programs of construction higher education and aAccredit programs meeting these standards through a rigorous, formal process of peer review.
Cost: $150.00
115 Members
Founded in: 1974

3820 **American Fence Association**
6404 International Parkway
Suite 2250-A
Plano, TX 75093
630-942-6598
800-822-4342; *Fax:* 314-480-7118;
www.americanfenceassociation.com
Social Media: Facebook, Twitter
Nate Prewitt, President
David Gregg, President Elect
Jamie R Turrentine, VP
Eddie Clark, Secretary
Susan Colson, Treasurer
The American Fence Association benefits the fence, deck and railing industry - as well as the consumer - by promoting the highest levels of professionalism, ethics and product standards by disseminating information and educating its members. With 31 member chapters serving the association, AFA offers several educational, certification options and networking opportunities to keep its members above and beyond their competition.
Cost: $365.00
2400 Members
Founded in: 1962

3821 **American Institute of Building Design**
7059 Blair Road NW
Suite 400
Washington, DC 20012
202-750-4900
800-366-2423; *Fax:* 866-204-0293
info@aibd.org; www.aibd.org

Social Media: Facebook, Twitter, LinkedIn, RSS

Steven Mickley, Executive Director
Whit Peterson, General Manager
David Pillsbury, President
Kevin Holdridge, Internal Vice President
Karen Kassik-Michelsohn, External Vice President

AIBD provides building designers with educational resources, and has developed nationwide design standards and a code of ethics for the building design profession. Today, AIBD is a nationally recognized association with professional and associate members in 48 states, throughout Canada and in Europe, Asia, Australia and the Bahamas. Its chartered state societies are active in their respective legislative arenas and work to promote public awareness of the bldg design profession.
Founded in: 1950

3822 American Institute of Constructors
19 Mantua Road
Mount Royal, NJ 08061

703-683-4999; *Fax:* 703-683-5480
info@professionalconstructor.org;
www.professionalconstructor.org
Social Media: Facebook, Twitter, LinkedIn

Greg Carender, President
Joseph Sapp, Executive Director
Charles L Sapp, Director, Association Management
Mark Hall, Treasurer
Terry Foster, Secretary

AIC is the organization that seeks to give Constructors the professional status they deserve. The Institute is the constructor's counterpart of professional organizations found in architecture, engineering, law and other fields. As such, the Institute serves as the national qualifying body of professional constructor. AIC membership identifies the individual as a true professional.
Founded in: 1971

3823 American Institute of Steel Construction
One East Wacker Drive
Suite 700
Chicago, IL 60601-1802

312-670-2400; *Fax:* 312-670-5403
ferch@aisc.org; www.aisc.org

Roger Ferch, President
Jacques Cattan, VP, Certification
John Cross, VP, Market Development & Finance
Scott Melnick, VP, Communications, Member Services
Charlie Carter, VP & Chief Structural Engineer

The American Institute of Steel Construction (AISC), headquartered in Chicago, is a not-for-profit technical institute and trade association serving the structural steel design community and construction industry in the United States. AISC's mission is to make structural steel the material of choice by being the leader in structural-steel-related technical and market-building activities, including: specification and code development, research, education, and tech assistance.
2.7M Members
Founded in: 1921

3824 American Iron and Steel Institute
25 Massachusetts Ave., NW
Suite 800
Washington, DC 20001

202-452-7100; www.steel.org
Social Media: Facebook, Twitter

Chuck Schmmit, Chairman
John Ferriola, Vice Chairman
Thomas J. Gibson, President, CEO
Lisa Harrison, SVP, Communications
David E. Bell, VP, Finance & Admin.

An association of North American steel producers that features steel information for consumers, engineers, and other professionals.
145 Members

3825 American Public Works Association
2345 Grand Blvd
Suite 700
Kansas City, MO 64108-2625

816-472-6100
800-848-2792; *Fax:* 816-472-1610
ddancy@apwa.net; www.apwa.net
Social Media: Facebook, Twitter, Youtube

Brian R Usher, President
Ann Daniels, Director/Credentialing
Brad Patterson, Chapter Membership Manager
Mark Leinwetter, Lead Development Manager
David Dancy, Director/Marketing

APWA exists to develop and support the people, agencies, and organizations that plan, build, maintain, and improve our communities. Just as communities count on their public works professionals, APWA strives to be the organization those professionals know they can count on. APWA offers the most comprehensive resources available in the areas of professional development tools, advocacy efforts, networking opportunities, and outreach activities.
26000 Members
Founded in: 1937

3826 American Society for Nondestructive Testing
1711 Arlingate Lane
PO Box 28518
Columbus, OH 43228-0518

614-274-6003
800-222-2768; *Fax:* 614-274-6899
wholliday@asnt.org; www.asnt.org
Social Media: Facebook, Twitter, LinkedIn, Youtube

Wayne Holliday, President
Mike Boggs, Quality Manager
Michael O'Toole, Manger/Conferences
Betsy Blazar, Manager/Marketing
Tim Jones, Manager/Publications

Technical society which is involved in nondestructive testing. ASNT publishes journals, including materials evaluation. The fall conference and quality testing show of this association is the society's largest annual show.
12000 Members
Founded in: 1941

3827 American Society of Heating, Refrigerating and Air-Conditioning Engineers
1791 Tullie Circle NE
Atlanta, GA 30329

404-636-8400
800-527-4723; *Fax:* 404-321-5478
ashrae@ashrae.org; www.ashrae.org
Social Media: Facebook, Twitter

T David Underwood, President
Timothy G Wentz, President Elect
Bjarne W Olesen, Treasurer
Walid Chakroun, Vice President
Jeff Littleton, Secretary

ASHRAE is a building technology society. The Society and its members focus on building systems, energy efficiency, indoor air quality and sustainability within the industry. Through research, standards writing, publishing and continuing education, ASHRAE shapes tomorrow's built environment today.
55000 Members
Founded in: 1894

3828 American Society of Professional Estimators
2525 Perimeter Place Drive
Suite 103
Nashville, TN 37214

615-316-9200
888-378-6283; *Fax:* 615-316-9800
SBO@aspenational.org; www.aspenational.org
Social Media: Facebook, Twitter

Marcene N. Taylor, ASPE President
Bruce D. Schlesier, 1st Vice President
Melvin D. Cowen, 2nd Vice President

The American Society of Professional Estimators was created with dedication and commitment to the idea of providing its members with tangible benefits.
2500 Members
Founded in: 1956

3829 American Subcontractors Association, Inc.
1004 Duke St.
Alexandria, VA 22314

703-684-3450; *Fax:* 703-836-3482
ASAoffice@asa-hq.com; www.asaonline.com
Social Media: Facebook, Twitter, LinkedIn, YouTube, Google+, RSS

Richard Bright, Chief Operating Officer
Colette Nelson, Chief Advocacy Officer
Marc Ramsey, Director, Communications
Linda Wilson, Director, Chapter Services
Robert Abney, Board of Directors

A nonprofit, national, membership trade association of constructionspecialty trade contractors, suppliers, and service providers in the United States and Canada.

3830 Asbestos Information and Training Centers
Georgia Institute of Real Estate
5784 Lake Forrest Drive
Atlanta, GA 30328

404-252-6768
800-633-3583; *Fax:* 404-257-0354
gire@learningrealestate.com;
www.learningrealestate.com
Social Media: Facebook, Twitter, RSS

Rebecca Fletcher, School Director
Mendalyn Harper, Information Central Manager
Jackie Townsend, Finance Director
Phil Avery, Finance Coordinator
Ned Kandul, Director, Art & Marketing

Sponsors the Regional Asbestos Information and Training Centers. The Centers provide information and training in identification and abatement of asbestos hazards with the ultimate goal of training contractors for eventual certification. Each center offers a variety of specialized courses including identification of asbestos hazards and possible remedies of problems and solutions for those involved in the asbestos hazard abatement process.
Founded in: 1959

3831 Asphalt Emulsion Manufacturers Association
Three Church Circle
PO Box 250
Annapolis, MD 21401

410-267-0023; *Fax:* 410-267-7546
krissoff@aema.org; www.aema.org
Social Media: Facebook

Archie Reynolds, President
Mark Ishee, Vice President
Todd Ryne, Secretary/Treasurer
Mark McCollough, Past President
Diane Franson, Director

The Asphalt Emulsion Manufacturers Association is the International Organization representing the asphalt emulsion industry. AEMA's

mission is to expand the use and applications of asphalt emulsions. Asphalt emulsions are the most environmentally sound, energy efficient and cost effective products used in pavement maintenance and construction.
150 Members
Founded in: 1973

3832 Asphalt Institute
2696 Research Park Dr
Lexington, KY 40511-8480

859-288-4960; *Fax:* 859-288-4999
info@asphaltinstitute.org;
www.asphaltinstitute.org
Social Media: Facebook, Twitter, LinkedIn, YouTube

Peter T Grass, President
Alexander Brown, Regional Director
Bob Horan, Regional Director
Mark Blow, Senior Regional Director
Bob Humer, Senior Regional Director

The Asphalt Institute is the international trade association of petroleum asphalt producers, manufacturers and affiliated businesses. Our mission is to promote the use, benefits and quality performance of petroleum asphalt, through engineering, research, marketing and educational activities, and through the resolution of issues affecting the industry.
113 Members
Founded in: 1919

3833 Associated Builders & Contractors, Inc.
440 1st St., N.W.
Ste., 200
Washington, DC 20001

202-595-1505
gotquestions@abc.org; www.abc.org
Social Media: Facebook, Twitter, LinkedIn, YouTube

Pamela Volm, Chairman
David Chapin, Chairman-Elect
Dan Brodbeck, Immediate Past Chairman
Anthony Stagliano, Treasurer
Michael Bellaman, President, CEO

A national construction industry trade association representing nearly 21,000 chapter members and whose activities include government representation, legal advocacy, education, workforce development, communications, technology,etc.
21000 Members
Founded in: 1950

3834 Associated Builders and Contractors
440 1st St., N.W.
Ste., 200
Washington, DC 20001
202-595-1505
gotquestions@abc.org; www.abc.org
Social Media: Facebook, Twitter, LinkedIn, Youtube

Pamela Volm, Chairman
David Chapin, Chairman-Elect
Dan Brodbeck, Immediate Past Chairman
Anthony Stagliano, Treasurer
Michael Bellaman, President, CEO
A national association representing merit shop construction and construction-related firms. ABC's membership represents all specialties within the U.S. construction industry and is comprised primarily of firms that perform work in the industrial and commercial sectors of the industry.
23000 Members
Founded in: 1950

3835 Associated Construction Distributors
1605 SE Deleware Avenue, Suite B
PO Box 14552
Ankeny, IA 50021

515-964-1335; *Fax:* 515-964-7668
acdi@acdi.net; www.acdi.net

Tom Goetz, Executive VP
Dave Hill, Director/Sales/Marketing
Jane Zieser, Controller
Linda Phipps, Meeting Manager

Associated Construction Distributors International, Inc. (ACDI) was founded when a group of independent, entrepreneurial businessmen came together and realized they had much to offer and much to learn. Sharing business information continues today at the core of the organization. It has allowed the members to succeed individually and as group. ACDI distributors account for nearly one billion dollars in the sale of materials and equipment to the construction industry.
34 Members
Founded in: 1968

3836 Associated Construction Publications
1200 Madison Ave
LL20
Indianapolis, IN 46225

317-423-7080
800-486-0014; *Fax:* 317-423-7094;
www.acppubs.com
Social Media: Facebook, Twitter, LinkedIn, RSS

Wayne Curtis, Publisher
Royce Morse, Production Director

Strives to assist the heavy construction industry with local and regional news on a nationwide basis.
14 Members
Founded in: 1938

3837 Associated Equipment Distributors
600 22nd Street
Suite 220
Oak Brook, IL 60523

630-574-0650
800-388-0650; *Fax:* 630-574-0132
info@aednet.org; www.aednet.org
Social Media: Facebook, Twitter, Google+, YouTube

Bob Henderson, EVP/COO
Jon Cruthers, VP, Sales/Publisher
Janet L Dixon, Director, Meetings & Conferences
Kim Phelan, Programs Director
Jenny Choe, Communications Director

Associated Equipment Distributors (AED) is an international trade association representing companies involved in the distribution, rental and support of equipment used in construction, mining, forestry, power generation, agriculture and industrial applications.
1200 Members
Founded in: 1919

3838 Associated General Contractors of America
2300 Wilson Blvd
Suite 300
Arlington, VA 22201

703-548-3118; *Fax:* 703-548-3119
info@agc.org; www.agc.org
Social Media: Facebook, Twitter, LinkedIn, RSS

Charles L Greco, President
Mark Knight, Senior Vice President
Art Daniel, Vice President
Joseph Stella, Treasurer
Stephen E Sandherr, Chief Executive Officer

The Associated General Contractors of America (AGC) is the leading association for the construction industry. Operating in partnership with its nationwide network of 95 chartered Chapters, AGC provides a full range of services satisfying the needs and concerns of its members, thereby improving the quality of construction and protecting the public interest.
33000 Members
Founded in: 1918

3839 Association of Equipment Manufacturers
6737 W Washington St
Suite 2400
Milwaukee, WI 53214-5647

414-272-0943; *Fax:* 414-272-1170
aem@aem.org; www.aem.org
Social Media: Twitter

John Patterson, Chair
Leif J Magnusson, Vice Chair
Dennis J Slater, Secretary
Goran Lindgren, Treasurer
Dennis Slater, President

Formed from the consolidation of the Construction Industry Manufacturers Association and Equipment Manufacturers Institute. The international trade and business development resource for companies that manufacture equipment, products and services used worldwide in the construction, agricultural, mining, forestry, and utility fields.
Founded in: 2002

3840 Association of Union Constructors (TAUC)
1501 Lee Highway
Suite 202
Arlington, VA 22209-1109

703-524-3336; *Fax:* 703-524-3364;
www.tauc.org

Steven Lindauer, Chief Executive Officer
David Acord, Communications Manager
Ben Cahoon, Data Systems Manager
Wayne Creasap, Health Director
Michael Dorsey, Industrial Relations Director

TAUC's mission is to act as an advocate for union contractors and enhance cooperation between the three entities involved in the successful completion of construction projects: the union, the contractor and the owner-client, the company for which the work is being completed. By encouraging this tripartite dialogue, many potential issues and delays are eliminated before work even begins.
5000+ Members
Founded in: 1969

3841 Association of the Wall and Ceiling Industry
513 West Broad Street
Suite 210
Falls Church, VA 22046
703-538-1722; *Fax:* 703-534-8307
info@awci.org; www.awci.org
Social Media: Facebook, Twitter, LinkedIn, Youtube

Steven Etkin, EVP/CEO
Brenton C Stone, Associate Publisher
Karen Bilak, Convention Director
Laura Porinchak, Communications Director
Annemarie Selvitelli, Education Director

Represents acoustics systems, ceiling systems, drywall systems, exterior insulation and finishing systems, fireproofing, flooring systems, insulation, and stucco contractors, suppliers and manufacturers and those in allied trades. The mission of the Association of the Wall and Ceiling Industry is to provide services and undertake activities that enhance the members' ability to operate a successful business.
2400 Members
Founded in: 1918

3842 **Barre Granite Association**
PO Box 481
Barre, VT 05641
802-476-4131; *Fax:* 802-476-4765
BGA@barregranite.org; www.barregranite.org
Social Media: Facebook, Twitter, LinkedIn, Pinterest

Robert Couture, President
John Castaldo, VP/Executive Directors

Manufacturers of cemetery monuments, mausoleums, statuary, landscape and architectural granite products. It has been estimated that one-third of the public and private monuments and mausoleums in America — and they are millions in number — are products of the Barre quarries and Barre's international community of sculptors, artisans, mechanics and laborers. All this has been largely accomplished since the closing decades of the last century.
35 Members
Founded in: 1889

3843 **Brick Industry Association**
1850 Centennial Park Drive
Suite 301
Reston, VA 20191
703-620-0010; *Fax:* 703-620-3928
brickinfo@bia.org; www.gobrick.com
Social Media: Facebook, Twitter, LinkedIn, Youtube, Pinterest

Ray Leonhard, President & CEO & CFO
Stephen Sears, COO & VP, Marketing
Sandy Speer, Executive Assistant
Judy Grandinetti, Accounting Manager
Susan Miller, VP, Environment, Health & Safety

National trade association representing distributors and manufacturers of clay brick and suppliers of related products and services. The Association is involved in a broad range of technical, research, marketing, government relations and communications activities. It is the recognized national authority on brick construction.
175 Members
Founded in: 1934

3844 **Bridge Grid Flooring Manufacturers Association**
201 Castle Drive
West Mifflin, PA 15122
412-469-3985; *Fax:* 419-257-0332;
www.abcdpittsburgh.org

Bill Ferko, President
Todd Carroll, Secretary
Jessica Saleh, Treasurer
Bill Ferko, Awards
Roxanne Podlipsky, Scholarships

Comprised of companies who manufacture steel grid flooring systems for bridges, and other companies with an interest in the steel grid market. The role of the Association is to promote the use of Grid Reinforced Concrete Bridge Decks through data collection, research/ development, and education.

3845 **Building Industry Association of Southern California**
24 Executive Park
Suite 100
Irvine, CA 92614
949-553-9500; *Fax:* 949-769-8943;
www.biasc.org
Social Media: Facebook, Twitter, LinkedIn

Michael Battaglia, President
Leonard Miller, Secretary/Treasurer
Daniel W Boyd, Immediate Past President

The Building Industry Association of Southern California is a nonprofit trade association representing companies involved in planning and building Southern California's communities. Our members are involved in all aspects of construction and green building - from architecture to roofing to landscape design.
1850 Members
Founded in: 1923

3846 **Building Material Dealers Association**
1006 SE Grand Street
Suite 301
Portland, OR 97214
503-208-3763
888-960-6329; *Fax:* 971-255-0790
bmda@bmda.com; www.bmda.com

Gwyn Matras, Executive Director, Executive Assistant, Supervisor, Research Department, Customer Service

BMDA provides Notice of Right to a Lien service for all states and Construction Lien service for Oregon and Washington. We offer current lien law manuals for Oregon and Washington, which assists our members with all areas of the construction lien laws. At BMDA, we believe attorneys who specialize in construction lien law are your best choice for answering legal questions. Therefore, we offer attorney referrals for Oregon and Washington. BMDA will not provide legal advice at any time.
3500 Members
Founded in: 1915

3847 **Building Stone Institute**
5 Riverside Drive, Bldg 2
PO Box 419
Chestertown, NY 12817
518-803-4336
866-786-6313; *Fax:* 518-803-4338;
www.buildingstoneinstitute.org
Social Media: Facebook

Jane Bennett, Executive Vice President
Kayla Carlozza, Association Services Coordinator
Gina De Nardo, Communications
Robert Barnes III, President
Aaron Hicken, Vice President

The Building Stone Institute works on behalf of the quarries, fabricators, retailers, importers, exporters, carvers, sculptors, restorers, designers, and installers that comprise our diverse membership. BSI provides programs and services that empower our member companies to offer the highest level of quality products and services. BSI is a not-for-profit trade association dedicated to serving its member firms, and providing educational materials and continuing education.
350 Members
Founded in: 1919

3848 **Building Trades Association**
6353 W. Rogers Circle
Unit 3
Boca Raton, FL 33487
800-326-7800
info@buildingtrades.com;
www.buildingtrades.com
Social Media: Facebook

An association made up of thousands of companies involved in all phases of the building and construction industries.

3849 **California Redwood Associates**
818 Grayson Road
Suite 201
Pleasant Hill, CA 94523
925-935-1499
888-225-7339; *Fax:* 925-935-1496
info@calredwood.org; www.calredwood.org
Social Media: Youtube

Christopher Grover, President

A trade association for redwood lumber producers.

3850 **Cedar Shake and Shingle Bureau**
PO Box 1178
Sumas, WA 98295-1178
604-820-7700; *Fax:* 604-820-0266
info@cedarbureau.org; www.cedarbureau.org

Lynne Christensen, Director of Operations
Barbara Enns, Accountant
Kelly Vaille, Marketing Coordinator
Christine Inglis, Customer Service
Sharron Beauregard, Project Coordinator

The Cedar Shake and Shingle Bureau is a non-profit organization that promotes the use of Certi-label cedar roofing and sidewall products. On June 9, 1915, at a meeting of the Trustees of the West Coast Lumber Manufacturers Association, it was agreed to establish a branch of the association to serve those members who manufactured shingles. Our influence grew, and as we survived both the Great Depression and World War II, manufacturers continued their quality commitment.
350 Members
Founded in: 1915

3851 **Construction Financial Management Association**
100 Village Blvd
Suite 200
Princeton, NJ 08540
609-452-8000
888-421-9996; *Fax:* 609-452-0474
info@cfma.org; www.cfma.org
Social Media: Facebook, Twitter, LinkedIn, Youtube

Stuart Binstock, President & CEO
Erica O'Grady, VP, Operations
Robert Rubin, VP, Finance & Administration
Brian Summers, VP, Content Management & Education
Brigitte Meinders, Director, Marketing

CFMA is the only organization dedicated to bringing together construction financial professionals and those partners serving their unique needs. CFMA serves members located throughout the US and Canada.
7000 Members
Founded in: 1981

3852 **Construction Industry Service Corporation**
2000 Spring Road
Suite 110
Oak Brook, IL 60523
630-472-9411
877-562-9411; *Fax:* 630-472-9413
Julia@cisco.org; www.cisco.org
Social Media: Facebook, Twitter, LinkedIn

Mark Maher, President
Joseph Benson, VP
Frank Furco, Treasurer
Loretta Molter, Secretary
Dan Allen, Executive Director

The Construction Industry Service Corporation (CISCO) is a non-profit labor management association bringing union construction labor and management representatives together to work cooperatively in order to better the construction industry as a whole. CISCO currently represents union contractors and workers in Cook, DuPage, Lake, Kane, Kendall and McHenry Counties.
14800 Members
Founded in: 1988

3853 **Construction Owners Association of America**
5000 Austell Powder Springs Rd
Suite 217
Austell, GA 30106
770-433-0820
800-994-2622; *Fax:* 404-577-3551

coaa@coaa.org; www.coaa.org
Social Media: Facebook, Twitter, LinkedIn

Kevin Lewis, President
Dean McCormick, Vice President
Gwen Glattes, Secretary/Treasurer
Ted Argyle, Past President
Stuart Adler, Director

National association dedicated to supporting project Owners' success in the design and construction of buildings and facilities through education, information and developing relationships within the industry. Comprised of public and private owners who manage facilities development and capital improvement projects.
530 Members
Founded in: 1994

3854 Construction Specifications Institute
110 South Union Street
Suite 100
Alexandria, VA 22314

703-684-0300
800-689-2900; *Fax:* 703-236-4600
csi@csinet.org; www.csinet.org
Social Media: Facebook, Twitter, LinkedIn, Youtube, Flickr

Lane J Beougher, President
Ronald L. Geren, President Elect
Ellen Kay Crews, Vice President
Kirby M. Davis, Vice President
Gary L. Beimers, Secretary

A national association dedicated to creating standards and formats to improve construction documents and project delivery. The organization is unique in the industry in that its members are a cross section of specifiers, architects, engineers, contractors and building materials suppliers.
15000 Members
Founded in: 1948

3855 Continental Automated Buildings Association (CABA)
1173 Cyrville Road
Suite 210
Ottawa, Canada, ON K1J 7S6

613-686-1814
888-798-2222; *Fax:* 613-744-7833
caba@caba.org; www.caba.org
Social Media: Facebook, Twitter, LinkedIn, YouTube

Ronald J Zimmer, President & CEO
Rawlson O'Neil King, Communications Director
Greg Walker, Research Director
George Grimes, Marketing & BD Consultant
Brenda Williamson, Database Administrator

The Continental Automated buildings Association (CABA) is a leading international, not for profit, industry organization that promoted advanced technologies in home and buildings. Its 350+ strong corporate members and 28,000+ individual industry contacts are leaders in advancing integrated home systems and building automation worldwide.
Founded in: 1988

3856 Deep Foundations Institute
326 Lafayette Avenue
Hawthorne, NJ 07506

973-423-4030; *Fax:* 973-423-4031
staff@dfi.org; www.dfi.org
Social Media: Facebook, LinkedIn

John Wolosick, President
Dan Brown, Vice President
Matthew Janes, Treasurer
Mike Wysockey, Secretary
Robert B. Bittner, Immediate Past President

DFI gathers professionals in the deep foundations sector of the construction industry, to create a place for discussion, inquiry and debate. In so doing, DFI brings the disciplines together where they have learned from each other, creating a better informed, more communicative foundations industry.
3000 Members
Founded in: 1976

3857 Design-Build Institute of America
1331 Pennsylvania Ave., NW
4th Floor
Washington, DC 20004

202-682-0110; *Fax:* 202-682-5877
dbia@dbia.org;
www.dbia.org/Pages/default.aspx
Social Media: Facebook, Twitter, LinkedIn

Timothy J. Heck, Chief Financial Officer
Louis J. Jenny, VP, Advocacy & Outreach
Lisa Washington, CAE, Executive Director/CEO
Allison Leisner, Coordinator
Richard Thomas, Dir., State/Local Legis. Affairs

An organization that defines, teaches, and promotes best practices in design-build and represents the entire design and construction industry.
Founded in: 1993

3858 Door & Access Systems Manufacturers Association International
1300 Sumner Avenue
Cleveland, OH 44115-2851

216-241-7333; *Fax:* 216-241-0105;
www.dasma.com

John H. Addington, Executive Director
R. Christopher Johnson, Assistant Executive Director
Joseph R. Hetzel, Technical Director
Louise M. Shellhammer, Administrative Assistant
Eva Brunk, Technical Assistant

Trade association of manufacturers of garage doors, rolling doors, high performance doors, garage door operators, vehicular gate operators, and access control products.
Founded in: 1996

3859 Elberton Granite Association
1 Granite Plaza
PO Box 640
Elberton, GA 30635

706-283-2551; *Fax:* 706-283-6380
granite@egaonline.com; www.egaonline.com

Manuel Fernadez, President

The Elberton Granite Association, Inc. is the largest trade association of granite quarriers and manufacturers in the United States. More than 250,000 granite memorials are manufactured annually by E.G.A. firms and shipped throughout the United States.
150 Members
Founded in: 1951

3860 Expanded Metal Manufacturers Association
800 Roosevelt Rd. Bldg. C
Suite 312
Glen Ellyn, IL 60137

630-942-6591; *Fax:* 630-790-3095
wlewis7@cox.net; www.emma-assoc.org

Randall Schievelbein, President
Jeff Church, Executive Vice President
Chris Steward, Immediate Past President
Wes Lewis, Technical Consultant
Mike Fernie, Secretary/Treasurer

Educational resources that promote the use of Expanded Metal which reduces scrap materials.
Founded in: 1938

3861 Hollow Metal Door and Buck Association
National Assn of Architectural Metal Manufacturer
800 Roosevelt Rd
Bldg C Suite 312
Glen Ellyn, IL 60137

630-942-6591; *Fax:* 630-790-3095
wlewis7@cox.net; www.naamm.org

Randall Schievelbein, President
Mike Fernie, Secretary/Treasurer
Tony Leto, Division Chair
Joseph Karpen, Division Vice Chair
Briana Gunn, Association Coordinator

The largest of four operating divisions of the National Association of Architectural Metal Manufacturers. HMMA is a group composed of companies that manufacture, distribute and promote the use of hollow metal door and frame products.
60 Members
Founded in: 1938

3862 Hollow Metal Manufacturers Association
800 Roosevelt Rd. Bldg. C
Suite 312
Glen Ellyn, IL 60137

630-942-6591; *Fax:* 630-790-3095
wlewis7@cox.net; www.hollowmetal.org

Randall Schievelbein, President
Jeff Church, Executive Vice President
Chris Steward, Immediate Past President
Wes Lewis, Technical Consultant
Mike Fernie, Secretary/Treasurer

Develops standards, conducts product performance testing and delivers education to promote the use of hollow metal doors and frames.
Founded in: 1938

3863 ICC: International Code Council
500 New Jersey Avenue, NW
6th Floor
Washington, DC 20001

888-422-7233
202-370-1800; *Fax:* 202-783-2348
webmaster@iccsafe.org; www.iccsafe.org
Social Media: Facebook, Twitter, LinkedIn, RSS, YouTube

Alex Olszowy III, President
M. Dwayne Garriss, VP
Jay Elbettar, P.E., CBO, Secretary/Treasurer
Guy Tomberlin, CBO, Immediate Past President
William Jeff Bechtold, Senior Building Official

The International Code Council is a member-focused association dedicated to helping the building safety community and construction industry provide safe, sustainable and affordable construction through the development of codes and standards used in the design, build and compliance process. Mission: To provide the highest quality codes, standards, products and services for all concerned with the safety and performance.
Founded in: 1994

3864 Interlocking Concrete Pavement Institute
14801 Murdock Stree
Suite 230
Chantilly, VA 20151

703-657-6900
800-241-3652; *Fax:* 703-657-6901
icpi@icpi.org; www.icpi.org
Social Media: Facebook, Twitter, LinkedIn, Youtube, Pinterest

David Pitre, Chairman
Matt Lynch, Chair-Elect
Mike Mueller, Secretary/Treasurer
Dave Carter, Immediate Past Chair
Elliot Bender, Member

Self governed, self funded autonomous association representing the interlocking concrete pavement industry in North America. Membership is

open to producers, contractors, suppliers, consultants and others who have an interest in the industry.
900+ Members
Founded in: 1993

3865 **International Door Association**
PO Box 246
West Milton, OH 45383
937-988-8042
800-355-4432; *Fax:* 937-698-6153
info@longmgt.com; www.doors.org
Social Media: Facebook, Twitter, LinkedIn, Youtube
Randy Oliver, President
Bill Gibson, Immediate Past President
Tim Mattews, Treasure, Industry Director
Flossie Mohler, Industry Member Vice President
Paul Peloquin, Dealer Member Vice President
The International Door Association plays an important role in the process of quality creation and control by providing helpful programs and services to those who sell, install, and service the superb products produced by the industry's list of manufacturers. Door and access systems dealers are the front line businesses that serve the customer face-to-face.
750 Members
Founded in: 1995

3866 **International Slurry Surfacing Association**
Three Church Circle
PO Box 250
Annapolis, MD 21401-1933
410-267-0023; *Fax:* 410-267-7546
krissoff@slurry.org; www.slurry.org
Social Media: Facebook, Twitter
Rusty Price, President
Carter Dabney, Vice President
Rex Eberly, Secretary
Eric Reimschiisel, Treasurer
Christine Deneuvillers, Immediate Past President
The International Slurry Surfacing Association (ISSA) is an international non-profit trade association comprised of contractors, equipment manufacturers, research personnel, consulting engineers and other industry professionals, working together to promote the concept of pavement preservation. ISSA promotes the highest standards of ethics and quality while providing its members with information, tech assistance and ongoing opportunities for networking and professional development.
Cost: $500.00
220+ Members
Founded in: 1963

3867 **International Zinc Association**
1822 East NC Highway 54
Suite 120
Durham, NC 27713
919-361-4647; *Fax:* 919-361-1957
contact@zinc.org; www.zinc.org
Social Media: Facebook, Twitter
A nonprofit global organization dedicated to the interests of zinc and its users.
Founded in: 1991

3868 **Interstates Construction Services**
1520 North Main
PO Box 260
Sioux Center, IA 51250
712-722-1662; *Fax:* 712-722-1667
bdev@interstates.com; www.interstates.com
Larry Den Herder, Chairman
Dave Crumrine, President
Catherine Bloom, Chief Financial Officer
Doug Post, President/Interstate Engineering
Jack Woelber, President/Control Systems
Combine the strengths of teams with processing industry expertise to develop the best solutions for clients' project needs. From the planning table to the plant floor, Interstates is with clients every step of the way. Assists with preliminary budgeting and help develop cost effective designs, setting the stage for a quick and efficient startup.
Founded in: 1953

3869 **Manufactured Housing Institute**
1655 North Fort Myer Road
Suite 104
Arlington, VA 22209
703-558-0400; *Fax:* 703-558-0401
info@mfghome.org;
www.manufacturedhousing.org
Social Media: Facebook, Twitter
Richard Jennison, President/CEO
Phyllis Knight, Vice Chair
Kevin Clayton, Secretary
Howard Walker, Treasurer
Lois Starkey, VP/Regulatory Affairs
MHI is the national trade organization representing all segments of the factory-built housing industry. MHI serves its membership by providing industry research, promotion, education and government relations programs, and by building and facilitating consensus within the industry.

3870 **Mason Contractors Association of America: Advancing the Masonry Industry**
1481 Merchant Drive
Algonquin, IL 60102
224-678-9709
800-536-2225; *Fax:* 224-678-9714;
www.masoncontractors.org
Social Media: Facebook, Twitter, LinkedIn
Mark Kemp, Chairman
Michael Sutter, Vice Chair
Paul Odom, Treasurer
Paul Oldham, Secretary
Michael Schmerbeck, Regional Vice President
The Mason Contractors Association of America (MCAA) is the national trade association representing mason contractors. The MCAA is committed to preserving and promoting the masonry industry by providing continuing education, advocating fair codes and standards, fostering a safe work environment, recruiting future manpower, and marketing the benefits of masonry materials.
1000 Members
Founded in: 1950

3871 **Masonry Society**
105 South Sunset Street
Suite Q
Longmont, CO 80501-6172
303-939-9700; *Fax:* 303-541-9215
info@masonrysociety.org;
www.masonrysociety.org
Social Media: LinkedIn
Scott Walkowicz, President
Jerry M Painter, President-Elect
Darrell McMillian, Vice President
Christine A. Subasic, Secretary/Treasurer
Phillip J. Samblanet, Executive Director
Dedicated to the advancement of scientific engineering, architechtural and construction knowledge of masonry. Promotes research and education and disseminates information on masonry materials, design, construction. Publishes newsletters, codes & specifications and material on masonry design.
700 Members
Founded in: 1977

3872 **Mechanical Contractors Association of America**
1385 Piccard Drive
Rockville, MD 20850
301-869-5800; *Fax:* 301-990-9690;
www.mcaa.org
Provides high-quality educational materials and programs for 2,500 firms involved in heating, air conditioning, refrigeration, plumbing, piping, and mechanical service.

3873 **Metal Building Manufacturers Association**
1300 Sumner Avenue
Cleveland, OH 44115-2851
216-241-7333; *Fax:* 216-241-0105;
www.mbma.com
Social Media: Twitter, LinkedIn
John H. Addington, General Manager
W. Lee Shoemaker, Ph.D., P.E., Dir., Research & Engineering
Jay D. Johnson, LEED AP, Dir., Architectural Services
Daniel J. Walker, P.E., Assistant General Manager
Vincent E. Sagan, P.E., Senior Staff Engineer
Promotes the design and construction of metal building systems in the low-rise, non-residential building marketplace.

3874 **Metal Construction Association**
8735 W. Higgins Rd.
Suite 300
Chicago, IL 60631
847-375-4718; *Fax:* 847-375-6488
mca@metalconstruction.org;
www.metalconstruction.org
Social Media: Facebook, Twitter, LinkedIn
Karl Hielscher, Chair
Norbert Schneider, Chair Elect
Todd E. Miller, Past Chair
Dale Nelson, Treasurer
Jim Bush, Director
An organization of manufacturers and suppliers whose metal products are used in structures.
Founded in: 1983

3875 **Metal Framing Manufacturers Association**
330 N Wabash Ave
Chicago, IL 60611
312-644-6610; *Fax:* 312-321-4098
MFMAstats@smithbucklin.com;
www.metalframingmfg.org
Mark Thorsby, Executive Director
Amanda Frjelich, Member Services
The Members of the Metal Framing Manufacturers Association (MFMA) focus on the manufacture of ferrous and nonferrous metal framing (continuous slot metal channel systems) which consist of channels with in-turned lips and associated hardware for fastening to the channels (Strut) at random points.
Founded in: 1981

3876 **Mississippi Valley Equipment Association**
11140 E Woodmen Rd
Falcon, CO 80831-8127
719-495-2283
800-388-9881; *Fax:* 719-495-3014
oholcombe@swassn.com; www.mvea.com
Social Media: Facebook
Jim C Herron, CEO
Olivia Holcombe, Director of Marketing
Cheinette Van Wyk, Administrative Manager
Jaclyn Parmer, Accounting Supervisor
Marge Tracy, Consumer Relations Supervisor

A regional affiliate of the North American Equipment Dealers Association provides members with a multitude of services designed to assist them in maintaining a profitable business operation.
165 Members
Founded in: 1941

3877 Modular Building Institute
944 Glenwood Station Ln
Suite 204
Charlottesville, VA 22901-1480

434-296-3288
888-811-3288; *Fax:* 434-296-3361
info@modular.org; www.mbinet.org
Social Media: Facebook, Twitter, LinkedIn, Youtube, Google+, Pinterest

Michael Bollero Sr., President
Harry Klukas, VP
Kathy Wilmot, VP Elect
Kelly Williams, Secretary
Christopher Peterson, Treasurer

The Modular Building Institute (MBI) is the international non-profit trade association serving modular construction. Members are manufacturers, contractors, and dealers in two distinct segments of the industry - permanent modular construction (PMC) and relocatable buildings (RB). Associate members are companies supplying building components, services, and financing.
211 Members
Founded in: 1983

3878 National Asphalt Pavement Association
5100 Forbes Blvd
Suite 200
Lanham, MD 20706—440

301-731-4748
888-468-6499; *Fax:* 301-731-4621
mcervarich@hotmix.org;
www.asphaltpavement.org
Social Media: Facebook, Twitter

Mike Acott, President
Ester Magorka, VP Awards/Marketing Programs
Audrey Copeland Ph.D., P.E., VP/Engineering
Jay Hansen, Executive Vice President
Kent Hansen P.E., Director/Engineering

The only trade association that represents the interests of the asphalt pavement producer and paving contractor on the national level with Congress, government agencies, and other national trade and business organizations. NAPA supports an active research program designed to answer questions about environmental issues and to improve the quality of asphalt pavements and paving techniques used in the construction of roads, streets, highways, parking lots, and environmental facilities.
1200 Members
Founded in: 1955

3879 National Association of Architectural Metal Manufacturers
800 Roosevelt Rd. Bldg. C
Suite 312
Glen Ellyn, IL 60137

630-942-6591; *Fax:* 630-790-3095
wlewis7@cox.net; www.naamm.org

Randall Schievelbein, President
Jeff Church, Executive Vice President
Chris Steward, Immediate Past President
Wes Lewis, Technical Consultant
Mike Fernie, Secretary/Treasurer

An association that represents a wide variety of architectural metal products for building construction.
Founded in: 1938

3880 National Association of Church Design Builders
1000 Ballpark Way
Suite 306
Arlington, TX 76011

817-200-2622
866-416-2232; *Fax:* 817-275-4519;
www.nacdb.com
Social Media: Facebook, Twitter

Dale Reiser, President
Steve Shehorn, Vice President
Amanda McFerren, Executive Director
Alexandria Gruhlkey, Administrator

An established, board-certified, nationwide association of firms committed to focusing on the ministry needs and styles of the churches they serve.

3881 National Association of Elevator Contractors
1298 Wellbrook Cir Ne
Suite A
Conyers, GA 30012-8031

770-760-9660
800-900-6232; *Fax:* 770-760-9714
info@naec.org; www.naec.org
Social Media: Facebook

Brian Farley, President
Bret Abels, Vice President
David Smarte, Secretary
Cory Hussey, Treasurer
Hugh Bertschin, Director

NAEC is an association of elevator contractors and suppliers serving primarily the interests of independent elevator contractors and independent suppliers of products and services; promoting safe and reliable elevator, escalator and short-range transportation and promoting excellence in the management of member companies.
634 Members
Founded in: 1950

3882 National Association of Home Builders
1201 15th Street NW
Washington, DC 20005

202-822-0200
800-368-5242; *Fax:* 202-266-8400
info@nahb.com; www.nahb.org
Social Media: Facebook, Twitter, LinkedIn, Google+, Pinterest

Rick Judson, Chairman
Kevin Kelly, First Vice Chair
Tom Woods, Second Vice Chair
Ed Brady, Third Vice Chair
Gerald M Howard, CEO

Represents the building industry by serving its members and affiliated state and local builders associations.
2200 Members
Founded in: 1942

3883 National Association of Women in Construction
327 S Adams Street
Fort Worth, TX 76104
817-877-5551
800-552-3506; *Fax:* 817-877-0324
nawic@nawic.org; www.nawic.org

Riki F. Lovejoy, CBT, CIT, President
Stephanie Crane, CIT, VP
Dede Hughes, EVP
Diana Sterrett, Bookkeeper
Lauri McCullough, Membership Coordinator

Founded by women working in the construction industry. The founders organized NAWIC to create a support network for women in construction.
5800 Members
Founded in: 1953

3884 National Association of the Remodeling Industry
PO Box 4250
Des Plaines, IL 60016

847-298-9200
800-611-6274; *Fax:* 847-298-9225
info@nari.org; www.nari.org
Social Media: Facebook, Twitter, YouTube, Pinterest

Fred Ulreich, CEO
Kevin Anundson, Chairman
Judy Mozen, President
Tom Miller, Treasurer
David Pekel, Secretary

NARI has an inclusive, encompassing purpose to; establish and maintain a firm commitment to developing and sustaining programs that expand and unite the remodeling industry; to ensure the industry's growth and security; to encourage ethical conduct, sound business practices and professionalism in the remodeling industry; and to present NARI as the recognized authority in the remodeling industry.
Founded in: 1935

3885 National Concrete Masonry Association
13750 Sunrise Valley Dr
Herndon, VA 20171-4662

703-713-1900; *Fax:* 703-713-1910
info@ncma.org; www.ncma.org
Social Media: Facebook, Twitter, LinkedIn, Pinterest

Robert Thomas, President
Brittaney R. Kamhong Thompson, Executive Administrator

Consists of manufacturers of concrete masonry products and suppliers of products to the industry. Offers a variety of technical of technical services and design aids through publications, computer programs, slide presentations and technical training.
Founded in: 1918

3886 National Conference of States on Building Codes & Standards
505 Huntmar Park Dr
Suite 210
Herndon, VA 20170-5103

703-437-0100; *Fax:* 703-481-3596
dbecker@ncsbcs.org; www.ncsbcs.org

Kevin Egilmez, Project Manager
Debbie Becker, Administrative Assistant

Serves as a forum for the interchange of information and provides technical services, education and training to our members to enhance the public's social, economic well-being through safe, durable, accessible and efficient buildings.
Founded in: 1967

3887 National Council of Acoustical Consultants
9100 Purdue Rd
Suite 200
Indianapolis, IN 46268

317-328-0642; *Fax:* 317-328-4629
info@ncac.com; www.ncac.com

Kenric Van Wyk P.E., President
Eric Reuter, VP Membership
Kerrie G. Standlee P.E., Immediate Past President
David Braslau, Director-at-Large

Strives to safeguard the interests of professional acoustical consulting firms. Managing physics

and psychoacoustics to provide optimum lisning environments.
130 Members
Founded in: 1962

3888 National Demolition Association
2025 M Street NW
Suite 800
Washington, DC 20036

202-367-1152
800-541-2412; *Fax:* 202-367-2152
info@demolitionassociation.com;
www.demolitionassociation.com
Social Media: Facebook, Twitter, LinkedIn

Peter Banks, President
Scott Knightly, VP
Christopher Godek, Secretary
John Adamo, Treasurer

Represents the demolition industry including demolition contractorsto foster goodwill and the exchange of ideas with the public, governmental agencies and contractors engaged in the demolition industry, and for manufacturers or suppliers of demolition equipment, supplies and services.
900 Members
Founded in: 1972

3889 National Electrical Contractors Association
3 Bethesda Metro Ctr
Suite 1100
Bethesda, MD 20814

301-657-3110; *Fax:* 301-215-4500
beth.margulies@necanet.org; www.necanet.org
Social Media: Facebook, Twitter, LinkedIn, Youtube, Flickr

John M Grau, CEO
Daniel G Walter, VP & COO
Traci Pickus, Secretary/Treasurer
Geary Higgins, VP, Labor Relations
Russell J Alessi, President, ELECTRI International

Represents a segment of the construction market comprised of electrical contracting firms.
70000 Members
Founded in: 1879

3890 National Environmental Balancing Bureau
8575 Grovemont Cir
Gaithersburg, MD 20877

301-977-3698
866-497-4447; *Fax:* 301-977-9589
jhuber@completecx.com; www.nebb.org

James Huber, President
Jean Paul Le Blance, President Elect
Robert , Linder, Past President
Jim Kelleher, Treasurer

NEBB is an international certification assocaition for firms that deliver high performance building systems. Members perform testing, adjusting and balancing (TAB) of heating, ventilating and air-conditioning systems, commission and retro-commission building systems commissioning, execute sound and vibration testing, and test and certify lab fume hoods and electronic and bio clean rooms. NEBB holds the highest standards in certification.
Founded in: 1971

3891 National Finishing Contractors Association
1 Parkview Plaza
Suite 610
Oakbrook Terrace, IL 60181

630-537-1042
866-322-3477; *Fax:* 630-590-5272
fca@finishingcontractors.org;
www.finishingcontractors.org
Social Media: Facebook, Twitter, LinkedIn

Anthony (Tony) Darkangelo, Chief Executive Officer

The Association represents contractors performing glazing work, flooring, drywalling and painting, among other finishing trades.

3892 National Hispanic Construction Association
1330 Locust Rd. NW
Washington, DC 20012-1319

214-566-2410
info@builtbylatinos.org;
www.builtbylatinos.org
Social Media: Facebook

John H. Martinez-D., Chairman

Association serving the interests of Hispanic construction professionals.

3893 National Housing Endowment
1201 15th St Nw
Washington, DC 20005

202-293-9072
800-368-5242; *Fax:* 202-266-8177
nhe@nahb.org;
www.nationalhousingendowment.org
Social Media: Facebook, Twitter, LinkedIn, Pinterest

Robert L Mitchell, Chairman
Roger Pastore, Chair-Elect
Robert Camp, Treasurer
Patsy R Smith, Secretary

Provides a permanaent source of funds to address long-term industry concerns at the national level including: supporting scholarship progams that encourage students to select home building and related fields as their life's work, assisting colleges and universities in the development of housing related curricula and activities, revitalizing the industry's labor pool and enhancing its professionalism through apprenticeship programs, seminars and continuing education.
Founded in: 1987

3894 National Lumber & Building Material Dealers Association
2025 M St NW
Suite 800
Washington, DC 20036-3309

202-367-1169
800-634-8645; *Fax:* 202-367-2169
info@dealer.org; www.dealer.org
Social Media: Facebook, Twitter, LinkedIn

JD Saunders, Chair
Scott Yates, Chair Elect
Scott Engquist, Treasurer
Chris Yenrick, Immediate Past Chair
Jonathan Paine, President

To advance the national agenda for America's building material suppliers.
6000 Members
Founded in: 1916

3895 National Organization of Minority Architects
1735 New York Avenue, NW
Suite 357
Washington, DC 20006

202-568-6682; www.noma.net
Social Media: Facebook, Twitter, LinkedIn

Kevin M Holland, President
Bryan Hudson, President Elect
Anzilla Gilmore, Vice President - South
Andrew Thompson, Vice President - North
Rod Henmi, Vice President - West

A national organization that strives to minimize the effects of racism in the architecture profession and also battles against apathy, bigotry, and abuse of the natural environment.
Founded in: 1971

3896 National Paint and Coatings Association
1500 Rhode Island Ave Nw
Washington, DC 20005

202-462-6272; *Fax:* 202-462-8549
npca@paint.org; www.paint.org
Social Media: Facebook, Twitter, LinkedIn

J Andrew Doyle, President
Thomas J Graves, VP, General Counsel
Allen Irish, Counsel/Director, Industry Affairs

Manufacturers of paints and industrial coatings and suppliers to the industry.
400+ Members
Founded in: 1887

3897 National Railroad Construction & Maintenance Association
500 New Jersey Ave NW
Suite 400
Washington, DC 20001

202-715-1264; *Fax:* 202-318-0867
info@nrcma.org; www.nrcma.org
Social Media: Facebook, Twitter, LinkedIn

Bill Dorris, Chairman
Chris Daloisio, Vice Chair
Mike Choat, Secretary/Treasurer
Chuck Baker, President
Keith Hartwell, Government Affairs

Members are railroad construction and maintenance contractors, engineering firms, manufacturing suppliers and professional associate firms.
100+ Members
Founded in: 1978

3898 National Ready Mixed Concrete Association
900 Spring St
Silver Spring, MD 20910-4015

301-587-1400
888-846-7622; *Fax:* 301-585-4219
info@nrmca.org; www.nrmca.org
Social Media: Facebook, Twitter, LinkedIn, YouTube

Allen Hamblen, Chairman
Ted Chandler, Vice Chair
Scott Parson, Secretary/Treasurer
Ric Suzio, Immediate Past Chairman

Our mission is to provide exceptional value for our members by responsibly representing and serving the entire ready mixed concrete industry through leadership, promotion, education and partnering; to ensure ready mixed concrete is the building material of choice.
1200 Members
Founded in: 1930

3899 National Roofing Contractors Association
10255 W. Higgins Road
Suite 600
Rosemont, IL 60018-5607

847-299-9070; *Fax:* 847-299-1183;
www.nrca.net
Social Media: Facebook, Twitter, LinkedIn, YouTube, Instagram, Google+

Richard M. Nugent, President
Lindy Ryan, Senior Vice President
Scott Baxter, Vice President
Dennis Conway, Vice President
Bob Kulp, Vice President

An association of roofing, roof deck, and waterproofing contractors; industry-related associate members; and international members worldwide.
3500 Members
Founded in: 1886

3900 National Slag Association
P.O Box 1197
Pleasant Grove, UT 84062

801-785-4535; *Fax:* 801-785-4539;
www.nationalslag.org

Members are processors of iron and steel slags for use as a aggregate in construction and manufacturing applications.
77 Members
Founded in: 1918

3901 National Stone, Sand & Gravel Association
1605 King St
Alexandria, VA 22314

703-525-8788
800-342-1415; *Fax:* 703-525-7782
jwilson@nssga.org; www.nssga.org
Social Media: Facebook, Twitter, LinkedIn, YouTube

Michael W Johnson, President & CEO
Gus Edwards, President Emeritus
Dennis F. Coker, Treasurer
Randy Lake, Secretary of the Board
Jennifer Lewis, Executive Administrator

Represents the crushed stone, sand and gravel — or aggregate — industries. Our members account for 90 percent of the crushed stone and 70 percent of the sand and gravel produced annually in the US.
570 Members
Founded in: 1985

3902 National Systems Contractors Association
3950 River Ridge DR NE
Suite B
Cedar Rapids, IA 52402

319-366-6722
800-446-6722; *Fax:* 319-366-4164
nsca@nsca.org; www.nsca.org
Social Media: Facebook, Twitter, LinkedIn, YouTube

Michael Hester, President
Ray Bailey, VP
Josh Shanahan, Treasurer
David Ferlino, Secretary
Chuck Wilson, Executive Director

A not for profit association representing the commercial electronic systems industry. Also a powerful advocate of all who work within the low voltage industry, including systems contractors/integrators, product manufacturers, consultants, sales representatives, a growing number of architects, specifying engineers and others.
2800 Members
Founded in: 1980

3903 National Terrazzo and Mosaic Association
P.O. Box 2605
Fredericksburg, TX 78624

800-323-9736; *Fax:* 888-362-2770
info@ntma.com; www.ntma.com

George Hardy, Executive Director

The association establishes national standards for all terrazzo floor and wall systems and provides complete specifications, color plates and general information to architects and designers at no cost.

3904 National Tile Contractors Association
626 Lakeland E Drive
PO Box 13629
Jackson, MS 39232

601-939-2071; *Fax:* 601-932-6117
webmaster@tile-assn.com; www.tile-assn.com
Social Media: Facebook, Twitter, LinkedIn, YouTube

James Woelfel, President
Martin Howard, First VP
Chris Walker, Second VP
Bart Bettiga, Executive Director
Jim Olson, Ass. Executive Director

Serving every segment of the industry, and is recognized as the largest and most respected tile contractors association in the world.
1000 Members
Founded in: 1947
Mailing list available for rent

3905 National Utility Contractors Association
3925 Chain Bridge Road
Suite 300
Fairfax, VA 22230

703-358-9300; *Fax:* 703-358-9307
nuca@nuca.com; www.nuca.com
Social Media: Facebook, Twitter, LinkedIn

Bonnie Williams, VP, Marketing & Communications
Will Brown, Director, Government Relations
Bill Hillman, CEO

A national association that provides a forum for continuing education and promotes effective public policy, through its grassroots network, to protect and enhance your industry.
1400 Members
Founded in: 1964

3906 North American Insulation Manufacturers Association
11 Canal Center Plaza
Suite 103
Alexandria, VA 22314-1548

703-684-0084; *Fax:* 703-684-0427;
www.naima.org

Kate Offringa, President/CEO
Angus Crane, EVP

Manufacturers of fiber glass, rock wool, and slag wool insulation products. NAIMA members manufacture the vast majority of fiber glass, rock and slag wool insulations produced and used in North America.
Founded in: 1933

3907 Northeastern Retail Lumber Association
585 N Greenbush Rd
Rensselaer, NY 12144

518-286-1010
800-292-6752; *Fax:* 518-286-1755
rferris@nrla.org; www.nrla.org

Jonas Kelly, Chair
Rita Ferris, President
Joe Miles, Chair Elect
Charles Handley, Vice Chair
Richard Tarr, Treasurer

A resource for industry members, consumers, and public officials independent lumber and building material suppliers and associated businesses in New York and the six New England states.
1150 Members
Founded in: 1894

3908 Operative Plasterers' and Cement Masons' International Association
11720 Beltsville Dr
Suite 700
Beltsville, MD 20705

301-623-1000; *Fax:* 301-623-1032
opcmiaintl@opcmia.org; www.opcmia.org

Patrick D Finley, General President
Earl F Hurd, General Secretary/Treasurer
Daniel E Stepano, EVP
Roger Bettermann, Vice President
Todd Lair, Vice President

Represents and trains plasterers and cement masonsn for the purpose of protecting and promoting the quality of the industry and the livelihood of the members.
Founded in: 1864

3909 Outdoor Power Equipment Institute
341 S Patrick St
Alexandria, VA 22314

703-549-7600; *Fax:* 703-549-7604
info@opei.org; www.opei.org
Social Media: Facebook, Twitter, LinkedIn

Kris Kiser, President & CEO
Lee Sowell, Chairman
Tim Merrett, Vice Chair
Daniel Ariens, Secretary/Treasurer

International trade association whose members are manufacturers of powered lawn and garden maintenance products, components and attachment supplies, as well as industry related services.
85 Members
Founded in: 1952

3910 Painting and Decorating Contractors of America
2316 Millpark Drive
Maryland Heights, MO 63043

314-514-7322
800-332-7322; *Fax:* 314-890-2068;
www.pdca.org
Social Media: Facebook, Twitter, LinkedIn, YouTube

David Ryker, Chair
Tony Severino, Vice Chair
Mark Adams, Treasurer
Richard Greene, MBA, CAE, CEO
Libby Loomis, Special Projects

PDCA exists to lead the industry by providing quality products, programs, services, and opportunities essential to the success of our members.
5M Members
Founded in: 1884

3911 Perlite Institute
2207 Forest Hills Drive
Suite A
Harrisburg, PA 17112

717-238-9723; *Fax:* 717-238-9985
info@perlite.org; www.perlite.org
Social Media: Facebook, LinkedIn

Matt Goecker, President
Matthew Malaghan, VP
Keith Hoople, Treasurer
Linda Chirico, Past President/Advisor

An international trade association which establishes product standards and specifications, and which encourages the development of new product uses through research.
183 Members
Founded in: 1949

3912 Pile Driving Contractors Association
33 Knight Boxx Road
Suite 1
Orange Park, FL 32065

904-215-4771
888-311-7322; *Fax:* 904-215-2977;
www.piledrivers.org
Social Media: Facebook, Twitter, LinkedIn

Eric Alberghini, President
Marty Corcoran, VP
Bill Marczewski, Treasurer
Eric Albergini, Secretary

An organization of pile driving contractors that advocates the incresed use of driven piles for deep foundations and earth retention systems. Promotes the use of driven pile solutions in all

cases where they are effective, support educational programs for engineers on the design and efficiency of driven piles and for contractors on improving installation procedures and give contractors a larger voice in establishing procedures and standards for pile installation and design.
450 Members
Founded in: 1996

3913 Pipe Fabrication Institute
511 Ave Of Americas
#601
New York, NY 10011

514-634-3434
866-913-3434; *Fax:* 514-634-9736
pfi@pfi-institute.org; www.pfi-institute.org

Jeff Huggard, Chairman
Tim Monday, Vice Chair
Greg Howell, Treasurer
Guy Fortin, Executive Director
Robert B Cottington, Legal Counsel

Members are companies producing sophisticated high temperature, high pressure piping systems that employ specialists from the United Association of Journeymen and Apprentices of the Plumbing and Pipe Fitting Industry. We exist solely for the purpose of ensuring a level of quality in the pipe fabrication industry that is without compromise.
65-70 Members
Founded in: 1913

3914 Portable Sanitation Association International
2626 E 82nd Street
Suite 175
Bloomington, MN 55425

952-854-8300
800-822-3020; *Fax:* 952-854-7560
info@psai.org; www.psai.org
Social Media: Facebook, Twitter, LinkedIn

Tim Petersen, President
Karen Holm, VP
Matt Sola, Secretary
Dwayne Siegmann, Treasurer

International trade association that represents firms engaged in the leasing, renting, selling and manufacturing of portable sanitation equipment, services and supplies for construction, recreation, emergency and other uses. Devoted to the proper handling of human waste by the most modern, sanitary means, giving the greatest concern to the preservation of an unspoiled environment.
550+ Members
Founded in: 1971

3915 Portland Cement Association
5420 Old Orchard Road
Skokie, IL 60077-1083

847-966-6200; *Fax:* 847-966-9781
info@cement.org; www.cement.org
Social Media: Facebook, Twitter, LinkedIn, YouTube

John Stull, Chair
Karl Watson Jr, Vice-Chair
James G Toscas, President/CEO
Steve Ambrose, Vice President, Sales and Marketing

The Portland Cement Association represents cement companies in the United States and Canada. It conducts market development, engineering, research, education, and public affairs programs.
Founded in: 1916

3916 Precast Prestressed Concrete Institute
200 W Adams St
Suite 2100
Chicago, IL 60606

312-786-0300; *Fax:* 312-621-1114
info@pci.org; www.pci.org
Social Media: Facebook, Twitter, LinkedIn, RSS

Robert Risser PE, President
Michelle Burgess, Managing Editor
Roger Becker PE, SE, Managing Director, R&D
Jeff Appel, Controller

Dedicated to fostering understanding and use of precast and prestressed concrete, maintains a full staff of techniocal and marketing specialists.
1400 Members
Founded in: 1954

3917 Professional Construction Estimators Association of America
PO Box 680336
Charlotte, NC 28216

704-484-1494
877-521-7232; *Fax:* 704-489-1495
pcea@pcea.org; www.pcea.org
Social Media: Facebook

Bill Barton, President
Glenn Hessee, President Elect
Derek Lanning, VP
Matt Solomon, Secretary
Wesley Ferree, Treasurer

Promotes construction estimating as a profession by upholding the code of ethics, and expanding public awareness.
1000 Members
Founded in: 1956

3918 Resilient Floor Covering Institute
115 Broad Street
Sutie 201
La Grange, GA 30240

301-340-8580
info@rfci.com; www.rfci.com
Social Media: Facebook, Pinterest

Douglas Wiegand, Executive Director

Industry trade association of North American manufacturers who produce resilient flooring products. Associate members of RFCI supply raw materials to the industry and manufacture installation and maintenance products.
21 Members
Founded in: 1975

3919 Retail Contractors Association
400 North Washington Street
Suite 300
Alexandria, VA 22314

800-847-5085
703-683-5637; *Fax:* 703-683-0018;
www.retailcontractors.org

Mike Wolff, President
Robert Moore, Vice President
Brad Bogart, Secretary/Treasurer
Steve Bachman, Director
Jack Grothe, Director

A national organization of retail contractors united to provide a solid foundation of ethics, quality, and professionalism within the retail construction industry.

3920 Roof Coatings Manufacturers Association
750 National Press Building
529 14th Street NW
Washington, DC 20045

202-207-0919; *Fax:* 202-223-9741
questions@roofcoatings.org;
www.roofcoatings.org
Social Media: LinkedIn

John Ferraro, Executive Director
Mike Fischer, Codes & Standard Director
Shawn Richardson, Communications Coordinator
Kelly Franklin, Industry Affairs Coordinator

Represents the interests of manufacturers of cold applied roof coatings, cements and waterproofing agents, as well as the suppliers of products, equipment and services to and for the industry.
70+ Members
Founded in: 1983

3921 Rubber Pavements Association
10000 N. 31st. Ave.
Suite D-408
Phoenix, AZ 85281-5738

480-517-9944
877-517-9944; *Fax:* 480-517-9959
mbelshe@rubberpavements.org;
www.rubberpavements.org

Cliff Ashcroft, VP
Mark Belshe, Executive Director
Guadalupe Dickerson, Office Manager

Dedicated to encouraging greater usage of high quality, cost effective asphalt pavements containing recycled tire rubber. Conducts national and international seminars.
20 Members
Founded in: 1985

3922 SPRI: Single Ply Roofing Industry
465 Waverley Oaks Road
Suite 421
Waltham, MA 02452

781-647-7026; *Fax:* 781-647-7222
info@spri.org; www.spri.org

Al Janni, President
Linda King, Managing Director

Comprised of manufacturers and marketers of sheet applied membrane roofing systems and components to the commercial roofing industry.
58 Members
Founded in: 1981

3923 Safety Glazing Certification Council
P.O. Box 730
Sackets Harbor, NY 13685

315-646-2234; *Fax:* 315-646-2297
erin@amscert.com; www.igcc.org

Don Boutelle, President
Bruce Kaskel, Vice President
Brian Burnet, Secretary
Bruce Kaskel, Treasurer

Nonprofit corporation that provides for the certifacation of safety glazing materials, comprised of safety glazing manufacturers and other parties concerned with public safety. SGCC is managed by a board of directors comprised of representatives from the safety glazing industry and the public interest sector.
105 Members
Founded in: 1977

3924 Scaffold Industry Association
400 Admiral Blvd
Kansas City, MO 64106-1508

602-257-1144
816-595-4860; *Fax:* 602-257-1166
info@scaffold.org; www.scaffold.org
Social Media: Facebook, Twitter, LinkedIn

Mike Russell, President
Frank Frietsch, Treasurer

Promotes safety by developing educational and informational material, conducting educational seminars and training courses, providing audio-visual programs and codes for safe practices, and other training and safety aids; to work with state, federal and other agencies in developing more effective safety standards; to reduce accidents, thereby reducing insurance costs; and to assist members in becoming more efficient and profitable in their businesses.
1000 Members
Founded in: 1972

3925 Screen Manufacturers Association
2850 S Ocean Boulevard
Suite 114
Palm Beach, FL 33480-6242
733-636-0672; *Fax:* 561-533-7466
Kathryn@SMAinfo.org; www.smainfo.org
Social Media: Twitter

Alan Gray, VP
Michael White-RiteScreen, President
Tammy Groft, Sales Manager

Manufacturers of insect screens, screen frames, window screens, detention screens, sliding screen doors, swinging screen doors, fiberglass insect screening and aluminum insect screening.
Cost: $1000.00
20 Members
Founded in: 1955

3926 Specialty Tools and Fasteners Distributors Association
500 Elm Grove Rd.
Suite 210
Elm Grove, WI 53122
262-784-4774
800-352-2981; *Fax:* 262-784-5059
info@stafda.org; www.stafda.org
Social Media: Facebook, LinkedIn

Rick Lamb, President
Rod Gowett, VP
Georgia Foley, Executive Director

International trade association composed of distributors and manufacturers and rep agents of light construction, industrial and related products. Members also include publishers of industry press serving the construction and industrial trades.
Cost: $350.00
2603 Members
Founded in: 1976

3927 Spray Polyurethane Foam Alliance
3827 Old Lee Hwy
Suite 101B
Fairfax, VA 22030
800-523-6154; *Fax:* 703-222-5816
info@sprayfoam.org; www.sprayfoam.org
Social Media: Facebook, Twitter

Bonnie Strickler, Chair
Dennis Vandewater, President
John Achille, VP
Richard Spiess, Secretary/Treasurer

A trade association representing interests associated with rigid and semi-rigid polyurethane foam products that are typically applied with spray equipment as roofing and insulation.
Founded in: 1987

3928 Steel Door Institute
30200 Detroit Road
Westlake, OH 44145
440-899-0010; *Fax:* 440-892-1404
info@steeldoor.org; www.steeldoor.org

Jeff Wherry, Managing Director

A voluntary, nonprofit business association that develops quality and performance standards for steel doors and frames.
Founded in: 1954

3929 Steel Joist Institute
234 W Cheves Street
Florence, SC 29501
843-407-4091; *Fax:* 843-626-5565
sji@steeljoist.org; www.steeljoist.org
Social Media: Twitter, LinkedIn

J Kenneth Charles III, Managing Director

Composed of active manufacturers, the SJI cooperates with government and business agencies to establish steel joint standards.
40 Members
Founded in: 1928

3930 Steel Window Institute
1300 Sumner Ave
Cleveland, OH 44115-2851
216-241-7333; *Fax:* 216-241-0105;
www.steelwindows.com

John Addington, Executive Director

An association of the leading manufacturers of windows made from either solid or formed sections of steel, and such related products as casings, trim, mechanical operators, screens, and moldings when manufactured and sold by members of the industry for use in conjunction with windows.
6 Members

3931 Structural Insulated Panel Association
P.O. Box 39848
Fort Lauderdale, FL 33339
253-858-7472; *Fax:* 253-858-0272
info@sips.org; www.sips.org
Social Media: Facebook, Twitter, RSS

Ard Smits, President
Jim Leroy, First VP
Mike Tobin, Second VP
David Tompos, Secretary/Treasurer

A trade association representing manufacturers, suppliers, fabriators, distributors, design professionals and builders committed to providing quality structural insulated panels for all segments of the construction industry.
250 Members
Founded in: 1990

3932 Stucco Manufacturers Association
2402 Vista Nobleza
Newport Beach, CA 92660-3545
949-640-9902; *Fax:* 949-701-4476
info@stuccomfgassoc.com;
www.stuccomfgassoc.com
Social Media: Facebook, Youtube

Kevin Wensel, President
Nick Brown, VP
Buck Buchanan, Secretary
Rui Bronze, Treasurer
Norma S Fox, Executive Director

Our main purpose is to promote the advantage of 3 coat colored cementitious stucco by educating the building industry and consumers.
50 Members
Founded in: 1957

3933 Subcontractors Trade Association
1430 Broadway
Suite 1600
New York, NY 10018
212-398-6220; *Fax:* 212-398-6224
hkita@stanyc.com; www.stanyc.com
Social Media: Facebook, Twitter, LinkedIn

Jerry Liss, President
Robert J Ansbro, VP
Robert Weiss, VP
Peter Cafiero, Treasurer
John A Finamore, Secretary

Members are specialty and supply companies in the construction industry. Our goal is to improve the economic well being of our members through representation, support and assistance through the process of legislation, legal action, public relations, education and other public information programs.
350+ Members
Founded in: 1966

3934 Textile Care Allied Trades Association
271 Route 46 West
Suite C-106
Fairfield, NJ 07004-2432
973-244-1790; *Fax:* 973-244-4455
info@tcata.org; www.tcata.org
Social Media: Facebook, Twitter, LinkedIn

Bryant Dunivan, President
Bryant Dunivan, President-Elect
David Cotter, Chief Executive Officer
Cheryl Paglia, Office Manager

Represents the interests of distributors and manufacturers of equipment and supplies for the cleaning industry.
Founded in: 1920

3935 The American Institute of Architects
1735 New York Ave., NW
Washington, DC 20006-5292
800-AIA-3837; *Fax:* 202-626-7547
docstechsupport@aia.org; www.aia.org
Social Media: Facebook, Twitter, LinkedIn, YouTube, RSS, Flickr

Based in Washington D.C., the AIA is the leading professional membership association for licensed architects, emerging professionals, and allied partners.
Founded in: 1857

3936 The Construction Specifications Institute
110 South Union Street
Suite 100
Alexandria, VA 22314
800-689-2900; *Fax:* 703-236-4600
csi@csinet.org; www.csinet.org
Social Media: Facebook, Twitter, LinkedIn, YouTube, Flickr

An organization that keeps and changes the standardization of construction language as it pertains to building specifications. It provides technical information and products, continuing education, professional conferences, and product shows.
Founded in: 1948

3937 Tile Contractors' Association of America
10434 Indiana Avenue
Kansas City, MO 64137
816-868-9300
800-655-8453; *Fax:* 816-767-0194
info@tcaainc.org; www.tcaainc.org

Ronald Schwartz, President/Chairman
Brian Castro, President Elect/Vice-Chairman
Lucinda Noel, Treasurer
Jennifer Panning, Immediate Past President
Brad Trostrud, Director

Union contractor association featuring; Architect/designer learning exchange, speakers, business meetings, new products and technology.
175 Members
Founded in: 1903

3938 Tile Roofing Institute
23607 Highway 99
Suite 2C
Edmonds, WA 98026
425-778-6162; *Fax:* 425-771-9588
info@tileroofing.org; www.tileroofing.org
Social Media: Facebook, Twitter, LinkedIn

Kevin Burlingame, Chairman
Chris Fenwick, Vice Chairman
Terry Johnson, Secretary/Treasurer
Cliff Taylor, Director

Manufacturers of clay and concrete roof tiles. Emphasis is on technical issues and codes that involve tile.
Founded in: 1971

3939 **Timber Frame Business Council**
46 Chambersburg
PO Box 60
Becket, MA 01223

413-623-8759
855-598-1803; *Fax:* 413-623-8759
info@timberframe.org; www.timberframe.org
Social Media: Facebook, Twitter

Jeff Arvin, Executive Director
Bruce Bode, President

Advances the business, communications and research interests of companies engaged in the timber framing industry.
Founded in: 1995

3940 **Timber Framers Guild**
12100 Sunset Hills Rd
PO Box 60
Becket, MA 01223

413-623-8759
855-598-1803; *Fax:* 413-623-8759
info@tfguild.org; www.tfguild.org
Social Media: Facebook, Twitter

Joel McCarty, Executive Director

The Guild is dedicated to establishing training programs for dedicated timber framers, disseminating information about timber framing and timber frame building design, displaying the art of timber framing to the public, and generally serving as a center of timber framing information for the professional and general public alike.
Cost: $85.00
1700 Members
Founded in: 1984

3941 **Truck Mixer Manufacturers Bureau**
900 Spring St
Silver Spring, MD 20910-4015

301-587-1400
888-846-7622; *Fax:* 301-587-1605
nmaher@cpmb.org; www.cpmb.org

Robert Garbini, President
Deana Angelastro, Executive Administrator

An association of ready mixed concrete truck manufacturers who have joined together in support of the ready mixed industry. TMMB members are required to manufacture equipment in accordance to the TMMB Standards.
Founded in: 1958

3942 **Western Building Material Association**
909 Lakeridge Drive SW
PO Box 1699
Olympia, WA 98507

360-943-3054
888-551-9262; *Fax:* 360-943-1219
wbma@wbma.org; www.wbma.org
Social Media: Facebook, Twitter, LinkedIn

Casey Voorhees, Executive Director
Stephanie Masters, Office Manager
Tom Rider, Manager Member Services

Regional trade association serving material dealers throughout the states of Alaska, Idaho, Montana, Oregon and Washington and a federated association of the National Lumber and Building Material Dealers Association.
600 Members
Founded in: 1903

Newsletters

3943

American Bar Association
321 N Clark St.
Chicago, IL 60654

www.americanbar.org/publications/under_construction

3944 **ACSM Bulletin**
American Congress on Surveying and Mapping
6 Montgomery Village Ave
Suite 403
Gaithersburg, MD 20879-3557

240-632-9716; *Fax:* 240-632-1321
ilse.genovese@acsm.net; www.acsm.net

Ilse Genovese, Editor

A bi-monthly professional magazine published by ACSM to inform the public about current developments taking place within the geospatial community.
Frequency: Bi-Monthly

3945 **AHW Reporter**
Duane Publishing
51 Park St
Dorchester, MA 02122-2643

617-282-4885; *Fax:* 617-282-0320;
www.rubblemakers.com

Herb Duane, Owner
Toby Duane, Director

Asbestos and hazardous waste information.

3946 **Asbestos & Lead Abatement Report**
Business Publishers
2222 Sedwick Dr
Suite 101
Durham, NC 27713

800-223-8720; *Fax:* 800-508-2592
custserv@bpinews.com; www.bpinews.com

Tracks the major legislative, regulatory and technological developments in asbestos and lead abatement industries. Includes highlights of major research studies on the effect of lead and asbestos on human health.
Cost: $371.54
Frequency: BiWeekly

3947 **Brick News**
Brick Industry Association
1850 Centennial Park Drive
Suite 301
Reston, VA 20191-1542

703-620-0010; *Fax:* 703-620-3928
brickinfo@bia.org; www.gobrick.com

Richard Jennison, President/CEO

News, information and programs of interest to brick distributors.

3948 **Building Products News**
Palgrave Macmillan
175 5th Ave
Suite 4
New York, NY 10010-7728

212-982-3900
888-330-8477; *Fax:* 212-307-5035;
www.macmillan.com

Winston Jeune, Director

A unique publication researching the commercial renovation and retrofit market.

3949 **Building Stone**
Building Stone Institute
5 Riverside Dr
Building 2
Chestertown, NY 12817

518-803-4336
866-786-6313; *Fax:* 518-803-4336;
www.buildingstoneinstitute.org

Duffe Elkins, President
Rob Teel, VP

State of the industry publication for architects, designers and people in the natural stone industries: granite, marble, limestone, etc.
Cost: $65.00
Frequency: Quarterly
Circulation: 17,000
Founded in: 1919

3950 **Building and Construction Market Forecast**
Reed Business Information
360 Park Ave S
New York, NY 10010-1737

646-746-6400; *Fax:* 646-756-7583
corporatecommunications@reedbusiness.com;
www.reedbusiness.com

Mark Kelsey, CEO
Stuart Whayman, CFO

Forecasts and analysis on the construction industry.
Cost: $187.00
6 Pages
Frequency: Monthly
Founded in: 1946

3951 **Concrete Pipe News**
American Concrete Pipe Association
8445 Freeport Parkway
Suite 350
Irving, TX 75063

972-506-7216; *Fax:* 972-506-7682
info@concrete-pipe.org;
www.concrete-pipe.org

Matt Childs, President
Josh Beakley, Technical Services Director
Wanda Cochran, Events Manager

Concrete Pipe News is designed to provide information on the use and installation of precast concrete pipe products for a wide variety of applications, including drainage and pollution control systems. Industry technology, research and trends are also important subjects of the publication. Readers include engineers, specifiers, public works officials, contractors, suppliers, vendors and members of the American Concrete Pipe Association.
Cost: $3.50
16 Pages
Frequency: Quarterly
Founded in: 1907

3952 **Construction Company Strategist**
Brownstone Publishers
149 5th Ave
10th Floor
New York, NY 10010

212-473-8200; *Fax:* 212-564-0465

Douglas Lowey, CEO
Andrew Shapiro, VP

Strategies, legal tips, and how-to advice for successfully managing a construction company in the 1990's. Features model contract language, forms, guidelines and more.
Cost: $269.00
Frequency: Monthly
Circulation: 180000
Founded in: 1971
Printed in 2 colors on matte stock

3953 **Construction Contractor**
Federal Publications
1100 13th Street NW
Washington, DC 20005

202-772-8295
888-494-3696; *Fax:* 202-772-8298
fedpubseminars.com

Michael Canavan, Director

Bi-weekly newsletter providing in-depth legal insight and analysis for all construction profes-

sionals.
Cost: $592.00
Frequency: BiWeekly

3954 Construction Equipment Monthly
Heartland Communications
1003 Central Avenue
PO Box 1052
Fort Dodge, IA 50501-1052

515-955-1600
800-247-2000; *Fax:* 515-574-2107
personnel@hlipublishing.com;
www.hlipublishing.com

Patrick Van Arnam, President
Gale McKinney, CFO

Listings by category, equipment and parts for sale.
Cost: $125.00
Frequency: Annual+
Founded in: 1988

3955 Construction Labor Report
Bureau of National Affairs
3 Bethesda Metro Center
Suite 250
Bethesda, MD 20814

800-372-1033; *Fax:* 800-253-0332
customercare@bna.com; www.bna.com

Donna Ives, VP Operations
Gregory McCaffery, President

A weekly information service that covers union-management relations in the construction industry, reporting on significant legislative, judicial, economic, management and union developments.
Cost: $1543.00
Frequency: Weekly
Circulation: 1600
ISSN: 0010-6836

3956 Constructor Newsletter
Associated General Contractors of America
2300 Wilson Blvd
Suite 400
Arlington, VA 22201

703-548-3118; *Fax:* 703-837-5400
info@agc.org; www.agc.org

Kristine Young, President
Joe Jarboe, SVP

Reports on contractors and items of interest to the construction community.
Frequency: Monthly
Circulation: 33000
Founded in: 1918

3957 Crow's Weekly Letter
CC Crow Publications
3635 N Farragut St
Portland, OR 97217-5954

503-241-7382; *Fax:* 503-646-9971
info@chadcrowe.com; www.chadcrowe.com

Chad Crowe, President

Weekly report on trends and prices in the wood products industry.
Cost: $285.00
12 Pages
Frequency: Weekly
Founded in: 1921
Printed in 4 colors on matte stock

3958 Demo-Memo
Duane Publishing
51 Park Street
PO Box 130
Dorchester, MA 02122

617-282-4885; *Fax:* 617-282-0320;
www.demolitionconsulting.com

Herbert Duane, President

Demolition news and information.

3959 Dodge Report & Bulletins
McGraw Hill
PO Box 182604
Columbus, OH 43272-1095

614-866-5769
877-833-5524; *Fax:* 614-759-3749
customer.service@mcgraw-hill.com;
www.mcgraw-hill.com

Jennifer Hayes, Editor
Harold McGraw III, President/CEO

Dodge Reports gives you the information you need to prepare a bid or enter negotiations. The detailed project information will also enable you to sell products or services.
Frequency: Daily
Founded in: 1884

3960 E-Catalyst Industry Update
Adhesive & Sealant Council
7101 Wisconsin Ave
Suite 990
Bethesda, MD 20814-4805

301-986-9700; *Fax:* 301-986-9795
data@ascouncil.org; www.ascouncil.org

Bill Allmond, President

3961 Environmental Building News
BuildingGreen
122 Birge St
Suite 30
Brattleboro, VT 05301-6703

802-257-7300; *Fax:* 802-257-7304
info@buildinggreen.com;
www.buildinggreen.com

Alex Wilson, Owner
Nadav Malin, President
Tristan Roberts, Editorial Director
Jennifer Atlee, Research Director

Featuring comprehensive, practical information on a wide range of topics related to sustainable building—from energy efficiency and recycled-content materials to land-use planning and indoor air quality.
Cost: $99.00
Frequency: Monthly
Founded in: 1992

3962 Hard Hat News
Lee Publications
6113 State Highway 5
PO Box 121
Palatine Bridge, NY 13428

518-673-3237
800-218-5586; *Fax:* 518-673-2699
info@leepub.com; www.leepub.com

Fred Lee, Owner
Wendell Jennings, Sales Manager

Construction and heavy equipment.
72 Pages
Frequency: Monthly

3963 Housing Marketing Report
CD Publications
8204 Fenton St
Silver Spring, MD 20910-4571

301-588-6380
800-666-6380; *Fax:* 301-588-6385
info@cdpublications.com;
www.cdpublications.com

Michael Gerecht, President
Charles Wisniowski, Editor

Concise analysis of national and regional housing markets, materials and supplies.
Cost: $469.00
Founded in: 1961
Mailing list available for rent: 2,000 names at $160 per M
Printed in on matte stock

3964 Indoor Air Quality Update
Aspen Publishers
76 Ninth Avenue
7th Floor
New York, NY 10011

212-771-0600
800-638-8437; *Fax:* 301-695-7931;
www.aspenlawschool.com

Mark Dorman, CEO
Gustavo Dobles, VP Operations

A guide to the practical control of building materials.
Cost: $440.00
Circulation: 20000
ISSN: 1040-5313

3965 Industry News
Modular Building Institute
944 Glenwood Station Ln
Suite 204
Charlottesville, VA 22901-1480

434-296-3288
888-811-3288; *Fax:* 434-296-3361
info@mbinet.org; www.mbinet.org

Tom Hardiman, Executive Director
Steven Williams, Operations Director

For members only.
Circulation: 650

3966 Machinery Outlook
Manfredi & Associates
20934 W Lakeview Pkwy
Mundelein, IL 60060-9502

847-949-9080; *Fax:* 847-949-9910
frank@manfredi.com;
www.machineryoutlook.com

Frank Manfredi, President
James Manfredi, Editor

A newsletter about and for the construction and mining machinery industry.
Cost: $550.00
14 Pages
Frequency: Monthly
Founded in: 1984
Printed in one color on matte stock

3967 Manufactured Structures Newsletter
Bobbitt Group
1710 S Gilbert Rd
Ste 1167
Mesa, AZ 85204
480-982-6173
wsbobbitt@hotmail.com;
www.thebobbittgroup.com
William Bobbitt, Editor/Publisher
Marci Bobbitt, Associate Editor/Business Manager

Covers all aspects of the automated building industry with a monthly collection of original feature stories profiling leading and emerging companies in the industry as well as other informative information on the industry, business tips, proven sales and marketing and featured editorials.
Frequency: Monthly
ISSN: 1068-4962
Founded in: 1969

3968 NAWIC Image
National Association of Women in Construction
327 S Adams Street
Fort Worth, TX 76104

817-877-5551
800-552-3506; *Fax:* 817-877-0324
nawic@nawic.org; www.nawic.org

Debra Gregoire, Presdient
Cindy Johnsen, VP

Management, trends and techniques in the construction business.
Cost: $50.00
Frequency: Bi-Monthly
Circulation: 6000

3969 NRCMA Biweekly Email Bulletin
National Railroad Construction & Maintenance Assoc
500 New Jersey Ave NW
Suite 400
Washington, DC 20001-2065

202-715-2919; *Fax:* 202-318-0867
info@nrcma.org; www.nrcma.org

Chuck Baker, President
Matt Ginsberg, Director of Operations
Frequency: Biweekly

3970 News Brief
Granite State Designers & Installers Association
53 Regional Drive
Ste 1
Concord, NH 03301-3520

603-228-1231; *Fax:* 603-228-2118
info@gsdia.org; www.gsdia.org

Carl Hagstrom, Director
Randy Orvis, Director

Newsletter for members of GSD1 relative to septic system design, installation and maintenance.
Cost: $150.00
Frequency: Monthly

3971 RCMA Newsletter
Roof Coatings Manufacturers Association
750 National Press Building
529 14th Street NW
Washington, DC 20045

202-207-0919; *Fax:* 202-223-9741
questions@roofcoatings.org;
www.roofcoatings.org

Steve Heinje, Director
Frequency: Quarterly

3972 Redwood Reporter
California Redwood Association
818 Grayson Road
Suite 201
Pleasant Hill, CA 94523

925-935-1499; *Fax:* 925-935-1496
info@calredwood.org; www.calredwood.org

Pamela Allsebrook, Publisher
Christopher Grover, President

Information about the redwood business of interest to redwood dealers.
8 Pages
Circulation: 8000

3973 Reed Construction Data
700 Longwater Drive
Norwell, MA 02061

770-209-3730
800-334-3509; *Fax:* 800-632-6732;
www.rsmeans.com

Offers statistical information for building contractors.

3974 SPEC-DATA Program
Construction Specifications Institute
110 S Union St
Ste 100
Alexandria, VA 22314-3351

703-684-0300
800-689-2900; *Fax:* 703-684-8436
csi@csinet.org; www.csinet.org

Walter Marlowe, CEO
Stacy Vail, Operations Director
Cost: $75.00
Frequency: Monthly

3975 Scaffold Industry Association Newsletter
Scaffold Industry Association
400 Admiral Blvd
Kansas City, MO 64106-1508

602-257-1144
866-687-7115; *Fax:* 602-257-1166
info@scaffold.org; www.scaffold.org

Steve Smith, President
Daryl Hare, Treasurer

Information on scaffold safety in the construction industry. Offers safe training programs for competent person and hazard awareness.
Cost: $65.00
Frequency: Monthly
Circulation: 1600
Founded in: 1972

3976 Scantlings
Timbers Framers Guild
PO Box 295
Alstead, NH 03602

559-834-8453
888-453-0879; *Fax:* 888-453-0879
info@tfguild.org; www.tfguild.org

Joel McCarty, Executive Director

It is a member benefit that is not available by subscription. Reports on timber framing events, news, business, and people.
Circulation: 1700
Founded in: 1984

3977 Specialty Tools and Fasteners Distributors Association Newsletter
Specialty Tools and Fasteners Distributors
PO Box 44
Elm Grove, WI 53122

262-784-4774
800-352-2981; *Fax:* 262-784-5059
info@stafda.org

Georgia Foley, President
Catherine Usher, Member Service Director

Members distribute or manufacture power equipment, anchors, fastening systems, drilling equipment and other related industrial supplies.
Circulation: 4,500
Founded in: 1976

3978 TAUC About Construction
The Association of Union Constructors
1501 Lee Highway
Suite 202
Arlington, VA 22209-1109

703-524-3336; *Fax:* 703-524-3364
dacord@tauc.org; www.tauc.org

Stephen R Lindauer, CEO
Kevin J Hilton, Senior VP

E-Newsletter containing exclusive TAUC content, with the latest collective bargaining agreements, wage rates, OSHA directives, legislative activity on Capitol Hill, and much more.
Frequency: Annual/May
Founded in: 1970

3979 TIDINGS Newsletter
Textile Care Allied Trades Association
271 Route 46 West
#D203
Fairfield, NJ 07004-2432

973-244-1790; *Fax:* 973-244-4455
info@tcata.org; www.tcata.org
Social Media: LinkedIn

Lawton Jones, President
Bryant Dunivan, President-Elect

Keeps members informed about relevant news in and affecting the industry, such as legislative/regulatory developments, benefits and services.

3980 Tilt-Up eNews
Tilt-Up Concrete Association
113 First Street W
PO Box 204
Mount Vernon, IA 52314-0204

319-895-6911; *Fax:* 320-213-5555
info@tilt-up.org; www.tilt-up.org

Ed Sauter, Executive Director
James Baty, Technical Director

A monthly newsletter published by the Tilt-Up Concrete Association, Tilt-Up eNews is free for members, however non-members can also sign up to receive these publications. The mission of the Tilt-Up Concrete Association is to expand and improve the use of Tilt-Up as the preferred construction method by providing education and resources that enhance quality and performance.
Cost: $25.00
Frequency: Quarterly
Circulation: 5500
Founded in: 1986
Printed in 4 colors on glossy stock

3981 Trade News
Specialty Tools and Fasteners Distributors Assn.
500 Elm Grove Rd.
Suite 210
Elm Grove, WI 53122

262-784-4774
800-352-2981; *Fax:* 262-784-5059
info@stafda.org; www.stafda.org
Social Media: Facebook, LinkedIn

Mike Kangas, President
Kramer Darragh, Vice President

Provides insight into the construction and industrial world, member news, Convention details, Trend Reports, and more.
4000 Attendees
Frequency: Monthly

3982 Under Construction
American Bar Assocation
321 N Clark St.
Chicago, IL 60654

www.americanbar.org/publications/under_construction

Jayne Czik, Editor
Ridgely Jackson, Associate Editor

Current legal topics in the construction industry and highlights from the ABA's Forum on Construction Law.
Frequency: 3x/year

3983 Western Building Material Association Newsletter
Western Building Material Association
PO Box 1699
Olympia, WA 98507-1699

360-943-3054
888-551-9262; *Fax:* 360-943-1219
wbma@wbma.org; www.wbma.org

38511 Pages
Frequency: Monthly
Circulation: 700
Printed in on matte stock

3984 World Fence News
World Fencing Data Center
6101 W Courtyard Dr
Building 3 Suite 115
Austin, TX 78730-5031

512-349-2536
800-231-0275; *Fax:* 512-349-2567
editor@worldfencenews.com;
www.worldfencenews.com

Roger Duke, Publisher
Rick Henderson, Editor

Includes the most up to date information on events, products, trends, and services that effect the industry.
Cost: $29.95
Frequency: Monthly
Circulation: 12500
Founded in: 1983

Magazines & Journals

3985 **ABC Today**
Associated Builders and Contractors
4250 Fairfax Dr
9th Floor
Arlington, VA 22203-1665
703-812-2000; *Fax:* 703-812-8201;
www.abc.org
Mike Bellaman, CEO
Todd Mann, COO
The purpose of this magazine is to offer industry updates on the latest trends and developments that affect general construction, labor, management, legislation, education, products and techniques for the building industry.
Cost: $36.00
Frequency: Monthly
Circulation: 25000
Founded in: 1950

3986 **American Painting Contractor**
Douglas Publications
2807 N Parham Road
Suite 200
Richmond, VA 23294
703-519-2341
800-223-1797; www.douglaspublications.com
Emily Howard, Editor
Jaimy Ford, Executive Editor
Features include business management, market research, decorating trends, techniques and developments in preparation and specialty coatings. News includes association activities, personnel changes and government actions.
Frequency: Monthly
Circulation: 25000
Founded in: 1985

3987 **American Public Works Magazine**
2345 Grand Blvd
Suite 700
Kansas City, MO 64108-2625
816-472-6100
800-848-2792; *Fax:* 816-472-1610
ddancy@apwa.net; www.apwa.net
Brian Van Norman, Director
David Dancy, Director of Marketing
Kevin Clark, Editor
International educational and professional association of public agencies, private sector companies, and individuals dedicated to providing high quality public works goods and services. The magazine is a forum for public works professionals, agencies and companies. It includes public works-related topics to public attention in local, state and federal areas.
Cost: $100.00
40 Pages
Frequency: Monthly
ISSN: 0092-4873
Founded in: 1937

3988 **Architectural Record**
McGraw-Hill Construction
2 Penn Plz
9th Floor
New York, NY 10121-2298
212-904-2594; *Fax:* 212-904-4256
william_hanley@mcgraw-hill.com;
www.mcgraw-hill.com
William Hanley, Editor
Lamar Clarkson, Editor
Provides original, reliable and useful information to the architectural marketplace worldwide, setting the standards for excellence in architectural design and presenting insights and practical solutions for current challenges in the design, building construction and business practices.
Cost: $49.00
Frequency: Monthly
Circulation: 102,000
ISSN: 0003-858X

3989 **Asphalt Magazine**
Asphalt Institute
2696 Research Park Dr
Lexington, KY 40511-8480
859-288-4960; *Fax:* 859-288-4999
info@asphaltinstitute.org;
www.asphaltinstitute.org
Social Media: Facebook, Twitter, LinkedIn
Peter Grass, President
Frequency: 3x/Year
Circulation: 18000

3990 **Automated Builder**
CMN Associates
2401 Grapevine Dr
Oxnard, CA 93036
805-351-5931
800-344-2537; *Fax:* 805-351-5755;
www.automatedbuilder.com/
Donald Carlson
Agnes Carlson, Circulation
Distributed free of charge in the US to executive and management personnel upon written request in companies that are production (big volume) site builders, panelized home manufacturers, modular home manufacturers, special unit manufacturers, component manufacturers and HUD-Code, modular, panelized and commercial building dealers.
Cost: $50.00
Frequency: Monthly
Circulation: 25000
ISSN: 0899-5540
Founded in: 1964
Printed in 4 colors on glossy stock

3991 **BUILDER**
Hanley-Wood
1 Thomas Cir NW
Suite 600
Washington, DC 20005-5811
202-452-0800; *Fax:* 202-785-1974
bthompson@hanleywood.com;
www.builderonline.com
Frank Anton, CEO
Hanley Wood, Publisher
Boyce Thompson, Editoral Director
BUILDER is the leading brand in residential new construction and serves as the magazine of the National Association of Home Builders (NAHB). For more than three decades, BUILDER has provided essential news, information and resources about products, technologies, trends, regulatory requirements and best practices to help home building professionals navigate challenges for success. BUILDER is the trusted source for top builders, architects and other industry professionals across the country.
Cost: $29.95
Frequency: Monthly
Circulation: 104852
ISSN: 0744-N93
Founded in: 1977
Mailing list available for rent: 100M names
Printed in 4 colors on glossy stock

3992 **Bonded Builders News**
Richard K Nicholson Enterprises
2201 Corporate Boulevard
Suite 100
Boca Raton, FL 33431-7337
561-278-6968
800-749-0381; *Fax:* 561-368-1781;
www.bondedbuilders.com
Whit Ward, President
Howard Head, Editor-in-Chief
Provides builders and developers with information involving new technologies and changing trends in the home building industry.
Cost: $18.00
Frequency: Quarterly
Circulation: 7000

3993 **Builder Insider**
PO Box 191125
Dallas, TX 75219-8105
214-988-9181
866-930-1950; *Fax:* 214-871-2931;
www.builderinsider.com
Michael Anderson, Editor
Independent trade publications covering the residential and light commercial building industry.
Cost: $12.00
28 Pages
Frequency: Monthly
Circulation: 5200
Founded in: 1976

3994 **Builders Trade Journal**
Lee Publications
6113 State Highway 5
PO Box 121
Palatine Bridge, NY 13428
518-673-3237
800-836-2888; *Fax:* 518-673-3245
info@leepub.com; www.leepub.com
Fred Lee, Editor
Wendell Jennings, Sales Manager
Edited for the building industry.
Frequency: Monthly
Founded in: 1982

3995 **Building Design & Construction**
Reed Business Information
360 Park Ave S
New York, NY 10010-1737
646-746-6400; *Fax:* 646-756-7583
corporatecommunications@reedbusiness.com;
www.reedbusiness.com
Mark Kelsey, CEO
Stuart Whayman, CFO
James Reed, Owner
Serves the needs of the design and construction professionals of commercial, industrial and institutional buildings that include new and retrofit projects. Geared towards the building team that includes professionals from building firms, owning firms and design firms.
Frequency: Monthly
Circulation: 76,005
Founded in: 1993

3996 **Building Environment Report**
IAQ Publications
7920 Norfolk Ave
Suite 900
Bethesda, MD 20814-2539
301-913-0115; *Fax:* 301-913-0119;
www.eschoolnews.com
Robert Morrow, Owner
Nancy David, Editor

Covers information to help manage building environmental hazards, meet environmental compliance requirements, protect building occupants, conference coverage and meetings of note.
Cost: $325.00
Frequency: Monthly
Circulation: 1,500

3997 Building Material Dealer
National Lumber & Building Material Dealers Assoc.
2025 M Street Nw
Ste 800
Washington, DC 20036
202-367-1169; *Fax:* 202-367-2169
info@dealer.org; www.dealer.org
Michael O'Brien, President
Scott Lynch, EVP
Content focuses on a mixture of regional and national news relating to governmental regulations, dealer and supplier news, meetings and seminars affecting the independent building retailer.
Frequency: Monthly
Circulation: 24,647

3998 Building Operating Management
Trade Press Publishing Corporation
2100 W Florist Avenue
Milwaukee, WI 53209-3799
414-228-7701; *Fax:* 414-228-1134;
www.tradepress.com
Brad Ehlert, Group Publisher
Brian Terry, Publisher
Serves the field of facilities management, encompassing commercial building: office buildings, real estate/property management firms, developers, financial institutions, insurance companies, apartment complexes, civic/convention centers, including members of the Building Owners and Managers Association
Cost: $120.00
Frequency: Monthly
Circulation: 70000
Founded in: 1954
Printed in 4 colors on glossy stock

3999 Building Stone Magazine
Building Stone Institute
5 Riverside Dr
Building 1
Chestertown, NY 12817
518-803-4336
866-786-6313; *Fax:* 518-803-4336;
www.buildingstoneinstitute.org
Social Media: Facebook
Duffe Elkins, President
Rob Teel, VP
State of the industry publication for architects, designers and people in the natural stone industries: granite, marble, limestone, etc.
Cost: $65.00
350 Members
Circulation: 18000
Founded in: 1919
Printed in 4 colors on glossy stock

4000 Building Supply Home Centers
Reed Business Information
360 Park Ave S
New York, NY 10010-1737
646-746-6400; *Fax:* 646-756-7583;
www.reedbusiness.com
Mark Kelsey, CEO
James Reed, Owner
For owners, manufacturers and other executives of the retail building market.
Cost: $60.00
Frequency: Monthly
Founded in: 1917

4001 Buildings: Facilities Construction & Management Magazine
Stamats Communications
PO Box 1888
Cedar Rapids, IA 52406-1888
319-364-6167
800-553-8878; *Fax:* 319-365-5421
info@stamats.com; www.stamats.com
Guy Wendler, CEO
Peter Stamats, EVP/CFO
Information on construction costs, building design, space planning, fire safety, environment solutions, energy effiency, accessibilty, security, and strategic facilities planning.
Cost: $70.00
Frequency: Monthly
Circulation: 56500
Founded in: 1906

4002 CIM Construction Journal
Construction Industries of Massachusetts
1500 Providence Highway Suite 14
PO Box 667
Norwood, MA 02062
781-551-0182; *Fax:* 781-551-0916
info@cimass.org; www.cimass.org
Mark Drummey, Editor/Publisher
John Pourbaix, Executive Director
Digest of horizontal public works projects.
Frequency: Weekly
Circulation: 2000
Founded in: 1921

4003 Carpenter
United Brotherhood of Carpenters & Joiners
6801 Placid St
Las Vegas, NV 89119-4205
702-938-1111; *Fax:* 702-938-1122
dshoemaker@carpenters.org;
www.ubcmillwrights.com
William Irwin, Executive Director
Contains news and information on the union and its members, the craft, and the construction industry as a whole.
Founded in: 1881

4004 Catholic Cemetery
National Catholic Cemetery Conference
1400 S Wolf Rd
Building # 3
Hillside, IL 60162
708-202-1242
888-850-8131; *Fax:* 708-202-1255;
www.ntriplec.com
Christine Kohut, Editor
Dennis Fairbank, Executive Director
News on products and manufacturers and also gives information on cemetery maintenance and repairs.
Frequency: Monthly
Circulation: 2100
Founded in: 1949

4005 Commerical Modular Construction
Emlen Publications/Modular Building Institute
1241 Andersen Dr
North Suite
San Rafael, CA 94901-5374
415-460-6185
800-965-8876; *Fax:* 415-460-6288;
www.emlenmedia.com
Eli Gage, Publisher
Ahavah Revis, Managing Editor
Contains articles on modular for architects, engineering and spec writers who need building product, specification and address information.

4006 Computer-Aided Engineering
Penton Media
1300 E 9th St
Suite 316
Cleveland, OH 44114-1503
216-696-7000; *Fax:* 216-696-6662
information@penton.com; www.penton.com
Sharon Rowlands, CEO
Database applications in design and manufacturing.
Cost: $50.00
96 Pages
Founded in: 1982

4007 Concrete InFocus
National Ready Mixed Concrete Association
900 Spring St
Silver Spring, MD 20910-4015
240-485-1139; *Fax:* 301-585-4219
info@nrmca.org; www.nrmca.org
Social Media: Facebook, LinkedIn, YouTube
Robert Garbini, President
Deana Angelastro, Executive Administrator
The top resource for industry news, trends, research, legislative articles and company profiles.
1200 Members
Frequency: Quarterly
Circulation: 5000+
Founded in: 1930

4008 Concrete Pressure Pipe Digest
American Concrete Pressure Pipe Association
3900 University Drive
Suite 110
Fairfax, VA 22030-2513
703-273-7227; *Fax:* 703-273-7230;
www.acppa.org
Richard Mueller, Chair
Mike Leathers, Vice Chair

4009 Concrete Pumping Magazine
American Concrete Pumping Association
606 Enterprise Dr
Lewis Center, OH 43035-9432
614-431-5618; *Fax:* 614-431-6944;
www.concretepumpers.com
Carl Walker, President
Christi Collins, Executive Director
Packed with articles on industry leaders, new products, and on-site examples.
Frequency: Quarterly
Circulation: 2,100

4010 Construction Bulletin
1200 Madison Ave
Indianapolis, IN 46225
317-423-7080; *Fax:* 317-422-7034;
www.acppubs.com
Greg Sitek, Editor
Kenny Veach, Advertising Sales Manager
Serves heavy highway and building construction.
Cost: $199.00
Frequency: Weekly
Circulation: 4000
ISSN: 0010-6720
Founded in: 1893

4011 Construction Dimensions
Association of the Wall and Ceiling Industry
513 W Broad St
Suite 210
Falls Church, VA 22046-3257
703-538-1600; *Fax:* 703-534-8307
info@awci.org; www.awci.org
Tim Wies, President
Jeffrey Burley, VP

A monthly magazine for manufacturers and suppliers in the wall and ceiling, and related industries. Construction Dimensions is the official publication of the Association of the Wall and Ceiling Industries International.
Cost: $ 40.00
115 Pages
Frequency: Monthly
Circulation: 23000
Founded in: 1918

4012 **Construction Distribution**
Cygnus Business Media
1233 Janesville Avenue
Fort Atkinson, WI 53538

800-547-7377
nancy.terrill@cygnusb2b.com;
www.cygnusb2b.com

Nancy Terrill, Publisher
Rebecca Wasieleski, Editor

Resource for product, marketing and management information for construction supply distributors and the manufacturers and reps who serve them.
Frequency: Quarterly
Circulation: 14,800
Founded in: 1966

4013 **Construction Equipment Distribution**
Associated Equipment Distributors
615 W 22nd St
Oak Brook, IL 60523-8807

630-574-0650
800-388-0650; *Fax:* 630-574-0132
info@aednet.org; www.aednet.org

Toby Mack, President
Mike Quirk, SVP

Offers valuable information for executives who sell and rent construction equipment.
Cost: $71.40
72 Pages
Frequency: Monthly
Circulation: 5500
Founded in: 1918

4014 **Construction Equipment Operation and Maintenance**
Construction Publications
PO Box 1689
Cedar Rapids, IA 52406-1689

319-366-1597; *Fax:* 319-362-8808

Clark Parks, Editor

Use and maintenance of construction equipment.
Cost: $10.00
24 Pages
Frequency: Monthly
Founded in: 1948

4015 **Construction Executive**
Associated Builders and Contractors
4250 Fairfax Drive
9th Floor
Arlington, VA 22203-1665

703-812-2000; *Fax:* 703-812-8201;
www.abc.org

Lisa A Nardone, Editor-in-Chief
Lauren Pinch, Assistant Editor
Mike Bellaman, CEO

Focus on commercial and industrial construction.
Cost: $24.00
Frequency: Monthly
Circulation: 49,000

4016 **Construction Industry International**
Quarto International
10 Whirling Dun
Collinsville, CT 06022-1239
Andrew Webster, Editor

Serves the administrative construction industry.
80 Pages
Frequency: Monthly
Founded in: 1975

4017 **Construction Specifier**
266 Elmwood Ave
Suite 289
Buffalo, NY 14222

716-572-5633
866-572-5633; *Fax:* 866-572-5677
sales@constructionspecifier.com;
www.constructionspecifier.com

Jill Kaletha, Editor

The offical magazine of Construction Specifications Institute. Focused on the job functions of its core readership-professionals involved in the specification process. Offers insight and analysis on industry topics through news, product announcements, legal columns, case studies and other research as well as providing in-depth features on industry-related issues.
Frequency: Monthly
Founded in: 1956
Printed in on glossy stock

4018 **Constructioneer**
Associated Construction Publication
30 Technology Pkwy S
Suite 100
Norcross, GA 30092-2925
770-209-3730
800-424-3996; *Fax:* 770-209-3712
rcdwebmaster@reedbusiness.com;
www.reedconstructiondata.com

Iain Melville, CEO
Steve Ritchie, VP Marketing
Marco Piovesan, VP Data

Information directed to construction industry of New York, Pennsylvania, New Jersey, and Delaware.
100 Pages
Frequency: Bi-Monthly
Circulation: 18889
Founded in: 1975
Printed in 4 colors on matte stock

4019 **Constructor Magazine**
Associated General Contractors of America
2300 Wilson Blvd
Suite 400
Arlington, VA 22201-5426

703-548-3118; *Fax:* 703-837-5400
info@agc.org; www.agc.org

Kristine Young, President
Joe Jarboe, SVP

Voice of the construction industry.
Frequency: Monthly
Circulation: 40,000
Founded in: 1918

4020 **Contractors Guide**
Painting and Decorating Contractors of America
1801 Park 270 Drive
Suite 220
St Louis, MO 63146-4020

314-514-7322
800-332-7322; *Fax:* 314-514-9417;
www.pdca.org

Darylene Dennon, Chair

What every painting and decorating contractor needs to know, organized for easy use by painting and decorating contractors of all sizes.
Cost: $68.00

4021 **Custom Home**
Hanley-Wood
1 Thomas Cir NW
Suite 600
Washington, DC 20005-5811

202-452-0800; *Fax:* 202-785-1974
fanton@hanleywood.com;
www.residentialarchitect.com

Frank Anton, CEO
Matt Flynn, CFO

Features materials, products, trends and the latest in designs for custom home construction.
Cost: $24.00
Frequency: 7 issues yearly
Circulation: 40000
Founded in: 1976

4022 **DBA Automated Builder Magazine**
CMN Associates
2401 Grapevine Dr
Oxnard, CA 93036

805-351-5931
800-344-2537; *Fax:* 805-351-5755
info@automatedbuilder.com;
www.automatedbuilder.com/

Don O Carlson, Editor/Publisher
Agnes Carlson, Circulation Manager

Magazine for manufacturers and suppliers who have a product line that is of interest to the factory-built housing industry. Covering all seven segments of US, Canadian and foreign housing industry, including: production builders; panelizers; component producers; modular; commercial modular; hud code; and all builder/dealers.
Frequency: Monthly
Circulation: 25000
ISSN: 0899-4450
Founded in: 1964

4023 **DFI Journal**
Deep Foundations Institute
326 Lafayette Avenue
Hawthorne, NJ 07506

973-423-4030; *Fax:* 973-423-4031
staff@dfi.org; www.dfi.org

Publishes practice-oriented, high quality papers related to broad area of Deep Foundations Engineering.
Frequency: Bi-Annual

4024 **Daily Construction Service**
Construction Market Data
142 Arena Street
El Segundo, CA 90245

310-322-9990; *Fax:* 858-573-0485

Jeanne Peterson, Editor

Offers valuable information for construction workers.
Cost: $365.00
Frequency: Monthly
Founded in: 1933

4025 **Daily Journal of Commerce**
Dolan Media Company/New Orleans Publishing Grp
111 Veterans Memorial Blvd., Suite 1440
3445 North Causeway Blvd., Suite 90
Metairie, LA 70005-3028

504-834-9292; *Fax:* 504-832-3435
djc@nopg.com; www.djcgulfcoast.com

Lisa Blossman, Publisher
Christian Moises, Editor
Anne Lovas, General Manager
Becky Naquin, Assistance Editor

Reports on building and engineering industries.
Cost: $456.00
Frequency: Monthly
Founded in: 1922

4026 **Deep Foundations Magazine**
Deep Foundations Institute

326 Lafayette Avenue
Hawthorne, NJ 07506

973-423-4030; *Fax:* 973-423-4031
dfihq@dfi.org; www.dfi.org

James Morrison, President
Virginia Fairweather, Executive Editor

Distributed to members.
Frequency: Quarterly
Circulation: 2753

4027 Demolition
National Demolition Association
16 N Franklin St
Suite 203
Doylestown, PA 18901-3536
215-348-4949
800-541-2412; *Fax:* 215-348-8422
info@demolitionassociation.com;
www.demolitionassociation.com

Don Rachel, President
Jeff Kroeker, VP

Trade publication for the demolition industry.
Cost: $40.00
Circulation: 5000
ISSN: 1522-5690
Founded in: 1972
Printed in 4 colors on matte stock

4028 Design Build
144 Lexington Street
Woburn, MA 01801

781-937-9265; *Fax:* 781-937-9241;
www.designbuild.construction.com

Gary Merrill, Sales Director
William Angelo, Editor-in-Chief

Received by all subscribers of Engineering News Record plus 7,500 owners identified by FW Dodge as having an interest in the design-build project delivery system, and 1,000 members of the Design-Build Institute of America.
84 Pages
Frequency: Quarterly
Circulation: 20000
ISSN: 1096-7095
Founded in: 1953

4029 Design Cost & Data
Rector Communications
2300 Chestnut St
Suite 340
Philadelphia, PA 19103-4398

215-963-9661; *Fax:* 215-963-9672;
www.rector.com

Marion Rector, Owner

Cost estimating magazine for architects, builders, developers, appraisers, specifiers, insurers and construction financiers.

4030 Design Lines
American Institute of Building Design
7059 Blair Rd NW
Suite 201
Washington, DC 20012

800-366-2423; *Fax:* 866-204-0293
info@aibd.org; www.aibd.org
Social Media: Facebook, Twitter, LinkedIn

Dan Sater, President
Alan Kent, Internal Vice President
Viki Wooster, External Vice President
Kerry Dick, Secretary/ Treasurer

Publication that focuses on issues, education, and events as they happen in the building design industry.
1500 Attendees
Frequency: Monthly
Founded in: 1950

4031 Design Solutions Magazine
Architectural Woodwork Institute
46179 Westlake Dr
Suite 120
Potomac Falls, VA 20165

571-323-3636; *Fax:* 571-323-3630
info@awinet.org; www.awinet.org

Robert Stout, President
Mike Bell, Vice President

Each issue showcases beautiful examples of fine architectural woodwork manufactured by AWI Manufacturing Member companies. With beautiful four-color images, crisp detailed drawings and thought provoking articles, Design Solutions offers our readers a bountiful resource that's sure to inspire and delight all.
Cost: $25.00
Frequency: Quarterly
Circulation: 27,000

4032 Dodge Construction News
McGraw Hill
2 Penn Plaza
9th Floor
New York, NY 10121-1299

212-904-3507; *Fax:* 212-904-2820
customerservice@mcgraw-hill.com;
www.mcgraw-hill.com

Jennifer Hayes, Editor
Harold McGraw, III, CEO/President

Consists of program edition and proceedings and recap edition for the National Conventions of the American Institute of Architects and Construction Specifications Institute.
Circulation: 86400
Founded in: 1884

4033 Door & Window Maker
Key Communications
PO Box 569
Garrisonville, VA 22463-0569

540-720-5584; *Fax:* 540-720-5687
key-com@glass.com; www.glass.com

Debra Levy, Owner
Brigid O'Leary, Assistant Editor
Frequency: 9 issues yearly
Circulation: 23,947
Founded in: 1993

4034 Engineering News Record
McGraw Hill
2 Penn Plaza
9th Floor
New York, NY 10121-2298

212-904-3507; *Fax:* 212-904-2820
scott_lewis@mcgraw-hill.com; www.enr.com

Richard Korman, Managing Senior Editor
Ilan Kapla, Senior Manager
Keith Wallace, Production Editor

Provides the news, analysis, commentary and data that construction industry professionals need to do their jobs more effectively. ENR is the national news magazine for the construction industry.
Cost: $82.00
Frequency: Weekly
Circulation: 60000
Founded in: 1874

4035 Environmental Design & Construction
Business News Publishing Company
2401 W Big Beaver Rd
Suite 700
Troy, MI 48084-3333

248-362-3700; *Fax:* 248-362-0317;
www.edcmag.com

Derrick Teal, Editor
Diana Brown, Publisher
Laura Zielinski, Associate Editor

Magazine dedicated to integrated high-performance buildings, and efficient and sustainable design and construction.
Founded in: 1926

4036 Equipment Today
Cygnus Business Media
1233 Janesville Avenue
Fort Atkinson, WI 53538

800-547-7377
becky.schultz@cygnuspub.com;
www.cygnusb2b.com

Becky Schultz, Editor

Contractors and other users of construction machinery. Editorial is focused on the selection, application and maintenance of equipment as well as new and improved product introductions. Accepts advertising.
Cost: $60.00
54 Pages
Frequency: Monthly
Circulation: 77,000
Founded in: 1966

4037 FW Dodge Northwest Construction
McGraw Hill
800 S Michigan St
Seattle, WA 98108-2655

206-378-4715
800-393-6343; *Fax:* 206-378-4741
support@construction.com;
www.construction.com

Keith Fox, President
Linda Brennan, VP Operations

Project news, plans, specifications and analysis data for the construction professional.
Cost: $40.00
Frequency: Monthly
Founded in: 1884

4038 Fabric Architecture
Industrial Fabrics Association International
1801 County Road B W
Roseville, MN 55113-4061

651-222-2508
800-225-4324; *Fax:* 651-631-9334
generalinfo@ifai.com; www.ifai.com

Stephen Warner, President
Chris Tschida, Editorial Manager

Strives to inform architects, designers, landscape architects, engineers and other specifiers about architectural fabric structures, the fibers and fabrics used to make them, their design possibilities, their construction, and issues regarding their applicability and acceptance.
Cost: $39.00
Frequency: Bi-monthly

4039 Facility Management Journal
International Facility Management Association
1 Greenway Plz
Suite 1100
Houston, TX 77046-0194

713-623-4362; *Fax:* 713-623-6124
ifma@ifma.org; www.ifma.org

Andrea Sanchez, Editor-in-Chief
Laurie Steiner, Senior Associate Editor

Covers industry economic, financial trends and the industries legislative, special emphasis on developments in technology.
Cost: $75.00
Circulation: 14000
Founded in: 1990

4040 Facility News Magazines
National Lead Abatement Council

PO Box 535
Olney, MD 20830

301-924-5490
800-590-6522; *Fax:* 301-924-0265

Stephen Weil, Publisher
Wendy Faxon, Editor

Information on facility maintenance management.
Cost: $36.00
20 Pages
Frequency: Monthly
Circulation: 7500
Founded in: 1981

4041 **Fenestration Magazine**
Ashlee Publishing
18 E 41st Street
20th Floor
New York, NY 10017-6009

212-376-7722; *Fax:* 212-376-7723;
www.fenestrationmagazine.com

Joel Bruinooge, Editor

Windows and door industry.
Cost: $40.00
80+ Pages
Frequency: 10x yearly
Circulation: 17,000
ISSN: 0895-450X

4042 **Fine Homebuilding**
Taunton Press
63 S Main St
Box 5506
Newtown, CT 06470-2344

203-426-8171; *Fax:* 203-426-3434;
www.taunton.com

Harrison McCampbell, Editor
Rob Yagid, Assistant Editor

Reviews of new equipment and related building materials and guidelines to successful work techniques and general industry news.
Cost: $37.95
Circulation: 308,000
Founded in: 1980

4043 **Floor Covering Installer**
Business News Publishing Company
22801 Ventura Blvd
#115
Woodland Hills, CA 91364

818-224-8035
818-224-8042; www.fcimag.com

John Moore, Editor
Jennifer Allen, Production Manager

Provides the varied information needed by those who engage in floor covering installation with how-to and skill-building articles, how-to-do-it photographic presentations, new installation product information, news of the industry, as well as how and where to get further training in various aspects of floor covering installation.
Frequency: Bi-Monthly
Circulation: 40,000

4044 **Foundation Drilling**
ADSC
8445 Freeport Parkway
Suite 325
Irving, TX 75063

469-359-6000; *Fax:* 469-359-6007
adsc@adsc-iafd.com; www.adsc-iafd.com

Tim Wies, President
Jeffrey Burley, VP

Written for foundation drilling and anchored earth retention contractors and their project managers, superintendents, foremen, civil and structural engineers, soils engineers, public engineering officials, architects, manufacturers and distributors of industry related equipments.
Frequency: 8x yearly
Circulation: 5000

4045 **Frame Building News**
F+W Media
38 E. 29th Street
New York, NY 10016

212-447-1400; *Fax:* 212-447-5231
contact_us@fwmedia.com;
www.fwpublications.com

David Nussbaum, CEO
Sara Domville, President

Edited for the diversified town & country builders of light-industrial, commercial, agricultural, and residential structures. The majority of the coverage is about post-frame structures. Readers look for the latest in post-frame research and techniques, building code information, equipment, and materials. Regular features include 'Builder Spotlight,' 'New Products,' 'Supplier News,' 'OSHA Updates,' 'Legal Issues,' 'Business Strategies,' and 'Calendar of Events.' Official magazine of NFBA.
56 Pages
Circulation: 19211
Founded in: 1952

4046 **Glass Digest**
Ashlee Publishing
18 E 41st Street
New York, NY 10017-6009

212-376-7722; *Fax:* 212-376-7723;
www.glassdigestmagazine.com/ashlee/glassdigest/index.html

Jordan Wright, Publisher

Merchandising/technical publication for the flat glass industry.
Cost: $25.00
140 Pages
Frequency: Monthly
Founded in: 1922

4047 **Hanley-Wood's Tools of the Trade**
Hanley Wood
1 Thomas Cir NW
Suite 600
Washington, DC 20005-5803

202-452-0800; *Fax:* 202-785-1974;
www.hanleywood.com

Frank Anton, CEO
Matt Flynn, CFO

The wide array of tools and equipment in the construction and renovation industries.
Cost: $36.00
Circulation: 65,000
Founded in: 1976

4048 **Home Builders Magazine**
Work-4 Projects
4819 Saint Charles Boulevard
Pierrefonds, QC H9H-3C7

514-620-2200; *Fax:* 514-620-6300
editor@work4.ca;
www.homebuildercanada.com/

Nachmi Artzy, Publisher
Cheryl Carvery, Sales

Specializes in educating readers on the latest installation tips, building techniques and materials that can be put into on-site practice everyday.
Cost: $30.00
Frequency: Bi-Monthly
Circulation: 23265
Founded in: 1988

4049 **Hot Mix Asphalt Technology**
National Asphalt Pavement Association
5100 Forbes Blvd
Suite 200
Lanham, MD 20706-4407

301-731-4748
888-468-6499; *Fax:* 301-731-4621
mcervarich@hotmix.org; www.hotmix.org

Mike Acott, President
Margaret Cervarich, VP Marketing/Public Affairs

The leading journal for the asphalt pavement contractor
Frequency: Bi-Monthly
Circulation: 10000

4050 **IEEE Power and Energy Magazine**
IEEE
445 Hoes Lane
Piscataway, NJ 08854

732-465-6480; *Fax:* - - 0
pels-staff@ieee.org; www.ieee-pels.org

Fran Zappulla, Staff Director, Publishing
Susan Hassler, Editor

Network analysis, system stability studies, fault protection and construction management.
Cost: $285.00
82 Pages
Frequency: Monthly
Circulation: 23000
ISSN: 1540-7977
Founded in: 1885
Mailing list available for rent
Printed in on glossy stock

4051 **InTents**
Industrial Fabrics Association International
1801 County Road B W
Roseville, MN 55113-4061

651-222-2508
800-225-4324; *Fax:* 651-631-9334
generalinfo@ifai.org; www.ifai.com

Stephen Warner, CEO
Chris Tschida, Editorial Manager

Promotes the use of tents and accessories to the special-event and general-rental industries.
Cost: $39.00
Frequency: Bi-Monthly
Circulation: 12,000

4052 **Insulation Outlook**
National Insulation Association
12100 Sunset Hills Road
Suite 330
Reston, VA 20190-3295

703-683-6422; *Fax:* 703-549-4838
editor@insulation.org; www.insulation.org

Michele Jones, EVP/CEO
Julie McLaughlin, Director of Publications

Contains information on new products, industry trends, asbestos abatement and installation practices.
Cost: $45.00
Frequency: Monthly
Circulation: 7000
Founded in: 1973
Printed in 4 colors on glossy stock

4053 **Interior Construction**
Ceilings & Interior Systems Construction Assn
1010 Jorie Boulevard
Suite 30
Oak Brook, IL 60223

630-584-1919; *Fax:* 866-560-8537;
www.cisca.org

Shirley Wodynski, Executive Director
Rick Reuland, Editor

Offers information designed to keep contractors abreast of the changes in interior construction.
Cost: $35.00
Frequency: Monthly
Circulation: 10000
Founded in: 1950

4054 **Interlocking Concrete Pavement Magazine**
Interlocking Concrete Pavement Institute
13921 Park Center Road
Suite 270
Herndon, VA 20171-3269

202-080-0285
800-241-3652; *Fax:* 202-408-0285
icpi@icpi.org; www.icpi.org

Ericka Giles, Editor
Charles McGrath, Executive Director
Cost: $5.00
32 Pages
Frequency: Quarterly
Circulation: 20,000
Founded in: 1993
Printed in 4 colors

4055 **Intermountain Contractor**
McGraw Hill
1114 W 7th Avenue
Suite 100
Denver, CO 80204

303-756-9995
800-393-6343; *Fax:* 303-756-4465
mark_shaw@mcgraw-hill.com;
www.intermountaincontractors.net

Seth Horositz, Publisher
Mark Shaw, Editor
For general contractors. Serves Colorado, Idaho, Montana, Utah and Wyoming.
Cost: $40.00
88 Pages
Frequency: Weekly
Circulation: 5,247

4056 **International Construction**
Primedia
3585 Engineering Drive
Suite 100
Norcross, GA 30092

678-421-3000
800-216-1423; www.primedia.com

Charles Stubbs, President
Kim Payne, SVP
Provides valuable information to help readers succeed in every aspect of their jobs, from planning strategies to targeting growth, from solving engineering problems to selecting the right equipment and materials.

4057 **Job-Site Supervisor**
FMI Corporation
5171 Glenwood Ave
Suite 200
Raleigh, NC 27612-3266

919-787-8400; *Fax:* 919-785-9320
webmasters@fminet.com; www.fminet.com

Hank Harris, President
Delivers articles on safety, regulations and management; with a special section that examines a challenging construction project. Editorial is presented from a field manager's point-of-view, including charts, graphs, illustrations and industry advice.
Cost: $179.00
Circulation: 4000
Founded in: 1953

4058 **Journal of Light Construction**
Hanley-Wood
186 Allen Brook Lane
Williston, VT 05495

802-879-3335
800-552-1951; *Fax:* 802-879-9384;
www.jlconline.com

Don Jackson, Editor
Rick Strachan, Publisher
Written for builders, remodelers, contractors and architects involved in the design and construction of residential and light commercial buildings. Accepts advertising.
Cost: $39.95
150 Pages
Frequency: Monthly
Circulation: 73000
ISSN: 1040-5224
Founded in: 1982
Mailing list available for rent: 70,000 names at $120 per M
Printed in 4 colors on glossy stock

4059 **Journal of Protective Coatings & Linings**
Technology Publishing Company
2100 Wharton St
Suite 310
Pittsburgh, PA 15203-1951

412-431-8300
800-837-8303; *Fax:* 412-431-5428
webmaster@paintsquare.com;
www.paintsquare.com

Marian Welsh, Publisher
Mary Chollet, Editor-in-Chief
The right tools to help you reach the protective and marine coatings industry.
Cost: $80.00
Frequency: Monthly
Circulation: 15,000
ISSN: 8755-1985

4060 **Kitchen & Bath Design News**
Cygnus Business Media
2 University Plaza
Suite 310
Hackensack, NJ 07601

201-487-7800; *Fax:* 201-487-1061
kathy.scott@cygnusb2b.com;
www.cygnusb2b.com

Eliot Sefrin, Editorial Director/Publisher
Scott, Director of Public Relations
Serving the kitchen and bath industry, a key niche within the residential construction and remodeling marketplace.
Frequency: Monthly
Circulation: 48667
Founded in: 1966

4061 **Manufactured Home Merchandiser**
RLD Group
PO Box 269149
Suite 800
Chicago, IL 60626-9149

312-236-3529; *Fax:* 312-236-4024

Herb Tider, President
Wayne Beamer, Editor
Offers information for home builders and professionals in the manufactured home industry.
Cost: $36.00
Frequency: Monthly
Circulation: 18600
Founded in: 1952

4062 **Masonry Magazine**
Mason Contractors Association of America
1481 Merchant Drive
Algonquin, IL 60102

224-678-9709
800-536-2225; *Fax:* 224-678-9714;
www.masoncontractors.org

Jeff Buczkiewicz, Executive Director
Tim O'Toole, Marketing Director
This periodical covers every aspect of the mason contractor profession, not only equipment and techniques but topics such as building codes and stanards.
Cost: $29.00
Frequency: Monthly
Circulation: 17,000

4063 **Metal Roofing**
F+W Media
38 E. 29th Street
New York, NY 10016

212-447-1400; *Fax:* 212-447-5231
contact_us@fwmedia.com;
www.fwpublications.com

David Nussbaum, CEO
Sara Domville, President
Circulation: 25000
ISSN: 1533-8711
Founded in: 1900
Printed in 4 colors on glossy stock

4064 **Midwest Contractor**
Associated Construction Publication
1200 Madison Ave
LL20
Indianapolis, IN 46225

317-423-7080
800-486-0014; *Fax:* 317-423-7094;
www.acppubs.com

Tad Smith, CEO
Greg Sitek, Managing Editor
Annual equipment buyers' guide, a complete cross reference listing of manufacturers, area distributors and their construction equipment lines.
Cost: $96.00
Founded in: 1905

4065 **Muir's Original Log Home Guide for Builders and Buyers**
Gary J Schroder
1101 SE 7th Ave
Grand Rapids, MN 55744-4087

218-326-4434
800-359-6614; *Fax:* 218-326-2529;
www.loghelp.com

Gary Schroeder, Owner
Allan Muir, Author
Log home industry.
Cost: $12.95
Frequency: Monthly
ISBN: 0-967786-90-8
Founded in: 1978

4066 **National Association of Demolition Contactors**
National Demolition Association
16 N Franklin Street
Suite 203
Doylestown, PA 18901

215-348-4949
800-541-2412; *Fax:* 215-348-8422
info@demolitionassociation.com;
www.demolitionassociation.com

Don Rachel, President
Jeff Kroeker, VP
Bimonthly magazine.
Cost: $40.00
Circulation: 5000
ISSN: 1522-5690
Founded in: 1969
Printed in 4 colors on matte stock

4067 **New England Construction**
Associated Construction Publication
1200 Madison Ave
LL20
Indianapolis, IN 46225
317-423-7080
800-486-0014; *Fax:* 317-423-7094;
www.acppubs.com
Tad Smith, CEO
Greg Sitek, Managing Editor
Complete reports on contracts awarded, low bids and proposed work; features on highway construction and earthmoving, land development projects, utility construction, industrial building construction in the six-state New England region.
Cost: $96.00
Frequency: Monthly
Circulation: 10490
Founded in: 1975

4068 **Northwest Construction**
McGraw Hill
800 S Michigan St
Seattle, WA 98108-2655
206-378-4715
800-393-6343; *Fax:* 206-378-4741
support@construction.com;
www.construction.com
Jeff Greisch, President
Heather McCune, Editor-in-Chief
A regional, monthly magazine with features on Washington and design construction projects. Accepts advertising.
Cost: $60.00
64 Pages
Frequency: Monthly
Circulation: 6,200
Founded in: 1997

4069 **Occupational Hazards**
Penton Media
1300 E 9th St
Suite 316
Cleveland, OH 44114-1503
216-696-7000; *Fax:* 216-696-6662
information@penton.com; www.penton.com
Sharon Rowlands, CEO
Analysis of qualified recipients who have indicated that they recommend, select and/or buy the safety equipment, fire protection and other occupational health products.
65 Pages
Frequency: Monthly
Circulation: 65,777
ISSN: 0029-7909
Founded in: 1892
Printed in 4 colors on glossy stock

4070 **Old House Journal**
Old House Journal Group
PO Box 420235
Palm Coast, FL 32142-235
800-826-3893; *Fax:* 978-283-4629
daposporos@homebuyerpubs.com;
www.oldhousejournal.com
Demetra Aposporos, Editor-in-Chief
Danielle Small, Advertising Manager
Covers restoration techniques for the pre-1939 home.
Cost: $27.00
Circulation: 140119
Founded in: 1999

4071 **Pacific Builder & Engineer**
Associated Construction Publication
30 Technology Pkwy S
Suite 100
Norcross, GA 30092-2925
770-209-3730
800-424-3996; *Fax:* 770-209-3712;
www.acppubs.com
Tad Smith, CEO
Greg Sitek, Managing Editor
For management level personnel in the highway and heavy construction and non-residential building industries in Washington, Oregon, Idaho, Montana and Alaska. Includes notice of bid calls, low bidders, contract awards on area projects; cost cutting construction methods, unusual techniques and equipment applications, analysis of market conditions and industry trends, new products and literature, general industry news and views, personal news and legal advice. Accepts advertising.
Cost: $50.00
Circulation: 100000
Founded in: 1902

4072 **Pavement**
Cygnus Business Media
1233 Janesville Avenue
Fort Atkinson, WI 53538
E-Mail: amy.schwandt@cygnusb2b.com;
www.cygnusb2b.com
Amy Schwandt, Publisher
Allan Heydorn, Editor/Associate Publisher
Reaches contractors in the pavement maintenance and commercial paving sector. Covers the four main segments of the market in each issue: sealcoating, striping, paving and sweeping.
Circulation: 18,500
Founded in: 1985

4073 **Period Homes**
Restore Media
5185 MacArthur Blvd NW
Suite 725
Washington, DC 20016
202-339-0744; *Fax:* 202-339-0749
info@restoremedia.com;
www.restoremedia.com
Michael Tucker, Chairman/CEO
Paul Kitzke, EVP
Peter Miller, President/Publisher
Lists sources of products for restoration and new construction of residential architecture.
Cost: $18.00
120 Pages
Circulation: 24,600
ISSN: 0898-0284

4074 **Products Finishing**
Scott Walker/Gardner Publications
6915 Valley Ln
Cincinnati, OH 45244-3153
513-527-8800
800-950-8020; *Fax:* 513-527-8801;
www.gardnerweb.com
Rick Kline, CEO
Serves the finishing field, including educational services, public administration and other manufacturing industries.
Cost: $89.00
Frequency: Monthly
Circulation: 42000
Founded in: 1928
Printed in 4 colors on glossy stock

4075 **Professional Builder**
Reed Business Information
2000 Clearwater Dr
Oak Brook, IL 60523-8809
630-288-8000; *Fax:* 630-288-8781;
www.reedbusiness.com
Iain Melville, CEO
Andrew Rak, SVP
New residential construction magazine with a more than 63 year tradition of providing builders the solutions they need to maximize profits.
Frequency: Monthly
Circulation: 127002
Founded in: 1931

4076 **Professional Door Dealer Magazine**
Virgo Publishing LLC
3300 N Central Ave
Suite 300
Phoenix, AZ 85012-2532
480-675-9925; *Fax:* 480-990-0819
danielle@vpico.com; www.vpico.com
Jenny Bolton, President
Educational resource for residential and commercial door and access-control professionals.
Circulation: 20000
Founded in: 1986
Printed in on glossy stock

4077 **Professional Remodeler**
Reed Business Information
360 Park Ave S
New York, NY 10010-1737
646-746-6400; *Fax:* 646-756-7583
corporatecommunications@reedbusiness.com;
www.reedbusiness.com
Iain Melville, CEO
Andrew Rak, SVP
Designed to accomodate the needs of residential remodelers and light commercial renovators and focuses on news, features, new products, tech-takes, and management and marketing approaches.
Frequency: Monthly
Circulation: 18131
Founded in: 2002

4078 **Professional Roofing**
National Roofing Contractors Association
10255 W Higgins Rd
Suite 600
Rosemont, IL 60018-5613
847-299-9070
800-323-9545; *Fax:* 847-299-1183
nrca@nrca.net; www.professionalroofing.net
William Good, EVP
Ambika-Punia Bailey, Editor
Chrystine Hanus, Associate Editor
Carl Good, Publisher
Articles on both technical and business aspects of professional roofing.
Cost: $35.00
3500 Members
Frequency: Monthly
Circulation: 16000
ISSN: 0896-5552
Founded in: 1886

4079 **Professional Spraying**
88-11th Avenue NE
Minneapolis, MN 55413
612-623-6000; *Fax:* 612-623-6580
CustomerService@graco.com; www.graco.com
Patrick McHale, President/CEO
James Graner, CFO
Targets new products, industry news, and trade literature.
Frequency: Monthly
Circulation: 40000
Founded in: 1926

4080 **Qualified Remodeler**
Cygnus Publishing
1233 Janesville Avenue
Fort Atkinson, WI 53538
920-563-6388; *Fax:* 920-563-1704
john.huff@cygnusb2b.com;
www.cygnusb2b.com
John Huff, Publisher
Serving contractors who specialize in residential and light commercial remodeling.
72 Pages
Frequency: Monthly
Circulation: 82000
Founded in: 1975
Mailing list available for rent: 84,000 names
Printed in 4 colors on glossy stock

4081 **RSI**
7300 N Linder Ave
Skokie, IL 60077
847-983-2000
roofingsidinginsulation@halldata.com;
www.rsimag.com
Delivers timely news, technical and business management information, including a monthly analysis of key industry trends and techniques to help roofing, siding and insulation contractors run progressive, profitable businesses
Cost: $36.00
64 Pages
Frequency: Monthly
Circulation: 23658
Founded in: 1945

4082 **Reed Bulletin**
Reed Business Informtion
30 Technology Parkway South
Suite 100
Norcross, GA 30092
800-424-3996
talisha.jackson@reedbusiness.com;
www.reedconstructiondata.com
Talisha Jackson, Media Contact
Provides contractors with project news and tools suppliers.

4083 **Reeves Journal**
Business News Publishing Company
23421 South Pointe Dr.
Suite 280
Laguna Hills, CA 92653
949-830-0881; *Fax:* 949-859-7845
ellyn@reevesjournal.com;
www.reevesjournal.com
Souzan Azar, Production
Ellyn Fishman, Publisher/Sales
Kati Larson, Advertising Sales
Jack Sweet, Editor
Reeves Journal, has been an invaluable tool for contractors & plumbing industry professionals for the last 85 years. Their goal is to address the regional opportunities and challenges facing PHC contractors, wholesalers and engineers in the 14 western United States.
Cost: $55.00
Frequency: Monthly
Circulation: 15,535
Founded in: 1922

4084 **Remodeling**
Hanley-Wood
1 Thomas Cir NW
Suite 600
Washington, DC 20005-5811
202-452-0800; *Fax:* 202-785-1974
rm@omeda.com; www.residentialarchitect.com
Frank Anton, CEO
Claire Conroy, Editorial Director
Jennifer Lash, Managing Editor
News on state-of-the-art in remodeling management, products, construction and techniques. Appeals to the residential and light commercial remodeling contractor.
Cost: $44.95
Frequency: Monthly
Circulation: 93612
Founded in: 1955

4085 **Rental Equipment Register**
17383 W Sunset Blvd
Suite A220
Pacific Plsds, CA 90272-4187
310-230-7160; *Fax:* 310-230-7169
michael.roth@penton.com
rermag.com
Michael Roth, Editor
Brandey Smith, Managing Editor
Edited for owners and managers of equipment rental and sales centers.
Cost: $45.00
125 Pages
Frequency: Monthly
Circulation: 21000
Founded in: 1886

4086 **Residential Architect**
Hanley-Wood
1 Thomas Cir NW
Suite 600
Washington, DC 20005-5811
202-452-0800
888-269-8410; *Fax:* 202-785-1974
jlash@hanleywood.com;
www.residentialarchitect.com
Frank Anton, CEO
Jennifer Lash, Managing Editor
Bruce Snider, Senior Editor
An award-winning national magazine focusing exclusively on the residential architecture profession.
Cost: $39.95
Frequency: 9x Yearly
Circulation: 22000
Founded in: 1976

4087 **Rock and Dirt**
174 4th St
Crossville, TN 38555-4303
931-484-5137
800-251-6776; *Fax:* 931-484-2532
subs@rockanddirt.com; www.rockanddirt.com
Mike Stone, Publisher
Comprehensive buy/sell publications for heavy construction. Primary target audiences worldwide are contractors and other heavy equipment buyers. A non-editorial tabloid, each issue contains display and classified ads that feature thousand of pieces of heavy machinery and related products and services. The magazine also has a large auction section.
Cost: $14.33
Circulation: 170,000
Founded in: 1950
Printed in 4 colors on newsprint stock

4088 **Roofing Contractor**
BNP Media
PO Box 5125
Naperville, IL 60540
630-554-2200; *Fax:* 630-554-3817
mward@illinoisroofing.com;
www.illinoisroofing.com
Focuses on coverage of new technology and its implementation in the field. Regular issues include equipment comparisons, new product information, safety tips and legal advice.
Frequency: Monthly
Circulation: 27205
Founded in: 1926

4089 **Rural Builder**
F+W Media
38 E. 29th Street
New York, NY 10016
212-447-1400; *Fax:* 212-447-5231
contact_us@fwmedia.com;
www.fwpublications.com
Scott Tappa, Editor
Focuses on the post frame and metal frame industry.
Cost: $18.94
64 Pages
Circulation: 32000
Founded in: 1952
Printed in 4 colors on glossy stock

4090 **Scaffold & Access**
Scaffold Industry Association
2001 E Campbell Avenue
Suite 101
Phoenix, AZ 85016
602-257-1144
866-687-7115; *Fax:* 602-257-1166;
www.scaffold.org
Steve Smith, President
Marty Coughlin, President Elect
Daryl Hare, Treasurer
Mike Russell, Secretary
The official publication of the SAIA. Striving to elevate the standard of practice in the scaffold and access industry by educating professionals on safety issues, better business practices and innovative solutions to difficult problems.
Frequency: Monthly

4091 **Services Magazine**
Building Service Contractors Association Int'l
401 N Michigan Avenue
22nd Floor
Chicago, IL 60611
312-321-5167
800-368-3414; *Fax:* 312-673-6735
info@bscai.org; www.bscai.org
Sally Schopmeyer, President
Kevin Rohan, VP
The Building Service Contractors Association International is the trade association serving the facility services industry through education, leadership, and representatiion.
Cost: $30.00
56 Pages
Frequency: Monthly
Circulation: 20,504
ISSN: 0279-0548
Founded in: 1981
Printed in 4 colors on glossy stock

4092 **Shelter**
Association Publications
1168 Vickery Ln
Suite 3
Cordova, TN 38016-1664
901-843-8226
James Powell, Editor
For the national distribution and retail segments of the building products industry.
Cost: $6.00
Frequency: Monthly
Founded in: 1962

4093 **Southern Building**
Southern Building Code Congress International
900 Montclair Rd
Birmingham, AL 35213-1206
205-591-1853
888-422-7233; *Fax:* 205-599-9871
webmaster@iccsafe.org; www.iccsafe.org
Gary Nichols, VP Operations

Publishes and maintains a set of model building codes called the Standard Codes. Also provides educational and technical support to the codes enforcement industry.
Cost: $25.00
40 Pages
Circulation: 12000
Founded in: 1943

4094 **Southwest Contractor**
McGraw Hill
4747 E Elliot Rd
Suite 29-339
Phoenix, AZ 85044

602-274-2155
800-393-6343; *Fax:* 602-631-3073
scott_blair@mcgraw-hill.com;
www.southwest.construction.com

Seth Horowitz, Publisher
Scott Blair, Editor

We cover all aspects of the commercial construction industry in Arizona, Nevada and New Mexico. Our mission is to provide news about the projects, the people and the events that affect the building and highway/heavy segments market.
Cost: $40.00
48 Pages
Frequency: Monthly
Circulation: 7000
Founded in: 1938

4095 **State of Seniors Housing**
American Seniors Housing Association
5225 Wisconsin Ave NW
Suite 502
Washington, DC 20015

202-237-0900; *Fax:* 202-237-1616;
www.seniorshousing.org

David Schless, President
Doris Maultsby, VP
Frequency: Yearly

4096 **Structural Insulated Panel**
Structural Insulated Panel Association
PO Box 1699
Gig Harbor, WA 98335

253-858-7472; *Fax:* 253-858-0272;
www.sips.org

Terry Dieken, President
Al Cobb, VP

A comprehensive, full color book on building with energy efficient SIPs.
Frequency: Quarterly
Circulation: 5000
Founded in: 1990

4097 **Structures**
Business Journal of Portland
851 Sw 6th Ave
Suite 500
Portland, OR 97204-1342

503-274-8733
866-246-0424; *Fax:* 503-219-3450
portland@bizjournals.com;
www.bizjournals.com/portland

Craig Wessel, Publisher

Special edition of The Business Journal that spotlights top construction projects and highlights the design, architecture and construction
Cost: $89.00
52 Pages
Frequency: Daily
Circulation: 400000
ISSN: 0742-6550
Printed in 4 colors on newsprint stock

4098 **Subcontractor**
Subcontractors Education Trust
1004 Duke St
Alexandria, VA 22314-3588

703-684-3450
800-221-0415; *Fax:* 703-836-3482
asaoffice@asa-hq.com; www.asaonline.com

Colette Nelson, EVP
Franklin Davis, Director Government Relations

News from the construction industry, including up-to-date information on legislative and regulatory affairs, and business news concerning the subcontracting industry.
24 Pages
Frequency: Quarterly
Circulation: 9000
Founded in: 1966
Printed in 2 colors

4099 **The Construction User**
The Association of Union Constructors
1501 Lee Highway
Suite 202
Arlington, VA 22209-1109

703-524-3336; *Fax:* 703-524-3364
dacord@tauc.org; www.tauc.org

Stephen R Lindauer, CEO
Kevin J Hilton, Senior VP

TAUC's official magazine, giving readers a fresh and thought-provoking perspective on union construction and the issues contractors, labor and owner-clients face on a daily basis.
Frequency: Monthly
Founded in: 1970

4100 **Tileletter**
National Tile Contractors Association
626 Lakeland E Drive
PO Box 13629
Jackson, MS 39232

601-939-2071; *Fax:* 601-932-6117
bart@tile-assn.com; www.tile-assn.com

Bart Bettiga, Executive Director
Lesley Goddin, Editor

A trade publication to the tile industry: contractors, distributors and manufacturers.
Cost: $35.00
100 Pages
Frequency: Monthly
Circulation: 20000
Mailing list available for rent: 20,000 names at $150 per M
Printed in on matte stock

4101 **Tiling & Decorative Surfaces**
Ashlee Publishing
18 E 41st Street
New York, NY 10017

212-376-7722; *Fax:* 212-376-7723;
www.ashlee.com

Jordan M Wright, President

Provides information about industry trends and events throughout the world including interviews with manufacturers, distributors and contractors, offering tips on successful merchandising and sales techniques. Issues include product listings and project articles.
Cost: $50.00
Frequency: Monthly
Circulation: 27181
Founded in: 1950

4102 **Tilt-Up TODAY**
Tilt-Up Concrete Association
113 First Street West
PO Box 204
Mount Vernon, IA 52314-0204

319-895-6911; *Fax:* 320-213-5555
info@tilt-up.org; www.tilt-up.org
Social Media: Facebook

Ed McGuire, President
Glenn Doncaster, President-Elect
Kimberly Corwin, Vice-President
Shane Miller, Treasurer
David Tomasula, Secretary

With continuing advancements in Tilt-Up innovation and architectural achievement, Tilt-Up TODAY highlights the wide variety of outstanding Tilt-Up construction that is taking place all across the world.
Frequency: Monthly
Founded in: 2005
Printed in 4 colors on glossy stock

4103 **Timber Framing**
Timbers Framers Guild
PO Box 295
Alstead, NH 03602

559-834-8453
888-453-0879; *Fax:* 888-453-0879
info@tfguild.org; www.tfguild.org

Joel McCarty, Executive Director

Contains in-depth articles on timber framing history, technology, theory, practice, design, and engineering, as well as the work of the guild and its members
Cost: $25.00
Frequency: Quarterly
Founded in: 1984

4104 **Timber Home Living**
Home Buyer Publications
4200 Lafayette Center Drive
Suite 100
Chantilly, VA 20151-1239

703-222-6951
800-850-7279; *Fax:* 703-222-3209
store@homebuyerpubs.com;
www.loghomeliving.com
Social Media: Facebook, LinkedIn

Lara Sloan, Publisher

For individuals wishing to plan, build, decorate, or design a log or timber frame home.
Cost: $3.99
Frequency: Bi-Monthly

4105 **Traditional Building**
Restore Media
45 Main Street
Suite 411
Brooklyn, NY 11201

718-636-0788; *Fax:* 718-636-0750
theditors@restoremedia.com;
www.traditional-building.com

Ray Shepherd, Production Manager
Clem Labine, Editor

Lists sources of products for restoration and new construction of traditional buildings.
Cost: $19.95
Frequency: Bi-Monthly
Circulation: 29,000
ISSN: 0898-0284
Founded in: 1988
Printed in on glossy stock

4106 **Underground Construction**
Oildom Publishing Company of Texas
PO Box 941669
Houston, TX 77094-8669

281-558-6930; *Fax:* 281-558-7029
oklinger@oildompublishing.com;
www.oildompublishing.com

Oliver Klinger, President & Publisher
Robert Carpenter, Editor
Cost: $25.00
Frequency: Monthly
Printed in 4 colors on glossy stock

4107 **Underground Focus**
Canterbury Communications

411 South Evergreen
Manteno, IL 60950

815-468-7814; *Fax:* 815-468-7644;
www.underspace.com

Ron Rosencrans, Editor-in-Chief
Paula Miller, Advertising Manager

People read Underground Focus magazine because it documents the importance of their work and helps them get the budgets to do the job. It powerfully dramatizes the need for underground damage prevention and excavation safety.
Cost: $25.00
46 Pages
Circulation: 18,000
ISSN: 1090-400X
Founded in: 1986
Printed in 2 colors

4108 Utility Contractor
3925 Chain Bridge Road
Suite 300
Fairfax, VA 22030

703-358-9300; *Fax:* 703-358-9307
bill@nuca.com; www.nuca.com

Bill Hillman, CEO

Serves the underground utility construction industry, including contractors, manufacturers, suppliers, engineering firms, municipal/public/private utilities, and others allied to the field.
Frequency: Monthly
Circulation: 20983
ISSN: 1098-0342
Founded in: 1967

4109 Walls & Ceilings
Business News Publishing Company
2401 West Big Beaver Road
Suite 700
Troy, MI 48084

248-362-3700; *Fax:* 248-362-5103
mark@wwcca.org; www.wconline.com

Lynette Barwin, Production Manager
John Wyatt, Editor
Mark Fowler, Editorial Directort

Information regarding management, building methods, technology, government regulations, consumer trends, and product information for the contractor involved in exterior finishes, waterproofing, insulation, metal framing, drywall, fireproofing, partitions, stucco and plaster.
Cost: $49.00
140 Pages
Frequency: Monthly
Circulation: 30000
Founded in: 1938
Printed in 4 colors

4110 Welding Journal
American Welding Society
550 NW 42nd Ave
Miami, FL 33126-5699

305-443-9353
800-443-9353; *Fax:* 305-443-7559
info@aws.org; www.aws.org

Annette O'Brien, Senior Editor
Mary Ruth Johnsen, Editor

Serves the metal working field, individuals and organizations engaged in welding, cutting or related processes and equipment for the fabrication, maintenance, design or repair of metal products.
Cost: $80.00
Frequency: Monthly
Circulation: 50,000
ISSN: 0043-2296
Founded in: 1919

4111 Western Builder
Western Builder Publishing Company
30 Technology Pkwy S
Suite 100
Norcross, GA 30092-2925

770-209-3730; *Fax:* 770-209-3712;
www.acppubs.com

Tad Smith, CEO
Greg Sitek, Editorial Director

Regional construction publication serving the heavy, highway and non-residential construction industry in Wisconsin and the Upper Peninsula of Michigan.
Cost: $53.00
Frequency: Monthly
Circulation: 100,000
Founded in: 1905

4112 Window & Door
National Glass Association
1945 Old Gallows Rd
Suite 750
Vienna, VA 22182

703-442-4890
866-342-5642; *Fax:* 703-442-0630;
www.glass.org

Philip James, President/CEO
Nicole Harris, VP

The focus is on technical, new product information, business management and industry issues which focus on manufacturing both new and replacement windows and doors.
Cost: $29.95
Circulation: 20000
Founded in: 1948

4113 Window Film Magazine
Key Communications
PO Box 569
Garrisonville, VA 22463

540-720-5584; *Fax:* 540-720-5687
boleary@glass.com;
www.windowfilmmag.com/

Debra Levy, Publisher
Penny Beverage, Assistant Editor
Katie Hodge, Editor

Provides industry news, supplier and film manufacturer profiles, technical and installation tips, as well as state-by-state legislative breakdowns and consumer marketing issues relevant to the film industry.
Cost: $35.00
Frequency: Monthly
Circulation: 7000

4114 Window World Magazine
Work-4 Projects
4819 St. Charles Boulevard
Pierrefonds, Quebec H9H-3C7

514-620-2200; *Fax:* 514-620-6300
editor@work4.ca;
www.homebuildercanada.com

Nachmi Artzy, Publisher

Provides new products, announcements, calendar events, and coverage of industry news, technical and maketing information to small and medium window and door manufacturers of North America.
Cost: $30.00
Frequency: Bi-Monthly
Circulation: 9,877

4115 Wrecking and Salvage Journal
Duane Publishing
51 Park St
Dorchester, MA 02122-2643

617-282-4885; *Fax:* 617-282-0320;
www.rubblemakers.com

Herb Duane, Owner
Toby Duane, Director

Business related information for those engaged in demolition and urban renewal.
Cost: $35.00
Frequency: Monthly
Circulation: 2500
Founded in: 1967

Trade Shows

4116 ACSM Annual Spring Conference
American Congress on Surveying and Mapping
6 Montgomery Village Avenue
Suite 403
Gaithersburg, MD 20879

240-632-9716; *Fax:* 240-632-1321
info@acsm.net; www.acsm.net

Curtis Sumner, Executive Director
Colleen Campbell, Conference Director

Four hundred booths of products and services offered by companies involved in the aerial mapping industry.
2000 Attendees
Frequency: Annual/April

4117 ACSM/APLS Annual Conference & Technology Exhibition
American Congress on Surveying & Mapping
6 Montgomery Village Avenue
Gaithersburg, MD 20879

240-632-9716; *Fax:* 240-632-1321
curtis.sumner@acsm.net; www.acsm.net

Curtis Sumner, Executive Director
Colleen Campbell, Conference Director

The American Congress on Surveying & mapping and the Arizona Professional Land Surveyors organizations have come together to produce this exhibition with four hundred booths of products and services offered by companies involved in the aerial mapping industry.
1500 Attendees
Frequency: Annual

4118 AEMA Annual Meeting
Asphalt Emulsion Manufacturers Association
3 Church Circle
PO Box 250
Annapolis, MD 21401-1933

410-267-0023; *Fax:* 410-267-7546
krissoff@aema.org; www.aema.org

Michael Krissoff, Executive Director

Representing close to 150 of the world's leading companies in the pavement preservation and rehabilitation industry. A combined annual meeting with the International Slurry Surfacing Association and the Asphalt Recycling & Reclaiming Association.
400 Attendees
Frequency: Annual/March

4119 AGC Building Contractors Conference
Associated General Contractors of America
2300 Wilson Blvd
Suite 400
Arlington, VA 22201

703-548-3119; *Fax:* 703-837-5405
meetings@agc.org; www.agc.org

Carolyn Coker, Executive Director
Joe Jarboe, SVP

One hundred and seventy-five exhibiors of heavy and light construction equipment, trucks, building materials, management services, computer

hardware and software. Contractors, subcontractors and trade professionals attend.
4500+ Attendees
Frequency: Annual

4120 **AIBD Annual Convention**
American Institute of Building Design
7059 Blair Rd NW
Suite 201
Washington, DC 20012
800-366-2423; *Fax:* 866-204-0293
info@aibd.org; www.aibd.org
Social Media: Facebook, Twitter, LinkedIn
Dan Sater, President
Alan Kent, Internal Vice President
Viki Wooster, External Vice President
Kerry Dick, Secretary/ Treasurer
Exhibition of 25 manufacturers, suppliers, distributors and plan publishers of building products including: roofing, windows, doors, floor covering, fire places, spas/jacuzzis, lumber, intercom systems, alarm systems and appliances; computer-aid design technology, computer hardware/software and plan publishers. Containing 30 booths and 30 exhibits.
1500 Attendees
Frequency: Annual/July
Founded in: 1950

4121 **AIC Annual Forum**
American Institute of Constructors
19 Mantua Road
Mount Royal, NJ 08061
703-683-4999; *Fax:* 703-683-5480
info@professionalconstructor.org;
www.professionalconstructor.org
Social Media: Facebook, Twitter, LinkedIn
Joseph Sapp, Executive Director
Greg Carender, President
Charles L. Sapp, Director, Association Management
Educational presentations from leading practitioners and educators in the world of construction, panel discussions with major voices in the industry, opportunities to network with other emerging leaders in the construction profession as they fine-tune their leadership skills.
Frequency: Annual
Founded in: 1971

4122 **AISC Annual Meeting**
American Institute of Steel Construction
1 E Wacker Drive
Suite 700
Chicago, IL 60601-2000
312-670-2400; *Fax:* 312-670-5403
ferch@aisc.org; www.aisc.org
Roger Ferch, President
Katey Lenihan, Meeting Planner
One hundred booths attended by structural engineers, steel fabricators, educators and construction managers. Those interested in the design fabrication and erection of structural steel for non-residential buildings and bridges.
100 Attendees
Frequency: Annual/September

4123 **APWA International Public Works Congress & Expo**
American Public Works Association
2345 Grand Boulevard
Suite 700
Kansas City, MO 64108-2625
816-472-6100
800-848-2792; *Fax:* 816-472-1610
ddancy@apwa.net; www.apwa.net
Brian Van Norman, Director
David Dancy, Director of Marketing
Offers the benefit of a variety of educational sessions, depth of the exhibit program and endless opportunities for networking. The latest cutting-edge technologies, managerial techniques and regulatory trends designed to keep you focused on the right solutions at the right time.
6500 Attendees
Frequency: Annual/September

4124 **APWA North American Snow Conference**
American Public Works Association
2345 Grand Boulevard
Suite 700
Kansas City, MO 64108-2625
816-472-6100
800-848-2792; *Fax:* 816-472-1610
ddancy@apwa.net; www.apwa.net
Brian Van Norman, Director
David Dancy, Director of Marketing
Education, technical and hands-on for snow and ice management.
1000 Attendees
Frequency: Annual/April
ISSN: 0092-4873

4125 **ASPE Annual Meeting and Estimators Summit**
American Society of Professional Estimators
2525 Perimeter Place Drive
Suite 103
Nashville, TN 37214
615-316-9200
888-378-6283; *Fax:* 615-316-9800
sbo@aspenational.org; www.aspenational.com
Marcene N. Taylor, President
Bruce D. Schlesier, 1st Vice President
Provides two days of presentations by nationally known speakers in the construction industry. ASPE's Technical Documents Committee prepares a book for each convention attendee that contains papers submitted by the speakers at these educational sessions.
Frequency: Annual/July

4126 **AWI Annual Meeting/Convention**
Architectural Woodwork Institute
46179 Westlake Dr
Suite 120
Potomac Falls, VA 20165
571-323-3636; *Fax:* 571-323-2330
info@awinet.org; www.awinet.org
Kimberly Kennedy, Meeting/Conventions Director
Robert Stout, President
Seminar, workshop and woodwork products such as casework, fixtures and panelings, equipment and supplies.
Frequency: Annual/October

4127 **Adhesive and Sealant Council Fall Convention**
Adhesive & Sealant Council
7101 Wisconsin Avenue
Suite 990
Bethesda, MD 20814
301-986-9700; *Fax:* 301-986-9795
data@ascouncil.org; www.ascouncil.org
Malinda Armstrong, Director, Meetings & Expositions
Frequency: October

4128 **AeroMat Conference and Exposition**
ASM International
9639 Kinsman Road
Materials Park, OH 44073-0002
440-338-5151
800-336-5152; *Fax:* 440-338-4634
natalie.nemec@asminternational.org;
www.asminternational.org
Stanley Theobald, Managing Director
Kelly Thomas, Exposition Account Manager
Natalie Nemec, Event Programming Manager
Conference for Aerospace Meterials Engineers, Structural Engineers and Designers. The annual event focuses on affordable structures and low-cost manufacturing, titanium alloy technology, advanced intermetallics and refractory metal alloys, materials and processes for space applications, aging systems, high strength steel, NDT evaluation, light alloy technology, welding and joining, and engineering technology. 150 exhibitors.
1500 Attendees
Frequency: Annual/June
Founded in: 1984

4129 **American Institute of Building Design Annual Convention**
American Institute of Building Design
7059 Blair Road NW
Suite 201
Washington, DC 20012
202-249-1407
800-366-2423; *Fax:* 202-249-2473
info@aibd.org; www.aibd.org
Dan Sater, President
A four day convention and trade show for residential design professionals.
Frequency: Annual/July

4130 **Annual Conference on Deep Foundations**
Deep Foundations Institute
326 Lafayette Avenue
Hawthorne, NJ 07506
973-423-4030; *Fax:* 973-423-4031
dfihq@dfi.org; www.dfi.org
James Morrison, President
Katie Criqui, Event Coordinator
The premier event for industry members from across the globe to gather and share experiences, exchange ideas and learn the current state-of-the-practice from various disciplines such as engineers, contractors, suppliers, manufacturers and academicians.
600 Attendees
Frequency: Annual/October
Founded in: 1975

4131 **Arrowhead Home and Builders Show**
Shamrock Productions
14552 Judicial Rd
Suite 111
Burnsville, MN 55306
952-431-9630; *Fax:* 952-431-9633
info@shamrockprod.com;
www.shamrockprod.com/dh.htm
Randy Schauer, President/CEO
Home building, remodeling, landscaping and more.
41960 Attendees
Frequency: Annual/April

4132 **Associated Builders and Contractors National Convention**
Associated Builders and Contractors
4250 N Fairfax Dr
9th Floor
Arlington, VA 22203
703-812-2000; *Fax:* 703-812-8200
meetings@abc.org; www.abc.org
Michael Bellaman, President/CEO
Tina Schneider, Meetings/Conventions Director
Exhibits for construction contractors, subcontractors, and associated trades.

4133 **Brick Show**
Brick Industry Association

1850 Centennial Park Drive
Suite 301
Reston, VA 20191-1525

703-620-0100; *Fax:* 703-620-3928
brickinfo@bia.org; www.bia.org

Susan Ludwig, Show Manager

The only national tradeshow and conference for the clay brick industry.
950 Attendees
Frequency: Annual/March

4134 **Builders Trade Show**
Maryland National Capital Building Industry Assn.
1738 Elton Road
Suite 200
Silver Spring, MD 20903-5730

301-445-5400; *Fax:* 301-445-5499;
www.mncbia.org

Jean Mathis, Events Director
Diane Swenson, EVP

Annual show and exhibits of construction equipment, supplies and services.

4135 **Building Industry Show**
Building Industry Assn. of Southern California
17444 Sky Park Circle
Irvine, CA 92614

949-553-9500; *Fax:* 949-769-8942;
www.buildingindustryshow.com

Wes Keusder, President

Annual show of about 400 exhibitors of products and services for the building industry.
8000+ Attendees
Frequency: Annual/November

4136 **Business Administration Conference**
National Ready Mixed Concrete Association
900 Spring Street
Silver Spring, MD 20910

301-587-1400
888-846-7622; *Fax:* 301-585-4219
info@nrmca.org; www.nrmca.org

Robert Garbini, President
Deana Angelastro, Executive Administrator

A 3-day educational program for financial, information technology, and human resources professionals in the construction and construction materials business.
Frequency: Annual/October

4137 **CFMA Annual Conference & Exhibition**
Construction Financial Management Association
100 Village Blvd
Suite 200
Princeton, NJ 08540

609-452-8000; *Fax:* 609-452-0474
info@cfma.org; www.cfma.org

Joseph Burkett, Chairman
Pat Cebelak, Treasurer

The source and resource for construction financial professionals.
6000 Attendees
Frequency: Annual/May

4138 **CONEXPO-CON/AGG**
Association of Equipment Manufacturers
6737 W Washington St
Suite 2400
Milwaukee, WI 53214-5647

414-272-0943
800-867-6060; *Fax:* 414-272-1170;
www.conexpoconagg.com

Ken Snover, Expo Managing Director
Jim Eldredge, Exhibits Coordinator

The international gathering place for the worldwide construction, aggregates and ready mixed concrete industries.
124M Attendees
Frequency: March/Every 3 Years
Founded in: 2002

4139 **Composites & Polycon**
American Composites Manufacturers Association
1010 North Glebe Road
Suite 450
Arlington, VA 22201

703-525-0511; *Fax:* 703-525-0743
info@acmanet.org; www.compositesworld.com

Lori Luchak, President

World's largest trade association serving the composites industry. Provides education and support for composites fabricators in the successful operation of businesses, and offers leading-edge services in regulatory compliance and formulation, education and training, management, and market expansion.
1.5M Attendees
Frequency: Annual/September

4140 **Coverings: The Ultimate Tile & Stone Experience**
NTP, Coverings Show Management
313 S Patrick Street
Alexandria, VA 22314

703-683-8500
800-687-7469; *Fax:* 703-836-4486
coverings@ntpshow.com; www.coverings.com

Karin Fendrich, COO

Showcasing the newest in tile and natural stone, the event provides opportunities for: continuing education, live demonstrations, networking and new business. 1200 international exhibitors, attracting 33,000+ distributors, retailers, fabricators, contractors, and design professionals.
33M Attendees
Frequency: Annual
Mailing list available for rent

4141 **Delmarva Ag & Construction Show**
Lee Publications
6113 State Highway 5
Palatine Bridge, NY 13428

518-732-2269
800-218-5586; *Fax:* 518-673-3237
info@leepub.com; www.leepub.com

Ken Maring, Trade Show Manager

Hundreds of agriculture and construction exhibitors with products and equipment. Skid steer rodeo for fun. Held at the Wicomico Youth and Civic Center in Maryland.
Frequency: Annual/December

4142 **Design & Construction Exposition**
Construction Association of Michigan
43636 Woodward
PO Box 3204
Bloomfield Hills, MI 48302

248-972-1000; *Fax:* 248-972-1001
marketing@cam-online.com;
www.cam-online.com

Ron Riegel, Exposition Manager
Jeanny Snowden, Marketing Coordinator

Annual show of 250 manufacturers, suppliers and distributors of construction industry equipment, supplies and services.
11M Attendees
Frequency: Annual/February
Founded in: 1985

4143 **EdCon & Expo**
Associated Builders and Contractors
4250 Fairfax Drive
9th Floor
Arlington, VA 22203-1665

703-812-2000; *Fax:* 703-812-8201
meetings@abc.org; www.abc.org

Michael Bellaman, CEO
Todd Mann, COO
Jason Daisey, CFO
1700 Attendees
Frequency: Annual/April

4144 **Elevator Escalator Safety Awareness Annual Meeting**
Elevator World
356 Morgan Avenue
Mobile, AL 36606

251-479-4514
800-730-5093; *Fax:* 251-479-7043
admin@elevator-world.com;
www.elevator-world.com

Linda Williams, Director of Administration
Patricia Cartee, Director of Operations

Meetings, discussions and exhibits on the safety of elevators.
Frequency: Annual/February

4145 **Environmental Management Conference and Exposition**
Environmental Information Association
6935 Wisconsin Avenue
Suite 306
Chevy Chase, MD 20815-6112

301-961-4999
888-343-4342; *Fax:* 301-961-3094
info@eia-usa.org; www.eia-usa.org

Kelly Rutt, Developement Manager
Brent Kynoch, Managing Director

Annual conference of 85-100 exhibitors of equipment, supplies and services for quantifying, managing or remediating environmental hazards in buildings and facilities.
1200 Attendees

4146 **Equipment Distributors Association Annual Meeting**
Associated Equipment Distributors
600 Hunter Dr
Suite 220
Oak Brook, IL 60523-8807

630-574-0650; *Fax:* 630-574-0132
info@aednet.org; www.aednet.org

Toby Mack, President/CEO
Janet Dixon, Convention & Meetings Director

A place where distributor, manufacturer and supplier executives meet, build relationships, do business, and learn new skills.
3.5M Attendees
Frequency: Annual/January

4147 **FENCETECH Convention & Expo**
American Fence Association
800 Roosevelt Rd
Building C-312
Glen Ellyn, IL 60137-5899

630-942-6598; *Fax:* 630-790-3095;
www.americanfenceassociation.com

Rod Wilson, President
Mike Robinson, Vice President

Four hundred and eighty booths for the fence industry. Educational opportunities that will inform you of the most up-to-date technology.
5883 Attendees
Frequency: Annual/January/February

4148 **GlassBuild America: Glass, Window & Door Expo**
National Glass Association

1945 Old Gallows Rd
Suite 750
Vienna, VA 22182

703-424-4890
866-342-5642; *Fax:* 703-442-0630;
www.glass.org

Philip James, President
Nicole Harris, VP

Provides one central showcase for the class processing equipment, window and door manufacturing equipment, and the latest technology for all types of glass and fenestration products used in residential and commercial construction and related applications.
Frequency: Annual/October

4149 Great Lakes Building Products Exposition
Michigan Lumber & Building Materials Association
5815 Executive Drive
Suite B
Lansing, MI 48911

517-394-5225; *Fax:* 517-394-5228;
www.thembsa.org

Jodi Barber, VP
Rick Seely, President

Offering new products and presentations on industry topics for the building material dealer and builders/contractors.
Frequency: Annual/January

4150 Hard Hat Show
Lee Publications
6113 State Highway 5
Palatine Bridge, NY 13428-0121

518-732-2269
800-218-5586; *Fax:* 518-673-3237
kmaring@leepub.com; www.leepub.com

Ken Maring, Trade Show Manager
Larry Price, Sales Manager
Beth Snyder, Trade Show Manager

The premier showcase for heavy construction in the Northeast sharing information about the latest innovations in the construction industry!
3.5M Attendees
Frequency: Annual/March
Founded in: 1989

4151 Home Improvement & Remodeling Exposition
Dmg World Media
325 Essjay Road
Suite 100
Williamsville, NY 14221

716-631-2266
800-274-6948; *Fax:* 716-631-2425;
www.dmgevents.com

Mark Carr, President

Featuring a spectacular garden, the latest in home technology, thousands of products, celebrity appearances and over 350 exhibits where consumers can find what they need to create their own unique spaces and put their special style to work.
60000 Attendees
Frequency: Annual/March

4152 IDA International Garage Door Expo
International Door Association
PO Box 246
West Milton, OH 45383-0246

937-988-8042
800-355-4432; *Fax:* 937-698-6153
info@longmgt.com; www.doors.org

Chris Long, Managing Director
Steve Smith, Accounting Manager

Workshops and Exhibits featuring the latest product innovations as well as the traditional products and services for which the industry is known for.
Frequency: Annual/April

4153 INTEX Expo System Construction Association
Association of the Wall and Ceiling Industry
513 W Broad Street
Suite 210
Falls Church, VA 22046

703-538-1600; *Fax:* 703-534-8307
info@awci.org; www.awci.org

Tim Wies, President
Jeffrey Burley, VP

The premier interior/exterior wall and ceiling commercial construction trade show. This annual show host exhibitors such as, wall and ceiling contractors, general contractors, architects, specifiers, suppliers, and distributors.
3000 Attendees
Frequency: Annual/April

4154 Independent Electrical Contractors National Convention
Independent Electrical Contractors
4401 Ford Avenue
Suite 1100
Alexandria, VA 22302

703-549-7351; *Fax:* 703-549-7448
info@ieci.org; www.ieci.org

Tim Welsh, Executive VP
Trayvia Watson, Meetings Manager

One hundred booths of electrical equipment, products and services.
1000 Attendees
Frequency: Annual/October

4155 International Builders Show
National Association of Home Builders
1201 15th Street NW
Washington, DC 20005

202-266-8200
800-368-5242; *Fax:* 202-266-8400
info@nahb.com; www.nahb.org

Gerald Howard, CEO

More than 1,600 suppliers, representing the most comprehensive showcase of home building products and services, are ready to demonstrate how their offerings can help you to corner the market.
90000 Attendees
Frequency: Annual/January

4156 International Conference Building Official
International Code Council
5360 Workman Mill Road
Whittier, CA 90601-2298

888-422-7233; *Fax:* 562-908-5524;
www.iccsafe.org

Jay Peters, Executive Director
Mark Johnson, SVP
1,2M Attendees
Frequency: Annual/September

4157 International Construction and Utility Equipment Exposition
Association of Equipment Manufacturers
6737 W Washington Street
Suite 2400
Milwaukee, WI 53214-5647

414-272-0943; *Fax:* 414-272-1170
aem@aem.org; www.aem.org

Sara Mooney Truesdale, Show Director
Paul Flemming, Exhibits Sales Manager

The only exposition for outdoor demonstrations of utility and construction equipment. Experience the newest technologies for their electric, phone, cable, water, sewer, gas, general construction, landscape, and government jobs.
15000 Attendees
Frequency: Annual/September

4158 International Thermal Spray Conference & Exposition
ASM International
9639 Kinsman Road
Materials Park, OH 44073

440-338-5151
800-336-5152; *Fax:* 440-338-4634
natalie.nemec@asminternational.org;
www.asminternational.org

Charles Hayes, Executive Director
Pamela Kleinman, Senior Event Manager

Global annual event attracting professional interested in thermal spray technology focusing on advances in HVOF, plasma and detonation gun, flame spray and wire arc spray processes, performance of coatings, and future trends. 150 exhibitors.
1000 Attendees
Frequency: Annual/May

4159 Lumber and Building Material Expo
Northeastern Retail Lumber Association
585 N Greenbush Road
Rensselaer, NY 12144

518-286-1010
800-292-6752; *Fax:* 518-286-1755
rferris@nrla.org; www.nrla.org

Donna Berger, Events Coordinator
Rita Ferris, President

Largest regional trade show in the lumber and building material industry. Retail lumber dealers in the Northeast are afforded the opportunity to interact with manufacturers, wholesalers, and distributors of lumber, building materials, and related technologies.
7000 Attendees
Frequency: Annual/February

4160 MBI World of Modular Conference
Modular Building Institute
944 Glenwood Station Ln
Suite 204
Charlottesville, VA 22901-1480

434-296-3288
888-811-3288; *Fax:* 434-296-3361
info@modular.org; www.modular.org

Steven Williams, Operations Director
Tom Hardiman, Executive Director

High-profile speakers, educational sessions, exhibits, discussion on trends in commercial modular, entertainment and prizes
500 Attendees
Frequency: Annual

4161 MCAA Annual Convention & Masonry Showcase
Mason Contractors Association of America
1481 Merchant Drive
Algonquin, IL 60102

224-678-9709
800-536-2225; *Fax:* 224-678-9714;
www.masoncontractors.org

Tim O'Toole, Marketing Director
Jeff Buczkiewicz, Executive Director

Featuring in-depth education seminars, high-profile international skills competitions and exhibit display. Attendees includes masonry contracting firms representing all facets of masonry installation, including the largest commercial, residential, institutional, landscape, paving, retaining, glass block, and stone contractors.
Frequency: Annual/March

4162 **MIACON Construction, Mining & Waste Management Show**
Finocchiaro Enterprises
2921 Coral Way
Miami, FL 33145

305-441-2865; *Fax:* 305-529-9217;
www.miacon.com

Michael Finocchiaro, President
Jose Garcia, VP
Justine Finocchiaro, Chief Operations

Annual show of 650 manufacturers, suppliers, distributors and exporters of equipment, machinery, supplies and services for the construction, mining and waste managment industries. There will be 600 booths.
10M Attendees
Frequency: Annual/October
Founded in: 1994

4163 **Metalcon International**
PSMJ Resources
10 Midland Avenue
Newton, MA 02458-1021

617-965-0055; *Fax:* 617-928-1670
metalcon@psmj.com; www.metalcon.com

Claire Kilcoyne, Show Manager
Suzanne Maher, Conference Director
Paula Parker, Exhibit Sales

Architects, builders, craftspeople, designers, framers, contractors, and other industry leaders will share their expertise, hone their skills, and make connections that will help their businesses reach new heights.
8000 Attendees
Frequency: Annual/October

4164 **NCSBCS/AMCBO Annual Conference**
Int'l Conference of State Bldg Codes & Standards
505 Huntmar Park Drive
Suite 210
Herndon, VA 20170

703-437-0100; *Fax:* 703-481-3596
dbecker@ncsbcs.org; www.ncsbcs.org

Kevin Egilmez, Project Manager
Carolyn Fitch, Membership Services

Providing a wide variety of technical and administrative information of immediate value to the nation's construction and code enforcement community, trade associations, information technology firms and professional societies, academicians, students, and elected officials regarding building codes administration and public safety.
Frequency: Annual/Sept-Oct

4165 **NECA Convention**
National Electrical Contractors Association
3 Bethesda Metro Center
Suite 1100
Bethesda, MD 20814

301-657-3110; *Fax:* 301-215-4500;
www.necanet.org

Russell Alessi, President
Katie Nolan, Convention Manager

The event brings the largest manufacturers, utilities, contractors, engineers, consultants, plant engineers, and distributors from all over North America and 31 foreign countries.
8000 Attendees
Frequency: Annual/September

4166 **NRCMA Conference**
National Railroad Construction & Maintenance Assoc
500 New Jersey Avenue NW
Suite 400
Washington, DC 20001

202-715-2919; *Fax:* 202-318-0867
info@nrcma.org; www.nrcma.org

Chuck Baker, President
Matt Ginsberg, Director of Operations

For railroad personnel, managers and purchasers in design, construction and maintenance. Information on breakthrough innovations in rail construction, railroad safety, new rail projects of national significance and more. 60-80 exhibitors.
750 Attendees
Frequency: Annual/January

4167 **NSSGA Dredging Seminar & Expo**
National Stone, Sand & Gravel Association
1605 King Street
Alexandria, VA 22314

703-525-8788
800-342-1415; *Fax:* 703-525-7782
jwilson@nssga.org; www.nssga.org

Jennifer Wilson, President/CEO
Cynthia McDowell, Conventions Director

Created to specifically meet the needs of aggregate producers who use dredges or have an interest in using dredges in the future. This seminar uses educational seminars, plant tours and manufacturer's exhibits to provide information useful to both novice and experienced dredgers.
Frequency: Annual/June

4168 **National Congress & Expo for Manufactured and Modular Housing**
Manufactured Housing Institute
2111 Wilson Boulevard
Suite 100
Arlington, VA 22201-3040

703-558-0400; *Fax:* 703-558-0401
info@mfghome.org;
www.manufacturedhousing.org

Thayer Long, President/CEO
Lisa Quinn Brechtel, VP/Executive Director

The opportunity to network with over 1500 industry captains who make a positive difference in the modular and manufactured housing industries.
Frequency: Annual/April

4169 **National Demolition Association Conference and Trade Show**
National Demolition Association
16 North Franklin Street
Suite 203
Doylestown, PA 18901

215-348-4949
800-541-2412; *Fax:* 215-348-8422
info@demolitionassociation.com;
www.demolitionassociation.com

Don Rachel, President
Jeff Kroeker, VP
1700 Attendees
Frequency: Annual

4170 **National Hardware Show**
Reed Exhibitions
383 Main Avenue
Norwalk, CT 06851

203-404-4800
888-425-9377; *Fax:* 203-840-9622
inquiry@hardware.reedexpo.com;
www.nationalhardwareshow.com

Richard Russo, Event Director
Juliana Van Der Beek, Sales Manager

The only housing after-market show, bringing together manufacturers and resellers of all products used to remodel, repair, maintain and decorate the home and its surroundings.
3M Attendees
Frequency: Annual/May

4171 **New England Home Show**
Dmg World Media
45 Braintree Hill Office Park
Suite 302
Braintree, MA 02184

781-849-0990
800-469-0990; *Fax:* 781-849-7544;
www.newenglandhomeshow.com

Laurie Myette, Show Manager
Amy Kimball, Administrative Assistant

Annual show of 379 exhibitors of homebuilding and improvement equipment, supplies and services, including bathroom and kitchen supplies, building materials, appliances, doors and windows, swimming pools, hot tubs and spas.
100M Attendees
Frequency: Annual/February

4172 **North American Quarry Recycling Show**
Lee Publications
6113 State Highway 5
PO Box 121
Palatine Bridge, NY 13428-0121

518-732-2269
800-218-5586; *Fax:* 518-673-3245;
www.leepub.com

Ken Maring, Trade Show Manager
Matt Stanley, Sales Manager

The North American Quarry Show is the largest trade show in North America for the aggregates industry.
Frequency: Annual/October

4173 **North American Steel Construction Conference**
American Institute of Steel Construction
One East Wacker Drive
Suite 700
Chicago, IL 60601

312-670-2400; *Fax:* 312-670-5403;
www.aisc.org

David Ratterman, General Counsel
Roger Ferch, President

A premier education event aimed at providing structural engineers, steel fabricators, erectors, and detailers with practical information and the latest design and construction techniques.
2300 Attendees
Frequency: Annual/April

4174 **Northwestern Building Products Expo**
Northwestern Lumber Association
5905 Golden Valley Road
Suite 110
Minneapolis, MN 55422-4528

763-544-6822
888-644-6822; *Fax:* 763-595-4060;
www.nlassn.org

Jodie Fleck, Director of Conventions
Paula Siewert, President

Building materials and their contractors attend this trade show and conference for continuing educataion and cammeraderie
1200 Attendees
Frequency: Annual

4175 **PACE: Paint and Coatings Expo**
Painting and Decorating Contractors of America
1801 Park 270 Drive
Suite 220
St Louis, MO 63146-4020

314-514-7322
800-332-7322; *Fax:* 314-514-9417;
www.pdca.org

Richard Greene, CEO
Libby Loomis, Event Coordinator

This mega show is the culmination of months of research and planning by members of the two professional associations (PDCA & SSPC), who joined forces in search of a 'one-stop shop' solution for convening the maximum number of industry professionals in the most cost-effective and productive way.
Frequency: Annual/January

4176 PowerGen
Scaffold Industry Association
2001 E Campbell Avenue
Suite 101
Phoenix, AZ 85016

602-257-1144
866-687-7115; *Fax:* 602-257-1166;
www.scaffold.org

Steve Smith, President
Marty Coughlin, President Elect
Daryl Hare, Treasurer
Mike Russell, Secretary

Companies from all sectors of the industry exhibit and attendees come together for a look at the industry with key emphasis on new solutions and innovations for the future.
Frequency: Annual/July

4177 RCMA Meeting
Roof Coatings Manufacturers Association
750 National Press Building
529 14th Street NW
Washington, DC 20045

202-207-0919; *Fax:* 202-223-9741
questions@roofcoatings.org;
www.roofcoatings.org

Steve Heinje, Director

An educational program focusing on Technical, Marketing, and regulatory updates regarding roof coatings.
100 Attendees
Frequency: Annual

4178 SIA Annual Convention & Exposition
Scaffold Industry Association
2001 E Campbell Avenue
Suite 101
Phoenix, AZ 85016

602-257-1144
866-687-7115; *Fax:* 602-257-1166;
www.scaffold.org

Steve Smith, President
Marty Coughlin, President Elect
Daryl Hare, Treasurer
Mike Russell, Secretary

Exhibits and classes on scaffold safety and education.
Frequency: Annual/July

4179 SIPA Annual Meeting & Conference
Structural Insulated Panel Association
PO Box 1699
Gig Harbor, WA 98335

253-858-7472; *Fax:* 253-858-0272;
www.sips.org
Social Media: Facebook, Twitter

Frank Baker, President

A valuable networking event for both longtime veterans and newcomers to the SIP industry. If you're a builder, architect, developer or entrepreneur interested in employing SIPs in your next commercial or residential project, you'll be interested in this conference
Frequency: Annual/April

4180 STAFDA Annual Convention & Trade Show
Specialty Tools and Fasteners Distributors Assn.
500 Elm Grove Rd.
Suite 210
Elm Grove, WI 53122

262-784-4774
800-352-2981; *Fax:* 262-784-5059
info@stafda.org; www.stafda.org
Social Media: Facebook, LinkedIn

Mike Kangas, President
Kramer Darragh, Vice President

Members distribute or manufacture power equipment, anchors, fastening systems, drilling equipment and other related industrial supplies.
4000 Attendees
Frequency: Annual/November

4181 Spray Foam Conference & EXPO
Spray Polyurethane Foam Alliance
4400 Fair Lakes Court
Suite 105
Fairfax, VA 22033

800-523-6154; *Fax:* 703-222-5816;
www.sprayfoam.org

Sig Hall, President
Bob Duke, Vice President
Peter Davis, Secretary/ Treasurer

Training and accreditation programs, general and breakout sessions, awards, networking receptions, and the exhibit hall
Frequency: Yearly
Founded in: 1987

4182 TAUC Annual Meeting
The Association of Union Constructors
1501 Lee Highway
Suite 202
Arlington, VA 22209-1109

703-524-3336; *Fax:* 703-524-3364
dacord@tauc.org; www.tauc.org

Stephen R Lindauer, CEO
Kevin J Hilton, Senior VP

The prime meeting of the year, bringing together our membership from around the country in a relaxed and informal setting. The meeting will provide an opportunity to network and meet our union contractors.
Frequency: Annual/May
Founded in: 1970

4183 TCA Annual Convention
Tilt-Up Concrete Association
113 First Street West
PO Box 204
Mount Vernon, IA 52314-0204

319-895-6911; *Fax:* 320-213-5555
info@tilt-up.org; www.tilt-up.org
Social Media: Facebook

Ed McGuire, President
Glenn Doncaster, President-Elect
Kimberly Corwin, Vice-President
Shane Miller, Treasurer
David Tomasula, Secretary

Tilt-up Concrete Association/TCA's annual convention that features intensive training and education seminars for contractors and engineers, as well as a trade show, building tour and focused sessions on marketing and architecturald design.
Frequency: Annual/October
Founded in: 2005

4184 Technology for Construction
Hanley-Wood
8600 Freeport Parkway
Suite 200
Irving, TX 75063

972-366-6300
866-962-7469; *Fax:* 972-536-6402
TCindric@hanleywood.com;
www.technologyforconstruction.com

Tom Cindric, Show Director
Jackie James, Show Manager
Todd Gilmore, Sales Manager

International conference and tradeshow focused on the technology needs and interests of architects and interior designers; civil engineers, contractors, builders, and construction managers, facility managers, building engineers, owners, GIS, surveyors and mapping professionals for private, commercial, institutional and government sectors.
33M Attendees
Frequency: Annual/January

4185 Utility Construction Expo
National Utility Contractors Association
3925 Chain Bridge Road
Suite 300
Fairfax, VA 22030

703-358-9300; *Fax:* 703-358-9307
bill@nuca.com; www.nuca.com

Bill Hillman, CEO
Bonnie Williams, VP

The latest technologies, products, and services being offered by the leading manufacturers and suppliers in the underground utility construction industry. Next trade show is scheduled to take place in Las Vegas, Nevada.
Frequency: Annual/February

4186 WBMA Annual Convention
Western Building Material Association
909 Lakeridge Drive SW
PO Box 1699
Olympia, WA 98507

360-943-3054
888-551-9262; *Fax:* 360-943-1219
wbma@wbma.org; www.wbma.org

One hundred and fourty booths of products stocked and sold by building material dealers.
1.6M Attendees
Frequency: Annual/November

4187 World Adhesive & Sealant Conference (WAC)
Adhesive & Sealant Council
7101 Wisconsin Avenue
Suite 990
Bethesda, MD 20814

301-986-9700; *Fax:* 301-986-9795
data@ascouncil.org; www.ascouncil.org

Malinda Armstrong, Director, Meetings & Expositions

International event drawing together industry stakeholders worldwide for three days of keynote addresses, technical courses, and networking opportunities.
Frequency: Every Four Years/April

4188 World of Asphalt Show & Conference
National Asphalt Pavement Association
5100 Forbes Boulevard
Suite 200
Lanham, MD 20706

301-731-4748
888-468-6499; *Fax:* 301-731-4621
mcervarich@hotmix.org; www.hotmix.org

Mike Acott, President
Margaret Cervarich, VP Marketing/Public Affairs

The leading trade show for the asphalt pavement industry, bringing together the Asphalt Pavement Conference and the People, Plants and Paving training program.
6000 Attendees

Directories & Databases

4189 **ANSI/SPRI Standard Field Test Procedure**
Single Ply Roofing Institute
411 Waverley Oaks Road
Suite 331B
Waltham, MA 02542

781-647-7026; *Fax:* 781-647-7222
info@spri.org; www.spri.org

Linda King, Managing Director

Standard Field Test Procedure for determining the withdrawal resistance of roofing fasteners.
Cost: $5.00
Frequency: Free to members

4190 **ANSI/SPRI Wind Design Standard**
Single Ply Roofing Institute
411 Waverley Oaks Road
Suite 331B
Waltham, MA 02452

781-647-7026; *Fax:* 781-647-7222
info@spri.org; www.spri.org

Linda King, Managing Director

Written for those who design, specify and install smooth-surfaced, low-slope flexible membrane roof systems.
Cost: $5.00
23 Pages

4191 **Affirmative Action Compliance Manual for Federal Contractors**
Bureau of National Affairs
1801 S Bell St
Arlington, VA 22202-4501

703-341-3000
800-372-1033; *Fax:* 800-253-0332
customercare@bna.com; www.bnabooks.com

Paul N Wojcik, CEO
Gregory C McCaffery, President

Employers and attorneys can more easily monitor and measure affirmative action requirements, implement policies, and quickly access other compliance information with this complete resource guide.
Cost: $611.00
Frequency: Monthly

4192 **Automated Builder: Top Component Producers Survey Issue**
Automated Builder
2401 Grapevine Dr
Oxnard, CA 93036

805-351-5931; *Fax:* 805-351-5755
info@automatedbuilder.com;
www.automatedbuilder.com

Don Carlson, Publisher

Over 100 leading industrialized building producers are profiled on the basis of sales. Top HUD-Code home producers, TOP pakelizers, TOP commercial modular builders. Features articles on technology, methods and machinery, sales and marketing for in-plant building.
Cost: $6.00
48 Pages
Frequency: Monthly
Circulation: 25000
ISSN: 0899-5540
Founded in: 1964

4193 **Blue Book of Building and Construction**
Contractors Register
PO Box 500
Jefferson Valley, NY 10535

914-450-0200
800-431-2584; *Fax:* 914-243-0287
info@thebluebook.com;
www.thebluebook.com
Social Media: YouTube

Jeff Fandl, Editor

Regional construction directories in most major markets throughout the US. Online, thebluebook.com provides easy access to continually updated information for each of our regional editions.
4500 Pages
Frequency: Annual
Circulation: 615,000
Founded in: 1913

4194 **Building & Construction Trades Department**
815 16th St NW
Suite 209
Washington, DC 20006-4101

202-347-1461; *Fax:* 202-628-0724;
www.bctd.org
Social Media: Facebook

Mark Ayers, President
Joseph Maloney, Secretary/Treasurer

Coordinates activity and provides resources to 15 affiliated trades unions in the construction industry.
386 Pages
Founded in: 1908

4195 **Building Materials Directory**
Underwriters Laboratories
333 Pfingsten Rd
Northbrook, IL 60062-2096

847-412-0136
877-854-3577; *Fax:* 847-272-8129
cec@us.ul.com; www.ul.com

Keith E Williams, CEO
John Drengenberg, Manager Consumer Affairs

Offers information on companies that have qualified to use the UL listing mark or classification marking on products that have been found to be in compliance with UL requirements.
Cost: $30.00
512 Pages
Frequency: Annual/February

4196 **Cedar Shake and Shingle Bureau Membership Directory/Buyer's Guide**
Cedar Shake & Shingle Bureau
PO Box 1178
Sumas, WA 98295-1178

604-820-7700; *Fax:* 604-820-0266;
www.cedarbureau.org

Jim Tuffin, Chairman
Len Taylor Jr., Vice-Chairman
Rav Dhaliwal, Secretary/Treasurer

About 102 member manufacturing mills in the Pacific Northwest and British Columbia, Canada; approximately 163 affiliated roofing applicators, builders, architects, remodelers and suppliers of related products and services.
Cost: $17.00
Frequency: SemiAnnual
Circulation: 450

4197 **Cement Americas**
Penton Media Inc
249 W 17th St
New York, NY 10011-5390

212-204-4200; *Fax:* 212-206-3622
steven.prokopy@penton.com;
www.penton.com

Sharon Rowlands, CEO

Offers 100 cement manufacturing companies in the United States, Canada, Mexico, Central and South America.
Cost: $78.00
225 Pages
Frequency: Annual
Circulation: 300
Mailing list available for rent
Printed in on glossy stock

4198 **Construction Equipment: Construction Giants Issue**
Reed Business Information
2000 Clearwater Dr
Oak Brook, IL 60523-8809

630-574-0825; *Fax:* 630-288-8781;
www.reedbusiness.com

Mark Kelsey, CEO
Stuart Whayman, CFO
Dan Olley, CIO

Listing of approximately 250 of the largest equipment-owning heavy construction contractors, engaged in earthmoving, paving, building and materials production owning over $10 million in equipment.
Frequency: Monthly
Circulation: 77010
Founded in: 1949

4199 **Construction Planning & Scheduling Manual**
National Insulation Association
Ste 330
12100 Sunset Hills Rd
Reston, VA 20190-3295

703-683-6422; *Fax:* 703-549-4838
niainfo@insulation.org; www.insulation.org

Melissa Jackson, Director of Publications
Beth Michaels, Vice President
Kristin DiDomenico, Vice President

This manual from the Associated General Contractors (AGC) was written to provide guidance to the contractor in the effective use of modern project management techniques. Its primary objective is to provide an educational tool that can be used within the construction industry to teach the concepts of construction planning and scheduling. The content of the book is written for all project personnel, from the working foreman to the project executive.
Cost: $155.00

4200 **Construction Specifier: Member Directory Issue**
Construction Specifications Institute
990 Canal Center Plaza
Suite 300
Alexandria, VA 22314

703-684-0300
800-689-2900; *Fax:* 703-684-8436
csi@csinet.org; www.csinet.org

Eugene A Valentine, President
W Richard Cooper, VP

Roster of construction specifiers certified by the institute and approximately 17,200 members.
Cost: $203.00
Frequency: Annual/January
Circulation: 19500

4201 **Constructor: AGC Directory of Membership and Services Issue**
Associated General Contractors of America
333 John Carlyle Street
Sutie 200
Alexandria, VA 22314

703-548-3118; *Fax:* 703-548-3119
constructinfo@riagc.org; www.agc.org

Donald Scott, Production Manager
Michael Kennedy, General Counsel
Norman Walton, Treasurer

List of more than 8,500 member firms and 24,000 national associate member firms engaged in building, highway, heavy, industrial, municipal utilities and railroad construction.
Frequency: Annual/July
Circulation: 34,000
ISSN: 0162-6191

4202 Directory of Architectural and Construction Information Resources
Grey House Publishing
4919 Route 22
PO Box 56
Amenia, NY 12501
518-789-8700
800-562-2139; *Fax:* 845-373-6390
books@greyhouse.com; www.greyhouse.com
Social Media: Facebook, Twitter
Richard Gottlieb, President
Leslie Mackenzie, Publisher
The leading desktop reference and preliminary research guide, featuring more than 10,000 building product manufacturers and their products.
194 Pages
Frequency: Annual
ISBN: 1-519250-00-0

4203 Directory of Building Codes & Regulations
National Conference of States on Building Codes
505 Huntmar Park Dr
Herndon, VA 20170-5103
703-437-0100
800-362-2633; *Fax:* 703-481-3596
Robert Wible, Executive Director
Carolyn Fitch, Membership Services
This directory is a comprehensive guide to the building codes and regulations adopted and enforced in each of the 50 states, Puerto Rico, the District of Columbia, and 53 major U. S. cities in 14 different code areas - building, mechanical, plumbing, electrical, energy conservation, gas, fire prevention, life safety, accessibility, one & two family, modular, ventilation/indoor air quality, manufactured home installation, and elevator.
Cost: $78.00
Frequency: Annual

4204 Dodge Construction Analysis System
McGraw-Hill
1221 Avenue of the Americas
New York, NY 10020-1095
212-512-2000
800-393-6343; *Fax:* 212-512-3840
webmaster@mcgraw-hill.com;
www.mcgraw-hill.com
Harold W McGraw III, CEO
Joseph A Scott, National Marketing Director
This database lists over 4 million time series for construction projects involving more than 200 structural types.

4205 Dodge DataLine
McGraw-Hill
1221 Avenue of the Americas
New York, NY 10020-1095
212-512-2000
800-393-6343; *Fax:* 212-512-3840
webmaster@mcgraw-hill.com;
www.mcgraw-hill.com
Harold W McGraw III, CEO
Joseph A Scott, National Marketing Director
Dodge DataLine offers the most advanced searching of project leads in the industry. You can search the largest U.S. database of 500,000+ active construction projects.
Frequency: Daily

4206 ENR Top 100 Construction Managers
Engineering News Record/McGraw Publishing
2 Penn Plaza
9th Floor
New York, NY 10121-2298
212-512-2000
888-877-8208; *Fax:* 212-512-4039
support@construction.com;
www.construction.com
Gary Graizzaro, Plant Manager
John J Kosowatz, Managing Editor
William G. Krizan, Assistant Managing Editor
List of the top 100 leading construction and program management firms with the largest dollar volume in new construction management contracts on a for-fee only basis and an at-risk basis in the previous year.
Cost: $250.00
Frequency: Annual/June
Circulation: 90000

4207 ENR Top 400 Contractors Sourcebook
Engineering News Record/McGraw Publishing
2 Penn Plaza
9th Floor
New York, NY 10121-2298
212-512-2000
888-877-8208; *Fax:* 212-512-4039
support@construction.com;
www.construction.com
Gary Graizzaro, Plant Manager
Joann Gonchar, Associate Editor
William G. Krizan, Assistant Managing Editor
Debra K. Rubin, Managing Senior Editor
Market analysis rankings of the largest U.S.-based general contractors in eight major industry sectors: general building, transportation, manufacturing, industrial process, petroleum, power, environmental and telecommunications.
Cost: $85.00
112 Pages

4208 ENR Top 600 Specialty Contractors Issue
Engineering News Record/McGraw Hill
2 Penn Plaza
9th Floor
New York, NY 10121-2298
212-512-2000; *Fax:* 212-512-4039
support@construction.com;
www.construction.com
Gary Graizzaro, Plant Manager
John J Kosowatz, Managing Editor
Lists of the 600 largest US specialty subcontractors with sub-lists of top firms in mechanical contracting, electrical, excavation-foundation, steel erection, rofing, sheet metal, demolition-wrecking, glazing curtain wall, masonry, concrete, utilities, painting, wall/ceiling and asbestos abatement.
Cost: $350.00
Frequency: Annual/September
Circulation: 90000

4209 ENR Top Owners Sourcebook
Engineering News Record/McGraw Hill
2 Penn Plaza
9th Floor
New York, NY 10121-2298
212-512-2000; *Fax:* 212-512-4039;
www.construction.com
Gary Graizzaro, Plant Manager
John J Kosowatz, Managing Editor
List of 700 companies that had the largest expenditures for building construction and building acquisition in the previous year.
Cost: $300.00
Frequency: Annual/December
Circulation: 90000

4210 Electrical Construction Materials Directory
Underwriters Laboratories
333 Pfingsten Rd
Northbrook, IL 60062-2096
847-412-0136
877-854-3577; *Fax:* 847-272-8129
cec@us.ul.com; www.UL.com
Keith E Williams, CEO
John Drengenberg, Manager Consumer Affairs
Companies that have qualified to use the UL listing mark or classification marking on or in connection with products which have been found to be in compliance with UL's requirements.
Cost: $30.00
Frequency: Annual
Printed in on glossy stock

4211 Fastener Selection Guide
Single Ply Roofing Institute
411 Waverley Oaks Road
Suite 331B
Waltham, MA 02452
781-647-7026; *Fax:* 781-647-7222
info@spri.org; www.spri.org
Linda King, Managing Director
Identifies the various fastener options for each desk type and typical pullout values.
Cost: $15.00

4212 Flexible Membrane Roofing: Guide to Specifications
Single Ply Roofing Institute
411 Waverley Oaks Road
Suite 331B
Waltham, MA 02452
781-647-7026; *Fax:* 781-647-7222
info@spri.org; www.spri.org
Linda King, Managing Director
Now in it's 7th edition, this is the most complete reference guide on materials, systems and designs for commerical roofing.
Cost: $50.00

4213 GreenSpec Directory
BuildingGreen
122 Birge Street
Suite 30
Brattleboro, VT 05301-6703
802-257-7300; *Fax:* 802-257-7304
info@buildinggreen.com;
www.buildinggreen.com
Alex Wilson, Owner
Nadav Malin, Editor
Daniel Woodbury, Publisher
Charlotte Snyder, Circulation Manager
Information on more than 1,850 green building products carefully screened by the editors of Environmental Building News. Directory listings cover more than 250 categories, from access flooring to zero-VOC paints. Included are product descriptions, environmental characteristics and considerations, and manufacturer contact information with internet addresses.
Cost: $89.00
464 Pages
ISBN: 1-929884-15-X

4214 MasterFormat
Construction Specifications Institute
110 South Union Street
Suite 100
Alexandria, VA 22314-3351
800-689-2900; *Fax:* 703-236-4600
csi@csinet.org; www.csinet.org

Social Media: Facebook, Twitter, LinkedIn, YouTube

Paul R. Bertram Jr., President
Gregory J. Markling, President-Elect
Mitch A. Miller, Vice President
Casey F. Robb, Vice President
Lane J. Beougher, Secretary

The reengineering of this industry standard sets the present and future pace for organizing construction communication. MasterFormat 2004 Edition simplifies the process of determining where specific subject matter is located.
Cost: $159.00
516 Pages
ISBN: 0-976239-90-6
Founded in: 2004

4215 NRCMA Membership Directory

National Railroad Construction & Maintenance Assoc
500 New Jersey Ave NW
Suite 400
Washington, DC 20001-2065

202-715-2919; *Fax:* 202-318-0867
info@nrcma.org; www.nrcma.org
Social Media: Facebook, Twitter, LinkedIn

Chuck Baker, President
Matt Ginsberg, Director of Operations
Jim Perkins, Chairman
Terry Benton, Vice Chairman

A book of the railroad contracting industry, lists all members of the NRC, including their technical specialities ang geographic regions of operation.
Cost: $35.00
Frequency: Free to Members

4216 Public Works Manual

Hanley-Wood
426 S Westgate Street
Addison, IL 60101

630-543-0870
800-524-2364; *Fax:* 630-543-3112
arozgus@hanleywood.com; www.pwmag.com

William D Palmer Jr., Editor-in-Chief
Amara Rozgus, Managing Editor
Sharon Glorioso, Associate Editor
Colette Palait, Editorial Assistant

Over 4,000 manufacturers and distributors of equipment, materials, services, computers and software used in the design, construction and maintenance of streets and highways, water systems, wastewater and solid wastes processing and recreation areas.
Cost: $30.00
Frequency: Annual
Circulation: 55000

4217 Roofing/Siding/Insulation: Trade Directory Issue

PO Box 1269
Skokie, IL 60076-8269

847-763-9594; *Fax:* 847-763-9694
roofingsidinginsulation@halldata.com; www.rsimag.com

Thomas Skernivitz, Editor
Jacke Lyttle, Publisher

Lists thousands of contractors, manufacturers and distributors of equipment and products.
Cost: $20.00
Frequency: Annual
Circulation: 22,000

4218 STAFDA Directory

Specialty Tools & Fasteners Distributors Assn
500 Elm Grove Rd.
Suite 210
Elm Grove, WI 53122

262-784-4774
800-352-2981; *Fax:* 262-784-5059
info@stafda.org; www.stafda.org
Social Media: Facebook, LinkedIn

Mike Kangas, President
Kramer Darragh, Vice President

This is a Who's Who of the industry. Listings include who makes over 900 different products: nearly 2,570 member addresses and contacts; brand names; fax numbers: 800 numbers; e-mail; www; and a recap of association services and activities.
500 Pages
Frequency: Annual
Circulation: 4500

4219 Scaffold Industry Association Directory & Handbook

Scaffold Industry Association
400 Admiral Blvd.
Kansas City, MO 64106-1508

816-595-4860
info@saiaonline.org; www.scaffold.org
Social Media: Facebook, Twitter, LinkedIn

Steve Smith, President
Marty Coughlin, President-Elect
Daryl Hare, Treasurer
Mike Russell, Secretary

The SIA Directory and Handbook contains complete membership information, company and individual listings. It also includes federal OSHA scaffold standards for general industry, construction and maritime, scaffold plank grading rules, map and listing of OSHA regional and area offices, scaffold standards for the state of California, glossary of scaffold terms, illustrations of various types of scaffolds, and codes of safe practices.
Cost: $125.00
355 Pages
Circulation: 5000

4220 Source: Buyer's Guide & Dealer Directory

Northeastern Retail Lumber Association
585 N Greenbush Rd
Rensselaer, NY 12144-9615

518-286-1010
800-292-6752; *Fax:* 518-286-1755
rferris@nrla.org; www.nrla.org
Social Media: Facebook

Rita Ferris, President
Tony Shepley, Chair
Jon Hallgren, Chair Elect
Jonas Kelly, Vice Chair

The industry's guide to names, addresses, phone numbers, fax numbers, and product lines of companies that comprise the independent retail lumber dealers of the Northeast.
Cost: $89.95
Frequency: Annual

4221 Sourcebook

Ray Publishing
P.O.Box 992
Morrison, CO 80465-0992

303-467-1776; *Fax:* 303-467-1777;
www.compositesworld.com

Judith Hazen, Publisher
Mike Mussleman, Managing Editor

A comprehensive directory of composites industry suppliers, manufacturers and service companies for the entire composites industry.
60 Pages
Founded in: 1993
Printed in 4 colors on glossy stock

4222 Store Fixture Buyers' Guide and Membership Directory

Nat'l Association of Store Fixture Manufacturers
3595 Sheridan
Suite 200
Hollywood, FL 33322

954-893-7300; *Fax:* 954-893-7500
nasfm@nasfm.org; www.nasfm.org
Social Media: Facebook, Twitter, LinkedIn

Jo Rossman, Senior Editor
Klein Merriman, Executive Director

This buyers' guide features the products and services of some 400 store fixture manufacturers. Contact information, plant size, number of employees, and company descriptions of all member manufacturers, plant listings by location, and contact and company information on products and services of 200 supplier members is included.
Cost: $175.00
80 Pages
Frequency: Free to Members

4223 Sweets Directory

Grey House Publishing/McGraw Hill Construction
1221 Avenue of the Americas
New York, NY 10020-1095

212-512-2000
800-442-2258; *Fax:* 212-512-3840
webmaster@mcgraw-hill.com;
www.mcgraw-hill.com
Social Media: Facebook, Twitter

Harold W McGraw III, CEO

The leading desktop reference and preliminary research guide, featuring more than 10,000 building product manufacturers and their products.
Cost: $145.00
950 Pages
Frequency: Annual
ISBN: 1-592378-50-1
Founded in: 1906

4224 ThomasNet

Thomas Publishing Company, LLC
User Services Department
5 Penn Plaza
New York, NY 10001

212-695-0500
800-699-9822; *Fax:* 212-290-7362
contact@thomaspublishing.com;
www.thomasnet.com
Social Media: Facebook, Twitter, LinkedIn

Carl Holst-Knudsen, President
Robert Anderson, VP, Planning
Mitchell Peipert, VP, Finance
Ivy Molofsky, VP, Human Resources

A way to reach qualified businesses that list their company information on ThomasNet.com. Detailed profiles promote their products, services, capabilities and brands carried. The ThomasNet.com web site is the most up-to-date compilation of 650,000 North American manufacturers, distributors, and service companies in 67,000 industrial categories.
Founded in: 1898

4225 Wind Design Guide

Single Ply Roofing Institute
411 Waverley Oaks Road
Suite 331B
Waltham, MA 02452

781-647-7026; *Fax:* 781-647-7222
info@spri.org; www.spri.org

Linda King, Managing Director

Wind Design Guide for Edge Systems Used with Low Slope Roofing Systems outlines design and construction of edge details for wind resistance, including test methods, calculations of design pressures and commentary.
Cost: $20.00

Industry Web Sites

4226 **http://gold.greyhouse.com**
G.O.L.D Grey House OnLine Databases
Grey House Publishing's online database platform, GOLD, offers Quick Search, Keyword Search and Expert Search for most business sectors including architecture, building and construction markets. The GOLD platform makes finding the information you need quick and easy - whether you're a novice searcher or an experienced database user. All of Grey House's directory products are available for subscription on the GOLD platform.

4227 **www.abc.org**
Associated Builders and Contractors
National trade association representing about 23,000 contractors, subcontractors, material suppliers and related firms from across the country and from all specialties in the construction industry.

4228 **www.acdi.net**
Associated Construction Distributors International
Cooperative association of independently owned and locally opearated distributors of specialty construction products and equipment.

4229 **www.acesystems.com**
AEC Systems International/Penton Media
Focuses on Internet/Intranet for the design, engineering and construction industries.

4230 **www.aednet.org**
Associated Equipment Distributors
Membership association of 1,200 independent distributors, manufacturers, and other organizations involved in the distribution of construction equipment and related products and services in North America and throughout the world.

4231 **www.agc.org**
Associated General Contractors of America
The voice of the construction industry, an organization of qualified construction contractors and industry related companies dedicated to skill, integrity and responsibility.

4232 **www.aibd.org**
American Institute of Building Design
Our members consist of professional building designers and architects, who have for the most part chosen residential design as the focus of their practice.

4233 **www.aisc.org**
American Institute of Steel Construction
Serving the structural steel industry in the US. Our purpose is to promote the use of structural steel through research activities, market development, education, codes and specifications, technical assistance, quality certifacation and standardization.

4234 **www.akropolis.net**
Akropolis
To enable firms at all levels of the design and building industry to operate more efficiently with the help of cutting edge technology solutions.

4235 **www.anodizing.org**
Aluminum Anodizers Council
Represents the interests of aluminum anodizers worldwide and is the principal trade organization for the anodizing industry in North America. It promotes the interests of its members through technical exchange, ongoing education, statistical data, market promotion, and industry representation.

4236 **www.apwa.net**
American Public Works Association
An international educational and professionals association of public agencies, private sector companies, and individuals dedicated to providing high quality public works goods and services.

4237 **www.aspenational.org**
American Society of Professional Estimators
Serving the construction estimators by providing education, fellowship and opportunity for professional development. ASPE represents individual members involved in the construction industry.

4238 **www.asphaltinstitute.org**
Asphalt Institute
Conducts education, research and engineering services related to asphaltic products; conducts seminars and sells publications and videos on asphalt technology.

4239 **www.asphaltpavement.org**
National Asphalt Pavement Association
The only trade association that exclusively represents the interest s of the Hot Mix Asphalt producer and paving contractor on the national level with Congress, government agencies, and other national trade and business organizations.

4240 **www.automatedbuilder.com**
CMN Associates
Association of manufacturers and suppliers who have a product line that is of interest to the manufactured and pre-fabricated housing industry.

4241 **www.awci.org**
Association of the Wall and Ceiling Industries
Represents acoustics systems, ceiling systems, drywall systems, exterior insulation and finishing systems, fireproofing, flooring systems, insulation, and stucco contractors, suppliers and manufacturers and those in allied trades.

4242 **www.build.com**
Build.com
Providing consumers, contractors and industry professionals with a valuable resource of products, service and information related to the building and home improvement industry.

4243 **www.buildingstone.org**
Building Stone Institute
Quarries, fabricators, dealers, installers and restorers of all types of natural stone. Membership dues based on sales volume.

4244 **www.calredwood.org**
California Redwood Association
A trade association for redwood lumber producers.

4245 **www.cfma.org**
Construction Financial Management Association
Non-profit organization dedicated to serving the financial professional in the construction industry.

4246 **www.cisco.org**
Construction Industry Service Corporation
Labor management association that promotes union construction, union contractors and union apprenticeship programs throughout Northeastern Illinois.

4247 **www.coaa.org**
Construction Owners Association of America
To act as a focal point and voice for the interests of owners in construction. Comprised of a diverse group of men and women representing construction owners.

4248 **www.concretepumpers.com**
American Concrete Pumping Association
Provides education, insurance, marketing and much more to companies involved with the concrete pumping industry. Our dedication to the concrete pumping industry has led us to become a key part in the education of safety and business management to everyone involved, from the operators to the management.

4249 **www.construction.com**
McGraw-Hill Construction
McGraw-Hill Construction (MHC), part of The McGraw-Hill Companies, connects people and projects across the design and construction industry, serving owners, architects, engineers, general contractors, subcontractors, building product manufacturers, suppliers, dealers, distributors and adjacent markets.

4250 **www.csinet.org**
Construction Specifications Institute
Our mission is to continuously improve the process of creating and sustaining the built environment. We do this by facilitating communication among all those involved in that process.

4251 **www.demolitionassociation.com**
National Association of Demolition Contractors
Representing the demolition industry including demolition contractors, formed to foster goodwill and the exchange of ideas with the public, governmental agencies and constractors engaged in the demolition industry. Also for manufacturers or suppliers of demolition equipment, supplies and services.

4252 **www.dfi.org**
Deep Foundations Institute
We can best be described as being a technical association of firms and individuals in the deep foundations and related industry. DFI covers the gamut of deep foundation construction and earth retention systems.

4253 **www.ebmda.org**
Eastern Building Material Dealers Association
Established to foster, protect and promote the welfare and best interest of its members engaged in the retail lumber and building materials business.

4254 **www.floorbiz.com**
Floor Biz
Internet's leading creator and operator of a vertical business community for the flooring industry. FloorBiz leverages the interactive features and global reach of the Internet to create a multi-national, targeted business community vertically integrated from consumer to manufacturer.

4255 **www.gobrick.com**
Brick Industry Association
A national trade association representing distributors and manufacturers of clay brick and suppliers of related products and services.

4256 **www.greyhouse.com**
Grey House Publishing
Authoritative reference directories for most business sectors including architecture, building and construction markets. Users can search the online databases with varied search criteria allowing for custom searches by product category, geographic area, sales volume, keyword, subject

and more. Full Grey House catalog and online ordering also available.

4257 **www.homeimprovement.com**
Hometime
Hometime is a home-improvement television show broadcast on public television, The Learning Channel and in syndication. A comprehensive online resource for your remodeling and home-improvement needs.

4258 **www.iccsafe.org**
International Code Council
Formerly known as the Building Officials and Code Administrators International, we publish codes that establish minimum performance requirements for all aspects of the construction industry.

4259 **www.icpi.org**
Interlocking Concrete Pavement Institute
Self governed, self funded, autonomous association representing the interlocking concrete pavement industry in North America. Membership is open to producers, contractors, suppliers, consultants and others who have an interest in the industry. As an industry voice, the membership represents a majority of concrete paver production in North America.

4260 **www.iilp.org**
International Institute for Lathe and Plaster
Federation of organizations representing contractors, unions and makers of lathing and manufacturing.

4261 **www.manufacturedhousing.org**
Manufactured Housing Institute
National trade organization representing all segments of the factory built housing industry. MHI serves its membership by providing industry research, promotion, education, and government relations programs, and by building and facilitating consensus within the industry.

4262 **www.masoncontractors.org**
Mason Contractors Association of America
Through strong programs, publications and services, the MCAA avtively promotes the interests of its members. By promoting the use of masonry, influencing resonable codes and standards, work force development and public affairs, the association advances the use of masonry.

4263 **www.masonrysociety.org**
Masonry Society
Dedicated to the advancement of scientific engineering, architechtural and construction knowledge of masonry. Promotes research and education and disseminates information on masonry materials, design, construction. Publishes a newsletter.

4264 **www.mbinet.org**
Modular Building Institute
Serving the commercial factory-built buildings industry on an international scale. Our regular members are manufacturers and dealers of commercial modular structures, while our associate members are companies supplying building components, services, and financing.

4265 **www.naamm.org**
Nat'l Assn of Architectural Metal Manufacturers
The largest of four operating divisions of the National Association of Architectural Metal Manufacturers. HMMA is a group composed of companies that manufacture, distribute and promote the use of hollow metal door and frame products.

4266 **www.nahb.org**
National Association of Home Builders
Represents the interests of concrete, log, modular, and panel manufacturers, builders, and suppliers.

4267 **www.nam.org**
National Association of Manufacturers
The nation's largest industrial trade association, representing small and large manufacturers in every industrial sector and in all 50 states.

4268 **www.nari.org**
National Association of the Remodeling Industry
A voice in the remodeling industry, NARI has an exclusive, encompasing purpose to; establish and maintain a firm commitment to developing and sustaining programs that expand and unite the remodeling industry; to ensure the industry's growth and security; to encourage ethical conduct, sound business practices and professionalism in the remodeling industry; and to present NARI as the recognized authority in the remodeling industry.

4269 **www.nationalslag.org**
National Slag Association
Members are processors of iron and steel slags for use as a aggregate in construction and manufacturing applications.

4270 **www.nawic.org**
National Association of Women in Construction
Founded by 16 women working in the construction industry. The founders organized NAWIC to create a support network for women in construction.

4271 **www.ncac.com**
National Council of Acoustical Consultants
Strives to safeguard the interests of professional acoustical consulting firms. Managing physics and psychoacoustics to provide optimum listning environments.

4272 **www.ncma.org**
National Concrete Masonry Association
Manufacturers of concrete masonry products and suppliers of products to the industry. Offers a variety of technical services and design aids through publications, computer programs, slide presentations and technical training.

4273 **www.ncsbcs.org**
National Conference of States on Building Codes
Serving as a forum for the interchange of information and provides technical services, education and training to our members to enhance the public's social, economic well-being through safe, durable, accessible and efficient buildings.

4274 **www.necanet.org**
National Electrical Contractors Association
Represents a segment of the construction market comprised of over 70,000 electrical firms.

4275 **www.newhomes.move.com**
HomeBuilder.com
The web's leading provider of information on newly built homes, with listings for over 125,000 new home and planned developments throughout the US. Supplier of media and technology solutions that promote and connect real estate professionals to consumers before, during and after a move.

4276 **www.nrcma.org**
National Railroad Construction & Maintenance Assn
Railroad construction and maintenance contractors, engineering firms, manufacturing suppliers and professional associate firms.

4277 **www.nrla.org**
Northeastern Retail Lumber Association
A resource for industry members, consumers, and public officials in dependent lumber and building material suppliers and associated businesses in New York and the six New England states.

4278 **www.nrmca.org**
National Ready Mixed Concrete Association
Our mission is to provide exceptional value for our members by responsibly representing and serving the entire ready mixed concrete industry through leadership, promotion, education and partnering; to ensure ready mixed concrete is the building material of choice.

4279 **www.nssga.org**
National Stone, Sand & Gravel Association
Represents the crushed stone, sand and gravel — or aggregate — industries. Our members account for 90 percent of the crushed stone and 70 percent of the sand and gravel produced annually in the US.

4280 **www.ntma.com**
National Terrazzo and Mosaic Association
Full service nonprofit trade association headquartered in Northern Virginia. The association establishes national standards for all terrazzo floor and wall systems and provides complete specifications, color plates and general information to architects and designers at no cost.

4281 **www.nuca.com**
National Utility Contractors Association
A national association that provides a forum for continuing education and promotes effective public policy, through its grassroots network, to protect and enhance your industry.

4282 **www.oikos.com**
Oikos
Devoted to serving professionals whose work promotes sustainable design and construction. Oikos is a Greek word meaning house. Oikos serves as the root for two English words: ecology and economy.

4283 **www.opcmia.org**
Operative Plasterers' & Cement Masons' Int'l Assn
Represents and trains plasterers and cement masons for the purpose of protecting and promoting the quality of our industry and the livelihood of our members.

4284 **www.opei.org**
Outdoor Power Equipment Institute
International trade association whose members are manufacturers of powered lawn and garden maintenance products, components and attachment supplies, as well as industry related services.

4285 **www.pbmdf.com**
Composite Panel Association
The association of North American wood and agrifiber based particle board and medium density fiberboard producers, to broaden the base of participation in industry outreach programs.

4286 **www.pci.org**
Precast Prestressed Concrete Institute
Dedicated to fostering greater understanding and use of precast and prestressed concrete, maintains a full staff of technical and marketing specialists.

4287 **www.perlite.org**
Perlite Institute
International trade association which establishes product standards and specifications, and which encourages the development of new product uses through research.

4288 **www.pfi-institute.org**
Pipe Fabrication Institute
Members are companies producing sophisticated high temperature, high pressure piping systems that employ specialists from the United Association of Journeymen & Apprentices of the Plumbing & Pipe Fitting Industry. We exist solely for the purpose of ensuring a level of quality in the pipe fabrication indusrty that is without compromise.

4289 **www.piledrivers.org**
Pile Driving Contractors Association
Organization of pile driving contractors that advocates the increased use of driven piles for deep foundations and earth retention systems. To do this we promote the use of driven pile solutions in all cases where they are effective, support educational programs for engineers on the design and efficiency of driven piles and for contractors on improving installation procedures. We also give contractors a larger voice in establishing procedures and standards for pile installation and design.

4290 **www.pipefitters537.org**
American Pipe Fittings Association
Trade association for any domestic corporation, firm or individual engaged in manufacture in the US or Canada of piping components and accessories, including pipe hangers and supports.

4291 **www.psai.org**
Portable Sanitation Association International
International trade association that represents firms engaged in the leasing, renting selling and manufacturing of portable sanitation equipment, services and supplies for construction, recreation, emergency and other uses. devoted to the proper handling of human waste by the most modern, sanitary means, giving the greatest concern to the preservation of an unspoiled environment.

4292 **www.reedconstructiondata.com**
First Source Online
Provides A/E/C professionals free access to the industry's most comprehensive, up-to-date library of formatted commercial building product information, plus manufacturers' addresses, telephone numbers, trade names, and regional distributors.

4293 **www.rfci.com**
Resilient Floor Covering Institute
Industry trade association of North American manufacturers who produce resilient flooring products. Associate members of RFCI supply raw materials to the industry and manufacture installation and maintenance products.

4294 **www.roofcoatings.org**
Roof Coatings Manufacturers Association
Represents the interests for manufacturers of cold applied roof coatings, cements and waterproofing agents, as well as the suppliers of products, equipment, and services to and for the industry. Currently RCMA boasts more than 70 member companies.

4295 **www.rubberpavements.org**
Rubber Pavements Association
Dedicated to encouraging greater usage of high quality, cost effective asphalt pavements containing recycled tire rubber. Conducts national and international seminars.

4296 **www.saiaonline.org**
Scaffold Industry Association
Promotes scaffold safety and education through its publications, conventions, tradeshows and training programs. Marketing of your product is available through the monthly magazine, convention and trade show.

4297 **www.sgcc.org**
Safety Glazing Certification Council
Provides for the certification of safety glazing materials, comprised of safety glazing manufacturers and other parties concerned with public safety. SGCC is managed by a board of directors comprised of representatives from the safety glazing industry and the public interest sector.

4298 **www.sips.org**
Structural Insulated Panel Association
A trade association representing manufacturers, suppliers, fabricators, distributors, design professionals and builders committed to providing quality structural insulated panels for all segments of the construction industry.

4299 **www.spri.org**
Single Ply Roofing Institute
Comprised of manufacturers and marketers of sheet applied membrane roofing systems and components to the commerical roofing industry.

4300 **www.stafda.org**
Specialty Tools & Fasteners Distributors Assn
International trade association composed of distributors and manufacturers and rep agents of light construction, industrial and related products. Members also include publishers of industry press serving the construction and industrial trades.

4301 **www.stanyc.com**
Subcontractors Trade Association
Members are specialty and supply companies in the construction industry. Our goal is to improve the economic well being of our members through representation, support and assistance through the process of legislation, legal action, public relations, education and other public information programs.

4302 **www.steelwindows.com**
Steel Window Institute
For United States manufacturers of windows made from hot-rolled, solid steel sections and such related products as castings, trim, mechanical operators, screens and moldings.

4303 **www.sweets.construction.com**
McGraw Hill Construction
In depth product information that lets you find, compare, select, specify and make purchase decisions in the industrial product marketplace.

4304 **www.swensongranite.com**
Swenson Granite Works
Family owned business that has been quarrying and cutting granite in New England since 1883.

4305 **www.tcaainc.org**
Tile Contractors Association of America
TCAA is an organization representing the finest union tile contractors in the United States. Founded in 1903, it is the only association which serves the needs of the union tile contractor.

4306 **www.tfguild.org**
Timber Framers Guild of North America
Dedicated to establishing training programs for dedicated timber framers, disseminating information about timber framing and timber frame building design, displaying the art of timber framing to the public, and generally serving as a center of timber framing information for the professional and general public alike.

4307 **www.thebluebook.com**
Contactors Register
Regional construction directories in most major markets throughout the US. Provides easy online access to continually updated information for each of our regional editions.

4308 **www.tile-assn.com**
National Tile Contractors Association
Serving every segment of the industry, and is recognized as the largest and most respected tile contractors association in the world.

4309 **www.tilt-up.org**
Tilt-up Concrete Association
Represents builders, engineers and suppliers involved with tilt-up concrete construction. Makes a continuing and increasingly important contribution to the success of each member through the most imaginative and efficient application of every appropriate skill, tool and service of the association.

4310 **www.wbma.org**
Western Building Material Association
Regional trade association serving building material dealers throughout the states of Alaska, Idaho, Montana, Oregon and Washington and a federated association of the National Lumber and Building Material Dealers Association.

4311 **www.wfca.org**
World Floor Covering Association
Shapes and defines public policy through agressive, national legislative advocacy on behalf of our members. Provides continuing professional educational programming through educational forums and the Regional Installation and Training Education (RITE) program.

4312 **www.windowanddoor.com**
WindowDoor.net
Anyone who is interested in window and door products can find the latest information on products, components and how-to information here.

Associations

4313 **AACC International**
3340 Pilot Knob Road
St. Paul, MN 55121

651-454-7250
800-328-7560; *Fax:* 651-454-0766
aacc@scisoc.org; www.aaccnet.org
Social Media: Facebook, Twitter, LinkedIn, Pinterest

Robert L. Cracknell, President
Lydia Tooker Midness, Chair
Laura M. Hansen, President Elect
Dave L. Braun, Treasurer

Formerly the American Association of Cereal Chemists, a non-profit organization of members who are specialists in the use of cereal grains in foods.
Founded in: 1915

4314 **AOAC International**
2275 Research Blvd
Suite 300
Rockville, MD 20850-3250

301-924-7077
800-379-2622; *Fax:* 301-924-7089
aoac@aoac.org; www.aoac.org
Social Media: Facebook, Twitter, LinkedIn

E James Bradford, CEO & Executive Director
Joyce L Schumacher, CFO
Delia A Boyd, Program Manager

Serves the communities of analytical sciences by providing the tools and porcesses necessary for community stakeholders to collaborate and through, consensus building, develop fit for purpose methods and services for assuring quality measurments.
3700 Members
Founded in: 1884

4315 **Acrylonitrile Group**
1250 Connecticut Ave NW
Suite 700
Washington, DC 20036-2657

202-419-1500; *Fax:* 202-659-8037
angroup@regnet.com; www.angroup.org

Robert J Fensterheim, Group Executive Director, President

Affiliated with the Synthetic Organic Chemical Manufacturers, (TAG) was formed under the Chemical manufacturers Association to do research. TAG represents producers and users of the industrial chemical used to make plastics, fibers and synthetic rubber products.
Founded in: 1960

4316 **Adhesion Society**
7101 Wisconsin Avenue
Suite 990
Bethesda, MD 20814

301-986-9700; *Fax:* 301-986-9795
Adhesionsociety@ascouncil.org;
www.adhesionsociety.org
Social Media: Twitter, LinkedIn

Anand Jagota, President
Gregory Schueneman, Vice President
Charles Shuster, Treasurer
Leonardo Lopez, Secretary

Supports all those who are involved in adhesion's role in coatings, compostie materials, biological tissues and bonded structures.
400 Members
Founded in: 1978

4317 **Alkyl Amines Council**
1850 M St NW
Suite 700
Washington, DC 20036

202-721-4100; *Fax:* 202-296-8120
info@socma.com; www.socma.com
Social Media: Facebook, Twitter, LinkedIn, YouTube

Lawrence D Sloan, President/CEO
Todd Brown, Director
Dolores Alonso, Senior Director

Data relating to production, processing and application.
6 Members
Founded in: 1921

4318 **Alkylphenols and Ethoxylates Research Council**
1250 Connecticut Ave NW
Suite 700
Washington, DC 20036

202-419-1500
866-273-7262; *Fax:* 202-659-8037
info@aperc.org; www.alkylphenol.org

Robert J Fensterheim, Executive Director

Monitors regulatory developments affecting manufacturers in the chemical industry
5 Members
Founded in: 1998

4319 **Alliance for Responsible Atmospheric Policy**
2111 Wilson Blvd
Suite 850
Arlington, VA 22201

703-243-0344; *Fax:* 703-243-2874
fay@alliancepolicy.org;
www.alliancepolicy.org
Social Media: Twitter

John Hurst, Chair
William McQuade, Vice Chair
Nanette Lockwood, Treasurer
Kevin Fay, Executive Director
Tonya Hunt, Finance & Membership Director

Made up of companies who rely on alternatives to ozone depleting chlorofluorocarbons(CFCs). Theses alternatives are HCPCs and HFCs, used primarily as refrigerants, speciality solvents, agents for foamed plastics.
300 Members
Founded in: 1980

4320 **American Association Textile Chemists and Colorists**
PO Box 12215
Research Triangle Park, NC 27709-2215

919-549-8141
800-360-5380; *Fax:* 919-549-8933
danielsj@aatcc.org; www.aatcc.org
Social Media: Facebook, Twitter, LinkedIn, Youtube

John Y Daniels, Executive VP
Debra Hibbard, Executive Assistant
Amy Holland, Office Manager
Bonnie Green, Membership Services
Suzanne Holmes, Program Manager/Technical Product

Supports all those working with colorants and chemical finishes for textile and related industries.
3000 Members

4321 **American Association for Clinical Chemistry**
900 Seventh Street, NW
Suite 400
Washington, DC 20001

202-857-0717
800-892-1400; *Fax:* 202-887-5093;
www.aacc.org
Social Media: Facebook, Twitter, LinkedIn, YouTube

Robert H Christensen, President
Steven H Wong, President Elect
Elizabeth L Frank, Secretary
Michael Bennett, Treasurer
Dennis J Dietzen, Director

AACC is an international scientific/medical society of clinical laboratory professionals, physicians, research scientists and other individuals involved with clinical chemistry and other clinical laboratory science related disciplines.
Founded in: 1948

4322 **American Association for Crystal Growth**
10922 Main Range Trail
Littleton, CO 80127

303-539-6907
888-506-1271; *Fax:* 303-600-5144
AACG@comcast.net; www.crystalgrowth.org

Robert Biefeld, President
Joan M Redwing, VP
Luis Zepeda-Ruiz, Treasurer
Mariya Zhuravleva, Secretary

Provides support for all professionals in the field of crystal and crystal growth.

4323 **American Association of Bioanalysts**
906 Olive Street
Suite 1200
Saint Louis, MO 63101-1448

314-241-1445; *Fax:* 314-241-1449
aab@aab.org; www.aab.org

Mark S Birenbaum PhD, Administrator

Professional association whose members are clinical laboratory directors, owners, supervisors, managers, medical technologists, medical laboratory technicians, physician office laboratory technicians, and phlebotomists.
Founded in: 1956

4324 **American Chemical Society**
1155 16th St NW
Washington, DC 20036

202-872-4600
800-227-5558; *Fax:* 202-872-4615
help@acs.org; www.acs.org
Social Media: Facebook, Twitter, LinkedIn, Google+

Madeleine Jacobs, CEO

Self-governed individual membership organization that provides a range of opportunities for peer interaction and career development, regardless of professional or scientific interests.
15900 Members
Founded in: 1876

4325 **American Chemistry Council**
700 Second St. NE
Washington, DC 20002

202-249-7000; *Fax:* 202-249-6100;
www.americanchemistry.com
Social Media: Facebook, Twitter, LinkedIn, Youtube

Calvin M Dooley, President & CEO
Raymond J O'Bryan, CFO & CAO
Dell Perelman, Chief of Staff & General Counsel
Anne Womack Kolton, VP, Communications
Roger D Bernstein, VP, State Affairs

Committed to improved environmental, health and safety performance through responsible care, common sense advocacy designed to address major public policy issues, health and environmental research and product testing.
190 Members

4326 **American Coatings Association**
1500 Rhode Island Ave Nw
Washington, DC 20005

202-462-6272; *Fax:* 202-462-8549
members@paint.org; www.paint.org
Social Media: Facebook

J. Andrew Doyle, President & CEO
Thomas J. Graves, Vice President, General Counsel
Allen Irish, Counsel/Director, Industry Affairs
Alison Keane, Vice President, Government Affairs
Robin Eastman Caldwell, Senior Government Affairs

Supports all those involved in the manufacturer of chemicals.
Founded in: 1903

4327 **American Coke & Coal Chemicals Institute**
25 Massachusetts Ave NW
Suite 800
Washington, DC 20001

724-772-1167; *Fax:* 866-422-7794
information@accci.org; www.accci.org

Ronald Schoen, Chairman
David Smith, Vice Chairman
Paul Saffrin, Secretary/Treasurer
David C. Ailor, President
Janis R. Deitch, Director of Administration

Formed by companies interested in establishing a forum to discuss and act upon issues of common concern to their industry. Today, ACCI represents 7 of the 8 independently owned and operated US merchant coke producers; several integrated steel companies which produce coke; and all 4 of the US and 1 Canadian coal chemical companies which refine coal tar. Nearly 50 companies contribute their knowledge and expertise to enhance the effectiveness of the Institute.
160 Members
Founded in: 1944

4328 **American College of Toxicology Annual Meeting**
1821 Michael Faraday Drive
Suite 300
Reston, VA 20190

703-547-0875; *Fax:* 703-438-3113;
www.actox.org
Social Media: Facebook, Twitter, LinkedIn

Mary Ellen Cosenza, President
Tracey Zoetis, MS, VP
Timothy McGovern, PhD, Treasurer
Timothy McGovern, PhD, Secretary
Carol C Lemire, Executive Director

Multidisciplinary society composed of professionals having a common interest in toxicology. Our mission is to educate and lead professionals in industry, government and related areas of toxicology and actively promote the exchange of information and perspectives on the current status of safety assessment and the application of new developments in toxicology. Annual meeting,education courses, symposia and exhibits.
500 Members
Founded in: 1979

4329 **American Fiber Manufacturers Association**
1530 Wilson Blvd
Suite 690
Arlington, VA 22209-2418

703-875-0432; *Fax:* 703-875-0907
afma@afma.org; www.afma.org

Paul O'Day, President
Robert Baker, VP
Frank Horn, President Economics Bureau Div

Trade association for US companies that manufacture synthetic and cellulosotic fibers.
33 Members
Founded in: 1933

4330 **American Hydrogen Association**
PO Box 4205
Mesa, AZ 85211

480-234-5070
webmaster@clean-air.org; www.clean-air.org
Social Media: Facebook, YouTube

Roy McAlister, President
Ben Ferguson, Vice President
Douglas Hawley, Secretary/Treasurer

Stimulates interest and helping to establish the renewable hydrogen energy economy.
Founded in: 1966

4331 **American Institute of Chemical Engineers**
120 Wall Street
FL 23
New York, NY 10005-4020

212-591-7338
800-242-4363; *Fax:* 203-775-5177
xpress@aiche.org; www.aiche.org
Social Media: Facebook, Twitter, LinkedIn

John Sofranko, Executive Director
William D Byers, President
Cathy Diana, Director Human Resources
Ken Gruber, Finance/IT Manager

A professional association of members that provide leadership in advancing the chemical engineering profession.
50000 Members
Founded in: 1908

4332 **American Institute of Chemists**
315 Chestnut St
Philadelphia, PA 19106-2702

215-873-8224; *Fax:* 215-629-5224
info@theaic.org; www.theaic.org

David Manuta, President
E Ray McAfee, President Elect
E Gerry Meyer, Secretary
J Stephen Duerr, Treasurer
Jerry Jasinski, Chairman

Supports all individual chemists and chemical engineers involved in the chemical industry.
Founded in: 1923

4333 **American Leather Chemists Association**
1314 50th Street
Suite 103
Lubbock, TX 79412

806-744-1798; *Fax:* 806-744-1785
alca@leatherchemists.org;
www.leatherchemists.org

Sarah Drayna, President
David Peters, VP
David Peters, VP Elect
Carol Adcock, Executive Secretary

Group of leather chemists interested in the development of methods that could be utilized to standardize both the supply and application of the tanning agents utilized by the industry
500 Members
Founded in: 1903

4334 **American Society Biochemistry and Molecular Biology**
11200 Rockville Pike
Suite 302
Rockville, MD 20852-3110

240-283-6600; *Fax:* 301-881-2080
asbmb@asbmb.org; www.asbmb.org
Social Media: Facebook, Twitter, LinkedIn, YouTube, Google+

Barbara A Gordon, Executive Director
Jennifer Dean, Director, Marketing
Ben Corb, Director, Public Affairs
Mary Ann Gunselman, Executive Assistant
Steve Miller, Deputy Executive Director and CFO

A professional and educational association for biochemists and molecular biologists which seeks to extend and utilize the fields of biochemistry and molecular biology.
13000 Members
Founded in: 1906
Mailing list available for rent

4335 **American Society for Mass Spectrometry**
2019 Galisteo Street, Building I-1
Santa Fe, NM 87505

505-989-4517; *Fax:* 505-989-1073
office@asms.org; www.asms.org
Social Media: Facebook, Twitter, LinkedIn

Jennifer Brodbelt, President
Vicki H. Wysocki, VP, Programs
Jack Henion, VP, Arrangements
Patrick R. Griffin, Treasurer
Yu Xia, Secretary

Formed to promote and disseminate knowledge of mass spectrometry and allied topics. Members come from academic, industrial and govermental laboratories. Their interests include advancement of techniques and instrumentation in mass spectrometry, as well as fundamental research in chemistry, geology, biological sciences and physics.
3500 Members
Founded in: 1969

4336 **American Society for Neurochemistry**
9037 Ron Den Lane
Windermere, FL 34786

407-909-9064; *Fax:* 407-876-0750
asnmanager@asneurochem.org;
www.asneurochem.org

Babette Fuss, PhD, President
Babette Fuss, President Elect
Sandra Hewett, Phd, Secretary
Jean Harry, PhD, Treasurer

Organized by US, Canadian and Mexican members of the International Society for Neurochemistry and incorporated in the District of Columbia. Membership dues are $75/year.
1000 Members
Founded in: 1969

4337 **American Society of Brewing Chemists**
3340 Pilot Knob Rd
St. Paul, MN 55121-2055

651-454-7250
800-328-7560; *Fax:* 651-454-0766
asbc@scisoc.org; www.asbcnet.org
Social Media: Facebook, Twitter, LinkedIn, Pinterest

Christina Schoenberger, President
Christine S White, President-Elect
Chris D Powell, Vice President
Thomas H Shellhammer, Past President
Robert Christiansen, Secretary
700 Members
Founded in: 1934

4338 Analytical, Life Science, and Diagnostics Association
500 Montgomery Street
Suite 400
Alexandria, VA 22314
703-647-6214; *Fax:* 703-647-6368
cstarke@alssa.org; www.alssa.org
Social Media: Facebook, Twitter, LinkedIn
Joseph D. Keegan, Chair
Tim Harkness, Vice Chair & Chair-Elect
Greg Herrema, Past Chairman
Michael J. Duff, President
ALSSA is the primary trade association for companies that supply instruments, chemical reagents, consumables and software used for analysis and measurement in chemistry and the life sciences.

4339 Association of Consulting Chemists and Chemical Engineers Inc.
A C C & C E
P.O. Box 902
Murray Hill, NJ 07974-0902
908-464-3182; *Fax:* 908-464-3182
accce@chemconsult.org;
www.chemconsult.org
Linda Townsend, Executive Secretary
Dr John Bonacci, Executive Director
The only organization of its kind that attracts qualified technical consultants of all kinds who assist their clients in creating and using chemical knowledge and technology.
150 Members
Founded in: 1928

4340 Association of Defensive Spray Manufacturers
906 Olive Street
Suite 1200
St Louis, MO 63101-1448
314-241-1445; *Fax:* 314-241-1449;
www.pepperspray.org
Mark S Birenbaum, Executive Director
To permit manufacturers of non lethal chemical weapons to join together to promote the industry as well as to address safety, quality control, marketing and other issues relevant to the industry
6 Members
Founded in: 1992

4341 Association of Official Racing Chemists
1021 Storrs Rd
Storrs, CT 06268
860-487-3755; *Fax:* 860-487-3756;
www.aorc-online.org
Dennis Hill, Executive Director
The international membership consits of individuals concerned with detection of drugs in racing samples.
200 Members
Founded in: 1947

4342 Basic Acrylic Monomer Manufacturers
17260 Vannes Court
Hamilton, VA 20158
540-751-2093; *Fax:* 540-751-2094;
www.bamm.net
Elizabeth K Hunt, Executive Director
Addresses the issues facing the basic acrylates. Also represents manufacturers and importers of acrylic acid and its esters.
5 Members
Founded in: 1986
Mailing list available for rent

4343 CIIT Centers for Health Research
Six Davis Drive
PO Box 12137
Research Triangle Park, NC 27709-2137
919-581-1200; *Fax:* 919-558-1400
wgreenlee@ciit.org; www.thehamner.org
Social Media: Twitter
John G. Dent, Ph.D., Chair & Treasurer
Charles E. Hamner, Jr., D.V.M., P, Vice Chair
William F. Greenlee, Ph.D., President/CEO
Joseph S. Pagano, M.D., Secretary
Jamie H. Wilkerson, CPA, CGMA, Assistant Treasurer
Studies toxicological and human health risk issues associated with the manufacture, distribution and disposal of industrial chemicals.
130 Members
Founded in: 1974

4344 Center for the Polyurethanes Industry
700 Second St., NE
Washington, DC 20002
202-249-7000; *Fax:* 202-249-6100
polyurethane.americanchemistry.com
Social Media: Facebook, Twitter
Calvin M. Dooley, President/CEO
Dell Perelman, Chief of Staff & General Council
Raymond J. O'Bryan, CFO/ Chief Administrative Officer
Bryan Zumwalt, Vice President of Federal Affairs
Nacole B. Hinton, Managing Director, HR
CPI of the American Chemistry Council promotes the sustainable growth of the polyurethane industry, by identifying and managing issues that could impact the industry, in cooperation with user groups. Members are producers and distributors of chemicals and equipment used to make polyurethane and manufacture polyurethane products.

4345 Chemical Coaters Association International
5040 Old Taylor Mill Rd
PMB 13
Taylor Mill, KY 41015
859-356-1030
800-926-2848; *Fax:* 513-624-0601
aygoyer@one.net; www.ccaiweb.com
Anne Goyer, Executive Director
A technical and professional organization that provides information and training on surface coating technologies. Users and suppliers of industrial cleaners, paints, coatings, and equipment.
1000 Members
Founded in: 1970
Mailing list available for rent

4346 Chemical Development and Marketing Association (CDMA)
330 N. Wabash Avenue
Suite 2200
Chicago, IL 60611
312-321-5145
800-232-5241; *Fax:* 312-673-6885
pdma@pdma.org;
www.cdmaonline.org/home.html
Theodre D. Goldman, President/Treasurer
Tom Regino, Executive Vice President
Eileen Strauss, Vice President/Webmaster
Maricy Bourgis, Vice President
A forum for networking, learning and sharing best practices in business development and marketing for the chemical and allied industries. Keeps members informed on commercial/business development and marketing as well as industrial marketing research via its two meetings per year (spring and fall), seminars and business schools.
Founded in: 1999

4347 Chemical Fabrics and Film Association
1300 Sumner Avenue
Cleveland, OH 44115-2851
216-241-7333; *Fax:* 216-241-0105;
www.chemicalfabricsandfilm.com
Charles Stockinger, Executive Secretary
International trade association representing manufacturers of polymer-based fabric and film products, used in the building and construction, automotive, fashion and many other industries.
40 Members
Founded in: 1927

4348 Chemical Heritage Foundation
315 Chestnut St
Philadelphia, PA 19106
215-925-2222; *Fax:* 215-925-1954
info@chemheritage.org;
www.chemheritage.org
Social Media: Facebook, Twitter, LinkedIn, Pinterest
Tom Tritton, President/CEO
Miriam Schaefer, Special Advisor to the President
Michael Meyer, Editor-in-Chief
An independent, nonprofit organization, CHF maintains major collections of instruments, fine art, photographs, papers, and books. We host conferences and lectures, support research, offer fellowships, and produce educational materials.
29 Members
Founded in: 1992

4349 Chemical Industry Data Exchange
401 North Michigan Avenue
Chicago, IL 60611-4267
312-321-5145; *Fax:* 312-212-5971
memberservices@cidx.org; www.cidx.org
JoAnne Norton, Executive Director
Laura Field, Communications
Promotes standards to improve the efficiency of transactions across the chemical industry supply chain. Members include chemical producers and companies active in the chemicals industry.

4350 Chemical Strategies Partnership
423 Washington St
4th Floor
San Francisco, CA 94111
415-421-3405; *Fax:* 415-421-3304;
www.chemicalstrategies.org
Jill Kauffman Johnson, Executive Director
Angeline Kung, Senior Associate
Aarthi Ananthanarayanan, Associate
Max Pike, Communications Associate
Mark Stoughton, Ph.D., Research Advisor
CSP seeks to reduce chemical use, waste, risks and cost through the transformation of the chemical supply chain by redefining the way chemicals are used and sold.
Founded in: 1978
Mailing list available for rent

4351 Chemtrec
1300 Wilson Blvd
Arlington, VA 22209-2323
703-741-5500
800-262-8200; *Fax:* 703-741-6086
chemtrec@chemtrec.com; www.chemtrec.com
A 24 hour emergency communication service center that helps fire fighters and emergency responders protect the public and helps shippers of hazardous materials comply with the US Department of Transportation regulations.
Founded in: 1971

4352 Chlorinated Paraffins Industry Association
1250 Connecticut Ave NW
Suite 700
Washington, DC 20036
202-419-1500; *Fax:* 202-659-8037
info@regnet.com; www.regnet.com/cpia
Robert J Fensterheim, Executive Director
Composed of manufacturers, distributors, and users of chlorinated paraffins, used in lubricants, plastics and flame retardants.
Founded in: 1970

4353 Chlorine Chemistry Division of the American Chemistry Counsil
700 Second St., NE
Washington, DC 20002
202-249-7000; *Fax:* 202-249-6100;
www.americanchemistry.com/s_chlorine/index.asp
Social Media: Facebook, Twitter
Calvin M. Dooley, President/CEO
Raymond J. O'Bryan, CFO & CAO
Robert J. Simon, Vice President, Chemical Products
Bryan Zumwalt, Vice President, Federal Affairs
Nacole B. Hinton, Managing Director, HR
This division represents major producers and users of chlorine in North America, working to promote and protect the sustainability of chlorine chemsitry processes, products and applications in accordance with the Responsible Care initiative.

4354 Chlorine Free Products Association
1304 S Main St
Algonquin, IL 60102-2757
847-658-6104; *Fax:* 847-658-3152
info@chlorinefreeproducts.org;
www.chlorinefreeproducts.org
Social Media: YouTube
Archie Beaton, Executive Director
A nonprofit association that's primary purpose is to promote total chlorine free policies, programs and technologies throughtout the world.

4355 Chlorine Institute
1300 Wilson Blvd
Suite 525
Arlington, VA 22209
703-894-4140; *Fax:* 703-894-4130
info@cl2.com; www.chlorineinstitute.org
Frank Reiner, President
Henry Ward, VP, Emergency Preparedness
Terry Cirone, VP Health, Environment
Robyn Kinsley, Director, Transportation
Anna Belousovitch, Project Coordinator
Supports the chlo-alkali industry and serves the public by promoting the safe handling of chlorine and caustic materials.
204 Members
Founded in: 1924

4356 Chlorobenzene Producers Association
1850 M St Nw
Suite 700
Washington, DC 20036-5810
202-721-4100; *Fax:* 202-296-8120
helmest@socma.com; www.socma.com
Social Media: Facebook, Twitter, LinkedIn, YouTube
Larry Sloan, President/CEO
David Doles, Treasurer
Gene Williams, Secretary
Addresses health and environmental issues in response to Environmental Protection Agency.
40 Members
Founded in: 1921

4357 Color Pigments Manufacturers Association
1850 M Street NW
Suite 730
Washington, DC 20036
202-465-4900; *Fax:* 202-296-8120
cpma@cpma.com; www.pigments.org
J Lawrence Robinson, President
An industry trade association representing color pigment companies in Canada, Mexico and the US. Represents small, medium, and large color pigments manufacturers accounting for 95% of the production of color pigments in North America
50 Members
Founded in: 1925

4358 Combustion Institute
5001 Baum Blvd
Suite 644
Pittsburgh, PA 15213-1851
412-687-1366; *Fax:* 412-687-0340
office@combustioninstitute.org;
www.combustioninstitute.org
Prof. Katrina Kohse-Hoinghaus, President
Prof. James F. Driscoll, VP, President Elect
Prof. Marcus Alden, Vice President Section Affairs
Prof. Reginald Mitchell, Secretary
Prof. Derek Dunn-Rankin, Treasurer
International organizaton with sections in several foreign countries including Canada. A non profit, educational organization with the purpose of promoting and disseminating knowledge in the field of combustion science.
4000 Members
Founded in: 1954

4359 Consumer Specialty Products Association
1667 k street,NW
Suite 300
Washington, DC 20006
202-872-8110; *Fax:* 202-223-2636
info@cspa.org; www.cspa.org
Social Media: Facebook, Twitter, LinkedIn, Flickr, Google+
Christopher Cathcart, President and CEO
Keith Fulk, Senior Vice President, Controller
Holly Schroeder SPHR, Director, Administrative Services
Phil Klein, Executive Vice President
Laura Madden, Director, Government Affairs
Supports all professionals involved in the manufacturer of chemical specialties.
Founded in: 1914
Mailing list available for rent

4360 Consumer Specialty Products Association
1667 K Street, NW
Suite 300
Washington, DC 20006-2501
202-872-8110; *Fax:* 202-223-2636
info@cspa.org; www.cspa.org
Social Media: Facebook, Twitter, LinkedIn, Flickr, Google+
Christopher Cathcart, President
Phil Klein, Executive Vice President
Colleen Creighton, Executive Director
Susan Little, Executive Director
Keith Fulk, Senior VP & Controller
Nonprofit organization composed of many companies involved in the formulation, manufacture, testing and marketing of chemical specialty products. Its line includes disinfectants that kill germs in homes, hospitals and restaurants, candles and fragrances that eliminate odors, pest management products for home and garden, cleaning products and much more.
200 Members
Founded in: 1914

4361 Council for Chemical Research
1120 Route 73
Suite 200
Mount Laurel, NJ 08054
856-439-0500; *Fax:* 856-439-0525;
www.ccrhq.org
Social Media: Facebook, LinkedIn
Dr. Jeffrey A Reimer, Chair
Dr. Eriv Lin, 1st Vice Chair
Dr. Jeff Robert, 2nd Vice Chair
Dr. Seth W. Snyder, President
Dr. Kelly O. Sullivan, Treasurer
Promotes cooperation in basic research and encourage high quality education in the chemical sciences and engineering. Membership represents industry, academia, and government.
200 Members
Founded in: 1980

4362 Council of Producers & Distributors of Agrotechnology
1730 Rhode Island Avenue
Suite 812
Washington, DC 20036
202-386-7407; *Fax:* 202-386-7409;
www.cpda.com
Dr Susan Ferenc, President
Diane Schute, Director of Communications
John Boling, Director of Legislative Affairs
Dr. Michael C White, Ph.D., J.D., Director, Regulatory Affairs
Melvin A. Moore-Adams, Administrative Coordinator
The voice of the generic pesticide, inert, adjuvant and surfactant manufacturer, as well as crop protection product formulators and distributors on federal legislative and regulatory issues affecting the crop protection industry.
56 Members
Founded in: 1975

4363 CropLife America
1156 15th St NW
Suite 400
Washington, DC 20005-1752
202-296-1585; *Fax:* 202-463-0474
Info@croplifeamerica.org;
www.croplifeamerica.org
Social Media: Facebook, Twitter, LinkedIn, Youtube
Jay Vroom, President and CEO
Beau Greenwood, Executive VP
Bill Kuckuck, Executive Vice President
Dr. Barbara Glenn, Senior Vice President, Science
Rachel Lattimore, Senior Vice President
A trade association of the manufacturers, formulators, and distributors of agricultural crop protection, pest control, and bitechnology products. Membership is composed of companies that produce, sell and distribute virtually all the active ingredients use in crop protection chemicals.
86 Members
Founded in: 1933
Mailing list available for rent

4364 Drug, Chemical & Associated Technologies Association
One Union St
Suite 208
Robbinsville, NJ 08691-3162
609-208-1888
800-640-3228; *Fax:* 609-208-0599

info@dcat.org; www.dcat.org
Social Media: Facebook, LinkedIn

George Svokos, President
Dr. Folker Ruchatz, First Vice President
Milton Boyer, Second Vice President
Joe Sutton, Third Vice President
David Beattie, Director

The not for profit, member supported business development association whose membership is comprimsed of companies that manufacture, distribute or provide services to the pharmaceutical, chemical, nutritional and related industries.
350 Members
Founded in: 1890

4365 **Embalming Chemical Manufacturers**
1370 Honeyspot Road Ext
Stratford, CT 06615-7115

Works to develop scientific, technological, and economic data about safety issues of the product.
Founded in: 1951

4366 **Emulsion Poylmers Council**
1250 Connecticut Ave NW
Suite 700
Washington, DC 20036-2657

202-419-1500; *Fax:* 202-659-8037
epc@regnet.com; www.regnet.com/epc/

Robert J Fensterheim, Executive Director

Represents regulatory professionals at companies which produce emulsion polymers, chemical compounds used in a variety of coating and other industril applications.
7 Members
Founded in: 1995

4367 **Ethylene Oxide Sterlization Association, Inc.**
PO Box 33361
Washington, DC 20033

866-235-5030; *Fax:* 202-557-3836
eosainfo@eosa.org; www.eosa.org

Jonathan Bull, President
Fenil Sutaria, Vice President
Robert Bogart, Treasurer
Chris Klosen, Secretary

EOSA is a non-profit organization that works to educate industry, regulators, and the public on the uses and benefits of ethylene oxide. EOSA also works to improve safety standards, foster industry communication, and provide a forum for issues related to ethylene oxide sterilization.
23 Members
Founded in: 1995

4368 **Federation of Analytical Chemistry and Spectroscopy Societies**
2019 Galisteo St
Building I-1
Santa Fe, NM 87505

505-820-1653; *Fax:* 505-989-1073;
www.facss.org
Social Media: Facebook, Twitter, LinkedIn

Greg Klunder, Governing Board Chairperson
Steven Ray, Governing Board Chairperson Elect
Cindy Lilly, Executive Assistant
Christopher Palmer, Secretary 2009-2013
Mark Druy, Treasurer 2013 - 2015

Exists to combine many small meetings previously organized bythe individual societies into one joint meeting that covers the whole field of Analytical Chemistry.
12 Members
Founded in: 1972

4369 **Federation of Societies for Coatings Technology**
1500 Rhode Island Ave., NW
Washington, DC 20005

202-462-6272; *Fax:* 202-462-8549
aca@paint.org; www.paint.org
Social Media: Facebook, Twitter, LinkedIn

J Andrew Doyle, President & CEO
Thomas J Graves, VP/General Counsel/Corporate Sec.
Allen Irish, Counsel / Director
Alison Keane, Vice President, Government Affairs
Jeff Wasikowski, Counsel

Provides technical education and professional development to its members and to the global industry through its multi-national constituent societies and collectively as a federation.
6000 Members
Founded in: 1922

4370 **Independent Liquid Terminals Association**
1005 North Glebe Road
Suite 600
Arlington, VA 22201

703-875-2011; *Fax:* 703-875-2018
info@ilta.org; www.ilta.org

Wayne N Driggers, Chairman
Jamie Coleman, Vice Chairman
Gregory J Pound, Treasurer/Secretary
Kim Breaux, Director
Sam Brown, Director

Provides members with essential informational tools to facilitate regulatory compliance and improve operations, safety and environmental performance.
80 Members
Founded in: 1974

4371 **Independent Lubricant Manufacturers Association**
400 N Columbus St
Suite 201
Alexandria, VA 22314

703-684-5574; *Fax:* 703-836-8503
ilma@ilma.org; www.ilma.org
Social Media: Facebook, Twitter

Frank H Hamilton III, President
Beth Ann Jones, Vice President
Dave Croghan, Treasurer
Barbara Kudis, Secretary
Barbara A Bellanti, Immediate Past President

Supports all those involved in the US and international independent lubricant industry.
Founded in: 1948

4372 **Institute for Polyacrylate Absorbents**
1850 M St NW
Suite 700
Washington, DC 20036

202-721-4100; *Fax:* 202-296-8120;
www.superabsorbents.com

C. Tucker Helmes Ph.D., Executive Director

Represents manufacturers and users of absorbent polymers made of cross-linked polyacrylates and manufacturers and users of acrylic acid or its salts. It addreses the scientific, regulatory and related issues which are likely to impact the manufacture, use and disposal of fluid-absorbing polyacrylates.
Founded in: 1985

4373 **International Cadmium Association**
168 Avenue de Tervuren BOX4
Brussels, VA 22066

202-776-0073; *Fax:* 202-776-0092
contact@cadmium.org; www.cadmium.org

Hugh Morrow, Consultant

Provides marketing research and promotion to the industry. Hosts seperate annual meetings in the United States and Europe.
30 Members
Mailing list available for rent

4374 **International Ozone Association: Pan American Group Branch**
PO Box 97075
Las Vegas, NV 89193

480-529-3787; *Fax:* 480-522-3080
infO3zone@io3a.org; www.ioa-pag.org

Robert Jarnis, Executive Director

Represents the interests of environmental and other scientific communities, application engineers, users, and manufacturers of ozone generation and contacting equipment.
810 Members
Founded in: 1973

4375 **MTI Communications**
Materials Technology Institute
1215 Ferk Ridge Parkway
Suite 206
St. Louis, MO 63141

314-576-7712; *Fax:* 314-576-6078
mtiadmin@mti-global.org; www.mti-global.org
Social Media: Twitter, LinkedIn

Paul Bancroft, Executive Director
Lindsey Skinner, Communications & Publications

Official newsletter of Materials Technology Institute, providing updates on member activities, meetings, and training announcement.
Frequency: 3x/Year
Founded in: 1977

4376 **Materials Technology Institute, Inc.**
1215 Fern Ridge Pkwy
Suite 206
St Louis, MO 63141

314-576-7712; *Fax:* 314-576-6078
mtiadmin@mti-global.org; www.mti-global.org
Social Media: Twitter, LinkedIn

Paul Whitcraft, Executive Director
Bryon Keelin, Operations Director
Lindsey Skinner, Communications & Publications

Provides leadership in materials technology for chemical processing to improve reliability, profitability and safety.
52 Members
Founded in: 1977

4377 **Methanol Institute**
225 Reinekers Lane
Suite 205
Alexandria, VA 22314

703-248-3636; *Fax:* 703-248-3997
MI@methanol.org; www.methanol.org
Social Media: Facebook, Twitter, LinkedIn

Gregory A. Dolan, CEO
Christopher D Chatterton, COO
Dom LaVigne, Director of Gov. & Public Affairs
Lawrence Navin, Sr. Manager, External Affairs & Ops
April Chan, Executive Manager

Our mission is to expand markets for the use of methanol as a chemical commodity and an energy fuel.
35 Members
Founded in: 1989

4378 **National Aerosol Association**
PO Box 5510
Fullerton, CA 92838
714-525-1518; *Fax:* 714-526-1295
NAA@nationalaerosol.com;
www.nationalaerosol.com
Harry Zechman, President
Steve Cook, Vice President
Bart Bastian, Past President
Craig Autry, Treasurer
Individuals, firms and agencies engaged in the development, manufacture, packaging, sale or distribution of aerosol products.
30 Members
Founded in: 1986

4379 **National Association of Chemical Recyclers**
1900 M Street NW
Washington, DC 20036
202-296-1725; *Fax:* 202-296-2530
Christopher Goebel, Executive Director
Members are companies whose primary business is the reclamation of solvents and other chemicals from industrial waste streams and recycling.
Founded in: 1979

4380 **National Chemical Credit Association**
500 Seneca Street
Suite 400
Buffalo, NY 14204-1963
844-462-6342; *Fax:* 716-878-0479
robert.gagliardi@abc-amega.com;
www.abc-amega.com
Social Media: Twitter, LinkedIn, YouTube, Google+
Don Peters, Contact
Glenn Lifrieri, Executive Board Co-Chair
Pam Kelley, Executive Board Past-Chair
Paulo Menezes, Treasurer
Gordon Miller, Member at Large
Members are major producers of basic chemicals and allied products.
100 Members
Founded in: 1938

4381 **National Pest Management Association**
10460 North Street
Fairfax, VA 22030
703-352-6762
800-678-6722; *Fax:* 703-352-3031;
www.npmapestworld.org
Social Media: Facebook, Twitter
H Russell Ives, President
Chuck Tindol, President-Elect
Bryan Cooksey, Jr., Treasurer
Dennis Jenkins, Secretary
William A Tesh, Immediate Past President
Represents the interests of its members and the structural pest control industry.
7000 Members
Frequency: October
Founded in: 1933

4382 **North American Catalysis Society**
PO Box 80262
Wilmington, DE 19880
302-695-2488; *Fax:* 302-695-8347
michael.b.damore@usa.dupont.com;
www.nacatsoc.org
Enrique Igle-sia, President
Bruce R. Cook, VP
Hong-Xin Li, Secretary
C. Y Chen, Treasurer
Fosters an interest in heterogeneous and homogeneous catalysis. Organizes national meetings. Members are chemists and chemical engineers engaged in the study and use of reactions involving catalysts. Publishes a newsletter.
1400 Members
Founded in: 1956
Mailing list available for rent: 3400 names

4383 **Pine Chemicals Association**
PO Box 17136
Fernandina Beach, FL 32035
404-994-6267; *Fax:* 404-994-6267
wjones@pinechemicals.org;
www.pinechemicals.org
Social Media: Facebook, Twitter, LinkedIn, YouTube
Charles W Morris, President/COO
Steve Violette, Chairman/CEO
Amanda Young, Executive Director
Mike Roberts, Vice-Chairman
Lee Godina, Chairman & CEO
An association of producers, processors and consumers of pine chemicals. Promotes innovative, safe and environmentally responsible practices to assure a reliable supply of high quality products.
50 Members
Founded in: 1947

4384 **Polyisocyanurate Insulation Manufacturers Association**
529 14th Street NW
Suite 750
Washington, DC 20045
301-654-0000; *Fax:* 301-951-8401
pima@pima.org; www.pima.org
Social Media: Facebook, Twitter
Renee Lamura, Director of Member Services
Jared O Blum, President
Represents the interests of polyisocyanurate manufacturers and suppliers to the industry. Efforts include education, environmental responsibility, government partnerships and energy conservation.
32 Members
Founded in: 1970
Mailing list available for rent

4385 **Polyurethane Foam Association**
334 Lakeside Plz
Loudon, TN 37774
865-657-9840; *Fax:* 865-381-1292
rluedeka@pfa.org; www.pfa.org
Pat Martin, Chairman
Robert Luedeka, Executive Director
Suppliers of raw material and equipment. Associate members are manufacturers of flexible polyurethane foam. Our mission is to educate customers and other groups about flexible polyurethane foam and promote its use in manufactured and industrial products. This includes providing facts on environmental, health and safety issues related to polyurethane foam to the membership of PFA, polyurethane foam users, regulatory officials, business leaders and the media.
63 Members
Founded in: 1980

4386 **Powder Coating Institute**
5040 Old Taylor Mill Rd
PMB 13
Taylor Mill, KY 41015
859-525-9988
800-988-COAT; *Fax:* 859-356-0908
pci-info@powdercoating.org;
www.powdercoating.org
Social Media: Facebook, Twitter, LinkedIn, Pinterest
John Cole, President
John Sudges, Vice President
Ron Cudzilo, Secretary/Treasurer
Bob Allsop, Director
John Cole, Secretary/ treasurer
A trade association representing suppliers of powder coating materials, equipment, and related products and services in North America.
325 Members
Founded in: 1981
Mailing list available for rent

4387 **Process Equipment Manufacturers Association**
201 Park Washington Ct
Falls Church, VA 22046
703-538-1796; *Fax:* 703-241-5603
info@pemanet.org; www.pemanet.org
Susan A. Denston, Executive Director & Secretary
Harry W. Buzzerd, Management Counsel
Charlie Ingram, Treasurer
Chuck Weilbrenner, President
Jay Brown, Vice-President
Manufacturers and suppliers of equipment for food, chemical, pulp and paper, water, wastewater processing.
50 Members
Founded in: 1960

4388 **Society of Chemical Manufacturers and Affiliates**
1850 M St Nw
Suite 700
Washington, DC 20036-5810
202-721-4100; *Fax:* 202-296-8120
info@socma.com; www.socma.com
Social Media: Facebook, Twitter, LinkedIn, YouTube
J. Steel Hutchinson, Chairman
Larry Sloan, President/ CEO
Tracy Devore, Manager
Tima Good, Account Executive
Sandra Lehrer, Senior Manager
Conducts workshops and seminars. Maintains a library on cancer policies and related subjects. Its member companies have more than 2,000 manufacturing sites and 100,000 employees.
300 Members
Founded in: 1921

4389 **Society of Cosmetic Chemists**
120 Wall St
Suite 2400
New York, NY 10005-4088
212-668-1500; *Fax:* 212-668-1504
scc@scconline.org; www.scconline.org
Social Media: Facebook, Twitter, LinkedIn
Guy Padulo, President
Dawn Burke-Colvin, Vice President
David Smith, Executive Director
Dawn Thiel Glaser, Secretary
Peter Tsolis, Treasurer
Supports all those involved in working with and developing cosmetic chemicals.
4000 Members
Founded in: 1945

4390 **Society of Toxicology**
1821 Michael Faraday Drive
Suite 300
Reston, VA 20190
703-438-3115; *Fax:* 703-438-3113
sothq@toxicology.org; www.toxicology.org
Social Media: Facebook, Twitter, LinkedIn, Pinterest, Google+
Peter L Goering, President
Patricia E Ganey, Vice President-Elect
Members are scientists concerned with the effects of chemicals on man and the environment. Promotes the acquisition and utilization of knowledge in toxicology, aids in the protection of public health and facilitates disciplines. The

society has a strong commitment to education in toxicology and to the recruitment of students and new members into the profession.
5000 Members
Founded in: 1961

4391 **Spray Polyurethane Foam Alliance**
3827 Old Lee Hwy.
#101B
Fairfax, VA 22030

800-523-6154; *Fax:* 703-222-5816
info@sprayfoam.org; www.sprayfoam.org
Social Media: Facebook, Twitter

Robert Duke, President
Dennis Vandewater, Vice President
Peter Davis, Secretary/Treasurer
Bill Baley, Board Member
Mac Sheldon, Board Member

A trade association representing interests associated with rigid and semi-rigid polyurethane foam products that are typically applied with spray equipment as roofing and insulation.
Founded in: 1987
Mailing list available for rent

4392 **The Electrochemical Society**
65 South Main St
Building D
Pennington, NJ 08534-2839

609-737-1902; *Fax:* 609-737-2743
esc@electrochem.org; www.electrochem.org
Social Media: Facebook, Twitter, LinkedIn

Roque J Calvo, Executive Director
Mary E. Yess, Deputy Executive Director
Dinia Agarwala, Interface Production manager
Karen Chmielewski, Finance Associate
Paul B. Cooper, Editorial Manager

An international nonprofit, educational organization concerned with a broad range of phenomena relating to electrochemical and solid-state science and technology. The Electrochemical Society has scientists and engineers in over 70 countries worldwide who hold individual membership, as well as roughly 100 corporations and laboratories that hold corporate membership.
8000 Members
Founded in: 1902

Newsletters

4393 **AAB Bulletin**
American Association of Bioanalysts
906 Olive Street
Suite 1200
Saint Louis, MO 63101-1448

314-241-1445; *Fax:* 314-241-1449
aab@aab.org; www.aab.org

Mark S Biernbaum PhD, Administrator

Newsletter that provides the latest information on meetings, conferences, legislative and regulatory issues and developments.
Frequency: Quarterly
Founded in: 1956

4394 **AACG Newsletter**
American Association for Crystal Growth
25 4th Street
Somerville, NJ 08876-3205

908-575-0649; *Fax:* 908-575-0794;
www.crystalgrowth.org

Candace Lynch, Chief Editor
Lara Keefer, Editor
Peter Schunemann, President
Robert Biefeld, Vice President

Technical articles and includes calendar of upcoming meetings.
Circulation: 600
ISSN: 1527-2389
Founded in: 1966
Printed in 4 colors on glossy stock

4395 **AATCC News**
PO Box 12215
Research Triangle Park, NC 27709-2215

919-549-8141
800-360-5380; *Fax:* 919-549-8933
danielsj@aatcc.org; www.aatcc.org
Social Media: Facebook, Twitter, LinkedIn

John Daniels, Executive VP
Debra Hibbard, Executive Assistant
Chris Leonard, Technical Director

Free, emailed newsletter providing up-to-date news and feature articles.
3000 Members

4396 **APE Newsletter**
Alkylphenois & Ethoxylates Research Council
1250 Connecticut Ave Nw
Suite 700
Washington, DC 20036-2657

202-419-1506
866-273-7262; *Fax:* 202-659-8037
angroup@regnet.com; www.angroup.org

Robert J Fensterheim, Editor

4397 **Adhesion Society Newsletter**
Adhesion Society
2 Davidson Hall
Blacksburg, VA 24061-0001

540-231-7257; *Fax:* 540-231-3971
adhesoc@vt.edu; www.adhesionsociety.org

Esther Brann, Manager

4398 **Advanced Coatings and Surface Technology**
John Wiley & Sons
111 River St
Hoboken, NJ 07030-5790

201-748-6000; *Fax:* 201-748-6088
info@wiley.com; www.wiley.com

William J Pesce, CEO

Provides intelligence service reports and puts into perspective significant developments in coatings and surface modification across a broad range of industry lines. ACT interprets developments ranging from traditional coating processes to chemical vapor deposition and iron beam methods, which offers interdisciplinary analyses of those that have true commercial potential.
Cost: $530.00
10 Pages
Frequency: Monthly
Founded in: 1807

4399 **Amber-Hi-Lites**
Rohm And Haas Company
100 S Independence Mall W
Suite 1A
Philadelphia, PA 19106-2399

215-592-3000; *Fax:* 215-592-3377;
www.rohmhaas.com

Raj L Gupta, CEO

Offers discussions of ion exchange resin use in fields of water conditioning.

4400 **Analytical Chemistry**
American Chemical Society
1155 16th St Nw
Suite 600
Washington, DC 20036-4892

202-872-4600
800-227-5558; *Fax:* 202-872-4615
service@acs.org; www.acs.org

Madeleine Jacobs, CEO
Elizabeth Zubritsky, Manager

Information and news on the chemical industry.
Founded in: 1876

4401 **Biochemistry**
American Chemical Society
1155 16th St Nw
Suite 600
Washington, DC 20036-4892

202-872-4600
800-333-9511; *Fax:* 202-872-4615
service@acs.org; www.acs.org

Madeleine Jacobs, CEO

News and information for the scientific community.
Cost: $137.00
Frequency: Weekly
Founded in: 1876

4402 **ChemEcology**
Chemical Manufacturers Association
1300 Wilson Boulevard
Arlington, VA 22209-2307

703-741-5502; *Fax:* 703-741-6807

Rebecca Swinehart, Editor

Issues on health, safety and the environment.

4403 **ChemWeek Association**
ChemWeek
110 William St
Suite 11
New York, NY 10038-3910

212-621-4900; *Fax:* 212-621-4800
ltattum@chemweek.com; www.chemweek.com

John Rockwell, VP
Joe Mennella, Global Sales Director

Comprehensive coverage of the latest developments, uses, production, distribution, and manufacturing of chemicals for all industries.
Cost: $159.00
Frequency: Monthly
Circulation: 20779
Founded in: 1977

4404 **Chemical Bond**
American Chemical Society
1155 16th St Nw
Suite 600
Washington, DC 20036-4892

202-872-4600
800-227-5558; *Fax:* 202-872-4615
service@acs.org; www.acs.org

Madeleine Jacobs, CEO

Covers organization activities.

4405 **Chemical Bulletin**
American Chemical Society
Ste 312
1400 Renaissance Dr
Park Ridge, IL 60068-1336

847-647-8405; *Fax:* 847-647-8364
chicagoacs@ameritech.net;
www.chicagoacs.org

Gail Wilkening, Office Manager

Highlights events and meetings of local chapters, profiles prominent society members, and reports on research and technological advancements in the field.
Cost: $20.00
Frequency: Monthly
Circulation: 5700

4406 **Chemical Economics Handbook Program**
SRI Consulting

4300 Bohannon Dr
Suite 200
Menlo Park, CA 94025-1042

650-384-4300; *Fax:* 650-330-1190;
www.sriconsulting.com

John Pearson, President/CEO

Ongoing multiclient program focusing on the chemical and allied products industries. History, status and projected trends for hundreds of chemicals, chemical raw materials, and end-use products. Service includes access to on-line data base and client inquiry privileges.
Cost: $12000.00
Frequency: Monthly
Founded in: 1946

4407 **Chemical Industries Newsletter**
SRI International
333 Ravenswood Ave
Menlo Park, CA 94025-3493

650-859-3711; *Fax:* 650-326-8916;
www.srifcu.org

Steve Bowles, President

Articles discuss the activities of SRI International Chemical Industries Centers.

4408 **Chemical Industry Monitoring**
Cyrus J Lawrence
1290 Avenue of the Americas
New York, NY 10006
Don Pattison, Editor

Prices and technological developments in the industry.

4409 **Chemical Product News**
US Dept. of Commerce, Business & Defense Service
200 Constitution Ave Nw
Washington, DC 20210-0001

202-693-5000; *Fax:* 202-219-8822;
www.dol.gov

Hilda L Solis, CEO

Offers information about chemical products and related issues.

4410 **Chemical Regulation Reporter**
Bureau of National Affairs
1801 S Bell St
Arlington, VA 22202-4501

703-341-3000
800-372-1033; *Fax:* 202-452-4084
customercare@bna.com; www.bnabooks.com

Paul N Wojcik, Chairman

A notification and reference service consisting of six binders that comprehensively covers federal chemical regulations.
Cost: $1103.00
Frequency: Weekly
Founded in: 1929

4411 **Chemical and Engineering News**
American Chemical Society
1155 16th St Nw
Suite 600
Washington, DC 20036-4892

202-872-4600
800-227-5558; *Fax:* 202-872-4615
service@acs.org; www.acs.org

Madeleine Jacobs, CEO

Covers news relating to chemical engineering and technology.
Frequency: Weekly
Circulation: 137,664
ISSN: 0009-2347
Founded in: 1876

4412 **Chemweek's Business Daily**
Chemical Week/Access Intelligence
110 William St
Suite 11
New York, NY 10038-3910

212-621-4900; *Fax:* 212-621-4800
ltattum@chemweek.com; www.chemweek.com

John Rockwell, VP
Joe Minnella, Global Sales Manager

Daily electronic newsletter covering the latest chemical industry business and financial news, including markets, pricing, regulatory and security issues, research, technologies and new services.
Cost: $1049.00
Frequency: Daily
Founded in: 2002
Printed in 4 colors

4413 **Chlor-Alkali Marketwire**
Chemical Week/Access Intelligence
110 William St
Suite 11
New York, NY 10038-3910

212-621-4900; *Fax:* 212-621-4800
ltattum@chemweek.com; www.chemweek.com

John Rockwell, VP
Joe Mennella, Global Sales Director

Weekly electronic newsletter covering chlor-alkali market sector, including market trends in supply and demand, pricing fluctuations, production rates in caristic soda and chlorine. Also covers vinyls, soda ash and related derivatives
Cost: $1699.00
Frequency: Weekly
Founded in: 2002
Printed in 4 colors

4414 **Chlorine Institute Newsletter**
Chlorine Institute
1300 Wilson Blvd
Arlington, VA 22209-2323

703-741-5760; *Fax:* 703-894-4130
aonna@cl2.com; www.chlorineinstitute.org

Arthur Dungan, President

Articles featuring safe handling of chlorine and caustic materials.
5 Pages
Printed in 2 colors on matte stock

4415 **Clinical & Forensic Toxicology News**
1850 K St NW
Suite 625
Washington, DC 20006-2215

202-857-0717
800-892-1400; *Fax:* 202-887-5093;
www.aacc.org
Social Media: Facebook, Twitter, LinkedIn, YouTube

Greg rd Miller, President
Nancy Sasavage, Ph.D., Editor
Robert Dofour, Treasury

Online only newsletter provides practical and timely information on the clinical, forensic, technical, and regulatory issues faced by toxicology laboratories.

4416 **Clinical Laboratory Strategies**
1850 K St NW
Suite 625
Washington, DC 20006-2215

202-857-0717
800-892-1400; *Fax:* 202-887-5093;
www.aacc.org
Social Media: Facebook, Twitter, LinkedIn, YouTube

Richard Flaherty, VP
Penelope Jones, Director

Online newsletter for laboratory directors and managers gives strategic information on how to better manage the changes faced in jobs every day.

4417 **Composites and Adhesives Newsletter**
T/C Press
223 S Detroit Street
PO Box 36006
Los Angeles, CA 90036

323-938-7023; *Fax:* 323-938-6923
tcpress@msn.com

Mark Albert, Editor-In-Chief
Sherry Baranek, Senior Editor
Tom Beard, Senior VP
Lori Beckman, Managing Editor

News about composites and adhesives industry. Accepts very limited and selective advertising.
Cost: $190.00
20 Pages
Frequency: Quarterly
Circulation: 300
ISSN: 0888-1227
Founded in: 1984

4418 **Electronic Chemicals News**
Chemical Week Associates
2 Grand Central Tower
140 E. 45th St., 40th Floor
New York, NY 10017

212-884-9528; *Fax:* 212-884-9514
lyn.tattum@ihs.com; www.chemweek.com

Lyn Tattum, Publisher & Director
Natasha Alperowicz, Executive Editor

Written for and about the chemicals industry and contains industry developments, environmental news, new products, and financial and corporate briefs.
Cost: $699.00

4419 **Government Affairs Update**
American Association for Clinical Chemistry
1850 K St NW
Suite 625
Washington, DC 20006-2215

202-857-0717
800-892-1400; *Fax:* 202-887-5093;
www.ashrae.org
Social Media: Facebook, Twitter, LinkedIn, YouTube

Richard Flaherty, VP
Penelope Jones, Director

Online government affairs newsletter presents a comprehensive summary of legislative and government news that affect clinical labs and manufacturers.

4420 **ILTA Newsletter**
Independent Liquid Terminals Association
1444 I St Nw
Suite 400
Washington, DC 20005-6538

202-842-9200; *Fax:* 202-326-8660
info@ilta.org; www.ilta.org

E David Doane, President

International trade association representing bulk liquid terminal companies that store commercial liquids in aboveground storage tanks and transfer products to and from oceangoing tank ships, tank barges, pipelines, tank trucks, and tank rail cars.
Frequency: Monthly
Circulation: 1200
Founded in: 1974
Printed in 2 colors on matte stock

4421 **Inside R&D**
John Wiley & Sons

111 River St
Hoboken, NJ 07030-5790

201-748-6000; *Fax:* 201-748-6088
info@wiley.com; www.wiley.com

William J Pesce, CEO

Weekly service offering information about current research and development, concentrating on new and significant developments that create new products/markets in the near-term and this are valuable to a company's bottom line.
Cost: $790.00
6 Pages
Frequency: Weekly
Founded in: 1807
Mailing list available for rent

4422 **Langmuir: QTL Biosystems**
American Chemical Society
1322 Pouseo de Peralta
Santa Fe, NM 87501

505-989-1907; *Fax:* 505-989-1979
service@acs.org; www.pubs.acs.org

David Whitten PhD, Editor

Edited for an audience involved with high-vacuum surface chemistry and spectroscopy, heterogeneous catalysis, all aspects of interface chemistry involving fluid interfaces and disperse systems.
Frequency: BiWeekly
Circulation: 1,200

4423 **North American Catalysis Society Newsletter**
PO Box 80262
Wilmington, DE 19880-262

302-695-2488; *Fax:* 302-695-8347
michael.b.damore@usa.dupont.com;
www.nacatsoc.org

Michael B D Amore, Editor
John N Armor, President
Gary McVicker, VP

Fosters an interest in heterogeneous and homogeneous catalysis. Organizes national meetings. Members are chemists and chemical engineers engaged in the study and use of reactions involving catalysts.
Cost: $45.00
38448 Pages
Frequency: Monthly
Founded in: 1956
Mailing list available for rent: 3,500 names at $160 per M

4424 **Pine Chemicals Association Newsletter**
3350 Riverwood Parkway SE
Suite 1900
Atlanta, GA 30339

770-984-5340; *Fax:* 404-994-6267
wjones@pinechemicals.org;
www.pinechemicals.org

Walter L Jones, President/COO
Gary Reed, Chairman/Board of Directors

An association of producers, processors and consumers of pine chemicals. Promotes innovative, safe and environmentally responsible practices to assure a reliable supply of high quality products.
Frequency: Quarterly

4425 **SOCMA Newsletter**
Synthetic Organic Chemical Manufacturers Assn
1850 M St Nw
Suite 700
Washington, DC 20036-5803

202-721-4100; *Fax:* 202-296-8120
info@socma.com; www.socma.com

Joseph Acker, President
Vivian Diko, Executive Assistant & CEO
Liesa Brown, Editor/Marketing/Communications

Offers information on the organic chemical industry.
10 Pages
Frequency: Bi-monthly
Founded in: 1921

Magazines & Journals

4426 **AATCC Review Journal**
PO Box 12215
Research Triangle Park, NC 27709-2215

919-549-8141
800-360-5380; *Fax:* 919-549-8933
danielsj@aatcc.org; www.aatcc.org
Social Media: Facebook, Twitter, LinkedIn

John Daniels, Executive VP
Debra Hibbard, Executive Assistant
Charles E Gavin, Treasurer
Chris Shaw, Advertising Sales

Covers fibers to finished products, and chemical synthesis to retail practices.
3000 Members

4427 **AICHE Journal**
American Institute of Chemical Engineers
3 Park Ave
New York, NY 10016-5991

212-591-7338
800-242-4363; *Fax:* 212-591-8888
CustomerService@aiche.org; www.aiche.org
Social Media: Facebook, Twitter, LinkedIn

June Wispelway, Executive Director
Steve Smith, Publications Director
Bette Lawler, Director of Operations
Neil Yeoman, Treasurer

Serves as a journal emcompassing data and results of the latest information in significant research and trends in the field.
Cost: $1250.00
Frequency: Monthly
ISSN: 0001-1541
Founded in: 1908

4428 **Accounts of Chemical Research**
American Chemical Society
1155 16th St NW
Suite 600
Washington, DC 20036-4892

202-872-4600
800-227-5558; *Fax:* 202-872-4615
service@acs.org; www.acs.org

Madeleine Jacobs, CEO

Chemical research and statistical information.
Cost: $526.00
Frequency: Monthly
Circulation: 159,000
Founded in: 1968

4429 **Advanced Coatings and Surface Technology**
605 3rd Avenue
9th Floor
New York, NY 10158

212-850-6824; *Fax:* 212-850-8643

4430 **American Laboratory**
International Scientific Communications
395 Oyster Pint Blvd.
#321
South San Francisco, CA 94080

650-243-5600
info@americanlaboratory.com;
www.americanlaboratory.com

Brian Howard, Editor-In-Chief
Robert G Sweeny, Publisher
Donna Frankel, Direcetor Of Editorial
Susan Messinger, Managing Editor

American Laboratory serves industry, university, government, independent and foundation research laboratories.
50 Pages
Frequency: Monthly
Circulation: 91611
ISSN: 0044-7749
Founded in: 1969
Printed in 4 colors on glossy stock

4431 **An Energy Efficient Solution**
Alliance for Responsible Atmoshperic Policy
2111 Wilson Blvd
Suite 850
Arlington, VA 22201-3001

703-243-0344; *Fax:* 703-243-2874
info@arap.org; www.arap.org

David Stirpe, Executive Director

4432 **Asia Pacific Chemicals**
Reed Chemical Publications
360 Park Avenue South
10th Floor
New York, NY 10010

713-525-2613
888-525-3255
jlucas@chemexpo.com;
www.reedchemicals.com

Stanley F Reed
Bernard Petersen, Sales Manager
Karen Yanard, Sales Executive
Alan Taylor, Editor

4433 **Asian Chemical News**
Reed Chemical Publications
360 Park Avenue South
10th Floor
New York, NY 10010

212-791-4208
888-525-3255
csc@icis.com; www.reedchemicals.com

Stanley F Reed
Bernard Petersen, Sales Manager
Karen Yanard, Sales Executive
Alan Taylor, Editor

4434 **CPI Purchasing**
Reed Business Information
2000 Clearwater Dr
Oak Brook, IL 60523-8809

630-574-0825; *Fax:* 630-288-8781
k.doyle@reedbusiness.com;
www.reedbusiness.com

Jeff Greisch, President
Kathy Doyle, Publisher

Trade magazine for purchasing professionals in the chemical/process industry. Accepts advertising.
Cost: $74.95
100 Pages
Circulation: 95078
Founded in: 1983

4435 **Cereal Chemistry**
AACC International

3340 Pilot Knob Rd
St. Paul, MN 55121-2055

651-454-7250
800-328-7560; *Fax:* 651-454-0766
aacc@scisoc.org; www.aaccnet.org

Les Copeland, Editor-In-Chief
F. William Collins, Senior Editor
Ian Batey, Associate Editor

Cereal chemistry explores raw materials, processes and products utulizing cereal.
Cost: $79.00
Frequency: Bi-Monthly
ISSN: 0009-0352

4436 Chemical Engineering
Chemical Week Associates
2 Grand Central Tower
140 East 45th Street,40th Floor
New York, NY 10017

212-884-9528; *Fax:* 212-884-9514
ltattum@chemweek.com; www.chemweek.com

Lyn Tattum, Publisher/Director
Robert Westervelt, Editor-In-Chief

Highlights include a calendar of related trade shows, new products listings, operations and maintenance techniques and marketing services ideas.
Cost: $59.00
Frequency: Monthly
Circulation: 69000
ISSN: 0009-2460
Founded in: 1902
Printed in 4 colors on glossy stock

4437 Chemical Engineering Progress
American Institute of Chemical Engineers
3 Park Ave
New York, NY 10016-5991

203-702-7660
800-242-4363; *Fax:* 203-775-5177
CustomerService@aiche.org; www.aiche.org

June Wispelwey, Executive Director
Marty Clancy, Director Membership/Cust. Service

Offers updated information for chemical engineers.
Cost: $245.00
Frequency: Quarterly
Founded in: 1908

4438 Chemical Equipment
Reed Business Information
301 Gibraltar Drive
PO Box 650
Morris Plains, NJ 07950-650

973-920-7000; *Fax:* 973-539-3476
privacymanager@reedbusiness.com;
www.reedbusiness.com

Bud Ramsey, Publisher
Geoffery Bridgman, Editor
Gerard Van de Aast, CEO/President

Chemical Equipment is for engineers, plant management personnel, maintenance engineering and others concerned with design, building, engineering, operating and maintaining chemical process plants.
Frequency: Monthly
Circulation: 106032
Founded in: 1959

4439 Chemical Equipment Literature Review
Reed Business Information
St 600
Rockaway
New Jersey, NJ 07866

973-920-7000
800-222-0289; *Fax:* 973-920-7531
plundy@reedbusiness.com;
www.reedbusiness.com

Geoff Bridgman, Editor
Gail Kirberger, Circulation Manager
Patrick Lundy, Publisher

Covers reviews of new catalogs and brochures on products for the chemical industry.
8 Pages
Frequency: Monthly
Circulation: 106038
Founded in: 1985

4440 Chemical Heritage
Chemical Heritage Foundation
315 Chestnut St
Philadelphia, PA 19106-2793

215-925-2222; *Fax:* 215-925-1954
info@chemheritage.org;
www.chemheritage.org

Michal Meyer, Editor

Dedicated to sharing the story chemistry and related sciences, technologies, and industries.
48 Pages
Circulation: 25000
ISSN: 0736-4555

4441 Chemical Intelligencer
Springer Verlag
233 Spring St
Suite 6
New York, NY 10013-1578

212-460-1500
800-777-4643; *Fax:* 212-460-1575
serviceny@springer.com; www.springer.com

William Curtis, President

Written for the scientist interested in the history and culture of chemistry. Includes articles and essays that develop and comment on the current directions and concerns in chemistry, new discoveries and experiments as well as present trends and opportunities in chemistry, philosophy and education.
Cost: $79.00
Frequency: Quarterly
Circulation: 1,000

4442 Chemical Management Review
Reed Chemical Publications
2 Wall St
26th Floor, Suite 13
New York, NY 10005-2044

212-732-3200; *Fax:* 212-791-4311
helga.tilton@chemicalmarketreporter.com;
www.reedchemicals.com

Stanley F Reed
Helga Tilton, Editor
Keith Jones, CEO/President
Jane Burgess, Marketing

Provides information for senior managers in the chemical industry and other industrial markets.
Cost: $195.00
Frequency: Monthly
Founded in: 1871
Printed in 4 colors on glossy stock

4443 Chemical Market Reporter
Schnell Publishing Company
2 Rector St
26th Floor
New York, NY 10006-1819

212-791-4267; *Fax:* 212-791-4321
editor@chemexpo.com; www.chemexpo.com

James Hannan, Publisher
Helga Tilton, Editor in Chief

Regular issue highlights include news of the week, coverage of pertinent industry trade shows/meetings, a review of new materials, and periodic insight reports on segments of the industry.
Cost: $109.00
Frequency: Weekly
Circulation: 14714

4444 Chemical Processing
Putman Media
1501 East Woodfield Road
Suite 400N
Schaumburg, IL 60173

630-467-1300; *Fax:* 630-467-0197
webmaster@putman.net;
www.putmanmedia.com

John Cappelletti, President & CEO
Tony D'Avino, Vice President & Publisher
Mark Rosenzweig, Editor-In-Chief
Amanda Joshi, Managing Editor

Carries technical overview and case history articles presented in a problem-solving environment geared to operations, engineering and R&D management. Topics include instrumentation, pumping, corrosion, heat transfer, mixing and energy conservation. Accepts advertising.
60 Pages
Frequency: Monthly
Circulation: 55000
ISSN: 0009-2630
Founded in: 1938
*Mailing list available for rent*at $130 per M
Printed in 4 colors

4445 Chemical Times & Trends
Allen Press
900 17th St NW
Washington, DC 20006-2106

202-872-8110; *Fax:* 202-872-8114
info@cspa.org; www.cspa.org

Christopher Cathcart, President
Keith Fulk, Vice President & Controller

Editorial focus emphasizes trends in legislation, industry events, packaging topics, and marketing concepts.
Cost: $27.00
Frequency: Quarterly
Circulation: 7000
Founded in: 1935

4446 Chemist
American Institute of Chemists
315 Chestnut St
Suite 420
Philadelphia, PA 19106-2702

215-873-8224; *Fax:* 215-925-1954
info@theaic.org; www.theaic.org

Davidah Manuta, President
Ray Mcafel, President-Elect
Jerry d Jasinski, Chair

Topics of professional, economic, social and legislative interest to individual chemists or chemical engineers.
Cost: $35.00
32 Pages
Frequency: Quarterly
Circulation: 5000
Founded in: 1923

4447 Chemistry Research in Technology
American Chemical Society
1155 16th St NW
Suite 600
Washington, DC 20036-4892

202-872-4600
800-227-5558; *Fax:* 202-872-4615
service@acs.org; www.acs.org

Madeleine Jacobs, CEO/Executive Director
Elizabeth Zubritsky, Manager

Information and research summaries of the latest in the chemical industry.
Cost: $49.00
Frequency: 1 Year 3 Issues
Founded in: 1876

4448 **Clinical Chemistry**
1850 K St NW
Suite 625
Washington, DC 20006-2215

202-857-0717
800-892-1400; *Fax:* 202-887-5093;
www.aacc.org
Social Media: Facebook, Twitter, LinkedIn, YouTube

Nadar Rifai, Editor-In-Chief
Tom Annesley, Deputy Editor
James Boyd, Deputy Editor

The leading forum for peer-reviewed, original research on innovative practices in today's clinical laboratory.

4449 **Clinical Laboratory News**
1850 K St NW
Suite 625
Washington, DC 20006-2215

202-857-0717
800-892-1400; *Fax:* 202-887-5093;
www.aacc.org
Social Media: Facebook, Twitter, LinkedIn, YouTube

Robert Christenson, President
Dennis Dietzen, Director
Elizabeth Frank, Secretary

News magazine that is the authoritative source for timely analysis of issues and trends affecting clinical laboratorians and clinical laboratories.
Founded in: 1948

4450 **Coatings World**
Rodman Publishing
70 Hilltop Rd
3rd Floor, Suite 3000
Ramsey, NJ 07446-1150

201-825-2552; *Fax:* 201-825-0553
info@rodpub.com;
www.nutraceuticalsworld.com

Rodman Zilenziger Jr, President
Matt Montgomery, VP

Cutting edge technical information and the most advanced and pertinent management and distribution techniques.
Frequency: 10 issues per y
Circulation: 17000
Founded in: 1964

4451 **Combustion and Flame**
Combustion Institute
5001 Baum Blvd.
Suite 635
Pittsburgh, PA 15213-1851

412-687-1366; *Fax:* 412-687-0340
office@combustioninstitute.org;
www.combustioninstitute.org

Barbara Waronek, Executive Administrator
Prof. Katherine Kohs-Hosinghaus, President
Derek Dunn-Rankin, Treasurer

A monthly publication that focuses on combustion phenomena and related topics.
6000 Members
Frequency: Monthly
Founded in: 1954

4452 **Compoundings Magazine**
Independent Lubricant Manufacturers Association
651 S Washington Street
Alexandria, VA 22314

703-684-5574; *Fax:* 703-836-8503
ilma@ilma.org; www.ilma.org

Tom Osborne, Editor
Martha Jolkovski, Director Publications & Advertising
Carla Mangone, Managing Editor

Association and marketing news, meetings and programs, as well as employment and business opportunities to the US and international independent lubricant industry.
Cost: $150.00
Frequency: Monthly
Circulation: 2050
ISSN: 1042-508X
Founded in: 1948
Printed in 4 colors on glossy stock

4453 **Energy Process**
American Institute of Chemical Engineers
3 Park Ave
New York, NY 10016-5991

212-591-7338
800-242-4363; *Fax:* 212-591-8888;
www.aiche.org

John Sofranko, Executive Director

Offers updated information for chemical engineers.
Cost: $20.00
Frequency: Quarterly

4454 **European Chemical News**
Reed Chemical Publications
Wall St
26th Floor, Suite 13
New York, NY 10005-2044

212-732-3200; *Fax:* 212-791-4311
jonathan.sismey@icis.com;
www.europeanchemicalnews.com

Stanley F Reed
Simon Platt, Director
Christopher Flook, Managing Director
Cost: $711.00
Frequency: Weekly
Circulation: 14112

4455 **European Journal of Clinical Chemistry and Clinical Biochemistry**
Walter De Gruyter
200 Saw Mill Road
Hawthorne, NY 1052

journalseek.net/

Water De Gruyler, Editor

Up-to-date information on the chemistry industry.
Frequency: Monthly

4456 **HAPPI Household and Personal Products Industry**
Rodman Publishing
70 Hilltop Rd
3rd Floor
Ramsey, NJ 07446-1150

201-825-2552; *Fax:* 201-825-0553
info@rodpub.com;
www.nutraceuticalsworld.com

Rodman Zilenziger Jr, President
Matt Montgomery, VP

Highlights current developments, marketing, production, formulations, technical innovations, packaging, and management problems. Includes in-depth news on developments abroad as well as in the United States.
Cost: $52.00
Frequency: Monthly
Circulation: 140000
Founded in: 1964

4457 **I&EC Research**
American Chemical Society
1155 16th St NW
Suite 600
Washington, DC 20036-4892

202-872-4600
800-227-5558; *Fax:* 202-872-4615
service@acs.org; www.acs.org

Madeleine Jacobs, CEO/Executive Director

Offers information and statistical updates for chemists.
Circulation: 4600
Founded in: 1876

4458 **IHS Chemical Week**
2 Grand Central Tower
140 E 45th St., 40th Fl.
New York, NY 10017

212-884-9528; *Fax:* 212-884-9514;
www.chemweek.com
Social Media: Facebook, Twitter, LinkedIn, YouTube

Lyn Tattum, Publisher
Robert Westervelt, Editor-in-chief

News and analysis from the chemical, petrochemical and specialty chemical industries.

4459 **Industrial & Engineering Chemistry Research**
American Chemical Society
1155 16th St NW
Suite 600
Washington, DC 20036-4892

202-872-4600
800-227-5558; *Fax:* 202-872-4615
help@acs.org; www.acs.org

Madeleine Jacobs, CEO/Executive Director
Judith Benham, Chair
Elizabeth Zubritsky, Manager

Features fundamental research, design methods, process design and development, product research and development for chemists and chemical engineers.
Circulation: 4600
Founded in: 1876

4460 **Inform**
American Oil Chemists' Society
2710 S Boulder
Urbana, IL 61802-6996

217-359-2344; *Fax:* 217-351-8091
keine@aocs.org; www.aocs.org

Lori Stewart, Publications Director
Kimmy Farris, Production Editor
Kethy Heine, Managing Editor
Patrick Donnelly, CEO

A member benefit that provides international news on fats, oils, surfactants, detergents, and related materials.
Cost: $175.00
100 Pages
Frequency: Monthly
Circulation: 4500
ISSN: 0897-8026
Founded in: 1990
Printed in 4 colors on glossy stock

4461 **International Laboratory**
International Scientific Communications
PO Box 870
Shelton, CT 06484-0870

203-926-9300; *Fax:* 203-926-9310
webmaster@iscpubs.com; www.iscpubs.com/

Brian Howard, Publisher
Robert G Sweeney, Publisher

International Laboratory serves the industry, universities, government, independent and foundation research laboratories.
50 Pages
Circulation: 50036
ISSN: 0010-2164
Founded in: 1971
Printed in 4 colors on glossy stock

4462 **International Laboratory Pacific Rim Edition**
International Scientific Communications

PO Box 870
Shelton, CT 06484-0870

203-926-9300; *Fax:* 203-926-9310
webmaster@iscpubs.com; www.iscpubs.com

Brian Howard, Publisher
Robert G Sweeney, Publisher

Edited for chemists and biologists throughout Far East Asia and Australia who have a professional interest in various aspects of modern laboratory practice and basic research.
40 Pages
Founded in: 1986

4463 **Journal of AOAC International**
AOAC International
481 N Frederick Ave
Suite 500
Gaithersburg, MD 20877-2450

301-924-7078
800-379-2622; *Fax:* 301-924-7089
aoac@aoac.org; www.aoac.org

James Bradford, Executive Director

Publishes fully refereed contributed papers in the fields of chemical and biological analysis: on original research on new techniques and applications, collaborative studies, authentic data of composition, studies leading to method development, meeting symposia, newly adopted AOAC approved methods and invited reviews.
Cost: $98.00

4464 **Journal of Analytical Toxicology**
Preston Publications
6600 W Touhy Ave
PO Box 48312
Niles, IL 60714-4516

847-647-2900; *Fax:* 847-647-1155;
www.prestonpub.com

Tinsley Preston, Owner
Dr. Bruce A. Goldberger, Editor
Maria Tamacho, Circulation Manager

An international publication for toxicologists, pathologists, analytical chemists, researchers, educators and others. Dedicated to the isolation, indentification, and quantification of potentially toxic substances. Emphasis is on the practical applications for use in clinical, forensic, industrial, and other toxicology laboratories, drug abuse testing, therapeutic drug monitoring, and environmental pollution. Includes new products and litrature, meetings and short courses.
Cost: $475.00
Frequency: 8 issues per ye
Circulation: 1148
Founded in: 1977
Mailing list available for rent: 9939 names at $125 per M

4465 **Journal of Biological Chemistry**
9650 Rockville Pike
Suite 300
Bethesda, MD 20814-3999

301-530-7150; *Fax:* 301-634-7126
publicaffairs@asbmb.org; www.asbmb.org

Herbert Taber, Editor
Barbara Gordon, Executive Director

Features research papers on biochemistry and molecular biology and other articles of interest to the professional.
Frequency: TriAnnual

4466 **Journal of Chemical Education**
Division of Chemical Education
Department of Chemistry
University of Georgia
Athens, GA 30602-2556

706-542-6559; *Fax:* 706-542-9454
norbert-pienta@jce.acs.org;
www.pubs.acs.orgorg
Social Media: Facebook, Twitter

Norbert J Oienta, Editor-in-Chief
Renee S. Cole, Associate Editor

Provides information about and examples of teaching techniques for classroom and laboratory, curricular innovations, chemistry content, and chemical education research.
Cost: $45.00
136 Pages
Frequency: Monthly
ISSN: 0021-9584
Founded in: 1924
Printed in on glossy stock

4467 **Journal of Chemical Information & Computer Sciences**
American Chemical Society
1155 16th St NW
Suite 600
Washington, DC 20036-4892

202-872-4600
800-227-5558; *Fax:* 202-872-4615
service@acs.org; www.acs.org

Madeleine Jacobs, CEO/Executive Director
George A. Milne, Editor

Offers the latest technological information and news directed at the chemical industry.
Cost: $27.00
Frequency: Bi-Monthly

4468 **Journal of Chemical Physics**
American Institute of Physics
2 Huntington Quadrangle
Suite 101
Melville, NY 11747-4502

516-576-2200; *Fax:* 516-349-7669
jcp@aip.org; www.aip.org

H. Frederick Dylia, Executive Director/CEO
Darlene Walters, Senior VP
John Haynes, VP Publishing

Targets both chemists and physicists involved in research and applications of chemical physics technology.
Frequency: Weekly
Circulation: 5,000

4469 **Journal of Chemical and Engineering Data**
American Chemical Society
180 Fitzpatrick Hall
University of Notre Dame
Notre Dame, IN 46556

574-631-1149; *Fax:* 516-349-9704
squarles@aip.org; www.aip.org

Joan F. Brennecke, Ph.D., Editor
Marc Brodsky, CEO

Offers the latest updates and new information in the chemical industry.
Cost: $458.00
Frequency: Weekly
Circulation: 5000
Founded in: 1931

4470 **Journal of Chromatographic Science**
Preston Publications
6600 W Touhy Ave
Niles, IL 60714-4516

847-647-2900; *Fax:* 847-647-1155
tpreston@prestonpub.com;
www.prestonpub.com

Tinsley Preston, Owner
Kevin Bailey, Managing Editor
Janice Gordon, Director Marketing

An international publication for scientists, analytical chemists, researchers, educators, and other allied to the field. Provides in depth information about analytical techniques, applications, sample preparation methods, systems problem solving, etc. Articles cover more practical information on all types of separations—gas, liquid, thin layer, supercritical fluid, electrophoresis, spectrometry, hyphenated methods, etc. any other single source. Also problem solving/troubleshooting answers.
Cost: $405.00
Frequency: Monthly
Circulation: 1000
Founded in: 1961

4471 **Journal of Colloid & Interface Science**
Academic Press
525 B St
Suite 1900
San Diego, CA 92101-4401

619-235-6336
800-321-5068; *Fax:* 619-699-6280;
www.aceparking.com

D.T. Wasan, Editor-in-Chief
Claudia Romas, Publisher

Presents chemical and physiochemical aspects of theory and practice of colloids.
Cost: $883.00
Frequency: Monthly
Circulation: 2000
Founded in: 1885

4472 **Journal of Medicinal Chemistry**
American Chemical Society
1155 16th St NW
Suite 600
Washington, DC 20036-4892

202-872-4600
800-227-5558; *Fax:* 202-872-4615
service@acs.org; www.acs.org

Madeleine Jacobs, CEO/Executive Director

Information on the chemistry industry, dealing with aspects directly pertaining to the medical profession.
Founded in: 1876

4473 **Journal of Organic Chemistry**
American Chemical Society
1155 16th St NW
Washington, DC 20036-4892

202-872-4600
800-227-5558; *Fax:* 202-872-4615
service@acs.org; www.acs.org

Madeleine Jacobs, CEO/Executive Director

Areas emphasized are the multiple facets of organic reactions, natural products, studies of mechanism, theoretical organic chemistry and the various aspects of spectroscopy related to organic chemistry.
Cost: $1260.00
Frequency: BiWeekly
Circulation: 8,500

4474 **Journal of Physical Chemistry**
American Chemical Society
GA Institute of Technology
Boggs Building
Atlanta, GA 30332

404-894-0293
800-227-5558; *Fax:* 404-894-0294;
www.pubs.acs.org

Mostafa A El-Sayed, Editor

Reports on both experimental and theoretical research dealing with the fundamental aspects of physical chemistry and chemical physics.
Frequency: Weekly
Circulation: 3774

4475 **Journal of Society of Cosmetic Chemists**
Society of Cosmetic Chemists

120 Wall St
Suite 2400
New York, NY 10005-4088

212-668-1500; *Fax:* 212-668-1504;
www.scconline.org

Theresa Cesario, Administrator
Mindy Goldstein, Journal Editor
Doreen Scelso, Publication Coordinator

Features highlight new products, processing techniques, safety issues, and pharmacological features.
Cost: $200.00
Circulation: 4200
Founded in: 1945

4476 **Journal of Surfactants and Detergents**
AOCS Press
12024 Vista Parke Drive
PO Box 200135
Austin, TX 78720-0135

512-331-2441; *Fax:* 512-331-2387

Michael F Cox, Editor-in-Chief

Reports on the development and performance of surfactants in all areas, from household detergents to industrial uses, as well as on the development and manufacture of other detergent ingredients and their formulation into finished products.
Cost: $85.00
Frequency: Quarterly
Circulation: 1,500

4477 **Journal of the American Chemical Society**
American Chemical Society
1155 16th St NW
Suite 600
Washington, DC 20036-4892

202-872-4600
800-227-5558; *Fax:* 202-872-4615
service@acs.org; www.acs.org

Madeleine Jacobs, CEO/Esecutive Director

Association news, member information and chemical industry information.
Cost: $125.00
Frequency: Weekly

4478 **Journal of the American Leather Chemists Association**
American Leather Chemists Association
1314 50th Street
Suite 103
Lubbock, TX 79412

806-744-1798; *Fax:* 806-744-1785
alca@leatherchemists.org;
www.leatherchemists.org

Carol Adcock, Executive Secretary
Cost: $175.00
Frequency: Monthly
Circulation: 500

4479 **Journal of the Electrochemical Society**
Electrochemical Society
65 S Main St
Building D
Pennington, NJ 08534-2839

609-737-1902; *Fax:* 609-737-2743
ecs@electrochem.org; www.electrochem.org

Roque J. Calvo, Executive Director
Annie Goedkoop, Publications Director
Paul B. Cooper, Editorial Manager

Leader in the field of solid-state and electrochemical science and technology. This peer-reviewed journal publishes an average of 450 pages of 70 articles each month. Articles are posted online, with a monthly paper edition following electronic publication. The ECS membership benefits package includes access to the electronic edition of this journal.
450 Pages
Frequency: Monthly
ISSN: 0013-4651

4480 **LCGC North America**
Advanstar Communications
Woodbridge Corporate Plaza
485 Route 1 S, Building F
Iselin, NJ 08830

732-225-9500; *Fax:* 732-225-0211
lcgcedit@lcgcmag.com;
www.lcgcmag.com/lcgc/
Social Media: Facebook

David Esola, VP/General Manager
Michael Tessalone, Group Publisher
Tria Deibert, Marketing Director

Includes product and literature reports along with meeting and seminar listings.
Cost: $67.00
100 Pages
Frequency: Monthly
Circulation: 56000
Founded in: 1987
Mailing list available for rent: 47,543 names at $155 per M
Printed in 4 colors on glossy stock

4481 **Laboratorio y Analisis**
Keller International Publishing Corporation
150 Great Neck Rd
Suite 400
Great Neck, NY 11021-3309

516-829-9210; *Fax:* 516-829-9306;
www.supplychainbrain.com

Terry Beirne, Publisher
Bryan DeLuca, Editor
Jerry Keller, President
Mary Chavez, Director of Sales

4482 **Lipids**
American Oil Chemists' Society
2710 S Boulder
Urbana, IL 61802-6996

217-359-2344; *Fax:* 217-351-8091
general@aocs.org; www.aocs.org

Jody Schonfeld, Publications Director
Pam Landman, Journals Coordinator
Kimmy Farris, Production Editor
Lori Stewart, Books and Publications
Jenna Tatar, Customer Service

Scientific journal features full-length original research articles, short communications, methods papers and review articles on timely topics. All papers are meticulously peer-reviewed and edited by some of the foremost experts in their respective fields.
Cost: $461.00
Frequency: Monthly
Circulation: 2400
Founded in: 1966

4483 **Nucleus**
American Chemical Society — Northeast
12 Corcoran Ave.
Burlington, MA 01803

800-872-2054
800-872-2054; *Fax:* 508-653-6329
webmaster@nesacs.org; www.nesacs.org

Vincent J Gale, Editor
Amy Tapper, Secretary
Anna Singer, Administrative Secretary
Liming Shao, Chair

Content includes local meeting announcements; news of members of the Northeastern Section, American Chemical Society; historical articles; book reviews; calender of events covering all chemistry disciplines in the area. No Company or product information is published. Advertising is accepted.
Frequency: Monthly
Circulation: 7500
Founded in: 1888
Printed in 2 colors on matte stock

4484 **PaintSquare**
PaintSquare
2100 Wharton Street
Suite 310
Pittsburgh, PA 15203

412-431-8300
800-837-8303; *Fax:* 412-431-5428
webmaster@paintsquare.com;
www.paintsquare.com
Social Media: Facebook, Twitter

Harold Hower, Publisher

Mission is to make PaintSquare a viable and useful tool to make your job easier and more efficient.
Founded in: 2002

4485 **Performance Chemicals Europe**
Reed Chemical Publications
Quadrant House, The Quadrant
Sutton, Surrey, UK SM2 5AS

212-732-3200
+44 20 8652 3335; *Fax:* 212-791-4311; *Fax:* +44 20 8652 3375
csc@icis.com;
www.performancechemicals.com

Stanley F Reed
Neil Sinclair, Director
Simon Platt, Director
Christopher Flook, Managing Director
Cost: $711.00

4486 **PetroChemical News**
William F Bland Co.
709 Turmeric Ln
Durham, NC 27713-3103

919-544-1717; *Fax:* 919-544-1999
pcn@petrochemical-news.com;
www.petrochemical-news.com

Susan Kensil, Editor
Michelle Zard, Circulation Director

Covers new plants and projects, awards of contracts, mergers and acquisitions, current technology, and related government actions.
Cost: $807.00
Frequency: Weekly
Founded in: 1963

4487 **Pine Chemicals Review**
Kriedt Enterprises
3803 Cleveland Ave.
New Orleans, LA 70119

504-482-3914; *Fax:* 504-482-4205
info@pinechemicalsreview.com;
www.pinechemicalsreview.com

Romney Richard, Publisher
Charley Richard, Editor

Pine Chemicals Review is the only trade journal covering pine and pulp chemicals within the naval stores industry. It is directed to producers and processors of pine gum and wood naval stores; pulp chemicals and pine derivative chemicals for the adhesives, coatings, printing ink, paper chemicals, flavor and fragrance.
Cost: $110.00
24 Pages
Frequency: Monthly
Circulation: 300
ISSN: 0164-4580
Founded in: 1890
Printed in 4 colors on glossy stock

4488 **Polyurethane Professional Development Program**
Center for the Polyurethanes Industry

1300 Wilson Blvd
Suite 990
Arlington, VA 22209-2307

703-841-0012; *Fax:* 703-841-0525;
www.polyurethane.org
Social Media: Facebook, Twitter

Calvin Dooley, President
Frequency: Yearly

4489 **Powder and Bulk Engineering**
CSC Publishing
1155 Northland Dr
St Paul, MN 55120-1288

651-287-5600; *Fax:* 651-287-5650;
www.cscpublishinginc.com

Richard R Cress, Publisher
Terry O'Neill, Editor
Katherine Davich, Senior Editor

Featured editorial includes technical articles, case histories, test centers, product news and literature, and industry news items.
Frequency: Monthly
Circulation: 35379
Founded in: 1986

4490 **Powder/Bulk Solids**
Reed Business Information
301 Gibraltar Drive
Box 650
Morris Plains, NJ 07950

973-920-7000; *Fax:* 973-539-3476
scrow@reedbusiness.com;
www.reedbusiness.com

Mark Kelsey, CEO

Equipment and technological news for dry particulates processors.
Cost: $74.95
Frequency: Monthly
Circulation: 45,070
ISSN: 8740-6653
Founded in: 1993

4491 **Proceedings of The Combustion Institute**
Combustion Institute
5001 Baum Blvd.
Suite 635
Pittsburgh, PA 15213-1851

412-687-1366; *Fax:* 412-687-0340
office@combustioninstitute.org;
www.combustioninstitute.org

Barbara Waronek, Executive Administrator
Prof. Katharina Kohse-Hoinghaus, President
Marcus Alden, VP
Derek Dunn-Rankin, Treasurer

Contains forefront contributions in fundamentals and applications of combustion science.
6000 Members
Frequency: Biennially
Founded in: 1954

4492 **Processing**
Putman Media Company
555 W Pierce Rd
Suite 301
Itasca, IL 60143-2626

630-467-1300; *Fax:* 630-467-0197
webmaster@putman.net; www.putman.net

John Cappelletti, CEO
Mike Bacidore, Editor-in-Chief
Tonia Becker, Publisher

Product areas covered include mechanical and pneumatic conveying, material handling, packaging, and storage. Each issue includes a specific editorial spotlight, product showcase and new literature section.
Frequency: Monthly
Circulation: 95035
ISSN: 0896-8659
Founded in: 1972
Printed in 4 colors

4493 **Quimica Latinoamericana**
Reed Chemical Publications
2 Wall St
26th Floor, Suite 13
New York, NY 10005-2044

212-732-3200
888-525-3255; *Fax:* 212-791-4311
cnihelp@cnionline.com;
www.quimicalatinoamericana.com/

Stanley F Reed
Christopher Flook, Publisher
Neil Sinclair, Managing Editor
Jeff Evans, CEO/President
Jing Huang, Project Manager

Publication of Latin American petrochemicals.

4494 **Soap/Cosmetics/Chemical Specialties**
Cygnus Publishing
445 Broad Hollow Road
Suite 21
Melville, NY 11747-3601
631-845-2700
800-308-6397; *Fax:* 631-845-2798
soap@erols.com; www.cygnuspub.com

Anita Hipius Shaw, Editor-in-Chief
Paul Bonaiuto, CFO
Kathy Scott, Director of Public Relations
John French, CEO

Includes tips on general management, purchasing, as well as new products and market trends, personal care, industrial and institutional markets, especially as they affect chemical, packing and equipment suppliers and their R and D professionals.
Cost: $30.00
Frequency: Monthly
Circulation: 6,491

4495 **Spray Technology & Marketing**
Industry Publications
3621 Hill Rd
Parsippany, NJ 07054-1001

973-331-9545; *Fax:* 973-331-9547
info@spraytechnology.com;
www.spraytechnology.com

Cynthia Hundley, Publisher
Michael L. SanGiovanni, Executive Editor
Shirleen Dorman, Editor

Features include articles on marketers, chemical and fragrance manufacturers and components manufacturers.
Frequency: Monthly
Circulation: 6,491
ISSN: 1055-2340
Founded in: 1954
Mailing list available for rent
Printed in 4 colors on glossy stock

4496 **Sulfuric Acid Today**
PO Box 3502
Covington, LA 70434

985-893-9692; *Fax:* 985-893-8693;
www.h2so4today.com

Earl B Heard, Publisher

Editorial covers industry news, engineering, technology and upcoming events.
Cost: $39.00
Frequency: SemiAnnual
Circulation: 5,000

4497 **Today's Chemist at Work**
American Chemical Society
1155 16th St NW
Washington, DC 20036-4892

202-872-4600
800-227-5558; *Fax:* 202-872-4615
service@acs.org; www.acs.org

Madeleine Jacobs, CEO/Executive Director
William F Carroll, VP

Covers reports on materials, new products, chemical education, analytical chemistry and instrumentation.
Cost: $18.00
Frequency: Monthly
Circulation: 120000
Founded in: 1876

Trade Shows

4498 **AACC International Annual Meeting**
3340 Pilot Knob Road
St. Paul, MN 55121-2055

651-454-7250
800-328-7560; *Fax:* 651-454-0766
aacc@scisoc.org; www.aaccnet.org
Social Media: Facebook, Twitter, LinkedIn

Robert L. Cracknell, President
Lydia Tooker Midness, Chair
Laura M. Hansen, President-Elect
Dave L. Braun, Treasurer

Formerly the American Association of Cereal Chemists, the AACC meeting offers the chance to come together, network with peers, discuss critical issues in the science and discover the methods of others.
Frequency: Annual/October

4499 **ACOS Annual Meeting & Expo**
American Oil Chemists' Society
2710 S Boulder
Urbana, IL 61802-6996

217-693-4813; *Fax:* 217-351-8091
meetings@aocs.org; www.aocs.org

Greg Hatfield, General Chairperson
Doreen Berning, Registration
Jeff Newman, Meeting Management/Logistics

The premier global science and business forum on fats, oils, surfactants, lipids and related materials. Includes oral and poster presentations, short courses, and exhibit, and networking with more than 1,600 colleagues from 60 countries.
2000 Attendees
Frequency: Annual/April-May

4500 **ACS Mid-Atlantic Regional Meeting**
American Chemical Society
1155 Sixteenth Street, NW
Washington, DC 20036

202-872-4600
800-227-5558; *Fax:* 989-835-8356
service@acs.org; www.acs.org

Madeleine Jacobs, CEO/Executive Director

Attend poster sessions, symposia and workshops to experience the most exciting and cutting-edge research in the field of chemistry.
1M Attendees
Frequency: Annual/Spring

4501 **ACS Spring & Fall National Meeting & Expos**
American Chemical Society
1155 Sixteenth Street NW
Washington, DC 20036

202-872-4600
800-227-5558; *Fax:* 202-776-8044
conf_vendorrel@acs.org; www.acs.org

Madeleine Jacobs, CEO/Executive Director

Symposia, poster sessions, and workshops around cutting-edge chemistry research.
1.2M Attendees
Frequency: Biennial

4502 ALCA Annual Meeting
American Leather Chemists Association
1314 50th Street
Suite 103
Lubbock, TX 79412

806-744-1798; *Fax:* 806-744-1785
alca@leatherchemists.org;
www.leatherchemists.org

Carol Adcock, Executive Secretary
100 Attendees

4503 AOAC International Annual Meeting & Expo
AOAC International
481 North Frederick Avenue
Suite 500
Gaithersburg, MD 20877-2417

301-924-7077
800-379-2622; *Fax:* 301-924-7089
aoac@aoac.org; www.aoac.org
Social Media: Facebook, LinkedIn

Lauren Chelf, Director, Meetings & Exposition

The meeting offers a diverse program of symposia, workshops, and poster and scientific sessions. Specific educational tracks are offered for analytical chemists, microbiologists, laboratory managers, and other laboratory personnel.
Frequency: August

4504 ASBC Annual Meeting
American Society of Brewing Chemists
3340 Pilot Knob Road
Saint Paul, MN 55121

651-454-7250
800-328-7560; *Fax:* 651-454-0766;
www.meeting.asbcnet.org
Social Media: Facebook, Twitter

Charles F. Strachan, President
Steven Nelson, Executive Officer
Karen Cummings, Director of Publications
A. Hope, VP Operations
300 Attendees
Frequency: June/Non-Members Fee
Founded in: 1934

4505 Agricultural Retailers Association Convention and Expo
Agricultural Retailers Association
1156 15th Street
Suite 500
Washington, DC 20005

202-457-0825
800-844-4900; *Fax:* 314-567-6808;
www.aradc.org

Daren Coppock, President/CEO
Richard Gupton, Sr. VP, Public Policy
Michelle Hummel, VP Marketing/Communications

Annual show of 120 manufacturers, suppliers and distributors of agricultural chemicals and fertilizers. Seminar, conference and banquet.
1200 Attendees
Frequency: Annual
Founded in: 1993

4506 American Assn of Textile Chemists & Colorists International Conference
American Assn of Textile Chemists & Colorists
PO Box 12215
Research Triangle Park, NC 27709-2215

919-549-8141
800-360-5380; *Fax:* 919-549-8933
danielsj@aatcc.org; www.aatcc.org

John Daniels, Executive VP
Debra Hibbard, Executive Assistant
Charles E Gavin, Treasurer

Colorants and chemical finishes for the textile trade are on display.
Frequency: Annual

4507 American Chemical Society: Southeastern Regional Conference & Exhibition
American Chemical Society
1155 16th Street NW
Washington, DC 20036

202-872-4600
800-227-5558; *Fax:* 202-872-4615
service@acs.org; www.acs.org

Madeleine Jacobs, CEO/Executive Director

Booths featuring exhibits of the chemicals industry.
Frequency: Annual

4508 American College of Toxicology Annual Meeting
9650 Rockville Pike
Bethesda, MD 20814

301-634-7840; *Fax:* 301-634-7852;
www.actox.org

Carol Lemire, Executive Director
Eve Gamzu Kagan, Asst. Executive Director

Education courses and scientific symposia, exhibits of contract laboratories, toxicology supplies and equipment and science journal publishing companies.
500 Attendees
Frequency: November

4509 American Institute Chemical Engineers Petrochemical Refining Expo
3 Park Avenue
New York, NY 10016-4363

212-591-8100
800-242-4363; *Fax:* 212-591-8888;
www.aiche.org
Social Media: Facebook, Twitter, LinkedIn

Marie Stewart, Director

A marketplace for materials used in processing chemicals.
20M Attendees
Frequency: April

4510 American Society Biochemistry and Molecular Biology Expo
American Society of Biochem & Molecular Biology
9650 Rockville Pike
Bethesda, MD 20814-3996

301-634-7145; *Fax:* 301-881-2080
asbmb@asbmb.org; www.asbmb.org

600 booths of products used in biomedical research.
8M Attendees

4511 Annual Green Chemistry & Engineering Conference
ACS Green Chemistry Institute
1155 16th Street NW
Washington, DC 20036

202-872-6102
800-227-5558; *Fax:* 202-872-4615
gci@acs.org; www.GCandE.org

Speakers, sessions, education, exhibits.
Frequency: Annual

4512 CPMA Conference
Color Pigments Manufacturers Association
300 N Washington St
Suite 105
Alexandria, VA 22314-2530

703-684-4044; *Fax:* 703-684-1795
cpma@cpma.com; www.pigments.org

J Lawrence Robinson, President

Brings together pigments manufacturers their suppliers and users, and others with an interest in color pigments including regulators, consultants, and exhibitors.
Frequency: Annual

4513 Chem Show: Chemical Process Industries Exposition
International Exposition Company
15 Franklin Street
Westport, CT 06880-5903

203-221-9232; *Fax:* 203-221-9260
info@chemshow.com; www.chemshow.com

Mark Stevens, Vice President
Jeff Stevens, Sales Vice President

Bringing together in one place major manufacturers of equipment, systems and services for the CPI. Product categories include; process equipment, fluid handling equipment and systems, solids handling equipment and sytems, engineered materials, instruments and controls, environmental and safety equipment and systems and services.
Frequency: Biennial/Oct
Founded in: 1915

4514 Chem-Distribution
PennWell Publishing Company
1421 S Sheridan Road
Tulsa, OK 74112-6619

918-835-3161
800-331-4463; *Fax:* 918-831-9834
headquarters@pennwell.com;
www.pennwell.com

Bill Pryor, CEO/President
Junior Isles, Publisher/Editor

Exhibits of technology for the distribution, transfer and storage of chemicals and petrochemicals.

4515 Chem-Safe
PennWell Conferences and Exhibitions
1421 S Sheridan Road
Tulsa, OK 74112-6619

918-835-3161
800-331-4463; *Fax:* 918-831-9834
headquarters@pennwell.com;
www.pennwell.com

Bill Pryor, CEO/President
Junior Isles, Publisher/Editor

Exhibits of environmental, safety and health technology for the chemical and process industries.

4516 Chlorine Institute Annual Meeting & Trade Show
Chlorine Institute
1300 Wilson Blvd
Arlington, VA 22209-2323

703-741-5760; *Fax:* 703-894-4130;
www.chlorineinstitute.org

Arthur Dungan, President
Frequency: Annual/Spring

4517 Conchem Exhibition and Conference
Reed Exhibition Companies
255 Washington Street
Newton, MA 02458-1637

617-584-4900; *Fax:* 617-630-2222

Elizabeth Hitchcock, International Sales

The international event featuring specialty additives and chemicals for the building industry.
Frequency: November

4518 **Consumer Specialty Products Association**
Chemical Specialties Products Association
900 17th Street NW
Suite 300
Washington, DC 20006

202-872-8110; *Fax:* 202-872-8114
info@cspa.org; www.cspa.org

Christopher Cathcart, President

Nonprofit organization trade show for the many companies involved in the formulation, manufacture, testing and marketing of chemical specialty products. 100 booths.
2M Attendees

4519 **Eastern Analytical Symposium & Exposition**
Eastern Analytical Symposium, Inc
PO Box 633
Montchanin, DE 19710-0633

610-485-4633; *Fax:* 610-485-9467
easinfo@aol.com; www.eas.org

Sheree Gold, Exposition Director

The world's leading community for analytcal chemists seeking education and career advancement. Technical programs, speakers, and the expo. 240 booths.
6M Attendees
Frequency: Annual

4520 **Electrochemical Society Meetings**
Electrochemical Society
65 S Main St
Building D
Pennington, NJ 08534-2827

609-737-1902; *Fax:* 609-737-2743
meetings@electrochem.org;
www.electrochem.org

Roque J Calvo, Executive Director
Colleen Keepser, Executive Administrator
Mary Yess, Deputy Executive Director
Corey Eberhart, Global Sales Director
Karen Baliff Ornstein, Marketing Manager

Providing a forum for exchanging information on the latest scientific and technical developments in the fields of electrochemical and solid-state science and technology. ECS meetings bring together scientists, engineers, and researchers from academia, industry, and government laboratories to share results and discuss issues on related topics through a variety of formats, such as oral presentations, poster sessions, panel discussions, and tutorial sessions.
8000 Members
Frequency: Biannual/Spring & Fall
Founded in: 1902

4521 **Federation of Spectroscopy Societies**
13 N Cliffe Drive
Wilmington, DE 19809-1623

302-656-0771

Dr. Edward Brame Jr, Show Manager

120 booths of analytical chemistry.
2M Attendees
Frequency: October

4522 **GlobalChem Conference and Exhibition**
1850 M St NW
Suite 700
Washington, DC 20036-5810

202-721-4100; *Fax:* 202-296-8120
info@socma.com; www.socma.com

Larry Sloan, President/CEO
Alicia Massey, Senior Manager

Provides information and interaction with experts on the U.S. Toxic Substances Control Act, emerging issues and trends in the product stewardship arena and equivalent international regulations.
6 Members
Founded in: 1985

4523 **ILTA Storage Tank & Bulk Liquid Terminal Int'l Operating Conf. & Trade Show**
Independent Liquid Terminals Association
1005 North Glebe Road
Suite 600
Arlington, VA 22201

703-875-2011; *Fax:* 703-875-2018
info@ilta.org; www.ilta.org

E David Doane, President
Melinda Whitney, Director/Government Affairs
Renita Gross, Director of Mtgs/Info. Services

Containing 202 booths and 161 exhibits.
2,700 Attendees
Frequency: June

4524 **IUPAC World Polymer Congress**
2 Davidson Hall
Blacksburg, VA 24061-0001

540-231-7257; *Fax:* 540-231-3971
adhesoc@vt.edu; www.adhesionsociety.org

Lynn Penn, President
Paul J Clark, Treasurer
Esther Brann, Manager

Enabling technologies for a safe, sustainable, healthy world.
400 Members
Founded in: 1978

4525 **InformexUSA**
1850 M St NW
Suite 700
Washington, DC 20036-5810

202-721-4100; *Fax:* 202-296-8120
info@socma.com; www.socma.com

Jill Aker, President

Serving businesses across a broad range of end-use markets such as pharmaceuticals, biopharmaceuticals, agrochemicals, adhesives, electronics, paints, and plastics. Utilizing an advisory committee, made up of industry executives and decision makers from across markets to help us make decisions that come directly from the chemical industry.
6 Members
Founded in: 1985

4526 **International Conference on the Methods and Applications**
American Nuclear Society
555 N Kensington Ave
La Grange Park, IL 60526-5592

708-352-6611
800-323-3044; *Fax:* 708-352-0499
advertising@ans.org; www.ans.org
Social Media: Facebook, Twitter, LinkedIn

Stephen Kuczynski, General Chair
Sedatel Goluoglu, Program Chair
Mikey Brady Raap, Treasurer

Of Radioanalytical Chemistry
10500 Members
Founded in: 1954

4527 **International Thermal Spray Conference & Exposition**
ASM International
9639 Kinsman Road
Materials Park, OH 44073

440-338-5151
800-336-5152; *Fax:* 440-338-4634
natalie.nemec@asminternational.org;
www.asminternational.org

Natalie Neme, Event Manager
Kelly Thomas, Exposition Account Manager

Global annual event attracting professional interested in thermal spray technology focusing on advances in HVOF, plasma and detonation gun, flame spray and wire arc spray processes, performance of coatings, and future trends. 150 exhibitors.
1000 Attendees
Frequency: Annual/May

4528 **Optimizing Your Lab Automation: Lessons from the Front Line**
1850 K St NW
Suite 625
Washington, DC 20006-2215

202-857-0717
800-892-1400; *Fax:* 202-887-5093;
www.aacc.org
Social Media: Facebook, Twitter, LinkedIn, YouTube

Robert Christenson, President
Steven Wong, President-Elect
Patricia Jones, Director

The premiere event for clinical laboratorians, industry representatives, and health care executives to network and get ahead.

4529 **PCA International Conference**
Pine Chemicals Associations, Inc
3350 Riverwood Parkway SE
Suite 1900
Atlanta, GA 30339

770-984-5340; *Fax:* 770-984-5341
wjones@pinechemicals.org;
www.pinechemicals.org

Walter L Jones, President/COO
Gary Reed, Chairman/Board of Directors
200 Attendees
Frequency: September

4530 **Powder Bulk Solids Conference and Expo**
Reed Business Information
2000 Clearwater Drive
Oak Brook, IL 60523

630-740-0825; www.reedbusiness.com

Angela Piermartini, Show Manager

1,300 booths.
11M Attendees
Frequency: May

4531 **Spray Foam Conference & EXPO**
Spray Polyurethane Foam Alliance
4400 Fair Lakes Court
Suite 105
Fairfax, VA 22033

800-523-6154; *Fax:* 703-222-5816
info@sprayfoam.org; www.sprayfoam.org

Sig Hall, President
Robert Duke, Vice President
Peter Davis, Secretary/Treasurer

Training and accreditation programs, general and breakout sessions, awards, networking receptions, and the exhibit hall.
Frequency: Annual/February
Founded in: 1987

4532 **TRADEWORX**
Chemical Specialties Products Association

900 17th Street NW
Suite 300
Washington, DC 20006

202-872-8110; *Fax:* 202-872-8114
info@cspa.org; www.cspa.org

Christopher Cathcart, President

Not-for-profit organization composed of many companies involved in the formulation, manufacture, testing and marketing of chemical specialty products.
2M Attendees
Frequency: May

Directories & Databases

4533 **Adhesives Digest**
International Plastics Selector/DATA Business Pub.
15 Inverness Way E
#6510
Englewood, CO 80112-5710

303-904-0407

A who's who directory of services and supplies to the industry.
Cost: $180.00
Frequency: Biennial

4534 **Advanced Coatings and Surface Technology**
John Wiley & Sons
111 River St
Hoboken, NJ 07030-5790

201-748-6000; *Fax:* 201-748-6088
info@wiley.com; www.wiley.com

William J Pesce, Chief Executive Officer

Offers information on coatings and surface technology, covering breakthroughs in traditional coating processes, chemical vapor deposition and ion beam methods.
Frequency: Full-text

4535 **American Coke & Coal Chemicals Institute Directory and By-Laws**
1140 Connecticut Ave NW
Suite 705
Washington, DC 20036-4011

202-452-7177; *Fax:* 202-496-9702
information@accci.org; www.recycle-steel.org

Chip Foley, VP
Charles Stewart, Chairman

Represents merchant oven coke producers, integrated coke producers, tar distillers, sales agents, and industry suppliers.
75 Pages
Founded in: 1944

4536 **American Laboratory Buyers Guide**
International Scientific Communications
PO Box 870
Shelton, CT 06484-0870

203-926-9300; *Fax:* 203-926-9310
webmaster@iscpubs.com; www.iscpubs.com

Brian Howard, Editor
Robert G Sweeny, Publisher

Manufacturers of and dealers in scientifi instruments, equipment, apparatus, and chemicals worldwide.
Cost: $25.00
Frequency: Annual

4537 **Available Chemicals Directory**
MDL Information Systems
3100 Central Expressway
Santa Clara, CA 05051-6608

408-764-2000
800-635-0064; *Fax:* 408-748-0175;
www.mdl-information-systems-inc.software.informer.com

Magnetic tape, covers approximately 240,000 commercially available chemicals, including organic, and inorganic chemicals.
Frequency: Semiannual

4538 **CEH On-Line**
SRI International
333 Ravenswood Ave
Menlo Park, CA 94025-3493

650-859-3711; *Fax:* 650-326-8916;
www.srifcu.org

Steve Bowles, President

Database containing economic data for more than 1300 major commodity and specialty chemical products.
Frequency: Full-text

4539 **CERCLIS Database of Hazardous Waste Sites**
Environmental Protection Agency
Ariel Rios Building
1200 Pennsylvania Avenue NW
Washington, DC 20460

202-272-0167
r9.info@epa.gov; www.epa.gov

Bob Zachariasiewicz, Acting Director
Shushona Hyson, Contact
Curt Spalding, Regional

Stands for Comprehensive Environmental Response, Compensation, and Liability Information System. This database contains information on more than 36,000 releases of hazardous substances reported to the US Environmental Protection Agency.
Frequency: Directory

4540 **CHEMEST**
Technical Database Services
62 W 39th Street
Rm 704
New York, NY 10018

212-245-0384; *Fax:* 212-556-0036

Mildred Green, Principal

This database contains information for estimating the properties of pharmaceuticals and chemicals of environmental concern.
Frequency: Properties

4541 **CLAIMS/Comprehensive Data Base**
IFI/Plenum Data Corporation
PO Box 1148
Madison, CT 06443

203-779-5301; *Fax:* 203-583-4521
info@ificlaims.com

Harry M Allcock, VP

This database contains enhanced indexing of the US chemical and chemically related patents included in the CLAIMS/UNITERM database.

4542 **Chem Source USA**
Chemical Sources International
PO Box 1824
Clemson, SC 29633

864-646-7840; *Fax:* 864-642-6168
information@chemsources.com;
www.chemsources.com

Mike Desing, Editor

Book containing information on where to obtain chemicals in the US and Canada.
Cost: $495.00
1700 Pages
Frequency: Annual January
Circulation: 10000
Founded in: 1958

4543 **Chem Sources International**
PO Box 1824
Clemson, SC 29633-1824

864-646-7840
800-222-4531; *Fax:* 864-646-6168
csinfo@chemsources.com;
www.chemsources.com

Mike Desing, Editor
Dale Krohn, Owner

The most comprehensive directory ever compiled on the world's chemical industry. Includes the products of more than 8,000 chemical firms spanning 128 countries.
Cost: $750.00
Frequency: Biennial
Founded in: 1958

4544 **Chemcyclopedia**
American Chemical Society
676 East Swedesford Road
Suite 202
Wayne, PA 19087-1612

610-964-8061; *Fax:* 610-964-8061
carroll@acs.org; www.acs.org
Social Media: 1

Madeleine Jacobs, Executive Director/CEO
Ken Carroll, Publisher

List of over 900 chemical manufacturers in the US.
Cost: $60.00
Frequency: Annual

4545 **Chemical Abstracts**
American Chemical Society
1155 16th St NW
Suite 600
Washington, DC 20036-4892

202-872-4600
800-227-5558; *Fax:* 202-872-4615
service@acs.org; www.acs.org

Madeleine Jacobs, CEO

Newsletter covering this branch of the American Chemical Society.
Frequency: Monthly

4546 **Chemical Exposure and Human Health**
McFarland & Company Publishers
PO Box 611
Jefferson, NC 28640-0611

336-246-4460
800-253-2187; *Fax:* 336-246-5018
info@mcfarlandpub.com;
www.mcfarlandpub.com

Cynthia Wilson, Editor

A list of organizations concerned with the effects of chemical exposure. Government exposure standards on over 300 chemicals.
Cost: $55.00
ISBN: 0-899508-10-3

4547 **Chemical Regulations and Guidelines System**
Network Management CRC Systems
11242 Waples Mill Road
Fairfax, VA 22030-6079

703-219-3865

This database contains citations, with abstracts, to US government statutes and federal guidelines.

4548 **Chemical Week: Financial Survey of the 300 Largest Companies in the US**
Chemical Week Associates

110 William St
New York, NY 10038-3910

212-621-4900; *Fax:* 212-621-4800;
www.chemweek.com

John Rockwell, Vice President

Offers information on over 300 chemical process companies in the United States.
Cost: $8.00
7 Pages
Frequency: Annual
Circulation: 50,615

4549 **DRI Chemical**
DRI/McGraw-Hill
24 Hartwell Ave
Lexington, MA 02421-3103

781-860-6060; *Fax:* 781-860-6002
support@construction.com;
www.construction.com

Keith Fox, President
Linda Brennan, VP Operations
Bob Stuono, Senior VP And General Manager

The coverage of this database encompasses the chemical industry in the United States, including imports and exports, inventories, production, sales, shipments and uses.

4550 **DRI Chemical Forecast**
DRI/McGraw-Hill
24 Hartwell Ave
Lexington, MA 02421-3103

781-860-6060; *Fax:* 781-860-6002
support@construction.com;
www.construction.com

Keith Fox, President

This time series contains over 700 quarterly forecasts on US supply and demand for more than 120 chemical products.

4551 **Directory of Bulk Liquid Terminal and Storage Facilities**
Independent Liquid Terminals Association
1005 North Glebe Road
Arlington, VA 22201

703-875-2011; *Fax:* 703-875-2018
info@ilta.org; www.ilta.org

E David Doane, President
Melinda Whitney, Director/Executive VP

Published annually in April.
Cost: $95.00

4552 **Directory of Chemical Producers: East Asia**
SRI Consulting/IHS Global
333 Ravenswood Ave
Menlo Park, CA 94025-3493

650-859-3711; *Fax:* 650-326-8916;
www.srifcu.org

Steve Bowles, President

Over 2,000 companies producing over 14,000 chemicals in 2,600 plant locations in Indonesia, Japan, Korea, Taiwan and the Philippines.
Cost: $1800.00
800 Pages
Frequency: Annual

4553 **Directory of Chemical Producers: U.S.**
SRI Consulting/IHS Global
333 Ravenswood Ave
Menlo Park, CA 94025-3493

650-859-3711; *Fax:* 650-326-8916;
www.srifcu.org

Steve Bowles, President

Over 1,500 United States basic chemical producers manufacturing almost 10,000 chemicals in commercial quantities at 4,500 plant locations. Providing comprehensive, accurate and timely coverage of the international chemical industry since 1961.
Cost: $1460.00
1100 Pages
Frequency: Annual

4554 **Directory of Chemical Producers: Western Europe**
SRI Consulting/IHS Global
333 Ravenswood Ave
Menlo Park, CA 94025-3493

650-859-3711; *Fax:* 650-326-8916;
www.srifcu.org

Steve Bowles, President

Covered are over 2,500 western European chemical producers, chemicals and plant locations.
Cost: $1930.00
Frequency: Annual
Circulation: 2,100

4555 **Directory of Custom Chemical Manufacturers**
Delphi Marketing Services
400 E 89th Street
Apartment 2J
New York, NY 10128-6728
Newman Giragosian, Editor

A list of over 280 custom chemical manufacturers.
Cost: $295.00
220 Pages

4556 **Directory of Suppliers of Services**
Independent Liquid Terminals Association
1005 North Glebe Road
Arlington, VA 22201

703-875-2011; *Fax:* 703-875-2018
info@ilta.org; www.ilta.org

E David Doane, President
Melinda Whitney, Director/Executive VP
Cost: $25.00

4557 **Environmental Fate Data Bases**
Syracuse Research Corporation
6225 Running Ridge Rd
North Syracuse, NY 13212-2510

315-452-8000
800-724-0451; *Fax:* 315-452-8100

Cheryl Wolfe, President

This database, consisting of 4 interrelated files of information on the fate of organic chemicals. The files include information in physical/chemical properties, degradation and transport, and monitoring for 16,000 chemicals.

4558 **Environmental Industry Yearbook and The Gallery**
Environmental Economics
1026 Irving Street
Philadelphia, PA 19107-6707

215-877-2063; *Fax:* 215-440-0116

More than 80 publicly traded companies, plus Fortune 500 firms that have an impact on environmental concerns.
Cost: $75.00
250 Pages
Frequency: SemiAnnual

4559 **Fine Chemicals Database**
Chemron
PO Box 2299
Paso Robles, CA 93447
210-340-8121
800-423-1148; *Fax:* 210-340-8123

This large database provides supplier information for more than 27,000 chemical products available from over 50 manufacturers and distributors in North America.
Frequency: Directory

4560 **Index to Chemical Regulations**
Bureau of National Affairs
1801 S Bell St
Arlington, VA 22202-4501

703-341-3000
800-372-1033; *Fax:* 800-253-0332
customercare@bna.com; www.bnabooks.com

Paul N Wojcik, Chairman
Gregory C McCaffery, President

A one-binder index containing more than 80,000 citations by chemical name to the Code of Federal Regulations and the Federal Register.
Cost: $988.00
Frequency: Monthly

4561 **Information Officers of Member Companies**
Chemical Manufacturers Association
1300 Wilson Boulevard
Arlington, VA 22209-2307

703-741-5502; *Fax:* 703-741-6807

Thomas J Gilroy, Associate Media Director

About 180 companies.
Frequency: Biennial

4562 **International Chemical Regulatory Monitoring System**
Ariel Research Corporation
4320 East West Highway
Suite 440
Bethesda, MD 20814-3319

301-951-2500; *Fax:* 301-986-1681;
www.3ecompany.com

John Wyatt, CEO

This database contains references to regulations and precautionary data on more than 100,000 chemical substances.
Frequency: Full-text

4563 **Kirk-Othmer Encyclopedia of Chemical Technology Online**
John Wiley & Sons
111 River St
Hoboken, NJ 07030-5790

201-748-6000
800-825-7550; *Fax:* 201-748-6088
info@wiley.com; www.wiley.com

Warren J Baker, President
Richard M Hochhauser, CEO

This comprehensive database offers complete text, citations, tables and abstracts of all 1,200 chapters in the 25-volume Encyclopedia of the same name. With no concurrent usage restriction, you can call up information covering the entire chemical industry and allied fields any time with a click of your mouse from the library, office or laboratory.

4564 **McCutcheons Functional Materials**
McCutcheons Division
P.O.Box 2249
New Preston Marble Dale, CT 06777-0249
201-652-2655; *Fax:* 201-652-3419
mcinfo@gomc.com; www.gomc.com

Michael Allured, Publisher

List of materials commonly used in conjunction with surfactants such as enzymes, lubricants, waxes, corrosion inhibitors, and other chemicals produced worldwide.
Cost: $40.00
Frequency: Monthly
Founded in: 1921

4565 **Multilingual Thesaurus of Geosciences**
Information Today

143 Old Marlton Pike
Medford, NJ 08055-8750

609-654-6266
800-300-9868; *Fax:* 609-654-4309
custserv@infotoday.com; www.infotoday.com

Thomas H Hogan, President
Roger R Bilboul, Chairman Of The Board

Represents the state of the art use of geoscience terminology by information centers around the world.
Cost: $99.00
654 Pages
ISBN: 1-573870-09-9

4566 OPIS/STALSBY Electric Power Industry Directory
OPIS/STALSBY
1255 Highway 70
Suite 32-N
Lakewood, NJ 08701

732-901-8800
877-210-4287; *Fax:* 732-901-9632;
www.opisnet.com

Karen England, Senior Editor
Karen Reng, Marketing Manager
Christine Kaniuk, Production/Advertising Coordinator

Provides detailed listings of over 1,200 companies and more than 2,700 personnel of the electric power industry. Company categories include producer, marketer, trader, broker, transmission, investor-owned, municipal, rural/co-op/fed/local government and independent. Personnel listings include sales/marketing, supply/purchasing, operations/transmissions, finance/treasury. Company listings include address, direct telephone, fax numbers and e-mails. CD-ROM $495.
Cost: $141.00
Frequency: 2 per year
Circulation: 625
Printed in 4 colors

4567 OPIS/STALSBY Petrochemicals Directory
OPIS/STALSBY
3349 State Route 138
Unit D
Wall Township, NJ 07719-9671

732-730-2500
877-210-4287; *Fax:* 732-280-0542;
www.ucg.com

Ben Brockwell, Manager
Karen Reng, Marketing Manager
Christine Kaniuk, Production/Advertising Coordinator
Bruce Levenson, Co-Founder

Provides detailed listings of over 2,100 companies and more than 7,000 personnel covering all segments of the petrochemical gas industry, including manufacturing, trading and distributing of petrochemicals. Company listings include addresses, telephone, fax, TLX, personal phone/fax numbers, cell phones and home addresses, area of responsibility and job titles. Five separate indices are provided for complete cross-referencing. CD-ROM $995.
Cost: $175.00
Frequency: 2 per year
Circulation: 425
Printed in 4 colors

4568 OPIS/STALSBY Petroleum Supply Americas Directory
OPIS/STALSBY
1255 Highway 70
Suite 32-N
Lakewood, NJ 08701

732-901-8800
877-210-4287; *Fax:* 732-901-9632;
www.opisnet.com

Karen England, Senior Editor
Karen Reng, Marketing Manager
Christine Kaniuk, Production/Advertising Coordinator

Helps traders, marketers and suppliers of crude oil, refined products and gas liquids to access detailed information on over 2,500 companies and 10,000 personnel in North, Central and South America. Company listings include company address, telephone, fax, TLX, personal phone/fax numbers, car phones, home addresses, area of responsibility and job title. Four separate indices are provided for complete cross-referencing. CD-ROM $995.
Cost: $235.00
Frequency: 2 per year
Circulation: 2,045
Printed in 4 colors

4569 OPIS/STALSBY Petroleum Supply Europe Directory
OPIS/STALSBY
1255 Highway 70
Suite 32-N
Lakewood, NJ 08701

732-901-8800
877-210-4287; *Fax:* 732-901-9632;
www.opisnet.com

Karen England, Senior Editor
Karen Reng, Marketing Manager
Christine Kaniuk, Production/Advertising Coordinator

Helps traders, marketers and suppliers of crude oil, refined products and gas liquids to access detailed information on over 1,500 companies and 6,600 personnel in Europe, Eastern Europe, Africa and the Middle East. Listings include company address, telephone, fax, TLX, personal phone/fax numbers, car phones, home addresses, area of responsibility and job titles. Four separate indices are provided for complete cross-referencing. CD-OM $995.
Cost: $190.00
Frequency: 2 per year
Circulation: 425
Printed in 4 colors

4570 OPIS/STALSBY Petroleum Terminal Encyclopedia
OPIS/STALSBY
1255 Highway 70
Suite 32-N
Lakewood, NJ 08701

732-901-8800
877-210-4287; *Fax:* 732-901-9632;
www.opisnet.com

Karen England, Senior Editor
Karen Reng, Marketing Manager
Christine Kaniuk, Production/Advertising Coordinator

Provides detailed listings of over 2,800 petroleum terminals. Information includes pipeline and rail interconnections and truck facilities for each terminal; berth, waterway and docking information for marine terminals; details on both public and private terminals for market analysis and exchange planning. Three separate indices are provided for complete cross-referencing. CD-ROM $995.
Cost: $245.00
Frequency: 2 per year
Circulation: 825
Printed in 4 colors

4571 OPIS/STALSBY Who's Who in Natural Gas
OPIS/STALSBY
1255 Highway 70
Suite 32-N
Lakewood, NJ 08701

732-901-8800
877-210-4287; *Fax:* 732-901-9632;
www.opisnet.com

Karen England, Senior Editor
Karen Reng, Marketing Manager
Christine Kaniuk, Production/Advertising Coordinator

Provides detailed listings of over 2,600 companies and more than 11,000 personnel covering all segments of the natural gas industry, including producers, processors, marketers, traders, transporters, major buyers, LDCs, brokers, gas storage, regulatory, etc. Company listings include addresses, telephone, fax, TLX, personal phone/fax numbers, car phones and home addresses, area of responsibility and job titles. Four separate indices are provided for complete cross-referencing. CD-ROM $995.
Cost: $200.00
Frequency: 2 per year
Circulation: 950
Printed in 4 colors

4572 Purchasing/CPI Edition: Chemicals Yellow Pages
Reed Business Information
2000 Clearwater Dr
Oak Brook, IL 60523-8809

630-574-0825; *Fax:* 630-288-8781;
www.reedbusiness.com

Jeff Greisch, President

Manufacturers and distributors of 10,000 chemicals and raw materials; manufacturers and distributors of containers and packaging.
Cost: $85.00
Frequency: Annual

4573 Refining & Gas Processing
Midwest Publishing Company
PO Box 4468
Suite E
Tulsa, OK 74159-0468

918-583-9999
800-829-2002; *Fax:* 918-587-9349
info@midwestdirectories.com;
www.midwestpub.com

Will L Hammack, Owner

Over 5,200 refineries, gas processing plants, engineering contractors, equipment manufacturers and supply companies.
Cost: $145.00
Frequency: Annual, May
Founded in: 1943

4574 Regulated Chemical Directory
Kluwer Academic Publishers
101 Philip Drive
Norwellk, MA 02061

617-871-6600; *Fax:* 617-871-6528
kluwer@wkap.com; www.hcirn.com

List of major federal and selected state and international regulatory and advisory sources of information regarding chemicals in the US, Canada, Australia, Germany and Israel.
Cost: $375.00
Frequency: Annual, January

4575 STN Easy
Chemical Abstracts Service

PO Box 3012
Columbus, OH 43210-0012
614-473-3600
800-848-6538; *Fax:* 614-447-3713
help@cas.org; www.cas.org

Easy web acccess to scientific research and patents. STN Easy provides access to more than 60 databases covering all types of sci/tech information including chemistry, life sciences, buisiness, MSDS, math/computer science, engineering, medicine, pharmaceuticals, general science, food and agriculture, and regulatory information.

4576 **Soap/Cosmetics/Chemical Specialties: Blue Book Issue**
Cygnus Publishing
445 Broad Hollow Road
Suite 21
Melville, NY 11747-3601
631-845-2700; *Fax:* 631-845-2723;
www.cygnuspub.com
Anita Shaw, Editor-in-Chief
Shelley Colwell, CFO
Paul Bonaiuto, CFO
Kathy Scott, Director of Public Relations

Sources of raw materials, equipment and services for the chemical, soap and cosmetics industries. Includes a list of trade associations.
Cost: $15.00
Frequency: Annual, April
Circulation: 19,000

Industry Web Sites

4577 **http://gold.greyhouse.com**
G.O.L.D Grey House OnLine Databases

Grey House Publishing's online database platform, GOLD, offers Quick Search, Keyword Search and Expert Search for most business sectors including chemical and agriculture markets. The GOLD platform makes finding the information you need quick and easy - whether you're a novice searcher or an experienced database user. All of Grey House's directory products are be available for subscription on the GOLD platform.

4578 **www.aaccnet.org**
American Association of Cereal Chemists

Nonprofit international organization of nearly 4,000 members who are specialists in the use of cereal grains in foods. AACC has been an innovative leader in gathering and disseminating scientific and technical information to professionals in the grain based foods industry worldwide for over 85 years.

4579 **www.accci.org**
American Coke & Coal Chemicals Institute Directory

For merchant oven coke producers, integrated coke producers, tar distillers, sales agents, and industry suppliers.

4580 **www.actox.org**
American College of Toxicology

Multidisciplinary society composed of professionals having a common interest in toxicology. Our mission is to educate and lead professionals in industry, government and related areas of toxicology by actively promoting the exchange of information and perspectives on the current status of safety assesment and the application of new developments in toxicology.

4581 **www.aiche.org**
American Institute of Chemical Engineers

Professional association of more than 50,000 members, providing leadership in advancing the chemical engineering profession. Members develop processes and design and operate manufacturing plants, as well as research the safe and environmentally sound manufacture, use and disposal of chemical products.

4582 **www.americanchemistry.com**
American Chemistry Council

Committed to improved environmental, health and safety performance through responsible care, common sense advocacy designed to address major public policy issues, health and environmental research and product testing.

4583 **www.aoac.org**
Association of Official Analytical Communities

Calender, publications and training courses. AOAC serves as the primary resource for timely knowledge exchange, networking and high quality laboratory information for its members.

4584 **www.aocs.org**
American Oil Chemists Society

Encourages advancement of technology and research in fats, oils and other associated substances.

4585 **www.asms.org**
American Society for Mass Spectrometry

Formed to disseminate knowledge of mass spectrometry and allied topics. Members come from academic, industrial and governmental laboratories. Their interests include advancement of techniques and instrumentation in mass specrometry, as well as fundamental research in chemistry, geology, biological sciences and physics.

4586 **www.chemheritage.org**
Chemical Heritage Foundation

An independent, nonprofit organization, CHF maintains major collections of instruments, fine art, photographs, papers, and books. We host conferences and lectures, support research, offer fellowships, and produce educational materials.

4587 **www.chemistry.org**
American Chemical Society

Encourages advancement in all branches of chemistry. There are 34 ACS divisions and 188 local sections.

4588 **www.chemtrec.org**
American Chemistry Council

Serves as a referral service for non-emergency health and safety information, maintains library and speakers bureaus. Offers 24 hour emergency communication service center for hazardous materials, material data sheets, lending library, audio-visual training programs.

4589 **www.coatingstech.org**
Federation of Societies for Coatings Technology

Provides technical education and professional development to its members and to the global industry through its multi-national constituent societies and collectively as a federation.

4590 **www.combustioninstitute.org**
Combustion Institute

A non-profit, educational, scientific society whose purpose is to promote and disseminate research combustion science.

4591 **www.csma.org**
Chemical Specialties Manufacturers Association

For companies involved in the formulation, manufacture, testing and marketing of chemical specialty products.

4592 **www.cspa.org**
Consumer Specialty Products Association

Nonprofit organization composed of many companies involved in the formulation, manufacture, testing and marketing of chemical specialty products. Our line includes disinfectants that kill germs in homes, hospitals and restaurants, candles that eliminate odors, pest management products for home and garden, cleaning products and much more.

4593 **www.dupont.com/nacs**
DuPont Experimental Station

For chemists and chemical engineers engaged in the study and use of reactions involving catalysts. Publishes a newsletter

4594 **www.electrochem.org**
Electrochemical Society

The society is an international nonprofit, educational organization concerned with phenomena relating to electrochemical and solid state science and technology. Members are individual scientists and engineers, as well as corporations and laboratories.

4595 **www.fibersource.com**
American Fiber Manufacturers Association

Trade association for US companies that manufacture synthetic and cellulostic fibers. The industry employs 30,000 people and produces over 9 billion pounds of fiber in the US. The association maintains close ties to other manufactured fiber trade associations worldwide.

4596 **www.greyhouse.com**
Grey House Publishing

Authoritative reference directories for most business sectors incluidng chemical and agricultural markets. Users can search the online databases with varied search criteria allowing for custom searches by product category, geographic area, sales volume, keyword, subject and more. Full Grey House catalog and online ordering also available.

4597 **www.ilta.org**
Independent Liquid Terminals Association

Representing bulk liquid terminal companies that store commercial liquids in aboveground storage tanks and transfer products to and from oceangoing tanks ships, tank barges, pipelines, tank trucks, and tank rail cars.

4598 **www.ioza.org**
International Ozone Assn-Pan American Group Branch

Not for profit educational association which performs its information sharing functions through sponsorship of international symposia, seminars, publications, and the development of personal relationships among ozone specialists throughout the world.

4599 **www.leatherchemists.org**
American Leather Chemists Association

Publishes the Journal of the American Leather Chemists Association where original research reports are published along with abstracts of foreign articles. A four-day technical meeting is held annually. Promotes the advancement of the knowledge of science and engineering in their application to the problems facing the leather and leather products industries.

4600 **www.methanol.org**
American Methanol Institute

Our mission is to expand markets for the use of methanol as a chemical commodity building block, a hydrogen carrier for fuel cell applications, and an alternative fuel. AMI was formed in 1989, during the height of the Clean Air Act debate, and worked to help create the highly successful reformulated gasoline program.

4601 www.mti-link.org
Materials Tech. Institute of the Chemical Process

MTI provides leadership in materials technology for chemical processing to improve reliability, profitability and safety.

4602 www.nacatsoc.org
North American Catalysis Society

Fosters an interest in heterogeneous and homogeneous catalysis. Organizes national meetings. Members are chemists and chemical engineers engaged in the study and use of reactions involving catalysts. Publishes a newsletter.

4603 www.pemanet.org
Process Equipment Manufacturers' Association

Organized in 1960, we represent more than 40 companies in the process equipment field. Member companies serve the liquid-solids separation, food processing, pulp and paper, waste water treatment industry and others.

4604 www.pestworld.org
National Pest Control Association

For over 65 years, the NPMA has represented the interests of its members and the structural pest control industry. Through the efforts of NPMA, the pest control industry is stronger, more professional, and more unified. Guiding its members and industry through legislative and regulatory initiatives on the federal and state levels, the creation of verifiable training, the changing technologies used by the industry, and public and media relations, NPMA has been a clear, positive voice.

4605 www.pfa.org
Polyurethane Foam Association

Educating customers and other groups about flexible polyurethane foam and to promote its use in manufactured and indutrial products. This includes providing facts on environmental, health and safety issues related to polyurethane foam to the memebership of PFA, polyurethane foam users, regulatory officials, business leaders and the media.

4606 www.pigments.org
Color Pigments Manufacturers Association

An industry trade association representing color pigment companies in Canada, Mexico and the US. Represents small, medium, and large color pigments manufacturers accounting for 95% of the production of color pigments in North America

4607 www.pima.org
Polyisocyanurate Insulation Manufacturers Assn

National association that advances the use of polyisocyanurate (polyiso) insulation. Polyiso is one of the nation's most widely used and cost-effective insulation products. PIMA's membership consiosts of manufacturers as well as suppliers to the industry.

4608 www.pinechemicals.org
Pine Chemicals Association

Association of producers, processors and consumers of pine chemicals. The PCA promotes innovative, safe and environmentally responsible practices to assure a reliable supply of high quality products.

4609 www.powdercoating.org
Powder Coating Institute

Founded in: 1981 as a nonprofit organization, PCI works to advance the utilization of powder coating as an economical, non-polluting and high quality finish for industrial and consumer products.

4610 www.scisoc.org/asbc
American Society of Brewing Chemists

News, information, member directory and publications.

4611 www.simaflavor.org
Flavor & Extract Manufacturers Assn of the US

Locates suppliers and manufacturers of rare chemicals and oils used in the flavor and fragrance industry.

4612 www.socma.com
Synthetic Organic Chemical Manufacturers Assn

Trade association serving the specialty batch and custom chemical industry since 1921. Its more than 320 member companies have more than 2,000 manufacturing sites and 100,000 employees. SOCMA members encompass every segment of the industry - and manufacture 50,000 products annually that are valued at $60 billion dollars.

4613 www.toxicology.org
Society of Toxicology

Members are scientists concerned with the effects of chemicals on man and the environment. Promotes the aquisition and utilization of knowledge in toxicology, aids in the protection of public health and facilitates disiplines. The society has a strong commitment to education in toxicology and to the recruitment of students and new members into the profession.

Associations

4614 **American Cleaning Institute**
1331 L St NW
Suite 650
Washington, DC 20005

202-347-2900; *Fax:* 202-347-4110
Info@CleaningInstitute.org;
www.cleaninginstitute.org
Social Media: Facebook, Twitter, LinkedIn, RSS Feed, SchoolTube, YouTube

Ernie Rosenberg, President & CEO
Helen Benz, CFO
Sandra Andrade, Program Coordinator, Meetings
Leonardo Bellisario, Govt. Affairs Coordinator
Melissa Bernardo, Manager of Sustainibility Programs

Nonprofit trade association representing manufacturers of household, industrial and institutional cleaning products; their ingredients and finished packaging. Dedicated to advancing public understanding of the safety and benefits of cleaning products and protecting the ability of its members to formulate products that best meet consumer needs.
100+ Members
Founded in: 1926
Mailing list available for rent

4615 **Association for Linen Management**
138 N Keeneland Dr.
Suite D
Richmond, KY 40475

859-624-0177
800-669-0863; *Fax:* 859-624-3580;
www.almnet.org
Social Media: Facebook, Twitter, Pinterest

Cindy Molko, President
James Manginin, Senior Vice President
Nathan Rivers, Vice President
Richard Bott, Treasurer
Kathy Harris, Director

Association for the advancement of professional development in the laundry institute.
Founded in: 1939

4616 **Building Service Contractors Association International**
330 N. Wabash Ave.
Suite 2000
Chicago, IL 60611

312-321-5167
800-368-3414; *Fax:* 312-673-6735
info@bscai.org; www.bscai.org
Social Media: LinkedIn

Chris Mundschenk, EVP/ CEO
Paul Greenland, President
Jim Harris, Jr, Treasurer
Tom Kruse, Vice President
Michael Diamond, Director

Trade association for companies offering security, maintenance and cleaning services. The international membership now represents over 10% of the association's professional membership.
Cost: $30.00
2500 Members
Founded in: 1965
*Mailing list available for rent*at $75 per M

4617 **Chlorine Free Products Association**
1304 S Main St
Algonquin, IL 60102-2757

847-658-6104; *Fax:* 847-658-3152
info@chlorinefreeproducts.org;
www.chlorinefreeproducts.org

Archie Beaton, Executive Director
Richard Albert, Technical Staff Manager
Dr. Kevin Lyons, Chief Procurement Officer
Frank Perkowski, President, Business Development
Jane Bloodworth, Business Manager

A nonprofit association that's primary purpose is to promote total chlorine free policies, programs and technologies throughtout the world.

4618 **Cleaning Equipment Trade Association**
PO Box 270908
Oklahoma City, OK 73137-0908

704-635-7362
800-441-0111; *Fax:* 651-982-0030
info@ceta.org; www.ceta.org

Linda Chappell, President
Curtis Brarber, Senior Vice President
Aaron Auger, Vice President
Kyle Notch, Secretary
Chad Rasmussen, Treasurer

International nonprofit reade association made up of manufacturers, distributors, and suppliers who coordinate their efforts to promote public awareness, professionalism, industry wide safety standards, and education for the advancement of the powered cleaning equipment industry.
300 Members
Founded in: 1996

4619 **Cleaning Management Institute**
125 Wolf Road Suite 112
Albany, NY 12205

800-225-4772; *Fax:* 847-982-1012
brant@issa.com; www.cminstitute.net
Social Media: Facebook, RSS

Maicah Ogburn, Director
Pat Harrington, Administrative Manager
Brant Insero, Training Sales Specialist
Matt Moberg, Training Development

CMI provides education, training and career improvement opportunities for building cleaning and maintenance professionals.
1000 Members
Founded in: 1964

4620 **Coin Laundry Association**
1 S. 660 Midwest Rd.
Suite 205
Oakbrook Terrace, IL 60181

630-953-7920
800-570-5629; *Fax:* 630-953-7925
info@coinlaundry.org; www.coinlaundry.org
Social Media: Facebook, Twitter, LinkedIn, YouTube, Google+

Brian Wallace, President & CEO
Craig Krichner, Chairman
Jeff Gardner, Chair Elect
Michael Sokolowski, EVP
James Whitmore, Vice-Chairman

Association for self-service laundry and dry cleaning industry.
2700+ Members
Founded in: 1960

4621 **Environmental Management Association**
Vickie Lewis, EMA President
38575 Mallast
Harrison Township, MI 48045

313-875-9450
866-999-4EMA; *Fax:* 586-463-8075
emadirector@gmail.com; www.emaweb.org
Social Media: Facebook, LinkedIn

Nancy Kapral, EMA Director
Vickie Lewis, President
Karen Terry-Johnson, VP & Membership Chair

Association for manufacturers, suppliers and distributors of sanitation maintenance supplies, products, services.
11 Members
Founded in: 1994

4622 **Halogenated Solvents Industry Alliance**
3033 Wilson Boulevard
Suite 700
Arlington, VA 22201

703-875-0683; *Fax:* 703-875-0675
info@hsia.org; www.hsia.org

Faye Graul, Executive Director

Represents the manufacturers of trichloroethynele, perchloroethylene and methylene chloride.

4623 **ISSA**
3300 Dundee Road
Northbrook, IL 60062

847-982-0800
800-225-4772; *Fax:* 847-982-1012
info@issa.com; www.issa.com
Social Media: Facebook, Twitter, LinkedIn

John Barrett, Executive Director
Alan R Tomblin, President
John Swigart, Secretary
John Barrett, Treasurer

The worldwide cleaning industry association.
5700+ Members
Founded in: 1923

4624 **International Drycleaners Congress**
9016 Oak Branch Dr.
Apex, NC 27502

919-363-5062; *Fax:* 919-387-8326;
www.idcnews.org

Manfred Wentz, Executive Director
Nobuyasu Igarashi, President

International organization for cleaners.
Founded in: 1959

4625 **International Kitchen Exhaust Cleaning Association**
100 N. 20th St.
Suite 400
Philadelphia, PA 19103

215-320-3876; *Fax:* 215-564-2175
information@ikeca.org; www.ikeca.org
Social Media: Facebook, Twitter, LinkedIn, YouTube

Kathy Slomer, President
Randall Rauth, President-Elect
Anne Levine, Secretary
Jesse Getz, Treasurer
Jack Grace, Immediate Past President

Promotes fire safety in restaurants through stringent standards and practices for contractors engaged in kitchen exhaust cleaning. Conducts a variety of educational programs, and works with influential code setting bodies such as the National Fire Protection Association to improve existing codes and regulations.
Founded in: 1989

4626 **International Maintenance Institute**
PO Box 751896
Houston, TX 77275

281-481-0869; *Fax:* 281-481-8337
iminst@swbell.net; www.imionline.org
Social Media: Facebook, Twitter, LinkedIn

George Masterson, Chairman
Gerard Goudreau, President
Joyce Rhoden, Executive Secretary
Edward Stedman, Secretary
Kevin O'Rourke, Treasurer

Focuses on plant workers and vendors who have products tailored to the maintenance industry.

The philosophy of the organization is to professionalize the maintenance function by helping maintenance managers to work smarter through the exchange of ideas and education.
2.5M Members
Founded in: 1960

4627 **Laundry and Dry Cleaning International**
14700 Sweitzer Lane
Laurel, MD 20707
301-622-1900
800-638-2627; *Fax:* 240-295-0685
techline@ifi.org; www.ifi.org
Patrick Jones, Manager
Sponsors and supports The League of Voter Education Political Action Committee.

4628 **Multi-Housing Laundry Association**
1500 Sunday Drive
Suite 102
Raleigh, NC 27607-5151
919-861-5579
800-380-3652; *Fax:* 919-787-4916
nshore@mla-online.com; www.mla-online.com
Social Media: Facebook, Twitter, LinkedIn
David Feild, Executive Director
Penny DePas CAE, Asst Exec Director/Conference Mgr
Furnishes information on tax and business development and promotes high business standards. Annual meetings held in June.
15M Members
Founded in: 1959

4629 **National Association of Diaper Services**
994 Old Eagle School Rd
Suite 1019
Wayne, PA 19087-1802
610-971-4850; *Fax:* 610-971-4859
nads@diapernet.org; www.diapernet.org
John Shiffert, Executive Director
The international professional trade association for the diaper service industry.
Founded in: 1938

4630 **National Association of Institutional Linen Management**
2130 Lexington Road
Richmond, KY 40475-7923
800-669-0863; *Fax:* 859-624-3580;
www.nailm.org
Jim Thacker, Executive Director
Seeks improvement of laundry technology. Conducts formal schools.
1.4M Members
Founded in: 1959

4631 **National Cleaners Association**
252 W 29th St
New York, NY 10001
212-967-3002
800-888-1622; *Fax:* 212-967-2240
info@nca-i.com; www.nca-i.com
Social Media: Facebook, LinkedIn, Pinterest
Debra Kravet, President
Nora Nealis, Executive Director
Simon Bai, Member Services Staff
Clint Lee, Member Services Staff
Vivian Benn, Office Staff
Professional trade association dedicated to the welfare of well groomed consumers and the professional cleaners who serve them. Elected officials, government angencies, consumer groups, fashion designers and major media outlets have recognized and responded to NCA's activities, reports and tradition of excellence.
4000 Members
Founded in: 1946

4632 **North East Fabricare Association**
P.O.Box 920
Pelham, NH 03076
603-635-0322
800-442-6848; *Fax:* 781-942-7393
peteblke@aol.com; www.nefabricare.com
Robert Joel, Vice-President
John Dallas, President
Yaahkov Cohn, Treasurer
John Dallas, Secretary
Serves cleaners in the New England, New Jersey and New York with information and news about the fabricare industry.
Founded in: 1992

4633 **Power Washers of North America**
PO Box 270634
Saint Paul, MN 55127
800-393-7962
800-393-7962; *Fax:* 651-213-0369;
www.pwna.org
Eric Clark, President
Tom Bickett, Treasurer
John Nearon, VP
Charlie Arnold, Secretary
Jackie Gavett, Executive Dir.
Developing and communicating high standards in ethical business practices, environmental awareness and safety through continuing education and active representation of the membership. PWNA educated and trained contractors raise the level of professionalism and value to their customers.
550 Members
Founded in: 1992
Mailing list available for rent: 500 names

4634 **Restoration Industry Association**
2025 M Street, NW
Suite 800
Rockville, MD 20852
202-367-1180
800-272-7012; *Fax:* 202-367-2180
info@restorationindustry.org;
www.restorationindustry.org
Social Media: Facebook, Twitter, LinkedIn
Scott Stamper, President
Chuck Violand, First Vice President
Mark Springer, Vice President
Jack A White, Secretary
Larry Holder, Treasurer
A trade association for cleaning and restoration professionals worldwide, and the foremost authority, trainer and educator in the industry.
1100 Members
Founded in: 1946

4635 **Rocky Mountain Fabricare Association**
2110 65th Ave.
Greely, CO 80634
970-330-0124
866-964-RFMA; *Fax:* 303-458-0002
info@rmfa.org; www.rmfa.org
Social Media: Facebook
Colleen Mulhern, Executive Director
Brad Ewing, Secretary/Treasurer
Jim Nixon, President
Enhancing the image and viability of the fabricare industry through education and development of the skills, talents and professionalism of its membership. Serves cleaners in Colorado, Utah and Wyoming.
900 Members

4636 **South Eastern Fabricare Association**
14700 Sweitzer Lane
Laurel, MD 20707
877-707-7332
877-707-7332; *Fax:* 912-355-3155
peter@sefa.org; www.sefa.org
Tim Morrow, President
Mark Watkins, VP-Alabama
Julia Campbell, Secretary
Wash Respress, Chairman
Russ Ballard, VP- South Carolina
Trade association that represents its members who have an interest in the dry cleaning and laundry industry.
900+ Members
Founded in: 1972
Mailing list available for rent

4637 **Southwest Drycleaners Association**
5750 Balcones Dr.
Suite 201
Austin, TX 78731
512-873-8195; *Fax:* 512-873-7423;
www.sda-dryclean.com
Social Media: Facebook, Twitter
Andrew Stanley, Executive Director
Michael E. Nesbit, CED, President
Douglas Johnson,CGCP, 1st Vice President
Amin Bata, CPD, 2nd Vice President
Jeff Schwarz, Sergeant at Arms
Serves cleaners in Louisiana, Mississippi, Missouri, Kansas, Arkansa, New Mexico, Oklahoma and Texas.

4638 **Sponge and Chamois Institute**
10024 Office Center Ave.
Suite 203
St. Louis, MO 63128
314-842-2230; *Fax:* 314-842-3999
scwaters@swbell.net;
www.chamoisinstitute.org
Jules Schwimmer, Executive Secretary
Members are dealers and suppliers of natural sponges and chamois leather.
Founded in: 1933

4639 **Uniform and Textile Service Association**
12587 Fair Lakes Cir
Fairfax, VA 22033-3822
703-247-2600
800-486-6745; *Fax:* 703-841-4750
info@utsa.com; www.utsa.com
David Hobson, President
Jennifer Kellar, Executive Coordinator
Larry Patton, Director Plant Operations
Deborah Hodges, Director Finance/Administration
Represents textile supply and service companies. Represents 95% of the annual sales generated by the uniform service industry and 65% of the annual sales generated by the linen supply industry. UTSA members provide, clean, and maintain reusable textile products, such as uniforms, sheets, table linen, shop and print towels, floor mats, mops and other items to thousands of businesses.
100 Members
Founded in: 1933

Newsletters

4640 **Bulletin**
Neighborhood Cleaners Association

252 W 29th St
New York, NY 10001-5271

212-967-3002; *Fax:* 212-967-2240
ncaiclean@aol.com; www.nca-i.com

Debra Kravet, President

Technical info for the dry cleaning industry. Government regulation compliance.
Frequency: Bi-Monthly

4641 Coin Laundry Association: Journal
Coin Laundry Association
1315 Butterfield Road
Suite 212
Downers Grove, IL 60515-5602

630-963-5547; *Fax:* 630-963-5864
info@coinlaundry.org; www.coinlaundry.org

Clay Pederson, Chairman
Brian Wallace, President
Bob Nieman, Editor
Laurie Moore, Circulation Manager
Bill Gilbert, Marketing Manager

Committed to offering coin-op owners the information necessary to become and remain competitive in today's changing market.
4 Pages
Frequency: Monthly
Founded in: 1960

4642 Fabricare News
Drycleaning & Laundrey Institute International
14700 Sweitzer lane
Laurel, MD 20707

301-622-1900
800-638-2627; *Fax:* 240-295-4200
techline@dlionline.org; www.dlionline.org
Social Media: Facebook

David MacHesny, President
Charlie Smith, Chair
Mary Scalco, CEO

Information of interest to dry cleaners and launderers.
8 Pages
Frequency: Monthly
Circulation: 5000
Founded in: 1883

4643 Maytag Commercial Newsletter
Whirlpool Corporation
553 Benson Road
Benton Harbor, MI 49022-2692

269-923-5000
800-344-1274; www.maytag.com

Mike Klosterman, Publisher
Debbie White, Executive Director

Self-service laundry industry news.
8 Pages
Frequency: BiWeekly

4644 Reclaimer
South Eastern Fabricare Association
7373 Hodgson Memorial Dr
Building 3, Suite C
Savannah, GA 31406-1595

912-355-3364
877-707-7332; *Fax:* 912-355-3155;
www.sefa.org

Billy Stewart, President
Ron McLamb, VP

A monthly newsletter dedicated to the service of the drycleaning industry.
Cost: $5.00
Frequency: Monthly
Circulation: 2200

Magazines & Journals

4645 American Coin-Op
Crain Communications Inc
360 N Michigan Ave
Suite 7
Chicago, IL 60601-3800

312-649-5200; *Fax:* 312-649-7937
info@crain.com; www.crain.com

Keith Crain, CEO

Offers operators, manufacturers and suppliers in-depth coverage of the latest industry trends, new products, energy-saving methods and management strategies.
Frequency: Monthly
Circulation: 17622
Mailing list available for rent

4646 American Drycleaner
Crain Communications Inc
360 N Michigan Ave
Suite 7
Chicago, IL 60601-3800

312-649-5200; *Fax:* 312-649-7937
info@crain.com; www.crain.com

Keith Crain, CEO

Brings news, expert advice and indepth features to drycleaning businesses and suppliers nationwide every month. Stories focus on management, equipment and operations to help owners build their skills and profits.
Frequency: Monthly
Circulation: 24217

4647 American Laundry News
Crain Communications Inc
360 N Michigan Ave
Suite 7
Chicago, IL 60601-3800

312-649-5200; *Fax:* 312-649-7937
info@crain.com; www.crain.com

Keith Crain, CEO

Focuses on the widely varied issues facing the industry: productivity, technology, labor, workplace safety, the environment and more.
Frequency: Monthly
Circulation: 15350
Founded in: 1974

4648 American Window Cleaner Magazine
12 Twelve Publishing Corporation
750-B NW Broad Street
Southern Pines, NC 28387

910-693-2644; *Fax:* 910-246-1681
info@awcmag.com; www.awcmag.com

Norman J Finegold, President

Information on new products, add-on businesses, association and convention news and safety.
Frequency: 6x/Year
Circulation: 8000

4649 Broom Brush & Mop
Rankin Publishing Company
204 E Main St
PO Box 130
Arcola, IL 61910-1416

217-268-0130; *Fax:* 217-268-4815
DRankin125@aol.com; www.ragsmag.com

Don Rankin, Owner
Harrell Kerkhoff, Editor
Ron White, Associate Editor

Reports on import and export totals as well as updates on new products and trade show coverage, also industry trends and market conditions.
Cost: $25.00
Frequency: Monthly
Circulation: 1,700
Founded in: 1912

4650 Brushware
Brushware
750-B NW Broad St
Southern Pines, NC 28387

910-693-2644; *Fax:* 910-246-1681
editors@brushwaremag.com;
www.brushwaremag.com/

Karen Grinter, Publisher
Norman J Finegold, President

Information on products that apply materials, clean and polish surfaces, covers also industry news, products, methods and trends, market reports, profiles and interviews.
Cost: $45.00
Circulation: 2000
Founded in: 1898

4651 Cleaner
COLE Publishing
1720 Maple Lake Dam Road
PO Box 220
Three Lakes, WI 54562

715-546-3346
800-257-7222; *Fax:* 715-546-3786;
www.cleaner.com

Ted Roulphe, Editor
Geoff Bruss, CEO

The latest tools and equipment promoting safety and efficiency, employment and environmental concerns, as well as industry profiles.
Cost: $15.00
Frequency: Monthly
Circulation: 24000
Founded in: 1979

4652 Cleaner Times
Advantage Publishing Company
1000 Nix Rd
Little Rock, AR 72211-3235

866-828-9267
800-525-7038; *Fax:* 501-280-9233
advpub@adpub.com; www.adpub.com

Charlene Yarbrough, Publisher
Gerry Plus, Circualtion Manager
Jim McMurry, Editor

Application, information, and productivity for persons engaged in the manufacturing, distribution, or the use of high pressure water systems and accessories. The emphasis is on safety, regulatory, which affect the industry as well as cleaning applications.
Cost: $36.00
72 Pages
Frequency: Monthly
Circulation: 25,000
ISSN: 1073-9602
Founded in: 1989
Printed in 4 colors on glossy stock

4653 Cleanfax Magazine
National Trade Publications
19 British Amer. Blvd. West
Latham, NY 12110-2197

518-783-1281; *Fax:* 518-783-1386;
www.cleanfax.com

Micah Ogburn, Publisher
Jeff Cross, Senio Editor
Barry Lovette, General Manager

Information on carpet cleaning, water and fire damage restoration, industry news and updates.
80 Pages
Frequency: Monthly
Circulation: 20,000
Founded in: 1981
Printed in 4 colors on glossy stock

4654 Cleaning & Restoration Magazine
Restoration Industry Association
9810 Patuxent Woods Dr
Suite K
Columbia, MD 21046-1595

443-878-1000
800-272-7012; *Fax:* 443-878-1010
info@restorationindustry.org;
www.restorationindustry.org

Donald E Manger, Executive Director
Patricia L Harman, Communications Director

Trade journal covering fire and water damage restoration, rug and textile cleaning, indoor air quality and business issues.
Frequency: Monthly
Circulation: 6000

4655 Commercial Floor Care
Business News Publishing Company
22801 Ventura Blvd
Suite 115
Woodland Hills, CA 91364-1230

818-224-8035
800-835-4398; *Fax:* 818-224-8042;
www.bnpmedia.com

Phil Johnson, Publisher
Jeffrey Stouffer, Editor
Amy Levin, Production Manager
Jim Michaelson, Associate Publisher

Dedicated to floor care in the commercial environment.
40 Pages
Frequency: Monthly
Circulation: 26700
Founded in: 1926
Printed in 4 colors on glossy stock

4656 Fabricare
Drycleaning & Laundry Institute International
14700 Sweitzer Lane
Laurel, MD 20707

301-622-1900
800-638-2627; *Fax:* 240-295-0685;
www.dlionline.org

Charlie Smith, Chairman
Jan Barlow, President
Dave MacHesny, President-Elect

The central publication of the International Fabricare Institute. This publication provides information, knowledge and education about drycleaning and laundry issues, the industry, as a whole, and the association.
8 Pages
Frequency: Monthly
Circulation: 8,000
Founded in: 1883

4657 ICS Cleaning Specialist
Business News Publishing Company
2401 West Big Beaver Road
Troy, MI 48054

818-224-8035
800-835-4398; *Fax:* 818-224-8042;
www.bnpmedia.com

Phil Johnson, Publisher
Evan Kessler, Publisher
Eric Fish, Editor
Amy Levin, Production Manager
Jim Michaelson, Associate Publisher

For carpet cleaning, restoration and floor care service providers.
68 Pages
ISSN: 1522-4708
Founded in: 1928
Printed in on glossy stock

4658 Industrial Launderer Magazine
Uniform & Textile Service Association
1501 Lee Hwy.kes Cir
Suite 304
Arlington, VA 22209

703-247-2600
800-486-6745; *Fax:* 703-841-4750

George Harrinton Jr, President

The authoritative source for information for the uniform and textile service industry. It provides practical guidance and assistance for businesses that rent, lease or sell uniforms and other textiles including linen supply.
Cost: $100.00
Frequency: Monthly
Circulation: 6000

4659 International Fabricare Institute
12251 Tech Rd
Silver Spring, MD 20904-1901

301-622-1900
800-638-2627; *Fax:* 301-236-9320
techline@ifi.org; www.ifi.org

William E Fisher, Publisher

The association of Professional Dry Cleaners, wetcleaners, and launderers. With its education, research, testing and professional training, IFI offers solutions that help member businesses provide expert garment care.
Founded in: 1883

4660 Journal of the Coin Laundering and Drycleaning Industry
Coin Laundry Association
1315 Butterfield Road
Suite 212
Downers Grove, IL 60515-5602

630-963-5547
800-570-5629; *Fax:* 630-963-5864
info@coinlaundry.org; www.coinlaundry.org

Brian Wallace, President
Clay Pederson, Chairman

The official voice of the coin laundry and drycleaning industry. It's the most cost effective way to reach over 28,000 small business entrepreneurs. Besides industry specific items these owners operate over 38,000 company vehicles, utilize business management materials and more. Accepts advertising.
52 Pages
Frequency: Monthly

4661 Maintenance Sales News
Rankin Publishing Company
204 E Main St
PO Box 130
Arcola, IL 61910-0130

217-268-4959
800-598-8083; *Fax:* 217-268-4815
drankin125@aol.com; www.ragsmag.com

Don Rankin, Owner
Linda Rankin, Co-Publisher
Harrell Kerkhoff, Editor
Rick Mullen, Editor

Information on selling techniques, business management, training, merchandise, and seminars.
Circulation: 18,000

4662 Maintenance Solutions
Trade Press Publishing Corporation
2100 W Florist Avenue
Milwaukee, WI 53209

414-228-7701; *Fax:* 414-228-1134
contact@facilitiesnet.com;
www.facilitiesnet.com
Dick Yake, Editoridal Director
Dan Hounsell, Editor
Brad Ehlert, VP Publisher
Robert Geissler, Publisher
Stephen Bolte, Publisher
How to articles and features designed to alleviate reader problems as well as new product information and applications.
Cost: $45.00
42 Pages
Frequency: Monthly
Circulation: 35000
ISSN: 1072-3560
Founded in: 1993

4663 Maintenance Supplies
Cygnus Publishing
3 Huntington Quadrangle
Suite 301N
Melville, NY 11747-3601

631-845-2700
800-308-6397; *Fax:* 720-945-2798
Rich.DiPaolo@cygnuspub.com;
www.cygnusb2b.com

Tracy Rossi, Publisher
Paul Mackler, President
Rich Di Paolo, Editor
Kathy Scott, Director of Public Relations
Elise Schafer, Assistant Editor

Case histories and general industry news, also supply distributors, new methods and equipment in the field.
Cost: $66.00
Frequency: Monthly
Circulation: 16,500
Founded in: 1966

4664 National Association of Institutional Linen Management News Magazine
2161 Lexington Rd
Suite 2
Richmond, KY 40475-7952

859-624-0177
800-669-0863; *Fax:* 859-624-3580;
www.nlmnet.org

Linda Fairbanks, Executive Director
Randy Wendland, Corporate Director

Offers information for cleaners of fine fabrics.
Frequency: Monthly

4665 Sanitary Maintenance
Trade Press Publishing Corporation
2100 W Florist Avenue
Milwaukee, WI 53201-3799

414-228-7701; *Fax:* 414-228-1134
info@tradepress.com; www.tradepress.com

Dick Yake, Editorial Director
Brian Terry, Publisher
Pat Foran, Editor
Robert Wisniewski, CEO

Business management, inventory control and product trends, also includes industrial paper products, cleaning chemicals, safety supplies, janitorial supplies and packaging products.
58 Pages
Frequency: Monthly
Circulation: 16052
ISSN: 0036-4436
Founded in: 1943

4666 Services Magazine
Building Service Contractors Association Int'l
401 N Michigan Avenue
22nd Floor
Chicago, IL 60611

312-321-5167
800-368-3414; *Fax:* 312-673-6735
info@bscai.org; www.bscai.org

Oliver Yandle, Executive VP/CEO
Karen Lawver, Director Membership Services

The Building Service Contractors Association International is the trade association serving the facility services industry through education,

leadership, and representatiion.
Cost: $30.00
56 Pages
Frequency: Monthly
Circulation: 20064
ISSN: 0279-0548
Founded in: 1981
Mailing list available for rent: 20000 names

4667 **Textile Rental Magazine**
Textile Rental Services Association
1800 Diagonal Rd
Suite 200
Alexandria, VA 22314-2842
703-519-0029
877-770-9274; *Fax:* 703-519-0026
trsa@trsa.org; www.trsa.org
Roger Cocivera, President/CEO
Jack Morgan, Editor
Steven Biller, Editorial Director
Packed with valuable tips and ideas.
Frequency: Monthly

4668 **Water Conditioning & Purification Magazine**
Publicom, Incorporated
2800 E. Ft. Lowell Road
Tucson, AZ 85716
520-323-6144; *Fax:* 520-323-7412
info@wcponline.com; www.wcponline.com
Kurt C. Peterson, Publisher
Sharon Peterson, Business Manager
Denise Roberts, Executive Editor
Water Conditioning & Purification Magazine(WC&P) has been the premier source for news, technical artticles and water science features sine 1959. We are committed to the water treatment industry. Our pro bono participation includes event and activity sponsorship, committe members, task force cahiras and association leadership.

Trade Shows

4669 **Association of Specialists in Cleaning & Restoration Convention**
Restoration Industry Association
9810 Patuxent Woods Drive
Suite K
Columbia, MD 21046-1595
443-878-1000
800-272-7012; *Fax:* 443-878-1010
info@restorationindustry.org; www.restorationindustry.org
Donald E Manger, Executive Director
Patricia L Harman, Communications Director
Annual convention and exhibits of carpet, upholstery and draperies cleaning and restoration equipment, duct cleaning supplies and services, 100+ booths.
600 Attendees
Frequency: Annual
Founded in: 1945

4670 **Building Service Contractors Association International Trade Show**
401 N Michigan Avenue
22nd Floor
Chicago, IL 60611
312-321-5167
800-368-3414; *Fax:* 312-673-6735
info@bscai.org; www.bscai.org
Oliver Yandle, Executive VP/CEO
Karen Lawver, Director Membership Services
Containing 400 booths and 185 exhibits.
2000 Attendees
Frequency: March/April
Founded in: 1965

4671 **Clean Show**
Riddle & Associates
1874 Piedmont Road
Suite 360
Atlanta, GA 30305
404-876-1988; *Fax:* 404-876-5121
info@cleanshow.com; www.cleanshow.com
John Riddle, Manager
Ann Howell, Communications
World's largest exposition for laundry, drycleaning and textile services industry featuring working equipment and educational program. Draws international attendance.
17000 Attendees
Frequency: Biennial, Odd Years
Founded in: 1977

4672 **Educational Congress for Laundering & Drycleaning**
Coin Laundry Association
1315 Butterfield Road
Suite 212
Downers Grove, IL 60515-5602
630-963-5547
800-570-5629; *Fax:* 630-963-5864
info@coinlaundry.org; www.coinlaundry.org
Brian Wallace, President
Clay Pederson, Chairman
Two thousand one hundred booths of equipment and products for the cleaning industry. Service schools and other events planned.
22M Attendees
Frequency: July

4673 **National Educational Exposition and Conference**
Environmental Management Association
Fishbones In Greektown
400 Monroe Street
Detroit, MI 48226-3333
Annual show of 15 manufacturers, suppliers and distributors of sanitation maintenance supplies, products, services.
150 Attendees

4674 **Power Clean**
Cleaning Equipment Trade Association
P0 Box 1710
Indian Trail, NC 28079
704-635-7362
800-441-0111; *Fax:* 704-635-7363; www.ceta.org
Troy Tranquill, President
Karl Loeffelholz, Manager
Annual show of 100 manufacturers and suppliers of cleaning equipment, high pressure washers and related component accessories and products.
1200 Attendees
Frequency: October, Dallas

4675 **Southern Drycleaners Show**
South Eastern Fabricare Association
P0 Box 912
Cumming, GA 30028
877-707-7332; *Fax:* 770-998-1441; www.sefa.org
Joel Deutsch, Manager
Trade show for the drycleaning industry with 120 exhibitors and 250 booths.
2500 Attendees
Frequency: August

4676 **Tex Care**
National Cleaners Association
252 W 29th Street
New York, NY 10001
212-967-3002; *Fax:* 212-967-2240
ncaiclean@aol.com; www.nca-i.com
Joseph Hallak, President
Ted Aveni, First Vice President
Containing 350 exhibits of interest to member cleaners.
5000+ Attendees
Frequency: April

Directories & Databases

4677 **Carpet Cleaners Institute of the Northwest Membership Roster**
147 SE 102nd Avenue
Portland, OR 97216-2703
503-253-9091
805-261-8222; *Fax:* 503-253-9172
info@ccinw.org; www.ccinw.org
Over 330 member companies involved in the carpet cleaning industry in Washington, Oregon, and Montana, USA and Alberta and British Columbia, Canada.
Frequency: Annual

4678 **Cleaning and Maintenance Management: Buyer's Guide Directory Issue**
National Trade Publications
13 Century Hill Drive
Latham, NY 12110-2197
518-783-1281; *Fax:* 518-783-1386
cmmonline.com
Alice J Savino, Group Publisher
Chris Sanford, Executive Editor
Over 500 manufacturers are profiled that supply equipment used in building maintenance and housekeeping.
Cost: $42.00
84 Pages
Frequency: Annual
Circulation: 42000
ISSN: 1051-5720
Founded in: 1966
Mailing list available for rent: 42M names at $125 per M
Printed in 4 colors on glossy stock

4679 **Coin Laundry Association of Suppliers**
Coin Laundry Association
1315 Butterfield Road
Downers Grove, IL 60515
630-963-5547
800-570-5629; *Fax:* 630-963-5864
info@coinlaundry.org; www.coinlaundry.org
Brian Wallace, President
Clay Pederson, Chairman
Bob Nieman, Editor
Kathy Sherman, Director Administration
Sue Lally, Director Membership
Lists over 500 manufacturers and suppliers of products and services to the coin and dry cleaning laundry industries.
2700+ Pages
Founded in: 1960

4680 **Inside Textile Service - Directories**
Uniform & Textile Service Association
12587 Fair Lakes Cir
Fairfax, VA 22033-3822
703-247-2600
800-486-6745; *Fax:* 703-841-4750; www.utsa.com
David Hobson, President
Jennifer Kellar, Executive Coordinator

The uniform and textile service industry's most comprehensive guide to US textile service companies. Includes contact data for UTSA's membership, and for hundreds of other textile service companies as well. Contains listings of all UTSA affiliated suppliers with catalog-like data on their products and services. Free to members.
Circulation: 3,000

4681 Textile Rental Services Association Roster
Textile Rental Services Association
1800 Diagonal Rd
Suite 200
Alexandria, VA 22314-2842

703-519-0029; *Fax:* 703-519-0026
trsa@trsa.org; www.trsa.org

Roger Cocivera, President
Scott Mallan, Finance Manager
Michael Wilson, Director Government Affairs
Jack Morgan, Editor

Offers a list of over 1,800 companies that supply linen, uniforms and other textile products to other industries.
1300 Pages
Founded in: 1913

Industry Web Sites

4682 http://gold.greyhouse.com
G.O.L.D Grey House OnLine Databases

Grey House Publishing's online database platform, GOLD, offers Quick Search, Keyword Search and Expert Search for most business sectors inlcuding the cleaning and laundry markets. Finding the information you need quick and easy - whether you're a novice searcher or an experienced database user. All of Grey House's directory products are available for subscription on the GOLD platform.

4683 www.ascr.org
Assn of Specialists in Cleaning and Restoration

For professionals involved in the cleaning and restoration of interior textiles and structures, including air handling systems.

4684 www.bscai.org
Building Service Contractors Association Int'l

For companies offering security, maintenance and cleaning services.

4685 www.ceta.org
Cleaning Equipment Trade Association

For manufacturers and suppliers of cleaning equipment, high pressure washers and related component accessories and products.

4686 www.cminstitute.net
Cleaning Management Institute

CMI provides education, training and career improvement opportunities for building cleaning and maintenance professionals.

4687 www.coinlaundry.org
Coin Laundry Association

For self-service laundry and dry cleaning industry. CLA is a not for profit trade association representing the 30,000 coin laundry owners in the US and the world.

4688 www.greyhouse.com
Grey House Publishing

Authoritative reference directories for most business sectors including cleaning and laundry markets. Users can search the online databases with varied search criteria allowing for custom searches by product category, geographic area, sales volume, keyword, subject and more. Full Grey House catalog and online ordering also available.

4689 www.ifi.org
International Fabricare Institute

With its education, research, testing and professional training, IFI offers solutions that help member businesses provide expert garment care.

4690 www.ikeca.org
International Kitchen Exhaust Cleaning Association

Education for members about safety, cleaning techniques and many other areas. Since its inception, IKECA, a not for profit trade association, has established stringent standards and practices for contractors engaged in kitchen exhaust clening, conducted a variety of educational programs, and worked with influential code setting bodies such as the National Fire Protection Association to improve existing codes and regulations.

4691 www.imionline.org
International Maintenance Institute

Focuses on plant workers and vendors who have products tailored to the maintenance industry. The philosophy of the organization is to professionalize the maintenace functiuon by helping maintenace managers to work smarter through the exchange of ideas and function.

4692 www.jriddle.com
Riddle & Associates

For the laundering, drycleaning and textile care industry - from single-owner coin-operated laundry and drycleaning establishments to giant industrial and institutional laundries. Our management capabilities work for any type of trade show - large or small. Our experience with heavy utility shows, and shows with highly technical requirements, gives us an expertise in these areas that is difficult to find.

4693 www.nailm.org
National Assn of Insurance Litigation Management

National educational and research group concerned primarily with the advancement of the art of manageing litigated claims.

4694 www.natclo.com
National Clothesline

News of interest to drycleaners. Links to regional and state associations, calendar of events.

4695 www.nca-i.com
Neighborhood Cleaners Association

Professional trade association dedicated to the welfare of well-groomed consumers and the professional cleaners and suppliers who serve them. for over 50 years, NCA has been at the vanguard of education, research and information distribution concerning garment and household fabric care. Elected officials, goverment agencies, consumer groups, fashion designers and major media outlets have recognized and responded to NCA's activities, reports and tradition of excellence.

4696 www.pwna.org
Power Washers of North America

Developing and communicating the highest standards in ethical business practices, environmental awareness and safety through continuing education and active representation of the membership. PWNA educated and trained contractors raise the level of professionalism and value to their customers.

4697 www.rmfa.org
Rocky Mountain Fabricare Association

Enhancing the image and viability of the fabricare industry through education and development of the skills, talents, and professionalism of its membership.

4698 www.sdahq.org
Soap and Detergent Association

Nonprofit tade association representing over 100 North American manufacturers of household, industrial and institutional cleaning products; their ingredients and finished packaging. Established in 1926, SDA is dedicated to advancing public understanding of the safety and benefits of cleaning products and protecting the ability of its members to formulate products that best meet consumer needs.

4699 www.sefa.org
South Eastern Fabricare Association

Trade association that represents its members who have an interest in the dry cleaning and laundry industry. The not for profit asscoiation provides value through education, research, legislative representation, industry specific information programs, products and services.

4700 www.uniforminfo.com
Uniform & Textile Service Association

Uniform companies provide more than just corporate apparel programs. Companies on this site offer a wide variety of products and services that will not only ensure that your unique corporate identity is conveyed consistently, but will help your workplace run more smoothly.

4701 www.utsa.com
Uniform & Textile Service Association

One stop place for important industry and UTSA news. It has complete information on upcoming events and activities, including online meeting brochures and secure online registration. Each department at UTSA has its own page where you will find information about committees, projects, regulations, and links to dozens of other pertinent sites such as the Clean Show or government sites.

Associations

4702 **Accuracy in Media**
4350 East West Highway
Suite 555
Bethesda, MD 20814

202-364-4401
800-787-4567; *Fax:* 202-364-4098
info@aim.org; www.aim.org
Social Media: Facebook, Twitter, LinkedIn, YouTube

Don Irvine, Chairman
Deborah Lambert, Director of Special Projects
Roger Aronoff, Editor
Cliff Kincaid, Dir. AIM Center

Accuracy in Media is a non-profit, grassroots citizens watchdog of the news media that critiques botched and bungled news stories and sets the record straight on important issues that have received slanted coverage.
3500 Members
Founded in: 1969

4703 **Advanced Television Systems Committee**
1776 K Street NW
8th Floor
Washington, DC 20006-2304

202-872-9160; *Fax:* 202-872-9161
atsc@atsc.org; www.atsc.org
Social Media: Facebook, Twitter

Mark Richer, President
Jerry Whitaker, Vice President
Lindsay Shelton Gross, Director, Communications
Daro Bruno, Office Manager

ATSC is an international, non-profit organzation developing voluntary standards for digital television.

4704 **Agricultural Comm. Excellence in Ag., Natural Resources and Life Sciences**
University of Florida
59 College Road
Taylor Hall
Durham, NH 03824

855-657-9544; *Fax:* 603-862-1585
ace.info@unh.edu; www.aceweb.org
Social Media: Facebook, LinkedIn, YouTube, Pinterest, RSS

Brad Beckman, President
Suzanne Steel, VP
Steve Miller, President-elect
Bob Furbee, Retirees Director
Holly Young, Executive Director

Members are writers, editors, broadcasters and communicators who are involved in the dissemination of agricultural, food sciences and natural resource information in land-grant colleges, federal and state agencies, international agencies and other private communications work.
700+ Members
Founded in: 1970

4705 **Alliance for Telecommunication Industry Solutions**
1200 G St NW
Suite 500
Washington, DC 20005

202-628-6380; *Fax:* 202-393-5453;
www.atis.org
Social Media: Twitter

Susan Miller, President/CEO
Andrew White, VP of Technology & Standards
Lauren Layman, VP of Marketing & Public Relations
Kris Rinne, Chairman
Bill Klein, VP Finance/Operations

Membership organization that provides the tools necessary for the industry to identify standards, guidelines and operating procedures that make the inoperability of existing and emerging telecommunications products and services possible.
1400 Members
Founded in: 1983

4706 **Alliance for Telecommunications Industry Solutions**
1200 G Street, NW
Suite 500
Washington, DC 20005

202-628-6380; www.atis.org
Social Media: Twitter, LinkedIn

Susan Miller, President & CEO
Thomas Goode, General Counsel
Lauren Layman, VP, Marketing and Public Relations
Andrew White, VP, Technology and Standards

A standards organization that develops technical and operational standards and solutions for the ICT industry.

4707 **American Communication Association**
College of Business Administration
The University of Northern Iowa
1227 W 27th Street
Cedar Falls, IA 50614-0125

209-667-3374
pdecaro@csustan.edu;
www.americancomm.org

Dr. Phillip J. Auter, Executive Director
Prof. Jim Parker, President
Vernon Humphrey, CFO
Myrene Augustin Magabo, Secretary
Dr. John Malalala, CIO

Founded for the purposes of fostering research and scholarship in all areas of human communication behavior, promoting and improving excellence in the pedagogy of communication, providing a voice in communication law and policy, providing evaluation and certification services for academic programs in communication study.
Founded in: 1993

4708 **American Public Communications Council**
3213 Duke Street
Suite 806
Alexandria, VA 22314

703-739-1322; *Fax:* 703-739-1324
APCC@apcc.net; www.apcc.net

Willard R. Nichols, President
Deborah Sterman, CFO
Helly Shareefy, Office Manager
Dan Collins, Corporate Counsel
Evelyn Bruggeman, Account Manager

Formed to promote and address, at the FCC and on Capitol Hill, the legal and regulatory issues facing payphone service providers.
1200 Members
Founded in: 1988

4709 **Armed Forces Communications & Electronics Association**
4400 Fair Lakes Ct
Fairfax, VA 22033-3899

703-631-6100
800-336-4583; *Fax:* 703-631-6169;
www.afcea.org
Social Media: Facebook, Twitter, LinkedIn, YouTube, Flickr

Kent Schneider, President/CEO
Nancy Temple, International Secretary
James L. Griggs, Jr., VP, CIO & CTO
Linda Gooden, Chairman
Patrick Miorin, EVP, CFO & International Treasurer

A non-profit membership association serving the military, government, industry, and academia as an ethical forum for advancing professional knowledge and relationships in the fields of communications, IT, intelligence, and global security.
31000 Members
Founded in: 1946

4710 **AscdiNatd**
131 NW First Avenue
Delray Beach, FL 33444

561-266-9016; *Fax:* 561-431-6302;
www.ascdi.com
Social Media: Facebook, Twitter, LinkedIn, YouTube

Rob Neumeyer, Board Member
Jerry Roberts, Board Member
Todd A. Bone, Board Member
Thomas Weltin, Board Member
Scott Fluty, Board Member

An international trade association made up of companies who providetechnology solutions, technical support, and value added services to the business community.

4711 **Association Media & Publishing**
12100 Sunset Hills Road
Suite 130
Reston, VA 20190

703-234-4063; *Fax:* 703-435-4390
info@associationmediaandpublishing.org
associationmediaandpublishing.org
Social Media: Facebook, Twitter, LinkedIn

Erin Pressley, President, BOD
Angel Alvarez-Mapp, Vice President, BOD
Kim Howard, CAE, Immediate Past President
Leslie McGee, Treasurer
John Falcioni, Assistant Treasurer

Serves the needs of association publishers, communications professionals and the media they create.
Founded in: 1963

4712 **Association for Business Communication**
181 Turner St, NW
Blacksburg, VA 24061
540-231-8460; *Fax:* 646-349-5297
abcoffice@businesscommunication.org
businesscommunication.org
Social Media: Facebook, Twitter

Kathy Rentz, First VP
Peter W. Cardon, Second VP
Nancy Schullery, President
Jim Dubinsky, Executive Dir.
Marilyn Buerkens, Office Manager

International organization commited to fostering excellence in business communication scholarship, research, education, and practice.
72 Members
Founded in: 1935

4713 **Association for Conservation Information**
Division of Fish Game and Wildlife
Po Box 400
Trenton, NJ 08625-0400

609-984-0837; *Fax:* 609-984-1414;
www.aci-net.org
Social Media: Facebook

Micah Holmes, President
Robin Cahoon, Vice-President
Kim Nix, Secretary
Judy Stokes Weber, Treasurer
Rachel Bradley, Board Member

Works to upgrade the quality of all forms of communication in and among agencies devoted to the

protection and management of natural resources and wildlife.
110 Members
Founded in: 1984

4714 Association for Educational Communications and Technology
320 W. 8th St.
Suite 101
Bloomington, IN 47404-3745

812-335-7675
877-677-2328; *Fax:* 812-335-7678
aect@aect.org
aect.site-ym.com
Social Media: Facebook, Twitter

Phillip Harris, Executive Director
Larry Vernon, Electronic Services
Brad Hokanson, President
Terri Lawson, Manager, Membership & Subscription

For audiovisual and instructional materials specialists, educational technologists, audiovisual and television production personnel, school media specialists.
2200 Members
Founded in: 1923
*Mailing list available for rent*at $159 per M

4715 Association for Information Systems
P.O. Box 2712
Atlanta, GA 30301-2712

404-413-7445
membership@aisnet.org
aisnet.org
Social Media: Facebook, Twitter, LinkedIn

Jody McGinness, Executive Director
Jason Thatcher, President
Mary C. Jones, Secretary
Matthew Nelson, Treasurer
Kevin D'Souza, VP of Communications

AIS members are academics with interest in information systems and related fields.
4300 Members
Founded in: 1994

4716 Association for Information and Image Management
1100 Wayne Avenue
Suite 1100
Silver Spring, MD 20910

301-587-8202
800-477-2446
aiim@aiim.org; www.aiim.org
Social Media: Facebook, Twitter, LinkedIn, YouTube, Google+, RSS

Paul Engel, Board Chair
Anthony Peleska, Vice Chair
Timothy Elmore, Immediate Past Chair
Daniel Antion, Treasurer
Mark Patrick, Executive Committee Member At Large

A nonprofit membership organization that provides education, marketresearch, certification, and standards for information professionals.

4717 Association for Interactive Marketing
1430 Broadway Avenue
8th Floor
New York, NY 10018

888-337-0008; *Fax:* 212-391-9233;
www.interactivehq.org

Kevin Noonan, Executive Director

AIM is a non-profit trade association for interactive marketers and service providers.

4718 Association for Multi-Media International
PO Box 1897
Lawrence, KS 66044

866-393-4264; *Fax:* 785-843-1274
hq@ami.org

Vanessa Reilly, Executive Director

The professional objectives of the AMI are to promote the safety and advancement of medical illustration and allied fields of visual communication, and to promote understanding and cooperation with the medical profession and related health science professions.
1M Members
Founded in: 1974

4719 Association for Postal Commerce
1800 Diagonal Rd.
Suite 320
Alexandria, VA 22314-2862

703-524-0096; *Fax:* 703-997-2414;
www.postcom.org

Gene Del Polito, President

National organization representing those who use, or who support, the use of mail as a medium for communication and commerce. Publishes a weekly newsletter covering postal policy and operational issues.
231 Members
Founded in: 1947

4720 Association for Service Managers International
11031 Via Frontera
Suite A
San Diego, CA 92127

239-275-7887
800-333-9786; *Fax:* 239-275-0794
info@afsmi.org; www.afsmi.org

J.B. Wood, President
Thomas Lah, Executive Director

A global organization dedicated to furthering the knowledge, understanding, and career development of executives, managers and professionals in the high technology service industry.
3000+ Members
Founded in: 1975

4721 Association for Women in Communications
3337 Duke Street
Alexandria, VA 22314

703-370-7436; *Fax:* 703-342-4311;
www.womcom.org
Social Media: Facebook, Twitter, LinkedIn, YouTube, Google+

Mitzie Zerr, Chair
Missy Kruse, Vice Chair
Pat Meads, Treasurer
Judy Arent-Morency, Immediate Past Chair
Lisa Angle, Secretary

An American professional organization for women in the communications industry.
Founded in: 1909

4722 Association of Alternative Newsmedia
116 Cass Street
Traverse City, MI 49684

703-470-2996; *Fax:* 866-619-9755
web@aan.org; www.altweeklies.com
Social Media: Facebook, Twitter, RSS, Google+

Blair Barna, President
Chuck Strouse, Vice President
Ellen Meany, Treasurer
Tiffany Shackelford, Executive Director
Jason Zaragoza, Deputy Director

A trade association of alternative weekly newspapers in North America.
Founded in: 1978

4723 Association of Cable Communicators
9259 Old Keene Mill Road
Suite #202
Burke, VA 22015

703-372-2215
800-210-3396; *Fax:* 703-782-0153
services@cablecommunicators.org;
www.cablecommunicators.org
Social Media: Facebook, Twitter, LinkedIn

Catherine Frymark, President
Catherine Frymark, Secretary
Steven R. Jones, Executive Dir.
Annie Howell, EVP, Communications
Catherine Frymark, Communications

ACC is the only national, professional organization specifically addressing the issues, needs and interests of the cable industry's communications and public affairs professionals.
Founded in: 1985

4724 Association of Federal Communications Consulting Engineers
PO Box 19333
Washington, DC 20036

941-329-6000; *Fax:* 703-591-0115;
www.afcce.org
Social Media: Facebook, Twitter, LinkedIn

Eric Wandel, President
Bob Weller, VP
David Layer, Secretary
Ronald Chase, Treasurer
David Snavely, Immediate Past President

An organization of professional engineering consultants serving the telecommunications industry.
250 Members
Founded in: 1948

4725 Association of Information Technology Professionals
1120 Route 73
Suite 200
Mount Laurel, NJ 08054-5113

856-380-6910
800-224-9371; *Fax:* 856-439-0525
aitp_hq@aitp.org; www.aitp.org
Social Media: Twitter, LinkedIn

Raja Singh, Chair
Carrie Drephal, Vice Chair, y

A professional association that focuses on information technology education for business professionals.
Founded in: 1951

4726 Association of Medical Illustrators
201 E. Main St.
Suite 1405
Lexington, KY 40507

866-393-4264; *Fax:* 859-514-9166
hq@ami.org; www.ami.org
Social Media: RSS Feed

Scott Weldon, Treasurer
Emily Shaw, Secretary
David Cheney, Chairman
Melanie Bowzer, Account Executive
Mark Schornak, President

An international organization of media professionals who promote, produce and utilize a wide range of presentation media.
1M Members
Founded in: 1944

4727 **Association of Professional Communication Consultants**
211 E 28th st
Tulsa, OK 74114-3329

918-743-4793; *Fax:* 918-745-0932;
www.consultingsuccess.org
Social Media: LinkedIn

Reva Daniel, Association Manager
Lee Johns, Treasurer

Professional community of communication consultants where members can increase their knowledge, grow their business and achieve high standards of professional practice. Services include professional development workshops, online newsletter and referral database and active listserve discussions.
200 Members
Founded in: 1982

4728 **Association of Schools of Journalism & Mass Communications**
234 Outlet Pointe Boulevard
Columbia, SC 29210-5667

803-798-0271; *Fax:* 803-772-3509
aejmchq@aol.com; www.asjmc.org

Brad Rawlins, President
Jan Slater, President Elect
Maryanne Reed, Vice-President
Ann Brill, Past President
Mary Jean Land, Executive Committee Representative

Promotes excellence in journalism and mass communication education. Non-profit, educational association composed of some 190 JMC programs at the college level. Eight international journalism and communication schools have joined the association in recent years.
202 Members
Founded in: 1917

4729 **Association of Teachers of Technical Writing**
Department Of Linguistics And Technical Comm.
1155 Union Circle #305298
Denton, TX 76203-5017

940-565-4458
sims@unt.edu; www.attw.org
Social Media: Facebook, Twitter, LinkedIn

Michelle Eble, President
Angela Haas, Vice-President
Brenda Sims, Secretary
Stuart Blythe, Treasurer
Huiling Ding, Member at Large

Provides communication among teachers of technical writing and develops technical communications as an academic discipline.
600 Members
Founded in: 1973

4730 **Association of Women in Communications**
3337 Duke Street
Alexandria, VA 22314

703-370-7436; *Fax:* 703-342-4311;
www.womcom.org
Social Media: Facebook, Twitter, LinkedIn, Youtube

Mitzie Zerr, Chair
Missy Kruse, Vice Chair
Pat Meads, Treasurer
Lisa Angle, Secretary
Judy Arent-Moreny, Immediate Past President

Professional organization that champions the advancement of women across all communications disciplines by recognizing excellence, promoting leadership and positioning its members at the forefront of the evolving communications era. Hosts an internal, bi-annual meeting.
3500 Members
Founded in: 1909
Mailing list available for rent

4731 **BioCommunications Association**
220 Southwind Lane
Hillsborough, NC 27278

919-245-0906
office@bca.org; www.bca.org
Social Media: Facebook, Twitter, LinkedIn, YouTube

Connie Johansen, RBP, President
Susanne Loomis, Vice President
James Koepfler, FBCA, Treasurer/Secretary
Susanne Loomis, FBCA, Immediate Past President
Karen M. Hensley, Director of Communication

An international association of photographers and media professionals who create and use quality images in visual communications for teaching, documentation and presentations in the life sciences and medicine.
Founded in: 1931

4732 **Cable in the Classroom**
25 Massachussetts Ave NW
Suite 100
Washington, DC 20001

202-222-2335; *Fax:* 202-222-2336
webmaster@ncta.com; www.ciconline.org
Social Media: Facebook, Twitter, LinkedIn

Frank Gallagher, Executive Director
Helen Chamberlin, Deputy Executive Director
Kat Stewart, Director, Strategic Initiatives
Beverly Hicks, Assistant Director

Promotes the visionary, sensible, responsible and effective use of cable's broaband technology, services, and content in teaching and learning. CIC also advocates digtial citizenship and supports the complimentary provision, by cable industry companies, of broadband and multichannel video services and educational content to the nation's schools.
Founded in: 1992

4733 **CanWest Media Sales**
121 Bloor Street East
Suite 1500
Toronto, ON M4W 3M5

416-967-1174; *Fax:* 416-967-1285
info@shawmedia.ca; www.shawmedia.ca

Barbara Williams, Executive Vice President
Christine Shipton, SVP/Chief Creative Officer
Troy Reeb, SVP, Global News & Station Ops
Dervla Kelly, VP, Marketing and Comm

Televison and newspaper advertising, marketing, and sales company.

4734 **Center for Communication**
110 East 23rd Street
Suite 900
New York, NY 10010

216-686-5005; *Fax:* 212-504-2632
info@cencom.org; www.cencom.org
Social Media: Facebook, Twitter, Youtube

David Barrett, Chairman
Tim Armstrong, CEO & chairman
Catherine Williams, Executice Dir.
Alaina Bendi, VP Membership/Business Development
Kate Stanley, Program Dir.

Exposes young people to the issues, the ethics, the people, and the creative product that defines the media business. Offers students interested in media careers a unique opportunity to learn about the world of communications.

4735 **Center for International Media Assistance**
1025 F Street NW
Suite 800
Washington, DC 20004

202-378-9700; *Fax:* 202-378-9407
CIMA@ned.org
cima.ned.org
Social Media: Facebook, Twitter

Mark Nelson, Senior Director
Don Podesta, Manager and Editor
Valerie Popper, Assist Program & Officer
Rosemary D'Amour, Associate Editor
Paul Rothman, Assistant Partnerships Officer

Provides information, builds networks, conducts research, and highlights the role media play in the creation and development of sustainable democracies.

4736 **Center for Media Literacy**
22837 Pacific Coast Highway
#472
Malibu, CA 90265

310-804-3985
cml@medialit.org; www.medialit.org
Social Media: YouTube

Elizabeth Thoman CHM, Founder
Tessa Jolls, President, CEO
Beth Thornton, Communications

An educational organization that provides leadership, public education, professional development and educational resources nationally and internationally.
Founded in: 1977

4737 **Communication Media Management Association**
www.cmma.org
Social Media: Facebook, Twitter, LinkedIn, RSS

Gregg Moss, President
Gregg Moss, President-Elect
Gerry Harris, Vice President
Thomas M. Densmore, Treasurer
Susan Kehoe, Secretary

Provides professional development and networking opportunities for communications media managers.
Founded in: 1946

4738 **CompTIA**
3500 Lacey Road
Suite 100
Downers Grove, IL 60515

630-678-8300
866-678-8300; *Fax:* 630-678-8384
techvoice@comptia.org; www.comptia.org
Social Media: Facebook, Twitter, LinkedIn, Google+, YouTube, Pinterest

Todd Thibodeaux, President/ Chief Executive Officer
Nancy Hammervik, Senior VP, Industry Relations
Kelly Ricker, SVP, Events and Education
David Sommer, Chief Financial Officer
Randy Gross, Chief Information Officer

A nonprofit trade association created by representatives of five microcomputer leaderships and is a provider of professional certifications for theinformation technology (IT) industry.

4739 **Computer and Communications Industry Association**
900 17th Street, NW
Suite 1100
Washington, DC 20006
202-783-0070; *Fax:* 202-783-0534;
www.ccianet.org
Social Media: Facebook, Twitter, RSS
Edward Black, President, CEO
Daniel Johnson, Vice President & General Counsel
Catherine Sloan, VP, Government Relations
Matthew Schruers, Vice President, Law & Policy
Dan O'Connor, Vice President, Public Policy
Association of computer product vendors and communications firms lobbying for free trade and open markets.

4740 **Consolidated Tape Association**
C/O New York Stock Exchange
11 Wall Street, 21st Floor
New York, NY 10005
212-656-2052; *Fax:* 212-656-5848
Patricia Hussey, Administrator
Members are stock exchanges and the National Association of Securities Dealers. CTA melds the reporting of transactions from the various stock exchanges.
9 Members
Founded in: 1974

4741 **Consortium for School Networking**
1025 Vermont Ave NW
Suite 1010
Washington, DC 20005-3599
202-861-2676
866-267-8747; *Fax:* 202-393-2011
info@cosn.org; www.cosn.org
Social Media: Facebook, Twitter, LinkedIn
Randy Wilhelm, CEO & Co-Founder
Michael Jamerson, Chair
Tom Ryan, Treasurer
Donna Williamson, Secretary
Walter l. Fox, Executive Director
Promotes the development and use of internet and information technologies for K-12 learning. Members are school districts, states, nonprofits and commercial organizations, all of whom share the goal of promoting the state of the art in computer networking technologies in schools.
450 Members
Founded in: 1992

4742 **Cooperative Communicators Association**
174 Crestview Dr
Bellefonte, PA 16823-8516
877-326-5994; *Fax:* 814-355-2452
CCA@communicators.coop;
www.communicators.coop
Social Media: Facebook, Twitter, YouTube, Flickr
Marian McLemore, President
Marian Douglas, Director
Nickie Sabo, Treasurer
Marian Douglas, Secretary
Chandra Allen, Director
A teaching and news tool for the Cooperative Communicators Association, CCA consists communicators, editors, photographers, graphics, designers, public relations specialists who work for cooperatives in 35 states, Canada and Poland.
350 Members
Founded in: 1953

4743 **Council of Communication Management**
65 Enterprise
Aliso Viejo, CA 92656
866-463-6226; *Fax:* 949-715-6931
info@thecommunicationexchange.org;
www.ccmconnection.com
Social Media: Facebook, Twitter, LinkedIn
Becky Healy, President
Jeff Kosiorek, VP
Kerrin Nally, Secretary
Barry Mike, Past President
Hannah Bauer, Director
Provides a network through which managers, consultants and educators, who work at the policy level in organizational communication can help one another advance the practice of communication in business.
270 Members
Founded in: 1955

4744 **Council of Science Editors**
10200 W 44th Ave.
Suite 304
Wheat Ridge, CO 80033
720-881-6046; *Fax:* 703-435-4390
CSE@CouncilScienceEditors.org;
www.councilscienceeditors.org
Social Media: Facebook, Twitter, LinkedIn
Angela Cochran, President
Barbara Gomez, Executive Vice President
Patricia K Baskin, President-Elect
Sarah Tegen, VP
Tim Cross, Past President
Membership consists of individuals concerned with writing, editing and publishing in the life sciences and related fields.
1200 Members
Founded in: 1957

4745 **Digital Media Association (DiMA)**
1050 17th St., NW
Suite 220
Washington, DC 20036
202-639-9509; www.digmedia.org
Lee Knife, Executive Director
Greg Barnes, General Counsel
Ann Brown, Communications Consultant
Aileen Atkins, SVP/General Counsel
Bill Way, VP/ General Counsel
National trade organization devoted primarily to the online audio and video industries, and more generally to commercially innovative digital media opportunities.

4746 **Drug Information Association**
800 Enterprise Road
Suite 200
Horsham, PA 19044-3595
215-442-6100; *Fax:* 215-442-6199
DIA@diahome.org; www.diahome.org
Social Media: Facebook, Twitter, LinkedIn, YouTube, Weibo, Digg, Reddit
Sandra A Milligan, MD, JD, President
John Roberts, Treasurer
Barbara Lopez Kunz, Global Chief Executive
Bayard Gardineer, CPA, CFO
Elizabeth Lincoln, MA, Worldwide Dir., HR
Provides a neutral global forum for the exchange and dissemination of information on the discovery, development, evaluation and utilization of medicines and related health care technologies. Through these activities the DIA provides development opportunities for its members.
20000 Members
Founded in: 1964

4747 **EDUCAUSE**
1150 18th St NW
Suite 900
Washington, DC 20036
202-872-4200; *Fax:* 202-872-4318
info@educause.edu; www.educause.edu
Social Media: Facebook, Twitter, LinkedIn, Flickr
Mark Luker, VP
EDUCAUSE is a nonprofit association whose mission is to advance higher education by promoting the intelligent use of information technology.
17M Members
Founded in: 1962

4748 **Eastern Communication Association**
600 Forbes Ave
340 College Hall
Pittsburgh, PA 15282
E-Mail: info@ecasite.org; www.ecasite.org
Social Media: Facebook, Twitter
J. Kanan Sawyer, President
Jason S. Wrench, Vice President
Benjamin R Bates, First Vice President Elect
Thomas R. Flynn, Immediate Past President
Ronald C. Arnett, Executive Director
A professional organization of scholars, teachers, and students of Communcation Studies.
Founded in: 1910

4749 **Electronic Retailing Association**
607 14th St., NW
Suite 530
Washington, DC 20005
703-841-1751
800-987-6462; *Fax:* 425-977-1036
webadmin@retailing.org; www.retailing.org
Social Media: Facebook, Twitter, LinkedIn, YouTube, Flickr
Julie Coons, President & CEO
Kevin S. Kelly, CFO & COO
Bill McClellan, VP, Govt Affairs
Dave Martin, VP, Marketing & Content
Cecilia Mason, Accounting Manager
To foster growth, development and acceptance of the rapidly growing direct response industry worldwide for the companies who use the power of electronic media to sell goods and services to the public.
Founded in: 1991
Mailing list available for rent

4750 **Enterprise Wireless Alliance (EWA)**
2121 Cooperative Way
Suite 225
Herndon, VA 20171
703-528-5115
800-482-8282; *Fax:* 703-524-1074
customerservice@enterprisewireless.org;
www.enterprisewireless.org
Mark Crosby, President/CEO
Andre Cote, Senior VP
Ila Dudley, EVP, Spectrum Solutions
Ron Franklin, Customer Service Manager
Karen Fouchie, Accounting Manager
Formerly ITA and AMTA, works to preserve spectrum rights and assets for enterprise wireless customers.
1200 Members
Founded in: 1953

4751 **Forest Industries Telecommunications**
1565 Oak St
Eugene, OR 97401
541-485-8441; *Fax:* 541-485-7556
license@landmobile.com;
www.landmobile.com
Social Media: Facebook, Twitter
Kevin Mc Carthy, President

Organized to assist the forest industry in radio matters before the FCC.
600 Members
Founded in: 1947

4752 **Forestry Conservation Communications Association**
122 Baltimore St.
Gettysburg, PA 17325
717-398-0815
844-458-0298; *Fax:* 717-778-4237;
www.fcca-usa.org
Chief Paul M. Leary, President
Roy Mott, VP
John McIntosh, Secretary/Treasurer
Matt Hogan, Executive Dir.
Michelle Fink, National Frequency Coordinator
Certified by the FCC as the radio frequency coordinator for the Forestry Conservation Radio Service.
200 Members
Founded in: 1944

4753 **Foundation for American Communications**
44 Avenue Road South
Suite 1200
Arlington, VA 22203
703-276-0100; *Fax:* 703-525-8277;
www.facsnet.org
John E Cox, CEO, President
Peter C McCarthy, Senior VP, COO
Paul Davis, Senior VP, Programs
Randy Reddick, Director
Christina Gardner, VP, Operations
A national non-profit educational organization with the mission of improving the quality of information reaching the public through the news.
Mailing list available for rent

4754 **Freedom Information Center**
133 Neff Annex University of Missouri
Columbia, MO 65211
573-882-4856; *Fax:* 573-884-6204
web.missouri.edu/~foiwww/
Social Media: Facebook, Twitter
Barbara A Petersen, President
Peter Scheer, VP
Katherine Garner, Secretary
Mal Leary, Treasurer
Maintains files documenting actions by government, media and society affecting the flow and content of information. Call or write for assistance with researching media topics or instruction in using access laws.
Founded in: 1989

4755 **Fulfillment Services Association of America**
3030 Malmo Drive
Arlington Heights, IL 60005-4728
847-364-1222; *Fax:* 847-364-1268
Frederick J Herzog, Executive VP
Formerly Association of Publishing and fulfillment services.
1450 Members
Founded in: 1986

4756 **Geospatial Information & Technology Association**
1360 University Ave. West
Suite 455
St. Paul, MN 55104-4086
E-Mail: president@gita.org; www.gita.org
Social Media: Facebook, Twitter, LinkedIn, YouTube
Mark Limbruner, President
Talbot J Brooks, Immediate Past President
Matthew Thomas, President Elect
Eric Hoogenraad, Secretary
Elizabeth Bialek, P.E., Treasurer
A nonprofit educational association dedicated to promoting the use and benefits of geospatial information technologies.

4757 **Health Industry Business Communications Council**
2525 E Arizona Biltmore Circle
Suite 127
Phoenix, AZ 85016
602-381-1091; *Fax:* 602-381-1093
info@hibcc.org; www.hibcc.org
Robert A Hankin PhD, President & CEO
DuWayne Schlittenhard, Chair
Patrick DeGrace, Immediate Past Chair
Greg Stivers, At Large
An industry-sponsored nonprofit council organized by major health care associations to develop a standard for data transfer using uniform bar code labeling, and later as the focal point for many other electronic data interchange standards.
12000 Members
Founded in: 1984

4758 **IEEE Communications Society**
www.comsoc.org
Social Media: Facebook, Twitter, LinkedIn, Tumblr, Instagram, Pinterest
Sergio Benedetto, President
Vijay Bhargava, Past President
Stan Moyer, Treasurer
Hikmet Sari, Vice President - Conferences
Susan Brooks, Executive Director
A diverse group of industry professionals with a common interest inadvancing all communications technologies.
Founded in: 1952

4759 **InfoComm International**
11242 Waples Mill Road
Suite 200
Fairfax, VA 22030
703-273-7200; *Fax:* 800-659-7469;
www.infocomm.org
Social Media: Facebook, Twitter, LinkedIn, Google+, YouTube, Flickr
Johanne Belanger, CPA, CA, LSC Chair
Matt Emerson, CTS, President
Craig Janssen, President-Elect
Gary Hall, CTS-D, CTS-I, Treasurer, Secretary
David Labuskes, CTS, RCDD, Executive Director, CEO
Educating, training, and certifying the communications industry.

4760 **Information Resources Group**
Ste A
2721 Industrial Dr
Jefferson City, MO 65109
573-632-6IRG
877-600- IRG; *Fax:* 877-295-7989;
www.irginc.net
Social Media: Facebook, Twitter, LinkedIn
Shyam Goel, President
A national organization that offers MIS and corporate professionals at over 150,000 companies throughout the United States.
1M Members

4761 **Information Systems Consultants**
4131 Idlevale Drive
Tucker, GA 30084
770-491-1500
800-832-7767
Nonprofit organization of small businesses and individuals providing consulting services to all industries and government.
350 Members
Founded in: 1986

4762 **Information Systems Management Benchmarking Consortium**
Houston, TX
281-440-5044
ismbc.org
Social Media: Facebook, Twitter
An international resource for business process research and metrics.
Founded in: 1992

4763 **Information Technology Industry Council**
1101 K St., NW
Suite 610
Washington, DC 20005
202-737-8888; *Fax:* 202-638-4922
info@itic.org; www.itic.org
Social Media: Facebook, Twitter, Google+, RSS, YouTube, Blog
Dean C. Garfield, President, CEO
Andy Halataei, SVP, Government Affairs
John Neuffer, SVP, Global Policy
Rick Goss, SVP, Environment and Sustainability
A.R. Trey Hodgkins, SVP, Public Sector
A Washington, D.C.-based trade association that represents companies from the information and communications technology (ICT) industry.
Founded in: 1916

4764 **Instructional Telecommunications Council**
426 C St., NE
Washington, DC 20002-5839
202-293-3110; *Fax:* 651-450-3679;
www.itcnetwork.org
Anne Johnson, Chair
Christine Mullins, Executive Director
Carol Spalding, Ed.D., Treasurer
Mickey Slimp, Executive Director
Loraine Schmitt, Chair-Elect
Members are educators and organizations involved in higher education instructional telecommunications and distance learning
500 Members
Founded in: 1977

4765 **Interactive Multimedia and Collaborative Communications Association**
PO Box 756
Syosset, NY 11797-0756
516-818-8184; *Fax:* 516-922-2170;
www.imcca.org
Social Media: Facebook, LinkedIn, RSS Feed
Carol Zelkin, Executive Director
Rick Snyder, Chairperson
Anne Hardwick, Treasurer
Ken Scaturro, Vice chairperson
David J. Danto, Dir., Emerging Technology
Provides a clearinghouse for the exchange of information between users, researchers, and providers in the field of teleconferencing.
1000 Members
Founded in: 1998

4766 **International Academy of Television Arts a nd Sciences**
25 West 52nd Street
New York, NY 10019
212-489-6969; *Fax:* 212-489-1946
iemmys@iemmys.tv; www.iemmys.tv
Social Media: Facebook, Twitter, YouTube
Fred Cohen, Chairman
Larry Gershman, Vice Chairman
Bruce Paisner, President & CEO
Simon Sutton, Secretary
Rainer Siek, Nominating Committee Chairman
Member based organization comprised of leading media and entertainment figures from over 50 countries and 500 companies from all sectors of television including internet, mobile and technology.
Founded in: 1969

4767 **International Association of Audio Informa tion Services**
1090 Don Mills Road
P.O. Box 847
Lawrence, KS 66044
416-422-4222
800-280-5325; *Fax:* 416-422-1622
info@iaais.org; www.iaais.org
Stuart Holland, President
Lori Kessinger, Chairperson
Marjorie Williams, 1st Vice President
Mark Dewitt, Awards Committee Chair
Lori Kesinger, Co-Chair
Encourages and supports the establishment and maintenance of audio information services that provide access to printed information for individuals who cannot read conventional print because of blindness or any other visual, physical, or learning disability.
Founded in: 1977

4768 **International Association of Audio Visual Communicators**
The Cindy Competitions
57 West Palo Verde Avenue
PO Box 270779
Flower Mound, TX 75027-0779
469-464-4180; *Fax:* 469-464-4170;
www.cindys.com
Social Media: Facebook, Twitter, LinkedIn, YouTube
Sheemon Wolfe, Contact
Members are audio-visual professionals using the media of film, video, slides, filmstrips, multi-image and interactive media to communicate information
5200 Members
Founded in: 1959

4769 **International Association of Business Communicators**
601 Montgomery St.
Suite 1900
San Francisco, CA 94111
415-544-4700
800-776-4222; *Fax:* 415-544-4747
service_centre@iabc.com; www.iabc.com
Social Media: Twitter, LinkedIn
Michael Ambjorn, Chair
Dianne Lynn Chase, Vice Chair
Carlos Fulcher, Executive Dir.
Mari Pavia, Dir., HR Administration
Aaron Heinrich, Dir. Of Communications
International knowledge network for professionals engaged in stategic business communication management.
13,00 Members
Founded in: 1970

4770 **International Association of Information Technology Asset Managers**
4848 Munson St. NW
Canton, OH 44718
330-628-3012
877-942-4826; *Fax:* 330-628-3289
info@iaitam.org; www.iaitam.org
Social Media: Facebook, Twitter, LinkedIn, YouTube
Barbara Rembiesa, President, Founder, CEO
The professional association for individuals and organizations involved in any aspect of IT Asset Management ("ITAM"), Software Asset Management ("SAM"), Hardware Asset Management, and the lifecycle processes supporting IT Asset Management in organizations of every size and industry across the globe.
Founded in: 2002

4771 **International Communication Association**
1500 21st Street, NW
PO Box 418950
Washington, DC 20036
202-955-1444; *Fax:* 202-955-1448
icahdq@icahdq.org; www.icahdq.org
Social Media: Facebook, Twitter, LinkedIn, Tumblr, Pinterest
Amy B Jordan, President
Peng Hwa Ang, President Elect
Peter Vorderer, Past President
Michael L. Haley, Executive Director
Sam Luna, Member Services Director
An academic association for scholars interested in the study, teaching, and application of all aspects of human and mediated communication.
Founded in: 1950

4772 **International Communications Association**
1500 21st St NW
Washington, DC 20036
202-955-1444; *Fax:* 202-955-1448
icahdq@icahdq.org; www.icahdq.org
Social Media: Facebook, Twitter, LinkedIn, Tumblr, Pinterest
Amy B Jordan, President
Peng Hwa Ang, President-Elect
Paula M Gardner, President-Elect-Select
Peter Vorderer, Immediate Past President
Francois Heinderyckx, Past President
International association for scholars interested in the study, teaching and application of all aspects of human mediated communication. ICA began as a small association of US reseachers and has matured into a international association with members in 65 countries.
3400+ Members
Founded in: 1950

4773 **International Communications Industry Association**
11242 Waples Mill Road
Suite 200
Fairfax, VA 22030
703-273-7200
800-659-7469; *Fax:* 703-278-8082
customerservice@infocomm.org;
www.infocomm.org
Social Media: Facebook, Twitter, LinkedIn, Flickr, YouTube, SlideShare
Johanne Belanger, CPA, CA, LSC Chair
Greg Jeffreys, Chair
Matt Emerson, President
Gary Hall, Secretary-Treasurer
David J. Labuskes, Executive Director
Centers on the technologies, products and systems for visual display, audio reproduction, video and audio production, interfacing and signal distribution, lighting, control systems, interactive display and audio presentation systems, remote video and web conferencing.

4774 **International Digital Enterprise Alliance**
1600 Duke St.
Suite 420
Alexandria, VA 22314
703-837-1070; *Fax:* 703-837-1072
info@idealliance.org; www.idealliance.org
Social Media: Facebook, Twitter, LinkedIn
Joe Duncan, Chairman
Marriott Winchester, Vice Chair
David J. Steinhardt, President & CEO
Frank Balser, VP of operations & Managing Dir.
Steve Bonoff, EVP
IDEAlliance programs and activities enable its members to strengthen their staff skills, participate in the development of standards, influence the development of tools and technologies, develop strategies and partnerships to deploy technology solutions, and position themselves as industry leaders.
200 Members
Founded in: 1966

4775 **International Documentary Association**
3470 Wilshire Boulevard
Suite 980
Los Angeles, CA 90010
213-232-1660; *Fax:* 213-232-1669
michael@documentary.org;
www.documentary.org
Social Media: Facebook, Twitter, LinkedIn, YouTube
Simon Kilmurry, Executive Director
Jon Curry, Office Manager/Membership Services
Akiva Gottlieb, Communications Manager
A nonprofit membership organization dedicated to supporting the efforts of nonfiction film and video makers throughout the United States and the world; promoting the documentary form; and expanding opportunities for the production, distribution, and exhibition of documentary.
2270 Members
Founded in: 1982

4776 **International Interactive Communications Society**
180 West 8th Ave
Suite 300
Eugene, OR 97401-2916
541-302-3777; *Fax:* 541-302-3778;
www.iste.org
Social Media: Facebook, Twitter, LinkedIn, YouTube
Kecia Ray, EdD, Chair
Matt Harris, EdD, Chair-Elect
Mia Williams, PhD, Secretary
Mila Thomas Fuller, Ed.D., Treasurer
Laurie Conzemius, At-Large Representative
Association of communications industry professionals dedicated to the advancement of interactive technologies. Provides a forum to share ideas, applications and techniques for effective use of interactive media.
3000 Members
Founded in: 1983
Mailing list available for rent: 8000 names

4777 **International Regional Magazine Association**
38 Burgess Ave.
Toronto, ON M4E 1W7
416-705-6884; *Fax:* 888-806-1533;
www.regionalmagazines.org
Chris Amundson, President
Penny Caldwell, VP
Shawn Dalton, Director
Joan Henderson, Director
Matt Holliday, Treasurer
IRMA provides a forum for regional magazine publishers to exchange ideas with the view to improving their respective publications.
250-3 Members
Founded in: 1960

4778 **International Society for Technology in Education**
180 W 8th Avenue
Suite 300
Eugene, OR 97401-2916
541-302-3777
800-336-5191; *Fax:* 541-302-3778
iste@iste.org; www.iste.org
Social Media: Facebook, Twitter, LinkedIn, YouTube, Pinterest
Kecia Ray, EdD, Chair
Matt Harris, EdD, Chair-Elect
Mia Williams, PhD, Secretary
Mila Thomas Fuller, Ed.D., Treasurer
Laurie Conzemius, At-Large Representative
A large nonprofit organization serving the technology-using educator.
10000 Members
Founded in: 1979

4779 **International Society of Business**
7159 Navajo Road
San Diego, CA 92119-1606
619-687-3450
Audio and videotape professionals.
Founded in: 1983

4780 **Internet Society**
1775 Wiehle Ave
Suite 201
Reston, VA 20190-5108
703-439-2120; *Fax:* 703-326-9881
isoc@isoc.org; www.isoc.org
Social Media: Facebook, Twitter, LinkedIn, YouTube, Google+
Terry Weigler, Manager
Gregory Kapfer, CFO
Nicole Armstrong, Sr. Events Manager
Jane Coffin, Dir.,Development Strategy
Members are technologists, developers, educators, researchers, government representatives, business people and other with an interest in internet technologies and applications.
20000 Members
Founded in: 1992

4781 **Land Mobile Communications Council**
2121 Cooperative Way
Suite 225
Herndon, VA 20171
703-528-5114; *Fax:* 703-524-1074
mark.crosby@enterprisewireless.org;
www.lmcc.org
Gregory Kunkle, President
Ralph Haller, VP
Mark Crosby, Secretary
A nonprofit association of organizations representing land mobile radio carriers and manufacturers equipment; LMCC membership represents diverse telecommunications sectors such as public safety, industrial/land transportation, private radio, specialized mobile radion and critical infrastructure.
Founded in: 1967

4782 **Local Media Association**
116 Cass Street
Traverse City, MI 49684
888-486-2466; *Fax:* 231-932-2985
hq@localmedia.org; www.localmedia.org
Social Media: Facebook, Twitter, LinkedIn, Tumblr, Instagram, Google+
Gordon Borrell, Board Chairman
Suzanne Schlicht, First Vice Chairman
Matt Coen, Second Vice Chairman
Mark Poss, Treasurer
Robert Brown, Secretary
A nonprofit, professional trade association specifically serving the local media industry.

4783 **Media Alliance**
1904 Franklin St
Suite 818
Oakland, CA 94612
510-684-6853; *Fax:* 510-238-8557
information@media-alliance.org;
www.media-alliance.org
Social Media: Facebook, Twitter
Tracy Rosenberg, Executive Director
Eloise Rose Lee, Program Director
A nonprofit training and resource center for media workers, community organizations and political activists.
Founded in: 1976

4784 **Media Communications Association-Internati onal**
PO Box 5135
Madison, WI 53705-0135
888-899-MCAI; *Fax:* 888-862-8150
loiswei@aol.com; www.mca-i.org
Social Media: Facebook, Twitter, LinkedIn, Google+
Jim Dufek, President
Brian Page, President-Elect
Art Kirsch, Treasurer
Liz De Nesnera, Secretary
Brian President, Past President
Global community that provides its members opportunities for networking, learning and career advancement. Members work in video, film, collaborative communication, distance learning, web design and creation, and all forms of interactive visual communication, along with associated crafts; serving businesses, nonprofit organizations, the government, educational institutions, the medical field, and electronic media. Chapters are throughout the US, with affiliates in Asia and Europe.
Founded in: 1970

4785 **Media Institute**
2300 Clarendon Blvd
Suite 602
Arlington, VA 22201
703-243-5700; *Fax:* 703-243-8808
info@mediainstitute.org;
www.mediainstitute.org
Social Media: Twitter, RSS Feed, You Tube
Patrick Maines, President
Richard T. Kaplar, Vice President
Susanna Coto, Director, Public Events
Wendy Wood, Webmaster
Non-profit research foundation specializing in communications policy isssues.
Founded in: 1979

4786 **Media Research Center**
1900 Campus Commons Drive
Suite 600
Reston, VA 20191
571-267-3500
800-672-1423; *Fax:* 571-375-0099;
www.mrc.org
Social Media: Facebook, Twitter
A politically conservative content analysis organization.
Founded in: 1987

4787 **Media Research Directors Association**
Ogilvy and Mather
309 W 49th Street
New York, NY 10019-7316
212-375-5502; www.mrda.org
Provides support for research and maintains library.

4788 **Minority Media and Telecommunications Coun cil**
3636 16th Street NW
Suite B 366
Washington, DC 20010
202-332-0500; *Fax:* 202-332-0503
info@mmtconline.org; www.mmtconline.org
Social Media: Twitter
Hon Julia L Johnson, Chairperson
Hon Deborah Taylor Tate, Vice Chair
David Honig, President
Ari Fitzgerald, Secretary
Ronald Johnson, Treasurer
National non-profit organization dedicated to promoting and oreserving equal opportunity and civil rights in the mass media, telecommunications and broadband industries, and closing the digital divide.

4789 **NTCA-The Rural Broadband Association**
4121 Wilson Boulevard
Suite 1000
Arlington, VA 22203
703-351-2000; *Fax:* 703-351-2001;
www.ntca.org
Shirley A. Bloomfield, CEO
Michael L. Viands, CFO
James M Dauby, President
Doug Boone, Vice President
William P Hegmann, Secretary/Treasurer
A nonprofit association representing small and rural telephone cooperatives and commercial companies.

4790 **National Association for Media Literacy Education**
10 Laurel Hill Drive
Cherry Hill, NJ 8003
888-775-2652
namle.net
Social Media: Facebook, Twitter, Google+, Flickr, RSS
David W Brown, President
Erin Reilly, 1st Vice President
Tony Streit, Treasurer
Joanne Parsont, Secretary
Lynda Bergsma, PhD, Past President
A national membership organization dedicated to media literacy as abasic life skill for the 21st century.
Founded in: 1997

4791 National Association for Multi-Ethnicity in Communications
50 Broad Street
Suite 1801
New York, NY 10004
212-594-5985; *Fax:* 212-594-8391
info@namic.com; www.namic.com
Social Media: Facebook, Twitter, LinkedIn, Instagram
Eglon E Simons, President/CEO
James Jones, VP Programs
Michelle L Rice, Chair
Mark DePietro, Treasurer
Jamie J. Rodriguez, Secretary
Works for diversity in the telecommunications industry.
2000 Members
Founded in: 1980

4792 National Association of Air Medical Communication Specialists
Po Box 19240
Topeka, KS 66619
877-396-2227; *Fax:* 866-827-2296
info@naacs.org; www.naacs.org
Social Media: Facebook, Twitter, LinkedIn
Steve Goff, President
Chris Forncrook, President-Elect
Mac Snead, Treasurer
Charles W Sheppard, MD, FACEP, At- Large Board Members
Garet Hickman, At- Large Board Members
Professional organization whose mission is to represent the air medical communications specialist on a national level through education, standardization and recognition.
200 Members

4793 National Association of Broadcasters
1771 N Street NW
Washington, DC 20036
202-429-5300
nab@nab.org; www.nab.org
Social Media: Facebook, Twitter, LinkedIn, YouTube
Gordon H. Smith, President, CEO
A trade association, workers union, and lobby group representing the interests of for-profit, over-the-air radio and television broadcasters in theUnited States.

4794 National Association of Communication Centers
commcenters.org
Social Media: Facebook
Marlina Davidson, Chair
Bonnie Wentzel, Vice Chair
Anand Rao, Vice Chair Elect
Russell Carpenter, Past Chair
Brandi Quesenberry, Secretary
An organization devoted to the support of communication centers on college and university campuses across the country.

4795 National Association of Hispanic Publications
529 14th St, NW.
Suite 923
Washington, DC 20045
202-662-7250; *Fax:* 703-610-9005
info@nahp.org; www.nahp.org
Social Media: Facebook, Twitter
Martha Mantoya, President
Angela Angulo, Vice President
Robert D Bush, Secretary
Ivan Cruz, Treasurer
Eddie Escobedo Jr., Vice Chair
Founded in: the belief that the most effective way to reach the more than 29 million Hispanic Americans in the country is through their own language.
234 Members
Founded in: 1982

4796 National Association of Independent Writers and Editors
P.O. Box 549
Ashland, VA 23005
804-767-5961
naiwe.com
Social Media: Facebook, Twitter
Janice Campbell, Director
A professional association for writers and editors, providing individual member websites and other benefits.
Founded in: 2007

4797 National Association of Media Women
601 Pennsylvania Avenue NW
South Building, Suite 900
Washington, DC 20004
800-556-2926; *Fax:* 202-403-3788
national@nawbo.org; www.nawbo.org
Social Media: Facebook, Twitter, LinkedIn, Google+, YouTube
Crystal Arredondo, Chair
Kathy Warnick, Secretary/ Treasurer
Teresa Meares, Treasurer
Darla Beggs, Immediate Past Chair
Jeanette Armbrust, Director
Sponsors studies, research and seminars to find solutions to problems and create opportunities for women. Presents annual awards.
300 Members
Founded in: 1975

4798 National Association of State Technology Directors
PO Box 11910
Lexington, KY 40578-1910
859-244-8186; *Fax:* 859-244-8001;
www.nastd.org
Jack Ries, President
Mark McCord, Executive Dir.
Pam Johnson, Meetings & Member Services Manager
Paul Czarnecki, Comm. & Research Specialist
Concerned with providing a forum for the exchange of ideas and practices and the development of a unified position on matters of national telecommunications policy and regulatory issues.
1000 Members
Founded in: 1978

4799 National Association of Telecommunications Officers and Advisors
3213 Duke St.
Suite 695
Alexandria, VA 22314
703-519-8035; *Fax:* 703-997-7080
info@natoa.org; www.natoa.org
Social Media: Facebook, Twitter, LinkedIn, RSS
Jodie Miller, Chair
Catherine Rice, Co-Chair
Tony Perez, President
Steve Traylor, Executive Director
Tonya Rideout, Deputy Director
A national association that represents the communications and interests of local governments, and those who advise local governments.
800 Members
Founded in: 1980

4800 National Cable & Telecommunications Association
25 Massachusetts Avenue, NW
Suite 100
Washington, DC 20001
202-222-2300; *Fax:* 202-222-2514
info@ncta.com; www.ncta.com
Social Media: Facebook, Twitter, LinkedIn
Michael Powell, President, CEO
Bruce Carnes, SVP, Finance & Administration
William Check, SVP, Science & Technology
Barbara York, SVP, Industry Affairs
Rick Chessen, SVP, Law & Regulatory Policy
Trade association for U.S. cable industry.

4801 National Cable and Telecommunications
25 Massachusetts Ave Nw
Suite 100
Washington, DC 20001-1434
202-222-2300; *Fax:* 202-222-2514
webmaster@ncta.com; www.ncta.com
Social Media: Facebook, Twitter, LinkedIn
Micheal Powell, President & CEO
Brian Dietz, Vice President, Communications
James M. Assey, Executive Vice President
K. Dane Snowden, Chief of Staff
Jill Luckett, Senior Vice President
3189 Members
Founded in: 1948

4802 National Captioning Institute
3725 Concorde Parkway
Suite 100
Chantilly, VA 20151
703-917-7600; *Fax:* 703-917-9853
info@ncicap.org; www.ncicap.org
Social Media: Facebook, Twitter, LinkedIn
Gene Chao, Chairman
Drake Smith, Chief Technology Officer
Jill Toschi, Vice President for Operations
Juan Mario Agudelo, Director, Sales & Marketing
Beth Nubbe, Director, Administration
Non-profit organization whose primary purposes are to deliver effective captioning services and encourage, develop and fund the continuing development of captioning, subtitling, and other media access services for the benefit of peopl who require additional access to the auditory and visual information.
Founded in: 1979

4803 National Communication Association
1765 N Street NW
Washington, DC 20036
202-464-4622; *Fax:* 202-464-4600
inbox@natcom.org; www.natcom.org
Social Media: Facebook, Twitter, YouTube, Blog
Kim Griffin, CPA, CFO
Nancy Kidd, Ph.D., Executive Director
Mark Fernando, Chief of Staff
Trevor Parry-Giles, Ph.D., Dir., Academic & Prof. Affairs
Michelle Randall, Dir., Conventions and Meetings
A not-for-profit membership-based scholarly society.
Founded in: 1914

4804 National Communications Association
1765 N Street NW
Washington, DC 20036
202-464-4622; *Fax:* 202-464-4600
inbox@natcom.org; www.natcom.org

Social Media: Facebook, Twitter, YouTube, NCA Blog

Nancy Kidd, Ph.D., Executive Director
Mark Fernando, Chief Of Staff
Kim Griffin, CPA, CFO
Wendy Fernando, Dir. Of Publications
Andy G. Riskind, Dir. Of Public Affairs

The NCA is the most dynamic and responsive of the communication-related organizations. It has achieved this prominance by serving the needs of departmental administrators in the communication arts and sciences.
7700 Members
Founded in: 1914
Mailing list available for rent

4805 National Council of Writing Program Administrators
Department of English
Miami University
Oxford, OH 45056

513-529-5221; *Fax:* 513-529-1392;
www.wpacouncil.org
Social Media: Facebook, Twitter, LinkedIn

John Tassoni, Chair
Susan Miller-Cochran, President
Dominic DelliCarpini, Vice President
Rita Malenczyk, Immediate Past President

National organization that fosters professional development, communication and community among college and university writing progrma administrators and other interested faculty.
700 Members
Founded in: 1975

4806 National Federation Abstracting & Information Services
801 Compass Way
Suite 201
Annapolis, MD 21401

443-221-2980; *Fax:* 443-221-2981
nfais@nfais.org; www.nfais.org
Social Media: Facebook, Twitter, LinkedIn

Mary Sauer-Games, President
Chris McCue, Past President
Chris Burghardt, President-Elect
Peter Simon, Treasurer
Lynn Willis, Secretary

Serves those groups that aggregate, organize, and facilitate access to information. To improve member capabilities and contribute to their ongoing success. Provides opportunities for education, advocacy, and a forum to address common interests.
60 Members
Founded in: 1958
Printed in on matte stock

4807 National Newspaper Association
900 Community Drive
Springfield, IL 62703

217-241-1400; *Fax:* 217-241-1301
membership@nna.org
nnaweb.org
Social Media: Facebook, Twitter, RSS

Matthew Paxton, President
Susan Rowell, Vice President
Dennis DeRossett, Chief Operating Officer
Tonda Rush, Director, Public Policy
Lynne Lance, Director, Membership Services

An association representing community newspapers, publishers, and editors. Lists resources, events, membership benefits, and jobs.
2100 Members
Founded in: 1885

4808 National Newspaper Publishers Association
1816 12th Street, NW
Washington, DC 20009

202-588-8764; *Fax:* 202-588-8960
admin@nnpa.org
nnpa.org
Social Media: Facebook, Twitter, Google+

Cloves C. Campbell, Chair
Mollie F. Belt, 1st Vice Chair
John B. Smith, Sr, 2nd Vice Chair
Lenora Alexander, Treasurer
Natalie Cole, Secretary

A trade association composed of more than 200 black newspapers in the United States and the Virgin Islands. It also created an electronic news service which enables newspapers to provide real time news and information to its national constituency.

4809 National Speakers Association
1500 S Priest Dr
Tempe, AZ 85281-6203

480-968-2552; *Fax:* 480-968-0911
memberservices@NSAspeaker.org;
www.nsaspeaker.org
Social Media: Facebook, Twitter, Google+, YouTube, Instagram

Stacy Tetschner, CAE, FASAE, CEO
William Peterson, MBA, Director Of Finance
Michelle Reynolds, Director of Member Experiences
Christie Turley, Director of Marketing, Consultant
Barbara Parus, Director of Publications

The leading organization for experts who speak professionally. NSA's members include experts in a variety of industries and disciplines, who reach audiences as trainers, educators, humorists, motivators, consultants, authors and more. NSA provides resources and education designed to advance the skills, integrity, and value of its members and speaking profession. NSA the voice of the speaking profession.
3500 Members
Founded in: 1973
Mailing list available for rent: 3200 names

4810 National Telemedia Council
1922 University Avenue
Madison, WI 53726

608-218-1182; *Fax:* 608-218-1183
ntelemedia@aol.com;
www.nationaltelemediacouncil.org

Marieli Rowe, Director

Promotes media literacy through workshops and telemediun.
Founded in: 1953

4811 National Translator Association
5611 Kendall Court
Suite 2
Arvada, CO 80002

303-378-8209; *Fax:* 303-465-4067
stcl@comcast.net;
www.nationaltranslatorassociation.org

Byron St. Clair, President
Arnold Cruze, Vice President
Alan Greager, Secretary/Treasurer

Dedicated to the preservation of free over-the-air TV in all geographical areas. It works to improve the technology of rebroadcast translators and regulatory climate which governs them. It continously promotes the concept of universal free over-the-air TV and reprsents the ineterests of translator operators before the FCC and other government agencies such as the Forest Service and the Bureau of Land Management. Membership is open to all individuals and organizations that are interested.
Founded in: 1967

4812 National Writers Association
www.nationalwriters.com

A nonprofit organization that provides education and an ethical resource for writers at all levels of experience. It also awards scholarships and provides no or low cost workshops and seminars.

4813 Networking Institute
PO Box 650037
West Newton, MA 02465-1928

617-965-3340; *Fax:* 617-965-2341
info@netage.com; www.netage.com

Jessica Lipnack, Owner
Jeffrey Stamps, Co-Founder
Carrie Kuempel, Director Training
Rich Carpenter, Strategy Advisor

Promotes networks to help people work together. Offers consulting services, educational workshops and seminars. To order: The Age of the Network and The TeamNet Factor call Oliver Wright productions at 800-343-0625.
Founded in: 1982

4814 New America Media Ethnic Media Association
209 9th St.
Suite 200
San Francisco, CA 94103

415-503-4170
communications@newamericamedia.org
newamericamedia.org

Sandy Close, Executive Editor & Director

An association for the promotion of ethnic media organizations.
Founded in: 1996

4815 Newspaper Association Managers
32 Dunham Road
Beverly, MA

978-338-2555
nammanagers.com

Lisa Hills, President
Layne Bruce, Vice President
Greg Sherrill, Immediate Past President
George White, Secretary
Tom Newton, Director

An organization of executives representing newspaper associations in the United States and Canada.

4816 Newspaper Association of America
4401 Wilson Blvd
Suite 900
Arlington, VA 22203-4195

571-366-1000; *Fax:* 571-366-1195
joan.mills@naa.org; www.naa.org
Social Media: Facebook, Twitter, LinkedIn, Google+, YouTube

Donna Barrett, Chairman
Stephen P Hills, Vice Chairman
Tony W Hunter, Secretary
Michael J. Klingensmith, Treasurer
Robert J Dickey, Past Chairman

Focuses on the major issues that affect today's newspaper industry public policy and legal matters, advertising revenue growth and audience development across the medium's broad portfolio of products and digital platforms.
2000 Members
Founded in: 1992

4817 North American Serials Interest Group
1902 Ridge Rd
West Seneca, NY 14224-3312

E-Mail: info@nasig.org; www.nasig.org

Joyce Tenney, President
Steve Kelley, Vice President/President-Elect
Shana McDanold, Secretary
Jennifer Arnold, Treasurer
Beverly Geckle, Treasurer-Elect

An independent organization taht promotes communication and sharing of ideas among all members of the serials information chain, anyone working with or concerned about serial publications.
1200 Members
Founded in: 1985

4818 Organization for the Promotion and Advance of Small Telecommunications Co.
21 Dupont Cir NW
Suite 700
Washington, DC 20036-1109

202-833-2775; *Fax:* 202-659-4619
membership@ncta.org; www.opastco.org

John Rose, President
Corey Watkins, Network Administrator

Protects the interests of small, rural, independent commercial telephone companies and cooperatives that have less than 50,000 access lines.
675 Members
Founded in: 1963

4819 PCIA- The Wireless Industry Association
500 Montgomery Street
Suite 500
Alexandria, VA 22314

703-971-7100
800-759-0300; *Fax:* 703-836-1608
andrewd@pcia.com; www.pcia.com
Social Media: Facebook, Twitter, LinkedIn

Thomas A. Murray, Chairman
Steven Marshall, Vice Chairman
David E Weisman, Treasurer
Jonathan S. Adelstein, President & CEO
Tim House, Vice President, External Relations

Represents companies that develop, own, manage and operate towers, commercial rooftops and other facilities for the provision of all types of wireless, broadcasting and telecommunications services.
3000 Members
Founded in: 1949

4820 Paley Center for Media
25 West 52nd Street
New York, NY 10019

212-621-6800; *Fax:* 212-621-6600
coman@paleycenter.org; www.paleycenter.org
Social Media: Facebook, Twitter, YouTube, Google+, Hulu

Maureen J Reidy, President, CEO
John Lanaway, Interim CFO
Maxim Thorne, Executive Vice President
Diane Lewis, Vice President, Public Affairs
Maureen J. Reidy, Chief Marketing Officer

Leads the discussion about the cultural, creative, and social significance of television, radio, and emerging platforms for the professional community and media-interested public.

4821 Personal Achievement Institute
1 Speaking Success Road
Box 6543
Kingman, AZ 86402-6543

928-753-5315
800-321-1225; *Fax:* 928-753-7554;
www.speakingsuccess.com

Burt Dubin, President

Education that provides advice and business strategies for both novices and experts in mastering the field of professional speaking. Free monthly newsletter is accessible through Website.
Founded in: 1978
Printed in one color on matte stock

4822 Portable Computer and Communications Association
PO Box 680
Hood River, OR 97031

541-490-5140; *Fax:* 413-410-8447
pcca@pcca.org; www.pcca.org

Gloria Kowalski, Director
Peter Rysavy, Executive Director

Represents firms, organizations, and individuals interested in moblie communications.
65 Members

4823 Public Relations Society of America
33 Maiden Ln.
11th Fl.
New York, NY 10038

212-460-1400; www.prsa.org
Social Media: Facebook, Twitter, LinkedIn, Pinterest, Tumblr

Kathy Barbour, Chair
Mark W. McClennan, Chair-Elect
Jane Dvorak, Treasurer
Marisa Vallbona, Secretary

The PRSA is the foremost professional development and standards and ethics body in the public relations industry.
22000 Members
Founded in: 1947

4824 Railway Systems Suppliers
13133 Professional Drive
Suite 100
Jacksonville, FL 32225

904-379-3366; *Fax:* 904-379-3941
rssi@rssi.org; www.rssi.org

John Paljug, President
N. Michael Choat, Executive Vice President
Walter Winzen, First Vice President
Franklin Brown, Second Vice President

A trade association serving the communication and signal segment of the rail transportation industry. Primary activity is to organize and manage a trade show for its members to exhibit their products and services.
260 Members
Founded in: 1966

4825 Real Estate Information Professionals Association
2501 Aerial Center Parkway
Suite 103
Morrisville, NC 27560

919-459-2070
801-999-1212; *Fax:* 919-459-2075;
www.reipa.org

Sarah Gillian, Executive Director

Supports professional information providers in the real estate industry.
110 Members
Founded in: 1995

4826 Religious Communication Association
Department of Communication
University of Texas at Tyler
3007 North Ben Wilson
Victoria, TX 77901

903-566-7093; *Fax:* 903-566-7287
wardm@uhv.edu; www.relcomm.org

Kristen Lynn Majocha, President
Mark A. E. Williams, Immediate Past President
Denise P Ferguson, First Vice President
Mark Allan Steiner, Second Vice President
Janie Harden Fritz, Executive Director

An academic society of individuals interested in the study of all aspects of public religious communication, members include teachers, students, clergy, broadcasters and other scholars and professionals.
210 Members
Founded in: 1973

4827 Republican Communications Association
PO Box 550
Washington, DC 20515

E-Mail: RCA@mail.house.gov;
www.rcaweb.org
Social Media: Facebook, Twitter, Google+

Lisa Boot, President
Neal Patel, Vice President
Shea Snider, Treasurer
Michael Tadeo, Social Director
Justin LaFranco, Social Director

Sponsors professional development and networking programs. Conducts seminars, briefings, and tours.
165 Members
Founded in: 1970

4828 Satellite Broadcasting and Communications Association
1100 17th Street NW
Suite 1150
Washington, DC 20036-4557

202-349-3620
800-541-5981; *Fax:* 202-349-3621
info@sbca.org; www.sbca.com
Social Media: Facebook, Twitter, LinkedIn, YouTube

Jeffrey Blum, Chairman
Andrew Reinsdorf, Vice Chairman
Joseph Widoff, Executive Director
Benjamin Rowan, Education Manager
Lisa Volpe McCabe, Director Public Policy and Outreach

The national trade organization representing all segments of the satellite industry. It is committed to expanding the utilization of satellite technology for the broadcast delivery of video, audio, data, music, voice, interactive and broadband services.
100 Members
Founded in: 1986

4829 Society for Technical Communication
9401 Lee Hwy
Suite 300
Fairfax, VA 22031-1803

703-522-4114; *Fax:* 703-522-2075
stc@stc.org; www.stc.org

Bernard Aschwanden, President
Jane Wilson, Treasurer
Adriane Hunt, Vice President
Alyssa Fox, Secretary
Chris Lyons, Executive Director

Seeks to advance the theory and practice of technical communication in all media. Presents awards and sponsors high school writing contests.
19000 Members
Founded in: 1953
Mailing list available for rent: 9000 names at $120 per M

4830 **Society of Satellite Professionals International**
250 Park Avenue
7th Floor
New York, NY 10177
212-809-5199; *Fax:* 212-825-0075
rbell@sspi.org; www.sspi.org
Social Media: Facebook, Twitter, LinkedIn, YouTube
Chris Stott, Chairman & CEO
Bryan McGuirk, COO
Dawn Harms, VP, Business Development
Tony Rayner, Chief Operating Officer
Members are individuals in the fields of businesss, education, entertainment, media, science and industry who share common interests in satellite technology.
1700 Members
Founded in: 1983

4831 **Society of Telecommunications Consultants**
13275 State Highway 89
PO Box 70
Old Station, CA 96071
530-335-7313
800-782-7670; *Fax:* 530-335-7360
stchdq@stcconsultants.org;
www.stcconsultants.org
Social Media: Facebook, Twitter, Pinterest
J. R Simmons, President
Elizabeth K English, Executive Vice President
Molly Zraik, Senior Vice President
The STC is an international organization of independent telecommunications and information technology consultants who serve clients in business and government
180 Members
Founded in: 1976

4832 **Telecommunications Benchmarking International Group**
4606 Fm 1960 Rd W
Suite 250
Houston, TX 77069-4617
281-440-5044
888-739-8244; *Fax:* 281-440-6677
tbig@benchmarkingnetwork.com;
www.benchmarkingnetwork.com
Mark Czarnecki, President
An association of contact center professionals within telecommunications companies dedicated to providing members with an opportunity to identify, document and establish best practices through benchmakring to increase value, effiencies, and profits.
3500+ Members
Founded in: 1976

4833 **Telecommunications Industry Association (TIA)**
1320 N. Courthouse Rd
Suite 200
Arlington, VA 22201-3834
703-907-7700; *Fax:* 703-907-7727
gseiffert@tiaonline.org; www.tiaonline.org
Thomas Stanton, Chair
Susan Schramm, Vice Chair
Jennifer Pentecost Sims, Treasurer
Grant Seiffert, President
Danielle Coffey, Vice President Government Affairs
The Telecommunications Industry Association/TIA represents providers of communications and information technology products and services for the global marketplace through its core competencies in standards development, domestic and international advocacy, as well as market development and trade promotion programs.

4834 **The Association of Business Information and Media Companies**
675 Third Avenue
Suite 2200
New York, NY 10017-5704
212-661-6360; *Fax:* 212-370-0736
info@abmmail.com; www.abmassociation.com
Social Media: Facebook, Twitter, LinkedIn, WordPress, YouTube
Doug Manoni, Chair
Doug Manoni, Vice Chair
Edward Keating, Treasurer
Ethan Eisner, Past Chair
Marion Minor, Secretary
An association that focuses on the integrated business-to-business media model—which includes print publications, events, digital media and business information.
Founded in: 1906

4835 **The Center for Media and Public Affairs**
933 N. Kenmore St.
Suite 405
Arlington, VA 22201
571-319-0029; *Fax:* 571-319-0029
rieckd@cmpa.com; www.cmpa.com
Social Media: Facebook, Twitter
Truman Anderson, Chairman of the Board
Dr. Robert Lichter, Founder, President
Nell Minow, Treasurer & Secretary of the Board
Donald Rieck, Executive Director
Dan Amundson, Research Director
A nonpartisan, nonprofit research organization in Washington, D.C.,conducting scientific studies of the news and entertainment media.
Founded in: 1985

4836 **The Energy Telecommunications and Electrical Association**
5005 W Royal Lane
Suite 116
Irving, TX 75063
972-929-3169
888-503-8700; *Fax:* 972-915-6040;
www.entelec.org
Social Media: Twitter, LinkedIn
William Gage, President
John Lapham, First Vice President
Jerry O Roberts, Second Vice President
Russel W Treat, Third Vice President
Richard Nation, Secretary-Treasurer
A user association focusing on communications and control technologies used by petroleum, natural gas, pipeline and electric utility companies.
Founded in: 1928

4837 **The International Foundation for Information Technology**
P. O. Box 907
Summit, NJ 07901-2508
www.if4it.com
Social Media: Facebook, Twitter, LinkedIn, Google+
A global industry best practices association that promotes the interests and career development of practitioners, educators, and students who wish to extend their knowledge and understanding of IT operations, management, and leadership.

4838 **Toastmasters International**
23182 Arroyo Vista
Rancho Santa Margarita
Mission Viejo, CA 92688-2620
949-858-8255
949-835-1300; *Fax:* 949-858-1207
newsletters@toastmasters.org;
www.toastmasters.org
Social Media: Facebook, Twitter
Jim Kokocki, DTM, International President
Mike Storkey, DTM, International President-Elect
Balraj Arunasalam, DTM, First Vice President
Lark Doley, DTM, Second Vice President
Mohammed Murad, DTM, Immediate Past Intl. President
Publishes educational articles on the subjects of communication and leadership. Topics include language, listening, humor, self-improvement, goal setting, success and logical thinking.
19500 Members
Founded in: 1924

4839 **United States Internet Service Providers**
700 12th St NW
Suite 700 E
Washington, DC 20005-4052
202-904-2351; www.usispa.org
John Albertine, President
Will serve both as the ISP community's representative during policy debates and as a forum in which members can share information and develop best practices for handling specific legal matters.
7 Members
Founded in: 1991

4840 **United States Telecom Association**
607 14th Street, NW
Suite 400
Washington, DC 20005
202-326-7300; *Fax:* 202-315-3603;
www.ustelecom.org
Social Media: Facebook, Twitter, LinkedIn, YouTube
Robert A Hunt, Chairman of the Board
Walter B. McCormick, Jr., President, CEO
Mark Kulish, SVP, Administration, CFO
Alan J. Roth, Senior Executive Vice President
Anne Veigle, SVP, Communications
A trade association that represents telecommunications-related businesses based in the United States.

4841 **United Telecom Council**
1129 20th Street
Suite 350
Washington, DC 20036
202-872-0030; *Fax:* 202-872-1331
bill.moroney@utc.org; www.utc.org
Social Media: Facebook, Twitter, LinkedIn
Connie Darshak, President/CEO
Kathleen Fitzpatrick, VP and General Counsel
Brett Kilbourne, Vice President, Government
Mike Oldak, Vice President, Strategy
Karnel Thomas, Vice President - Member & Industry
Represents organizations using telecommunications in their operations before various federal and state legislative and regulatory agencies, particularly the FCC
1500 Members
Founded in: 1948

4842 **Utility Communicaotrs International**
150 Mark Trai
Sandy Springs, GA 30328
970-368-2021; *Fax:* 512-864-7203
info@utilitycommunicators.com;
www.utilitycommunicators.com
Social Media: Facebook, Twitter, LinkedIn
Brian Phillips, President
Jeff Rogers, Vice President
Jennifer Moffatt, Treasurer
Jerry Cargile, Board
Eunice Tanjuaquio Bray, Board

International organization comprimsed of advertising, public relations and marketing professionals from electric, gas and water utilities, energy companies, telephone companies, advertising and public relations agencies, and suppliers who communicate for and about the utility and energy industries.
400 Members
Founded in: 1922

4843 Wikibon
5 Mount Royal Ave.
Suite 280
Marlborough, MA 1752

774-463-3400; *Fax:* 774-463-3405
wikibon.org
Social Media: Facebook, Twitter, LinkedIn, Blog

A professional community solving technology and business problems through an open source sharing of free advisory knowledge.
Founded in: 2007

4844 Wireless Communications Association International
1333 H St NW
Suite 700 W
Washington, DC 20005-4754

202-452-7823; *Fax:* 202-452-0041;
www.wcai.com
Social Media: Facebook, Twitter, LinkedIn

Fred Campbell, President

The non-profit trade and professional association for the Wireless Broadband industry. Mission is to advance the interests of the wireless carriers that provide high-speed data, internet, voice and video services on broadband spectrum through land-based systems using reception/transmit devices in all broadband spectrum bands.
250 Members
Founded in: 1987

4845 Wireless Dealers Association
9746 Tappenbeck Dr
Houston, TX 77055-4102

713-467-0077
800-624-6918
contact@wirelessindustry.com;
www.wirelessindustry.com

Robert Hutchinson, President

Business association made up of cellular and wireless communications agents, dealers, resellers, carriers, manufacturers, distributors and importers.
2500 Members
Founded in: 1986

4846 Women in Cable and Telecommunications
2000 K Street, NW
Suite 350
Washington, DC 20006
202-827-4794; *Fax:* 202-450-5596
membership@wict.org; www.wict.org
Social Media: Facebook, Twitter, YouTube

Maria E. Brennan, CAE, President & CEO
Mary Meduski, Immediate Past Chair
Gail Mackinnon, Treasurer
Michelle Rice, Governance Chair
Parthavi Das, Chief of Staff

Provides opportunitites for leadership, networking, and advocacy in the industry.
4600 Members
Founded in: 1979

4847 World Teleport Association
250 Park Avenue
Suite 14B
New York, NY 10177

646-291-6166; *Fax:* 212-825-0075
icf@intelligentcommunity.org;
www.intelligentcommunity.org
Social Media: Facebook, Twitter, YouTube

Robert Bell, Executive Director

Promotes the understanding, development, and use of eleports as a means to achieve economic, political and social progress locally, regionally and worldwide.
606 Members
Founded in: 1985

Newsletters

4848 411 Newsletter
United Communications Group
11300 Rockville Pike
Suite 1100
Rockville, MD 20852-3030

301-287-2700; *Fax:* 301-816-8945
webmaster@ucg.com; www.ucg.com

Benny Dicecca, President

Business newsletter for professionals in the communications industry.
Cost: $339.00
Founded in: 1977

4849 ATTW Bulletin
Association of Teachers of Technical Writing
Department of Linguistics and Technical Comm
1155 Union Circle #305298
Denton, TX 76203-5017

940-565-4458
sims@unt.edu; www.attw.org

Barbara Sims, Executive Secretary

Publishes news about members, the association, and the profession as well as bibliographic resources for teachers, teaching techniques, suggested assignments, implications of current research for the classroom, opinions on professional issues, notices and highlights of conferences, calls for papers and proposals, job announcements, and other information that will interest new and experienced teachers in undergraduate or graduate curricula.
Frequency: Semi-Annual

4850 Advertising & Newspaper Media
Newspaper Association of America
4401 Wilson Blvd
Suite 900
Arlington, VA 22203-4195

571-366-1000; *Fax:* 571-366-1195
joan.mills@naa.org; www.naa.org

Reggie Hall, Senior VP

Electronic newsletters delivers retail, national and classified advertising ideas plus updates on your most important customers. If your job responsibilities include any type advertising revenue you need to be a subscriber.
Frequency: Monthly

4851 Bandwidth Minutes and IP Transport Markets Will Capacity Traders Succeed?
Probe Research
3 Wing Drive
Suite 240
Cedar Knolls, NJ 07927-1000

973-285-1500; *Fax:* 973-285-1519;
www.proberesearch.com

We look into capacity exchanges and determine how they add value, whter participants will find exchanges useful, what are the presequisites for a robust capacity market, what are the risk to telcos if they use exchanges, and what do the exchanges need to do in order to increase trading volume.

4852 Bandwidth Pricing Trends
Probe Research
3 Wing Drive
Suite 240
Cedar Knolls, NJ 07927-1000

973-285-1500; *Fax:* 973-285-1519;
www.proberesearch.com

Provides an analysis of the trends in capacity pricing and the expected effects on demand. It provides a view of the drivers that determine what the bandwidth cost will be on a particular route. Also looks at how these determinants have contributes to the level of price erosion each of the routes analyzed.

4853 Big Ideas Newsletter
Newspaper Association of America
4401 Wilson Blvd
Suite 900
Arlington, VA 22203-4195
571-366-1000; *Fax:* 571-366-1195
joan.mills@naa.org; www.naa.org

Reggie Hall, Senior VP

Designed especially for smaller market newspapers, featuring ways to increase revenues, cut costs or otherwise improve your newspaper.
Frequency: Bi-Monthly

4854 Brandwidth Supply and Demand Analysis WIT IP Traffic Demand Update
Probe Research
3 Wing Drive
Suite 240
Cedar Knolls, NJ 07927-1000

973-285-1500; *Fax:* 973-285-1519;
www.proberesearch.com

Provides an analysis of the bandwidth supply and demand on number of interregional routes. Describes methodology of building up the bandwidth supply and demand picture on these routes. Analyzes what the supply and demand balance is on these routes. Concludes what the business ramifications are for ISPs and backbone providers, banks and vendors.

4855 Broadband Wireless
Probe Research
3 Wing Drive
Suite 240
Cedar Knolls, NJ 07927-1000

973-285-1500; *Fax:* 973-285-1519;
www.proberesearch.com

In this bulletin, we take a look into is going on with terrestrial fixed wireless last mile solutions in the MMDS, LMDS spectrums. LMDS is emerging as the next platform for CLECs. However, these CLECs will be entering the market at the end of a long line of competitors in many cities.

4856 Business Publisher
JK Publishing

3105 N Newhall Street
Milwaukee, WI 53211

414-332-1625; *Fax:* 414-332-0916

John Kenney, Editor
Jean O'Brien, Circulation Manager

Offers information and full coverage of the magazine and business/trade publishing industry.
Cost: $335.00
8 Pages
Frequency: BiWeekly

4857 CMA Newsletter
College Media Advisers
University
#300
Memphis, TN 38152

512-471-5084; *Fax:* 901-678-4798;
www.collegemedia.org

Ken Rosenauer, Publisher

Provides news and information to those who advise/supervise college media run by students (i.e. newspapers, magazines, yearbooks, radios, and TV stations).
Cost: $60.00
6 Pages
Circulation: 750
Founded in: 1954

4858 Cantu's Newsletter
Cantu's Comedy Newsletter
PO Box 210495
San Francisco, CA 94121

415-668-2402
info1@HumorMall.com; www.humormall.com

John Cantu, Publisher

Articles of interest to public speakers, writers, comedians, comedy writers.
Cost: $29.95
Circulation: 3000
Founded in: 1999

4859 Chamber Executive
American Chambers of Congress Exec Communications
4875 Eisenhower Ave
Suite 250
Alexandria, VA 22304-4850

703-998-0072; *Fax:* 703-212-9512
webmaster@acce.org; www.acce.org

Mick Flemming, Manager

Newsletter aimed at management level communications professionals.
Cost: $99.00
12 Pages
Founded in: 1914
Mailing list available for rent
Printed in 4 colors on matte stock

4860 Circulation Update E-Newsletter
Newspaper Association of America
4401 Wilson Blvd
Suite 900
Arlington, VA 22203-4195

571-366-1000; *Fax:* 571-366-1195
joan.mills@naa.org; www.naa.org
Social Media: Facebook, Twitter

Reggie Hall, Senior VP

Focused on newspaper executives with responsibility for marketing their newspapers to readers. You will find a balance of recent headline stories, consumer marketing research, information about your retailers, and regulatory information blended with success stories and resources to help you in your mission of building circulation and readership.
Frequency: Weekly

4861 Classified Communications Newsletter
PO Box 4242
Prescott, AZ 86302

520-778-6788
classa@northlink.com

Agnes Franz, Publisher

Information and ad-writing tips for small budget advertisers. Both display and word classifieds addressed. Will also review books on advertising and marketing.
Cost: $35.00
8 Pages
Frequency: Monthly
Circulation: 2000
Founded in: 1989
Printed in 2 colors on glossy stock

4862 Communication Briefings
Briefings Publishing Group
1101 King St
Suite 110
Alexandria, VA 22314-2944

703-548-3800; *Fax:* 703-684-2136;
www.communicationbriefings.com

William G Dugan, Group Publisher
Susan Marshall, Executive Editor
Lois Willingham, Marketing Manager
Charles Blakeney, Owner

This newsletter provides subscribers with communications ideas and techniques to use to persuade clients, and motivate employees.
Cost: $79.00
8 Pages
Frequency: Monthly
Circulation: 55000
Founded in: 1981

4863 Communications Business Daily
Warren Communications News
2115 Ward Ct Nw
Washington, DC 20037-1209

202-872-9200
800-771-9202; *Fax:* 202-318-8350
info@warren-news.com;
www.warren-news.com

Brig Easley, Manager
Daniel Warren, President/Editor
Founded in: 1945

4864 Communications Concepts
Communication Concepts
508 Mill Stone Dr
Beavercreek, OH 45434-5840

937-426-8600; *Fax:* 937-429-3811
cci.dayton@pobox.com;
www.communication-concepts.com

Rodger L Southworth, President

Ideas and methods for professional communications.

4865 DBS Report
Kagan World Media
1 Lower Ragsdale Dr
Building One, Suite 130
Monterey, CA 93940-5749

831-624-1536
800-307-2529; *Fax:* 831-625-3225
info@kagan.com; www.kagan.com

Tim Baskerville, President
Cost: $1045.00
Frequency: Monthly
Founded in: 1969

4866 Daily Deal
Vicki King
105 Madison Avenue
New York, NY 10016

212-313-9200
888-667-3325
customerservice@thedeal.com;
www.thedeal.com

Mickey Hernandez, Advertising Sales
Elena Freed, Marketing

Reports and analyzes all the aspects of the booming, high stakes world of the deal economy. Areas of coverage include mergers and aquisitions, private equity, venture capital and bankruptcies.
Cost: $498.00
26 Pages
Frequency: Daily
Circulation: 40893
Founded in: 1999

4867 EHS News Briefs
Newspaper Association of America
4401 Wilson Blvd
Suite 900
Arlington, VA 22203-4195

571-366-1000; *Fax:* 571-366-1195
joan.mills@naa.org; www.naa.org

Reggie Hall, Senior VP

These news briefs spotlight what is happening in Congress, the Administration, Courts and around the industry.
Frequency: Weekly

4868 Emerging Media Report
Knight MediaCom International
2400 Kettner Boulevard
Suite 237
San Diego, CA 92101

619-338-9885; *Fax:* 619-338-9886
knightsmedia@hotmail.com;
www.knightmedia.com

Covers VR, TV, CD, PC, and entertainment marketing.
Founded in: 1978

4869 Fusion Magazine
Newspaper Association of America
4401 Wilson Blvd
Suite 900
Arlington, VA 22203-4195

571-366-1000; *Fax:* 571-366-1195
joan.mills@naa.org; www.naa.org

Reggie Hall, Senior VP

This newsletter focuses on the business of diversity within the newspaper industry. In it you will find new strategies for making diversity work in advertising, news and editorial, circulation, marketing, production, human resources and the business office.
Frequency: Quarterly

4870 Growing Audience E-Newsletter
Newspaper Association of America
4401 Wilson Blvd
Suite 900
Arlington, VA 22203-4195

571-366-1000; *Fax:* 571-366-1195
joan.mills@naa.org; www.naa.org

Reggie Hall, Senior VP

This newsletter provides an unparalleled array of information to keep you informed on the most current newspaper readership issues, experiments, results, ideas, successes and failures.
Frequency: Weekly

4871 Information Broker
Burwell Enterprises

5619 Plumtree Drive
Dallas, TX 75252

972-331-1951; *Fax:* 972-733-1951;
www.burwellinc.com

Helen Burwell, Publisher
Jeanne Paulino, Marketing Director

Covers fee-based information services for practitioners and users of information services. Accepts advertising.
Cost: $40.00
12 Pages
Frequency: Bi-Monthly
Circulation: 500
Printed in one color on matte stock

4872 **Intercom**
Society for Technical Communication
9401 Lee Hwy
Suite 300
Fairfax, VA 22031-1803

703-522-4114; *Fax:* 703-522-2075
stc@stc.org; www.stc.org

Susan Burton, Executive Director
Anita Dosik, Publications Director
Maurice P. Martin, Editor
Antoinette DeSalvo, Marketing Coordinator
Suzanna Laurent, President

A monthly magazine offering Society members with information and articles on communication industry trends and activities.
Cost: $95.00
Circulation: 20000
Founded in: 1957
Mailing list available for rent: 1000 names at $120 per M

4873 **Labor & Employment Law Letter**
Newspaper Association of America
4401 Wilson Blvd
Suite 900
Arlington, VA 22203-4195

571-366-1000; *Fax:* 571-366-1195
joan.mills@naa.org; www.naa.org

Reggie Hall, Senior VP

This newsletter offers readers information on critical employment issues facing the newspaper industry.
Frequency: Bi-Monthly

4874 **Lifestyle Media-Relations Reporter**
InfoCom Group
5900 Hollis Street
Suite L
Emeryville, CA 94608

510-596-9300
800-959-1059; www.infocomgroup.com

This newsletter offers information on media placement in lifestyle and consumer media.
Cost: $369.00
Frequency: Monthly
Founded in: 1980

4875 **MAPNetter**
Architecture Technology Corporation
9977 Valley View Rd
Suite 300
Eden Prairie, MN 55344-3586

952-829-5864; *Fax:* 952-829-5871
info@atcorp.com; www.atcorp.com
Social Media: Facebook

Kenneth Thurber, President

Monthly newsletter covering important developments in the field of factory communication systems.
Cost: $432.00
12 Pages
Frequency: Monthly
Founded in: 1981

4876 **MRC Cyberalert**
Media Research Center
325 S Patrick St
Alexandria, VA 22314-3501

703-683-9733
800-672-1423; *Fax:* 703-683-9736
mrc@mediaresearch.org; www.mrc.org
Social Media: Facebook

Brent Bozell, CEO

A news-daily report which documents and exposes liberal media bias. MRC is the nation's leading media watchdog.
Cost: $29.00
Frequency: Monthly
Circulation: 13000
Founded in: 1987

4877 **Marketing Library Services**
Information Today
143 Old Marlton Pike
Medford, NJ 08055-8750

609-654-6266
800-300-9868; *Fax:* 609-654-4309
custserv@infotoday.com; www.infotoday.com

Thomas H Hogan, President
Roger R Bilboul, Chairman of the Board

Provides information professional in all types of libraries with specfic ideas for marketing their services.
Cost: $79.95
Frequency: Bi Monthly
ISSN: 0896-3908

4878 **Marketing New Media**
Kagan World Media
1 Lower Ragsdale Dr
Building One, Suite 130
Monterey, CA 93940-5749

831-624-1536
800-307-2529; *Fax:* 831-625-3225
info@kagan.com; www.kagan.com

Tim Baskerville, President
Tom Johnson, Marketing Manager

News of the Marketing New Media. Three month trial available.
Cost: $795.00
Frequency: Monthly
Founded in: 1878

4879 **Media Access**
WGBH Educational Foundation
PO Box 200
Boston, MA 02134-1008

617-300-2000; *Fax:* 617-300-1032
feedback@wgbh.org; www.wgbh.org

Jonathan Abbott, President
Russell Peotter, Owner
Mary Cotton, Owner

Includes information on NCAM's research and development projects, which strive to make media and technology accessible to disabled populations.
2 Pages
Circulation: 15000
Founded in: 1951
Printed in 2 colors on matte stock

4880 **Media File**
Media Alliance
1904 Franklin St
Suite 500
Oakland, CA 94612-2926

510-832-9000; *Fax:* 510-238-8557;
www.media-alliance.org

Tracy Rosenberg, Executive Director
Eloise Rose Lee, Program Director

Information about media and media workers.
8 Pages
Frequency: Quarterly

4881 **Media Law Reporter**
Bureau of National Affairs
1801 S Bell St
Arlington, VA 22202-4501

703-341-3000
800-372-1033; *Fax:* 800-253-0332
customercare@bna.com; www.bnabooks.com

Paul N Wojcik, CEO

A weekly reference service containing the full-text of federal and state court decisions and selected agency rulings affecting newspapers, magazines, radio, television, film and other media.
Cost: $1856.00
Frequency: Weekly
ISSN: 0148-1045
Founded in: 1929

4882 **Media Mergers & Acquisitions**
Kagan World Media
1 Lower Ragsdale Dr
Building One, Suite 130
Monterey, CA 93940-5749

831-624-1536
800-307-2529; *Fax:* 831-625-3225
info@kagan.com; www.kagan.com

Tim Baskerville, President
Tom Johnson, Marketing Manager

Where it all comes together. Exclusive scorecard of deals done by media companies. Dollar amounts, multiples paid, trends captured in succinct summaries of complex transactions. Three month trial available.
Cost: $795.00
Frequency: Monthly
Founded in: 1969

4883 **Media Sports Business**
Kagan World Media
1 Lower Ragsdale Dr
Building One, Suite 130
Monterey, CA 93940-5749

831-624-1536; *Fax:* 831-625-3225
info@kagan.com; www.kagan.com

Tim Baskerville, President
Tom Johnson, Marketing Manager
Cost: $945.00
Frequency: Monthly
Founded in: 1969

4884 **Motion Picture Investor**
Kagan World Media
1 Lower Ragsdale Dr
Building One, Suite 130
Monterey, CA 93940-5749

831-624-1536
800-307-2529; *Fax:* 831-625-3225
info@kagan.com; www.kagan.com

Tim Baskerville, President
Tom Johnson, Marketing Manager
Cost: $845.00
Frequency: Monthly
Founded in: 1969

4885 **NAMIC E-Newsletter**
Natl Assoc for Multi-Ethnicity in Communications
320 West 37th Street
8th Floor
New York, NY 10018

212-594-5985; *Fax:* 212-594-8391
info@namic.com; www.namic.com
Social Media: Facebook, Twitter

Kathy A Johnson, President
James Jones, VP Programs

For members only, provides timely and useful national and local information about industry-related issues, trends and events
Frequency: Bi-Monthly

4886 **NFAIS e-Notes**
National Federation Abstracting & Info Services
1518 Walnut St
Suite 1004
Philadelphia, PA 19102

215-893-1561; *Fax:* 215-893-1564
nfais@nfais.org; www.nfais.org
Social Media: Facebook, Twitter, LinkedIn

Bonnie Lawlor, Executive Director
Jill O'Neil, Director Communications

Membership organization for all organizations that create, aggregate or provide ease of access to credible information.
80 Members
Frequency: Monthly
Founded in: 1958

4887 **Newspaper Investor**
Kagan World Media
1 Lower Ragsdale Dr
Building One, Suite 130
Monterey, CA 93940-5749

831-624-1536
800-307-2529; *Fax:* 831-625-3225
info@kagan.com; www.kagan.com

Tim Baskerville, President
Tom Johnson, Marketing Manager
Cost: $845.00
Frequency: Monthly
Founded in: 1969

4888 **Online Publishing Update E-Newsletter**
Newspaper Association of America
4401 Wilson Blvd
Suite 900
Arlington, VA 22203-4195

571-366-1000; *Fax:* 571-366-1195
joan.mills@naa.org; www.naa.org

Reggie Hall, Senior VP

A round-up of news, research, industry trends, best practices and more, focusing on items of interest to newspaper and digital media executives. Online Publishing Update e-newsletter is published every Monday, Wednesday and Friday.
Frequency: 3x/Weekly

4889 **Pacific Dialogue**
Robert Miko
33 Ferry Ct
Stratford, CT 06615

203-378-2803
bmiko@pacificdialogue.com;
www.pacificdialogue.com

Robert Miko, Publisher

Corporate communications of the Pacific Region.
Cost: $196.00
4 Pages
Frequency: Weekly
Circulation: 1,000

4890 **Party Line**
Party Line Publishing Company
35 Sutton Place
New York, NY 10022-2464

212-755-3487; *Fax:* 212-755-4859;
www.partylinepublishing.com

Morton Yarmon, Publisher
Betty Yarmon, Editor
Betty Yarmon, Marketing

Weekly media placement newsletter with up-to-date news of the media for public relations executives in all aspects of business, hospitals, publishers and associations.
Cost: $200.00
Frequency: Weekly
Circulation: 2000
Founded in: 1960
*Mailing list available for rent*at $100 per M
Printed in 2 colors on matte stock

4891 **Pay TV Newsletter**
Kagan World Media
126 Clock Tower Place
Carmel, CA 93923-8746

831-624-1536; *Fax:* 831-625-3225
info@kagan.com; www.kagan.com

George Niesen, Editor
Tom Johnson, Marketing Manager
Cost: $845.00
Frequency: Monthly

4892 **SIGNAL Connections**
4400 Fairfax Lakes Court
Fairfax, VA 22033

703-631-6100
800-336-4583; *Fax:* 703-631-6169
promo@afcea.org; www.afcea.org
Social Media: Facebook, Twitter, LinkedIn

Richard K Ackerman, Editor in Chief

Bridges the gap between issues of SIGNAL by providing additional news and feature articles about the industry and the Association.
Frequency: Monthly

4893 **Satellite Week**
Warren Communications News
2115 Ward Ct Nw
Washington, DC 20037-1209

202-872-9200
800-771-9202; *Fax:* 202-318-8350
info@warren-news.com;
www.warren-news.com

Brig Easley, Manager
Daniel Warren, President/Editor
Founded in: 1945

4894 **Smaller Market E-Newsletter**
Newspaper Association of America
4401 Wilson Blvd
Suite 900
Arlington, VA 22203-4195

571-366-1000; *Fax:* 571-366-1195
joan.mills@naa.org; www.naa.org
Social Media: Facebook, Twitter

Reggie Hall, Senior VP

Stay ahead of industry news and trends with the latest reports outlining how to improve your smaller market newspaper. Also receive a synopsis on new NAA products and services and how they can benefit smaller market newspapers.
Frequency: Monthly

4895 **Speech Technology Magazine**
2628 Wilhite Court
Suite 100
Lexington, KY 40503

859-278-2223
877-993-9767; *Fax:* 859-278-7364;
www.speechtechmag.com/

John Kelly, Publisher & Editor
Sheila Willison, Circulation Director
Stephanie Owens, Associate Editor
Devon Taylor, Magazine Sales
Kerrie Porath, Sales Coordinator

Divided into four sections: applications, technology, new products, and a special focus section. Authors from the field contribute their expertise to this trade magazine.
73 Pages
Frequency: Fortnightly
Circulation: 25000
Founded in: 1996

4896 **Telecom A.M.**
Warren Communications News
2115 Ward Ct Nw
Washington, DC 20037-1209

202-872-9200
800-771-9202; *Fax:* 202-318-8350
info@warren-news.com;
www.warren-news.com

Brig Easley, Manager
Daniel Warren, President/Editor
Founded in: 1945

4897 **Telemarketing Update: The Regulations and the Impact**
Newspaper Association of America
4401 Wilson Blvd
Suite 900
Arlington, VA 22203-4195

571-366-1000; *Fax:* 571-366-1195
joan.mills@naa.org; www.naa.org
Social Media: Twitter

Reggie Hall, Senior VP

Perspective on the Federal Telemarketing Regulations and an explanation of how newspapers are being impacted by the changes. What's working and what's not and what the Federal Government has in store for newspapers.

4898 **Television A.M.**
Warren Communications News
2115 Ward Ct Nw
Washington, DC 20037-1209

202-872-9200
800-771-9202; *Fax:* 202-318-8350
info@warren-news.com;
www.warren-news.com

Brig Easley, Manager
Daniel Warren, President/Editor
Founded in: 1945

4899 **The RCA News**
Grove City College
Attn: Daniel Brown
100 Campus Drive, Box 3014
Grove City, PA 16127

724-458-3793
dsbrown@gcc.edu;
www.americanrhetoric.com/rca

Daniel S Brown, Newsletter Editor
Ken Danielson, Executive Secretary
Janie Harden Fritz, President

A newsletter for the academic society of individuals interested in the study of all aspects of public religious communication, members include teachers, students, clergy, broadcasters and other scholars and professionals.
210 Members
Founded in: 1973

4900 **Washington Internet Daily**
Warren Communications News
2115 Ward Ct Nw
Washington, DC 20037-1209

202-872-9200
800-771-9202; *Fax:* 202-318-8350
info@warren-news.com;
www.warren-news.com

Brig Easley, Manager
Daniel Warren, President/Editor
Founded in: 1945

Magazines & Journals

4901 **15 Minutes Magazine.Com**
7334 173rd Street
Fresh Meadows, NY 11366-1428

718-969-0404; *Fax:* 718-591-3660
editor@15minutesmagazine.com;
www.15minutesmagazine.com

Tim Boxer, Editor/Publisher
Nina Boxer, Associate Editor
Bernie Ilson, PR Consultant
Stanley Donen, Founder
Michael Fredo, Owner

Monthly magazine online covering society benefits, with reviews of arts and entertainment, travel and new products. Targets 715,000 readers in affluent market
Cost: $50.00
Frequency: Monthly
Circulation: 4,45,000
Founded in: 1999
Printed in 4 colors

4902 **AV Video and Multimedia Producer**
Knowledge Industry Publications
701 Westchester Ave
Suite 101W
West Harrison, NY 10604-3077

914-328-9157; *Fax:* 914-328-9093;
www.kipinet.com/av_mmp/

Ollie Bieniemy, Publisher

Covers product development, graphics and animation, software and equipment, and industry news for readers involved in professional production, multimedia production, and presentation technology.
Cost: $53.00
Frequency: Monthly
Circulation: 100,000

4903 **Archive Magazine**
Luerzer's Archive Inc
410 Park Avenue
Suite 1530
New York, NY 10022-9441

212-941-2496; *Fax:* 212-941-5490
office@showcase.com;
www.lurzersarchive.com
Social Media: Twitter, LinkedIn

Walter Lurzer, Editor

Read by advertising agency executives in 35 countries, archive presents tv commercials and print ads that are currently running around the world.
Frequency: 6x a year
Circulation: 40000

4904 **Business Communications Review**
BCR Enterprises
3025 Highland Pkwy
Suite 200
Downers Grove, IL 60515-5668

630-986-1432
800-227-1234; *Fax:* 630-323-5324;
www.bcr.com

Offers a complete package of the latest information for persons associated with the communications industry.
Cost: $46.00
80 Pages
Frequency: Monthly

4905 **Communication World**
Int'l Association of Business Communicators
601 Montgomery Street
Suite 1900
San Francisco, CA 94111

415-544-4700; *Fax:* 415-544-4747
cwmagazine@iabc.com; www.iabc.com

Natasha Nicholson, Executive Editor
Sue Khodarahmi, Managing Editor
Sue Cavallaro, Production Editor

Covers the leatest in communication research, technology and trends through in-depth reports and insightful interviews.
Cost: $150.00
Frequency: Bi-Monthly
Circulation: 13,000
ISSN: 0744-7612
Founded in: 1982
Printed in on matte stock

4906 **Communications ASP**
Technology Marketing Corporation
1 Technology Plz
Norwalk, CT 06854-1936

203-852-6800
800-243-6002; *Fax:* 203-853-2845
tmc@tmcnet.com; www.tmcnet.com

Rich Tehrani, CEO

Communication solution magazine.
Cost: $2000.00
Frequency: Monthly
Founded in: 1972

4907 **Communications Arts**
Coyne & Blanchard
110 Constitution Dr
Menlo Park, CA 94025-1107

650-326-6040
800-688-1971; *Fax:* 650-326-1648
ca@commarts.com; www.commarts.com

Patrick Coyne, Publisher/Editor

The leading professional journal in the US on graphic arts, commercial photography, illustration and interactive design. Features profile individuals, studios, and agencies with examples of their work. Accepts advertising.
Cost: $53.00
140 Pages
Frequency: 1 Year 8 Issues
Circulation: 74,834
ISSN: 0010-3519
Founded in: 1959
Printed in on glossy stock

4908 **Communications Daily**
Warren Publishing
2115 Ward Ct NW
Washington, DC 20037-1209

202-872-9200
800-771-9202; *Fax:* 202-318-8350
info@warren-news.com;
www.warren-news.com

Brig Easley, Manager
Daniel Warren, President/Editor

Covers the entire spectrum of the telephone, data communications, broadcasting, cable TV, electronic information distribution, cellulars, PCS and satellite.
Cost: $4295.00
Frequency: Daily
Founded in: 1945

4909 **Computers in Libraries**
Information Today
143 Old Marlton Pike
Medford, NJ 08055-8750

609-654-6266
800-300-9868; *Fax:* 609-654-4309
custserv@infotoday.com; www.infotoday.com

Thomas H Hogan, President
Roger R Bilboul, Chairman of the Board

Coverage of news and issues in the field of library information technology. Focuses on practical applications of technology in community, school, academic and special libraries. Includes discussions of the impact of emerging computer technologies on library systems and services and on the library community itself.
Cost: $99.95
Frequency: 10 issues/yr
Mailing list available for rent: 4M names
Printed in 4 colors on glossy stock

4910 **Digital Magic**
PennWell Publishing Company
10 Tara Boulevard
5th Floor
Nashua, NH 03062-2800

603-891-0123; *Fax:* 603-891-0539;
www.penwell.com

Dennis Allen, Publisher

Insights on new technology trends and techniques, covers the latest in hardware and software products to keep digital effects professional competitive and up to date.
Cost: $19.95
Frequency: Bi-Monthly
Circulation: 30,000

4911 **Documentary**
International Documentary Association
1201 W 5th St
Suite M270
Los Angeles, CA 90017-1476

213-534-3600; *Fax:* 213-534-3610
michael@documentary.org;
www.documentary.org

Michael Lumpkin, Executive Director
Jon Curry, Office Manager
Cindy Chyr, Development

Offers essential information and keeps readers on track with the industry.
Cost: $45.00
Frequency: Quarterly

4912 **Extra!**
Fairness & Accuracy in Publishing
112 W 27th Street
New York, NY 10001

212-633-6700; *Fax:* 212-727-7668
fair@fair.org; www.fair.org

Deborah Thomas, Publisher
Jeff Cohen, Founder

Progressive media criticism.
Cost: $21.00
Frequency: Bi-monthly
Circulation: 21800
Founded in: 1987

4913 **Folio: Magazine for Magazine Management**
Red 7 Media, LLC
10 Norden Place
Norwalk, CT 06855

203-854-6730; *Fax:* 203-854-6735
tsilber@red7media.com; www.foliomag.com

Stefanie Botelho, Associate Editor
Kerry Smith, President/CEO
Dan Trombetto, Group Creative Director
Tony Silber, General Manager
John Ellertson, Director Advertising Sales Manager

Written for the people who run the nation's magazines. Offers authoritative intelligence on the magazine market to enable industry professionals to navigate the widening range of strategic options. Every issue delivers features on the people and technologies that are transforming the magazine business, along with useful columns and departments, thought-provoking analysis and tactical advice for building successful maga-

zines.
Cost: $96.00
Frequency: Monthly
Circulation: 11550
Founded in: 1971

4914 **Government Video**
Miller Freeman Publications
810 7th Ave
27th Fl, Suite 4
New York, NY 10019-5818
212-636-2700; *Fax:* 212-636-2750
sedorusa@optonline.net;
www.governmentvideo.com
Gary Rhodes, International Sales Manager
Articles on audio, video production and technologies, training and presentation, multimedia, video conferencing, and medical and scientific applications.
Frequency: Monthly
Circulation: 18,000

4915 **IEEE Wireless Communications**
IEEE Communications Society
3 Park Ave
17th Floor
New York, NY 10016-5997
212-705-8920; *Fax:* 212-705-8999
publications@comsoc.org; www.ieee.org
Laura Book, Manager
Jack Howell, Executive Director
An interdisciplinary bimonthly magazine, covers technical and policy issues relating to personal, location-independent communications in all media and at all protocol layers.
Frequency: Bi-Monthly

4916 **Information Week**
UBM LLC
600 Community Drive
Manhasset, NY 11030
516-562-5000; *Fax:* 516-562-5036;
www.informationweek.com
Rob Preston, VP/Editor In Chief
Laurianne McLaughlin, Editor In Chief
Fritz Nelson, VP/Editorial Director
Delivers breaking news, blogs, high-impact image galleries, proprietary research as well as analysis on IT trends, a whitepaper library, video reports and interactive tools, al i a 24/7 environment.
Circulation: 440,000

4917 **International Communications Association**
1500 21st St NW
Washington, DC 20036-1000
202-955-1444; *Fax:* 202-955-1448
publications@icahdq.org; www.icahdq.org
M Haley, Executive Director
Wolfgang Donfback, Administrative Assistant
Colleen Brady, Administrative Assistant
James Danowski, Secretary
Bi-monthly newsletter that supports all students and professionals in the international communications industry.
Cost: $30.00
Circulation: 3500
Founded in: 1950
Printed in on matte stock

4918 **Journal of Applied Communications**
Agricultural Communicators in Education
University of Florida
PO Box 110810
Gainesville, FL 32611
352-392-9588; *Fax:* 352-392-8583
ace@ifas.ufl.edu;
www.aceweb.org/jac/jac.html
Amanda Aubuchon, Managing Editor
Mark Tucker, Executive Editor
A peer-reviewed professional journal which accepts original contributions about communications, research, innovations and other pertinent information. The Journal is provided to all members, libraries and other interested people.
Cost: $75.00
Frequency: Quarterly
Circulation: 700
ISSN: 1051-0834
Founded in: 1990

4919 **Journal of Open Computing**
Association for Communication Administration
1765 N Street NW
Washington, DC 20036
202-464-4622; *Fax:* 202-464-4600;
www.natcom.org

4920 **Journal of the Association of Information Systems**
Association for Information Systems
Case Western Reserve University
P.O. Box 2712
Atlanta, GA 30301-2712
404-413-7445; *Fax:* 404-413-7443
publications@aisnet.org; www.aisnet.org
Suprateek Sarker, Editorn-in-Chief
Jody McGinness, Executive Director
Jason Thatcher, President
Publishes the highest quality scholarship in the field of information systems. Covers all aspects of Information Systems and Information Technology. Publishes rigorously developed and forward looking conceptual and empirical contributions.Encourages multidisciplinary and nontraditional approaches.
Frequency: Quarterly

4921 **Journal of the Relgious Communication Association**
Department of Communication & Rhetorical Studies
340 College Hall
600 Forbes Ave
Pittsburgh, PA 15282
E-Mail: owner@americanrhetoric.com;
www.americanrhetoric.com/rca
Kathleen Edelmayer, President
Matthew Melton, VP
The JCR addresses the concerns of the religious communicator and the communication scholar and includes reviews of current publications in the field of religious communication. The journal is semi-annual and is included with membership.
Circulation: 675

4922 **MAIL: Journal of Communication Distribution**
Gold Key Box 2425
Milford, PA 18337
607-746-7600; *Fax:* 607-746-2750
mailmagazine@msn.com; www.mailomg.com
Offers updated information on electronic mail and mail messaging systems.
Cost: $6.00
105 Pages
Frequency: Monthly

4923 **Managing Media Relations in a Crisis**
NACHA: The Electronic Payments Association
13450 Sunrise Valley Drive
Suite 100
Herndon, VA 20171
703-561-1100; *Fax:* 703-787-0996
info@nacha.org; www.nacha.org
Janet O Estep, CEO
Marcie Haitema, Chairperson
Designed to assist your organization to develop, test and execute a crisis communication plan. With this guide, you will understand how to address issues, whom to call and in what order to alert them, which vendors you can count on to help and how to develop a means to track the crisis as it grows or abates.
Cost: $30.00

4924 **Media Studies Journal**
Columbia University, Freedom Forum Media Center
2960 Broadway
New York, NY 10027-6902
212-854-1754; *Fax:* 212-678-4817;
www.columbia.edu
Lee C Bollinger, President
Aimed at scholars, practitioners and commentators. Offers information on mass communications issues involving the media and the public at large.
Cost: $20.00
Frequency: Quarterly
Circulation: 9000
Founded in: 1754

4925 **Novedades USA**
Echo Media
900 Circle 75 Pkwy SE
Suite 1600
Atlanta, GA 30339-6014
770-955-3346
sales@echo-media.com; www.echo-media.com
Michael Puffer, CEO
Stacey Reece, VP
Frequency: Weekly
Circulation: 100,000
Founded in: 1986
Printed in 4 colors on newsprint stock

4926 **Presstime Magazine**
Newspaper Association of America
4401 Wilson Blvd
Suite 900
Arlington, VA 22203-4195
571-366-1000; *Fax:* 571-366-1195
joan.mills@naa.org; www.naa.org
Social Media: Twitter
Reggie Hall, Senior VP
The flagship publication reaches top executives across all departments with information about the issues that affect newspaper operations today and in the future.
Frequency: Monthly
Mailing list available for rent

4927 **Professional Journal: Sbusiness Publication**
AFSM International
11031 Via Frontera
Suite A
San Diego, CA 92127-1709
858-673-3055
800-333-9786; *Fax:* 239-275-0794
info@afsmi.org; www.afsmi.org
JB Wood, President
Thomas Lah, Executive Director
A global organization dedicated to furthering the knowledge, understanding, and career development of executives, managers, and professionals in the high-technology services and support industry as well as to provide leadership and direction that helps our individual and corporate

members expand their capabilities to meet the growing complexities and challenges of the industry. Sbusiness publication is distributed bi-monthly serving international decision makers.
Cost: $ 95.00
114 Pages
Circulation: 10000
ISSN: 1049-2135
Founded in: 1975
Printed in 4 colors on matte stock

4928 **Publishers Weekly**
PO Box 51593
Harlan, IA 51593

800-278-2991; *Fax:* 712-733-8019
pwycustserv@cdsfulfillment.com;
www.publishersweekly.com
Social Media: Facebook, Twitter

Jim Milliot, Co-Editorial Director
Michael Coffey, Co-Editorial Director
Diane Roback, Children's Book Editor
Louisa Ermelino, Reviews Director
Calvin Reid, News Editor

PW is the international journal of book publishing and bookselling including business news, reviews and bestseller lists targeted at publishers, booksellers, librarians and literary agents.
Frequency: Weekly
Founded in: 1872

4929 **Red Herring: The Business of Technology**
Red Herring
1900 Alameda De Las Pulgas
Suite 1
San Mateo, CA 94403-1222

650-428-2900; *Fax:* 650-428-2901
info@redherring.com; www.redherring.com

Alex Vieux, Publisher
Christopher Alden, Editorial Director
Joel Dreyfuss, Editor-in-Chief

Offers information on new and rising companies, as well as current industrial technology issues and topics.
Frequency: Weekly
Circulation: 45000
Founded in: 1993

4930 **Replication News**
Miller Freeman Publications
810 7th Ave
27th Fl, Suite 4
New York, NY 10019-5818

212-636-2700; *Fax:* 212-636-2750
sedorusa@optonline.net;
www.governmentvideo.com
Social Media: Facebook, Twitter

Gary Rhodes, International Sales Manager

Information on electronic and recording media through news coverage and analysis to provide executives with the market for strategic business planning.
Frequency: Monthly
Circulation: 16,490
Mailing list available for rent

4931 **SIGNAL Magazine**
4400 Fair Lakes Court
Fairfax, VA 22033-3899

703-631-6100
800-336-4583; *Fax:* 703-631-6133
promo@afcea.org; www.afcea.org
Social Media: Facebook, Twitter, LinkedIn

Robert K Ackerman, Editor in Chief

International news magazine serving the critical information needs of government, military and industry professionals active in the fields of command, control, communications, computers, intelligence, surveillance and reconnaissance (C4ISR); information security, research and development; electronics; and homeland security.
Frequency: Monthly
Circulation: 90000

4932 **Signal Magazine**
Armed Forces Communications & Electronics Assoc
4400 Fair Lakes Court
Fairfax, VA 22033-3899

703-631-6100
800-336-4583; *Fax:* 703-631-6405
service@afcea.org; www.afcea.org
Social Media: Facebook, Twitter, LinkedIn

Kent Schneider, President/CEO
Becky Nolan, Executive VP
John A Dubia, Executive VP

4933 **Speaker Magazine**
National Speakers Association
1500 S Priest Dr
Tempe, AZ 85281-6203

480-968-2552; *Fax:* 480-968-0911
andrea@nsaspeaker.org; www.nsaspeaker.org

Ronald Culberson, President

Trends, issues and perspectives about and for the professional speaking industry.
Cost: $49.00
Frequency: 10x/Year

4934 **TV Guide**
United Video Satellite Group
1211 Avenue of the Americas
4th Floor
New York, NY 10036-8701

212-852-7500; *Fax:* 212-852-4914

Richard Porter, Publisher

Focuses on all aspects of network, cable and pay television programming and how it affects and reflects their audience.
Cost: $39.88
Frequency: Weekly
Circulation: 13mm

4935 **TV Technology**
IMAS Publishing
PO Box 1214
Falls Church, VA 22041

703-998-7600; *Fax:* 703-998-2966;
www.tvtechnology.com

Steven Dana, President
Tom Butts, Editor
Eric Trabb, Publisher
Kwentin Keenan, Circulation Manager
Bob Moses, Executive Director

News of a technical nature covering topics ranging from regulatory developments through maintenance and new products.
Cost: $39.95
Frequency: Fortnightly
Circulation: 37,000
Founded in: 1978

4936 **TechTrends**
Assn. for Educational Communications & Technology
320 West 8th Streete
Suite 101
Bloomington, IN 47404
812-335-7675
877-677-2328; *Fax:* 812-335-7678
aect@aect.org
aect.site-ym.org
Social Media: Facebook, Twitter

Charles B. Hodges, Editor-in-Chief
Phillip Harris, Executive Editor
Brad Hokanson, President

Provides a medium of information exchange for professionals in media management programs.
Cost: $125.00
Frequency: Bi-Monthly
Circulation: 3500
ISSN: 8756-3894

4937 **Television International Magazine**
Television International Magazine
PO Box 2473
Universal City, CA 91610-8471

323-462-1099; *Fax:* 702-939-4725
tvi@smart90.com; www.tvimagazine.com

Josie Cory, Publisher
Mark Soval, Advertising Director

News and information regarding the television industry, includes the who's who of the business; geared toward the executives and professionals of the industry.
Cost: $129.00
Frequency: Monthly
Circulation: 16000
Founded in: 1956
Printed in 4 colors on glossy stock

4938 **xchange**
Virgo Publishing LLC
3300 N Central Ave
Suite 300
Phoenix, AZ 85012-2532

480-675-9925; *Fax:* 480-990-0819
mikes@vpico.com; www.vpico.com
Social Media: Twitter, LinkedIn

Jenny Bolton, President

Provides in-depth, executive-level news and analysis regarding strategy, technology and regulation to help communications service providers create new revenue, lower costs and achieve sustainable business models.
Cost: $75.00
Frequency: Monthly
Circulation: 35,003
Founded in: 1986

Trade Shows

4939 **AFCEA TechNet International**
Armed Forces Communications and Electronics Assn
4400 Fair Lakes Court
Fairfax, VA 22033-3899

703-631-6200
800-564-4220; *Fax:* 703-654-6931
technetinternational@jspargo.com;
www.afcea.org
Social Media: Facebook, Twitter, LinkedIn

Paul doCarmo, Sales Manager
Connie Shaw, Sales Manager

This event draws commanders and staff from every branch of the military, including warfighting integration organizations charged with the most critical responsibilities of synthesizing military power on land, at sea, and in the air.
7500 Attendees
Frequency: June

4940 **AM&AA Summer Conference**
Alliance of Merger and Acquisition Advisors
150 North Michigan Avenue
Suite 2700
Chicago, IL 60601

877-844-2535; *Fax:* 312-729-9800;
www.amaaonline.com

Ainsley Emerson, Director

Premier international organization serving the educational and resource needs of the middle market and M&A profession.
Frequency: Annual

4941 **ATTW Conference**
Association of Teachers of Technical Writing
Department of Linguistics and Technical Comm
1155 Union Circle #305298
Denton, TX 76203-5017

940-565-4458
sims@unt.edu; www.attw.org

Bill Davidson, President
Brenda Sims, Secretary
600 Members
Frequency: Annual/April
Founded in: 1973
Mailing list available for rent

4942 **American Public Communications Council Conference & Expo**
American Public Communications Council
625 Slaters Lane
Suite 104
Alexandria, VA 22314

703-739-1322; *Fax:* 703-739-1324;
www.apcc.net

Willard Nichols, President
Michael Bright, Director
Conference, luncheon and 100 exhibits of public communications equipment and information including, pay phones, internet, atm, multimedia and more. Discussions include lobbying, the political climate, legal regulatory and legislative updates.
Founded in: 1988

4943 **Association for Business Communication Annual Symposium**
Po Box 6143
Nacogdoches, TX 75962-0001

936-468-6280; *Fax:* 646-468-6281;
www.businesscommunication.org

Nancy Schullery, President
Workshop and displays from textbook publishers, speech and business writing, technical publications and corporate communication.
400 Attendees
Founded in: 1935

4944 **DISA Customer Partnership AFCEA Technology Showcase**
Armed Forces Communications and Electronics Assn
4400 Fair Lakes Court
Fairfax, VA 22033

703-631-6200
800-564-4220; *Fax:* 703-654-6931;
www.afcea.org
Social Media: Facebook, Twitter, LinkedIn

Paul doCarmo, Assistant Director/Exhibit Sales
Connie Shaw, Exhibit Sales Account Manager
This conference facilitates a continuing interface with customers and strategic partners by allowing attendees to benefit from the perspective of DoD (Department of Defense) and industry speakers. It offers information sessions that provide a forum for questions, concerns and problem resolution.
1200 Attendees
Frequency: April-May

4945 **Entelec Conference & Expo**
Energy Telecommunications and Electrical Assoc
5005 W Royal Lane
Suite 116
Irving, TX 75063

972-929-3169
888-503-8700; *Fax:* 972-915-6040
info@entelec.org; www.entelec.org

Michael Burt, President
James Coulter, VP
To bring together communications and control technology professionals from the petroleum, natural gas, pipeline, and electric utility companies for three days of quality training, seminars, exhibits and networking.
Frequency: Annual/May

4946 **Graphic Communications Conference of the Int'l Brotherhood of Teamsters**
1900 L Street NW
Washington, DC 20036

202-462-1400; *Fax:* 202-721-0600
webmessenger@gciu.org; www.gciu.org

James Hoff, President
Robert Lacey, Secretary/Treasurer
Combines three independent shows: Printing XPO, Type-X, and Art-X and gives you a complete overview of the most recently introduced technologies and the newest information in the field of graphic arts.
15000 Members
Founded in: 1983

4947 **LandWarNet Conference**
Armed Forces Communications and Electronics Assn
4400 Fair Lakes Court
Fairfax, VA 22033

703-631-6200
800-564-4220; *Fax:* 703-654-6931;
www.afcea.org
Social Media: Facebook, Twitter, LinkedIn

Nathan Wills, Account Manager
Thousands of key communications/information technology buyers and influencers attend the conference every year. This is an opportunity to network with the best and develop crucial relationships with some of the Army's most influential decision-makers.
3700 Attendees
Frequency: August

4948 **MILCOM**
Armed Forces Communications and Electronics Assn
4400 Fair Lakes Court
Fairfax, VA 22033

703-631-6200
800-564-4220; *Fax:* 703-654-6931;
www.afcea.org
Social Media: Facebook, Twitter, LinkedIn

Paul doCarmo, Assistant Director/Exhibit Sales
Connie Shaw, Exhibit Sales Account Manager
For over 20 years, MILCOM has been the premeir international conference for military communications, with over 3,000 attendees every year. It attracts decision-makers from government, military, academia and industry, including heads of multi-national forces from around the globe, all who contribute key technologies decisions and investments for their agency.
3000 Attendees
Frequency: October

4949 **Mailcom**
The Art & Science of Mail Communications
Po Box 7045
Philadelphia, PA 19149

732-280-8865; *Fax:* 732-280-7854
ljhumphries@msn.com; www.mailcom.org

Lance Humphries, Managing Director
Learn how business communications can become strategic corporate tools
9000 Attendees
Frequency: Oct Las Vegas
Mailing list available for rent

4950 **NAA Annual Convention**
Newspaper Association of America
4401 Wilson Boulevard
Suite 900
Vienna, VA 22203-1867

571-366-1000; *Fax:* 571-366-1195
joan.mills@naa.org; www.naa.org

James Moroney, President
Donna Barret, Treasurer
This event will welcome industry executives from across the country and is the opportunity for senior level newspaper professionals to learn, share ideas and network. The agenda will showcase the strategies and tactics necessary to address the key issues of revenue, audience, digital and infrastructure.
Frequency: Annual
Mailing list available for rent

4951 **NAMIC Conference**
Natl Assoc for Multi-Ethnicity in Communications
320 West 37th Street
8th Floor
New York, NY 10018

212-594-5985; *Fax:* 212-594-8391
info@namic.com; www.namic.com
Social Media: Facebook, Twitter, LinkedIn

Kathy A Johnson, President
James Jones, VP Programs
Educational forum focused on leadership development, corporate diversity and inclusion, digital media and multi-ethnic content and programming. Content emphasizes diversity as a strategic business imperative
700 Attendees
Frequency: Annual

4952 **NFAIS Annual Conference**
National Federation Abstracting & Info Services
1518 Walnut St
Suite 1004
Philadelphia, PA 19102

215-893-1561; *Fax:* 215-893-1564
nfais@nfais.org; www.nfais.org

Bonnie Lawlor, Executive Director
Jill O'Neil, Director Communications
300 Attendees
Frequency: February/March

4953 **NSA Convention**
National Speakers Association
1500 S Priest Dr
Tempe, AZ 85281-6203

480-968-2552; *Fax:* 480-968-0911;
www.nsaspeaker.org

Ronald Culberson, President
1500 Attendees
Frequency: Annual

4954 **National Hispanic Market Trade Show and Media Expo (Se Habla Espanol)**
Hispanic Business
425 Pine Avenue
Santa Barbara, CA 93117-3709

805-964-4554; *Fax:* 805-964-5539
info@hispanstar.com; www.expomediainc.com
Social Media: Facebook, Twitter, LinkedIn

John Pasini, Cfo/Coo

Annual show of 100 exhibitors of market/research, media, advertising, public relations, information services and recruitment.
1500 Attendees

4955 PRSA International Conference
Public Relations Society of America
33 Maiden Ln.
11th Fl.
New York, NY 10038

212-460-1400
Social Media: Facebook, Twitter, LinkedIn, Reddit, Tumblr

Kathy Barbour, Chair

Actionable best practices are the focus of this annual event.

4956 Toastmasters Trade Show
Toastmasters International
PO Box 9052
Mission Viejo, CA 92690-9052

949-858-8255
949-835-1300; *Fax:* 949-858-1207
newsletters@toastmasters.org;
www.toastmasters.org

Focuses on communication in general and public speaking in particular. Topics include language, listening, humor, self improvement, goal setting, success and logical thinking.
2M Attendees
Frequency: August

Directories & Databases

4957 ACCE Communications Council Directory
4875 Eisenhower Ave
Suite 250
Alexandria, VA 22304-4850

703-998-0072; *Fax:* 703-212-9512
webmaster@acce.org; www.acce.org
Social Media: Facebook, Twitter, LinkedIn

Michael Flemming, President

Offers member information on the council activities.
Frequency: Annual+
Founded in: 1914

4958 Adweek Directory
Prometheus Global Media
770 Broadway
New York, NY 10003-9595

212-493-4100; *Fax:* 646-654-5368;
www.prometheusgm.com

Richard D. Beckman, CEO
Jame A. Finkelstein, Chairman
Madeline Krakowsky, Vice President Circulation
Tracy Brater, Executive Director Creative Service

Adweek Directories Online is where you will find searchable databases with comprehensive information on ad agencies, brand marketers and multicultural media.
Frequency: Annual
Circulation: 800
Founded in: 1981

4959 American Showcase Illustration
Luerzer's Archive Inc
Ste 1530
410 Park Ave
New York, NY 10022-9441

212-941-2496; *Fax:* 212-941-5490;
www.lurzersarchive.com

Walter Lurzer, Editor

Illustrators and graphic designers.
Mailing list available for rent

4960 Association for Educational Communications and Technology Membership Directory
Assn. for Educational Communications & Technology
320 W. 8th Street
Suite 101
Bloomington, IN 47404

812-335-7675
877-677-2328; *Fax:* 812-335-7678
aect@aect.org
aect.site-ym.org
Social Media: Facebook, Twitter

Brad Hokanson, President
Phillip Harris, Executive Director

5,000 audiovisual and instructional materials specialists, educational technologists, audiovisual and television production personnel, school media specialists
Frequency: Annual

4961 Bacon's Newspaper & Magazine Directories
Cision U.S., Inc.
322 South Michigan Avenue
Suite 900
Chicago, IL 60604

312-263-0070
866-639-5087
info.us@cision.com
us.cision.com

Joe Bernardo, President & CEO
Heidi Sullivan, VP & Publisher
Valerie Lopez, Research Director
Jessica White, Research Director
Rachel Farrell, Research Manager

Two volume set listing all daily and community newspapers, magazines and newsletters, news service and syndicates, syndicated columnists, complete editorial staff listings of each publication provided, covers U.S., Canada, Mexico, and Carribean.
Cost: $350.00
4,700 Pages
Frequency: Annual
ISSN: 1088-9639
Founded in: 1951
Printed in one color on matte stock

4962 Bacon's Radio/TV/Cable Directory
Cision U.S., Inc.
332 South Michigan Avenue
Suite 900
Chicago, IL 60604

312-263-0070
866-639-5087
info.us@cision.com; www.us.cision.com

Joe Bernardo, President & CEO
Heidi Sullivan, VP & Publisher
Valerie Lopez, Research Director
Jessica White, Research Director
Rachel Farrell, Research Manager

Includes comprehensive coverage for contact and programming information for more than 3,500 televsion networks, cable networks, television syndicators, television stations, and cable systems in the United States and Canada.
Cost: $350.00
Frequency: Annual
ISSN: 1088-9639
Printed in one color on matte stock

4963 Burrelle's Media Directory
BurrellesLuce
75 E Northfield Rd
Livingston, NJ 07039-4532

973-992-6600
800-631-1160; *Fax:* 973-992-7675;
www.burrellesluce.com
Social Media: Facebook, Twitter, LinkedIn

Robert C Waggoner, CEO

Approximately 60,000 media listings in North America. Listings cover newspapers, magazines (trades and consumer), broadcast, and internet outlets.
Cost: $795.00
Frequency: Annual

4964 Corporate Yellow Book
Leadership Directories
104 5th Ave
New York, NY 10011-6901

212-627-4140; *Fax:* 212-645-0931
corporate@leadershipdirectories.com;
www.leadershipdirectories.com

David Hurvitz, CEO

Contact information for over 48,000 executives at over 1,000 companies and 6,000 subsidiaries and divisions, and more than 9,000 board members and their outside affiliations.
Cost: $360.00
1,400 Pages
Frequency: Quarterly
ISSN: 1058-2908
Founded in: 1986
Mailing list available for rent: 50,000 names at $105 per M

4965 Film & Video Finder
Information Today
143 Old Marlton Pike
Medford, NJ 08055-8750

609-654-6266
800-300-9868; *Fax:* 609-654-4309
custserv@infotoday.com; www.infotoday.com

Thomas H Hogan, President
Roger R Bilboul, Chairman Of The Board

Contains information on 130,000 films and videos. The most comprehensive reference available to educational films and videos. A three volume hardbound set.
Cost: $295.00
6434 Pages
Frequency: Annual
ISBN: 0-937548-29-4

4966 Gale Database of Publications and Broadcast Media
Gale/Cengage Learning
PO Box 09187
Detroit, MI 48209-0187

248-699-4253
800-877-4253; *Fax:* 248-699-8049
gale.galeord@cengage.com; www.gale.com
Social Media: Facebook, Twitter, LinkedIn

Patrick C Sommers, President

This media directory contains thousands of listings for radio and television stations and cable companies.
Founded in: 2008

4967 Gale's Ready Reference Shelf
Gale/Cengage Learning
PO Box 09187
Detroit, MI 48209-0187

248-699-4253
800-877-4253; *Fax:* 248-699-8049
gale.galeord@cengage.com; www.gale.com
Social Media: Facebook, Twitter, LinkedIn

Patrick C Sommers, President

Gale's Ready Reference Shelf allows you to search the entire database of integrated content at one time and the data updates are automatic allowing the user to access the latest information available.

4968 Gebbie Press All-in-One Directory
Gebbie Press

PO Box 1000
New Paltz, NY 12561-0017

845-255-7560; *Fax:* 845-256-1239;
www.gebbieinc.com

Mark Gebbie, Editor/Publisher

TV and radio stations, daily and weekly newspapers, consumer and trade magazines, black and Hispanic media, news syndicates, networks, AP/UPI bureaus. Compact spiral bound 6x9 inches.
Cost: $140.00
500 Pages
Frequency: Also on Disk
Founded in: 1970

4969 Hudson's Washington News Media Contacts Directory
Grey House Publishing
4919 Route 22
PO Box 56
Amenia, NY 12501

518-789-8700
800-562-2139; *Fax:* 845-373-6390
books@greyhouse.com; www.greyhouse.com
Social Media: Facebook, Twitter

Leslie Mackenzie, Publisher
Richard Gottlieb, President

A comprehensive guide to the entire Washington, D.C. press corps, broken down into categories.
Cost: $289.00
350 Pages
ISBN: 1-592378-53-6
Printed in one color on matte stock

4970 Hudson's Washington News Media Contacts - Online Database
Grey House Publishing
4919 Route 22
PO Box 56
Amenia, NY 12501

518-789-8700
800-562-2139; *Fax:* 845-373-6390
gold@greyhouse.com;
www.gold.greyhouse.com
Social Media: Facebook, Twitter

Leslie Mackenzie, Publisher
Richard Gottlieb, President

With 100% verification of data, Hudson's is the most accurate, most up-to-date source for media contacts in our nation's capital. With the largest concentration of news media in the world, having access to Washington's news media will get your message heard by these key media outlets.

4971 Journalism and Mass Communication Directory
AEJMC
234 Outlet Pointe Boulevard
Suite A
Columbia, SC 29210-5667

803-798-0271; *Fax:* 803-772-3509
aejmchq@aol.com; www.aejmc.org
Social Media: Facebook, Twitter, LinkedIn

Kyo Hum, President

Over 3,000 professionals, academics and graduate students; more than 400 journalism and mass communications schools and departments in four-year colleges and universities, including 200 members of the Association of Schools of Journalism and Mass Communication.
Cost: $25.00
Frequency: Annual
Circulation: 5000
Founded in: 1983
Mailing list available for rent

4972 Kagan Media Index
Kagan World Media
126 Clock Tower Place
Carmel, CA 93923-8746

831-624-1536; *Fax:* 831-625-3225
info@kagan.com; www.kagan.com

George Niesen, Editor
Tom Johnson, Marketing Manager

The most comprehensive collection of media industry databases found anywhere. Current estimates of industry growth for a dozen different media businesses, shown on a 145-line spreadsheet, projected forward and updated monthly. Three month trial available.
Cost: $795.00
Frequency: Monthly

4973 M Street Radio Directory
M Street Corporation
81 Main Street, Suite 2
PO Box 442
Littleten, NH 03561
603-444-5720
800-248-4242; *Fax:* 603-444-2872
ww.mstreet.net

Cathy Devine, Research Director
Kelli Grisez, Operations Manager
Frank Saxe, Senior Editor

Approximately 14,000 AM and FM radio stations in the US and Canada.
Cost: $79.00
Frequency: Annual
Printed in on matte stock

4974 News Media Directories
PO Box 316
Mount Dora, FL 32757

352-589-9020
800-749-6399; *Fax:* 866-586-7020;
www.newsmediadirectories.com

Dean Highberger, Editor

Directory for lists, daily papers, new services, magazines, weekly papers, special publications and radio stations. We have directories covering eight states , Alabama, Florida, Georgia, Mississippi, North Carolina, Ohio, South Carolina and Tennessee. Also, we have a condensed southeast edition. Listings include address, phone, fax, e-mail, and key associates.
Frequency: Annual

4975 News Media Yellow Book
Leadership Directories
104 5th Ave
New York, NY 10011-6901

212-627-4140; *Fax:* 212-645-0931
newsmedia@leadershipdirectories.com;
www.leadershipdirectories.com
Social Media: Facebook, Twitter

David Hurvitz, CEO
James M Petrie, Associate Publisher

Contact information for over 39,000 journalists at over 2,500 new services, networks, newspapers, television, radio stations, as well as independent journalists and syndicated columnists.
Cost: $325.00
1,200 Pages
Frequency: Quarterly
ISSN: 1071-8931
Founded in: 1989
Mailing list available for rent: 32,000 names at $125 per M

4976 O'Dwyer's Directory of Public Relations Firms
JR O'Dwyer Company
271 Madison Ave
Suite 600
New York, NY 10016-1013

212-679-2461; *Fax:* 212-683-2750
jack@odwyerpr.com; www.odwyerpr.com

Jack O'Dwyer, Publisher
Kevin McCauley, Editor
Sharlene Spingler, Associate Publisher

Exclusive ranking of public relations firms and lists more than 1,700 firms in the US and 55 countries.
Cost: $125.00
400 Pages
Frequency: Annual
Founded in: 1968

4977 Pocket Media Guide
Media Distribution Services
307 W 36th St
Department P
New York, NY 10018-6519

212-279-4800
800-637-3282; *Fax:* 212-643-0576;
www.mdsconnect.com

Dan Cantelmo, President

Designed to fit easily into a wallet, the palm size guide includes names and addresses, with phone numbers, of more than 700 major print and media in North America, plus a calendar, annual media statistics, and a publicity primer.
40 Pages
Frequency: Annual

4978 Power Media Selects
Broadcast Interview Source
2233 Wisconsin Ave NW
Suite 301
Washington, DC 20007-4132

202-333-5000
800-932-7266; *Fax:* 202-342-5411;
www.expertclick.com

Mitchell Davis, Owner
Alan Caruba, Production Manager

Approximately 3,000 media contacts throughout the US, including newswire services, syndicates, syndicated columnists, national newspapers, magazines, radio and television talk shows, etc.
Cost: $166.50
Frequency: Annual

4979 Sound & Communications
Testa Communications
25 Willowdale Avenue
Port Washington, NY 11050-3779

516-767-2500; *Fax:* 516-767-9335

David Silverman, Editor
Bob Beoder, Advertising Manager

The systems magazine for contractors and consultants who design, specify, sell, and install audio and display systems. Installation profiles, news, business and product updates, incisive theory and applications reporting.
Cost: $15.00
Frequency: Monthly
Circulation: 23,000
Founded in: 1955

Industry Web Sites

4980 http://gold.greyhouse.com
G.O.L.D Grey House OnLine Databases

Grey House Publishing's online database platform, GOLD, offers Quick Search, Keyword Search and Expert Search for most business markets including boradcasting, communications and media markets. The GOLD platform makes finding the information you need quick and easy - whether you're a novice searcher or an experienced database user. All of Grey House's directory products are available for subscription on the GOLD platform.

4981 **www.acce.org**
American Chamber of Commerce Executives
National organization uniquely serving individuals involved in the management of chambers of all sizes. Chamber executives and their staffs can capitalize on a wealth of information, leadership, skill development, management techniques and innovative program offerings. Also works diligently to upgrade the economic status and professional standing of those active in the chamber field.

4982 **www.adweek.com**
Adweek
Leading decision makers in the advertising and marketing field go to Adweek.com every day for breaking news, insight, buzz, opinion, analysis, research and classifieds. The resources of all six regional editions of Adweek, as well as the national edition of Brandweek are combined with the knowledge of our editors and the multimedia-interactive capabilities of the Web to deliver vital information quickly and effectively to our target audience.

4983 **www.aim.org**
Accuracy in Media
Nonprofit, grassroots citizens watchdog of the news media that critiques botched and bungled news stories and sets the record straight on important issues that have recieved slanted coverage.

4984 **www.americomm.org**
American Communication Association
Founded for the purposes of fostering research and scholorship in all areas of human communication behavior, promoting and improving excellence in the pedagogy of communication, providing a voice in communication law and policy, and providing evaluation and certification services for academic programs in communication study.

4985 **www.amta.org**
Antenna Measurement Techniques Association
Nonprofit professional organization, open to individuals with an interest in antenna measurements. Areas of interest include: measurement facilities, unique or innovative measurement techniques, test instrumentation and systems, RCS measurements, compact range design and evaluation, near-field techniques and their applications, and the practical aspects of measurement problems problems and their solutions.

4986 **www.apcc.net**
American Public Communications Council
APCC proudly offers offers a wide array of services to the public communications industry, from Perspectives magazine to our annual trade show to our involvement in legal and regulatory issues. This site is a place for the public to find out about our industry and for our members to learn of legal and regulatory developments, to become aware of APCC programs events, and to have a forum for discussion.

4987 **www.apco911.org**
Association of Public-Safety Communications
The world's oldest and largest professional organization dedicated to the enhancement of public safety communications and to serving its more than 15,000 members, the people who use public safety communications systems and services.

4988 **www.attw.org**
Association of Teachers of Technical Writing
Provides communication among teachers of technical writing and develops technical communications as an academic discipline.

4989 **www.bowker.com**
Reed Reference Publishing RR Bowker
Offers, in four separate volumes, syndicates, newspapers, radio and television stations, feature writers, photographers, illustrators and internal house organs.

4990 **www.consultingsuccess.org**
Assn of Professional Communication Consultants
Professional community where communication consultants increase their knowledge, grow their business, achieve high standards of professional practice. APCC's mission is to support members as they help clients reach their goals through better communication.

4991 **www.digmedia.org**
Digital Media Association
National trade organization devoted primarily to the online audio and video industries, and more generally to commercially innovative digital media opportunities.

4992 **www.drudgereport.com**
Links to international news sources and columnists.

4993 **www.entelec.org**
Energy Telecommunications and Electrical Assoc
A user association focusing on communications and control technologies used by petroleum, natural gas, pipeline and electric utility companies.

4994 **www.greyhouse.com**
Grey House Publishing
Authoritative reference directories for most business sectors including broadcasting, communications and meida markets. Users can search the online databases with varied search criteria allowing for custom searches by product category, geographic area, sales volume, keyword, subject and more. Full Grey House catalog and online ordering also available.

4995 **www.iaais.org**
Int'l Association of Audio Information Services
Formerly the National Association of Radio Reading Services, we are an organization of services that provide audio access to information for people who are print disabled. People served are blind, visually impared, learning disabled or physically disabled.

4996 **www.iabc.com**
Int'l Association of Business Communications
International knowledge network for professionals engaged in strategic business communication management. IABC links communicators in a global network that inspires, establishes and supports the highest professional standards.

4997 **www.icahdq.org**
International Communications Association
International association for scholars interested in the study, teaching and application of all aspects of human mediated communication.

4998 **www.iics.org**
International Interactive Communication Society
For communications industry professionals dedicated to the advancement of interactive technologies. Provides a forum to share ideas, applications amd techniques for effective use of interactive media.

4999 **www.iste.org**
International Society for Technology in Education
Nonprofit professional organization with a worldwide membership of leaders and potential leaders in educational technology.

5000 **www.kagan.com**
Kagan World Media
For those interested in investments in radio and TV stations and publicly held companies.

5001 **www.kausfiles.com**
Kausfiles
Site for journalists and media specialists.

5002 **www.liberty.uc.wlu.edu**
Journalism Resources
Lists of newspapers, film resources, jobs and internships and political advocacy groups.

5003 **www.missouri.edu/~foiwww**
Affiliation of University of Missouri
Maintains files documenting actions by government, media and society affecting the flow and content of information. Call or write for assistance with researching media topics or instruction in using access laws.

5004 **www.netage.com**
Networking Institute
Promotes networks to help people work together. Offers consulting services, educational workshops and seminars.

5005 **www.nfais.org**
National Federation Absrtacting & Info Services
Serves those groups that aggregate, organize, and facilitate access to information. To improve member capabilities and contribute to their ongoing success. Provides opportunities for education, advocacy, and a forum to address common interests.

5006 **www.nsaspeaker.org**
National Speakers Association
The leading organization for experts who speak professionally. NSA's 4000 members include experts in a variety of industries and disciplines, who reach audiences as trainers, educators, humorists, motivators, consultants, authors and more. NSA provides resources and education designed to advance the skills, integrity, and value of its members and speaking profession. NSA the voice of the speaking profession.

5007 **www.postcom.org**
Association for Postal Commerce
National Organization representing those who use, or support the use, of mail as a medium for communication and commerce. Postcom publishes a weekly newsletter covering postal policy and operational issues.

5008 **www.poynter.org**
Poynter Online
Poynter Institute is dedicated to teaching and inspiring journalists and media leaders. Promotes excellence and integrity in the practice of craft and in the practical leadership of successful businesses.

5009 **www.regionalmagazines.org**
International Regional Magazine Association
Promotes the interests of international and regional magazine professionals.

5010 **www.retailing.org**
Electronics Retailing Association
For infomercial producers, marketers, product developers, broadcasters and other industries serving the infomercial market.

5011 **www.speakingsuccess.com**
Personal Achievement Institute

5012 **www.theabc.org**
Association for Business Communication
International organization commited to fostering excellence in business communication scholarship, research, education, and practice.

5013 **www.toastmasters.org**
Toastmasters International
Publishes educational articles on the subjects of communication and leadership. Topics include language, listening, humor, self-improvement, goal setting, success and logical thinking.

5014 **www.wgbh.org**
WGBH Educational Foundation
WGBH productions are seen and heard on stations around the country.

Associations

5015 **AIM Global**
One Landmark North, 20399 Route 19
Suite 203
Cranberry Township, PA 16066
724-934-4470; *Fax:* 724-742-4476
info@aimglobal.org; www.aimglobal.org
Social Media: Facebook, Twitter, LinkedIn, Pinterest
Chuck Evanhoe, President & CEO
Don Ertel, North America Chapter Rep.
Mary Lou Bosco, Chief Operating Officer
Cynthia Troup, Communications & Marketing
International trade association representing automatic identification and mobility technology solution providers.
Founded in: 1972

5016 **ARMA International**
11880 College Blvd
7th Floor
Overland Park, KS 66210
913-341-3808
800-422-2762; *Fax:* 913-341-3742
headquarters@armaintl.org; www.arma.org
Social Media: Facebook, Twitter, LinkedIn
Julie J. Colgan, CRM, President
Brenda Prowse, CRM, Treasurer
Fred Pulzello, CRM, President-Elect
Komal Gulich, CRM, Chair / Immediate Past President
A not-for-profit professional association and the authority on managing records and information.
11000 Members
Founded in: 1955

5017 **Alpha Micro Users Society**
210 N Iris Avenue
Rialto, CA 92376-5727
909-874-6214; *Fax:* 909-874-2143
info@amus.org; www.computerhistory.org
Jeff Kreider, President
An organization supported by members to promote the uses of computers manufactured by Alpha Micro Products of Irvine, California. This basic purpose has expanded, over the years, from merely a focal point for the exchange of technical information on its use and versatility, to promotion of products (Software and Hardware) from Alpha Micro and various third party organizations having an interest in users of Alpha Micro computers.
125 Members
Founded in: 1978

5018 **American Association for Artificial Intelligence**
2275 East Bayshore Road
Suite 160
Palo Alto, CA 94303
650-328-3123; *Fax:* 650-321-4457;
www.aaai.org
Alan Mackworth, President
Ted Senator, Treasurer/Secretary
Nonprofit society devoted to advancing the scientific understanding of the mechanisims underlying thought and intellegent behavior and their embodiment in machines.
6000 Members
Founded in: 1979
Mailing list available for rent

5019 **American Council for Technology**
3040 Williams Dr
Suite 610
Fairfax, VA 22031-4618
703-208-4800; *Fax:* 703-208-4805
act-iac@actgov.org; www.actgov.org
Social Media: Facebook, Twitter, LinkedIn, YouTube
Ken Allen, Executive Director
Don Arnold, Director
April Davis, Director Of Member Service
Jim Beaupre, Director, ACT-IAC Academy
Don Becker, Associate Director, Communications
A non-profit educational organization established to assist government in acquiring and using information technology, resources effectively and efficiently. Working with all levels of the government, ACT provides education, programming, and networking opportunities that enhance and advance the government IT profession.
50000 Members
Founded in: 1978

5020 **American Medical Informatics Association**
4720 Montgomery Lane
Suite 500
Bethesda, MD 20814-6052
301-657-1291; *Fax:* 301-657-1296;
www.amia.org
Social Media: Facebook, Twitter, LinkedIn, YouTube, Flickr
Kevin M. Fickenscher, MD, CPE,, AMIA President and CEO
Sara Ward, Executive Assistant
Karen Greenwood, Executive Vice President & COO
Ross D. Martin, MD, MHA, Vice President Corporate Relations
Jeffrey Williamson, M.Ed, Vice President, Education
Support all those involved with commercial and scientific medical informatics software and hardware, supplies and services. Hosts annual trade show.
3200 Members
Founded in: 1990
Mailing list available for rent: 2000 names

5021 **American Society for Information Science and Technology**
8555 16th Street
Suite 850
Silver Spring, MD 20910
301-495-0900; *Fax:* 301-495-0810
asis@asis.org; www.asist.org
Social Media: Facebook, Twitter, LinkedIn
Andrew Dillon, President
Vicki Gregory, Treasurer
Richard Hills, Executive Director
William Senn, Chapter Assembly Director
Naresh Agarwal, Deputy Chapter Assembly Director
ASIS&T has been the society for information professionals leading the search for new and better theories, techniques, and technologies to improve access to information.
4000 Members
Founded in: 1937

5022 **American Society for Precision Engineering**
PO Box 10826
Raleigh, NC 27605-0826
919-839-8444; *Fax:* 919-839-8039;
www.aspe.net
Alexander H. Slocum, President
John S. Taylor, Vice President
Thomas A. Dow, Executive Director
Ilka Lee, Publications and Office Manager
Wendy Shearon, Meetings & Membership Manager
Members are from academia, industry and government, and include professionals in engineering, materials science, physics, chemistry, mathematics and computer science. Multidisciplinary professional and technical society concerned with precision engineering research and development, design and manufacturing of high accuracy components and systems.
Founded in: 1985

5023 **Armed Forces Communications & Electronics Association (AFCEA)**
4400 Fair Lakes Ct
Fairfax, VA 22033-3899
703-631-1397
800-336-4583; *Fax:* 703-631-4693
service@afcea.org; www.afcea.org
Social Media: Facebook, Twitter, LinkedIn, Google+, YouTube
Kent Schneider, President/CEO
Becky Nolan, Executive VP
John A Dubia, Executive VP
A non-profit membership association serving the military, government, industry, and academia as an ethical forum for advancing professional knowledge and relationships in the fields of communications, IT, intelligence, and global security.
31000 Members
Founded in: 1946

5024 **Association for Computing Machinery**
2 Penn Plz
Suite 701
New York, NY 10121-0799
212-868-5716
800-342-6626; *Fax:* 212-944-1318
acmhelp@acm.org; www.acm.org
Social Media: Facebook, Twitter, LinkedIn, YouTube
John R White, Executive Director/CEO
Patricia Ryan, Deputy Exec Director Operations/COO
Wayne Graves, Director of Information Systems
Russell Harris, Director of Financial Services
Association for advancing the skills of information technology professionals and for interpreting the impact of information technology on society.
80000 Members
Founded in: 1947

5025 **Association for Educational Communications and Technology**
320 W. 8th St
Suite 101
Bloomington, IN 47404
812-335-7675
877-677-2328; *Fax:* 812-335-7678
aect@aect.org
aect.site-ym.com
Social Media: Facebook, Twitter
Brad Hokanson, President
Phillip Harris, Executive Director
Larry Vernon, Electronic Services
Terri Lawson, Manager. Membership & Subscription
A professional association of thousands of educators and others whose activities are directed towards improving instruction through technology.
Founded in: 1923

5026 **Association for Information and Image Management International**
1100 Wayne Avenue
Suite 1100
Silver Spring, MD 20910
301-587-8202
800-477-2446; *Fax:* 301-587-2711
aiim@aiim.org; www.aiim.org

Social Media: Facebook, Twitter, LinkedIn, YouTube

John F. Mancini, President and CEO
Felicia Dillard, CFO
Atle Skjekkeland, Chief Operating Officer
Peggy Winton, Vice President and CMO
Georgina Clelland, Director, Events

Global authority on enterprise content management (ECM). ECM Technologies are used to create, capture, customize, deliver, and manage information to support business process.
Founded in: 1943

5027 **Association for Services Management International**
11031 Via Frontera
Suite A
San Diego, CA 92127

239-275-7887
800-333-9786; *Fax:* 239-275-0794
info@afsmi.org; www.afsmi.org

JB Wood, President
Thomas Lah, Executive Director

Provides the knowledge, fellowship and career connections that customer services and support managers for technology based products and solutions needed for professional and career development.
Cost: $375.00
Frequency: Membership Fee
Founded in: 1975

5028 **Association for the Advancement of Computing in Education**
P.O. Box 719
Waynesville, NC 28786

828-246-9558; *Fax:* 828-246-9557
info@aace.org; www.aace.org
Social Media: Facebook

Dr Gary H Marks, Executive Director

An international, educational and professional nonprofit organization dedicated to the advancement of the knowledge, theory and quality of learning and teaching at all levels with information technology.
Founded in: 1981

5029 **Association of Information Technology Professionals**
1120 Route 73
Suite 200
Mount Laurel, NJ 08054-5113

856-380-6910
800-224-9371; *Fax:* 856-439-0525
aitp_hq@aitp.org; www.aitp.org
Social Media: Twitter, LinkedIn

Raja Singh, Chair
Carrie Drephal, Vice Chair

Comprised of career minded individuals who seek to expand their potential employers, employees, managers, programmers, and many others. The organization seeks to provide avenues for all their members to be teachers as well as students and to make contacts with other members in the IS field, all in an effort to become more marketable in rapidly changing, technological careers.
Founded in: 1951

5030 **Business Software Alliance**
20 F Street, NW
Suite 800
Washington, DC 20001

202-872-5500; *Fax:* 202-872-5501
info@bsa.org; www.bsa.org
Social Media: Facebook, Twitter, LinkedIn, YouTube

Victoria A. Espinel, President and CEO
Jodie L. Kelley, General Counsel and SVP
Matthew Reid, Senior Vice President
Scott Van Hove, CFO and Vice President

An organization dedicated to promoting a safe and legal digital world. BSA educates consumers on software management and copyright protection, cyber security, trade, e-commerce and other internet related issues.
Founded in: 1988

5031 **Business Technology Association**
12411 Wornall Road
Suite 200
Kansas City, MO 64145-1212

816-941-3100
800-325-7219; *Fax:* 816-941-2829
info@bta.org; www.bta.org
Social Media: Facebook, Twitter, LinkedIn

Rob Richardson, President
Brent Hoskins, Executive Director
Valerie Briseno, Marketing Manager
Elizabeth Marvel, Associate Editor
Brian Smith, Membership Sales Representative

Serving independent dealers, value-added resellers, systems integrators, manufacturers and distributors in the business equipment and systems industry. BTA helps its members profit through a wide variety of services, including free legal advice and guidance; business benchmarking studies and reports; information on the latest news, trends, and products in the industry.
Founded in: 1926

5032 **CEMA: Computer Event Marketing Association**
1512 Weiskopf Loop
Round Rock, TX 78664-6128

512-310-8330; *Fax:* 512-682-0555;
www.cemaonline.com
Social Media: Facebook, Twitter, LinkedIn

Kimberley Gishler, President & CEO
Chris Meyer, Vice President
Heather Shatz, Treasurer
Ashley Muntan, Secretary
Kimberley Gishler, Executive Director

Serving marketing professionals in the high technology industry. CEMA has grown to represent the interest of marketing communications professionals in the information technology industry.
500 Members
Frequency: $275-$775 Membership Fee
Founded in: 1990

5033 **Carnegie Mellon University: Information Networking Institute**
4616 Henry Street
Pittsburgh, PA 15213

412-268-7195; *Fax:* 412-268-7196
ini@cmu.edu; www.ini.cmu.edu
Social Media: Facebook, Twitter, LinkedIn, YouTube, Google+

Dena Haritos-Tsamitis, Director
Terri Weinberg, Administrative Assistant
Tracey Bragg, Business & Enrollment Manager
Sean O'Leary, Manager

Established as the nation's first research and education center devoted to Information Networking. INI focuses on professional degree programs that combine technologies, economics, and policies of global communication networks and information security.
300 Members
Founded in: 1989

5034 **CompTIA**
3500 Lacey Road
Suite 100
Downers Grove, IL 60515
630-678-8300
866-835-8020; *Fax:* 630-678-8384
info@comptia.org; www.comptia.org
Social Media: Facebook, Twitter, LinkedIn, YouTube, Flickr

MJ Shoer, Chairman
Frank Vitagliano, Vice Chair
Todd Thibodeaux, President and CEO
Nancy Hammervik, Senior Vice President, Industry
David Sommer, Chief Financial Officer

CompTIA is a trade association representing the international technology community. Its goal is to provide a unified voice, global advocacy and leadership, and to advance industry growth through standards, professional competence, education and business solutions.
20000 Members
Founded in: 1984

5035 **Computer Assisted Language Instruction Consortium**
Texas State University
214 Centennial Hall
San Marcos, TX 78666

512-245-1417; *Fax:* 512-245-9089
info@calico.org; www.calico.org
Social Media: Twitter

Robert Fischer, Executive Director
Esther Horn, Manager

A professional organization involved in language teaching and technology.
780 Members
Founded in: 1983

5036 **Computer Security Institute**
350 Hudson Street
Suite 300
New York, NY 10014

415-947-6320; *Fax:* 415-905-2218
csi@ubm.com; www.gocsi.com
Social Media: Facebook, Twitter, LinkedIn

Robert Richardson, Director
Nancy Baer, Marketing Manager
Mary Griffin, Membership Director
Fran Timmerman, Operations Manager

The world's leading membership organization specifically dedicated to serving and training the information, computer and network security professional.
Cost: $224.00
Frequency: Membership Fee
Founded in: 1974

5037 **Computerized Medical Imaging**
National Biomedical Research Foundation
37th and O Streets, N.W
Washington, DC 20057

202-687-0100; *Fax:* 202-687-1662
ledley@nbrf.georgetown.edu;
www.georgetown.edu
Social Media: Facebook, Twitter, LinkedIn, YouTube, Flickr

Blaire V Mossman, Chief Administrator
Dr. John J. DeGioia, Ph.D, President
William J Doyle, Chair
Thomas Parkes, S.J, Vice Chair

Formerly the Computerized Radiology Society. A source for the exchange of information concerning the medical use of computerized tomography in radiological diagnosis.
Founded in: 1798

5038 **Computing Research Association**
1828 L Street
Suite 800
Washington, DC 20036-4632

202-234-2111; *Fax:* 202-667-1066
info@cra.org; www.cra.org
Social Media: Facebook, Twitter, YouTube

J Strother Moore, Chair, Board of Directors
Ronald Brachman, Treasurer
Laura M. Haas, Vice Chair, Board of Directors

Susan B. Davidson, Chair, Board of Directors
Andrew Bernat, Executive Director

Our mission is to seek to strengthen research and advanced education in computing and allied fields.
200 Members
Founded in: 1972

5039 Data Interchange Standards Association (DISA)
7600 Leesburg Pike
Suite 430
Falls Church, VA 22043-2004

703-970-4480
888-363-2334; *Fax:* 703-970-4488
info@disa.org; www.disa.org
Social Media: Twitter, LinkedIn

Jerry C. Connors, President
Jim Taylor, Chair
Stephanie Fetzer, Vice Chair
Jim Leach, Treasurer
Jonathan Lyon, Secretary

Nonprofit home for the development of cross-country electronic business interchange standards.
350+ Members
Founded in: 1986

5040 Data Management Association
One State Street Plaza
27th Floor
New York, NY 10004

414-607-0979; *Fax:* 262-546-0794
help@sourcemedia.com;
www.information-management.com
Social Media: Facebook, Twitter, LinkedIn, Google+

Tony Carrini, Director of Business Development
Peggy Schecter, Publisher
David Weldon, Editorial-in-Chief
Eric Kavanagh, DM Radio Host

A vendor independent professional organization dedicated to the advancement of data asset management concepts.
Founded in: 1986

5041 Electronics Industries Alliance
2500 Wilson Boulevard
Arlington, VA 22201

703-907-7500; *Fax:* 703-907-7602;
www.eia.org

Dave McCurdy, President/CEO
Charles L Robinson, COO
James Shiring, Secretary/Treasurer

A national trade organization that includes a full spectrum of U.S. manufacturers. The alliance is a partnership of electronic and high-tech associations and companies whose mission is promoting the market development and competitiveness of the U.S. high-tech industry through domestic and international policy efforts.
1300 Members
Founded in: 1952

5042 Enterprise Computing Solutions
26024 Acero
Mission Viejo, CA 92691-2768

949-609-1980; *Fax:* 949-609-1981
cbulter@thinkecs.com; www.thinkecs.com

David Buttler, President
Cheryl Butler, CFO
John Foley, CTO

A leading provider of IT infrastructure solutions for Fortune 500 and mid-tier companies throughout California. ECS builds sophisticated IT infrastructure solutions for mission-critical applications, provides enterprise storage solutions that ensure data protection and business continuity, and delivers state-of-the-art server solutions for optimal computing capacity.
500 Members
Founded in: 1995

5043 Independent Computer Consultants Association (ICCA)
11131 S Towne Sq
Suite F
St Louis, MO 63123-7817

314-892-1675; *Fax:* 314-487-1345
execdirector@icca.org; www.icca.org

Joyce Burkard, Executive Director

Provides professional development opportunities and business support programs for independent computer consultants. Chapters are in many major metropolitan areas representing consulting firms nationwide.
1000 Members
Founded in: 1977

5044 Information Resources Management Association
701 E Chocolate Ave
Suite 200
Hershey, PA 17033-1240

717-533-8845; *Fax:* 717-533-8661
member@irma-international.org;
www.irma-international.org

Jan Travers, Executive Director
Sherif Kamel, Communications Director

An international professional organization dedicated to advancing the concepts and practices of information resources management in modern organizations. The primary objective of IRMA is to assist organizations and professionals in enhancing the overall knowledge and understanding of effective information resources management in the early 21st century and beyond.
Mailing list available for rent

5045 Information Systems Audit & Control Association (ISACA)
3701 Algonquin Rd
Suite 1010
Rolling Meadows, IL 60008-3124

847-253-1545; *Fax:* 847-253-1443
news@isaca.org; www.isaca.org
Social Media: Facebook, Twitter, LinkedIn

Susan Caldwell, CEO

With members in more than 160 countries, ISACA is a recognized worldwide leader in IT governance, control, security and assurance. Sponsors international conferences, publishes the thw ISACA Journal and develops international information systems auditing and control standards.
75000 Members
Founded in: 1967

5046 Information Technology Management Institute
PO Box 890
Merrifield, VA 22116

703-208-9610; *Fax:* 703-208-9604
info@itm-inst.com; www.itm-inst.com

Dr. Diane Murphy, CEO/Founder

Association for information technology organizations primarily in the US.
90 Members
Founded in: 1996

5047 Institute of Electrical & Electronics Engineers Computer Society
2001 L Street N.W.
Suite 700
Washington, DC 20036-4928

202-371-0101; *Fax:* 202-728-9614
help@computer.org; www.computer.org
Social Media: Facebook, Twitter, LinkedIn, YouTube, Google+

Angela R Burgess, Executive Director
Anne Marie Kelly, Director, Governance
Chris Jensen, Director of Marketing and Sales
Ray Kahn, Director of Information Technology
John G. Miller, Director of Finance and Accounting

Supports all those involved in use and design of multimedia hardware, software and systems in industry, business, academia and the arts.
10000 Members
Founded in: 1946

5048 International Association for Computer Systems Security
6 Swarthmore Lane
Dix Hills, NY 11746-4829

631-499-1616; *Fax:* 631-462-9178
iacssjalex@aol.com; www.iacss.com

Robert J Wilk, President/Founder

Offers a testing program and upholds professional ethics. Supports education through workshops and sponsors lectures.
Founded in: 1981

5049 International Association of Knowledge Engineers
973 Russell Avenue
Gaithersburg, MD 20879-3292

301-948-5390; *Fax:* 301-926-4243;
www.isko.org

Milton White, Owner
Julie Walker-Lowe, Executive Director

An international association of computer professionals concerned with designing reasoning machines and computer systems to receive, organize and maintain human knowledge.
Founded in: 1987

5050 International Society for Technology in Education
180 W 8th Avenue
Eugene, OR 97401-2916

541-302-3777
800-336-5191; *Fax:* 541-302-3778
iste@iste.org; www.iste.org
Social Media: Facebook, Twitter, LinkedIn, YouTube, Pinterest

Kekia Ray, EdD, Chair
Mila Thomas Fuller, Ed.D, Treasurer
Mia Williams, PhD, Secretary
Brian Lewis, M.A., CAE, Chief Executive Officer
Jessica Medaille, Chief Membership Officer

A large nonprofit organization serving the technology-using educator.

5051 International Technology Law Association/ ITechLaw
7918 Jones Branch Drive
Suite 300
McLean, VA 01880-6200

703-506-2895; *Fax:* 703-579-4366
memberservices@itechlaw.org;
www.itechlaw.org
Social Media: Facebook, Twitter, LinkedIn

Jenna Karadbil, President
Susan Barty, Vice President
Robert Weiss, Treasurer
Christian Frank, Secretary
Charles Morgan, Assistant Secretary

Computer Law Association changed its identity to ITechLaw to better reflect its global activities and expanded focus. Providing benefit to the worldwide community of information technology law professionals.
2000 Members
Founded in: 1971

5052 Internet Alliance
1615 L Street NW
Suite 1100
Washington, DC 20036-5624

202-861-2407
tammy@internetalliance.org;
www.internetalliance.my

Kris Larsen, Manager
Kaye Caldwell, California Policy Director

Formerly the Interactive Services Association, the Alliance has been the only consisted voice representint internet companies in the 50 states. We have a proven track record of blocking or mitigating privacy and anti-spam legislation, and a high level of expertise in the Internet state tax area.
Founded in: 1999

5053 NaSPA: Association for Corporate Computing Technical Professionals
NaSPA
7044 S 13th Street
Oak Creek
Milwaukee, WI 53154

414-908-4945; *Fax:* 414-768-8001
j.tucker@naspa.com; www.naspa.com
Social Media: LinkedIn

Scott Sherer, Chairman
Leo Wrobel, President / Director
Sharon Wrobel, Director / Secretary / Treasurer
Radi Shourbaji, VP of Marketing
Edward J. Krueger, Director of Membership Services

Our mission is to serve the means to enhance the status and promote the advancement of all network and systems professionals; nurture member's technical and managerial knowledge and skills and many more.
50000 Members
Founded in: 1986

5054 National Association of Computer Consultant Businesses
1420 King St
Suite 610
Alexandria, VA 22314-2750

703-838-2050; *Fax:* 703-838-3610
staff@naccb.org; www.naccb.org
Social Media: Facebook, Twitter, LinkedIn

Susan Thaden, Chair
Chris Walters, President
Jim Carteris, Vice-President
Tom Nunn, Treasurer
Mark Roberts, Chief Executive Officer

Members are companies providing technical support services to clients such as programming, systems analysis and software/hardware engineering.
300 Members
Founded in: 1987

5055 National BDPA
9500 Arena Drive
Suite 106
Largo, MD 20774

301-584-3135; *Fax:* 301-560-8300
info@bdpa.org; www.bdpa.org
Social Media: Facebook, Twitter, LinkedIn

Earl Pace, Founder
Mike Williams, President
Pamela Mathews, Vice President
Teresa Williams, Vice President, Member Services

Association for the professional advancement of African Americans and other minorities in information technology and related STEM industries.
Founded in: 1975

5056 Online Audiovisual Catalogers
Minnesota State University
Memorial Library 3097
PO Box 8419
Mankota, MN 56002-2645

507-892-2147; *Fax:* 904-620-2719
gerhart@u.washington.edu; www.olacinc.org
Social Media: RSS

Stacie A Traill, President
Annie Glerum, Vice President/Presidnet Elect
Jennifer Eustis, Secretary
Autumn Faulkner, Treasurer/Membership Coordinator
Marcy A. Strong, Newsletter Editor

To establish and maintain a group that could speak for catalogers of audiovisual materials. Provides a means for exchange of information, continuing education, and communication among catalogers of audiovisual materials and with the Library of Congress. Maintaining a voice with the bibliographic utilities that speak for catalogers of audiovisual materials, works toward common understanding of AV cataloging practices and standards.
Founded in: 1980

5057 Open Applications Group
PO Box 4897
Marietta, GA 30061-4897

404-402-1962; *Fax:* 801-740-0100
inquiry@oagi.org; www.openapplications.org

David M Connelly, CEO
Mike Rowell, Chief Architect
Ralph Hertlein, VP, Operations
Jim Wilson, Chemical Industry Architect
Michelle Rascoe, Business Manager

A not-for-profit open standards group building process-based XML standards for both B2B and A2A integration.
Founded in: 1994

5058 Optical Society of America
2010 Massachusetts Ave Nw
Washington, DC 20036-1023

202-223-8130; *Fax:* 202-223-1096
info@osa.org; www.osa.org
Social Media: Facebook, Twitter, LinkedIn, YouTube

Philip Russell, President
Eric Mazur, Vice President
Georges Bayz, Treasurer
Elizabeth A. Rogan, Chief Executive Officer
Philip Russell, President

The Optical Society of America (OSA) was organized to increase and diffuse the knowledge of optics, pure and applied; to promote the common interests of investigators of optical problems, of designers and of users of optical apparatus of all kinds; and to encourage cooperation among them. The purposes of the Society are scientific, technical and educational.
Cost: $95.00
15000 Members
Frequency: Membership Fee
Founded in: 1916

5059 Personal Computer Memory Card International Association
2635 N 1st St
Suite 218
San Jose, CA 95134-2048

408-433-2273; *Fax:* 408-433-9558;
www.pcmcia.org
Social Media: Facebook

Patrick Maher, Executive Director
Ken Stufflebeam, President
Brian Ikeya, Secretary
Jim Koser, Treasurer

Created to establish standards for Integrated Circuit cards and to promote interchangeability among mobile computers where ruggedness, low power, and small size were critical.
200+ Members
Founded in: 1989

5060 Polar Microsystems
Po Box 403
Huntingdon Valley, PA 19006

215-676-1590; *Fax:* 215-676-1596;
www.polarmicro.com

Doug C Baer, Senior Systems Engineer

Provides consulting services that enable our clients to advance their businesses through full utilization of the Apple Macintosh hardware and software platform.

5061 Portable Computer and Communications Association
PO Box 680
Hood River, OR 97031

541-490-5140; *Fax:* 413-410-8447;
www.pcca.org

Peter Rysavy, Executive Director

Represents firms, organizations and individuals interested in mobile communications. PCCA publishes information, standards, software and other materials.
Cost: $100.00
75 Members
Frequency: Individual Membership Fee
Founded in: 1992

5062 Society For Modeling Simulation International
2598 Fortune Way
Suite I
Vista, CA 92081

858-277-3888; *Fax:* 858-277-3930
scs@scs.org; www.scs.org
Social Media: Facebook, LinkedIn

Lin Zhang, President
Bjorn Johansson, Treasurer
Oletha Darensburg, Executive Director
Vicki Pate, Publications Manager & Editor
Aleah Hockridge, Conferences Director

The only technical Society dedicated to advancing the use of modeling & simulation to solve real-world problems. SCS is the principal technical society devoted to the advancement of simulation and allied computer arts in all fields.
Cost: $55.00
Frequency: Regular Membership Dues
Founded in: 1952

5063 Society for Imaging Science and Technology
7003 Kilworh Lane
Springfield, VA 22151-4088

703-642-9090; *Fax:* 703-642-9094
info@imaging.org; www.imaging.org

Geoff J Woolfe, President
Steven J Simske, Executive VP
Scott Silence, Treasurer
Ingeborg Tastl, Secretary
Suzanne E. Grinnan, Executive Director

Our goal is to keep members aware of the latest scientific and technological developments in the field of imaging through conferences, journals and other publications. We focus on imaging in all its aspects, with particular emphasis on silver halide, digital printing, electronic imaging, photofinishing, image preservation, image assessment, pre-press technologies and hybrid imaging systems.
2000+ Members
Founded in: 1947

5064 **Society for Information Display**
1475 S Bascom Ave
Campbell, CA 95008-4006

408-879-3901; *Fax:* 408-879-3833
office@sid.org; www.sid.org
Social Media: Facebook, Twitter, LinkedIn, YouTube

Amal Ghosh, President
Helge Seetzen, Treasurer
Takatoshi Tsujimura, Secretary
Dave Eccles, VP-Americas
Bao Ping Wang, VP -Asia

Representing the international and local display communities. Offers opportunites to network, recieve information and publications and news about trade shows.
6000 Members
Founded in: 1962

5065 **Society for Materials Engineers and Scientists**
3440 E University Drive
Phoenix, AZ 85034

602-470-5700; *Fax:* 602-437-8497
general.inquiries@asm.com; www.asm.com
Social Media: Twitter

Chuck D del Prado, President and CEO
Peter A.M Van Bommel, Member of the Management Board
Per Ove Hansson, General Manager Thermal Products
Tominori Yoshida, General Manager Plasma Products
Fokko LeutScher, Vice President of Front-end Global

A leading supplier of semiconductor process equipment in both front and back end markets. The Company possesses a strong technological base, state-of-the-art manufacturing facilities, a competent and qualified workforce and a highly trained, strategically distributed support network.
Founded in: 1968

5066 **Society of Manufacturing Engineers International**
1 SME Drive
Po Box 930
Dearborn, MI 48121

313-425-3000
800-733-4763; *Fax:* 313-425-3401
service@sme.org; www.sme.org
Social Media: Facebook, Twitter, LinkedIn, YouTube, Google+

Wayne F Frost, CMfgE, President
Jeffrey M Krause, CEO
Wayne F. Frost, CMfgE, Vice President
Dean L. Bartles, PhD, FSME, Secretary/Treasurer
Nancy S. Berg, Executive Director/General Manager

An association that provides information on various automated and computerized systems.
33 Members
Founded in: 1932

5067 **Software Engineering Institute**
4500 Fifth Avenue
Pittsburgh, PA 15213-2612

412-268-5800; *Fax:* 412-268-5758
customer-relations@sei.cmu.edu; www.sei.cmu.edu
Social Media: Facebook, Twitter, LinkedIn, YouTube

Paul D Nielsen, CEO
Clyde Chittister, Chief Operating Officer

A federally funded research and development center sponsored by the U.S. Department of Defense through the Office of the Under Secretary of Defense for Acquisition, Technology, and Logistics. Supports all those engineers involved in the software industry.

5068 **Software Management Network**
55 Madison Avenue
STE400
Morristown, CA 07960

973-285-3264; *Fax:* 973-538-0503;
www.softwaremanagement.com

Nicholas Zvegintzov, President/Chief Technical Officer
Judith Marx Golub, VP/CFO

A publishing, consulting, and training group that serves professional software teams responsible for working, installed software systems. Its unique mission is to make available the most effective resources for managing active software.
Founded in: 1996

5069 **Uni Forum Association**
PO Box 3177
Annapolis, MD 21403

410-715-9500
800-333-8649; *Fax:* 240-465-0207
afedder@uniforum.org; www.uniforum.org

Alan Fedder, President
Deborah Murray, VP
John Lehmann, Board Member
Phil Hughes, Board Member
Paul Wolotsky, Board Member

Professional association for end users, developers and vendors. Promotes and exchanges information about the practices and benefits of open technologies and related hardware, software, applications and standards.
Founded in: 1981

5070 **Vmebus International Trade Association**
9100 Paseo del Vita
Oklahoma City, OK 73131

480-837-7486
info@vita.com; www.vita.com
Social Media: Facebook, Twitter, LinkedIn

Jerry Gipper, Executive Director
Jing Kwok, Technical Director
Ray Alderman, Chairman of the Board

Association for manufacturers of microcomputer boards, hardware, software, military products, controllers, bus interfaces and other accessories compatible with VMEbus architecture.
Cost: $2500.00
150 Members
Frequency: Regular Membership Fee
Founded in: 1981

Newsletters

5071 **AAR Newsletter**
School of Information Technology & Engineering
University of Ottawa
800 King Edward Avenue
Ottawa, Canada

613-562-5738; *Fax:* 613-562-5664
pieper@mcs.anl.gov; www-unix.mcs.anl.gov

Gail W Pieper, Editor
Mary Dzielski, Secretary
Janet Werner, Executive Secretary

Represents research notes and problem sets, discusses software advances and announces conferences and workshops.
Frequency: Quarterly

5072 **ADAIC News**
Ada Information Clearinghouse
201 ILR Extension Building
Cornell University
Ithaca, NY 14853-3901

607-255-2763
800-949-4232
northeastada@cornell.edu; www.northeastada.org

Susan Carlson, Publisher
Lorrie Fessenden, Administrative Assistant

Information on Ada-an internationally standardized, general purpose computer language used in a variety of applications includes news of the Ada community.
Circulation: 20,000
Founded in: 2001

5073 **AEC Automation Newsletter**
Technology Automation Services
PO Box 3593
Englewood, CO 80155-3593

303-770-1728; *Fax:* 303-770-3660;
www.aec-me.com

Jeff Rowe, Editor
David Weisberg, Circulation Director
Randall S Newton, Editor-In-Chief
W Bradley Holtz, Group Publisher
Joel N Orr, Senior Editor

Reports on computer hardware and software issues relevant to architectural design, civil engineering, structural design, process plant design and geographic information management. Includes articles on software developments, new computer hardware, business issues, operating systems, application software, networking and technology developments.
Cost: $235.00
16 Pages
Frequency: Monthly
Founded in: 1977
Printed in one color on matte stock

5074 **AI Interactions**
Academy of International Business
Michigan State University
7 Eppley Center
East Lansing, MI 48824-1121

517-432-4336; *Fax:* 517-432-1009
ciber@msu.edu
aib.msu.edu

G Tomas M Hult, Executive Secretary
Tunga Kiyak, Managing Director
Irem Kiyak, Treasurer

Calls for papers, meeting notices and membership news of interest to professors of international business around the world.
Circulation: 3000
Mailing list available for rent: 3000 names at $250 per M

5075 **AIMatters**
AIM Global
One Landmark North, 20399 Route 19
Suite 203
Cranberry Township, PA 16066

724-934-4470; *Fax:* 724-934-4495
info@aimglobal.org; www.aimglobal.org
Social Media: Facebook, Twitter, LinkedIn

Chuck Evanhoe, President & CEO
Cynthia Troup, Communciations & Marekting

Topics include AIDC, RFID, NFC, RTLS, Internet of Things, and mobile computing.
900+ Members
Frequency: Quarterly
Founded in: 1972
Mailing list available for rent

5076 **Acronyms**
Computer Laboratory Michigan State University

40F Computer Ctr
East Lansing, MI 48824-1042

517-355-3600; *Fax:* 517-355-5176

Linda Dunn, Publisher

A listing of procedures, policies, hardware and software for computer users.
Frequency: Quarterly

5077 **Advanced Office Technologies Report**
DataTrends Publications
Po Box 4460
Leesburg, VA 20177-8541

703-779-0574
800-766-8130; *Fax:* 703-779-2267
info@stemcellresearchnews.com;
www.stemcellresearchnews.com

Paul G Ochs, Owner

Offers information on products, technological breakthroughs and industry developments in office automation technology.
Frequency: Full-text

5078 **Alpha Forum**
Pinnacle Publishing
316 N Michigan Avenue
Suite 300
Chicago, IL 60601

312-272-2401
800-493-4867; *Fax:* 312-960-4106
pinpub@ragan.com; www.pinpub.com

Brent Smith, Publisher
David Stevenson, Editor

Technical newsletter for application developers and users. Hands-on articles with specific usage and programming techniques, tips and product updates.
16 Pages
Frequency: Monthly
Circulation: 8000
Founded in: 1990
Mailing list available for rent
Printed in 2 colors on matte stock

5079 **Applications Software**
Thomson Media
1 State St
27th Floor
New York, NY 10004-1481

212-825-8445; *Fax:* 212-843-9600

James Malkin, President/CEO
William Johnson, CFO

General business management and word processing, reference services, custom services and CD-ROM services.
Frequency: Monthly

5080 **Artificial Intelligence Letter**
Kluwer Academic Publishers
101 Philip Drive
Norwell, MA 02061-1677

781-871-6600; *Fax:* 781-871-6528

Masoud Yazdani, Publisher

Provides a forum for the work of researchers and application developers from artificial intelligence, cognitive science and related disciplines.
Circulation: 625

5081 **Bits and Bytes Review**
Bits and Bytes Computer Resources
623 Iowa Ave
Whitefish, MT 59937-2336

406-862-7280
800-361-7280; *Fax:* 406-862-1124
Info@bitsbytescomputer.com;
www.bitsbytescomputer.com

John J Hughes, Owner

Resources and products for the academic field.
Cost: $56.90
Frequency: Monthly

5082 **Branch Automation News**
Phillips Publishing
7811 Montrose Road
Potomac, MD 20854

301-340-2100
feedback@healthydirections.com;
www.healthydirections.com

Strategies for planning, implementing and managing bank technology.
Cost: $495.00
Circulation: 1000
Founded in: 1974
Mailing list available for rent: 30342 names at $125 per M
Printed in 2 colors on matte stock

5083 **Business Computer Report**
Guidera Publishing Corporation
3 Myrtle Bank Road
Hilton Head Island, SC 29926-1809
Lawrence C Oakley, Editor

Hands-on review of business related software, as well as hardware, primarily for the PC world (as opposed to the MAC World). Readers are primarily owners of small to medium-sized businesses.
Cost: $95.00
8 Pages
Frequency: Monthly
Circulation: 125,000
Printed in one color on matte stock

5084 **Business Software News**
110 N Bell Avenue
Suite 300
Shawnee, OK 74801-6967

405-275-3100; *Fax:* 405-275-3101;
www.techradar.com/news/software/business-software

Shari Bodger, Publisher
Melody Wrinkle, Editor
Shari Bodger, Marketing Manager

Offers updated information on computer software, marketing and technology news. Columnists address networks, sales and management with every issue including independent, comparative software reviews.
Cost: $40.00
8 Pages
Circulation: 1000
Founded in: 1991
Printed in 4 colors on matte stock

5085 **C/C & Users Journal**
Miller Freeman Publications
2800 Campus Drive
San Mateo, CA 94403

650-513-4300
800-365-1364; *Fax:* 650-513-4601
cuj@neodata.com; www.cuj.com

Peter Westerman, Publisher
Jon Erickson, Editorial Director
Jessica Marty, Director of Marketing
Amy Stephens, Managing Editor

Information for intermediate and advanced C and C++ programmers. Includes programming techniques, tutorials and software reviews.
Cost: $29.95
Frequency: Monthly
Circulation: 39,048
Founded in: 1988

5086 **C/Net News.Com**
CNET
100 Pine St
Suite 1775
San Francisco, CA 94111-5127

415-409-8900; *Fax:* 415-395-9254;
www.ccolaw.com

Therese Cannata, Partner
John Morris, Editor
Christina Koukkos, Managing Editor

Provides information for high end audiences in the market for tech news, including the IS community, the technology business itself and the financial community.
Frequency: Daily
Founded in: 1992

5087 **COM-SAC: Computer Security, Auditing & Controls-Quarterly**
Management Advisory Services & Publications
PO Box 81151
Wellesley Hills, MA 02481-0001

781-235-2895; *Fax:* 781-235-5446
info@masp.com; www.masp.com

A quarterly journal of in-depth tutorials in computer security, auditing and Corporate and IT Governance plus the most comprehensive digest service of all publications in the above fields.
Cost: $70.00
8 Pages
Founded in: 1972
Mailing list available for rent
Printed in 2 colors on matte stock

5088 **COMDEX Show Daily**
Key 3 Media Group
795 Folsom Street
6th Floor
San Francisco, CA 94107-1243

415-905-2300; *Fax:* 415-905-2329;
www.medialiveinternational.com

Sean Cassidy, Marketing Manager
Robert Priest-Heck, President/CEO

Tabloid newspaper of computer related exhibits.
Frequency: Daily
Circulation: 3445

5089 **CPA Technology Advisor**
Harcourt Brace Professional Publishing
9720 Carroll Centre Rd
Suite 1900
San Diego, CA 92126-4551

858-271-7390
800-831-7799; www.hbpp.com

Bruce Ta, Owner
Frank Peterson, Editor

Concise unbiased recommendations on hardware and software for CPA's.
Cost: $19.00

5090 **Client/Server Economics Letter**
Computer Economics
2082 Business Center Drive
Suite 240
Irvine, CA 92612

949-831-8700; *Fax:* 949-442-7688;
www.computereconomics.com

Frank Scavo, President
Dan Husiak, VP

Economic look at the client/server revolution. Provides critical economic data on costs and risks of client/server computing, backed up with research and presentation-quality graphs and tables. Provides the information you need to make sound business decisions.
Cost: $395.00
Frequency: Daily
Founded in: 1978

5091 **Comp-U-Fax Computer Trends Newsletter**
Microcomputers Software and Consulting
28 S 12th Avenue
Mount Vernon, NY 10550-2913
Bob James, Publisher
Corporate information resource newsletter.

5092 **Computer Aided Design Report**
CAD/CAM Publishing
7100 N Broadway
Suite 2-P
Denver, CO 80221
303-482-2813; *Fax:* 303-484-3610
info@cadcamnet.com; www.cadcamnet.com
Randall Newton, Editor
Uses of computers by engineers in the manufacturing trades.
Cost: $195.00

5093 **Computer Architecture**
IEEE Computer Society
1730 Massachusetts Avenue NW
Washington, DC 20036-1992
202-371-1013; *Fax:* 202-728-9614
Henry Ayling, Publisher
Lee Blue, Production Manager
Current trends in computer networks, hardware description languages, performance.
Circulation: 2303

5094 **Computer Business**
Round Table Association SAB
5340 W 57th Street
Los Angeles, CA 90056-1339
310-649-2846
A Hassan, Publisher/Editor
J Hassan, Circulation Manager
Best computer/communications articles of previous month, briefly abstracted.
Cost: $20.00

5095 **Computer Economics Report**
Computer Economics
2082 Business Center Drive
Suite 240
Irvine, CA 92612
949-831-8700; *Fax:* 949-442-7688;
www.computereconomics.com
Frank Scavo, President
Dan Husiak, VP
Written from an end-user perspective, this monthly newsletter provides analyses of new IBM technologies, plus acquisition and financial management strategies. Regular features include cost comparisons, price/performance analysis, new product forecasts, and evaluations of acquisition techniques for medium and large computer systems.
Cost: $595.00
Frequency: Monthly
Founded in: 1978

5096 **Computer Industry Report**
International Data Corporation
5 Speen Street
Framingham, MA 01701
508-872-8200
leads@idc.com; www.idc.com/
Kirk Campbell, President/CEO
Research and analysis of the computer processing industry.
Founded in: 1964

5097 **Computer Integrated Manufacture and Engineering**
Lionheart Publishing
2555 Cumberland Pkwy Se
Suite 299
Atlanta, GA 30339-3921
770-432-2551; *Fax:* 770-432-6969
Explores cutting edge developments in manufacturing systems operation management.
Circulation: 24,000

5098 **Computer Modeling and Simulation in Engineering**
Sage Science Press
2455 Teller Rd
Newbury Park, CA 91320-2234
805-499-9774
800-818-7243; *Fax:* 805-499-0871
info@sagepub.com; www.sagepub.com
Blaise R Simqu, CEO/President
Publishes application-oriented papers that utilize computer modeling and simulation techniques to understand and resolve industrial problems or processes that are of immediate and contemporary interest.
Frequency: Monthly

5099 **Computer Protocols**
Worldwide Videotex
PO Box 3273
Boynton Beach, FL 33424-3273
561-738-2276
markedit@juno.com; www.wvpubs.com
Mark Wright, Editor/President
Linda Dera, Marketing Manager
Linda Dera, Circulation Manager
Covers news and developments of bridges, gateway and LAN. Coverage also provided on the development of internal protocols.
Cost: $165.00
Frequency: Monthly
Circulation: 30000
Founded in: 1981

5100 **Computer Reseller News**
CMP Publications
One Jericho Plaza
Jericho, NY 11753-1680
516-562-5000; *Fax:* 516-562-7243
shadowram@mcimail.com; www.crn.com
John Russell, Publisher
Computer news for resellers and distributors.

5101 **Computer and Communications Buyer**
Technology News of America Company
PO Box 20008
New York, NY 10025-1510
212-222-1123; www.eintelligence.com
Annotated statistical reports on capital equipment. $450.00 outside of United States.
Cost: $395.00
8 Pages
Frequency: Monthly
ISSN: 1042-4296
Founded in: 1984
Mailing list available for rent

5102 **Computer and Computer Management News and Developments**
Management Advisory Services & Publications
PO Box 81151
Wellesley Hills, MA 02481-0001
781-235-2895; *Fax:* 781-235-5446
info@masp.com; www.masp.com
Newsletter aimed at the management level of the computer industry.

5103 **Computers & Security**
Elsevier Science
6277 Sea Harbor Drive
Orlando, FL 32887
407-345-4020
877-839-7126; *Fax:* 407-363-1354
usjcs@elsevier.com; www.elsevier.com
Andrew Fletcher, Publisher
E Schultz, CEO/President
Ann Dudley, Circulation Manager
Carl Lampert, Editor
International newsletter for the management of computer and information security.
Circulation: 1500

5104 **Computers & Structures**
Elsevier Science
PO Box 945
New York, NY 10010-945
212-989-5800
888-437-4636; *Fax:* 212-633-3680
usinfo@sciencedirect.com;
www.sciencedirect.com
Keith Lambert, Publisher/Editor
Analyzes the many relationships between computer technology and the different fields of engineering.
Circulation: 1500
Founded in: 1962

5105 **Computers, Foodservice and You**
Mike Pappas
Po Box 338
Raton, NM 87740-0338
575-445-9811; *Fax:* 575-445-3080
Mike Pappas, Owner
A newsletter focusing on computers for the hospitality industry.
Cost: $119.00
16 Pages
Frequency: Bi-Monthly
Circulation: 450
Printed in one color on matte stock

5106 **DM Direct**
220 Regency Court
Suite 210
Brookfield, WI 53045
262-784-0444; *Fax:* 262-782-9489;
www.dmreview.com
Tony Carrini, Associate Publisher
In this e-mail newsletter you will find articles, online columnists, news and industry events exclusive to you, the online reader. Our goal is to ensure that DM Direct provides the information you need to compete in the business intelligence, data warehousing and analytics marketplace.

5107 **DP Budget**
Computer Economics
2082 Business Center Drive
Suite 240
Irvine, CA 92612
949-831-8700; *Fax:* 949-442-7688;
www.computereconomics.com
Frank Scavo, President
Dan Husiak, VP
Report analyzing DP expenses, salary issues and acquisition costs. Focuses on increasing productivity and improving the return on your DP investment.
Cost: $495.00
Frequency: Monthly

5108 **DPFN**
Directory & Database Publishers Forum & Network

352 Seventh Avenue
New York, NY 10001-546

212-643-5458
845-358-8034; www.dpfn.com

Barry Lee, Membership Chair
Jeff Fandl, President

Contains events, seminar information, publishers story, industry snapshots, and news pertaining to the industry. Members are large and small directory publishers, vendors to the trade and consultants. Provides networking opportunities and exposure to industry experts through their meetings and workshops.
Founded in: 1990
Printed in on matte stock

5109 Data Channels
Phillips Publishing
7811 Montrose Road
Potomac, MD 20854

301-340-2100
feedback@healthydirections.com;
www.healthydirections.com

Source of intelligence for executives making data communications decisions. Accepts advertising.
Cost: $397.00
9 Pages

5110 Data Security Management
Auerbach Publications
535 5th Avenue
Room 806
New York, NY 10017-3610

800-737-8034;
www.auerbach-publications.com

Rich O'Hanley, Editor

Technical and management information for security managers, networks and systems administrators and data center managers.
Cost: $495.00
Frequency: Bi-Monthly
Circulation: 1,500
ISSN: 1096-7907
Printed in on matte stock

5111 Dental Computer Newsletter
Andent
1000 N Avenue
Waukegan, IL 60085

847-223-5077
info@andent.net; www.andent.net

For and by an international group of Dentists, Physicians and allied health professionals interested in computers. Emphasis is on the practical use of all brands of computers for the professional office.
Cost: $25.00
Frequency: Quarterly
Circulation: 3100

5112 Digital Directions Report
Computer Economics
2082 Business Center Drive
Suite 240
Irvine, CA 92612

949-831-8700; *Fax:* 949-442-7688;
www.computereconomics.com

Frank Scavo, President

Provides details on the financial ramifications of future DEC products. The information is critical for decision makers involved with cost-control, strategy planning and new product analysis.
Cost: $525.00
Frequency: Monthly

5113 Directory of Top Computer Executives
Applied Computer Research
Po Box 41730
Phoenix, AZ 85080

602-216-9100
800-234-2227; *Fax:* 602-548-4800
tara@topitexecs.com; www.acrhq.com

Computer performance and management.
Cost: $370.00
Circulation: 1000
ISSN: 0193-9920
Founded in: 1972
Printed in one color on matte stock

5114 Document Imaging Report
Corry Publishing
5539 Peach Street
Erie, PA 16509

814-380-0025; *Fax:* 814-864-2037
corrypub@corrypub.com; www.corrypub.com

john Coiston, Publisher
Terry Peterson, CEO
Micole Hykes, Editor
Karrie Boocious, Marketing
Melinda Fadden, Circulation Manager

Timely and actionable information on electronic imaging applications, products and user implementation.
Frequency: Monthly
Circulation: 43000

5115 Dvorak Developments
Freelance Communications
PO Box 666
Ridgway, CO 81432

970-626-2255

Randy Cassingham, Publisher

Promotes the use of the Dvorak keyboard for typewriters and computers. Dvorak is more ergonomic than the common Qwerty keyboard. Accepts advertising.
8 Pages

5116 E-News
Patricia Seybold Group
Po Box 240565
Boston, MA 02129

617-742-5200
800-826-2424; *Fax:* 617-742-1028
feedback@psgroup.com; www.psgroup.com

Patricia Seybold, Founder/CEO

E-mail newsletter includes perspectives on the e-commerce industry, research and upcoming events.

5117 EDI News
Phillips Publishing
7811 Montrose Road
Potomac, MD 20854

301-340-2100
feedback@healthydirections.com;
www.healthydirections.com

Electronic data interchange marketplace information.
Cost: $397.00
9 Pages

5118 Education Technology News
Business Publishers
2222 Sedwick Dr
Suite 101
Durham, NC 27713

800-223-8720; *Fax:* 800-508-2592
custserv@bpinews.com; www.bpinews.com

Information on educational hardware and software, trends in computer-aided teaching and computer uses in the classroom.
Cost: $217.00
Circulation: 500
Founded in: 1963

5119 Electronic Education Report
Simba Information
60 Long Ridge Rd
Suite 300
Stamford, CT 06902-1841

203-325-8193
888-297-4622; *Fax:* 203-325-8915
info@simbanet.com; www.simbanet.com

Linda Kopp, Publisher

News and analysis from a business perspective on software, multimedia/CD-ROM, videodisc, distance learning, Internet/online services and educational videocassettes.
Cost: $625.00
Founded in: 1989

5120 Electronic Marketing News
Software Assistance International
PO Box 750
Morris Plains, NJ 07950-0750

973-644-0022; *Fax:* 973-539-3253

George Papov, Editor

Supplier of electronic catalogs to business and industries.
Circulation: 6,000

5121 End-User Computing Management
Auerbach Publications
535 5th Avenue
Room 806
New York, NY 10017-3610

800-737-8034; *Fax:* 212-297-9176

Kim Hovan Kelly, Publisher

Technical and mangement information.
Cost: $495.00
Frequency: BiWeekly
Circulation: 1,000

5122 Federal Computer Week
101Communications
3141 Fairview Park Drive
#777
Falls Church, VA 22042-4507

703-876-5100; *Fax:* 703-876-5126;
www.fcw.com

Anne Armstrong, Publisher
Jeff Calore, General Manager

The Federal Computer Week provides practical news, analysis and insight on how to buy, build and manage technology in government.
Circulation: 93000

5123 Forestry Computer Applications
Michaelsen's Micro Magic Publishers
PO Box 7332
Fredericksburg, VA 22404-7332
Nancy Michaelsen, Publisher

Offers news and information on computers and electronics used in the forestry services industry, including manufacturing, building, construction and architecture.
Cost: $29.95

5124 Frontline
Computer Security Institute
600 Harrison Street
San Francisco, CA 94107

415-947-6320; *Fax:* 818-487-4550;
www.gocsi.com

Robert Richardson, Editorial Director
Chris Keating, Director

This quarterly newsletter is to improve the security practices of your entire organization to increase end-user awareness of critical security topics pertaining to them.
Cost: $1860.00
4 Pages
Frequency: Annual Subscription

5125 GCN Tech Edition
Post Newsweek Tech Media
10 G St Ne
Suite 500
Washington, DC 20002-4228

202-772-2500
866-447-6864; *Fax:* 202-772-2511;
www.gcn.com

David Greene, President
Tom Temin, Editor-in-Chief
Kirstin Crane, Marketing Manager
Bar Blaskowsky, Circulation Manager

Evaluates performance, cost and applications of hardware, software, peripheral and communication products available to government agencies and businesses.
Cost: $95.00
Circulation: 87500
Founded in: 1998
Printed in on glossy stock

5126 Government Computer News
Reed Business Information
2000 Clearwater Dr
Oak Brook, IL 60523-8809

630-574-0825; *Fax:* 630-288-8781;
www.reedbusiness.com

Jeff Greisch, President

The national newspaper of government computing.
Cost: $53.00
55 Pages
Frequency: Monthly
Founded in: 1982

5127 Graphic Communications Today
IDEA Alliance
1421 Prince Street
Suite 230
Alexandria, VA 22314-2805

703-837-1070; *Fax:* 703-837-1072;
www.idealliance.org

Alan Kotok, Editor
David Steinhardt, CEO

Electronic commerce, direct marketing, printing and paper aspects, and graphics updates.
Frequency: Daily
Circulation: 200
Founded in: 1966

5128 HIS Insider
United Communications Group
11300 Rockville Pike
Street 1100
Rockville, MD 20852-3030

301-287-2700; *Fax:* 301-816-8945
webmaster@ucg.com; www.ucg.com

Benny Dicecca, President

News and reports on new hospital and clinical information system technologies, upcoming vendor merger acquisitions, analyses of telecommunicaiton systems used in health care.
Cost: $427.00
Frequency: Weekly
Founded in: 1977

5129 IN SYNC Magazine
Agate Publishing
21 West 26th Street
New York, NY 10010

847-475-4457
seibold@agatepublishing.com;
www.agatepublishing.com

Doug Seibold

News and how-to for distributed and cooperative applications. Particularly how to link multiple computer systems to gain best advantage from each.
Cost: $8.00
Circulation: 1000

5130 IS Budget
Computer Economics
2082 Business Center
Dr. Ste 240
Irvine, CA 92612

949-831-8700; *Fax:* 949-442-7688;
www.computereconomics.com

Frank Scavo, President
Dan Husiak, VP

Tackles today's toughest IS budgeting issues head-on with exhaustively researched line-item cost comparisons by type of industry, installation size, company revenue and type of expenditure. Regular features include MIS spending comparisons, analyses of budgeting issues and inside information on vendor discounts.
Cost: $495.00
Frequency: Monthly
Founded in: 1978

5131 Independent Computer Consultants Newsletter
Independent Computer Consultants Association
11131 S Towne Sq
Suite F
St Louis, MO 63123-7817

314-892-1675; *Fax:* 314-487-1345
execdirector@icca.org; www.icca.org

Joyce Burkard, Executive Director

Promotes professional standards in the industry. Conducts educational programs and maintains local chapters in many major cities. Available to members only.
Circulation: 1000
Founded in: 1976
Mailing list available for rent: 1200 names at $500 per M
Printed in 2 colors

5132 Inside the Internet
Cobb Group
115 6th Ave
Dayton, KY 41074-1111

859-291-1146
800-733-2040; *Fax:* 859-655-2482
tomherman@cobbinc.com; www.cobbinc.com

Tom Herman, President
Adam Browning, Production Manager

Practical advice and instructions for Internet users.

5133 Intelligence: The Future of Computing
Intelligence
PO Box 20008
New York, NY 10025-1510

212-222-1123
800-638-7257; www.eintelligence.com

Edward Rosenfeld, Editor/Publisher

Provides coverage of advanced computing: neutral networks, AI, genetic algorithms, fuzzy systems, wavelets, et. al., and the Net, the Web, Nanotechnologies quanteum, molecular and DNA computing.
Cost: $395.00
8 Pages
Frequency: Monthly
ISSN: 1042-4296
Founded in: 1984
Printed in one color on matte stock

5134 International Spectrum
International Spectrum Magazine & Conferences
8956 Fox Drive
Suite 102
Thornton, CO 80260

720-259-1356; *Fax:* 603-250-0664
nathan@intl-spectrum.com;
www.intl-spectrum.com

Nathan Rector, President
Monica Giobbi, Manager
Clif Oliver, Editor

Trade magazine for PICK/UNIX/DOS computer industry which covers hardware, software and peripherals. Company produces major trade show held annually in Southern California and regional exhibitions and conferences across the country.
88 Pages
Frequency: 6 issues/Yr
Circulation: 50,000
Founded in: 1982
Mailing list available for rent: 80M names
Printed in 4 colors on glossy stock

5135 Managing Human Resource Information Systems
Institute of Management and Administration
1 Washington Park
Suite 1300
Newark, NJ 07102

212-244-0360; *Fax:* 973-622-0595;
www.ioma.com

Covers management issues critical to building and maintaining state-of-the-art HRIS software, hardware, and Internet/intranet activities. It is intended to help control costs of HRIS, make better use of new technologies, migrate HRIS from mainframe, mini, and client/server systems.
Cost: $259.00
Frequency: Monthly
Circulation: 180000
Founded in: 1982

5136 Micro Publishing
Cygnus Publishing
445 Broad Hollow Road
Melville, NY 11747

631-845-2700
800-308-6397; *Fax:* 631-845-2798;
www.cygnuspub.com

James Cavuoto, Publisher
Nancy Whelan, Advertising/Sales
Kenneth Spears, Production
Mark Erikson, Circulation Manager
Paul Bonaiuto, CFO

A newsletter for hardware and software vendors that examines the micro-based publishing systems market, including workstation publishing, printers, scanners, networks, technology and data-based publishing, production methods and page layout software. The editorials consists of microcomputer publishing product reviews, notes, and trend analysis, and new product announcements.
Cost: $295.00
10 Pages
Frequency: Monthly
Printed in on matte stock

5137 Network Economics Letter
Computer Economics
5841 Edison Place
Carlsbad, CA 92008-6500

760-438-8100
800-326-8100; *Fax:* 760-431-1126;
www.computereconomics.com

Bruno Bassi, Publisher
Don Trevillian, Editor

Provides an executive overview for MIS and network professionals who are involved in network strategic planning and implementation. It covers such topics as comparative analysis of hardware and software systems, cost of ownership studies,

analysis of emerging protocols and standards and cost-saving opportunities.
Cost: $395.00
Frequency: Monthly

5138 **OSINetter Newsletter**
Architecture Technology Corporation
9977 Valley View Rd
Suite 300
Eden Prairie, MN 55344-3586
952-829-5864; *Fax:* 952-829-5871
info@atcorp.com; www.atcorp.com
Noel Schmidt, Executive VP
Covers products and company activity in the area of open systems interconnection.
Cost: $50.00
Founded in: 1955

5139 **Official Memory News**
Phillips Publishing
7811 Montrose Road
Potomac, MD 20854
301-340-2100
feedback@healthydirections.com;
www.healthydirections.com
Provides the latest news and analysis on OSI standards developments. Accepts advertising.
Cost: $497.00
9 Pages
Founded in: 1974

5140 **Open Systems Economics Letter**
Computer Economics
2082 Business Center Drive
Suite 240
Irvine, CA 92612
949-831-8700; *Fax:* 949-442-7688;
www.computereconomics.com/
Dan Husiak, Vo
Frank Scavo, President
Addresses the critical economic issues associated with the worldwide transformation to open systems. In a concise, monthly format, this report provides the information that you must have to successfully adopt an open systems strategy, manage your transition to open standards, and protect your corporate investment in new technology.
Cost: $395.00
Frequency: Monthly

5141 **Optical Memory News**
Phillips Publishing
7811 Montrose Road
Potomac, MD 20854
301-340-2100
feedback@healthydirections.com;
www.healthydirections.com
Provides the latest news and analysis on the optical storage marketplace from vendor perspective. Accepts advertising.
Cost: $397.00
9 Pages
Frequency: BiWeekly
Printed in one color on matte stock

5142 **Product Data Management Report**
CAD/CAM Publishing
7100 N Broadway
Suite 2-P
Denver, CO 80221
303-482-2813; *Fax:* 303-484-3610
info@cadcamnet.com; www.cadcamnet.com
Randall Newton, Editor
Devoted to product data management software and systems that are used by major manufacturing firms to store, control, and distribute CAD and other engineering data.
Cost: $345.00

5143 **Public and Policy**
American Public Human Services Association
1133 19th St NW
Suite 400
Washington, DC 20036
202-682-0100; *Fax:* 202-204-0071;
www.aphsa.org
Tracy Wareing, Executive Director
Frequency: Bimonthly

5144 **Rapid Prototyping Report**
CAD/CAM Publishing
2880 Stone Trail Dr
Bethesda, MD 20817-4556
240-425-4004; *Fax:* 301-365-4586
info@cadcamnet.com; www.cadcamnet.com
Geoff Smith-Moritz, Editor
L Wolf, Production Manager
Gives in-depth objective appraisals of strengths and weaknesses of rapid prototyping technology. Includes applications on how RP technology is used in the industry.
Cost: $295.00
Frequency: Monthly

5145 **Report on IBM**
DataTrends Publications
Po Box 4460
Leesburg, VA 20177-8541
703-779-0574; *Fax:* 703-779-2267;
www.stemcellresearchnews.com
Paul G Ochs, Owner
For information technology professionals.
Cost: $495.00
Founded in: 1983

5146 **Retail Price Week**
Personal Technology Research
63 Fountain Street
#400
Framingham, MA 01702-6262
508-875-5858
Casey Dworkin, Publisher
Product-specific advertising and pricing data on microcomputer software, perhipherals and desktop retail commodities.
Frequency: Weekly
Circulation: 300

5147 **Semiconductor Economics Report**
Relayer Group
8232 E Buckskin Trail
Scottsdale, AZ 85255-2132
Howard Dicken, Publisher
Economics in the microelectronics industry.

5148 **Small Business Systems**
Charles Moore Associates
277 Alexander Street
Suite 410
Rochester, NY 14607
585-325-5242; *Fax:* 585-325-5242
Charles Moore, Editor
Nancy Hannigan, Circulation Manager
Case histories which apply computers to solve small business problems.

5149 **Softletter**
Mercury Group
990 Washington Street
Suite 308 S
Dedham, MA 02026
781-518-8600
860-663-0552; *Fax:* 301-816-8945
customer@softletter.com; www.softletter.com
Merrill R Chapman, Publisher
Gail Wertheimer, Editor
Rick Chapman, Marketing Manager
Ruth Greenfield, Director
Trends in the microcomputer software industry.
Cost: $596.00
Frequency: Fortnightly
ISSN: 0882-3499
Founded in: 1983
Printed in 2 colors

5150 **Softrader**
Amerasia Group
PO Box 53114
Indianapolis, IN 46253-0114
Ben Yanto, Publisher
Shareware public domain programs guide. Accepts advertising.
16 Pages
Frequency: BiWeekly

5151 **Software Economics Letter**
Computer Economics
5841 Edison Place
Carlsbad, CA 92008-6500
760-438-8100
800-326-8100; *Fax:* 760-431-1126;
www.computereconomics.com
Bruno Bassi, Publisher
Don Trevillian, Editor
Devoted to management and cost control of software investments. Provides the corporate user and information systems communities with a concise analysis of software issues. Profiles the latest trends in software and software licensing and includes analysis of vendor policies and practices.
Cost: $395.00
Frequency: Daily

5152 **Step-By-Step Electronic Design**
Dynamic Graphics
6000 N Forest Park Drive
Peoria, IL 61614-3592
309-688-8851; *Fax:* 309-688-6579;
www.dgi.com
Tom Biederbeck, Editor
Kris Elwell, Publisher
Alan Meckler, CEO/President
Mike Demilt, Marketing
Marcy Slane, Manager
For electronic designers, illustrators and prepress professionals, how-to articles with step-by-step techniques.
Cost: $36.00
Circulation: 24000
Founded in: 1995

5153 **System Development**
Applied Computer Research
PO Box 41730
Phoenix, AZ 85080
602-216-9100
800-234-2227; *Fax:* 602-548-4800
tara@topitexecs.com; www.acrhq.com
Philip Howard, Publisher
Allen Howard, CEO
Tara Saenz, Circulation Manager
Improvement ideas and techniques for software development.
Cost: $630.00
12 Pages
Frequency: Bi-annually
Founded in: 1971
Mailing list available for rent: 20M names at $105 per M
Printed in one color on matte stock

5154 **Systems Reengineering Economics Letter**
Computer Economics

2082 Business Center Drive
Suite 240
Irvine, CA 92612

949-831-8700; *Fax:* 949-442-7688;
www.computereconomics.com

Frank Scavo, President
Dan Husiak, VP

Economic look at the re-engineering explosion, delivering critical information on the methods, costs and risks of systems and business process re-engineering. Updates on the analyses, data, opinions, and case studies you need to make sound business decisions and capitalize on your re-engineering process.
Cost: $395.00
Frequency: Daily
Founded in: 1978

5155 TechTarget
TechTarget
117 Kendrick St
Suite 800
Needham Heights, MA 02494-2728

781-657-1000
888-274-4111; *Fax:* 781-657-1100
info@techtarget.com; www.techtarget.com

Greg Strakosch, CEO
Don Hawk, President
Lisa Johnson, VP Marketing
Catherine Engelke, Direector Public Relations

IBM iSeries focused media. The IBM e-Server iSeries (formerly the AS/400) is considered to be the world's most often used multi-user business computer. The installed base worldwide is huge and will get bigger, fueled by incresed Web development. The iSeries come with an integrated Web application server and all the tools needed to build internet, intranet, extranet, and e-commerce sites quickly and will figure promenently into IT strategy and implementation for years to come.
Frequency: Monthly
Founded in: 1999

5156 Technology Advertising & Branding Report
Simba Information
60 Long Ridge Rd
Suite 300
Stamford, CT 06902-1841

203-325-8193
888-297-4622; *Fax:* 203-325-8915
info@simbanet.com; www.simbanet.com

Linda Kopp, Publisher

Offers news, statistics and analysis of advertising strategies in the technology industry. Provides competitive information on the advertising and marketing activities of computer hardware and software companies. Helps computer publishers target advertising sales by reporting the plans of computer advertisers. Shows computer advertisers how to get best buys.
Cost: $549.00
8 Pages

5157 Techweek
Metro States Media
1156 Aster Avenue
#B
Sunnyvale, CA 94086-6810

408-249-8300; *Fax:* 408-249-0727;
www.techweek.com

John Leggett, Publisher

Provides articles for the local high technology industry programmers. Includes information about the internet, finances, job market, and new products for technology professionals.
Frequency: BiWeekly
Circulation: 100,000

5158 TidBITS
TidBITS
50 Hickory Road
Ithaca, NY 14850

E-Mail: ace@tidbits.com; www.tidbits.com

Adam Engst, Publisher
Tonya Engst, Managing Editor
Jeff Carlson, Managing Editor

Online newsletter and web site, devoted to the person behind the most personal of personal computers, the Macintosh. TidBITS relates events and products to real life uses and concerns. New TidBITS issues go out every Monday night; breaking news and important updates appear on the web site more frequently.
Frequency: Weekly
Circulation: 150000
Founded in: 1990

5159 Wireless LAN
Information Gatekeepers
1340 Soldiers Field Rd
Suite 3
Brighton, MA 02135-1000

617-782-5033
800-323-1088; *Fax:* 617-782-5735
info@igigroup.com; www.igigroup.com

Paul Polishuk, CEO
Cathey Mallen, Production Manager
Brian Mark, Newsletter Managing Editor
Bev Wilson, Managing Editor
Yesim Taskor, Controller

LAN technological trends and market opportunities.
Cost: $695.00
Frequency: Monthly
Founded in: 1977

5160 Work Process Improvement Today
Recognition Technologies Users Association
75 Federal Street
Suite 901
Boston, MA 02110-1413

617-426-1167
800-99 -2974; *Fax:* 617-521-8675;
www.tawpi.org

Dan Bllida, Editor
Debra Sanderson, Publisher
Frank Moran, Owner

Accepts advertising.
Cost: $60.00
Circulation: 10000

5161 iACTion Newsletter
American Council for Technology
3040 Williams Dr
Suite 610
Fairfax, VA 22031-4618

703-208-4800; *Fax:* 703-208-4805
act-iac@actgov.org; www.actgov.org

Ken Allen, Executive Director
Frequency: Monthly

Magazines & Journals

5162 2600 Magazine
PO Box 752
Middle Island, NY 11953

631-751-2600; *Fax:* 631-474-2677
webmaster@2600.com; www.2600.com/

Emanuel Golstein, Editor

Written for computer hackers.
Cost: $20.00
Frequency: Quarterly
Founded in: 1984

5163 ACM QUEUE
1515 Broadway
17th Floor
New York, NY 10036-5701

212-869-7440
800-342-6626; *Fax:* 212-302-5826
acmhelp@acm.org; www.acm.org

Mark Mandelbaum, Director Publication
John R White, Associate Director
Robert Okajima, Associate Director
Alain Chesnais, Founder
Liliana Cintron, Administrative Assistant

Published by the Association for Computing Machinery.
Circulation: 25000
Founded in: 1947

5164 AFSM International Professional Journal and High-Technology Service Mgmt.
AFSM International
11031 Via Frontera
Suite A
San Diego, CA 92127-1709

858-673-3055
800-333-9786; *Fax:* 239-275-0794
info@afsmi.org; www.afsmi.org

John Shoenewald, Executive Director
Jb Wood, President/Ceo

For trade association members.
Cost: $150.00
86 Pages
Frequency: Monthly
Circulation: 20000
Founded in: 1975
Printed in 4 colors on glossy stock

5165 AI Expert
Miller Freeman Publications
2655 Seely Avenue
San Jose, CA 95134

408-943-1234; *Fax:* 408-943-0513

Regina Star Ridley, Editor

Practical applications of artificial intelligence in any field.
Cost: $37.00
42 Pages
Frequency: Monthly
Founded in: 1986

5166 AI Magazine
American Association for Artificial Intelligence
445 Burgess Drive
Menlo Park, CA 94025-3442

650-328-3123; *Fax:* 650-321-4457;
www.aimagazine.org

David Leake, Editor
David M Hamilton, Managing Editor
Michael Wellman, Book Review Editor
Carol McKenna Hamilton, Executive Director, AAAI
Alanna Spencer, Director

Quarterly issued magazine, available through AAAI membership. AI Magazine features articles regarding research in the field of artificial intelligence.
128 Pages
Frequency: Quarterly
Circulation: 7000
ISSN: 0738-4602
Founded in: 1980
Printed in on matte stock

5167 ASR News
Voice Information Associates

P.O.Box 2861
Acton, MA 01720-6861

978-266-1966; *Fax:* 978-263-3461;
www.asrnews.com

Walt Tetschner, Publisher and Editor

Developments in products, marketing, technology, and investments in the automatic speech recognition industry.
Cost: $345.00
Frequency: Monthly
Founded in: 1990

5168 Advanced Imaging
Cygnus Publishing
3 Huntington Quadrangle
Suite 301N
Melville, NY 11747-3601

631-845-2700
800-308-6397; *Fax:* 631-845-2736;
www.advancedimagingmag.com

Dave Brambert, Publisher
Larry Adams, Editor-in-Chief
Paul Mackler, CEO

The only international magazine specifically designed to meet the needs of professionals using all forms of electronic imaging technologies. Offering monthly coverage of imaging application solutions for medical/diagnostic, industrial machine vision, government/security, and scientific imaging markets.
Frequency: Monthly
Circulation: 44009
Founded in: 1966

5169 Aixpert
IBM Corporation
1133 Westchester Avenue
White Plains
New York, NY 10604-3406

914-423-3000; *Fax:* 866-722-9226;
www.ibm.com

George Noren, Editor-in-Chief

Provides timely up-to-date technical material to help developers plot, develop, and enhance applications for IBM AIX products.
Frequency: Quarterly
Circulation: 10,000

5170 Aldus Magazine
Aldus Corporation
801 N 34th Street
Seattle, WA 98103-8882
Carla Noble, Publisher
Harry Edwards, Editor

Supports and educates graphics professionals using ALDUS software. Covers tips, tricks and how-to pointers for maximizing PageMaker, Freehand, PhotoStyler and Persuasion. Also covers trends in electronic publishing.
Cost: $ 24.00
68 Pages
Frequency: 8 per year
Circulation: 220,000
Founded in: 1989

5171 Algorithmica
Springer Verlag
233 Spring St
New York, NY 10013-1578

212-460-1500; *Fax:* 212-460-1575
service@springer-ny.com;
www.springer-ny.com

William Curtis, President
D T Lee, Managing Editor
Rubin Wang, Managing Editor

Provides an in-depth look into distributed computing, parellel processing, automated design, and software tools.
Cost: $1008.00
Frequency: Quarterly
Circulation: 1000
Founded in: 1855

5172 Analysis Solutions
ConnectPress
2530 Camino Entrada
Santa Fe, NM 87505-4807

505-474-5000; *Fax:* 505-474-5001;
www.isentia.com

Carolyn Mascarenas, Publisher

Design analysis and optimization for ANSYS technology users. Covers engineering simulation, acousitc analysis, model meshing, new products and case studies.
Cost: $90.00
Frequency: Quarterly
Circulation: 27,575

5173 Application Development Trends
600 Worcester Road
Suite 301
Framingham, MA 01702

508-875-6644; *Fax:* 508-875-6622;
www.adtmag.com

Sheryl Katz, Publisher
Michael Alexander, Editorial-in-Chief
Tracy S. Cook, Marketing Director
Christina Schaller, Managing Editor

The number one information source on today's key application development options delivering a high powered, management-oriented editorial that covers the application development industry in greater depth and breadth than any other publication.
Frequency: Monthly
Circulation: 45000
Founded in: 1998

5174 Applied Computing Technologies
9041 Executive Park Dr
Suite 222
Knoxville, TN 37923-4603

865-675-0508; *Fax:* 865-694-9096

Peyman Dehkordi, Owner

5175 Applied Optics
Optical Society of America
2010 Massachusetts Ave Nw
Washington, DC 20036-1023

202-223-8130; *Fax:* 202-223-1096
info@osa.org; www.osa.org

Elizabeth Rogan, Executive Director

5176 Automatic ID News
Advanstar Communications
641 Lexington Ave
8th Floor
New York, NY 10022-4503

212-951-6600; *Fax:* 212-951-6793
info@advanstar.com; www.advanstar.com

Joseph Loggia, CEO

Information for decision-makers in all industries seeking definitive information about automatic data collection technology. The technology includes optical, magnetic, radio frequency and voice recognition systems and peripherals.
Frequency: Monthly
ISSN: 0890-9768

5177 BAM Publications
BAM Publications
3470 Buskirk Avenue
Pleasant Hill, CA 94523-4340
925-932-5900

Dennis Erokan, Editor

Provides regionally focused product and channel news to computer products and services.
Cost: $120.00
60 Pages
Frequency: Monthly
Founded in: 1988

5178 Better Channel
ABCD: The Microcomputer Industry Association
450 E 22nd Street
Suite 230
Lombard, IL 60148-6158

630-268-1818; *Fax:* 630-268-1384

John Venator, Executive VP

A professional magazine that is exclusively dedicated to representing and serving all segments of the microcomputer industry. Accepts advertising.
Cost: $150.00
32 Pages
Frequency: Monthly

5179 CADALYST
Advanstar Communications
641 Lexington Ave
8th Floor
New York, NY 10022-4503

212-951-6600; *Fax:* 212-951-6793
info@advanstar.com; www.advanstar.com

Joseph Loggia, CEO

Expert coverage of the latest developments in auto CAD systems, their products and the various CAD applications.
Cost: $4.00
Frequency: Monthly
Circulation: 70000

5180 CALICO Journal
Texas State University
214 Centennial Hall
San Marcos, TX 78666

512-245-1417; *Fax:* 512-245-9089
info@calico.org; www.calico.org

Robert Fischer, Editor

Devoted to the dissemination of information concerning the application of technology to language teaching and language learning. The CALICO Journal is fully refereed and publishes articles, research studies, reports, software reviews, and professional news and announcements.
Cost: $85.00
Frequency: 3x/Year
Circulation: 800
ISSN: 0742-7778

5181 CASE Strategies
Cutter Information Corporation
37 Broadway
Suite 1
Arlington, MA 02474-5500

781-648-1950; *Fax:* 781-648-1950;
www.cutter.com

Verna Allee, Senior Consultant

Implementation strategies, reviews and case studies in areas of computer-aided systems engineering.
Cost: $295.00

5182 CBT Solutions
SB Communications
183 Whiting Street
#15
Hingham, MA 02043-3845

781-749-2151; www.cbtsolutions.com

Steve Blumberg, Publisher

Featured editorials include advanced technology in the past and future, interactive web programs,

new methods to access and control information, and personal profiles.
Frequency: Bi-Monthly
Circulation: 15,000

5183 **CD-ROM Enduser**
Disc Company
6609 Rosecroft Pl
Falls Church, VA 22043-1828
Linda Helgerson, Editor

For people who use CD-ROM applications.
Cost: $3.00
Frequency: Monthly
Founded in: 1989

5184 **CD-ROM Librarian**
Mecklermedia Corporation
20 Ketchum Street
Westport, CT 06880-5808

203-226-6967; *Fax:* 203-454-5840

Alan Meckler, Editor

A periodical intended for the library professional.
Cost: $80.00
Frequency: Monthly
Founded in: 1986

5185 **CHANCE: New Directions for Statistics and Computing**
Springer Verlag
233 Spring St
New York, NY 10013-1578

212-460-1500; *Fax:* 212-460-1575
service@springer-ny.com;
www.springer-ny.com

William Curtis, President
John E Rolph, Editor
Derk Haank, CEO
Peter Hendriks, President of Marketing
Rubin Wang, Managing Editor

Covers both statistics and computing. Designed for everyone who has an interest in the analysis of data. The informal style highlights and encourages sound statistical practice.
Cost: $7.00
Frequency: Monthly
Circulation: 4500
Founded in: 1842

5186 **CRN**
UBM LLC
550 Cochituate Road
First Floor-West Wing, Suite 5
Framingham, MA 01701

508-416-1100; www.crn.com

Kelley Damore, VP/Editorial Director
Steven Burke, Editor
Jane O'Brien, Managing Editor

Delivers strategic information and useful business tools that Solution Providers and other Channel professionals
Cost: $89.00
Frequency: BiWeekly
Circulation: 95,072

5187 **Cadence**
Miller Freeman Publications
2655 Seely Avenue
San Jose, CA 95134

408-468-8603; *Fax:* 408-468-1902
info@gartner.com; www.gartner.com

Johanna Kleppe, Publisher
Kathleen Maher, Managing Editor
Michael Fister, CEO
Tom McCall, Senior Director Public Relations
Michael Bingle, Director

For users of Autocad - a construction/architecture program.
Cost: $6.00
Circulation: 72664

5188 **Catalyst**
Western Center for Microcomputers
1259 El Camino Real
#275
Menlo Park, CA 94025

650-855-8064;
www.home.earthlink.net/~thecatalyst/index.html

Sue Swezey, Editor
Robert Scott, Chief Information Officer

Reporting on both the increasing sophistication of technology and the increasing complexity special education. We've covered the profound changes in the lives of children and adults with special needs as they have benefited from computer use, as well as on the obstacles confronting them and those who serve them.
Cost: $18.00
Frequency: Quarterly

5189 **Christian Computing**
PO Box 319
Belton, MO 64012-0319

800-456-1868; *Fax:* 800-456-1868;
www.ccmag.com

Steve Hewitt, Editor-in-Chief
Frequency: Monthly
Founded in: 1989

5190 **CircuiTree**
Business News Publishing Company
1050 IL Route 83
Suite 200
Bensenville, IL 60106-1096
630-377-5909
circuitree.com

Katie Rotella, Manager
Tom Esposito, Group Publisher
Darryl Seland, Associate Publisher/
Karl Dietz, Technical Editor
Cost: $64.00
Frequency: Monthly
Circulation: 12000
Founded in: 1926

5191 **Civic.com**
FCW Government Technology Group
3141 Fairview Park Drive
Suite 777
Falls Church, VA 22042-4507

Fax: 703-876-5126; www.fcw.com

Edith Holmes, President
Steve Vito, Publisher
Agnes Vanek, Circulation Director
Margo Dunn, Production Manager
Anne Armstrong, Editor

A print magazine and electronic companion designed for volume IT buyers, chief information officers and IT planners in state and local government.

5192 **CleanRooms Magazine**
PennWell Publishing Company
98 Spit Brook Rd
Suite 100
Nashua, NH 03062-5737

603-891-0123; *Fax:* 603-891-9294
johnh@pennwell.com; www.pennwell.com

Christine Shaw, VP
James Enos, Publisher
Angela Godwin, Managing Editor
Steve Smith, News Editor
Bob Johnson, National Sales Manager

Serves the contamination control and ultrapure materials and process industries. Written for readers in the microelectronics, pharmaceutical, biotech, health care, food processing and other user industries. Provides technology and business news and new product listings.
Cost: $97.00
Frequency: Monthly
Circulation: 35031
Founded in: 1987

5193 **Com-SAC, Computer Security, Auditing & Controls**
Management Advisory Services & Publications
PO Box 81151
Wellesley Hills, MA 02481-0001

781-235-2895; *Fax:* 781-235-5446
info@masp.com; www.masp.com

A quarterly journal of in-depth tutorials in computer security, auditing and the most comprehensive digest service of all publications in computer security and controls.
Cost: $98.00
Frequency: Quarterly
Founded in: 1973

5194 **Common Knowledge**
230 W Monroe St
Suite 220
Chicago, IL 60606-4802
312-416-3656
800-777-6734; *Fax:* 312-201-9588;
www.knowledgenetworks.com

Kris Neeley, Publisher

Features interviews with industry experts, case studies, tutorials, the latest industry news and overviews of management concerns.
Frequency: Quarterly
Circulation: 15,000

5195 **Communications of the ACM**
Association for Computing Machinery
2 Penn Plz
Suite 701
New York, NY 10121-0799

212-868-5716
800-342-6626; *Fax:* 212-944-1318
acmhelp@acm.org; www.acm.org

Jerry Ashton, President
John R White, CEO
Edward Grossman, Publisher
Diane Crawford, Executive Editor
Brian Hebert, Marketing/Communications Manager

Technical magazine covering developments in computer science for professional scientific and business dp, systems programming, database techniques and more.
Cost: $17.00
Frequency: Monthly
Circulation: 82,867
Founded in: 1947

5196 **CompactPCI Systems**
CompactPCI Systems
13253 La Montana
Dr 207
Fountain Hills, AZ 85268-5328

480-967-5581; *Fax:* 480-837-6466;
www.compactpci-systems.com

Mike Hopper, Publisher
Joe Pavlat, Editor

Features application success stories that demonstrate how and where CompactPCI technology has provided solutions.
Circulation: 20000

5197 **Component Development Strategies**
Cutter Information Corporation

37 Broadway
Suite 1
Arlington, MA 02474-5500

781-648-1950
800-964-5118; *Fax:* 781-648-1950
press@cutter.com; www.cutter.com

Karen Coburn, President and CEO
Tom Welsh, Senior Consultant
Hillel Glazer, Senior Consultant
Ron Blitstein, Director

Editorial content covers the latest information and technology on object-oriented programming, databases, and analysis and design.
Cost: $2400.00
Frequency: Monthly
Founded in: 1991

5198 **CompuServe Magazine**
5000 Arlington Centre Blvd
Columbus, OH 43220-5439

614-326-1002
800-848-8199
webcenters.netscape.compuserve.com/menu/

Offers updated and statistical information for computer professionals.

5199 **Computer**
IEEE Computer Society
10662 Los Vaqueros Circle
P. O. Box 3014
Los Alamitos, CA 90720-1314

714-821-8380
800-272-6657; *Fax:* 714-821-4010
volunteer.services@computer.org;
www.computer.org/

Matt Loeb, Publisher
Doris L. Carver, Editor in Chief
Bill Schilit, Associate Editor
Judi Prow, Managing Editor
Jim Sanders, Senior Editor

Information on late breaking news, business trends, and a variety of technology specific departments.
Cost: $63.00
Frequency: Monthly
Circulation: 84340
Founded in: 1988

5200 **Computer Business Review**
ComputerWire
245 5th Avenue
4th Floor
New York, NY 10016

212-770-0409; *Fax:* 212-686-2626;
www.computerwire.com/cbr

Jake Sharp, Publisher
Micheal Danzon, CEO
Jason Stamper, Editor

Company profiles, computer market coverage and technology trends and news for investors and professionals in the computer, communications and microelectronics industries.
Cost: $195.00
Frequency: Monthly
Circulation: 20450
Founded in: 1984

5201 **Computer Buyer's Guide & Handbook**
Bedford Communications
1410 Broadway
21st Floor
New York, NY 10018-5008

212-807-8220; *Fax:* 212-807-1098;
www.techworthy.com

Ed Brown, Owner

A guide to buying peripherals and software, as well as general advice and news on the world of computing.
Cost: $36.00
128 Pages
Frequency: Monthly
Circulation: 50000
Founded in: 1981

5202 **Computer Design**
PennWell Publishing Company
10 Tara Boulevard
5th Floor
Nashua, NH 03062-2800

603-891-0123; *Fax:* 603-891-0514;
www.computer-design.com

John Carroll, Group Publisher

Each issue contains in-depth articles and timely features written by experienced senior editors who concentrate on the critical technologies, components and tools needed to design microprocessor and computer based OEM products and systems.
Frequency: Monthly
Circulation: 105,028

5203 **Computer Graphics Review**
Primedia
Po Box 12901
Shawnee Mission, KS 66282-2901

913-341-1300; *Fax:* 913-514-6895;
www.penton.com

Eric Jacobson, Senior VP

To identify and interpret significant technological and business developments.
Cost: $48.00
120 Pages
Frequency: Monthly
Founded in: 1986

5204 **Computer Graphics World**
PennWell Publishing Company
98 Spit Brook Rd
Nashua, NH 03062-5737

603-891-0123
800-225-0556; *Fax:* 603-891-9294
phil@pennwell.com; www.pennwell.com

Christine Shaw, VP
Jenny Donelan, Managing Editor

Covers specific applications of computer graphics, written by users and vendors of equipment and services to the industry. The magazine of 3D computer graphics for engineering and animation professionals.
Frequency: Monthly
Founded in: 1978
Printed in 4 colors on glossy stock

5205 **Computer Industry Almanac**
304 W White Oak
Arlington Heights, IL 60005

847-758-3687; *Fax:* 847-758-3686
ej@c-i-a.com; www.c-i-a.com

Egil Juliussen, President

Annual reference book for and about the computer industry. The Almanac has ranking and awards of products, people and companies. Includes salary information, market forecasts, technology trends and directories of companies, publications, market research firms, associations and trade shows.
Cost: $45.00
Frequency: Annual

5206 **Computer Journal**
Oxford University Press
2001 Evans Rd
Cary, NC 27513-2010

919-677-0977
800-852-7323; *Fax:* 919-677-2673;
www3.oup.co.uk/computer_journal/

F Leroy, Editorial Assistant:
F Murtagh, Editor-in-Chief
Julie Gribben, Special Sales Manager

Provides information on web sites, personal computers, hardware, software and online uses.
Cost: $920.00
Circulation: 18000

5207 **Computer Language**
600 Harrison Street
6th Floor
San Francisco, CA 94107

415-947-6000; *Fax:* 415-941-6055

Computer news and information.

5208 **Computer Link Magazine**
Millennium Publishing
100 Mobile Dr
Suite 1
Rochester, NY 14616-2145

585-797-4399
info@computerlinkmag.com; www.techny.com

Justin Ziemniak, Editor-in-Chief

Website reviews, employment opportunities, and women's involvement in the technology age. Includes reports on the Western New York computer market.
Cost: $20.00
Frequency: Monthly
Circulation: 20000

5209 **Computer Manager**
Story Communications
116 N Camp Street
Seguin, TX 78155-5600

830-303-3328; *Fax:* 830-372-3011
story@storycomm.com;
www.storycommunications.com

James M Story, Publisher
K Wiemann, Circulation Manager

Information to help corporate end users purchase computers and communications equipment easily.
Frequency: Quarterly
Circulation: 50000

5210 **Computer Price Guide**
Computer Merchants
22 Saw Mill River Road
Hawthorne, NY 10532-1533

914-347-0290; *Fax:* 914-347-0292

Svend Hartmann, Publisher

Market trends and developments, prices on used IBM computer equipment.
Cost: $70.00
Frequency: Quarterly
Circulation: 3500

5211 **Computer Security Journal**
Computer Security Institute
600 Harrison Street
San Francisco, CA 94107
415-947-6320
866-271-8529; *Fax:* 415-947-6023;
www.gocsi.com

Russell Kay, Publisher
Chris Keating, Director
Robert Richardson, Editorial Director
Nancy Baer, Marketing Manager

Keeps you informed with comprehensive, practical articles, case studies, reviews and commentaries written by knowledgeable computer

security professionals.
Cost: $25.00
Frequency: Quarterly
Circulation: 3000
Founded in: 1974

5212 **Computer Security, Auditing and Controls (COM-SAC)**
Management Advisory Services & Publications
PO Box 81151
Wellesley Hills, MA 02481-0001

781-235-2895; *Fax:* 781-235-5446
info@masp.com; www.masp.com

Indepth tutorials in computer security and auditing and the most comprehensive digest service of all publications in computer security, auditing and internal controls. Security hardware-software news.
Cost: $98.00
Frequency: Quarterly
ISSN: 0738-4262
Founded in: 1973
Printed in on glossy stock

5213 **Computer Shopper**
Segal Company
1 Battery Park Plz
New York, NY 10004-1487

212-858-1000; *Fax:* 212-251-5490
info@segalco.com

Glenn E Siegel

A buyer's guide of sorts, listing the latest information and equipment for the world of computers.

5214 **Computer Survival Journal**
Enterprise Publishing
Po Box 328
Blair, NE 68008-0328

402-426-2121; *Fax:* 402-426-2227
mrhoades@enterprisepub.com;
www.enterprisepub.com

Mark Rhoades, President
Dave Smith, Production Manager
Tracy Prettyman, Business Manager

Reviews and features on all areas of computer, office and home products (hardware and software). Also includes information on cellular phones, TV's and appliances, home electronics and television.
Cost: $250.00
50 Pages

5215 **Computer Technology Review**
West World Productions
420 N Camden Dr
Beverly Hills, CA 90210-4507

310-276-9500
888-889-3130; *Fax:* 310-276-9874
sinan@kanatsiz.com; www.wwpi.com

Yuri R Spiro, Publisher

Computer Technology Review is an all-inclusive tabloid that covers the full spectrum of new and emerging technologies vital to systems integrators, high-end VARS, and OEM.
Cost: $10.00
60 Pages
Frequency: Monthly
Circulation: 64044
ISSN: 0278-9647
Founded in: 1981
Printed in 4 colors on matte stock

5216 **Computer User Magazine**
Key Professional Media
220 S 6th St
Suite 500
Minneapolis, MN 55402-4501

612-339-7571
800-788-0204; *Fax:* 612-333-5806
info@computeruser.com;
www.computeruser.com

Nat Opperman, President
Elizabeth Millard, Associate Publisher

For small to medium-size business professionals and computer owners, ComputerUser is published in 13 markets nationally.
Cost: $14.00
60 Pages
Frequency: Monthly
Circulation: 64000
Founded in: 1981
Printed in 4 colors on newsprint stock

5217 **Computer World/Focus**
PO Box 9171
Framingham, MA 01701-9171
Joe Maglitta, Feature Editor

A comprehensive magazine offering information on the computer industry.

5218 **Computer-Aided Engineering**
Penton Media
1300 E 9th St
Cleveland, OH 44114-1503

216-696-7000; *Fax:* 216-696-6662
caenetmaster@penton.com; www.penton.com

Jane Cooper, Marketing

Applications, news, trends and products for CAD/CAM technology as applied in manufacturing, electronics, architectural and construction industries.
Cost: $50.00
Frequency: Monthly
Circulation: 56,062

5219 **Computers User**
220 S 6th Street
Suite 500
Minneapolis, MN 55042

612-339-7571; www.computeruser.com

David Needle, Editor
Matt Kusilek, Publisher

End user computer magazine for business and professional users of PC and Macintosh computers, software and peripherals.
Cost: $24.99
Frequency: Monthly

5220 **Computers and Biomedical Research**
Academic Press
1901 E South Campus Drive
Suite 1195
Salt Lake City, UT 84112-9359

801-581-6461; *Fax:* 801-585-5414;
www.aoce.utah.edu

T Allan Pryor, Editor
Liz McCoy, Executive Assistant
Brynn Roundy, Executive Secretary

Information on application of computer technology in biomedical research for medical professionals. Evaluates and discusses various techniques. Accompanied by photographs, charts, graphs and figures.
Cost: $325.00
Frequency: 6 per year
Circulation: 1,425

5221 **Computers in the Schools**
Taylor & Francis Group LLC
325 Chestnut St
Suite 800
Philadelphia, PA 19106-2614

215-625-8900
800-354-1420; *Fax:* 215-625-2940
haworthorders@taylorandfrancis.com;
www.taylorandfrancis.com

Kevin Bradley, President

Articles emphasize the practical aspect of any application but also tie theory to practice, relate present accomplishments to past efforts and future trends, identify conclusions and their implications and discuss the theoretical and philosophical basis for the application.
Frequency: Quarterly

5222 **Computertalk**
Computertalk Associates
492 Norristown Road
Suite 160
Blue Bell, PA 19422

610-825-7686; *Fax:* 610-825-7641
wal@computertalk.com;
www.computertalk.com

William A Lockwood Jr, President
Maggie L Lockwood, Director of Publications

Profiles on various sytems available for pharmacists purchasing and using computers.
Cost: $50.00
Frequency: Monthly
Circulation: 32,000
Founded in: 1980
Printed in 4 colors on glossy stock

5223 **Computerworld**
CW Publishing
One Speen Street
PO Box 9171
Framingham, MA 01701-4653

508-879-0700
800-343-6474; *Fax:* 508-626-2705
editor@computerworld.com;
www.computerworld.com

Mitch Betts, Executive Editor
Don Tennant, VP/Editor in Chief
Matt Sweeney, CEO

For computer professionals who evaluate and implement information systems.
Cost: $99.99
170 Pages
Circulation: 170000
Founded in: 1967

5224 **Computing Surveys**
Association for Computing Machinery
One Astor Place
1515 Broadway
New York, NY 10036-5701

212-869-7440
800-342-6626; *Fax:* 212-302-5826
acmhelp@acm.org; www.acm.org

Mark Mandelbaum, Director Publication
John R. White, CEO
Gul Agha, Editor in Chief
Robert Okajima, Associate Director
Alain Chesnais, Founder

Carefully planned and presented introductions to complex issues, supported by exhaustive and comprehensive notations on the relevant literature.
Cost: $170.00
Frequency: Quarterly
Founded in: 1947

5225 **Computing in Science & Engineering**
American Institute of Physics
2 Huntington Quad
Melville, NY 11747-4502

516-576-2200; *Fax:* 516-349-7669;
www.aip.org

Darlene Walters, Senior VP
Angela Burgess, Publisher
Georgann Carter, Marketing Manager

Computer science's interdisciplinary juncture with physics, astronomy and engineering.
Cost: $55.00

5226 **Control Solutions**
PennWell Publishing Company
1421 S Sheridan Rd
Tulsa, OK 74112-6619

918-831-9421
800-331-4463; *Fax:* 918-831-9476;
www.pennwell.com

Robert Biolchini, President
Ron Kuhfeld, Editor-in-Chief

Represents control technology for engineers and engineering manage4ment.

5227 **Cryptosystems Journal**
Cryptosystems Journal
485 Middle Holland Road
Holland, PA 18966-2870
Tony Patti, Publisher/Editor

Unique international journal devoted to implementation of cryptographic systems on IBM-PC's and compatibles.

5228 **Cyber Defense Magazine**
PO Box 71748
Phoenix, AZ 85050

480-990-0407
866-487-6652; *Fax:* 480-990-7306;
www.cyberdefensemagazine.com

John Riccio, Publisher
Curt Blakeney, Editor

Computer/Network security magazine.
Cost: $31.00
64 Pages
Frequency: 12 issues
Circulation: 64,000
Founded in: 2003
Printed in 4 colors on glossy stock

5229 **DBMS-Database Management Systems**
Miller Freeman Publications
2655 Seely Avenue
San Jose, CA 95134

408-943-1234; *Fax:* 408-943-0513

Phillip Chapnick, Publisher
David Kohman, Editor

Covers the database and database applications marketplace.
Circulation: 69,029

5230 **DG Review**
Data Base Publications
9390 Research Blvd
Suite 300
Austin, TX 78759-7374

512-418-9590; *Fax:* 512-418-8165;
www.bancvue.com

Gabe Krajicek, CEO
Gloria Trent, Editor

For Data General and compatible computer users.
Cost: $48.00
64 Pages
Frequency: Monthly
Founded in: 1981

5231 **DM Review**
Powell Publishing Company
16655 W Bluemound Rd
Suite 201
Brookfield, WI 53005-5935

262-780-0202; *Fax:* 414-771-8058;
www.b-eye-network.com

Ron Powell, Owner
Val Latzke, Editor
Jean Schauer, Editor in Chief
Mary Jo Nott, Executive Editor

Provides a wealth of knowledge through columns by top industry experts, data warehouse success stories, timely and informative articles, third-party product reviews, and executive interviews.
Frequency: Monthly
Circulation: 75012
Founded in: 1994

5232 **DSP Engineering**
13253 La Montana Dr
Suite 207
Fountains Hills, AZ 85268

480-967-5581; *Fax:* 480-837-6466;
wwwdspengineering.com

Rosemary Kristoff, VP
Phyllis Thompson, Circulation Manager
Patrick Hopper, VP Marketing
Mike Hopper, Publisher

5233 **Data Bus**
AM Publications
PO Box 20044
Saint Petersburg, FL 33742

727-577-5500; *Fax:* 727-576-0622
ampubs@aol.com

Al Martino, Publisher/Editor

Contains new product reviews, trade literature and personnel announcements.
Frequency: Monthly
Circulation: 24000

5234 **Data Communications**
McGraw Hill
PO Box 182604
Columbus, OH 43272

614-866-5769; *Fax:* 614-759-3759
customer.service@mcgraw-hill.com;
www.mcgraw-hill.com

Kevin Harold, Publisher
Steve Weiss, Production Manager

Networking magazine edited for the technical managers responsible for the implementation and integration of computer information networks.
Cost: $5.00
Circulation: 112,941

5235 **Data Sources**
Ziff Davis Publishing Company
28 E 28th St
New York, NY 10016-7940

212-503-5772
info@ziffdavis.com; www.ziffdavis.com

Steve Weitzner, CEO
Leo Greisman, General Counsel
Stephen Hicks, General Counsel
Steve Horowitz, COO
Cost: $240.00
Frequency: Monthly
Circulation: 700000
Founded in: 1981

5236 **Data Storage**
PennWell Publishing Company
PO 91372
Calabasas, CA 91372

818-348-1240; *Fax:* 818-348-1742;
www.datastorage.com

Becky Adams, Publisher
David Simpson, Editor
Kevin Komiega, Senior Editor

Features news and information on all types of systems such as magnetic disk drives, media and magnetic tape drives, CD-ROM, optical, magneto-optical, holographic and nonvolatile semiconductor storage devices.
Frequency: Monthly
Circulation: 15,140

5237 **Data to Knowledge**
Business Rule Solutions
2476 Bolsover Street
#488
Houston, TX 77005-2518

713-681-1651; *Fax:* 604-681-7223
datatoknow@brsolutions.com;
www.brcommunity.com

Gladys S W Lam, Publisher
Ronald G Ross, Executive Editor
Keri Anderson Healy, Editor
Marie Yang, Director, Marketing & Business Dev
John Hall, Technology Review Editor

Provides analysis, news and tutorials for data management professionals, data administrators, DBA's and other involved in the planning, design and construction of large-scale information systems.
Circulation: 4603
Founded in: 1973

5238 **Database Searcher**
Mecklermedia Corporation
11 Ferry Lane W
Westport, CT 06880-5808
Alan Meckler, Editor

Covers online and micro-computer techniques.
Cost: $95.00
Frequency: Monthly
Founded in: 1985

5239 **Datamation**
Reed Business Information
2000 Clearwater Dr
Oak Brook, IL 60523-8809

630-574-0825; *Fax:* 630-288-8781;
www.reedbusiness.com

Jeff Greisch, President
William Semich, Editor-in-Chief

The magazine that interprets products, events and technologies for computer professionals in large companies worldwide.
Cost: $4.00
Circulation: 189,101

5240 **Design Automation**
Miller Freeman Publications
2655 Seely Avenue
San Jose, CA 95134

408-943-1234; *Fax:* 408-943-0513

Lindsey Vereen, Editor

Targeted to computer design engineers.
Frequency: Monthly

5241 **Designfax**
NP Communications, LLC
2500 Tamiami Trail N
Nokomis, FL 34275

941-966-9521; *Fax:* 941-966-2590
mfoley@nelsonpub.com; www.designfax.net

Mike Foley, Editor
John W Holmes, National Sales Manager

eMagazine whose primary content focuses on the latest exciting applications and products for Electrical/Electronic, Mechanical, Motion Control, Fluid Power, and Materials engineering, including articles on powerful software programs that serve as a primary engineering tool.
Cost: $54.00
Frequency: Weekly
Circulation: 128,000
Founded in: 1979
Printed in 4 colors on glossy stock

5242 **Desktop Engineering**
Helmers Publishing
174 Concord Street
PO Box 874
Peterborough, NH 03458
603-924-9631; *Fax:* 603-924-4004
jgooch@deskeng.com; www.deskeng.com
Brian Vaillancourt, Publisher
Anthony J Lockwood, Editorial Director
Bill Fahy, Circulation Director
Carol Laughner, Marketing Director
Magazine providing design solutions from concept throughout manufacture, focuses on hardware, software, and technologies for hands-on design engineers and engineering management in the manufacturing solutions throughout extensive product reviews, comparisions, technology updates, real-world application stories, news, product resource guides, and new product reports.
60 Pages
Frequency: Monthly
Circulation: 63000
ISSN: 1085-0422
Founded in: 1995
Printed in 4 colors on glossy stock

5243 **Distributed Computing Monitor**
Patricia Seybold Group
Po Box 240565
Boston, MA 02129
617-742-5200
800-826-2424; *Fax:* 617-742-1028
feedback@psgroup.com; www.psgroup.com
Patricia Seybold, Founder/CEO
The editors give advanced technologists and strategic technology architects the technical details and business perspective necessary to sell upper management on how, why and when to implement the leading edge.
Frequency: Monthly
Founded in: 1978

5244 **E-doc**
Association for Information and Image Management
1100 Wayne Avenue
Suite 1100
Silver Spring, MD 20910-5603
301-587-8202
800-477-2446; *Fax:* 301-587-2711
aiim@aiim.org; www.aiim.org
Jan Andersson, Chair
Robert Zagami, Vice Chair
Peggy Winton, Marketing Director
Association magazine on electronic document management.
Circulation: 40000
Founded in: 1943

5245 **EServer Magazine**
IBM Corporation
220 S 6th Street
Suite 500
Minneapolis, MN 55402
612-339-7571; *Fax:* 612-336-9220;
www.eservercomputing.com
Doug Rock, Editor/Publisher
Mari Adamson-Bray, Marketing Manager
Kelly McManus, Production Manager
New products and services, technological information, and related topics that benefit the decision makers in the optimization and management of these systems are included.
80 Pages
Frequency: Monthly
Circulation: 45000
ISSN: 1074-7082
Founded in: 1993
Printed in 4 colors on glossy stock

5246 **Educational Technology**
Educational Technology Publications
700 Palisade Avenue
PO Box 1564
Englewood Cliffs, NJ 07632-564
201-871-4007
800-952-2665; *Fax:* 201-871-4009
edtecpubs@aol.com;
www.bookstoread.com/etp
Lawrence Lipsitz, Publisher/Editor
Systematic design of software and applications, and their impact on the educational community worldwide. Emphasis on computer-based instruction, the Internet, multimedia, electronic performance support, television and videoconferencing.
Cost: $139.00
Frequency: Bi-annually
ISSN: 0013-1962
Founded in: 1960
Printed in on glossy stock

5247 **Educational Technology Research and Development**
Assn. of Educational Communications & Technology
320 W. 8th Street
Suite 101
Bloomington, IN 47404
812-335-7675
877-677-2328; *Fax:* 812-335-7678
aect@aect.org
aect.site-ym.com
Social Media: Facebook, Twitter
Tristan E. Johnson, Editor-in-Chief
Brad Hokanson, President
Phillip Harris, Executive Director
Includes scholarly articles on communcations, technology and instructional development news.
Cost: $75.00
Frequency: Bi-Monthly
ISSN: 1042-1629
Founded in: 1923
Mailing list available for rent: 6000 names at $150 per M

5248 **Educational Technology Review**
AACE International
PO Box 3728
Norfolk, VA 23514
757-623-7588; *Fax:* 703-977-8760
info@aace.org; www.aace.org
Gary H Marks, Editor
Promotes the use of information technology in education. New products including software, hardware and related materials.
Cost: $38.00
Founded in: 1981

5249 **Electronic Design**
Penton Media
1300 E 9th St
Suite 310
Cleveland, OH 44114-1503
216-696-7000; *Fax:* 216-696-6662
information@penton.com; www.penton.com
Jane Cooper, Marketing
David B Nussbaum, CEO
Celebrating 50 years of innovation, this authoritative magazine provides leading-edge technical information to electronic and engineering managers around the world.
Cost: $105.00
Circulation: 145000
Founded in: 1890

5250 **Embedded Systems Programming**
Miller Freeman Publications
600 Harrison Street
6th Floor
San Francisco, CA 94107
415-947-6000; *Fax:* 415-947-6055;
www.mfi.com
Frequency: Monthly
Circulation: 45,000
Founded in: 1986

5251 **Enterprise Management Issues**
AFCOM
742 E Chapman Ave
Orange, CA 92866-1644
714-997-7966; *Fax:* 714-997-9743
afcom@afcom.com; www.afcom.com
Jill Eckhaus, President
Content includes an in-depth cover story and features on current developments and the impact of advancing technology. Regular departments are devoted to automation issues and data processing news.
Frequency: Bi-Monthly
Circulation: 4,000

5252 **European Sources and News**
SSC Group
3126 Woodley Road NW
Washington, DC 20008-3448
202-232-0822; *Fax:* 202-337-5354;
www.neweurope.eu
Robert Snyder, Publisher
Steve Solomon, Editor
Provides European resellers, VAR, systems integrators and OEM with information on product sources and reseller management strategies.
Circulation: 49000

5253 **Federal Computer Week**
FCW Government Technology Group
3141 Fairview Park Drive
Suite 777
Falls Church, VA 22042-4507
703-876-5100
866-293-3194; *Fax:* 703-876-5126;
www.fcw.com
Jeffrey Calore, General Manager, Sales & Marketing
Anne Armstrong, Publisher
John Zyskowski, Senior Editor
The markets leading newspaper for influential users and volume buyers of federal information technology.
Cost: $100.00
48 Pages
Frequency: Weekly
Circulation: 100000
Founded in: 1987

5254 **Foghorn**
FOG Publications
PO Box 1030
Dixon, CA 95620-1030
Gale Rhoades, Editor
For users of 16 and 32 bit systems.
Cost: $30.00
64 Pages
Frequency: Monthly
Founded in: 1985

5255 **GEOWorld**
Bel-Av Communications
359 Galahad Road
Bolingbrook, IL 60440-2108
E-Mail: tdanielson@geoplace.com;
www.geoplace.com
Jo Treadwell, VP/Group Publisher
Todd Danielson, Editor
Offers a wealth of knowledge through features, news and commentary covering the geospatial industry. Covers local and federal government,

emergency management, infrastructure, natural resource management, industry trends and onnovations and much more.
Cost: $72.00
Frequency: Monthly
Circulation: 25,000

5256 Game Developer Magazine
Think Services
600 Harrison Street
6th Floor
San Francisco, CA 94107
www.gdmag.com
Simon Carless, Publisher
Brandon Sheffield, Editor-In-Chief
Jeffrey Fleming, Production Editor
Written specifically for creators of entertainment software, provides technical and industry information to professional game developers. Features articles written by professional game developers on cutting-edge game development techniques in the areas of graphics and AI programming, audio design and engineering, art and animation.
Cost: $49.95
Frequency: Monthly
Circulation: 35,000
Founded in: 1971

5257 Genealogical Computing
Ancestry
360 W 4800 N
Provo, UT 84604-5675
801-705-7000
800-262-3787; *Fax:* 801-705-7001;
www.myfamily.com
Timothy P Sullivan, CEO
Elizabeth Kelley Kerstens, Managing Editor
Jennifer Browning, Senior Editor
For readers who use computers and technology to organize and enhance their research into accounts of ancestries and descent.
Cost: $25.00
Frequency: Quarterly

5258 Gilder Technology Report
Gilder Publishing
291 Main St
Suite A
Great Barringto, MA 01230-1608
413-644-2100; *Fax:* 413-644-2123
info@gilder.com; www.gildertech.com
George Gilder, Editor in Chief
Focuses on the ascendence of the telecoms and the centrality of the Internet.
Cost: $195.00
Frequency: Monthly
Founded in: 1995

5259 Global Technology Business
Global Technology Business Publishing
1157 San Antonio Road
Mountain View, CA 94043
650-934-2300; *Fax:* 650-934-2306;
www.gtbusiness.com
Alex Vieux, Publisher
Laurence Scott, Editor
Bob Beauchamp, CEO
Emphasizes the business aspects of the global computer and communications industries through corporate strategies, financial performance, technological directions.
Frequency: Monthly
Circulation: 45000

5260 Global Techventures Report
Miller Freeman Publications
2655 Seely Avenue
San Jose, CA 95134
408-943-1234; *Fax:* 408-943-0513
Annie Feldman, Publisher
Editorial content profiles vital capital investments and start-up companies, and addresses a variety of legislation, security and communication issues as they relate to today's technology.
Frequency: SemiMonthly

5261 Government Best Buys
FCW Government Technology Group
3141 Fairview Park Drive
Suite 777
Falls Church, VA 22042-4507
703-876-5100
866-293-3194; *Fax:* 703-876-5126;
www.fcw.com
Edith Holmes, President
John Stein Monroe, Editor-in-Chief
Christopher J. Dorobek, Executive Editor
Covers the hardware and software products available to government buyers on agency contracts and the General Services Administration schedule.
Founded in: 1987

5262 Hard Copy Observer
Lyra Research
320 Nevada Street 1st Floor
PO Box 9143
Newtonville, MA 02640-9143
617-454-2600; *Fax:* 617-454-2601;
www.lyra.com
Charles LeCompte, President
Ann Priede, Director of Marketing
Carolyn ODonnell, Director of Marketing
News on the latest products, market news, supplies, end-user reponse and product testing for the computer printer industry.
Cost: $617.00
80 Pages
Frequency: Monthly
Founded in: 1991

5263 Heller Report on Educational Technology Markets
Nelson B Heller & Associates
810 S Alfred Street
#1
Alexandria, VA 22314
303-209-9410; *Fax:* 303-209-9444
info@hellerreports.com;
www.hellerreports.com
Anne Wujcik, Publisher/Managing Editor
Information on the marketing of technology and telecommunications equipment to educators at all levels.
Cost: $395.00
Frequency: Monthly
Circulation: 1,100

5264 Home Networking News
111 Spleen
Suite 200
Framingham, MA 01701-2000
508-663-1500; *Fax:* 508-663-1599
kmoyes@ehpub.com; www.ehpub.com
Kenneth Moyes, CEO/Publisher
Cindy Tazis, Editor
Elizabeth Cruze, Marketing Manager
Christine Ayers, Circulation Manager
Cost: $14.95
Frequency: Monthly
Circulation: 100000
Founded in: 1994

5265 IEEE Computational Science & Engineering
IEEE Computer Society
PO Box 3014
Los Alamitos, CA 90720-1314
714-821-8380; *Fax:* 714-821-4010
mloeb@computer.org
computer.org
Matt Loeb, Publisher
Scott Andresen, Editor
Monette Velasco, Production Manager
Paul Croll, Treasurer
David Grier, VP Publications
Developments in computation and algorithms, high-performance evaulation, and visualization techniques in the computational science field.
Cost: $98.00
Frequency: Quarterly
Circulation: 5713
Founded in: 1946

5266 IEEE Computer
IEEE Computer Society
10662 Los Vaqueros Circle
PO Box 3014
Los Alamitos, CA 90720-1314
714-218-8380
800-272-6657; *Fax:* 714-821-4010
aburgess@computer.org; www.computer.org
Angela Burgess, Executive Director
Marilyn Potes, Managing Editor
Rakesh Gupta, Editor in Chief
Paul Croll, Treasurer
David Grier, VP Publications
Examines a wide range of computer-related technologies. Written and refereed by experts, it features articles on the latest developments in computer technology, applications and research in the computer field.
Cost: $37.00
Circulation: 85930
Founded in: 1946

5267 IEEE Computer Graphics and Applications
IEEE Computer Society
10662 Los Vaqueros Circle
PO Box 3014
Los Alamitos, CA 90720-1314
714-821-8380
800-272-6657; *Fax:* 714-821-4010
help@computer.org; www.computer.org/
Angela Burgess, Executive Director
Sandy Brown, Marketing Director
Robin Baldwin, Managing Editor
Christine Kelly, Staff Editor
Tammi Titsworth, Staff Editor
Focuses on the design and use of computer graphics and systems. Addresses topics such as solid modeling, animation, CAD/CAM, tools for rendering graphics and graphics in medicine, science and business.
Cost: $70.00
Circulation: 10028
Founded in: 1946

5268 IEEE Computer Society of Computing Software Magazine
Po Box 3014
Los Alamitos, CA 90720-1314
714-821-8380; *Fax:* 714-821-4010
volunteer.services@computer.org;
www.computer.org
Angela Burgess, Executive Director
Warren Harrison, Treasurer
Paul Croll, Treasurer
David Grier, VP Publications

Offers information on the latest software programs for computer professionals.
Circulation: 10000
Founded in: 1945

5269 IEEE Expert
IEEE Computer Society
10662 Los Vaqueros Circle
PO Box 3014
Los Alamitos, CA 90720
714-821-8380
800-272-6657; *Fax:* 714-821-4010
volunteer.services@computer.org;
www.computer.org
Crystal Shif, Managing Editor
Angela Burgess, Executive Director
Matthew Bertholf, Advertising Manager
Sandy Brown, Senior Business Development Manager
Paul Croll, Treasurer
Accepts advertising.
Cost: $58.00
Circulation: 3,463
Founded in: 1986

5270 IEEE Intelligent Systems
IEEE Computer Society
10662 Los Vaqueros Circle
PO Box 3014
Los Alamitos, CA 90720-1314
714-821-8380
800-272-6657; *Fax:* 714-821-4010
volunteer.services@computer.org;
www.computer.org
Angela Burgess, Executive Director
Paul Croll, Treasurer
Doris L Carver, Editor-in-Chief
David Grier, VP Publications
Features emphasize advanced research that is ready to be used in the real world. Departments include interviews, books and product reviews, opinion pieces, and conference calendars.
Cost: $47.00
Circulation: 15355
Founded in: 1946

5271 IEEE Network
Institute of Electrical & Electronics Engineers
3 Park Ave
17th Floor
New York, NY 10016-5997
212-419-7900; *Fax:* 212-752-4929
society-info@ieee.org; www.ieee.org
Daniel J Senese, CEO
Dr. Warren Gifford, Editor
Technical magazine serving both users and designers of multimedia hardware, software and systems in industry, business, academia and the arts.
Circulation: 14388
Founded in: 1871

5272 IEEE Transactions on Computers
IEEE Computer Society
10662 Los Vaqueros Circle
PO Box 3014
Los Alamitos, CA 90720
714-821-8380; *Fax:* 714-821-4010
help@computer.org; www.computer.org
Jean-Luc Gaudidt, Editor-in-Chief
Angela Burgess, Treasurer
Paul Croll, Treasurer
David Grier, VP Publications
Includes technical research reports and papers on the theory, design and applications of computer systems.
Cost: $72.00
Frequency: Monthly
Circulation: 8000
Founded in: 1979

5273 ISACA Journal
Information Systems Audit & Control Association
3701 Algonquin Rd
Suite 1010
Rolling Meadows, IL 60008-3124
847-253-1545; *Fax:* 847-253-1443
publication@isaca.org; www.isaca.org
Susan Caldwell, CEO
Provides professional development information to those spearheading IT governance and those involved with information systems audit, control and security
Cost: $75.00
Circulation: 35000
Founded in: 1969
Printed in 4 colors

5274 ISR: Intelligent Systems Report
Lionheart Publishing
2555 Cumberland Pkwy SE
Suite 299
Atlanta, GA 30339-3921
770-432-2551; *Fax:* 770-432-6969
llewellyn@lionhrtpub.com;
www.lionhrtpub.com
John Llewellyn, Publisher
Marvin Diamond, Advertising Sales Manager
Provides an in-depth look into the integration and application of advanced decision support technologies including artificial intelligence, speech recognition, neural networks, fuzzy logic, expert systems, multimedia and virtual reality, and artificial life.
Frequency: Monthly

5275 Imaging World
American Business Media
1300 Virginia Drive
Suite 400
Fort Washington, PA 19034-3297
215-643-8000; *Fax:* 215-643-8159;
www.imaging-world.com
Robert Boucher Jr, President/CEO
Dan Marsh, Publisher, Eyecare Business
Stephanie De Long, Editor-in-Chief, Eyecare
Serves the needs of vendors wishing to reach the North American market for electronic imaging and document-based information management and workflow.
Frequency: Monthly
Circulation: 75000
Founded in: 1997

5276 InTech Computing Magazine
ISA Services
67 Alexander Drive
PO Box 12277
Research Triangle Park, NC 27709
919-549-8411; *Fax:* 919-549-8288
info@isa.org; www.isa.org
Gregory Hale, Editor
Richard T Simpson, Publisher
Key source of information on automating manufacturing processes.
Cost: $45.00
Frequency: Monthly
Founded in: 1945
Printed in 4 colors on glossy stock

5277 Info Log Magazine
BBS Press Service
785-286-4272; *Fax:* 239-992-4862
Alan Bechtold, Editor
A comprehensive magazine offering the latest information on aspects of the computer industry.
Frequency: Monthly
Founded in: 1982

5278 Information Display
Ste 114
1475 S Bascom Ave
Campbell, CA 95008-0628
408-977-1013; *Fax:* 408-977-1531
office@sid.org; www.sid.org
Ken Werner, Editor
Jenny Needham, Circulation Manager
Shigeo Nikoshiba, CEO/President
A magazine published by the Society for Information Display.
Cost: $55.00
Frequency: Monthly
Circulation: 12000
Founded in: 1964

5279 Information Management Magazine
ARMA International
11880 College Blvd
Suite 450
Overland Park, KS 66215
913-341-3808
800-422-2762; *Fax:* 913-341-3742
hq@arma.org; www.arma.org
Marilyn Bier, Executive Director
Jody Becker, Associate Editor
The leading source of information on topics and issues central to the management of records and information worldwide. Each issue features insightful articles written by experts in the management of records and information.
Cost: $115.00
Frequency: Bi-monthly
Circulation: 11000
ISSN: 1535-2897
Mailing list available for rent: 9000 names
Printed in 4 colors on glossy stock

5280 Information Systems Management
Auerbach Publications
3701 Algonquin Road
Suite 1010
Rolling Meadows, IL 60008
847-253-1545; *Fax:* 847-253-1443
publication@isaca.org; www.isaca.org
Debra Cutts, Marketing
Jen Blader, Editorial
Susan Caldwell, CEO
Coverage includes information technology developments and business applications, financial issues, IS staff development, and relationships with business management.
Cost: $75.00
Frequency: Bi-monthly
Circulation: 40,000
ISSN: 1058-0530
Founded in: 1969

5281 Information World Review
143 Old Marlton Pike
Medford, NJ 08055-8750
609-654-7777; *Fax:* 609-654-4309
Offers a full overview of the computer industry overseas.

5282 InformationWEEK
CMP Publications
600 Community Dr
Manhasset, NY 11030-3810
516-562-5000; *Fax:* 516-562-5036;
www.cmp.com
Stephanie Stahl, Editor-in-Chief
Mike Friedenberg, Publisher
For information systems management.
Frequency: Weekly
Circulation: 440,000
Founded in: 1985

5283 Infostor
PennWell Publishing Company

98 Spit Brook Rd
Nashua, NH 03062-5737

603-891-0123; *Fax:* 603-891-9294
mark@pennwell.com; www.pennwell.com

Christine Shaw, VP
Jill Davis, Marketing Communications

News and information for enterprise storage professionals.
Cost: $120.00
Frequency: Monthly
Circulation: 38000
Founded in: 1997

5284 Infoworld Magazine
Infoworld
501 Second Street
San Francisco, CA 94107

847-291-5217
feedback@infoworld.com;
www.infoworld.com/

Bob Ostrow, President/Publisher
Paul Calento, VP Marketing
Kevin McKean, Chairman
Steve Fox, Editor-in-Chief
Kathy Badertscher, Executive Managing Editor

Offers information for computer professionals.
Frequency: Weekly

5285 Inside DPMA
Data Processing Management Association
505 Busse Highway
Park Ridge, IL 60068-3143

847-825-0880; *Fax:* 847-825-1693

Paul Zuziak, Editor

A monthly newspaper for the DPMA and the information management profession. Accepts advertising.
Cost: $16.00
Frequency: Monthly
Founded in: 1988

5286 Inside Technology Training
Ziff Davis Publishing Company
500 Unicorn Park Drive
Woburn, MA 01801

781-938-2600
editor@itrain.com; www.itrain.com/

Nancy J Weingarten, Publisher

Targets management level executives, technology trainers, information technology training managers, CIO's and independent training consultants. Includes reports on new software, new media and new career paths. Also features designed to help training managers create and successfully implement strategy training and reskilling programs that anyone on any level can use.
Frequency: 10 per year
Circulation: 40,000

5287 Inside Visual Basic
ZD Journals
500 Canal View Boulevard
Rochester, NY 14623-2800

585-407-7301; *Fax:* 585-240-7760;
www.zdjournals.com

Jon Pyles, Publisher

Authors discuss subjects covering the building and creating of external objects, as well as topics surrounding class development. The publication informs readers of Visual Basic online resources, and addresses real world questions reagrding controls written in the program, uses of the status bar and extending functions capabilities.
Frequency: Monthly

5288 Integrated System Design
Verecom Group
954 San Rafael Avenue
Mountain View, CA 94043-1926

650-988-9677; www.isdmag.com

James Uhl, Publisher
Richard Wallace, VP

Articles are written by designers who explain unique methods for solving design challenges. Publication supplies information on design methodologies and the use of tools and semiconductor capabilities.
Frequency: Monthly
Circulation: 58082

5289 Intelligent Enterprise
Miller Freeman Publications
411 Boral Avenue
#100
San Mateo, CA 94402-3522

650-573-3210; *Fax:* 650-655-4350;
www.intelligententerprise.com

David Kalman, Publisher

Each issue provides detailed analyses of the products, trends and strategies that help accelerate the creation of the enterprise's information infrastructure. Topics include: business intelligence; enterprise resource planning; knowledge management; transaction processing and performance monitoring; applications and systems management.
Frequency: 18 per year
Circulation: 103,000

5290 Interactions
Association for Computing Machinery
2 Penn Plz
Suite 701
New York, NY 10121-0799

212-868-5716
800-342-6626; *Fax:* 212-944-1318
acmhelp@acm.org; www.acm.org

Mark Mandelbaum, Director Publication
Jonathan Arnowitz, Editors in Chief

Editorial content covers business, design, methods and tools, book previews, conference previews and current events pertaining to designers, developers and researchers.
Founded in: 1947

5291 International Journal of IT Standards and Standardization Research
Information Resources Management Association
701 E Chocolate Ave
Suite 200
Hershey, PA 17033-1240

717-533-8879; *Fax:* 717-533-8661
members@irma-international.org;
www.irma-international.org

Jan Travers, Executive Director
Koichi Asatani, Associate Editors
Carl Cargill, Associate Editor
Tineke Egyedi, Associate Editor
Richard Hawkins, Associate Editor

An authoritative source and information outlet for the diverse community of IT standards researchers, publishing research findings with the goal of advancing knowledge and research in all aspects of IT standards and standardization in modern organizations.
Cost: $115.00
Frequency: Semi-Annual
ISSN: 1539-3062

5292 International Journal of Information and Communication Technology Education
Information Resources Management Association
701 E Chocolate Ave
Suite 200
Hershey, PA 17033-1240

717-533-8879; *Fax:* 717-533-8861
member@irma-international.org;
www.irma-international.org

Jan Travers, Executive Director
Tonya Barrier, Associate Editor
Dencho Batanov, Associate Editor
David Carbonara, Associate Editor
Martin Crossland, Associate Editor

Includes new applications of technology for teaching and learning, and document those practices that contribute irrefutable verification of information technology education as a discipline.
Cost: $115.00
Frequency: Quarterly
ISSN: 1550-1876
Printed in

5293 Iris Universe: Magazine of Visual Computing
Silicon Graphics
1500 Crittenden Lane
Mountain View, CA 94043

650-960-1980
800-800-7441; *Fax:* 650-932-6102;
www.sgi.com

Warren C Pratt, CEO/President
Gaye Graves, Features Editor
Anne Marie Gambelin, Publisher
Dominic Martinelli, Chief Information Officer

Written to appeal to all users of computer visualization, from the most technically oriented to the novice. Devoted to cutting edge techniques and technology used and presents the best in new products available.
Frequency: Quarterly
Founded in: 1981

5294 Journal of American Society for Information Science
John Wiley & Sons
111 River St
Hoboken, NJ 07030-5790

201-748-6000; *Fax:* 201-748-6088
info@wiley.com; www.wiley.com

William J Pesce, CEO
Richard M Hochhauser, CEO

Communications, management, applications, economics, and other news of interest in the science field.
Cost: $95.00
72 Pages
Frequency: Bi-Monthly

5295 Journal of Imaging Science and Technology
Society for Imaging Science & Technology
7003 Kilworh Lane
Springfield, VA 22151-4088

703-642-9090; *Fax:* 703-642-9094
info@imaging.org; www.imaging.org

George T.C. Chin, Editor
Donna Smith, Managing Editor

Provides the imaging community documentation of a broad range of research, development, and applications in imaging. The selection of papers reflects the role of IS&T as the window on imaging, promoting communication and understanding across the boundaries of the many disciplines involved in modern imaging.
Cost: $95.00
Circulation: 2000
ISSN: 1062-3701
Founded in: 1947

5296 Journal of Interactive Learning Research
AACE International

1 Morton Drive
Suite 500
Charlottesville, VA 22903

434-977-5029; *Fax:* 434-977-5431
info@aace.org; www.aace.org

John Self, Editor

Reports on the research, developments, applications, and integration of intelligent computer technologies in education.
Frequency: Quarterly
Circulation: 3M

5297 Journal of Object-Oriented Programming
SIGS Publications
9121 Oakdale Avenue
Chatsworth, CA 91311

818-734-1520; *Fax:* 818-734-1522;
www.101com.com

Richard S Weiner, Editor
Mike Valenti, Executive Vice President

Provides an international forum for research, developments, applications, and new products in the field.
Circulation: 3,50,000
Founded in: 1998

5298 KM World
Information Today
143 Old Marlton Pike
Medford, NJ 08055-8750

609-654-6266
800-300-9868; *Fax:* 609-654-4309
custserv@infotoday.com; www.infotoday.com

Thomas H Hogan, President
Roger R Bilboul, Chairman of the Board

Serves the knowledge management industry by offering components and processes, including success stories, designed to improve business.
Cost: $23.95
Mailing list available for rent: 4M names
Printed in 4 colors on glossy stock

5299 LAN Magazine
Miller Freeman Publications
600 Harrison Street
6th Fl
San Francisco, CA 94107

415-947-6000; *Fax:* 415-947-6055;
www.mfi.com

Covers Local Area Networks.
Cost: $20.00
180 Pages
Frequency: Monthly
Founded in: 1986

5300 Law Office Computing
James Publishing
PO Box 25202
Santa Ana, CA 92799-5202

714-755-5450; *Fax:* 714-751-5508;
www.jamespublishing.com

Jamie Tyo, Managing Editor
Amanda Flatten, Editor & Publisher
Jim Pawell, Marketing and Circulation

Legal software reviews, productivity enhancing tips and resources to improve law office automation.
Cost: $39.00
Founded in: 1981

5301 Learning and Leading with Technology
International Society for Technology in Education
180 W 8th Avenue
Eugene, OR 97401-2916

541-302-3777
800-336-5191; *Fax:* 541-302-3778
iste@iste.org; www.iste.org

Don Knezek, CEO
Leslie Conery, Deputy CEO

Authors and teachers include school and state administrators, classroom and lab teachers, tech coordinators, and teachers educators. Most are involved in tech-purcahsing decisions for their school and district. Every issue of L&L includes: a feature subject of broad appeal, articles about using tech in specific subject areas, lesson plans, reproducible worksheets, professional development advice, and referral to supplementary information on the L&L web site at www.iste.org.
Cost: $89.00
Circulation: 17000
ISSN: 1082-5754
Founded in: 1989

5302 Library Software Review
Sage Publications
Vanderbilt University
419 21st Avenue S
Nashville, TN 37240-0001

615-343-6094; *Fax:* 615-343-8834
info@sagepub.com; www.sagepub.com

Marshall Breeding, Editor

Provides the library professional with information necessary to make intelligent software evaluation, procurement, integration and installation decisions. Issues review software and software books and periodicals.
Cost: $52.00
Frequency: Quarterly
Circulation: 1M

5303 Link-Up Digital
Information Today
143 Old Marlton Pike
Medford, NJ 08055-8750

609-654-6266
800-300-9868; *Fax:* 609-654-4309
custserv@infotoday.com; www.infotoday.com

Thomas H Hogan, President
Roger R Bilboul, Chairman Of The Board

A web-only product featuring articles, reviews and more for users and producers of electronic information products and services.
Mailing list available for rent: 4M names
Printed in 4 colors on glossy stock

5304 MD Computing
Springer Verlag
175 5th Ave
New York, NY 10010-7703

212-477-8200; *Fax:* 212-473-6272;
www.mdcomputing.com

Nhora Cortes-Comerer, Executive Editor
Kelley Suttenfield, Assistant Editor

Provides comprehensive and up-to-date information about the various segments of medical and healthcare informatics, such as clinical computing, health care information and delivery systems, telemedicine, radiology, and many others.
Cost: $69.00
74 Pages
Frequency: Bi-Monthly
Circulation: 19,771
ISSN: 0724-6811
Printed in 4 colors on glossy stock

5305 MacWeek
MacWorld Communications
501 2nd St
San Francisco, CA 94107-1496

415-243-0505; *Fax:* 415-442-0766

Mike Kisseberth, CEO
David Ezequelle, Publisher
Rick Lepage, President

Covers Apple's Macintosh computers. Accepts advertising.
Cost: $99.00
72 Pages
Frequency: 44 per year
Founded in: 1987

5306 MacWorld Magazine
Mac Publishing
501 2nd St
San Francisco, CA 94107-1496

415-243-0505; *Fax:* 415-442-0766
letters@macworld.com; www.macworld.com

Mike Kisseberth, CEO
Dan Miller, Executive Editor
Scholle Sawyer McFarland, Senior Editor
Dan Frakes, Senior Writer

The ultimate resource for Mac professionals and savvy Mac users. Each issue is packed with practical how-tos, in-depth features, the latest troubleshooting tips and tricks, industry news, future trends and more.
Cost: $19.97
Frequency: Year Subscription

5307 Marketing Computers
V&U
770 Broadway
F18
New York, NY 10003-9595

646-654-5000; *Fax:* 646-654-5374;
www.marketingcomputers.com

Donna Tapellini, Editor
Tony DiCamillo, Publisher

Edited for advertising and marketing executives in the high-tech industries. The publication covers interpretive news, timely big picture features, departments and analysis by staff editors and industry experts.
Cost: $149.00
100 Pages
Frequency: Weekly
Circulation: 15484

5308 Mobile Office
4845 West 111th Street
Alsip, IL 60658

708-636-5400; *Fax:* 708-636-8637
sales@mobileofficeinc.com
mobileofficeinc.com

Jeff Hecox, Editor

Office equipment, computer technology and information.

5309 Motion System Distributor
Penton Media
1300 E 9th St
Cleveland, OH 44114-1503

216-696-7000; *Fax:* 216-696-6662
information@penton.com; www.penton.com

Jane Cooper, Marketing
David B. Nussbaum, CEO
Larry Berardinis, Editor

Provides selling and technical information to individuals and distributors, specializing in power transmission, motion control and fluid products.
Frequency: Monthly
Circulation: 54000
Founded in: 1892

5310 NCR Connection
Publications & Communications

505 Cypress Creek Road
Suite B
Cedar Park, TX 78613

512-250-9023; *Fax:* 512-331-3900

Mary Wilson, Editor

For users of NCR computer systems.
Cost: $92.00
32 Pages
Frequency: Monthly
Founded in: 1983

5311 **NEWS 3X/400**
Duke Communications International
221 E 29th Street
Loveland, CO 80538-2769

970-634-4700; *Fax:* 970-667-2321

Tim Fixmer, Publisher
Trish Faubion, Editor

Leading technical journal for IBM Systems.
Cost: $119.00
220 Pages
Frequency: 16 per year
Circulation: 31,000
Founded in: 1982

5312 **Network Support Magazine**
Technical Enterprises
7044 S 13th Street
Oak Creek, WI 53154-1429

414-768-8000; *Fax:* 414-768-8001
customercare@naspa.com; www.naspa.com

Denise Rockhill, Publisher/Advertising Sales
Rachael Zimmerman, Editor
Matthew Jossart, Art Director

The most comprehensive how to publication in the industry. Orientedtoward professionals involved with a myriad of computing technologies and discusses the topic of importance in mainframe, host based and network oriented environments.
Cost: $5.00
68 Pages
Frequency: Monthly
Circulation: 50,000
Founded in: 1987

5313 **Network World**
Network World
118 Turnpike Road
Southborough, MA 01772-9108

508-756-6400
800-622-1108; *Fax:* 508-460-1192;
www.networkworld.com

Evilee T Ebb, CEO/Publisher
John Gallant, CFO
Dylan Smith, CFO

For network IS professionals with direct responsibility for planning and managing their companies network computing environment.
Cost: $129.00
100 Pages
Frequency: Weekly
Circulation: 170,000
Founded in: 1986

5314 **Newmedia Age**
HyperMedia Communications
PO Box 299
Brooklin, ME 04616

207-359-6573
800-935-0040; *Fax:* 207-359-9809
support@hypernet.com

Ben Calica, Editor

Covers new products and technology trends in audio and video computing.
Cost: $24.00
Frequency: Quarterly
Circulation: 40,000

5315 **OfficeWorld News**
366 Ramtown Greenville Road
Howell, NJ 07731-2789

732-785-5976; *Fax:* 732-785-1347

William Urban, Publisher
Kim Chandlee McCabe, Editor-in-Chief

Provides a diverse population of business products resellers the news and information to best serve the needs of small, mid and large business customers. Provides insight into partnering with their peers in this diverse marketplace.
Frequency: Monthly
Circulation: 31,500
Printed in 4 colors on glossy stock

5316 **PC Arcade**
Softdisk Publishing
606 Common Street
Shreveport, LA 71101-3437

318-218-8718; *Fax:* 318-221-8870

Al Vekovius, President
Ronda Farries, Circulation Director

Publisher of software subscriptions for DOS, Windows and Macintosh computers.
Cost: $19.95
Frequency: Monthly
Founded in: 1990

5317 **PC Sources**
Ziff Davis Publishing Company
500 Unicorn Park Drive
Woburn, MA 01801

781-938-2600; *Fax:* 781-938-2626
info@ziffdavis.com; www.ziffdavis.com

Peter McKie, Editor
Robert F Callahan, CEO
Michael J Miller, Editor-in-chief
Stephen Hicks, General Counsel

Serves experienced PC users.
Cost: $149.75
Frequency: Monthly
Founded in: 1985

5318 **PC Systems and Support**
Technical Enterprises
7044 S 13th Street
Oak Creek, WI 53154

414-325-3366; *Fax:* 414-768-8001

Scott Sherer, President
Amy Birschbach, Editor

Offers solutions with tutorials on hardware and software implementation/upgrade techniques, workstation customization, integration and optimization. The how-to material presented each month guides those professionals in evaluating, selecting, acquiring, implementing, and supporting PC distributed resources. Presents in-depth technical information that can be applied at work.

5319 **PC Techniques**
Coriolis Group
14455 N Hyden Road
Suite 220
Scottsdale, AZ 85260

480-483-0192

Keith Weiskamp, Publisher
Jeff Duntemann, Editor

Covers information on a wide variety of computer systems and language technology.
Cost: $22.00
104 Pages
Frequency: Bi-Monthly
Founded in: 1990

5320 **Pen Computing Magazine**
Aeon Publishing Group
PO Box 408
Plainview, NY 11803-0408

www.pencomputing.com

Conrad H Blickenstorfer, Editor-in-Chief
Howard Borgen, Publisher
Wayne Laslo, Advertising Manager

In-depth coverage of pen technology, wireless communications and mobile computing.
Cost: $18.00
Frequency: Monthly
Circulation: 79515
Founded in: 1993

5321 **Physicians & Computers**
Moorhead Publications
600 S Waukegan Road
#200
Lake Forest, IL 60045-2672

847-615-8333;
www.physicians-computers.com

Tom Moorhead, Publisher

Provides physicians with information on computer advances helpful in the private practice of medicine. Practice management, current medical and nonmedical software, computer diagnostics, etc.
Cost: $50.00
Frequency: Monthly

5322 **Powerbuilding Developer's Journal**
SYS-CON Publications
135 Chestnut Ridge Rd
Montvale, NJ 07645-1152

201-782-9600
800-513-7111; *Fax:* 201-782-9601;
www.pbdj.sys-con.com

Fuat Kircaali, Publisher

Covers provide an advanced look at Powerbuilder techniques, new products, reader feedback and interaction, and training in the Powerbuilder language.
Frequency: Monthly
Circulation: 20000

5323 **Precision Engineering Journal**
Elsevier Science Publishing
6277 Sea Harbor Drive
Orlando, FL 32887-4800

407-345-4020
877-839-7126; *Fax:* 407-363-1354
usjcs@elsevier.com; www.elsevier.com
/www.aspe.net

W T Estler, Editor-in-Chief
D G Chetwynd, Editor
T. Moriwaki, Co-Editor
Bill Godfrey, Chief Information Officer

Provides an integrated approach to all subjects related to the development, design, manufacture, and application of high-precision machines, systems, and components. International news, reviews, conference reports, informed comment, and a calendar of forthcoming events complete the spectrum of coverage designed to keep readers abreast with a fast-moving technology.
Cost: $1014.00
ISSN: 0141-6359
Founded in: 1979

5324 **Processor**
Peed Corporation
PO Box 85518
Lincoln, NE 68501-5518

402-479-2141
800-819-9014; *Fax:* 402-479-2120
feedback@processor.com; www.processor.com

Susy Miller, Publisher
Rhonda Peed, CEO

Information on computer products and services.
Cost: $26.00
84 Pages
Frequency: Weekly
Founded in: 1978

5325 Products for Document Management
Acron Publishing
1306 Gaskins Road
Richmond, VA 23233-4919
804-754-2101; *Fax:* 804-754-1534
Irwin Posner, Publisher
News and reviews of latest technology and applications for document management world, including hardware, software, supplies and services.
Frequency: Quarterly
Circulation: 10.963

5326 RIS/Retail Info Systems News
Edgell Communications
4 Middlebury Boulevard
Randolph, NJ 07869-4221
973-252-0100; *Fax:* 973-252-9020;
www.risnews.com
Andrew Gaffney, Publisher
Jeff Zabe, Circualtion Manager
Gabriele A. Edgell, CEO
Gerald C Ryerson, President
Updates on the latest development in retail management technologies with articles that focus on the application of managerial and hi-tech advancements.
Frequency: Monthly
Founded in: 1984
Printed in 4 colors on glossy stock

5327 RTC
RTC Group
27312 Calle Arroyo
San Juan Capistrano, CA 92675-2768
949-443-4400; *Fax:* 949-489-8502
johnr@rtcgroup.com; www.rtcgroup.com
John Reardo, Publisher
Provides information to answer real life questions about the open systems computer market. Also news, product updates, tech updates and standard tracking.
Frequency: Monthly
Circulation: 29,500

5328 Real Time Graphics
Computer Graphic Systems Development Corporation
2483 Old Middlefield Way
#140
Mountain View, CA 94043-2330
650-903-4920; *Fax:* 650-967-5252;
www.cgsd.com
Roy Latham, Owner
In-depth information on the technology of real time graphics, VR, simulations and coverage of industry news.
Cost: $205.00
Frequency: Monthly
Circulation: 1M

5329 Real-Time Engineering
Micrology PBT
2618 S Shannon
Tempe, AZ 85282-2936
480-967-5581; *Fax:* 480-968-3446
micrology@aol.com;
www.realtime-engineering.com
John Black, Editor-in-Chief
Focuses on software and operating systems.
Frequency: Quarterly
Circulation: 10,000

5330 Red Herring: The Business of Technology
Red Herring Communications
1550 Bryant St
Suite 450
San Francisco, CA 94103-4832
415-486-2819; *Fax:* 415-865-2280
info@redherring.com; www.redherring.com

5331 Report on Healthcare Information Management
Aspen Publishers
1101 King Street
#444
Alexandria, VA 22314
703-683-4100; *Fax:* 703-739-6517;
www.aspenlawschool.com
Mike Brown, Publisher
H. Stephen Lieber, CEO/President
Timothy B Clark, Marketing & Business Dev
System development, clinical information systems, cost-effective clinical integration, data collection, network security and confidentiality for the health care industry.
Cost: $358.00
Frequency: Monthly

5332 Retail Systems Alert
Retail Systems Alert Group
377 Elliot Street
PO Box 332
Newton Upper Falls, MA 02464
617-527-4626; *Fax:* 617-527-8102;
www.retailsystems.com
Tom Friedman, President
Hideo Funamoto, Contributing Editor
Provides updated information on automation news and trends, including decision systems, information systems implementation, in-store merchandise management, and case studies of retailers.
Cost: $295.00
8 Pages
Frequency: Monthly
Founded in: 1988

5333 Retail Systems Reseller
Edgell Communications
4 Middlebury Boulevard
Suite 1
Randolph, NJ 07869-1111
973-252-0100; *Fax:* 973-252-9020;
www.edgellcommunications.com
michael Kachmar, Publisher
Joe Skorupa, Editor-in-Chief
Gabriele Edgell, CEO
Gerald C. Ryerson, President
John Chiego, Vice President
Offers information to retailers, dealers, systems integraters, VARs, VADs, etc., on retail technology for small to mid-size retailers.
Cost: $190.00
Frequency: Monthly
Founded in: 1984

5334 RetailTech
Progressive Grocer Associates
23 Old King's Highway South
Darien, CT 06820-4538
646-654-7561; *Fax:* 203-656-3800
info@progressivegrocer.com;
www.progressivegrocer.com
John Failla, Publisher
Jenny McTaggart, Senior Editor
Stephen Dowdell, Editor-in-Chief
Joseph Tarnowski, Tech Editor, Equipment & Design
Editoral content covers software, computer peripherals, communications, electronic retailing, point-of-sale systems, networking, data warehousing, logistics/distribution systems, and the Internet.
Cost: $99.00
Frequency: Monthly

5335 Robot Explorer
Appropriate Solutions
85 Grove Street
PO Box 458
Peterborough, NH 03458
603-924-6079; *Fax:* 603-924-8668;
www.appropriatesolutions.com
Raymond Cote, Editor
Targets the world of non-industrial robots. From eight-legged walking machines exploring Antarctic volcanoes, to microscopic nano-machines, Robot Explorer provides practical construction details and fascinating reviews of current technology.
Cost: $14.95
Circulation: 500

5336 SCO Magazine
600 Community Drive
Manhasset, NY 11030-3847
516-562-5836; *Fax:* 516-562-5466
H Newton Barrett, Publisher

5337 SIGNAL Magazine
4400 Fair Lakes Center
Fairfax, VA 22033-3899
703-631-6100
800-336-4583; *Fax:* 703-631-6169
bmowery@afcea.org; www.afcea.org
Beverly Mowery, Associate Publisher
Robert K Ackerman, Editor-in-Chief
A news magazine targeted to serve the critical information needs of government, military and industry professionals active in the fields of command, control, communications, computers, intelligence, surveillance and reconnaissance, or C4ISR; information security; research and development; electronics; and homeland security.
Cost: $56.00
Frequency: Monthly/Year Subscription
Mailing list available for rent

5338 SQL Forum Online
Informant Communications Group
10519 E Stockton Boulevard
Suite 100
Elk Grove, CA 95624-9703
916-863-3700; *Fax:* 916-379-0610;
www.informant.com
Forrest Freeman, Owner
Tom Bondur, Publisher
Written for data-base professionals to share and exchange ideas. Has papers and articles that are filled with answers to common data-base questions.
Frequency: Monthly

5339 Sawtooth News
Sawtooth Technologies
1500 Skokie Boulevard
Suite 510
Northbrook, IL 60062
847-239-7300; *Fax:* 847-239-7301
info@sawtooth.com; www.sawtooth.com
Nicole Garneau, Editor
Articles on computer aided telephone interviewing, computer interviewing, conjoint analysis, and other advanced research techniques.
Founded in: 1995

5340 Scan Tech News
Reed Business Information

2000 Clearwater Dr
Oak Brook, IL 60523-8809

630-574-0825; *Fax:* 630-288-8781;
www.reedbusiness.com

Jeff Greisch, President

Updates in trends in ADC technology and standards, the latest news from leading industry events, and product developments that streamline the flow of essential information in industrial settings.
Frequency: Monthly
Circulation: 82M

5341 **Scan: Data Capture Report**
Corry Publishing
5905 Beacon Hill Lane
Erie, PA 16509

814-380-0025; *Fax:* 814-864-2037
rickm@scandcr.com;
www.rmgenterprises.com/

Larry Roberts, CEO and Publisher
(Jon) Rick Morgan, President and Editor

Developments in bar code scanning, biometric identification, electronic commerce and areas of automatic data capture.
Cost: $597.00
Frequency: Fortnightly
Founded in: 1996

5342 **Scientific Computing & Automation**
Reed Business Information
2000 Clearwater Dr
Oak Brook, IL 60523-8809

630-574-0825; *Fax:* 630-288-8781;
www.reedbusiness.com

Jeff Greisch, President

Provides the scientists working in industrial/analytical labs, clinical labs, life science labs and electronics R&D labs with information on developments in computing and automation technology for the laboratory.
Cost: $60.00
Frequency: Monthly
Circulation: 50,059

5343 **Scientific Computing & Instrumentation**
Reed Business Information
45 E 85th St
4th Floor
New York, NY 10028-0957

212-772-8300; *Fax:* 630-288-8686
subsmail@reedbusiness.com;
www.scimag.com

Lawrence S Reed
Suzanne Tracy, Editor in Chief

5344 **Semiconductor Magazine**
Semiconductor Equipment & Materials International
3081 Zanker Road
San Jose, CA 95134

408-943-6900; *Fax:* 408-428-9600
semihq@semi.org; www.semi.org

T Buehler, Editor-in-Chief
Chris Bucholtz, Editor
Marie Claussell, Circulation Manager
Barbara Wietzel, Marketing Manager

Covers the technical and business information needs of inportant worldwide semiconductor manufacturers, including captive manufacturers, merchant manufacturers, research and development laboratories, equipment suppliers, government/military installations and consortiums.
Cost: $125.00
Frequency: Monthly
Founded in: 1980

5345 **Sensors Magazine**
Advanstar Communications
275 Grove Street
Suite 2-130
Newton, MA 02466

603-924-5400; *Fax:* 603-924-5401;
www.sensormag.com

Barbara Goode, Group Editorial Director
Stephanie Henkel, Executive Editor
Jill Thiry, Group Publishing Director

Source among design and production engineers of information on sensor technologies and products, and topic integral to sensor-based systems and applications. Provides practical and in-depth yet accessible information on sensor operation, design, application, and implementation within systems. Covers the effective use of state-of-the-art resources and tools that enable readers to get the maximum benefit from their use of sensors.
Frequency: Monthly
Circulation: 66676
Founded in: 1999

5346 **Serverworld Magazine**
Publications & Communications
11675 Jollyville Rd
Suite 150
Austin, TX 78759

512-250-9023
800-678-9724; *Fax:* 512-331-3900
pci@pcinews.com; www.pcinews.com

David Wohlbrueck, Editor
Gary Pittman, CEO/President
Bill Lifland, VP Operations

Dedicated to Hewlett-Packard computing.
Cost: $45.00
60 Pages
Frequency: Monthly
Founded in: 1979

5347 **Simulation**
Simulation Councils
PO Box 17900
San Diego, CA 92177-7900

858-277-3888; *Fax:* 858-277-3930
info@scs.org; www.scs.org

William Gallagher, Publisher
Richard Fujimoto, Editor-in-Chief
Steve Branch, Executive Director

Information on computer simulation including, applications, methodologies and techniques of computer simulation.
Cost: $195.00
Frequency: Monthly
Circulation: 3800
Founded in: 1952

5348 **Small Business Advisor: Software News**
Software News Publishing Company
110 N Bell Avenue
Suite 300
Shawnee, OK 74801-6967

405-275-3100
800-456-0864; *Fax:* 405-275-3101;
www.cpatechadvisor.com

Sharie Dodgen, Publisher
Melody Wrinkle, Manager
Isaac OBannon, Manager
Thomson Reuters, Executive Editor

Published for advisers to small businesses and for software installers for small businesses.
Cost: $48.00
Circulation: 50000
Founded in: 1991

5349 **Smart Reseller**
Ziff Davis Publishing Company
500 Unicorn Park Drive
Woburn, MA 01801-4874

781-938-2600; *Fax:* 781-938-2626;
www.smartreseller.com

Sloan Seymour, Publisher

Identifies the most lucrative new business opportunities and details how to profitably take advantage of them. In-depth business management strategies and trusted new technology solutions-based reviews.
Frequency: SemiMonthly
Circulation: 60M

5350 **Software Development**
Miller Freeman Publications
2655 Seely Avenue
San Jose, CA 95134

408-943-1234
800-227-4675; *Fax:* 408-943-0513

Veronica Costanza, Publisher
Nicole Freeman, Editor
Laura Merling, Executive Director

For corporate developers and technical managers involved in the development of software applications within the industries.
Circulation: 73297

5351 **Software Digest**
National Software Testing Laboratories
670 Sentry Pkwy
2nd Floor
Blue Bell, PA 19422-2325

610-832-8400; *Fax:* 610-941-9952
info@nstl.com; www.nstl.com

Lowrenie Goldstein, Publisher
Andrew Froning, Editor

Independent and comparative ratings on IBM PC software. All categories tested free of bias. No advertising is accepted.
Frequency: Monthly
Founded in: 1983

5352 **Solid Solutions**
ConnectPress
551 W Cordova Road
Suite 701
Santa Fe, NM 87505-4100

505-474-5000; *Fax:* 505-474-5001
info@solidprofessor.com; www.solidmag.com

Dale Bennie, Publisher

Covers the latest market developments and tracks the growth of SolidWorks software in the CAD/CAM/CAE market. Reviews of workstations, 3D printers, and Windows NT graphic accelerators.
Cost: $99.00
Frequency: Monthly

5353 **Solutions Integrator**
International Data Group
3 Post Office Sq
4th Floor
Boston, MA 02109-3939

617-423-9030; *Fax:* 617-423-0240;
www.solutionsintegrator.com

Bob Carrigan, CEO
Joel Shore, Editor-In-Chief

Provides accessment of technology, IT buying practices and plans, business strategies and vendor technology roadmaps.
Circulation: 90000

5354 **Speech Recognition Update**
CI Publishing

PO Box 570730
Tarzana, CA 91357-730

818-708-0962
888-632-7419; *Fax:* 818-345-2980
info@tmaa.com; www.tmaa.com

William S Meisel, President
Bill Meisel, Editor

News and analysis of speech recognition markets, companies and technologies.
Cost: $195.00
Frequency: Monthly
Founded in: 1993

5355 **Storage Management Solutions**
West World Productions
420 N Camden Dr
Beverly Hills, CA 90210-4507

310-276-9500; *Fax:* 310-276-9874;
www.wwpi.com

Yuri R Spiro, Publisher/CEO
Steve Schone, Circulation Manager

Articles on tutorials, case studies, lab tests and new products that offer solutions to issues of data accessibility, availablity and protection and network storage.
Cost: $10.00
72 Pages
Frequency: Monthly
Circulation: 64044
ISSN: 1097-5152
Founded in: 1995
Printed in 4 colors on glossy stock

5356 **Studio City**
Resource Central
4126 Pennsylvania Avenue
Suite 3
Kansas City, MO 64111-3018
Tom Weishaar, President

Information on using the multimedia package Hyper Studio, mailed on 3.5 inch disk, 6 times a year. Available in Macintosh and Apple II versions.
Frequency: Bi-Monthly

5357 **Sun Observer**
Publications & Communications
11675 Jollyville Rd
Suite 150
Austin, TX 78759

512-250-9023
800-678-9724; *Fax:* 512-331-3900
pci@pcinews.com; www.pcinews.com

Gary Pittman, CEO/President
Robert Martin, Editor

Journal of news and information devoted to the users of Sun Microsystems.
Cost: $14.95
80 Pages
Founded in: 1980

5358 **Supply Chain Systems Magazine**
Helmers Publishing
174 Concord Street
P O Box 874
Peterborough, NH 03458-1291

603-924-9631; *Fax:* 603-924-7408;
www.scs-mag.com

David Andrewso, Publisher/Editorial
Bill Fahy, Circulation Director
Paul Quinn, Editor/Senior Writer

Educates its readers about the benefits and bast practices of supply chain management in manufacturing and service industries. We educate our readers about how e-business, Enterprises Resource Planning, asset management, data capture, warehouse management and management can be integrated to create effective and efficient supply chain systems.
60 Pages
Frequency: Weekly
Circulation: 53000
Founded in: 1979
Printed in 4 colors on glossy stock

5359 **Synapps**
Synergis Technologies
472 California Rd
Quakertown, PA 18951-2463

215-643-6620; *Fax:* 215-536-9249
marketingsupport@synergis.com;
www.synergis.com

Barbara White, VP

Information for professional management of AutoCAD systems and includes application articles.
Frequency: Quarterly
Circulation: 25000

5360 **Sys Admin**
CMP Media
4601 West 6th Street
Suite B
Lawrence, KS 66046

785-841-1631; *Fax:* 785-841-2047
samag@neodata.com; www.sysadminmag.com

Edwin Rothrock, Publisher
Amber Ankerholz, Editor
Gary Marshall, President
Bob Cucciniello, Marketing
Deirdre Blake, Managing Editor

SYS ADMIN serves the Unix and Linux system administration market.
Cost: $43.00
100 Pages
Frequency: Monthly
Circulation: 29121
Founded in: 1992
Printed in on glossy stock

5361 **Systems Development Management**
Auerbach Publications
535 5th Avenue
Room 806
New York, NY 10017-3610

800-737-8034; *Fax:* 212-297-9176;
www.auerbach-publications.com

Rich O'Hamley, Publisher
Janet Butler, Editor

Technical and managerial information on systems development.
Cost: $495.00
Frequency: Bi-Monthly
Circulation: 1,000
ISSN: 1096-7893
Printed in on matte stock

5362 **Systems Integration**
Reed Business Information
360 Park Ave S
New York, NY 10010-1737

646-746-6400; *Fax:* 646-756-7583
slebris@reedbusiness.com;
www.reedbusiness.com

John Poulin, CEO
Thomas Temin, Editor
James Reed, Owner
Jim Casella, CEO

Covers trade and developments for mini-micro based computer systems.
Cost: $75.00
Frequency: Monthly
Founded in: 1968

5363 **TAAR: The Automated Agency Report**
Automation Management Group
4964 Sundance Square
Boulder, CO 80301-3739

303-581-0525; www.taan.com

Rick Morgan, Editor

Covers trends, developments and news, reviews new and current technology, and offers ideas and profiles on the productivity benefits.
Cost: $175.00
Frequency: Monthly

5364 **Tech Week**
1156 Aster Avenue
Suite B
Sunnyvale, CA 94086

408-249-8300; *Fax:* 408-249-0727

5365 **Techlinks**
3350 Riverwood Parkway
Suite 1900
Atlanta, GA 30339

678-627-8157; *Fax:* 678-627-8159

5366 **Technical Services Quarterly**
Taylor & Francis Group LLC
325 Chestnut St
Suite 800
Philadelphia, PA 19106-2614

215-625-8900
800-354-1420; *Fax:* 215-625-2940
haworthorders@taylorandfrancis.com;
www.taylorandfrancis.com

Kevin Bradley, President

This journal publishes up to the minute information that technical services professionals and paraprofessionals need in order to successfully negotiate changes in the field and take full advantage of automated systems that ultimately make collections more accessible to users.
Frequency: Quarterly

5367 **Technical Support Magazine**
Technical Enterprises
7044 S 13th Street
Oak Creek, WI 53154

414-908-4945; *Fax:* 414-768-8001
customercare@naspa.com; www.naspa.com

Rachael Zimmerman, Editor
Denise Rockhill, President

Provides tips and techniques for MVS, VM and VSE mainframe operating systems and NT environments. It also examines security and system performance, product installation experiences and a host of other related enterprise concerns.
68 Pages
Frequency: Monthly
Circulation: 50,000
Founded in: 1986
Printed in 4 colors on glossy stock

5368 **Technical Training**
American Society for Training & Development
1640 King St
Box 1443
Alexandria, VA 22314-2743

703-683-8100; *Fax:* 703-683-8103
customercare@astd.org; www.astd.org

Tony Bingham, President

Industry trends, technologies and techniques within computer, manufacturing, telecommunications and government industries.
Cost: $59.00
Frequency: Bi-Monthly
Circulation: 11M

5369 **Technology & Learning**
Tech & Learning

1111 Bayhill Drive
Suite 125
San Bruno, CA 94066

650-238-0260; *Fax:* 650-238-0263
techlearning@nbmedia.com;
www.techlearning.com

Allison Knapp, Publisher
Kevin Hogan, Editorial Director
Christine Weiser, Managing Editor

Serves the K-12 education community with practical resources and expert strategies for transforming education through integration of digital technologies. Often used as a professional development tool to help educators across the board get up to speed with the newest technologies and products in order to best prepare students for the global digital workforce.
Frequency: Monthly
Circulation: 81000
Founded in: 1971
Printed in on glossy stock

5370 **Technology and Practice Guide**
ABA Publishing
321 N Clark St
Chicago, IL 60654-7598

312-988-5000
800-285-2221; *Fax:* 312-988-5280
askaba@abanet.org; www.abanet.org

Tommy H Wells Jr, President

Helps law professionals of general practice in making decisions about legal information management and technology.
Cost: $18.00
Frequency: SemiAnnual
Circulation: 13,477

5371 **Techscan: The Managers Guide to Technology**
Richmond Research
266 W 37th St
PO Box 537
New York, NY 10018-6609

212-594-9795
techscan@pipeline.com

Larry Richmond, President

Information and insights on how various new technologies, products and design techniques are used to solve business problems.
Cost: $87.50
Frequency: Monthly
Circulation: 2,500

5372 **Text Technology: The Journal of Computer Text Processing**
McMaster University
1280 Main Street W
Hamilton, On 0

905-525-9140; *Fax:* 905-577-6930
buckleyj@mcmaster.ca
texttechnology.mcmaster.ca

Joanne Buckley, Editor
Edie Rasmussen, Editor

Tips, techniques and programs for TEXT, Icon, Macintosh and other software and word-processing programs, desktop publishing and Internet as they apply to educational applications.
Cost: $45.00
Frequency: Quarterly
Circulation: 800

5373 **Trends in Computing**
Scientific American
415 Madison Ave
New York, NY 10017-7934

212-451-8200
800-333-1199; *Fax:* 212-832-2998
webmaster@sciam.com; www.sciam.com

Gretchen G Teichgraeber, CEO
Elias Arnett, Owner

Targets computer managers and professionals.
Cost: $24.97
Frequency: Annual+
Founded in: 1845

5374 **Unisys World/Network Computing News**
Publications & Communications
505 Cypress Creek Road
Suite B
Cedar Park, TX 78613-1868

512-250-9023; *Fax:* 512-331-3900

Larry Storer, Editor

Dedicated to the users and OEMs of convergent technologies products.
Cost: $48.00
24 Pages
Frequency: Monthly
Founded in: 1983

5375 **Varindustry Products**
VIPublishing
30506 Palos Verdes Drive W
Rancho Palos Verdes, CA 90275-4471
Kenneth Allen, Editor

Focuses on new products and services.
Frequency: Monthly
Founded in: 1990

5376 **Vision Systems Design**
PennWell Publishing Company
98 Spit Brook Rd
5th Floor
Nashua, NH 03062-5737

603-891-0123; *Fax:* 603-891-9294
cholton@pennwell.com; www.pennwell.com

Christine Shaw, VP
Andrew Wilson, Editor
Bonnie Heines, Managing Editor

Each issue discusses the development of leading edge industrial, scientific, medical, military, and aerospace machine vision applications.
Cost: $85.00
Frequency: Monthly
Circulation: 32000
Founded in: 1910
Mailing list available for rent
Printed in 4 colors

5377 **Visual Basic Programmer's Journal**
Fawcette Technical Publications
2600 S El Camino Real
Suite 300
San Mateo, CA 94403-2381

650-378-7100
800-848-5523; *Fax:* 650-853-0230;
www.fawcette.com/vsm/

James Fawcette, President
Tina Fontenot, Marketing
Karin Becker, Associate Publisher
Karen Koenen, Sr. Circulation Director

Provides technical news on how to increase productivity and process applications more efficiently.
Cost: $71.40
Frequency: Monthly
Circulation: 109874
Founded in: 1990

5378 **WINDOWS Magazine**
CMP Publications
600 Community Dr
Manhasset, NY 11030-3810

516-562-5000; *Fax:* 516-562-5995

Scott Wolfe, Publisher

Offers the latest information and updates for the WINDOWS user.

5379 **Wall Street Computer Review**
Miller Freeman Publications
1199 S Belt Line Rd
Suite 100
Coppell, TX 75019-4666

972-906-6500; *Fax:* 972-419-7825

Elizabeth Katz, Publisher
Pavan Sahgal, Editor

For financial and investment professionals and individual investors.
Cost: $5.00
Circulation: 34,000

5380 **Waters**
Waters Information Services
270 Lafayette St
Suite 700
New York, NY 10012-3311

212-925-6990; *Fax:* 212-925-7585
jkotz@riskwaters.com; www.watersinfo.com

Andrew Delaeny, Editor-in-Chief
Phil Albinus, Editor
John Waters, CEO
Farrell McManus, Advertising Manager

Articles on technology applications leading strategic business success, career enhancements and workplace changes.
Cost: $240.00
Frequency: Monthly
Circulation: 20000
Founded in: 1993

5381 **Windows & Dot Net**
Duke Communications International
221 E 29th Street
Loveland, CO 80538

970-663-4700
800-621-1544; *Fax:* 970-667-2321
CorporateCustomerService@penton.com;
www.penton.com

Bart Taylor, Group Publisher
Kim Paulsen, Publisher
David B. Nussbaum, CEO
Cost: $49.95
Frequency: Monthly
Circulation: 100000
Founded in: 1982

5382 **Windows Developer's Journal**
600 Harrison Street
San Francisco, CA 94107

415-947-6000; *Fax:* 415-947-6027;
www.wdj.com

John Dorsey, Editor in Chief
Kerry Gates, Publisher
Holly Vessichelli, Director of Marketing
Deirdre Blake, Managing Editor

Publication for professional Windows developers.
Founded in: 1990

5383 **Windows NT Magazine**
Duke Communications International
221 E 29th Street
PO Box 447
Loveland, CO 80539-447

970-663-4700
800-621-1544; *Fax:* 970-203-2996;
www.winntmag.com

Mark Smith, Publisher
Karen Forster, Manager
John Savill, Manager

Serves technical decision makers using the Windows NT application, and related systems.
Cost: $49.95
Frequency: Monthly
Circulation: 75000

5384 **Windows/DOS Developer's Journal**
R&D Associates
6701 W 121st Street
Suite 310
Overland Park, KS 66209

913-491-0345; *Fax:* 785-841-2624;
www.rndassociates.com

Ron Burk, Editor

Information for professional Windows and DOS programmers.
Cost: $29.00
Frequency: Monthly
Circulation: 22000
Founded in: 1996

5385 **Windowspro Magazine**
Ziff Davis Publishing Company
500 Unicorn Park Drive
Woburn, MA 01801

781-938-2600; *Fax:* 781-938-2626;
www.windowspro.com

Jason Young, Publisher
Jacquelyn Gavron, Editor-in-Chief

Serves technology-experts responsible for Windows NT based support. Includes technologies, products, solutions, and how-to instructions.
Frequency: Monthly
Circulation: 150,000

5386 **Wired**
Wired News
520 3rd St
1st Floor
San Francisco, CA 94107-6805

415-276-8400
800-769-4733; *Fax:* 415-276-8500
info@wired.com; www.wired.com

Evan Hansen, Editor-in-Chief
Jeremy Barna, Production Manager
Alison Macondray, General Manager
Drew Schutte, Publisher

Focuses on people and ideas behind digital technology.
Frequency: Monthly
Circulation: 305097

5387 **Workstation News**
Data Base Publications
9390 Research Blvd
Suite 300
Austin, TX 78759-7374

512-418-9590; *Fax:* 512-418-8165;
www.bancvue.com

Gabe Krajicek, CEO

Aimed at workstation users and volume buyers.
Frequency: Monthly
Founded in: 1990

Trade Shows

5388 **AAAI National Conference**
American Association for Artificial Intelligence
445 Burgess Drive
Menlo Park, CA 94025-3442

650-328-3123
800-968-1738; *Fax:* 650-321-4457;
www.aaai.org

Keri Vasser Harvey, Senior Conference Coordinator
Corina Anzaldo, Conference Coordinator

The conference provides a forum for a broad range of topics, including knowledge representation and automated reasoning, planning, machine learning and data mining, autonomous agents, robotics and machine perception, probabilistic inference, constraint satisfaction, search and game playing, natural language processing, neural networks, multi-agent systems, computational game theory and cognitive modeling.
1.2M Attendees
Frequency: July
Founded in: 1980

5389 **ACT Management of Change Conference**
American Council for Technology
3040 Williams Drive
Suite 610
Fairfax, VA 22031

703-208-4800; *Fax:* 703-208-4805
act-iac@actgov.org; www.actgov.org

Kelly Olsen, Conference Director

For government and industry executives who are interested in unleashing the tremendous innovation potential of their organizations. It will explore the processes and effects of creative ideas, experiments and ventures that hold the promise of a better and safer America.
Frequency: June

5390 **AIA Business Conference**
Automated Imaging Association
900 Victors Way
Suite 140
Ann Arbor, MI 48108

734-994-6088
800-994-6099; *Fax:* 734-994-3338
jburnstein@robotics.org;
www.machinevisiononline.org

Jeff Burnstein, Executive Director

The annual AIA Business Conference has become the machine vision industry's most important networking event. The Conference gathers top industry executives to do business with their peers and hear presentations on issues affecting the global economy in general and the machine vision industry specifically.
300+ Attendees
Frequency: February

5391 **AIIM Annual Expo Conference & Exposition**
Association for Information and Image Management
1100 Wayne Avenue
Suite 1100
Silver Spring, MD 20910

301-587-8202
800-477-2446; *Fax:* 301-587-2711
aiim@aiim.org; www.aiim.org

Jan Andersson, Chair
Robert Zagami, Vice Chair

The largest enterprise content & document management conference and exposition showcasing the technologies and solutions that provide intelligence behind information. For more than 50 years, this annual event attracts business professionals and executive management seeking the latest technologies.
Frequency: May

5392 **AIM Summit**
AIM Global
One Landmark North, 20399 Route 19
Suite 203
Cranberry Township, PA 16066

724-934-4470; *Fax:* 724-934-4495
info@aimglobal.org; www.aimglobal.org
Social Media: Facebook, Twitter, LinkedIn

Mary Lou Bosco, Chief Operating Officer
Chuck Evanhoe, President & CEO
Cynthia Troup, Communciations & Marketing

An opportunity for experts and professionals in automatic identification and data capture to discuss and share ideas and trends.
Frequency: Annual
Founded in: 1972

5393 **AMIA Annual Symposium**
American Medical Informatics Association
4915 St Elmo Avenue
Suite 401
Bethesda, MD 20814

301-657-1291; *Fax:* 301-657-1296
mail@amia.org; www.amia.org

Charles P Friedman, Meeting Chairman
Karen Greenwood, Executive Vice President

Features an outstanding program of scientific papers, posters, tutorials and other educational events that provide information about cutting-edge work in medical informatics.
2000 Attendees
Frequency: Annual/October
Founded in: 1977

5394 **ARMA International Conference & Expo**
ARMA International
11880 College Blvd
Suite 450
Overland Park, KS 66215

913-341-3808
800-422-2762; *Fax:* 913-341-3742
hq@arma.org; www.arma.org/conference

Carol Jorgenson, Meetings/Education Coordinator
Wanda Wilson, Senior Manager, Conferences
Elizabeth Zlitni, Exposition Manager

Conference, seminar, workshop, banquet, award ceremony and 175 exhibits of micrographics, optical disk, automated document storage and retrieval systems and more technology of interest to information professionals.
3500 Attendees
Frequency: Annual
Founded in: 1956

5395 **ASIS&T Annual Meeting**
American Society for Information Science & Techn.
1320 Fenwick Lane
Suite 510
Silver Spring, MD 20910

301-495-0900; *Fax:* 301-495-0810
asis@asis.org; www.asis.org

Richard B Hill, Executive Director
Nancy Roderer, President

Focus on the diversity of perspectives and insights from all those participating in the information science and technology community, as they generate innovative ideas, define theoretical concepts or work out the nuts and bolts of implementing well-tested ideas in new ways and in new settings.
Frequency: Annual/Oct-Nov

5396 **ASPE Annual Meeting**
American Society for Precision Engineering

PO Box 10826
Raleigh, NC 27605-0826

919-839-8444; *Fax:* 919-839-8039;
www.aspe.net

Erika Deutsch Layne, Meetings Manager
Thomas A Dow, Chairman

Offering the latest in precision engineering research through presentations from national and international speakers. Participants in the Annual Meeting have the opportunity to exchange ideas with internationally renowned experts in the field.
Frequency: Annual/Oct-Nov

5397 AWWA Annual Conference and Exposition
American Water Works Association
6666 W Quincy Avenue
Denver, CO 80235

303-794-7711
800-926-7337; *Fax:* 303-347-0804
info@montana-awwa.org; www.awwa.org

Nilaksh Kothari, President
Jack W. Hoffbuhr, Executive Director

The source of knowledge and information for water professionals who work to improve the quality and supply of drinking water in North America and beyond. You'll learn from industry experts in the field, hear about cutting edge research and exceptional best practices, and have the opportunity to ask questions, seek advice, and interact with other water professionals regarding both universal topics and items specifically focused to meet your needs.
Frequency: Annual/June

5398 AWWA Information Management & Technology Conference
American Water Works Association
6666 W Quincy Avenue
Denver, CO 80235

303-794-7711
800-926-7337; *Fax:* 303-347-0804;
www.awwa.org

Nilaksh Kothari, President
Jack W. Hoffbuhr, Executive Director

This event is North America's premier conference in the area of water supply information management technology and applications for the water and wastewater industry.
Frequency: March

5399 Association For Services Management World Conference Expo
AFSM International
11031 Via Frontera
Suite A
San Diego, CA 92127

239-275-7887
800-333-9786; *Fax:* 239-275-0794
info@afsmi.org; www.afsmi.org

John Schoenewald, Executive Director
Jb Wood, President/Ceo

World's largest gathering of executives in the services and support industry.
Frequency: October

5400 Association of College Unions International Conference
Association of College Unions International
120 W 7th Street
One City Centre, Suite 200
Bloomington, IN 47404-3925

812-245-2284; *Fax:* 812-245-6710
acui@acui.org; www.acui.org

Rich Steele, President
Marsha Herman-Betzen, Executive Director

Educational programs, speakers, and exhibits and the opportunity for attendees to connect and network.
Frequency: April
Founded in: 1914

5401 Autodesk Expo
AEC Systems International/Penton Media
1300 E 9th Street
Cleveland, OH 44114

800-451-1196; *Fax:* 610-280-7106
sales@acesystems.com; www.acesystems.com

Philip McKay, Manager

Highlights AutoCAD and related products from Autodesk and third party developers. 500 exhibits.
20M Attendees
Frequency: May

5402 BDPA Annual Technology Conference
National BDPA
9500 Arena Drive
Suite 106
Largo, MD 20774

301-584-3135; *Fax:* 301-560-8300
info@bdpa.org; www.bdpa.org
Social Media: Facebook, Twitter, LinkedIn

Earl Pace, Founder
Mike Williams, President
Pamela Mathews, Vice President
Teresa Williams, Vice President, Member Services
Founded in: 1975

5403 Bentley MicroStation Mail
AEC Systems International/Penton Media
1300 E 9th Street
Cleveland, OH 44114

800-451-1196; *Fax:* 610-280-7106
sales@acesystems.com; www.acesystems.com

Philip McKay, Manager

Showcases a comprehensive line-up of intergrated design, facility management and GIS solutions built around MicroStation software. 500 exhibits.
20M Attendees
Frequency: May

5404 CALICO Annual Conference
Computer Assisted Language Instruction Consortium
Southwest Texas State University
116 Centennial Hall
San Marcos, TX 78666

512-245-1417; *Fax:* 512-245-8298
info@calico.org; www.calico.org

Robert Fischer, Executive Director
Esther Horn, Manager

Providing a forum for discussions of state-of-the-art educational technology and its applications to the more effective teaching and learning of languages. The symposia accommodate workshops, papers, demonstrations, panels, and special interest groups for participants at all levels of expertise.
450 Attendees
Frequency: May

5405 CLA World Computer and Internet Law Congress Conference
Computer Law Association
3028 Javier Road
Suite 402
Fairfax, VA 22031

703-560-7747; *Fax:* 703-207-7028;
www.cla.org

Barbara Fieser, Executive Director

This conference will provide you with proven strategies and best practices that will enable you to effectively address your existing clients' IT-related challenges and problems and seek out clients whom you can assist with knowledge you will gain from the conference.
2000+ Attendees
Frequency: May

5406 CSI Annual Computer Securtiy Conference & Exhibition
CMP Media/Computer Security Institute Services
600 Community Drive
Manhasset, NY 11030

516-562-5000
866-271-8529; *Fax:* 818-487-4550;
www.cmp.com

Jennifer Stevens, Conference Manager
Kimber Heald, Registration Manager
Annette Campo, Manager

The exhibition features 150 security vendors, from the industry leaders to the up-and coming, displaying the latest security technologies.
950 Attendees
Frequency: November

5407 CUMREC
Educause
4772 Walnut Street
Suite 206
Boulder, CO 80301-2538

303-449-4430; *Fax:* 303-440-0461
info@educause.edu; www.educause.edu

Beverly Williams, Director of Conference Activities
Lisa Gesner, Assistant Director of Marketing

Higher education administrative technology conference. The purpose of CUMREC is to provide a forum for higher education professionals to share their expertise and experiences with computer systems in our ever changing world of technology. The CUMREC annual conference, founded in 1956, is devoted to promoting the understanding and use of information technology in higher education.
3M Attendees
Frequency: May
Founded in: 1956

5408 Comdex Spring and Fall Shows
MediaLive International
795 Folsom Street
6th Floor
San Francisco, CA 94107-1243

415-905-2300; *Fax:* 415-905-2FAX;
www.medialiveinternational.com

Eric Faurot, VP
Marco Pardi, Exhibit Sales

COMDEX is the global marketplace for the IT industry. Buyers and sellers from around the world converge to learn how best to use technology to solve their business challenges and remain competitive. COMDEX is where hardware manufacturers, software vendors and service providers launch new products, where thought-leaders discuss industry trends, and where the media reports on the latest in the IT industry and considers its future.
100M+ Attendees
Frequency: November

5409 CompTIA Annual Breakaway Conference
CompTIA
1815 S Meyers Road
Suite 300
Oakbrook Terrace, IL 60181-5228

630-678-8300; *Fax:* 630-678-8384
breakaway@comptia.org; www.comptia.org

John A Venator, President/CEO
Karen Lukasik, VP Operations
Laurel Chivari, VP Marketing & Communications

Rachel Fabro, Public Relations Specialist
Robert Kramer, VP Public Policy

The annual CompTIA Breakaway conference is the computing industry's premier partnering event. The conference focuses on business-building solutions, networking forums, and the latest industry trends and technologies.
Frequency: Annual/August

5410 Design Automation Conference
Design Automation
5405 Spine Road
Suite 102
Boulder, CO 80301

303-530-4333; *Fax:* 303-530-4334
feedback@dac.com; www.dac.com

Kevin Lepine, Co-President
Lee Wood, Co-President
Nannette Jordan, Registration Coordinator

The premier Electronic Design Automation (EDA) and silicon solution event. DAC features over 50 technical sessions covering the latest in design methodologies and EDA tool developments, and an Exhibition and Demo Suite area with over 250 of the leading EDA, silicon, and IP Providers.
11M+ Attendees
Frequency: June

5411 ESRI Southwest Users Group Conference
Southwest Users Group
18727 Nadal Street
Canyon Country, CA 91351

www.swuggis.org

Interface with ESRI users to learn about the latest technologies and discuss ESRI software-related topics.
Frequency: Annual

5412 Embedded Systems Conference
CMP Media Headquarters
600 Community Drive
Manhasset, NY 11030

516-562-5000; www.esconline.com

Christian Fahlen, Senior Conference Manager
Ardis Gough, Conference Manager
Kara Pistochini, Conference Assistant
Annette Campo, Manager

The only conference to focus on the art and science of microcomptroller and microprocessor based development, covering the needs of real-time software engineers.
2.7M Attendees
Frequency: September
Mailing list available for rent

5413 FOSE
Post Newsweek Tech Media
10 G Street NE
Suite 500
Washington, DC 20002-4228

202-772-2500
800-791-FOSE; *Fax:* 202-772-2511;
www.ntpshow.com

Lauri Nichols, Trade Show Operations Manager
Melanie Woodfolk, Show Marketing Manager
David Greene, President

Largest information technology exposition serving the government marketplace.
4000 Attendees
Frequency: April

5414 Graph Expo & Convention
Graphic Arts Show Company
1899 Preston White Drive
Reston, VA 20191

703-264-7200; *Fax:* 703-620-9187
info@gasc.org; www.gasc.org

Kelly Kilga, Conference/Show Operations Director
Lilly Kinney, Conference Manager

The largest, most comprehensive prepress, printing, converting and digital equipment trade show and conference in the Americas.
40000 Attendees
Frequency: October

5415 Graphics of the Americas
Printing Association of Florida
6275 Hazeltine National Drive
Orlando, FL 32822

407-240-8009
800-331-0461; *Fax:* 407-240-8333;
www.flprint.org

Anne Gaither, Convention Director
Michael H Streibig, Staff Executive

We are the second largest Graphic Arts and Converting show in America. We give you two vital markets — southeast US and Latin America: Mexico, South America, Central America and the Caribbean. Our 28 year track record reflects our success with both exhibitors and show visitors.
20000 Attendees
Frequency: Feb

5416 Healthcare Information and Management Systems Society Conference
Healthcare Information and Management Systems
230 E Ohio
Suite 500
Chicago, IL 60611-3269

312-664-4467; *Fax:* 312-664-6143
kmalone@himss.org; www.himss.org

Karen Malone, Director of Meetings
John Daniels, Vice President

An opportunity to learn the latest industry intelligence, find solutions to your most pressing professional challenges, and network with your peers. Pre-conference workshops and education session, see industry newsmakers, explore the latest technologies in more than 600 exhibits and earn continuing education credit and certification.
20000 Attendees
Frequency: February

5417 IAAP International Convention and Education Forum
Int'l Association of Administrative Professionals
10502 NW Ambassador Drive
Kansas City, MO 16415

816-891-6600; *Fax:* 816-891-9118
tgoodall@iaap-hq.org; www.iaap-hq.org

Inge Hafkemeyer, Convention/Meetings/Exhibit Manager
Don Bretthauer, Executive Director

An opportunity to showcase your product or service to this important audience. Office Expo exhibitors include major office product manufacturers, publishers, software vendors, staffing firms, gift suppliers, paper companies, and many more.
2000 Attendees
Frequency: July

5418 IAPP Privacy and Data Security Academy Expo
Internet Alliance
1111 19th Street NW
Suite 1180
Washington, DC 20035-5782

202-284-4380; *Fax:* 202-955-8081;
www.internetalliance.my

Emily T Hackett, Executive Director
Katy Caldwell, California Policy Director

The conference will showcase the latest thinking on important privacy issues in healthcare, financial services, technology and marketing. Attendees will gain a deeper understanding of strategies and tools required to meet today's privacy challenges.
1000 Attendees
Frequency: October
Founded in: 1981

5419 IEEE SoutheastCon
IEEE Meeting & Conference Management (MCM)
445 Hoes Lane
Piscataway, NJ 08854

732-562-3878
800-678-4333; *Fax:* 732-971-1203
conference-services@ieee.org; www.ieee.org

A student conference, technical conference, and business meeting.
800 Attendees
Frequency: Annual

5420 IRMA Annual Conference
Information Resources Management Association
701 E Chocolate Avenue
Suite 200
Hershey, PA 17033

717-533-8879; *Fax:* 717-533-8661
member@irma-international.org;
www.irma-international.org

Mehdi Khosrow-Pour PhD, President
Sherif Kamel PhD, Communications Director
Gerald Grant PhD, IRMA Doctoral Symposium Director
Lech Janczewski PhD, IRMA World Representative Director
Paul Chalekian, IRMA United States Representative

Provides forums for researchers and practitioners to share leading-edge knowledge in the global resource information management area. Various seminars, conventions and conferences, and other training programs are offered by IRMA throughout the year.
Frequency: May

5421 IS&T/SPIE Annual Symposium Electronic Imaging
International Society for Optical Engineering
1000 20th Street
PO Box 10
Bellingham, WA 98227-6705

360-763-3290; *Fax:* 360-647-1445
customerservice@spie.org; www.spie.org

Giordano B Beretta, Director
Robert L Stevenson, Co-Director
Eugene Arthurs, Executive Director
Amy Nelson, Manager

Electronic Imaging's top-notch technical program gathers the world's prominent experts to discuss and push the forefront of imaging technology and it's applications.
1200 Attendees
Frequency: Annual/January

5422 ISACA International Conference
Information Systems Audit & Control Association

3701 Algonquin Road
Suite 1010
Rolling Meadows, IL 60008

847-253-1545; *Fax:* 847-253-1443
conference@isaca.org; www.isaca.org

Sandy Arens, Registration

The International Conference has long been recognised throughout the world for providing in-depth coverage of the leading-edge technical and managerial issues facing IT governance, control, security and assurance professionals.
Frequency: June

5423 **Industrial Virtual Reality**
Reed Exhibitions
US Consumer Show Division
225 Wyman Street
Waltham, MA 02451

781-622-8616; *Fax:* 781-622-8042
inquiry@sport.reedexpo.com;
www.reedexpo.com

Elizabeth Hitchcock, International Sales

The first trade show focusing on industrial applications of virtual reality and tele-existence.
Frequency: June

5424 **Information Technology Week**
Information Week/CMP Media
600 Community Drive
Manhasset, NY 11030

516-562-5000; *Fax:* 516-562-5036;
www.informationweek.com

Lisa Monvigner, Events Associate Director
Stephanie Iannuzzi, Sr. Marketing Manager
Michael Friedenberg, Publisher

A forum for computer technicians and professionals.
Frequency: May
Mailing list available for rent

5425 **International Conference on Methods for Surveying Hard-To-Reach Populations**
American Association for Public Opinion Research
111 Deer Lake Road
Suite 100
Deerfield, IL 60015

847-205-2651; *Fax:* 847-480-9282;
www.aapor.org
Social Media: Facebook, Twitter, LinkedIn

Paul Lavrakas, President
Rob Santos, VP/President-Elect
Scott Keeter, Secretary-Treasurer

The conference will address both the statistical and survey design aspects of including hard to reach groups. Researchers will report findings from censuses and surveys and other research related to the identification, definition, measurement, and methodologies for surveying and enumerating undercounted populations.
850 Attendees
Frequency: Annual
Mailing list available for rent: 1000 names at $400 per M

5426 **International Conference on Software Engineering**
Software Engineering Institute
Carnegie Mellon University
Pittsburgh, PA 15213-3890

412-687-7700; *Fax:* 412-268-6257;
www.sei.cmu.edu

Paul Nielsen, CEO
Clyde Chittister, COO
Douglas Schmidt, Deputy Dir Research

ICSE is the premier software engineering conference, providing a forum for researchers, practitioners and educators to present and discuss the most recent innovations, trends, experiences, and concerns in the field of software engineering.
800 Attendees
Frequency: May

5427 **International Consumer Electronics Show (CES)**
Consumer Technology Association
1919 South Eads Street
Arlington, VA 22202

703-907-7600
866-858-1555; *Fax:* 703-907-7675
cta@cta.tech; www.cta.tech

Gary Shapiro, President & CEO
David Hagan, Chairman

The largest annual consumer technology tradeshow offering a wealth of opportunity for your business.
Frequency: Annual

5428 **International Spectrum MultiValue Conference & Exhibition**
International Spectrum
715 J Street
Suite 301
San Diego, CA 92101-2478

619-515-9930; *Fax:* 619-515-9933
editor@intl-spectrum.com;
www.intl-spectrum.com

Monica Giobbi, President
Gus Giobbi, Chairman

A conference and exhibition showcasing MultiValue products and services.
6M Attendees
Frequency: March

5429 **Interop Conference**
Interop
C/O MediaLive International
795 Folsom Street, 6th Floor
San Francisco, CA 94107-1243

415-905-2300; *Fax:* 415-905-2FAX;
www.interop.com

Jennifer Sioteco, Sr. Operations Manager
Lenny Heymann, General Manager

Provides you an overview of the robust conference offerings, workshops and tutorials, and special programs.
60000 Attendees

5430 **Java One Conference**
Sun Microsystems
4150 Network Circle
Santa Clara, CA 95054
650-960-1300
866-382-7151; www.java.sun.com

Jonathan Schwartz, President/CEO
Anil Gadre, Chief Executive Officer

Gain knowledge and Java technology education directly from Sun Microsystems, Inc. and other industry leaders. Get expert advice on solving the most common Java challenges. Benefit from four full days of content. Choose from hundreds of technical sessions and test drive real-world Java technology solutions.
5000 Attendees
Frequency: June

5431 **MacWorld Conference & Expo**
MacWorld 2010
PO Box 3221
Boston, MA 02241
805-290-1341
800-645-EXPO; *Fax:* 805-654-1676
macworld2010@rcsreg.com;
www.macworld.com/expo

Annual show with hundreds of exhibitors of Mac equipment, supplies and services. Provides education, networking and thought leadership that professionals and consumers alike need to get the most from their technology investment.
65000 Attendees
Frequency: Annual

5432 **Marketechnics**
Food Marketing Institute
2345 Crystal Drive
Suite 800
Arlington, VA 22202

202-452-8444; *Fax:* 202-429-4519;
www.fmi.org

Tim Hammonds, CEO

Provides a once-a-year opportunity to hear, see and discuss new technologies and their impact on the supply chain, store operations and marketing/merchandising strategies.
7000 Attendees
Frequency: Jan-Feb

5433 **NACCB Annual Conference**
National Association of Computer Consultants
1420 King Street
Suite 610
Alexandria, VA 22314

703-838-2050; *Fax:* 703-838-3610
susan@naccb.org; www.naccb.org

Susan Donohoe, Director of Programs/Public Policy
Beth Berman, Program & Administrative Coord.

The only educational, networking, and leadership event exclusively for the IT Services Industry. The NACCB conference provides a platform where IT services firms connect to address issues and solutions most affecting business today.
Frequency: Annual/November
Founded in: 1988

5434 **National Ergonomics Conference and Exposition**
Continental Exhibitions
370 Lexington Avenue
Suite 1407
New York, NY 10017-6503

212-370-5005; *Fax:* 212-370-5699
information@ergoexpo.com;
www.ergoexpo.com

Larry L Elyea, Executive Program Director
Pedro Caceres, Senior VP of Operations

The NECE maximizes your time and effort by providing direct contact with industry leaders that comprise our speaker faculty, direct contact with leading providers of ergonomics products and services, and direct contact with your peers at networking receptions during the exposition.
Frequency: Nov-Dec

5435 **Object World Conference**
Object Management Group/IDG Management
111 Speen Street
PO Box 9107
Framingham, MA 01701-9514

800-225-4698; *Fax:* 508-872-8237;
www.omg.com

Mary DeCristoforo, Conference Director
David Elliott, Exhibit Sales Manager

An annual conference sponsored by the Object Management Group and IDG Management Group to advance object-oriented technology in commercial software development. The event features tutorials and conference sessions.
6.5M Attendees
Frequency: October

5436 **Optical Fiber Communications Conference**
Optical Society of America

2010 Massachusetts Avenue NW
Washington, DC 20036

202-238-8130; *Fax:* 202-416-6140
info@ofcconference.org; www.ofcnfoec.org

Colleen Morrison, Media Relations Director
Melissa Russell, Exhibit Sales Director
Colleen Morrison, Media Relations Manager
Angela Stark, Director Communications

Provides leading edge, peer reviewed educational programming along with a high powered, commerce driven exhibition. This unique combination attracts the field's most progressive professionals and exhibiting companies.
13111 Attendees
Frequency: March
Founded in: 1916

5437 PCB Design Conference West
UP Media Group
2400 Lake Park Dr Se
Suite 440
Smyrna, GA 30080-7695

678-589-8800; *Fax:* 678-589-8850
askarbek@upmediagroup.com;
www.pcbwest.com

Alyson Skarbek, Show Operations Manager
Andy Shaughnessy, Conference Chairperson
Brooke Anglin, Exhibit Sales Manager

The first and only conference 100% dedicated to the needs of the PCB designer.
750 Attendees
Frequency: March

5438 PIMA Leadership Conference
Paper Industry Management Association
4700 W Lake Avenue
Glenview, IL 60025-1485

847-375-6860
877-527-5973; *Fax:* 732-460-7333
info@pimaweb.org; www.pima-online.org

Carol Waugh, Meetings Manager
Julie Weir, Account Manager
Mary Cornell, Account Manager

Three-day conference to bring together IT and process control professionals from around the world to share their knowledge of information technology in the pulp and paper industry and to promote systems applications. The only IT conference planned for and by IT professionals.
500 Attendees
Frequency: Annual/June

5439 Pacific Telecommunications Council Conference: PTC Conference
Pacific Telecommunications Council
2454 S Beretania Street
3rd Floor
Honolulu, HI 96826-1596

808-941-3789; *Fax:* 808-944-4874
snakama@ptc.org; www.ptc.org

Sharon Nakama, Conference Director
Dolores Fung, Conference/Seminar Coordinator
Claudine Naruse, Conference/Seminar Coordinator
Justin Riel, Conference/Seminar Assistant

Provides an opportunity to learn and to analyze current issues. Registrants from the ranks of senior corporate officers and management, experts from law and consulting firms, noted analysts and scholars, and technical experts provide a wide diversity of ideas.
1500 Attendees
Frequency: January

5440 SC: High Performance Networking & Computing
Hall-Erickson
98 E Naperville Road
Westmont, IL 60559

630-639-9185; *Fax:* 630-434-1216;
www.sc-conference.org

William Kramer, Conference General Chair
Barbara Horner-Miller, Conference Deputy Chair

The world's leading conference on high performance computing, networking and storage. Representatives from many technical communities together to exchange ideas, celebrate past successes and plan for the future.
6000 Attendees
Frequency: Annual/November
Founded in: 1988

5441 SCSC: Summer Simulation Multiconference
Society for Modeling and Simulation International
PO Box 17900
San Diego, CA 92177-7900

858-277-3888; *Fax:* 858-277-3930
scs@scs.org; www.scs.org

Steve Branch, Executive Director
Mark Yen, Event Coordinator

Focusing on Innovative Technologies for Simulation this year. Modeling and Simulation is a very critical area for supporting Research and Development as well as competitiveness worldwide; new technologies are enabling new use of M&S and increasing its impact in new areas; SCSC provides an international forum for presenting the state of the art in the international simulation community.
600 Attendees
Frequency: July

5442 SID International Symposium, Seminar and Exhibition
Society for Information Display
610 S 2nd Street
San Jose, CA 95112

408-977-1013; *Fax:* 408-977-1531
office@sid.org; www.sid.org

Mark Goldfab, Conference Coordinator
Bill Klein, Symposium Coordinator
Kate Dickie, Exhibition/Sponsorship Sales Mgr.
Danielle Rocco, Exhibition/Sponsorship Coordinator
Jenny Needham, Manager

The premier international gathering of scientists, engineers, manufacturers and users in the electronic display industry. The event provides access to a wide range of technology and applications from high-definition flat-panel displays using both emissive and liquid-crystal technology to the latest in OLED displays and large-area projection-display systems.
6000 Attendees
Frequency: May
Founded in: 1962

5443 SIGGRAPH Conference
Association for Computing Machinery
2 Penn Plaza
Suite 701
New York, NY 10121-0701

212-626-0500
800-342-6626; *Fax:* 212-944-1318
acmhelp@acm.org; www.siggraph.org

Dino Schweitzer, Conference Chief Staff Executive
James Mohler, Conference Chairperson

The annual conference and its year round initiatives provide unique crossroads for a diverse community of researchers, developers, creators, educators and practitioners. Our continuing mission is to be the premier annual conference on leading edge theory and practice of computer graphics and interactive techniques, inspiring progress through education, excellence, and interaction.
50000 Attendees
Frequency: July-August

5444 SMC: Spring Simulation Multiconference
Society for Modeling and Simulation International
PO Box 17900
San Diego, CA 92177-7900

858-277-3888; *Fax:* 858-277-3930
sbranch@scs.org; www.scs.org

Drew Hamilton, Conference General Chair
Steve Branch, Executive Director

Bringing together eight symposia and providing a forum for academia, industry, business and government covering a wide variety of disciplines and domains that utilize modeling and simulation to present their work in a unique setting.
400 Attendees
Frequency: April

5445 Seybold Seminars
MediaLive International
795 Folsom Street
6th Floor
San Francisco, CA 94107-1243

415-905-2300; *Fax:* 415-905-2FAX;
www.medialiveinternational.com

Jackie Rees, Program Director
Cynthia Wood, Conference Content Director

Four focused conferences; Chicago, New York, San Francisco, that will deliver new solutions, emerging technologies and real world examples of businesses that have successfully implemented new digital publishing workflow and content management strategies.
21000 Attendees
Frequency: Sept, Oct, Nov

5446 TAWPI Annual Forum & Exposition
Association for Work Process Improvement
185 Devonshire Street
Suite M102
Boston, MA 02110-1407

617-426-1167
800-998-2974; *Fax:* 617-521-8675
info@tawpi.org; www.tawpi.org

Sandra Savage, Conference Planner
Jenny Star, Director Business Development
Tonya Gregoire, Director Business Development

Leading event for technology and management professionals in data capture, mail, imaging, payment/remittance, document and forms processing.
1500 Attendees
Frequency: July

5447 TechNet International
Armed Forces Communications and Electronics Assn
4400 Fair Lakes Court
Fairfax, VA 22033

703-631-6100
800-336-4583; *Fax:* 703-631-6405;
www.afcea.org

Kent Schneider, President/CEO
Becky Nolan, Executive VP
John A Dubia, Executive VP

An annual event representing top government, industry and military professionals in the fields of communications, electronics, intelligence, information systems, imaging and multi-media.
Frequency: Annual/June

5448 **UNITE Golden Opportunities Annual Technology Conference**
UNITE
21523 Harper Avenue
St Clair Shores, MI 48080-2209
586-443-6901; *Fax:* 586-443-6902
cathmurphy39@hotmail.com; www.unite.org
Catherine Murphy, Conference Chair
George Gray, Conference Vice Chair
Held in mid October. Development and use of information technology. Pre-registration for full conference attendees: $1,095; daily attendees: $740.
Frequency: October

5449 **Usenix Annual Technical Conference**
Usenix
2560 9th Street
Suite 215
Berkeley, CA 94710-2573
510-528-8649; *Fax:* 510-548-5738
conference@usenix.org; www.usenix.org
Jennifer Joost, Conference Manager
Devon Shaw, Administrative Assistant
Andrew Gustafson, Administrative Assistant
Dan Klein, Director
John Arrasjid, Secretary
A 5 day training running alongside a 3 day conference program filled with the latest research, security breakthroughs, sessions devoted to Linux and open source software and practical approaches to the puzzles and problems you wrestle with.
3M Attendees
Frequency: June

5450 **Vue/Point Conference**
Graphic Arts Show Company
1899 Preston White Drive
Reston, VA 20191
703-264-7200; *Fax:* 703-620-9187
info@gasc.org; www.gasc.org
Kelly Kilga, Conference/Show Operations Director
Lilly Kinney, Administrative Assistant
Erin Omwake, Administrative Assistant
Deborah Vieder, Director of Communications
The only interactive, peer-to-peer conference event in the graphic communications industry.
Frequency: April

5451 **WMC: Western Simulation Multiconference**
Society for Modeling and Simulation International
PO Box 17900
San Diego, CA 92177-7900
858-277-3888; *Fax:* 858-277-3930
sbranch@scs.org; www.scs.org
Steve Branch, Executive Director
Mark Yen, Events & Publications Coordinator
15 booths of technical and scientific papers.
300+ Attendees
Frequency: January

5452 **Westec Exposition**
Society of Manufacturing Engineers
One SME Drive
Dearborn, MI 48121
313-425-3000
800-733-4763; *Fax:* 408-428-9600
service@sme.org; www.sme.org
Ana Christiansen, Exposition Marketing
Leslie Schade, Exhibitor Services
The West Coast's definitive manufacturing event, showcasing crucial breakthroughs in machine tools, production methods, materials and management strategies. More than 450 exhibitors.
1500 Attendees
Frequency: Annual

5453 **Western Conference & Exposition**
Armed Forces Communications and Electronics Assn
4400 Fair Lakes Court
Fairfax, VA 22033
703-631-1397; *Fax:* 703-818-9177
gmcgovern@afcea.org; www.afcea.org
Gina McGovern, Patron/Sponsor Director
Kim Couranz, Senior Vice President
Booz Hamilton, Senior Vice President
Largest event on the West Coast for communications, electronics, intelligence, information systems, imaging, military weapon systems, aviation, shipbuilding, and more. Featuring the people you need to hear from, the products and services you need to do your job, and the critical issues of today and tomorrow.
7000 Attendees
Frequency: January

Directories & Databases

5454 **ACM-SIGGRAPH Computer Graphics Education Directory**
Association for Computing Machinery
1515 Broadway
17th Floor
New York, NY 10036-8901
212-869-7440
800-342-6626; *Fax:* 212-944-1318
acmhelp@acm.org; www.acm.org
Lynn D'Addesio-Kraus, Production Manager
Roma Simon, Associate Director
Robert Okajima, Associate Director
Alain Chesnais, Founder
Liliana Cintron, Administrative Assistant
Compiled to create a unified site where educators, students, and others can find information about computer graphics educational programs, computer graphics curriculum, computer graphics text.
Cost: $20.00
0 Pages
Frequency: Biennial

5455 **ARMA International's Buyers Guide**
ARMA International
11880 College Blvd
Suite 450
Overland Park, KS 66215
913-341-3808
800-422-2762; *Fax:* 913-341-3742
hq@arma.org; www.arma.org/conference
75-100 companies listed. Free.

5456 **AV Market Place**
Information Today
143 Old Marlton Pike
Medford, NJ 08055-8750
609-654-6266
800-300-9868; *Fax:* 609-654-4309
custserv@infotoday.com; www.infotoday.com
Thomas H Hogan, President
Roger R Bilboul, Chairman Of The Board
The complete business directory of audio, audio visual, computer systems, film, video, and programming with industry yellow pages. The only guide needed to find more than 7,500 companies that create, apply or distribute AV equipment and services for business, education, science, and government.
Cost: $199.95
1700 Pages
Frequency: February
ISBN: 1-573871-87-7

5457 **CD-ROM Databases**
Worldwide Videotex
PO Box 3273
Boyton Beach, FL 33424
561-738-2276
markedit@juno.com; www.wvpubs.com
Contains information on currently marketed databases available on CD-ROM.
Frequency: Directory

5458 **CD-ROMs in Print**
Thomson Gale
PO Box 09187
Detroit, MI 48209-0187
248-699-4253
800-877-4253; *Fax:* 248-699-8049;
www.galegroup.com
Patrick C Sommers, President
Rich Foley, Account Manager
Judy Roberts, Account Manager
Maria Moffre, Product Manager
International guide to CD-ROM, Cdi, 3Do, Mmcd, Cd32, Multimedia, Laserdisc and Electronic Products.
Cost: $205.00
Circulation: 13,000
ISBN: 0-787671-33-9

5459 **Computer Database**
Information Access Company
362 Lakeside Drive
Foster City, CA 94404-1171
650-378-5200
800-227-8431; *Fax:* 650-378-5368;
www.iacnet.com
Robert Howells, President
Comprehensive database offering over 500,000 citations, with abstracts, to literature from over 150 trade journals, industry newsletters and platform-specific publications covering the computer, telecommunications and electronics industries.

5460 **Computer Industry Almanac**
Computer Industry Almanac
304 W White Oak
Arlington Heights, IL 60005-3201
847-758-3687; *Fax:* 847-758-3686;
www.c-i-a.com
Egil Juliussen, Editor
Karen Petska-Juliussen, Editor
A reference book about the computer industry.
Cost: $63.00
800 Pages
Frequency: Annual
ISBN: 0-942107-08-X

5461 **Computer Industry Market Intelligence System**
Hart-Hanks Market Intelligence
9980 Huennekens St
Suite 100
San Diego, CA 92121-2917
858-625-4800; *Fax:* 858-452-6857;
www.hartehanksmi.com
Terry Olson, CEO
Randy Ilas, Product Management Director
Database of more than 250,000 business locations with mainframe, mini or micro computer systems.

5462 **Computer Review**
Computer Review

19 Pleasant St
Gloucester, MA 01930-5937

978-283-2100
info@computerreview.com;
www.computerreview.com

George Luhowy, Owner

Your personal business tool for mining the Knowledge economy. This is a well organized hardcopy directory with a daily online monitor. It shows you what's happening in 12,000 companies from 77 technology sectors.
Cost: $495.00
750 Pages
Frequency: Annual
ISBN: 0-914730-02-9
ISSN: 0093-416X

5463 **DACS Annotated Bibliography**
Data & Analysis Center for Software
775 Daedalian Drive
Rome, NY 13441-4909

315-334-4905
800-214-7921; *Fax:* 315-334-4964
cust-liasn@dacs.dtic.mil; www.iac.dtic.mil

Thomas McGibbon, Director

Offers citations on over 9,000 technical reports, articles, papers and books concerned with software development and engineering.
Cost: $60.00
400 Pages

5464 **DIALOG Publications**
Dialog, Thomas Business
11000 Regency Parkway
Suite 10
Cary, NC 27511

919-462-8600
800-3DI-ALOG; *Fax:* 919-468-9890;
www.dialog.com

Mike Eastwood, VP Finance & Administration
Al Zink, VP Human Resources
Roy Martin, CEO

Offers descriptions of DIALOG system and database publications that are available for purchase.

5465 **DP Directory**
525 Goodale Hill Rd
Glastonbury, CT 06033-4022

860-659-1065
al@dpdirectory.com; www.dpdirectory.com

Al Harberg, President

Offers mailing lists for the computer trade as well as information on the value and uses of press releases for marketers.

5466 **Datapro Directory of Microcomputer Hardware**
S. Karger Publishers
26 W Avon Road
PO Box 529
Farmington, CT 06085

860-675-7834
800-828-5479; *Fax:* 860-675-7302
karger@snet.net; www.libri.ch

Martin Buess, Managing Director
Andrea Murdoch, CEO
Monika Augstburger, Account Manager
Marianne Dill, Manager Customer Service

Offers valuable information on over 1,500 manufacturers of microcomputers and peripheral equipment.
Cost: $675.00
1000 Pages
Frequency: Monthly
ISSN: 1074-3308

5467 **Directory of Computer and High Technology Grants**
Research Grant Guides
PO Box 1214
Loxahatchee, FL 33470-1214

561-795-6129

Richard M Eckstein, Author

Offers information on over 750 foundations and corporations that award grants to nonprofit organizations for computers, computer training and software.
Cost: $52.50
200 Pages
Frequency: Biennial
ISBN: 0-945078-07-2

5468 **Directory of Library Automation Software, Systems and Services**
Information Today
143 Old Marlton Pike
Medford, NJ 08055-8750

609-654-6266
800-300-9868; *Fax:* 609-654-4309
custserv@infotoday.com; www.infotoday.com

Thomas H Hogan, President
Roger R Bilboul, Chairman Of The Board

Recognized as the primary reference source for software packages used in automating libraries. This entirely new expanded 2004-2005 edition provides detailed descriptions of hundreds of currently available microcomputer, minicomputer, and mainframe software packages and services.
Cost: $89.00
351 Pages
Frequency: Bi-Annually
Founded in: 1983

5469 **Directory of Simulation Software**
Society for Modeling and Simulation International
4838 Ronson Ct
PO Box 17900
San Diego, CA 92177-7900

858-277-3888; *Fax:* 858-277-3930
info@scs.org; www.scs.org

Amy Shapiro, Publications Manager & Editor
Steve Branch, Executive Director

About 200 simulation software packages and their suppliers.
Cost: $40.00
Frequency: Annual
Circulation: 2,000
Mailing list available for rent

5470 **Directory of Top Computer Executives**
Applied Computer Research
PO Box 41730
Phoenix, AZ 85080

602-216-9100
800-234-2227; *Fax:* 602-548-4800;
www.acrhq.com

Contains the names of more than 52,000 of the most influential information technology managers in the US and Canada. Entepreneurs and corporate executives have used this data base to build successful businesses for over 30 years.
Cost: $245.00
Frequency: Semi-Annual
Founded in: 1972

5471 **Directory of US Government Software for Mainframes and Microcomputers**
US National Technical Information Service
5285 Port Royal Road
Springfield, VA 22161

703-605-6000
800-553-6847; *Fax:* 703-605-6900
info@ntis.gov; www.ntis.gov

Patrik Ekstr"m, Business Development Manager
Reuel Avila, Managing Director

Contains descriptions of some 550 mainframe and microcomputer programs made available from more than 100 federal agencies, or their contractors since 1984. The directory is an essential reference tool for users who wish to tap the wealth of U.S. Government software.
Cost: $65.00
174 Pages
Frequency: Annual
ISBN: 0-934213-37-2

5472 **Electronic Imaging an Image Processing: An Assessment of Technology & Products**
Richard K Mill & Associates
5880 Live Oak Parkway
Suite 270
Norcross, GA 30093-1707

770-416-0006; *Fax:* 770-416-0052

Richard K Miller, Editor/President
Kelli D Washington, Editor-in-Chief

List of producers and suppliers of electronic imaging computer software and hardware.
Cost: $485.00
ISBN: 0-896711-12-9

5473 **Guide to Free Films, Flimstrips and Slides**
Educators Progress Service
214 Center St
Randolph, WI 53956-1497

920-326-3126
888-951-4469; *Fax:* 920-326-3127
questions@freeteachingaids.com;
www.freeteachingaids.com

Kathy Nehmer, President

Offers sources for films, filmstrips, slide sets, audiotapes and videotapes.
Cost: $37.95
135 Pages
Frequency: Annual
ISBN: 0-877083-51-7

5474 **Hoover's Guide to Computer Companies**
Hoover's
5800 Airport Blvd
Austin, TX 78752-3826

512-374-1187
800-486-8666; *Fax:* 512-374-4501
customersupport@hoovers.com;
www.hoovers.com

David Mather, President
Paul Pellman, Executive VP Marketing/Products

250 of the largest public and private computer industry companies in in-depth profiles.
Cost: $34.95
737 Pages
Frequency: Annual
ISBN: 1-878753-80-0

5475 **IT Computer Economics Report Journal**
Computer Economics
2082 Business Center Drive
Suite 240
Irvine, CA 92612

949-831-8700; *Fax:* 949-442-7688;
www.computereconomics.com

Frank Scavo, President
Dan Husiak, VP

Provides decision makers throughout the world with timely insights into the management of information systems.
Frequency: Monthly
Founded in: 1978

5476 Index to AV Producers & Distributors 10th Edition
Information Today
143 Old Marlton Pike
Medford, NJ 08055-8750
609-654-6266
800-300-9868; *Fax:* 609-654-4309
custserv@infotoday.com; www.infotoday.com
Thomas H Hogan, President
Roger R Bilboul, Chairman Of The Board
Contains over 23,500 producers and distributors of AV materials of all kinds. This handy softbound volume is an indispensible tool for buyers of audiovisual materials of all kinds.
Cost: $89.00
626 Pages
ISBN: 0-937548-30-8

5477 Internet & Personal Computing Abstracts Journal
Information Today
143 Old Marlton Pike
Medford, NJ 08055-8750
609-654-6266
800-300-9868; *Fax:* 609-654-4309
custserv@infotoday.com; www.infotoday.com
Thomas H Hogan, President
Roger R Bilboul, Chairman Of The Board
This comprehensive database contains over 150,000 citations, with abstracts to reviews of commentaries on the use and applications of microcomputers and software packages.
Cost: $235.00
Frequency: Quarterly
Circulation: 10,000
Founded in: 1980

5478 Inventor's Desktop Companion: A Guide to Successfully Marketing Ideas
Visible Ink Press/Gale Research
PO Box 09187
Detroit, MI 48209-0187
248-699-4253
800-877-GALE; *Fax:* 248-699-8049
Patrick C Sommers, President
Offers information on agencies and organizations of interest to inventors, including regional and national associations, university innovation research centers and business incubators for the computer and desktop industries.
Cost: $24.95
470 Pages

5479 Micro Publishing Report's Directory of Desktop Publishing Suppliers
Cygnus Publishing
PO Box 803
Fort Atkinson, WI 53538-0803
920-000-1111
800-547-7377; *Fax:* 920-563-1699
rich.reiff@cygnuspub.com;
www.cygnusb2b.com
John French, CEO
Tom Martin, Director of Public Relations
Kathy Scott, Director of Public Relations
Paul Bonaiuto, CFO
Offers valuable information on over 200 suppliers of microcomputer systems for desktop publishing.
Cost: $35.00
30 Pages
Frequency: Annual

5480 Microcomputer Market Place
Random House
202 E 50th St
New York, NY 10022
212-572-6120
Offers information on manufacturers and suppliers of computer equipment and accessories.
Cost: $29.95
795 Pages

5481 Microprocessor Integrated Circuits
DATA Digest
321 Inverness Drive South
Englewood, CO 80112
303-790-0600
800-525-7052; www.ihs.com
Jerre Stead, Chair/CEO
Michael Armstrong, Director
Offers a list of over 185 manufacturers and distributors of microprocessor integrated circuits.
Cost: $205.00
Frequency: SemiAnnual

5482 Microsoft Applications and Systems Forums
Microsoft Corporation
1 Microsoft Way
Redmond, WA 98052-8300
425-882-8080
800-426-9400; *Fax:* 425-936-7329;
www.microsoft.com
Steve Ballmer, CEO
This database provides an exchange of information and tips on Microsoft computer systems for participants.

5483 Modern Machine Shop's Handbook for Metalworkingi Industries on CD-ROM
Gardner Publications
6915 Valley Ln
Cincinnati, OH 45244-3153
513-527-8800
800-950-8020; *Fax:* 513-527-8801;
www.gardnerweb.com
Rick Kline Sr, CEO
John Campos, Manager
Brian Wertheimer, Account Manager
Eddie Kania, Sales Manager
Provides a balanced blend of traditional and modern topics. In addition to containing a wide range of reference tables covering all aspects of machining, composition of materials, and dimensions of tooling and machine components.
Cost: $55.00
2368 Pages
ISBN: 1-569903-55-7
Founded in: 2002

5484 National Directory of Bulletin Board Systems
Penton Media
1300 E 9th St
Suite 316
Cleveland, OH 44114-1503
216-696-7000; *Fax:* 216-696-6662
information@penton.com; www.penton.com
Jane Cooper, Marketing
Computer bulletin board systems that display notices of special events or new products are profiled.
Cost: $45.00
400 Pages
Frequency: Annual

5485 NetWire
Novell
165 Nantasket Beach Avenue
Hull, MA 02045
78- 9-5 17
800-453-2167; *Fax:* 781-925-6545
john@netwire.com
netwire.com
This database concentrates on Novell computer software and hardware information.

5486 Online Networks, Databases & Bulletin Boards on Assistive Technology
ERIC Document Reproduction Service
7420 Fullerton Road
Suite 110
Springfield, VA 22153-2852
703-440-1400
800-443-ERIC; *Fax:* 703-440-1408
Directory of electronic networks that focus on technology-related services.

5487 Orion Blue Book: Computer
Orion Research Corporation
14555 N Scottsdale Rd
Suite 330
Scottsdale, AZ 85254-3487
480-951-1114
800-844-0759; *Fax:* 480-951-1117
orion@orionbluebook.com;
www.orionbluebook.com
Roger Rohrs, Owner
63,053 products listed from 1970's to present. Over 1,000 manufacturers listed.
695 Pages
Frequency: Annual
Founded in: 1985

5488 PC-Link
America Online
8619 Westwood Center Drive
Suite 200
Vienna, VA 22182-2238
pclink.com.eg
Provides access to a variety of databases and computer services of interest to users of IBM and compatible computers running MS-DOS.
Frequency: Directory

5489 ParaTechnology Directory of Systems and Network Integrators
ParaTechnology
1215 120th Ave NE
Suite 101
Bellevue, WA 98005-2135
425-453-0676
800-377-2021; *Fax:* 425-453-0338;
www.eside.org
One thousand computer system and network integrators in North America.
Cost: $495.00
Frequency: Annual

5490 Personal Computing Directory
Resources
PO Box 1067
Cambridge, MA 02238-1067
Directory of services and supplies to the industry.
Cost: $29.95
Frequency: Annual

5491 Pocket Guides to the Internet: Telnetting
Information Today

143 Old Marlton Pike
Medford, NJ 08055-8750

609-654-6266
800-300-9868; *Fax:* 609-654-4309
custserv@infotoday.com; www.infotoday.com

Thomas H Hogan, President
Roger R Bilboul, Chairman Of The Board

Logon information and resources available via telnetting.
Cost: $9.95

5492 Q-Link
America Online
8619 Westwood Center Drive
Suite 200
Vienna, VA 22182-2238

800-227-6364; *Fax:* 540-265-2135

Anne Botsford

This database consists of several files of general interest news and information for users of Commodore computers.
Frequency: Full-text

5493 Shareware Magazine: PC SIG's Encyclopedia of Shareware Section
Shareware Magazine
1030 E Duane Avenue
Suite D
Sunnyvale, CA 94086-2624

408-733-8900

Offers a variety of software programs for the IBM PC and its compatibles.
Cost: $19.95
Frequency: Bi-Monthly

5494 SoftBase
Information Resources
PO Box 8120
Berkeley, CA 94707-8120

510-525-6220; *Fax:* 510-525-1568;
www.searchsoftbase.com

Ruth K Koolish, Editor

It produces software products, services and companies abstracted from more than 200 business, computer, technical, trade and consumer publications.
Frequency: Monthly

5495 Software Encyclopedia
R R Bowker LLC
630 Central Ave
New Providence, NJ 07974-1506

908-286-0288
888-269-5372; *Fax:* 908-464-3553
info@bowker.com; www.bowker.com

R R Bowker

A comprehensive easy to navigate guide filled with detailed information on microcomputer software. Listings of over 44,600 software programs from 4,646 publishers and distributors are fully annotated to facilitate research and acquisition.
Frequency: 2 Volume set
ISBN: 0-835249-69-0

5496 Software Engineering Bibliography
Kaman Sciences Corporation
258 Genesse Street
Utica, NY 13502

315-732-1955; www.dacs.com

Citation for over 15,000 technical reports, articles, theses, papers and books concerned with software technology.
Cost: $30.00
Frequency: Annual

5497 Software Life Cycle Tools Directory
Data & Analysis Center for Software
PO Box 1400
Rome, NY 13442-1400

315-334-4905
800-214-7921; *Fax:* 315-334-4964
cust-liasn@dacs.dtic.mil;
www.iac.dtic.mil/dacs

Offers sources of more than 400 software packages for software engineering and maintenance.
Cost: $40.00
500 Pages

5498 Telecom Internet Directory
Information Gatekeepers Group
1340 Soldiers Field Rd
Suite 302
Brighton, MA 02135-1000

617-782-5033
800-323-1088; *Fax:* 617-782-5735
info@igigroup.com; www.igigroup.com

Paul Polishuk, CEO
Bev Wilson, Controller
Yesim Taskor, Controller

Developed to help find information in telecommunications efficiently and timely manner. A wide range of researchers, market analysts, information specialists, librarians and others will find the directory useful in finding information about telecommunications on the Internet.
Cost: $195.00

5499 Top 100 Service Companies
Coordinated Service
20A Court Street
Groton, MA 01450-4217

978-448-2472

100 of the largest US based independent computer service companies.

5500 UNISYS World Software Directory
Publications & Communications
Cypress Creek Road
Suite B
Cedar Park, TX 78613

512-250-9023

Offers valuable information on suppliers of computer software packages compatible with UNISYS Corporation computer systems.
140 Pages
Frequency: SemiAnnual
Circulation: 650

5501 Uplink Directory
Virginia A Ostendorf
PO Box 2896
Littleton, CO 80161-2896

303-797-3131

Directory of services and supplies to the industry.

5502 User's Directory of Computer Networks
Digital Press
129 Parker Street
Maynard, MA 01754-2199

978-493-1770

Offers a list of hosts, site contacts and administrative domains.
Cost: $35.95
630 Pages

Industry Web Sites

5503 http://gold.greyhouse.com
G.O.L.D Grey House OnLine Databases

Grey House Publishing's online database platform, GOLD, offers its Quick Search, Keyword Search and Expert Search for most business sectors including comupter and data processing markets. The GOLD platform makes finding the information you need quick and easy - whether you're a novice searcher or an experienced database user. All of Grey House's directory products are available for subscription on the GOLD platform.

5504 www.4w.com
Information Analytics

Dedicated to the non-profit professional development of information systems managers, directors and analysts.

5505 www.aaai.org
American Association for Artificial Intelligence

A scientific society devoted to advancing the scientific understanding of the mechanisms underlying thought and intelligent behavior and their embodiment in machines.

5506 www.aace.org
Assn for the Advancement of Computing in Education

Promotes the use of computers and the internet in educational settings.

5507 www.adweek.com
Adweek

Leading decision makers in the advertising and marketing field go to Adweek.com every day for breaking news, insight, buzz, opinion, analysis, research and classifieds. The resources of all six regional editions of Adweek, as well as the national edition of Brandweek are combined with the knowledge of our online editors and the multimedia-interactive capabilities of the web to deliver vital information quickly and effectively to our target audience.

5508 www.afsmi.org
Association for Services Management International

Provides the knowledge, fellowship and career connections that customer services and support managers for technology based products and solutions needed for professional and career development.

5509 www.aiim.org
Association for Information and Image Management

The leading international organization focused on helping users to understand the challenges associated with managing documents, content, and business processes.

5510 www.aimglobal.org
AIM Global

International trade association representing automatic identification and mobility technology solution providers.

5511 www.aitp.org
Association of Information Technology Professional

Comprised of career minded individuals who seek to expand their potential employers, employees, managers, programmers and many others. This organization seeks to provide avenues for all their members to be teachers as well as students and to make contacts with other members in the IS field, all in an effort to become more marketable in rapidly changing technological careers.

5512 www.apple.com
Apple

Official web site for Apple; Macintosh computers and software.

5513 **www.asm.com**
Society for Materials Engineers and Scientists

A leading supplier of semiconductor process equipment in both front and back end markets. The Company possesses a strong technological base, state-of-the-art manufacturing facilities, a competent and qualified workforce and a highly trained, strategically distributed support network.

5514 **www.bsa.org**
Business Software Alliance

An organization dedicated to promoting a safe and legal digital world. BSA educates consumers on software management and copyright protection, cyber security, trade, e-commerce and other internet related issues.

5515 **www.bta.org**
Business Technology Association

Serving independent dealers, value added resellers, system integrators, manufacturers and distributors in the business equipment and system industry. BTA helps its members profit through a wide variety of services, including free legal advice and guidance; business benchmarking studies and reports; information on the latest news, trends, and products in the industry.

5516 **www.calico.org**
Computer Assisted Language Instruction Consortium

For language teachers, linguists, courseware developers and governments who are interested in teaching languages with the use of computer assisted instruction.

5517 **www.comptia.org**
CompTIA

Representing the international technology community. The goal is to provide a unified voice, global advocacy and leadership and to advance industry growth through standards, professional competence, education and business solutions.

5518 **www.devx.net**
DevX

The leading provider of technical and services that enable corporate application development teams to efficiently conquer development challenges and keep projects moving.

5519 **www.disa.org**
Data Interchange Standards Association

Many industries are looking to develop and implement eXtensible Markup Language (XML) specifications to eliminate paperwork, improve data accuracy, increase productivity, and reduce operating costs. This effort requires technical and administrative support. DISA can help.

5520 **www.greyhouse.com**
Grey House Publishing

Authoritative reference directories for most business sectors incluidng computer and data processing markets. Users can search the online databases with varied search criteria allowing for custom searches by product category, geographic area, sales volume, keyword, subject and more. Full Grey House catalog and online ordering also available.

5521 **www.guide.sbanetweb.com**
Guide to Computer Vendors

Planning and project management involved in the installation and implementation of client server accounting systems. We provide consulting assitance to a wide range of services such modeling agencies, publishing firms as well as manufacturing and distributors.

5522 **www.icca.org**
Independent Computer Consultants Association

Represents a wide variety of information technology consultants who provide consulting, implementation, support, training, strategic planning, and business analysis services.

5523 **www.internet.com**
Internet.Com/Mecklermedia

A leading source of global Internet news, and analyses. To learn about Internet.com's latest activities.

5524 **www.intl-spectrum.com**
International Spectrum

The independent source of information for users and vendors of IBM's UniVerse and UniData; jBASE International's jBASE; Northgate information Solutions Reality; ONgroup's ONware; Raining Data's D3, mvBASE and mvEnterprise; Revelation Software's Opensight and VIA Systems UniVision Databases.

5525 **www.ioma.com**
IOMA

Supports managers involved in building and maintaining state-of-the-art HRIS software, hardware, and Internet/intranet activities. Publishes newsletter.

5526 **www.irga.com**
International Reprographic Association

Provides a framework for the exchange of information and support for the reprographic industry. The IRgA continues to be the only independent association serving the reprographics industry and the AEC community.

5527 **www.iste.org**
International Society for Technology in Education

A worldwide membership of leaders and potential leaders in educational technology. We are dedicated to providing leadership and service to improve teaching and learning by advancing the effective use of technology in K-12 education and teacher education. We provide our members with information, networking opportunities, and guidance as they face the challenge of incorporating computers, the Internet, and other new technologies into their schools.

5528 **www.openapplications.org**
Open Applications Group

A open standards group building process-based XML standards for both B2B and A2A integration.

5529 **www.pcca.org**
Portable Computer and Communications Association

A forum for disparate industries to meet, learn about each other, and collaborate on the interaction of the multiple technologies involved in wireless solutions.

5530 **www.polarmicro.com**
Polar Microsystems

Provides consulting services that enable our clients to advance their businesses through full utilization of the Apple Macintosh hardware and software platform.

5531 **www.sei.cmu.edu**
Software Engineering Institute

Works closely with defense and government organizations, industry, and academia to continually improve software-intensive systems.

5532 **www.sme.org**
Automated Systems Technical Group/SME

This group harnesses the power of information technology for advancing product development and design, manufacturing automation, enterprise integration, and communication throughout the product life cycle and supply chain.

5533 **www.spie.org**
International Society for Optical Engineering

Serves the international technical community as the premier provider of education, information, and resources covering optics, photonics, and their applications.

5534 **www.thinkecs.com**
Enterprise Computing Solutions

A leading provider of IT infrastructure solutions for Fortune 500 and mid-tier companies throughout California. ECS builds sophisticated IT infrastructure solutions for mission critical applications, provides enterprise storage solutions that ensure data protection and business continuity and delivers state of the art server solutions for optimal computing capacity.

5535 **www.unf.edu/library**
University of North Florida, Carpenter Library

For catalogers of audiovisual materials and electronic resources. Provides information exchange, continuing education, and works toward a common understanding of practices and standards.

5536 **www.vita.com**
VMEbus International Trade Association

For manufacturers of microcomputer boards, hardware, software, military products, controllers, bus interfaces and other accessories compatible with VMEbus architecture. VITA is an incorporated, nonprofit organization of vendors and users having a common market interest.

5537 **www.webdeveloper.com**
Mecklermedia/Internet.Com

Information on maintaining and growing business web sites and intranets.

5538 **www1.hp.com**
Hewlett Packard /Compaq

The official Web site for the Compaq PCs.

Associations

5539 Association of Progressive Rental Organizations
1540 Robinhood Trail
Austin, TX 78703-2624

512-794-0095
800-204-2776; *Fax:* 512-794-0097
cferguson@rtohq.org; www.rtohq.org
Social Media: Facebook, Twitter, YouTube, Flickr

Bill Keese, Executive Director
Gary Ferriman, President
Jonathan Rose, Secretary
Gopal Reddy, First Vice President
Mark Connelly, Second Vice President

Members include television, appliance and furniture dealers who rent merchandise with an option to purchase.
2000 Members
Founded in: 1980

5540 Consumer Electronics Forum
CompuServe Information Service
5000 Arlington Center Boulevard
Columbus, OH 43220

614-457-8600
800-848-8199

Offers valuable information on electronic consumer products, including audio, video and satellite systems and radar detectors.

5541 Consumer Technology Association
1919 S Eads St.
Arlington, VA 22202

703-907-7600
866-858-1555; *Fax:* 703-907-7675
cta@cta.tech; www.cta.tech
Social Media: Facebook, Twitter, LinkedIn, Google+

Gary Shapiro, President & CEO

Formerly the Consumer Electronics Association (CEA), the organization provides valuable and innovative member-only resources including: exclusive information and unparalleled market research, networking opportunities with business advocates and leaders, up-to-date educational programs and technical training, exposure in extensive promotional programs, and representation from the voice of the industry.
2200 Members

5542 Custom Electronic Design & Installation Association
7150 Winton Drive
Suite 300
Indianapolis, IN 46268

317-328-4336
800-669-5329; *Fax:* 317-735-4012
info@cedia.org; www.cedia.org
Social Media: Facebook, Twitter, YouTube

Larry Pexton, Chairman
Dennis Erskine, Vice Chairman
Federico Bausone, Immediate Past Chairman
Richard Millson, Secretary
David Humphries, Treasurer

A global authority in the home technology industry that provides access to industry-leading education, certification, research, and consumer awareness.
3500 Members

5543 Electronic Industries Alliance
2500 Wilson Boulevard
Arlington, VA 22201-3834

703-907-7500; *Fax:* 703-907-7500;
www.eia.org

Ronald L Turner, Chairman
Mike Kennedy, Vice Chairman
Dave McCurdy, President/CEO
Neal McDonald, Senior Coordinator
James Shiring, Secretary/Treasurer

Trade organization representing the entire spectrum of manufacturers and consumer manufacturers involved in electronic products.
1.5M Members
Founded in: 1924

5544 Electronic Retailing Association
607 14th Street, NW
Suite 530
Washington, DC 20005

703-841-1751
800-987-6462; *Fax:* 425-977-1036
webadmin@retailing.org; www.retailing.org
Social Media: Facebook, Twitter, LinkedIn, YouTube, Flickr

Julie Coons, CEO
Cecilia Mason, Accounting Manager
Bill McClellan, Vice President, Government Affairs
Dave Martin, VP, Marketing and Content
Vi Paynich, Content Manager

The trade association that represents the leaders of direct response: members who maximize revenues through electronic retailing on television, online and on radio. ERA strives to protect the regulatory and legislative climate of direct response while ensuring a favorable landscape that enhances e-retailers' ability to bring quality products and services to the consumer.
Founded in: 1990

5545 Electronic Security Association
6333 North State Highway 161
Suite 350
Irving, TX 75038

972-807-6800
888-447-1689; *Fax:* 972-807-6883;
www.esaweb.org
Social Media: Facebook, Twitter, LinkedIn

Marshall Marinace, President
Dee Ann Harn, Vice President
Merlin Guilbeau, Executive Director
Jon Sargent, Secretary
Steve Paley, Treasurer

A nonprofit trade association that represents, promotes, and enhances the growth and professional development of the electronic life safety, security, and integrated sytems industry.
Founded in: 1948

5546 Entertainment Consumers Association
www.theeca.com

Hal Halpin, Founder & President

Non-profit representing the interests of consumers of digital entertainment in the US and Canada.

5547 IEEE Consumer Electronics Society
3 Park Ave.
17th Floor
New York, NY 10016-5997

212-419-7900; *Fax:* 212-752-4929
ckobert@ieee.org
cesoc.ieee.org

Charlotte Kobert, Executive Administrator

Organization for the advancement of the theory and practice of electronic engineering in consumer electronics.
5000 Members

5548 The Repair Association
E-Mail: ggbyrne@repair.org
repair.org

Gay Gordon-Byrne, Press Contact

Advocacy group for repair industry professionals and the Right to Repair movement.
Founded in: 2013

Newsletters

5549 Consumer Electronic and Appliance News
Kasmar Publications
41905 Boardwalk
Suite L
Palm Desert, CA 92221

800-253-9992
800-253-9992; *Fax:* 760-723-2876;
www.kasmarpub.com

Donald Martin, Editor

Home entertainment, consumer electronics and major appliances.
28 Pages
Founded in: 1970

5550 Consumer Electronics Daily
Warren Communications News
2115 Ward Court NW
Washington, DC 20037

800-771-9202
newsroom@warrennews.com
consumerelectronicsdaily.com

Daily coverage of the consumer electronics marketplace featuring original reporting and analysis.
Frequency: Daily

5551 Twice: This Week in Consumer Electronics
Reed Business Information
360 Park Ave S
15th Floor
New York, NY 10010-1737

646-746-6400
800-826-6270; *Fax:* 646-756-7583
mgrand@reedbusiness.com;
www.reedbusiness.com

John Poulin, CEO
Jeff Greisch, Editor/CEO/President
Stephen F Smith, Editor-in-Chief
James Reed, Owner
Patricia Kennedy, Production Manager

Features include industry news, statistics, financial reports and new product trends and announcements.
Cost: $94.90
Frequency: Monthly
Circulation: 41000

Magazines & Journals

5552 AudioXpress
Audio Amateur Publications
PO Box 876
Peterborough, NH 03458

603-924-9464
888-924-9465; *Fax:* 603-924-9467
editorial@audioxpress.com;
www.audioxpress.com

Edward Dell, Publisher

Focuses on the developments in sound production and enhancements in audio equipment and contains information on the construction of new and modification of existing audio equipment. Projects include schematics, parts lists and instructions necessary for completion aimed at electronic engineers and hobbyists.
Cost: $34.95
72 Pages
Frequency: Monthly
Circulation: 11000
ISSN: 1548-6028
Founded in: 2001
Printed in 4 colors on glossy stock

5553 CTA 5 Technology Trends to Watch
Consumer Technology Association
1919 S Eads St.
Arlington, VA 22202
703-907-7600
866-858-1555; *Fax:* 703-907-7675;
www.cta.tech
Gary Shapiro, President & CEO
Annual prediction of which products and services will transform consumers' lives.
Frequency: Annual

5554 CTA Corporate Report
Consumer Technology Association
1919 S Eads St.
Arlington, VA 22202
703-907-7600
866-858-1555; *Fax:* 703-907-7675;
www.cta.tech
Gary Shapiro, President & CEO
Annual publication looking at the Association's accomplishments and goals.
Frequency: Annual

5555 CTA Digital America
Consumer Technology Association
1919 S Eads St.
Arlington, VA 22202
703-907-7600
866-858-1555; *Fax:* 703-907-7675;
www.cta.tech
Gary Shapiro, President & CEO
Annual snapshot of the state of the U.S. consumer technology industry.
Cost: $995.00
Frequency: Annual

5556 IEEE Consumer Electronics Magazine
IEEE Consumer Electronics Society
3 Park Ave.
17th Floor
New York, NY 10016-5997
212-419-7900; *Fax:* 212-752-4929
saraju.mohanty@unt.edu
cesoc.ieee.org/publications/ce-magazine.html
Saraju Mohanty, Editor in Chief
Magazine of IEEE Consumer Electronics Society.

Trade Shows

5557 Augmented World Expo
AugmentedReality.org
www.augmentedworldexpo.com
Social Media: Facebook, Twitter, YouTube
Ori Inbar, CEO
Showcase for technologies making the world more interactive: augmented reality; virtual reality; and wearable technology.
4000 Attendees

5558 Consumer Electronics Show
Consumer Technology Association
1919 S Eads St.
Arlington, VA 22202
703-907-7600
866-858-1555; *Fax:* 703-907-7675
cta@cta.tech; www.cta.tech
Gary Shapiro, President & CEO
World's premier consumer technology event.
177K Attendees
Frequency: Annual

5559 Electronic Entertainment Expo
Entertainment Software Association
601 Massachusetts Ave. NW
Suite 300
Washington, DC 20001
www.e3expo.com
Social Media: Facebook, Twitter, flickr
Ori Inbar, CEO
Video game industry showcase featuring technology debuts and product launches.
50000 Attendees

5560 Electronics Reuse Conference
PC Rebuilders & Recyclers
773-545-7575
sc@pcrr.com; www.ereuseconference.com
Sarah Cade, Conference Director
Computer refurbishment, repair and recycling.
Founded in: 2003

Industry Web Sites

5561 repair.org
The Repair Association
E-Mail: ggbyrne@repair.org
repair.org
Gay Gordon-Byrne, Press Contact
Advocacy group for repair industry professionals and the Right to Repair movement.
Founded in: 2013

Associations

5562 **Aesthetics' International Association**
310 E. Interstate 30
Suite B107
Garland, TX 75043

972-203-8530
877-968-7539; *Fax:* 972-962-1480;
www.aestheticsassociation.com

Patricia Strunk, President
Michelle D'Allaird, Vice President
Michelle D'Allaird, VP, Director of Education
Saundra S. Brown, VP, Director of Operations
Melissa Lawrence, Membership Director

The association for the advancement of education and public awareness on aesthetics. Paramedical aesthetics and body spa therapy. Professionals from the medical, paramedical and beauty industries working together for the most advanced techniques for the patients and clients.
Founded in: 1972

5563 **Allied Beauty Association (ABA)**
145 Traders Blvd. E.
Suites 26&27
Mississauga, ON IL4Z3L3

800-268-6644; *Fax:* 905-568-1581
abashows@abacanada.com
abacanada.com
Social Media: Facebook, Twitter, LinkedIn

Marc Speir, Executive Director

Manufacturers and distributors of the professional beauty industry that serve Canada.
Founded in: 1957

5564 **American Association for Esthetics Education**
310 E. Interstate 30
Suite B107
Garland, TX 75043

312-321-6809
877-968-7539; www.aestheticsassociation.com
Social Media: Facebook, Twitter, YouTube

Patricia Strunk, President
Michelle D'Allaird, Vice President
Michelle D'Allaird, VP, Director of Education
Melissa Lawrence, Membership Director

Provides access to educational experts, methods for increasing profits, and infomation on the latest products and techniques.
Cost: $105.00
Founded in: 1972

5565 **American Association of Cosmetology Schools**
9927 E. Bell Road
Suite 110
Scottsdale, AZ 85260

480-810-0431
800-831-1086; *Fax:* 480-905-0993
jim@beautyschools.org;
www.beautyschools.org
Social Media: Facebook, Twitter, LinkedIn, YouTube

Jim Cox, Executive Director
Lisa Zarda, General Manager
Sandra Bruce, Director
Lynelle Lynch, Secretary
Frank Trieu, Treasurer

Association open to all privately owned cosmetology schools.
1100 Members
Founded in: 1924

5566 **American Beauty Association**
4330 Gaines Ranch Loop
Austin, TX 78735

512-872-2830
800-868-4265; *Fax:* 312-245-1080
support@beautyassociation.org
beautyassociation.org
Social Media: Facebook, Twitter, YouTtbe, Google+, Instagram, P

Pablo Arellano Jr., President
Myriam Clifford, VP
Bruce Selan, First VP
Lydia Sarfati, Second VP
George Schaeffer, Secretary

ABA members are manufacturers, manufacturer reps and consultants in the professional beauty industry. Associate members are made up of trade publications, distributors and salons. The ABA's mission is to expand, serve and protect the interests of the professional beauty industry.
200 Members
Founded in: 1985

5567 **American Cosmetics Manufacturers Association**
1050 17th St. NW
Suite 600
Washington, DC 20036-4702

202-441-7500; www.acma.us
Social Media: Facebook, Twitter, YouTube, Google+

An association to support the export of American-made cosmetics and personal care products.

5568 **American Hair Loss Association**
23679 Calabasas Road
#682
Calabasas, CA 91301-1502

www.americanhairloss.org

The American Hair Loss Association is the only national, non-profit membership organization dedicated to educating the public, healthcare professionals, main stream media and legislators about the emotionaally devastating disease of hair loss (alopecia). Committed to the prevention and treatment of hair loss, the ALHA is dedicated to supporting research that will ultimately treat and cure thoses who suffer from this silent epidemic.

5569 **American Hair Loss Council**
30 South Main
Shenandoah, PA 17976

412-765-3666; *Fax:* 412-765-3669
info@ahlc.org; www.ahlc.org
Social Media: Facebook, Twitter, LinkedIn

Susan Kettering, Executive Director

The nation's only, unbiased, not for profit agency, dedicated to sorting through this information, discovering what works and what doesn't,a nd presenting our findings to the consumer.

5570 **American Society of Hair Restoration Surgery**
225 W. Wacker Drive
Suite 650
Chicago, IL 60606

312-981-6760; *Fax:* 312-981-6787
info@cosmeticsurgery.org;
www.cosmeticsurgery.org
Social Media: Facebook, Twitter, LinkedIn

Michael J Will, MD, DDS, FAC, President
Robert A Shumway, MD, FACS, President-Elect
Joe Niamtu, III, DMD, Secretary
Robert H Burke, MD, DDS, FACS, Treasurer
Jane Petro, MD, Immediate Past President

Comprised of physicians specializing in hair loss, dedicated to promulgating the highest standards of medical practice and medical ethics. Provides continuing education to physicians specializing in hair transplant surgery and gives the public the latest information on medical and surgical treatments for hair loss.
1600 Members

5571 **American Society of Perfumers**
PO Box 1256
Piscataway, NJ 08855-1256

201-500-6101; *Fax:* 877-732-0090
info@perfumers.org; www.perfumers.org
Social Media: Facebook, Twitter, LinkedIn, Pinterest

Christopher Diienno, President
Roger Howell, Vice-President
John Gamba, Treasurer
James Krivda, Secretary
Linda Chinery, Director

Nonprofit organization fosters and encourages the art and science of perfumery in the US while promoting professional exchange and a high standard of professional conduct within the fragrance industry. The ASP holds yearly symposiums in the New York City area where leading members of the fragrance industry are invited to speak and present information on all aspects of the industry.
Founded in: 1947

5572 **Association Accredited Cosmetology Schools**
5201 Leesburg Pike
Falls Church, VA 22041-3244
Ronald Smith, Publisher

Association for those concerned with cosmetology.
6 Members

5573 **B-cause**
PO Box 4814
Poughkeepsie, NY 12601

845-431-6670; www.bcause.org
Social Media: Facebook

Rudy Sprogis, Founder/President

Non-profit organization that advances charitable causes for salon owners and beauty industry professionals.
Founded in: 2000

5574 **BOBSA**
PO Box 25173
San Francisco, CA 94128

650-863-3491; *Fax:* 858-712-1934
bobsaone.org
Social Media: Facebook, Twitter, LinkedIn

Sam Ennon, President

Representing beauty store operators in the ethnic health and beauty-care industry.

5575 **Chain Drug Marketing Association**
43157 W Nine Mile Road
PO Box 995
Novi, MI 48376-0995

248-449-9300; *Fax:* 248-449-9396
support@chaindrug.com; www.chaindrug.com
Social Media: Facebook, Twitter, LinkedIn, YouTube, Pinterest

Jack Walker, Chairman
Jim Devine, President
Jim Salley, Treasurer
Judy Aspinall, Secretary

Members are regional drug chains from across North ASmerica Association markets over 800 products under the name Quality Choice to its members.
101 Members
Founded in: 1926

5576 **Consumer Healthcare Products Association**
1625 Eye Street, NW
Suite 600
Washington, DC 20006-2105
202-429-9260; *Fax:* 202-223-6835
eassey@chpa-info.org; www.chpa-info.org
Social Media: Twitter, YouTube, Pinterest
Paul L. Sturman, Chair
Scott Melville, President/CEO
John F. Gay, Vice President, Government Affairs
Tiffany Currie, Controller
Susan M DiBartolo, Manager, IT, Database & Website
Promotes industry growth through consumer understanding, appreciation, and acceptance of responsible self-care in America's health care system by developing and sustaining a climate that provides consumers with convenient access to safe and effective nonprescription medicines and other self-care products marketed without undue restrictions.
Founded in: 1881

5577 **Cosmetic Executive Women**
159 West 25th Street
8th Floor
New York, NY 10001
212-685-5955
646-929-8000; *Fax:* 212-685-3334
ksweeney@cew.org; www.cew.org
Social Media: Facebook, Twitter, LinkedIn, YouTube
Carlotta Jacobson, President
Kelly McPhilliamy, Treasurer
Jill Scalamandre, Chairwoman
Barbara Kotlikoff, Vice Chairwomen
Heidi Manheimer, Vice Chairwomen
To advance the professional growth and leadership development of women in the beauty industry.
4000 Members
Founded in: 1954

5578 **Cosmetic Industry Buyers and Suppliers**
36 Lakeville Road
New Hyde Park, NY 11040
516-775-0220; *Fax:* 516-328-9789
cibsmail@cibsonline.com;
www.cibsonline.com
Social Media: LinkedIn
Rafael Cruz, President
Jo_anne Greco, Vice President
Myoschi. T Oriol, Treasurer
Nick LoPrinzi, Director
Laura Carey, Director
Members are individuals providing and obtaining essential oils, chemicals, packaging and other goods for the cosmetic industry.
800 Members
Founded in: 1948

5579 **Cosmetologists Chicago**
440 S. LaSalle Street
Suite 2325
Chicago, IL 60611-4255
312-321-6809
800-648-2505; *Fax:* 312-673-6612
info@americasbeautyshow.com;
www.chicagomidwestbeautyshow.com
Social Media: Facebook, Twitter, YouTube, Pinterest
Denise Provenzano, President
Larry Silvestri, First VP
Robert Passage, Second Vice President
Karen Gordon, Secretary
Joseph Cartagena, Immediate Past President
A beauty voice and presenter of cosmetology shows.

5580 **Cosmetology Advancement Foundation**
PO Box 811
FDR Station
New York, NY 10150
212-750-2412; *Fax:* 212-593-0862
nalcopr@aol.com
cosmetology.org
Norma A. Lee, Executive Director
Members represent the professional beauty industry's varied constituencies: cosmetologists, salon owners, cosmetology schools, distributors, manufacturers, associations and professional publications. CAF works through the All-Industry Summit to identify issues that affect the future growth and development of the industry.

5581 **Drug, Chemical & Associated Technologies Association**
One Union St
Suite 208
Robbinsville, NJ 08691-3162
609-208-1888
800-640-3228; *Fax:* 609-208-0599
mtimony@dcat.org; www.dcat.org
George Svokos, Executive Director
Laura Kuhen, Project Coordinator
Lyra Myers, Finance Officer
Dr. Folker Ruchatz, First Vice President
Jeanne Motola, Administrative Assistent
The premier business development association whose membership is comprised of companies that manufacture, distribute or provide services to the pharmaceutical, chemical, nutritional and related industries.
Founded in: 1890

5582 **Esthetics Manufacturers and Distributors Alliance**
401 N Michigan Avenue
Chicago, IL 60611
312-215-5120
800-868-4265; *Fax:* 312-245-1080
Paul Dykstra, Executive Director
Paul Scott Premo, President
Charles Mizelle, VP
Mark Lees, Chairman
Julianne Bendel, Manager
A member of the American Beauty Association, whose members are manufacturers of specific products related to the professional beauty industry. EMDA is dedicated to meeting the needs of skin care and body care manufacturers and distributors and the salons they service. The mission of the American Beauty Association and all of its sub-groups is to expand, serve and protect the interests of the professional beauty industry.
40 Members
Founded in: 1993

5583 **Fragrance Foundation**
621 2nd Avenue
2nd Floor
New York, NY 10016
212-725-2755; *Fax:* 646-786-3260
info@fragrance.org; www.fragrance.org
Social Media: Facebook, Twitter, LinkedIn, YouTube
Elizabeth Mushmanno, President
Marc Blaison, Executive VP
Nonprofit, educational arm of the international fragrance industry. Devotes its energies to creating an atmosphere of understanding and appreciation of the benefits and pleasures of fragrance in all its many forms.
160 Members
Founded in: 1949

5584 **Fragrance Materials Association of the US**
1620 I St NW
Suite 925
Washington, DC 20006-4076
202-293-5800; *Fax:* 202-463-8998;
www.fmafragrance.org
Social Media: Facebook, Twitter
Glenn Roberts, Executive Director
Daniel J Carey, VP
Robert Bedoukian, Secretary
Stephen A Block, Treasurer
90 Members
Founded in: 1927

5585 **Fragrance Research Fund**
621 2nd Avenue
2nd Floor
New York, NY 10016
212-725-2755; *Fax:* 646-786-3260
info@fragrance.org; www.fragrance.org/
Social Media: Facebook, Twitter, YouTube
Elizabeth Mushmanno, President
Marc Blaison, Executive VP
Theresa Molnar, Executive Director
Amy Rubins, Special Projects and Events
Lilia Nicoletti, Director of Office Operations
Offers financial support for doctors and clinical researchers. Bestows awards.
Founded in: 1949

5586 **Handmade Cosmetic Alliance**
www.handmadecosmeticalliance.org
Advocating for state and federal legislation that supports the growing handmade cosmetics and soap industry.
Founded in: 2007

5587 **Independent Cosmetic Manufacturers and Distributors**
21925 Field Parkway
Suite 205
Deer Park, IL 60010
847-991-4499
800-334-2623; *Fax:* 847-991-8161
info@icmad.org; www.icmad.org
Social Media: Facebook, Twitter, LinkedIn
Pam Busiek, President/CEO
Sheila Sebor, VP Operations
Vance Seaton, Executive Assistant
Stan Katz, Chairman Emeritus
Karen Acker, Director
Represents cosmetic manufacturers, distributors and suppliers to industry. Mission: to represent, educate and foster the growth and profitability of entrepreneurial companies in the cosmetic and personal care industries worldwide.
540 Members
Founded in: 1974

5588 **Indoor Tanning Association (ITA)**
2025 M St, NW
Suite 800
Washington, DC 20036
888-377-0477; *Fax:* 202-367-2142;
www.theita.com
Social Media: Facebook, Twitter, LinkedIn
Dan Humiston, President
John Overstreet, Executive Director
Dan Humiston, President
Karen Bentlage, Public Relations
Represents indoor tanning manufacturers, distributors, facility owners and members from other support industries.
1000+ Members
Founded in: 1999

5589 **International Aloe Science Council**
8630 Fenton Street
Suite 918
Silver Spring, MD 20910-3818

734-476-9690; *Fax:* 301-588-1174;
www.iasc.org

Steven Dentali, President
Jasen Lavoie, President-Elect
Charlie Metcalfe, Treasurer
Walt Jones, Director
Roger Poore, Chairman

Explores the use of aloe in cosmetic industries, hair products, herb preparations, pharmaceuticals and drinks.
300 Members
Founded in: 1981

5590 **International Association of Color Manufacturers**
1101 17th Street NW
Suite 700
Washington, DC 20036

202-293-5800; *Fax:* 202-463-8998
info@iacmcolor.org; www.iacmcolor.org
Social Media: LinkedIn

Glenn Roberts, Executive Director
David R. Carpenter, President & Treasurer
Rohit Tibrewala, Secretary

Actively represents the interests of the regulated color industry by demonstrating the safety of color additives and promotes the industry's economic growth by participating in new color approvals, regulatory and legislative issues that affect the industry worldwide.
15 Members
Founded in: 1972

5591 **International Fragrance Association North America**
1655 Fort Myer Dr.
Suite 875
Arlington, VA 22209

571-317-1500; *Fax:* 571-312-8033
info@ifrana.org
ifrana.org
Social Media: Facebook, Twitter, Pinterest

Jennifer Abril, President
Megan Ekstrom, Director, Government Affairs
Suzanne Hartigan, Director, Sci. Pol'y & Reg. Affairs

Part of the International Fragrance Association network, IFRA North America advocates for the interests of companies in the fragrance manufacturing and fragrance materials supply trades.
60 Members
Founded in: 2011

5592 **International Perfume Bottle Association**
PO Box 1299
Paradise, CA 95967

E-Mail: paradise@sunset.net;
www.perfumebottles.org
Social Media: Facebook

Jeffrey Sanfilippo, President
Teri Wirth, Vice President
Lillie Gold, Membership Secretary
Steven Shulman, Treasurer
Madeleine Winkelmann, Recording Secretary

Worldwide non-profit organization of people who collect and deal in the variety of perfume containers.
Cost: $45.00
2000+ Members
Founded in: 1988

5593 **International SPA Association**
2365 Harrodsburg Road
Suite A325
Lexington, KY 40504

859-226-4326
888-651-4772; *Fax:* 859-226-4445
ispa@ispastaff.com; www.experienceispa.com
Social Media: Facebook, Twitter, LinkedIn, YouTube

Michael Tompkins, Chair
Ella Stimpson, Vice Chair
Jennifer Wayland-Smith, Vice Chairman
Todd Shaw, Secretary/ Treasurer

International community of spa professionals, product manufacturers and service providers.
Cost: $530.00
Founded in: 1990

5594 **International SalonSpa Business Network**
4712 E 2nd St
#445
Belmont Shore, CA 90803

562-453-3995; *Fax:* 866-444-5139
salonspanetwork.org
Social Media: Facebook, Twitter, Google+

Rhoda Olsen, President
Eric Bakkan, Vice President
Pat Neville, Vice President
Larry Walt, Treasurer
Charles Penzone, Secretary

The association strives to unify the industry and drive it to become more politically active. Members share information, conduct roundtables and help each other recruit, train and retain their staffs.
60+ Members

5595 **Nail Manufacturers Council**
Professional Beauty Association
15825 N. 71st Street
Suite 100
Scottsdale, AZ 85254-1521

480-281-0424
800-468-2274; *Fax:* 480-905-0708
info@probeauty.org; www.probeauty.org/nmc
Social Media: Facebook, Twitter, LinkedIn, YouTube, Pinterest

Reuben Carranza, Chair
Scott Buchanan, Chairman
Bruce Selan, Treasurer

The NMC comprises the leading manufacturers of nail care products sold to, and used in, professional salons. Members cooperate with the association to assure the dissemination of education, training, and technical information concerning nail care products. The NMC has been active in working with international, federal, and state bodies to maintain high professional standards and ensure the safety of industry professionals and their customers, as well as the communities they serve.
50 Members
Founded in: 1990

5596 **National Accrediting Commission of Cosmetology Arts & Sciences(NACCAS)**
4401 Ford Avenue
Suite 1300
Arlington, VA 22302

703-600-7600; *Fax:* 703-379-2200
naccas@naccas.org
naccas.org

Tony Mirando, Executive Director
Eddie Broomfield, Assistant to Executive Director

To accredit post-secondary cosmetology schools and programs.
1050 Members

5597 **National Beauty Culturists' League (NBCL)**
25 Logan Circle N.W.
Washington, DC 20005

202-332-2695; *Fax:* 202-332-0940
mercedestoregano@hotmail.com;
www.nbcl.info

Dr. Katie B. Catalon, President

Continuing education and higher learning degree program that serves as a unifying force and a catalyst for professionalism, excellence and growth of the beauty industry.
Founded in: 1940

5598 **National Coalition of Estheticians Manufacturers/Distributors Assns.**
484 Spring Avenue
Ridgewood, NJ 07450-4624

201-670-4100; *Fax:* 201-670-4265
nceaorg@aol.com; www.ncea.tv

Susanne S Warfield, Executive Director

Represents and promotes the esthetic and related professions industry by sharing information, building consensus and providing a unified voice on behalf of the industry.
7000+ Members
Founded in: 2000

5599 **National Cosmetology Association**
15825 N. 71st Street
#100
Scottsdale, AZ 85254-1521

480-281-0424
800-468-2274; *Fax:* 480-905-0708;
www.probeauty.org
Social Media: Facebook, Twitter, LinkedIn, YouTube, Pinterest, Instagram

Reuben Carranza, Chair
Beth Hickey, Vice Chair
Steve Sleeper, Executive Director
Rachel Molepske, Manager of Leadership Operations
Eric Z Horn, CMP, Associate Executive Director

Nationwide community of salon professionals, connected by a common passion for learning, growing and raising the professionalism of the entire salon industry. As a group we have a storng voice in our communities, our industry and with our government because ithe NCA is for everyone in the professional salon industry. Members have access to education, fashion events, community service and inurance — all the tools needed to build your career.
30000 Members

5600 **National Interstate Council of State Boards of Cosmetology**
7622 Briarwood Cir
Little Rock, AR 72205-4811

501-227-8262; *Fax:* 501-227-8212
dnorton@nictesting.org; www.nictesting.org

Kay Kendrick, President
Betty Leake, Vice President
Wayne Kindle, Secretary/ Treasurer

Merger of National Council of State Boards of Cosmetology and Interstate Council of State Boards of Cosmetology. Persons commissioned by the state governments to administer cosmetology laws and examine applicants for cosmetology licenses.
3200 Members
Founded in: 1950

5601 **National Latino Cosmetology Association NLCA**
7925 W Russell Rd
PO Box 401044
Las Vegas, NV 89140
702-448-5020
877-658-3801; *Fax:* 702-448-8993
marketing@nlcamerican.org
nlcamerican.org
Social Media: Facebook, Twitter, Pinterest
Julie Zepeda, President/ CEO
Gustavo Castillo, Executive Producer
Mark Sejvar, Marketing Manager
Unites beauty professionals, including salon/spa owners, licensed cosmetologists, barbers, estheticians, nail technicians, students, distributors and manufacturers representing the interests of the beauty industry on a global level.
Founded in: 2006

5602 **Personal Care Products Council**
1620 L Street
Suite 1200
Washington, DC 20036-4702
202-331-1770; *Fax:* 202-331-1969;
www.personalcarecouncil.org
Social Media: Facebook, Twitter, LinkedIn, YouTube
Pamela Bailey, President
Mark Pollak, VP
Cheryl Mason, Secretary
The leading national trade association representing the global cosmetic and personal care products industry. Member companies manufacture, distribute, and supply the vast majority of finished personal care products marketed in the U.S.
600 Members
Founded in: 1894

5603 **Professional Beauty Association**
15825 N 71st Street
Suite 100
Scottsdale, AZ 85254
480-281-0424
800-468-2274; *Fax:* 480-905-0708;
www.probeauty.org
Social Media: Facebook, Twitter, LinkedIn, YouTube
Scott Buchanan, Chair
Reuben Carranza, Vice Chair
Bruce Selan, Treasurer
A non-profit trade association that represents the interests of the professional beauty industry from manufacturers and distributors to salons and spas. Offers business tools, education, advocacy, networking and more to improve individual businesses and the industry as a whole.

5604 **Professional Beauty Foundation**
13034 Saticoy Avenue
N Hollywood, CA 91605
800-211-4872; www.probeautyfederation.org
A nonprofit organization made up of professional beauty organizations dedicated to promote and protect the professional beauty industry as it relates to government laws and regulation.

5605 **RIFM: Research Institute for Fragrance Materials**
50 Tice Boulevard
Woodcliff Lake, NJ 07677
201-689-8089; *Fax:* 201-689-8090
rifm@rifm.org; www.rifm.org
Social Media: Facebook, Twitter, LinkedIn, Pinterest
Sean G. Traynor, Ph.D, President (Chair)
Robert H. Bedoukian, Ph.D, President (Vice Chair)
David C. Shipman, Group Vice President (Treasurer)
Steven Hicks, Secretary
Michael Carlos, President (Fragrance Division)
Evaluates and distributes scientific data on the safety of fragrance raw materials found in cosmetics, perfumes, shampoos, acndles, air fresheners and other personal products, to encourage uniform safety standards. Membership is open to all companies that manufacture , sell, distribute or engage in business related to the fragrance industry for at least one year.
Founded in: 1966

5606 **Regulatory Affairs Professionals Society**
5635 Fishers Lane
Suite 550
Rockville, MD 20852-3048
301-770-2920; *Fax:* 301-841-7956
raps@raps.org; www.raps.org
Social Media: Facebook, Twitter, LinkedIn, YouTube, Google+, Flickr
Rainer Voelksen, Chairman of the Board
Martha A Brumfield, PhD, President
Todd Chermak, RPh, PhD, President-Elect
Salma Michor, Secretary/ Treasurer
Don Boyer, BSc, RAC, FRAPS, Director
The foremost worldwide member organization creating and upholding standards of ethica, credentialing and education for the regulatory affairs profession within the health product sector.
10000 Members
Founded in: 1976

5607 **Scent Marketing Institute**
7 Fox Meadow Road
New York, NY 10583
646-236-4606; *Fax:* 914-470-2416
info@scentmarketing.org;
www.scentmarketing.org
Social Media: Facebook, Twitter, LinkedIn, YouTube
Harald H Vogt, Founder/Chief Marketer
Avery Gilbert PhD, Chief Scientist
Provides networking, educational and marketing support to our member companies and supplies information about scent marketing to the press, marketing, advertising and branding agencies and brand owners.
Founded in: 2004

5608 **Sense of Smell Institute**
621 2nd Avenue
2nd Floor
New York, NY 10016
212-725-2755; *Fax:* 646-786-3260
info@fragrance.org; www.senseofsmell.org
Social Media: Facebook, Twitter
Elizabeth Mushmanno, President
Provides information resources to the public, members of the media, corporate and academic sectors. Also sponsors and conducts educational and public outreach programs to increase awareness of the important role the sense of smell plays in our lives.
Founded in: 1949

5609 **Society of Clinical and Medical Hair Removal**
2424 American Lane
Madison, WI 53704-3102
608-443-2470; *Fax:* 608-443-2474
homeoffice@scmhr.org; www.scmhr.org
Social Media: Facebook, Twitter, Google+
William A. Moore, President
Fadia Hoyek, Executive Vice President
Carol Crowley, Vice President
Lisa Birket, Treasurer
Denise MacIsaace, Secretary
An international non profit organization with members in the United States, Canada, Australia, Japan and beyond. Supports all methods of hair removal and is dedicated to the research of new technology that will keep its members at the pinnacle of thier professsion, offering safe, effective hair removal to their clients.
600 Members
Founded in: 1985

5610 **Society of Cosmetic Chemists**
120 Wall St
Suite 2400
New York, NY 10005-4088
212-668-1500; *Fax:* 212-668-1504
scc@scconline.org; www.scconline.org
Social Media: Facebook, Twitter, LinkedIn
Guy Padulo, President
Dawn Burke, Vice President
Peter Tsolis, Treasurer
Dawn Burke-Colvin, Secretary
Dawn Thiel Glase, Secretary
Dedicated to the advancement of cosmetic science, the Society strives to increase and disseminate scientific information through meetings and publications. By promoting research in cosmetic science and industry, and by setting high ethical, professional and educational standards, we reach our goal of improving the qualifacations of cosmetic scientists.
4000 Members
Founded in: 1945

5611 **The Day Spa Association**
2863 Hedberg Drive
Union City, NJ 07087
877-851-8998; *Fax:* 855-344-8990
dayspaassociation.com
Social Media: Facebook, Google+
Allan Share, President & Executive Director
Open to day spas, spa salons, individuals working in the spa industry and companies supplying products and services to the industry. Its aim is to unify and support the spa industry.
900 Members

5612 **Women in Flavor & Fragrance Commerce**
3301 State Route 66
Suite 205
Neptune, NJ 07753-2705
732-922-0500; *Fax:* 732-922-0560
info@wffc.org; www.wffc.org
Social Media: Facebook, LinkedIn
Amy Marks-Mcgee, President
Kay Murano, Ph.D., Vice President
Bea Hornedo, Secretary
Erica Lermond Mcdonnell, Treasurer
This organization was borne out of a recognized need for a networking, education and support system for women in our industry. Providing a center of education, camaraderie, support, and networking.
300 Members
Founded in: 1982

Newsletters

5613 **American Society of Perfumers Newsletter**
PO Box 1551
West Caldwell, NJ 07004
201-991-0040; *Fax:* 201-991-0073
info@perfumers.org; www.perfumers.org
Social Media: Twitter
Marvel Fields, President

Information on upcoming events, industry news, fragrance related issues and special articles.
Founded in: 1947

5614 FDC Reports: Rose Sheet
FDC Reports
5550 Friendship Boulevard
Suite 1
Chevy Chase, MD 20815-7256

301-657-9830
800-332-2181; *Fax:* 301-664-7238;
www.fdcreports.com

Brooke Mcmanus, Editor
Susan Easton, Publisher
Mike Squires, President
Shaun Smith, Marketing
Nicole Tesschamts, Circulation Manager

For executives in the cosmetics, toiletries, fragrances and skin care industries. Provides, coverage of the regulatory and legal environment for cosmetics, major scientific developments and testing methods product marketing news, new product launches; promotions and advertising, retail weekly trademark listings, mergers and acquisitions and developments in the European community.
Cost: $1050.00
Frequency: Weekly
ISSN: 0279-1110
Founded in: 1939

5615 Perfume Bottle Quarterly
PO Box 1299
Paradise, CA 95967

E-Mail: paradise@sunset.net;
www.perfumebottles.org

Ed Lefkowith, President
Anne Conrad, Publications Chair

Features association news bottle photos, people, literature reviews, trade events, and classified ads. Providing a tremendous resource of knowledge about our field, PBQ is essential to staying current on information, events, and people of the field.
24 Pages
Frequency: Quarterly
Founded in: 1997
Printed in 4 colors

5616 Society of Cosmetic Chemists Newsletter
Society of Cosmetic Chemists
120 Wall St
Suite 2400
New York, NY 10005-4088

212-668-1500; *Fax:* 212-668-1504
scc@scconline.org; www.scconline.org

Randy Wickett, Ph.D, President
Joseph Dallal, Vice President
Guy Padulo, Vice President-Elect
Dawn Burke-Colvin, Secretary
Tony O'Lenick, Treasurer

Issued once a month providing up-to-date information about activities within the SCC and contemporary issues in international arbitration and mediation.
3600 Members
Founded in: 1945

5617 WFFC Newsletter
Women in Flavor & Fragrance Commerce
3301 State Route 66
Suite 205
Neptune, NJ 07753-2705

732-922-0500; *Fax:* 732-922-0560
info@wffc.org; www.wffc.org

Joanne Kennedy, President
Celine Roche, Vice President
Kathryn Bardsley, Secretary
Anne Marie Api, Treasurer

This organization was borne out of a recognized need for a networking, education and support system for women in our industry. Providing a center of education, camaraderie, support, and networking.
300 Members
Founded in: 1982

Magazines & Journals

5618 Beauty Fashion
Ledes Group
286 Madison Ave
Suite 200
New York, NY 10017-6407

212-840-8800; *Fax:* 212-840-7246;
www.beautyfashion.com

John Ledes, Owner
Michelle Krell Kydd, Marketing

The authoritative magazine in the field of cosmetics, toiletries, fragrances and personal care.
Cost: $25.00
131 Pages
Frequency: Monthly
Circulation: 18672
ISSN: 0005-7487
Printed in 4 colors on glossy stock

5619 Beauty Fashion: Body/Bath/Sun Issue
Beauty Fashion
16 E 40th Street
New York, NY 10016

212-328-6789; *Fax:* 212-840-7246;
www.beautyfashion.com
Social Media: Facebook

Offers listings of body/bath and sun products as well as manufacturers and US distributors.
Cost: $25.00
Frequency: Annual
Circulation: 17,000

5620 Beauty Fashion: CTFA Convention Issue
Beauty Fashion
16 E 40th Street
New York, NY 10016

212-328-6789; *Fax:* 212-840-7246;
www.beautyfashion.com

Offers various suppliers of goods and services to the cosmetics industry manufacturers represented at Cosmetic, Toiletry and Fragrance Association convention.
Cost: $25.00
Frequency: Annual
Circulation: 17,000

5621 Beauty Fashion: Cosmetics Issue
Beauty Fashion
16 E 40th Street
New York, NY 10016

212-328-6789; *Fax:* 212-840-7246;
www.beautyfashion.com

Offers listings of color cosmetics products for women as well as manufacturers and US distributors.
Cost: $25.00
Frequency: Annual
Circulation: 17,000

5622 Beauty Fashion: Women's Fragrance Issue
Beauty Fashion
16 E 40th Street
New York, NY 10016-5101

212-328-6789; *Fax:* 212-840-7246;
www.beautyfashion.com/

Michelle Kre Kydd, Marketing
Veronica Kelly, Circulation Manager
Adelaide Farah, Editor

Offers listings of women's fragrance products including perfumes, eau de toilettes, and colognes as well as manufacturers and US distributors.
Cost: $25.00
Frequency: Monthly
Circulation: 17000

5623 Beauty Fashion: Women's Treatment Issue
Beauty Fashion
Ste 700
286 Madison Ave
New York, NY 10017-6407
212-840-8800; *Fax:* 212-840-7246;
www.beautyfashion.com/

Adelaide Farah, Group Editorial Director
Veronica Kelly, Subscription
Michelle Krell Kydd, Marketing

Offers listings of products and manufacturers and US distributors of cosmetics called treatment products.
Cost: $25.00
Frequency: Monthly

5624 Beauty Forum NAILPRO
Creative Age Publications
7628 Densmore Ave
Van Nuys, CA 91406-2042

818-782-7560
800-442-5667; *Fax:* 818-782-7450
dayspa@creativeage.com;
www.creativeage.com

Linda Lewis, Editor
Linda Kossoff, Marketing Manager

NAILPRO for a number of markets in Europe.
Cost: $22.00
Frequency: Monthly
Founded in: 1971

5625 Beauty Inc.
Fairchild Publications
7 W 34th St
New York, NY 10001-8100

212-630-3880
800-289-0273; *Fax:* 212-630-3868
customerservice@fairchildpub.com;
www.fairchildpub.com

Mary Berner, President
Jenny B. Fine, Editor-in-Chief
Sarah Murphy, Publisher

The ONLY resource for the global beauty supply chain-from the suppliers and manufacturers who develop the products to the retailers who influence purchase. Packed with immediate actionable information and inspiration.
Cost: $ 60.00
Frequency: Monthly
Circulation: 40056

5626 Beauty Packaging
Rodman Publishing
70 Hilltop Rd
3rd Floor
Ramsey, NJ 07446-1150

201-825-2552; *Fax:* 201-825-0553
info@rodpub.com;
www.nutraceuticalsworld.com

Rodman Zilenziger Jr, President
Matt Montgomery, VP

Covering all types of packaging. Beauty Packaging is published for executives involved in the

personal care, cosmetic and fragrance industry.
Cost: $40.00
Circulation: 17387
Founded in: 1965

5627 Beauty Store Business
Creative Age Publications
7628 Densmore Ave
Van Nuys, CA 91406-2042
818-782-7560
800-442-5667; *Fax:* 818-782-7450
dayspa@creativeage.com;
www.creativeage.com
Linda Lewis, Editor
Linda Kossoff, Marketing Manager
Products, news and trends for open-line and professional beauty stores and distributors.
Cost: $22.00
Frequency: Monthly
Founded in: 1971

5628 Cosmetic Ingredient Review
1101 17th St NW
Suite 310
Washington, DC 20036-4720
202-331-0651; *Fax:* 202-331-0088
cirinfo@cir-safety.org; www.cir-safety.org
Alan Andersen, Executive Director
Wilma F. Bergfeld, Chairman
Assesses the safety of ingredients used in cosmetics in an unbiased manner and publishes the result in open, peer written literature.
Cost: $100.00
Frequency: Annual+
Founded in: 1976

5629 Cosmetic World
Ledes Group
286 Madison Ave
Suite 200
New York, NY 10017-6407
212-840-8800; *Fax:* 212-840-7246;
www.cosmeticworld.com
John Ledes, Owner
Dorene Kaplan, Managing Editor
Current industry events, legislation, management changes and corporate activities, as well as marketing developments and financial analysis.
Cost: $175.00
Frequency: Weekly
Circulation: 5397

5630 Cosmetics & Toiletries
Allured Publishing Corporation
336 Gundersen Dr
Suite A
Carol Stream, IL 60188-2403
630-653-2155; *Fax:* 630-653-2192
customerservice@allured.com;
www.allured.com
Janet Ludwig, President
Linda Knott, Director Of Operations
This magazine presents a full range of products covering the international cosmetic technology field - including the magazine, a tradeshow, conferences, books and extensive Web sites. The magazine brings the most current technologies in formulating, research, regulations and new ingredients. It also delivers for you a devoted readership base of cosmetic chemists and scientists around the world.
Cost: $98.00
110 Pages
Frequency: Monthly
Circulation: 15,000
ISSN: 0361-4387
Printed in 4 colors on glossy stock

5631 DaySpa Magazine
Creative Age Publications
7628 Densmore Ave
Van Nuys, CA 91406-2042
818-782-7560
800-442-5667; *Fax:* 818-782-7450
dayspa@creativeage.com;
www.creativeage.com
Linda Lewis, Editor
Linda Kossoff, Marketing Manager
Powerful ideas to build your spa business.
Cost: $22.00
Frequency: Monthly
Founded in: 1971

5632 Delicious Living
New Hope Natural Media
1401 Pearl St
Suite 200
Boulder, CO 80302-5346
303-939-8440; *Fax:* 303-939-9886
info@newhope.com; www.newhope.com
Social Media: Facebook, Twitter
Fred Linder, President
Pamela Emanoil, Advertising Manager
A trusted health and wellness resource for more than 25 years.
Cost: $12.99
Frequency: Monthly

5633 Dermascope Magazine
Aesthetics International Association
2611 N Belt Line Rd
Suite 101
Mesquite, TX 75182-9301
972-203-8530
800-961-3777; *Fax:* 972-226-2339;
www.dermascope.com
William Strunk, Publisher
Rachel Valma, Circulation Director
Casey Fore, Editor
The official publication for the advancement of education and public awareness. Variety of articles on skin care, makeup, body spa therapy and paramedical articles where medical and beauty specialists interact.
Cost: $45.00
Frequency: Monthly
Circulation: 80000
Founded in: 1972

5634 Global Cosmetic Industry
Allured Publishing Corporation
336 Gundelsen Drive
Suite A
Carol Stream, IL 60188-2755
630-653-2155; *Fax:* 630-597-0118;
www.gcimagazine.com
Jeff Falk, Editor in Chief
Kim Jednachowski, Sales/Account Manager
The business information resource for marketers, brand managers, manufacturers and executives in the global beauty industry. Industry professionals look to GCI for the strategies, trends, analyses and market data that translate into brand impact.
Circulation: 36,500

5635 Happi
Rodman Publishing
70 Hilltop Rd
3rd Floor
Ramsey, NJ 07446-1150
201-825-2552; *Fax:* 201-825-0553
info@rodpub.com;
www.nutraceuticalsworld.com
Rodman Zilenziger Jr, President
Matt Montgomery, VP
Serves the manufacturers and fillers of cosmetics, toiletries, fragrances, pharmaceuticals, detergents and chemical specialties inclusing household cleaning products and others product lines allied to the field.
Founded in: 1964

5636 Health Products Business
Cygnus Publishing
2 Huntington Quad
Suite 301n
Melville, NY 11747-4618
631-845-2700; *Fax:* 631-845-2723
feedback@magazines.com;
www.healthproducts.com
Susanne Alberto, Editor/Features
Bruce Leftakels, Publisher
This is a trade magazine that covers news and trends in the natural health products industry vitamins, herbs, dietary supplements and other products. Publishes annual raw materials directory and purchasing guide. Target audience, natural products retail store owners, buyers and managers. Qualified subscription only.
Founded in: 1996

5637 Inside Cosmeceuticals
Virgo Publishing LLC
3300 N Central Ave
Suite 300
Phoenix, AZ 85012-2532
480-675-9925; *Fax:* 480-990-0819
peggyj@vpico.com; www.vpico.com
Jenny Bolton, President
An online information source exploring emerging product trends and scientific research designed to support the growth and development of the cosmeceuticals market. Visited by manufacturers, marketers and formulators of healthy and innovative cosmetics and personal care products. Mailing list available for rent: 17000+ names at $var per M

5638 Inspire
Creative Age Publications
7628 Densmore Ave
Van Nuys, CA 91406-2042
818-782-7560
800-442-5667; *Fax:* 818-782-7450
dayspa@creativeage.com;
www.creativeage.com
Linda Lewis, Editor
Linda Kossoff, Marketing Manager
America's most popular line of hairstyling books.
Cost: $22.00
Frequency: Monthly
Founded in: 1971

5639 Journal of Essential Oil Research/JEOR
Allured Publishing Corporation
336 Gundersen Dr
Suite A
Carol Stream, IL 60188-2403
630-653-2155; *Fax:* 630-653-2192
customerservice@allured.com;
www.allured.com
Janet Ludwig, President
Linda Knott, Director Of Operations
Forum for the publication of essential oil research and analysis.
Cost: $660.00
Frequency: 6x/Year

5640 Launchpad
Creative Age Publications
7628 Densmore Ave
Van Nuys, CA 91406-2042
818-782-7560
800-442-5667; *Fax:* 818-782-7450

dayspa@creativeage.com;
www.creativeage.com

Linda Lewis, Editor
Linda Kossoff, Marketing Manager

News and features about new products for hair, nails, makeup, skincare and tools for beauty professionals.
Cost: $22.00
Frequency: Monthly
Founded in: 1971

5641 LiveSpa Magazine
International Spa Association
2365 Harrodsburg Road
Suite A325
Lexington, KY 40504

888-651-4772; *Fax:* 859-226-4445
ispa@ispastaff.com; www.experienceispa.com
Social Media: Facebook, Twitter

Lynne Walker McNees, President
Deborah Waldvogel, Chairman
Jennifer Wayland-Smith, Vice Chairman
Ella Stimpson, Secretary/ Treasurer

ISPA's consumer magazine, explores a variety of fascinating and useful spa topics and answer spa-goer questions. Insights coming straight from the experts, LiveSpa provides consumers with the practical information they need to better embrace this important aspect of their overall wellness routine. (Also available in digital format)
Cost: $530.00

5642 MedEsthetics
Creative Age Publications
7628 Densmore Ave
Van Nuys, CA 91406-2042

818-782-7560
800-442-5667; *Fax:* 818-782-7450
dayspa@creativeage.com;
www.creativeage.com

Linda Lewis, Editor
Linda Kossoff, Marketing Manager

News, features and education about noninvasive cosmetic therapies, trends, products and equipment for medical professionals and spa owners/managers in the U.S.
Cost: $22.00
Frequency: Monthly
Founded in: 1971

5643 NAILPRO
Creative Age Publications
7628 Densmore Ave
Van Nuys, CA 91406-2042

818-782-7560
800-442-5667; *Fax:* 818-782-7450
dayspa@creativeage.com;
www.creativeage.com

Linda Lewis, Editor
Linda Kossoff, Marketing Manager

The magazine for nail professionals.
Cost: $22.00
Frequency: Monthly
Founded in: 1971

5644 Nails Magazine
Bobit Business Media
3520 Challenger St
Torrance, CA 90503

310-533-2400; *Fax:* 310-533-2507;
www.nailsmag.com

Dedicated to the success of nail professionals.
Cost: $34.50
Frequency: Bi-Monthly
Circulation: 4,500

5645 Perfume 2000 Magazine
Nathalie Publishing Corp
444 Brickell Avenue
Suite 510
Miami, FL 33131

305-669-4602; *Fax:* 305-669-6116;
www.perfume2000.com

Bernard Pommier, Circulation Manager
Joseph P Quick, Publisher

Provides an inside look at the American and international prefume industry.
Cost: $18.00
Frequency: Bi-Monthly
ISSN: 1081-7220

5646 Perfumer & Flavorist
Allured Publishing Corporation
336 Gundersen Dr
Suite A
Carol Stream, IL 60188-2403

630-653-2155; *Fax:* 630-653-2192
customerservice@allured.com;
www.allured.com

Janet Ludwig, President
Linda Knott, Director Of Operations

Helps readers to analyze global trends, discover new ingredients and innovations, and keep up-to-date with industry news and analysis.
Cost: $135.00
Frequency: 8 Issues + 3 Bonus Issues

5647 Proud Magazine
PO Box 19510
Chicago, IL 60619-0510

708-633-6328; *Fax:* 708-633-6329;
www.ahbai.org

Joe Dudley, Senior President
Jory Luste, President
Nathaniel Bronner, Jr. Executive VP

AHBAI reresents leading, African American-owned companies manufacturing ethnic hair care and beauty products. Members serve African Americans through employment, scholarships and education.

5648 Pulse Magazine
International Spa Association
2365 Harrodsburg Road
Suite A325
Lexington, KY 40504

888-651-4772; *Fax:* 859-226-4445
ispa@ispastaff.com; www.experienceispa.com
Social Media: Facebook, Twitter

Lynne Walker McNees, President
Deborah Waldvogel, Chairman
Jennifer Wayland-Smith, Vice Chairman
Ella Stimpson, Secretary/ Treasurer

The magazine for the spa professional. An in-depth look at the latest spa industry trends or tips on balancing your personal and professional life. At Pulse, our goal is to be a source for spa business solutions as well as a medium for personal exploration.
Cost: $530.00

5649 Rite Aid Be Healthy & Beautiful
Drug Store News Consumer Health Publications
425 Park Ave
New York, NY 10022-3526

212-756-5220
800-766-6999; *Fax:* 212-756-5250
jtanzola@lf.com; www.drugstorenews.com

Lebhar Friedman, Publisher

Provides health and beauty tips to millions of women who visit Rite Aid stores.
Frequency: Quarterly
Circulation: 450,000
Founded in: 2002

5650 SalonOvation Magazine
Milady Publishing Company
5 Southside Dr
Clifton Park, NY 12065-3870

518-280-9500
800-998-1498; *Fax:* 518-373-6200
esales@thomsonlearning.com;
www.delmarlearning.com

Shannon Melldady, Owner
Donna Lewis, Executive Marketing Director
Ron Schlosser, President/CEO

Dedicated to furthering the education of new and established beauty professionals, available by paid subscription to cosmetology students, and practicing massage therapists, cosmetologists, nail technicians, barber-stylists and estheticians.
Cost: $20.00
Frequency: Monthly
Circulation: 80000
Founded in: 1945

5651 Scent Marketing Digest
7 Fox Meadow Road
Scarsdale, NY 10583

646-236-4606; *Fax:* 914-470-2416
info@scentmarketing.org;
www.scentmarketing.org

Harald H Vogt, Founder/Chief Marketer
Avery Gilbert PhD, Chief Scientist

The essential blog for Scent Marketing resources, industry experts, scent developers and scent solution providers.

5652 The Colorist
Creative Age Publications
7628 Densmore Ave
Van Nuys, CA 91406-2042

818-782-7560
800-442-5667; *Fax:* 818-782-7450
dayspa@creativeage.com;
www.creativeage.com

Linda Lewis, Editor
Linda Kossoff, Marketing Manager

The latest in haircolor trends, techniques, products and fashion.
Cost: $22.00
Frequency: Monthly
Founded in: 1971

5653 The Link
30 South Main
Shenandoah, PA 17976

412-765-3666; *Fax:* 412-765-3669
info@ahlc.org; www.ahlc.org

Susan Kettering, Executive Director

The voice of the American Hair Loss Council.

5654 WWD Beauty Biz
Fairchild Publications
7 W 34th St
New York, NY 10001-8100

212-630-3880
800-289-0273; *Fax:* 212-630-3868
customerservice@fairchildpub.com;
www.fairchildpub.com

Mary Berner, President
Jenny B. Fine, Editor-in-Chief
Sarah Murphy, Publisher

The premier guide to the beauty industry. Provides in-depth coverage and analysis on all aspects of the industry, including trends, brands, retailers, and personalities driving both the general comsumer and insider sides of the business.
Cost: $60.00
Frequency: Monthly
Circulation: 40056

Trade Shows

5655 AACS Annual Convention
9927 E. Bell Road
Suite 110
Scottsdale, AZ 85260

480-810-0431
800-831-1086; *Fax:* 480-905-0993
jim@beautyschools.org;
www.beautyschools.org
Social Media: Facebook, Twitter

Jim Cox, Executive Director
Lisa Zarda, General Manager

Association open to all privately owned cosmetology schools.
1100 Members
Founded in: 1924

5656 AACS Annual Convention & Expo
American Association of Cosmetology Schools
9927 E. Bell Road
Suite 110
Scottsdale, AZ 85260

480-281-0431
800-831-1086; *Fax:* 480-905-0993
jim@beautyschools.org;
www.beautyschools.org

Jim Cox, Executive Director
Lisa Zarda, General Manager

An opportunity to bring your professional team together to lead your school into the future. Education tracks, ckasses, social events, and the expo hall complete the experience.
Frequency: Annual/Fall

5657 AHBAI Mid-Year Conference
American Health & Beauty Aids Institute
PO Box 19510
Chicago, IL 60619-0510

708-633-6328; *Fax:* 708-633-6329;
www.ahbai.org

Joe Dudley, Senior President
Jory Luste, President
Nathaniel Bronner, Jr. Executive VP

AHBAI reresents leading, African American-owned companies manufacturing ethnic hair care and beauty products. Members serve African Americans through employment, scholarships and education.

5658 Aesthetics' and Spa World Conference
Aesthetics' International Association
2611 N Belt Line Road
Suite 140
Sunnyvale, TX 75182

972-038-8530
800-961-3777; www.dermascope.com/aia

Networking, workshops, classes, exhibitors and more for the aesthetics' and spa professionals.
2000 Attendees

5659 America's Beauty Show
America's Beauty Show
401 N Michigan Avenue
Chicago, IL 60611

312-321-6809
800-648-2505; *Fax:* 312-321-0575
info@americasbeautyshow.com;
www.americasbeautyshow.com

Pat Dwyer, Tradeshow Logisitics Manager
Ingrid Qualls, Tradeshow Sr Coordinator

Evaluate new products, meet with distributors, continuing education classes on the show floor, and purchase product.
Frequency: Annual/March

5660 America's Expo for Skin Care & Spa
Allured Publishing Corporation
336 Gundersen Drive
Suite A
Carol Stream, IL 60188-2403

630-653-2155; *Fax:* 630-653-2192
customerservice@allured.com;
www.allured.com

Janet Ludwig, President
Linda Knott, Director of Operations

Interactive exhibition focuses on professional skin care and spa services. Showcases the newest products, services and technologies from industry manufacturers and suppliers.
Frequency: May

5661 American Society of Perfumers Annual Symposium
PO Box 1551
West Caldwell, NJ 07004

201-991-0040; *Fax:* 201-991-0073
info@perfumers.org; www.perfumers.org
Social Media: Twitter

Marvel Fields, President

All about Perfumery with special guest perfumers speaking about creativity and honors to those who help build our industry.
Founded in: 1947

5662 Annual Scientific Meeting and Technology Showcase
Society of Cosmetic Chemists
120 Wall St
Suite 2400
New York, NY 10005-4088

212-668-1500; *Fax:* 212-668-1504
scc@scconline.org; www.scconline.org

Randy Wickett, Ph.D, President
Joseph Dallal, Vice President
Guy Padulo, Vice President-Elect
Dawn Burke-Colvin, Secretary
Tony O'Lenick, Treasurer

Furthering the interest and recognition of cosmetic scientists.
3600 Members
Founded in: 1945

5663 Annual Scientific Seminar
Society of Cosmetic Chemists
120 Wall St
Suite 2400
New York, NY 10005-4088

212-668-1500; *Fax:* 212-668-1504
scc@scconline.org; www.scconline.org

Randy Wickett, Ph.D, President
Joseph Dallal, Vice President
Guy Padulo, Vice President-Elect
Dawn Burke-Colvin, Secretary
Tony O'Lenick, Treasurer

Providing information and forums for the exchange of ideas and new developments in cosmetic research and technology.
3600 Members
Founded in: 1945

5664 Association of Image Consultants Annual Global Conference
Association of Image Consultants International
1000 Westgate Drive
Suite 252
Saint Paul, MN 55114

651-290-7468; *Fax:* 651-290-2266
info@aici.org; www.aici.org
Social Media: Facebook, Twitter

Jane Seaman, President
Riet De Vlieger, President-Elect
Gail Morgan, Secretary
Chris Fulkerson, Treasurer
Eric Ewald, Executive Director

Conference and industry related exhibits.
Founded in: 1991

5665 Beacon
Professional Beauty Association
15825 N. 71st Street
Suite 100
Scottsdale, AZ 85254

480-281-0424
800-468-2274; *Fax:* 480-905-0708
info@probeauty.org; www.probeauty.org/nmc

Max Wexler, Chair
Scott Buchanan, Vice Chair
Bruce Selan, Treasurer

Beacon is held annually to provide the nation's top cosmetology students with the guidance to achieve maximum career success. Beacon students attend the most celebrated industry events during PBA Beauty Week, and benefit from specially designed educational sessions to help them embark on a successful career path.
50 Members
Founded in: 1989

5666 Beauty Exposition USA
Beauty Expo USA
10725 Midwest Industrial Blvd
Saint Louis, MO 63132

314-426-6333; *Fax:* 314-426-6335
btexpo@yahoo.com; www.beautyexpousa.com

Leon Beatty, Owner
Ann Park, Marketing Director

Hair and beauty supply trade show with a mission of connecting buyers and exhibitors for concentrated business exchanges. Training for retailers in product knowledge and display methods.
2,000 Attendees
Frequency: Annual/Winter

5667 Beauty Supply Show: West Coast
West Coast Beauty Supply
5001 Industrial Way
Benicia, CA 94510

707-484-4800
800-233-3141; *Fax:* 707-748-4623
info@westcoastbeauty.com;
www.westcoastbeauty.com

Jennifer Coleman, Director
Wayne Clark, President
Jane West, Principal

200 booths of the newest and the best beauty products for the individual and business.
15M Attendees
Frequency: March

5668 CDMA Education & Trade Show
Chain Drug Marketing Association
43157 W Nine Mile Road
PO Box 995
Novi, MI 48376-0995

248-499-9300; *Fax:* 248-449-9396;
www.chaindrug.com
Social Media: Facebook, Twitter, LinkedIn

James Devine, President
Judy Aspinall, VP
John Devine, VP of Store

Hundreds of exhibitors and thousands of buyers from regional chains, regional wholesalers, and independent pharmacies.
Frequency: Annual
Founded in: 1926

5669 CEA Annual Convention
Cosmetology Educators of America
9927 E. Bell Road
Suite 110
Scottsdale, AZ 85260
480-810-0431
800-831-1086; *Fax:* 480-905-0993
jim@beautyschools.org;
www.beautyschools.org
Social Media: Facebook, Twitter
Jim Cox, Executive Director
Lisa Zarda, General Manager
Chris Cox, Member services Manager
Association open to all privately owned cosmetology schools.
1100 Members
Founded in: 1924

5670 CHPA Annual Executive Conference
Consumer Health Care Products Association
900 19th St NW
Suite 700
Washington, DC 20006-2105
202-429-9260; *Fax:* 202-223-6835
eassey@chpa-info.org; www.chpa-info.org
Scott Melville, President and CEO
Katie Bernard, State Legislative Analyst
Roman Blazauskas, VP
Chelsea Crutti, Associate Director, State Gov
Join top healthcare executives from across the nation and participate in high-level education sessions focused on the industry's rapidly shifting environment.

5671 Capitol Hill Visits
Professional Beauty Association
15825 N. 71st Street
Suite 100
Scottsdale, AZ 85254
480-281-0424
800-468-2274; *Fax:* 480-905-0708
info@probeauty.org; www.probeauty.org/nmc
Max Wexler, Chair
Scott Buchanan, Vice Chair
Bruce Selan, Treasurer
PBA takes Capitol Hill by storm each year. Armed with talking points about issues such as tip-tax reform, association health plans and more, members meet with their Congressional representatives.
50 Members
Founded in: 1989

5672 Circle of Champions
Premiere Show Group
444 Brickell Avenue
Suite 510
Miami, FL 33131
305-669-4602; *Fax:* 305-669-6116
magazine@perfume2000.com;
www.perfume2000.com
Bernard Pommier, Circulation Manager
Joseph P Quick, Publisher
Rewarding the best of the perfume industry.
Frequency: Bi-Monthly

5673 Cosmetic Science Symposium & Expo
Personal Care Products Council
1101 17th Street NW
Suite 300
Washington, DC 20036-4702
202-331-1770; *Fax:* 202-331-1969;
www.personalcarecouncil.org
Social Media: Facebook, Twitter, LinkedIn, YouTube
Pamela Bailey, President
Mark Pollak, VP
Cheryl Mason, Secretary
Attracts industry leaders and decision-makers and offers personal care products industry staff one-stop shopping for information about Microbiology, Quality Assurance, Safety, and Environmental. The Science Symposium is a great opportunity to learn from the experts and meet colleagues and friends in the industry. Also features the Cosmetic Science Expo.
525 Members
Founded in: 1894

5674 Cosmoprof North America
Professional Beauty Association
15825 N 71st Street
Suite 100
Scottsdale, AZ 85254
800-468-2274; *Fax:* 480-905-0708
Cpnainfo@probeauty.org;
www.cosmoprofnorthamerica.com
Social Media: Facebook, Twitter, LinkedIn
Jen Ingalls, Trade Show Manager
Nathan Miner, Sales Manager
Melissa Coe, Registration Manager
Bonnie Bonadeo, Director Education
Best in hair,cosmetics,packagin and style. Attracted 25,000 professionals from 32 countries with 760 exhibitors.
10M Attendees
Frequency: July
Founded in: 2002

5675 DCAT Western Education Conference
Drug, Chemical & Associated Technologies
1 Washington Boulevard
Suite 7
Robbinsville, NJ 08691
609-448-1000
800-640-3228; *Fax:* 609-448-1944
brooke@dcat.org; www.dcat.org
Brooke DiGiuseppe, Meeting Services
Margaret Timony, Executive Director
Gain important insights into issues and trends that will affect the future of the nutrition and health industry. Participate in discussion on key business issues with industry experts.

5676 Elements Showcase
Skylight West
500 West 36th Street
New York, NY 10018
E-Mail: info@elements-showcase.com;
www.elements-showcase.com
Social Media: Facebook, Twitter, LinkedIn, YouTube
Showcasing diverse range of cosmetic products. Get to know the latest product range and services that will be displayed by leading and well known companies from every corner of the world.

5677 Emerging Issues Conference
Personal Care Products Council
1101 17th Street NW
Suite 300
Washington, DC 20036-4702
202-331-1770; *Fax:* 202-331-1969;
www.personalcarecouncil.org
Social Media: Facebook, Twitter, LinkedIn, YouTube
Pamela Bailey, President
Mark Pollak, VP
Cheryl Mason, Secretary
Regulations being considered in California have an impact on every manufacturer and consumer in the United States. Water, waste, air, packaging, ingredients, recycling, new technology, whatever the issue, the discussions often begin in this state. The Council will host an annual Emerging Issues Conference focusing on the many challenges we see on the horizon for our industry.
525 Members
Founded in: 1894

5678 Engredea
New Hope Natural Media
1401 Pearl St
Suite 200
Boulder, CO 80302-5346
303-939-8440; *Fax:* 303-939-9886
info@newhope.com; www.newhope.com
Social Media: Facebook, Twitter
Fred Linder, President
Pamela Emanoil, Advertising Manager
Encompassing the world of ingredients, Engredea brings together the community of leading suppliers and manufacturers to source new ingredients, packaging, technologies, equipment, and services. Cultivating innovation for tomorrow's best-selling products across food/beverage, dietary supplement and nutricosmetic categories by offering exhibits, formulation demos, networking events and education opportunities for the industry.
Frequency: Monthly

5679 Extracts: Essentials for Spa, Home, & Travel
George Little Management
10 Bank Street
Suite 1200
White Plains, NY 10606
914-486-6070
800-292-4560; *Fax:* 914-948-6289
laura_woodward@glmshows.com;
www.extractsny.com/www.glmshows.com
Rita Malek, Show Manager
Laura Anne Woodward, Show Coordinator
George Little II, President
Paula Bertolotti, Sales Manager
EX-TRACTS: Essentials for Spa, Home and Travel is co-located with the International Hotel/Motel Restaurant Show® (IH/MRS). Presenting the finest Apparel & Accessories, Aromatherapy Products & Candles, Baby and Cildren's Spa Products, Bathrobes and Loungewear, Business Services, Cosmetics, Cosmeceuticals, Home Environment Products, Essential Oils, Frangrances, Home Spa Electrics, Massage/Reflexology, Men's Spa Products, Music & Recordings.
10000 Attendees
Frequency: Nov
Founded in: 1997

5680 Extracts: New Discoveries in Beauty and Wellness
George Little Management
10 Bank Street
Suite 1200
White Plains, NY 10606
914-486-6070
800-292-4560; *Fax:* 914-948-6289;
www.extractsny.com
Rita Malek, Show Manager
Laura Anne Woodward, Show Coordinator
George Little II, President
Paula Bertolotti, Sales Manager
EXTRACTS® at the NYIGF is a unique, high-quality environment, showcasing the most innovative personal care and wellness products for the gift industry: aromatherapy, bath & bodycare, cosmetics, beauty accessories, candles, home fragrances, massage oils, music & recordings, natural/organic products, perfumes, potpourri and skincare.
43M Attendees
Frequency: Jan/Aug
Founded in: 1997

5681 **Face & Body Spa & Healthy Aging**
Allured Publishing
444 Brickell Avenue
Suite 510
Miami, FL 33131

305-669-4602; *Fax:* 305-669-6116
magazine@perfume2000.com;
www.perfume2000.com

Bernard Pommier, Circulation Manager
Joseph P Quick, Publisher

Spa professionals gather at Face & Body for practical business solutions, trend information and the latest offerings and insights from leading industry suppliers.
Frequency: Bi-Monthly
ISSN: 1081-7220

5682 **Face & Body Spa Conference & Expo**
Allured Business Media
336 Gundersen Drive
Suite A
Carol Stream, IL 60188-2403

630-653-2155; *Fax:* 630-653-2192
fbmw@allured.com; www.faceandbody.com
Social Media: Facebook

Maureen Nolimal, Account Executive
Sandy Chapin, Group Show Director
Mary Richter, Event Coordinator
Andrew Blood, Exhibits Coordinator

Skin care professionals gather at the Face & Body Midwest for practical business solutions, education, treatments, trends, products and equipment, as well as the latest offerings and insights from leading industry suppliers.
Frequency: Annual

5683 **General Merchandise/Health and Beauty Care Conference**
Food Marketing Institute
2345 Crystal Drive
Suite 800
Arlington, VA 22202-2709

202-452-8444; *Fax:* 202-429-4519
fmi@fmi.org; www.fmi.org
Social Media: Facebook, Twitter, LinkedIn, you Tube

Don McWhirter, Owner

Annual show of 150 exhibitors of health and beauty care products.
3000 Attendees

5684 **HAIRCOLOR USA**
International Beauty Show Group
757 Thrid Ave
5th Floor
New York, NY 10017

212-895-8200; *Fax:* 212-895-8209;
www.beautyshows.com
Social Media: Facebook, Twitter, YouTube

Mike Boyce, Show Manager
Rick Rosalina, Operations
Nicole Peck, Media partnerships

0
1500 Attendees
Frequency: June

5685 **Health & Beauty America**
HBA
350 Hudson St
Ste 300
New York, NY 10014

609-759-4700; *Fax:* 347-962-3889;
www.hbaexpo.com
Social Media: Facebook, Twitter, LinkedIn

Jack Gonzalez, Director Health/Beauty Events
Caitlin Carragee, Sales Coordinator

America's largest industry-specific educational conference and exposition for cosmetics, toiletries, fragances and personal care.
16500 Attendees

5686 **ICMAD Annual Meeting**
Independent Cosmetic Manufacturers & Distributors
444 Brickell Avenue
Suite 510
Miami, FL 33131

305-669-4602; *Fax:* 305-669-6116
magazine@perfume2000.com;
www.perfume2000.com

Bernard Pommier, Circulation Manager
Joseph P Quick, Publisher

Information about programs and services available to help companies succeed in the beauty and personal care industries.
ISSN: 1081-7220

5687 **ISPA Conference & Expo**
International Spa Association
2365 Harrodsburg Road
Suite A325
Lexington, KY 40504

888-651-4772; *Fax:* 859-226-4445
ispa@ispastaff.com; www.experienceispa.com
Social Media: Facebook, Twitter, LinkedIn, YouTube

Lynne Walker McNees, President
Deborah Waldvogel, Chairman
Jennifer Wayland-Smith, Vice Chairman
Ella Stimpson, Secretary/ Treasurer

The largest ISPA event of the year for spa professionals. The expectation of Conference attendees is to provide spa owners, directors, managers and suppliers with cutting edge tips on where the industry is headed and how to ensure that business is sustainable. Also brings together the leading suppliers in the industry to network with spa decision makers.

5688 **ISSE Long Beach**
Professional Beauty Association
15825 N. 71st Street
Suite 100
Scottsdale, AZ 85254

480-281-0424
800-468-2274; *Fax:* 480-905-0708
info@probeauty.org; www.probeauty.org/nmc

Max Wexler, Chair
Scott Buchanan, Vice Chair
Bruce Selan, Treasurer

The International Salon and Spa Expo is the biggest cash-and-carry beauty show on the West Coast. ISSE Long Beach delivers valuable technical education, quality manufacturers on the exhibit floor and a professionals-only atmosphere.
50 Members
Founded in: 1989

5689 **ISSE Midwest**
Professional Beauty Association
15825 N. 71st Street
Suite 100
Scottsdale, AZ 85254

480-281-0424
800-468-2274; *Fax:* 480-905-0708
info@probeauty.org; www.probeauty.org/nmc

Max Wexler, Chair
Scott Buchanan, Vice Chair
Bruce Selan, Treasurer

The International Salon and Spa Expo is the biggest cash-and-carry beauty show. ISSE delivers valuable technical education, quality manufacturers on the exhibit floor and a professionals-only atmosphere.
50 Members
Founded in: 1989

5690 **Intercoiffure America-Canada**
Creative Age Publications
7628 Densmore Ave
Van Nuys, CA 91406-2042

818-782-7560
800-442-5667; *Fax:* 818-782-7450
dayspa@creativeage.com;
www.creativeage.com

Deborah Carver, President and CEO
Mindy Rosiejka, VP and COO
Barbara Shepherd, Circulation Director

Creative Age Publications is the association management firm for Intercoiffure America-Canada, the premier organization for salon owners.
Frequency: Monthly
Founded in: 1971

5691 **International Beauty Show**
International Beauty Show Group
757 Third Avenue
5th Floor
New York, NY 10017

212-895-8200
800-736-7170; *Fax:* 212-895-8209;
www.ibsnewyork.com
Social Media: Facebook, Twitter, LinkedIn, YouTube

Deborah Carver, Founder
Rick Rosalina, Operations

Annual exposition of hair and skin care products manufacturers and beauty technicians. Held in New York city.
75000 Attendees
Frequency: March

5692 **International Congress of Esthetics & Spa**
310 E. Interstate 30
Suite B107
Garland, TX 75043

972-203-8530
877-968-7539; *Fax:* 972-962-1480
AIAtheKey@aol.com;
www.aestheticsassociation.com

Deborah Carver, Founder
Michelle D'Allaird, VP, Director of Education
Melissa Guillette, Director of Operations

The association for the advancement of education and public awareness on aesthetics. Paramedical aesthetics and body spa therapy. Professionals from the medical, paramedical and beauty industries working together for the most advanced techniques for the patients and clients.
Founded in: 1972

5693 **International Perfume Bottle Association Annual Convention**
PO Box 1299
Paradise, CA 95967

E-Mail: paradise@sunset.net;
www.perfumebottles.org
Social Media: Facebook

Deborah Carver, Founder
Walter Jones, Vice President
Peggy Tichenor, Membership Secretary
Janet Ziffer, Treasurer
Barbara W. Miller, Recording Secretary

The most exciting event in perfume bottle collecting. A three-day extravaganza featuring the world's premiere exhibition and sale with the field's leading dealers featuring thousands of bottles and an internationally recognized auction. The convention draws together collectors and dealers from around the world.
2000+ Members

5694 Medical Device Submission & Compliance Strategies for the U.S. Market
5635 Fishers Lane
Suite 550
Rockville, MD 20852-3048

301-770-2920; *Fax:* 301-770-2924
raps@raps.org; www.raps.org
Social Media: Facebook, Twitter, LinkedIn, YouTube

Susan E. James, Chairman of the Board
Cecilia Kimberlin, President
Paul Brooks, President-elect
Leigh M. Vaughan, Secretary/ Treasurer
Linda Bowen, Director

Featuring an expert panel of industry professionals and US Food and Drug Administration (FDA) regulators, this RAPS workshop will provide critical information on navigating the medical device submission process and creating compliance strategies for products for the US market.
10000 Members
Founded in: 1976

5695 Mid American Beauty Classic
Premiere Show Group
444 Brickell Avenue
Suite 510
Miami, FL 33131

305-669-4602; *Fax:* 305-669-6116
magazine@perfume2000.com;
www.perfume2000.com

Bernard Pommier, Circulation Manager
Joseph P Quick, Publisher

Beauty trade show for members of the professional beauty industry. Hair Show, Nail Show, Skincare Show.
Frequency: Bi-Monthly
ISSN: 1081-7220

5696 NAHA
Professional Beauty Association
15825 N. 71st Street
Suite 100
Scottsdale, AZ 85254

480-281-0424
800-468-2274; *Fax:* 480-905-0708
info@probeauty.org; www.probeauty.org/nmc

Max Wexler, Chair
Scott Buchanan, Vice Chair
Bruce Selan, Treasurer

The North American Hairstyling Awards (NAHA) is the most prestigious photographic beauty competition in North America, celebrating the artistry and skill of the professional salon industry. Individuals are recognized in 13 categories of excellence, including the Student Hairstylist of the Year, during a star-studded Awards Ceremony.
50 Members
Founded in: 1989

5697 NAILPRO Competitions
Creative Age Publications
7628 Densmore Ave
Van Nuys, CA 91406-2042

818-782-7560
800-442-5667; *Fax:* 818-782-7450
dayspa@creativeage.com;
www.creativeage.com

Deborah Carver, President and CEO
Mindy Rosiejka, VP and COO
Barbara Shepherd, Circulation Director

Nail artists from all over the world compete at trade shows all over the U.S. for a chance to be the best and win the coveted annual NAILPRO Cup.
Frequency: Monthly
Founded in: 1971

5698 NAILPRO Nail Institute
Creative Age Publications
7628 Densmore Ave
Van Nuys, CA 91406-2042

818-782-7560
800-442-5667; *Fax:* 818-782-7450
dayspa@creativeage.com;
www.creativeage.com

Deborah Carver, President and CEO
Mindy Rosiejka, VP and COO
Barbara Shepherd, Circulation Director

Practical marketing education helps nail professionals build their businesses.
Frequency: Monthly
Founded in: 1971

5699 NAILPRO Sacramento
Creative Age Publications
7628 Densmore Ave
Van Nuys, CA 91406-2042

818-782-7560
800-442-5667; *Fax:* 818-782-7450
dayspa@creativeage.com;
www.creativeage.com

Deborah Carver, President and CEO
Mindy Rosiejka, VP and COO
Barbara Shepherd, Circulation Director

The industry's hottest nails-only trade show spotlights new products and innovative techniques for nail technicians from top manufacturers.
Frequency: Monthly
Founded in: 1971

5700 NBCL Annual Convention
National Beauty Culturalists' League
25 Logan Circle NW
Washington, DC 20005-3725

202-332-2695; *Fax:* 202-332-0940;
www.nbcl.org

Dr. Katie B Catalon, President
Dr. William Lindsay, Executive Manager

One hundred booths of beauty industry associates, manufacturing companies and other businesses.
Frequency: July

5701 NBJ Summit
New Hope Natural Media
1401 Pearl St
Suite 200
Boulder, CO 80302-5346

303-939-8440; *Fax:* 303-939-9886
info@newhope.com; www.newhope.com
Social Media: Facebook, Twitter

Fred Linder, President
Pamela Emanoil, Advertising Manager

The premier leadership event for progressive nutrition industry CEOs, investors and thought leaders. It has provided unparalleled education and a tremendous venue for thoughtful leaders to establish strategic relationships and grow the potential of their businesses.
Frequency: Monthly

5702 Natural Products Association MarketPlace
New Hope Natural Media
1401 Pearl St
Suite 200
Boulder, CO 80302-5346

303-939-8440; *Fax:* 303-939-9886
info@newhope.com; www.newhope.com
Social Media: Facebook, Twitter

Fred Linder, President
Pamela Emanoil, Advertising Manager

An intimate trade show for the natural and healthy products industries. Topics cover advocacy, retail training and trends, standards and industry regulation, marketing, sustainability, and other relevant, timely topics direct from industry experts and business leaders.
Frequency: Monthly

5703 Natural Products Expo
New Hope Natural Media
1401 Pearl St
Suite 200
Boulder, CO 80302-5346

303-939-8440; *Fax:* 303-939-9886
info@newhope.com; www.newhope.com
Social Media: Facebook, Twitter

Fred Linder, President
Pamela Emanoil, Advertising Manager

Where new products turn into record profits. Join in an experience with exhibits from different companies showcasing the newest products in natural and specialty foods, organic, health and beauty, natural living, supplements and pet products.
Frequency: Monthly

5704 Nutracon
New Hope Natural Media
1401 Pearl St
Suite 200
Boulder, CO 80302-5346

303-939-8440; *Fax:* 303-939-9886
info@newhope.com; www.newhope.com

Fred Linder, President
Pamela Emanoil, Advertising Manager

The premier education and networking conference for the health and nutrition industry. Provides relevant insights for innovation based on science and technology, case studies and market intelligence. Gain an understanding of the impact of next generation ingredients, emerging markets, consumer trend data and regulatory constraints.
Frequency: Monthly

5705 PBA Beauty Week
Professional Beauty Association
15825 N. 71st Street
Suite 100
Scottsdale, AZ 85254

480-281-0424
800-468-2274; *Fax:* 480-905-0708
info@probeauty.org; www.probeauty.org/nmc

Max Wexler, Chair
Scott Buchanan, Vice Chair
Bruce Selan, Treasurer

PBA Beauty Week is North America's largest, most inclusive beauty event, offering unlimited networking, education, and professional growth opportunities to all sectors of the beauty industry. This week of beauty also features the North American Hairstyling Awards, Best Practice Club, City of Hope and Beacon. PBA Beauty Week is produced by the Professional Beauty Association in cooperation with Cosmoprof North America.
50 Members
Founded in: 1989

5706 PBA Symposium
Professional Beauty Association
15825 N. 71st Street
Suite 100
Scottsdale, AZ 85254

480-281-0424
800-468-2274; *Fax:* 480-905-0708
info@probeauty.org; www.probeauty.org/nmc

Max Wexler, Chair
Scott Buchanan, Vice Chair
Bruce Selan, Treasurer

PBA Symposium provides the upper-level business education, unlimited networking and powerful industry research. Held annually during PBA Beauty Week, this three-day educational

summit will inspire and educate salon owners and licensed professionals to take their businesses and careers, as well as the entire industry, to the next level.
50 Members
Founded in: 1989

5707 **Paperboard Packaging Council Annual Convention**
Independent Cosmetic Manufacturers & Distributors
444 Brickell Avenue
Suite 510
Miami, FL 33131
305-669-4602; *Fax:* 305-669-6116
magazine@perfume2000.com; www.perfume2000.com
Bernard Pommier, Circulation Manager
Joseph P Quick, Publisher
Industry leaders specializing in sustainability, the economy, and education will come together to impart their knowledge, experience, and business predictions.
Frequency: Bi-Monthly
ISSN: 1081-7220

5708 **Perfumers Choice Awards**
The American Society of Perfumers
444 Brickell Avenue
Suite 510
Miami, FL 33131
305-669-4602; *Fax:* 305-669-6116
magazine@perfume2000.com; www.perfume2000.com
Bernard Pommier, Circulation Manager
Joseph P Quick, Publisher
Excellence in fragrance creation takes center stage.
Frequency: Bi-Monthly
ISSN: 1081-7220

5709 **Personal Care Products Council Annual Meeting**
Personal Care Products Council
1101 17th Street NW
Suite 300
Washington, DC 20036-4702
202-331-1770; *Fax:* 202-331-1969; www.personalcarecouncil.org
Social Media: Facebook
Round-tables, R&D, business strategy, and learning panels, along with companies with exhibits of supplies and raw materials for the cosmetic industry.
Frequency: Annual

5710 **Personal Care Products Council Legal & Regulatory Conference**
Personal Care Products Council
1101 17th Street NW
Suite 300
Washington, DC 20036-4702
202-331-1770; *Fax:* 202-331-1969; www.personalcarecouncil.org
Social Media: Facebook, Twitter, LinkedIn, YouTube
Pamela Bailey, President
Mark Pollak, VP
Cheryl Mason, Secretary
The premier annual meeting for industry general counsel and legal staff, regulatory affairs staff, and outside counsel representing member companies. Held each year exclusively for Council members.
525 Members
Founded in: 1894

5711 **Professional Beauty Association Annual Convention**
Professional Beauty Association
15825 N 71st Street
Suite 100
Scottsdale, AZ 85254
480-281-0424
800-468-2274; *Fax:* 480-905-0708
cpna@probeauty.org; www.probeauty.org
Steven Sleeper, Executive Director
Eric Z Horn, Director Sales/Show Manager
Annual show of 700 exhibitors of industry related equipment, supplies and services.
10M Attendees

5712 **Proud Lady Beauty Show**
PO Box 19510
Chicago, IL 60619-0510
708-633-6328; *Fax:* 708-633-6329; www.ahbai.org
Clyde Hammond, Senior President
Jory Luste, President
Nathaniel Bronner, Jr. Executive VP
The Beauty Professionals Marketplace
Founded in: 1981

5713 **RAPS Executive Development Program at the Kellogg School of Management**
5635 Fishers Lane
Suite 550
Rockville, MD 20852-3048
301-770-2920; *Fax:* 301-770-2924
raps@raps.org; www.raps.org
Social Media: Facebook, Twitter, LinkedIn, YouTube
Susan E. James, Chairman of the Board
Cecilia Kimberlin, President
Paul Brooks, President-elect
Leigh M. Vaughan, Secretary/ Treasurer
Linda Bowen, Director
Strong business skills are essential to your success and the ability of your company to survive in a volatile and competitive regulatory environment. This program brings the opportunity to cultivate your business management skills through vigorous discussions with some of the world's best business professors in an intimate learning environment.
10000 Members
Founded in: 1976

5714 **RAPS; The Regulatory Convergence**
5635 Fishers Lane
Suite 550
Rockville, MD 20852-3048
301-770-2920; *Fax:* 301-770-2924
raps@raps.org; www.raps.org
Social Media: Facebook, Twitter, LinkedIn, YouTube
Susan E. James, Chairman of the Board
Cecilia Kimberlin, President
Paul Brooks, President-elect
Leigh M. Vaughan, Secretary/ Treasurer
Linda Bowen, Director
Delivers the knowledge, competence development and resources you need to design effective solutions to complex challenges, seize opportunities and lead.
10000 Members
Founded in: 1976

5715 **Salon Focus**
Advanstar Communications
641 Lexington Avenue
8th Floor
New York, NY 10022
212-951-6600; *Fax:* 212-951-6793
info@advanstar.com; www.advanstar.com
Joseph Loggia, CEO
Thomas Ehardt, EVP and CFO
Chris Demoulin, EVP
Educational and exhibiting forum for the Southwest professional salon industry. 140 booths.
6.5M Attendees
Frequency: November

5716 **Scent World Expo**
7 Fox Meadow Road
Scarsdale, NY 10583
646-236-4606; *Fax:* 914-470-2416
info@scentmarketing.org; www.scentmarketing.org
Harald H Vogt, Founder/Chief Marketer
Avery Gilbert PhD, Chief Scientist
Learn about the latest scent technology, fragrance trends and success stories. Members of the scent marketing industry, executives from marketing and branding firms as well as consumer goods companies, hotels/ cruise ships, cosmetic companies and other end users of scent. A wonderful lineup of speakers, with top researchers, creative marketing & branding gurus, innovative perfumers and dynamic scent professionals. Take your business to the next level.

5717 **Spring Management and Financial Aid Conference**
9927 E. Bell Road
Suite 110
Scottsdale, AZ 85260
480-810-0431
800-831-1086; *Fax:* 480-905-0993
jim@beautyschools.org; www.beautyschools.org
Social Media: Facebook, Twitter
Jim Cox, Executive Director
Lisa Zarda, General Manager
Chris Cox, Member services Manager
Association open to all privately owned cosmetology schools.
1100 Members
Founded in: 1924

5718 **Techniques**
New Dimensions Advertising
47 W Main Street
Mechanicsburg, PA 17055-6262
717-697-4181
800-845-4694; *Fax:* 717-790-9441
Triennial show of 25 exhibitors of cosmetics and accessories.
1500 Attendees

5719 **The Makeup Show**
E-Mail:
Focuses on and celebrates the art of makeup and networking. Strengthening the working capability and build a professional network for all the people from the makeup artistry community.

5720 **Welcome to Our World**
Professional Beauty Association
15825 N. 71st Street
Suite 100
Scottsdale, AZ 85254
480-281-0424
800-468-2274; *Fax:* 480-905-0708
info@probeauty.org; www.probeauty.org/nmc
Max Wexler, Chair
Scott Buchanan, Vice Chair
Bruce Selan, Treasurer
The professional beauty industry invites Congress for its annual makeover each year. While Congress enjoys the beauty services, members push legislative issues important to the industry.
50 Members
Founded in: 1989

5721 **West Coast Spring Style and Beauty Show**
West Coast Beauty Supply

5001 Industrial Way
Benicia, CA 94510

707-484-4800
800-233-3141; *Fax:* 707-748-4623;
www.westcoastbeauty.com

Paul Eggert, Show Director
Wayne Clark, President
John Golliher, Manager

200 booths.
15M Attendees
Frequency: March

5722 World International Nail and Beauty Association
1221 N Lake View Ave
Anaheim, CA 92807

714-779-9892
800-541-9838; *Fax:* 714-779-9971
dkellenberger@inmnails.com

David Kellenberger

Represents industry, promotes effective use of products, sponsors competition and bestows awards. Also offers world championship competitions for nails, hair and makeup.
13000 Members
Founded in: 1981

Directories & Databases

5723 Beauty Fashion: Men's Issue
Beauty Fashion
16 E 40th Street
New York, NY 10016

212-328-6789
0; *Fax:* 212-840-7246;
www.beautyfashion.com
Social Media: Facebook

Debra Davis, Advertising Director
Adelaide Farah, Editorial Director

Offers listings of men's fragrances, toiletries and related products as well as manufacturers and US distributors.
Cost: $25.00
Frequency: Annual
Circulation: 17,000

5724 Complete Directory of Cosmetic Specialties
Sutton Family Communications & Publishing Company
920 State Route 54 East
Elmitch, KY 42343

270-276-9500
jlsutton@apex.net

Theresa Sutton, Editor
Lee Sutton, General Manager

Print-out from database of wholesalers, manufacturers, distributors, importers and close-out houses. Database is updated daily to guarantee the most current and up-to-date sources available.
Cost: $39.50
100+ Pages

5725 Complete Directory of Personal Care Items
Sutton Family Communications & Publishing Company
920 State Route 54 East
Elmitch, KY 42343

270-276-9500
jlsutton@apex.net

Theresa Sutton, Editor
Lee Sutton, General Manager

Print-out from database of wholesalers, manufacturers, distributors, importers and close-out houses. Database is updated daily to guarantee the most current and up-to-date sources available.
Cost: $39.50
100+ Pages

5726 Cosmetics & Toiletries: Cosmetic Bench Reference
Allured Publishing Corporation
336 Gundersen Dr
Suite A
Carol Stream, IL 60188-2403

630-653-2155; *Fax:* 630-653-2192
customerservice@allured.com;
www.allured.com

Janet Ludwig, President
Linda Knott, Director Of Operations

Offers a full list of cosmetics ingredient suppliers.
Cost: $95.00
Frequency: Biennial

5727 Cosmetics & Toiletries: Who's Who in R&D Directory Issue
Allured Publishing Corporation
336 Gundersen Dr
Suite A
Carol Stream, IL 60188-2403

630-653-2155; *Fax:* 630-653-2192
customerservice@allured.com;
www.allured.com

Janet Ludwig, President
Linda Knott, Director Of Operations

Offers a list of cosmetic manufacturers and consultants for product development, legal, safety and regulatory assistance.
Cost: $25.00
Frequency: Annual
Circulation: 3,200

5728 Fragrance Foundation Reference Guide
Fragrance Foundation
545 5th Ave
Suite 900
New York, NY 10017-3636

212-779-9058; *Fax:* 212-779-9058
info@fragrance.org; www.fragrance.org

Terry Molnar, Executive Director
Mary Lapsansky, VP

Over 1100 fragrances are listed that are available in the US, with dates of introduction and description, alphabetically indexed with company name, address and phone number.
Cost: $60.00
112 Pages
Frequency: Annual

5729 Fragrance and Olfactory Dictionary
Fragrance Foundation
545 5th Ave
Suite 900
New York, NY 10017-3636

212-779-9058; *Fax:* 212-779-9058
info@fragrance.org; www.fragrance.org

Terry Molnar, Executive Director
Mary Lapsansky, VP

Definitions of ingredients, techniques, language of fragrance and olfactory references.
Cost: $7.00
32 Pages

5730 Passion
Milady Publishing Company
5 Southside Dr
Clifton Park, NY 12065-3870

518-280-9500
800-998-1498; *Fax:* 518-373-6200
esales@thomsonlearning.com;
www.delmarlearning.com
Social Media: Twitter

Shannon Melldady, Owner
Donna Lewis, Executive Marketing Director
Ron Schlosser, President/CEO

A Salon Professionals Handbook for Building a Successful Business
Cost: $20.00
Frequency: Monthly
Circulation: 80000
Founded in: 1945

5731 Perfume 2000
Perfume 2000
444 Brickell Avenue
Suite 510
Miami, FL 33131

305-374-6849; *Fax:* 305-374-6850
ana@perfume2000.com;
www.perfume2000.com

Ana Murias, Public Relations

Comprehensive database; services encourage industry networking and integration.

5732 RIFM Database of Fragrance & Flavor Materials
50 Tice Boulevard
Woodcliff Lake, NJ 07677

201-689-8089; *Fax:* 201-689-8090
rifm@rifm.org; www.rifm.org/nd

A comprehensive source offering safety evaluations and toxicology data on more than 4,500 fragrance and flavor materials. Operated in full cooperation with Flavor & Extracts Manufacturing Association (FEMA).
Founded in: 1966

5733 Who's Who: Membership Directory of the Cosmetic, Toiletry & Fragrance Assn
Personal Care Products Council
1101 17th Street NW
Suite 300
Washington, DC 20036-4702

202-331-1770; *Fax:* 202-331-1969;
www.personalcarecouncil.org

Gwen Hallill, Director Publications/Comm
Pamela Bailey, President

About 500 member companies of the cosmetics industry.
Cost: $75.00
Frequency: Annual, June

Industry Web Sites

5734 http://gold.greyhouse.com
G.O.L.D Grey House OnLine Databases

Grey House Publishing's online database platform, GOLD, offers Quick Search, Keyword Search and Expert Search for most business sectors including beauty, cosmetics, perfumes and personal care markets. The GOLD platform makes finding the information you need quick and easy - whether you're a novice searcher or an experienced database user. All of Grey House's directory products are available for subscription on the GOLD platform.

5735 www.abbies.org
American Beauty Association

Works to expand, serve and protect the interests of the professional beauty industry.

5736 www.ahbai.org
American Health and Beauty Aids Institute

Trade association representing leading Black-owned companies manufacturing ethnic hair care and beauty products that feature the

Proud Lady symbol. Members serve Black America through employment, scholarships and education of consumers on recycling their dollars into the Black community.

5737 **www.bbsi.org**
Beauty and Barber Supply Institute

Our members are wholesaler-distributors, manufacturers and manufacturers' representatives from around the world. Our mission is to maximize the potential of the salon industry.

5738 **www.beautyworks.com/aia**
Aestheticis International Association

For the advancement of education and public awareness on aesthetics. Paramedical aesthetics and body spa therapy. Professionals from the medical, paramedical and beauty industries working together for the most advanced techniques for the patients and clients.

5739 **www.cew.org**
Cosmetic Executive Women

Nonprofit trade organization of approximately 1,500 executives in the beauty, cosmetics, fragrance and related industries. Based in New York City, CEW has associated organizations in France and the United Kingdom. As a leading trade organization in the beauty industry, CEW helps develop the career contacts, knowledge and skills of its members so that they may advance on both professional and personal levels.

5740 **www.cosmeticindex.com**
CosmeticIndex.Com
www.cosmeticindex.com

Online source for cosmetics, resources and services.

5741 **www.cosmeticsinfo.org**
Personal Care Products Council
1620 L St. NW
Suite 1200
Washington, DC 20036

202-331-1770; *Fax:* 202-331-1969
Social Media: Facebook, Twitter

Lezlee Westine, President & CEO
Thia Breen, Chair

Information about safety, testing and regulation of cosmetics and personal care products. Sponsored by the Personal Care Products Council.

5742 **www.greyhouse.com**
Grey House Publishing

Authoritative reference directories for most business segments incluidng beauty, cosmetic, perfume and personal care markets. Users can search the online databases with varied search criteria allowing for custom searches by product category, geographic area, sales volume, keyword, subject and more. Full Grey House catalog and online ordering also available.

5743 **www.iacmcolor.org**
International Association of Color Manufacturers

Actively represents the interests of the regulated color industry by demonstrating the safety of color additives and to promote the industry's economic growth by participating in new color approvals, regulatory and legislative issues that affect the industry worldwide.

5744 **www.iasc.org**
International Aloe Science Council

Nonprofit trade organization for the Aloe Vera Industry world-wide. Its membership includes Aloe growers, processors, finished goods manufacturers, marketing companies, insurance companies, equipment suppliers, printers, sales organizations, physicians, scientists and researchers.

5745 **www.icmad.org**
Independent Cosmetic Manufacturers & Distributors

Information on government consumers and the media. Provides group programs for product liability.

5746 **www.inmnails.com**
World International Nail and Beauty Association

Promotes effective use of products, sponsors competition and bestows awards. Also offers world championship competitions for nails, hair and makeup.

5747 **www.isnow.com**
Cosmetologists Chicago

Voice of the salon industry. For over eight decades, we have been a beauty authority and presenter of the Chicago Midwest Beauty Show. We are stylists, estheticians, color technicians, salon owners, educators and nail technicians.

5748 **www.perfumers.org**
American Society of Perfumers

Nonprofit organization fostering and encouraging the art and science of perfumery in the US while promoting professional exchange and a high standard of professional conduct within the fragrance industry. The ASP holds symposiums in the New York City area where leading members of the fragrence community are invited to speak and present information on all aspects of the industry.

5749 **www.personalcarecouncil.org**
Personal Care Products Council

Provides a complete range of services that support the personal care products industry's needs and interests in the scientific, legal, regulatory, legislative and international fields. CTFA strives to ensure that the personal care products industry has the freedom to pursue creative product development and compete in a fair and responsible marketplace.

5750 **www.salonprofessionals.org**
National Cosmetology Association

Nationwide community of 30,000 salon professionals, connected by a common passion for learning, growing and raising the professionalim of the entire salon industry. As a group, we have a strong voice in our communities, our industry and with our government because the NCA is for everyone in the professional community. Members have access to education, fashion events, community service and insurance — all the tools needed to build your career.

Associations

5751 **ACA International**
Association of Credit and Collection Professionals
PO Box 390106
Minneapolis, MN 55439-0106

952-926-6547; *Fax:* 952-926-1624
aca@acainternational.org;
www.acainternational.org
Social Media: Facebook, Twitter, LinkedIn, YouTube

Lucia Lebens, director

International trade organization of credit and collection professionals providing a variety of accounts receivable management services to over 1,000,000 credit grantors.
5300 Members
Founded in: 1995
Mailing list available for rent

5752 **Advertising Media Credit Executives Association**
PO Box 433
Louisville, KY 40201

502-582-4327; *Fax:* 502-582-4330
amcea@amcea.org; www.amcea.org
Social Media: Facebook

Norman Taylor, President
Kimberly Archibald Russell, VP
Newt Collins, Secretary - Treasurer
Vickie Bolinger, Immediate Past President
Sandra Lawson, Directors

A non-profit organization that exists to serve the media credit manager. Directed and managed by professionals just like you, media credit managers who volunteer for various projects to benefit the industry and our association.
Founded in: 1953

5753 **Affordable Housing Tax Credit Coalition**
1090 K Street NW
12th Floor
Washington, DC 20006

202-661-7698; *Fax:* 202-661-2299
info@taxcreditcoalition.org;
www.taxcreditcoalition.org
Social Media: Facebook, Twitter, LinkedIn, YouTube

Jeff Whiting, Chairman
Todd Crow, President
Tony Alfieri, First VP
Joseph Hagan, President Emeritus
Michael Novogradac, VP

Plays a major role in assuring the conitinuance of the low income housing tax credit, with the primary goal of achieving permanent extension of the low income housing tax credit program.
105 Members
Founded in: 1988

5754 **American Bankruptcy Institute**
66 Canal Center Plaza
Suite 600
Alexandria, VA 22314-1546

703-739-0800; *Fax:* 703-739-1060
info@abiworld.org; www.abiworld.org
Social Media: Facebook, Twitter, LinkedIn, YouTube

Samuel Gerdano, Executive Director
Felicia S Turner, Deputy Executive Director
Patricia A Redmond, Chairman
James Patrick Shea, President
Brian L Shaw, Immediate Past President

Multidisiplinary, nonpartisan organization dedicated to research and education on matters related to insovency. Engaged in numerous educational and research activities as well as the production of a number of publications both for the insolvency practitioner and the public.
11700 Members
Founded in: 1982

5755 **American Financial Services Association**
919 18th Street NW
Suite 300
Washington, DC 20006-5517

202-296-5544
info@afsamail.org; www.afsaonline.org
Social Media: Facebook, Twitter, LinkedIn, Google+

Chris Steinebert, President/CEO
Gary L. Phillips, Chairman
Nathan D. Benson, Member
Dietmar W. Exler, VP

A national trade association for market funded providers of financial services to consumers and small businesses.
400 Members
Founded in: 1916

5756 **American Recovery Association**
5525 N MacArthur Boulevard
Suite 135
Irving, TX 75038

972-755-4755; *Fax:* 972-870-5755
homeoffice@americanrecoveryassn.org;
www.repo.org
Social Media: Facebook, LinkedIn, Google+

Jerry Wilson, President
David Handschin, VP
Bennett Deese, Secretary/Treasurer

Approximately 500 offices around the US, Canada and Germany, providing repossesion services around the world.
280 Members
Founded in: 1965

5757 **BCCA**
550 W Frontage Rd
Suite 3600
Northfield, IL 60093-1243

847-881-8757; *Fax:* 847-784-8059
info@bccacredit.com; www.bccacredit.com
Social Media: Facebook, Twitter, LinkedIn

Mary Collin, CEO
Jamie Smith, Director of Operations
Cindy Laser, Sales/Membership

BCCA is the media industry's credit association that functions as a central clearing house for credit information on advertisers, agencies and buying services, both locally and nationally. Also provides an Electronic Media Credit Application (EMCAPP.com) to members that helps streamline the application process. One app in one location!
600 Members
Founded in: 1972

5758 **Broadcast Cable Credit Association**
550 W Frontage Rd
Suite 3600
Northfield, IL 60093-1243

847-881-8757; *Fax:* 847-784-8059
info@bccacredit.com; www.bccacredit.com
Social Media: Facebook, Twitter, LinkedIn

Mary Collin, CEO
Cheryl Ingram, Chairman
Dalton Lee, Secretary
John Drain, SVP, Finance

Subsidiary of the Media Financial Management Association. BCCA provides industry specific credit reports on individual agencies, advertisers or buying services both national and local. These reports may be obtained upon request online and by phone or fax. Its mission is to provide tools and services that will allow members to perform their functions to the best of their abilities, and help them achieve a profitable bottom line.
600 Members
Founded in: 1972

5759 **Business Products Credit Association**
P.O. Box 5003
St. Paul, MS 55101-7003

651-998-9609
info@bcpa.org; www.bcpa.org
Social Media: Facebook, Twitter, LinkedIn

Heidi Piche, President
Sandra Sandra, Secretary
Matt Shillerstrom, Treasurer
Marie Strawser, Program Director
Bob Kunzer, Information Director

Credit Trade Association for manufacturers and wholesalers.
Founded in: 1875

5760 **CDC Consumer Debt Counseling**
831 W. Morse Blvd.
Winter Park, FL 32789

314-647-9006
800-820-9232; *Fax:* 407-599-5954;
www.consumerdebtcounselors.org

Philip Johnston, President
Melissa Towel, Advisor
Janice Diaz, Customer Care

Nonprofit provider of quality, face-to-face and telephone budget and debt counseling education.
Founded in: 1998

5761 **Capital Markets Credit Analysts Society**
25 N Broadway
Tarrytown, NY 10591

914-332-0040; *Fax:* 914-332-1541
cmcas@cmcas.org; www.cmcas.org
Social Media: Facebook

Stuart Plesser, President
Kelly Byrne, Account Manager
Bikas Tomkoria, Treasurer
Claudia Calderon, Secretary

A professional society whose membership consists primarily of managers and analysts in credit risk departments that directly support their employers' capital market activities.
500 Members
Founded in: 1989
Mailing list available for rent

5762 **Coalition of Higher Education Assistance Organizations**
1101 Vermont Ave NW
Suite 400
Washington, DC 20005-3586

202-289-3910; *Fax:* 202-371-0197
hwadsworth@wpllc.net; www.coheao.com

Maria Livolsi, President
Carl Perry, VP
Lori Hartung, Treasurer
Tom Schmidt, Secretary

Focus is on legislative and regulatory advocacy for Federal Perkins and other campus based student loan programs.
365 Members
Founded in: 1981

5763 **Commercial Finance Association**
370 7th Ave. Ste. 1801
7 Penn Plz
New York, NY 10001-3979

212-792-9390; *Fax:* 212-564-6053
info@cfa.com; www.cfa.com
Social Media: Facebook, Twitter, LinkedIn, YouTube

Patrick Trammell, President
D. Michael Monk, Vice President - Finance

Andrea Petro, First Vice President
Robert Trojan, CEO
David Grende, VP

Trade group of the asset-based, financial services industry, with members throughout the US, Canada and around the world. Members include the asset-based lending arms of domestic and foreign commercial banks, small and large independent finance companies, floor plan financing organizations, factoring organizations and financing subsidiaries of major industrial corporations. CFA membership is by organization, not by individual.
Founded in: 1944

5764 Commercial Mortgage Securities Association
20 Broad St
7th Floor
New York, NY 10005

212-509-1844; *Fax:* 646-884-7569
info@crefc.org; www.crefc.org
Social Media: Facebook, Twitter, LinkedIn

Stephen Renna, CEO
Ed DeAngelo, VP
Michael Flood, VP

International trade organization for the commercial real estate capital markets. Also represents and promotes an orderly and ethical global institutional secondary market for the sale of commercial mortgage loans and equity investments.
309 Members
Founded in: 1994

5765 Consumer Credit Industry Association
6300 Powers Ferry Road
Suite 600-286
Atlanta, GA 30339

678-858-4001
webmaster@cciaonline.com;
www.cciaonline.com

Tom Keepers, Executive VP
John Euwema, VP Legislative Regulatory Counsel
Stephanie Neal, Director of Member Services

To preserve, promote and enhance the availability, utility and integrity of insurance and related products and services delivered in connection with financial transactions.
140 Members
Founded in: 1951

5766 Consumer Credit Insurance Association
6300 Powers Ferry Road
Suite 600-286
Atlanta, GA 30339

678-858-4001; *Fax:* 312-939-8287
webmaster@cciaonline.com;
www.cciaonline.com

Jim Pangburn, President
Dick Williams, Chairman
Michelle Dicks, General Counsel

To preserve, promote and enhance the availability, utility and integrity of insurance and related products and services delivered in connection with financial transactions.
140 Members
Founded in: 1951

5767 Credit Union National Association
601 Penn Ave
NW South Building, Suite 600
Washington, DC 20004-2601

202-628-5777
800-356-9655; *Fax:* 202-638-7734;
www.cuna.org
Social Media: Facebook, Twitter, YouTube

Susan Newton, Executive Director
Pat Sowick, VP
Richard Dines, Senior State and League Affairs
Alicia Valencia Erb, League Relations
Shellee Mitchell, Executive Assistant

The premier trade association in the financial services arena. Supports, protects, unifies and advances the credit union movement.

5768 FCIB
Finance, Credit, International Business Assoc.
8840 Columbia 100 Pkwy
Columbia, MD 21045-2158

410-423-1840
888-256-3242; *Fax:* 410-740-5574
fcib_info@fcibglobal.com;
www.fcibglobal.com
Social Media: Twitter, LinkedIn

Marta Chacon-Martinez, Director
Mike Mino, CCE, Chairman
Ron Shepherd, Director, Membership & Business

FCIB enjoys an international reputation as the premier Association of executives in finance, credit and international business, providing critical export credit and collections insight, practical advice and intelligence to companies of all sizes - from Fortune 500 multi-nationals to medium and small private companies. With international credit management and trade finance professionals in 55 countries around the world, FCIB offers unique networking and educational opportunities
1200 Members
Founded in: 1919

5769 Farm Credit
7951 East Maplewood Ave.
Suite 200
Greenwood Village, CO 80111

E-Mail: ask@farmcredit.com;
www.farmcreditnetwork.com
Social Media: Facebook, Twitter, YouTube, Pinterest, Instagram

Todd Van Hoose, President & CEO
Curtis Hancock, Chairman

Farm Credit member organizations provide credit to farmers, ranchers and rural communities for agriculture and infrastructure projects.
Founded in: 1916

5770 International Association of Commercial Collectors
4040 W 70th Street
Minneapolis, MN 55435

952-925-0760
800-859-9526; *Fax:* 952-926-1624
iacc@commercialcollector.com;
www.commercialcollector.com
Social Media: LinkedIn

Tom Brenan, President
Greg Cohen, Vice President
Paul Eisenberg, Treasurer
Lee Vandenheuvel, Immediate Past President
Marc Bressler, Director

International trade association comprised of collection specialists and commercial attorneys, with members throughout the US and 20 international countries. IACC's mission is to promote the commercial collection profession by providing IACC members with the resources to excel in the industry.
350 Members
Founded in: 1970

5771 International Energy Credit Association
1120 Route 73
Suite 200
Mt. Laurel, NJ 08054

856-380-6854; *Fax:* 856-439-0525
mbiordi@ahint.com; www.ieca.net
Social Media: Facebook, Twitter, LinkedIn, RSS

Gary Nicholson, EVP
Michele Biordi, Executive Director
Zachary Starbird, President
James Hawkins, First Vice President
Amanda Kenly, Past President

The oldest international industry credit association in the United States. Membership includes companies located in the Uited States, Canada, most Western European countries, Mexico, South America and Asia.
700 Members
Founded in: 1923

5772 Jewelers Board of Trade
95 Jefferson Blvd
Warwick, RI 02888-1046

401-467-0055; *Fax:* 401-467-1199
jbtinfo@jewelersboard.com;
www.jewelersboard.com
Social Media: Twitter

Dione Kenyen, President

A not for profit jewelry trade association whose primary function is to compile and disseminate accurate and reliable credit information among its members as to the financial standing, credit history and background of dealers of jewelry and related products.
3200 Members
Founded in: 1884

5773 Mortgage Bankers Association
1919 M Street NW
5th floor
Washington, DC 20036
202-557-2700
800-793-6222
membership@mortgagebankers.org;
www.mba.org
Social Media: Facebook, Twitter, LinkedIn, YouTube

David H Stevens, President and CEO
Marcia Davies, COO
Michael Fratantoni, Chief Economist/ SVP
Bill Killmer, SVP, Legislative & Pol. Affairs
Thomas T. Kim, SVP, Commercial/Multifamily

Representing the real estate finance industry, MBA serves its membership by representing their legislative and regulatory interests before the US Congress and federal agencies; by meeting their educational needs through programs and a range of periodicals and publications; and by supporting their business interests with a variety of research initiatives and other products and services.
2900 Members
Founded in: 1918

5774 NACUSO
3419 Via Lido
#135
Newport Beach, CA 92663

949-645-5296
888-462-2870; *Fax:* 949-645-5297
info@nacuso.org; www.nacuso.org

Jack Antonini, President/CEO
Mark Zook, Chairman
Mike Atkins, Secretary
400 Members
Founded in: 1984

5775 **National Association of Consumer Credit**
PO Box 20871
Columbus, OH 43220-871

614-326-1165; *Fax:* 614-326-1162
nacca2007@sbcglobal.net;
www.naccaonline.org

Joe Mulberry, President
Mike Larsen, First VP
Brian Landis, Second VP
Carri Grube-Lybarker, Secretary/treasurer

Improving the supervision of consumer credit agencies; facilitating the administration of laws governing these agencies by providing a forum for the exchange of information, ideas and experiences among public officials having supervision of such agencies and changes with the administration of such laws; facilitating intercommunication among its members and developing standard information collection concerning consumer credit agencies in each state.
55 Members
Founded in: 1935

5776 **National Association of Credit Management**
8840 Columbia 100 Pkwy
Columbia, MD 21045-2100

410-740-5560; *Fax:* 410-740-5574
robins@nacm.org; www.nacm.org
Social Media: Facebook, Twitter, LinkedIn, Pinterest, RSS

Rocky Thomas, CCE, Chairperson
Gary Gaudette, CCE, ICCE, Chairman/elect
Kevin Quinn, Director
Jay Snyder, CCE, ICCE, Director

NACM and its network of affiliated associations are the leading resource for credit and financial management information and education, delivering products and services which improve the management of business credit and accounts receivable. Our collective voice has influenced legislative results concerning commercial business and trade credit to our nation's policy makers for more than 100 years, and continues to play an active part in legislative issues pertaining to business credit.
18000 Members
Founded in: 1896

5777 **National Association of Credit Union Service Organizations**
PMB 3419 Via Lido
Suite 135
Newport Beach, CA 92663

949-645-5296
888-462-2870; *Fax:* 949-645-5297
info@nacuso.org; www.nacuso.org

Jack Antonini, President/CEO
Mark Zook, Chairman
Mike Atkins, Secretary

Leading professional trade association for credit unions and CUSO's seeking to provide a full aray of services, such as mortgages, business lending and business lending depository services, trust services, investments and insurance to their members and non members alike.
412 Members
Founded in: 1984

5778 **National Association of Federal Credit Unions**
3138 10th St N
Arlington, VA 22201-2160

703-522-4770
800-336-4644; *Fax:* 703-524-1082
lcorbin@nafcu.org; www.nafcu.org
Social Media: Facebook, Twitter, LinkedIn, YouTube

Fred Becker, President
Alicia Hosmer, VP, Marketing
Ed Templeton, Chair/Director-at-Large
Richard L Harris, Vice Chair/Region V Director
Jeanne Kucey, Treasurer

A respected and influential trade association that exclusively represents the interest of federal credit unions before the federal government and the public.
804 Members
Founded in: 1967

5779 **National Association of State Credit Union Supervisors**
1655 Fort Myer Dr
Suite 300
Arlington, VA 22209-3108

703-528-8351
800-728-7927; *Fax:* 703-528-3248
offices@nascus.org; www.nascus.org
Social Media: Twitter

Lucy Ito, President/CEO
Tammy Gentilini, State Programs Coordinator
Patrick Keefe, Vice President, Communications
Steve Pleger, Chairman
Mary Ellen O'Neill, Chairman-Elect

State chartered credit unions and state credit union supervisors.
900 Members
Founded in: 1965

5780 **National Chemical Credit Association**
500 Seneca Street
Suite 400
Buffalo, NY 14209-1963

716-887-9527
844-937-3268; *Fax:* 716-878-0479
robert.gagliardi@abc-amega.com;
www.ncca1.org
Social Media: Twitter, LinkedIn, YouTube, Google+

Glenn Lifrieri, Executive Board Chair

Members are major producers of basic chemicals and allied products.
100 Members
Founded in: 1938

5781 **National Council of Postal Credit Unions**
PO Box 160
Del Mar, CA 92014-0160

858-792-3883; *Fax:* 858-792-3884
ncpcu@ncpcu.org; www.ncpcu.org

Kevin A Yaeger, Chairman
Rebecca Cuddy, Vice Chair
Sidney Parfait, Treasurer
Neil Crean, Secretary

Organized to represent the special interests of postal credit unions.
160 Members
Founded in: 1984

5782 **National Credit Reporting Association**
701 E. Irving Park Rd
Suite 306
Roselle, IL 60712

630-539-1525; *Fax:* 630-539-1526
tclemans@ncrainc.org; www.ncrainc.org
Social Media: Facebook, Twitter, LinkedIn

Terry W Clemans, Executive Director
Jan Gerber, Office & Members Services Manager

Purpose is to promote the general welfare of its members. Also provides leadership in education, legislation, ethics and enhanced vendor's relation
150 Members
Founded in: 1992

5783 **National Credit Union Administration**
1775 Duke St
Alexandria, VA 22314-6115

703-518-6300
800-755-1030; *Fax:* 703-518-6539
consumerassistance@ncua.gov; www.ncua.gov
Social Media: Facebook, Twitter, YouTube

Debbie Matz, Chairman

Governed by a three member board appointed by the President and confirmed by the US Senate, this independent federal agency charters and supervises federal credit unions. NCUA, with the backing of the full faith and credit of the US government, operates the National Credit Union Share Insurance Fund, insuring the savings of 80 million account holders in all federal credit unions and many state chartered credit unions.
82M Members
Founded in: 1970

5784 **National Federation of Community Development Credit Unions**
39 Broadway
Suite 2140
New York, NY 10006-3063

212-809-1850
800-437-8711; *Fax:* 212-809-3274
info@cdcu.coop; www.cdcu.coop
Social Media: Facebook, Twitter, LinkedIn

Cathie Mahon, President/CEO
Eben Sheaffer, CFO/Chief Investment Officer
Pablo DeFilippi, CUDE, VP, Membership & BD
Pamela Owens, CUDE, Vice President, Programs
Ysemny (Nachi) Abood, Technical Assistance Specialist

Serve and represent financial cooperatives in low income communities. Members are community based credit unions. Provides training and management support to CDCU's and asists groups in organizing new credit unions.
200 Members
Founded in: 1974

5785 **National Foundation for Credit Counseling**
2000 M Street NW
Suite 505
Washington, DC 20036

202-677-4300
800-338-2227; www.nfcc.org
Social Media: Facebook, Twitter, YouTube

Susan C Keating, CEO
Paul Weiss, Chief Of Staff/CFO
Lydia Sermons-Ward, Senior VP Marketing

Sets the standard for quality credit counseling, debt reduction services and education for financial wellness.
1200 Members

5786 **National Installment Lenders Association**
PO Box 65615
Washington, DC 20035

nilaonline.org
Social Media: Facebook, Twitter, YouTube

An organization formed to educate people about the advantages of installment loans as sources of consumer credit over credit cards, payday loans and other financial products.
Founded in: 2008

5787 **National Rural Lenders Association**
2402 E 44th Place
Tulsa, OK 74105

918-430-3956; *Fax:* 918-550-8293
nrla-usda.org

Stephen Van Sickle, Chairman
Greg O'Donnell, Executive Director

The NRLA is an advocate for United States Department of Agriculture lending programs to support rural development.

5788 **New York Media Credit Group**
500 Seneca Street
Suite 400
Buffalo, NY 14209
716-887-9547
844-937-3268; *Fax:* 716-878-0479
robert.gagliardi@abc-amega.com;
www.ny-media.com
Social Media: Twitter, LinkedIn, YouTube, Google+
Glenn Lifrieri, Executive Board Chair
One of the most active credit association for media credit professionals today. Many of the members are from major media including cable television, sports and news cable TV, and radio.
Founded in: 1938

5789 **Risk Management Association**
One Liberty Place
1801 Market St
Suite 300
Philadelphia, PA 19103-1613
215-446-4000
800-677-7621; *Fax:* 215-446-4101
customers@rmahq.org; www.rmahq.org
Social Media: Facebook, Twitter, LinkedIn
Dwight Overturf, CFO
William F Githens, President/CEO
Maurice H Hartigan II, President/CEO
Reid Adamson, Senior VP
William S Aichele, President/CEO
Champions risk management while also monitoring emerging trends. Our strong relationship with members and regulators helps us develop new risk management techniques, innovative products and education and training programs geared to risk management professionals at different stages of their careers.
3000 Members
Founded in: 1914

Newsletters

5790 **AHTCC News**
Affordable Housing Tax Credit Coalition
401 9th Street NW
Suite 900
Washington, DC 20004
202-585-8162; *Fax:* 202-585-8080
info@taxcreditcoalition.org;
www.taxcreditcoalition.org
Joseph Hagan, President
Frequency: Monthly

5791 **ARA News & Views**
American Recovery Association
5525 N MacArthur Boulevard
Suite 135
Irving, TX 75038
972-755-4755; *Fax:* 972-870-5755
homeoffice@americanrecoveryassn.org;
www.repo.org/
Mary Jane Hogan, President
Paul Hallock
Provides news, information and coverage of the recovery industry. Free to members only in print. Available to all others online
28 Pages
Frequency: Quarterly
Founded in: 1965

5792 **Bankcard Barometer**
RAM Research Group
320 E 72nd St
Suite 9C
New York, NY 10021
212-724-7535; *Fax:* 212-208-4384
info@investmentTechnologies.com;
www.investmenttechnologies.com
Brian Rom, Owner
Robert B McKinley, Publisher
Reports on the pricing and performance of US bank credit card portfolios. Trendline charts follow deliquency, charge-offs, attrition, payment rates, bankruptcy rates, fraud losses, interest yield, operating expenses, net interest margin and return on assets.
Cost: $1295.00
40 Pages
Frequency: Monthly
Founded in: 1986
Printed in 4 colors

5793 **Bankcard Dispatch**
RAM Research Group
999 Vanderbilt Beach Road
2nd Floor
Naples, FL 34108
239-325-5300
staff@ramresearch.com; www.cardweb.com
Robert B McKinley, Editor
Covers the entire payment card industry as it affects the US market. Comprehensive periodical is prepared for payment card executives.
Cost: $1295.00
40 Pages
Frequency: Monthly
Printed in 4 colors

5794 **Bankcard Update**
RAM Research Group
999 Vanderbilt Beach Road
2nd Floor
Naples, FL 34108
239-325-5300
staff@ramresearch.com; www.cardweb.com
Robert B McKinley, Editor/chairman
Updated printed report and CD-ROM on quarterly statistics of the top US issuers. Covers hundreds of portfolios comprising more than 95 percent of the US market. Subscription includes both the printed version and CD-ROM.
Cost: $ 1295.00
40 Pages
Frequency: Monthly
Founded in: 1986
Printed in 4 colors

5795 **Capitol Watch**
National Association of Credit Unions
3138 10th St N
Arlington, VA 22201-2149
703-522-4770
800-336-4644; *Fax:* 703-524-1082;
www.nafcu.org
Social Media: Facebook, Twitter, YouTube
Fred Becker, President
Alicia Hosmer, VP, Marketing
This members only electronic format newsletter is NAFCU's monthly communication for credit unions with assets of $50 million or less.

5796 **Collection Agency Report**
First Detroit Corporation
30033 Paul Ct
Warren, MI 48092-1805
586-573-0045
800-366-5995; *Fax:* 586-573-9219
ascace@firstdetroit.com; www.firstdetroit.com
Albert Scace, President
Patricia Herrick, Marketing Manager
Patricia Herrick, Circulation Manager
Provides financially oriented news on the collection agency and bad debt buying industries worldwide.
Cost: $420.00
8 Pages
Frequency: Monthly
ISSN: 1052-4029
Founded in: 1988
*Mailing list available for rent*at $110 per M

5797 **Communicator**
Consumer Data Industry Association
1090 Vermont Ave Nw
Suite 200
Washington, DC 20005-4964
202-371-0910; *Fax:* 202-371-0134
cdia@cdiaonline.org; www.cdiaonline.org
Norm Magnuson, VP
Alicia Payne, Contact
Comprehensive online news about the consumer reporting industry, legislation, member news and schedule of industry events. Members only benefit.
16 Pages
Frequency: Monthly
Circulation: 3000
Founded in: 1906

5798 **Consumer Bankruptcy News**
LRP Publications
Po Box 24668
West Palm Beach, FL 33416-4668
561-622-6520
800-341-7874; *Fax:* 561-622-2423
custserv@lrp.com; www.lrp.com
Kenneth Kahn, President
Keeps readers up-to-date on the latest news and cases involving consumer bankruptcy. A must-have for every bankruptcy professional.
Cost: $290.00
Mailing list available for rent
Printed in 2 colors on matte stock

5799 **Covering Credit Newsletter**
Covering Credit
13 Calle Larspur
Rancho Santa Margarita, CA 92688
949-460-7609; *Fax:* 949-460-7609
newsletter@coveringcredit.com;
www.coveringcredit.com
Social Media: Facebook, LinkedIn
Michael C Dennis, Communications Advisor
Steve Kozack, Financial Consultant
Intended for business professionals dealing with credit risk management and/or commercial debt collection and their advsiors. Free and online.
Frequency: Monthly
Founded in: 1989

5800 **Credit Union News Watch**
Credit Union National Association
601 Penn Ave
NW South Building, Suite 600
Washington, DC 20004
202-628-5777
800-356-9655; *Fax:* 202-638-7729;
www.cuna.org
Social Media: Facebook, Twitter
Susan Newton, Executive Director
Pat Sowick, VP
Richard Dines, Senior State and League Affairs Dir
Alicia Valencia Erb, League Relations
Shellee Mitchell, Executive Assistant
Offers news and reports on credit and lending services.
Cost: $50.00
Frequency: Weekly
Founded in: 1970

5801 **Credit Union Report**
Callahan & Associates
1001 Connecticut Ave Nw
Suite 1001
Washington, DC 20036-5523
202-223-3920
800-446-7453; *Fax:* 202-223-1311
pubs@creditunions.com; www.callahan.com
Nader Moghaddam, President/CEO
Keeps an eye on the future, providing stategic vision for every level of credit union management. Each issue includes leading-edge ideas from the industry's top consultants and CEO's, as well as financial trend analysis to help credit unions operate more effectively. Available in print and electronic formats.
Cost: $149.00
Frequency: Monthly

5802 **Credit Union Times**
33-41 Newark Street
2nd Floor
Hoboken, NJ 07030
201-526-1230
800-543-0874; *Fax:* 201-526-1260
subscriptions@cutimes.com;
www.cutimes.com
Social Media: Facebook, Twitter, LinkedIn
Sarah Snell Cooke, Editor in Chief
Sarah Snell Cooke, Publisher/Editor in Chief
Donald Shoultz, Managing Editor
Reports on marketing, regulation, technology and developing trends.
Cost: $120.00
Frequency: Weekly
Circulation: 9337
Printed in 4 colors on matte stock

5803 **Inside MBS & ABS**
Inside Mortgage Finance Publishers
7910 Woodmont Ave
Suite 1000
Bethesda, MD 20814-7019
301-951-1240; *Fax:* 301-656-1709
service@imfpubs.com; www.imfpubs.com
Social Media: Twitter, LinkedIn, YouTube
Guy Cecala, Owner
John Bancroft, Managing Editor
If you're involved in issuing, underwriting, investing, research, rating or trading mortgage-backed securities and asset-backed securities, this publication is for you.
Cost: $1699.00
Founded in: 1984

5804 **Jumbo Rate News**
Bauer Financial
2655 S Le Jeune Rd
Suite 1A
Coral Gables, FL 33134-5827
305-445-9500
800-388-6686; *Fax:* 305-445-6775
customerservice@bauerfinancial.com;
www.bauerfinancial.com
Karen L Dorway, President/CEO
Each issue contains over 1,000 separate Jumbo CD rates in seven categories from over 200 creditworthy banks and thrifts nationwide. Includes star ratings, wire transfer fees, deposit requirements and financial highlights for each institution.
Cost: $4150.00
Frequency: Weekly
Founded in: 1986
Printed in 2 colors on matte stock

5805 **MBA Newslink**
Mortgage Bankers Association
1717 Rhode Island Avenue NW
Suite 400
Washington, DC 20036
202-557-2700
mbsnewslink@mortgagebankers.org;
www.mortgagebankers.org
Social Media: Facebook, Twitter, LinkedIn, YouTube
David H Stevens, President/CEO
Marcia Davies, Chief of Staff/SVP
Learn the latest residential, commercial, and multifamily real estate finance news. Hear what's happening at MBA, read special features that provide vital facts and insight into industry trends, news from Washington, DC and more.
Cost: $69.95
Frequency: Daily
Circulation: 54,000

5806 **NACM E-News**
National Association of Credit Management
8840 Columbia 100 Pkwy
Columbia, MD 21045-2100
410-740-5560; *Fax:* 410-740-5574
robins@nacm.org; www.nacm.org
Social Media: Facebook, Twitter, LinkedIn
Toni Drake, Chairperson
Chris Meyers, Chairman Elect
Kevin Quinn, Director
Jay Snyder, Director
News items of interest to credit and business professionals. Free online.

5807 **National Mortgage News**
Thomson Financial Publishing
1 State St
27th Floor
New York, NY 10004-1481
212-803-8333
800-221-1809; *Fax:* 800-235-5552
custserv@thomsonmedia.com;
www.nationalmortgagenews.com
Social Media: Facebook, Twitter, LinkedIn
Timothy Murphy, Group Publisher
Mortgage information, legislation and news.
Cost: $228.00
Frequency: Weekly
Printed in 2 colors on newsprint stock

5808 **Newsbreak**
First Entertainment Credit Union
PO Box 100
Hollywood, CA 90078
323-851-3673
888-800-3328; *Fax:* 323-874-1397
mail@firstent.org; www.firstent.org
Social Media: Facebook, Twitter, You tube
Charles A Bruen, President/CEO
Provides industry, resources and investment news and information for the First Entertainment Credit Union member. Free online.
Frequency: Quarterly

5809 **SNL Daily ThriftWatch**
SNL Financial
212 7th Street NE
Charlottesville, VA 22902
434-977-1600
866-296-3743; *Fax:* 434-977-4466;
www.snl.com
Mike Chin, President
Provides the information that thrift executives and investors require to stay on top of the industry. Available in print and electronic formats.
5 Pages
Frequency: Daily
Founded in: 1987

5810 **Scope**
International Association of Commercial Collectors
4040 W 70th St
Minneapolis, MN 55435-4104
952-925-0760
800-859-9526; *Fax:* 952-926-1624
iacc@commercialcollector.com;
www.commercialcollector.com
Social Media: LinkedIn
Johon Yursha, President
Tammy Schoenberg, Executive Director
Jessica Hartman, Director
Sara Bobrowski, IACC Coordinator
Randy Frazee, Board Treasurer
Provides updates on developments in the industry, important legislative and legal issues, and IACC events and resources. Free to members only.
350 Members
Frequency: Monthly
Circulation: 350
Founded in: 1970
Printed in on glossy stock

5811 **Trade Vendor Quarterly**
Blakeley & Blakeley
2 Park Plaza
Suite 400
Irvine, CA 92614
949-260-0611; *Fax:* 949-260-0613
administrator@vendorland.com;
www.vendorlaw.com
Scott Blakey, Esq.
Highlights developments in commercial, creditors' rights, e-commerce and bankruptcy law of interest to the credit and financial professional. Free online.
Frequency: Quarterly

Magazines & Journals

5812 **Affordable Housing Finance**
Hanley Wood
300 Montgomery Street
Suite 1060
San Francisco, CA 94104
415-315-1241; *Fax:* 415-315-1248
ahf@omeda.com; www.housingfinance.com
Social Media: Facebook, Twitter
John McManus, Editorial Director
Jerry Ascierto, Editor in Chief
Offers practical information on obtaining debt and equality financing from federal, state, and local governments as well as private resources. In-depth coverage on the federal low-income housing tax credit program, tax-exempt bond financing, corporate tax credit investigation.
Cost: $83.00
88 Pages
Frequency: Monthly
Circulation: 9000
Founded in: 1993
Printed in 4 colors on glossy stock

5813 **American Bankruptcy Institute Journal**
American Bankruptcy Institute
44 Canal Center Plz
Suite 404
Alexandria, VA 22314-1546
703-739-0800; *Fax:* 703-739-1060
Support@abiworld.org; www.abiworld.org
Social Media: Facebook, Twitter, LinkedIn
James Markus, President
Patricia Redmond, President-elect
Margaret Howard, VP Research
Brian Shaw, VP Membership

Benefit to ABI members. Written by experts in the insolvency community, the Journal addresses timely issues involving consumer bankruptcy, the intersection of state laws and the Bankrupcy Code, valuation, turnaround management concerns, recent legislative developments, the US trustee system and more. Available in print or online.
Cost: $225.00
Frequency: 1 Year 10 Issue
Circulation: 10500
Founded in: 1982
Printed in 5 colors on matte stock

5814 **Apartment Finance Today Magazine**
Hanley Wood LLC
One Thomas Circle, NW
Suite 600
Washington, DC 20005
202-452-0800; *Fax:* 202-785-1974;
www.hanleywood.com
Peter Goldston, CEO
Frank Anton, Vice Chairman
Provides in-depth and unbiased reporting and insightful analysis for owners, developers and asset managers
80 Pages
ISSN: 1097-4059
Founded in: 1995
Printed in 4 colors on glossy stock

5815 **Business Credit Magazine**
National Association of Credit Management
8840 Columbia 100 Pkwy
Columbia, MD 21045-2100
410-740-5560; *Fax:* 410-740-5574
robins@nacm.org; www.nacm.org
Social Media: Facebook, Twitter, LinkedIn
Toni Drake, Chairperson
Chris Meyers, Chairman/elect
Kevin Quinn, Director
Jay Snyder, Director
Serves those responsible for extending business and trade credit and overseeing risk management for their companies. Keeps individuals up-to-date on cutting-edge trands and important legislative, bankruptcy, business ethics, trade finance, asset protection, benchmarking and scoring issues.
Frequency: 9x/Year
Circulation: 22000

5816 **Card Technology**
Thomson Financial Publishing
Thomson Reuters
3 Times Square
New York, NY 10036
646-223-4000
general.info@thomsonreuters.com;
www.tfn.com
Thomas H Glocer, Chief Executive Officer
Store-value cards, optical-memory cards, biometrics, cards on the Internet, cards for electronic data storage, and devices used with these cards in banking, government, telecommunications, transportation and education.
Cost: $ 98.00
Frequency: Monthly
Circulation: 25000
Founded in: 1961
Printed in 4 colors on glossy stock

5817 **Collections & Credit Risk**
Thomson Financial Publishing
1 State St
27th Floor
New York, NY 10004-1481
212-803-8200
800-221-1809; *Fax:* 800-843-9600
custserv@sourcemedia.com;
www.creditcollectionsworld.com
Darren Waggoner, Chief Editor
Melissa Buonos, National Sales Manager
Focuses on news and trends of strategic and competitive importance to collections and credit policy executives. Covers the credit risk industry's growth, diversification and technology in both commercial and consumer credit.
Cost: $98.00
66 Pages
Frequency: Monthly
Circulation: 25000
Founded in: 1996

5818 **Commercial Collection Guidelines for Credit Grantors**
International Association of Commercial Collectors
4040 W 70th St
Minneapolis, MN 55435-4104
952-925-0760
800-859-9526; *Fax:* 952-926-1624
iacc@commercialcollector.com;
www.commercialcollector.com
Social Media: LinkedIn
John Yursha, President
Tammy M. Schoenberg, Executive Director
Jessica Hartman, Director
Sara Bobrowski, IACC Coordinator
Randy Frazee, Board Treasurer
Helps to assist commercial account credit managers and their staffs in evaluating receivables and collecting accounts. Topics include internal credit control, credit granting and collecting and professional commercial collection service.
Cost: $70.00
350 Members
Frequency: Monthly
Founded in: 1970

5819 **Credit & Financial Management Review**
Credit Research Foundation
1812 Baltimore Blvd
Suite H
Westminster, MD 21157
443-821-3000; *Fax:* 443-821-3627;
www.crfonline.org
Lyle Wallis, President
Referred journal that publishes original material concerned with all aspects of credit, accounts receivable and customer financial relationships. It is devoted to the improvement and further development of the theory and practice of credit management.
Cost: $80.00
56 Pages
Frequency: Quarterly
Circulation: 3000
Printed in 2 colors

5820 **Credit Card Management**
Thomson Financial Publishing
Thomas Reuters
3 Times Square
New York, NY 10036
646-223-4000
800-782-5555; *Fax:* 646-223-8593;
www.tfn.com
Thomas H Glocer, Chief Executive Officer
Information on the major developments in the credit card industry.
Cost: $98.00
74 Pages
Frequency: Monthly
Circulation: 19000
Printed in 4 colors on glossy stock

5821 **Credit Professional**
Credit Professionals International
10726 Manchester Rd
Suite B
St Louis, MO 63122-1320
314-821-9393; *Fax:* 314-821-7171
creditpro@creditprofessionals.org;
www.creditprofessionals.org
Sue Heusing, President
Rhonda McKinney, VP
Charlotte Rancilio, Editor
A bi-annual magazine published by Credit Professionals International.
Cost: $15.00
Frequency: Bi-annually
Circulation: 550
Founded in: 1989

5822 **Credit Union Magazine**
Credit Union National Association
601 Penn Ave
NW South Building, Suite 600
Washington, DC 20004
202-628-5777
800-356-9655; *Fax:* 202-638-7729
webservices@cuna.org; www.cuna.org
Social Media: Facebook, Twitter
Daniel A Mica, CEO
Tom Dorety, Vice Chairman
Kathy Kuehn, Manager Periodicals
The role and operations of modern credit unions.
Cost: $50.00
100 Pages
Frequency: Monthly
Circulation: 34401
ISSN: 0011-1066
Printed in 4 colors on glossy stock

5823 **Federal Credit Union Magazine**
National Association of Federal Credit Unions
3138 10th St N
Arlington, VA 22201-2149
703-522-4770
800-336-4644; *Fax:* 703-524-1082
fbecker@nafcu.org; www.nafcu.org
Social Media: Facebook, Twitter, YouTube
Fred Becker, President
Alicia Hosmer, VP, Marketing
Written for CEO's, senior staff and volunteers of Federal Credit Unions. Offers legislative and regulatory news, as well as technology and operational issues. Call for rates.
50 Pages
Circulation: 1500
ISSN: 1043-7789
Founded in: 1967
Printed in 4 colors on glossy stock

5824 **News and Views**
Advertising Media Credit Executives Association
8840 Columbia 100 Parkway
Columbia, MD 21045-2158
410-992-7609; *Fax:* 410-740-5574
amcea@amcea.org; www.amcea.org
Sheila Wroten, President
Mary Younger, VP
Vickie Bolinger, Director
Our magazine reports on current trends and legal issues while offering tips on customer service, time management and collections.
Frequency: Quarterly
Founded in: 1953

Trade Shows

5825 **AMCEA Conference**
Advertising Media Credit Executives Association

8840 Columbia 100 Parkway
Columbia, MD 21045-2158

410-992-7609; *Fax:* 410-740-5574
amcea@amcea.org; www.amcea.org

Sheila Wroten, President
Kimberly Riley, VP
Vickie Bolinger, Director

The conference encompasses four days and is a networking extravaganza. Top attorneys discuss bankruptcy and legal issues. We invite advertising agencies to discuss network buying and liability problems.
Frequency: Annual

5826 **Credit Union Executive Society Annual Convention: CUES**
5510 Research Park Drive
Madison, WI 53711-5377

608-712-2664
800-252-2664; *Fax:* 608-271-2303
cues@cues.org; www.cues.org
Social Media: Facebook, Twitter, LinkedIn

Fred Johnson, CEO/President

Offers a rainbow of marketing and technology topics, as well as a supplier showcase, geared toward board members.
Frequency: June
Founded in: 1962

5827 **Credit Union National Association Governmental Affairs Conference**
Credit Union National Association
601 Penn Ave
NW South Building, Suite 600
Washington, DC 20004

202-628-5777
800-356-9655; *Fax:* 202-638-7729;
www.cuna.org
Social Media: Facebook, Twitter

Susan Newton, Executive Director
Pat Sowick, VP
Richard Dines, Senior State and League Affairs Dir
Alicia Valencia Erb, League Relations
Shellee Mitchell, Executive Assistant

Annual conference held in Washington, DC, with a focus on legislative issues impacting credit unions.
Frequency: February

5828 **Credit Union National Association Future Forum**
601 Penn Ave
NW South Building, Suite 600
Washington, DC 20004

202-628-5777
800-356-9655; *Fax:* 202-638-7729;
www.cuna.org
Social Media: Facebook, Twitter

Susan Newton, Executive Director
Pat Sowick, VP
Richard Dines, Senior State and League Affairs Dir
Alicia Valencia Erb, League Relations
Shellee Mitchell, Executive Assistant

Convention and annual general meeting with exhibit hall, educational sessions, and other events.
Frequency: September

5829 **Defense Credit Union's Annual Conference**
Defense Credit Union Council
601 Pennsylvania Avenue NW
South Building, Suite 600
Washington, DC 20004

202-638-3950; *Fax:* 202-638-3410
admin@dcuc.org; www.dcuc.org

Conference and exhibits of equipment, supplies and services for credit unions that serve Department of Defense personnel with problems peculiar to military installations and personnel.
200 Attendees
Frequency: August

5830 **Education Credit Union Council Annual Conference**
Education Credit Union Council
PO Box 7558
Spanish Fort, AL 36577-7558

251-626-3399; *Fax:* 251-626-3565;
www.ecuc.org

Lorraine B Zerfas, Executive Director

Any CEOs, directors, committee members and top management active in the operations of any credit union that serves the educational community who want to achieve professional excellence should attend. Interact with peers from across the US serving the fields of education, introduce executive staff and managers to credit union ideas and philosophy on a national level and discuss issues important to your credit union in the coming year.
Frequency: February

5831 **Finance, Credit & International Business Global Conference**
Finance, Credit & International Business
8840 Columbia 100 Parkway
Columbia, MD 21045-2158

410-423-1840
888-256-3242; *Fax:* 410-423-1845
fcib_info@fciglobal.com; www.fcibglobal.com
Social Media: Twitter, LinkedIn

Annual gathering of international credit and finance professionals draws upon the combined expertise of financial executives from all regions of the world to provide attendees with practical insight for managing in a rapidly evolving international environment.
Frequency: November

5832 **Fleet/Lease Remarketing**
S&A Conferences Group
Westview At Weston
301 Cascade Pointe Lane
Cary, NC 27513

800-608-7500; *Fax:* 919-674-6027;
www.autoremarketing.com
Social Media: Facebook, Twitter, LinkedIn

Ron Smith, President

Executive conference focused on remarketing strategies for manufacturer, bank, finance, commercial and rental fleet/lease vehicles.
Frequency: February

5833 **International Association of Commercial Collectors Annual Convention**
4040 W 70th Street
Minneapolis, MN 55435

952-925-0760
800-859-9526; *Fax:* 952-926-1624
iacc@commercialcollector.com;
www.commercialcollector.com
Social Media: LinkedIn

John Yursha, President
Tammy M. Schoenberg, Executive Director

International trade association comprised of more than 230 collection specialists and 140 commercial attorneys, with members throughout the US and 20 international countries. IACC's mission is to promote the commercial collection profession by providing IACC members with the resources to excel in the industry.
350 Members
Frequency: January
Founded in: 1970

5834 **Legal Issues & Regulatory Compliance Conference**
Mortgage Bankers Association
1717 Rhode Island Avenue NW
Suite 400
Washington, DC 20036

202-557-2700
meetings@mortgagebankers.org;
www.mortgagebankers.org
Social Media: Facebook, Twitter, LinkedIn, YouTube

David H Stevens, President/CEO
Marcia Davies, Chief of Staff/SVP

Learn about all the legal and regulatory developments facing the industry.
Frequency: Annual/May

5835 **NFCC Leaders Conference**
National Foundation for Credit Counseling
2000M Street NW
Suite 505
Washington, DC 20036

202-677-4300
800-388-2227; www.nfcc.org
Social Media: Facebook, Twitter, YouTube

Susan C Keating, President/CEO
Paul Weiss, CFO/ Chief Of Staff
William Binzel, Chief Counsel

Three-day conference to discuss credit counseling industry practices, trends and issues.
300 Attendees
Frequency: Annual/Fall
Founded in: 1965

5836 **NRLA Annual Conference**
National Rural Lenders Association
2402 E 44th Place
Tulsa, OK 74105

918-430-3956; *Fax:* 918-550-8293
media@nrla-usda.org
nrla-usda.org

Greg O'Donnell, Executive Director

Hear from, and interact with, policy makers.
Frequency: Annual
Founded in: 2015

5837 **National Association of Credit Management: Annual Credit Congress**
National Association of Credit Management
8840 Columbia 100 Parkway
Columbia, MD 21045

410-740-5560; *Fax:* 410-740-5574
robins@nacm.org; www.nacm.org
Social Media: Facebook, Twitter, LinkedIn

Toni Drake, Chairperson
Chris Meyers, Chairman/elect
Kevin Quinn, Director
Jay Snyder, Director

The event for the business credit and financial professional offering relevant, timely educational offerings, including industry specific programs, over 100 specialized service providers on the expo floor, showcasing the latest products and services, countless networking and relationship-building events to facilitate the sharing of knowlege and expertise.
18000 Members
2000 Attendees
Frequency: May/June

5838 **National Fraud Issues Conference**
Mortgage Bankers Association
1717 Rhode Island Avenue NW
Suite 400
Washington, DC 20036

202-557-2700
meetings@mortgagebankers.org;
www.mortgagebankers.org

Social Media: Facebook, Twitter, LinkedIn, YouTube

David H Stevens, President/CEO
Marcia Davies, Chief of Staff/SVP

The forum where industry professionals can learn about the issues related to the growing incidence and complexity of mortgage fraud.
Frequency: Annual/March

5839 National Mortgage Servicing Conference & Expo
Mortgage Bankers Association
1717 Rhode Island Avenue NW
Suite 400
Washington, DC 20036

202-557-2700
meetings@mortgagebankers.org;
www.mortgagebankers.org
Social Media: Facebook, Twitter, LinkedIn, YouTube

David H Stevens, President/CEO
Marcia Davies, Chief of Staff/SVP

Provides the opportunity to reach key servicing executives from residential mortgage companies and showcase the product offerings, network with key decision makers, and obtain qualified leads that can help reach goals.
Frequency: Annual/February

5840 National Policy Conference
Mortgage Bankers Association
1717 Rhode Island Avenue NW
Suite 400
Washington, DC 20036

202-557-2700
meetings@mortgagebankers.org;
www.mortgagebankers.org
Social Media: Facebook, Twitter, LinkedIn, YouTube

David H Stevens, President/CEO
Marcia Davies, Chief of Staff/SVP

Brings together key officials, cabinet members and special guest speakers to address these critical issues.
Frequency: Annual/March

5841 National Technology in Mortgage Banking Conference
Mortgage Bankers Association
1717 Rhode Island Avenue NW
Suite 400
Washington, DC 20036

202-557-2700
meetings@mortgagebankers.org;
www.mortgagebankers.org
Social Media: Facebook, Twitter, LinkedIn, YouTube

David H Stevens, President/CEO
Marcia Davies, Chief of Staff/SVP

Forum to learn about the newest industry solutions and how they can increase your company's competitive edge. The conference focuses on relevant topics, including legal / regulatory updates, eMortgages, investor reporting changes and technology advances such as mobile computing.
Frequency: Annual/March

5842 Risk Management Conference
Risk Management Association
1801 Market Street
Suite 300
Philadelphia, PA 19103-1628

215-446-4000
800-677-7621; *Fax:* 215-446-4100
customers@rmahq.org; www.rmahq.org

William F Githens, President/CEO
Kathleen M Beans, Public Relations Manager

Educates and helps risk management professionals develop new techniques and learn about new innovative products at different stages of their careers. Mailing list available for exhibitors and sponsors only.
800 Attendees
Frequency: October

Directories & Databases

5843 AMCEA Member Handbook & Roster
Advertising Media Credit Executives Association
8840 Columbia 100 Parkway
Columbia, MD 21045-2158

410-992-7609; *Fax:* 410-740-5574
amcea@amcea.org; www.amcea.org

Sheila Wroten, President
Kimberly Riley, VP
Vickie Bolinger, Director

Inside you will find direct telephone numbers to every credit manager in our association along with numbers for credit references and fax inquiries. We also include their e-mail addresses and computer hardware and software information.

5844 American Recovery Association Directory
American Recovery Association
5525 N MacArthur Boulevard
Suite 135
Irving, TX 75038

972-755-4755; *Fax:* 972-870-5755
homeoffice@americanrecoveryassn.org;
www.repo.org

Mary Jane Hogan, President
Tom Crosby, Secretary/Treasurer

Contain's listings of ARA's members, offices and services. Available in hardcopy and electronic formats.
308 Pages
Frequency: Annual
Founded in: 1965

5845 Banksearch Book
Sheshunoff Information Services
2801 Via Fortuna
Suite 600
Austin, TX 78746-7970

512-472-4000
800-477-1772; www.smslp.com

Gabrielle Sheshunoff, CEO

Offers information on savings and loans, savings banks and credit unions with assets over 10 million. Customized for your institutution type: bank thrift, bank holding company or credit union. You buy only the data you want — by state, region or nation.
Cost: $295.00
Frequency: Annual

5846 Business Products Credit Association
BCPA
607 Westridge Drive
O'Fallon, MO 63366

636-924-5775; *Fax:* 636-754-0567
service@bpca.org; www.bpca.org

BPCA has a database of over 400,000 companies and their payment histories. This is available to members over the Internet.

5847 Callahan's Credit Union Directory
Callahan & Associates
1001 Connecticut Ave NW
Suite 1001
Washington, DC 20036-5523

202-223-3920
800-446-7453; *Fax:* 202-223-1311;
www.callahan.com

Sean Hession, CEO
Charles Filson, Chairman
Jay Johnson, EVP
Alix Patterson, COO

This directory turns raw data into research, giving you the tools you need to keep up with the credit union industry. Access all the credit union information found in the print edition through the Online Edition on this website. In a special Users Area only for purchasers of the print edition, you can access updated finacials four times a year, conduct searches on key information and save those search results to return to over and over again. Real time updates directly from our database.
Cost: $135.00
Frequency: Annual

5848 Collection Agency Directory
First Detroit Corporation
PO Box 5025
Warren, MI 48090-5025

586-573-0045
800-366-5995; *Fax:* 586-573-9219;
www.firstdetroit.com

Albert W Scace, Publisher

Offers information and statistics on nearly 900 collection agencies throught the world.
Cost: $347.00
301 Pages
Frequency: Annual, Paperback
ISSN: 1058-983X
Founded in: 1991
Mailing list available for rent: 11,000 names at $150 per M
Printed in one color on matte stock

5849 Credit
American Financial Services Association
919 18th Street NW
Suite 300
Washington, DC 20006-5517

202-296-5544
sharrison@afsamail.org; www.afsaonline.org
Social Media: Twitter

Chris Steinebert, President/CEO

Focuses on breaking developments on legislative and regulatory issues on the federal and state levels, as well as consumer education initiatives, industry news, news inside AFSA and information on meetings and conferences. Free online access.
1500 Pages
Frequency: Bi-Monthly

5850 Credit Card and Check Fraud: A Stop-Loss Manual
Fraud & Theft Information Bureau
9770 S. Military Trail
Suite 380
Boynton Beach, FL 33436

561-737-8700; *Fax:* 561-737-5800
sales@fraudandtheftinfo.com;
www.fraudandtheftinfo.com

Larry Schwartz, Founder and Director
Pearl Sax, Founder and Director

The Fraud And Theft Information Bureau is the leading consultant on credit card and check fraud control and loss prevention — and the publisher of related manuals and fraud-blocker data bases
Cost: $199.95
300 Pages
Founded in: 1982

5851 Credit Union Cooperatives
Callahan & Associates

1001 Connecticut Ave NW
10th Floor
Washington, DC 20036-5523

202-223-3920
800-446-7453; *Fax:* 202-223-1311;
www.callahan.com

Sean Hession, CEO
Charles Filson, Chairman
Jay Johnson, EVP
Alix Patterson, COO

Your source for information on credit union service organizations (CUSOs) and other cooperative providers to the credit industry. The directory has up-to-date contact names, addresses and phone numbers for more than 700 CUSOs and their associated credit unions. Use this publication to compare services offered by CUSOs or if you're looking to start or expand an existing CUSO.
Cost: $165.00

5852 **Credit Union Directory**
National Credit Union Administration
1775 Duke St
Suite 4206
Alexandria, VA 22314-6115

703-518-6300
800-755-1030; *Fax:* 703-518-6539
consumerassistance@ncua.gov; www.ncua.gov
Social Media: Facebook, Twitter, YouTube

Debbie Matz, Chairman

Federal credit and state-chartered credit unions are the focal point of this directory. Free online.
Frequency: Annual

5853 **Credit Union Financial Yearbook**
Callahan & Associates
1001 Connecticut Ave NW
Washington, DC 20036-5523

202-223-3920
800-446-7453; *Fax:* 202-223-1311;
www.callahan.com

Sean Hession, CEO
Charles Filson, Chairman
Jay Johnson, EVP
Alix Patterson, COO

Each quarter Callahan publishes a comprehensive study on the state of the industry that includes detailed financials for all credit unions over $50 million. The third quarter edition is published in 3 volumes based on asset size. Fourth quarter edition is based on total assets for the year. Asset sizes considered are $50 to $100 million, $100 - $250 million and over $250 million.
Cost: $565.00
Frequency: Complete Year Price

5854 **Defense Credit Union Directory**
Defense Credit Union Council
601 Pennsylvania Ave NW
Suite 600
Washington, DC 20004-2601

202-638-3950; *Fax:* 202-638-3410
admin@dcuc.org; www.dcuc.org

Roland Arteata, President

Listing of about 360 credit unions with membership consisting wholly or partly of the military and civilian personnel of the United States and worldwide.
Cost: $150.00
60 Pages
Frequency: Biennial
Founded in: 1963

5855 **Directory of Venture Capital & Private Equity Firms - Online Database**
Grey House Publishing
4919 Route 22
PO Box 56
Amenia, NY 12501

518-789-8700
800-562-2139; *Fax:* 845-373-6390
gold@greyhouse.com
http://gold.greyhouse.com
Social Media: Facebook, Twitter

Leslie Mackenzie, Publisher
Richard Gottlieb, Editor

Packed with need-to-know information, this database offers immediate access to 2,300 VC firms, over 10,000 managing partners, and over 11,500 VC investments.
Frequency: Annual

5856 **Directory of Venture Capital and Private Equity Firms**
Grey House Publishing
4919 Route 22
PO Box 56
Amenia, NY 12501

518-789-8700
800-562-2139; *Fax:* 845-373-6390
books@greyhouse.com; www.greyhouse.com
Social Media: Facebook, Twitter

Richard Gottlieb, President
Leslie Mackenzie, Publisher

Offers access to over 2,300 domestic and international venture capital and private equity firms, with detailed contact information and extensive data on investment and funds.
Cost: $685.00
1200 Pages
Frequency: Annual
ISBN: 1-592372-72-4

5857 **Dun's Credit Guide**
Dun & Bradstreet Information Service
103 John F Kennedy Pkwy
Short Hills, NJ 07078-2708

973-921-5500
800-234-3867; *Fax:* 908-665-5803;
www.dnb.com
Social Media: Facebook, Twitter, LinkedIn, YouTube

Sara Mathew, CEO
James Fernandez, EVP and COO

Providing a dollar-specific credit guideline on manufacturers, wholesalers and retailers, this database is updated continuously for the interested business person.

5858 **National Credit Union Administration Directory**
National Credit Union Administration
1775 Duke St
Suite 4206
Alexandria, VA 22314-6115

703-518-6300; *Fax:* 703-518-6539
ociomail@ncua.gov; www.ncua.gov

Debbie Matz, Chairman

Directory of credit unions governed by a three member board appointed by the President and confirmed by the US Senate, by the independent federal agency that charters and supervises federal credit unions. NCUA, with the backing of the full faith and credit of the US government, operates the National Credit Union Share Insurance Fund, insuring the savings of 80 million account holders in all federal credit unions and many state chartered credit unions.

5859 **Thomson Credit Union Directory**
4709 Golf Road
Skokie, IL 60076-1231

847-676-9600
800-321-3373; *Fax:* 847-933-8101
custserv@accuitysolutions.com;
www.accuitysolutions.com

Hugh Johnes IV, President and CEO
Kerry Hewson, EVP
Jay Ryan, Head of Sales

Semi-annual directory that includes valuable industry statistics, a quick telephone lookup index of all credit unions and a resource guide featuring vendors within the credit union marketplace. Includes over 12,500 major credit unions and 5,500 branches, with asset rankings, membership totals and more. Published in partnership with the Credit Union National Association.
Cost: $199.00
Frequency: January/July
ISBN: 1-563103-24-9

5860 **Who's Who in Credit and Financial**
New York Credit and Financial Management Assn
520 8th Avenue
New York, NY 10018-6507

212-695-4807

Directory of services and supplies to the industry.

5861 **World Council of Credit Unions Directory**
World Council of Credit Unions
5710 Mineral Point Road
Madison, WI 53705

608-395-2000; *Fax:* 608-395-2001
mail@woccu.org; www.woccu.org

Pepi Dougherty, Executive
Mike Muckian, Marketing & Communications

Lists over 100 World Council of Credit Union leaders and member organizations in each of seven confederations. African, Asian, Australian, Canadian, Caribbean, Latin-American and the United States.

Industry Web Sites

5862 **http://gold.greyhouse.com**
G.O.L.D Grey House OnLine Databases

Grey House Publishing's online database platform, GOLD, offers Quick Search, Keyword Search and Expert Search for most business sectors including banking, credid and lending service markets. The GOLD platform makes finding the information you need quick and easy - whether you're a novice searcher or an experienced database user. All of Grey House's directory products are available for subscription on the GOLD platform.

5863 **www.aacul.org**
American Association of Credit Union Leagues

Voluntary membership association for credit union leagues that are members of the Credit Union National Association. AACUL provides representation, products, services and programs to its members.

5864 **www.abiworld.org**
American Bankruptcy Institute

ABI is the largest multi-diciplinary, non-partisan organization dedicated to research and education on matters related to insolvency. The ABI membership provides a forum for the exchange of ideas and information. ABI is engaged in numerous educational and research activities, as well as the production of a number of publications both for the insolvency practitioner and the public.

5865 **www.afsaonline.com**
American Financial Services Association

National trade association for market funded providers of financial services to consumers and small businesses. These providers offer an array of finacial services, including unsecured personal loans, automobile loans, home equity loans and credit cards through specialized bank institutions.

5866 **www.amcea.org**
Advertising Media Credit Executives Association
Improving the professionalism, principles, understanding and techniques of media credit management by encouraging the exchange of ideas, methods and procedures within the membership. Providing additional education and training in the business fundamentals of media credit and credit policies and in the related areas of finance, accounting, law and economics for the purpose of enhancing the career development of members.

5867 **www.bccacredit.com**
Broadcast Cable Credit Association
Subsidiary of the Broadcast Cable Financial Management Association. BCCA provides industry specific credit reports on individual agencies, advertisers, or buying services (national and local).

5868 **www.bpca.org**
Business Products Credit Association
Nonprofit trade association for credit personnel of manufacturers, wholesalers and factors. The national credit group consists of discount stores, superstores, commercial stationers, printing and publications, business machines, computer peripherals and software, plus mass merchandisers. In addition, BPCA has groups on school supply, janitorial/sanitary supplies, fine pens/promotional products.

5869 **www.cdiaonline.org**
Consumer Data Industry Association
Trade association representing consumer information companies that provide fraud prevention and risk management products, credit and mortgage reports, tenant and employment screening services, check fraud and verifacation services and collection services. Sets industry standards and provides education for it's members. Provides educational materials for consumers regarding their credit rights and how consumer credit reporting agencies can better serve their needs.

5870 **www.cfa.com**
Commercial Finance Association
Trade group of the asset-based financial services industry, with members throughout the US, Canada and around the world. Members include the asset-based lending arms of domestic and foreign commercial banks, small and large independent finance companies, floor plan financing organizations, factoring organizations and financing subsidiaries of major industrial corporations.

5871 **www.collector.com**
American Collectors Association
International trade organization of credit and collection professionals that provides a variety of accounts recievable management services.

5872 **www.commercialcollector.com**
International Association of Commercial Collectors
International trade association comprised of more than 230 collection specialists and 140 commercial attorneys, with members throughout the US and 20 international countries. IACC's mission is to promote the commercial collection profession by providing IACC members with the resources to excel in the industry.

5873 **www.creditunions.com**
Callahan & Associates
National credit union research and consulting firm specializing in financial publications and analysis software, strategic planning and investment management.

5874 **www.crfonline.org**
Credit Research Foundation
Independent, member run organization, consisting of a dynamic community of like minded business professionals with a vested interest in improving and fostering the field of business credit — more specifically, the practices and technologies of business credit.

5875 **www.cues.org**
Credit Union Executives Society
For credit union executives, we serve to advance the professional development of CEOs, senior management and directors.

5876 **www.cuna.org**
Credit Union National Association
The premier trade association in the financial services arena. Supports, protects, unifies and advances the credit union movement.

5877 **www.ecuc.org**
Education Credit Union Council
Dedicated to providing educational and networking opportunities to credit unions who serve educational communities, industry teachers, administrators, students, support staff and others in the educational community.

5878 **www.electran.org**
Electronic Transaction Association
International trade association serving the needs of organizations offering transaction processing products and services.

5879 **www.fcibglobal.com**
FCIB
Provider of products and services to many small, medium and large size exporters as well as major multinational corporations in 30 countries around the world.

5880 **www.firstent.org**
First Entertainment Credit Union
Nonprofit institution serves as the financial resource for the entertainment community to more than 700 entertainment based companies.

5881 **www.fraudandtheftinfo.com**
Fraud & Theft Information Bureau
Provides problem solving, crime prevention, money saving manuals and fraud blocker databases.

5882 **www.greyhouse.com**
Grey House Publishing
Authoritative reference directories for most business sectors including banking, credit and lending service markets. Users can search the online databases with varied search criteria allowing for custom searches by product category, geographic area, sales volume, keyword, subject and more. Full Grey House catalog and online ordering also available.

5883 **www.mbaa.org**
Mortgage Bankers Association of America
Representing the real estate finance industry, MBA serves its membership by representing their legislative and regulatory interests before the US Congress and federal agencies; by meeting their educational needs through programs and a range of periodicals and publications; and by supporting their business interests with a variety of research initiatives and other products and services.

5884 **www.nacm.org**
National Association of Credit Management
Promotes honest and fair dealings in credit transactions, fosters and encourages research in the field of credit.

5885 **www.ncua.gov**
National Credit Union Administration
Governed by a three-member board appointed by the President and confirmed by the US Senate, this is the independent federal agency that charters and supervises the nation's federal credit unions.

5886 **www.nfcc.org**
National Foundation for Credit Counceling
National nonprofit credit counseling oranization with 1,200 offices helping 1.5 million households annually. Identify NFCC members (Consumer Credit Counseling Service CCCS) by the NFCC member seal representing high standards, free and low-cost confidential services.

5887 **www.repo.org**
American Recovery Association
Approximately 500 offices throughout the US, Canada and Germany, providing repossesion services around the world.

5888 **www.rmahg.org**
Risk Management Association
Financial services association that champions best practices in risk management, monitors emerging trends, develops new risk management techniques, innovative products, and education and training programs geared to risk management professionals.

Associations

5889 ATM Industry Association

www.atmia.com
Social Media: Facebook, Twitter, LinkedIn, YouTube

Mike Lee, Chief Executive Officer
Sharon Lane, Global Director, Finance
Dana Benson, Dir., Conferences & Sponsorships
Amanda Hardy, Marketing Director, Europe
David Tente, Executive Director, USA

Alliance promoting the proliferation of automated teller machines, ATMs and cash.
5000 Members
Founded in: 1997

5890 Advanced Network & Services

2600 South Road
Suite 44-193
Poughkeepsie, NY 12601

845-795-2090; *Fax:* 845-795-2180
contact@advanced.org; www.advanced.org
Social Media: Facebook, Twitter, LinkedIn

William Howle, Chairman of the Board
Allan Weis, Founder/President/Managing Director
Kristin Mortensen, Secretary/Treasurer

A nonprofit corporation dedicated to advancing education by accelerating the use of computer networking applications and technology.
Mailing list available for rent

5891 American e-Commerce Association

www.aeaus.com

Computer training, e-commerce education, membership, recognition, endorsement, and evaluation services.

5892 Armed Forces Communications and Electronics Association (AFCEA)

4400 Fair Lakes Court
Fairfax, VA 22033-3899

703-631-6100
800-336-4583; *Fax:* 703-631-6169;
www.afcea.org
Social Media: Facebook, Twitter, LinkedIn, Google+, Flickr, YouTube

Linda Gooden, Chair of the Board of Directors
Brig Gen John Meincke, Vice Chair, B.O.D.
LtGen Robert M. Shea, President, CEO
Pat Miorin, CPA, EVP, CFO, Int. Treasurer
Mike Warlick, Vice President, Defense Operations

A nonprofit international organization that serves its members by providing a forum for the ethical exchange of information and is dedicated to increasing knowledge through the exploration of issues relevant to information technology, communication, and electronics for the defense, homeland security and intelligence communities.

5893 Business Software Alliance

20 F Street, NW
Suite 800
Washington, DC 20001

202-872-5500; *Fax:* 202-872-5501
info@bsa.org; www.bsa.org
Social Media: Facebook, Twitter, LinkedIn, YouTube, RSS

Steven Dietz, Chair
Bruce Sewell, Vice Chair
Bradford Smith, Secretary
Scott Taylor, Treasurer

An organization dedicated to promoting a safe and legal digital world. BSA educates consumers on software management and copyright protection, cyber security, trade, e-commerce and other internet related issues.
Founded in: 1988

5894 Center for Internet Security

31 Tech Valley Drive
Suite 2
East Greenbush, NY 12061

518-266-3460; *Fax:* 518-283-3216
contact@cisecurity.org; www.cisecurity.org
Social Media: Facebook, Twitter, LinkedIn, Blog, YouTube

John M Giiligan, Chairman
Jack Arthur, Treasurer
Deirdre O' Callaghan, Chief Counsel and Secretary
Jane Holl Lute, CEO
Steven J Spano, President and CEO

A nonprofit organization that provides products and resources that help partners achieve security goals through expert guidance and cost-effective solutions.

5895 CompTIA

3500 Lacey Road
Suite 100
Downers Grove, IL 60515

630-678-8300
866-835-8020; *Fax:* 630-678-8384
techvoice@comptia.org; www.comptia.org
Social Media: Facebook, Twitter, LinkedIn, Pinterest, Google+, YouTube

Todd Thibodeaux, President, CEO
Charles Eaton, CEO, Educational Foundation
Ann Batko, SVP, Marketing
Kelly Ricker, SVP, Events and Education
David Sommer, Chief Financial Officer

A nonprofit trade association created by representatives of five microcomputer leaderships and is a provider of professional certifications for theinformation technology (IT) industry.

5896 Council on CyberSecurity

1700 North Moore Street
Suite 2100
Arlington, VA 22209
703-600-1935
info@counciloncybersecurity.org;
www.cisecurity.org
Social Media: Facebook, Twitter, LinkedIn

John M Giiligan, Chairman
Jack Arthur, Treasurer
Deirdre O' Callaghan, Chief Counsel and Secretary
Jane Holl Lute, CEO
Steven J Spano, President and CEO

Organization that mobilizes a broad community of stakeholders to identify, validate, promote and sustain the adoption of cybersecurity best practice.

5897 Cyber Security Research Alliance

401 Edgewater Place
Suite 600
Wakefield, MA 1880

781-876-8860
aobrien@cybersecurityresearch.org;
www.cybersecurityresearch.org

Julian Warrick, Interim President
Steven Kester, Treasurer
Claire Vishik, Secretary

A nonprofit organization founded by industry stakeholders as a forum develop R & D strategy to address grand challenges in cyber security, and to facilitate public-private partnerships that define a more focused, coordinated, and concerted approach to cyber security research and development.

5898 Cyber, Space, & Intelligence Association

703-855-3917
richcoleman1@gmail.com
cyberspaceintel.org

Richard Coleman, Chairman, President and Founder
Tidal W. (Ty) McCoy, Senior Executive
Timothy J. Evans, Senior Advisor
Founded in: 2011

5899 Cybersecurity Association

127 Segre Place
Santa Cruz, CA 95060

831-426-9827
paul.hoffman@cybersecurity.org;
www.cybersecurity.org

Organization focused on testing the security capabilities and performance of firewalls, intrusion prevention systems and other similar security equipment.

5900 High Technology Crime Investigation Association

3288 Goldstone Drive
Roseville, CA 95747

916-408-1751; *Fax:* 916-384-2232
info@htcia.org; www.htcia.org
Social Media: Facebook, Twitter, LinkedIn

Carol Hutchings, Executive Director
Jimmy Garcia, Public Relations
Elisa Hutchings, Membership Inquiries

A nonprofit professional organization devoted to the prevention, investigation, and prosecution of crimes involving advanced technologies.
Founded in: 1984

5901 ISACA

3701 Algonquin Road
Suite 1010
Rolling Meadows, IL 60008

847-253-1545; *Fax:* 847-253-1443;
www.isaca.org
Social Media: Facebook, Twitter, LinkedIn, Google+

A nonprofit, independent association that advocates for professionals involved in information security, assurance, risk management and governance.
Founded in: 1969

5902 Information Systems Security Association

12100 Sunset Hills Road
Suite 130
Reston, VA 20190

866-349-5818
703-234-4077; *Fax:* 703-435-4390;
www.issa.org
Social Media: Facebook, Twitter, LinkedIn

Ira Winkler, President
Andrea C. Hoy, Vice President
Kevin D. Spease, Treasurer/CFO
Bill Danigelis, Secretary
Anne Rogers, Director

A nonprofit, international professional organization of informationsecurity professionals and practitioners.

5903 InfraGard

E-Mail: infragardmembership@leo.gov;
www.infragard.org
Social Media: RSS

A nonprofit organization serving as a public-private partnership between U.S. businesses and the Federal Bureau of Investigation.

5904 **Institute for Security, Technology, and Society**
7 Maynard Street
Sudikoff Laboratory
Hanover, NH 03755
603-646-0700; *Fax:* 603-646-1672
info.ists@dartmouth.edu;
www.ists.dartmouth.edu
Social Media: Facebook, Twitter, Flickr, YouTube, iTunes
Organization dedicated to pursuing research and education to advance information security and privacy throughout society.
Founded in: 2000

5905 **Intelligence and National Security Alliance**
Ballston Metro Center Office Towers
901 North Stuart Street, Suite 205
Arlington, VA 22203
703-224-4672; *Fax:* 703-224-4681;
www.insaonline.org
Social Media: Facebook, Twitter, LinkedIn, Google+, Flickr, YouTube
John Negroponte, Chairman of the Board
Joseph R. DeTrani, President
Charles E. Allen, SeniorIntelligenceAdvisor
Chuck Alsup, Vice Presidentof Policy
Robert Joseph, Senior NationalSecurity Advisor
A nonprofit, non-partisan, public-private organization that works to promote and recognize the highest standards within the national security and intelligence communities. Members include current and former high-ranking intelligence, military and government agency leaders, analysts, and experts from industry and academia.
Founded in: 1979

5906 **Internet Merchants Association**
E-Mail: info@imamerchants.org;
www.imamerchants.org
Social Media: Facebook
Fred Neff, President
Scott Cole, Vice-President
Doyle Carver, Secretary
Andy Sollofe, Treasurer
Develops, promotes, and protects the economic vitality of internet merchants through a positive business environment and fosters a climate in whichcommerce, industry, and technology will flourish.

5907 **Internet Security Alliance**
703-907-7090
admin@isalliance.org; www.isalliance.org
Tim McKnight, Board Chairman
Jeff Brown, Board Vice Chairman
Gary McAlum, Board Second Vice Chairman
Larry Clinton, President, CEO
Julie Taylor, Board Member
A nonprofit organization that acts as a forum for information sharing and leadership on information security, and it lobbies for corporate securityinterests.

5908 **National Cyber Security Alliance**
www.staysafeonline.org
Social Media: Facebook, Twitter, LinkedIn, Google+, YouTube
Jacqueline Beauchere, Board President
Michael Kaiser, Executive Director
Tiffany Barrett, Director
Kara Wright, Director of Digital Strategy
Betty Hallman, Director, Development
A nonprofit, public-private partnership working with the Departmentof Homeland Security (DHS), private sector sponsors, and nonprofit collaboratorsto promote cyber security awareness for home users, small and medium size businesses, and primary and secondary education.

5909 **National Cyber-Forensics & Training Alliance**
2000 Technology Drive
Suite 450
Pittsburgh, PA 15219
412-802-8000; *Fax:* 412-802-8510
info@ncfta.net; www.ncfta.net
A nonprofit corporation focused on identifying, mitigating, and neutralizing cyber crime threats through strategic alliances and partnerships with Subject Matter Experts (SME) in the public, private, and academic sectors.

5910 **National CyberWatch Center**
301 Largo Road
Largo, MD 20774
E-Mail: tkepner@nationalcyberwatch.org;
www.nationalcyberwatch.org
Social Media: Facebook, Twitter, LinkedIn, YouTube
Anita Shelton, Administrative Associate
Bob Spear, Senior Advisor
Casey W O'Brien, Executive Director
Costis Toregas, Director, Business Development
An organization of higher education institutions, public and private schools, businesses, and government agencies focused on collaborative efforts to advance cybersecurity education and strengthen the national cybersecurity workforce.

5911 **National Cybersecurity and Communications Integration Center**
245 Murray Lane SW
Building 410
Washington, DC 20598
888-282-0870; www.us-cert.gov/nccic
Social Media: Twitter, RSS
Serves as a central location where a diverse set of partners involved in cybersecurity and communications protection coordinate and synchronize their efforts. Partners include other government agencies, the private sector, and international entities.

5912 **National Initiative for Cybersecurity Careers and Studies**
E-Mail: NICCS@hq.dhs.gov
niccs.us-cert.gov
Robin Williams, Chief
A national resource for cybersecurity awareness, education, careers, and training.

Newsletters

5913 **ATM Industry Association Global Newsletter**
www.atmia.com/media/atmia-global-newsletter/
Social Media: Facebook, LinkedIn, YouTube
Mike Lee, Chief Executive Officer
Sharon Lane, Global Director, Finance
Dana Benson, Dir., Conferences & Sponsorships
Amanda Hardy, Marketing Director, Europe
David Tente, Executive Director, USA
Alliance promoting the proliferation of automated teller machines, ATMs and cash.
5000 Members
Founded in: 1997

5914 **Center for Internet Security**
31 Tech Valley Drive
Suite 2
East Greenbush, NY 12061
518-266-3460; *Fax:* 518-283-3216
contact@cisecurity.org
msisac.cisecurity.org/newsletters
Social Media: Facebook, Twitter, LinkedIn, Blog, YouTube
William F. Pelgrin, President, CEO
Thomas Duffy, SVP, Operations and Services
Laura Iwan, SVP, Programs
Julie Evans, Chief Operating Officer
Al Szesnat, Chief Financial Officer
A nonprofit organization that provides products and resources that help partners achieve security goals through expert guidance and cost-effective solutions.

5915 **Dot.COM**
Business Communications Company
25 Van Zant Street
Suite 13
Norwalk, CT 06855-1713
203-853-4266; *Fax:* 203-853-0348
sales@bccresearch.com; www.bccresearch.com
Louis Naturman, Publisher
C Toenne, Editor
Updates readers on the commercial use of the Internet and related platforms.
Cost: $38.00

5916 **E-Healthcare Market Reporter**
Health Resources Publishing
1913 Atlantic Ave
Suite 200
Manasquan, NJ 08736-1067
732-292-1100
888-843-6242; *Fax:* 732-292-1111
info@themcic.com; www.hin.com/ehealth.html
Robert K Jenkins, Publisher
Judith Granel, Marketing
John Russel, Editor
Brett Powell, Regional Director
Alice Burron, Director
A bi-monthly covering strategies, new products, innovation, privacy issue, business solutions, service available, vendor news and comparative for implementing sales and marketing on the internet.
Cost: $397.00
Frequency: Fortnightly
ISSN: 1098-5654
Founded in: 1988

5917 **Internet Alliance Cyberbrief**
Internet Alliance
1615 L Street NW
Suite 1100
Washington, DC 20036-5624
202-861-2407
tammy@internetalliance.org;
www.internetalliance.my
Tammy Cota, Executive Director
Coverage of public policy changes in government, enhancing consumer satisfaction in interactive services, and education.
Frequency: Weekly

5918 **Internet Business**
Information Gatekeepers
1340 Soldiers Field Rd
Suite 3
Brighton, MA 02135-1000
617-782-5033
800-323-1088; *Fax:* 617-782-5735
info@igigroup.com; www.igigroup.com
Paul Polishuk, CEO
Hui Pan, Chief Analyst, Editor in Chief
Bev Wilson, Managing Editor
Covers the rapid developments in the industry.
Cost: $695.00
Frequency: Monthly

5919 **Internet World**
Mecklermedia Corporation

20 Ketchum Street
Westport, CT 06880

212-260-0758; *Fax:* 203-454-5840
bbesch@mecklermedia.com

Bill Besch, Publisher

Internet industry news, product reviews and technical reports, with an emphasis on Internet technology, hardware, management and security.
Cost: $160.00
Frequency: Weekly
Circulation: 98,947

5920 Mealey's Litigation Report: Cyber Tech & E -Commerce
LexisNexis Mealey's
555 W 5th Avenue
Los Angeles, CA 90013

213-627-1130
mealeyinfo@lexisnexis.com;
www.lexisnexis.com/mealeys

Tom Hagy, VP/General Manager
Maureen McGuire, Editorial Director
Mark Rogers, Editor

The Report covers disputes arising from e-commerce. The report tracks emerging legal issues, including: Internet security, data destruction and/or alteration, defamation on the Web, software errors, hardware failure, electronic theft, e-mail trespass, online privacy, government action, shareholder lawsuits, Internet jurisdiction issues, file sharing (copyright) disputes and much more.
Cost: $999.00
100 Pages
Frequency: Monthly
Founded in: 1999

5921 Online Reporter
G2 Computer Intelligence
PO Box 7
Glen Head, NY 11545-1616

516-759-7025; *Fax:* 516-759-7028
news@g2news.com; www.g2news.com

Maureen O'Gara, Publisher

Information on recent developments on the Internet through news briefs and a section called Chat Room. Includes information on e-commerce, Java and network security.
Cost: $695.00
Frequency: Weekly

5922 Privacy Journal
P.O. Box 28577
Providence, RI 02908

401-274-7861; *Fax:* 401-274-4747
orders@privacyjournal.net;
www.privacyjournal.net

Robert Ellis Smith, Publisher

An independent monthly on privacy in a computer age.
Cost: $65.00
Frequency: Monthly
ISSN: 0145-7659
Founded in: 1974
Printed in one color

5923 The CyberSkeptic's Guide to Internet Research
Information Today
143 Old Marlton Pike
Medford, NJ 08055-8750

609-654-6266
800-300-9868; *Fax:* 609-654-4309
custserv@infotoday.com; www.infotoday.com

Thomas H Hogan, President
Roger R Bilboul, Chairman Of The Board

A monthly subscription newsletter in print, that explores and evaluates free and low cost Web sites and search strategies to help you use the Internet and stay up to date.
Cost: $164.95
ISSN: 1085-2417

Magazines & Journals

5924 Active Server Developer's Journal
ZD Journals
500 Canal View Boulevard
Rochester, NY 14623-2800

585-407-7301; *Fax:* 585-214-2387
asp@zdjournals.com; www.asdj.com

Jon Pyles, Publisher
Taggard Andrews

Addresses such issues as database publishing, creating hack-proof files and getting the most out of server-side components. Special sections focus on client-side solutions, covering the basics and taking an in-depth look at more detailed techniques.
Cost: $149.00
Frequency: Monthly

5925 Electronic Commerce Advisor
Thomson Reuters
195 Broadway # 4
New York, NY 10007-3124

646-822-2000
800-231-1860; *Fax:* 646-822-2800
trta.lei-support@thomsonreuters.com;
www.ria.thomsonreuters.com

Elaine Yadlon, Plant Manager
Thomas H Glocer, CEO & Director
Robert D Daleo, Chief Financial Officer
Kelli Crane, Senior Vice President & CIO

Offers the latest in electronic commerce covering what's available and how to select and employ the best technology without costly trial-and-error mistakes. Information on EDI, e-mail, fax gateways, Internet, encryption, VANs, procurement cards, imaging, voice response, remote computering and other related information.
Cost: $155.00
Circulation: 4500
Founded in: 1940

5926 ISACA
3701 Algonquin Road
Suite 1010
Rolling Meadows, IL 60008

847-253-1545; *Fax:* 847-253-1443;
www.isaca.org/journal/pages/default.aspx
Social Media: Facebook, Twitter, LinkedIn

A nonprofit, independent association that advocates for professionals involved in information security, assurance, risk management and governance.
Founded in: 1969

5927 Information Security
International Computer Security Association
117 Kendrick Street
Suite 800
Needham, MA 02494

781-657-1000; *Fax:* 781-657-1100
lwalsh@infosecuritymag.com;
www.infosecuritymag.com

Andrew Briney, VP
Lawrence Walsh, Editor
Michael S Mimoso, Senior Editor
Gabrielle DeRussy, Advertising Sales
Susan Rastellini Smith, Product Management

Articles and analysis of information-security issues such as media, entwork and virus protection, internet security and encryption reports.
Cost: $100.00
Frequency: Monthly
Circulation: 60000
Founded in: 1999

5928 Information Systems Security
Auerbach Publications
2494 Bayshore Boulevard
Suite 201
Dunedin, FL 34698

703-891-6781
800-737-8034; *Fax:* 703-891-0782
institute@isc2.org; www.isc2.org
Social Media: Facebook, Twitter, YouTube

David Shearer, COO
Debra Taylor, CFO
John Colley, Chairman
Debra Taylor, Chief Financial Officer
Hord Tipton, Executive Director

Facts and experience, expert opinion on directions in security, public policy, computer crime and ethics related to the information security field.
Cost: $175.00
Circulation: 1500
Founded in: 2003

5929 Internet Security Alliance
703-907-7090
admin@isalliance.org;
www.isalliance.org/isa-publications

Tim McKnight, Board Chairman
Jeff Brown, Board Vice Chairman
Gary McAlum, Board Second Vice Chairman
Larry Clinton, President, CEO
Julie Taylor, Board Member

A nonprofit organization that acts as a forum for information sharing and leadership on information security, and it lobbies for corporate securityinterests.

Trade Shows

5930 ATM Industry Association
www.atmia.com/conferences/usa
Social Media: Facebook, LinkedIn, YouTube

Mike Lee, Chief Executive Officer
Sharon Lane, Global Director, Finance
Dana Benson, Dir., Conferences & Sponsorships
Amanda Hardy, Marketing Director, Europe
David Tente, Executive Director, USA

Alliance promoting the proliferation of automated teller machines, ATMs and cash.
5000 Members
Founded in: 1997

5931 CompTIA
3500 Lacey Road
Suite 100
Downers Grove, IL 60515

630-678-8300; *Fax:* 630-678-8384
techvoice@comptia.org;
www.comptia.org/events
Social Media: Facebook, Twitter, LinkedIn, Pinterest, Google+, YouTube

Todd Thibodeaux, President, CEO
Charles Eaton, CEO, Educational Foundation
Ann Batko, SVP, Marketing
Kelly Ricker, SVP, Events and Education
David Sommer, Chief Financial Officer

A nonprofit trade association created by representatives of five microcomputer leaderships and is a provider of professional certifications for theinformation technology (IT) industry.

5932 Cyber Security Summit
www.cybersecuritysummit.org
Social Media: Facebook, Twitter, LinkedIn

Andrew Borene, Esq., Chair

Because of the scope of cyber threats, the Summit endeavors to bring together all stakeholders - in-

dustry, government and academia - to improve cyber security.
Frequency: Annual
Founded in: 2011

5933 **DMD New York Conference & Expo**
Direct Marketing Conferences
20 Academy Street
Norwalk, CT 06850-4032

203-854-9166
800-969-6566
connecticut@dmdays.com; www.dmdays.com

Direct Marketing Days New York offers new ideas in media, creative, database, eCommerce and technology. Hundreds of exhibits showcase the newest technologies, products and services. Over 85 sessions and 25 consultation centers led by A level speakers. Network with top-level executives.
Frequency: Annual/June

5934 **GovSec**
National Trade Productions
313 S Patrick Street
Alexandria, VA 22314

703-838-8500; *Fax:* 703-836-4486;
www.govsecinfo.com

Denise Medved, General Manager

Provides a full spectrum of security solutions for federal, state, and local governments tasked with developing comprehensive strategies that address physical security, information security and cyber security needs. Educational programs held in conjunction with displays of a wide variety of security products and services designed specifically for government users.
Frequency: Annual/May

Directories & Databases

5935 **ATM Industry Association**

www.atmia.com/directory-of-atm-services
Social Media: Facebook, LinkedIn, YouTube

Mike Lee, Chief Executive Officer
Sharon Lane, Global Director, Finance
Dana Benson, Dir., Conferences & Sponsorships
Amanda Hardy, Marketing Director, Europe
David Tente, Executive Director, USA

Alliance promoting the proliferation of automated teller machines, ATMs and cash.
5000 Members
Founded in: 1997

Industry Web Sites

5936 **www.bsa.org**
Business Software Alliance

An organization dedicated to promoting a safe and legal digital world. BSA educates consumers on software management and copyright protection, cyber security, trade, e-commerce and other internet related issues.

5937 **www.cisecurity.org**
Center for Internet Security

Helps organizations around the world effectively manage the risks related to internet security.

5938 **www.nga.org/cms/statecyber**
National Governors Association
Hall of the States
444 N Capitol St., Suite 267
Washington, DC 20001-1512

202-624-5300; *Fax:* 202-624-5313;
www.nga.org
Social Media: Facebook, Twitter

Gov. Gary Herbert, Utah, Chair
Gov. Terry McAuliffe, Virginia

Tools and resources to help states improve their cybersecurity policies and practices. Provided by the National Governors Association.

Associations

5939 **Advertising Mail Marketing Association**
Advertising Mail Marketing Association
1333 F Street NW
Suite 710
Washington, DC 20004-1108

202-347-0055; *Fax:* 202-347-0789;
www.amma.org
Social Media: Facebook, Twitter, LinkedIn

Gene A DelPolito, Publisher
Chad W Robbins, Editor

For those who use mail for fundraising or business purposes.
Founded in: 1947

5940 **American Marketing Association**
311 S Wacker Dr
Suite 5800
Chicago, IL 60606-6629

312-542-9000
800-262-1150; *Fax:* 312-542-9001;
www.marketingpower.com
Social Media: Facebook, Twitter, LinkedIn, YouTube, Pinterest, Google+

Rob Malcolm, Chairperson
Valarie Zeithaml?, Chairperson-elect
Mary Garrett, Vice President Finance/Secretary?
Ric Sweeney, Immediate Past Chairperson

A professional association for individuals and organizations involved in the practice, teaching and study of marketing worldwide.
40000 Members
Founded in: 1953

5941 **American Teleservices Association**
3815 River Crossing Parkway
Suite 20
Indianapolis, IN 46240

317-816-9336
877-779-3974; *Fax:* 317-218-0323
contact@ataconnect.org; www.ataconnect.org

Tim Searcy, CEO

Represents the call centers, trainers, consultants and equipment suppliers that initiate, facilitate and generate telephone, Internet and e-mail sales, service and support.
240 Members

5942 **Art Directors Club**
106 W 29th St
New York, NY 10001-5301

212-643-1440; *Fax:* 212-643-4266
info@adcglobal.org; www.adcglobal.org
Social Media: Facebook, Twitter, LinkedIn, Pinterest

Ami Brophy, CEO
Jon Kamen, VP
Vickie Peslak, Second VP
Thomas Mueller, Secretary
Myrna Davis, Executive Director

An international nonprofit organization of leading creatives in advertising, graphic design, interactive media, broadcast design, typography, packaging, environmental design, photography, illustration and related disciplines.
1200 Members
Founded in: 1920
Mailing list available for rent

5943 **Association of Direct Marketing Agencies**
Cohn & Wells
350 Hudson Street
New York, NY 10014-4504

212-192-2278; *Fax:* 212-302-6714;
www.cyberdirect.com/ADMA

John A Greco Jr, President/CEO

Members are direct response advertising agencies.
100 Members

5944 **Association of Hispanic Advertising Agencies**
8280 Willow Oaks Corporate Drive
Suite 600
Fairfax, VA 22031

703-745-5531
info@ahaa.org; www.ahaa.org
Social Media: Facebook, Twitter, LinkedIn, YouTube, Storify

Aldo Quevedo, Chair
Horacio Gavilan, Executive Director
Fulvia Lee, Program Manager
Gabriela Alcantara-Diaz, Treasurer
Carlos Santiago, Secretary

Trade organization for promoting the Hispanic marketing and advertising industry.
Founded in: 1996

5945 **Association of Teleservices International**
222 South Westmonte Drive
Suite 101
Altamonte Springs, FL 32714

866-896-ATSI; *Fax:* 407-774-6440
admin@atsi.org
atsi.org
Social Media: Facebook, Twitter, LinkedIn

Jeff Zindel, President
Doug Robbins, Vice President
Josue Leon, VP- Secretary
JoAnn Fussell, VP- Treasurer
Gary Edwards, Director

An international trade association established by and for entrepreneurs in the TeleServices business. It provides a wide variety of services to businesses, governmental agencies, local emergency respondents and the general public.
35000 Members
Founded in: 1942

5946 **Business Marketing Association: Atlanta**
13 Corporate Square
Suite 100
Atlanta, GA 30329

404-641-9417
800-664-4262; *Fax:* 312-822-0054
info@bmaatlanta.com; www.bmaatlanta.com
Social Media: Facebook, Twitter

Ed King, President-Elect
John Wiley, Marketing & Public Relations
Barry Mirkin, Development & Research
Stacey Krizan, Membership/Education/Certification
Joe Noonan, Programs Co-Chair

The Atlanta chapter of the BMA includes marketing executives from a variety of industries and backgrounds including research, advertising, promotions, events, Web development, printing and more. The BMA offers an information-packed Web site, online skills-building, marketing certification programs, and industry surveys and papers. In addition, members have the opportunity to interact with peers at seminars, participate in chapter training programs and the BMA Annual Conference.

5947 **Business Marketing Association: Boston**
246 Hampshire Street
Cambridge, MA 02130

617-418-4000
800-664-4262; *Fax:* 312-822-0054
info@thebmaboston.com;
www.thebmaboston.com/

Michael Lewis, President
Will Robinson, VP Public Relations
Matthew Mamet, VP Internet Marketing
Larry Perreault, VP Finance
Chris Perkett, VP Programming

BMA Boston helps members improve their ability to manage business-to-business marketing and communications for greater productivity and profitability by providing unique access to information, ideas, and the experience of peers. The BMA offers an information-packed Website, online skills-building, marketing certification programs, and industry surveys and papers. In addition, members have the opportunity to interact with peers at seminars, chapter training programs and the BMA Annual Conference.

5948 **Cable & Telecommunications Association for Marketing**
120 Waterfront Street
Suite 200
National Harbor, MD 20745

301-485-8900; *Fax:* 301-560-4964
info@ctam.com; www.ctam.com
Social Media: Facebook, Twitter, LinkedIn, YouTube

Mark Greatrex, Chair
Jamia Bigalow, Vice Chairman
Bob Benya, President/ CEO
Todd Esenwein, Director of Business Services
Zell Murphy, SVP Finance & Administration

Provides marketing knowledge and industry scale to help its membersmanage the future and drive business results. Also provides consumer research, an interactive executive innovation series, conferences and awards.

5949 **Color Marketing Group**
1908 Mount Vernon Avenue
Alexandria, VA 22301

703-329-8500; *Fax:* 703-535-3190
sgriffis@colormarketing.org;
www.colormarketing.org
Social Media: Facebook, Twitter, LinkedIn, Google+, Pinterest

John West, CMG, President
Heather Beland, CMG, Vice President Marketing
Geraldine Chmiel, Secretary
Art Schmehling, Treasurer
Sharon Griffis, Executive Director

A nonprofit international association of color designers involved in the use of color as it applies to the profitable marketing of goods and services.
1300 Members
Founded in: 1962

5950 **Digital Analytics Association**
401 Edgewater Place
Suite 600
Wakefield, WA 1880

781-876-8933; *Fax:* 781-224-1239;
www.digitalanalyticsassociation.org
Social Media: Facebook, Twitter, LinkedIn, Google+

Casey Carey, President
Eric Feinberg, Vice President
Steve Petitpas, Vice President-Marketing
Mike Levin, Executive Director
Jacki Conn, Education Manager

A global organization of practitioners, corporations, vendors, marketing and public relations

agencies, consultants, academics, and more involved in the growing digital analytics industry.
Founded in: 2004

5951 Digital Concepts for Business
PO Box 745
Suite 102
Crystal Lake, IL 60039-0745
815-575-0089; *Fax:* 847-458-5134
info@dcfb.com; www.dcfb.com
Social Media: Facebook, Twitter, LinkedIn, Google+, Pinterest
Mary Owens, Owner
Provides services to companies throughout the US and is dedicated to providing high-quality business communcations solutions using the latest hardware and software for both PC and Macintosh.
Founded in: 1996

5952 Direct International
1501 3rd Avenue
New York, NY 10028-2101
212-861-4188; *Fax:* 212-986-3757
Alfred Goodloe, President
Offers publications and services for the international direct marketing executive.

5953 Direct Marketing Association
1120 Avenue of the Americas
New York, NY 10036-6700
212-768-7277; *Fax:* 212-302-6714
thedma.org
Social Media: Facebook, Twitter, LinkedIn
Thomas J. Benton, Chief Executive Officer
Bob Greco, SVP of Operations, Finance & Events
Peggy Hudson, SVP, Government Affairs
Linsay Hutter, SVP, Communications
Xenia Boone, JD, SVP, General Counsel
Advances and protects responsible data-driven marketing.

5954 Direct Selling Association
1667 K St NW
Suite 1100
Washington, DC 20006-1660
202-452-8866; *Fax:* 202-452-9010
info@dsa.org; www.wfdsa.org
Social Media: Facebook, Twitter, RSS
Neil H Offen, President
Douglas L DeVos, Vice Chairman
Neil H Offen, President
John A Addison Jr, Director
Mark Bosworth, Director
National trade of the leading firms that manufacture and distribute goods and services sold directly to consumers. Members of the association are copanies including many well-known brand names. The association's mission is to protect, serve and promote the effectiveness of member companies and the independent business people they represent.
Founded in: 1978

5955 Direct-to-Direct Marketing Association Council for Hispanic Marketing
Direct Marketing Association
1120 Avenue of the Americas
New York, NY 10036-6700
212-768-7277; *Fax:* 212-768-6714
thedma.org
Allison Longley, Manager
Provides education, information and networking opportunities for direct marketing professionals targeting the Hispanic market.
120 Members
Founded in: 1992

5956 EMarketing Association
40 Blue Ridge Dr
Charlestown, RI 02813
800-496-2950; *Fax:* 408-884-2461
admin@emarketingassociation.com; www.emarketingassociation.com
Social Media: Facebook, Twitter, LinkedIn
Robert Fleming, President
Todd Daum, VP
John Hastings, VP
Linda Jaffe, VP
An international association of emarketing professionals. Members include government, companies, professionals and students involved with the emarketing arena.

5957 Internet Marketing Association
10 Mar Del Rey
San Clemente, CA 92673
949-443-9300; *Fax:* 949-443-2215
info@imanetwork.org
imanetwork.org
Social Media: Facebook, Twitter, LinkedIn, YouTube, RSS, Google+
Sinan Kanatsiz, CIM, Chairman/ Founder
Matthew Langie, Vice Chairman, Education
Rachel Reenders, CIM, Executive Director
David Steinberg, CIM, VP of Business Alliances
Vince Walden, Finance Director
A professional organization that has gained more than 900,000 members in fields including sales, marketing, business ownership, programming and creative development. It provides a platform where proven Internet marketing strategies are demonstrated and shared to increase members value to their organizations.
90000 Members
Founded in: 2001

5958 Life Insurance Direct Marketing Association
3227 S. Cherokee Lane
Suite 1320
Woodstock, GA 30188
770-516-0207
866-890-LEAD
info@lidma.org
lidma.org
Social Media: Facebook, Twitter, LinkedIn
Pat Wedeking, Chair
Byron Udell, President
Patrick M Bowen, CLU, VP, Senior Account Manager
Staci Birk, Director
Cynthia Farrow, Secretary/ Treasurer
A nonprofit organization dedicated specifically to supporting businesses and professionals active in direct sales of term life insurance products to consumers.

5959 Mail Advertising Service Association
1800 Diagonal Road
Suite 320
Alexandria, VA 22314-2862
703-836-9200; *Fax:* 703-548-8204
webmaster@epicomm.org; www.mfsanet.org
Social Media: Facebook, Twitter, LinkedIn, YouTube, Pinterest, Google+
Ken Garner, President and CEO
Tom Saggiomo, Vice Chairman
John Rafner, Second Vice Chairman
Wayne Marshall, Treasurer
Supports all those involved in the mailing, addressing, and inserting industries.
Founded in: 2014

5960 Mailing & Fulfillment Service Association
One Meadowlands Plaza
Suite 1511
East Rutherford, NJ 07073
201-634-9600; *Fax:* 703-548-8204
webmaster@epicomm.org; www.mfsanet.org
Social Media: Facebook, Twitter, LinkedIn, YouTube, Pinterest, Google+
Ken Garner, President
Bill Stevenson, Director Marketing
The national trade association for the mailing and fulfillment services industry.
Founded in: 2014

5961 Midwest Direct Marketing Association
P.O. Box 75
Suite S256
Andover, MN 55304
763-607-2943; *Fax:* 763-753-2240
office@mdma.org; www.mdma.org
Ed Harrington, Manager
Ben DuBois, Director
Dedicated to the advancement of professional and ethical practice of direct response marketing by members throughout the Upper Midwest.
600 Members
Founded in: 1960

5962 Mobile Marketing Association
41 E 11th St
11th floor
New York, NY 10003
646-257-4515
northamerica@mmaglobal.com; www.mmaglobal.com
Social Media: Facebook, Twitter, LinkedIn, Google+
John Costello, President
Jack Philbins, Co-Founder, President and CEO
Carolyyn Everson, VP, Global Marketing
A global nonprofit trade association comprised of more than 800 member companies that strive to accelerate the transformation and innovation of marketing through mobile, driving business growth with closer and stronger consumerengagement.
800 Members

5963 Mobile Marketing Research Association
216 W. Jackson Blvd.
Suite 625
Chicago, IL 60606
312-252-2502; www.mmra-global.org
Social Media: Facebook, Twitter, LinkedIn, Pinterest
Rebecca West, President
Rick West, Vice President
Mark Michelson, Executive Director
Sheila Gidley, Director of Operations
Jan Willem Smulders, Treasurer
A global trade association dedicated to the promotion and development of professional standards and ethics for conducting marketing research on mobile devices.
Founded in: 2011

5964 Multi-Level Marketing International Association
119 Stanford Ct
Irvine, CA 92612
949-854-0484
info@mlmia.com; www.mlmia.com
Social Media: Facebook, Twitter
Doris Wood, President Emeritus
Carrol Leclerc, President, Canada
Tom Leffler, VP of Support Board

Michael L. Sheffield, Co-Founder
Linda Bruno, Secretary
A nonprofit professional trade organization representing all sectors of the networking marketing industry on a worldwide basis.

5965 North American Farmers' Direct Marketing Association
62 White Loaf Road
Southampton, MA 1073
Fax: 413-233-4285
Charlie @ Whiteloafridge.com; www.farmersinspired.com
Social Media: Facebook, Twitter, Pinterest, YouTube
Cynthia Chiles, President/ Chair
Charlie Touchette, Executive Director
Becky Walters, VP of Membership
Ben Beaver, VP of Education
Mike Dunn, Treasurer/ Finance Team Chair
A membership association that advances the prosperity of its members and the farm direct marketing industry through networking, participation, education, and innovation.

5966 Professional Association of Customer Engagement
8500 Keystone Crossing
Suite 480
Indianapolis, IN 46240
317-816-9336; www.paceassociation.com
Social Media: Facebook, Twitter, LinkedIn, YouTube, RSS
Michael Rauscher, Chair
Barbra Merwin, Vice Chairman
Tom Rocca, Chief Executive Officer
Susan Burt, Finance Director
Angie Brown, Operations Director
A nonprofit trade organization dedicated exclusively to the advancement of companies that utilize contact centers as an integral channel of operations.

5967 Society of Publication Designers
27 Union Square West
Suite 207
New York, NY 10003
212-223-3332; *Fax:* 212-223-5880
mail@spd.org; www.spd.org
Social Media: RSS
Tim Leong, President
David Curcurito, Vice President
Allyson Torrisi, Vice President
Keisha Dean, Executive Director
Leah Bailey, Treasurer
An organization dedicated to promoting and encouraging excellence in editorial design. Members include art directors, designers, photo editors, editors, and graphics professionals.
Founded in: 1965

Newsletters

5968 Business Owner
Mailing & Fulfillment Service Association
1421 Prince Street
Suite 410
Alexandria, VA 22314-2806
703-836-9200; *Fax:* 703-548-8204
mfsa-mail@mfsanet.org; www.mfsanet.org
David L Perkins Jr, Editor
Developed specifically to communicate with owners and CEOs on issues unique to them. You'll receive a wealth of knowledge on growing your business, tax issues, insurance, estate planning, management, finance and much more.
Frequency: Bi-Monthly

5969 Career News Update
American Marketing Association
311 S Wacker Dr
Suite 5800
Chicago, IL 60606-6629
312-542-9000
800-262-1150; *Fax:* 312-542-9001; www.marketingpower.com
Dennis Dunlap, CEO
You'll receive the latest career and hiring advice as well as useful job resources and employment listings.
Frequency: Monthly

5970 Daily News E-Mail (3D)
Direct Marketing Association
1120 Avenue of the Americas
New York, NY 10036-6700
212-768-7277; *Fax:* 212-302-6714
customerservice@the-dma.org; www.the-dma.org
Lawrence M Kimmel, CEO
Delivers the essential news, research, hot trends, and technological developments from the nations leading newspapers, trade publications, and the government all in an easy-to-read, time-saving format

5971 Direct Response
Direct Marketing Center
21171 S. Western Ave
Suite 260
Torrance, CA 90501
310-212-5727; *Fax:* 310-212-5773; www.directmarketingcenter.net
Craig Huey, President/Publisher
Kent Komae, Editor
Direct marketing information.
Cost: $79.00
Frequency: Monthly

5972 Direct Selling Association International Bulletin
World Federation of Direct Selling Associations
1667 K St Nw
Suite 1100
Washington, DC 20006-1660
202-452-8866; *Fax:* 202-452-9010
info@wfdsa.org; www.wfdsa.org
Neil H Offen, President
Association activities, legislation affecting direct selling and trends.
Circulation: 1200

5973 Direction
Direct Marketing Consultants
705 Franklin Tpke
Allendale, NJ 07401-1637
201-327-9213
Hugh P Curley, Publisher
How to' information on motivating buying decisions via more creative use of direct mail, sales promotion, newsletters, and other marketing tools.
Cost: $40.00
Circulation: 3800

5974 Empoyment Points
Mailing & Fulfillment Service Association
1421 Prince Street
Suite 410
Alexandria, VA 22314-2806
703-836-9200; *Fax:* 703-548-8204
mfsa-mail@mfsanet.org; www.mfsanet.org
The content is written for business owners and operators who want to stay informed about current employment issues. The editorial is targeted on human resource issues and employment practices in the mailing and fulfillment services industry.
Frequency: 4x/Year
Circulation: 2000

5975 Fred Goss' What's Working in Direct Marketing
United Communications Group
11300 Rockville Pike
Street 1100
Rockville, MD 20852-3030
301-287-2700; *Fax:* 301-816-8945
webmaster@ucg.com; www.ucg.com/
Benny Dicecca, President
Direct response marketing-all forms.
Cost: $242.00
Founded in: 1977

5976 Friday Report
Hoke Communications
224 7th Street
Garden City, NY 11530-5771
516-746-6700
800-229-6700; *Fax:* 516-294-8141
dmmagazine@aol.com; www.directmarketingmag.com
Henry R Hoke, Publisher
Joseph D Gatti, Editor
Stuart W Boysen, President
Edson Georges, Mailing Systems Manager
Weekly newsletter of direct marketing.
Cost: $165.00
8 Pages
Frequency: Weekly
Founded in: 1951

5977 General Encouragement, Motivation and Inspirational Handbook
Economics Press
12 Daniel Road
Fairfield, NJ 07004-2565
973-227-1224; *Fax:* 973-227-3558
info@epinc.com; www.epinc.com
Allan Yahalen, President
Rob Gilbert, Editor
Cost: $20.00
24 Pages
Frequency: Monthly
Circulation: 200000
Mailing list available for rent: 200,000 names
Printed in 4 colors on matte stock

5978 Inside Mail Order
Mellinger Company
PO Box 956
Santa Clarita, CA 91380-9056
661-259-2303; *Fax:* 805-257-4840; www.tradezone.com
BL Mellinger III, Publisher
A newsletter offering the latest information to businesses on marketing and advertising through direct mail.

5979 Mail Order Digest & Washington Newsletter
National Mail Order Association
2807 Polk St Ne
Minneapolis, MN 55418-2954
612-788-1673; *Fax:* 612-788-1147
editor@nmoa.org; www.nmoa.org
John Schulte, President
J Bradley, Editor
Paul Muchnick, Founder Director
Contains information of interest to small to midsize mail marketers including new products available, money saving techniques, industry contacts, help for beginners, new concepts for mail order selling, and postal changes and regula-

tions.
Cost: $99.00
Frequency: Monthly
Circulation: 7000
Founded in: 1972

5980 **Marketing Academics Newsletter**
American Marketing Association
311 S Wacker Dr
Suite 5800
Chicago, IL 60606-6629

312-542-9000
800-262-1150; *Fax:* 312-542-9001;
www.marketingpower.com

Dennis Dunlap, CEO

This newsletter provides news and information that affect and inform this important constituency. It reviews Academic Council activities, profiles Academic SIGS and highlights upcoming events.

5981 **Marketing Matters Newsletter**
American Marketing Association
311 S Wacker Dr
Suite 5800
Chicago, IL 60606-6629
312-542-9000
800-262-1150; *Fax:* 312-542-9001;
www.marketingpower.com

Dennis Dunlap, CEO

This e-newsletter updates readers on the latest happenings in the marketing profession through news briefs, indepth features and interviews.
Frequency: 2x/Monthly

5982 **Marketing Power Newsletter**
American Marketing Association
311 S Wacker Dr
Suite 5800
Chicago, IL 60606-6629

312-542-9000
800-262-1150; *Fax:* 312-542-9001;
www.marketingpower.com

Dennis Dunlap, CEO

This update of the latest news, research and trends in the marketing industry and allied fields.
Frequency: Weekly

5983 **Marketing Researchers Newsletter**
American Marketing Association
311 S Wacker Dr
Suite 5800
Chicago, IL 60606-6629

312-542-9000
800-262-1150; *Fax:* 312-542-9001;
www.marketingpower.com

Dennis Dunlap, CEO

This e-newsletter provides members with content designed to educate and inform researchers or any member interested in marketing research topics.

5984 **Marketing Through Leaders Newsletter**
American Marketing Association
311 S Wacker Dr
Suite 5800
Chicago, IL 60606-6629

312-542-9000
800-262-1150; *Fax:* 312-542-9001;
www.marketingpower.com

Dennis Dunlap, CEO

These articles focus on the issues and concepts that shape marketing today and tomorrow.
Frequency: Monthly

5985 **Memo to Mailers**
US Postal Service
475 Lenfant Plz Sw
Room 10523
Washington, DC 20260-1805

202-268-2900
800-275-8777; *Fax:* 202-268-6436
mmailers@usps.com; www.usps.com

Robert F Gardner, Manager

Carries information and news about the Postal Service as well as value added information about using the mail effectively and efficiently. Also offers information to mail center managers on ways to cut costs.
8 Pages
Frequency: Daily
Circulation: 100000

5986 **Nonprofit Mailers Foundation**
125 Michigan Avenue NE
#239
Washington, DC 20017-1004

202-628-4380

Esther Huggins, Manager

Promotes welfare of groups using nonprofit mail rates for communications and fundraising.
600 Pages
Founded in: 1982

5987 **PD&D Direct Mail List**
Chilton Way
Radnor, PA 19089-0001

973-920-7782; *Fax:* 973-607-5492
Tom Lynch, Group Publisher
Christina Schmidt, Publisher
Don Grennan, Director of Marketing
Jeff Reinke, Editorial Director
David Mantey, Editor

This list is a proven response vehicle for product promotion, seminar announcements and trade show promotions.

5988 **PostScripts**
Mailing & Fulfillment Service Association
1421 Prince Street
Suite 410
Alexandria, VA 22314-2806

703-836-9200; *Fax:* 703-548-8204
mfsa-mail@mfsanet.org; www.mfsanet.org

Leo Raymond, Editor

Each issue of PostScripts highlights a theme relevant to mailing or fulfillment operations, such as production management or information technology.
Frequency: 18x/Year
Circulation: 2800

5989 **Postal Points**
Mailing & Fulfillment Service Association
1421 Prince Street
Suite 410
Alexandria, VA 22314-2806

703-836-9200; *Fax:* 703-548-8204
mfsa-mail@mfsanet.org; www.mfsanet.org

Leo Raymond, Editor

Deals exclusively with current and pending postal and delivery issues. Here you will find the facts and analysis of developing postal issues.
Frequency: 18x/Year

5990 **Target Market News**
Target Market News
228 S Wabash Ave
Suite 210
Chicago, IL 60604-2383

312-408-1867; *Fax:* 312-408-1867
info@targetmarketnews.com;
www.targetmarketnews.com

Ken Smikle, President
Hallie Mummert, Editor

News and developments in the areas of black consumer marketing and black-oriented media.
Cost: $40.00
12 Pages
Frequency: Monthly
Founded in: 1988

5991 **TeleResponse**
InfoCision Management
325 Springside Dr
Akron, OH 44333-4504

330-668-1400; *Fax:* 330-668-1401;
www.infocision.com

Carl Albright, CEO

Specializes in making outbound sales calls for the infomercial, catalog and direct marketing industries.

5992 **Telephone Selling Report**
Business By Phone
13254 Stevens Street
Omaha, NE 68137-1728

402-455-1111
800-326-7721; *Fax:* 402-896-3353
arts@businessbyphone.com;
www.businessbyphone.com

Art Sobczak, Production Manager

For businesses that use the phone to prospect, service and sell. How-to information on getting through screens; creating interest-grabbing openings; closes that work; overcoming tough objections; and beating call reluctance. Accepts advertising inserts.
Cost: $109.00
8 Pages
Frequency: Monthly
Mailing list available for rent: 2M names
Printed in 2 colors

5993 **Venture Views & News**
Venture Communications
60 Madison Ave
New York, NY 10010-1600

212-447-5247; *Fax:* 212-576-1129
sales@ven.com; www.venturedirect.com

Rachel Krasny, Editor
Richard Baumer, CEO/President
Neal Mandel, Group Division Sales Manager
Michael Platt, Founder

News and practical advice in the field of direct response marketing.
Frequency: Weekly
Founded in: 1983

5994 **What's Working in DM and Fulfillment**
United Communications Group
11300 Rockville Pike
Suite 1100
Rockville, MD 20852-3030

301-816-8950
800-929-4824; *Fax:* 301-816-8945
webmaster@ucg.com; www.ucg.com/

Barbara W Kaplowitz, Publisher
Monica Brown, Circulation Manager

Tested tips, tactics and techniques for direct marketers in all industries, news, legislative updates and winning (and losing) DM ideas including hard costs and how to's.
Cost: $242.00
8 Pages
Founded in: 1977
*Mailing list available for rent*at $125 per M
Printed in 2 colors on matte stock

Magazines & Journals

5995 **BtoB Magazine**
Ad Age Group/ Division of Crain Communications
711 3rd Ave
New York, NY 10017-4014
212-210-0785; *Fax:* 212-210-0200
info@crain.com; www.crain.com
Norm Feldman, Manager
Dedicated to integrated business to business marketing. Every page is packed with substance news, reports, technologies, benchmarks, best practices served up by the most knowledgeable journalists.
Frequency: Monthly
Circulation: 45000

5996 **Chief Marketer**
Penton Media, Inc.
249 W 17th Street
New York, NY 10011
212-204-4200; www.penton.com
Social Media: Facebook, Twitter, LinkedIn
Tyler T. Zachehm, Co-CEO
Anup Bagaria, Co-CEO
Nicola Allais, EVP & CFO
Jasmine Alexander, SVP & CIO
Chief Marketer provides fresh, multi-disciplined approaches to direct marketing, events, advertising research, and promotional marketing.
Frequency: Monthly
Founded in: 1976

5997 **Customer Interface**
Advanstar Communications
6200 Canoga Avenue
2nd Floor
Woodland Hills, CA 91367
818-593-5000; *Fax:* 818-593-5020
info@advanstar.com; www.advanstar.com
Joseph Loggia, President
Chris DeMoulin, VP
Susannah George, Marketing Director
Magazine for decision-makers actively involved in planning, managing or operating a business call center.
Cost: $39.00
104 Pages
Circulation: 50000
Founded in: 1992

5998 **Dateline: DMA**
Direct Marketing Association
11 W 42nd Street
New York, NY 10036-8002
212-391-9683; *Fax:* 212-768-4546
Offers comprehensive information on the Direct Marketing Association, trends in the industry, technological advances and more for the marketing and advertising professional.

5999 **Direct**
Chief Marketer
249 W 17th Street
New York, NY 10011
212-204-4200; www.chiefmarketer.com
Social Media: Facebook, Twitter, LinkedIn
Beth Negus Viveiros, Managing Editor
Brian Quinton, Executive Editor
Patricia Odell, Managing Editor
Richard Levey, Senior Writer
Larry Riggs, Senior Editor
Information Resource for Direct Marketers.
Frequency: Monthly
Founded in: 1976

6000 **Direct Marketing News**
Haymarket Media, Inc.
114 W 26th St.
4th Fl.
New York, NY 10001
646-638-6000; www.dmnews.com
Lee Maniscalco, Chairman & CEO
Ginger Conlon, Editor-in-Chief
Valuable information on the newest trends in direct marketing, catalog statistics and advertising information for persons working in the direct mail industry.
Cost: $148.00
Frequency: Monthly
ISSN: 1187-7111
Founded in: 1979

6001 **Journal of Direct Marketing**
John Wiley & Sons
111 River St
Hoboken, NJ 07030-5790
201-748-6000
800-825-7550; *Fax:* 201-748-6088
info@wiley.com; www.wiley.com
William J Pesce, CEO
Richard M Hochhauser, CEO
Publication featuring research articles from some of the best minds in the field of direct marketing. Offers creative ideas for marketing products, analysis of what works, pioneering research from the nation's top universities, articles from other direct marketing publications and special reports on overseas direct marketing.
Cost: $1000.00
Frequency: Quarterly
Founded in: 1807

6002 **Journal of International Marketing**
American Marketing Association
311 S Wacker Dr
Suite 5800
Chicago, IL 60606-6629
312-542-9000
800-262-1150; *Fax:* 312-542-9001;
www.marketingpower.com
Dennis Dunlap, CEO
Presents scholarly and managerially relevant articles on international marketing.

6003 **Journal of Marketing**
American Marketing Association
311 S Wacker Dr
Suite 5800
Chicago, IL 60606-6629
312-542-9000
800-262-1150; *Fax:* 312-542-9001;
www.marketingpower.com
Dennis Dunlap, CEO
The premier broad based scholarly journal of the marketing discipline that focuses on substantive issues in marketing and marketing management.

6004 **Journal of Marketing Research**
American Marketing Association
311 S Wacker Dr
Suite 5800
Chicago, IL 60606-6629
312-542-9000
800-262-1150; *Fax:* 312-542-9001;
www.marketingpower.com
Dennis Dunlap, CEO
Covers a wide range of marketing research concepts, methods and applications. You'll read about new techniques, contributions to knowledge based on experimental methods and developments in related fields that have a bearing on marketing research.

6005 **Journal of Public Policy & Marketing**
American Marketing Association
311 S Wacker Dr
Suite 5800
Chicago, IL 60606-6629
312-542-9000
800-262-1150; *Fax:* 312-542-9001;
www.marketingpower.com
Dennis Dunlap, CEO
Each issue features a wide ranging forum for the research, findings and discussion of marketing subjects related to business and government.

6006 **Marketing Health Services**
American Marketing Association
311 S Wacker Dr
Suite 5800
Chicago, IL 60606-6629
312-542-9000
800-262-1150; *Fax:* 312-542-9001;
www.marketingpower.com
Dennis Dunlap, CEO
Specifically aimed at senior level healthcare marketers and managers, offers targeted information, practical strategies and thought provoking commentary to help achieve your goals and shape your vision.
Frequency: Quarterly

6007 **Marketing Management**
American Marketing Association
311 S Wacker Dr
Suite 5800
Chicago, IL 60606-6629
312-542-9000
800-262-1150; *Fax:* 312-542-9001;
www.marketingpower.com
Dennis Dunlap, CEO
Focuses on strategic marketing issues that marketing managers face every day.
Frequency: 6x/Year

6008 **Marketing News**
American Marketing Association
311 S Wacker Dr
Suite 5800
Chicago, IL 60606-6629
312-542-9000
800-262-1150; *Fax:* 312-542-9001;
www.marketingpower.com
Dennis Dunlap, CEO
Covers the industry's basics, the core concepts around which winning programs are built.

6009 **Marketing Research**
American Marketing Association
311 S Wacker Dr
Suite 5800
Chicago, IL 60606-6629
312-542-9000
800-262-1150; *Fax:* 312-542-9001;
www.marketingpower.com
Dennis Dunlap, CEO
Researchers and managers count on this quarterly resource to help stay on top of current methodologies and issues, management concerns and the latest books and software.
40000 Members
Frequency: Quarterly

6010 **Multichannel Merchant**
Chief Marketer
249 W 17th Street
New York, NY 10011
212-204-4200; www.chiefmarketer.com
Social Media: Facebook, Twitter, LinkedIn
Beth Negus Viveiros, Managing Editor
Brian Quinton, Executive Editor

Patricia Odell, Managing Editor
Richard Levey, Senior Writer
Larry Riggs, Senior Editor

Exclusively serves online merchants and catalog companies, as well as retailers, manufacturers and wholesale/distributors.
Frequency: Monthly
Founded in: 1976

6011 Operations & Fulfillment
Primedia
Po Box 12901
Shawnee Mission, KS 66282-2901

913-341-1300
800-775-3777; *Fax:* 913-514-6895;
www.penton.com

Eric Jacobson, Senior VP
Glenn Laudenslager, Marketing Manager
Leslie Bacon, Publisher
Leonard Roberto, Circulation Manager
John French, President

Provides executives information they can't get anywhere else and reach executives and managers with purchasing authority in all areas of operations management. Information on direct to customer fulfillment..
Cost: $36.00
Frequency: Monthly
Founded in: 1905

6012 Politically Direct
Direct Marketing Association
1120 Avenue of the Americas
New York, NY 10036-6700

212-768-7277; *Fax:* 212-302-6714
customerservice@the-dma.org;
www.the-dma.org

Lawrence M Kimmel, CEO

Published both in print and digital, this newsletter on DMA advocacy efforts keeps DMA members informed and involved in the politics and policies that impact them today and ahead of the curve on developments that will affect them tomorrow.
Frequency: Quarterly

6013 Promo
Chief Marketer
249 W 17th Street
New York, NY 10011

212-204-4200; www.chiefmarketer.com
Social Media: Facebook, Twitter, LinkedIn

Beth Negus Viveiros, Managing Editor
Brian Quinton, Executive Editor
Patricia Odell, Managing Editor
Richard Levey, Senior Writer
Larry Riggs, Senior Editor

Promo Magazine covers the Promotions and the Promotional Marketing Industry.
Frequency: Monthly
Founded in: 1976

6014 Target
North American Publishing Company
1500 Spring Garden St
Suite 1200
Philadelphia, PA 19130-4094

215-238-5300; *Fax:* 215-238-5342
editor.tm@napco.com;
www.targetmarketingmag.com

Ned S Borowsky, CEO
Peggy Hatch, Publisher
Lois Boyle, President

This monthly magazine is the authoritative information source for direct marketers with hands-on, how-to-do-it, ideas you can take to the bank.
Cost: $24.95
Frequency: Monthly
Circulation: 35000
Founded in: 1977

Mailing list available for rent
Printed in 4 colors on glossy stock

6015 Telemarketing Magazine
Technology Marketing Corporation
1 Technology Plz
Norwalk, CT 06854-1936

203-852-6800
800-243-6002; *Fax:* 203-853-2845
tmc@tmcnet.com; www.tmcnet.com

Rich Tehrani, CEO
Linda Driscoll, Editor/VP
Rich Tehrani, President/Editor-in-Chief

Serves telemarketing, marketing, customer service, sales and telecommunications professionals. Features legislative updates, new product and service releases, techniques and beginner information.
Cost: $49.00
Frequency: Monthly
Founded in: 1972

Trade Shows

6016 &Then
Direct Marketing Association
1120 Avenue of the Americas
New York, NY 10036-6700

212-768-7277; *Fax:* 212-302-6714
thedma.org/events

The Direct Marketing Association's annual event.
Frequency: Annual

6017 Annual Conference and Mailing Fulfillment Expo
Mailing & Fulfillment Service Association
1421 Prince Street
Suite 410
Alexandria, VA 22314-2806

703-836-9200; *Fax:* 703-548-8204
mfsa-mail@mfsanet.org; www.mfsanet.org

Ken Garner, President
Jennifer Root, Director
Bill Stevenson, Director Marketing

Quality educational sessions, industry specific exhibit hall, networking and more.
Frequency: Annual

6018 Annual Conference for Catalog and Multichannel Merchants
PRISM Business Exhibitions
11 River Bend Drive South
Stamford, CT 06907

203-358-9900
800-927-5007; *Fax:* 203-358-5816
registration@prismb2b.com;
www.accmshow.com

Ed Berkowitz, Sales Director
Angela Eastin, Group Show Director

Co-presented by the Direct Marketing Association and Multichannel Merchant Magazine, ACCM offers the latest advances, technology and information and solutions for cataloger, retailers and multichannel merchants.
Frequency: May

6019 Business-to-Business Database Marketing Conference
Interlect Events
11 Riverbend Drive S
Stamford, CT 06907

203-852-4200
http://www.importexporthelp.com/b2b-lists.htm

Robin Altman, Contact

The only database marketing conference that is focused exclusively on business-to-business marketing database strategies and tactics. 40 tabletop exhibits.
500 Attendees
Frequency: Fall

6020 DMA Annual Conference & Exhibition
Direct Marketing Association
1120 Avenue of Americas
New York, NY 10036-6700

212-768-7277; *Fax:* 212-302-6714
dmaconferences@the-dma.org;
www.the-dma.org

Lawrence M Kimmel, CEO
Julie A Hogan, SVP Conferences/Events

Brings together thousands of practitioners and experts from the entire marketing continuum to discuss solutions and best practices to achieve optimal channel mix and integration that lead to measurable results and increase real-time customer engagement.
12000 Attendees
Frequency: October

6021 DMD New York Conference & Expo
Direct Marketing Conferences
20 Academy Street
Norwalk, CT 06850-4032

203-854-9166
800-969-6566
connecticut@dmdays.com; www.dmdays.com

Direct Marketing Days New York offers new ideas in media, creative, database, eCommerce and technology. Hundreds of exhibits showcase the newest technologies, products and services. Over 85 sessions and 25 consultation centers led by A level speakers. Network with top-level executives.
Frequency: Annual/June

6022 Email Evolution Conference
Direct Marketing Association
1120 Avenue of Americas
New York, NY 10036-6700

212-768-7277; *Fax:* 212-302-6714
dmaconferences@the-dma.org;
www.the-dma.org

Julie A Hogan, SVP Conference/Events
Lawrence M Kimmel, CEO

Focuses on the ever-changing and evolving world of email marketing, providing attendees with the best ways to capitalize on the high ROI this low-cost communication tool can provide both on its own, and integrated with social, search, mobile, video and other email enhancers.
10M Attendees
Frequency: Annual/February

6023 Internet Telephony Conference & EXPO (East or West)
Technology Marketing Corporation (TMCnet)
One Technology Plaza
Norwalk, CT 06854

203-852-6800
800-243-6002; *Fax:* 203-853-2845
tmc@tmcnet.com; www.tmcnet.com

Frank Coppola, Conference Team
Lorna Lyle, Conference Team
Tim Zaccagnini, Conference Team
Kevin Lake, Exhibit Sales
Natasha Barbera, Operations Contact

The world's foremost forum on IP and VoIP, and all things telephony: workshops, training courses, focused tracks, and exhibitors.
Frequency: East/West - Winter/Fall

6024 MFSA Mailing and Fulfillment Expo
Mailing & Fulfillment Service Association

1421 Prince Street
Suite 100
Alexandria, VA 22314-2805

703-369-9200
800-333-6272; *Fax:* 703-548-8204;
www.mfsanet.org

Eric Casey, Manager
David Weaver, President

Annual exposition of suppliers to mailing and fulfillment companies. Containing 60 booths and 50 exhibits.
250 Attendees
Frequency: June
Mailing list available for rent

6025 **MFSA Midwinter Executive Conference**
Mailing & Fulfillment Service Association
1421 Prince Street
Suite 410
Alexandria, VA 22314-2806

703-836-9200; *Fax:* 703-548-8204
mfsa-mail@mfsanet.org; www.mfsanet.org

Ken Garner, President
Jennifer Root, Director
Bill Stevenson, Director Marketing

Will address financial operations and business valuation, marketing your own company, the changing world of postal regulations, technology in fulfillment, building a sales team, being strong in digital printing and the landscape of employment law.

6026 **Mailer Strategies Conference**
Mailing & Fulfillment Service Association
1421 Prince Street
Suite 410
Alexandria, VA 22314-2806

703-836-9200; *Fax:* 703-548-8204
mfsa-mail@mfsanet.org; www.mfsanet.org

Ken Garner, President
Jennifer Root, Director
Bill Stevenson, Director Marketing

This conference will focus solely on postal issues that are important to your operations.

6027 **Marketing in the Millennium**
Florida Direct Marketing Association
8851 NW 10th Pl
Plantation, FL 33322-5007

954-472-6374
800-520-FDMA; *Fax:* 954-472-8165;
www.fdma.org

Beth Kaufman, Manager

Yearly exhibit of legislative updates and more for members of the direct marketing industry.
Frequency: February
Founded in: 1999

6028 **NCDM Conference**
Direct Marketing Association
1120 Avenue of Americas
New York, NY 10036-6700

212-768-7277; *Fax:* 212-302-6714
dmaconferences@the-dma.org;
www.the-dma.org

Julie A Hogan, SVP Conference/Events
Lawrence M Kimmel, CEO

Presents industry experts and hard-hitting case studies from a variety of verticles, such as financial services, retail, automotive, publishing, non-profit and many more, who will share the latest strategies and methodologies in gathering, analyzinf, leveraging and protecting the most valuable business asset-the customer database.
10M Attendees
Frequency: Annual/December

6029 **National Catalog Operations Forum**
Primedia
9800 Metcalf Avenue
Overland Park, KS 66212

913-341-1300; *Fax:* 913-967-1898;
www.catalogmailers.org

Robin Altman, Contact

The only major national conference devoted exclusively to the sharing of vital catalog operations information. This conference is dedicated to the crucial background of the catalog business, and brings operations management together to meet and learn; 140 booths.
1.2M+ Attendees
Frequency: April/May

6030 **National Conference on Operations & Fulfillment (NCOF)**
Direct Marketing Association
1120 Avenue of Americas
New York, NY 10036-6700

212-768-7277; *Fax:* 212-302-6714
dmaconferences@the-dma.org;
www.the-dma.org

Julie A Hogan, SVP Conference/Events
Lawrence M Kimmel, CEO

Focuses on innovative solutions for the warehouse, distribution, operations, and ecommerce needs in the ever-changing world of operations and fulfillment.
10M Attendees
Frequency: Annual/April

6031 **New York Nonprofit Conference**
Direct Marketing Association
1120 Avenue of Americas
New York, NY 10036-6700

212-768-7277; *Fax:* 212-302-6714
dmaconferences@the-dma.org;
www.the-dma.org

Julie Hogan, SVP Conference/Events

Discover which acknowledgement programs work best and why, increase revenue with membership options-as well as traditional fundraising appeals, learn how the Internet and e-mail campaigns can improve fundraising, lower costs and increase advocacy.
10M Attendees

Directories & Databases

6032 **Adweek Directory**
Prometheus Global Media
770 Broadway
New York, NY 10003-9595

212-493-4100; *Fax:* 646-654-5368;
www.prometheusgm.com

Richard D. Beckman, CEO
James A. Finkelstein, Chairman
Madeline Krakowsky, Vice President Circulation
Tracy Brater, Executive Director Creative Service

Adweek Directories Online is where you will find searchable databases with comprehensive information on ad agencies, brand marketers and multicultural media.
Frequency: Annual
Circulation: 800
Founded in: 1981

6033 **Annual Guide to Telemarketing**
Marketing Logistics
1460 Cloverdale Avenue
Highland Park, IL 60035-2817

847-831-1575

Arnold Fishman, Editor

About 400 telemarketing services bureaus in the United States.
Cost: $475.00
Frequency: Irregular

6034 **Art Directors Annual**
Art Directors Club
106 W 29th St
New York, NY 10001-5301

212-643-1440; *Fax:* 212-643-4266
info@adcglobal.org; www.adcglobal.org

Ami Brophy, CEO
Myrna Davis, Executive Director

Innovative advertising, design, publishing, photography, illustration, film, video, and interactive media.
Cost: $65.00
520 Members
Circulation: 7,000
Mailing list available for rent

6035 **Associations Yellow Book**
Leadership Directories
104 5th Ave
New York, NY 10011-6901

212-627-4140; *Fax:* 212-645-0931
associations@leadershipdirectories.com;
www.leadershipdirectories.com

David Hurvitz, CEO
James M Petrie, Associate Publisher

Contact information for over 41,000 officers and board members at 1,000 trade and professional associations, coalitions, PACs, and foundations.
Cost: $245.00
1,300 Pages
Frequency: SemiAnnual
ISSN: 1054-4070
Founded in: 1991
Mailing list available for rent: 37,000 names at $125 per M

6036 **Catalog Success**
North American Publishing Company
4001 S Business Park Avenue
Marshfield, WI 54449-9027

715-387-3400; *Fax:* 715-486-4185;
www.catalogsuccess.com

Putting marketing management to the test.
Frequency: Monthly
ISSN: 1524-2307
Printed in 4 colors

6037 **Corporate Yellow Book**
Leadership Directories
104 5th Ave
New York, NY 10011-6901

212-627-4140; *Fax:* 212-645-0931
corporate@leadershipdirectories.com;
www.leadershipdirectories.com

David Hurvitz, CEO

Contact information for over 48,000 executives at over 1,000 companies and more than 9,000 board members and their outside affiliations.
Cost: $360.00
1,400 Pages
Frequency: Quarterly
ISSN: 1058-2098
Founded in: 1986
Mailing list available for rent: 50,000 names at $105 per M

6038 **Customer Interaction Solutions**
Technology Marketing Corporation
1 Technology Plz
Norwalk, CT 06854-1936

203-852-6800
800-243-6002; *Fax:* 203-853-2845;
www.tmcnet.com

Rich Tehrani, CEO
Tracy Schelmetic, Editor

Over 1100 domestic and foreign suppliers of equipment products and services to the telecommunications/telemarketing industry.
Cost: $25.00
Frequency: Annual/December/89 Pages
Founded in: 1982
Mailing list available for rent: 63,000 names at $25 per M

6039 **D&B Million Dollar Database**
Dun & Bradstreet Information Service
3 Sylvan Way
Parsippany, NJ 07054-3822

973-605-6000
800-526-0651; *Fax:* 973-605-9630

160,000 public and private businesses with either a net worth of 500,000 or more, 250 emplyees at that location or 25,000,000 or more in sales volume.

6040 **D&B Million Dollar Database: International**
Dun & Bradstreet Information Service
3 Sylvan Way
Parsippany, NJ 07054-3822

973-605-6000
800-526-0651; *Fax:* 973-605-9630

50,000 top corporations, utilities, transportation companies, bank and trust companies, stock brolers, mutual and stock insurance companies, wholesalers, retailers, and domestic susidiaries of foreign corporations.

6041 **Direct Mail Service**
Information Resource Group
50495 Corporate Drive
Suite 112
Shelby Township, MI 48315-3132

586-726-6237

This database offers over 1,000,000 MIS and corporate professionals at over 150,000 companies throughout the United States.
Cost: $150.00

6042 **Direct Selling World Directory**
World Federation of Direct Selling Association
1776 K St NW
Suite 600
Washington, DC 20006-2304

202-546-5330; *Fax:* 202-463-4569;
www.dsa.org

Over 50 direct selling associations and over 1,000 associated member companies are offered in this comprehensive directory.
90 Pages
Frequency: Annual

6043 **Directory of Mail Order Catalogs**
Grey House Publishing
4919 Route 22
PO Box 56
Amenia, NY 12501

518-789-8700
800-562-2139; *Fax:* 845-373-6390
books@greyhouse.com; www.greyhouse.com
Social Media: Facebook, Twitter

Leslie Mackenzie, Publisher
Richard Gottlieb, Editor

The premier source of information on the mail order catalog industry. Covers over 13,000 consumer and business catalog companies with 44 different product chapters from Animals to Toys and Games.
Cost: $395.00
1900 Pages
Frequency: Annual
ISBN: 1-592373-96-8
Founded in: 1981

6044 **Directory of Mail Order Catalogs - Online Database**
Grey House Publishing
4919 Route 22
PO Box 56
Amenia, NY 12501

518-789-8700
800-562-2139; *Fax:* 845-373-6390
gold@greyhouse.com
http://gold.greyhouse.com
Social Media: Facebook, Twitter

Leslie Mackenzie, Publisher
Richard Gottlieb, Editor

Reach over 10,000 consumer catalog companies in one easy-to-use source with The Directory of Mail Order Catalogs - Online Database. Filled with business-building detail, each company profile gives you the information you need to access that organization quickly and easily. Listings provide key contacts, sales volume, employee size, printing information, circulation, list data, product descriptions and much more.
Frequency: Annual
Founded in: 1981

6045 **Directory of Major Mailers**
North American Publishing Company
1500 Spring Garden St
Suite 1200
Philadelphia, PA 19130-4094

215-238-5300; *Fax:* 215-238-5342

Ned S Borowsky, CEO

Offers over 7,500 major direct mailers and the key players with their names, addresses, phones and fax numbers, executive contacts, types of business, and the size of the house file. The Directory also contains actual reproductions of these mailings - letters, envelopes, order cards, brochures, etc. You'll see what was mailed, what worked and what didn't.
Cost: $395.00
Frequency: Annual
Founded in: 1994
Mailing list available for rent
Printed in one color on matte stock

6046 **International Job Finder: Where the Jobs are Worldwide**
Planning/Communications
7215 Oak Ave
River Forest, IL 60305-1935

708-366-5200
888-366-5200; *Fax:* 708-366-5280
dl@planningcommunications.com;
www.planningcommunications.com

Daniel Lauber, President

Describes in detail over 1,200 print and online sources of jobs outside the USA; newsletters, magazines, directories, web sites, online job databases, resume banks, email job alerts, and salary surveys.
Cost: $19.95
384 Pages
Frequency: Every 4 Years
Circulation: 8,000
ISBN: 1-884587-10-0
Founded in: 2002
Printed in one color on matte stock

6047 **Nonprofit Sector Yellow Book**
Leadership Directories
104 5th Ave
New York, NY 10011-6901

212-627-4140; *Fax:* 212-645-0931
info@leadershipdirectories.com;
www.leadershipdirectories.com

David Hurvitz, CEO
James M Petrie, Associate Publisher

Contact information for over 51,000 nonprofit executives and trustees at over 1,300 nonprofit organizations, including foundations, colleges and universities, museums, performing arts group and centers, medical institutions, library systems, preparatory schools, and charitable service organizations.
Cost: $245.00
1,200 Pages
Frequency: SemiAnnual
ISSN: 1520-9148
Founded in: 1999
Mailing list available for rent: 45,000 names at $125 per M

6048 **Nonprofits Job Finder: Where the Jobs are in Charities and Nonprofits**
Planning/Communications
7215 Oak Ave
River Forest, IL 60305-1935

708-366-5200
888-366-5200; *Fax:* 708-366-5280
dl@planningcommunications.com;
www.planningcommunications.com

Daniel Lauber, President

Describes in detail over 1,500 sources of jobs in the nonprofit sectors job database online, resume banks, email job alerts, directories, salary surveys, newsletters, and magazines.
Cost: $17.95
300 Pages
Circulation: 6,000
ISBN: 1-884587-06-2
Founded in: 2005
Printed in one color on matte stock

6049 **Who's Who: MASA Buyer's Guide to Blue Ribbon Mailing Services**
Mailing & Fulfillment Service Association
1421 Prince Street
Suite 410
Alexandria, VA 22314-2806

703-836-9200; *Fax:* 703-548-8204
mfsa-mail@mfsanet.org; www.mfsanet.org

Ken Garner, President
Bill Stevenson, Director Marketing

Offers a detailed listing of suppliers of equipment, products and services to the direct mail industry, most containing a description of the specific products they provide.
Frequency: Annual

6050 **Yellow Pages & Directory Report**
Simba Information
11200 Rockville Pike
Suite 504
Rockville, MD 20852

240-747-3096
877-352-2021; *Fax:* 340-747-3004
dgoddard@imslocalsearch.com;
www.yellowpagesanddirectoryreport.com
Social Media: Facebook, Twitter, LinkedIn

David Goddard, EVP/Senior Analyst/Editor
Kyle Kroll, President

Covers directory publishing, advertising, printing and releases from national yellow pages accounts.
Cost: $695.00

Industry Web Sites

6051 **http://gold.greyhouse.com**
G.O.L.D Grey House OnLine Databases

Grey House Publishing's online database platform, GOLD, offers Quick Search, Keyword Search and Expert Search for most business sectors including direct marketing and public relations markets. The GOLD platform makes finding the information you need quick and easy - whether you're a novice searcher or an experienced database user. All of Grey House's directory products are available for subscription on the GOLD platform.

6052 **www.adweek.com**
Adweek
Leading decision makers in the advertising and marketing field go to Adweek.com everyday for breaking news, insight, buzz, opinion, analysis, research and classifieds. The resources of all six regional editions of Adweek, as well as the national edition of Brandweek are combined with the knowledge of our online editors and the multimedia-interactive capabilities of the web to deliver vital information quickly and effectively to our target audience.

6053 **www.amma.org**
Advertising Mail Marketing Association
Represents the interests of those who use mail for fundraising or business purposes.

6054 **www.ataconnect.org**
American Teleservices Association
Represents the call centers, trainers, consultants and equipment suppliers that initiate, facilitate and generate telephone, Internet and e-mail sales, service and support.

6055 **www.cadm.org**
Chicago Association of Direct Marketing
Promotes the interests of Chicago's direct marketing professionals. Fosters member development through business, educational and social opportunities and provides a high-quality forum for the exchange of ideas by direct marketing professionals.

6056 **www.cyberdirect.com/ADMA**
Cohn & Wells
Members are direct response advertising agencies.

6057 **www.dmad.org**
Direct Marketing Association of Detroit
Not for profit organization dedicated to providing networking and educational opportunities to a dymamic group of direct marketing professionals. It is the premier resource for direct response marketing information, and is committed to recognizing outstanding direct marketing achievements in the Detroit area.

6058 **www.dmnews.com**
Haymarket Media, Inc.
114 W 26th St.
4th Fl.
New York, NY 10001
646-638-6000
Ginger Conlon, Editor-in-Chief
Al Urbanski, Senior Editor
Natasha Smith, Senior Editor
Direct Marketing News covers the latest trends, proven strategies and essential technologies.

6059 **www.dsa.org**
Direct Selling Association
National trade association of the leading firms that manufacture and distribute goods and services sold directly to consumers. More than 150 companies are members of the association, including many well-known brand names. The association's mission is to protect, serve and promote the effectiveness of member companies and the independent business people they represent.

6060 **www.fraudandtheftinfo.com**
Fraud & Theft Information Bureau
Provides problem solving, crime prevention, money saving manuals and fraud blocker databases.

6061 **www.greyhouse.com**
Grey House Publishing
Authoritative reference directories for most business sectors includng direct marketing and public relations markets. Users can search the online databases with varied search criteria allowing for custom searches by product category, geographic area, sales volume, keyword, subject and more. Full Grey House catalog and online ordering also available.

6062 **www.ims-lists.com/links**
IMS Direct Marketing Links
Professional associations links.

6063 **www.marketingpower.com**
American Marketing Association
A professional association for individuals and organizations involved in the practice, teaching and study of marketing worldwide.

6064 **www.mdma.org**
Midwest Direct Marketing Association
Advancing the professional and ethical practice of direct response marketing by members throughout the Upper Midwest. The MDMA seeks to accomplish this by sponsoring educational and professional networking events to share and encourage the best practices in telemarketing, direct mail and online marketing techniques and strategies.

6065 **www.mfsanet.org**
Mailing & Fulfillment Service Association
The national trade association for the mailing and fulfillment services industry.

6066 **www.nedma.com**
New England Direct Marketing Association

6067 **www.nmoa.org**
National Mail Order Association
Offers the stongest and lowest cost means for people to come together for the purpose of conducting business and creating sales. Small to medium sized organizations come for education, information, ideas, resources and new contacts.

6068 **www.the-dma.org**
Direct Marketing Association
Trade association in the direct marketing field with more than 3,500 member companies from the United States and 54 foreign nations. Included are catalogers, direct marketers from consumer to business-to-business, publishers, retail stores as well as service industries that support them.

Associations

6069 Advanced Network & Services
1225 Eye Street, NW
Suite 550
Washington, DC 20005
845-795-2090; *Fax:* 845-795-2180
consumerbankers.com
Social Media: Facebook, Twitter, LinkedIn
Wiliam Howle, Chair
Ross Elect, Chair Elect
Timothy Wennes, Past Chair
A nonprofit corporation dedicated to advancing education by accelerating the use of computer networking applications and technology.
Mailing list available for rent

6070 Advertising Specialty Institute
4800 Street Rd
Trevose, PA 19053-6698
215-953-4000
800-546-1350; *Fax:* 215-953-3045
customerservice@asicentral.com;
www.asicentral.com
Social Media: Facebook, Twitter, LinkedIn, YouTube, Instagram, Pinterest
Norman Unger Cohn, Chairman
Timothy Andrews, President & CEO
Steve Bright, EVP/General Counsel
Rob Watson, SVP, Marketing
Vince Bucolo, Chief Operating Officer
Advertising Specialty Institute provides distributors, suppliers and decorators in the advertising specialty industry with catalogs, information directories, newsletters, magazines, web sites and databases, and offers interactive e-commerce, marketing and selling tools.
26000 Members
Founded in: 1950

6071 Alliance for Public Technology
919 18th St NW
Suite 900
Washington, DC 20006-5512
480-624-2500; *Fax:* 202-263-2960;
www.apt.org
Sylvia Rosenthal, Executive Director
Matthew Bennett, Policy Director
A nonprofit membership organization based in Washington, DC.

6072 American Public Communications Council
3213 Duke Street
Suite 806
Alexandria, VA 22314
703-739-1322
800-868-2722; *Fax:* 703-739-1324
apcc@apcc.net; www.apcc.net
Mason Harris, State Assistant Director
Troy Lee, Additional Director
Michael Bright, At-Large Director
Donald Goens, At-Large Director
Aims to protect and expand domestic and foreign markets for public communications and provide business opportunities for members.
Founded in: 1988

6073 American Registry for Internet Numbers
3635 Concorde Parkway
Suite 200
Chantilly, VA 20151-1130
703-227-9840; *Fax:* 703-227-0676
hostmaster@arin.net; www.arin.net
John Curran, President
Paul Andersen, Treasurer
Timothy Denton, Secretary
Manage the internet numbering resources for North America focused completely on serving our members and the Internet community at large.

6074 American e-Commerce Association
www.aeaus.com
Computer training, e-commerce education, membership, recognition, endorsement, and evaluation services.

6075 Association for the Advancement of Computing in Education
P.O. Box 719
Waynesville, NC 28786
757-623-7588; *Fax:* 828-246-9557
info@aace.org; www.aace.org
International, educational and professional nonprofit organization dedicated to the advancement of the knowledge, theory and quality of learning and teaching at all levels with information technology. Encourages scholarly inquiry related to information technology and research results through publications, conferences, societies and chapters plus inter-organizational projects.
Founded in: 1981

6076 Association of Internet Researchers
910 W. Van Buren St.
Suite 142
Chicago, IL 60607-3523
www.aoir.org
Social Media: Facebook, Twitter
Lori Kendall, President
Jennifer Stromer-Galley, Vice-President
Michael Zimmer, Treasurer
Andrew Herman, Secretary
A learned society dedicated to the advancement of the transdisciplinary field of Internet Studies.

6077 Business Marketing Association: Boston
246 Hampshire Street
Cambridge, MA 02130
617-418-4000
800-664-4262; *Fax:* 312-822-0054
info@thebmaboston.com;
www.thebmaboston.com/
Michael Lewis, President
Will Robinson, VP Public Relations
Matthew Mamet, VP Internet Marketing
Larry Perreault, VP Finance
Chris Perkett, VP Programming
BMA Boston helps members improve their ability to manage business-to-business marketing and communications for greater productivity and profitability by providing unique access to information, ideas, and the experience of peers. The BMA offers an information-packed Website, online skills-building, marketing certification programs, and industry surveys and papers. In addition, members have the opportunity to interact with peers at seminars, chapter training programs and the BMA Annual Conference.

6078 Business Software Alliance
20 F Street, NW
Suite 800
Washington, DC 20001
202-872-5500; *Fax:* 202-872-5501
info@bsa.org; www.bsa.org
Social Media: Facebook, Twitter, LinkedIn, YouTube, RSS
Steven Dietz, Chair
Bruce Sewell, Vice Chair
Bradford Smith, Secretary
Scott Taylor, Treasurer
An organization dedicated to promoting a safe and legal digital world. BSA educates consumers on software management and copyright protection, cyber security, trade, e-commerce and other internet related issues.
Founded in: 1988

6079 CTIA-The Wireless Association
1400 16th Street, NW
Suite 600
Washington, DC 20036
202-785-0081; www.ctia.org
Social Media: Facebook, Twitter, LinkedIn
Meredith Attwell Baker, President/ CEO
Michael Altschul, Sr. VP, General Counsel
Scott Bergmann, Vice President, Regulatory Affairs
Heather Blanchard, Director, Internet Development
Rocco Carlitti, VP, Finance & Administration
An industry trade group that represents the international wireless telecommunications industry.

6080 Consumer Technology Association (CTA)
1919 South Eads Street
Arlington, VA 22202
703-907-7600
866-858-1555; *Fax:* 703-907-7675
cta@cta.tech; www.cta.tech
Social Media: Facebook, Twitter, LinkedIn, Google+
Gary Shapiro, President & CEO
David Hagan, Chairman
Mike Fasulo, Vice Chairman
Glenda MacMullin, Treasurer
Jacqueline Black, Secretary
Formerly known as the Consumer Electronics Association (CEA), the association provides valuable and innovative member-only resources including: exclusive information and unparalleled market research, networking opportunities with business advocates and leaders, up-to-date educational programs and technical training, exposure in extensive promotional programs, and representation from the voice of the industry.
2000 Members

6081 EMarketing Association
40 Blue Ridge Dr
Charlestown, RI 02813
401-315-2194; *Fax:* 408-884-2461
service@emarketingassociation.com;
www.emarketingassociation.com
Social Media: Facebook, Twitter, LinkedIn
Robert Fleming, President
Todd Daum, VP
John Hastings, VP
Linda Jaffe, VP
An international association of emarketing professionals. Members include government, companies, professionals and students involved with the emarketing arena.

6082 Electronic Retailing Association
607 14th Street, NW
Suite 530
Washington, DC 20005
703-841-1751
800-987-6462; *Fax:* 425-977-1036
webadmin@retailing.org; www.retailing.org
Social Media: Facebook, Twitter, LinkedIn, Flickr, YouTube
Julie Coons, CEO
Christopher Hearing, Treasurer
Babak Azad, Member of the Board
To foster growth, development and acceptance of the rapidly growing direct response industry worldwide for the companies who use the power of electronic media to sell goods and services to the public.

6083 **Entertainment Software Association**
601 Massachusetts Ave. NW
Suite 300
Washington, DC 20001
E-Mail: esa@theesa.com; www.theesa.com
Social Media: Facebook, Twitter
Michael D. Gallagher, President and CEO
The trade association of the video game industry.
Founded in: 2000

6084 **Hispanic Chamber of E-Commerce**
750 B St
Ste. 3308
San Diego, CA 92101
858-768-2483; *Fax:* 858-456-5238
info@hiscec.com; www.hiscec.com
Social Media: Facebook, YouTube
Tayde Aburto, Founder
Claudia Garcia, Founder/Chief Education Officer
Lisa Maino, Founder & CEO
German M Bravo, Founder/Chief Technology Officer
Rodrigo Gomez, Founder/Market Intelligence
The Hispanic Chamber of E-Commerce is a B2B membership-based national business association focused on providing tools and solutions to members to increase their presence online.
200 Members
Founded in: 2008

6085 **Information Systems Security Association**
12100 Sunset Hills Road.
Suite 130
Reston, VA 20190
703-234-4077
866-349-5818; *Fax:* 703-435-4390;
www.issa.org
Social Media: Facebook, Twitter, LinkedIn, YouTube, Google+
Andrea C. Hoy, CISM, CISSP, MBA, President
Justin White, Vice President
Anne Rogers, Secretary/ Director of Operations
Pamela Fusco, Treasurer/ Chief Financial Officer
Frances Alexander, Director
A nonprofit, international professional organization of information security professionals and practitioners.

6086 **International Society for Technology in Education**
180 W 8th Avenue
Eugene, OR 97401-2916
541-302-3777
800-336-5191; *Fax:* 541-302-3778
iste@iste.org; www.iste.org
Social Media: Facebook, Twitter, LinkedIn, YouTube, Pinterest
Kecia Ray, EdD, Chair
Matt Harris, EdD, Chair-Elect
Mia Wiiliams, PhD, Secretary
Mila Thomsa Fuller, Ed.D, Treasurer
A large nonprofit organization serving the technology-using educator.
12M Members
Founded in: 1979

6087 **Internet Marketing Association**
10 Mar Del Rey San
Clemente, CA 92673
949-443-9300; *Fax:* 949-443-2215
info@imanetwork.org; www.imanetwork.org
Social Media: Twitter, LinkedIn
Rachel Reenders, CIM Account Executive
Sinan Kanatsiz, CIM, Chairman and Founder
Matthew Langie, CIM, Vice Chairman of Education
Jeff Marcoux, Director
David Krauss, Director
A professional internet marketing group that provides educational resources on effective internet marketing strategies to business professionals.

6088 **Internet Merchants Association**
E-Mail: info@imamerchants.org;
www.imamerchants.org
Social Media: Facebook
Fred Neff, President
Scott Cole, Vice-President
Doyle Carver, Secretary
Andy Sollofe, Treasurer
Develops, promotes, and protects the economic vitality of internet merchants through a positive business environment and fosters a climate in whichcommerce, industry, and technology will flourish.

6089 **Internet Society**
1775 Wiehle Ave
Suite 201
Reston, VA 20190-5158
703-439-2120; *Fax:* 703-326-9881
isoc@isoc.org; www.isoc.org
Kathryn Brown, President/ CEO
Gregory Kapfer, CFO
Technologists, developers, educators, researchers, government representatives, and business people.
16000 Members
Founded in: 1992

6090 **Internet Society**
1775 Wiehle Avenue
Suite 201
Reston, VA 20190-5108
703-439-2120
isoc@isoc.org; www.internetsociety.org
Social Media: Facebook, Twitter, LinkedIn
Kathryn Brown, President/ CEO
Ms. Nicole Armstrong, Senior Events Manager
Howard Baggott, Senior Events Manager
Brenda Boggs, Senior Drupal Developer
Andre Copelin, Chief of Staff
An international, nonprofit organization that provides leadership in Internet related standards, education, and policy.
Founded in: 1992

6091 **National E-Commerce Association**
PO Box 2825
Peoria, AZ 85380
www.ecommerceassoc.com
The National E-Commerce Association provides an ear and a voice for the E-Commerce industry at the local, state and federal level. In addition to this, we have and will continue to negotiate the most aggressive pricing on goods and services for our members.
Founded in: 1980

6092 **NetSuite Ecommerce**
2955 Campus Drive
Suite 100
San Mateo, CA 94403-2511
650-627-1000
877-638-7848; *Fax:* 650-627-1001
info@netsuite.com; www.netsuite.com
Social Media: Facebook, Twitter, LinkedIn, YouTube
Evan Goldberg, Co-Founder/Chief Technology Officer
Zach Nelson, CEO
Jim McGeever, President/COO
Ron Gill, Chief Financial Officer
Fred Studer, Chief Marketing Officer
NetSuite E-commerce provides you with the tools you need to drive growth in your e-commerce channel and streamline and automate your business operations.
10000 Members
Founded in: 1998

6093 **US Internet Industry Association**
PO Box 302
Luray, VA 22835
540-742-1928; www.usiia-net.org
Dennis C. Hayes, Chairman
David P. McClure, President/ CEO
Michael McKeehan, Chair Public Policy
Christian Dawson, Chair, Web Hosting Council
Stephen B. May, Chief Technology Officer
A nonprofit North American trade association for Internet commerce, content and connectivity.
Founded in: 1994

6094 **Uniform Code Council**
Princeton Pike Corporate Center
1009 Lenox Drive Suite 202
Lawrenceville, NJ 08648
609-620-0200; *Fax:* 609-620-1200;
www.gs1us.org
Social Media: Facebook, Twitter, LinkedIn
Robert W Carpenter, President/CEO
Laura DiSciullo, SVP, Solutions
Gayle (Jones) Reilich, SVP, Customer Engagement
Yegneswaran Kumar, SVP/CFO
Siobhan O'Bara, SVP, Industry Engagement
Barcodes, eCommerce and data synchronization, to EPC/RFID and business process automation standards.
Frequency: Members 280,000
Founded in: 1974

6095 **Women in eCommerce**
PO Box 550856
Fort Lauderdale, FL 33355-0856
954-625-6606
877-947-3337
heidi@wecai.org; www.wecai.org
Social Media: Facebook, Twitter, LinkedIn
Suzannah Richards, President
Rosana Santos, President Elect
Ellen Sue Burton, VP/Logistics & Hospitality
Racheli Smilovitz, VP/Professional Development
Dalila J. Grohowski, VP/Membership Development
The original business and social networking community for social and professional networking and business development for successful women who want to take their businesses to a new level offline and online. We offer tools, resources and networking opportunities to build a strong foundation for future growth and expansion.
Founded in: 2001

6096 **eCommerce Merchants Trade Association**
917-388-1698; www.ecmta.org
Brandon Dupsky, Managing Director
Jonathan Garriss, Executive Director
eCommerce Merchants is a trade association founded by a group of online retailers who realized that by working together they could enjoy the premium services and discounted pricing normally available to very large companies.
Founded in: 2005

6097 **eMarketing Association**
40 Blue Ridge Dr
Suite 129
Charlestown, RI 02813
800-496-2950; *Fax:* 408-884-2461
service@eMarketingAssociation.com;

www.emarketingassociation.com
Social Media: Facebook, Twitter, LinkedIn

Chris Baggott, CEO
Bert DuMars, C-Founder/CEO
Murray Gaylord, VP/Marketing
Jeff Hilmire, President
Simms Jenkins, Founder & Principal

The eMA provides marketing resources, services, research, certifications, educational programs and events to its members and the marketing community. The eMA works with a number of organizations, companies and governments on issues related to e-commerce, multi-channel marketing and legislative issues.~
Founded in: 1997

Newsletters

6098 **APT News**
Alliance for Public Technology
919 18th St Nw
Suite 1000
Washington, DC 20006-5512

202-263-2970; *Fax:* 202-263-2960;
www.apt.org

Sylvia Rosenthal, Executive Director
Frequency: Bi-Monthly

6099 **Dot.COM**
Business Communications Company
25 Van Zant Street
Suite 13
Norwalk, CT 06855-1713

203-853-4266; *Fax:* 203-853-0348
sales@bccresearch.com; www.bccresearch.com

Louis Naturman, Publisher
C Toenne, Editor

Updates readers on the commercial use of the Internet and related platforms.
Cost: $38.00

6100 **E-Healthcare Market Reporter**
Health Resources Publishing
1913 Atlantic Ave
Suite 200
Manasquan, NJ 08736-1067

732-292-1100
888-843-6242; *Fax:* 732-292-1111
info@themcic.com; www.hin.com/ehealthcare

Robert K Jenkins, Publisher
Judith Granel, Marketing
John Russel, Editor
Brett Powell, Regional Director
Alice Burron, Director

A bi-monthly covering strategies, new products, innovation, privacy issue, business solutions, service available, vendor news and comparative for implementing sales and marketing on the internet.
Cost: $397.00
Frequency: Fortnightly
ISSN: 1098-5654
Founded in: 1988

6101 **E-News**
Patricia Seybold Group
Po Box 240565
Boston, MA 02129

617-742-5200
800-826-2424; *Fax:* 617-742-1028
feedback@psgroup.com; www.psgroup.com

Patricia Seybold, Founder/CEO

E-mail newsletter includes perspectives on the e-commerce industry, research and upcoming events.

6102 **Ecommerce @lert**
ZD Journals
500 Canal View Boulevard
Rochester, NY 14623-2800

585-407-7301; *Fax:* 585-214-2387;
www.ecommercealert.com
Social Media: Facebook, Twitter, LinkedIn

Bob Artner, Managing Editor

Explores the emerging digital and online technology used in sales management, as well as the companies in the forefront of this change.
Cost: $495.00

6103 **Electronic Commerce News**
Phillips Publishing
PO Box 60037
Potomac, MD 20859

301-208-6787; *Fax:* 301-424-2098
htreat@phillips.com; www.ectoday.com

Heather Treat, Publisher
Stuart Zipper, Editor
Diane Schwartz, Publisher
Laurie Hofmann, Director of Marketing

Provides business strategies for the extended enterprise with the latest technological development and opportunities.
Cost: $597.00
Frequency: Weekly

6104 **Higher Education Technology News**
Business Publishers
2222 Sedwick Dr
Suite 101
Durham, NC 27713

800-223-8720; *Fax:* 800-508-2592
custserv@bpinews.com; www.bpinews.com

Provides timely, independent coverage of the issues surrounding technology in a higher educational setting. Offers news from federal and state government, the business world and others educators.
Cost: $307.00
8 Pages
Founded in: 1963

6105 **International Cyber Centers**
Probe Research
3 Wing Drive
Suite 240
Cedar Knolls, NJ 07927-1000

973-285-1500; *Fax:* 973-285-1519;
www.proberesearch.com

Strategic positioning and product portfolios of major domestic and international carriers in collocation, Web hosting, applications hosting, e-commerce, IP-centric data, managed services and other value added offerings. Examines the global square footage race in building or upgrading what are variously known as Internet centers, data centers or cyber centers worldwide. Profiles of several key players are included in the bulletin issue.

6106 **Internet Alliance Cyberbrief**
Internet Alliance
1615 L Street NW
Suite 1100
Washington, DC 20036-5624

202-861-2407; www.internetalliance.org

Tammy Cota, Executive Director

Coverage of public policy changes in government, enhancing consumer satisfaction in interactive services, and education.
Frequency: Weekly

6107 **Internet Business**
Information Gatekeepers
1340 Soldiers Field Rd
Suite 3
Brighton, MA 02135-1000

617-782-5033
800-323-1088; *Fax:* 617-782-5735
info@igigroup.com; www.igigroup.com

Paul Polishuk, CEO
Hui Pan, Chief Analyst, Editor in Chief
Bev Wilson, Managing Editor

Covers the rapid developments in the industry.
Cost: $695.00
Frequency: Monthly

6108 **Internet Business Advantage**
ZD Journals
500 Canal View Boulevard
Rochester, NY 14623-2800

585-407-7301; *Fax:* 585-214-2387
iba@zdjournals.com; www.zdjournals.com

Bob Artner, Editor-in-Chief

Keeps readers up-to-date of technological advances and new services available on the Internet. Reviews new products and provides tips on businss applications.
Cost: $295.00

6109 **Internet Media Investor**
Kagan World Media
126 Clock Tower Place
Carmel, CA 93923-8746

831-624-1536
800-307-2529; *Fax:* 831-625-3225
info@kagan.com; www.kagan.com
Social Media: Facebook, Twitter, LinkedIn, YouTube

George Niesen, Editor
Tom Johnson, Marketing Manager

Follows public stocks and private deals, analyzes publicly held interactive multimedia companies, tracks key industry subgroups through Kagan stock averages that relate companies by product lines, projects growth of new TV and data networks, programming and technology. Provides economic modeling of new corporate ventures and interprets announcements and events. Three month trial is available.
Cost: $1095.00
Frequency: Monthly
Founded in: 1969

6110 **Internet World**
Mecklermedia Corporation
20 Ketchum Street
Westport, CT 06880

212-260-0758; *Fax:* 203-454-5840

Bill Besch, Publisher

Internet industry news, product reviews and technical reports, with an emphasis on Internet technology, hardware, management and security.
Cost: $160.00
Frequency: Weekly
Circulation: 98,947

6111 **Internetweek**
CMP Media
600 Community Drive
Manhasset, NY 11030-3847

516-562-5000; *Fax:* 516-562-5554;
www.internetweek.com

Mike Azzara, Publisher

News and coverage of the latest trends in electronic commerce and intranet application platforms, the effects of high technology on daily production, changing regulations and operating standards, the best tools and practices, and related business and financial news.
Cost: $143.00
Frequency: Weekly
Circulation: 161264

6112 **Manufacturing Automation**
Vital Information Publications
754 Caravel Lane
Foster City, CA 94404-1712

650-345-7018; www.sensauto.com

Peter Adrian, Owner
Gary Kuba, Marketing Director

Provides market research data and vital information about key products, applications, and technologies for a wide range of industrial automation segments, such as CAD/CAM, supply chain management, e-Commerce solutions, enterprise resource planning, automation software, manufacturing technology, industrial controls, and manufacturing systems.

6113 **Mass Storage News**
Corry Publishing
2840 W 21st Street
Erie, PA 16506

814-838-0025; *Fax:* 814-838-0035
terryp@corrypub.com; www.corrypub.com

Terry Peterson, Publisher

News on optical disk based imaging and storage systems, new products, technical developments and industry developments.
Cost: $597.00
Frequency: BiWeekly
Circulation: 1,500

6114 **Mealey's Litigation Report: Class Actions**
LexisNexis Mealey's
555 W 5th Avenue
Los Angeles, CA 90013

213-627-1130
mealeyinfo@lexisnexis.com;
www.lexisnexis.com/mealeys

Tom Hagy, VP/General Manager
Maureen McGuire, Editorial Director
David Elreth, Editor
This report will provide in-depth coverage of class action litigation involving mass torts and beyond - including consumer law, employment law, securities litigation and e-commerce disputes. Get the latest on: hard-to-find filings, notice plans, fairness hearings, class certification rulings, settlements, trial news and verdicts, attorney fee news, appeals, breaking news stories, new complaints, Supreme Court battles, and much more.
Cost: $1195.00
100 Pages
Frequency: Semi-Monthly
Founded in: 1997

6115 **Mealey's Litigation Report: Cyber Tech & E -Commerce**
LexisNexis Mealey's
555 W 5th Avenue
Los Angeles, CA 90013

213-627-1130
mealeyinfo@lexisnexis.com;
www.lexisnexis.com/mealeys

Tom Hagy, VP/General Manager
Maureen McGuire, Editorial Director
Mark Rogers, Editor

The Report covers disputes arising from e-commerce. The report tracks emerging legal issues, including: Internet security, data destruction and/or alteration, defamation on the Web, software errors, hardware failure, electronic theft, e-mail trespass, online privacy, government action, shareholder lawsuits, Internet jurisdiction issues, file sharing (copyright) disputes and much more.
Cost: $999.00
100 Pages
Frequency: Monthly
Founded in: 1999

6116 **Mobile Internet**
Information Gatekeepers
1340 Soldiers Field Rd
Suite 3
Brighton, MA 02135-1000

617-782-5033
800-323-1088; *Fax:* 617-782-5735
info@igigroup.com; www.igigroup.com

Paul Polishuk, CEO
Hui Pan, Chief Analyst, Editor in Chief
Bev Wilson, Managing Editor

Covers worldwide developments in 3G wireless networks, with an emphasis on the worldwide PCS/GSM/CDMA markets.
Cost: $695.00
Frequency: Monthly
Founded in: 1977

6117 **Multimedia & Internet Training Newsletter**
Brandon Hall Resources
690 W Fremont Ave
#9C
Sunnyvale, CA 94087-4200

408-736-2335; www.brandon-hall.com
Social Media: Facebook, Twitter, LinkedIn

Mike Cooke, CEO
Rachel Ashkin, COO
Michael Rochelle, CSO

The latest in multimedia news, virtual clasroom reports, insight into web-based training, and technology tutorial. Job bank listings, upcoming events, seminars, and tips and techniques.
Cost: $189.00
Frequency: Monthly
Circulation: 900

6118 **Online & CD-ROM Review**
Information Today
1308 W Main
University of Illinois
Urbana, IL 61801

217-333-1074
800-248-8466; *Fax:* 217-762-3956
custserv@infotoday.com; www.infotoday.com/

Martha Williams, Editor
Thomas H Hogan, CEO/President
Heather Rudolph, Marketing
Inge Coffey, Circulation Manager

Covers the use and management of online and CD-ROM services, the training and education of online and CD-ROM users, creation and marketing of databases, and new development in search aids.
Cost: $115.00
Frequency: Monthly
Circulation: 4745

6119 **Online Libraries & Microcomputers**
Information Intelligence
PO Box 31098
Phoenix, AZ 31098

602-996-2283; www.phoenix-intel.com

George Machovec, Managing Editor

Examines new library online and automation applications with reviews of new software and hardware, industry news and trends, and upcoming related events.
Cost: $62.50
9 Pages
Frequency: 10 per year
ISSN: 0737-7770
Founded in: 1983

6120 **Online Newsletter**
Information Intelligence
PO Box 31098
Phoenix, AZ 85046-1098

602-996-2283; www.phoenix-intel.com

Richard S Huleatt, Editor

Covers all aspects of online and CD-ROM developments throughout the world. Regular feature sections include news and events, mergers and acquisitions, people in the news, telecommunications, and networks. Editoral reflects product development and its impact on users, and provides listings of upcoming events related to this industry.
Cost: $62.50
9 Pages
Frequency: 10 per year
ISSN: 0194-0694
Founded in: 1983

6121 **Online Reporter**
G2 Computer Intelligence
PO Box 7
Glen Head, NY 11545-1616

516-759-7025; *Fax:* 516-759-7028;
www.g2news.com

Maureen O'Gara, Publisher

Information on recent developments on the Internet through news briefs and a section called Chat Room. Includes information on e-commerce, Java and network security.
Cost: $695.00
Frequency: Weekly

6122 **Privacy Journal**
P.O. Box 28577
Providence, RI 02908

401-274-7861; *Fax:* 401-274-4747
orders@privacyjournal.net;
www.privacyjournal.net

Robert Ellis Smith, Publisher

An independent monthly on privacy in a computer age.
Cost: $65.00
Frequency: Monthly
ISSN: 0145-7659
Founded in: 1974
Printed in one color

6123 **Report on Electronic Commerce**
Telecommunications Reports International
1333 H Street NW
#100 E
Washington, DC 20005-4707

202-842-3022; *Fax:* 202-842-1875;
www.tr.com

Jerry Ashworth, Editor
Brian Hammond, Managing Editor

Provides insiths on the latest developments in EDI, EFT, EBT, digital cash, home shopping and baking, value-added networks, and transaction processing. Offers articles, analysis and case studies regarding financial and business transaction over the Internet.
Cost: $745.00
Frequency: BiWeekly

6124 **Sysop News and Cyberworld Report**
BBS Press Service
5610 SW 10th Avenue
Topeka, KS 66604-2104

785-286-4272; *Fax:* 785-271-0192
alanbenchtold@sysop.com; www.sysop.com

Alan R Bechtold, Publisher
Debbie Boos, Owner

Online industry news and updates, Web site reviews, event announcements, Web design basics, Internet-based applicaitons, business solutions and various technical articles of interest.
Cost: $59.95
Frequency: Weekly
Circulation: 18M

6125 **TechTarget**
TechTarget
117 Kendrick St
Suite 800
Needham Heights, MA 02494-2728

781-657-1000
888-274-4111; *Fax:* 781-657-1100
info@techtarget.com; www.techtarget.com

Greg Strakosch, CEO
Don Hawk, President
Lisa Johnson, VP Marketing
Catherine Engelke, Direcctor Public Relations

IBM iSeries focused media. The IBM e-Server iSeries (formerly the AS/400) is considered to be the world's most often used multi-user business computer. The installed base worldwide is huge and will get bigger, fueled by incresed Web development. The iSeries comes with an integrated Web application server and all the tools needed to build internet, intranet, extranet, and e-commerce sites quickly and will figure prominently into IT strategy and implementation for years to come.
Frequency: Monthly
Founded in: 1999

6126 **The CyberSkeptic's Guide to Internet Research**
Information Today
143 Old Marlton Pike
Medford, NJ 08055-8750

609-654-6266
800-300-9868; *Fax:* 609-654-4309
custserv@infotoday.com; www.infotoday.com

Thomas H Hogan, President
Roger R Bilboul, Chairman Of The Board

A monthly subscription newsletter in print, that explores and evaluates free and low cost Web sites and search strategies to help you use the Internet and stay up to date.
Cost: $164.95
ISSN: 1085-2417

6127 **Trade Vendor Quarterly**
Blakeley & Blakeley
2 Park Plaza
Suite 400
Irvine, CA 92614

949-260-0611; *Fax:* 949-260-0613;
www.vendorlaw.com

Scott Blakey, Esq.

Highlights developments in commercial, creditors' rights, e-commerce and bankruptcy law of interest to the credit and financial professional. Free online.
Frequency: Quarterly

6128 **Web Review**
Miller Freeman Publications
600 Harrison Street
San Francisco, CA 94107
650-573-3210

Veronica Costanza, Publisher

Timely and practical information on the practice of Internet development as well as news on the latest techniques and technologies.
Frequency: BiWeekly
Circulation: 12M

6129 **Webdeveloper.com**
Mecklermedia Corporation
23 Old Kings Hwy S
Darien, CT 06820-4541

203-662-2800; *Fax:* 203-655-4686
info@WebMediaBrands.com;
www.webmediabrands.com

Alan M Meckler, CEO
Mike Demiot, Marketing Manager

Product reviews, practical techniques, codes, tools and tips for Internet professionals who design, develop and maintain Web sites and Internet services.
Frequency: Daily

6130 **West Side Leader/Green Leader**
Leader Publications
3075 Smith Rd
Suite 204
Akron, OH 44333-4454

330-665-0909
888-945-9595; *Fax:* 330-665-9590
webmaster@akron.com; www.akron.com

Kathryn Core, Editor
Kathleen Collins, Managing Editor
Maria Lindsay, Assistant Editor

Weekly newspapers.
Cost: $10.00
Circulation: 53000

Magazines & Journals

6131 **Active Server Developer's Journal**
ZD Journals
500 Canal View Boulevard
Rochester, NY 14623-2800

585-407-7301; *Fax:* 585-214-2387
asp@zdjournals.com; www.asdj.com

Jon Pyles, Publisher
Taggard Andrews

Addresses such issues as database publishing, creating hack-proof files and getting the most out of server-side components. Special sections focus on client-side solutions, covering the basics and taking an in-depth look at more detailed techniques.
Cost: $149.00
Frequency: Monthly

6132 **Bio & Software and Internet Report**
Mary Ann Liebert
140 Huguenot St # 3
3rd Floor
New Rochelle, NY 10801-5215

914-740-2100; *Fax:* 914-740-2101
info@liebertpub.com; www.liebertpub.com
Social Media: Facebook, Twitter, LinkedIn

Mary A Liebert, Owner
Gerry Elman, Editor-in-Chief
Robert A Bohrer, Executive Editor
Judith Gunn Bronson, Managing Editor

News and reviews of all areas of scientific computing, including software, hardware and network products.
Cost: $1554.00
ISSN: 1527-9162
Founded in: 1980

6133 **Boardwatch Magazine**
Penton Media
1300 E 9th St # 316
Cleveland, OH 44114-1503

216-696-7000; *Fax:* 216-696-6662;
www.penton.com

Jane Cooper, Marketing
David Icopf, Editorial Director

Editorial coverage for communications service providers.
Cost: $72.00
Frequency: Monthly
Circulation: 50,000
ISSN: 1054-2760
Founded in: 1987
Mailing list available for rent: 50,000 names at $250 per M

6134 **BtoB Magazine**
Ad Age Group/ Division of Crain Communications
711 3rd Ave
New York, NY 10017-4014

212-210-0785; *Fax:* 212-210-0200
info@crain.com; www.crain.com

Norm Feldman, Manager

Dedicated to integrated business to business marketing. Every page is packed with substance news, reports, technologies, benchmarks, best practices served up by the most knowledgeable journalists.
Frequency: Monthly
Circulation: 45000

6135 **Card Technology**
Thomson Financial Publishing
1 State St
27th Floor
New York, NY 10004-1481

212-825-8445
800-221-1809; *Fax:* 212-843-9622
custserv@thomsonmedia.com;
www.cardtechnology.com

Daniel Wolfe, Editor in Chief
Austin Kilgore, Managing Editor
Ed McKinley, Independent Sales Organizations
Hope Lerman, National Sales Manager

Store-value cards, optical-memory cards, biometrics, cards on the Internet, cards for electronic data storage, and devices used with these cards in banking, government, telecommunications, transportation and education.
Cost: $ 98.00
Frequency: Monthly
Circulation: 25000
Printed in 4 colors on glossy stock

6136 **Computer & Online Industry Litigation Reporter**
Andrews Publications
175 Strafford Avenue
Building 4, Suite 140
Wayne, PA 19087-3331

610-225-0510
800-345-1101; *Fax:* 610-225-0501;
www.andrewspub.com

John Backe, Publisher

Editorial covers telecommuncations and the Internet for attorneys and professionals in the legal field.
Cost: $850.00

6137 **Computer Gaming World**
Ziff Davis Publishing Company
101 2nd St # 900
8th Floor
San Francisco, CA 94105-3650

415-547-8000; *Fax:* 415-547-8777
info@ziffdavis.com; www.ziffdavis.com

Dale Strang, Manager
Matt Leone, Editor
Paul Fusco, Sales Director
Bobby Markowitz, Marketing Director
Stephen Hicks, General Counsel

Reviews commercially available and on-line games. Features interviews with game designers, as well as strategy tips, contests and news.
Cost: $98.88
Frequency: Monthly
Circulation: 212783

6138 **Computer Journal**
Las Vegas Computer Journal

2232 S Nellis Boulevard
#169
Las Vegas, NV 89104-6213

702-270-4656; *Fax:* 702-432-6204;
www.internetsurfer.com

Johanna Nezhoda, Publisher

Spotlights Web news, site reviews, interface tools and commentary on the changing face of computing.
Cost: $24.95
Frequency: Monthly
Circulation: 25M

6139 **Computer Music Journal**
MIT Press
3 Cambridge Ctr # 23
Cambridge, MA 02142-1613

617-499-3200; *Fax:* 617-621-0856
journals-orders@mit.edu; www.adoptaboat.org

Miguel Suarez, Manager
Keeril Makan, Managing Editor

Tutorials and research articles, news and reviews of computer music systems, hardware and software for music sound, digital audio, signal processing and multimedia.
Cost: $82.00
120 Pages
Frequency: Quarterly
Circulation: 5000
Founded in: 1926

6140 **Computer Service & Repair Magazine**
Searle Publishing Company
5511 Morning Glory Ln
#210-110
Littleton, CO 80123-2701

303-730-3006
810-797-8708; *Fax:* 303-797-0276;
www.independentcable.com

Robert Searle, Publisher
Roderick Robles, Associate Publisher

Information on the maintenance and repair of computer systems. Reviews new products and technology.

6141 **Corporate Help Desk Solutions**
Gartner Group
Po Box 10212
Stamford, CT 06904-2212
203-964-0096; *Fax:* 203-316-6488
help@gartner.com; www.gartner.com
Social Media: Facebook, Twitter, LinkedIn

Jean Hall, CEO
Gene Hall, CEO/President
David Godfrey, Marketing/Circulation
Robin Kranich, SVP Human Resources

Key technologies, management practices and techniques for the most cost-effective help desk solutions.
Cost: $395.00
Frequency: Monthly
Founded in: 1979

6142 **Customer Interaction Solutions**
Technology Marketing Corporation
1 Technology Plz
Norwalk, CT 06854-1936

203-852-6800
800-243-6002; *Fax:* 203-853-2845
tmc@tmcnet.com; www.tmcnet.com

Rich Tehrani, CEO
Tracey Schelmetic, Managing Editor
Erik D Lounsbury, Editorial Director

Magazine devoted to teleservices and e-services outsourcing, marketing and consumer management issues.
Frequency: Monthly
Founded in: 1982

6143 **Customer Interface**
Advanstar Communications
6200 Canoga Avenue
2nd Floor
Woodland Hills, CA 91367

818-593-5000; *Fax:* 818-593-5020
info@advanstar.com; www.advanstar.com

Joseph Loggia, President
Chris DeMoulin, VP
Susannah George, Marketing Director

Business management resource for senior and mid-level decision makers who are responsible for call centers, customer contact and customer service initiatives. We are stewards for the industry as we prepare it for continued transformation and growth.
Circulation: 50,000
Founded in: 1988

6144 **CyberDealer**
Meister Publishing Company
37733 Euclid Ave
Willoughby, OH 44094-5992

440-942-2000
800-572-7740; *Fax:* 440-975-3447;
www.meisternet.com

Gary Fitzgerald, President

Helps agricultural dealerships better manage their operations.
Frequency: 6 per year

6145 **Desktop Video Communications**
BCR Enterprises
950 York Road
#203
Hinsdale, IL 60521-8609

630-789-6700; *Fax:* 630-323-5324;
www.bcr.com

Fred Knight, Publisher/Editor-in-Chief

Useful information for communications and informations systems managers, line managers, system developers and integrators, value-added resellers, and software vendors.
Frequency: Bi-Monthly
Circulation: 30M

6146 **Digital Travel**
Jupiter Communications Company
627 Broadway
2nd Floor
New York, NY 10012-2612

212-533-8885; *Fax:* 212-780-6075;
www.jup.com

Eva Papoutsakis, Editor
Marla Kammer, Managing Director
Ellen Daley, Managing Director
Charles Rutstein, Chief Operating Officer

Editorial includes the latest information and technology in agencies, airlines, lodging, ticketing, mapping, Web advertising, transaction processing, revenue models, demographics, and full-service sites.
Cost: $595.00
Frequency: Monthly

6147 **E-Business Advisor**
Advisor Media
P.O.Box 503350
San Diego, CA 92150-3350

858-278-5600
800-336-6060; *Fax:* 858-278-0300;
www.e-businessadvisor.com

John L Hawkins, Editorial Director
Jane Falla, Senior Editor
Brian Dunning, Technical Editor

E-Business Advisor is the monthly magazine presenting the best innovation, strategies, and practices for e-business leaders. It is an independent guide for the team of business and technical managers within an enterprise responsible for strategic innovation, planning, design, implementation, and management of e-business and e-commerce solutions.
Cost: $49.00
68 Pages
Circulation: 60000
ISSN: 1098-8912
Founded in: 1983
Mailing list available for rent: 60000 names at $175 per M

6148 **E-Content**
Information Today
143 Old Marlton Pike
Medford, NJ 08055-8750

609-654-6266
800-300-9868; *Fax:* 609-654-4309
custserv@infotoday.com; www.infotoday.com

Thomas H Hogan, President
Roger R Bilboul, Chairman Of The Board

Delivers essential research, reporting, news and analysis of content related issues. It is essential reading for executive and professionals involved in content creation, management, acquisition, organization and distribution in both commercial and enterprise environments.
Cost: $115.00
Frequency: 10 issues/yr
Mailing list available for rent: 4M names
Printed in 4 colors on glossy stock

6149 **ESchool News**
IAQ Publications
7920 Norfolk Ave # 900
Suite 900
Bethesda, MD 20814-2539

301-913-0115; *Fax:* 301-913-0119
gdowney@eschoolnews.com;
www.eschoolnews.com

Robert Morrow, Owner

Guide to buying and updating classroom technology for K-12 educators. Product information listings, industry updates and related reports. Covers grant writing and funding, as well as government legislation regarding education.
Cost: $90.00

6150 **Electronic Commerce Advisor**
Thomson Reuters
195 Broadway # 4
New York, NY 10007-3124

646-822-2000
800-231-1860; *Fax:* 646-822-2800
trta.lei-support@thomsonreuters.com;
www.ria.thomsonreuters.com

Elaine Yadlon, Plant Manager
Thomas H Glocer, CEO & Director
Robert D Daleo, Chief Financial Officer
Kelli Crane, Senior Vice President & CIO

Offers the latest in electronic commerce covering what's available and how to select and employ the best technology without costly trial-and-error mistakes. Information on EDI, e-mail, fax gateways, Internet, encryption, VANs, procurement cards, imaging, voice response, remote computering and other related information.
Cost: $155.00
Circulation: 4500
Founded in: 1940

6151 **Electronic Mail & Messaging Systems**
Business Research Publications
1333 H Street NW
Suite 100 East
Washington, DC 20005-4707

202-364-6473
800-822-6338; *Fax:* 202-842-1875

Rod Kuckro, Editor-in-Chief

Exclusive biweekly intelligence technology applications, products and market trends in elec-

tronic mail, computer fax, wireless messaging and the Internet.
Cost: $595.00
Frequency: BiWeekly

6152 **Electronic Publishing**
PennWell Publishing Company
98 Spit Brook Rd # LI-1
Nashua, NH 03062-5737

603-891-0123; *Fax:* 603-891-9294
genepri@pennwell.com; www.pennwell.com

Christine Shaw, VP
Keith V. Hevenor, Editor

For those who communicate in print, including service bureaus, printers, prepress houses and desktop publishers, it provides latest products, news and related developments.
Cost: $59.00
Frequency: Monthly
Circulation: 68441
Founded in: 1910

6153 **Electronic Retailer Magazine**
Electronic Retailing Association
2000 14th St N # 300
Suite 300
Arlington, VA 22201-2573

703-841-1751
800-987-6462; *Fax:* 703-841-1860
contact@retailing.org; www.retailing.org

Julie Coons, CEO
Vitisia Paynich, Editor-in-Chief
Tom Dellner, Executive Editor

Delivers news updates, exclusives, industry research, educational features and in-depth converage of issues relating to government affairs, legal aspects, concepts and products, production, media-buying as well as all back end services.
Frequency: Monthly
Circulation: 21000

6154 **Emediaweekly**
Mac Publishing
501 2nd St
San Francisco, CA 94107-1496

415-243-0505
800-288-6848; *Fax:* 415-442-0766
sitehelp@macworld.com; www.macworld.com
Social Media: Facebook, Twitter, YouTube

Mike Kisseberth, CEO

Covers the creation, technologies, applications and hardware for the publishing spectrum, including print, Web, multimedia, CD and digital video. Emphasis on hardware and software products, along with analysis, reviews, and buyer's guides.
Cost: $125.00
Frequency: Weekly

6155 **Explore the Net with Internet Explorer**
ZD Journals
500 Canal View Boulevard
Rochester, NY 14623-2800

585-407-7301; *Fax:* 585-214-2386
etn_editor@zdjournals.com;
www.zdjournals.com

Joelle Martin, Publisher

Informs readers of new features and how they may be used; covering such concepts as browser upgrades, compatibility issues, authoring tools and connection utilities. Regular departments showcase the 'site of the month,' in addition to reviewing other sites that have attractive interfaces and are valuable resources.
Cost: $49.00
Frequency: Monthly

6156 **Ezine - WECommerce News**
Women in eCommerce
PO Box 550856
Fort Lauderdale, FL 33355-0856

954-625-6606
877-947-3337
heidi@wecai.org; www.wecai.org

Suzannah Richards, President
Rosana Santos, President Elect
Ellen Sue Burton, VP/Logistics & Hospitality
Racheli Smilovitz, VP/Professional Development
Dalila J. Grohowski, VP/Membership Development

Helping women do business on the web.
Founded in: 2001

6157 **GEOWorld**
Bel-Av Communciations
359 Galahad Rd
Bolingbrook, IL 60440-2108

www.geoplace.com

Jo Treadwell, VP/Group Publisher
Todd Danielson, Editor

Offers a wealth of knowledge through festures, news and commentary covering the geospatial industry. Covers local and federal government, emergency management, infrastructure, natural resource management, industry trends and innovations and more.
Cost: $72.00
Frequency: Monthly
Circulation: 25000

6158 **Genealogical Computing**
Ancestry
360 W 4800 N
Provo, UT 84604-5675

801-705-7000
800-262-3787; *Fax:* 801-705-7001;
www.myfamily.com
Social Media: Facebook, Twitter

Timothy P Sullivan, CEO
Matthew Wright, Contributing Editor
David C Moon, CEO
Mary-Kay Evans, Director, Public Relations

For readers who use computers and technology to organize and enhance their research into accounts of ancestries and descent.
Cost: $25.00
Frequency: Quarterly

6159 **Geospatial Solutions**
Advanstar Communications
201 Sandpointe Ave # 600
Suite 500
Santa Ana, CA 92707-8700

714-513-8400; *Fax:* 714-513-8680;
www.geospatial-solutions.com

Mike Weldon, Plant Manager

Practical applications of geographic information systems and technologies for planning, developing, preserving, analyzing and managing environments.
Frequency: Monthly
Circulation: 30000
Founded in: 1987

6160 **Harlow Report: Geographic Information Systems**
Advanced Information Management Group
905 Thistledown Lane
Birmingham, AL 35244-3361

334-982-9203
chris@geoint.com; www.theharlowreport.com/

Chris Harlow, Publisher/Editor

Key management issues and new software highlights, service providers and users for the geographic information systems industry.
Cost: $190.00
Frequency: Monthly
Founded in: 1982

6161 **Heller Report on Internet Strategies for Education Markets**
Nelson B Heller & Associates
9933 Lawler Avenue
#502
Skokie, IL 60077-3708

800-525-5811
877-435-5373; *Fax:* 303-209-9444
info@hellerreports.com;
www.hellerreports.com
Social Media: Facebook, Twitter

Nelson B Heller, President/Publisher
Emily Garner, Sales/Marketing Director

Covers Internet hardware, software and services for educational use. Discusses the funding and deadlines relevant to the products and services offered through the Internet.
Cost: $397.00
12 Pages
Frequency: Monthly
Circulation: 500
Founded in: 1981
Printed in 2 colors

6162 **IEEE Internet Computing**
IEEE Computer Society
PO Box 3014
Los Alamitos, CA 90720-1314

714-821-8380
800-272-6657; *Fax:* 714-821-4010
volunteer.services@computer.org;
www.computer.org/internet
Social Media: Facebook, Twitter, LinkedIn, YouTube

Angela Burges, Executive Director
Davis Hennage, CEO/President
Steve Woods, Production Manager
Sandy Brown, Marketing
Steve Woods, Production Manager

Provides a technology roadmap for high-end users and application developers, as well as a venue for standards, case histories, and new ideas. Essays, interview, and roundtable discussions adress the Internet's impact on engineering practice. Describes Internet tools, technologies, and application-oriented research.
Cost: $28.00
Frequency: Quarterly
Circulation: 11265
Founded in: 1946

6163 **IT Cost Management Strategies**
Computer Economics
2082 Business Center Dr
Suite 240
Irvine, CA 92612

949-831-8700; *Fax:* 949-442-7688;
www.computereconomics.com

Frank Scavo, President
Dan Husiak, VP

Covers budgeting, financial news, computer programming, marketing and management for management information systems directors as a planning assistant.
Frequency: Monthly
Founded in: 1978

6164 **ITS World**
Advanstar Communications
859 Willamette Street
Eugene, OR 97401-2918

541-431-0026; *Fax:* 541-344-3514;
www.itsworld.com

Phillip Arndt, Publisher

Articles on industry news, current issues that affect Intelligent Transportation Systems, practical

advice, applications, new and existing technology, and new product information.
Cost: $35.00
Frequency: 9 per year
Circulation: 15,124

6165 **Information Display**
Palisades Institute for Research Services
2 Shadybrook Lane
Norwalk, CT 06854

203-853-7069; *Fax:* 203-855-9769
office@sid.org; www.sid.org

Kenneth I Werner, Editor
Shigeol Mikoshiba, President/CEO

State-of-the-art developments in electronic, electromechanical and hardcopy display equipment; input and output technologies; storage media; human factors and display standards; entrepreneurship, marketing and management; and manufacturing.
Cost: $36.00
Frequency: Monthly
Circulation: 11000
Founded in: 1962
Printed in 4 colors

6166 **Information Retrieval & Library Automation**
Lomond Publications
PO Box 88
Mount Airy, MD 21771-0088

202-362-1361; *Fax:* 202-362-6156

Thomas Hattery, Publisher

New technology, products and equipment that improve information systems and library services, for science, social, social science, law, medicine, academic institutions and the public.
Cost: $75.00
Frequency: Monthly

6167 **Information Security**
International Computer Security Association
117 Kendrick Street
Suite 800
Needham, MA 02494

781-657-1000; *Fax:* 781-657-1100
lwalsh@infosecuritymag.com;
www.infosecuritymag.com

Andrew Briney, VP
Lawrence Walsh, Editor
Michael S Mimoso, Senior Editor
Gabrielle DeRussy, Advertising Sales
Susan Rastellini Smith, Product Management

Articles and analysis of information-security issues such as media, entwork and virus protection, internet security and encryption reports.
Cost: $100.00
Frequency: Monthly
Circulation: 60000
Founded in: 1999

6168 **Information Systems Security**
Auerbach Publications
2494 Bayshore Boulevard
Suite 201
Dunedin, FL 34698

703-891-6781
800-737-8034; *Fax:* 703-891-0782
institute@isc2.org; www.isc2.org
Social Media: Facebook, Twitter, YouTube

David Shearer, COO
Debra Taylor, CFO
John Colley, Chairman
Debra Taylor, Chief Financial Officer
Hord Tipton, Executive Director

Facts and experience, expert opinion on directions in security, public policy, computer crime and ethics related to the information security field.
Cost: $175.00
Circulation: 1500
Founded in: 2003

6169 **Inside the Internet**
ZD Journals
500 Canal View Boulevard
Rochester, NY 14623-2800

585-407-7301; *Fax:* 585-214-2387
int@zdjournals.com; www.zdjournals.com

Joelle Martin, Publisher

Information and hands-on instruction for applications along with some pictorial explanation.
Cost: $49.00
Frequency: Monthly

6170 **Internet & Intranet Business and Technology Report**
Computer Technology Research Corporation
6 N Atlantic Wharf
Charleston, SC 29401-2115

843-766-5293; *Fax:* 843-853-7210;
www.ctrcorp.com

Edward Wagner, Publisher

Reports on international news, historical profiles of the impact of various applications, and developing standards and regulations. Topics covered include domain registration, Webcasting and the market for Internet e-mail.
Cost: $390.00
Frequency: Monthly

6171 **Internet Business**
Ziff Davis Publishing Company
28 E 28th St
New York, NY 10016-7940

212-503-5772

Steve Weitzner, CEO
Adam Gordon, VP

Provides in-depth information and analysis on Internet products, techniques and tools, based on comparative lab testing and real world experience. Feature articles address technology segments that optimize an Internet strategy such as firewalls, authoring tools, etc., and how-to columns look at technical issues surrounding Web site development.
Cost: $24.99
Frequency: Monthly

6172 **Internet Business Strategies**
Gartner Group
Po Box 10212
Stamford, CT 06904-2212

203-964-0096; *Fax:* 203-316-6488
info@gartner.com; www.gartner.com
Social Media: Facebook, Twitter, LinkedIn
Jean Hall, CEO
Eugene Hall, CEO
David Godfrey, Senior Vice President
John Gardner, President
Robin Kranich, SVP Human Resources

Helps readers make informed decisions about how to use the Internet to deploy electronic commerce and interactive initiatives.
Cost: $395.00
Frequency: Weekly
Circulation: 10,000
Founded in: 1993

6173 **Internet Reference Service Quarterly**
Taylor & Francis
325 Chestnut Street
Suite 800
Philadelphia, PA 19106

800-354-1420; *Fax:* 215-625-2940;
www.tandf.co.uk

Brenda Reeb, Editor

Designed to function as a comprehensive information source librarians can turn to and count on for keeping up-to-date on emerging technological innovations, while emphasizing theoretical, research, and practical applications of Internet-related information services, sources and resources.
Cost: $82.00
Frequency: Quarterly
Circulation: 3000
ISSN: 1087-5301
Founded in: 1978

6174 **Internet Shopper**
Mecklermedia Corporation
20 Ketchum Street
Westport, CT 06880-5908

203-662-2800; *Fax:* 203-454-5840;
www.internetshopper.com

Susan Leiterstein, Publisher

Edited for consumers who purchas products and services direct from Interet Web sites. Covers online malls, computers and electronics, stocks, books, home furnishings, music and more. Reviews the best sites within their categoreis and includes tips on how to conduct safe and effective online transactions.
Frequency: Daily

6175 **Internet Telephony**
Technology Marketing Corporation
1 Technology Plz
Norwalk, CT 06854-1936
203-852-6800
800-243-6002; *Fax:* 203-853-2845
tmc@tmcnet.com; www.tmcnet.com

Rich Tehrani, CEO
Richard Tehrani, President/Group Publisher
Shirley A. Russo, Circulation Director

News and departments focus on providing readers with information they need to learn about and purchase the equipment, software and services necessary for Internet telephony, through the convergence of voice, video, fax and data.
Frequency: Monthly
Circulation: 28024
Founded in: 1972

6176 **Internet World**
Mecklermedia Corporation
20 Ketchum Street
Westport, CT 06880-5908

203-226-6967; *Fax:* 203-454-5840

Corey Friedman, Publisher
Michael Neubarth, Editor

For noncommercial and commercial uses of Internet and the National Research and Education Network.
Cost: $5.00
Circulation: 256883
Founded in: 1971

6177 **Journal of Electronic Imaging**
International Society for Optical Engineering
1000 20th Street
Bellingham, WA 98225-10

360-676-3290; *Fax:* 360-647-1445
customerservice@spie.org; www.spie.org

Kristin Lewotsky, Executive Editor
Winn Hardin, Senior Editor
Michael Brownell, Contributing Editors
Amy Nelson, Manager

Timely information about evolving imaging technologies, including image acquistions, image data storage, image data display, image visualization, image processing, image data communciations, hard copy output and multime-

dia systems.
Cost: $135.00
Frequency: Quarterly
Circulation: 1500
Founded in: 1992

6178 **Journal of Internet Law**
Apen Publishers
400 Hamilton Avenue
Palo Alto, CA 94301-1809

650-328-6561; *Fax:* 650-327-3699;
www.gcfw.com

Mark F Radcliffe, Editor-in-Chief

Discusses strategies utilized by top intellectual property, computer law and information technology industry experts.
Frequency: Monthly

6179 **Journal of Research on Computing in Education**
International Society for Technology in Education
180 W 8th Avenue
Eugene, OR 97401-2916

541-302-3777
800-336-5191; *Fax:* 541-302-3778
iste@iste.org; www.iste.org

Don Knezek, CEO
Leslie Conery, Deputy CEO

Covers computer research and developments relating to all levels of education. Articles define the state of current and future use of technology in education.
Cost: $79.00
Frequency: Quarterly
Circulation: 4500
Founded in: 1989
Mailing list available for rent

6180 **Journal of Technology in Human Services**
Taylor & Francis
325 Chestnut Street
Suite 800
Philadelphia, PA 19106

800-354-1420; *Fax:* 215-625-2940;
www.tandf.co.uk

Dick Schoech PhD, Editor

Explores the potentials of computer and telecommunciations technologies in mental health, developmental disability, welfare, addictions, education, and other human services.
Cost: $120.00
Frequency: Quarterly
ISSN: 1522-8835
Founded in: 1978
Mailing list available for rent
Printed in one color on matte stock

6181 **KM World**
Information Today
18 Bayview Street
PO Box 1358
Camden, ME 04843-1358

207-236-8524; *Fax:* 207-236-6452
webmaster@kmworld.com;
www.kmworld.com
Social Media: Facebook, Twitter, LinkedIn

Hugh McKellar, Editor in Chief
Sandra Haimila, Managing Editor
Michael V Zarrello, Advertising Director
Andy Moore, Publisher
David Panara, Sales Manager

Serves content, document and knowledge of management market to help improve business performance.
Circulation: 56000

6182 **MacTech**
Xplain Corporation
PO Box 5200
Westlake Village, CA 91359-5200

805-494-9797; *Fax:* 805-494-9798
custservice@mactech.com; www.mactech.com
Social Media: Twitter

Neil Ticktin, Publisher
Dave Mark, Executive Editor
Edward Marczak, Executive Editor
David Allen, Production Manager

Provides web developers and network administrators with the most technically advanced information for them to combat the needs of the industry. How to articles, technically oriented product reviews with a Mac focus.
Cost: $19.95
Frequency: Monthly
ISBN: 3-212874-88-7
ISSN: 1067-8360
Founded in: 1984
Printed in on glossy stock

6183 **On the Internet**
Rickard Group
1775 Wiehle Ave
Suite 201
Reston, Va 20190-5108

703-439-2120
editor@isoc.org; www.isoc.org
Social Media: Facebook, Twitter, LinkedIn, YouTube

Wendy Rickard Bollentin, Publisher
Internet information for technologists, developers, educators, researchers, government representatives, and business people.
Cost: $22.00
Frequency: Bi-Monthly
Circulation: 9M

6184 **Optical Technology 21st Century**
Frames Data
PO Box 2141
Skokie, Il 60077

800-739-7555
847-763-9532
customerservice@framesdata.com;
www.framesdata.com

Skip Johnson, President
Hunter Noell, Business Development Manager
Movement of product electronically; computerization of office functions, lab work, testing procedures and equipment; information on the Internet, optical Web sites, and onlines services.
Cost: $299.00
Frequency: Quarterly
Circulation: 19M

6185 **PCAI**
Knowledge Technology
PO Box 30130
Phoenix, AZ 85046

602-971-1869; *Fax:* 602-971-2321;
www.pcai.com/pcai

Terry Hengl, Publisher
Daniel W Rasmus, Editorial Advisor
Don Barker, Senior Editor
Robin Okun, VP of Marketing
Information necessary to help managers, programmers, executives and other professionals understand the unfolding realm of artificial intelligence and intelligent applications.
Cost: $24.00
Founded in: 1987

6186 **PDN's Pix**
VNU Business Media
30 E 23rd St # 5
New York, NY 10010-4442

212-673-1100; *Fax:* 212-673-7074;
www.vnu.com

Penny Vane, Owner
Rob Ruijter, CFO
Covers the world of electronic digital imaging to help readers use new imaging technology and the Web, digital meda, image capture and transfer.
Cost: $19.94
Circulation: 51753
Founded in: 1964

6187 **Virus Bulletin**
Virus Bulletin
590 Danbury Road
Ridgefield, CT 06877-2722
203-438-7714; *Fax:* 203-431-8165

Richard Ford, Editor
Victoria Lammer, Production Manager

An international journal addressing computer viruses, Trojan horses and other malicious programs. Emphasis is placed on providing technical and procedural countermeasures for businesses using computers.
Cost: $35.00

6188 **WWWiz Magazine**
WWWiz Corporation
8840 Warner Avenue
Suite 200
Fountain Valley, CA 92708

714-848-9600; *Fax:* 714-375-2493;
www.wwwiz.com

Don Hamilton, Editor-in-Chief
Vivian Hamilton, Managing Editor

WWWiz is a publication focused on the internet with content aimed entrepenuers and business professionals. We interview people who have found success in internet business along with articles pertaining to legal issues, marketing, technology, travel, and other special interest areas.
Cost: $28.00
Frequency: Monthly
Circulation: 120000
Founded in: 1995

6189 **Wall Street & Technology**
Miller Freeman Publications
11 West 19th Street
New York, NY 10011

212-780-0400; *Fax:* 212-600-3045;
www.wallstreetandtech.com

Michael Friedenberg, Group Publisher
Richard Rosenblatt, CEO/President
Kerry Massaro, Editor-in-Chief
Anne Marie Miller, Senior VP/Sales & Marketing

Editoral emphasis on the automation of brokerage houses and money management firms.
Frequency: Monthly
Circulation: 21226

6190 **Web Builder**
Fawcette Technical Publications
2600 S El Camino Real # 300
Suite 300
San Mateo, CA 94403-2381

650-378-7100
800-848-5523; *Fax:* 650-853-0230
customerservice@fawcette.com;
www.ftponline.com

James Fawcette, President
Karen Koenen, Sr. Circulation Director
John Sutton, Executive VP
Susan Ogren, Marketing Manager
Henry Allain, President

Highly technical, code-sensitive articles that cover all that goes into designing interfaces for sophisticated Internet/Intranet applications. Fea-

tures a case-study approach to finding out who is using which Web sites and how.
Cost: $32.96
Frequency: Monthly

6191 **Web Content Report**
Lawrence Ragan Communications
316 N Michigan Ave # 400
Suite 400
Chicago, IL 60601-3773

312-960-4100
800-493-4867; *Fax:* 312-960-4106
cservice@ragan.com; www.ragan.com

Jim Ylisela, Publisher
Mark Ragan, CEO/President
Kasia Chalko, Marketing Director Events
Frank Bleers, Marketing Director Publisher

Outlines ways to attract visitors to a Web site, and be able to then monitor and evaluate the traffic on the home page. New developments in Web technology, how products can be sold on sites, budgeting matters and communicaiton with management.
Cost: $269.00
Frequency: Monthly
Founded in: 1996
Printed in 2 colors on matte stock

6192 **Web Guide Monthly**
H&S Media
430 Oak Grove Street
Suite 100
Minneapolis, MN 55403-3234

612-990-3203; *Fax:* 612-879-1082
wdorn@webguidemag.com;
www.webguidemag.com

Dan Beaver, Publisher

Examines and evaluates useful tools that merge the Internet with everyday life, at work and at home. Sites are sorted into categories, and are referenced in an index.
Cost: $34.95
Frequency: Monthly
Circulation: 120M

6193 **Web Techniques**
Miller Freeman Publications
411 Borel Avenue
#100
San Mateo, CA 94402-3516

650-573-3210; *Fax:* 650-655-4250
editors@web-techniques.com;
www.webtechniques.com

Manny Sawit, Publisher
Deirdre Blake, Managing Editor

Latest information, tips and techniques to Web site developers. Contains information on new products and the latest information about the ever-changing world of Web development.
Cost: $34.95
Frequency: Monthly
Circulation: 100M

6194 **Webserver Online Magazine**
Computer Publishing Group
1340 Centre Street
Newton Centre, MA 02459-2499

617-641-9101; *Fax:* 617-641-9102
editor@cpg.com; www.cpg.com

S Henry Sacks, CEO/President
Doug Pryor, Editorial Director
Carol Flanagan, Marketing Manager
Tina Jackson, Circulation Manager
S Sacks, Publisher

Source for information Web professionals who need to get the most ot of their Web development and deployment efforts. Technology and industry news, systems and network adminsitration issues, the latest in Web tools, and a guide to new products, services and resources.
Frequency: Monthly
Founded in: 1989

6195 **WirelessWeek.com**
PO Box 266008
Highlands Ranch, CO 80163-6008

303-470-4800; *Fax:* 303-470-4892
subsmail@reedbusiness.com;
www.wirelessweek.com

Gerard Van de Aast, CEO
Debby Denton, Publisher
Rhonda Wickham, Editor -in- Chief
Glenn Comar, Marketing Director

Trade Shows

6196 **American Public Communications Council Conference & Expo**
625 Slaters Lane
Suite 104
Alexandria, VA 22314

703-739-1322; *Fax:* 703-739-1324
apcc@apcc.net; www.apcc.net

Wilard Nichols, President
Deborah Sterman, CFO
Dan Collins, Corporate Counsel

Conference, luncheon and 100 exhibits of public communications equipment and information including, pay phones, internet, atm, multimedia and more.
Founded in: 1988

6197 **DMD New York Conference & Expo**
Direct Marketing Conferences
20 Academy Street
Norwalk, CT 06850-4032

203-854-9166
800-969-6566
connecticut@dmdays.com; www.dmdays.com

Direct Marketing Days New York offers new ideas in media, creative, database, eCommerce and technology. Hundreds of exhibits showcase the newest technologies, products and services. Over 85 sessions and 25 consultation centers led by A level speakers. Network with top-level executives.
Frequency: Annual/June

6198 **E-Sports & Business Services Show at the Super Show**
Communications & Show Management
1450 NE 123rd Street
North Miami, FL 33161

305-893-8771; *Fax:* 305-893-8783;
www.bizbash.com
Social Media: Facebook

David Adler, CEO and Founder
Richard Aaron, President
Chad Kaydo

Retailers, distributors, wholesalers, importers/exporters and other buyers of sports related products come for 10,000 exhibits of sports apparel, footwear, accessories and e-commerce products and services.
100k Attendees
Frequency: January

6199 **EcomXpo**
Wordwide Business Research
535 5th Ave
8th Floor
New York, Ny 10017

888-482-6012; *Fax:* 646-200-7535
info@ecomxpo.com; www.ecomxpo.com

Rick Worden, Chairman and CEO
Steve Goldring, Managing Director

An educationally focused, online virtual trade show designed specifically for search, affiliate and interactive marketers.
Frequency: July

6200 **How To Make A Living On-line**
Women in eCommerce
PO Box 550856
Fort Lauderdale, FL 33355-0856

954-625-6606
877-947-3337
heidi@wecai.org;
www.wecai.org/3909/how-to-make-a-living-on line/

Suzannah Richards, President
Rosana Santos, President Elect
Ellen Sue Burton, VP/Logistics & Hospitality
Racheli Smilovitz, VP/Professional Development
Racheli Smilovitz, VP/Professional Development

An action packed, content-rich luncheon on the topic of internet marketing.
Founded in: 2001

6201 **Info Today Conference**
Information Today
143 Old Marlton Pike
Medford, NJ 08055-8758

609-654-6266
800-300-9868; *Fax:* 609-654-4309
custserv@infotoday.com; www.infotoday.com

Thomas H Hogan, Publisher/President
Roger R Bilboul, Chairman Of The Board

Users of online information services, electronic databases and the Internet. 200 booths.
6M Attendees
Frequency: May
Founded in: 1980
Mailing list available for rent: 5000 names

6202 **International Consumer Electronics Show (CES)**
Consumer Technology Association
1919 South Eads Street
Arlington, VA 22202

703-907-7600
866-858-1555; *Fax:* 703-907-7675
cta@cta.tech; www.cta.tech

Gary Shapiro, President & CEO
David Hagan, Chairman

The CES reaches across global markets, connects the industry and enables consumer electronics to grow and thrive. International CES is owned and prroduced by the Consumer Electronics Association (CEA).
Frequency: Annual

6203 **Internet Communications Exposition**
IDG Expositions
1400 Providence Highway
Norwood, MA 02062

508-879-6700

6204 **National Conference on Operations & Fulfillment (NCOF)**
Direct Marketing Association
1120 Avenue of Americas
New York, NY 10036-6700

212-768-7277; *Fax:* 211-302-6714
dmaconferences@the-dma.org;
www.the-dma.org

Julie A Hogan, SVP Conference/Events
Lawrence M Kimmel, CEO

Focuses on innovative solutions for the warehouse, distribution, operations, and ecommerce needs in the ever-changing world of operations and fulfillment.
10M Attendees

6205 **Sporting Goods Manufacturers Markets**
1150 17th Street NW
8th Floor
Washington, DC 20036-1604
202-775-1762; *Fax:* 202-296-7462
info@sgma.com; www.sgma.com
Tom Cove, President/CEO
Gregg Harrlety, VP
Kalinda Mathis, Director Marketing
Retailers, distributors, wholesalers, importers/exporters and other buyers of sports related products come for 10,000 exhibits of sports apparel, footwear, accessories and e-commerce products and services.
80000 Attendees
Frequency: Biannual/Spring/Fall

6206 **SuiteWorld User Conference**
NetSuite Ecommerce
2955 Campus Drive
Suite 100
San Mateo, CA 94403-2511
650-627-1000; *Fax:* 650-627-1001
info@netsuite.com; www.netsuite.com
Evan Goldberg, Co-Founder/Chief Technology Officer
Zach Nelson, President & CEO
SuiteWorld provides customers, users and partners with the opportunity to gain insights, inspiration and hands-on training to run your business smarter and faster on NetSuite.
10000 Members
Founded in: 1998

6207 **VoIP 2.0**
Technology Marketing Corporation
One Technology Plaza
Norwalk, CT 06854
203-852-6800
800-243-6002; *Fax:* 203-853-2845;
www.itexpo.com
Frequency: October, San Diego

6208 **eM Conference**
91 Point Judith Road
Suite 129
Narragansett, RI 02882
800-496-2950; *Fax:* 408-884-2461
service@eMarketingAssociation.com;
www.emarketingassociation.com
Chris Baggott, CEO
Bert DuMars, C-Founder/CEO
Murray Gaylord, VP/Marketing
Jeff Hilmire, President
Simms Jenkins, Founder & Principal
The Power of eMarketing Conference offers an unparalleled experience in best practices, case histories and processes for social, email and search marketing.
Frequency: Annual/April
Founded in: 1997

Directories & Databases

6209 **Adweek Directory**
Prometheus Global Media
770 Broadway
New York, NY 10003-9595
212-493-4100; *Fax:* 646-654-5368;
www.prometheusgm.com
Richard D. Beckman, CEO
James A. Finkelstein, Chairman
Madeline Krakowsky, Vice President Chairman
Tracy Brater, Executive Director Creative Service
Adweek Directories Online is where you will find searchable databases with comprehensive information on ad agencies, brand marketers and multicultural media.
Frequency: Annual
Circulation: 800
Founded in: 1981

6210 **America Online**
8619 Westwood Center Drive
Suite 200
Vienna, VA 22182-2238
800-227-6364; *Fax:* 540-265-2135
Jack Daggitt, Director
Anne Botsford
This multi-faceted information service provides complete access to a variety of databases and computer services of interest to users of Macintosh and Apple II computers. Databases included in this systems range from Computing & Software to Lifestyles & Interests.
Frequency: Full-text

6211 **Boardwatch Magazine Directory of Internet Service Providers**
Penton Media
1300 E 9th St # 316
Cleveland, OH 44114-1503
216-696-7000; *Fax:* 216-696-6662;
www.penton.com
Jane Cooper, Marketing
Bill McCarthy, Editorial Director
Reviews various Internet providers and lists different programs available through their individual companies who operate in the US and Canada.
Cost: $72.00
Frequency: Monthly
Circulation: 70,000

6212 **Fulltext Sources Online**
Information Today
143 Old Marlton Pike
Medford, NJ 08055-8750
609-654-6266
800-300-9868; *Fax:* 609-654-4309
custserv@infotoday.com; www.infotoday.com
Thomas H Hogan, President
Roger R Bilboul, Chairman Of The Board
A directory of periodicals accessible online in full text through 28 aggregator products. Lists over 22,000 newspapers, journals, newsletters, newswires, and transcripts.
Cost: $145.00
Frequency: Biannually Jan & July
ISBN: 1-573872-23-7

6213 **Global Business Directory**
Women in eCommerce
PO Box 550856
Fort Lauderdale, FL 33355-0856
954-625-6606
877-947-3337
heidi@wecai.org; www.wecai.org
Suzannah Richards, President
Rosana Santos, President Elect
Ellen Sue Burton, VP/Logistics & Hospitality
Racheli Smilovitz, VP/Professional Development
Racheli Smilovitz, VP/Professional Development
30 member institutions; also lists free resources, global network and internet resources.
Founded in: 2001

6214 **IQ Directory Adweek**
Prometheus Global Media
770 Broadway
New York, NY 10003-9595
212-493-4100; *Fax:* 646-654-5368;
www.prometheusgm.com
Richard D. Beckman, CEO
James A. Finkelstein, Chairman
Madeine Krakowsky, Vice President Circulation
Tracy Brater, Executive Director Creative Service
Profile of companies at the leading edge of digital marketing, has the specifics you'll need to investigate, launch and/or expand your digital presence. Profiles over 2,200 interactive agencies, web developers, brand marketers, online media, CD-ROM developers, POP/Kiosk designers and multimedia creative companies
Founded in: 1981

6215 **Internet Blue Pages**
Information Today
143 Old Marlton Pike
Medford, NJ 08055-8750
609-654-6266
800-300-9868; *Fax:* 609-654-4309
custserv@infotoday.com; www.infotoday.com
Thomas H Hogan, President
Roger R Bilboul, Chairman Of The Board
The Guide to Federal Government Web Sites is the leading guide to federal government information on the web. Includes over 1,800 annotated agency listings, arranged in the US Government Manual style to help you find the information you need.
Cost: $34.95
464 Pages
ISBN: 0-910965-43-9

6216 **Key Guide to Electronic Resources: Language and Literature**
Information Today
143 Old Marlton Pike
Medford, NJ 08055-8750
609-654-6266
800-300-9868; *Fax:* 609-654-4309
custserv@infotoday.com; www.infotoday.com
Thomas H Hogan, President
Roger R Bilboul, Chairman Of The Board
Part of the ongoing topic related series of reference guides is an evaluative directory of electronic reference sources in the fields of language and literature.
Cost: $39.50
120 Pages
ISBN: 1-573870-20-x

6217 **On-Line Networks, Databases & Bulletin Boards on Assistive Technology**
ERIC Document Reproduction Service
7420 Fullerton Road
Suite 110
Springfield, VA 22153-2852
703-440-1400
800-443-ERIC; *Fax:* 703-440-1408
Directory of electronic networks that focus on technology-related services.

6218 **Professional Trade Association Membership**
Local Hispanic Chamber of Commerce
1424 K Street NW
Suite 401
Washington, DC 20005
202-715-0494
membership@ushcc.com; www.ushcc.com
Javier Palomarez, President & CEO
DeVere Kutscher, Chief of Staff & VP of Strategy
The USHCC is a not-for-profit (501(c)6) organization founded in 1979 to foster Hispanic eco-

nomic development and to create sustainable prosperity for the benefit of American society.
Founded in: 1979

6219 Trade Show News Network
Tarsus Group plc
16985 W Bluemound Road
Suite 210
Brookfield, WI 53005

262-782-1900; *Fax:* 603-372-5894
rwimberly@tsnn.com; www.tsnn.com

Rachel Wimberly, Editor-in-Chief
John Rice, Sales & Business Development
Arlene Shows, Marketing Manager

The world's leading online resource for the trade show, exhibition and event industry since 1996. TSNN.com owns and operates the most widely consulted event database on the internet, containing data about more than 19,500 trade shows, exhibitions, public events and conferences.
13900 Members
Frequency: Bi-Monthly
Founded in: 1196

Industry Web Sites

6220 http://gold.greyhouse.com
G.O.L.D Grey House OnLine Databases
Grey House Publishing's online database platform, GOLD, offers Quick Search, Keyword Search and Expert Search for most business sectors including e-commerce and internet markets. The GOLD platform makes finding the information you need quick and easy - whether you're a novice searcher or an experienced database user. All of Grey House's directory products are available for subscription on the GOLD platform.

6221 www.aace.org
Association for the Advancement of Computing in Ed
Promotes the use of computers and the internet in educational settings.

6222 www.adsl.com/adsl_forum.html
Information about ADSL, Asymmetric Digital Subscriber Line, a system that provides high-speed Internet connections

6223 www.apcc.net
American Public Communications Council
APCC Proudly offers a wide array of services to the public communications industry, from Perspectives magazine to our annual trade show to our involvement in legal and regulatory issues. This site is a place for the public to find out about our industry and for our members to learn of legal and regulatory developments, to become aware of APCC programs and events and to have a forum for discussion.

6224 www.bsa.org
Business Software Alliance
An organization dedicated to promoting a safe and legal digital world. BSA educates consumers on software management and copyright protection, cyber security, trade, e-commerce and other internet related issues.

6225 www.cabledatacomnews.com/cmic.htm
Cable modems

6226 www.computercpa.com
Accountant's Home Page
Provides information on general accounting for manufacturing, contstruction, service, not-for-profit, e-commerce and more.

6227 www.conferences.calendar.com/
Academic conferences, symposia, courses and workshops.

6228 www.ditialmx.com/wires/
Integrated Services Digital Network

6229 www.greyhouse.com
Grey House Publishing
Authoritative reference directories for most business sectors incluidng e-commerce and internet markets. Users can search the online databases with varied search criteria allowing for custom searches by product category, geographic area, sales volume, keyword, subject and more. Full Grey House catalog and online ordering also available.

6230 www.hayes.com/prodinfo/adsl/intro.html
Information about ADSl, Asymmetric Digital Subscriber Line, a system that provides high-speed Internet connections

6231 www.internets.com
Internets.com
Searchable database and related industry links.

6232 www.iste.org
International Society for Technology in Education
Nonprofit professional organization with a worldwide membership of leaders and potential leaders in educational technology.

6233 www.sdl.com/en/wcm/
eMarketing Association
SDL Tridion R5, the core product, provides complete Web content management and content delivery capabilities, focusing on ease-of-use for all content contributors, site managers and power users.

6234 www.shop.com
Altura International
CatalogCity.com is a powerful and flexible e-commerce technology. This site includes recognized brand names such as Blair, Bombay, Chef's Catalog, Fisher-Price, Gump's by Mail, Hammacher Schlemmer, Ross-Simmons, The Sharper Image, and many more.

6235 www.spie.org
International Society for Optical Engineering
Serves the international technical community as the premier provider of education, information, and resources covering optics, photonics, and their applications.

6236 www.wecommercenews.com
Women in eCommerce
A qualified audience of women looking for e-commerce solutions, information and tolls to run their online endeavors.

Associations

6237 **American Automatic Control Council**
3640 Col Glenn Hwy
Dayton, OH 45435
937-775-5062; *Fax:* 937-775-3936
pmisra@cs.wright.edu; www.a2c2.org
Tariq Samad, President
Glenn Y Masada, President-elect
Linda Bushnell, Treasurer
B.Wayne Bequette, Secretary
Supports all those involved in the manufacturer and distribution of automatic controls. Hosts annual trade show.

6238 **Association for High Technology Distributors**
N19 W24400 Riverwood Drive
Waukesha, WI 53188
262-696-3645
800-488-4845
ahtd@ahtd.org; www.ahtd.org
Social Media: Twitter, LinkedIn
Thomas Swenton, President
Bryan Roeesler, Executive Director
Brian Lepsis, VP
John Pirner, Secretary/Program Chair
Paul Burk, Treasurer
Works to increase productivity and profitability of high technology automation solutions, providers and manufacturers.
250 Members
Founded in: 1985

6239 **Association of Edison Illuminating Companies**
600 18th Street N
PO Box 2641
Birmingham, AL 35291
205-257-2530; *Fax:* 205-257-2540
aeicdir@bellsouth.net; www.aeic.org
Terry H Waters, Executive Director/Secretary
Len Holland, Manager AEIC Services
Becky Neel, Administrative Assistant
Cindy McLeod, Administrative Assistant
Association of electric utilities concerned with generating, transmitting and distributing electricity. This organization supplies information and support to the industry.
165 Members
Founded in: 1885

6240 **Bioelectromagnetics Society**
2412 Cobblestone Way
Frederick, MD 21702-2626
301-663-4252; *Fax:* 301-694-4948
office@bems.org; www.bems.org
Social Media: Facebook, Twitter
Gloria Parsley, Executive Director
Richard Nuccitelli, VP
Jonna Wilen, Secretary
Nonprofit organization and international resource for excellence in scientific research, knowledge and understanding of the interaction of electromagnetic fields with biological systems. Members are biological and physical scientists, physicians and engineers interested in the interactions of nonionizing radiation with biological systems.
400 Members
Founded in: 1978

6241 **Contract Services Association of America**
1000 Wilson Boulevard
Suite 1800
Arlington, VA 22209
703-243-2020; *Fax:* 703-243-3601
info@csa-dc.org; www.pscouncil.org
Barry Cullen, President
Colleen Preston, Senior VP
Represents the government services contracting industry. Membership ranges from small businesses and corporations servicing federal and state government in numerous capacities. CSA acts to foster the effective implementation of the government's policy of reliance on the private sector for support services. Largest DOD association of service contractors.
650 Members
Founded in: 1965

6242 **EOS/ESD Association, Inc. (DBA ESD Association)**
Electrostatic Discharge Association
7900 Turin Road
Building 3
Rome, NY 13440-2069
315-339-6937; *Fax:* 315-339-6793
info@esda.org; www.esda.org
Social Media: Facebook, Twitter, LinkedIn
Terry Welsher, President
Gianluca Boselli, Sr. VP
Ginger Hansel, VP
Lisa Pimpinella, Director of Operations
EOS/ESD Association is a professional voluntary association dedicated to advancing the theory and practice of electrical overstress and electrostatice avoidance. The Association expands EOS/ESD awareness through atandards development, educational programs, local chapters, publications, tutorials, certification and symposia.
Cost: $60.00
2000+ Members
Frequency: Bi-Monthly
Founded in: 1982

6243 **Edison Electric Institute**
701 Pennsylvania Avenue NW
Washington, DC 20004-2696
202-508-5000; *Fax:* 202-508-5360
feedback@eei.org; www.eei.org
Social Media: Facebook, Twitter, YouTube
Thomas R Kuhn, President
David Owens, Executive VP
Brian Wolff, Senior VP, External Affairs
The association of U.S. Shareholder-owned electric companies.
180 Members
Founded in: 1933

6244 **Electric Association**
40 Shuman Blvd
Suite 247
Naperville, IL 60563-8446
630-305-3050; *Fax:* 630-305-3056
cspaeth@eachicago.org; www.eachicago.org
Social Media: Facebook, LinkedIn
Mark Gibson, President
Rick Jamerson, Vice President
Steven Anixter, Treasurer
Thomas Scherzer, Secretary
Provides members of the electrical industry of Chicagoland and their employees with formal educational opportunities, professional development, information exchange, and member services.
Founded in: 1926

6245 **Electric Power Research Institute**
3420 Hillview Avenue
Palo Alto, CA 94304
650-855-2121
800-313-3774; *Fax:* 650-855-2954
askepri@epri.com; www.epri.com
Social Media: Facebook, Twitter, LinkedIn, YouTube, Flikr
Gil C Quiniones, Chairman
Michael W Howard, President/CEO
Nonprofit, energy research consortium for the benefit of utility members, their customers and society. Mission is to provide science and technology-based solutions of indispensable value to our global energy customers by managing a far-reaching program of scientific research, technology development and product implementation.
660 Members
Founded in: 1973

6246 **Electrical Apparatus Service Association**
1331 Baur Boulevard
St Louis, MO 63132-1903
314-993-2220; *Fax:* 314-993-1269
easainfo@easa.com; www.easa.com
Social Media: Facebook, Twitter, LinkedIn, YouTube
Mike Dupuis, Chair
Linda J Raynes CAE, President/CEO
Richard Tutka, Finance Manager
An international trade organization of electromechanical sales and service firms in 58 countries. Provides members with a means of keeping up to date on materials, equipment, and state of the art technology.
2100 Members
Founded in: 1937
Mailing list available for rent

6247 **Electrical Association**
One Energy Center
40 Shuman Boulevard, Suite 247
Naperville, IL 60563
630-305-3050; *Fax:* 630-305-3056
cspaeth@eachicago.org; www.eachicago.org
Social Media: Facebook, LinkedIn
Mark Gibson, President
Rick Jamerson, Vice President
Steven Anixter, Treasurer
Thomas Scherzer, Secretary
Provides members of the electrical industry of Chicagoland and their employees with formal educational opportunities, professional development, information exchange and member services

6248 **Electrical Equipment Representatives Association**
638 W 39th Street
Kansas City, MO 64111
816-561-5323
800-728-2272; *Fax:* 816-561-1991
info@eera.org; www.eera.org
Kier Cooper, President
Rob Rigsby, President Elect
Jennifer Tibbetts, VP
Bobby Cox, Secretary
Doug Softy, Treasurer
Provides technically competent, hands-on, local representation for companies providing products and services to the electric power industry.

6249 Electrical Generating Systems Association
1650 S Dixie Hwy
Suite 400
Boca Raton, FL 33432-7461

561-750-5575; *Fax:* 561-395-8557;
www.egsa.org
Social Media: Facebook

Ed Murphy, President
Charlie Habic, VP
David Brown, Secretary/Treasurer

A trade association made up of companies in the USA and around the world that design, manufacture, sell, distribute, rent, specify, service and use on site power equipment.
600 Members
Founded in: 1965

6250 Electrical Safety Foundation International
1300 N 17th Street
Suite 900
Arlington, VA 22209

703-841-3229; *Fax:* 703-841-3329
info@esfi.org; www.esfi.org
Social Media: Facebook, Twitter, LinkedIn, YouTube

Stephen Sokolow, Chairman
John Engel, Vice Chairman
Kevin Cosgriff, Treasurer
Patrick Davin, Secretary

The mission of the Electrical Safety Foundation International (ESFI) is to advocate electrical safety in the home and in the workplace in order to reduce electrically-related fatalities, injuries and property loss.
Founded in: 1994

6251 Electrochemical Society
65 S Main St
Building D
Pennington, NJ 08534-2827

609-737-1902; *Fax:* 609-737-2743
ecs@electrochem.org; www.electrochem.org
Social Media: Facebook, Twitter, LinkedIn

Roque J. Calvo, Executive Director/CEO
Dinia Agarwala, Graphic Designer
Marcelle Austin, Board Relations Specialist
Rob Gerth, Director, Mktg. & Digital Eng.
Annie Goedkoop, Director of Publications Production

Members are electrochemists and professionals in related industries.
8000 Members
Founded in: 1902

6252 Electronic Industries Association
2214 rock Hill Rd
Suite 170
Herndon, VA 20170

571-323-0294; *Fax:* 571-323-0245;
www.eia.org
Social Media: LinkedIn, YouTube

Ronald L Turner, Chairman
Mike Kennedy, Vice Chairman
Dave McCurdy, President
Charles Robinson, Chief Operating Officer
James Shiring, Secretary/Treasurer

Is a national trade organization that includes the full spectrum of U.S. manufacturers.
1300 Members

6253 Electronic Technicians Association
5 Depot St
Greencastle, IN 46135-8024

765-653-8262
800-288-3824; *Fax:* 765-653-4287
eta@eta-i.org; www.eta-i.org
Social Media: Facebook, Twitter, LinkedIn, YouTube, Google+

Fred Weiss, Chairman
John Baldwin, Vice Chairman
Joseph LaGanga, Secretary
Ira Wiesenfeld, Treasurer
William Brinker, Communications Division Chair

Association for electronics technicians worldwide offering over 70 certifications.
5000 Members
Founded in: 1978

6254 IPC: Association Connecting Electronics
3000 Lakeside Dr
Suite 309 S
Bannockburn, IL 60015-1249

847-615-7100; *Fax:* 847-615-7105
webmaster@ipc.org; www.ipc.org
Social Media: Facebook, Twitter, LinkedIn, YouTube, Google+, RSS

John W. Mitchell, President & CEO
Tom Sandman, CFO
Dave Bergman, VP, International Relations
John Hassleman, VP, Government Relation
Sanjay Huprikar, VP, Member Success

A trade association for the printed circuit boards and electronics assembly industries, offering programs and resources to board manufacturers and electronic assemblers, designers, industry suppliers and original equipment manufacturers.
2700 Members
Founded in: 1957

6255 Independent Electrical Contractors Association
4401 Ford Ave
Suite 1100
Alexandria, VA 22302-1464

703-549-7351
800-456-4324; *Fax:* 703-549-7448
info@ieci.org; www.ieci.org
Social Media: Facebook, Twitter, LinkedIn, YouTube, Instagram, Flickr

Thayer Long, Executive Vice President/CEO
Vernice Howard, CFO
Alicia Johnson, Office Manager
Bruna Patio, Staff Accountant

The mission of IEC is to create success among independent electrical contractors by developing a professional workforce, communicating clearly with government, promoting ethical business practices, and providing leadership for the electrical industry.
73000 Members
Founded in: 1957

6256 Institute of Electrical and Electronics Engineers
3 Park Ave.
17th Fl.
New York, NY 10016-5997

212-419-7900; *Fax:* 212-752-4929;
www.ieee.org
Social Media: Facebook, Twitter, LinkedIn, YouTube, Google+

Howard E. Michel, President & CEO
E. James Prendergast, Executive Director

Supports all those involved in the field of electrical engineering. Publishes newsletter and hosts trade show.
430K Members
Founded in: 1963

6257 Institute of Electrical/Electronic
3 Park Ave
17th Floor
New York, NY 10016-5997

732-562-3878; *Fax:* 732-562-6046
ieee-mce@ieee.org; www.ieee.org
Social Media: Facebook, Twitter, LinkedIn, YouTube, Google+

Moshe Kam, President and CEO
Roger Pollard, Director and Secretary
Dr Mohamed El-Hawary, Director/Secretary
365K Members
Founded in: 1963

6258 Instrumentation and Measurement Society
3 Park Ave
17th Floor
New York, NY 10016-5997

212-419-7900; *Fax:* 732-981-0225
webmaster@ieee.org; www.ieee-ims.org
Social Media: Twitter, LinkedIn

Reza Zoughi, President
Ruth A. Dyer, Executive VP
Dario Petri VP Finance Committee
Dr Mohamed El-Hawary, Director/Secretary

A subsidiary of the Institute of Electrical and Electronics Engineers. Provides support to scientists and technicians who design and develop electrical and electronic measuring instruments and equipment.
36000 Members
Founded in: 1980

6259 Instrumentation, Systems, and Automation Society
67 Alexander Drive
Box 12277
Research Triangle Park, NC 27709

919-549-8411; *Fax:* 919-549-8288
info@isa.org; www.isa.org
Social Media: Facebook, Twitter, LinkedIn, YouTube, Flickr

Ken Baker, President
Patrick Gouhin, Executive Director
Debbie Eby, Executive Assistant
Leo Staples, Treasurer

Nonprofit, educational organization connecting people and ideas in automation. The Society fosters advancement in the theory, design, manufacture, and use of sensors, instruments, computers, and systems for automation in a wide variety of applications.
33000 Members
Founded in: 1945

6260 International Brotherhood of Electrical Workers
900 7th St. NW
Washington, DC 20001

202-833-7000; *Fax:* 202-728-7676;
www.ibew.org
Social Media: Facebook, Twitter, YouTube, Flickr, Vimeo

Lonnie R. Stephenson, President
Salvatore J. Chilia, Secretary/Treasurer

Among the largest unions in the AFL-CIO, the IBEW represents electrical workers in many fields, from railroads to telecommunications.

6261 International Electrical Testing Association
3050 Old Centre Ave.
Suite 102
Portage, MI 49024

269-488-6382
888-300-6382; *Fax:* 269-488-6383

neta@netaworld.org; www.netaworld.org
Social Media: Facebook, LinkedIn, YouTube

Melissa Richard, Finance and Business Manager
Jayne Tanz, Executive Director
Ron Widup, 1st VP
Lynn Hamrick, Secretary
John White, Treasurer

Defines the standards by which electrical equipment is deemed safe and reliable. Creates specifications, procedures, testing and requirements for commissioning new equipment and testing the reliability and performance of existing equipment.
2000 Members
Founded in: 1972

6262 International Institute of Connector and Interconnection
3000 Lakeside Drive
Bannockburn, IL 60015

E-Mail: info@iicit.org; www.iicit.org

Dale Reed, Content Editor

Dedicated to the spread of technological information throughout the industry. In a time of global competition, success depends on communicating technological breakthroughs, innovations and changes in specifications to engineers, designers, specifiers, consultants and other professionals using your product or services.
2640 Members
Founded in: 1958

6263 International League of Electrical Associations
P.O. Box 24
Mumford, NY 14511

585-538-6350; *Fax:* 585-538-6166
inco@ileaweb.org; www.ileaweb.org
Social Media: LinkedIn

Chris Price, President
Robert Morris, VP
Kirstie Steves, Secretary
Barbette Cejalvo, Treasurer

An organization of professional electric association and electric league managers from more than thirty US and seven Canadian cities.
Founded in: 1936

6264 International Magnetics Association
Eight South Michigan Avenue
Suite 1000
Chicago, IL 60603-3310

312-456-5590; *Fax:* 312-580-0165;
www.intl-magnetics.org

August Sisco, Chair
Lowell Bosley, President
George Orenchak, Secretary/Treasurer

Is the worldwide trade association representing manufacturers of magnetic materials, distributors and fabricators, suppliers to the magnetics industry and others with an interest in magnetics.
35 Members
Founded in: 1959

6265 International Microwave Power Institute
PO Box 1140
Mechanicsville, VA 23111-5007

804-559-6667; *Fax:* 804-559-4087
info@impi.org; www.impi.org
Social Media: Facebook, Twitter

Molly Poisant, President
Ben Wilson, Vice President
Dorin Bolder, Secretary
Amy Lawson, Treasurer

To be the global organization that provides a forum for the exchange of information on all aspects of microwave and RF heating technologies.
Founded in: 1966

6266 Laser Institute of America
13501 Ingenuity Dr
Suite 128
Orlando, FL 32826-3009

407-380-1553
800-345-2737; *Fax:* 407-380-5588
lia@lia.org; www.lia.org
Social Media: Facebook, Twitter, LinkedIn, Google+

Robert Thomas, President
Stephen Capp, Treasurer
Paul Denny, Secretary

The Laser Institute of America is the professional membership society dedicated to fostering lasers, laser applications and safety worldwide.
1200 Members
Founded in: 1968

6267 Laser and Electro-Optic Manufacturers
123 Kent Road
Pacifica, CA 94044-3923

650-738-1492; *Fax:* 650-738-1769
info@leoma.com; www.leoma.com

John Ambroseo, President
Breck Hitz, Executive Director
Lynn Strickland, Treasurer
Brian Lula, Secretary

Is the trade association for North American manufacturers of lasers and associated electro-optics equipment.
Founded in: 1986

6268 National Association of Electrical Distributors
1181 Corporate Lake Drive
St. Louis, MO 63132

314-991-9000
888-791-2512; *Fax:* 314-991-3060
memberservices@naed.org; www.naed.org
Social Media: Facebook, Twitter, LinkedIn, YouTube

Tom Naber, President
Michelle McNamara, VP/Executive Director
Sheila Logan, Office & Executive Manager

Supports manufacturers and distributors of electrical components, supplies and equipment. Publishes directory.
Founded in: 1997

6269 National Electrical Contractors
3 Bethesda Metro Ctr
Suite 1100
Bethesda, MD 20814-5372

301-657-3110; *Fax:* 301-215-4500
beth.margulies@necanet.org; www.necanet.org
Social Media: Facebook, Twitter, LinkedIn, YouTube

John M Grau, CEO
Geary Higgins, VP, Labor Relations
Dan Walter, Vice President and COO
Beth Ellis, Executive Director

Represents a segment of the construction market comprised of over 70,000 electrical contracting firms.
65000 Members
Founded in: 1901

6270 National Electrical Manufacturers Representatives Association
28 Deer Street
Suite 302
Portsmouth, NH 03801

914-524-8650
800-446-3672; *Fax:* 603-319-1667
nemra@nemra.org; www.nemra.org
Social Media: Twitter, LinkedIn

Kenneth Hooper, President
Kirsty Stebbins, Manager of Marketing
Sue Todd, Office Manager

Promotes the function of the independent manufacturer's representative as the most effective way to market electrical products. Increases the income of the rep's firm employees and sales staff by increasing the value of the rep firm to owners and customers. Offers educational opportunities that help representatives strengthen the management, technical and professional capabilities of their firms. Promotes communication between independent electrical representatives and manufacturing partners.

6271 National Electronics Service Dealers Association
3000-A Landers St,
Fort Worth, TX 76107
817-921-9061
800-797-9197; *Fax:* 817-921-3741
info@nesda.com; www.nesda.com
Social Media: Facebook

Ben Fowler, President
Jerrell Helms, Vice President
Wayne Markman, Secretary
George Weiss, Treasurer

Trade association supporting professionals within the electronics business who repair appliances, consumer electronic equipment and computers.
8 Members
Founded in: 1950

6272 National Rural Electric Cooperative Association
4301 Wilson Blvd
Suite 1
Arlington, VA 22203-1860

703-907-5500; *Fax:* 703-907-5526;
www.nreca.org
Social Media: Twitter

Glenn English, CEO

Organized specifically to overcome World War II shortages of electric construction materials, to obtain insurance coverage for newly constructed rural electric cooperatives, and to mitigate wholesale power problems. Since those early days, NRECA has been an advocate for consumer owned cooperatives on energy and operational issues as well as rural community and economic development.
1000 Members
Founded in: 1942

6273 National Systems Contractors Association
3950 River Ridge Drive NE
Cedar Rapids, IA 52402
319-366-6722
800-446-6722; *Fax:* 319-366-4164
nsca@nsca.org; www.nsca.org
Social Media: Facebook, Twitter, LinkedIn, YouTube

Michael Hester, President
Ray Bailey, Vice President
Josh Shanahan, Treasurer
David Ferlino, Secretary
Chuck Wilson, Executive Director

Represents the commercial electronic systems industry. Serves as an advocate for all those who work within the low-voltage industry, including systems contractors/integrators, product manufacturers, consultants, sales representatives and a growing number of architects, specifying engineers and others.
2800 Members
Founded in: 1980

6274 North American Electric Reliability Corporation
3353 Peachtree Road, N.E
Suite 600 North Tower
Atlanta, GA 30326

404-446-2560
info@nerc.com; www.nerc.com

Gerry W. Cauley, President/CEO
Mark Rossi, SVP/Chief Reliability Officer
Marcus H. Sachs, SVP/Chief Security Officer
Charles A. Berardesco, SVP/General Counsel/Corp Secretary
Michael Walker, SVP/CFO/CAO/Treasurer

Principal organization for coordinating and promoting North America's electrical supplies, demands and reliability issues.
11 Members
Founded in: 1968

6275 North Central Electrical League
2901 Metro Dr
Suite 203
Bloomington, MN 55425-8699

952-854-4405
800-925-4985; *Fax:* 952-854-7076
dale@ncel.org; www.ncel.org
Social Media: Facebook, Twitter, LinkedIn, Flickr

Dan Paulson, Chair
Ed Studniski, Vice Chair
Dale Yohnke, Executive Director
Nikki Borgen, Manager - Membership Engagement
Eryka Pluff, Coordinator - Member Benefits

Trade association representing all segments of the electrical industry in the Upper Midwest.
1500 Members
Founded in: 1936

6276 Power Sources Manufacturers Association
PO Box 418
Mendham, NJ 07945-0418

973-543-9660; *Fax:* 973-543-6207
power@psma.com; www.psma.com
Social Media: LinkedIn

Ernie Parker, Chairman
Eric Persson, President
Stephen Oliver, VP
Michel Grenon, Secretary/Treasurer

The PSMA is a not-for-profit organization incorporated in the state of California. The purpose of the Association shall be to enhance the stature and reputation of its members and their products, improve their knowledge of technological and other developments related to power sources, and to educate the entire electronics industry, plus academia, as well as government and industry agencies as to the importance of, and relevant applications for, all types of power sources and conversion devices.
155 Members
Founded in: 1985

6277 Relay and Switch Industry Association
2500 Wilson Boulevard
Arlington, VA 22201

703-907-8024; *Fax:* 703-875-8908
narm@ecaus.org; www.ec-central.org/RSIA

Robert Willis, President
James Kaplan, Chairman and CEO

Represents the electronics industry sector comprised of companies that manufacturer, produce or market relay and switch technologies and products.
Founded in: 1947

6278 SMMA: The Motor & Motion Association
PO Box P182
South Dartmouth, MA 02748

508-979-5935; *Fax:* 508-979-5845
info@smma.org; www.smma.org

Paul Murphy, President
Matt French, Vice President
Steve Herrmann, Secretary/Treasurer

Trade association for the electric motor and motion control industry in North America. The voice of the motor and motion industry providing a forum for education, communication, research and networking.
120 Members
Founded in: 1975

6279 Semiconductor Equipment and Materials International
3081 Zanker Road
San Jose, CA 95134

408-943-6900; *Fax:* 408-428-9600
semihq@semi.org; www.semi.org
Social Media: Twitter, LinkedIn

Yong Han Lee, Chairman
Tetsuo Tsuneishi, Vice Chairman
Mary G. Puma, Secretary/Treasurer
Denny McGuirk, President/CEO
Laith Altimime, President, SEMI Europe

Global industry association serving the manufacturing supply chains for the microelectronic, display and photovoltaic industries.
2300 Members
Founded in: 1970

6280 Semiconductor Industry Association
1101 K Street NW
Suite 450
Washington, DC 20005

202-446-1700
866-756-0715; *Fax:* 202-216-9745
mailbox@sia-online.org; www.sia-online.org
Social Media: Facebook, Twitter

John Neuffer, President/CEO
Latoya Arnold, Executive Assistant/Office Manager
Jimmy Goodrich, Vice President, Global Policy
Joe Pasetti, Director, Government Affairs
Dan Rosso, Communications Manager

Trade association representing the US microchip industry. Provides a forum for working collectively to enhance the competitiveness of the US chip industry.
70 Members
Founded in: 1977

6281 Society of Manufacturing Engineers
1 SME Drive
Dearborn, MI 48128

313-425-3000
800-733-4763; *Fax:* 313-425-3400
service@sme.org; www.sme.org
Social Media: Facebook, Twitter, LinkedIn, YouTube, Google+, RSS

Wayne F. Frost, CMfgE, President
Jeffrey M. Krause, Chief Executive Officer
Kathleen Borgula, Human Resources
Erica Ciupak, Information Technology
Debbie Clark, Governance

Supports all those engineers involved in electrical manufacturing. Hosts trade show.
25K Members
Founded in: 1932

6282 Surface Mount Technology Association
5200 Willson Rd
Suite 215
Edina, MN 55424-1316

952-920-7682; *Fax:* 952-926-1819
joann@smta.org; www.smta.org
Social Media: Facebook, Twitter, LinkedIn, YouTube, Google+

Bill Barthel, President
Eileen Hibbler, VP of Membership
Raiyomand Aspandiar, Ph.D., VP Technical Programs
Michelle Ogihara, VP Communications
Richard Henrick, Secretary

Network of professionals building skills, sharing practical experience and developing solutions in electronic assembly technologies and related business operations.
3200 Members
Founded in: 1984

6283 U.S. Department of Energy
1000 Independence Ave. SW
Washington, DC 20585

202-586-5000; *Fax:* 202-586-4403;
www.energy.gov
Social Media: Facebook, Twitter

Dr. Ernest Moniz, Secretary of Energy
Dr. Elizabeth Sherwood-Randall, Deputy Secretary of Energy

The Energy Department is responsible for the transformation of the nation's energy system through the application of the latest science and technology solutions.

Newsletters

6284 Advanced Battery Technology
Seven Mountains Scientific
913 Tressler Street
PO Box 650
Boalsburg, PA 16827

814-466-6559; *Fax:* 814-466-2777
jo@7ms.com; www.7ms.com

E Thomas Chesworth, Technical Editor
Josephine Chesworth, Managing Editor

The oldest, most widely read international newsletter reporting on battery technology, marketing and industry events including new products and financial news. Accepts advertising. Print and online versions available.
Cost: $ 180.00
Circulation: 1000
Printed in 4 colors on matte stock

6285 Cleanroom Markets Newsletter
McIlvaine Company
191 Waukegan Rd
Suite 208
Northfield, IL 60093-2743

847-784-0012; *Fax:* 847-784-0061
editor@mcilvainecompany.com;
www.mcilvainecompany.com

Robert McIlvaine, Owner
Robert Mclvaine, President
Marilyn McIlvaine, EVP

Information on clean rooms markets worldwide.
Cost: $460.00
8 Pages
Frequency: Monthly
Printed in on newsprint stock

6286 Cleanroom Technology Newsletter
McIlvaine Company

191 Waukegan Rd
Suite 208
Northfield, IL 60093-2743

847-784-0012; *Fax:* 847-784-0061;
www.mcilvainecompany.com

Robert McIlvaine, Owner
Robert McIvaine, President
Marilyn McIlvaine, EVP

Information on clean room technology.

6287 Continuous Improvement
James Publishing
PO Box 25202
Santa Ana, CA 92799-5202

714-755-5450
800-394-2626; *Fax:* 714-751-2709
customer-service@jamespublishing.com;
www.jamespublishing.com

Jim Pawell, Founder and President
Stephen Sicillan, Editor

Tutorial and news on new quality assurance technologies and ISO 9000, QS 9000 and ISO 14000.
Cost: $20.00
Circulation: 2000

6288 Currents
Electrical Apparatus Service Association
1331 Baur Boulevard
Saint Louis, MO 63131-1903

314-993-2220; *Fax:* 314-993-1269
easinfo@easa.com; www.easa.com

Kevin Toor, Chairman
William Gray, Vice Chairman
Kenneth Gralow, Secretary Treasurer

Provides information on EASA's programs, seminars, technical articles and industry trends and events. Members receive a copy each month.
Frequency: Monthly
Circulation: 2000+

6289 Display Technology News
Business Communications Company
49 Walnut Park
Building 2
Wellesley, MA 02481

781-489-7301
866-285-7215; *Fax:* 781-253-3933
sales@bccresearch.com; www.bccresearch.com
Social Media: Facebook, Twitter

Greg Lindberg, Chairman and CEO
Bridgett Hurley, CMO
Kevin Fitzgerald, Editorial Director
Sharon Blank, Sales Director
Mark McCarthy, Operations Director

Market reports and technology updates of topics such as news materials, news applications, patents, technology transfer, processing and equipment.
Cost: $500.00
Frequency: Monthly
Founded in: 1971

6290 Document Imaging Report
Corry Publications
5340 Fryling Road
Knowledge Park, Suite 300
Erie, PA 16510

814-897-9000; *Fax:* 814-899-5583
corrypub@corrypub.com; www.corrypub.com

Nicole Hykes, Editor
John Toiston, Publisher
Carry Procious, Marketing
Mindy Sadden, Circulation Manager

Presents the most timely and actionable information on electronic imaging applications, products and user implementation.
Frequency: Monthly
Circulation: 50

6291 EA Extra
Electrical Association of Philadelphia
527 Plymouth Road
Suite 408
Plymouth Meeeting, PA 19462-1641

610-825-1600; *Fax:* 610-825-1603
electric@eap.org; www.eap.org
Social Media: Facebook, Twitter, YouTube

Kevin Lane, President
Joe Henry, Vice President
Kim Schneider, Treasurer
Kenneth Hull, Secretary

Carries information on industry trends, events, educational and business opportunities, economic briefings, member happening, mergers, and member benefit updates.
450 Members
Founded in: 1917

6292 Electrical Connection
Electrical Association of Rochester
PO Box 20219
Rochester, NY 14602-0219

585-538-6350; *Fax:* 585-538-6166;
www.eawny.com

Joe Lengen, President
Bonnie Curran, First VP
Coreg Merrill, Secretary/Treasurer
Kirstie Steves, Executive Director

Contains information on upcoming events, recaps past events, a message from the President, the current calendar and much more.
Frequency: Quarterly
Founded in: 1924

6293 Electrical Product News
Business Marketing & Publishing
PO Box 7457
Wilton, CT 06897

203-834-9959; www.epnweb.com
Social Media: Facebook

George Young, Editor/Publisher

Accepts advertising.
Cost: $39.50
20 Pages
Frequency: Monthly
Circulation: 3500
Printed in 2 colors on newsprint stock

6294 Electro Manufacturing
Worldwide Videotex
PO Box 3273
Boynton Beach, FL 33424-3273

561-738-2276
markedit@juno.com; www.wvpubs.com

Computer and electronic technologies used to help improve manufacturing efficiency.
Cost: $165.00

6295 Executive Newsline
Electric Power Research Institute
PO Box 10412
Palo Alto, CA 94303-0813

650-855-2000
800-313-3774; *Fax:* 650-855-2954
askepri@epri.com; www.epri.com
Social Media: Facebook, Twitter, LinkedIn, YouTube, Flikr

Steven R Specker, CEO
Jackie Turner, Communications Manager
Don Kintner, Communications Manager
Rick Langley, Director

Contains brief highlights of EPRI science and technology developments and announcements of interest to utility executives.

6296 Global Electronics
Pacific Studies Center
222B View Street
Mountain View, CA 94041-1344

650-969-1545; *Fax:* 650-961-9818

Leonard Siegel, Editor

News items detailing the industry throughout the world and the social, environmental and military implications of production and application.
Cost: $1.00
Circulation: 400

6297 IEEE Transactions on Applied Superconductivity
IEEE Instrumentation and Measurement Society
67 Alexander Drive
PO Box 12277
Research Triangle Park, NC 27709

919-549-8411; *Fax:* 919-549-8288
info@isa.org; www.isa.org
Social Media: Facebook, Twitter, LinkedIn

Ken Baker, President
Patrick Gouhin, Executive Director
Jerry Clemons, Department VP
Leo Staples, Treasurer

Concentrates on materials and their applications to electronics and power systems where superconductivity is central to the work.

6298 IEEE Transactions on Mobile Computing
IEEE Instrumentation and Measurement Society
67 Alexander Drive
PO Box 12277
Research Triangle Park, NC 27709

919-549-8411; *Fax:* 919-549-8288
info@isa.org; www.isa.org
Social Media: Facebook, Twitter, LinkedIn

Ken Baker, President
Patrick Gouhin, Executive Director
Jerry Clemons, Department VP
Leo Staples, Treasurer

Research papers are presented in this publication dealing with mobile computing, wireless networks, reliability, quality assurance, distributed systems architecture and high-level protocols.
Frequency: Quarterly

6299 IFAC Newsletter
American Automatic Control Council
3640 Col Glenn Hwy
Dayton, OH 45435

937-775-5062; *Fax:* 937-775-3936
pmisra@cs.wright.edu; www.a2c2.org

John Watkins, Editor

It contains up-to-date information about forthcoming IFAC events as well as brief announcements of other IFAC related activities. It is sent free of charge to NMO's, IFAC Affiliates and libraries.
Frequency: Bi-Monthly

6300 Inside FERC
McGraw Hill
PO Box 182604
Columbus, OH 43272

720-485-5000
877-833-5524; *Fax:* 614-759-3749
customer.service@mcgraw-hill.com;
www.mcgraw-hill.com
Social Media: Facebook, Twitter, LinkedIn, YouTube

Harold McGraw, President and CEO
Jack Callahan, Executive VP/CFO
John Berisford, EVP, Human Resources

Provides coverage of the Federal Energy Regulatory Commission's activities and federal regula-

tions.
Cost: $975.00
14 Pages
Frequency: Monthly
Founded in: 1884

6301 Inside NRC
McGraw Hill
PO Box 182604
Columbus, OH 43272

614-304-4000
877-833-5524; *Fax:* 614-759-3749
customer.service@mcgraw-hill.com;
www.mcgraw-hill.com
Social Media: Facebook, Twitter, LinkedIn, YouTube

Harold McGraw, President and CEO
Jack Callahan, Executive VP/CFO
John Berisford, EVP, Human Resources

Focuses exclusively on the US Nuclear Regulatory Commission.
Cost: $1310.00
13 Pages
Founded in: 1800

6302 SMT Trends
New Insights
303 Vallejo Street
Crockett, CA 94525-1237

510-787-2273; *Fax:* 415-389-8671

Michael New, Publisher/Editor

Marketing and business news for the surface mount industry. Covers component and packaging trends, CAD, CAE, pick and place, robotics and test inspection.
Printed in one color on matte stock

6303 SMTA News
Surface Mount Technology Association
5200 Wilson Road
Suite 215
Minneapolis, MN 55424

952-920-7682; *Fax:* 952-926-1819
joann@smta.org; www.smta.org

Dan Baldwin, President
Marie Cole, VP Tech Programs
Kola Akinade, Secretary
Hal Hendrickson, Treasurer

6304 Seven Mountain Scientific
PO Box 650
Boalsburg, PA 16827-651

814-466-6559; *Fax:* 814-466-2777
abt@7ms.com; www.7ms.com

E Thomas Chesworth, President

Industry news in battery and fuel cell technology, marketing and industry events including new products, electric vehicle, R&D and environmental news.
Cost: $180.00
ISSN: 0001-8627
Founded in: 1965

6305 Tech Notes
National Technical Information Service
5301 Shawnee Rd
Alexandria, VA 22312

703-605-6000; *Fax:* 703-605-6900
info@ntis.gov; www.ntis.gov
Social Media: Facebook, Twitter

Bruce Borzino, Director
Patrik Ekstrom, Business Development Manager
Reuel Avila, Managing Director

Describes new processes, equipment, materials and techniques developed by Federal laboratories.
Cost: $8.00

6306 Threshold Newsletter
Electrostatic Discharge Association
7900 Turin Road
Building 3
Rome, NY 13440-2069

315-339-6937; *Fax:* 315-339-6793
info@esda.org; www.esda.org
Social Media: Facebook, LinkedIn, YouTube

Donn Bellmore, President
Leo G. Henry, Sr. VP
Terry Welsher, VP
Lisa Pimpinella, Director of Operations
Donn Pritchard, Treasurer

Benefits of ESD membership include a subscription to the Threshold Newsletter in addition to other Association activities and programs such as educational tutorials and seminars; the EOS/ESD Symposium; participation in local chapters; discounts on Association standards and other publications; extensive networking; membership roster, and participation in standards development.
2000+ Members
Founded in: 1982

6307 Transformers for Electronic Circuits
Power Sources Manufacturers Association
PO Box 418
Mendham, NJ 07945-0418

973-543-9660; *Fax:* 973-543-6207
power@psma.com; www.psma.com

Dusty Becker, Chairman
Carl Blake, President
Jim Marinos, VP
Michel Grenon, Secretary/Treasurer

It is a complete, one-stop guide to transformer and inductor design and applications for everyone who designs, builds, or uses power magnetics components. Combines analysis and synthesis, and all theory is related to the solution of real world problems.
Cost: $100.00
155 Members
Founded in: 1985

6308 Update
Power Sources Manufacturers Association
PO Box 418
Mendham, NJ 07945-0418

973-543-9660; *Fax:* 973-543-6207
power@psma.com; www.psma.com
Social Media: LinkedIn

Dusty Becker, Chairman
Carl Blake, President
Jim Marinos, VP
Michel Grenon, Secretary/Treasurer

PSMA Update is published and distributed via e-mail quarterly by the Power Sources Manufacturers Association.
Frequency: Quarterly
Circulation: 2700

6309 Vision
Society of Manufacturing Engineers
1 SME Drive
PO Box 930
Dearborn, MI 48128

313-425-3000
800-733-4763; *Fax:* 313-425-3400
service@sme.org; www.sme.org

Paul Bradley, President
Mark Tomlinson, Executive Director/CEO

The newsletter highlights the latest developments in the machine vision industry including applications, techniques and methods.
Cost: $85.00
Frequency: Quarterly
Circulation: 1100
ISSN: 1544-3531

6310 Wafer News Confidential
PennWell Publishing Company
98 Spit Brook Rd
Suite L1-1
Nashua, NH 03062-5737

603-891-0123
800-225-0556; *Fax:* 603-891-9294
ATD@PennWell.com; www.pennwell.com

Christine Shaw, VP
Barbara Pennwell, CEO/President

Provides semiconductor equipment industry executives with information on developments, trends, news and market insights.
Cost: $15.00
Frequency: Monthly
Founded in: 1910

Magazines & Journals

6311 Bioelectromagnetics Journal
John Wiley & Sons
2412 Cobblestone Way
Frederick, MD 21702-3519

301-663-4252; *Fax:* 301-694-4948
office@bems.org; www.bems.org

James Lin, Editor in Chief
Carmela Marino, Associate Editor
Andrei Pakhomov, Associate Editor

It is a peer-reviewed, internationally circulated scientific journal that specializes in reporting original data on biological effect and applications of electromagnetic fields that range in frequency from zero hertz static fields) to the terahertz undulations of visible light.
Frequency: 6x yearly

6312 Contact
1000 McKee Street
Batavia, IL 60510-1682

630-879-6000; *Fax:* 630-879-0867

Steve Wilcox, Editor

Application of electric motor controls to electrically operated machinery and equipment.
Circulation: 4,000

6313 Control Solutions
PennWell Publishing Company
1421 S Sheridan Rd
Tulsa, OK 74112-6619

918-835-3161
800-331-4463; *Fax:* 918-831-9497
Headquarters@PennWell.com;
www.pennwell.com

Robert Biolchini, President
Ron Kuhfeld, Editor-in-Chief
Frequency: Monthly

6314 Diesel & Gas Turbine Worldwide
Diesel & Gas Turbine Publications
20855 Watertown Rd
Suite 220
Waukesha, WI 53186-1873

262-754-4100; *Fax:* 262-754-4175;
www.dieselspec.com

Michael Osenga, President
Lynne Diefenbach, Advertising Manager

Concentrates its editorial on the design, packaging, operation and maintenance of medium and slow-speed, high output diesel, natural gas and gas turbine engine systems used in the electrical power generation, cogeneration, oil and gas, marine propulsion and railroad markets throughout the world.
Cost: $65.00
Frequency: 10x yearly
Circulation: 22,000
Founded in: 1969

6315 ECN Magazine
Reed Business Information

360 Park Ave S
4th Floor
New York, NY 10010-1737

646-746-6400; *Fax:* 646-756-7583
subsmail@reedbusiness.com;
www.reedbusiness.com

John Poulin, CEO
Aimee Kalnoskas, Editor
Steve Wirth, Publisher Director
James Reed, Owner

Provides product solutions for designed engineers in the electronics industry.
Cost: $96.19
Frequency: Monthly

6316 **EE Product News**
Penton Media
1166 Avenue of the Americas/10th Fl
New York, NY 10036

212-204-4200
CorporateCustomerService@penton.com;
www.penton.com

David Kieselstien, CEO
Nicola Allais, CFO
Jasmine Alexander, CIO

Source of information on new products necessary to successfully design, assemble and test prototypes of commercial, industrial, military and aerospace electronic products.
Frequency: Monthly
Circulation: 111968
Founded in: 1892

6317 **EE: Evaluation Engineering**
Nelson Publishing
2500 Tamiami Trl N
Nokomis, FL 34275-3476

941-966-9521
800-226-6113; *Fax:* 941-966-2590
pmilo@evaluationengineering.com;
www.healthmgttech.com
Social Media: Facebook, Twitter

Kristine Russel, President
Phil Colpas, Managing Editor

Magazine devoted exclusively to companies that test, evaluate, design and manufacture electronic products and equipment.
Cost: $43.00
84 Pages
Frequency: Monthly
Founded in: 1962
Mailing list available for rent: 65,000 names
Printed in 4 colors on glossy stock

6318 **ElectriCITY**
Electric Association
40 Shuman Boulevard
Suite 247
Naperville, IL 60563

630-305-3050; *Fax:* 630-305-3056
cspaeth@eachicago.org; www.eachicago.org

Mark Gibson, President
Rick Jamerson, Vice President
Steven Anixter, Treasurer
Thomas Scherzer, Secretary
Founded in: 1925

6319 **ElectriCITY Magazine**
Electric Association
40 Shuman Boulevard
Suite 247
Naperville, IL 60563-8446

630-305-3050; *Fax:* 630-305-3056
admin@eachicago.org; www.eachicago.org
Social Media: Facebook, LinkedIn

Mark Gibson, President
Rick Jamerson, Vice President
Steven Anixter, Treasurer
Thomas Scherzer, Secretary
Bob Porter, Secretary

Corporate news, timely articles, career announcements, product line changes, industry-dates calendars, career placement services, and government legislation updates; circulation across the Midwest.
Frequency: Quarterly

6320 **Electric Co-op Today**
National Rural Electric Cooperative Association
4301 Wilson Blvd
Suite 1
Arlington, VA 22203-1860

703-907-5500; *Fax:* 703-907-5526;
www.nreca.org
Social Media: Twitter

Glenn English, CEO

Devoted to accurate, critical coverage of electric cooperative developments and electric cooperative industry news, unavailable in any other publication. The only weekly publication covering electric cooperative industry news, legislation and regulation, and community and economic development. Each issue highlights what you need to know to understand key industry issues clearly, quickly, and easily.
Cost: $40.00
Frequency: Weekly
Founded in: 1994

6321 **Electric Light & Power**
PennWell Publishing Company
1421 S Sheridan Rd
Tulsa, OK 74112-6619

918-835-3161
800-331-4463; *Fax:* 918-831-9497
Headquarters@PennWell.com;
www.pennwell.com

Serves the North American Electric Utility Industry including electric power generation, delivery, and information technology operations in investor-owned electric utilities.
Frequency: Monthly
ISSN: 0013-4120
Founded in: 1902

6322 **Electric Perspectives**
Edison Electric Institute
701 Pennsylvania Avenue NW
Washington, DC 20004-2696

202-508-5000; *Fax:* 202-508-5360
feedback@eei.org; www.eei.org
Social Media: Facebook, Twitter, YouTube

Thomas R Kuhn, President
David Owens, Executive VP Business Operations
Brian Wolff, Senior VP, External Affairs

Written and edited specifically for management-level employees at shareholder-owned electric utilities.
Frequency: Bi-Monthly
Circulation: 15,000
ISSN: 0364-474X

6323 **Electrical Apparatus**
Barks Publications
400 N Michigan Ave
Suite 900
Chicago, IL 60611-4164

312-321-9440; *Fax:* 312-321-1288
info@barks.com; www.barks.com

Horace Barks, Owner
Elsie Dickson, Associate Publisher
Horace Barks, CEO
Joseph Hoff, Manager

Serves the electromechanical and electronic maintenance and application industries, including manufacturing plants, institutional facilities and service companies.
Cost: $45.00
Frequency: Monthly
Circulation: 15500
Founded in: 1969

6324 **Electrical Construction & Maintenance**
Primedia
1166 Avenue of the Americas/10th Fl
New York, NY 10036

212-204-4200
CorporateCustomerService@penton.com;
www.penton.com

David Kieselstien, CEO
Nicola Allais, CFO
Jasmine Alexander, CIO

Owners and company officials, engineers, electrical personnel, electrical inspectors, architects and designers, purchasing and other related personnel.
Circulation: 104344

6325 **Electrical Contractor Magazine**
National Electrical Contractors Association
3 Bethesda Metro Ctr
Suite 1100
Bethesda, MD 20814-5372

301-657-3110; *Fax:* 301-215-4500
beth.margulies@necanet.org; www.necanet.org
Social Media: Facebook, Twitter, LinkedIn, YouTube

John M Grau, CEO
Dan Walter, VP and COO
Michael Thompson, Secretary/Treasurer

The magazine has been the complete information source for electrical construction professionals. Its goal is to serve all participants in the power and integrated building systems industries. It delivers the latest information in the areas of power, communications and controls in both high voltage and low voltage applications to electrical contractors who compete in residential, commercial, industrial and institutional market segments of the construction arena.
Circulation: 85,000
Founded in: 1939

6326 **Electrical Distributor Magazine**
National Association of Electrical Distributors
1181 Croporate Lake Drive
St Louis, MO 63132

314-991-9000
888-791-2512; *Fax:* 314-991-3060
info@naed.org; www.naed.org
Social Media: Facebook, Twitter, YouTube

Robert Reynolds, Chairman
Tom Naber, President and CEO

An informative, insightful publication that offers electrical distributors the latest information affecting their business. Subscriptions are free to NAED members.

6327 **Electrical Wholesaling**
Primedia
1166 Avenue of the Americas/10th Fl
New York, NY 10036

212-204-4200
CorporateCustomerService@penton.com;
www.penton.com

David Kieselstien, CEO
Nicola Allais, CFO
Jasmine Alexander, CIO

Offers information on manufacturers, suppliers, prices and marketing of electrical products.
Cost: $25.00
Frequency: Monthly
Circulation: 22,500
Founded in: 1905

6328 Electricity Today
1885 Clements Road
Unit 218
Pickering, Canada, ON L1W-3V4

905-686-1040; *Fax:* 905-686-1078;
www.electricity-today.com

Randy Hurst, Publisher

Electricity Today is a leading electrical transmission and distribution magazine distributed free of charge to North American T&D electric utility engineering, construction and maintenance personnel, and high voltage T&D consulting engineers.

6329 Electronic Design
Penton Media
1166 Avenue of the Americas/10th Fl
New York, NY 10036

212-204-4200
CorporateCustomerService@penton.com;
www.penton.com

David Kieselstien, CEO
Nicola Allais, CFO
Jasmine Alexander, CIO

Celebrating 50 years of innovation, this authoritative source provides leading-edge information to electronic and engineering managers around the world.

6330 Fringe Ware Review
Fringe Ware
PO Box 49921
Austin, TX 78765-4858

512-444-2393

Paco Nathan, Co-Founder
Don Lebkowsky, Co-Founder
Monte McCarter, Art Director
Tiffany Lee Brown, Assistant Editor

Stories and review on electronic products made by smaller producers.
Cost: $4.00
Founded in: 1992

6331 High Tech News
Electronic Technicians Association International
5 Depot St
Greencastle, IN 46135-8024

765-653-8262
800-288-3824; *Fax:* 765-653-4287
eta@eta-i.org; www.eta-i.org
Social Media: Facebook, Twitter, LinkedIn

Teresa Maher, CSS, President
Cindy Reed, Financial Director
Richard Glass, CETsr, CEO Emeritus

Exclusive bi-monthly publication of ETA International, and a subscription is included with each individual membership. Each issue features information on the changing electronics industry: specialty techniques & technology, trends, qualification opportunities and educational advice.
4500 Members
Frequency: Bi-Monthly
Circulation: 10000
Founded in: 1978

6332 IEEE Instrumentation and Measurement Magazine
IEEE Instrumentation and Measurement Society
67 Alexander Drive
PO Box 12277
Research Triangle Park, NC 27709

919-549-8411; *Fax:* 919-549-8288
info@isa.org; www.isa.org
Social Media: Facebook, Twitter, LinkedIn

Kim Fowler, Editor-in-Chief

This publication is included in member dues, it contains applications-oriented articles and news nominations, awards, highlights of conferences, Technical Committee news, book reviews, tutorials and contributions from the membership.
Frequency: Quarterly

6333 IEEE Sensors Journal
IEEE Instrumentation and Measurement Society
67 Alexander Drive
PO Box 12277
Research Triangle Park, NC 27709

919-549-8411; *Fax:* 919-549-8288
info@isa.org; www.isa.org
Social Media: Facebook, Twitter, LinkedIn

Ken Baker, President
Patrick Gouhin, Executive Director
Jerry Clemons, Department VP
Leo Staples, Treasurer

Specializes in the theory, design, fabrication, manufacturing and applications of devices for sensing and transducing physical, chemical and biological phenomena.
Frequency: Bi-Monthly

6334 IEEE Transactions on Intelligent Transportation Systems
IEEE Instrumentation and Measurement Society
67 Alexander Drive
PO Box 12277
Research Triangle Park, NC 27709

919-549-8411; *Fax:* 919-549-8288
info@isa.org; www.isa.org
Social Media: Facebook, Twitter, LinkedIn

Ken Baker, President
Patrick Gouhin, Executive Director
Jerry Clemons, Department VP
Leo Staples, Treasurer

This journal contains basic and applied research to expand the knowledge base on transportation for improved design, management and control of future transportation systems.
Frequency: Quarterly

6335 IEEE Transactions on Nanotechnology
IEEE Instrumentation and Measurement Society
67 Alexander Drive
PO Box 12277
Research Triangle Park, NC 27709

919-549-8411; *Fax:* 919-549-8288
info@isa.org; www.isa.org
Social Media: Facebook, Twitter, LinkedIn

Ken Baker, President
Patrick Gouhin, Executive Director
Jerry Clemons, Department VP
Leo Staples, Treasurer

The journal is devoted to the dissemination of new results and discussions related to understanding the physical basis and engineering applications of phenomena at the nanoscale level.
Frequency: Quarterly

6336 Industrial Laser Solutions
PennWell Publishing Company
98 Spit Brook Rd
Nashua, NH 03062-5737

603-891-0123
80- 2-5 05; *Fax:* 603-891-9294;
www.pennwell.com

Christine Shaw, VP
David Belforte, Editor

For all industries that use industrial lasers.
Cost: $260.00
45 Pages
Frequency: Monthly
Circulation: 10,000
ISSN: 1523-4266
Founded in: 1986

6337 Industrial Market Place
Wineberg Publications
7842 Lincoln Avenue
Skokie, IL 60077

847-676-1900
800-323-1818; *Fax:* 847-676-0063
info@industrialmktpl.com;
www.industrialmktpl.com

Eliot Wineberg, President
Jackie Bitensky, Editor

Has advertisements on machinery, industrial and plant equipment, services and industrial auctions in each issue.
Cost: $175.00
60 Pages
Frequency: Bi-Monthly
Circulation: 14,000
Founded in: 1951
Printed in 4 colors on glossy stock

6338 Interface Magazine
Electrochemical Society
65 S Main St
Building D
Pennington, NJ 08534-2827

609-737-1902; *Fax:* 609-737-2743
ecs@electrochem.org; www.electrochem.org

Christine Garzon, President
Tetsuya Osaka, Sr. VP
Harikila Deligianni, Secretary
Christina Bock, Treasurer

Is an authoritative accessible publication for those in the field of solid-state and electrochemical science and technology which contains technical articles about the latest developments in the field, and presents news and information about and for members of ECS.
Cost: $40.00
Frequency: Quarterly
Circulation: 9000
ISSN: 1064-8208
Founded in: 1902
Printed in 4 colors

6339 Journal of Laser Applications
Laser Institute of America
13501 Ingenuity Dr
Suite 128
Orlando, FL 32826-3009

407-380-1553
800-345-2737; *Fax:* 407-380-5588
lia@lia.org; www.lia.org
Social Media: Facebook, Twitter, LinkedIn

Klaus Loeffler, President
Stephen Capp, Treasurer
Robert Thomas, Secretary

The official journal of the Laser Institute of America and serves as the major international forum for exchanging ideas and information in disciplines that apply laser technology. Internationally known editors, reviewers, and columnists deliver the latest results of their research worldwide, dealing with the diverse, practical applications of photonic technology.
Cost: $410.00

6340 Journal of Lightwave Technology
IEEE Instrumentation and Measurement Society
67 Alexander Drive
PO Box 12277
Research Triangle Park, NC 27709

919-549-8411; *Fax:* 919-549-8288
info@isa.org; www.isa.org
Social Media: Facebook, Twitter, LinkedIn

Ken Baker, President
Patrick Gouhin, Executive Director
Jerry Clemons, Department VP
Leo Staples, Treasurer

The Journal is concerned with research, applications and methods used in all aspects of lightwave technology and fiber optics.
Frequency: Monthly

6341 Journal of Microwave Power and Electromagnetic Energy
International Microwave Power Institute
PO Box 1140
Mechanicsville, VA 23111-5007

804-559-6667; *Fax:* 804-559-4087
info@impi.org; www.impi.org

Bob Schiffmann, President
Ben Wilson, Vice President
Dorin Bolder, Secretary
Amy Lawson, Treasurer

The quarterly, technical journal of the Institute published by the Industrial, Scientific, Medical and Instrumentation (ISMI) section. Designed for the information needs of professionals specializing in the research and design of industrial and bio-medical applications, the Journal exemplifies the highest standards of scientific and technical information on the theory and application of electromagnetic power.
Cost: $250.00
Frequency: Quarterly

6342 Journal of the Electrochemical Society
Electrochemical Society
65 S Main St
Building D
Pennington, NJ 08534-2827

609-737-1902; *Fax:* 609-737-2743
ecs@electrochem.org; www.electrochem.org

Roque J Calvo, President

This peer reviewed journal publishes 60 articles each month. Articles are posted online, with a monthly paper edition following electronic publication. The ECS membership benefits package includes access to the electronic edition of this journal. Free with membership.
Cost: $110.00
Frequency: Monthly
Circulation: 8300
ISSN: 0013-4651
Founded in: 1902

6343 LIA Today
Laser Institute of America
13501 Ingenuity Dr
Suite 128
Orlando, FL 32826-3009

407-380-1553
800-345-2737; *Fax:* 407-380-5588
lia@lia.org; www.lia.org
Social Media: Facebook, Twitter, LinkedIn

Klaus Loeffler, President
Stephen Capp, Treasurer
Robert Thomas, Secretary

Includes articles on the latest industry news to keep members and other laser professionals current on important issues that impact the laser community. Readers of LIA TODAY consist of production managers, supervisors, safety professionals, researchers, end-users, laser physicians and nurses.
Frequency: Bi-Monthly
Circulation: 5000

6344 Laser Tech Briefs
Associated Business Publications International
317 Madison Avenue
New York, NY 10017

212-490-3999; *Fax:* 212-986-7864;
www.abpi.net

Domenic Mucchetti, CEO
Josheph Pramberger, President
Luke Schnirring, Executive VP

For purchasers of laser/optical products.
Circulation: 40,000

6345 Lighting Dimensions
Primedia Business
249 W 17th St
New York, NY 10011-5382

212-206-1894
800-827-3322; *Fax:* 212-514-3719;
www.lightingdimensions.com
Social Media: Facebook, Twitter

Doug MacDonald, Group Publisher
David Johnson, Associate Publisher
Marian Sandberg-Dierson, Editor
Ellen Lampert-Greaux, Consulting Editor
Jennifer Hirst, Art Director

Trade publication for lighting professionals in film, theatre, television, concerts, clubs, themed environments, architectural, commercial, and industrial lighting. Sponsors of the LDI Trade Show and the Broadway Lighting Master Classes.
Cost: $34.97
Frequency: Monthly
Circulation: 14,177
Founded in: 1989

6346 Market Trends
Electronic Industries Association
2500 Wilson Boulevard
Arlington, VA 22201-3834

703-907-7500; *Fax:* 703-907-7767

Statistical information and marketing trends in the electronics industry.
Cost: $195.00
Frequency: Monthly

6347 Motion Control
ISA Services
P.O. Box 787
Williamsport, PA 17703

570-567-1982
800-791-8699; *Fax:* 570-320-2079
briefingsweborders@publishersserviceasso;
www.douglaspublications.com

Janine Nunes, Editor
Edward Mueller, Publisher

Information for those who design and maintain motion control systems.
56 Pages
Frequency: Monthly
Circulation: 16,490
ISSN: 1058-4644
Founded in: 1985
Printed in 4 colors on glossy stock

6348 NETA World
International Electrical Testing Association
Po Box 687
Morrison, CO 80465-0687

303-697-8441
888-300-6382; *Fax:* 303-697-8431
neta@netaworld.org; www.netaworld.org
Social Media: Facebook, YouTube

Mose Ramieh, President
David Huffman, First VP
Ron Widup, Second VP
John White, Treasurer
Walter Cleary, Secretary

Features articles of interest to electrical testing and maintenance companies, consultants, engineers, architects, and plant personnel directly involved in electrical testing and maintenance. Free with membership.
Frequency: Quarterly

6349 Power Conversion & Intelligent Motion
Primedia
1166 Avenue of the Americas/10th Fl
New York, NY 10036

212-204-4200
CorporateCustomerService@penton.com;
www.penton.com

David Kieselstien, CEO
Nicola Allais, CFO
Jasmine Alexander, CIO

Directed to engineers, designers and manufacturers of power electronic and electronic motion control components, subsystems and systems. Feature articles interpret trends and innovation in these subjects.
Circulation: 31,113

6350 Power Engineering International
PennWell Publishing Company
1421 S Sheridan Rd
Tulsa, OK 74112-6619

918-831-9421
800-331-4463; *Fax:* 918-831-9476
headquarters@pennwell.com;
www.pennwell.com

Robert Biolchini, President

Serves the global electric power generation and transmission industry.
Frequency: Monthly
Circulation: 34000
ISSN: 1069-4994
Founded in: 1896

6351 Powerline Magazine
Electrical Generating Systems Association
1650 S Dixie Hwy
Suite 500
Boca Raton, FL 33432-7461

561-750-5575; *Fax:* 561-395-8557;
www.egsa.org
Social Media: Facebook

Debra Laurentis, President
Edward Murphy, VP
Bob Hafich, Secretary/Treasurer

Focuses on the entire on-site power generation industry.
Cost: $5.00
Frequency: Bi-Monthly

6352 ProService Magazine
National Electronics Service Dealers Association
3608 Pershing Ave
Fort Worth, TX 76107-4527

817-921-9061
800-797-9197; *Fax:* 817-921-3741
webmaster@nesda.com; www.nesda.com
Social Media: Facebook

Ben Fowler, President
Jerrell Helms, Vice President
Wayne Markman, Secretary
George Weiss, Treasurer

Published for members of NESDA/ISCET.
24 Pages
Frequency: Bi-Monthly

6353 Process Heating
Business News Publishing Company
155 Pfingsten Road
Suite 205
Deerfield, IL 60015

847-405-4000; *Fax:* 248-502-1001
PHeditors@bnpmedia.com;
www.process-heating.com
Social Media: Facebook, Twitter

Anne Armel, Publisher
Linda Becker, Associate Publisher & Editor
Beth McClelland, Production Manager

Magazine covers heat processing at temperatures up to 1000 degrees F at end user and OEM plants in 9 industries. Follow us at twit-

ter.com/ProcessHeating, www.facebook.com/ProcessHeating
Circulation: 25000
Founded in: 1994

6354 **RE Magazine**
National Rural Electric Cooperative Association
4301 Wilson Blvd
Suite 1
Arlington, VA 22203-1860
703-907-5500; *Fax:* 703-907-5526;
www.nreca.org
Social Media: Twitter
Glenn English, CEO
Editorial content covers utility operations, deployment of the latest industry products and services; a showcase of new products, services, and catalogs; online resources; safety; member(customer) services; business and management trends; marketing tools; community and economic development; local leaders and rural issues; co-op personnel news; and politics and regulatory policies impacting electric co-ops.
Cost: $43.00
Frequency: Monthly
Founded in: 1942

6355 **Rural Electrification**
National Rural Electric Cooperative Association
4301 Wilson Blvd
Arlington, VA 22203-1860
703-907-5500; *Fax:* 703-907-5526;
www.nreca.org
Social Media: Twitter
Glenn English, CEO
Serves people involved in the rural electric cooperative industry including generation and transmission cooperatives, distribution systems and public utility district members of NRECA; electric equipment manufacturers; US Congress, state and federal regulatory agencies and commissions; and others allied to the field.
Cost: $85.00
Frequency: Monthly
Founded in: 1942

6356 **Service Contractor Magazine**
Contract Services Association of America
1000 Wilson Boulevard
Suite 1800
Arlington, VA 22209
703-243-2020; *Fax:* 703-243-3601
info@csa-dc.org; www.pscouncil.org
Barry Cullen, President
Colleen Preston, Senior VP
Focuses on industry developments, regulatory and legislative issues, and any issues encountered in the process of competing for and securing contracts, such as changes in the acquisitions or procurement process. It tailors its content exclusively to government contractors.
Frequency: Bi-Annual

6357 **Standard for Certification of Electrical Testing Technicians**
International Electrical Testing Association
Po Box 687
Morrison, CO 80465-0687
303-697-8441
888-300-6382; *Fax:* 303-697-8431
neta@netaworld.org; www.netaworld.org
Social Media: Facebook, YouTube
Mose Ramieh, President
David Huffman, First VP
Ron Widup, Second VP
John White, Treasurer
Walter Cleary, Secretary
Specifying requisite levels of training, experience, and education for the evaluator of electrical power equipment is an important test procedure itself. The requirements parallel those of the National Skill Standards Board in Washington, DC, which promulgates for various occupations.
Cost: $55.00
36 Pages

6358 **Standard for Electrical Maintenance Testing of Dry-Type Transformers**
International Electrical Testing Assocaition
Po Box 687
Morrison, CO 80465-0687
303-697-8441
888-300-6382; *Fax:* 303-697-8431
neta@netaworld.org; www.netaworld.org
Social Media: Facebook, YouTube
Mose Ramieh, President
David Huffman, First VP
Ron Widup, Second VP
John White, Treasurer
Walter Cleary, Secretary
This Standard has been an individual section within the NETA document entitled Maintenance Testing Specifications for Electrical Power Distribution Equipment and Systems since 1975. The Maintenance Testing Specifications along with NETA's Acceptance Testing Specifications have long been in general use by organizations and individuals involved with testing of electrical apparatus.
Cost: $55.00
18 Pages

6359 **Standard for Electrical Maintenance Testin g of Liquid-Filled Transformers**
International Electrical Testing Association
PO Box 687
Morrison, CO 80465-0687
303-697-8441
888-300-6382; *Fax:* 303-697-8431
neta@netaworld.org; www.netaworld.org
Social Media: Facebook, YouTube
Mose Ramieh, President
David Huffman, First VP
Ron Widup, Second VP
John White, Treasurer
Walter Cleary, Secretary
The Standard has been an individual section within the NETA document entitled Maintenance Testing Specifications for Electrical Power Distribution Equipment and Systems since 1975. The Maintenance Testing Specifications along with NETA's Acceptance Testing Specifications have long been in general use by organizations and individuals involved with testing of electrical apparatus.
Cost: $55.00
21 Pages

Trade Shows

6360 **AHTD Trade Show**
Association for High Technology Distributors
N19 W24400 Riverwood Drive
Waukesha, WI 53188
262-696-3645
800-488-4845
ahtd@ahtd.org; www.ahtd.org
Social Media: Twitter, LinkedIn
Neil Montogomery, President
John Pirner, Vice President
Thomas Swenton, Secretary
Brian Lepsis, Treasurer
Works to increase productivity and profitability of high technology automation solutions, providers and manufacturers.
250 Members
Frequency: Annual/September
Founded in: 1985

6361 **American Control Conference**
American Automatic Control Council
2145 Sheridan Road
Evanston, IL 60208-3118
847-491-8175; *Fax:* 847-491-4455
aacc@ece.northwestern.edu; www.a2c2.org
R. Russell Reinehart, President
Tariq Samad, President-elect
Jordan Berg, Treasurer
B.Wayne Bequette, Secretary
Covers a broad range of topics relevant to the theory and practice of control and automation, including robotics, manufacturing, guidance and control, power systems, process control, identification and estimation, signal processing, modeling and advanced simulation.
800 Attendees
Frequency: Annual/June

6362 **Annual Connector & Interconnection Technology Symposium and Trade Show**
International Institute of Connector and Intercon
PO Box 20002
Sarasota, FL 34276
941-929-1806
800-854-4248; *Fax:* 941-929-1807
info@iicit.org; www.iicit.org
Dale Reed, Content Editor
Offers the opportunity to meet with other connector/interconnection industry users and vendors to learn about the latest advances in interconnection technology in the areas of radio frequency interconnection, quality, high speed connectors, personal computer interconnections, automotive Interconnections, materials, finishes, and platings, test methods, automation, surface mount technology, fiber optics, spaceflight connector technology, and medical applications.

6363 **Annual Legislative & Regulatory Roundtable**
Electronic Industries Association
2214 rock Hill Rd
Suite 170
Herndon, VA 20170
571-323-0294; *Fax:* 571-323-0245;
www.eia.org
Social Media: LinkedIn, YouTube
Gail Tannenbaum, CMP, Manager Meetings
Panel topics in the past have included Broadband, Tax, Trade, Environment, Defense, Space, and the Congressional Leadership Agenda.
Frequency: Annual/August

6364 **Applied Power Electronics Conference & Exposition (APEC)**
Power Sources Manufacturers Association
PO Box 418
Mendham, NJ 07945-0418
973-543-9660; *Fax:* 973-543-6207
power@psma.com; www.psma.com
Social Media: LinkedIn
Dusty Becker, Chairman
Carol Blake, President
Jim Marinos, VP
Michel Grenon, Secretary/Treasurer
APEC continues the long-standing tradition of addressing issues of immediate and long-term interest to the practicing power electronics engineer.
1000 Attendees

6365 **Bioelectromagnetics - Stun Gun Mini Symposium**
Bioelectromagnetics Society
2412 Cobblestone Way
Frederick, MD 21702-3519

301-663-4252; *Fax:* 301-694-4948
office@bems.org; www.bems.org

David Black, President
Gloria Parsley, Executive Director

The focus of this symposium will be the technology, physiology and potential adverse side effects of the use of electronic weapons or stun guns, which are rapidly being deployed in military and police use.
Frequency: Annual/June

6366 **Bioelectromagnetics - U.S. Air Force Workshop**
Bioelectromagnetics Society
2412 Cobblestone Way
Frederick, MD 21702-3519

301-663-4252; *Fax:* 301-694-4948
office@bems.org; www.bems.org

David Black, President
Gloria Parsley, Executive Director

Will focus on the use of molecular biology to identify changes in genes and proteins that may lead to physiological, pathological, or behavioral events.
Frequency: Annual/June

6367 **Bioelectromagnetics Society Meeting**
Bioelectromagnetics Society
2412 Cobblestone Way
Frederick, MD 21702-3519

301-663-4252; *Fax:* 301-694-4948
office@bems.org; www.bems.org

David Black, President
Gloria Parsley, Executive Director
Richard Nuccitelli, VP

This is a joint meeting of The Bioelectromagnetics Society and The European BioElectromagnetics Association. Topics will be: Electric Fields, Human Studies, Exposure Assessment, Dosimetry, In Vitro ELF, Epidemiology, Unique EMF Signals, Medical applications, Mechanisms, Electromagnetic Therapy.
400 Attendees
Frequency: Annual/June

6368 **CSA Winter Meeting**
Contract Services Association of America
1000 Wilson Boulevard
Suite 1800
Arlington, VA 22209

703-243-2020; *Fax:* 703-243-3601
info@csa-dc.org; www.pscouncil.org

Barry Cullen, President
Colleen Preston, Senior VP

This one day workshop is a free flowing exchange of information with real time interaction and information exchange.
Frequency: Annual/January

6369 **Coherence and Electromagnetic Fields in Biological Systems**
Bioelectromagnetics Society
2412 Cobblestone Way
Frederick, MD 21702-3519

301-663-4252; *Fax:* 301-694-4948
office@bems.org

David Black, President
Gloria Parsley, Executive Director
Richard Nuccitelli, VP

Highlights of the symposium organized by the Institute of Radio Engineering and Electronics, the Academy of Sciences of the Czech Republic and others are expected to include biophysical principles of coherence, role of endogenous EMF in the organization of biological systems, biophysical mechanisms of interaction of biological systems with EMF and more.
Frequency: Annual/July

6370 **Consulting Electrical Engineers(CEE) Technical Forum & Table-Top**
Electric Association
One Energy Center,40 Shuman Boulevard
Suite 247
Naperville, IL 60563

630-305-3050; *Fax:* 630-305-3056
admin@eachicago.org; www.eachicago.org
Social Media: Facebook, LinkedIn

Mark Gibson, President
Rick Jamerson, VP
Steven Anixter, Treasurer
Thomas Scherzer, Secretary

This event will feature a free technical forum for engineers, specifiers, and designers on Short Circuit analysis, Coordination, and Arc Flash Hazard analysis using conventional and computerized methods. The Table Top tradeshow will feature 45 vendors and their latest technology.
Frequency: Annual/May

6371 **EASA Annual Convention**
Electrical Apparatus Services Association
1331 Baur Boulevard
Saint Louis, MO 63131-1903

314-993-2220; *Fax:* 314-993-1269
easainfo@easa.com; www.easa.com

Linda Raynes, President/CEO
Anne Vogel, Executive Secretary

Provides members with a means of keeping up to date on materials, equipment, and state-of-the-art technology. 100+ exhibitor booths.
2500 Attendees
Frequency: Annual/June
Mailing list available for rent

6372 **EDS: Where the Electronics Industry Connects**
Electronics Distributions Show Corporation
2214 Rock Hill Road
Suite 170
Herndon, VA 20170

312-648-1140; *Fax:* 312-648-4282
eds@edsconnects.com; www.edsconnects.com
Social Media: LinkedIn

Gretchen Oie-Weghorst, Director
Gerald M Newman, Executive VP

Attendees are manufacturers of electronic components who sell their products through electronics distributors. Provides networking and meeting opportunities, and opens doors to new business. Hundreds of exhibits, thousands of attendees.
6M Attendees
Frequency: Annual/May
Founded in: 1937

6373 **EEI Annual Convention/Expo**
Edison Electric Institute
701 Pennsylvania Avenue NW
Washington, DC 20004-2696

202-508-5000; *Fax:* 202-508-5360
feedback@eei.org; www.eei.org
Social Media: Facebook, Twitter, YouTube

Thomas Kuhn, President
David Owens, Executive VP Business Operations
Brian Wolff, Senior VP, External Affairs
1000 Attendees
Frequency: Annual/June

6374 **EEI Financial Conference**
Edison Electric Institute
701 Pennsylvania Avenue NW
Washington, DC 20004-2696

202-508-5000; *Fax:* 202-508-5335
feedback@eei.org; www.eei.org
Social Media: Facebook, Twitter, YouTube

Thomas Kuhn, President
David Owens, Executive VP Business Operations
Brian Wolff, Senior VP, External Affairs

Provides a unique forum for exchange of ideas and experience; and to give you insight into emerging critical issues.
Frequency: Annual/November

6375 **EERA Annual Meeting**
Electrical Equipment Representation
638 W 39th Street
Kansas City, MO 64111

816-561-5323
800-728-2272; *Fax:* 816-561-1249
info2005@eera.org; www.eera.org

Vince Brown III, President
Brad Cahoon, President Elect
Don Shirk, VP
Kier Cooper, Secretary
Rob Rigsby, Treasurer
Frequency: Annual/April

6376 **EGSA Annual Spring Convention**
Electrical Generating Systems Association
1650 S Dixie Highway
Suite 500
Boca Raton, FL 33432

561-750-5575; *Fax:* 561-398-8557;
www.egsa.org
Social Media: Facebook

Cara Clark, Director Conventions/Meetings
Bob Breese, Director of Education

Offers educational sessions covering a broad range of issues effecting the on-site power industry.
Frequency: Annual/March

6377 **EIA's Congressional Technology Forum**
Electronic Industries Association
2214 rock Hill Rd
Suite 170
Herndon, VA 20170

571-323-0294; *Fax:* 571-323-0245;
www.eia.org
Social Media: LinkedIn, YouTube

Gail Tannenbaum, CMP, Manager Meetings

Discusses the issues most relevant for the electronics and high-tech industries.
Frequency: Annual/October

6378 **Electri...FYI**
Electrical Association of Rochester
PO Box 20219
Rochester, NY 14602-0219

585-538-6350; *Fax:* 585-538-6166;
www.eawny.com

Ed Langschwager, President
Joe Lengen, First VP
Rich Monroe, Secretary/Treasurer
Kirstie Steves, Executive Director

Upstate Electrical Show. 120+ exhibitors. Free entry.
2000 Attendees
Frequency: Tri-Annual

6379 **Electric West Conference**
PRIMEDIA Business Exhibitions

11 River Bend Drive S
PO Box 4232
Stamford, CT 06907-0232

203-358-9900; *Fax:* 203-358-5816;
www.primediaevents.com

David Small, Show Director
Tara Keating-Magee, Show Coordinator

Educational sessions attract electrical professionals from contracting companies, industrial plants, consulting engineering firms, datacom installers and electricians. Presentations focus on such topics as power quality, lighting, the NEC, project management, claims management and fiber optics. Also provides in-depth coverage of National Electrical Code changes that directly impact the work of electrical professionals. 250 Exhibitors.
6000 Attendees
Frequency: Annual/March

6380 **Energy - Exhibit Promotions Plus**
US Department of Energy/US Dept. of Defense/GSA
11620 Vixens Path
Ellicott City, MD 21042

301-596-3028; *Fax:* 410-997-0764;
www.epponline.com

Harve Horowitz, President
Kevin Horowitz, Senior Association Manager

Energy is an exclusive Federal Grant sponsored annual educational forum and exhibition.
1000+ Attendees
Frequency: Annual/August

6381 **Fall Technical and Marketing Conference**
Electrical Generating Systems Association
1650 S Dixie Highway
Suite 500
Boca Raton, FL 33432

561-750-5575; *Fax:* 561-395-8557;
www.egsa.org
Social Media: Facebook

Cara Clark, Director Conventions/Meetings
Bob Breese, Director of Education

Will focus on technical presentations and marketing efforts.
Frequency: Annual/September

6382 **IETA Annual Technical Conference**
International Electrical Testing Association
106 Stone Street
Morrison, CO 80465

303-697-8441
888-300-6382; *Fax:* 303-697-8431
neta@netaworld.org; www.netaworld.org
Social Media: Facebook, YouTube

Mose Ramieh, President
David Huffman, First VP
Ron Widup, Second VP
John White, Treasurer
Walter Cleary, Secretary

Targets the electrical testing industry.
Frequency: Annual/March

6383 **IFAC World Congress**
American Automatic Control Council
3640 Col Glenn Hwy
Dayton, OH 45435

937-775-5062; *Fax:* 937-775-3936
pmisra@cs.wright.edu; www.a2c2.org

R. Russell Reinehart, President
Tariq Samad, President-elect
Jordan Berg, Treasurer
B.Wayne Bequette, Secretary

You will have the opportunity to take part in the wide spectrum of categories for technical presentations, including plenary lectures, survey papers, regular papers of both lecture and poster session types, panel discussions and case studies.
Frequency: Annual/July

6384 **ILEA Annual Conference**
International League of Electrical Association
12165 West Center Road
Suite 59
Omaha, NE 68144

402-330-7227; *Fax:* 402-330-7283
info@ileaweb.org; www.ileaweb.org
Social Media: LinkedIn

Monique DeBoer, President
Chris Price, VP
Kirstie Steves, Secretary
Barbette Cejalvo, Treasurer

Provides a venue through which information and ideas exchanged and by encouraging all members to attend and share ideas.
Frequency: Annual/July

6385 **IMA Spring Meeting**
International Magnetics Association
8 S Michigan Avenue
Suite 1000
Chicago, IL 60603-3310

312-456-5590; *Fax:* 312-580-0165;
www.intl-magnetics.org

August Sisco, Chair
Lowell Bosleyeo, President
George Orenchak, Secretary/Treasurer

Promote the worldwide growth, development, and use of magnetic materials through: collection and dissemination of global trade statistics, publication of industry standards and user and industry education.
Frequency: Annual/May

6386 **IMAPS International Symposium on Microelectronics**
International Microelectronics & Packaging Society
611 2nd Street NE
Washington, DC 20002

202-548-4001
888-464-6277; *Fax:* 202-548-6115
imaps@imaps.org
http://www.imaps.org

Michael O'Donoghue, Executive Director
Ann Bell, Manager Marketing/Communications

Symposium for the microelectronics and electronics packaging industries. Features a powerful technical program, progressive professional development courses and many forums to share the latest developments in microelectronics. Comprehensive exhibition of materials and equipment for the industry.
3000 Attendees
Frequency: Annual/September

6387 **IMPI Annual Symposium**
International Microwave Power Institute
PO Box 1140
Mechanicsville, VA 23111

804-596-6667; *Fax:* 804-559-4087
info@impi.org; www.impi.org

Bob Schiffman, President
Ben Wilson, Vice President
Dorin Bolder, Secretary
Amy Lawson, Treasurer

Brings together researchers from across the globe to share the latest findings related to non-communications uses of microwave energy.
Frequency: Annual/June

6388 **IPC Printed Circuits Expo**
IPC: Association Connecting Electronics
3000 Lakeside Drive
Suite 309 S
Bannockburn, IL 60015

847-615-7100; *Fax:* 847-615-7105;
www.ipc.org
Social Media: Facebook, Twitter, LinkedIn, YouTube

Robert Ferguson, Chairman
Stephen Pudles, Vice Chairman
Don Schroeder, Secretary/Treasurer

Meet with everyone who designs, manufactures, and assembles printed circuit boards and electronics assemblies.
Frequency: Annual/February

6389 **ISA Expo**
ISA
67 Alexander Drive
Box 12277
Research Triangle Park, NC 27709

919-549-8411; *Fax:* 919-549-8288
info@isa.org; www.isa.org
Social Media: Facebook, Twitter, LinkedIn

Tracey Berrett-Noble, Event Manager
Rodney Jones, Conference Coordinator
Cyrus Taft, Program Chair
Dale Lee, Director Convention Services
Tracey Berrett, Manager Convention Services

Features the latest and most extensive products and services exhibition, a strategically relevant technical conference, and a prominent continuing education and training program. With practitioners from over 70 countries. Offers the most complete automation and control experience in today's marketplace.
15000 Attendees
Frequency: Annual/October

6390 **ISA Fugitive Emissions LDAR Symposium and Training**
Instrumentation, Systems, and Automation Society
67 Alexander Drive
Box 12277
Research Triangle Park, NC 27709

919-549-8411; *Fax:* 919-549-8288
info@isa.org; www.isa.org
Social Media: Facebook, Twitter, LinkedIn

Dale Lee, Director Convention Services
Tracey Berrett, Manager Convention Services

Covers topics including, but not limited to leak detection repair methods and fugitive emissions management systems. Industry experts in leak detection and repair will discuss implementations and improvements in LDAR programs in plant facilities.
Frequency: Annual/May

6391 **Innovation in Power Generation Measurement & Control Conference**
Instrumentation, Systems, and Automation Society
67 Alexander Drive
Box 12277
Research Triangle Park, NC 27709

919-549-8411; *Fax:* 919-549-8288
info@isa.org; www.isa.org
Social Media: Facebook, Twitter, LinkedIn

Denny Younie, Conference General Chair
Rodney Jones, Conference Coordinator
Cyrus Taft, Program Chair
Dale Lee, Director Convention Services
Tracey Berrett, Manager Convention Services

Dedicated to instrumentation and control in the fossil and nuclear power generation industry. This year's conference includes approximately 50 technical papers presented in 8 sessions over two and a half days, a vendor exhibition area, 5 training courses, several ISA committee meet-

ings, and the EPRI I&C Interest Group meeting and a Sunday evening welcome reception.
Frequency: Annual/June

6392 **International Conference and Exhibition on Device Packaging**
International Microelectronics & Packaging Society
611 2nd Street NE
Washington, DC 20002

202-548-4001
888-464-6277; *Fax:* 202-548-6115
imaps@imaps.org; www.imaps.org

Jim Drehle, President
Michael O'Donoghue, Executive Director
Steve Capp, Treasurer
Lawrence J Rexing, Secretary

Will provide a comprehensive technical program addressing the challenges of applications, and the latest developments in packaging for emerging devices, circuits, MEMS, sensors as well as materials and processes.
Frequency: Annual/March

6393 **International Congress Applications of Lasers and Electro-Optics**
Laser Institute of America
13501 Ingenuity Drive
Suite 128
Orlando, FL 32826-3204

407-380-1553
800-345-2737; *Fax:* 407-380-5588
icaleo@laserinstitute.org;
www.laserinstitute.org
Social Media: Facebook, Twitter, LinkedIn

Klaus Loeffler, President
Yongfeng Lu, President Elect
Stephen Capp, Treasurer
Robert Thomas, Secretary

Provides an international forum for the exchange of technical information between the people in the industrial, government and academic communities who apply laser/electro-optic technologies and the scientists, engineers and technicians engaged in developing these technologies. Accepts advertising.
5M Attendees
Frequency: Annual/October

6394 **International Instrumentation Symposium**
Instrumentation, Systems, and Automation Society
67 Alexander Drive
Box 12277
Research Triangle Park, NC 27709

919-549-8411; *Fax:* 919-549-8288
info@isa.org; www.isa.org
Social Media: Facebook, Twitter, LinkedIn

Denny Younie, Conference General Chair
Rodney Jones, Conference Coordinator
Cyrus Taft, Program Chair
Dale Lee, Director Convention Services
Tracey Berrett, Manager Convention Services

Provides an outstanding opportunity to gain valuable technical information and training in the traditional areas of measurements/sensors, instrumentation systems, data and advanced system/sensor technology as well as innovative papers in many other state of the art areas.
Frequency: Annual/May

6395 **International Laser Safety Conference**
Laser Institute of America
13501 Ingenuity Drive
Suite 128
Orlando, FL 32826

407-380-1553
800-345-2737; *Fax:* 407-380-5588
lia@laserinstitute.org; www.laserinstitute.org
Social Media: Facebook, Twitter, LinkedIn

Klaus Loeffler, President
Yongfeng Lu, President Elect
Stephen Capp, Treasurer
Robert Thomas, Secretary

A comprehensive four-day conference covering all aspects of laser safety practice and hazard control. Technical sessions and workshops will address developments in regulatory, mandatory and voluntary safety standards for laser products and laser use.
Frequency: Annual/March

6396 **International Symposium on Bioenergetics and Bioelectrochemistry**
Bioelectromagnetics Society
2412 Cobblestone Way
Frederick, MD 21702-3519

301-663-4252; *Fax:* 301-694-4948
office@bems.org; www.bems.org

David Black, President
Gloria Parsley, Executive Director
Richard Nuccitelli, VP
Phil Chadwick, Treasurer
Jonna Wilen, Secretary

Covers analytical chemistry.
Frequency: Annual/June

6397 **Joint Conference on Decision and Control & European Control Conference**
American Automatic Control Council
3640 Col Glenn Hwy
Dayton, OH 45435

937-775-5062; *Fax:* 937-775-3936
pmisra@cs.wright.edu; www.a2c2.org

R. Russell Reinehart, President
Tariq Samad, President-elect
Jordan Berg, Treasurer
B.Wayne Bequette, Secretary

Dedicated to the advancement of the theory and practice of systems and control. It brings together an international community of experts to discuss the state-of-the-art, new research results, perspectives of future developments, and innovative applications relevant to decision making, control, automation, and related areas.
Frequency: Annual/December

6398 **Laser Institute of America**
Laser Institute of America
13501 Ingenuity Drive
Suite 128
Orlando, FL 32826

407-380-1553; *Fax:* 407-380-5588
lia@lia.org; www.lia.org
Social Media: Facebook, Twitter, LinkedIn

Klaus Loeffler, President
Stephen Capp, Treasurer
Robert Thomas, Secretary

Devoted to the field of laser applications and laser safety in both medical and industrial fields.

6399 **Magnetism Conference: Institute of Electrical/Electronics Engineers**
Courtesy Associates
2000 L Street NW
Suite 710
Washington, DC 20036

202-331-2000; *Fax:* 202-331-0111;
www.magnetism.org

Paul Crowell, Chair
Yumi Ljiri, Treasurer
Brian Maranville, Publicity

Conference brings together scientists and engineers interested in recent developments in all branches of fundamental and applied magnetism. Emphasis is placed on experimental and theoretical research in magnetism, the properties and synthesis of new magnetic materials and advances in magnetic technology. Program consists of invited and contributed papers.
1.1M Attendees
Frequency: Annual/October

6400 **Meeting of the Electrochemical Society**
Appliance Manufacturer
65 South Main Street
Building D
Pennington, NJ 08534

609-737-1902; *Fax:* 609-737-2743
ecs@electrochem.org; www.electrochem.org

Christine Garzon, President
Tetsuya Osaka, Sr. VP
Harikila Deligianni, Secretary
Christina Bock, Treasurer

Has become the leading society for solid-state and electrochemical science and technology. ECS has 8000 scientists and engineers in over 75 countries worldwide who hold individual membership, as well as roughly 100 corporations and laboratories who hold corporate membership.
Frequency: Annual/May
Founded in: 1902

6401 **Mid-Atlantic Electrical Exposition**
S&L Productions
1916 Crain Highway S
Suite 16
Glen Burnie, MD 21061-5572

410-863-1180
888-532-3669; *Fax:* 410-863-1187

Triennial show and 150 exhibits with 200 booths of electrical supplies, hardware and services.
3000 Attendees
Frequency: Annual/October
Founded in: 2000

6402 **NAED Annual Meeting**
National Association of Electrical Distributors
1181 Corporate Lake Drive
St Louis, MO 63132

314-991-9000
888-791-2512; *Fax:* 314-991-3060
info@naed.org; www.naed.org
Social Media: Facebook, Twitter

Tom Naber, President and CEO
Michelle McNamara, Senior VP

The only event to bring the entire industry together in the same place at the same time. In addition to offering strong topical and informational programming, the NAED Annual Meeting provides distributors access to the top management of more than 225 electrical product suppliers.

6403 **NECA**
National Electrical Contractors Association
3 Bethesda Metro Center
Suite 1100
Bethesda, MD 20814

301-657-3110; *Fax:* 301-215-4500;
www.necanet.org
Social Media: Facebook, Twitter, LinkedIn, YouTube

Russell Alessi, President
John Grau, CEO
Dan Walter, VP and COO
Michael Thompson, Secretary/Treasurer

Brings the largest manufacturers, utilities, contractors, engineers, consultants, plant engineers, and distributors from all over North America and 31 foreign countries.
8000 Attendees
Frequency: Annual/September

6404 NEMA Annual Meeting
National Electrical Manufacturers Association
1300 North 17th Street
Suite 1752
Rosslyn, VA 22209

703-841-3200; *Fax:* 703-841-5900;
www.nema.org
Social Media: Facebook, Twitter, LinkedIn, You tube

Evan Gaddis, President

Provides a forum for the standardization of electrical equipment, enabling consumers to select from a range of safe, effective and compatible electrical products.
Frequency: Annual/November
Founded in: 1926

6405 NEMRA Annual Conference
Nat'l Electrical Mfgs Representatives Association
28 Deer Street
Suite 302
Portsmouth, NH 03801

914-524-8650
800-446-3672; *Fax:* 603-319-1667
nemra@nemra.org; www.nemra.org
Social Media: Twitter, LinkedIn

Mark Gibson, Chairman
Greg reynolds, Chairman Elect
Greg Baker, Secretary/Treasurer

Provides a forum for the standardization of electrical equipment, enabling consumers to select from a range of safe, effective, and compatible electrical products.
Frequency: Annual/March

6406 NORTHCON
Electronic Conventions
8110 Airport Boulevard
Los Angeles, CA 90045-3119

800-877-2668; *Fax:* 310-641-5117

Donna Ybarra, Show Manager

400 booths featuring exhibits of components and microelectronics instrumentation.
6057 Attendees
Frequency: Annual/October

6407 NOx Emissions & Source Monitoring Technical Conference and Training
Instrumentation, Systems, and Automation Society
67 Alexander Drive
Box 12277
Research Triangle Park, NC 27709

919-549-8411; *Fax:* 919-549-8288
info@isa.org; www.isa.org
Social Media: Facebook, Twitter, LinkedIn

Denny Younie, Conference General Chair
Rodney Jones, Conference Coordinator
Cyrus Taft, Program Chair
Dale Lee, Director Convention Services
Tracey Berrett, Manager Convention Services

Will present experiences with the measurement and control of low level NOx emissions, new concepts for NOx reduction techniques, and innovative monitoring systems. Presenters will participate in Q&A sessions, panel discussions, and be accessible throughout the two days to answer your questions.
Frequency: Annual/August

6408 NRECA's Annual Meeting
National Rural Electric Cooperative Association
4301 Wilson Boulevard
Suite 1
Arlington, VA 22203-1860

703-907-5500; *Fax:* 703-907-5514;
www.electric.coop

Glenn L English, CEO

The national service organization dedicated to representing the national interests of cooperative electric utilities and the consumers they serve. An advocate for consumer-owned cooperatives on energy and operational issues as well as rural community and economic development.
Frequency: Annual/February
Founded in: 1942

6409 NSCA Systems Integration Expo
National Systems Contractors Assocaition
3950 River Ridge Drive NE
Cedar Rapids, IA 52402

319-366-6722
800-446-6722; *Fax:* 319-366-4164
nsca@nsca.org; www.nsca.org
Social Media: Facebook, Twitter, LinkedIn, YouTube

Injolf de Jonh, President
Kelley McCarthy, Vice President
Michael Hester, Treasurer
Ron Bailey, Secretary

Dedicated to building connections between the people, knowledge and new ideas of the commercial electronic systems industry. A leading not-for-profit association representing the commercial electronic systems industry. A powerful advocate of all who work within the low-voltage industry, including systems contractors/integrators, product manufacturers, consultants, sales representatives, a growing number of architects, engineers and others. 600 exhibitors
11000 Attendees
Frequency: Annual/March

6410 National Electrical Equipment Show
Reed Exhibition Companies
255 Washington Street
Suite 275
Newton, MA 02458-1649

617-584-4900; *Fax:* 617-630-2222

Mike Rusbridge, Chairman/CEO

Serves the electrical and electronic industries.
7.5M Attendees
Frequency: Annual/March

6411 National Electrical Wire Processing Technology Expo
Expo Productions
510 Hartbrook Drive
Hartland, WI 53029

262-367-5500
800-367-5520; *Fax:* 262-367-9956
cheryl@epishows.com;
www.electricalwireshow.com
Social Media: Facebook

Cheryl L Luck, Sales Manager
Jay Partington, Show Manager

Only trade show tailored expressly to the electrical wire cable processing industry.
2000 Attendees
Frequency: Annual/May

6412 National Lighting Fair
Dallas Market Center
2100 N Stemmons Freeway
Suite 1000
Dallas, TX 75207-3009

214-556-6100; *Fax:* 214-655-6100
Charlie Sullivan, Executive Director
Cindy Morris, Chief Operating Officer

250 booths.
5M Attendees
Frequency: Annual/February

6413 National Professional Service Convention
National Electronics Service Dealers Association
3608 Pershing Avenue
Fort Worth, TX 76107

817-921-9061; *Fax:* 817-921-3741
npsc@nesda.com; www.nesda.com
Social Media: Facebook

PAtricia Bohon, Trade Show Manager

Annual show of 55 manufactures, suppliers and distributor of electronics, receivers, recorders, and supplies, software, telecommunications equipment, computers, videocassette recorders, parts and accessories, business forms, warranty companies and magazines/associations. Containing 100 booths and 70 exhibits.
950 Attendees
Frequency: Annual/July
Founded in: 1964

6414 Pacific International Conference on Applications of Lasers and Optics
Laser Institute of America
13501 Ingenuity Drive
Suite 128
Orlando, FL 32826

407-380-1553; *Fax:* 407-380-5588
lia@laserinstitute.org; www.laserinstitute.org
Social Media: Facebook, Twitter, LinkedIn

Milan Brandt, Conference General Chair

Will focus on growth and application of lasers and optics in the Pacific region.
Frequency: Annual/April

6415 Power-Gen International Trade Show
Electrical Generating Systems Association
1650 S Dixie Highway
Suite 500
Boca Raton, FL 33432

561-750-5575; *Fax:* 561-395-8557;
www.egsa.org

Cara Clark, Director Conventions/Meetings
Bob Breese, Director of Education

This is a special section of a larger show where we concentrate booths of firms that make, sell, and distribute on-site power products.
Frequency: Annual/December

6416 Product Safety and Liability Conference
National Electrical Manufacturers Association
1300 North 17th Street
Suite 1752
Rosslyn, VA 22209

703-841-3200; *Fax:* 703-841-5900;
www.nema.org
Social Media: Facebook, Twitter, LinkedIn, YouTube

Evan Gaddis, President
Tom Hixon, Vice President

Provides a forum for the standardization of electrical equipment, enabling consumers to select from a range of safe, effective and compatible electrical products.
Frequency: Annual/September

6417 Reliability and Maintenance Symposium
Consulting Services

1768 Lark Lane
Cherry Hill, NJ 08003-3215

856-428-2342; *Fax:* 856-616-9315
vrmonshaw@ieee.org; www.rams.org

V R Monshaw, Administrator
Raymond Sears, Treasurer
Patrick Dallosta, Secretary, Treasurer

The symposium offers the opportunity to explore and learn more about this and other related R&M subjects. 50 booths.
1M Attendees
Frequency: Annual/January

6418 Rocky Mountain Electronics Expo
Conference and Management Specialists
138 Garfield St
Denver, CO 80206-5517

303-568-8028; *Fax:* 303-799-0678

Karen Hone, Executive Director

Annual show and exhibits of products and services related to the hi-tech electronics industry.

6419 SESHA Annual Symposium
Semiconductor Environmental, Safety & Health Assn
1313 Dolly Madison Boulevard
Suite 402
McLean, VA 22101

703-790-1745; *Fax:* 703-790-2672
sesha@burkinc.com
seshaonline.org

John D Cox, President
Brett Burk, Co-Founder
Glenn Tom, Co-Founder

For individuals employed within the electronics and related high technology industries with an interest in environmental, health and safety issues.
1235 Attendees
Frequency: Annual/May
Founded in: 1978

6420 SMMA: Fall Technical Conference
SMMA: The Motor & Motion Association
PO Box P182
South Dartmouth, MA 02748

508-979-5935; *Fax:* 508-979-5845
info@smma.org; www.smma.org

Elizabeth B Chambers, Executive Director
William Chambers, Operations Director

Provide members and prospective members the opportunity to interact with industry colleagues. Attendees learn about industry trends and technologies, identify new supplier partners and network with other motor and drives professionals.
120 Attendees
Frequency: Annual/November

6421 SMMA: Spring Management Conference
SMMA: The Motor & Motion Association
PO Box P182
S Dartmouth, MA 02748

508-979-5935; *Fax:* 508-979-5845
info@smma.org; www.smma.org

Elizabeth B Chambers, Executive Director
William Chambers, Operations Director

Provide members and prospective members the opportunity to interact with industry colleagues. Attendees learn about industry trends and technologies, identify new supplier partners and network with other motor and drives professionals.
80 Attendees
Frequency: Annual/May

6422 SMTA International
Surface Mount Technology Association
5200 Wilson Road
Suite 215
Minneapolis, MN 55424

952-920-7682; *Fax:* 952-926-1819
joann@smta.org; www.smta.org

Dan Baldwin, President
Marie Cole, VP Technical Programs
Kola Akinade, Secretary
Hal Hendrickson, Treasurer

A network of professionals who build skills, share practical experience and develop solutions in electronics assembly technologies and related business operations.
1200 Attendees
Frequency: Annual/October

6423 SOUTHCON
Electronic Conventions
12340 Rosecrans Avenue
Suite 100
Manhattan Beach, CA 90266

310-524-4100
800-877-2668; *Fax:* 310-643-7328;
www.southcon.org

Donna Ybarra, Show Manager

Companies attending represent a major cross-section of the electronics industry including consumer, computer, medical, automotive and others. Offers conference sessions, in-depth technical sessions, product demonstrations and exhibits by vendors.
10M Attendees
Frequency: Annual/March

6424 TechAdvantage Conference
National Rural Electric Cooperative Association
4301 Wilson Boulevard
Suite 1
Arlington, VA 2203-1860

703-907-5500; *Fax:* 703-907-5514

Glenn L English, CEO

The only utility industry trade show exclusively for electric cooperative network management; engineering and operations; information services and technology; and purchasing employees.

6425 Upper Midwest Electrical Expo
North Central Electrical League
2901 Metro Drive
Suite 203
Bloomington, MN 55425

952-854-4405
800-925-4985; *Fax:* 952-854-7076
dale@ncel.org; www.ncel.org

Jeff Keljik, Chair
Chuck Healy, Vice Chair
Dan Paulson, Treasurer
Dale Yohnke, Secretary

Unites our electrical industry by providing vital industry commerce, educational discussion forums and offering various outlets for peer interaction. NCEL is the bridge between industry sectors and our electrical industry joins together to develop, expand and to protect all stakeholder interests in our Upper MIdwest Electrical Industry.
10213 Attendees
Frequency: Every 2 Years

6426 eastec Exposition
Society of Manufacturing Engineers
Deerborn, MI 48128

313-425-3000
800-763-4763; www.sme.org

500 booths of new technologies in equipment, materials and products used in the manufacture of semiconductors and flat panel displays.
8M Attendees
Frequency: Annual/October

Directories & Databases

6427 Buyer's Guide and Member Services Directory
Diesel & Gas Turbine Publications
1650 S Dixie Highway
Suite 500
Boca Raton, FL 33432

561-750-5575; *Fax:* 561-395-8557;
www.egsa.org

Donald M Ferreira, Director Publications
George Rowley, Director of Education

It is the ultimate gen-set industry buyer's guide, because the members are listed in one or more of 23 different product categories. Each member's listing also shows whether they sell, rent, and/or service equipment.
Cost: $6.00
Frequency: Annual

6428 Circuits Assembly: Buyers' Guide Issue
Miller Freeman Publications
600 Harrison Street
Suite 400
San Francisco, CA 94107-1391

Fax: 415-905-2239

Ron Daniels, Editor-in-Chief

List of suppliers of products and services to the surface mount industry; representatives and distributors.
Cost: $7.00
Frequency: Annual, November
Circulation: 40,500

6429 Compressor Tech Two
Diesel & Gas Turbine Publications
20855 Watertown Rd
Suite 220
Waukesha, WI 53186-1873

262-754-4100; *Fax:* 262-832-5075;
www.dieselspec.com

Michael Osenga, President
Phil Burnside, Editor-in-Chief
Brent Haight, Managing Editor
Kara Kane, Advertising Manager
Sheila Lizdas, Circulation Manager

Covers the operation, application and design of gas compression systems, as used in the gas gathering, transportation, storage, processing and related industries worldwide. Featured are new products, new technologies and interesting new applications related to gas compression systems and components.
Cost: $45.00
Frequency: 6 per year
Circulation: 13,000
Founded in: 1996

6430 Diesel Progress: International Edition
Diesel & Gas Turbine Publications
20855 Watertown Rd
Suite 220
Waukesha, WI 53186-1873

262-754-4100; *Fax:* 262-832-5075;
www.dieselspec.com

Michael Osenga, President
Michael J Brezonick, Editor-in-Chief
Katie Evans, Advertising Sales Manager

Covers the design of engine-powered equipment manufactured outside of North America. This includes various types of mobile on-and-off-highway equipment including construction, mining, forestry, agricultural and turf maintenance vehicles, trucks and buses; specialty vehicles; pleasure boats; and generator, pump and compressor set manufacturers. Editorial focus is on new

products and technology for these markets.
Cost: $40.00
Frequency: 6 per year
Circulation: 12,000
ISSN: 1091-3696
Founded in: 1981

6431 Diesel Progress: North American Edition
Diesel & Gas Turbine Publications
20855 Watertown Rd
Suite 220
Waukesha, WI 53186-1873

262-754-4100; *Fax:* 262-832-5075;
www.dieselspec.com

Michael Osenga, President
Patricia May, Advertising Sales Manager

Published for those concerned with the design, distribution and service of equipment powered by diesel, gasoline, or alternatively fueled engines. This includes all types of mobile on-and-off-highway equipment and stationary equipment. Markets covered include: construction, mining, forestry, agricultural and turf maintenance equipment; trucks and buses; pleasure boats; and generator, pump and compressor sets. Editorial focus is on new products and technology for these markets.
Cost: $75.00
Frequency: Monthly
Circulation: 30,000
ISSN: 1091-370X
Founded in: 1935

6432 Directory of Electrical Wholesale Distributors
Penton
249 W. 17th Street
New York, NY 10011

212-204-4200; www.penton.com

Sharon Reynolds, CEO

Features a full search and download capabilities, you can easily assess your current distributor network and look for new distributors for your products. Search by MSA market, location square footage, employee count and many other critical variables. The handy main house and branch cross-reference brings the ever-changing electrical distribution market into focus. Using the simple search functions, you can build and download highly targeted lists in just seconds.
Frequency: Cd-Rom

6433 EASA Yearbook
Electrical Apparatus Services Association
1331 Baur Boulevard
Saint Louis, MO 63131-1903

314-993-2220; *Fax:* 314-993-1269
easainfo@easa.com; www.easa.com

Kevin Toor, Chairman
William Gray, Vice Chairman
Kenneth Gralow, Secretary/Treasurer
Cost: $100.00
267 Pages
Mailing list available for rent

6434 Electrical Construction Materials Directory
Underwriters Laboratories
2600 N.W. Lake Rd
Camas, WA 98607

877-854-3577; *Fax:* 360-817-6278
cec@us.ul.com; www.UL.com

Keith E Williams, CEO
John Drengenberg, Manager Consumer Affairs

Offers information on companies that have qualified to use the UL listing mark or classification marking with products that have been found to be in compliance with UL regulations.
Cost: $40.00
912 Pages
Frequency: Annual
Printed in on glossy stock

6435 Electrical Distributor
National Association of Electrical Distributors
1181 Corporate Lake Drive
St. Louis, MO 63132

314-991-9000
888-791-2512; *Fax:* 314-991-3060
info@naed.org; www.naed.org

Robert Reynolds, Chair
Clarence Martin, Chair Elect

List of manufacturers and distributors of electrical components, supplies and equipment.
Cost: $295.00
Frequency: Biennial
Circulation: 3,500

6436 Electrical Equipment Representatives Association Membership Directory
Electrical Equipment Representatives Association
638 W 39th Street
Kansas City, MO 64111
816-561-5323
800-728-2272; *Fax:* 816-561-1249;
www.eera.org

Scott Whitehead, President
Vince Brown, President Elect
Brad Cahoon, Vice-President
Don Shirk, Secretary
Kier Cooper, Treasurer

More than 105 manufacturers representatives of electrical equipment companies.
Frequency: Annual, October
Founded in: 1948

6437 Engineers Relay Handbook
Relay and Switch Industry Association
2500 Wilson Boulevard
Arlington, VA 22201

703-907-8025; *Fax:* 703-875-8908
narm@ecaus.org; www.ec-central.org/RSIA

Dave Baicjaome, Chairman
Jeffrey Boyce, Director Business Development
Rodd Ruland, Director Business Development
Steve Lane, General Manager

In summary, special effort has been made by the editors to cover specification parameters in sufficient detail to provide systems and product design engineers with all the information they need to obtain the correct types of relays for their applications.
Cost: $60.00
Frequency: Annual

6438 Global Sourcing Guide
Diesel & Gas Turbine Publications
20855 Watertown Rd
Suite 220
Waukesha, WI 53186-1873

262-754-4100; *Fax:* 262-832-5075;
www.dieselspec.com

Michael Osenga, President
Michael J Mercer, Managing Editor
Kara Kane, Publication Manager
Christa Stern, Production Manager
Sheila Lizdas, Circulation Manager

The Global Sourcing Guide is one of the premier references and purchasing guides for the power systems and components industry. Covering products and systems used across the mobile and stationary engine-powered equipment industries, this guide incorporates information in a wide range of classifications.
Cost: $110.00
Frequency: Annual
Founded in: 1935

6439 High-Performance Composites Directory
Ray Publishing
PO Box 992
Morrison, CO 80465-0992

303-467-1776; *Fax:* 303-467-1777;
www.compositesworld.com

Judith Hazen, Publisher
Mike Mussleman, Managing Editor

The publisher of High-Performance Composites and Composites Technology magazines and well as the Sourcebook Industry directory and special design and application guides.
60 Pages
Founded in: 1993
Printed in 4 colors on glossy stock

6440 Indoor Electrical Safety Check Booklet
Electrical Safety Foundation International
1300 N 17th Street
Suite 1847
Rosslyn, VA 22209

703-413-3209; *Fax:* 703-841-3329
info@esfi.org; www.electrical-safety.org

Grant J Carter, Chair
David Tallman, Vice Chair
Michael Clendenin, Executive Director
Barbara R Guthrie, Secretary

Instructions on running an electrical safety audit of your home and at the same time learn about electrical inspections, circuit maps, power audits, and potential electrical hazards and safety tips from your circuit breaker or fuse panel to your outlets, power cords and extension cords, light bulbs, space heaters, ground fault circuit interrupters (GFCIs), arc fault circuit interrupters (AFCIs), batteries, and much more.

6441 NEMA Database
National Electrical Manufacturers Association
1300 17th St N
Suite 1752
Rosslyn, VA 22209-3806

703-841-3200; *Fax:* 703-841-5900;
www.nema.org

Evan R Gaddis, CEO
Tom Hixon, VP

This database offers time series on orders, shipments and unfilled orders for 6 major segments of the electrical manufacturing industry.

6442 National Electrical Manufacturers Representatives Association Locator
National Electrical Manufacturers Rep Assoc
28 Deer Street
Suite 302
Portsmouth, NH 03801

914-524-8650
800-446-3672; *Fax:* 603-319-1667
nemra@nemra.org; www.nemra.org

Michael Gorin, Chairman
Mark Gibson, Chair Elect
Greg Reynolds, Secretary/Treasurer

Approximately 1,000 electrical manufacturers representative companies.
Cost: $200.00
Frequency: Annual

6443 National Electronic Distributors Association Membership Directory
National Electronic Distributors Association

1111 Alderman Dr
Suite 400
Alpharetta, GA 30005-4175

678-393-9990; *Fax:* 678-393-9998;
www.nedassoc.org

Brian McNally, President
Michael Knight, President Elect
Robin Gray, Executive VP

Approximately 300 member distributors and 180 member manufacturers of electronics products, plus 1,100 branch offices.

6444 **On-Site Power Generation: A Reference Book**
Electrical Generating Systems Association
1650 S Dixie Hwy
Suite 400
Boca Raton, FL 33432-7461

561-750-5575; *Fax:* 561-395-8557;
www.egsa.org

Jalane Kellough, Executive Director
George Rowley, Director of Education

This book contains the most complete and up-to-date technical information covering on-site electrical power generation.
Cost: $95.00
600 Pages

6445 **Outdoor Electrical Safety Check Booklet**
Electrical Safety Foundation International
1300 N 17th Street
Suite 1847
Rosslyn, VA 22209

703-413-3209; *Fax:* 703-841-3329
info@esfi.org; www.electrical-safety.org

Grant J Carter, Chair
David Tallman, Vice Chair
Michael Clendenin, Executive Director
Barbara R Guthrie, Secretary

Use this handy booklet to learn about available electrical safety devices, and the safety rules related to hot tubs, spas and pools, extension cords, electrical lawn and garden products, battery operated products and power tool safety.

6446 **Product and Supplier Information**
Electrical Generating Systems Association
1650 S Dixie Hwy
Suite 400
Boca Raton, FL 33432-7461

561-750-5575; *Fax:* 561-395-8557;
www.egsa.org

Jalane Kellough, Executive Director
George Rowley, Director of Education

EGSA publishes a new Buyer's Guide and Member Services Directory listing every member.

6447 **SMMA: Directory**
SMMA: Small Motors & Motion Association
PO Box P182
S Dartmouth, MA 02748

508-979-5935; *Fax:* 508-979-5845
info@smma.org; www.smma.org

Elizabeth Chambers, Executive Director
William Chambers, Operations Director

Manufacturers, suppliers and users of fractional and subfractional horsepower electric motors.
Founded in: 1975

6448 **Transmission and Distribution: Specifiers and Buyers Guide Issue**
Penton
249 W. 17th Street
New York, NY 10011

212-204-4200
CorporateCustomerService@penton.com;
www.penton.com

Sharon Rowlands, CEO

List of manufacturers and distributors of equipment for electric power transmission and distribution.
Cost: $20.00
Frequency: Annual, September
Circulation: 49,000

6449 **Wholesale Source Directory of Electrical Products, Supplies & Accessories**
Sutton Family Communications & Publishing Company
155 Sutton Lane
Fordsville, KY 42343

270-740-0870
jlsutton@apex.net;
www.suttoncompliance.com

Theresa Sutton, Editor
Lee Sutton, General Manager

Listings include names, addresses, phone/fax numbers and product descriptions for wholesale distributors, importers, manufacturers, close-out houses and liquidators. Every item needed to become an electrical contractor, open an electrical store or sell this type of merchandise in a hardware store, flea market or other market. Daily updated laser printed copy. Price includes shipping and handling.
Cost: $57.20
100+ Pages
Founded in: 1977

Industry Web Sites

6450 **http://gold.greyhouse.com**
G.O.L.D Grey House OnLine Databases

Grey House Publishing's online database platform, GOLD, offers Quick Search, Keyword Search and Expert Search for most business sectors including electrical markets. The GOLD platform makes finding the information you need quick and easy - whether you're a novice searcher or an experienced database user. All of Grey House's directory products are available for subscription on the GOLD platform.

6451 **www.7ms.com**
Seven Mountains Scientific

Industry news in battery technology, marketing and industry events including new products, electric vehicles, R&D and environmental news.

6452 **www.ahtd.org**
Association for High Technology Distributors

Works to increase productivity and profitability of high technology automation solutions, providers and manufacturers.

6453 **www.bioelectromagnetics.org**
Bioelectromagnetics Society

International resource for excellence in scientific research, knowledge and understanding of the interaction of electromagnetic fields with biological systems. Members of the society are biological and physical scientists, physicians and engineers interested in the interactions of nonionizing radiation with biological systems.

6454 **www.construction.com**
McGraw-Hill Construction

McGraw-Hill Construction (MHC), part of The McGraw-Hill Companies, connects people and projects across the design and construction industry, serving owners, architects, engineers, general contractors, subcontractors, building product manufacturers, suppliers, dealers, distributors and adjacent markets.

6455 **www.csa-dc.org**
Contract Services Association of America

Represents the government services contracting industry in Washington, DC. Members range from small businesses to large corporations servicing federal and state government in numerous capacities. CSA acts to foster effective implementation of the government's policy of reliance on the private sector for support services.

6456 **www.eachicago.org**
Electric Association

Its purpose is to serve as the umbrella organization for the various electrical disciplines in the Chicagoland area.

6457 **www.easa.com**
Electrical Apparatus Service Association

An international trade organization of electromechanical sales and service firms in 58 countries. Provides members with a means of keeping up to date on materials, equipment, and state-of-the-art technology

6458 **www.ec-central.org/RSIA**
Relay and Switch Industry Association

The purpose and aims shall be to encourage the advancement of the art and science of making and using those switching devices generally known as relays; to promote and further interest of relay manufacturers consistent with the best interest of relay users; to create a spirit of mutual esteem, respect and recognition among members, and between the members and their customers and suppliers.

6459 **www.eei.org**
Edison Electric Institute

Advocates public policy, expands market opportunities and provides strategic business information for the shareholder-owned electric utility industry. Find out more about EEI's members, upcoming meetings, career opportunities and products and services.

6460 **www.eera.org**
Electrical Equipment Representatives Association

Sales agents for manufacturers of electrical equipment used by utilities. Mission is to advance the quality and increase effectiveness of manufacturer's representatives in the electrical equipment industry.

6461 **www.electric-find.com**
Electric Find

A directory/search engine for the electrical construction industry. Search results have been screened by electrical professionals.

6462 **www.electrochem.org**
Electrochemical Society

The society is an international nonprofit, educational organization concerned with phenomena relating to electrochemical and solid state science and technology. Members are individual scientists and engineers, as well as corporations and laboratories.

6463 **www.epri.com**
Electric Power Research Institute

Research relating to the production, transmission, distribution and utilization of electric power.

6464 **www.esda.org**
Electrostatic Discharge Association

Dedicated to advancing the theory and practice of electrostatic discharge avoidance.

6465 **www.ewh.ieee.org**
Instrumentation and Measurement Society

A subsidiary of the Institute of Electrical and Electronics Engineers. Provides support to scientists and technicians who design and develop electrical and electronic measuring instruments and equipment.

6466 **www.greyhouse.com**
Grey House Publishing

Authoritative reference directories for most business sectors incluidng electrical markets. Users can search the online databases with varied search criteria allowing for custom searches by product category, geographic area, sales volume, keyword, subject and more. Full Grey House catalog and online ordering also available.

6467 **www.icea.net**
Insulated Cable Engineers Association

Professional organization dedicated to developing cable standards for the electric power, control and telecommunications industries. Ensures safe, economical and efficient cable systems utilizing proven state-of-the-art materials and concepts. ICEA documents are of interest to cable manufacturers, architects and engineers, utility and manufacturing plant personnel, telecommunication engineers, consultants and OEMs.

6468 **www.imaps.org**
International Microelectronics & Packaging Society

Dedicated to the advancement and growth of the use of microelectronics and electronic packaging through public and professional education, dissemination of information by means of symposia, workshops and conferences and promotion of the Society's portfolio of technologies.

6469 **www.impi.org**
International Microwave Power Institute

IMPI's members include scientists, researchers, lab technicians, product developers, marketing managers and a variety of other professionals in the microwave industry. The Institute serves the information needs of all specialists working with dielectric (microwave and RF) heating sytems, and was expanded in 1977 to meet the information needs relating to consumer microwave ovens and related products.

6470 **www.ipc.org**
IPC:Association Connecting Electronics

Works to develop standards in circuit board assembly equipment. Brings together all players in the electronic interconnection industry, including designers, board manufacturers, assembly companies, suppliers and original equipment manufacturers. Offers workshops, conferences, meetings and online communications.

6471 **www.ncel.org**
North Central Electrical League

Trade association representing all segments of the electrical industry in the Upper Midwest.

6472 **www.necanet.org**
National Electrical Contractors Association

Represents a segment of the construction market comprised of over 70,000 electrical firms.

6473 **www.nerc.com**
North American Electric Reliability Council

Voluntary organization promoting bulk electric system reliability and security.

6474 **www.netaworld.org**
International Electrical Testing Association

Defines the standards by which electrical equipment is deemed safe and reliable. Creates specifications, procedures, testing and requirements for commissioning new equipment and testing the reliability and performance of existing equipment.

6475 **www.nsca.org**
National Systems Contractors Association

Not-for-profit association representing the commercial electronic systems industry. Serves as an advocate for all those who work within the low-voltage industry including systems contractors/integrators, product manufacturers, consultants, sales representatives and a growing number of architects, specifying engineers and others.

6476 **www.platts.com**
Electrical World

The latest trends in utility engineering and IT, equipment and services, best business practices and critical industry thinking. For managers, engineers and technicians who plan, design, build, maintain and upgrade electric T&D systems around the world.

6477 **www.psma.com**
Power Sources Manufacturers Association

Worldwide membership consists of manufacturers of power sources and conversion equipment. Nonprofit association strives to integrate the resources of the power sources industry to more effectively and profitably serve the needs of the power sources users, providers and PSMA members. Educates the electronics industry and others on the relevant applications for power sources and conversion devices.

6478 **www.semi.org**
Semiconductor Equipment & Materials International

Strengthens the performance of member companies through lobbying, promotion, education and statistical research.

6479 **www.seshaonline.org**
Semiconductor Environmental, Safety & Health Assn

Members are individuals employed within the electronics and related high technology industries with an interest in environmental, health and safety issues.

6480 **www.sia-online.org**
Semiconductor Industry Association

Trade association representing the US microchip industry.

6481 **www.smma.org**
SMMA: Small Motors & Motion Association

Trade association for the electric motor and motion control industry in Northern America. The voice of the motor and motion industry providing a forum for education, communication, research and networking.

6482 **www.smta.org**
Surface Mount Technology Association

A network of professionals building skills, sharing practical experience and developing solutions in electronic assembly technologies and related business operations.

6483 **www.sweets.construction.com**
McGraw Hill Construction

In depth product information that lets you find, compare, select, specify and make purchase decisions in the industrial product marketplace.

Associations

6484 **AG Electronic Association**
10 S Riverside Plaza
Suite 1220
Chicago, IL 60606-3710

312-321-1470; *Fax:* 312-321-1480
age@agelectronicsassn.org;
www.agelectronicsassn.org

Darrin Dollinger, Marketing Manager

Identifies, develops & or facilitates appropriate action aimed at furthering the compatibility & interchangeability of electronics and information systems used in agriculture.

6485 **AVS Science & Technology Society**
125 Maiden Ln
15th Floor
New York, NY 10038

212-248-0200; *Fax:* 212-248-0245
ricky@avs.org; www.avs.org
Social Media: Facebook, Twitter, LinkedIn

Ivan G. Petrov, President
Gregory J. Exarhos, Treasurer
Yvonne Towse, Managing Director
Joseph E Greene, Clerk/Secretary
Peter Burke, Financial Administrator

Supports all those involved with all aspects of science and technology through research, education, new products, publications and conferences.
5500 Members
Founded in: 1953

6486 **Aircraft Electronics Association**
3570 Ne Ralph Powell Rd
Lees Summit, MO 64064-2360

816-347-8400; *Fax:* 816-347-8405
info@aea.net; www.aea.net
Social Media: Facebook, Twitter, LinkedIn, Flickr, YouTube

Paula Derks, President
Debra McFarland, Executive Vice President
Mike Adamson, VP, Member Programs & Education
Linda Adams, VP, Member Services
Aaron Ward, Director of Information Services

AEA represents aviation businesses, including repair stations that specialize in maintenance, repair and installation of avionics and electronic systems in general aviation aircraft.
1250 Members
Founded in: 1957
Mailing list available for rent

6487 **American Electronics Association**
5201 Great America Parkway
Santa Clara, CA 95054

408-987-4200
800-284-4232; *Fax:* 408-987-4298;
www.aeanet.org

John V Harker, Chairman
William T Archey, President/CEO
Samuel J Block, VP/Controller
Tim Bennett, COO/EVP

Works to foster a healthy business climate by providing services, education and research programs.
3500 Members
Founded in: 1943

6488 **AmericanAssociationofElectronic Reporters and Transcribers**
P.O. Box 9826
Wilmington, DE 19809

302-765-3510
800-233-5306; *Fax:* 302-241-2177
sherry@aaert.org; www.aaert.org
Social Media: Facebook, Twitter, LinkedIn

Geoffrey Hunt, President
Steve Townsend, Vice President
Richard Russell, Treasurer
K.C. Corbin, Secretary
Michael F. Tannen, CSEP, Executive Director

A national professional association that deals with the electronic court reporting.

6489 **Armed Forces Communications and Electronics Association (AFCEA)**
4400 Fair Lakes Ct
Fairfax, VA 22033-3899

703-631-6100
800-336-4583; *Fax:* 703-631-6169;
www.afcea.org
Social Media: Facebook, Twitter, LinkedIn, Flickr, YouTube, Google+, Slid

LtGen Robert M. Shea, USMC (Ret.), President
LTG John R. Wood, USA (Ret.), Executive VP
Pat Miorin, CPA, EVP/CFO/Treasurer
James L. Griggs Jr., VP/CIO/CTO
Tina Jordan, VP, Region and Chapter Outreach

A non-profit membership association serving the military, government, industry, and academia as an ethical forum for advancing professional knowledge and relationships in the fields of communications, IT, intelligence, and global security.
30000 Members
Founded in: 1946

6490 **Association for Electronics Manufacturing**
1 SME Drive
PO Box 930
Dearborn, MI 48121

313-425-3000
800-733-4763; *Fax:* 313-425-3400
service@sme.org; www.sme.org
Social Media: Facebook, Twitter, LinkedIn, YouTube, Google+

Wayne F. Frost, CMfgE, President
Jeffrey M. Krause, Chief Executive Officer
Kathleen Borgula, Human Resources
Erica Ciupak, Information Technology
Debbie Clark, Governance

Represents the electrical manufacturers.
3.6M Members
Founded in: 1932

6491 **Electrical Apparatus Service Association**
1331 Baur Blvd.
St. Louis, MO 63132

314-993-2220; *Fax:* 314-993-1269
easainfo@easa.com; www.easa.com
Social Media: Facebook, Twitter, LinkedIn, YouTube

Linda J. Raynes, CAE, President & CEO
Anne Vogel, Executive Secretary
Richard Tutka, Finance Manager
Randy D. Joslin, Communications Manager
Tyler Voss, Membership Specialist

An international trade organization of more than 1,900 electromechanical sales and service firms in 62 countries that provides members with a meansof keeping up to date on materials, equipment, and state-of-the-art technology.

6492 **Electronic Components Industry Association**
1111 Alderman Drive
Suite 400
Alpharetta, GA 30005

678-393-9990; *Fax:* 678-393-9998
jwood@ecianow.org; www.ecianow.org
Social Media: Facebook, Twitter, LinkedIn, YouTube

Blair Haas, Chair
Ed Smith, Chair Elect
John Denslinger, President and CEO
Victor Meijers, VP, Marketing & Comm.
Barney Martin, VP, Industry Practices

Organization made up of electronic component manufacturers, their manufacturer representatives and authorized distributors that provides resources and opportunities for members to improve their business performance while enhancing the industry's overall capacity for growth and profitability.

6493 **Electronic Industries Alliance**
2500 Wilson Boulevard
Arlington, VA 22201-3834

703-907-7500; *Fax:* 703-907-7500;
www.eia.org

Ronald L Turner, Chairman
Mike Kennedy, Vice Chairman
Dave McCurdy, President/CEO
Neal McDonald, Senior Coordinator
James Shiring, Secretary/Treasurer

Trade organization representing the entire spectrum of manufacturers and consumer manufacturers involved in electronic products.
1.5M Members
Founded in: 1924

6494 **Electronic Security Association**
6333 North State Highway 161
Suite 350
Irving, TX 75038

972-807-6800
888-447-1689; *Fax:* 972-807-6883;
www.esaweb.org
Social Media: Facebook, Twitter, LinkedIn

Marshall Marinace, President
Dee Ann Harn, Vice President
Merlin Guilbeau, Executive Director
Jon Sargent, Secretary
Steve Paley, Treasurer

A nonprofit trade association that represents, promotes, and enhances the growth and professional development of the electronic life safety, security, and integrated sytems industry.
Founded in: 1948

6495 **Electronic Transactions Association**
1101 16th Street NW
Suite 402
Washington, DC 20036

202-828-2635
800-695-5509; *Fax:* 202-828-2639
meghan.cieslak@electran.org;
www.electran.org
Social Media: Facebook, LinkedIn, YouTube, Flickr

Debra Rossi, President
Jeff Rosenblatt, Treasurer
Mary Albert, Director of Regulatory Affairs
Jeff Sloan, Secretary
Grant Carlson, Government Affairs Coordinator

ETA is the international trade association serving the needs of organizations offering transaction processing products/services.
400M Members
Founded in: 1990

6496 **Electronics Representatives Association**
300 W Adams St
Suite 617
Chicago, IL 60606-5109
312-419-1432
800-776-7377; *Fax:* 312-419-1660
info@era.org; www.era.org
David Norris, President
Dan Parks, CPMR, Chairman
Chuck Tanzola, SVP, Fiscal & Legal
Provides services and benefits to electronic industry manufacturers and manufacturers' representatives.
Cost: $48.00
450 Members
Founded in: 1935

6497 **Electronics Technicians Association International**
5 Depot Street
Greencastle, IN 46135
765-653-8262
800-288-3824; *Fax:* 765-653-4287
eta@eta-i.org; www.eta-i.org
Social Media: Facebook, Twitter, LinkedIn, YouTube, Google+
Teresa Maher, CSS, President
Bryan Allen, CSM, CSS, Vice President
Richard Glass, CETsr, CEO Emeritus
Delores Andrews, Staff Support
Emily Hatfield, Research & Development
Association for electronic technicians worldwide offering over 70 certifications.
4500 Members
Founded in: 1978

6498 **ElectronicTransactionAssociation**
1101 16th Street NW
#402
Washington, DC 20036
202-828-2635
800-695-5509
meghan.cieslak@electran.org; www.electran.org
Social Media: Facebook, LinkedIn, YouTube, Flickr
Debra Rossi, President
Jeff Rosenblatt, Treasurer
Mary Albert, Director of Regulatory Affairs
Jeff Sloan, Secretary
Grant Carlson, Government Affairs Coordinator
International trade association for the payment processing industry.
Founded in: 1990

6499 **Federated Rural Electric**
77100 US Highway 71
PO Box 69
Jackson, MN 56143-0069
507-728-8366
800-321-3520; *Fax:* 507-728-8366
info@federatedrea.coop; www.federatedrea.coop
David A. Hansen, President
Dave Meschke, Vice-President
Darvin Voss, Secretary
Bruce Brockmann, Director
Glenn Dicks, Director
A distribution electric utility.
Founded in: 1935

6500 **IEEE Photonics Society**
445 Hoes Lane
Piscataway, NJ 08855-1331
732-562-3926; *Fax:* 732-562-8434
C.Jannuzzi@ieee.org; www.photonicssociety.org
Dalma Novak, President
Paul Juodawlkis, VP Membership
Catrina Coleman, VP Publications
Christopher Jannuzzi, Executive Director
Douglas Razzano, Associate Executive Director
A leading professional network of 7,000+ members that provide access to technical information.
Founded in: 1965

6501 **IEEE Power Electronics Society**
E-Mail: m.p.kelly@ieee.org; www.ieee-pels.org
Social Media: Twitter, LinkedIn
Philip Krein, History Chair
Michael P. Kelly, Executive Director
Donna Florek, Tech Community Program Specialist
Michael Markowycz, Tech Community Program Specialist
Jo-Ellen Snyder, Tech Community Program Specialist
A society of the Institute of Electrical and Electronics Engineers (IEEE) that focuses on the developmnet of power electronics technology.
7000 Members

6502 **IPC Association**
3000 Lakeside Drive
105 N
Bannockburn, IL 60015
847-615-7100; *Fax:* 847-615-7105
answers@ipc.org; www.ipc.org
Social Media: Facebook, Twitter, LinkedIn, YouTube, Google+, RSS
Marc Peo, Chairman
Joseph Joe O'Neil, Vice Chairman
John W. Mitchell, President/ CEO
Mikel H. Williams, Secretary/ Treasurer
Stephen Steve Pudles, Immediate Past Chairman
A trade association that standardizes the assembly and production requirements of electronic equipment and assemblies.

6503 **IPC: Association Connecting Electronics**
3000 Lakeside Drive
105 N
Bannockburn, IL 60015
847-615-7100; *Fax:* 847-615-7105
webmaster@ipc.org; www.ipc.org
Social Media: Facebook, Twitter, LinkedIn, YouTube, Google+, RSS
Marc Peo, Chairman
Joseph Joe O'Neil, Vice Chairman
John W. Mitchell, President/ CEO
Mikel H. Williams, Secretary/ Treasurer
Jennifer Sandahl, Controller
A trade association for the printed circuit boards and electronics assembly industries, offering programs and resources to board manufacturers and electronic assemblers, designers, industry suppliers and original equipment manufacturers.
2000 Members
Founded in: 1957

6504 **Independent Distributors of Electronics Association**
116 Helen Highway
#2900
Cleveland, GA 30528
714-670-0200; *Fax:* 714-670-0201
info@IDofEA.org; www.idofea.org
Social Media: Facebook, Twitter, LinkedIn
Paul Romano, President
Dan Ellsworth, Vice President
Homey Shoroogh, Secretary/ Treasurer
Brian Wilson, Executive Board member
Jason Jowers, Executive Board member
A global trade association comprised of organizations for independent distributors to find relevant information and to participate in advancing industry ethics, ensuring customer satisfaction, establishing standards, and promoting education.

6505 **Independent Electrical Contractors**
4401 Ford Avenue
Suite 1100
Alexandria, VA 22302
703-549-7351
800-456-4324; *Fax:* 703-549-7448
info@ieci.org; www.ieci.org
Social Media: Facebook, Twitter, LinkedIn, YouTube, Flickr, Instagram
Mark Gillespie, National President
Bruce Seilhammer, National Senior Vice President
Thayer Long, Executive Vice President/CEO
Vernice Howard, Chief Financial Officer
Bruna Patio, Staff Accountant
A national trade association for merit shop electrical and systems contractors.
Founded in: 1957

6506 **Instrumentation & Measurement Society**
www.ieee-ims.org
Social Media: Facebook, Twitter, LinkedIn
Reza Zoughi, President
Ruth A Dyer, Executive VP
Dario Petri, VP Finance
Alessandra Flammini, VP Conferences
Mark Yeary, VP Publications
A professional society of the IEEE whose field of interest is the science, technology, and application of instrumentation and measurement.

6507 **Instrumentation and Measurement Society**
799 N Beverly Glen
Los Angeles, CA 90077
310-446-8280; *Fax:* 732-981-0225
bob.myers@ieee.org; www.ewh.ieee.org
Robert Myers, Executive Director
Lee Myers, Assistant Director
Robert Rassa, President
Barry Oakes, VP Finance
A subsidiary of the Institute of Electrical and Electronics Engineers. Provides support to scientists and technicians who design and develop electrical and electronic measuring instruments and equipment.
6500+ Members
Founded in: 1950

6508 **International Electrical Testing Association**
3050 Old Centre Ave.
Suite 102
Portage, MI 49024

269-488-6382; *Fax:* 269-488-6383
mrichard@netaworld.org; www.netaworld.org
Social Media: Facebook, LinkedIn, YouTube

Dave Huffman, President
Ron Widup, 1st Vice President
Jim Cialdea, 2nd Vice President
Jayne Tanz, Executive Director
Melissa Richard, Finance and Business Manager

Establishes standards, publishes specifications, accredits independent, third-party, electrical testing companies, certifies test technicians, and promotes the services of association members.

6509 **International Federation of Air Traffic Safety Electronics Associations**
E-Mail: info@ifatsea.org; www.ifatsea.org

Daniel Boulet, President
Theodore Kiritsis, Vice-President

Federation represents the interests of air traffic safety electronics personnel.
50 Members
Founded in: 1972

6510 **International Microelectronics and Electronic Packaging**
611 2nd Street NE
Washington, DC 20002

202-548-4001
888-464-6277; *Fax:* 919-287-2339
imaps@imaps.org; www.imaps.org

Michael O'Donoghue, Executive Director
Jennifer Davis, Office Assistant
Brian Schieman, Director Information Technology
Ann Bell, Manager Marketing/Communications
Brianne Lamm, Membership & Events Manager

Promotes interaction among technologies of ceramics, thin and thick films, semiconductor packaging, surface mount technology, multichip modules, semiconductor devices and monolithic circuits. Dedicated to the advancement and growth of the use of microelectronics and electronic packaging through education. Disseminates information through symposia, workshops and conferences.
11000 Members
Founded in: 1967

6511 **International SEMATECH**
257 Fuller Road
Albany, NY 12203

518-437-8686; *Fax:* 512-356-3135
rcollier@sunypoly.edu; www.sunycnse.com

Alain Kaloyeros, Founding President/CEO
Walter Gerald Barber, President/Chief Admin Officer
Scott Bateman, CFO
Patricia Bucklin, Vice President for Administration
Richard Collier, Director for Student Affairs

A global consortium of leading semiconductor manufacturers who engage in cooperative precompetitive efforts to improve semiconductor manufacturing technology through the support of their members.
Founded in: 2004

6512 **International Society of Certified Electronic Technicians**
3000-A Landers St.,
Fort Worth, TX 76107-5642

817-921-9101
800-946-0201; *Fax:* 817-921-3741
info@iscet.org; www.iscet.org

Pete Founding PresidentCEO, President
Daniel Champion, Vice President
Mack Blakely, Executive Director
Rich Reid, Secretary
John Wilkins, Treasurer

Helps train, prepare, and test technicians in the electronics and appliance service industry.
Founded in: 1965

6513 **International Society of Certified Electronic Technicians**
3000-A Landers St.,
Fort Worth, TX 76107-5642

817-921-9101
800-946-0201; *Fax:* 817-921-3741
info@iscet.org; www.iscet.org

Pete Rattigan, President
Daniel Champion, Vice President
Mack Blakely, Executive Director
Rich Reid, Secretary
John Wilkins, Treasurer

Seeks to provide awareness of and services to certified electronics technicians. Provides educational materials in electronics training to schools, technical institutes and junior colleges. Offers certification programs for electronics technicians in associate and journeyman levels.
46000 Members
Founded in: 1965

6514 **Minerals, Metals & Materials Society**
184 Thorn Hill Road
Warrendale, PA 15086-7514
724-776-9000
800-759-4867; *Fax:* 724-776-3770
webmaster@tms.org; www.tms.org
Social Media: Facebook, LinkedIn, YouTube

James Robinson, Executive Director
Adrianne Carolla, Deputy Executive Director
Nancy Lesko, Executive & Board Administrator
Marleen Schrader, Accounting & HR Specialist
Paul Zappas, Information Technology Manager

Supports all those in the minerals, metals and materials industries with education, publications, trade shows and conferences.
Founded in: 1971

6515 **Mobile Electronics Retailers Association**
85 Flagship Drive
Suite F
North Andover, MA 1845
800-949-6372
info@merausa.org; www.merausa.org

Mike Anderson, Chairman
Chris Cook, President
Mike Bartells, Advisory Board
Tony Dehnke, Advisory Board
Joe Forcella, Advisory Board

Focuses on education and networking opportunities designed to advance the professionalism and profitability of the mobile electronics industry.
Founded in: 1992

6516 **National Electrical Manufacturers Association**
1300 North 17th Street
Suite 900
Arlington, VI 22209

703-841-3200; www.nema.org
Social Media: Facebook, Twitter, LinkedIn, YouTube, Google+, Instagram

Donald J. Hendler, Chairman
Maryrose Sylvester, Vice Chairman
Kevin J. Cosgriff, President
Donald R. Leavens, PhD., Vice President and Chief Economist
John Caskey, Assistant VP, Operations

Develops standards for the electrical manufacturing industry.
Founded in: 1926

6517 **National Electronic Distributors Association**
2211 South 47th Street
Suite 400
Phoenix, AZ 85034

678-393-9990
800-408-8353; *Fax:* 678-393-9998
customer.care@avnet.com
avnetexpress.avnet.com
Social Media: Facebook, Twitter, LinkedIn, YouTube

Ed Smith, President
Rick Hamada, CEO
Debbie Conyers, Director Marketing
Barney Martin, VP Industry Practices

Conducts research and offers educational programs for wholesale distributors of electronic components.
Founded in: 1921
Mailing list available for rent

6518 **National Electronics Service Dealers Association**
3608 Pershing Ave
Fort Worth, TX 76107-4527

817-921-9061
800-797-9197; *Fax:* 817-921-3741
info@nesda.com; www.nesda.com

Mack Blakely, Executive Director
Sheila Fredrickson, Dir Communications/Info Technology
Patricia Bohon, Membership & Trade Show Coordinator
James Keesler, Associate Editor/Graphic Designer
Margaret Vazquez, Bookkeeper/Administrative Assistant

A national trade association for professionals in the business of repairing consumer electronics equipment, appliances, and computers. NESDA has an e-mail group of members and manufacturers that communicate daily for information sharing. NESDA also has an annual convention and trade show.
600 Members
Founded in: 1950

6519 **National Marine Electronics Association**
692 Ritchie Highway
Suite 104
Severna Park, MD 21146

410-975-9425; *Fax:* 410-975-9450
info@nmea.org; www.nmea.org
Social Media: Facebook

Johnny Lindstrom, Chairman
Mike Spyros, Vice Chairman
Mark Reedenauer, President & Executive Director
Michael S. Quarders, Treasurer
Jules Rutstein, Secretary

Is the unifying force behind the entire marine electronics industry, bringing together all aspects of the industry for the betterment of all in our business.
400 Members
Founded in: 1957

6520 **National Rural Electric Cooperative Association**
4301 Wilson Blvd.
Arlington, VA 22203

703-907-5500; www.nreca.coop
Social Media: Facebook, Twitter, LinkedIn, YouTube

Jo Ann Emerson, Chief Executive Officer
Kirk Johnson, SVP of Government Relations
Peter Baxter, SVP
Marc Breslaw, Executive Director
Jeffrey Connor, Chief of Staff and COO

An organization that represents the interests of over 900 electric cooperatives in the United States to various legislatures.
Founded in: 1933

6521 **Optical Society of America**
2010 Massachusetts Ave Nw
Washington, DC 20036-1023

202-223-8130; *Fax:* 202-223-1096
info@osa.org; www.osa.org
Social Media: Facebook, Twitter, LinkedIn, YouTube

Philip Russell, President
Eric Mazur, Vice President
Elizabeth A. Rogan, Chief Executive Officer
Sean Bagshaw, COO/CIO
Tracy Schario, Chief External Relations Officer

The Optical Society of America (OSA) was organized to increase and diffuse the knowledge of optics, pure and applied; to promote the common interests of investigators of optical problems, of designers and of users of optical apparatus of all kinds; and to encourage cooperation among them. The purposes of the Society are scientific, technical and educational.
15000 Members
Founded in: 1916

6522 **Power Electronics Society**
799 N Beverly Glen
Los Angeles, CA 90077
310-446-8280; *Fax:* 310-446-8390
bob.myers@ieee.org; www.pels.org

Michael P. Kelly, Executive Director
Donna Florek, Program Specialist
Michael Markowycz, Program Specialist
Jo-Ellen Snyder, Tech Community Program Specialist
Grant Pitel, Volunteer PELS Webmaster

A subsidiary of the Institute of Electrical & Electronics Engineers. Supports professionals working in the field of power electronics technology.
5000 Members
Founded in: 1987

6523 **Power Sources Manufacturers Association**
PO Box 418
Mendham, NJ 07945-0418

973-543-9660; *Fax:* 973-543-6207
power@psma.com; www.psma.com
Social Media: LinkedIn

Ernie Parker, Chairman
Eric Persson, President
Stephen Oliver, VP
Michel Grenon, Secretary/ Treasurer

The PSMA is a not-for-profit organization incorporated in the state of California. The purpose of the Association shall be to enhance the stature and reputation of its members and their products, improve their knowledge of technological and other developments related to power sources, and to educate the entire electronics industry, plus academia, as well as government and industry agencies as to the importance of, and relevant applications for, all types of power sources and conversion devices.
155 Members
Founded in: 1985

6524 **SPIE**
1000 20th St.
Bellingham, WA 98225-6705

360-676-3290
888-504-8171; *Fax:* 360-647-1445
CustomerService@SPIE.org; www.spie.org
Social Media: Facebook, Twitter, LinkedIn, RSS, YouTube, Blogspot

Dr. H. Philip Stahl, President
Mr. William Arnold, Immediate Past President
Prof Toyohiko Yatagai, President Elect
Dr. Robert A Lieberman, Vice President
Brian Lula, Secretary/ Treasurer

A nonprofit international professional society for optics and photonics technology.
Founded in: 1955

6525 **Semiconductor Environmental, Safety & Health Association**
1313 Dolly Madison Boulevard
Suite 420
McLean, VA 22101

703-790-1745; *Fax:* 703-790-2672
sesha@burkinc.com; www.seshaonline.org

Hilary Matthews, President
Raymond McDaid, Secretary
Brian Sherin, Treasurer
Karl Albrecht, Secretary

Members are individuals employed within the electronics and related high technology industries with an interest in environmental, health and safety issues.
1500 Members
Founded in: 1978

6526 **Semiconductor Equipment and Materials International**
3081 Zanker Road
San Jose, CA 95134

408-943-6900; *Fax:* 408-428-9600
semihq@semi.org; www.semi.org

Yong Han Lee, Chairman
Tetsuo Tsuneishi, Vice Chairman
Denny McGuirk, President/CEO
Richard Salsman, CFO/VP, Operations
Peter Gillespie, Chief Marketing Officer

An international trade association representing firms supplying equipment, materials and services to the semiconductor industry. Strengthens the performance of members through promotion, lobbying, education and statistical research.
2300 Members
Founded in: 1970

6527 **Semiconductor Industry Association**
1101 K Street NW
Suite 450
Washington, CA 20005

202-446-1700
866-756-0715; *Fax:* 202-216-9745
mailbox@sia-online.org; www.sia-online.org

John Neuffer, President and CEO
Jimmy Goodrich, Vice President, Global Policy
Mike Williams, Chief Financial Officer
Joe Pasetti, Director, Government Affairs
Dan Rosso, Communications Manager

Trade association representing the US microchip industry. Provides a forum for working collectively to enhance the competitiveness of the US chip industry.
70 Members
Founded in: 1977

6528 **Society of Manufacturing Engineers**
1 SME Drive
PO Box 930
Dearborn, MI 48128

313-425-3000
800-733-4763; *Fax:* 313-425-3400
service@sme.org; www.sme.org
Social Media: Facebook, Twitter, LinkedIn, Google+, RSS

Wayne F. Frost, President
Jeffrey M. Krause, Chief Executive Officer
Kathleen Borgula, Human Resources
Erica Ciupak, Information Technology
Julie Duff, Finance

Supports all engineers in electronics manufacturing. Publishes quarterly newsletter.
70M Members
Founded in: 1932

6529 **Surface Mount Technology Association**
5200 Willson Rd
Suite 215
Minneapolis, MN 55424-1316

952-920-7682; *Fax:* 952-926-1819
joann@smta.org; www.smta.org
Social Media: Facebook, Twitter, LinkedIn

Bill Barthel, President
JoAnn Stromberg, Executive Administrator
Eileen Hibbler, VP Membership
Raiyomand Aspandiar, Ph.D., VP Technical Programs
Debbie Carboni, VP Expos

Network of professionals building skills, sharing practical experience and developing solutions in electronic assembly technologies and related business operations.
3200 Members
Founded in: 1984

6530 **Tobacco Vapor Electronic Cigarette Association**
1005 Union Center Dr.
Suite F
Alpharetta, GA 30004

888-998-8322
info@tveca.com; www.tveca.com
Social Media: Facebook, Twitter, LinkedIn, Google+

Ray Story, CEO
Keith Nelson, US Chief Political Officer
Thomas R. Kiklas, CFO
Chrissy Keheley, Secretary
Christopher Fowler, CTO/Web Development

A nonprofit organization dedicated to create a sensible and responsible electronic cigarette market by providing the media, legislative bodies, andconsumers with education, communication, and research.

6531 **Universal Association of Computer and Electronics Engineers**
42 Broadway
Suite 12-217
New York, NY 10004

212-901-3781; *Fax:* 212-901-3786
support@uacee.org; www.uacee.org

A registered nonprofit society to promote research.

6532 **Video Electronics Standards Association**
1754 Technology Dr.
Suite 238
San Jose, CA 95110

408-982-3850; *Fax:* 408-669-0976
moderator@vesa.org; www.vesa.org
Social Media: Twitter, YouTube

Alan Kobayashi, Chairman
Syed Athar Hussain, Vice Chairman
Richard Hubbard, Secretary/ Treasurer
Bill Lempesis, Executive Director
Joan White, Membership Services Manager

An international nonprofit corporation standards body for computer graphics.

6533 **Wheatland Rural Electric Association**
P. O. Box 1209
Wheatland, WY 82201

307-322-2125
800-344-3351; *Fax:* 307-322-5340;
www.wheatlandrea.com
Social Media: Facebook

Robert Brockman, President
Bill Teter, Vice-President
Britt Wilson, Secretary/ Treasurer
Sandra Hranchak, Director
Jack Finnerty, Director

Home power usage calculations, product and new service information,and youth scholarships.
Founded in: 1936

Newsletters

6534 **AEA Monthly News**
American Electronics Association
5201 Great America Parkway
Santa Clara, CA 95054

408-987-4200
800-284-4232; *Fax:* 408-987-4298;
www.aeanet.org

John V Harker, Chairman
William T Archey, President/CEO
Samuel J Block, VP/Controller
Tim Bennett, COO/EVP

AEA Advancing the Business of Technology, Access to Investors, State, Federal & International Lobbying, Insurance Services, Government Procurement, Business Networking, Foreign Market Access, Select Business Services, Executive Education.
Frequency: Monthly

6535 **AEA by the Bay**
American Electronics Association
5201 Great America Parkway
Santa Clara, CA 95054

408-987-4200
800-284-4232; *Fax:* 408-987-4298;
www.aeanet.org

John V Harker, Chairman
William T Archey, President/CEO
Samuel J Block, VP/Controller
Tim Bennett, COO/EVP

Newsletter for the AEA Bay Area Council.
Frequency: Monthly

6536 **AEA's Californica Monday Morning Report**
American Electronics Association
5201 Great America Parkway
Santa Clara, CA 95054

408-987-4200
800-284-4232; *Fax:* 408-987-4298;
www.aeanet.org

John V Harker, Chairman
William T Archey, President/CEO
Samuel J Block, VP/Controller
Tim Bennett, COO/EVP

A weekly report of what is going on in Californica policy relating to the high-tech industry, and how to change it.
Frequency: Weekly

6537 **American Electronics Association Impact**
American Electronics Association
5201 Great America Parkway
Santa Clara, CA 95054-1122

408-987-4200; *Fax:* 408-970-8565;
www.aeanet.org

William Archey, President

Representing the electronics software and information technology industries. Covers business and management issues for electronics executives.
Frequency: Monthly
Circulation: 25000
Founded in: 1945

6538 **Currents**
Electrical Apparatus Service Association
1331 Baur Blvd.
St. Louis, MO 63132

314-993-2220; *Fax:* 314-993-1269
easainfo@easa.com; www.easa.com
Social Media: Facebook, Twitter, LinkedIn

Linda J Raynes, President/CEO
Dale Shuter, Meetings/Expositions Manager

EASA is a trade association recognized internationally as the leader in the electrical and mechanical apparatus sales, service and repair industry.
Frequency: Monthly
Circulation: 2000+
Founded in: 1933

6539 **Electronic Advertising Marketplace Report**
Simba Information
PO Box 4234
Stamford, CT 06907-0234

203-258-8193; *Fax:* 203-358-5825
simbainfo@simbanet.com; www.simbanet.com

Linda Kopp, Editor
Donna Devall, Marketing Director
Joyce Brigish, Circulation Manager

Provides news, analysis and opinion for the emerging business of electronic advertising and shopping and commerce. Discover how publishers, telephone companies, distributors, and retailers are now using information technologies to build the information infrastructure that will reach new customers and match buyers with sellers. Covers electronic marketing, new electronic classified and transactional services, the role of the Internet, electronic yellow pages, etc.
Cost: $499.00
Frequency: BiWeekly

6540 **Electronic Education Report**
Simba Information
PO Box 4234
Stamford, CT 06907-0234

203-258-8193; *Fax:* 203-358-5825
simbainfo@simbanet.com; www.simbanet.com

Megan St. John, Manager
Patrick Quinn, Editor

Provides information on the multi-billion dollar market for electronic instructional materials. Includes company rankings, financial profiles, sales and distrbution trends, funding and adoptions, enrollement and demographics, trademark and copyright issues, strategic alliances and mergers.
Cost: $445.00
Frequency: BiWeekly

6541 **Electronic Imaging Report**
Phillips Publishing
7811 Montrose Road
Potomac, MD 20854

301-340-2100
feedback@healthydirections.com;
www.healthydirections.com

Written for top-level executives interested in learning how imaging technology can streamline their operations, cut their overhead costs and boost their competitiveness. Accepts advertising.
Cost: $397.00
9 Pages
Frequency: BiWeekly

6542 **Electronic Information Report**
Simba Information
PO Box 4234
Stamford, CT 06907-234

203-258-8193; *Fax:* 203-358-5825
simbainfo@simbanet.com; www.simbanet.com

Linda Kopp, Editor
Charlie Friscia, Marketing Director

The original information industry newsletter. Every week, this report monitors, analyzes, and reports on trends and developments in information services. It covers new storage and distribution media, databases, electronic publishing, value-added fax, online, multimedia and voice services. Readers will receive up-to-the-minute news written from a product, financial and marketing viewpoint.
Cost: $685.00
Frequency: 46 Issues Per Y
Founded in: 1989

6543 **Electronic Materials Technology News**
Business Communications Company
25 Van Zant Street
Suite 13
Norwalk, CT 06855-1713

203-853-4266; *Fax:* 203-853-0348
sales@bccresearch.com; www.bccresearch.com

Louis Naturman, President
Marc Favrean, Editor
Alan Hall, Editorial Director
Thomas Abraham, VP Research
Marc Favreau, VP Development

Reports on electronic materials and processes, patents, companies involved, trends and business opportunities.
Cost: $35.00
Founded in: 1971

6544 **Electronics Manufacturing Engineering**
Society of Manufacturing Engineers
1 SME Drive
PO Box 930
Dearborn, MI 48128

313-425-3000
800-733-4763; *Fax:* 313-425-3400
service@sme.org; www.sme.org

Mark Tomlinson, Executive Director/General Manager
Greg Sheremet, Publisher
Bob Harris, Director Finance

Covers various aspects of electronics manufacturing.
Cost: $60.00
8 Pages
Frequency: Quarterly
Circulation: 2147
Mailing list available for rent: 18190 names at $95 per M
Printed in 2 colors on matte stock

6545 **IEEE All-Society Periodicals Package(ASPP)**
Power Electronics Society
799 N Beverly Glen
Los Angeles, CA 90077

310-446-8280; *Fax:* 310-446-8390
bob.myers@ieee.org; www.pels.org

Jerry Hudgins, President
Robert Myers, Executive Director
Steven Leeb, Treasurer
Ronald Harley, VP Operations

Provides access to our core collection of engineering, electronics, and computer science periodicals.

6546 **ISCET Update**
Int'l Society of Certified Electronics Technicians
3608 Pershing Ave
Fort Worth, TX 76107-4527

817-921-9101
800-946-0201; *Fax:* 817-921-3741
info@iscet.org; www.iset.org

Ed Clingman, Administrator
Sheila Fred, Editor
Brian Gibbson, Circulation Manager

News and information for the electronics community.
Frequency: Monthly
Circulation: 1300

6547 **Integrated Circuit Manufacturing Synopsis**
Semiconductor Equipment & Materials International
3081 Zanker Road
San Jose, CA 95134

408-943-6900; *Fax:* 408-428-9600
semihq@semi.org; www.semi.org

Maggie Hershey, Manager
Anne Miller, Author
Victoria Hadfield, Executive VP/President, N America

An illustrated booklet that provides an excellent introduction to the semiconductor industry and makes a great handout for new employee orientation or as a resource for industry suppliers. It is easy to understand and free of technical terminology.
Cost: $15.75
35 Pages

6548 **Manufacturing Market Insider**
JBT Communications
PO Box 782
Needham Heights, MA 02494-0006

781-444-2154; *Fax:* 781-455-8409;
www.mfgmkt.com

John B Tuck, Publisher/Editor
Ann Connors, Circulation Manager

Specializes in contract manufacturing of electronics. Includes acquisitions, expansions, financial results and contract awards announced by contract manufacturers of electronics.
Cost: $420.00
8 Pages
Frequency: Monthly
ISSN: 1072-8651
Founded in: 1991
Printed in one color on matte stock

6549 **Military & Aerospace Electronics**
PennWell Publishing Company
98 Spit Brook Rd
Suite L1-1
Nashua, NH 03062-5737

603-891-0123; *Fax:* 603-891-9294
ATD@PennWell.com; www.pennwell.com

Christine Shaw, VP
Tobias Naegele, Editor

Engineering newspaper written exclusively for military-aeronautical electronic systems designers, buyers and project managers.
Cost: $10.00
Frequency: Monthly
Circulation: 48,100
Founded in: 1910

6550 **Optics & Photonics News (OPN)**
Optical Society of America
2010 Massachusetts Ave Nw
Washington, DC 20036-1023

202-223-8130; *Fax:* 202-223-1096
info@osa.org; www.osa.org

Elizabeth Rogan, Executive Director

Optics & Photonics/OPN is a monthly magazine that keeps members up to date on technical innovations, industry news, OSA activities and much more. OPN promotes the generation application, archiving and worldwide dissemination of knowledge in optics and photonics.
Frequency: Monthly
Circulation: 17000
Mailing list available for rent

6551 **SITE**
American Electronics Association
5201 Great America Parkway
Santa Clara, CA 95054

408-987-4200
800-284-4232; *Fax:* 408-987-4298;
www.aeanet.org

John V Harker, Chairman
William T Archey, President/CEO
Samuel J Block, VP/Controller
Tim Bennett, COO/EVP

Brings High-Tech HR professionals important information about compensation and benefits, employment law, relevant legislation, education and training.
Frequency: Bi-Monthly

6552 **SouthWest Technology Report**
Communications
PO Box 23899
Tempe, AZ 85285-3899

480-345-1118; *Fax:* 480-345-1119

Walter J Schuch, Publisher

Focused on business and technology news related to high tech and electronics companies and organizations based in the Southwestern United States.
Cost: $69.00
8 Pages
Frequency: Monthly
Printed in one color on matte stock

6553 **Technician Association News**
Electronic Technicians Association International
5 Depot St
Greencastle, IN 46135-8024

765-653-8262
800-288-3824; *Fax:* 765-653-4287
eta@eta-i.org; www.eta-i.org

Dick Glass, President
Brianna Pinson, Office Manager

A professional and trade journal servicing electronic technicians nationwide. Lists new certified electronics technicians, technical repair services, upcoming seminars and satellite training sessions.
Frequency: Monthly
ISSN: 1092-9592
Founded in: 1978
Printed in 2 colors

6554 **Technology News Today**
American Electronics Association
5201 Great America Parkway
Santa Clara, CA 95054

408-987-4200
800-284-4232; *Fax:* 408-987-4298;
www.aeanet.org

John V Harker, Chairman
William T Archey, President/CEO
Samuel J Block, VP/Controller
Tim Bennett, COO/EVP
Melissa La vigna, Contact

Aims to benefit investors with exclusive information on high-tech industry trends available only through AEA's extensive research, legislative monitoring and high-leveled networking capabilities.
Frequency: Quarterly

Magazines & Journals

6555 **Advancing Microelectronics**
ISHM-Microelectronics Society
611 2nd street NE
Washington Dc, DC 20002

202-548-4001
888-464-6277; *Fax:* 202-548-6115
imaps@imaps.org; www.imaps.org

For the Microelectronics Society.
Circulation: 4010

6556 **Applied Microwave & Wireless**
Noble Publishing Corporation
1334 Meridian Rd
Thomasville, GA 31792

229-377-0587; *Fax:* 229-377-0589;
www.noblepub.com

Joseph White, Publisher
Randy W Rhea, CEO

Edited for the RF and microwave professional.
Cost: $30.00
Frequency: Monthly
Circulation: 26287
ISSN: 1075-0207
Founded in: 1994

6557 **Avionics News Magazine**
Aircraft Electronics Association
3570 Ne Ralph Powell Rd
Lees Summit, MO 64064-2360

816-347-8400; *Fax:* 816-478-3100
info@aea.net; www.aea.net

Paula Derks, President
Tracy Lykins, Editor
Linda Adams, Managing Editor

This publication is the voice of the general aviation electronics industry. It is recognized as one of the leading publications for the latest information in avionics technology. Subscriptions are complimentary within North America, however, subscribers must be employed within the aviation industry to receive the magazine.
Cost: $132.00
Frequency: Monthly
Mailing list available for rent

6558 **Channel Magazine**
Semiconductor Equipment & Materials International

3081 Zanker Road
San Jose, CA 95134-4080

408-943-6900; *Fax:* 408-428-9600
semihq@semi.org; www.semi.org

Karen Savala, Publisher
Steve Buehler, Editor

A forum for equipment and material suppliers committed to the environment, health and safety as a Global Care member.
Founded in: 1970

6559 **Circuits Assembly**
Circuit Assembly
18 Thomas Street
Irvine, CA 92618-2777

949-855-7887; *Fax:* 949-855-4298
sales@circuitassembly.com;
www.circuitassembly.com

Laura Brown Sims, Associate Publisher

Devoted to the global electronics assembly industry.
Frequency: Monthly

6560 **CleanRooms Magazine**
PennWell Publishing Company
98 Spit Brook Rd
Nashua, NH 03062-5737

603-891-0123
800-225-0556; *Fax:* 603-891-9294
jhaystead@pennwell.com; www.pennwell.com

Christine Shaw, VP
Angela Godwin, Managing Editor
Heidi Barns, Circulation Manager
Lisa Bergevin, Marketing
James Enos, Publisher

Serves the contamination control and ultrapure materials and process industries. Written for readers in the microelectronics, pharmaceutical, biotech, health care, food processing and other user industries. Provides technology and business news and new product listings.
Frequency: Monthly
Circulation: 35031
Founded in: 1987

6561 **CommVerge**
Reed Business Information
2000 Clearwater Dr
Oak Brook, IL 60523-8809

630-574-0825; *Fax:* 630-288-8781;
www.reedbusiness.com

Jeff Greisch, President

The world leading publisher and information provider. Provides a range of communication and information channels, magazines, exhibitions, directories, online media, marketing services across five continents. Prestige brands in leading positions in key business sectors we deliver unrivalled access to business professionals across a diverse range of industries.

6562 **Computer Business Review**
ComputerWire
150 Post Street
#520
San Francisco, CA 94108-4707

415-274-8290; *Fax:* 415-274-8281;
www.computerwire.com/cbr

Tim Langford, Publisher

Company profiles, computer market coverage and technology trends and news for investors and professionals in the computer, communications and microelectronics industries.
Cost: $195.00
Frequency: Monthly
Circulation: 23M

6563 **Computer-Aided Engineering**
Penton Media
1300 E 9th St
Cleveland, OH 44114-1503

216-696-7000; *Fax:* 216-696-6662
caenetmaster@penton.com; www.penton.com

Jane Cooper, Marketing

Applications, news, trends and products for CAD/CAM technology as applied in manufacturing, electronics, architectural and construction industries.
Cost: $50.00
Frequency: Monthly
Circulation: 56,062

6564 **Control Solutions**
PennWell Publishing Company
1421 S Sheridan Rd
Tulsa, OK 74112-6619

918-831-9421
800-331-4463; *Fax:* 918-831-9476
headquarters@pennwell.com;
www.pennwell.com

Robert Biolchini, President
Ron Kuhfeld, Editor-in-Chief
Frequency: Monthly
Founded in: 1910

6565 **Dealerscope**
North American Publishing Company
1500 Spring Garden St
Suite 1200
Philadelphia, PA 19130-4094

215-238-5300
800-627-2689; *Fax:* 215-238-5342
webmaster@napco.com; www.napco.com

Ned S Borowsky, CEO
Rhoda Dixon, Circulation Manager
Eric Schwartz, President/Publishing Dir

Dedicated to delivering peer-based knowledge and experience, Dealerscope is the ultimate vehicle for presenting product and service solutions to the consumer.
Frequency: Monthly
Founded in: 1958

6566 **Digital America**
Consumer Technology Assocation (CTA)
1919 South Eads Street
Arlington, VA 22202

703-907-7600
866-858-1555; *Fax:* 703-907-7675
cta@cta.tech; www.cta.tech

Cindy Stevens, Senior Director, Publications
Gary Shapiro, President & CEO
David Hagan, Chairman
Mike Fasulo, Vice Chairman
Glenda MacMullin, Treasurer

Annual publication covering state of the industry analysis, including market research, data and analysis.
Cost: $995.00
Frequency: Annual
Circulation: 1000

6567 **ECN Magazine**
Reed Business Information
360 Park Ave S
4th Floor
New York, NY 10010-1737

646-746-6400; *Fax:* 646-756-7583
subsmail@reedbusiness.com;
www.reedbusiness.com

John Poulin, CEO
James Reed, Owner

Provides product solutions for design engineers in the electronics industry.
Circulation: 117923
Founded in: 1957

6568 **EDN Asia**
Reed Business Information
45 E 85th St
4th Floor
New York, NY 10028-0957

212-772-8300; *Fax:* 630-288-8686;
www.edn.com/

Lawrence S Reed
Mike Pan, Editor
Robin Peter Lange, Managing Editor
Raymond Wong, Publishing Director
Chen Wai Chun, Publisher

A source for all the design features, technology trends, design ideas, hands-on applications and product updates.
Frequency: Monthly
Circulation: 30000
Founded in: 1990

6569 **EDN China**
Reed Business Information
45 E 85th St
4th Floor
New York, NY 10028-0957

212-772-8300; *Fax:* 630-288-8686
john.dodge@reedbusiness.com;
www.reedbusiness.com

Lawrence S Reed
William Zhang, Publisher Director
John Mu, Executive Editor
Stephen D. Moylan, President

A source for design, development, & applications information foe electronics engineers & managers.
Frequency: Monthly
Circulation: 30018
Founded in: 1946

6570 **EDN Europe**
Reed Business Information
45 E 85th St
4th Floor
New York, NY 10028-0957

212-772-8300; *Fax:* 630-288-8686
gprophet@reedbusiness.com;
www.edninteractive.com

Lawrence S Reed
Martin Savery, Publisher
Graham Prophet, Editor

A focused product specific to, and unique in, its own region, that draws on a unique international network of editorial expertise. EDN serves design engineers, providing exactly the information they need to conceive and create tomorrow's electronic products.
Circulation: 35,024

6571 **EE Product News**
Penton Media
1300 E 9th St
Cleveland, OH 44114-1503

216-696-7000; *Fax:* 216-696-6662
information@penton.com; www.penton.com

Jane Cooper, Marketing
David B. Nussbaum, CEO

Source of information in new products necessary to successfully design, assemble and test prototypes of commerical, industrial, military and aerospace electronic products.
Frequency: Monthly
Circulation: 111968
Founded in: 1892

6572 **EE: Evaluation Engineering**
Nelson Publishing
2500 Tamiami Trl N
Nokomis, FL 34275-3476

941-966-9521
800-226-6113; *Fax:* 941-966-2590;
www.healthmgttech.com

A Verner Nelson, Owner
Michael Hughes, Sales

Magazine devoted exclusively to companies that test, evaluate, design and manufacture electronic products and equipment.
Cost: $43.00
84 Pages
Frequency: Monthly
Founded in: 1962
Mailing list available for rent: 65,000 names
Printed in 4 colors on glossy stock

6573 Electromagnetic News Report
Seven Mountains Scientific
913 Tressler Street
PO Box 650
Boalsburg, PA 16827

814-466-6559; *Fax:* 814-466-2777
enr@7ms.com; www.7ms.com

Josephine Chesworth, Managing Editor
E Thomas Chesworth, Technical Editor
Patrick D. Elliott, Production Manager

Offers industry news and technical articles of interest to readers as well as a calendar of events, product news and EMI publications.
Cost: $90.00
40 Pages
Circulation: 1000
ISSN: 0270-4935
Founded in: 1972
Printed in 4 colors on matte stock

6574 Electronic Business
Reed Business Information
5525 Sierra Rd
Building N
San Jose, CA 95132-3421

408-926-6340; *Fax:* 408-345-4400
subsmail@reedbusiness.com;
www.reedbusiness.com

Donald Reed, Owner
Kathleen Doler, Editor-in-Chief
James A Casella, CEO
Shahrokh Rad, Owner
Salina Le Bris, Corporate Communications/PR
Frequency: Monthly
Circulation: 65732
Founded in: 1975

6575 Electronic Components
Global Sources
7341 Washington Avenue
Suite C
Whittier, CA 90602

562-945-4612; *Fax:* 562-945-4192;
www.globalsources.com

Anna Maria Anguiano, Account Manager
Mark Sanderson, Publisher
Dan Katz, Managing Director
Cost: $75.00
Frequency: Monthly
Founded in: 1971

6576 Electronic Design
Penton Media
1300 E 9th St
Cleveland, OH 44114-1503

216-696-7000; *Fax:* 216-696-6662
information@penton.com; www.penton.com

Jane Cooper, Marketing
Mark David, Editor in Chief
Janet Connors, Marketing

Celebrating 50 years of innovation, this authoritative source provides leading-edge technical information to electronic and engineering managers around the world.
Frequency: Monthly
Circulation: 145000
Founded in: 1892

6577 Electronic Packaging & Production
Reed Business Information
1350 E Touhy Avenue
Des Plaines, IL 60018

630-320-7000; *Fax:* 630-288-8686;
www.reedbusiness.com

Vicky Steen, Publisher
Michael Sweeney, Editorial Director

Edited for engineers and managers who are involved in packaging designed, printed circuit board fabrication and assembly, and production testing of electronic circuits, systems, products and equipment.

6578 Electronic Products
Hearst Business Communications
645 Stewart Ave
Garden City, NY 11530-4769

516-227-1300; *Fax:* 516-227-1342
ralphr@electronicproducts.com;
www.elecprod2.com

Todd Christenson, Publisher
Gail Meyer, Production Manager
R Pell, Editor-in-Chief

News about developments in electronic components and equipment.
Frequency: Monthly
Circulation: 123767
Founded in: 1958
Mailing list available for rent: 123767 names
Printed in 4 colors on glossy stock

6579 Electronic Products Magazine

www.electronicproducts.com

Electronic products and product technology news from an engineering standpoint.

6580 Electronics Manufacturing Engineering
Society of Manufacturing Engineers
1 SME Drive
PO Box 930
Dearborn, MI 48128

313-425-3000
800-733-4763; *Fax:* 313-425-3400
service@sme.org; www.sme.org

Mark Tomlinson, Executive Director/General Manager
Greg Sheremet, Publisher
Bob Harris, Director Finance

For manufacturing engineers and managers involved with electronics manufacturing.
Circulation: 3,300

6581 High Density Interconnect
CMP Media
600 Community Drive
Manhasset, NY 11030

516-562-5000; *Fax:* 415-947-6090;
www.cmp.com

6582 High Tech News
Electronic Technicians Association International
5 Depot St
Greencastle, IN 46135-8024

765-653-8262
800-288-3824; *Fax:* 765-653-4287
eta@eta-i.org; www.eta-i.org
Social Media: Facebook, Twitter, LinkedIn

Teresa Maher, CSS, President
Chrissy Baker, Marketing Coordinator
Richard Glass, CETsr, CEO Emeritus

Exclusive bi-monthly publication of ETA International, and a subscription is included with each individual membership. Each issue features information on the changing electronics industry: specialty techniques & technology, trends, qualification opportunities and educational advice.
4500 Members
Frequency: Bi-Monthly
Circulation: 10000
Founded in: 1978

6583 IEEE Control Systems Magazine
IEEE Control Systems Society (CSS)
445 Hoes Lane
PO Box 1331
Piscataway, NJ 08854-1331

732-981-0060; *Fax:* 732-981-1721
society-info@ieee.org; www.ieee.org

Dennis S Bernstein, Editor
Susan Schneiderman, Business Development Manager

Focuses on applications of technical knowledge and concentrates on industrial implementations, design tools, technology review, control education and applied research. Geared towards readers with many different responsibilities including applied research, device design, product development and design including software and semiconductor components.
Cost: $210.00
Founded in: 1973
Mailing list available for rent

6584 Journal of Microelectronics & Electronic Packaging
International Microelectronics & Electronic Pack.
611 2nd Street NE
Washington, DC 20002

202-548-4001
888-464-6277; *Fax:* 202-548-6115
imaps@imaps.org; www.imaps.org

Fred D Barlow III PhD, Editor-in-Chief

6585 Journal of Microelectronics and Electronic Packaging
International Microelectronics & Electronics
611 2nd Street NE
Washington, DC 20002

202-548-4001
888-464-6277; *Fax:* 202-548-6115
impas@imaps.org; www.imaps.org

Michael O'Donoghue, Executive Director
Rick Mohn, Operations Manager
Brian Schieman, Director Information Technology
Ann Bell, Manager Marketing/Communications

Dedicated to publishing peer-reviewed papers in microelectronics, multichip module technologies, electronic packaging, electronic materials, surface mount and other related technologies, interconnections, RF and microwaves, wireless communications, manufacturing, design, test, and reliability.
Cost: $35.00

6586 Journal of Microwave Power and Electromagnetic Energy
International Microwave Power Institute
PO Box 1140
Mechanicsville, VA 23111-5007

804-559-6667; *Fax:* 804-559-4087
info@impi.org; www.impi.org
Social Media: Facebook, Twitter

Molly Poisant, Executive Director

The quarterly, technical journal of the Institute published by the Industrial, Scientific, Medical and Instrumentation (ISMI) section. Designed for the information needs of professionals specializing in the research and design of industrial and bio-medical applications, the Journal exemplifies the highest standards of scientific and technical information on the theory and application of electromagnetic power.
Cost: $250.00
Frequency: Quarterly

6587 Laser Focus World
PennWell Publishing Company

98 Spit Brook Rd
Nashua, NH 03062-5737

603-891-0123; *Fax:* 603-891-9294
allisono@pennwell.com; www.pennwell.com

Christine Shaw, Publisher
Carol Settino, Managing Editor

The world of optoelectronics.
Cost: $150.00
173 Pages
Frequency: Monthly
Circulation: 70004
Founded in: 1965
Printed in 4 colors on glossy stock

6588 **Modeling Power Devices and Model Validation**
Power Sources Manufacturers Association
PO Box 418
Mendham, NJ 07945-0418

973-543-9660; *Fax:* 973-543-6207
power@psma.com; www.psma.com

Dusty Becker, Chairman
Carl Blake, President
Jim Marinos, VP

This report consists of two parts, one devoted to modeling, and the other, model validation. The first article in the report reviews commonly used device models used in circuit simulations, and applies these to simulation designed power converters and rectifers. The second article establishes processes by which the features and accuracy of a model are determined by simulating the results of test circuits containing power devices and comparing these results with the results of actual measurements
Cost: $20.00
155 Members
Founded in: 1985

6589 **Optics Letters**
Optical Society of America
2010 Massachusetts Ave Nw
Washington, DC 20036-1023

202-223-8130; *Fax:* 202-223-1096
info@osa.org; www.osa.org

Elizabeth Rogan, Executive Director

Offers rapid dissemination of new results in all areas of optics with short, original, peer-reviewed communications. Optics Letters covers the latest research in optical science, including atmospheric optics, quantum electronics, Fourier optics, integrated optics, and fiber optics.
Frequency: 24 issues per year
ISSN: 0146-9592

6590 **Power Conversion & Intelligent Motion**
Primedia
Po Box 12901
Shawnee Mission, KS 66282-2901

913-341-1300; *Fax:* 913-514-6895;
www.penton.com

Eric Jacobson, Senior VP
Sam Davis, Editor

Directed to engineers, designers and manufacturers of power electronic and electronic motion control components, subsystems and systems. Feature articles interpret trends and innovation in these subjects.
Circulation: 31,113

6591 **Power Electronics Technology**
Penton Media, Inc
249 W 17th Street
New York, NY 10011

212-204-4200
bill.baumann@penton.com;
www.powerelectronics.com

Bill Baumann, Group Publisher
Sam Davis, Editor-in-Chief

Formerly PCIM Power Electronic Systems, delivers timely information to professionals in the power electronic industry.
Frequency: Monthly
Circulation: 36,000
Founded in: 1975

6592 **Printed Circuit Fabrication**
CMP Media
600 Community Drive
Manhasset, NY 11030

516-562-5000; *Fax:* 415-947-6090

6593 **ProService**
Int'l Society of Certified Electronics Technicians
3608 Pershing Ave
Fort Worth, TX 76107-4527

817-921-9101
800-946-0201; *Fax:* 817-921-3741
info@iscet.org; www.iset.org

Ed Clingman, Administrator
Shiela Fredrickson, Publisher

A bi-monthly magazine published by the International Society of Certified Electronics Technicians.
24 Pages
Founded in: 1965

6594 **ProService Magazine**
National Electronics Service Dealers Association
3608 Pershing Ave
Fort Worth, TX 76107-4527

817-921-9061
800-797-9197; *Fax:* 817-921-3741
webmaster@nesda.com; www.nesda.com

Brian Gibson, President
Don Cressin, VP
Mack Blakely, Executive Director
Fred Paradis, CSM, Treasurer
Wayne Markman, Secretary

For members of NESDA/ISCET, and a printed magazine is mailed to the membership address on file in April and August.
Frequency: Bi-Monthly

6595 **RTOHQ: The Magazine**
Association of Progressive Rental Merchandise
1540 Robinhood Trail
Austin, TX 78703-2624

512-794-0095
800-204-APRO; *Fax:* 512-794-0097
cferguson@rtohq.org; www.rtohq.org

Bill Keese, Executive Director
John C Cleek, President
Bill Kelly, Secretary
Frequency: Bi-Monthly
Circulation: 11000

6596 **Representor Magazine**
Electronics Representatives Association
300 W Adams St
Suite 617
Chicago, IL 60606-5109

312-527-3050
800-776-7377; *Fax:* 312-527-3783
info@era.org; www.era.org

Tom Shanahan, Executive VP
Bob Walsh, President

Devoted to fulfilling the management, informational, educational and communications needs of representatives and manufacturers in the electronics industry.
Cost: $15.00
450 Members
Frequency: Quarterly
Founded in: 1935

6597 **Review of the Electronic and Industrial Distribution Industries**
National Electronic Distributors Association
1111 Alderman Dr
Suite 400
Alpharetta, GA 30005-4175

678-393-9990; *Fax:* 678-393-9998
admin@nedassoc.org; www.nedassoc.org

Robin B Gray Jr, Executive VP
Debbie Conyers, Director Marketing
Barney Martin, VP Industry Practices

Contains academic articles on topics pertinent to our members' business. Leading electronic and industrial distribution academicians provides the content. Offers insightful articles aimed at improving industry practices. $12.00 per volume or $20.00 for an annual subscription.
Cost: $20.00
Frequency: Bi-Annually

6598 **SIGNAL Magazine**
Armed Forces Communications and Electronics Assn
4400 Fair Lakes Ct
Fairfax, VA 22033-3899

703-631-1397
800-336-4583; *Fax:* 703-631-4693;
www.afcea.org

Kent Schneider, President/CEO
Becky Nolan, Executive VP
John A Dubia, Executive VP

Is a international news magazine serving the critical information needs of government, military and industry professionals active in the fields of command, control, communications, computers, intelligence, surveillance and reconnaissance (C4ISR); information security; research and development; electronics; and homeland security.
Frequency: Monthly

6599 **Sensors Magazine**
Questex Media
275 Grove St
Suite 2-130
Auburndale, MA 02466-2275

617-219-8300
888-552-4346; *Fax:* 617-219-8310
jmcmahon@questex.com; www.questex.com

Kerry C Gumas, CEO
Stephanie Henkel, Executive Editor

Source among design and production engineers of information on sensor technologies and products, and topic integral to sensor-based systems and applications. Provides practical and in-depth yet accessible information on sensor operation, design, application, and implementation within systems. Covers the effective use of state-of-the-art resources and tools that enable readers to get the maximum benefit from their use of sensors.
Cost: $99.00
Frequency: Monthly
Circulation: 75000
Founded in: 1984

6600 **Tech Briefs**
Associated Business Publications International
1466 Broadway
Suite. 910
New York, NY 10036-7309

212-490-3999; *Fax:* 212-986-7864
alfredo@abpi.net; www.techbriefs.com

Dominic Mucchetti, CEO
Hugh Dowling, Circualtion Manager
Linda Bell, Chief Editor

Serves design engineers, managers and scientists in the industries of electronics, industrial equipment, computers, communications, bio-medical, transportation/automotive, power and energy,

materials, chemicals and many more related fields.
Cost: $75.00
Frequency: Monthly
Founded in: 1958

6601 Test & Measurement World
Reed Business Information
275 Washington St
Suite 275
Newton, MA 02458-1611

617-964-3030; *Fax:* 617-558-4470;
www.designnews.com

Rick Nelson, Chief Editor
Deborah M Sargent, Managing Editor
Russ Pratt, Publisher

The magazine on test, measurement and inspection in the electronics industry
Frequency: Monthly
Circulation: 65000
Founded in: 1981
Mailing list available for rent

6602 The Minerals, Metals & Materials Society/ Journal of Electronic Materials
Minerals, Metals & Materials Society
184 Thorn Hill Road
Warrendale, PA 15086-7528

724-776-9000
800-759-4867; *Fax:* 724-776-3770;
www.tms.org

Suzanne Mohney, Editor-In-Chief

Reports on the science and technology of electronic materials, while examining new applications for semiconductors, magnetic alloys, insulators, optical and display materials.
Cost: $131.00
11000 Members
Frequency: Monthly
Circulation: 1400
ISSN: 0361-5235
Founded in: 1957
Printed in 2 colors on glossy stock

6603 Wideband
Advanstar Communications
641 Lexington Ave
8th Floor
New York, NY 10022-4503

212-951-6600; *Fax:* 212-951-6793
info@advanstar.com; www.advanstar.com

Joseph Loggia, CEO

Covers accessories, equipment, services, products, and an anlysis of major market trends, industry news, statistics, new products, and personnel changes are featured in every issue.
Frequency: SemiMonthly
Circulation: 26,000

Trade Shows

6604 AEA Annual Convention & Trade Show
Aircraft Electronics Association
4217 S Hocker
Independence, MO 64055

816-373-6565; *Fax:* 816-478-3100
info@aea.net; www.aea.net

Paula Derks, President
Debra McFarland, VP
Tracy Lykins, Director Communications
Mark Gibson, Administration/Meeting Management

Annual show of 131 exhibitors of industry related equipment and supplies.
1500 Attendees
Frequency: Annual
Founded in: 1957

6605 AFCEA Sponsored Conferences/Symposia
Armed Forces Communications and Electronics Assn
4400 Fair Lakes Court
Fairfax, VA 22033-3899

703-631-6100
800-336-4583; *Fax:* 703-631-6405;
www.afcea.org

Kent Schneider, President/CEO
Becky Nolan, Executive VP
John A Dubia, Executive VP

Offers problem solving and networking opportunities through exhibits, technical panels, and featured speakers. Decision-makers from around the world attend AFCEA conferences for hands-on demonstrations, question-and-answer sessions and system solutions.

6606 AFCEA TechNet Asia-Pacific
Armed Forces Communications and Electronics Assn
4400 Fair Lakes Court
Fairfax, VA 22033-3899

703-631-6200
800-654-4220; *Fax:* 703-654-6931
technet@jspargo.com; www.afcea.org

Paul doCarmo, Assistant Director/Exhibit Sales
Connie Shaw, Exhibit Sales Account Manager

Military, government and industry communications and electronics professionals gather to see exhibits of communications and electronics equipment, supplies and services. Seminar, conference, dinner and luncheon. Co-sponsored by AFCEA International and AFCEA Hawaii.
2000 Attendees
Frequency: Nov 7-9
Founded in: 1985

6607 AFCEA TechNet International
Armed Forces Communications and Electronics Assn
4400 Fair Lakes Court
Fairfax, VA 22033-3899

703-631-6200
800-564-4220; *Fax:* 703-654-6931;
www.afcea.org

Paul doCarmo, Sales Manager
Connie Shaw, Sales Manager

This event draws commanders and staff from every branch of the military, including warfighting integration organizations charged with the most critical responsibilities of synthesizing military power on land, at sea, and in the air.
7500 Attendees
Frequency: June

6608 AFCEA/USNI West Conference & Exposition
Armed Forces Communications and Electronics Assn
4400 Fair Lakes Court
Fairfax, VA 22033

703-631-6200
800-564-4220; *Fax:* 703-654-6931
west@jspargo.org; www.afcea.org

Paul doCarmo, Assistant Direct/Exhibit Sales
Connie Shaw, Exhibit Sales Account Manager

Over 350 of the industry's most recognized defense and technology organizations showcase their technology products and services to top decision-makers from the US Pacific Fleet, Naval Station San Diego, Space & Warfare Command, Naval Base Coronado, Camp Pendleton Marine Corps Base and many other west coast military and government facilities.
6000 Attendees
Frequency: January
Founded in: 1980

6609 APRO Rent-To-Own Convention & Trade Show
1504 Robin Hood Trail
Austin, TX 78703

512-794-0095
800-204-APRO; *Fax:* 512-794-0097;
www.rtohq.org

Shannon Strunkec, President
John C Cleek, First VP
Jeannie Hutchison, Program Coordinator
Bill Keese, Manager

Seminar, reception and tours, plus 280 exhibits of products and services of interest to rent to own dealers: stereos, televisions, furniture, fabric protection and more.
1400 Attendees
Frequency: Annual

6610 ASM/TMS Spring Symposium
Minerals, Metals & Materials Society
184 Thorn Hill Road
Warrendale, PA 15086-7514

724-776-9000; *Fax:* 724-776-3770
foundation@tms.org; www.tms.org

Tresa Pollock, President
Brajendra Mishra, VP
Alexander Scott, Executive Director
John Parsey, Financial Planning Officer
Marc DeGraef, Director Information Technology

This symposium, organized by the local chapters of TMS and ASM, will focus on materials for extreme environments, with sessions on materials characterization in three dimensions, structural materials for high temperature, materials for space applications, and materials by design.
Frequency: May

6611 ATE and Instrumentation West
Miller Freeman Publications
600 Harrison Street
Suite 400
San Francisco, CA 94107-1391

415-905-2354; *Fax:* 415-905-2232

Steve Schulderfrei, Trade Show Director

Geared to the test and measurement of electronics.
5.8M Attendees
Frequency: January

6612 AVS Annual Symposium & Exhibition
AVS Science & Technology Society
125 Maiden Lane
15th Floor
New York, NY 10038

212-248-0200; *Fax:* 212-248-0245;
www.avs.org

Christie R Marrian, President
John Coburn, Treasurer
Joseph E Greene, Clerk/Secretary
Yvonne Towse, Executive Director

Promotes communication, dissemination of knowledge, recommended practices, research, and education in the use of vacuum and other controlled environments to develop new materials, process technology, devices, and related understanding of material properties for the betterment of humanity.
Frequency: Annual/February

6613 AVS International Symposium and Exhibition
AVS Science & Technology Society

120 Wall Street
32nd Floor
New York, NY 10005-3993

212-248-0200; *Fax:* 212-248-0245
angela@avs.org; www.avs.org

Christie R Marrian, President
John Coburn, Office Manager
Nancy Schultheis, Office Manager
Joseph E Greene, Clerk/Secretary
Yvonne Towse, Executive Director

This conference has been developed to address cutting edge issues associated with vacuum science and technology in both the research and manufacturing communities. The equipment exhibition is one of the largest in the world and provides an excellent opportunity to view the latest products and services offered by over 200 participating companies.
3000 Attendees

6614 All-Service Convention
Electronic Technicians Association International
5 Depot Street
Greencastle, IN 46135
765-653-4301
800-288-3824; *Fax:* 765-653-4287
eta@eta-i.org; www.eta-i.org

Teresa Maher, President
Chrissy Baker, Marketing Coordinator

Appliances and electronic service products and services. Third party administrators. Certification exams and study materials. Tools and test equipment. Containing 40 booths and 50 exhibits.

6615 Annual Legislative & Regulatory Roundtable
Electronic Industries Alliance
2500 Wilson Boulevard
Arlington, VA 22201-3834

703-907-7500
703-907-7500; www.eia.org

Gail Tannenbaum, CMP, Manager Meetings/Industry Relations
Frequency: Annual/August

6616 Asia Card Technology Exhibition
Reed Exhibition Companies
383 Main Avenue Suite 3
PO Box 6059
Norwalk, CT 06851

203-840-4800; *Fax:* 203-840-9628

Emily Hackett, Executive Director
Peter DiLeo, Marketing Director
Deborah Luongo, Conference Manager

Trade professionals see exhibits on computers and electronics.
Frequency: Annual

6617 Assembly Northeast Exhibition
Reed Exhibition Companies
383 Main Avenue Suite 3
PO Box 6059
Norwalk, CT 06851

203-840-4800; *Fax:* 203-840-9628

Emily Hackett, Executive Director
Peter DiLeo, Marketing Director
Deborah Luongo, Conference Manager
Gregg Vautrin, CEO

Assembly industry equipment, supplies and services for engineers and managers from electronic and automated assembly operations.
1365 Attendees
Frequency: Annual
Founded in: 1999

6618 Assembly Technology Exposition
Reed Exhibition Companies
383 Main Avenue Suite 3
PO Box 6059
Norwalk, CT 06851

203-840-4800
800-267-3796; *Fax:* 203-840-9686;
www.atexpo.com

Emily Hackett, Executive Director
Peter DiLeo, Marketing Director
Deborah Luongo, Conference Manager

525 exhibitors with robotics, vision systems, electronics and production machinery of interest to engineers and managers from automated assembly plants.
14000 Attendees
Frequency: Annual
Founded in: 1979

6619 Assembly West Exhibition
Reed Exhibition Companies
383 Main Avenue Suite 3
PO Box 6059
Norwalk, CT 06851

203-840-4800; *Fax:* 203-840-9628

Emily Hackett, Executive Director
Peter DiLeo, Marketing Director
Deborah Luongo, Conference Manager
Gregg Vautrin, CEO

Assembly industry equipment, supplies and services for engineers and managers from electronic and automated assembly operations.
3000 Attendees
Frequency: Annual

6620 Automated Manufacturing Exposition: New England
TEC
2001 Assembly Street
Suite 204
Columbia, SC 29201

803-779-7123; www.amexpo.com/newengland

Tony Smith, Founder
Rafael Pastor, Chairman/CEO
Richard Carr, President/Vice Chairman
Jerry Schneider, Chief Financial Officer

In addition to the exhibits, the conference will feature seminars that focus on topics such as continuous improvement and lean manufacturing.

6621 CEO Summit
Consumer Technology Association (CTA)
1919 S Eads Street
Arlington, VA 22202

703-907-7600
866-858-1555; *Fax:* 703-907-7675
cesreg@cta.tech; www.ces.tech

Gary Shapiro, President & CEO
David Hagan, Chairman

An invite-only event that presents a rare opportunity to network in a qualified, executive-only environment, to gather insight helpful to your business and to focus on the issues most critical to the industry.
Frequency: Annual

6622 CES Unveiled
Consumer Technology Association
1919 South Eads Street
Arlington, VA 22202

703-907-7600
866-858-1555; *Fax:* 703-907-7675
cta@cta.tech; www.cta.org

Gary Shapiro, President & CEO
David Hagan, Chairman

Held in major tech cities around the world, this event brings together industry experts, tech startups and electronics professionals for a chance to network with peers and showcase ideas.
Frequency: Annual

6623 CLEO/QELS Conference
Optical Society of America
2010 Massachusetts Avenue NW
Washington, DC 20036-1012

202-223-8130; *Fax:* 202-223-1096
info@osa.org; www.osa.org

Elizabeth A Rogan, Executive Director

Is a unique conference that gathers distringuished leaders to discuss the latest research in the fields of optics and photonics. The conference includes application-focused forums, educational sessions and an applications-oriented exhibit.
Frequency: May

6624 COM Conference of Metallurgists
Minerals, Metals & Materials Society
184 Thorn Hill Road
Warrendale, PA 15086-7514

724-776-9000; *Fax:* 724-776-3770
foundation@tms.org; www.tms.org

Tresa Polloc, President
Brajendra Mishra, VP
Alexander Scott, Executive Director
John Parsey, Financial Planning Officer
Marc DeGraef, Director Information Technology

Topic: Challenges for the Metals and Materials Industry. This conference will feature symposia on computational analysis in hydrometallurgy; nickel and cobalt; pipelines for the 21st century; materials degradation: innovation, inspection, control, and rehabilitation; light metals; fuel cell and hydrogen technologies; recruitment and early career development programs; and the treatment of gold ores.
Frequency: August

6625 CONNECTIONS - The Digital Living Conference and Showcase
Parks Associates
5310 Harvest Hill Road
Suite 235, Lock Box 162
Dallas, TX 75230-5805

972-490-1113
800-727-5711
info@parksassociates.com;
www.connectionsconference.com

Tricia Parks, Founder and CEO
Stuart Sikes, President
Farhan Abid, Research Analyst
Bill Ablondi, Director, Home Systems Research
John Barrett, Director of Research

This conference attracts over 500 executives focused on innovative consumer technology solutions. The unique conference and showcase highlights consumer and industry research from Parks Associates, showcases key players and new technologies, and delivers insight and recommendations for new business models and opportunities in digital media/content, mobile applications and services, connected consumer electronics, broadband and value-added services, and home systems.
Frequency: Annual
Founded in: 1986
Mailing list available for rent

6626 Ceramic Interconnect and Ceramic Microsystems
International Microelectronics & Electronics
611 2nd Street
Washington, DC 20002

202-548-4001
888-464-6277; *Fax:* 202-548-6115
imaps@imaps.org; www.imaps.org

Michael O'Donoghue, Executive Director
Rick Mohn, Operations Manager
Brian Schieman, Director Information

Technology
Ann Bell, Manager Marketing/Communications
Frequency: April

6627 **DistribuTech Conference**
PennWell Conferences and Exhibitions
350 Post Oak Blouevard
Suite 205
Houston, TX 77056
713-621-8833; *Fax:* 713-963-6284;
www.pennwell.com
Bob Biolchini, CEO
Is the leading automation and information technology conference and exhibition in the utility industry; and provides the best resources, tools and networking opportunities relating to electric utility automation and control systems, IT, T&D engineering, power and delivery equipment, and water utility technology.
3000 Attendees
Frequency: January

6628 **EASA Conference**
Electrical Apparatus Service Association
1331 Baur Boulevard
Saint Louis, MO 63132-1903
314-993-2220; *Fax:* 314-993-1269
easainfo@easa.com; www.easa.com
Social Media: Facebook, Twitter, LinkedIn
Linda J Raynes, President/CEO
Dale Shuter, Meetings/Expositions Manager
EASA is a trade association recognized internationally as the leader in the electrical and mechanical apparatus sales, service and repair industry.
2000+ Attendees
Frequency: Annual, June
Founded in: 1933

6629 **EIA's Congressional Technology Forum**
Electronic Industries Alliance
2500 Wilson Boulevard
Arlington, VA 22201-3834
703-907-7500; *Fax:* 703-907-7500;
www.eia.org
Gail Tannenbaum, CMP, Manager Meetings/Industry Relations
Frequency: October

6630 **EOS/ESD Symposium & Exhibits**
Electrostatic Discharge Association
7900 Turin Road
Building 3
Rome, NY 13440-2069
315-339-6937; *Fax:* 315-339-6793
info@esda.org; www.esda.org
Social Media: Facebook, LinkedIn
Donn Bellmore, President
Leo G. Henry, Sr. VP
Terry Welsher, VP
Lisa Pimpinella, Director of Operations
Donn Pritchard, Treasurer
International technical forum on electrical overstress and electrostatic discharge that features research, technology, and solutions to increase understanding, enhance quality and reliability, reduce and control costs, and improve yields and productivity.
2000+ Members
1M Attendees
Frequency: September
Founded in: 1982

6631 **ETA Annual Meeting and Expo**
Electronic Transactions Association
1101 16th Street NW
Suite 402
Washington, DC 20036
202-828-2635
800-695-5509; *Fax:* 202-828-2639;
www.electran.org
Jennifer Leo, Meetings Manager
Kurt Strawhecker, Managing Director
Steve Carnevale, Senior Vice President
Featuring valuable networking opportunities, outstanding speakers and educational seminars.
Frequency: April, Las Vegas

6632 **ETA Expo Network**
Electronic Transactions Association
1101 16th Street NW
Suite 402
Washington, DC 20036
202-828-2635
800-695-5509; *Fax:* 202-828-2639;
www.electran.org
Jennifer Leo, Meetings Manager
Kurt Strawhecker, Managing Director
Steve Carnevale, Senior Vice President
Offers conference events that focus specifically on delivering need to know education to ISOs and sales agents. ETA created these meetings to increase educational and business development opportunities for the industry. These affordable and easily accessible conferences are the ideal opportunity to increase your knowledge and meet new business partners.

6633 **East Coast Video Show**
Expocon Management Associates
363 Reef Road
PO Box 915
Fairfield, CT 06430-0915
203-882-1300; *Fax:* 203-256-4730
Diane Stone, Show Director
8000 Attendees

6634 **Electronic Distribution Show and Conference**
Electronic Distribution Show Corporation
222 S Riverside Plaza
Suite 2160
Chicago, IL 60606-6160
312-648-1140; *Fax:* 312-648-4282
eds@edsc.org; www.edsc.org
Gretchen Oie-Weghorst, Show Manager
Gretchen Oie, Manager
Annual conference and exhibits of 500 manufacturers of electronic components who sell through distribution. Containing 700 booiths and 500 exhibits.
10M Attendees
Frequency: May

6635 **Electronic Imaging East**
Miller Freeman Publications
600 Harrison Street
Suite 400
San Francisco, CA 94107-1391
415-905-2354; *Fax:* 415-905-2232
Stephen Schuldenfrei, Trade Show Director
300 booths consisting of electrical equipment and services.
5.3M Attendees
Frequency: October

6636 **Electronic Imaging West**
Miller Freeman Publications
600 Harrison Street
Suite 400
San Francisco, CA 94107-1391
415-905-2534; *Fax:* 415-905-2232
Stephen Schuldenfrei, Trade Show Director
Exhibits of equipment, supplies and services for the computer and electronics industries.
3M Attendees

6637 **Electronic Materials Conference**
Minerals, Metals & Materials Society
184 Thorn Hill Road
Warrendale, PA 15086-7514
724-776-9000; *Fax:* 724-776-3770
foundation@tms.org; www.tms.org
Tresa Pollock, President
Brajendra Mishra, VP
Alexander Scott, Executive Director
John Parsey, Financial Planning Officer
Marc DeGraef, Director Information Technology
This conference will provide a forum for topics of current interest and significance related to the preparation and characterization of electronic materials. Individuals actively engaged or interested in electronic materials research and development are encouraged to submit an abstract or attend the meeting. A technological exhibition will also be held.
Frequency: June

6638 **Electronic West: Annual Western Electrical Exposition Conference**
Continental Exhibitions
370 Lexington Avenue
Suite 1401
New York, NY 10017
212-370-5005; *Fax:* 212-370-5699
10000 Attendees

6639 **Embedded Systems Conference - West**
Miller Freeman Publications
600 Harrison Street
Suite 400
San Francisco, CA 94107
415-905-2354; *Fax:* 415-905-2220;
www.esconline.com
Lisa Ostrom, Electronics Show Director
Christian Fahlen, CEO
This is an ideal forum to learn relevant new skills, and about the latest technologies and products; to network with industry experts, vendors and your peers; and to discover an exhibits floor featuring leading companies showcasing cutting edge products.
13000 Attendees
Frequency: March

6640 **Executive Leadership Forum & Board of Governors Meeting**
Electronic Industries Alliance
2500 Wilson Boulevard
Arlington, VA 22201-3834
703-907-7500; *Fax:* 703-907-7500;
www.eia.org
Gail Tannenbaum, CMP, Manager Meetings/Industry Relations
Frequency: February, California

6641 **IMPI Annual Symposium**
International Microwave Power Institute
7076 Drinkard Way
PO Box 1140
Mechanicsville, VA 23111
804-596-6667; *Fax:* 804-559-4087
info@impi.org; www.impi.org
Social Media: Facebook, Twitter
Bob Schiffmann, President
Ben Wilson, VP
dorin Boldor, Secretary
Amy Lawson, Treasurer
Juan Aguilar, Editor in Chief
Brings together researchers from across the globe to share the latest findings related to non-communications uses of microwave energy.
Frequency: Annual/June

6642 **IS&T/SPIE's Electronic Imaging**
International Society for Optical Engineering
1000 20th Street
PO Box 10
Bellingham, WA 98227-0010
360-763-3290; *Fax:* 360-647-1445
meetinginfo@spie.org; www.spie.org
Electronic Imaging's top-notch technical program gathers the world's most prominent experts to discuss and push the forefront of imaging technology and it's applications.
1200 Attendees
Frequency: Annual/January

6643 **Industry Wide Service and Retail Convention**
Electronic Technicians Association International
5 Depot Street
Greencastle, IN 46135
765-653-4301
800-288-3824; *Fax:* 765-653-4287
eta@eta-i.org; www.eta-i.org
Teresa Maher, President
Brianna Pinson, Office Manager
Three groups united to offer the largest schedule of business management and technical seminars and trade show for educators, servicers and retailers. Thirty booths.
200 Attendees
Frequency: February

6644 **Innovate! and Celebrate**
Consumer Technology Association (CTA)
1919 South Eads Street
Arlington, VA 22202
703-907-7600
866-858-1555; *Fax:* 703-907-7675
cta@cta.tech; www.cta.org
Gary Shapiro, President & CEO
David Hagan, Chairman
Bringing together CTA members, industry thought leaders, and industry professionals for networking and learning opportunities.

6645 **International Conference on Trends in Welding Research**
Minerals, Metals & Materials Society
184 Thorn Hill Road
Warrendale, PA 15086-7514
724-776-9000; *Fax:* 724-776-3770
foundation@tms.org; www.tms.org
Tresa Pollock, President
Brajendra Mishra, VP
Alexander Scott, Executive Director
John Parsey, Financial Planning Officer
Marc DeGraef, Director Information Technology
This conference will feature five days of technically intensive programming focusing on both fundamental and applied topics related to welding and joining. Top researchers from industry, government, and academia will present the latest in experimental and modeling developments.
Frequency: May

6646 **International Symposium for Testing & Failure Analysis**
ASM International
9639 Kinsman Road
Materials Park, OH 44073
440-338-5151
800-336-5152; *Fax:* 440-338-4634
kim.schaefer@asminternational.org; www.asminternational.org
Kim Schaefer, Event Manager
Kelly Thomas, Exposition Account Manager
Annual event focusing on microelectronic and elcetronic device failure analysis, techniques, EOS/ESD testing and descretes aimed at failure analysis engineers and managers, technisians and new failure analysis engineers. 200 exhibitors.
1100 Attendees
Frequency: Annual/November

6647 **Materials, Science & Technology**
Minerals, Metals & Materials Society
184 Thorn Hill Road
Warrendale, PA 15086-7514
724-776-9000; *Fax:* 724-776-3770;
www.tms.org
Tresa Pollock, President
Brajendra Mishra, VP
Alexander Scott, Executive Director
John Parsey, Financial Planning Officer
Marc DeGraef, Director Information Technology
Offers a materials science and applied technology event unlike any other.
Frequency: September

6648 **NCSLI Workshop & Symposium**
NCSL
1800 30th Street
Suite 305 B
Boulder, CO 80301
303-440-3339; *Fax:* 303-440-3384
info@ncsli.org; www.ncsli.org
Harry J Moody, President
William T Pound, Executive Director
Will provide a forum to discuss the impact of these advances have had on metrology, as well as other related issues. Please join us as we reflect on how far and fast metrology has progressed over the past quarter of a century and to discuss its future needs and directions.
1200 Attendees
Frequency: August, Washington

6649 **NEDA Executive Conference**
National Electronic Distributors Association
1111 Alderman Drive
Suite 400
Alpharetta, GA 30005-4175
678-393-9990; *Fax:* 678-393-9998
admin@nedassoc.org; www.nedassoc.org
Francis Flynn Jr, President
Robin B Gray Jr, Executive VP
Debbie Conyers, Director Marketing
Barney Martin, VP Industry Practices
Frequency: November

6650 **NMEA Convention & Expo**
National Marine Electronics Association
Seven Riggs Avenue
Severna Park, MD 21146
410-975-9425; *Fax:* 410-975-9450
info@nmea.org; www.nmea.org
Mark Young, Chairman
Jules Rutstein, Vice Chairman
Beth Kahr, Executive Director
Michael Cerchiaro, Treasurer
Christopher Harley, Secretary
Frequency: October

6651 **NPSC Meeting**
National Electronics Service Dealers Association
3608 Pershing Avenue
Fort Worth, TX 76107-4527
817-921-9061
800-797-9197; *Fax:* 817-921-3741
webmaster@nesda.com; www.nesda.com
Brian Gibson, President
Don Cressin, VP
Mack Blakely, Executive Director
Fred Paradis, CSM, Treasurer
Wayne Markman, Secretary
Featuring Training, Sponsored Meal Events, Meetings, and Opportunities to Network with other service professionals as well as key service industry representatives.
Frequency: July

6652 **Northwest Electronics Technology Conference**
Electronic Conventions Management
8110 Airport Boulevard
Los Angeles, CA 90045-3119
310-215-3976
800-877-2668; *Fax:* 310-641-5117
northcon@ieee.org; www.nedme.com
James Lipman, PhD, Conference Director
Sue Kingston, Trade Show Manager
Offers a concentrated technical conference with complimenting exhibits. It provides a venue where those involved with the design, production and marketing of electronics-related products can converge in a real time, interactive atmosphere.
7000 Attendees
Frequency: May

6653 **OEMBoston**
Canon Communications
11444 W Olympic Boulevard
Suite 900
Los Angeles, CA 90064-1549
310-445-4200; *Fax:* 310-445-4299;
www.oemboston.com
William F Cobert, President/CEO
Diane O'Conner, Trade Show Director
Dan Cutrone, Show Marketing Director
The creation of two seperate shows, OEM Electronics and OEMed, the OEMBoston is accessible to thousands of electronics and medical OEMs, who can benefit from the combination of the two shows. The different product classification found at this show include Contract Manufacturing, Electronics Components, Component Fabrication, Production/Assembly Equipment, Packaging Equipment & Supplies, Tubing and more. Held at the Bayside Expo Center in Boston, Massachusetts.
1604 Attendees
Frequency: September

6654 **OFC/NFOEC Conference**
Optical Society of America
2010 Massachusetts Avenue NW
Washington, DC 20036-1012
202-223-8130; *Fax:* 202-223-1096
info@osa.org; www.osa.org
Elizabeth A Rogan, Executive Director
With more than 750 presentations focused on the industry's hottest topics, FTTx and ROADMs at the top of the list, the conference again established itself as the leading technical conference for optical communications. OFC/NFOEC is the show to present new product and corporate announcements.
15000 Attendees
Frequency: March
Founded in: 1916

6655 **OSA Technical Conference**
Optical Society of America
2010 Massachusetts Avenue NW
Washington, DC 20036-1012
202-223-8130; *Fax:* 202-223-1096
info@osa.org; www.osa.org
Elizabeth A Rogan, Executive Director
Connect with the most accomplished international scientists, researchers, engineers and business leaders as they shape the future of optics, photonics, and laser science.
Frequency: October

6656 **PhAST Conference**
Optical Society of America
2010 Massachusetts Avenue NW
Washington, DC 20036-1012

202-223-8130; *Fax:* 202-223-1096
info@osa.org; www.osa.org

Elizabeth A Rogan, Executive Director
Will feature previews of new application areas, access to industry innovators and discussions of the engineering ideas behind new products.
Frequency: May

6657 **SEMI Expo CIS**
Semiconductor Equipment & Materials International
3081 Zanker Road
San Jose, CA 95134

408-943-6900; *Fax:* 408-428-9600
semihq@semi.org; www.semi.org

Scott Smith, Public Relations Manager
Will highlight CIS as a region with huge potential and a new developing market for the world semiconductor equipment and materials manufacturers.
Frequency: September

6658 **SESHA Annual Symposium**
Semiconductor Environmental, Safety & Health Assn
1313 Dolly Madison Boulevard
Suite 402
McLean, VA 22101

703-790-1745; *Fax:* 703-790-2672
sesha@burkinc.com
seshaonline.org

Bernie First, President
Brett Burk, Co-Founder
Glenn Tom, Co-Founder
Brian Sherin, Treasurer
Karl Albrecht, Secretary
For individuals employed within the electronics and related high technology industries with an interest in environmental, health and safety issues.
1235 Attendees
Frequency: May
Founded in: 1978

6659 **SOUTHCON**
Electronic Conventions
12340 Rosecrans Avenue
Suite 100
Manhattan Beach, CA 90266

310-524-4100
800-877-2668; *Fax:* 310-643-7328;
www.southcon.org

Susan Kingston, Show Manager
Companies attending represent a major cross-section of the electronics industry including consumer, computer, medical, automotive and others. Offers conference sessions, in-depth technical sessions, product demonstrations and exhibits by vendors.
10M Attendees
Frequency: March

6660 **Semiconductor**
Semiconductor Equipment & Materials International
3081 Zankeer Road
San Jose, CA 95134

408-943-6900; *Fax:* 408-428-9600
semihq@semi.org; www.semi.org

Scott Smith, Public Relations Manager
The future of the European Semiconductor Industry.
Frequency: June

6661 **Service & Retail Convention**
Electronic Technicians Association International
5 Depot Street
Greencastle, IN 46135

765-653-4301
800-288-3824; *Fax:* 765-653-4287
eta@eta-i.org; www.eta-i.org

Teresa Maher, President
Brianna Pinson, Office Manager

6662 **Southeastern Technology Week**
TEC
2001 Assembly Street
Suite 204
Columbia, SC 29201

803-779-7123; *Fax:* 803-772-9964;
www.teconline.com

6663 **Strategic Leadership and Networking Forum**
Electronic Transactions Association
1101 16th Street NW
Suite 402
Washington, DC 20036

202-828-2635
800-695-5509; *Fax:* 202-828-2639;
www.electran.org

Jennifer Leo, Meetings Manager
Kurt Strawhecker, Managing Director
Steve Carnevale, Senior Vice President
A unique event designed to help executives thrive in the new payments industry. The Forum goes far beyond fundamental education to tackle the strategic, big-picture issues that today's payment executives and CEOs deal with each day. ETA takes a distinct approach to executive education and has adopted interactive formats conducive to peer-to-peer learning and business-to-business networking.

6664 **Strategic Materials Conference**
Semiconductor Equipment & Materials International
3081 Zanker Road
San Jose, CA 95134

408-943-7805; *Fax:* 408-428-9600;
www.semi.org

Anna Morais, Conference Contact
Hear about new business models, emerging players, green requirements and the the diverse partnerships in the semiconductor materials sector; the latest market trends, forecasts, best-practices, and discussions.
12000 Attendees
Frequency: May, Singapore

6665 **TABES Technical Business Exhibition & Symposium**
Huntsville Association of Technical Societies
3414 Governors Dr SW
PO Box 1964
Huntsville, AL 35805

256-882-1234; *Fax:* 205-837-4275;
www.hats.org/society

J Tardy, Manager
John Young, Treasurer
Brings new business into the community.
10000 Attendees
Founded in: 1969

6666 **Tech Advantage Exposition**
National Rural Electric Cooperative Association
4301 Wilson Blouevard
Arlington, VA 22203

703-907-5500; *Fax:* 703-907-5528;
www.nreca.org

Gary Pfann, Conference Contact
Barbara Christiana, Expo Contact
11000 Attendees

6667 **Technology & Standards Forum**
Consumer Technology Association (CTA)
1919 S Eads Street
Arlington, VA 22202

703-907-7600
866-858-1555; *Fax:* 703-907-7675
cta@cta.tech; www.cta.tech

Gary Shapiro, President & CEO
David Hagan, Chairman
Focus on development of emerging industry standard, contribute your company's viewpoint, and gain networking opportunities. Take advantage of valuable opportunities to interface with industry technical leaders as they consider, develop, and finalize, crucial CE standards.

6668 **Winter Break**
Consumer Technology Association (CTA)
1919 South Eads Street
Arlington, VA 22202
703-907-7600
866-858-1555; *Fax:* 703-907-7675
cta@cta.tech; www.cta.tech

Gary Shapiro, President & CEO
David Hagan, Chairman
Attendees can focus on the development of emerging industry standards, contribute their company's viewpoints, and gain networking opportunities. Interface with industry technical leaders as they consider, develop, and finalize crucial CE standards.

6669 **westec Exposition**
Society of Manufacturing Engineers
One SME Drive
Dearborn, MI 48121

313-425-3000
800-733-4763; *Fax:* 408-428-9600
service@sme.org; www.sme.org

Ana Christiansen, Exposition Marketing
Leslie Schade, Exhibitor Services
The West Coast's definitive manufacturing event, showcasing crucial breakthroughs in machine tools, production methods, materials and management strategies. More than 450 exhibitors.
1500 Attendees
Frequency: Annual

Directories & Databases

6670 **Antenna Book**
Electronic Technicians Association International
5 Depot St
Greencastle, IN 46135-8024

765-653-8262
800-288-3824; *Fax:* 765-653-4287
eta@eta-i.org; www.eta-i.org

Dick Glass, President
Brianna Pinson, Office Manager
Written by professional technicians who have worked closely with antennas, this two book series is the ultimate study guide for technicians seeking certification through ETA-I's Video Distribution, Certified Satellite Installer and TVRO programs. It can also serve as study materials for electronics classes, employee training, or as a quick reference guide your whole shop can use

Includes shipping & handling.
Cost: $33.00
ISBN: 1-891749-14-5
Printed in on matte stock

6671 **Battery Report**
Power Sources Manufacturers Association
PO Box 418
Mendham, NJ 07945-0418
973-543-9660; *Fax:* 973-543-6207
power@psma.com; www.psma.com
Dusty Becker, Chairman
Carl Blake, President
Jim Marinos, VP
Is a comprehensive report describing the state-of-the-art, current problems and R&D needs for numerous battery systems. The report also includes battery global market trends, status of electric/hybrid vehicle battery development and UN requirements for shipping lithium.
Cost: $125.00
155 Members
Founded in: 1985

6672 **ERA Rep Locator**
Electronics Representatives Association
444 N Michigan Avenue
Suite 1960
Chicago, IL 60611
312-527-3050
800-776-7377; *Fax:* 312-527-3783
info@era.org; www.era.org
Mark Motsinger, Chairman
Dave Rossi, Vice Chairman
Mike Kunz, President
Raymond J Hall, EVP/CEO
William R Warfield, Director Finance/Operations
Manufacturers match your products and territories with qualified, professional representatievs firms. The Locator lists ERA member companies with informtion on size of firm, territories covered, type of products represented and customer bases.
Cost: $90.00
Frequency: Annually

6673 **Electronic Buyers News: Specialized and Local/Regional Directory**
CMP Publications
600 Community Dr
Manhasset, NY 11030-3810
516-562-5000; *Fax:* 516-562-5123
Hailey McKeefry, Editor
List of about 325 distributors of electronic products and supplies operating on less than national scale, or offering only one or a few produst nationwide.

6674 **Electronic Buyers News: Top 50 Distributors Issue**
CMP Publications
600 Community Dr
Manhasset, NY 11030-3810
516-562-5000; *Fax:* 516-562-5123
David Gabel, Editor
List of electronic distributors ranked by annual gross sales.

6675 **Electronic Distribution Directory**
Electronic Distribution Show Corporation
222 S Riverside Plz
Suite 2160
Chicago, IL 60606-6112
312-648-1140; *Fax:* 312-648-4282
eds@edsc.org; www.edsconnects.com
Gretchen Oie, Manager

6676 **Electronic Industries Association: Trade Directory and Membership List**
Electronic Industries Alliance
2500 Wilson Boulevard
Arlington, VA 22201-3834
703-907-7500; *Fax:* 703-907-7501;
www.eia.org
Dave McCurdy, President/CEO
Charles L Robinson, Chief Operating Officer
More than 1,200 member companies in the electronic manufacturing industry.
Frequency: Annual

6677 **Electronic Materials & Process Handbook**
International Microelectronics & Electronics
611 2nd Street NE
Washington, DC 20002
202-548-4001
888-464-6277; *Fax:* 202-548-6115
imaps@imaps.org; www.imaps.org
Charles A Harper, Editor
Ronald M Sampson, Editor
Offers guidance on insulations, conductors, and semiconductor materials, defines critical manufacturing parameters, and shows how these parameters can be combined to create successful electronic devices.
Cost: $80.00
ISBN: 0-070542-99-6

6678 **Electronic Representatives Directory**
Harris Publishing Company
360 B Street
Idaho Falls, ID 83402-1938
208-524-4217; *Fax:* 208-522-5241
customerservice@harrispublishing.com;
www.harrispublishing.com
Directory of services and supplies to the industry.
Cost: $25.00
320 Pages
Frequency: Annual
Circulation: 7,500

6679 **Electronics Manufacturers Directory on Diskette**
Harris InfoSource International
2057 E Aurora Rd
Twinsburg, OH 44087-1938
330-425-4481
800-888-5900; *Fax:* 330-487-5368;
www.harrisinfo.com
David Wilkof, VP
Diskette. Covers approximately 1,000,000 manufacturers of electronic equipment and products.
Cost: $329.00
Frequency: Annual

6680 **North American Directory of Contract Electronic Manufacturers**
Miller Freeman Publications
600 Harrison Street
Suite 400
San Francisco, CA 94107-1391
Fax: 415-905-2239; www.cassembly.com
Kimberly Cassidy, Editor
Over 1,350 electronics manufacturers facilities in the United States, Canada, and Mexico.
Cost: $295.00
Frequency: Annual

6681 **ProService Directory and Yearbook**
National Electronics Service Dealers Association
3608 Pershing Ave
Fort Worth, TX 76107-4527
817-921-9061
800-797-9197; *Fax:* 817-921-3741
webmaster@nesda.com; www.nesda.com
Clyde Nabors, Publisher
Wallace Harrison, Editor
Mary Margaret Merill, Production Manager
The yearbook is an annual resource listing for servicers. This directory is sent each January to current members.
Frequency: Annual

6682 **Product Source Guide for Electronic Devices**
Reed Business Information
275 Washington St
Newton, MA 02458-1611
617-964-3030; *Fax:* 617-558-4470
sales@eb-mag.com; www.designnews.com
Donald Swanson, Editor
List of over 4,000 manufacturers and suppliers of equipment and materials used in the production, testing, and packaging of electronic devices and systems.
Cost: $25.00
Frequency: Annual

6683 **Source Book**
Armed Forces Communications and Electronics Assn
4400 Fair Lakes Ct
Suite 100
Fairfax, VA 22033-3899
703-631-1397
800-336-4583; *Fax:* 703-631-4693;
www.afcea.org
Kent Schneider, President/CEO
Becky Nolan, Executive VP
John A Dubia, Executive VP
The Source Book published in the January issue, contains the company profiles and contacts of AFCEA's corporate members. It is the who's who of C$ISR and homeland secuity organizations. The annual Security Directory, published in the February issue, focuses on security solutions and the organizations that provide them.
31000 Members
Founded in: 1946

6684 **Who's Who in Electronics Buyer's Guide**
Harris Publishing Company
360 B Street
Idaho Falls, ID 83402-1938
208-524-4217; *Fax:* 208-522-5241
customerservice@harrispublishing.com;
www.harrispublishing.com
A list of over 15,000 manufacturers and distributors of electronics products in five regional volumes.
Cost: $65.00
Frequency: Annual
Circulation: 60,000

Industry Web Sites

6685 **http://gold.greyhouse.com**
G.O.L.D Grey House OnLine Databases
Grey House Publishing's online database platform, GOLD, offers Quick Search, Keyword Search and Expert Search for most business sectors including electronics markets. The GOLD platform makes finding the information you need quick and easy - whether you're a novice searcher or an experienced database user. All of Grey House's directory products are available for subscription on the GOLD platform.

6686 www.afcea.org
Armed Forces Communications and Electronics Assn
An association that represents the professional communications, electronics, intelligence and information systems community.

6687 www.aprovision.org
Association of Progressive Rental Organizations
Members include television, appliance and furniture dealers who rent merchandise with an option to purchase.

6688 www.cta.tech
Consumer Technology Association (CTA)

6689 www.era.org
Electronics Representatives Association
Provides services and benefits to electronic industry manufacturers representatives.

6690 www.eta-i.org
Electronic Technicians Association International
A worldwide professional association founded by electronics technicians and servicing dealers.

6691 www.ewh.ieee.org
Instrumentation and Measurement Society
A subsidiary of the Institute of Electrical and Electronics Engineers. Provides support to scientists and technicians who design and develop electrical and electronic measuring instruments and equipment.

6692 www.greyhouse.com
Grey House Publishing
Authoritative reference directories for most business sectors including electronic markets. Users can search the online databases with varied search criteria allowing for custom searches by product category, geographic area, sales volume, keyword, subject and more. Full Grey House catalog and online ordering also available.

6693 www.imaps.org
International Microelectronics & Packaging Society
Dedicated to the advancement and growth of the use of microelectronics and electronic packaging through public and professional education, dissemination of information by means of symposia, workshops and conferences and promotion of the Society's portfolio of technologies.

6694 www.ipc.org
IPC-Association Connecting Electronics Industries
Works to develop standards in circuit board assembly equipment. Brings together all players in the electronic interconnection industry, including designers, board manufacturers, assembly companies, suppliers and original equipment manufacturers. Offers workshops, conferences, meetings and online communications.

6695 www.iscet.org
Int'l Society of Certified Electronics Technicians
Designed to measure the degree of theoretical knowledge and technical proficiency of practicing technicians.

6696 www.nesda.com
National Electronics Service Dealers Association
A national trade association for professionals in the business repairing consumer electronics equipment, appliances, and computers. NESDA has an e-mail group of over 600 members and manufacturers that communicate daily for information sharing. NESDA also has an annual convention and trade show.

6697 www.nmea.org
National Marine Electronics Association
The unifying force behind the entire marine electronics industry, bringing together all aspects of the industry for the betterment of all in the business.

6698 www.psma.com
Power Sources Manufacturers Association
Worldwide membership consists of manufacturers of power sources and conversion equipment. Nonprofit association strives to integrate the resources of the power sources industry to more effectively and profitably serve the needs of the power sources users, providers and PSMA members. Educates the electronics industry and others on the relevant applications for power sources and conversion devices.

6699 www.semi.org
Semiconductor Equipment & Materials International
Strengthens the performance of member companies through lobbying, promotion, education and statistical research.

6700 www.seshaonline.org
Semiconductor Environmental, Safety & Health Assn
Members are individuals employed within the electronics and related high technology industries with an interest in environmental, health and safety issues.

6701 www.sia-online.org
Semiconductor Industry Association
Trade association representing the US microchip industry.

6702 www.sme.org
Society of Manufacturing Engineers
Represents the electrical manufacturers.

6703 www.smta.org
Surface Mount Technology Association
A network of professionals building skills, sharing practical experience and developing solutions in electronic assembly technologies and related business operations.

Associations

6704 ASM International/Materials Information Society
9639 Kinsman Rd
Materials Park, OH 44073-0002
440-338-5151
800-336-5152; *Fax:* 440-338-4634
memberservicecenter@asminternational.org; www.asminternational.org
Social Media: Facebook, Twitter, LinkedIn
Dr. Sunniva R. Collins, FASM, President
Jon D. Tirpak, P.E., FASM, Vice-President
Craig D. Clauser, P.E., Treasurer
Managing Director, Terry F. Mosier
The society for materials engineers and scientists, a worldwide network dedicated to advancing industry, technology and applications of metals and materials.
35000 Members
Founded in: 1913

6705 ASME/International Gas Turbine Institute
Three Park Avenue
New York, NY 10016-5990
973-882-1170
800-843-2763
infocentral@asme.org; www.asme.org
Julio Guerrero, President
Thomas G. Loughlin, Executive Director
James W. Coaker, Secretary/Treasurer
David Soukup, Managing Director Operations
William Garofalo, Assistant Treasurer
Supports all those involved with engineering and energy technology.
12500 Members
Founded in: 1958

6706 ASTM International
100 Barr Harbor Drive
PO Box C700
W Conshohocken, PA 19428-2959
610-832-9500; *Fax:* 610-832-9555
service@astm.org; www.astm.org
Social Media: Facebook, Twitter, LinkedIn, RSS, Youtube
Ronald J. Ebelhar, Chairman
D. Thomas Marsh, Vice Chairman
James A. Thomas, President
Not-for-profit organization that provides a global forum for the development and publication of voluntary consensus standards for materials, products, systems and services. Members are users, producers, consumers and representatives of academia and government. Formerly known as the American Society for Testing and Materials.
30000 Members
Founded in: 1898

6707 AVS Science & Technology Society
125 Maiden Ln
15th Floor
New York, NY 10038-4714
212-248-0200; *Fax:* 212-248-0245
ricky@avs.org; www.avs.org
Ricky Baldeo, Office Services Coordinator
Peter Burke, Financial Administrator
Angela Klink, Member Services Administrator
Jeannette DeGennaro, Exhibition & Sales Manager
Yvonne Towse, Managing Director
AVS is a resource for scientists, engineers, industrialists, students and educators.
6000 Members
Founded in: 1963

6708 Abrasive Engineering Society
144 Moore Rd
Butler, PA 16001-1312
724-282-6210; *Fax:* 724-234-2376
aes@abrasiveengineering.com; www.abrasiveengineering.com
Doug Haynes, President
Ted Giese, Executive Director
Dedicated to promoting technical information about abrasives minerals and their uses including abrasives grains and products such as grinding wheels, coated abrasives and thousands of other related tools and products that serve manufacturing and the consumer.
500 Members
Founded in: 1957

6709 Accreditation Board for Engineering and Technology
415 North Charles Street
Suite 1050
Baltimore, MD 21201
410-347-7700; *Fax:* 410-625-2238
info@abet.org; www.abet.org
Michael Milligan, Executive Director, CEO
Joe Sussman, PhD, F.ASME, Chief Accreditation Officer, CIO
Lance Hoboy, MBA, CAE, CFO/COO
Danielle Baron, Senior Director
Rochelle Williams, PhD, Director, Programs and Events
Accreditation of engineering, technology and applied science educational programs.
31 Members
Founded in: 1932

6710 Acoustical Society of America
2 Huntington Quad
Suite 1N01
Melville, NY 11747-4505
516-576-2360; *Fax:* 516-576-2377
asa@aip.org
acousticalsociety.org
Christy K. Holland, President
Lily M. Wang, VP
Susan E. Fox, Executive Director
James F. Lynch, Editor-in-Chief
Christopher J. Struck, Standards Director
Supports all those involved with the acoustics industry.
7000 Members
Founded in: 1929

6711 Adhesive & Sealant Council
7101 Wisconsin Ave
Suite 990
Bethesda, MD 20814-4805
301-986-9700; *Fax:* 301-986-9795
data@ascouncil.org; www.ascouncil.org
Social Media: Twitter, LinkedIn, RSS
William Allmond, President
Valeryia Mikharava, Director, Finance and Admin.
Malinda Armstrong, Director, Meetings & Expositions
Mark Collatz, Director, Regulatory Affairs
Steve Duren, Senior Director, Member Services
A North American trade association dedicated to representing the adhesive and sealant industry. ASC is bound by the collective efforts of its members, and strives to improve the industry operating environment and strengthen its member companies.
124 Members
Founded in: 1958

6712 Air & Waste Management Association
420 Fort Duquesne Blvd.
Pittsburgh, PA 15222-1435
412-232-3444
800-270-3444; *Fax:* 412-232-3450
info@awma.org; www.awma.org
Social Media: Facebook, Twitter, LinkedIn
Dallas Baker, President
Stephanie Glyptis, Executive Director
Carrie Hartz, Conferences & Events Planner
Gloria Henning, Education Programs Coordinator
Nancy Bernheisel, Publications Coordinator
Professional organization that provides training, information, and networking opportunities to environmental professionals.

6713 Alpha Pi Mu
3005 Lancaster Drive
Blacksburg, VA 24060
540-553-2043
office@alphapimu.com; www.alphapimu.com
Dr. Wafik H Iskander, President
Sarah Lam, Executive Vice President
Dr. C. Patrick Koelling, Executive Director
Dr. Wafik H Iskander, Vice President
Dr. S. Balachandran, Treasurer
An honor society for Industrial and Systems Engineering students.
Founded in: 1949

6714 American Academy of Environmental Engineers & Scientists
147 Old Solomons Island Road
Suite 303
Annapolis, MD 21401-7003
410-266-3311; *Fax:* 410-266-7653
info@aaees.org; www.aaees.org
Social Media: Facebook, Twitter, LinkedIn, Youtube, Flickr
Burk Kalweit, Executive Director
Howard B. LaFever, President
Dr. Robert Williams, President-Elect
C. Hunter Nolen, Vice President
Joyce Dowen, Executive Assistant
Periodical for environmental engineers, environmental engineer professionals, as well as environmental engineering services, and scientists in the environmental field.
2500 Members
Founded in: 1955

6715 American Association of Engineering Societies
1801 Alexander Bell Drive
Reston, VA 20191
202-296-2237
888-400-2237; *Fax:* 202-296-1151
dbateson@aaes.org; www.aaes.org
Dr. James L. Melsa, Chairman
Alyse Stofer, Vice Chair
Wendy Cowan, CAE, Executive Director/Secretary
Mark W. Woodson, P.E., Treasurer
Association for national, U.S. organizations concerned with engineering and related fields.
14 Members
Founded in: 1979

6716 American Automatic Control Council
Northwestern University
3640 Col Glenn Highway
Dayton, OH 45435
937-775-5062; *Fax:* 937-775-3936
pmisra@cs.wright.edu; www.a2c2.org
Tariq Samad, President
Linda Bushnell, Treasurer
B. Wayne Bequette, Secretary
Pradeep Misra, Secretary

Supports industry of automatic controls producers.
1M Members
Founded in: 1960

6717 American Council of Engineering Companies
1015 15th St
8th floor NW
Washington, DC 20005-2605

202-347-7474; *Fax:* 202-898-0068
acec@acec.org; www.acec.org
Social Media: Facebook, Twitter, Pinterest

Ralph W. Christie, Chairman
Harvey M. Floyd, Senior Vice Chair and Treasurer
David A. Raymond, President and CEO
Mary Ann Emely, VP, Operations & Membership
Steven Hall, Vice President, Government Affairs

Membership includes US firms engaged in a range of engineering works. Mission is to contribute to the nation's prosperity through advancing the interests of member firms.
55000 Members
Founded in: 1905

6718 American Crystallographic Association
Ellicott Station
PO Box 96
Buffalo, NY 14205-0096

716-898-8690; *Fax:* 716-898-8695
aca@hwi.buffalo.edu;
www.amercrystalassn.org
Social Media: Twitter

Christopher Cahill, President
Tom Terwilliger, Vice President
William L. Duax, Chief Executive Officer
S.N. Rao, Chief Financial Officer
Kristina Vitale, Membership Secretary

Supports all those involved with hardware, software, and x-ray equipment for the crystal industry.
2200 Members
Founded in: 1949

6719 American Design Drafting Association
105 East Main Street
Newbern, TE 38059

731-627-0802; *Fax:* 731-627-9321
okparker@adda.org; www.adda.org
Social Media: Facebook, Twitter, LinkedIn, Google+

Rick Frymyer, Chairman
Richard Button, Governor
Alex Devereux, Vice President
Olen K Parker, Executive Director
Donna Brenton, Administrative Manager

An individual membership society for the design drafting community across all industries.
Founded in: 1948

6720 American Engineering Association, Inc.
533 Waterside Blvd.
Monroe Township, NJ 08831

201-664-6954
aea@aea.org; www.aea.org

Richard F. Tax, President
Charles Fischer, Vice President
Jenny Blackford, Marketing Director
Laurie Johnson, Office Assistant

As a national nonprofit professional association the AEA is a voice for engineers. The AEA, Inc. is dedicated to the enhancement of the engineering profession and U.S. Engineering capabilities. AEA is a strong advocate for providing opportunities for US engineers and is involved in issues of utilization, skill enhancement, loss of jobs, offshore manufacturing, layoffs, and many others that affect the lives and professional welfare of our engineers.
Founded in: 1979

6721 American Helicopter Society
2701 Prosperity Avenue
Suite 210
Fairfax, VA 22031

703-684-6777
855-247-4685; *Fax:* 703-739-9279
staff@vtol.org; www.vtol.org
Social Media: Facebook, Twitter, LinkedIn, YouTube, RSS

Mick Maurer, Chair
Leanne Caret, President
Mike Hirschberg, Executive Director
Kay Yosua Brackins, Deputy Executive Director
David Renzi, Director

The professional society for the advancement of vertical flight technology and its useful application throughout the world.
Founded in: 1943

6722 American Indian Science and Engineering Society
2305 Renard SE
Suite 200
Albuquerque, NM 87106

505-765-1052; *Fax:* 505-765-5608;
www.aises.org
Social Media: Facebook, Twitter, LinkedIn, YouTube, Instagram

Richard Stephens, Chair
Dr. Twyla Baker-Demaray, Vice-Chair
Marlene Watson, Secretary
Dr. James May, Treasurer
Sarah Echohawk, Chief Executive Officer

A nonprofit professional association with the goal of increasing American Indian and Alaskan Native representation in the fields of engineering, science, and other related technology disciplines.
3500 Members
Founded in: 1977

6723 American Institute of Chemical Engineers
120 Wall Street
FL 23
New York, NY 10005-4020

203-702-7660
800-242-4363; *Fax:* 203-775-5177;
www.aiche.org
Social Media: Facebook, Twitter, LinkedIn, YouTube, Flickr, Slideshare

Maria Burka, President
Kimberly Ogden, Secretary
Andre Da Costa, Treasurer
June Wispelwey, Executive Director

Professional association providing leadership in advancing the chemical engineering profession. Members are those who develop processes and design and operate manufacturing plants, as well as researchers who assure the safe and environmentally sound manufacture, use and disposal of chemical products.
50000 Members
Founded in: 1908

6724 American Institute of Physics
1 Physics Ellipse
College Park, MD 20740-3841

301-209-3100; *Fax:* 301-209-0843
dylla@aip.org; www.aip.org

Louis J. Lanzerotti, Chair
Robert G. W. Brown, Chief Executive Officer
Gigi Swartz, Chief Financial Officer
Margaret Wiley, Senior Executive Secretary
Liz Dart Caron, Senior Director

Presents original research in high performance polymer science and technology. Primarily applications-driven, with a major focus on the molecular structure/processability/property relationship with regard to the specified applications.
1931 Members
Founded in: 1931

6725 American Iron and Steel Institute
25 Massachusetts Avenue, NW
Suite 800
Washington, DC 20001

202-452-7100; www.steel.org
Social Media: Facebook, Twitter, YouTube

Chuck Schmitt, Chairman
John Ferriola, Vice Chairman
Kevin M. Dempsey, SVP, Public Policy, General Counsel
David E Bell, VP, Finance and Administration
Lisa Harrison, SVP, Communications

Steel information for consumers, engineers, and other professionals.
125 Members
Founded in: 1855

6726 American Nuclear Society
555 N Kensington Ave
La Grange Park, IL 60526-5592

708-352-6611
800-323-3044; *Fax:* 708-352-0499;
www.ans.org
Social Media: Facebook, Twitter, LinkedIn

Eugene S. Grecheck, President
Andrew C. Klein, Vice President
Robert C. Fine, JD, CAE, Executive Director
Staci B. Levy, CPA, Director, Finance
Tari Marshall, Department Director

Serves its members in their efforts to develop and safely apply nuclear science and technology for public benefit through knowledge exchange, professional development, and enhanced public understanding.
Founded in: 1954

6727 American Oil Chemists Society
2710 S. Boulder
Urbana, IL 61802

217-359-2344; *Fax:* 217-351-8091
general@aocs.org; www.aocs.org
Social Media: Facebook, Twitter, LinkedIn, Blogger

M. Trautmann, President
B. Hendrix, VP
Patrick J. Donnelly, Chief Executive Officer
Jamie Lourash, Data Services Coordinator
Jeffry L. Newman, Senior Director, Programs

A global forum to promote the exchange of ideas, information, and experience, to enhance personal excellence, and to provide high standards of quality among those with a professional interest in the science and technology of fats, oil, surfactants, and related materials.
5400+ Members
Founded in: 1909

6728 American Oil Chemists' Society (AOCS)
2710 S Boulder Drive
PO Box 17190
Urbana, IL 61803-6996

217-359-2344; *Fax:* 217-351-8091
general@aocs.org; www.aocs.org
Social Media: Facebook, Twitter, LinkedIn, Blogger

M. Trautmann, President
B. Hendrix, VP
Patrick J. Donnelly, Chief Executive Officer
Jamie Lourash, Data Services Coordinator
Jeffry L. Newman, Senior Director, Programs

AOCS is a global scientific society open to all individuals and corporations who are interested in fats, oils, surfactants, detergents and related materials. AOCS is a trusted source of information for its members and thousands of non-members from more than 90 countries worldwide.
4500 Members
Founded in: 1909
Mailing list available for rent

6729 **American Society for Engineering Education**
1818 N St NW
Suite 600
Washington, DC 20036-2476

202-331-3500; *Fax:* 202-265-8504
prism@asee.org; www.asee.org

Norman Fortenberry, Executive Director
Joe Dillon, Managing Director, Finance/CFO
Keith Mounts, Chief Information Officer (CIO)
Ashok Agrawal, Managing Director
Patti Greenawalt, Managing Director, Member Services

Supports all those educators in the engineering technology fields.
12000 Members
Founded in: 1893

6730 **American Society for Precision Engineering**
PO Box 10826
Raleigh, NC 27605-0826

919-839-8444; *Fax:* 919-839-8039;
www.aspe.net

Byron R. Knapp, President
Robert D. Grejda, Vice President
Thomas A. Dow, ASPE Executive Director
Ilka Lee, Publications and Office Manager
Wendy Shearon, Meetings & Membership Manager

Members are from academia, industry and government, and include professionals in engineering, materials science, physics, chemistry, mathematics and computer science. Multidisciplinary professional and technical society concerned with precision engineering research and development, design and manufacturing of high accuracy components and systems. Member and nonmember rates for annual meetings, spring and summer topical meetings, books and video tapes. Membership is $65 regular, $30 student.
Founded in: 1986

6731 **American Society for Quality**
600 N Plankinton Avenue
PO Box 3005
Milwaukee, WI 53201-3005

414-272-8575
800-248-1946; *Fax:* 414-272-1734
help@asq.org; www.asq.org
Social Media: Facebook, Twitter, LinkedIn, YouTube, Google+

Cecilia L. Kimberlin, Chair
Bill Troy, Chief Executive Officer
Eric Hayler, Treasurer
Sue Campbell, Executive Assistant

ASQ's mission is to facilitate continuous improvement and increase customer satisfaction. Promotes quality principles, concepts and technologies. Provides information, contacts and opportunities to make things better in the workplace, in communities and in people's lives.
100M Members
Founded in: 1946

6732 **American Society for the Geoprofessional Business Association (ASFE)**
1300 Piccard Dr.
LL14
Rockville, MD 20850

301-565-2733; *Fax:* 301-589-2017
info@geoprofessional.org; www.asfe.org
Social Media: Facebook, Twitter, LinkedIn, YouTube, RSS

Gordon M. MathesonE, President
Joel G. Carson, Executive Director
Sara Menase, Program Manager
Barb Nappy, Director of Events
Charles L. Head, P.E., P.G., Secretary/Treasurer

Not-for-profit trade association. Supports all employees of engineering companies.
300 Members
Founded in: 1969

6733 **American Society of Agricultural and Biological Engineers**
2950 Niles Rd
St Joseph, MI 49085-8607

269-429-0300
800-371-2723; *Fax:* 269-429-3852
hq@asabe.org; www.asabe.org

Mary Leigh Wolfe, President
Darrin Drollinger, Executive Director
Joann McQuone, Executive Assistant
Mark Zielke, Senior Director
Dolores Landeck, Director of Public Affairs

Holds annual meetings and conferences and publishes journals related to agricultural engineering, biological engineering and food process engineering.
8500 Members
Founded in: 1907

6734 **American Society of Certified Engineering**
PO Box 1348
Flowery Branch, GA 30542

770-967-9173; *Fax:* 770-967-8049;
www.ascet.org

Russell E Freier, Chairman
Leo Saenz, CET, President
Kurt Schuler, Secretary/Treasurer

Strives to obtain recognition of engineering technicians as essential to the engineering scientific team. Provides a forum for discussion of employment issues and improvement of the professional status of engineering technicians.
2000 Members
Founded in: 1964

6735 **American Society of Civil Engineers**
1801 Alexander Bell Dr
Reston, VA 20191-4382

703-295-6300
800-548-2723; *Fax:* 703-295-6222
cybrarian@asce.org; www.asce.org/
Social Media: Facebook, Twitter, LinkedIn, YouTube, Google+

Robert D. Stevens, President
Dennis D. Truax, Ph.D., P.E., Treasurer
Randall M. Perkinson, P.E., Assistant Treasurer
Thomas W. Smith III, ENV SP, CAE, Secretary

Professional association of engineers and scientists working in civil and structural engineering, applied mechanics and engineering science, aeronautics and astronautics.
Founded in: 1852

6736 **American Society of Gas Engineers**
P.O. Box 66
Artesia, CA 90702

562-455-9417
asgecge@aol.com; www.asge-national.org

Jerry Moore, Executive Director
Mike O'Donnell, President
Ray Maddock, Vice President
Chad Johnson, Treasurer

Supports all engineers in the gas industry.
Founded in: 1954

6737 **American Society of Heating, Refrigerating , and Air Conditioning Engineers**
1791 Tullie Circle, N.E.
Atlanta, GA 30329

404-636-8400
800-527-4723; *Fax:* 404-321-5478
ashrae@ashrae.org; www.ashrae.org
Social Media: Facebook, Twitter, YouTube

T. David Underwood, President
Walid Chakroun, Ph.D., P.E., Vice President
Patricia T. Graef, P.E., Vice President
James K. Vallort, Vice President
Jeff H. Littleton, Secretary

Global society that focuses on building systems, energy efficiency,indoor air quality, refrigeration, and sustainability.

6738 **American Society of Heating, Refrigeration & Air-Conditioning Engineers**
1791 Tullie Cir Ne
Atlanta, GA 30329-2398

404-636-8400
800-527-4723; *Fax:* 404-321-5478
ashrae@ashrae.org; www.ashrae.org

T. David Underwood, President
Walid Chakroun, Ph.D., P.E., Vice President
Patricia T. Graef, P.E., Vice President
James K. Vallort, Vice President
Jeff H. Littleton, Secretary

An international organization that fulfills its mission of advancing heating, ventilation, air conditioning and refrigeration to serve humanity and promote a sustainable world through research, standards writing, publishing and continuing education.
55000 Members
Founded in: 1894

6739 **American Society of Mechanical Engineers**
Three Park Ave
New York, NY 10016-5902

973-882-1170
800-843-2763; *Fax:* 202-429-9417
infocentral@asme.org; www.asme.org

Mark Goldsmith, President
Webb Marner, Secretary/Treasurer

To promote and enhance the technical competency and professional well-being of the members, and through quality programs and activities in mechanical engineering, better enable its practitioners to contribute to the well being of human kind
12000 Members
Founded in: 1880

6740 **American Society of Naval Engineers**
1452 Duke Street
Alexandria, VA 22314-3458

703-836-6727; *Fax:* 703-836-7491
asnehq@navalengineers.org;
www.navalengineers.org

Anthony W. Lengerich, USN, President
Mr. Mike D'Amato, Vice President
Dr. William H. Luebke, Vice President

VADM Paul E. Sullivan, USN (Ret.), Vice President
Dr. Leigh McCue, Executive Dir/Secretary/Treasurer

Naval engineering includes all arts construction and sciences as applied in research, development design, construction, operation, maintenance, and logistic support of: surface/sub-surface ships and marine craft.
Founded in: 1888

6741 **American Society of Petroleum Operations Engineers**
301 East Culpeper Street
Culpeper, VA 22701

703-768-4159
800-918-8962; www.aspoe.org
Social Media: Facebook, Twitter, LinkedIn, YouTube, Google+, Instagram, P

John B Stanley, President
Gerald Holton, VP
Harry Lyon, Executive VP
Coles Marsh, Treasurer
Cheryl George, Secretary

Works to stimulate interest from the academic world in the qualifications necessary to become a Petroleum Operations Engineer.
Founded in: 1976

6742 **American Society of Plumbing Engineers**
6400 Shafer Ct.
Suite 350
Rosemont, IL 60018-4914

847-296-0002; *Fax:* 773-695-9007
info@aspe.org; www.aspe.org

Mitch Clemente, CPD, President
Billy Smith, FASPE Executive Director / CEO
Donald Thurner, Director of Finance & Admin.
Stacey A. Kidd, Director of Membership & Meetings
Richard Albrecht, Director of Information Technology

Supports all those engineers in the plumbing industry.
7500 Members
Founded in: 1964

6743 **American Society of Safety Engineers**
520 N. Northwest Hwy
Park Ridge, IL 60068

847-699-2929; *Fax:* 847-768-3434
customerservice@asse.org; www.asse.org

Michael Belcher, CSP, President
James D. Smith, M.S., CSP, Senior VP
Stephanie A. Helgerman, CSP, VP of Finance
Fred J. Fortman, Secretary and Executive Director

The oldest and largest professional safety organization. Its members manage, supervise and consult son safety, health, and environmental issues in industry, insurance, government and education.
30000 Members
Founded in: 1911

6744 **American Society of Sanitary Engineering**
18927 Hickory Creek Drive
Suite 220
Mokena, IL 60448

708-995-3019; *Fax:* 708-479-6139;
www.asse-plumbing.org

Douglas A. Marian, President
Dana Colombo, Vice President
Scott Hamilton, Executive Director
Conrad Jahrling, Staff Engineering Supervisor
Benjamin Ryan, Communications Editor

Members are from all segments of the plumbing industry, including contractors, engineers, inspectors, journeymen, apprentices and others who are involved in various segments of the industry. Provides information, an opportunity to exchange ideas, solve problems and offers a forum where all sides can express their views.
300 Members

6745 **American Water Works Association**
6666 W. Quincy Ave.
Denver, CO 80235

303-794-7711
800-926-7337; *Fax:* 303-347-0804;
www.awwa.org
Social Media: Facebook, Twitter, LinkedIn, YouTube

David B. LaFrance, Chief Executive Officer
Paula I. MacIlwaine, Deputy Chief Executive Officer
Kevin Mann, Chief Financial Officer
Kevin Turntine, Chief Information Officer
Susan Franceschi, Chief Membership Officer

An international nonprofit scientific and educational association founded to improve water quality and supply.
50000 Members
Founded in: 1881

6746 **Applied Technology Council**
201 Redwood Shores Parkway
Suite 240
Redwood City, CA 94065

650-595-1542; *Fax:* 650-593-2320
atc@atcouncil.org; www.atcouncil.org

James A. Amundson, President
Victoria Arbitrio, Vice President
William Staehlin, Secretary/Treasurer
Jon A. Heintz, Executive Director
Scott D. Schiff, Director of Projects

Nonprofit, tax-exempt corporation established through the efforts of the Structural Engineers Association of California. ATC's mission is to develop and promote state-of-the-art, user-friendly, engineering resources and applications for use in mitigating the effects of natural and other hazards on the built environment.
300 Members
Founded in: 1973

6747 **Association for Computing Machinery**
2 Penn Plaza
Suite 701
New York, NY 10121-0701

212-626-0500
800 342-6626; *Fax:* 212-944-1318
acmhelp@acm.org; www.acm.org
Social Media: Facebook, Twitter, LinkedIn, YouTube, Google+

Alexander L Wolf, President
Vicki L. Hanson, Vice President
John R. White, Executive Director and CEO
Erik R Altman, Secretary/Treasurer
Erik R Altman, Secretary/Treasurer

A U.S.-based international learned society for computing.

6748 **Association for Facilities Engineering**
8200 Greensboro Drive
Suite 400
McLean, VA 22102

571-395-8777; *Fax:* 571-766-2142
Info@AFE.org; www.afe.org

Dennis M Hydrick, President
Wayne P. Saya Sr., CPE, Executive Director
Scott Klahne, Director, Government Liaison
Gabriella Rosales, Manager, Professional Development
Charlie Clunk, Administrative Assistant

Provides education, certification, technical information and other relevant information for plant and facility engineering operations and maintenance professionals worldwide.
5000 Members
Founded in: 1954

6749 **Association for Iron & Steel Technology (AIST)**
186 Thorn Hill Rd
Warrendale, PA 15086-7528

724-814-3000; *Fax:* 724-814-3001
memberservices@aist.org; www.aist.org
Social Media: Facebook, Twitter, LinkedIn, YouTube

George J. Koenig, President
Wendell L. Carter, First Vice President
Randy C. Skagen, Second Vice President
Joseph Dzierzawski, Treasurer
Ronald E. Ashburn, Secretary

The Association for Iron & Steel Technology (AIST) is an international technical association representing iron and steel producers, their allied suppliers and related academia. The association is dedicated to advancing the technical development, production, processing and application of iron and steel.
13800 Members
Founded in: 2004

6750 **Association for Women in Science**
1667 K Street NW
Suite 800
Washington, DC 20006

202-588-8175
awis@awis.org; www.awis.org
Social Media: Facebook, Twitter, LinkedIn

Bahija Jallal, President
Robert Powell, Secretary
Pamela Marrone, Treasurer
Janet Bandows Koster, Executive Director & CEO
Meredith Gibson, Chief Operations Officer

Provides support for female scientists and bioengineers. Also dedicated to achieving equity and full participation for women in science, mathematics, engineering and technology.
5000 Members
Founded in: 1971
Mailing list available for rent

6751 **Association for the Advancement of Cost Engineering**
1265 Suncrest Towne Centre Drive
Suite 100
Morgantown, WV 26505-1876

304-296-8444
800-858-2678; *Fax:* 304-291-5728
info@aacei.org
web.aacei.org
Social Media: Facebook, Twitter, LinkedIn

Ms Julie K Owen, President
Charity A. Golden, MBA CIA CCT, Executive Director
Penny Whoolery, Manager, Certification
Jennie Amos, Director
Amanda Bliss, Certification Administrator

Leading-edge society for cost estimators, cost engineers, schedulers project managers, and project control specialists.
7000 Members
Founded in: 1956

6752 **Association of Building Officials and Code Administrators**
500 New Jersey Ave
6th Floor
Washington, DC 20001-2070

202-370-1800
888-422-7233; *Fax:* 202-783-2348

webmaster@iccsafe.org; www.iccsafe.org
Social Media: Facebook, Twitter, LinkedIn

Alex Olszowy III, President
M. Dwayne Garriss, Vice President
Jay Elbettar, P.E., CBO, Secretary/Treasurer
Dominic Sims, CEO
John Belcik, COO/CFO

An independent nonprofit organization which conducts a voluntary program of evaluation of both traditional and innovative building materials, products and systems for compliance with BOCA National Codes.
14000 Members
Founded in: 1994

6753 **Association of Energy Engineers**
3168 Mercer University Drive
Suite 420
Atlanta, GA 30341

770-447-5083; *Fax:* 770-446-3969
info@aeecenter.org; www.aeecenter.org

Dr. Scott Dunning, President
Albert Thumann, P.E., C.E.M., Executive Director
Bill Younger, Secretary
Paul Goodman, Treasurer
Angie Quarles, Assistant to the Executive Director

Membership organization of professionals and certification programs in the fields of energy efficiency, utility deregulation, facility management, plant engineering and environmental compliance. Offers seminars, conferences, books to critical buyer-seller, networking trade shows, job listings and certification programs.
8000+ Members
Founded in: 1977

6754 **Association of Environmental & Engineering Geologists**
1100-H Brandywine Blvd.
Suite 575
Zanesville, OH 43701

303-757-2926
844-331-7867; *Fax:* 740-452-2552
aeg@aegweb.org; www.aegweb.org

Dale C. Andrews, President
Kathy Troost, Vice President
Kevin Richards, Treasurer
Cynthia Palomares, Secretary

Meets the professional needs of geologists who are applying their scientific training and experience to the broad field of civil and environmental engineering. Mission is to provide leadership in the development and application of geologic principles and knowledge to serve engineering, environmental and public needs.
Founded in: 1957

6755 **Association of State Dam Safety Officials**
239 S. Limestone
Lexington, KY 40508

859-550-2788
info@damsafety.org; www.damsafety.org
Social Media: Facebook, Twitter, LinkedIn, YouTube

Jim Pawloski, President
Jon Garton, Secretary
Roger Adams, P.E, Secretary
Jon Garton, Secretary
Dusty Myers, Treasurer

Provides outreach programs and a forum for the exchange of information to advance and improve the safety of dams.
Founded in: 1983

6756 **Association of Technology, Management, and Applied Engineering**
275 North York Street
Suite 401
Elmhurst, IL 60126

630-433-4514
atmae@atmae.org; www.atmae.org
Social Media: Facebook, Twitter, LinkedIn, YouTube

John Hausoul, Executive Director
Kelly Schild, Director, Accreditation
Angie Coleman, Conference Manager
Alyssa Ebersole, Membership and Journal Coordinator

Provides support to all those involved in the industrial technology industry. Hosts trade shows and publishes various materials.
1000+ Members
Founded in: 1967
Mailing list available for rent

6757 **Audio Engineering Society**
551 Fifth Ave.
Suite 1225
New York, NY 10176

212-661-8528; *Fax:* 212-682-0477;
www.aes.org
Social Media: Facebook, Twitter, LinkedIn, YouTube, Google+

Andres Mayo, President
Michael Fleming, VP, Central Region, USA/Canada
David W Scheirman, VP, Western Region, USA/Canada
Ron Streicher, Secretary
Garry Margolis, Treasurer

Worldwide professional association for professionals and students involved in the audio industry.

6758 **Biomedical Engineering Society**
8201 Corporate Dr
Suite 1125
Landover, MD 20785-2224

301-459-1999
877-871-2637; *Fax:* 301-459-2444
info@bmes.org; www.bmes.org
Social Media: Facebook, Twitter, LinkedIn

Richard T. Hart, PhD, President
Edward L. Schilling, III, Executive Director
Doug Beizer, Communications Director
Michele Surricchio Ciapa, Education Director
Terry Young, BMES Career Connections Director

Supports all those involved in the biomedical engineering industry.
3800 Members
Founded in: 1968

6759 **Carnegie Mellon University: Information Networking Institute**
Carnegie Mellon University
Electrical & Computer Engineering Department
4616 Henry Street
Pittsburgh, PA 15213

412-268-7195; *Fax:* 412-268-7196
ini@cmu.edu; www.ini.cmu.edu
Social Media: Facebook, Twitter, LinkedIn, YouTube, Instagram, Google+, F

Dr. Dena Haritos Tsamitis, Director
Mike Niederberger, Business/Finance Administrator
Donald Shields, Director Development
Dean Haritos Tsamitis, Director Information Networking
Sean O'Leary, Manager

Focusing on professional degrees programs combining economics, technologies and global communication networks - information security policies.
Founded in: 1989

6760 **Cold Regions Research and Engineering Laboratory**
US Army Corps of Engineers
72 Lyme Road
Hanover, NH 03755-1290
603-646-4100; *Fax:* 603-646-4278
info@crrel.usace.army.mil;
www.crrel.usace.army.mil/welcome
James L Wuebben, PE, Director
Dr Mary Albert, Research Mechanical Engineer

The mission of this Laboratory is to understand the characteristics of the cold regions of the world and to apply this knowledge to make it easier for people to live and work in those regions. For example, CRREL engineers have conducted a long-term program on the correct design of roofs in heavy snowfall areas.

6761 **Cold-Formed Steel Engineers Institute**
25 Massachusetts Avenue, N.W.
Suite 800
Washington, DC 20001

202-263-4488
866-465-4732; *Fax:* 202-452-1039
info@cfsei.org; www.cfsei.org

Jennifer Zabik, P.E., S.E, Chairman
Robert Warr, P.E, Vice Chairman
Jennifer Zabik, Vice Chairman

Produces safe and efficient designs for commercial and residential structures with cold-formed steel.
Founded in: 1849

6762 **Construction Financial Management Association**
100 Village Blvd.
Suite 200
Princeton, NJ 8540

609-452-8000
888-421-9996; *Fax:* 609-452-0474
info@cfma.org; www.cfma.org
Social Media: Facebook, Twitter, LinkedIn, YouTube

Stuart Binstock, President/ CEO
Brian Summers, VP, Content Strategy & Education
Ariel Sanchirico, Director, Online Learning
Erica O'Grady, CAE, Vice President, Operations
Robert Rubin, CPA, Vice President, Finance & Admin

Support and networking for construction financial professionals within the United States.
Founded in: 1981

6763 **Construction Management Association of America**
7926 Jones Branch Drive
Suite 800
McLean, VA 22102-3303

703-356-2622; *Fax:* 703-356-6388
info@cmaanet.org; www.cmaanet.org
Social Media: Facebook, Twitter, LinkedIn, YouTube

Rebecca Jones, Chair
Sandy Hamby, AIA, CCM, Vice Chair
Tim Murchison, JD, CCM, Vice Chair
Brian Ott, CCM, Vice Chair
Tim Murchison, JD, CCM, Vice Chair

A nonprofit and non-governmental professional association serving the construction management industry.
11000 Members
Founded in: 1982

6764 Construction Owners Association of America
5000 Austell Powder Springs Road
Suite 217
Austell, GA 30106
770-433-0820
800-994-2622; *Fax:* 404-577-3551
coaa@coaa.org; www.coaa.org
Social Media: Facebook, Twitter, LinkedIn
Kevin Lewis, President
Dean McCormick, Vice President
Lisa DeGolyer, Chief Executive, Conferences & Edu
Valerie Delaney, Chief Executive, Finance & Ops
Donna Heavener, Director
A national organization of public and private owners who manage facilities development and capital improvement projects.

6765 CorrConnect
GSG Inc
www.gsgsystems.com
Joshua Bane, Project Manager
An online resource center for training modules on corrosion.
Founded in: 2007

6766 Council of Engineer and Scientific Specialty Board
PO Box 1448
Annapolis, MD 21401-1448
410-266-3766; *Fax:* 410-721-1746
wanderson@cesb.org; www.cesb.org
William C Anderson PE DEE, Executive Director
Accredits engineering, science and technology certification programs from professional to technician certificates.
Founded in: 1990
Mailing list available for rent

6767 Electric Power Research Institute
3420 Hillview Avenue
Palo Alto, CA 94304
650-855-2121
800-313-3774
orders@epri.com; www.epri.com
Social Media: Facebook, Twitter, LinkedIn, YouTube
Gil C Quiniones, Chair
Pat K. Vincent-Collawn, Vice Chair
Michael W Howard, President/ Chief Executive Officer
Tom Alley, Vice President, Generation
Pamela J. Keefe, SVP, CFO and Treasurer
A nonprofit organization that conducts research on issues related to the electric power industry in the USA.
Founded in: 1965

6768 Engineering Workforce Commission
1801 Alexander Bell Drive
Reston, VA 20191
202-296-2237
888-400-2237; *Fax:* 202-296-1151
dbateson@aaes.org; www.ewc-online.org
Dan Batson, Director
AAES's Engineering Workforce Commission monitors engineering job stats that help universities, corporations, and government set salary, hiring, enrollment, and degree trends in the marketplace. It publishes three major surveys per year that are regarded as the most accurate, objective and timely reports about the engineering workforce: Degrees, Enrollments, and Salaries.
35 Members
Founded in: 1950

6769 Environmental Information Association
6935 Wisconsin Ave
Suite 306
Chevy Chase, MD 20815-6112
301-961-4999
888-343-4342; *Fax:* 301-961-3094
info@eia-usa.org; www,eia-usa.org
Kevin Cannan, President
Steve Fulford, Vice President
Brent Kynoch, Managing Director
Kim Goodman, Membership and Marketing Manager
Kelly Rutt, Development and Comm. Manager
Nonprofit organization dedicated to providing environmental information to individuals, members and industry. Disseminates information on the abatement of asbestos and lead-based paint, indoor air quality, safety and health issues, analytical issues and environmental site assessments.

6770 Ergosyst Associates
4840 W 15th Street
Suite 1012
Lawrence, KS 66049
785-842-7334; *Fax:* 785-842-7348
John Burch, Publisher
Association for those interested in economics/human factors.

6771 Eta Kappa Nu
445 Hoes Lane
Piscataway, NJ 08854
732-465-5846
800-406-2590
info@hkn.org
hkn.org
Evelyn Hirt, President
S.K. Ramesh, President-Elect
Ronald Jensen, Treasurer
Eta Kappa Nu (HKN) is the electrical and computer engineering honor society of the Institute of Electrical and Electronics Engineers (IEEE).
Founded in: 1904

6772 Federation of Materials Societies
910 17th St NW
Suite 800
Washington, DC 20006-2606
202-296-9282; *Fax:* 202-833-3014;
www.materialsocieties.org
Betsy Houston, Executive Director
Petr Vanysek, President
Promotes cooperation among societies concerned with the understanding, development and application of materials and processes.
700K Members
Founded in: 1972

6773 ICC Evaluation Service
3060 Saturn Street
Suite 100
Whittier, CA 92821
562-699-0541
800-423-6587; *Fax:* 562-695-4694
es@icc-es.org; www.iccsafe.org
Social Media: Facebook, Twitter, LinkedIn
Alex Olszowy III, President
M. Dwayne Garriss, Vice President
Jay Elbettar, P.E., CBO, Secretary/Treasurer
Dominic Sims, CEO
John Belcik, COO/CFO
An independent, nonprofit organization that conducts a voluntary program of evaluation of both traditional and innovative building materials, products and systems for compliance with the three major model codes in the United States.
Founded in: 2003

6774 Illuminating Engineering Society of North America
120 Wall Street
17th Floor
New York, NY 10005
212-248-5000; *Fax:* 212-248-5018
ies@ies.org; www.ies.org
Clayton Gordon, Marketing Manager
Nicole DeGirolamo, Executive Assistant
Samuel Fontanez, Senior Art Director
Robert Horner, Director of Public Policy
Samantha Schwirck, Senior Associate Editor, LD+A
To advance knowledge and disseminate information for the improvement of the lighted environment to the benefit of society. Publishes a monthly magazine; Lighting Design & Applications.
7000 Members
Founded in: 1906

6775 Industrial Designers Society of America
555 Grove St.
Suite 200
Herndon, VA 20170
703-707-6000; *Fax:* 703-787-8501
idsa@idsa.org; www.idsa.org
Social Media: Facebook, Twitter, LinkedIn, Pinterest, Vimeo Flickr
John Barratt, Chairman
Daniel Martinage, CAE, Executive Director
Karen Berube, Senior Creative Director
Lisa Brenner, CPA, Director of Finance & Accounting
Jordan Fleger, Member Relations Coordinator
The IDSA is the world's oldest, largest, member-driven society for product design, industrial design, interaction designs, human factors, ergonomics, design research, design management, university design and related fields.

6776 Industrial Fabrics Association International
1801 County Road B W
Roseville, MN 55113-4061
651-222-2508
800-225-4324; *Fax:* 651-631-9334
generalinfo@ifai.com; www.ifai.com
Social Media: Facebook, Twitter, LinkedIn, YouTube
Stephen Warner, CEO
JoAnne Ferris, Marketing Director
A not-for-profit trade association whose member companies represent the international specialty fabrics marketplace, who facilitates the development, application and promotion of products manufactures by the diverse membership.
2000 Members

6777 Industrial Research Institute
2200 Clarendon Boulevard
Suite 1102
Arlington, VA 22201
703-647-2580; *Fax:* 703-647-2581;
www.iriweb.org
Tom Kavassalis, Chairman
Edward Bernstein, President
Ana Escobar, Associate, Executive & Publications
Lee Green, Vice President, Knowledge Creation
Pamela R. Hanner, Manager, Web & IT
The mission is to enhance the effectiveness of technological innovation industry.
200 Members
Founded in: 1938

6778 **Institute of Biological Engineering**
3493 Lansdowne Drive
Suite 2
Lexington, KE 40517

859-977-7450; *Fax:* 859-271-0607
info@ibe.org; www.ibe.org
Social Media: Facebook, LinkedIn

Jeong Yeol Yoon, President
Prem Parajuli, Secretary
Melanie Correll, Treasurer

A nonprofit professional organization which encourages inquiry and interest in the field of biological engineering.

6779 **Institute of Industrial Engineers**
3577 Parkway Lane
Suite 200
Norcross, GA 30092

770-449-0460
800-494-0460; *Fax:* 770-441-3295
cs@iienet.org; www.iienet.org
Social Media: Facebook, Twitter, LinkedIn, YouTube, Google+

Don Greene, CEO
Donna Calvert, COO
Nancy LaJoice, Director of Membership
Pam Patterson, Membership Administrator
Elaine Schwartz, Membership Administrator

Supports all industrial engineers with training, education, publications, conferences, etc.
15000 Members
Founded in: 1948

6780 **Institute of Noise Control Engineering**
12100 Sunset Hills Rd.
Suite 130
Reston, VA 20190

703-234-4073; *Fax:* 703-435-4390
ibo@inceusa.org; www.inceusa.org

Gordon Ebbitt, President
Joseph M. Cuschieri, Executive Director
George C. Maling, Jr., Managing Director Emeritus
Deane Jaeger, Treasurer
Karl B. Washburn, Secretary

Supports those involved with hearing protection, modal analysis, and signal processing.
1200 Members

6781 **Institute of Transportation Engineers**
1627 Eye Street, NW
Suite 600
Washington, DC 20006

202-785-0060; *Fax:* 202-785-0609
ite_staff@ite.org; www.ite.org
Social Media: Facebook, Twitter, LinkedIn, YouTube, Instagram, Google+

W. Hibbett Neel, International President
John J Kennedy, International Vice President
Zaki Mustafa, Immediate Past President
Colleen L Hill-Stramsak, International Director
Dean J Kaiser, International Director

An international educational and scientific association of transportation professionals who are responsible for meeting mobility and safety needs.
13199 Members
Founded in: 1930

6782 **Instrument Society of America**
67 T.W. Alexander Drive
PO Box 12277
Research Triangle Park, NC 27709

919-549-8411; *Fax:* 919-549-8288
info@isa.org; www.isa.org
Social Media: Facebook, Twitter, LinkedIn, YouTube, Flickr, Google+

Richard W. Roop, President
Michelle Anderson, Human Resources Manager
Eugenia Bell, Production Coordinator
Patrick J Gouhin, Executive Director/CEO
James W Keaveney, Treasurer

A nonprofit technical society for engineers, technicians, businesspeople, educators and students who work, study or are interested in industrial automation and pursuits related to it, such as instrumentation.
30000 Members
Founded in: 1945

6783 **Instrumentation and Measurement Society**
799 N Beverly Glen
Los Angeles, CA 90077

310-446-8280; *Fax:* 732-981-0225
bob.myers@ieee.org
http://sites.ieee.org/

Michael P. Kelly, Executive Director
Donna Florek, Program Specialist
Michael Markowycz, Program Specialist
Jo-Ellen Snyder, Tech Community Program Specialist
Grant Pitel, Volunteer PELS Webmaster

A subsidiary of the Institute of Electrical and Electronics Engineers. Provides support to scientists and technicians who design and develop electrical and electronic measuring instruments and equipment.
6500 Members
Founded in: 1950

6784 **Insulated Cable Engineers Association**
PO Box 2694
Alpharetta, GA 30023

770-830-0369
info@icea.net; www.icea.net

Lauri J Hiivala, President
Webmaster

Professional organization dedicated to developing cable standards for the electric power, control and telecommunications industries. Ensures safe, economical and efficient cable systems utilizing proven, state-of-the-art materials and concepts. ICEA documents are of interest to cable manufacturers, architects and engineers, utility and manufacturing plant personnel, telecommunication engineers, consultants and OEMs.
Founded in: 1925

6785 **International Association for Radio, Telec ommunications and Electromagnets**
600 N. PLANKINTON AVE
Suite 301
Milwaukee, WI 53201

888-722-2440
888-722-2440; *Fax:* 414-765-8661
info@exemplarglobal.org; www.narte.org
Social Media: Facebook, Twitter, LinkedIn, YouTube, Google+

Peter Holtmann, President & Chief Executive Officer
Sal Agnello, General Manager, iNARTE

A worldwide, nonprofit, professional association which certifies qualified engineers and technicians in the fields of Telecommunications, Electromagnetic Compatibility/Interference (EMC/EMI), Product Safety (PS), Electrostatic Discharge control (ESD) and Wireless Systems Installation.

6786 **International Facility Management Association**
800 Gessner Rd.
Ste. 900
Houston, TX 77024-4257

713-623-4362; *Fax:* 713-623-6124
ifma@ifma.org; www.ifma.org
Social Media: Facebook, Twitter, LinkedIn, YouTube, Flickr, RSS

Michael D. Feldman, FMP, CM, Chair
Maureen Ehrenberg, FRICS, CRE, First Vice Chair
Tony Keane, CAE, President/CEO
John Perry, Chief Operating Officer
Aaron Clark, Vice President, Corporate Services

International association for facility management professionals.
22659 Members
Founded in: 1978

6787 **International Reprographic Association**
401 N Michigan Avenue
Chicago, IL 60611

708-218-7755; *Fax:* 312-527-6705
ed.avis@irga.com; www.irga.com
Social Media: LinkedIn

Tony Militano, President
Steve Andrikut, Vendor Director
Ed Avis, Managing Director
Michael Shaw, Director
Joe Williamson, Director

Represents entrepreneurial businesses serving the wide-format imaging needs of graphic arts, architectural, engineering, manufacturing, corporate, legal, retail, and POP industries.
Founded in: 1927

6788 **International Society Weighing/Measurement**
13017 Wisteria Drive
#341
Germantown, MD 20874

240-753-4397; *Fax:* 866-285-3512
staff@iswm.org; www.iswm.org

James Baxter, President
Jerry Finnegan, Vice President
Jamie Notter, Executive Director

Supports all those involved in the weighing and measurement industry.

6789 **International Society for Optical Engineering**
1000 20th Street
P O Box 10
Bellingham, WA 98225-6705

360-676-3290
888-504-8171; *Fax:* 360-647-1445
spie@spie.org; www.spie.org/
Social Media: Facebook, Twitter, LinkedIn, RSS, YouTube, Blogspot

Katerina Svanberg, President
William Arnold, Vice President
Brian Lula, Ssecretary/Treasurer
Eugene Arthurs, CEO

Serves the international, technical community as the premier provider of education, information, and resources covering optics, photonics, and their applications.
16000 Members
Founded in: 1955

6790 **Investigative Engineers Association**
10001 W Oakland Park Blvd.
Suite 301
Sunrise, FL 33351

954-530-0715
844-217-6975; *Fax:* 954-537-4942

jhogge@ienga.net; www.ienga.net
Social Media: Facebook, Twitter, LinkedIn

Lewis W Ernest, Advisor
James R Hogge, CEO
Tom Hogge, President
Nancy Pashkoff, Marketing Director
Tammy Lane, National Director

Consists of independent forensic engineering firms nationwide and abroad.

6791 Materials Research Society
506 Keystone Dr
Warrendale, PA 15086-7573

724-779-3003; *Fax:* 724-779-8313
info@mrs.org; www.mrs.org

Oliver Kraft, President
Kristi S. Anseth, Vice President
Sean J. Hearne, Secretary
Michael R. Fitzsimmons, Treasurer
Todd M. Osman, Executive Director

The Materials Research Society is a not-for-profit organization that brings together scientists, engineers and research managers from industry, government, academia and research laboratories to share findings in the research and development of new materials of technological importance. The Materials Research Society promotes communication for the advancement of interdisciplinary materials research to improve the quality of life.
16000 Members
Founded in: 1973

6792 NACE International
1440 S Creek Drive
Houston, TX 77084-4906

281-228-6200
800-797-6223; *Fax:* 281-228-6300
firstservice@nace.org; www.nace.org
Social Media: Facebook, Twitter, LinkedIn, YouTube, Google+, Instagram

Jim Feather, President
A. I. Sandy Williamson, Vice President
D. Terry Greenfield, Treasurer
Bob Chalker, CEO

Advances the knowledge of corrosion engineering and science in all major industries through education, certification, standards, publications, and public awareness.
21000 Members
Founded in: 1943

6793 National Academy of Engineering
500 5th Street NW
Washington, DC 20001

202-334-3200; *Fax:* 202-334-2290;
www.nae.edu
Social Media: Twitter, LinkedIn, YouTube

C. D. Mote, Jr., President
Alton D. Romig, Jr., Executive Officer
Mary Lee Berger-Hughes, Membership Director
Joan Zaorski, Director of Finance
Randy Atkins, Senior Program Officer

Promotes public understanding of the role that engineering plays in the technical fields. Sponsors programs aimed at meeting national needs in the field. Encourages research.
2000 Members
Founded in: 1964

6794 National Association of Fire Equipment Distributors
180 N. Wabash Avenue
Suite 401
Chicago, IL 60601

312-461-9600; *Fax:* 312-461-0777
dharris@nafed.org; www.nafed.org
Social Media: LinkedIn, YouTube

Ed Hugill, President
Danny Harris, Executive Director/CEO
Norbert Makowka, Vice President, Technical
Tamara Matthews, Communications Manager
Socorro Garcia, Office Manager

Improves the economic environment, business performance, and technical competence in the fire protection industry.
Founded in: 1963

6795 National Association of Minority Engineers
701 West Stadium Ave.
Suite 130
West Lafayette, IN 47907

765-494-4936; *Fax:* 407-629-2502
namepa@namepa.org; www.namepa.org

Virginia Booth Womack, President and Executive Director
Darryl A. Dickerson, Treasurer
Alaine M. Allen, Secretary
Jahi Sauk Simbai, Treasurer
Ivan Favila, Secretary

Provides a communication network among college-level administrators of minority engineering programs.
575 Members

6796 National Board of Boiler and Pressure Vessel Inspectors
1055 Crupper Ave
Columbus, OH 43229-1108

614-888-8320; *Fax:* 614-888-0750
information@nationalboard.org;
www.nationalboard.org

Don Tanner, Executive Director
Connie Homer, Senior Executive Secretary

Membership is composed of chief boiler inspectors of states, major US cities and Canadian provinces having boiler laws.
55 Members
Founded in: 1919

6797 National Council of Examiners for Engineering and Surveying
280 Seneca Creek Road
Seneca, SC 29678

864-654-6824
800-250-3196; *Fax:* 864-654-6033;
www.ncees.org
Social Media: Facebook, Twitter, LinkedIn, YouTube, RSS, Google+

Michael Conzett, P.E., President
Jerry Carter, Chief Executive Officer
Davy McDowell, P.E., Chief Operating Officer
Tim Miller, P.E., Director of Exam Services
Donna Moss, SHRM-CP, PHR, Director of Human Resources

Promotes uniform standards of registration and coordinates interstate registration of engineers and surveyors.
68 Members
Founded in: 1920

6798 National Electrical Contractors Association
3 Bethesda Metro Center
Suite 1100
Bethesda, MD 20814

301-657-3110; *Fax:* 301-215-4500;
www.necanet.org
Social Media: Facebook, Twitter, LinkedIn, YouTube, Flickr

John M Grau, Chief Executive Officer
Daniel G Walter, Vice President & COO
Beth Ellis, Exe. Dir., Convention/Exposition
Michael Johnston, Executive Director
Bill Triplett, Executive Director

A trade association in the United States that represents the electrical industry.
Founded in: 1901

6799 National Environmental Balancing Bureau
8575 Grovemont Cir
Gaithersburg, MD 20877-4121

301-977-3698
866-497-4447; *Fax:* 301-977-9589
karen@nebb.org; www.nebb.org

Jean-Paul Le Blanc, President
Glenn Fellman, Executive Vice President
Tiffany J. Suite, Operations Manager
Sheila Simms, Manager of Certifications
Leonard Maiani, Technical Director

NEBB is an international certification association for firms that deliver high performance building systems. Members perform testing, adjusting and balancing (TAB) of heating, ventilating and air-conditioning systems, commission and retro-commission building systems commissioning, execute sound and vibration testing, and test and certify lab fume hoods and electronic and bio clean rooms. NEBB holds the highest standards in certification.
Founded in: 1971

6800 National Fire Protection Association
1 Batterymarch Park
Quincy, MA 02169-7471

617-770-3000
800-844-6058; *Fax:* 617-770-0700;
www.nfpa.org
Social Media: Facebook, Twitter, LinkedIn, YouTube, Flickr, Google+

Ernest J Grant, Chair
Randolph W Tucker, First Vice Chair
Jim Pauley, President/ CEO
Julie Lynch, Vice President, Talent & Culture
Bruce H. Mullen, Executive Vice President and CFO

Publishes fire and building safety standards including the NationalElectrical Code.
Founded in: 1896

6801 National Institute for Certification in Technologies
1420 King St
Alexandria, VA 22314-2750

703-548-1518
888-476-4238; *Fax:* 703-682-2756
certify@nicet.org; www.nicet.org
Social Media: Facebook, LinkedIn

Greg Cagle, SET, Chair
Thomas J. Frericks, Jr., CT, Vice-Chair
Michael A. Clark, Chief Operating Executive
Regina L. Stevenson, Director, Administrative Services
Gloria Mathson, Manager, General Services

Issues certification to engineering technicians and technologists who voluntarily apply for certification and satisfy competency criteria through examinations and verification of work experience.
113K Members
Founded in: 1961

6802 National Society of Black Engineers
205 Daingerfield Road
Alexandria, VA 22314

703-549-2207; *Fax:* 703-683-5312
info@nsbe.org; www.nsbe.org
Social Media: Facebook, Twitter, LinkedIn, Pinterest, Google+

Neville Green, National Chair
Candice M Dixon, Vice Chairperson
Justin Brown, National Parliamentarian
Jennifer Jasper, National Secretary
Carl Mack, Executive Director

Supports all black technical professionals involved in the manufacturing engineering industry.
15000 Members
Founded in: 1971

6803 **National Society of Professional Engineers**
1420 King St
Alexandria, VA 22314-2794
703-684-2800; *Fax:* 703-836-4875;
www.nspe.org
Social Media: Facebook, Twitter, LinkedIn
Tim Austin, P.E., F.NSPE, President
Thomas C. Roberts, P.E., F.NSPE, Vice President
Julia M. Harrod, P.E., F.NSPE, Treasurer
Mark Golden, FASAE, CAE, Executive Director and Secretary
The mission of the Society is to promote the ethical, competent and licensed practice of engineering and to enhance the professional, social and economic well-being of its members.
60000 Members
Founded in: 1934

6804 **North American Die Casting Association**
3250 N. Arlington Heights Rd
Ste 101
Arlington Heights, IL 60004
847-279-0001; *Fax:* 847-279-0002
nadca@diecasting.org; www.diecasting.org
Daniel Twarog, President
The organization serves as the voice of the industry, promoting growth and enhancing member's ability to compete domestically in the global marketplace.
3700 Members
Founded in: 1989

6805 **North American Manufacturing Research Institute**
1 SME Drive
Dearborn, MI 48128
313-425-3000
800-733-4763; *Fax:* 313-425-3400
service@sme.org; www.sme.org
Social Media: Facebook, Twitter, LinkedIn, Google+, RSS
Wayne F. Frost, President
Jeffrey M. Krause, Chief Executive Officer
Kathleen Borgula, Human Resources
Erica Ciupak, Information Technology
Julie Duff, Finance
Members are engaged in manufacturing, research and technology development.
180 Members
Founded in: 1973

6806 **Order Of The Engineer**
PO Box 25473
Scottsdale, AZ 85255-0107
866-364-7464; *Fax:* 480-585-6418
orderofeng@gmail.com;
www.order-of-the-engineer.org
Paula Ostaff, Executive Director
An association for graduate and professional engineers in the United States that emphasizes pride and responsibility in the engineering profession.

6807 **Pi Tau Sigma**
www.pitausigma.net
Dr. Mun Young Choi, President
Dr. Gloria J Wiens, Eastern Region Vice-President
Dr. Alex Moutsoglou, National Secretary-Treasurer
Dr. Chris Wilson, Central Region Vice-President
Dr. Darryl James, Western Region Vice-President
An International Mechanical Engineering Honor Society.
Founded in: 1947

6808 **Professional Engineers in Private Practice**
1420 King Street
Alexandria, VA 22314-2750
703-684-2800; *Fax:* 703-836-4875;
www.nspe.org
Social Media: Facebook, Twitter, LinkedIn
Terrance N Glunt, Chair
Larry L Britt, PE, Chair-Elect
Steve M Theno, PE, Secretary
Addresses the concerns of individual engineers in private practice, primarily working in design for construction. Offers resources, standard contracts, newsletters and management guidance in the forms of videos, books, and newsletters.
24M Members
Founded in: 1956

6809 **Railway Engineering: Maintenance Suppliers Association**
500 New Jersey Ave. NW
Suite 400
Washington, DC 20001
202-715-2921; *Fax:* 202-204-5753
info@remsa.org; www.remsa.org
Trent Marshall, President
Bruce R. Wise, Vice President
Alan D. Reynolds, Secretary/Treasurer
David Tennent, Executive Director, REMSA
C. David Soule, CEM, Director of Trade Shows, REMSA
Members are distributors and manufacturers of railway machinery supplies and services.
225 Members
Founded in: 1965

6810 **Refrigeration Service Engineers Society**
1911 Rohlwing Road
Suite A
Rolling Meadows, IL 60008-1397
847-297-6464
800-297-5660; *Fax:* 847-297-5038
general@rses.org; www.rses.org
Social Media: Facebook, Twitter, LinkedIn, RSS
Harlan Krepcik, CMS, RCT, Intl President
Michael J. Thompson, CMS, Intl Vice President
Nick Reggi, CMS, RCT, Intl Secretary/Treasurer
Roger M. Hensley, CMS, RCT, Board Chairman
Steve Wright, Sr., CMS, RCT, International Sergeant at Arms
A leading education, training and certification association for heating, ventilation, air conditioning and refrigeration professionals. RSES credentials include the SM/CM/CMS exam series as well as one of the largest EPA Section 608 certification programs in the industry.
15231 Members
Founded in: 1933

6811 **Reliability Engineering and Management Institute**
1077 N Highland
Tucson, AZ 85721
520-626-8324; *Fax:* 520-621-8191
dimitri@u.arizona.edu; www.u.arizona.edu
Michele Norin, VP for IT/CIO
Christian Schreiber, Chief Information Security Officer
Derek Masseth, Deputy Chief Info Officer/CTO
Thomas C Bourgeois, Executive Director
Kay Stevens Beasock, Director, Communications/Marketing
Supports all engineers and managers who deal with the issue of Reliability Engineering. Provides publications, training, education, new techniques and product forums and two annual conference.
Founded in: 1963
Mailing list available for rent: 44000 names

6812 **Research Council on Structural Connections**
Sargent & Lundy
55 E Monroe Street
Chicago, IL 60603-5780
312-269-2000; *Fax:* 312-269-3681
rshaw@steelstructures.com;
www.boltcouncil.org
Ray Tide, Chairman Executive Committee
Geoff Kulak, Vice Chairman
Charles Carter, Chairman Membership/Funding
Emile Troup, Secretary/Treasurer
Researches the effects of stress on bolted and riveted joints for its member companies and institutions.
45 Members
Founded in: 1946

6813 **Robotics Industries Association**
900 Victors Way
Suite 140
Ann Arbor, MI 48108
734-994-6088; *Fax:* 734-994-3338
webmaster@robotics.org; www.robotics.org
Social Media: Facebook, Twitter, LinkedIn, Google+
Stuart Shepherd, Chairperson
Jeff Burnstein, President
Dana Whalls, Vice President
Bob Doyle, Director of Communications
Alex Shikany, Director, Market Analysis
Trade group organized specifically to serve the robotics industry. Member companies include leading robot manufacturers, users, system integrators, component suppliers, research groups and consulting firms. Trade show is held every two years.
250+ Members
Founded in: 1974

6814 **Science and Technology Society**
125 Maiden Ln
15th Floor
New York, NY 10038
212-248-0200; *Fax:* 212-248-0245
ricky@avs.org; www.avs.org
Christie R Marrian, President
John Coburn, Treasurer
Joseph E Greene, Clerk/Secretary
Supports all those in the vacuum industry, especially scientists and engineers.
6000 Members
Founded in: 1953

6815 **Sigma Phi Delta**
438 Smithfield Street
East Liverpool, OH 43920-1723
330-385-5287
webmaster@sigphi.org; www.sigphi.org
Social Media: Facebook, Twitter, LinkedIn
Alixandre R. Minden PE, PMP, Grand President
Eric J. Pew, Grand VP
Tyler S Condon, Treasurer
Joshua J. Lester, Director of Alumni Relations
Erik N. Schultz, Director of Chapter Development
A professional and social fraternity in engineering.
7200 Members
Founded in: 1924

6816 Society for Experimental Mechanics
7 School St
Bethel, CT 06801-1855
203-790-6373; *Fax:* 203-790-4472
sem@sem1.com; www.sem.org
Social Media: Facebook, Twitter, YouTube

Peter Ifgu, President
Emmanuel Gdoutos, Vice President
Jon Rogers, Treasurer
Tom Proulx, Executive Director

Supports all those involved with general experimental mechanics and the measurement of stresses and strains in metals and other materials.
Founded in: 1943

6817 Society for the Advancement of Material and Process Engineering
1161 Parkview Drive
Suite 200
Covina, CA 91724-3759
626-331-0616
800-562-7360; *Fax:* 626-332-8929
sampe@sampe.org; www.sampe.org
Social Media: Facebook, Twitter, LinkedIn

Gregg Balko, Executive Director
Mike Keilty, Controller
Dr Scott Beckwith, Technical Director

An international professional member society, provides information on new materials and processing technology either via technical forums, journal publications, or books in which professionals in this field can exchange ideas and air their views.
Founded in: 1944

6818 Society of Allied Weight Engineers
5734 E. Lucia Walk
Long Beach, CA 90803-4015
562-596-2873; *Fax:* 562-596-2874
exdirector@sawe.org; www.sawe.org

Anthony Primozich, President
Robert Hundl, Executive VP
Rick Watkins, Senior VP
Jerry L. Pierson, VP Training
Ronald Fox, Executive Director

Consists of engineers in the aerospace, shipbuilding, land vehicles, offshore and allied industries.
800 Members
Founded in: 1941

6819 Society of American Military Engineers
607 Prince St
Alexandria, VA 22314-3117
703-549-3800
800-336-3097; *Fax:* 703-684-0231
webmanager@same.org; www.same.org

Jane C. Penny, President
Col. Kurt Ubbelohde, F.SAME, Vice President
Gen. Joseph Schroedel, P.E.,, Executive Director
Desyre, Jones, Senior Operations & Admin Manager
Belle Febbraro, Program Manager

Brings together professional engineers and those in engineering related fields to improve and increase the engineering capabilities of the nation and to exchange and advance the knowledge of engineering technologies, applications and practices.
20000 Members
Founded in: 1920

6820 Society of Automotive Engineers
1200 G St., NW
Suite 800
Washington, DC 20005
202-463-7318; *Fax:* 202-463-7319;
www.sae.org
Social Media: Facebook, Twitter, LinkedIn, Google+

Frank Menchaca, Chief Product Officer
Dana M Pless, Chief Financial Officer
David L Schutt, Chief Executive Officer
George Bradley, Esq., General Counsel
Sandra L. Dillner, Director of Human Resources

Advances mobility in land, sea, air, and space.
Founded in: 1905

6821 Society of Broadcast Engineers
9102 North Meridian Street
Suite 150
Indianapolis, IN 46260
317-846-9000; www.sbe.org
Social Media: Facebook, Twitter, LinkedIn, YouTube, Blogger

Jerry Massey, President
James E. Leifer, CPBE, Vice President
John Poray, CAE, Executive Director
Megan Clappe, Certification Director
Debbie Hennessey, Sustaining Member Manager

A professional organization for engineers in broadcast radio and television.
5500 Members

6822 Society of Fire Protection Engineers
9711 Washingtonian Blvd
Suite 380
Gaithersburg, MD 20878
301-718-2910; *Fax:* 240-328-6225
foundation@sfpe.org; www.sfpe.org
Social Media: Facebook, Twitter, LinkedIn, YouTube, RSS

Michael Madden, P.E., FSFPE, President
Milosh Puchovsky, P.E., FSFPE, President Elect
Jack Poole, P.E., FSFPE, Secretary-Treasurer
Nicole Testa Boston, CAE, Ex-Officio
David Barber, Director

The largest professional society for fire safety engineers.
4500 Members
Founded in: 1971

6823 Society of Hispanic Professional Engineers
323-725-3970
703-373-7930
shpenational@shpe.org
shpe.org
Social Media: Facebook, Twitter, LinkedIn, YouTube, Instagram

Barry Cordero, Chair
Miguel Alemany, Vice Chair
Yuliana Porras Mendoza, Secretary
Ernesto Felix, Treasurer
Rodrigo T. Garcia, President

A national organization of professional engineers to serve as rolemodels in the Hispanic community.
Founded in: 1974

6824 Society of Manufacturing Engineers
1 SME Drive
Dearborn, MI 48128
313-425-3000
800-733-4763; *Fax:* 313-425-3400
service@sme.org; www.sme.org
Social Media: Facebook, Twitter, LinkedIn, Google +, RSS, YouTube

Wayne F. Frost, President
Jeffery M. Krause, Chief Executive Officer
Dean L. Bartles, PhD, FSME, President-Elect
Sandra L. Bouckley, Vice President
Thomas R. Kurfess, PhD, FSME, PE, Treasurer

Professional society dedicated to advancing scientific knowledge in the field of manufacturing and to applying its resources for researching, writing, publishing and disseminating information.
70M Members
Founded in: 1932

6825 Society of Naval Architects and Marine Engineers
99 Canal Center Plaza
Suite 310
Alexandria, VA 22314
703-997-6701; *Fax:* 703-997-6702;
www.sname.org

Erik Seither, Executive Director
Jodi Lane, Executive Administrative
Mike Hall, Director Of Membership
Carole Herzog, Membership Coordinator
Susan Evans Grove, Director Of Content

A global professional society that provides a forum for the advancement of the engineering profession as applied to the marine field.
8500 Members
Founded in: 1893

6826 Society of Petroleum Engineers
222 Palisades Creek Dr.
Richardson, TX 75080
972-952-9393
800-456-6863; *Fax:* 972-952-9435
spedal@spe.org; www.spe.org
Social Media: Facebook, Twitter, LinkedIn, Instagram, YouTube

Helge Hove Haldorsan Statoil, President
Roland Moreau, Vice President, Finance
Dan Hill, Director For Academia
David Curry, Technical Director
Trey Shaffer, Technical Director

To provide the means for collection, dissemination and exchange of technical information concerning the development of oil and gas resources, subsurface fluid flow and production of other materials through well bores for the public benefit.
64000 Members
Founded in: 1957

6827 Society of Rheology
American Institute of Physics
2 Huntington Quadrangle
Suite 1N01
Meville, NY 11747-4502
516-576-2471; *Fax:* 516-576-2223
rheology@aip.org; www.rheology.org

Greg McKenna, President
Gareth H. McKinley, Vice President
Albert Co, Secretary
Montgomery T. Shaw, Treasurer
Ralph H. Colby, Editor

Composed of physicists, chemists, biologists, engineers, and mathematicians interested in advancing and applying rheology, which is defined as the science of deformation and flow of matter.
1700 Members

6828 Society of Tribologists and Lubrication Engineers
840 Busse Hwy
Park Ridge, IL 60068-2376
847-825-5536; *Fax:* 847-825-1456
information@stle.org; www.stle.org

Dr. Martin N. Webster, President
Dr. Eli Erdemir, Vice President
Mr. Michael Anderson, Secretary
Mr. Greg Croce, Treasurer
Mr. James Arner, Director

Strives to advance the science of lubrication tribology and related arts and sciences. Sponsors courses and an annual meeting.
4400 Members
Founded in: 1960

6829 Society of Women Engineers
203 N La Salle Street
Suite 1675
Chicago, IL 60601

877-793-4636
hq@swe.org
societyofwomenengineers.swe.org
Social Media: Facebook, Twitter, LinkedIn, YouTube, Instagram, Google+

Colleen M. Layman, President
Jessica Rannow, President Elect
Stephanie Loete, Secretary
Cindy Hoover, Treasurer
Mary Perkinson, Director Of Advocacy

An organization that stimulates women to achieve full potential in careers as engineers.

6830 Tau Beta Pi Association
PO Box 2697
Knoxville, TN 37901-2697

865-546-4578; *Fax:* 865-546-4579;
www.tbp.org
Social Media: Facebook, Twitter, WordPress

Joseph P. Blackford, President
Norman Pih, Vice President
Curtis D. Gomulinski, Exec. Dir./ Sec-Treasurer & Editor
James D. Froula, Secretary-Treasurer Emeritus
Susan L. R. Holl, Councillor

The National Engineering honor society recognizes engineering students of superior scholarship and exemplary character and practitioners of engineering. The organization includes 230 collegiate chapters and 16 alumnus chapters.
525K Members
Founded in: 1885

6831 The American Association for Wind Engineers
1415 Blue Spruce Drive
Suite 3
Fort Collins, CO 80524

970-498-2334; *Fax:* 970-221-3124
aawe@aawe.org; www.aawe.org

Dr. Partha Sarkar, President
Dr. Greg Kopp, President Elect
Dr. Steve C. S. Cai, Secretary/ Treasurer
Dr. David O Prevatt, Board of Directors
Dr. Anne Cope, Board of Directors

A nonprofit professional organization that promotes and disseminates technical information in the research community.
Founded in: 1995

6832 The American Society For Nondestructive Testing
1711 Arlingate Lane
Columbus, OH 43228-0518

614-274-6003
800-222-2768; *Fax:* 614-274-6899
pwhite@asnt.org; www.asnt.org
Social Media: Facebook, Twitter, LinkedIn, YouTube

Amy Bereson, Executive Director
Michelle Thomas, Executive Dir. Admin. Assistant
Heather Cowles, Senior Manager
Pat White, Membership Coordinator
Debbie Segor, Sections Coordinator

A technical society for nondestructive testing professionals.
Founded in: 1941

6833 The Associated General Contractors of America
2300 Wilson Blvd.
Suite 300
Arlington, VA 22201

703-548-3118
800-242-1767; *Fax:* 703-837-5405
info@agc.org; www.agc.org
Social Media: Facebook, Twitter, LinkedIn

Charles L. Greco, President
Art Daniel, Senior Vice President
Mark Knight, Vice President
Joseph Stella, Treasurer
Stephen E. Sandherr, Executive Director

Trade association for the construction industry.
26000 Members

6834 The Order of the Engineer, Inc.
PO Box 25473
Scottsdale, AZ 85255-0107

866-364-7464; *Fax:* 480-585-6418;
www.order-of-the-engineer.org

Kenneth McGowan, Chair
Paula Ostaff, Executive Director

Association for graduate and professional engineers emphasizing pride and responsibility.
Founded in: 1970

6835 Theta Tau
1011 San Jacinto
Suite 205
Austin, TX 78701

512-482-1904
800-264-1904; *Fax:* 512-472-4820
central.office@thetatau.org; www.thetatau.org
Social Media: Facebook, Twitter, LinkedIn

Michael Livingston, Grand Regent
Justin Wisemen, Grand Vice Regent
Rachael Stensrud, Grand Scribe
J. Matthew Clark, Grand Treasurer

A professional fraternity in engineering. Founded at the University of Minnesota. Purpose of the fraternity is to develop and maintain a high standard of professional interest among its members, and to unite them in a strong bond of fraternal fellowship.
30000 Members
Founded in: 1904

6836 TheTire Society
810 E. 10th St.
Lawrence, KS 66044

785-865-9403
800-627-0326; *Fax:* 785-843-6153
tst@allenpress.com; www.tiresociety.org

Saied Taheri, President
Randy Jenniges, Vice President
Ric Mousseau, Past President
Michell Hoo Fatt, Secretary
Rusty Adams, Treasurer

A professional engineering society that increases and disseminates knowledge as it pertains to the science and technology of tires.

6837 United Engineering Foundation
16 Copper Penny Road
Flemington, NJ 08822-5540

E-Mail: engfnd@aol.com;
www.uefoundation.org

Ian Sadler, President
Patrick J. Natale, Executive Director

Supports research in engineering science and seeks to advance the profession of engineering.
19 Members
Founded in: 1904

6838 United Engineering Trustees
16 Copper Penny Road
Flemington, NJ 08822-5540

www.uefoundation.org

Ian Sadler, President
Patrick J. Natale, Executive Director

Aims to advance engineering arts and sciences.
Founded in: 1904

Newsletters

6839 AEG News
Assn. of Environmental & Engineering Geologists
1100-H Brandywine Boulevard
Suite 575
Zanesville, OH 43701

303-757-2926
844-331-7867; *Fax:* 740-452-2552
aeg@aegweb.org; www.aegweb.org

Dale C. Andrews, President
Kathy Troost, Vice President
Kevin Richards, Treasurer
Cynthia Palomares, Secretary

Includes reports of committee activities, section news, and other news items of interest to the profession.
Frequency: Quarterly

6840 AIP History Newsletter
American Institute of Physics
1 Physics Ellipse
College Park, MD 20740-3841

301-209-3100; *Fax:* 301-209-0843
dylla@aip.org; www.aip.org

Marc Brodsky, CEO
Margaret Wiley, Senior Executive Secretary
Benjamin Snavely, AIP Corporate Secretary
Melissa Poleski, Assistant To Corporate Secretary

Our Newsletter reports on work in the history of physics (and allied fields such as astronomy and geophysics), carried out at the American Institute of Physics and elsewhere. It includes lists of recent publications in the history of modern physics, and reports on papers deposited in archives worldwide.

6841 ASFE Newslog
ASFE/The Geoprofessional Business Association
8811 Colesville Rd
Suite G106
Silver Spring, MD 20910-4343

301-565-2733; *Fax:* 301-589-2017
info@asfe.org; www.asfe.org

David Gaboury, President

Information on geo professional, environmental, and civil engineering firms. Past issues are available through the online store. Electronic copies are always free to members.

6842 ASGE Newsletter
American Society of Gas Engineers
P.O. Box 66
Artesia, CA 90702

562-455-9417
asgecge@aol.com; www.asge-national.org

Jerry Moore, Executive Director
Mike O'Donnell, President
Ray Maddock, Vice President
Chad Johnson, Treasurer

Keeps members current on events and issues facing the Gas Appliance Industry. Features articles that address new technologies and trends.
Founded in: 1954

6843 ASTM International Business Link
ASTM International
PO Box C700
W Conshohocken, PA 19428-0700

610-832-9500; *Fax:* 610-832-9555
service@astm.org; www.astm.org

James A Thomas, President

Provides information on the topics connecting the business and technical communities.
Frequency: Semi-Annual

6844 Access ASTM International
ASTM International
PO Box C700
W Conshohocken, PA 19428-0700

610-832-9500; *Fax:* 610-832-9555
service@astm.org; www.astm.org

James A Thomas, President
John Pace, Manager
Jeff Adkins, Manager
Fran Dougherty, Administrative Assistant

Periodic update for ASTM's global customers.
Frequency: Semi-Annual

6845 American Automatic Control Council Newsletter
AACC Secretariat
2145 Sheridan Road
Evanston, IL 60208-3118

847-491-8175; *Fax:* 847-491-4455
aacc@ece.northwestern.edu; www.a2c2.org

Bonnie Heck, Publisher
William Levine, President
A Ulsoy, Vice-President

Automatic control council information.
4 Pages
Frequency: Quarterly
Founded in: 1961

6846 BMES Bulletin
Biomedical Engineering Society
8401 Corporate Dr
Suite 140
Hyattsville, MD 20785-2263

301-459-1999; *Fax:* 301-459-2444
info@bmes.org; www.bmes.org

Barbara Dunlevy, Executive Director
Heather Comstock, Meeting Manager

The Bulletin presents bioengineering science articles, student chapter news, Society and public policy announcements, employment opportunities, and a calendar of conference and events. It is also a forum for member opinions through editorials and letters.
Cost: $30.00
Frequency: Monthly
Circulation: 3500
Founded in: 1969
Printed in 2 colors on matte stock

6847 Bulletin of Tau Beta Pi
Tau Beta Pi Association
PO Box 2697
Knoxville, TN 37901-2697

865-546-4578; *Fax:* 865-546-4579;
www.tbp.org

R E Hawks, Editor

The purpose of The Bulletin is to disseminate news and information about Tau Beta Pi of special interest to the collegiate chapters. It is an important vehicle for the annual repetition of instructions from the Executive Council and national headquarters to the chapters on election and initiation procedures and for the exchange of chapter project ideas and experience.
Frequency: 3x Annually
Founded in: 1925

6848 Computer Integrated Manufacture and Engineering
Lionheart Publishing
506 Roswell St Se
Suite 220
Marietta, GA 30060-4101

770-422-3139; *Fax:* 770-432-6969
lpi@lionhrtpub.com; www.lionhrtpub.com/

Marvin Diamond, Advertising Sales Manager

Explores cutting edge developments in manufacturing systems operation management.
Circulation: 24000

6849 Cross Connection Protection Devices
American Society of Sanitary Engineering
901 Canterbury Rd
Suite A
Westlake, OH 44145-1480

440-835-3040; *Fax:* 440-835-3488;
www.asse-plumbing.org

James Bickford, President
Donald Summers, First VP
John Flader, Treasurer

Summary of backflow conditions and method of eliminating or minimizing their possible dangers.
Cost: $15.00

6850 E-Catalyst Industry Update
Adhesive & Sealant Council
7101 Wisconsin Ave
Suite 990
Bethesda, MD 20814-4805

301-986-9700; *Fax:* 301-986-9795
data@ascouncil.org; www.ascouncil.org

William Allmond, President

6851 Echoes Newsletter
Acoustical Society of America
2 Huntington Quad
Suite 1N01
Melville, NY 11747-4505

516-576-2360; *Fax:* 516-576-2377
asa@aip.org; www.acousticalsociety.org

Charles E Schmid, President

Covers current and topical happenings of general interest and features articles about current research and personalities. Distributed free to members.
Frequency: Quarterly

6852 Engineering Department Management and Administration Report
Institute of Management and Administration
3 Bethesda Metro Center
Suite 250
Bethesda, MD 20814

703-341-3500; *Fax:* 800-253-0332;
www.ioma.com

Focuses on improving efficiency and productivity.
Cost: $245.00
16 Pages
Frequency: Monthly

6853 Engineering Times
National Society of Professional Engineers
1420 King St
Alexandria, VA 22314-2794

703-684-2800; *Fax:* 703-836-4875
webmaster@nspe.org; www.nspe.org

Larry Jacobson, Executive Director/Secretary
Robert Grey, President

Reports on issues affecting the engineering profession; featured monthly series on ethics. Free to members.
Cost: $30.00
24 Pages

6854 High-Tech Materials Alert
Technical Insights
605 3rd Avenue
New York, NY 10158

212-850-6824
800-245-6217; *Fax:* 212-850-8643

Kenneth Kovaly, Publisher

Opportunities in advanced materials.
Cost: $867.00
12 Pages

6855 Highpoints Newsletter
American Academy of Environmental Engineers
147 Old Solomons Island Road
Suite 303
Annapolis, MD 21401-7003

410-266-3311; *Fax:* 410-266-7653
info@aaees.org; www.aaees.org

Newsletter providing news and updates on Academy activities, as well as general industry information and news.
Frequency: Monthly

6856 Hufact Quarterly: A Current Awareness Resource
Ergosyst Associates
123 W 8th Street
Suite 210
Lawrence, KS 66044-2687

Fax: 785-842-7348

John Burch, Publisher

Covers economics/human factors.
Cost: $100.00

6857 IE News: Ergonomics
Institute of Industrial Engineers
3577 Parkway Lane
Suite 200
Norcross, GA 30092

770-449-0460
800-494-0460; *Fax:* 770-441-3295
cs@iienet.org; www.iienet.org

Don Greene, CEO
Donna Calvert, COO

Newsletter for Ergonomics Division.
4 Pages
Frequency: Quarterly
Founded in: 1948

6858 IE News: Facilities Planning and Design
Institute of Industrial Engineers
25 Technology Pkwy S
Suite 150
Norcross, GA 30092-2946

770-449-0461; *Fax:* 770-263-8532

Dona Brown, Publisher

Accepts advertising.
4 Pages

6859 IE News: Operations Research
Institute of Industrial Engineers
25 Technology Pkwy S
Suite 150
Norcross, GA 30092-2946

770-449-0461; *Fax:* 770-263-8532

Dona Brown, Publisher

News for industrial engineers. Accepts advertising.
4 Pages

6860 **IE News: Quality Control and Reliability Engineering**
Institute of Industrial Engineers
25 Technology Pkwy S
Suite 150
Norcross, GA 30092-2946

770-449-0461; *Fax:* 770-263-8532

Dona Brown, Publisher

Association news.
4 Pages

6861 **Innovators Digest**
InfoTeam
PO Box 15640
Plantation, FL 33318-5640

954-473-9560; *Fax:* 954-473-0544

Merton Allen, Editor

A multidisciplinary publication covering developments in science, engineering, products, markets, business development, manufacturing and other technological developments having industrial or commercial significance.
Frequency: Bi-Annual

6862 **Instrumentation Newsletter**
National Instruments
6504 Bridge Point Parkway
Austin, TX 78730-5017

512-389-9119
888-280-7645; *Fax:* 512-794-8411
info@natinst.com; www.natinst.com

Gail Folkins, Managing Editor
John Graff, Vice President of Sales
James Truchard, President
Frequency: Quarterly
Circulation: 150000
Founded in: 1976

6863 **Last Word**
American Council of Engineering Companies
1015 15th St
8th Floor NW
Washington, DC 20005-2605

202-347-7474; *Fax:* 202-898-0068
acec@acec.org; www.acec.org
Social Media: Facebook, Twitter

Dave Raymond, President
Ann Randstapter, Editor
Sheila Mahoutchian, Marketing Manager
Mary Jaffe, Director, Publications
Alan Crockett, Director, Public Relations

Independent private practice engineering companies.
Cost: $90.00
2 Pages
Frequency: Monthly
Circulation: 5800
Founded in: 1905
Printed in on glossy stock

6864 **Leadership and Management in Engineering**
American Society of Civil Engineers
1801 Alexander Bell Dr
Suite 100
Reston, VA 20191-4382

703-295-6300
800-548-2723; *Fax:* 703-295-6222
cybrarian@asce.org; www.asce.org

D Wayne Klotz, President

A cutting-edge periodical focusing on the art and practice of management and leadership in the civil engineering community.
Frequency: Quarterly

6865 **Licensure Exchange**
National Council of Examiners for Engineering
280 Seneca Creek Road
PO Box 1686
Clemson, SC 29633

864-654-6824
800-250-3196; *Fax:* 864-654-6033;
www.ncees.org

Keri Anderson, Editor
Ashley Cheney, Treasurer
David Widmer, Treasurer
Theodore Sack, Vice President

Provides information, opinion, and ideas regarding the licensure of engineers and land surveyors.
Frequency: Bi-Monthly

6866 **Nuclear News**
American Nuclear Society
555 N Kensington Ave
La Grange Park, IL 60526-5592

708-352-6611; *Fax:* 708-352-0499;
www.ans.org

Jack Tuohy, Executive Director

Covers the latest developments in the nuclear field, a large part of which concerns nuclear energy - in particular, the 104 operating U.S. nuclear power plants, and another 334 operating elsewhere around the globe.
Cost: $365.00
Frequency: Monthly
Founded in: 2005

6867 **Plumbing Systems & Design**
American Society Of Plumbing Engineers
2980 S River Rd
Des Plaines, IL 60018-4203

773-693-2773; *Fax:* 773-695-9007;
www.psdmagazine.org/

Tom Govedarica, Executive Publisher
Gretchen Pienta, Managing Editor
Maria Barriga, Circulation Manager
Jill Dirksen, Technical Director
David Ropinski, Graphic Designer

Industry leading technical publication with ASPE news and features. Free to ASPE members and subscribers.
Cost: $150.00
Circulation: 25500
Printed in 4 colors on glossy stock

6868 **Power**
McGraw Hill
PO Box 182604
Columbus, OH 43272-1095
720-485-5000
877-833-5524; *Fax:* 614-759-3749;
www.mcgraw-hill.com

Harold McGraw, Chairman and President
Jack Callahan, Executive VP

Published for engineers who design, construct, operate and maintain power operating facilities in cogeneration and independent power plants in electric utilities. Accepts advertising.
Cost: $50.00
Frequency: Monthly
Founded in: 1888

6869 **Rheology Bulletin**
Society of Rheology
2 Huntington Quadrangle
Suite 1N01
Meville, NY 11747-4502

516-576-2471; *Fax:* 516-576-2223
rheology@aip.org; www.rheology.org

Faith Morrison, President
Jeffrey Giacomin, Vice President
Albert Co, Secretary
Montgomery Shaw, Treasurer

To inform members of the Society affairs and matters of general interest to rheologists.
Frequency: 2x yearly

6870 **Robotics Today**
Society of Manufacturing Engineers
1 Sme Drive
Dearborn, MI 48128

313-425-3000
800-733-4763; *Fax:* 343-425-3400
service@sme.org; www.sme.org

Paul Bradley, President
Mark Tomlinson, CEO and Executive Director
Dennis Bray, Vice President
Michael Molner, Secretary/Treasurer

Reports on robotics used in manufacturing.
Cost: $60.00
8 Pages
Frequency: Quarterly
*Mailing list available for rent*at $95 per M
Printed in 2 colors on matte stock

6871 **SAWE Technical Papers**
Society of Allied Weight Engineers
5734 E. Lucia Walk
Long Beach, CA 90803-4015

562-596-2873; *Fax:* 562-596-2874
exdirector@sawe.org; www.sawe.org

Patrick Brown, President
Jeffrey Cerro, Executive VP
Ronald Fox, Executive Director

The Technical Paper Index.
Frequency: Every 3 Years

6872 **Systems**
Institute of Industrial Engineers
25 Technology Pkwy S
Suite 150
Norcross, GA 30092-2946

770-449-0461; *Fax:* 770-263-8532

SL Browder, Publisher

Newsletter for IIE's society.
4 Pages
Frequency: Quarterly

6873 **The AOCS Newsletter**
American Oil Chemists' Society
2710 S Boulder Drive
P.O. Box 17190
Urbana, IL 61803-6996

217-359-2344; *Fax:* 217-351-8091
general@aocs.org; www.aocs.org
Social Media: Facebook, Twitter, LinkedIn

Gloria Cook, Senior Director, Finance
Jeffry L. Newman, Senior Director, Programs

The AOCS Newsletter is sent electronically each month to approximately 4,200 AOCS members and 10,000 other related industry professionals. It contains the latest AOCS news, including discounted offers, upcoming meeting information and registration details, AOCS press releases, and technical services updates.
4500 Members
Frequency: Annual/April-May
Founded in: 1909

6874 **Tribology Letters**
Kluwer Academic/Plenum Publishers
840 Busse Highway
Park Ridge, IL 60068-2376

847-825-5536; *Fax:* 847-825-1456
information@stle.org; www.stle.org

Karl Phipps, Associate Managing Editor

Devoted to the development of the science of Tribology and to its applications. It also serves as the depository for new information on the mechanical properties of surfaces.
Frequency: 95x Yearly

6875 **Velocitus Officers Newsletter**
Theta Tau

815 Brazos
Suite 710
Austin, TX 78701

512-482-1904
800-264-1904; *Fax:* 512-472-4820
central.office@thetatau.org; www.thetatau.org

Michael T Abraham, Executive Director
Dana Wortman, Grand Treasurer
Brandon J Satterwhite, Western Regional Director
Matthew Clark, Treasurer

Available by request via email or calling our 800 number.

Magazines & Journals

6876 AFE Facilities Engineering Journal
Association for Facilities Engineering
8160 Corporate Park Drive
#125
Cincinnati, OH 45242-3309

513-489-2473; *Fax:* 513-247-7422
Info@AFE.org; www.afe.org

Gabriella Jacobs, Communications Manager
Bob Kruhm, Advertising Manager
Patrick Janszen, Art Director
Michael Ireland, Executive Director

Information on maintenance management, energy conservation, safety and security, computerized maintenance management systems, environmental compliance, telecommunications and related issues.
Cost: $225.00
Frequency: Monthly
Circulation: 6000
ISSN: 1088-5900
Founded in: 1956
Mailing list available for rent: 10000 names at $100 per M
Printed in 4 colors on glossy stock

6877 ASEE Prism
American Society for Engineering Education
1818 N St NW
#600
Washington, DC 20036-2476

202-331-3500; *Fax:* 202-265-8504
pubsinfo@asee.org; www.asee.org

Frank L Huband, Executive Director
Mary Dalheim, Editor
Sherra E. Kerns, President

Geared towards educators in the engineering technology fields.
Frequency: Monthly
Circulation: 12000
Founded in: 1893

6878 ASME News
American Society of Mechanical Engineers
3 Park Ave
New York, NY 10016-5902

212-591-7000
800-843-2763; *Fax:* 212-591-8676
infocentral@asme.org; www.asme.org

Virgil R Carter, CEO
John G Falcioni, Managing Director
David Soukup, Managing Director

News, profiles and more from the American Society of mechanical engineers.
Cost: $125.00
Frequency: Monthly
Circulation: 125000
Founded in: 1880
Printed in 4 colors on matte stock

6879 ASTM Standardization News
ASTM International
100 Barr Harbor Drive
PO Box C700
W Conshohocken, PA 19428-2959

610-832-9500
610-832-9500; *Fax:* 610-832-9555
service@astm.org; www.astm.org

James A Thomas, President
Jeff Grove, Vice President

The official magazine of ASTM International, SATM Standardization news reports events in materials research and standardization.
Cost: $18.00
88 Pages
Frequency: Monthly
Circulation: 35000
Founded in: 1898

6880 AWIS Magazine
Association for Women in Science
1667 K Street NW
Suite 800
Washington, DC 20006

202-588-8175
awis@awis.org; www.awis.org
Social Media: Facebook, Twitter, LinkedIn

Janet Bandows Koster, Executive Director

Focuses on issues relevant to women scientists. Contains articles about current events, career advancement, financial planning, work-life balance, and creating a diverse work environment.
Frequency: Quarterly
Circulation: 3500

6881 Advanced Materials & Processes
ASM International
9639 Kinsman Rd
Materials Park, OH 44073

440-338-5151
800-336-5152; *Fax:* 440-338-4634;
www.asminternational.org

Ed Kubel, Senior Editor
Julie Kalista, Editor
Joanne Miller, Production Manager

AM&P, the monthly technical magazine from ASM International, is designed to keep readers aware of leading-edge developments and trends in engineering materials - metals and alloys, engineering polymers, advanced ceramics, and composites - and the methods used to select, process, fabricate, test, and characterize them.
36000 Members
Frequency: Monthly
Circulation: 32M
Founded in: 1977

6882 Aerospace Engineering
400 Commonwealth Drive
Warrendale, PA 15096-1

724-776-4841; *Fax:* 724-776-9765;
www.sae.org

JE Robertson PE, President
Robert E Spitzer, VP Aerospace
Raymond Morris, Executive Vice President
Richard Schaum, VP Automotive
Andrew Brown, Treasurer

Serves the international aerospace design and manufacturing field which consists of producers of airliners, helicopters, spacecraft, missiles, and power plants, propulsion systems, avionics, electronic/electrical systems, parts and components.
Cost: $75.00
Circulation: 28440
Founded in: 1905

6883 American Consulting Engineer
American Council of Engineering Companies
1015 15th St
8th Floor NW
Washington, DC 20005-2605

202-347-7474; *Fax:* 202-898-0068
acec@acec.org; www.acec.org
Social Media: Facebook, Twitter

David A Raymond, President

American Consulting Engineer serves engineers and surveyors who are employed by Consulting Engineering Firms, Architectural & Engineering Firms, and Surveying Firms.
Cost: $45.00
42 Pages
Frequency: Monthly
Circulation: 15841
ISSN: 1050-2203
Founded in: 1905
Printed in 4 colors on glossy stock

6884 Annals of Biomedical Engineering
Biomedical Engineering Society
8201 Corporate Dr
Suite 1125
Landover, MD 20785-2224

301-459-1999
877-871-2637; *Fax:* 301-459-1999
info@bmes.org; www.bmes.org

Edward L. Schilling, Executive Director
Barbara Colburn, Membership Director
Heather Comstock, Meeting Manager

Presents original research in the following areas: tissue and cellular engineering and biotechnology; biomaterials and biological interfaces; biological signal processing and instrumentation; biomechanics, rheology, and molecular motion; dynamical, regulatory, and integrative biology; transport phenomena, systems analysis and electrophysiology; imaging.
Frequency: Monthly

6885 Automotive Engineering International
Society of Automotive Engineers
400 Commonwealth Dr
Warrendale, PA 15086-7511

724-776-4841
877-606-7323; *Fax:* 724-776-5760
magazines@sae.org; www.saesections.org

Richard O Schaum, President
Kevin Jost, Editor
J Robertson, President

For engineers involved in the auto design industry.
Cost: $120.00
125 Pages
Frequency: Monthly
Circulation: 124451
Founded in: 1905

6886 Biomedical Engineering Society
8401 Corporate Dr
Suite 140
Hyattsville, MD 20785-2263

301-459-1999; *Fax:* 301-459-2444
info@bmes.org; www.bmes.org

Barbara Dunlevy, Executive Director
Heather Comstock, Meeting Manager

Of interest to those in the biomedical engineering field. To promote the increase of biomedical engineering knowledge and its utilization.
Cost: $175.00
Frequency: Monthly
Founded in: 1968
Printed in 8 colors on matte stock

6887 Bridge
National Academy of Engineering

500 5th Street NW
Washington, DC 20001

202-334-3200; *Fax:* 202-334-2290;
www.nae.edu

Charles M. Vest, President
Laura Mersky, Senior Executive Assistant

Solicited articles only. News related to the organization
Frequency: Quarterly
Circulation: 6500
Founded in: 1954

6888 CET Magazine
American Society of Certified Engineering
PO Box 1348
Flowery Branch, GA 30542-0023

770-967-9173; *Fax:* 770-967-8049;
www.ascet.org

Russell E Freier, Chairman
Leo Saenz, CET, President
Kurt Schuler, Secretary/Treasurer

It contains technical, educational, notices of upcoming events, employment opportunities, legislative and informational articles. Also included are national, regional and local society news, reports and activities.
32 Pages
Frequency: Bi-Monthly
Founded in: 1964
Printed in one color

6889 Chemical & Engineering News
American Chemical Society
1155 16th St Nw
Suite 600
Washington, DC 20036-4892

202-872-4600
800-227-5558; *Fax:* 202-872-4615
service@acs.org; www.acs.org

Madeleine Jacobs, CEO

Professional magazine which covers all areas of interest to the chemical community, including business, science and government.
Frequency: Weekly
Founded in: 1934

6890 Civil Engineering
American Society of Civil Engineers
1801 Alexander Bell Dr
Reston, VA 20191-4382

703-295-6300
800-548-2723
703-295-6300; *Fax:* 703-295-6222
member@asce.org; www.asce.org

D Wayne Klotz, President
Virginia Fairweather, Editor-in-Chief
Anne Powell, Editor

Comprised of news, information and updates for the civil engineering industry.
Cost: $180.00
Frequency: Monthly
Circulation: 107,000
Founded in: 1855
Printed in 4 colors

6891 Clientship
American Council of Engineering Companies
1015 15th St
8th Floor NW
Washington, DC 20005-2605

202-347-7474; *Fax:* 202-898-0068
acec@acec.org; www.acec.org
Social Media: Facebook, Twitter

Dave Raymond, President
Frequency: Monthly

6892 Community Matters
Accreditation Board for Engineering & Technology
111 Market Place
Suite 1050
Baltimore, MD 21202-4012

410-347-7700; *Fax:* 410-625-2238
info@abet.org; www.abet.org

Phillip E. Borrowman, President
Larry A. Kaye, President-Elect/VP
Frequency: Monthly
Founded in: 1932

6893 Composites Technology
Ray Publishing
P.O.Box 992
Morrison, CO 80465-0992

303-467-1776; *Fax:* 303-467-1777;
www.raypubs.com

Judith Ray Hazen, Publisher/Editor
Michael Musselman, Managing Editor
Donna K. Dawson, Senior Editor
Susan Rush, Copy Editor
Dirk Weed, Global Sales Manager

To provide comprehensive coverage of the composites industry by focusing on the design, engineering, manufacture and performance of products made from this type of material. Particular attention is given to the transfer of technology from traditional end-use markets into high-volume commercial and industrial arenas.
Cost: $15.00
44 Pages
Circulation: 24000
ISSN: 1083-4117
Founded in: 1993
Printed in 4 colors on glossy stock

6894 Composites in Manufacturing
Society of Manufacturing Engineers
1 SME Drive
PO Box 930
Dearborn, MI 48121

313-425-3000
800-733-4763; *Fax:* 313-425-3400
service@sme.org; www.sme.org

Mark Tomlinson, Executive Director/General Manager
Greg Sheremet, Publisher
Bob Harris, Director Finance

Covers various aspects of composite materials used in manufacturing.
Frequency: Bi-Annual
Circulation: 20000
Founded in: 1932
Mailing list available for rent: 13727 names at $95 per M

6895 Computer-Aided Engineering
Penton Media
249 W. 17th Street
New York, NY 10011

216-696-7000; *Fax:* 216-696-6662
information@penton.com; www.penton.com

Sharon Rowlands, CEO

Database applications in design and manufacturing.
Cost: $50.00
96 Pages
Founded in: 1982

6896 Computing in Science & Engineering
American Institute of Physics
2 Huntington Quad
Suite 1NO1
Melville, NY 11747-4502

516-576-2200; *Fax:* 516-349-7669;
www.aip.org

Darlene Walters, Senior VP
Angela Dombroski, CEO
Randolph Nanna, Publisher

Computer science's interdisciplinary juncture with physics, astronomy and engineering.
Cost: $42.00
Frequency: Monthly
Founded in: 1931

6897 Consulting-Specifying Engineer
Reed Business Information
360 Park Avenue South
New York, NY 10010

646-746-6400
877-422-4637; *Fax:* 630-288-8781
e-letters@reedbusiness.com;
www.reedbusiness.com

Jeff Greisch, President
Jim Crockett, Chief Editor
Scott Siddens, Senior Editor

Serves engineering management and engineering personnel who perform mechanical and/or electrical engineering activities.
100 Pages
Frequency: Monthly
Circulation: 46,157
ISSN: 0892-5046
Founded in: 1958
Printed in 4 colors on glossy stock

6898 Control Solutions
PennWell Publishing Company
1421 S Sheridan Rd
Tulsa, OK 74112-6619

918-831-9421
800-331-4463; *Fax:* 918-831-9476;
www.pennwell.com

Robert Biolchini, President
Ron Kuhfeld, Editor-in-Chief

A highly diversified, business-to-business media company providing authoritative print and online publications, conferences and exhibitions, research, databases, online exchanges and information products to strategic global markets.
Founded in: 1910

6899 Corrosion Journal
NACE International
1440 S Creek Dr
Houston, TX 77084-4906

281-492-0535; *Fax:* 281-228-6300;
www.nace.org

Angela Jarrell, Managing Editor
Suzanne Moreno, Editorial Assistant

Recognized internationally as the world's leading research journal devoted exclusively to furthering corrosion science and engineering
Cost: $150.00
Frequency: Monthly
Circulation: 7800

6900 Cost Engineering Journal
AACE International
1265 Suncrest Towne Centre Drive
Morgantown, WV 26501-1876

304-296-8444
800-858-2678; *Fax:* 304-291-5728
info@aacei.org; www.aacei.org

Michael R. Nosbisch, President
Marlene Hyde, President-Elect

International journal of cost estimation, cost/schedule control, and project management read by cost professionals around the world to get the most up-to-date information about the profession.
Frequency: Monthly

6901 Cutting Tool Engineering
CTE Publications

40 Skokie Blvd
Suite 395
Northbrook, IL 60062-1698

847-498-9100; *Fax:* 847-559-4444
alanr@jwr.com; www.ctemag.com

John W Roberts, CEO
Don Nelson, CEO
Alan Rooks, Director

Serves manufacturing plants in the metal working industries.
Cost: $65.00
72 Pages
Frequency: Monthly
Circulation: 34871
ISSN: 0011-4189
Founded in: 1955
Printed in 4 colors on glossy stock

6902 Design News
Reed Business Information
225 Wyman St
Waltham, MA 02451-1216

781-734-8000; *Fax:* 781-290-3178;
www.reedbusiness.com

Mark Finklestein, President
Karen Auguston Field, CFO
Stuart Whayman, CFO
Tracey Farina, Marketing,
Reck Allis, Circulation Manager

A magazine devoted exclusively to engineering design.
Frequency: Monthly
Circulation: 170114
Founded in: 1958
Printed in 4 colors on glossy stock

6903 EE: Evaluation Engineering
Nelson Publishing
2500 Tamiami Trl N
Nokomis, FL 34275-3476

941-966-9521
800-226-6113; *Fax:* 941-966-2590;
www.healthmgttech.com

Kristine Russel, President
Phil Colpas, Managing Editor

Magazine devoted exclusively to companies that test, evaluate, design and manufacture electronic products and equipment.
Cost: $43.00
84 Pages
Frequency: Monthly
Circulation: 80000
Founded in: 1962
Mailing list available for rent: 65,000 names
Printed in 4 colors on glossy stock

6904 Energy Engineering Journal
The Fairmont Press, Association of Energy Engineer
4025 Pleasantdale Road
Suite 420
Atlanta, GA 30340

770-447-5083; *Fax:* 770-446-3969
info@aeecenter.org; www.aeecenter.org

Jennifer Vendola, Accountant
Ruth Whitlock, Executive Admin

Engineering solutions to cost efficiency problems and mechanical contractors who design, specify, install, maintain, and purchase non-residential heating, ventilating, air conditioning and refrigeration equipment and components.
Cost: $160.00
Circulation: 8000

6905 Energy Services Marketing Institute News
Association of Energy Engineers
4025 Pleasantdale Rd
Suite 420
Atlanta, GA 30340-4264

770-447-5083; *Fax:* 770-446-3969
info@aeecenter.org; www.aeecenter.org

Eric A. Woodroof, President
Gary Hogsett, President-Elect
Paul Goodman, Treasurer
Laurie Wiegand-Jackson, Secretary

Subjects addressed include IPMVP Management and Verification Standard; Performance Contracting; Energy Project Financing and Energy Procurement.
Frequency: 3x Yearly

6906 Engineering Automation Report
Technology Automation Services
PO Box 3593
Englewood, CO 80155-3593

303-689-9099; *Fax:* 303-770-3660;
www.automationworl.com

David Weisberg, Publisher
Steve Weisberg, Editor
Dave White, President

Internet/intranet technologies for use in engineering design are covered along with software news.
Cost: $235.00
Frequency: Monthly

6907 Engineering News Record
McGraw Hill
2 Penn Plaza
9th Floor
New York, NY 10121-2298

212-904-3507; *Fax:* 212-904-2820
scott_lewis@mcgraw-hill.com; www.enr.com

Richard Korman, Managing Senior Editor
Ilan Kapla, Senior Manager
Keith Wallace, Production Editor

Provides the news, analysis, commentary and data that construction industry professionals need to do their jobs more effectively. ENR is the national news magazine for the construction industry.
Cost: $82.00
Frequency: Weekly
Circulation: 60000
Founded in: 1874

6908 Engineering and Mining Journal
Primedia Business
29 N Wacker Drive
10th Floor
Chicago, IL 60606-2802

312-726-2802; *Fax:* 312-726-2574
pjohnson@mining-media.com;
www.mining-media.com

Peter Johnson, Publisher
Steve Fiscor, Managing Editor
Russ Carter, Managing Editor
Victor Matteucci, National Sales Manager

Serves the field of mining including exploration, development, milling, smelting, refining of metals and nonmetallics.
Cost: $79.00
Circulation: 20589
Founded in: 1989
Mailing list available for rent
Printed in 4 colors

6909 Engineering in Medicine and Biology
445 Hoes Lane
Piscataway, NJ 08854-1331

732-981-0060
800-678-4333; *Fax:* 732-981-1721
customer-service@ieee.org;
www.spectrum.ieee.org/ieeemedia

DesirTe de Myer, Managing Editor
John Enderle, Editor
Susan Schneiderman, Business Development

Focuses on up-to-date biomedical engineering applications for engineers who are at the forefront of electrotechnology innovation.
Cost: $300.00
Circulation: 7983
ISSN: 0739-5175
Founded in: 1988

6910 Environmental Engineer and Scientist
American Academy of Environmental Engineers
147 Old Solomons Island Road
Suite 303
Annapolis, MD 21401-7003

410-266-3311; *Fax:* 410-266-7653
info@aaees.org; www.aaees.org

Burk Kalweit, Executive Director
J. Sammi Olmo, Manager, Special Projects

Articles dealing with environmental engineering practice issues and history.
Cost: $10.00
Frequency: Quarterly
Circulation: 12000
Founded in: 1955
Mailing list available for rent

6911 Environmental and Engineering Geosciences
Assn. of Environmental & Engineering Geologists
1100-H Brandywine Boulevard
Suite 575
Zanesville, OH 43701

303-757-2926
844-331-7867; *Fax:* 740-452-2552
aeg@aegweb.org; www.aegweb.org

Dale C, Andrews, President
Kathy Troost, Vice President
Kevin Richards, Treasurer
Cynthia Palomares, Secretary

Presents reviewed technical papers and discussions and book reviews related to the general field of engineering geology.
Frequency: Quarterly

6912 Experimental Mechanics
Society for Experimental Mechanics
2455 Teller Road
Thousand Oaks, CA 91320-1855

800-818-7243; *Fax:* 805-499-0871
info@sagepub.com; www.sagepub.com

Thomas W Proulx, Publisher
N R Sottos, Editor
Hugh Bruck, Associate Tech Editor

Concentrates on advanced research and development. EM is the archival publication of the Society and is recognized as one of the many journals in engineering mechanics. Members receive free electronic access.
Cost: $767.04
Frequency: Quarterly
Circulation: 4500
Founded in: 1965

6913 Experimental Techniques
Society for Experimental Mechanics
7 School St
Bethel, CT 06801-1855

203-790-6373; *Fax:* 203-790-4472
sem@sem1.com; www.sem.org

Kathy Ramsey, Manager
Thomas Proulx, Executive Director

Focused on the techniques utilized in experimental mechanics. ET includes Society news, peer-reviewed technical articles and notes, new

product information and much more. All members receive a printed copy of the journal and free electronic access.
Cost: $145.00
48 Pages
Circulation: 4000
Founded in: 1943
Printed in 4 colors on glossy stock

6914 **Exponent**
Iowa Engineering Society
100 Court Ave
#102
Des Moines, IA 50309-2257

515-284-7055; *Fax:* 515-284-7301
ies@iaengr.org; www.iaengr.org

David Scott, Executive Director
Brian E Roth, President

Supplies the Iowa engineering society members with vital information on issues and activities such as state legislation, education, ethics.
Cost: $6.00
26 Pages
Frequency: Quarterly
Circulation: 1000

6915 **Facilities Engineering Journal**
Association for Facilities Engineering
8160 Corporate Park Drive
Suite 125
Cincinnati, OH 45242

513-489-2473; *Fax:* 513-247-7422
Info@AFE.org; www.afe.org

Gabriella Jacobs, Editor/Communications Manager

Provides you with practical, in-depth information on the key issues you face on the job every day.

6916 **Fiberoptic Product News**
Reed Business Information
100 Enterprise Drive
Suite 600
Rockaway, NJ 07866-912

973-920-7000; *Fax:* 973-920-7534;
www.fpnmag.com

Steve Wirth, VP/Group Publisher
Diane Himes, Editor
Kim Potts, Managing Editor
Ernest Worthman, Technical Editorial Director
R Reed, Owner

Edited for designers, engineers, researchers and management personnel who design, install and the buy the products and services that make up the fiberoptic marketplace.
Frequency: Monthly
Circulation: 35000
Founded in: 1986
Printed in 4 colors on glossy stock

6917 **Fusion Science and Technology**
American Nuclear Society
555 N Kensington Ave
La Grange Park, IL 60526-5592

708-352-6611; *Fax:* 708-352-0499;
www.ans.org

Jack Tuohy, Executive Director
E James Reinsch, President-Elect/VP
Harry Bradley, Executive Director
William F Naughton, Treasurer

Is the source of information on fusion plasma physics and plasma engineering, fusion plasma enabling science and technology, fusion nuclear technology and material science, fusion applications, fusion design and system studies.
Cost: $1425.00
Frequency: 8x Yearly
Founded in: 2005

6918 **Geotechnical Fabrics Report**
Industrial Fabrics Association International
1801 County Road B W
Roseville, MN 55113-4061

651-222-2508
800-225-4324; *Fax:* 651-631-9334
generalinfo@ifai.com; www.ifai.com

Stephen Warner, CEO
Chris Kelsey, Editor
Susan.B Smeed, Assistant Circulation Manager
Miller Weldmaster, Director
JoAnne Ferris, Director of Marketing

Peer reviewed technical journal for civil engineers using geosynthetics in road construction, erosion control, hazardous waste, drainage, containment and reinforcement.
Cost: $49.00
Circulation: 16000
ISSN: 0882-4983
Founded in: 1982
Printed in 4 colors on glossy stock

6919 **Geotechnical Testing Journal**
ASTM International
PO Box C700
W Conshohocken, PA 19428-0700

610-832-9500; *Fax:* 610-832-9555
service@astm.org; www.astm.org

James A Thomas, President
Jeff Adkins, Manager
Fran Dougherty, Administrative Assistant

Provides a high quality publication that informs the profession of new developments in soil and rock testing and related fields; provides a forum for the exchange of information, particularly that which leads to the development of new test procedures; and to stimulate active participation of the profession in the work of ASTM International Committee D18 on Soil and Rock and related information.
Cost: $229.00
Frequency: Bi-Monthly

6920 **Global Design News**
Reed Business Information
360 Park Avenue South
New York, NY 10010

646-746-6400
877-422-4637; *Fax:* 630-288-8781
e-letters@reedbusiness.com;
www.reedbusiness.com

Jeff Greisch, President
Jim Crockett, Chief Editor
Scott Siddens, Senior Editor

Publication includes articles that cover the key product areas necessary for product development; reports on new technologies in the OEM industries, developments in the field of engineering design; and regular features on European product listings, technique and system updates.
Circulation: 30173
Founded in: 1958

6921 **Heat Transfer Engineering**
Taylor & Francis Group Ltd
2 Park Square
Milton Park
Abingdon Oxford UK OX14 4RN

4.40207E+12; *Fax:* 4.40207E+12;
www.tandf.com.uk

James Edward, Publisher
Afshin Ghajar, Editor-in-Chief
Jack Taylor, Owner

Information on refereed papers of original work, state-of-the-art reviews, articles on new developments in equipment and practices and news items on people and companies in the field.

6922 **Hispanic Engineer & Information Technology**
Career Communications Group
729 E Pratt St
Suite 504
Baltimore, MD 21202-3302

410-244-7101; *Fax:* 410-752-1837;
www.ccgmag.com

Jean Hamilton, Chief Financial Officer
Vishal Thakkar, Director of Marketing
Diane Jones, Director of Marketing
Christy Flemming, Director

Devoted to science and technology and to promoting opportunities in those fields for Hispanic Americans.
Cost: $13.00
56 Pages
ISSN: 1088-3452
Founded in: 1982
Printed in 4 colors on glossy stock

6923 **Hydraulics & Pneumatics**
Penton Media
249 W. 17th Street
New York, NY 10011

212-204-4200; *Fax:* 216-696-6662
hp@penton.com; www.penton.com

Sharon Rowlands, CEO
Nicola Allais, Executive VP

Issues highlight the application of new hydraulic and pneumatic components, new equipment research and listings, new design and literature innovations in fluid power and motion control systems.
Cost: $65.00
Frequency: Monthly
Circulation: 49,878
Founded in: 1892

6924 **ID International Design**
F&W Publications
38 E 29th St
Floor 3
New York, NY 10016-7911

212-447-1400; *Fax:* 212-447-5231;
www.printmag.com

Joyce Rutter Kaye, VP
Julie Lasky, Editor - in - chief
Nicole Martin, Circualtion Manager
Barbara Schmitz, VP

The issues include news and features on computers, new technologies, case studies, design management, materials, aesthetics, new components and design trends. They also cover new sources, a calendar of events, personnel news, book reviews and products.
Cost: $30.00
Circulation: 19852
Founded in: 1954

6925 **IIE Solutions**
Institute of Industrial Engineers
3577 Parkway Lane
Suite 200
Norcross, GA 30092

770-449-0460
800-494-0460; *Fax:* 770-441-3295
cs@iienet.org; www.iienet.org

Don Greene, CEO
Donna Calvert, Chief Operating Officer

Listings, literature and news for executive engineers.
Cost: $66.00
Frequency: Monthly
Circulation: 26276
Founded in: 1948

6926 **InTents**
Industrial Fabrics Association International

1801 Country Road BW
Roseville, MN 55113

651-222-2508
800-225-4324; *Fax:* 651-631-9334;
www.ifai.com

Peter F. McKernan, Chairman
Kevin Yonce, Vice Chairman

Promotes the use of tents and accessories to the special-event and general rental industries.
Cost: $39.00
Frequency: Bi-Monthly
Circulation: 12,000

6927 **Industrial Equipment News**
TCC Media Group
90 W Aftan Avenue
#117
Yardley, PA 19067

267-519-1705
800-733-1127
todd@ien.com; www.ien.com

Todd Baker, President

Serves the industrial field including manufacturing, mining, utilities, construction, transportation,governmental establishments, and educational services.
Frequency: Monthly
Circulation: 205000
ISSN: 0019-8258
Founded in: 1933

6928 **Inform**
American Oil Chemists' Society
2710 S Boulder Drive
P.O. Box 17190
Urbana, IL 61803-6996

217-359-2344; *Fax:* 217-351-8091
general@aocs.org; www.aocs.org
Social Media: Facebook, Twitter, LinkedIn

Gloria Cook, Senior Director, Finance & Operatio
Jeffry L. Newman, Senior Director, Programs

Inform magazine is an AOCS member benefit providing international news on fats, oils, surfactants, detergents, and related materials.
4500 Members
Frequency: Annual/April-May
Founded in: 1909

6929 **Innovation**
Industrial Designers Society of America
45195 Business Court
Suite 250
Dulles, VA 20166-6717

703-707-6000; *Fax:* 703-787-8501
idsa@idsa.org; www.idsa.org

Clive Roux, CEO
Annette Butler, Executive Assistant
Kaycee Childress, Marketing
Roxann Henze, Press, Media & Public Relations

IDSA is the world's oldest, largest, member-driven society for product design, industrial design, interaction design, human factors, ergonomics, design research, design management, universal design and related design fields. IDSA publishes Innovation, a quarterly on design. IDSA's charitable arm, the Design Foundation, supports the dissemination of undergraduate scholarships annually to further industrial design education.
Cost: $50.00
Frequency: Quarterly
Circulation: 3500
Founded in: 1965

6930 **Interface Magazine**
Electrochemical Society
65 S Main St
Building D
Pennington, NJ 08534-2827

609-737-1902; *Fax:* 609-737-2743
interface@electrochem.org;
www.electrochem.org

Roque J Calvo, Executive Director
Mary E. Yess, Deputy Executive Director

Editorial material contains news, reviews, advertisements and articles on technical matters in the fields of electrochemical and solid state science and technology.
Cost: $61.97
Frequency: Quarterly
Circulation: 8000
Founded in: 1902

6931 **International Dredging Review**
PO Box 1487
Fort Collins, CO 80522-1487

970-416-1903; *Fax:* 970-416-1878
editor@dredgemag.com; www.dredgemag.com

Judith Powers, Publisher/Editor
Leonard F Cors, Business Manager
Nelson Spencer, Business Manager
Julia Leach, Production Manager

Targeted to dredging company executives, project managers and dredge crew members, suppliers and service people such as pump manufacturers, hydrographic surveyors, consulting engineers, etc.
Cost: $85.00
Circulation: 3300
ISSN: 0737-8181
Founded in: 1981
Mailing list available for rent
Printed in 4 colors on glossy stock

6932 **Iron & Steel Technology**
Association for Iron & Steel Technolgy (AIST)
186 Thorn Hill Rd
Warrendale, PA 15086-7528

724-814-3000; *Fax:* 724-814-3001
memberservices@aist.org; www.aist.org
Social Media: Facebook, Twitter, LinkedIn

Ron Ashburn, Executive Director
Lori Wharrey, Board Administrator
Chris McKelvey, Assistant Board Administrator

The official monthly publication of AIST, this is the premier technical journal for metallurgical, engineering, operating and maintenance personnel in the global iron and steel industry.
Cost: $20.00
Frequency: Monthly
Circulation: 9500

6933 **JSME International Journal**
American Society of Mechanical Engineers
3 Park Ave
New York, NY 10016-5902

212-591-7000
800-843-2763; *Fax:* 212-591-8676
infocentral@asme.org; www.asme.org

Victoria Rockwell, President
Marc Goldsmith, President-Elect
David Soukup, Managing Director Operations

Provides advanced scientific and technological information for the mechanical engineering industry to facilitate the international exchange and transfer of technology.
Cost: $200.00
Frequency: Monthly

6934 **Journal of Applied Mechanics**
American Society of Mechanical Engineers
3 Park Ave
New York, NY 10016-5902

212-591-7000
800-843-2763; *Fax:* 212-591-8676
infocentral@asme.org; www.asme.org

Victoria Rockwell, President
Marc Goldsmith, President-Elect

To serve as a vehicle for the communication of original research results of permanent interest in all branches of mechanics.
Cost: $60.00
Frequency: Bi-Monthly
ISSN: 0021-8936

6935 **Journal of Biomechanical Engineering**
American Society of Mechanical Engineers
3 Park Ave
New York, NY 10016-5902

212-591-7000
800-843-2763; *Fax:* 212-591-8676
infocentral@asme.org; www.asme.org

Victoria Rockwell, President
Marc Goldsmith, President-Elect

Reports research results involving the application of mechanical engineering and knowledge, skills and principles to the conception, design, development, analysis, and operation of biomechanical systems, including; artificial organs and prostheses; bioinstrumentation and measurements; bio-heat transfer; biomaterials; biomechanics; bioprocess engineering; cellular mechanics; design and control of biological systems, and physiological systems.
Frequency: Bi-Monthly
ISSN: 0148-0731

6936 **Journal of Construction Engineering and Management**
American Society of Civil Engineers
1801 Alexander Bell Dr
Reston, VA 20191-4382

703-295-6300
800-548-2723; *Fax:* 703-295-6222
cybrarian@asce.org; www.asce.org

D Wayne Klotz, President

Quality papers that aim to advance the science of construction engineering, to harmonize construction practices with design theories, and to further education and research in construction engineering and management.

6937 **Journal of Engineering Education**
American Society for Engineering Education
1818 N St NW
Suite 600
Washington, DC 20036-2476

202-331-3500; *Fax:* 202-265-8504
pubsinfo@asee.org; www.asee.org

Frank L Huband, Executive Director

It serves as an archival record of scholarly research in engineering education.
Frequency: Quarterly
ISSN: 1069-4730

6938 **Journal of Engineering for Industry**
American Society of Mechanical Engineers
3 Park Ave
New York, NY 10016-5902

212-591-7000
800-843-2763; *Fax:* 212-591-8676
infocentral@asme.org; www.asme.org

Virgil R Carter, CEO
David Soukup, Managing Director
William T Cousins, President

Covers interfaces of mechanical engineering.
Frequency: Quarterly
Circulation: 2162
Founded in: 1880

6939 **Journal of Forensic Sciences**
ASTM International
PO Box C700
W Conshohocken, PA 19428-0700

610-832-9500; *Fax:* 610-832-9555
service@astm.org; www.astm.org

James A Thomas, President
Jeff Adkins, Manager
Fran Dougherty, Administrative Assistant

Is the official publication of the American Academy of Forensic Sciences (AAFS). It is devoted to the publication of original investigations, observations, scholarly inquiries, and reviews in the various branches of the forensic sciences.
Cost: $249.00
Frequency: Bi-Monthly

6940 **Journal of Management in Engineering**
American Society of Civil Engineers
1801 Alexander Bell Dr
Reston, VA 20191-4382

703-295-6300
800-548-2723; *Fax:* 703-295-6222
cybrarian@asce.org; www.asce.org

D Wayne Klotz, President

Examines contemporary issues associated with leadership and management for the twenty-first century civil engineer.

6941 **Journal of Materials Engineering and Performance**
ASM International
9639 Kinsman Road
Materials Park, OH 44073-0002

440-338-5151
800-336-5152; *Fax:* 440-338-4634;
www.asminternational.org

Jeane Deatherage, Administrator
Charles Hayes, Executive Director
Virginia Shirk, Executive Assistant

Peer-reviewed journal that publishes contributions on all aspects of materials selection, design, characterization, processing and performance testing. The journal for solving day-to-day engineering challenges - especially those involving components for larger systems.
Cost: $1965.00
Frequency: Bi-Monthly
Circulation: 305
Founded in: 1992

6942 **Journal of Petroleum Technology**
Society of Petroleum Engineers
PO Box 833836
Richardson, TX 75083-3836

972-529-9300
800-456-6863; *Fax:* 972-952-9435
spedal@spe.org; www.spe.org

Giovanni Paccaloni, President
Bill Cobb, VP Finance
John E Bethancourt, Director Management/Information
Ian Gorman, Director Production/Operations
Niki Bradbury, Managing Director

A suite of peer-reviewed, discipline-centered journals; books written by the industry's most honored professionals; and an online, 35,000-paper library.
Cost: $15.00
Frequency: Monthly

6943 **Journal of Phase Equilibria**
ASM International
9639 Kinsman Rd
Materials Park, OH 44072

440-338-5151
800-336-5152; *Fax:* 440-338-4634;
www.asminternational.org

Jeane Deatherage, Administrator
Charles Hayes, Executive Director
Virginia Shirk, Executive Assistant

Peer-reviewed journal that contains basic and applied research results, evaluated phase diagrams, a survey of current literature, and comments or other material pertinent to the previous three areas. The aim is to provide a broad spectrum of information concerning phase equilibria for the materials community.
Cost: $1965.00
Frequency: Bi-Monthly
Circulation: 305

6944 **Journal of Process Control**
Butterworth Heinemann
313 Washington Street
Suite 302
Newton, MA 02458-1626

617-928-5460; *Fax:* 617-928-5494

JD Perkins, Editor
T McAvoy, Regional Editor

Covers the application of control theory, operations research, computer science and engineering principles to the solution of process control problems.

6945 **Journal of Quality Technology**
American Society for Quality
600 N Plankinton Avenue
PO Box 3005
Milwaukee, WI 53201-3005

414-272-8575
800-248-1946; *Fax:* 414-272-1734
help@asq.org; www.asq.org

Roberto M Saco, President
Mike Adams, Director
Erica Gumieny, Sales
Fay Spano, Communications/Media Relations

Published by the American Society for Quality, the JQT is a quarterly, peer-reviewed journal that focuses on the subject of quality control and the related areas of reliability and similar disciplines.
Cost: $30.00
100M Members
Frequency: Quarterly
Founded in: 1946

6946 **Journal of Rheology**
Society of Rheology
2 Huntington Quadrangle
Suite 1N01
Meville, NY 11747-4502

516-576-2471; *Fax:* 516-576-2223
rheology@aip.org; www.rheology.org

Faith A. Morrison, President
A. Jeffrey Giacomin, Vice President
Frequency: Bi-Monthly

6947 **Journal of Surfactants and Detergents (JSD)**
American Oil Chemists' Society
2710 S Boulder Drive
P.O. Box 17190
Urbana, IL 61803-6996

217-359-2344; *Fax:* 217-351-8091
general@aocs.org; www.aocs.org
Social Media: Facebook, Twitter, LinkedIn

Gloria Cook, Senior Director, Finance
Jeffry L. Newman, Senior Director, Programs

Since 1998, JSD has remained dedicated to the practical and theoretical aspects of oleochemical and petrochemical surfactants, soaps and detergents. This growing quarterly scientific journal publishes peer-reviewed research papers, and reviews related to surfactants and detergents technologies.
4500 Members
Frequency: Annual/April-May
Founded in: 1909

6948 **Journal of Testing and Evaluation**
ASTM International
PO Box C700
W Conshohocken, PA 19428-0700

610-832-9500; *Fax:* 610-832-9555
service@astm.org; www.astm.org

James A Thomas, President
Jeff Adkins, Manager
Fran Dougherty, Administrative Assistant

Provides a multidisciplinary forum for applied sciences and engineering.
Cost: $249.00
Frequency: Bi-Monthly

6949 **Journal of Thermal Spray Technology**
ASM International
9639 Kinsman Rd
Materials Park, OH 44072-9603

440-338-5151
800-336-5152; *Fax:* 440-338-4634;
www.asminternational.org

Jeane Deatherage, Administrator
Charles Hayes, Executive Director
Virginia Shirk, Executive Assistant

Peer-reviewed journal which publishes contributions on all aspects, fundamental and practical, of thermal spray science, including processes, feedstock manufacture, testing and characterization. As the primary vehicle for thermal spray information transfer, its mission is to synergize the rapidly advancing thermal spray industry and related industries by presenting research and development efforts leading to advancements in implementable engineering applications of the technology.
Cost: $1577.00
Frequency: Bi-Monthly
Circulation: 680
Founded in: 1952

6950 **Journal of the Acoustical Society of America**
Acoustical Society of America
2 Huntington Quad
Suite 1N01
Melville, NY 11747-4505

516-576-2360; *Fax:* 516-576-2377
asa@aip.org; www.acousticalsociety.org

Charles E Schmid, President

Distributed free to members.
Cost: $1545.00
7000 Pages
Frequency: Monthly

6951 **Journal of the American Oil Chemists' Society (JAOCS)**
American Oil Chemists' Society
2710 S Boulder Drive
P.O. Box 17190
Urbana, IL 61803-6996

217-359-2344; *Fax:* 217-351-8091
general@aocs.org; www.aocs.org
Social Media: Facebook, Twitter, LinkedIn

Gloria Cook, Senior Director, Finance
Jeffry L. Newman, Senior Director, Programs

Since 1947, the Journal of the American Oil Chemists' Society has been the leading source for technical papers related to the fats and oils industries. JAOCS is a monthly, peer-reviewed journal devoted to fundamental and practical research, production, processing, packaging and distribu-

tion in the growing field of fats, oils, proteins and other related substances.
4500 Members
Frequency: Annual/April-May
Founded in: 1909

6952 **Journal of the Electrochemical Society**
Electrochemical Society
65 S Main St
Building D
Pennington, NJ 08534-2827

609-737-1902; *Fax:* 609-737-2743
ecs@electrochem.org; www.electrochem.org

Roque J Calvo, Executive Director
Mary E. Yess, Deputy Executive Director
Roque Calvo, Manager

Contains technical papers covering basic research and technology.
Cost: $63.00
Circulation: 8300
Founded in: 1902

6953 **LD&A**
Illuminating Engineering Society of North America
120 Wall Street
17th Floor
New York, NY 10005

212-248-5000; *Fax:* 212-248-5017
ies@ies.org; www.ies.org

Denis Lavoie, President
Chip Israel, Vice President

A magazine for professionals involved in the art, science, study, manufacture, teaching and implementation of lighting. LD&A is designed to enhance and improve the practice of lighting. Free to members.
Cost: $44.00
Frequency: Monthly
Circulation: 7000
ISSN: 0360-6325
Mailing list available for rent: 8000 names

6954 **LEUKOS, The Journal Of IES**
Illuminating Engineering Society of North America
120 Wall Street
17th Floor
New York, NY 10005

212-248-5000; *Fax:* 212-248-5017
ies@ies.org; www.ies.org

Denis Lavoie, President
Chip Israel, Vice President

LEUKOS serves members of the IES, the lighting community, and the public. The journal contains international technical developments of current interest and lasting importance relating to illuminating engineering and lighting design. Free to members, online.
Cost: $250.00
Frequency: Quarterly
ISSN: 1550-2729
Mailing list available for rent: 8000 names

6955 **Lighting Design & Application**
Illuminating Engineering Society of North America
120 Wall St
17th Floor
New York, NY 10005-4001

212-248-5000; *Fax:* 212-248-5017
iesna@iesna.org; www.ies.org

Denis Lavoie, President
Chip Israel, Vice President

Is a magazine for professionals involved in the art, science, study, manufacture, teaching and implementation of lighting. LD+A is designed to enhance and improve the practice of lighting. Every issue of LD+A includes feature articles on design projects, technical articles on the science of illumination, new product developments, industry trends, news of the Illuminating Engineering Society and vital information about the illuminating profession.
Cost: $32.00
Frequency: Monthly
Circulation: 8000
ISSN: 0360-6325

6956 **Lipids**
American Oil Chemists' Society
2710 S Boulder Drive
P.O. Box 17190
Urbana, IL 61803-6996

217-359-2344; *Fax:* 217-351-8091
general@aocs.org; www.aocs.org
Social Media: Facebook, Twitter, LinkedIn

Gloria Cook, Senior Director, Finance
Jeffry L. Newman, Senior Director, Programs

Introduced in 1966, Lipids is a premier journal published in the lipid field today. This monthly scientific journal features full-length original research articles, short communications, methods papers and review articles on timely topics. All papers are meticulously peer-reviewed and edited by some of the foremost experts in their respective fields.
4500 Members
Frequency: Annual/April-May
Founded in: 1909

6957 **Low Temperature Physics**
200 Huntington Quadrangle
Suite 1N01
Melville, NY 11747-4502

516-516-2270; *Fax:* 516-349-9704

6958 **Machine Design**
1300 E 9 Street
Cleveland, OH 44114-2518

216-696-7000
847-763-9670; *Fax:* 216-696-0177
mdeditor@penton.com;
www.machinedesign.com

Leland Teschler, Editor
Ken Korane, Managing Editor
Bobbie Macy, Circulation Manager

The only magazine for applied technology for design engineering edited for design engineers and engineering managers. It covers new products and design practices in the fields of mechanical, electromechanical, electronics, motion control and process engineering.
Circulation: 180000
Founded in: 1929

6959 **Maintenance Solutions**
Trade Press Publishing Corporation
2100 W Florist Avenue
Milwaukee, WI 53209

414-228-7701; *Fax:* 414-228-1134
contact@facilitiesnet.com;
www.facilitiesnet.com/

Dick Yake, Editorial Director
Dan Hounsell, Editor
Brad R. Ehlert, VP
Brian Terry, Publisher
Renee Gryzkewicz, Associate Editor

How to articles and features designed to alleviate reader problems as well as new product information and applications.
Cost: $45.00
42 Pages
Frequency: Monthly
Circulation: 35000
ISSN: 1072-3560
Founded in: 1993

6960 **Maintenance Technology**
Applied Technology Publications
1300 S Grove Ave
Suite 105
Barrington, IL 60010-5246

847-382-8100; *Fax:* 847-304-8603;
www.mt-online.com

Jane Alexander, Editor-in-Chief
Rick Carter, Executive Editor
Randy Buttstadt, Director of Creative Services

Maintenance Technology magazine serves the business and technical information needs of managers and engineers responsible for assuring availability of plant equipment and systems. It provides readers with articles on advanced technologies, strategies, tools, and services for the life-cycle management of capital assets.
Frequency: Monthly
Circulation: 50,827
Mailing list available for rent: 35,263 names at $$15 per M

6961 **Marine Fabricator**
Industrial Fabrics Association International
1801 County Road B W
Roseville, MN 55113-4061

651-222-2508
800-225-4324; *Fax:* 651-631-9334
generalinfo@ifai.com; www.ifai.com

Peter F. McKernan, Chairman
Kevin Yonce, Vice Chairman

Educates and informs 5,000 marine shop professionals and also provides reportage that reflects the innovations and trends of the industry.
Cost: $34.00
Frequency: Bi-Monthly

6962 **Material Handling Business**
Penton Media
249 W. 17th Street
New York, NY 10011

212-204-4200; *Fax:* 216-696-6662
information@penton.com; www.penton.com

Sharon Rowlands, CEO
Nicola Allais, Executive VP
Antoinette Sanchez Perkins, Circulation Manager

Journal written for design engineering managers, system integrates, material handling distributors and manufacturing sales executives.
86 Pages
Circulation: 92836
Founded in: 1892
Printed in 4 colors on glossy stock

6963 **Materials Performance**
NACE International
1440 S Creek Dr
Houston, TX 77084-4906

281-492-0535
800-797-6223; *Fax:* 281-228-6300
stephanie.garner@nace.org; www.nace.org

Oliver Moghissi, President
Kevin Garrity, Vice President

Provides current news and features, practical data, and information on new products and services in the corrosion industry.
Frequency: Monthly
Circulation: 22000
Founded in: 1943

6964 **Materials at High Temperatures**
Butterworth Heinemann
313 Washington Street
Newton, MA 02458-1626

617-928-5460; *Fax:* 781-933-6333

T Suzuki, Co-Editor
TB Gibbons, Co-Editor

Serves the needs of those developing and using materials for high temperature applications in the power, chemical, engine, processing and furnace industries.

6965 **Measurements and Control News**
Measurements and Data Corporation
100 Wallace Avenue
Suite 100
Sarasota, FL 34237

941-954-8405; *Fax:* 941-366-5743

Ken Kemski, Editor-in-Chief
Kristine Burmester, Associate Editor

Serves engineers, technichians, scientists, and other professionals involved in the recommendation and specification, of instuments and devices for measurement, inspection, testing, analysis, computing, and control.
Frequency: Bi-Monthly

6966 **Medical Equipment Designer**
Adams Business Media
6001 Cuchran Road
Suite 300
Cleveland, OH 44139

216-249-9444; *Fax:* 440-248-0187;
www.medicaldesigner.com

Terry Person, Publisher
Steve Wafalosky, Publisher

Published for the design function as it relates specifically to medical manufacturing and design of materials, components and complete systems.
1004 Pages
Frequency: Bi-Monthly
Circulation: 15,000
Founded in: 1985
Printed in 4 colors on glossy stock

6967 **Medical Physics**
2 Huntington Quadrangle
Suite 1N01
Melville, NY 11747

516-576-2200; *Fax:* 516-576-2481;
www.aip.org

Bill Hendee, Editor
Founded in: 1931

6968 **Microwave and RF**
Penton Media
45 Eisenhower Drive
5th Floor
Paramus, NJ 07652

201-452-2400
800-829-9028; *Fax:* 201-845-2493;
www.mwrf.com

Jack Browne, Publisher/Editor
Dawn Prior, Editorial Assistant

Dedicated to educating senior level design engineers, engineering managers, both domestic and foreign, who work all types of microwave systems, subsystems and components.
Cost: $81.00
Frequency: Monthly
Circulation: 47000
Founded in: 1967
Mailing list available for rent
Printed in on glossy stock

6969 **Modern Materials Handling**
Reed Business Information
275 Washington St
Newton, MA 02458-1611

617-964-3030; *Fax:* 617-630-3925
support@designnews.com;
www.designnews.com

Peter Boniface, Publisher
Raymond Kulwiec, Editor
James A Casella, CEO
Jason Cassidy, VP
Greg Flores, Senior Vice President

The magazine for managers and engineers responsible for handling materials and managing inventories in manufacturing, warehousing and distribution.
Frequency: 14x Yearly
Founded in: 1977
Printed in 4 colors on glossy stock

6970 **Motion Control**
ISA Services
Po Box 12277
Resrch Trngle P, NC 27709-2277

919-549-8411; *Fax:* 919-549-8288
info@isa.org; www.isa.org

Pat Gouhin, Executive Director

Information for those who design and maintain motion control systems.
Cost: $54.00
56 Pages
Circulation: 41000
ISSN: 1058-4644
Founded in: 1945
Printed in 4 colors on glossy stock

6971 **Motion System Distributor**
Penton Media
249 W. 17th Street
New York, NY 10011

212-204-4200
800-249-9365; *Fax:* 216-696-6662
information@penton.com; www.penton.com

Sharon Rowlands, CEO
Nicola Allais, Executive VP
Larry Berardinis, Editor

Provides selling and technical information to individuals and distributors specializing in power transmission, motion control and fluid products.
Cost: $65.00
Frequency: Monthly
Circulation: 54,000
Founded in: 1892

6972 **NSBE Magazine**
National Society of Black Engineers
1454 Duke Street
Alexandria, VA 22314-3403

703-549-2207; *Fax:* 703-683-5312
office@nsbe.org; www.nsbe.org

Pamela D Sharif, Publisher
Carl Mack, Manager
George Bowman, Manager

Coverage of all aspects of manufacturing engineering, geared towards black technical professionals.
Cost: $30.00
Circulation: 100000
Printed in 4 colors on glossy stock

6973 **Naval Engineers Journal**
American Society of Naval Engineers
1452 Duke Street
Alexandria, VA 22314-3458

703-836-6727; *Fax:* 703-836-7491
asnehq@navalengineers.org;
www.navalengineers.org

Susan King, Editor

It contains technical papers authored by professionals engaged in naval and related engineering fields. Its high quality content is sought by those with an interest in topics of importance to the advancement of naval engineering.
Frequency: Quarterly

6974 **New Equipment Digest**
Penton Media
1300 E 9th St
Cleveland, OH 44114-1503

216-696-7000; *Fax:* 216-696-1752
information@penton.com; www.penton.com

Sharon Rowlands, CEO
Dave Madonia, Publisher
Robert.F King, Editor
Nicola Allais, Executive VP & CEO

New Equipment Digest serves the general industrial field which includes manufacturing, processing, engineering services, construction, transportation, mining, public utilities, wholesale distributors, educational services, libraries and governmental establishments.
Cost: $65.00
Frequency: Monthly
Circulation: 206006
Founded in: 1936

6975 **Noise Control Engineering Journal**
Institute of Noise Control Engineering
62 Timberline Drive, Arlington Branch
PO Box 3206
Poughkeepsie, NY 12603-0206

845-462-4006; *Fax:* 845-463-0201;
www.ince.org

Alan Marsh, Editor

Includes articles on hearing protection, modal analysis, and signal processing. Information is refereed, authoritative, and technical.
Cost: $110.00
Frequency: Bi-Monthly
Circulation: 2,000
ISSN: 0736-2501

6976 **Noise/News International**
Institute of Noise Control Engineering
9100 Purdue Road
Suite 200
Indianapolis, IN 46268

317-735-4063
ibo@inceusa.org; www.inceusa.org

James K Thompson, President
Rich Peppin, Advertising/Expo Manager

Contains not only news items but also feature articles on a wide variety of topics of broad interest in noise control engineering.
Cost: $60.00
Frequency: Quarterly
ISSN: 1021-643X

6977 **Nuclear Science and Engineering**
American Nuclear Society
555 N Kensington Ave
La Grange Park, IL 60526-5592

708-352-6611; *Fax:* 708-352-0499;
www.ans.org

Jack Tuohy, Executive Director
E James Reinsch, President-Elect/VP
Harry Bradley, Executive Director
William F Naughton, Treasurer

The journal is widely recognized as an outstanding source of information on research in all scientific areas related to the peaceful use of nuclear energy and radiation. Technical papers, notes, critical reviews, and computer code abstracts are presented.
Cost: $1200.00
Frequency: 9x Yearly
Founded in: 1956

6978 **Nuclear Technology**
American Nuclear Society
555 N Kensington Ave
La Grange Park, IL 60526-5592

708-352-6611; *Fax:* 708-352-0499;
www.ans.org

Jack Tuohy, Executive Director
E James Reinsch, President-Elect/VP
Harry Bradley, Executive Director
William F Naughton, Treasurer

Leading international publication reporting on new information in all areas of the practical application of nuclear science. Topics include all aspects of reactor technology: operations, safety materials, instrumentation, fuel, and waste man-

agement. Also covered are medical uses, radiation detection, production of radiation, health physics, and computer applications.
Cost: $1315.00
Frequency: Monthly
Founded in: 2005

6979 **Off-Highway Engineering**
SAE
400 Commonwealth Dr
Warrendale, PA 15086-7511

724-776-4841; *Fax:* 724-776-5760;
www.saesections.org

Richard O Schaum, President
Mark Davies, Editor-In-Chief

Off-Highway Engineering serves the international off highway design and manufacturing field which consists of producers of construction, lawn and garden, agricultural equipment, and industrial vehicles. Also served are makers of engines and parts and components and others allied to the field.
Cost: $70.00
66 Pages
Circulation: 16308
ISSN: 1074-6919
Founded in: 1905
Printed in 4 colors on glossy stock

6980 **Optics and Spectroscopy**
Optical Society of America
2010 Massachusetts Ave Nw
Washington, DC 20036-1023

202-223-8130; *Fax:* 202-223-1096
info@osa.org; www.osa.org

Elizabeth Rogan, Executive Director
Elizabeth Nolan, Chief Publishing Officer

Optics and Spectroscopy covers such topics as multiphoton spectroscopy, phase conjugation, holography, scattering, and quantum electronics.
Frequency: Monthly
Founded in: 1916

6981 **PM Engineer**
Business News Publishing Company
2401 W Big Beaver Road
Suite 700
Troy, MI 48084

248-362-3700; www.bnpmedia.com

Katie Rotella, Manager

Provides technical sheets, manufacturer product brochures, news features and analysis of useful industry information on the engineering and design of plumbing, piping, hydronics, cooling/heating, and fire protection/sprinkler systems. Free to trade engineers.
Cost: $64.00
80 Pages
Frequency: Monthly
Circulation: 25000
Founded in: 1970
Printed in 4 colors on glossy stock

6982 **PT Design**
Penton Media
1300 E 9th St
Cleveland, OH 44114-1503

216-696-7000; *Fax:* 216-696-1752
information@penton.com; www.penton.com

Sharon Rowlands, CEO
David Madonia, Publisher

Blends state-of-the-art motion system designs with traditional electrical and mechanical technology for the system designer. Also features articles on new products and technology, industry trends and application ideas.
Cost: $ 65.00
Frequency: Monthly
Circulation: 54000
Founded in: 1892

6983 **PT Distributor**
Reed Business Information
2000 Clearwater Dr
Oak Brook, IL 60523-8809

630-288-8000; *Fax:* 630-288-8781;
www.reedbusiness.com

Mark Kelsey, Global CEO
Jeff DeBalko, President, Media Division

provides information on selling techniques, fiscal and personnel management, purchasing, improving profits, training, and inventory and warehousing control.
Cost: $30.00
Frequency: Bi-Monthly
Circulation: 10,000

6984 **Pharmaceutical Engineering**
Int'l Society for Pharmaceutical Engineering
600 N Westshore Blvd.
Suite 900
Tampa, FL 33609

813-960-2105; *Fax:* 813-264-2816
ask@ispe.org; www.ispe.org

Charles DiMarco, Director of Marketing
Danielle Hould, Communications Manager
Angie Brumley, Publications Coordinator
Valerie Adams, Advertising Sales Coordinator

Journal is published bi-monthly for members only and is considered by ISPE members to be the number one member benefit. Feature articles provide practical application and specification information on the design, construction, supervision and maintenance of process equipment, plant systems, instrumentation and facilities.
Circulation: 13138

6985 **Plant Engineering**
Reed Business Information
8878 Barrons Blvd
Littleton, CO 80129-2345

303-470-4000
800-446-6551; *Fax:* 303-470-4691
subsmail@reedbusiness.com;
www.reedbusiness.com

Tim Myers, Executive
Bobbie Wisniewski, Advertising Production Manager
Rick Ellis, Circulation Manager
Rick Dunn, Editor
Jim Silvestri, Managing Editor

Provides a constant reminder of engineering products and services and helps keep your company at the top of your customers' minds.
Frequency: Monthly
Circulation: 100034
Founded in: 1947

6986 **Plant Services**
Putman Media
555 W Pierce Rd
Suite 301
Itasca, IL 60143-2626

630-467-1301
800-984-7644; *Fax:* 630-467-0197;
www.putman.net

John Cappelletti, CEO
Mike Bacidore, Editor-in-Chief
Mike Brenner, Group Publisher
Keith Larson, VP Content

The newsletters reach a monthly world wide audience of more than 150,000 professionals responsible for optimizing the productivity and insuring the reliability of manufacturing plants, facilities and utilities in North America and across the globe.
Cost: $96.00
Frequency: Monthly
Circulation: 80100
ISSN: 0199-8013
Founded in: 1938

Mailing list available for rent: 10,000 names
Printed in 4 colors on glossy stock

6987 **Plastics Engineering**
Society of Plastics Engineers
13 Church Hill Rd
Newtown, CT 06470

203-775-0471; *Fax:* 203-775-8490
info@4spe.org; www.4spe.org

Susan Oderwald, Executive Director

A communication to SPE's global audience of plastics professionals about current developments in the industry, technology, and activities of the Society.
Frequency: Monthly

6988 **Plumbing Engineer**
Delta Communications
1167 W Bluemound Road
Wauwatosa, WI 53226

262-542-8820; *Fax:* 262-542-9111
delta@deltacommunications.com;
www.deltairaq.net

Edwin Scott, Editor

Offers news and updates to plumbing engineers and manufacturers.
Cost: $35.00
Frequency: Monthly
Founded in: 1973

6989 **Plumbing Standard Magazine**
American Society of Sanitary Engineering
901 Canterbury Rd
Suite A
Cleveland, OH 44145-1480

440-835-3040; *Fax:* 440-835-3488;
www.asse-plumbing.org

Ken Van Wagnen, Manager
Donald Summers, First VP
Steve Silber, Second VP
Scott Hamilton, Third VP
Shannon Corcoran, Executive Director

This magazine includes technical articles, current information on codes, standards, and other developments in the plumbing industry and related fields. Free with membership.
Cost: $12.00
Frequency: Quarterly

6990 **Powder Diffraction**
International Center for Diffraction Data
12 Campus Boulevard
Newton Square, PA 19073-3200

610-325-9814; *Fax:* 610-325-9823
info@icdd.com; www.icdd.com

Timothy Fawcett, Executive Director
Cathyann Colaiezzi, Managing Editor
Theresa Kahmer, Publication Manager

A quarterly journal devoted to the use of the powder method for material characterization is available on annual subscription. The journal focus is on materials. Characterization employing x-ray powder diffraction and related techniques.
Cost: $90.00
Frequency: Quarterly
Founded in: 1941

6991 **Powder and Bulk Engineering**
CSC Publishing
1155 Northland Dr
St Paul, MN 55120-1288

651-287-5600; *Fax:* 651-287-5650;
www.cscpublishinginc.com

Richard R Cress, Publisher
Terry O' Neill, Editor

Featured editorial includes technical articles, case histories, test centers, product news and literature, and industry news items.
Cost: $100.00
Frequency: Monthly

6992 **Power Engineering International**
PennWell Publishing Company
1421 S Sheridan Rd
Tulsa, OK 74112-6619
918-835-3161
800-331-4463; *Fax:* 918-831-9497
candiced@pennwell.com; www.pennwell.com
Robert Biolchini, President
Brian Schimmoller, Managing Editor
Serves the global electric power generation and transmission industry.
Cost: $180.00
Frequency: Monthly
ISSN: 1069-4994
Founded in: 1896

6993 **Precision Engineering**
Elsevier Science
PO Box 10826
Raleigh, NC 27605-0826
919-839-8444; *Fax:* 919-839-8039;
www.aspe.net
W T Estler, Editor-in-Chief
Is the foremost international journal devoted to the study of ultra-high precision engineering and metrology.

6994 **Printed Circuit Design**
CMP Media
240 West 35th Street
New York, NY 10001
516-562-5000; *Fax:* 415-947-6090;
www.cmp.com
David Levin, CEO

6995 **Process Heating**
Business News Publishing Company
155 Pfingsten Road
Suite 205
Deerfield, IL 60015
847-405-4000; *Fax:* 248-502-1001
PHeditors@bnpmedia.com;
www.process-heating.com
Social Media: Facebook, Twitter
Anne Armel, Publisher
Linda Becker, Associate Publisher & Editor
Beth McClelland, Production Manager
Magazine covers heat processing at temperatures up to 1000 degrees F at end user and OEM plants in 9 industries. Follow us at twitter.com/ProcessHeating, www.facebook.com/ProcessHeating
Circulation: 25000
Founded in: 1994

6996 **Processing**
Putman Media
PO Box 698
Birmingham, AL 35243
888-431-2877; *Fax:* 205-408-3797
webmaster@grandviewmedia.com;
www.grandviewmedia.com
Dennis Van Milligen, Editor in Chief
Mike Wasson, Publisher
Offers information on printing, publishing and processing. Information is given on the latest technology in these and other desktop industries.
Cost: $15.00
53 Pages
Frequency: Monthly
Founded in: 1960

6997 **Product Design and Development**
Reed Business Information
301 Gibraltar Drive
Box 650
Morris Plains, NJ 07950
973-292-5100; *Fax:* 630-288-8686;
www.reedbusiness.com
Stuart Whayman, CFO

6998 **Product Development Best Practices Report**
Management Roundtable
92 Crescent St
Waltham, MA 02453-4315
781-891-8080; *Fax:* 781-398-1889;
www.pharmcentric.com
Stewart Maws, Owner
The goal of this publication is to help firms market, manufacture and design better products at a lower rate.
Cost: $219.00
Frequency: Monthly

6999 **Professional Safety Journal**
American Society of Safety Engineering
1800 E Oakton Street
Des Plaines, IL 60018
847-699-2929; *Fax:* 847-768-3434
customerservice@asse.org; www.asse.org
Social Media: Facebook, Twitter, LinkedIn
Fred Fortman, Executive Director
Bruce Sufranski, Finance/Controller Director
Diane Hurns, Manager Public Relations Department
Sally Madden, Human Resources Manager
The American Society of Safety Engineers (ASSE) is the oldest professional safety society committed to protecting people, property and the environment. ASSE has more than 32,000 occupational safety, health and environmental (SH&E) professional members who manage, supervise, research and consult on safety, health, transportation and the environment in all industries, government, labor and education.
34000 Members
Frequency: Monthly
Circulation: 40,000
Founded in: 1911

7000 **Quality Engineering**
American Society for Quality
600 N Plankinton Avenue
PO Box 3005
Milwaukee, WI 53201-3005
414-272-8575
800-248-1946; *Fax:* 414-272-1734
help@asq.org; www.asq.org
Roberto M Saco, President
Paul E Borawski, CEO
Erica Gumieny, Sales
Fay Spano, Communications/Media Relations
Co-published with Taylor and Francis, this journal is for professional practitioners and researchers whose goal is quality engineering improvements and solutions.
Cost: $34.75
100M Members
Frequency: Quarterly/Members Price
Founded in: 1946

7001 **Quality Management Journal**
American Society for Quality
600 N Plankinton Avenue
PO Box 3005
Milwaukee, WI 53201-3005
414-272-8575
800-248-1946; *Fax:* 414-272-1734
help@asq.org; www.asq.org
Roberto M Saco, President
Paul E Borawski, CEO
Erica Gumieny, Sales
Fay Spano, Communications/Media Relations
Published by the American Society for Quality, the QMT is a quarterly, peer-reviewed journal that focuses on the subject of quality management practice and provides a discussion forum for both practitioners and academics in the area of research.
Cost: $50.00
100M Members
Frequency: Quarterly
Founded in: 1946

7002 **Quality Progress**
American Society for Quality
600 N Plankinton Avenue
PO Box 3005
Milwaukee, WI 53201-3005
414-272-8575
800-248-1946; *Fax:* 414-272-1734
help@asq.org; www.asq.org
Roberto M Saco, President
Paul E Borawski, CEO
Erica Gumieny, Sales
Fay Spano, Communications/Media Relations
Published by the American Society for Quality, the QP is a peer-reviewed journal that focuses on the subject of quality control, discussing the usage and implementation of quality principles including the subject areas of organizational behavior, knowledge management and process improvement.
Cost: $55.00
100M Members
Founded in: 1946

7003 **RSES Journal**
Refrigeration Service Engineers Society
1666 Rand Rd
Des Plaines, IL 60016-3552
847-297-6464
800-297-5660; *Fax:* 847-297-5038
general@rses.org; www.rses.org
Social Media: Facebook, Twitter, LinkedIn
Robert Sherman, President
Lawrence Donaldson, Vice President
Wes Maxfield, Secretary Treasurer
Providing quality technical content in digital and printed forms that can be applied on the job site.
Frequency: Monthly
Circulation: 15231

7004 **Radwaste Solutions**
American Nuclear Society
555 N Kensington Ave
La Grange Park, IL 60526-5592
708-352-6611; *Fax:* 708-352-0499;
www.asn.org
Jack Tuohy, Executive Director
E James Reinsch, President-Elect/VP
Harry Bradley, Executive Director
William F Naughton, Treasurer
Cal Poly, Vice President
Containing articles that discuss practical approaches and solutions to everyday problems and issues in all fields of radioactive waste management and environmental restoration.
Cost: $455.00
Frequency: Bi-Monhtly
Founded in: 2005

7005 **Reliability Engineering and Management Proceedings**
7340 N La Oesta Ave
Tucson, AZ 85704-3119
520-621-6120; *Fax:* 520-621-8191
dimitri@u.arizona.edu; www.u.arizona.edu
Dimitri B Kececioglu, Owner
Proceedings where over 15 leading corporations present their latest techniques in this field.
Cost: $50.00
Frequency: Annual+
Circulation: 50

Founded in: 1963
Mailing list available for rent: 43000 names at $152 per M

7006 **Repro Report**
International Reprographic Association
401 N Michigan Avenue
Chicago, IL 60611

312-245-1026; *Fax:* 312-527-6705
info@irga.com; www.irga.com

Bryan Thomas, President
Dan Stephens, Executive Director
Steve Bova, Executive Director
Ben Barclay, Director of Operations

Articles on blueprint service companies, engineering equipment manufacturers and suppliers.
Cost: $150.00
Circulation: 1000
Founded in: 1927

7007 **Research-Technology Management**
Industrial Research Institute
2300 Clarendon Boulevard
Suite 400
Arlington, VA 22201-3331

703-647-2580; *Fax:* 703-647-2581
information@iriweb.org; www.iriweb.org

Martha Collins, Chairman
Daniel Abramowicz, Chairman-Elect
Edward Bernstein, President
James Euchner, Editor-in-Chief
Maryanne Gobble, Managing Editor

As the official journal of IRI, Research-Technology Management, is the bi-monthly, peer-reviewed journal, providing authoritative, practitioner-oriented articles for technology leaders.
200 Members
Frequency: 6x Yearly
Circulation: 1800
ISSN: 0895-6308
Founded in: 1938

7008 **Resource**
American Society of Agricultural Engineers
2950 Niles Rd
St Joseph, MI 49085-8607

269-429-0300
800-371-2723; *Fax:* 269-429-3852
hq@asabe.org; www.asabe.org

Ronald McAllister, President
Donna Hull, Publication Director

Accepts advertising.
Cost: $75.00
Circulation: 9000
ISSN: 1076-3333
Founded in: 1907
Printed in on matte stock

7009 **Review of Scientific Instruments**
American Institute of Physics
2 Huntington Quadrangle
Melville, NY 11747-4502

516-576-2200; *Fax:* 516-349-7669
rsi@aip.org; www.aip.org

Darlene Walters, Senior VP
Douglas LaFrenier, Marketing Director

Presents original articles on new principles, devices and techniques in scientific instrumentation.
Cost: $90.00
Frequency: Monthly
Circulation: 3100
Founded in: 1931

7010 **Robotics and Computer-Intergrated Manufacturing**
Elsevier Science
PO Box 945
New York, NY 10159

212-895-5800; *Fax:* 212-633-3680
usinfo-f@elsevier.com; www.elsevier.com

Nam P Sata, Editor
A. Sharon, Chief Executive Officer
Bill Godfrey, Chief Information Officer
David Clark, Senior Vice President

Contains original papers on theoretical, applied and experimental robotics and computer-integrated manufacturing, with emphasis on flexible manufacturing systems.
Cost: $1156.00
Circulation: 2500
Founded in: 1880

7011 **SAMPE Journal**
Society for the Advancement of Material & Process
1161 Park View Drive
Suite 200
Covina, CA 91724-3751

626-331-0616
800-562-7360; *Fax:* 626-332-8929
sampeibo@sampe.org; www.sampe.org
Social Media: Facebook, LinkedIn

Dr Scott Beckwith, Technical Editor
Jennifer Stephens, Production Manager
Patty Hunt, Advertising Rep

An informative and acclaimed publication provides a steady stream of technical articles, industry and international technical news, product and new literature announcements, book reviews, technical events calendars, and local SAMPE information. This publication is mailed complimentary to all SAMPE members.
Cost: $82.00
Frequency: Bi-Monthly

7012 **SAWE Weight Engineers Handbook**
Society of Allied Weight Engineers
5734 E. Lucia Walk
Long Beach, CA 90803-4015

562-596-2873; *Fax:* 562-596-2874
exdirector@sawe.org; www.sawe.org

Patrick Brown, President
Jeffery Cerro, Executive VP
Ronald Fox, Executive Director
Robert Ridenour, VP Publications
Clint Bower, Executive VP

Contains technical information on materials, engineering formulas as well as other reference materials.
Cost: $100.00
348 Pages
Frequency: Periodic

7013 **SPE Drilling & Completion**
Society of Petroleum Engineers
PO Box 833836
Richardson, TX 75083-3836

972-529-9300
800-456-6863; *Fax:* 972-952-9435
spedal@spe.org; www.spe.org

Giovanni Paccaloni, President
Bill Cobb, VP Finance
John E Bethancourt, Director Management/Information
Ian Gorman, Director Production/Operations
Niki Bradbury, Managing Director

Features papers covering bit technology, completions, drilling fluids and operations, equipment and instrumentation, perforation and sand control, simulations tubulars, well control, and work over well construction related topics.
Cost: $30.00
Frequency: Quarterly

7014 **SPE Journal**
Society of Petroleum Engineers
PO Box 833836
Richardson, TX 75083-3836

972-529-9300
800-456-6863; *Fax:* 972-952-9435
spedal@spe.org; www.spe.org

Giovanni Paccaloni, President
Bill Cobb, VP Finance
John E Bethancourt, Director Management/Inforamtion
Ian Gorman, Director Production/Operations
Niki Bradbury, Managing Director

Includes full length technical papers covering all aspects of petroleum technology. SPE Journal covers the theories and emerging concepts that will become the new technologies of tomorrow.
Cost: $60.00
Frequency: Quarterly

7015 **SPE Production & Facilities**
Society of Petroleum Engineers
PO Box 833836
Richardson, TX 75083-3836

972-529-9300
800-456-6863; *Fax:* 972-952-9435
spedal@spe.org; www.spe.org

Giovanni Paccaloni, President
Bill Cobb, VP Finance
John E Bethancourt, Director Management/Information
Ian Gorman, Director Production/Operations
Niki Bradbury, Managing Director

It includes papers on artificial lift, chemical treatments, design and operation of surface facilities and downhole equipment, formation damage control, fracturing, gas production and storage, offshore operations, production logging and optimization systems, sand control, separation and processing, and work over-production improvement.
Cost: $30.00
Frequency: Quarterly

7016 **SPE Reservoir Evaluation & Engineering**
Society of Petroleum Engineers
PO Box 833836
Richardson, TX 75083-3836

972-529-9300
800-456-6863; *Fax:* 972-952-9435
spedal@spe.org; www.spe.org

Giovanni Paccaloni, President
Bill Cobb, VP Finance
John E Bethancourt, Director Management/Information
Ian Gorman, Director Production/Operations
Niki Bradbury, Managing Director

The journal covers a wide range of topics, including the following: Reservoir Engineering.
Cost: $40.00
Frequency: Bi-Monthly

7017 **Sea Technology Magazine**
Compass Publications, Inc.
1501 Wilson Blvd
Suite 1001
Arlington, VA 22209-2403

703-524-3136; *Fax:* 703-841-0852
seatechads@sea-technology.com;
www.sea-technology.com
Social Media: Facebook, Twitter

Amos Bussmann, President/Publisher
Joy Carter, Circulation Manager
Meghan Ventura, Managing Editor

Worldwide information leader for marine/offshore business, science and engineering. Read in more than 110 countries by management, engineers, scientists and technical personnel working in industry, government and education.
Cost: $40.00
Frequency: Monthly
Circulation: 16304

ISSN: 0093-3651
Founded in: 1960
*Mailing list available for rent*at $80 per M
Printed in 4 colors

7018 Software Quality Professional
American Society for Quality
600 N Plankinton Avenue
PO Box 3005
Milwaukee, WI 53201-3005

414-272-8575
800-248-1946; *Fax:* 414-272-1734
help@asq.org; www.asq.org

Roberto M Saco, President
Paul E Borawski, CEO
Erica Gumieny, Sales
Fay Spano, Communications/Media Relations

Published by the American Society for Quality, the SQP is a quarterly, peer-reviewed journal for software development professionals that focuses on the subject of quality practice principles in the implementation of software and the development of software systems.
Cost: $45.00
100M Members
Frequency: Quarterly
Founded in: 1946

7019 TEST Engineering & Management
Mattingley Publishing Company
3756 Grand Ave
#205
Oakland, CA 94610-1545

510-839-0909; *Fax:* 510-839-2950;
www.mattingley-publ.com

Eve Mattingley, Owner
Nora Archambeau, Advertising Sales Manager

Includes mechanical testing, environmental simulation, and related technologies in industry, government, testing labs, and universities.
Cost: $45.00
Frequency: Monthly
Circulation: 9500
ISSN: 0193-4120
Founded in: 1959
Printed in 4 colors on glossy stock

7020 The Bent
Tau Beta Pi Association
PO Box 2697
Knoxville, TN 37901-2697

865-546-4578
800-250-3196; *Fax:* 865-546-4579;
www.tbp.org
Social Media: Facebook

James D Froula, Executive Director/Editor
Dr. Larry Simonson, President

The official publication of the Tau Beta Pi Association - the engineering honor society and the world's largest engineering organization.
Cost: $10.00
Frequency: Quarterly
Circulation: 87000
ISSN: 0005-884x

7021 The Bridge
IEEE-Eta Kappa Nu
445 Hoes Lane
Piscataway, NJ 08854

732-465-5846
800-406-2590
info@hkn.org;
www.ieee.org/education_careers/education/ieee_hkn/bridge

Steve Watkins, Editor-in-Chief
Nancy Ostin, Managing Editor

The award-winning digital magazine of the IEEE-HKN.
Frequency: 3x/year

7022 Tribology & Lubrication Technology
Society of Tribologists & Lubrication
840 Busse Hwy
Park Ridge, IL 60068-2376

847-825-5536; *Fax:* 847-825-1456
information@stle.org; www.stle.org

Ed Salek, Executive Director
Karl Phipps, Associate Editor
Dr Neil Canter, Contributing Editor

Technical magazine that serves an audience of interdisciplinary professionals from industry, academic institutions and government. Included in this group are scientists, engineers, corporate leaders, researchers and product developers, plant managers and maintenance professionals, sales and marketing people and more.
Frequency: Monthly
Circulation: 7,000

7023 Tribology Transaction
Society of Tribologists & Lubrication
840 Busse Hwy
Park Ridge, IL 60068-2376

847-825-5536; *Fax:* 847-825-1456
information@stle.org; www.stle.org

Ed Salek, Executive Director

Provides you with new and useful reports and analysis of every aspect of tribology and lubrication presented by renowned authors from around the globe. Available online as well.
Frequency: Quarterly

7024 US Black Engineer & Information Technology
Career Communications Group
729 E Pratt St
Suite 504
Baltimore, MD 21202-3302

410-244-7101; *Fax:* 410-752-1837;
www.ccgmag.com

Jean Hamilton, Chief Financial Officer
Lango Deen, Technology Editor
Antonio Watson, VP Sales
Guy Madison, Publisher
Diane Jones, Director of Marketing

Devoted to engineering, science, and technology and to promoting opportunities in those fields for Black Americans.
Cost: $26.00
84 Pages
Frequency: Quarterly
Circulation: 100,000
ISSN: 1088-3444
Printed in 4 colors on glossy stock

7025 VXI Journal
30233 Jefferson Avenue
Saint Clair Shores, MI 48282

586-415-6500; *Fax:* 586-415-4882

Magazine is geared towards test engineers who are using or considering VXI bus systems and equipment.
Frequency: Quarterly
Circulation: 8000

7026 Way Ahead Magazine
Society of Petroleum Engineers
PO Box 833836
Richardson, TX 75083-3836

972-529-9300
800-456-6863; *Fax:* 972-952-9435
spedal@spe.org; www.spe.org

Giovanni Paccaloni, President
Bill Cobb, VP Finance
John E Bethancourt, Director
Management/Information
Ian Gorman, Director Production/Operations
Niki Bradbury, Managing Director

Designed for and written by young professionals in the oil and gas industry. In it, you will find items of particular interest to the younger members of our industry, including articles on the current state of the job market, how to improve communication skills, and what SPE young professionals are doing will be.
Frequency: 3x Yearly

7027 Weighing & Measurement
Key Markets Publishing Company
4729 Charles Street
PO Box 5867
Rockford, IL 61125-0867

815-636-7739

David M Mathieu, Publisher

Articles on new products, industry news, previews and reviews of events, and technical approaches to measurement.
Frequency: Bi-Monthly
Circulation: 12,000

7028 Wireless Design & Development
Reed Business Information
301 Gibraltar Drive
PO Box 650
Morris Plains, NJ 07950-0650

973-292-5100; *Fax:* 973-292-0783;
www.wirelessdesignmag.com

Wayne Curtis, Group Publisher
Kim Stokes, Editor

Edited for wireless component and system design engineers in the commercial RF and microwave market.
Frequency: Monthly

Trade Shows

7029 AACE Annual Meeting
Association of Cost Engineering
1265 Suncrest Towne Centre Drive
Morgantown, WV 26505-1876

304-296-8444
800-858-2678; *Fax:* 304-291-5728
info@aacei.org; www.aacei.org

Jennie Amos, Marketing/Meetings Manager

See and hear outstanding technical presentations, panel discussions, workshops, tours, and guest speakers
Frequency: Annual/June

7030 ACA Annual Meeting & Exhibition
American Crystallographic Association
Ellicott Station
PO Box 96
Buffalo, NY 14205-0096

716-898-8690; *Fax:* 716-898-8695
aca@hwi.buffalo.edu;
www.AmerCrystalAssn.org

Thomas Koetzle, President
George Philip, Vice President

75 manufacturers exhibits of commercial hardware and software, and x-ray equipment. In addition to the exhibition, take advantage of workshops, and scientific and poster sessions.
1000 Attendees
Frequency: Annual
Founded in: 1955

7031 AEE Globacon
Association of Energy Engineers
4025 Pleasantdale Road
Suite 420
Atlanta, GA 30340

770-447-5083; *Fax:* 770-446-3969
ashley@aeecenter.org; www.aeecenter.org

Ashley Clark, Exhibits Manager
Patricia Ardavin, Conference Registration

Director
Michelle Oxner, Conference Speakers Director
Lauren Lake, Event & Marketing Director
Bill Kent, Sponsorship Programs

Decision makers from business, industry and government coming together to seek integrated solutions to assure secure and affordable power supplies, effective management practices of both energy and overall operations costs, and exploring new technologies. The multi-track conference offer opportunity to learn about innovative and cost-conscious strategies, compare energy supply options, network, and workshops. Expo includes the Northeast Green Showcase by Energy Star.
8.2M Attendees
Mailing list available for rent

7032 **AEG Annual Meeting**
Assn. of Environmental & Engineering Geologists
1100-H Brandywine Boulevard
Suite 575
Zanesville, OH 43701

303-757-2926
844-331-7867; *Fax:* 740-452-2552
aeg@aegweb.org; www.aegweb.org

Dale C. Andrews, President
Frequency: Annual

7033 **AHR Expo**
Refrigeration Service Engineers Society
1666 Rand Road
Des Plaines, IL 60016-3552

847-297-6464
800-297-5660
webmaster@rses.org; www.rses.org

Robert Sherman, Intl President
Lawrence Donaldson, Intl Vice President

Attracts thousands of attendees from all facets of the industry, including contractors, engineers, dealers, distributors, wholesalers, OEM's, architects and builders, industrial plant operators, facility owners and managers, agents and reps.
Frequency: Annual/January

7034 **AISTech Conference & Exposition**
Association for Iron & Steel Technology
186 Thorn Hill Rd
Warrendale, PA 15086-7528

724-814-3000; *Fax:* 724-814-3001
info@aist.org; www.aist.org

Ronald E Ashburn, Executive Director
Brian Bliss, Technology Programs Manager
Karen Hickey, Publications Manager/Editor
Mark Didiano, Finance & Administration Manager
Stacy Varmecky, Membership Services Manager

Featuring technologies from across the globe, allowing steel producers to compete in today's global market. Submit technical papers for presentation at the event. 300 exhibitors. Registration starts at $425.
7000 Attendees
Frequency: Annual/Spring

7035 **AMSE International Manufacturing Science & Engineering Conference**
American Society of Mechanical Engineers
Three Park Avenue
New York, NY 10016-5990

973-882-1167
800-843-2763
infocentral@asme.org; www.asme.org

Victoria Rockwell, President

The MSEC highlights cutting edge manufacturing research in technical paper, poster and panel sessions.
3200 Attendees
Frequency: Annual/Fall
*Mailing list available for rent*at $125 per M

7036 **ANS Annual Meeting**
American Nuclear Society
555 North Kensington Avenue
La Grange Park, IL 60526

708-352-6611; *Fax:* 708-352-0499;
www.ans.org

Dr Lawrence Papay, General Chair
Dr Atambir Rao, Technical Program Chair
Harry Bradley, Executive Director
Frequency: Annual/June

7037 **AOCS Annual Meeting & Expo**
American Oil Chemists Society
2710 S Boulder
Urbana, IL 61802-6996

217-359-2344; *Fax:* 217-351-8091
general@aocs.org; www.aocs.org

Joy McClaugherty, Conference Contact
Jodey Schonfeld, Publications
Frequency: Annual/April-May

7038 **APPA Annual Conference & Exposition**
Association of Higher Education Facilities
1643 Prince Street
Alexandria, VA 22314-2818

703-684-1446; *Fax:* 703-549-2772
katy@appa.org; www.appa.org

E. Lander Medlin, Executive VP
Anita Dosik, Publications Manager
Ted Weidner, CAPPA Event Contact

Discussions and programs centered around today's educational facilities professionals: gain insight on current trends and conditions, identify challenges and solutions being implemented by industry experts, CEU and networking opportunities, and the innovative showcase of exhibitors.
Frequency: Annual

7039 **ASA Annual Meeting & Noise-Con**
Acoustical Society of America
2 Huntington Quadrable
Suite 1NO1
Melville, NY 11747

516-576-2360; *Fax:* 516-576-2377
asa@aip.org; www.acousticalsociety.org

Charles E Schmid, Executive Director
Elaine Moran, ASA Office Manager
Mardi Hastings, President
700 Attendees
Frequency: Annual/Spring

7040 **ASA: Drive Systems-Control Units-Automation**
Stygar Associates
1202 Allanson Road
Mundelein, IL 60060

847-566-4566; *Fax:* 847-566-4580
estygariii@aol.com; www.stygarassociates.com

376 exhibitors of hydraulic and pneumatic elements, compressed air systems, automation components, openloop and measuring controls.
40000 Attendees
Frequency: Biennial

7041 **ASCE Annual Civil Engineering Conference & Exposition**
American Society of Civil Engineers
1801 Alexander Bell Drive
Reston, VA 20191-4400

703-295-6000
800-548-2723; *Fax:* 703-295-6144
conf@asce.org; www.asce.org

Mark Geiger, Sr Coor, Exhibits & Meeting Svcs
Heather Doughlin, Sr Mgr, Conferences & Meeting Svcs
Kathy Caldwell, President

175 exhibits of industry related products and services, seminars, workshops and banquet plus continuing education classes.
3000 Attendees
Frequency: Annual/Fall
Founded in: 1879

7042 **ASCE Annual Meeting**
American Society of Certified Engineering
PO Box 1348
Flowery Branch, GA 30542-0023

770-967-9173; *Fax:* 770-967-8049;
www.ascet.org

Russell E Freier, Chairman
Leo Saenz, CET, President
Kurt Schuler, Secretary/Treasurer
Frequency: Annual/June

7043 **ASCE's Annual Civil Engineers Conference**
American Society of Civil Engineers
1801 Alexander Bell Drive
Reston, VA 20191-4400

703-295-6000
800-548-2723; *Fax:* 703-295-6144;
www.asce.org

Phil Gaughan, President

Focus on the challenges faced by companies and agencies already implementing the next generation of infrastructure in Water (e.g. dams, desalination, and recycling) and Transportation (e.g. seaports, rail, and roads). 100 booths.
24M Attendees
Frequency: Annual/October

7044 **ASEE Annual Conference & Exposition**
American Society for Engineering Education
1818 N Street NW
Suite 600
Washington, DC 20036-2476

202-331-3500; *Fax:* 202-265-8504
pubsinfo@asee.org; www.asee.org

Patti Greenawalt, Director Meetings/Conventions
Frank Huband, Executive Director
Frequency: Annual/June

7045 **ASFE Fall Meeting**
ASFE/The Geoprofessional Business Association
8811 Colesville Road
Suite G106
Silver Springs, MD 20910

301-565-2733; *Fax:* 301-589-2017
info@asfe.org; www.asfe.org

John P Bachner, Executive VP
David Gaboury, President
Frequency: Annual/Fall

7046 **ASFE Spring Meeting**
ASFE/The Geoprofessional Business Association
8811 Colesville Road
Suite G106
Silver Springs, MD 20910

301-565-2733; *Fax:* 301-589-2017
info@asfe.org; www.asfe.org

John P Bachner, Executive VP
David Gaboury, President
Frequency: Annual/Spring

7047 **ASFE Winter Leadership Conference**
ASFE/The Geoprofessional Business Association

8811 Colesville Road
Suite G106
Silver Springs, MD 20910

301-565-2733; *Fax:* 301-589-2017
info@asfe.org; www.asfe.org

John Bachner, Executive VP
David Gaboury, President
Frequency: Annual/January

7048 ASGE National Conference
American Society of Gas Engineers
P.O. Box 66
Artesia, CA 90702

562-455-9417
asgecge@aol.com; www.asge-national.org

Jerry Moore, Executive Director
Mike O'Donnell, President
Ray Maddock, Vice President
Chad Johnson, Treasurer

Where members meet to discuss the most current events and issues facing the Gas Appliance industry. Allows individuals to learn about new technology and to network with other Gas Industry Professionals.
Frequency: Annual
Founded in: 1954

7049 ASM Heat Treating Society Conference & Exposition
ASM International/Materials Information
9639 Kinsman Road
Materials Park, OH 44073

440-338-5151
800-336-5152; *Fax:* 440-338-4634
pamela.kleinman@asminternational.org; www.asminternational.org

Pamela Kleinma, Senior Manager, Events
Kellye Thomas, Exposition Account Manager
Dr. Mark Smith, President

Conference and exhibits of heat treating equipment and supplies plus information of interest to metallurgists, manufacturing, research and design technical professionals. 300 exhibitors.
3500 Attendees
Frequency: Bi-Annual
Founded in: 1974

7050 ASM Materials Science & Technology (MS&T)
ASM International
9639 Kinsman Road
Materials Park, OH 44073-0002

440-338-5151
800-336-5152; *Fax:* 440-338-4634
pamela.kleinman@asminternational.org; www.asminternational.org

Pamela Kleinman, Senior Manager, Events
Kelly Thomas, Exposition Account Manager
Dr. Mark Smith, President

Annual event focusing on testing, analysis, characterization and research of materials such as engineered materials, high performance metals, powdered metals, metal forming, surface modification, welding and joining. 350 exhibitors.
4,000 Attendees
Frequency: Annual/October
Founded in: 2005

7051 ASME Annual Meeting
American Society of Mechanical Engineers
Three Park Avenue
New York, NY 10016

973-882-1170
800-843-2763; *Fax:* 212-591-7856
infocentral@asme.org; www.asme.org

Melissa Torres, Meetings Manager
Mary Jakubowski, Meetings Manager
Marc Goldsmith, President
Frequency: Annual/June

7052 ASME Gas Turbine Users Symposium (GTUS)
American Society of Mechanical Engineers/IGTI
6525 The Corners Pkwy
Suite 115
Norcross, GA 30092

404-847-0072; *Fax:* 404-847-0151
igtiprogram@asme.org; www.asme.org/igti

Smita Solanki, Coordinator, IGTI Conferences
Kristen Barranger, Manager, IGTI Conferences & Expos
Michael Ireland, Managing Director

A show focused on the role gas turbines will play in meeting the nation's future energy demands, provides the information related to gas turbine operations, maintenance, advances, and design.
2000 Attendees
Frequency: Annual

7053 ASNT Fall Conference & Quality Testing Show
American Society for Nondestructive Testing
1711 Arlingate Lane
PO Box 28518
Columbus, OH 43228-0518

614-274-6003
800-222-2768; *Fax:* 614-274-6899; www.asnt.org

Michael O'Toole, Sernior Manager, Conferences
Jacquie Guinta, Meeting Coordinator
Ruth Staat, Exhibit/Event Supervisor

Seminar, conference and 150 exhibits of nondestructive testing equipment, services, supplies and laboratory representatives. Holds a smaller conference in the spring.
3000 Attendees
Frequency: Annual/Fall

7054 ASPE Technical Symposium
American Society of Plumbing Engineers
8614 Catalpa Avenue
Suite 1007
Chicago, IL 60656-1116

773-693-2773; *Fax:* 773-695-9007
info@aspe.org; www.aspe.org

Pat Delaney, Convention/Symposium Information
Stan Wolson, Executive Director

For professional plumbing engineers, designers and contractors to improve their skills, learn original design concepts and make important networking contacts to help them stay abreast of current trends, codes and technologies.
Frequency: Annual/October

7055 ASPE's Annual Meeting
American Society for Precision Engineering
PO Box 10826
Raleigh, NC 27605-0826

919-839-8444; *Fax:* 919-839-8039; www.aspe.net

Erika Deutsch-Layne, Meetings Manager

Offers the latest in precision engineering research through presentations from national and international.
Frequency: Annual/October

7056 ATCE
Society of Petroleum Engineers
PO Box 833836
Richardson, TX 75083-3836

972-529-9300
800-456-6863; *Fax:* 972-952-9435
spedal@spe.org; www.spe.org

Giovanni Paccaloni, President
Bill Cobb, VP Finance
John E Bethancourt, Director
Management/Information
Ian Gorman, Director Production/Operations
Niki Bradbury, Managing Director
40482 Attendees
Frequency: Annual/October

7057 ATMAE Annual Conference
Association of Technology, Management, and AE
275 North York Street
Suite 401
Elmhurst, IL 60126

630-433-4514
atmae@atmae.org; www.atmae.org

John Hausoul, Executive Director
Angie Coleman, Conference Manager
Cost: $550.00

7058 AVS International Symposium & Exhibition
American Vacuum Society
125 Maiden Lane
15th Floor
New York, NY 10038

212-248-0200; *Fax:* 212-248-0245
jeannette@avs.org; www.avs.org

Jeannette DeGennaro, Exhibition & Sales Coordinator
Angela Klink, Membership Services Coordinator
Heather Korff, Events/Office Coordinator AVS West
Yvonne Towse, Managing Director
Angus Rockett, President

The Symposium and Exhibition has been developed to address cutting-edge issues associated with the vacuum science and technology in both the research and manufacturing communities. It offers a week long forum for exchange, topical conferences, courses, training, career workshops and networking. Over 200 booths of the latest products and services around vacuum science and technology.
3000 Attendees
Frequency: Annual

7059 AVS International Symposium and Exhibition
AVS Science & Technology Society
120 Wall Street
32nd Floor
New York, NY 10005-3993

212-248-0200; *Fax:* 212-248-0245
david_aspnes@avs.org; www.avs.org

David E Aspnes, President
Christie R Marrian, President-Elect
John Coburn, Treasurer
Joseph J Greene, Clerk/Secretary
Yvonne Towse, Executive Director

This has been developed to address cutting-edge issues associated with vacuum science and technology in both the research and manufacturing communities. The Symposium is a week long forum for science and technology exchange featuring papers from technical divisions and technology groups, and topical conferences on emerging technologies.
3000 Attendees
Founded in: 1953

7060 AVS New Mexico Chapter Annual Symposium Short Courses/Vendor Show
AVS Science & Technology Society

120 Wall Street
32nd Floor
New York, NY 10005-3993

212-248-0200; *Fax:* 212-248-0245
david_aspnes@avs.org; www.avs.org

David E Aspnes, President
Christie R Marrian, President-Elect
John Coburn, Treasurer
Joseph J Greene, Clerk/Secretary
Yvonne Towse, Executive Director
Frequency: Annual/May

7061 **Adhesion Society Annual Meeting**
Adhesion Society
2 Davidson Hall-0201
Blacksburg, VA 24061

540-231-7257; *Fax:* 540-231-3971
adhesoc@vt.edu; www.adhesionsociety.org

Ken Shull, Program Chair
Leonardo Lopez, Exhibition Chair
Esther Brann, Office Manager

Engineers, chemists, biologists, mathematicians, physicists, physicians and dentists visit exhibits relating to the study of adhesion's role in coatings, composite materials, the function of biological tissues, and the performance of bonded structures.
400 Attendees
Frequency: Annual/February

7062 **Adhesive & Sealant Fall Convention**
Adhesive & Sealant Council
7101 Wisconsin Avenue
Suite 990
Bethesda, MD 20814
301-986-9700; *Fax:* 301-986-9795
data@ascouncil.org; www.ascouncil.org

Malinda Armstrong, Director, Meetings & Expositions
William Allmond, President
Frequency: Annual/October

7063 **AeroMat Conference and Exposition**
ASM International
9639 Kinsman Road
Materials Park, OH 44073-0002

440-338-5151
800-336-5152; *Fax:* 440-338-4634;
www.asminternational.org

Kim Schaefer, Event Manager
Kelly Thomas, Exposition Account Manager
Mark F Smith, President
Stanley Theobald, Managing Director

Conference for Aerospace Materials Engineers, Structural Engineers and Designers. The annual event focuses on affordable structures and low-cost manufacturing, titanium alloy technology, advanced intermetallics and refractory metal alloys, materials and processes for space applications, aging systems, high strength steel, NDT evaluation, light alloy technology, welding and joining, and engineering technology. 150 exhibitors.
1500 Attendees
Frequency: Annual/June
Founded in: 1984

7064 **Airlines Engineering Committee**
Aeronautical Radio
2551 Riva Road
Annapolis, MD 21401-7435

410-266-4000; *Fax:* 410-266-4040

Daniel Martinec, Director Avionics

Commercial airline and other transport aircraft avionics engineers.
800 Attendees
Frequency: October

7065 **American Society for Engineering Education Conference and Exposition**
American Society for Engineering Education
1818 N State Street
Suite 600
Washington, DC 20036

202-331-3500; *Fax:* 202-265-8504
conferences@asee.org; www.asee.org

Patti Greenawalt, Director Conventions/Meetings
Jennifer Atkinson, Meetings Assistant
Kathi J Springer, Manager Exhibits/Sponsorships
Frank Huband, Executive Director

Annual conference of 150 publishers, manufacturers, producers, suppliers, designers of scientific instrumentation and distributors. Exhibits include publications, engineering supplies and equipment, computers, software and research companies all products and services related to engineering education.
1700 Attendees
Frequency: Annual/June

7066 **American Society of Plumbing Engineers Meeting**
American Society of Plumbing Engineers
2980 S River Road
Des Plaines, IL 60018

847-296-0002; *Fax:* 773-695-9007
info@aspe.org; www.aspe.org

Cliff Reis, Managing Director of Education
Jim Kendzel, Executive Director

Biennial meeting and exhibits for the plumbing engineering industry. 600 booths.
7000 Attendees
Founded in: 1964

7067 **American Society of Safety Engineers Professional Development Conference**
American Society of Safety Engineers
1800 E Oakton Street
Des Plaines, IL 60018

847-699-2929; *Fax:* 847-768-3434
customerservice@asse.org; www.asse.org

Terri Norris, President
James Smith, Vice President/ Finance
Diane Hurns, Manager Public Relations Department

Annual conference and expo of 250 manufacturers and suppliers of safety equipment and health products.
3500 Attendees
Frequency: Annual/June

7068 **Annual Applied Reliability Engineering and Product Assurance**
The University of Arizona
Aerospace and Mechanical Engineering Department
Building 119, PO Box 210119
Tucson, AZ 85721-0119

520-215-5511; *Fax:* 520-621-8191;
www.u.arizona.edu/~dimitri

Dimitri B Kececioglu PE, Professor Aerospace/Mechanical Eng.
Frequency: Annual/July

7069 **Annual Canadian Conference on Intelligent Systems**
Robotics Industris Association
900 Victors Way
PO Box 3724
Ann Arbor, MI 48106

734-994-6088; *Fax:* 734-994-3338
webmaster@robotics.org; www.robotics.org

Don Vincent, Executive VP
Brian Huse, Director Marketing/PR
Jim Adams, Manager of Public Relations
Sharon Adams, Accounting Manager

Canada's leading showcase of research excellence and breakthroughs in robotics and intelligent systems, featuring technology displays, demonstrations, presentations and workshops.
Frequency: Annual/June

7070 **Annual Lean Management Solutions Conference**
Institute of Industrial Engineers
3577 Parkway Lane
Suite 200
Norcross, GA 30092

770-449-0460
800-494-0460; *Fax:* 770-441-3295
cs@iienet.org; www.iienet.org

Gregg Griffith, Marketing Director
Don Greene, CEO

Will enable you to significantly improve performance, reduce costs, and increase customer satisfaction. With over 60 presentations and new tracks in MRO, Food Processing, Aviation, Healthcare, and Product Design, you will find what you need.
Frequency: Annual/December

7071 **Annual Lean Six Sigma Conference**
American Society for Quality
600 N Plankinton Avenue
PO Box 3005
Milwaukee, WI 53201-3005

414-272-8575
800-248-1946; *Fax:* 414-272-1734
help@asq.org; www.asq.org

Paul Borawski, CEO
James Rooney, Chair
Erica Gumieny, Sales
Fay Spano, Communications/Media Relations

An exclusive two-day briefing and networking event designed by and for the top practitioners in the Six Sigma community.
100M Members
Frequency: Annual/February
Founded in: 1946

7072 **Annual Meeting of the Society of Rheology**
Socieety of Rheology
2 Huntington Quadrangle
Suite 1N01
Meville, NY 11747-4502

516-576-2471; *Fax:* 516-576-2223
rheology@aip.org; www.rheology.org

A. Jeffrey Giacomin, VP
Faith Morrison, President
Frequency: Annual/October

7073 **Annual Physical Electronics Conference**
AVS Science & Technology Society
120 Wall Street
32nd Floor
New York, NY 10005-3993

212-248-0200; *Fax:* 212-248-0245
david_aspnes@avs.org; www.avs.org

David E Aspnes, President
Christie R Marrian, President-Elect
John Coburn, Treasurer
Joseph J Greene, Clerk/Secretary
Nancy Schultheis, Office Manager

Will provide a forum for the dissemination and discussion of new research results in the physics and chemistry of surfaces and interfaces. The conference will continue to emphasize fundamental science in materials systems, including metals, semiconductors, insulators and biomaterials.
Frequency: Annual/June

7074 **Annual Quality Audit Conference**
American Society for Quality
600 N Plankinton Avenue
PO Box 3005
Milwaukee, WI 53201-3005
414-272-8575
800-248-1946; *Fax:* 414-272-1734
help@asq.org; www.asq.org
Paul Borawski, President
James Rooney, Chair
Topics of interest include: new innovating audit/process approaches, value added involvement, corporate expectations, corporate/social responsibility, auditing in the overall corporate scheme.
100M Members
Frequency: Annual/October
Founded in: 1946

7075 **Annual RSES Conference & Expo**
Refrigeration Service Engineers Society
1666 Rand Road
Des Plaines, IL 60016-3552
847-297-6464
800-297-5660
webmaster@rses.org; www.rses.org
Robert Sherman, Intl President
Lawrence Donaldson, Intl Vice President
Frequency: Annual/September

7076 **Annual Service Quality Conference**
American Society for Quality
600 N Plankinton Avenue
PO Box 3005
Milwaukee, WI 53201-3005
414-272-8575
800-248-1946; *Fax:* 414-272-1734
help@asq.org; www.asq.org
James Rooney, President
Paul E Borawski, CEO
Erica Gumieny, Sales
Fay Spano, Communications/Media Relations
The sessions we plan will help you to navigate through unpredictable consumer behavior and increasing competition to build a strong foundation for reaching superior levels of quality service.
100M Members
Frequency: Annual/September
Founded in: 1946

7077 **Annual Simulation Solutions Conference**
Institute of Industrial Engineers
3577 Parkway Lane
Suite 200
Norcross, GA 30092
770-449-0460
800-494-0460; *Fax:* 770-441-3295
cs@iienet.org; www.iienet.org
Greg Griffith, Marketing Director
Don Greene, CEO
You will have a rich menu of over forty presentations by successful practitioners of simulation in transportation and military applications; management strategies; manufacturing; lean scheduling and operations; healthcare; simulation skills; supply chain, material handling, and distribution; and service and business processes.
Frequency: Annual/May

7078 **Annual World Conference on Quality and Improvement**
American Society for Quality
600 N Plankinton Avenue
PO Box 3005
Milwaukee, WI 53201-3005
414-272-8575
800-248-1946; *Fax:* 414-272-1734
help@asq.org; www.asq.org
James Rooney, President
Paul E Borawski, CEO
Erica Gumieny, Sales
Fay Spano, Communications/Media Relations
Conference focuses on quality and improvement with more than 2,000 exhibits and attendees. Keynote speakers and sessions discuss quality tools, techniques and methodologies. Provides the opportunity for members to meet and network with colleagues in the industry.
100M Members
Frequency: Annual/May
Founded in: 1946

7079 **Atlantic Design & Manufacturing**
Canon Communications
11444 W Olympic Boulevard
Suite 900
Los Angeles, CA 90064-1549
310-445-4200; *Fax:* 310-445-4299;
www.cancom.com
Diane O'Conner, Trade Show Director
Dan Cutrone, Show Marketing Manager
Serves the East Coast's dynamic design, process, and manufacturing marketplace. This exposition, recently acquired by Canon Communications, is now co-located with Medical Design and Manufacturing East. Product classifications include: Coatings and Finishes, Composites, Computer Aided Design/Computer Aided Manufacturing, Electrical/Electronic, Electric Optical Components and Equipment, Engineered Safety Products, Engineering Management and Tools, Fasteners, Fluid Media, Fluid Power and Control.
Frequency: Annual/May

7080 **Atomic Layer Deposition**
AVS Science & Technology Society
120 Wall Street
32nd Street
New York, NY 10005-3993
212-248-0200; *Fax:* 212-248-0245
david_aspnes@avs.org; www.avs.org
David E Aspnes, President
Chrisitie R Marrian, President-Elect
John Coburn, Treasurer
Joseph J Greene, Clerk/Secretary
Nancy Schultheis, Office Manager
Conference will be a three-day meeting, dedicated to the science and technology of atomic layer controlled deposition of thin films, in particular atomic layer deposition.
Frequency: Annual/August

7081 **BMES Annual Fall Meeting**
Biomedical Engineering Society
8201Corporate Drive
Suite 1125
Landover, MD 20785-2224
301-459-1999
877-871-BMES; *Fax:* 301-459-2444
info@bmes.org; www.bmes.org
Richard Waugh, President
Edward Schilling, Executive Director
Debra Tucker, Meetings Director
Frequency: Annual/September

7082 **Design Part Show**
Job Shop Company
16 Waterbury Road
Prospect, CT 06712-1215
800-317-0474; www.jobshoptechnology.com
Gerald Schmidt, President
Jennifer Bryda, Production Manager
The show is designed to attract the highest caliber engineers and buyers from your major DEM product manufacturers.
2000 Attendees
Frequency: Annual/April
Founded in: 1999

7083 **ESTECH, IEST's Annual Technical Meeting and Exposition**
American Institute of Physics
One Physics Ellipse
College Park, MD 20740-3843
301-209-3100
dylla@aip.org; www.aip.org
H. Frederick Dylia, Executive Director/CEO
John Haynes, Vice President Publishing
Benjamin Snavely, AIP Corporate Secretary
Melissa Poleski, Assistant To Corporate Secretary
Will feature a cutting-edge technical program, hot-topic tutorials, must attend Working Group meetings, and a state-of-the-art exposition.
Frequency: Annual/May

7084 **Earth and Space**
American Society of Civil Engineers
1801 Alexander Bell Drive
Reston, VA 20191
703-295-6000
800-548-2723; *Fax:* 703-295-6222
webmaster@asce.org; www.asce.org
Patricia Galloway, President
Lawrence Roth, Deputy Executive Director
Patrick Natale, Secretary/Treasurer
You will be among experts from a variety of disciplines and have ample, enjoyable opportunities to discuss exploration, engineering, construction, and operations in challenging environments on Planet Earth, in Space, and on other planetary bodies such as the Moon and Mars.
Frequency: Annual/March

7085 **Electric West**
PRIMEDIA Business Exhibitions
11 River Bend Drive S
PO Box 4949
Stamford, CT 06907-0949
203-358-9900; *Fax:* 203-358-5816;
www.primediaevents.com
Liza Wylie, Show Director
Mandy Ferreira-Nunez, Operations Manager
Educational sessions attract electrical professionals from contracting companies, industrial plants, consulting engineering firms, datacom installers and electricians. Presentations focus on such topics as power quality, lighting, the NEC, project management, claims management and fiber optics. Also provides in-depth coverage of National Electrical Code changes that directly impact the work of electrical professionals.
Frequency: Annual/March

7086 **European Symposium of the Protein Society**
American Institute of Physics
One Physics Ellipse
College Park, MD 20740-3843
301-209-3100
dylla@aip.org; www.aip.org
H. Frederick Dylla, Executive Director/CEO
John Haynes, Vice President Publishing
Benjamin Snavely, AIP Corporate Secretary
Melissa Poleski, Assistant To Corporate Secretary

The meeting features sessions on nanotechnology, biosensors and proteins as materials, proteomics, protein networks and systems biology. membrane proteins and diseases, protein folding and diseases, protein flexibility, and molecular recognition.
Frequency: Annual/May

7087 **Finishing Expo**
Society of Manufacturing Engineers
1 SME Drive
PO Box 930
Dearborn, MI 48121

313-425-3000
800-733-4763; *Fax:* 313-425-3400
service@sme.org; www.sme.org

Mark Tomlinson, Executive Director/General Manager
Paul Bradley, President
Bob Harris, Director Finance

The conference will include workshops, tutorials, and technical sessions. 200 booths.
25M Attendees

7088 **General Convention**
Sigma Phi Delta
438 Smithfield Street
East Liverpool, OH 43920-1723

330-385-5287
webmaster@sigphi.org; www.sigphi.org

Derek R Troy, Grand President
Alixandre R Minden, Grand VP
Steven A Weiss, Communications Director
Edward A Hurst, Treasurer
Levon Haig Barsoumian, Executive Secretary

Includes a tentative schedule of business sessions, symposiums and events.
Frequency: Annual/July

7089 **GeoFlorida**
Geo-Institute, American Society of Civil Engineers
1801 Alexander Bell Drive
Reston, VA 20191-4400

703-295-6350; *Fax:* 703-295-6351
stacey.gardiner@tggroup.com
content.geoinstitute.org

Stacey Gardiner, Conference Director
Greory DiLoreto, President- Elect
Mark Rusnica, Deputy Executive Director

The annual geo-conference of the Geo-Institute of ASCE. Presents developments in geotechnical engineering analysis, modeling and design; opportunities to share knowledge, learn about innovations and emerging technologies; panel discussions, technical sessions, lectures, short courses, workshops and student competition; and an extensive exhibit hall.
Frequency: Annual

7090 **GlobalCon Conference & Expo**
Association of Energy Engineers
4025 Pleasantdale Rd
Suite 420
Atlanta, GA 30340-4264

770-447-5083; *Fax:* 770-446-3969
info@aeecenter.org; www.aeecenter.org
Social Media: Facebook, Twitter, LinkedIn, YouTube

Eric A. Woodroof, President
Gary Hogsett, President Elect
Bill Younger, Secretary
Paul Goodman, C.P.A., Treasurer

Designed specifically to facilitate those seeking to expand their knowledge of fast-moving developments in the energy field, explore promising new technologies, compare energy supply options, and learn about innovative and cost-conscious project implementation strategies.
8.2M Members
Founded in: 1977

7091 **Government Affairs Briefing**
North American Die Casting Association
241 Holbrook Drive
Wheeling, IL 60090-5809

847-279-0001; *Fax:* 847-279-0002
twarog@diecasting.org; www.diecasting.org

Daniel Twarog, President

Will provide you with important information in the following informative sessions, state of US manufacturing, trade and global competition, metalcasting research programs, health care & other worker issues, new air standards & other environmental issues.
Frequency: Annual/June

7092 **IDSA National Conference**
Industrial Designers Society of America
45195 Business Court
Suite 250
Sterling, VA 20166-6717
703-707-6000; *Fax:* 703-787-8501
idsa@idsa.org; www.idsa.org

Clive Roux, CEO
Bob Swartz, Executive Director
Kaycee Childress, Marketing
Roxann Henze, Press, Media & Public Relations

IDSA is the world's oldest, largest, member-driven society for product design, industrial design, interaction design, human factors, ergonomics, design research, design management, universal design and related design fields. IDSA organizes the renowned International Design Excellence Award competition annually; hosts the International Design Conference and five regional conferences each year.
800 Attendees
Frequency: Annual/August

7093 **IES Annual Meeting**
Illuminating Engineering Society of North America
120 Wall Street
17th Floor
New York, NY 10005

212-248-5000; *Fax:* 212-248-5018
ies@ies.org; www.ies.org

William Hanley, Executive VP
Marianne Conrad, Director Member Services
400 Attendees
Frequency: Annual

7094 **IFAI Annual Expo**
Industrial Fabrics Association International
1801 Country Road BW
Roseville, MN 55113

651-222-2508
800-225-4324; *Fax:* 651-631-9334
generalinfo@ifai.com; www.ifai.com

Todd Lindemann, VP Conference Manger
Stephen Warner, President

A trade event in the Americas for the technical textiles and specialty fabrics industry.
Frequency: Annual/September

7095 **IFAI Outlook**
Industrial Fabrics Association International
1801 Country Road BW
Roseville, MN 55113

651-222-2508
800-225-4324; *Fax:* 651-631-9334
generalinfo@ifai.com; www.usifi.com

Todd Lindemann, VP Conference Manger
Stephen Warner, President

Will bring industry leaders together to discuss important issues and challenges faced by the United States textile industry.
Frequency: Annual/May

7096 **IIE Annual Conference**
Institute of Industrial Engineers
3577 Parkway Lane
Suite 200
Norcross, GA 30092

770-449-0460
800-494-0460; *Fax:* 770-441-3295
cs@iienet.org; www.iienet.org

Greg Griffith, Marketing Director
Don Greene, CEO

With over 600 content filled presentations and expert speakers, it is the productivity event of the year. Discover the latest tools, techniques and solutions from top professionals in the field. Network with peers, decision makers, and leaders during the conference.
1,100 Attendees
Frequency: Annual/May

7097 **IPTC**
Society of Petroleum Engineers
PO Box 833836
Richardson, TX 75083-3836

972-529-9300
800-456-6863; *Fax:* 972-952-9435
spedal@spe.org; www.spe.org

Giovanni Paccaloni, President
Bill Cobbs, VP Finance
John E Berthancourt, Director Management/Information
Ian Gorman, Director Production/Operations
Niki Bradbury, Managing Director

The theme for the conference is Sustaining World Growth - Technology and People. A new meeting brought to you by four leading industry societies (AAPG, EAGE, SEG, and SPE). Natural gas will be a major focus of this meeting.
Frequency: Annual/November

7098 **IRI Annual Meeting**
Industrial Research Institute
2200 Clarendon Boulevard
Suite 1102
Arlington, VA 22201

703-647-2580; *Fax:* 703-647-2581;
www.iriweb.org

Robert Kumpf, Chairman
Ryan Dirkx, Chairman-Elect
Edward Bernstein, President
Frequency: Annual/May

7099 **IRgA Annual Convention and Trade Show**
International Reprographic Association
401 N Michigan Avenue
Chicago, IL 60611

312-673-4805; *Fax:* 312-321-5150
info@irga.com; www.irga.com

Robert Roperti, President
Dan Mulrooney, VP
Steve Bova, Executive Director

You will gain first hand knowledge and experience from technical sessions presented by experts in their field, access to the latest products and services available to enhance your company's performance at the trade show, re-establish contacts and connections as you interact with peers to find out how they are handling the latest challenges.
Frequency: Annual/May

7100 **ISWM Annual Conference & Expo**
International Society of Weighing & Measurement
1801 Alexander Bell Avenue
Reston, VA 20191

703-295-6350; *Fax:* 703-295-6351
staff@iswm.org
content.geoinstitute.org

Kate Fitzgerald CMP, Director of Meetings

150 booths; presentations from industry leaders; workshops, panels, and discussions.
1.8M Attendees

7101 International Code Council Annual Conference
BOCA Evaluation Services
500 New Jersey Avenue
6th Fl
Washington, DC 20001-2070
888-422-7233; *Fax:* 202-783-2348
webmaster@iccsafe.org; www.iccsafe.org
James Brothers, President
William Dupler, Vice President
The conference features the Final Action Hearings, the Education Program, the Annual Business Meeting, the International Code Council Expo and networking opportunities with your peers in the building safety and fire prevention fields.
Frequency: Annual/September

7102 International Conference on Construction Engineering/Management
American Society for Civil Engineers
1801 Alexander Bell Drive
Reston, VA 20191
703-295-6000
800-548-2723; *Fax:* 703-295-6222
webmaster@asce.org; www.asce.org
Patricia Galloway, President
Lawrence Roth, Deputy Executive Director
Patrick Natale, Secretary/Treasurer
Frequency: Annual/October

7103 International Conference on Deburring and Surface Finishing
Abrasive Engineering Society
144 Moore Road
Butler, PA 16001
724-282-6210; *Fax:* 724-234-2376
aes@abrasiveengineering.com;
www.abrasiveengineering.com
Doug Haynes, President
Ted Giese, Executive Director
The program, which is part of series of international conferences, is scheduled for June. This conference will include a Technical Exhibition and Tours. A special course on deburring and surface finishing will be taught following the conference.
Frequency: Annual/June

7104 International Conference on Metallurgical Coatings and Thin Films
AVS Science & Technology Society
120 Wall Street
32nd Floor
New York, NY 10005-3993
212-248-0200; *Fax:* 212-248-0245
david_aspnes@avs.org; www.avs.com
David E Aspnes, President
Christie R Marrian, President-Elect
John Coburn, Treasurer
Joseph J Greene, Clerk/Secretary
Steve Sukman, Executive Vice President
Internationally recognized as a vibrant technical conference that integrates fundamentals and applied research focused on thin film deposition, characterization, and advanced surface modification techniques leading-edge technology.
Frequency: Annual/May

7105 International Symposium for Testing & Failure Analysis
ASM International
9639 Kinsman Road
Materials Park, OH 44073
440-338-5151
800-336-5152; *Fax:* 440-338-4634;
www.asminternational.org
Jaime Creighton, Event Manager
Kelly Thomas, Exposition Account Manager
Annual event focusing on microelectronic and electronic device failure analysis, techniques, EOS/ESD testing and desecrates aimed at failure analysis engineers and managers, technicians and new failure analysis engineers. 200 exhibitors.
1100 Attendees
Frequency: Annual/November

7106 International Symposium on Advances in Abrasives Technology
Abrasive Engineering Society
141 Moore Road
Butler, PA 16001
724-826-6210; *Fax:* 742-234-2376
aes@abrasiveengineering.com;
www.abrasiveengineering.com
Doug Haynes, President
Ted Giese, Executive Director
Jointly sponsored by the International Committee for Abrasives Technology and the Japan Society for Abrasive Technology, which has conducted eight international conferences on abrasives technologies. Topics including abrasive machining, finishing, assessment of grinding performance, machine tools and systems, coolant and other topics.
Frequency: Annual/November

7107 International Thermal Spray Conference & Exposition
ASM International
9639 Kinsman Road
Materials Park, OH 44073
440-338-5151
800-336-5152; *Fax:* 440-338-4634
natalie.nemec@asminternational.org;
www.asminternational.org
Pamela Kleinman, Event Manager
Kelly Thomas, Exposition Account Manager
Global annual event attracting professional interested in thermal spray technology focusing on advances in HVOF, plasma and detonation gun, flame spray and wire arc spray processes, performance of coatings, and future trends. 150 exhibitors.
1000 Attendees
Frequency: Annual/May

7108 International Workshop on Deep Inelastic Scattering - DIS05
American Institute of Physics
One Physics Ellipse
College Park, MD 20740-3843
301-209-3100
dylla@aip.org; www.aip.org
H. Frederick Dylla, Executive Director/CEO
Benjamin Snavely, Senior Executive Secretary
Benjamin Snavely, AIP Corporate Secretary
Melissa Poleski, Assistant to Corporate Secretary
The aim of these workshops is to review the progress in the field of DIS and QCD and to discuss and lay the groundwork for the future. DIS 2005 will bring together about 250 experimentalists and theorists. The workshop format will involve plenary sessions with review talks and parallel working group sessions with shorter contributions.
Frequency: Annual/April

7109 LIGHTFAIR International Trade Show
Illuminating Engineering Society of North America
120 Wall Street
17th Floor
New York, NY 10005
212-248-5000; *Fax:* 212-248-5018
ies@ies.org; www.ies.org
William Hanley, Executive VP
Marianne Conrad, Director Member Services
Denis Lavoie, President
23000 Attendees
Frequency: Annual

7110 MCAA Annual Conference
Mechanical Contractors Association of America
1385 Piccard Drive
Rockville, MD 20850-4340
301-869-5800; *Fax:* 301-990-9690;
www.mcaa.org
Lonnie Coleman, MCAA President
Containing 100 booths and 95 exhibits. Education sessions, leadership and keynote presentations, exhibitions.

7111 MIACON Construction, Mining & Waste Management Show
Finocchiaro Enterprises
2921 Coral Way
Miami, FL 33145
305-441-2865; *Fax:* 305-529-9217;
www.miacon.com
Michael Finocchiaro, President
Jose Garcia, VP
Justine Finocchiaro, Chief Operations
Annual show of 650 manufacturers, suppliers, distributors and exporters of equipment, machinery, supplies and services for the construction, mining and waste managment industries. There will be 600 booths.
10M Attendees
Frequency: Annual/October
Founded in: 1994

7112 Meeting of the Acoustical Society of America
Acoustical Society of America
2 Huntington Quandrangle
Suite 1N01
Melville, NY 11747-4502
516-576-2360; *Fax:* 516-576-2377
asa@aip.org; www.acousticalsociety.org
William A Kuperman, President
William A Yost, President-Elect
Mark F Hamilton, VP
Donna L Neff, VP Elect
Charles E Schmid, Executive Director
Frequency: Annual/May

7113 Metalcasting Congress
North American Die Casting Association
241 Holbrook Drive
Wheeling, IL 60090-5809
847-279-0001; *Fax:* 847-279-0002
twarog@diecasting.org; www.diecasting.org
Daniel Twarog, President
With the wide range of opportunities for technology transfer, it promises to be the industry's premier show. The American Foundry Society and the North American Die Casting Association are joining together.
Frequency: Annual/April

7114 Mid-Atlantic Job Shop Show
Edward Publishing

16 Waterbury Road
Prospect, CT 06712-1215

203-758-6658; *Fax:* 203-758-4476; www.jobshoptechnology.com

Jennifer Bryda, Production Manager

The show is designed to attract the highest caliber engineers and buyers from your major DEM product manufacturers. There will be 260 exhibitors and booths.
2500 Attendees
Frequency: Annual/May
Founded in: 1999

7115 NACE International Annual Conference & Expo (CORROSION)
NACE International
1440 S Creek Drive
Houston, TX 77084-4906

281-228-6200
800-797-6223; *Fax:* 281-228-6300
firstservice@nace.org; www.nace.org

Oliver Moghissi, President
Bob Chalker, Executive Director

World's largest conference dedicated to Corrosion control and prevention
5000 Attendees
Frequency: Annual

7116 NADCA Sales Training
North American Die Casting Association
241 Holbrook Drive
Wheeling, IL 60090-5809

847-279-0001; *Fax:* 847-279-0002
twarog@diecasting.org; www.diecasting.org

Daniel Twarog, President

NADCA will be providing a one day seminar to address the challenges we face in today's marketplace.
Frequency: Annual/June

7117 NSPE Annual Convention and Expo
National Society of Professional Engineers
1420 King Street
Alexandria, VA 22314-2794

703-684-2800
888-285-2853; *Fax:* 703-836-4875
webmaster@nspe.org; www.nspe.org

Katrina Robinson, Marketing Manager

The National Society of Professional Engineers is the only engineering society that represents individual engineering professionals and licensed engineers across all disciplines. Founded in 1934, NSPE serves some 60,000 members and the public through 53 state and territorial societies and more than 500 chapters nationally and internationally. The conference brings together the decision makers of engineering companies and business owners nationwide to network and discuss issues of importance.
700 Attendees
Frequency: Annual/July
Mailing list available for rent: 50,000+ names at $130 per M

7118 National Industrial Automation, Integration & Control Show
Reed Exhibition Companies
383 Main Avenue Suite 3
PO Box 6059
Norwalk, CT 06851-1543

203-840-4800; *Fax:* 203-840-5805
inquiry@reedexpo.com; www.reedexpo.com

Peter DiLeo, Marketing Director
Mike Rusbridge, CEO
Domonic Shine, Chief Information Officer

Annual show of 200 exhibitors of chemical engineering and processing, electronics, machinery equipment, supplies and services.
19M Attendees

7119 National Quality Education Conference
American Society for Quality
600 N Plankinton Avenue
PO Box 3005
Milwaukee, WI 53201-3005

414-272-8575
800-248-1946; *Fax:* 414-272-1734
help@asq.org; www.asq.org

James Rooney, Chair
Paul E Borawski, CEO
Erica Gumieny, Sales
Fay Spano, Communications/Media Relations

Provides teachers, administrators, and support personnel opportunities to examine continuous improvement principles used in education. It provides resources and best practices to help you address requirements of No Child Left Behind, while helping you increase student achievement and improve overall performance.
100M Members
Frequency: Annual/November
Founded in: 1946

7120 Northern American Material Handling Show & Forum
Appliance Manufacturer
5900 Harper Road
Suite 105
Solon, OH 44139-1935

440-349-3060
800-345-1815; *Fax:* 440-498-9121
cmiller@mhia.org; www.mhia.com

Carol Miller, Senior Director Marketing
Frequency: Bi-Annual

7121 Northwest Plant Engineering & Maintenance Show and Conference (NWPE)
Cygnus Expositions
3167 Skyway Court
Fremont, CA 94539

510-543-3131; *Fax:* 510-354-3159
showinfo@proshows.com
facilitiesexpo.com

Erin Sparks, Marketing Manager
Paul Bonaiuto, CFO
Kathy Scott, Director of Public Relations

Annual show of 233 exhibitors of low-tech cleaning systems, high-tech computerized maintenance management systems, diagnostic problem software, indoor air quality controllers and related products and services.
5000 Attendees
Frequency: Annual/May

7122 Nuclear and Emerging Technologies for Space
555 N Kensington Ave
La Grange Park, IL 60526-5592

708-352-6611
800-323-3044; *Fax:* 708-352-0499
advertising@ans.org; www.ans.org
Social Media: Facebook, Twitter, LinkedIn

Jack Tuohy, Executive Director
James S Tulenko, VP
William F Naughton, Treasurer

Positive collaborative environment and series of discussion forums and technical showcasing.
10500 Members
Founded in: 1954

7123 OTC Expo
Society of Petroleum Engineers
PO Box 833836
Richardson, TX 75083-3836

972-529-9300
800-456-6863; *Fax:* 972-952-9435
spedal@spe.org; www.spe.org

Giovanni Paccaloni, President
Bill Cobbs, VP Finance
John E Bethancourt, Director Management/Information
Ian Gorman, Director Production/Operations
Niki Bradbury, Managing Director
51300 Attendees

7124 Pacific Design & Manufacturing
Canon Communications
11444 W Olympic Boulevard
Suite 900
Los Angeles, CA 90064-1549

310-445-4200; *Fax:* 310-445-4299; www.pacdesignshow.com

Diane O'Conner, Trade Show Director
Dan Cutrone, Show Marketing Manager

The Pacific Design Engineering show is the most comprehensive event serving the West Coast's design, process and manufacturing marketplace. Product classifications include Coatings & Finishes, Composites, Computer Aided Design/Computer Aided Manufacturing, Electrical/Electronic, ElectroOptical Components & Equipment, Engineered Safety products, Engineering Management & Tools and more. Held at the Anaheim Convention Center in Anaheim, California.
35970 Attendees
Frequency: Annual/January

7125 Plant & Facilities Expo (PFE)
Association of Energy Engineers
4025 Pleasantdale Road
Suite 420
Atlanta, GA 30340

770-447-5083; *Fax:* 770-446-3969
info@aeecenter.org; www.aeecenter.org

Ruth Whitlock, Executive Director
Jennifer Vendola, Accountant

Seek solutions for plant and facility needs. Vendors have an opportunity to meet prospective customers, reacquaint themselves with existing customers, and network with other vendors.
5000 Attendees
Frequency: October

7126 ProMat
Material Handling Industry of America
8720 Red Oak Blvd
Suite 201
Charlotte, NC 28217

704-676-1190
800-345-1815; *Fax:* 704-676-1199; www.mhia.org

Tom Carbott, Exhibiting Information
Terri Heisey, Educational Conference & Seminar

You can compare the latest solutions essential to the productivity of your manufacturing, warehousing, and distribution operations. The material handling & logistics solutions you discover at ProMat will help you differentiate your product, improve customer service and increase overall corporate profitability. 700 exhibits.
Frequency: Annual

7127 Professional Development Conference & Exposition
1800 E Oakton Street
Des Plaines, IL 60018

847-699-2929; *Fax:* 847-768-3434
customerservice@asse.org; www.asse.org
Social Media: Facebook, Twitter, LinkedIn

Fred Fortman, Executive Director
Bruce Sufranski, Finance/Controller Director

Diane Hurns, Manager Public Relations Department
Sally Madden, Human Resources Manager

The American Society of Safety Engineers (ASSE) is the oldest professional safety society committed to protecting people, property and the environment. ASSE has more than 32,000 occupational safety, health and environmental (SH&E) professional members who manage, supervise, research and consult on safety, health, transportation and the environment in all industries, government, labor and education.
34000 Members
4,000 Attendees
Founded in: 1911

7128 **REMSA and AREMA Meeting**
Railway Engineering: Maintenance Supplies Assn
500 New Jersey Avenue
Suite 400
Washington, DC 20001

202-715-2921; *Fax:* 202-204-5753
home@remsa.org; www.remsa.org

Philip Hoffman, President
John Fox, VP
David Soule, Executive Director
Ronald C Olds, Secretary/Treasurer

Holding the exhibits and technical conference simultaneously in Louisville give added benefit to REMSA members.
Frequency: Annual/September

7129 **REMSA and NRC: Synergy in Action**
Railway Engineering: Maintenance Supplies Assn
500 New Jersey Avenue
Suite 400
Washington, DC 20001

202-715-2921; *Fax:* 202-204-5753
home@remsa.org; www.remsa.org

Philip Hoffman, President
John Fox, VP
David Soule, Executive Director
Ronald C Olds, Secretary/Treasurer

Members and other industry suppliers discuss their products, services and equipment with attendees representing a broad spectrum of railroaders: transits, short lines, commuter and Class I railroads. There were 56 exhibiting companies.
Frequency: Annual/January

7130 **RSES Annual Conference and HVAC Technology Expo**
Refrigeration Service Engineers Society
1666 Rand Road
Des Plaines, IL 60016-3552

847-297-6464
800-297-5660
general@rses.org; www.rses.org
Social Media: Facebook, Twitter, LinkedIn

Lawrence Donaldson, Intl. Executive Vice President
Josh Flaim, Operations Manager
Jean Birch, Conference & Seminar Manager

80 booths consisting primarily of products and services.

7131 **RoboBusiness Conference and Exposition**
American Institute of Physics
One Physics Ellipse
College Park, MD 20740-3843

301-209-3100
dylla@aip.org; www.aip.org

H. Frederick Dylla, Executive Director/CEO
John Haynes, Vice President Publishing
Benjamin Snavely, AIP Corporate Secretary
Melissa Poleski, Assistant To Corporate Secretary

Focuses on the business development and technical issues involved with the commercial application of mobile robotics and intelligent systems technology to develop entirely new markets and product categories, open additional lines of business and enhance existing product lines.
Frequency: Annual/May

7132 **SAFETY Expo**
American Society of Safety Engineers
1800 E Oakton Street
Des Plaines, IL 60018

847-699-2929; *Fax:* 847-768-3434
info@asse.org; www.asse.org

Terri Norris, President
Kathy Seabrook, Senior Vice President
Diane Hurns, Manager Public Relations Department

A full 3-day conference featuring more than 200 sessions, an exposition with 300 exhibitors, special pre- and post-conference seminars, conference proceedings on CD, numerous networking events and more.
Frequency: Annual/July

7133 **SAMPE Tech Conference**
Society for the Advancement of Material & Process
1161 Park View Drive
Suite 200
Covina, CA 91724-3751

626-331-0616
800-562-7360; *Fax:* 626-332-8929
sampeibo@sampe.org; www.sampe.org
Social Media: Facebook, LinkedIn

Gregg Balko, Executive Director
Rosemary Loggia, Conference/Exhibits Manager
Priscilla Heredia, Conference/Symposia Assistant Mgr

Known for its excellent conference programs. Featuring expert speakers and industry insiders, the information take-away from this event is invaluable to M&P professionals.
Frequency: Annual/October

7134 **SME Annual Meeting**
Society of Manufacturing Engineers
1 SME Drive
PO Box 930
Dearborn, MI 48121

313-425-3000
800-733-4763; *Fax:* 313-425-3400
service@sme.org; www.sme.org

Mark Tomlinson, Executive Director/General Manager
Greg Sheremet, Publisher
Bob Harris, Director Finance

Bringing together hundreds of SME members to interact and exchange ideas with their fellow practitioners. This yearly forum offers technical training, special sessions for members, and a celebration of the best that manufacturing has to offer through our International Honor Awards Banquet.
Frequency: Annual/June

7135 **STL Annual Meeting**
Society of Tribologists & Lubrication
840 Busse Highway
Park Ridge, IL 60068-2376

847-825-5536; *Fax:* 847-825-1456
information@stle.org; www.stle.org

Merle Hedland, Meetings Manager

Expect more than 300 technical and practical presentations will be selected for the Calgary program.
Frequency: Annual/May

7136 **Street & Area Lighting Conference**
Illuminating Engineering Society of North America
120 Wall Street
17th Floor
New York, NY 10005

212-248-5000; *Fax:* 212-248-5018
ies@ies.org; www.ies.org

William Hanley, Executive VP
Valerie Landers, Director Member Services
500 Attendees
Frequency: Annual

7137 **TBP Annual Convention**
Tau Beta Pi Association
PO Box 2697
Knoxville, TN 37904-2697

865-546-4578; *Fax:* 865-546-4579;
www.tbp.org
Social Media: Facebook, LinkedIn

James D Froula, Executive Director
Larry Simonson, President
James Froula, Executive Director

A convention at which members conduct the official business of the Association, network with engineers from around the country, and participate in a recruiting fair.
500+ Attendees

7138 **Texoma Regional Education & Training Conference**
Society of American Military Engineers
607 Prince Street
Alexandria, VA 22314-3117

703-549-3800
800-336-3097; *Fax:* 703-684-0231
webmanager@same.org; www.same.org

Dr Robert D Wolff, Executive Director
Ann McLeod, Director of Meetings
Jenni Ford, CPA, Director Finance/Accounting

Will provide opportunities to attend SAME sponsored sessions as well as TSPE sponsored training sessions. This diversity of training venues is intended to provide the attendee with exposure to a wide variety of topics and will provide a beneficial learning experience.
Frequency: Annual/June

7139 **Total Product Development**
American Supplier Institute
17333 Federal Drive
Suite 220
Allen Park, MI 48101-3614

313-336-8877
800-462-4500; *Fax:* 313-336-3187;
www.amsup.com

Dr Genichi Taguchi, Executive Director

Annual show and exhibits relating to the encouragement of change in US industry through development and implementation of advanced manufacturing and engineering technologies.
200 Attendees

7140 **UNYVAC's Co-Sponsored Symposium**
AVS Science & Technology Society
120 Wall Street
32nd Floor
New York, NY 10005-3993

212-248-0200; *Fax:* 212-248-0245
david_aspnes@avs.org; www.avs.org

David E Aspnes, President
Christie R Marrian, President-Elect
John Coburn, Treasurer
Joseph J Greene, Clerk/Secretary
Nancy Schultheis, Office Manager

Topic: Functional Coatings and Surface Engineering. Will provide a forum for training and

discussion of the physics and chemistry of functional coatings and surfaces.
Frequency: Bi-Annual

7141 **West Coast Energy Management Congress EMC**
Association of Energy Engineers
4025 Pleasantdale Road
Suite 420
Atlanta, GA 30340
770-447-5083; *Fax:* 770-446-3969
info@aeecenter.org; www.aeecenter.org
Jennifer Vendola, Accountant
Ruth Whitlock, Executive Admin
Specifically for business, industrial and institutional energy users. It brings together the top experts in all areas of the field to help you set a clear, optimum path to both energy cost control and energy supply security.
Frequency: Annual/June

7142 **Winter Meeting and Nuclear Technology Expo**
American Nuclear Society
555 North Kensington Avenue
La Grange Park, IL 60526
708-352-6611; *Fax:* 708-352-0499;
www.ans.org
Thomas A Christopher, General Co-Chair
Michael Wallac, General Co-Chair
Topic: Talk About Nuclear Differently: A Good Story Untold.
Frequency: Annual/November

7143 **World Energy Engineering Congress**
Association of Energy Engineers
4025 Pleasantdale Road
Suite 420
Atlanta, GA 30340
770-447-5083; *Fax:* 770-446-3969
info@aeecenter.org; www.aeecenter.org
Jennifer Vendola, Accountant
Ruth Whitlock, Executive Admin
A comprehensive forum where participants can fully assess the big picture and see exactly how the economic and market forces, new technologies, regulatory developments and industry trends all merge to shape their critical decisions on their organizations' energy and economic future.
Frequency: Annual/September

Directories & Databases

7144 **AEG Annual Directory**
Assn. of Environmental & Engineering Geologists
1100-H Brandywine Boulevard
Suite 575
Zanesville, OH 43701
303-757-2926
844-331-7867; *Fax:* 740-452-2552
aeg@aegweb.org; www.aegweb.org
Dale C. Andrews, President
Kathy Troost, Vice President
Contains member and Association information.

7145 **ANS Buyers Guide**
American Nuclear Society
555 N Kensington Ave
La Grange Park, IL 60526-5592
708-352-6611; *Fax:* 708-352-0499;
www.ans.org
Jack Tuohy, Executive Director
E James Reinsch, President-Elect/VP
Harry Bradley, Executive Director
William F Naughton, Treasurer
Buyer's Guide Directory lists approximately 1150 suppliers of products and services to the nuclear industry. This comprehensive listing contains approximately 500 categories representing the wide range of nuclear components and services available today.
Cost: $110.00
Frequency: Annual
Founded in: 2005

7146 **ASME Database**
American Society of Mechnical Engineers
3 Park Ave
Suite 21
New York, NY 10016-5990
212-591-7000
800-843-2763; *Fax:* 212-591-7674
infocentral@asme.org; www.asme.org
Victoria Rockwell, President
Warren Leonard, Managing Director Operations
Virgil Carter, Executive Director
Provides proven direct mail buyers and selection options that enable you to customize lists to achieve your objective.

7147 **AWWA Buyer's Guide**
American Water Works Association
6666 W Quincy Ave
Denver, CO 80235-3098
303-794-7711
800-926-7337; *Fax:* 303-347-0804;
www.awwa.org
Jerry Stevens, President
David LaFrance, Executive Director
The official resource guide to water industry products and services.

7148 **Advanced Energy Design Guide for Small Office Buildings**
Illuminating Engineering Society of North America
120 Wall St
17th Floor
New York, NY 10005-4001
212-248-5000; *Fax:* 212-248-5017
ies@ies.org; www.ies.org
William Hanley, Executive VP
Valerie Landers, Director Member Services
Provides a sensible approach by including practical products and readily-available, off-the-shelf technology. The Guide offers you all the tools you need to create an energy-efficient building where the owners will see a 30 percent energy savings compared to buildings that only meet the minimum requirements of Standard 90.1.
Cost: $47.00
390 Pages
Founded in: 2004

7149 **American Association of Cost Engineers Membership Directory**
Association for Total Cost Management
209 Prairie Avenue
#100
Morgantown, WV 26501-5949
Fax: 304-291-5728
Andy Dowd, Executive Director
Member directory.
Cost: $35.00
100 Pages
Frequency: Annual

7150 **American Society for Engineering Education Membership Directory**
1818 N St NW
Suite 600
Washington, DC 20036-2476
202-331-3500; *Fax:* 202-265-8504
f.huband@asee.org; www.asee.org
Frank L Huband, Executive Director
Offers information on over 10,000 colleges and university engineering professors and personnel, practicing engineers and industry executives who are members of the ASEE.
200 Pages
Frequency: Annual
Circulation: 10,000

7151 **American Society of Civil Engineers Official Register**
1801 Alexander Bell Dr
Suite 100
Reston, VA 20191-4382
703-295-6300
800-548-2723; *Fax:* 703-295-6222
conf@asce.org
http://www.asce.org
D Wayne Klotz, President
Provides ready access to governing documents, statistics, and general information about ASCE for leadership, members, and staff.
Cost: $24.00
640 Pages
Frequency: Annual
ISBN: 0-784407-73-8
Founded in: 2005

7152 **BMES Membership Directory**
Biomedical Engineering Society
8201 Corporate Dr
Suite 1125
Landover, MD 20785-2224
301-459-1999
888-871-BMES; *Fax:* 301-459-2444
info@bmes.org; www.bmes.org
Richard Waugh, President
Debra Tucker, Meeting Manager
Edward Schilling, Executive Director
A directory listing members' names, mailing addresses, telephone numbers, e-mail addresses, areas of specialization, as well as indexes of professional interest and geographic location.
Frequency: Annual

7153 **Basics of Code Division Multiple Access (CDMA)**
International Society for Optical Engineering
PO Box 10
Bellingham, WA 98227-0010
360-676-3290; *Fax:* 360-647-1445
customerservice@spie.org; www.spie.org
Raghuveer Rao, Editor
Sohail Dianat, President
Amy Nelson, Manager
This text, aimed at the reader with a basic background in electrical or optical engineering, covers CDMA fundamentals: from the basics of the communication process and digital data transmission, to the concepts of code division multiplexing, direct sequence spreading, diversity techniques, the near-far effect, and the IS-95 CDMA standard form.
Cost: $35.00
120 Pages
ISBN: 0-819458-69-4

7154 **CED Directory of Engineering and Engineering Technology Programs**
Mississippi State University

PO Box 6046
Mississippi State, MS 39762-6046

662-258-8122; *Fax:* 662-325-8733

Mike Mathews, Editor

Over 150 colleges and universities with cooperative education programs in engineering and engineering technology are listed.
Cost: $50.00
250 Pages
Frequency: Biennial

7155 CRC Press
2000 NW Corporate Boulevard
Boca Raton, FL 33431

561-994-0555
800-272-7737; *Fax:* 772-998-0876
techsupport@crcpress.com; www.crcpress.com

Eleanor Riemer, Publisher
Emmett Dages, CEO

Publisher in science, medicine, environmental science, forensic, engineering, business, technology, mathematics, and statistics. Our food science and nutrition books and our journal, Critical Reviews in Food and Nutrition, are well established and respected publications in the food science industry.

7156 CSA Engineering
Cambridge Scientific Abstracts
7200 Wisconsin Ave
Suite 601
Bethesda, MD 20814-4890

301-961-6700; *Fax:* 301-961-6790
service@csa.com; www.csa.com

Andrew M Snyder, President
Martin Nowicki, Editor, Engineering

This database offers information on more than 500,000 citations, with abstracts, to international periodical and other research literature covering all fields of engineering and science.
Cost: $945.00
Frequency: Monthly

7157 Coolant Filtration-Additional Technologies
Society of Tribologists & Lubrication
840 Busse Hwy
Park Ridge, IL 60068-2376

847-825-5536; *Fax:* 847-825-1456
information@stle.org; www.stle.org

Ed Salek, Executive Director

The text covers coolant cleaning and handling for metalworking operations where coolants are used as part of the process. The publication also provides the latest thinking on specific metalworking applications with some comprehensive guidelines. 76 illustrations.
Cost: $56.00
223 Pages

7158 Design-Build Project Delivery (ACEC)
American Council of Engineering Companies
1015 15th St
8th Floor NW
Washington, DC 20005-2605

202-347-7474; *Fax:* 202-898-0068
acec@acec.org; www.acec.org
Social Media: Facebook, Twitter

Dave Raymond, President
Howard Messner, Executive Director

Guide for firms considering design/build projects. Analyzes risks, steps and milestones necessary for successful completion of design/build projects.

7159 Directory of Accredited Engineering & Technology Certification Programs
Council of Engineer and Scientific Specialty Board
PO Box 1448
Annapolis, MD 21404-1488

410-266-3766; *Fax:* 410-721-1746
academy@aaee.net; www.cesb.org

Ronald Council, Owner
William C Anderson PE DEE, Executive Director

Provides a description of existing programs for persons interested in being certified and for those seeking an objective assessment of an expert's capability and competence.

7160 Directory of Engineering Document Sources
Global Engineering Documents
15 Inverness Way E
Englewood, CO 80112-5710

303-900-0600
800-854-7179; *Fax:* 303-397-2740
CustomerCare@ihs.com; www.global.ihs.com

Charles Picasso, CEO

Offers over 10,000 document initialisms and acronyms for governmental, military and industry specifications and related publications.
Cost: $145.00
274 Pages
Frequency: Annual

7161 Directory of Engineers in Private Practice
National Society of Professional Engineers
1420 King St
Suite 500
Alexandria, VA 22314-2794

703-684-2800; *Fax:* 703-836-4875
webmaster@nspe.org; www.nspe.org

Larry Jacobson, Executive Director

Consulting engineering firms and individuals who are members of the Society's Professional Engineers in Private Practice division.
Cost: $85.00
260 Pages
Frequency: Annual

7162 Directory of Iron and Steel Plants
186 Thorn Hill Rd
Warrendale, PA 15086-7528

724-814-3000; *Fax:* 724-814-3001
memberservices@aist.org; www.aist.org

Ronald E Ashburn, Executive Director
William A Albaugh, Technology Programs Manager
Joann Cantrell, Publications Manager/Editor
Mark Didiano, Finance & Administration Manager
Stacy Varmecky, Membership Communications Manager

The Directory lists more than 2,000 companies and 17,500 individuals. Featuring data on essentially ever steel producer in the USA, Canada and Mexico, including names and titles of executive, engineering, maintenance and operating personnel. Also includes an alpha listing of all major equipment, product and service providers to the international iron and steel industry, and a listing of associations affiliated with the industry, with complete geo-indexing. Softbound book with CD.
Cost: $95.00
ISBN: 1-935117-00-1

7163 EI Page One
Engineering Information
1 Castle Point Ter
Hoboken, NJ 07030-5906

201-356-6800
800-221-1044; *Fax:* 201-356-6801
eicustomersupport@elsevier.com; www.ei.org

This database contains a table of contents listing citations to more than 350,000 journal articles and conference papers and proceedings in all fields of engineering.

7164 ENR: Top International Design Firms Issue
McGraw Hill
1221 Avenue of the Americas
47th Floor
New York, NY 10020-1095

212-512-2000; *Fax:* 212-512-3840
webmaster@mcgraw-hill.com;
www.mcgraw-hill.com

Harold W McGraw III, CEO

Offers a list of over 200 design firms competing outside their own national borders who received largest dollar volumes in foreign contracts.
Cost: $270.00
Frequency: Annual
Circulation: 900,000

7165 Energy Engineering: Directory of Software for Energy Managers and Engineers
Fairmont Press
700 Indian Trail Lilburn Rd NW
Lilburn, GA 30047-6862

770-925-9388; *Fax:* 770-381-9865;
www.fairmontpress.com

Brian Douglas, President

Directory of services and supplies to the industry.
Cost: $15.00
Circulation: 8,500
ISSN: 0199-8895

7166 Manufacturer and Repair Directory
National Board of Boiler & Pressure Vessel
1055 Crupper Ave
Columbus, OH 43229-1108

614-888-0750; *Fax:* 614-888-0750
information@nationalboard.org;
www.nationalboard.org

Don Tanner, Manager
Connie Homer, Senior Executive Secretary

Manufacturers of boilers, pressure vessels, or other pressure-retaining items who are authorized to register these items with the National Board, Repair organizations holding National Board certificates of authorization for use of either the R, VR, or NR stamps.

7167 Mechanical Contractor Directory Marketing
Mechanical Contractors Association America
1385 Piccard Dr
Rockville, MD 20850-4329

301-869-5800; *Fax:* 301-990-9690
webmaster@mcaa.org; www.mcaa.org

John Gentille, Executive VP
John Gentille, Executive VP

7168 Plumbing Directory
American Society of Sanitary Engineering
901 Canterbury Rd
Suite A
Cleveland, OH 44145-1480

440-835-3040; *Fax:* 440-835-3488;
www.asse-plumbing.org

Ken Van Wagnen, Manager
Sara Marxen, Compliance Coordinator
Steven Hazzard, Staff Engineer

Contains more than 4,000 plumbing words and terms, abbreviations, cross references, helpful charts and illustrations, solar energy terms. A great teaching tool for plumbing and related fields.
Cost: $21.00

7169 **Research, Training, Test, and Production Reactor Directory**
American Nuclear Society
555 N Kensington Ave
La Grange Park, IL 60526-5592

708-352-6611; *Fax:* 708-352-0499;
www.asn.org

Jack Tuohy, Executive Director
E James Reinsch, President-Elect/VP
Harry Bradley, Executive Director
William F Naughton, Treasurer
Cal Poly, Vice President

This comprehensive directory includes administrative, operational, and technical data for all nonpower reactors in the United States.
Cost: $400.00
876 Pages
ISBN: 0-894485-12-1
Founded in: 1988

7170 **Tau Beta Pi Information Book**
Tau Beta Pi Association
PO Box 2697
Knoxville, TN 37901-2697

865-546-4578; *Fax:* 865-546-4579;
www.tbp.org
Social Media: Facebook, LinkedIn

Larry Simonson, President
Solange Dao, VP
Curtis D. Gomulinski, Executive Director/Treasurer

The book also serves as a reference to membership and alumni giving statistics as well as names of past and present officers, fellows, scholars, and other award winners.
Frequency: Yearly

7171 **US Abrasives Industry Directory**
Abrasive Engineering Society
144 Moore Rd
Butler, PA 16001-1312

724-282-6210; *Fax:* 724-234-2376
aes@abrasiveengineering.com;
www.abrasiveengineering.com

Ted Giese, Owner

Though the scene for industrial abrasive manufacturers has changed significantly over the last decade, the US continues as one of the world's largest manufacturers of abrasive products developing new abrasive grains and products that set international standards for quality and performance.

7172 **Wage & Benefit Survey**
North American Die Casting Association
241 Holbrook Drive
Wheeling, IL 60090-5809

847-279-0001; *Fax:* 847-279-0002
twarog@diecasting.org; www.diecasting.org

Daniel Twarog, President

This survey provides a comprehensive look at 13 different job classifications of hourly wage earners, how they are compensated, what benefits they receive and how practices vary by company size and location.
Cost: $200.00
42 Pages
Founded in: 2004

7173 **Who's Who in Environmental Engineering**
American Academy of Environmental Engineers
147 Old Solomons Island Road
Suite 303
Annapolis, MD 21401-7003

410-266-3311; *Fax:* 410-266-7653
info@aaees.org; www.aaees.org

Burk Kalweit, Executive Director
Howard B. LaFever, President
Dr. Robert Williams, President-Elect

A recognized reference for industry, consultants, recruiters, attorneys and health professionals who need to identify and locate experts in the environmental engineering profession.
Cost: $75.00
Frequency: Annual
Mailing list available for rent

7174 **World Directory of Nuclear Utility Management**
American Nuclear Society
555 N Kensington Ave
La Grange Park, IL 60526-5592

708-352-6611; *Fax:* 708-352-0499;
www.ans.org

Jack Tuohy, Executive Director
E James Reinsch, President-Elect/VP
Harry Bradley, Executive Director
William F Naughton, Treasurer

Is a handy desk reference listing key personnel at nuclear utility headquarters and nuclear plant sites, including plant managers, maintenance superintendents, radwaste managers, contacts for purchasing and public relations, and more.
Cost: $850.00
249 Pages
Founded in: 2005

Industry Web Sites

7175 **http://gold.greyhouse.com**
G.O.L.D Grey House OnLine Databases
Grey House Publishing's online database platform, GOLD, offers Quick Search, Keyword Search and Expert Search for most business sectorc incluidng engineering markets. The GOLD platform makes finding the information you need quick and easy - whether you're a novice searcher or an experienced database user. All of Grey House's directory products are available for subscription on the GOLD platform.

7176 **www.aacei.org**
Association for Advancement of Cost Engineering
Individuals interested in applying scientific principals to the solution of problems.

7177 **www.aaee.org**
American Association for Employment in Education
Provides information and other resources to assist colleges and universities in the employment of education.

7178 **www.aaees.org**
American Academy of Environmental Engineers
Improves the standards of environmental engineering. Certifies those with the special knowledge of environmental engineering and supplies a list of certified engineers to the public. Publishes reference books and other matters of interest for the profession.

7179 **www.aaes.org**
American Association of Engineering Societies
A multidisciplinary organization dedicated to advancing the knowledge, understanding and practice of engineering in the public interest.

7180 **www.abet.org**
Accreditation Board for Engineering and Technology
Accreditation of engineering, technology and applied science educational programs.

7181 **www.abrasiveengineering.org**
Abrasive Engineering Society
Dedicated to promoting technical information about abrasives minerals and their uses including abrasives grains and products such as grinding wheels, coated abrasives and thousands of other related tools and products that serve manufacturing and the consumer.

7182 **www.acec.org**
American Council of Engineering
Membership includes more than 5,800 US firms engaged in a range of engineering works. Mission is to contribute to the nation's prosperity through advancement of the business interests of member firms.

7183 **www.acesystems.com**
AEC Systems International/Penton Media
Focuses on Internet/Intranet for the design, engineering and construction industries.

7184 **www.aea.org**
American Engineering Association, Inc.
Dedicated to the enhancement of the engineering profession and U.S. Engineering capabilities.

7185 **www.aeecenter.org**
Association of Energy Engineers
Source of information on the field of energy efficiency, utility deregulation, plant engineering, facility management and environmental compliance. Membership includes more than 8,000 professionals and certification programs. Offers seminars, conferences, job listings and certification programs.

7186 **www.aegweb.org**
Association of Engineering Geologists
Meets the professional needs of geologists who are applying their scientific training and experience to the broad field of civil and environmental engineering. Mission is to provide leadership in the development and application of geologic principles and knowledge to serve engineering, environmental and public needs.

7187 **www.aes.org**
Audio Engineering Society
Professional society devoted to audio technology. Membership includes leading engineers, scientists and other authorities in the field. Serves its members, the industry and the public by stimulating and facilitating advances in the constantly changing field of audio.

7188 **www.aiche.org**
American Institute of Chemical Engineers
Professional association of more than 50,000 members, providing leadership in advancing the chemical engineering profession. Members are those who develop processes and design and operate manufacturing plants, as well as researchers who assure the safe and environmentally sound manufacture, use and disposal of chemical products.

7189 **www.akropolis.net**
Akropolis
Directory of architects, engineers, designers, construction professionals and others in related fields. Web portal to showcase modules and applications developed by our company.

7190 **www.aocs.org**
American Oil Chemists Society

Largest international society focused on the science and technology of fats, oils, lipids, and related substances.

7191 **www.ascet.org**
American Society of Certified Engineering
Strives to obtain recognition of engineering technicians as essential to the engineering scientific team. Provides a forum for discussion of employment issues and improvement of the professional status of engineering technicians.

7192 **www.asem.org**
American Society for Engineering Management
Strives to promote the profession of engineering management as well as assisting its members in developing and improving their skills as practicing managers of engineering and technology. Members are from academic, field, industrial and governmental organizations.

7193 **www.asfe.org**
ASFE
Not-for-profit trade association. Helps geoprofessional, environmental and civil engineering firms profit through professionalism.

7194 **www.asnt.org**
American Society for Nondestructive Testing
Helps create a safer world by serving the nondestructive testing professions and promoting NDT technologies through publishing, certification, research and conferencing.

7195 **www.aspe.net**
American Society for Precision Engineering
Technical society emphasizing research, design, development, manufacture and measurement of high accuracy components and systems. Members come from the fields of engineering, materials science, physics, chemistry, mathematics and computer science, and work in industry, academia and national labs.

7196 **www.asq.org**
American Society for Quality
ASQ's mission is to facilitate continuous improvement and increase customer satisfaction. Promotes quality principles concepts and technologies. Provides information, contacts and opportunities to make things better in the workplace, in communities and in people's lives.

7197 **www.asse-plumbing.org**
American Society of Sanitary Engineering
Members are from all segments of the plumbing industry, including contractors, engineers, inspectors, journeymen, apprentices and others involved in the industry. Provides information, the opportunity to exchange ideas, solve problems and offers forum where all sides can express their views.

7198 **www.astm.org**
ASTM International
Not-for-profit organization providing a global forum for development and publication of voluntary consensus standards for materials, products, systems and services. Over 30,000 members from 100 nations include producers, users, consumers and representatives of academia and government. Formerly known as the American Society for Testing and Materials.

7199 **www.atcouncil.org**
Applied Technology Council
A nonprofit, tax-exempt corporation established through the efforts of the Structural Engineers Association of California. ATC's mission is to develop and promote state-of-the-art, user-friendly engineering resources and applications for use in mitigating the effects of natural and other hazards on the built environment.

7200 **www.construction.com**
McGraw-Hill Construction
McGraw-Hill Construction (MHC), part of The McGraw-Hill Companies, connects people and projects across the design and construction industry, serving owners, architects, engineers, general contractors, subcontractors, building product manufacturers, suppliers, dealers, distributors and adjacent markets.

7201 **www.eia-usa.org**
Environmental Information Association
Nonprofit organization dedicated to providing environmental information to individuals, members and the industry. Disseminates information on the abatement of asbestos and lead-based paint, indoor air quality, safety and health issues, analytical issues and environmental site assessments.

7202 **www.electrochem.org**
Electrochemical Society
The society is an international nonprofit, educational organization concerned with phenomena relating to electrochemical and solid state science and technology. Members are individual scientists and engineers, as well as corporations and laboratories.

7203 **www.ewh.ieee.org**
Instrumentation and Measurement Society
A subsidiary of the Institute of Electrical and Electronics Engineers. Provides support to scientists and technicians who design and develop electrical and electronic measuring instruments and equipment.

7204 **www.greyhouse.com**
Grey House Publishing
Authoritative reference directories for most business sectors incluidng engineering markets. Users can search the online databases with varied search criteria allowing for custom searches by product category, geographic area, sales volume, keyword, subject and more. Full Grey House catalog and online ordering also available.

7205 **www.icc-es.org**
ICC Evaluation Service
An independent, nonprofit organization that conducts a voluntary program of evaluation of both traditional and innovative building materials, products and systems for compliance with the three major model codes in the United States.

7206 **www.iccsafe.org**
International Code Council
Nonprofit membership association with more than 16,000 members who span the building community, from code enforcement officials to materials manufacturers. Dedicated to preserving the public health, safety and welfare in the built environment through the effective use and enforcement of model codes.

7207 **www.icea.net**
Insulated Cable Engineers Association
Professional organization dedicated to developing cable standards for the electric power, control and telecommunications industries. Ensures safe, economical and efficient cable systems utilizing proven state-of-the-art materials and concepts. ICEA documents are of interest to cable manufacturers, architects and engineers, utility and manufacturing plant personnel, telecommunication engineers, consultants and OEMs.

7208 **www.iienet.org**
Institute of Industrial Engineers
Founded in: Columbus, Ohio as the American Institute of Industrial Engineers.

7209 **www.irga.com**
International Reprographic Association
Represents entrepreneurial businesses serving the wide-format imaging needs of graphic arts, architectural, engineering, manufacturing, corporate, legal, retail, and POP industries.

7210 **www.manufacturing.net**
Manufacturing Marketplace
Manufacturing industry news and resources for the engineering, design, purchasing, logistics and distribution professional.

7211 **www.materialsocieties.org**
Federation of Materials Societies
Promotes cooperation among societies concerned with the understanding, development and application of materials and processes.

7212 **www.mt-online.com**
Applied Technology Publications
MT-online.com is the premier source of capacity assurance and best practice solutions for manufacturing, process and service operations worldwide. Online home of Maintenance Technology magazie, the dynamic MT-online.com portal serves the critical technical, business and professional-development needs of engineers, managers and technicians from across all industrial, institutional and commercial sectors.

7213 **www.nace.org**
National Association of Corrosion Engineers
Conducts research on corrosion control. Sponsors short courses annually at universities.

7214 **www.nationalboard.org**
National Board of Boiler & Pressure Vessel Inspec.
Membership is composed of chief boiler inspectors of states, major US cities and Canadian provinces having boiler laws.

7215 **www.naval.org**
American Society of Naval Engineers
Includes all arts construction and sciences as applied in research, development design, construction, operation, maintenance, and logistic support of surface/sub-surface ships and marine craft.

7216 **www.ncees.org**
Natl Council of Examiners for Engineering & Survey
Promotes uniform standards of registration and to coordinate interstate registration of engineers and surveyors.

7217 **www.nspe.org**
National Society of Professional Engineers
The mission of the Society is to promote the ethical, competent and licensed practice of engineering and to enhance the professional, social and economic well-being of its members.

7218 **www.remsa.org**
Railway Engineering-Maintenance Suppliers Assn
Members are distributors and manufacturers of railway track machinery supplies and services.

7219 **www.reta.com**
Refrigerating Engineers & Technicians Association
Seeks to upgrade the skills and knowledge of experienced members. Offers home-study courses on refrigeration and air conditioning.

7220 **www.rses.org**
Refrigeration Service Engineers Society
RSES is the leading training and education association for heating, ventilation, air conditioning and refrigeration professionals. It is a non-profit organization of 25,000 members in 421 chapters in the US and Canada, as well as affiliate organizations in other countries.

7221 **www.same.org**
Society of American Military Engineers
Brings together professional engineers and those in engineering-related fields to improve and increase the engineering capabilities of the nation, and to exchange and advance the knowledge of engineering technologies, applications, and practices.

7222 **www.sawe.org**
Society of Allied Weight Engineers
Consists of engineers in the aerospace industry.

7223 **www.sme.org**
Society of Manufacturing Engineers
Members are engaged in manufacturing, research and technology development.

7224 **www.spe.org**
Society of Petroleum Engineers
To provide the means for collection, dissemination and exchange of technical information concerning the development of oil and gas resources, subsurface fluid flow and production of other materials through well bores for the public benefit. To provide opportunities through its programs for interested individuals to maintain and upgrade their individual technical competence in the aforementioned areas for the public benefit.

7225 **www.steelnews.com**
Association for Iron and Steel Technology (AIST)
SteelNews.com is a publication created by the Association for Iron and Steel Technology (AIST) for the steel community. The site features daily updates of the latest global headlines.

7226 **www.sweets.construction.com**
McGraw Hill Construction
In depth product information that lets you find, compare, select, specify and make purchase decisions in the industrial product marketplace.

7227 **www.tbp.org**
Tau Beta Pi Association
The National Engineering honor society recognizes engineering students of superior scholarship and exemplary character and practitioners of engineering. Founded in 1885, the world's largest engineering organization includes 218 collegiate chapters and 220 alumnus chapters.

7228 **www.thetatau.org**
Theta Tau
A professional fraternity in engineering. Founded at the Univerity of Minnesota. Purpose of the fraternity is to develop and maintain a high standard of professional interest among its members, and to unite them in a strong bond of fraternal fellowship.

7229 **www.u.arizona.edu/n aimitril**
Reliability Engineering and Management Institute
This is an annual conference on Reliability Engineering and Management of all types of products. Over 15 leading corporations present their latest techniques in this field, and the proceedings thereof are published.

7230 **www.uefoundation.org**
United Engineering Foundation
Aims to advance engineering arts and sciences.

7231 **www.usace.army.mil**
US Army Corps of Engineers
Information on flood control, environmental protection, disaster response, military construction and support of others through the sharing of engineering expertise with other agencies, state and local governments, academia and foreign nations.

Associations

7232 **ASFE/The Geoprofessional Business Association**
8811 Colesville Rd
Suite G106
Silver Springs, MD 20910-4343
301-565-2733; *Fax:* 301-589-2017
info@geoprofessional.org;
www.geoprofessional.org
Social Media: Facebook, Twitter, LinkedIn, YouYube, RSS
Gordon M. Matheson, President
Laura R. Reinbold, P.E., President-Elect
John P. Bachner, Executive Vice President
Charles L. Head, P.E., P.G., Secretary/Treasurer
Joel G. Carson, Executive Director
Not-for-profit trade association. Supports all employess of engineering companies.
300 Members
Founded in: 1969

7233 **Academy for Educational Development**
1825 Connecticut Ave Nw
Washington, DC 20009-5728
202-884-8978; *Fax:* 202-884-8997
rjohn@aed.org;
www.pciaonline.org/academy-educational-development-aed
Social Media: Facebook, Twitter, YouTube
Edward W. Russell, Chairman of the Board
Roberta N. Clarke, Vice Chairman of the Board
Rebecca Logan, President and CEO
A nonprofit organization working globally to improve education, health, civil society and economic development-the foundation of thriving societies.
Founded in: 1961

7234 **Adirondack Council**
103 Hand Ave, Suite 3
PO Box D-2
Elizabethtown, NY 12932-0640
877-873-2240; *Fax:* 518-873-6675
info@adirondackcouncil.org;
www.adirondackcouncil.org
Social Media: Facebook, Twitter, YouTube, Flickr
Robert K. Kafin, Chair
Lee Keet, Vice-Chair
Meredith Prime, Vice-Chair
Curt R. Welling, Treasurer
Virginia M. Lawrence, Secretary
Research, education and advocacy to protect the natural character and communities of the Adirondack Park. Also publishes an annual State of Park Report and quarterly newsletters.
Founded in: 1975
Mailing list available for rent

7235 **African American Environmentalist Association**
1629 K Street, NW
Suite 300
Washington, DC 20006
443-569-5102
africanamericanenvironmentalist@msn.com
aaenvironment.Blogspot.com
Social Media: Facebook, Twitter, LinkedIn, YouTube, RSS
Norris McDonald, President
Derry Bigby, Vice President
Dedicated to providing energy and environmental information and educating the African American community.

7236 **Agricultural Research Institute**
1034 Miner Farm Road
PO Box 90
Chazy, NY 12921
518-846-7121; *Fax:* 518-846-8445;
www.whminer.com
Social Media: Facebook, Google +
Richard J. Grant Ph.D, President
Kirk E. Beattie, Vice President
Rachel Dutil, Secretary
Joseph C. Burke Ph.D, Trustees
Richard Eakins, Trustees
Institutions concerned with environmental issues, pest control, agricultural meteorology, biotechnology, food irradiation, agricultural policy, research and development, food safety, technology transfer and remote sensing.
125 Members

7237 **Air & Waste Management Association**
420 Fort Duquesne Boulevard
One Gateway Center, 3rd Floor
Pittsburgh, PA 15222-1435
412-232-3444
800-270-3444; *Fax:* 412-232-3450
info@awma.org; www.awma.org
Social Media: Facebook, Twitter, LinkedIn
Dallas Baker, President
Brad Waldron, QEP, CHMM, President Elect
Michael Miller, Immediate Past President
Nancy Meilahn Fowler, Treasurer
Stephanie Glyptis, Secretary/ Executive Director
Supports all those involved with the environment, specifically the air and waste management industry. Publishes a magazine.
9000 Members
Founded in: 1907

7238 **Air Pollution Control Association**
420 Fort Duquesne Boulevard
One Gateway Center, 3rd Floor
Pittsburgh, PA 15222-1435
412-232-3444
800-270-3444; *Fax:* 412-232-3450
info@awma.org; www.awma.org
Social Media: Facebook, Twitter, LinkedIn
Dallas Baker, President
Brad Waldron, QEP, CHMM, President Elect
Michael Miller, Immediate Past President
Nancy Meilahn Fowler, Treasurer
Stephanie Glyptis, Secretary/ Executive Director
Association for the environment and conservation industry.
9000 Members
Founded in: 1907

7239 **Alliance for Bio-Integrity**
54 North Park Street
Fairfield, IA 52556
206-888-4852
info@biointegrity.org; www.biointegrity.org
Steven M Druker, Executive Director
A nonprofit organization dedicated to the advancement of human and environmental health through sustainable and safe technologies.

7240 **Alliance to Save Energy**
1850 M Street, NW
Suite 610
Washington, DC 20036
202-857-0666; www.ase.org
Social Media: Facebook, Twitter, LinkedIn, RSS, Google+, Flickr, YouTube
Sen Jeanne Shaheen, Honorary Chair
Jane Palmieri, Co-Chair
Sen Chris Coons, Honorary Vice Chair
Sen. Rob Portman, Honorary Vice Chair
Sen-Susan Collins, Honorary Board Member
Promotes energy efficiency to achieve a healthier economy, a cleaner environment, and greater energy security.

7241 **America the Beautiful Fund**
P.O. Box 6007
Indianapolis, IN 46206-6007
202-638-1649
800-421-4225; *Fax:* 888-421-4351
katie@america-the-beautiful.org;
www.americanfunds.com
Nanine Bilski, President
Kathleen Rehicaldt, Program Director
Daniel Schneider, Secretary
Groups and private citizens that improve the quality of the environment.
1M Members
Founded in: 1965

7242 **American Association for Aerosol Research (AAAR)**
12100 Sunset Hills Road
Suite 130
Reston, VA 20190
703-437-4377
800-485-3106; *Fax:* 856-439-0525
info@aaar.org; www.aaar.org
Jay Turner, President
Sheryl Ehrman, Vice President
Allen Robinson, Vice President Elect
Linsey Marr, Treasurer
Suresh Dhaniyala, Secretary
AAAR is a nonprofit professional organization for scientists and engineers who wish to promote and communicate technical advances in the field of aerosol research. The Association fosters the exchange of information among members and with other disciplines through conferences, symposia and publication of a professional journal. Committed to the development of aerosol and its application to important social issues, AAAR offers an international forum for education, communication and networking.
1000 Members
Founded in: 1982

7243 **American Bird Conservancy**
4249 Loudoun Ave.
P.O. Box 249
The Plains, VA 20198-2237
540-253-5780
888-247-3624; *Fax:* 540-253-5782;
www.abcbirds.org
Warren F. Cooke, Chair
V Richard Eales, Treasurer & Vice Chair
William H. Leighty, Vice Chair
William F. Sheehan, Vice Chair
George H. Fenwick, President
A nonprofit membership organization dedicated to the conservation of wild birds and their habitats in the Americas.
Founded in: 1980

7244 **American Council on Science and Health**
1995 Broadway
Suite 202
New York, NY 10023-5882
212-362-7044
866-905-2694; *Fax:* 212-362-4919
acsh@acsh.org; www.acsh.org
Social Media: Facebook, Twitter, YouTube
Hank Campbell, President
Cheryl Martin, Director Of Development
Dr. Gilbert Ross, M.D., Medical Director
Ruth Kava Ph.D, Senior Nutrition Fellow
Lila Abassi M.D., Director Of Medicine
A consumer education organization providing the public with scientifically accurate evalua-

tions of food, chemicals, the environment and health.
Founded in: 1978

7245 **American Farmland Trust**
1150 Connecticut Avenue
Suite 600
The Plains, VA 20036

800-431-1499; *Fax:* 202-659-8339
halthouse@farmland.org; www.farmland.org
Social Media: Facebook, Twitter, LinkedIn, Pinterest

Barton H. Thompson, Jr., Chair
John Hardin Jr., Vice Chair
William Cohan, Treasurer
Ralph Grossi, Interim President
Susan Sink, VP, Dev. & Ext. Affair

An organization that protects farmland and ranch land in the UnitedStates, promotes environmentally sound farming practices and keeps farmers on the land.
Founded in: 1980

7246 **American Fisheries Society**
5410 Grosvenor Ln
Suite 110
Bethesda, MD 20814-2199

301-897-8616; *Fax:* 301-897-8096
sjohnston@fisheries.org; www.fisheries.org
Social Media: Facebook, Twitter, vimeo, flickr

Bob Hughes, President
Donna L. Parrish, President-Elect
Ronald J. Essig, First Vice President
Joe Margraf, Second Vice President
John Boreman, Past President

Supports all those involved in the fishing industry, specifically environmental issues that the profession addresses.
8500 Members
Founded in: 1870

7247 **American Forests**
1220 L Street NW
Suite 750
Washington, DC 20005

202-737-1944
info@americanforests.org;
www.americanforests.org
Social Media: Facebook, Twitter

Ann Nichols, Chair
Bruce Lisman, Vice Chair
Roderick DeArment, Treasurer
Scott Steen, President & CEO
Peter Hutchins, Vice President/ COO

The oldest national nonprofit conservation organization in the U.S.that advocates for the protection and expansion of forests.
Founded in: 1990

7248 **American Institute of Hydrology**
1230 Lincoln Drive
Carbondale, IL 62901

618-453-7809
aih@engr.siu.edu; www.aihydrology.org

Dr. Mustafa M. Aral, President
Dr. Rao S. Govindaraju, President-Elect
Dr. John L. Nieber, VP For Academic Affairs
John W. Balay, VP For Institute Development
Ed A. Baquerizo, VP For International Affairs

Registers and certifies hydrologists and hydrogeologists, provides a forum to discuss national and international issues, and provides educational courses.
1000 Members
Founded in: 1981

7249 **American Nuclear Society**
555 N Kensington Ave
La Grange Park, IL 60526-5592

708-352-6611
800-323-3044; *Fax:* 708-352-0499
advertising@ans.org; www.ans.org
Social Media: Facebook, Twitter, LinkedIn

Eugene S. Grecheck, President
Andrew C. Klein, Vice President/President-Elect
Steven A. Arndt, Treasurer
Michaele C. Brady Raap, Immediate Past President
Robert C. Fine, JD, CAE, Executive Director

Supports all those involved in the fields of radioactive waste management, removal, handling, disposal, treatment, cleanup and environmental restoration.
10500 Members
Founded in: 1954

7250 **American Phytopathological Society**
3340 Pilot Knob Road
Saint Paul, MN 55121-2097

651-454-7250
800-328-7560; *Fax:* 651-454-0766
aps@scisoc.org; www.apsnet.org
Social Media: Facebook, Twitter, LinkedIn, Pinterest

Sally A. Miller, President
Timothy D. Murray, President-Elect
Mary E. Palm, Vice President
Steven A. Slack, Treasurer
David M. Gadoury, Internal Communications Officer

Scientific organization that studies plant diseases and their control.
4500 Members
Founded in: 1908

7251 **American Public Works Association**
2345 Grand Blvd
Suite 700
Kansas City, MO 64108-2625

816-472-6100
800-848-2792; *Fax:* 816-472-1610;
www.apwa.net
Social Media: Facebook, Twitter, YouTube

Mr. Brian R. Usher, PWLF, President
Mr.Ronald J. Calkins, PE, PWLF, President Elect
Richard F. Stinson, Director, Region I
Mr. Harry L. Weed, II, PWLF, Director, Region II
William Barney Mills, Jr., Director, Region III

International educational and professional association of public agencies, private sector companies, and individuals dedicated to providing high quality public works, goods and services. APWA provides a forum brings important public works-related topics to public attention in local, state, and federal areas. Mailing list for members only.
Cost: $100.00
26000 Members
Founded in: 1937

7252 **American Shore and Beach Preservation Association**
5460 Beaujolais Lane
Fort Myers, FL 33919

239-489-2616; *Fax:* 239-362-9771
managing@asbpa.org; www.asbpa.org
Social Media: Facebook, Twitter

Anthony P. Pratt, President
Russell Boudreau, Vice President
Nicole Elko Ph.D, Vice President
Phillip Roehrs, Vice President
Brad Pickel, Treasurer

Federal, state and local government agencies and individuals interested in conservation, development and restoration of beaches and shorefronts.
1M Members
Founded in: 1926

7253 **American Society for Environmental History**
UW Interdisciplinary Arts and Sciences Program
1900 Commerce Street
Tacoma, WA 98402

206-343-0226; *Fax:* 206-343-0249
info.aseh@gmail.com; www.aseh.net

Kathleen Brosnan, President
Graeme Wynn, Vice President/ President Elect
Jay Tylor, Secretary
Mark Madison, Treasurer
Emily Greenwald, Executive Committee

ASEH members are techers and researchers with an interest in human ecology and environmental history.
1200 Members
Founded in: 1976

7254 **American Society for Photogammetry and Remote Sensing (ASPRS)**
5410 Grosvenor Lane
Suite 210
Bethesda, MD 20814-2160

301-493-0290; *Fax:* 301-493-0208
asprs@asprs.org; www.asprs.org
Social Media: Facebook, Twitter

Dr. E. Lynn Usery, President
Dr. Charles K. Toth, CP, President-Elect
Ms. Rebecca A. Morton, CP, Vice President
Dr. A. Stewart Walker, CP, Immediate Past President
Mr. Gregory Brunner, National Director

Supports all those involved in mapping, photogrammetry, environmental management, remote sensing, geographic infromation, and natural resources.
6000 Members
Founded in: 1934

7255 **American Society of Agronomy**
5585 Guilford Rd.
Madison, WI 53711-1086

608-273-8080; *Fax:* 608-273-2021
headquarters@sciencesocieties.org;
www.agronomy.org
Social Media: Facebook, Twitter, LinkedIn

Newell Kitchen, President
Kenneth Barbarick, President-Elect

Supports educators and scientists interested in the impacts of environmental perturbations on the biological and physical sciences.
10000 Members
Founded in: 1907

7256 **American Society of Mining and Reclamation**
American Society of Mining and Reclamation
1800 South Oak Street
Suite 100
Champaign, IL 61820

217-333-9489
217-493-7847; *Fax:* 859-335-6529
rdarmody@illinois.edu; www.asmr.us
Social Media: Facebook

Robert Darmody, Executive Secretary
Pete Stahl, President
Kimery Vories, President Elect

Dissemination of technical information relating to the reclamation of lands disturbed by mineral extraction. Members yearly issue is paid out of

proceeding. Membership dues $50 regular $10 students.
Founded in: 1973

7257 **American Society of Safety Engineers**
520 N. Northwest Hwy
Park Ridge, IL 60068

847-699-2929; *Fax:* 847-768-3434
info@asse.org; www.asse.org
Social Media: Facebook, Twitter, LinkedIn, Instagram

Michael Belcher, CSP, President
Thomas F. Cecich, CSP, CIH, President-Elect
James Smith, M.S., CSP, Senior Vice President
Fred J. Fortman, Jr., Secretary and Executive Director
Stephanie A. Helgerman, CSP, Vice President, Finance

The oldest and largest professional safety organization. Its members manage, supervise and consult on safety, health, and environmental issues in industry, insurance, government and education.
30000 Members
Founded in: 1911

7258 **Animal Protection and Rescue League**
302 Washington St.
#404
San Diego, CA 92103

858-999-2343
info@aprl.org; www.aprl.org
Social Media: Facebook, Twitter, YouTube

A nonprofit organization that influences animal protection legislation, conducts rescues of abused factory farmed animals and educates people abouthumane eating.
Founded in: 2003

7259 **Aquatic Plant Management Society**
7922 NW
71st Street
Gainesville, FL 32653

Fax: 601-634-5502
dpetty@ndrsite.com; www.apms.org
Social Media: Facebook, LinkedIn

Rob Richardson, President
John Madsen, President-Elect
John Rodgers, Vice-President
Jeremy Slade, Treasurer
Jeff Schardt, Secretary

An international organization of scientists, educators, students, commercial pesticide applicators, administrators, and concerned individuals interested in the management and study of aquatic plants.
Founded in: 1961

7260 **Association for Environmental Health and Sciences (AEHS) Foundation, Inc.**
150 Fearing Street
Amherst, MA 01002

413-549-5170; *Fax:* 413-549-0579;
www.aehsfoundation.org

Paul T Kostecki, PhD, Executive Director
Brenna Lockwood, Managing Director
Sierra Pelletier, Program Assistant
Ed Calabrese, Editor-In-Chief
Denise Leonard, Managing Editor

AEHS Foundation is a multi-disciplinary association providing a forum for individual professionals concerned with soil protection and cleanup. Fields represented include chemistry, geology, hydrogeology, law, engineering, modeling, toxicology, regulatory science, public health and public policy.
600 Members
Founded in: 1989

7261 **Association for Population/Family Planning Libraries & Information Conference**
Family Health International Library
PO Box 13950
Research Triangle Park, NC 27709

919-447-7040; www.aplici.org

Yan Fu, President
Alli Buehler, Vice-President
Jill Leonard, Treasurer
Liz Nugent, Recording Secretary
Debra Dickson, Past President

Offers support for all those involved in issues concerning population and family planning, including publications, training and conferences.
Frequency: Annual

7262 **Association of Environmental & Engineering Geologists**
1100-H Brandywine Blvd.
Suite 575
Zanesville, OH 43701

303-757-2926
844-331-7867; *Fax:* 740-452-2552
aeg@aegweb.org; www.aegweb.org
Social Media: Facebook, Twitter

Dale C. Andrews, President
Kathy Troost, Vice Rpesident
Kevin Richards, Treasurer
Cynthia Palomares, Secretary

Meets the professional needs of geologists who are applying their scientific training and experience to the broad field of civil and environmental engineering. Mission is to provide leadership in the development and application of geologic principles and knowledge to serve engineering, environmental and public needs.
3000 Members
Founded in: 1957
Mailing list available for rent: 3000 names at $100 per M

7263 **Association of Environmental Engineering and Science Professors**
1211 Connecticut Ave NW,
Suite 650
Washington, DC 20036

202-640-6591; *Fax:* 217-355-9232
bschorr@aeesp.org; www.aeesp.org

Gregory W. Characklis, President
Peter J. Vikesland, President-Elect
Linda K. Weavers, Vice President
Ching Hua Huang, Secretary
Andrea Ferro, Treasurer

Individuals working or teaching in the field of environmental engineering, including water quality and treatment, air quality, air pollution control and solid and hazardous waste management.
700 Members
Founded in: 1963

7264 **Association of Environmental and Resource Economists**
13006 Peaceful Terrace
Silver Spring, MD 20904
202-559-8998; *Fax:* 202-559-8998
info@aere.org; www.aere.org

W.L (Vic) Adamowicz, President
Dr. Richard G. Newell, Vice President
Prof. Sarah West, Secretary
Dr. Dallas Burtraw, Treasurer
Prof. Elena G. Irwin, Board Of Director

AERE serves as an information resource for economists involved in natural resources policy planning and research. It was estabilshed as a way to exchange ideas, stimulate research, and promote graduate research in environmental economics.
900 Members
Founded in: 1979

7265 **Association of Fish & Wildlife Agencies**
1100 First Street NE
Suite 825
Washington, DC 20002

202-838-3474; *Fax:* 202-350-9869
info@fishwildlife.org; www.fishwildlife.org
Social Media: Facebook, Twitter

Ron Regan, Executive Director
Dave Chanda, President
Nick Wiley, Vice President
Carol Bambrey, Association Council
Glenn Normandeau, Secretary/Treasurer

The organization that represents all of North America's fish and wildlife agencies that promotes sound management and conservation, and speaks with a unified voice on important fish and wildlife issues.
Founded in: 1902

7266 **Association of State Floodplain Managers**
575 D'Onofrio Drive
Suite 200
Madison, WI 53719

608-828-3000; *Fax:* 608-828-6319
Larry@floods.org; www.floods.org
Social Media: Facebook, Twitter, Google+

Larry Larson, Director Emeritus
Maria Cox Lamm, Vice Chair
Leslie Durham, Secretary
Karen McHugh, Treasurer
Ingrid Danler, Deputy Director

Promotes common interest in flood damage abatement, supports environmental protection for floodplain areas, provides education on floodplain management practices and policy and urges incorporating multi-objective management approaches to solve local flooding problems.
6500 Members
Founded in: 1977

7267 **Association of Zoos and Aquariums**
8403 Colesville Rd
Suite 710
Silver Spring, MD 20910-6331

301-562-0777; *Fax:* 301-562-0888
membership@aza.org; www.aza.org
Social Media: Facebook, Twitter

Dennis E Pate, Executive Director & CEO
Steve Burns, Chair-Elect
Dennis W. Kelly, Vice-Chair
Jim Breheny, Director
Lynn Clements, Director

A nonprofit organization dedicated to the advancement of accredited zoos and aquariums in the areas of animal care, wildlife conservation, education and science.
200 Members
Founded in: 1924

7268 **Center for Biological Diversity**
P.O. Box 710
Tucson, AZ 85702-0710

520-623-5252
866-357-3349; *Fax:* 520-623-9797
center@biologicaldiversity.org;
www.biologicaldiversity.org
Social Media: Facebook, Twitter, YouTube, Instagram

Marcey Olajos, Board Chair
Stephanie Zill, Treasurer
Robin Silver, Secretary
Paula Simmonds, Director, Development
Mike Stark, Communications Director

National U.S. group using science, law, and creative media to protect the lands, waters, and climate that species need to survive.

7269 **Center for Environmental Philosophy**
1155 Union Circle
#310980
Denton, TX 76203-5017
940-565-2727; *Fax:* 940-565-4439
cep@unt.edu; www.cep.unt.edu
Graduate program in environmental ethics at the University of NorthTexas.

7270 **Center for Food Safety**
660 Pennsylvania Ave, SE
#302
Washington, DC 20003
202-547-9359; *Fax:* 202-547-9429
office@centerforfoodsafety.org;
www.centerforfoodsafety.org
Social Media: Facebook, Twitter, Pinterest, YouTube
Andrew Kimbrell, Executive Director
Rebecca Spector, West Coast Director
Adam Keats, Senior Attorney
Cristina Stella, Staff Attorney
Amy Van Saun, Legal Fellow
A U.S. environmental, nonprofit organization based in Washington, D.C.

7271 **Center for a Livable Future**
Johns Hopkins Bloomberg School of Public Health
615 N Wolfe St., W7010
Baltimore, MD 21205-2179
410-502-7578; *Fax:* 410-502-7579
clf@jhsph.edu;
www.jhsph.edu/research/centers-and-institutes
Social Media: Facebook, Twitter, YouTube
Robert Lawrence, Director
Polly Walker, Senior Fellow
Shawn McKenzie, Associate Director
Research and programs for a secure, equitable and resilient food system.

7272 **Center for a New American Dream**
POBox797
Charlottesville, VA 22902
301-891-3683
newdream@newdream.org;
www.newdream.org
Social Media: Facebook, Twitter, YouTube, Pinterest
Casey Williams, Interim Executive Director
Edna Rienzi, Program Director
Guinevere Higgins, Director Of Development
Lisa Mastny, Publications Director
A nonprofit organization that helps Americans reduce and shift their consumption to improve quality of life, protect the environment, and promote social justice.
Founded in: 1997

7273 **Citizens Campaign for the Environment**
225-A Main Street
Farmingdale, NY 11735
516-390-7150; *Fax:* 516-390-7160
farmingdale@citizenscampaign.org;
www.citizenscampaign.org
Social Media: Facebook, Twitter, YouTube, RSS, Blog
Adrienne Esposito, Executive Director
Brian Smith, Associate Exe. Dir.
Mary Ellen Dour, Education & Financial Director
Sarah Eckel, Policy Director
Jacob McCaffery, Outreach Dir.
Works to protect the environment and public health with the supportof members in New York and Connecticut.
Founded in: 1985

7274 **Citizens' Climate Lobby**
1330 Orange Ave
#300
Coronado, CA 92118
619-437-7142
ccl@citizensclimatelobby.org
citizensclimatelobby.org
Social Media: Facebook, Twitter, Instagram, YouTube, Google+
Marshall Saunders, Founder/ President
Mark Reynolds, Executive Director
Steve Valk, Communications Director
Amy Bennett, Director, Operations
Danny Richter, Legislative Director
An international grassroots environmental group that trains and supports volunteers to build relationships with their Members of Congress in order to influence climate policy.

7275 **Coastal Conservation Association**
6919 Portwest Dr
Suite 100
Houston, TX 77024-8049
713-626-4234
800-201-FISH; *Fax:* 713-626-5852
ccantl@joincca.org; www.joincca.org
Social Media: Facebook, Twitter, RSS
Degraaf Adams, Executive Board, Texas
Bill Bird, Executive Board, Florida
Stan Brogdon, Executive Board, Washington
Robert Donlin, Executive Board, South Carolina
Jim Flannery, Executive Board , Maryland
Seeks to advance protection and conservation of all marine life. Conducts seminars and bestows awards.
85000 Members
Founded in: 1977

7276 **Committee for a Constructive Tomorrow**
P.O. Box 65722
Washington, DC 20035
202-429-2737; www.cfact.org
Social Media: Facebook, Twitter, RSS, YouTube
David Rothbard, President/ Co-Founder
Craig Rucker, Executive Director, Co-Founder
Marc Morano, Director of Communications
Duggan Flanakin, Director of Policy Research
Christina Wilson Norman, Development Officer
A conservative Washington, D.C.-based nonprofit organization that promotes a positive voice on environment and development issues.

7277 **Community Alliance with Family Farmers**
PO Box 363
Davis, CA 95617-363
530-756-8518; *Fax:* 530-756-7857
info@caff.org; www.caff.org
Social Media: Facebook, Twitter, YouTube
Rich Collins, Board Chair
Carol Presley, Vice Chair
Judith Redmond, Secretary
Vicki Williams, Treasurer
Diane Del Signore, Executive Director
Non-profit organization that advocates for California's family farmers and sustainable agriculture. Strives to build on shared values around food and agriculture, and work together in practical, on-the-ground programs. Parterships create locally based economic vitality, improved human and environmental health, and long-term sustainability of family farms.
Cost: $47.95

7278 **Conservation Education Association**
Department of Conservation
PO Box 180
Jefferson City, MO 65102-0180
573-751-4115; *Fax:* 573-751-4467;
www.aheia.com
John Hoskins, Director
Lorna Domke, Outreach/Education
Tom Cwyner, Editor
Focuses on conservation and the importance of protecting the environment.
Founded in: 1937

7279 **Conservation Fund**
1655 N. Fort Myer Drive
Suite 1300
Arlington, VA 22209-3199
703-525-6300; *Fax:* 703-525-4610
webmaster@conservationfund.org;
www.conservationfund.org
Social Media: Facebook, Twitter, LinkedIn, YouTube
J. Rutherford Seydel II, Chairman
R. Michael Leonard, Vice Chairman
Lawrence A. Selzer, President and CEO
Richard L. Erdmann, Executive VP and General Counsel
David K. Phillips, Jr., Treasurer, Executive VP & CFO
Works with private and public agencies and organizations to protect wildlife habitats, historic sites and parks.
Founded in: 1985

7280 **Conservation International**
2011 Crystal Dr
Suite 500
Arlington, VA 22202-3787
703-341-2400
800-429-5660
community@conservation.org;
www.conservation.org
Social Media: Facebook, Twitter, YouTube, Instagram, RSS
Peter Seligmann, Chairman of the Board & CEO
Rob Walton, Chairman Of Executive Committee
Harrison Ford, Vice Chair
Andr, Esteves, Vice Chair
Dawn Arnall, Board Member
Mission is to conserve the Earth's living heritage-our global biodiversity-and to demonstrate that human societies are able to live harmoniously with nature.
60M Members
Founded in: 1987

7281 **Conservation Law Foundation**
62 Summer Street
Boston, MA 02110-1016
617-350-0990
e-info@clf.org; www.clf.org
Social Media: Facebook, Twitter, LinkedIn, RSS, Instagram, Pinterest, Goo
Sara Molyneaux, Chair
Gordan Hall III, Vice Chair
Peter Nessen, Vice Chair
Eugene H. Clapp, Treasurer
Bradley Campbell, President
An environmental advocacy organization based in New England that advocates on behalf of the region's environment and its communities.
Founded in: 1966

7282 Conservation Treaty Support Fund
3705 Cardiff Road
Chevy Chase, MD 20815
301-654-3150
800-654-3150; *Fax:* 301-652-6390;
www.conservationagreementfund.org
George A Furness Jr, President
Frederick E. Morris
John C. Goldsmith
Promotes awareness, understanding and support of conservation treaties and their goals. Through the International Endangered Species Treaty, the Wetlands Convention, and other conservation agreements, more than 150 nations are committed to work together to preserve the wildlife and habitats that are our shared natural heritage.
Founded in: 1986

7283 Conservation and Preservation Charities of America
1100 Larkspur Landing Circle
Suite 340
Larkspur, CA 94939
800-626-6685; www.conservenow.org
Patrick Mcguire, President
CPCA is a consortium of environmental stewardship organizations. CPCA acts as a central focus for charitable giving dedicated to the protection of the natural habitat and historic treasures. Sponsors workplace giving campaigns in support of its member organizations.

7284 Defenders of Wildlife
1130 17th Street, NW
Washington, DC 20036
202-682-9400
800-385-9712
defenders@mail.defenders.org;
www.defenders.org
Social Media: Facebook, Twitter, RSS, YouTube, Flickr
Winsome Dunn McIntosh, Chair
Susan Wallace, Vice Chair
Mark Caylor, Treasurer
Caroline Gabel, Secretary
Jamie Rappaport Clark, President, CEO
A nonprofit conservation organization based in the United States that protects all animals and plants native to North America in their natural communities.
Founded in: 1947

7285 Earth Island Institute
2150 Allston Way
Suite 460
Berkeley, CA 94704-1375
510-859-9100; *Fax:* 510-859-9091
arch@earthisland.org; www.earthisland.org
Social Media: Facebook, Twitter, YouTube
Michael Mitrani, President
Martha Davis, Vice President
Kenneth Brower, Vice President
Jennifer Snyder, Secretary
Alex Giedt, Treasurer
Seeks to prevent destruction of environment and sponsors fund drives and activist projects to protect wildlife.
33M Members
Founded in: 1985

7286 Earth Policy Institute
1350 Connecticut Avenue NW
Suite 403
Washington, DC 20036
202-496-9290; *Fax:* 202-496-9325
epi@earthpolicy.org; www.earth-policy.org
Social Media: Facebook, Twitter, RSS
Judith Gradwohl, Chairman
Lester R. Brown, Founder, President
Reah JaniseKauffman, Co-Founder, VP
Janet Larsen, Director of Research
J. Matthew Roney, Research Associate
An independent nonprofit environmental organization based in Washington D.C. in the United States.
Founded in: 2001

7287 Earth Regeneration Society
1442A Walnut Street
#57
Berkeley, CA 94709-1405
510-527-9716; *Fax:* 510-559-8410;
www.earthregenerationsociety.org
Alden Bryant, President
Cynthia Johnson, Secretary
Glen A. Frendel, Executive Director
Alden Bryant, Acting Treasurer
Dolores Huerta, Board Of Director
Organized to develop and study scientific and practical solutions to environmental issues.

7288 Earth Society Foundation
238 East 58th Street
Suite 2400
New York, NY 10022
212-832-3659
800-3EA-THDA
earthsociety1@hotmail.com;
www.earthsocietyfoundation.org
Social Media: Facebook
Helen Garland, Chairperson
Thomas C. Dowd, President
Tom Dowd, VP
News of interest in environmental and sociological issues. Purpose is to promote Earth Day and the Earth Trustee agenda; Every individual and institution should seek choices in ecology, economics, and ethics that will eliminate pollution, poverty, and violence.

7289 Earth's Birthday Project
PO Box 1536
Santa Fe, MN 87504-1536
505-986-6040
800-698-4438; *Fax:* 505-395-9410
info@earthsbirthday.org;
www.earthsbirthday.org
Social Media: Facebook, Twitter
Albert Scharf, President
Richard Murray, Treasurer
Mary Hofstedt, Secretary
Clifford Ross, Executive Director
Alia Munn, Operations Director
A U.S. based educational nonprofit organization that inspires wonder, learning, and care of the natural world in children, teachers, and parents.
Founded in: 1989

7290 Earthjustice
50 California St.
Suite 500
San Francisco, CA 94111
800-584-6460; *Fax:* 415-217-2040
headquarters@earthjustice.org
earthjustice.org
Social Media: Facebook, Twitter
Trip Van Noppen, President
Drew Caputo, VP, Litig., Lands/Wildlife/Oceans
Abigail Dillen, VP, Litigation, Climate & Energy
Lisa Garcia, VP, Litigation, Healthy Communities
Martin Hayden, VP, Litigation, Policy/Legislation
Non-profit environmental law organization.
Founded in: 1971

7291 Ecological and Toxicological Association of Dyes
Stadthausgasse 18
4051 Basel
Switzerland
616-909-966; *Fax:* 616-914-278;
www.etad.com
Jill Aker, President
Represents the interests of manufacturers and formulators of dyes in the region with regard to environmental and health hazards in the manufacture, processing, shipment, use and disposal of thier products.
Founded in: 1974

7292 Energy & Environmental Research Center
University of North Dakota
15 N 23rd St., Stop 9018
Grand Forks, ND 58202-9018
701-777-5000; *Fax:* 701-777-5181
Social Media: Facebook, Twitter, LinkedIn, Google+, YouTube, Flickr
Thomas A. Erickson, Director
John A. Harju, Ass. Dir., Strategic Relationships
Erin M. O'Leary, Ass. Dir., Business & Operations
Edward N. Steadman, Ass. Dir., Research
Michael J. Holmes, Dep. Ass. Dir., Research
The EERC conducts research on fossil, renewable and altenative fuels, as well as pollution prevention and environmental cleanup.
Founded in: 1951

7293 Energy Action Coalition
www.energyactioncoalition.org
Social Media: Facebook, Twitter, RSS, Flickr, YouTube, Vimeo
Lydia Avila, Executive Director
Kristina Banks, Operations Coordinator
Sean Estelle, National Divestment Campaigner
Tina Johnson, Sr. Dir of Env. Justice & Programs
Kendall Mackey, National Tar Sands Organizer
A North American nonprofit organization made up of 50 partner organizations in the U.S. and Canada that runs campaigns to build the youth and student clean energy movement and advocate for changes on local, state, national, andinternational levels in North America.

7294 Environmental & Energy Study Institute
1112 16th Street, NW
Suite 300
Washington, DC 20036
202-628-1400; *Fax:* 202-204-5244
alaporte@eesi.org; www.eesi.org
Social Media: Facebook, Twitter, YouTube, Google+
Jared Blum, Board Chair
Shelley Fidler, Board Secretary/Treasurer
Richard L. Ottinger, Board Chair Emeritus
Quincalee Brown, Executive Director
Frances S. Buchholzer, Director
A non-profit organization dedicated to promoting environmentally sustainable societies.
Founded in: 1984

7295 Environmental Alliance for Senior Involvement
PO Box 250
Milford, CT 06460
203-779-0024; *Fax:* 203-779-0025
easi@easi.org; www.easi.org
Thomas Benjamin, President
Roy Geiger, VP Administration
Peggy Knight, VP Programs
Engaging senior volunteers to use their experience in the restoration and maintenance of envi-

ronmentally sound environments. International network.
Founded in: 1990

7296 **Environmental Assessment Association**
PO Box 879
Palm Springs, CA 92263
877-743-6806
877-810-5643; *Fax:* 760-327-5631
info@eaa-assoc.org; www.eaa-assoc.org
Social Media: LinkedIn
Bill C. Merrell Ph.D , CEI, National Education Director
Supports all those involved in environmental assessment, including training and education, publications, conferences and research resources.

7297 **Environmental Bankers Association**
1827 Powers Ferry Rd.
Building 14, Suite 100
Atlanta, GA 30339
678-619-5045
800-966-7475; *Fax:* 678-229-2777
eba@envirobank.org; www.envirobank.org
Sharon Valverde, President
Georgina Dannatt, Vice President
Richard Belyea, Secretary
David Lambert, Treasurer
Julie Kilgore, Affiliate Chair
EBA voting members are banks, trust companies, credit unions, savings and loan associations, and other financial services organizations with an interest in environmental risk management and related issues. Active participants are bankers from Trust or Credit offices with responsibility for environmental liability, and financial services officers with environmental interests. Affiliate members are from law firms, consulting and insurance organizations.
Founded in: 1994

7298 **Environmental Business Association**
126 State Street
3rd Floor
Albany, NY 12207-1637
518-432-6400; *Fax:* 518-432-1383;
www.eba-nys.org
John L. Cusack, President
Linda R. Shaw, Vice President
Martha M. Holstein, Secretary
Ronald J. Beruta, Treasurer
Robert Hall, Director
EBA members represent all segments of the environmental industry—consultants, labaoratories, remediation companies, disposal firms, recyclers and technology innovators. EBA facilitates arrangements and information exchange among members to develop business opportunities. Services include sponsoring seminars, monthly meetings, industry trends, changes in technology and legislation.
Founded in: 1989

7299 **Environmental Compliance Institute**
165 Sherwood Ave
Farmingdale, NY 11735
631-414-7757
866-670-5366; *Fax:* 631-843-6331
pbany@c2g.us; www.c2g.us
Attorneys and corporations interested in environmental law and federal regulations governing waste disposal and other matters related to the environment.

7300 **Environmental Council of the States(ECOS)**
50 F Street NW
Suite 350
Washington, DC 20001
202-266-4920; *Fax:* 202-266-4937
ecos@ecos.org; www.ecos.org
Martha Rudolf, President
John Linc Stine, Vice President
Elizabeth Dieck, Secretary-Treasurer
John Stine, Committe Chair, Air
Sara Parker Pauley, Committe Chair, Water
Improving the capability of State environmental agencies and their leaders to protect and improve human health and the environment of the United States of America.

7301 **Environmental Design Research Association**
1760 Old Meadow Road
Suite 500
McLean, VA 22102
703-506-2895; *Fax:* 703-506-3266
edra@telepath.com; www.edra.org
Social Media: Facebook, Twitter, LinkedIn
Gowri Betrabet Gulwadi, Chair
Lynne Manzo, Chair-Elect
Paula Horrigan, Secretary
Shauna Mallory-Hill, Treasurer
Rula Awwad-Rafferty, Ex- Officio
Is to advance the art and science of environmental design research, to improve understanding of the interrelationships between people and their built and natural surroundings, and to help create environments responsive to human needs. EDRA members are designers and other professionals with an interest in environmental design research.
700 Members
Founded in: 1968

7302 **Environmental Industry Association**
4301 Connecticut Ave Nw
Suite 300
Washington, DC 20008-2304
202-244-4700
800-424-2869; *Fax:* 202-966-4824
wa@envasns.org; www.oneia.ca
Social Media: Facebook
Bruce Parker, President
Supports all those involved with technology of recycling, resource recovery and sanitary landfills. Publishes magazine.

7303 **Environmental Information Association**
6935 Wisconsin Ave
Suite 306
Chevy Chase, MD 20815-6112
301-961-4999
888-343-4342; *Fax:* 301-961-3094
info@eia-usa.org; www.eia-usa.org
Kevin Cannan, President
Chris Gates, President Elect
Steve Fulford, Vice President
Robert De Malo, Secretary
Kyle Burroughs, Treasurer
Nonprofit organization dedicated to providing environmental information to individuals, members and industry. Disseminates information on the abatement of asbestos and lead-based paint, indoor air quality, safety and health issues, analytical issues and environmental site assessments.

7304 **Environmental Law Institute**
1730 M Street NW
Suite 700
Washington, DC 20036-4919
202-939-3800
800-433-5120; *Fax:* 202-939-3868
law@eli.org; www.eli.org
Social Media: Facebook, Twitter, LinkedIn
Scott Fulton, President
Scott Schang, Executive Vice President
Martin Dickinson, VP Development
John V. Pendergrass, Acting VP, Research & Policy
Loretta Reinersmann, VP, Finance & Administration
Supports all those involved in environmental issues from a legal perspective, fostering the exchange of ideas and solutions for pressing environmental issues.

7305 **Environmental Mutagen Society**
1821 Michael Faraday Drive
Suite 300
Reston, VA 20190
703-438-8220; *Fax:* 703-438-3113
emshq@ems-us.org; www.emgs-us.org
Suzanne M. Morris, President
Bevin P. Engelward, Vice President
Barbara L. Parsons, Secretary
Barbara S. Shane, Treasurer
Marguerite Leishman, Executive Director
Members are scientists of diverse backgrounds and varied interests working in the field of molecular genetics and mutagenesis, whether in academia, industry or government. Focus is to encourage the study mutagens in the human environment particularly as they affect public health.
1500 Members
Founded in: 1969

7306 **Environmental and Energy Study Institute**
1112 16th Street, NW
Suite 300
Washington, DC 20036
202-628-1400; *Fax:* 202-204-5244;
www.eesi.org
Social Media: Facebook, Twitter, YouTube, Google+
Jared Blum, Board Chair
Richard L. Ottinger, Chaise-Emeritus
Shelley Fidler, Board Secretary/Treasurer
Quincalee Brown, Executive Director
Frances S. Buchholzer, Director
Educating Congress on energy efficiency and renewable energy; advancing innovative policy solutions.
Founded in: 1984

7307 **Federation of Environmental Technologists**
W175 N11081 Stonewood Dr.
Ste 203
Germantown, WI 53022-4771
262-437-1700; *Fax:* 262-437-1702
info@fetinc.org; www.fetinc.org
Social Media: Facebook, LinkedIn
Jeff Nettesheim, Board Chair
Cheryl Moran, President
Patrick Rego, Vice President
Anthony Montemurro, Treasurer
Barbara Hurula, Executive Director
Educational Seminars and Courses on Environmental, Health and Safety topics throughout the year around the state of Wisconsin for business and industry. Annual conference and exhibition held each October in Wisconsin.
700 Members
Founded in: 1981

7308 Floodplain Management Association
PO Box 712080
Santee, CA 92072-2080

760-936-3676; *Fax:* 619-749-9524
admin@floodplain.org; www.floodplain.org
Social Media: Facebook, LinkedIn, YouTube

Mark Seits, Chair
Maria Lorenzo Lee, Vice Chair
John Powderly, Secretary
George Booth, Treasurer
Andrew Trelease, Director

A nonprofit educational association established to promote the reduction of flood losses and to encourage the protection and enhancement of nautral floodplain values through the use of effective wetland management strategies and engineering technolgies.
Founded in: 1990

7309 Forest History Society
701 William Vickers Ave
Durham, NC 27701-3162

919-682-9319; *Fax:* 919-682-2349
recluce2@duke.edu; www.foresthistory.org
Social Media: Facebook, Twitter, LinkedIn, Flickr

Hayes Brown, Chairman
Kent Gilges, Co-Vice Chairman
Chris Zinkhan, Co-Vice Chairman
Henry I. Barclay III, Treasurer
Steven Anderson, Secretary & President

Nonprofit, educational institution that explores the history of the environment, forestry and conservation.
2000 Members
Founded in: 1946

7310 Forestry, Conservation Communications Association
122 Baltimore Street
Gettysburg, PA 17325

717-778-4237
844-458-0298; *Fax:* 717-398-0815
david.steinour@frequencycoordination.org; www.fcca.info

Chief Paul M. Leary (ret.), President
Roy Mott, Vice President
John McIntosh, Secretary/Treasurer
Ralph Haller, Executive Director
Janet Muncy, Financial Assistant

Association for manufacturers or suppliers of forestry and conservation communications equipment, systems and procedures.

7311 Friends of the Earth USA
1100 15th St. NW
11th Fl.
Washington, DC 20005

202-783-7400
877-843-8687; *Fax:* 202-783-0444;
www.foe.org
Social Media: Facebook, Twitter, LinkedIn, Instagram, Pinterest, Flickr

Erich Pica, President

Global organization of environmental activists.

7312 Friends of the Trees Society
PO Box 165
Hot Springs, MT 59845

406-741-5809
friendsofthetrees@yahoo.com;
www.friendsofthetrees.net

Michael Pilarski, Founder & Director

Nonprofit organization helping tree lovers worldwide.
Founded in: 1978

7313 GREENGUARD Environmental Institute
2211 Newmarket Parkway
Suite 110
Marietta, GA 30067

888-485-4733; *Fax:* 770-980-0072
environment@ul.com; www.greenguard.org

An industry-independent organization that aims to protect human health and improve quality of life by enhancing indoor air quality and reducing people's exposure to chemicals and other pollutants.

7314 Global Water Policy Project
E-Mail: info@globalwaterpolicy.org;
www.globalwaterpolicy.org

Promotes the preservation and sustainable use of Earth's fresh water through research, writing, outreach, and public speaking.

7315 Green Zionist Alliance
PO Box 1176
Long Beach, NY 11561

347-559-4492
info@aytzim.org; www.aytzim.org

Rabbi Michael Cohen, Co-founder
David Krantz, Board of Director
Susan Levine, Board of Director
Netta Schmeidler, Board of Director
Pesach Stadlin, Board of Director

A North America-based nonprofit organization that works to educate and mobilize people around the world for Israel's environment, to protect Israel's environment and support its environmental movement.
Founded in: 2001

7316 Greenpeace USA
702 H St NW
Suite 300
Washington, DC 20001-3876

202-462-1177
800-722-6995; *Fax:* 202-462-4507
goa@wdc.greenpeace.org;
www.greenpeaceusa.org
Social Media: Facebook, Twitter, YouTube

John Passacantando, CEO
Ellen McPeake, COO

Leading independent campaigning organization that uses non-violent direct action and creative communication to expose global environmental problems and to promote solutions that are essential to a green and peaceful future.
2.5M Members
Founded in: 1971

7317 Honor The Earth
PO Box 63
607 Main Ave,
Callaway, MN 56521

218-375-3200
info@honorearth.org; www.honorearth.org
Social Media: Facebook, Twitter

A nonprofit organization founded to raise awareness and financial support for Indigenous environmental justice.
Founded in: 1993

7318 Institute for Energy and Environmental Research
6935 Laurel Ave.
Suite 201
Takoma Park, MD 20912

301-270-5500; *Fax:* 301-270-3029
info@ieer.org
ieer.org
Social Media: Facebook, Twitter, RSS

Arjun Makhijani, President, Senior Engineer
Sadaf Rassoul Cameron, Vice President
David Close, Ph.D., Treasurer, Secretary
Annie Makhijani, Project Scientist
Christina Mills, Staff Scientist

Focuses on the environmental safety of nuclear weapons production, ozone layer depletion, and other issues relating to energy.
Founded in: 1987

7319 Institute for Environmental Auditing
City Office Park
Tritton Road
Lincoln LNS7AS

152-254-0069; *Fax:* 152-254-0090
info@iema.net; www.iema.net
Social Media: Twitter, LinkedIn, Google+

Dr Diana Montgomery FIEMA, Chairman
Richard Powell OBE, Executive Director
Tim Balcon, Chief Executive
Martin Baxter FIEMA, CEnv, Executive Director Policy
Dave Stanley. FIEMA, Cenv, Director

A professional organization of environmental auditors.
100 Members

7320 Institute for World Resource Research
PO Box 50303
Palo Alto, CA 94303-0303
630-910-1551; *Fax:* 202-729-7610;
www.globalwarming.net

BJ Jefferson, Advertising/Sales

Supports those involved in all phases of developments in forestry and reforestation of northern nations including the US, Canada, Russia, Sweden, Finland, Norway, China, Japan and others. Its goal is to increase the worldwide understanding of the ecological and economic roles of the northern forest regions of the world.

7321 Institute of Environmental Sciences and Technology
2340 S Arlington Heights Rd.
Suite 620
Arlington Heights, IL 60005

847-981-0100; *Fax:* 847-981-4130
information@iest.org; www.iest.org
Social Media: Facebook, Twitter, LinkedIn

Wei Sun, President
Ahmad Soueid, President-Elect

Is an international professional society that serves members and the industries they represent through education and the development of recommended practices and standards.
Founded in: 1953

7322 Institute of Gas Technology
1700 S Mount Prospect Rd
Des Plaines, IL 60018-1804

847-768-0500; *Fax:* 847-768-0501
publicrelations@gastechnology.org;
www.gastechnology.org
Social Media: Twitter, LinkedIn, YouTube

David Carroll, President & CEO
Ronald Snedic, Vice President/ Corporate Devel.
Jim Ingold, Vice President, Finance
Edward Johnston, VP, Research Operations
Paul Armstrong, Director

Supports all those involved in the gas industry worldwide, including energy industry production, consumption, reserves, imports and prices.

7323 Institute of Scrap Recycling Industries
1615 L St NW
Suite 600
Washington, DC 20036-5664

202-662-8500; *Fax:* 202-626-0900
isri@isri.org; www.isri.org

Social Media: Facebook, Twitter, LinkedIn, Instagram

Doug Kramer, Chairman
Mark Lewon, Chair Elect
Brian Shine, Vice Chair
Gary Champlin, Secretary Treasurer
Robin K. Wiener, President

Supports all those involved in the scrap processing and recycling industry.
165 Members
1987 Attendees

7324 International Association for Food Protection

6200 Aurora Ave
Suite 200W
Des Moines, IA 50322-2864

515-276-3344
800-369-6337; *Fax:* 515-276-8655
info@foodprotection.org;
www.foodprotection.org
Social Media: Facebook, Twitter, LinkedIn

Alejandro S. Mazzotta, President
Linda J. Harris, President-Elect
Mickey Parish, Vice President
Tim Jackson, Secretary
David W. Tharp, Executive Director

Nonprofit, educational association of food protection professionals. The association is dedicated to the education and service of its members, specifically, as well as industry personnel.
3400 Members
Founded in: 1911

7325 International Association of Wildland Fire

1418 Washburn Street
Missoula, MT 59801

406-531-8264
888-440-4293
iawf@iawfonline.org; www.iawfonline.org
Social Media: Facebook, Twitter, LinkedIn

Tom Zimmerman, President
Alan Goodwin, Vice President
David Moore, Treasurer
Kathy Clay, Secretary
Timothy Brown, Board Member

IWAF members are academics and professionals with an interest in wildland fires.
800 Members
Founded in: 1990

7326 International Council on Nanotechnology - ICON

214-494-2071
icon.rice.edu

Vicki Colvin, Executive Director
Kristen Kulinowski, Director

A portal for information about the environmental, health, and safety aspects of nanotechnology.

7327 International Ecotourism Society

427 North Tatnall Street
Wilmington, DE 19801-2230

202-506-5033; *Fax:* 202-789-7279
info@ecotourism.org; www.ecotourism.org
Social Media: Facebook, Twitter, YouTube

Kelly Bricker, Chair
Tony Charters, Vice Chair
Neal Inamdar, Director Finance/Administration

Society members include park managers, tour operators, conservation professionals, and others with an interest in the development of ecology-centered tourism.
900 Members
Founded in: 1990

7328 International Lead Zinc Research Organization

1822 NC Highway 54 East
Suite 120
Durham, NC 27713

919-361-4647; *Fax:* 919-361-1957
rputnam@ilzro.org; www.ilzro.org

Stephen Wilkinson, President
Frank Goodwin, VP Materials Sciences
Scott Mooneyham, Treasurer
Rob Putnam, Director Communications

ILZRO members are miners and refiners of lead and zinc. Trade association of the lead and zinc industry worldwide. Focus on research and development to detect new uses for the metals and refine existing uses.
Founded in: 1958

7329 International Society for Ecological Economics

15 River Street
#204
Boston, MA 02108

703-790-1745; *Fax:* 703-790-2672
secretariat@ecoeco.org
http://www.isecoeco.org/
Social Media: Facebook, Twitter, LinkedIn, Google+, Pinterest

Dr. Marina Fischer-Kowalski, President
Sabine O'Hara, President-Elect
Anne Carter Aitken, Treasurer
Bina Agarwal, Past President
Rashid Hassan, Board of Director

Members are researchers, academics, and other professionals who study the impact of economic models and policies on the environment.
750 Members
Founded in: 1989

7330 Isaak Walton League

707 Conservation Lane
Gaithersburg, MD 20878

301-548-0150
800-453-5463; *Fax:* 301-548-0146
info@iwla.org; www.iwla.org
Social Media: Facebook, Twitter, LinkedIn, Google+, Pinterest

Jodi Arndt Labs, Chair
Shawn Gallagher, President
Jeff Deschamps, Vice President
Jim Storer, Secretary
Walter Lynn Jr., Treasurer

Protects America's outdoors through education, community-based conservation, and promoting outdoor recreation.
37000 Members
Founded in: 1922

7331 Keep America Beautiful

1010 Washington Boulevard
Stamford, CT 6901

203-659-3000; *Fax:* 203-659-3001
info@kab.org; www.kab.org
Social Media: Facebook, Twitter, Tumblr, YouTube, Pinterest

Howard Ungerleider, Chairman
Tom Waldeck, Treasurer
Thomas H. Tamoney, Jr., Secretary
Shannon Reiter, President
Gregory H. Ray, Senior Vice President

Nonprofit organization that builds and sustains vibrant communities.
Founded in: 1953

7332 League of Conservation Voters

1920 L Street, NW
Suite 800
Washington, DC 20036

202-785-8683; *Fax:* 202-835-0491;
www.lcv.org
Social Media: Facebook, Twitter, YouTube, Flickr

Carol Browner, Chair
Sherwood Boehlert, Vice Chair
Trip Van Noppen, Treasurer
Carrie Clark, Secretary
Gene Karpinski, President

A political advocacy organization that advocates for sound environmental policies and elects pro-environmental candidates who will adopt and implement such policies.

7333 Marine Technology Society

1100 H St., Nw
Suite LL-100
Washington, DC 20005

202-717-8705; *Fax:* 202-347-4302
membership@mtsociety.org;
www.mtsociety.org
Social Media: Facebook, Twitter, LinkedIn, YouTube

Ray Toll, President
Donna Kocak, President-Elect
Andy Clark, VP of Industry and Technology
Liesl Hotaling, VP of Education and Research
Justin Manley, VP of Gov. & Public Affairs

Addresses coastal zone management, marine, mineral and energy resources, marine environmental protection, and ocean engineering issues.
2M Members
Founded in: 1963

7334 Midwest for Environmental Science and Public Policy

1845 N Farwell Avenue
Suite 100
Milwaukee, WI 53202

414-271-7280; *Fax:* 414-273-7293;
www.mcespp.org

Patrice Ann Morrow, Chair
Jeffery A Foran, President/CEO

For citizens concerned with environmental protection.

7335 NORA: Association of Responsible Recyclers

7250 Heritage Village Plaza,
Suite 201
Gainesville, VA 20155

703-753-4277; *Fax:* 703-753-2445
sparker@noranews.org; www.noranews.org

Bill Hinton, President
Chris Bergstrom, Executive Vice President
Roy Schumacher, Vice President
Brandon Velek, Past President
Ellie Bruce, Board Of Director

Is a trade association representing the interests of companies in the United States engaged in the safe recycling of used oil, antifreeze, waste water and oil filters.
Founded in: 1984

7336 National Association for Environmental Management

1612 K St NW
1002
Washington, DC 20006-2830

202-986-6616
800-391-6236; *Fax:* 202-530-4408
programs@naem.org; www.naem.org
Social Media: Facebook, Twitter, LinkedIn

Rick Taylor, President
Kris Morico, 1st Vice President
Mark Hause, 2nd Vice President
Alan Leibowitz, Treasurer
Stephen Evanoff, Ex-Officio Member - Past President

Dedicated to advancing the profession of environmental management and supports the profes-

sional corporate and facility environmental manager.
1000+ Members
Founded in: 1990

7337 National Association for PET Containers
7310 Turfway Road
Suite 550
Florence, KY 41042
859-372-6635; *Fax:* 707-935-1998
n4mayshun@napcor.com; www.napcor.com
Social Media: Facebook
Rick Moore, Executive Director
Resa Dimino, Director Of Public Policy
Kate Eagles, Project Director
National association for the PET plastic industry. Promotes the use of PET plastic packaging and facilitates the recycling of PET containers.
Frequency: Bi-Monthly
Founded in: 1987

7338 National Association of Environmental Professionals
PO Box 460
Collingswood, NJ 08108
856-283-7816; *Fax:* 856-210-1619
naep@bowermanagementservices.com; www.naep.org
Social Media: Facebook, LinkedIn
Brock Hoegh, CEP, President
David Dickson, Vice President
Courtney Arena, Treasurer
Kristin Bennett, Secretary
Harold Draper,D.Sc., CEP, Immediate Past President
Our mission is to be the interdisciplinary organization dedicated to developing the highest standards of ethics and proficiency in the environmental professions. Our members are public and private sector professionals who promote excellence in decision-making in light of the environmental, social, and economic impacts of those decisions.

7339 National Association of Local Government Environmental Professionals
1001 Connecticut Avenue
Suite 405
Washington, DC 20036-1532
202-337-4503; *Fax:* 202-429-5290
nalgep@nalgep.org; www.nalgep.org
Social Media: Facebook
Ellen Walkowiak, Chair
John Stufflebean, Vice Chair
Douglas MacCourt, Treasurer
Lee Ilan, Secretary
Chris Bird, Director
Is a national organization representing local government professionals responsible for environmental compliance and the development of local environmental policy. NALGEP brings together local environmental officials to share information on practices, conduct policy projects, promote environmental training and education, and communicate the view of local officials on national environmental issues.
150 Members
Founded in: 1993

7340 National Audubon Society
225 Varick Street
New York, NY 10014
212-979-3000
webmaster@audubon.org; www.audubon.org
Social Media: Facebook, Twitter, YouTube
Conserves and restores natural ecosystems, focusing on birds, other wildlife, and their habitats for the benefit of humanity and the earth's biological diversity.
50000 Members
Founded in: 1992

7341 National Center for Appropriate Technology
3040 Continental Drive
Butte, MT 59702
406-494-4572
800-275-6228; *Fax:* 406-494-2905;
www.ncat.org
Social Media: Facebook, Twitter, LinkedIn, RSS, Pinterest
Gene Brady, Chairman
Randall Chapman, Vice Chairman
Jeannie Jertson, Secretary
Brian Castelli, Treasurer
John Colgan, Commissioner
Their mission is to help people by championing small-scale, local, and sustainable solutions to reduce poverty, promote healthy communities, and protect natural resources.
Founded in: 1976

7342 National Conference of Local Environmental Health Administrators
1010 South Third Street
Dayton, WA 99328
509-382-2181; *Fax:* 360-382-2942
David_Riggs@co.columbia.wa.us; www.ncleha.org
A professional association for supervisors, administrators and managers of environmental health programs in local agencies.

7343 National Council for Science and the Environment
1101 17th Street NW
Suite 250
Washington, DC 20036
202-530-5810; *Fax:* 202-628-4311
NCSE@NCSEonline.org; www.ncseonline.org
Social Media: Facebook, Twitter, LinkedIn, YouTube, Flickr
Peter Saundry, Ph.D., Executive Director
Andi Glashow, Director, Finance
Sudeep Vyapari, Ph.D., Associate Executive Director
Jessica Soule, Director, EnvironMentors
David Blockstein, Ph.D., Senior Scientist, Dr. Education
A U.S. based nonprofit organization that improves the scientific basis for environmental decision-making.

7344 National Environmental Balancing Bureau
8575 Grovemont Circle
Gaithersburg, MD 20877-4121
301-977-3698
866-497-4447; *Fax:* 301-977-9589
karen@nebb.org; www.nebb.org
Jean-Paul Le Blanc, President
Jim Kelleher,, President-Elect
Donald E. Hill, Vice President
Jim Whorton, Treasurer
James Huber, Past President
NEBB is an international certification assocaition for firms that deliver high performance building systems. Members perform testing, adjusting and balancing (TAB) of heating, ventilating and air-conditioning systems, commission and retro-commission building systems commissioning, execute sound and vibration testing, and test and certify lab fume hoods and electronic and bio clean rooms. NEBB holds the highest standards in certification.
Founded in: 1971

7345 National Environmental Development Association
One Thomas Circle NW
10th Floor
Washington, DC 20006
202-332-2933; *Fax:* 202-530-0659;
www.nedacap.org
Phil Clapp, President
Steve Hellem, Executive Director
NEDA members are companies and other organizations concerned with balancing environmental and economic interests to obtain both a clean environment and a strong economy.
Founded in: 1973

7346 National Environmental, Safety and Health Training Association
2700 N. Central Avenue
Suite 900
Phoenix, AZ 85004-1147
602-956-6099; *Fax:* 602-234-1867
neshta@neshta.org; www.neshta.org
Social Media: Facebook, Twitter, LinkedIn, Google+, Pinterest, Tumblr
Myrtle I. Turner-Harris, President
Jeffery K. Dennis,CET, CSP, CHMM, Vice President
Dave Owings,CET, General Manager
Bruce V. Guiliani,CET, CSP, Dir. Of Saftey Loss & Prevention
David L. Galt, Managing Editor for Safety
A non-profit educational society for environmental, safety, health and other technical training and adult education professionals. Mission is to promote trainer competency through trainer skills training, continuing education, voluntary certification, peer networking and the adoption of national and international training and trainer standards.
Founded in: 1977

7347 National Institutes for Water Resources
47 Harkness Road
Pelham, MA 10002
413-253-5686; *Fax:* 413-253-1309
tracy@uidaho.edu
niwr.net
Jeffery Allen, President
Reagan Waskom, President-Elect
John Tracy, Secretary-Treasurer
NIWRD represents state and territorial Water Research Institutes and Centers in collective activities to implement the provisions of the Water Resources Act of 1984, and subsequesnt federal legislation. NIWR networks these separate institutes into a coordinated unit, represented by 8 regional groupings, and facilitates the response of the Water Research Institutes and its membership to other mutual concerns and interests in water resources.
54 Members
Founded in: 1974

7348 National Parks Conservation Association
777 6th St. NW
Suite 700
Washington, DC 20001-3723
202-223-6722
800-628-7275; *Fax:* 202-454-3333
npca@npca.org; www.npca.org
Social Media: Facebook, Twitter
Theresa Pierno, President & CEO
Advocates for the preservation of America's national parks and historical sites.
Founded in: 1919

7349 **National Registry of Environmental Professionals**
PO Box 2099
Glenview, IL 60025
847-724-6631; *Fax:* 847-724-4223
nrep@nrep.org; www.nrep.org
Social Media: Facebook, Twitter, LinkedIn, YouTube
Scott Spear, Executive Chairperson
Richard Young, PhD, REM, P, Executive Director
Edward C. Beck, PhD, REM, PE,, Director
Charles J. McAfee, REM, CEA,, Director
Marie Hunter , REM, Director
To promote legal and professional recognition of individuals possessing education, training and experience as environmental managers, engineers, technologists, scientists and technicians-and to consolidate that recognition in one centralized source-so that the public, government, employers and insurers can justify the importance and acceptance of such individuals to carry out operations and management of environmental activities.
17000 Members
Founded in: 1983
Mailing list available for rent

7350 **National Society of Environmental Consultants**
PO Box 460
Collingswood, NJ 08108
856-283-7816; *Fax:* 856-210-1619
naep@bowermanagementservices.com; www.naep.org
Brock Hoegh, CEP, President
David Dickson, Vice President
Courtney Arena, Treasurer
Kristin Bennett, Secretary
Harold Draper,D.Sc., CEP, Immediate Past President
Supports all activities of environmental consultants.
600 Members
Founded in: 1992

7351 **National Solid Wastes Management Association**
4301 Connecticut Ave NW
Suite 300
Washington, DC 20008-2304
202-244-4700
800-424-2869; *Fax:* 202-966-4824
wa@envasns.org; www.wasterecycling.org
Social Media: Facebook, Twitter, Google +
Sharon H. Kneiss, President
Kevin Kraushaar, Esq., CAE, VP, Gov. Affairs & Chapters
Christopher Doherty, VP, Communications
Sheila R. Alkire, Director, Education
Tiffany Jones, Director, Certification
Supports all those involved in the environment industry, especially the handling, transportation and disposal of infectious wastes.

7352 **National Wildlife Federation**
PO Box 1583
Merrifield, VA 22116-1583
703-438-6000
800-822-9919; *Fax:* 703-438-3570; www.nwf.org
Social Media: Facebook, Twitter, LinkedIn, YouTube
Bruce Wallace, Chair
Paul Beaudette, Eastern Vice Chair
Clark Bullard, Central Vice Chair
Kent Salazar, Western Vice Chair
Brian Bashore, Director
Encourages management of natural resources. Gives financial aid to local groups and graduate studies. Conducts guided nature trail tours, produces programs and sponsors competitions.
4.5MM Members
Founded in: 1936

7353 **National Wildlife Refuge Association**
1001 Connecticut Ave. NW
Suite 905
Washington, DC 20036
202-417-3803
nwra@refugeassociation.org
refugeassociation.org
Social Media: Facebook, Twitter, LinkedIn, RSS
Rebecca Rubin, Chair
Donal O'Brien, Vice Chair
David Houghton, President
Anne Truslow, VP, Chief Operating Officer
Desiree Sorenson-Groves, VP, Government Affairs
An independent membership organization that works to conserve American wildlife.

7354 **National Woodland Owners Association**
374 Maple Avenue East
Suite 310
Vienna, VA 22180-4718
703-255-2700
800-470-8733; *Fax:* 703-281-9200; www.woodlandowners.org
Keith A. Argow, President
Dick Courter, Chairman
Phil Gramelspacher, Vice Chairman
Provides timely information about forestry and forest practices with news from Washington,DC and state capitals. Written for non-industrial land owners. Includes state landowner association news.
39M Members
Founded in: 1983

7355 **Native Forest Council**
PO Box 2190
Eugene, OR 97402
541-688-2600; *Fax:* 541-461-2156
info@forestcouncil.org
forestcouncil.org
Social Media: Facebook, Twitter, Vimeo, YouTube
Bill Barton, Board of Director
Allan Branscomb, Board of Director
Calvin Hececta, Board of Director
Timothy Hermach, Board of Director
Timothy Moxley, Board of Director
Provides news and resources for the protection of publicly owned lands from logging, mining, grazing, drilling, and off-road vehicles.
Founded in: 1987

7356 **Natural Resources Defense Council**
40 W 20th St
New York, NY 10011-4231
212-727-2700; *Fax:* 212-727-1773
nrdcinfo@nrdc.org; www.nrdc.org
Social Media: Facebook, Twitter, YouTube, Tumblr, RSS
Daniel R. Tishman, Chair
Frederick A.O. Schwarz Jr., Chair Emeritus
Wendy K. Neu, Vice Chair
Alan F. Horn, Vice Chair
Patricia Bauman, Vice Chair
Dedicated to the wise management of natural resources through research, public education and the development of effective public policies.
50000 Members
Founded in: 1970

7357 **Nature's Classroom**
19 Harrington Rd.
Charlton, MA 1507
508-248-2741
800-433-8375; *Fax:* 508-248-2745
info@naturesclassroom.org; www.naturesclassroom.org
Social Media: Facebook
A nonprofit outdoor environmental education program.

7358 **NatureServe**
4600 N. Fairfax Dr.
7th Floor
Arlington, VA 22203
703-908-1800; *Fax:* 703-229-1670
info@natureserve.org; www.natureserve.org
Social Media: Facebook, Twitter, LinkedIn, YouTube, Vimeo, Flickr, RSS
Mary Klein, President/ CEO
Lori Scott, Chief Information Officer
Ravi Shankar, CFO/ COO
Leslie Honey, VP, Conservation Services
Don Kent, Director of Network Relations
A nonprofit organization that provides proprietary wildlife conservation-related data, tools, and services to private and government clients, partner organizations, and the public.
Founded in: 1974

7359 **Negative Population Growth**
2861 Duke St.
Suite 36
Alexandria, VA 22314
703-370-9510; *Fax:* 703-370-9514; www.npg.org
Social Media: Facebook, Twitter, LinkedIn, RSS, YouTube
Donald Mann, President
Craig Lewis, Executive Vice President
Tracy Canada, Deputy Director
Diane Saco, Board of Director
Sharon Marks, Board of Director
A membership organization in the United States that works on overpopulation issues and advocates a gradual reduction in U.S. and world population.
Founded in: 1972

7360 **North American Association for Environmental Education**
2000 P Street NW
Suite 540
Washington, DC 20036
202-419-0412; *Fax:* 202-419-0415
info@naaee.org; www.naaee.org
Social Media: Facebook
Jose Pepe Marcos-Iga, President
Judy Braus, Executive Director
Susan McGuire, Secretary
Mary Ford, Treasurer
Flisa Stevenson, At-Large Board Member
Purpose is to assist and support the work of individuals and groups engaged in environmental education, research and service.
1500 Members
Founded in: 1971

7361 **North American Chapter - International Society for Ecological Modelling**
550 M Ritchie Highway
PMB 255
Severna Park, MD 21146
E-Mail: webmaster@isemna.org; www.isemna.org
Sven E. Jorgensen, President
Tarzan Legovic, Secretary-General
David A. Mauriello, Treasurer

Brian D. Faith, President, North America
Guy Larocque,, Secretary, North America

Promotes the international exchange of general knowledge, ideas and scientific results in the area of the application of systems analysis and simulation to ecology, environmental science and natural resource management using mathematical and computer modelling of ecological systems.
150 Members
Founded in: 1983

7362 **North American Lake Management Society**
PO Box 5443
Madison, WI 53705-443
608-233-2836; *Fax:* 608-233-3186
info@nalms.org; www.nalms.org
Social Media: Facebook, LinkedIn, Flickr

Reed Green, President
Julie Chambers, President-Elect
Sara Peel, Secretary
Mike Perry, Treasurer
Terry McNabb, CLM, Past President

Members are academics, lake managers and others interested in furthering the understanding of lake ecology. The North American Lake Management Society's mission is to forge partnerships among citizens, scientists and professionals to foster the management and protection of lakes and reservoirs for today and tomorrow. Please call for rate information.
1700 Members
Founded in: 1980

7363 **Oceana**
1350 Connecticut Ave.
5th Fl.
Washington, DC 20036
202-833-3900; *Fax:* 202-833-2070
info@oceana.org
oceana.org
Social Media: Facebook, Twitter, Instagram, YouTube, Google+

Andrew Sharpless, Chief Executive Officer
Simon Sidamon-Eristoff, Chair

Environmental organization focused solely on the protection and restoration of the world's oceans.
Founded in: 2001

7364 **Organic Seed Alliance**
PO Box 772
Port Townsend, WA 98368-0772
360-385-7192; *Fax:* 360-385-7455
info@seedalliance.org; www.seedalliance.org
Social Media: Facebook, Twitter

Sebastian Aguilar, President
Atina Diffley, Vice President
Sean Schmidt, Secretary
Zea Sonnabend, Treasurer
Micaela Colley, Executive Director

Organic Seed Alliance suppports the ethical development and stewardship of the genetic resources of agricultural seed.
25M Members
Founded in: 1975

7365 **Plant Growth Regulation Society of America**
Rhone-Poulenc, Ag Company
1018 Duke Street
Alexandria, VA 22314
703-836-4606; *Fax:* 706-883-8215
dmancini@ashs.org; www.pgrsa.org
Social Media: Facebook, Twitter, RSS

Dr. Carl Sams, President
Dr. Holly Little, 1st Vice President
Mr. Michael Rethwisch, 2nd Vice President
Dr. Tim Spann, Past President
Dr. Chris Gunter, Secretary

Functions as a nonprofit educational and scientific organization.
325 Members
Founded in: 1973

7366 **Rachel Carson Council**
8600 Irvington Avenue
Bethesda, MD 20817
301-214-2400
office@rachelcarsoncouncil.org
rachelcarsoncouncil.org
Social Media: Twitter

Diana Post, Executive Director
David B McGrath, Treasurer
Dr Diana Post, Secretary

Library and clearinghouse on pesticide toxicity, lower risk alternatives for pest control, and Rachel Carson. Produces publications and sponsors conventions/meetings on these topics, issues newsletter. Nonprofit.
Founded in: 1965

7367 **Rainforest Action Network (RAN)**
425 Bush St.
Suite 300
San Francisco, CA 94108
415-398-4404
answers@ran.org; www.ran.org
Social Media: Facebook, Twitter, YouTube

Noel R. Natividad, Chief Operating Officer
Lindsey Allen, Executive Director

Environmental organization focused on forest systems.

7368 **Renewable Fuels Association**
425 Third Street, SW
Suite 1150
Washington, DC 20024
202-289-3835; *Fax:* 202-289-7519
info@ethanolrfa.org; www.ethanolrfa.org
Social Media: Facebook, Twitter, LinkedIn, YouTube, Google+, Instagram

Randall Doyal,, Chairman
Mick Henderson, Vice Chairman
Jim Seurer, Treasurer
Bob Dinneen, President
Geoff Cooper, Senior Vice President

Members are companies and individuals involved in the production and use of ethanol.
55 Members
Founded in: 1981

7369 **Renewable Natural Resources Foundation**
6010 Executive Boulevard
5th Floor
Bethesda, MD 20852-3827
301-493-9101; *Fax:* 301-770-9104
info@rnrf.org; www.rnrf.org
Social Media: Facebook, Twitter

Richard A. Engberg, Chairman
John E. Durrant, Vice-Chairman
Robert D. Day, Executive Director
Sarah Gerould, Director
Erik Hankin, Director

A consortium of professional and scientific societies whose members are concerned with the advancement of research, education, scientific practice and policy formulation for the conservation, replenishment and use of the earth's renewable natural resources.
14 Members
Founded in: 1972

7370 **Resource Policy Institute**
1525 Selby Avenue
Ste. 304
Los Angeles, CA 90024-5796
310-470-9711; www.bu.edu/hrpi

Dr Arthur Purcell, Director/Founder

Education, and consulting research group concerned with environmental policies, technologies, and management strategies..
Founded in: 1975

7371 **Safe Buildings Alliance**
Metropolitan Square
655 15th Street NW
Suite 1200
Washington, DC 20005-5701
202-879-5120; *Fax:* 202-638-2103
sba.lfpc.org

Association of building products companies that formerly manufactured asbestos-containing materials for building construction. Its main focus is to provide public information on issues relating to asbestos in building. SBA promotes a reasonable, safe response to the problem of asbestos in buildings, including the development of uniform, objective Federal and State standards for asbestos identification and abatement, nonremoval alternatives and the regulation of inspectors.
Founded in: 1984

7372 **Sagamore Institute of the Adirondacks Inc**
Great Camp Sagamore
PO Box 40
Raquette Lake, NY 13436-0040
315-354-5311; *Fax:* 315-354-5851
info@greatcampsagamore.org;
www.greatcampsagamore.org
Social Media: Facebook, YouTube

Garet Livermore, Executive Director
Bob Henisler, Superintendant
Dr. Jeffery Flagg, Program Director
Hannah Gibbons, Program Manager
Andrew Gillcrist, Director Of Family Programs

Non-profit 501c3 National Historic Landmark, former retreat of the Vanderbilts, offering educational programs on history, ecology and culture of the Adirondack Park.

7373 **Sierra Club**
85 Second St.
2nd Fl.
San Francisco, CA 94105
415-977-5500; *Fax:* 415-977-5797
information@sierraclub.org;
www.sierraclub.org
Social Media: Facebook, Twitter

Michael Brune, Executive Director
Lou Barnes, Chief Financial Officer

Founded in: 1892, the largest environmental organization in the United States campaigns for the protection of endangered species, habitat conservation, environmental protection and an end to the use of fossil fuels.
Founded in: 1892

7374 **Silicones Environmental Health and Safety**
700 Second St., NE
Washington, DC 20002
202-249-7000; *Fax:* 202-249-6100;
www.sehsc.com
Social Media: Facebook, Twitter

Calvin M. Dooley, President
Dell Perelman, Chief Of Staff & General Counsel
Raymond J. O'Bryan, Chief Financial Officer
Nacole B. Hinton, Managing Director
Anne Womack Kolton, VP Of Communications

A not-for-profit trade association comprised of North American silicone chemical producers and importers.
6 Members
Founded in: 1971

7375 **Society for Ecological Restoration International**
1017 O Street NW
Washington, DC 20001

202-299-9518; *Fax:* 270-626-5485
info@ser.org; www.ser.org
Social Media: Facebook, Twitter, LinkedIn

Alan Unwin, Chair
Cara R. Nelson, Vice Chair
Stuart Allison, Secretary
Jim Hallet, Treasurer
James Aronson, Representative - At- Large

SER members are academics, scientists, environmental consultants, government agencies and others with an interest in ecological restoration.
2300 Members
Founded in: 1988

7376 **Society for Environmental Geochemistry and Health**
4698 S Forrest Avenue
Springfield, MO 65810

417-851-1166; *Fax:* 417-881-6920
DRBGWIXSON@aol.com; www.segh.net

Dr Chaosheng Zhang, President
Dr Chaosheng Zhang, European Chair
Kyoung-Woong Kim, Asia/Pacific Chair
Anthea Brown, Membership Secretary/Treasurer
Malcolm Brown, Secretary

Promotes a multi-disciplinary approach to research in fields of geochemistry and health to facilitate and expand communication among scientists within these disciplines and to advance knowledge in the area.
400 Members
Founded in: 1971

7377 **Society for Human Ecology**
College of the Atlantic
105 Eden Street
Bar Harbor, ME 04609-0180

207-801-5630; *Fax:* 207-288-3780
info@societyforhumanecology.org;
www.societyforhumanecology.org
Social Media: Facebook, Twitter

Rob Dyball, President
Lee Cerveny, Second Vice President
Chiho Watanabe, Third Vice President-International
Rob Lilieholm, Treasurer
Barbara Carter, Secretary

SHE members are academics, scientists, health professionals and others with an interest in studying the interrelationship of man's actions and his environment.
150 Members
Founded in: 1981

7378 **Society for Occupational and Environmental Health**
111 North Bridge Road
#21-01 Peninsula Plaza
Singapore 179098

E-Mail: oehsadmin@gmail.com;
www.oehs.org.sg

Dr. Lee Lay Tin, President
Mr. Eric Ng, Vice President
Kam Wai Kuen, Honorary Secretary
Dr. Lucy Leong, Honorary Treasurer
Dr. Gregory Chan, Committee Members

Members include physicians, hygienists, economists, laboratory scientists, academicians, labor and industry representatives, or anyone interested in occupational and/or environmental health. Serves as a forum for the presentation of scientific data and the exchange of information among members; sponsors conferences and meetings which address specific problem areas and policy questions.
300 Members
Founded in: 1972

7379 **Society of Environmental Toxicology and Chemistry**
229 South Baylen Street
2nd Floor
Pensacola, FL 32502

850-469-1500; *Fax:* 888-296-4136
setac@setac.org; www.setac.org
Social Media: Facebook, Twitter, LinkedIn

Paul van den Brink, President
Tim Canfield, Vice President
Fred Heimbach, Treasurer

Is a professional society established to promote the use of multidisciplinary approaches to solving problems of the impact of chemicals and technology on the environment. SETA members are professionals in the fields of chemistry, toxicology, biology, ecology, atmospheric sciences, health sciences, earth sciences, and environmental engineering.
4000 Members
Founded in: 1979

7380 **Society of Exploration Geophysicists**
8801 South Yale
Suite 500
Tulsa, OK 74137-3575

918-497-5500
877-778-5463; *Fax:* 918-497-5557
web@seg.org; www.seg.org
Social Media: Facebook, Twitter, LinkedIn

Mary Fleming, Executive Director
Vladimir Grechka, Editor

The Society of Exploration Geophysicists/SEG is a not-for-profit organization that promotes the science of geophysics and the education of applied geophysicists. SEG fosters the expert and ethical practice of geophysics in the exploration and development of natural resources, in characterizing the near surface, and in mitigating earth hazards.
Founded in: 1930

7381 **Soil and Plant Analysis Council**
347 North Shores Circle
Windsor, CO 80550

970-686-5702
rmiller@lamar.colostate.edu;
www.spcouncil.com

Rao Mylavarapu, President
Robert Mikkelsen, Vice President
Rigas Karamanos, Past President
Robert Miller, Secretary/Treasurer
Brad Joern, Individual Class Member

Supports all those involved in the analysis of soil and plants.

7382 **Soil and Water Conservation Society**
945 SW Ankeny Rd
Ankeny, IA 50023-9764

515-289-2331
800-843-7645; *Fax:* 515-289-1227
swcs@swcs.org; www.swcs.org
Social Media: Facebook, Twitter, LinkedIn

Mark Berkland, President
Jon Scholl, Vice-President
Mike Collins, Secretary
Susan Meadows, Treasurer
Wendi Goldsmith, NE Region Director

SWCS is a nonprofit scientific and educational organization that serves as an advocate for conservation professionals and for science-based conservation practice, programs, and policy.
5000+ Members
Founded in: 1943

7383 **Southeastern Association of Fish and Wildlife Agencies**
27 Sylwood Place
Jackson, MS 39209

601-668-6916; *Fax:* 850-893-6204
crayhopkins@bellsouth.net; www.seafwa.org

Bob Ziehmer, President
Gordon Myers, Vice President
Robert Barham, Secretary/Treasurer
Nick Wiley, Past President
Ed Carter, At Larger Executive Board Member

An organization whose members are the state agencies with primary responsibility for management and protection of the fish and wildlife resources in 16 states, Puerto Rico and the US Virgin Islands.
18 Members
Founded in: 1947

7384 **Steel Recycling Institute**
680 Andersen Drive
Pittsburgh, PA 15220-2700

412-922-2772
800-876-7274; *Fax:* 412-922-3213;
www.recycle-steel.org
Social Media: Facebook, Twitter, YouTube, Google+

William H Heenan Jr, President

Promotes steel recycling and works to forge a coalition of steelmakers, can manufacturers, legislators, government officials, solid waste managers, business and consumer groups.
Founded in: 1988

7385 **Student Conservation Association**
4245 North Fairfax Drive
Suite 825
Arlington, VA 22203

703-524-2441; *Fax:* 603-543-1828;
www.thesca.org
Social Media: Facebook, Twitter, YouTube

Jamie Berman Matyas, President and CEO
Karen Davis, SVP & Chief Advancement Officer
Aimee Dobrzeniecki, Chief Financial Officer
Barbara Gonzalez-McIntosh, Chief Counsel
Laura Herrin, Senior VP, Programs

To build the next generation of conservation leaders and inspire lifelong stewardship of our environment and communities by engaging young people in hands-on service to the land.
35000 Members
Founded in: 1957

7386 **Surfaces in Biomaterials Foundation**
1000 Westgate Drive
Suite 252
St Paul, MN 55114-8679

651-290-6267; *Fax:* 651-290-2266
memberservices@surfaces.org;
www.surfaces.org
Social Media: Twitter, LinkedIn

Dr. Aylvin A. Dias, President
Chander Chawla, President-Elect
Bill Theilacker, Vice President
Mark Smith PhD, Treasurer
Joe McGonigle, Secretary

Dedicated to exploring creative solutions to technical challenges at the BioInterface by fostering education and multidisciplinary cooperation among industrial, academic, clinical and regulatory communities.
250 Members

7387 **Test Boring Association**
181 Beagle Club Road
Washington, PA 15301

722- 22- 299
888-267-4647; *Fax:* 724-228-2992

jrselvoski@testboringservices.com;
www.testboring.com

Patrizia Zita, Management Executive

Contractors engaged in test boring and core drilling.
Founded in: 1941

7388 The African Wild Dog Conservancy
208 N California Ave.
Silver City, NM 88061

E-Mail: lycaonpictus@awdconservancy.org;
www.awdconservancy.org

A nonprofit, non-governmental organization working with local communities, and national and international stakeholders to conserve the African wilddog through scientific research and education.
Founded in: 2001

7389 The Center for International Environmental Law
1350 Connecticut Avenue NW
Suite #1100
Washington, DC 20036

202-785-8700; *Fax:* 202-785-8701
info@ciel.org; www.ciel.org
Social Media: Facebook, Twitter, LinkedIn, RSS

Carroll Muffett, President/ CEO
Jeffrey Wanha, Dir., Finance & Admin.
Marcos A. Orellana, Director, Human Rights
Cameron Aishton, Administrator
Kevin Parker, Development Director

Nonprofit organization that provides environmental legal services in international and comparative environmental law.

7390 The Indoor Air Institute
2548 Empire Grade
Santa Cruz, CA 95060

831-426-0148; *Fax:* 831-426-6522
info@IndAir.org
indair.org

Hal Levin, President
William Fisk, Vice President
William Nazaroff, Vice President

Supports all those involved with indoor air quality and climate with training, education, resource materials and an annual conference.

7391 The Marine Mammal Center
2000 Bunker Road
Fort Cronkhite
Sausalito, CA 94965-2619

415-289-7325
415-289-SEAL
info@tmmc.org;
www.marinemammalcenter.org
Social Media: Facebook, Twitter, RSS, Pinterest, YouTube

Marci Davis, Chief Financial Officer
Dr. Jeff Boehm, Executive Director
Nancy Sackson, Dir., Marketing & Development
Rachel Bergren, Education Director
Heather Groninger, Human Resources Director

A private, nonprofit U.S. organization established for the purpose of rescuing, rehabilitating, and releasing marine mammals who are injured, ill, or abandoned.
Founded in: 1975

7392 The Nature Conservancy
4245 North Fairfax Drive
Suite 100
Arlington, VA 22203-1606

703-841-5300
800-628-6860
members@tnc.org; www.nature.org
Social Media: Facebook, Twitter, LinkedIn, Google+, Flickr

Craig O. McCaw, Chairman
James E. Rogers, Vice Chair
Frank e. Loy, Secretary
Mark R. Tercek, President & CEO
Muneer A. Satter, Treasurer

The leading conservation organization working around the world to protect ecologically important lands and waters for nature and people. Addresses the most pressing conservation threats at the largest scale.
Founded in: 1984

7393 The School for Field Studies
100 Cummings Center
Suite 534-G
Beverly, MA 1915

978-741-3567
800-989-4418; *Fax:* 978-922-3835
jcramer@fieldstudies.org;
www.fieldstudies.org
Social Media: Facebook, Twitter, LinkedIn, YouTube, Google+, Flickr

Terry Andreas, Chairman Of Board
James A. Cramer, President
Leslie Granese, B.A, Vice President
Carrie Camp, B.S, Chief Finance Officer
Yizette Colon, M.B.A, Accounting Manager

Creates transformative study abroad experiences through field-basedlearning and research.
Founded in: 1980

7394 The Wilderness Society
1615 M St NW
Washington, DC 20036-3258

202-833-2300
800-843-9453; *Fax:* 202-429-3945
member@tws.org
wilderness.org
Social Media: Facebook, Twitter, LinkedIn, Pinterest, YouTube

Jamie Williams, President
Thomas Tepper, VP, Finance & Administration
Melyssa Watson, Vice President, Conservation
Kitty Thomas, VP, Communications & Marketing
Ame Hellman, VP, Philanthropy

An American nonprofit organization that is dedicated to protecting wilderness areas as national public lands in the United States.
200M Members
Founded in: 1935

7395 Union of Concerned Scientists
Two Brattle Sq.
Cambridge, MA 02138-3780

617-547-5552; *Fax:* 617-864-9405;
www.ucsusa.org
Social Media: Facebook, Twitter, Google+

James J. McCarthy, Chair
Peter A. Bradford, Vice Chair
James S. Hoyte, Treasurer
Thomas H. Stone, Secretary
Kenneth Kimmell, President

A nonprofit science advocacy organization based in the United States.

7396 United Association of Used Oil Services
318 Newman Road
Sebring, FL 33870-6702

941-655-3880
800-877-4356

Established to be an effective presence in dealing with regulations and to provide a network for those with an interest in the collection and proper disposition of used lubricating oils.
Founded in: 1987

7397 Water Environment Federation
601 Wythe St
Alexandria, VA 22314-1994

703-684-2400
800-666-0206; *Fax:* 703-684-2492
inquiry@wef.org; www.wef.org
Social Media: Facebook, Twitter

Paul Bowen, President
Rick Warner, President-Elect
Jenny Hartfelder, Vice President
Ed McCormick, Immediate Past President
Ralph Exton, Treasurer

Supports those involved in issues that affect the international water environment.
79 Members
ISSN: 1044-9943
Founded in: 1928

7398 Water Quality Association
4151 Naperville Rd
Lisle, IL 60532-3696

630-505-0160; *Fax:* 630-505-9637
wqa@wqa.org; www.wqa.org
Social Media: Facebook, Twitter, YouTube

David Westman, MBA, CAE, CPA, Interim Executive Director
Pauli Undesser, MWS, Deputy Executive Director
Ken G. Kabira, Associate Executive Director
Susan Barkach, Business Operations Director
Larry Deutsch, Marketing & Communications Director

An international, nonprofit trade association representing retail/dealers and manufacturer/suppliers in the point of use/entry water quality improvement industry. Membership benefits and services include technical and scientific information, educational seminars and home correspondence course books, professional certification and discount services.
2.5M Members
Founded in: 1974

7399 Wilderness Society
1615 M St NW
Washington, DC 20036-3258

202-833-2300
800-843-9453; *Fax:* 202-429-3945
member@tws.org; www.wilderness.org
Social Media: Facebook, Twitter, LinkedIn, Pinterest, YouTube

Jamie Williams, President
Thomas Tepper, VP, Finance & Administration
Melyssa Watson, Vice President, Conservation
Kitty Thomas, VP, Communications & Marketing
Ame Hellman, VP, Philanthropy

Establishes the land ethic as a basic element of the American culture and educates people on the importance of wilderness preservation and land protection.
200M Members
Founded in: 1935
Mailing list available for rent: 178000 names at $90 per M

7400 Wildlife Conservation Society
2300 Southern Boulevard
Bronx, NY 10460

718-220-5100; *Fax:* 718-584-2625
membership@wcs.org; www.wcs.org
Social Media: Facebook, Twitter, YouTube, Google+, Instagram

Ward W. Woods, Chair
Edith McBean, Vice Chair
Gordon B. Pattee, Vice Chair
Brian J. Heidtke, Treasurer
Andrew H. Tisch, Secretary

Supports all those involved in the conservation of wildlife, especially the most rare and endangered species.

7401 **Wildlife Habitat Council**
8737 Colesville Road
Suite 800
Silver Spring, MD 20910

301-588-8994; *Fax:* 301-588-4629
whc@wildlifehc.org; www.wildlifehc.org
Social Media: Facebook, Twitter, LinkedIn, YouTube, Flickr

Margaret O'Gorman, President
Josiane Bonneau, Sr. Director
Linda Duvall, Director, Finance & HR
Monica Keller, Director, Marketing & Comm.
Thelma Redick, Sr. Director

Supports corporate, government and conservation leaders from around the globe involved in environmental stewardship.
120+ Members
Founded in: 1988

7402 **Wildlife Management Institute**
4426 VT Route 215N
Cabot, VT 05647

802-563-2087; *Fax:* 802-563-2157
wmisw@together.net;
www.wildlifemanagementinstitute.org

Richard E McCabe, Executive VP
Scot J Williamson, VP
Carol J Peddicord, Finance Manager
Robert L Byrne, Wildlife Program Coordinator
Ronald R Helinski, Conservation Policy Specialist

Supports all those involved with the challenges of modern conservation.

7403 **Wildlife Society**
5410 Grosvenor Ln
Suite 200
Bethesda, MD 20814-2144

301-897-9770; *Fax:* 301-530-2471
tws@wildlife.org; www.wildlife.org
Social Media: Facebook, Twitter, LinkedIn

Michael Hutchins, Executive Director
Laura Bies, Director, Government Affairs
Jane Jorgensen, Office and Finance Manager
Yanin Walker, Operations Manager

Supports all those involved in wildlife conservation, including wildlife artists, environmental consultants, conservation groups, scientific associations and natural resource companies, industry groups and government agencies.
9000 Members
Founded in: 1937

7404 **Women's Council on Energy and the Environment**
PO Box 33211
Washington, DC 20033-0211

202-997-4512; *Fax:* 202-478-2098;
www.wcee.org
Social Media: Facebook, Twitter, Pinterest

Robin Cantor, President
Mary Brosnan-Sell, Vice President
Alice Grabowski, Secretary
Barbara Tyran, Treasurer
Joyce Chandran, Executive Director

Supports women involved in the environmental community with education, research, new trend information and several publications.

7405 **World Research Foundation**
PO Box 20828
Sedona, AZ 86341

928-284-3300; *Fax:* 928-284-3530
info@wrf.org; www.wrf.org
Social Media: Facebook, Twitter, Google+

Steven A Ross, President

A unique, international, health information network, so that people could be informed of all available treatments around the world, and so that they could have the freedom to choose, based on complete and in-depth information.
41000 Members
Founded in: 1984

7406 **World Resources Institute**
10 G St NE
Suite 800
Washington, DC 20002-4252

202-729-7600; *Fax:* 202-729-7686
front@wri.org
wri.org
Social Media: Facebook, Twitter, LinkedIn, YouTube, RSS

James A. Harmon, Chairman
Harriet C. Babbitt, Vice Chair
Susan Tierney, Vice Chair
Afsaneh M. Beschloss, President & CEO
Frances Beinecke, Former President

Compiles information, conducts research, publishes the Environmental Almanac and more.
Founded in: 1982

7407 **World Society for the Protection of Animals**
Nelson Tower Building
450 Seventh Avenue, 31st Floor
New York, NY 10123

646-783-2200; *Fax:* 212-564-4250
info@worldanimalprotection.us.org;
www.worldanimalprotection.org
Social Media: Facebook, Twitter, YouTube

Robert S. Cummings, President
John Bowen, Secretary
Carter Luke, Treasurer

International animal protection news reports. Lobbies for effective animal welfare laws and provides educational material.
12 Members

7408 **World Wildlife Fund**
1250 24th Street, NW
Washington, DC 20037

800-963-0993
membership@wwfus.org;
www.worldwildlife.org
Social Media: Facebook, Twitter, YouTube, Instagram, Google+

Neville Isdell, Chair
Carter Roberts, President & CEO
Margaret Ackerley, Senior VP & general Counsel
Brad Ack, Senior VP, Oceans
Suzanne Apple, Senior VP, Pvt Sector Engagement

Supports all those involved in maintaining wildlife and their environment. Monitors human development, and seeks to influence public opinion and policy makers in favor of ecologically sound practices.
4M Members
Founded in: 1961

7409 **Worldwatch Institute**
1400 16th Street NW
Suite 430
Washington, DC 20036

202-745-8092; *Fax:* 202-478-2534
worldwatch@worldwatch.org;
www.worldwatch.org
Social Media: Facebook, Twitter, LinkedIn, RSS, YouTube, Flickr

Ed Groark, Chair
Robert Charles Friese, Vice Chair
John Robbins, Treasurer
Nancy Hitz, Secretary
Barbara Fallin, Dir., Finance & Administration

Analyzes interdisciplinary environmental data from around the world, providing information on how to build a sustainable society.
Founded in: 1974

Newsletters

7410 **AEESP Newsletter**
2303 Naples Court
Champaign, IL 61822

217-398-6969; *Fax:* 217-355-9232;
www.aeesp.org

Joanne Fetzner, Business Secretary

Official newsletter of the Association of Environmental Engineering and Science Professors. Topics cover the scope and diversity of challenges faced in environmental engineering and science.
Frequency: Quarterly

7411 **AEG News**
Assn. of Environmental & Engineering Geologists
1100-H Brandywine Boulevard
Suite 575
Zanesville, OH 43701

303-757-2926
844-331-7867; *Fax:* 740-452-2552
aeg@aegweb.org; www.aegweb.org
Social Media: Facebook, Twitter

Dale C. Andrews, President
Kathy Troost, Vice President
Kevin Richard, Treasurer
Cynthia Palomares, Secretary

Connecting Professionals, Practice and the Public.
3000 Members
Founded in: 1957
Mailing list available for rent: 3000 names at $100 per M

7412 **AERE Newsletter**
Association of Environmental and Resource
1616 P St Nw
Suite 400
Washington, DC 20036-1434

202-328-5157; *Fax:* 202-939-3460
voigt@rff.org; www.aere.org

Marilyn Voigt, Executive Secretary
Ralph Metts, President

Includes policy essays, meeting announcements, calls for papers, new publications, research reports, position announcements and other information of interest to AERE members and environmental economists in general.
Frequency: Semi-Annual

7413 **AIH Bulletin**
American Institute of Hydrology
1230 Lincold Drive
Carbondale, IL 62901

618-453-7809
aih@engr.siu.edu; www.aihydrology.org

Cathy Lipsett, Owner
Cathryn Seaburn, Manager

Newsletter for the American Institute of Hydrology, providing information designed to improve professional skills and abilities of its members, the professional community and the public at large.
Frequency: Quarterly

7414 **APLIC Communicator**
Family Health International Library
PO Box 13950
Research Triangle Park, NC 27709

919-447-7040; www.aplici.org

Claire Twose, President
Lori Rosman, Vice-President
Joann Donatiello, Treasurer

Read by population and reproductive health information specialists, librarians, and documentalists.
Frequency: Annual

7415 ASBPA Newsletter
American Shore & Beach Preservation Association
5460 Beaujolais ch Road
Fort Myers, FL 33919
239-489-2616; *Fax:* 239-362-9771
exdir@asbpa.org; www.asbpa.org
Social Media: Facebook, Twitter
Harry Simmons, President
Nicole Elko, Secretary
Brad Pickel, Treasurer
Kate Gooderham, Editor
Federal, state and local government agencies and individuals interested in conservation, development and restoration of beaches and shorefronts.
1M Members
Founded in: 1926

7416 ASEH News
American Society for Environmental History
UW Interdisciplinary Arts and Sciences Program
1900 Commerce Street
Tacoma, WA 98402
206-343-0226; *Fax:* 206-343-0249
director@aseh.net; www.aseh.net
John McNeill, President
Gregg Mitman, Vice President/ President Elect
Ellen Stroud, Secretary
Mark Madison, Treasurer
Updated and timely information on current environmental issues and their historical background, as well as Society news and events.
1200 Members
Founded in: 1976

7417 ASFE Newslog
ASFE/The Geoprofessional Business Association
8811 Colesville Rd
Suite G106
Silver Springs, MD 20910-4343
301-565-2733; *Fax:* 301-589-2017
info@asfe.org; www.asfe.org
John P Bachner, Executive VP
Information on geo professional, environmental, and civil engineering firms. Past issues are available through the online store. Electronic copies are always free to members.
Cost: $240.00
16 Pages
Frequency: 6/Year
Circulation: 5000

7418 ATTRAnews
National Center for Appropriate Technology
3040 Continental Drive
PO Box 3838
Butte, MT 59702
406-494-4572
800-275-6228; *Fax:* 406-494-2905;
www.ncat.org
Social Media: Facebook, Twitter, LinkedIn
Eugene Brady, Chairman
Kathleen Hadley, Executive Director
ATTRAnews brings you up to date on the latest developments in sustainable agriculture, what's happening at the USDA and with Sustainable Agriculture Working Groups around the country. ATTRAnews features events and opportunities in sustainable agriculture, information on funding and financing, and it keeps you current on programs and policies that can affect your future.
Frequency: 6x/Year
Founded in: 1976

7419 Advisor
Great Lakes Commission
2805 S Industrial Hwy
Suite 100
Ann Arbor, MI 48104-6791
734-971-9135; *Fax:* 734-971-9150;
www.glc.org
Tim Eder, Executive Director
Cook Havtrkamp, Author
Covers economic and environmental issues of the Great Lakes region with a special focus on activities of the Great Lakes Commission.
12 Pages
Frequency: Quarterly
Founded in: 1955
Printed in one color on matte stock

7420 Air Water Pollution Report's Environment Week
Business Publishers
8737 Colesville Road
Suite 1100
Silver Spring, MD 20910-3928
301-876-6300
800-274-6737; *Fax:* 301-589-8493
custserv@bpinews.com; www.bpinews.com
Leonard A Eiserer, Publisher
Beth Early, Operations Director
David Goeller, Editor
Provides a balanced, insightful update on the week's most important environmental news from Washington, D.C.
Cost: $595.00
Frequency: Weekly
Founded in: 1963

7421 Annual Research Program Report
National Institutes for Water Resources
niwr.net
Paul Joseph Godfrey, PhD, Executive Director

7422 Aquatic Plant News
Aquatic Plant Management Society
PO Box 821265
Vicksburg, MS 39182-1265
Fax: 601-634-5502
dpetty@ndrsite.com; www.apms.org
Social Media: Facebook, LinkedIn
Linda Nelson, President
Terry Goldsby, VP
Sherry Whitaker, Treasurer
Aquatic Plant News is produced 3 times each year, and is distributed primarily by email.
Frequency: 3x/Year
Founded in: 1961

7423 Asbestos & Lead Abatement Report
Business Publishers
8737 Colesville Road
Suite 1100
Silver Spring, MD 20910-3928
301-876-6300
800-274-6737; *Fax:* 301-589-8493
custserv@bpinews.com; www.bpinews.com
Leonard Eiserer, Publisher
Contains articles on regulation compliance, environmental trends, and business opportunities.
Cost: $382.00
Frequency: Monthly
Founded in: 1963

7424 BNA's Environmental Compliance Bulletin
Bureau of National Affairs
1801 S Bell St
Arlington, VA 22202-4501
703-341-3000
800-372-1033; *Fax:* 800-253-0332
customercare@bna.com; www.bnabooks.com
Paul N Wojcik, CEO
Gregory C McCaffery, President
Water and air pollution, waste management and regulatory updates, as well as a summary of selected regulatory actions and a list of key environmental compliance dates.
Cost: $649.00
Frequency: Annual+
Founded in: 1929

7425 BankNotes
Environmental Bankers Association
510 King St
Suite 410
Alexandria, VA 22314-3212
703-549-0977; *Fax:* 703-548-5945
eba@envirobank.org; www.envirobank.org
Rick Ferguson, President
Sharon Valverde, Vice President
Scott Beckerman, Treasurer
Stephen Richardson, Secretary
Timely information on the EBA, read by bank and non-bank financial institutions, insurers, asset management firms and those who provide services to them. Covers environmental risk issues, risk management, development, and due diligence policies and procedures.
Frequency: Bi-Monthly

7426 Biosolids Technical Bulletin
Water Environment Federation
601 Wythe St
Alexandria, VA 22314-1994
800-666-0206; *Fax:* 703-684-2492;
www.wef.org
Social Media: Facebook, Twitter
Matt Bond, President
Cordell Samuels, President-Elect
Sandra Ralston, Vice President
Chris Browning, Treasurer
Jeff Eger, Secretary and Executive Director
A must have for anyone involved in residuals and biosolids management. The latest treatment processes, odor management, beneficial use options, environmental management systems, or public outreach approaches.
79 Members
ISSN: 1044-9943
Founded in: 1928

7427 Bulletins
World Research Foundation
41 Bell Rock Plz
Sedona, AZ 86351-8804
928-284-3300; *Fax:* 928-284-3530
laverne@wrf.org; www.wrf.org
Steven A Ross, President
Updates on recent research including topics involving health information pertinent to the World Research Foundation.
Frequency: Quarterly

7428 CCA Newsletter
Coastal Conservation Association
6919 Portwest Dr
Suite 100
Houston, TX 77024-8049
713-626-4234
800-201-FISH; *Fax:* 713-626-5852
ccantl@joincca.org; www.joincca.org
Social Media: Twitter
David Cummins, President

Contains timely updates from CCA state chapters and bulletins on developing fisheries issues.
85000 Members
Founded in: 1977

7429 CCHEST Newsletter
Council on Certification of Health, Environmental
2301 W. Bradley Avenue
Champaign, IL 61821

217-359-9263; *Fax:* 217-359-0055
cchest@cchest.org; www.cchest.org
Social Media: Facebook, Twitter, LinkedIn

Margaret M. Carroll, President
Carl W. Heinlein, Vice President
Emory E. Knowles III, Treasurer

Keeps members up to date on events, OSHA news and the latest safety courses.
Frequency: Annual
Mailing list available for rent: 20,000 names

7430 Capitol Connect
Society of Chemical Manufacturers & Affiliates
1850 M St Nw
Suite 700
Washington, DC 20036-5803

202-721-4100; *Fax:* 202-296-8120
info@socma.org; www.socma.org

Larry Brotherton, Ph.D., Chair
Dave Hurder, Vice Chair
Davide DeCuir, Treasurer
J. Steel Hutchinson, Secretary

Government relations newsletter covering a range of environmental, safety, security, chemicals management and trade topics.
10 Pages
Frequency: Bi-Weekly

7431 ChemStewards
Society of Chemical Manufacturers & Affiliates
1850 M St Nw
Suite 700
Washington, DC 20036-5803

202-721-4100; *Fax:* 202-296-8120
info@socma.org; www.socma.org

Larry Brotherton, Ph.D., Chair
Dave Hurder, Vice Chair
Davide DeCuir, Treasurer
J. Steel Hutchinson, Secretary

e-Newsletter focusing on ChemStewards Training Opportunities, upcoming events, and the latest program news.
10 Pages
Frequency: Bi-Weekly

7432 Clean Water Report
CJE Associates
Silver Spring, MD 20910-3928

301-589-5103
800-274-6737; *Fax:* 301-589-8493
custserv@bpinews.com; www.bpinews.com

Follows the latest news from the EPA, Congress, the states, the courts, and private industry. A key information source for environmental professionals, covering the important issues of ground and drinking water, wastewater treatment, wetlands, drought, coastal protection, non-point source pollution, agrichemical contamination and more.
8 Pages

7433 Climate Change News
Environmental & Energy Study Institute
122 C Street NW
Suite 630
Washington, DC 20001

202-628-1400; *Fax:* 202-628-1825
eesi@eesi.org; www.eesi.org
Social Media: Facebook, Twitter, YouTube

Jared Blum, Board Chair
Shelley Fidler, Board Treasurer
Richard L. Ottinger, Board Chair Emeritus

Recounts the top climate science, business, and politics stories of the week and includes a list of upcoming events and pending federal legislation.
Founded in: 1984

7434 Composting News
McEntee Media Corporation
9815 Hazelwood Ave
Strongsville, OH 44149-2305

440-238-6603; *Fax:* 440-238-6712
ken@recycle.cc; www.recycle.cc

Ken Mc Entee, Owner

The latest in composting, wood waste recycling and organics management in a monthly newsletter.
Cost: $83.00
Frequency: Monthly
Circulation: 2000
Founded in: 1990

7435 Conservation Commission News
New Hampshire Association of Conservation Comm.
54 Portsmouth Street
Concord, NH 03301-5486

603-225-3431; *Fax:* 603-228-0423

Marjory Swope, Publisher

Encourage conservation and appropriate use of New Hampshire's natural resources by providing assistance to New Hampshire's municipal conservation commissions and by facilitating communication among commissions and between commissions and other public and private agencies involved in conservation.
Cost: $5.00
8 Pages
Frequency: Quarterly
Circulation: 1,650
Printed in one color on matte stock

7436 Convention Proceedings
Society for Human Ecology
College of the Atlantic
105 Eden Street
Bar Harbor, ME 04609-0180

207-288-5015; *Fax:* 207-288-3780
carter@ecology.coa.edu;
www.societyforhumanecology.org

Barbara Carter, Assistant to Executive Director

7437 Cosecha Mensual
National Center for Appropriate Technology
3040 Continental Drive
PO Box 3838
Butte, MT 59702

406-494-4572
800-275-6228; *Fax:* 406-494-2905;
www.ncat.org
Social Media: Facebook, Twitter, LinkedIn

Eugene Brady, Chairman
Kathleen Hadley, Executive Director

NCAT's Spanish-language electronic newsletter on sustainable agriculture. Subscribers enjoy news items and reviews of Spanish-language resources.
Frequency: Monthly
Founded in: 1976

7438 Council on Women in Energy and Environmental Leadership Newsletter
Association of Energy Engineers
4025 Pleasantdale Rd
Suite 420
Atlanta, GA 30340-4264

770-447-5083; *Fax:* 770-446-3969
info@aeecenter.org; www.aeecenter.org
Social Media: Facebook, Twitter, LinkedIn, YouTube

Eric A. Woodroof, President
Gary Hogsett, President Elect
Bill Younger, Secretary
Paul Goodman, C.P.A., Treasurer

Addressing the high cost of energy, present and future sources of energy, and the impact of energy on the environment.
8.2M Members
Founded in: 1977

7439 Daily Environment Report
Bureau of National Affairs
1801 S Bell St
Arlington, VA 22202-4501

703-341-3000
800-372-1033; *Fax:* 800-253-0332
customercare@bna.com; www.bnabooks.com

Paul N Wojcik, CEO
Gregory C McCaffery, President

A 40-page daily report providing comprehensive, in-depth coverage of national and international environmental news. Each issue contains summaries of the top news stories, articles, and in-brief items, and a journal of meetings, agency activities, hearings and legal proceedings. Coverage includes air and water pollution, hazardous substances, and hazardous waste, solid waste, oil spills, gas drilling, pollution prevention, impact statements and budget matters.
Cost: $ 3537.00
40 Pages
Frequency: Daily
ISSN: 1060-2976

7440 Digital Traveler
International Ecotourism Society
733 15th Street NW
Suite 1000
Washington, DC 20005

202-547-9203; *Fax:* 202-387-7915;
www.ecotourism.org

Martha Honey, Executive Director
Amos Bien, Director International Programs
Neal Inamdar, Director Finance/Administration

Regular updates about TIES work and programs.
Frequency: Monthly

7441 E&P Environment
Pasha Publications
1616 N Fort Myer Dr
Suite 1000
Arlington, VA 22209-3107

703-528-1244
800-424-2908; *Fax:* 703-528-1253;
www.newsletteraccess.com

Harry Baisden, Group Publisher
Jerry Grisham, Editor

Reports on environmental regulations, advances in technology and litigation aimed specifically at the exploration and production segments of the oil and gas industry.
Cost: $395.00

7442 E-Scrap News
Resource Recycling
PO Box 42270
Portland, OR 97242-270

503-233-1305; *Fax:* 503-233-1356
info@resource-recycling.com;
www.resource-recycling.com

Jerry Powell, Publisher/Editor
Andrew Santosusso, Managing Editor
Betsy Loncar, Circulation Director

Monthly newsletter covering all aspects of recovering, recycling, and managing electronics scrap. Coverage includes market prices and trends, collection events, product stewardship developments and global trends.
Cost: $99.00
6 Pages
Frequency: Monthly
Circulation: 1000
ISSN: 1536-3856
Founded in: 1983
Mailing list available for rent: 40,000 names at $100 per M
Printed in 2 colors on matte stock

7443 ECOMOD Newsletter
International Society for Ecological Modelling
University of California, Animal Sciences Dept
One Shields Avenue
Davis, CA 95616-8521
530-752-5362; *Fax:* 530-752-0175;
www.isemna.org
Wolfgang Pittroff, Secretary-General
Information on conferences, workshops and symposia that promote the systems philosophy in ecological research and teaching. Members frequently contribute articles.
Frequency: Quarterly

7444 EH&S Software News Online
Donley Technology
PO Box 152
Colonial Beach, VA 22443-152
804-224-9427
800-201-1595; *Fax:* 804-224-7958;
www.ehssoftwarenews.com
John Donley, Editor
Reports on news and upgraded software products, database, and on-line systems from commercial developers and government resources.
Cost: $125.00
Founded in: 1988

7445 EMS Newsletter
Environmental Mutagen Society
1821 Michael Faraday Drive
Suite 300
Reston, VA 20190
703-438-8220; *Fax:* 703-438-3113
emshq@ems-us.org; www.ems-ph.org
Kathleen Hill, Editor
Barbara Parsons, Editor
Cathy Klein, Editor
Current scientific research, policies, and guidelines for the causes and consequences of damage to the genome and epigenome.
Frequency: Bi-Annual

7446 Economic Opportunity Report
Business Publishers
2222 Sedwick Dr
Suite 101
Durham, NC 27713
800-223-8720; *Fax:* 800-508-2592
custserv@bpinews.com; www.bpinews.com
Antipoverty news coverage and analysis which gives insight into developments that affect social programs.
Cost: $383.00
Frequency: Weekly

7447 Environment Reporter
Bureau of National Affairs
1801 S Bell St
Arlington, VA 22202-4501
703-341-3000
800-372-1033; *Fax:* 800-253-0332
customercare@bna.com; www.bnabooks.com
Paul N Wojcik, CEO
Gregory C McCaffery, President
A weekly notification and reference service covering the full-spectrum of legislative, administrative, judicial, industrial and technological developments affecting pollution control and environmental protection.
Cost: $3776.00
Frequency: Weekly
ISSN: 0013-9211
Founded in: 1929

7448 Environmental Design Research Association Newsletter
Environmental Design Research Association
PO Box 7146
Edmond, OK 73083-7146
405-330-4863; *Fax:* 405-330-4150
edra@telepath.com; www.edra.org
Janet Singer, Executive Director
Document collection includes pdfs of full papers that have appeared in the annual EDRA conference proceedings.
Frequency: Annual

7449 Environmental Engineers and Managers Institute Newsletter
Association of Energy Engineers
4025 Pleasantdale Rd
Suite 420
Atlanta, GA 30340-4264
770-447-5083; *Fax:* 770-446-3969
info@aeecenter.org; www.aeecenter.org
Social Media: Facebook, Twitter, LinkedIn, YouTube
Eric A. Woodroof, President
Gary Hogsett, President Elect
Bill Younger, Secretary
Paul Goodman, C.P.A., Treasurer
Keeps members ahead on trends, upcoming conferences, industry leaders, jobs, relevant publications and more.
8.2M Members
Founded in: 1977

7450 Environmental Health Newsletter
International Lead Zinc Research Organization
2525 Meridian Parkway, Suite 100
PO Box 12036
Durham, NC 27713
919-361-4647; *Fax:* 919-361-1957;
www.ilzro.org
Stephen Wilkinson, President
Frank Goodwin, VP Materials Sciences
Scott Mooneyham, Treasurer
Rob Putnam, Director Communications
Information on environmental health sciences, use of technology, rules, and public education.
Frequency: Quarterly

7451 Environmental Nutrition
52 Riverside Drive
Suite 15A
New York, NY 10024
212-362-0424
800-424-7887; *Fax:* 212-362-2066
betty@environmentalnutrition.com;
www.environmentalnutrition.com
Betty Goldblatt, Publisher
Susan Male Smith, Editor
Monthly nutrition newsletter on nutrition and health. Written and edited by registered dietitians.
Cost: $24.00
Frequency: Monthly
Circulation: 50000
Founded in: 1977
Printed in 2 colors on matte stock

7452 Environmental Policy Alert
Inside Washington Publishers
1919 S Eads St
Suite 201
Arlington, VA 22202-3028
703-418-3981
800-424-9068; *Fax:* 703-416-8543;
www.iwpnews.com
Alan Sosenko, Owner
Adresses the legislative news and provides reports on the federal environmental policy process.
Cost: $560.00
Founded in: 1980

7453 Environmental Problems & Remediation
InfoTeam
PO Box 15640
Plantation, FL 33318-5640
954-473-9560; *Fax:* 954-473-0544
infoteamma@aol.com
Merton Allen, Editor
Concerned with environmental problems and effects, the methods and approaches for mitigation and remediation. Covers air pollution; surface and ground water pollution; wastewater; soil contamination; waste recycling; medical wastes; landfills and waste sites; stack gases; combustion and incineration; earth warming and more.

7454 Environmental Regulatory Advisor
JJ Keller
3003 W Breezewood Lane
Neenah, WI 54956-368
920-722-2848
800-327-6868; *Fax:* 800-727-7516
sales@jjkeller.com; www.jjkeller.com
Webb Shaw, Editor
Robert Keller, CEO
Covers developments at the EPA.
Founded in: 1953

7455 Environotes Newsletter
Federation of Environmental Technologists
PO Box 624
Slinger, WI 53086-0624
414-540-0070; *Fax:* 262-644-7106
info@fetinc.org; www.fetinc.org
Triese Haase, Administrator
Educating and Developing Excellence in Environmental Professionals
Frequency: Monthly

7456 Facility Managers Institute Newsletter
Association of Energy Engineers
4025 Pleasantdale Rd
Suite 420
Atlanta, GA 30340-4264
770-447-5083; *Fax:* 770-446-3969
info@aeecenter.org; www.aeecenter.org
Social Media: Facebook, Twitter, LinkedIn, YouTube
Eric A. Woodroof, President
Gary Hogsett, President Elect
Bill Younger, Secretary
Paul Goodman, C.P.A., Treasurer
Online newsletter addresses subjects such as the Integrated Approach to plant management, secu-

rity and safety issues, and overall facility management.
8.2M Members
Founded in: 1977

7457 Fibre Market News
GIE Media
4012 Bridge Avenue
Cleveland, OH 44113-3320

216-961-4130
800-456-0707; *Fax:* 216-961-0364

Richard Foster, Publisher
Daniel Sandoval, Editor

Covers the international paper recycling industry. Trends, markets, expansions, economics covered in an in-depth fashion. Also have weekly fax update covering late-breaking news.
Cost: $115.00
16 Pages
Frequency: BiWeekly

7458 ForeFront
National Registry of Environmental Professionals
PO Box 2099
Glenview, IL 60025

847-724-6631; *Fax:* 847-724-4223
nrep@nrep.org; www.nrep.org
Social Media: Facebook, Twitter, LinkedIn

Richard A Young, PhD, Executive Director
Edward Beck, PhD, Senior Director
Carol Schellinger, Director
Christopher Young, Director of Operation
Marie Hunter, Director

Information on continuing education, certification, and recognition for the professionals who help understand and study the environment.
20000 Members
Frequency: Bi-Monthly
Founded in: 1987

7459 Forest History Society
Forest History Society
701 William Vickers Ave
Durham, NC 27701-3162

919-682-9319; *Fax:* 919-682-2349
recluce2@duke.edu; www.foresthistory.org

Steven Anderson, President
R Scott Wallinger, Chairman
Yvan Hardy, Co-Vice Chairman
Mark Wilde, Co Vice-Chairman

Nonprofit educational institution that explores the history of the environment, forestry and conservation.

7460 From the Ground Up
Ecology Center
117 Division Street
Ann Arbor, MI 48104-1523

734-761-3186; *Fax:* 734-663-2414;
www.ecocenter.org

Ted Sylvester, Editor
Mike Wallad, President
Michael Garfield, Director

Progressive environmental news from southeast Michigan.
Cost: $30.00
32 Pages
Frequency: Monthly
Circulation: 5000
Founded in: 1970
Printed in 4 colors on newsprint stock

7461 GRAS Flavoring Substances 25
Flavor & Extract Manufacturers Association
1620 I Street NW
Suite 925
Washington, DC 20006

202-293-5800; *Fax:* 202-462-8998;
www.femaflavor.org
Social Media: YouTube, RSS Feed

Ed R. Hays, Ph.D., President
George C. Robinson, III, President Elect
Mark Scott, Treasurer
Arthur Schick, VP & Secretary
John Cox, Executive Director

The 25th publication by the Expert Panel of the Flavor and Extract Manufacturers Association provides an update on recent progress in the consideration of flavoring ingredients generally recognized as safe under the Food Additive Amendment.
123 Members
Frequency: Biennial
Founded in: 1909

7462 Global Environmental Change Report
Aspen Publishers
76 Ninth Avenue
7th Floor
New York, NY 10011
212-771-0600
800-638-8437; www.aspenlawschool.com

Mark Dorman, CEO
Gustavo Dobles, VP Operations

News and analysis of policy, science and industry developments in the areas of global warming and acid rain.
Cost: $447.00
Frequency: BiWeekly

7463 HazTECH News
Haztech News
14120 Huckleberry Lane
Silver Spring, MD 20906

301-871-3289; *Fax:* 301-460-5859

Cathy Dombrowski, Editor/Publisher

Describes technologies for hazardous waste management, site remediation, industrial wastewater treatment and VOC control.
Cost: $385.00
8 Pages
Frequency: Bi-Weekly
Printed in one color

7464 Hazardous Materials Intelligence Report
World Information Systems
PO Box 535
Cambridge, MA 02238-535

617-492-3312; *Fax:* 617-492-3312
members.aol.com/socejp/hmir.html

Richard S Golob, Publisher
Roger B Wilson Jr, Editor

Provides news analysis on environmental business, hazardous materials, waste management, pollution prevention and control. Covers regulations, legislation and court decisions, new technology, contract opportunities and awards and conference notices.
Cost: $375.00
Frequency: Weekly
Circulation: 50000

7465 Hazardous Materials Transportation
Bureau of National Affairs
1801 S Bell St
Arlington, VA 22202-4501

703-341-3000
800-372-1033
customercare@bna.com; www.bnabooks.com

Gregory C McCaffery, President
Paul N Wojcik, Chairman

A two-binder service containing the full-text of rules and regulations governing shipment of hazardous material by rail, air, ship, highway and pipeline, including DOT's Hazardous Materials Tables and EPA's rules for its hazardous waste tracking system.
Cost: $933.00
Frequency: Monthly

7466 Hazardous Waste Report
Aspen Publishers
7201 McKinney Cir
Frederick, MD 21704-8356

301-698-7100
800-638-8437; *Fax:* 212-597-0335;
www.aspenlawschool.com

Paul Gibson, Publisher
Sally Almeria, Editor
Bruce Becker, CEO/President
Tom Ceodi, Marketing

Provides information on industry news.
Cost: $875.00
8 Pages
Founded in: 1958

7467 Health Facts and Fears.com
American Council on Science and Health
1995 Broadway
2nd Floor
New York, NY 10023-5882

212-362-7044; *Fax:* 212-362-4919
acsh@acsh.org; www.acsh.org

Dr Elizabeth Whelan, President
Jeff Stier, Associate Director

Daily e-mail blast on the latest public health news and junk science scares.
Frequency: Weekly

7468 IES Quarterly Newsletter
International Ecotourism Society
733 15th Street NW
Suite 1000
Washington, DC 20005

202-547-9203; *Fax:* 202-387-7915;
www.ecotourism.org

Martha Honey, Executive Director
Amos Bien, Director International Programs
Neal Inamdar, Director Finance/Administration

Offering information on advocacy uniting communities, conservation, and sustainable travel.
Frequency: Quarterly

7469 Industrial Health & Hazards Update
InfoTeam
PO Box 15640
Plantation, FL 33318-5640

954-473-9560; *Fax:* 954-473-0544

Merton Allen, Editor

Covers occupational safety, health, hazards, and disease, mitigatioin and control of hazardous situations; waste recycling and treatment; environmental pollution and control; product safety and liability; fires and explosions; plant and computer security,; air pollution; surface and ground water; wastewater; soil gases; combustion and incineration; earth warming; ozone layer depletion; electromagnetic radiation; toxic materials; and many other related topics.

7470 Infectious Wastes News
National Solid Wastes Management Association
4301 Connecticut Ave Nw
Suite 300
Washington, DC 20008-2304

202-966-4701; *Fax:* 202-966-4818
wa@envasns.org; www.wasterecycling.org

Bruce Parker, President

A publication by the Environmental industry association geared toward providing readers with

timely news and information about the handling, transportation and disposal of infectious wastes.
Frequency: BiWeekly

7471 **Integrated Environmental Assessment and Management**
Society of Environmental Toxicology and Chemistry
1013 N 12th Ave
Pensacola, FL 32501-3306
850-437-1901; *Fax:* 850-469-9778
rparrish@setac.org; www.edwardjones.com
Rodney Parrish, Executive Director
Focuses on the application of science in environmental decision-making, regulation, and management, including aspects of policy and law, and the development of scientifically sound approaches to environmental problem solving.
Frequency: Quarterly

7472 **Integrated Waste Management**
1801 S Bell Street
Arlington, VA 22202
212-512-3916
800-372-1033; *Fax:* 212-512-2723;
www.bna.com
Gregory C McCaffery, President
Paul N Wojcik, Chairman
Articles geared toward integration of solid waste management.
Cost: $745.00
8 Pages
Frequency: BiWeekly

7473 **Interface Newsletter**
Society for Environmental Geochemistry and Health
4698 S Forrest Avenue
Springfield, MO 65810
417-885-1166; *Fax:* 417-881-6920
drbgwixson@wixson.com; www.segh.net
Bobby Wixson, Director Membership

7474 **International Environment Reporter**
Bureau of National Affairs
1801 S Bell St
Arlington, VA 22202-4501
703-341-3000
800-372-1033; *Fax:* 800-253-0332
customercare@bna.com; www.bnabooks.com
Gregory C McCaffrey, President
Paul N Wojcik, Chairman
A four-binder information and reference service covering international environmental law and developing policy in the major industrial nations.
Cost: $2555.00

7475 **Journal of Science and Sustainability**
National Registry of Environmental Professionals
PO Box 2099
Glenview, IL 60025
847-724-6631; *Fax:* 847-724-4223
nrep@nrep.org; www.nrep.org
Social Media: Facebook, Twitter, LinkedIn
Richard A Young, PhD, Executive Director
Edward Beck, PhD, Senior Director
Carol Schellinger, Director
Christopher Young, Director of Operation
Marie Hunter, Director
Digital journal serving sustainability professionals worldwide.
20000 Members
Frequency: Semi-Annual
Circulation: 50,000
Founded in: 1987

7476 **Marine Conservation News**
Center for Marine Conservation
2029 K Street
Washington, NW 20006
202-750-0574
800-519-1541; *Fax:* 202-872-0619;
www.cmc-ocean.org
Rose Bierce, Publisher
Roger Rufe, President
Stephanie Drea, VP Commun
Matt Schatzle, VP Membership & Development
Wanda Cantrell, Manager
Updates members of CMC on the organization projects and activities.
24 Pages
Frequency: Quarterly
Circulation: 100000
Printed in 2 colors on matte stock

7477 **McCoy's Hazardous Waste Regulatory Update**
McCoy & Associates
25107 Genesee Trail Road
Suite 200
Golden, CO 80228-4173
303-526-2674; *Fax:* 303-526-5471
info@mccoyseminars.com;
www.mccoyseminars.com/contact.cfm
Offers a complete text of the federal hazardous waste regulations, summaries, interpretations and indexes.
Founded in: 1983

7478 **McCoy's Regulatory Analysis Service**
McCoy & Associates
25107 Genesee Trail Road
Golden, CO 80401-5708
303-526-2674; *Fax:* 303-526-5471
info@mccoyseminars.com;
www.mccoyseminars.com
Provides timely, in-depth analyses of hazardous waste regulations within 10 working days after their publication in the Federal Register.
Cost: $550.00
Founded in: 1983

7479 **Mealey's Litigation Report: Insurance**
LexisNexis Mealey's
555 W 5th Avenue
Los Angeles, CA 90013
213-627-1130
mealeyinfo@lexisnexis.com;
www.lexisnexis.com/mealeys
Tom Hagy, VP/General Manager
Maureen McGuire, Editorial Director
Vivi Gorman, Editor
Shawn Rice, Co-Editor
The report tracks declaratory judgment actions regarding coverage for litigation arising from long-tail claims, including environmental contamination and latent damage and injury allegedly caused by asbestos, tox chemicals and fumes, lead, breast implants, medical devices, construction defects, and more. Key issues: allocation, occurrence, policy exclusion, choice of law, discovery, duty to defend, notice, trigger of coverage and known loss.
Founded in: 1984

7480 **Montana Green Power Update**
National Center for Appropriate Technology
3040 Continental Drive
PO Box 3838
Butte, MT 59702
406-494-4572
800-275-6228; *Fax:* 406-494-2905;
www.ncat.org
Social Media: Facebook, Twitter, LinkedIn
Eugene Brady, Chairman
Kathleen Hadley, Executive Director
This free monthly electronic newsletter contains the latest success stories in renewable energy development in the state of Montana, hot tips, information on financing and tax incentives, upcoming events, and links to stories from regional and national sources as featured on the Montana Green Power web site.
Frequency: Monthly
Founded in: 1976

7481 **Motor Carrier Safety Report, HAZMAT Transp ortation Report**
J.J. Keller & Associates, Inc.
3003 Breezewood Lane
PO Box 368
Neenah, WI 54957-0368
920-722-2848
800-327-6868; *Fax:* 800-727-7516
sales@jjkeller.com; www.jjkeller.com
Stephanie Hallman, Business Development
The nation's leader in risk and regulatory management solutions, including printed publications, videos, and online training for workplace safety, hazardous materials, transportation, human resources, and environmental safety.
Cost: $90.00
12 Pages
Frequency: Monthly
ISSN: 1056-3164
Founded in: 1953

7482 **NAESCO Newsletter**
National Association of Energy Service Companies
1615 M St NW
Suite 800
Washington, DC 20036-3213
202-822-0950; *Fax:* 202-822-0955
info@naesco.org; www.naesco.org
Terry E Singer, Executive Editor
Michael Hamilton, Marketing Manager
Mary Lee Berger-Hughes, Publisher
Targets energy service companies, electric and gas utilities amd other energy providers. Highlights industry news and features energy conservation.
Circulation: 200
Founded in: 1985

7483 **NCAT Action**
National Center for Appropriate Technology
3040 Continental Drive
PO Box 3838
Butte, MT 59702
406-494-4572
800-275-6228; *Fax:* 406-494-2905;
www.ncat.org
Social Media: Facebook, Twitter, LinkedIn
Eugene Brady, Chairman
Kathleen Hadley, Executive Director
Action is a quarterly newsletter featuring local solutions for a sustainable future. Each issue focuses on a different topic, providing information that will help you move toward a more sustainable lifesytle in your home and in your community. Action features thought-provoking commentary, informative news stories, and extensive resource lists compiled by NCAT's expert professional staff.
Frequency: Quarterly
Founded in: 1976

7484 **NORA News**
NORA: an Association of Responsible Recyclers
5965 Amber Ridge Rd
Haymarket, VA 20169-2623
703-753-4277; *Fax:* 703-753-2445
sparker@noranews.org; www.noranews.org
Scott Parker, Executive Director

7485 **National Association of Conservation Districts**
National Association of Conservation Districts
509 Capitol Ct. NE
Washington, DC 20002-4937

202-547-6223; *Fax:* 202-547-6450;
www.nacdnet.org
Krysta Harden, CEO
Bob Cordova, Second Vice President

Highlights forestry issues of importance to districts and to showcase district-related forestry projects and success stories. Funded through a cooperative agreement between NACD and the U.S. Forest Service.
Cost: $35.00
12 Pages
Frequency: Monthly
Circulation: 25000
Founded in: 1937

7486 **Nature's Voice**
National Resources Defense Council
40 W 20th St
New York, NY 10011-4231

212-727-2700; *Fax:* 212-727-1773
nrdcinfo@nrdc.org; www.nrdc.org
Social Media: Facebook, Twitter, YouTube

Frances Beinecke, President
Daniel R. Tishman, Chair
Frederick A.O. Schwarz Jr., Chair Emeritus
Adam Albright, Vice Chair
Patricia Bauman, Vice Chair

Environmental news and activism, using law, science and the support of more than 1 million members and online activists to protect the plante's wildlife and wild places and to ensure a healthy environment for all living things.
50000 Members
Founded in: 1970

7487 **Networker**
National Center for Appropriate Technology
3040 Continental Drive
PO Box 3838
Butte, MT 59702

406-494-4572
800-275-6228; *Fax:* 406-494-2905;
www.ncat.org
Social Media: Facebook, Twitter, LinkedIn

Eugene Brady, Chairman
Kathleen Hadley, Executive Director

The newsletter is compiled by the LIHEAP Clearinghouse, and NCAT project. Stories highlight state energy assistance program and low-income energy news.
Frequency: Quarterly
Founded in: 1976

7488 **News Flash**
National Association of Local Government
1333 New Hampshire Ave Nw
Suite 400
Washington, DC 20036-1532

202-887-4107; *Fax:* 202-393-2866
nalgep@spiegelmcd.com; www.nalgep.org

Kenneth E Brown, Executive Director
David Dickson, Projects Manager

Brings together noteworthy funding opportunities, conferences, legislative tracking on climate change and highlights projects completed on the federal or local level.
Frequency: Bi-Weekly

7489 **Noise Regulation Report**
Business Publishers
2222 Sedwick Dr
Suite 101
Durham, NC 27713

800-223-8720; *Fax:* 800-508-2592
custserv@bpinews.com; www.bpinews.com

Exclusive coverage of airport, highway, occupational and open space noise, noise control and mitigation issues.
Cost: $511.00
10 Pages
Frequency: 12 per year
Printed in on matte stock

7490 **Nuclear Monitor**
Nuclear Information & Resource Services
1424 16th Street NW
Suite 404
Washington, DC 20036-2239

202-328-0002; *Fax:* 202-462-2183
nirsnet@nirs.org; www.nirs.org
Social Media: Twitter, YouTube

Michael Mariotte, Editor
Linda Gunder, Media Manager

NIRS and WISE merged the Nuclear Monitor and WISE News Communique into a new Nuclear Monitor. Now available as an international edition.
Cost: $250.00
12 Pages
Frequency: 18 issues per y
Circulation: 1200
Founded in: 1978
Printed in one color on matte stock

7491 **Nuclear Waste News**
Business Publishers
2222 Sedwick Dr
Suite 101
Durham, NC 27713

800-223-8720; *Fax:* 800-508-2592
custserv@bpinews.com; www.bpinews.com

Worldwide coverage of the nuclear waste management industry including waste generation, packaging, transport, processing and disposal.
Cost: $697.00
10 Pages
Frequency: 25 per year
Mailing list available for rent
Printed in 2 colors on matte stock

7492 **Outdoor News Bulletin**
Wildlife Management Institute
4426 VT Route 215N
Cabot, VT 05647

802-563-2087; *Fax:* 802-563-2157
wmisw@together.net;
www.wildlifemanagementinstitute.org

Richard E McCabe, Executive VP
Scot J Williamson, VP
Carol J Peddicord, Finance Manager
Robert L Byrne, Wildlife Program Coordinator
Ronald R Helinski, Conservation Policy Specialist

Reports on select, significant issues, circumstances and other information that bear on the professional management of wildlife and related natural resources.

7493 **RESTORE**
Society for Ecological Restoration
1017 O Street NW
Washington, DC 20001

202-299-9518; *Fax:* 270-626-5485
info@ser.org; www.ser.org

Steve Whisenant, Chair
Cara R. Nelson, Vice Chair
Mary Travaglini, Treasurer
Alan Unwin, Secretary

Weekly e-bulletin. Contains articles of interest to people in the field of restoration ecology, and is an indispensable way to keep up with what's happening in the world of ecological restoration, rounding up all the latest, breaking news from around the world on a wide variety of restoration-related issues. Available in electronic form only.
Frequency: Semi-Annual

7494 **Recycling Markets**
NV Business Publishers Corporation
43 Main St
Avon By the Sea, NJ 07717-1051

732-502-0500; *Fax:* 732-502-9606;
www.nvpublications.com

Ted Vilardi, Owner
Anna Dutko, Managing Editor
Tom Vilardi, President/Publisher
Ted Vilardi Jr., Co-Publisher

Contains profiles on recycling mills, as well as large users and generators of recycled materials for the broker, dealers and processors of paper stock, scrap metal, plastics and glass.
Cost: $180.00
Frequency: Weekly
Circulation: 3315
Printed in 4 colors on newsprint stock

7495 **Resource Conservation & Recovery Act: A Guide to Compliance**
McCoy & Associates
13701 W Jewell Avenue
Suite 202
Lakewood, CO 80228-4173

303-870-0835; *Fax:* 303-989-7917

Drew McCoy, Publisher
Deborah McCoy, President

Land disposal restrictions for hazardous waste.
300 Pages
Frequency: Annual

7496 **Resource Development Newsletter**
University of Tennessee
PO Box 1071
Knoxville, TN 37996-1071

865-974-1000; *Fax:* 865-974-7448
rpdavis@utk.edu

Alan Barefield, Publisher

Community development information.
4 Pages
Frequency: Quarterly
Circulation: 2000
Founded in: 1794
Printed in one color on matte stock

7497 **Resource Recovery Report**
PO Box 3356
Warrenton, VA 20188-1956

540-347-4500
800-627-8913; *Fax:* 540-349-4540
rwill@coordgrp.com;
www.alexandriava.gov/resourcerecovery

Richard Will, Production Manager

Covers all alternatives to landfills, i.e., recycling, energy recovery, composting in North America, Government, industry, associations, universities, etc. are included.
Cost: $227.00
12 Pages
Frequency: Monthly
Mailing list available for rent: 12M names
Printed in one color on matte stock

7498 **SEG Extra**
Society of Exploration Geophysicists

8801 South Yale
Suite 500
Tulsa, OK 74137-3575

918-497-5500; *Fax:* 918-497-5557
web@seg.org; www.seg.org
Social Media: Facebook, Twitter, LinkedIn

Mary Fleming, Executive Director
Vladimir Grechka, Editor

eNewsletter, delivering the most relevant, up-to-date information pertaining directly to SEG members and stakeholders.
Founded in: 1930

7499 SOCMA Newsletter
Society of Chemical Manufacturers & Affiliates
1850 M St Nw
Suite 700
Washington, DC 20036-5803

202-721-4100; *Fax:* 202-296-8120
info@socma.org; www.socma.org

Larry Brotherton, Ph.D., Chair
Dave Hurder, Vice Chair
Davide DeCuir, Treasurer
J. Steel Hutchinson, Secretary

Provides the specialty, batch and custom chemical industry with the latest regulatory, legislative and commerce news in a convenient newsletter exclusively compiled for members.
10 Pages
Frequency: Bi-Weekly

7500 Salt & Highway Deicing Newsletter
Salt Institute
700 N Fairfax St
Suite 600
Alexandria, VA 22314-2085

703-549-4648; *Fax:* 703-548-2194
info@saltinstitute.org; www.saltinstitute.org

Richard L Hanneman, President
Tammy Goodwin, Director
Mark OKeefe, Director of Communications

A quarterly e-newsletter published by the Salt Institute that focuses on highway uses of salt.
Frequency: Quarterly
Circulation: 77000
Founded in: 1914
Printed in on glossy stock

7501 Salt and Trace Minerals Newsletter
Salt Institute
700 N Fairfax St
Suite 600
Alexandria, VA 22314-2085

703-549-4648; *Fax:* 703-548-2194
info@saltinstitute.org; www.saltinstitute.org

Richard L Hanneman, President

E-Newsletter containing information on animal nutrition.
Frequency: Quarterly
Circulation: 77000
Founded in: 1914
Printed in on glossy stock

7502 SmartBrief
American Wind Energy Association
1501 M Street NW
Suite 1000
Washington, DC 20005

202-383-2500; *Fax:* 202-383-2505
windmail@awea.org; www.awea.org
Social Media: Facebook, Twitter, YouTube

Ned Hall, Chair
Thomas Carnahan, Chair-Elect
Gabriel Alonso, Secretary
Don Furman, Treasurer
Vic Abate, Past Chair

Delivers quickly digestible summaries of the day's wind energy-related stories from across the media, keeps readers informed about the industry, and allows readers to stay on top of what's being said about it.
2400 Members

7503 Society Update
American Society of Safety Engineers
1800 E Oakton Street
Des Plaines, IL 60018

847-699-2929; *Fax:* 847-768-3434
customerservice@asse.org; www.asse.org
Social Media: Facebook

Terrie S. Norris, President
Richard A. Pollock, President Elect
Kathy Seabrook, Senior Vice President
Fred J. Fortman, Jr., Secretary & Executive Director
James D. Smith, Vice President, Finance

Highlights the latest Society news, activities, upcoming events and notable member achievements.
30000 Members
Founded in: 1911

7504 Society of Chemical Manufacturers & Affiliates Newsletter
1850 M St NW
Suite 700
Washington, DC 20036-5803

202-721-4100; *Fax:* 202-296-8120
info@socma.org; www.socma.org

Larry Brotherton, Ph.D., Chair
Dave Hurder, Vice Chair
Davide DeCuir, Treasurer
J. Steel Hutchinson, Secretary

Newsletter tailored to provide industry executives with the most up-to-date information on events hosted or sponsored by SOCMA.
10 Pages
Frequency: Bi-Weekly

7505 State Recycling Laws Update
Raymond Communications
5111 Berwin Road
Suite no#115
College Park, MD 20740

301-345-4237; *Fax:* 301-345-4768;
www.raymond.com

Lorah utter, Editor
Bruce Popka, Vice President of Communications
Allyn Weet, Circulation Manager

Contains analysis and reports, provides coverage of recycling legislation affecting business, as well as the outlook on future legislation across the states and Canada. Also publishes special reports on related topics, for example, Transportation Packaging and the Environment.
Cost: $367.00
Frequency: Monthly
Circulation: 200
Founded in: 1991

7506 Superfund Week
Pasha Publications
8737 Colesville Road
Suite 1100
Silver Spring, MD 20910-3928

301-589-5103
800-274-6737; *Fax:* 301-589-8493
custserv@bpinews.com; www.bpinews.com

Harry Baisden, Group Publisher
Michael Hopps, Editor

Reporting the most recent developments in Congress, the EPA, and other government offices affecting hazardous waste investigations and cleanups in the federal Superfund and RCRA programs. Contains progress reports on specific cleanup sites in federal and state programs.
Cost: $525.00
Frequency: Weekly
Founded in: 1963

7507 SurFACTS in Biomaterials
Surfaces in Biomaterials Foundation
1000 Westgate Drive
Suite 252
St Paul, MN 55114-8679

651-290-7487; *Fax:* 651-290-2266
memberservices@surfaces.org;
www.surfaces.org

Steven Goodman, Executive Editor
Janeyy Duntley, Managing Editor

Dedicated to exploring creative solutions to technical challenges at the BioInterface by fostering education and multidisciplinary cooperation among industrial, academic, clinical and regulatory communities.
Frequency: Bimonthly

7508 The Current
Women's Council on Energy and the Environment
PO Box 33211
Washington, DC 20033-0211

202-997-4512; *Fax:* 202-478-2098;
www.wcee.org
Social Media: Facebook, Twitter

Ronke Luke, President
Mary Brosnan-Sell, Secretary
Robin Cantor, Vice President
Alice Grabowski, Treasurer
Joyce Chandran, Executive Director

Keeps members up to date on energy and environmental issues to foster the professional development.

7509 The Dirt
Land and Water
Po Box 1197
Fort Dodge, IA 50501-1197

515-576-3191; *Fax:* 515-576-2606;
www.landandwater.com
Social Media: Facebook

Amy Dencklau, Publisher
Shanza Dencklau, Assistant Editor
Rasch M. Kenneth, President

eNewsletter including information relating to the erosion control and water management industry such as: feature stories, industry news, conferences, expert tips and video clips, new products and more. Striving to keep readers up-to-date on all current happenings and relevant information beyond the pages of Land and Water Magazine.
Cost: $20.00
72 Pages
Circulation: 20000
Founded in: 1959
Mailing list available for rent: 20M names
Printed in 4 colors on glossy stock

7510 The Forest Timeline
Forest History Society
701 William Vickers Ave
Durham, NC 27701-3162

919-682-9319; *Fax:* 919-682-2349
recluce2@duke.edu; www.foresthistory.org
Social Media: Facebook, Twitter

L. Michael Kelly, Chairman
Robert Healy, Co-Vice Chairman
Mark Wilde, Co-Vice Chairman
Henry I. Barclay III, Treasurer
Steven Anderson, Secretary & President

E-newsletter to keep the public informed of FHS news and activities.
2000 Members
Founded in: 1946

7511 The Networker
National Center for Appropriate Technology

3040 Continental Drive
PO Box 3838
Butte, MT 59702

406-494-4572
800-275-6228; *Fax:* 406-494-2905;
www.ncat.org
Social Media: Facebook, Twitter, LinkedIn

Gene Brady, Chairman
Randall Chapman, Vice Chairman
George Ortiz, Chairman Emeritus
Jeannie Jertson, Secretary
Brian Castelli, Treasurer

Compiled by the LIHEAP Clearinghouse, an NCAT project. Stories highlight state energy assistanc program and low-income energy news.
Founded in: 1976

7512 **The Resource**
National Association of Conservation Districts
509 Capitol Ct. NE
Washington, DC 20002-4937

202-547-6223; *Fax:* 202-547-6450;
www.nacdnet.org

Krysta Harden, CEO
Bob Cordova, Second Vice President

NACD's print publication provides in depth coverage of the association's recent activities and features columns by the NACD CEO and President, in addition to guest and partnership columns.
Cost: $35.00
12 Pages
Frequency: Monthly
Circulation: 25000
Founded in: 1937

7513 **The Soil Plant Analyst**
Soil and Plant Analysis Council
347 North Shores Circle
Windsor, CO 80550

970-686-5702
rmiller@lamar.colostate.edu;
www.spcouncil.com/

Rigas Karamanos, President
Robert Miller, Secretary/Treasurer
Rao Mylavarapu, Vice President

Quarterly newsletter dedicated to the Agricultural Laboratory Industry.
Cost: $80.00
Circulation: 250

7514 **WEF Highlights**
Water Environment Federation
601 Wythe St
Alexandria, VA 22314-1994

800-666-0206; *Fax:* 703-684-2492;
www.wef.org
Social Media: Facebook, Twitter

Matt Bond, President
Cordell Samuels, President-Elect
Sandra Ralston, Vice President
Chris Browning, Treasurer
Jeff Eger, Secretary and Executive Director

Covers current Federation activities, Member Association news, and items of concern to the water quality field.
79 Members
ISSN: 1044-9943
Founded in: 1928

7515 **Washington Environmental Protection Report**
Callahan Publications
PO Box 1173
Mc Lean, VA 22101-1173
703-356-1925; *Fax:* 703-356-9614
sue@newsletteraccess.com;
www.newsletteraccess.com

Vincent Callahan, Editor

Twice-monthly letter on contracting opportunities, legislation, research and development, and rules and regulations for the nation's environmental programs. The war on pollution, in all its forms, is coming to the forefront of federal priorities and could be the answer to the many economic problems facing America.
Cost: $190.00
8 Pages
Frequency: Bi-monthly
Founded in: 1990
Printed in one color

7516 **Waste Handling Equipment News**
Lee Publications
6113 Strate Highway 5
PO Box 121
Palatine Bridge, NY 13428
518-673-3237
800-218-5586; *Fax:* 518-673-2381
mstanley@leepub.com;
www.wastehandling.com

Fred Lee, Publisher
Matt Stanley, Sales Manager
Holly Rieser, Editor

Addresses equipment needs of owners and operating managers involved in construction demolition, asphalt/concrete recycling, wood waste recycling, scrap metal recycling and composting. Every issue features editorial on new equipment, equipment adaptations, site stories, and news focused on our targeted segment of the recycling industry.
Frequency: Monthly
Circulation: 14000
Founded in: 1993
Printed in on newsprint stock

7517 **Waste News**
Crain Communications
1155 Gratiot Ave.
Detroit, MI 48207-2997

313-446-6000; www.crain.com

Keith Crain, Chairman
Rance Crain, President
Mary Kay Crain, Treasurer/Assistant Secretary
Merrilee P. Crain, Secretary/Assistant Treasurer

Trade publication covering the solid waste industry.
Frequency: Bi-Weekly
Circulation: 52838
Founded in: 1995

7518 **Waste Recovery Report**
Icon: Information Concepts
211 S 45th St
Philadelphia, PA 19104-2995

215-349-6500; *Fax:* 215-349-6502
wasterec@aol.com; www.wrr.icodat.com

Alan Krigman, Publisher/Editor

Contains information on waste-to-energy, recycling, composting and other technologies.
Cost: $60.00
6 Pages
Frequency: Monthly
Circulation: 500
ISSN: 0889-0072
Founded in: 1975

7519 **Water Environment Laboratory Solutions**
Water Environment Federation
601 Wythe St
Alexandria, VA 22314-1994

800-666-0206; *Fax:* 703-684-2492;
www.wef.org
Social Media: Facebook, Twitter

Matt Bond, President
Cordell Samuels, President-Elect
Sandra Ralston, Vice President
Chris Browning, Treasurer
Jeff Eger, Secretary and Executive Director

Focuses on day-to-day concerns regarding equipment use, sample tracking, and quality control, as well as discussing certification issues, staff management approaches, and new and revised analytical methods.
79 Members
ISSN: 1044-9943
Founded in: 1928

7520 **Water Environment Regulation Watch**
Water Environment Federation
601 Wythe St
Alexandria, VA 22314-1994

800-666-0206; *Fax:* 703-684-2492;
www.wef.org
Social Media: Facebook, Twitter

Matt Bond, President
Cordell Samuels, President-Elect
Sandra Ralston, Vice President
Chris Browning, Treasurer
Jeff Eger, Secretary and Executive Director

Monthly snapshot of Washington's water quality activities. Provides concise reports of related bills, regulations, legal decisions, congressional hearings, and other federal government actions, following key issues from introduction to final determination.
79 Members
ISSN: 1044-9943
Founded in: 1928

7521 **Weather & Climate Report**
Nautilus Press
1056 National Press Building
Washington, DC 20045-2001

202-347-6643

John R Botzum, Editor

Reports on federal actions which impact weather, climate research and global changes in climate.

7522 **Weekly Harvest**
National Center for Appropriate Technology
3040 Continental Drive
PO Box 3838
Butte, MT 59702

406-494-4572
800-275-6228; *Fax:* 406-494-2905;
www.ncat.org
Social Media: Facebook, Twitter, LinkedIn

Eugene Brady, Chairman
Kathleen Hadley, Executive Director

This e-newsletter is a Web digest of sustainable agriculture news, resources, events and funding opportunities gleaned from the Internet and featured on the website.
Frequency: Weekly
Founded in: 1976

7523 **World Research News**
World Research Foundation
41 Bell Rock Plz
Sedona, AZ 86351-8804

928-284-3300; *Fax:* 928-284-3530
laverne@wrf.org; www.wrf.org

LaVerne Boeckman, Co-Founder
Steven Ross, Co-Founder

Health information that is collected, categorized and disseminated in an independent and unbiased manner. Including allopathic medicine alongside complementary and alternative medicine... ancient and traditional techniques and healing therapies as well as the latest medical technology.
Frequency: Quarterly

7524 **World Wildlife Fund: Focus**
World Wildlife

PO Box 97180
Washington, DC 20090-7180

202-293-4800; *Fax:* 202-293-9211;
www.worldwildlife.org

Kathryn S Fuller, CEO
Jennifer Seeger, Chief Financial Officer
Michael Bauer, Chief Financial Officer
Marcia Marsh, Chief Operating Officer

WWF projects are highlighted around the world in 450 national parks and nature reserves, with emphasis on coverage of programs and activities in the US.
8 Pages
Frequency: Monthly
Founded in: 1960

7525 **eNotes**
National Association of Conservation Districts
509 Capitol Ct. NE
Washington, DC 20002-4937

202-547-6223; *Fax:* 202-547-6450;
www.nacdnet.org

Krysta Harden, CEO
Bob Cordova, Second Vice President

NACD's weekly news briefs.
Cost: $35.00
12 Pages
Frequency: Monthly
Circulation: 25000
Founded in: 1937

Magazines & Journals

7526 **ACCA Insider**
Air Conditioning Contractors of America
2800 Shirlington Rd
Suite 300
Arlington, VA 22206-3607

703-575-4477
info@acca.org; www.acca.org
Social Media: Facebook, Twitter, LinkedIn, YouTube

Paul Stalknecht, President & CEO

Offering targeted news to ACCA members.

7527 **ASNT Annual Fall Conference**
American Society for Nondestructive Testing
1711 Arlingate Lane
PO Box 28518
Columbus, OH 43228

614-274-6003
800-222-2768; *Fax:* 614-274-6899;
www.asnt.org

Tim Jones, Senior Manager, Publications
Wayne Holliday, Executive Director

Research, reviews and information of nondestructive testing materials. Provides members and subscribers the latest news and technical information concerning this industry.
Cost: $75.00
12000 Members
90 Pages
Frequency: Monthly
Circulation: 13000
ISSN: 0025-5327
Founded in: 1942
Printed in 4 colors on glossy stock

7528 **Aerosol Science and Technology (AS&T)**
American Association for Aerosol Research
15000 Commerce Parkway
Suite C
Mount Laurel, NJ 08054

856-439-9080; *Fax:* 856-439-0525
info@aaar.org; www.aaar.org

Peter McMurry, Editor-In-Chief
Tami C Bond, Editor
Warren H Finlay, Editor

AS&T is the offficial journal of AAAR. It publishes the results of theoretical and experimental investigations into aerosol phenomena and closely related material as well as high-quality reports on fundamental and applied topics.
Cost: $1214.00

7529 **Agronomy Journal**
American Society of Agronomy
5585 Guilford Rd.
Madison, WI 53711-1086
608-273-8080; *Fax:* 608-273-2021
headquarters@sciencesocieties.org;
www.agronomy.org
Social Media: Facebook, Twitter, LinkedIn

Newell Kitchen, President
Kenneth Barbarick, President-Elect

Journal of agriculture and natural resource sciences. Articles convey original research in soil science, crop science, agroclimatology, agronomic modeling, production agriculture, instrumentation, and more.
10000 Members
Founded in: 1907

7530 **American Environmental Laboratory**
International Scientific Communications
30 Controls Drive
PO Box 870
Shelton, CT 06484-0870

203-926-9300; www.iscpubs.com

Brian Howard, Editor
Robert G Sweeny, Publisher

Laboratory activities, new equipment, and analysis and collection of samples are the main topics.
Cost: $282.42
Frequency: Monthly
Circulation: 185000

7531 **American Forests**
Po Box 2000
Suite 800
Washington, DC 20013-2000

202-737-1944; *Fax:* 202-955-4588
info@amfor.org; www.americanforests.org

Deborah Gangloff, Executive Director

A publication that offers our members the best in conservation news. Articles include different perspectives on current environmental issues, stories on wildlife restoration projects, updates on forest management practices, and ways to engage the conservation movement in your community.
Cost: $25.00
Frequency: Quarterly
Founded in: 1875

7532 **American Waste Digest**
Charles G Moody
226 King St
Pottstown, PA 19464-9105

610-326-9480
800-442-4215; *Fax:* 610-326-9752
awd@americanwastedigest.com;
www.americanwastedigest.com

Carasue Moody, Publisher
Shannon Costa, Circulation Manager
J. Robert Tagert, Sales Manager

Provides reviews on new products, profiles on sucessful waste removal businesses, and provides discussion on legislation on municipal regulations on recycling.
Cost: $24.00
86 Pages
Frequency: Monthly
Circulation: 33000
Printed in 4 colors on glossy stock

7533 **Archives of Environmental Health**
Society for Occupational and Environmental Health
111 North Bridge Road #21-01
Peninsula Plaza
Singapore 179098

703-556-9222; *Fax:* 703-556-8729;
www.oehs.org

Laura Degnon, Manager

Publishing new research based on the most rigorous methods and discussion to put this work in perspective for public health, public policy, and sustainability, the Archives addresses such topics of current concern as health significance of chemical exposure, toxic waste, new and old energy technologies, industrial processes, and the environmental causation of disease.
Frequency: Bi-Monthly

7534 **Bio-Mineral Times**
Allen C Forter & Son
3450 W Central Avenue
#328
Toledo, OH 43606-1418

419-535-6374; *Fax:* 419-535-7008
info@nviro.com; www.nviro.com

Bonnie Hunter, Publisher
James McHugh, Chief Financial Officer

Issues focus on environmental legislation efforts, regulation compliance, and finding answers to the mechanics and practical applications of the distribution and management of biosolids derived products.
Frequency: Quarterly
Circulation: 25,000

7535 **CONNECT Magazine**
Association of Zoos and Aquariums
8403 Colesville Rd
Suite 710
Silver Spring, MD 20910-6331
301-562-0777; *Fax:* 301-562-0888;
www.aza.org
Social Media: Facebook, Twitter

L. Patricia Simmons, Chair
Tom Schmid, Chair-Elect
Jackie Ogden, PhD, Vice-Chair

Window to the professional zoo and aquarium world. Magazine features fascinating stories that explore trends, educational initiatives, member achievements and conservation efforts.
200 Members
Founded in: 1924

7536 **CSA News**
American Society of Agronomy
5585 Guilford Rd.
Madison, WI 53711-1086

608-273-8080; *Fax:* 608-273-2021
headquarters@sciencesocieties.org;
www.agronomy.org
Social Media: Facebook, Twitter, LinkedIn

Newell Kitchen, President
Kenneth Barbarick, President-Elect

The official magazine for members of the American Society of Agronomy, Crop Science Society of America, and Soil Science Society of America.
10000 Members
Founded in: 1907

7537 **Crop Science**
American Society of Agronomy

5585 Guilford Rd.
Madison, WI 53711-1086

608-273-8080; *Fax:* 608-273-2021
headquarters@sciencesocieties.org;
www.agronomy.org
Social Media: Facebook, Twitter, LinkedIn

Newell Kitchen, President
Kenneth Barbarick, President-Elect

Publishes original research in crops and turfgrass science.
10000 Members
Founded in: 1907

7538 Crops & Soils
American Society of Agronomy
5585 Guilford Rd.
Madison, WI 53711-1086

608-273-8080; *Fax:* 608-273-2021
headquarters@sciencesocieties.org;
www.agronomy.org
Social Media: Facebook, Twitter, LinkedIn

Newell Kitchen, President
Kenneth Barbarick, President-Elect

The magazine for certified crop advisors, agronomists, and soil scientists. Focuses on solutions to the daily challenges facing those working in the field and features information on new technology and products, company strategies, CEU articles and quizzes, and regulatory and industry news.
10000 Members
Founded in: 1907

7539 E/Environmental Magazine
28 Knight St
Norwalk, CT 06851-4719

203-854-5559
800-967-6572; *Fax:* 203-866-0602
info@emagazine.com; www.emagazine.com

Jim Motavalli, Editor
Karen Soucy, Associate Publisher
Doug Moss, Publisher & Executive Dir
Brita Belli, Director
Trudy Hodenfield, Operations Manager

Providing information about environmental issues and sharing ideas and resources so that readers can live more sustainable lives and connect with ongoing efforts for change. Covers everything environmental, from big issues like climate change, renewable energy and toxins and health, to the topics that directly impact our readers' daily lives; how to eat right and stay healthy, where to invest responsibly and how to save energy at home.
Cost: $19.95
Circulation: 185,000
Founded in: 1988

7540 EI Digest: Hazardous Waste Marketplace
Environmental Information
PO Box 390266
Minneapolis, MN 55439

952-831-2473; *Fax:* 952-831-6550;
www.envirobiz.com

Cary Perket, President

Focused on serving the market information needs of the commercial hazardous waste management sector. Included those involved in recycling and re-use, energy recovery, waste treatment, and waste disposal. Provides compilations and analysis of the commercial markets for hazardous waste energy recovery, fuel blending, incineration, landfill and solvent recovery. Also undertakes special reports on chemical distributors, RCRA metal recyclers and wastewater treatment.
ISSN: 1042-251X
Founded in: 1983
Printed in 2 colors

7541 EM
Air & Waste Management Association
420 Fort Duquesne Boulevard
One Gateway Center, 3rd Floor
Pittsburgh, PA 15222-1435

412-652-2458; *Fax:* 412-232-3450
info@awma.org; www.awma.org
Social Media: Facebook, Twitter, LinkedIn

Jeffry Muffat, President
Merlyn L. Hough, President Elect
Mike Kelly, Secretary/ Executive Director
Amy Gilligan, Treasurer
Dallas Baker, Vice President

A&WMA's magazine for environmental managers, explores a range of issues affecting the industry with timely, provocative articles and regular columns written by leaders in the field. Keeps readers informed of coverage of regulatory changes, EPA research, new technologies, market analyses, environment, health, and safety issues, new products, professional development opportunities, and more.
9000 Members
Founded in: 1907

7542 Earth First! Journal
PO Box 964
Lake Worth, FL 33460
561-320-3840
collective@earthfirstjournal.org
earthfirstjournal.org
Social Media: Facebook, Twitter, Google+, Reddit

Quarterly voice of the radical environmental movement.
Frequency: Quarterly
Founded in: 1979

7543 Earth Island Journal
2150 Allston Way
Suite 460
Berkeley, CA 94704-1375

510-859-9100; *Fax:* 510-859-9091;
www.earthisland.org
Social Media: Facebook, Twitter, YouTube

Martha Davis, President
Kenneth Brower, Vice President
Michael Hathaway, Vice President
Jennifer Snyder, Secretary
Alex Giedt, Treasurer

Combines investigative journalism and thought-provoking essays that make the subtle but profound connections between the environment and other contemporary issues. The Journal's unique brand of environmental journalism is a key resource for anyone eager to help protect our shared planet.
33M Members
Founded in: 1985

7544 Ecological Economics, The ISEE Journal
International Society for Ecological Economics
15 River Street
#204
Boston, MA 02108

703-790-1745; *Fax:* 703-790-2672
secretariat@ecoeco.org; www.ecoeco.org
Social Media: Facebook, Twitter

John Gowdy, President
Bina Agarwal, President-Elect
Anne Aitken, Managing Editor

Concerned with extending and integrating the study and management of ecology and economics. This integration is necessary because conceptual and professional isolation have led to economic and environmental policies which are mutually destructive rather than reinforcing in the long term.
750 Members
Founded in: 1989

7545 Ecological Management & Restoration
Society for Ecological Restoration International
1017 O Street NW
Washington, DC 20001
202-299-9518; *Fax:* 270-626-5485
info@ser.org; www.ser.org
Social Media: Facebook

Steve Whisenant, Chair
Cara R. Nelson, Vice Chair
Mary Travaglini, Treasurer
Alan Unwin, Secretary

Aims to bridge the gap between the ecologist's perspective and field manager's experience. Answers the growing need among land managers for reliable, relevant information and acknowledges the need for two-way communication in devising new hypotheses, sound experimentation, effective treatments and reliable monitoring.
2300 Members
Frequency: Quarterly
Founded in: 1988

7546 Economics of Energy and Environmental Policy (EEEP)
International Association for Energy Economics
28790 Chagrin Blvd
Suite 350
Cleveland, OH 44122-4642

216-464-5365; *Fax:* 216-464-2737
iaee@iaee.org; www.iaee.org
Social Media: Facebook, LinkedIn

Mine Yucel, President
Lars Bergman, President-Elect
David L. Williams, Executive Director

Policy oriented, focusing on all policy issues in the interface between energy and environmental economics. Provides a research-based, scholarly, yet easily read and accessible source of information on contemporary economic thinking and analysis of energy and environmental policy.
3400 Members
Founded in: 1977

7547 Energy Engineering
Association of Energy Engineers
4025 Pleasantdale Rd
Suite 420
Atlanta, GA 30340-4264

770-447-5083; *Fax:* 770-446-3969
info@aeecenter.org; www.aeecenter.org

Albert Thumann, Executive Director
Ruth Whitlock, Executive Admin
Albert Thumann, Executive Director
Ruth Marie, Managing Editor

Engineering solutions to cost efficiency problems and mechanical contractors who design, specify, install, maintain, and purchase non-residential heating, ventilating, air conditioning and refrigeration equipment and components.
Circulation: 8000
Founded in: 1976

7548 Environ: A Magazine for Ecologic Living and Health
Environ
1616 Seventeenth Street
Suite 468
Denver, CO 80202

303-285-5543; *Fax:* 303-628-5597;
www.environcorp.com

Suzanne Randegger, Publisher/Editor
Ed Randegger, Co-Publisher/Ad Director

John Haasbeek, Senior Manager
Chris Keller, Managing Director

Designed to keep health and ecology conscious readers aware of circumstances hazardous to human health, and provide alternatives - practical, political, and global. Coverage of environmental legislation, ecologic food-growing practices and certification, geographically and climatically safe and hazardous locations, and a view of today's health problems with active solutions. Supported by screened advertisers.
Cost: $15.00
40 Pages
Frequency: Quarterly

7549 **Environment**
Helen Dwight Reid Educational Foundation
1319 18th Street NW
Washington, DC 20036-1802

202-296-6267; *Fax:* 202-296-5149
brichman@heldref.org; www.heldref.org

Douglas Kirkpatrick, Publisher
Barbara Richman, Editor
Fred Huber, Circulation Manager
Emily Tawlowski, Marketing Manager
Steve Hellem, Executive Director

Analyzes the problems, places, and people where environment and development come together, illuminating concerns from the local to the global. Articles and commentaries from researchers and practitioners who provide a broad range of international perspectives. Also features in-depth reviews of major policy reports, conferences, and environmental education initiatives, as well as guides to the best Web sites, journal articles, and books.
Cost: $51.00
Frequency: Monthly
Circulation: 11,408
Founded in: 1956

7550 **Environmental & Engineering Geoscience**
Assn. oF Environmental & Engineering Geologists
1100-H Brandywine Boulevard
Suite 575
Zanesville, OH 43701

303-757-2926
844-331-7867; *Fax:* 740-452-2552
aeg@aegweb.org; www.aegweb.org
Social Media: Facebook, Twitter

Dale C. Andrews, President
Kathy Troost, Vice President

Publishes peer reviewed manuscripts that address issues relating to the interaction of people with hydrologic and geologic systems. Theoretical and applied contributions are appropriate, and the primary criteria for acceptance are scientific and technical merit.
3000 Members
Founded in: 1957
Mailing list available for rent: 3000 names at $100 per M

7551 **Environmental Business Journal**
Environmental Business International
4452 Park Boulevard Suite 306
PO Box 371769
San Diego, CA 92116-1769

619-295-7685; *Fax:* 619-295-5743;
www.ebiusa.com

Grant Ferrier, Publisher
Dan Johnson, Manager

An overview piece, segment analysis by country, profiles of domestic and foreign firms, financial data on listed environmental companies in the region, the latest developments on government initiatives and regulations, company news and projects are included in the features of this publications.
Cost: $495.00
Founded in: 1988
Printed in 2 colors

7552 **Environmental Communicator**
North American Association for Environmental
2000 P St NW
Suite 540
Washington, DC 20036-6921

202-419-0412; *Fax:* 202-419-0415
email@naaee.org; www.naaee.org

Brian Day, Executive Director

A publication of the North American Association for EE. Feature articles, association news, affiliate news, op-ed pieces, announcements on new EE resources, available jobs, and future events and opportunities.
Frequency: Bi-Monthly

7553 **Environmental Engineering Science**
Mary Ann Liebert
140 Huguenot St
New Rochelle, NY 10801-5215

914-740-2100; *Fax:* 914-740-2101
info@liebertpub.com; www.liebertpub.com

Mary A Liebert, Owner
Dumpnico Grosso, Editor-in-Chief
Stephanie Paul, Production Editor
Lisa Cohen, Associate Editors

Publishing studies of innovative solutions to problems in air, wter, and land contamination and waste disposal. Features applications of environmental engineering and scientific discoveries, policy issues, environmental economics, and sustainable development.
Cost: $330.00
Frequency: Monthly
Circulation: 1800
ISSN: 1092-8758
Founded in: 1980

7554 **Environmental Forensics**
AEHS Foundation Inc
150 Fearing Street
Amherst, MA 01002

413-549-5170; *Fax:* 413-549-0579;
www.aehsfoundation.org

Paul T Kostecki, PhD, Executive Director

An international publication offering scientific studies that explore source, fate, transport and ecological effects of environmental contamination, with contamination being delineated in terms of chemical characterization, biological influence, responsible parties and legal consequences.
600 Members
Founded in: 1989

7555 **Environmental Geochemistry and Health**
Society for Environmental Geochemistry and Health
4698 S Forrest Avenue
Springfield, MO 65810

417-885-1166; *Fax:* 417-881-6920;
www.segh.net

Bobby Wixson, Director Membership

Publishes original research papers, short communications, reviews and topical special issues across the broad field of environmental geochemistry. Coverage includes papers that directly link health and the environment.
Frequency: Quarterly

7556 **Environmental History (EH)**
UW Interdisciplinary Arts and Sciences Program
1900 Commerce Street
Tacoma, WA 98402

206-343-0226; *Fax:* 206-343-0249
director@aseh.net; www.aseh.net

John McNeill, President
Gregg Mitman, Vice President/ President Elect
Ellen Stroud, Secretary
Mark Madison, Treasurer

The world's leading scholarly journal in environmental history. Brings together scholars, scientists, and practitioners from a wide array of disciplines to explore changing relationships between humans and the environment over time.
1200 Members
Founded in: 1976

7557 **Environmental Practice**
National Association of Environmental Professional
PO Box 2086
Bowie, MD 20718-2086

888-251-9902; *Fax:* 301-860-1141;
www.naep.org

John Perkins, Editor

Incorporates original research articles, news of issues and of the NAEP, and opinion pieces. Of interest to private consultants, academics, and professionals in federal, state, local, and tribal governments, as well as in corporations and non-governmental organizations. Reports on historic and contemporary environmental issues that help inform current practices.
Frequency: Quarterly

7558 **Environmental Protection**
Stevens Publishing Corporation
5151 Belt Line Rd
10th Floor
Dallas, TX 75254-7507

972-687-6700; *Fax:* 972-687-6767;
www.eponline.com

Craig S Stevens, President
Dana Cornett, President/COO
Randy Dye, Publisher
Sherleen Mahoney, Editor
Margaret Perry, Circulation Director

The comprehensive online information resource for environmental professionals.
Circulation: 63000
Founded in: 1925

7559 **Environmental Science and Technology**
American Chemical Society
1155 16th St Nw
Washington, DC 20036-4892

202-872-4600
800-227-5558; *Fax:* 202-872-4615
service@acs.org; www.acs.org

Madeleine Jacobs, CEO/Executive Director

Publishes news and research in diverse areas of environmental science and engineering.
Cost: $156.00
110 Pages
Frequency: Monthly
Circulation: 13000
Founded in: 1966

7560 **Environmental Times**
Environmental Assessment Association
1224 N Nokomis NE
Alexandria, MN 56308

320-763-4320
info@eaa-assoc.org; www.iami.org/eaa.html

Robert Johnson, Executive Director

This publications contents contain environment conferences and expos, industry trends, federal regulations related to the environment and industry assessments.
Cost: $19.95
24 Pages
Circulation: 7000
Founded in: 1972
Printed in 4 colors on newsprint stock

7561 **Environmental Toxicology and Chemistry**
Society of Environmental Toxicology and Chemistry
1013 N 12th Ave
Pensacola, FL 32501-3306

850-437-1901; *Fax:* 850-469-9778
rparrish@setac.org; www.edwardjones.com

Chad Stacy, Manager

Dedicated to furthering scientific knowledge and disseminating information on environmental toxicology and chemistry, including the application of these sciences to risk management. Provides a forum for professionals in academia, business, and government.

7562 **Environmental and Molecular Mutagenesis**
Environmental Mutagen Society
1821 Michael Faraday Drive
Suite 300
Reston, VA 20190

703-438-8220; *Fax:* 703-438-3113
emshq@ems-us.org; www.ems-ph.org

Publishes original research articles on environmental mutangenesis. Manuscripts published in the six general areas of mechanisms of mutagenesis, genomics, DNA damage, replication, recombination and repair, public health, and DNA technology.
Frequency: 8/year

7563 **ExecutiveBrief**
Synthetic Organic Chemical Manufacturers Assn
1850 M St Nw
Suite 700
Washington, DC 20036-5803

202-721-4100; *Fax:* 202-296-8120
info@socma.org; www.socma.org

Joseph Acker, President
Vivian Diko, Executive Assistant & CEO
Charlene Patterson, Editor

Provides quality content on software development, outsourcing, project and risk management.

7564 **Fisheries**
American Fisheries Society
5410 Grosvenor Ln
Suite 110
Bethesda, MD 20814-2199

301-897-8616; *Fax:* 301-897-8096;
www.fisheries.org

Gus Rassam, Executive Director
Charles Moseley, Journals Manager

Peer reviewed articles that address contemporary issues and problems, techniques, philosophies and other areas of interest to the general fisheries profession. Monthly features include letters, meeting notices, book listings and reviews, environmental essays and organization profiles.
Cost: $76.00
50 Pages
Frequency: Monthly
Founded in: 1870
Mailing list available for rent: 8500 names at $250 per M

7565 **Forest History Today**
Forest History Society
701 William Vickers Ave
Durham, NC 27701-3162

919-682-9319; *Fax:* 919-682-2349
recluce2@duke.edu; www.foresthistory.org
Social Media: Facebook, Twitter

L. Michael Kelly, Chairman
Robert Healy, Co-Vice Chairman
Mark Wilde, Co-Vice Chairman
Henry I. Barclay III, Treasurer
Steven Anderson, Secretary & President

Providing members of FHS with engaging writings in forest history and staying updated with current FHS activities.
2000 Members
Founded in: 1946

7566 **Fusion Science and Technology**
American Nuclear Society
555 N Kensington Ave
La Grange Park, IL 60526-5592

708-352-6611
800-323-3044; *Fax:* 708-352-0499
advertising@ans.org; www.ans.org
Social Media: Facebook, Twitter, LinkedIn

Jack Tuohy, Executive Director
James S Tulenko, VP
William F Naughton, Treasurer

Information on fusion plasma physics and plasma engineering, fusion plasma enabling science and technology, fusion nuclear technology and material science, fusion applications, fusion design and system studies. Plasma and fusion energy physics, tokamak experiments, stellarators, next step burning plasma experiments, target fabrications and technology for inertial confinement fusion, inertial fusion science and applications, tritium science and technology, and more.
10500 Members
Founded in: 1954

7567 **Geophysics**
Society of Exploration Geophysicists
8801 South Yale
Suite 500
Tulsa, OK 74137-3575

918-497-5500; *Fax:* 918-497-5557
web@seg.org; www.seg.org
Social Media: Facebook, Twitter, LinkedIn

Mary Fleming, Executive Director
Vladimir Grechka, Editor

An archival journal encompassing all aspects of research, exploration, and education in applied geophysics.
Founded in: 1930

7568 **Hauler**
Hauler Magazine
166 S Main Street
PO Box 508
New Hope, PA 18938

800-220-6029
800-220-6029; *Fax:* 215-862-3455
mag@thehauler.com; www.thehauler.com

Thomas N Smith, Publisher/Editor
Barbara Gibney, Circulation Manager
Leslie T Smith, Marketing Director

Dedicated to the refuse and solid waste industry. It is the acknowledged leader in the new and used refuse truck and equipment marketplace, and now lists hundreds of new and used trash trucks, trailers, containers, services, plus parts and accessories from the best suppliers in the industry.
Cost: $12.00
Frequency: Monthly
Circulation: 18630
Founded in: 1978

7569 **Hazardous Management**
Ecolog
1450 Don Mills Road
Don Mills, Ontario M3B-2X7

416-442-2292
888-702-1111; *Fax:* 416-442-2204;
www.hazmatmag.com

Lynda Reilly, Publisher

The latest environmental regulations and programs as well as the evolving technology and equipment needed to achieve compliance.
Cost: $39.50
Frequency: Bi-Monthly
Circulation: 16,000
ISSN: 0843-9303
Founded in: 1989
*Mailing list available for rent*at $250 per M
Printed in 4 colors on glossy stock

7570 **Hazardous Waste Consultant**
Aspen Publishers
8400 east cresent parkway
6 floor greenwood village
Lakewood, CO 80111

720-528-4270
800-638-8437; *Fax:* 212-597-0335

A unique approach to hazardous waste issues. It is written by engineers and regulatory specialists who have an extensive background in the field and understand the problems that industry, consultants, and regulators face.
Cost: $475.00

7571 **Human Ecology Review**
Society for Human Ecology
College of the Atlantic
105 Eden Street
Bar Harbor, ME 04609-0180

207-288-5015; *Fax:* 207-288-3780
carter@ecology.coa.edu;
www.societyforhumanecology.org

Barbara Carter, Assistant to Executive Director

Publishes peer-reviewed research and theory on the interaction between humans and the environment and other links between culture and nature, essays and applications relevant to human ecology, book reviews, and relevant commentary, announcements, and awards.
Frequency: Semi-Annual

7572 **Human and Ecological Risk Assessment**
AEHS Foundation Inc
150 Fearing Street
Amherst, MA 01002
413-549-5170; *Fax:* 413-549-0579;
www.aehsfoundation.org

Paul T Kostecki, PhD, Executive Director

Devoted to providing a framework for professionals researching and assessing developments in both human and ecological risk assessment.
600 Members
Founded in: 1989

7573 **Hydrological Science and Technology**
American Institute Of Hydrology
300 Village Green Circle
Suite 201
Smyrna, GA 30080

770-269-9388; www.aihydro.org

Cathy Lipsett, Owner
Cathryn Seaburn, Manager

Peer-reviewed international journal covering research and practical studies on hydrological science, technology, water resources and related topics including water, air and soil pollution and hazardous waste issues. Communicating ideas, findings, methods, techniques and summaries of interesting projects or investigations in the area of hydrology.
Frequency: Quarterly

7574 **IEEE Power and Energy Magazine**
IEEE
PO Box 1331
Piscataway, NJ 08855
732-981-0061; *Fax:* 732-981-9667
society-info@ieee.org; www.ieee.org
Mel Olken, Editor
Susan Schneiderman, Business Development
Dedicated to disseminating information on all matters of interest to electric power engineers and other professionals involved in the electric power industry. Feature articles focus on advanced concepts, technologies, and practices associated with all aspects of electric power from a technical perspective in synergy with nontechnical areas such as business, environmental, and social concerns.
Cost: $260.00
82 Pages
Frequency: Monthly
Circulation: 23000
ISSN: 1540-7977
Founded in: 2003
Mailing list available for rent
Printed in on glossy stock

7575 **Identifying Business Risks & Opportunities**
World Resources Institute
10 G St NE
Suite 800
Washington, DC 20002-4252
202-729-7600; *Fax:* 202-729-7610
front@wri.org; www.wcdassessment.org
Jonathan Lash, President

7576 **Indoor Air Journal**
The Indoor Air Institute
2548 Empire Grade
Santa Cruz, CA 95060
831-426-0148; *Fax:* 831-426-6522
info@IndAir.org
indair.org
Hal Levin, President
William Fisk, Vice President
William Nazaroff, Vice President
Providing a location for reporting original research results in the broad area defined by the indoor environment of non-industrial buildings. The results will provide the information to allow designers, builders, owners and operators to provide a healthy and comfortable environment for building occupants. Health effects, monitoring and modelling, source characterization, ventilation and other environmental control techniques, thermal comfort, and public policy.

7577 **Indoor Environment Review**
IAQ Publications
7920 Norfolk Ave
#900
Bethesda, MD 20814-2539
301-913-0115; *Fax:* 301-913-0119;
www.eschoolnews.com
Robert Morrow, Owner
New technology, research and legislation concerning all indoor air and water quality issues.
Frequency: Monthly
Circulation: 10000

7578 **Industrial Safety & Hygiene**
Business News Publishing Company
2401 W. Big Beaver Road
Suite 700
Troy, MI 48084
847-763-9534; *Fax:* 847-763-9538
ishn@halldata.com; www.ishn.com
Randy Green, Publisher/ West Coast Manager
Dave Johnsen, Editor
Maureen Brady, Managing Editor/Project Editor
Vince Miconi, Production Manager
Lydia Stewart, Inside Sales/Classifides
A business-to-business trade publication targeted at key safety, health and industrial hygiene buying influencers at manufacturing facilities of all sizes. Designed for the busy professionals with early mail dates and short articles backed by dynamite graphics. Each issue is packed with vital editorial on OSHA and EPA regulations, ho-to features, safety and health management topics, and the latest product news. For safety and health managers at high-hazard worksites.

7579 **Industrial Wastewater**
Water Environment Federation
601 Wythe St
Alexandria, VA 22314-1994
800-666-0206; *Fax:* 703-684-2492;
www.wef.org
Social Media: Facebook, Twitter
Matt Bond, President
Cordell Samuels, President-Elect
Sandra Ralston, Vice President
Chris Browning, Treasurer
Jeff Eger, Secretary and Executive Director
Discusses relevant regulatory and legal issues, provides examples of real-world treatment options, and offers suggestions on minimizing waste and preventing pollution.
79 Members
ISSN: 1044-9943
Founded in: 1928

7580 **Inside EPA**
Inside Washington Publishers
1919 S Eads St
Arlington, VA 22202-3028
703-418-3981
800-424-9068; *Fax:* 703-416-8543
support@iwpnews.com; www.iwpnews.com
Alan Sosenko, Owner
Gives timely information on all facets of waste, water, air, and other environmental regulatory programs.
Frequency: Weekly
Founded in: 1980

7581 **Inside Waste**
John Cupps Associates
2757 13th Street
Sacramento, CA 95818-2907
916-448-5272; *Fax:* 916-448-7862
John A Cupps, Publisher/Editor
The waste trade spans a diverse range of activities, from waste collection to resource recovery to landfilling. The operating environment varies from state to state, between urban and rural areas, and even among different councils. Inside Waste brings this all together, covering all the news, projects, contracts and issues that matter to the waste trade.
Frequency: Monthly

7582 **Integrated Environmenal Assessment and Management**
SETAC
1013 N 12th Ave
Pensacola, FL 32501-3306
850-437-1901; *Fax:* 850-469-9778
setac@setac.org; www.setac.org
Social Media: Facebook, Twitter, LinkedIn
Paul van den Brink, President
Tim Canfield, Vice President
Fred Heimbach, Treasurer
Bridges the gap between scientific research and its application in environmental decision-making, regulation, and management.
4000 Members
Founded in: 1979

7583 **International Dredging Review**
PO Box 1487
Fort Collins, CO 80522-1487
970-416-1903; *Fax:* 970-416-1878
editor@dredgemag.com; www.dredgemag.com
Judith Powers, Publisher
Julia Leach, Business Manager
Nelson Spencer, Business Manager
Targeted to dredging company executives, project managers and dredge crew members, suppliers and service people such as pump manufacturers, hydrographic surveyors, consulting engineers, etc.
Cost: $85.00
Frequency: Monthly
Circulation: 3300
ISSN: 0737-8181
Founded in: 1967

7584 **International Environmental Systems Update**
CEEM
3975 University Drive
Suite 230
Fairfax, VA 22030-3223
703-437-9000
800-745-5565; *Fax:* 703-437-9001;
www.qsuonline.com
Paul Scicchitano, Publisher
Suzanne Leonard, Senior Editor
Provides information covering the emerging environmental issues that affect business and industry around the globe including competitive advantages, global updates, strategies, management systems and company profiles.
Cost: $ 390.00
24 Pages
Frequency: Monthly
Circulation: 50000
ISSN: 1079-0837
Founded in: 1994
Mailing list available for rent
Printed in 2 colors on matte stock

7585 **International Journal of Phytoremediation**
AEHS Foundation Inc.
150 Fearing Street
Amherst, MA 01002
413-549-5170
888-540-2347; www.aehsfoundation.org
Paul T Kostecki, PhD, Executive Director
Devoted to the publication of current laboratory and field research describing the use of plant systems to remediate contaminated environments. Designed to link professionals in the many environmental disciplines involved in the development, application, management, and regulation of emerging phytoremediation technologies.
600 Members
Frequency: Quarterly
Founded in: 1989

7586 **International Journal of Wildland Fire**
International Association of Wildland Fire
4025 Fair Ridge Drive
Fairfax, VA 22033
785-423-1818; *Fax:* 785-542-3511
sandy@iawfonline.org; www.iawfonline.org
Social Media: Facebook, Twitter
Sacha Dick, Programs Manager
Mikel Robinson, Executive Director
Online journal publishing new and significant papers that advance basic and applied research concerning wildland fire. Aims to publish quality papers on a broad range of wildland fire issues, and has an international perspective, since

wildland fire plays a major social, economic, and ecological role around the globe.
Frequency: Quarterly

7587 **Journal of Air & Waste Management Association**
Air & Waste Management Association
1 Gateway Center
3rd Floor
Pittsburgh, PA 15222-1435

412-652-2458
800-270-3444; *Fax:* 412-232-3450
info@awma.org; www.awma.org
Social Media: Facebook, Twitter, LinkedIn

Andy Knopes, Production Manager/Editor
Richard Sherr, Execetive Director

Intended to serve those occupationally involved in air pollution control and waste management through the publication of timely and reliable information. Descriptions of contemporary advances in air quality and waste management science and technology for use in improving environmental protection.
Cost: $330.00
Frequency: Monthly
Circulation: 3500
ISSN: 1047-3289
Founded in: 1907

7588 **Journal of Environmental Economics and Management**
Association of Environmental and Resource
1616 P St Nw
Suite 400
Washington, DC 20036-1434

202-328-5125; *Fax:* 202-939-3460
info@aere.org; www.aere.org

Devoted to the publication of theoretical and empirical papers concerned with the linkage between economic systems and environmental and natural resources systems. The top journal in natural resources and environmental economics, it concentrates on the management and/or social control of the economy in its relationship with the management and use of natural resources and the natural environment.
Frequency: Bi-Monthly

7589 **Journal of Environmental Education**
Heldref Publications
1319 18th St Nw
Washington, DC 20036-1802

202-296-6267; *Fax:* 202-296-5149
jee@heldref.org; www.heldref.org

James Denton, Executive Director
J. Heldref, Editor

Details how best to present environmental issues and how to evaluate programs already in place for primary through university level and adult students. Publishes material that advances the instruction, theory, methods, and practice of environmental education and communication. Subject areas include the sciences, social sciences, and humanities.
Cost: $58.00
Frequency: Quarterly
Circulation: 1250
Founded in: 1970

7590 **Journal of Environmental Engineering**
American Society of Civil Engineers
1801 Alexander Bell Dr
Reston, VA 20191-4382

703-295-6300
800-548-2723
703-295-6300; *Fax:* 703-295-6222
webmaster@asce.org; www.asce.org

D Wayne Klotz, President
M. Kathy Banks, Editor

Emphasizes on the implementaion of effective and safe methods for handling, transporting, and treating waste materials.
Cost: $308.00
Frequency: Monthly
Circulation: 2,500
Founded in: 1852

7591 **Journal of Environmental Geochemistry and Health**
Society for Environmental Geochemistry & Health
4698 S Forrest Avenue
Springfield, MO 65810

417-851-1166; *Fax:* 417-881-6920
DRBGWIXSON@aol.com; www.segh.net

Prof. Xiangdong Li, President
Prof. Andrew Hursthouse, European Chair
Kyoung-Woong Kim, Asia/Pacific Chair
Anthea Brown, Membership Secretary/Treasurer
Malcolm Brown, Secretary

Publishes original research papers, research notes and reviews across the broad field of environmental geochemistry.
400 Members
Founded in: 1971

7592 **Journal of Environmental Health**
National Environmental Health Association
720 S Colorado Blvd
Suite 970S
Denver, CO 80246-1926

303-756-9090; *Fax:* 303-691-9490
staff@neha.org; www.neha.org
Social Media: Facebook, Twitter, LinkedIn

Nelson Fabian, Executive Director
Julie Collins, Research
Kim Brandow, Marketing/Sales Manager
Larry Marcum, Managing Director
Bob Custard, Manager

A practical journal containing information on a variety of environmental health issues.
Cost: $90.00
5000 Members
70 Pages
Frequency: 10 per year
Circulation: 20,000
ISSN: 0022-0892
Founded in: 1937
Printed in 4 colors on glossy stock

7593 **Journal of Environmental Quality**
American Society of Agronomy
5585 Guilford Rd.
Madison, WI 53711-1086

608-273-8080; *Fax:* 608-273-2021
headquarters@sciencesocieties.org;
www.agronomy.org
Social Media: Facebook, Twitter, LinkedIn

Newell Kitchen, President
Kenneth Barbarick, President-Elect

Papers are grouped by subject matter and cover water, soil, and atmospheric research as it relates to agriculture and the environment.
10000 Members
Founded in: 1907

7594 **Journal of Food Protection**
International Association for Food Protection
6200 Aurora Ave
Suite 200W
Des Moines, IA 50322-2864

515-276-3344
800-369-6337; *Fax:* 515-276-8655
info@foodprotection.org;
www.foodprotection.org
Social Media: Facebook, Twitter, LinkedIn

Isabel Walls, President
Katherine M.J. Swanson, President-Elect
Don Schaffner, Vice President
Don Zink, Secretary
David W. Tharp, Executive Director

Each issue contains scientific research and authoritative review articles reporting on a variety of topics in food science pertaining to food safety and quality.
3400 Members
Founded in: 1911

7595 **Journal of Intelligent Material Systems and Structures**
Sage Journals Online
www.jim.sagepub.com

Dan Inman, Editor-In-Chief

An international peer reviewed journal that publishes the highest quality original research. JIMSS reports on the results of experimental or theoretical work on any aspect of intelligent materials systems and/or structures research also called smart structure, smart materials, active materials, adaptive structures and adaptive materials.
Cost: $995.00
80 Pages
Frequency: Monthly
ISSN: 1045-389X
Printed in 2 colors on matte stock

7596 **Journal of Natural Resources & Life Sciences Education**
American Society of Agronomy
5585 Guilford Rd.
Madison, WI 53711-1086

608-273-8080; *Fax:* 608-273-2021
headquarters@sciencesocieties.org;
www.agronomy.org
Social Media: Facebook, Twitter, LinkedIn

Newell Kitchen, President
Kenneth Barbarick, President-Elect

Today's educators look here for the latest teaching ideas in the life sciences, natural resources, and agriculture.
10000 Members
Founded in: 1907

7597 **Journal of Plant Registrations**
American Society of Agronomy
5585 Guilford Rd.
Madison, WI 53711-1086

608-273-8080; *Fax:* 608-273-2021
headquarters@sciencesocieties.org;
www.agronomy.org
Social Media: Facebook, Twitter, LinkedIn

Newell Kitchen, President
Kenneth Barbarick, President-Elect

Publishes cultivar, germplasm, parental line, genetic stock, and mapping population registration manuscripts.
10000 Members
Founded in: 1907

7598 **Journal of Soil and Water Conservation**
Soil and Water Conservation Society
945 SW Ankeny Rd
Ankeny, IA 50023-9764

515-289-2331
800-843-7645; *Fax:* 515-289-1227
pubs@swcs.org; www.swcs.org

Oksana Gieseman, Director of Publications

The JSWC is a multidisciplinary journal of natural resource conservation research, practice, policy, and perspectives. The journal has two sections: the A Section containing various departments and features and the Research Section containing peer-reviewed research papers.
Cost: $99.00
Frequency: Bimonthly
Circulation: 2000

ISSN: 0022-4561
Founded in: 1945

7599 Journal of Wildlife Management
Wildlife Society
5410 Grosvenor Ln
Suite 200
Bethesda, MD 20814-2197

301-897-9770; *Fax:* 301-530-2471
tws@wildlife.org; www.wildlife.org
Social Media: Facebook, Twitter, LinkedIn

Michael Hutchins, Executive Director

One of the world's leading scientific journals covering wildlife science, management and conservation.
Founded in: 1937

7600 Journal of the Air Pollution Control Association
Air Pollution Control Association
1 Gateway Center 3rd Floor
420 Fort Duquesne Blvd.
Pittsburgh, PA 15222-1435

412-232-3444
800-270-3444; *Fax:* 412-232-3450
info@awma.org; www.awma.org/
Social Media: Facebook, Twitter, LinkedIn

Tim Keener, Technical Editor-in-Chief
George Hidy, Co-Editor
Jeffrey Brook, Associate Editor

A comprehensive journal offering information to the environment and conservation industry.
Cost: $95.00
Frequency: Monthly
Circulation: 700
Founded in: 1907

7601 Journal of the American Society of Mining and Reclamation
American Society of Mining and Reclamation
1800 South Oak Street
Suite 100
Champaign, IL 61820

217-333-9489; *Fax:* 859-335-6529
rdarmody@illinois.edu; www.asmr.us

Robert Darmody, Executive Secretary
Pete Stahl, President
Kimery Vories, President Elect
Richard Barnhisel, Editor-in-Chief

The official journal of the ASMR, offering professional insights and trends on reclamation.
Founded in: 1973

7602 Journal of the IEST
Institute of Environmental Sciences and Technology
2340 S Arlington Heights Rd.
Suite 620
Arlington Heights, IL 60005

847-981-0100; *Fax:* 847-981-4130
information@iest.org; www.iest.org

Wei Sun, President
Ahmad Soueid, President-Elect

Official publication of the Institute of Environmental Sciences and Technology.
Frequency: Annual

7603 Journal of the U.S. SJWP
Water Environment Federation
601 Wythe St
Alexandria, VA 22314-1994

800-666-0206; *Fax:* 703-684-2492;
www.wef.org
Social Media: Facebook, Twitter

Matt Bond, President
Cordell Samuels, President-Elect
Sandra Ralston, Vice President
Chris Browning, Treasurer
Jeff Eger, Secretary and Executive Director

Electronic publication. Purpose is to share the fresh thinking of today's young scientists with the entire water quality community. In addition to the benefit of research exchange, students are mentored in scientific writing and publication.
79 Members
ISSN: 1044-9943
Founded in: 1928

7604 Lake & Reservoir Management
North American Lake Management Society
PO Box 5443
Madison, WI 53705

608-233-2836; *Fax:* 608-233-3186
info@nalms.org; www.nalms.org
Social Media: Facebook, LinkedIn, Flickr

Bev Clark, President
Reesa Evans, Secretary

Publishes original studies relevant to lake and reservoir management. Papers address the management of lakes and reservoirs, their watersheds and tributaries, along with limnology and ecology needed for sound supervision of these systems.
Frequency: Quarterly

7605 LakeLine Magazine
North American Lake Management Society
PO Box 5443
Madison, WI 53705-443

608-233-2836; *Fax:* 608-233-3186
info@nalms.org; www.nalms.org

Bev Clark, President
Reesa Evans, Secretary
Linda Green, Treasurer

Contains news, commentary and articles on topics affecting lakes, reservoirs and watersheds. Organized around a theme, like control of invasive species or resolving recreational conflicts, each issue becomes a valued resource for lake users and advocates.
Frequency: Quarterly

7606 Land and Water Magazine
Land and Water
Po Box 1197
Fort Dodge, IA 50501-1197

515-576-3191; *Fax:* 515-576-2606;
www.landandwater.com
Social Media: Facebook

Amy Dencklau, Publisher
Shanza Dencklau, Assistant Editor
Rasch M. Kenneth, President

Edited for contractors, engineers, architects, government officials and those working in the field of natural resource management and restoration from idea stage through project completion and maintenance.
Cost: $20.00
72 Pages
Circulation: 20000
Founded in: 1959
Mailing list available for rent: 20M names
Printed in 4 colors on glossy stock

7607 MSW Management
Forester Communications
2946 De La Vina street
Santa Barbara, CA 93105

805-682-1300; *Fax:* 805-682-0200
customerservice@forester.net;
www.foresterpress.com

Daniel Waldman, Publisher/President
John Trotti, Group Editor

Provides municipal solid waste professionals with general news on facility construction, financing, new equipment and revenue issues.
Cost: $94.95
Circulation: 25000
Founded in: 1990

7608 Marine Technology Society Journal
Marine Technology Society
1100 H St., Nw
Suite LL-100
Washington, DC 20005

202-717-8705; *Fax:* 202-347-4302
membership@mtsociety.org;
www.mtsociety.org
Social Media: Facebook, Twitter, LinkedIn

Jerry Boatman, President
Drew Michel, President-Elect
Jerry Wilson, VP of Industry and Technology
Jill Zande, VP of Education and Research
Justin Manley, VP of Gov. & Public Affairs

Publishes the highest caliber, peer-reviewed papers on subjects of interest to the society; marine technology, ocean science, marine policy and education. Dedicated to publishing timely special issues on emerging ocean community concers while also showcasing general interest and student-authored works.
2M Members
Founded in: 1963

7609 National Woodlands Magazine
National Woodland Owners Association
374 Maple Avenue East
Suite 310
Vienna, VA 22180-4718

703-255-2700
800-470-8733; *Fax:* 703-281-9200;
www.woodlandowners.org
Social Media: Facebook

Keith A. Argow, President
Dick Courter, Chairman
Eric Johnson, National Woodlands Editor

7610 Natural History Magazine
American Museum of Natural History
79th St & Central Park W
New York, NY 10024

212-769-5400; *Fax:* 212-769-5009
communications@amnh.org;
www.library.amnh.org

Michael J Novacek, CEO
Victor W Fazio, Editor

Chronicled the major expeditions and research findings by curators at the American Museum of Natural History and at other natural history museums and science centers. Mission of this magazine is to promote public understanding and appreciation of nature and science.
Cost: $55.00

7611 Natural Resources & Environment
American Bar Association
321 N Clark St
Chicago, IL 60654-7598

312-988-5000
800-285-2221; *Fax:* 312-988-5280
askaba@abanet.org; www.abanet.org
Social Media: Facebook, Twitter

Lori Lyons, Staff Editor
Christine LeBel, Executive Editor

Practical magazine on the latest developments in the field of natural resources law for the ABA Section of Environment, Energy, and Resources.
Cost: $80.00
64 Pages
Frequency: Quarterly
ISSN: 0822-3812
Printed in 4 colors

7612 North American Elk: Ecology & Management
Wildlife Management Institute

1146 19th St NW
Suite 700
Washington, DC 20036-3727

202-973-7710; *Fax:* 202-785-1348;
www.wildlifemanagementinstitute.org

Dale E Towell, Editor

7613 Northeast Sun
NE Sustainable Energy Association
50 Miles St
Greenfield, MA 01301-3255

413-774-6051; *Fax:* 413-774-6053
nesea@nesea.org; www.nesea.org

David Barclay, Executive Director
Paul Horowitz, Chairman

Includes articles by leading authorities on sustainable energy practices, energy efficiency and renewable energy.
Frequency: Quarterly
Circulation: 5000
Founded in: 1974

7614 Nuclear News
American Nuclear Society
555 N Kensington Ave
La Grange Park, IL 60526-5592

708-352-6611
800-323-3044; *Fax:* 708-352-0499
advertising@ans.org; www.ans.org
Social Media: Facebook, Twitter, LinkedIn

Jack Tuohy, Executive Director
James S Tulenko, VP
William F Naughton, Treasurer

The flagship membership publication of the American Nuclear Society, the recognized credible advocate for advancing and promoting nuclear science and technology.
10500 Members
Founded in: 1954

7615 Nuclear Science and Engineering
American Nuclear Society
555 N Kensington Ave
La Grange Park, IL 60526-5592

708-352-6611
800-323-3044; *Fax:* 708-352-0499
advertising@ans.org; www.ans.org
Social Media: Facebook, Twitter, LinkedIn

Jack Tuohy, Executive Director
James S Tulenko, VP
William F Naughton, Treasurer

The research journal of the American Nuclear Society, widel recognized as an outstanding source of information on research in all scientific areas related to the peaceful use of nuclear energy and radiation. Technical papers, notes, critical reviews, and computer code abstracts are presented.
10500 Members
Founded in: 1954

7616 Nuclear Technology
American Nuclear Society
555 N Kensington Ave
La Grange Park, IL 60526-5592

708-352-6611
800-323-3044; *Fax:* 708-352-0499
advertising@ans.org; www.ans.org
Social Media: Facebook, Twitter, LinkedIn

Jack Tuohy, Executive Director
James S Tulenko, VP
William F Naughton, Treasurer

The leading international publication reporting on new information in all areas of the practical application of nuclear science. Topics include all aspects of reactor technology; operations, safety materials, instrumentation, fuel, and waste management. Also covered are medical uses, radiation detection, production of radiation, health physics, and computer applications.
10500 Members
Founded in: 1954

7617 Occupational Health and Safety
Stevens Publishing Corporation
5151 Belt Line Rd
10th Floor
Dallas, TX 75254-7507

972-687-6700; *Fax:* 972-687-6767;
www.ohsonline.com

Craig S Stevens, President
Dana Cornett, President/COO
Randy Dye, Publisher
Jerry Laws, Editor
Margaret Perry, Circulation Director

Practical advice on how to keep the workplace safe from hazards and in full compliance with ever-changing laws and regulations. Delivering the most up-to-date info for professionals in the health, safety, industrial hygiene, environmental, security and fire protection fields with in-depth features, new product releases and more!
Circulation: 63000
Founded in: 1925

7618 Oceana
1350 Connecticut Ave.
5th Fl.
Washington, DC 20036

202-833-3900
membership@oceana.org
oceana.org/publications/magazine

Suzannah Evans, Interim Editor
Brianna Elliott, Online Content Editor

The magazine of Oceana, the largest environmental organization focused solely on ocean conservation.

7619 OnEarth
National Resources Defense Council
40 W 20th St
New York, NY 10011-4231

212-727-2700; *Fax:* 212-727-1773
nrdcinfo@nrdc.org; www.nrdc.org
Social Media: Facebook, Twitter, YouTube

Frances Beinecke, President
Daniel R. Tishman, Chair
Frederick A.O. Schwarz Jr., Chair Emeritus
Adam Albright, Vice Chair
Patricia Bauman, Vice Chair

Publication exploring the challenges that confront our world, the solutions that promise to heal it, and the way we can use those solutions to improve our homes, our health, our communities, and our future.
50000 Members
Founded in: 1970

7620 Outdoor America
Isaak Walton League
707 Conservation Lane
Gaithersburg, MD 20878

301-548-0150; *Fax:* 301-548-0146
general@iwla.org; www.iwla.org

David Hoskins, Executive Director

Entertaining and educational articles about the conservation work of IWLA members. Also provides in-depth coverage of broader conservation issues such as national energy policy, urban sprawl, and wetland loss.
Cost: $36.00
Frequency: Quarterly
Circulation: 37000
ISSN: 0021-3314

7621 Photogrammetric Engineering & Remote Sensing (PE&RS)
ASPRS
5410 Grosvenor Lane
Suite 210
Bethesda, MD 20814-2160
301-493-0290; *Fax:* 301-493-0208
asprs@asprs.org; www.asprs.org
Social Media: Facebook, Twitter

Jaws Plasker, Exec. Director

The official journal for imaging and geospation information science and technology.
6000 Members
Founded in: 1934

7622 Phytopathology
American Phytopatholgical Society
3340 Pilot Knob Road
Saint Paul, MN 55121-2097

651-454-7250
800-328-7560; *Fax:* 651-454-0766
aps@scisoc.org; www.apsnet.org

Greg Grahek, Director of Marketing

The premier international journal for publication of articles on fundamental research that advances understanding of the nature of plant diseases, the agents that cause them, their spread, the losses they cause, and measures that can be used to control them.
Frequency: Monthly
Circulation: 1200
ISSN: 0031-949X
Printed in 4 colors

7623 Plant Disease
American Phytopatholgical Society
3340 Pilot Know Road
Saint Paul, MN 55121-2097

651-454-7250
800-328-7560; *Fax:* 651-454-0766
aps@scisoc.org; www.apsnet.org

Greg Grahek, Director of Marketing

Leading international journal for rapid reporting of research on new diseases, epidemics, and methods of disease control. Covers basic and applied research, which focuses on practical aspects of disease diagnosis and treatment.The popular Disease Notes section contains brief and timely reports of new diseases, new disease outbreaks, new hosts, and pertinent new observations of plant diseases and pathogens worldwide.
Frequency: Monthly
Circulation: 1200
ISSN: 0191-2917

7624 Plastics Recycling Update
Resource Recycling
PO Box 42270
Portland, OR 97242-270

503-233-1305; *Fax:* 503-233-1356
pru@resource-recycling.com;
www.resource-recycling.com

Jerry Powell, Publisher

The only magazine in North America focusing exclusively on polymer recovery efforts. A superb source for marketing recycling equipment and services and offers an excellent means of sourcing new suppliers of recovered plastics. The authority in plastic recycling market analysis, coverage of the latest legislation, industry news and views, and technical specs on the latest equipment.
Cost: $59.00
6 Pages
Frequency: Monthly
Circulation: 1000
ISSN: 1052-4908
Founded in: 1981
Mailing list available for rent: 40,000 names at $100 per M
Printed in one color on matte stock

7625 Pollution Engineering
Business News Publishing Company

2401 W Big Beaver Rd
Suite 700
Troy, MI 48084-3333

248-362-3700; *Fax:* 248-362-0317;
www.bnpmedia.com
Social Media: Facebook, Twitter

Mitchell Henderson, CEO
Roy Bigham, Managing Editor
Seth Fisher, Products Editor

Providing must read information for today's Engineers and Consulting Engineers in Pollution Control for; Air, Wastewater, and Remediation Hazardous Solid Waste. Up-to-date information on regulatory requirements, coverage of economic benefits of environmental control techniques, and up-to-date information on innovative and cost-effective environmental equipment, products, technology and services.
Frequency: Monthly
ISSN: 0032-3640
Founded in: 1969

7626 **Pollution Equipment News**
Rimbach Publishing
8650 Babcock Blvd
Suite 1
Pittsburgh, PA 15237-5010

412-364-5366
800-245-3182; *Fax:* 412-369-9720
info@rimbach.com; www.rimbach.com
Social Media: Facebook, Twitter

Norberta Rimbach, President
Karen Galante, Circulation Manager
Paul Henderson, VP of Sales and Marketing

Provides information to those responsible for selecting products and services for air, water, wastewater and hazardous waste pollution abatement.
Frequency: Bi-Annually
Circulation: 91000
Founded in: 1968

7627 **Pollution Prevention Northwest**
US EPA
Ariel Rios Building
1200 Pennsylvania Avenue NW
Washington, DC 20460

202-272-0167; www.epa.gov

Bob Zachariasiewicz, Acting Director

Articles include recent information on source reduction and sustainable technologies in industry, transportation, consumer, agriculture, energy, and the international sector.
Frequency: Monthly
Circulation: 12000
Founded in: 1970

7628 **Popular Science**
2 Park Ave
9th Floor
New York, NY 10016-5614

212-779-5000; *Fax:* 212-986-2656
letters@popsci.com; www.popsci.com

Greg Hano, Publisher
Robert Novick, General Manager

A leading source of science and technology news, with insightful commentary on the new innovations, and even scientific takes on the hottest Hollywood stories.
Cost: $48.00
Frequency: Monthly
Founded in: 1964

7629 **Pumper**
COLE Publishing
PO Box 220
Three Lakes, WI 54562-220

715-546-3346; *Fax:* 715-546-3786
info@pumper.com; www.pumper.com
Social Media: Facebook, Twitter, YouTube

Ted Rulseh, Editor
Jeff Bruss, President

Emphasis on companies, individuals and industry events while focusing on customer service, environmental issues and employment trends.
Cost: $16.00
Frequency: Monthly
Circulation: 20,740
Founded in: 1978

7630 **Radwaste Solutions**
American Nuclear Society
555 N Kensington Ave
La Grange Park, IL 60526-5592

708-352-6611
800-323-044; *Fax:* 708-352-0499
advertising@ans.org; www.ans.org/advertising

Jack Tuohy, Executive Director
Sarah Wells, Editor
Harry Bradley, Executive Director
Gloria Naurocki, Membership & Marketing
Mary Beth Gardner, Scientific Publications

The magazine of radioactive waste management and facility remediation. Serving the nuclear waste management and cleanup business segments of the industry. Also included are articles on radwaste management programs and practices outside the US, as well as guest editorials and letters to the editor, shorter thought-pieces, and articles on recent academic/technical advances detailing their immediate or planned practical applications.
Cost: $455.00
Frequency: Fortnightly
Circulation: 2000
Founded in: 1954
Printed in on matte stock

7631 **Recharger Magazine**
1050 E Flamingo Rd
Suite 237
Las Vegas, NV 89119-7427

702-438-5557; *Fax:* 702-873-9671
info@rechargermag.com;
www.rechargermag.com
Social Media: Facebook, Twitter

Phyllis Gurgeview, Publisher
Amy Turner, Managing Editor
Brenda Potts, Circulation Manager
Becky Fenton, Manager
Amy Weiss, Director

Information on remanufacturing imaging supplies including articles that cover business and marketing, technical updates, association and industry news, and company profiles. Related features focus on supply sales and equipment service.
Cost: $45.00
250 Pages
Frequency: Monthly
Circulation: 8000
ISSN: 1053-7503
Printed in 4 colors

7632 **Reclamation Matters**
American Society of Mining and Reclamation
1800 South Oak Street
Suite 100
Champaign, IL 61820

217-333-9489; *Fax:* 859-335-6529
asmr@insightbb.com; www.asmr.us
Social Media: Facebook

Robert Darmody, Executive Secretary
Pete Stahl, President
Kimery Vories, President Elect
Richard Barnhisel, Editor-in-Chief

The official magazine of ASMR.
500 Members
ISSN: 2328-8744
Founded in: 1973

7633 **Recycling Laws International**
Raymond Communications
P.O.Box 4311
Silver Spring, MD 20914-4311

301-345-4237; *Fax:* 301-345-4768
circulation@raymond.com; www.raymond.com

Lorah Utter, Editor
Allyn Sweet, Circulation Manager
Michele Raymond, President

Covers recycling, takeback, green labeling policy for business in 35 countries. Also contains a country page document that is updated annually.
Cost: $485.00
200 Pages
Circulation: 150
Founded in: 1991

7634 **Recycling Product News**
Baum Publications
2323 Boundary Road
#201
Vancouver, BC 0

604-291-9900; *Fax:* 604-291-1906
webadmin@baumpub.com;
www.baumpub.com

Engelbert J Baum, Publisher
Keith Barker, Editor

Published for the recycling center operators and other waste mangers, articles discuss technology and new products.
Circulation: 14000

7635 **Recycling Today**
GIE Media
4012 Bridge Avenue
Cleveland, OH 44113-3320

216-961-4130
800-456-0707; *Fax:* 216-961-0364
info@recyclingtoday.com;
www.recyclingtoday.com/
Social Media: Facebook, Twitter

James R Keefe, Group Publisher
Brian Taylor, Editor
Richard Foster, CEO
Debbie Kean, Manager

Published for the secondary commodity processing/recycling market.
Cost: $30.00
Frequency: Monthly
Circulation: 15000

7636 **Renewable Resources Journal**
Renewable Natural Resources Foundation
5430 Grosvenor Ln
Suite 220
Bethesda, MD 20814-2193

301-493-9101; *Fax:* 301-493-6148
info@rnrf.org; www.rnrf.org

Robert D Day, Executive Director
Ryan M Colker, Programs Director
Chandru Krishna, Circulation

Provides information of general interest concerning public policy issues related to natural resources management. Comprised of contributed and solicited articles on a wide range of natural resource issues, news items about RNRF's members, notices of significant meetings, editorials, and commentaries.
Cost: $25.00
32 Pages
Frequency: Quarterly
Circulation: 1800
ISSN: 0738-6532

Founded in: 1975
Printed in 2 colors on matte stock

7637 **Resource Recycling**
Resource Recycling
PO Box 42270
Portland, OR 97242-270

503-233-1305; *Fax:* 503-233-1356
info@resource-recycling.com;
www.resource-recycling.com

Jerry Powell, Editor/Publisher
Rick Downing, Graphic Designer
Suzette Ducharme, Graphic Designer
Mary Lynch, Executive Editor

The nation's leading recycling and composting magazine. This monthly journal focuses on efforts in the US and Canada to recover materials from homes and businesses for recycling. Accepts advertising.
Cost: $52.00
64 Pages
Frequency: Monthly
Circulation: 14000+
ISSN: 0744-4710
Founded in: 1982
Printed in 4 colors on glossy stock

7638 **Restoration Ecology**
Blackwell Science
350 Main St
Malden, MA 02148-5089

781-388-8250; *Fax:* 781-388-8210
subscrip@bos.blackwellpublishing.com;
www.blackwellpublishing.com

Amy Yodaniss, VP
Richard Hobbs, Editor

Provides the most recent developments in the ecological and biological restoration field for both the fundamental and practical implications of restorations.
Cost: $200.00
Frequency: Quarterly
Circulation: 2000
Founded in: 1897

7639 **Restoration Ecology Journal**
Society for Ecological Restoration International
1017 O Street NW
Washington, DC 20001

202-299-9518; *Fax:* 270-626-5485
info@ser.org; www.ser.org
Social Media: Facebook

Steve Whisenant, Chair
Cara R. Nelson, Vice Chair
Mary Travaglini, Treasurer
Alan Unwin, Secretary

Primary emphases are: research on restoration and ecological principles that help explain restoration processes, descriptions of techniques that the authors have pioneered and that are likely to be of use to other practicing restorationists, desriptions of setbacks and surprises encountered during restoration and the lessons learnt, analytical opinions, and reviews of articles that summarize literature on specialized aspects of restoration.
2300 Members
Frequency: Bi-Monthly
Founded in: 1988

7640 **Review of Environmental Economics and Policy (REEP)**
Association of Environmental and Resource Economis
13006 Peaceful Terrace
Silver Spring, MD 20904

202-559-8998; *Fax:* 202-559-8998
info@aere.org; www.aere.org

Catherine L. Kling, President
Sarah L. Stafford, Secretary
Juha Siikamaki, Treasurer
Wiktor L. Adamowicz, Vice President

Designed for broad appeal to economists and others in academia, government, the private sector, and the advocacy world who share a common interest in environmental and natural resource policy. Rather than focusing on technical and methodological aspects of research, articles will focus on the broad lessons that can be learned, for environmental and resource economics or for public policy, from broader lines of research.
900 Members
Founded in: 1979

7641 **Risk Policy Report**
Inside Washington Publishers
1919 S Eads St
Suite 1400
Arlington, VA 22202-3028

703-418-3981; *Fax:* 703-415-8543
support@iwpnews.com; www.iwpnews.com

Alan Sosenko, Owner
David Clarke, Editor

Contains analysis, great perspectives, industry news, policymaking profiles and a calendar of events.
Cost: $295.00
Frequency: Monthly
Founded in: 1980

7642 **SETAC Globe**
Society of Environmental Toxicology and Chemistry
1013 N 12th Ave
Pensacola, FL 32501-3306

850-437-1901; *Fax:* 850-469-9778
rparrish@setac.org; www.edwardjones.com

Chad Stacy, Manager
Greg Schifer, Manager

Stay up to date on the latest firm news, and learn about the companies followed with Edward Jones.
Frequency: Bi-Monthly

7643 **SOLAR TODAY**
American Solar Energy Society
4760 Walnut Street
Suite 106
Boulder, CO 80301-2843

303-443-3130; *Fax:* 303-443-3212
ases@ases.org; www.ases.org
Social Media: Facebook, Twitter, LinkedIn

David G. Hill, Chair
Bill Poulin, Treasurer
Jason Keyes, Secretary
Jeff Lyng, Immediate Past Chair

Trusted source for the latest technology, policy advances and analysis. Brings together ASES' professional members as contributors and readers, amid the community of ASES chapters nationwide, to publish industry-leading editorial.
ISSN: 1042-0630

7644 **Science Magazine**
American Assn for the Advancement of Science
1200 New York Avenue NW
Washington, DC 20005-3941

202-266-6721; *Fax:* 202-371-9227
membership@aaas.org; www.aaas.org
Social Media: Facebook, Twitter

Kathy Fishback, Publication Services Director

The world's leading outlet for scientific news, commentary, and cutting-edge research. Available online and in print, Science Magazine continues to publish the very best in scientific research, news, and opinion.

7645 **Scrap Magazine**
Institute of Scrap Recycling Industries
1615 L St NW
Suite 600
Washington, DC 20036-5664

202-662-8500; *Fax:* 202-626-0900
isri@isri.org; www.isri.org

John Sacco, Chairman
Jerry I. Simms, Chair Elect
Douglas Kramer, Vice Chair
Mark R. Lewon, Secretary Treasurer

Providing practical and useful information to scrap professionals through articles and columns that will increase the profitability of their businesses. The editorial content is designed to stimulate- to help scrap professionals manage all aspects of their businesses more successfully.
165 Members
1987 Attendees

7646 **Security Products**
Stevens Publishing Corporation
5151 Belt Line Rd
10th Floor
Dallas, TX 75254-7507

972-687-6700; *Fax:* 972-687-6767;
www.secprodonline.com

Craig S Stevens, President
Dana Cornett, President/COO
Randy Dye, Publisher
Ralph Jensen, Editor-In-Chief
Margaret Perry, Circulation Director

Leading new product and technology resource for security dealers, integrators and end users seeking comprehensive product-related information.
Circulation: 63000
Founded in: 1925

7647 **Shore & Beach**
American Shore and Beach Preservation Association
5460 Beaujolais Lane
Fort Myers, FL 33919

239-489-2616; *Fax:* 239-362-9771
exdir@asbpa.org; www.asbpa.org
Social Media: Facebook, Twitter

Harry Simmons, President
Kate Gooderham, Executive Director
Lesley Ewing, Editor
Beth Sciaudone, Managing Editor
Ken Gooderham, Production

Information and articles regarding management of shores and beaches.
1M Members
Founded in: 1926

7648 **Sierra**
85 Second St.
2nd Fl.
San Francisco, CA 94105-3459

E-Mail: sierra.magazine@sierraclub.org;
www.sierraclub.org/sierra
Social Media: Facebook, Twitter, Pinterest, Instagram

Jason Mark, Editor-in-Chief
Tracy Cox, Art Director

The official magazine of the Sierra Club.
Cost: $3.95
Frequency: Bimonthly
Circulation: 1000000
ISSN: 0161-7362

7649 **Soil Science Society of America Journal**
American Society of Agronomy
5585 Guilford Rd.
Madison, WI 53711-1086

608-273-8080; *Fax:* 608-273-2021
headquarters@sciencesocieties.org;

www.agronomy.org
Social Media: Facebook, Twitter, LinkedIn

Newell Kitchen, President
Kenneth Barbarick, President-Elect

Publishes basic and applied soil research in agricultural, forest, wetlands, urban settings and more.
10000 Members
Founded in: 1907

7650 **Soil Survey Horizons**
American Society of Agronomy
5585 Guilford Rd.
Madison, WI 53711-1086

608-273-8080; *Fax:* 608-273-2021
headquarters@sciencesocieties.org;
www.agronomy.org
Social Media: Facebook, Twitter, LinkedIn

Newell Kitchen, President
Kenneth Barbarick, President-Elect

Informs and entertains with research updates, soil problems and solutions, history of soil survey, and personal essays from the lives of soil scientists in the field.
10000 Members
Founded in: 1907

7651 **Soil and Sediment Contamination**
AEHS Foundation Inc.
150 Fearing Street
Suite 21
Amherst, MA 01002

413-549-5170
888-540-2347; www.aehs.com

Paul T Kostecki, PhD, Executive Director

Focuses on soil and sediment contamination from; sludges, petroleum, petrochemicals, chlorinated hydrocarbons, pesticides, and lead and other heavy metals. Offers detailed descriptions of all the latest and most efficient offsite and in situ remediation techniques, strategies for assessing health effects and hazards, and tips for dealing with everyday regulatory and legal issues. Assess, mitigate, and solve rural and urban soil contamination problems.
Frequency: Bi-Monthly

7652 **Solid Waste & Recycling**
Southam Environment Group
1450 Don Mills Road
Don Mills, ON 0

905-305-6155
888-702-1111; *Fax:* 416-442-2026
bobrien@solidwastemag.com;
www.solidwastemag.com

Brad O'Brien, Publisher
Bibi Khan, Circualtion Manager
Guy Crittenden, Editor-in-Chief

Emphasizes municipal and commercial aspects of collection, handling, transportation, hauling, disposal and treatment of solid waste , including incineration, recycling and landfill technology.
Cost: $29.95
Frequency: Weekly
Circulation: 10000

7653 **Solid Waste Report**
Business Publishers
2222 Sedwick Dr
Suite 101
Durham, NC 27713

800-223-8720; *Fax:* 800-508-2592
custserv@bpinews.com; www.bpinews.com

Comprehensive news and analysis of legislation, regulation and litigation in solid waste management including resource recovery, recycling, collection and disposal. Regularly features international news, state updates and business trends.
Cost: $567.00
Founded in: 1963

7654 **TIDE**
Coastal Conservation Association
6919 Portwest Dr
Suite 100
Houston, TX 77024-8049

713-626-4234
800-201-FISH; *Fax:* 713-626-5852
ccantl@joincca.org; www.joincca.org
Social Media: Twitter

David Cummins, President

The official magazine of the CCA.
85000 Members
Founded in: 1977

7655 **The Leading Edge**
Society of Exploration Geophysicists
8801 South Yale
Suite 500
Tulsa, OK 74137-3575

918-497-5500; *Fax:* 918-497-5557
web@seg.org; www.seg.org
Social Media: Facebook, Twitter, LinkedIn

Mary Fleming, Executive Director
Vladimir Grechka, Editor

A gateway publication, introducing new geophysical theory, instrumentation, and established practices to scientists in a wide range of geoscience disciplines. Most material is presented in a semitechnical manner that minimizes mathematical theory and emphasizes practical application. Also serves as SEG's publication venue for official society business.

7656 **The Plant Genome**
American Society of Agronomy
5585 Guilford Rd.
Madison, WI 53711-1086

608-273-8080; *Fax:* 608-273-2021
headquarters@sciencesocieties.org;
www.agronomy.org
Social Media: Facebook, Twitter, LinkedIn

Newell Kitchen, President
Kenneth Barbarick, President-Elect

Electronic journal providing leadership of the latest advances and breakthroughs in plant genomics research.
10000 Members
Founded in: 1907

7657 **Tree Farmer Magazine, the Guide to Sustaining America's Family Forests**
American Forest Foundation
1111 19th St NW
Suite 780
Washington, DC 20036

202-463-2700; *Fax:* 202-463-2785
info@forestfoundation.org;
www.forestfoundation.org

Tom Martin, President & CEO
Brigitte Johnson APR, Director Communications, Editor

The official magazine of ATFS, this periodical provides practical, how-to and hands-on information and techniques, and services to help private fore landowners to become better stewards, save money and time, and add to the enjoyment of their land.

7658 **Vadose Zone Journal**
American Society of Agronomy
5585 Guilford Rd.
Madison, WI 53711-1086

608-273-8080; *Fax:* 608-273-2021
headquarters@sciencesocieties.org;
www.agronomy.org
Social Media: Facebook, Twitter, LinkedIn

Newell Kitchen, President
Kenneth Barbarick, President-Elect

Focuses on multidisciplinary research in the unsaturated zone appealing to a diverse group of scientists and engineers.
10000 Members
Founded in: 1907

7659 **Washington Environmental Compliance Update**
M Lee Smith Publishers
PO Box 5094
Bentwood, TN 37024-5094

615-737-7517
800-274-6774

F Lee Smith, Publisher
Douglas S Little, Editor

Review of environmental laws.
Cost: $225.00
8 Pages
Frequency: Daily
Mailing list available for rent
Printed in 2 colors on matte stock

7660 **Waste Age**
Environmental Industry Association
4301 Connecticut Ave NW
#300
Washington, DC 20008-2304

202-966-4701; *Fax:* 202-966-4818
contact@envasns.org; www.wasterecycling.org
Social Media: Facebook, Twitter, YouTube

Bruce Parker, President
Patricia-Ann Tom, Editor
Laura Magliola, Marketing Manager
Christine Hutcherson, Director Member Services
Alice Jacobsohn, Director Education

Contents focus on new system technologies, recycling, resource recovery and sanitary landfills with regular features on updates in the status of government regulations, new products, guides, company profiles, exclusive survey information, legislative implications and news.
Frequency: Monthly
Circulation: 38000

7661 **Waste Age's Recycling Times**
Environmental Industry Association
4301 Connecticut Ave NW
#300
Washington, DC 20008-2304

202-966-4701; *Fax:* 202-966-4818
rct@envasns.org; www.wasteage.com

Bruce Parker, President
Wendy Angel, Assistant Editor
Gregg Herring, Group Publisher

Features municipalities, recycling goals and rates, program innovations, waste habits, and new materials being recycled.
Cost: $99.00
Frequency: Monthly
Circulation: 5000

7662 **Water & Wastes Digest**
Scranton Gillette Communications
3030 W Salt Creek Lane
Suite 201
Arlington Heights, IL 60005-5025

847-391-1000; *Fax:* 847-390-0408
nsimeonova@sgcmail.com;
www.scrantongillette.com
Social Media: Facebook, Twitter, LinkedIn

Neda Simeonova, Editorial Director
Caitlin Cunningham, Managing Editor

Serves readers in the water and/or wastewater industries. These people work for municipalities, in industry, or as engineers. They design, specify,

buy, operate and maintain equipment, chemicals, software and wastewater treatment services.
Cost: $40.00
128 Pages
Frequency: Monthly
Circulation: 101000
ISSN: 0043-1181
Founded in: 1961

7663 Water Environment & Technology (WE&T)
Water Environment Federation
601 Wythe St
Alexandria, VA 22314-1994

800-666-0206; *Fax:* 703-684-2492;
www.wef.org
Social Media: Facebook, Twitter

Matt Bond, President
Cordell Samuels, President-Elect
Sandra Ralston, Vice President
Chris Browning, Treasurer
Jeff Eger, Secretary and Executive Director

Premier magazine for the water quality field. Provides information on what professionals demand; cutting-edge technologies, innovative solutions, regulatory and legislative impacts, and professional development.
79 Members
ISSN: 1044-9943
Founded in: 1928

7664 Water Environment Research (WER)
Water Environment Federation
601 Wythe St
Alexandria, VA 22314-1994

800-666-0206; *Fax:* 703-684-2492;
www.wef.org
Social Media: Facebook, Twitter

Matt Bond, President
Cordell Samuels, President-Elect
Sandra Ralston, Vice President
Chris Browning, Treasurer
Jeff Eger, Secretary and Executive Director

Original, fundamental and applied research in all scientific and technical areas related to water quality, pollution contro, and management.
79 Members
ISSN: 1044-9943
Founded in: 1928

7665 Water Quality Products
Scranton Gillette Communications
3030 W Salt Creek Lane
Suite 201
Arlington Heights, IL 60005

847-391-1000; *Fax:* 847-390-0408;
www.wqpmag.com
Social Media: Facebook, Twitter

Neda Simeonova, Editorial Director
Dennis Martyka, VP/Group Publisher
Kate Cline, Managing Editor

Provides balanced editorial content including developments in water conditioning, filtration and disinfection for residential, commercial and industrial systeme.
Cost: $40.00
68 Pages
Frequency: Monthly
Circulation: 19000
ISSN: 1092-0978
Founded in: 1995

7666 Wildfire Magazine
International Association of Wildland Fire
4025 Fair Ridge Drive
Fairfax, VA 22033

785-423-1818; *Fax:* 785-542-3511
sandy@iawfonline.org; www.iawfonline.org

Sacha Dick, Programs Manager
Mikel Robinson, Executive Director

Addresses the needs of chiefs and wildland forestry managers by providing a unique international prospective. Each issue focuses on the demand of leaders responsible for managing and controlling wildland fires. Readers are the top decision makers and leaders who have influence over purchasing equipment, supplies and contracted services. Readership includes fire chiefs, governmental agencies, private sector professionals, consultants and contractors.
Frequency: Monthly

7667 Wildlife Conservation Magazine
2300 S Boulevard
Bronx, NY 10460

718-220-5121
800-786-8226; *Fax:* 718-584-2625
magazine@wcs.org;
www.wildlifeconservation.org/

Debby Bahler, Editor
Diana Warren, Advertising Director
4teve Sanderson, President

A national nature and science magazine. Contains stunning photography, conservation news and special updates on endangered species. Learn how to help protect local wildlife, and the secrets of the world's rarest and most mysterious animals.
Cost: $19.95
96 Pages
Circulation: 150000
Founded in: 1895

7668 World Resource Review
SUPCON International
International Headquarters 2W381
75th Street
Naperville, IL 60565-9245

630-910-1551; *Fax:* 630-910-1561
syshen@megsinet.net; www.globalwarming.net

Dr. Sinyan Shen, Production Manager

For business and government readers, provides expert worldwide reviews of global warming and extreme events in relation to the management of natural, mineral and material resources. Subjects include global warming impacts on agriculture, energy, and infrastructure, monitoring of changes in resources using remote sensing, actions of national and international bodies, global carbon budget, greenhouse budget and more.
Cost: $72.00
Frequency: Quarterly
Circulation: 12000
ISSN: 1042-8011

7669 World Wastes: The Independent Voice
Communication Channels
6151 Powers Ferry Road NW
Atlanta, GA 30339-2959

770-953-4805; *Fax:* 770-618-0348

Bill Wolpin, Editor
Jerrold France, President Argus Business

Reaches individuals and firms engaged in the removal and disposal of solid wastes.
Cost: $48.00
Frequency: Monthly
Circulation: 36,000

7670 World Water
Water Environment Federation
601 Wythe St
Alexandria, VA 22314-1994

800-666-0206; *Fax:* 703-684-2492;
www.wef.org
Social Media: Facebook, Twitter

Matt Bond, President
Cordell Samuels, President-Elect
Sandra Ralston, Vice President
Chris Browning, Treasurer
Jeff Eger, Secretary and Executive Director

International magazine for the water quality industry. Provides the most cutting-edge and helpful information on global water issues.
79 Members
ISSN: 1044-9943
Founded in: 1928

7671 World Water Reuse & Desalination
Water Environment Federation
601 Wythe St
Alexandria, VA 22314-1994

800-666-0206; *Fax:* 703-684-2492;
www.wef.org
Social Media: Facebook, Twitter

Matt Bond, President
Cordell Samuels, President-Elect
Sandra Ralston, Vice President
Chris Browning, Treasurer
Jeff Eger, Secretary and Executive Director

Becoming the global news and information resource for the water reuse and quality industries. Provides the most up-to-date and innovative information on all facets of global water reuse and desalination issues.
79 Members
ISSN: 1044-9943
Founded in: 1928

Trade Shows

7672 AAAR Annual Conference
American Association for Aerosol Research
15000 Commerce Parkway
Suite C
Mount Laurel, NJ 08054

856-439-9080
877-777-6753; *Fax:* 856-439-0525
info@aaar.org; www.aaar.org

William Nazaroff, President
Barbara Turpin, Vice President
Barbara Wyslouzil, Vice President Elect
Murray Johnston, Treasurer
CY Wu, Secretary

Benefit from learning about the latest advances across the full frontier of aerosol science and technology. An excellent opportunity to renew old acquaintances and to meet new colleagues.
1000 Members
Founded in: 1982

7673 AAAR Annual Meeting
American Association for Aerosol Research
15000 Commerce Parkway
Suite C
Mount Laurel, NJ 08054

856-439-9080; *Fax:* 856-439-0525
dbright@ahint.com; www.aaar.org

Lynn Russell, Program Chair
Melissa Baldwin, Executive Director

Exibits related to aerosol research in areas including industrial process, air pollution, and industrial hygiene. Over 600 professionals attend.
600 Attendees
Frequency: Annual, October

7674 AAAS Annual Meeting
Renewable Natural Resources Foundation
5430 Grosvenor Ln
Bethesda, MD 20814-2193

301-493-9101; *Fax:* 301-493-6148
info@rnrf.org; www.rnrf.org

Howard N. Rosen, Chairman
Richard A. Engberg, Vice-Chairman
Robert D. Day, Executive Director

The most important general science venue for a growing segment of scientists and engineers.
14 Members
Founded in: 1972

7675 **ACCA Annual Meetings**
Air Conditioning Contractors of America
2800 Shirlington Rd
Suite 300
Arlington, VA 22206

703-575-4477
info@acca.org; www.acca.org
Social Media: Facebook, Twitter, LinkedIn, YouTube

Paul T Stalknecht, President & CEO

Where America's most successful HVACR, building services, and energy professionals come together to share, learn, and collaborate. Options for learning how to take your business to the next levels of profitability and success.
Frequency: February/March

7676 **ACE Annual Conference**
Air & Waste Management Association
420 Fort Duquesne Boulevard
One Gateway Center, 3rd Floor
Pittsburgh, PA 15222-1435

412-652-2458; *Fax:* 412-232-3450
info@awma.org; www.awma.org
Social Media: Facebook, Twitter, LinkedIn

Jeffry Muffat, President
Merlyn L. Hough, President Elect
Mike Kelly, Secretary/ Executive Director
Amy Gilligan, Treasurer
Dallas Baker, Vice President

Environmental professionals from around the world to the outstanding technical program, exhibits of the latest products and services, and networking and professional development opportunities.
9000 Members
Founded in: 1907

7677 **AEESP Annual Meeting**
Association of Environmental Engineering and
2303 Naples Court
Champaign, IL 61822

217-398-6969; *Fax:* 217-355-9232
joanne@aeesp.org; www.aeesp.org

Joanne Fetzner, Business Secretary

With the Water Environment Federation
Frequency: Fall

7678 **AERE Summer Conference**
Association of Environmental and Resource
1616 P Street NW
Suite 600
Washington, DC 20036

202-328-5125; *Fax:* 202-939-3460
voigt@rff.org; www.aere.org

Marilyn Voigt, Executive Director

nonprofit international professional association for economists working on the environment and natural resources.
850 Members
350 Attendees
Frequency: January
Founded in: 1979

7679 **APLIC Annual Conference**
Family Health International Library
PO Box 13950
Research Triangle Park, NC 27709

919-447-7040; www.aplici.org

Claire Twose, President
Lori Rosman, Vice-President
Joann Donatiello, Treasurer

Focuses on current issues in communication, information, and resource technology and management.
Frequency: Annual

7680 **APWA International Public Works Congress & Expo**
American Public Works Association
2345 Grand Boulevard
Suite 700
Kansas City, MO 64108-2625

816-472-6100
800-848-2792; *Fax:* 816-472-1610
ddancy@apwa.net; www.apwa.net

Peter King, Executive Director
David Dancy, Director Of Marketing

Offers the benefit of a variety of educational sessions, depth of the exhibit program and endless opportunities for networking. The latest cutting-edge technologies, managerial techniques and regulatory trends designed to keep you focused on the right solutions at the right time.
6500 Attendees
Frequency: Annual/September
ISSN: 0092-4873
Founded in: 1894

7681 **ASAS Annual Meeting**
American Society of Animal Science
1111 N Dunlap Avenue
Savoy, IL 61874

217-356-9050; *Fax:* 217-398-4119; www.asas.org

Paula Schultz, Meetings Coordinator
Lorena Nicholas, General Meeting Information
Kim Surles, Exhibits/Advertising
Jerry Baker, Executive Director

This meeting serves as an international forum to gather vital information for the future of the animal agriculture industry. A cutting-edge scientific program in food science, animal health, dairy production, beef nutrition, swine nutrition, reproduction, companion animals, and many other diverse interests.
3500 Attendees
Frequency: July/Non-Members Fee
Founded in: 1908

7682 **ASBPA Coastal Summit**
American Shore & Beach Preservation Association
5460 Beaujolais Lane
Fort Myers, FL 33919

239-489-2616; *Fax:* 239-362-9771
exdir@asbpa.org; www.asbpa.org
Social Media: Facebook, Twitter

Tony Pratt, President
Nicole Elko, Vice President
Cameron Perry, Treasurer
Derek Brockbank, Executive Director

information and articles regarding management of shores and beaches.
1M Members
Founded in: 1926

7683 **ASBPA National Coastal Conference**
American Shore and Beach Preservation Association
5460 Beaujolais Lane
Fort Myers, FL 33919

239-489-2616; *Fax:* 239-362-9771
managing@aspba.org; www.asbpa.org
Social Media: Facebook, Twitter

Tony Pratt, President
Kate Gooderham, Executive Director
Nicole Elko, Secretary
Russell Boudreau, VP
Brad Pickel, Treasurer

Federal, state and local coastal policy and legal issues, shoreline processes and coastal management, shoreline projects and global coastal issues are discussed.
1M Members
Founded in: 1926

7684 **ASEH Annual Meeting**
American Society for Environmental History
119 Pine Street
Suite 301
Seattle, WA 98101

206-343-0226; *Fax:* 206-343-0249; www.aseh.net

Lisa Mighetto, Acting Executive Director

Individuals and groups all over the world will attend to collaborate on ways to live better with nature, and to make a better world for all outside of traditional political structures and older models of environmentalism.
Frequency: Spring, Texas

7685 **ASES National Solar Conference**
American Solar Energy Society
4760 Walnut Street
Suite 106
Boulder, CO 80301-2843

303-443-3130; *Fax:* 303-443-3212
ases@ases.org; www.ases.org
Social Media: Facebook, Twitter, LinkedIn

David G. Hill, Chair
Bill Poulin, Treasurer
Jason Keyes, Secretary
Jeff Lyng, Immediate Past Chair

America's premier educational event for solar energy professionals. The conference introduces you to the leaders, innovators and technologies moving the industry forward.
ISSN: 1042-0630

7686 **ASES National Solar Tour**
American Solar Energy Society
4760 Walnut Street
Suite 106
Boulder, CO 80301-2843

303-443-3130; *Fax:* 303-443-3212
ases@ases.org; www.ases.org
Social Media: Facebook, Twitter, LinkedIn

David G. Hill, Chair
Bill Poulin, Treasurer
Jason Keyes, Secretary
Jeff Lyng, Immediate Past Chair

The largest grassroots solar event in history. Offers participants the opportunity to tour homes and buildings to see how neighbors are using solar energy, energy efficiency and other sustainable technologies to reduce their monthly utility bills and help tackle climate change.
ISSN: 1042-0630

7687 **ASFE Fall Meeting**
ASFE/The Geoprofessional Business Association
8811 Colesville Road
Suite G106
Silver Springs, MD 20910

301-565-2733; *Fax:* 301-589-2017
info@asfe.org; www.asfe.org

John P Bachner, Executive VP

Providing geotechnical, geologic, environmental, construction materials engineering and testing, and related professional services information and education.
Frequency: Annual/Fall

7688 **ASFE Spring Meeting**
ASFE
8811 Colesville Road
Suite G106
Silver Springs, MD 20910

301-565-2733; *Fax:* 301-589-2017
info@asfe.org; www.asfe.org

John P Bachner, Executive VP

Provides geotechnical, geologic, environmental, construction materials engineering and testing,

and related professional services information and education.
Frequency: Annual/Spring

7689 ASFE Winter Leadership Conference
ASFE/The Geoprofessional Business Association
8811 Colesville Road
Suite G106
Silver Springs, MD 20910

301-565-2733; *Fax:* 301-589-2014
info@asfe.org; www.asfe.org

John Bachner, Executive VP

ASFE's leaders meet to finish priorities for the current year and determine the direction of ASFE for the coming year.
Frequency: Annual/January

7690 ASFPM Annual Conference
Association of State Floodplain Managers
2809 Fish Hatchery Road
Suite 204
Madison, WI 53713

608-274-0123; *Fax:* 608-274-0696
memberhelp@floods.org; www.floods.org

Larry Larson, Executive Director
Alison Stierli, Manager
Diane Brown, Manager

Focus on floodproofing techniques, materials, floodproofing and elevation contractors, current issues and programs, new federal tax impications and the various means of funding floodproofing projects. implications.
Frequency: Annual

7691 ASFPM Annual National Conference
Association of State Floodplain Managers
2809 Fish Hatchery Rd
Suite 204
Madison, WI 53713-5020

608-274-0123; *Fax:* 608-274-0696
Larry@floods.org; www.floods.org
Social Media: Facebook

Sally McConkey, Chair
William Nechamen, Vice Chair
Alan J. Giles, Secretary
John V. Crofts, Treasurer

The national conferences all community, state and federal floodplain managers plan to attend. Many of the most important consulting firms and product vendors associated with floodplain management attend.
6500 Members
Founded in: 1977

7692 ASMA Annual Meeting
American Society of Mining and Reclamation
1800 South Oak Street
Suite 100
Champaign, IL 61820

217-333-9489; *Fax:* 859-335-6529
asmr@insightbb.com; www.asmr.us
Social Media: Facebook

Robert Darmody, Executive Secretary
Pete Stahl, President
Kimery Vories, President Elect

Approximately 30 exhibitors.
Frequency: Annual
Founded in: 1973

7693 ASMR Meeting & Conference
American Society of Mining and Reclamation
1800 South Oak Street
Suite 100
Champaign, IL 61820-6974

859-335-6529
asmr@insightbb.com; www.asmr.us

Robert Darmody, Executive Secretary
Pete Stahl, President
Kimery Vories, President Elect

Promoting the advancement of basic and applied reclamation science through research and technology transfer.
Founded in: 1973

7694 ASPRS Annual Conference
American Society for Photogammetry/Remote Sensing
5410 Grosvenor Lane
Suite 210
Bethesda, MD 20814-2160

301-493-0290; *Fax:* 301-493-0208
asprs@asprs.org; www.asprs.org

Dr. Carolyn J. Merry, Ph.D., President
Roberta Lenczowski, VP
Dr. Donald Laurer, Treasurer
James Plasker, Executive Director

One hundred exhibits of mapping, photogrammetry, environmental management, remote sensing, geographic information, natural resources and much more.
6000 Members
2000 Attendees
Founded in: 1934

7695 AWEA Offshore Windpower Conference Exhibition
American Wind Energy Association
1501 M Street NW
Suite 1000
Washington, DC 20005

202-383-2500; *Fax:* 202-383-2505
windmail@awea.org; www.awea.org
Social Media: Facebook, Twitter, YouTube

Ned Hall, Chair
Thomas Carnahan, Chair-Elect
Gabriel Alonso, Secretary
Don Furman, Treasurer
Vic Abate, Past Chair

Brings together exhibitors and attendees from all over the world who are interested in becoming players in this new and highly promising market.
2400 Members

7696 Aerosol/ Atmospheric Optics: Visibility and Air Pollution
A&WMA
420 Fort Duquesne Boulevard
One Gateway Center, 3rd Floor
Pittsburgh, PA 15222-1435

412-652-2458; *Fax:* 412-232-3450
info@awma.org; www.awma.org
Social Media: Facebook, Twitter, LinkedIn

Jeffry Muffat, President
Merlyn L. Hough, President Elect
Mike Kelly, Secretary/ Executive Director
Amy Gilligan, Treasurer
Dallas Baker, Vice President

Provide a technical forum on advances in the scientific understanding of the effects of aerosols.
9000 Members
Founded in: 1907

7697 Air Quality Measurement Methods and Technology
A&WMA
420 Fort Duquesne Boulevard
One Gateway Center, 3rd Floor
Pittsburgh, PA 15222-1435

412-652-2458; *Fax:* 412-232-3450
info@awma.org; www.awma.org
Social Media: Facebook, Twitter, LinkedIn

Jeffry Muffat, President
Merlyn L. Hough, President Elect
Mike Kelly, Secretary/ Executive Director
Amy Gilligan, Treasurer
Dallas Baker, Vice President

Explore advances in measurement technology, data quality assurance, and data uses.
9000 Members
Founded in: 1907

7698 Air and Waste Management Association Annual Conference and Exhibition
Air and Waste Management Association
1 Gateway Center
3rd Floor
Pittsburgh, PA 15222-1435

412-652-2458
800-270-3444; *Fax:* 412-232-3450
info@awma.org; www.awma.org

Deborah Hilfman, Show Manager
Robert Greenbaum, Exhibit Manager

Environmental professionals from all sectors of the economy including colleges, universities, natural resource manufacturing and process industries, consultants, local state, provincial, regional and federal governments, construction, utilities industries. Over 300 exhibits of envirnomental control products.
6000 Attendees

7699 American Meteorological Society Annual Meeting
Renewable Natural Resources Foundation
5430 Grosvenor Ln
Bethesda, MD 20814-2193

301-493-9101; *Fax:* 301-493-6148
info@rnrf.org; www.rnrf.org

Howard N. Rosen, Chairman
Richard A. Engberg, Vice-Chairman
Robert D. Day, Executive Director

Technology in research and operations, how we got here and where we're going.
14 Members
Founded in: 1972

7700 American Occupational Health Conference & Exhibits
Slack
4930 Del Ray Avenue
Bethesda, MD 20814

301-654-2055; *Fax:* 301-654-5920
member@gastro.org; www.gastro.org

Robert Greenberg, Executive Vp
Michael Stolar, Senior Vp

400 exhibits of pharmaceuticals, equipment, software and supplies for health professionals, offices and labs.
4500 Attendees

7701 American Society of Safety Engineers Professional Development Conference
American Society of Safety Engineers
1800 E Oakton Street
Des Plaines, IL 60018

847-699-2929; *Fax:* 847-768-3434
customerservice@asse.org; www.asse.org

Fred Fortman, Executive Director
Jim Drzewiecki, Finance/Controller Director
Diane Hurns, Manager Public Relations Department

Annual conference and expo of 250 manufacturers and suppliers of safety equipment and health products.
3500 Attendees
Frequency: June

7702 **American Water Resources Association Annual Water Resource Conference**
Renewable Natural Resources Foundation
5430 Grosvenor Ln
Bethesda, MD 20814-2193

301-493-9101; *Fax:* 301-493-6148
info@rnrf.org; www.rnrf.org

Howard N. Rosen, Chairman
Richard A. Engberg, Vice-Chairman
Robert D. Day, Executive Director

Brings together a diverse group of water resource professionals from across the state. Presenting a unique opportunity for water resource practitioners from diverse disciplines to gether and interact together.
14 Members
Founded in: 1972

7703 **Annual EcoFarm Conference**
Community Alliance with Family Farmers
PO Box 363
Davis, CA 95617-363

530-756-8518; *Fax:* 530-756-7857
info@caff.org; www.caff.org
Social Media: Facebook, Twitter, YouTube

Carol Presley, Board Chair
Pete Price, Vice President
Judith Redmond, Secretary
Vicki Williams, Treasurer

Oldest and largest ecological agricultural gathering in the West, meets every year to create, maintain, and promote healthy, safe, and just food farming systems. Myriad opportunities for networking with colleagues, discovering the newest ecological agricultural delvelopment and techniques, and building skills for individuals and together as a community.

7704 **Annual International Conference on Soil, Water, Energy, and Air**
AEHS Foundation Inc
150 Fearing Street
Amherst, MA 01002

413-549-5170; *Fax:* 413-549-0579;
www.aehsfoundation.org

Paul T Kostecki, PhD, Executive Director

Live equipment demonstrations augment the exhibition hall, bringing real world application to the technical theory presented in the sessions. An exciting opportunity for all those concerned with the challenge of developing creative, cost-effective assessments and solutions that can withstand the demands of regulatory requirements.
600 Members
Founded in: 1989

7705 **Annual International Conference on Soils, Sediments, Water and Energy**
AEHS Foundation Inc
150 Fearing Street
Amherst, MA 01002

413-549-5170; *Fax:* 413-549-0579;
www.aehsfoundation.org

Paul T Kostecki, PhD, Executive Director

Live equipment demonstrations augment the exhibition hall, bringing real world application to the technical theory presented in the sessions. An exciting opportunity for all those concerned with the challenge of developing creative, cost-effective assessments and solutions that can withstand the demands of regulatory requirements.
600 Members
Founded in: 1989

7706 **Annual National Ethanol Conference**
Renewable Fuels Association
425 Third Street, SW
Suite 1150
Washington, DC 20024

202-289-3835; *Fax:* 202-289-7519
info@ethanolrfa.org; www.ethanolrfa.org
Social Media: Facebook, Twitter

Chuck Woodside, Chairman
Neill McKinstray, Vice Chairman
Randall Doyal, Treasurer
Walter Wendland, Secretary

Delivers accurate, timely information on marketing, legislative and regulatory issues facing the ethanol industry. Industry leaders and experts address accelerating innovation in technology, marketing, logistics and feedstocks for the production of advanced ethanol.
55 Members
Founded in: 1981

7707 **Annual Odors and Air Pollutants Conference**
Water Environment Federation
601 Wythe St
Alexandria, VA 22314-1994

800-666-0206; *Fax:* 703-684-2492;
www.wef.org
Social Media: Facebook, Twitter

Matt Bond, President
Cordell Samuels, President-Elect
Sandra Ralston, Vice President
Chris Browning, Treasurer
Jeff Eger, Secretary and Executive Director

Topics covered include; odor and emission Control Systems, Biological odor control, innovative technologies, design of odor control systems, collection systems tunnel ventilation, emission from biosolids, fate and odor modeling, and many more.
79 Members
ISSN: 1044-9943
Founded in: 1928

7708 **Annual SWCS International Conference**
Soil and Water Conservation Society
945 SW Ankeny Rd
Ankeny, IA 50023-9764

515-289-2331
800-843-7645; *Fax:* 515-289-1227
swcs@swcs.org; www.swcs.org

Bill Boyer, President
Dan Towery, Vice-President
Clark Gantzer, Secretary
Jerry Pearce, Treasurer

Considering Ecology, Economics and Ethics.
5000+ Members
Founded in: 1943

7709 **Aquatic Plant Management Society Annual Meeting**
Aquatic Plant Management Society
PO Box 821265
Vicksburg, MS 39182-1265

Fax: 601-634-2398
dpetty@ndrsite.com; www.apms.org
Social Media: Facebook, LinkedIn

Linda Nelson, President
Terry Goldsby, VP
Sherry Whitaker, Treasurer
Jeff Schardt, Secretary
Greg Aguillard, Director

An international organization of educators, scientists, commercial pesticide applicators, administrators and individuals interested in aquatic plant species and plant management.
Founded in: 1961

7710 **Biennial International Conference on Petroleum Geophysics**
Society of Exploration Geophysicists
8801 South Yale
Suite 500
Tulsa, OK 74137-3575

918-497-5500; *Fax:* 918-497-5557
web@seg.org; www.seg.org
Social Media: Facebook, Twitter, LinkedIn

Mary Fleming, Executive Director
Vladimir Grechka, Editor

Continuing education courses, exhibitions and networking.
Founded in: 1930

7711 **BioInterface**
Surfaces in Biomaterials Foundation
1000 Westgate Drive
Suite 252
Saint Paul, MN 55114

651-290-6295; *Fax:* 651-290-2266
memberservices@surfaces.org;
www.surfaces.org

Bill Monn, Executive Director
Larry Salvati, President

One of the best technical and most stimulating conferences in the field of biomaterials science. Connect, share and learn by relaxed contact with fellow attendees. Be enriched by the science, and the high quality of interaction that is fostered by the unique blend of industry, academic, regulatory and clinical attendees.
150 Attendees
Frequency: Annual/Fall

7712 **CONTE Conference on Nuclear Training and Education**
555 N Kensington Ave
La Grange Park, IL 60526-5592

708-352-6611
800-323-3044; *Fax:* 708-352-0499
advertising@ans.org; www.ans.org
Social Media: Facebook, Twitter, LinkedIn

Jack Tuohy, Executive Director
James S Tulenko, VP
William F Naughton, Treasurer

Topics of interest include knowledge retention, industry training practices, workforce development, government support, partnerships with colleges and universities, applications of technology to training, and training for next generation of nuclear plants.
10500 Members
Founded in: 1954

7713 **Conference of the Brazilian Association for Aerosol Research**
American Association for Aerosol Research
15000 Commerce Parkway
Suite C
Mount Laurel, NJ 08054

856-439-9080
877-777-6753; *Fax:* 856-439-0525
info@aaar.org; www.aaar.org

William Nazaroff, President
Barbara Turpin, Vice President
Barbara Wyslouzil, Vice President Elect
Murray Johnston, Treasurer
CY Wu, Secretary

Opportunity to meet with other aerosol scientists and learn of the latest advances in all frontiers of aerosol science and technology. Meet new colleagues, and network with academia, government, and industry researchers.
1000 Members
Founded in: 1982

7714 **Conference on the Applications of Air Pollution Meteorology**
A&WMA

420 Fort Duquesne Boulevard
One Gateway Center, 3rd Floor
Pittsburgh, PA 15222-1435

412-652-2458; *Fax:* 412-232-3450
info@awma.org; www.awma.org
Social Media: Facebook, Twitter, LinkedIn

Jeffry Muffat, President
Merlyn L. Hough, President Elect
Mike Kelly, Secretary/ Executive Director
Amy Gilligan, Treasurer
Dallas Baker, Vice President

Topics dealing with ALL aspects of air pollution meteorology ranging from the microscale to the global scale and including field and laboratory measurements, instrumentation, theoretical studies, numerical modeling, evaluation studies and applications. Also on transport and dispersion modeling systems, urban meteorology and dispersion, and regional to global scale transport and dispersion.
9000 Members
Founded in: 1907

7715 Downscaling Climate Models for Planning
A&WMA
420 Fort Duquesne Boulevard
One Gateway Center, 3rd Floor
Pittsburgh, PA 15222-1435

412-652-2458; *Fax:* 412-232-3450
info@awma.org; www.awma.org
Social Media: Facebook, Twitter, LinkedIn

Jeffry Muffat, President
Merlyn L. Hough, President Elect
Mike Kelly, Secretary/ Executive Director
Amy Gilligan, Treasurer
Dallas Baker, Vice President
9000 Members
Founded in: 1907

7716 EBA Annual Meeting
Environmental Business Association
1150 Connecticut Avenue NW
9th Floor
Washington, DC 20036-4129

202-624-4363; *Fax:* 202-828-4130
wbode@bode.com

William H Bode, President

Learn more about the research, development and demonstration activities in fuel cells, hydrogen production delivery and storage technologies.
Frequency: June

7717 EBA Semi-Annual Meeting
Environmental Bankers Association
510 King Street
Suite 410
Alexandria, VA 22314
703-549-0977
800-966-7475; *Fax:* 703-548-5945;
www.envirobank.org

D J Telego, Executive Co-Director

Network with peers in the bank and non-bank financial institutions, insurers, asset management firms and those who provide services to them. Learn more about environmental risk management, sustainable development, and due diligence policies and procedures in financial institutions.
Frequency: January, June

7718 EDRA Annual Meeting
Environmental Design Research Association
PO Box 7146
Edmond, OK 73083-7146

405-304-4863; *Fax:* 403-330-4150
edra@telepath.com; www.edra.org

Janet Singer, Executive Director

Providing information about the advancement and dissemination of environmental design research, improving understanding of the interrelationships between people, their built and natural surroundings, and creating environments responsive to human needs.
Frequency: Spring-Summer

7719 EHS Management Forum
National Assoc. for Environmental Management
1612 K St NW
Suite 1102
Washington, DC 20006-2830

202-986-6616
800-391-6236; *Fax:* 202-530-4408
programs@naem.org; www.naem.org
Social Media: Facebook, Twitter, LinkedIn

Kelvin Roth, President
Stephen Evanoff, 1st Vice President
Debbie Hammond, 2nd Vice President
Frank Macielak, Secretary and Treasurer

The largest annual gathering of EHS and sustainability decision-makers. Three days of interactive breakout sessions and keynote presentations, the Forum is the best opportunity for professional networking, benchmarking, and best-practice sharing available to EHS and sustainability practitioners today.
1000+ Members
Founded in: 1990

7720 EIA's National Conference & Exposition
Environmental Information Association
6935 Wisconsin Ave
Suite 306
Chevy Chase, MD 20815-6112

301-961-4999
888-343-4342; *Fax:* 301-961-3094
info@eia-usa.org; www.eia-usa.org

Dana Hudson, President
Mike Schrum, President Elect
Kevin Cannan, Vice President
Joy Finch, Secretary
Chris Gates, Treasurer

Providing the environmental industry with the information needed to remain knowledgeable, responsible, and competitive in the environmental health and safety industry.

7721 EMS Annual Meeting
Environmental Mutagen Society
1821 Michael Faraday Drive
Suite 300
Reston, VA 20190

703-438-8220; *Fax:* 703-438-3113
emshq@ems-us.org; www.ems-ph.org

Tonia Masson, Executive Director
Suzanne Morris, Secretary
Barbara Shane, Treasurer

Environmental Impacts on the Genome and Epigenome; Mechanisms and Risks.
Frequency: Spring

7722 EPRI-A&WMA Workshop on Future Air Quality Model Development Needs
American Association for Aerosol Research
15000 Commerce Parkway
Suite C
Mount Laurel, NJ 08054

856-439-9080
877-777-6753; *Fax:* 856-439-0525
info@aaar.org; www.aaar.org

William Nazaroff, President
Barbara Turpin, Vice President
Barbara Wyslouzil, Vice President Elect
Murray Johnston, Treasurer
CY Wu, Secretary

Designed to bring together researchers from academia, government and private institutions, industry, and other stakeholders to brainstorm on various air quality model development needs and to develop a comprehensive research agenda that can be used by the community to help guide research plans and to promote collaboration amongst researchers.
1000 Members
Founded in: 1982

7723 ESTC Annual Convention
International Ecotourism Society
PO Box 96503 #34145
Washington, DC 20090-6503

202-506-5033; *Fax:* 202-789-7279
info@ecotourism.org; www.ecotourism.org
Social Media: Facebook, Twitter, YouTube

Kelly Bricker, Chair
Tony Charters, Vice Chair
Neal Inamdar, Director Finance/Administration

Highlighting global challenges and local opportunities, supporting sustainable development of tourism and promoting solutions that balance conservation, communities and sustainable travel.
900 Members
Founded in: 1990

7724 ESTECH 2017
Institute of Environmental Sciences and Technology
2340 S Arlington Heights Rd.
Suite 620
Arlington Heights, IL 60005

847-981-0100; *Fax:* 847-981-4130
information@iest.org; www.iest.org

Wei Sun, President
Ahmad Soueid, President-Elect

Single source of contamination control knowledge for the industry. Participate in exceptional continuing education training courses and interactive working group meetings.
800 Attendees
Frequency: Spring
Founded in: 1953

7725 ETAD Annual Meeting
Ecological and Toxicological Association of Dyes
1850 M Street NW
Suite 700
Washington, DC 20036

202-721-4154; *Fax:* 202-296-8120;
www.etad.com

Dr C Tucker Helmes, Executive Director

Cooperate with ETAD member companies and value chain for the benefit of health and the environment. Learn more about environmental regulations.
Frequency: Spring

7726 Effective Cover Cropping in the Midwest
Soil and Water Conservation Society
945 SW Ankeny Rd
Ankeny, IA 50023-9764

515-289-2331
800-843-7645; *Fax:* 515-289-1227
swcs@swcs.org; www.swcs.org

Bill Boyer, President
Dan Towery, Vice-President
Clark Gantzer, Secretary
Jerry Pearce, Treasurer

Targeted to farmers and cover crop service providers. Provides a forum for farmers to exchange information, discuss opportunities for collaboration, and learn about new and successful practices related to cover crops. Goal of this conference is to get farmers together to learn how to effectively manage cover crops in a way that

enhances soil quality, keeps nutrients in the fields, and increases the bottom line.
5000+ Members
Founded in: 1943

7727 **Enviro Expo**
Industrial Shows Northeast
333 Trapelo Road
Belmont, MA 02478-1856
617-489-2302
800-543-5259; *Fax:* 781-489-5534;
www.enviroexpo.com
Social Media: Facebook, Twitter, LinkedIn

Russ Ryan, President
Diane Fisher, Show Manager

A single stop responsible family-oriented event, designed to educate and entertain. Variety of products and services that specialize in; health & wellness, transportation, home & garden, renewable energy, and Eco fashions.
5,000 Attendees
Frequency: May
Founded in: 1987

7728 **Environmental Technology Expo**
Association of Energy Engineers
4025 Pleasantdale Road
Suite 420
Atlanta, GA 30340
770-447-5083; *Fax:* 770-446-3969
info@aeecenter.org; www.aeecenter.org

Ruth Whitlock, Executive Admin
Jennifer Vendola, Accountant

Annual show and exhibits of air and water pollution contrasts, waste-to-energy services information, asbestos abatement and monitoring instruments and equipment.
Frequency: October

7729 **FET Annual Meeting**
Federation of Environmental Technologists
PO Box 624
Slinger, WI 53086-0624
414-540-0070; *Fax:* 262-644-7106
info@fetinc.org; www.fetinc.org

Triese Haase, Administrator

Attend the program, visit the exhibitions and hear from keynote speakers on relevant environmental topics.
Frequency: March

7730 **FET-Federation Of Environmental Technologist, Inc.**
Federation of Environmental Technologists
W175 N11081 Stonewood Dr.
Ste 203
Germantown, WI 53022-4771
262-437-1700; *Fax:* 262-437-1702
info@fetinc.org; www.fetinc.org

Dan Brady, Board Chair
Mark Steinberg, President
Dave Seitz, Vice President
Anthony Montemurro, Treasurer
Jeffrey Nettesheim, Secretary

Educational Seminars and Courses on Environmental, Health and Safety topics throughout the year around the state of Wisconsin for business and industry.
700 Members
Founded in: 1982

7731 **Fish Wildlife Agencies Association Southeast**
8005 Freshwater Farms Road
Tallahassee, FL 32309
850-893-1204; *Fax:* 850-893-6204
seafwa@aol.com; www.seafwa.org

Robert Brently, Executive Secretary

Fifteen booths.
1,000 Attendees
Frequency: October

7732 **Forestry, Conservation Communications Association Annual Meeting**
Forestry, Conservation Communications Association
Hall of the States
444 N Capitol
Washington, DC 20001
202-624-5416; *Fax:* 202-751-9099

Joe Friend, Executive Director

Annual meeting and exhibits of forestry and conservation communications equipment, systems and procedures.

7733 **Global Warming International Conference & Expo**
SUPCON International
PO Box 5275
Woodridge, IL 60517-0275
630-910-1551; *Fax:* 630-910-1561
syshen@megsinet.net; www.globalwarming.net

Environmental and energy technology, global warming mitigation, journals, publications and software, greenhouse gas measurements, alternative vehicles and alternative energy. Containing 100 booths and exhibits.
2000 Attendees
Frequency: April Boston

7734 **GlobalCon Conference & Expo**
Association of Energy Engineers
4025 Pleasantdale Rd
Suite 420
Atlanta, GA 30340-4264
770-447-5083; *Fax:* 770-446-3969
info@aeecenter.org; www.aeecenter.org
Social Media: Facebook, Twitter, LinkedIn, YouTube

Eric A. Woodroof, President
Gary Hogsett, President Elect
Bill Younger, Secretary
Paul Goodman, C.P.A., Treasurer

Designed specifically to facilitate those seeking to expand their knowledge of fast-moving developments in the energy field, explore promising new technologies, compare energy supply options, and learn about innovative and cost-conscious project implementation strategies.
8.2M Members
Founded in: 1977

7735 **Green Industry Conference - GIC**
Professional Lawncare Network, Inc (PLANET)
950 Herndon Parkway
Suite 450
Herndon, VA 20170
703-736-9666
800-395-2522; *Fax:* 703-736-9668
info@gie-expo.com;
www.landscapeprofessionals.org

Held in conjunction with the GIE+EXPO, the conference offers leadership series, workshops, educational opportunities, events, and new member orientation.
Frequency: Annual

7736 **Healthy Buildings Conference & Exhibition**
The Indoor Air Institute
2548 Empire Grade
Santa Cruz, CA 95060
831-426-0148; *Fax:* 831-426-6522
info@IndAir.org
indair.org

Hal Levin, President
William Fisk, Vice President
William Nazaroff, Vice President

Issues addressed relate to indoor air quality and its impact on health. The main focus is on buildings as confined spaces where we spend around 90% of our life.

7737 **Heating with Biomass;**
Environmental & Energy Study Institute
122 C Street NW
Suite 630
Washington, DC 20001
202-628-1400; *Fax:* 202-628-1825
eesi@eesi.org; www.eesi.org
Social Media: Facebook, Twitter, YouTube

Jared Blum, Board Chair
Shelley Fidler, Board Treasurer
Richard L. Ottinger, Board Chair Emeritus

Win-Win for Households, Economic Development, Energy Security. Learn about how clean, renewable, efficient biomass heating can contribute to job creation, economic development, and energy security in communities across the country, as well as ways in which policies can help overcome some of the existing challenges and barriers to biomass use in the residential, commercial, and institutional sectors.
Founded in: 1984

7738 **HydroVision**
HCI Publications
410 Archibald Street
Kansas City, MO 64111-3001
816-931-1311; *Fax:* 816-931-2015;
www.hcipub.com

Leslie Eden, Manager

Focusing on asset management, civil works and dam safety, new development, ocean/ tidal/ stream power, operations and maintenance, policies and regulations, and water resources.
1,600 Attendees
Frequency: July-August

7739 **IAWF Annual Meetings**
International Association of Wildland Fire
4025 Fair Ridge Drive
Fairfax, VA 22033
785-423-1818; *Fax:* 785-542-3511;
www.iawfonline.org
Social Media: Facebook, Twitter

Sacha Dick, Programs Manager
Mikel Robinson, Executive Director

Participants represent a wide range of organizations, disciplines, and countries. Conference program includes workshops, invited speakers, oral and poster presentations, panels, and vendor displays.

7740 **ILZRO Annual Meeting**
International Lead Zinc Research Organization
2525 Meridian Parkway, Suite 100
PO Box 12036
Durham, NC 27713-2036
919-361-4647; *Fax:* 919-361-1957;
www.ilzro.org

Stephen Wilkinson, President
Frank Goodwin, VP Materials Sciences
Scott Mooneyham, Treasurer
Rob Putnam, Director Communications

Focused on new technology and its role in managing risks in the production and use of lead, the drivers for health and environmental legislation and their likely future direction, trends, threats

and opportunities in the global lead/zinc market, in particular those arising from the increasing desire for more low emission vehicles. Enabling delegates to meet a wide cross-section of key players in the lead producing and consuming countries.
Frequency: November

7741 **ISEE Annual Meetings**
International Society for Ecological Economics
1313 Dolley Madison Boulevard
Suite 402
McLean, VA 22101

703-790-1745; *Fax:* 703-790-2672;
www.iseepi.org
Social Media: Facebook, Twitter, LinkedIn

Heide Scheiter-Rohland, Director Membership

Provides an excellent opportunity for members to meet other ecological economists, test their ideas by presenting papers, and participate in the governance of the Society.
Frequency: Summer or Fall

7742 **ISEMNA Annual Meeting**
International Society for Ecological Modelling
University of California, Animal Sciences Dept
One Shields Avenue
Davis, CA 95616-8521

530-752-5362; *Fax:* 530-752-0175
webmaster@isemna.org; www.isemna.org

Wolfgang Pittroff, Secretary-General
David Mauriello, Treasurer

Providing a forum for scientists from around the world to exchange ideas, theories, concepts, methodologies, and results from ecological modelling that address these important issues.
Frequency: August

7743 **IWA-WEF Wastewater Treatment Modelling Seminar**
Water Environment Federation
601 Wythe St
Alexandria, VA 22314-1994

800-666-0206; *Fax:* 703-684-2492;
www.wef.org
Social Media: Facebook, Twitter

Matt Bond, President
Cordell Samuels, President-Elect
Sandra Ralston, Vice President
Chris Browning, Treasurer
Jeff Eger, Secretary and Executive Director

With stricter effluent limits for nutrients and other contaminants, and concerns about plant efficiency, climate change, and emerging contaminants, there is a drive for new, more sophisticated application of modeling. Objective is to present recent findings and successful case studies with the aim of bringing together different approaches.
79 Members
ISSN: 1044-9943
Founded in: 1928

7744 **IWLA National Convention**
Izaak Walton League
707 Conservation Lane
Gaithersburg, MD 20878

301-548-0150
800-453-5463; *Fax:* 301-548-0146
general@iwla.org; www.iwla.org
Social Media: Facebook, Twitter

Jim A. Madsen, President
Robert Chapman, Vice President
Marj Striegel, Secretary
Walter Lynn Jr., Treasurer

Explore how Izaak Walton League members can make a difference for the future of America's great rivers, and the people and wildlife that depend on them.
37000 Members
Founded in: 1922

7745 **Instructional Technology for Occupational Safety and Health Professionals**
Nat. Environmental, Safety & Health Training Assoc
2700 N. Central Avenue
Suite 900
Phoenix, AZ 85004-1147

602-956-6099; *Fax:* 602-956-6399
neshta@neshta.org; www.neshta.org

Design, develop, deliver, evaluate and manage workplace safety and health training programs. Prepare and give a 15-minute presentation on a relevant workplace health and safety topic. The presentation will include skills and techniques learned in the course; however you will be encouraged to also bring materials that you are currently working on to use as a reference.
Founded in: 1977

7746 **Int'l Conference on Southern Hemisphere Meteorology & Oceanography**
Renewable Natural Resources Foundation
5430 Grosvenor Ln
Bethesda, MD 20814-2193

301-493-9101; *Fax:* 301-493-6148
info@rnrf.org; www.rnrf.org

Howard N. Rosen, Chairman
Richard A. Engberg, Vice-Chairman
Robert D. Day, Executive Director

An interdisciplinary forum for presentations of our current state of knowledge, as well as motivating new research and applications within the variety of disciplines related to weather and climate of the ocean and atmosphere.
14 Members
Founded in: 1972

7747 **Inter-American Dialogue on Water Management**
Water Environment Federation
601 Wythe St
Alexandria, VA 22314-1994

800-666-0206; *Fax:* 703-684-2492;
www.wef.org
Social Media: Facebook, Twitter

Matt Bond, President
Cordell Samuels, President-Elect
Sandra Ralston, Vice President
Chris Browning, Treasurer
Jeff Eger, Secretary and Executive Director

The most prominent water encounter in the region. Gathering a wide myriad of sectors, government officials, national and international cooperation agency representatives, stakeholders, and practitioners in water management in the Americas. Address the need to evolve towards an inter-generation dialogue to embrace water management challenges beyond sectoral barriers that we have built in recent generations.
79 Members
ISSN: 1044-9943
Founded in: 1928

7748 **International Association for Energy Economics Conference**
International Association for Energy Economics
28790 Chagrin Boulevard
Suite 350
Cleveland, OH 44122-4630

216-464-5365; *Fax:* 216-464-2737
iaee@iaee.org; www.iaee.org

David Williams, Executive Director
John Jimison, Managing Director

Semi-annual conference and exhibits relating to energy economics including publications, consultants, energy database software.
325 Attendees

7749 **International Conference & Exhibition on Liquefied Natural Gas (LNG)**
Institute of Gas Technology
1700 S Mount Prospect Rd
Des Plaines, IL 60018-1804

847-768-0664; *Fax:* 847-768-0669;
www.gastechnology.org
Social Media: Facebook, Twitter, LinkedIn, YouTube

David Carroll, President & CEO
Ronald Snedic, Vice President/ Corporate Dev
Paul Chromek, General Counsel & Secretary

A landmark strategic, technical and commercial event for leaders, experts and committed professionals of the worldwide LNG Industry.

7750 **International Conference On Air Quality- Science and Application**
A&WMA
420 Fort Duquesne Boulevard
One Gateway Center, 3rd Floor
Pittsburgh, PA 15222-1435

412-652-2458; *Fax:* 412-232-3450
info@awma.org; www.awma.org
Social Media: Facebook, Twitter, LinkedIn

Jeffry Muffat, President
Merlyn L. Hough, President Elect
Mike Kelly, Secretary/ Executive Director
Amy Gilligan, Treasurer
Dallas Baker, Vice President

One of the most prominent forums for discussing the latest scientific developments, applications and implications for policy and other uses. An important feature it that it brings together scientists and other stakeholders from the air pollution, climate change, policy and health communities.
9000 Members
Founded in: 1907

7751 **International Conference on Facility Operations-Safeguards Interface**
555 N Kensington Ave
La Grange Park, IL 60526-5592

708-352-6611
800-323-3044; *Fax:* 708-352-0499
advertising@ans.org; www.ans.org
Social Media: Facebook, Twitter, LinkedIn

Jack Tuohy, Executive Director
James S Tulenko, VP
William F Naughton, Treasurer

New methods, products, instructions and ideas for the nuclear science and technology safety field.
10500 Members
Founded in: 1954

7752 **International Conference on Ground Penetrating Rador GPR**
Society of Exploration Geophysicists

8801 South Yale
Suite 500
Tulsa, OK 74137-3575

918-497-5500; *Fax:* 918-497-5557
web@seg.org; www.seg.org
Social Media: Facebook, Twitter, LinkedIn

Mary Fleming, Executive Director
Vladimir Grechka, Editor

Devoted to the development of ground penetrating radar. Presents the most recent technical information and case studies on ground penetrating radar for engineers, scientists, and end users.
Founded in: 1930

7753 **International Conference on Indoor Air Quality and Climate**
International Academy of Indoor Air Sciences
343 Soquel Avenue
PMB 312
Santa Cruz, CA 95062

831-426-0148; *Fax:* 831-426-6522;
www.indoorair2002.org

Multidisciplinary event involving participants from medicine, engineering, architecture and related fields. The conference will cover all aspects of Indoor Air Quality and Climate and the effects on human health, comfort and productivity. Cutting-edge research results will be presented, including ways to achieve an optimal indoor environment in a sustainable manner. Will address a variety of indoor environments, residential, office, school, industrial, commercial and transport.
Frequency: June-July

7754 **International Hazardous Materials Response Teams Conference**
International Association of Fire Chiefs
4025 Fair Ridge Drive
Suite 300
Fairfax, VA 22033-2868

703-273-0911; *Fax:* 703-273-9363
thicks@iafc.org; www.iafc.org
Social Media: Facebook, Twitter, LinkedIn

Mark Light, Executive Director & CEO
Lisa Yonkers, Director, Conferences & Education
Jason Nauman, Education & Learning Manager
Leanne Shroeder, Conference Manager

Also known as the IAFC Hazmat Conference. One of the largest gatherings of hazmat responders, facilitating new ideas. Dedicated exhibit hours and events, and indoor and outdoor exhibits.
Frequency: Annual

7755 **International High-Level Radioactive Waste Management**
555 N Kensington Ave
La Grange Park, IL 60526-5592

708-352-6611
800-323-3044; *Fax:* 708-352-0499
advertising@ans.org; www.ans.org
Social Media: Facebook, Twitter, LinkedIn

Jack Tuohy, Executive Director
James S Tulenko, VP
William F Naughton, Treasurer

Subject coverage includes site characterization, analogue studies, geochemical studies, disruptive events, spent fuel and high-level-waste transportation, engineered barrier systems, design and testing, disposal containers, and waste form. Performance assessment and regulatory issues are also addressed.
10500 Members
Founded in: 1954

7756 **International Society for Environmental Epidemiology Meeting**
American Association for Aerosol Research
15000 Commerce Parkway
Suite C
Mount Laurel, NJ 08054

856-439-9080
877-777-6753; *Fax:* 856-439-0525
info@aaar.org; www.aaar.org

William Nazaroff, President
Barbara Turpin, Vice President
Barbara Wyslouzil, Vice President Elect
Murray Johnston, Treasurer
CY Wu, Secretary

Discussion of problems unique to the study of health and the environment.
1000 Members
Founded in: 1982

7757 **International Symposium on Environmental Geochemistry**
Society for Environmental Geochemistry & Health
4698 S Forrest Avenue
Springfield, MO 65810

417-851-1166; *Fax:* 417-881-6920
DRBGWIXSON@aol.com; www.segh.net

Prof. Xiangdong Li, President
Prof. Andrew Hursthouse, European Chair
Kyoung-Woong Kim, Asia/Pacific Chair
Anthea Brown, Membership Secretary/Treasurer
Malcolm Brown, Secretary

Convey expertise in a range of scientific fields, such as geochemistry, biology, engineering, geology, hydrology, epidemiology, chemistry, medicine, nutrition and toxicology.
400 Members
Founded in: 1971

7758 **International Topical Meeting on Nuclear Plant Instrumentation**
555 N Kensington Ave
La Grange Park, IL 60526-5592

708-352-6611
800-323-3044; *Fax:* 708-352-0499
advertising@ans.org; www.ans.org
Social Media: Facebook, Twitter, LinkedIn

Jack Tuohy, Executive Director
James S Tulenko, VP
William F Naughton, Treasurer

Control and Human Machine Interface Technologies
10500 Members
Founded in: 1954

7759 **International Workshop on Seismic Anisotropy**
Society of Exploration Geophysicists
8801 South Yale
Suite 500
Tulsa, OK 74137-3575

918-497-5500; *Fax:* 918-497-5557
web@seg.org; www.seg.org
Social Media: Facebook, Twitter, LinkedIn

Mary Fleming, Executive Director
Vladimir Grechka, Editor

Cover both theoretical and applied aspects of seismic anisotropy in earth sciences. Focusing on applications of anisotropic models and methods in exploration & development of both conventional and unconventional Oil & Gas reservoirs, earthquake seismology, and reservoir monitoring using seismic anisotropy and microseismic.
Founded in: 1930

7760 **Joint International Conference PBC/SEGH**
Society for Environmental Geochemistry & Health
4698 S Forrest Avenue
Springfield, MO 65810

417-851-1166; *Fax:* 417-881-6920
DRBGWIXSON@aol.com; www.segh.net

Prof. Xiangdong Li, President
Prof. Andrew Hursthouse, European Chair
Kyoung-Woong Kim, Asia/Pacific Chair
Anthea Brown, Membership Secretary/Treasurer
Malcolm Brown, Secretary

On behalf of the Pacific Basin Consortium and the Society for Environmental Geochemistry and Health (Asia/ Pacific region)
400 Members
Founded in: 1971

7761 **MEGA Symposium**
A&WMA
420 Fort Duquesne Boulevard
One Gateway Center, 3rd Floor
Pittsburgh, PA 15222-1435

412-652-2458; *Fax:* 412-232-3450
info@awma.org; www.awma.org
Social Media: Facebook, Twitter, LinkedIn

Jeffry Muffat, President
Merlyn L. Hough, President Elect
Mike Kelly, Secretary/ Executive Director
Amy Gilligan, Treasurer
Dallas Baker, Vice President

Addresses issues related to power plant air emissions through the combined efforts of four key industry payers. Update seasoned professionals and provide an excellent learning experience for early career engineers.
9000 Members
Founded in: 1907

7762 **MTS TechSurge, Oceans in Action**
Marine Technology Society
1100 H St., Nw
Suite LL-100
Washington, DC 20005

202-717-8705; *Fax:* 202-347-4302
membership@mtsociety.org;
www.mtsociety.org
Social Media: Facebook, Twitter, LinkedIn

Jerry Boatman, President
Drew Michel, President-Elect
Jerry Wilson, VP of Industry and Technology
Jill Zande, VP of Education and Research
Justin Manley, VP of Gov. & Public Affairs

Learn how government agencies and universities are supporting both current and emerging oceanographic operations worldwide. Discover how marine science, technology, engineering, products and services come together to support real-world issues around the globe, including piracy, disaster monitoring and recovery, prediction and forecast of ocean properties, coastal restoration, hypoxia, harmful algal blooms, fisheries and much more.
2M Members
Founded in: 1963

7763 **Middle East Geosciences Conference & Exhibition**
Society of Exploration Geophysicists
8801 South Yale
Suite 500
Tulsa, OK 74137-3575

918-497-5500; *Fax:* 918-497-5557
web@seg.org; www.seg.org
Social Media: Facebook, Twitter, LinkedIn

Mary Fleming, Executive Director
Vladimir Grechka, Editor
Founded in: 1930

7764 **NAAEE Annual Meeting**
North American Association for Environmental

2000 P Street NW
Suite 540
Washington, DC 20036

202-419-0412; *Fax:* 202-419-0415;
www.naaee.org

William H Dent, Jr, Executive Director
Barbara Eager, Conference Coordinator
Paul Werth, Owner

Concurrent sessions, plenary sessions and networking, as well as workshops, field experiences and special events.
Frequency: Fall

7765 **NAEP Annual Meeting**
National Association of Environmental Professional
PO Box 2086
Bowie, MD 20718-2086

301-860-1140
888-251-9902; *Fax:* 301-860-1141;
www.naep.org

Sandi Worthman, Administrator

Learn unbiased information on environmental practices.
Frequency: Spring

7766 **NALGEP Annual Meetings**
National Association of Local Government
1333 New Hampshire Avenue NW
Washington, DC 20036

202-638-6254; *Fax:* 202-393-2866
nalgep@spiegelmcd.com; www.nalgep.org

Kenneth Brown, Executive Director
David Dickson, Project Manager

Discussion of congressional issues
Frequency: Regional Workshops

7767 **NALMS Symposium**
North American Lake Management Society
4513 Vernon Boulevard, Suite 100
PO Box 5443
Madison, WI 53705-443

608-233-2836; *Fax:* 608-233-3186
nalms@nalms.org; www.nalms.org

Bev Clark, President
Reesa Evans, Secretary
Linda Green, Treasurer

A collection of professional presentations, general workshops and non-stop discussions on managing lakes and reservoirs. Vendors are present with the latest lake management tools displayed. Scientific and environmental minds will offer a variety of relevant topical subject matter to be covered in breakout educational sessions, and networking opportunities will allow for collaboration with lake property association members and other interested parties.
1700 Members
Frequency: Annual/October
Founded in: 1980

7768 **NAPE**
Society of Exploration Geophysicists
8801 South Yale
Suite 500
Tulsa, OK 74137-3575

918-497-5500; *Fax:* 918-497-5557;
www.napeexpo.com
Social Media: Facebook, Twitter, LinkedIn

Mary Fleming, Executive Director
Vladimir Grechka, Editor

Provides a marketplace for the buying, selling and trading of oil and gas products and producing properties via exhibit booths. Brings prospects and producing properties, capital formation, services and technologies all together in one location, creating an environment to establish strategic alliances for doing business and initiating purchases and trades.
Founded in: 1930

7769 **NEHA Annual Educational Conference and Exhibition**
National Environmental Health Association
720 S Colorado Boulevard
Suite 970-S
Denver, CO 80246-1925

303-756-9090; *Fax:* 303-691-9490
staff@neha.org; www.neha.org

Toni Roland, Conference Coordinator
Kim Brandow, Managing Director
Larry Marcum, Managing Director
Bob Custard, Manager
Jill Cruickshank, Communications Manager

The National Environmental Health Association (NEHA) is a unique organization representing all professionals in environmental health. NEHA offers credentials, publications, training, Journal of Environmental Health, and discounts for members. Each year NEHA conducts the Annual Educational Conference and Exhibition, this year it will be at the Minneapolis Hilton in Minneapolis, MN.
2000 Attendees
Frequency: June-July

7770 **NEHA Annual Meeting**
National Conference of Local Environmental Health
c/o NEHA, 720 S Colorado Boulevard
South Tower, Suite 970
Denver, CO 80246-1925

303-756-9090; *Fax:* 303-691-9490
nfabian@neha.org
http://www.neha.org

Nelson E Fabian, Executive Director

Held with the National Environmental Health Association.
Frequency: June

7771 **NESHTA Annual Meetings**
National Environmental, Safety and Health Training
PO Box 10321
Phoenix, AZ 85064-0321

602-956-6099; *Fax:* 602-956-6399
info@neshta.org; www.neshta.org

Charles L Richardson, Executive Director
Joan J Jennings, Manager Association Services
Suzanne Lanctot, Manager Certification/Membership

The network for academic, government, industrial, utility and consulting trainers and training managers responsible for protecting public health, workers, and our physical environment.
Frequency: June

7772 **NGWA Ground Water Summit & GWPC Spring Meeting**
Renewable Natural Resources Foundation
5430 Grosvenor Ln
Bethesda, MD 20814-2193

301-493-9101; *Fax:* 301-493-6148
info@rnrf.org; www.rnrf.org

Howard N. Rosen, Chairman
Richard A. Engberg, Vice-Chairman
Robert D. Day, Executive Director

Innovate and Integrate.
14 Members
Founded in: 1972

7773 **NIWR Annual Conference**
National Institutes for Water Resources
47 Harkness Road
Pelham, MA 10002

413-253-5686; *Fax:* 413-253-1309
tracy@uidaho.edu
niwr.net

Jeffery Allen, President
Reagan Waskom, President-Elect
John Tracy, Secretary-Treasurer

Water Resource Institute directors and associate directors are invited to join for the annual meeting.
54 Members
Founded in: 1974

7774 **NORA Semi-Annual Meetings**
NORA: Association of Responsible Recyclers
5965 Amber Ridge Road
Haymarket, VA 20169

703-753-4277; *Fax:* 703-753-2445
sparker@noranews.org; www.noranews.org

Scott D Parker, Executive Director
Jim Letteney, Vice President

The liquid recycling industry's premier networking and education event.
Frequency: May, November

7775 **NREP Annual Meetings**
National Registry of Environmental Professionals
PO Box 2099
Glenview, IL 60025

847-724-6631; *Fax:* 847-724-4223
nrep@nrep.org; www.nrep.org

Richard A Young, PhD, Executive Director

Certification preparatory workshops, technical papers and special seminars.
1000 Attendees
Frequency: Semi-Annual
Mailing list available for rent

7776 **National Environmental Balancing Bureau Meeting**
National Environmental Balancing Bureau
8575 Grovemont Circle
Gaithersburg, MD 20877-4121

301-977-3698; *Fax:* 301-977-9589

Michael Dolim, VP

Annual meeting and exhibits of testing and balancing equipment, supplies and services.

7777 **National Fish & Wildlife Conservation Congress**
Association of Fish & Wildlife Agencies
444 N Capitol St NW
Suite 725
Washington, DC 20001-1553

202-624-7890; *Fax:* 202-624-7891
info@fishwildlife.org; www.fishwildlife.org
Social Media: Facebook, Twitter

Jon Gassett, President
Jeff Vonk, Vice President
Dave Chanda, Secretary/ Treasurer
Curtis Taylor, Past President

Bring together leading fish and wildlife scientists, government leaders, federal, provincial, state and local fish and wildlife agencies, conservation organizations and anglers and hunters to participate in discussions and debates about the future of fish and wildlife resources in North America.
Founded in: 1902

7778 **National Flood Risk Management; Flood Risk Summit**
Association of State Floodplain Managers

2809 Fish Hatchery Rd
Suite 204
Madison, WI 53713-5020

608-274-0123; *Fax:* 608-274-0696
Larry@floods.org; www.floods.org
Social Media: Facebook

Sally McConkey, Chair
William Nechamen, Vice Chair
Alan J. Giles, Secretary
John V. Crofts, Treasurer

Invitation-only. Soliciting feedback and providing updates to local, state, regional, and federal officials and the private sector on vital national policies currently under construction at the Federal level.
6500 Members
Founded in: 1977

7779 National FloodProofing Conference and Exposition Levees and Beyond
Association of State Floodplain Managers
2809 Fish Hatchery Rd
Suite 204
Madison, WI 53713-5020

608-274-0123; *Fax:* 608-274-0696
Larry@floods.org; www.floods.org
Social Media: Facebook

Sally McConkey, Chair
William Nechamen, Vice Chair
Alan J. Giles, Secretary
John V. Crofts, Treasurer

Making Wise Choices Highlighting the various floodproofing methods, products, techniques, programs, funding sources, and issues that have developed. Showcasing the state-of-the-art in materials, services, equipment, accessories and techniques.
6500 Members
Founded in: 1977

7780 National Planning Conference
Renewable Natural Resources Foundation
5430 Grosvenor Ln
Bethesda, MD 20814-2193

301-493-9101; *Fax:* 301-493-6148
info@rnrf.org; www.rnrf.org

Howard N. Rosen, Chairman
Richard A. Engberg, Vice-Chairman
Robert D. Day, Executive Director

Hosted by the American Planning Association.
14 Members
Founded in: 1972

7781 National Quail Symposium
Wildlife Habitat Council
8737 Colesville Road
Suite 800
Silver Spring, MD 20910

301-588-8994; *Fax:* 301-588-4629
whc@wildlifehc.org; www.wildlifehc.org
Social Media: Facebook, YouTube

Greg Cekander, Chairman
Lawrence A Selzer, Vice Chairman
Kevin Butt, Secretary-Treasurer

Highlight the diversity in conservation of quails. Serve as an excellent venue to publish current research and advance quail conservation.
120+ Members
Founded in: 1988

7782 National Real Estate Environmental Conference
National Society of Environmental Consultants
PO Box 12528
San Antonio, TX 78212-0528

210-225-2897
800-486-3676; *Fax:* 956-225-8450

Annual conference and exhibits related to the environmentally responsible use of real estate.

7783 National Water Monitoring Conference
Renewable Natural Resources Foundation
5430 Grosvenor Ln
Bethesda, MD 20814-2193

301-493-9101; *Fax:* 301-493-6148
info@rnrf.org; www.rnrf.org

Howard N. Rosen, Chairman
Richard A. Engberg, Vice-Chairman
Robert D. Day, Executive Director

National forum provides an exceptional opportunity for federal, state, local, tribal, volunteer, academic, private, and other water stakeholders to exchange information and technology related to water monitoring, assessment, research, protection, restoration, and management, as well as to develop new skills and professional networks.
14 Members
Founded in: 1972

7784 North American Environmental Field Conferences & Expositions
1230 Lincoln Drive
Carbondale, IL 62901

618-453-7809
aih@engr.siu.edu; www.aihydrology.org

Emitt C. Witt, III, President
Marzi Sharfaei, Secretary
T. Allen J. Gookin, Treasurer

Interactive indoor workshops, presented by some of the world's foremost authorities in the field, discussing cutting-edge field-based technologies and methods for environmental site characterization, sampling monitoring and remediation. Hands-on interactive outdoor workshops and equipment demos featuring the latest environmental field methods and equipment.
1000 Members
Founded in: 1981

7785 North American Wildlife and Natural Resources Conference
Wildlife Management Institute
1101 14th Street NW
Suite 801
Washington, DC 20005

202-371-1808; *Fax:* 202-408-5059;
www.wildlifemanagementinstitute.org

Meeting the challenges of modern conservation. Industry leaders dedicated to the conservation, enhancement and management of North America's wildlife and other natural resources.

7786 Ocean Sciences Meeting
Renewable Natural Resources Foundation
5430 Grosvenor Ln
Bethesda, MD 20814-2193

301-493-9101; *Fax:* 301-493-6148
info@rnrf.org; www.rnrf.org

Howard N. Rosen, Chairman
Richard A. Engberg, Vice-Chairman
Robert D. Day, Executive Director

Largest worldwide conference in the geophysical sciences, attracting Earth and space scientists, educators, students and policy makers. Meeting showcases current scientific theory focused on discoveries that will benefit humanity and ensure a sustainable future for our planet.
14 Members
Founded in: 1972

7787 Oceans MTS/IEEE Conference
Marine Technology Society
1100 H St., Nw
Suite LL-100
Washington, DC 20005

202-717-8705; *Fax:* 202-347-4302
membership@mtsociety.org;
www.mtsociety.org
Social Media: Facebook, Twitter, LinkedIn

Jerry Boatman, President
Drew Michel, President-Elect
Jerry Wilson, VP of Industry and Technology
Jill Zande, VP of Education and Research
Justin Manley, VP of Gov. & Public Affairs

The major international forum for scientists, engineers, and responsible ocean users to present the latest research results, ideas, developments, and applications in Oceanic Engineering and Marine Technology.
2M Members
Founded in: 1963

7788 Offshore Technology Conference
Marine Technology Society
1100 H St., Nw
Suite LL-100
Washington, DC 20005

202-717-8705; *Fax:* 202-347-4302
membership@mtsociety.org;
www.mtsociety.org
Social Media: Facebook, Twitter, LinkedIn

Jerry Boatman, President
Drew Michel, President-Elect
Jerry Wilson, VP of Industry and Technology
Jill Zande, VP of Education and Research
Justin Manley, VP of Gov. & Public Affairs

The world's foremost event for the development of offshore resources in the fields of drilling, exploration, production and environmental protection. A worldwide forum for the exchange of technical information vital to exploration and development of ocean resources.
2M Members
Founded in: 1963

7789 Plant Growth Regulation Society of America Annual Conference
Rhone-Poulenc, Ag Company
1018 Duke Street
Alexandria, VA 22314

703-836-4606; *Fax:* 706-883-8215
Social Media: Facebook, Twitter

Dr Eric A Curry, President
Dr Louise Ferguson, VP
Dr Ed Stover, Secretary

Highlights the latest in basic and applied research in plant growth regulation including hormone binding, stress physiology and plant growth regulator application.
325 Members
Founded in: 1973

7790 Residuals and Biosolids Conference
Water Environment Federation
601 Wythe St
Alexandria, VA 22314-1994

800-666-0206; *Fax:* 703-684-2492;
www.wef.org
Social Media: Facebook, Twitter

Matt Bond, President
Cordell Samuels, President-Elect
Sandra Ralston, Vice President
Chris Browning, Treasurer
Jeff Eger, Secretary and Executive Director

Highlights beneficial reuse options, science, and technologies currently available to leverage biosolids as a valuable resource.
79 Members
ISSN: 1044-9943
Founded in: 1928

7791 SEG Annual Meeting
Society of Exploration Geophysicists

PO Box 702740
Tulsa, OK 74170-2740

918-497-5500; *Fax:* 918-497-5557
web@seg.org; www.seg.org/index.shtml

Mary Fleming, Executive Director
Vladimir Grechka, Editor

The world's largest oil, energy and mineral exposition showcasing cutting-edge technology for use in exploration and associated industries. It is the premier venue for individuals to meet and discuss new geophysical technologies and their uses.
9300 Attendees
Frequency: October

7792 **SEGH Annual Meetings**
Society for Environmental Geochemistry and Health
4698 S Forrest Avenue
Springfield, MO 65810

417-885-1166; *Fax:* 417-881-6920;
www.segh.net

Bobby Wixson, Director Membership

Environmental determinants of quality of life, including water resources, sediments and soil pollution and climate change, engineered solutions to hazardous waste including treatment of hazardous substances and regulatory solutions and approaches to hazardous substances, and all other environmental quality and human health issues.
Frequency: Summer-Fall

7793 **SER Annual Meeting**
Society for Ecological Restoration
285 West 18th Street #1
Tucson, AZ 85701

520-622-5485; *Fax:* 520-622-5491
info@ser.org; www.ser.org

Mary Kay C LeFevour, Executive Director
Jane Cripps, Membership
Julie St John, Communications
Dennis Martinez, Founder
Val Schaefer, Secretary

Provides members (and non-members) with the opportunity to exchange ideas and information, participate in activities such as workshops and field trips, reconnect with friends and colleagues, and make new acquaintances.
Frequency: Fall

7794 **SER World Conference on Ecological Restoration**
Society for Ecological Restoration
1017 O Street NW
Washington, DC 20001

202-299-9518; *Fax:* 270-626-5485
info@ser.org; www.ser.org

Steve Whisenant, Chair
Cara R. Nelson, Vice Chair
Mary Travaglini, Treasurer
Alan Unwin, Secretary

Provide members and non-members with the opportunity to exchange ideas and information, participate in activities such as workshops and field trips, reconnect with friends and colleeagues, and make new acquaintances.
Frequency: Semi-Annual

7795 **SETAC Annual Meeting**
Society of Environmental Toxicology and Chemistry
1010 N 12th Street
Pensacola, FL 32501-3367

850-469-1500; *Fax:* 850-469-9778
rparrish@setac.org; www.setac.org

Rodney Parrish, Executive Director
Greg Schifer, Manager

Information and collaboration on environmental toxicology and chemistry.
Frequency: Fall

7796 **SHE Bi-Ennial Meetings**
Society for Human Ecology
College of the Atlantic
105 Eden Street
Bar Harbor, ME 04609-0180

207-288-5015; *Fax:* 207-288-3780
carter@ecology.coa.edu;
www.societyforhumanecology.org

Barbara Carter, Assistant to Executive Director

Brings together scholars and practitioners associated with the study and practice of human ecology because of the importance of the disciplines' philosophy and applications in developing mutually beneficial solutions for society and the environment. A platform for sharing knowledge on present status and approaches for sustainable development.

7797 **SOCMA Annual Meeting**
Synthetic Organic Chemical Manufacturers Assn
1850 M Street NW
Suite 700
Washington, DC 20036

202-721-4100; *Fax:* 202-296-8120
info@socma.com; www.socma.com

Joseph Acker, President
Vivian Diko, Executive Assistant & CEO
Charlene Patterson, Director Human Resources

Industry leaders come together.
Frequency: Early Spring

7798 **SOEH Annual Meeting**
Society for Occupational and Environmental Health
6728 Old McLean Village Drive
McLean, VA 22101

703-556-9222; *Fax:* 703-556-8729
soeh@degnon.org; www.soeh.org

George K Degnon, CAE, Executive Director

Topic will be international aspects of pesticide exposure and health, and key interest areas for presentations and posters will be; chronic health effects from pesticide exposure, agricultural worker surveillance and biomonitoring studies, good models of integrated pesticide management and involvement of community members, and much more.
Frequency: Spring

7799 **Science, Politics, and Policy: Environmental Nexus**
National Association of Environmental Professional
PO Box 460
Collingswood, NJ 08108

856-283-7816; *Fax:* 856-210-1619
naep@bowermanagementservices.com;
www.naep.org
Social Media: Facebook, LinkedIn

Paul Looney, President
Harold Draper, Vice President
Joseph F. Musil Jr., Treasurer
Robert P. Morris Jr., Secretary

NEPA and Decision Making, program on what happens after NEPA documents are prepared, and how that information is useful to their preparation. Also a program on Advance Topics in Visual Resource Impact Assessment.

7800 **SeminarFest**
American Society of Safety Engineers
1800 E Oakton Street
Des Plaines, IL 60018

847-699-2929; *Fax:* 847-768-3434
customerservice@asse.org; www.asse.org
Social Media: Facebook

Terrie S. Norris, President
Richard A. Pollock, President Elect
Kathy Seabrook, Senior Vice President
Fred J. Fortman, Jr., Secretary & Executive Director
James D. Smith, Vice President, Finance

Pass your ASP, CSP, OHST and CHST exams with confidence by taking our certification preparation workshops. Earn a certificate of completion in Safety Management & the Executive Program in Safety Management. Develop business acument, leadership and training skills. Measure safety effectiveness and review safety management approaches. Also participate in technical and topical seminars.
30000 Members
Founded in: 1911

7801 **Sino-European Symposium on Environment and Health (SESH)**
Society for Environmental Geochemistry & Health
4698 S Forrest Avenue
Springfield, MO 65810

417-851-1166; *Fax:* 417-881-6920
DRBGWIXSON@aol.com; www.segh.net

Prof. Xiangdong Li, President
Prof. Andrew Hursthouse, European Chair
Kyoung-Woong Kim, Asia/Pacific Chair
Anthea Brown, Membership Secretary/Treasurer
Malcolm Brown, Secretary

Provides an opportunity for a direct communication between experts from China and the rest of the world.
400 Members
Founded in: 1971

7802 **Smart Energy Summit**
Parks Associates
5310 Harvest Hill Road
Suite 235, Lock Box 162
Dallas, TX 75230-5805

972-490-1113
800-727-5711
info@parksassociates.com;
www.parksassociates.com

Tricia Parks, Founder and CEO
Stuart Sikes, President
Farhan Abid, Research Analyst
Bill Ablondi, Director, Home Systems Research
John Barrett, Director of Research

Smart Energy Summit is an annual three-day event that examines the opportunities and technical business requirements inherent in the consumer programs and advanced systems and services made possible by Smart Grids and Residential Energy Management solutions.
Frequency: Annual
Founded in: 1986

7803 **Soil and Water Conservation Society Annual International Conference**
Soil and Water Conservation Society
945 SW Ankeny Road
Ankeny, IA 50021-9764

515-289-2331
800-843-7645; *Fax:* 515-289-1227;
www.swsc.org

Craig A Cox, Executive VP

Explores ways to improve the linkages among conservation science, policy and application at local, national, and international scales. The conference will provide participants an opportunity

to teach skills, learn techniques, compare successes, and improve understanding.
1200 Attendees
Frequency: Annual

7804 **Spatial Cognition for Architectural Design Symposium**
Environmental Design Research Association
1760 Old Meadow Road
Suite 500
McLean, VA 22102

703-506-2895; *Fax:* 703-506-3266;
www.edra.org
Social Media: Facebook, Twitter, LinkedIn

Nick Watkins, Chair
Mallika Bose, Chair-Elect
Vikki Chanse, Secretary
Shauna Mallory-Hill, Treasurer
Kate O'Donnell, Executive Director(ex-officio)

Addresses the theoretical and methodological achievements of the cognitive and computational disciplines in the domain of architectural design. A dialogue between scientists from design research and educational disciplines is sought with the aim to identify how such application of knowledge may provide real benefit for the theory and professional practice of architectural design.
700 Members
Founded in: 1968

7805 **Sustainability in Public Works Conference**
2345 Grand Blvd
Suite 700
Kansas City, MO 64108-2625

816-472-6100
800-848-2792; *Fax:* 816-472-1610;
www.apwa.net
Social Media: Facebook, Twitter, YouTube

Diane M. Linderman, President
Elizabeth Treadway, President Elect
Richard F. Stinson, Director, Region I
Edward A. Gottko, Director, Region II
William Barney Mills, Jr., Director, Region III

International educational and professional association of public agencies, private sector companies, and individuals dedicated to providing high quality public works, goods and services. APWA provides a forum brings important public works-related topics to public attention in local, state, and federal areas. Mailing list for members only.
26000 Members
Founded in: 1937

7806 **Sustainable Water Management Conference**
Water Environment Federation
601 Wythe St
Alexandria, VA 22314-1994

800-666-0206; *Fax:* 703-684-2492;
www.wef.org
Social Media: Facebook, Twitter

Matt Bond, President
Cordell Samuels, President-Elect
Sandra Ralston, Vice President
Chris Browning, Treasurer
Jeff Eger, Secretary and Executive Director

Will focus on large-scall sustainability issues related to water supply and management topics such as water conservation, urban planning and design, and sustainable utilities, infrastructure, and communities.
79 Members
ISSN: 1044-9943
Founded in: 1928

7807 **Take It Back**
Raymond Communications
5111 Berwin Road
#115
College Park, MD 20740

301-345-4237; *Fax:* 301-345-4768;
www.raymond.com

Michele Raymond, Publisher/Editor

The conference brings in the top recycling policy experts from around the world to brief customers. We also have practical sessions with case histories on such issues as packaging design, design for environment in electronics, and lifecycle issues.
150 Attendees
Frequency: March
Founded in: 1996

7808 **Teaming With Wildlife Fly-In Day**
Association of Fish & Wildlife Agencies
444 N Capitol St NW
Suite 725
Washington, DC 20001-1553

202-624-7890; *Fax:* 202-624-7891
info@fishwildlife.org; www.fishwildlife.org
Social Media: Facebook, Twitter

Jon Gassett, President
Jeff Vonk, Vice President
Dave Chanda, Secretary/ Treasurer
Curtis Taylor, Past President

Join in supporting funding for the State & Tribal Wildlife Grants Program, the nation's CORE program for preventing fish and wildlife from becoming endangered in every state and territory.
Founded in: 1902

7809 **The Utility Management Conference**
Water Environment Federation
601 Wythe St
Alexandria, VA 22314-1994

800-666-0206; *Fax:* 703-684-2492;
www.wef.org
Social Media: Facebook, Twitter

Matt Bond, President
Cordell Samuels, President-Elect
Sandra Ralston, Vice President
Chris Browning, Treasurer
Jeff Eger, Secretary and Executive Director

Water and wastewater managers and professionals will gather to be part of the latest approaches, practices, and techniques in all aspects of utility management.
79 Members
ISSN: 1044-9943
Founded in: 1928

7810 **Thermal Treatment Technologies/ Hazardous Waste Combustors**
A&WMA
420 Fort Duquesne Boulevard
One Gateway Center, 3rd Floor
Pittsburgh, PA 15222-1435

412-652-2458; *Fax:* 412-232-3450
info@awma.org; www.awma.org
Social Media: Facebook, Twitter, LinkedIn

Jeffry Muffat, President
Merlyn L. Hough, President Elect
Mike Kelly, Secretary/ Executive Director
Amy Gilligan, Treasurer
Dallas Baker, Vice President

Brings together industry experts from around the world to share experiences, lessons learned and new ideas on how to best operate thermal treatment facilities.
9000 Members
Founded in: 1907

7811 **Topical Meeting on the Technology of Fusion Energy (TOFE)**
555 N Kensington Ave
La Grange Park, IL 60526-5592

708-352-6611
800-323-3044; *Fax:* 708-352-0499
advertising@ans.org; www.ans.org
Social Media: Facebook, Twitter, LinkedIn

Jack Tuohy, Executive Director
James S Tulenko, VP
William F Naughton, Treasurer

Providing a forum for sharing the exciting new progress that has been made in fusion research as well as presenting the future of national and worldwide fusion programs. Draws together scientists, engineers, and students from various countries.
10500 Members
Founded in: 1954

7812 **Underwater Intervention Conference**
Marine Technology Society
1100 H St., Nw
Suite LL-100
Washington, DC 20005

202-717-8705; *Fax:* 202-347-4302
membership@mtsociety.org;
www.mtsociety.org
Social Media: Facebook, Twitter, LinkedIn

Jerry Boatman, President
Drew Michel, President-Elect
Jerry Wilson, VP of Industry and Technology
Jill Zande, VP of Education and Research
Justin Manley, VP of Gov. & Public Affairs

The conference is of interest to a number of diverse marine industries, including offshore oil and gas, marine construction, shipwreck exploration, ocean mining and marine salvage. Presentation tracks include cable, remote intervention, commercial diving, and shipwreck salvage, among others.
2M Members
Founded in: 1963

7813 **Utility Working Conference and Vendor Technology Expo**
555 N Kensington Ave
La Grange Park, IL 60526-5592

708-352-6611
800-323-3044; *Fax:* 708-352-0499
advertising@ans.org; www.ans.org
Social Media: Facebook, Twitter, LinkedIn

Jack Tuohy, Executive Director
James S Tulenko, VP
William F Naughton, Treasurer

Dedicated to identifying innovations in all areas of nuclear power plant operations. The functional area tracks/ sessions bring together professionals with different perspectives focusing on current issues and innovations.
10500 Members
Founded in: 1954

7814 **WINDPOWER Conference and Exhibition**
American Wind Energy Association (AWEA)
1501 M Street NW
Suite 1000
Washington, DC 20005

202-383-2500; *Fax:* 202-383-2505
windmail@awea.org;
www.windpowerexpo.org

Denise Bode, Chief Executive Officer
Pam Poisson, Chief Financial Officer
Britt Theismann, Chief Operating Officer
Rob Gramlich, Senior VP, Public Policy
Peter Kelley, VP, Public Affairs

The WINDPOWER Conference & Exhibition is produced by the American Wind Energy Associ-

ation to provide a venue for the wind industry to network, do business, and solve problems. Recognized as one of the fastest-growing trade shows in the U.S., WINDPOWER includes nearly 1,400 exhibiting companies, thousands of qualified wind energy professionals, engaging educational information and unmatched networking opportunities and special events.
2500 Members
20000 Attendees
Frequency: Annual

7815 WSSA Annual Meeting
Weed Science Society of America
PO Box 7050
Lawrence, KS 66044

785-429-9622
800-627-0629; *Fax:* 785-843-1274;
www.wssa.net

Rhonda Green, Registration Coordinator

Usually held during the first full week of February in the United States or Canada. These Meetings provide a venue for the exchange of research and educational ideas and for discussion and activity on society business.
1M Attendees
Frequency: February
Founded in: 1956

7816 Waterpower XIII
HCI Publications
410 Archibald Street
Kansas City, MO 64111-3001

816-931-1311; *Fax:* 816-931-2015;
www.hcipub.com

Leslie Eden, Manager

The conference offers industry professionals a forum in which to share new ideas and approaches to move hydropower forward as the world's leading source of renewable energy. Containing 120 booths.
1,000 Attendees
Frequency: July-August

7817 Wildlife Habitat Council Annual Symposium
Wildlife Habitat Council
8737 Colesville Road
Suite 800
Silver Spring, MD 20910

301-588-8994; *Fax:* 301-588-4629
whc@wildlifehc.org; www.wildlifehc.org

Bill Howard, President
Martha Gruelle, Program Manager
Linda Duvall, Accounting Manager
Tiffany Msonthi, Executive Assistant

The annual symposium brings together corporate, government and conservation leaders from around the globe for informative sessions, exhibits and field trips on environmental stewardship.
400 Attendees
Frequency: November

7818 Wildlife Society Annual Conference
Wildlife Society
5410 Grosvenor Lane
Suite 200
Bethesda, MD 20814-2144

301-897-9770; *Fax:* 301-530-2471
tws@wildlife.org; www.wildlife.org

Lisa Moll, Program Assistant/Membership

Hear from industry leaders to discuss new and evolving trends and innovations in wildlife management and conservation, learn about the latest research from original research and techniques presented by wildlife professionals, connect with colleagues at the largest gathering of wildlife professionals in North America.
1200 Attendees
Frequency: September
Founded in: 1994

7819 Windpower Conference
American Wind Energy Association
1501 M Street NW
Suite 1000
Washington, DC 20005

202-383-2500; *Fax:* 202-383-2505
windmail@awea.org; www.awea.org
Social Media: Facebook, Twitter, YouTube

Ned Hall, Chair
Thomas Carnahan, Chair-Elect
Gabriel Alonso, Secretary
Don Furman, Treasurer
Vic Abate, Past Chair
2400 Members

Directories & Databases

7820 A Guide to Internet Resources
American Assoc for the Advancement of Science
1200 New York Avenue NW
Washington, DC 20005-3941

202-266-6721; *Fax:* 202-371-9227
membership@aaas.org; www.aaas.org

Nathan E Bell, Editor

Free online document provides a starting point for finding internet resources. Topics include internet resources for math, science, health, english, software, grants, shareware, and much more.

7821 ACCA Membership Directory
Air Conditioning Contractors of America
2800 Shirlington Rd
Suite 300
Arlington, VA 22206-3607

703-575-4477
info@acca.org; www.acca.org
Social Media: Facebook, Twitter, LinkedIn, YouTube

Paul Stalknecht, President & CEO

7822 ACSH Media Update
American Council on Science and Health
1995 Broadway
2nd Floor
New York, NY 10023-5882

212-362-7044; *Fax:* 212-362-4919
acsh@acsh.org; www.acsh.org

Elizabeth Whelan, President
Jeff Stier, Director of Publications
Alyssa Pelish, Director of Publications
Gilbert Ross, Executive Director
Frequency: Semi-Annual

7823 Aboveground Storage Tank Management and SP CC Guide
ABS Group
PO Box 846304
Dallas, TX 75284-6304

Fax: 301-921-0264

7824 Acid Rain
Watts, Franklin
90 Sherman Turnpike
Danbury, CT 06816

203-797-3500
800-621-1115; *Fax:* 203-797-3657

Lists over 4,000 citations, with abstracts, to the worldwide literature on the sources of acid rain and its effects on the environment.

7825 Alternative Energy Network Online
Environmental Information Networks
119 S Fairfax Street
Alexandria, VA 22314-3301

703-548-1202

Reports on news of all energy sources designed as alternatives to conventional fossil fuels, including wind, solar and alcohol fuels.
Frequency: Full-text

7826 American Recycling Market: Directory/Reference Manual
Recycling Data Management Corporation
PO Box 577
Ogdensburg, NY 13669-0577

315-785-9072

Offers information, in three volumes, encompassing over 15,000 recycling companies and centers.
Cost: $175.00
1000 Pages
Frequency: Annual
ISSN: 0885-2537

7827 Business and the Environment: A Resource Guide
Island Press
1718 Connecticut Ave NW
Suite 300
Washington, DC 20009-1148

202-232-7933; *Fax:* 202-234-1328
info@islandpress.org; www.islandpress.org

Chuck Savitt, President
Allison Pennell, Editor

List of approximately 185 business and environmental educators working to integrate environmental issues into management, research, education and practices.
Cost: $60.00

7828 Canadian Environmental Directory
Grey House Publishing
4919 Route 22
PO Box 56
Amenia, NY 12501
518-789-8700
800-562-2139; *Fax:* 845-373-6390
books@greyhouse.com; www.greyhouse.com
Social Media: Facebook, Twitter

Leslie Mackenzie, Publisher
Tannys Williams, Managing Editor

Canada's most complete national listing of environmental associations and organizations, government regulators and purchasing groups, product and service companies, special libraries, and more.
Cost: $315.00
900 Pages
ISBN: 1-592372-24-9
Founded in: 1981

7829 Carcinogenicity Information Database of Environmental Substances
Technical Database Services
10 Columbus Circle
New York, NY 10019-1203

212-556-0001; *Fax:* 212-556-0036

This database contains test results on the carcinogenic and mutagenic effects of approximately 1000 substances of environmental or health concerns.

7830 Conservation Directory
National Wildlife Federation
11100 Wildlife Center Dr
Reston, VA 20190-5362

703-438-6000
800-822-9919; *Fax:* 703-438-3570
info@nwf.org; www.nwf.org

Mark Van Putten, CEO

Federal agencies, national and international organizations and state government agencies.
Cost: $20.00
500 Pages
Frequency: Annual

7831 **Department of Energy Annual Procurement and Financial Assistance Report**
US Department of Energy
1000 Independence Ave SW
Washington, DC 20585-0001
202-586-5000; *Fax:* 202-586-0573;
www.energy.gov
Mary Lein, Manager
Offers a list of universities, research centers and laboratories that represent the Department of Energy.
Frequency: Annual

7832 **Directory of Environmental Websites: Online Micro Edition**
US Environmental Directories
PO Box 65156
Saint Paul, MN 55165-0156
612-331-6050;
www.geocities.com/usenvironmentaldirectories
Roger N McGrath, Publisher
John C Brainard, Editor
The Directory is a complete guide to the environmental movement on the Internet, provides a concise, practical listing of over 190 of the major Internet addresses of the Environmental Movement. A clear, understandable and comprehensive guide to national and international environmental organizations, directories, networks and services on the Internet.
Cost: $25.75
48 Pages
ISSN: 1096-3316
Founded in: 1998

7833 **Directory of International Periodicals & Newsletters on Built Environments**
Division of Mineral Resources
PO Box 3667
Charlottesville, VA 22903-0667
434-951-6341; *Fax:* 434-951-6365;
www.ulrichsweb.com
Scott Richeson, Programs Director
More than 1,400 international periodicals and newsletters that cover architectural design and the building industry, and the aspects of the environment that deal with the industry are covered.
Cost: $6.00
29 Pages

7834 **EDOCKET**
Environmental Protection Agency
1200 Pennsylvania Avenue NW
Mail Code 3213A
Washington, DC 20460
202-260-2090; *Fax:* 202-566-0545
r9.info@epa.gov; www.epa.gov
An electronic public docket and on-line comment system designed to expand access to documents in EPA's major dockets.
Frequency: Full-text

7835 **EH&S Compliance Auditing & Teaching Software Report**
Donley Technology
PO Box 152
Colonial Beach, VA 22443-0152
804-224-9427
800-201-1595; *Fax:* 804-224-7958
donleytech@donleytech.com;
www.donleytech.com
Elizabeth Donley, Editor
Profiles 25 software packages for achieving and maintaining compliance, including detailed product descriptions, tables comparing system features, and contact information.
Cost: $195.00
240 Pages
Frequency: Every 2 Years
ISBN: 1-891682-08-3
Founded in: 1997
Printed in on matte stock

7836 **EMS Membership Roster**
Environmental Mutagen Society
1821 Michael Faraday Drive
Suite 300
Reston, VA 20190
703-438-8220; *Fax:* 703-438-3113
emshq@ems-us.org; www.ems-ph.org
Tonia Masson, Executive Director
Suzanne Morris, Secretary
Barbara Shane, Treasurer
Frequency: Irregular

7837 **Ecology Abstracts**
Cambridge Scientific Abstracts
7200 Wisconsin Ave
Suite 601
Bethesda, MD 20814-4890
301-961-6700
800-843-7751; *Fax:* 301-961-6790
service@csa.com; www.csa.com
Andrew M Snyder, President
Theodore Caris, Publisher
Robert Hilton, Editor
Mark Furneaux, VP Marketing
Angela Hitti, Production Manager
This large database updated continuously, offers over 150,000 citations, with abstracts, to the worldwide literature available on ecology and the environment.
Cost: $945.00
Frequency: Monthly

7838 **Education for the Earth: A Guide to Top Environmental Studies Programs**
Peterson's Guides
202 Carnegie Center
#2123
Princeton, NJ 08540-6239
800-338-3282; *Fax:* 609-869-4531
Colleges and universities that offer programs in environment and conservation are listed.
Cost: $10.95
192 Pages

7839 **Educational Communications**
Educational Communications
PO Box 351419
Los Angeles, CA 90035-9119
310-559-9160; *Fax:* 310-559-9160
ECNP@aol.com; www.ecoprojects.org
Nancy Pearlman, Editor/Executive Director
Directory of over 6,500 environmental organizations worldwide are the focus of this comprehensive directory. Over 400 1/2 hour television shows on the environment. Environmental directions - radio has over 1,500 interviews with ecological experts. Monthly newsletter, TV and radio series about ecological problems and solutions; promotion of ecotourem. Audo/video cassettes available.
Cost: $20.00
244 Pages
Frequency: Annual Paperback
Founded in: 1957
Mailing list available for rent

7840 **El Environmental Services Directory**
Environmental Information Networks
7301 Ohms Lane
Suite 460
Eding, MN 55439
952-831-2473; *Fax:* 952-831-6550
customerservice@envirobiz.com;
www.envirobiz.com
Cary Perket
James Rue, Secretary
Marshall Sanders, Manager
Bruce McGranahan, Director
Waste-handling facilities, transportation and spill response firms, laboratories and the broad scope of environmental services. Online versions are also available.
Cost: $1250.00
Frequency: Biennial
ISSN: 1053-475N
Founded in: 1984

7841 **Emergency Response Directory for Hazardous Materials Accidents**
Odin Press
PO Box 536
New York, NY 10021-0011
212-605-0338
Pamela Lawrence, Editor
Over 1,000 federal, state and local governmental agencies, chemical manufacturers and transporters, hotlines and strike teams, burn care centers, civil defense and disaster centers and other organizations concerned with the containment and cleanup of chemical spills and other hazardous materials accidents.
Cost: $36.00
Frequency: Biennial

7842 **Energy Statistics Spreadsheets**
Institute of Gas Technology
1700 S Mount Prospect Rd
Des Plaines, IL 60018-1804
847-768-0664; *Fax:* 847-768-0669;
www.gastechnology.org
Carol L Worster, Manager
Edward Johnston, Managing Director
The coverage of this database encompasses worldwide energy industry statistics, including production, consumption, reserves, imports and prices.

7843 **Energy User News: Energy Technology Buyers Guide**
Chilton Company
300 Park Ave
Suite 19
New York, NY 10022-7409
212-751-3596; *Fax:* 212-443-7701;
www.chiltonfunds.com
Richard L Chilton Jr, Owner
Lisa Czachor, Director
Mary Morse, Senior Vice President
A list of about 1,500 manufacturers, dealers and distributors of energy conservation and used equipment.
Cost: $10.00
Frequency: Annual
Circulation: 40,000

7844 **Environmental Bibliography**
International Academy at Santa Barbara
5385 Hollister Avenue
#210
Santa Barbara, CA 93111
805-683-8889; *Fax:* 805-965-6071
info@iasb.org; www.iasb.org
Gloria Lindfield, Executive Assistant
Hilary Eastman, Manager
Tom Seidenstein, Chief Operating Officer
Over 615,000 citations are offered in this database, aimed at scientific, technical and popular

periodical literature dealing with the environment.
Cost: $1750.00
ISSN: 1053-1440
Founded in: 1972

7845 **Environmental Cost Estimating Software Report**
Donley Technology
PO Box 152
Colonial Beach, VA 22443-0152
804-224-9427
800-201-1595; *Fax:* 804-224-7958
donleytech@donleytech.com;
www.donleytech.com
Elizabeth Donley, Editor
John Donley, Editor
Profiles 20 software packages for estimating the cost of environmental projects, including detailed product descriptions, tables comparing system features, and contact information.
Cost: $195.00
162 Pages
ISBN: 1-891682-05-9
Founded in: 1996
Printed in on matte stock

7846 **Environmental Health & Safety Dictionary**
ABS Group
PO Box 846304
Dallas, TX 75284-6304
Fax: 301-921-0264
Lydia Simpson, Manager

7847 **Environmental Law Handbook**
ABS Group
PO Box 846304
Dallas, TX 75284-6304
Fax: 301-921-0264

7848 **Environmental Protection Agency Headquarters Telephone Directory**
Environmental Protection Agency
1200 Pennsylvania Avenue NW
Pittsburgh, PA 15250-7954
412-442-4000; *Fax:* 202-512-2250;
www.epa.gov/customerservice/phonebook
Ken Bowman, Executive Director
Directory of services and supplies to the industry.
Cost: $15.00
400 Pages

7849 **Environmental Resource Handbook**
Grey House Publishing
4919 Route 22
PO Box 56
Amenia, NY 12501
518-789-8700
800-562-2139; *Fax:* 845-373-6390
books@greyhouse.com; www.greyhouse.com
Social Media: Facebook, Twitter
Leslie Mackenzie, Publisher
Richard Gottlieb, Editor
The most up-to-date and comprehensive source for Environmental Resources and Statistics. Included is contact information for resource listings in addition to statistics and rankings on hundreds of important topics such as recycling, air and water quality, climate, toxic chemicals and more.
Cost: $155.00
1200 Pages
ISBN: 1-592371-95-7
Founded in: 1981

7850 **Environmental Resource Handbook - Online Database**
Grey House Publishing
4919 Route 22
PO Box 56
Amenia, NY 12501
518-789-8700
800-562-2139; *Fax:* 845-373-6390
gold@greyhouse.com
http://gold.greyhouse.com
Social Media: Facebook, Twitter
Leslie Mackenzie, Publisher
Richard Gottlieb, Editor
With a subscription to Environmental Resource Handbook - Online Database, you'll have immediate access to over 7,000 associations, organizations & government agencies, awards & honors, conferences & trade shows, foundations & charities, national parks & wildlife refuges, research centers & educational programs, legal resources and much more.
Founded in: 1981

7851 **Environmental Statutes**
Government Institutes
4 Research Place
Suite 200
Rockville, MD 20850-3226
301-921-2323; *Fax:* 301-921-0264;
www.govinst.com
Two-volume set. Complete and exact text of the statues and amendments made by Congress concerning environmental law.
Cost: $125.00
1678 Pages
Frequency: Paperback
ISBN: 0-865879-33-8

7852 **Fibre Market News: Paper Recycling Markets Directory**
Recycling Media Group GIE Publishers
4012 Bridge Avenue
Cleveland, OH 44113-3320
216-961-4130
800-456-0707; *Fax:* 216-961-0364;
www.giemedia.com
Dan Moreland, Executive Vice President
A list of over 2,000 dealers, brokers, packers and graders of paper stock in the United States and Canada.
Cost: $28.00
Frequency: Annual
Circulation: 3,000

7853 **Floodplain Management: State & Local Programs**
Association of State Floodplain Managers
2809 Fish Hatchery Rd
Suite 204
Fitchburg, WI 53713-5020
608-274-0123; *Fax:* 608-274-0696
memberhelp@floods.org; www.floods.org
Larry A Larson, Executive Director
Alison Stierli, Member Services Coordinator
Anita Larson, Member Services
Mark Riebau, Project Manager
Diane Brown, Manager
The most comprehensive source assembled to date, this report summarizes and analyzes various state and local programs and activities.
Cost: $25.00

7854 **Geothermal Progress Monitor**
Office of Geothermal Technologies EE-12
1000 Independence Avenue SW
Washington, DC 20585-0001
202-586-1361; *Fax:* 202-586-8185
Allan J Jelacic, Director
Lists of operating, planned and under construction geothermal electric generating plants; geothermal articles and publications; federal and state government employees active in geothermal energy development.
Frequency: Annual

7855 **Grey House Safety & Security Directory**
Grey House Publishing
4919 Route 22
PO Box 56
Amenia, NY 12501
518-789-8700
800-562-2139; *Fax:* 845-373-6390
books@greyhouse.com; www.greyhouse.com
Social Media: Facebook, Twitter
Leslie Mackenzie, Publisher
Richard Gottlieb, Editor
Kristen Thatcher, Production Manager
Comprehensive guide to the safety and security industry, including articles, checklists, OSHA regulations and product listings. Focuses on creating and maintaining a safe and secure enviroment, and dealing specifically with hazardous materials, noise and vibration, workplace preparation and maintenance, electrical and lighting safety, fire and rescue and more.
Cost: $165.00
1600 Pages
ISBN: 1-592373-75-5
Founded in: 1981

7856 **Handling Dyes Safely - A Guide for the Protection of Workers Handling Dyes**
ETAD North America
1850 M St NW
Suite 700
Washington, DC 20036-5810
202-721-4100; *Fax:* 202-296-8120;
www.etad.com
Jill Aker, President

7857 **Hazardous Materials Guide**
JJ Keller
PO Box 368
Neenah, WI 54957-0368
920-722-2848
800-327-6868; *Fax:* 800-727-7516
contactus@jjkeller.com; www.jjkeller.com
Webb Shaw, Editor
A complete reference guide of hazardous materials regulations.

7858 **Hazardous Materials Information Resource System**
One Church Street
Suite 200
Rockville, MD 20850
301-577-1842; *Fax:* 301-738-2330
CAPT Michael J. Macinski, Commanding Officer
CAPT Robert W. Farr, Executive Officer
HMCM Robert E. Searles, II, Command Master Chief
The Hazardous Materials Information Resource System is a Department of Defense (DOD) automated system developed and maintained by the Defense Logistics Agency. HMIRS is the central repository for Material Safety Data Sheets (MSDS) for the United States Government military services and civil agencies.

7859 **Hazardous Waste Guide**
JJ Keller
PO Box 368
Neenah, WI 54957-0368
920-722-2848
800-327-6868; *Fax:* 800-727-7516
contactus@jjkeller.com; www.jjkeller.com
Webb Shaw, Editor

Contains word-for-word regulations.

7860 Hydro Review: Industry Sourcebook Issue
HCI Publications
410 Archibald St
Kansas City, MO 64111-3288

816-931-1311; *Fax:* 816-931-2015
hci@aol.com; www.hcipub.com

Leslie Eden, President
List of over 800 manufacturers and suppliers of products and services to the hydroelectric industry in the US and Canada.
Cost: $20.00
180 Pages
Frequency: Annual December
Circulation: 5000
Founded in: 1984
Printed in 4 colors on glossy stock

7861 IES Membership Directory
International Ecotourism Society
733 15th Street NW
Suite 1000
Washington, DC 20005

202-547-9203; *Fax:* 202-387-7915;
www.ecotourism.org

Martha Honey, Executive Director
Amos Bien, Director International Programs
Neal Inamdar, Director Finance/Administration
Frequency: Annual

7862 International Directory of Human Ecologists
Society for Human Ecology
College of the Atlantic
105 Eden Street
Bar Harbor, ME 04609-0180

207-288-5015; *Fax:* 207-288-3780;
www.societyforhumanecology.org

Barbara Carter, Assistant to Executive Director
Frequency: Irregular

7863 LEXIS Environmental Law Library
Mead Data Central
9443 Springboro Pike
Dayton, OH 45401

888-223-6337; *Fax:* 518-487-3584;
www.lexis-nexis.com

Andrew Prozes, CEO
Rebecca Schmitt, Chief Financial Officer
This database contains decisions related to environmental law from the Supreme Court and other legislative bodies.
Frequency: Full-text

7864 NIWR Member Directory
National Institutes for Water Resources
47 Harkness Road
Pelham, MA 10002

413-253-5686; *Fax:* 413-253-1309
godfrey@tei.umass.edu
snr.unl.edu/NIWR

Paul Joseph Godfrey, PhD, Executive Director

7865 National Directory of Conservation Land Trusts
Land Trust Alliance
1319 F Street NW
Suite 501
Washington, DC 20004-1106

202-638-4725; *Fax:* 202-638-4730
info@lta.org; www.lta.org

More than 1,200 nonprofit land conservation organizations at the local and regional levels are profiled.
Cost: $12.00
210 Pages
Frequency: Biennial

7866 National Environmental Data Referral Service
US National Environmental Data Referral Service
1825 Connecticut Avenue NW
Washington, DC 20235-0003

202-606-4089

More than 22,200 data resources that have available data on climatology and meteorology, ecology and pollution, geography, geophysics and geology, hydrology and limnology, oceanography and transmissions from remote sensing satellites.
Frequency: Quarterly

7867 National Organic Directory
Community Alliance with Family Farmers
PO Box 363
Davis, CA 95617-0363

530-756-8518
800-892-3832; *Fax:* 530-756-7857
info@caff.org; www.caff.org

Wriiten for all sectors of the booming organic food and fiber industry. Offers international listing with full contact information and extensive, cross-referenced index - Also provides regulatory updates, essays by industry leaders and other ressources.
Cost: $47.95
324 Pages
Frequency: Annual
Circulation: 2,500
ISBN: 1-891894-04-8
Founded in: 1983

7868 POWER
US Department of Energy
Forrestal Building
5H - 021
Washington, DC 20585-0001

202-646-5095; *Fax:* 202-586-1605;
www.eren.doe.gov

Timothy Unruh, Program Manager
A large database offersing information on all forms of energy, including fossil, nuclear, solar, geothermal and electrical.

7869 Pollution Abstracts
Cambridge Scientific Abstracts
7200 Wisconsin Ave
Suite 601
Bethesda, MD 20814-4890

301-961-6700; *Fax:* 301-961-6790
service@csa.com; www.csa.com

Andrew M Snyder, President
Ted Caris, Publisher
Evelyn Beck, Editor
Mark Furneaux, VP Marketing
Angela Hitti, Production Manager
This database offers information on environmental pollution research and related engineering studies.
Cost: $985.00
Frequency: Monthly

7870 Public Citizen Organizations
Public Citizen
215 Pennsylvania Ave SE
Suite 3
Washington, DC 20003-1188

202-544-4985; *Fax:* 202-547-7392
cmep@citizen.org

Bob Ritter, Manager
Patricia Lovera, Organizer
Ronald Taylor, Manager
We provide many publications regarding nuclear safety, nuclear waste, water, food, and energy deregulation.
Frequency: Annual

7871 RIFM/FEMA Fragrance and Flavor Database
Flavor & Extract Manufacturers Association
1620 I Street NW
Suite 925
Washington, DC 20006

202-293-5800; *Fax:* 202-462-8998;
www.femaflavor.org
Social Media: YouTube, RSS Feed

Ed R. Hays, Ph.D., President
George C. Robinson, III, President Elect
Mark Scott, Treasurer
Arthur Schick, VP & Secretary
John Cox, Executive Director
The Database currently contains over 50,000 references and more than 103,000 human health and environmental studies.
Frequency: Annual
Founded in: 1909

7872 Recycling Today: Recycling Products & Services Buyers Guide
Recycling Today GIE Publishers
4012 Bridge Avenue
Cleveland, OH 44113-3320

216-961-4130; *Fax:* 216-961-0364
http://www.recyclingtoday.com

Richard Foster, President
James Keefe, Publisher
Mark Phillips, Editor
Rosalie Slusher, Circulation Director
Jami Childs, Production Manager
Directory of services and supplies to the industry.
Cost: $19.95
Frequency: Annual
Circulation: 22,000

7873 Using Multiobjective Management to Reduce Flood Losses in Your Watershed
Association of State Floodplain Managers
2809 Fish Hatchery Rd
Suite 204
Fitchburg, WI 53713-5020

608-274-0123; *Fax:* 608-274-0696
memberhelp@floods.org; www.floods.org

Larry A Larson, Executive Director
Alison Stierli, Manager
Diane Brown, Manager
Introduction to multiobjective management and planning process that helps a community select suitable flood loss reduction measures.
Cost: $15.00

7874 Waste Manifest Software Report
Donley Technology
PO Box 152
Colonial Beach, VA 22443-0152

804-224-9427
800-201-1595; *Fax:* 804-224-7958
donleytech@donleytech.com;
www.donleytech.com

Elizabeth Donley, Editor
Profiles 30 software packages for solid and hazardous waste management, including detailed product descriptions, tables comparing system features, and contact information.
Cost: $97.50
118 Pages
ISBN: 1-891682-01-6
Founded in: 1996
Printed in on matte stock

7875 Water Environment and Technology Buyers Guide/Yearbook
Water Environment Federation

601 Wythe St
Alexandria, VA 22314-1994

703-684-2400
800-666-0206; *Fax:* 703-684-2492;
www.wef.org

Bill Bertera, Executive Director

Offers listings of the Water Environment Federation and consultant members.
Cost: $28.00
Frequency: Annual
ISSN: 1044-9943

7876 **Weather America**
Grey House Publishing
4919 Route 22
PO Box 56
Amenia, NY 12501

518-789-8700
800-562-2139; *Fax:* 845-373-6390
books@greyhouse.com; www.greyhouse.com
Social Media: Facebook, Twitter

Leslie Mackenzie, Publisher
Richard Gottlieb, Editor

Provides extensive climatological data for over 4,000 places throughout the United States - states, counties, cities, and towns. Included are rankings across the US for precipitation, snowfall, fog, humidity, wind speed and more.
Cost: $175.00
2020 Pages
ISBN: 1-891482-29-7
Founded in: 1981

7877 **Who's Who in Training**
National Environmental, Safety and Health Training
5320 N 16th Street
Suite 114
Phoenix, AZ 85016-3241

602-956-6099; *Fax:* 602-956-6399
info@neshta.org; www.neshta.org

Charles L Richardson, Executive Director
Joan J Jennings, Manager Association Services
Suzanne Lanctot, Manager Certification/Membership
Frequency: Annual

7878 **Wilderness Preservation: A Reference Handbook**
ABC-CLIO
PO Box 1911
Santa Barbara, CA 93116-1911

805-705-9339

Offers a list of agencies and organizations concerned with wilderness preservation.

7879 **World Directory of Environmental Organizations**
California Institute of Public Affairs
PO Box 189040
Sacramento, CA 95818-9040

916-442-2472; *Fax:* 916-442-2478;
www.interenvironment.org

Over 2,500 governmental, intergovernmental and United Nations organizations are covered.
Cost: $47.00
232 Pages

7880 **Your Resource Guide to Environmental Organizations**
Smiling Dolphin Press
4 Segura
Irvine, CA 92612-1726

Information is offered, in three separate sections, on non-governmental organizations, federal agencies and state agencies that address environmental concerns.
Cost: $15.95
514 Pages

Industry Web Sites

7881 **The Environmental Literacy Council**
1625 K St. NW
Suite 1020
Washington, DC 20006

202-296-0390; *Fax:* 202-822-0991
enviroliteracy.org
Social Media: Facebook, LinkedIn

Roger A. Sedjo, Chairman
Kathleen Berry, President

The Council provides resources on environmental topics for teachers and students.

7882 **http://gold.greyhouse.com**
G.O.L.D Grey House OnLine Databases

Grey House Publishing's online database platform, GOLD, offers Quick Search, Keyword Search and Expert Search for most business sectors including environment and conservation markets. The GOLD platform makes finding the information you need quick and easy - whether you're a novice searcher or an experienced database user. All of Grey House's directory products are available for subscription on the GOLD platform.

7883 **www.adirondackcouncil.org**
Adirondack Council

Research, education and advocacy to protect the natural character and communities of the Adirondack Park. Also publishes an annual State of Park Report and quarterly newsletters.

7884 **www.aeecenter.org**
Association of Energy Engineers

Source of information on the field of energy efficiency, utility deregulation, plant engineering, facility management and environmental compliance. Membership includes more than 8,000 professionals and certification programs. Offers seminars, conferences, job listings and certification programs.

7885 **www.aga.org**
American Gas Association

Association for the natural gas industry.

7886 **www.america-the-beautiful-fund.org**
America the Beautiful Fund

Groups and private citizens that improve the quality of the environment.

7887 **www.apwa.net**
American Public Works Association

The American Public Works Association is an international educational and professional association of public agencies, private sector companies, and individuals dedicated to providing high quality public works goods and services. APWA provides a forum in which public works professionals competency, increase the performance of their agencies and companies, and bring important public works-related topics to public attention in local, state, and federal areas. Mailing list for members only.

7888 **www.ases.org**
American Solar Energy Society

Individuals and professionals working in the field of solar energy and conservation.

7889 **www.asfe.org**
ASFE

Not-for-profit trade association. Helps geoprofessional, environmental and civil engineering firms profit through professionalism.

7890 **www.audbon.org**
National Audubon Society

Conserves and restores natural ecosystems, focusing on birds, other wildlife, and thier habitats for the benefit of humanity and the earth's biological diversity.

7891 **www.bisoncentral.com**
National Bison Association

The National Bison Association was formed to promote the production, marketing, and preservation of bison.

7892 **www.blr.com**
Business & Legal Reports

Provides essential tools for safety and environmental compliance and training needs

7893 **www.cbemw.org**
Citizens for a Better Environment

For citizens concerned with environmental protection. Maintains library.

7894 **www.cnie.org/nle**
National Library for the Environment

Environment-related information: daily environment and congressional news, upcoming conferences, education resources and congressional research reports.

7895 **www.conservation.state.mo.us**
Department of Conservation

Focuses on conservation and the importance of protecting the environment.

7896 **www.conservationfund.org**
Conservation Fund

Works with private and public agencies and organizations to protect wildlife habitats, historic sites and parks.

7897 **www.conservationtreaty.org**
Conservation Treaty Support Fund

Promotes awareness, understanding and support of conservation treaties and their goals.

7898 **www.construction.com**
McGraw-Hill Construction

McGraw-Hill Construction (MHC), part of The McGraw-Hill Companies, connects people and projects across the design and construction industry, serving owners, architects, engineers, general contractors, subcontractors, building product manufacturers, suppliers, dealers, distributors and adjacent markets.

7899 **www.earthisland.org/ei**
Earth Island Institute

Seeks to prevent destruction of environment and sponsors fund drives and activist projects to protect wildlife.

7900 **www.earthsite.org**
Earth Society Foundation

News of interest in environmental and sociological issues. Purpose is to promote Earth Day and the Earth Trustee agenda.

7901 **www.eia-usa.org**
Environmental Information Association

Nonprofit organization dedicated to providing environmental information to individuals, members and the industry. Disseminates information on the abatement of asbestos and lead-based paint, indoor air quality, safety and health issues, analytical issues and environmental site assessments.

7902 **www.epa.gov**
US Environmental Protection Agency

7903 **www.ethenolrfa.org**
Renewable Fuels Association

Members are companies and individuals involved in the production and use of ethanol.

7904 www.femaflavor.org
Flavor & Extract Manufacturers Assn of the US
1620 I Street NW
Suite 925
Washington, DC 210006
202-293-5800; *Fax:* 202-463-8998
Ed R. Hayes, President
George C. Robinson III, President Elect
Mark Scott, Treasurer
Arthur Schick, Vice President & Secretary
FEMA is comprised of flavor manufacturers, flavor users, flavor ingredient suppliers, and others with an interest in the U.S. flavor industry. FEMA works with legislators and regulators to assure that the needs of members and consuemr are continuously addressed and is committed to assuring a substantial supply of safe flavoring substances.

7905 www.floods.org
Association of State Floodplain Managers
Promotes common interest in flood damage abatement, supports environmental protection for floodplain areas, provides education on floodplain management practices and policy, and urges incorporating multi-objective management, approaches to solve local flooding problems.

7906 www.greyhouse.com
Grey House Publishing
Authoritative reference directories for most business sectors including environment and conservation markets. Users can search the online databases with varied search criteria allowing for custom searches by product category, geographic area, sales volume, keyword, subject and more. Full Grey House catalog and online ordering also available.

7907 www.ia-usa.org
National BioEnergy Industries Association

7908 www.iaee.org
International Association for Energy Economics
Association for those involved in energy economics including publications, consultants, energy database software.

7909 www.iaia.org
International Association for Impact Assessment
IAIA provides a forum for the exchange of the ideas and experiences to stimulate innovation in assessing, managing and mitigating the consequences of development.

7910 www.iwla.org
Isaak Walton League
Conducts research and education on river ecosystems and healthy fisheries.

7911 www.joincca.org
Coastal Conservation Association
Seeks to advance protection and conservation of all marine life. Conducts seminars and bestows awards.

7912 www.lib.duke.edu/forest/
Forest History Society
Non-profit educational institution that explores the history of the environment, forestry, and conservation.

7913 www.members.aol.com/rccouncil
Rachael Carson Council
Seeks to promote awareness of the problems of environmental contamination and by serving as an information clearing house on chemical contaminates, especially pesticides.

7914 www.mtsociety.org
Marine Technology Society
Addresses coastal zone management, marine mineral and energy resources, marine environmental protection, and ocean engineering issues.

7915 www.nacdnet.org
National Association of Conservation Districts
Association for those interested in the environment.

7916 www.naem.org
National Association for Environmental Management
Dedicated to advancing the profession of environmental management and supports the professional corporate and facility environmental manager.

7917 www.nalms.org
North American Lake Management Society
Members are academics, lake managers and others interested in furthering the understanding of lake ecology.

7918 www.napcor.com
National Association for Pet Container Resources
National trade association which promotes the recycling of food containers made from PET plastic (containers with recycle code #1).

7919 www.nationalwoodlands.org
National Woodland Owners Association
Provides timely information about forestry and forest practices with news from washington,Dc and state capitals. written for non-industrial land owners. Includes state landowner association news.

7920 www.ncat.org
National Center for Appropriate Technology
A resource center for information and expertise on methods of promoting conservation and energy self sufficiency. The term, appropriate technology, is defined as a small-scale, environmentally sound, low-cost, locally based approach to problems with an emphasis on self help.

7921 www.neha.org
National Environmental Health Association
Association for suppliers of environmental educational materials.

7922 www.noaa.gov
National Oceanic and Atmospheric Administration
National weather forecasts, statistics, searchable databases, agency directory and links to related agencies and sites.

7923 www.pollutiononline.com
Pollution Online
For vendors and professionals in pollution equipment and control industries. News, product information, links to related web sites and business information.

7924 www.purezone.com
PureZone
Devoted to indoor air quality. Discussion forum moderated by industry experts on topics such as sensors and transducers technology.

7925 www.recycle-steel.srs
Steel Recycling Institute
Promotes steel recycling and works to forge a coalition of steelmakers, can manufacturers, legislators, government officials, solid waste managers, business and consumer groups.

7926 www.rnrf.org
Renewable Natural Resources Foundation
A consortium of professional and scientific societies whose members are concerned with the advancement of research, education, scientific practice and policy formulation for the conservation, replenishment and use of the earth's renewable natural resources.

7927 www.sca-inc.org
Student Conservation Association

7928 www.socma.com
Silicone Health Council
Coordinates health, environmental and safety programs. Conveys scientifically sound information about silicones.

7929 www.sweets.construction.com
McGraw Hill Construction
In depth product information that lets you find, compare, select, specify and make purchase decisions in the industrial product marketplace.

7930 www.techknow.org
TechKnow
Lists environmentally friendly remediation and ozone-depleting substance management resources.

7931 www.terrassa.pnl.gov:2080/hydrology
Hydrology Web
Lists of related internet resource lists.

7932 www.usace.army.mil
US Army Corps of Engineers
Information on flood control, environmental protection, disaster response, military construction and support of others through the sharing of engineering expertise with other agencies, state and local governments, academia and foreign nations.

7933 www.woodlandowners.org
National Woodland Owners Association
Provides timely information about forestry and forest practices with news from washington,Dc and state capitals. written for non-industrial land owners. Includes state landowner association news.

7934 www.wqa.org
Water Quality Association
An international nonprofit trade association representing retail/dealers and manufacturer/suppliers in the point of use/entry water quality improvement industry. Membership benefits and services include technical and scientific information, educational seminars and home correspondence course books, professional certification and discount services.

Associations

7935 AMC Institute
1940 Duke Street
Suite 200
Alexandria, VA 22314

703-570-8954; *Fax:* 856-439-0525
info@amcinstitute.org; www.amcinstitute.org

Tina Wehmeir, Chief Executive Officer
Greg Schultz, Chair
Fred Stringfellow, Chair-Elect
Michael Payne, Treasurer
Jeanne Sheehy, Secretary

AMCs are professional service firms that provide executive, administrative, and financial management; strategic counsel planning; membership development; public affairs and lobbying; education and professional development; statistical research; meetings management; and marketing and communication services.
175 Members
Founded in: 2006

7936 American Business Media
675 Third Avenue
Suite 2200
New York, NY 10017-5704

212-661-6360; *Fax:* 212-370-0736
info@abmmail.com; www.siia.net
Social Media: Facebook, Twitter, LinkedIn

Doug Manoni, Chair
Marion Minor, Secretary
Edward Keating, Treasurer
Ethan Eisner, Immediate Past Chair
Ty Bobit, Board Member

An association for business-to-business information providers, including producers of print publications, Web sites, trade shows and other media.
200+ Members
Founded in: 1906

7937 American Society of Association Executives
1575 I St NW
Washington, DC 20005-1103

202-371-0940
888-950-2723
Flickr; *Fax:* 202-371-8315
service@asaenet.org; www.asaenet.org
Social Media: Facebook

Abe Eshkenazi, Chairman
Scott D. Wiley , FASAE, CAE, Chair-Elect
Susan K. Neely , CAE, Immediate Past President
Matthew R. Shay, CAE, Secretary/Treasurer
Lori M. Anderson, CAE, Board Member

ASAE is the premier source of learning, knowledge and future-oriented research for the association and nonprofit profession, and provides resources, education, ideas and advocacy to enhance the power and performance of the association and nonprofit community.
21M Members
Founded in: 1920

7938 Association of Collegiate Conference and Special Events
Colorado State University
S. College Avenue
Suite 3B
Fort Collins, CO 80525

970-449-4960; *Fax:* 970-449-4965
info@acced-i.org; www.acced-i.org
Social Media: Facebook, Twitter, LinkedIn

Trish Carlson, President
Lisa Beringer Salazar, CCEP, President-Elect
Daniel L. Dykstra, Immediate Past President
Jim Hodges, Treasurer
Mary Kay Baker, CCEP, Director

Members are college and university conference and special events directors, professionals and others who design, market and coordinate conferences and special events.
1400 Members
Founded in: 1980

7939 Association of International Meeting Planners
2547 Monroe Street
Dearborn, MI 48124-3013

313-563-0360; *Fax:* 972-702-3070

Meeting planners.
40 Members
Founded in: 1986

7940 Association of Science-Technology Centers
818 Connecticut Avenue, NW
7th Floor
Washington, DC 20006-2734

202-783-7200; *Fax:* 202-783-7207
info@astc.org; www.astc.org
Social Media: Facebook, Twitter, LinkedIn

Chevy Humphrey, Chair
Linda Conlon, Chair-Elect
Joanna Haas, Secretary
David Chesebrough, Treasurer
Kate Bennett, Director

Organization of science centers and museums dedicated to futhering the public understanding of science among increasingly diverse audiences. Encourges excellence and innovation in informal science learning by serving and linking its members worldwide and advancing their common goals.
550 Members
Founded in: 1973

7941 CEMA
1512 Weiskopf Loop
Round Rock, TX 78664-6128

512-310-8330; *Fax:* 510-682-0555;
www.cemaonline.com

Erika Brunke, Executive Director
Olga Rosenbrook, Member Services
Alexia Henrie, Secretary
Trinette R Cunningham, Executive Staff

Professionals from the event, trade show and marketing communications industry. Striving to be the definitive resource for event marketing professionals in the information technology industry.
250 Members
Founded in: 1990

7942 Center for Exhibition Industry Research
12700 Park Central Dr
Suite 750
Dallas, TX 75251-1526

972-687-9242; *Fax:* 972-692-6020
info@ceir.com; www.ceir.org
Social Media: Facebook, LinkedIn

Britton Jones, Chair
Aaron Bludworth, Vice Chair
Dennis Slater, immediate Past Chair
Steve Moster, Secretary/Treasurer
David Audrain, Director

The Center for Exhibition Industry Research is an apolitical, nonprofit orgnization with the dual mission of producing research that supports the unique features and value of exhibitors; then, using that research and other tools to promote the image and growth of the exhibition industry

7943 Connected International Meeting
9200 Bayard Place
Fairfax, VA 22032

512-684-0889; *Fax:* 267-390-5193
susan2@cimpa.org; www.cimpa.org

Andrea Sigler, President/CEO

Members are conference and convention planners with a certificate in convention management. Specializes in planning meetings events, incentives, using the internet.
8000 Members
Founded in: 1982

7944 Convention Industry Council
700 N Fairfax Street
Alexandria, VA 22314

571-527-3116; *Fax:* 571-527-3105
cichq@conventionindustry.org;
www.conventionindustry.org
Social Media: Facebook, Twitter, LinkedIn, YouTube

David Dubois, CMP, CAE, Chair
Bonnie Fedchock, CAE, Vice Chair
Bob Gilbert, CHME CHBA, Immediate Past Chair
Vicki Hawarden, CMP, Board Member At-Large
Kimberly Miles, CMP, Board Member At-Large

An organization that represents individuals as well as 15,000 firms and properties involved in the meetings, conventions and exhibitions industries.
98000 Members
Founded in: 1949

7945 Convention Liaison Council
10200 W 44th Avenue
Suite 310
Wheat Ridge, CO 80033-2840

303-420-2902; *Fax:* 303-422-8894
clc@resourcenter.com; www.clc.org

Francine Butler, Executive VP

Members are associations which are directly involved in the convention, exposition, trade show and meeting industry.

7946 Display Distributors Association
Modern Display
424 S 700 E
Salt Lake City, UT 84102-2864

801-355-7427; *Fax:* 801-521-3040

Members are distributors of display equipment.
16 Members
Founded in: 1950

7947 Event Service Professionals Association
191 Clarksville Road
Princeton Junction, NJ 08550

609-799-3712; *Fax:* 609-799-7032
info@espaonline.org; www.espaonline.org
Social Media: Facebook, Twitter, LinkedIn

Denise I. Suttle,CMP, President
Madonna Carr, CMP, President-Elect
Paul Ruby, CMP, 1st Vice President
Kathy Denkenberger, 2nd Vice President
Amy Cabe, Treasurer

Dedicated to elevating the event and convention service profession and to preparing members, through education and networking, for their pivotal role in innovating and successful event execution.
400 Members
Founded in: 1988

7948 **Exhibit Designers & Producers Association**
10 Norden Place
Norwalk, CT 06855

203-852-5698; *Fax:* 203-854-6735
jprovost@edpa.com; www.edpa.com

Robert Campbell, President
Kelli Glasser, VP, Finance & Administration
Gwen Hill, VP, Education
Donna Shultz, VP, Member Services
Dave Flory, VP, Member Development

Internationally recognized, national trade association with corporate members from 18 countries that are engaged in the design, manufacture, transport, installation and service of displays and exhibits primarily for the trade show industry. EDPA's purpose is to champion the prosperity of member businesses.
400+ Members
Founded in: 1956

7949 **Exhibit and Event Marketers Association**
2214 NW 5th St.
Bend, OR 97701

541-317-8768; *Fax:* 541-317-8749
tsea@tsea.org; www.tsea.org

Amanda Helgemoe, President
Michael Mulry, Vice President
Glenda Brundgardt, Treasurer
Chris Griffin, Secretary
Jim Wurm, Executive Director

Supports marketing and management professionals.

7950 **Exposition Service Contractors Association**
5068 West Plano Parkway
Suite 300
Plano, TX 75093

972-447-8212
877-792-3722; *Fax:* 972-447-8209;
www.esca.org

Jay Atherton, President
Lenny Servedio, President-Elect
Julia Smith, Vice President
Richard P. Curran, Secretary/Treasurer
Bruce Nable, Immediate Past President

Annual guide to exposition service is distributed annually and lists safety regulations and building rules in major US convention centers.
120 Members
Founded in: 1970

7951 **Healthcare Convention & Exhibitors Association**
1100 Johnson Ferry Rd NE
Suite 300
Atlanta, GA 30342-1733

678-298-1183; *Fax:* 404-385-5595
hcea@kellencompany.com; www.hcea.org
Social Media: Facebook, Twitter, LinkedIn

Christine Farmer, President
Don Schmid, MBA, CME/H, President-Elect
Kyle Wood, Vice President
Sue Huff, Secretary/Treasurer
Diane Benson, CTSM, Immediate Past President

Trade association of organizations involved in health care exhibiting or providing services to health care conventions, exhibitions, and/or meetings.
600 Members
Founded in: 1930

7952 **Hospitality Sales & Marketing Association International**
7918 Jones Branch Drive
Suite 300
McLean, VA 22102

703-506-3280; *Fax:* 703-506-3266
info@hsmai.org; www.hsmai.org
Social Media: Facebook, Twitter, LinkedIn, Google+

Rob Torres, Chair
Jeff Senior, Chair-Elect
Marina MacDonald, Vice Chair
Mark Thompson, CHBA, CHSE, Secretary/Treasurer
Barb Bowden, CRDE, Immediate Past Chairman

The hospitality industry's source for knowledge, community, and recognition for leaders committed to professional development, sales growth, revenue optimization, marketing and branding.
7000 Members
Founded in: 1927

7953 **International Association for Exhibition Management**
12700 Park Central Dr.
Suite 308
Dallas, TX 75251-1313

972-458-8002; *Fax:* 972-458-8119
info@iaee.com; www.iaee.com
Social Media: Facebook, Twitter, LinkedIn, YouTube

Megan Tanel, CEM, Chairperson
Julia Smith, CEM, CTA, Chair-Elect
Daniel McKinnon, CEM, Secretary/Treasurer
Jonathan Skip Cox, Immediate Past Chairperson
Vicki Bedi, Director

Members are managers of shows, exhibits and expositions; associate members are industry suppliers.
3500 Members
Founded in: 1928

7954 **International Association for Modular Exhibitry**
155 W Street
Suite 3
Wilmington, MA 01887-3064

978-988-1200

Irving Sacks, Executive Director

Members are companies that promote the use of modular exhibits for trade shows and museums.
47 Members
Founded in: 1987

7955 **International Association of Exhibitions and Events**
12700 Park Central Dr.
Suite 308
Dallas, TX 75251

972-458-8002; *Fax:* 972-458-8119
info@iaee.com; www.iaee.com
Social Media: Facebook, Twitter, LinkedIn, YouTube

Megan Tanel, Chairperson
Daniel McKinnon, Secretary/Treasurer

Represents the interests of both those who produce trade shows and exhibitions, and those who provide the exhibition industry with products and services.
9000 Members
Founded in: 1928

7956 **International Association of Assembly Management**
635 Fritz Dr
Suite 100
Coppell, TX 75019-4462

972-906-7441
800-935-4226; *Fax:* 972-906-7418
mike.meyers@iaam.org; www.iaam.org

Dexter King, Executive Director
Robyn Williams, First Vice President

Members are managers of auditoriums, arenas, convention centers, stadiums and performing arts centers.
400 Members
Founded in: 1924

7957 **International Association of Conference Centers**
35 East Wacker Drive
Suite 850
Chicago, IL 60601

312-224-2580; *Fax:* 312-644-8557
info@iacconline.org
http://www.iacconline.org/
Social Media: Facebook, Twitter, LinkedIn

Alex Caba□as, President
Rachael Bartlett, Vice President, UK
TJ Fimmano, Vice President, USA
Sean Anderson, Director
Lotta Boman, Director

Facilities-based organization which advances the understanding and awareness of conference centers as distinct within the training, education, hospitality and travel fields.
377 Members
Founded in: 1981

7958 **International Association of Fairs and Expositions**
3043 E Cairo
PO Box 985
Springfield, MO 65802

417-862-5771
800-516-0313; *Fax:* 417-862-0156
iafe@fairsandexpos.com;
www.fairsandexpos.com
Social Media: Facebook, Twitter, YouTube

John Sykes, CFE, Chair
Kent Hojem, CFE, 1st Vice Chair
Becky Brashear, CFE, 2nd Vice Chair
Jim Tucker, President
John Hanschen, Director at large

The International Association of Fairs and Expositions (IAFE) is a voluntary, non-profit corporation whose members provide services and products that promote the overall development and improvement of fairs, shows, expositions, and allied fields.
Founded in: 1885

7959 **International Congress and Convention Association**
PO Box 6833
Freehold, NJ 07728-6833

732-851-6603; *Fax:* 732-851-6584
n.america@iccaworld.org; www.iccaworld.com

Martin Sirk, Chief Executive Officer
Joanne H. Joham, Regional Director, North America

Representing events specialists in more than 90 countries.
1000+ Members
Founded in: 1963

7960 International Festivals and Events Association
2603 W Eastover Ter
Boise, ID 83706-2800

208-433-0950; *Fax:* 208-433-9812
nia@ifea.com; www.ifea.com

Cindy Lerick, Chair
Guy LaFlamme, Chair-Elect
James L. Holt, CFEE, Immediate Past Chair
William O'Toole, CFEE, Secretary
Michael Berry, CFEE, President & CEO

A voluntary association of events, event producers, event suppliers, and related professionals and organizations whose common purpose is the production and presentation of festivals, events, and civic and private celebrations.
2000 Members
Founded in: 1956

7961 International Laser Display Association
7062 Edgeworth Drive
Orlando, FL 32819

407-797-7654; *Fax:* 503-344-3770
mail@laserist.org; www.laserist.org

Christine Jenkin, President
Abdulwahab Baghdadi, 3rd Dimension EvenTech
Brian Gonzalez, Individual Member

ILDA members are individuals involved in the laser entertainment and display industry.
Founded in: 1986

7962 International Special Events Society
330 M Wabash Ave.
Suite 2000
Chicago, IL 60611-4267

312-321-6853
800-688-4737; *Fax:* 312-673-6953
info@ises.com; www.ises.com

Jodi Collen, CSEP, President
Judy Brillhart, President-Elect
Ingrid Nagy, CSEP, Treasurer
Sara Hunt, CSEP, Secretary
Kevin White, CSEP, Immediate Past President

Professionals in over a dozen countries representing special event producers, caterers, decorators, florists, destination management companies, rental companies, special effects experts, tent suppliers, audio-visual technicians, party and convention coordinators, ballon artists, educators, journalists, hotel sales managers, specialty entertainers, convention center managers and more.
4000 Members
Founded in: 1987

7963 Meeting Professionals International
3030 LBJ Fwy
Suite 1700
Dallas, TX 75234-2759

972-702-3000; *Fax:* 972-702-3065
feedback@mpiweb.org; www.mpiweb.org
Social Media: Facebook, Twitter, LinkedIn

Paul Van DeVenter, President & CEO
Michael Woody, Chief Operating Officer
Daniel Gilmartin, Chief Financial Officer
Darren Temple, Chief Business Dev Officer

MPI members manage meetings and related activities for association, corporations, and educational institutions, or provide goods and services to the meetings industry.
1900 Members
Founded in: 1972

7964 National Association for Campus Activities
13 Harbison Way
Columbia, SC 29212

803-732-6222
800-845-2338; *Fax:* 803-749-1047
info@naca.org; www.naca.org
Social Media: Facebook, Twitter, Instagram, YouTtube, Pinterest

Steve Westbrook, Director Student Affairs
Alan Davis, Executive Director
Gordon Schell, Manager/Member Services
Dawn Thomas, Director/Educational/Events
Erin Wilson, Manager Communications

Largest collegiate organization for campus activities. Purpose is to assist in marketing entertainment services to educational institutions and providing student leadership development programs and services.
1100 Members
Founded in: 1960

7965 National Association of Agricultural Fair Agencies
MI State Department of Agriculture
PO box 40627
Nashville, TN 37204

615-837-5081; *Fax:* 517-373-9146;
www.nasda.org

Director Greg Ibach, President
Comm. Michael Strain, 1st Vice President
Comm. Steven Reviczky, 2nd Vice President
Director Jeff Witte, Secretary-Treasurer
Scott Enright, Past President

U.S. and Canadian representatives of state/provincial agencies that are responsible for the support of education and agricultural fairs.
Founded in: 1966

7966 National Association of Consumer Shows
147 Se 102nd Ave
Portland, OR 97216-2703

503-253-0832
800-728-6227; *Fax:* 503-253-9172;
www.publicshows.com
Social Media: Facebook, Twitter

Mark Adams, President
Marc McIntosh, Treasurer
Mark Concilla, Secretary
Carolyn Alt, Director
Jim Fricke, Director

Nonprofit organization dedicated to furthering the interests of consumer show producers and suppliers.
265 Members
Founded in: 1987

7967 National Association of Display Industries
4651 Sheridan Street
Suite 200
Hollywood, FL 33021

954-893-7300; *Fax:* 954-893-7500
nadi@nadi-global.com; www.nadi-global.com

Klein Merriman, Executive Director
Tracy Dillon, Director Communications

Sponsors seminars and annual contests. Conducts research programs and maintains placement services.
400 Members
Founded in: 1937

7968 National Association of Professional Organizers
1120 Route 73
Suite 200
Mount Laurel, NJ 08054-2212

856-380-6828; *Fax:* 856-439-0525
napo@napo.net; www.napo.net
Social Media: Facebook, Twitter, Pinterest, Flickr, YouTube

Ellen Faye , CPO, COC, President
Susie Hayman, Secretary
Lisa Mark , CPO, Treasurer
Danielle Liu, MPA, CPO, Director
Elizabeth Dodson, Corp Associate Members Director

Members are time, productivity and organization management consultants.
1800 Members
Founded in: 1985

7969 National Catholic Educational Exhibitors
2621 Dryden Road
Suite 300
Dayton, OH 45439

937-293-1415
888-555-8512; *Fax:* 937-293-1310
cynpleg@aol.com; www.ncee.org

Peter Li, Executive Director

A group for companies that provide products or services for Catholoc education.
500 Members
Founded in: 1950

7970 National Coalition of Black Meeting Planners
700N Fairfax Street
Suite 510
Alexandria, VA 22314

571-527-3110; *Fax:* 301-860-0500
info@ncbmp.org; www.ncbmp.com

Ana Aponte-Curtis, Chair
Kevin J. Johnson, President
JoAnn S. Brown, Vice President
Stephanie Marshall, CMP, Secretary
Myron L. Hardiman, Treasurer

Nonprofit organization dedicated to the training needs of African American meeting planners.
Founded in: 1983

7971 North American Farm Show Council
590 Woody Hayes Drive
Room 232
Columbus, OH 43210

614-292-4278; *Fax:* 614-292-9448
gamble.19@osu.edu;
www.farmshowcouncil.org

Chip Blalock, President
Chuck Gamble, Secretary-Treasurer
David Zimmerman, 1st Vice President
Matt Jungmann, 2nd Vice President
Dennis Alford, Immediate Past-President

Strives to improve the value of its member shows through education, communication and evaluation. The overall goal is to provide the beest possible marketing showcase for exhibitors for agricultural equipment and related products to the farmer/rancher/producer customer.
37 Members
Founded in: 1972

7972 Professional Convention Management Association
35 East Wacker Drive
Suite 500
Chicago, IL 60601-2105

312-423-7262
877-827-7262; *Fax:* 312-423-7222

communications@pcma.org; www.pcma.org
Social Media: Facebook, Twitter, LinkedIn

Ray Kopcinski, CMP, Chair
William Reed , FASAE, CMP, Chair-Elect
Mary Pat Heftman, Secretary-Treasurer
Christopher Wehking, CMP, Immediate Past Chair
Martin Balogh, Director

PCMA delivers superior and innovative education, to promote the value of professional convention management.
6100 Members
Founded in: 1957

7973 **Professional Show Managers Association**
41 Applewood Lane
Avon, CT 06001

860-677-0094; *Fax:* 860-286-0787
info@rdpgroup.com; www.psmashows.org
Social Media: Facebook, LinkedIn

Dordy Fontinel, President
Christine Palmer, Vice President
Frank Gaglio, Secretary/Treasurer
Nancy Johnson, Immediate Past President
Bart Caple, Director
Founded in: 1987

7974 **Religious Conference Management Association**
7702 Woodland Drive
Suite 120
Indianapolis, IN 46278

317-632-1888; *Fax:* 317-632-7909
rcma@rcmaweb.org; www.rcmaweb.org
Social Media: Facebook, LinkedIn, YouTube

Harry R. Schmidt, Executive Director/CEO Dean
Dean Jones, Director of Conferenec & Events
Judy Valenta, Special Projects Cooordinator
Debbie Hochstetler, Director of Finance

Provides members with a wealth of resources designed specifically to enhance their professionalism and overall effectiveness as religious leaders.
3200 Members
Founded in: 1972

7975 **Society of Government Meeting Professionals**
PO Box 321025
Alexandria, VA 22320

703-549-0892; *Fax:* 703-549-0708;
www.sgmp.org
Social Media: LinkedIn, YouTube

Maggie McGowan, CGMP, CMP, President
Michelle Milligan, First Vice President
James Lynton, CGMP, 2nd Vice President
Brett Sterenson, Treasurer
Maurine Hill, Secretary

Trade association for government meeting planners and exhibitors.
3100 Members
Founded in: 1981

7976 **Society of Independent Show Organizers**
2601 Ocean Park Blvd
Suite 200
Santa Monica, CA 90405-5250

310-450-8831
877-937-7476; *Fax:* 310-450-9305;
www.shomex.com
Social Media: Facebook, Twitter, LinkedIn

David Audrain, Chairman
Rick McConnell, Vice Chair
Charles McCurdy, Treasurer
Tony Calanca, Secretary
Lewis R. Shomer, Executive Director
200 Members
Founded in: 1990

7977 **Visitor Studies Association**
2885 Sanford Ave SW
Suite 18100
Grandville, MI 49418

740-872-0566; *Fax:* 301-637-3312
info@visitorstudies.org;
www.visitorstudies.org
Social Media: Facebook, Twitter, LinkedIn

Joe Heimlich, President
Kimberly Kiehl, President-elect
Dave Ucko, Vice President, Organizational Dev
Bob Breck, Vice President, Outreach
Jessica Luke, Vice President, Professional Dev

Members are professionals at various institutions interested in studying audience experiences at museums, zoos, parks, etc. Promotes research in visitor participation and application of such research to programming and policy.
365 Members
Founded in: 1990

Newsletters

7978 **ACOMmodate**
Association for Convention Operations Management
191 Clarksville Road
Princeton Junction, NJ 08550

609-799-3712; *Fax:* 609-799-7032;
www.espaonline.org

Lynn McCullough, Executive Director

Includes news, networking ideas, and articles of professional interest.
Frequency: Quarterly

7979 **Affiliate Connection**
International Festivals and Events Association
2603 W Eastover Ter
Boise, ID 83706-2800

208-433-0950; *Fax:* 208-433-9812
craig@ifea.com; www.ifea.com

Steven Schmader, President
Nia Forster, VP/Marketing
Craig Sarton, Director

The IFEA newsletter provides information and news 24 hours a day, 7 days a week, keeping members, suppliers and affialiates up-to-date and current.
2000 Members
Frequency: Monthly
Founded in: 1956

7980 **Annual Conference Abstracts**
Visitor Studies Association
8175-A Sheridan Boulevard
Suite 362
Arvada, CO 80003-1928

303-467-2200; *Fax:* 303-467-0064
info@visitorstudies.org;
www.visitorstudies.org

Alan Friedman, President
Ellen Cox, Treasurer
Jessica Luke, Treasurer
Frequency: Annual

7981 **Aviso**
American Association of Museums
1575 Eye Street NW
Suite 400
Washington, DC 20005-1113

202-289-1818; *Fax:* 202-289-6578
membership@aam-us.org; www.aam-us.org

Ford Bell, President
Kim Igone, VP Policy & Program

Reports on musuems in the news, federal legislation affecting museums, upcoming seminars and workshops, fedel grant deadlines and AAM activities and services.
Frequency: Monthly
Mailing list available for rent

7982 **CEMA Communicator**
Computer Event Marketing Association
1512 Weiskopf Loop
Round Rock, TX 78664-6128

512-310-8330; *Fax:* 978-443-4715;
www.cemaonline.com

Mitch Ahiers, President

Newsletter posted directly on the Internet.
Frequency: Monthly
Founded in: 1990

7983 **ESCA Voice Newsletter**
Exhibition Services and Contractors Association
2260 Corporate Circle
Suite 400
Henderson, NV 80914

702-319-9561
877-792-3722; *Fax:* 702-450-7732
askus@esca.org; www.esca.org

Susan L Schwartz, Director Communications
Cynthia Kelly, Accounting Manager
Frequency: Quarterly

7984 **Exhibition Perspectives**
American Academy of Equine Art
c/o Kentucky Horse Park
4089 Iron Works Parkway
Lexington, KY 40511

859-281-6031; *Fax:* 859-281-6043;
www.aaea.net

Julie Buchanan, Director
Frequency: Annual

7985 **HCEA Edge**
Healthcare Convention & Exhibitors Association
5775 Peachtree Dnwdy Rd
Building G, Suite 500
Atlanta, GA 30342-1556

404-252-3663; *Fax:* 404-252-0774
hcea@kellencompany.com; www.hcea.org

Eric Allen, Executive Vice President

News and events of the trade association of over 600 organizations involved in healthcare exhibiting or providing services to healthcare conventions, exhibitions and/or meetings.
Frequency: Monthly, Members Only

7986 **IEG Endorsement Insider**
IEG

640 N La Salle Dr
Suite 600
Chicago, IL 60654-3186

312-944-1727
800-834-4850; *Fax:* 312-944-1897
valuationservices@sponsorship.com;
www.sponsorship.com

Lesa Ukman, CEO
John Ukman, Publisher

A newsletter covering the use of sports and entertainment personalities for endorsements, appearances and other marketing purposes.
Cost: $295.00
Frequency: Monthly

7987 IEG Sponsorship Report
IEG
640 N La Salle Dr
Suite 600
Chicago, IL 60654-3186

312-944-1727
800-834-4850; *Fax:* 312-944-1897
ieg@sponsorship.com; www.sponsorship.com

Lesa Ukman, CEO
John Ukman, Publisher
Bart Zautcke, CEO
Brad Smith, Marketing

Newsletter on sports, arts, event, entertainment and cause marketing.
Cost: $415.00
8 Pages
Frequency: Biweekly
Circulation: 15000
Founded in: 1982

7988 NAAFA Newsletter
National Association of Agricultural Fair Agencies
MI State Department of Agriculture
PO Box 30017
Lansing, MI 48909

517-373-9766; *Fax:* 517-373-9146

Carol Carlson, Secretary/Treasurer
Frequency: Annual

7989 NAFSC Brochure
North American Farm Show Council
590 Woody Hayes Drive
Columbus, OH 43210-6131

614-292-4278; *Fax:* 614-292-9448
gamble19@osu.edu; www.worldagexpo.com

Dennis Alford, First VP
Chuck Gamble, Secretary-Treasurer

The North American Farm Show Council strives to improve the value of its member shows through education, communication and evaluation. The goal of the Council is to provide the best possible marketing showcase for the exhibitors of agricultural equipment & related products.
Frequency: Bi-Ennial
Founded in: 1972

7990 NCEE News
National Catholic Educational Exhibitors
2621 Dryden Road
Suite 300
Dayton, OH 45439

937-293-1415
888-555-8512; *Fax:* 937-293-1310
cynpleg@aol.com; www.ncee.org

Peter Li, Executive Director

A regular newsletter for the exclusive use of NCEE members. Each issue brings messages from the NCEE president and the NCEA Convention and Exposition Director; market and association updates, and the Exhibition Planning Calendar

7991 Newsbytes
Meeting Professionals International
3030 Lbj Fwy
Suite 1700
Dallas, TX 75234-2759

972-702-3000; *Fax:* 972-702-3070
feedback@mpiweb.org; www.mpiweb.org

Bruce Mac Millan, President
Frequency: Weekly

7992 Newsletter
American Academy of Equine Art
c/o Kentucky Horse Park
4089 Iron Works Parkway
Lexington, KY 40511

859-281-6031; *Fax:* 859-281-6043;
www.aaea.net

Julie Buchanan, Director
Frequency: Semi-Annual

7993 Workshop Brochure
American Academy of Equine Art
c/o Kentucky Horse Park
4089 Iron Works Parkway
Lexington, KY 40511

859-281-6031; *Fax:* 859-281-6043;
www.aaea.net

Julie Buchanan, Director
Frequency: Annual

Magazines & Journals

7994 American Speaker
Briefings Publishing Group
1101 King St
Suite 110
Alexandria, VA 22314-2944

703-548-3800
800-722-9221; *Fax:* 703-684-2136;
www.briefings.com

Aram Bakshian Jr, Editor-in-Chief
Alan Douglas, President

An updateable loose leaf product geared to amateur and polished public speakers. The product has tips on speaking, model speeches, and filler material for all speaking needs.
Cost: $395.00
Frequency: Monthly
Founded in: 1992
Mailing list available for rent: 14000 names at $125 per M
Printed in 2 colors on matte stock

7995 Association Conventions & Facilities
Coastal Communications Corporation
2700 N Military Trail
Suite 120
Boca Raton, FL 33431

561-989-0600; *Fax:* 561-989-9509
ccceditor@att.net;
www.themeetingmagazines.com

Harvey Grotsky, Publisher/Editor-In-Chief
Susan Wycoff Fell, Managing Editor
Susan Gregg, Managing Editor

Edited for association meeting planners with the responsibility for staging and planning meetings, conferences and conventions, for site selection, specifying accommodations and transportation. Issues provide in-depth focus on sites and transportation, current legislation, seminar and training oprtions, budget and cost controls, and destination reports.
Cost: $60.00
Frequency: BiMonthly
Circulation: 20,500
ISSN: 2162-8831
Founded in: 2008

7996 Association Meetings
Primedia
Po Box 12901
Shawnee Mission, KS 66282-2901

913-341-1300; *Fax:* 913-514-6895;
www.penton.com

Eric Jacobson, Senior VP
Larry Keltto, Editor

Directed to association executive directors and meeting planners with the objective of aiding the planning, site selection, and organization of meetings and conventions.
Cost: $223.65
Circulation: 20065
Printed in 4 colors

7997 Convene Magazine
Professional Convention Management Association
2301 S Lake Shore Dr
Suite 1001
Chicago, IL 60616-1419

312-423-7262
877-827-7262; *Fax:* 312-423-7222
communications@pcma.org; www.pcma.org

Deborah Sexton, President/CEO
Kati S Quigley CMP, Chairman of Board
Barry L Smith, Chair Board of Trustees

The leading meetings industry trade publication for education content and timely, relevant information from the Professional Convention Management Association
Frequency: Monthly
Circulation: 35000

7998 Convention South
2001 W First Street
2001 West First Street
Gulf Shores, AL 36542

251-968-5300; *Fax:* 251-968-4532
info@conventionsouth.com;
www.conventionsouth.com

J Talty O'Connor, Editor/Publisher
Kristen S McIntosh, VP/Executive Editor
Pamela Redden, Marketing Services Manager
Suzanne Kellams, Manager, Circulation Development

For planners of meetings, conferences, seminars and similar events that are held in the South
Frequency: Monthly
Circulation: 18000
ISSN: 1074-0627
Founded in: 1983
Printed in 4 colors on glossy stock

7999 Corporate & Incentive Travel
Coastal Communications Corporation
2700 N Military Trail
Suite 120
Boca Raton, FL 33431

561-989-0600; *Fax:* 561-989-9509
ccceditor1@att.net;
www.themeetingmagazines.com

Harvey Grotsky, Publisher/Editor-In-Chief
Susan Wyckoff Fell, Managing Editor
Susan Gregg, Managing Editor

The magazine for corporate meetings and incentive travel planners. In-depth editorial focus on site selection, accommodations and transportation, current legislation, conference, seminar and training facilities, budget and cost controls, and destination reports. Regular features highlight industry news and developments, trends and personalities, meeting values, facilities, and destinations.
Frequency: Monthly
Circulation: 40,000
Founded in: 1983

8000 Corporate Meetings & Incentives
Primedia

Po Box 12901
Shawnee Mission, KS 66282-2901

913-341-1300; *Fax:* 913-514-6895;
www.penton.com

Eric Jacobson, Senior VP
Melissa Fromento, Publisher

Senior executives guide to decision-making.
138 Pages
Frequency: Monthly
Circulation: 34246
Founded in: 1980
Printed in 4 colors on glossy stock

8001 **ESCA Extra Magazine**
Exhibition Services and Contractors Association
2260 Corporate Circle
Suite 400
Henderson, NV 80914

702-319-9561
877-792-3722; *Fax:* 702-450-7732
askus@esca.org; www.esca.org

Susan L Schwartz, CEM, Executive Director
Heather Geldner, Accounting Manager
Cynthia Kelly, Accounting Manager
Frequency: Monthly

8002 **EXPO Magazine**
Expo Magazine
7015 College Blvd
Overland Park, KS 66211-1579

913-469-1185
800-444-4388; *Fax:* 913-469-0806
expo@halldata.com; www.expoweb.com

Cam Bishop, President
Donna Sanford, Publisher
Danica Tormohlen, Editor-in-Chief

Magazine for exposition managment.
Cost: $48.00
134 Pages
Circulation: 7500
ISSN: 1046-3925
Founded in: 1989
Printed in 4 colors on glossy stock

8003 **Event Solutions**
Virgo Publishing LLC
3300 N Central Ave
Suite 300
Phoenix, AZ 85012-2532

480-675-9925; *Fax:* 480-990-0819
mikes@vpico.com; www.vpico.com

Jenny Bolton, President

Topics featured include decor, themes, high tech support, indoor facility equipment, food and beverage ideas, special effects, new products, and financial issues and regulations. Provides corporate, product and even profiles with suggestions from experts in the field.
Cost: $45.00
Frequency: Monthly
Circulation: 25,000

8004 **Events World**
International Special Events Society: Indiana
401 North Michigan Avenue
Chicago, IL 60611-4267

312-321-6853
800-688-4737; *Fax:* 312-673-6953
info@ises.com; www.ises.com

Kevin Hacke, Executive Director
Kristin Prine, Operations Director

Editorial contents include practical information on each of the seven disciplines, news on promotions, job banks, people in the industry, ISES activities and events, technology trends, and global vision information about environmental, legal and political issues relating to the special events industry.
Frequency: Monthly
Circulation: 20000
Founded in: 1987

8005 **Exhibit Builder**
Exhibit Builder
22900 Ventura Boulevard #245
PO Box 4144
Woodland Hills, CA 91365

818-225-0100
800-356-4451; *Fax:* 818-225-0138;
www.exhibitbuilder.net

Jill Brookman, CEO/President
Judy Pomerantz, Managing Editor
Jollen Ryan, Circulation Manager
Scott Gray, Editors

Devoted to the business and technical interest of the designers and fabricators of exhibits for trade shows, museums and point of purchase displays, includes application articles, new products, and new technology for creating booths.
Cost: $40.00
72 Pages
Frequency: Annual+
Circulation: 15000
ISSN: 0887-6878
Founded in: 1983
Printed in 4 colors on glossy stock

8006 **Exhibit Marketing Magazine**
Eaton Hall Publishing
256 Columbia Turnpike
Florham Park, NJ 07932-1231

973-514-5900
800-746-9646; *Fax:* 973-514-5977
info@eatonhall.com; www.eatonhall.com

Scott Goldman, Publisher

Eaton Hall is a publishing and trade show firm which specializes in bringing buyers and sellers together.
Cost: $5.00
52 Pages
Frequency: Quarterly
Circulation: 31000
Founded in: 1990
Printed in 4 colors on glossy stock

8007 **Exhibitor**
Exhibitor Magazine Group
Po Box 368
Suite 745
Rochester, MN 55903-0368

507-289-6556
888-235-6155; *Fax:* 507-289-5253
webmaster@exhibitoronline.com;
www.exhibitoronline.com

Lee Knight, Owner
John Pavek, VP Publishing
Cara Schulz, National Sales Manager
Nicole Brudos Ferrara, Managing Editor
Whitney Archibald, Editor

The magazine for trade show and event marketing management.
Cost: $78.00
122 Pages
Frequency: Monthly
Circulation: 30000
ISSN: 0739-6821
Founded in: 1982
Printed in 4 colors on glossy stock

8008 **Facilities & Destinations**
Bedrock Communications
650 1st Ave
7th Floor
New York, NY 10016-3240

212-532-7088; *Fax:* 212-213-6382
mikecaffin@aol.com;
www.facilitiesonline.com

Stella Johnson, Senior Executive Editor
Timothy Herrick, Director

Serves the association meeting industry defined as finance, banking, health, education,religious, trade, labor, fraternal, manufacturing, civic, social, professional, government/military, association management companies, independent meeting planners, destination management companies, trade show/event production companies and other groups who use the facilities industry for meetings, conferences, exhibitions, trade shows and conventions.
45 Pages
Circulation: 34000+
Founded in: 1988

8009 **Facilities & Event Management**
Bedrock Communications
650 1st Ave
7th Floor
New York, NY 10016-3240

212-532-7088; *Fax:* 212-213-6382
mikecaffin@aol.com;
www.facilitiesonline.com

Michael Caffin, Managing Editor
Glen O'Grady, Director
Timothy Herrick, Director

Editorial articles solve problems based on industry facts and statistics and coverage encompasses various segments of the facilities industry, including: convention centers, exhibition halls, hotel/conference centers, civic centers, arenas, stadiums, arts centers, etc. Monthly features detail facility business activity and provide coverage of the products and services available.
Subscription, $48.00
Cost: $4.95
52 Pages
Frequency: Monthly
Circulation: 30000
ISSN: 1524-0258

8010 **Fairs and Expositions**
International Association of Fairs & Expositions
3043 E Cairo
PO Box 985
Springfield, MO 65802

417-862-5771
800-516-0313; *Fax:* 417-862-0156;
www.fairsandexpos.com

Jim Tucker, President
Steve Siever, Director
Max Willis, Editor

The source of information for fair trends, innovative ideas and association activities.
Frequency: 10/year
Founded in: 1885

8011 **Feed and Grain**
Cygnus Business Media
1233 Janesville Avenue
Fort Atkinson, WI 53538

920-563-6388; *Fax:* 920-563-1702;
www.feedandgrain.com

Arlette Sambs, Publisher
Jackie Roembke, Editor

Committed to providing targeted editorial that addresses the specific needs of its readers. Subscribers consist of feed manufacturers, integrated livestock operators, pet food manufacturers, soybean processors, builders, designers and millwrights, as well as businesses such as rice mills, country and terminal elevators, flour mills, brew-

eries and distilleries.
Cost: $48.00
Frequency: Bi-Monthly
Circulation: 15700
Founded in: 1966
Mailing list available for rent: 16,505 names at $100 per M
Printed in 4 colors on glossy stock

8012 IE - Business of International Events Magazine
International Festivals and Events Association
2603 W Eastover Ter
Boise, ID 83706-2800

208-433-0950; *Fax:* 208-433-9812
craig@ifea.com; www.ifea.com

Steven Schmader, President
Nia Forster, VP/Marketing
Craig Sarton, Director

IFEA'S quarterly magazine that provides members with the latest news and features focusing on current trends and topics, events, resources and more.
2000 Members
Founded in: 1956

8013 Inside Events
Trio Communications
8899 Beverly Boulevard
#408
Los Angeles, CA 90048-2431

310-888-8566; *Fax:* 310-888-1866

Elisabeth Familian, Publisher
Articles include area listings of sites and vendors for any type of gathering. Profiles the creative ideas of industry professionals.
Frequency: Quarterly
Circulation: 20,000

8014 Insurance & Financial Meetings Management
Coastal Communications Corporation
2700 N Military Trail
Suite 120
Boca Raton, FL 33431-6394

561-989-0600; *Fax:* 561-989-9509
ccceditor@att.net;
www.themeetingmagazines.com

Harvey Grotsky, Publisher/Editor-In-Chief
Susan Wyckoff Fell, Managing Editor
Susan Gregg, Managing Editor

The executive source for planning meetings and incentives for the financial and insurance sectors. With regular features and special focus on site selection, destinations, industry-related studies and activities, motivational and incentive programs, program and event planning.
Frequency: Monthly
Circulation: 40,000
Founded in: 1983

8015 Insurance Conference Planner
Primedia
Po Box 12901
Shawnee Mission, KS 66282-2901

913-341-1300
866-505-7173; *Fax:* 913-514-6895;
www.penton.com

Eric Jacobson, Senior VP
Melissa Fromento, Publisher

Meeting and incentive strategies for the financial services industry.
148 Pages
Frequency: Monthly
Circulation: 8005
Founded in: 1965
Printed in 4 colors on glossy stock

8016 Laserist
International Laser Display Association
7062 Edgeworth Drive
Orlando, FL 32819

407-797-7654; *Fax:* 503-344-3770
president@laserist.org; www.laserist.org

Tim Walsh, President
Patrick Murphy, Executive Director

Providing the latest news about the art and technology of laser displays
Frequency: Quarterly
Founded in: 1986

8017 Medical Meetings
Primedia
11 Riverbend Dr S
Stamford, CT 06907-2524

203-316-8178; *Fax:* 203-358-5812;
www.meetingsnet.com

Betsy Bair, Editor Director
Melissa Framento, Publisher

International guide for health care and meeting planners.
106 Pages
Frequency: Monthly
Circulation: 10,823
Founded in: 1973
Printed in 4 colors on glossy stock

8018 Meeting Professionals
Meeting Professionals International
3030 LBJ Fwy
Suite 1700
Dallas, TX 75234-2759

972-702-3000; *Fax:* 972-702-3070
feedback@mpiweb.org; www.mpiweb.org

Bruce MacMillan, President
Eric Rozenberg CMP,CMM, Vice Chairman Administration

Furthers the professional development and education of all those who participate in the meetings industry.
Cost: $99.00
Frequency: Monthly
Circulation: 28,000
Founded in: 1972

8019 Meetings & Conventions
Reed Business Information
500 Plaza Drive
Secaucus, NJ 07094

201-021-1960; *Fax:* 201-902-2053
lcioffi@ntmllc.com;
www.meetings-conventions.com

Bernard Lynch, Associate Editor
Lori Cioffi, Editor in Chief
Loren G. Edelstein, Executive Editor
Allen Sheinman, Managing Editor
Lisa Grimaldi, Senior Editor

Serves the corporate and independent travel and meeting planner with features on meeting facilities, hotels/airports/car rental, incentive travel options, trade show coverage, entertainment/leisure options and industry news.
Cost: $70.00
Frequency: Monthly
Circulation: 70013
Founded in: 1965

8020 Meetings Industry
Dunn Enterprises
513 Commerce Dr
Upper Marlboro, MD 20774-7434

301-249-4600; *Fax:* 301-249-9100;
www.jtdunn.com

Barbara Cox, Owner
Robert Lantang, Graphic Designer

Profiles meetings sites and accomodations for meetings of all sizes. Includes personnel appointments of other meeting planners.
Circulation: 35000

8021 Programming Magazine
National Association for Campus Activities
13 Harbison Way
Columbia, SC 29212-3401

803-732-6222
800-845-2338; *Fax:* 803-749-1047
info@naca.org; www.naca.org

Glenn Farr, Editor
Erin Wilson, Circulation

Features cover facilities and financial management, promotions, and student development to help plan a wide range of events.
Cost: $70.00
Circulation: 4300
Founded in: 1960

8022 Religious Conference Manager
Religious Conference Management Association
7702 Woodland Drive
Suite 120
Indianapolis, IN 46228-6150

317-632-1888; *Fax:* 317-632-7909
rcma@rcmaweb.org; www.rcmaweb.org

Eric Allen, Executive Director

Presents timely information for the meeting professional. Content focuses on current trends and features educational articles and news within this specialized field.
Frequency: Bi-Monthly

8023 Resorts, Hotels, Meetings & Incentives
Publishing Group
PO Box 318
Trumbull, CT 06611-0318

860-279-0149

John Mortimer, Publisher

Editorial contents include in-depth articles on industry trends, budgeting, planning tips, and profiles of the top meeting facilities in the world.
Frequency: Monthly
Circulation: 58,601

8024 Special Events Magazine
Primedia Publication
17383 W Sunset Blvd
Suite A220
Pacific Plsds, CA 90272-4187

310-230-7160
800-543-4116; *Fax:* 310-230-7168
lhurley@specialevents.com;
www.specialevents.com

Lisa Hurley, Editor
Lisa Perrin, President, Chief Executive Officer
Wanda McKnight, Sales Manager

Resource for event professionals who design and produce special events (including social, corporate and public events) in hotels, resorts, banquet facilities and other venues.
Cost: $48.43
Frequency: Monthly
Circulation: 2000+
Founded in: 1982

8025 Tradeshow & Exhibit Manager
Goldstein & Associates
2117 Highland Avenue
Louisville, KY 40204

502-548-3188; *Fax:* 502-742-8749;
www.goldsteinandassociates.com

Steve Goldstein, Publisher

Featured articles focus on the issues, trends and products of interest connected to the tradeshow

industry. Topics include security, boothmanship, legislation and shipping.
Cost: $80.00
Circulation: 14600

8026 **Tradeshow Week**
Reed Business Information
5700 Wilshire Boulevard
Suite 120
Los Angeles, CA 90036-5804
323-576-6600; *Fax:* 323-965-2407;
www.tradeshowweek.com
Amy Lacey, Marketing Director
Adam Schaffer, Publisher
Michael Hart, Editor-in-Chief
Carlos Lopez, Production Director
Heidi Genoist, Senior Associate Editor
For corporate exhibit managers, independent show managers, special event and meeting planners, association show managers and industry suppliers. Focuses on changing trends, new ideas and issues shaping the exposition industry in the US/Canada and abroad. Each issue contains a national and international show calendar.
Cost: $439.00
Frequency: Weekly
Circulation: 2394
Founded in: 1971
Printed in 4 colors on matte stock

8027 **Visitor Studies Today**
Visitor Studies Association
8175-A Sheridan Boulevard
Suite 362
Arvada, CO 80003-1928
303-467-2200; *Fax:* 303-467-0064
info@visitorstudies.org;
www.visitorstudies.org
Alan Friedman, President
Ellen Cox, Treasurer
Jessica Luke, Treasurer
Frequency: 3/year

Trade Shows

8028 **AAEA Annual Meetings**
American Academy of Equine Art
c/o Kentucky Horse Park
4089 Iron Works Parkway
Lexington, KY 40511
859-281-6031; *Fax:* 859-281-6043;
www.aaea.net
Shelley Hunter, Executive Director
Julie Buchanan, President
Frequency: April, September

8029 **AAM Annual Meeting & MuseumExpo**
American Alliance of Museums
2451 Crystal Dr.
Suite 1005
Arlington, VA 22202
202-289-1818; *Fax:* 202-289-6578
membership@aam-us.org; www.aam-us.org
Andrea Streat, Director, Meetings & Events
The largest gathering of museum professionals in the world.
Frequency: Annual/May

8030 **ASTC Annual Conference & Exhibit Hall**
Association of Science/Technology Centers
1025 Vermont Avenue NW
Suite 500
Washington, DC 20005-6310
202-783-7200; *Fax:* 202-783-7207
conference@astc.org; www.astc.org
Cindy Kong, Director, Meetings & Conferences
Wendy Pollock, Dir, Research, Pubs, Exhibitions
Sheryl Thorpe, Manager, Conference & Exhibit Hall
Provides science center professionals from across the world a forum to exchange ideas and discuss the field's leading issues. With over 100 conference sessions, participants are challenged to explore ways of making science centers more essential to their communities.
1500 Attendees
Founded in: 1973

8031 **Affordable Meetings Exposition and Conference**
George Little Management
10 Bank Street
Suite 1200
White Plains, NY 10606-1954
914-486-6070
800-272-7469; *Fax:* 914-948-6180
customer_relations@glmshows.com;
www.glmshows.com
Susan Sloan, Show Manager
George Little II, President
Focuses on the needs of meeting planners from all types and sizes of organizations who are responsible for producing successful yet cost effective meetings. 430 booths.
3M Attendees
Frequency: September

8032 **Association of Collegiate Conference & Events Directors Conference**
Assn of Collegiate Conference & Events Directors
1301 S College Avenue
Fort Collins, CO 80523-8037
877-502-2233; *Fax:* 970-491-0667
acced@colostate.edu
acced-i.edu
Deborah Blom, Executive Director
Monica Nesbit Schultz, Marketing/Sales Manager
Workshop, conference, banquet and luncheon plus exhibits of conference and special event planning supplies, equipment and service information.
1300 Attendees
Frequency: March
Founded in: 1980

8033 **Business to Business Exposition**
Trade Shows West
2880 S Main
Suite 110
Salt Lake City, UT 84115
801-485-0176; *Fax:* 801-485-0241
16000 Attendees

8034 **Conventions and Expositions**
American Society of Association Executives
1575 I Street NW
Washington, DC 20005-1105
202-262-2723; *Fax:* 202-626-8825
Judy Comeaux, Advertising
John Young, Production
Exposition planners trade show; 500-700 booths.
2-5M Attendees
Frequency: March

8035 **ESC Semi-Annual Meetings**
Exhibition Services and Contractors Association
2260 Corporate Circle
Suite 400
Henderson, NV 80914
702-319-9561
877-792-3722; *Fax:* 702-450-7732
askus@esca.org; www.esca.org
Susan L Schwartz, CEM, Executive Director
Heather Geldner, Accounting Manager
Cynthia Kelly, Accounting Manager
December Meeting with International Association for Exposition Management and Summer Educational Conference.
Frequency: December, Summer

8036 **ESCA's Summer Educational Conference**
Exhibition Services & Contractors Association
2340 E Trinity Mills Road
Suite 100
Carrollton, TX 75006
469-574-0698
877-792-ESCA; *Fax:* 469-574-0697;
www.esca.org
Designed to give attendees the opportunity to advance their knowledge and to have an impact on the shape of the exhibition industry's future, as well as to network. Three session tracks, interactive forums and roundtables, speakers, and exhibits.
Frequency: Annual

8037 **ESPA Annual Conference**
Event Service Professionals Association
191 Clarksville Road
Princeton Junction, NJ 08550
609-799-3712; *Fax:* 609-799-7032
info@espaonline.org; www.espaonline.org
Social Media: Facebook, Twitter, LinkedIn
Lynn McCullough, Executive Director
Diane Galante, Meeting Planner
Elizabeth Roe, Association Coordinator
Meghan Higgins, Public Relations Manager
Conference geared specifically to the event and convention services industry.
Frequency: Annual

8038 **Exhibit Ideas Show**
Exhibit Builder
1600 Golf Road
Suite 550
Rolling Meadows, IL 60008-4273
800-638-6396; *Fax:* 847-280-0771
Russ Eisenhardt, Show Manager
Jill Brookman, Publisher
Marketplace for products, services and technologies for exhibit builders and buyers. Elements included in trade show, museum and point of purchase booth construction are displayed, as are portable, modular and custom exhibit systems. 700 booths.
20M Attendees
Frequency: April

8039 **Exhibit Industry Conference & Exposition**
Trade Show Exhibitors Association
McCormick Place, 2301 S Lake Shore Drive
Suite 1005
Chicago, IL 60616
312-842-8732; *Fax:* 312-842-8744
tsea@tsea.org; www.tsea.org
Stephen Schuldenfrei, President
Emily Burger, Sales Manager
Frequency: July

8040 **Exhibitor Conference**
Exhibitor Magazine Group

98 E Naperville Road
Westmont, IL 60559

630-434-7779
800-752-6312; *Fax:* 630-434-1216
exhibitorshow@heiexpo.com;
www.exhibitorshow.com

Carol Fojtik, Managing Director/Sr VP

Conference program combined with exhibit hall featuring latest products and resources shaping the future of exhibiting and corporate event programs. Anyone responsible for planning, managing or implementing trade show or corporate event marketing functions should attend. Conference is held annually in Las Vegas, NV.
5M Attendees
Frequency: March
Founded in: 1989

8041 **HCEA Annual Meeting**
Healthcare Convention & Exhibitors Association
1100 Johnson Ferry Rd NE
Suite 300
Atlanta, GA 30342-1733

404-252-3663; *Fax:* 404-252-0774
hcea@kellencompany.com; www.hcea.org

Eric Allen, Executive Vice President
Jackie Beaulieu, Associate Director

Cost varies; approximately 50 booths; 800 attendees.
200 Attendees
Frequency: Annual

8042 **HCEA Marketing Summit**
Healthcare Convention & Exhibitors Association
1100 Johnson Ferry Rd NE
Suite 300
Atlanta, GA 30342-1733

404-252-3663; *Fax:* 404-252-0774
hcea@kellencompany.com; www.hcea.org

Eric Allen, Executive Vice President
Jackie Beaulieu, Associate Director

Cost varies; no exhibits; 200-250 attendees.
200 Attendees
Frequency: Annual

8043 **IAAM Annual Conference & Trade Show**
International Association of Assembly Managers
635 Fritz Drive
Suite 100
Coppell, TX 75019-4442

972-906-7441
800-935-4226; *Fax:* 972-906-7418;
www.iaam.org

Kristie Todd, Membership & Exposition Coordinator
JoAnn Ramsey, Exhibition Manager

Members are managers of auditoriums, arenas, convention centers, stadiums and performing arts centers, coming together for education and networking opportunities, expert speakers, and exhibits.
3000 Attendees
Frequency: Annual/
Founded in: 1925
Mailing list available for rent: 2800 names at $300 per M

8044 **IAEE Expo! Expo!**
International Assn of Exhibitions and Events
12700 Park Central Drive
Suite 308
Dallas, TX 75251

972-458-8002; *Fax:* 972-458-8119
news@iaee.com; www.iaee.com

Annual show of 250 exhibitors of conventions and visitor bureaus, hotels, travel airlines, car rental, shippers, insurance, computer hardware and software, service contractors, printing products, specialty advertisement products, photography equipment and audio-visual equipment.
2500 Attendees
Frequency: Annual/December
Founded in: 1928

8045 **IAEM Semi-Annual Meetings**
International Association for Exhibition Mgmt
8111 LBJ Freeway, Suite 750
PO Box 802425
Dallas, TX 75251-1313

972-458-8002; *Fax:* 972-458-8119;
www.iaee.com

Steven G Hacker, CAE, President
Cathy Breden, CAE CMP, SVP
Susan Brower, Director Marketing/Communications

Annual show of 250 exhibitors of conventions and visitor bureaus, hotels, travel airlines, car rental, shippers, insurance, computer hardware and software, service contractors, printing products, specialty advertisement products, photography equipment and audio-visual equipment.
2200 Attendees
Frequency: June, December

8046 **IAFE Annual Meeting**
International Association of Fairs & Expositions
3043 E Cairo
PO Box 985
Springfield, MO 65802

417-862-5771
800-516-0313; *Fax:* 417-862-0156
iafe@fairsandexpos.com;
www.fairsandexpos.com

Jim Tucker, President
Steve Siever, Director

Many branch divisions of the IAFE within the United States and Canada have their own annual meetings where members can meet, have access to resources, programs and workshops.
5000 Attendees
Frequency: Fall, Neveda
Founded in: 1885

8047 **IBTM America**
800-417-8646
203-840-5636
ibtmamerica@reedexpo.com;
www.ibtmamerica.com
Social Media: Facebook, Twitter, LinkedIn, Instagram, Pinterest, YouTube

Jaime McAuley, Event Director

IBTM's 8 global and regional events are showcases for the meetings and events industry.

8048 **IFEA Annual Convention and Expo**
International Festivals and Events Associations
2603 W Eastover Terrace
Boise, ID 83706

208-433-0950; *Fax:* 208-433-9812;
www.ifea.com

Steve Wood Schmader, President
Nia Forster, VP/Marketing
Shauna Spencer, Director

Unites hundreds of the world's leading festivals and events, suppliers, media, sponsors and related industry professionals to share information on every aspect of event production through in-depth workshops, round-table discussions and networking.
2000 Members
800 Attendees
Frequency: Fall
Founded in: 1956

8049 **ILDA Conference**
International Laser Display Association
7062 Edgeworth Drive
Orlando, FL 32819

407-797-7654; *Fax:* 503-344-3770;
www.laserist.org

Tim Walsh, President
Patrick Murphy, Executive Director

One of the world's largest exhibitions of entertainment technology. Features international exhibitors from the fields of lighting, lasers, audio, video and staging.
70000 Attendees
Founded in: 1986

8050 **International Technology Meetings & Incentives Conference**
Techno-Savvy Meeting Professional
9200 Bayard Place
Fairfax, VA 22032-2103

703-978-6287; *Fax:* 703-978-5524
cimpa@cimpa.org; www.cimpa.org

Andrea Sigler, President

Containing 100 booths and 100 exhibits.
Frequency: November

8051 **MPI Semi-Annual Meetings**
Meeting Professionals International
3030 LBJ Freeway
Suite 1700
Dallas, TX 75234

972-023-3000; *Fax:* 972-702-3070
feedback@mpiweb.org; www.mpiweb.org

Colin C Rorrie, Jr PhD CAE, President/CEO
Frequency: Summer, Winter

8052 **NAAFA Semi-Annual Meetings**
National Association of Agricultural Fair Agencies
MI State Department of Agriculture
PO Box 30017
Lansing, MI 48909

517-373-9766; *Fax:* 517-373-9146

Carol Carlson, Secretary/Treasurer
Frequency: Summer, Winter

8053 **NAFSC Annual Meeting**
North American Farm Show Council
590 Woody Hayes Drive
Columbus, OH 43210-6131

614-292-4278; *Fax:* 614-292-9448
gamble19@osu.edu; www.worldagexpo.com

Dennis Alford, First VP
Chuck Gamble, Secretary/Treasurer
Frequency: May
Founded in: 1972

8054 **NCEE Annual Meeting**
National Catholic Educational Exhibitors
2621 Dryden Road
Suite 300
Dayton, OH 45439

937-293-1415
888-555-8512; *Fax:* 937-293-1310
bthomas@peterli.com

Bret Thomas, Executive Director

In conjunction with the National Catholic Educational Association.
Frequency: March

8055 **PCMA Annual Meeting**
Professional Convention Management Association

2301 S Lake Shore Dr
Suite 1001
Chicago, IL 60616-1419

312-423-7262
877-827-7262; *Fax:* 312-423-7222
communications@pcma.org; www.pcma.org

Deborah Sexton, President/CEO
Kati S Quigley CMP, Chairman of Board
Barry L Smith, Chair Board of Trustees
3000 Members

8056 RCMA Conference & Exposition
Religious Conference Management Association
7702 Woodland Drive
Suite 120
Indianapolis, IN 46228-6150

317-632-1888; *Fax:* 317-632-7909
rcma@rcmaweb.org; www.rcmaweb.org

Eric Allen, Executive Director
Frequency: Annual

8057 The Special Event Annual Conference & Exhibition
Special Event Magazine
PO Box 8987
Malibu, CA 90265-8987

708-486-0731
866-486-0731; *Fax:* 310-317-0264
registration@penton.com;
www.specialevents.com

Sharon Morabito, Group Show Director
Tara Melingonis, Conference Manager
Kim Romano, Special Events Manager
Wanda McKnight, Sales Manager
Dacia Coppola, Show Coordinator

Brings together those in the special events industry for new product displays, education, networking and learning. 275 booths.
3M Attendees
Frequency: Annual/January

8058 VSA Annual Meeting
Visitor Studies Association
8175-A Sheridan Boulevard
Suite 362
Arvada, CO 80003-1928

303-467-2200; *Fax:* 303-467-0064
info@visitorstudies.org;
www.visitorstudies.org

Alan Friedman, President
Ellen Cox, Treasurer
Jessica Luke, Treasurer
Frequency: Summer

Directories & Databases

8059 Association Management: Convention Bureau and Convention Hall Issue
American Society of Association Executives
1575 Eye St NW
Washington, DC 20005-1103

202-626-2700; *Fax:* 202-371-8825
publicpolicy@asaenet.org; www.asaenet.org

A list of halls, centers, auditoriums, arenas and visitors bureaus in the United States and Canada.
Cost: $4.00
Circulation: 20,000

8060 Audarena International Guide & Facility Buyers Guide
VNU Business Publications
49 Music Sq W
4th Floor
Nashville, TN 37203-3213

615-321-4251; *Fax:* 615-320-0454
Research@billboard.com; www.billboard.com

Ken Schlager, Executive Editor
Mitch Tebo, Directory Marketing Director
George Van, President
Monica Herrera, Manager
Bill Werde, Director
Cost: $99.00
310 Pages
Frequency: October

8061 CEMA Member Directory and Meeting Planner
Computer Event Marketing Association
1512 Weiskopf Loop
Round Rock, TX 78664-6128

512-310-8330; *Fax:* 510-682-0555;
www.cemaonline.com

Erika Brunke, Executive Director
Olga Rosenbrook, Member Services

All event managers and primary IA members.
500 Pages
Founded in: 1990

8062 Constitution and Membership Roster
National Association of Agricultural Fair Agencies
MI State Department of Agriculture
PO Box 30017
Lansing, MI 48909

517-373-9766; *Fax:* 517-373-9146

Carol Carlson, Secretary/Treasurer
Frequency: Annual

8063 Corporate and Incentive Travel: Official
2700 N Military Trl
Suite 120
Boca Raton, FL 33431-6394

561-989-0600; *Fax:* 561-989-9509;
www.themeetingmagazines.com/corporate-incentive-travel

Harvey Grotsky, President

8064 HCEA Directory of Healthcare Meetings and Conventions
Healthcare Convention & Exhibitors Association
5775 Peachtree Dnwdy Rd
Building G, Suite 500
Atlanta, GA 30342-1556

404-252-3663; *Fax:* 404-252-0774
hcea@kellencompany.com; www.hcea.org

Eric Allen, Executive Director
Carol Wilson, Director Meetings

Information on 6,000 health care meetings, available to members only.
500 Pages
Founded in: 1930

8065 IAFE Directory
International Association of Fairs & Expositions
3043 E Cairo
PO Box 985
Springfield, MO 65802

417-862-5771
800-516-0313; *Fax:* 417-862-0156
iafe@fairsandexpos.com;
www.fairsandexpos.com

Jim Tucker, President
Steve Siever, Director

A annual reference guide giving members access to their associate members' products, services, and business activities.
1300 Members
Frequency: Annual
Founded in: 1885

8066 IEG Sponsorship Sourcebook
IEG
640 N La Salle Dr
Suite 450
Chicago, IL 60654-3186

312-944-1727
800-834-4850; *Fax:* 312-944-1897
ieg@sponsorship.com; www.sponsorship.com

Lesa Ukman, CEO
John Ukman, Publisher
Alicia Fidler, Product Manager

A directory of sponsors, properties, agencies and suppliers from th most active sponsors to the hottest sponsorship opportunities. Contains the critical data you need to make smart sponsorship connections.
Cost: $299.00
468 Pages
Frequency: Annual
ISBN: 0-944807-43-7
Printed in on glossy stock

8067 MPI Membership Directory
Meeting Professionals International
3030 Lbj Fwy
Suite 1700
Dallas, TX 75234-2759

972-702-3000; *Fax:* 972-702-3070
feedback@mpiweb.org; www.mpiweb.org

Bruce Mac Millan, President
Frequency: Annual

8068 Meetings and Conventions: Gavel International Directory Issue
Reed Travel Group
500 Plaza Dr
Suite C
Secaucus, NJ 07094-3619

201-902-1800; *Fax:* 207-319-1628

Alina Dalmau, Editor
Lori Cioffi, Manager

Lists over 4,000 convention halls and hotels in the United States, suitable for meetings.
Cost: $35.00
Frequency: Annual
Circulation: 80,000

8069 NCEE Membership Directory
National Catholic Educational Exhibitors
2621 Dryden Road
Suite 300
Dayton, OH 45439

937-293-1415
888-555-8512; *Fax:* 937-293-1310
bthomas@peterli.com

Bret Thomas, Executive Director
Frequency: Annual

8070 Nationwide Directory of Corporate Meeting Planners
Reed Reference Publishing RR Bowker
121 Chanlon Road
New Providence, NJ 07974-1541

908-665-2834; *Fax:* 908-464-3553
info@bowker.com; www.bowker

Offers valuable information on over 12,000 corporations that hold regular, off-site meetings arranged by over 18,000 corporate meeting planners.
Cost: $297.00
1140 Pages
Frequency: Annual

8071 **Official Meeting Facilities Guide**
Reed Travel Group
500 Plaza Dr
Suite C
Secaucus, NJ 07094-3619

201-902-1800; *Fax:* 201-902-2053

Virginia Nonneman, Editor
Lori Cioffi, Manager

One thousand national and international meeting facilities, primarily hotels in the US.
Cost: $45.00
Frequency: SemiAnnual
Circulation: 18,500

8072 **Protocol**
Protocol Directory
101 W 12th St
Suite PH-H
New York, NY 10011-8142
212-633-6934; *Fax:* 212-633-6934
noemail@councilofprotocolexecutives.org;
www.councilofprotocolexecutives.org

Edna Greenbaum, Editor

Approximately 4,000 suppliers of products and services used by planners of executive meetings, special events and other entertainment.
Cost: $60.00
Frequency: 1 issue
Founded in: 1989
Printed in on matte stock

8073 **Sports Market Place Directory - Online Database**
Grey House Publishing
4919 Route 22
PO Box 56
Amenia, NY 12501

518-789-8700
800-562-2139; *Fax:* 845-373-6390
gold@greyhouse.com
http://gold.greyhouse.com
Social Media: Facebook, Twitter

Leslie Mackenzie, Publisher
Richard Gottlieb, Editor

For over 20 years, this comprehensive, up-to-date directory provides current key information about the people, organizations and events involving the sports industry including, contact information and key executives for single sports organizations, multi-sport organizations, media, sponsors, college sports, manufacturers, trade shows and more.
Founded in: 1981

8074 **Trade Show Exhibitors Association: Membership Directory**
Trade Show Exhibitors Association
2301 S Lake Shore Dr
Suite 1005
Chicago, IL 60616-1419

312-842-8732; *Fax:* 541-317-8749
tsea@tsea.org; www.tsea.org

Steve Schuldenfrei, President
Emily Burger, Sales Manager

About 1,900 members of the Trade Show Exhibitors Association.
Cost: $55.00
Frequency: Annual February

8075 **Trade Show News Network**
Tarsus Group plc
16985 W Bluemound Road
Suite 210
Brookfield, WI 53005

262-782-1900; *Fax:* 603-372-5894
rwimberly@tsnn.com; www.tsnn.com

Rachel Wimberly, Editor-in-Chief
John Rice, Sales & Business Development
Arlene Shows, Marketing Manager

The world's leading online resource for the trade show, exhibition and event industry since 1996. TSNN.com owns and operates the most widely consulted event database on the internet, containing data about more than 19,500 trade shows, exhibitions, public events and conferences.
13900 Members
Frequency: Bi-Monthly
Founded in: 1196

8076 **TradeShow & Exhibit Manager's Buyer's Guide**
2117 Highland Avenue
Louisville, KY 40204

502-548-3188; *Fax:* 502-742-8749;
www.goldsteinandassociates.com

Steve Goldstein, Publisher

Over 1,000 suppliers of products and services to the trade show industry are profiled.
Cost: $60.00
150 Pages
Frequency: Annual
Circulation: 12,000

8077 **Tradeshow Week Exhibit Manager**
Goldstein & Associates
2117 Highland Avenue
Louisville, KY 40204

502-548-3188; *Fax:* 502-742-8749;
www.goldsteinandassociates.com

Steve Goldstein, Publisher

For exhibit managers.
Cost: $80.00
Frequency: Bi-Monthly
Founded in: 1983

8078 **Tradeshow Week's Tradeshow Services Directory**
Business Information Publication
5700 Wilshire Blvd
Suite 120
Los Angeles, CA 90036-7209

323-549-4100; *Fax:* 323-965-2407;
www.tradeshowweek.com

Tina George-Reyes, Editor
Adam Schaffer, Publisher

Offers information on designers, builders, carriers and decorators involved in tradeshow and convention industries.
Cost: $95.00
300 Pages
Frequency: Annual

8079 **VSA Membership Directory**
Visitor Studies Association
8175-A Sheridan Boulevard
Suite 362
Arvada, CO 80003-1928
303-467-2200; *Fax:* 303-467-0064
info@visitorstudies.org;
www.visitorstudies.org

Alan Friedman, President
Ellen Cox, Treasurer
Jessica Luke, Treasurer
Frequency: Annual

8080 **Who's Who in Exposition Management**
International Assn for Exhibition Management
PO Box 802425
Dallas, TX 75380-2425

972-216-1511; *Fax:* 972-458-8119

Over 1,500 show manager members and 1,500 associate members.
Cost: $225.00
Frequency: Annual June

8081 **Worldwide Tradeshow Schedule**
1700 K Street NW
Suite 403
Washington, DC 20006-3810

202-463-4088

Over 110 international trade fairs are listed in all major industrial sectors.
10 Pages

Industry Web Sites

8082 **http://gold.greyhouse.com**
G.O.L.D Grey House OnLine Databases

Grey House Publishing's online database platform, GOLD, offers Quick Search, Keyword Search and Expert Search for most business sectors including exhibit and meeting planning markets. The GOLD platform makes finding the information you need quick and easy - whether you're a novice searcher or an experienced database user. All of Grey House's directory products are available for subscription on the GOLD platform.

8083 **www.aacei.org**
Association for Advancement of Cost Engineering

Association for Advancement of Cost Engineering provides its members with the resources they need to enhance their performance and ensure continued growth and success. Serves cost management professionals: cost management and engineers, project managers, planners and schedulers, estimators and bidders, and value engineers.

8084 **www.acced-i.colostate.edu**
Colorado State University

Members are college and university conference and special events directors, profesionals and others who design, market and coordinate conferences and special events.

8085 **www.acmenet.org**
Association for Convention Marketing Executives

Annual meetings for marketing and sales executives.

8086 **www.acomonline.org**
Association for Convention Operations Management

Dedicated to advancing the practice of convention services management in the meetings industry, and to preparing CSM professionals for their critical role in the growth and success of their organizations.

8087 **www.cimpa.org**
Connected Int'l Meeting Professionals Association

Members are conference and convention planners with a certificate in convention management. Specializes in planning meetings events, incentives, using the internet.

8088 **www.clc.org**
Convention Liaison Council

Members are associations which are directly involved in the convention, exposition, trade show and meeting industry.

8089 **www.edpa.com**
Exhibit Designers & Producers Association

Exhibit Designers and Producers Association is an internationally recognized national trade association with more than 370 corporate members from 18 countries that are engaged in the design, manufacture, transport, installation and service of display and exhibits primarily for the trade show industry

8090 **www.edsc.org**
Electronic Distribution Show Corporation
Attendees are manufacturers of electronic components who sell their products through electronics distributors.

8091 **www.esca.org**
Exposition Service Contractors Association
Guide to exposition service is distributed annually and lists safety regulations and building rules in major US convention centers.

8092 **www.greyhouse.com**
Grey House Publishing
Authoritative reference directories for most business sectors including exhibit and meeting planning markets. Users can search the online databases with varied search criteria allowing for custom searches by product category, geographic area, sales volume, keyword, subject and more. Full Grey House catalog and online ordering also available.

8093 **www.hcea.org**
Healthcare Convention & Exhibitors Association
Trade association of over 700 organizations involved in health care exhibiting or providing services to health care conventions, exhibitions and/or meetings.

8094 **www.iaam.org**
International Association of Assembly Managers
Members are managers of auditoriums, arenas, convention centers, stadiums and performing arts centers.

8095 **www.iacc.online.org**
International Association of Conference Centers
A facilities-based organization which advances the understanding and awareness of conference centers as distinct within the training, education, hospitality and travel fields.

8096 **www.iaem.org**
Int'l Association for Exposition Management
Members are managers of shows, exhibits and expositions; associate members are industry suppliers.

8097 **www.moderndisplay.com**
Modern Display
Members are distributors of display equipment.

8098 **www.mpiweb.org**
Meeting Planners International
Meeting industry professionals who plan and/or manage meetings, trade shows and conferences for corporations, educational institutions and associations.

8099 **www.naca.org**
National Association for Campus Activities
Largest collegiate organization for campus activities.

8100 **www.nceeonline.org**
National Catholic Educational Exhibitors
A group for companies that provide products or services for Catholoc education.

8101 **www.pcma.org**
Professional Convention Management Association
Features emphasize solutions of practical and logistical problems concerning business travel, the hospitality/hotel industry, and related event planning topics

8102 **www.publicshows.com**
National Association of Consumer Shows
Non-profit organization dedicated to furthering the interests of consumer show producers and suppliers.

8103 **www.rcmaweb.org**
Religious Conference Management Association
Provides members with a wealth of resources designed specifically to enhance their professionalism and overall effectiveness as religious leaders.

8104 **www.sgmp.org**
Society of Government Meeting Planners
Trade association for government meeting planners and exhibitors.

8105 **www.tsea.org**
Trade Show Exhibitors Association
Provides knowledge to marketing and management professionals.

Associations

8106 ACA International
Association of Credit and Collection Professionals
4040W 70th Street
Minneapolis, MN 55435
952-926-6547; *Fax:* 952-926-1624
aca@acainternational.org;
www.acainternational.org
Social Media: Facebook, Twitter, LinkedIn, YouTube, The Hub

Mark Neeb, President

International trade organization of over 5,300 credit and collection professionals providing a variety of accounts receivable management services to over 1,000,000 credit grantors.

8107 About US Association for Financial Counseling and Planning Education
1940 Duke Street
Suite 200
Alexandria, VA 22314

703-684-4484; *Fax:* 703-684-4485
rwiggins@afcpe.org; www.afcpe.org
Social Media: Facebook, Twitter, LinkedIn

Michael Gutter, President
Barry Wilkinson, Past President
Jinhee Kim, President-Elect
Brenda Vaughn, Secretary
Leslie Green-Pimentel, Treasurer

AFCPE is a non-profit professional organization created to promote the education and training of the professional in financial management.
810 Members
Founded in: 1983

8108 Alliance of Merger & Acquisition Advisors
222 North LaSalle Avenue
Suite 300
Chicago, IL 60601

312-856-9590
877-844-2535; *Fax:* 312-729-9800
info@amaaonline.org; www.amaaonline.com
Social Media: Facebook, Twitter, LinkedIn, Google+

Michael Nall, CM&AA, CGMA, Founder and Managing Director
Diane Niederman, VP Business Development
Amie Schneider, Director of Operations
Dylan Whitcher, CM&AA, Business Development Manager
Maxie Gallegos, Social Media & Marketing Specialist

AM&AA is the premier International Organization serving the educational and resource needs of the middle market M&A profession.
Founded in: 1998

8109 Alliance of Merger and Acquisition Advisors
222 North LaSalle Avenue
Suite 300
Chicago, IL 60601

312-856-9590
877-844-2535; *Fax:* 312-729-9800
info@amaaonline.org; www.amaaonline.com
Social Media: Facebook, Twitter, LinkedIn, Google+

Michael Nall, CM&AA, CGMA, Founder and Managing Director
Diane Niederman, VP Business Development
Amie Schneider, Director of Operations
Dylan Whitcher, CM&AA, Business Development Manager
Maxie Gallegos, Social Media & Marketing Specialist

A national organization serving the educational and resource needs of the M&A profession.
200 Members
Founded in: 1999

8110 Allied Financial Adjusters Conference
956 S. Bartlett Road
Suite 321
Bartlett, IL 60103

800-843-1232; *Fax:* 888-949-8520
alliedfinanceadjusters@gmail.com;
www.alliedfinanceadjusters.com
Social Media: Facebook, LinkedIn, YouTube

George Badeen, President
Jamie Hernandez, First Vice President
James Osselburn, Second Vice President
Elisa Schmid, Executive Secretary
Bryan Finn, Treasurer

Membership is composed of professsional liquidators, repossessors and skip tracers. Membership fee varies with size of populations of the city served.
200 Members
Founded in: 1936

8111 American Association of Individual Investors
625 N Michigan Ave
Suite 1900
Chicago, IL 60611-3151

312-280-0170
800-428-2244; *Fax:* 312-280-9883
members@aaii.com; www.aaii.com

James B Cloonan, Ph.D., CEO

An independent, nonprofit corporation formed in 1978 for the purpose of assisting individuals in becoming effective managers of their own assets through programs of education, information and research.
13000 Members
Founded in: 1978

8112 American Association of Residential Mortgage Regulators
1025 Thomas Jefferson Street NW
Suite 500 East
Washington, DC 20007

202-521-3999; *Fax:* 202-833-3636
efreundel@aarmr.org; www.aarmr.org

Cindy Begin, President
Charlie Fields, Vice President
Don DeBastiani, Treasurer
Louisa Broudy, Secretary
David A. Saunders, Executive Director

Members are state employees responsible for administration or residential mortgage oversight. Primary members include model legislation and best practices.
100 Members
Founded in: 1989

8113 American Bankers Association
1120 Connecticut Avenue NW
Washington, DC 20036-3902

202-663-5000
800-226-5377; *Fax:* 202-828-4540
custserv@aba.com; www.aba.com
Social Media: Facebook, Twitter, LinkedIn, YouTube, Google+, Instagram

John A. Ikard, Chairman
R. Daniel Blanton, Chairman-Elect
Dorothy A. Savarese, Vice Chairman
G. William Beale, Treasurer
Frank Keeting, President and CEO

Brings together all categories of banking institutions to best represent the interests of this rapidly changing industry. It's membership — which includes community, regional and money center banks and holding companies, as well as savings associations, trust companies and savings banks, makes ABA one of the largest banking trade associations in the country.
Founded in: 1875

8114 American Bankruptcy Institute
66 Canal Center Plaza
Suite 600
Alexandria, VA 22314-1546

703-739-0800; *Fax:* 703-739-1060
support@abiworld.org; www.abiworld.org
Social Media: Facebook, Twitter, LinkedIn, Flickr

Patricia A. Redmond, Chairman
James Patrick Shea, President
Brian L. Shaw, Immediate Past President
Jeffrey N. Pomerantz, President Elect
Douglas E. Deutsch, Vice President-Research / Grants

Multidisiplinary, nonpartisan organization dedicated to research and education on matters related to insovency. Engaged in numerous educational and research activities as well as the production of a number of publications both for the insolvency practitioner and the public.
11700 Members
Founded in: 1982

8115 American Benefits Council
1501 M St. NW
Suite 600
Washington, DC 20005

202-289-6700; *Fax:* 202-289-4582;
www.americanbenefitscouncil.org

James A. Klein, President
Lynn D. Dudley, SVP, Global Retirement & Comp. Pol.
Katy Spangler, SVP, Health Policy

On behalf of its members - benefit plan sponsors or service providers - advocates for employer-sponsored benefit programs in Washington.

8116 American Council of Life Insurance
101 Constitution Ave NW
Suite 700
Washington, DC 20001-2133

202-624-2000
877-674-4659
contact@acli.com; www.acli.com
Social Media: Facebook, Twitter, YouTube

Dirk Kempthorne, President & Chief Executive Officer
Larry Burton, CEO
Brian Waidmann, Chief of Staff
Gary E. Hughes, Executive Vice President
David C. Turner, Executive Vice President

Works to advance the interests of the life insurance industry and to provide effective government relations. Conducts investment and social research programs.
631 Members
Founded in: 1976

8117 American Education Finance Association
8365 S Armadillo Trail
Evergreen, CO 80439

303-674-0857; *Fax:* 303-670-8986;
www.aefa.cc

Ed Steinbecher, Executive Director

AEFA encourages communications among groups and individuals in the education finance field, including academicians, researchers, policy makers and practitioners. Serving as a forum for a broad range of issues and concerns, AEFA concerns include traditional school finance concepts, issues of public policy, and teaching school finance.
650 Members
Founded in: 1975
Mailing list available for rent

8118 **American Finance Association**
350 Main Street
Malden, MA 02148
781-388-8599
800-835-6770; *Fax:* 781-388-8232
cs-membership@wiley.com; www.afajof.org
Social Media: Facebook, Twitter
Patrick Bolton, President
Campbell R. Harvey, President Elect
David Scharfstein, Vice President
James (Jim) Schallheim, Executive Secretary and Treasurer
Kenneth J. Singleton, Editor of the Journal of Finance
Seeks to improve public understanding of financial problems and to provide for exchange of ideas.
11500 Members
Founded in: 1939

8119 **American Financial Services Association**
919 18th Street NW
Suite 300
Washington, DC 20006-5517
202-296-5544
info@afsamail.org; www.afsaonline.org
Social Media: Facebook, Twitter, LinkedIn, Google+
Andrew Stuart, Chair
Nathan D. Benson, Chair-Elect
Gary Phillips, Immediate Past Chair
Chris Stinebert, President & CEO
Jeffery D. Adams, Executive Vice President
The American Financial Services Association is the national trade association for market funded providers of financial services to consumers and small business. These providers offer an array of financial services, including unsecured personal loans, automotive loans, home equity loans and credit cards through specialized bank institutions
400 Members
Founded in: 1916

8120 **American Society of Appraisers**
11107 Sunset Hills Rd
Suite 310
Reston, VA 20190
703-478-2228
800-272-8258; *Fax:* 703-742-8471
asainfo@appraisers.org; www.appraisers.org
Social Media: Facebook, Twitter, YouTube
Linda B. Trugman, ASA, International President
Susan Golashovsky, ASA, International Vice President
Sharon A. Desfor, ASA, International Secretary/Treasurer
Gary L. Smith, ASA, MGA, International Past President
Gary Snowdon, ASA, Region 1 Governor
Professional association of appraisers of all kinds.
6500 Members
Founded in: 1936

8121 **American Society of Military Comptrollers**
415 N Alfred St
Alexandria, VA 22314-2269
703-549-0360
800-462-5637; *Fax:* 703-549-3181; www.asmconline.org
Social Media: Facebook, Twitter, LinkedIn
Mr. Craig Bennett, President
Gretchen Anderson, Vice President
Mr. Mike Ramsey, Vice President
Mr. Richard Voigt, Vice President
Ann-Cecile M. McDermott, Vice President
ASMC is the successor to the Society of Military Accountants and Statisticians.
18000 Members
Founded in: 1948

8122 **American Trucking Association**
950 North Glebe Road
Suite 210
Arlington, VA 22203-4181
703-838-1700
nafc@trucking.org; www.truckline.com
Social Media: Facebook, Twitter, YouTube
Pat Thomas, Chairman
Kevin Burch, First Vice Chairman
David Manning, Second Vice Chairman
Bill Graves, President & CEO
John M. Smith, Secretary
ATA's mission is to serve and represent the trucking industry with a single, united voice to influence policies beneficial to the industry; promote safety on America's highways; improve the industry's image, efficiency, and competitiveness; educate the public about the critical role trucking plays in the economy
1000 Members
Founded in: 1933

8123 **Association for Financial Professionals**
4520 East West Hwy
Suite 750
Bethesda, MD 20814-3319
301-907-2862; *Fax:* 301-907-2864; www.afponline.org
Social Media: Facebook, Twitter, LinkedIn, YouTube
Anthony Scaglione, CTP, Chairman
Roberta Eiseman, CTP, Vice Chairman
Jeff Johnson, CTP, CPA, Vice Chairman
Ann Anthony, CTP, Board of Director
Terry Crawford, CTP, Board of Director
Association of 12,000 financial professionals. Please call for our publication listings or visit us online.
14000 Members
Founded in: 1979

8124 **Association for Financial Technology**
10813 Pleasant Valley Road
Frazeysburg, OH 43822
614-895-1208; *Fax:* 614-895-3466
aft@aftweb.com; www.aftweb.com
Social Media: Twitter, LinkedIn
Wade Arnold, President
Russ Bernthal, Immediate Past President & Scholars
Xan Kasprzak, Vice President & Program Committee
James R. Bannister, Executive Director
Susan Hurley, Managing Director
Trade association for companies providing services to the financial industry. Our members provide systems, applications and outsourcing services to 90% of America's banks. Vendors of computer hardware, software and ancilliary products and services are also welcome.
52 Members
Founded in: 1975

8125 **Association for Management Information in Financial Services**
14247 Saffron Circle
Carmel, IN 46032
317-815-5857; *Fax:* 317-815-5877
ami2@amifs.org; www.amifs.org
Social Media: Facebook, Twitter, LinkedIn
Robert McDonald, President
Kevin Link, Executive Director
Meg Foster, Executive Vice President
Krissa Hatfield, Assistant Executive Director
The Association for Management Information in Financial Services is the preeminent organization for management information professionals in the financial services industry.
300 Members
Founded in: 1980

8126 **Association for the Advancement of Cost Engineering**
1265 Suncrest Towne Centre Drive
Morgantown, WV 26505-1876
304-296-8444; *Fax:* 304-291-5728
info@aacei.org; www.aacei.org
Social Media: Twitter, LinkedIn
Ms Julie K. Owen, CCP, PSP, President
Mr John C. Livengood, President-Elect
Mr James E. Krebs, PE, CCP, VP - Administration
Mr. Joseph W. Wallwork. PE, CCP,CFCC, VP - Finance
Dr. Dan Melamed CCP, EVP, VP -TEC
The leading-edge professional society for cost estimators, cost engineers, schedulers project managers, and project control specialists.
7000 Members
Founded in: 1956

8127 **Association of Commercial Finance Attorneys**
Kennedy Covington Lobdell & Hickman, LLP
214 N Tryon St
22nd Floor
Charlotte, NC 28202-2367
704-350-7721
acfa@acfalaw.org; www.acfalaw.org
Alison Manzer, President
R. Marshall Grodner, Vice President
Janet Nadile, Vice President
Paul Ricotta, Treasurer
Kenneth Lewis, Secretary
ACF members are attorneys specializing in commercial finance and bankruptcy law. ACFA provides continuing education and publishes material relevant to the field for its members.
350 Members
Founded in: 1958

8128 **Association of Finance and Insurance Professionals**
4104 Felps Drive
Suite H
Colleyville, TX 76034-5868
817-428-2434; *Fax:* 817-428-2534
info@afip.com; www.afip.com
Social Media: Facebook, Twitter, LinkedIn
Deb Hankins, Manager
Linda J Robertson, Senior Vice President
A nonprofit educational foundation that serves the needs of in-dealership finance and insurance personnel for the automobile, RV, commercial truck and equipment, motorcycle, and motorized sports industries while assisting the lenders, vendors and independent general agents who support the F&I function.
Founded in: 1989
Mailing list available for rent

8129 **Association of Government Accountants**
2208 Mount Vernon Avenue
Alexandria, VA 22301-1314
703-684-6931
800-AGA-7211; *Fax:* 703-548-9367
agacgfm@agacgfm.org; www.agacgfm.org
Social Media: LinkedIn
Ann M. Ebberts, MS, PMP, Chief Executive Officer
John E. Homan, MBA, CGFM, 2015-2016 National President

Cristina Barbudo, MS, CPA, Director of Finance
Katya Silver, Director of Professionals
Maryann Malesardi, Director of Communications/Journal

AGA is an educational association dedicated to enhancing public financial management by serving the professional interests of governmental managers and public accounting firms.
15000 Members
Founded in: 1950

8130 BCCA
550 W Frontage Rd
Suite 3600
Northfield, IL 60093-1243

847-881-8757; *Fax:* 847-784-8059
info@bccacredit.com; www.bccacredit.com
Social Media: LinkedIn

Ralph Bender , CFO, Chairman
Timothy Mulvaney, Vice Chair
Mary M. Collins, President & CEO
Robert Damon, Secretary
Cindy Pekrul, Treasurer

BCCA is the media industry's credit association that functions as a central clearing house for credit information on advertisers, agencies and buying services, both locally and nationally. Also provides an Electronic Media Credit Applicationi (EMCAPP.com) to members that helps streamline the application process. One app in one location
600 Members
Founded in: 1972

8131 Bond Market Foundation
360 Madison Avenue
New York, NY 10017-7111

646-637-9067; *Fax:* 646-637-9120

Micah Green

The Bond Market Foundation is a charitable and educational not for profit (501-c-3) association. The Foundation develops and enhances the public's access to quality saving and investor education in addition to providing credible non-proprietary research capacity and expert discussion on public issues relevant to the bond markets. The Bond Market Foundation is partner to the Securities Industry and Financial Markets Association (SIFMA).

8132 Broadcast Cable Credit Association
550 W Frontage Rd
Suite 3600
Northfield, IL 60093-1243

847-881-8757; *Fax:* 847-784-8059
info@bccacredit.com; www.bccacredit.com
Social Media: Twitter, LinkedIn

Ralph Bender , CFO, Chairman
Timothy Mulvaney, Vice Chair
Mary M. Collins, President & CEO
Robert Damon, Secretary
Cindy Pekrul, Treasurer

Subsidiary of the Media Financial Management Association. BCCA provides credit information, education, and netwroking opportunities which enables members to efficiently manage credit risk and increase profitability.
600 Members
Founded in: 1972

8133 CFA Institute
560 Ray C. Hunt Drive
PO Box 3668
Charlottesville, VA 22903

434-951-5499
800-247-8132; *Fax:* 434-951-5262
info@cfainstitute.org; www.cfainstitute.org
Social Media: Facebook, Twitter, LinkedIn, YouTube, Google+, Instagram

Beth Hamilton- Keen, CFA, Chair, Board of Governors
Frederic P. Lebel, CFA, Vice Chair
Aaron Low, CFA, Immediate Past Chair
Paul Smith, CFA, President & CEO
John L. Bowman , CFA, Managing Director

CFA Institute is the global, non-profit professional association that administers the Chartered Financial Analyst curriculum and examination program worldwide and sets voluntary, ethics-based professional and performance-reporting standards for the investment industry.
70000 Members
Founded in: 1990

8134 CRE Finance Council
20 Broad St
7th Ffloor
New York, NY 10005

Fax: 646-884-7569
info@crefc.org; www.crefc.org
Social Media: Facebook, Twitter, LinkedIn

Gregory Michaud, Chairman
Matthew Borstein, Chairman-Elect
Nik Chillar, Membership Committee Chair
Daniel E. Bober, Treasurer
Stephen M. Renna, President & CEO

International trade organization for the commercial real estate capital markets. Also represents and promotes an orderly ans ethical global institutional secondary market for the sale of commercial mortgage loans and equity investments.
309 Members
Founded in: 1994

8135 Coalition of Higher Education Assistance Organizations
1101 Vermont Ave NW
Suite 400
Washington, DC 20005-3586

202-289-3910; *Fax:* 202-371-0197
hwadsworth@wpllc.net; www.coheao.com

Maria Livolsi, President
Carl Perry, Vice President
Tom Schmidt, Secretary
Lori Hartung, Treasurer
Robert Perrin, Past President

Focus is on legislative and regulatory advocacy for Federal Perkins and other campus based student loan programs.
365 Members
Founded in: 1981

8136 Commercial Finance Association
370 7th Avenue
Suite 1801
New York, NY 10001

212-792-9390; *Fax:* 212-564-6053
info@cfa.com; www.cfa.com
Social Media: Facebook, Twitter, LinkedIn, YouTube

Michael Coiley, Chairman of the Board
Patrick Trammel, President
Andrea Petro, First Vice President
D. Michael Monk, Vice President - Finance
David Grende, Vice President

Trade group of the asset based financial services industry, with members throughout the US, Canada and around the world. Members include the asset based lending arms of domestic and foreign commercial banks, small and large independent finance companies, floor plan financing organizations, factoring organizations and financing subsidiaries of major industrial corporations. CFA membership is by organization, not by individual.
300 Members
Founded in: 1944

8137 Defense Credit Union Council
601 Pennsylvania Ave NW
South Building, Suite 600
Washington, DC 20004-2601

202-638-3950; *Fax:* 202-638-3410
admin@dcuc.org; www.dcuc.org
Social Media: Facebook, Twitter

Denise Floyd, Chairman & At Large Representative
Gordon A. Simmons, 1st Vice Chair
Frank Padak, 2nd Vice Chair
Michael Kloiber, Secretary & Air Force Rep.
Craig Chamberlin, Treasurer & Marine Corps Rep

Organizations of credit unions whose membership consists wholly or in part of personnel of the US Department of Defense, both military and civilians.
14 m Members
Founded in: 1963

8138 EMTA - Emerging Markets Trade Association
360 Madison Avenue
17th Floor
New York, NY 10017

646-289-5410; *Fax:* 646-289-5429
awerner@emta.org; www.emta.org

Mark L. Coombs, Co-Chair
Robert H. Milam, J.P, Co-Chair
Brian Weinstein, Vice Chair
Alberto Agrest, Vice Chair
Marcel Naime, Vice Chair

EMTA is the principal trade group for the Emerging Markets trading and investment community and is dedicated to promoting the orderly development of fair, efficient, and transparent trading markets for Emerging Markets into the global capital markets.
Founded in: 1990

8139 Emerging Markets Private Equity Association
1077 30th St. NW
Suite 100
Washington, DC 20007

202-333-8171
support@empea.org
empea.org
Social Media: Facebook, Twitter, LinkedIn

Robert W. van Zwieten, President & CEO
Shannon Stroud, VP, Programs & Business Development
Randy Mitchell, VP, Strategic Engagement
Ann Marie Plubell, VP, Regulatory Affairs

A nonprofit organization that supports private equity investors in emerging markets with data and market intelligence.

8140 Evangelical Council for Financial Accountability
440 W Jubal Early Dr
Auite 100
Winchester, VA 22601-6319

540-535-0103
800-323-9473; *Fax:* 540-535-0533
info@ecfa.org; www.ecfa.org
Social Media: Facebook, Twitter, LinkedIn, YouTube

Michael Little, Chair
Michael Batts, Vice Chair
Kenneth Larson, Secretary
Richard A. Alvis, Treasurer
Thomas Addington, Board Member

Helps organizations earn the public's trust through developing and maintaining standards of accountability that convey ethical practices.
1500 Members
Founded in: 1979

8141 **FSC/DISC Tax Association**
3 Bethesda Metro Center
Suite 250
Bethesda, MD 20814-5377
703-341-3500
800-372-1033; *Fax:* 914-328-5757
blawhelp@bna.com; www.bna.com
Social Media: Facebook, Twitter
Michele Harris, Principal
Joan Fisher, Vice President
Sri Rajan, Manager
The only organization operating on a national level devoted to educational interests of companies that have set up a foreign sales corporation.
300 Members
Founded in: 1982

8142 **Financial & Security Products Association (FSPA)**
1024 Mebane Oaks Road
Suite 273
Mebane, NC 27302
919-648-0664
800-843-6082; *Fax:* 919-648-0670
info@fspa1.com; www.fspa1.com
Linda Abell, Chairman
L. A. Smith, President
Gene Polito, Vice President
Kevin Callahan, Secretary/Treasurer
Joe Petchulat, Director
Independent dealers, manufacturers and associates whose outstanding products and services give financial institutions a crucial edge in performance, efficiency and economy.
Founded in: 1973

8143 **Financial Executives International**
1250 Headquarters Plaza
West Tower, 7th Floor
Morristown, NJ 07960
973-765-1000; *Fax:* 973-765-1018
membership@financialexecutives.org;
www.financialexecutives.org
Social Media: Facebook, Twitter, LinkedIn, YouTube, Google+
Taylor Hawes, Sr., Chair
Donald Robillard, Jr., Vice Chair
Gregory Ulferts, National Secretary
Ann Flatz, National Treasurer
Marie N. Hollein, CTP, President and CEO
A professional organization of individuals performing the duties of CFO, Controller, Treasurer or VP of Finance. Has an annual budget of $6.5 million.
15M Members
Founded in: 1931

8144 **Financial Management Association International**
University of South Florida
4202 E Fowler Ave
BSN 3331
Tampa, FL 33620-5500
813-974-2084; *Fax:* 813-974-3318
fma@coba.usf.edu; www.fma.org
Jay R. Ritter, President
David Denis, President-Elect
Brad Barber, Vice President- Program
John Graham, Vice President- Elect
Andrea J. Heuson, Treasurer
The mission of the FMA is to broaden the common interests between academicians and practitioners, provide opportunities for professional interaction between and among academicians, practitioners and students, promote the development and understanding of basic and applied research and of sound financial practices, and to enhance the quality of education in finance.
3000 Members
Founded in: 1970

8145 **Financial Managers Society**
1 North LaSalle Street
Suite 3100
Chicago, IL 60602-4003
312-578-1300
800-275-4367; *Fax:* 312-578-1308
info@fmsinc.org; www.fmsinc.org/cms
Sydney K. Garmong, Chairman
John Westwood, Vice Chairman
Alan Renfroe, Immediate Past President
Dick Yingst, President
Darrell E. Blocker, Director- At- Large
Is the only individual membership society exclusively serving the technical and professional needs of today's bank, thrift and credit union financial officers.
1600 Members
Founded in: 1948

8146 **Financial Markets Association**
333 Second Street NE
#104
Washington, DC 20002
202-547-6327
dp-fma@starpower.org; www.fmaweb.org
Peter Wadkins, President
Geoffrey Gowey, Vice President
Robert J Tum-Suden, Treasurer
Carlene Crnkovich, Secretary
A world-class organization of Foreign Exchange, Money Market, and Derivative traders, salespersons, brokers, vendors, and corporate participants organized for the purpose of education, promotion, fellowship, and advancement of the wholesale market within the United States.
300 Members
Founded in: 1958

8147 **Financial Planning Association**
7535 E. Hampden Avenue
Suite 600
Denver, CO 80231
303-759-4900
800-322-4237; *Fax:* 303-759-0749
info@onefpa.org; www.plannersearch.org
Social Media: Facebook, Twitter, LinkedIn
Marv Tuttle, Executive Director
Ian McKenzie, Managing Director/Publishing
Lauren Schadle CAE, Associate Executive Director/COO
FPA is the professional membership association that represents the financial planning community.
29000 Members
Founded in: 2000

8148 **Financial Services Technology Consortium**
600 13th Street NW
Suite 400
Washington, DC 20005
202-289-4322; *Fax:* 202-628-2558
bits@fsround.org; www.bits.org
Christopher F. Feeney, President
Nancy Guglielmo, Vice President
Andrew Kennedy, Senior Program Manager
Josh Magri, Regulatory Counsel
Denise Miller, Executive & Comm. Assistant
Association of leading North American-based financial institutions, technology vendors, independent research organizations and government agencies. Goal is to promote interoperable, open-standard technologies that provide critical infrastructures for the finacial services industry.
Founded in: 1993

8149 **Financial Services Roundtable**
600 13th Street NW
Suite 400
Washington, DC 20005
202-289-4322; *Fax:* 202-628-2558
info@fsroundtable.org; www.fsroundtable.org
Social Media: Twitter, LinkedIn, YouTube
Frederick H Waddel, Chairman
Ajaypal S. Banga, Chairman-Elect
Larry Zimpleman, Immediate Past Chairman
Kessel Stelling, Treasurer
Richard K. Davis, Director
Mission is to be the premier executive forum for the leaders of the financial services industry; to provide powerful legislative and regulatory advocacy; to enhance the industry's public reputation; and led by BITS, to promote best practices and a strong infrastrucutre in technology.
Founded in: 1993

8150 **Financial Services Technology Consortium**
600 13th Street NW
Suite 400
Washington, DC 20005
202-289-4322; *Fax:* 202-628-2558
bits@fsround.org; www.bits.org
Christopher F. Feeney, President
Nancy Guglielmo, Vice President
Andrew Kennedy, Senior Program Manager
Josh Magri, Regulatory Counsel
Denise Miller, Executive & Comm. Assistant
FSTC sponsors product testing, development programs, and other projects to ensure the continued viability of new technologies in the financial sector.
Founded in: 1993

8151 **Financial Services Technology Network**
411 Borel Ave
Ste 620
San Mateo, CA 94402
312-782-4951; *Fax:* 312-580-0165
fstn@gss.net; www.fsnweb.com
Social Media: Facebook, Twitter, LinkedIn
Kathleen Luleasile, Executive Director
Dale Smith, President
Kathy Johnson, Secretary/Treasurer

8152 **Financial Women International**
1027 W Roselawn Avenue
Roseville, MN 55113
651-487-7632
866-807-6081; *Fax:* 651-489-1322
info@fwi.org; www.fwi.org
Melissa Curzon, President
Cindy Hass, VP
Carleen DeSisto, Secretary
FWI is dedicated to developing leaders, accelerating careers, and generating results for professionals in the banking and financial services industry.
1000 Members
Founded in: 1921

8153 **Fraud & Theft Information Bureau**
9770 S Military Trail
Suite 380
Boynton Beach, FL 33436
561-737-8700; *Fax:* 561-737-5800
sales@fraudandtheftinfo.com;
www.fraudandtheft.com
Larry Schwartz, Founder/Director
Pearl Sax, Founder/Director
A leading consultant on credit card and check fraud control and loss prevention, and the pub-

lisher of related manuals and fraud-blocker data bases.
Founded in: 1982

8154 Futures Industry Association
2001 Pennsylvania Ave NW
Suite 600
Washington, DC 20006-1823

202-446-5460; *Fax:* 202-296-3184
info@fia.org; www.fia.org
Social Media: Facebook, Twitter, LinkedIn, Flickr

Gerald Corcoran, Chairman & CEO
M. Clark Hutchison, Treasurer
Emily Portney, Secretary
Craig Abruzzo, Managing Director
Antoine Babule, Managing Director

Representative of all organizations that have an interest in the futures market.
180 Members
Founded in: 1955

8155 Global Association of Risk Professionals
111 Town Square Place
14th Floor
Jersey City, NJ 07310-2778

201-719-7210; *Fax:* 201-222-5022
Memberservices@garp.com; www.garp.com
Social Media: Facebook, Twitter, LinkedIn, Google+, YouTube

William Martin, Chairman
Jacques Longerstaey, Chairman Compensation Committee
Dr. Ren, Stulz, Chairman Governance Committee
Victor Ng, Chairman Adult & Risk Committee
Richard Apostolik, President & CEO

GARP's international membership includes a varity of professionals from the finance industry who share a common interest in financial risk management practice and research.
52330 Members
Founded in: 2000

8156 Government Finance Officers Association
203 N La Salle St
Suite 2700
Chicago, IL 60601-1216

312-977-9700; *Fax:* 312-977-4806
inquiry@gfoa.org; www.gfoa.org
Social Media: Facebook, Twitter, LinkedIn, YouTube

Heather A. Johnston, President
Marc Gonzales, President-Elect
Bob Eichem, Past President
Robert Bishop, Director Of Finance
Lori A. Economy-Scholler, Chief Financial Officer

The purpose of the Government Finance Officers Association is to enhance and promote the professional management of governments for the public benefit by identifying and developing financial policies and practices and promoting them through education, training and leadership.
17300 Members
Founded in: 1906

8157 Healthcare Billing and Management Association
2025 M Street NW
Suite 800
Washington, DC 20036

877-640-4262; *Fax:* 202-367-2177
info@hbma.org; www.hbma.org
Social Media: Facebook, Twitter, LinkedIn, YouTube

Andre Williams, Executive Director
Zoe Fuller, Operations & Administration
Caroline Fabacher, Program Coordinator
Ellie Hurley, Event Services
David Merli, Advertising/ Sales

Members are companies providing third-party medical billing services.
500 Members
Founded in: 1993
Mailing list available for rent

8158 Healthcare Financial Management Association
3 Westbrook Corporate Center
Suite 600
Westchester, IL 60154

708-531-9600
800-252-4362; *Fax:* 708-531-0032
webmaster@hfma.org; www.hfma.org
Social Media: Facebook, Twitter, LinkedIn, YouTube

Joseph J. Fifer, FHFMA, CPA, CEO & President
Edwin P. Czopek, FHFMA, CPA, CA, Senior Vice President
Susan Brenkus, Vice President, Human Resources
Richard L Gundling, Vice President, Healthcare
Tod Nelson, Vice President, Education

Brings perspective and clarity to the industry's complex issues for the purpose of preparing our members to succeed. Through our programs, publications and partnerships we enhance the capabilities that strengthen not only individual careers, but also the organizations from which our members come.
40000 Members

8159 Initiatives of Change, USA
2201 West Broad Street
Suite 200
Richmond, VA 23220-2022

804-305- 176; *Fax:* 804-358-1769
support@web.iofc.org; www.us.iofc.org
Social Media: Facebook, Twitter

H. Alexander Wise, Chairman
Patrick T. Mcnamara, Executive Vice Chairman
William S. Elliott, Executive Director
Valerie Lemmie, Treasurer
Anjum A. Ali, Secretary

Is the national voice for lenders and investors engaged in the reverse mortgage business.
Founded in: 1997
Mailing list available for rent

8160 Institute for Divorce Financial Analysts
2224 Sedwick Road
Suite 102
Durham, NC 27713

989-631-3605
800-875-1760; *Fax:* 919-287-2952
info@institutedfa.com; www.institutedfa.com
Social Media: Twitter, LinkedIn

The Institute for Divorce Financial Analysts (IDFAT) is the premier national organization dedicated to the certification, education and promotion of the use of financial professionals in the divorce arena.
Founded in: 1993

8161 Institute of Internal Auditors
247 Maitland Ave
Altamonte Springs, FL 32701-4201

407-937-1111; *Fax:* 407-937-1101
customerrelations@theiia.org; www.theiia.org
Social Media: Facebook, Twitter, LinkedIn

Lawrence J. Harrington, Chairman of the Board
J. Michael Joyce Jr. CIA , CRMA, Chairman of North American Board
Richard F. Chambers, CIA, CGAP, C, President and CEO

Independent, objective assurance and consulting activity designed to add value to an organization's operations. It helps an organization accomplish its objectives by bringing a systematic, disciplined approach to evaluate and improve the effectiveness of risk management, control and governance processes. Representation from more than 100 countries.
10000 Members
Founded in: 1941

8162 Institute of International Finance
1333 H St NW
Suite 800 E
Washington, DC 20005-4770

202-857-3600; *Fax:* 202-775-1430
info@iif.com; www.iif.com
Social Media: Facebook, YouTube

Douglas J. Flint, Chairman
Roberto E Setubal, Vice Chairman
Walter Kielholz, Vice Chairman
Marcus Wallenberg, Vice Chairman and Treasurer
Timothy D. Adams, President and CEO

Members are primarily international, commercial banks that focus on middle-income countries by communicating with the debtor countries, international financial institutions and regulatory agencies in order to improve the process of international lending.
450 Members
Founded in: 1983

8163 Institute of Management & Administration
3 Bethesda Metro Center
Suite 250
Bethesda, MD 20814-5377

800-372-1033
703-341-3500; *Fax:* 800-253-0332
blawhelp@bna.com; www.ioma.com
Social Media: Facebook, Twitter, YouTube

Gregory C. McCaffery, President & CEO
Sue Martin, Chief Operating Officer
Paul Albergo, Bureau Chief
Joe Breda, Executive Vice President - Product
Daniel M. Fine, Executive Vice President-Strategy

An independent source of exclusive business management information for experienced senior and middle management professionals.

8164 Institute of Management Accountants
10 Paragon Drive
Suite 1
Montvale, NJ 07645-1760

201-573-9000
800-638-4427; *Fax:* 201-474-1600
ima@imanet.org; www.imanet.org
Social Media: Facebook, Twitter, LinkedIn, YouTube

Benjamin R. Mulling CMA, CPA, CITP, Chair
Joseph A. Vincent CMA, Chair- Emeritus
Marc P. Palker CMA, Chair- Elect
Jeffrey C Thomson, President & CEO
Atul Kumar Agarwal, Director

To provide a dynamic forum for management accounting and finance professionals to develop and advance their careers through certification, research and practice development, education, networking, and the advocacy of the highest ethical and professional practices.
65000 Members
Founded in: 1919

8165 **Institutional Shareholder Services**
101 Federal St.
Suite 2105
Boston, MA 02110

646-680-6350; *Fax:* 301-556-0491;
www.issgovernance.com

Gary Retelny, President & CEO
Stephen Harvey, Chief Revenue Officer
Nancy Adler, Head of Marketing
Chris Cernich, Deputy Director Of Global Research
Mark Brockway, Head of the ISS Corporate Services

Leading provider of independent and impartial research on coporations and their shareholders.
500 Members
Founded in: 1972

8166 **Interactive & Newsmedia Financial**
MFM, 550 W. Frontage Road
Ste. 3600
Northfield, IL 60093

847-716-7000; *Fax:* 847-716-7004
info@mediafinance.org; www.infe.org
Social Media: Twitter, LinkedIn

Mary M. Collins, President & CEO
Chad Richardson, Chairman
Dalton A. Lee, Vice Chairman
Jamie L. Smith, MFM/BCCA Director of Operations
Arcelia Pimentel, MFM Membership Manager & Sales

Focuses on newspaper financial management, with members representing most North American newpaper companies, as well as many offshore. INFE's activities include publishing, conferences, workshops, industry surveys and studies, and offers members networking opportunities.
1200 Members
Founded in: 1961

8167 **International Association of Financial Engineers**
555 Eight Avenue
Suite 1902
New York, NY 10018

646-736-0705; *Fax:* 646-417-6378
main@iafe.org; www.iaqf.org

David Jaffe, Executive Director

The IAFE is a not-for-profit, professional society dedicated to fostering the profession of quantitative finance by providing platforms to discuss cutting-edge and pivotal issues in the field. Its composed of individual academic and practioners from banks, broker dealers, hedge funds, pension funds, asset managers, technology firms, regulators, accounting, consulting and law firms and universities worldwide.
Founded in: 1992

8168 **International Association of Purchasing**
45 Woodside W
Patchogue, NY 11772

631-654-2384; *Fax:* 516-475-2754

A professional organization dedicated to the advancement of world trade. Membership is open to buyers, purchasing managers, executives and all individuals that may be involved or have an interest in the important function of buying goods and services on the global market. A nonprofit organization.
1600 Members
Founded in: 1985

8169 **International Society of Financiers**
64 Brookside Drive
Hendersonville, NC 28792-9207

828-698-7805; *Fax:* 828-698-7806;
www.insofin.com

Ronald I Gershen, Chairman/President

A professional society of brokers, consultants, investors and corporate lenders active in financial projects and transactions. ISF provides an exclusive and confidential forum for member-to-member exchange and business networking.
300 Members
Founded in: 1979

8170 **International Swaps and Derivatives Association**
360 Madison Ave
16th Floor
New York, NY 10017

212-901-6000; *Fax:* 212-901-6001
isda@isda.org; www.isda.org

Eric Litvack, Chairman
Richard Prager, Vice Chairman
Keith Bailey, Secretary
Diane Genova, Treasurer
Yasunobu Arima, Director

Represents firms, primarily financial institutions, corporations and government entities who deal in privately-negoiated derivatives, as well as firms who provide services to such institutions. ISDA's, mission is to encourage the productive development of interest rate, currency, commodity, and equity swaps as financial products.
Founded in: 1985

8171 **International Union of Housing Finance**
Rue Jacques de Lalaing 28
B-1040 Brussels
Belgium

322-231-0371; *Fax:* 322-230-8245
info@housingfinance.org;
www.houseingfinance.org

Dale Bottom, Secretary General

Disseminates information in housing finance policies and techniques worldwide.
107 Members
Founded in: 1914

8172 **Investment Company Institute**
1401 H St NW
Suite 1200
Washington, DC 20005

202-326-5800
webmaster@ici.org; www.ici.org
Social Media: Facebook, Twitter, LinkedIn, vimeo.com

F.William McNabb III, Chairman
Gregory E. Johnson, Vice Chairman
Paul Schott Stevens, President & CEO
Peter H Gallary, Chief Operating Officer
Donald C Auerbach, Chief Government Affairs Officer

Acts to represent members in matters of legislation, taxation, regulation, economic research and marketing and public information regarding investments and mutual funds.
9400+ Members
Founded in: 1940

8173 **Investment Recovery Association**
638 W 39th Street
Kansas City, MO 64111

816-561-5323
800-728-2272; *Fax:* 816-561-1991
jmale@swassn.com; www.invrecovery.org

Barry Street, President
Sean Byro, Senior Vice President
Kelly May, Secretary
Todd Thompson, Treasurer
Paul Hoffman, Director

Helps fulfill an important role by bringing people together from disparate industries...all focused on sharing best IR practices and improving the knowledge and skills necessary to properly perform the wide-ranging responsibilities required of investment recovery practitioners.

8174 **Latin American Private Equity and Venture Capital Association**
589 Eighth Ave.
18th Fl.
New York, NY 10018

646-315-6735
lavca.org
Social Media: Twitter, LinkedIn

Cate Ambrose, President & Executive Director
Ivonne Cuello, Director, Bus. Dev. & Strategy

A nonprofit organization that supports the growth of the private equity and venture capital industry in Latin America.
170+ Members

8175 **Media Financial Management Association**
550 W. Frontage Road
Suite 3600
Northfield, IL 60093

847-716-7000; *Fax:* 847-716-7004
info@mediafinance.org;
www.mediafinance.org
Social Media: Twitter, LinkedIn

Mary M. Collins, President & CEO
Chad Richardson, Chairman
Dalton A. Lee, Vice Chairman
Jamie L. Smith, MFM/BCCA Director of Operations
Arcelia Pimentel, MFM Membership Manager & Sales

Professional society of more than 1,300 of media's top financial, MIS Credit and HR executives, plus associates in auditing, data processing, software development, law, tax and credit and collections.
1200 Members
Founded in: 1961

8176 **Mortgage Bankers Association of America**
1919 M Street NW
5th Floor
Washington, DC 20036

202-557-2700
800-793-6222
membership@mortgagebankers.org;
www.mortgagebankers.org

David H Stevens, President & CEO
Marcia Davies, Chief Operating Officer
Michael Fratantoni, Chief Economist. Enior VP
Peter J. Grace, Senior Vice President
Bill Kilmer, Senior Vice President

Association for all state and local MBA officers.
2200 Members

8177 **Mutual Fund Education Alliance**
100 NW Englewood Rd
Suite 130
Kansas City, MO 64118-4076

816-454-9422; *Fax:* 816-454-9322
mfea@mfea.com; www.mfea.com
Social Media: Facebook, Twitter

Michelle Smith, Executive Director

Conducts public education and public relation activities in an effort to acquaint investors, industry organizations and government agencies with direct market funds.
Founded in: 1971

8178 Mutual Fund Investors Association
85 Wells Avenue
Suite 109
Newton, MA 02459
617-321-2200
800-492-6868; *Fax:* 61 -32 -221
info@adviserinvestments.com;
www.kobren.com
Daniel P Weiner, Chair & CEO
David Thorne, President
James H. Lowell, Chief Investment Officer
Chris Keith, Senior Vice President
Jeffrey DeMaso, Director Of Research
Association for those interested in information and rates for mutual funds, investments, stocks and bonds.
Founded in: 1994

8179 NACHA - Electronic Payments Association
2550 Wasser Terrace
Suite 400
Herndon, VA 20171
703-561-1100; *Fax:* 703-787-0996;
www.nacha.org
Social Media: Facebook, Twitter, LinkedIn
Janet O Estep, CEO
Deb Evans-Doyle, Sr Director Conference Marketing
Julie Hedlund, Sr Director Electronic Commerce
Michael Herd, Director Public Relations
NACHA is a trade association that forms the cooperative foundation for the automated clearing house (ACH) payments system through a network of 21 ACH associations nationwide. It also provides marketing and educational members through direct memberships and a network of regional payment associations.
Founded in: 1974

8180 Nat'l Institute of Pension Administrators
330 N Wabash Ave
Suite 2000
Chicago, IL 60611-7621
800-999-6472
800-999-6272; *Fax:* 312-673-6609
nipa@nipa.org; www.nipa.org
Social Media: LinkedIn
Patrick M. Shelton, President
Michelle Marsh, President Elect and CFO
Joseph Burt, Chief financial Officer
Robert Chin, Director
Ralph DelSesto, Director
The Institute is responsible for the formation Of professional standards, an ongoing education program consisting of workshops and home study courses, and awards of the APA and the APR designations by examination and experience.
1000 Members
Founded in: 1983

8181 National Aircraft Finance Association
PO Box 1570
Edgewater, MD 21037
410-571-1740; *Fax:* 410-571-1780
info@nafa.aero; www.nafa.aero
Social Media: Facebook, Twitter, LinkedIn
David Jarvis, President
Chris Miller, Vice President
Ford Von Weise, Vice President
Karen Griggs, Executive Director
Anthony Kioussis, Secretary
A non-profit corporation dedicated to promoting the general welfare of individual and organization providing aircraft financing and loans secured by aircraft; to improve the industry's service to the public; to work with government agencies to foster a greater understanding of our member's needs.
95 Members
Founded in: 1969

8182 National Association of Affordable Housing Lenders
1667 K St NW
Suite 210
Washington, DC 20006
202-293-9850; *Fax:* 202-293-9852
naahl@naahl.org; www.naahl.org
Buzz Roberts, President & CEO
Paul Haaland, Chief Operating Officer
Sara Olson, Administrative Assistant
Is the only association devoted to increasing private capital lending and investment in low and moderate income communities.
800 Members
Founded in: 1977

8183 National Association of Bankruptcy Trustees
One Windsor Cove
Suite 305
Columbia, SC 29223
803-252-5646
800-445-8629; *Fax:* 803-765-0860
info@nabt.com; www.nabt.com
Richard D. Nelson, President
Dwayne Murray, President Elect
Ronald R. Peterson, Vice President
Brian L. Budsberg, Treasurer
Raymond J. Obuchowski, Secretary
The majority of the members of the NABT are Chapter 7 trustees who primarily liquidate non-exempt assets for the benefit of creditors.
1200 Members
Founded in: 1982

8184 National Association of Certified Valuators and Analysts
5217 South State Street
Suite 400
Salt Lake City, UT 84107
801-486-0600
800-677-2009; *Fax:* 801-486-7500
nacva1@nacva.com; www.nacva.com
Pamela Bailey, Executive Advisory Board
Melissa Bizyak, Executive Advisory Board
Parnell Black, Executive Advisory Board
Rod Burket, Executive Advisory Board
Mark Hanson, Executive Advisory Board
Global, professional association that supports the business valuation and litigation consulting disciplines within the CPA and professional communities. Along with its training and certification programs, NACVA offers a range of support services, reference materials, software, and customized databases to enhance the professional capabilities and capacities of its members.
6500 Members
Founded in: 1990

8185 National Association of Corporate Treasurers
12100 Sunset Hills Road
Suite 130
Reston, VA 20190-3221
703-437-4377; *Fax:* 703-435-4390
nact@nact.org; www.nact.org
Social Media: LinkedIn
Ramon Yi, Chairman
Mary Dean Hall, President
Joseph C. Sullivan, Vice-President
Ruud Roggekamp, Secretary/Treasurer
Thomas C. Deas, Immediate Past Chairman
Members are corporate chief financial officers, treasurers or assistant treasurers.
825 Members
Founded in: 1982

8186 National Association of Development Companies
1725 Desales St NW
Suite 504
Washington, DC 20036
202-349-0070; *Fax:* 202-349-0071;
www.nadco.org
Social Media: Facebook, Twitter, Stumbleupon
Sally Robertson, Chairman
Mary Mansfield, Vice Chair
Randy Griffin, Treasurer
Pat MacKrell, Secretary
Barbara Vohryzek, President & CEO
Provides long term, fixed asset financing to small businesses.
135 Members
Founded in: 1981

8187 National Association of Division Order Analysts
PO Box 2300
Less Summit, MO 64063
972-715-4489
administrator@nadoa.org; www.nadoa.org
Social Media: Facebook, Twitter, LinkedIn
Jason Lucas, President
Mary Sons, Vice President
Nancy Cemino, CDOA, 2nd Vice President
Angela Korthauer, Treasurer
Kim Henderson, CDOA, Corresponding Secretary
Division order analysts are petroleum and gas company employees or independent consultants responsible for royalty working interest and overiding royalty payments. Offers a certification program providing education, training and testing for qualified applicants desiring to attain Certified Divison Order Analyst credentials.
900 Members
Frequency: 4
Founded in: 1974

8188 National Association of Equipment Leasing Brokers
100 North 20th Steet
Suite 400
Philadelphia, PA 19103
800-996-2352; *Fax:* 215-564-2175
info@naelb.org; www.naelb.org
Social Media: Facebook, Twitter, LinkedIn, YouTube
Joe Casey, Executive Director
Laura Huestis, Associate Director
Broker-oriented association.
500 Members
Founded in: 1990

8189 National Association of Federal Credit Unions
3138 10th St N
Arlington, VA 22201-2149
703-522-4770
800-336-4644; *Fax:* 703-524-1082;
www.nafcu.org
Social Media: Facebook, Twitter
B. Dan Berger, President
Anthony W. Demangone, Vice President
Carolyn Sable, Executive Assistant
Leann Obermeir, Executive Assistant
Martin Breland, Region II Director
Trade association exclusively represents the interests of federal credit unions before the federal government and the public. Provides members with representation, information, education and assistance to meet the challenges that coopera-

tive financial institutions face in today's economic environment. Stands as a national forum for the federal credit union community where new ideas, issues, concerns and trends can be identified, discussed and resolved.
Founded in: 1967

8190 National Association of Independent Public Finance Advisors
19900 MacArthur Boulevard
Suite 1100
Irvine, CA 92612
630-896-1292
844-770-6262; *Fax:* 209-633-6265
rhoban@naipfa.com; www.naipfa.com
Jeanine Rogers Caruso, President
Terri Heaton, Vice President
Bruce A. Kimmel, CIPFA, Secretary
Micheal Sudsina, CIPFA, Treasurer
Shelly Aronson,CIPFA, Director at large
A professional organization limited to firms that specialize in providing financial advice on bond sales and financial planning on public projects of public agencies. Promotes the common interests of independent advisory firm members.
48 Members
Founded in: 1989

8191 National Association of Investors Corporation
711 W 13mile Road
Suite 900
Madison Heights, MI 48071
248-654-3047
877-275-6242; *Fax:* 248-583-4880
webmaster@betterinvesting.org;
www.betterinvesting.org
Social Media: Facebook, Twitter
Roger H Ganser, Chairman
Kamie Zaracki, CEO
Stephen Sanborn, Treasurer
Gary Ball, Director
Robert Brooker, Director
Strives to counsel and teach investing techniques and sound investment procedures to interested people.
23000 Members
Founded in: 1951

8192 National Association of Local Housing Finance Agencies
2025 M St NW
Suite 800
Washington, DC 20036
202-367-1197; *Fax:* 202-367-2197
info@nalhfa.org; www.nalhfa.org
Ron Williams, President
W.D Morris, Vice President
Vivian Benjamin, Treasurer
Tom Cummings, Secretary
Kurt Creager, Director
The National Association of Local Housing Finance Agencies, founded in 1982, is the national association of professionals working to finance affordable housing in the broader community development context at the local level. As a non-profit association, NALHFA is an advocate before Congress and federal agencies on legislative and regulatory issues affecting affordable housing and provides technical assistance and educational opportunities to its members and the public.
Founded in: 1982

8193 National Association of Personal Financial Advisors
8700 W. Bryn Mawr Avenue
Suite 700 N
Chicago, IL 60631
847-483-5400
888-333-6659; *Fax:* 847-483-5415
info@napfa.org; www.napfa.org
Geoffrey Brown, CEO
Mardi Lee, Assistant to CEO
Bevin Callan, Member Services Senior Manager
Laura J Maddalone, Controller
Members are financial planners who are compensated only by fees. NAPFA members are prohibited from receiving any type of product-related compensation, such as sales commissions. Members do not sell products nor do they direct sales to parties with whom they have financial interests.
2400 Members
Founded in: 1983

8194 National Association of Publicly Traded Partnerships
1200 19th Street, NW
Suite 700
Washington, DC 20036
202-973-2400
800-621-8390; *Fax:* 202-973-2401
inquiries@navigant.com;
www.mlpassociation.org
Social Media: LinkedIn, YouTube
William M Goodyear, Chairman And CEO
Thomas A. Glidehaus, Director
Cynthia A. Glassman, Phd, Director
Julie M. Howard, Director & Navigant CEO
Stephan A. James, Director
A trade association representing publicly traded limited partnerships (and publicly traded LLCs taxed partnerships) and those who work with them.
Founded in: 1983
Mailing list available for rent

8195 National Association of Review Appraisers & Mortgage Underwriters
810 N Farrell Drive
Palm Springs, CA 92262
760-327-5284
877-743-6805; *Fax:* 760-327-5631
support@assoc-hdqts.org; www.naramu.org
Social Media: LinkedIn
Jerry M. Green, Owner
Gary R. Vermaat, President
Robert e. Runyan, Vice President
Association for professionals who review real estate appraisals and underwrite real estate mortgages. The association offers the CRA, Certified Review Appraiser and RMU, Registered Mortgage Underwriter, professional designation.
2852 Members
Founded in: 1975
Mailing list available for rent: 3500 names at $75 per M

8196 National Association of Sales Professionals
555 Friendly Street
Bloomfield Hills, MI 48341
480-596-6634
866-365-1520; *Fax:* 248-254-6757;
www.nasp.com
Social Media: Facebook, Twitter, LinkedIn
Rod Hairston, CEO & Chairman
Idris Grant, President and COO
Tonia Revere, Director
Sabine Grant, Vice President
Amanda Ritz, Membership, director & advisor

Members are companies who purchase structured settlements, lottery annuities, and similar periodic payment plans from their beneficiaries.
Founded in: 1991

8197 National Association of State Budget Officers
444 N Capitol St NW
Suite 642
Washington, DC 20001
202-624-5382; *Fax:* 202-624-7745
spattison@nasbo.org; www.nasbo.org
Social Media: Facebook, Twitter, LinkedIn
Scott D. Pattison, Executive Director
Stacy Mazer, Senior Staff Associate
Brian Sigritz, Director of State Fiscal Studies
Michael Streepey, Fiscal Policy Analyst
Kathryn Vesey White, Director, Member Relations
Membership limited to three budget officers per state. Affiliated with the National Governors Association.
160 Members
Founded in: 1945

8198 National Association of Tax Professionals
PO Box 8002
Appleton, WI 54912-8002
800-558-3402
800-558-3402; *Fax:* 800-747-0001
natp@natptax.com; www.natptax.com
Jo Ann Schoen, EA, President
Jean Millerchip,EA,CPF, Vice-President
Gerard F. Cannito CPA,CPF, Treasurer
Praticia(Ann) Mcneer EA, Secretary
Dorothy Atchison, EA, Director
The National Association of Tax Professionals (NATP) is a nonprofit professional association founded in 1979 and is committed to excellence in the tax profession. Our national headquarters is located in Appleton, Wisconsin and employs 42 professionals and 25 instructors. NATP was formed to serve professionals who work in all areas of tax practice and has more than 19,500 members nationwide.
24000 Members
Founded in: 1979

8199 National Association of Trade Exchanges
926 easterm Avenue
Malden, MA 02148
617-763-3311
bartertrainer@aol.com; www.natebarter.com
Social Media: Facebook, LinkedIn
Anne Weiser, President
Ric Zampatti, Vice President
Rolf Wilkin, Director
Maurya Lane, Director
Kim Ames, Secretary
NATE offers their members additional benefits such national and regional meetings and accreditation opportunities.
80 Members
Founded in: 1984

8200 National Automotive Finance Association
7037 Ridge Road
Suite 300
Hanover, MD 21076-1343
410-712-4036
800-463-8955; *Fax:* 410-712-4038
inquire@nafassociation.com;
www.nafassociation.com
Social Media: LinkedIn
Steve Hall, Chairman
Mark Floyd, President
Scot Seagrave, Vice President

Ian Anderson, Vice President
Gary Schultz, Secretary

NAF Association serves companies and professionals in the non-prime auto lending industry.
85 Members
Founded in: 1996

8201 National Bankers Association
1513 P St Nw
Washington, DC 20005

202-588-5432; *Fax:* 202-588-5443
eholliday@nationalbankers.org;
www.nationalbankers.org

Preston Pinkett III, Chairman
B. Doyle Mitchell, Immediate Past Chairman
Michael A. Grant, President
Cynthia N. Day, Secretary
Neill S. Wright, Treasurer

Association for banks owned or controlled by minority group persons or women.
15000 Members
Founded in: 1927

8202 National Community Capital Association
Public Ledger Building, 620 Chestnut Street
Suite 572
Philadelphia, PA 19106

215-923-4754; *Fax:* 215-923-4755
info@opportunityfinance.net; www.ofn.org
Social Media: Facebook, Twitter, LinkedIn, www.vimeo.com

Trinita Logue, Chair President
Eric Belsky, Executive Director
John Berdes, President/CEO
Keith Bisson, Program Management & Development
Lori Chatman, Vice Chair

Provides support for nonprofit, revolving loan funds that lend capital and offer technical assistance in distressed and disenfranchised communities.
52 Members
Founded in: 1986

8203 National Credit Union Administration
1775 Duke St
Alexandria, VA 22314-6115

703-518-6300; *Fax:* 703-518-6539
ociomail@ncua.gov; www.ncua.gov

Michael Fryzel, Manager

Governed by a three member board appointed by the President and confirmed by the US Senate, this independent federal agency charters and supervises federal credit unions. NCUA, with the backing of the full faith and credit of the US government, operates the National Credit Union Share Insurance Fund, insuring the savings of 80 million account holders in all federal credit unions and many state chartered credit unions.

8204 National Defined Contribution Council
307 Waverley Oaks Rd.
Waltham, MA 02452

781-693-7500; *Fax:* 866-904-9666;
www.zoominfo.com
Social Media: Facebook, Twitter, LinkedIn

Yonaton Stern, CEO & Chief Scientist
Eugenia Gillan, Vice President of Engineering
Steve Hill, Chief Financial Officer
Hila Nir, Vice President of Production Mgt.
Philip Garlick, VP, Corporate Development

NDCC is dedicated to the promotion and protection of the defined contribution industry and the public it serves. The Council specifically addresses the legislative needs of the defined contribution industry's plan service providers.
300 Members
Founded in: 1995

8205 National Federation of Municipal Analysts
PO Box 14893
Pittsburgh, PA 15234

412-341-4898; *Fax:* 412-341-4894
lgood@nfma.org; www.nfma.org
Social Media: Twitter, LinkedIn

Jeffery Burger, Chairman
Susan Dushock, Vice Chairman
Jennifer Johnston, Treasurer
Lisa Washburn, Secretary
Lisa Good, Executive Director

Promotes the profession of municipal credit analysts through educational programs, industry, communications and related programming.
1000 Members
Founded in: 1997

8206 National Finance Adjusters
PO Box 2652
Glenville, NY 12325

623-516-1018; *Fax:* 410-728-2528
info@nfacoop.com; www.nfacoop.com

Burton Greenwood Jr, Secretary/Treasurer
Jack S Barnes, Executive Director

Members are collateral recovery specialists.

8207 National Futures Association
300 S. Riverside Plaza
#1800
Chicago, IL 60606-6615

312-781-1300; *Fax:* 312-781-1467
information@nfa.futures.org;
www.nfa.futures.org

Christopher K. Hehmeyer, Chairman
Michael C. Dawley, Vice Chair
Leo Melamed, Chaise & CEO
Scott A. Cordes, President
Gerald F. Corcoran, Chief Executive Officer

Association for corporations and firms that are registered with the Commodity Futures Trading Commission.

8208 National Home Equity Mortgage Association
42484 Bellagio Drive
Bermuda Dunes, CA 92203

760-772-5806; www.nhema.org

Jeffrey Zeltzer, Principal

Mission is to promote the growth and recognition of the home equity lending industry.
300 Members
Founded in: 1974

8209 National Institute of Pension Administrators
330 N Wabash Ave
Suite 2000
Chicago, IL 60611-7621

800-999-6472; *Fax:* 312-673-6609
nipa@nipa.org; www.nipa.org
Social Media: LinkedIn

Patrick M. Shelton, GBA, President
Michelle Marsh, QKA, President Elect and CFO
Joseph Burt, Chief Financial Officer
Darren Holsy, Executive Committee Member-at-Large
Laura Rudzinski, Executive Director

The mission is to enhance professionalism in the retirement plan industry
1000 Members
Founded in: 1983

8210 National Investment Company Service Association
8400 Westpark Drive
2nd Floor
McLean, VA 22102

508-485-1500; *Fax:* 508-488-1560
info@nicsa.org; www.nicsa.org
Social Media: Facebook, Twitter, LinkedIn, Google+

George Batejan, Chairman
Dan Houlihan, Vice Chairman
Barry Benjamin, Treasurer
Steve Avera, Co-Chair
Jim Fitzpatrick, President

NICSA works to facilitate and promote leadership and innovation within the operations sector of the mutual fund industry.
10000 Members
Founded in: 1962

8211 National Pawnbrokers Association
891 Keller parkway
Suite 220
Keller, TX 76248

817-337-8830; *Fax:* 817-337-8875
info@nationalpawnbrokers.org;
www.nationalpawnbrokers.org
Social Media: Facebook, Twitter, Youtube

Larry Nuckols, President
Tim Collier, Vice President
Robert Anderson, Treasurer
Kathleen barbee, Secretary
Edward Bean, Director

NPA was founded to unite all pawnbrokers in their common efforts to improve the image of the industry, educate the public, adn disseminate professional information and assistance.
2000 Members
Founded in: 1987

8212 National Vehicle Leasing Association
N83 W13410 leon road
Menomonee Falls, WI 53051

414-533-3300
800-225-6852; *Fax:* 410-712-4038
info@nvla.org; www.nvla.org
Social Media: LinkedIn

Ben Carfrae, CVLE, Past President
PJ McMahon, CVLE, President/Treasurer
Terry L. Bowlder, 1st Vice president
David Blassingame, 2nd Vice President
Scott Crawford, CVLE, Director

Fosters education, publishing, conferences, legal services, advancement and industry relations certification.
500 Members
Founded in: 1968

8213 National Venture Capital Association
25 Massachusetts Avenue NW
Suite 730
Washington, DC 20001

202-864-5920; *Fax:* 202-864-5930
info@nvca.org; www.nvca.org
Social Media: Facebook, Twitter, LinkedIn, Youtube

Jon Callaghan, Chairman
Venky Ganesan, Chair-Elect
Scott Kupar, Treasurer
John Backus, Secretary
Maria Cirino, At Large

National trade association that represents venture capital firms. Activities include advocacy, professional development, networking and research.
450 Members
Founded in: 1973

8214 Neighborhood Reinvestment Corporation
5111 North Scottsdale Road
Suite 201
Scottsdale, AZ 85250
800-808-3372; *Fax:* 480-994-4456
sales@federalregister.com;
www.federalregister.com

Supplies training, grants, developmental assistance, and a range of other technical services designed to help the local partnerships achieve substantially self-reliant neighborhoods. The goal is to improve a neighborhood's housing and physical conditions, build a positive community image, and establish a healthy real estate market and a core of neighbors capable of managing the continued health of their neighborhood.
Founded in: 1978

8215 Partnership for Philanthropic Planning
233 McCrea St
Suite 300
Indianapolis, IN 46225
317-269-6274; *Fax:* 317-269-6268
info@pppnet.org;
www.charitablegiftplanners.org
Social Media: Facebook, Twitter, LinkedIn, YouTube, flickr

Gregory Sharkey, Chair
Melanie Norton, Chair-elect
Alexandra Brovey, Treasurer
Thomas H. Armstrong, Secretary
Michael Kenyon, President and CEO

Members are professionals involved in the process of planning and cultivating charitable gifts.
11500 Members
Founded in: 1988

8216 RMA - Risk Management Association
1801 Market Street
Suite 300
Philadelphia, PA 19103-1628
215-446-4137
800-677-7621; *Fax:* 215-446-4100
customers@rmahq.org; www.rmahq.org

J Tol Broome Jr, Chairman
Helga Houston, Vice Chairman
Nancy J. Foster, Immediate Past Chair
William F Githens, President & CEO
H. Lynn Harton, Director

Seeks to improve the risk management capabilities and principles of commercial lending and credit functions, loan administration and asset management in commercial banks and other financial industries.
17500 Members
Founded in: 1914

8217 Retirement Industry Trust Association
4251 Pasadena Circle
Sarasota, FL 34233
941-724-0900; *Fax:* 301-577-6476;
www.ritaus.org

Mary L. Mohr, Executive Director

8218 Securities Industry and Financial Markets Association (SIFMA)
1101 New York Ave NW
8th Floor
Washington, DC 20005
202-962-7300; *Fax:* 202-962-7305
webmaster@sifma.org; www.sifma.org
Social Media: Twitter, LinkedIn, Youtube, Google+

William A. Johnstone, Chairman
John F.W Rogers, Chair-elect
Timothy C. Scheve, Vice Chair
Gerad McGraw, Treasurer
Kenneth E Bentson Jr, President & CEO

SIFMA's mission is to champion policies and practices that benefit investors and issuers, expand and perfect global capital markets, and foster the development of new products and services. SIFMA provides an enhanced member network of access and forward-looking services, as well as premiere educational resources for the professionals within the industry and the investors whom they serve.

8219 Security Traders Association
1115 Broadway
Suite 1110
New York, NY 10010
646-699-5996; *Fax:* 212-321-3449
sta@securitytraders.org;
www.securitytraders.org
Social Media: Facebook, Twitter, LinkedIn, Instagram

Rory O'Kane, Chairman
Jim Toes, President & CEO
John Russell, Vice Chairman
Jon Schneider, Treasurer
Doug Clark, Secretary

Members involved in the securities industry.
7000 Members
Founded in: 1934

8220 Small Business Investor Alliance
1100 H Street NW
Suite 1200
Washington, DC 20005
202-628-5055; *Fax:* 202-628-5080
info@sbia.org; www.sbia.org
Social Media: Twitter, LinkedIn

Mike Blackburn, Chairman
JD White, Chair-Elect
Jeri Harman, Vice Chairman
Carolyn Galiette, Secretary
Brett Palmer, President

Trade association representing federally licensed venture capital firms and small private equity firms.
400 Members
Founded in: 1958

8221 Society for Information Management
1120 Royte73
Ste 200
Mount Laurel, NJ 08054-5113
800-387-9746
800-387-9746; *Fax:* 856-439-0525
sim@simnet.org; www.simnet.org
Social Media: Facebook, Twitter, LinkedIn, www.multiview.com

Eric Gorham, Chairman
Kevin More, Vice Chairman
Caren Shiozaki, Treasurer/Secretary
Jim Knight, Chair Emeritus
Kevin Sauer, Director, Chapter Representative

SIM was formed to enhance international recognition of information as a basic organizational resource and to promote the effective utilization and management of this resource towards the improvement of management performance. It attempts to enhance communications between IS executives and the senior executives responsible for management of the business enterprise.
3000 Members
Founded in: 1969

8222 Society of Financial Examiners
12100 Sunset Hills Rd
Suite 130
Reston, VA 20190-3221
703-234-4140
800-787-7633; *Fax:* 888-436-8686
sofe@sofe.org; www.sofe.org
Social Media: Facebook, LinkedIn

L Brackett, Executive Director
Judy Estus, Administrator
Annete Knief, President
James Katman, Treasurer
Mark Murphy, Secretary

Is a professional society for examiners of insurance companies, banks, savings and loans, and credit unions.
1600 Members
Founded in: 1973

8223 Society of Quantitative Analysts
1450 Western avenue
Suite 101
Albany, NY 12203
518-694-3157
800-918-7930
sqa@sqa-us.org; www.sqa-us.org
Social Media: Facebook, LinkedIn

Peg DioRio, President
Inna Okounkova, Vice President
Kennith N. Hightower, Secretary
Randy O' Toole, Treasurer
Indrani De, CFA PRM, Past President

SQA is concerned with the application of new and innovative techniques for finance, with particular emphasis on the use of quantitative techniques in investment management.
350 Members
Founded in: 1989

8224 Stable Value Investment Association
1025 Connecticut Avenue NW
Suite 1000
Washington, DC 20036
202-580-7620
800-327-2270; *Fax:* 202-580-7621
info@StableValue.org; www.stablevalue.org
Social Media: Twitter, LinkedIn

Marc Magnoli, Chair

Members are firms and individuals with a professional interest in savings for retirement.
Founded in: 1990

8225 State Debt Management Networking
2760 Research Park Drive
Lexington, KY 40511
859-244-8175; *Fax:* 859-244-8053
nast@csg.org; www.sdmn.org

Hon. Manju Ganeriwala, Chair
Steve Wisloski, Vice-chair
Laura Lockwood-Mccall, Director, Debt Management
Ellen Evans, Deputy Treasurer Debt Management
Robert L. Watson, Assistant Director

SDMN members are state officials concerned with the insurance or management of state debt. The purpose is to enhance debt management practices throough training, development of educational materials, and data collection and dissemination
50 Members
Founded in: 1991

8226 State Risk and Insurance Management Association
PO Box 13777
Austin, TX 78711
304-766-2646
robert.a.fisher@wv.gov; www.strima.org

Robert Fischer, President

STRIMA members are state government risk and insurance managers.
50 Members
Founded in: 1974

8227 **Tax Executives Institute**
1200 G St NW
Suite 300
Washington, DC 20005

202-638-5601; *Fax:* 202-638-5607;
www.tei.org

Timothy Mc Cormally, Executive Director
Deborah K Gaffney, Director Conference Planning
Deborah C Giesey, Director Administration

A professional organization of corporate tax executives. Membership is open to corporate officers and employees chargesd with administering their company's tax affairs.
7000 Members
Founded in: 1944

8228 **The Fiduciary & Investment Risk Management Association**
P.O.Box 507
Stockbridge, GA 30281-0507

678-565-6211; *Fax:* 678-565-8788
info@thefirma.org; www.thefirma.org
Social Media: Facebook, Twitter, LinkedIn

Bruce K Goldberg, CTA, CPA, President
Jennifer De Vries, CTA, Vice President
David Jonke CTA, CPA, Secretary
John L. Clark, Director
Daniele G Nicotra, Director-Compliance

Members are audit and compliance professionals.
820 Members
Founded in: 1989

8229 **The Resource Centre for Religious Institutes**
8824 Cameron Street
Silver Spring, MD 20910

301-589-8143; *Fax:* 301-589-2897
trcri@trcri.org; www.trcri.org
Social Media: Facebook, Twitter, www.blogspot.com

Fr. Thomas Carkhuff, OSC, President
Sr. Lynn McKenzie, OSB, Vice-President
Daniel J. Ward, OSB, JCL, JD, Executive Director
Sr. Margaret Ma Cosgrove, BVM, Treasurer
Sr. Margaret Perron, RJM, Secretary

The leading resource and provider of education, services, and information to meet the current and emerging stewardship needs of all religious institutes throughout the United States.
Founded in: 1981

8230 **Urban Homesteading Assistance Board**
120 Wall St
20th Floor
New York, NY 10005

212-479-3300; *Fax:* 212-344-6457
webmaster@uhab.org; www.uhab.org
Social Media: Facebook, Twitter, Youtube

Andrew Reicher, Executive Director
Anya Irons, Director Of Operations
Charles Laven, President
Janice Lancaster, Office Manager
Julie Harris, Director

The oldest provider of technical assistance to homesteading and sweat equity groups in the country. Promotes homesteading as an important component of comprehensive self-help housing programs. Provides technical assistance and training in self-help housing rehabilitation and managment to low income tenants, cooperative shareholders and homesteaders.
8 Members
Founded in: 1973

8231 **Wall Street Technology Association**
620 Shrewsbury Ave
Suite C
Tinton Falls, NJ 07701

732-530-8808; *Fax:* 732-530-0020
info@wsta.org; www.wsta.org
Social Media: Facebook, Twitter, LinkedIn

John Killeen, President
Chris Randazzo, 1st Vice President
Joseph Weitekamp, 2nd Vice President
Ronald F. Ries, Treasurer
Michael Maffattone, Secretary

Nonprofit educational organization that focuses on technologies, operational approaches, and business issues for the global financial community.
2600+ Members
Founded in: 1967

8232 **Wall Street Technology Association (WSTA)**
620 Shrewsbury Ave
Suite C
Tinton Falls, NJ 07701

732-530-8808; *Fax:* 732-530-0020
info@wsta.org; www.wsta.org
Social Media: Facebook, Twitter, LinkedIn

John Killeen, President
Chris Randazzo, 1st Vice President
Joseph Weitekamp, 2nd Vice President
Ronald F. Ries, Treasurer
Michael Maffattone, Secretary

Nonprofit educational organization that focuses on technologies, operational approaches, and business issues for the global financial community.
2800+ Members
Founded in: 1967

8233 **Washington Municipal Treasurers Associaion**
2601 Fourth Avenue
Suite 800
Seattle, WA 98121-1280

206-625-1300
hstewart@mrsc.org; www.wmta-online.com

Stpehanie McKanzie, President
Elizabeth Alba, President-Elect
Philip Steffan, Secretary
Gwen Pilo, Treasurer
Cheryl Grant, Director

Mission is to promote the profession of municipal treasurers through education, mutual support, professional recognition, and legislative advocacy.
Founded in: Was

Newsletters

8234 **AARMR Newsletter**
American Association of Residential Mortgage
1025 Thomas Jefferson Street NW
Suite 500 East
Washington, DC 20007

202-521-3999; *Fax:* 202-833-3636
efreundel@aarmr.org; www.aarmr.org

David A Saunders, Executive Director
Erika Freundel, Manager Of Member Services
Frequency: Quarterly

8235 **AEFA Newsletter**
American Education Finance Association
8365 S Armadillo Trail
Evergreen, CO 80439

303-674-0857; *Fax:* 303-670-8986;
www.aefa.cc

Ed Steinbacher, Executive Director
Frequency: Quarterly

8236 **AFCPE Newsletter**
Association for Financial Counseling and Planning
2112 Arlington Avenue
Suite H
Upper Arlington, OH 43221

614-485-9650; *Fax:* 614-485-9621;
www.afcpe.org

Sharon Burns, PhD, Executive Director
Frequency: Quarterly

8237 **AMI Bulletin**
Assn for Management Information in Financial Svcs
14247 Saffron Circle
Carmel, IN 46032

317-518-5857; *Fax:* 317-518-5877
ami2@amifs.org; www.amifs.org

Robert McDonald, President
Kevin Link, Executive Director

News, calendars, events, and industry articles.
Frequency: Quarterly

8238 **Airline Financial News**
PBI Media
1201 Seven Locks Road
Suite 300
Potomac, MD 20854-2931

301-354-1400
800-777-5006; *Fax:* 301-309-3847;
www.aviationtoday.com

Richard Koulbanis, Publisher

Provides information for CEO's financial directors, operations managers, engine aircraft manufacturers and suppliers on financial, market development, buying, leasing and aircraft transactions.
Cost: $697.00
Frequency: Weekly
Circulation: 1850

8239 **Annual Statement Studies**
RMA - Risk Management Association
6147 Ridge Ave
Suite 2300
Philadelphia, PA 19128-2627

215-482-3222
800-677-7621; *Fax:* 215-446-4101
customers@rmahq.org; www.rmahq.org

Angelo Roma, Owner
William F Githens, Director Member Relations
Dwight Overturf, CFO/Information Technology Officer
Florence J Wetzel, COO/Administrative Officer
John Rumm, Executive Director
Frequency: Annual

8240 **Asset-Backed Alert**
Harrison Scott Publications
5 Marine View Plz
Suite 301
Hoboken, NJ 07030-5722

201-386-1491; *Fax:* 201-659-4141
info@hspnews.com; www.hspnews.com

Andy Albert, Owner
Tom Ferris, Editor
Daniel Cowles, CEO/President
Barbara Bannace, Marketing
Joan Tassie, Operations Director

A weekly newsletter on the securitization of consumer and corporate receivables.
Cost: $2297.00
10 Pages
Frequency: Weekly
Circulation: 2178
ISSN: 1520-3700
Founded in: 1988
Printed in 4 colors on matte stock

8241 BNA Pension & Benefits Reporter
Bureau of National Affairs
1801 S Bell St
Arlington, VA 22202-4501
703-341-3000
800-372-1033; *Fax:* 800-253-0332
customercare@bna.com; www.bnabooks.com
Gregory C McCaffrey, President
Paul N Wojcik, Chairman
Covers latest pension developments stemming from the passage of ERISA and its amendments, plus pension and welfare benefit regulations, standards, enforcement actions, court decisions, legislative and administrative actions, agency options, and employee benefit trust fund requirements.
Cost: $1448.00
Frequency: Weekly
Founded in: 1929
Printed in on matte stock

8242 Back-Office Bulletin
United Communications Group
Two Washingtonian Center
9737 Washingtonian Blvd Suite 100
Gaithersburg, MD 20878-7364
301-287-2700; *Fax:* 301-287-2039;
www.ucg.com
Daniel Brown, Publisher
For financial operations professionals.
Founded in: 1970

8243 Bandwidth Investor
Kagan World Media
1 Lower Ragsdale Dr
Building 1, Suite 130
Monterey, CA 93940-5749
831-624-1536; *Fax:* 831-625-3225
info@kagan.com; www.kagan.com
Tim Baskerville, President/CEO
Harvey Kraft, Circulation/Marketing Manager
Cost: $1195.00
Frequency: Monthly
Founded in: 1969

8244 Bank 13D Dictionary
SNL Securities
PO Box 2124
Charlottesvle, VA 22902-2124
434-977-1600; *Fax:* 434-977-4466
isales@snl.com; www.snl.com
Todd Davenport, Editor
Reid Nagle, Chief Operating Officer
Nick Cafferillo, Chief Operating Officer
Adam Hall, Managing Director
For banks, thrifts, investors, investment bankers, law firms, consultants and regulatory agencies. Contains all active 13D filings and related filings for every public traded bank in the country, including those which trade on the 'pink sheets.'
Frequency: Quarterly
Founded in: 1987

8245 Benefax
SNL Securities
PO Box 2124
Charlottesvle, VA 22902-2124
434-977-1600; *Fax:* 434-977-4466
isales@snl.com; www.snl.com
Keith Davis, Editor
Reid Nagle, Chief Operating Officer
Nick Cafferillo, Chief Operating Officer
Adam Hall, Managing Director
For bank and thrift executives. Contains only summaries of available information.
1 Pages
Frequency: Monthly
Founded in: 1987

8246 Bondweek
Institutional Investor
225 Park Ave S
7th Floor
New York, NY 10003-1605
212-224-3300; *Fax:* 212-224-3197
iieditor@institutionalinvestor.com;
www.institutionalinvestor.com
Christopher Brown, CEO
Erik Kolk, Publisher
Deirdre Brennan, Managing Editor
Nick Ferris, Group Marketing Director
Coverage of stocks, bonds and investments for the financial professional and consumer, information includes rates.
Cost: $2245.00
Frequency: 51 issues per y
Founded in: 1967

8247 Broadcast Banker/Broker
Kagan World Media
1 Lower Ragsdale Dr
Building One,Suite 130
Monterey, CA 93940-5749
831-624-1536
800-307-2529; *Fax:* 831-625-3225
info@kagan.com; www.kagan.com
Tim Baskerville, President
Tom Johnson, Marketing Manager
A readers guide to equity deals and debt financing for radio and TV Station buying and selling analyzed. Key details on station trades with critical yardsticks of value. Three month trial is available.
Cost: $925.00
Frequency: Monthly

8248 Broadcast Investor
Kagan World Media
126 Clock Tower Place
Carmel, CA 93923-8746
831-624-1536; *Fax:* 831-624-5882
info@kagan.com; www.kagan.com
George Niesen, Editor
Tom Johnson, Marketing Manager
The newsletter on investments in radio and TV stations and publicly held companies. Comprehensive analysis of cash flow multiples and trends that impact value. Three month trial available.
Cost: $895.00
Frequency: Monthly

8249 Broker Magazine
Thomson Media
1 State St
27th Floor
New York, NY 10004-1481
212-825-8445
800-221-1809; *Fax:* 800-235-5552;
www.sourcemedia.com
Timothy Murphy, Publisher
James Malkin, Director of Sales
Melissa Sefic, Director of Sales
Features on training, motivation, technology, legislation and marketing
Frequency: Monthly
Circulation: 750000

8250 Budget Processors in the States
National Association of State Budge Officers
444 N Capitol St NW
Suite 642
Washington, DC 20001-1512
202-624-5382; *Fax:* 202-624-7745
spattison@nasbo.org; www.nasbo.org
Frequency: Bi-Ennial

8251 Bull & Bear Financial Report
PO Bo 917179
Longwood, FL 32791
954-781-3455
800-336-2855; *Fax:* 954-781-5865;
www.thebullandbear.com
David J Robinson, Publisher/Editor
Dozens of original articles by leading investment pros with investment information on precious metals, commodities, mutual funds, currencies, economic trends and monetary survival.
Circulation: 55000

8252 Bulletin Newsletter
EMTA - Trade Association for the Emerging Markets
360 Madison Avenue
17th Floor
New York, NY 10017
646-289-5410; *Fax:* 646-289-5429
awerner@emta.org; www.emta.org
Michael M Chamberlin, Executive Director
Aviva Werner, General Counsel
Jonathan Murno, Managing Director
Suzette Ortiz, Office Manager
Monika Forbes, Administrative Assistant
Frequency: Quarterly

8253 CFMA Building Profits
Construction Financial Management Association
29 Emmons Drive
Princeton, NJ 08540
609-452-8000; *Fax:* 609-452-0474
pwristen@cfma.org; www.cfma.org
Paula Wristen, Editor
Sarah Patt, Sales/Advertising Director
William Schwab, President
The leading source of education and information about financial management within the construction industry. The only magazine dedicated to helping financial managers in the construction business find practical solutions to emerging issues in the industry. Accepts advertising.
32 Pages
Circulation: 6500

8254 CIPFA Newsletter
National Association of Independent Public Finance
PO Box 304
Montgomery, IL 60538-0304
630-896-1292
800-624-7321; *Fax:* 209-633-6265;
www.naipfa.com
Roseanne M Hoban, Executive Director
Frequency: Quarterly

8255 Cable Program Investor
Kagan World Media

126 Clock Tower Place
Carmel, CA 93923-8746

831-624-1536; *Fax:* 831-624-5882
info@kagan.com; www.kagan.com

George Niesen, Editor
Tom Johnson, Marketing Manager

Covers the economics of basic cable programming networks. Numbers, perspective unavailable from any other source. Programmers applaud its accuracy. Three month trial available.
Cost: $845.00
Frequency: Monthly

8256 **Cable TV Finance**
Kagan World Media
126 Clock Tower Place
Carmel, CA 93923-8746

831-624-1536
800-307-2529; *Fax:* 831-624-5882
info@kagan.com; www.kagan.com

George Niesen, Editor
Tom Johnson, Marketing Manager
Tim Baskerville, CEO/President

Cable's financial bible. Analyzes sources of funding for cable TV. Selling and buying of cable systems. Financing strategies and trends. Exclusive surveys of capital sources. Three month trial available.
Cost: $995.00
Frequency: Monthly
Founded in: 1969

8257 **Cable TV Investor**
Kagan World Media
1 Lower Ragsdale Dr
Building One, Suite 130
Monterey, CA 93940-5749

831-624-1536
800-307-2529; *Fax:* 831-625-3225
info@kagan.com; www.kagan.com

Tim Baskerville, President
Tom Johnson, Marketing Manager

Readers road map to cable stock trends. Chart service tracking stock price movements of 37 publicly held cable TV companies. Each graph shows two years of stock price activity. Three month trial available.
Cost: $945.00
Frequency: Monthly

8258 **Card News**
Phillips Publishing
7811 Montrose Road
Potomac, MD 20854

301-340-2100
feedback@healthydirections.com;
www.healthydirections.com

Covering the financial card marketplace.

8259 **Client Information Bulletin**
WPI Communications
55 Morris Ave
Suite 300
Springfield, NJ 07081-1422

973-467-8700; *Fax:* 973-467-0368
info@wpicomm.com; www.wpicomm.com

Steve Klinghoffer, Owner
Marilyn Lang, Chairman

Bulletin for lawyers and CPAs to distribute to clients to keep them informed on tax matters. This original publication which has been helping accountants build their practices since 1952, has been redesigned. Covers important new tax developments, general business principals, financial planning, estate planning and other related topics.

8260 **Collection Agency Report**
First Detroit Corporation
PO Box 5025
Warren, MI 48090-5025

586-573-0045
800-366-5995; *Fax:* 586-573-9219;
www.firstdetroit.com

Albert Scace, President
Petricia Herrick, Marketing Manager

Provides financially oriented news on the collection agency and bad debt buying industries worldwide.
Cost: $289.00
8 Pages
Frequency: Monthly
ISSN: 1052-4029
Mailing list available for rent: 5000 names at $110 per M

8261 **Commercial Mortgage Alert**
Harrison Scott Publications
5 Marine View Plz
Suite 301
Hoboken, NJ 07030-5722

201-386-1491; *Fax:* 201-659-4141
info@hspnews.com; www.hspnews.com

Andy Albert, Owner
Tom Ferris, Director
Michelle Lebowitz, Director

A weekly newsletter on the securitization of consumer and corporate receivables.
Cost: $1497.00
10 Pages
Frequency: Weekly
Circulation: 500
ISSN: 1520-3700
Printed in 4 colors on matte stock

8262 **Conference Executive Summaries**
Society for Information Management
401 N Michigan Avenue
Chicago, IL 60611

312-215-5190; *Fax:* 312-245-1081;
www.simnet.org

Jim Luisi, Executive Director
Frequency: Semi-Annual

8263 **Conversion Candidates List**
SNL Securities
PO Box 2124
Charlottesvle, VA 22902-2124

434-977-1600; *Fax:* 434-977-4466
isales@snl.com; www.snl.com

Chris Smith, Editor
Reid Nagle, Chief Operating Officer
Nick Cafferillo, Chief Operating Officer
Adam Hall, Managing Director

For thrift executives, individual investors and institutional investors. Lists mutual thrifts that are in a position to convert to stock ownership by offering shares for sale.
Frequency: Monthly
Founded in: 1987

8264 **Conversion Watch**
SNL Securities
PO Box 2124
Charlottesvle, VA 22902-2124

434-977-1600; *Fax:* 434-977-4466
isales@snl.com; www.snl.com

Chris Smith, Editor
Nick Cafferillo, Chief Operating Officer
Adam Hall, Managing Director

Delivered via fax whenever new activity is announced, including rumored, pending, announced and completed activity. Provides relevant data from conversion-related filings, including eligible record dates, offering size, Pro Formas, opening and closing dates for the subscription, asset size, net worth and rating of the thrift.
Cost: $1200.00
5 Pages
Frequency: Annual+
Founded in: 1987

8265 **Cost Control News**
Siefer Consultants
PO Box 1384
Storm Lake, IA 50588-1384

712-732-7340; *Fax:* 712-732-7906
info@siefer.com; www.siefer.com/

Dan Siefer, Publisher

Cost cutting opportunities for financial institutions.
Cost: $297.00
8 Pages
Founded in: 1981

8266 **Credit Collections News**
SourceMedia
550 W Van Buren
Suite 1100
Chicago, IL 60607-6680

312-913-1334; *Fax:* 312-913-1340;
www.sourcemedia.com

John Stewart, Publisher
Melissa Sefic, Director of Sales

Analysis of the global economy, current industry trends and policies, as well as problems commonly encountered in credit collections.
Frequency: Monthly

8267 **Credit Union Journal**
SourceMedia
224 Datura Street
Suite 615
West Palm Beach, FL 33401

561-832-2929; *Fax:* 561-832-2939;
www.cujournal.com

Frank J Dierkmann, Publisher/Editor
Tim O'Hara, Co-Publisher

JournalScan to review recent credit union developments, industry news articles, an agenda of upcoming meetings, deadlines and events and Washington Watch covering the latest news in Washington DC.
Frequency: Weekly
Circulation: 5300

8268 **Credit Union Management**
Credit Union Executives Society
PO Box 14167
Madison, WI 53714-167

608-271-2664
800-252-2664; *Fax:* 608-271-2303
cues@cues.org; www.cues.org

Mary Arnold, Publisher
Theresa Sweeney, Editor
Fred Johnson, CEO/President
Cost: $93.00
Frequency: Monthly
Printed in 4 colors on glossy stock

8269 **Credit and Collection Manager's Letter**
Bureau of Business Practice
76 Ninth Avenue
7th Floor
New York, NY 10011

212-771-0600; *Fax:* 212-771-0885;
www.aspenlawschool.com
Social Media: Facebook, Twitter, LinkedIn

Mark Dorman, CEO
Gustavo Dobles, VP Operations

Hands-on information for improving the credit and collection departments in both commercial and consumer markets.
Frequency: SemiMonthly
Circulation: 9380

8270 **Daily Tax Report**
Bureau of National Affairs
1801 S Bell St
Arlington, VA 22202-4501

703-341-3000
800-372-1033; *Fax:* 800-253-0332
customercare@bna.com; www.bnabooks.com

Paul N Wojcik, CEO

A daily tax notification service that covers legislative, regulatory, judicial and policy developments on a national basis, designed to give tax professionals rapid notification and comprehensive coverage of those developments.
Cost: $3215.00
Frequency: Daily
ISSN: 0092-6884

8271 **Debit Card News**
SourceMedia
224 Datura Street
Suite 615
West Palm Beach, FL 33401

561-832-2929; *Fax:* 561-832-2939;
www.cujournal.com

Don Davis, Editor

Marketing, pricing, different card applications, smart cards, point-of-sale and other electronic banking activities.
Frequency: SemiMonthly

8272 **Declined Contribution Market Insights**
National Defined Contribution Council
9101 E Kenyon
Suite 300
Denver, CO 80237-0467

303-770-5353; *Fax:* 303-770-1812;
www.ndcconline.org

Al Brust, Executive VP
Frequency: Annual

8273 **Equipment Leasing & Finance**
Equipment Leasing And Finance Association
1825 K Street NW
Suite 900
Washington, DC 20006

202-238-3400; *Fax:* 202-238-3401;
www.elfaonline.org

Amy Vogt, Managing Editor

As the flagship publication of the Equipment Leasing and Finance Association, Equipment Leasing & Finance is the trusted leader, bringing readers unrivaled coverage of the people, trends and issues that have an impact on the $628 billion equipment finance industry. Information of funding sources, portfolio management, sales and marketing strategy, large ticket leasing, transportation leasing, the computer leasing market, remarketing equipment, and the role of the equipment manager.
Frequency: 6x/Year
Circulation: 10000
Founded in: 1961
Printed in 4 colors on glossy stock

8274 **Executive Brief**
Society for Information Management
401 N Michigan Avenue
Chicago, IL 60611

312-215-5190; *Fax:* 312-245-1081;
www.simnet.org

Jim Luisi, Executive Director
Frequency: Quarterly

8275 **Executive Compensation Review for Commercial Banks**
SNL Securities
PO Box 2124
Charlottesvle, VA 22902-2124

434-977-1600; *Fax:* 434-977-4466;
www.snlnet.com

Keith Davis, Editor
Nick Cafferillo, Chief Operating Officer
Reid Nagle, Publisher
Mark Outlaw, Advertising Director
Adam Hall, Managing Director

For banks, regulatory agencies and executive recruiters. Includes detailed compensation and benefit information for the top 5 officers of all publicly traded banks, thrifts, REITs and insurance companies.
550 Pages
Frequency: Annual
Founded in: 1988

8276 **Executive Compensation Review for Insurance Companies**
SNL Securities
PO Box 2124
Charlottesvle, VA 22902-2124

434-977-1600; *Fax:* 434-977-4466;
www.snlnet.com

Keith Davis, Editor
Nick Cafferillo, Chief Operating Officer
Reid Nagle, Publisher
Mark Outlaw, Advertising Director
Pat LaBua, Subscription Manager

For insurance companies, investment analysts, service providers to the insurance industry and regulators. Includes detailed compensation and benefit information for the top 5 officers of all publicly traded banks, thrifts, REITs and insurance companies.
200 Pages
Frequency: Annual
Founded in: 1997

8277 **Executive Compensation Review for REITs**
SNL Securities
PO Box 2124
Charlottesvle, VA 22902-2124

434-977-1600; *Fax:* 434-977-4466
isales@snl.com; www.snl.com

Keith Davis, Editor
Chandler Spears, Chief Operating Officer
Nick Cafferillo, Chief Operating Officer
Adam Hall, Managing Director

For REITs, REIT service providers, investment companies, executive recruiters and regulators. Annual data digests that include detailed compensation and benefit information for the top 5 officers of all publicly traded banks, thrifts, REITs and insurance companies.
Cost: $495.00
Frequency: Monthly
Founded in: 1987

8278 **Executive Compensation Review for Thrift Institutions**
SNL Securities
PO Box 2124
Charlottesvle, VA 22902-2124

434-977-1600; *Fax:* 434-977-4466
isales@snl.com; www.snl.com

Keith Davis, Editor
Nick Cafferillo, Chief Operating Officer
Adam Hall, Managing Director

For thrifts, regulatory agencies and executive recruiters. Annual data digests that include detailed compensation and benefit information for the top 5 officers of all publicly traded banks, thrifts, REITs and insurance companies.
Cost: $495.00
Frequency: Monthly
Founded in: 1987

8279 **Export Finance Letter**
International Business Affairs Corporation
5523 Brite Dr
#346
Bethesda, MD 20817-6304

301-907-8647; *Fax:* 301-907-8650;
www.internationalrelationsedu.org

Richard Barovick, Owner

A report on government and private resources in US Export & Import Finance, Payments and Risk Management.
Founded in: 1979

8280 **FEI Briefing**
Financial Executives Institute
200 Campus Drive
PO Box 674
Forham Park, NJ 07932

973-360-0177; *Fax:* 973-765-1023;
www.fei.org

P Norman Roy, Publisher
Christopher Allen, Editor
Colleen Sayther Cunningham, CEO/President
Christopher Allen, Marketing
Lucinda Arsenio, Secretary

Up-to-date news for treasurers and controllers of large corporations.
Circulation: 14000
Founded in: 1931

8281 **FSR Newsletter**
Financial Services Roundtable
1001 Pennsylvania Ave Nw
Suite 500 S
Washington, DC 20004-2508

202-628-2455; *Fax:* 202-289-1903
info@fsround.org; www.fsround.org

Steve Bartlett, CEO
Frequency: Monthly

8282 **Federal Securities Act**
Matthew Bender and Company
744 Broad St
Newark, NJ 07102-3885

973-820-2000
800-227-9597; *Fax:* 937-865-1284
info.in@lexisnexis.com; www.lexisnexis.com

Kent Frankstone, Manager
Rebecca Schmitt, Chief Financial Officer

A comprehensive, up-to-date treatise on the Securities Act of 1933 and all amendments thereto, as well as the application of the Trust Indenture Act of 1939.

8283 **Fee Income Report**
Siefer Consultants
PO Box 1384
Storm Lake, IA 50588-1384

712-732-7340; *Fax:* 712-732-7906
info@siefer.com; www.siefer.com

Dan Siefer, Publisher

Fee income news and opportunities for financial institutions.
Cost: $297.00
8 Pages
Frequency: Monthly
Founded in: 1981

8284 **Fidelity Insight**
Mutual Fund Investors Association
20 William St
Suite 200
Wellesley, MA 02481-4138

781-235-1560
800-586-4727; www.kobren.com

Eric Kobren, President
Chris Keith, Senior Vice President
Todd Peters, Senior Vice President

Offers information and rates for mutual funds, investments, stocks and bonds.
Cost: $127.00
8 Pages
Frequency: Monthly
Founded in: 1985

8285 Finance Company Weekly
SNL Securities
PO Box 2124
Charlottesvle, VA 22902-2124

434-977-1600; *Fax:* 434-977-4466
isales@snl.com; www.snl.com

David Meadors, Editor
Nick Cafferillo, Chief Operating Officer
Adam Hall, Managing Director

Weekly news on publicly and privately traded finance companies. Includes consumer, commercial, credit card companies, pawn shops and leasing companies. Summarizes recent industry earnings announcement, trends, registration statements and performance rankings.
Cost: $396.00
10 Pages
Frequency: Weekly
Founded in: 1987

8286 Financial Management Association International (FMA)
University of South Florida
4202 E Fowler Ave
Tampa, FL 33620-9951

813-974-2011; *Fax:* 813-974-5530
fma@coba.usf.edu OR info@fma.org; www.usf.edu

Judy L Genshaft, President
William Christie, Financial Management Editor
Keith M Howe, Journal of Applied Finance Editor
James Schallheim, FMA Survey Synthesis Series Editor
John Finnerty, Editor FMA Online

Financial books, textbooks, databases, newspapers, research services, software and related products and services.
Frequency: Quarterly
Founded in: 1970

8287 Financial Managers Update
Financial Managers Society
100 W Monroe
Suite 810
Chicago, IL 60603

312-578-1300
800-275-4367; *Fax:* 312-578-1308
info@fmsinc.org; www.fmsinc.org/cms

Dick Yingst, President/CEO
Jennifer Vimarco, Professional Development Director
Jennifer Doak, Director of Marketing

The latest accounting and regulatory information related to financial institutions, as well as news and trends. Includes a regulatory check list.
8 Pages
Circulation: 1400
Mailing list available for rent
Printed in one color

8288 Financial NetNews
Institutional Investor
488 Madison Ave
15th Floor
New York, NY 10022-5701

212-303-3100
800-115-9196; *Fax:* 212-224-3491
iieditor@institutionalinvestor.com; www.institutionalinvestor.com

Dahlia Weinman, Publisher
Deirdre Brennan, Editor
Nick Ferris, Marketing Manager
Chris Brown, CEO/President

Businesses and their Web sites, providing up-to-date information on networkings and assessment of industry trends and mistakes.
Frequency: Weekly

8289 Financial News
Financial News Corporation
PO Box 1769
Jacksonville, FL 32201-1769

904-356-2466; *Fax:* 904-353-2628
editorial@jaxdailyrecord.com; www.jaxdailyrecord.com

James F Bailey Jr, Publisher
Angie Campbell, Business Manager
Karen Mathis, Managing Editor

Business and legal information for financial institutions.
Cost: $89.00
Frequency: Daily

8290 Financial Planning Advisory
WPI Communications
55 Morris Ave
Suite 300
Springfield, NJ 07081-1422

973-467-8700
800-323-4995; *Fax:* 973-467-0368
info@wpicomm.com; www.wpicomm.com

Steve Klinghoffer, Owner
Marilyn Lang, Chairman

Offers institutions and businesses information on financial planning and campaigns.
Founded in: 1952

8291 Financial Services
8180 Corporate Park Drive
Suite 305
Cincinnati, OH 45242-3309

513-591-0149; *Fax:* 513-527-3141

Linda Niesz, Publisher

National and regional news for members.
Cost: $7.00
6 Pages
Frequency: Monthly

8292 Financial Services Daily
SNL Securities
PO Box 2124
Charlottesvle, VA 22902-2124

434-977-1600; *Fax:* 434-977-4466
isales@snl.com; www.snl.com

David Meadors, Editor
Nick Cafferillo, Chief Operating Officer
Adam Hall, Managing Director

Daily fax of news headlines on finance companies, mortgage banks, investment advisors and brokers/dealers, plus divident and earnings announcements, stock highlights and index values, registration statements and ownership filings.
6 Pages
Frequency: Daily
Founded in: 1987

8293 Financial Services M&A Insider
SNL Securities
PO Box 2124
Charlottesvle, VA 22902-2124

434-977-1600; *Fax:* 434-977-4466
isales@snl.com; www.snl.com

L Vencil, Editor
Reid Nagle, Chief Operating Officer
Nick Cafferillo, Chief Operating Officer
Adam Hall, Managing Director

Fax: newsletter featuring in-depth articles and the latest financial information on financial services M&A activity. Covers mortgage banks, finance companies, investment advisors and broker/dealers. Analyzes industry trends and specific market and ownership changes to identify potential consolidation activity.
Cost: $695.00
10 Pages
Frequency: Monthly
Founded in: 1987

8294 Financial Women Today
Financial Women International
1027 W Roselawn Avenue
Roseville, MN 55113

651-487-7632
866-807-6081; *Fax:* 651-489-1322
info@fwi.org; www.fwi.org

Melissa Curzon, President
Cindy Hass, VP
Carleen DeSisto, Secretary

Covers financial services industry trends, as well as women's issues and association news.
1000 Members
Circulation: 10,000
Founded in: 1921

8295 First Friday
ASCU
PO Box 5488
Madison, WI 53705-0488

608-238-2646; *Fax:* 608-238-2646

C Barle, Publisher

Market research and statistics.
Cost: $35.00
6 Pages
Frequency: Monthly
Founded in: 1973
Mailing list available for rent: 11,000 names at $60 per M
Printed in on matte stock

8296 Fiscal Survey of the States
National Association of State Budget Officers
444 N Capitol St Nw
Suite 642
Washington, DC 20001-1556

202-624-8020; *Fax:* 202-624-7745
spattison@nasbo.org; www.nasbo.org

Scott Pattison, Executive Director
Frequency: Semi-Annual

8297 Focus on Accountability
Evangelical Council for Financial Accountability
440 W Jubal Early Dr
Suite 130
Winchester, VA 22601

540-535-0103
800-323-9473; *Fax:* 540-535-0533
info@ecfa.org; www.ecfa.org

Dan Busby, President
Kim Sandretzky, Vice President, Communications
2250 Members
Frequency: Quarterly
Circulation: 30000
Founded in: 1979

8298 Forecaster
Forecaster Publishing Company
19623 Ventura Blvd
Tarzana, CA 91356-2918

818-345-4421; *Fax:* 818-345-0468

John Kamin, Owner
Brian Kamin, CEO/President

Analyzes lucrative speculations in unusual areas. Researches gold, silver, coins, gems, property, antiques, interest rates, business cycles, economic advice, tax strategies, wine, guns, collector cars and more.
Cost: $180.00
8 Pages
Frequency: Weekly

ISSN: 0095-294X
Founded in: 1962
*Mailing list available for rent*at $170 per M
Printed in 2 colors on matte stock

8299 **Fund Directions**
Financial Communications Company
225 Park Avenue S
New York, NY 10003
212-953-3500
800-715-9195; *Fax:* 212-224-3699
customerservice@iinews.com;
www.funddirections.com
Colin Minnihan, Publisher
Wendy Connett, Executive Editor
Amy Cohen, Managing Editor
Kevin Francella, Plant Manager
Kim Lemmonds, Marketing Director
Trends in the rapidly changing fund environment and analysis of key issues in fund governance.
Frequency: Monthly
Circulation: 2500

8300 **Futures Market Alert**
Robbins Trading Company
8700 W Bryn Mawr Ave
Seventh Floor, S Tower
Chicago, IL 60631-3530
773-380-9700
800-453-4444; *Fax:* 773-380-9701
info@robbinstrading.com;
www.rabjohnsnef.com
Reginold Rabjohns, Partner
Covers futures trading.

8301 **Global Money Management**
Institutional Investor
225 Park Ave S
7th Floor
New York, NY 10003-1605
212-224-3300
800-543-4444; *Fax:* 212-224-3197
iieditor@institutionalinvestor.com;
www.institutionalinvestor.com
Christopher Brown, President/CEO
Deirdre Brennan, Managing Editor
Stuart Wise, Senior Editor
Nick t Ferris, Group Marketing Director
Money management news. Accepts advertising.
Cost: $11.95
Frequency: Fortnightly
Founded in: 1967

8302 **Gold Newsletter**
Blanchard and Company
2400 Jefferson Hwy
Suite 600
New Orleans, LA 70121-3838
504-835-0029
800-877-8847; *Fax:* 504-837-4884
gnlmail@jeffersoncompanies.com;
www.neworleansconference.com
James Blanchard, President
Brien Lundin, CEO
Offers information and news for the financial community on stocks, bonds and investment opportunities.
Cost: $198.00
Frequency: Monthly
Founded in: 1971

8303 **Government Affairs Bulletin**
Financial Services Roundtable
1001 Pennsylvania Ave Nw
Suite 500 S
Washington, DC 20004-2508
202-628-2455; *Fax:* 202-289-1903
info@fsround.org; www.fsround.org
Steve Bartlett, CEO
Frequency: Monthly

8304 **Government Finance Officers Association Newsletter**
Government Finance Officers Association
203 N La Salle St
Suite 2700
Chicago, IL 60601-1216
312-977-9700; *Fax:* 312-977-4806
inquiry@gfoa.org; www.gfoa.org
Jeffrey L Esser, Executive Director
Karen Utterback, Editor/Research & Consulting
Rebecca Russum, Senior Editor Technical Services
Barbara Mollo, Director Operations & Marketing
John Jurkash, CFO/Financial Administration
The purpose of the Government Finance Officers Association is to enhance and promote the professional management of governments for the public benefit by identifying and developing financial policies and practices and promoting them through education, training and leadership. Membership includes a twice-monthly newsletter in addition to specialty newsletters on cash management, accounting, auditing, and financial reporting.
17300 Pages
Founded in: 1906

8305 **HBMA Newsletter**
Healthcare Billing and Management Association
1540 South Coast Highway
Suite 203
Laguna Beach, CA 92651
877-640-4262
http://www.hbma.org
Bradley Lund, Executive Director
Paul Myers, Director of Education
Frequency: Monthly

8306 **HFMA's Leadership E-Newsletter**
Healthcare Financial Management Association
Two Westbrook Corporate Center
Suite 700
Westchester, IL 60154-5700
708-319-9600
800-252-4362; *Fax:* 708-531-0032;
www.hfma.org/leadership
Robert Fromberg, Editor-in-Chief
Maggie Van Dyke, Product Manager & Editor
Chris Burke, Advertising Manager
Kurt Belisle, Sponsorhip Manager
Showcases examples of how leading healthcare organizations are driving down costs, enhancing quality, and collaborating across disciplines and care sites. The initiative highlightes innovative providers. Subscription includes a twice-yearly print publication, monthly e-newsletter, webcasts, and exclusive invites.
Frequency: Monthly
Circulation: 32900

8307 **HFMA's The Business of Caring**
Healthcare Financial Management Association
Two Westbrook Corporate Center
Suite 700
Westchester, IL 60154-5700
708-319-9600
800-252-4362; *Fax:* 708-531-0032;
www.hfma.org/boc
Robert Fromberg, Editor-in-Chief
Maggie Van Dyke, Product Manager & Editor
Chris Burke, Advertising Manager
Kurt Belisle, Sponsorhip Manager
Helps nurse managers navigate the business side of health care to become successful hospital leaders. Topics discussed include: budgeting, workforce management, cost containment, and IT implementation. Available Free Online.
Frequency: Quarterly

8308 **Hedge Fund Alert**
Harrison Scott Publications
5 Marine View Plz
Suite 301
Hoboken, NJ 07030-5722
201-386-1491; *Fax:* 201-659-4141
info@hspnews.com; www.hspnews.com
Andy Albert, Owner
Tom Ferris, Editor
Howard Kapiloff, Managing Editor
Barbara Eannace, Advertising Director
Michelle Lebowitz, Director
A weekly newsletter on the securitization of consumer and corporate receivables.
Cost: $2097.00
10 Pages
Frequency: Weekly
Circulation: 500
ISSN: 1520-3700
Printed in 4 colors on matte stock

8309 **High Yield Report**
American Banker-Bond Buyer
1 State St
27th Floor
New York, NY 10004-1561
212-803-8450
800-367-3989; *Fax:* 212-843-9624;
www.sourcemedia.com
Jim Malkin, CEO
Mario DiUbaldi, Director of Sales
Melissa Sefic, Director of Sales
The only financial publication dealing exclusively with high yield corporate debt and distressed bank debt.
Cost: $795.00
Frequency: Weekly
Circulation: 350

8310 **Housing Finance Report**
National Assn. of Local Housing Finance Agencies
2025 M St Nw
Suite 800
Washington, DC 20036-2422
202-367-1197; *Fax:* 202-367-2197;
www.noca.org
Greg Brown, Editor
Karen Thompson, Production Manager
This newsletter covers major developments in housing finance in the Congress, federal agencies and private sector. It also gives highlights new and innovative activities of ALHFA members.
Circulation: 450
Founded in: 1982

8311 **IBC's Money Fund Report**
IBC Financial Data
1 Research Dr
Westborough, MA 01581-3922
508-616-5567; *Fax:* 508-616-5511
info@imoneynet.com; www.imoneynet.com/
Kenneth Bohlin, Publisher
Peter Crane, Editor
Randy Wood, CEO
Claudia Missert, marketin
Compiles yield, average maturity and portfolio data for each money fund along with summary information for more than a dozen categories.
Cost: $3125.00
Frequency: Weekly
Circulation: 200
Founded in: 1975
Printed in 2 colors on matte stock

8312 **IE News: Financial Services**
Institute of Industrial Engineers
25 Technology Pkwy S
Suite 150
Norcross, GA 30092-2946

770-449-0461; *Fax:* 770-263-8532

Offers full coverage of the financial community pertaining to engineering and industrial corporations.

8313 **IHS Haystack Standard Standards**
Information Handling Services
15 Inverness Way E
Englewood, CO 80112-5710

303-790-0600
800-525-7052; *Fax:* 303-754-3940;
www.ihs.com

Jerre L Stead, CEO
Michael Armstrong, Director
Frequency: Daily

8314 **IPO Reporter**
Securities Data Publishing
1290 6th Avenue
36th Floor
New York, NY 10104-0101

212-765-5311; *Fax:* 212-957-0420

Ted Weissberg, Group Publisher

Reliable news, data and analysis. Provides the most comprehensive coverage available, including a detailed calendar of upcoming deals; new IPOs filled with the SEC; valuation information; comaparison data; company name and locationas well as names of underwriters, auditors and counsels.
Frequency: Weekly

8315 **IRA Reporter**
Universal Pensions
PO Box 979
Brainerd, MN 56401-0979

218-855-0565
800-346-3860; *Fax:* 218-829-4814

Thomas G Anderson, President
Jennifer M Norquist, Editor

Discusses IRS rulings, regulations, legislation and other industry news and trends relating to IRA's.
Cost: $115.00
8 Pages
Frequency: Monthly
Printed in on glossy stock

8316 **ISDA Newsletter**
International Swaps and Derivatives Association
360 Madison Ave
16th Floor
New York, NY 10017-7126

212-901-6000; *Fax:* 212-901-6001
isda@isda.org; www.isda.org

Robert Pickel, CEO
Ruth Ainslie, Director Communications
Corrine Gerasley, Director Administration
Frequency: 5/year

8317 **Insurance M&A Newsletter**
SNL Securities
One SNL Plaza
PO Box 2124
Charlottesville, VA 22902

434-977-1600; *Fax:* 434-977-4466
subscriptions@snl.com; www.snl.com

L Todd Vencil, Editor
Reid Nagle, Chief Operating Officer
Nick Cafferillo, Chief Operating Officer
Adam Hall, Managing Director

For investment bankers, analysts, insurance investors, insurance company executives and insurance regulators. Features in-depth articles and the latest financial information on insurance mergers and acquisitions activity.
Cost: $998.00
15 Pages
Frequency: Fortnightly
Founded in: 1987

8318 **Interactive Mobile Investor**
Kagan World Media
126 Clock Tower Place
Carmel, CA 93923-8746

831-624-1536; *Fax:* 831-625-3225
info@kagan.com; www.kagan.com

George Niesen, Editor
Tom Johnson, Marketing Manager
Cost: $945.00
Frequency: Monthly

8319 **Interactive TV Investor**
Kagan World Media
126 Clock Tower Place
Carmel, CA 93923-8746

831-624-1536; *Fax:* 831-625-3225
info@kagan.com; www.kagan.com

George Niesen, Editor
Tom Johnson, Marketing Manager
Cost: $895.00
Frequency: Monthly

8320 **International Financier Newsletter**
International Society of Financiers
PO Box 398
Naples, NC 28760

828-698-7805; *Fax:* 828-698-7806;
www.insofin.com

Ronald I Gershen, Chairman/President
Frequency: Monthly

8321 **International Securitization & Structured Finance**
WorldTrade Executive
2250 Main Street Suite 100
PO Box 761
Concord, MA 01742-761

978-287-0301; *Fax:* 978-287-0302
info@wtexec.com; www.wtexec.com

Jill McKenna, Production Manager
Gary Brown, CEO
Scott stutbar, Editor
John Margel, Marketing
Heather Margel, Circulation Manager

A twice monthly report devoted exclusively to asset-backed securities in international markets. Covers all aspects of international asset-backed securitization, including innovative product trends, issuer considerations, regulatory matters, and tax and accounting considerations. Examines what is working in emerging markets and spotlights unique US transactions.
Cost: $1333.00

8322 **International Wealth Success**
PO Box 1866
Merrick, NY 11566

516-378-3922
800-323-0548; *Fax:* 516-766-5919

Tyler G Hicks, Publisher

Monthly newsletter giving sources and techniques for financing a variety of small businesses - import-export, mail order, real estate, home-based activities, etc. Gives specific, hands-on methods for beginners to start and own a successful business of their own.
Cost: $24.00
16 Pages
Frequency: Monthly
Mailing list available for rent: 100 M names at $75 per M
Printed in 2 colors on matte stock

8323 **Internet Media Investor**
Kagan World Media
126 Clock Tower Place
Carmel, CA 93923-8746

831-624-1536; *Fax:* 831-625-3225
info@kagan.com; www.kagan.com

George Niesen, Editor
Tom Johnson, Marketing Manager
Cost: $945.00
Frequency: Monthly

8324 **Investing in Crisis**
KCI Communications
1750 Old Meadow Road
Suite 301
McLean, VA 22102

703-905-8000
800-832-2330; *Fax:* 703-905-8100
service@kci-com.com;
www.kcicommunications.com

Allie Ash Jr, Publisher

Offers information on investments, low-risk bonds, stocks and campaigns for businesses in times of economic survival.
Cost: $195.00
80 Pages

8325 **Investment Dealers' Digest**
Thomson Financial Publishing
195 Broadway
Suite 4
New York, NY 10007-3124

646-822-2000; *Fax:* 646-822-2800;
www.thomson.com

Elaine Yadlon, Plant Manager
James Smith, Chief Operating Officer

Corporation financing, market conditions, financial techniques and organizational strategies.
Frequency: Weekly
Circulation: 6255

8326 **Investment News**
Crain Communications Inc
711 3rd Ave
Suite 3
New York, NY 10017-9214

212-210-0171; *Fax:* 212-210-0237
info@crain.com; www.investmentnews.com

Rance Crain, President

Provides news vital to their businesses, including news affecting their clients investments and reports about the growing financial advisory industry and the companies that serve it.
Frequency: Weekly
Circulation: 61000
Founded in: 1916

8327 **Investment Quality Trends**
IQ Trends
2888 Loker Avenue East
Suite 116
Carlsbad, CA 92010

866-927-5250; *Fax:* 866-927-5251
info@iqtrends.com; www.iqtrends.com

Michael Minney, Publisher
Kelley Wright, Managing Editor
Geraldine Weiss, Publisher Emeritus

Investment newsletter specializing in high-quality, divident-paying blue chip stocks, macro-economics, and market outlook.
Cost: $310.00
12 Pages
Frequency: Bi-monthly
Founded in: 1966

8328 **Investment Recovery Association**
638 W 39th Street
Kansas City, MO 64111

816-561-5323
800-728-2272; *Fax:* 816-561-1991
ira@invrecovery.org; www.invrecovery.org

David Rupert CMIR, President
Al Kidney CMIR, VP

Helps fulfill an important role by bringing people together from disparate industries...all focused on sharing best IR practices and improving the knowledge and skills necessary to properly perform the wide-ranging responsibilities required of investment recovery practitioners.
Cost: $300.00
16 Pages
Frequency: Monthly
Circulation: 900

8329 **Investor Relations Newsletter**
Kennedy Information
1 Pheonix Mill Lane
Floor 3
Petersborough, NH 03458

603-924-1006
800-531-0007
bookstore@kennedyinfo.com;
www.kennedyinfo.com

Gerald Murray, Editor

Provides practical, hands on strategy and tactics for the investor relations professional.
Cost: $295.00
Frequency: Monthly
ISSN: 1535-5802
Founded in: 1970

8330 **John Bollinger's Capital Growth Letter**
Bollinger Capital Management
Po Box 3358
Manhattan Beach, CA 90266-1358

310-798-8855
800-888-8400; *Fax:* 310-798-8858
bbands@bollingerbands.com;
www.bollingerbands.com

John Bollinger, Owner

Covers stocks, bonds, precious metals, commodities, the dollar and the international markets. Utilizes a technically driven asset allocation approach and investment recommendations. The online service is a monthly newsletter with a weekly update.
Cost: $300.00
12 Pages
Frequency: Monthly
Circulation: 500
Founded in: 1980
Printed in 2 colors

8331 **John Bollinger's Group Power**
Bollinger Capital Management
Po Box 3358
Manhattan Beach, CA 90266-1358

310-798-8855
800-888-8400; *Fax:* 310-798-8855
BBands@BollingerBands.com;
www.bollingerbands.com

John Bollinger, Owner
Dorit Kehr, Contact

Electronic daily newsletter available everyday via email or on Bollinger's home page. Provides group analysis using a group structure, provides a wide array of marketing statistics designed to assist the investor in making market timing and investment decisions.
Frequency: Daily

8332 **Jumbo Rate News**
Bauer Financial
Gables International Plaza
PO Box 143520
Coral Gables, FL 33114

800-388-6686; *Fax:* 800-230-9569
customerservice@bauerfinancial.com;
www.bauerfinancial.com

Karen L Dorway, President/CEO
Caroline Jervey, Editor

Each issue contains over 1,000 separate Jumbo CD rates in seven categories from over 200 creditworthy banks and thrifts nationwide. Includes star ratings, wire transfer fees, deposit requirements and financial highlights for each institution.
Cost: $445.00
Frequency: Weekly
Founded in: 1983
Printed in 2 colors on matte stock

8333 **Kagan Media Investor**
Kagan World Media
126 Clock Tower Place
Carmel, CA 93923-8746

831-624-1536
800-307-2529; *Fax:* 831-625-3225
info@kagan.com; www.kagan.com

George Niesen, Editor
Tom Johnson, Marketing Manager
Robin Flynn, Senior VP

News of the Kagan Media Investor. Three month trial available.
Cost: $1195.00
Frequency: Monthly
Founded in: 1969

8334 **Kagan Media Money**
Kagan World Media
1 Lower Ragsdale Dr
Bldg 1 Suite 130
Monterey, CA 93940-5749

831-624-1536; *Fax:* 831-625-3225
info@kagan.com; www.kagan.com

George Niesen, Editor
Harvey Kraft, Marketing Manager
Tim Baskerville, CEO
Harvey Kraft, Circulation Manager
Sandy Borthwick, Communications Manager

Analysts dissect deals, anticipate trends, project revenues, track financings and value the debt and equity of hundreds of privately held and publicly traded advertising, broadcasting, cable TV, digital TV, home video, Internet media, motion picture, newspaper, pay TV, professional sports and wireless telecommunications companies in the US and abroad.
Cost: $1245.00
Frequency: Monthly
Founded in: 1969

8335 **Kagan Music Investor**
Kagan World Media
126 Clock Tower Place
Carmel, CA 93923-8746

831-624-1536; *Fax:* 831-625-3225
info@kagan.com; www.kagan.com

George Niesen, Editor
Tom Johnson, Marketing Manager

News and analysis for investors in the music industry.
Cost: $945.00
Frequency: Monthly

8336 **Kiplinger Tax Letter**
Kiplinger Washington Editors
1729 H St Nw
Washington, DC 20006-3924

202-887-6400
800-544-0155; *Fax:* 202-778-8976
sub.services@kiplinger.com;
www.kiplinger.com

Knight Kiplinger, VP
Steven D Ivins, Editor

Biweekly tax letter for investors, business owners and managers. Covers current developments in Congress, IRS and the courts.
Cost: $54.00
4 Pages
Circulation: 125000
Mailing list available for rent
Printed in one color

8337 **Latin American Finance & Capital Markets**
WorldTrade Executive
PO Box 761
Concord, MA 01742-0761

978-287-0301; *Fax:* 978-287-0302
info@wtexec.com; www.wtexec.com

Alison French, Production Manager

An action-oriented report on treasury management, tax, legal, accounting and other operational issues that impact doing business in Latin America. Provides an independent assessment of local capital markets.
Cost: $595.00
Frequency: Twice monthly

8338 **Limelight eNewsletter**
Wall Street Teechnology Association
521 Newman Springs Road
Suite 12
Lincroft, NJ 07738

732-530-8808; *Fax:* 732-530-0020
info@wsta.org; www.wsta.org

Phyllis Lampell, Executive Director
JoAnn Cooper, Executive Director
Frequency: Monthly
Circulation: 14000

8339 **Long Term Investing**
Concept Publishing
5202 Humphreys Road
Lake Park, GA 31636

229-257-0367; *Fax:* 229-219-1097;
www.newconceptspublishing.com

Jim Dovan, Publisher
David Coleman, Editor
Madris Gutierrez, Editor-in-Chief
Andrea DePasture, Senior Editor

Offers full coverage of long term stocks, bonds and investments.
Cost: $98.00
12 Pages
Frequency: Monthly
Circulation: 600
Founded in: 1998
Printed in one color on matte stock

8340 **MAR/Hedge**
Managed Account Reports
1250 Broadway
26th Floor
New York, NY 10001

212-213-6202
800-638-2525; *Fax:* 212-213-1870
subs@marhedge.com; www.marhedge.com

Greg Newton, Publisher
Randall Devere, Editor-in-Chief
Lisa McErlane, Director of Marketing
Gary Lynch, President/Publisher

The first newsletter to cover the field of hedge funds in its entirety with industry news, in-depth articles and reviews of hedge fund managers and fund of funds and rankings of these managers and fund of funds.
Cost: $1195.00
16 Pages
Frequency: Monthly

Circulation: 300
Founded in: 1994
Printed in 2 colors on matte stock

8341 **Managing 401(k) Plans**
Institute of Management and Administration
1 Washington Park
Suite 1300
Newark, NJ 07102
212-244-0360; *Fax:* 973-622-0595;
www.ioma.com
The definitive resource for HR and Financial Department managers looking to run the best plan for their company.
Cost: $429.00

8342 **Managing Credit, Receivable & Collections**
Institute of Management and Administration
1 Washington Park
Suite 1300
Newark, NJ 07102
212-244-0360; *Fax:* 973-622-0595;
www.ioma.com
Accelerate receivables and learn what technology and techniques are working best.
Cost: $269.00
Frequency: Monthly

8343 **Media Mergers & Acquisitions**
Kagan World Media
126 Clock Tower Place
Carmel, CA 93923-8746
831-624-1536; *Fax:* 831-624-5882
info@kagan.com; www.kagan.com
George Niesen, Editor
Tom Johnson, Marketing Manager
Where it all comes together. Exclusive scorecard of deals done by media companies. Dollar amounts, multiples paid, trends captured in succinct summaries of complex transactions. Three month trial available.
Cost: $795.00
Frequency: Monthly

8344 **Merger Strategy Report**
SNL Securities
PO Box 2124
Charlottesvle, VA 22902-2124
434-977-1600; *Fax:* 434-977-4466;
www.snlnet.com
Erik Winthrow, Editor
John Minor, Editor
Reid Nagle, Publisher
Mark Outlaw, Advertising Director
Nick Cafferillo, Chief Operating Officer
For bank and thrift executives, with a regional M&A recap; list of deals; ranking of advisors and lawyers.
5 Pages
Frequency: Quarterly
Founded in: 1995

8345 **Mergers & Acquisitions Executive Compensation Review**
SNL Securities
One SNL Plaza
PO Box 2124
Charlottesvle, VA 22902-2124
434-977-1600; *Fax:* 434-977-4466
isales@snl.com; www.snl.com
John Minor, Editor
Michael Spears, Advertising
Mike Scott, Mergers/Acquisitions
Nick Cafferillo, Chief Operating Officer
Adam Hall, Managing Director
For banks, thrifts, investment banks, law firms that advise on mergers, executives at banks expecting to merge and personnel and compensation specialists. Provides compensation information on the executives of banks that have entered into agreements to be acquired.
Cost: $495.00
10 Pages
Frequency: Monthly
Founded in: 1987

8346 **Micro Ticker Report**
Waters Information Services
PO Box 2248
Binghamton, NY 13902-2248
607-770-8535; *Fax:* 607-723-7151
Dennis Waters, Publisher
Andrew Delaney, Editor
Covers the financial quotation industry.

8347 **Money Management Letter**
Institutional Investor
225 Park Ave S
12th Floor
New York, NY 10003-1605
212-224-3300; *Fax:* 212-224-3197
iieditor@institutionalinvestor.com;
www.institutionalinvestor.com
Christopher Brown, CEO
Tom Lamont, Editor
This newsletter offers businesses information on investments, stocks, bonds, low-risk campaigns and financial planning opportunities.

8348 **Mortgaged Backed Securities Letter**
American Banker-Bond Buyer
1 State St
26th Floor
New York, NY 10004-1483
212-803-8350; *Fax:* 212-843-9600;
www.securitiesindustry.com
John Del Mauro, VP
Tom Steinert-Threlkeld, Director
Provides coverage of structured finance and includes comprehensive listings of asset backed securities.
Frequency: Weekly
Circulation: 4200

8349 **Motion Picture Investor**
Kagan World Media
126 Clock Tower Place
Carmel, CA 93923-8746
831-624-1536; *Fax:* 831-625-3225
info@kagan.com; www.kagan.com/
George Niesen, Editor
Tom Johnson, Marketing Manager
Cost: $845.00
Frequency: Monthly
Founded in: 1969

8350 **NACHA Operating Rules & Guidelines**
NACHA: The Electronic Payments Association
13450 Sunrise Valley Drive
Suite 100
Herndon, VA 20171
703-561-1100; *Fax:* 703-787-0996
info@nacha.org; www.nacha.org
Janet O Estep, CEO
Marcie Haitema, Chairperson
Reflects the results of the Rules Simplification initiative. PReviously organized around major topics, the simplified Rules framework is structured around the rights and responsibilities of participants in the ACH Network.
Cost: $78.00
Frequency: Annual

8351 **NADOA Newsletter**
National Association of Division Order Analysts
2805 Oak Trail Court
Suite 6312
Arlington, TX 76016
972-715-4489
administrator@nadoa.org; www.nadoa.org
Lynn S McCord, Administrator
Frequency: Bi-Monthly

8352 **NALHFA Newsletter**
National Association of Local Housing Finance
2025 M St Nw
Suite 800
Washington, DC 20036-2422
202-367-1197; *Fax:* 202-367-2197
john_murphy@nalhfa.org; www.noca.org
John C Murphy, Executive Director
Scott Lynch, Association Manager
Kim McKinon, Coordinator Membership
Frequency: Bi-Monthly

8353 **NAPFA Newslink**
National Association of Personal Financial Advisor
3250 N Arlington Heights Road
Suite 109
Arlington Heights, IL 60004
847-483-5400
800-366-2732; *Fax:* 847-483-5415
info@napfa.org; www.napfa.org
Ellen Turf, CEO
Margery Wasserman, Director Conference
Frequency: Quarterly

8354 **NASDAQ Subscriber Bulletin**
National Association of Securities Dealers
1212newyork anenue
suite950
Washington, DC 20005-1516
202-371-5535; *Fax:* 202-371-5536
Margo Porter, Publisher
Richard DeLouise, Editor
Pamela Anderson, Executive
Developments in the NASDAQ market.

8355 **NATRI Newsletter**
National Association for Treasurers of Religious
8824 Cameron Street
Silver Springs, MD 20910
301-587-7776; *Fax:* 301-589-2897;
www.natri.org
Laura Reicks, Publisher
Lorelle Elcock, Associate Director Finance
Frequency: Bi-Monthly

8356 **NICSA News**
National Investment Company Service Association
36 Washington Street
Suite 70
Wellesley Hills, MA 02481
781-416-7200; *Fax:* 781-416-7065
info@nicsa.org; www.nicsa.org
Barbara V Weidlich, President
Keith Dropkin, Director Operations
Doris Jaimes, Registrar
Sheila Kobaly, Events Manager
Chris Ludent, IT Manager
Frequency: Quarterly

8357 **National Mortgage News**
Thomson Financial Publishing

1 State St
27th Floor
New York, NY 10004-1481

212-825-8445
800-235-5552; *Fax:* 212-292-5216;
www.nationalmortgagenews.com/

Timothy Murphy, Group Publisher
Mark Fogarty, Editorial Director
Paul Muolo, M&A/Data Editor
Timothy Reifschneider, Advertising Director
Jose Thomas, Manager

Mortgage information, legislation and news.
Cost: $228.00
Frequency: Weekly
Circulation: 5000
Printed in 2 colors on newsprint stock

8358 Network Newsletter
Society for Information Management
401 N Michigan Avenue
Chicago, IL 60611

312-215-5190; *Fax:* 312-245-1081;
www.simnet.org

Jim Luisi, Executive Director
Frequency: Bi-Monthly

8359 Newspaper Investor
Kagan World Media
1 Lower Ragsdale Dr
Building One, Suite 130
Monterey, CA 93940-5749

831-624-1536
831-625-3225; *Fax:* 831-625-3225
info@kagan.com; www.kagan.com

Tim Baskerville, President
Tom Johnson, Marketing Manager
Cost: $845.00
Frequency: Monthly
Founded in: 1969

8360 OTC Chart Manual
Standard & Poor's Corporation
55 Water St
New York, NY 10041-0003

212-438-1000; *Fax:* 212-438-0299;
www.standardandpoors.com

Deven Sharma, President

Charts on over 800 OTC stocks.

8361 Origination News
4709 Golf Road
Skokie, IL 60076

847-676-9600
800-321-3373; *Fax:* 847-933-8101
custserv@accuitysolutions.com;
www.accuitysolutions.com

Timothy Murphy, Group Publisher
Mark Fogarty, Editorial Director
Jose Thomas, Manager
Malcolm Taylor, Managing Director

Information for mortgage industry executives on mortgage brokers, mortgage bankers and mortgage executives in commercial banks, savings banks, savings and loan associations and credit unions.
Cost: $78.00
Frequency: Monthly

8362 Pawnbroker News
National Pawnbrokers Association
P.O.Box 508
Keller, TX 76244-0508

817-491-4554; *Fax:* 817-491-8770
info@NationalPawnbrokers.org;
www.nationalpawnbrokers.org

Bob Benedict, CAE, Executive Director
Emmett Murphy, Director
Teresa Congleton, Administrative Assistant
Frequency: 8/year

8363 Pink Comparison Report
SNL Securities
PO Box 2124
Charlottesvle, VA 22902-2124

434-977-1600; *Fax:* 434-977-4466;
www.snlnet.com

Maria Moyer, Editor
Reid Nagle, Publisher
Mark LaBua, Subscription Manager
Mark Outlaw, Advertising Director
Nick Cafferillo, Chief Operating Officer

For CEOs, CFOs and IRCs of banks. Compares a subscribing bank or thrift's consolidated financial and market performance to other banks and thrifts chosen by the subscriber and banks and thrifts of similar asset size and location.
40 Pages
Frequency: Quarterly

8364 Private Equity Week
Securities Data Publishing
40 W 57th St
New York, NY 10019-4001

212-484-4701; *Fax:* 212-956-0112;
www.sdponline.com

Jennifer Reed, Editor-in-Chief
Edward Cortese, Marketing Executive

News of the past week and forecast of the weeks to come for investors.
Cost: $780.00
Frequency: Weekly

8365 Private Placement Letter
Securities Data Publishing
1290 6th Avenue
36th Floor
New York, NY 10104-101

212-765-5311; *Fax:* 212-957-0420
custserv@sourcemedia.com;
www.privateplacementletter.com/

John Toth, Publisher
Ronald Cooper, Editor-in-Chief
Lauren Klopacs, Marketing Manager
Mark Cialdella, Circulation Manager
David Harkey, Advertising Manager

Highly sophisticated information on the debt private placement market including senior and mezzanine level debt.
Cost: $1395.00

8366 Proceedings of the National Conference on Planned Giving
National Committee on Planned Giving
233 S McCrea St
Suite 400
Indianapolis, IN 46225-1068

317-269-6274; *Fax:* 317-269-6276;
www.ncpg.org

Tanya Howe Johnson, President
Sandra Kerr, Director Government Education
Barbara Owens, Director Membership
Kathryn J Ramsey, Director Meetings
Kurt Reusze, Manager Education/Technology
Frequency: Annual

8367 Quality Performance Report
Managed Account Reports
220 5th Avenue
19th Floor
New York, NY 10001-7708

212-213-6202
800-638-2525; *Fax:* 212-213-6273;
www.marhedge.com

Randall Devere, Editor-in-Chief
Lois Peltz, Editor
Gary Lynch, President
Lisa McErlane, Marketing

The pre-eminent source of qualitative and quantitative information on global managed derivatives. Delivers in-depth analysis on the performance of the trading advisors in MAR's qualified database. Now covering over 500 trading advisors and programs.
Cost: $299.00
Frequency: Quarterly
Circulation: 400
Founded in: 1913
Printed in 2 colors on matte stock

8368 REIT Daily Fax
SNL Securities
One SNL Plaza
PO Box 2124
Charlottesvle, VA 22902-2124

434-977-1600; *Fax:* 434-293-0407
isales@snl.com; www.snl.com

Amy Woolard, Editor
Nick Cafferillo, Chief Operating Officer
Alan Zimmerman, Publisher
Pat LaBua, Customer Service Director
Adam Hall, Managing Director

Newsletter designed specifically for REIT industry professionals and investors. Features important industry events, condensed news stories, recent capital offerings and the latest market information.
4 Pages
Frequency: Daily
Founded in: 1987

8369 REIT Performance Graph
SNL Securities
One SNL Plaza
PO Box 2124
Charlottesvle, VA 22902-2124

434-977-1600; *Fax:* 434-977-4466
subscriptions@snl.com; www.snl.com

Steve Arnold, Vice Chairman, CFO
Chandler Spears, Editor
Keven Lindemann, Real Estate
Gregg Amonette, General Media
Nick Cafferillo, Chief Operating Officer

For publicly traded REITs and REIT service providers. Compares the investment performance of a publicly traded REIT to a specific SNL index or to a selected peer group and the appropriate broad multi-industry index. Covers a 5-year period or the period beginning with the IPO date.
Cost: $399.00
1 Pages
Founded in: 1987

8370 Real Estate Alert
Harrison Scott Publications
5 Marine View Plz
#301
Hoboken, NJ 07030-5722

201-386-1491; *Fax:* 201-659-4141
info@hspnews.com; www.hspnews.com

Andy Albert, Owner
Bob Mura, Editor
Barbara Eannaci, Marketing Manager
Michelle Lebowitz, Director

Information on investment opportunities in institutional grade commercial real estate, includes sales acquisitions and personnel changes.
Cost: $1597.00
Frequency: Weekly
Circulation: 650
Founded in: 1989

8371 Real Estate Finance Today
Mortgage Bankers Association of America
1919 Pennsylvania Avenue NW
Washington, DC 20006-3404

202-557-2700
info@mortgagebankers.org;
www.mortgagebankers.org

Information on anticipating industry trends, regulatory changes, economic outlook, federal and

state legislation and trends in the secondary mortgage industry.
Cost: $100.00
Frequency: Monthly
Circulation: 1500
Founded in: 1939

8372 Real-Estate Alert
Harrison Scott Publications
5 Marine View Plz
Suite 301
Hoboken, NJ 07030-5722

201-386-1491; *Fax:* 201-659-4141
info@hspnews.com; www.hspnews.com

Andy Albert, Owner
Tom Ferris, Director
Michelle Lebowitz, Director

A weekly newsletter on the securitization of consumer and corporate receivables.
Cost: $1497.00
10 Pages
Frequency: Weekly
Circulation: 600
ISSN: 1520-3700
Printed in 4 colors on matte stock

8373 Reducing Benefits Costs
Institute of Management and Administration
1 Washington Park
Suite 1300
Newark, NJ 07102

212-244-0360; *Fax:* 973-622-0595;
www.ioma.com

Provides information on controlling benefit costs.
Cost: $245.00
16 Pages
Frequency: Monthly

8374 Regional Economic Digest
Federal Reserve Bank of Kansas City
925 Grand Avenue
Kansas City, MO 64198-0001

816-881-2970
800-333-1010; *Fax:* 816-881-2569
http://ideas.repec.org

Thomas Davis, Publisher
Bob Regan, Editor

A review of financial and economic conditions in the Tenth District. Includes articles of regional interest, statistics on District commercial banks and the area economy and results of a survey of agricultural credit conditions.
32 Pages

8375 Regulatory Risk Monitor
United Communications Group
11300 Rockville Pike
Street 1100
Rockville, MD 20852-3030

301-287-2700; *Fax:* 301-816-8945
webmaster@ucg.com; www.ucg.com

Benny Dicecca, President

Updates banking officials, credit union, compliance officers, attorneys and auditors with current independent news and guidance.
Founded in: 1970

8376 Report on Financial Analysis, Planning & Reporting
Institute of Management and Administration
1 Washington Park
Suite 1300
Newark, NJ 07102

212-244-0360; *Fax:* 973-622-0595;
www.ioma.com

FARP regularly covers performance measurements effective use of new FASB, IRS and SEC financial and accounting requirements for all industries, shows managers the best way to evaluate business opportunities, how to read and evaluate capital budgets, earbug reports and analysts see the big picture through the use of new financial tools such as Economic Value Assets and Shareholder Valuations models.
Cost: $269.00
Frequency: Monthly

8377 Retirement Plans Bulletin
Universal Pensions
PO Box 979
Brainerd, MN 56401

218-855-0565
800-346-3860; *Fax:* 218-829-4814

Thomas G Anderson, President
Jennifer M Norquist, Editor

Digests IRS technical jargon on IRA's and qualified plans and translates it into understandable articles and advice for financial organizations.
Cost: $89.00
10 Pages
Frequency: Monthly
Printed in 2 colors on glossy stock

8378 SNL Bank M&A DataSource
SNL Securities
One SNL Plaza
PO Box 2124
Charlottesvle, VA 22902-2124

434-977-1600; *Fax:* 434-977-4466
subscriptions@snl.com; www.snl.com

John Minor, Publisher
Eric Hoffer, Editor
John McCune, Banks/Thrifts Manager
Michael Spears, Advertising
Nick Cafferillo, Chief Operating Officer

For investment bankers, investment companies, banks, thrifts, consultants and broker/dealers. Includes all merger and acquisition activity involving a bank or thrift as a buyer or seller.
Founded in: 1987

8379 SNL Branch Migration DataSource
SNL Securities
PO Box 2124
Charlottesvle, VA 22902-2124

434-977-1600; *Fax:* 434-977-4466;
www.snlnet.com

Melissa Hobson, Editor
John Minor, Editor
Reid Nagle, Publisher
Mark Outlaw, Advertising Director
Nick Cafferillo, Chief Operating Officer

For investment bankers, investment companies, banks, thrifts, consultants and regulatory agencies. Re-assigns bank and thrift branch deposits to account for all M&A activity that has occurred since the last regulatory release.
Frequency: Annual
Founded in: 1991

8380 SNL Corporate Performance Graphs for Banks
SNL Securities
One SNL Plaza
PO Box 2124
Charlottesvle, VA 22902-2124

434-977-1600; *Fax:* 434-977-4466
subscriptions@snl.com; www.snl.com

Will Wick, Editor
James Record, Editor
John McCune, Banks/Thrifts Manager
Michael Spears, Advertising
Nick Cafferillo, Chief Operating Officer

For publicly traded banks, law firms, accountants and consulting firms. Includes a 5-year comparison of an institution's stock to both a selected peer group index and a broad multi-industry index.
1 Pages
Founded in: 1987

8381 SNL Financial DataSource
SNL Securities
One SNL Plaza
PO Box 2124
Charlottesvle, VA 22902-2124

434-977-1600; *Fax:* 434-977-4466
subscriptions@snl.com; www.snl.com

Steve Tomasi, Editor
Steve Ferguson, Editor
Edward Metz, Financial
Michael Spears, Advertising
Nick Cafferillo, Chief Operating Officer

For investment bankers, investment companies, banks, thrifts, institutional investors, consultants and broker/dealers. Available in six separate interactive modules that contain data for equity research, industry trend analysis, peer group comparisons and identification of investment and acquisition opportunities.
Founded in: 1987

8382 SNL Mutual Thrift Conversion Investors Kit
SNL Securities
One SNL Plaza
PO Box 2124
Charlottesvle, VA 22902-2124

434-977-1600; *Fax:* 434-977-4466
subscriptions@snl.com; www.snl.com

Chris Smith, Editor
Reid Nagle, Publisher
John McCune, Banks/Thrifts Manager
Michael Spears, Advertising
Nick Cafferillo, Chief Operating Officer

For thrift executives, individual investors and institutional investors. Contains a set of articles explaining the mechanics of mutual-to-stock conversion and the 'how-to' of investing, reviewing profitability of conversion investments and outlining regulatory issues that affect conversions.
Cost: $495.00
100 Pages
Frequency: Monthly
Founded in: 1987

8383 SNL Pink Quarterly
SNL Securities
PO Box 2124
Charlottesvle, VA 22902-2124

434-977-1600; *Fax:* 434-977-4466;
www.snlnet.com

Maria Moyer, Editor
Reid Nagle, Publisher
Mark Outlaw, Advertising Director
Pat LaBua, Subscription Manager
Nick Cafferillo, Chief Operating Officer

For investment companies, banks and thrifts, broker/dealers and individual investors. Contains detailed financial and market information on all banks and thrifts traded on the OTC bulletin boards and by market makers, as well as in-depth analysis of this sector.
240 Pages
Frequency: Quarterly
Founded in: 1995

8384 SNL Securities Thrift Performance Graph
SNL Financial
PO Box 2124
Charlottesvle, VA 22902-2124

434-977-1600; *Fax:* 434-977-4466;
www.snlnet.com

Reid Nagle, Publisher
John Racine, Editor
Mark Outlaw, Advertising Director
Pat Labua, Subscription Manager
Jeff Sternberg, Production Editor

SNL Securities is a research and publishing company that focuses on banks, thrifts, REITs insurance companies, and specialized, financial service companies. Founded in 1987, SNL securities has become the authority for information on financial institutions.

8385 SNL Securities Bank Comparison Report
SNL Securities
PO Box 2124
Charlottesvle, VA 22902-2124

434-977-1600; *Fax:* 434-977-4466;
www.snlnet.com

Mona Thompson, Editor
Dan Oakey, Editor
Keith Davis, Editor
Reid Nagle, Publisher
Nick Cafferillo, Chief Operating Officer

For CEOs, CFOs and IRCs of banks. Compares a subscribing bank's consolidated financial and market performance to that of banks and thrifts of similar asset size and location.
40 Pages
Frequency: Quarterly
Founded in: 1987

8386 SNL Securities Thrift Comparison Report
SNL Securities
PO Box 2124
Charlottesvle, VA 22902-2124

434-977-1600; *Fax:* 434-977-4466;
www.snlnet.com

Dave Spence, Editor
Reid Nagle, Publisher
Mark Outlaw, Advertising Director
Pat LaBua, Subscripton Manager
Nick Cafferillo, Chief Operating Officer

Report for CEOs, CFOs and IRCs of thrifts and major corporate stockholders. Illustrates and compares a subscribing thrift's consolidated financial and market performance to thrifts of similar asset size and location.
40 Pages
Frequency: Quarterly
Founded in: 1988

8387 Secured Leader
Commercial Finance Association
Ste 1801
7 Penn Plz
New York, NY 10001-3979

212-594-3490; *Fax:* 212-564-6053
info@cfa.com; www.cfa.com

Bruce H Jones, Executive Director
Theodore Kompa, President

Only publication devoted exclusively to the asset-based financial services industry. Editorial matter is directed toward practitioners of asset-based financing. Accepts advertising.
Cost: $56.00
76 Pages
Circulation: 5000
Founded in: 1944

8388 Securities Industry News
Source Media
1 State St
27th floor
New York, NY 10004-1561

212-803-8200
800-221-1809; *Fax:* 212-843-9608
custserv@sourcemedia.com;
www.sourcemedia.com

James M Malkin, CEO
Michael Eggebrecht, Managing Editor
Edward Hanasik, Marketing Director
Omar Asmar, Art Director
David Greenough, VP/Business Technology Group

Securities Industry News is a weekly newspaper in the global securities and financial markets that delivers original, time-critical news and analysis to senior decision-makers in charge of operations, technology, processing services, and compliance in the global securities and financial markets.
Cost: $575.00
Frequency: 42 Issues Annually

8389 Securities Week
McGraw Hill
PO Box 182604
Columbus, OH 43272

614-304-4000
877-833-5524; *Fax:* 614-759-3759
customer.service@mcgraw-hill.com;
www.mcgraw-hill.com

Michael Ocrant, Managing Editor
Harold McGraw, CEO

Information on firms and exchanges strategy plans, new hires, events and issues, as well as legislation and legal rulings impacting the securities industry.
Frequency: Weekly
Founded in: 1884

8390 Shareholder Satisfaction Survey
National Investment Company Service
36 Washington Avenue
Suite 70
Wellesley Hills, MA 02481

781-416-7200; *Fax:* 781-416-7065
info@nicsa.org; www.nicsa.org

Barbara V Weidlich, President
Keith Dropkin, Director Operations
Doris Jaimes, Registrar
Sheila Kobaly, Events Manager
Chris Ludent, IT Manager
Frequency: Annual

8391 Special Stock Report
Wall Street Transcript
67 Wall Street
9th Floor
New York, NY 10005-3701

212-952-7400
800-246-7673; *Fax:* 212-668-9842
twsteditor@twst.com; www.twst.com

Andrew Pickup, President/CEO
Doug Estadt, Online Editor
Andrew Pickup, Publisher
Jason Flatt, Marketing

Monthly stock pick based on research, interviews, and data contained in the wall st. transcript.
Cost: $399.00
Frequency: Monthly
Circulation: 7274
Founded in: 1963

8392 Specialty Lender
SNL Securities
PO Box 2124
Charlottesvle, VA 22902-2124

434-977-1600; *Fax:* 434-977-4466;
www.snlnet.com

Dave Meadors, Editor
Jim Allen, Editor
L Todd Vencil, Editor
Reid Nagle, Publisher
Nick Cafferillo, Chief Operating Officer

For executives of specialty lending companies, banks and thrifts which have specialty lending operations, heads of captive finance companies, investors, investment bankers and equity analysts. Provides news, analysis and financial and market information about specialty lenders, focusing on credit management and access to capital.
40 Pages
Frequency: Monthly
Founded in: 1996

8393 Specialty Lender Performance Graph
SNL Securities
PO Box 2124
Charlottesvle, VA 22902-2124

434-977-1600; *Fax:* 434-977-4466;
www.snlnet.com

David Meadors, Editor
Reid Nagle, Publisher
Mark Outlaw, Advertising Director
Pat LaBua, Subscription Manager
Nick Cafferillo, Chief Operating Officer

For publicly traded specialty lenders and specialty lender service providers. Compares the investment performance of a specialty lender to a specific SNL index or to a selected peer group and the appropriate broad multi-industry index. Covers a 5-year period or the period beginning with the IPO date.
Frequency: By request
Founded in: 1997

8394 Streaming Media Investor
Kagan World Media
126 Clock Tower Place
Carmel, CA 93923-8746

831-624-1536; *Fax:* 831-624-5882
info@kagan.com; www.kagan.com

George Niesen, Editor
Tom Johnson, Marketing Manager

News of the Streaming Media Investor. Three month trial available.
Cost: $895.00
Frequency: Monthly

8395 TV Program Investor
Kagan World Media
126 Clock Tower Place
Carmel, CA 93923-8746

831-624-1536
800-307-2529; *Fax:* 831-625-3225
info@kagan.com; www.kagan.com

George Niesen, Editor
Harvy Kraft, Marketing Manager
Tim Baerville, CEO/President
Robert Naylor, Circulation Manager
Cost: $895.00
Frequency: Monthly
Founded in: 1969

8396 Tax Management Compensation Planning
1250 23rd Street NW
Washington, DC 20037-1164

202-337-7240
800-223-7270; *Fax:* 202-496-6013

David McFarland, President
Glenn Davis, Managing Editor

Nearly 40 portfolios, each focusing on specific tax, labor and other aspects of qualified and non-qualified retirement plans, employee welfare benefit plans, executive compensation, employment taxes and accounting for deferred compensation. Offers practitioner-authored articles, analysis of recent developments and decisions, and insightful comments from leading practitioners on the latest planning strategies.
Cost: $837.00
Frequency: Monthly

8397 Taxpractice
Tax Analysts

6830 North
Fairfax Drive
Arlington, VA 22213-1001

703-533-4400
800-955-2444; *Fax:* 703-533-4444
webmaster@tax.org; www.tax.org

Thomas F Field, Publisher
Jill Biden, Vice President

Contains comprehensive coverage of IRS rulings, court decisions, tax law changes and other topics of interest.
Cost: $749.00
Frequency: Weekly
Circulation: 2200
Founded in: 1970

8398 **TheStreet Ratings, Inc.**
14 Wall Street
15th Floor
New York, NY 10005

212-321-5000
800-289-9222; *Fax:* 212-321-5016
letters@thestreet.com; www.thestreet.com

Dave Kansas, Editor-in-Chief

Information on what is happening on Wall Street, along with mutual fund and economic news, stock quotes, market summaries, and analyses of key indicators.
Cost: $69.95
Frequency: Daily

8399 **Thrift 13D Dictionary**
SNL Securities
PO Box 2124
Charlottesvle, VA 22902-2124

434-977-1600; *Fax:* 434-977-4466;
www.snlnet.com

Todd L Davenport, Editor
Reid Nagle, Publisher
Mark Outlaw, Advertising Director
Pat LaBua, Subscription Manager
Nick Cafferillo, Chief Operating Officer

Contains all active 13D filings and related filings for every publicly traded bank in the country, including those which trade on the pink sheets.
250 Pages
Frequency: Quarterly

8400 **Thrift Performance Graph**
SNL Securities
One SNL Plaza
PO Box 2124
Charlottesvle, VA 22902-2124

434-977-1600; *Fax:* 434-977-4466
subscriptions@snl.com; www.snl.com

Will Wick, Editor
James Record, Editor
John McCune, Banks/Thrifts Manager
Michael Spears, Advertising
Nick Cafferillo, Chief Operating Officer

Compares investment performance of a publicly traded Thrift company to a specific SNL index or to a selected peer group and the appropriate broad multi-industry index. Graph covers a 5-year period or the period beginning with the IPO date. For publicly traded thrifts, law firms, accountants and consulting firms.
1 Pages
Founded in: 1987

8401 **Trading Technology Week**
Waters Information Services
270 Lafayette St
Suite 700
New York, NY 10012-3311

212-925-6990; *Fax:* 212-925-7585
eugene.grygo@incisivemedia.com;
www.dealingwithtechnology.com

Tim Weller, CEO
Eugene Grygo, Editor
Adrian Goulbourn, Publisher
Lillian Lopez, Production Manager
Melissa Jao, Business Development Manager

Information covering the latest applications, platforms and strategies in trading room systems and proprietary execution.
Cost: $2025.00
Frequency: Weekly
Founded in: 2000

8402 **Transactions**
AACE International
209 Prairie Ave
Suite 100
Morgantown, WV 26501-5934

304-296-8444
800-858-2678; *Fax:* 304-291-5728
info@aacei.org; www.aacei.org

Andrew Dowd, Executive Director
Megan McCulla, Asst Manager
Jenny Alms, Marketing Manager
Cost: $65.00
Frequency: Monthly
Circulation: 5000
Founded in: 1956

8403 **Turning Points**
Concept Publishing
PO Box 500
York, NY 14592-500

800-836-4575
800-836-4575; *Fax:* 585-243-3148
publishing@conceptpub.com;
www.conceptpub.com

Jim Dovan, Publisher
David Coleman, Editor

Economic news.
Cost: $198.00
2 Pages
Circulation: 600
Founded in: 1974
Printed in one color on matte stock

8404 **VOD Investor**
Kagan World Media
126 Clock Tower Place
Carmel, CA 93923-8746

831-624-1536
800-307-2529; *Fax:* 831-625-3225
info@kagan.com; www.kagan.com

George Niesen, Editor
Tom Johnson, Marketing Manager
Robin Flynn, Senior VP

News of the VOD Investor. Three month trial available.
Cost: $1045.00
Frequency: Monthly
Founded in: 1969

8405 **Video Investor**
Kagan World Media
126 Clock Tower Place
Carmel, CA 93923-8746

831-624-1536; *Fax:* 831-624-5882
info@kagan.com; www.kagan.com

George Niesen, Editor
Tom Johnson, Marketing Manager

Authoritative look inside the business of renting and selling video cassettes. Exclusive estimates of retail and wholesale transactions and inventories. Tracking movies into the home. Three month trial is available.
Cost: $ 795.00
Frequency: Monthly

8406 **Wall Street Technology Association Enewsletter**
620 Shrewsbury Ave
Suite C2
Tinton Falls, NJ 07701

732-530-8808; *Fax:* 732-530-0020
info@wsta.org; www.wsta.org
Social Media: Facebook, Twitter, LinkedIn

John Killeen, President
Phyllis Lampell, Executive Director
JoAnn Cooper, Executive Director

Nonprofit educational organization that focuses on technologies, operational approaches, and business issues for the global financial community.
2000+ Members
Frequency: Monthly
Circulation: 14000+
Founded in: 1967

8407 **Water Investment Newsletter**
US Water News
230 Main St
Halstead, KS 67056-1913

316-835-2222
800-251-0046; *Fax:* 316-835-2223;
www.uswaternews.com

Thomas Bell, Owner
Toni Young, Chairman

News, features and profiles of shareholder owned water supply and treatment companies. General news on water-related investment opportunities with stock portfolio.
Cost: $140.00
8 Pages
Frequency: Monthly
ISSN: 1049-443X
Printed in one color on matte stock

8408 **Wireless Market Stats**
Kagan World Media
1 Lower Ragsdale Dr
Building One, Suite 130
Monterey, CA 93940-5749

831-624-1536
800-307-2529; *Fax:* 831-625-3225
info@kagan.com; www.kagan.com

Tim Baskerville, President
Tom Johnson, Marketing Manager

News of the Wireless Market Stats. Three month trial available.
Cost: $1095.00
Frequency: Monthly
Founded in: 1969

8409 **Wireless Telecom Investor**
Kagan World Media
1 Lower Ragsdale Dr
Bldg 1, Suite 130
Monterey, CA 93940-5749

831-624-1536
800-307-2529; *Fax:* 831-625-3225
info@kagan.com; www.kagan.com

Tim Baskerville, President
Harvey Kraft, Director of Marketing
George Niesen, Editor
Robert Naylor, Circulation Manager
Sandie Borthwick, Publisher

Exclusive analysis of private and public values of wireless telecommunications companies, including cellular telephone, ESMR and PCS. Exclusive databases of subscribers, market penetrations, market potential, industry growth. Catching super-fast growth in a capsule. Three month trial available.
Cost: $1095.00
Frequency: Monthly
Founded in: 1970

8410 Wireless/Private Cable Investor
Kagan World Media
126 Clock Tower Place
Carmel, CA 93923-8746

831-624-1536; *Fax:* 831-624-5882
info@kagan.com; www.kagan.com

George Niesen, Editor
Tom Johnson, Marketing Manager

The original bible of the wireless cable, multipoint distribution pay TV industry. Published continuously since 1972, this newsletter is the window on cable competition. Three month trial available.

Magazines & Journals

8411 AAII Journal
American Association of Individual Investors
625 N Michigan Avenue
Chicago, IL 60611

312-280-0170
800-428-2244; *Fax:* 312-280-9883
members@aaii.com; www.aaii.com

James Cloonan, Chairman
James Cloonan, Founder

Journal focusing on personal finance, specifically investing in stocks and mutual funds and portfolio management.
Cost: $29.00
40 Pages
Circulation: 170000
ISSN: 0192-3315
Founded in: 1978

8412 AG Lender
Food 360/Vance Media
10901 W 84th Ter
Lenexa, KS 66214-1631

913-438-5721
800-808-2623; *Fax:* 913-438-0697
rkeller@vancepublishing.com;
www.vancepublishing.com

Cliff Becker, VP

AG Lender magazine reaches key agricultural financial leaders with editorial material geared to their business success.
Frequency: Monthly
Circulation: 1700
Founded in: 1923

8413 AGA Today
Association of Government Accountants
2208 Mount Vernon Ave
Alexandria, VA 22301-1314

703-562-0900
800-242-7211; *Fax:* 703-548-9367
agacgfm@agacgfm.org; www.agacgfm.org

Relmond Van Daniker, Executive Director

This publication acts as a clearinghouse for current government financial management information.
Frequency: Bi-Weekly
Circulation: 12,000

8414 Accounting and Business Review World
Scientific Publishing Company
1060 Main Street
River Edge, NJ 07661-2013
201-487-9655; *Fax:* 201-487-9656

Ed Yang Hoong Pang

Aims to provide a forum for the publication of accounting and business research papers which are of interest to educators, students and practitioners.
Cost: $60.00

8415 Affiliate Forum
NACHA: Electronic Payments Association
13665 Dulles Technology Dr
Suite 300
Herndon, VA 20171-4607

703-561-1100; *Fax:* 703-787-0996
info@nacha.org; www.nacha.org

Janet O Estep, CEO

8416 Alert
Defense Credit Union Council
601 Pennsylvania Ave NW
South Building, Suite 600
Washington, DC 20004-2601

202-638-3950; *Fax:* 202-638-3410;
www.dcuc.org

Roland Arteata, President
Frequency: Monthly

8417 Annual Institute Journal
National Association of Division Order Analysts
2805 Oak Trail Court
Suite 6312
Arlington, TX 76016

972-715-4489
administrator@nadoa.org; www.nadoa.org

Lynn S McCord, Administrator
Frequency: Annual

8418 Armed Forces Comptroller
American Society of Military Comptrollers
415 N Alfred St
Alexandria, VA 22314-2269

703-549-0360
800-462-5637; *Fax:* 703-549-3181;
www.asmconline.org

Robert Hale, Executive Director
Frequency: Quarterly

8419 Asset Management
ASMC
170 Avenue at the Common
PO Box 7930
Shrewsbury, NJ 07702-4803

732-389-8700; *Fax:* 732-389-8701;
www.djassetmanagement.com

Barry Vinocur, Publisher

Departments include a mutual fund snapshot, a variable annuity databank, asset allocation, a journal watch and much more. Also offering topical features of interest to industry professionals.
Frequency: Bi-Monthly
Circulation: 30,000

8420 Asset Protection: Offshore Tax Reports
Offshore Press
4500 W 72nd Ter
Shawnee Mission, KS 66208-2824

913-362-9667; *Fax:* 913-432-7174;
www.offshorepress.com

Vernon K Jacobs, President
Cost: $120.00
Frequency: Weekly
Founded in: 1981

8421 Barter News
PO Box 3024
Mission Viejo, CA 92690-1024

949-831-0607; *Fax:* 949-831-9378
bmeyer@barternews.com;
www.barternews.com

Bob Meyer, Publisher/Editor
Michael Mercier, VP
Fredrick Fuest, COO
Julia Homer, CFO

Industry news is covered including listings of CEO's and CFO's and editorials. An in-depth look into the changes and evolution of barter, and shows how-to profitability use barter to increase the bottom line.
Cost: $40.00
96 Pages
Frequency: Quarterly
Circulation: 30,000
Founded in: 1980
Printed in 4 colors on glossy stock

8422 Business Credit
National Association of Credit Management
8840 Columbia 100 Pkwy
Columbia, MD 21045-2100

410-740-5560; *Fax:* 410-740-5574
robins@nacm.org; www.nacm.org

Robin Schauseil, President
Jim Vanghel, Vice President

For professionals responsible for extending credit and collecting receivables. Topics include business law, lein law, technology, credit management, collections, deductions, fraud, credit risk, credit scoring, outsourcing, information services, trade finance and more.
Cost: $54.00
72 Pages
Circulation: 32000
Founded in: 1896
Printed in 4 colors on matte stock

8423 Business Finance
Duke Communications International
221 E 29th Street
PO Box 3438
Loveland, CO 80539-3438

970-634-4700; *Fax:* 970-593-1050
info@businessfinancemag.com;
www.businessfinancemag.com

David Blansfield, Publisher
Laurie Brannen, Editor-in-Chief
Meg Waters, Managing Editor
Matthew Weiner, Associate Publisher
Bruce Lynn, Managing Partner

Articles cover a broad range of topics from accounting to the Internet, from benchmarking to best practices, and cost management to career management.
Frequency: Monthly
Circulation: 50000

8424 CEIR - Quarterly National Economic Reports
National Association of Certified Valuation
1111 Brickyard Road
Suite 200
Salt Lake City, UT 84106-5401

303-698-1883
800-677-2009
sherril@nacva.com; www.navca.co.uk

Pamela R Bailey, Executive Director
Parnell Black, MBA CPA CVA, CEO
Roberto Castro, Director Business Development
Dean Dinas, Director Economic Research
Brien K Jones, General Manager Conferences
Frequency: Quarterly

8425 CMBA World
Commerical Mortgage Securities Association
30 Broad St
28th Floor
New York, NY 10004-4119

212-509-1844; *Fax:* 212-509-1895
info1@cmbs.org; www.cmbs.org

Dottie Cunningham, CEO
Frequency: Quarterly

8426 Collections & Credit Risk
Thomson Financial Publishing

1 State St
27th Floor
New York, NY 10004-1481

212-825-8445
800-221-1809; *Fax:* 212-803-1592;
www.creditcollectionsworld.com

Sharon Rowlands, President/CEO
Louis Eccleston, Marketing Director
Catherine Ladwig, Editor
Darren Waggoner, Executive Editor
Jose Thomas, Manager

Focuses on news and trends of strategic and competitive importance to collections and credit policy executives. Covers the credit risk industry's growth, diversification and technology in both commercial and consumer credit.
Cost: $98.00
66 Pages
Frequency: Monthly
Circulation: 25000
ISSN: 1093-1260
Founded in: 1961
Printed in 4 colors on glossy stock

8427 Collector Magazine
ACA International
PO Box 390106
Minneapolis, MN 55439-106

952-926-6547; *Fax:* 952-926-1624
aca@acainternational.org;
www.acainternational.org

Timothy Dressen, Editor/Director Comm
Gary Rippentrop, CEO
Anne Rosso, Associate Editor

Brings you vital, up to the minute information on industry trends, regulations and legislation each month.
Cost: $70.00
Frequency: Monthly
Circulation: 6000
Founded in: 1939

8428 Computerized Investing
American Association of Individual Investors
625 N Michigan Avenue
Chicago, IL 60611

312-280-0170
800-428-2244; *Fax:* 312-280-9883
mambers@aaii.com; www.aaii.com

James Cloonan, Chairman

Offers information on computed investing, stocks and bonds.
Cost: $40.00
Founded in: 1978

8429 Consumer Finance Law Quarterly Report
Conference on Consumer Finance Law
Oklahoma City University School of Law
2501 N Blackwelder
Oklahoma City, OK 73106

405-208-5363; *Fax:* 405-208-5089
ccflqr@lec.okcu.edu; www.ccfonline.org

Alvin C Harrell, Executive Director
Frequency: Quarterly

8430 Contingency Planning & Management
Witter Publishing Corporation
84 Park Avenue
Flemington, NJ 08822

908-788-0343; *Fax:* 908-788-3782;
www.WitterPublishing.com

Steve Biggers, Publisher
Andy Hagg, Editor
Andrew Witter, President

Serves the fields of financial/banking, manufacturing industrial, transportation, utilities, telecommunications, health care, government, insurance and other allied fields.
Founded in: 1996

8431 Controller's Quarterly
Institute of Management Accountants
10 Paragon Dr
Suite 1
Montvale, NJ 07645-1774

201-573-9000
800-638-4427; *Fax:* 201-474-1600
ima@imanet.org; www.imanet.org

Paul Sharman, President
Sandra Richtermeyer, Chair
Frequency: Monthly

8432 Corporate Controller
Thomson Reuters
195 Broadway
New York, NY 10007-3124

646-822-2000
800-231-1860; *Fax:* 646-822-2800
trta.lei-support@thomsonreuters.com;
www.ria.thomsonreuters.com

Elaine Yadlon, Plant Manager
Thomas H Glocer, CEO & Director
Robert D Daleo, Chief Financial Officer
Kelli Crane, Senior Vice President & CIO

Includes health care costs, cash management, executive compensation and environmental insurance as well as regular columns on tax planning, technology advances, and innovative business trends.
Frequency: Bi-Monthly
Circulation: 3500

8433 Corporate Risk Management
Oster Communications
219 Main St
Cedar Falls, IA 50613-2742

319-277-1271; *Fax:* 319-277-7481

Merrill Oster, President

Written for financial decision makers.
48 Pages
Frequency: Monthly
Founded in: 1989

8434 Cost Engineering Journal
AACE International
209 Prairie Avenue
Suite 100
Morgantown, WV 26501-5934

304-296-8444
800-858-2678; *Fax:* 304-291-5728
info@aacei.org; www.aacei.org

Marvin Gelhausen, Managing Editor
Noah Kinderknecht, Editor

International journal of cost estimation, cost/schedule control, and project management read by cost professionals around the world to get the most up-to-date information about the profession.
Frequency: Monthly

8435 Cost Management Update
Institute of Management Accountants
10 Paragon Dr
Suite 1
Montvale, NJ 07645-1774

201-573-9000
800-638-4427; *Fax:* 201-474-1600
ima@imanet.org; www.imanet.org

Paul Sharman, President
Sandra Richtermeyer, Chair
Frequency: Monthly

8436 Credit Card Management
Thomson Financial Publishing
1 State St
27th Floor
New York, NY 10004-1481

212-825-8445
800-535-8403; *Fax:* 800-235-5552
custserv@sourcemedia.com;
www.cardforum.com

James Daly, Editor
Sharon Rowlands, President/CEO
Louis Eccleston, Marketing Director
Jose Thomas, Manager

Information on the major developments in the credit card industry.
Cost: $98.00
74 Pages
Frequency: Monthly
Circulation: 19000
Founded in: 1962
Printed in 4 colors on glossy stock

8437 Credit Scoring
Credit Research Foundation
8840 Columbia 100 Pkwy
Suite 100
Columbia, MD 21045-2100

410-740-5499; *Fax:* 410-740-4620
crf_info@crfonline.org; www.crfonline.org

Terry Callahan, President
Michael Durant, Vice-Chairman

8438 Credit Union Executive Journal
Credit Union National Association
Po Box 431
Madison, WI 53701-0431

608-231-4000
800-356-9655; *Fax:* 608-231-1869
dorothy@cuna.org; www.cuna.org

Daniel A Mica, CEO

Techniques and concepts available in management, finance, marketing, lending, human resources and technology for credit unions.
Cost: $202.00
Circulation: 2400
Founded in: 1930

8439 Credit Union Magazine
Credit Union National Association
5710 Mineral Point Road
Madison, WI 53705-4454

800-356-9655; *Fax:* 608-231-4263
dorothy@cuna.org; www.cuna.org

Daniel A Mica, CEO
Tom Dorety, Vice Chairman
Bill Merrick, Managing Editor

The role and operations of modern credit unions.
Cost: $50.00
100 Pages
Frequency: Monthly
Circulation: 32776
ISSN: 0011-1066
Founded in: 1981
Printed in 4 colors on glossy stock

8440 Credit Union Technology
Credit Union Technology
110-64 Queens Boulevard
#106
Forest Hills, NY 11375-6347

718-793-9400; *Fax:* 718-793-9414;
www.cutmag.com

Andrew Mallon, Publisher

Information on improving customer service through technological advances.
Cost: $36.00
24 Pages
Frequency: Bi-Monthly
Circulation: 6000
ISSN: 1054-7304
Founded in: 1991
Printed in 4 colors on glossy stock

8441 **Credit and Collection Survey**
Broadcast Cable Credit Association
550 W Frontage Rd
Suite 3600
Northfield, IL 60093-1243

847-881-8757; *Fax:* 847-784-8059
info@bccacredit.com; www.bccacredit.com

Mary Collin, CEO
Jamie Smith, Director of Operations
Rachelle Brooks, BCCA Sales
Frequency: Bi-Ennial

8442 **DC Advocate**
National Defined Contribution Council
9101 E Kenyon
Suite 300
Denver, CO 80237-0467

303-770-5353; *Fax:* 303-770-1812;
www.ndcconline.org

Al Brust, Executive VP
Frequency: Quarterly

8443 **Disclosure Record**
Newsfeatures
8511 249th Street
Jamaica, NY 11426-2105
Jack Lotto, Editor

Full texts of corporate and financial news reports.
Cost: $50.00
8 Pages
Frequency: Monthly
Founded in: 1973

8444 **Electronics Payment Journal**
NACHA: Electronic Payments Association
13665 Dulles Technology Dr
Suite 300
Herndon, VA 20171-4607

703-561-1100; *Fax:* 703-787-0996
info@nacha.org; www.nacha.org

Janet O Estep, CEO
Deb Evans-Doyle, Senior Director Conference Mktg
Julie Hedlund, Senior Director Electronic Commerce
Michael Herd, Director Public Relations
Priscilla Holland, AAP, Senior Director Corporate Pymts

8445 **Estate Planning Review**
2700 Lake Cook Road
Riverwoods, IL 60015-3867

847-267-7000
800-224-8299; *Fax:* 800-224-8299;
www.support.cch.com

Robert Becker, President and CEO
Cost: $275.00
Frequency: Monthly
Founded in: 1913

8446 **Examiner**
Society of Financial Examiners
174 Grace Blvd
Altamonte Spgs, FL 32714-3210

407-682-4930
800-787-7633; *Fax:* 407-382-3175;
www.sofe.org

Pauline Keyes, Owner
Stephen J Szypula, Financial Administrator
Frequency: Quarterly

8447 **F & I Management Technology**
Association of Finance and Insurance Professionals
4112 Southwood E
Colleyville, TX 76034

817-428-2434; *Fax:* 817-428-2534;
www.afip.com

David N Robertson, Executive Director

8448 **Federal Credit Union Magazine**
National Association of Federal Credit Unions
3138 10th St N
Arlington, VA 22201-2160

703-522-4770
800-336-4644; *Fax:* 703-524-1082
fbecker@nafcu.org; www.nafcu.org

Fred Becker, President

Written for CEO's, senior staff and volunteers of Federal Credit Unions. Offers legislative and regulatory news, as well as technology and operational issues. Call for rates.
50 Pages
Circulation: 1500
ISSN: 1043-7789
Founded in: 1967
Printed in 4 colors on glossy stock

8449 **Financial Analysts Journal**
CFA Institure
Po Box 3668
Charlottesville, VA 22903-0668

434-951-5499
800-247-8132; *Fax:* 434-951-5262
info@cfainstitute.org; www.cfainstitute.org

John Rogers, CEO
Rodney N Sullivan, Associate Editor

To advance the knowledge and understanding of the practice of investment management through the publication of high-quality, practitioner-relevant research
Founded in: 1945

8450 **Financial Executive**
Financial Executives International
200 Campus Dr
Suite 8
Florham Park, NJ 07932-1007

973-236-0177
800-336-0773; *Fax:* 973-765-1018;
www.financialexecutives.com

Jim Abel, President
Ellen Heffes, Managing Editor
Colleen S Cunningham, President
Maria O'Grady, Marketing Manager

Addresses accounting and treasury subjects, as well as overall strategies in corporate financial mangement.
Cost: $74.39
72 Pages
Frequency: Monthly
Circulation: 16500
ISSN: 0895-4186
Founded in: 1931
Printed in 4 colors on glossy stock

8451 **Financial Management Journal**
Financial Management Association International
4202 E Fowler Ave
BSN 3331
Tampa, FL 33620-9951

813-974-2084; *Fax:* 813-974-3318
info@fma.org; www.fma.org

Jack S Rader, Executive Director
Jeffrey Coles, Advisory Editor
John Graham, Advisory Editor
Michael Lemmon, Advisory Editor
Jay Ritter, Advisory Editor

Financial Management serves both academicians and practitioners who are concerned with the financial management of non-financial businesses, financial institutions, and public and private not-for-profit organizations. The journal serves the profession by publishing significant new scholarly research in finance that is of the highest quality.
Frequency: Quarterly

8452 **Financial Manager**
Broadcast Cable Financial Management Association
550 W Frontage Rd
Suite 3600
Northfield, IL 60093-1243

847-716-7000; *Fax:* 847-784-8059
info@bccacredit.com; www.bcfm.com
Mary Collins, President
Jamie Smith, Director of Operations
Rachelle Brooks, BCCA Sales

A bi-monthly magazine published by the Broadcast Cable Financial Management Association.
Cost: $69.00
36 Pages
Circulation: 300
Mailing list available for rent: 1100 names at $495 per M

8453 **Financial Manager/Credit Topics**
Broadcast Cable Credit Association
550 W Frontage Rd
Suite 3600
Northfield, IL 60093-1243

847-881-8757; *Fax:* 847-784-8059
info@bccacredit.com; www.bccacredit.com

Mary Collin, CEO
Jamie Smith, Director of Operations
Rachelle Brooks, BCCA Sales
Frequency: Bi-Monthly

8454 **Financial Planning & Counseling Journal**
Association for Financial Counseling and Planning
2112 Arlington Avenue
Suite H
Upper Arlington, OH 43221

614-485-9650; *Fax:* 614-485-9621;
www.afcpe.org
Sharon Burns, PhD, Executive Director
Frequency: Semi-Annual

8455 **Financial Planning Digest**
Harcourt Brace Professional Publishing
6277 Sea Harbor Drive
Orlando, FL 32887

407-345-2000; *Fax:* 407-345-3016;
www.smartbrief.com

Angelita Streeter, Editor
Paul Amidei, Managing Editor

Estate, retirement, insurance planning tips and strategies, practice management insight, book reviews and legislation updates.
Cost: $99.00
Frequency: Monthly

8456 **Financial Review Magazine**
NFR Communications
4948 Washburn Avenue S
Minneapolis, MN 55410

612-929-8110; *Fax:* 612-929-8146;
www.nfrcom.com

Tom Bengtson, Editor
Jackie Hilgert, Production Manager

Trade publication covering the commercial banking industry in the upper midwest. Designed for the decision-maker in the bank.
Frequency: 25 per year

8457 **Financial Services Quarterly**
SNL Securities

One SNL Plaza
PO Box 2124
Charlottesvle, VA 22902-2124

434-977-1600; *Fax:* 434-977-4466
subscriptions@snl.com; www.snl.com

Pam Askea, Editor
Dan Oakey, Editor
Michael Spears, Advertising
Edward Metz, Financial Services
Nick Cafferillo, Chief Operating Officer

Comprehensive reference guide available on finance companies, mortgage banks, investment advisors and securities brokers/dealers. In-depth company profiles and financial data on these publicly traded companies and summary financials on thousands of non-public financial services companies.
Cost: $696.00
400 Pages
Frequency: Quarterly
Founded in: 1987

8458 Financier
Bank Administration Institute
1 N Franklin St
Chicago, IL 60606-3598

312-553-4600; *Fax:* 312-683-2373
info@bai.org; www.bai.org

Deborah Bianucci, CEO
Willard Rappleye Jr, Executive Vice President
Ann Barcroft, Executive Vice President
Anne Matsumoto, Managing Director

Forum of ideas for the private sector.
Cost: $5.00
Circulation: 32,000

8459 Forbes Global
Forbes Media LLC.
60 5th Ave
New York, NY 10011-8868

212-620-2200; *Fax:* 212-620-1857
readers@forbes.com; www.forbes.com

Malcolm S Forbes Jr, CEO
Bruce Rogers, VP Marketing
Paul Maidment, Executive Editor
Michael Smith Maidment, VP, GM Operations

A magazine giving detailed information about business and finance.
Frequency: Monthly

8460 Forbes Magazine
Forbes Media LLC.
60 5th Ave
11th Floor
New York, NY 10011-8868

212-620-2200; *Fax:* 212-620-1857
customerservice@forbes.com;
www.forbes.com

Malcolm S Forbes Jr, CEO
Bruce Rogers, VP Marketing
Paul Maidment, Executive Director
Micheal Smith Maidment, VP, GM Operations

A magazine giving detailed information about business and finance.
Cost: $4.95
304 Pages
Founded in: 1917

8461 Futures Industry
Futures Industry Association
2001 Pennsylvania Ave NW
#600
Washington, DC 20006-1823

202-223-1528; *Fax:* 202-296-3184
info@futuresindustry.org;
www.futuresindustry.org

John Damgard, President/CEO
Erin Kairys, Manager
Will Acworth, Editor
Roselia Marmolejos, Administrative Assistant

Front and back office operations, marketing, research, money management, regulatory and brokerage issues from a domestic and international perspective.
Circulation: 15000
Founded in: 1955

8462 Futures Magazine
Oster Communications
219 Main St
Suite 6
Cedar Falls, IA 50613-2742

319-277-1271; *Fax:* 319-277-7481;
www.futuresmag.com

Merrill Oster, President
Ginger Szala, Publisher

News, analysis, and strategies for futures, options and derivatives traders. Descriptions include annual sourcebook directory of exchange, contract, company and product information.
Cost: $39.00
Frequency: Monthly
Circulation: 60000
Founded in: 1972

8463 Global Custodian
Asset International
125 Greenwich Avenue
Greenwich, CT 06830

203-295-5015; *Fax:* 203-629-5024;
www.globalcustodian.com

Dominic Hobson, Editor-in-Chief
Charles Ruffel, Executive Editor
Meredith Hughes, Publisher
Alix Hughes, Sales Director

An in-depth perspective on the business of international investing, custody and clearing, and directory-type data on industry participants and trends. Provides investment professionals with an analysis of the strength and weaknessed of the players and systems that underlie international investing.
Cost: $185.00
Circulation: 30,488
Founded in: 1989

8464 Global Finance
7 E 20th St.
New York, NY 10003

www.gfmag.com
Social Media: Facebook, Twitter, LinkedIn

Joseph Giarraputo, Publisher & Editorial Director

The magazine offers analysis, articles and data to help corporate leaders, bankers and investors make decisions.
Frequency: Monthly
Circulation: 50,050
Founded in: 1987

8465 Global Investment Magazine
Global Investment Technology
820 2nd Ave
4th Floor
New York, NY 10017-4504

212-370-3700; *Fax:* 212-370-4606
info@globalinv.com; www.globalinv.com

Micheal Horton, Publisher
Pierre-Yves Sacchi, Managing Director

Portfolio management, trading and global asset services, and a wide range of issues pertaining to institutional portfolio management strategies and decision making in the US and cross-border markets.
Frequency: Quarterly
Circulation: 15000

8466 Global Investment Technology
Global Investment Technology
820 2nd Ave
4th Floor
New York, NY 10017-4504

212-370-3700; *Fax:* 212-370-4606
info@globalinv.com; www.globalinv.com

Micheal Horton, Publisher
Pavan Sehgal, Managing Director
Pierre-Yves Sacchi, Managing Director

The strategic business interests of top-level decision makers as well as their operations and systems professionals.
Cost: $695.00
Circulation: 1800
Founded in: 1990

8467 Healthcare Financial Management
2 Westbrook Corporate Ctr #700
Westchester, IL 60154-5723

708-531-9614; *Fax:* 708-531-0032;
www.hfma.org

Richard L Clarke, President

8468 IBIS Review
Charles D Spencer
250 S Wacker Drive
#600
Chicago, IL 60606-5800

312-993-7900; *Fax:* 312-993-7910;
www.ibisnews.com

Charles D Spencer, Publisher
Celia Cruz, Owner

For the individual responsible for the compensation and benefits of employees working abroad. Topics include pensions and profit-sharing plans, stock purchase and savings plans, death and disability benefits, health care coverage, termination indemnities, executive renumeration plans, investments, and expatriate plans.
Frequency: Monthly
Circulation: 1500

8469 IMA Focus
Institute of Management Accountants
10 Paragon Dr
Suite 1
Montvale, NJ 07645-1774

201-573-9000
800-638-4427; *Fax:* 201-474-1600
ima@imanet.org; www.imanet.org

Paul Sharman, President
Frequency: Bi-Monthly

8470 INSIGHT
Society of Financial Examiners
174 Grace Blvd
Altamonte Spgs, FL 32714-3210

407-682-4930
800-787-7633; *Fax:* 407-682-3175;
www.sofe.org

Pauline Keyes, Owner
Stephen J Szypula, Financial Administrator
Frequency: Monthly

8471 ISM Info Edge
Institute for Supply Management
2055 E Centennial Circle
PO Box 22160
Tempe, AZ 85285-2160

480-752-6276
800-888-6276; *Fax:* 480-752-7890
infocenter@ism.ws; www.ism.ws

Paul Novak, CPM, CEO
Holly LaCroix Johnson, Senior Vice President
Deborah Webber, SVP
Jean McHale, Manager
Frequency: Quarterly

8472 Inside Mortgage Finance
Inside Mortgage Finance Publishers

7910 Woodmont Ave
Suite 1010
Bethesda, MD 20814-7019

301-951-1240
800-570-5744; *Fax:* 301-656-1709
service@imfpubs.com;
www.insidemortgagefinance.com

John Bancroft, CEO & Publisher
John Bancroft, Vice President & Executive Editor
Paul Muolo, Managing Editor
Mari Mullane, Director, Marketing
Tony Cecala, Production Manager

Residential finance industry news and related trade literature. Includes extensive rankings from top originators to the leading private mortgage insurers.
Cost: $889.00
12 Pages
Frequency: Weekly
ISSN: 8756-0003
Founded in: 1984
Printed in 2 colors on matte stock

8473 **Inside Supply Management**
Insitute for Supply Management
2055 E Centennial Circle
PO Box 22160
Tempe, AZ 85285-2160

480-752-6276
800-888-6276; *Fax:* 480-752-7890
infocenter@ism.ws; www.ism.ws

Paul Novak, CPM, CEO
Holly LaCroix Johnson, Senior Vice President
Deborah Webber, SVP
Jean McHale, Manager
Frequency: Monthly

8474 **Institute of Management & Administration Newsletter**
Institute of Management and Administration
1 Washington Park
Suite 1300
Newark, NJ 07102

212-244-0360; *Fax:* 973-622-0595;
www.ioma.com

Information for those involved in international sales. Regular monthly features.

8475 **Institutional Investor**
225 Park Ave. S
New York, NY 10003

212-224-3300
info@institutionalinvestor.com;
www.institutionalinvestor.com
Social Media: Facebook, Twitter, LinkedIn, Google+, StockTwits

Diane Alfano, Chairman
David E. Antin, Chief Executive Officer
Allison Adams, Publisher

Authoritative financial news for institutional investors.

8476 **Insurance & Financial Meetings Managment**
Coastal Communications Corporation
2700 N Military Trail
Suite 120
Boca Raton, FL 33431

561-989-0600; *Fax:* 561-989-9509
ccceditor@att.net;
www.themeetingmagazines.com

Harvey Grotsky, Publisher/Editor-In-Chief
Susan Wycoff Fell, Managing Editor
Susan Gregg, Managing Editor

The executive source for planning meetings and incentives for the financial and insurance sectors. With regular features and special focus on site selection, destinations, industry-related studies and activities, motivational and incentive programs, program and event planning.
Frequency: Monthly
Circulation: 40,000
Founded in: 1983

8477 **International Journal of Supply Chain Management**
Institute for Supply Management
2055 E Centennial Circle
PO Box 22160
Tempe, AZ 85285-2160

480-752-6276
800-888-6276; *Fax:* 480-752-7890
infocenter@ism.ws; www.ism.ws

Paul Nocak, CPM, CEO
Holly LaCroix Johnson, Senior Vice President
Deborah Webber, SVP
Jean McHale, Manager
Frequency: Quarterly

8478 **Investor Relations Business**
Securities Data Publishing
40 W 57th St
New York, NY 10019-4001

212-484-4701; *Fax:* 212-956-0112
sdp@tfn.com

Matthew Greco, Editor
Edward Cortese, Marketing Executive

News updates, career opportunities and personnel announcements for CEO's, CFO's, treasurers and directors of corporations.
Cost: $415.00
Frequency: Bi-Monthly

8479 **Journal of Applied Finance**
Financial Management Association International
4202 E Fowler Ave
BSN 3331
Tampa, FL 33620-9951

813-974-2084; *Fax:* 813-974-3318
info@fma.org; www.fma.org

Jack S Rader, Executive Director
Ali Fatemi, Editor
Reena Aggarwal, Associate Editor
James S Ang, Associate Editor
Robert F Bruner, Associate Editor

Launched in 2001, JAF publishes easy-to-read pieces that focus on financial practice and education - a standard reference for those seeking knowledge on the new developments in applied finance.
Frequency: Bi-Annual

8480 **Journal of Asset Protection**
Thomson Reuters
195 Broadway
New York, NY 10007-3124

646-822-2000
800-231-1860; *Fax:* 646-822-2800
trta.lei-support@thomsonreuters.com;
www.ria.thomsonreuters.com

Elaine Yadlon, Plant Manager
Thomas H Glocer, CEO & Director
Robert D Daleo, Chief Financial Officer
Kelli Crane, Senior Vice President & CIO

Information on shielding personal and business assets from creditors, third party attachments and government claims.
Cost: $195.00
Frequency: Bi-Monthly
Circulation: 2,000

8481 **Journal of Cost Management**
Thomson Reuters
195 Broadway
New York, NY 10007-3124

646-822-2000
800-231-1860; *Fax:* 646-822-2800
trta.lei-support@thomsonreuters.com;
www.ria.thomsonreuters.com

Elaine Yadlon, Plant Manager
Thomas H Glocer, CEO & Director
Robert D Daleo, Chief Financial Officer
Kelli Crane, Senior Vice President & CIO

Information on cost management techniques and manufacturing technology. Provides essays and or research papers by professionals and educators.
Cost: $210.00
Frequency: Monthly
Circulation: 5000
Founded in: 1940

8482 **Journal of Education Finance**
American Education Finance Association
5249 Cape Leyte Drive
Sarasota, FL 34242-1805

941-349-7580

Information and news to educational organizations on financial investing and prospecting.
150 Pages
Frequency: Quarterly
Circulation: 700
Founded in: 1978

8483 **Journal of Finance**
American Finance Association
Haas School of Business
Berkley, CA 94720-1900

510-642-2397; *Fax:* 510-525-6246
pyle@haas.berkley.edu; www.afajof.org

Robert F Stambaugh, Editor
Anat R Admati, Associate Editors
Wendy Washburn, Editorial Assistant
David H Pyle, Business Manager

Covers theory and practice in the field of finance.
Frequency: Bi-Monthly
Circulation: 10000+
Founded in: 1939

8484 **Journal of Financial Planning**
4100 E Mississippi Avenue
Suite 400
Denver, CO 80246

303-759-4900
800-322-4237; *Fax:* 303-759-0749
journal@fpanet.org; www.fpanet.org

Marvin W Tuttle CAE, Executive Director/CEO
Ian McKenzie, Managing Director/Publishing

A comprehensive financial publication offering information and news on financial planning, investing and prospecting.
Cost: $90.00
Frequency: Monthly
Circulation: 50,000
Founded in: 1979

8485 **Journal of Fixed Income**
Institutional Investor
488 Madison Ave
16th Floor
New York, NY 10022-5701

212-303-3100
800-945-2034; *Fax:* 212-224-3491
iieditor@institutionalinvestor.com;
www.institutionalinvestor.com/

Allison Adams, Publisher
Brian Bruce, Editor
Anne O'Brien, Marketing

Reporting on analysis of theories and ideas involving fixed income.
Cost: $370.00
Frequency: Quarterly
Circulation: 2500
Founded in: 1967

8486 **Journal of Gift Planning**
National Committee on Planned Giving

233 S McCrea St
Suite 400
Indianapolis, IN 46225-1068

317-269-6274; *Fax:* 317-269-6276;
www.ncpg.org

Tanya Howe Johnson, President
Sandra Kerr, Director Government Education
Barbara Owens, Director Membership Manager
Kathryn J Ramsey, Director Meetings
Kurt Reusze, Manager Education/Technology
Frequency: Quarterly

8487 Journal of Government Financial Management
Association of Government Accountants
2208 Mount Vernon Ave
Alexandria, VA 22301-1314

703-562-0900
800-242-7211; *Fax:* 703-548-9367
agacgfm@agacgfm.org; www.agacgfm.org

Relmond Van Daniker, Executive Director

Provides valuable information for governmental decision makers. Examines budgeting, accounting, auditing and date process developments.
Frequency: Quarterly
Circulation: 14,769

8488 Journal of Healthcare Administrative Management
American Association of Healthcare Administrative
11240 Waples Mill Rd
Suite 200
Fairfax, VA 22030-6078

703-934-0164; *Fax:* 703-359-7562
moayad@aaham.org; www.aaham.org

Sharon Geller, Executive Director
Linda Sheaffer, Chair
Frequency: Quarterly

8489 Journal of Investing
Institutional Investor
1900 Preston Road
#267-310
Plano, TX 75093-5175

214-495-9533; *Fax:* 212-224-3491
info@iijournals.com; www.iijournals.com

Brian Bruce, Editor-in-Chief
Allison Adams, Publisher
Anne O'Brien, Director of Marketing

Features equity investments, fixed income investing, security valuation and related investment vehicles.
Cost: $360.00
Frequency: Quarterly
Circulation: 2500
Founded in: 1967

8490 Journal of Mutual Fund Services
Securities Data Publishing
600 Atlantic Avenue
Boston, MA 02210-2211

617-723-6400; *Fax:* 617-624-7200;
www.dalbar.com

Ken Heath, Publisher
Kathleen Whalen, Managing Director

Focuses on backroom operations of the mutual fund industry, with directories featuring transfer assets, fund accountants, custodians, attorneys and other service personnel.
Cost: $795.00
Frequency: 8 per year

8491 Journal of Performance Management
Assn for Management Information in Financial Svcs
14247 Saffron Circle
Carmel, IN 46032

317-815-5857; *Fax:* 317-815-5877
ami2@amifs.org; www.amifs.org

Robert McDonald, President
Kevin Link, Executive Director
Cost: $200.00
Frequency: 3x/Year
Circulation: 350

8492 Journal of Portfolio Management
Institutional Investor
488 Madison Ave
16th Floor
New York, NY 10022-5701

212-303-3100
800-437-9997; *Fax:* 212-224-3491
iieditor@institutionalinvestor.com;
www.institutionalinvestor.com/

Allison Adams, Publisher
Peter Bernstein, Editor
Anne O'Brien, Marketing Manager

Ideas and concepts in the practice and theory of portfolio management.
Cost: $430.00
Frequency: Quarterly
Circulation: 5000
Founded in: 1975

8493 Journal of Taxation
Thomson Reuters
195 Broadway
New York, NY 10007-3124

646-822-2000
800-231-1860; *Fax:* 646-822-2800
trta.lei-support@thomsonreuters.com;
www.ria.thomsonreuters.com

Elaine Yadlon, Plant Manager
Thomas H Glocer, CEO & Director
Robert D Daleo, Chief Financial Officer
Kelli Crane, Senior Vice President & CIO

Information on tax developments and trends, revenue rulings, court decisions and legislative and administrative actions of significance to the sophisticated tax professional.
Cost: $315.00
Frequency: Monthly
Circulation: 12000
ISSN: 0022-4863
Founded in: 1984
Printed in on glossy stock

8494 Legislative Currents
American Association of Healthcare Administrative
11240 Waples Mill Rd
Suite 200
Fairfax, VA 22030-6078

703-934-0164; *Fax:* 703-359-7562
moayad@aaham.org; www.aaham.org

Sharon Geller, Executive Director
Linda Sheaffer, Chair
Frequency: Bi-Monthly

8495 MS Quarterly Journal
Society for Information Management
401 N Michigan Avenue
Chicago, IL 60611

312-215-5190; *Fax:* 312-245-1081;
www.simnet.org

Jim Luisi, Executive Director
Frequency: Quarterly

8496 Management and Technology
Association of Finance and Insurance Professionals
412 Southwood E
Colleyville, TX 76034

817-428-2434; *Fax:* 817-428-2534;
www.afip.com

David N Robertson, Executive Director

8497 Market Survey
International Swaps and Derivatives Association
360 Madison Ave
16th Floor
New York, NY 10017-7126

212-901-6000; *Fax:* 212-901-6001
isda@isda.org; www.isda.org

Robert Pickel, CEO
Ruth Ainslie, Director Communications
Corrine Greasley, Director Administration
Frequency: Semi-Annual

8498 Money
1271 Avenue of the Americas
32nd Floor
New York, NY 10020-1300

212-759-4094; *Fax:* 212-522-0773

8499 Mortgage Originator
Pfingsten Publishing
3990 Oldtown Avenue
Suite A203
San Diego, CA 92110

619-223-9989
800-995-2090; *Fax:* 619-223-9943;
www.mortgageoriginator.com

Chuck Hirsch, Publisher
David Robinson, Editor
Andy Strasser, Marketing Manager
Sue Burns, Circulation Director

Information on sales and marketing issues, correspondent management, retail mortgage, bankers and wholesale originators.
Cost: $58.00
Circulation: 19,500
ISSN: 1070-5708
Founded in: 1998
Printed in 4 colors on glossy stock

8500 Mortgage Servicing News
Thomson Financial Publishing
1 State St
27th floor
New York, NY 10004-1481

212-825-8445
800-221-1809; *Fax:* 212-292-5216;
www.mortgageservicingnews.com

Timothy Murphy, Publisher
Mark Fogarty, Editorial Director
Robert Cullen, CEO

Information on cross serving techniques, legislative decisions, management strategies, and professional profiles.
Cost: $98.00
Frequency: Monthly
Circulation: 20000

8501 NABTalk
National Association of Bankruptcy Trustees
One Windsor Cove
Suite 305
Columbia, SC 29233

803-252-5646
800-445-8629; *Fax:* 803-765-0860
info@nabt.com; www.nabt.com

Carol H Webber, Executive Director
Frequency: Quarterly

8502 NAPFA Advisor Magazine
National Association of Personal Financial Advisor

3250 N Arlington Heights Road
Suite 109
Arlington Heights, IL 60004

847-483-5400
800-366-2732; *Fax:* 847-483-5415
info@napfa.org; www.napfa.org

Ellen Turf, CEO
Margery Wasserman, Director Conferences
Frequency: Monthly

8503 NATE Update
National Association of Trade Exchange
8836 Tyler Road
Mentor, OH 44060
440-205-5378; *Fax:* 440-205-5379;
www.nate.org

Thomas H McDowell, Executive Director

8504 Natinal Pawnbroker Magazine
National Pawnbrokers Association
P.O.Box 508
Keller, TX 76244-0508

817-491-4554; *Fax:* 817-481-8770
info@NationalPawnbrokers.org;
www.nationalpawnbrokers.org

Bob Benedict, CAE, Executive Director
Emmett Murphy, Director
Teresa Congleton, Administrative Assistant
Frequency: Quarterly

8505 National Association of Investors Corporation
Po Box 220
Royal Oak, MI 48068-0220

248-583-6242
887-ASK-NAIC; *Fax:* 248-583-4880

Kathleen Zaracki, CEO
Adam Ritt, Editor

Articles on counseling and teaching investing techniques. Magazine is included with membership.
100 Pages
Frequency: Monthly
Circulation: 250,000
Founded in: 1951
Printed in 4 colors on glossy stock

8506 Nelson's World's Best Money Managers
Nelson Publishing
2500 Tamiami Trl N
Nokomis, FL 34275-3476

941-966-9521; *Fax:* 941-966-2590
webmaster@nelsonpub.com;
www.healthmgttech.com

A Verner Nelson, Owner
George G Lindsey, COO
Kevin T Black, VP Database

A special quarterly report extracted from the Nelson Investment Manager Database which ranks the top investment managers by performance results in each of 200 categories.
Cost: $245.00
200 Pages
Frequency: Quarterly

8507 Newspaper Financial Executive Journal
Interactive & Newsmedia Financial Executives
14237 Bookcliff Court
Suite 200
Purcellville, VA 20132

703-421-4060; *Fax:* 703-421-4068;
www.infe.org

Jeff Hood, President

Trade publication for financial management of newspapers. More than 800 members.
Frequency: Weekly
Circulation: 1000
Founded in: 1947

8508 OCC Quarterly Journal
Comptroller of the Currency
250 E St Sw
250 E Street SW
Washington, DC 20219-0001

202-874-5000
800-613-6743; *Fax:* 202-874-4490
Webmaster@occ.treas.gov; www.occ.treas.gov

John C Dugan, CEO
Nancy K Jones, Administrative Assistant
Ruth Montgomery, Administrative Assistant
Teri Pote, Program Manager

Significant actions and policies of the Office of Comptroller of the Currency, the agency that regulates national banks. Legal interpretations, merger decisions, speeches and testimony and statistical and structural data on national banks are included.
Cost: $100.00
132 Pages
Frequency: Quarterly
Circulation: 6500
Founded in: 1863

8509 Pensions & Investments
Crain Communications
360 N Michigan Ave
Chicago, IL 60601-3800

312-649-5200; *Fax:* 312-649-7937
info@crain.com; www.crain.com

Keith Crain, CEO

Delivers critical financial news to executives responsible for the investment of large institutional assets such as pension funds, endowments and foundations.
Frequency: Monthly
Circulation: 52000

8510 Plan Horizons
National Institute of Pension Administrators
401 N Michigan Avenue
Suite 2200
Chicago, IL 60611-4267

800-999-6472
nipa@nipa.org; www.nipa.org

Laura J Rudzinski, Executive Director
Frequency: Quarterly

8511 Professional Collector
Pohly & Partners
27 Melcher Street
2nd Floor
Boston, MA 02210

617-451-1700; *Fax:* 617-338-7767;
www.pohlypartners.com

Karen English, Editor
Piania Pohly, CEO/President
Annie Swearingven, Marketing Manager

Information on the latest technology, legislation and other issues affecting the debt collections industry.
Cost: $24.95
Frequency: Quarterly
Circulation: 148000
Printed in 4 colors

8512 Purchasing
Reed Business Information
225 Wyman St
Waltham, MA 02451-1216

781-734-8000
800-446-6551; *Fax:* 781-290-3201
subsmail@reedbusiness.com;
www.reedbusiness.com

Mark Finklestein, President
Kathy Doyle, CFO
Stuart Whayman, CFO

Information for purchasing personnel in industry.
Frequency: bi-monthly
Circulation: 95,078
Founded in: 1915
Printed in 4 colors on glossy stock

8513 REIT Securities Monthly
SNL Securities
PO Box 2124
Charlottesvle, VA 22902-2124

434-977-1600; *Fax:* 434-977-4466;
www.snlnet.com

Eden Rood, Editor
Reid Naglews, Chief Operating Officer
Nick Cafferillo, Chief Operating Officer
Adam Hall, Managing Director

Features sector analysis and interviews with industry leaders, as well as coverage of REIT investing and capital raising. The source for REIT and real estate investors, analysts and executives.
50 Pages
Frequency: Monthly

8514 RMA Journal
RMA - Risk Management Association
6147 Ridge Ave
Suite 2300
Philadelphia, PA 19128-2627

215-482-3222
800-677-7621; *Fax:* 215-446-4101
customers@rmahq.org; www.rmahq.org

Angelo Roma, Owner
William F Githens, Director Member Relations
Dwightce J Overturf, CFO/Information Technology Officer
Florence J Wetzel, COO/Administrative Officer
Dom DiBernardi, Associate Director
Frequency: Monthly

8515 Regional Review
Federal Reserve Bank of Boston
600 Atlantic Ave
Boston, MA 02210-2204

617-973-3397
800-248-0168; *Fax:* 617-973-4292
boston.library@bos.frb.org; www.bos.frb.org

Joyce Hannan, Manager
Cathy E Minehan, President/CEO
Jane Katz, Editor

Reliable and balanced discussions of economic issues. It is addressed to the opinion leaders of New England's business and government community.
Frequency: Quarterly
Circulation: 21000
Founded in: 1913

8516 Registered Representative
Primedia
Po Box 12901
Shawnee Mission, KS 66282-2901

913-341-1300
866-505-7173; *Fax:* 913-514-6895
rgcs@pbsub.com; www.penton.com

Eric Jacobson, Senior VP
Rich Santos, Group Publisher

Magazine for retail stockbrokers that presents highly focused career-oriented editorials. Accepts advertising.
Cost: $59.00
Frequency: Monthly
Circulation: 108067
Founded in: 1976
Printed in 4 colors on glossy stock

8517 Report on Business
Institute for Supply Management
2055 E Centennial Circle
PO Box 22160
Tempe, AZ 85285-2160
480-752-6276
800-888-6276; *Fax:* 480-752-7890
infocenter@ism.ws; www.ism.ws
Paul Novak, CFM, CEO
Holly LaCroix Johnson, Senior Vice President
Deborah Webber, SVP
Jean McHale, Manager
Frequency: Monthly

8518 Research
Financial Communications Company
PO Box 7588
San Francisco, CA 94120
415-621-0220; *Fax:* 415-621-0735;
www.researchmag.com
Robert Tyndall, Publisher
Bill Nieder, Managing Director
Joseph Geraci, Managing Director
Corporate profiles, investment information, and reports on building and keeping client base.
Cost: $35.00
Frequency: Monthly
Circulation: 65,227

8519 Responsible Owner
Institute for Responsible Housing Preservation
401 9th St NW
Suite 900
Washington, DC 20004-2145
202-585-8000; *Fax:* 202-457-5355
info@housingpreservation.org
Kathryn Holmes, VP
Frequency: Monthly

8520 Reverse Mortgage Advisor
National Reverse Mortgage Lenders Association
1625 Massachusetts Ave Nw
Suite 601
Washington, DC 20036-2212
202-939-1780; *Fax:* 202-265-4435;
www.nrmlaonline.org
Peter H Bell, Executive Director
Glenn Petherick, Director Communications
Frequency: Quarterly

8521 Secondary Marketing Executive Magazine
Zackin Publications
100 Willenbrock Road
Oxford, CT 06478
203-262-4670
800-325-6745; *Fax:* 203-262-4680
info@secondarymarketingexec.com;
www.secondarymarketingexec.com
Social Media: Facebook, Twitter
Michael Bates, Publisher
Patrick Barnard, Editor
Vanessa Williams, Business Development
Delivers news, analysis and how-to advice to people involved in the buying and selling of mortgage loans and servicing rights nationwide.
Frequency: Monthly
Founded in: 1986

8522 Secured Lender
Commercial Finance Association
Ste 1801
7 Penn Plz
New York, NY 10001-3979
212-594-3490; *Fax:* 212-564-6053
info@cfa.com; www.cfa.com
Bruce H Jones, Executive Director
Theodore Kompa, President
Eileen M. Wubbe, Assistant Editor
Edward R. Fallon, Editorial Consultant
Linda C. Mohr, Production Manager
Provides in-depth reporting on federal and state legislation affecting the industry, legal notes on a wide range of issues, a full caladar year of industry workshops, meetings and seminars, personnel shifts, industry news and reviews of publications covering the industry. Discouted subscription rates for members.
Cost: $56.00
Frequency: 6 issues per ye
Circulation: 27000
Founded in: 1944
Printed in 4 colors on glossy stock

8523 Small Business Update
Institute of Management Accountants
10 Paragon Dr
Suite 1
Montvale, NJ 07645-1774
201-573-9000
800-638-4427; *Fax:* 201-474-1600
ima@imanet.org; www.imanet.org
Paul Sharman, President
Frequency: Monthly

8524 Stable Times
Stable Value Investment Association
2121 K St Nw
Suite 800
Washington, DC 20037-1801
202-261-6530
800-327-2270; *Fax:* 202-261-6527
info@StableValue.org; www.stablevalue.org
Andrew Cohen, Editor
Frequency: Quarterly

8525 Strategic Finance
Institute of Management Accountants
10 Paragon Dr
Suite 1
Montvale, NJ 07645-1774
201-573-9000
800-638-4427; *Fax:* 201-474-1600
ima@imanet.org; www.imanet.org
Paul Sharman, President
Frederick Schea, Chair-Emeritus
Sandra Richtermeyer, Chair-Elect
Jeffrey Thomson, President & CEO
IMA's award winning magazine that provides the latest information about practices and trends in finance, accounting, and information management that will impact members and their jobs.
Cost: $195.00
Frequency: Monthly
Printed in 4 colors on glossy stock

8526 Tax Executive
Tax Executives Institute
1200 G St NW
Suite 300
Washington, DC 20005-3833
202-638-5601; *Fax:* 202-638-5607;
www.tei.org
Timothy Mc Cormally, Executive Director
Deborah K Gaffney, Director Conference Planning
Deborah C Giesey, Director Administration
Karina Horesky, Coordinator Membership
Fred F Murray, General Counsel
Frequency: Bi-Monthly

8527 Tax Lawyer
American Bar Association Section of Taxation
321 N Clark St
Chicago, IL 60654-7598
312-988-5000
800-285-2221; *Fax:* 312-988-6281
askaba@abanet.org; www.abanet.org
Louis A. Mezzullo, Editor-in-Chief
William H. Lyons, Managing Editor
Journal of scholarly articles written by highly respected tax attorneys and professors. It provides key reports by Section committees and task forces, and student notes and comments on timely topics.
Frequency: Quarterly

8528 Taxes: the Tax Magazine
CCH
2700 Lake Cook Rd
Riverwoods, IL 60015-3867
847-940-4600
800-835-5224; *Fax:* 773-866-3095
taxes@cch.com; www.cch.com
Mike Sabbatis, President
Douglas M Winterrose, Vice President & CFO
Jim Bryant, EVP Software Products
Information on legal, accounting and economic aspects of federal and state taxes.
Cost: $245.00
Frequency: Monthly
Circulation: 10000
Founded in: 1913

8529 The Wall Street Journal
www.wsj.com
Social Media: Facebook, Twitter, LinkedIn, Google+, YouTube
Gerard Baker, Editor-in-Chief
International English-language business newspaper.
Circulation: 2.4m
ISSN: 0099-9660
Founded in: 1889

8530 ThriftInvestor
SNL Securities
One SNL Plaza
PO Box 2124
Charlottesvle, VA 22902
434-977-1600; *Fax:* 434-977-4466
isales@snl.com; www.snl.com
Mark Saunders, Editor
Pat LaBua, Customer Service
Michael Spears, Advertising Director
Nick Cafferillo, Chief Operating Officer
Adam Hall, Managing Director
Timely articles by industry experts on topics such as conversions, investment opportunities and government regulations. Source for important financial news, investor filings, conversion data and current financial and market information on all publicly traded thrifts.
Cost: $495.00
80 Pages
Frequency: Monthly
Founded in: 1987

8531 Ticker Magazine
Wall Street Teechnology Association
521 Newman Springs Road
Suite 12
Lincroft, NJ 07738
732-530-8808; *Fax:* 732-530-0020
info@wsta.org; www.wsta.org
JoAnn Cooper, Managing Editor
Features articles that provide practical suggestions for technology professionals in the financial community, evaluate costs and benefits of

alternate technologies, and disseminate news about the association
Frequency: Quarterly
Circulation: 14000

8532 Trader's World Magazine
Halliker's
2508 W Grayrock St
Springfield, MO 65810-2165
417-882-9697; *Fax:* 417-886-5180
publisher@tradersworld.com;
www.tradersworld.com
Lawrence Jacobs, Owner
Information on stock indexes, techniques of trading, exchange activities and current developments.
Cost: $19.95
64 Pages
Frequency: Quarterly
Circulation: 12000
ISSN: 1045-7690
Founded in: 1989
Printed in 4 colors on glossy stock

8533 Traders Magazine
Securities Data Publishing
40 W 57th St
11th Floor
New York, NY 10019-4001
212-484-4701; *Fax:* 212-956-0112
Ken Heath, Publisher
Edward Cortese, Marketing Executive
Focuses on industry news, market and regulatory trends and the firms and individuals who shape the equities market.
Frequency: Monthly
Circulation: 6,000

8534 Trusts and Estates
PRIMEDIA Intertec-Marketing & Professional Service
Po Box 12901
Shawnee Mission, KS 66282-2901
913-341-1300; *Fax:* 913-514-6895;
www.penton.com
Eric Jacobson, Senior VP
Rorie Sherman, Editor in Chief
Thrupthi Reddy, Editor
Rich Santos, Group Publisher
Features updates on trust department operations, estates and life insurance, wills, federal tax notes and current literature.
Cost: $199.00
Frequency: Monthly
Circulation: 14730
Founded in: 1886

8535 Value Examiner
National Association of Certified Valuation
1111 Brickyard Road
Suite 200
Salt Lake City, UT 84106-5401
801-486-0600
800-677-2009; *Fax:* 801-486-7500
nacva1@nacva.com; www.nacva.com
Parnell Black, CEO
Frequency: Bi-Monthly

8536 Venture Capital Journal
Securities Data Publishing
40 W 57th St
New York, NY 10019-4001
212-484-4701; *Fax:* 212-956-0112
sdp@tfn.com
Merry Logan, Associate Publisher
Edward Cortese, Marketing Executive
Provides information on recent issues, monitors current companies and looks at companies who have recently gone public.
Cost: $1025.00
Frequency: Monthly
Circulation: 1500

8537 Wall Street Computer Review
Miller Freeman Publications
1199 S Belt Line Rd
Suite 100
Coppell, TX 75019-4666
972-906-6500; *Fax:* 972-419-7825
Elizabeth Katz, Publisher
Pavan Sahgal, Editor
For financial and investment professionals and individual investors.
Cost: $5.00
Circulation: 34,000

8538 Washington Alert
Institute for Responsible Housing Preservation
401 9th St NW
Suite 900
Washington, DC 20004-2145
202-585-8000; *Fax:* 202-457-5355
info@housingpreservation.org;
www.nixonpeabody.com
Kathryn Holmes, VP
Brian Moynihan, Communications Manager
Frequency: Irregular

8539 Washington Update
National Association of Affordable Housing Lenders
1667 K St NW
Suite 905
Washington, DC 20006-1612
202-293-9850; *Fax:* 202-293-9852
naahl@naahl.org; www.naahl.org
Judy Kennedy, President
Frequency: Monthly

Trade Shows

8540 AACE Annual Meeting
AACE International
209 Prairie Avenue
Suite 100
Morgantown, WV 26501-5934
304-296-8444
800-858-2678; *Fax:* 304-291-5728
info@aacei.org; www.aacei.org
Andrew S Dowd Jr, Executive Director
Jennie Amos la, Marketing/Meetings Manager
Frequency: June

8541 AAHAM Annual Meeting
American Association of Healthcare Administrative
11240 Waples Mill Road
Suite 200
Fairfax, VA 22030
703-281-4043; *Fax:* 703-359-7562
moayad@aaham.org; www.aaham.org
Robert Debiase, National President
Linda Sheaffer, Chair
Frequency: October

8542 AARMR Annual Meeting
American Association of Residential Mortgage
1255 23rd Street NW
Suite 200
Washington, DC 20037
202-521-3999; *Fax:* 202-883-3636;
www.aarmr.org
Christopher Murphy, Executive Director
Frequency: Fall

8543 ABA Annual Convention, Business Expo & Director' Forum
American Bankers Association
1120 Connecticut Avenue NW
Washington, DC 20036
202-635-5000
800-BAN-KERS
custserv@aba.com; www.aba.com
Gail Kolakowski, VP Bus Development & Show Manager
Event for CEOs, presidents and other C-level executives from financial services firms across the nation, offering a products and services showcases, lanches and announcements, sessions focused on strategies and tactics for success, regulatory updates, effective leadership, and more.
Frequency: Annual

8544 ACA Annual International Convention & Exposition
American Credit Association International
PO Box 390106
Minneapolis, MN 55439
952-926-6547; *Fax:* 952-926-1624
aca@acainternational.org;
www.acainternational.com
Gary D Rippentorp CAE, CEO
Cathy Berg, Director Meetings
Annual international convention and exposition for credit and collection professionals.
Frequency: July

8545 AEFA Annual Meeting
American Education Finance Association
8365 S Armadillo Trail
Evergreen, CO 80439
303-674-0857; *Fax:* 303-670-8986;
www.aefa.cc
Ed Steinbecher, Executive Director
Frequency: March

8546 AGA Annual Meeting
Association of Government Accountants
2208 Mount Vernon Avenue
Alexandria, VA 22301
703-684-6931
800-242-7211; *Fax:* 703-548-9367;
www.agacgfm.org
Relmond P Van Daniker, Executive Director
Marie S Force, Director Communications
Susan Fritzlen, Deputy Exeucutive Director
Brian Watkins, Manager
Pamella Shaw, Accounting Manager
Frequency: July

8547 AMIFS Annual Profitability & Performance Measurement Conference
Assn for Management Information in Financial Svcs
14247 Saffron Circle
Carmel, IN 46032
317-815-5857; *Fax:* 317-815-5877
ami2@amifs.org; www.amifs.org
Robert McDonald, President
Kevin Link, Executive Director
Krissa Hatfield, Assistant Executive Director

3-day conference consisting of one day of workshops, and two days of educational sessions. 10 exhibitors.
Frequency: Annual/April

8548 **ASMC Annual Meeting**
American Society of Military Comptrollers
415 N Alfred Street
Alexandria, VA 22314-4650
703-549-0360
800-462-5637; *Fax:* 703-549-3181;
www.asmconline.org
James F McCall, Executive Director
Frequency: May

8549 **American Bankers Association Annual Convention & Banking Industry Forum**
American Bankers Association
1120 Connecticut Avenue NW
Washington, DC 20036-3902
202-635-5000; *Fax:* 202-663-5210
http://www.aba.com
Edward Yingling, President/CEO
Annual convention and 200 exhibitors of systems and products for the banking industry.
5000 Attendees

8550 **American Bankers Association National Agricultural Bankers Conference**
1120 Connecticut Avenue NW
Washington, DC 20036-3902
800-226-5377
custserv@aba.com; www.aba.com
Edward Yingling, President/CEO
Diane M Casey-Landry, COO/Senior Executive VP
1M Attendees
Frequency: Novembe

8551 **American Bankers Association: Bank Operations & Technology Conference**
American Bankers Association
1120 Connecticut Avenue NW
Washington, DC 20036-3902
202-635-5000; *Fax:* 202-663-5210
Edward Yingling, President/CEO
Diane M Casey-Landry, COO/Senior Executive VP
Designed to address hot topics for bank operations professinals, covers critical issues and provides insights into the practical applications of bank technology
2600 Attendees
Frequency: April

8552 **American Bankers Association: National Bank Card Conference**
American Bankers Association
1120 Connecticut Avenue NW
Washington, DC 20036-3902
202-635-5000; *Fax:* 202-663-5210
http://www.aba.com
Edward Yingling

8553 **Appraisers Association of America National Conference**
Appraisers Association of America
386 Park Avenue S
Suite 2000
New York, NY 10016-8804
212-889-5404; *Fax:* 212-889-5503
twniem@appraisersassoc.org;
www.appraisersassoc.org
Beth Weingast, President
Exhibits of interest to appraisers, workshops, and presentations.

8554 **Association for Financial Professionals Annual Conference**
Association for Financial Professionals
4520 East West Highway
Suite 750
Bethesda, MD 20814
301-907-2862; *Fax:* 301-907-2864;
www.AFPonline.org
Loren Starr, Chairman
James Gilligan, Vice Chairman
Karen E Ball, Marketing Director
Workshop and 642 exhibits of lockboxes, check processing systems, computers, investments, pensions, foreign exchange, consulting, mergers, aquistions and more information of interest to finacial professionals.
6000 Attendees
Frequency: November
Founded in: 1979

8555 **BCCA Annual Meeting**
Broadcast Cable Credit Association
550 Frontage Road
Suite 3600
Northfield, IL 60093
847-881-8757; *Fax:* 847-784-8059
info@bccacredit.com; www.bccacredit.com
Mary Collins, President/CEO
Jamie Smith, Director of Operations
Rachelle Brooks, BCCA Sales
Frequency: May

8556 **CCFL Semi-Annual Meetings**
Conference on Consumer Finance Law
Oklahoma City University School of Law
2501 N Blackwelder
Oklahoma City, OK 73106
405-521-5363; *Fax:* 405-521-5089;
www.theccfl.com
Alvin C Harrell, Executive Director
Held with American Bar Association.
Frequency: Spring, Summer

8557 **CDFA Annual Meeting**
Council of Development Finance Agencies
301 NW 63rd Avenue
Suite 500
Oklahoma City, OK 73116
405-848-6059; *Fax:* 405-842-3299
info@cdfa.net; www.cdfa.net
Stan Provus, Training Director
Don Conkle, Manager
Frequency: Fall

8558 **CDVCA Annual Conference**
Community Development Venture Capital Alliance
330 Seventh Avenue
19th Floor
New York, NY 10001
212-594-6747; *Fax:* 212-594-6717
info@cdvca.org; www.cdvca.org
Kerwin Tesdell, President
Gary Brooks, Managing Director
Attended by management of social venture capital funds; those thinking of starting funds; investors in social venture capital funds; economic development professionals; banking and investment professionals; foundation representatives and policy makers and government professionals.
Frequency: March

8559 **CFA Institute Annual Conference**
CFA Institute
560 Ray C Hunt Drive
Charlottesville, VA
434-951-5499
800-247-8132; *Fax:* 434-951-5262
info@cfainstitute.org; www.cfainstitute.org
Jeffrey Diermeier, President/CEO
Provides an unparalleled look at the trends and investment issues critical to success in today's global marketplace
Frequency: April

8560 **CIFA Semi-Annual Meetings**
Council of Infrastructure Financing Authorities
805 15th Street NW
Suite 500
Washington, DC 20005
202-371-9694; *Fax:* 202-371-6601;
www.cifanet.org
Richard T Farrell, Executive Director
Richard T Farrell, Executive Director
Letitia Chambers, Owner
Legislative Conference, Spring & Workshop, Fall

8561 **CMSA Annual Meeting**
Commercial Mortgage Securities Association
30 Broad Street
28th Floor
New York, NY 10004
212-509-1844; *Fax:* 212-509-1895
info1@cmbs.org; www.cmbs.org
Dottie Cunningham, CEO
Frequency: Winter

8562 **CORFAC Semi-Annual Meetings**
Corporate Facility Advisors
2000 N 15th Street
Suite 101
Arlington, VA 22201
703-528-3500; *Fax:* 703-528-0113
info@corfac.com; www.corfac.com
Thomas P Bennett, Executive Director
Bill Hawkins, Treasurer
Robert Tillsley, Secretary
Frequency: February, September

8563 **CRF Annual Meeting**
Credit Research Foundation
8840 Columbia Parkway
Suite 100
Columbia, MD 21045-2117
410-740-5499; *Fax:* 410-740-4620
crf_info@crfonline.org; www.crfonline.org
Alex Behm, Chairman
Michael Durant, Vice-Chairman
Frequency: May

8564 **California Accounting & Business Show**
Flagg Management
353 Lexington Avenue
New York, NY 10016
212-286-0333; *Fax:* 212-286-0086
flaggmgmnt@msn.com; www.flaggmgmt.com
Russell Flagg, President
150 exhibitors of investment management systems, databases, real-time and on-line systems. Global and US markets, Windows, PC and client/server systems. New income opportunities for CPAs in California with the change to commissionable financial services. The show is free; the conference is $40 per day and offers CPE sessions. Sponsored by the California CPA Education Foundation.
Frequency: Annual

8565 **Credit Union Executives Expo**
Credit Union Executives Society
Po Box 14167
Madison, WI 53708-0167

608-712-2664
800-252-2664; *Fax:* 608-271-2303;
www.cues.org

Fred Johnson, President/CEO

Expo is held in conjunction with CUES Marketing, Operations and Technology Conference, where the top marketers and operations professionals in the industry gather.
500 Attendees
Frequency: May
Founded in: 1962

8566 **DCUC Annual Meeting**
Defense Credit Union Council
601 Pennsylvania Avenue NW
South Building, Suite 600
Washington, DC 20004-2601

202-638-3950; *Fax:* 202-638-3410;
www.dcuc.org

Frequency: August

8567 **EMTA Annual Meeting**
EMTA - Trade Association for the Emerging Markets
360 Madison Avenue
18th Floor
New York, NY 10017

646-637-9100; *Fax:* 646-637-9128
awerner@emta.org; www.emta.org

Michael M Chamberlin, President
Aviva Werner, Managing Director
Jonathan Murno, Managing Director
Suzette Ortiz, Office Manager
Monika Forbes, Administrative Assistant
Frequency: December

8568 **FMS Annual Meeting**
Financial Managers Society
100 W Monroe Street
Suite 810
Chicago, IL 60603-1959

312-781-1300
800-275-4367; *Fax:* 312-578-1308
diane@fmsinc.org; www.fmsinc.org

Richard A Yingst, President/CEO
Jennifer Doak, Director Marketing
Diane Walter, VP/Director Professional Dev
Frequency: June

8569 **FPA Annual Meeting**
Financial Planning Association
4100 E Mississippi Avenue
Suite 400
Denver, CO 80246

303-759-4900
800-322-4237; *Fax:* 303-759-0749
info@fpanet.org; www.fpanet.org

Martin W Tuttle CAE, Executive Director/CEO
Ian McKenzie, Managing Director Publishing
Frequency: Fall

8570 **FPA Experience: The Annual Conference of the Financial Planning Community**
Financial Planning Association
7535 East Hampden Avenue
Suite 600
Denver, CO 80231

303-759-4900
800-322-4237; *Fax:* 303-759-0749;
www.fpaannualconference.org

Social Media: Facebook, Twitter, LinkedIn, FPA Connect

The event provides networking and professional development opportunities, as well as exhibits.
24000 Members
3000 Attendees
Frequency: Annual/Fall
Founded in: 2000

8571 **FSR Semi-Annual Meetings**
Financial Services Roundtable
1001 Pennsylvania Avenue NW
Suite 500 S
Washington, DC 20004

202-289-4322; *Fax:* 202-628-2507
info@fsround.org; www.fsround.org

Steve Bartlett, President/CEO
Frequency: Spring, Fall

8572 **FSTC Annual Meeting**
Financial Services Technology
44 Wall Street
12th Floor
New York, NY 10005

212-711-1400; *Fax:* 646-349-3629;
www.fstc.org

Zachary Tumin, Executive Director
Frequency: Spring

8573 **Fiduciary and Risk Management Association Annual Meeting**
Fiduciary and Risk Management Association
PO Box 48297
Athens, GA 30604

706-354-0083; *Fax:* 706-353-3994
info@thefirma.org; www.thefirma.org

Hale Mast, Executive Director
Deborah A Austin, VP

To educate, support and promote risk management professionals and improve the effectiveness of risk management for the fiduciary and investment service industry.
Frequency: Spring

8574 **FinEXPO**
Miller Freeman Publications
1975 W El Camino Real
Suite 307
Mountain View, CA 94040-2218

Fax: 650-966-8934

Sixty exhibitors of full range of systems, software, service and solutions that financial and information system decision makers need to meet the challenges of today and the future.
2000 Attendees

8575 **Financial Management Association International Annual Meeting**
University of South Florida
College of Business Administration/BSN 3331
4202 E Fowler Avenue
Tampa, FL 33620-5500

813-974-2084; *Fax:* 813-974-3318;
www.fma.org/

Jonathan Karpoff, President Director
Jacqueline Garner, Vice President Financial Education
Rawley Thomas, VP Practitioner Services
Kenneth Eades, Vice President Global Services
Anthony Saunders, Vice President Annual Meeting

Annual meeting and exhibits of financial management related equipment, supplies and services.
Frequency: October

8576 **Financial Women International Annual Conference**
Financial Women International
1027 W Roselawn Avenue
Roseville, MN 55113

651-487-7632
866-807-6081; *Fax:* 651-489-1322
info@fwi.org; www.fwi.org

Melissa Curzon, President
Cindy Hass, VP
Carleen DeSisto, Secretary
Frequency: September

8577 **HBMA Annual Meeting**
Healthcare Billing and Management Association
1540 South Coast Highway
Suite 203
Laguna Beach, CA 92651

877-640-4262
http://www.hbma.org

Bradley Lund, Executive Director
Paul Myers, Director of Education
Frequency: March

8578 **HMFA's ANI: The Healthcare Finance Conference**
Healthcare Finance Management Association
100 W Monroe Street
Suite 1001
Chicago, IL 60603

312-541-0567; *Fax:* 312-541-0573;
www.hfma.org/events/ani

Access to education programs, speaker sessions and hundreds of vendors, as well as networking and best practices sharing opportunities.

8579 **HMFA's Virtual Healthcare Finance Conference & Career Fair**
Healthcare Finance Management Association
100 W Monroe Street
Suite 1001
Chicago, IL 60603

312-541-0567; *Fax:* 312-541-0573
virtualhcfc@hfma.org; www.hfma.org

Access live education programs and on-demand sessions from your office. Keynote speakers and presenters, and a virtual exhibit hall and career fair.

8580 **IMA Annual Meeting**
Institute of Management Accountants
10 Paragon Drive
Suite 1
Montvale, NJ 07645-1718

201-573-9000
800-638-4427; *Fax:* 201-474-1600
ima@imanet.org; www.imanet.org

John Brausch, Chair
Frederick Schea, Chair-Emeritus
Sandra Richtermeyer, Chair-Elect
Jeffrey Thomson, President & CEO
1500 Attendees
Frequency: July

8581 **IRHP Meeting/Conference**
Institute for Responsible Housing Preservation
401 Ninth Street NW
Suite 900
Washington, DC 20004

202-858-8000; *Fax:* 202-585-8080
info@housingpreservation.org;
www.housingpreservation.org

Linda D Kirk, Executive Director
Frequency: January

8582 **ISM Annual Meeting**
Institute for Supply Management
2055 E Centennial Circle
PO Box 22160
Tempe, AZ 85285-2160

480-752-6276
800-888-6276; *Fax:* 480-752-7890
infocenter@ism.ws; www.ism.ws

Paul Novak, CPM, CEO
Holly LaCroix Johnson, Senior Vice President
Deborah Webber, SVP
Jean McHale, Manager
3000 Attendees
Frequency: May

8583 **NAAHL Annual Meetings**
National Association of Affordable Housing Lenders
1300 Connecticut Avenue NW
Suite 905
Washington, DC 20036

202-293-9850; *Fax:* 202-293-9852
naahl@naahl.org

Judith A Kennedy, President/CEO
Frequency: Winter, Spring

8584 **NABT Semi-Annual Meetings**
National Association of Bankruptcy Trustees
One Windsor Cove
Suite 305
Columbia, SC 29233

803-252-5646
800-445-8629; *Fax:* 803-765-0860
info@nabt.com; www.nabt.com

Carol H Webster, Executive Director
Frequency: August

8585 **NACM's Credit Congress and Exposition**
National Association of Credit Management
8840 Columbia 100 Parkway
Columbia, MD 21045-2282

410-740-5560; *Fax:* 410-740-5574
robins@nacm.org; www.nacm.org

Jim Vanghel, Vice President
Robin Schauseil, President
Annual exhibits of relevance to credit and financial executives.
2500 Attendees
Frequency: June

8586 **NACVA Annual Consultants' Conference**
Nat'l Association of Certified Valuation Analysts
1111 Brickyard Road
Suite 200
Salt Lake City, UT 84106-5401

801-486-0600
800-677-2009; *Fax:* 801-486-7500
nacva1@nacva.com; www.nacva.com

Parnell Black, CEO
750 Attendees
Frequency: June

8587 **NADOA Annual Meeting**
National Association of Division Order Analyst
2805 Oak Trail Court
Suite 6312
Arlington, TX 76016

972-715-4489
administrator@nadoa.org; www.nadoa.org

Lynn S McCord, Administrator
Frequency: September

8588 **NAELB Annual Meeting**
National Association of Equipment Leasing Brokers
304 W Liberty Street
Suite 201
Louisville, KY 40202

800-996-2352; www.naelb.org

Carol Davis, Administrator
Frequency: May

8589 **NAFC Annual Meeting**
National Accounting and Finance Council
2200 Mill Road
Alexandria, VA 22314

703-838-1915
nafc@trucking.org; www.truckline.com

David Hershey, Executive Director
500 Attendees
Frequency: June

8590 **NAFCU Annual Conference and Exhibition**
National Association of Federal Credit Unions
3138 10th Street N
Suite 300
Arlington, VA 22201-2149

703-224-4770
800-336-4644; *Fax:* 703-524-1082
http://www.nafcu.org

Jerome Bruce, Exhibits/Advertising Manager
Fred Becker, President
Annual show of 150 manufacturers and suppliers of complete range of financial products and services. 175 booths.

8591 **NALHFA Semi-Annual Meetings**
National Association of Local Housing Finance
2025 M Street NW
Suite 800
Washington, DC 20036-3309

202-367-1197; *Fax:* 202-367-2197
john_murphy@nalhfa.org; www.nalhfa.org

John C Murphy, Executive Director
Scott Lynch, Association Manager
Kim McKinon, Coordinator Membership
Frequency: Spring, Fall

8592 **NAPFA Annual Meeting**
National Association of Personal Financial Advisor
3250 N Arlington Heights Road
Suite 109
Arlington Heights, IL 60004

847-483-5400
800-366-2732; *Fax:* 847-483-5415
info@napfa.org; www.napfa.org

Ellen Turf, CEO
Margery Wasserman, Director Conferences
800 Attendees
Frequency: May

8593 **NAPTP Meeting/Conference**
Nat'l Assoc of Publicly Traded Partnerships
805 15th Street NW
Suite 500
Washington, DC 20005

202-973-4515; *Fax:* 202-973-3101;
www.ptpcoalition.org

Mary Lyman, Executive Director
Frequency: February

8594 **NASBO Annual Meeting**
National Association of State Budget Officers
444 North Capitol Street NW
Suite 642
Washington, DC 20001

202-624-5382; *Fax:* 202-624-7745
spattison@nasbo.org; www.nasbo.org

Scott Pattison, Executive Director
Lauren Cummings, Manager Member Relations
Frequency: Summer

8595 **NATP National Conference & Expo**
National Association of Tax Professionals
PO Box 8002
Appleton, WI 54912

920-749-1040
800-558-3402; *Fax:* 800-747-0001
natp@natptax.com; www.natptax.com

Annual conference and exhibits of computer hardware, tax accounting and planning software, tax research information, tax forms, one-write accounting, financial planning information, office products and business equipment.
Frequency: Annual

8596 **NATRI National Conference**
National Association for Treasurers of Religious
8824 Cameron Street
Silver Springs, MD 20910

301-587-7776; *Fax:* 301-589-2897
natri@natri.org; www.natri.org

Barbara Matteson, Executive Director
Helen Burke, Associate Director
Frequency: November

8597 **NCPG Annual Meeting**
National Committee on Planned Giving
233 McCre Street
Suite 400
Indianapolis, IN 46225-1030

317-269-6274; *Fax:* 317-269-6276;
www.ncpg.org

Tanya Howe Johnson, President/CEO
Sandra Kerr, Director Government Education
Barbara Owens, Director Membership/Manager HR
Kathryn J Ramsey, Director Meetings
Kurt Reusze, Manager Education/Technology
1700 Attendees

8598 **NDCC Semi-Annual Meetings**
National Defined Contribution Council
9101 E Kenyon
Suite 300
Denver, CO 80237-0467

303-770-5353; *Fax:* 303-770-1812;
www.ndcconline.org

Al Brust, Executive VP
Frequency: Spring, Fall

8599 **NICSA Annual Meeting**
National Investment Company Service Association
36 Washingtn Street
Suite 70
Wessesley Hills, MA 02481

781-416-7200; *Fax:* 781-416-7065
info@nisca.org; www.nisca.org

Barbara V Weidlich, President
Keith Dropkin, Director Operations
Doris Jaimes, Registrar
Sheila Kobaly, Events Manager
Chris Ludent, IT Manager
Frequency: February

8600 **NIPA Semi-Annual Meetings**
National Institute of Pension Administrators

401 N Michigan Avenue
Suite 2200
Chicago, IL 60611-4267

800-999-6472
nipa@nipa.org; www.nipa.org

Laura J Rudzinski, Executive Director
Frequency: Winter, Spring

8601 **NPA Annual Meeting**
National Pawnbrokers Association
PO Box 1040
Roanoke, TX 76262

817-491-4554; *Fax:* 817-491-8770
info@NationalPawnbrokers.org;
www.nationalpawnbrokers.org

Bob Benedict, CAE, Executive Director
Emmett Murphy, Director
Teresa Congleton, Administrative Assistant
1000 Attendees
Frequency: Summer

8602 **National Association of Review Appraisers & Mortgage Underwriters Convention**
National Assn of Review Appraisers/Mortgage Under.
1224 N Nokomis NE
Alexandria, MN 56308

320-763-7626; *Fax:* 320-763-9290
nara@iami.org; www.iami.org

Robert G Johnson, Executive Director

Annual convention of real estate related information and services. Containing 50-75 booths, as well as environmental, home inspection, and construction inspection.
450 Attendees
Frequency: October
Founded in: 1962
Mailing list available for rent: 2500 names at $75 per M

8603 **Payments**
NACHA: Electronic Payments Association
13450 Sunrise Valley Drive
Suite 100
Herndon, VA 20171

703-561-1100; *Fax:* 703-787-0996
info@nacha.org; www.nacha.org

Marcie Haitema, Chairperson
Janet O Estep, CEO

The premier source for payments professionals from across industries and around the globe to get the most vital and actionable information needed to help address the myraid of issues and opportunities in today's rapidly changing environment.
1000 Attendees
Frequency: Annual/April-May

8604 **Private Equity Analyst Global Investing Conference**
Asset Alternatives
170 Linden Street
2nd Floor
Wellesley, MA 02482-7919

781-235-4565; *Fax:* 781-304-1440;
www.assetalt.com

Lisa Hughs, Production Manager

Hundreds of institutional investors, private equity managers, and deal sources to debate the merits of funds of funds and regional funds for investing in Western and Eastern Europe, Latin America, Asia, the Middle East, and elsewhere.

8605 **Risk Management Association's Annual Conference**
Risk Management Association
1801 Market St
Suite 300
Philadelphia, PA 19103-1628

215-446-4000
800-677-7621; *Fax:* 215-446-4100
customers@rmahq.org; www.rmahq.org

Kevin Blakely, President/CEO
Sonny Lyles, Vice Chair

Educates and helps risk management professionals develop new techniques and learn about new innovative products at different stages of their careers.
800 Attendees
Frequency: September/October

8606 **SFE Annual Meeting**
Society of Financial Examiners
174 Grace Boulevard
Altamonte Springs, FL 32714

407-682-4930
800-787-7633; *Fax:* 407-682-3175;
www.sofe.org

Paula Keyes, Executive Director
Stephen J Szypula, Financial Administrator
500 Attendees

8607 **SIM Annual Meeting**
Society for Information Management
401 N Michigan Avenue
Chicago, IL

312-215-5190; *Fax:* 312-245-1081;
www.simnet.org

Jim Luisi, Executive Director
Frequency: Fall

8608 **SQA Annual Meeting**
Society of Quantitative Analysts
25 North Broadway
Tarry Town, NY 10591

914-332-0040; *Fax:* 914-332-1541
cmcas@cmcas.org; www.cmcas.org

Stuart Ganes, President
Frequency: May

8609 **STA's Annual Conference & Business Meeting**
Security Traders Association
777 Post Road
Suite 200
Darien, CT 06820

203-202-7680; *Fax:* 203-202-7681;
www.securitytraders.org

John C Giesea, President & CEO

Keynote speakers, discussions on trading issues, regulatory updates, exchange topics, and exhibits.
1700 Attendees
Frequency: Annual

8610 **Securities Industry and Financial Markets Association (SIFMA) Annual Meeting**
1101 New York Avenue NW
8th Floor
Washington, DC 20005

202-962-7300; *Fax:* 202-962-7305;
www.sifma.org

T Timothy Ryan Jr, President/CEO
Randy Snook, Senior Managing Director/EVP
Donald D Kittell, CFO

The Securities Industry and Financial Markets Association/SIFMA Annual Meeting and Conference program addresses a variety of topics that may include competitiveness of the U.S. capital markets, global exchange consolidation, regulatory and legal initiatives, and trends in the fixed-income and capital markets.

8611 **Southern Finance Association**
University of Florida
Mowry Road, Building 116
PO Box 110811
Gainesville, FL 32611-0811

352-392-5930; *Fax:* 352-392-7902;
www.aceweb.org

Dr. Robert Radcliffe, Show Manager
Twenty five ooths.
1.4M Attendees
Frequency: November

8612 **Success Forum**
International Association for Financial Planning
2 Concourse Parkway NE
Suite 800
Atlanta, GA 30328-5588

770-351-9600
800-945-IAFP; *Fax:* 770-668-7758

J Patrick Tinley, CEO

Annual show and exhibits of financial services equipment, supplies and services.
2500 Attendees

8613 **TEI Annual Meeting**
Tax Executives Institute
1200 G Street NW
Suite 300
Washington, DC 20005-3814

202-638-5601; *Fax:* 202-638-5607
dgaffney@tei.org; www.tei.org

Timothy J McNormally, Executive Director
Deborah K Gaffney, Director Conference Planning
Deborah C Giesey, Director Administration
Karina Horesky, Coordinator Membership
Fred F Murray, General Counsel/Dir Tax Affairs
Frequency: April

8614 **Venture Capital & Health Care Conference**
Asset Alternatives
170 Linden Street
2nd Floor
Wellesley, MA 02482-7919

781-235-4565; *Fax:* 781-304-1440;
www.assetalt.com

Lisa Hughs, Production Manager

This annual gathering of top investors, deal sources, entrepreneurs, Wall Street analysts, and senior health care executives explores the latest trends in health care services, devices, and medical information systems.
Circulation: 0

Directories & Databases

8615 **AACE Directory**
Assoc. for the Advancement of Cost Engineering
209 Prairie Ave
Suite 100
Morgantown, WV 26501-5934

304-296-8444
800-858-2678; *Fax:* 304-291-5728
info@aacei.org; www.aacei.org

Andrew Dowd, Executive Director
Megan McCulla, Asst Manager
Charla Miller, Staff Director Education
Carol S Rogers, Manager Finance
Frequency: Annual

8616 **AEFA Membership Directory**
American Education Finance Association

8365 S Armadillo Trail
Evergreen, CO 80439

303-674-0857; *Fax:* 303-670-8986;
www.aefpweb.org

Ed Steinbecher, Executive Director
Frequency: Annual

8617 ALERT
AuTex Systems
11 Farnsworth Street
Boston, MA 02210-1210

617-345-2000

A database offering all available information on securities and securities trading information.

8618 ATLAS
Technical Data
11 Farnsworth Street
Boston, MA 02210-1210

617-345-2000

Contains a variety of financial data and analyses of 7 major government bond markets.

8619 All-Quotes
545 Madison Avenue
Suite 1400
New York, NY 10022-4219

Fax: 212-425-6895

Offers real-time and delayed quotes, and price and volume history for about 100,000 stocks, options and commodities.

8620 Almanac of Business and Industrial Financial Ratios
Pearson Education
1 Lake St
Upper Saddle Rv, NJ 07458-1813

201-236-7000
800-947-7700; *Fax:* 201-236-7696;
www.prenhall.com

Will Ethridge, President

Profiles corporate performance in two analytical tables for a variety of industries.
Cost: $69.95
Frequency: Annual

8621 American Banker On-Line
American Banker-Bond Buyer
1 State St
27th Floor
New York, NY 10004-1561

212-803-8450
207-581-3042; *Fax:* 207-581-3015;
www.sourcemedia.com

Jim Malkin, CEO
Mario DiUbaldi, Publisher
Phil Roosevelt, Editor
Carole Lambert, Sales/Marketing Director
Stacy Weinstein, Production Director

World wide web edition of daily financial services newspaper. Journal available.

8622 American Financial Directory
4709 Golf Road
Skokie, IL 60076

847-676-9600
800-321-3373; *Fax:* 847-933-8101
custserv@accuitysolutions.com;
www.accuitysolutions.com

Marideth Johnson, Manager, Marketing/Communications
Malcolm Taylor, Managing Director
Cost: $523.00
Frequency: January/July
Circulation: 41300
ISBN: 1-563103-47-8

8623 American Society of Appraisers Directory
American Society of Appraisers
11107 Sunset Hills Rd
Suite 310
Reston, VA 20190

703-478-2228
800-272-8258; *Fax:* 703-742-8471
asainfo@appraisers.org; www.appraisers.org
Social Media: Facebook, Twitter, LinkedIn, YouTube

Jane Grimm, Executive VP
Susan Fischer, Governance Manager
Jack Washbourn, President

Directory of association members who are accredited appraisers.
Cost: $12.50
5000 Members
Circulation: 8,000
Founded in: 1936
Mailing list available for rent: 5,000 names at $200 per M

8624 American Stock Exchange Fact Book
Publications Department
86 Trinity Pl
New York, NY 10006-1817

212-308-0046; *Fax:* 212-306-2160

Neal Wolkoff, CEO

Lists addresses, telephone and fax numbers and ticker symbols of every listed company. Historical statistics and all-time trading records for equities, with a list of every stock option, index option and derivative security traded on the American Stock Exchange.
Cost: $20.00
Frequency: Annual
Circulation: 10,000
Founded in: 1994

8625 American Stock Exchange Guide
CCH
2700 Lake Cook Rd
Riverwoods, IL 60015-3867

847-940-4600
800-835-5224; *Fax:* 773-866-3095;
www.cch.com

Mike Sabbatis, President
Douglas M Winterrose, Vice President & CFO
Jim Bryant, EVP Software Products

Volume 1 lists a directory of officials, members, organizations and securities; Volume 2 lists by-laws and rules of the exchange.
Cost: $570.00

8626 Asia Pacific Securities Handbook
Reference Press
6448 E Highway 290
Suite E104
Austin, TX 78723-1041

512-331-1815; *Fax:* 512-374-4501

Dan Capper, President

Offers stock information on the exchanges in Australia, Bangladesh, China, Hong Kong, India, Indonesia, Japan, Malaysia, Nepal, New Zealand, Pakistan, Taiwan, Sri Lanka, and Thailand.
Cost: $99.95
250 Pages
Founded in: 1993

8627 Bank Mergers & Acquisitions Yearbook
SNL Securities
PO Box 2124
Charlottesvle, VA 22902-2124

434-977-1600; *Fax:* 434-977-4466;
www.snlnet.com

John Minor, Editor
Nick Cafferillo, Chief Operating Officer
Christie Atkinson, Editor
Reid Nagle, Publisher
Mark Outlaw, Advertising Director

For bank and thrift CEOs, CFOs, investment banks, merger and acquisition advisors, law firms, accounting firms and individual investors. Covers all bank and thrift merger activity from the previous year, state-by-state reviews of all private sector whole-bank and whole-thrift transactions, branch sales, merger conversions and government-assisted transactions announced in that year.
150 Pages
Frequency: Annual
Founded in: 1994

8628 Bank Securities Monthly
SNL Securities
212 7th Street NE
Charlottesville, VA 22902

434-977-1600; *Fax:* 434-977-4466
subscriptions@snlnet.com; www.snlnet.com

Mike Chinn, President
Steve Tomasi, Editor
Reid Nagle, Publisher
Mark Outlaw, Senior Vice President

Provides current financial, market and merger information on publicly traded banks. News highlights of the past month and comprehensive industry articles addressing topics such as bank investment opportunities, capital structure and earnings prospects.
70 Pages
Frequency: Monthly

8629 Bloomberg Business News
499 Park Ave
New York, NY 10022-1240

212-893-5555; *Fax:* 212-369-5966;
www.bloomberg.com

Kim Bang, Manager
Matthew Winkler, Editor

A 24-hour global news service available exclusively on The Bloomberg. All stories are fully integrated into The Bloomberg's newsminder which instantly alerts you to developments in all stock and bond markets.

8630 Bloomberg Financial Markets Commodities News
PO Box 888
Princeton, NJ 08542-0888

609-279-3000; *Fax:* 609-279-2028

Michael Bloomberg, Publisher
Matthew Winkler, Editor
Beth Mazzeo, Global Products

A leading multimedia distributor of news, information, data and analysis, providing information on everything from capital markets and airline schedules to employment opportunities and luxury goods.
Cost: $795.00
Frequency: Monthly

8631 Bond Buyer's Municipal Marketplace
Thomson Financial Publishing
4709 Golf Road
6th Floor
Skokie, IL 60076-1231

847-778-8037

James L Nowell, Editor

Offers information on firms and personnel in the municipal bond industry, including municipal

bond dealers, chief finance officers of municipalities which issue bonds, and attorneys specializing in the field of municipal finance.
Cost: $185.00
937 Pages
Frequency: Semiannual

8632 Bonds Data Base
ADP Data Services
42 Broadway
Suite 1730
New York, NY 10004-1617

212-406-2820

This database, update daily, contains historical prices and trading volumes for more than 33,000 corporate, government and agency bonds.

8633 Bowser Directory of Small Stocks
Bowser Report
PO Box 6278
Newport News, VA 23606-0278

757-877-5979; *Fax:* 757-595-0622
Ministocks@aol.com;
www.thebowsersreport.com

Cindy Bowser, Editor

Lists 14 fields of information on over 700 low-priced stocks.
Cost: $89.00
35 Pages
Frequency: Monthly
ISSN: 1053-0908

8634 Bridge Information System
717 Office Parkway
Saint Louis, MO 63141-7115

314-567-8100
800-325-3282; *Fax:* 314-432-5391

Tony Bridge, Manager

This large database contains real-time, last sale and quote data on all listed and unlisted stocks, options, futures and foreign securities.

8635 Bull and Bear's Directory of Investment Advisory Newsletters
Bull & Bear Financial Report
PO Box 917179
Longwood, FL 32791-7179

407-682-6170; www.thebullandbear.com

David J Robinson, President

Advice from investment advisory newsletters on various investment areas, small-cap stocks, global and domestic stock markets, mutual funds, precious metals and economy.
Cost: $29.00
48 Pages
Frequency: Annual
Circulation: 55,000
Founded in: 1974

8636 Business and Financial News Media
Larriston Communications
PO Box 20229
New York, NY 10025-1518

310-871-0563

Sheila Gordon, Editor

Lists over 300 daily newspapers with at least 50,000 in circulation and a business or finance correspondent; television stations and all-news radio stations in the largest 40 markets.
Cost: $89.00
175 Pages
Frequency: Annual

8637 CDA/Wiesenberger Investment Companies Service
CDA Investment
1355 Piccard Drive
Suite 200
Rockville, MD 20850-4300

Jay Nadler, Editor

Lists 5,000 open and closed mutual funds, unit trusts and investment companies listing policies and objectives, history, and statistical information of the company.
1500 Pages
Frequency: Annual

8638 CIN: Corporation Index System
Office of Applications & Reports Services
450 5th Street NW
Washington, DC 20001-2739

202-942-0020

David Weiss, Manager

Lists 1,580 active companies registered under the Investment Company Act of 1940. Information is extend to include related underwriters and advisers and 800 number.
Cost: $90.00
Frequency: Monthly

8639 CISCO
CISCO
170 W Tasman Dr
San Jose, CA 95134-1706

408-526-4000
805-553-6387; *Fax:* 408-853-3683
dljones@cisco-futures.com; www.cisco.com

Frank A Calderoni, Executive VP

Contains technical analyses and prices of commodities futures, and currencies.

8640 CUSIP Master Directory
Standard & Poor's Corporation
55 Water St
New York, NY 10041-0003

212-438-1000; *Fax:* 212-438-0299

Deven Sharma, President

Official listings of numbers and descriptions for more than 1,500,000 stocks, bonds and warrants of 100,000 issuers, including corporations and municipalities of the United States and Canada.
Cost: $1900.00
Frequency: Annual

8641 Commodity Futures Trading Commission Geographic Directory
Three Lafayette Centre
1155 21st Street NW
Washington, DC 20581

202-418-5000; *Fax:* 202-418-5521;
www.cftc.org

Offers information on corporations and firms that are registered with the Commodity Futures Trading Commission.
Cost: $25.00

8642 Corporate Finance Sourcebook
National Register Publishing
430 Mountain Ave.
Suite 400
New Providence, NJ 07974

800-473-7020; *Fax:* 908-673-1189
NRPeditorial@marquiswhoswho.com;
www.financesourcebook.com

Contains a variety of information on the financial services industry. Listings include securities research analysts, major private lenders, mergers and acquisitions, commercial finance firms, pension managers and leasing companies.
Cost: $425.00
1600 Pages
Frequency: Annual

8643 Corporate Venturing Directory & Yearbook
Asset Alternatives
170 Linden Street
Wellesley, MA 02482

781-304-1400; *Fax:* 781-304-1440;
www.corporateventuring.com

Dave Barry, Senior Editor
Barbara Bissonnette, VP Marketink/Sales

Features the most comprehensive data ever essembled on corporations participating in venture-backet deals, and the young companies they're financing.
Cost: $495.00
Frequency: Annual
Printed in on matte stock

8644 Cost Engineers Notebook
AACE International
209 Prairie Ave
Suite 100
Morgantown, WV 26501-5934

304-296-8444
800-858-2678; *Fax:* 304-291-5728
info@aacei.org; www.aacei.org

Andrew Dowd, Executive Director
Megan McCulla, Asst Manager
Charla Miller, Staff Director Education
Carol S Rogers, Manager Finance
Frequency: Irregular

8645 Credit Decisioning Study
Credit Research Foundation
8840 Columbia Pkwy
Suite 100
Columbia, MD 21045-2100

410-740-5499; *Fax:* 410-740-4620
crf_info@crfonline.org; www.crfonline.org

Terry Callahan, President
Michael Durant, Vice-Chairman

8646 Current Market Snapshot
CompuServe Information Service
5000 Arlington Centre Blvd
Columbus, OH 43220-5439

614-326-1002
800-848-8199

Offers information on up-to-date stock prices foreign currency data, and general market statistics.

8647 DIAL/DATA
Track Data Corporation
95 Rockwell Pl
Brooklyn, NY 11217-1105

718-522-7373; *Fax:* 718-260-4324
info@trackdata.com; www.trackdata.com

Martin Kaye, CEO
Stan Stern, Senior Vice President

This database contains current and historical data on securities, options and commodities.

8648 DRI Commodities
DRI/McGraw-Hill
11000 Regency Parkway
Suite 400
Cary, NC 27511

919-462-8600; *Fax:* 919-468-9890;
www.profound.com

This database contains more than 51,000 daily time series of price and trading data for major commodities traded on makrets in the US, Canada, London and Singapore.

8649 DRI Transportation
DRI/McGraw-Hill

11000 Regency Parkway
Suite 400
Cary, NC 27511

919-462-8600; *Fax:* 919-468-9890;
www.profound.com

This large database contains over 15,000 weekly, monthly, and annual time series on commodity traffic by mode, carrier operations and financial data.

8650 DRI US Bonds
DRI/McGraw-Hill
11000 Regency Parkway
Suite 400
Cary, NC 27511

919-462-8600; *Fax:* 919-468-9890;
www.profound.com

This financial database contains daily time series of current and historical prices, yields and fundamental financial information for more than 60,000 dealer-priced debt issues.

8651 Daily Foreign Exchange Analysis & Updates
Technical Data
11 Farnsworth Street
Boston, MA 02210-1210

617-345-2000

This database offers daily reports from major world financial centers including, currency forecasts, analysis of the US bond and money markets, currency reports and the trends of the New York foreign exchange market.
Frequency: Full-text

8652 Dick Davis Digest
Dick Davis Publishing
P.O.Box 2049
Salem, MA 01970-6249

954-733-3996; *Fax:* 954-733-8559
editorial@dickdavis.com; www.dickdavis.com

Steven Halpern, Publisher/Editor
Lorianne Kiesl, Marketing Director
Donald Hanrahan, Owner

The digest excerpts over 400 newsletters and the research reports from leading Wall Street analysts and compiles this information into a 12 page compendium of what leading financial advisors currently recommend.
Cost: $165.00
Frequency: BiWeekly

8653 Directory of Buyout Financing Sources
Securities Data Publishing
40 W 57th St
New York, NY 10019-4001
212-484-4701; *Fax:* 212-956-0112
sdp@tfn.com; www.sdponline.com

Ted Weissberg, Editor-in-Chief
Deborah Chieglis, Advertising Manager
Edward Cortese, Marketing Executive

Over 700 sources of financing, including senior lenders, equity and mezzanine providers in the United States and international avenues, with detailed information on industry, geographic and invetment size preferances and recent activity for each firm.

8654 Directory of Defense Credit Union
Defense Credit Union Council
601 Pennsylvania Ave NW
Suite 600
Washington, DC 20004-2601

202-638-3950; *Fax:* 202-638-3410
dcucl@cuna.com; www.dcuc.org

Roland Arteata, President
Frequency: Bi-Ennial

8655 Directory of Manufacturers' Sales
Manufacturers' Agents National Association
PO Box 3467
Laguna Hills, CA 92654-3467

949-859-4040; *Fax:* 949-855-2973;
www.manaonline.org

Joseph Miller, President
Susan Strouse, Secretary, Treasurer
Alane LaPlante, Director

Association for independent agents and firms representing manufacturers and other businesses in specified territories on a commission basis, including consultants and associate member firms interested in the manufacturer/agent method of marketing.
Cost: $129.00
Frequency: Annual
Circulation: 25,000

8656 Directory of Mastercard and Visa Credit Cards
Todd Publications
PO Box 635
Nyack, NY 10960-0635

845-358-6213; *Fax:* 845-358-1059
toddpublications.com

Barry Klein, Editor

Offers information on 500 credit cards from 200 banks across the country.
Cost: $50.00
1000 Pages
Frequency: Biennial
Circulation: 5,000
Founded in: 1994
Mailing list available for rent: 200 names at $50 per M

8657 Directory of Mutual Funds
Investment Company Institute
100 F Street
Washington, DC 20549
202-942-8088

Sue Duncan, Editor
Cost: $5.00
247 Pages
Frequency: Annual

8658 Directory of Venture Capital & Private Equity Firms - Online Database
Grey House Publishing
4919 Route 22
PO Box 56
Amenia, NY 12501

518-789-8700
800-562-2139; *Fax:* 845-373-6390
gold@greyhouse.com
http://gold.greyhouse.com
Social Media: Facebook, Twitter

Leslie Mackenzie, Publisher
Richard Gottlieb, Editor

Packed with need-to-know information, this database offers immediate access to 2,300 VC firms, over 10,000 managing partners, and over 11,500 VC investments.
Frequency: Annual

8659 Directory of Venture Capital and Private Equity Firms
Grey House Publishing
4919 Route 22
PO Box 56
Amenia, NY 12501

518-789-8700
800-562-2139; *Fax:* 845-373-6390
books@greyhouse.com; www.greyhouse.com
Social Media: Facebook, Twitter

Leslie Mackenzie, Publisher
Richard Gottlieb, Editor

Offers access to over 2,300 domestic and international venture capital and private equity firms, including detailed contact information and extensive data on investments and funds.
Cost: $685.00
1200 Pages
Frequency: Annual
ISBN: 1-592372-72-4

8660 Dow Jones Business and Finance Report
Dow Jones & Company
PO Box 300
Princeton, NJ 08543-0300

609-520-4000
http://www.dowjones.com

This large database offers financial news and information on developments in business and industry, domestic and international economies, and the stock market.
Frequency: Full-text

8661 Dow Jones Futures and Index Quotes
Dow Jones & Company
PO Box 300
Princeton, NJ 08543-0300

609-520-4000

This database, updated continuously, offers current and historical stock quotations for more than 80 contracts from major North American stock exchanges.

8662 Dow Jones Text Library
Dow Jones & Company
PO Box 300
Princeton, NJ 08543-0300

609-520-4000
http://www.dowjones.com

This large database offers business and financial news covering more than 6,000 US companies, 700 Canadian companies and 50 industries.
Frequency: Full-text

8663 E-Z Telephone Directory of Brokers and Banks
106 7th Street
Garden City, NY 11530-5796
516-294-0350; *Fax:* 516-294-0356

MJ Gentile, Editor

Security brokers, banks, and financial organizations in the New York area are listed in this directory.
Cost: $90.00
200 Pages
Frequency: SemiAnnual
Circulation: 10,000
Printed in on matte stock

8664 ECFA Member List
Evangelical Council for Financial Accountability
440 W Jubal Early Dr
Suite 130
Winchester, VA 22601

540-535-0103
800-323-9473; *Fax:* 540-535-0533
dan@ecfa.org; www.ecfa.org

Dan Busby, President
John Van Drunen, Executive Vice President
Kim Sandretzky, Vice President, Communications

ECFA is an accrediting organization whose mission is "enhancing trust in christ-centered churches and ministries."
2250 Members
Founded in: 1979

8665 EMARKET
International Financial Corporation

1818 H St NW
Washington, DC 20433-0001

202-473-1000; *Fax:* 202-974-4384;
www.ifc.org

Robert Zoellich, President

This database offers over 1,000 weekly, annual and monthly time series on company stocks from over 18 developing countries.

8666 Evans Economics Analysis and Commentary
Evans Economics
1660 L Street NW
Suite 207
Washington, DC 20036-5603

This database reports on changes in economic activity to all major financial markets. Over 20 files are listed that provide the forecasts and reports on the effect of economic variables on debt and equity markets.
Frequency: Full-text

8667 Financial Ratios for Manufacturing Corporations Database
US Department of Commerce
Herbert Rm 4885
Washington, DC 20230-0001

202-690-7650; *Fax:* 202-482-0325;
www.access.gpo.gov

Pam Nacci

This database provides 20 quarterly seasonally adjusted financial and operating ratios for selected two- and three-digit SIC groups in the manufacturing sector.
Cost: $85.00
Frequency: Series

8668 Financial Services Canada
Grey House Publishing
4919 Route 22
PO Box 56
Amenia, NY 12501

518-789-8700
800-562-2139; *Fax:* 845-373-6390
books@greyhouse.com; www.greyhouse.com
Social Media: Facebook, Twitter

Leslie Mackenzie, Publisher
Richard Gottlieb, Editor

With over 18,000 organizations and hard-to-find business information, Financial Services Canada is the most up-to-date source for names and contact information of industry professionals, senior executives, portfolio managers, financial advisors, agency bureaucrats and elected representatives.
Cost: $325.00
900 Pages
ISBN: 1-592372-78-3
Founded in: 1981

8669 Financial Yellow Book
Leadership Directories
104 5th Ave
New York, NY 10011-6901

212-627-4140; *Fax:* 212-645-0931
financial@leadershipdirectories.com;
www.leadershipdirectories.com

David Hurvitz, CEO
James M Petrie, Associate Publisher

Contact information for over 26,000 executives at public and private financial institutions, and over 5,000 board members and their outside affiliations.
Cost: $245.00
900 Pages
Frequency: Semiannual
ISSN: 1058-2878
Founded in: 1987
Mailing list available for rent: 20,000 names at $95 per M

8670 Financing Your Business in Eastern Europe
WorldTrade Executive
PO Box 761
Concord, MA 01742-0761

978-287-0301; *Fax:* 978-287-0302
info@wtexec.com; www.wtexec.com

Alison French, Production Manager

Provides reliable information on financing sources, including local and international banks, capital markets, venture capital funds, and government sources
Cost: $135.00

8671 FirstList
Vision Quest Publishing
37308 12th Street
Phoenix, AZ 86086

928-451-4445
mergers@firstlist.com
http://www.firstlist.com

A Robert Weicherding, President

Information is offered in this directory covering companies that are candidates for merger or acquisition, buyers seeking acquisitions, sources of financinf, equity or debt financing and joint venture and licensing opportunities. Also available on-line and the Internet.
Cost: $350.00
120 Pages
Frequency: 8 per year

8672 Ford Data Base
Ford Investor Services
11722 Sorrento Valley Rd
Suite 1
San Diego, CA 92121-1021

858-755-1327; *Fax:* 858-455-6316
info@fordequity.com; www.fordequity.com

Tim Alward, President

This database offers 80 financial data items for each of 2,000 leading common stocks.

8673 Futures Magazine Sourcebook
Oster Communications
5081 Olympic Boulevard
Erlanger, KT 41018

319-277-1271; www.futuresmag.com

Ginger Szala, Group Publisher/Editorial Director
Daniel P Collins, Managing Editor
Christine Birkner, Associate Editor

This issue deals with exchanges in futures and options contracts, including commodities, foreign currencies, stock indexes and international financial coverage.
Cost: $22.00
130 Pages
Frequency: Annual
Circulation: 60,000

8674 Hulbert Guide to Financial Newsletters
Dearborn Financial Publishing
155 Wacker Avenue
Chicago, IL 60606

312-836-4400

Matt Schiff, Owner
Kathleen A Welton, VP

Lists over 100 financial newsletters offering descriptions and evaluation of model portfolios.
Cost: $27.95
574 Pages
Frequency: Biennial

8675 IBC/Donoghue's Money Fund Report/ Electronic
290 Eliot Street
#9104
Ashland, MA 01721-2351

This valuable database offers information and analyses of trends and developments in the money market mutual funds industry.
Frequency: Full-text

8676 IBC/Donoghue's Mutual Funds Almanac
290 Eliot Street
#9104
Ashland, MA 01721-2351
Ann V Needle, Editor

Over 2,400 load and no load mutual funds, including equity, bond and municipal funds.
Cost: $39.95
Circulation: 25,000

8677 Insider Trading Monitor Database
CDA Investment
3265 Meridian Parkway
Suite 130
Fort Lauderdale, FL 33331-3506

954-384-1500

More than 12,500 companies and all insider security transactions reported to the US Securities and Exchange Commission, FDIC, Toronto Stock Exchange and OTS.
Frequency: Daily

8678 Insiders' Chronicle
CDA Investment
3265 Meridian Parkway
Suite 130
Fort Lauderdale, FL 33331-3506
954-384-1500

Robert Gabele, Editor

Publicly held companies in whose securities there has been significant buying or selling by executive officers, directors, and those who hold 10% or more of its shares.
15 Pages

8679 International Financial Statistics
International Monetary Fund
700 19th St NW
Washington, DC 20431-0002

202-623-7000; *Fax:* 202-623-4661
publications@imf.org; www.imf.org

Masood Ahmed, VP
Kathleen Tilmans, Secretary
Olivier Blanchard, Secretary
Christine Lagarde, Managing Director

Offers informaiton on more than 23,000 annual, quarterly and monthly time series of economic and dinancial statistics on over 200 countries.

8680 International Investor's Directory
Asset International
125 Greenwich Avenue
Suite 5
Greenwich, CT 06830-5512
203-629-5015; *Fax:* 203-629-5024

Eric Laursen, Editor

Directory of services and supplies to the industry.
Cost: $235.00
735 Pages
Frequency: Annual

8681 Investment Blue Book
Securities Investigations
PO Box 888
Woodstock, NY 12498-0888

845-679-2300

Lists over 6,000 brokers and dealers in tax shelter plans; 2,000 sponsors of tax shelter products and

suppliers of service to the industry and mutual funds information.
Cost: $145.00
350 Pages
Frequency: Irergular
Circulation: 10,000

8682 Investment Recovery Association Directory
Investment Recovery Association
5800 Foxridge Drive
Suite 115
Mission, KS 66202-2338

913-624-4597; *Fax:* 913-262-0174

Jane Male, Editor

Directory of services and supplies to the industry.
Cost: $250.00
Frequency: Annual
Circulation: 400

8683 Investor Relations Resource Guide
National Investor Relations Institute
8045 Leesburg Pike
Suite 600
Vienna, VA 22182

571-633-0532; *Fax:* 703-506-3571
info@niri.org; www.niri.org

Melissa Jones, Editor
Ariel Finno, Director Research

Lists about 110 investment counseling firms, 50 financial investment associations and 40 financial investment service firms such as publishers of magazines and newsletters.
Cost: $50.00
83 Pages
Frequency: Annual

8684 Japanese Investment in the Midwest
Japan-America Society of Greater Cincinnati
441 Vine Street
Cincinnati, OH 45202-2821

513-579-3114; *Fax:* 513-579-3101;
www.patent-pros.com

Jack Adams, Executive Director

A list of more than 400 Japanese manufacturing firms in the states of Illinois, Indiana, Kentucky, Michigan, Ohio, and Tennessee.
Cost: $40.00
30 Pages
Frequency: Annual

8685 Lipper Marketplace
Lipper, A Thomson Reuters Company
3 Times Square
New York, NY 10036

646-223-4000
800-782-5555
salesinquiries@thomsonreuters.com;
www.lippermarketplace.com

James C Smith, Chief Executive Officer
Stephane Bello, Chief Financial Officer
David W Craig, President, Finance
Robert D Daleo, Vice Chairman
Susan Taylor Martin, President, Reuters Media

This powerful web-based solution opens the door to highly targeted prospects by putting the tools to identify your market at your fingertips. Designed with the input of institutional investment professionals, MarketPlace not only helps you qualify your prospects, it also gives you the cutting-edge competitive intelligence you need to transform your prospects into clients.

8686 Loan Broker: Annual Directory
Ben Campbell, Publisher
917 S Park Street
Owosso, MI 48867-4422

Lists approximately 800 loan brokers, private funding sources and business financing services operating in the continental United States.
Cost: $59.95
Frequency: Annual
Circulation: 3,000

8687 MJK Commodities Database
MJK Associates
1289 S Park Victoria Drive
Suite 205
Milpitas, CA 95035-6974

Fax: 408-941-3404

Offers information on United States and Canadian commodities; internatinal monetary markets; futures indexes and stock index futures.

8688 Mentor Support Group Directory
National Association of Certified Valuation
1111 Brickyard Road
Suite 200
Salt Lake City, UT 84106-5401

801-486-0600
800-677-2009; *Fax:* 801-486-7500
nacva1@nacva.com; www.nacva.com

Parnell Black, CEO
Frequency: Annual

8689 Merger & Acquisition Sourcebook Edition
Quality Services Company
5290 Overpass Road
Suite 126
Santa Barbara, CA 93111-3009

805-964-7841; *Fax:* 805-964-1073

Walter Jurek, Editor
Nancy Rothlein, Production Manager

Contains complete information on the previous years' merger and acquisitions actuary.
Cost: $350.00

8690 Merger Yearbook
Securities Data Publishing
40 W 57th St
11th Floor
New York, NY 10019-4001

212-484-4701; *Fax:* 212-956-0112
sdp@tfn.com; www.sdponline.com

Ted Weissberg, Editor-in-Chief
Deborah Chieglis, Advertising Manager
Edward Cortese, Marketing Executive

Information on tens of thousands of announces and completed deals plus charts giving awards information on industry rankings and transactions.

8691 Merger and Corporate Transactions Database
Securities Data Publishing
1180 Raymond Boulevard
Suite 5
Newark, NJ 07102-4107

This database contains more than 85,000 records on transactions involving mergers, acquisitions, divestitures leveraged buyouts and stock repurchases.
Frequency: Full-text

8692 Mergers & Acquisitions Yearbook
American Banker-Bond Buyer
1 State St
27th Floor
New York, NY 10004-1561

212-803-8450
800-367-3989; *Fax:* 212-843-9624;
www.sourcemedia.com

Jim Malkin, CEO
Mario DiUbaldi, Publisher
Phil Roosevelt, Editor
Carole Lambert, Sales/Marketing Director
Stacy Weinstein, Production Director

Annual yearbook detailing all bank merger and acquisition activity for the previous year. Includes sale price, financial and legal advisors and governmental information.
Cost: $175.00
Frequency: Annual

8693 Mergers and Acquisitions Handbook
National Association of Division Order Analysts
2805 Oak Trail Court
Suite 6312
Arlington, TX 76016

972-715-4489
administrator@nadoa.org; www.nadoa.org

Lynn S McCord, Administrator
Frequency: Annual

8694 Money Market Directory of Pension Funds and their Investment Managers
Money Market Directories
PO Box 1608
Charlottesville, VA 22902-1608

434-977-1450
800-446-2810; *Fax:* 434-979-9962;
www.mmdaccess.com

Tom Lupo, Manager
John Martin, Production Manager
Dennis Thurston, Publications

Over 44,000 tax-exempt funds with over $1,000,000 in assets, and about 1,800 investment management services including bank trust departments and insurance companies, each handling at least $25,000,000 in tax-exempt funds.
Cost: $1150.00
2000 Pages
Frequency: Annual January
Circulation: 8,500
ISBN: 0-939712-31-8
ISSN: 0736-6051
Founded in: 1970

8695 Money Source Book
Business Information Network
15851 Dallas Parkway
Suite 600
Dallas, TX 75248

972-982-8686

Over 1,500 traditional and non-traditional sources of business capital with an emphasis on the south-central United States.
Cost: $24.95
200 Pages
Frequency: Annual
Circulation: 20,000

8696 MoneyData
Technical Data
11 Farnsworth Street
Boston, MA 02210-1210

617-345-2000

This database offers a full line of information on money markets.

8697 MoneyWatch
McCarthy, Crisanti & Maffei
71 Broadway
New York, NY 10006-2601

212-675-5880; *Fax:* 212-509-7389

This database offers valuable information on the money market, including economic indicators.
Frequency: Full-text

8698 Morningstar
Morningstar

225 W Washington Street
Chicago, IL 60602

312-384-4000; *Fax:* 312-696-6001
productinfo@morningstar.com;
www.morningstar.com

Joe Mansueto, Chairman & CEO
Chris Boruff, President, Software Division
Peng Chen, President, Global Investment Div.
Bevin Desmond, President, International Operations
Scott Cooley, Chief Financial Officer

Morningstar provides data on approximately 330,000 investment offerings, including stocks, mutual funds, and similar vehicles, along with real-time global market data on more than 5 million equities, indexes, futures, options, commodities, and precious metals, in addition to foreign exchange and Treasury markets. Morningstar also offers investment management services and has more than $167 billion in assets under advisement and management.

8699 Mutual Fund Encyclopedia
Dearborn Financial Publishing
155 Wacker Drive
Chicago, IL 60606

312-836-4400

Gerald W Perritt, Author

Directory of services and supplies to the industry.
Cost: $35.95
600 Pages
Frequency: Annual

8700 Mutual Fund/Municipal Bond
Interactive Data Corporation
10 Post Office Sq
39th Floor
Boston, MA 02109-4695
617-428-1600
info@interactivedata.com;
www.interactivedata.com

James Murawski, Manager

This database contains over 3,000 time series of price data for municipal bonds held in the portfolios of selected mutual funds.

8701 NADOA Directory
National Association of Division Order Analysts
2805 Oak Trail Court
Suite 6312
Arlington, TX 76016

972-715-4489
administrator@nadoa.org; www.nadoa.org
Lynn S McCord, Administrator
Frequency: Annual

8702 NALHFA Membership Directory
National Associatin of Local Housing Finance
2025 M St NW
Suite 800
Washington, DC 20036-2422

202-367-1197; *Fax:* 202-367-2197;
www.noca.org

John C Murphy, Executive Director
Scott Lynch, Association Manager
Kim McKinon, Coordinator Membership
Frequency: Annual

8703 NASBO Newsletter
National Association of State Budget Officers
444 N Capitol St NW
Suite 642
Washington, DC 20001-1556

202-624-8020; *Fax:* 202-624-7745
spattison@nasbo.org; www.nasbo.org

Scott Pattison, Executive Director
Lauren Cummings, Manager Member Relations

8704 NASD Manual
CCH
2700 Lake Cook Rd
Riverwoods, IL 60015-3867

847-940-4600
800-835-5224; *Fax:* 773-866-3095;
www.cch.com

Mike Sabbatis, President
Douglas M Winterrose, Vice President & CFO
Jim Bryant, EVP Software Products

Officials, members, by-laws and rules of NASD.
Founded in: 1913

8705 NATRI Membership Directory
National Association for Treasurers of Religious
8824 Cameron Street
Silver Springs, MD 20910

301-587-7776; *Fax:* 301-589-2897;
www.natri.org

Laura Reicks, Executive Director
Lorelle Elcock, Associate Director Finance
Frequency: Annual

8706 National Bankers Association: Roster of Minority Banking Institutions
National Bankers Association
1513 P St NW
Washington, DC 20005-1909

202-588-5432; *Fax:* 202-588-5443
webmaster@nationalbankers.org;
www.nationalbankers.org

Michael Grant, President
Floyd Weekes, Chairman

About 140 banks owned or controlled by minority group persons or women.
Cost: $5.00
Frequency: Annual October

8707 National Credit Union Administration Directory
National Credit Union Administration
1775 Duke St
Suite 4206
Alexandria, VA 22314-6115

703-518-6300; *Fax:* 703-518-6539
ociomail@ncua.gov; www.ncua.gov

Michael Fryzel, Chairman
Sarah Vega, Executive Director

Directory of credit unions governed by a three member board appointed by the President and confirmed by the US Senate, by the independent federal agency that charters and supervises federal credit unions. NCUA, with the backing of the full faith and credit of the US government, operates the National Credit Union Share Insurance Fund, insuring the savings of 80 million account holders in all federal credit unions and many state chartered credit unions.

8708 National Directory of Investment Newsletters
GPS
PO Box 372
Morrisville, PA 19067-8372

215-295-8700;
www.investmentnewsletterdirectory.com

George T Scilieber, Editor

Lists over 800 newsletters dealing with investments and financial planning and their publishers.
Cost: $49.95
60 Pages
Frequency: Biennial

8709 North American Financial Institutions Directory
4709 Golf Road
Skokie, IL 60076

847-676-9600
800-321-3373; *Fax:* 847-933-8101
custserv@accuitysolutions.com;
www.accuitysolutions.com

Marideth Johnson, Manager, Marketing/Communications
Malcolm Taylor, Managing Director
Cost: $460.00
Circulation: 31850

8710 PC Bridge
Bridge Information Systems
717 Office Parkway
Saint Louis, MO 63141-7115

314-567-8100; *Fax:* 314-432-5391

Tony Bridge, Manager

This database delivers real-time market information, monitoring up to 100 symbols per page on 10 available pages.

8711 Pacific Stock Exchange Guide
CCH
2700 Lake Cook Rd
Riverwoods, IL 60015-3867

847-940-4600
800-835-5224; *Fax:* 773-866-3095;
www.cch.com

Mike Sabbatis, President
Douglas M Winterrose, Vice President & CFO
Jim Bryant, EVP Software Products

Lists officials, members, member organizations; by-laws and rules of the Pacific Stock Exchange.
Cost: $405.00

8712 Pensions & Investments: Investment Managers
Crain Communications
711 3rd Ave
New York, NY 10017-4014

212-210-0785; *Fax:* 212-210-0465
jmurphy@crain.com

Norm Feldman, Manager
Chris Battaglia, Publisher

List of over 1,050 banks, insurance companies, investment advisors and other investment management organizations.
Cost: $40.00
Frequency: Annual May
Circulation: 41,000

8713 Pensions & Investments: Master Trust, Custody and Global Custody Banks
Crain Communications
711 3rd Ave
New York, NY 10017-4014

212-210-0785; *Fax:* 212-210-0465
jmurphy@crain.com

Norm Feldman, Manager
Chris Battaglia, Publisher

List of banks with master trust/master custodial assets and global custody assets.
Cost: $10.00
Frequency: Annual October
Circulation: 41,000

8714 Philadelphia Stock Exchange Guide
CCH

2700 Lake Cook Rd
Riverwoods, IL 60015-3867

847-940-4600
800-835-5224; *Fax:* 773-866-3095;
www.cch.com

Mike Sabbatis, President
Douglas M Winterrose, Vice President & CFO
Jim Bryant, EVP Software Products

Lists officials, members, member organizations, securities, by-laws and rules of the Exchange.
Cost: $350.00
Frequency: Monthly

8715 **Pratt's Guide to Private Equity & Venture Capital Sources**
Thomson Reuters
3 Times Square
New York, NY 10036

646-223-4431
800-782-5555
rpp.americas@thomsonreuters.com;
www.thomsonreuters.com

James C Smith, Chief Executive Officer
Stephane Bello, Chief Financial Officer
David W Craig, President, Finance
Robert D Daleo, Vice Chairman
Susan Taylor Martin, President, Reuters Media

This is the definitive reference source to actively investing private equity and venture capital firms operating around the world. Pratt's Guide is available in both hard copy and online format - the latter being continually updated with new fund-raising data, new investment and exit data and new contact information.

8716 **Professional Investor Report**
Dow Jones & Company
PO Box 300
Princeton, NJ 08543-0300

609-520-4000

Offers information on unusual stock trading activity taking place on the New York and American stock exchanges and the National Market System portion of the OTC market.

8717 **Quarterly Financial Report**
GE Information Services
401 N Washington Street
Rockville, MD 20850-1707

301-388-8284; *Fax:* 301-294-5501

Cathy Ge, Owner

This unique database offers information on financial estimates for US enterprises within 31 industry classifications.

8718 **RSP Funding for Nursing Students and Nurses**
Reference Service Press
5000 Windplay Dr
Suite 4
El Dorado Hills, CA 95762-9319

916-939-9620; *Fax:* 916-939-9626
info@rspfunding.com; www.rspfunding.com

Gail Schlachter, Owner
R David Weber, Manager
Martin Sklar, Manager

You can find out about the more than 600 scholarships, fellowships, loans, loan repayment programs, forgivable loans, grants, awards, prizes and interships set aside specifically to support study, research, creative activities, past accomplishments, future projects, professional development and traineeships. This is more than twice the number of nursing related funding programs covered in any other source.
Cost: $30.00
210 Pages
Frequency: Biennial
ISBN: 1-588410-95-1
Founded in: 1998

8719 **Registry of Financial Planning Practitioners**
International Association for Financial Planning
1580 W. El Camino Real
Suite 10
Mountain View, CA 94040

877-794-9511
650-390-6400; *Fax:* 650-989-2131
customer.service@trademarkia.com;
www.trademarkia.com

J Patrick Tinley, CEO
Alexander Esq, Owner

Directory of services and supplies to the industry.
80 Pages
Frequency: Annual

8720 **Research Reports**
National Committee on Planned Giving
233 S McCrea St
Suite 400
Indianapolis, IN 46225-1068

317-269-6274; *Fax:* 317-269-6276;
www.ncpg.org

Tanya Howe Johnson, President
Sandra Kerr, Director Government Education
Barbara Owens, Director Membership/Manager HR
Kathryn J Ramsey, Director Meetings
Kurt Reusze, Manager Education/Technology
Frequency: Irregular

8721 **Roster of Minority Financial Institutions**
US Department of the Treasury
401 14th Street SW
Room 523C
Washington, DC 20024-2106

202-874-5740; *Fax:* 202-874-6907

Robert Jones, Editor

About 170 commercial, minority-owned and controlled financial institutions participating in the Department of the Treasury's Minority Bank Deposit program.
Frequency: Biennial

8722 **S&P MarketScope Database**
Standard & Poor's Corporation
55 Water St
New York, NY 10041-0003

212-438-1000; *Fax:* 212-438-0299

Deven Sharma, President

Over 5,000 companies are listed in the Reference Section of Standard and Poors database offering names, addresses, background information and current and historical financial information.

8723 **Secondary Marketing Executive Directory of Mortgage Technology**
LDJ Corporation
P.O.Box 2180
Waterbury, CT 06722-2180

203-755-0158; *Fax:* 203-755-3480

David Zackin, Publisher
John Florian, Editor

A who's who directory of technology products and services to the real estate finance industry.
Cost: $5.00
Frequency: Annual
Circulation: 21,000

8724 **Service Directory**
National Association for Treasurers of Religious
8824 Cameron Street
Silver Springs, MD 20910

301-587-7776; *Fax:* 301-589-2897;
www.natri.org

Laura Reicks, Executive Director
Lorelle Elcock, Associate Director Finance
Frequency: Annual

8725 **Sheshunoff Bank & S&L Quarterly**
Sheshunoff Information Services
2801 Via Fortuna
Suite 600
Austin, TX 78746-7970

512-472-4000
800-477-1772; *Fax:* 512-305-6575
sales@smslp.com; www.smslp.com

Gabrielle Sheshunoff, CEO

Overview of the financial health of the banking industry and of every bank and S&L in the nation. Information includes CAMEL, fachois, asset quality, earnings, and rotation.
Cost: $543.00
Frequency: Quarterly

8726 **Sheshunoff Banking Organization Quarterly**
Sheshunoff Information Services
2801 Via Fortuna
Suite 600
Austin, TX 78746-7970

512-472-4000
800-456-2340; *Fax:* 512-305-6575
gsheshunoff@smslp.com; www.smslp.com

Gabrielle Sheshunoff, CEO

Offers ownership structure for all bank holding companies and overview and ratings for bank holding companies and their brinking subs.
Cost: $499.00
Frequency: Quarterly

8727 **Small Business Investment Company Directory and Handbook**
International Wealth Success
PO Box 186
Merrick, NY 11566-0186

516-766-5850
800-323-0548; *Fax:* 516-766-5919
admin@iwsmoney.com; www.iwsmoney.com
Social Media: Facebook, LinkedIn

Tyler G Hicks, President

Lists more than 400 small business investment companies that invest in small businesses to help them prosper. Also gives tips on financial management in business.
Cost: $20.00
135 Pages
Frequency: Annual
ISBN: 1-561503-12-6
Founded in: 1975

8728 **Speakers Bureau Directory**
National Association of Certified Valuation
1111 Brickyard Road
Suite 200
Salt Lake City, UT 84106-5401

801-486-0600
800-677-2009; *Fax:* 801-486-7500
nacva1@nacva.com; www.nacva.com

Parnell Black, CEO
Frequency: Annual

8729 **Standard & Poor's Directory of Bond Agents**
Standard & Poor's Corporation
55 Water St
New York, NY 10041-0003

212-438-1000; *Fax:* 212-438-0299

Deven Sharma, President

A list of paying agents, registrars, co-registrars and conversion agents for 30,000 corporate and municipal bonds are included.
Cost: $1250.00

8730 Standard & Poor's Security Dealers of North America
Standard & Poor's Financial Services, LLC
401 East Market Street
PO Box 1608
Charlottesville, VA 22902

434-977-1450
800-446-2810; *Fax:* 434-979-9962;
www.mmdwebaccess.com

Deven Sharma, President

The most comprehensive guide to brokerage and investment banking firms in the US and Canada. The directory contains all the facts you need for conveniently locating firms and facilitating transactions.
Cost: $498.00
Frequency: 2x/Year

8731 State Expenditure Report
National Association of State Budget Officers
444 N Capitol St NW
Suite 642
Washington, DC 20001-1556

202-624-8020; *Fax:* 202-624-7745;
www.nasbo.org

Scott Pattison, Executive Director
Lauren Cummings, Manager Member Relations
Frequency: Annual

8732 TA Guide & Checklist
National Investment Company Service Association
36 Washington Street
Suite 70
Wellesley Hills, MA 02481

781-416-7200; *Fax:* 781-416-7065;
www.nisca.org

Barbara V Weidlich, President
Keith Dropkin, Director Operations
Doris Jaimes, Registrar
Sheila Kobaly, Events Manager
Chris Ludent, IT Manager
Frequency: Annual

8733 TRW Trade Payment Guide
TRW Business Credit Services
500 City Pkwy W
Orange, CA 92868-2913

714-385-7000
800-344-0603; *Fax:* 714-938-2586

Approximately 2,500,000 credit active business locations.
Frequency: Quarterly

8734 Tax Directory
Tax Analysts
6830 N Fairfax Drive
Arlington, VA 22213-1001

703-533-4400
800-955-3444; *Fax:* 703-533-4664
taxdir@tax.org; www.tax.org

Amie Chant, Editor
Thomas F Field, Vice President
Jill Biden, Vice President

A reference tool that provides users with comprehensive listings of federal, state and private sector tax professionals. Now in three sections - Government Officials, Corporate Tax Managers and International Officials.
Cost: $ 399.00
960 Pages
Frequency: Quarterly
Circulation: 2,000
ISSN: 0888-1243

8735 Tax Free Trade Zones of the World
Matthew Bender and Company
11 Penn Plz
Suite 5101
New York, NY 10001-2006

212-000-1111

Eric Blood, Data Processing

Covers over 450 free trade zones, transit zones, free perimeters and free ports. The emphasis is placed on tax advantages of each.
Cost: $280.00
1000 Pages

8736 Technical Resources Handbook
National Association of Certified Valuation
1111 Brickyard Road
Suite 200
Salt Lake City, UT 84106-5401

801-486-0600
800-677-2009; *Fax:* 801-486-7500
nacva1@nacva.com; www.nacva.com

Parnell Black, CEO
Frequency: Annual

8737 TheStreet Ratings Guide to Bond & Money Market Mutual Funds
Grey House Publishing
4919 Route 22
PO Box 56
Amenia, NY 12501

518-789-8700
800-562-2139; *Fax:* 845-373-6390
books@greyhouse.com; www.greyhouse.com
Social Media: Facebook, Twitter

Leslie Mackenzie, Publisher
Richard Gottlieb, Editor

Each quarterly edition provides ratings and analyses of more than 4,200 fixed income funds, more than any other publication, including corporate bond funds, municipal bond funds, mortgage security funds, money market funds, global bond funds, and government bond funds.
Cost: $249.00
600 Pages
Frequency: Quarterly
Founded in: 1981

8738 TheStreet Ratings Guide to Common Stocks
Grey House Publishing
4919 Route 22
PO Box 56
Amenia, NY 12501

518-789-8700
800-562-2139; *Fax:* 845-373-6390
books@greyhouse.com; www.greyhouse.com
Social Media: Facebook, Twitter

Leslie Mackenzie, Publisher
Richard Gottlieb, Editor

Each quarterly edition provides reliable insight into the risk-adjusted performance of over 7,500 common stocks listed on the NYSE, AMEX, and NASDAQ, more than any other publication. This user-friendly guide offers step-by-step guidance for users to find out which type of stocks are best for them, and quickly and easily points the user to the best performing stocks in that category.
Cost: $249.00
600 Pages
Frequency: Quarterly
Founded in: 1981

8739 TheStreet Ratings Guide to Exchange-Traded Funds
Grey House Publishing
4919 Route 22
PO Box 56
Amenia, NY 12501

518-789-8700
800-562-2139; *Fax:* 845-373-6390
books@greyhouse.com; www.greyhouse.com
Social Media: Facebook, Twitter

Leslie Mackenzie, Publisher
Richard Gottlieb, Editor

The intuitive, consumer-friendly ratings allow investors to instantly identify those funds that have historically done well and those that have under-performed the market. Identifies top-performing exchange-traded funds based on risk category, type of fund, and overall risk-adjusted performance.
Cost: $249.00
600 Pages
Frequency: Quarterly
Founded in: 1981

8740 TheStreet Ratings Guide to Stock Mutual Funds
Grey House Publishing
4919 Route 22
PO Box 56
Amenia, NY 12501

518-789-8700
800-562-2139; *Fax:* 845-373-6390
books@greyhouse.com; www.greyhouse.com
Social Media: Facebook, Twitter

Leslie Mackenzie, Publisher
Richard Gottlieb, Editor

Offers ratings and analyses on more than 8,000 equity mutual funds, including growth funds, index funds, balanced funds and sector or international funds - more than any other publication.
Cost: $249.00
600 Pages
Frequency: Quarterly
Founded in: 1981

8741 TheStreet Ratings Ultimate Guided Tour of Stock Investing
Grey House Publishing
4919 Route 22
PO Box 56
Amenia, NY 12501

518-789-8700
800-562-2139; *Fax:* 845-373-6390
books@greyhouse.com; www.greyhouse.com
Social Media: Facebook, Twitter

Leslie Mackenzie, Publisher
Richard Gottlieb, Editor

This user-friendly guide provides a step-by-step introduction to stock investing designed for the beginning to intermediate investor. Starting with the basics of stock investing and ending with an evaluation of the user's risk tolerance and the identification of the types of stocks that best match their needs, this easy-to-navigate guide pulls together all of the information necessary to educate the consumer on how to get the best start in investing.
Cost: $249.00
600 Pages
Frequency: Quarterly
Founded in: 1981

8742 Trading Volume Survey
EMTA - Trade Association for the Emerging Markets
360 Madison Avenue
18th Floor
New York, NY 10017

646-637-9100; *Fax:* 646-637-9128
awerner@emta.org; www.emta.org

Michael M Chamberlin, Executive Director
Aviva Werner, Managing Director
Jonathan Murno, Managing Director
Suzette Ortiz, Office Manager
Monika Forbes, Administrative Assistant
Frequency: Quarterly

8743 Trusts & Estates: Directory of Trust Institutions Issue
Primedia
PO Box 12901
Shawnee Mission, KS 66282-2901
913-341-1300; *Fax:* 913-514-6895;
www.penton.com
Eric Jacobson, Senior VP
Offers a list of about 5,000 trust departments in the United States and Canadian banks.
Cost: $82.00
Frequency: Annual January
Circulation: 12,200

8744 Valuation Compilation
National Association of Certified Valuation
1111 Brickyard Road
Suite 200
Salt Lake City, UT 84106-5401
801-486-0600
800-677-2009; *Fax:* 801-486-7500
nacva1@nacva.com; www.nacva.com
Parnell Black, CEO
Frequency: Bi-Ennial

8745 Venture Capital: Where to Find it
National Association of Small Business Investment
1199 N Fairfax Street
Suite 200
Alexandria, VA 22314-1437
703-549-2100
Jeanette D Smith, Editor
Directory of services and supplies to the industry.
Frequency: Annual

8746 Weiss Ratings Consumer Box Set
Grey House Publishing
4919 Route 22
PO Box 56
Amenia, NY 12501
518-789-8700
800-562-2139; *Fax:* 845-373-6390
books@greyhouse.com; www.greyhouse.com
Social Media: Facebook, Twitter
Leslie Mackenzie, Publisher
Richard Gottlieb, Editor
Each guide in the Weiss Ratings Consumer Box Set is packed with accurate, unbiased information, including helpful, step-by-step Worksheets & Planners. The set consists of Consumer Guides to Variable Annuities, Elder Care Choices, Medicare Supplement Insurance, Medicare Prescription Drug Coverage, Homeowners Insurance, Automobile Insurance, Long-Term Care Insurance, and Term Life Insurance.
Cost: $249.00
600 Pages
Frequency: Quarterly
Founded in: 1981

8747 Weiss Ratings Guide to Banks & Thrifts
Grey House Publishing
4919 Route 22
PO Box 56
Amenia, NY 12501
518-789-8700
800-562-2139; *Fax:* 845-373-6390
books@greyhouse.com; www.greyhouse.com
Social Media: Facebook, Twitter
Leslie Mackenzie, Publisher
Richard Gottlieb, Editor
Offers accurate, intuitive safety ratings your patrons can trust; supporting ratios and analyses that show an institution's strong & weak points; identification of the Weiss Recommended Companies with branches in your area and more.
Cost: $249.00
600 Pages
Frequency: Quarterly
Founded in: 1981

8748 Weiss Ratings Guide to Credit Unions
Grey House Publishing
4919 Route 22
PO Box 56
Amenia, NY 12501
518-789-8700
800-562-2139; *Fax:* 845-373-6390
books@greyhouse.com; www.greyhouse.com
Social Media: Facebook, Twitter
Leslie Mackenzie, Publisher
Richard Gottlieb, Editor
This new reference tool provides accurate financial strength ratings of the 7,800 credit unions in the United States.
Cost: $249.00
600 Pages
Frequency: Quarterly
Founded in: 1981

8749 Weiss Ratings Guide to Health Insurers
Grey House Publishing
4919 Route 22
PO Box 56
Amenia, NY 12501
518-789-8700
800-562-2139; *Fax:* 845-373-6390
books@greyhouse.com; www.greyhouse.com
Social Media: Facebook, Twitter
Leslie Mackenzie, Publisher
Richard Gottlieb, Editor
Weiss Ratings Guide to Health Insurers is the first and only source to cover the financial stability of the nation's health care system, rating the financial safety of more than 6,000 health maintenance organizations (HMOs) and all of the Blue Cross Blue Shield plans - updated quarterly to ensure the most accurate, up-to-date informations.
Cost: $249.00
600 Pages
Frequency: Quarterly
Founded in: 1981

8750 Weiss Ratings Guide to Life & Annuity Insurers
Grey House Publishing
4919 Route 22
PO Box 56
Amenia, NY 12501
518-789-8700
800-562-2139; *Fax:* 845-373-6390
books@greyhouse.com; www.greyhouse.com
Social Media: Facebook, Twitter
Leslie Mackenzie, Publisher
Richard Gottlieb, Edtior
Each easy-to-use edition provides independent, unbiased ratings on the financial strength of 1,000 life and annuity insurers, including companies providing life insurance, annuities, guaranteed investment contracts (GICs) and other pension products.
Cost: $249.00
600 Pages
Frequency: Quarterly
Founded in: 1981

8751 Weiss Ratings Guide to Property & Casualty Insurers
Grey House Publishing
4919 Route 22
PO Box 56
Amenia, NY 12501
518-789-8700
800-562-2139; *Fax:* 845-373-6390
books@greyhouse.com; www.greyhouse.com
Social Media: Facebook, Twitter
Leslie Mackenzie, Publisher
Richard Gottlieb, Editor
Updated quarterly, this publication is the only resource that provides independent, unbiased ratings and analyses on the 2,400 insurers offering auto & homeowners, business, worker's compensation, product liability, medical malpractice and other professional liability insurance in the United States.
Cost: $249.00
600 Pages
Frequency: Quarterly
Founded in: 1981

8752 Who's Who in Economic Development Directory
International Economic Development Council (IEDC)
734 15th St NW
Suite 900
Washington, DC 20005-1013
202-223-7800; *Fax:* 202-223-4745;
www.iedconline.org
Jeffrey Finkle, CEO
Jon Roberts, Managing Director
Jackie Gibson, Project Manager
Charles Stein, Founder
A listing of over 2,500 Council members and other certified individuals. Directory is limited to international coverage.
200 Pages
Frequency: Annual

8753 Who's Who in Venture Capital
Grey House Publishing
4919 Route 22
PO Box 56
Amenia, NY 12501
518-789-8700
800-562-2139; *Fax:* 845-373-6390
books@greyhouse.com; www.greyhouse.com
Social Media: Facebook, Twitter
Leslie Mackenzie, Publisher
Richard Gottlieb, Editor
Provides immediate access to nearly 10,000 principals, partners and managing directors heading the world's Venture Capital and Private Equity firms. The listings contain comprehensive profile information including partner and firm names, titles, education, professional background, directorships and full contact information.
Cost: $295.00
643 Pages
Founded in: 1981

8754 World Emerging Stock Markets
Probus Publishing Company
1333 Burbridge Parkway
Burbridge, IL 60521
Directories of stock markets in Central and South America, Middle East and Europe.
Cost: $59.95

8755 Yearbook of Education Finance
American Education Finance Association
8365 S Armadillo Trail
Evergreen, CO 80439
303-674-0857; *Fax:* 303-670-8986;
www.aefa.cc
Ed Steinbecher, Executive Director
Information and updates for educational institutions and organizations regarding financial investing, prospecting and fundraising.
Frequency: Annual

Industry Web Sites

8756 **http://gold.greyhouse.com**
G.O.L.D Grey House OnLine Databases
Grey House Publishing's online database platform, GOLD, offers Quick Search, Keyword Search and Expert Search for most business sectors including financial services and banking markets. The GOLD platform makes finding the information you need quick and easy - whether you're a novice searcher or an experienced database user. All of Grey House's directory products are available for subscription on the GOLD platform.

8757 **www.aacei.org**
Association for Advancement of Cost Engineering
Association for those interested in the financial aspects of engineering all aspects of cost management.

8758 **www.aaii.com**
American Association of Individual Investors
An independent nonprofit corporation formed in 1978 for the purpose of assisting individuals in becoming effective managers of their own assets through programs of education, information and research.

8759 **www.abiworld.org**
American Bankruptcy Institute
Provides a multi-disiplinary, non-partisan organization dedicated to research and education on matters related to insolvency. Provides a forum for the exchange of ideas and information. ABI is engaged in numerous educational and research activities, as well as the production of a number of publications both for the insolvency practitioner and the public.

8760 **www.acainternational.org**
ACA International
Formerly know as the American Collectors Association, is the association of credit and collection professionals. Founded in 1939, it has over 5,300 members, including third party collection agencies, attorneys, credit grantors and vendor affiliates. Headquartered in Minneapolis, ACA serves members in the US and Canada plus 58 other countries worldwide.

8761 **www.aefa.org**
American Education Finance Association
Encourages communications among groups and individuals in education financial fields.

8762 **www.afponline.org**
Association for Financial Professionals
Association of 12,000 financial professionals.

8763 **www.afsaonline.com**
American Financial Services Association
National trade association for market funded providers of financial services to consumers and small businesses. These providers offer an array of finacial services, including unsecured personal loans, automobile loans, home equity loans and credit cards through specialized bank institutions.

8764 **www.agacgfm.org**
Association of Government Accountants
AGA is an educational association dedicated to enhancing public financial management by serving the professional interests of governmental managers and public accounting firms.

8765 **www.appraisalinstitute.org**
Appraisal Institute
Promotes a code of ethics and uniform standards of the real estate appraisal practice. Publishes periodicals, books and appraisal-related materials, and sponsors courses and seminars.

8766 **www.appraisers.org**
American Society of Appraisers
Professional association of appraisers of all kinds.

8767 **www.bcfm.com**
Broadcast Cable Financial Management Association
Professional association for TV, radio and cable CEOs, bueiness managers, HR, MIS controllers and financial personnel, as well as associate members in legal, audit and related fields.

8768 **www.bma.net.org**
Bank Marketing Association
Association for suppliers of industry related products and services.

8769 **www.communitycapital.org**
National Community Capital Association
Provides support for non-profit revolving loan funds that lend capital and offer technical assistance in distressed and disenfranchised communities.

8770 **www.dbcams.com**
FCSI Industry Web Sites
A resource for the financial industry, including stock exchanges, news, pricing services, research, information and more.

8771 **www.ecfa.org**
Evangelical Council for Financial Accountability
Helps Christ-centered organizations earn the public's trust through developing and maintaining standards of accountability that convey God-honoring ethical practices.

8772 **www.federalregister.com**
Neighborhood Reinvestment Corporation
Supplies training, grants, developmental assistance, and a range of other technical services designed to help the local partnerships achieve substantially self-reliant neighborhoods. The goal is to improve a neighborhood's housing and physical conditions, build a positive community image, and establish a healthy real estate market and a core of neighbors capable of managing the continued health of their neighborhood.

8773 **www.fei.org**
Financial Executives International
A professional organization of individuals performing the duties of C.F.O., Controller, Treasurer or Vice President of Finance.

8774 **www.financialratingsseries.com**
Grey House Publishing
Financial Ratings Series Online combines the strength of Weiss Ratings and TheStreet Ratings to offer the library community with a single source for financial strength ratings and financial planning tools covering Banks, Insurers, Mutual Funds and Stocks. This powerful database will provide the accurate, independent information consumers need to make informed decisions about their financial planning.

8775 **www.fma.org**
Financial Management Association
Strives to facilitate exchanges of ideas among persons in financial management.

8776 **www.fmsinc.org**
Financial Managers Society
Provides technical information and education to financial officers in banks, thrifts and credit unions.

8777 **www.globalpurchasing.org**
International Association of Purchasing Managers
A professional organization dedicated to the advancement of world trade, membership is open to buyers, purchasing managers, executives and all individuals that may be involved or have an interest in the important function of buying goods and services on the global market. A NON-PROFIT organization..

8778 **www.greenwood.com**
Greenwood Publishing Group
Business and professional publishing, academic books in Business, Finance, Business Law, and Applied Economics management.

8779 **www.greyhouse.com**
Grey House Publishing
Authoritative reference directories for most business sectors including financial services and banking markets. Users can search the online databases with varied search criteria allowing for custom searches by product category, geographic area, sales volume, keyword, subject and more. Full Grey House catalog and online ordering also available.

8780 **www.houisingfinance.org**
Int'l Union of Housing Finance Institutions
Disseminates information in housing finance policies and techniques worldwide.

8781 **www.iami.org**
National Association of Review Appraisers
Association for professionals who review real estate appraisals and underwrite real estate mortgagers. The association offers the CRA, Certified Review Appraiser and RMU, Registered Mortgage Underwriter, professional designation.

8782 **www.ici.org**
Investment Company Institute
Acts to represent members in matters of legislation, taxation, regulation, economic research and marketing and public information regarding investments and mutual funds.

8783 **www.investavenue.com**
Invest Avenue
Online magazine featuring articles from leading professionals in the finacial world, current news and analysis. Newsletter can be e-mailed on request.

8784 **www.invrecovery.org**
Investment Recovery Association
Association for manufacturers of services and supplies to the industry.

8785 **www.irrc.org**
Investor Responsibility Research Center
Acts to publish reports and analyses of social issues and public policy affecting corporation and investors.

8786 **www.kobren.com**
Mutual Fund Investors Association
Association for those interested in information and rates for mutual funds, investments, stocks and bonds.

8787 **www.marketresearch.com**
Research Reports
Search financial services reports from over 350 sources. Updated daily.

8788 **www.mfea.com**
Mutual Fund Education Alliance
Conducts public education and public relation activities in an effort to acquaint industry, organizations and government agencies with direct market funds.

8789 **www.mortgagepress.com**
National Mortgage Professional
Information on new products, industry news, personnel announcements and calendar of events.

8790 **www.nact.org**
National Association of Corporate Treasurers
Members are corporate chief financial officers, treasurers or assistant treasurers.

8791 **www.nadco.org**
National Association of Development Companies
Provides long-term fixed asset financing to small businesses.

8792 **www.nafa-us.org**
National Aircraft Finance Association
Members are lending institutions involved in aircraft financing.

8793 **www.nafcunet.org**
National Association of Federal Credit Unions
Association for manufacturers and suppliers of complete range of financial products and services.

8794 **www.nasbic.org**
Nat'l Assn of Small Business Investment Companies
Trade Association representing federally licensed ventures capital firms, Email, and business investment companies.

8795 **www.natptax.com**
National Association of Tax Professionals
The National Association of Tax Professionals (NATP) is a nonprofit association dedicated to excellence in taxation and related financial services. NATP was formed to serve professionals who work in all areas of tax practice. Members include Enrolled Agents, Certified Public Accountants, individual practitioners, accountants, attorneys, and financial planners.

8796 **www.nchffa.com**
National Council of Health Facilities Finance
To serve the common interests and enhance the effectiveness of member Authorities through communication, education and advocacy.

8797 **www.nfa.future.org**
National Futures Association
Association for corporations and firms that are registered with the Commodity Futures Trading Commission.

8798 **www.nfa.org**
National Finance Adjusters
Serves collateral recovery specialists.

8799 **www.nfma.org**
National Federation of Municipal Analysts
Promotes the profession of municipal credit analysts through educational programs, industry, communications and related programming.

8800 **www.nibesa.com**
National Independent Bank Equipment & Systems Assn
Association of financial security equipment nationwide. Annual convention and showcase and monthly newsletter.

8801 **www.nipa.org**
National Institute of Pension Administrators
Enhancing professionalism in the retirement plan industry through education.

8802 **www.nvca.org**
National Venture Capital Association
Corporations, corporate financiers and private individuals who invest private capital in young companies on a professional basis.

8803 **www.nvla.org**
National Vehicle Leasing Association
Fosters education, publishing, conferences, legal services, advancement and industry relations certification.

8804 **www.plunkettresearch.com/finance/index.htm**
Plunkett Research
Free section of company web site provides an synopsis of trends in the finacial industry and a glossary of terms.

8805 **www.securitytraders.org**
Security Traders Association
Serves the securities industry.

8806 **www.snl.com**
SNL Securities
News articles on banks and thrifts, insurance and other financial services. Also features vital company information.

8807 **www.theiia.org**
Institute of Internal Auditors
International organization composed of internal auditors, corporate executives and board members. Contact and current development information.

8808 **www.thestreet.com**
TheStreet Ratings, Inc.
Publisher of ratings guides.

8809 **www.uhab.org**
Urban Homesteading Assistance Board
Information on affordable housing and self reliance. Activities include advocacy, organizing, classroom and on-site training, direct technical assistance, development consulting, development and sponsorship of new co-ops and services to member co-ops that include bookkeeping, insurance, legal services, bulk purchasing, newsletters and IT services.

8810 **www.wsta.org**
Wall Street Technology Association
White papers on the latest in technology for IT professionals working in the finacial field. Resource guide for industry products and services and information on seminars and conferences included.

Associations

8811 American Albacore Fishing Association
4364 Bonita Rd., Box 311
Bonita, CA 91902

619-941-2307; *Fax:* 619-863-5046
nataliewebster@americanalbacore.com
americanalbacore.com

Tim Thomas, President
Carl Nish, Vice President
Jack Vantress, Treasurer
Jack Webster, Secretary

A nonprofit representing commercial pole and line vessels that advocates for a sustainable tuna fishery.

8812 American Crappie Association
125 Ruth Avenue
Benton, KY 42025

270-395-4204; *Fax:* 270-395-4381
office@crappieusa.com; www.crappieusa.com
Social Media: Facebook

Darrell VanVactor, President
Charles Rogers, VP
Larry Crecelius, Public Relations Director
Jim Perry, Secretary/Treasurer
Dan Wagoner, Member

For all crappie anglers, from weekend fishermen to tournament pros. Influencing national manufacturers to produce more and better crappie fishing products, establishing a voice and lobby for crappie anglers everywhere and elevating the sport of crappie fishing to its rightful place in the limelight.
Cost: $20.00
Frequency: Individual Membership

8813 American Fisheries Society
5410 Grosvenor Ln
Suite 110
Bethesda, MD 20814

301-897-8616; *Fax:* 301-897-8096
sjohnston@fisheries.org; www.fisheries.org
Social Media: Facebook, Twitter, vimeo, flickr

Bob Hughes, President
Donna L. Parrish, President-Elect
Ronald J. Essig, First Vice President
Joe Margraf, Second Vice President
John Boreman, Past President

AFS promotes scientific research and enlightened management of resources for optimum use and enjoyment by the public. It also encourages a comprehensive education for fisheries scientists and continuing on-the-job training
Cost: $100.00
8500 Members
Frequency: Membership Fee
Founded in: 1870
Mailing list available for rent: 8500 names

8814 American Fly Fishing Trade Association
321 East Main St.
Suite 300
Bozeman, MO 59715

406-522-1556; *Fax:* 406-522-1557;
www.affta.com
Social Media: Facebook

Ben Bulis, President
Tucker Ladd, Chairman

A sole trade organization for the fly fishing industry. The mission is to promote the sustained growth of the fly fishing industry.
400 Members
Founded in: 2003
Mailing list available for rent

8815 American Institute of Fishery Research Biologists
205 Blades Road
Havelock, NC 28532

www.aifrb.org
Social Media: Facebook, Twitter, LinkedIn, Stumbleupon, www.digg.com

Tom Keegan, President
Allen Shimada, Treasurer
Barbara Warkentine, Secretary
Sarah Fox, Executive Editor
Linda Jones, Past President

A professional organization founded to promote conservation and proper utilization of fishery resources through application of fishery science and related sciences.
1000 Members
Founded in: 1956

8816 American Littoral Society
18 Hartshorne Drive
Suite #1
Highlands, NJ 07732

732-291-0055; *Fax:* 732-291-3551
driepe@nyc.rr.com; www.littoralsociety.org
Social Media: Facebook, Twitter, Stumbleupon

Tim Dillingham, Executive Director
Kathleen Gasienica, President
Peter Hetzler, Vice President
Gregory Quirk, Treasurer
Sameul Huber, Secretary

Dedicated to the environmental well-being of coastal habitat.
5000+ Members
Frequency: Membership Fee: $30-$35
Founded in: 1961
Mailing list available for rent

8817 American Shrimp Processors Association
PO Box 4867
EIN #72-6029637
Biloxi, MS 39535

857-445-4165; *Fax:* 228-385-2565
info@fundraise.com; www.fundraise.com
Social Media: Facebook, Twitter

Nate Drouin, CEO
Kurt Schneider, Chief Operating Officer
Kevin Bedell, Chief Technical Officer
Ivan Sifrim, UX Developer
Nick Alekhine, Developer

A non-profit trade organization designed to represent U.S. shrimp processors in all aspects of business. Allowing processors and related industries to work together to foster a business and technological climate in which its members can prosper while providing the highest quality product to its customers.
Founded in: 1964

8818 American Sportfishing Association
1001 North Fairfax St.
Suite 501
Alexandria, VA 22314

703-519-9691; *Fax:* 703-519-1872
info@asafishing.org; www.asafishing.org
Social Media: Facebook, Twitter

Mike Nussman, President & CEO
Scott Gudes, VP, Government Affairs
Diane Carpenter, VP, Operations & CFO
Glenn Hughes, VP, Industry Relations
Jill Calabria, Membership Director

The Association advocates for fish, anglers and the sportfishing industry.
Founded in: 1933

8819 Association of Fish and Wildlife Agencies
1100 First Street NE
Suite 825
Washington, DC 20002

202-838-3474; *Fax:* 202-350-9869
info@fishwildlife.org; www.fishwildlife.org
Social Media: Facebook, Twitter

Ron Regan, Executive Director
Dave Chanda, President
Nick Wiley, Vice President
Carol Bambrey, Association Council
Glenn Normandeau, Secretary/Treasurer

The organization that represents all of North America's fish and wildlife agencies that promotes sound management ans conservation, and speaks with a unified voice on important fish and wildlife issues.
Founded in: 1902

8820 Association of Smoked Fish Processors
c/o Shuster Labs
85 John Road
Canton, MA 02120

781-821-2200
800-444-8705; *Fax:* 781-821-9266
info@shusterlabs.com; www.shusterlabs.com

Members are food processors with an interest in smoked fish.
Founded in: 1963

8821 Association of Zoos and Aquariums
8403 Colesville Rd
Suite 710
Silver Spring, MD 20910-3314

301-562-0777; *Fax:* 301-562-0888
membership@aza.org; www.aza.org
Social Media: Facebook, Twitter

Dennis E. Pate, Executive Director & CEO
Steve Burns, Chair-Elect
Dennis W. Kelly, Vice-Chair
Jim Breheny, Director
Lynn Clements, Director

A nonprofit organization dedicated to the advancement of accredited zoos and aquariums in the areas of animal care, wildlife conservation, education and science.
200 Members
Founded in: 1924

8822 At-Sea Processors Association
4039 21st Ave W
Suite 400
Seattle, WA 98199

206-285-5139; *Fax:* 206-285-1841
jgilmore@atsea.org; www.atsea.org

Stephanie Madsen, Executive Director
Paul MacGregor, General Counsel
Jim Gilmore, Public Affairs Director
Ed Richardson, PhD., Resource Economist
Melinda Madson Schmidt, Program Coordinator

A trade association representing seven copmanies that own and operate 19 U.S. flag cathcer/processor vessels that participate principally in the Alaska pollack fishery and west coast Pacific whiting fishery.
Cost: $500.00
7 Members
Frequency: Membership Fees Vary
Founded in: 1985

8823 **Atlantic States Marine Fisheries Commission**
1050 N. Highland St.
Suite 200 A-N
Arlington, VA 22201

703-842-0740; *Fax:* 703-842-0741
info@asmfc.org; www.asmfc.org
Social Media: Facebook, Twitter

Dr. Louis B. Daniel III, Chair
Douglas E Grout, Vice Chair
John M.R Bull, Commissioner
Laura C. Leach, Director
Cecelia Butler, Human Resources Administrator

The commission was formed by the fifteen Atlantic coast states. It serves as a deliberative body, coordinating the conservation and management of the states shared near shore fishery resources.
45 Members
Founded in: 1942

8824 **Bass Anglers Sportsman Society**
3500 Blue Lake Drive
Suite 330
Birmingham, AL 35243

334-272-9530
877-227-7872; *Fax:* 334-279-7148
bassmaster@emailcustomerservice.com;
www.bassmaster.com
Social Media: Facebook, Twitter

Dean Kassel, President
Chris Horton, Associate Director

A service organization for bass fishermen. It protects and preserves the fishing environment, reports on the newest products and techniques, and provides an arena for professional and amateur fishing competitions.
Cost: $14.95
600M Members
Frequency: Annual Membership Fee
Founded in: 1972

8825 **Blue Water Fishermen's Association**
PO Box 779
Forked River, NJ 08731-0779

609-891-8672; *Fax:* 732-279-4522
bwfa@usa.net; www.bwfa-usa.org
Social Media: Facebook, Twitter, LinkedIn, Stumbleupon

Nelson R Beideman, Executive Director

Non-profit organization of companies and individuals representing fishermen, Captains, vessel owners, docks, dealers, suppliers and related service businesses.
Founded in: 1990

8826 **California Fisheries & Seafood Institute**
1521 I St
Sacramento, CA 95814

916-441-5560; *Fax:* 916-446-1063
Info@calseafood.net; www.calseafood.net

Kevin Joyce, President
Dave Rudie, 1st Vice President
Steve Foltz, Treasurer
Sal Balestrieri, Vice President-Legislative
Kathleen Halson, Vice President-Promotion

Regional trade organization representing members of the consumer seafood supply industry.
130+ Members
Founded in: 1954

8827 **California Salmon Council**
PO Box 2255
Folsom, CA 95763-2255

916-933-7050; *Fax:* 916-933-7055
info@calkingsalmon.org;
www.calkingsalmon.org

Greg Ambiel, Chairman
Bill Dawson, Vice-Chairman

Represents the marketing interests of California's commercial salmon fishermen. It creates consumer awareness and demand for California King Salmon.
Founded in: 1989

8828 **Catfish Farmers of America**
1100 Highway 82 E
Suite 202
Indianola, MS 38751

662-887-2699; *Fax:* 662-887-6857;
www.catfishfarmersofamerica.com
Social Media: Facebook, Twitter

Hugh Warren, President

Represents the largest aquaculture industry in the United States. Represents the interests of farm-raised catfish industry of farmers, processors, feed mills, researchers and supplier industries.
Cost: $40.00
Frequency: Membership Fee
Founded in: 1968

8829 **FishAmerica Foundation**
1001 North Fairfax St.
Suite 501
Alexandria, VA 22314

703-519-9691; *Fax:* 703-519-1872
fafgrants@asafishing.org;
www.fishamerica.org
Social Media: Facebook, Twitter, Youtube

Gregg Walner, Chairman
Dave Bulthuis, Vice Chairman
Donn Schaible, Secretary
Jim Hubbard, Treasurer
Jeff Marble, Immediate Past President

The sportfishing industry's trade association, committed to looking out for the interests of the entire sportfishing community.
650+ Members
Founded in: 1962

8830 **Fishermen's Marketing Association**
1585 Heartwood Drive
Suite E
McKinleyville, CA 95519
707-840-0182; *Fax:* 707-840-0539
fma@trawl.org; www.trawl.org

Peter Leipzig, Executive Director

Represents commercial groundfish and shrimp fishermen from San Pedro, California to Bellingham, Washington. The mission is to engage in activities which promote stable prices and an orderly flow of wholesome seafood to the consumer
60 Members
Founded in: 1952

8831 **Fishing Vessel Owners Association**
4005 20th Ave W
Room 232
Seattle, WA 98199

206-284-4720; *Fax:* 206-283-3341;
www.fvoa.org

Per Odegaard, President
Paul Clampitt, Vice-President
John Crowley, Secretary/Treasurer
Robert D. Alverson, Manager
Miachel Offerman, Trustee

Trade association of longline vessel operators which promotes safety at sea, habitat-friendly gear with minimum bycatch and ensures competitive pricing.
Founded in: 1914

8832 **Garden State Seafood Association**
212 W State St
Trenton, NJ 08608

609-898-1100; *Fax:* 609-898-6070
gregdidomenico@gardenstateseafood.org;
www.gardenstateseafood.org
Social Media: Facebook, Twitter

Ernie Panacek, President
Jeffrey Reichel, Vice-President
Greg DiDomenico, Executive Director
Rick Marks, Washington D.C. Representative
Scot Mackey, Trenton Representative

Dedicated to assure that New Jersey's marine resources are managed responsibly and are able to be enjoyed by anglers and seafood consumers for generations.
Founded in: 1999

8833 **Great Lakes Fishery Commission**
2100 Commonwealth Blvd
Suite 100
Ann Arbor, MI 48105

734-662-3209; *Fax:* 734-741-2010
info@glfc.org; www.glfc.int
Social Media: Facebook, Twitter

Michael Hansen, Chairman
Dale Burkett, Director
Steve Domeracki, Manager
Robert (Bob) Lambe, Executive Secretary
Ted Treska, Information Manager

The commission has two major responsibilities; to develop coordinated programs of research on the Great Lakes and to formulate and implement a program to eradicate or minimize sea lamprey populations in the Great Lakes.
Founded in: 1955
Mailing list available for rent

8834 **Gulf and Caribbean Fisheries Institute (GCFI)**
2796 Overseas Highway
Suite 119
Marathon, FL 33050

305-289-2330; *Fax:* 305-289-2334
bob.glazer@gcfi.org; www.gcfi.org
Social Media: Facebook

Gracia Garcia-Moliner, Chairman
Nancy Brown-Peterson, Vice Chair
LeRoy Cresswel, Executive Secretary
Mel Goodwin, PhD, Treasurer
Bob Glazer, Executive Director

Provides information exchange among governmental, non-governmental, academic and commerical users of marine resources in the Gulf and Carribean Region
950 Members
Founded in: 1947

8835 **Gulf of Mexico Fishery Management Council**
2203 N Lois Avenue
Suite 1100
Tampa, FL 33607

813-348-1630
888-833-1844; *Fax:* 813-348-1711
gulfcouncil@gulfcouncil.org;
www.gulfcouncil.org
Social Media: Facebook

Doug Gregory, Executive Director
Carrie Simons, Deputy Executive Director
Charlene Ponce, Public Information Officer
Cathy Readinger, Administrative Officer
Beth Hager, Financial Assistant

The council preserves fishery plans which are designed to manage fishery resources from where

state waters end out to the 200 mile limit of the Gulf of Mexico.
Founded in: 1976

8836 **ICFA-USA**
internationalcarpfishingassociation.com
David Moore, ICFA USA Representative
The International Carp Fishing Association promotes carp angling worldwide.
Founded in: 2004

8837 **International Institute of Fisheries Economics and Trade**
Dept of Agricultural & Resource Economic
Oregon State University
Corvallis, OR 97331-3601
541-737-1416; *Fax:* 541-737-2563
iifet@oregonstate.edu;
www.oregonstate.edu/dept/iifet
Ann L Shriver, Executive Director
Dr. Rebecca Metzner, President
Dr. Ralph Townsend, President-Elect
Kara Keenan, Assistant
An international group of economists, government managers, private industry members, and others interested in the exchange of research and information on marine resource issues. Founded to promote interaction and exchange between people from all countries and professional disciplines about marine resource economics and trade issues.
Founded in: 1982

8838 **National Fisheries Institute**
7918 Jones Branch Dr
Suite 700
Mc Lean, VA 22102-3319
703-752-8890; *Fax:* 703-752-7583
admin@SIRFonline.org; www.sirfonline.org
Social Media: Facebook, Twitter, LinkedIn
Russ Mentzer, Chairman
Eric Bloom, Director
Jim Bonnvie, Director
Pete Cardone, Director
Dan DiDonato, Director
Members are farmers, food processors and food distributors with an interest in aquaculture.
Founded in: 1964

8839 **National Seafood Educators**
PO Box 93
Shamokawa, WA 98647
206-546-6410; *Fax:* 206-546-6411
Information@SeafoodEducators.com;
www.seafoodeducators.com
Evie Hansen, Founder
The goal is to educate and inform the public about the many health benefits of a seafood diet. National Seafood Educators has also consulted with many seafood retail businesses on how to sell, store and prepare wholesome seafood.
Founded in: 1977

8840 **National Shellfisheries Association**
c/o US EPA, Atlantic Ecology Division
27 Tazewell Drive
Narragansett, RI 02880
631-653-6327; *Fax:* 631-653-6327
webmaster@shellfish.org; www.shellfish.org
Karolyn Mueller Hansen, President
Steven M. Allen, President-Elect
Shirley Baker, Vice-President
Lisa Milke, Secretary
John Scarpa, Treasurer
An international organization of scientists, management officials and members of industry, all deeply concerned with the biology, ecology, production, economics and management of shellfish resources-clams, oysters, mussels, scallops, snails, shrimp, lobsters, crabs, among many other species of commercial importance.
Cost: $85.00
1000 Members
Frequency: Membership Fee
Founded in: 1908

8841 **North Carolina Fisheries Association**
PO Box 335
Bayboro, NC 28515-0335
252-745-0225; *Fax:* 252-745-0258
peggy@ncfish.org; www.ncfish.org
Brent Fulcher, Chairman
Karolyn Mueller Hansen, President
Leslie Daniel, Treasurer
Peggy C. Page, Accounting Manager
Lauren Morris, Membership and Operations Manager
Non-profit trade organization created to facilitate the promotion of North Carolina families, heritage and seafood through accessible data about the commercial fishing industry. NCFA lobbies Local, State, and Federal legislators and engages in a wide scope of public awareness projects.
Founded in: 1952

8842 **Pacific Coast Federation of Fishermen's Association**
Building 991, Marine Drive, Crissy Field
PO Box 29370
San Francisco, CA 94129-0370
415-561-5080; *Fax:* 415-561-5464
fish1ifr@aol.com; www.pcffa.org
Zeke Grader, Executive Director
David Bitts, President
Vivian Helliwell, Watershed Conservation Director
Glen Spain, Northwest Regional Director
Mitch Farro, Fishey Enhancement Director
Commercial fishermen's organizations from California to Alaska. Works to prevent and improve the resources of the commercial fishing industry, protect rivers from herbicide and pesticide applications that may threaten salmon populations, maintain activity within the industry, regain local control over fisheries management.
22 Members
Founded in: 1976

8843 **Pacific Seafood Processors Association**
1900 West Emerson Place
Suite 205
Seattle, WA 98119
206-281-1667; *Fax:* 206-283-2387
info@pspafish.net; www.pspafish.net
Glenn Reed, President
Nancy Diaz, Administrative Assistant
Trade association to foster a better public understanding of the seafood industry and its value to the regional and national economies.
25 Members
Founded in: 1914

8844 **Recreational Fishing Alliance**
Po Box 3080
New Gretna, NJ 08224
609-404-1060
888-564-6732; *Fax:* 609-294-3812;
www.joinrfa.org
Jim Donofrio, Executive Director
John DePersenaire, Researcher
Jim Martin, West Coast Regional Director
Gary Caputi, Corporate Relations Director
An organization that supports and fights back against federal government state legislatures impose unreasonable restrictions on our ability to enjoy recreational fishing.
Frequency: $35/Membership

8845 **Southeastern Fisheries Association**
1118-B Thomasville Rd.
Tallahassee, FL 32303
850-224-0612; *Fax:* 850-222-3663;
www.seafoodsustainability.us
Bob Jones, Executive Director
To defend, preserve and enhance the commercial fishing industry in the southeastern United States for present participants as well as future generations through all legal means.
Founded in: 1952

8846 **The International Game Fish Association**
300 Gulf Stream Way
3rd Fl.
Dania Beach, FL 33004
954-927-2628; *Fax:* 954-924-4299;
www.igfa.org
Rob Kramer, President
Michael J. Myatt, Chief Operating Officer
A nonprofit organization that advocates for a sustainable game fishing industry.

8847 **West Coast Seafood Processors Association**
1618 SW 1st Ave
Suite 318
Portland, OR 97201
503-227-5076; *Fax:* 503-296-2824
rod.wcseafood@gmail.com; www.wcspa.com
Rod Moore, Executive Director
Susan Chambers, Deputy Director
Kim Lowman, Executive Assistant
Serves the needs of the shore-based seafood processors in California, Oregon and Washington, helping them to face and survive economic, environmental and regulatory challenges.
13 Members

8848 **Women's Fisheries Network**
2442 NW Market Street
#243
Seattle, WA 98107
206-789-1987; *Fax:* 206-789-1987;
www.fis.com/wfn
Nancy Munro, President
Men and women dedicated to education of issues confronting the fishing and seafood industry.
2000 Members
Founded in: 1993

Newsletters

8849 **American Sportfishing**
American Sportfishing Association
1001 North Fairfax Street
Suite 501
Alexandria, VA 22314
703-519-9691; *Fax:* 703-519-1872
info@asafishing.org; www.asafishing.org
Social Media: Facebook
Mike Nussman, President/CEO
Joyce Anderson-Logan, Executive Assistant
Gordon Robertson, Vice President
Diane Carpenter, Chief Financial Officer
Provides a broader view of the activities of ASA and our partners. Includes information about industry news, events, perspectives and trends that affect the sportfishing community.
Frequency: Bi-Monthly

8850 **Aquaculture North America**
Capamara Communications

815 1st Ave
#301
Seattle, WA 98104

250-474-3982
800-936-2266; *Fax:* 250-478-3979
jeremy@capamara.com; www.naqua.com

Peter Chetteburgh, Editor-in-Chief
Jeremy Thain, Sales Manager
James Lewis, Production Department

Follows the trends, issues, people and events that have set the pace for the fastest growing agribusiness sector on the continent. Coverage is relevant to all finfish and shellfish species grown in North America plus special reports from other regions around the world.
Cost: $27.95
Frequency: Bi-monthly
Circulation: 4000
Founded in: 1985

8851 Briefs
American Institute of Fishery Research Biologists
205 Blades Road
Havelock, NC 28532
www.aifrb.org

John Butler, Editor
John Merriner, Production Editor

It is intended to communicate the professional activities and accomplishments of the Institute, its District, and Members; the results of research; the effects of management; unusual biological events; matters affecting the profession; political problems and other matters of importance to the fishery community.
Frequency: Bi-Monthly

8852 Commercial Fisheries News
Compass Publications
Deer Isle, ME

800-989-5253; *Fax:* 207-348-1059
comfish@fish-news.com; www.fish-news.com

Richard W Martin, Publisher
Susan Jones, Editor

Provides the latest waterfront news along with coverage of the state and federal rules and regulations affecting the harvest of all the region's major species. Regular features include lobster and fish market reports, a safety column, new boats, the enforcement report, and the popular and effective classifieds section.
Cost: $21.95
72 Pages
Frequency: Monthly
Circulation: 9223
ISSN: 0273-6713
Founded in: 1978
Printed in 4 colors on n stock

8853 Crow's Nest
Casamar Group/Holdings
8082 Firethorn Lane
Las Vegas, NV 89123

702-792-6868; *Fax:* 702-792-6668;
www.casamargroup.com

Malu Marigomen, Executive Director

An in-depth report on the status of the Tuna Industry
Frequency: Monthly

8854 Currents
Women's Fisheries Network
2422 NW Market Square
Seattle, WA 98107

206-789-1987; *Fax:* 206-789-1987;
www.fis.com/wfn

Debbie Slotivg, Editor
Ron Gawith, Owner

Features current topics in fisheries, members' activities, upcoming events and chapter reports.
Frequency: Monthly

8855 Fish Farming News
Compass Publications
Deer Isle, ME

800-989-5253; *Fax:* 207-348-1059
comfish@fish-news.com; www.fish-news.com

Richard W Martin, Publisher
Susan Jones, Editor

The business newspaper for the U.S. aquaculture industry. Readers are aquaculture professionals who are directly or indirectly involved in the business of growing fish and seafood products. Encompassing all major farm raised species (finfish, shellfish and aquatic plants) both marine (saltwater) and fresh water aquaculture.
Cost: $21.95
72 Pages
Frequency: Monthly
Circulation: 9223
ISSN: 0273-6713
Founded in: 1978
Printed in 4 colors on n stock

8856 Fishermen's News
PCFFA
Building 991, Marine Drive
PO Box 29370
San Francisco, CA 94129-0370

415-561-5080; *Fax:* 415-561-5464
fish1ifr@aol.com; www.pcffa.org

Zeke Grader, Executive Director
Chuck Wise, President

Oldest publication in the west coast commercial fishing industry. Deals with resource protection and policy issues of great importance to the fishing industry, as well as with critical Congressional issues which affect us all.
22 Members
Founded in: 1976

8857 IIFET Newsletter
International Institute of Fisheries Economics
Dept of Agricultural & Resource Economic
Oregon State University
Corvallis, OR 97331-3601

541-737-1439; *Fax:* 541-737-2563
iifet@oregonstate.edu;
www.oregonstate.edu/dept/iifet

Provides conference listings, news items, and information on new publications and the activities of members.
20 Pages
Frequency: Semi-Annual
ISSN: 1048-9509

8858 Littorally Speaking
American Littoral Society Northeast Chapter
28 W 9th Rd
Broad Channel, NY 11693-1112

718-318-9344; *Fax:* 718-318-9345;
www.alsnyc.org

Don Riepe, Executive Director

A digest of environmental concerns

8859 Makin' Waves Quarterly Newsletter
Recreational Fishing Alliance
PO Box 3080
New Gretna, NJ 08224
609-404-1060
888-564-6732; *Fax:* 609-294-3812;
www.joinrfa.org

James Donofrio, Executive Director
Gary Caputi, Corporate Relations Director
Courtney Howell Thompson, Marketing Coordinator/PR

This RFA paper has proven that fish and fishermen are not the only variables in the equation of fisheries management.
Frequency: $35/Membership

8860 NSA Newsletter
National Shellfisheries Association
c/o US EPA, Atlantic Ecology Division
27 Tazewell Drive
Narragansett, RI 02880

401-782-3155; *Fax:* 401-782-3030
news@shellfish.org; www.shellfish.org

Dr Evan Ward, Editor

Current issues and concerns in shellfish research and in the shellfish industry, including details regarding upcoming meetings, employment listings, and gossip items for our Metamorphoses column.

8861 National Shellfisheries Association Quarterly Newsletter
National Shellfisheries Association
C/O US EPA, Atlantic Ecology Division
27 Tazewell Drive
Narragansett, RI 02880

631-653-6327; *Fax:* 631-653-6327;
www.shellfish.org

R. LeRoy Creswell, President
Christopher V. Davis, President-Elect
George E. Flimlin, VP & Program Chair
Marta Gomez-Chiarri, Secretary

An informative newsletter for the shellfish industry, shellfish managers and shellfish researchers.
Cost: $85.00
1000 Members
Frequency: Membership Fee
Founded in: 1908

8862 PSPA Update
Pacific Seafood Processors Association
1900 W Emerson Pl
Suite 205
Seattle, WA 98119-1649

206-281-1667; *Fax:* 206-283-2387
info@pspafish.net; www.pspafish.net

Glenn Reed, President

Daily news update for major seafood processing companies with operations in Alaska and Washington.
25 Members
Founded in: 1914

8863 Tradewinds
North Carolina Fisheries Association
PO Box 12303
New Bern, NC 28561
252-633-2288; *Fax:* 252-633-9616
peggy@ncfish.org; www.ncfish.org

Sean McKeon, President
Peggy C Page, Bookkeeper

Members only newspaper, which includes special bulletins regarding legislative issues and various articles concerning fisheries issues.
24 Pages
Frequency: Bi-Monthly

8864 Wheel Watch
Fishing Vessel Owners Association
4005 20th Ave W
Room 232, West Wall Bldg
Seattle, WA 98199-1273

206-284-4720; *Fax:* 206-283-3341;
www.fvoa.org

Robert D. Alverson, Manager
Carol M. Batteen, Executive Assistant

Brings you up-to-date with regards to action of the Halibut Commission, North Pacific Council, Pacific Council, and market information.
Frequency: Quarterly

Magazines & Journals

8865 Aquaculture North America
Capamara Communications
PO Box 1409
Arden, NC 28704
250-474-3982
877-687-0011; *Fax:* 250-478-3979
aquaculturenorthamerica.com
Gregory J Gallagher, Editor/Publisher
Rebekah Craig, Circulation Manager
Brenda Jo McManama, Advertising/Sales
Earning the respect of aquaculture industry professionals throughout the world who hold its trade publications in high regard.
Cost: $24.00
96 Pages
Frequency: Annually/Summer
Circulation: 5000
ISSN: 0199-1388
Founded in: 1968

8866 Atlantic Fisherman
Advocate Media Publishing
181 Brown's Point Road
Nova Scotia B0K-1H0
902-485-1990
800-236-9526; *Fax:* 902-485-6353;
www.atlanticfisherman.com
Social Media: Twitter
Susan Purdy, Publications Manager
Provides news for the commercial fisherman in the four Atlantic provinces of Canada. Includes prespectives from the unions, the government and the fishermen themselves.
Cost: $16.00
Frequency: Monthly
Circulation: 9950

8867 Bass Times
Bass Anglers Sportsman Society
3500 Blue Lake Drive
Suite 330
Birmingham, AL 35243
334-272-9530
877-227-7872; *Fax:* 334-279-7148;
www.bassmaster.com
Social Media: Facebook, Twitter
Dean Kassel, President
Chris Horton, Associate Director
Each issue includes; detailed, in-depth tips & techniques, bass biology, conservation news, BASS Federation Nation news, Bassmaster Tournament Trail coverage, and Legislation coverage.
Cost: $14.95
600M Members
Frequency: Annual Membership Fee
Founded in: 1972

8868 Catfish Journal
Catfish Farmers of America
6311 Ridgewood Road
Suite W404
Jackson, MS 39211
601-977-9559; *Fax:* 601-977-9632;
www.uscatfish.com
Social Media: Facebook, Twitter
Mike McCall, Editor
Sandra Goff, Production Manager
News on catfish production, processing, feed manufacturing and research.
Frequency: Monthly

8869 Connect Magazine
American Zoo and Aquarium Association
8403 Colesville Rd
Suite 710
Silver Spring, MD 20910-6331
301-562-0777; *Fax:* 301-562-0888;
www.aza.org
Jim Maddy, Executive Director
Kris Vehrs, Executive Director
Muri Dueppen, Marketing
For the professional zoo and aquarium world. This magazine features fascinating stories that explore trends, educational initiatives, member achievements and conservation efforts.
200 Members
Frequency: Monthly
Circulation: 6000

8870 Esox Angler
Esox Angler
PO Box 895
Hayward, WI 54843
715-638-2311; www.esoxhunter.com
Jack Burns, Senior Editor
Rob Kimm, Editor
A muskie and pike magazine for the world's muskie and pike anglers. Articles focusing on proven techniques and new ideas from top name anglers, as well as regular guys who are catching lots of fish.

8871 Fish Sniffer
3201 Eastwood Road
Sacramento, CA 95821
916-685-2245; *Fax:* 916-685-1498
danielbacher@fishsniffer.com;
www.fishsniffer.com
Social Media: Facebook
Dan Bacher, Editor
Cal Kellogg, Associate Editor
Current fishing reports, weather conditions, fishing news, photos, boats for sale, what and where to fish and much more.
Cost: $29.00
Frequency: Bi-Weekly

8872 Fisheries
American Fisheries Society
5410 Grosvenor Ln
Suite 110
Bethesda, MD 20814-2199
301-897-8616; *Fax:* 301-897-8096;
www.fisheries.org
Social Media: Facebook, Twitter
Gus Rassam, Executive Director
Myra Merritt, Office Administrator
Peer reviewed articles that address contemporary issues and problems, techniques, philosophies and other areas of interest to the general fisheries profession. Monthly features include letters, meeting notices, book listings and reviews, environmental essays and organization profiles.
Cost: $106.00
50 Pages
Frequency: Monthly
Circulation: 9800
Founded in: 1870
Mailing list available for rent: 8500 names at $250 per M

8873 Fishermen's News
Philips Publishing Group
2201 W Commodore Way
Seattle, WA 98199-1298
206-284-8285; *Fax:* 206-284-0391
circulation@rhppublishing.com;
www.pacmar.com
Peter Philips, Publisher
Lisa Albers, Editor
Maggie Cheung, Circulatiom Manager
Covers commercial fishing activity, market trends, gear and boat building news, political news and financial matters related to the industry.
Founded in: 1945

8874 Fly Fisherman
InterMedia Outdoors Inc
PO Box 420235
Palm Coast, FL 32142-0235
212-852-6600; www.flyfisherman.com
Social Media: Facebook, Twitter
Jeff Paro, President
From the deepest bass ponds, wildest rivers or abundant saltwater flats, America's fishing sportsmen rely on this magazine to provide them with the newest techniques, tools and tips whenever and wherever they need this information.
Cost: $19.95
Frequency: Annually
Founded in: 1969

8875 IAFWA Proceedings
International Association of Fish and Wildlife
444 N Capitol St NW
Suite 725
Washington, DC 20001-1553
202-638-7999; *Fax:* 202-638-7291
info@iafwa.org; www.statenet.com
Wayne Muhlstein, VP
Eric Schwaab, Resource Director
Reports on the business transacted by the Association at its March meeting held in conjunction with the North American Wildlife and Natural Resources Conference and at its September annual conference.

8876 In-Fisherman
InterMedia Outdoors Inc
PO Box 420235
Palm Coast, FL 420235
218-829-1648
ross.purnell@imoutdoors.com;
www.in-fisherman.com
Social Media: Facebook, Twitter
Ross Purnell, Editor
Written for the avid freshwater angler. In each issue, you'll find detailed instructions and demonstrations on catching, cleaning, and eating your favorite species of fish, and reports on the latest scientific studies concerning fish and habitat conservation.
Cost: $12.00
Frequency: 8x/year
Founded in: 1975

8877 Island Fisherman
610 Azalea Place
Campbell River
BC Canada V9W 7H2
250-923-0939
ifmm@shaw.ca;
www.islandfishermanmagazine.com
Larry E Stefanyk, Founder/Publisher
Bob Jones, Editor
Covering the west coast of British Columbia from the Queen Charlottes to Victoria on Vancouver Island. Covering saltwater and freshwater fishing with how to and where to tips to help you find the big one or just experience what the west coast of British Columbia has to offer.
Cost: $40.00
Frequency: Monthly
Founded in: 2001

8878 Journal of Aquatic Animal Health
American Fisheries Society

5410 Grosvenor Ln
Suite 110
Bethesda, MD 20814-2199

301-897-8616; *Fax:* 301-897-8096;
www.fisheries.org
Social Media: Facebook, Twitter

Bill Fisher, President
John Boreman, President-Elect
Bob Hughes, First Vice President
Donna Parrish, Second Vice President

International journal publishing original research on diseases affecting aquatic life, including effects, treatments and prevention.
Cost: $100.00
8500 Members
Frequency: Membership Fee
Founded in: 1870

8879 Marine and Coastal Fisheries: Dynamics, Management, and Ecosystem Science
American Fisheries Society
5410 Grosvenor Ln
Suite 110
Bethesda, MD 20814-2199

301-897-8616; *Fax:* 301-897-8096;
www.fisheries.org
Social Media: Facebook, Twitter

Bill Fisher, President
John Boreman, President-Elect
Bob Hughes, First Vice President
Donna Parrish, Second Vice President

Online publication focusing on marine, coastal, and estuarine fisheries.
Cost: $100.00
8500 Members
Frequency: Membership Fee
Founded in: 1870

8880 Marlin
World Publications
460 N Orlando Avenue
Suite 200
Winter Park, FL 32789

407-628-4802; *Fax:* 407-628-7061;
www.marlinmag.com/www.worldpub.net

Dave Ferrell, Editor
Glen Hughes, Group Publisher
Terry Snow, Owner

The bible for big-game fishermen. It is written for the most affluent anglers who need to know what is happening around the world regarding offshore fishing. It is the who's who of the sport, written in the voice of the sportfisherman, one-on-one to a peer, as a member of this elite fraternity. Marlin magazine will continue to be the No. 1 buy in big-game fishing by delivering the best targeted edit to the wealthiest boat-owning saltwater fishermen in the world.
Cost: $24.95
Frequency: 8x/year
Circulation: 40,000

8881 National Fisherman
Diversified Business Communications
Po Box 7437
Portland, ME 04112-7437

207-842-5600; *Fax:* 207-842-5503
editor@nationalfisherman.com;
www.nationalfisherman.com
Social Media: Facebook, Twitter

Nancy Hasselback, President/CEO
Lincoln Bedrosian, Senior Editor

Regional coverage of boats, fishing gear, environmental developments, technology, new products, and fishery resource information
Cost: $19.95
Frequency: Monthly
Circulation: 38,000
Founded in: 1903

8882 North American Journal of Aquaculture
American Fisheries Society
5410 Grosvenor Ln
Suite 110
Bethesda, MD 20814-2199

301-897-8616; *Fax:* 301-897-8096;
www.fisheries.org
Social Media: Facebook, Twitter

Gus Rassam, Executive Director
Myra Merritt, Office Administrator

Publishes research in all areas of fish culture.
Cost: $38.00
Frequency: Quarterly
ISSN: 1548-8454

8883 North American Journal of Fisheries Management
American Fisheries Society
5410 Grosvenor Ln
Suite 110
Bethesda, MD 20814-2199

301-897-8616; *Fax:* 301-897-8096;
www.fisheries.org
Social Media: Facebook, Twitter

Bill Fisher, President
John Boreman, President-Elect
Bob Hughes, First Vice President
Donna Parrish, Second Vice President

Promotes communication among managers. Published with a focus on maintenance, enhancement, and allocation of resources.
Cost: $100.00
8500 Members
Frequency: Membership Fee
Founded in: 1870

8884 Outdoor Journal
American Crappie Association
125 Ruth Avenue
Benton, KY 42025

270-395-4204; *Fax:* 270-395-4381
office@crappieusa.com; www.crappieusa.com

Darrell VanVactor, President
Larry Crecelius, Public Relations Director

Features news and updates on memberships, events, tournaments, and more for crappie anglers from amateurs to professionals.
Frequency: Annually
Circulation: 60000

8885 Pacific Fishing
Pacific Fishing
1000 Andover Park E
Seattle, WA 98188-7632

206-324-5644; *Fax:* 206-324-8939;
www.pacificfishing.com

Michael Daigle, Owner
Jon Holland, Editor
Duane Brady, es & Marketing Manager

Serving owners and operators of commercial fishing boats throughout the world's most productive ocean, from Alaska to the tropical Pacific. Our readers also include crew members, processors, fisheries managers, suppliers, seafood brokers and distributors, educators, and others who want serious information about the business of hauling up food from the Pacific.
Cost: $15.00
Frequency: Monthly
Circulation: 7160
Founded in: 1980

8886 SaltWater
Time, Inc.
2 Park Avenue
New York, NY 10016

212-221-1212; *Fax:* 212-779-5999
editor@saltwatersportsman.com;
www.saltwatersportsman.com

David DiBenedetto, Editor
Gerald Bethge, Executive Editor
Jason Y Wood, Managing Editor
Karl Anderson, Senior Editor

A publication on salt-water sport fishing. Each monthly issue contains exciting feature stories, columns, award-winning color photos covering both big- and small-game fishing, the newest techniques, tackle, boats and equipment, and the latest developments in conservation and fishery management.
Founded in: 1939

8887 Saltwater Sportsman
World Publications
460 N Orlando Avenue
Suite 200
Winter Park, FL 32789

407-628-4802; *Fax:* 407-628-7061;
www.marlinmag.com/www.worldpub.net
Social Media: Facebook, Twitter

Dave Ferrell, Editor
Glen Hughes, Group Publisher
Terry Snow, Owner

Designed for serious recreational salt water fishermen who demand the most accurate and detailed information available on inshore and offshore fishing from boats. Articles cover the entire spectrum of boat and tackle rigging, tactics and methods for catching game fish, travel, boat and equipment reviews, U.S. regional/ local coverage, and fisheries management and conservation.
Cost: $24.95
Frequency: 8x/year
Circulation: 40,000

8888 Sea Technology Magazine
Compass Publications, Inc.
1501 Wilson Blvd
Suite 1001
Arlington, VA 22209-2403

703-524-3136; *Fax:* 703-841-0852
oceanbiz@sea-technology.com;
www.sea-technology.com
Social Media: Twitter

Amos Bussmann, President/Publisher
Joy Carter, Circulation Manager
Meghan Ventura, Managing Editor

Worldwide information leader for marine/offshore business, science and engineering. Read in more than 110 countries by management, engineers, scientists and technical personnel working in industry, government and education.
Cost: $40.00
Frequency: Monthly
Circulation: 16304
ISSN: 0093-3651
Founded in: 1960
*Mailing list available for rent*at $80 per M
Printed in 4 colors

8889 Seafood Business
Diversified Business Communications
121 Free Street
PO Box 7438
Portland, ME 04112-7437

207-842-5542
mlarkin@divcom.com;
www.seafoodbusiness.com
Social Media: Facebook, Twitter, LinkedIn

Mary Larkin, Publisher
Fiona Robinson, Associate Publisher, Editor
James Wright, Associate Editor
Melissa Wood, Assistant Editor

Focuses on the business of buying and selling seafood and provides seafood buyers with the tools and analysis they need to make educated safood buying decisions.
Frequency: Monthly
Circulation: 15,000
Founded in: 1982

8890 Sport Fishing
World Publications
460 N Orlando Avenue
Winter Park, FL 32789
407-628-4802; *Fax:* 407-628-7061
editor@sportfishingmag.com; www.sportfishingmag.com
Social Media: Facebook, Twitter
Glenn Hughes, Group Publisher
Bruce Miller, Circulation VP
Terry Snow, Owner
Written for the passionate angler who must have in-depth, cutting-edge information on the latest techniques, the hottest locations and the newest equipment to maximize his day on the water, Sport Fishing magazine is the source for saltwater fishing information.
Cost: $19.97
Frequency: 10x/year
Circulation: 150,000
Founded in: 2001

8891 The Fisherman
326 12th Street
1st Floor
New Westminster, BC V3M-4H6
604-669-5569; *Fax:* 604-688-1142
fisherman@ufawu.org; www.thefisherman.ca
Social Media: Facebook, Twitter, YouTube
Sean Griffin, Editor
Suzanne Thomson, Advertising Manager
Covering saltwater and freshwater fishing from Maine through Delaware Bay. Local fishing reports.
Frequency: Monthly
Circulation: 8000

8892 Transactions of the American Fisheries Society
American Fisheries Society
5410 Grosvenor Ln
Suite 110
Bethesda, MD 20814-2199
301-897-8616; *Fax:* 301-897-8096; www.fisheries.org
Gus Rassam, Executive Director
Myra Merritt, Office Administrator
The Society's highly regarded international journal of fisheries science features results of basic and applied research in genetics, physiology, biology, ecology, population dynamics, economics, health, culture, and other topics germane to marine and freshwater finfish and shellfish and their respective fisheries and environments
Cost: $43.00
Frequency: Bi-Monthly
ISSN: 0002-8487
Founded in: 1872

Trade Shows

8893 ASA Sportfishing Summit
American Sportfishing Association
225 Reinekers Lane
Suite 420
Alexandria, VA 22314
703-519-9691; *Fax:* 703-519-1872
info@asafishing.org; www.asafishing.org
Mary Jane Williamson, Communications Director
Amy Yohanes, Administrative Services Manager
Membership meeting and premier networking event. From special sessions, to busiess workshops to association committee meeting, the Summit provides a wide-range of opportunities to gain information on the most relevant issues facing the sportfishing industry.
Frequency: October

8894 ASA/Eastern Fishing & Outdoor Exposition
American Sportfishing Association
1001 North Fairfax Street
Suite 501
Alexandria, VA 22314
703-519-9691; *Fax:* 703-519-1872
info@asafishing.org; www.asafishing.org
Social Media: Facebook
Mike Nussman, President/CEO
Joyce Anderson-Logan, Executive Assistant
Gordon Robertson, Vice President
Diane Carpenter, Chief Financial Officer
The finest sportsmen's expos on the East Coast. The best outdoor gear, accessories and resources for fishing, boating, hunting, adventure and travel are available at these shows. The only sport shows where 100 percent of the proceeds go to safeguarding and promoting the enduring social, economic and conservation values of America's outdoor heritage.
Frequency: Bi-Monthly

8895 AZA Regional Conference
American Zoo and Aquarium Association
8403 Colesville Road
Suite 710
Silver Spring, MD 20910-3314
301-562-0777; *Fax:* 301-562-0888; www.aza.org
Jim Maddy, President
Kris Vehrs, Executive Director
Jill Nicoll, Marketing
Exhibits, workshops and discussions about the industry.
200 Members
Founded in: 1924

8896 Annual Fish Baron's Ball
North Carolina Fisheries Association
PO Box 12303
New Bern, NC 28561
252-745-0225; *Fax:* 252-633-9616
peggy@ncfish.org; www.ncfish.org
Billy Carl Tillett, Chairman
Sherrill Styron, Vice Chairman
Sean McKeon, President
Janice Smith, Treasurer
Attendees getting together for an evening of great seafood and fun, and participate in the silent auction. Program proceeds go toward Association-related activities.
Founded in: 1952

8897 CFA Fish Farming Trade Show
Catfish Farmers of America
1100 Highway 82 E
Suite 202
Indianola, MS 38751
662-887-2699; *Fax:* 662-887-6857; www.catfishfarmersamerica.org
America's largest fish farming equipment expo.
Frequency: February

8898 Catfish Farmers of America Annual Convention & Research Symposium
Catfish Farmers of America
1100 Highway 82 E
Suite 202
Indianola, MS 38751-2251
662-887-2699; *Fax:* 662-887-6857; www.catfishfarmersofamerica.org
Hugh Warren, President
Opportunity to launch new products, meet new buyers, learn emerging trends and access the North American seafood market.
Frequency: Membership Fee
Founded in: 1968

8899 Eastern Fishing & Outdoor Expo
Eastern Fishing & Outdoor Expositions
PO Box 4720
Portsmouth, NH 00380
603-431-4315; *Fax:* 603-431-1971
info@sportshows.com; www.sportshows.com
Paul Fuller, President/Show Director
Judy L Chapman, Assistant Show Director
Partnership with American Sportfishing Association. Exhibitors representing the entire spectrum of saltwater sportfishing. This includes inshore to offshore, light tackle to big-game tackle, and everything in between. Fishermen will see and touch the latest from major tackle manufacturers and buy the latest tackle from local retailers at special show prices.

8900 Fish Expo Workboat Atlantic
National Fisherman/Diversified Bus. Communications
121 Free Street
PO Box 7437
Portland, ME 04112
207-425-5608; *Fax:* 207-842-5509; www.fishexpoatlantic.com
Bob Callahan, Show Director
Heather Palmeter, Show Coordinator
Newest products and technology, attend free seminars and workshops, talk to technical experts, and find the best deals on equipment and gear.
6,000 Attendees
Frequency: April

8901 Fly-Fishing Retailer World Trade Expo
VNU Expositions/Business Media
770 Broadway
New York, NY 10003
646-545-5100
nielsen.com/us/en.html
Andy Tompkins, Show Director
Peter Devin, Group Show Director
Where brands are launched, innovations are unveiled and connections are made. Designed for the specialty fly-fishing industry, Fly-Fishing Retailer World Trade Expo connects a targeted audience to conduct business in a professional yet friendly atmosphere.
Frequency: August
Founded in: 1998

8902 IAFWA Annual Meeting
International Association of Fish and Wildlife
444 North Capitol Street NW
Suite 725
Washington, DC 20001
202-624-7890; *Fax:* 202-624-7891; www.fishwildlife.org
Gary T Myers, Executive Director
Cindy Delaney, Meetings Coordinator
Wayne Muhlstein, VP
Providing many opportunities to hear from our nation's wildlife conservation leaders, partners, and management experts. The meeting is our response to the need for national consensus on

state-by-state fish and wildlife management issues.
250 Attendees
Frequency: September

8903 **ICAST**
American Sportfishing Association
225 Reinekers Lane
Suite 420
Alexandria, VA 22314

703-519-9691; *Fax:* 703-519-1872
mdelvalle@asafishing.org; www.asafishing.org

Maria del Valle, ICAST Director
Kenneth Andres, ICAST Associate

The sportfishing industry's largest trade event is a major catalyst for sales and a terrific networking opportunity for the sportfishing community.

8904 **IIFET Biennial International Conference**
IIFET
Dept of Agricultural & Resource Economic
Oregon State University
Corvallis, OR 97331-3601

541-737-1416; *Fax:* 541-737-2563
iifet@oregonstate.edu;
www.oregonstate.edu/dept/iifet

Ann L Shriver, Executive Director
Dr. Rebecca Metzner, President
Dr. Ralph Townsend, President-Elect

An important forum for members and others to learn about important research developments in seafood trade, aquaculture, and fisheries management issues. Attended by fisheries social scientists, managers, and industry members from all of the world's fishing areas. Provides participants with unparalleled opportunities to interact with the world's foremost fisheries economists in both formal and informal settings. Learn more about fishing and aquaculture activities across the globe.
Founded in: 1982

8905 **IPHC Annual Meeting**
Pacific Seafood Processors Association
1900 West Emerson Place
Suite 205
Seattle, WA 98119-1649

206-281-1667; *Fax:* 206-283-2387
nancy@pspafish.net; www.pspafish.net

Glenn Reed, President

Annual members meeting to discuss catch limits each year.
25 Members
Founded in: 1914

8906 **International Boston Seafood Show**
Diversified Business Communications
PO Box 7437
Portland, ME 04112-7437

207-842-5504; *Fax:* 207-842-5505
customerservice@divcom.com;
www.bostonseafood.com

Diane Vassar, Promotions Director
David Lowell, President

This event attracts top-tier buyers and sellers of seafood. You will find exhibit categories representing every aspect of seafood including; seafood, seafood equipment, services and organizations and seafood packaging.
20M Attendees
Frequency: March/Silver Pkg $250

8907 **International Convention of Allied Sportfishing Trades (ICAST)**
American Sportfishing Association
1001 North Fairfax Street
Suite 501
Alexandria, VA 22314

703-519-9691; *Fax:* 703-519-1872
info@asafishing.org; www.asafishing.org
Social Media: Facebook

Mike Nussman, President/CEO
Joyce Anderson-Logan, Executive Assistant
Gordon Robertson, Vice President
Diane Carpenter, Chief Financial Officer

World's largest sportfishing trade show, representing the cornerstone of the sportfishing industry, driving sportfishing companies' product sales year round and is the showcase for the latest innovations in gear and accessories.
Frequency: Bi-Monthly

8908 **International Fly Tackle Dealer Show**
American Fly Fishing Trade Association
901 Front St.
Suite B-125
Louisville, CO 80027

303-604-6132; *Fax:* 303-604-6162;
www.affta.com

Randi Swisher, President
Gary Berlin, Business Manager
Jim Klug, Chairman

The largest international gathering of fly fishing manufacturers, retailers, sales reps, media and fly fishing organizations in the world. Best venue to meet with the industry, people, products, innovations, emerging trends and the leading brand presentations, latest gear, equipment, waders, fly like, tippet and accessories for the upcoming season.
400 Members
Founded in: 2003

8909 **International West Coast Seafood Show**
Diversified Business Communications
PO Box 7437
Portland, ME 04112-7437

207-842-5500; *Fax:* 207-842-5503
mlarkin@divcom.com;
www.westcoastseafood.com

Mary Larkin, VP Seafood Expositions

A total resource for seafood industry leaders; showcases the latest seafood products and equipment from the US, Pacific Rim and beyond.
Frequency: October
Founded in: 1996

8910 **NSA Annual Meeting**
National Shellfisheries Association
c/o US EPA, Atlantic Ecology Division
27 Tazewell Drive
Narragansett, RI 02880

401-782-3155; *Fax:* 401-782-3030
news@shellfish.org; www.shellfish.org

Dr Lou D'Abramo, President
Christopher Davis, Treasurer

A time and place to interact with other associations and industry people.
Frequency: Spring

8911 **National River Rally**
American Sportfishing Association
225 Reinekers Ln
Suite 420
Alexandria, VA 22314-2875

703-519-9691; *Fax:* 703-519-1872
info@asafishing.org; www.fishamerica.org

Mike Nussman, President/CEO
Diane Carpenter, CFO
Gordon Robertson, Vice President

The premier national event to come together to learn, inspire and celebrate the passionate work of all things rivers and watersheds. Trainings, field trips and a deeply moving River Heroes awards banquet honoring incredible River leaders.
650+ Members
Founded in: 1962

8912 **Pacific Marine Expo**
Diversified Business Communications
121 Free Street
PO Box 7437
Portland, ME 04112

207-425-5608; *Fax:* 207-842-5509;
www.pacificmarineexpo.com

Bob Callahan, Show Director
Heather Palmeter, Show Coordinator

A trade show dedicated to the pacific maritime industry that provides a gathering of marine products and services. With nearly 500 manufacturers and distributors showcasing the latest technologies and thousands of products for all commercial vessels, tugs, barges, boat building, marine construction, passenger vessels, seafood processing plants and more, PME is the best source for all marine business needs.
6,000 Attendees
Frequency: November

8913 **Seafood Processing America**
Catfish Farmers of America
1100 Highway 82 E
Suite 202
Indianola, MS 38751-2251

662-887-2699; *Fax:* 662-887-6857;
www.catfishfarmersofamerica.org

Hugh Warren, President

Opportunity to launch new products, meet new buyers, learn emerging trends and access the North American seafood market.
Frequency: Membership Fee
Founded in: 1968

8914 **Sportfishing Summit**
American Sportfishing Association
1001 North Fairfax Street
Suite 501
Alexandria, VA 22314

703-519-9691; *Fax:* 703-519-1872
info@asafishing.org; www.asafishing.org
Social Media: Facebook

Mike Nussman, President/CEO
Joyce Anderson-Logan, Executive Assistant
Gordon Robertson, Vice President
Diane Carpenter, Chief Financial Officer

Where industry leaders met to discuss the issues impacting recreational fishing.
Frequency: Bi-Monthly

Directories & Databases

8915 **AZA Membership Directory**
American Zoo and Aquarium Association
8403 Colesville Rd
Suite 710
Silver Spring, MD 20910-3314

301-562-0777; *Fax:* 301-562-0888
membership@aza.org; www.aza.org
Social Media: Facebook, Twitter

L. Patricia Simmons, Chair
Tom Schmid, Chair-Elect
Jackie Ogden, Ph.D, Vice-Chair

Accredited institutions, professional affiliates, professional fellows, commercial members, related facilities and conservation partners receive one complimentary copy as a membership benefit.
Cost: $50.00
200 Members
Frequency: Annual
Founded in: 1924

8916 **Angling America Database**
PO Box 22567
Alexandria, VA 22304

www.anglingamerica.com
Stephen Aaron, Director
Austin Ducworth, Director
The most searchable database for fishing charters and guides across America.

8917 **Commercial Marine Directory & Fish Farmers Phone Book/ Directory**
Compass Publications
Deer Isle, ME

800-989-5253; *Fax:* 207-348-1059
comfish@fish-news.com; www.fish-news.com
Richard W Martin, Publisher
Susan Jones, Editor
Go-to-reference tools for commercial fishermen and fish farmers. Comprehensive listing of suppliers providing essential goods and services and convenient industry yellow pages.
Cost: $21.95
72 Pages
Frequency: Monthly
Circulation: 9223
ISSN: 0273-6713
Founded in: 1978
Printed in 4 colors on n stock

8918 **IIFET Membership Directory**
International Institute of Fisheries Economics
Dept of Agricultural & Resource Economic
Oregon State University
Corvallis, OR 97331-3601

541-737-1416; *Fax:* 541-737-2563
iifet@oregonstate.edu; www.orst.edu/dept/iifet
Social Media: Facebook, Twitter, LinkedIn, YouTube, Flickr
Ann L Shriver, Executive Director
Kara Kennan, Assistant Executive Director
This handbook lists all members with complete contact information, including an e-mail directory, plus areas of interest. Regular updates are provided with the newsletter.
Frequency: Biennial

8919 **Who's Who in the Fish Industry**
Urner Barry Publications
PO Box 389
Toms River, NJ 08754-0389
732-240-5330
800-932-0617; *Fax:* 732-341-0891
sales@urnerbarry.com; www.urnerbarry.com
Jay Bailey, Sales Manager
Janice Brown, Advertising Manager
The source for buying and selling contacts in the North American Seafood Industry. This 2006-2007 edition is fully updated and verified, boasting over 6,000 listings of seafood companies in the US and Canada. The directory boasts detailed information about each company listed such as products handled, contact names, product forms, product origin, sales volume, company website and much more.
Cost: $199.00
800 Pages
Frequency: Annual
ISSN: 0270-1600
Founded in: 1979

Industry Web Sites

8920 **http://gold.greyhouse.com**
G.O.L.D Grey House OnLine Databases
Grey House Publishing's online database platform, GOLD, offers Quick Search, Keyword Search and Expert Search for most business sectors including fishing and food markets. The GOLD platform makes finding the information you need quick and easy - whether you're a novice searcher or an experienced database user. All of Grey House's directory products are available for subscription on the GOLD platform.

8921 **www.asafishing.org**
American Sportfishing Association
Manufacturers and importers of fishing tackle and allied products. Promotes fishing for children and adults. Compiles statistics. Sponsors National Fishing Week.

8922 **www.fish307.com/links.htm**
This site provides links to Lake George Regional Web Sites, Fishing Charters, International Web Sites related to fishing.

8923 **www.fishhoo.com**
Fishhoo search Index for Fishermen. The internet's best fishing resources. There are 2991 links to choose from and translate to: French, German and Spanish.

8924 **www.greyhouse.com**
Grey House Publishing
Authoritative reference directories for most businsee sectors including fishing and food markets. Users can search the online databases with varied search criteria allowing for custom searches by product category, geographic area, sales volume, keyword, subject and more. Full Grey House catalog and online ordering also available.

8925 **www.internets.com/sfishing.htm**
Fishing Databases Search Engines.

8926 **www.nauticalworld.com**
Dedicated to bringing all related web sites within easy access to watersports enthusiasts. This search engine has been designed to locate advertiser's information within Nautical World but will also offer access to other watersport related web sites as well. Offers sections on marine electronics and hardware, sailing, boats, dock supplies, fishing accessories, diving accessories, industry news, watersports, weather forecasting and more.

8927 **www.nfi.org**
National Fishing Institute
Promotes the shipping and production of fishery products in international trade.

8928 **www.ospafish.net**
Pacific Seafood Processors Association
Trade association for the onshore processors in Oregon, Washington and Alaska.

8929 **www.pcffa.org**
Pacific Coast Federation of Fishermen's Assoc
Commercial fishermen's organizations from California to Alaska. Works to prevent and improve the resources of the commercial fishing industry, protect rivers from herbicide and pesticide applications that may threaten salmon populations, maintain activity within the industry, regain local control over fisheries management.

8930 **www.web.mit.edu/seagrant/www/wfn.html**
Women's Fisheries Network
Men and women dedicated to education of issues confronting the fishing and seafood industry. Conducts educational programs.

Associations

8931 **AACC International**
3340 Pilot Knob Road
St. Paul, MN 55121

651-454-7250
800-328-7560; *Fax:* 651-454-0766
aacc@scisoc.org; www.aaccnet.org
Social Media: Facebook, Twitter, LinkedIn

Robert L. Cracknell, President
Lydia Tooker Midness, Chair
Laura M. Hansen, President-Elect
Dave L. Braun, Treasurer

Formerly the American Association of Cereal Chemists, a non-profit organization of members who are specialists in the use of cereal grains in foods.
Founded in: 1915

8932 **ASI Food Safety Consultants**
7625 Page Avenue
St. Louis, MO 63133

314-725-2555
800-477-0778; *Fax:* 314-727-2563
info@asifood.com; www.asifood.com
Social Media: Facebook, Twitter, LinkedIn

Tom Huge, President
Gary Huge, Vice President
Jane Griffith, Technical Director
Jeff Capell, GMP, Technical Director
Jeanette Huge, Director

A full service provider of food safety audits, GMP audits, seminars and HACCP setups, as well as HACCP verification. Thoroughly addresses every vital concern of your valuable facility including food safety, pest control, employee practices and facility conditions.
Founded in: 1930

8933 **Academy of Nutrition and Dietics**
120 S Riverside Plaza
Suite 2000
Chicago, IL 60606-6995

312-899-0040
800-877-1600
info@eatright.org; www.eatright.org
Social Media: Facebook, Twitter, LinkedIn, Pinterest, Youtube

The American Dieteric Association is the World's largest organization of food and nutrition professionals. ADA is committed to improving the nation's health and advancing the profession of dietetics through research, education and advocacy.
75000 Members
Founded in: 1917
Mailing list available for rent

8934 **Agribusiness Council**
P.O Box 5565
Washington, DC 20016

202-296-4563; *Fax:* 202-887-9178
info@agribusinesscouncil.org;
www.agribusinesscouncil.org

Lyndon B. Jhonson, President

Organization dedicated to strengthening US agro-industrial competitiveness through programs which highlight international trade and development potentials as well as broad issues which encompass several individual agribusiness sectors and require a food systems approach.
Founded in: 1967

8935 **Agricultural & Applied Economics Association**
555 E. Wells St.
Suite 1100
Milwaukee, WI 53202

414-918-3190; *Fax:* 414-276-3349
Info@aaea.org; www.aaea.org
Social Media: Facebook, Twitter, LinkedIn

Jill McClusky, President
Jayson Lusk, President-Elect
Michael Boland, Director
Hayley Chouinard, Director
Keith H. Koble, Director

A not-for-profit association serving the professional interests of members working in agricultural and broadly related fields of applied economics. Will be the leading organization for professional advancement in, knowledge about agricultural, development, environmental, food and consumer, natural resource, regional, rural, and associated areas of applied economics and business.
Cost: $150.00
4M Members
Frequency: Regular Membership Fee
Founded in: 1910

8936 **Agricultural Education National HQ**
National FFA Organization
6060 FFA Drive
PO Box 68960
Indianapolis, IN 46268-0960

317-802-6060
888-332-2668
orders@ffa.org; www.ffa.org
Social Media: Facebook, Twitter

Dr. Steve A. Brown, National FFA Advisor, Board Chair
Sherene R. Donaldson, National FFA Executive Secretary
Nancy J. Trivette, National FFA Organization Treasurer
W. Dwight Armstrong, CEO
Josh Bledose, Chief Operating Officer

Headquarters of the National FFA Organization, the organization's mission is to prepare students for successful careers and a lifetime of informed choices in the global agriculture, food, fiber and natural resources systems.
507M Members
Founded in: 1928

8937 **Agricultural Retailers Association**
1156 15th St NW
Suite 500
Washington, DC 20005

202-457-0825
800-844-4900; *Fax:* 202-457-0864
ara@aradc.org; www.aradc.org
Social Media: Facebook, Twitter

Darren Coppock, President & CEO
Richard Gupton, Senior Vice President
Donnie Taylor, Vice President
Brian Reuwee, Director of Comm. and Marketing
David McKnight, Director of Member services

Nonprofit trade organization representing the interests of retailers across the United States on legislative and regulatory issues on Capitol Hill.
1200 Members
Frequency: Membership Dues Vary
Founded in: 1993

8938 **Allied Purchasing**
PO Box 1249
Mason City, IA 50402-1249

800-247-5956; *Fax:* 800-635-3775
kbamrick@alliedpurchasing.com;
www.alliedpurchasing.com
Social Media: Facebook, LinkedIn

Brian Janssen, President/CFO
Steve Husome, Executive Vice President
Kari Mondt, Senior Account Manager
Nicole Reisdorfer, Senior Account Manager
Kim Bamrick, Account Manager

A member owned not-for-profit buying organization established to negotiate favorable purchasing programs in part because we offer quantity purchases and prompt payment to suppliers. Purchases equipment, supplies, ingredients, and services for, dairy, soft drink, bottled water, water treatment and brewery industries.
Cost: $50.00
1200 Members
Frequency: Membership: 1 Share Stock
Founded in: 1937

8939 **Allied Trades of the Baking Industry**
c/o Cereal Food Processors
2001 Shawnee Mission Parkway
Mission Woods, KS 66205

913-890-6300
t.miller@cerealfood.com; www.atbi.org

Rick McGrath, President
Tom McCurry, First Vice President
John Hellman, Second Vice President
Tom McCurry, Secretary/Treasurer

An organization which exists to serve the grain-based food industry through cooperation between a large cross-section of suppliers to the wholesale manufacturers that each day provide our country with bread, rolls, cereals, cakes, cookies, crackers, tortillas and any number of other items that incorporate grains as their base. Values the relationships which have been built between the supplier and the manufacturer over the nearly 90 years since its inception.
Cost: $50.00
Frequency: Annual Dues
Founded in: 1920

8940 **Aluminum Foil Container Manufacturers Association**
10 Vecilla Lane
Hot Springs Village, AR 71909

440-781-5819; *Fax:* 440-247-9053
info@afcma.org; www.afcma.org

Coke Williams, Executive Secretary

Represents leading manufacturers of aluminum foil containers in the United States and Canada. The Association has worked to promote aluminum foil as a superior packaging material since the beginning.
13 Members
Founded in: 1955

8941 **American Agricultural Law Association**
American Agricultural Economics Association
PO Box 5861
Columbia, SC 29250

803-728-3200; *Fax:* 360-423-2287
ellenberg@aglaw-assn.org;
www.aglaw-assn.org

Jesse J. Richardson Jr, President
Anne 'Beth' Crocker, President-elect
Kristy Thomason Ellenberg JD, Executive Director
Justin Schneider, Director
Amber Miller, Director

The only national professional organization focusing on the legal needs of the agricultural community. Crossing traditional barriers, it offers an independent forum for investigation of innovative and workable solutions to complex agricultural law problems. This role has taken on greater importance in the midst of the current international and environmental issues reshaping agri-

culture and the impending technological advances which promise equally dramatic changes.
600 Members
Founded in: 1980

8942 American Angus Association
3201 Frederick Ave
St Joseph, MO 64506
816-383-5100; *Fax:* 816-233-9703
angus@angus.org; www.angus.org
Social Media: Facebook, Twitter

Steve Olson, President
Jim Sitz, Vice President
Richard Wilson, Interim CEO
Richard Wilson, Chief Financial Officer
Chris Stallo, Vice President of Operations

To provide programs, services, technology and leadership to enhance the genetics of the Angus breed, broaden its influence within the beef industry, and expand the market for superior tasting, high-quality Angus beef worldwide. Achieve Angus excellence through information, increase beef demand with Angus equity, identify and implement relevant technologies, optimize resources, and create opportunities.
Cost: $80.00
30+M Members
Frequency: Membership Fees Vary
Founded in: 1883

8943 American Association of Candy Technologist
711 W Water St.
PO Box 266
Princeton, WI 54968
920-295-6959; *Fax:* 920-295-6843
aactinfo@gomc.com; www.aactcandy.org
Social Media: LinkedIn

Judy Cooley, President
Adam Lechter, First Vice President
Mike Gordon, Second Vice President
Lynn Wieland, Secretary
Mike Allured, Treasurer

A premier professional group of individual technologists, operations personnel, educators, students, business staff and others dedicated to the advancement of the confectionery industry.
Cost: $60.00
Frequency: Membership Fee
Founded in: 1947

8944 American Association of Crop Insurers
1 Massachusetts Ave NW
Suite 800
Washington, DC 20001-1401
202-789-4100; *Fax:* 202-408-7763
aaci@mwmlaw.com; www.cropinsurers.com

Mike Mc Leod, Executive Director
David Graves, Manager/Secretary
Jahi Sauk Simbai

AACI is widely recognized on Capitol Hill as the leading source of crop insurance information and advice on legislative and administrative proposals. AACI is a member of a coalition of groups in Washington working together to improve the risk management options for America's farmers.
15 Members
Frequency: Membership Fee

8945 American Association of Grain Inspection and Weighing Agencies
PO Box 26426
Kansas City, MO 64196
816-569-4020; *Fax:* 816-221-8189
info@aagiwa.org; www.aagiwa.org

David Ayers, President
Tom Dahl, Vice President
David Reeder, Secretary/ Treasurer

Established to provide a liaison between the Federal Grain Inspection Service and designated agencies.
50 Members
Founded in: 1964

8946 American Association of Meat Processors
One Meating Place
Elizabethtown, PA 17022
717-367-1168; *Fax:* 717-367-9096
aamp@aamp.com; www.aamp.com
Social Media: Facebook, Twitter, YouTube, Google+

Erica Hering, President
Louis Muench, 1st Vice President
Marty Manion, CAE, Executive Director
Diana Dietz, Communications Manager
Jane Frey, Accounting & Finances, Dues Billing

Membership consists of small to medium sized meat, poultry and food businesses including, slaughterers, processors, wholesalers, home food service businesses, deli and catering operators and suppliers to the industry. AAMP is affiliated with 32 state, regional and provincial associations.
1400 Members
Founded in: 1939

8947 American Association of Nutritional Consultants
220 Parker St.
Warsaw, IN 46580
574-269-6165
888-828-2262; *Fax:* 574-268-2120
registrar@aanc.net; www.aanc.net
Social Media: Facebook, Twitter, Pinterest

Wendell Whitman, Owner

Promotes ethical standards in the field of nutrition consultants, and those who hold bachelor's degrees in the health related fields.
Cost: $60.00
Frequency: Annual Membership Fee
Founded in: 1985

8948 American Bakers Association
1300 I St NW
Suite 700 West
Washington, DC 20005
202-789-0300; *Fax:* 202-898-1164
info@americanbakers.org;
www.americanbakers.org
Social Media: Twitter, LinkedIn, Youtube, Stationerswidows

Rich Scalise, Chairman of the Board
Fred Penny, First Vice Chairman
Bradley K. Alexander, Second Vice Chairman
Robb MacKie, President & CEO
Lee Sanders, Secretary

A long and dedicated history of representing the interests of the wholesale baking industry before the U.S. Congress, federal agencies, state legislatures and agencies, and international regulatory authorities.
300 Members
Frequency: Membership Dues Vary
Founded in: 1897

8949 American Beekeeping Federation
3525 Piedmont Rd
Bldg 5 Suite 300
Atlanta, GA 30305
404-760-2875; *Fax:* 404-240-0998
info@abfnet.org; www.abfnet.org

Gene Brandi, President
Tim May, Vice President
Regina Robuck, Executive Director
Susan Reu, Membership Coordinator

A national organization that continually works in the interest of all beekeepers, large or small, and those associated with the industry to ensure the future of the honey bee. Members share a common interest to work toward better education and information for all segments of the industry in the hope of increasing chances for survival in today's competitive world.
4700 Members
Frequency: Membership Fees Vary
Founded in: 1943

8950 American Berkshire Association
2637 Yeager Road
West Lafayette, IN 47906
765-497-3618; *Fax:* 765-497-2959
berkshire@nationalswine.com;
www.americanberkshire.com
Social Media: Facebook

Lorraine Hoffman, President
John Baker, Vice President
Merrill Smith, Secretary
Steve Brown, Treasurer

The official national registry for the Berkshire breed of pigs. The ABA promotes the Berkshire breed of hogs, and maintains breed purity through registration of purebred Berkshires. Dedicated Berkshire breeders focus on delivering the superior meat quality that drives the popularity of Berkshire pork among discerning culinary experts.
300+ Members
Founded in: 1998

8951 American Beverage Association
1101 Sixteenth Street NW
Washington, DC 20036
202-463-6732; *Fax:* 202-659-5349
info@ameribev.org; www.ameribev.org
Social Media: Facebook, Twitter, YouTUBE

Rodger L. Collins, Chair
Jeffrey Honickman, Vice Chair
Susan Neely, President
Mark Hammond, Chief Financial Officer
Ralph D. Crowley Jr., Treasurer

The national voice for the non-alcoholic refreshment beverage industry, providing a neutral forum in which members convene to discuss common issues while maintaining their tradition of spirited competition in the American marketplace. Also serving as liaison between the industry, government and the public, and providing a unified voice in legislative and regulatory matters.
Founded in: 1919

8952 American Beverage Licensees Association
5101 River Rd
Suite 108
Bethesda, MD 20816-1560
301-656-1494; *Fax:* 301-656-7539
info@ablusa.org; www.ablusa.org
Social Media: Facebook, Twitter, RSS

Warren Scheidt, President
Terry Harvath, Vice President
John D. Bodnovich, Executive Director
Susan Day Duffy, Director of Trade Relations & Ops
Jessica Anders, Manager, Comm. & PR

An association representing off-premise licensees in the open or license states and on-premise proprietors in markets across the nation. ABL was created after the merger of the National Association of Beverage Retailers (NABR) and the National Licensed Beverage Association (NLBA).
17000 Members
Founded in: 2002

8953 American Brahman Breeders Association
3003 S Loop W
Suite 520
Houston, TX 77054

713-349-0854; *Fax:* 713-349-9795
abba@brahman.org; www.brahman.org
Social Media: Facebook, Twitter, YouTube, Instagram

J. D. Sartwelle, Jr., President
George Kempfer, Vice President
Chris Shivers, Executive Vice President
Armelinda Ibarra, Recording Secretary/Office Manager
Teresa Dominguez, Administrative Assistant

American Brahman is a beef crossbreeding organization that plays a big role in the United States and beyond.
Founded in: 1924

8954 American Center for Wine, Food & the Arts
500 First Street
Napa, CA 94559

707-259-1600
888-512-6742; *Fax:* 707-257-8601;
www.copia.org

Arthur Jacobus, President
Kurt Nystrom, COO
Larry Tsai, Chief Marketing Officer

A non-profit discovery center whose mission is to explore and celebrate the cultural significance of wine, food and the arts.

8955 American Cheese Society
2696 S. Colorado Blvd
Suite 570
Denver, CO 80222-5954

720-328-2788; *Fax:* 720-328-2786
info@cheesesociety.org;
www.cheesesociety.org
Social Media: Facebook, Twitter, LinkedIn, YouTube

Peggy Smith, Chair
Dick Roe, President
Jeff Jirik, Vice President
Nora Weiser, Executive Director
Jane Bauer, Education & Outreach Manager

The Society's membership includes farmstead, artisanal and specialty cheesemakers; academicians and enthusiasts; marketing and distribution specialists; food writers and cookbook authors and specialty foods retailers from the United States, Canada and Europe.
800 Members
Founded in: 1983

8956 American Council on Science and Health
1995 Broadway
Suite 202
New York, NY 10023-5882

212-362-7044
866-905-2694; *Fax:* 212-362-4919
acsh@acsh.org; www.acsh.org
Social Media: Facebook, Twitter, Youtube

Nigel Bark, M.D., Chairman
Hank Campbell, President
Josh Bloom, Director of Chemical Science
Gilbert Ross, Senior Director
Josh Bloom, Ph.D., Director

A consumer education organization providing the public with scientifically accurate evaluations of food, chemicals, the environment and health.
Founded in: 1978

8957 American Culinary Federation
180 Center Place Way
St Augustine, FL 32095

904-824-4468
800-624-9458; *Fax:* 904-940-0741
acf@acfchefs.net; www.acfchefs.org
Social Media: Facebook, Twitter, Flickr, RSS

Thomas J. Macrina, President
Heidi Cramb, Executive Director
Amy Thomason, Administrative Project Manager
Jayme Booth, Project Coordinator
Jennifer Manley, Director of Marketing and Comm.

A professional, not-for-profit organization for chefs and cooks. The principal goal of the founding chefs remains true to ACF today_to promote the professional image of American chefs worldwide through education among culinarians at all levels, from apprentices to the most accomplished certified master chefs.
19000 Members
Founded in: 1929

8958 American Dairy Association Mideast
5950 Sharon Woods Blvd
Columbus, OH 43229

614-890-1800
800-292-MILK; *Fax:* 614-890-1636
info@drink-milk.com; www.drink-milk.com
Social Media: Facebook, Twitter, Youtube, Pinterest

Scott Higgins, CEO
Jenny Hubble, Vice President of Communication

We represent dairy farmers and serve as the local affiliate for the American Dairy Association and the National Dairy Council. We work closely with Dairy Management Inc. and the Milk Processors Education Program to extend national dairy promotion programs to the local level.
3800 Members
Founded in: 1915

8959 American Dairy Council
Interstate Place II
100 Elwood Davis Road
North Syracuse, NY 13212

315-472-9143; *Fax:* 315-472-0506
dairyinfo@adadc.com; www.adadc.com
Social Media: Facebook, Twitter, YouTube, Instagram

Richard Naczi, Director

To economically benefit diary farmers by encouraging the consumption of milk and diary products through advertising, education and promotion, to reach consumers with product benefits and advantages.
Founded in: 1915
Mailing list available for rent

8960 American Dairy Products Institute
126 N. Addison Avenue
Elmhurst, IL 60126

630-530-8700; *Fax:* 630-530-8707
info@adpi.org; www.adpi.org

Doug Wilke, President
Jerry O'Dea, Vice President
David Thomas, Chief Executive Officer
Dan Meyer, Director of Technical Services
Beth Holcomb, Director of Member Communications

An association for manufactured dairy products, including dry milks, whey, lactose, evaporated and condensed milk. ADPI's main purpose is to effectively communicate the many positive attributes and benefits of our members' products. Additionally, we serve our membership by offering the most current industry information available and by collaborating with dairy associations to represent members' interests before state and federal regulatory agencies.
150 Members
Founded in: 1986

8961 American Dairy Science Association
1800 S. Oak Street
Suite 100
Champaign, IL 61820-6974

217-356-5146; *Fax:* 217-398-4119
adsa@assochq.org; www.adsa.org

Susan Duncan, President
Lou Armentano, Vice President
Peter Studney, Executive Director
Vicki Paden, Administrative Assistant
Cara Tharp, Executive Assistant/Event Coor.

Organization of professional researchers. Publishes journals and holds annual member meetings.
4000 Members
Founded in: 1896

8962 American Dry Bean Board
www.americanbean.org

Health benefits of beans, bean salad recipes, healthy bean soup recipes, and bean facts.

8963 American Egg Board
1460 Renaissance Drive - Ste 301
PO Box 738
Park Ridge, IL 60068

847-296-7043; *Fax:* 847-296-7007
aeb@aeb.org; www.aeb.org
Social Media: Twitter

Joanne Ivy, CEO
Elisa Maloberti, Consumer Information Coordinator

U.S. egg producer's link to the consumer in communicating the value of the incredible egg. As the egg industry's promotion arm, AEB's foremost challenge is to convince the American public that the egg is still one of nature's most nearly perfect foods. AEB's basic task is to improve the demand for shell eggs, egg products, as well as spent fowl throughout the United States.
300 Members
Founded in: 1976

8964 American Emu Association
510 W Madison Street
Suite 2
Ottawa, IL 61350

541-332-0675
info@aea-emu.org; www.aea-emu.org
Social Media: Facebook

Tony Citrhyn, President
Terry Turner, Vice President
Joylene Reavis, Secretary
Susan Wright, Treasurer
Richard Merrow, Parliamentarian

A national, member driven, non-profit agricultural association dedicated to the emu industry. AEA promotes public awareness of emu products, fosters research and publishes a bi-monthly newsletter and several industry brochures. Represents an alternative agricultural industry, dominated by the small farmer, who is committed to humane and environmentally positive practices that produce high quality, beneficial products.
Cost: $100.00
1,700 Members
Frequency: Membership Fee
Founded in: 1989

8965 American Farm Bureau Federation
600 Maryland Ave SW
Suite 1000W
Washington, DC 20024

202-484-3600; *Fax:* 202-484-3604
webmaster@fb.org; www.fb.org

Social Media: Facebook, Twitter, YouTube, Google+, RSS, Pintere

Bob Stallman, President
Julie Anna Potts, Executive VP & Treasurer
Lynne Finnerty, Director
Jean Bennis, Executive Assistant

An independent, non-governmental, voluntary organization governed by and representing farm and ranch families united for the purpose of analyzing their problems and formulating action to achieve educational improvement, economic opportunity and social advancement and, thereby, to promote the national well-being. The voice of agricultural producers at all levels.
3MM Members
Founded in: 1919
Mailing list available for rent

8966 American Forage and Grassland Council
PO Box 867
Berea, KY 40403

800-944-2342; *Fax:* 859-623-8694
info@afgc.org; www.afgc.org
Social Media: Facebook, Twitter, YouTube

Gary Wilson, President
Mark Kennedy, Vice President
Robert Shoemaker, Senior Vice President
Tom Keene, Secretary/Treasurer

An international organization with the primary objective to promote the profitable production and sustainable utilization of quality forage and grasslands.
Cost: $30.00
3,000 Members
Frequency: Annual Dues
Mailing list available for rent: 2400+ names

8967 American Frozen Food Institute
2000 Corporate Ridge, Blvd.
Suite 1000
McLean, VA 22102

703-821-0770; *Fax:* 703-821-1350
info@affi.com; www.affi.com

Joseph Clayton, Interim President
Kraig R. Naasz, CEO
Kathleen R. Greco, Chief Administrative Officer
Tom Kearney, Chief Financial Officer
Karim Kadrie, Director of Finance

AFFI is the national trade association the promotes and represents the interests of all segments of the frozen food industry.
500 Members
Founded in: 1942

8968 American Guernsey Association
1224 Alton Darby Creek Road
Suite G
Columbus, OH 43228

614-864-2409; *Fax:* 614-864-5614
info@usguernsey.com; www.usguernsey.com
Social Media: Facebook

David Trotter, President & District 2
Duane Schuler, 1st Vice President & District 4
David Coon, 2nd Vice President & District 1
Brian Schnebly, Executive Secretary
Deb Hoffman, Office Manager

Promotes programs and services to the dairy industry.
36 Members
Founded in: 1877

8969 American Herb Association
PO Box 1673
Nevada City, CA 95959

530-265-9552; *Fax:* 530-274-3140;
www.ahaherb.com

Kathi Keville, Director
Robert Brucia, Co-Director
Marion Wyckoff, Secretary

An association of Medical Herbalists. Membership is open to anyone interested in herbs and includes the AHA Quarterly. The goals of the AHA are to promote the understanding, acceptance and ecological use of herbs.
Cost: $20.00
Frequency: Membership Fee
Founded in: 1981

8970 American Herbal Products Association
8630 Fenton St
Suite 918
Silver Spring, MD 20910

301-588-1171; *Fax:* 301-588-1174
ahpa@ahpa.org; www.ahpa.org

Graham Rigby, Chair
Michael McGuffin, President
Maged Sharaf, Chief Science Officer
Merle Zimmermann, PhD, Chief Information Analyst
Monica Kendrick, Office and Finance Administrator

The national trade association which represents manufacturers, importers and distributors of herbs and herbal products. AHPA seeks self-regulation, establishment of standards and rules of ethical conduct, member enrichment and public outreach.
Cost: $1000.00
300 Members
Frequency: Membership Fees Vary
Founded in: 1983

8971 American Hereford Association
PO Box 014059
Kansas City, MO 64101
816-842-3757; *Fax:* 816-842-6931
aha@hereford.org; www.hereford.org
Social Media: Facebook

Craig Huffhines, Executive VP
Jack Ward, Chief Operating Officer
Leslie Mathews, Chief Financial Officer
Angie Stump Denton, Director of Communications
Stacy Sanders, Director of Records Department

Association for people in the Hereford cattle industry.
8M Members
Founded in: 1986

8972 American Honey Producers Association
PO Box 435
Mendon, UT 84325

281-900-9740; *Fax:* 403-463-2583
cassie@AHPAnet.com;
www.americanhoneyproducers.org

Randy Verhoek, President
Darren Cox, VP
Cassie Cox, Executive Secretary
Kelvin Adee, Treasurer

Represents the interests of major US honey producers and pollinators.
Cost: $150.00
700 Members
Frequency: Membership Fees Vary
Founded in: 1969

8973 American Institute for Cancer Research
1759 R Street, NW
Washington, DC 20009

202-328-7744
800-843-8114; *Fax:* 202-328-7226
aicrweb@aicr.org; www.aicr.org
Social Media: Facebook, Twitter, Pinterest

Melvin Hutson, Chairman
Lawrence Pratt, Vice Chairman
Marilyn Gentry, President
Kelly B. Browning, Chief Executive Officer
Susan Pepper, Secretary/Treasurer

First organization to focus research on the link between diet and cancer and translating the results into practical information for the public. AICR helps people make choices that reduce their chances of developing cancer.
Founded in: 1982

8974 American Institute of Baking
1213 Bakers Way
PO Box 3999
Manhattan, KS 66505-3999

785-537-4750
800-633-5137; *Fax:* 785-537-1493
sales@aibonline.org; www.aibonline.org
Social Media: Facebook, Twitter, LinkedIn

Andre Biane, President/ CEO
Tom Ogle, Chief Financial Officer
Maureen Olewnik, SVP, Food Safety Services
Susan Hancock, VP, Innovation & PD
Brian Strouts, Vice President, Baking

A nonprofit corporation founded by the North American wholesale andretail baking industries as a technology transfer center for bakers and food processors.
Founded in: 1919

8975 American Institute of Food Distribution
10 Mountain View Road
Suite S125
Upper Saddle River, NJ 07458

201-791-5570; *Fax:* 201-791-5222
questions@foodinstitute.com;
www.foodinstitute.com
Social Media: Facebook, Twitter, LinkedIn

Dean Erstad, Chairman
Brian Todd, President/CEO
Donna L. George, President and COO
Susan T. Borra, Senior Vice President
Peter R. Lavoy, Former President & CEO

The best source for timely, current, and relevant information about the food industry. A nonprofit organization for providing information on the hottest topics and latest trends, reports and studies, and industry analysts to answer member inquiries.
Cost: $725.00
2700 Members
Frequency: Annual Membership Fee
Founded in: 1928

8976 American Institute of Wine & Food
P.O. Box 973
Belmont, CA 94002-0973

415-508-6790
info@aiwf.org; www.aiwf.org
Social Media: Facebook

Frank Giaimo, National Chair
Mary Chamberlin, National Vice Chair
Drew Jaglom, National Secretary
George Linn, National Treasurer
Joyce Kucharvy, Director

The American Institute of Wine & Food is one of the few national organizations with the unique combination membership of dedicated wine and food enthusiasts and professionals. Wine and food enthusiasts get to meet and learn from reowned chefs, winemakers, authors, culinary historians, and food producers, while industry professionals have the opportunity to know and understand their core consumers
Cost: $75.00
6000+ Members
Founded in: 1981

8977 **American International Charolais Association**
11700 NW Plaza Circle
Kansas City, MO 64153
816-464-5977; *Fax:* 816-464-5759
north@charolaisusa.com;
www.charolaisusa.com

Larry Lehman, President
Bill Nottke, Vice President
Robb Creasey, Treasurer
John Chism, Secretary
J. Neil Orth, Executive VP

The official registry of Charolais and Charbray cattle in the United States.
2,900 Members

8978 **American Jersey Cattle Association**
6486 E Main Street
Reynoldsburg, OH 43068-2362
614-861-3636; *Fax:* 614-861-8040;
www.usjersey.com
Social Media: Facebook, Twitter

Neal Smith, Executive Secretary & CEO
Whittney Smith, Administrative Assistant
Vickie White, Treasurer and Office Manager
Cindy Watson, Assistant to the Treasurer

They improve and promote the Jersey cattle breed.
Founded in: 1868

8979 **American Livestock Conservancy**
33 Hillsboro St
PO Box 477
Pittsboro, NC 27312
919-542-5704; *Fax:* 919-545-0022
albc@albc-usa.org;
www.livestockconservancy.org
Social Media: Facebook, Blogger, Youtube

Charles R Bassett, Executive Director
Don T Schrider, Communications Director
Jeannette Beranger, Research/Technical Program Manager
Anneke Jakes, Breed Registry Manager

Ensuring the future of agriculture through genetic conservation and the promotion of endangered breeds of livestock and poultry. A non profit membership organization working to protect over 180 breeds of livestock and poultry from extinction.
Cost: $30.00
Frequency: Membership Fee
ISSN: 1064-1599
Founded in: 1977

8980 **American Meat Institute**
1150 Connecticut Ave NW
12th Floor
Washington, DC 20036
202-587-4200; *Fax:* 202-587-4300;
www.meatami.com
Social Media: Facebook, Twitter, LinkedIn

Barry Carpenter, President & CEO
Ron Nunnery, Chief Financial Officer
Eric Mittenthal, Vice President, Public Affairs
Scott Goltry, Vice President, Regulatory Affairs
Susan Backus, Executive Director

AMI keeps its fingers on the pulse of legislation, regulation and media activity that impacts the meat and poultry industry and provides rapid updates and analyses to its members to help them stay informed. Also conducts scientific research through its Foundation designed to help meat and poultry companies improve their plants and their products.
300 Members
Frequency: Membership Fees Vary
Founded in: 1906

8981 **American Meat Science Association**
201 W Springfield Ave
Suite 1202
Champaign, IL 61820
217-356-5370
800-517-AMSA; *Fax:* 888-205-5834; *Fax:* 217-356-5370
information@meatscience.org;
www.meatscience.org
Social Media: Facebook, Twitter, LinkedIn, Vimeo

Bucky Gwartney, Ph.D., President
Steve Campano, Treasurer
Betsy L. Booren, Chair
Thomas Powell, Executive Director
Casey B. Frye, Treasurer

AMSA fosters community and professional development among individuals who create and apply science to efficiently provide safe and high quality meat.

8982 **American Mushroom Institute**
1284 Gap Newport Pike
Suite 800
Avondale, PA 19311
610-268-7483; *Fax:* 610-268-8015
ami@mwmlaw.com;
www.americanmushroom.org

Joseph G. Poppiti, Chairman
Don Needham, Chairman Elect
Curtis Jurgensmeyer, Vice Chair/ Treasurer
Stephen Anania, Secretary
Laura Phelps, President

This organization is comprised of mushroom growers, associate businesses and suppliers who represent growers and coordinate industry research.
Founded in: 1955

8983 **American Oil Chemists' Society**
2710 S. Boulder
Urbana, IL 61802-6996
217-359-2344; *Fax:* 217-351-8091
general@aocs.org; www.aocs.org
Social Media: Facebook, Twitter, LinkedIn, Blogger

M. Trautmann, President
B. Hendrix, Vice President
N. Widlak, Secretary
D. Bibus, Treasurer
P. Donnelly, Chief Executive Officer

Largest international society focused on the science and technology of fats, oils, lipids and related substances.
Cost: $10.00
5400 Members
Frequency: Membership Dues Vary
Founded in: 1909

8984 **American Ostrich Association**
PO Box 166
Ranger, TX 75158
972-968-8546; *Fax:* 936-333-6142
aoa@ostriches.org; www.ostriches.org

Joel Brust, President
Boyd Clark, Vice President
Sharon Birmingham, Secretary/ Treasurer
Carol Garnett, Director at large

Organization that provides leadership for the ostrich industry and its future through the promotion of ostrich products.
Cost: $150.00
Frequency: Membership Fee
Founded in: 1988

8985 **American Peanut Council**
1500 King St
Suite 301
Alexandria, VA 22314
703-838-9500; *Fax:* 703-838-9508
info@peanutsusa.com; www.peanutsusa.com
Social Media: Facebook, Twitter

Patrick Archer, President

The council was formed through a merger of the National Peanut Council and the National Peanut Council of America. Serving as a forum for all segments of the peanut industry to discuss issues which impact the production, utilization and marketing of peanuts and peanut products worldwide.
Founded in: 1997

8986 **American Peanut Research and Education Society**
2360 Rainwater Road
UGA/NESPAL Building
Tifton, GA 31793
229-329-2949; *Fax:* 229-386-7371
kim.cutchins@apresinc.com;
www.apresinc.com

Naveen Puppala, President
Kimberly J. Cutchins, Executive Officer
Kimberly J. Cutchins, Executive Officer
Jeffrey Pope, Board Representative
Howard Valentine, Director of Science & Technology

The purpose of this Society is to instruct and educate the public on the properties, production, and use of the peanut through the organization and promotion of public discussion groups, forums, lectures, and other programs or presentations to the interested public.
Cost: $80.00
550 Members
Frequency: Organizational Fee: $100
Founded in: 1968

8987 **American Pie Council**
PO Box 368
Lake Forest, IL 60045
www.piecouncil.org
Social Media: Facebook, Twitter, Pinterest, YouTube

The Pie Council is dedicated to preserving America's pie heritage.

8988 **American Pomological Society**
102 Tyson Building
University Park, PA 16802
814-863-6163; *Fax:* 814-237-3407;
www.americanpomological.org

Peter Hirst, President
Michele Warmund, 1st Vice-President
Marvin Pritts, 2nd Vice-President
Richard Marini, Secretary
Robert Crassweller, Treasurer/ Business Manager

The oldest fruit organization in North America, to foster the science and practice of fruit growing and variety development.
Cost: $40.00
1000 Members
Frequency: Annual Membership Fee
Founded in: 1848

8989 **American Poultry Association**
PO Box 306
Burgettstown, PA 15021
724-729-3459
AmPoultryAssoc@yahoo.com;
www.amerpoultryassn.com

Dave Anderson, President
John Monaco, Vice President
Pat Horstman, Secretary/Treasurer
Dave Anderson, Director at large

The mission of the association is to promote and protect the standard bred poultry industry in all its phases. To encourage and protect poultry shows as being the show window of the industry, an education for both breeders and the public and a means of interesting young future breeders.
Cost: $25.00
Frequency: Annual Membership

8990 American Seafood Institute
25 Fairway Circle
Hope Valley, RI 02832
401-491-9017; *Fax:* 401-491-9024;
www.americanseafood.org
Colleen Coyne, Director

8991 American Seed Trade Association
1701 Duke Street
Suite 275
Alexandria, VA 22314
703-837-8140; *Fax:* 703-837-9365
infi@amseed.org; www.amseed.com
Social Media: Facebook, Twitter, Youtube, Googleplus
Andy Lavigna, President & CEO
Bernice Slutsky, Senior Vice President
Jane Demarchi, Vice President
Rick Dunkle, Senior Director
Michelle Kohn, Director
Producers of seeds for planting purposes. Consists of companies involved in seed production and distribution, plant breeding and related industries in North America.
850 Members
Frequency: Membership Fees Vary
Founded in: 1883

8992 American Sheep Industry Association
9785 Maroon Circle
Suite 360
Englewood, CO 80112
303-771-3500; *Fax:* 303-771-8200
eatlamb@wildblue.net; www.sheepusa.org
Social Media: Facebook, Twitter
Burton Pfliger, President
Mike Corn, Vice President
Peter Orwick, Executive Director
Rita Kourlis Samuelson, Director of Wool Marketing
Paul Rodgers, Deputy Director of Policy
A federation of state associations dedicated to the welfare and profitability of the sheep industry.
8000+ Members
Founded in: 1865

8993 American Shrimp Processors Association
PO Box 4867
EIN #72-6029637
Biloxi, MS 39535
228-806-9600; *Fax:* 228-385-2565
director@americanshrimp.com;
www.americanshrimp.com
Social Media: Facebook, Twitter, Pinterest, YouTube, Instagram
Andrew Blanchard, President
Jonathan McLendon, Vice President
Scott Young, Secretary/Treasurer
Ivan Sifrim, UX Developer
Nick Alekhine, Developer
A non-profit trade organization designed to represent U.S. shrimp processors in all aspects of business. Allowing processors and related industries to work together to foster a business and technological climate in which its members can prosper while providing the highest quality product to its customers.
Founded in: 1964

8994 American Society for Enology and Viticulture
PO Box 1855
Davis, CA 95617-1855
530-753-3142; *Fax:* 530-753-3318
society@asev.org; www.asev.org
Social Media: Twitter, LinkedIn
Mark Greenspan, President
Nichola Hall, First Vice President
Dr. James Harbertson, Second Vice President
Tom Collins, Secretary/ Treasurer
Linda Bisson, AJEV Science Editor
A tax exempt professional society dedicated to the interests of enologists, viticulturists, and others in the fields of wine and grape research and production throughout the world.
2400+ Members
Founded in: 1950

8995 American Society for Horticultural Science
1018 Duke Street
Alexandria, VA 22314
703-836-4606; *Fax:* 703-836-2024
webmaster@ashs.org; www.ashs.org
Social Media: Facebook, Twitter, LinkedIn, Pinterest
Curt Rom, Chair
John Dole, President
Michael W. Neff, Executive Director
Heather Hilko, Membership
A cornerstone of research and education in horticulture and an agent for active promotion of horticultural science.
2500+ Members
Frequency: Membership Fees Vary
Founded in: 1903

8996 American Society for Parenteral and Enteral Nutrition
8630 Fenton Street
Suite 412
Silver Spring, MD 20910
301-587-6315; *Fax:* 301-587-2365
aspen@nutritioncare.org;
www.nutritioncare.org
Social Media: Facebook, Twitter, LinkedIn, YouTube
Gordon Sacks, President
Charlene W. Compher, President-Elect
M. Molly McMahon, Vice President
Phil Ayers, Secretary/Treasurer
Albert Barrocas, Director
Advancing the science and practice of clinical nutrition and metabolism. An interdisciplinary organization whose members are involved in the provision of clinical nutrition therapies, including parenteral and enteral nutrition.
6400+ Members
Founded in: 1976

8997 American Society of Agricultural Consultants
605 Columbus Ave South
New Prague, MN 56071
952-758-5811; *Fax:* 952-758-5813
asac@gandgcomm.com;
www.agconsultants.org
Social Media: Facebook, Twitter, LinkedIn, YouTube
Russell Morgan, CAC, Principal
Norman Brown, President-Elect
Den Gardner, Executive Vice President
Kristy Mach, Associate
Roy Ferguson, Director
An association representing the full range of agricultural consultants which serves as an information, resource, and networking base for its members.
181 Members
Founded in: 1963

8998 American Society of Agronomy
5585 Guilford Road
Madison, WI 53711-5801
608-273-8080; *Fax:* 608-273-2021
membership@agronomy.org;
www.agronomy.org
Social Media: Facebook, Twitter, LinkedIn
Jean L. Steiner, President
David B. Mengel, President-elect
Ellen G.M. Bergfeld, Chief Executive Officer
Wes Meixelsperger, Chief Financial Officer
Sara Uttech, Senior Manager
Society members are dedicated to the conservation and wise use of natural resources to produce food, feed, and fiber crops while maintaining and improving the environment. Membership is tax deductible. ASA is seen as a progressive, scientific society.
11000 Members
Founded in: 1907

8999 American Society of Animal Science
PO Box 7410
Champaign, IL 61826-7410
217-356-9050; *Fax:* 217-568-6070
asas@asas.org; www.asas.org
Social Media: Facebook, Twitter, Youtube
Dr. Michael L. Looper, President
Dr. Debora Hamernik, President-Elect
Dr. Todd A. Armstrong, Foundation Trustee Chair
Dr. James Sartin, Editor-in-chief
Dr. Phillip S. Miller, Recording Secretary
A professional organization for animal scientists designed to help members provide effective leadership through research, extension, teaching and service for the dynamic and rapidly changing livestock and meat industries.
5000+ Members
ISSN: 0021-8812
Founded in: 1908

9000 American Society of Baking
7809 N Chestnut Avenue
Kansas City, MO 64119
800-713-0462; *Fax:* 888-315-2612
info@asbe.org; www.asbe.org
Social Media: Facebook, Twitter, LinkedIn
Ramon Rivera, Chairman
Mario Somoza, 1st Vice Chairman
Wendi Ebbing, 2nd Vice Chairman
Bill Zimmerman, 3rd Vice Chairman
Teresa Ruder, Secretary/ Treasurer
Formerly known as the American Society of Bakery Engineers, a professional society comprised of members in either engaged in, involved with, or interested in wholesale or large scale bakery production. The purpose is to promoted the advancement of baking science technology through the exchange of information and interaction among baking industry professionals.
Cost: $135.00
2900 Members
Frequency: Membership Fee
Founded in: 1924

9001 American Society of Brewing Chemists
3340 Pilot Knob Rd
St. Paul, MN 55121
651-454-7250; *Fax:* 651-454-0766
asbc@scisoc.org; www.asbcnet.org
Social Media: Facebook, Twitter, LinkedIn
Christina Schoenberger, President
Christine S. White, President-Elect
Chris D. Powell, Vice President

Robert Christiansen, Secretary
Kelly A. Tretter, Treasurer-Elect

ASBC is dedicated to ensuring the highest quality, consistency and safety of malt-based beverages and their ingredients. Analytical, scientific process control methods, problem solving on industry-wide issues, scientific support to evaluate raw materials for optimum performance, and professional development opportunities.
Cost: $233.00
750+ Members
Frequency: Membership Fee
Founded in: 1934

9002 **American Society of Farm Managers and Rural Appraisers**
950 S Cherry St
Suite 508
Denver, CO 80246-2664

303-758-3513; *Fax:* 303-758-0190
hevans@asfmra.org; www.asfmra.org
Social Media: Facebook, Twitter, LinkedIn

Fred L. Hepler, President
Merrill E. Swanson, President-Elect
Michael J. Krause, First Vice President
LeeAnn E. Moss, Academic Vice President
Jake Minton, District II Vice President

Protects and promotes the interest of members before government, regulatory bodies, and other organizations, enhances member opportunities for professional development and interation with peers, improves ethics, standards and quality of service offered by members, promotes awareness and confidence, and recruits and maintains a highly qualified, professional membership.
Cost: $175.00
Frequency: Membership Fees Vary
Founded in: 1929

9003 **American Society of Sugar Cane Technologists**
LSU AgCenter
Sturgis Hall #128
Baton Rouge, LA 70803

225-578-6930; *Fax:* 225-578-1403
assct@assct.org; www.assct.org

Bruce McManus, President, Florida
Wallace Millet, President, Louisiana

With branches in Florida and Louisiana, the Society is dedicated to the study and advancement of the cane sugar industry in the United States.

9004 **American Soybean Association**
12125 Woodcrest Executive Drive
Suite 100
Saint Louis, MO 63141-5009

314-576-1770
800-688-7692; *Fax:* 314-576-2786
membership@soy.org; www.soygrowers.com
Social Media: Facebook, Twitter, Youtube, Feedburner

Wade Cowan, President
Ray Gaesser, Chairman
Richard Wilkins, 1st Vice President
Ron Moore, Secretary
Davie Stephens, Treasurer

A primary focus of the American Association is policy development and implementation and to improve US soybean farmer profitability.
21000 Members
Founded in: 1920

9005 **American Spice Trade Association**
1101 17th St NW
Suite 700
Washington, DC 20036

202-331-2460; *Fax:* 202-463-8998
info@astaspice.org; www.astaspice.org

Greg Lightfood, President
Vinayak Narin, Vice President/ Secretary
Matt Meilander, Treasurer
Frank Collette, Associate Group Director
Cheryl Deem, Executive Director

ASTA, The voice of the US spice industry, works to ensure the supply of clean, safe spice, shape public policy on behalf of the global industry and advance the business interests of its members.
Frequency: Membership Dues Vary
Founded in: 1907

9006 **American Sugar Alliance**
2111 Wilson Blvd
Suite 700
Arlington, VA 22201

703-351-5055; *Fax:* 703-351-6698
info@sugaralliance.org;
www.sugaralliance.org
Social Media: Facebook, Twitter, YouTube, Pinterest

Don Phillips, Trade Adviser
Vickie Meyer, Executive Director
Jack Roney, Dir.Economics & Policy Analysis
Phillip W. Hayes, Director of Media Relations
Laura Gouge, Special Projects Coordinator

The American Sugar Aliance is a national coalition of sugarcane and sugarbett farmers, processors, refiners, suppliers, workers and others dedicated to preserving a strong domestic sugar industry.
Frequency: Membership Fee
Founded in: 1983

9007 **American Sugar Beet Growers Association**
1156 15th St NW
Suite 1101
Washington, DC 20005

202-833-2398; *Fax:* 240-235-4291
info@americansugarbeet.org;
www.americansugarbeet.org
Social Media: Facebook

John Snyder, President
Ruthann Geib, Vice President
Luther Markwart, Executive Vice President
Galen Lee, Vice President
Mark Olson, Treasurer

The purpose of the organization is to unite sugarbeet growers in the United States and promote the common interest of state and regional beet grower associations, which include legislative and international representation and public relations.
10000 Members

9008 **American Sugar Cane League**
PO Drawer 938
206 E Bayou Rd.
Thibodaux, LA 70301

985-448-3707; *Fax:* 985-448-3722;
www.amscl.org
Social Media: Facebook, Twitter, LinkedIn, YouTube, Pinterest

Michael Melancon, President
James H. Simon, General Manager

A Louisiana nonprofit involved in research, promotion and education in support of the state's sugar industry.
Founded in: 1922

9009 **American Veal Association**
2900 NE Brooktree Lane
Suite 200
Gladstone, MO 64119

816-556-3169
info@americanveal.com;
www.americanveal.com
Social Media: Facebook, Twitter, Digg, Stumbleupon,Reddit

Jurian Bartelse, President
Dr. Adnan Aydin, Vice President
Chris Landwehr, Treasurer
Dale Bakke, Secretary

Provides information on veal production practices, industry facts, a tour of a modern veal barn and educational materials. Promoting the American veal industry, and encouraging communications and distributing information pertinent to the veal industry.
1300 Members
Founded in: 1984

9010 **American Wholesale Marketers Association**
11311 Sunset Hills Road
Reston, VA 20190

703-208-3358
800-482-2962; *Fax:* 703-573-5738
info@cdaweb.net; www.cdaweb.net
Social Media: Facebook, Twitter

Scott Ramminger, President & CEO
Robert Pignato, IOM, Senior Vice President & COO
Anne Holloway, Vice President Government Affairs
Jane Berzan, Vice President of Strategy
Bob Gatty, Vice President, Communications

International trade organization working on behalf of convenience distributors in the U.S. Associate members include manufacturers, brokers, retailers and others allied to the convenience product industry. Typical products purchased and sold by convenience distributors include candy, tobacco, snacks, beverages, health and beauty care items, general merchandise, foodservice and groceries.
530 Members
Frequency: Membership Dues
Founded in: 1942

9011 **American Wine Society**
P.O. Box 889
Scranton, PA 18501

888-297-9070; www.americanwinesociety.org
Social Media: Facebook, Twitter, LinkedIn

Kristin Casler Kraft, President
Joseph Broski, Vice President
David Falchuk, Executive Director
Jay Bileti, Director, Member Services

The oldest and largest consumer based wine education organization in North America. A non-profit, educational, consumer-oriented organization for those interested in learning more about all aspects of wine.
5000 Members
Frequency: Membership Dues Vary
Founded in: 1967

9012 **Animal Agriculture Alliance**
2101 Wilson Blvd
Suite 916-B
Arlington, VA 22201

703-562-5160; *Fax:* 703-524-1921
info@animalagalliance.org;
www.animalagalliance.org
Social Media: Facebook, Twitter

Kay Johnson Smith, President & CEO
Morgan Hawley, Executive Assistant to President
Hannah Thompson, Communications Director
Shakera Daley, Administrative Assistant
Casey Whitaker, Communications Coordinator

The animal Agriculture Alliance is a 501 (c)(3) education foundation. The alliance's mission is to support and promote animal agricultural practices that provide for farm animal well-being through sound science and public education.
3000 Members
Founded in: 1987

9013 Apple Processors Association
1701 K Street NW
Suite 650
Washington, DC 20006
202-785-6715; *Fax:* 202-331-4212
pweller@agriwashington.org;
www.appleprocessors.org
Social Media: Facebook

Andrea Ball, President
Paul S. Weller Jr., EVP Communications
Elizabeth Johnson, VP, Food & Nutrition Policy
Jacquie Ball, Director of Administration

A national association of companies that manufacture quality apple products from whole apples. Members are either apple grower/processor cooperatives, or proprietary firms.
25 Members
Founded in: 1987

9014 Apple Products Research & Education Council
1100 Johnson Ferry Road
Suite 300
Atlanta, GA 30342
404-252-3663; *Fax:* 404-252-0774;
www.appleproducts.org

Formerly known as The Processed Apples Institute. We are producers of processed apple products; suppliers of equipment, packaging or ingredients to the industry and brokers and concentrate manufacturers.
80 Members
Founded in: 1951

9015 Association for Dressings & Sauces
1100 Johnson Ferry Road
Suite 300
Atlanta, GA 30342
678-298-1181; *Fax:* 404-252-0774
ads@kellencompany.com;
www.dressings-sauces.org
Social Media: Facebook, Twitter, YouTube, Pinterest

Pam Chumley, President
Jeannie Milewski, Executive Director
Jacque Knight, Membership/Administration Manager

This association is comprised of manufacturers of mayonnaise, salad dressings and condiment sauces, as well as industry suppliers. Its purpose is to serve the best interests of industry members, its customers, and consumers of its products.
184 Members
Founded in: 1926
Mailing list available for rent

9016 Association for Packaging and Processing Technologies
Packaging Machinery Manufacturers Institute
11911 Freedom Drive
Suite 600
Reston, VA 20190
703-243-8555
888-275-7664; *Fax:* 703-243-8556
pmmiwebhelp@pmmi.org; www.pmmi.org
Social Media: Facebook, Twitter, LinkedIn, YouTube

Charles D. Yuska, President
Katie Bergmann, Senior Vice President
Corinne G Mulligan, Executive Assistant
Caroline Abromavage, Director, Operations
Monjur Alam, Data Analyst

Members manufacture packaging and packaging-related converting machinery in the United States and Canada. PMMI's vision is to be the leading global resource for packaging. Its mission is to improve and promote members' abilities to meet the needs of their customers.
500+ Members
Founded in: 1933

9017 Association of American Feed Control Officials
Purdue University
1800 S. Oak Street
Suite 100
Champaign, IL 61820-6974
217-356-4221; *Fax:* 217-398-4119
aafco@aafco.org; www.aafco.org
Social Media: Facebook

Tim Darden, President
Doug Lueders, President-Elect
Ali Kashani, Secretary/Treasurer
Mark LeBlanc, Sr. Director
Richard Teneyck, Sr. Director

A voluntary membership association of local, state and federal agencies charged by law to regulate the sale and distribution of animal feeds and animal drug remedies.
54 Members
Founded in: 1909

9018 Association of American Seed Control Officials
Utah Department of Agriculture and Food
350 N Redwood Road
PO Box 146500
Salt Lake City, UT 84114-6500
801-538-7182; *Fax:* 801-538-7189
walshm@purdue.edu; www.seedcontrol.org

Jim Drews, President
Johnny Zook, 1st Vice President
Greg Stordahl, 2nd Vice President
Greg Helmbrecht, Treasurer
John Heaton, Secretary

The AASCO's purpose is to promote and establish basic requirements of a state seed law which shall serve as guidelines for member states, to promote and foster uniformity of procedures and policies by member states, to exchange problems and solutions or ideas and suggestions, to coordinate action and cooperate, and to impress and create a sense of mutual understanding between members and other organizations that are concerned with orderly legal merchandising of high quality seed.
Founded in: 1949

9019 Association of Correctional Food Service Affiliates
PO Box 10065
Burbank, CA 91510
818-843-6608; *Fax:* 818-843-7423
philip.atkinson@co.hennepin.mn.us;
www.acfsa.org
Social Media: Facebook, Twitter, Shutterfly

Laurie Maurino, President
Timothy Thielman, Vice President
Carlos Salazar Jr., Vice President Elect/Treasurer
Linda Mills, RDN, FADA, Secretary
Jon Nichols, Executive Director

An international non-profit organization dedicated to the professional growth of our many nation's correctional foodservice employees. Association members are foodservice professionals employed in correctional facilities and agencies within federal, state and municipal prison/jail systems. Members are employed within government and commercially operated facilities within the United States, Canada, and an expanding international market.
Cost: $50.00
1300 Members
Frequency: Dues up to $150
Founded in: 1969

9020 Association of Food Industries
3301 State Route 66
Building C, Suite 205
Neptune, NJ 07753
732-922-3008; *Fax:* 732-922-3590
info@afius.org; www.afius.org
Social Media: Facebook

Fred Mortati, Chair
Stephen O'Mara, 1st Vice Chair
James Libby, 2nd Vice Chair
John Sessler, Treasurer
Joe Fragola, Secretary

Promotes free trade and commerce in the food industry. Offers information and education on customs and usage of trade in the food markets and represents member interests in government.
Cost: $1040.00
800 Members
Frequency: Membership Dues Vary
Founded in: 1906

9021 Association of Food and Drug Officials
2550 Kingston Rd
Suite 311
York, PA 17402
717-757-2888; *Fax:* 717-650-3650
afdo@afdo.org; www.afdo.org
Social Media: Twitter

Stephen Stich, President
Stan Stromberg, President-elect
Steven Mandernach, Vice-President
Steven Moris, Secretary/Treasurer
Joseph Corby, Executive Director

Promotes the enforcement of laws and regulations at all levels of government. Fosters understanding and cooperation between industry and regulators. Develops model laws and regulations and seeks their adoption.
800 Members
Frequency: Membership Dues Vary
Founded in: 1896

9022 Association of Fruit and Vegetable Inspection
PO Box 588
Williamston, NC 27892
252-792-1672; *Fax:* 252-792-4787
ronnie.wynn@ncagr.gov; www.afvisa.org

Jack Dantzler, President
Russell Beamsley, Vice President
Carrie Porterfield, Second Vice President
Dennis Clary, Treasurer
Laura Thomas, Secretary

An organization of shipping point inspection programs that advocates for more uniformity between states.
Founded in: 1986

9023 Association of Seafood Importers
Empress International
10 Harbor Park Drive
Port Washington, NY 11050-4681
516-621-5900
800-645-6244; *Fax:* 516-621-8318

Burt C Faure

Membership is comprised of seafood importers focusing on problems facing the industry.

9024 Association of Smoked Fish Processors
85 John Road
Canton, MA 02021
781-821-2200
800-444-8705; *Fax:* 781-821-9266
info@shusterlabs.com; www.shusterlabs.com

This association provides technical consulation and services to the smoked fish and seafood industry. Services include recall manuals, plant audits, product evaluations, process evaluation, process evaluation, microbiological testing, analytical testing. HACCP plan development and plan ventilation.

9025 **At-Sea Processors Association**
4039 21st Ave W
Suite 400
Seattle, WA 98199
206-285-5139; *Fax:* 206-285-1841;
www.atsea.org
Stephanie Madsen, Executive Director
Paul MacGregor, General Counsel
Jim Gilmore, Public Affairs Director
A trade association representing seven copmanies that own and operate 19 U.S. flag cathcer/processor vessels that participate principally in the Alaska pollack fishery and west coast Pacific whiting fishery.
Cost: $500.00
7 Members
Frequency: Membership Varies
Founded in: 1985

9026 **Bakery Equipment Manufacturers and Allieds (BEMA)**
10740 Nall Avenue
Suite 230
Overland Park, KS 66211
913-338-1300; *Fax:* 913-338-1327
info@bema.org; www.bema.org
Social Media: Facebook, Twitter
KERWIN BROWN, President & CEO
Terry Bartsch, Chairman
Allen Wright, 1st Vice Chairman
Don Osborne, 2nd Vice Chairman
Paul Lattan, 3rd Vice Chairman
Through the exchange of information, active involvement on committees and participation in educational seminars, BEMA members are continually able to increase the efficiency and sophistication of their equipment while keeping design in adherence with Baking Industry Standarts Committee (BISSC) codes. Continually improving the efficiency of production and establishing sanitation standards.
208 Members
Frequency: Annual Membership Dues
Founded in: 1918

9027 **Baking Industry Sanitation Standards Committee**
PO Box 3999
Manhattan, KS 66505-3999
866-342-4772
785-537-4750; *Fax:* 785-537-1493
bissc@bissc.org; www.bissc.org
James Munyon, President
Jon Anderson, Board Member
Develops and promotes sanitation standards for the design and construction of bakery equipment. Offers certification and third party verification programs for the member companies whose equipment conforms to the BISSC standards.
125 Members
Founded in: 1949

9028 **Beef Industry Food Safety Council**
Attn: Deb Cole
9110 E. Nichols Ave
Centennial, CO 80112
303-850-3320; *Fax:* 303-770-6921
dcole@beef.org; www.bifsco.org
Deborah Cole, Administrative Coordinator
Gary Voogt, President
Forrest Roberts, CEO
Luisa Munsee, Treasurer
Bill Donald, VP
BIFSCo brings together representatives from all segments of the beef industry to develop industry-wide, science-based strategies to solve the problem of food borne pathogens.

9029 **Beef and Lamb New Zealand**
PO Box 121
Wellington, NZ 6140
644-473-9150
800-233-352; *Fax:* 644-474-0800
enquiries@beeflambnz.com;
www.beeflambnz.com
Social Media: Facebook, Twitter, LinkedIn, Youtube, Pinterest
Dr. Scott Champion, Chief Executive Officer
Cros Spooner, Chief Operating Officer
Andrew Morrison, Director
Anne Munro, Director
Kirsten Bryant, Director
Funded by livestock producers through levies on all beef, sheep and goats slaughtered and on all wool sold. This income is used primarily to market New Zealand wool and meat worldwide, to maintain and extend trade access for New Zealand wool and meat, to provide solutions that will help improve New Zealand farm returns, and to provide technology to the wool industry.

9030 **Beer Institute**
Beer Institute
440 First Street NW
Suite 350
Washington, DC 20001
202-737-2337
800-379-2739; *Fax:* 202-737-7004
info@beerinstitute.org; www.beerinstitute.org
Social Media: Facebook, Twitter
James A. McGreevy III, President & CEO
Sandra Castro, Manager, Administration
Joy Dubost, Senior Director
Denise A. Dunckel, Vice President, Public Affairs
Susan Haney, Vice President of Operations
The national trade association for the brewing industry. Representing both big and small brewers as well as importers and industry suppliers.
Founded in: 1986

9031 **Beet Sugar Development Foundation**
800 Grant Street
Suite 300
Denver, CO 80203
303-832-4460; *Fax:* 303-832-4468
Tom@bsdf-assbt.org; www.bsdf-assbt.org
J.W. Schorr, President
T.D. Knudsen, First Vice President
J. Dean, Second VP
T.K. Schwartz, Executive Vice President/Secretary
Aimee Dokes, Administrative Assistant
Association specializing in beet sugar research and the advertisement of seed companies.
Cost: $100.00
13 Members
Frequency: Membership Fee/Max. $450

9032 **Biodynamic Farming & Gardening Association**
1661 N Water Street
Suite 307
Milwaukee, WI 53202
262-649-9212; *Fax:* 262-649-9213
info@biodynamics.com;
www.biodynamics.com
Social Media: Facebook
Robert Karp, Executive Director
Thea Maria Calson, Director of Programs
Jessica St. John, Director of Operations
Rebecca Briggs, Communications Coordinator
Ken Keffer, Program Assistant
A non-profit, membership organization open to the public with a purpose to foster knowledge of the practices and principles of the biodynamic method of agriculture, horticulture, and forestry in the North American continent and to advance the applications of this method through educational activities such as research, lectures, conferences; publishing literature on the biodynamic methods, and supporting consultation and extension services to farmers, gardeners, and foresters.
Cost: $45.00
Frequency: 6 per year
Circulation: 1000+
Founded in: 1938

9033 **Biscuit & Cracker Manufacturers' Association**
6325 Woodside Court
Suite 125
Columbia, MD 21046
443-545-1645; *Fax:* 410-290-8585
dvanlaar@thebcma.org; www.thebcma.org
Social Media: Facebook, Twitter, Googel+
Dave Van Laar, President
Vanessa Vial, Comm. & eLearning Manager
Kathy Kinter Phelps, Member & Edu. Services Mgr
Todd Wallin, Treasurer
Kathy Kinter Phelps, Secretary
An international trade organization representing the entire spectrum of companies in the manufacturing of cookies and crackers and suppliers to theindustry.
Founded in: 1901

9034 **Blue Diamond Growers**
1701 C Street
Sacramento, CA 95811
916-442-0771
800-987-2329; *Fax:* 916-446-8461
feedback@bdgrowers.com;
www.bluediamondgrowers.com
Social Media: Facebook, Twitter, Youtube, Pinterest
Dan Cummings, Chairman of the Board
Dale Van Groningen, Vice Chairman
Mark Jansen, President & CEO
Don Yee, Director-at-large
Mel Machado, Director, Member relations
The world's largest tree nut processing and marketing company. Building markets and creating new products, uses, and opportunities for members.

9035 **Board of Trade of Wholesale Seafood**
7 Dey Street
Room 801
New York, NY 10007-3223
212-732-4340; *Fax:* 212-732-6644;
www.aboutseafood.com
Social Media: Facebook, Twitter, Googelplus
Albert Altesnan, President/Administrator
Credit exchange and collection agency for wholesale seafood merchants and producers, in the US and Canada.
Founded in: 1931

9036 **Bread Bakers Guild of America**
670 West Napa Street
Suite B
Sonoma, CA 95476
707-935-1468; *Fax:* 707-935-1672
info@bbga.org; www.bbga.org
Social Media: Facebook, Twitter
Jeff Yankellow, Board Chair
Phyllis Enloe, Board Vice Chair
Neale Creamer, Treasurer
Cathy Wayne, Director of Operations
Jill Valavanis, Administrative Assistant
Well known in the baking community as the go-to educational resource for substantive, accurate information on the craft of making bread. The definitive resource on all aspects of artisan baking in America, supporting and fostering the

growth of the artisan baking community. Defining and upholding the highest professional standarts, and celebrating the craft and the passion of the artisan baker.
1300 Members
Founded in: 1993

9037 Brewers Association
1327 Spruce Street
Boulder, CO 80302

303-447-0816
888-822-6273; *Fax:* 303-447-2825
info@brewersassociation.org;
www.homebrewersassociation.org
Social Media: Facebook, Twitter

Sam Calagione, Chair
Gary Fish, Vice Chair
Mark Edelson, Treasurer/Secretary
Katie Brown, Finance Assistant
Tom Clark, Finance Director

The goal of the BA is to promote and protect small and independent American brewers, their craft beers and the community of brewing enthusiasts.
43000 Members
Founded in: 1978

9038 Brown Swiss Association
800 Pleasant St
Beloit, WI 53511-5456

608-365-4474; *Fax:* 608-365-5577
info@brownswissusa.com;
www.brownswissusa.com
Social Media: Facebook

Lee Barber, President
Tome Portner, Vice President
David Wallace, Executive Secretary
David Gunter, Director
Annissa Jones, Bookkeeper

Membership is comprised of key dairy industry leaders and dairy producers who are on the cutting edge of the world's latest agricultural technology.
800 Members
Founded in: 1880

9039 Brown Swiss Cattle Breeder's Association
800 Pleasant Street
Beloit, WI 53511

608-365-4474; *Fax:* 608-365-5577
info@brownswissusa.com;
www.brownswissusa.com
Social Media: Facebook

Lee Barber, President
Tom Portner, Vice President
David Wallace, Exec. Secretary
David Gunter, Director
Annissa Jones, Bookkeeper

Registers about 10,000 animals per year and promotes and expands the Brown Swiss breed with programs that assist the membership and industry to compete favorably in the market place.
800 Members
Founded in: 1880

9040 CCFMA Annual Convention
Conference Caterers & Food Manufacturers Assoc.
1205 Spartan Drive
Madison Heights, MI 48071

248-982-5379
ccfma@ymail.com; www.mobilecaterers.com

See the changes in the industry, learn tools to help business succeed and grow, and network with peers.
Frequency: Annual/October
Founded in: 1964

9041 Calaveras Winegrape Alliance
P.O. Box 2492
Murphys, CA

209-728-9467
866-806-9463
calaveraswines@att.net;
www.calaveraswines.org
Social Media: Facebook, Twitter, Pinterest

Dedicated to increasing the awareness of all wines produced in Calaveras County and/or produced from Calaveras grapes.

9042 California Walnuts
101 Parkshore Dr.
Ste. 2503
Folsom, CA 95630

916-932-7070; *Fax:* 916-932-7071
info@walnuts.org; www.walnuts.org
Social Media: Facebook, Twitter, YouTube, Pinterest

Dennis A. Balint, Executive Director

Established to represent walnut growers and handlers. The board promotes usage of walnuts in the U.S. through publicity, product promotions and production research and education programs.
Founded in: 1948
Mailing list available for rent

9043 Calorie Control Council
2611 Winslow Dr Ne
Atlanta, GA 30305-3777

678-608-3200; *Fax:* 404-252-0774
webmaster@caloriecontrol.org;
www.caloriecontrol.org

An international non-profit association representing the low-calorie food and beverage industry. The Council seeks to provide an effective channel of communication among its members, the public and government officials, and to assure that scientific, medical and other pertinent research and information is developed and made available to all interested parties.
60 Members
Founded in: 1966

9044 Can Manufacturers Institute
1730 Rhode Island Ave NW
Suite 1000
Washington, DC 20036

202-232-4677; *Fax:* 202-232-5756;
www.cancentral.com
Social Media: Facebook, Twitter, LinkedIn

Robert Budway, President

Serves as the voice of the metal can making industry, providing a forum for members to advocate common industry problems to legislative and regulatory agencies whose activities impact the metal can market, to address issues of common concern, and to promote cost-effectively the benefits of the can to protect and grow the market.
35 Members
Founded in: 1939

9045 Canned Foods
PO Box 5258
Madison, WI 53705-0000

608-231-2250; *Fax:* 608-231-6952;
www.cannedveggies.org

Gene Kroupa, Executive Director

An educational and promotional organization of vegetable canners whose goals are to raise the awareness of consumer and food service buyers regarding canned vegetables.
80 Members
Founded in: 1977

9046 Canola Council of Canada
167 Lombard Avenue Suite 400
Winnipeg, Manitoba
Canada R3B 0T6

204-982-2100
866-834-4378; *Fax:* 204-942-1841
admin@canola-council.org;
www.canolacouncil.org

Patti Miller, President
Jim Everson, Vice President, Gov Relations
Bruce Jowett, Vice President, Market Development
Curtis Rempel, Vice President, Crop Production
Cari Mell, Comptroller

Representing canola growers, input suppliers, researchers, processors and marketers of canola and its products.

9047 Cape Cod Cranberry Growers Association
1 Carver Square Boulevard
PO Box 97
Carver, MA 02330

508-866-7878; *Fax:* 508-866-4220
info@cranberries.org; www.cranberries.org

Brad Morse, President
Gary Garretson, 1st Vice President
Keith Mann, 2nd Vice President
Carolyn DeMoranville, Secretary/ Treasurer
Brian Wick, Executive Director

Established to standardize the measure with which cranberries are sold, the CCCGA is one of the country's oldest farmers' organizations. Giving growers both a single voice and a collective strength in promoting the cranberry industry, and working to ensure that cranberry farming can survive urbanization and the open space and clean water, vital to growing, will be preserved.
Founded in: 1888

9048 Carneros Wine Alliance
PO Box 189
Vineburg, CA 95487

707-812-1919
info@carneros.com; www.carneros.com
Social Media: Facebook, Twitter

Anne Moller-Racke, Chair
Heidi Soldinger, Vice Chair
T. J. Evans, Treasurer
Alison Crowe, Board of Director
Carla Bosco, Secretary

A nonprofit association of wineries and grape-owners in the Carneros American Viticultural Area (AVA).

9049 Center for Food Safety & Applied Nutrition
5100 Paint Branch Parkway
College Park, MD 20740

888-723-3366
http://www.fda.gov/AboutFDA/CentersOffices/OfficeofFoods/CFSAN/

Provides services to consumers, domestic and foreign industry and other outside groups regarding field programs; agency administrative tasks; scientific analysis and support; and policy, planning and handling of critical issues related to food and cosmetics.

9050 Cheese Importers Association of America
204 E Street NE
Washington, DC 20002

202-547-0899; *Fax:* 202-547-6348
info@theciaa.org; www.theciaa.org

Thomas Gellert, President
Dominique Delugeau, First Vice President
Ken Olsson, 2nd Vice President

Philip Marfuggi, Treasurer
Daniel Schnyder, Secretary

Helps facilitate the efficient import of dairy products from around thw world into the United States. The CIAA endeavors to support dairy trade, within the context of compliance with international trade agreements and all applicable US regulations, and maintains active contacts with government officials worldwide in order to further the objectives of the organization and its members.
150 Members
Founded in: 1942

9051 Cherry Marketing Institute
12800 Escanaba Drive
Suite A
Dewitt, MI 48820

925-838-5454; *Fax:* 925-838-2311
info@choosecherries.com;
www.choosecherries.com
Social Media: Facebook, Twitter

Philip Korson II, President
Fred Tubbs, Chairman
Chris Dunkel, Manager

Association representing the cherry industry. Provides promotional material to food service operators, brokers, retailers and manufacturers.
Founded in: 1988
Mailing list available for rent

9052 Chocolate Manufacturers Association
1101 30th Street NW
Suite 200
Washington, DC 20007

202-534-1440; *Fax:* 202-337-0637
info@candyUSA.com;
www.thestoryofchocolate.com

Dennis Whalen, Chairman
Louise Hilsen, Vice Chairman
Alison Bodor, Executive Vice President
Susan S. Smith, SVP, Communications
Liz Clark, VP Government Affairs

The trade group for manufacturers and distributors of cocoa and chocolate products in the United States. The association was founded to fund and administer research, promote chocolate to the general public and serve as an advocate of the industry before Congress and government agencies.
9 Members
Founded in: 1884

9053 Citrus Industry Magazine
5053 NW Hwy 225-A
Ocala, FL 34482

352-671-1909; *Fax:* 888-957-2226;
www.citrusindustry.net
Social Media: Facebook

Ernie Ness, Editor

Association for citrus grower organizations and other trade associations within the industry.
Founded in: 1920
Mailing list available for rent

9054 Coca-Cola Bottlers Association
3282 Northside Parkway
Suite 200
Atlanta, GA 30327

404-872-2258; *Fax:* 404-872-2869
ccba.atl@gmail.com; www.ccbanet.com

Hank Flint, President
M. Trevor Messinger, Vice President
Mark Francouer, Treasurer
Ann Burton, CFO
John Gould, Executive Director & CEO

Assisting members in reducing costs and improving efficiency, the Association acts as a servicing arm and agent on behalf of participating Bottlers to meet their needs in numerous areas, including procurement, employee benefits, insurance programs and retirement plans. Also serves as a primary mechanism for fostering the exchange of ideas and information within the Coca-Cola system.
Founded in: 1913

9055 Coffee, Sugar and Cocoa Exchange
New York Board of Trade
1 N End Avenue
New York, NY 10282-1101

212-748-4000; *Fax:* 212-748-4039;
www.csce.com

Acts as a financial exchange where futures and options are traded, the CSCE provides hedging and investing, opportunities in the coffee, sugar, cocoa and dairy markets.

9056 Colombia Coffee Federation
140 E 57th Street
New York, NY 10022

212-421-8300; *Fax:* 212-758-3816;
www.cafedecolombia.com/en/familia

John Boden, Manager
Founded in: 1964

9057 Commercial Food Equipment Service Association
3605 Centre Circle
Fort Mill, SC 29715

336-346-4700; *Fax:* 336-346-4745
asidders@cfesa.com; www.cfesa.com
Social Media: Facebook, LinkedIn, MySpace, YouTube

Paul Toukatly, President
John Schwindt, Vice President
Gary Potvin, Vice President
Wayne Stoutner, Treasurer
David Hahn, Secretary

The trade association of professional service and parts distributors. Helps members meet the challenges of the industry and ensure customer satisfaction.
450 Members
Founded in: 1963
Mailing list available for rent

9058 Communicating for America
112 E Lincoln Avenue
Fergus Falls, MN 56537

218-739-3241
800-432-3276; *Fax:* 218-739-3832
memberbenefits@cainc.org;
www.communicatingforamerica.org

Milt Smedsrud, Chairman
Patty Strickland, President & COO
Wayne Nelson, President
Stephen Rufer, Vice President & General Counsel
Roger Gussiaas, Vice President

Strives to promote health, well-being and advancement of people in agriculture and agribusiness.
40M Members
Founded in: 1972

9059 Communication and Agricultural Education
Oklahoma State University
301 Umberger Hall
Manhattan, KS 66506

785-532-5804; *Fax:* 785-532-5633
commdept@ksu.edu;
www.communications.ksu.edu
Social Media: Facebook, Twitter, Youtube, Foursquare

Beth Holz, President
Wyatt Betchel, First VP
Megan Brouk, Second VP
Amanda Spoo, Secretary
Brittney Machado, Treasurer

The Mission of National ACT is to build relationships among agricultural communication professionals and college students and faculty, to provide professional and academic development for members and to promote agriculture through communications efforts.
Founded in: 1970

9060 Composite Can and Tube Institute
50 S Pickett Street
Suite 110
Alexandria, VA 22304-7206

703-823-7234; *Fax:* 703-823-7237
ccti@cctiwdc.org; www.cctiwdc.org

Kristine Garland, Executive VP
Janine Marczak, Associate Manager, Events
Wayne Vance, Association Counsel

CCTI is an international nonprofit trade association representing the interests of manufacturers of composite paperboard cans, containers, canisters, tubes, cores, edgeboard and related or similar composite products and suppliers to those manufacturers of such items as paper, machinery, adhesives, labels and other services and materials.
Founded in: 1933

9061 Concord Grape Association
1 Cliffstar Avenue
Dunkirk, NY 14048

716-366-6100
info@concordgrape.org;
www.concordgrape.org

Pam Chumley, Executive Director
Linda Whitley, Contact

The Concord Grape Association represents processors of Concord grapes and manufacturers of products derived from them. The organization operates as the Concord Grape Section under the umbrella of the Juice Products Association (JPA), which represents the juice and juice products industry in the U.S. and overseas. Members handle more than the majority of the Concord grapes processed annually in the United States.
Founded in: 1956

9062 Consultants Association for the Natural Products Industry (CANI)
PO Box 4014
Clovis, CA 93613

559-325-7192; *Fax:* 559-325-7195
info@cani-consultants.org;
www.cani-consultants.org
Social Media: LinkedIn

Karena K. Dillon, President
Robert Forbes, Vice President
Ginni Garner, Treasurer
Sheldon Baker, Director
Kathy Francis, SECRETARY

Committed to working individually and collectively, to enhance the growth and integrity of the natural products industry by providing professional expertise and objective counsel to our clients. These specialized services contribute to the prosperity and values of the individual business as well as the industry as a whole.
Founded in: 1991

9063 Convenience Caterers & Food Manufacturers Association
1205 Spartan Drive
Madison Heights, MI 48071

248-982-5379
ccfma@ymail.com; www.mobilecaterers.com

Dedicated to the best interests of the growing industrial catering industry and to a commitment of excellence in service to catering truck operators, the food service industry, and the public. An in-

ternational association representing food service professionals who are anxious to improve mobile catering operations.
Founded in: 1964

9064 Cookware Manufacturers Association
PO Box 531335
Birminghan, AL 35253-1335
205-592-0389; *Fax:* 205-599-5598
hrushing@usit.net; www.cookware.org
Jay Zilinskas, President
Gene Karlson, VP
Hugh J Rushing, Executive VP
Represents manufactures of cookware and bakeware in the US and Canada. Publishes consumer guides to cookware and engineering standards for industry.
21 Members
Founded in: 1922

9065 Corn Refiners Association
1701 Pennsylvania Avenue N.W.
Suite 950
Washington, DC 20006
202-331-1634; *Fax:* 202-331-2054
comments@corn.org; www.corn.org
Social Media: Facebook, Twitter, Stumbleupon, Digg
Audrae Erickson, President
Shannon Weiner, Executive Assistant
Bob Adams, Director Public Affairs
Pat Saks, Assistant Director
Supports carbohydrate research programs through grants to colleges, government laboratories and private research centers.
8 Members
Founded in: 1913

9066 Council for Agricultural Science and Technology
4420 West Lincoln Way
Ames, IA 50014-3447
515-292-2125; *Fax:* 515-292-4512
cast@cast-science.org; www.cast-science.org
Social Media: Facebook, Twitter, LinkedIn, YouTube, Schooltube
David Songstad, President
Mark Armfelt, President-Elect
Kent G. Schescke, Executive Vice President
Dan Gingerich, Treasurer
Melissa Sly, Director of Council Operations
Assembles, interprets and communicates science based information regionally, nationally and internationally on food, fiber, agriculture, natural resources, and related societal and environmental issues.
2000+ Members
Founded in: 1972

9067 Council for Responsible Nutrition
1828 L St NW
Suite 510
Washington, DC 20036-5114
202-204-7700; *Fax:* 202-204-7701
webmaster@crnusa.org; www.crnusa.org
Social Media: Twitter, Googleplus
Steve Mister, President & CEO
Judy Blatman, Senior Vice President
Mike Greene, Vice President, Gov Relations
James C. Griffiths, Vice President, Scientific
Andrea Wong, Ph.D., Vice President, Science
The leading trade association representing dietary supplement manufacturers and ingredient suppliers. Member companies manufacture popular national brands as well as the store brands marketed by major supermarkets, drug store and discount chains. All members also agree to adhere to voluntary guidelines for manufacturing, marketing and CRN's Code of Ethics.
70 Members
Founded in: 1973

9068 Council of Supply Chain Management Professionals
333 E Butterfield Rd
Suite 140
Lombard, IL 60148
630-574-0985; *Fax:* 630-574-0989
cscmpadmin@cscmp.org; www.cscmp.org
Social Media: Facebook, Twitter, LinkedIn, YouTube
Heather Sheehan, Chair
Theodore Stank, Chair-Elect
Kevin Smith, Vice Chair
Mary Long, Secretary & Treasurer
CSCMP's mission is to lead the evolving supply chain management profession by developing, advancing, and disseminating supply chain knowledge and research.
10000 Members
Founded in: 1963

9069 Crop Insurance and Reinsurance Bureau
440 First St NW
Suite 500
Washington, DC 20001
202-544-0067; *Fax:* 202-330-5255
mtorrey@cropinsurance.org; www.cropinsurance.org
Sheri Bane, Chairwoman
Ron Rutledge, Vice-Chairman
Mike Torrey, Executive Vice President
Tara Smith, Federal Affairs Vice President
Zane Vaughn, Treasurer
National trade association made up of insurance providers and related organizations that provide a variety of insurance products for our nation's farmers.
Founded in: 1964

9070 Crop Life America
1156 15th St NW
Washington, DC 20005
202-296-1585; *Fax:* 202-463-0474
info@croplifeamerica.org; www.croplifeamerica.org
Social Media: Facebook, Twitter, LinkedIn, YouTube
Jay Vroom, President
William Kuckuck, Executive VP & COO
Dr. Barbara Glenn, Senior Vice President
Rachel Lattimore, Senior Vice President
Doug Nelson, Senior Advisor
A trade association of manufacturers and distributors of agriculture crop protection and pest control products.
74 Members
Founded in: 1933

9071 Crop Science Society of America
5585 Guilford Rd.
Madison, WI 53711-5801
608-273-8080; *Fax:* 608-273-2021
membership@sciencesocieties.org; www.crops.org
Social Media: Facebook, Twitter, LinkedIn
Roch E. Gaussoin, President
Michael A. Grusak, President-Elect
Ellen G.M. Bergfeld, CEO
Dedicated to the conservation and wise use of natural resources to produce food, feed, and fiber crops while maintaining and improving the environment. Continuously evolving and modifying it's educational offerings to support the changing needs of its members.
5000+ Members
Founded in: 1956

9072 Dairy Farmers of America
10220 N Ambassador Dr
Kansas City, MO 64153
816-801-6455
888-332-6455; *Fax:* 816-801-6456
webmail@dfamilk.com; www.dfamilk.com
Social Media: Facebook, Twitter, LinkedIn, YouTube
Rick Smith, President & CEO
John McDaniel, Senior Vice President
Alex Bachelor, Senior Vice President
Randy McGinnis, Senior Vice President & COO
David Meyer, Senior Vice President, Finance
A milk marketing cooperative and dairy food processor dedicated to delivering value to members through secure markets, competitive pricing and increasing value throughout the entire diary chain.
Founded in: 1998

9073 Dairy Management, Inc.
O'Hare International Center
10255 W Higgins Rd
Suite 900
Rosemont, IL 60018-5616
847-803-2000
800-853-2479; *Fax:* 847-803-2077; www.dairy.org
James Ahlem, Chair
Skip Hardie, Secretary
Thomas P. Gallagher, Chief Executive Officer
Barbara O'Brien, President
Mollie Waller, Chief Communication Officer
This association aims to provide the sale and consumption of milk and milk products in the US.
Founded in: 1980

9074 Dairy and Food Industries Supply Association
1451 Dolley Madison Boulevard
McLean, VA 22101-3879
703-883-0515; *Fax:* 703-761-4334
John Martin, President
Burce D'Agostino, Vice President
Mary O'Dea, Communications Manager
Trade association of almost 800 suppliers to the food, beverage, dairy, pharmaceutical and related sanitary processing industries.

9075 Diamond of California
1050 S Diamond Street
Stockton, CA 95205
209-467-6000; *Fax:* 209-467-6788; www.diamondnuts.com
Brian J. Discoll, President & CEO
Ray Silcock, Executive Vice President & CFO
Lloyd J. Jhonson, Executive Vice President
David Colo, Executive Vice President & COO
Stephen Kim, Senior Vice President
Walnut growers' association with Diamond guarantees a market for their crops and provides the company with high quality walnuts. Diamond provides information and resources to help growers to produce the best nuts in the world.
1900 Members
Founded in: 1912

9076 Distillers Grains Technology Council
University of Louisville
3327 Elings Hall
Ames, IA 50011
515-294-4019
800-759-3448; *Fax:* 502-852-1577
karosent@iastate.edu; www.distillersgrains.org
Dr. Kurt Rosentrater, Executive Director/CEO
A non-profit organization that stresses the importance of utilization of distillers co-products in animal feeds. We address the production and product quality issues that are known to impact

the market acceptability and production costs of these products.
7 Members
Founded in: 1945

9077 Dr. Pepper Bottlers Association
PO Box 906
Rowlett, TX 75030-0906

972-475-7397; *Fax:* 972-475-5290
Social Media: Facebook, Twitter, Googleplus

Bill Elmore Jr, President
James Lee, Vice President
Scott Chase, Secretary/ Director
Bill Yarbrough, Treasurer/ Director

Represents 430 bottlers for the Dr. Pepper Company.

9078 Drug, Chemical & Associated Technologies Association
One Union St.
Suite 208
Robbinsville, NJ 08691

609-208-1888
800-640-3228; *Fax:* 609-208-0599
mtimony@dcat.org; www.dcat.org

George Svokos, President
Dr. Folker Ruchatz, Sr. Vice President
Milton Boyer, 2nd Vice President
Christopher Rayfield, VP-Pharmaceutical Services Industry
David Beattie, VP-Biotechnology

The premier business development association whose membership is comprised of companies that manufacture, distribute or provide services to the pharamceutical, chemical, nutritional and related industries.
Founded in: 1890

9079 Eastern Frosted and Refrigerated Foods Association
17 Park St
Wanaque, NJ 07465

973-835-1710; *Fax:* 973-835-1708
efra@efraweb.org; www.efraweb.org

Hans Ketels, President
Paul Raguso, 1st Vice President
Ken Atkinson, 2nd Vice President
Jody Avallone, Director
Mike Ryan, Executive Director

Brings together all related segments of the frozen food industry; brokers, warehousing, manufacturers, transportation, distributors, packaging/labeling and retailers. Constantly gathering information for members from authoritative national and regional sources, other members, and publication editorials affecting the industry.
65 Members
Founded in: 1937

9080 Eastern Perishable Products Association
61 Woodhollow Road
PO Box 478
Colts Neck, NJ 07722

973-831-4100; *Fax:* 973-831-8100;
www.eppainc.org
Social Media: Facebook

Fred D'Agostino, President
Barry Kahn, Chairman
Robert Carley, Vice President
Stan Futoran, Vice President
Tom Tracy, Secretary

Regional association with national and international recognition. The EPPA keeps the industry current with the trends, new products, packaging, programs, changes and technical advances that are so dynamic in todays marketplace through projects, publications and activities.
130 Members

9081 Electric Foodservice Council
180 Raymond Court
PO Box 142156
Fayetteville, GA 30214

770-461-3870; *Fax:* 770-461-7799
krhutchinson1@msn.com;
www.foodservicecouncil.org

Billy Griffis, President
Jim Wixson, Senior Vice President
Roshena Ham, Secretary
Mitzi Shanks, Treasurer

Unique organization designed to bring together utilities, equipment manufacturers, trade allies, and foodservice operators who are committed to the advancement of the foodservice industry.
Founded in: 1987

9082 Farmer Direct Foods Inc.
511 Commercial
PO Box 326
Atchison, KS 66002

913-367-4422
800-372-4422; *Fax:* 913-367-4443;
www.farmerdirectfoods.com

Mark Fowler, President / Chief Executive Officer
Marcia Walters, Accounting Manager
Justin Howie, Plant Operations Manager

A producer owned cooperative marketing corporation formed in 1988 with the mission to develop white wheat markets for wheat producers.
125 Members
Founded in: 1988

9083 Fermenters International Trade Association
PO Box 1373
Valrico, FL 33595

813-685-4261; *Fax:* 813-681-5625;
www.fermentersinternational.org
Social Media: Facebook, Twitter

Dee Roberson, Executive Director
Bill Metzger, Editor

Manufacturers, wholesalers, retailers, authors and editors having a commercial interest in the beer and wine trade. Offers publications to members only.
200+ Members
Founded in: 1976

9084 Fertilizer Institute
425 Third Street, SW
Suite 950
Washington, DC 20024

202-962-0490; *Fax:* 202-962-0577
information@tfi.org; www.tfi.org
Social Media: Facebook, Twitter, LinkedIn

Chris Jahn, President
Pamela Guffain, Vice President, Member Services
Kathy Mathers, Vice President, Public affairs
Monica Conway, Executive Assistant to President
Carol Dorrough, Director, Administration & Finance

Members include brokers, producers, importers, dealers and manufacturers of fertilizer and fertilizer-related equipment.
325 Members
Founded in: 1969

9085 Fishermens Marketing Association
1585 Heartwood Drive
Suite E
McKinleyville, CA 95519

707-840-0182; *Fax:* 707-840-0539
fma@trawl.org
trawl.org

Peter Leipzig, Executive Director

An organization made up of fishermen which promotes stable prices and an orderly flow of wholesome seafood to the consumer.
Founded in: 1952

9086 Flavor & Extract Manufacturers Association (FEMA)
1101 17th St NW
Suite 700
Washington, DC 20036

202-293-5800; *Fax:* 202-463-8998;
www.femaflavor.org
Social Media: YouTube, RSS Feed

Kevin Renskers, President
Timothy Webster, President Elect
John Cavallo, Vice President & Secretary
John Cox, Executive Director
Gary Smith, Treasurer

Comprised of flavor manufacturers, flavor users, flavor ingredient suppliers, and others with an interest in the U.S. flavor industry. Working with legislators and regulators to assure that the needs of members and consumers are continuously addressed. FEMA is committed to assuring a substantial supply of safe flavoring substances.
123 Members
Founded in: 1909

9087 Food & Nutrition Service
3101 Park Center Drive
Alexandria, VA 22302

703-305-2062; *Fax:* 703-305-2312;
www.fns.usda.gov
Social Media: Facebook, Twitter, Flickr, YouTube

Audrey Rowe, Administrator
Kevin Concannon, Under Secretary
Dr. Janey Thronton, Deputy under Secretary
Telora Dean, Associate Administrator & COO
Rich Lucas, Deputy Administrator

Provides children and needy families better access to food and a more healthful diet through its food assistance programs and comprehensive nutrition education efforts. FNS also works to empower program participants with knowledge of the link between diet and health.
Founded in: 1969
Mailing list available for rent

9088 Food Allergy Research & Education
7925 Jones Branch Dr.
Suite 1100
McLean, VA 22102
703-691-3179
800-924-4040; *Fax:* 703-691-2713
faan@foodallergy.org; www.foodallergy.org
Social Media: Facebook, Twitter, Youtube, Flickr, Pinterest

Janet Atwater, Chairman
Elliot S. Jaffe, Chairman Emeritus
Robert Nichols, Vice Chair
James R. Baker, Jr., Chief Executive Officer
Michael Lade, Treasurer

The only nonprofit organization in the United States devoted solelyto patient education for food allergies. Mission is to create public awareness about food allergies and anaphylaxis, to provide education, and to advance research on behalf of all those affected by food allergy.
Cost: $30.00
22000 Members
Frequency: 6 per year
Founded in: 1991

9089 Food Distribution Research Society
PO Box 441110
Fort Washington, MD 20749-1110
301-292-1970; *Fax:* 706-542-0739
Jonathan_baros@ncsu.edu; www.fdrsinc.org

Dawn Thilmany, President
Kynda Curtis, President-Elect

Randall D. Little, Vice President Communication
Alba J. Collart, Vice President Education
Ronald L. Rainey, Vice President Logistics & Outreach

Food distribution research society encourages research, serves as an information clearinghouse and encourages implementation of research. The Society organizes conferences and meetings for industry, academic and government leaders within the food industry sector.
Founded in: 1967

9090 Food Export Association of the Midwest USA
309 West Washington
Suite 600
Chicago, IL 60606

312-334-9200; *Fax:* 312-334-9230
info@foodexportusa.org; www.foodexport.org
Social Media: Facebook

Tim F Hamilton, Executive Director
Lauren Swartz, Deputy Director
John Belmont, Communications Manager
Suzanne Milshaw, International Marketing Program

A non-profit organization that promotes the export of food and agricultural products from the northeast region of the United States. The organization has been helping exporters of northeast food and agricultural products sell their products overseas since it was first organized.
Founded in: 1973

9091 Food Industry Association Executives
664 Sandpiper Bay Dr., SW
Sunset Beach, NC 28468

910-575-3423; *Fax:* 815-550-1731
bev@mgmt57.com; www.fiae.net

Jamie Pfhul, Chairwoman
Ellie Taylor, Vice Chairwoman
Bev Lynch, President
Pat Davis, Vice President, State Government
Brian Jordan, Secretary/Treasurer

Sponsors meetings, activities, publications and services to advance the knowledge and professionalism of the food industry association executive, and serves as a vehicle for the advancement of the food industry's agenda.
125 Members
Founded in: 1927

9092 Food Industry Suppliers Association
1207 Sunset Drive
Greensboro, NC 27408

336-274-6311; *Fax:* 336-691-1839
stella@fisanet.org; www.fisanet.org

Bob Morava, President
Brad Myers, Vice President
Joe Allman, Director
Chad Hawkins, Director
Andrew Mahoney, Director

Trade association dedicated to promoting distribution in serving high purity industries. Membership includes independent distributors and manufacturers who go to market through distribution. Members serve customers in food, beverage, personal care, pharmaceutical, Bio-Pharm and other high purity industries.
245 Members
Founded in: 1968
Mailing list available for rent

9093 Food Information Service Center
21050 SW 93rd Lane Road
Dunnellon, FL 34431

352-489-8919
800-443-5820; *Fax:* 352-489-8919
fcsgroup@artdc.net

James Allen Mixon, President

Publishes technical assistance manuals for operating congregate feeding food service programs. Reaches market through direct mail and publicity.
Founded in: 1957

9094 Food Marketing Institute
2345 Crystal Drive
Suite 800
Arlington, VA 22202

202-452-8444; *Fax:* 202-429-4519;
www.fmi.org
Social Media: Facebook, Twitter, LinkedIn, YouTube

Jerry Garland, Chair
Leslie G. Sarasin Esq., CAE, President & CEO
Rob Bartels, Vice-Chair
Russell T. Lund III, Vice-Chair
Joseph Sheridan, Vice-Chair

Food Marketing Institute (FMI) conducts programs in public affairs, food safety, research, education and industry relations on behalf of food retailers and wholesalers in the United States and around the world. FMI's U.S. members operate approximately 26,000 retail food stores and 14,000 pharmacies. Their combined annual sales volume of $680 billion represents three-quarters of all retail food store sales in the United States.
1500 Members
Founded in: 1977
Mailing list available for rent

9095 Food Processing Suppliers Association
1451 Dolley Madison Blvd
Suite 101
Mc Lean, VA 22101-3850

703-761-2600; *Fax:* 703-761-4334
info@fpsa.org; www.fpsa.org
Social Media: Facebook, Twitter, LinkedIn

Gil Williams, Chairman, Vice Chair
David Seckman, President & CEO
Robyn Roche, CFO
Scott Gregory, Treasurer

FPSA members are organized in vertical industry councils which focus association programs on specific concerns and needs that are unique to that industry sector. Membership permits companies to participate in as many industry councils as appropriate at no additional cost.
510 Members
Founded in: 2005

9096 Food Processors Suppliers Association
1451 Dolly Madison Boulevard
Suite 101
McLean, VA 22101-3850

703-761-2600; *Fax:* 703-761-4334
info@fpsa.org; www.fpsa.org
Social Media: Facebook, Twitter, LinkedIn

Gil Williams, Chairman, Vice Chair
David Seckman, President & CEO
Robyn Roche, CFO
Scott Gregory, Treasurer

MISA offers its members an opportunity to project a common and uniform stance on important industry issues, particularly in the regulatory and machinery safety and hygienic standards area.
500+ Members
Founded in: 1983

9097 Foodservice & Packaging Institute
7700 Leesburg Pike
Suite 421
Falls Church, VA 22043

703-592-9889; *Fax:* 703-592-9864
ldyer@fpi.org; www.fpi.org
Social Media: Facebook, Twitter, LinkedIn

Lynn Dyer, President
Natha Dempsey, Vice President
Jennifer Goldman, Membership & Meetings Manager

A national association comprised of manufacturers and suppliers of single-use foodservice packaging products.
25 Members
Founded in: 1933

9098 Foodservice Consultants Society International
PO Box 4961
Louisville, KY 40204

502-379-4122; *Fax:* 519-856-0648
info@fcsi.org; www.fcsi.org
Social Media: Facebook, Twitter

William Taunton, Chair
Wade Koehler, Executive Director
Kimberly Kissel, DIRECTOR OF EDUCATION
Mrs. Penny Price, DIRECTOR OF MEMBER SERVICES
James Petersen, SECRETARY/ TREASURER

Professional organization offering design and management consulting services, specialized in the foodservice and hospitality industry across the world.
Founded in: 1955

9099 Foodservice Sales and Marketing Association
Grocery Manufactures Association
1801-J York Road
Suite 384
Lutherville, MD 21093

410-715-4084
800-617-1170; *Fax:* 888-668-7496
info@fsmaonline.com; www.fsmaonline.com
Social Media: Facebook, Twitter, LinkedIn, Youtube

Rick Abraham, President & CEO
Sharon Boyle, Vice President
Stuart Wolff, Chairman
Dan Cassidy, CEO of Key Imapact Sales
Jessica Muffoletto, Manager, Membership & Meetings

Advances the interests of the food, beverage and consumer products industry on key issues that effect the ability of brand manufacturers their products profitably and deliver superior value to the consumer.
250 Members
Founded in: 2003

9100 Fresh Mushrooms - Nature's Hidden Treasure
2880 Zanker Road
Suite 203
San Jose, CA 95134

408-432-7210; *Fax:* 408-432-7213
info@mushroomcouncil.org;
www.mushroomcouncil.org
Social Media: Facebook, Twitter, YouTube, Pinterest, Google+, R

Carla Blackwell-Mckinney, Vice Chair
Robert Crouch, Secretary

Plays an important role in the national promotion of fresh mushrooms through consumer public relations, foodservice communications and retail communications.
Founded in: 1993
Mailing list available for rent

9101 Fresh Produce Association of the Americas
590 East Frontage Road
PO Box 848
Nogales, AZ 85621

520-287-2707; *Fax:* 520-287-2948
info@freshfrommexico.com;
www.freshfrommexico.com

Alejandro Canelos, Chairman
Matt Mandel, Chairman Elect

Represents more than 125 member companies involved in growing, harvesting, marketing and importing of Mexican produce entering the US at Nogales, Arizona.
125 Members
Founded in: 1944

9102 Fresh Produce and Floral Council
2400 E. Katella Ave.
Ste. 330
Anaheim, CA 92806

714-739-0177; *Fax:* 714-739-0226
info@fpfc.org; www.fpfc.org

Brad Martin, Chairman
Marvin Quebec, Chair Elect
Carissa Mace, President
Connie Stukenberg, Treasurer/Secretary
Amy Wun, Manager Member Programs

Provides unique networking and business growth opportunities for professionals in the produce and floral industries in California. Members include growers, snippers, wholesalers, brokers, distributors and retailers of produce and/or floral items.
500 Members
Founded in: 1965

9103 Frozen & Refrigerated Association of the North East
PO Box 6377
Wolcott, CT 06716-0377

203-597-7215; *Fax:* 203-879-0594
frane@frane.org; www.frane.org
Social Media: Facebook

Jim Wright, Chair
Donna Maglio, Executive Chair
Jason Adams, Director
Sal Marrocco, Vice-President
John Powers, Director

Non-profit regional trade association, representing the ever changing frozen and refrigerated industries throughout the Northeast. It remains one of the largest and most active associations in the United States and is affiliated with the National Frozen & Refrigerated Association (NFRA).
135 Members
Founded in: 1955

9104 Future Food
101 Finsbury Pavement
London, UK EC2A 1RS

203-002-3002; *Fax:* 203-003-3003
prteam@marcusevans.com;
www.marcusevans.com
Social Media: Facebook, Twitter, LinkedIn, Googleplus,vimeo

European events and publications for food industry.
Founded in: 1983

9105 Ginseng Board of Wisconsin
668 Maratech Avenue
Suite E
Marathon, WI 54448

715-443-2444; *Fax:* 715-443-2444
ginseng@ginsengboard.com;
www.ginsengboard.com

Joe Heil, President

Representing Wisconsin Ginseng producers as the worldwide leader of the American Ginseng industry, committed to the advertising, promotion and the sale of Wisconsin Ginseng, the purest ginseng in the world. Working to improve the health and wellness of consumers while suporting the sustainability of the industry and the rural economy associated with it.
Founded in: 1986

9106 Glass Packaging Institute
1220 North Fillmore Street
Suite 400
Arlington, VA 22201

703-684-6359; *Fax:* 703-546-0588
info@gpi.org; www.gpi.org
Social Media: Facebook, Twitter

Andres Lopez, Chairman
Lynn M. Bragg, President
John Riordan, Director
Sanjay Gandhi, Director
John Gallo, Director

Represents the North American glass container industry. Through GPI, glass container manufacturers speak with one voice to advocate industry standards, promote sound environmental policies and educate packaging professionals. Member companies manufacture glass containers for food, beverage, cosmetic and many other products.
Founded in: 1919

9107 Global Cold Chain Alliance
1500 King Street
Suite 201
Alexandria, VA 22314-2730

703-373-4300; *Fax:* 703-373-4301
email@gcca.org; www.gcca.org
Social Media: Facebook, Twitter, LinkedIn

Corey Rosenbuch, President & COO
Megan Costello, Vice President of Member & Industry
Rita Haley, Executive Assistant and Manager
Richard Tracy, Vice President
Tori Miller Liu, Director of Information Systems

The Global Cold Chain Alliance (GCCA) is committed to building and strengthening the temperature-controlled supply chain around the world. As part of that mission, GCCA provides specialized cold chain advisory services to government agencies, organizations, and associations through its core partner, the World Food Logistics Organization (WFLO)
900 Members
Frequency: Membership Dues Vary
Founded in: 1891

9108 Glutamate Association: US
1010 Wiconsin Ave. NW
Ste. 350
Washington, DC 20007

202-384-1840; *Fax:* 202-384-1850
info@watsongreenllc.com; www.msgfacts.com
Social Media: Facebook, Twitter, LinkedIn

Lisa Watson, Executive Director

(TGA) ia an association of manufacturers,national marketers,and processed food users of glutamic acid and its salts, principally the flavor enhancer, monosodium glutamat (MSG). TGA seeks to povide an effective channel of communcation among its members, the public,the media,the scientific community, foof professionals and government officials about the use and safety of glutamates.
12 Members
Founded in: 1977

9109 Golden Gold Chain Alliance
1500 King Street
Suite 201
Alexandria, VA 22314-2730

703-373-4300; *Fax:* 703-373-4301
email@gcca.org; www.gcca.org
Social Media: Facebook, Twitter, LinkedIn

Corey Rosenbuch, President & COO
Megan Costello, Vice President of Member & Industry
Rita Haley, Executive Assistant and Manager
Richard Tracy, Vice President
Tori Miller Liu, Director of Information Systems

The Global Cold Chain Alliance (GCCA) is committed to building and strengthening the temperature-controlled supply chain around the world. As part of that mission, GCCA provides specialized cold chain advisory services to government agencies, organizations, and associations through its core partner, the World Food Logistics Organization (WFLO)
900 Members
Founded in: 1891

9110 Grocery Manufacturers Association
1350 Eye (I) Street NW
Suite 300
Washington, DC 20005

202-639-5900; *Fax:* 202-639-5932
info@gmaonline.org; www.gmaonline.org
Social Media: Facebook, Twitter, RSS

Advances the interests of the food, beverage and consumer products industry on key issues that affect the ability of brand manufacturers to market their products profitably and deliver superior value to the consumer.
Founded in: 1908

9111 Hand in Hand Foundation
PO Box 67351
Scott's Valley, CA 95067
831-438-3736; *Fax:* 831-535-6331
adoptions@handinhand.us;
www.handinhandfoundation.com

David Boschen, Director
Melissa Thomas, Case Worker
April Pao, Case Worker
Kristi VanPykren, Case Worker
Katie Garcia, Office Administrator

Not for profit that solicits food and donations for the needy.
Founded in: 1971

9112 Hazelnut Council
424 2nd Avenue W
Seattle, WA 98119

206-270-4321; *Fax:* 206-270-4656
info@hazelnutcouncil.org;
www.hazelnutcouncil.org

The Hazenut Council represents the world's leading hazelnut producers, importers and distributors.

9113 Healthy Water Association
PO Box 1417
Patterson, CA 95363

408-897-3023; *Fax:* 408-897-3028
paulmason@mgwater.com;
www.mgwater.com/hwa.shtml

Paul Mason, President

Serves the bottled water industry.

9114 Herb Growing and Marketing Network
PO Box 245
Silver Spring, PA 17575-0245

717-393-3295; *Fax:* 717-393-9261
herbworld@aol.com; www.herbworld.com

Maureen Rogers, Director

The largest trade association for the herb industry.
Cost: $48.00
1000+ Members
Founded in: 1990

9115 Herb Research Foundation
5589 Arapahoe Ave
Suite 205
Boulder, CO 80303

303-449-2265; *Fax:* 303-449-7849
info@herbs.org; www.herbs.org

Rob McCaleb, President

Provides scientific based and traditional information about use and safety of herbs for health. Fee based hotline, information packs and literature are available to all.
Founded in: 1983
Mailing list available for rent

9116 **Herb Society of America**
9019 Kirtland Chardon Rd
Kirtland, OH 44094

440-256-0514; *Fax:* 440-256-0541
herbs@herbsociety.org; www.herbsociety.org
Social Media: YouTube, Wordpress

Katrinka Morgan, Executive Director
Amy Rogers, Administrative Assistant
Robin Siktberg, Editor/Horticulturist
Brent DeWitt, Editor/Graphic Designer
Karen Frandanisa, Accountant

An organization that focuses on educating its members and the public on the cultivation of herbs and the study of their history and uses, both past and present.
Founded in: 1933

9117 **Holstein Association USA**
1 Holstein Place
PO Box 808
Brattleboro, VT 05302-0808

802-254-4551
800-952-5200; *Fax:* 802-254-8251;
www.holsteinusa.com
Social Media: Facebook, Twitter, YouTube

Glen E. Brown, President
Gordie Cook, Vice President
Barbara Casna, Treasurer
John M. Meyer, Executive Secretary
John S. Burket, Board of Directors

The world's largest dairy cattle breed organization offering information services to all dairy producers.
Founded in: 1903

9118 **Home Baking Association**
10841 S Crossroads Drive
Suite 105
Parker, CO 80138

785-478-3283; *Fax:* 785-478-3024;
www.homebaking.org
Social Media: Facebook, Twitter, Flickr, Wordpress

Kent Symms, President
Sam Garlow, First Vice President
Eric Wall, Second Vice President

Promoting home baking by providing educators tools and knowledge to perpetuate future generations of home bakers.
Founded in: 1951
Mailing list available for rent

9119 **Hospitality Link**
866 SE 14th Terrace
Suite 128
Deerfield Beach, FL 33441

954-579-1802; *Fax:* 954-421-1046
info@hospitalitylink.com;
www.hospitalitylink.com
Social Media: LinkedIn

Provides consulting for food technology.

9120 **Hydroponic Society of America**
PO Box 1183
El Cerrito, CA 94530

510-926-2908; www.lisarein.com/hydroponics

Joseph O Brien, President

The scientific and educational arm of the hydroponic community. The H.S.A. is rooted in science and physics, plant physiology and photo-biology and the other 16 disciplines required to understand the complexity of the science known as hydroponics. The H.S.A. separates the fiction from the fact, and the truth from the mythology.
Founded in: 1976

9121 **Independent Bakers Association**
PO Box 3731
Washington, DC 20027-0231

202-333-8190; *Fax:* 202-337-3809
independentbaker@yahoo.com;
www.independentbaker.net
Social Media: Twitter, LinkedIn

Ron Cardey, Chairman
Joe Davis, First Vice Chair
Scott Barth, Second Vice Chair
Brian Stevenson, Secretary
Heidi Brenner, Treasurer

National trade association of mostly family owned wholesale bakeries and allied industry trades. Protects the interests of independent wholesale bakers from antitrust and anti-competitive mergers and acquisitions; pressures Congress to support market-oriented farm commodity programs, seeking representation to consider federal labor, tax and environmental law.
400 Members
Founded in: 1968

9122 **Indian River Citrus League**
7925 20th Street
Vero Beach, FL 32966

772-562-2728; *Fax:* 772-562-2577
info@ircitrusleague.org
ircitrusleague.org

Rusty Varn, Board of Director
Trey Smith, Board of Director
Scott Lambeth, Board of Director
Daniel R. Richey, Board of Director
Daniel Scott, Board of Directors

Organization of growers in the area. Newsletters, links and contactinformation.
Founded in: 1807

9123 **Institute of Food Science and Engineering**
2650 North Young Avenue
Fayetteville, AR 72704

479-575-4040; *Fax:* 479-575-2165;
www.uark.edu/depts/ifse

Steve Brooks, President & CEO
Dr. Jean Francois Meullent, Director
Dr. Donald Freeman, Advisory Board
Dr. Patti Landers, Advisory Board
Don McCaskill, Advisory Board

Serves as the primary entity in Arkansas for research, graduate education and extension to help ensure that; food supply is high quality, wholesome, safe and nutritious, value is added to raw agricultural products to enhance economic development of the state, region and nation, and the nutritional needs of society are understood, communicated and met.

9124 **Institute of Food Technologists**
525 W Van Buren
Suite 1000
Chicago, IL 60607

312-782-8424
800-438-3663; *Fax:* 312-782-8348
info@ift.org; www.ift.org
Social Media: Facebook, Twitter, LinkedIn, Youtube

Robert Gravani, Chairman
Colin Dennis, President
John Neil Coupland, President-Elect
Christie Tarantino, Executive Vice President
Robert Gravani, Treasurer

A nonprofit scientific society working in food science, food technology, and related professions in industry, academia and government.
18000 Members
Founded in: 1939

9125 **Institute of Food and Agricultural Sciences (IFAS)**
University of Florida
PO Box 110180
Gainesville, FL 32611-0180

352-392-1971; www.ifas.ufl.edu
Social Media: Facebook, Twitter

Ruth Borger, Assistant Vice President
Jenny Mooney, Manager

A federal-state-county partnership throughout Florida, dedicated to improving your life by developing and providing knowledge in agriculture, natural resources, and life sciences.
Founded in: 1906

9126 **Institute of Packaging Professionals**
One Parkview Plaza
Suite 800
Oakbrook Terrace, IL 60181

630-544-5050
800-432-4085; *Fax:* 630-544-5055
info@iopp.org; www.iopp.org
Social Media: Facebook, Twitter, LinkedIn, YouTube

Jane Chase, Chair
Toby Wingfield, Treasurer
Dan Alexander, Vice Chair
Robert Meisner, EVP - Education & Certification
Suzanne Simmons, Executive VP-Membership

Information regarding the packaging industry internationally.

9127 **Institute of Shortening & Edible Oils**
1319 F Street NW
Suite 600
Washington, DC 20004

202-783-7960; *Fax:* 202-393-1367
contactus@iseo.org; www.iseo.org

Robert L. Collette, President
Diana L. Stare, Office Administrator

A trade association representing the refiners of edible fats and oils in the United States. Members represent approximately 90-95 percent of the edible fats and oils produced domestically that are used in baking and frying fats (shortening), cooking and salad oils, margarines, spreads, confections and toppings, and ingredients in a wide variety of foods.
Founded in: 1936

9128 **International Dairy-Deli-Bakery Association (IDDBA)**
636 Science Drive
Madison, WI 53711-1073

608-310-5000; *Fax:* 608-238-6330
iddba@iddba.org; www.iddba.org

A nonprofit trade association providing education, training, and marketing resources for food retailers, manufacturers, brokers, distributors, and other interested professionals.
Founded in: 1964

9129 **International Association for Color Manufacturers**
1101 17th Street NW
Suite 700
Washington, DC 20036

202-293-5800; *Fax:* 202-463-8998
info@iacmcolor.org; www.iacmcolor.org
Social Media: LinkedIn

David R Carpenter, President & Treasurer
Rohit Tibrewala, President-Elect & Secretary
Bobby Gruber, Director

Philip Kaczmarski, Director
Sue Ann McAvoy, Director

The IACM is a trade association that represents the manufacturers and end-users of coloring substances that are used in foods. Members include producers and users of both certified and exempt colors.
Founded in: 1972

9130 International Association of Culinary Professionals
1221 Avenue of the Americas
42nd Floor
New York, NY 10020

646-358-4957
866-358-4951; *Fax:* 866-358-2524
info@iacp.com; www.iacp.com
Social Media: Facebook, Twitter, Youtube, Vimeo

Martha Holmberg, Chief Executive Officer
Shani Phelan, Member Progams and Ops Manager
Glenn Mack, Chair
Kendra McMurray, CMP, Director, Conferences and Events

IACP connects culinary professionals with the people, places, and knowledge they need to succeed. IACP is a worldwide forum for the development and exchange of information, knowledge, and inspiration within the professional food and beverage community. This organization of creative and talented professionals is engaged in and committed to excellence in the food industry.
3000+ Members
Founded in: 1978

9131 International Association of Ice Cream and Vendors
3601 East Joppa Road
Baltimore, MD 21234

410-931-8100; *Fax:* 410-931-8111
info@iaicdv.org; www.iaicdv.org
Social Media: Facebook, Twitter, Stumbleupon, Gmail

Hoss Rafaty, President
Taylor Dubord, Executive Director
Michelle Franklin, Vice President
Nick Nikbakht, Secretary-Treasurer

Members are manufacturers and distributors of ice cream novelties and street vendors.
Founded in: 1969

9132 International Association of Milk Control Agencies
Department of Dairy Agriculture
Division of Dairy Industry Services
Albany, NY 12235-0001

518-457-3880; *Fax:* 518-485-5816;
www.nasda.org/cms

Charles Huff, Secretary/Treasurer

Founded to improve the effectiveness and uniformity of regulation among the economic regulatory agencies and to provide a forum for exchange of information.
Founded in: 1935

9133 International Association of Operative Millers
12351 W. 96th Terrace
Suite 100
Lenexa, KS 66215

913-338-3377; *Fax:* 913-338-3553
info@iaom.info; www.iaom.info/about/
Social Media: Facebook, Twitter, LinkedIn

Roy Loepp, President
Brad Allen, Vice President
Melinda Farris, Executive Vice President
Stephen Doyle, Treasurer
Brad Beckwith, Director

An international organization, comprised of flour millers, cereal grain and seed processors and allied trades representatives and companies devoted to the advancement of technology in the flour milling, cereal grain processing industries.
1500 Members
Founded in: 1896

9134 International Banana Society
1901 Pennsylvania Ave NW
Suite 1100
Washington, DC 20006-3412

202-303-3400; *Fax:* 202-303-3433;
www.bananas.org
Social Media: Facebook, LinkedIn, Youtube

A trade organizatoin consisting of members engaged in teh business of importing bananas into the United States. Provides a forum for members to discuss common and technical issues pertaining to banana production, distribution, and marketing.
Founded in: 1982

9135 International Beverage Dispensing Equipment Association
PO Box 248
Reisterstown, MD 21136

410-602-0616
877-404-2332; *Fax:* 410-486-6799
ibdea@cornerstoneassoc.com; www.ibdea.org
Social Media: Facebook, LinkedIn, Youtube

An international non-profit trade association representing companies that sell, lease, rent, manufacture and service beverage dispensing equipment and supplies. Members are companies that provide equipment, related products and services to restaurants, bars, taverns, hospitals, schools and other institutions.
250+ Members
Founded in: 1971

9136 International Bottled Water Association
1700 Diagonal Rd
Suite 650
Alexandria, VA 22314

703-683-5213
800-928-3711; *Fax:* 703-683-4074
info@bottledwater.org; www.bottledwater.org
Social Media: Facebook, Twitter, YouTube

Bryan Shinn, Chairman
Joe Bell, Vice Chairman
Joseph Doss, President
Robert R. Hirst, Vice President
Shayron Barnes-Selby, Treasurer

The leading voice of the bottled water industry and serves to protect the interests of bottled water bottlers, distributors and suppliers.
Founded in: 1958

9137 International Chewing Gum Association
1001 G Street NW
Suite 500 West
Washington, DC 20001

E-Mail: information@gumassociation.org;
www.gumassociation.org

Andy Pharoah, President

The leading voice of the chewing gum industry. ICGA continues to gain recognition and credibility among decision-makers across the globe.

9138 International Council on Hotel, Restaurant and Institutional Education
2810 N Parham Road
Suite 230
Richmond, VA 23294

804-346-4800; *Fax:* 804-346-5009
info@chrie.org; www.chrie.org
Social Media: Facebook, Twitter, LinkedIn

Maureen Brookes, President
Margaret Steiskal, Vice President
Kathy McCarty, Chief Executive Officer
Wanda Costen, Secretary
Stephanie Hein, Treasurer

A marketplace for facilitating exchanges of information, ideas, research, products and services related to education, training and resource development for the hospitality and tourism industry (food, lodging, recreation and travel services). Serving as the hospitality and tourism education network, striving to unite educators, industry executives and associations.
1400 Members
Founded in: 1946

9139 International Dairy Foods Association
1250 H Street NW
Suite 900
Washington, DC 20005

202-737-4332; *Fax:* 202-331-7820
membership@idfa.org; www.idfa.org
Social Media: Facebook, Twitter, YouTube, Blog, Smartbrief

Patricia Stroup, Chair
Jeffery Kaneb, Vice Chair
Michael Walls, Secretary
Mike Reidy, Treasurer
Connie Tipton, President and CEO

Represents the nation's dairy manufacturing and marketing industries and their suppliers. IDFA is composed of three constituent organizations; Milk Industry Foundation, National Cheese Institute, and the International Ice Cream Association.
550 Members

9140 International Dairy-Deli-Bakery Association
636 Science Drive
PO Box 5528
Madison, WI 53705-0528

608-310-5000; *Fax:* 608-238-6330
iddba@iddba.org; www.iddbanet.org

William J. Klump, Chairman
David Leonhardi, Executive Vice Chairman
John Cheesman, Vice Chairman
Jewel Hunt, Treasurer

IDDBA members meet the challenges of today's business world by exchanging information and ideas, participating in educational programs and networking.
Founded in: 1964

9141 International Flight Services Association
1100 Johnson Ferry Road
Suite 300
Atlanta, GA 30342

404-252-3663; *Fax:* 404-252-0774
ifsa@kellencompany.com; www.ifsanet.com
Social Media: Facebook, Twitter, LinkedIn, YouTube

David Loft, Chairperson
Pam Suder Smith, President
Jane Bernier -Tran, Vice President
Paul Platamone, Treasurer
Denise Poole, Secretary

Represents the $14 billion inflight and travel catering industry. Activities include annual confer-

ences, trade shows, seminars and training events around the world.
400 Members
Founded in: 1965

9142 International Food Additives Council
1100 Johnson Ferry Road
Suite 300
Atlanta, GA 30342
404-252-3663; *Fax:* 404-252-0774
jrogers@kellencompany.com;
www.foodadditives.org

An international trade association of food additives manufacturers and businesses having interest in food additives.

9143 International Food Information Council Foundation
1100 Connecticut Ave NW
Suite 430
Washington, DC 20036
202-296-6540; *Fax:* 202-296-6547
info@foodinsight.org; www.foodinsight.org
Social Media: Facebook, Twitter, LinkedIn

David B. Schmidt, President & CEO
Geraldine McCann, COO
Marianne Smith Edge, Senior VP, Nutrition & Food Safety
Andy Benson, VP, International Relations
Kimberly Reed, President

Dedicated to the mission of effectively communicating science-based information on health, nutrition and food safety for the public good. Independent and non-profit, bringing together, working with, and providing information to consumers, health and nutrition professionals, educators, government officials, and food, beverage, and agricultural industry professionals.
33 Members
Founded in: 1985

9144 International Food Processors Association
200 Daingerfield Road
Suite 100
Alexandria, VA 22314-2884
703-684-1080; *Fax:* 703-548-6563

9145 International Food Service Brokers Association
1101 Pennsylvania Avenue
Washington, DC 20004
www.foodbrokers.org
1500 Members
ISSN: 0884-7185
Founded in: 1956

9146 International Food Service Editorial Council
7 Point Place
PO Box 491
Hyde Park, NY 12538
845-229-6973; *Fax:* 845-229-6973
ifec@ifeconline.com; www.ifeconline.com
Social Media: Facebook, Twitter

Sam Oches, President
Cathy Holley, Vice President
Bill Schreiber, Secretary
Rachel Tracy, Treasurer
Carol Lally, Executive Director

A networking association that fosters the open exchange of information and the building of productive working relationships among foodservice editor and publicist members. Conferences and other activities offer professional development as well as opportunities to make new contacts and gain hands-on-experience of the food cultures and personalities in cities where conferences are held.
265 Members
Founded in: 1956

9147 International Food Service Executives Association
4955 Miller Street
Suite 107
Wheat Ridge, CO 80033
800-893-5499
ifseahqoffice@gmail.com; www.ifsea.com
Social Media: Facebook

David Orosz, Chairman

Professional association with members from the food service and hospitality profession. IFSEA's mission is to enhance the careers of its members through food service certification, education seminars, networking, student mentorships and community service. Members inclued executive chefs, restaurant owners, catering directors, equipment manufacturers, food suppliers, military, professionals new to the industry and students.
3000 Members
Founded in: 1901

9148 International FoodService Manufacturers Association
180 North Stetson Avenue
Suite 850
Chicago, IL 60601
312-540-4400; *Fax:* 312-540-4401
ifma@ifmaworld.com; www.ifmaworld.com
Social Media: Facebook, LinkedIn, YouTube

Richard Ferranti, Chairman
Joe Bybel, First Vice Chairman
Kevin Delahunt, Vice Chairman
Ben Shanley, Vice Chairman
Don Davis, Treasurer

Member companies of the IFMA can capitalize on opportunities, tackle challenges, as well as gain new customer contact and networking opportunities, education and training that helps company sales force build market share, and leadership roles in such initiatives as GS1.
650 Members
Founded in: 1952

9149 International Foodservice Distributors Association
1410 Spring Hill Road
Suite 210
McLean, VA 22102
703-532-9400; *Fax:* 703-538-4673;
www.ifdaonline.org
Social Media: Twitter, LinkedIn

Thomas A. Zatina, Chairman
James Crawford, Vice Chairman
Mark S. Allen, President & CEO
Jonathan Eisen, Senior Vice President
Andrew Mercier, Treasurer

Trade association comprised of food distribution companies that supply independent grocers and food service operations throughout the US, Canada and 19 other countries.
135 Members
Founded in: 2003

9150 International Foodservice Distributors Ass
1410 Spring HIll Road
Suite 210
McLean, VA 22102
703-532-9400; *Fax:* 703-538-4673;
www.ifdaonline.org
Social Media: Twitter, LinkedIn

Thomas A. Zatina, Chairman
James Crawford, Vice Chairman
Mark S. Allen, Jr., President/ CEO
Andy Mercier, Treasurer
Jonathan Eisen, SVP, Government Relations

9151 International Glutamate Technical Committee
5775 Peachtree Dunwoody Rd NE
Atlanta, GA 30342
404-252-3663; *Fax:* 404-252-3663;
www.aspartame.org

Andrew Ebert PhD, Chairman
Judy Rogers, Contact

Members are associations that are engaged in the manufacture, sale and commercial use of glutamates.
8 Members
Founded in: 1965

9152 International HACCP Alliance
120 Rosenthal Center
2471 TAMU
College Station, TX 77843-2471
979-862-3643; *Fax:* 979-862-3075
kharris@tamu.edu; www.haccpalliance.org

Ranzell Nickelson, Chairman
Rosemary Mucklow, Vice Chairman
Robert Hibbert, Treasurer/ Secretary
Rafael Rivera, Past Chairman
Rena Pietrami, Board of Directors

Provides a uniform program to assure safer meat and poultry products.
Founded in: 1994

9153 International Herb Association
PO Box 5667
Jacksonville, FL 32247-5667
904-399-3241; *Fax:* 904-396-9467;
www.iherb.org

Matthias Reisen, President
Dianna Nance, Vice President
Karen O'Brien, Secretary
Marge Powell, Treasurer
Davy Dabney, Chairman

Supports herb businesses and educates the public.
Founded in: 1986

9154 International Institute of Fisheries Economics & Trade
213 Ballard Hall
Corvallis, OR 97331-3601
541-737-2942; *Fax:* 541-737-2563
osuweb@lists.orst.edu;
www.oregonstate.edu/dept/IIFET

Dr. Dan Holland, President
Dr. Claire Armstrong, President-elect
Ann L. Shriver, Executive Director
Kara Keenan, Assistant

Promotes discussion, research projects and sponsors educational courses. Publications available.
400 Members
Founded in: 1982

9155 International Maple Syrup Institute
5072 Rock St. RR#4
Spencerville, ON K0E 1X0
613-658-2329; *Fax:* 877-683-7241
agrofor@ripnet.com;
www.internationalmaplesyrupinstitute.com

Richard Norman, President
Yvon Poitras, Vice President
Steve Selby, Treasurer
Dave Chapeskie, Executive Director

Members are producers, processors, industry suppliers and others interested in promoting the industry.
15M Members
Founded in: 1975

9156 **International Natural Sausage Casing Association**
12100 Sunset Hills Road
Suite 130
Reston, VA 20190

703-234-4112; *Fax:* 703-435-4390;
www.insca.org

David Blanga, Chairman
Elliot Simon, Vice Chairman
Michael Mayo, Treasurer

The only international association for the natural sausage casing industry. Members include producers, suppliers and brokers of natural casing products.
265+ Members
Founded in: 1965

9157 **International Olive Council**
Principe de Vergara
154
Spain, MD 28002

491-590-3638; *Fax:* 491-563-1263
iooc@internationaloliveoil.org;
www.internationaloliveoil.org

Jean Louis Barjol, Executive Director

The world's only international intergovernmental organization in the field of olive oil and table olives. The Council is a decisive player in contributing to the sustainable and responsible development of olive growing and serves as a world forum for discussing policymaking issues and tackling present and future challenges.
Founded in: 1959

9158 **International Organization of the Flavor Industry (IOFI)**
Flavor & Extract Manufacturers Association
1101, 17th Street NW
Suite 700
Washington, DC 20036

202-293-5800; *Fax:* 202-462-8998;
www.femaflavor.org

Kevin Renskers, President
Timothy Webster, President Elect
John Cavallo, Vice President & Secretary
John Cox, Executive Director
Gary Smith, Treasurer

FEMA staff monitors regulations that impact flavor and extracts all around the world.
Frequency: Annual
Founded in: 1909
Mailing list available for rent

9159 **International Packaged Ice Association**
238 East Davis Blvd.
Suite 213
Tampa, FL 33606

813-258-1690
800-742-0627; *Fax:* 919-251-2783
jane@packagedice.com;
www.packagedice.com

John Smibert, Chairman
Tommy Sedler, Vice Chairman/ Treasurer
Dann Ades, Secretary/ Assistant Treasurer
Mike Ringstaff, Conference Chairman
Bo Russell, Immediate Past Chairman

A trade association representing manufacturers and distributors of packaged ice and manufacturers of ice making equipment.
400 Members
Frequency: Call For Membership Info
Founded in: 1917

9160 **International Society of Beverage Technologists(ISBT)**
14070 Proton Rd
Suite 100, LB 9
Dallas, TX 75244-3601

972-233-9107; *Fax:* 972-490-4219
office@bevtech.org; www.bevtech.org

Brian Stegmann, President
Cloeann Durham, 1st Vice President
Sieg Mueller, 2nd Vice President
Larry Hobbs, Executive Director
Jessica Anacker, Director

Enhance promotione, development and dissemination of knowledge relating to art and science of beverage technology. Focus ares include beverage formulation, production, packaging and more. We provide forums, stimulate the uise of science in the industry, encourage and foster research.

9161 **International Warehouse Logistics Association**
2800 S River Rd
Suite 260
Des Plaines, IL 60018

847-813-4699; *Fax:* 847-813-0115
email@iwla.com; www.iwla.com

Rob Doyle, Chairman
Mark DeFabis, Vice Chairman
Steve DeHaan, President & CEO
Clifford Otto, Treasurer
Frank Anderson, Secretary

A trade association of warehouse logistics providers that helps members run high-quality, profitable busineses. IWLA focuses on the warehouse logistics business, providing ideas and information that make it easier for member companies to succeed.
Founded in: 1891

9162 **Interstate Professional Applicators Association**
PO Box 1420
Milton, WA 98354-1420

253-922-9437; *Fax:* 253-922-3788

Provides education and information for the professional horticultural applicator. Legislative work involves the states of Washington, Oregon, Idaho in the area of laws and regulations.

9163 **Iowa Meat Processors Association**
PO Box 334
Clarence, IA 52216

563-452-3329; *Fax:* 563-452-2141
execdirector@iowameatprocessors.org;
www.iowameatprocessors.org

Tom Taylor, President
Merrill Angell, 1st Vice President
Dave Burma, 2nd Vice President
Jason Ludwig, 3rd Vice President
Marcia Richmann, Executive Directors

An organization comprised of beef, pork, wild game, and poultry processors and allied businesses from throughout the state of Iowa. Members include slaughterers, food service companies, packers, locker operators, butcher shops, ham manufacturers, smokehouse owners, wholesalers, custom operations, retail operations, and companies that supply goods and services to the meat industry.

9164 **Islamic Food and Nutrition Council of America (IFANCA)**
777 Busse Hwy
Park Ridge, IL 60068

847-993-0034; *Fax:* 847-993-0038;
www.ifanca.org

Social Media: Facebook, Twitter, LinkedIn, Youtube,stumbleupon,digg,frien

Zeshan Sadek, Director International Services
Mujahid Masood, Ph.D., Senior Food Scientist

A non-profit Islamic organization dedicated to promote halel food and the institution of halel.
Founded in: 1982

9165 **Italian Trade Agency**
Italian Trade Commission
33 E 67th St
New York, NY 10065-5949

212-980-1500; *Fax:* 212-758-1050
newyork@ice.it; www.italtrade.com

Pace Marisa, Executive Secretary
Augusta Smargiassi, Senior Deputy Trade Commissioner
Antonio Lucarelli, Senior Trade Commission

The Italian government agency entrusted with the promotion of trade, business opportunities and industrial cooperation between Italian and foreign companies. It supports the internationalisation of Italian firms and their consolidation in foreign markets.

9166 **Italian Wine and Food Institute**
One Grand Central Place
60 East 42nd St. Suite 2214
New York, NY 10165

212-867-4111; *Fax:* 212-867-4114
iwfi@aol.com;
www.italianwineandfoodinstitute.com

Lucio Caputo, President
Vincent Giampaolo, VP

Members are producers, distributors and marketers of Italian wines and foods.
Founded in: 1983

9167 **Juice Products Association**
750 National Press Building
529 14th Street NW
Washington, DC 20045

202-785-3232; *Fax:* 202-223-9741
jpa@kellencompany.com;
www.juiceproducts.org

Richard E Cristol, President
Carol Freysinger, Executive Director
Patricia Faison, Technical Director
Darrell McCook, Meetings Manager
Jim Wolters, Account Coordinator

The trade association for the fruit and juice products industry, including juice processors, packers, extractors, brokers as well as marketers of fruit juices and vegetable juices, juice beverages, fruit jams, jellies and preserves and similar products. JPA also represents juice industry suppliers and food testing laboratories and includes firms engaged in the trading of frozen concentrated orange juice futures and/or options on behalf of JPA processor members.
135 Members
Founded in: 1957

9168 **LaSalle Food Processing Association**
108 S Broadway
PO Box 97
La Salle, MN 56056-0097

507-375-3408; *Fax:* 507-642-3077

Pat Thiner, Manager

A meat packers trade association.

9169 **Leafy Greens Council**
PO Box 143
Waterport, NY 14571

716-517-0248; www.leafy-greens.org

Ray Clark, Executive Director
Robert Strube, President

Purpose is to improve the marketing and increase consumption through national promotions, to ed-

ucate consumers about the nutritional values of leafy greens through media campaigns, to represent member interests to government, and to provide networking opportunities for members. Members represent growers, shippers, brokers, terminal market operators, and suppliers.
117 Members
Founded in: 1974

9170 Les Amis d'Escoffier Society of New York, Inc.
787 Ridgewood Road
Millburn, NJ 07041

212-414-5820; *Fax:* 973-379-3117;
www.escoffier-society.com

Mark Arnao, President
George McNeill, First Vice President
Jay Jones, Secretary
Kurt Keller, TREASURER

Providing opportunitites for members' delight and edification and also generate gains in the perfection of the art of fine dining. Membership consists of chefs de cuisine, hotel executives, restaurateurs and business executives.
Founded in: 1936

9171 Livestock Marketing Association
10510 NW Ambassador Drive
Kansas City, MO 64153

816-891-0502
800-821-2048; *Fax:* 816-891-0552
lmainfo@lmaweb.com; www.lmaweb.com
Social Media: Facebook, Twitter

Tim Starks, Chairman
Dan Harris, President
BRIAN GLICK, DIRECTOR
Mark Mackey, Chief Executive Officer
SHERI CRIST, INTERIM CHIEF FINANCIAL OFFICER

Committed to the support and protection of the local livestock auction markets. LMA is the voice for the auction markets on legislative and regulatory issues and in providing member services to maintain successful, viable marketing businesses and better service to all of the livestock producers who sell at auction.

9172 Machalek Communications, Inc.
Machalek Communications
12550 W Frontage Road
Suite 220
Burnsville, MN 55337

952-736-8000
800-846-5520; *Fax:* 866-490-8834
info@machalek.com; www.machalek.com
Social Media: Facebook, LinkedIn

Andrea McChalek, President/CEO
Deanna Morin, Vice Pres. of Business Development
Krista Gardner, Office Manager
Maria Palmer, Lead Graphic and Web Designer

Includes over 20 employees and publishes seven nationwide postcard advertising decks. Distributes more then 100 million postcards per year to over 800,000 qualified buyers. Company has furthermore evolved to include additional sales lead generation services including list rental, mail, and internet marketing.
25 Members
Founded in: 1987
Mailing list available for rent

9173 Maraschino Cherry and Glace Fruit Processors
3301 State Route 66
Neptune, NJ 07753

732-922-3008

Richard Sullivan, Executive VP

9174 Master Brewers Association of the Americas
3340 Pilot Knob Rd.
St. Paul, MN 55121

651-454-7250; *Fax:* 651-454-0766
mbaa@mbaa.com; www.mbss.com
Social Media: Facebook, Twitter, LinkedIn, Pinterest

Amy Hope, Executive Vice President

Global association for the advancement of the brewing and allied industries.
3000 Members
Founded in: 1887

9175 Material Handling Industry of America
8720 Red Oak Blvd
Suite 201
Charlotte, NC 28217-3996

704-676-1190; *Fax:* 704-676-1199
dvarner@mhi.org; www.mhi.org
Social Media: Facebook, Twitter, LinkedIn, YouTube

Dave Young, Executive Chairman
John Paxton, President
Gregg E. Goodner, Vice President
George Prest, CEO
Donna Varner, Executive Administrator

The complexity of managing supply chains that span continents and dominate markets demands strategies, equipment and systems that are agile, adaptable, and aligned. With product lifescycles shortening and worldwide competition increasing, success depends on effective material handling and logistics solutions for the global supply chain. Being able to deliver the right product to the right market at the right time.

9176 Meat & Livestock Australia
Level 1, 40 Mount Street
Locked Bag 991
North Sydney, NS 2060

294-639-333; *Fax:* 294-639-393
info@mla.com.au; www.mla.com.au
Social Media: Facebook, Twitter, YouTube

Michele Allan, Chairman
Richard Norton, Managing Director
Lucinda Corrigan, Director
Geoffrey Maynard, Director
John McKillop, Director

Providing marketing and research and development services to cattle, sheep and goat producer members and the broader red meat industry to help them meet community and consumer expectations. MLA is committed to fostering world leadership for the Australian red meat and livestock industry for creating opportunities for its stakeholders, the environment, red meat consumers and the community.
30000 Members
Founded in: 1998

9177 Meat & Livestock Australia, North American Region
1401 K Street NW
Suite 602
Washington, DC 20005

202-521-2551; *Fax:* 202-521-2699
info@mlana.com; www.australian-meat.com
Social Media: Facebook, Twitter, YouTube

David Pietsch, Regional Manager, North America
Scott Hansen, Managing Director

Providing marketing and research and development services to cattle, sheep and goat producer members and the broader red meat industry to help them meet community and consumer expectations. MLA is committed to fostering world leadership for the Australian red meat and livestock industry for creating opportunities for its stakeholders, the environment, red meat consumers and the community.
30000 Members
Founded in: 1998

9178 Meat Import Council of America
1901 Fort Myer Dr
Suite 1110
Arlington, VA 22209

703-522-1910
800-522-1910; *Fax:* 703-524-6039
lauriebryant@micausa.org; www.micausa.org

Kim Holzner, Chairman
David Rind, Vice Chairman
Donald E. Stewart, Treasurer
Laurie I. Bryant, Executive Director & Secretary

To foster the trade, commerce and interests of importers and exporters of fresh and/or frozen and/or cured and/or cooked and/or canned meats.
130 Members
Founded in: 1962

9179 Meat Trade Institute
213 South Avenue East
Spencer Savings Bank Building
Cranford, NJ 07016

908-276-5111; *Fax:* 212-279-4016
sflannagan@sprintmail.com;
www.spcnetwork.com/mti/

John J. Calcangno, President

A full-time fully-staffed trade association serving meat and poultry industries in the northeast. The Institute seeks to build and strengthen the relationships of its members with government, labor, and all other segments of the meat and poultry industry.

9180 Mid-Atlantic Canners Association
316 S Front Street
Hamburg, PA 19526

610-562-3061; *Fax:* 610-562-0281

Robert Crosswell, Crosswell
D Seibert, VP Finance

Mid Atlantic Canners Association is a cooperative soft drink canning facility for the Coca-Cola system. All of the national Coca-Cola Company brands are canned, packaged and shipped by truck to various Coca-Cola franchised distributors located throughout the northeast United States.

9181 Mid-Atlantic Dairy Association
325 Chestnut St
Suite 600
Philadelphia, PA 19106

215-627-8800; *Fax:* 215-627-8887
dairyspot@milk4u.org; www.dairyspot.com
Social Media: Facebook, Twitter, LinkedIn, Youtube, Pinterest, Googleplus

Patty Purcell, CEO

Mid-Atlantic Dairy Association is one of 19 state and regional promotion organizations working under the umbrella of the United Dairy Industry Association. Working to bring a fully integrated national promotion program to the Mid-Atlantic region.
Mailing list available for rent

9182 Mid-States Meat Association
1335 Dublin Rd
Suite 10
Columbus, OH 43215-1000

614-459-5188; *Fax:* 614-442-5516;
www.midstatesmeat.org

Kristin Mullins, Executive Director
100 Members

9183 **Midwest Dairy Association**
2015 Rice St
St Paul, MN 55113

651-488-0261
800-642-3895; *Fax:* 651-488-0265
snewell@midwestdairy.com;
www.midwestdairy.com
Social Media: Facebook, Twitter, Youtube, Pinterest

Mike Kruger, CEO

Works on behalf of dairy farmers to increase dairy sales, foster innovation and inspire consumer confidence in dairy products and practices.
210M Members
Founded in: 1940

9184 **Midwest Food Processors Association**
4600 American Pkwy
Suite 210
Madison, WI 53718-8334

608-255-9946; *Fax:* 608-255-9838
info@mwfpa.org; www.mwfpa.org
Social Media: Facebook, Twitter, LinkedIn

Nick George, President
Brian Elliot, Director of Communications
Robin Fanshaw, Manager
Brian Deschane, Director of Operations

Trade association that advocates on behalf of food processing companies and affiliated industries in Illinois, Minnesota, and Wisconsin. Influencing public policy and making the Midwest a great place for food processors to do business. Advocating, educating, communicating, and facilitating.
Founded in: 1905

9185 **Missouri Grocers Association**
315 North Ken Avenue
Springfield, MO 65802

417-831-6667; *Fax:* 417-831-3907
cmcmillian@missourigrocers.com;
www.missourigrocers.com
Social Media: Facebook

Erick Taylor, Chairman
John Porter, President
Mike Beal, Vice President
Chuck Murfin, III, Treasurer
Dan Shaul, State Director

Committed to the growth and profitability of its members by providing proactive state and federal legislative and regulatory representation, effective communication, beneficial member services, and education of industry innovations.

9186 **Mushroom Council**
2880 Zanker Road
Suite 203
San Jose, CA 95134

408-432-7210; *Fax:* 408-432-7213
info@mushroomcouncil.org;
www.mushroomcouncil.org
Social Media: Facebook, Twitter, YouTube, Pinterest, Google+, R

Carla Blackwell-Mckinney, Vice Chair
Robert Crouch, Secretary

Plays an important role in the national promotion of fresh mushrooms through consumer public relations, foodservice communications and retail communications.
Founded in: 1993

9187 **National Advisory Group**
19111 Detroit Road
Suite 201
Rocky River, OH 44116

440-250-1583
info@nagconvenience.com; www.nag-net.com
Social Media: Facebook

Ben Jatlow, Chairman
Mary Banmiller, President

Mission is to provide industry retail leaders a peer-to-peer forum for the exchange of ideas to improve their business performance.
Founded in: 1992

9188 **National Agri-Marketing Association**
11020 King Street
Suite 205
Overland Park, KS 66210

913-491-6500; *Fax:* 913-491-6502
agrimktg@nama.org; www.nama.org
Social Media: Facebook, Twitter, LinkedIn, YouTube, Flickr

Marvin Kokes, President
Matt Coniglio, 1st Vice President
Amy Bugg, Vice President
Amber Harrison, Vice President
Amy Bradford, Secretary/Treasurer

The nation's largest association for professionals in marketing and agribusiness.
Cost: $170.00
3500 Members
Frequency: Membership Dues
Founded in: 1957

9189 **National Agriculture Day**
11020 King St
Suite 205
Overland Park, KS 66210

913-491-1895; *Fax:* 913-491-6502
info@agday.org; www.agday.org
Social Media: Facebook, Twitter, YouTube, Flickr

Curt Blades, Chair
Annette Degnan, Vice Chair
Lynn Henderson, Board of Director
Tres Bailey, Board of Director
Colin Woodall, Board of Director

An organization uniquely composed of leaders in the agriculture, food and fiber communities dedicated to increasing the public awareness of agriculture's vital role in our society.
Founded in: 1973

9190 **National Alcohol Beverage Control Association**
4401 Ford Avenue
Suite 700
Alexandria, VA 22302-1433

703-578-4200; *Fax:* 703-820-3551
nabca.info@nabca.org; www.nabca.org
Social Media: Facebook, Twitter, Youtube, Google

Stephen Larson, Chairman
Stephanie O'Brien, Chairman-Elect
James M. Sgueo, President & CEO
Jeffrey R. Anderson, Board of Director
Andrew J. Deloney, Board of Director

It is the mission of the National Alcohol Beverage Control Association to support and benefit alcohol control systems by providing research, fostering relationships, and managing resources to address policy for the responsible sale and consumption of alcohol beverages. Members include control jurisdictions, supplier members and industry trade associations.
175 Members
Frequency: Membership Dues Vary
Founded in: 1938

9191 **National Aquaculture Association**
PO Box 12759
Tallahassee, FL 32317

850-216-2400; *Fax:* 850-216-2480
naa@thenaa.net
thenaa.net

Jim Parsons, President
Sebastian Belle, Vice President
Adam Hater, Secretary
Rick Martin, Treasurer

A producer-based, non-profit trade association dedicated to advocacy for U.S. aquaculture.

9192 **National Association for the Specialty Food Trade**

www.specialtyfood.com
Social Media: Facebook, Twitter, LinkedIn, YouTube, Pinterest

Nonprofit business trade association established to foster trade, commerce, and interest in the specialty food industry.
Founded in: 1952

9193 **National Association of Agricultural Educators**
University of Kentucky
300 Garrigus Building
Lexington, KY 40546-0215

859-257-2224
800-509-0204; *Fax:* 859-323-3919
naae@uky.edu; www.naae.org
Social Media: Facebook, Twitter

Charlie Sappington, President
Terry Rieckman, President-Elect
Jay Jackman, Executive Director
Alissa Smith, Associate Executive Director
Linda Berry, Staff Support Associate

A federation of 50 affiliated state vocational agricultural teacher associations. The mission is to provide agricultural education for the global community through visionary leadership, advocacy and service.
7600 Members
Founded in: 1948

9194 **National Association of Animal Breeders**
PO Box 1033
Columbia, MO 65205

573-445-4406; *Fax:* 573-446-2279
naab-css@naab-css.org; www.naab-css.org

Charles Sattler, Chairman
Dr. Nate Zwald, Vice-Chairman
Gordon A. Doak, President
Gordon A. Doak, Secretary/Treasurer
Gordon A. Doak, Secretary/Treasurer

Unite those individuals and organizations engaged in the artificial insemination of cattle and other livestock into an affiliated federation operating under self-imposed standards of performance and to conduct and promote the mutual interest and ideals of its members. Members are farmer co-ops and others interested in livestock improvement.
Founded in: 1946

9195 **National Association of Beverage Importers Inc.**
529 14th St NW
Suite 1183
Washington, DC 20045

202-393-6224; *Fax:* 202-393-6595;
www.bevimporters.org

John F. Beaudette, Chairman
Michael J. Rudy, Chairman of the Committee
Stacey M. Tank, Vice Chairman
William T. Earle, President
Marc P. Goodrich, Treasurer

Trade association representing US importers of alcohol beverages, representing the interests of importers of alcohol beverages on issues that have a principal impact on importers, and cooperating with other trade associations on issues that impact all alcohol beverages whether imported or domestic.
Founded in: 1934

9196 National Association of Concessionaires
180 N. MICHIGAN AVENUE
Suite 2215
Chicago, IL 60601
312-236-3858; *Fax:* 312-236-7809
info@naconline.org; www.naconline.org
Social Media: Facebook, LinkedIn
John Evans Jr., Chairman
Jeff Scudillo, Presdient
Terry Conlon, President-Elect
Dan Borschke, Executive Vice President
Andrew Cretors, Treasurer
Trade association for the recreation and leisure-time food and beverage concessions industry. Providing members with information and services that maintain and enhance the standards of excellence and professionalism within the recreation and leisure time food, beverage and related services industry.
800 Members
Founded in: 1944

9197 National Association of Convenience Stores
1600 Duke St
7th Floor
Alexandria, VA 22314
703-684-3600
800-684-3600; *Fax:* 703-836-4564
nacs@nacsonline.com; www.nacsonline.com
Social Media: Facebook, Twitter, LinkedIn, YouTube
Henry Armour, President & CEO
Lyle Beckwith, Sr. VP, Government Relations
Michael Davis, V.P., Member Services
Shirley Jaffe, V.P.,Business Operations
Bob Hughes, V.P., Supplier Relations
Providing news, information and resources to the convenience and petroleum retail stores.
4000 Members
Founded in: 1961

9198 National Association of Flavors and Food Ingredient Systems
3301 State Route 66
Building C, Suite 205
Neptune, NJ 07753
732-922-3218; *Fax:* 732-922-3590
info@naffs.org; www.naffs.org
Dave Adams, Chair
Christine Daley, President
Pia Henzi, President-Elect
Cynthia Astrack, Vice President
Chris Williams, Vice Presdient
A broad-based trade association of manufacturers, processors and suppliers of fruits, flavors, syrups, stabilizers, emulsifiers, colors, sweeteners, cocoa and related food ingredients. Its associate membership is open to all companies that provide products and services to the food industry.
120 Members
Founded in: 1917

9199 National Association of Margarine Manufacturers
E-Mail: NAMM@kellencompany.com; www.iheartbutterytaste.com
Social Media: Facebook, Twitter, Pinterest
Information and recipes about buttery soft spread margarines.

9200 National Association of Pizzeria Operators
909 S 8th Street
Suite 200
Louisville, KY 40203
502-736-9532; *Fax:* 502-736-9502
dwyatt@pizzatoday.com; www.napo.com
Social Media: Facebook, Twitter, Youtube
Joe Straughan, President
Mary Sullivan, Membership Coordinator
Mission is to create and foster a community of independent and small chain pizzeria operators and their industry suppliers where doing business with another is mutually beneficial.
1100+ Members
Founded in: 1984
Mailing list available for rent: 25000 names

9201 National Association of State Departments of Agriculture
4350 North Fairfax Drive
Suite 910
Arlington, VA 22203
202-296-9680; *Fax:* 703-880-0509
nasda@nasda.org; www.nasda.org
Social Media: Facebook, Twitter
Greg Ibach, President
Michael Strain, 1st Vice President
Steven Reviczky, 2nd Vice President
Jeff Witte, Secretary/Treasurer
Chuck Ross, Director at large
Mission is to represent the state departments of agriculture in the development, implementation, and communication of sound public policy and programs which support and promote the American agricultural industry, while protecting consumers and the environment.
Founded in: 1915

9202 National Association of Wheat Growers
415 Second Street NE
Suite 300
Washington, DC 20002-4993
202-547-7800; *Fax:* 202-546-2638
wheatworld@wheatworld.org; www.wheatworld.org
Social Media: Facebook, Twitter, YouTube
Wayne Hurst, President
Erik Younggren, 1st Vice President
Bing Von Bergen, 2nd Vice President
Paul Penner, Secretary/ Treasurer
Dana Peterson, CEO
A nonprofit partnership of US wheat growers who, by combining their strengths, voices and ideas, are working to ensure a better future for themselfves, their industry and the general public. Focusing on the policies of the US government that affect the livelihoods of US wheat producers.
Founded in: 1950

9203 National Association of Wholesalers - Distributors
1325 G Street NW
Suite 1000
Washington, DC 20005-3100
202-872-0885; *Fax:* 202-785-0586
naw@naw.org; www.naw.org
Social Media: Facebook, Twitter, YouTube
Dirk Van Dongen, President
Jade West, Senior Vice President
James A. Anderson, Junior Vice President
Joy Goldman, Vice President-Administrative
Ron Schreibman, SVP-Strategic Direction
Representing the wholesale distributor industry. NAW is active in these areas: government relations and political action; research and education; and group purchasing. In addition the association operates the Wholesaler-Distributor Political Action Committee, the Distribution Research & Education Foundation, and the NAW Service Corporation.

9204 National Bar and Restaurant Association
307 W Jackson Avenue
Oxford, MS 38655
662-236-5510; *Fax:* 202-331-2429; www.bar-restaurant.com
Jennifer Robinson, COO
Laura Speakes, Financial Affairs VP
Founded by Nightclub and Bar magazine, the association's mission is to provide discounts, services and networking opportunities enabling restaurant, bar and hospitality professionals to increase revenues and profits through innovative promotions, marketing and management.
Founded in: 1924

9205 National Barbecue Association
P.O. Box 9686
Naperville, IL 60567-9686
331-444-7347
888-909-2121; *Fax:* 502-589-3602
info@nbbqa.org; www.nbbqa.org
Social Media: Facebook, Twitter, LinkedIn, Youtube
Linda Orrison, President
Dave Raymond, President-Elect
Patrick Murty, Treasurer
Bonnie Gomez, Secretary
Jeff Allen, Executive Director
Mission is to provide the barbeque community with a visionary, beneficial, and responsive association. NBBQA's goals are to promote the art and enjoyment of barbecue, facilitate the effective networking of industry resources and to foster new business opportunities.
Founded in: 1991

9206 National Beer Wholesalers Association
1101 King Street
Suite 600
Alexandria, VA 22314-2944
703-683-4300; *Fax:* 703-683-8965
info@nbwa.org; www.nbwa.org
Social Media: Facebook, Twitter, YouTube, Flickr
Greg LaMantia, Chair
Craig A Purser, President & CEO
Wendy Huerter, Executive Assistant
Patti Rouzie, VP Membership and Meetings
Kathleen Joyce, Communications Director
NBWA represents the interests of America's 2,850 independent, licensed beer distributors which service every congressional district and media market in the country.
Founded in: 1938
Mailing list available for rent

9207 National Bison Association
8690 Wolff Ct
200
Westminster, CO 80031

303-292-2833; *Fax:* 303-845-9081
david@bisoncentral.com;
www.bisoncentral.com
Social Media: Facebook

Bruce Anderson, President
Roy Liedtke, Vice-President
Jason Moore, Secretary/Treasurer
Dave Carter, Executive Director
Dick Gehring, Director at Large

Bringing together stakeholders to celebrate the heritage of American bison/buffalo, educating, and creating a sustainable future for our industry.
900 Members
Founded in: 1975

9208 National Bulk Vendors Association
1202 East Maryland Avenue
Suite 1k
Phoenix, AZ 85014

888-628-2872; *Fax:* 480-302-5108
admin@nbva.org; www.nbva.org
Social Media: Facebook

Judi Heston, President
Shawn Dumphy, Vice President
Carl Morcate, Treasurer
John P. Winters, Secretary
George Wells, Membership Chair

A national, not-for-profit trade association comprised of the manufacturers, distributors and operators of bulk vending machines and products.
Founded in: 1950

9209 National Cattlemen's Beef Association
9110 E. Nichols Ave.
#300
Centennial, CO 80112

303-694-0305; *Fax:* 303-694-2851
customerservice@beef.org; www.beef.org
Social Media: Facebook, Twitter

Forrest Roberts, CEO
John Queen III, President
Thad Larson, Director

Consumer focused, producer directed organization representing the largest segment of the nation's food and fiber industry.
28000 Members
Founded in: 1898
Mailing list available for rent

9210 National Cherry Growers and Industries Foundation (NCGIF)
2667 Reed Road
Hood River, OR 97031

541-386-5761; *Fax:* 541-386-3191
info@maraschinocherries.org
maraschinocherries.org
Social Media: Facebook, LinkedIn, YouTube, Pinterest

B J Thurlby, President
Idell Dunn, Assessment Supervisor
Andrew Willis, Promotion Director
Cheryl Kroupa, Marketing Director

Formed for the purpose of having a unified effort from the processed cherry industry to lobby against excessive cherry imports. The foundation compiles and distributes to members a yearly statistical publication of information regarding cherry production, utilization, and sales, both import and export.
Founded in: 1948

9211 National Coffee Association
45 Broadway
Suite 1140
New York, NY 10006

212-766-4007; *Fax:* 212-766-5815
info@ncausa.org; www.ncausa.org
Social Media: Facebook, Twitter, LinkedIn

Bruce Goldsmith, Chairman
John DeMuria, Vice Chairman
William (Bill) Murray, President & CEO
William M. Cortner, Secretary
Thrisha Andrews, Administrative Assistant

Established on the behalf of the coffee companies in the United States. Respond to external issues and represent the coffee industry before the legislative and executive branches of government.
200 Members
Founded in: 1911

9212 National Confectioners Association
1101 30th Street NW
Suite 200
Washington, DC 20007

202-534-1440; *Fax:* 202-337-0637
info@candyUSA.com; www.candyusa.com
Social Media: Facebook, Twitter, LinkedIn, YouTube, Pinterest, Instagram

Peter W. Blommer, Chairman
Michael G. Rosenberg, Vice Chairman
John H. Downs, Jr., President
Martino Caretto, Vice President
John E. Brooks, Jr., Treasurer

Representing the entire confection industry, offering education and leadership in manufacturing, technical research, public relations, retailing practices, government relations, and statistical analyses.
Founded in: 1884

9213 National Confectionery Sales Association
Spitfire House
3135 Berea Road
Cleveland, OH 44111

216-631-8200; *Fax:* 216-631-8210
info@candyhalloffame.org
candyhalloffame.org/NCSA/contact.shtml
Social Media: Facebook, Twitter

Joe Muck, Chairman
John A. Leipold Jr., President
Russell Berg, Director
David Fleischer, Director
Anthony P. Cognetti, Treasurer

Dedicated to furthering positive growth and acceptance of confectionery and allied products by education, open and frank dialogue, and recognition of peers' notable accomplishments. The Associations' responsibility to principals, customers, members and the community is to represent their products and services professionally and ethically in all relationships.
375 Members
Founded in: 1899

9214 National Conference of State Liquor Administrators
543 Long Hill Road
Gurnee, IL 60031

847-721-6410; www.ncsla.org

Jerry W. Waters, Sr, President
Matthew D. Botting, 1st Vice President
Richard Haymaker, 2nd Vice President
A. Keith Burt, 3rd Vice President
Pamela Frantz, Executive Director

Promoting the enactment of the most effective and equitable types of state alcoholic beverage control laws, to devise and promote the use of methods which provide the best enforcement of the particular alcoholic beverage control laws in each state, to work for the adoption of uniform laws, and to promote harmony with the federal government in its administration.

9215 National Conference on Interstate Milk Shipments
PO Box 108
Monticello, IL 61856

217-762-2656
ncims.bordson@gmail.com; www.ncims.org

Dr. Stephen Beam, Chair
David E. Latten, Vice Chair
Marlena G. Bordson, Executive Secretary
Beth Briczinski, Board Member
Ken Anderson, Board Member

The goal is to assure the safest possible milk supply for all the people. The NCIMS is governed by an executive board comprised of representatives from state and local regulatory agencies from three geographical regions; FDA, USDA, industry and laboratories and academia.
Founded in: 1940

9216 National Corn Growers Association
632 Cepi Drive
Chesterfield, MO 63005

636-733-9004; *Fax:* 636-733-9005
corninfo@ncga.com; www.ncga.com
Social Media: Facebook, Twitter, Pinterest

Brent Hostetler, Chair
Jessica Brown, CMP, Meetings Manager
Ellen Campen, Bookkeeper
Chris Novak, Chief Executive Officer
Kathy Baker, Executive Assistant

Mission is to create and increase opportunities for corn growers. The Association will continue to be the recognized leader working in cooperation with its suppliers and customers to maintain sustainability and to achieve new business and profit opportunities for those it represents.
32300 Members
Founded in: 1957
Mailing list available for rent

9217 National Council of Chain Restaurants
1101 New York Ave NW
Washington, DC 20005

202-783-7971
800-673-4692; *Fax:* 202-737-2849
info@nrf.com; www.nccr.net
Social Media: Twitter

KIP TINDELL, Chairman
MINDY F. GROSSMAN, Vice Chairman
MATTHEW R. SHAY, President & CEO
CARLEEN KOHUT, EVP, CEO
VICKI CANTRELL, SVP, COMMUNITIES AND EXECUTIVE DIRE

The leading trade association exclusively representing chain restaurant companies. Working to advance sound public policy that best serves the interests of restaurant businesses and the millions of people they employ.
Founded in: 1965

9218 National Council of Farmer Cooperatives
50 F Street NW
Suite 900
Washington, DC 20001

202-626-8700; *Fax:* 202-626-8722;
www.ncfc.org
Social Media: Facebook, Twitter, Flickr

Charles Conner, President/ CEO
Marlis Carson, SVP, Legal, Tax
Justin Darisse, Vice President, Communications
Lisa Van Doren, Vice President & Chief of Staff
Kevin Natz, Vice President

Regional and national farmer cooperatives.
Founded in: 1929

9219 **National Country Ham Association**
PO Box 948
Conover, NC 28616

828-466-2760
800-820-4426; *Fax:* 828-466-2770
eatham@countryham.org;
www.countryham.org

Allan Benton, President

Encourages promotion, development and improvement of the businesses of country ham carvers and encourages the use of country carved meats through co-operative methods of production, promotion, education and advertisement.
53 Members
Founded in: 1992

9220 **National Dairy Council**
Interstate Place II
100 Elwood Davis Road
North Syracuse, NY 13212

315-472-9143; *Fax:* 315-472-0506
ndc@dairyinformation.com;
www.nationaldairycouncil.org
Social Media: Facebook, Twitter, Pinterest

This association operates under the auspices of the United Dairy Industry Association. NDC provides timely, scientifically sound nutrition information to the media, physicians, dietitians, nurses, educators, consumers and others concerned about fostering a healthier society.
Founded in: 1915
Mailing list available for rent

9221 **National Farmers Organization**
528 Billy Sunday Road
Suite 100, P.O. Box 2508
Ames, IA 50010

800-247-2110
nfo@nfo.org; www.nfo.org
Social Media: Facebook, YouTube

Paul Olson, President, Chairman
Paul Riniker, Vice President

Members represent a cross-section of both conventional and organic production—grain growers, cattle and hog producers and dairymen and women.

9222 **National Farmers Union**
20 F Street NW
Suite 300
Washington, DC 20001

202-554-1600; *Fax:* 202-554-1654;
www.nfu.org
Social Media: Facebook, Twitter, LinkedIn, YouTube, Flickr

Roger Johnson, President
Jeff Knudson, Senior VP, Operations
Chandler Goule, SVP, Programs
Donn Teske, Vice President
Maria Miller, Executive Director

A national federation of state Farmers Union organizations in the United States.
Founded in: 1902

9223 **National Federation of Coffee Growers of Colombia**
140 E 57th St
New York, NY 10022-2765

212-271-8802; www.federaciondecafeteros.org

This organization is comprised of coffee growers from Colombia whose goal is to promote Colombian coffee in the US.

9224 **National Frozen & Refrigerated Foods Association Inc.**
4755 Linglestown Road Suite 300
PO Box 6069
Harrisburg, PA 17112

717-657-8601; *Fax:* 717-657-9862
info@nfraweb.org; www.nfraweb.org
Social Media: Facebook, Twitter, LinkedIn

H V Skip Shaw Jr, President/CEO
Jeff Rumachik, Executive Vice President/COO
Julie W. Henderson, Vice President of Communications
Jessica Kurtz, Vice President of Finance
Dayna Jackson, Director of Membership

NFRA is a non-profit trade association representing all segments of the frozen the frozen and refrigerated foods industry. Heaquartered in Harrisburg, PA, NFRA is the sponsor of March National Frozen Food Month, June Dairy Month, and the Summer Favorites Ice Cream novelties promotion as well as the October Cool Food for Kids educational outreach program. NFRA holds the annual National Frozen & Refrigerated Foods Convention in October.
400 Members
Founded in: 1945

9225 **National Frozen Dessert and Fast Food Association**
9614 Tomstown Road
Waynesboro, PA 17268

800-535-7748

This association is made up of small, independent owners and operators of ice cream and fast food establishments.

9226 **National Grape Co-Operative/Welch's**
2 South Portage Street
Westfield, NY 14787

716-326-5200; *Fax:* 716-326-5494
nationalinfo@welchs.com; www.welchs.com
Social Media: Facebook, Twitter

Joseph C Falcone, President

More than just an organization of grape growers, stringent quality growing and harvesting standards, viticultural research, and aggressively funding new product development, manufacturing and marketing programs of Welch's.
Founded in: 1897

9227 **National Honey Board**
11409 Business Park Circle
Suite 210
Firestone, CO 80504-9200

303-776-2337; *Fax:* 303-776-1177
honey@nhb.org; www.honey.com
Social Media: Facebook, Twitter, YouTube, Pinterest, Google+, I

Jill Clark, Chairperson
Mark Mammen, Vice Chairperson
Margaret Lombard, Chief Executive Officer
Eric S. Wenger, Secretary/Treasurer
Douglas Hauke, Producers

Conducts research, advertising and promotion programs to help maintain and expand domestic and foreign markets for honey.
Founded in: 1987
Mailing list available for rent

9228 **National Honey Packers & Dealers Association**
3301 Route 66
Suite 205, Building C
Neptune, NJ 07753

732-922-3008; *Fax:* 732-922-3590
info@nhpda.org; www.nhpda.org

Bob Bauer, Executive Vice President

Comprised of US packers, importers and foreign exporters.

9229 **National Hot Dog and Sausage Council**
1150 Connecticut Avenue, NW
12th Floor
Washington, DC

202-587-4200; www.hot-dog.org
Social Media: Facebook, YouTube, Pinterest

Janet Riley, President
Eric Mittenthal, Vice President, Public Affairs

Conducts scientific research to benefit hot dog and sausage manufacturers.
Founded in: 1994

9230 **National Hot Pepper Association**
400 NW 20th Street
Fort Lauderdale, FL 33311-3818

954-565-4972; *Fax:* 954-566-2208
peppergal@mindspring.com

Networking among industry and private members. Education and information sharing.

9231 **National Ice Cream Mix Association**
2101 Wilson Blvd
Suite 400
Arlington, VA 22201

703-243-5630; *Fax:* 703-841-9328
nicma@nmpf.org; www.icecreammix.org

Joe Duscher, President
Pat Galloway, Vice President
Jamie Jonker, Vice President, Scientific Regs
Bob Kmetz, Treasurer
Tom Balmer, Executive Director

This group is made up of manufacturers of soft-serve ice cream, ice milk, shakes and other dessert mixes.
Founded in: 1926

9232 **National Ice Cream Retailers Association**
1028 W Devon Avenue
Elk Grove Village, IL 60007

847-301-7500
866-303-6960; *Fax:* 847-301-8402
info@nicra.org; www.nicra.org
Social Media: Facebook

Carl Chaney, President, President Elect
Jim Oden, Vice President
Lynda Utterback, Executive Director
Jill Curran, Secretary/Treasurer

NICRA is a trade organization whose members are in the retail ice cream and frozen dessert business. NICRA will associate with similar associations dedicated to the same interests, facilitate communication and education that both newcomers and veterans in the industry desire to be successful.
500 Members
Founded in: 1933
Mailing list available for rent

9233 **National Mango Board**
3101 Maguire Blvd
Suite 111
Orlando, FL 32803

407-629-7318
877-MAN-OS 1; www.mango.org
Social Media: Facebook, Twitter, Pinterest, YouTube

Lucy Keith, Consumer Media
Susan Hughes, Foodservice
Kristine Concepcion, Mango Industry Contact
Katie Ola, Trade Media
Wendy McManus, Retail Contact

A national promotion and research organization which is supported by assessments from domestic and imported mangos.

9234 National Meat Canners Association
1150 Connecticut Avenue, NW
12th Floor
Washington, DC 20036

202-587-4200; *Fax:* 202-587-4300
webmaster@meatami.com; www.meatami.org
Social Media: Facebook, Twitter, LinkedIn

Nick Merigolli, Chairman
Greg Benedict, Vice-Chairman
Barry Carpenter, President & CEO
J. Michael Townsley, Treasurer
John Vatri, Secretary

AMI is the national trade association representing companies that process 70 percent of U.S. meat and their suppliers throughout America.

9235 National Milk Producers Federation
2101 Wilson Blvd
Suite 400
Arlington, VA 22201

703-243-6111; *Fax:* 703-841-9328
info@nmpf.org; www.nmpf.org
Social Media: Facebook, Twitter, Flickr, YouTube

Randy Mooney, Chairman
Ken Nobis, 1st Vice Chairman
Adrian Boer, 2nd Vice Chairman
Mike McCloskey, 3rd Vice Chairman
Pete Kappelman, Treasurer

Develops and carries out policies that advance the well being of dairy producers and the cooperatives they own. Provides a forum through which dairy farmers and their cooperatives formulate policy on national issues that affect milk production and marketing.
Founded in: 1916
Mailing list available for rent

9236 National Oilseed Processors Association
1300 L St NW
Suite 1020
Washington, DC 20005

202-842-0463; *Fax:* 202-842-9126
nopa@nopa.org; www.nopa.org

Thomas A. Hammer, President
David J. Hovermale, Executive Vice President
David C. Ailor, Executive Vice President
Jeanne L. Seibert, Office Administrator

Represents firms engaged in the actual processing of oilseeds, and associate firms who are consumers of vegetable oil or oilseed meal, including some refiners and mixed feed manufacturers.
Founded in: 1929

9237 National Onion Association
822 7th St
Suite 510
Greeley, CO 80631

970-353-5895; *Fax:* 970-353-5897;
www.onions-usa.org
Social Media: Twitter, Pinterest

Shawn Hartley, President
John Rietveld, Vice President
Doug Stanley, 2nd Vice President
Wayne Mininger, Executive Vice President
Monna Canaday, Administrative Assistant

Represents interests of US onion producers. Informational lobbying and generic promotional headquarters for fresh dry bulb onion growers. Provides connections for networking and education exchange.
600 Members
Founded in: 1913
Mailing list available for rent

9238 National Pasta Association
750 National Press Building
529 14th Street NW
Washington, DC 20045

202-591-2459; *Fax:* 202-591-2445
info@ilovepasta.org; www.ilovepasta.org

Greg Pearson, Chairman
Bastiaan DeZeeuw, Vice Chairman
Jim Meyer, Treasurer
Peter Bisaccia, Board Member
Randy Gilbertson, Board Member

To increase the consumption of pasta, to promote the development of sound public policy and, act as a center of knowledge for the industry.
Founded in: 1904

9239 National Peanut Board
3350 Riverwood Parkway
Suite 1150
Atlanta, GA 30339
678-424-5750
866-825-7946; *Fax:* 678-424-5751
peanuts@nationalpeanutboard.org;
www.nationalpeanutboard.org
Social Media: Facebook, Twitter, Pinterest

Bob H. White, Chairman
Monty Rast, Vice Chairman
Gayle White, Treasurer
Ed White, Secretary
Gregory Gill, Board Member

A farmer-funded national research, promotion and education check-off program. Through NPB, growers from across the United States come together to contribute to the research and promotion of USA-grown peanuts.

9240 National Pecan Shellers Association
1100 Johnson Ferry Road
Suite 300
Atlanta, GA 30342

678-298-1189; *Fax:* 404-591-6811
npsa@kellencompany.com;
www.ilovepecans.org
Social Media: Facebook, Twitter, Pinterest

The NPSA is the trade association for the pecan shelling and processing industry. The association is dedicated to educating culinary and health professionals, food technologists, educators and the general public about the health benefits, nutritional value, variety of uses and all-around great taste of pecans.

9241 National Pork Board
1776 NW 114th St.
Des Moines, IA 50325

800-456-7675
info@pork.org; www.pork.org

John Johnson, Chief Operating Officer

Uniting pork producers for the future of the pork industry.

9242 National Pork Producers Council
122 C Street NW
Suite 875
Washington, DC 20001

202-347-3600; *Fax:* 202-347-5265
warnerd@nppc.org; www.nppc.org
Social Media: Facebook, Twitter, LinkedIn, Swinecast, Pinterest, Flickr

Ron Prestage, President
John Weber, President-Elect
Ken Maschhoff, Vice President
Kent Bang, Board Member
Cory Bollum, Board Member

Conducts public-policy outreach on behalf of its 43 affiliated state associations, enhancing opportunities for the success of US pork producers and other industry stakeholders by establishing the US pork industry as a consistent and responsible supplier of high-quality pork to the domestic and world markets.

9243 National Potato Council
1300 L St NW
Suite 910
Washington, DC 20005

202-682-9456; *Fax:* 202-682-0333
spudinfo@nationalpotatocouncil.org;
www.nationalpotatocouncil.org
Social Media: Facebook, Twitter, Youtube

DAN LAKE, President
JIM TIEDE, First Vice President
LARRY ALSUM, Vice President, Finance
DOMINIC LAJOIE, VP Environmental Affairs
Dwayne Weyers, Vice President, Growers

Represents US potato growers on federal legislative and regulatory issues.
6000 Members
Founded in: 1948

9244 National Poultry & Food Distributors Association
2014 Osborne Road
Saint Marys, GA 31558
770-535-9901; *Fax:* 770-535-7385
kkm@npfda.org; www.npfda.org
Social Media: Facebook, Twitter, LinkedIn

Marc Miro, President
Ted Rueger, Vice President
Lee Wilson, Treasurer
Kristin McWhorter, Executive Director

To promote the poultry and food distributors, processors and allied industries by bringing them together and providing a forum to foster long term business relationships.
210 Members
Founded in: 1967

9245 National Renderers Association
500 Montgomery Street
Suite 310
Alexandria, VA 22314
703-683-0155; *Fax:* 571-970-2279
renderers@nationalrenderers.com;
www.nationalrenderers.org
Social Media: Twitter

Gerald F. Smith Jr., Chairman
Ross Hamilton, First Vice Chairman
Tim Guzek, Second Vice Chairman
Nancy Foster, President
Marty Covert, Convention Coordinator

Representing members' interests to regulatory and other governmental agencies, promoting the greater use of animal by-products and fostering the opening and expansion of trade between foreign buyers and North American exporters.
Founded in: 1933

9246 National Restaurant Association Educational Foundation
2055 L. St. NW
Washington, DC 20036

202-315-4102
800-424-5156
wsafstrom@nraef.org; www.nraef.org
Social Media: Facebook, Twitter, Youtube

Denise Marie Fugo, Chair
Mike Gibbons, Vice Chair
Dawn Sweeney, President & CEO
Rob Gifford, Executive Vice President
Michael Hickey, Treasurer

NRAEF is the philanthropic foundation of the National Restaurant Association. Committed to enhancing the restaurant industry's service to the public through education, community engagement and promotion of career opportunities.
Founded in: 1987

9247 **National Restaurant Association**
2055 L. St. NW
Suite 700
Washington, DC 20036
202-331-5900
800-424-5156; *Fax:* 202-331-2429;
www.restaurant.org
Social Media: Facebook, Twitter, YouTube
Jack Crawford, Chair
Joe Kadow, Vice Chair
Dawn Sweeney, President & CEO
Jeff Davis, Treasurer
Striving to help members build customer loyalty, find financial success and provide rewarding careers in foodservice.
60000 Members
Founded in: 1919

9248 **National Seafood Educators**
PO Box 93
Skamokawa, WA 98647
206-546-6410; *Fax:* 206-546-6411
information@seafoodeducators.com;
www.seafoodeducators.com
Evie Hansen, Founder
Goal is to educate and inform the public about the many health benefits of a seafood diet. Also has consulted with many seafood retail businesses on how to sell, store, and prepare wholesome seafood.
Founded in: 1977

9249 **National Seasoning Manufacturers Association Inc**
8905 Maxwell Dr
Suite 200
Potomac, MD 20854
301-765-9675; *Fax:* 301-299-7523
alsmeyerfood@isp.com
Dick Alsmeyer PhD, Executive Director
Food seasoning manufacturers, producers of meat curing compounds, flavors, supplies, services, and equipment used for the seasoning and preserving of food.
23 Members
Founded in: 1972

9250 **National Shellfisheries Association**
National Marine Fisheries Service Laboratory
Oxford, MD 21654
631-653-6327; *Fax:* 631-653-6327
webmaster@shellfish.org; www.shellfish.org
Karolyn Mueller Hansen, President
Steven Allen, President-Elect
Shirley Baker, Vice President
Lisa Milke, Secretary
John Scarpa, Treasurer
Organization comprised of scientists, public health workers, shellfish producers and fishery administrators to promote and advance shellfisheries research and the application of results to the shellfish industry.
1M Members
Founded in: 1908

9251 **National Society on Healthcare Foodservice**
455 S. 4th Street
Suite 650
Louisville, KY 40202
888-528-9552; *Fax:* 502-589-3602
info@healthcarefoodservice.org;
www.healthcarefoodservice.org
Social Media: Facebook, Twitter, LinkedIn, YouTube
Laura Watson, President
Lisette Coston, President-Elect
Jacqueline Sikoski, Secretary
Robert Darrah, Treasurer
Julie Jones, Treasurer-Elect
The only professional society dedicated to professionals and suppliers in the self-operated healthcare foodservice industry- those facilities who choose to keep their foodservice departments on staff, instead of outsourcing them to third-party contractors.

9252 **National Sunflower Association**
2401 46th Avenue SE
Suite 206
Mandan, ND 58554-4829
701-328-5100
888-718-7033; *Fax:* 701-328-5101
larryk@sunflowernsa.com;
www.sunflowernsa.com
Social Media: Facebook, YouTube
John Sandbakken, Executive Director
Tina Mittlesteadt, Manager
A non-profit commodity organization working on problems and opportunities for the improvement of all members. Members include growers and the support industry.
20000 Members
Founded in: 1981

9253 **National Turkey Federation**
1225 New York Avenue NW
Suite 400
Washington, DC 20005
202-898-0100; *Fax:* 202-898-0203
info@turkeyfed.org; www.eatturkey.com
Social Media: Facebook, Twitter, Youtube, Pinterest
John Burkel, Chairman
Gary Cooper, Vice Chairman
Joel Brandenberger, President
Damon Wells, Vice President
Jihad Douglas, Secretary-Treasurer
(NTF) is the national Advocate for all segments of the $8 billion turkey industry, providing services and conducting activities that increase demand for its members' products. The federation also protects and enhances its members' ability to effectively and profitably provide wholesome, high quality, nutritious turkey products.
264 Members
Founded in: 1939

9254 **National WIC Association**
2001 S St NW
Suite 580
Washington, DC 20009
202-232-5492; *Fax:* 202-387-5281
douglasg@nwica.org; www.nwica.org
Social Media: Facebook, Twitter, Pinterest
Douglas Greenaway, President & CEO
Cecilia Richardson, Staff/Nutrition Program Director
DuWvaughn P. Francois, Office Manager
Robert A. Lee, Development Manager
Martelle Esposito, Government Affairs Manager
Members are geographic state, Native American state and local agency directors of the Special Supplement nutrition program for women, infants and children.
900 Members
Founded in: 1983

9255 **National Watermelon Promotion Board**
1321 Sundial Point
Winter Springs, FL 32708
407-657-0261
877-599-9595; *Fax:* 407-657-2213
info@watermelon.org; www.watermelon.org
Social Media: Facebook, Twitter, RSS, YouTube, Instagram
Mark Arney, Executive Director
Rebekah Dossett, Director of Operations
Megan McKenna, Dir., Marketing
Stephanie Barlow, Director of Communications
Andrea Smith, Industry Affairs Manager
Increase consumer demand for fresh watermelon through promotion, research, and educational programs.
Founded in: 1989

9256 **National Yogurt Association**
Washington, DC
703-245-7698
info@aboutyogurt.com
aboutyogurt.com
Becky O'Grady, Co-Chairman
Gustavo Valle, Co-Chairman
Kraig R. Naasz, President
Non-profit representing the nation's yogurt manufacturers and marketers.

9257 **Natural Marketing Institute**
272 Ruth Road
Harleysville, PA 19438
215-513-7300; *Fax:* 215-513-1713
Nancy.White@NMIsolutions.com;
www.NMIsolutions.com
Social Media: Facebook, Twitter, LinkedIn
Maryellen Molyneaux, President
George Ward, Vice President Strategic Consulting
John Devries, Vice President Strategic Consulting
Diane Ray, Vice President of Strategy
Kathryn Schulte, Director Project Management
NMI is an international strategic marketing consultancy specializing in health, wellness, sustainability and healthy aging with full-service consulting and market research services.
Founded in: 1989

9258 **Natural Products Association**
1773 T Street, NW
Washington, DC 20009
202-223-0101
800-966-6632; *Fax:* 202-223-0250
natural@NPAinfo.org; www.npainfo.org
Social Media: Facebook, Twitter, LinkedIn, Pinterest, Googleplus
Jon Fiume, President Elect
Jain Drinkwalter, Chair
Roxanne Green, President
Daniel Fabricant, Executive Director & CEO
Mark LeDoux, Treasurer
The nation's largest and oldest non-profit organization dedicated to the natural products industry. NPA unites a diverse membership, from the smallest health food store to the largest dietary supplement manufacturer.
1900+ Members
Founded in: 1936

9259 **New York Apple Association**
7645 Main Street
PO Box 350
Fishers, NY 14453-0350
585-924-2171; *Fax:* 585-924-1629;
www.nyapplecountry.com
Social Media: Facebook, Twitter
Jim Allen, President
Julia Stewart, Communications
Molly Golden, Director of Marketing
Linda Quinn, Media Representative
Ellen Mykins, Accounting
The New York Apple Association is a non-profit trade association representing over 600 commercial apple growers in New York State. The apple industry produces about 25 million bushels each year at a value of approximately $137 million, making it one of the largest sectors in New York agriculture.
600 Members
Founded in: 1950

9260 **North American Association of Food Equipment Manufacturers**
161 N Clark Street
Suite 2020
Chicago, IL 60601

312-821-0201; *Fax:* 312-821-0202
info@nafem.org; www.nafem.org
Social Media: Facebook

Michael L. Whiteley, President
Kevin Fink, President-Elect
Joseph Carlson, CFSP, Secretary/Treasurer
Deirdre Flynn, Executive Vice President
Genny Bertalmio, Office Manager

The North American Association of Food Equipment Manactures (NAFEM) is a trade association of more than 625 foodservice equipment and supplies manufacturers that provide products for food preparation, cooking, storage and table service providers. NAFEM's biennial trade show attracts approximately 20,000 foodservice professionals and features more than 600 North American manufacturers.
625 Members

9261 **North American Blueberry Council**
80 Iron Point Circle
Suite 114
Folsom, CA 95630

916-983-2279; *Fax:* 916-983-9370
info@nabcblues.org; www.nabcblues.org

Bob Carini, President
Tom Bodtke, First Vice President
Tom Avinelis, Second Vice President
Art Galletta, Treasurer
Ken Patterson, Secretary

A non-profit association with the important role of acting as a voice for the highbush blueberry industry.
Founded in: 1965

9262 **North American Farm Show Council**
590 Woody Hayes Drive
Columbus, OH 43210

614-292-4278; *Fax:* 614-292-9448
gamble.19@osu.edu; www.worldexpo.com

Dennis Alford, President
Chip Blalock, 1st Vice President
David Zimmerman, 2nd Vice President
Chuck Gamble, Secretary/Treasurer

Strives to improve the value of its member shows through education, communication and evaluation. The overall goal is to provide the best possible marketing showcase for exhibitors of agricultural equipment and related products to the farmer/rancher/producer customer.
Founded in: 1972

9263 **North American Limousin Foundation**
6 Inverness Court East
Suite 260
Englewood, CO 80112-5595

303-220-1693; *Fax:* 303-220-1884
limousin@nalf.org; www.nalf.org
Social Media: Facebook, Twitter

Chad Settje, President
Bret Begert, Vice President
Jim Bob Hendrickson, Secretary
Dexter Edwards, Treasurer
Mark Anderson, Executive Director

Register, promote and research on Limousin beef cattle.
4000 Members
Founded in: 1968

9264 **North American Meat Association**
1150 Connecticut Avenue, NW
12th Floor
Washington, DC 20036

202-640-5333
800-368-3043; *Fax:* 202-318-4078
info@meatassociation.com;
www.meatinstitute.org
Social Media: Twitter, LinkedIn

Mike Hesse, Co-Chairman
Brian Coelho, Co-President
Barry Carpenter, President & CEO
Phil Kimball, CAE, Executive Director
Sabrina Moore, Director, Meetings

Provides its members unique one-on-one assistance resolving regulatory issues. Mission is to be proactive and responsive in serving members both individually and collectively.
Founded in: 2012

9265 **North American Millers' Association**
600 Maryland Ave SW
Suite 825 West
Washington, DC 20024

202-484-2200; *Fax:* 202-488-7416
generalinfo@namamillers.org;
www.namamillers.org
Social Media: Facebook

Dan Dye, Chairman
Mark Kolkhorst, Vice Chairman
James A. McCarthy, President & CEO
James A. Bair, Vice President
Sherri Lehman, Director of Government Relations

Trade association representing the wheat, corn, oat and rye milling industry. NAMA members operate one hundred and seventy mills in thirty-eight states and Canada. Their aggregate production of more than one hundred and sixty million pounds per day is approximately ninety-five percent of the industry capacity in the U.S.
Founded in: 1902

9266 **North American Natural Casing Association**
494 Eighth Avenue
Suite 805
New York, NY 10001

212-695-4980; *Fax:* 212-695-7153
nanca18hq@yahoo.com; www.nanca.org

Barbara Negron, President
Phil Schwartz, Vice President
Mike Wallace, Secretary
Eric Svendsen, Treasurer

To obtain legislation favorable to the industry's interests and prevent or change legistation deemed harmful at the local, state and federal levels, including protection from unfair trade practices by foreign countries, and working with member governments to ease trade. Also addresses common industry problems encountered by management in the production, distribution and financial function of the naturasl casing industry.

9267 **North American Olive Oil Association**
3301 Route 66
Suite 205, Building C
Neptune, NJ 07753

732-922-3008; *Fax:* 732-922-3590
info@naooa.org; www.naooa.org
Social Media: Facebook, Twitter

Eryn Balch, Executive Vice President

Committed to supplying North American consumers with quality products in a fair and competitive environment; to fostering a clear understanding of the different grades of olive oil; and to expounding the benefits of olive oil in nutrition, health, and the culinary arts.
Founded in: 1989

9268 **Northeast Fresh Foods Alliance**
1189R N Main Street
Randolph, MA 02368

781-963-9726; *Fax:* 781-963-5829

Brian Long, President
Bob Ogan, Executive VP
Chris Bruhn, First VP
Paul Sullivan, Secretary
Paul Palumbo, Treasurer
350 Members
Founded in: 1979

9269 **Northern Nut Growers Association, Inc.**

www.northernnutgrowers.org

Robert Stehli, President
Tim Ford, Vice President
Jeanne Romero-Severson, Treasurer
Tom Molnar, Secretary

The Association brings together people interested in growing nut trees, from amateurs to tree breeders.
Founded in: 1910

9270 **Northwest Cherry Briners Association Inc.**
2667 Reed Rd
Hood River, OR 97031
E-Mail: director.orgcouncil@gmail.com;
www.orgcouncil.com

Carl Payne, VP Tech Services

Association of briners of sweet cherries in the northwestern US. The organization works to inform briners of regulatory decisions and current practices affecting brining operations.
8 Members
Founded in: 1936

9271 **Northwest Food Processors Association**
8338 NE. Alderwood Road
Suite 160
Portland, OR 97220
503-327-2200; *Fax:* 503-327-2201
info@nwfpa.org; www.nwfpa.org
Social Media: Facebook, Twitter, LinkedIn

Kurt McKnight, Chair
Debbie Radie, Chair Elect
Steven Rowe, Vice Chair
David McGiverin, President
Greg Satrum, Director

NWFPA is an advocate for members interests and a resource for enhancing the food processing industry in Oregon, Washington and Idaho.
350 Members
Founded in: 1914

9272 **Northwest Meat Processors Association**
2380 NW Roosevelt St
Portland, OR 97210-2323

503-226-2758; *Fax:* 503-224-0947
haysmgmt@pipeline.com

Dennis Hays, Executive Director
250 Members
Founded in: 1962

9273 **Organic Alliance**
Organic Alliance International
Asheville, NC 28804

828-337-6114; www.organicalliance.org

An alliance of people, businesses and organizations working together to promote the goodness of organics and help to make it available to all.

9274 **Organic Crop Improvement Association International (OCIA)**
1340 North Cotner Boulevard
Lincoln, NR 68505-1838

402-477-2323; *Fax:* 402-477-4325
info@ocia.org; www.ocia.org

Jack Geiger, President
Susan Linkletter, 1st Vice President
Joel Koskan, 2nd Vice President
Demetria Stephens, Secretary
Jeff Kienast, Treasurer

An accredited world leader in the certified organic industry, provides certification, education and research services to thousands of organic farmers, processors and handlers from 20 countries in North, Central and South America and Asia.
3500 Members
Founded in: 1985

9275 **Organic Trade Association**
28 Vernon St
Suite 413
Brattleboro, VT 05301

802-275-3800; *Fax:* 802-275-3801
info@ota.com; www.ota.com
Social Media: Facebook, Twitter, LinkedIn

Melissa Hughes, President
Kim Dietz, Vice President
Tony Bedard, Treasurer
Sarah Bird, Secretary
Laura Batcha, Chief Executive Officer

A business association for the organic industry in North America. OTA's mission is to encourage global sustainability through promoting and protecting the growth of diverse organic trade.
1400 Members
Founded in: 1985
Mailing list available for rent

9276 **Ozark Food Processors Association**
2650 N Young Avenue
Fayetteville, AR 72704

479-575-4607; *Fax:* 479-575-2165
ofpa@uark.edu
ofpa.uark.edu

Jason Hayward, President
Andrea Dunigan, Vice President
Dr. Renee Threlfall, Secretary
Steve Crider, Board Member
Jared Brooks, Board Member

This association is comprised of regional food processors and national suppliers for the food service industry.
90 Members
Founded in: 1906

9277 **Pacific Coast Shellfish Growers Association**
120 State Ave NE
#142
Olympia, WA 98501

360-754-2744; *Fax:* 360-754-2743;
www.pcsga.net
Social Media: Facebook, Flickr

Margaret Pilaro Barrette, Executive Director
Connie Smith, Projects Manager
Mary Middleton, Executive Assistant

Members grow a wide variety of healthy, sustainable shellfish including oysters, clams, mussels, scallops and geoduck. PCSGA works on behalf of its members on a broad spectrum of issues, including environmental protection, shellfish safety, regulations, technology, and marketing.
Founded in: 1930

9278 **Paperboard Packaging Council**
1350 Main Street
Suite 1508
Springfield, MA 01103-1670

413-686-9191; *Fax:* 413-747-7777
paperboardpackaging@ppcnet.org;
www.ppcnet.org
Social Media: Facebook, Twitter, LinkedIn, YouTube

Kyle Eldred, Chair
Charles Johnson, Vice Chair
Ben Markens, President
Lou Kornet, Vice President
Steven Levkoff, Treasurer

Trade association serving converters and suppliers of all forms of paperboard packaging, including folding cartons, rigid boxes, paper cylinders, and laminated small flute containers.
Founded in: 1929

9279 **Peanut and Tree Nut Processors Association**
PO Box 2660
Alexandria, VA 22301

301-365-2521; *Fax:* 301-365-7705
ptnpa.org
Social Media: Twitter

Brian Ezell, Chairman
JOEL PERKINS, Vice Chairman
Michael J. Valentine, Secretary/Treasurer
Jeannie Shaughnessy, Executive Director
Trish Schechtman, Oepratiions/Membership Manager

Representing the owners and operators of companies (large and small) who shell, process, salt and/or roast peanuts and tree nuts. In addition, our members also supply equipment and services that are critical to our industry.
Founded in: 1939

9280 **Pear Bureau Northwest**
4382 SE International Way
Suite A
Milwaukie, OR 97222-4635

503-652-9720; *Fax:* 503-652-9721
info@usapears.com; www.usapears.com
Social Media: Facebook, Twitter, LinkedIn, YouTube, Pinterest

Kevin D. Moffitt, President & CEO
Linda Bailey, VP of Operations
Kathy Stephenson, Director Marketing Communications

A non-profit marketing organization that promotes, advertises and develops markets for fresh pears grown in Oregon and Washington. Through professional representatives in the U.S. and around the world, the Bureau coordinates activities designed to increase awareness and consumption of fresh USA Pears, facilitating research on behalf of the Northwest pear industry relative to consumer awareness and preferences, nutritional benefits and emerging global markets.
1600 Members
Founded in: 1931

9281 **Pickle Packers International Inc.**
1101 17th Street NW
Suite 700
Washington, DC 20036

202-331-2465; *Fax:* 202-463-8998;
www.ilovepickles.org
Social Media: Facebook

Sponsors research, represents industry before government agencies, produces educational materials, and provides superior networking opportunities to members. Members inlude processors, salters, green shippers, brokers, growers, seed companies, ingredient and equipment manufacturers, packaging suppliers, and those providing goods and services to the industry.
Founded in: 1896

9282 **Popcorn Board**
330 N Wabash Avenue
Suite 2000
Chicago, IL 60611

312-644-6610; *Fax:* 312-527-6783
info@popcorn.org; www.popcorn.org
Social Media: Facebook, Twitter, Blog

A non-profit organization funded by US popcorn processors to raise awareness of popcorn as a versatile, whole-grain snack.
Founded in: 1943

9283 **Printing Industries of America**
301 Brush Creek Road
Warrendale, PA 15086

412-741-6860
800-910-4283; *Fax:* 412-741-2311
printing@printing.org; www.printing.org
Social Media: Facebook, Twitter, LinkedIn, Pinterest, Googleplus

David A. Olberding, Chairman
Bradley L. Thompson II, 1st Vice Chairman
MR CURT KREISLER, 2nd Vice Chairman
Michael L. Wurst, Treasurer
BRYAN T. HALL, Secretary

Members are companies printing labels for food or consumer products.
40 Members
Founded in: 1887

9284 **Produce Marketing Association**
1500 Casho Mill Road
PO Box 6036
Newark, DE 19711

302-738-7100; *Fax:* 302-731-2409
solutionctr@pma.com; www.pma.com
Social Media: Facebook, Twitter, Flickr, YouTube, Xchange

Cathy Burns, President
Bryan Silbermann, CEO
Tony Parassio, Chief Operating Officer
Yvonne Bull, CFO
Robert J. Whitaker, Ph.D., Chief Science & Technology Officer

Providing business solutions that strengthen and lead the global produce community, PMA has set the standard for quality events with the annual convention and continues to revolutionize one of the world's most vibrant industries.
100 Members
Founded in: 1949

9285 **Professional Farmers of America**
6612 Chancellor Dr.
Cedar Falls, IA 50613

319-277-1278
800-772-0023; *Fax:* 319-827-1792
editors@profarmer.com; www.profarmer.com

Mike Walsten, VP
Merrill Oster, Executive Director
Rich Posson, Editor

Provides farmers with marketing strategies and market-trend data, as well as seminars and home study courses.
25M Members
Founded in: 1972

9286 **Quality Bakers of America Cooperative**
1275 Glenlivet Drive
Suite 100
Allentown, PA 18106-3107
973-263-6970; *Fax:* 973-263-0937
info@qba.com; www.qba.com
Providing members with access to sources of appropriate services in order to maintain the highest product quality and sanitation standards.
Founded in: 1922

9287 **Quality Chekd Dairies**
901 Warrenville Rd
Suite 405
Lisle, IL 60532
800-222-6455; *Fax:* 630-717-1126
qchekd@qchekd.com; www.qchekd.com
Peter Horvath, President
Mary DeMarco, Accounting & Admin Manager
Steve Drabek, Human Resource & Training Director
Laura Moehs, Training & Admin Coordinator
Chuck Yarris, Quality & Food Safety Director
A cooperative of dairy foods processors who use the Quality Checked trademark on their products and engage in group purchasing of ingredients and supplies.
Founded in: 1944

9288 **Raisin Administration Committee**
2445 Capitol Street
Suite 200
Fresno, CA 93721-2236
559-225-0520; *Fax:* 559-225-0652
info@raisins.org; www.raisins.org
Gary Schulz, President
Debbie Powell, Sr. Vice President of Operations
Larry Blagg, Sr. Vice President of Marketing
Ron Degiuli, Vice President of Accounting
Administrative board of growers and packers of raisins.

9289 **Red Angus Association of America**
4201 N Interstate 35
Denton, TX 76207-3415
940-387-3502; *Fax:* 888-829-6069
info@redangus.org; www.redangus.org
Social Media: Facebook
Kim Ford, President
Twig Marston, CEO
Jeanene McCuistion, Accounting Director
Kevin Miller, 1st Vice President
Bob Morton, 2nd Vice President
Dedicated to providing its members with excellence and innovation in leadership, service, information and education. An association for breeders of Red Angus cattle.
2000 Members
Founded in: 1954

9290 **Refrigerated Foods Association**
3823 Roswell Road
Suite 208
Marietta, GA 30062
678-426-8175; *Fax:* 678-550-4504
info@refrigeratedfoods.org;
www.refrigeratedfoods.org
Steve Loehndorf, President
Wes Thaller, Vice President
Josh Knott, Secretary
Kenneth Funger, Treasurer
Megan Levin, Executive Director
An organization of manufacturers and suppliers of refrigerated prepared foods united by a common interest; to advance and safeguard the industry. Members include manufacturers and suppliers of wet salads, refrigerated entrees and side dishes, dips, desserts, soups, and ethnic foods, as well as companies engaged in business operations related to the refrigerated foods industry.
200+ Members
Founded in: 1980

9291 **Research and Development Associates for Military Food and Packaging Systems**
16607 Blanco Rd
Suite 501
San Antonio, TX 78232
210-493-8024; *Fax:* 210-493-8036
hqs@militaryfood.org; www.militaryfood.org
Social Media: Facebook
Bill McCreary, Chairman
Daniel Weil, Vice Chairman
John Q. McNulty, Executive Director
Jan Cook, Director of Administration
Kimberly Addison Sanford, Marketing Events Coordinator
To provide the safest and highest food service to the US Armed Forces by linking industry, government and academics.
700 Members
Founded in: 1946

9292 **Retail Bakers of America**
15941 Harlem Avenue
#347
Tinley Park, IL 60477
800-638-0924; *Fax:* 800-638-0924
Info@retailbakersofamerica.org;
www.americanbanker.com/conferences/retail
Social Media: Facebook
Richard Reinwald, Chairman
Paul Sapienza, Secretary
Dale A. Biles, Treasurer
Comprised of retail bakeries, allied suppliers and other industry members. The purpose is to offer our members knowledge and resources to enhance business operations through learning opportunities, shared best practices, networking and industry communication.
2000 Members
Founded in: 1918

9293 **Retail Confectioners International**
2053 S. Waverly
Ste. C
Springfield, MO 65804
417-883-2775
800-545-5381; *Fax:* 417-883-1108
info@retailconfectioners.org;
www.retailconfectioners.org
Social Media: Facebook, Twitter, YouTube
Brian Pelletier, President
Judith Hilliard McCarthy, 1st Vice President
Steve Vande Walle, 2nd Vice President
John Asher, III, 3rd Vice President
Angie Burlison, Secretary/Treasurer
Providing education, promotion and legislative services to our members who are manufacturing retailers of quality boxed chocolate and other confectionery products throughout the U.S., Canada and overseas.
600 Members
Founded in: 1917

9294 **Rocky Mountain Bean Dealers Association**
PO Box 1285
Elizabeth, CO 80107
303-646-8883; *Fax:* 720-306-2878
rmbean@revealmail.com
Vickie Root, Executive Director
This organization is dedicated to advancing the general interest of its members and the industry.

9295 **Rocky Mountain Food Industry Association**
PO Box 1083
Arvada, CO 80001-1083
303-830-7001; *Fax:* 303-424-7114;
www.rmfia.org
Mary Lou Chapman, President/CEO
The trade organization for the Colorado and Wyoming grocery industry, representing retail grocers, convenience stores, and their wholesale suppliers. The association serves as a voice for its members with state legislatures, US Congress and the various governmental agencies that regulate the food industry.
500 Members
Founded in: 1917

9296 **Roundtable of Food Professionals**
4363 Larwin Avenue
Cypress, CA 90630
714-562-5088; *Fax:* 714-670-2965;
www.rfporg.org
Barb Colucci, President
Jenny Rosoff, President-Emeritus
David Stennes, VP
Stephany Rosenthal, Membership Co-Chair
Provide opportunities for development and career expansion within the whole spectrum of the food industry.
50 Members
Founded in: 2002

9297 **Royal Crown Bottlers Association**
515 Eline Ave
St Matthews, KY 40207-3655
502-896-0861; *Fax:* 502-896-0861
Stephanie Garling, Executive Director
Represents franchised Royal Crown bottlers.
100 Members
Founded in: 1964

9298 **Salt Institute**
405 5th Ave. South
Suite 7C
Naples, FL 34102-6515
239-231-3305; *Fax:* 239-330-1492
jorge@saltinstitute.org; www.saltinstitute.org
Social Media: Facebook, Twitter, YouTube
Lori Roman, President
Morton Satin, Vice President
Jorge Amselle, Director of Communication
Wilfrid Nixon, VP Science and the Environment
A source of authoritative information about salt and its more than 14,000 known users. Provides public information and advocates on behalf of its members, including use of the website.
Founded in: 1914

9299 **Santa Gertrudis Breeders International**
PO Box 1257
Kingsville, TX 78364
361-592-9357; *Fax:* 361-592-8572
sgbi@sbcglobal.net; www.santagertrudis.com
Social Media: Facebook, Twitter, Googleplus
Curtis Salter, President
Deanna Parker, Secretary/Treasurer
John E. Ford, Executive Director
The original American beef breed. Custom built for the range and market, these cattle have proven themselves worldwide to be a hardy and profitable breed from the mountains of Montana and Mexico to the tropics and deserts of Argentina and Australia. Worldwide, cattlemen are getting results using Santa Gertrudis genetics.
Founded in: 1950

9300 **School Nutrition Association**
120 Waterfront St
Suite 300
National Harbor, MD 20745

301-686-3100
800-877-8822; *Fax:* 301-686-3115
servicecenter@schoolnutrition.org;
www.schoolnutrition.org
Social Media: Digg

Jean Ronnei, President
Becky Domokos-Bays, President-Elect
Lynn Harvey, Vice President
Linda Eichenberger, Secretary/Treasurer
Patricia Montague, CEO

This is a national, nonprofit professional organization representing members who provide high quality, low-cost meals to students across the country.
55000 Members
Founded in: 1946

9301 **Sioux Honey Association**
301 Lewis Boulevard
PO Box 388
Sioux City, IA 51101
712-258-0638; *Fax:* 712-258-1332;
www.suebeehoney.com
Social Media: Facebook, Twitter, Pinterest

David Allibone, President/CEO

Established by five beekeepers so that they could market their honey at greater profit through sharing services and equipment, processing and packing facilities and complete marketing and sales organizations.
315 Members
Founded in: 1921

9302 **Small Farm Resource**

www.farminfo.org

Contains a wide variety of information useful to those with small farms and rural property.
Founded in: 1995

9303 **Snack Food Association**
1600 Wilson Blvd
Suite 650
Arlington, VA 22209
703-836-4500
800-628-1334; *Fax:* 703-836-8262
sfa@sfa.org; www.sfa.org
Social Media: Facebook, Twitter, LinkedIn, Youtube, Flickr

Tom Dempsey, CEO
Liz Wells, Vice President, Meetings & Events
Paul Downey, Director of Finance and Admin
David Walsh, Director, Government Affairs
Meegan Smith, Director, Communications & Marketin

Representing snack manufacturers and suppliers worldwide. Serving as the voice for the snack industry before government, researches and compiles annual snack sales and consumer data, educates manufacturers on technological advances in equipment and raw ingredients and provides technical support to its members through direct assistance, videos, seminars and publications.
800 Members
Founded in: 1937

9304 **Society for Laboratory Automatic and Screening**
100 Illinois Street
Suite 242
St. Charles, IL 60174

630-256-7527
877-990-7527; *Fax:* 630-741-7527
slas@slas.org; www.slas.org
Social Media: Facebook, Twitter, LinkedIn, YouTube

Dean Ho, President
Richard Eglen, Vice President
Mike Snowden, Treasurer
Michele A. Cleary, Secretary
Alastair Binnie, Director

Supports research and discovery in pharmaceutical biotechnology and the agrichemical industry that utilize biomolecular screening procedures.
2000+ Members
Founded in: 1994

9305 **Society of Commercial Seed Technologists**
653 Constitution Avenue NE
Washington, DC 200002

202-870-2412; *Fax:* 607-273-1638
scst@seedtechnology.net;
www.seedtechnology.net

Barbara Cleave, President
David Stimpson, VP
Steve Beals, Director at Large
DaNell Jamieson, Director-at-Large
Heidi Jo Larson, Director-at-Large

A organization comprised of commercial, independent and government seed technologists. Developed over the years into a progressive organization that trains and provides accreditation of technologists, conducts research studies and proposes rule changes, and serves as an important resource to the seed industry.
Founded in: 1922

9306 **Southeast United Dairy Industry Association**
5340 W Fayetteville Rd
Atlanta, GA 30349-5416

678-833-0580
800-343-4693; *Fax:* 770-996-6925;
www.southeastdairy.org
Social Media: Facebook, Twitter, YouTube, Pinterest

Amanda Trice, Director of IR & Communications
Rebecca Egseiker, Assistant Director of Communication

Provides a wealth of information for milk and dairy consumers, media, school and health professionals and dairy farmers.
6000 Members
Founded in: 1971
Mailing list available for rent

9307 **Southeastern Dairy Foods Research Center**
NCSU Department of Food Science
PO Box 7624
Raleigh, NC 27695

919-515-4197; *Fax:* 919-513-0014
fbns.ncsu.edu/
Social Media: Facebook, Twitter, YouTube

Chris Daubert, Department Head

One of six National Centers funded and managed by Dairy Management Incorporated. The mission is to conduct research to develop and apply new technologies for value-added processing of fluid milk and its components into dairy products and ingredients with improved safety, quality or expanded functionalities.
Founded in: 1988

9308 **Southern Peanut Farmers Federation**
1025 Sugar Pike Way
Canton, GA 30115

770-751-6615
lpwagner@comcast.net;
www.southernpeanutfarmers.org

Formed to educate American consumers about the US peanut industry and its products.
Founded in: 1998

9309 **Southern Peanut Growers**
1025 Sugar Pike Way
Canton, GA 30115
770-751-6615
lpwagner@comcast.net;
www.peanutbutterlovers.com
Social Media: Facebook, Twitter, YouTube, Pinterest

Leslie Wagner, Executive Director

A nonprofit trade association representing peanut farmers in Georgia, Alabama, Florida and Mississippi. Formed to educate American consumers about the US peanut industry and its products.
6000 Members
Founded in: 1980
Mailing list available for rent

9310 **Southern US Trade Association**
701 Poydras Street
Suite 3845
New Orleans, LA 70139

504-568-5986; *Fax:* 504-568-6010
susta@susta.org; www.susta.org
Social Media: Facebook

Bernadette Wiltz, Executive Director
Danielle Viguerie, Marketing Director
Missie Lindsey, Marketing Coordinator
Tina Meshell, Office Manager
Troy Rosamond, Deputy Director & Financial Directo

A non-profit agricultural export trade development association comprised of the Departments of Agriculture of the 15 southern states and the Commonwealth of Puerto Rico.
Founded in: 1973

9311 **Soy Protein Council**
1255 23rd Street NW
Washington, DC 20037

202-467-6610; *Fax:* 202-833-3636;
www.spcouncil.org
Social Media: Facebook, Twitter

David A Saunders, Executive VP
Elroy Wolff, General Counsel

Primary purpose is to promote the growth and interests of the soy protein industry and broaden the acceptance of soy products as key components of the worldwide food system.
Founded in: 1971

9312 **Soyfoods Association of North America**
1050 17th Street, NW
Suite 600
Washington, DC 20036

202-659-3520
info@soyfoods.org; www.soyfoods.org
Social Media: Facebook, Twitter, YouTube, Pinterest

Kate Leavltt, President
Helen Kor, Vice President
Kate Leavitt, Treasurer
Nancy Chapman, Executive Director

A trusted advocate in providing information about the health benefits and nutritional advantages of soy consumption. Encouraging

sustainability, integrity and growth of the soyfoods industry through members.
50+ Members
Founded in: 1978

9313 Specialty Coffee Association of America
117 W. 4th St,
Suite 300
Santa Ana, CA 92701

562-624-4100; *Fax:* 562-624-4101
info@scaa.org; www.scaa.org
Social Media: Facebook, Twitter, YouTube

Tracy Allen, President
Ben Pitts, Vice President
Heather Perry, 2nd Vice President
Guy Burdett, Secretary/Treasurer
Colleen Anunu, Director

One of the primary functions is to set the industry's standards for growing, roasting and brewing. Members of the SCAA include coffee retailers, roasters, producers, exporters and importers, as well as manufacturers of coffee equipment and related products.
2500+ Members
Founded in: 1982
Mailing list available for rent

9314 Specialty Food Association and Fancy Food Show
136 Madison Avenue
12th Floor
New York, NY 10016

646-878-0301; *Fax:* 212-482-6459;
www.specialtyfood.com
Social Media: Facebook, Twitter, LinkedIn, YouTube

Mike Silver, Chair
Shawn McBride, Vice Chair
Ann Daw, President
Becky Renfro Borbolla, Treasurer
Matt Neilsen, Secretary

A business trade association to foster trade, commerce and interest in the specialty food industry. Composed of domestic and foreign manufacturers, importers, distributors, brokers, retailers, restaurateurs, caterers and others in the specialty foods business.
3000+ Members
Founded in: 1952

9315 Sugar Association
1300 L Street NW
Suite 1001
Washington, DC 20005

202-785-1122; *Fax:* 202-785-5019
sugar@sugar.org; www.sugar.org
Social Media: Facebook, Twitter, Pinterest

Andrew Briscoe, President/CEO
P. Courtney Gaine, VP, Scientific Affairs
Cheryl Digges, VP Public Policy & Education
Lisa Swanson, Administrative Assistant

Promoting the consumption of sugar through sound scientific principles while maintaining an understanding of the benefits that sugar contributes to the quality of wholesome foods and beverages.
Founded in: 1943

9316 Switzerland Cheese Association
704 Executive Blvd
Suite I
Valley Cottage, NY 10989-2010

845-268-2460; *Fax:* 845-268-9991

Paul U Schilt, CEO

9317 Tea Association of the USA
362 Fifth Avenue
Suite 801
New York, NY 10001

212-986-9415; *Fax:* 212-697-8658
info@teausa.com; www.teausa.com
Social Media: Facebook, Twitter

Joe Simrany, President

Association of companies dedicated to the interests and growth of the US tea industry.
100 Members
Founded in: 1899
Mailing list available for rent

9318 Tea Board of India
14 B.T.M. Sarani
Kolkata, KO 700001

332-235-1331; *Fax:* 332-221-5715;
www.teaboard.gov.in

Santosh Sarangi, Chairman
A.K Das, Deputy Chairman
Sumita Lahiri, Personal Secretary to Chairman
A. Rajan, Secretary
Joydip Biswas, Deputy Director

This association promotes Indian tea and develops new markets for tea in the US and Canada.
Founded in: 1953

9319 The American Dairy Association Indiana, Inc.
9360 Castlegate Drive
Indianapolis, IN 46256

317-842-3060
800-225-6455; *Fax:* 317-842-3065
osza@winnersdrinkmilk.com;
www.indianadairycouncil.org
Social Media: Facebook, Twitter, LinkedIn, YouTube, Pinterest, Instagram

Donald Gurtner, President
Paul Mills, Vice President
Steve Phares, Treasurer
Anita Schmitt, Secretary

A not-for-profit organization which promotes the sale and consumption of diary foods.
Founded in: 1915

9320 The Biscuit & Cracker Manufacturers' Association
6325 Woodside Court
Suite 125
Columbia, MD 21046

443-545-1645; *Fax:* 410-290-8585;
www.thebcma.org
Social Media: Facebook, LinkedIn

David Van Laar, President
Kathy Kinter Phelps, Membership & Education Manager
Vickie Clancy, Meetings Assistant
Dennis Loalbo, Technical Advisor
Blake Hutzley, Technical Advisor

International trade organization representing the entire spectrum of companies involved in the manufacturing of biscuits and crackers and the suppliers to the baking industry. Our mission is to bring unparalled educational training programs and networking opportunities to members of the cookie and cracker industry.
250 Members
Founded in: 1901

9321 The Catfish Institute
6311 Ridgewood Road
Suite W404
Jackson, MS 39211

601-977-9559; *Fax:* 662-887-6857
catfishinfo@uscatfish.com;
www.uscatfish.com
Social Media: Facebook, Twitter, Youtube, Pinterest

Butch Wilson, President
Roger Barlow, Executive Vice-President

Represents the largest aquaculture industry in the United States. Represents the interests of the farm-raised catfish industry of farmers, processors, feed mills, researchers, and supplier industries. Promotes the many healthy, great tasting uses for genuine U.S. Farm-Raised Catfish.
Cost: $40.00
Frequency: Membership Fees
Founded in: 1986
Mailing list available for rent

9322 The Cranberry Institute
PO Box 497
Carver, MA 02330

508-866-1118; *Fax:* 508-866-1199
cinews@cranberryinstitute.org;
www.cranberryinstitute.org

Kevin Hatton, Chairman
Bob Wilson, Vice Chairman
Steve Berlyn, Secretary/Treasurer

A nonprofit that supports cranberry growers and the cranberry industry.
Founded in: 1951

9323 The Food and Beverage Association of America
111 East 14th Street
Suite 390
New York, NY 10003

212-344-8252; *Fax:* 212-504-9536
office@fbassoc.com; www.fbassoc.com
Social Media: Facebook, LinkedIn, YouTube

Steven V. Gattullo, President
Sean Cassidy, First Vice President
Gus Montesantos, Second Vice President
Guy Salisch, Secretary
Daniel Saalman, Treasurer

A nonprofit, philanthropic, trade organization for executives of the food and beverage industries of the New York metropolitan area.
Founded in: 1956

9324 The Industry Council for Research on Packaging and the Environment
SoanePoint, 6-8 Market Place
Reading
Berkshire RG1 2EG

118-925-5991; *Fax:* 202-833-3636;
www.incpen.org
Social Media: Facebook, Twitter

Steve Young, President

A research organization, which draws together an influential group of companies who share a vision of the future where all production, distribution, and consumption are sustainable. Aiming to ensure policies on packaging makes a positive contribution to sustainability, encourages the industry to minimize the environmental impact of packaging and continuously improve packaging, and explain the role of packaging in society.
Founded in: 1974

9325 The National Chicken Council
1152 15th Street NW
Suite 430
Washington, DC 20005-2622

202-296-2622; *Fax:* 202-293-4005
ncc@chickenusa.org;
www.nationalchickencouncil.org
Social Media: Facebook, Twitter

Michael J. Brown, President
Ashley Peterson, Senior Vice President
Mary M. Colville, VP of Government Affairs
Tom Super, Vice President of Communications
Margaret A. Ernst,, Senior Director

National, non-profit trade association representing the US chicken industry. Promoting and protecting the interests of the chicken industry and acts as the industry's voice before Congress and federal agencies. Members include chicken producer/processors, poultry distributors, and allied industry firms.
150+ Members
Founded in: 1954

9326 The National Confectioners' Association
1101 30th Street, NW
Suite 200
Washington, DC 20007

202-534-1440; *Fax:* 202-337-0637
info@CandyUSA.com; www.candyusa.com
Social Media: Facebook, Twitter, LinkedIn, Flickr, Pinterest, YouTube

Robert M. Simpson, Jr., Chairman
Peter W. Blommer, Vice Chairman
John H. Downs, Jr., President/ CEO
Joseph Vittoria, Treasurer
Martino Caretto, Vice President

Advances, protects, and promotes the confectionery industry.
Founded in: 1884

9327 The Peanut Institute
PO Box 70157
Albany, GA 31708-0157

229-888-0216
888-873-2688; *Fax:* 229-888-5150;
www.peanut-institute.org
Social Media: Facebook, Twitter, YouTube

A nonprofit that supports nutrition research and advocates for the peanut's place in healthful lifestyles.

9328 Today's Market Prices
www.todaymarket.com

A user friendly information center that provides within its market prices service, daily price information on more than 200 fruit, vegetables, and herbs from the most important wholesale markets of the USA, Canada, Mexico, and Europe.
Founded in: 1996

9329 Tortilla Industry Association
1600 Wlison Blvd
Suite 650
Arlington, VA 22209

800-944-6099; *Fax:* 800-944-6177
info@tortilla-info.com; www.tortilla-info.com

Criss Cruz, Chairman
Jim Kabbani, Executive Director
Dana Beall, Secretary

Members include companies engaged in manufacturing tortillas and suppliers, food brokers and Mexican restaurant owners.
175 Members
Founded in: 1886

9330 U.S. Meat Export Federation
1855 Blake Street
Suite 200
Denver, CO 80202

303-623-6328; *Fax:* 303-623-0297
migoe@usmef.org; www.usmef.org
Social Media: Facebook, Twitter, YouTube

Leann Saunders, Chair
Roel Andriessen, Chair-elect
Bruce Schmoll, Vice Chair
Dennis Stiffler, Treasurer/ Secretary
Philip M. Seng, President, CEO

A nonprofit trade association working to create new opportunities and develop existing international markets for U.S. beef, pork, lamb, and veal.

9331 U.S. Poultry & Egg Association
1530 Cooledge Road
Tucker, GA 30084-7303

770-493-9401; *Fax:* 770-493-9257
info@uspoultry.org; www.uspoultry.org
Social Media: Facebook, Twitter, LinkedIn, Google+, YouTube

John Starkey, President
Charles Olentine, PhD, Executive Vice President
Gwen Venable, Vice President of Communications
Jason Rivera, Vice President, IT
Barbara Jenkins, Vice President - Education Programs

Represents producers and processors of broilers, turkeys, eggs and breeding stock, as well as allied companies.
Founded in: 1947

9332 U.S. Wheat Associates
3103 10th Street, North
Suite 300
Arlington, VA 22201

202-463-0999; *Fax:* 703-524-4399
info@uswheat.org; www.uswheat.org
Social Media: Facebook, Twitter, YouTube, Flickr

Brian O'Toole, Chairman
Jason Scott, Vice Chairman
Roy Motter, Past Chairman
Alan Tracy, President
Mike Miller, Secretary-Treasurer

Supports the sale of wheat by offering education for overseas buyers, onsite training services, promotes trade policies, and consumer promotion.

9333 US Animal Health Association
4221 Mitchelle Ave.
Saint Joseph, MO 64507

816-671-1144; *Fax:* 816-671-1201
usaha@usaha.org; www.usaha.org
Social Media: Facebook, Twitter

Dr. Stephen Crawford, President
Dr. Bruce King, President-Elect
Dr. David Schmitt, First Vice President
Dr. Boyd Parr, Second Vice President
Mrs. Barbara Determan, 3rd Vice President

Seeks to prevent, control and eliminate livestock diseases.
1400 Members
Founded in: 1897

9334 US Apple Association
8233 Old Courthouse Rd
Suite 200
Vienna, VA 22182

703-442-8850; *Fax:* 703-790-0845
info@usapple.org; www.usapple.org
Social Media: Facebook, Twitter, Youtube

Jim Bair, President & CEO
Diane Kurrle, Senior Vice President
Jessa Allen, Director, Membership & Communicatons
Wendy Brannen, Director,Consumer Health
Niza Strike, Office manager

Providing all segments of the US apple industry the means to profitably produce and market apples and apple products. Committed to serving the entire US apple industry by representing the industry on national issues, increasing the demand for apples and apple products, and providing information on matters pertaining to the apple industry.
440 Members
Founded in: 1970

9335 US Beet Sugar Association
1156 15th St NW
Suite 1019
Washington, DC 20005

202-296-4820
800-872-0127; *Fax:* 202-331-2065;
www.beetsugar.org

James Johnson, President
Elin Peltz, VP
Claudia Tidwell, Director of Administration
Hillary Fabrico, Government Affairs Assistant
Cassie Bladow, Director of Government Affairs

Beet sugar processing companies make up the membership of this association.
Founded in: 1911

9336 US Canola Association
600 Pennsylvania Ave SE
Suite 320
Washington, DC 20003

202-969-8113; *Fax:* 202-969-7036
info@uscanola.com; www.uscanola.com
Social Media: Facebook, Twitter, YouTube

Ryan Pederson, President
Jeff Scott, First VP
Robert Rynning, Second Vice President

Works to support and advance US canola production, marketing, processing and use through government and industry relations. Striving to develop and implement agricultural policies, promote efficient production of the crop, and develop markets for US canola products.
Founded in: 1989

9337 US Grains Council
20 F Street, NW
Suite 600
Washington, DC 20001

202-789-0789; *Fax:* 202-898-0522
grains@grains.org; www.grains.org
Social Media: Facebook, Twitter, Youtube, Flickr

Alan Tiemann, Chairman
Chip Councell, Vice Chairman
Thomas Sleight, President & CEO
Debra Keller, Secretary/Treasurer
Jim Raben, At-Large Director

Develops export markets for US barley, corn, grain sorghum and related products. Members include producer organizations and agribusinesses with a common interest in developing export markets.
100 Members
Founded in: 1960

9338 US Meat Export Federation
1855 Blake St
Suite 200
Denver, CO 80202

303-623-6328; *Fax:* 303-623-0297;
www.usmef.org

Leann Saunders, Chair
Roel Andriessen, Chair-elect
Bruce Schmoll, Vice Chair
Dennis Stiffler, Treasurer/ Secretary
Philip M. Seng, President, CEO

A trade association working to create new opportunities and develop existing international markets for U.S. beef, pork, lamb and veal.
160 Members
Founded in: 1996

9339 US Poultry & Egg Association
1530 Cooledge Rd
Tucker, GA 30084-7303

770-938-6915; *Fax:* 770-493-9257;
www.poultryegg.org
Social Media: Facebook

Gary Cooper, Chairman
John Starkey, President
Carol 9anson, Executive Assistant

Representing the entire industry as an All Feather association. Membership includes producers and processors of broilers, turkeys, ducks, eggs, and breeding stock, as well as allied companies.
Cost: $300.00
600 Members
Frequency: Membership Dues
Founded in: 1947

9340 USA Hops
PO Box 1207
301 W Prospect Place
Moxee, WA 98936

509-453-4749; *Fax:* 509-457-8561
info@usahops.org; www.usahops.org

Supports commercial hop producers in US Pacific Northwest.

9341 USA Rice Federation
2101 Wilson Boulevard
Suite 610
Arlington, VA 22201

703-236-2300; *Fax:* 703-236-2301
riceinfo@usarice.com; www.usarice.com
Social Media: Facebook, Twitter, RSS, YouTube, Pinterest

A national association representing producers, millers and allied businesses advancing the use and consumption of U.S. grown rice.

9342 United Agribusiness League
54 Corporate Park
Irvine, CA 92606

800-223-4590; *Fax:* 949-975-1671
membership@unitedag.org; www.unitedag.org
Social Media: Facebook

Brian Edmonds, Chairman
Anthony Vollering, Vice Chairman
A.J. Cisney, Treasurer
Les Graulich, Director
Jerry Pogorzelski, Director

Creating a community for agribusiness—networking and education.
Founded in: 1983

9343 United Braford Breeders
www.brafords.org

Organization that registers Braford cattle in the United States.

9344 United Egg Producers
1720 Windward Concourse
Alpharetta, GA 30005

770-360-9220; *Fax:* 770-360-7058;
www.unitedegg.org
Social Media: Facebook, Twitter

Chad Gregory, President & CEO
David Inall, Senior Vice President
Sherry Shedd, Vice President of Finance
Oscar Garrison, Director of Food Safety
Derreck Nassar, Director of Operations

UEP is a Capper-Volstead cooperative of egg farmers from all across the United States and representing the ownership of all the nation's egg-laying hens.
Founded in: 1968

9345 United Food and Commercial Workers International Union
1775 K St Nw
Washington, DC 20006

202-223-3111; *Fax:* 202-466-1562
ssmith@ufcw.org; www.ufcw.org
Social Media: Facebook, Twitter, YouTube, Flickr

Anthony Marc Perrone, President
Patrick J O'Neill, Secretary/Treasurer
Paul Meinema, Executive VP
Esther lopez, Executive VP
Wayne E. Hanley, Executive VP

UFCW is North America's neighborhood union, members standing together to improve the lives and livelihoods of workers, families and communities.
1.4 M Members
Founded in: 1979

9346 United Fresh Produce Association
1901 Pennsylvania Ave NW
Suite 1100
Washington, DC 20006

202-303-3400; *Fax:* 202-303-3433
united@unitedfresh.org; www.unitedfresh.org
Social Media: Facebook, Twitter, LinkedIn

Brian W. Kocher, Chairman
Tony Freytag, Chairman-Elect
Lisa J. Strube, Secretary/Treasurer
Miriam Wolk, Vice President of Membership
Jeff Oberman, Vice President, Trade Relations

A trade association committed to driving the growth and success of produce companies ans their partners. Represents the interests of member companies throughout the global, fresh produce supply chain, including family-owned, private and publicly trade businesses as well as regional, national and international companies.
Founded in: 1987

9347 United Soybean Board
16305 Swingley Ridge Rd
Suite 150
Chesterfield, MO 63017

636-530-1777
800-989-8721; *Fax:* 636-530-1560
ydock@unitedsoybean.com;
www.unitedsoybean.org
Social Media: Facebook, Twitter, YouTube

Jim Stillman, Chairman
Jim Call, Vice Chair
John Becherer, CEO
Lewis Brainbridge, Secretary
Bob Haselwood, Treasurer

Mission is to ensure that US soy is of the highest quality and the most competitive in a global marketplace.
Founded in: 1972
Mailing list available for rent

9348 United States Cane Sugar Refiners
1730 Rhode Island Ave NW
#608
Washington, DC 20036-3101

202-331-1458

Joseph Cox, President

9349 United States Potato Board
4949 S. Syracuse St.
#400
Denver, CO 80237

303-369-7783; *Fax:* 303-369-7718;
www.uspotatoes.com
Social Media: Facebook, Twitter, LinkedIn, YouTube, Pinterest, Instagram

Rob Davis, Chairman
Blair Richardson, President & CEO
Diana LeDoux, VP,Finance/Information Technology
David Fraser, VP, Industry Communciations
John Toaspern, Vice President, International

The nation's potato marketing organization. The central organizing force in implementing programs that will increase demand for potatoes, providing the ideas, information, tools and inspiration for the industry to unite in achieving common goals.
Founded in: 1971

9350 United States Tuna Foundation
1101 17th St NW
Suite 609
Washington, DC 20036-4718

202-857-0610; www.tunafacts.com

Desiree Filippone, Manager

Serves as an umbrella organization representing the various interests of the U.S. canned tuna industry. Representing the internationaln and domestic interests to federal and state regulations, to national legislation, to domestic marketing.
Founded in: 1976

9351 Vegetarian Awareness Network/VEGANET
4041G Hadley Road,
Suite 101
South Plainfield, NJ 07080

908-769-1160
800-872-8343; *Fax:* 908-769-1171
jasmineburroughs@wfcinc.com;
www.wholefoodsmagazine.com
Social Media: Facebook, Twitter, LinkedIn

Howard V. Wainer, President

Networks to promote healthful living, environmental healing, and respect for all life; to advance public awareness of the advantages of the increasingly popular vegetarian lifestyle; to enhance the visibility and accessibility of vegetarian products and services; and to facilitate the formation and expansion of local vegetarian organizations.
Founded in: 1980

9352 Vegetarian Resource Group
PO Box 1463
Baltimore, MD 21203

410-366-8343; *Fax:* 410-366-8804
vrg@vrg.org; www.vrg.org
Social Media: Facebook, Twitter

Debra Wasserman, Director

An organization dedicated to educating the public on vegetarianism and the interrelated issues of health, nutrition, ecology, ethics, and world hunger.
15000 Members
Founded in: 1982
Mailing list available for rent

9353 Vidalia Onion Committee
100 Vidalia Sweet Onion Drive
PO Box 1609
Vidalia, GA 30474

912-537-1918; *Fax:* 912-537-2166
info@vidaliaonion.org; www.vidaliaonion.org
Social Media: Facebook, Twitter, YouTube, Pinterest

Aries Haygood, Chairman
Michael E. Hively, Vice Chairman
Myrtle S. Jones, Secretary

Promote growth, distribution and awareness of this one of a kind crop.
225 Members
Founded in: 1931

9354 **Vinegar Institute**
1100 Johnson Ferry Road
Suite 300
Atlanta, GA 30342

404-252-3663; *Fax:* 404-252-0774
vidsmith@kellencompany.com;
www.versatilevinegar.org
Social Media: Facebook

Pamela A Chumley, President
Jeannie Milewski, Executive Director

Manufacturers and bottlers of vinegar and suppliers to the industry are the members of this association. Publications available only to members.
Founded in: 1967

9355 **Walnut Council**
1007 N 725 W
West Lafayette, IN 47906-9431

765-583-3501; *Fax:* 765-583-3512
walnutcouncil@walnutcouncil.org;
www.walnutcouncil.org

Jerry Van Sambeek, President
Dan Harris, Vice President
Liz Jackson, Executive Director
Bill Hoover, Treasurer
John Katzke, Quartermaster

Representing woodland owners, foresters, forest scientists and wood producing industry representatives. The purpose is to assist in the technical transfer of forest research to field applications, help build and maintain bettermarkets for wood products and nut crops.
1000 Members
Founded in: 1970

9356 **Western Dairy Association**
12000 Washington
Suite 175
Thornton, CO 80241

303-451-7711
800-274-6455; *Fax:* 303-451-0411
info@westerndairyassociation.org;
www.westerndairyassociation.org
Social Media: Facebook, Twitter, YouTube

Rick Podtburg, Chairman
Jim Webb, Vice-Chairman
Ron Shelton, Secretary
Tim Bernhardt, Treasurer
Cindy Haren, Chief Executive Officer

Leading dairy farmer members and the industry in a world class direction of partnerships and business resulting in economic viability, new innovations in dairy products and building stronger community commitment to dairy farms and dairy families.
Founded in: 1936

9357 **Western Growers Association**
17620 Fitch Street
Irvine, CA 92614
949-863-1000
800-333-4942; *Fax:* 949-863-9028
info@wga.com; www.wga.com

Stephen J. Barnard, Chairman
Bruce C. Taylor, Senior Vice Chairman
Victor Smith, Vice Chairman
John S. Manfre, Secretary
Mark J. Teixeria, Treasurer

Association for growers, shippers, packers, brokers and distributors of fruits and vegetables in California and Arizona.
3000 Members
Founded in: 1926

9358 **Western U.S. Agricultural Trade Association**
4601 NE 77th Ave
Suite 240
Vancouver, WA 98662

360-693-3373; *Fax:* 360-693-3464
export@wusata.org; www.wusata.org

Andy Anderson, Executive Director
Janet Kenefsky, Deputy Director
Tricia Walker, FundMatch Manager
Betsy Green, Branded Coordinator
Robin Koss, Branded Coordinator

Exporting resource for agribusinesses based in the Western United States.
200 Members
Founded in: 1980

9359 **Western United States Agricultural Trade Association**
4601 NE 77th Avenue
Suite 240
Vancouver, WA 98662

360-693-3373; *Fax:* 360-693-3464
export@wusata.org; www.wusata.org

Andy Anderson, Executive Director
Janet Kenefsky, Deputy Director
Tricia Walker, FundMatch Manager
Betsy Green, Branded Coordinator
Robin Koss, Branded Coordinator

This organization offers information and support to increase exports of US agricultural products.
200 Members
Founded in: 1980

9360 **Wheat Foods Council**
51 Red Fox Lane
Unit D
Ridgway, CO 81432
970-626-9828; *Fax:* 303-840-6877
wfc@wheatfoods.org; www.wheatfoods.org
Social Media: Facebook, Twitter

Don Brown, Chair
Debi Rogers, Vice Chair
Tim O'Connor, President
Gayle Veum, Vice President
Reid Christopherson, Treasurer/Secretary

An industry-wide partnership dedicated to increasing wheat and other grain foods consumption through nutrition information, education, research and promotional programs.
Founded in: 1972

9361 **Wild Blueberry Association of North America**
PO Box 100
Old Town, ME 04468

207-570-3535; *Fax:* 207-581-3499
wildblueberries@gwi.net;
www.wildblueberries.com
Social Media: Facebook, Twitter, Youtube, Pinterest, Googleplus

Ragnar Kamp, President
Mike Collins, Marketing Manager

Represents processors and growers of wild blueberries in Eastern Canada and Maine. The Association is focused on the generic promotion of wild blueberries around the world. It offers promotional materials, joint funding, product development, assistance, seminars, newsletters, supplier lists and ongoing support to users of wild blueberries in all retail, manufacturing, food service and bakery trade segments.
Founded in: 1981

9362 **Wine & Spirits Wholesalers of America, Inc**
805 15th Street NW
Suite 430
Washington, DC 20005
202-371-9792; *Fax:* 202-789-2405
Info@wswa.org; www.wswa.org
Social Media: Facebook, Twitter, YouTube, RSS

Craig Wolf, President and CEO
Jim Rowland, Senior VP, Government Affairs
Dawson Hobbs, Vice President, State Affairs
Reilly O Connor, Vice President, Government Affairs
Catherine McDaniel, Vice President, Government Affairs

Wine & Spirits Wholesalers of America, inc.(WSWA) is the national trade organization representing the wholesale tier of the wine and spirits industry. It is dedicated to advancing the interests and independence of wholesale distributors and brokers of wine and spirits.
450 Members
Founded in: 1943

9363 **Wine Appreciation Guild**
360 Swift Ave
Unit 30-40
S San Francisco, CA 94080

650-866-3020
800-239-9463; *Fax:* 650-866-3029
info@wineappreciation.com;
www.wineappreciation.com

James Mackey, Manager
Jason Simon, Manager
Jeff Szczesney, Contact
Hamlin Endicott, Contact
Amy Decker, Contact

Formed as the official successor in the distribution of wine accessories, and the publication and distribution of books and educational materials.
1500 Members
Founded in: 1973

9364 **Wine Institute**
425 Market St
Suite 1000
San Francisco, CA 94105

415-512-0151; *Fax:* 415-356-7569
info@wineinstitute.org; www.wineinstitute.org

Robert Koch, President/CEO
Kaye Clement, Executive Assistant
Betty Easter, Receptionist
Steve Gross, VP State Relations
Nancy Light, VP Communications

Dedicated to initiating and advocating state, federal and international public policy to enhance the environment for the responsible consumption and enjoyment of wine.
887 Members
Founded in: 1934

9365 **Wine and Spirits Shippers Association**
11800 Sunrise Valley Dr
Suite 332
Reston, VA 20191

703-860-2300
800-368-3167; *Fax:* 703-860-2422
info@wssa.com; www.wssa.com
Social Media: Facebook, Twitter, LinkedIn

V. James Andretta, Jr., Chairman Emeritus
Louis Healey, President
Howard Jacobs, Vice President
Alison Leavitt, Managing Director
Heather Randolph, Director of Operations

A non-profit shippers association composed of importers and exporters of beverages and allied products. Provides members, importers and ex-

porters with efficient and economical ocean transportation and other logestic services.
400 Members
Founded in: 1976

9366 Wine and Spirits Wholesalers of America, Inc.
805 15th Street, NW
Suite 430
Washington, DC 20036

202-371-9792; *Fax:* 202-789-2405
Info@wswa.org; www.wswa.org
Social Media: Facebook, Twitter, YouTube, RSS

Brien Fox, Chairman
Alan Dreeben, Immediate Past Chairman
Doug Epstein, Vice Chairman
Carmine Martignetti, Senior VP
Sydney Ross, Treasurer

National trade organization representing the wholesale branch of the wine and spirits industry.
450 Members
Founded in: 1943

9367 Women in Flavor & Fragrance Commerce
Association of Food Industries
3301 Route 66
Suite 205, Building C
Neptune, NJ 07753

732-922-0500; *Fax:* 732-922-0560
info@wffc.org; www.wffc.org
Social Media: Facebook, LinkedIn

Amy Marks-Mcgee, President
Kay Bardsley-Murano, Vice President
BEA HORNEDO, Secretary
ERICA LERMOND MCDONNELL, Treasurer
Dolores Avezzano, Sales Manager

Provides a center of education, camaraderie, support and networking opportunities for women in our industry. Our membership encompasses women involved is sales, purchasing, customer service as well as technical and laboratory careers. WFFC has timely seminars as well as social and networking opportunities for our members and the industry as a whole.
300 Members
Founded in: 1982

Newsletters

9368 AAMPlifier Bulletin
American Association of Meat Processors
One Meating Place
Elizabethtown, PA 17022

717-367-1168; *Fax:* 717-367-9096
aamp@aamp.com; www.aamp.com

Contains a wealth of information on industry trends, important national news, Association activities, and operational information to keep members fully informed about events affecting their business.
Frequency: Bi-Monthly
Founded in: 1939

9369 ABL Insider
American Beverage Licensees Association
5101 River Rd
Suite 108
Bethesda, MD 20816-1560

301-656-1494; *Fax:* 301-656-7539
info@ablusa.org; www.ablusa.org

Lyle Fitzsimmons, Editor

The voice of America's beer, wine & spirits retailers.
Frequency: Monthly

9370 ADPI Weekly Newsletter
American Dairy Products Institute
116 N York Street
Suite 200
Elmhurst, IL 60126

630-530-8700; *Fax:* 630-530-8707
info@adpi.org; www.adpi.org

Electronic communication of industry news, regulatory developments, and association matters.
Frequency: Weekly
Circulation: 1000

9371 AFFI Newsletter
American Frozen Food Institute
2000 Corporate Ridge
Suite 1000
McLean, VA 22102-7862

703-821-0770; *Fax:* 703-821-1350
info@affi.com; www.affi.com

Kraig R Naasz, President/CEO
Jason Bassett, Director Legislative Affairs
Chuck Fuqua, VP Communications
Robert L Garfield, SVP Public Policy/Intl Affairs
Frequency: Weekly

9372 AHA Quarterly
American Herb Association
PO Box 1673
Nevada City, CA 95959-1673

530-265-9552; *Fax:* 530-274-3140;
www.ahaherb.com

Kathi Keville, Director
Robert Brucia, Co-Director
Marion Wyckoff, Secretary

Reports on the latest scientific studies, new herb, aromatherapy, cooking and gardening books, international herb news, legal and environmental issues, herb-related events and conferences.
Cost: $20.00
20 Pages
Frequency: w/Membership
Founded in: 1981

9373 AICR Newsletter
American Institute for Cancer Research
1759 R St NW
Washington, DC 20009-2570

202-328-7744
800-843-8114; *Fax:* 202-328-7226
aicrweb@aicr.org; www.aicr.org

Marilyn Gentry, President

Explains current cancer research, provides recipes and menu ideas for healthy eating, and offers practical advice to lower cancer risk.
Frequency: Quarterly
Circulation: 1.6MM
Founded in: 1982

9374 ALBC News
American Livestock Breeds Conservancy
15 Hillsboro Street
PO Box 477
Pittsboro, NC 27312

919-542-5704; *Fax:* 919-545-0022
albc@albc-usa.org; www.albc-usa.org

Marjorie Bender, Prog. Coord./Research
Don Schrider, Communication Director
Charles Bassett, Executive Director
Angelique Thompson, Operations Manager
Jennifer Kendall, Communications Director

Breeders directory; annual conference; catalog of publications available.
Cost: $30.00
20 Pages
Circulation: 3000
ISSN: 1064-1599
Founded in: 1977
Printed in one color on matte stock

9375 AMSA eNews
American Meat Science Association
2441 Village Green Pl
Champaign, IL 61822-7676

800-517-AMSA; *Fax:* 888-205-5834; *Fax:* 217-356-5370
information@meatscience.org;
www.meatscience.org

William Mikel, President
Scott J. Eilert, President Elect
Casey B. Frye, Treasurer

Published for all AMSA members every other week, including member news and meat science information updates.

9376 APIS
CITA International
3464 W Earll Drive
Suites E & F
Phoenix, AZ 85017

602-447-0480; *Fax:* 602-447-0305
esam@citainternational.com;
www.citainternational.com

EM Morsy, Editor
PE Pederson, Advertising/Sales

The international bulletin for specialty livestock, pet animal and ag-chem product developments.
Frequency: Quarterly
Founded in: 1988

9377 ASBC Newsletter
American Society of Brewing Chemists
3340 Pilot Knob Rd
Eagan, MN 55121-2055

651-454-7250; *Fax:* 651-454-0766
asbc@scisoc.org; www.asbcnet.org

Steven C Nelson, VP

Contains the annual meeting program, lists of ASBC committees and reports, and local section news.
Frequency: Quarterly
Circulation: 800+
Founded in: 1934

9378 ASTA Advocate
American Spice Trade Association
2025 M St NW
Suite 800
Washington, DC 20036-2422
202-367-1127; *Fax:* 202-367-2127
info@astaspice.org; www.astaspice.org

Donna Tainter, President
Roger Clarke, Vice President/ Secretary
Gaspare Colletti, Treasurer
David Howe, Associate Group Director

Electronic newsletter designed to keep members informed about the spice industry, events impacting the industry and ASTA activities. ASTA Advocate is ASTA's regulatory newsletter.
Frequency: Membership Dues Vary
Founded in: 1907

9379 Agri Times Northwest
Sterling Ag
PO Box 189
Pendleton, OR 97801

541-276-7845; *Fax:* 541-276-7964;
www.agritimes.com/

Virgil Rupp, CEO/President
Sterling Allen, Publisher/Marketing Director

Regional agricultural newspaper.
Cost: $20.00
16 Pages
Circulation: 3700
Printed in 4 colors on newsprint stock

9380 Agri-Pulse
International Dairy Foods Association

1250 H Street NW
Suite 900
Washington, DC 20005

202-737-4332; *Fax:* 202-331-7820
membership@idfa.org; www.idfa.org
Social Media: Facebook, Twitter, YouTube, Blog

Connie Tipton, President & CEO
Mike Nosewicz, Chair
Brian Perry, Vice Chair
Jon Davis, Secretary
Ed Mullins, Treasurer

The latest information and news in agricultural information. Investigating several aspects of the food, fuel, feed and fiber industries, looking at the economic, statistical and financial trends and evaluate the changes impacting businesses.
550 Members
Frequency: Weekly

9381 **Alcoholic Beverage Control Fast: From the State Capitals**
Wakeman Walworth
PO Box 7376
Alexandria, VA 22307-7376

703-768-9600; *Fax:* 703-768-9690;
www.statecapitals.com/alcoholbev.html

Keyes Walworth, Publisher

Covers binge drinking laws, internet sales, advertising, taxes, bottle bills, Sunday sales laws, license regulation, drunk driving laws, under-age drinking, mini-bottles and other state laws affecting beer, liquor and wine distribution.
4 Pages
Frequency: Weekly
Founded in: 1962
Printed in one color on matte stock

9382 **Alcoholic Beverage Executives' Newsletter International**
Patricia Kennedy
PO Box 3188
Omaha, NE 68103-1088

402-397-5514; *Fax:* 402-397-3843

Patricia Kennedy, Editor

Current news of the wine, beer, and distilled spirits marketplace, and provides information and ideas for the marketing and advertising campaigns of these beverages.
Cost: $275.00
Frequency: Weekly
ISSN: 0889-3510

9383 **American Agriculturist**
Farm Progress Companies
255 38th Avenue
Suite P
St Charles, IL 60174-5410

630-462-2224
800-441-1410
jvogel@farmprogress.com;
www.farmprogress.com/american-agriculturist/

John Vogel, Editor
Willie Vogt, Cororate Editorial Director
Dan Crummett, Executive Editor

Serves Northeast producers with information to help them maximize their productivity and profitability. Each issue is packed with information, ideas, news and analysis.
Cost: $29.65
Frequency: Monthly
Founded in: 1842

9384 **American Bakers Association Bulletin**
American Bakers Association
1350 I Street NW
Suite 1290
Washington, DC 20005-3305

202-789-0300; *Fax:* 202-898-1164
kkotche@americanbakers.org;
www.americanbakers.org

Kelly Kotche, Communications/Membership Manager
Paul Abenante, President/CEO

The association's newsletter that covers the conventions.
Frequency: Semi-Annual

9385 **American Beekeeping Federation Newsletter**
American Beekeeping Federation
3525 Piedmont Rd
Bldg 5 Suite 300
Atlanta, GA 30305-1509

404-760-2875; *Fax:* 404-240-0998
info@abfnet.org; www.abfnet.org

Regina Robuck, Executive Director

ABF-member benefit to inform members about ABF activities and happenings in the beekeeping industry.
24 Pages
Frequency: Bi-Monthly
Circulation: 1,200
Founded in: 1943

9386 **American Herb Association Quarterly Newsletter**
American Herb Association
PO Box 1673
Nevada City, CA 95959-1673

530-265-9552; *Fax:* 530-274-3140;
www.ahaherb.com

Kathi Keville, Director
Robert Brucia, Co-Director
Marion Wyckoff, Secretary

Updates and news on the herbal industry, such as; new scientific herbal and aromatherapy studies, plants interaction with ecology, reports on legal issues about herbs, a calendar of herbal and aromatherapy events, and a media report listing the herbal stories in the media.
Cost: $20.00
Frequency: Membership Fee
Founded in: 1981

9387 **American Institute of Baking Technical Bulletin**
American Institute of Baking
PO Box 3999
Manhattan, KS 66505-3999

785-537-4750
866-342-4772; *Fax:* 785-565-6060
bissc@bissc.org; www.bissc.org

James Munyon, President

Developed to keep the baking and allied trades apprised of current trends in ingredients, products, equipment, processing, packaging, nutrition and research.
Frequency: Monthly

9388 **American Meat Institute: Newsletter**
American Meat Institute
1150 Connecticut Ave Nw
Suite 1200
Washington, DC 20036-4126

202-587-4200; *Fax:* 202-587-4300;
www.meatami.com

J Patrick Boyle, CEO
Janet Riley, Editor
Ayoka Blandford, Marketing Manager

Subscription includes news of legislative and government regulations and actions relevant to the meat industry.
Frequency: Quarterly
Circulation: 3000
Founded in: 1906

9389 **American Society of Agricultural Consultants News**
American Society of Agricultural Consultants
950 S Cherry Street
Suite 508
Denver, CO 80246-2664

303-758-3514; *Fax:* 303-758-0190;
www.agconsultants.org

Deborah Wiig, Editor

Informs ASAC members of news regarding members, events, education and government issues.
8-12 Pages
Frequency: Quarterly
Circulation: 200
Founded in: 1963
Printed in on newsprint stock

9390 **American Soybean Association Newsletter**
American Soybean Association
12125 Woodcrest Executive
Suite 100
Creve Coeur, MO 63141-5009

314-576-1770
800-688-7692; *Fax:* 314-576-2786
bcallanan@soy.org; www.soygrowers.com

Steve Censky, CEO
Neal Bredehoeft, President
Bob Metz, VP

Mission is to improve US soybean farmer profitability.
Frequency: Monthly
Founded in: 1920
Printed in 4 colors on glossy stock

9391 **Angus Beef Bulletin**
American Angus Association
3201 Frederick Ave
St Joseph, MO 64506-2997

816-383-5100; *Fax:* 816-233-9703
angus@angus.org; www.angus.org
Social Media: Facebook, Twitter

Joe Hampton, Chair
Jarold Callahan, Vice Chair
Phil Trowbridge, Treasurer

To provide programs, services, technology and leadership to enhance the genetics of the Angus breed, broaden its influence within the beef industry, and expand the market for superior tasting, high-quality Angus beef worldwide. Achieve Angus excellence through information.
Cost: $80.00
30+M Members
Frequency: Membership Fees Vary
Founded in: 1883

9392 **Association of American Seed Control Officials Bulletin**
Utah Department of Agriculture
801 Summit Crossing Place
Suite C
Gastonia, NC 28054

704-810-8877; *Fax:* 704-853-4109;
www.seedcontrol.org

Ron Pence, President
John Heaton, Services Director
Brenda Ball, Second VP
Brenda Ball, Second VP
Greg Helmbrecht, Treasurer

Seed laws in the US and Canada.
Frequency: Annual

9393 Association of Food Industries Newsletter
Association of Food Industries
3301 State Route 66
Suite 205, Building C
Neptune, NJ 07753-2705

732-922-3008; *Fax:* 732-922-3590
info@naooa.org; www.naooa.org

Robert Bauer, President

Offers information & education on customs and usage of trade in the food industry and current events in the business.
Founded in: 1906

9394 BEMA Newsletter
Bakery Equipment Manufacturers Association
10740 Nall Avenue
Suite 230
Overland Park, KS 66211

913-338-1300; *Fax:* 913-338-1327
info@bema.org; www.bema.org

Published by BEMA, to keep members informed about the latest baking and food industry news.
Frequency: Quarterly

9395 Bakers Band Together to Demand Relief-ABA Calls for March on Washington
American Bakers Association
1120 Connecticut Avenue NW
Washington, DC 200036

800-226-5377; www.aba.com

Robb Mac Kie, President
Frequency: Monthly

9396 Beer Marketer's Insights Newsletter
Beer Marketer's Insights
49 E Maple Ave
Suffern, NY 10901-5507

845-624-2337; *Fax:* 845-624-2340;
www.beerinsights.com

Benj Steinman, President

Reports on the competitive battle among brewers for a share of the beer market. Analyzes recent legislation and factors that affect the industry.
Frequency: Monthly

9397 Beer Perspectives
National Beer Wholesalers Association
1101 King Street
Suite 600
Alexandria, VA 22314-2965

703-683-4300; *Fax:* 703-683-8965
info@nbwa.org; www.nbwa.org
Social Media: Facebook, Twitter

Craig A Purser, President & CEO
Michael Johnson, EVP
Rebecca Spicer, VP Public Affairs/Chief
Paul Pisano, SVP Industry Affairs/Gen. Counsel

NBWA's newsletter reporting legislative, regulatory and industry news of importance to beer distributors.
Frequency: Bi-Weekly

9398 Beer Statistics News
Beer Marketer's Insights
49 E Maple Ave
Suffern, NY 10901-5507

845-624-2337; *Fax:* 845-624-2340;
www.beerinsights.com

Benj Steinnan, CEO/President
Jerry Curley, Circulation Manager

Supplies data for major brewers' shipments in 39 reporting states.
Cost: $450.00
Frequency: Annual+

9399 Beverage Digest
Beverage Digest
PO Box 621
Bedford Hills, NY 10507-0621

914-244-0700; *Fax:* 914-244-0774
order@beverage-digest.com;
www.beverage-digest.com

John Sicher, Editor/Publisher
Tom Fine, Managing Editor

Authoritative publication covering the non-alcoholic beverages industry.
Cost: $675.00
Frequency: 22 issues per y
Founded in: 1982

9400 Beverage World Periscope
Keller International Publishing Corporation
150 Great Neck Rd
Suite 400
Great Neck, NY 11021-3309

516-829-9722; *Fax:* 516-829-9306;
www.supplychainbrain.com

Terry Beirne, Publisher
Bryan DeLuca, Editor
Jerry Keller, President
Mary Chavez, Director of Sales

Analysis of developments as they occur in the beverage marketplace, presented in a tightly-written, four-color tabloid format, makes this a unique newsletter. This publication limits advertising to tabloid or standard pages.
Frequency: Monthly
Circulation: 33000
Founded in: 1882

9401 Bottled Water Reporter
Bottled Water Association
1700 Diagonal Road
Suite 650
Alexandria, VA 22314-2844
703-683-5213; *Fax:* 703-683-4074
mbusetti@bottledwater.org;
www.bottledwater.org

Sabrina Hicks, Editor

Trade news.

9402 Brewers Bulletin
PO Box 677
Thiensville, WI 53092

262-242-6105; *Fax:* 262-242-5133
bulletindigest@milwpc.com

Thomas Volke, President

Brewing industry newspaper.
Cost: $53.00
Circulation: 550
Founded in: 1907

9403 Brown Swiss Bulletin
Brown Swiss Cattle Breeder's Assoc of the USA
800 Pleasant St
Beloit, WI 53511-5456

608-365-4474; *Fax:* 608-365-5577
info@brownswissusa.com;
www.brownswissusa.com

David Wallace, Executive Secretary
Charlotte Muenzenberg, Sup't of Records
Leonard Johnson, Genetic Programs/Show Manager
Cost: $25.00
Frequency: Monthly
ISSN: 0007-2516

9404 Bu$Iness of Herbs
Herb Growing and Marketing Network
PO Box 245
Silver Spring, PA 17575-0245

717-393-3295; *Fax:* 717-393-9261
herbworld@aol.com; www.herbworld.com

Finds a wide variety of articles that will help with marketing, growing and genergal business issues. Has profiles of herb businesses and how they've created a business that allows them to support themselves with their passion.
Cost: $48.00
Frequency: Monthly

9405 Business of Herbs
Northwind Farm Publications
439 Ponderosa Way
Jemez Springs, NM 87025-8036

505-829-3448; *Fax:* 505-829-3449;
www.herbworld.com/businessofherbs.htm

David Oliver, Publisher
Paula Oliver, Editor

News of interest for herb growers and marketers. Covers all aspects of the herb industry and offers book reviews, events calendar, new products, business profiles, sources, resources, networking and more. Geared to small businesses.
Cost: $24.00
48 Pages
Frequency: Bi-Monthly
Circulation: 2,500
Printed in one color on matte stock

9406 Calorie Control Commentary
Calorie Control Council
2611 Winslow Dr Ne
Atlanta, GA 30305-3777

678-608-3200; *Fax:* 404-252-0774
webmaster@caloriecontrol.org;
www.caloriecontrol.org

Timely information on low-calorie and reduced-fat foods and beverages, weight management, physical activity and healthy eating.
60 Members
Founded in: 1966

9407 Cameron's Foodservice Marketing Reporter
Cameron's Publications
5423 Sheridan Drive
PO Box 676
Williamsville, NY 14231

519-586-8785; *Fax:* 519-586-8816
mail@cameronpub.com;
www.cameronpub.com

Successful promotion and advertising case histories for the restaurant and hotel industry.

9408 Can Shipments Report
Can Manufacturers Institute
1730 Rhode Island Ave Nw
Suite 1000
Washington, DC 20036-3112

202-232-4677; *Fax:* 202-232-5756;
www.cancentral.com

Robert Budway, President
Shawn Relly, Editor/Publisher

Provides a summary of the past year's accomplishments, as well as a look at the strategy to fulfill goals in the coming year.
Frequency: Annual
Founded in: 1938

9409 Capitol Line-Up
American Association of Meat Processors

PO Box 269
Elizabethtown, PA 17022

717-367-1168; *Fax:* 717-367-9096
aamp@aamp.com; www.aamp.com

Tom K Inboden, President
Jon Frohling, First VP
Daniel T Weber, Second VP

Deals strictly with governmental affairs in the industry. Keeps AAMP members up to date with the latest news about government affairs from Congress and key agencies in Washington, as well as state legislatures and state regulatory bodies.
Frequency: 26x Yearly

9410 Catering Service Idea Newsletter
Prosperity & Profits Unlimited
PO Box 416
Denver, CO 80201

303-573-5564

A Doyle, Editor

Catering service business ideas and possibilities.

9411 Center of the Plate
American Culinary Federation
180 Center Place Way
St Augustine, FL 32095-8859

904-824-4468
800-624-9458; *Fax:* 904-825-4758
acf@acfchefs.net; www.acfchefs.org

Heidi Cramb, Executive Director
Kay Orde, Editor
Joachim Buchner, CEO
Michael Feierstein, Administrative Assistant
Bryan Hunt, Graphic Designer

Official membership newsletter of the American Culinary Federation.
Cost: $50.00
Frequency: Monthly
Circulation: 25,000
Founded in: 1956

9412 Cereal Foods World
AACC International
3340 Pilot Knob Rd
Eagan, MN 55121-2055

651-454-7250
800-328-7560; *Fax:* 651-454-0766
aacc@scisoc.org; www.aaccnet.org

Amy Hope, Publisher
Jody Grider, Executive Editor
Jordana Anker, Managing Editor
Greg Grahek, Director, Publications

Covers grain-based food science, technology, and new product development. Includes articles that focus on advances in grain-based food science and the application of these advances to product development and food production practices.
Frequency: Bimonthly
ISSN: 0146-6283

9413 Champagne Wines Information Bureau
KCSA
800 2nd Avenue
5th Floor
New York, NY 10017-4709

212-682-6300
800-642-4267; *Fax:* 212-697-0910
info@champagnes.com;
www.champagnes.com

Jean-Louis Carbonnier, Editor
Herbert L Corbin, President/CEO

Representative of Comite Interprofessionnel duVinde Champagne, Epernay, France.
4 Pages
Circulation: 10000
Printed in one color on matte stock

9414 Cheese Reporter
Cheese Reporter Publishing Company
2810 Crossroads Dr
Suite 3000
Madison, WI 53718-7972

608-246-8430; *Fax:* 608-246-8431
info@cheesereporter.com;
www.cheesereporter.com

Dick Groves, Publisher/Editor
Kevin Thome, Marketing Director
Betty Mertes, Circulation Manager

Leading weekly publication serving manufacturers and marketers of cheese, butter, ice cream, yogurt and other fermented milk foods, whey and other dairy processors.
Cost: $150.00
16 Pages
Frequency: Weekly
Circulation: 2000
ISSN: 0009-2142
Founded in: 1876
Printed in 4 colors on n stock

9415 Coffee Reporter
National Coffee Association
15 Maiden Ln
Suite 1405
New York, NY 10038-5113

212-766-4007; *Fax:* 212-766-5815
info@ncausa.org; www.ncausa.org

Robert F Nelson, President
Joseph F DeRupo, Communications/PR Director

Contains news of NCA activities and programs, new product development and market trends in both the U.S. and global coffee industry, regulatory action affecting the U.S. coffee industry and statistical data on ICO prices and U.S. retail prices. A single copy subscription is supplied free of charge to members, non-eligible parties for membership the cost is $40.00
Cost: $65.00
Frequency: Quarterly

9416 Coffee, Sugar and Cocoa Exchange Daily Market Report
New York Board of Trade
1 North End Avenue
New York, NY 10282-1101

212-748-4000
877-877-8890; *Fax:* 212-748-4039
webmaster@nybot.com; www.nybot.com

Leonel Fern ndez, President

Offers market reports on the stock market exchange covering foods and specific food investing.

9417 Communique
CHRIE
2810 N Parham Road
Suite 230
Richmond, VA 23294

804-346-4800; *Fax:* 804-346-5009
info@chrie.org; www.chrie.org
Social Media: Facebook, Twitter, LinkedIn

Susan Fournier, President
Josette Katz, Vice President
Chris Roberts, Secretary
John Drysdale, Treasurer
Kathy McCarty, CEO

Council on Hotel, Restaurant, and Institutional Educations informational newsletter.
Cost: $45.00
Frequency: Monthly

9418 Concessionworks Newsletter
National Association of Concessionaires
35 E Wacker Dr
Suite 1816
Chicago, IL 60601-2270

312-236-3858; *Fax:* 312-236-7809
scross@naconline.org; www.naconline.org

Charles A Winans, Executive Director

For members with updates on association happenings, feature articles, new member listings, product news and industry updates.
Founded in: 1944

9419 Country World Newspaper
Echo Publishing Company
401 Church Street
PO Box 596
Sulphur Springs, TX 75483

903-885-8663
800-245-2149; *Fax:* 903-885-8768;
www.countryworldnews.com

Scott Keys, Publisher
Lori Cope, Editor
Jim Horton, Advertising Manager

A newspaper offering agricultural information to farmers, ranchers, dairyfarmers, and agribusinesses.
Cost: $24.00
36 Pages
Frequency: Weekly
Circulation: 16200
Founded in: 1981
Printed in 4 colors on newsprint stock

9420 Crop Protection Management
2892 Crescent Avenue
Eugene, OR 97408

541-343-5641
800-874-3276; *Fax:* 541-686-0248

Jeff Powell, Publisher

This newsletter covers all aspects of crop management and protection, including pesticides, agricultural chemicals and legislation.
Frequency: 5 per year

9421 Daily Advocate
Thomson Newspapers
PO Box 220
Greenville, OH 45331-220

937-548-3151; *Fax:* 937-548-3913
webmaster@dailyadvocate.com;
www.dailyadvocate.com

Gary Lamberg, Publisher
Bob Robinson, Editor
Ken Bowen, Circulation Manager
Ashley Fritz, Graphic Designer
Barb Wilson, Business Manager

Farming interests, grain, livestock. Sections on senior citizens, farmers, builders, religion, sports, as well as special sections on agriculture and home improvement.
Cost: $117.00
Frequency: Daily
Founded in: 1883

9422 Dairy Council Digest
National Dairy Council
Interstate Place II
100 Elwood Davis Road
North Syracuse, NY 13212

315-472-9143; *Fax:* 315-472-0506
ndc@dairyinformation.com;
www.nationaldairycouncil.org
Social Media: Facebook, Twitter

Provides a comprehensive review of research on topics ranging from the benefits of dairy foods in child nutrition, to dairy's potential protective role for metabolic syndrome and type 2 diabetes.
Frequency: Bi-Monthly
Founded in: 1915

9423 **Dairy Industry Newsletter**
Eden Publishing Company
10255 W Higgins Road
Suite 900
Rosemont, IL 60018-4924

312-240-2880;
www.dairyindustrynewsletter.com

Resource serving all sectors of the dairy industry. Reports on commercial, trade, political and market information.
8 Pages
Frequency: 25x Yearly
Printed in 2 colors on glossy stock

9424 **Dairy Market Report**
American Butter Institute
2101 Wilson Boulevard
Suite 400
Arlington, VA 22201

703-243-5630; *Fax:* 703-841-9328
AMiner@nmpf.org; www.nmpf.org/ABI

Peter Vitaliano, Editor

9425 **Dairy Profit Weekly**
DairyBusiness Communications
6437 Collamer Road
East Syracuse, NY 13057-1031

315-703-7979
800-334-1904; *Fax:* 315-703-7988;
www.dairybusiness.com

Dave Natzke, Editorial Director
Joel Hastings, Publisher
Eleanor Jacobs, Regional Editor

Latest information, tips, and trends.
Cost: $179.00
4 Pages
Frequency: Weekly
Circulation: 1700
Printed in 2 colors on newsprint stock

9426 **Dairy-Deli-Bake Digest**
International Dairy-Deli-Bakery Association
636 Science Drive
PO Box 5528
Madison, WI 53705-0528

608-310-5000; *Fax:* 608-238-6330
IDDBA@iddba.org; www.iddbanet.org

Carol Christison, Executive Director

Packed with practical how-to information to help readers run a successful business. Features new management trends, new products, reports, reviews, association news, features, and consumer attitudes and trends.
Frequency: Monthly
Founded in: 1964

9427 **Dairy-Deli-Bake Wrap-Up**
International Dairy-Deli-Bakery Association
636 Science Drive
PO Box 5528
Madison, WI 53705-0528

608-310-5000; *Fax:* 608-238-6330
IDDBA@iddba.org; www.iddbanet.org

Carol Christison, Executive Director

Covers IDDBA's seminars, expositions, member news, awards, and programs and services.
Frequency: Quarterly
Founded in: 1964

9428 **Distributor News**
Food Industry Suppliers Association
1207 Sunset Drive
Greensboro, NC 27408

336-274-6311; *Fax:* 336-691-1839
stella@fisanet.org; www.fisanet.org

David Brink, President
Bob Morava, Vice President

FISA's official newsletter, publishing industry happenings and business management information.
245 Members
Frequency: Quarterly
Founded in: 1968

9429 **Doane's Agricultural Report**
Doane Agricultural Services
77 Westport Plz
Suite 250
St Louis, MO 63146-3121

314-569-2700
866-647-0918; *Fax:* 314-569-1083;
www.doane.com

Dan Manternach, Editor

Provides information to US farmers and agricultural professionals. Doane keeps you up to date on factors affecting your farm program benefits and production costs too.
Frequency: Weekly

9430 **FDRS Newsletter**
Food Distribution Research Society
PO Box 441110
Fort Washington, MD 20749

301-292-1970; *Fax:* 301-292-1787
Jonathan_baros@ncsu.edu
fdrs.tamu.edu

John Park, President
Ron Rainey, President-Elect
Kellie Raper, Secretary/ Treasurer
Jennifer Dennis, Director
Stan Ernst, Director

Reports on Society events and happenings as well as related news from the industry and abroad.
Frequency: Quarterly

9431 **FPA Update**
Flexible Packaging Association
971 Corporate Blvd
Suite 403
Linthicum, MD 21090-2253

410-694-0800; *Fax:* 410-694-0900
fpa@flexpack.org; www.flexpack.org

Marla Donahue, President

Updating membership as well as the industry on FPA activities, events and accomplishments throughthe FPA Update, which is included within Flexible Packaging magazine.
Frequency: Monthly

9432 **FSC Newsletter**
Food Safety Consortium
110 Agriculture Building
University of Arkansas
Fayetteville, AR 72701

479-575-5647; *Fax:* 479-575-7531
fsc@cavern.uark.edu; www.fsconsortium.net

Dave Edmark, Communications Manager

A production of the three member schools of the consortium; University of Arkansas, Iowa State University and Kansas State University.
Frequency: Monthly
Founded in: 1988

9433 **FYI ASTA**
American Spice Trade Association
2025 M St NW
Suite 800
Washington, DC 20036-2422

202-367-1127; *Fax:* 202-367-2127
info@astaspice.org; www.astaspice.org

Donna Tainter, President
Roger Clarke, Vice President/ Secretary
Gaspare Colletti, Treasurer
David Howe, Associate Group Director

Electronic newsletter designed to keep members informed about the spice industry, events impacting the industry and ASTA activities. The resource for members looking for information about ASTA, our programs and services.
Frequency: Membership Dues Vary
Founded in: 1907

9434 **Federal Focus**
Natural Products Association
2112 E 4th St
Suite 200
Santa Ana, CA 92705-3816

714-460-7732
800-966-6632; *Fax:* 714-460-7444;
www.npainfo.org
Social Media: Facebook, Twitter, LinkedIn

John F. Gay, Executive Director & CEO
Jeffrey Wright, President

Provides information and alerts from the federal and state agencies that affect the industry.
1900+ Members
Frequency: Monthly
Founded in: 1936

9435 **Fence Post**
423 Main Street
Windsor, CO 80550-5129

970-686-5691
800-275-5646; *Fax:* 970-686-5694;
www.thefencepost.com

Jim Eisberry, President
Gary Sweeney, Publisher
Luke Gonzales, Business Manager
Tom Vilsack, Secretary

Farming news and reports.
Cost: $39.00
Frequency: Weekly

9436 **Food Allergy News**
Food Allergy & Anaphlaxis Network
11781 Lee Jackson Mem Hwy
Suite 160
Fairfax, VA 22033-3309

703-691-3179
800-929-4040; *Fax:* 703-691-2713;
www.foodallergy.org

Anne Munoz-Furlong, President
Andreia Miller, Editor

Allergy newsletter with two pages of allergy-free recipes, coping strategies, research and studies.
Cost: $30.00
12 Pages
Circulation: 28000
ISSN: 1075-4318
Founded in: 1991
Printed in 2 colors on glossy stock

9437 **Food Industry Futures: A Strategy Service**
CRS
PO Box 430
Fayetteville, NC 28302

910-486-9059; *Fax:* 910-486-9058

Ian Cuthill, Publisher, Editor

Includes new developments concerning management or marketing practices, mergers and acquisitions, economics, trade policies, etc. It covers the industry from farm and retail stores, mostly in the US but also internationally. Accepts advertising.
Cost: $150.00
4 Pages

9438 **Food Industry Newsletter**
Newsletters

PO Box 342730
Bethesda, MD 20827-2730

301-469-8507; *Fax:* 301-469-7271
foodltr@aol.com

Ellis Meredith, Publisher
Ray Marsili, Editor
Alice Corcoran, Circulation Manager

Concise, objective report for busy food executives, covering major food industry developments, including mergers and acquisitions, new trends and products, corporate and marketing strategies, etc. In addition to 22 regular issues a year, subscription also includes Special Food Marketing Reports on timely matters.
Cost: $245.00
Frequency: twice monthly except Aug.
Founded in: 1972

9439 **Food Insight**
International Food Information Council
1100 Connecticut Ave Nw
Suite 430
Washington, DC 20036-4120

202-296-6540; *Fax:* 202-296-6547
foodinfo@ific.org; www.ific.org

Dave Schmidt, President
Nick Alexander, Associate Editor
Michael Hayes, Copy Editor
8 Pages
Frequency: 6 issues per ye
Circulation: 45000
Printed in 4 colors on glossy stock

9440 **Food Institute Report**
American Institute of Food Distribution
1 Broadway
2nd Floor
Elmwood Park, NJ 07407-1844

201-791-5570; *Fax:* 201-791-5222;
www.foodinstitute.com

Brian Todd, President
Mike Slattery, Chairman
Michael Sansolo, Senior Vice President
Joe Crocker, Vice Chairman
Donna George, Treasurer

Membership includes a subscription to The Food Institute Report, an in-depth weekly digest that delivers insights on new products, crop markets, legislation, customer demographics, mergers, food industry statistics, competitors and market trends.
Frequency: Weekly
Circulation: 3000
Founded in: 1928

9441 **Food Merchants Advocate**
New York State Food Merchant
130 Washington Ave
Albany, NY 12210-2220

518-463-0300; *Fax:* 518-462-5474;
www.nyscar.org

Christopher Pellnat, Editor

A tabloid newspaper for food retailers.
Cost: $10.00
Frequency: Monthly

9442 **Food Safety Professional**
Carpe Diem
208 Floral Vale Boulevard
Yardley, PA 19067

215-860-7800; *Fax:* 215-860-7900;
www.foodquality.com

Paul Juestrich, Production Manager
Ken Potuznik, Director
Lisa Dionne, Creative Director

The Food Safety Professional is a quarterly publication of The antional Registry of Food Safety Professionals. Practical hands on article and advice form the experts will keep you informed of the latest technique an technologies in food safety.'
Cost: $20.00
Frequency: Quarterly
Circulation: 30,000

9443 **Food Trade News**
Best-Met Publishing
5537 Twin Knolls Rd
Suite 438
Columbia, MD 21045-3270

410-730-5013; *Fax:* 410-740-4680
office@best-met.com; www.best-met.com

Jeff Metzger, Publisher
Terri Maloney, Editor
Beth Pripstein, Office Manager
Cost: $63.00
Frequency: Monthly
Printed in one color on matte stock

9444 **Food World Information Services**
Best-Met Publishing Company
5537 Twin Knolls Rd
Suite 438
Columbia, MD 21045-3270

410-730-5013; *Fax:* 410-740-4680
tmaloney@best-met.com; www.best-met.com

Jeff Metzger, Publisher
Terri Maloney, Editor
Beth Pripstein, Office Manager
Richard J. Bestany, President

Provides market data for Baltimore, Washington, Central Pennsylvania and Philadelphia
Frequency: Monthly
Printed in on newsprint stock

9445 **Food for Thought**
D/FW Grocers Association
3044 Old Denton Rd
Suite 111, PMB 323
Carrollton, TX 75007

214-731-3132
800-791-6590; *Fax:* 469-574-5252
info@dfwga.net; www.dfwga.net

Offers information on grocery retailing and items of interest to members of the Grocers Association.
Frequency: Quarterly
Circulation: 1,000
Founded in: 1947

9446 **FoodTalk**
Pike & Fischer
PO Box 25277
Alexandria, VA 22313

703-548-3146; *Fax:* 703-548-3017
info@setantapublishing.com;
www.setantapublishing.com

Declan Couroy, Editor/Publisher

Sanitation tips for food workers.
Cost: $120.00
Frequency: Quarterly
Circulation: 5000
Founded in: 1987
Printed in 2 colors on matte stock

9447 **Friday Notes**
Council for Agricultural Science and Technology
4420 West Lincold Way
Ames, IA 50014-3447

515-292-2125; *Fax:* 515-292-4512
cast@cast-science.org; www.cast-science.org

John Bonner, Executive VP
Lynette Allen, Assistant Editor

Electronic newsletter featuring lead articles on current topics being discussed in agriculture, congressional updates, and advance announcements of upcoming CAST publications and activities.
Frequency: 48x Yearly
Founded in: 1972

9448 **GRAS Flavoring Substances 25**
Flavor & Extract Manufacturers Association
1620 I Street NW
Suite 925
Washington, DC 20006

202-293-5800; *Fax:* 202-462-8998;
www.femaflavor.org
Social Media: YouTube, RSS Feed

Ed R. Hays, Ph.D., President
George C. Robinson, III, President Elect
Mark Scott, Treasurer
Arthur Schick, VP & Secretary
John Cox, Executive Director

The 25th publication by the Expert Panel of the Flavor and Extract Manufacturers Association provides an update on recent progress in the consideration of flavoring ingredients generally recognized as safe under the Food Additive Amendment.
Frequency: Biennial
Founded in: 1909

9449 **Global Food Marketer**
Food Export USA
309 West Washington
Suite 600
Chicago, IL 60606

312-334-9200; *Fax:* 312-334-9230
info@foodexportusa.org;
www.foodexportusa.org

Tim F Hamilton, Executive Director
Daleen D Richmond, Deputy Director

Newsletter for US exporters, containing useful articles, updates on overseas market conditions and trends, marketing tips, a column by a food export helpline counselor, and calendar of upcoming events.
Frequency: Bi-Monthly
Founded in: 1973

9450 **Gourmet News**
Oser Communications Group
1877 N Kolb Road
Tuscon, AZ 85715

520-721-1300; www.gourmetnews.com

Rocelle Aragon, Editor
Kate Seymour, Senior Associate Publisher

The authoritative voice, and publication of choice for thousands of professionals in the gourmet and specialty food business. Reports timely and trustworty stories about events, issues, trends and other happenings within the trade.
Cost: $65.00
Frequency: Monthly
Circulation: 23100
Founded in: 1991

9451 **Grayson Report**
Grayson Associates
30728 Paseo Elegancia
San Juan Cpstrn, CA 92675-5426

949-487-9970; *Fax:* 949-487-9975;
www.graysonassociates.com

Suzanne Grayson, President
Robert Grayson, Director

Marketing analysis of the packaged goods industry.
Founded in: 1970

9452 **Grocery Manufacturers of America:**
Grocery Manufacturers Association of America

1350 I St Nw
Suite 300
Washington, DC 20005-3377

202-337-9400; *Fax:* 202-639-5932
info@gmaonline.org; www.gmabrands.com

Pamela G Bailey, CEO
Jeff Nedelman, VP Communications

Focuses on the productivity and public policy issues affecting our industry.
Founded in: 1908

9453 Herd on the Hill
National Meat Association
1970 Broadway
Suite 825
Oakland, CA 94612

510-763-1533; *Fax:* 510-763-6186
staff@nmaonline.org; www.nmaonline.org

Robert Rebholtz, Chairman
Larry Vad, President
Marty Evanson, Vice President
Mike Hesse, Secretary
Brian Coelho, Treasurer

Provides up-to-date information on what's happening in Washington in relation to the meat and poultry industry.
600 Members
Frequency: Weekly
Founded in: 1946

9454 Home Baking Association Newsletter
Home Baking Association
10841 S Crossroads Drive
Suite 105
Parker, CO 80135

785-478-3283; *Fax:* 785-478-3024;
www.homebaking.org
Social Media: Facebook, Twitter, Flickr

Striving to bring a wide variety of educational materials that benefit the community of Bakers and Baking Educators worldwide. Newsletter includes the latest tips, recipes and baking resources.
Frequency: Monthly

9455 Hot Sheet
Fresh-Cut Produce Association
1600 Duke Street
Suite 440
Alexandria, VA 22314

530-756-8900; *Fax:* 530-756-8901;
www.fresh-cuts.org

Jerry Gorny, President
Sean Handerhan, Marketing Director

A newsletter containing technical information, marketing news and exhibit information on the produce trade. Serves over 500 members.
Cost: $35.00
Frequency: Monthly
Circulation: 23,000
Founded in: 1987

9456 Hotel, Restaurant, Institutional Buyers Guide
Urner Barry Publications
PO Box 389
Toms River, NJ 08754

732-240-5330
800-932-0617; *Fax:* 732-341-0891
help@urnerbarry.com; www.urnerbarry.com/

Paul B Brown Jr, President
Sheila M Deane, Marketing Manager
Richard A. Brown, VP

Reports on perishable food prices, meat, seafood, fruits, vegetables and others compiled for the metropolitan New York, New Jersey and Connecticut markets.
Cost: $86.00
4 Pages
Frequency: Weekly
Circulation: 120
ISSN: 0270-4161
Founded in: 1858

9457 Hotel, Restaurant, Institutional Meat Price Report
Urner Barry Publications
PO Box 389
Toms River, NJ 08754-2741

732-240-5330
800-932-0617; *Fax:* 732-341-0891
help@urnerbarry.com; www.urnerbarry.com

Paul B Brown Jr, President
Karen Mick, Circulation Director

Current meat and poultry pricing for the hotel, restaurant and institutional buyers.
Cost: $174.00
Frequency: Weekly
Circulation: 200
ISSN: 1067-3962
Founded in: 1858

9458 IAFIS Global Food MegaTrends
International Assn of Food Industry Suppliers
1451 Dolley Madison Boulevard
Suite 101
McLean, VA 22101

703-761-2600; *Fax:* 703-761-4334
info@fpsa.org; www.fpsa.org

George Melnykovich, President
Andrew Drennan, VP

A quarterly bulletin covering international news and its effect on the food processing and packaging industries.

9459 IBDEA Report
International Beverage Dispensing Association
3837 Naylors Lane
Baltimore, MD 21208

410-602-0616
877-404-2332; *Fax:* 410-486-6799
ibdea@cornerstoneassoc.com; www.ibdea.org

Official newsletter of the International Beverage Dispensing Association, offering the latest news and technologies in the industry.
Frequency: Quarterly

9460 IDDBA & YOU
International Dairy-Deli-Bakery Association
636 Science Drive
PO Box 5528
Madison, WI 53705-0528

608-310-5000; *Fax:* 608-238-6330
IDDBA@iddba.org; www.iddbanet.org

Carol Christison, Executive Director

E-Newsletter designed for deli and bakery supermarket management and in-store staff teams. A fact-filled relevant resource on deli and bakery trends, timely sales data, merchandising ideas, training, new products, seminars, experts, news, and programs.
Frequency: Monthly
Founded in: 1964

9461 IDDBA Legis-Letter
International Dairy-Deli-Bakery Association
636 Science Drive
PO Box 5528
Madison, WI 53705-0528

608-310-5000; *Fax:* 608-238-6330
IDDBA@iddba.org; www.iddbanet.org

Carol Christison, Executive Director

Formerly IDDA UPDATE, a membership benefit. Highlights recent legislative bills and reports, FDA activities, and topical issues such as state action on bst, NLEA, and HACCP.
Frequency: Monthly
Founded in: 1964

9462 IFSEA Infusion
International Food Service Executives
4955 Miller Street
Suite 107
Wheat Ridge, CO 80033

800-893-5499
hq@ifsea.com; www.ifsea.com
Social Media: Facebook

Barbara Sadler, Chairwoman
Fred Wright, Chair-Elect
David Orosz, Treasurer

Official newsletter of the IFSEA focusing on the happenings and news, as well as industry tips and recipes.
Frequency: Monthly

9463 INsight
Southern US Trade Association
701 Poydras St
Suite 3725
New Orleans, LA 70139-4596

504-568-5986; *Fax:* 504-568-6010
susta@susta.org; www.susta.org

Troy Rosamond, Financial Director
Bernadette Wiltz, Deputy Director

Providing the latest exporting information.
Frequency: Quarterly
Founded in: 1973

9464 Ice Cream Reporter
Ice Cream Reporter
Hilton Terrace
Willsboro, NY 12996

518-963-4333; *Fax:* 518-963-4999

Howard Waxman, Publisher/Editor

News for ice cream executives.
Cost: $395.00
Frequency: Monthly
Founded in: 1987

9465 Independent Bakers Association Newsletter
Independent Bakers Association
Georgetown Station
PO Box 3731
Washington, DC 20027-0231

202-333-8190; *Fax:* 202-337-3809
independentbaker@yahoo.com;
www.independentbaker.net

Updating Washington legislative and regulatory actions and analyzing pro-business positions impacting on wholesale baking, allied industry operations.
Frequency: Monthly

9466 Insight
Retailer's Bakery Association
14239 Park Central Drive
Laurel, MD 20707-5261

301-725-2149
800-638-0924; *Fax:* 301-725-2187
Info@RBAnet.com; www.rbanet.com

Bernard Reynolds, Publisher
Stewart Taylor, Convention Director
Katrina Cooley, Marketing & Communications Director

Member newsletter for baking industry professionals.
8 Pages
Frequency: Monthly
Founded in: 1918
Printed in 2 colors on matte stock

9467 **International Association of Food**
1451 Dolley Madison Boulevard
Suite 101
McLean, VA 22101
703-761-2600; *Fax:* 703-761-4334
info@fpsa.org; www.fpsa.org
George Melnykovich, President
Andrew Drennan, VP
Dairy food and beverage industries, and related sanitary processing industries addressing the marketing and business information needs of the food supply channel.
Founded in: 1983
Mailing list available for rent

9468 **IoPP update**
Institute of Packaging Professionals
Ste 123
1833 Centre Point Cir
Naperville, IL 60563-4848
630-544-5050
800-432-4085; *Fax:* 630-544-5005
info@iopp.org; www.iopp.org
Social Media: Facebook, Twitter, LinkedIn, YouTube
Edwin Landon, Executive Director
Patrick Farrey, General Manager
Stan Zelesnik, Director Education
Robert DePauw, Finance Manager
Kelly Staley, Member Services Manager
Emailed newsletter of the Institute of Packaging Professionals.
Frequency: Bi-Weekly

9469 **Kane's Beverage Week**
Whitaker Newsletters
313 S Avenue
#340
Fanwood, NJ 07023-1364
800-359-6049; *Fax:* 908-889-6339
Joel Whitaker, Publisher
News on marketing, economic and regulatory factors affecting the alcohol beverage industry.
Cost: $499.00
6 Pages
Frequency: Quarterly
ISSN: 0882-2573

9470 **Kashrus Magazine**
Yeshiva Birkas Revuen
PO Box 204
Brooklyn, NY 11230
718-336-8544; *Fax:* 718-336-8550
webmaster@kashrusmagazine.com;
www.kashrusmagazine.com
Rabbi Yosef Wikler, Editor
Vaad Hakashrut, Director
Rabbi Levin, Executive Director
Regular, complete update on Kosher food mislabelings, dairy/nondairy status, kosher supervision standards, newly certified products and food technology, travel and Jewish life.
Cost: $18.00
88 Pages
Circulation: 10000
Founded in: 1980
Printed in 4 colors on glossy stock

9471 **Kettle Talk**
Retail Confectioners International
2053 S Waverly Ave
Suite 204
Springfield, MO 65804-2414
417-883-2775
800-545-5381; *Fax:* 847-724-2719
info@retailconfectioners.org;
www.retailconfectioners.org
Terry Craft, President
Terry Hickling, Chairman of Marketing
Dan Malley, VP
Membership newsletter, including confection recipes. Also regional meetings.
Frequency: Monthly
Circulation: 550
Founded in: 1917
Printed in on matte stock

9472 **Kiplinger Agricultural Letter**
Kiplinger Washington Editors
1729 H St Nw
Washington, DC 20006-3924
202-887-6400
800-544-0155; *Fax:* 202-778-8976
sub.services@kiplinger.com;
www.kiplinger.com
Knight Kiplinger, VP
Kevin McCormally, Editorial Director
Fred Frailey, Editor
David Harrison, Manager
Forecasts and judgments on wages, income, food packaging, processing and marketing techniques.
Cost: $56.00
Founded in: 1923

9473 **Kitchen Times**
Howard Wilson and Company
PO Box 290
Waukegan, IL 60079-0290
708-339-5111
800-245-7224; *Fax:* 708-210-2069;
www.hwilson.com
Howard Wilson, Publisher/Editor
News on food and cooking.
Cost: $33.00
8 Pages
Frequency: Monthly
Founded in: 1959

9474 **Lean Trimmings**
National Meat Association
1970 Broadway
Suite 825
Oakland, CA 94612-2299
510-763-1533; *Fax:* 510-763-6186
staff@nmaonline.org; www.nmaonline.org
Barry Carpenter, CEO
Jen Kempis, Operations Manager
Covers industry regulations, new technology and export news, as well as labor issues and business strategy.
Frequency: Weekly
Founded in: 1946
Printed in one color on matte stock

9475 **Legislative Onion Outlet**
Legislative Onion Outlet
822 7th St
Suite 510
Greeley, CO 80631-3941
970-353-5895; *Fax:* 970-353-5897
info@onions-usa.org; www.onions-usa.org
Wayne Mininger, Executive VP
Tanya Fell, Public/Industry Relations
An annual bulletin published by the National Onion Association.
Circulation: 600
Founded in: 1913
Mailing list available for rent: 600 names

9476 **Link Newsletter**
R&D Associates
16607 Blanco Road
Suite 1506
San Antonio, TX 78232-1940
210-493-8024; *Fax:* 210-493-8036
hqs@militaryfood.org; www.militaryfood.org
David Dee, Editor
Food packaging, food processing and foodservice industry.
300 Pages
Frequency: Quarterly

9477 **Loan Trimmings & Herd on the Hill**
1970 Broadway Avenue
Suite 825
Oakland, CA 94612-2299
510-763-1533; *Fax:* 510-763-6186;
www.nmaonline.org
Barry Carpenter, Executive Director
Jen Kempis, Associate Director
Frequency: Weekly
Circulation: 600

9478 **Make It Tasty**
Prosperity & Profits Unlimited
PO Box 416
Denver, CO 80201-0416
303-573-5564
AC Doyle, Publisher
Spice company blends food business newsletter with salt-free, herb and spice blend recipes.
Founded in: 1996

9479 **Making a Difference**
National FFA Organization
6060 FFA Drive
PO Box 68960
Indianapolis, IN 46268-0960
317-802-6060
888-332-2668
membership@ffa.org; www.ffa.org
Steve A. Brown, National FFA Advisor
Marion D. Fletcher, National FFA Organization Treasurer
Resource for Agriculture teachers. It features news from FFA and Team Ag Ed, teaching resources, ideas, inspiration and more.
507M Members
Founded in: 1928

9480 **Market News**
Meat & Livestock Australia
1401 K Street NW
Suite 602
Washington, DC 20005
202-521-2551; *Fax:* 202-521-2699
info@mla.com.au; www.mla.com.au
Social Media: Facebook, Twitter, YouTube
Don Heatley, Chairman
David Palmer, Managing Director
Bernie Bindon, Director
Chris Hudson, Director
eNewsletter presents the latest market news from Australia and key international markets.
30000 Members
Frequency: Weekly
Founded in: 1998

9481 **Meat & Poultry**
Meat Trade Institute
213 South Avenue East
Spencer Savings Bank Building
Cranford, NJ 07016
908-276-5111; *Fax:* 212-279-4016;
www.spcnetwork.com/mti/
John Calcangno, President
A respected newsletter which keeps readers abreast of membership information and all news pertinent to Institute members. Available online.
Frequency: Monthly

9482 **Meat and Livestock Weekly**
Meat & Livestock Australia

1401 K Street NW
Suite 602
Washington, DC 20005

202-521-2551; *Fax:* 202-521-2699
info@mla.com.au; www.mla.com.au
Social Media: Facebook, Twitter, YouTube

Don Heatley, Chairman
David Palmer, Managing Director
Bernie Bindon, Director
Chris Hudson, Director

eNewsletter providing the latest news, analysis and trends for domestic and export markets, including information on buyer and competitor activity and trends.
30000 Members
Frequency: Weekly
Founded in: 1998

9483 **More Beef from Pastures**
Meat & Livestock Australia
1401 K Street NW
Suite 602
Washington, DC 20005

202-521-2551; *Fax:* 202-521-2699
info@mla.com.au; www.mla.com.au
Social Media: Facebook, Twitter, YouTube

Don Heatley, Chairman
David Palmer, Managing Director
Bernie Bindon, Director
Chris Hudson, Director

eNewsletter designed to keep readers up-to-date with the latest developments in the MLA More Beef from Pastures program.
30000 Members
Frequency: Quarterly
Founded in: 1998

9484 **NAFEM online**
N. American Assn. of Food Equipment Manufacturing
161 N Clark Street
Suite 2020
Chicago, IL 60601

312-821-0201; *Fax:* 312-821-0202
info@nafem.org; www.nafem.org

Steven R. Follett, President
Thomas R. Campion, President-Elect
Michael L. Whiteley, Secretary/Treasurer
Deirdre Flynn, Executive Vice President

The latest and greatest NAFEM and industry news to all NAFEM members. e-Newsletter.
Frequency: Monthly

9485 **NAMA Newsletter**
North American Millers' Association
600 Maryland Ave SW
Suite 825 W
Washington, DC 20024

202-484-2200; *Fax:* 202-488-7416
generalinfo@namamillers.org;
www.namamillers.org

Betsy Faga, President
James Bair, VP

Trade association representing the wheat, corn, oat and rye milling industry. NAMA members operate one hundred and seventy mills in thirty-eight states and Canada. Their aggregate production of more than one hundred and sixty million pounds per day is approximately ninety-five percent of the industry capacity in the U.S.
Frequency: Monthly
Circulation: 250

9486 **NCA Annual Convention**
National Coffee Association
15 Maiden Ln
Suite 1405
New York, NY 10038-5113

212-766-4007; *Fax:* 212-766-5815
info@ncausa.org; www.ncausa.org

Robert F Nelson, President
Steven M Wolfe, Membership/Marketing Director

The coffee event of the year, industry executives from all over the world get together to learn from the most current educational sessions, see old friends and meet new ones.
Frequency: Annual/March
Founded in: 1911

9487 **NFRA Update**
National Frozen & Refrigerated Foods Association
4755 Linglestown Road Suite 300
PO Box 6069
Harrisburg, PA 17112

717-657-8601; *Fax:* 717-657-9862
info@nfraweb.org; www.nfraweb.org

H V Skip Shaw Jr, President/CEO
Jeff Romachik, Executive VP/COO
Marlene Barr, VP Membership

NFRA's main communication tool in keeping members informed of upcoming frozen and refrigerated food promotions and Association meetings and resources. Also covers local associations, members' personnel changes and member news such as the introduction of new products and facility expansions.
Frequency: Monthly
Circulation: 2300

9488 **NICRA Bulletin**
National Ice Cream Retailers Association
1028 W Devon Avenue
Elk Grove Village, IL 60007

847-301-7500
866-303-6960; *Fax:* 847-301-8402
info@nicra.org; www.nicra.org

Lynn Dudek, President
Dan Messer, VP

Information to assist you with Practical Advice on Daily Operations, Industry Trends, Tax Related Articles, Legislative Issues, Association News, Labeling Information, and more.
Frequency: Monthly
Circulation: 500

9489 **NPA Fact of the Week**
Natural Products Association
2112 E 4th St
Suite 200
Santa Ana, CA 92705-3816

714-460-7732
800-966-6632; *Fax:* 714-460-7444;
www.npainfo.org
Social Media: Facebook, Twitter, LinkedIn

John F. Gay, Executive Director & CEO
Jeffrey Wright, President

Emailed to Congressional staffers who handle health issues for their representative or senator. Highlights the latest news, research and trends in dietary supplements and the natural products industry.
1900+ Members
Frequency: Weekly
Founded in: 1936

9490 **NPA NOW**
Natural Products Association
2112 E 4th St
Suite 200
Santa Ana, CA 92705-3816

714-460-7732
800-966-6632; *Fax:* 714-460-7444;
www.npainfo.org
Social Media: Facebook, Twitter, LinkedIn

John F. Gay, Executive Director & CEO
Jeffrey Wright, President

Provides members with important association and industry news on a timely basis.
1900+ Members
Frequency: 6x Yearly
Founded in: 1936

9491 **NPFDA NEWS**
National Poultry & Food Distributors
2014 Osborne Road
Saint Marys, GA 31558

770-535-9901; *Fax:* 770-535-7385
kkm@npfda.org; www.npfda.org

Chris Sharp, President
Al Acunto, Vice President
Marc Miro, Treasurer
Kristin McWhorter, Executive Director

Brings the latest information about NPFDA members- featuring Member Spotlights, government regulations and upcoming industry events.
Frequency: Monthly
Founded in: 1967

9492 **NSA Newsletter**
National Shellfisheries Association
National Marine Fisheries Service Laboratory
Oxford, MD 21654

631-653-6327; *Fax:* 631-653-6327
webmaster@shellfish.org; www.shellfish.org

R. LeRoy Creswell, President
Christopher V. Davis, President-Elect
George E. Flimlin, VP & Program Chair
Marta Gomez-Chiarri, Secretary
Sandra E. Shumway, Editor

Current issues and concerns in shellfish research and in the shellfish industry, including details regarding upcoming meetings, employment listings, and column.
1M Members
Frequency: Quarterly
Founded in: 1908

9493 **National Automatic Merchandising**
National Automatic Merchandising Association
20 N Wacker Dr
Suite 3500
Chicago, IL 60606-3102

312-346-0370
800-331-8816; *Fax:* 312-704-4140
dmathews@vending.org; www.vending.org

Richard Geerdes, President
Craig Hesch NCE, Senior Vice Chairman
Brad Ellis NCE, Vice Chairman

Serves food and refreshment, vending, contract foodservice management and office coffee service industries.
2500 Members
Founded in: 1936

9494 **National Conference on Interstate Milk Shipments**
National Conference on Interstate Milk
123 Buena Vista Drive
Frankfort, KY 40601-8770

502-695-0253; *Fax:* 502-695-0253;
www.ncims.org

Leon Townsend, Executive Secretary
Marlena Bordson, Chair
Founded in: 1946

9495 **National Fertilizer Solutions Association Newsletter**
339 Consort Drive
Manchester, MO 63011-4439
636-256-6650; *Fax:* 636-256-4901
Kelly O'Brien-Wray, Publisher
Fred Speckmann, Editor
Accepts advertising.
90 Pages

9496 **National Honey Market News**
US Department of Agriculture
21 N 1st Avenue
#224
Yakima, WA 98902-2663
509-575-2494; *Fax:* 509-457-7132
FVInfo@ams.usda.gov;
www.ams.usda.gov/fv/mncs
Linda Verstrate, Publisher
Michael Jarvis, Director
Current honey market information and colony conditions in the US.
Cost: $24.00
10-12 Pages
Frequency: Monthly

9497 **National Hot Pepper Association**
400 NW 20th Street
Fort Lauderdale, FL 33311-3818
954-565-4972; *Fax:* 954-566-2208;
www.peppergal.com
Robert J Payton, Publisher
Betty Payton, Editor
Networking among industry and private members. Education and information sharing.
Cost: $20.00
28 Pages
Frequency: Quarterly
Printed in on matte stock

9498 **National Nutritional Foods Association Today**
National Nutritional Foods Association
2112 E 4th St
Suite 200
Santa Ana, CA 92705-3816
949-622-6272
800-966-6632; *Fax:* 949-622-6266;
www.nnfa.org
Amanda Thomason, Editor/Publications Manager
Paul Bennett, CEO/President
Nonprofit trade organization dedicated to protecting and advancing the natural products industry for both retailers and suppliers.
Cost: $48.00
Frequency: Monthly
Circulation: 8000
Founded in: 1936

9499 **National Onion Association Newsletter**
National Onion Association
822 7th St
Suite 510
Greeley, CO 80631-3941
970-353-5895; *Fax:* 970-353-5897
info@onions-usa.org; www.onions-usa.org
Wayne Mininger, Executive VP
Kim Reddin, Public/Industry Relation
Newsletter published by and only for the National Onion Association.
Frequency: Monthly
Circulation: 600
Founded in: 1913
Mailing list available for rent: 600 names

9500 **National Seasoning Manufacturers Newsletter**
National Seasoning Manufacturers Association
2527 Mill Race Road
Frederick, MD 21701-6812
301-694-0419; *Fax:* 301-299-7523
alsmeyerfood@isp.com
Dick Alsmeyer PhD, Executive Director
Frequency: Quarterly

9501 **National Shellfisheries Association News**
Long Island University/Southampton College
Natural Sciences Division
Southampton, NY 11968
631-283-4000; *Fax:* 631-287-8054
Sandra Shumway, Production Manager
Eric Lang, Owner
Newsletter focusing on information for public health workers, shellfish producers and fishery administrators.
Cost: $125.00
Circulation: 1000
Mailing list available for rent: 1M names
Printed in one color on matte stock

9502 **National Young Farmer Educational News**
National FFA Organization
PO Box 68960
6060 FFA Drive
Alexandria, VA 22309-160
317-802-6060
888-332-2668; *Fax:* 800-366-6556
aboutffa@ffa.org; www.ffa.org
Wayne Sprick, Publisher
Larry Case, CEO
Tabloid which receives articles and information from state associations as well as information from the National Association.
12 Pages
Founded in: 1928

9503 **Natural News Update**
Natural Products Association
2112 E 4th St
Suite 200
Santa Ana, CA 92705-3816
714-460-7732
800-966-6632; *Fax:* 714-460-7444;
www.npainfo.org
Social Media: Facebook, Twitter, LinkedIn
John F. Gay, Executive Director & CEO
Jeffrey Wright, President
A weekly news and information resource, offering the latest news, federal activity, association announcements and research.
1900+ Members
Frequency: Weekly
Founded in: 1936

9504 **Nebraska Alfalfa Dehydrators Bulletin**
Nebraska Alfalfa Dehydrators Association
8810 Craig Dr
Shawnee Mission, KS 66212-2916
913-648-6800; *Fax:* 913-648-2648;
www.nebada.org
Wanda L Cobb, Executive VP
Market Information on Alfalfa Pellets, Meal, Cubes, and Hay.
Frequency: Weekly
Founded in: 1941

9505 **News in a Nutshell**
National Peanut Board
2839 Paces Ferry Road
Suite 210
Atlanta, GA 30339-5769
678-424-5750
866-825-7946; *Fax:* 678-424-5751
peanuts@nationalpeanutboard.org;
www.nationalpeanutboard.org
Social Media: Facebook, Twitter, YouTube, Flickr
George Jeffcoat, Chairman
Cindy Belch, Vice Chairman
John Harrell, Secretary
Vic Jordan, Treasurer
e-Newlsetter from the National Peanut Board with news about everything peanut.
Frequency: Bi-Weekly

9506 **No-Till Farmer**
Lessiter Publications
PO Box 624
Brookfield, WI 53008-0624
262-782-4480
800-645-8455; *Fax:* 262-782-1252
info@lesspub.com; www.lesspub.com
Donna Schwierske, Manager
Frank Lessiter, Accounting Manager
Michael Storts, Accounting Manager
Management information for farmers interested in conservation tillage.
Cost: $37.95
16 Pages
Frequency: Monthly
Circulation: 5500
ISSN: 0091-9993
Founded in: 1984
Mailing list available for rent: 5,000 names at $90m per M
Printed in 2 colors on glossy stock

9507 **Organic Business News**
Hotline Printing & Publishing
PO Box 161132
Atamonte Springs, FL 32716-1132
407-628-1377; *Fax:* 407-628-9935;
www.hotlineprinting.com/obn.html
Dennis Blank, Publisher/Editor
Christine Blank, Senior Editor
Leading industry publication that tracks the latest government actions, policy trends and financial development in development in the organic food business.
Cost: $110.00
12 Pages
Printed in 2 colors

9508 **Organic Trade Association Newsletter**
Organic Trade Association
60 Wells Street
PO Box 547
Greenfield, MA 01302
413-774-7511; *Fax:* 413-774-6432
info@ota.com; www.ota.com
Christine Bushway, Executive Director/CEO
Linda Lutz, Membership Manager
Laura Batcha, Marketing/Public Relations Director
Members are businesses involved in the organic agriculture and products industry. Seeks to promote the industry and establish production and marketing standards. Also publishes The Organic Page: North American Resource Directory

9509 **Packer**
Vance Publishing

400 Knightsbridge Parkway
Lincolnshire, IL 60069

847-634-2600; *Fax:* 847-634-4379
info@vancepublishing.com;
www.vancepublishing.com

William C Vance, Chairman
Peggy Walker, President
News and information on fresh fruit and vegetable marketing.

9510 **Pear Newsletter**
Pear Bureau Northwest
4382 SE International Way
Suite A
Milwaukie, OR 97222-4627

503-652-9720; *Fax:* 503-652-9721
info@usapears.com; www.usapears.com

Kevin Moffitt, President/CEO
Cristie Mather, Communciations Manager
Frequency: Monthly

9511 **Peterson Patriot**
Peterson Patriot Printers-Publishers
202 Main Street
Peterson, IA 51047

712-295-7711; *Fax:* 712-295-7711
Roger Stoner, Publisher
Jane Stoner, Editor

Agricultural news.
Cost: $18.00
12 Pages
Frequency: Weekly
Circulation: 549

9512 **Practical Gourmet**
Linick Group
Gourmet Building 7 Putter Lane
PO Box 102
Middle Island, NY 11953-0102

631-924-3888
roger@practicalgourmet.com;
www.practicalgourmet.com

Gaylen Andrews, Publisher/Editor
Roger Dextor, VP/Director of PR
Barbara Deal, Marketing Manager
Andrew Linick, Manager
Bill Bruzy, Contributing Editor

Since 1982, the focus of this upscale monthly publication is on providing 'healthy dining trends for the affluent traveler' 45 plus; includes feature articles and in-depth interviews with award winning chefs, wineries/tastings, honoring 2-5 star restaurants with PG's Gold Taste Dining Awards, upscale hotels, properties, resorts, spas, cruises/yachting, airlines, ground operators, food festivals/contests, cooking schools and worldwide culinary events.
Cost: $48.00
36 Pages
Frequency: Monthly
Circulation: 210,000
Founded in: 1975
Mailing list available for rent: 210 M names at $110 per M
Printed in 4 colors on glossy stock

9513 **Produce Merchandiser**
United Fresh Fruit & Vegetable Association
1901 Pennsylvania Ave Nw
Suite 1100
Washington, DC 20006-3412

202-862-4989; *Fax:* 202-303-3433
united@uffva.org; www.uffva.org

Thomas E Stenzel, CEO
Information on promotion and consumer issues.

9514 **Product Alert**
Marketing Intelligence Service
482 N Main St
Canandaigua, NY 14424-1049

585-374-6326
800-836-5710; *Fax:* 585-374-5217;
www.productscan.com

Christine Dengler, Marketing/Sales Manager

A twice-monthly briefing on new packaged goods introduced in North America. Featuring product pictures and descriptions with indexing provided in two convenient formats. Also available in a twice monthly, international version.
Cost: $795.00
Frequency: Fortnightly

9515 **RBA Newsbrief**
Retail Bakers of America
202 Village Circle
Suite 1
Slidell, LA 70458

985-643-6504
800-638-0924; *Fax:* 985-643-6929
Info@RBAnet.com; www.rbanet.com
Social Media: Facebook

Felix Sherman, Sr., President
Kenneth Downey, Sr., 1st Vice President
Marlene Goetzeler, 2nd Vice President
Dale A. Biles, Treasurer
Susan Nicolais, CAE, Secretary

Distributed electronically to RBA members, containing articles gathered from an expansive list of sources.
2000 Members
Frequency: Weekly
Founded in: 1918

9516 **Regulatory Register**
American Butter Institute
2101 Wilson Boulevard
Suite 400
Arlington, VA 22201

703-243-5630; *Fax:* 703-841-9328
AMiner@nmpf.org; www.nmpf.org/ABI

Randy Mooney, Chairman
Dave Fuhrmann, Secretary
Clyde Rutherford, 1st Vice Chairman
Cornell Kasbergen, 2nd Vice Chairman
Ken Nobis, Treasurer

A publication for dairy cooperatives and producers which details recent regulatory activity directly impacting the operation of their farms and manufacturing facilities. Highlights the following areas of regulatory affairs; animal health, food safety, nutrition, standards and labeling, and environment and energy.
31 Members
Founded in: 1908

9517 **Research Report for Foodservice**
1 Bridge St
Irvington, NY 10533-1550

914-591-4297
info@restaurantchains.net;
www.restaurantchains.net

James Santo, President

Market research company that provides contact information for companies in the foodservice industry. Our two primary brands are RestaurantChains.net, a directory of company profiles and sales leads for US restaurant chains, and FoodserviceReport.com; a weekly bulletin on new US restaurant openings and changes of ownership.
3600 Members
Founded in: 1996
Mailing list available for rent: 80000 names

9518 **Restaurant Chain Growth**
Research Report for Foodservice
1 Bridge St
Irvington, NY 10533-1550

914-591-4297
info@restaurantchains.net;
www.restaurantchains.net

James Santo, President

Providing the reader with proprietary information.
3600 Members
Frequency: Weekly
Founded in: 1996
Mailing list available for rent: 80000 names

9519 **Restaurants and Institutions**
Reed Business Information
125 Park Avenue
23rd Floor
New York, NY 10017

212-309-8100; *Fax:* 212-309-8187;
www.rimag.com

A magazine for restaurant professionals faced with fast-paced consumer demands, government regulations, health concerns and evolving food trends in a variety of market segments. R&I keeps these professionals informed and offers menu advice to prepare for new customers and business growth.

9520 **Salad Special**
Refrigerated Foods Association
2971 Flowers Rd S
Suite 266
Chamblee, GA 30341-5403

770-452-0660; *Fax:* 770-455-3879
info@refrigeratedfoods.org;
www.refrigeratedfoods.org

Terry Dougherty, Executive Director

A newsletters covering technical and marketing aspects of the industry, including news of projects, conventions and expositions.
Frequency: Monthly
Founded in: 1980

9521 **Salt & Trace Mineral Newsletter**
Salt Institute
700 N Fairfax St
Suite 600
Alexandria, VA 22314-2085

703-549-4648; *Fax:* 703-548-2194
info@saltinstitute.org; www.saltinstitute.org

Richard L Hanneman, President
Martina Moran, Director
Tammy Goodwin, Director
Mark OKeefe, Director of Communications

Information on animal nutrition.
Circulation: 3000
Founded in: 1940
Printed in on glossy stock

9522 **Seafood Price-Current**
Urner Barry Publications
PO Box 389
Toms River, NJ 08754-389

732-240-5330
800-932-0617; *Fax:* 732-341-0891
help@urnerbarry.com; www.urnerbarry.com

Paul B Brown Jr, President
Karen Mick, Circulation Director

Spot market prices of the most widely traded fresh and frozen fin and shellfish items.
Cost: $383.00
8 Pages
Frequency: Weekly
Circulation: 1500
ISSN: 0270-4170
Founded in: 1858

9523 **Seafood Trend Newsletter**
Seafood Trend

8227 Ashworth Ave N
Seattle, WA 98103-4434

206-523-2280; *Fax:* 206-526-8719
seafoodtrend@aol.com

Ken Talley, Editor/Publisher

Provides information, statistics and economic facts and figures pertaining to the seafood market.
Cost: $235.00
4 Pages
Circulation: 400
ISSN: 1057-2708
Founded in: 1984
Printed in 2 colors on matte stock

9524 **Shelby Report of the Southeast**
Shelby Publishing Company
517 Green St Nw
Gainesville, GA 30501-3300

770-534-8380; *Fax:* 770-535-0110
shelbpub@bellsouth.net;
www.shelbypublishing.com

Ron Johnston, President
Chuck Gilmer, Editor
Carol Tomaseski, Circulation Manager
Ileen Bloch, VP Publishing

A newsletter offering information on the retail and wholesale food trade.
Cost: $36.00
Frequency: Monthly
Circulation: 25,201
Founded in: 1966
Printed in on newsprint stock

9525 **Shrimp News International**
Aquaculture Digest
9450 Mira Mesa Boulevard
#B562
San Diego, CA 92126-4850

Fax: 858-271-0324

Robert Rosenberry, Editor

Publishes reports and directories on the world's shrimp industry.
Cost: $95.00
24 Pages
Frequency: Biweekly
Mailing list available for rent
Printed in one color on matte stock

9526 **Signals Newsletter**
Association for Communications Excellence
University of Florida
PO Box 110811
Gainesville, FL 32611-0811

Fax: 352-392-8583
ace@ifas.ufl.edu; www.aceweb.org

Features news of interest to members. Includes articles with a professional development focus; updates from special interest groups, states and regions; announcements about upcoming workshops and conferences; and write-ups about members' awards and accomplishments, job changes and more.

9527 **Soft Drink Letter**
Whitaker Newsletters
313 S Avenue
#203
Fanwood, NJ 07023-1364

908-889-6336
800-359-6049; *Fax:* 908-889-6339;
www.att.net

Joel Whitaker, Editor

For managers and owners of bottling and soft drink and water companies.
Cost: $349.00
Printed in one color

9528 **Speedy Bee**
Fore's Honey Farms
PO Box 998
Jesup, GA 31598

912-427-4018; *Fax:* 912-427-8447

Troy Fore, Editor

Honey and beekeeping industry news.
Cost: $17.25
16 Pages
Frequency: Monthly
Circulation: 4000
ISSN: 0190-6798
Founded in: 1972
Printed in on newsprint stock

9529 **Spiceletter**
American Spice Trade Association
2025 M St Nw
Suite 800
Washington, DC 20036-2422

202-367-1127; *Fax:* 202-367-2127;
www.iamss.org

Cheryl Deem, Executive Director
Frequency: Bi-Monthly

9530 **Spirited Living: Dave Steadman's Restaurant Scene**
5301 Towne Woods Rd
Coram, NY 11727-2808

631-736-0436; *Fax:* 631-736-0436

Dave Steadman, Editor

Newsletter published biweekly except January, July, and August.
Cost: $75.00

9531 **Sunflower Week in Review**
National Sunflower Association
2401 46th Avenue SE
Suite 206
Mandan, ND 58554-4829

701-328-5100
888-718-7033; *Fax:* 701-328-5101
larryk@sunflowernsa.com;
www.sunflowernsa.com
Social Media: Facebook, YouTube

Larry Kleingartner, Executive Director

Provides the latest news regarding sunflower information, conveniently summarized with highlights and data to keep you informed.
Frequency: Weekly
Founded in: 1981

9532 **Supermarket News**
Fairchild Publications
750 3rd Ave
New York, NY 10017-2703

212-630-4000
877-652-5295; *Fax:* 212-630-3563;
www.fairchildpub.com

Mary G Berner, CEO
David Merrefield, VP, Editorial Director
David Orgel, Editor-in-Chief
Dan Bagan, Publishing Director

A weekly guide aimed at retailers, wholesalers, manufacturers and others in the food industry.
Cost: $23.00
Frequency: Weekly
Circulation: 36346
Founded in: 1892

9533 **THE LINK**
R & D Associates for Military Food & Packaging
16607 Blanco Rd
Suite 501
San Antonio, TX 78232-1940

210-493-8024; *Fax:* 210-493-8036;
www.militaryfood.org

Barney Guarino, Chairman
Jim Merryman, Vice Chairman
Tim Zimmerman, President
Bill McCreary, Executive Vice President
Jim Fagan, Executive Director

Provides pertinent data available and will keep readers informed of the activities of major government agencies.
Frequency: Quarterly
Founded in: 1946

9534 **TecAgri News**
Clark Consulting International
PO Box 68
Park Ridge, IL 60068-0068

847-836-5100; *Fax:* 847-792-7565
warren.clark@ccimarketing.com;
www.tecagrinews.com

Warren E Clark, President

News on new technology in agriculture reaching large computerized family farmers.
Cost: $1200.00
Frequency: Weekly
Circulation: 100,000
Founded in: 1986
Mailing list available for rent: 2.1M names at $250 per M

9535 **Technical E-News**
Refrigerated Foods Association
1640 Powers Ferry Road
Bldg. 2, Suite 200A
Marietta, GA 30067

770-303-9905; *Fax:* 770-303-9906
info@refrigeratedfoods.org;
www.refrigeratedfoods.org

Brian Edmonds, President
George Bradford, Vice President
Steve Loehndorf, Secretary
Wes Thaller, Treasurer

Contains the latest technical and regulatory news affecting the industry.
200+ Members
Frequency: Bi-Monthly
Founded in: 1980

9536 **The Business Owner**
Retail Bakers of America
202 Village Circle
Suite 1
Slidell, LA 70458

985-643-6504
800-638-0924; *Fax:* 985-643-6929
Info@RBAnet.com; www.rbanet.com
Social Media: Facebook

Felix Sherman, Sr., President
Kenneth Downey, Sr., 1st Vice President
Marlene Goetzeler, 2nd Vice President
Dale A. Biles, Treasurer
Susan Nicolais, CAE, Secretary

Publication delivering basic business advice and know-how for today's small and mid-size business proprietor. Each issue delivers knowledge in the areas of business strategy, profit and cash flow maximization, risk reduction and avoidance, insurance, sales and marketing, advertising and branding.
2000 Members
Frequency: 6x Yearly
Founded in: 1918

9537 **The Business of Herbs**
Herb Growing and Marketing Network
PO Box 245
Silver Spring, PA 17575-0245

Fax: 717-393-9261
herbworld@aol.com; www.herbnet.com

Maureena Rogers, Editor

Information on commercial cultivation of herbs and marketing. Also regulatory information, calender of events, business notes.
40 Pages
Frequency: Monthly

Circulation: 2,000
Founded in: 1990

9538 The Coffee Reporter
National Coffee Association
45 Broadway
Suite 1140
New York, NY 10006

212-766-4007; *Fax:* 212-766-5815
info@ncausa.org; www.ncausa.org
Social Media: Facebook, Twitter, LinkedIn

Dub Hay, Chairman
John E. Boyle, Vice Chairman
Richard Emanuele, Secretary
Robert F. Nelson, President & CEO

National Coffee Association's official online newsletter.
Frequency: Weekly

9539 The Culinary Insider
American Culinary Federation
180 Center Place Way
St Augustine, FL 32095-8859

904-824-4468
800-624-9458; *Fax:* 904-825-4758
acf@acfchefs.net; www.acfchefs.org
Social Media: Facebook, Twitter

Michael Ty, President
Thomas J. Macrina, Secretary
James Taylor, Treasurer

ACF's electronic newsletter featuring the latest culinary news, events, continuing education opportunities and more.
19000 Members
Founded in: 1929

9540 The Exchange
Agricultural & Applied Economics Association
555 E. Wells St.
Suite 1100
Milwaukee, WI 53202-6600

414-918-3190
Info@aaea.org; www.aaea.org

Robert P. King, President
Richard Sexton, President-Elect
Bruce A. Babcock, Director
Jayson Lusk, Director
Lori Lynch, Director

Bi-monthly electronic newsletter published by AAEA for members only. The content of the newsletter includes association announcements, membership news, and updates from the profession.
Cost: $150.00
4M Members
Frequency: Regular Membership Fee
Founded in: 1910

9541 Today's Grocer
Florida Grocer Publications
PO Box 430760
S Miami, FL 33243

305-661-0792
800-440-3067; *Fax:* 305-661-6720;
www.todaysgrocer.com

Jack Nobles, Publisher
Dennis Kane, Editor

Provides the latest food industry news and trends to Florida, Georgia, Alabama, Louisiana, Mississippi and the Carolinas.
Cost: $29.00
24 Pages
Frequency: Monthly
Circulation: 19500
ISSN: 1529-4420
Founded in: 1968
Printed in 4 colors on newsprint stock

9542 US Beer Market
Business Trend Analysts/Industry Reports
2171 Jericho Tpke
Suite 200
Commack, NY 11725-2937

631-462-5454
800-866-4648; *Fax:* 631-462-1842;
www.bta-ler.com

Charles J Ritchie, Executive VP
Donna Priani, Marketing Director

Profiles markets for premium, superpremium, popular and light beers.
Cost: $1495.00
Founded in: 1978

9543 USA Rice Daily
USA Rice Federation
4301 N Fairfax Drive
Suite 425
Arlington, VA 22203

703-226-2300; *Fax:* 703-236-2301
riceinfo@usarice.com; www.usarice.com

Jamie Warshaw, Chairman

The latest news on issues and activities for the U.S. rice industry.

9544 Uncorked
California Wine Club
2175 Goodyear Ave Suite 102
PO Box 3699
Ventura, CA 93006-3699
805-504-4330
800-777-4443; *Fax:* 800-700-1599
info@cawineclub.com; www.cawineclub.com

Bruce Boring, Publisher
Judy Reynolds, Editor

8 page newsletter that describes featured winery. It provides an upclose and personal look at a small boutique California winery.
Circulation: 10000
Founded in: 1990

9545 Update
National FFA Organization
6060 FFA Drive
PO Box 68960
Indianapolis, IN 46268-0960

317-802-6060
888-332-2668
membership@ffa.org; www.ffa.org

Steve A. Brown, National FFA Advisor
Marion D. Fletcher, National FFA Organization Treasurer

The National FFA's newsletter for State Staff and Advisors. Find important news, information and program updates.
507M Members
Founded in: 1928

9546 Urner Barry's Price-Current
Urner Barry Publications
PO Box 389
Toms River, NJ 08754-0389

732-240-5330
800-932-0617; *Fax:* 732-341-0891
help@urnerbarry.com; www.urnerbarry.com

Paul B Brown Jr, President
Sheila M Deane, Marketing Manager

Daily market price report serving the poultry and egg industries.
Cost: $415.00
8 Pages
Frequency: Daily
Circulation: 3,000
ISSN: 0273-9992

9547 Urner Barry's Price-Current West Coast Edition
Urner Barry Publications
PO Box 389
Toms River, NJ 08754

732-240-5330
800-932-0617; *Fax:* 732-341-0891
help@urnerbarry.com; www.urnerbarry.com/

Paul Brown Jr, President
Sheila M Deane, Marketing Manager
Richard A. Brown, VP

Reports changes in price and market conditions of poultry and eggs on the West Coast.
Cost: $444.00
8 Pages
Frequency: Daily
Circulation: 3000
ISSN: 0273-5016
Founded in: 1858

9548 Urner Barry's Yellow Sheet
Urner Barry Publications
PO Box 389
Toms River, NJ 08754

732-240-5330
800-932-0617; *Fax:* 732-341-0891
help@urnerbarry.com; www.urnerbarry.com

Paul B Brown Jr, President
Richard A Brown, VP/Treasurer

Market price report of timely unbiased meat quotes to help pinpoint the latest trading levels of beef, pork, lamb, veal, meat by-products, carcasses and boxed cuts.
Cost: $559.00
8 Pages
Frequency: Daily
Circulation: 1500
ISSN: 1066-8195
Founded in: 1858

9549 Vegetarian Times
Active Interest Media
300 Continental Blvd
Suite 650
El Segundo, CA 90245-5067

310-356-4100; *Fax:* 310-356-4110
editor@vegetariantimes.com;
www.amedia.com

Efrem Zymbalist III, CEO
John Robles, Marketing Manager

Inspiring everyone to eat healthier, live greener, and be happier.
Cost: $19.95
Frequency: Monthly
Founded in: 1999

9550 Vinotizie Italian Wine Newsletter
Italian Trade Commission
499 Park Ave
6th Floor
New York, NY 10022-1240

212-980-1500; *Fax:* 212-758-1050;
www.italtrade.com/ice

Michelle Jones, Editor

This newsletter discusses developments in the Italian wine industry and market, as well as reviews of imported wines from Italy.
Frequency: Bi-Monthly

9551 WSSA Newsletter
Weed Science Society of America
P.O.Box 7065
Lawrence, KS 66044-7065

785-429-9622
800-627-0629; *Fax:* 785-843-1274
wssa@allenpress.com; www.wssa.net

David Shaw, Editor
Michael E Foley, Publications Director

Subscription is included in the annual dues.
Cost: $5.00
Frequency: Quarterly/Non-Member Fee

9552 **Washington Association of Wine Grape Growers**
PO Box 716
Cashmere, WA 98815

509-782-8234; *Fax:* 509-782-1203
info@wawgg.org; www.wawgg.org

Vicky Scharlau, Executive Director
Paul Champoux, Business Manager
Debbie Sands, Business Manager
Janet Heath, Office Manager
Julie Lindholm, Director

Guidance in research and education, and maintaining leadership in local, state and national wine grape issues.
Cost: $115.00
Founded in: 1983

9553 **Washington Report Newsletter**
National Chicken Council
1015 15th Street NW
Suite 930
Washington, DC 20005-2622

202-081-1339; *Fax:* 202-293-4005
ncc@chickenusa.org;
www.nationalchickencouncil.org

George Watts, President
William P Roenigk, Senior VP
Richard L Lobb, Communications Director
Margaret Ernst, Director Meetings/Membership Comm.

NCC's weekly, member's only newsletter provides information on current statistics, as well as information on economic, trade, and marketing developments, updates on regulatory, legislative, technology, and other industry issues and news
Frequency: Weekly
Circulation: 5000
Founded in: 1954

9554 **Webster Agricultural Letter**
Webster Communications Corporation
1530 Key Blvd
Suite 401W
Arlington, VA 22209-1531

703-525-4512; *Fax:* 703-852-3534;
www.agletter.com

James C Webster, Editor/CEO

Agricultural politics and policy issues.
Cost: $397.00
6 Pages
Frequency: Fortnightly
ISSN: 1073-4813
Founded in: 1980
Printed in one color on matte stock

9555 **Weekly Insiders Dairy & Egg Letter**
Urner Barry Publications
PO Box 389
Toms River, NJ 08754

732-240-5330
800-932-0617; *Fax:* 732-341-0891
help@urnerbarry.com; www.urnerbarry.com

Paul B Brown Jr, President
Randy Pesciotta, Editor
Janice Brown, Advertising

Statistical newsletter of storage stocks of whole, liquid and dried eggs, slaughter and consumption figures and retail selling prices as well as critical data on butter, margarine and cheese.
Cost: $24.00
4 Pages
Frequency: Weekly
Circulation: 10000
ISSN: 0270-4153
Founded in: 1858

9556 **Weekly Insiders Poultry Report**
Urner Barry Publications
PO Box 389
Toms River, NJ 08754-389

732-240-5330
800-932-0617; *Fax:* 732-341-0891
help@urnerbarry.com; www.urnerbarry.com

Paul B Brown Jr, President
Sheila M Deane, Marketing Manager

Statistical news of broiler eggs set and hatched, current chicken and fowl slaughter, storage holdings and competing red meat availability.
Cost: $190.00
4 Pages
Frequency: Weekly
Circulation: 230
ISSN: 0160-4910
Founded in: 1858

9557 **Weekly Insiders Turkey Report**
Urner Barry Publications
PO Box 389
Toms River, NJ 08754-389

732-240-5330
800-932-0617; *Fax:* 732-341-0891
help@urnerbarry.com; www.urnerbarry.com

Paul B Brown Jr, President
Sheila M Deane, Marketing Manager
Richard A. Brown, VP Treasurer
Michael W. O'Shaughnessy, Secretary

Statistical report containing slaughter figures, consumption patterns, US Storage Stock Estimates and comparative weekly prices.
Cost: $173.00
4 Pages
Frequency: Weekly
Circulation: 230
ISSN: 0160-4910
Founded in: 1858

9558 **Weekly Livestock Reporter**
Weekly Livestock
PO Box 7655
Fort Worth, TX 76111-0655

817-838-0106; *Fax:* 817-831-3117
service@weeklylivestock.com;
www.weeklylivestock.com

Ted Gouldy, Publisher
Phil Stoll, Editor

Offers comprehensive weekly information for cattle farmers and livestock agricultural professionals.
Cost: $18.00
Frequency: Weekly
Circulation: 10000
Founded in: 1897

9559 **Weekly Weather and Crop Bulletin**
NOAA/USDA Joint Agricultural Weather Facility
1400 Independence Ave SW
Washington, DC 20250

202-720-2791
jawfweb@oce.usda.gov; www.noaa.gov

Robert Keeney, Administrator
David Miscus, Managing Editor

Provides a vital source of information on weather, climate and agricultural developments worldwide, along with detailed charts and tables of agrometeorological information that is appropriate for the season.
Frequency: Weekly
Circulation: 1500
Founded in: 1807

9560 **Western Hemisphere Agriculture and Trade Report**
US Department of Agriculture
Room 112-A
US Department of Agriculture
Washington, DC 20250-3810

202-012-2000; *Fax:* 202-690-4915
webmaster@usda.gov; www.usda.gov

Miriam Stuart, Publisher
Abraham Lincoln, Chief Information Officer
Chris Smith, Chief Information Officer
Matt Paul, Director of Communications
Ramona Romero, General Counsel

Information on current and projected agricultural production and trade trends for North, Central, South America and the Caribbean. Includes information on trade agreements and blocks in the Hemisphere.
Founded in: 1862

9561 **What's News in Organic**
Organic Trade Association
60 Wells Street
PO Box 547
Greenfield, MA 01302

413-774-7511; *Fax:* 413-774-6432
info@ota.com; www.ota.com
Social Media: Facebook, Twitter, LinkedIn

Matt McLean, President
Sarah Bird, Vice President
Todd Linsky, Secretary
Kristen Holt, Treasurer

Includes a feature focusing on a hot topic for the industry, a pertinent quotation, and a world of news section outlining brief news related to the industry. Electronic publication.
Frequency: Quarterly
Founded in: 1985

9562 **Wine on Line Food and Wine Review**
Enterprise Publishing
PO Box 328
Blair, NE 68008-0328

402-426-2121; *Fax:* 402-426-2227
mrhoades@enterprisepub.com;
www.enterprisepub.com

Mark Rhoades, President
Dave Smith, Production Manager
Tracy Prettyman, Business Manager

Reviews, feature articles and information on all areas of food and wine, including restaurants, hotels, trains and airlines. Accepts advertising.
Cost: $100.00
10 Pages
Frequency: Monthly

9563 **fridayfeedback**
Meat & Livestock Australia
1401 K Street NW
Suite 602
Washington, DC 20005

202-521-2551; *Fax:* 202-521-2699
info@mla.com.au; www.mla.com.au
Social Media: Facebook, Twitter, YouTube

Don Heatley, Chairman
David Palmer, Managing Director
Bernie Bindon, Director
Chris Hudson, Director

Providing a weekly wrap-up of market information, industry news and updates, and on-farm information including tools and calculators, and producer case studies.
30000 Members
Frequency: Weekly
Founded in: 1998

Magazines & Journals

9564 **ABF E-Buzz**
American Beekeeping Federation

3525 Piedmont Rd
Bldg 5 Suite 300
Atlanta, GA 30305-1509

404-760-2875; *Fax:* 404-240-0998
info@abfnet.org; www.abfnet.org

Regina Roebuck, Executive Director
Gene Brandi, President

A member benefit published electronically to inform members about ABF activities and happenings in the beekeeping industry.
Cost: $35.00
Frequency: Membership Fees Vary
Founded in: 1943

9565 ABL Insider
American Beverage Licensees Association
5101 River Rd
Suite 108
Bethesda, MD 20816-1512

301-656-1494; *Fax:* 301-656-7539
rogers@ablusa.org; www.ablusa.org
Social Media: Facebook, Twitter

Chuck Ferrar, President
Ray Cox, Vice President
Harry Klock, Vice President
Victor Pittman, Vice President
Robert Sprenger, Vice President

A publication of the American Beverage Licensees, the voice of America's beer, wine, and spirits retailers.
17000 Members
Founded in: 2002

9566 AHA Quarterly
American Herb Association
PO Box 1673
Nevada City, CA 9595-1673

530-265-9552; *Fax:* 530-274-3140;
www.ahaherb.com

Kathi Keville, Editor/Director
Mindy Green, Associate Editor

Contains news bulletins, scientific studies, book reviews, research in the field and networking between members. Also offers directories of herb education and mail order sources of herbs.
Cost: $20.00
20 Pages
Frequency: Quarterly
Circulation: 1000
Founded in: 1981
Printed in on matte stock

9567 ASMC Sales & Marketing Magazine
Association of Sales & Marketing Companies
1010 Wisconsin Avenue NW, #900
9th Floor
Washington, DC 20007

202-337-9351; *Fax:* 202-337-4508
info@asmc.org; www.ama.org

Jamie DeSimone, Dir, Marketing/Member Services

Reports on the progress and change in the food broker profession.
Cost: $25.00
450 Pages
Frequency: Bi-Annual
ISSN: 0884-7185
Founded in: 1904
Printed in 4 colors

9568 AWS Wine Journal
American Wine Society
P.O. Box 889
Scranton, PA 18501

888-297-9070; www.americanwinesociety.org
Social Media: Facebook, Twitter, LinkedIn

David Falchek, Executive Director
Kristin Casler Kraft, President

Contains articles on all aspects of wine appreciation, wine making, wine destinations, and wine & food. Articles provide a wide range of exciting stories and educational information.
Frequency: Quarterly
Founded in: 1967
Mailing list available for rent: 3000 names

9569 AgProfessional Magazine
Agricultural Retailers Association
1156 15th St NW
Suite 500
Washington, DC 20005-1745

202-457-0825
800-844-4900; *Fax:* 202-457-0864;
www.agprofessional.com
Social Media: Twitter, YouTube

Provides editorial and advertising for agronomic and business management solutions specifically to agricultural retailers/distributors, professional farm managers and crop consultants.
1200 Members
Frequency: Membership Dues Vary
Founded in: 1993

9570 Agri Marketing Magazine
Henderson Communications LLC
1422 Elbridge Payne Rd
Suite 250
Chesterfield, MO 63017-8544

636-728-1428; *Fax:* 636-777-4178
info@agrimarketing.com;
www.agrimarketing.com

Lynn Henderson, Owner

Covers the unique interests of corporate agribusiness executives, their marketing communications agencies, the agricultural media, ag trade associations and other ag related professionals.
Frequency: Monthly
Circulation: 8000
Founded in: 1962

9571 Agribusiness Fieldman
Western Agricultural Publishing Company
4969 E Clinton Way
Suite 104
Fresno, CA 93727-1549

559-252-7000
888-382-9772; *Fax:* 559-252-7387
westag@psnw.com; www.westagpubco.com

Paul Baltimore, Publisher
Randy Bailey, Editor
Robert Fujimoto, Assistant Director

For the professional agricultural consultant, featuring the latest information on chemical regulation, pest control techniques and feature stories on PCA and PCO community.

9572 Airline Catering International
International Inflight Food Service Association
5775 Peachtree-Dunwoody Road, Building G
Suite 500
Atlanta, GA 30342
404-252-3663; *Fax:* 404-252-0774
ifsa@kellencompany.com; www.ifsanet.com
Social Media: Facebook, Twitter, LinkedIn, YouTube

Sandra Pineau, President
Ken Samara, VP

A review of inflight catering and galley equipment. Provides expert coverage and analysis of next-generation galley technology through to the latest menu development trends and eco-friendly food packaging initiatives. Offers a fresh take on the fast-moving and specialized inflight catering market.
400 Members
Frequency: Bi-Annually
Founded in: 1965

9573 Alaska Fisherman's Journal
Diversified Business Communications
PO Box 7437
Portland, ME 04112-7437

207-842-5600; *Fax:* 207-842-5503;
www.divbusiness.com

Nancy Hasselback, CEO
Randy Le Shane, Production Manager
Mike Lodato, Publisher
Neil Casey, Advertising Coordinator
Stephanie Wendel, Audience Development Manager

Primary publication serving the North Pacific commercial fishing fleet in the world's healthiest and most lucrative commercial fishing region.
Cost: $21.00
Frequency: Monthly
Circulation: 10,000
ISSN: 0164-8330

9574 Alimentos Balanceados Para Animales
WATT Publishing Company
122 S Wesley Ave
Mt Morris, IL 61054-1451

815-734-7937; *Fax:* 815-734-4201;
www.wattnet.com

Clayton Gill, Editorial Director
James Watt, Owner

For feed industry professionals in Latin America.
Cost: $42.00
Circulation: 9471
ISSN: 0274-5571
Founded in: 1917
Printed in 4 colors on glossy stock

9575 All About Beer
501 Washington St
Suite H
Durham, NC 27701-2169

919-530-8150
800-999-9718; *Fax:* 919-530-8160
editor@allaboutbeer.com;
www.allaboutbeer.com

Julie Bradford, Publisher
Natalie Abernethy, Circulation Manager

Quality beers, breweries and restaurants.
Cost: $19.99

9576 Allied Tradesman
Allied Trades of the Baking Industry
2001 Shawnee Mission Pkwy
Mission Woods, KS 62205

707-935-0103; *Fax:* 707-935-0174;
www.atbi.org

Gary Cain, President
Tim Miller, Secretary, Treasurer
Brad Hahn, Secretary, Treasurer
Matt Ungashick, Secretary
Bruce Criss, Vice President
Frequency: Monthly
Circulation: 500
Founded in: 1920

9577 Almond Facts
Blue Diamond Growers
1802 C Street
PO Box 1768
Sacramento, CA 95811

916-442-0771; *Fax:* 916-325-2880
feedback@bdgrowers.com;
www.bluediamond.com

Robert Donovan, CFO
Douglas D Youngdahl, CEO/President

The latest news affecting Blue Diamond and the almond industry with Almond Facts magazine. Service to Blue Diamond's grower-owners, also

available online.
Cost: $25.00
Frequency: Bi-Monthly
Founded in: 1910
Printed in 4 colors

9578 American Beefalo World Registry
30 Stevenson Road
#5
Laramie, WY 82070

307-745-3505
866-374-2297; *Fax:* 307-745-3505;
www.abwr.org

Offers information for beef and cattle farmers.

9579 American Brewer
1049 B Street
PO Box 510
Hayward, CA 94543-510

510-886-7418; *Fax:* 510-538-7644
info@ambrew.com; www.ambrew.com

Bill Owens, Publisher
Greg Kitsock, Editor

A magazine covering the business of beer.
Cost: $50.00
Frequency: Quarterly
Founded in: 1979

9580 American Fruit Grower
Meister Publishing Company
37733 Euclid Ave
Willoughby, OH 44094-5992

440-942-2000
800-572-7740; *Fax:* 440-975-3447;
www.meisternet.com

Gary Fitzgerald, President
Joe Monahan, Group Publisher
Fran Mihalik, Circulation Manager

Specialized production and marketing information and industry-wide support for fruit growers.
Cost: $19.95
66 Pages
Frequency: Monthly
Circulation: 37,000
Founded in: 1931

9581 American Journal of Enology and Viticulture
American Society for Enology and Viticulture
1784 Picasso Avenue Suite D
PO Box 2160
Davis, CA 95617-2160

530-753-3142; *Fax:* 530-753-3318;
www.ajevonline.org

Judith McKibben, Managing Editor

Full-length research papers, literature reviews, research notes and technical briefs on various aspects of enology and viticulture, including wine chemistry, sensory science, process engineering, wine quality assessments, microbiology, methods development, plant pathogenesis, diseases and pests of grape, rootstock and clonal evaluation, effect of field practices and grape genetics and breeding.
Frequency: Quarterly
Mailing list available for rent

9582 American Red Angus Magazine
Red Angus Association of America
4201 N Interstate 35
Denton, TX 76207-3415

940-387-3502; *Fax:* 888-829-5573
info@redangus.org; www.redangus.org
Social Media: Facebook

Joe Mushrush, President
Greg Comstock, CEO

The most comprehensive resource guide to the Red Angus breed. Keep informed about a breed that is focused on economic value, efficiency and quality.
2000 Members
Founded in: 1954

9583 American Small Farm Magazine
560 Sunbury Rd
Suite 6
Delaware, OH 43015-8692

740-363-2395; *Fax:* 740-369-9526
sales@smallfarm.com; www.smallfarm.com

Marti Smith, Information
Andy Stevens, Editor

Published for the owner/operator of farms from five to three hundred acres. Focuses on production agriculture including alternative and sustainable farming ideas and technology, case studies, small farm lifestyle and tradition.
Cost: $18.00
ISSN: 1064-7473

9584 American Vegetable Grower
Meister Media Worldwide
37733 Euclid Ave
Willoughby, OH 44094-5992

440-942-2000
800-572-7740; *Fax:* 440-975-3447;
www.meisternet.com

Gary Fitzgerald, President
Ken Hall, Communications Manager
Josep W Monahan, Publisher
Fran Mihalik, Circulation manager

Information source for commercial vegetable growers.
Cost: $19.95
Frequency: Monthly
Circulation: 34772
Founded in: 1931

9585 American Wholesale Marketers Association/ Convenience Distribution
American Wholesale Marketers Association
2750 Prosperity Ave
Suite 530
Fairfax, VA 22031-4338

703-208-3358
800-482-2962; *Fax:* 703-573-5738
info@awmanet.org; www.cdaweb.net

Scott Ramminger, Publisher Executive Editor
Joan Fay, Editor + Associate Publisher

A magazine specifically targeted toward convenience distributors. Our readers are involved in the purchase and sale of candy, tobacco, snacks, beverages, health and beauty care items, general merchandise, foodservice, groceries and more.
Cost: $36.00
Frequency: Monthly/Non-Members Fee
Circulation: 11,000
ISSN: 1083-9313
Printed in 4 colors on glossy stock

9586 Angus Journal
American Angus Association
3201 Frederick Ave
St Joseph, MO 64506-2997

816-383-5100; *Fax:* 816-233-9703
angus@angus.org; www.angus.org
Social Media: Facebook, Twitter

Joe Hampton, Chair
Jarold Callahan, Vice Chair
Phil Trowbridge, Treasurer

To provide programs, services, technology and leadership to enhance the genetics of the Angus breed, broaden its influence within the beef industry, and expand the market for superior tasting, high-quality Angus beef worldwide. Achieve Angus excellence through information.
Cost: $80.00
30+M Members
Frequency: Membership Fees Vary
Founded in: 1883

9587 Applied Economic Perspectives and Policy
Agricultural & Applied Economics Association
555 E. Wells St.
Suite 1100
Milwaukee, WI 53202-6600

414-918-3190
Info@aaea.org; www.aaea.org

Robert P. King, President
Richard Sexton, President-Elect
Bruce A. Babcock, Director
Jayson Lusk, Director
Lori Lynch, Director

Publishes articles that synthsize, integrate, and analyze areas of current applied economic research within the mission of the AAEA as well as stimulate linkages between sub-fields of agricultural and applied economics.
Cost: $ 150.00
4M Members
Frequency: Regular Membership Fee
Founded in: 1910

9588 Applied Engineering in Agriculture
American Society of Agricultural Engineers
2950 Niles Rd
St Joseph, MI 49085-8607

269-429-0300
800-371-2723; *Fax:* 269-429-3852
hq@asabe.org; www.asabe.org

Mark D Zielke, CEO
Donna Hull, Pubilcation Director

Focus is on agricultural equipment, farm buildings, electrification, soil conservation, irrigation and food engineering.
26 Pages
Frequency: Monthly
Circulation: 9000
Founded in: 1907

9589 Aquaculture Magazine
Achill River Corporation
PO Box 2329
Asheville, NC 28802-2329

828-687-0011; *Fax:* 828-681-0601;
www.aquaculturemag.com

Gregory J Gallagher, Editor/Publisher
Doinita Ciociovei, Circulation Manager
Joseth Strickland, Advertisement Manager

Focus emphasizes the production, processing, and marketing of aquatic organisms and plant life.
Founded in: 1968

9590 Arbor Age
Green Media
1030 W Higgins Road
Suite 230
Park Ridge, IL 60068

847-720-5600; *Fax:* 847-720-5601;
www.arborage.com

John Kmitta, Senior Editor

Targets arborists in the commercial, municipal and utility sectors. Content is provided by a wide range of green industry experts, including professional arborists, academicians, instructors, consultants, government bodies and research organizations.
43 Pages
Frequency: 9x Yearly
Circulation: 16,500
Founded in: 1981
Printed in 4 colors on glossy stock

9591 Atlantic Control States Beverage Journal
Club & Tavern

3 12th Street
Wheeling, WV 26003-3276

304-232-7620; *Fax:* 304-233-1236

Arnold Lazarus, Editor

A magazine for the alcoholic beverage industry. Serving bars, restaurants, clubs and industry personnel with West Virginia, Virginia, and North Carolina state editions. Includes states' liquor price lists.

9592 Automatic Merchandiser
Cygnus Business Media
1233 Janesville Avenue
Fort Atkinson, WI 53538

800-547-7377; www.vendingmarketwatch.com

Gary Thom, Publisher

Serves the business management, marketing, technology and product information needs of its readers.
Cost: $66.00
84 Pages
Frequency: Monthly
Circulation: 14000
Founded in: 1937
Mailing list available for rent: 16004 names at $150 per M
Printed in 4 colors on newsprint stock

9593 Bake Magazine
Sosland Publishing Company
4801 Main St
Suite 100
Kansas City, MO 64112-2513

816-756-1000; *Fax:* 816-756-0494; www.sosland.com

John Unrein, Editor
John Sonderegger, Publisher
Troy Ashby, Associate Publisher

Focuses on wholesale baking, specialty bakeries, and retail bakeries.
Cost: $25.00
Frequency: Annual

9594 Baker's Rack
Retail Bakers of America
202 Village Circle
Suite 1
Slidell, LA 70458

985-643-6504
800-638-0924; *Fax:* 985-643-6929
Info@RBAnet.com; www.rbanet.com
Social Media: Facebook

Felix Sherman, Sr., President
Kenneth Downey, Sr., 1st Vice President
Marlene Goetzeler, 2nd Vice President
Dale A. Biles, Treasurer
Susan Nicolais, CAE, Secretary

Reaching retail baking professionals and the baking industry as a whole. Articles are submitted from industry experts who understand the unique interests and needs of today's retail baker.
2000 Members
Frequency: Quarterly
Founded in: 1918

9595 Bakery Production and Marketing
245 W 17th Street
1350 E Toughy Avenue
New York, NY 10011

212-414-1160; *Fax:* 212-337-7198; www.cahners.com

Doug Krumrei, Editor
Stuart Whayman, CFO

Dedicated to delivering sensible ideas for profitable baking with editorial that addresses solutions and opportunities found within retail, instore, food service and intermediate wholesale bakeries.
Cost: $70.00
Frequency: Monthly
Circulation: 31,000

9596 Baking & Snack
Sosland Publishing Company
4801 Main St
Suite 100
Kansas City, MO 64112-2513

816-756-1000; *Fax:* 816-756-0494; www.sosland.com

Dan Malovany, Editorial Director
Lauri Gorton, Executive Editor
Joanie Spences, Managing Editor
Mike Gude, Director, Publishing

Magazine published with a focus on food processing & in-plant operations.
Circulation: 31000
Founded in: 1922

9597 Baking and Snack
Paul Lattan
4800 Main Street
Suite 100
Kansas City, MO 64112-2504

816-756-1000; *Fax:* 816-756-0494
bbcservice@sosland.com; www.bakingbusiness.com

Steve Barne, Editor
Laurie Gorton, Executive Editor

A magazine offering information on baking equipment and ingredients for the commercial baker.
Frequency: Monthly
Circulation: 12,494
Founded in: 1922

9598 Bar & Beverage Business Magazine
Mercury Publications
1839 Inkster Boulevard
Winnipeg, Ma 0

204-954-2085; *Fax:* 204-954-2057
webmaster@mercury.mb.ca; www.mercury.mb.ca/

Frank Yeo, Publisher
Robert Thompson, National Account Manager
Kelly Gray, Editor
Angie Finnbogason, Circulation Manager
Carly Peters, Editorial Production Manager

The buying and selling of beverages, operator profiles, new products, product merchandising and trends.
Cost: $35.00
Frequency: Quarterly
Circulation: 16923
Founded in: 1948
Mailing list available for rent

9599 Bartender Magazine
Foley Publishing Corporation
PO Box 157
Spring Lake, NJ 07762

732-449-4499; *Fax:* 732-974-8289
barmag@aol.com; www.bartender.com
Social Media: Facebook, Twitter

Raymond Foley, Publisher
Jaclyn Wilson Foley, Editor

Serves all full-service drinking establishments, including individual restaurants, hotels, motels, bars, taverns, lounges and all other full service on premise licenses.
76 Pages
Frequency: Quarterly
Circulation: 104000
Founded in: 1979
Printed in 4 colors on glossy stock

9600 Bee Culture
AI Root Company
PO Box 706
Medina, OH 44258-0706

330-725-6677
800-289-7668; *Fax:* 330-725-5624
weboptout@rootcandles.com; www.rootcandles.com

John Root, President
Kathy Summers, Production Manager

Honey bees and their keeping for beginners and experienced apiculturists. Accepts advertising, press releases, new products, and book reviews.
Cost: $21.50
64 Pages
Circulation: 12000
ISSN: 1071-3190
Founded in: 1863
Printed in 4 colors on matte stock

9601 Beer, Wine & Spirits Beverage Retailer
Oxford Publishing
Ste 1
1903b University Ave
Oxford, MS 38655-4150

662-236-5510
800-247-3881; *Fax:* 662-236-5541; www.nightclub.com

Ed Meek, Publisher
Michael Harrelson, Editor
Jennifer Parsons, Marketing
Jennifer Robinson, COO
Adam Alson, Founder

Beverage Retailer serves retail establishments in the beer, wine and spirits industries, including liquor, package and wine stores and others allied to the field.
Cost: $30.00
52 Pages
Frequency: Monthly
Circulation: 19985
Founded in: 1997
Printed in 4 colors on glossy stock

9602 Beverage Dynamics
The Beverage Information Group
17 High Street
2nd Floor
Norwalk, CT 06851

203-855-8499
lzimmerman@m2media360.com; www.bevinfogroup.com

Liza Zimmerman, Editor-in-Chief
Jeremy Nedelka, Managing Editor

Provides a unique and essential communciations link between suppliers and chain and independent retailers in the off-premise market (liquor stores, supermarkets, beverage outlets, etc)
Cost: $35.00
Frequency: Bi-Monthly
Founded in: 1934

9603 Beverage Industry
Stagnito Communications
2401 W Big Beaver Road
Suite 700
Troy, MI 48084

847-763-9534; *Fax:* 847-763-9538
bi@halldata.com; www.bevindustry.com
Social Media: Facebook, Twitter, LinkedIn

Steve Pintarelli, Publisher
Jessica Jacobsen, Editor
Stephanie Cernivec, Managing Editor

Provides the most in-depth information about the beverage market including production, technology and distribution. The changing industry demands a change leader and BI fills that role by reporting behind the scenes of the gigantic 65 bil-

lion market.
Cost: $40.00
Frequency: Monthly
Circulation: 28000
Founded in: 1946

9604 **Beverage Journal**
Michigan Licensed Beverage Association
920 N Fairview Ave
Lansing, MI 48912-3238

517-374-9611
877-292-2896; *Fax:* 517-374-1165
info@mlba.org; www.mlba.org

Lou Adado, CEO
Catherine Pavick, Executive Director

Offers information on the alcoholic beverage industry/retail sales
Cost: $52.00
Frequency: Monthly
ISSN: 1050-4427
Printed in on glossy stock

9605 **Beverage Media**
Beverage Media Group
152 Madison Avenue
Suite 600
New York, NY 10016

212-571-3232; *Fax:* 212-571-4443;
www.bevnetwork.com

Journal offering information on the liquor, wine and beer trade. New products & promotions, industry news and current trends.
Cost: $119.00
Frequency: Monthly

9606 **Beverage Network**
4437 Concord Lane
Skokie, IL 60076-2605

617-497-0062; *Fax:* 617-812-7740
sales@bevnet.com; www.bevnet.com

Organization of beverage distributors dealing with specialty, nonalcoholic products.

9607 **Beverage Retailer Magazine**
Oxford Publishing
Ste 1
1903b University Ave
Oxford, MS 38655-4150

662-236-5510
800-247-3881; *Fax:* 662-236-5541;
www.bevindustry.com

Ed Meek, Publisher
Brenda Owen, Editor
Ruth Ann Wolfe, Circualtion Manager

A magazine covering the off-premise market for retailers in the wine, beer and spirits business.
Cost: $30.00
Frequency: Monthly
Circulation: 25000
Founded in: 1920
Printed in 4 colors on glossy stock

9608 **Biodynamics**
Biodynamic Farming & Gardening Association
PO Box 944
East Troy, WI 53120-0944

262-649-9212
info@biodynamics.com;
www.biodynamics.com
Social Media: Facebook

Charles Beedy, Contact

A membership publication providing a thoughtful collection of original articles centered on a theme of interest to the biodynamic community. Voices from the community, discussion of the biodynamic preparations, regional, national, and international news and updates, event overviews, book and film reviews, organizational updates, seasonal recipes, columns and more.
Cost: $45.00
Frequency: 6 per year
Circulation: 1000+

9609 **Bison World Magazine**
National Bison Association
8690 Wolff Ct
200
Westminster, CO 80234

303-292-2833; *Fax:* 303-845-9081
david@bisoncentral.com;
www.bisoncentral.com

Jim Matheson, Assistant Director
Dave Carter, Executive Director

Featured articles and regular departments cover all aspects of raising bison and what's happening in this exciting industry. Available with all levels of membership with the association.
Frequency: Quarterly
Circulation: 1000

9610 **Body, Mind & Spirit Magazine**
PO Box 95
Dogsland, SK

306-356-4634; *Fax:* 306-356-4634;
www.saskworld.com/bodymindspirit

Jeni Mayer, Publisher
Adele Azar-Rucquoi, Contributing Writers
Frequency: Quarterly

9611 **Bottled Water Reporter**
International Bottled Water Association
1700 Diagonal Rd
Suite 650
Alexandria, VA 22314-2870

703-683-5213
817-719-6197; *Fax:* 703-683-4074
ibwainfo@bottledwater.org;
www.bottledwater.org

Joseph Doss, Publisher/President

Covers IBWA events and programs while highlighting new technologies and equipment within the industry, taking notice of personnel changes and reporting on the latest industry statistical data. It also features useful articles on management, operations and marketing specific to the bottled water industry.
Cost: $50.00
74 Pages
Circulation: 2500
Founded in: 1958
Printed in 4 colors on glossy stock

9612 **Brahman Journal**
American Brahman Breeders Association
915 12th Street
Suite 520
Houston, TX 77054

979-826-4347; *Fax:* 979-826-2007
info@brahmanjournal.com;
www.brahmanjournal.com
Social Media: Facebook

Victoria Lambert, Editor
Brandy Barnes, Field Representative
Mandy Chambers, Assistant Editor

Provides timely, useful information about one of the largest. most dynamic and most influential breeds of beef cattle in the world. Each issue reports on American Brahman and International Brahman shows, American Brahman and international Brahman events, Brahman sales and Brahman history, as well as pertinent cattle industry news, technical articles and the latest research as it pertains to the Brahman Breed and its followers.
Cost: $25.00
Frequency: Monthly
Circulation: 7000
Founded in: 1971

9613 **Brandpackaging**
Independent Publishing Company
P.O.Box 3116
Saint George, UT 84771-3116

435-656-1555
800-808-7449; *Fax:* 435-656-1511;
www.independentpublishing.com

Josh Warburton, President/Publisher
Circulation: 5500
Founded in: 1996

9614 **Brewers Digest**
Siebel Publishing Company
Business Office
PO Box 677
Thiensville, WI 53092-6026
915-877-3319; *Fax:* 915-877-3319

Thomas Volke, Publisher
Dori Whitney, Editor

The gamut of operational, production, buying, engineering, and packaging issues affecting brewing companies and enterprises.
Cost: $20.00
70 Pages
Frequency: Monthly
Circulation: 3000
ISSN: 0006-971X
Founded in: 1926
Printed in 4 colors on glossy stock

9615 **Business of Herbs**
Northwind Farm Publications
439 Ponderosa Way
Jemez Springs, NM 87025-8036

505-829-3448; *Fax:* 505-829-3449;
www.herbworld.com/businessofherbs.htm

Paula Oliver, Publisher
David Oliver, Editor

Primarily for herb businesses and those keenly interested in herbs and botanicals.
Cost: $4.00

9616 **Calf News (Cattle Feeder Magazine)**
1531 Kensington Boulevard
Garden City, KS 67846

620-276-7844; *Fax:* 620-275-7333
steve@calfnews.com; www.calfnews.net

Betty Jo Gigot, Editor & Publisher
Patti Wilson, Sales Manager
Larisa Willrett, Copy Editor/Circulation
Kathie Bedolli, Director

This magazine offers the latest information to cattle breeders and feeders.
Cost: $33.00
Circulation: 6,352
Founded in: 1964

9617 **Candy Industry**
Stagnito Communications
155 Pfingsten Road
Suite 205
Deerfield, IL 60015

847-205-5660; *Fax:* 847-205-5680;
www.stagnito.com

Harry Stagnito, President
Korry Stagnito, Publishing Director
Sue Ravenscraft, VP Circulation

Magazine serving chocolate and confectionary manufacturers.
Cost: $59.00
Frequency: Monthly
Founded in: 1944
Printed in 4 colors on glossy stock

9618 **Capital Press**
Press Publishing Company

PO Box 2048
Salem, OR 97308-2048

503-364-4431
800-882-6789; *Fax:* 503-370-4383;
www.capitalpress.com

Carl Sampson, Managing Editor
Elaine Shein, Editor/Publisher
Mike O'Brien, Circulation/General Manager

For the agricultural and forest community of the Pacific Northwest.
Cost: $44.00
60 Pages
Frequency: Weekly
Circulation: 37000
Founded in: 1928
Printed in 4 colors on newsprint stock

9619 Carnetec
1415 N Dayton
Chicago, IL 60622

312-266-3311; *Fax:* 312-266-3363
annica@meatingplace.com; www.carnetec.com

Ryan Pfister, Product Manager

Spanish language magazine reaching executives in the Latin American meat and poultry processing industry. Helps improve the manufacturing process, equipment, sanitation, safety and technology.

9620 Carrot Country
Columbia Publishing
8405 Ahtanum Rd
Yakima, WA 98903-9432

509-248-2452
800-900-2452; *Fax:* 509-248-4056;
www.carrotcountry.com

Brent Clement, Editor/Publisher
Mike Stoker, Publisher

Includes information on carrot production, grower and shipper feature stories, carrot research, new varieties, market reports, spot reports on overseas production and marketing and other key issues and trends of interest to US and Canadian carrot growers.
Cost: $10.00
Frequency: Quarterly
Circulation: 2700
Founded in: 1975
Printed in 4 colors on glossy stock

9621 Cereal Chemistry
AACC International
3340 Pilot Knob Rd
St. Paul, MN 55121-2055

651-454-7250
800-328-7560; *Fax:* 651-454-0766
aacc@scisoc.org; www.aaccnet.org

Les Copeland, Editor-In-Chief
F. William Collins, Senior Editors
Ian Batey, Associate Editors

The premier international archival journal in cereal science. Juried, original research exploring topics that range from raw materials, processes, products utilizing cereal, to oilseeds, pulses, as well as analytical procedures, technological tests and fundamental research in the cereals area.
Cost: $79.00
Frequency: Bi-Monthly
Circulation: 3539
ISSN: 0009-0352
Founded in: 1915

9622 Cereal Foods World
AACC International
3340 Pilot Knob Rd
Eagan, MN 55121-2055

651-454-7250
800-328-7560; *Fax:* 651-454-0766;
www.scientificsocieties.org

Steven Nelson, VP
Bernie Bruinsma, Chair of Board
Laura Hansen, Treasurer

A leading source of information on grain-based food science, technology, and new product development. Includes articles that focus on advances in grain-based food science and the application of these advances to product development and current food production practices.
Cost: $48.00
Frequency: Bi-Monthly
Circulation: 4500
ISSN: 0146-6283
Founded in: 1956

9623 Cheers
Jobson Publishing Corporation
100 Avenue of the Americas
Suite 9
New York, NY 10013-1678

212-274-7000; *Fax:* 212-431-0500;
www.jobson.com

Michael J Tansey, CEO

Every issue is designed to help on-premise operators enhance the profitability of their beverage operations.

9624 Cheese Market News
Quarne Publishing
PO Box 620244
Middleton, WI 53562

608-831-6002; *Fax:* 608-831-1004
squarne@cheesemarketnews.com;
www.cheesemarketnews.com

Susan Quarne, Publisher
Kate Sander, Editorial Director

Weekly trade news for the nation's cheese and dairy/deli business
Cost: $105.00
16 Pages
Frequency: Weekly
Circulation: 2200
ISSN: 0891-1509
Founded in: 1981
Mailing list available for rent: 2200 names at $500 per M
Printed in 4 colors on newsprint stock

9625 Chef
Talcott Communications Corporation
20 W Kinzie St
Suite 1200
Chicago, IL 60654-5827

312-849-2220
800-229-1967; *Fax:* 312-849-2174;
www.talcott.com

Daniel Von Rabenau, Executive Director
Robert S Benes, Senior Editor

Information on food production and presentation, includes chef profiles, trend studies, marketing information and restaurant profiles.
Cost: $32.00
Circulation: 40,000
ISSN: 1087-061X
Founded in: 1956
Printed in 4 colors on glossy stock

9626 Chemical and Pharmaceutical Press
C&P Press
90 william strret
5th Floor
New York, NY 10106-2899

212-326-6760
800-544-7377; *Fax:* 646-733-6010;
www.pharmpress.com

Dr. Mary Conway, Executive Editor
Bron Zienkiewicz, Sales/Marketing
Sonia Tighe, Publisher

Supplies chemical information to professionals involved with the sale, application, storage or regulations of agricultural or ornamental and turf pesticides. Information is available in either reference book form or on computer disc. Complete product labels, MSDS's and indexes are included.
Founded in: 1984

9627 Choices
Agricultural & Applied Economics Association
555 E Wells Street
Suite 1100
Milwaukee, WI 53202

414-918-3190; *Fax:* 414-276-3349
info@aaea.org; www.choicesmagazine.org

Walter J Armbruster, Editor
James Novak, Associate Editor

Provides current coverage regarding economic implications of food, farm, resource, or rural community issues directed toward a broad audience. Publishes thematic groupings of papers and individual papers.
Frequency: Quarterly
ISSN: 0886-5558
Founded in: 1910
Printed in 4 colors on glossy stock

9628 Citograph
Western Agricultural Publishing Company
4969 E Clinton Way
#104
Fresno, CA 93727-1549

559-252-7000; *Fax:* 559-252-7387;
www.westapub.com

Paul Baltimore, Publisher

The oldest continuous citrus-specific publication in the world. Stories centering on all aspects of citrus production from planting to harvest and all maintenance in between. Lemons, limes, oranges, avocados — all citrus is included.

9629 Citrus & Vegetable Magazine
Vance Publishing
400 Knightsbridge Parkway
Lincolnshire, IL 60069

847-634-2600; *Fax:* 847-634-4379
info@vancepublishing.com;
www.vancepublishing.com

William C Vance, Chairman
Peggy Walker, President

Delivers profitable production and management strategies to commerical citrus and vegetable growers in Florida.
Cost: $45.00
Frequency: Monthly
Circulation: 12004

9630 CleanRooms Magazine
PennWell Publishing Company
98 Spit Brook Rd
Suite 100
Nashua, NH 03062-5737

603-891-0123; *Fax:* 603-891-9294
info@pennwell.com; www.pennwell.com

Christine Shaw, VP
James Enos, Publisher
Adam Japker, CEO

Serves the contamination control and ultrapure materials and process industries. Written for readers in the microelectronics, pharmaceutical, biotech, health care, food processing and other user industries. Provides technology and business news and new product listings.
Founded in: 1987

9631 Communications in Soil Science and Plant Analysis
Marcel Dekker
270 Madison Avenue
New York, NY 10016

212-696-9000
800-228-1160; *Fax:* 212-685-4540;
www.dekker.com

Harry A Mills, Editor
Marcel Dekker, President

All aspects of soil science and crop production in all climates.
Cost: $567.00
120 Pages
Circulation: 23500
ISSN: 0010-3624
Founded in: 1963

9632 Concession Profession
National Association of Concessoinaires
35 East Wacker Drive
Suite 1816
Chicago, IL 60601-2270

312-236-3858; *Fax:* 312-236-7809
info@naconline.org; www.naconline.org
Social Media: Facebook, LinkedIn

Charles A Winans, Executive Director
Susan M Cross, Communications Director
Barbara Aslan, Membership Services Manager

The NAC member magazine devoted to the recreational and leisuretime food and beverage concessions industry, featuring news briefs, feature articles, association news and advertising opportunities.
800 Members
Founded in: 1944

9633 Concession Professsion
National Association of Concessoinaires
35 E Wacker Dr
Suite 1816
Chicago, IL 60601-2270

312-236-3858; *Fax:* 312-236-7809
scross@NAConline.org; www.naconline.org
Social Media: Facebook, LinkedIn

John Evans, Jr., President
Jeff Scudillo, President-Elect
Ron Krueger II, Board Chairman

Devoted to the recreational and leisuretime food and beverage concessions industry, featuring news briefs, feature articles, association news and advertising opportunities.
Frequency: Bi-Annual
Printed in 4 colors

9634 Convenience Store Decisions
Harbor Communications
19111 Detroit Road
Suite 201
Rocky River, OH 44116

440-250-1538; *Fax:* 440-333-1892;
www.csdecisions.com

Jeff Donohoe, Owner
Jay Gordon, Editor

For buyers, directors, field managers, owners and executives in the convenience store business. Free to qualified subscribers.
180 Pages
Frequency: Monthly
Circulation: 40000+
Founded in: 1892

9635 Cooking for Profit
CP Publishing
PO Box 267
Fond du Lac, WI 54936

920-923-3700; *Fax:* 920-923-6805
comments@cookingforprofit.com;
www.cookingforprofit.com

Colleen Phalen, Editor-in-Chief/Publisher

Paid subscription trade magazine targeted to foodservice owners, managers and chefs. Each month features current trends in food preparation with step-by-step recipes and photographs; effective management techniques; and the latest in foodservice equipment — all written by industry experts. Also features in-depth profiles of a successful foodservice operation.
Cost: $26.00
28 Pages
Frequency: Monthly
Circulation: 75000
Founded in: 1932
Printed in 4 colors on glossy stock

9636 Cooperative Grocer
361 East College Street
Iowa City, IA 52240-267

319-466-9029; *Fax:* 866-600-4588
cooperativegrocer.coop

Dave Gutknecht, Editor
Dan Nordley, Publisher
Don McLemore, CEO

Trade magazine by and for people working with consumer cooperative grocery stores.
Founded in: 1999

9637 Cotton Farming
One Grower Publishing
5118 Park Avenue
Suite 111
Memphis, TN 38117-5710

901-767-4020; *Fax:* 901-767-4026;
www.cottonfarming.com
Social Media: Twitter, Flickr

Lia Guthrie, Publisher/VP
Tommy Horton, Editor

Serving the industry, providing the latest news and technology information.
Frequency: Monthly
Founded in: 1937

9638 Country Folks
Lee Publications
6113 State Highway 5
PO Box 121
Palatine Bridge, NY 13428-121

518-673-2269
800-218-5586; *Fax:* 518-673-3245
subscriptions@leepub.com;
www.countryfolks.com

Frederick Lee, Publisher
Marjorie Struckle, Editor
Bruce Button, President
Janet Button, Marketing Manager
Tom Mahoney, Sales Manager

Agricultural news from national, state and local levels. Some features on farm and agricultural industry, rural interest, etc.
Cost: $12.00
75 Pages
Frequency: Weekly
Circulation: 27000

9639 Country Living
Arens Corporation
PO Box 69
Covington, OH 45318-0069

937-473-2020; *Fax:* 937-473-2500
garyg@arenspub.com; www.arenspub.com

Gary Godfrey, Publisher/President
Don Selanders, Sales Manager
Connie Didier, Circulation Manager

Current news and features devoted to the agricultural industry.
Cost: $1395.00
Frequency: Monthly
Circulation: 17500
Founded in: 1950

9640 Country Woman
Reiman Publications
5400 S 60th St
Greendale, WI 53129-1404

414-423-0100
800-344-6913; *Fax:* 414-423-1143
editors@countrywomanmagazine.com;
www.countrywomanmagazine.com

Barbara Newton, President
Ann Kaiser, Editor

Offers recipes, stories, profiles and articles pertaining to the country woman.
Cost: $14.98
68 Pages
Founded in: 1965

9641 Critical Reviews in Food and Nutrition
CRC Press
6000 Broken Sound Pkwy NW
Suite 300
Boca Raton, FL 33487-5704

561-994-0555
800-272-7737; *Fax:* 561-989-9732
techsupport@crcpress.com; www.crcpress.com

Emmett Dages, CEO
Susan Lee, Editor
Founded in: 1913

9642 Culinary Trends
Culinary Trends Publications
6285 Spring St
Number 107
Long Beach, CA 90808

714-826-9188; *Fax:* 714-826-0333
Editor@culinarytrends.net;
www.culinarytrends.net

Fred Mensigna, Publisher
Jean Hutchins, Director

Information for food and beverage managers along with managers of hotels and restaurants.
Cost: $21.00
Frequency: Quarterly
Circulation: 10000
Founded in: 1993

9643 DDBC News
Dairy, Deli, Bakery Council of Southern California
PO Box 1872
Whittier, CA 90609

562-947-7016; *Fax:* 562-947-7872;
www.ddbcformation.org

Bob Dreffler, CEO
Dave Daniel, Editor
Susan Steele, Circulation Manager

Serves the deli, dairy, bakery and meat industry.
Cost: $25.00
Frequency: Monthly
Circulation: 5000
ISSN: 0011-7862
Founded in: 1960
Printed in 4 colors on glossy stock

9644 DFA Leader
Dairy Farmers of America

10220 N Ambassador Dr
Kansas City, MO 64153-1367

816-801-6455
888-332-6455; *Fax:* 816-801-6456
webmail@dfamilk.com; www.dfamilk.com
Social Media: Facebook, Twitter, LinkedIn, YouTube

Randy Mooney, Chairman of the Board
George Mertens, Vice Chairman
Tom Croner, Secretary/ Treasurer

Provides members with information about DFA and the dairy industry, along with features on members whose innovative ideas are worth emulating.
Frequency: Quarterly
Founded in: 1998

9645 Dairy Foods Magazine
Business News Publishing
1050 IL Route 83
Suite 200
Bensenville, IL 60106-1096

630-377-5909; *Fax:* 630-227-0527;
www.dairyfoods.com

Katie Rotella, Manager
David Phillips, Executive Editor
Marina Mayer, Executive Editor
Scott Wolters, Director
Barb Szatko, Regional Sales Manager

Dairy Foods serves the dairy industry by analyzing and reporting on technologies trends and issues and how they affest North America's processors of milk, cheese, frozen deserts and cultured products. Current issues and qualification forms for free subsciptions will be available to attendees. Dairy Foods is part of BNP Food Group.
Frequency: Weekly
Circulation: 20000
Founded in: 1926
Printed in 4 colors on glossy stock

9646 Dairy Today
AgWeb
30 S 15th Street
Suite 900
Philadelphia, PA 19102-4826

215-557-8900; *Fax:* 215-568-4436
jdickrell@farmjournal.com; www.agweb.com

Bill Newham, Publisher
Jim Dickrell, Editor

A trusted source of dairy information for its subscriber base of US dairy producers.
Frequency: Monthly
Circulation: 65000
Founded in: 1989

9647 Dairy, Food and Environmental Sanitation
International Association for Food Protection
6200 Aurora Ave
Suite 200W
Urbandale, IA 50322-2864

515-276-3344
800-369-6337; *Fax:* 515-276-8655
info@foodprotection.org;
www.foodprotection.org

David W Tharp, Executive Director
Vickie Lewandowski, VP
Isabel Walls, Secretary

Published as the general membership publication by the International Association for Food Protection, each issue contains referred articles on applied research, applications of current technology and general interest subjects for food safety professionals. Regular features include industry and association news, an industry related product section and a calendar of meetings, seminars and workshops.Updates of government regulations and sanitary design is also featured. All members receive DFES.
Cost: $227.00
Frequency: Monthly
Circulation: 3000
ISSN: 1043-3546
Mailing list available for rent: 3000+ names at $150 per M
Printed in 4 colors

9648 Dietitian's Edge
Rodman Publishing
70 Hilltop Rd
3rd Floor
Ramsey, NJ 07446-1150

201-825-2552; *Fax:* 201-825-0553
info@rodpub.com;
www.nutraceuticalsworld.com

Rodman Zilenziger Jr, President
Matt Montgomery, VP

9649 Drovers Journal
Vance Publishing
400 Knightsbridge Parkway
Lincolnshire, IL 60069

847-634-2600; *Fax:* 847-634-4379
info@vancepublishing.com;
www.vancepublishing.com

William C Vance, Chairman
Peggy Walker, President

Recognized as the beef industry leader for more than 30 years, valued for its management, production and marketing information.
Cost: $60.00
Frequency: Monthly
Circulation: 91715
Founded in: 1937

9650 Eastern Milk Producer
Eastern Milk Producers Cooperative Association
PO Box 6966
Syracuse, NY 13217-6966

315-437-1225

Bob Stronach, Editor
Trish Stokes, Production Manager

Communicates to members of the association dairy issues, farm issues, association events and policy.
Cost: $13.00
20 Pages
Frequency: Monthly

9651 Egg Industry
WATT Publishing Company
303 N Main Street
Suite 500
Rockford, IL 61101

815-966-5400; *Fax:* 815-966-6416
tokeefe@wattnet.net; www.wattnet.com

James Watt, Chairman/CEO
Greg Watt, President/COO
Terrence O'Keefe, Editor

Reports on trends, production practices, processing, marketing and economics, and is regarded as the standard for information on current issues, personalities and emerging technology. A pivotal source of news, data and information for innovators and decision-makers in the buying centers of companies producing eggs and further-processed products.
Cost: $36.00
Frequency: Monthly
Circulation: 1553
Founded in: 1917

9652 El Restaurante Mexicano
Maiden Name Press
PO Box 2249
Oak Park, IL 60303

708-267-0023
kfurore@restmex.com; www.restmex.com
Social Media: Facebook

A quarterly magazine featuring industry specific food news, features restaurant profiles and new product information for personnel of restaurants serving mexican/southwestern menu items nationwide.
Cost: $108.00
Circulation: 27000
ISSN: 1091-5885
Founded in: 1997
Printed in 4 colors on glossy stock

9653 Europe Agriculture and Trade Report
USDA Economic Research Service
1800 M Street NW
Washington, DC 20036-5831

202-203-3935
800-999-6779
service@ers.usda.gov; www.ers.usda.gov

Susan Offutt, Administrator
Leslee Lowstuter, Central Operations Staff Director
Thomas McDonald, Publishing/Communications
Suchada Langley, Global Agricultural Markets Branch
Ron Bianchi, Associate Director

An important resource for agribusiness and researchers.
Circulation: 2000

9654 Executive Guide to World Poultry Trends
WATT Publishing Company
303 N Main Street
Suite 500
Rockford, IL 61101

815-966-5400; *Fax:* 815-966-6416;
www.wattnet.com

James Watt, Chairman/CEO
Greg Watt, President/COO
Jeff Swanson, Publishing Director

Packed with facts and figures that give a full overview of the world poultry market.
Frequency: Annual

9655 FEDA News & Views
Foodservice Equipment Distributors Association
2250 Point Boulevard
Suite 200
Elgin, IL 60123

224-293-6500; *Fax:* 224-293-6505
feda@feda.com; www.feda.com

Ray Herrick, EVP/Publisher/Editor-in-Chief
Stacy Ward, Editor

Keep updated with the latest issues within the dealer community. Well-read among the FEDA membership, and includes stories on dealers, letters to the editor on industry issues, the President's message, and other items of interes to both dealers and manufacturer.
Cost: $160.00
Frequency: Bi-Monthly
Founded in: 1933

9656 FFA New Horizons
National FFA Organization
6060 FFA Drive
Indianapolis, IN 46268

317-802-4235
800-772-0939

newhorizons@ffa.org;
www.ffanewhorizons.org

Jessy Yancey, Association Editor
Christina Carden, Associate Production Director
Julie Woodard, FFA Publications Manager

The official member magazine of the FFA is published bimonthly and mailed to more than 525,000 readers. Each issue contains information about agricultural education, career possibilities, chapter and individual accomplishments and news on FFA. Now available online.
100 Pages
ISSN: 1069-806x
Founded in: 1928
Printed in 4 colors

9657 Fancy Foods & Culinary Products
Talcott Communications Corporation
20 W Kinzie St
12th Floor
Chicago, IL 60654-5827

312-849-2220
888-545-3676; *Fax:* 312-849-2174
fancyfood@talcott.com; www.talcott.com

Daniel Von Rabenau, Executive Director
Natalie Hamm Noblitt, Editor

Specialty food stores, department store specialty food departments, gift departments, confection stores, independent groceries and supermarket chains, gift basket retailers, cookware and kitchen stores, cooking school gift stores, cheese stores, coffee and tea stores brokers/representatives/manufacturers/importers/wholesalers/distributors and others allied to the field.
Cost: $26.00
Frequency: Monthly
Circulation: 23,000
ISSN: 1521-5156
Founded in: 1983

9658 Fastline Catalog
Fastline Media Group
4900 Fox Run Road
P.O. Box 248
Buckner, KY 40010-0248

502-222-0146
800-626-6409; *Fax:* 502-222-0615;
www.fastline.com
Social Media: Facebook, Twitter, YouTube, Flickr

William G Howard, President
Susan Arterburn, Marketing Director
Pat Higgins, Vice President, Sales

Nationwide and regional picture buying guides for the farming industry.
Frequency: Monthly
Founded in: 1978

9659 Feedback
Meat & Livestock Australia
1401 K Street NW
Suite 602
Washington, DC 20005

202-521-2551; *Fax:* 202-521-2699
info@mla.com.au; www.mla.com.au
Social Media: Facebook, Twitter, YouTube

Don Heatley, Chairman
David Palmer, Managing Director
Bernie Bindon, Director
Chris Hudson, Director

The red meat and livestock industry journal, featuring on-farm updates and market information for the north, south-east and south-west areas of Australia.
30000 Members
Frequency: 9x Yearly
Founded in: 1998

9660 Fine Foods Magazine
Griffin Publishing Group
201 Oak Street
Suite A
Pembroke, MA 02359

781-294-4700; *Fax:* 781-829-0134;
www.griffinpublishinginc.com

Stephen Griffin, President

A magazine offering information on the Northeast specialty, ethnic and prepared foods business.
Frequency: Monthly

9661 Fisheries
American Fisheries Society
5410 Grosvenor Ln
Suite 110
Bethesda, MD 20814-2199

301-897-8616; *Fax:* 301-897-8096;
www.fisheries.org

Gus Rassam, Executive Director
Myra Merritt, Office Administrator

Peer reviewed articles that address contemporary issues and problems, techniques, philosophies and other areas of interest to the general fisheries profession. Monthly features include letters, meeting notices, book listings and reviews, environmental essays and organization profiles.
Cost: $106.00
50 Pages
Frequency: Monthly
Circulation: 9800
Founded in: 1870
Mailing list available for rent: 8500 names at $250 per M

9662 Food & Drug Packaging
Stagnito Communications
210 S 5th Street
Suite 202
Saint Charles, IL 60174

847-205-5660; *Fax:* 630-377-1678;
www.fdp.com

Edwin Landon, Publisher
Vince Miconi, Advertising Production Manager
George Misko, Regional Sales Manager
Catherine Wynn, Sales Manager

Food and Drug Packaging serves industries engaged in packaging food, beverages, pharmaceuticals, cosmetics and consulting/engineering firms.
Frequency: Monthly
Circulation: 75140
Founded in: 1959

9663 Food Aid Needs Assessment
US Department of Agriculture
200 Independence Ave SW
Washington, DC 20201-0007

202-690-7650; *Fax:* 202-219-0942

Gene Mathia, Branch Chief

This annual report assesses the food situation in 60 developing countries. Most of the data are presented by region; crisis countries are covered individually.

9664 Food Arts Magazine
M Shanken Communications
387 Park Ave S
8th Floor
New York, NY 10016-8872

212-684-4224; *Fax:* 212-684-5424;
www.cigaraficionado.com

Marvin Shanken, Publisher
Julie Mautner, President

A publication serving the fine food service industry is edited for restauranteurs, chefs, food and beverage directors and caterers.
Frequency: Monthly
Circulation: 50000
Founded in: 1972
Printed in 4 colors on glossy stock

9665 Food Channel Trend Wire
Noble & Associates
2155 W Chesterfield Blvd
Springfield, MO 65807-8650

417-875-5000
800-545-4087; *Fax:* 417-875-5051;
www.noble.net

Robert Noble, CEO

Designed to make the food industry professionals food trend experts. Encapsulates trend information from more than 125 food and consumer publications each month. Provides insights into emerging food trends.
Cost: $195.00
Circulation: 2000

9666 Food Distribution Research Society News
Silesia Companies
PO Box 441110
Fort Washington, MD 20749-1110

301-292-1970; *Fax:* 706-542-0739;
www.fdrsinc.org

John Strovinsky, Publisher
Wojciech Florkowski, Editor

Food distribution research society encourages research, serves as an information clearinghouse and encourages implementation of research. The Society organizes conferences, and meetings for industry, academic and government leaders within the food industry sector.
Cost: $65.00
16 Pages
Circulation: 150
Founded in: 1960
Mailing list available for rent: 150 names

9667 Food Engineering
Business News Publishing Company
1050 IL Route 83
Suite 200
Bensenville, IL 60106-1096

630-377-5909; *Fax:* 947-763-9538;
www.foodengineering.com
Social Media: Facebook, Twitter

Patrick Young, Publisher & District Sales Manager
Paul Kelly, District Sales Manager
Brian Gronowski, District Sales Manager
Wayne Wiggins Jr, District Sales Manager
Carolyn Dress, Inside & Online Sales Manager

A publication offering information on all facets of the food industry, from ingredients to food packaging and processing.
Cost: $64.00
Frequency: Monthly
Circulation: 15000
Founded in: 1926

9668 Food Management
Penton Publishing Company
1300 E 9th St
Suite 1020
Cleveland, OH 44114-1514

216-861-0360; *Fax:* 216-696-0836
information@penton.com;
www.food-management.com

Preston L Vice, CFO
Adrian Meredith, CFO
David Brodowski, General Manager
Denise Walde, Senior Production Manager

Combines the industry's most comprehensive circulation package with an editorial mix that emphasizes business management strategies and ideas, food trends and recipes and in-depth news analysis in a contemporary feature magazine.
90 Pages
Frequency: Monthly

Circulation: 47899
ISSN: 0091-018X
Founded in: 1892
Printed in 4 colors on glossy stock

9669 **Food Processing**
555 W Pierce Road
Suite 301
Itasca, IL 60143

630-467-1300; *Fax:* 630-467-1124;
www.foodprocessing.com

Lily Modjeski, Sales Manager
Patricia Donatiu, Circulation Manager
Dave Fusaro, Editor-in-Chief
Steve Slankis, Group Publisher
Anetta Gauthier, Production Manager

Information on food equipment, packaging material and other supplies and services.
Frequency: Monthly
Circulation: 65000
Founded in: 1938

9670 **Food Product Design**
Virgo Publishing LLC
3300 N Central Ave
Suite 300
Phoenix, AZ 85012-2532

480-675-9925; *Fax:* 480-990-0819
peggyj@vpico.com;
www.foodproductdesign.com

Jenny Bolton, President

Publication distributed to product development professionals and corporate management executives at food and beverage manufacturing and foodservice companies.
Circulation: 20000
Founded in: 1986
Printed in on glossy stock

9671 **Food Production/Management Magazine**
CTI Publications
2823 Benson Mill Rd
Sparks Glencoe, MD 21152-9575

410-308-2080; *Fax:* 410-308-2079;
www.ctipubs.com

Randy Gerstmyer, Publisher/Editor

Serves those in the canning, glasspacking, freezing and aseptic packaged food industries. Readers include corporate executives and staff personnel responsible for direction of management, operations, production, engineering, packaging, research and development. Accepts advertising.
Cost: $40.00
32 Pages
Frequency: Monthly
Circulation: 4482
ISSN: 0191-6181
Founded in: 1878
Mailing list available for rent: 4500 names at $675 per M
Printed in 4 colors on glossy stock

9672 **Food Protection Trends**
International Association for Food Protection
6200 Aurora Ave
Suite 200W
Urbandale, IA 50322-2864

515-276-3344
800-369-6337; *Fax:* 515-276-8655
info@foodprotection.org;
www.foodprotection.org

David W Tharp, Executive Director
Vickie Lewandowski, VP
Isabel Walls, Secretary

Each issue contains articles on applied research, applications of current technology and general interest subjects for food safety professionals. Regular features include industry and association news, and industy-related products section and a calendar of meetings, seminars and workshops. Updates of government regulations and sanitary design are also featured.
Cost: $227.00
Frequency: Monthly
Circulation: 9000
ISBN: 0-362028-X -
Founded in: 1911
Mailing list available for rent
Printed in 4 colors on glossy stock

9673 **Food Quality**
Wiley-Blackwell
111 River Street
Hoboken, NJ 07030-5774

856-380-4117
800-322-9373; www.foodquality.com

The established authority in the market as the science-based news magazinw focused on quality, assurance, safety, and security in the food and beverage industry.
Cost: $195.00
66 Pages
Frequency: Monthly
Circulation: 21000
ISSN: 1092-7514
Founded in: 1994
Mailing list available for rent: 15,000 names at $195 per M
Printed in 4 colors on glossy stock

9674 **Food Safety Magazine**
Target Group
1945 W Mountain St
Glendale, CA 91201-1258

818-842-4777; *Fax:* 818-769-2939
info@foodsafetymagazine.com;
www.foodsafetymagazine.com
Social Media: Facebook, Twitter, LinkedIn

Don Meeker, Owner/CEO
Andrea Karges, Circulation Manager
Barbara VanRenterghem, Editorial Director

Publicaton is for food safety and quality assurance/control professionals at food and beverage processors, food service companies and agri-food laboratories worldwide. These decision makers implement science-based food safety strategies and systems to prevent, control, test and verify that chemical, microbiological and physical hazards do not enter the food supply.
Cost: $19.00
Frequency: Monthly
Circulation: 20,000
Founded in: 1980

9675 **Food Service Equipment & Supplies Specialist**
Reed Business Information
2000 Clearwater Dr
Oak Brook, IL 60523-8809

630-574-0825; *Fax:* 630-288-8781;
www.reedbusiness.com

Jeff Greisch, President
Maureen Slocum, Publisher
Judy Erickson, Group Circulation Manager
Stuart Whayman, CFO

Magazine for professionals who specify, sell and distribute food service equipment, supplies and furnishings.
Cost: $69.95
Frequency: Monthly
Circulation: 22,740
Founded in: 1948
Printed in 4 colors on glossy stock

9676 **Food Technology**
Institute of Food Technologists
525 W Van Buren
Suite 1000
Chicago, IL 60607-3842

312-782-8424; *Fax:* 312-782-8348
info@ift.org; www.ift.org

Bob Swientek, Editor-in-Chief

The leading publication addressing all facets of food science and technology. Its in-depth and balance coverage includes the latest research developments, industry news, consumer product innovations, and professional opportunities.
Cost: $190.00
Frequency: Monthly
Circulation: 18000
ISSN: 0015-6639

9677 **Food Trade News**
Best-Met Publishing
5537 Twin Knolls Rd
Suite 438
Columbia, MD 21045-3270

410-730-5013; *Fax:* 410-740-4680
jmetzger@best-met.com; www.best-met.com

Jeff Metzger, Publisher
Terri Maloney, Editor
Nina Weiland, VP
Beth Pripstein, Office Manager
Richard J Bestany, Advertising Director

A magazine aimed at the players in the food distribution industry.

9678 **Food World**
Best-Met Publishing Company
5537 Twin Knolls Rd
Suite 438
Columbia, MD 21045-3270

410-730-5013; *Fax:* 410-740-4680
jmetzger@best-met.com; www.best-met.com

Jeff Metzger, Publisher
Jeffrey W. Metzger, Publisher
Beth Pripstein, Office Manager
Richard J. Bestany, President

Regional food trade newspaper covering the Mid-Atlantic market
Frequency: Monthly
Printed in on newsprint stock

9679 **FoodService and Hospitality**
Kostuch Publications
Two City Place Drive
Suite 200 PMB 2004
Saint Louis ario, MO 63141-3P6

314-812-2565; *Fax:* 314-835-0044
wgilchri@ix.netcom.com;
www.foodserviceworld.com

Mitch Kostuch, President
Rosanna Caira, Publisher/Editor
Wendy Gilchrist, Director Business Development
Phoebe Fung, Owner
Owen Knowlton, Director

Canada's only national specialty business magazine reaching owners,managers and buyers in all sections of the foodservice industry.
Cost: $50.00
Frequency: Monthly
Circulation: 25,000
Printed in on glossy stock

9680 **FoodTalk**
Pike & Fischer
PO Box 25277
Alexandria, VA 22313

703-548-3146; *Fax:* 703-548-3017
info@setantapublishing.com;
www.setantapublishing.com

Declan Couroy, Editor/Publisher

Sanitation tips for food workers.
Cost: $120.00
Frequency: Quarterly
Circulation: 5000
Founded in: 1987
Printed in 2 colors

9681 **Foodservice Equipment & Supplies**
Reed Europe
2000 Clearwter Drive
Oak Brook, IL 60523
630-320-7000
800-446-6551; *Fax:* 630-288-8282;
www.fesmag.com
Maureen Slocum, Publisher
Mitchell Schechter, Editor-in-Chief
Edited for readers outside the US who are employed in firms that manufacture food and beverage products.
Frequency: Monthly
Founded in: 1948

9682 **For Fish Farmers**
Mississippi Cooperative Extension Service
PO Box 9690
Mississippi State, MS 39762-9690
662-325-3174; *Fax:* 601-857-2358
Martin W Bunson, Editor
A magazine offering information that addresses the concerns of fish farmers.
Frequency: Quarterly

9683 **Fresh Cup Magazine**
Fresh Cup Publishing Company
537 SE Ash Street Suite 300
PO Box 14827
Portland, OR 97293
503-236-2587
800-868-5866; *Fax:* 503-236-3165;
www.freshcup.com
Ward Barbee, Publisher
Jan Weigel, President
Julie Beals, Marketing
Bill Berninger, Circulation Manager
Natalie Caceres, Marketing Coordinator
Cost: $60.00
80 Pages
Frequency: Monthly
Circulation: 15000
Founded in: 1992
Printed in 4 colors on glossy stock

9684 **Fresh Cut Magazine**
Great American Publishing
75 Applewood Drive, Suite A
PO Box 128
Sparta, MI 49345
616-887-9008; *Fax:* 616-887-2666;
www.freshcut.com
Matt McCallum, Publisher
Scott Christie, Managing Editor
The only publication covering all sectors of the international value-added produce industry. Growers, processors, retailers and foodservice professionals all find information relating to their day-to-day operations in the pages of Fresh Cut magazine.
Cost: $15.00
40 Pages
Frequency: Monthly
ISSN: 1072-2831
Founded in: 1993
Printed in 4 colors on glossy stock

9685 **Frozen Food Digest, Inc.**
271 Madison Ave
Suite 1402-A
New York, NY 10016-1014
212-557-8600; *Fax:* 212-986-9868
Saul Beck, President/Hall of Fame Member
Cost: $45.00
Circulation: 16000
Founded in: 1985

9686 **Fruit Country**
Clintron Publishing
PO Box 30998
Spokane, WA 99223-3016
509-248-2452
800-869-7923; *Fax:* 509-458-3547;
www.agpowermag.com
Clintke Withers, Publisher
John M Dahlin, Editor
Tyson Graff, Circualtion Manager
Written for and about growers, their operations and their needs. Stories on growers and shippers, developments and trends in the fruit industry, human interest stories and politics, new products, chemicals and supplies, avant garde management techniques, cultural practices and tips on profitability. Advertising equipment and services to the fruit industry and distribution system.
Cost: $12.00
Frequency: Monthly
Circulation: 11500
Founded in: 1976

9687 **Futures Magazine**
Futures Magazine
111 W Jackson Blvd
7th Floor
Chicago, IL 60604-4139
312-977-0999; *Fax:* 312-846-4638
dcollins@futuresmag.com; www.aip.com
Steve Lown, Manager
Daniel P Collins, Editor
Gabby Mouizerh, Production Manager
Steve Lown, Manager
Agriculture commodities charted by various technical studies, plus analysis.
Cost: $39.00
24 Pages
Frequency: Monthly
Circulation: 60,000
Founded in: 1972

9688 **Game Bird Gazette**
Allen Publishing
970 East
3300 South
Salt Lake City, UT 84106
801-485-1299
memberservices@gamebird.com;
www.gamebird.com
George Allen, Editor
All about keeping, breeding and raising pheasants, quails, partridges, peacocks, doves, pigeons, waterfowl and gamebirds of all kinds.
Cost: $23.95
45 Pages
Frequency: Monthly
Founded in: 1940

9689 **Gourmet Retailer Magazine**
3301 Ponce De Leon Blvd
Suite 300
Coral Gables, FL 33134-7273
305-273-0437
800-765-9797; *Fax:* 305-446-2868
info@gourmetretailer.com;
www.gourmetretailer.com
Edward Loeb, Publisher
Michael Keighley, Editorial Director
Laura Everage, Managing Editor
Shari Levenson, Marketing Manager
Kathy Colwell, Advertising Production Manager
Frequency: Monthly
Circulation: 25000
Founded in: 1979

9690 **Grape Grower**
Western Agricultural Publishing Company
4969 E Clinton Way
#104
Fresno, CA 93727-1549
559-252-7000
888-382-9772; *Fax:* 559-252-7387
westag@westagpubco.com;
www.westagpubco.com
Paul Baltimore, Publisher
Randy Bailey, Editor
Robert Fujimoto, Assistant Editor
The West's most widely read authority on the cultivation of table grapes, raising grapes and wine grapes. All aspects of production are covered with the most current university, government and private research.
Mailing list available for rent

9691 **Greenhouse Product News**
Scranton Gillette Communications
3030 W Salt Creek Lane
Suite 201
Arlington Heights, IL 60005-5025
847-391-1000; *Fax:* 847-390-0408
bbellew@sgcmail.com; www.gpnmag.com
Bob Bellew, VP/Group Publisher
Tim Hodson, Editorial Director
Jasmina Radjevic, Managing Editor
Features the industry's leading Buyer's Guide directory, the PGR table and the bookstore are just a few of the reasons the industry's buyers keep coming back.
Cost: $30.00
Frequency: Monthly
Circulation: 19000
Mailing list available for rent: 19,000 names

9692 **Griffin Report: Market Studies**
Griffin Publishing Company
201 Oak Street
Pembroke, MA 02359
781-829-4700; *Fax:* 781-829-0134;
www.griffinreport.com
Mike Berger, Editor
Kevin Griffin, Vice President
Karen Harty, Vice President
Julie Mignosa, Office Manager
This report offers statistics on the leading chain and multi-store independent grocers in the northeast.
Cost: $42.00
Frequency: Monthly
Founded in: 1966
Mailing list available for rent: 10,000 names at $350 per M
Printed in on newsprint stock

9693 **Grocers Report**
Super Markets Productions
PO Box 6124
San Rafael, CA 94903-124
415-479-0211; *Fax:* 415-479-0211
Lori Abrams, CEO
JM Adlman, Publisher
Joan Adams, Circulation Manager
Offers information on the retail grocery industry.
Cost: $10.00
Frequency: Quarterly
Circulation: 18000
Founded in: 1978
Printed in 4 colors on glossy stock

9694 **Growertalks Magazine**
Ball Publishing

622 Town Road
PO Box 1660
West Chicago, IL 60186

630-231-3675
888-888-0013; *Fax:* 630-231-5254
info@ballpublishing.com;
www.growertalks.com

Chris Beytes, Editor/Publisher
Jennifer Zurko, Associate Editor

Specializes in the publishing of horticulture information, primarily related to floriculture production and marketing.
Frequency: Monthly
Circulation: 12000
Founded in: 1937

9695 Growing for Market
Fairplain Publications
PO Box 3747
Lawrence, KS 66046

785-748-0605
800-307-8949; *Fax:* 785-748-0609;
www.growingformarket.com

Lynn Byczynski, Editor/Publisher
Roger Yepsen, Author

A monthly periodical for small-scale farmers, market gardeners, and grower of vegetables, fruits, herbs and flowers. Offers news and ideas about organic production, pest control, tools and equipment and direct marketing.
Cost: $ 30.00
20 Pages
Frequency: Monthly
Circulation: 4000
ISSN: 1060-9296
Founded in: 1992

9696 Guernsey Breeders' Journal
Purebred Publishing Inc
7616 Slate Ridge Blvd
Reynoldsburg, OH 43068-3126

614-575-4620; *Fax:* 614-864-5614
khenson@usguernsey.com;
www.usguernsey.com

Katie Henson, Editor

The oldest dairy breed magazine published by a US breed organization. Contents range across current management trends, breeder stories and events withing the Guernsey industry in the US and worldwide.
Cost: $20.00
Frequency: 10x Yearly

9697 Health Products Business
Cygnus Publishing
445 Braod Hollow Road
Melville, NY 11747-3669

631-845-2700
800-308-6397; *Fax:* 631-845-2723
micheal.schiavitz@cygnuspub.com;
www.healthproducts.com

Bruce Ceftakes, Publisher/Sales
Micheal Schiavetta, Editor
Christian Biscuiti, Assistant Editor

This is a trade magazine that covers news and trends in the natural health products industry including vitamins, herbs, dietary supplements and other products. Publishes annual raw materials directory and purchasing guide, as well as other speciality issues. Targets natural products retail store owners, buyers and managers. Qualified subsciption only.
ISSN: 0149-9602

9698 Herb Quarterly
EGW Publishing Company
4075 Papazian Way
Suite 204
Fremont, CA 94538-4372

510-668-0268; *Fax:* 510-668-0280
info@egw.com; www.herbquarterly.com

Chris Slaughter, VP
Jennifer Barrett, Editor

Each issue introduces readers to new herbs and fascinating herbal lore; provides tips on hard to grow varieties and medicinals; showcases gardens from around the world; and tempts the palate with seasonal menus and tantalizing recipes built around herbs and edible flowers.
Cost: $19.97
68 Pages
Frequency: Quarterly
Circulation: 36753
Founded in: 1978
Printed in 4 colors on matte stock

9699 Hereford World
American Hereford Association
PO Box 014059
Kansas City, MO 64101

816-842-3757; *Fax:* 816-842-6931
aha@hereford.org; www.hereford.org

Craig Huffhines, Executive VP
Trade magazine for breeders of registered Hereford cattle. Articles and columns provide in-depth information about the beef industry.
Frequency: Monthly
Circulation: 9500
Founded in: 1742

9700 Honey Producer
American Honey Producers Association
PO Box 162
Power, MT 59468

406-463-2227; *Fax:* 406-463-2583
beeguy4jensen@yahoo.com;
www.americanhoneyproducers.org

Lyle Johnston, Editor

Highlights current industry news, publishes submitted articles from the scientific community, informs of legal battles being fought in Washington,'DC, provides cmoplete AHPA convention schedules.
Cost: $20.00
Frequency: Quarterly
ISSN: 1091-3394

9701 Hospitality News Featuring Coffee Talk
PO Box 21027
Salem, OR 97307-1027

503-390-8343
800-685-1932; *Fax:* 503-390-8344;
www.hospnews.com

Kerri R Goodman-Small, Publisher
Miles Small, Editor-in-Chief

Serves restaurants, lodges, health care facilities, schools, clubs,casinos, caterers, and culinary and beverage marketplaces nationally.
Circulation: 30000
ISSN: 1084-2551
Founded in: 1988
Printed in on newsprint stock

9702 Hotline Magazine
International Food Service Executives
4955 Miller Street
Suite 107
Wheat Ridge, CO 80033

800-893-5499; www.ifsea.com
Social Media: Facebook

Barbara Sadler, Chairwoman
Fred Wright, Chair-Elect
David Orosz, Treasurer

IFSEA's membership magazine that focuses on all things IFSEA and food service. Also available electronically.
Frequency: Bi-Annually

9703 IAFIS Reporter
International Assn of Food Industry Suppliers
1451 Dolley Madison Boulevard
Suite 101
McLean, VA 22101

703-761-2600; *Fax:* 703-761-4334
info@fpsa.org; www.fpsa.org

George Melnykovich, President
Andrew Drennan, VP

Happenings and trends in the food and dairy industry.
Founded in: 1983

9704 IGA Grocergram
Pace Communications
PO Box 13607
Greensboro, NC 27415-3607

336-378-6065; *Fax:* 336-275-2864
info@pacecommunications.com;
www.pacecommunications.com

Bonnie McElveen, CEO
Wes Isley, Chief Financial Officer
Leigh Klee, Chief Financial Officer
Ed Calfo, Executive Vice President

Edited for IGA retailers and wholesalers throughout the US. Focuses on training, merchandising, display, promotion, and advertising and marketing techniques. Also addresses financial and personnel management and innovations in store engineering and development.
Cost: $24.00
Frequency: Monthly

9705 Import Statistics
Association of Food Industries
3301 State Route 66
Suite 205, Building C
Neptune, NJ 07753-2705

732-922-3008; *Fax:* 732-922-3590
info@afius.org; www.naooa.org

Robert Bauer, President
Cost: $40.00
Frequency: Annual+
Circulation: 1200
Founded in: 1906

9706 In Good Taste
Specialty Coffee Association of America
302 5th Avenue
5th Floor
New York, NY 10001

646-733-6000
800-544-7377; *Fax:* 646-733-6010;
www.pharmpress.com

Ted R Lingle, Editor

This periodical offers business, promotional and educational advice in the areas of cultivation, processing, preparation and marketing of specialty coffee.
Frequency: Monthly

9707 Industria Alimenticia
Stagnito Communications
155 Pfingster Road
Suite 205
Deerfield, IL 60015

847-205-5660; *Fax:* 847-205-5680;
www.stagnito.com

Harry Stagnito, President
Elsa Rico, Director/Editor
Mary Mazur, Circulation

Information source for Latin American food and beverage processors
Cost: $85.00
Printed in 4 colors on glossy stock

9708 Inform
American Oil Chemists' Society
2710 S. Boulder
PO Box 17190
Urbana, IL 61802-6996
217-359-2344; *Fax:* 217-351-8091
general@aocs.org; www.aocs.org
Social Media: Facebook, Twitter
E. Dumelin, President
D. Myers, Vice President
S. Erhan, Secretary
T. Kemper, Treasurer
The monthly business and scientific magazine of AOCS, providing international news on fats, oils, surfactants, detergents, and related materials.
Cost: $10.00
5400 Members
Frequency: Membership Dues Vary
Founded in: 1909

9709 Insider Magazine
American Correctional Food Service Affiliates
210 N Glenoaks Blvd
Suite C
Burbank, CA 91502
818-843-6608; *Fax:* 818-843-7423;
www.acfsa.org
Jon Nichols, Executive Director
Contains news pertaining to correctional foodservice activities of the Association and fellow members, as well as industry-specific educational articles.
56 Pages
Frequency: Quarterly
Circulation: 1500
Founded in: 1969
Printed in 4 colors on glossy stock

9710 Institute of Food and Nutrition
HealthComm International
9770 44th Avenue
N.W. Suite 100
Gig Harbor, WA 98332
253-851-3943
800-692-9400; *Fax:* 253-851-9749
info@metagenics.com; www.metagenics.com
Jeffrey Bland, President/Chief Science Officer
Jeffrey Katke, Chairman of the Board/CEO
Carl Mickey Moore, Co-Chief Operating Officer
Janice Moore, Co-Chief Operating Officer
Matthew Tripp, VP of Research & Development
Founded in: 1983

9711 Intermountain Retailer
Utah Food Industry Association
1578 W 1700 S
Suite 100
Salt Lake City, UT 84104-3489
801-973-9517
800-423-6636; *Fax:* 801-972-8712;
www.utfood.com
James Olsen, President
Meik Rapp, Editor
This annual guide offers information on brokers in Utah that are serving the retail food industry.
Cost: $25.00
48 Pages
Frequency: Annual+
Circulation: 1200
Founded in: 1896

9712 International Journal of Food Engineering
Reed Business Information
360 Park Ave S
New York, NY 10010-1737
646-746-6400; *Fax:* 646-756-7583
corporatecommunications@reedbusiness.com;
www.reedbusiness.com
John Poulin, CEO
Peter Havens, Publisher
James Reed, Owner
Devoted to engineering disciplines related to processing foods. The areas of interest include heat, mass transfer and fluid flow in food processing; food microstructure development and characterization; application of artificial intelligence in food research; food biotechnology, and more.
Frequency: Annual
Circulation: 15,000

9713 International Product Alert
Marketing Intelligence Service
482 N Main St
Canandaigua, NY 14424-1049
585-374-6326
800-836-5710; *Fax:* 585-374-5217;
www.productscan.com
Tom Vierhile, Executive Editor
Sherry Meeker-Barton, Editor-in-Chief
Reports the introduction of new food, beverage, health & beauty aides, household & pet products outside of North America. Reports include full product descriptions and selected illustrations of products and advertising backup.
Cost: $700.00

9714 Italian Cooking and Living
Italian Culinary Institute
302 5th Avenue
9th Floor
New York, NY 10001
212-899-9057
888-742-2373; *Fax:* 212-889-3907
irene@italiancookingandliving.com;
www.italiancookingandliving.com
Paolo Villoresi, Publisher
Irene De Gasparis, Associate Publisher
Charles Pennino, Owner
American magazine devoted to Italian cuisine/culture/travel
Founded in: 2001

9715 JAOCS
American Oil Chemists' Society
2710 S. Boulder
PO Box 17190
Urbana, IL 61802-6996
217-359-2344; *Fax:* 217-351-8091
general@aocs.org; www.aocs.org
Social Media: Facebook, Twitter
E. Dumelin, President
D. Myers, Vice President
S. Erhan, Secretary
T. Kemper, Treasurer
The leading source for technical papers related to the fats and oils industries. A peer-reviewed journal devoted to fundamental and practical research, production, processing, packaging and distribution in the growing field of fats, oils, proteins and other related substances.
Cost: $10.00
5400 Members
Frequency: Membership Dues Vary
Founded in: 1909

9716 Journal of Animal Science
American Society of Animal Science
2441 Village Green Pl
Champaign, IL 61822-7676
217-356-9050; *Fax:* 217-398-4119
susanp@assochq.org; www.asas.org
Meghan Wulster-Radcli, Executive Director
Susan Pollack, Managing Editor/Editorial Director
The official journal of the American Society of Animal Science, JAS publishes results of original research in Genetics, Growth and Physiology, Nutrition, Production, Products, and Special Topics. JAS consistently ranks in the top tier in the category of Agriculture, Dairy, and Animal Sciences
Frequency: Monthly
Circulation: 3500
ISSN: 0021-8812
Founded in: 1908
Printed in on glossy stock

9717 Journal of Business Logistics
Council of Supply Chain Management Professionals
333 E Butterfield Rd
Suite 140
Lombard, IL 60148-5617
630-574-0985; *Fax:* 630-574-0989
cscmpadmin@cscmp.org; www.cscmp.org
Social Media: Facebook, Twitter, LinkedIn, YouTube
Rick Blasgen, President & CEO
Sue Paulson, Executive Assistant
Nancy Nix, Chair
Rick J. Jackson, Chair-Elect
Theodore Stank, Secretary & Treasurer
Provides a forum for the dissemination of original thoughts, research, and best practices within the logistics and supply chain arenas. Provides readers with new and helpful information, new supply chain management theory or techniques, research generalizations, creative views and sytheses of dispersed concepts, and articles in subject areas which have significant current impact on thought and practice in logistics and supply chain management.
10000 Members
Founded in: 1963

9718 Journal of Child Nutrition & Management
School Nutrition Association
120 Waterfront St
Suite 300
National Harbor, MD 20745-1142
301-686-3100
800-877-8822; *Fax:* 301-686-3115
servicecenter@schoolnutrition.org;
www.schoolnutrition.org
Helen Phillips, President
Sandy Ford, President-Elect
Leah Schmidt, Vice President
Beth Taylor, Secretary/Treasurer
Features up-to-date research articles on significant issues affecting child nutrition and school foodservice management. Provides timely and relevant insights into the many challenges and opportunities surrounding child nutrition programs. Information facilitates decision-making and serves as evidence of how effective child nutrition programs are.
55000 Members
Frequency: Monthly
Founded in: 1946

9719 Journal of Dairy Science
American Dairy Science Association

2441 Village Green Pl
Champaign, IL 61822-7676

217-356-5146; *Fax:* 217-398-4119
adsa@assochq.org; www.adsa.org

Michael Mangino, Senior Editor
Sharon Frick, Secretary
Diane Hekken, Secretary
Richard Pursley, Secretary, Treasurer

Research in dairy cattle production and dairy food products.
Cost: $110.00
Frequency: Monthly
Founded in: 1990

9720 Journal of Environmental Quality
American Society of Agronomy
5585 Guilford Road
Madison, WI 53711-1086

608-273-8080; *Fax:* 608-273-2021
headquarters@agronomy.org;
www.agronomy.org
Social Media: Facebook, Twitter, LinkedIn

Newell Kitchen, President
Kenneth Barbarick, President-Elect

Papers are grouped by subject matter and cover water, soil, and atmospheric research as it relates to agriculture and the environment.
11000 Members
Founded in: 1907

9721 Journal of Food Distribution Research
Food Distribution Research Society
PO Box 441110
Fort Washington, MD 20749

301-292-1970; *Fax:* 301-292-1787
Jonathan_baros@ncsu.edu
fdrs.tamu.edu

John Park, President
Ron Rainey, President-Elect
Kellie Raper, Secretary/ Treasurer
Jennifer Dennis, Director
Stan Ernst, Director

Publishes articles that cover every aspect of our modern food system. JFDR is a peer reviewed journal published exlusively online.
Frequency: 3x Yearly

9722 Journal of Food Protection
International Association for Food Protection
6200 Aurora Ave
Suite 200W
Des Moines, IA 50322-2864

515-276-3344
800-369-6337; *Fax:* 515-276-8655
info@foodprotection.org;
www.foodprotection.org
Social Media: Facebook, Twitter, LinkedIn

Isabel Walls, President
Katherine M.J. Swanson, President-Elect
Don Schaffner, Vice President
Don Zink, Secretary
David W. Tharp, Executive Director

Each issue contains scientific research and authoritative review articles reporting on a variety of topics in food science pertaining to food safety and quality.
3400 Members
Founded in: 1911

9723 Journal of Food Science
Institute of Food Technologists
525 W Van Buren St
Suite 1000
Chicago, IL 60607-3842

312-782-8424; *Fax:* 312-782-8348
info@ift.org; www.ift.org

Barbara Byrd Keenan, Executive VP
Daryl B Lund, Editor-in-Chief

IFT's premier science journal, containing peer-reviewed reports of original research and critical reviews of all aspects of food science.
Frequency: 9x Yearly
Founded in: 1936

9724 Journal of Foodservice Business Research
Taylor & Francis Group LLC
325 Chestnut St
Suite 800
Philadelphia, PA 19106-2614

215-625-8900
800-354-1420; *Fax:* 215-625-2940;
www.taylorandfrancis.com

Kevin Bradley, President

Features articles from international experts in various disciplines, including management, marketing, finance, law, food technology, nutrition, psychology, information systems, anthropology, human resources, and more.
Frequency: Quarterly

9725 Journal of Hospitality & Tourism Research
CHRIE
2810 N Parham Road
Suite 230
Richmond, VA 23294

804-346-4800; *Fax:* 804-346-5009
info@chrie.org; www.chrie.org
Social Media: Facebook, Twitter, LinkedIn

Susan Fournier, President
Josette Katz, Vice President
Chris Roberts, Secretary
John Drysdale, Treasurer
Kathy McCarty, CEO

Offers high quality refereed articles which advance the knowledge base of the hospitality field. Articles on empirical research, theoretical developments and innovative methodologies are guided by an editor and a review board consisting of leading hospitality and tourism researchers.
Frequency: Quarterly

9726 Journal of Hospitality and Tourism Education
CHRIE
2810 N Parham Road
Suite 230
Richmond, VA 23294

804-346-4800; *Fax:* 804-346-5009
info@chrie.org; www.chrie.org
Social Media: Facebook, Twitter, LinkedIn

Susan Fournier, President
Josette Katz, Vice President
Chris Roberts, Secretary
John Drysdale, Treasurer
Kathy McCarty, CEO

A refereed, interdisciplinary quarterly magazine designed to serve the needs of all levels of hospitality and tourism education through the presentation of issues and opinions pertinent to the field.
Frequency: Quarterly

9727 Journal of Natural Resources & Life Sciences Education
American Society of Agronomy
5585 Guilford Road
Madison, WI 53711-1086

608-273-8080; *Fax:* 608-273-2021
headquarters@agronomy.org;
www.agronomy.org
Social Media: Facebook, Twitter, LinkedIn

Newell Kitchen, President
Kenneth Barbarick, President-Elect

Today's educators look here for the latest teaching ideas in the life sciences, natural resources, and agriculture. Articles are written by and for educators in extension, universities, industry, administration, and grades k-12.
11000 Members
Founded in: 1907

9728 Journal of Packaging
Institute of Packaging Professionals
Ste 123
1833 Centre Point Cir
Naperville, IL 60563-4848

630-544-5050
800-432-4085; *Fax:* 630-544-5005
info@iopp.org; www.iopp.org
Social Media: Facebook, Twitter, LinkedIn, YouTube

Edwin Landon, Executive Director
Patrick Farrey, General Manager
Stan Zelesnik, Director Education
Robert DePauw, Finance Manager
Kelly Staley, Member Services Manager

Serves the entire packaging community's educational needs. The Journal is a resource for professional analysis of all packaging issues. Available online only, it is a forum that covers issues in depth.
Frequency: Daily

9729 Journal of Plant Registrations
Crop Science Society of America
5585 Guilford Rd.
Madison, WI 53711-1086

608-273-8080; *Fax:* 608-273-2021;
www.crops.org
Social Media: Facebook, Twitter, LinkedIn

Maria Gallo, President
Jeffrey Volenec, President-Elect
Ellen G.M. Bergfeld, CEO

Publishes cultivar, germplasm, parental line, genetic stock, and mapping population registration manuscripts.
4700 Members
Frequency: Monthly
Founded in: 1955

9730 Journal of Shellfish Research
National Shellfisheries Association
National Marine Fisheries Service Laboratory
Oxford, MD 21654

631-653-6327; *Fax:* 631-653-6327
webmaster@shellfish.org; www.shellfish.org

R. LeRoy Creswell, President
Christopher V. Davis, President-Elect
George E. Flimlin, VP & Program Chair
Marta Gomez-Chiarri, Secretary
Sandra E. Shumway, Editor

The international journal promoting all aspects of shellfish research.
1M Members
Frequency: Monthly
Founded in: 1908

9731 Journal of Sugar Beet Research
Beet Sugar Development Foundation
800 Grant Street
Suite 300
Denver, CO 80203

303-832-4460; *Fax:* 303-832-4468
aa@bsdf-assbt.org; www.bsdf-assbt.org

Fosters all phases of sugarbeet and beet sugar research, promotes the dissemination of relevant scientific knowledge, and strives to maintain high standards of ethics, and to cooperate with other organizations having objectives beneficial to the beet sugar industry.
Frequency: Quarterly
ISSN: 0899-1502

9732 Journal of Surfactants and Detergents (JSD)
American Oil Chemists' Society

2710 S. Boulder
PO Box 17190
Urbana, IL 61802-6996

217-359-2344; *Fax:* 217-351-8091
general@aocs.org; www.aocs.org
Social Media: Facebook, Twitter

E. Dumelin, President
D. Myers, Vice President
S. Erhan, Secretary
T. Kemper, Treasurer

A scientific journal dedicated to the practical and theoretical aspects of oleochemical and petrochemical surfactants, soaps, and detergents.
Cost: $10.00
5400 Members
Frequency: Membership Dues Vary
Founded in: 1909

9733 Journal of the American Dietetic Association
Elsevier Health Publishing
1600 John F Kennedy Blvd
Suite 1800
Philadelphia, PA 19103-2398

215-239-3900; *Fax:* 215-239-3990;
www.elsevier.com

Michael Hansen, CEO
Jason Swift, Editor
Ryan Lipscomb, Department Editor
Linda Van Horn, Editor-in-Chief

A premier source for the practice and science of food, nutrition, and dietetics. The Journal focuses on advancing professional knowledge across the range of research and practice issues such as: nutritional science, medical nutrition therapy, public health nutrition, food science and biotechnology, foodservice systems, leadership and management and dietetics education.
Cost: $229.00
Frequency: Monthly/Subscription
ISSN: 0002-8223

9734 Journal of the American Oil Chemists' Society
American Oil Chemists' Society
2710 S Boulder
Urbana, IL 61802-6996

217-359-2344; *Fax:* 217-351-8091
general@aocs.org; www.aocs.org

Jody Schonfeld, Publications Director
Pam Landman, Journals Coordinator
Kimmy Farris, Production Editor

The leading source for technical papers related to the fats and oils industries. A peer-reviewed journal devoted to fundamental and practical research, production, processing, packaging and distribution in the growing field of fats, oils, proteins and other related substances
Frequency: Monthly
Founded in: 1947

9735 Journal of the American Pomological Society
103 Tyson Building
University Park, PA 16802-4200

814-863-6163; *Fax:* 814-237-3407
bardenja@vt.edu;
www.americanpomological.org

Dr John Barden, Editor

The Journal contains refereed technical articles and a wide variety of applied articles relating to fruit varieties.
Frequency: Quarterly/Free to Members

9736 Journal of the American Society for Horticultural Science
American Society for Horticultural Science
1018 Duke Street
Alexandria, VA 22314

703-836-4606; *Fax:* 703-836-2024
journal@ashs.org; www.ashs.org

Michael Neff, Publisher/Executive Director

A peer-reviewed publication of results of orginal research on horticultural plants and their products or directly related research areas. Its prime function is communication of mission-oriented, fundamental research to other researchers.
Cost: $85.00
Frequency: Bi-Monthly
ISSN: 0003-1062
Founded in: 1903
Mailing list available for rent: 2500 names at $100 per M

9737 Journal of the Association of Food and Dru g Officials
Association of Food and Drug Officials
2550 Kingston Rd
Suite 311
York, PA 17402-3734

717-757-2888; *Fax:* 717-755-8089
afdo@afdo.org; www.afdo.org

Denise Rooney, Executive Director

News and the latest legislation for the Food and Drug Association.
Founded in: 1937

9738 Kosher Today
1428 36th street
219
Brooklyn, NY 11218

718-854-4460; *Fax:* 718-854-4474
info@koshertoday.com;
www.koshertoday.com/

Menachem Lubinsky, CEO
Bill Springer, Account Executive
Christine Salmon, Account Executive
Karyn Gilbert, Marketing Manager

Covers the kosher food industry.
28 Pages
Frequency: Weekly
Circulation: 20000
Founded in: 1984
Printed in 4 colors on newsprint stock

9739 Lean Trimmings Prime
National Meat Association
1970 Broadway
Suite 825
Oakland, CA 94612

510-763-1533; *Fax:* 510-763-6186
staff@nmaonline.org; www.nmaonline.org

Robert Rebholtz, Chairman
Larry Vad, President
Marty Evanson, Vice President
Mike Hesse, Secretary
Brian Coelho, Treasurer

Brings a broad range of topics and essential association information to the membership and beyond.
600 Members
Frequency: Weekly
Founded in: 1946

9740 Lipids
American Oil Chemists' Society
2710 S. Boulder
PO Box 17190
Urbana, IL 61802-6996

217-359-2344; *Fax:* 217-351-8091
general@aocs.org; www.aocs.org
Social Media: Facebook, Twitter

E. Dumelin, President
D. Myers, Vice President
S. Erhan, Secretary
T. Kemper, Treasurer

A premier journal in the lipid field, published monthly, featuring full-length original research articles, short communications, methods papers, and review articles on timely topics.
Cost: $10.00
5400 Members
Frequency: Membership Dues Vary
Founded in: 1909

9741 Logistics Journal
Transportation Intermediaries Association
1625 Prince St
Suite 200
Alexandria, VA 22314-2883

703-299-5700; *Fax:* 703-836-0123
info@tianet.org; www.tianet.org

Robert Voltmann, President
Nancy King, Marketing Manager

Education and policy organization for North American transportation intermediaries. The only national association representing the interests of all third party transportation service providers. Members include logistics management firms, property brokers, perishable commodities brokers, freight forwarders, intermodal marketers and ocean and air forwarders.
Frequency: Monthly
Circulation: 1000
Founded in: 1978

9742 Manufacturing Confectioner
MC Publishing
711 W Water Street
PO Box 266
Princeton, WI 54968

920-295-6969; *Fax:* 920-295-6843
mcinfo@gomc.com; www.gomc.com

Eric Schmoyer, President
Michael Allured, Publisher/Editor-in-Chief

The worldwide business, marketing and technology journal of the candy, chocolate, confectionery, cough drop, and sweet baked goods industry. Provides in-depth coverage of news, industry statistics, sales and marketing, ingredients, equipment and services.
Cost: $65.00
Frequency: Monthly
Founded in: 1921

9743 Meat & Poultry
Sosland Publishing Company
4801 Main St
Suite 100
Kansas City, MO 64112-2513

816-756-1000; *Fax:* 816-756-0494;
www.sosland.com

Joel Crews, Editorn-in-Chief
Kimberlie Clyma, Managing Editor
Dave Crost, Publisher

Serves meat, poultry and seafood processors, wholesalers-distrubuters, slaughterers, fabricators, cutters, meat buyers, and rendering and pet food manufacturers.
Frequency: Monthly
Circulation: 21,000
Founded in: 1955
Printed in 4 colors on glossy stock

9744 Meat Marketing and Technology
Marketing & Technology Group
1415 N Dayton St
Suite 115
Chicago, IL 60642-7033

312-266-3311; *Fax:* 312-266-3363
webinars@meatingplace.com;
www.meatingplace.com

Mark Lefens, Owner
Dan Allen, Editor-at-Large
Jim Goldberg, VP Sales/Marketing
John Gregerson, Editor
Deborah Silver, Managing Editor

Provides information on meat processing, retail, slaughtering and fabricating and rendering.
Cost: $40.00
Frequency: Monthly
Circulation: 20,009
Founded in: 1993
Printed in 4 colors on glossy stock

9745 Meat Science
American Meat Science Association
2441 Village Green Pl
Champaign, IL 61822-7676

800-517-AMSA; *Fax:* 888-205-5834; *Fax:* 217-356-5370
information@meatscience.org; www.meatscience.org

William Mikel, President
Scott J. Eilert, President Elect
Casey B. Frye, Treasurer

The official journal of AMSA. Peer-reviewed resource is the best way to stay current on the latest research in meat science across all meat products and in all aspects of meat production and processing. Available online or in print.

9746 Midwest Food Service News
Pinnacle Publishing
316 N Michigan Avenue
Suite 300
Chicago, IL 60601

312-272-2401
800-493-4867; *Fax:* 312-960-4106
pinpub@ragan.com; www.midwestfoodservicenews.com

Keith Hadley, Publisher
Joanne Cooper, Editor

Communicates directly and exclusively with restaurant and food service operations in Indiana, Kentucky, Michigan, Ohio, Pennsylvania and West Virginia.
52 Pages
Frequency: Bi-Monthly
Circulation: 40,000
Founded in: 1982
Printed in 4 colors on newsprint stock

9747 Military Grocer
Downey Communications
4800 Montgomery Lane
Suite 710
Bethesda, MD 20814-3461

301-718-7600; *Fax:* 301-718-7604

Richard T Carroll, Publisher
Loretta M Downey, CEO

Serves defense commissary employees worldwide.
Frequency: 5 per year
ISSN: 1058-8620
Printed in 4 colors on glossy stock

9748 Milk and Liquid Food Transporter
Glen Street Publications
W4652 Glen Street
Appletone, WI 54913

920-749-4880; *Fax:* 920-749-4877; www.glenstreet.com

Jane Plout, Publisher

Information for owners, operators and managers of companies that haul milk or other liquid foods in sanitary or food grade tankers. Publication covers maintenance, association news, state of the industry, business management, and activities of independent haulers.
16 Pages
Frequency: Monthly
Circulation: 4768
Founded in: 1960
Printed in 4 colors on glossy stock

9749 Milling & Baking News
Sosland Publishing Company
4801 Main St
Suite 100
Kansas City, MO 64112-2513

816-756-1000; *Fax:* 816-756-0494; www.sosland.com

Morton Sosland, Editor-in-Chief
Josh Sosland, Editor
Neil N Sosland, Executive Editor
Eric Schroeder, Managing Editor
Jeff Gelski, Associate Editor

This magazine is aimed at baking, milling and food processing industries.
Cost: $135.00
Frequency: Monthly
Circulation: 4032

9750 Milling Journal
3065 Pershing Court
Decatur, IL 62526

217-877-9660
800-728-7511; *Fax:* 217-877-6647
webmaster@grainnet.com; www.grainnet.com

Jim Camillo, Editor
Mark Avery, Publisher
Kay Merryfield, Circulation Manager
Jody Sexton, Editorial Assistant
Deb Coontz, Sales Manager

Mailed to all active AOM members in the US, Canada, and internationally, including wheat flour/corn mills and corn/oilseed processors in US and Canada.
Frequency: Quarterly
Circulation: 1217

9751 Missouri Grocer
Missouri Grocers Association
315 North Ken Avenue
Springfield, MO 65802-6213

417-831-6667; *Fax:* 417-831-3907
cmcmillian@missourigrocers.com; www.missourigrocers.com
Social Media: Facebook

Erick Taylor, President
John Porter, Vice President
Mike Beal, Treasurer
Linda Ryan, Chairperson

Referred to as the pre-convention issue. Highlights the exhibitors, sponsors, awardees and events that will be taking place during the Annual Convention and Merchandising Show.

9752 Modern Baking
Penton Media
330 N Wabash
Suite 2300
Chicago, IL 60611

E-Mail: katie.martin@penton.com
modern-baking.com

Jerry Rymont, VP Penton Food Group
Katie Martin, Chief Editor
Matt Reynolds, Group Managing Editor

Provides the latest product and service information to the $20 billion in-store and $14.9 billion retail baking and foodservice markets.
Cost: $75.00
112 Pages
Frequency: Monthly
Circulation: 27000
ISSN: 0897-6201
Founded in: 1987
Mailing list available for rent: 27,000 names
Printed in 4 colors on glossy stock

9753 Modern Brewery Age
Business Journals
50 Day Street
S Norwalk, CT 06854-3100

203-853-6015; *Fax:* 203-852-8175
pete@breweryage.com; www.breweryage.com

Peter VK Reid, Editor
Britton Jones, President
Arthur Heilman, Circulation Manager

A magazine for the wholesale and brewing industry.
Cost: $95.00
Frequency: Quarterly
Founded in: 1933

9754 Modern Brewery Age: Tabloid Edition
Business Journals
50 Day Street
#5550
Norwalk, CT 06854-3100

203-853-6015; *Fax:* 203-852-8175

Peter VK Reid, Editor

Brewery industry tabloid.
Cost: $85.00
Frequency: Weekly

9755 Monthly Price Review
Urner Barry Publications
PO Box 389
Toms River, NJ 08754

732-240-5330
800-932-0617; *Fax:* 732-341-0891
help@urnerbarry.com; www.urnerbarry.com

Paul B Brown Jr, President
Karen Mick, Circulation Director

Lists price of eggs, turkeys, chickens, fowl, butter, margarine, cheese and concentrated milk products for the month and compares the monthly average to the previous year.
Cost: $149.00
Frequency: Monthly
Circulation: 310
ISSN: 0566-3628
Founded in: 1858

9756 Mushroom News
American Mushroom Institute
1284 Gap Newport Pike
Suite 2
Avondale, PA 19311-9503

610-268-7483; *Fax:* 610-268-8015; www.americanmushroom.org

Sara Manning, Manager
Mark Wach, Chairman
Laura Phelps, President
Bill Barber, Publisher

For growers and scientists in mushroom production.
Cost: $275.00
Frequency: Monthly
Founded in: 1956

9757 NACS Magazine
National Association of Convenience Stores
1600 Duke St
Suite 700
Alexandria, VA 22314-3436

703-684-3600; *Fax:* 703-836-4564
bmoyer@nacsonline.com; www.nacsonline.com

Hank Armour, President
Ben Moyer, Advertising Manager

Delivered to all members, this magazine reaches a majority of the convenience and petroleum marketing channel of trade.
Frequency: Monthly
Circulation: 27,632

9758 **NAEDA Equipment Dealer**
North American Equipment Dealers Association
1195 Smizer Mill Rd
Fenton, MO 63026-3480

636-349-5000; *Fax:* 636-349-5443
naeda@naeda.com; www.naeda.com
Social Media: Twitter, LinkedIn

Paul Kindinger, President/CEO
Michael Williams, VP, Government Relations/Treasurer
Terry Leath, Executive Assistant
Roger Gjellstad, First Vice Chair
Lester Killebrew, Chairman

Featuring articles about successful dealers, new products, new technology, industry news, insurance loss control solutions and top management tips.
Cost: $40.00
5000 Members
Frequency: Monthly
Circulation: 9,500
Founded in: 1900
Printed in 4 colors on glossy stock

9759 **NWAC News: Thad Cochran National Warmwater Aquaculture Center**
127 Experiment Station Road
Stoneville, MS 38776-197

662-686-3273; *Fax:* 662-686-3320
javery@drec.msstate.edu;
www.msstate.edu/dept/tcnwac

Jimmy Avery, Editor
J Lee, CEO/President
Frequency: Monthly
Circulation: 1200
Founded in: 1998
Printed in 3 colors on matte stock

9760 **Nation's Restaurant News**
Lebhar-Friedman
425 Park Ave
Suite 6
New York, NY 10022-3526

212-756-5088; *Fax:* 212-838-9487
info@lf.com; www.nrn.com

Heather Martin, Manager
Michael Cardillo, VP Sales

Serves commercial and onsite food service and lodging establishments including restaurants, schools, universities, hospitals, nursing homes and other health and welfare facilities, hotels and motels with food service, government installations, clubs and other related firms.
Cost: $44.95
Circulation: 85999
Founded in: 1925
Mailing list available for rent: 100,000 names at $100 per M
Printed in 4 colors on matte stock

9761 **National Confectionery Sales Association Annual Journal**
Teresa Tarantino
10225 Berea Road, Suite B
Cleveland, OH 44102

216-631-8200; *Fax:* 216-631-8210
ttarantino@mail.propressinc.com;
www.candyhalloffame.com

Tony Rufrano, President
Steve Foster, Executive Director

Annual membership listing and biographies of Candy Hall of Fame industees.
Cost: $25.00
76 Pages
Founded in: 1997
Printed in 4 colors on matte stock

9762 **National Culinary Review**
American Culinary Federation
180 Center Place Way
St Augustine, FL 32095-8859

904-824-4468
800-624-9458; *Fax:* 904-825-4758
acf@acfchefs.net; www.acfchefs.org

Heidi Cramb, Executive Director

A monthly magazine that is circulated by paid subscription. ACF members receive this publication as a benefit of membership in the American Culinary Federation. The National Culinary Review contains chef-tested recipes, industry news, and culinary techniques and is an educational resource for everyone interested in food preparation.
Cost: $50.00
Frequency: 10x Yearly
Circulation: 25,000
Founded in: 1932

9763 **National Farmers Union News**
National Farmers Union
11900 E Cornell Ave
Aurora, CO 80014-6201

303-368-7300
800-347-1961; *Fax:* 303-368-1390;
www.nfu.org

David Frederickson, President
Rae Price, Publications Editor

A grass roots structure in which policy positions are initiated locally. The goal is to sustain and strengthen family farm and ranch agriculture.
Cost: $30.00
Frequency: Monthly
Founded in: 1902

9764 **National Fisherman**
Diversified Business Communications
PO Box 7437
Portland, ME 04112-7437

207-842-5600; *Fax:* 207-842-5503
info@divcom.com; www.divbusiness.com

Nancy Hasselback, President/CEO
Randy Le Shane, VP Operations
Nancy Gelette, VP Operations
Stephnie Wendel, Circulation Manager

The most widely read commercial fishing magazine and the only commercial fishing publication providing national coverage and national circulation.
Cost: $22.95
Frequency: Monthly
Circulation: 38000
ISSN: 0027-9250
Founded in: 1949

9765 **National Food Processors Association State Legislative Report**
National Food Processors Association
1350 Eye St NW
Suite 300
Washington, DC 20005-3377

202-393-0890
800-355-0983; *Fax:* 202-639-5932;
www.nfpa-food.org

Cal Dooley, CEO
Lisa Weddig, Executive Director
Tammy Morgan, Contact
Frequency: Monthly
Circulation: 345
Founded in: 1901

9766 **National Hog Farmer**
7900 International Dr
Suite 300
Minneapolis, MN 55425-2562

952-851-4710; *Fax:* 952-851-4601
nationalhogfarmer.com/

Dale Miller, Editor
Tom Vilsack, Secretary
JoAnn DeSmet, Marketing
Robert Moraczewski, Senior Vice President

Offers production information for hog farming business managers.
Frequency: Monthly
Circulation: 84000
Founded in: 1960
Mailing list available for rent: 84M names
Printed in 4 colors on glossy stock

9767 **National Provisioner**
Stagnito Communications
155 Pfingster Road
Suite 205
Deerfield, IL 60015

847-205-5660; *Fax:* 847-205-5680;
www.nationalprovisioner.com

Ned Bardic, Publisher
Barbara Young, Editor
Tommy Howell, Marketing
Vito Laudati, Business Development Manager
Diana Rotman, Sales Manager

Magazine for meat, poultry, prepared food processors.
Cost: $85.00
Frequency: Monthly
Circulation: 25000
Founded in: 1912

9768 **Natural Foods Merchandiser**
New Hope Natural Media
1401 Pearl St
Suite 200
Boulder, CO 80302-5346

303-939-8440
800-431-1255; *Fax:* 303-939-9886
info@newhope.com; www.newhope.com

Fred Linder, President
Marty Traynor, Editor
Lynne Brenner, Human Resources Executive

Natural Foods Merchandiser features a comprehensive overview of the industry, the latest reports on new ingredients and formulations, market news, new product releases and many other features specifically designed for the retailmarket. It offers the information and the products retailers require to succeed in the competitive natural products marketplace.
65 Pages
Frequency: Monthly
Circulation: 15,000
ISSN: 0164-335x
Founded in: 1979
Printed in 4 colors on glossy stock

9769 **Natural Products INSIDER**
Virgo Publishing LLC
3300 N Central Ave
Suite 300
Phoenix, AZ 85012-2532

480-675-9925; *Fax:* 480-990-0819;
www.naturalproductsinsider.com

Jenny Bolton, President

Official magazine for SupplySide. Provides timely information and news for marketers, manufacturers and formulators of dietary supplements, functional foods and personal care. The website also offers exclusive resources and offers, free weekly e-newsletters and a searchable news archive.
Mailing list available for rent: 15000+ names at $var per M

9770 **Natural Products Marketplace**
Virgo Publishing LLC
3300 N Central Ave
Suite 300
Phoenix, AZ 85012-2532

480-675-9925; *Fax:* 480-990-0819
peggyj@vpico.com; www.vpico.com

Jenny Bolton, President

Publication discussing the dietary supplement, food and personal care industries, focusing on the latest news, products and trend analysis to keep retailers informed and ahead of the competition.
Mailing list available for rent: 15000+ names at $var per M

9771 **Nightclub & Bar Magazine**
Oxford Publishing
Ste 1
1903b University Ave
Oxford, MS 38655-4150

662-236-5510
800-247-3881; *Fax:* 662-236-5541
ed@oxpub.com; www.nightclub.com

Ed Meek, Publisher
Taylor Rau, Editor
Jennifer Parsons, Marketing
Jennifer Robinson, CEO/President
Adam Alson, Founder

A monthly publication covering the nightclub and bar hospitality industry.
Cost: $30.00
Frequency: Monthly
Circulation: 30000
Printed in 4 colors on glossy stock

9772 **North Africa and Middle East International Agricultural and Trade Report**
US Department of Agriculture
1301 New York Avenue NW
#612
Washington, DC 20005-4701

202-219-0724; *Fax:* 202-219-0942

Michael Kurrzig, Editor

Information on current and projected agriculture production and trade in North Africa and the Middle East. Reports include trade and production data and highlight US and European trade with the region.
Frequency: Annual

9773 **North American Deer Farmers Magazine**
North American Deer Farmers Association
104 S Lakeshore Dr
Lake City, MN 55041-1641

651-345-5600; *Fax:* 651-345-5603
info@nadefa.org; www.nadefa.org

Shawn Schafer, Executive Director
Dave McQuaig, First VP
Glenn Dice Jr, Second VP

National association of deer farming and ranching. Membership dues are $75-195 which include this quarterly magazine.
Frequency: Quarterly
Circulation: 1000
ISSN: 1084-0583
Founded in: 1983
Mailing list available for rent
Printed in on glossy stock

9774 **North American Journal of Aquaculture**
American Fisheries Society
5410 Grosvenor Ln
Suite 110
Bethesda, MD 20814-2199

301-897-8616; *Fax:* 301-897-8096;
www.fisheries.org

Gus Rassam, Executive Director
Myra Merritt, Office Administrator

Formerly published as The Progressive Fish-Culturist. The focus is on culture of all aquatic organisms that are of importance to North American culturists. Topics include, but are not limited to, nutrition and feeding, broodstock selection and spawning, drugs and chemicals, health and water quality, and testing new techniques and equipment for the management and rearing of aquatic species
Cost: $38.00
Frequency: Quarterly
ISSN: 1548-8454

9775 **Northeast DairyBusiness**
DairyBusiness Communications
6437 Collamer Road
East Syracuse, NY 13057-1031

315-703-7979
800-334-1904; *Fax:* 315-703-7988;
www.dairybusiness.com

Eleanor Jacobs, Editor
Susan Harlow, Managing Editor

Business resource for successful milk producers. Devoted exclusively to the business and dairy management needs of milk producers in the 12 northeastern states.
Cost: $38.95
51 Pages
Frequency: Monthly
Circulation: 17,500
ISSN: 1523-7095
Founded in: 1904
Printed in 4 colors on glossy stock

9776 **Northwest Palate Magazine**
Pacifica Publishing
PO Box 10860
Portland, OR 97296

503-224-6039
800-398-7842; *Fax:* 503-222-5312
http://www.northwestpalate.com

Cameron Nagel, Publisher/Editor
Angie Jabine, Owner
Ericka Burke, Owner

Regional magazine that focuses on food, wine and travel. Coverage includes restaurants, destinations and the wines of the Pacific Northwest states and British Columbia.
Cost: $15.00
56 Pages
Frequency: 6 issues per ye
Circulation: 45000
ISSN: 0892-8363
Founded in: 1987
Printed in 4 colors on glossy stock

9777 **Nut Grower**
Western Agricultural Publishing Company
4969 E Clinton Way
Suite 104
Fresno, CA 93727-1549

559-252-7000
888-382-9772; *Fax:* 559-252-7387;
www.westagpubco.com

Paul Baltimore, Publisher
Randy Bailey, Editor
Robert Fujimoto, Assistant Editor

Covers production topics, the latest in research developments, and crop news on almonds, walnuts, pistachios, pecans and chestnuts.

9778 **Nutraceuticals World**
Rodman Publishing
70 Hilltop Rd
3rd Floor
Ramsey, NJ 07446-1150

201-825-2552; *Fax:* 201-825-0553
info@rodpub.com;
www.nutraceuticalsworld.com

Rodman Zilenziger Jr, President
Matt Montgomery, VP

Articles about many aspects of the market, from dietary supplements to functional foods to nutritional beverages, and everything in between.
Frequency: Monthly
Circulation: 12010

9779 **Nutrition Action Healthletter**
Center for Science in the Public Interest
1875 Connecticut Avenue NW
Suite 300
Washington, DC 20009

202-332-9110; *Fax:* 202-265-4954
cspi@cspinet.org; www.cspinet.org

Stephen B Schmidt, Editor-in-Chief
Chris Schmidt, Customer Service Manager
Michael Jacobson, Executive Director
Jamie Jonker, Director Regulatory Affairs

A magazine covering food and nutrition, the food industry, and relevant government regulations.
Cost: $32.00
16 Pages
Circulation: 800000
Founded in: 1971
Mailing list available for rent: 700,000 names at $90 per M
Printed in 4 colors on matte stock

9780 **On-Campus Hospitality**
Executive Business Media
825 Old Country Road
PO Box 1500
Westbury, NY 11590

516-334-3030; *Fax:* 516-334-8959
ebm-mail@ebmpubs.com; www.ebmpubs.com

Murry H Greenwald, President/Publisher
Paul Ragusa, Managing Editor

College and university food service operations and outlets and related purchasing and administrative offices.
Cost: $30.00
Circulation: 9,445
ISSN: 0887-431X
Founded in: 1979
Printed in 4 colors

9781 **Onboard Services**
International Publishing Company of America
664 La Villa Dr
Miami Springs, FL 33166-6030

305-887-1700
800-525-2015; *Fax:* 305-885-1923;
www.onboard-services.com

Alexander Morton, Owner
George Hulcher, Contributing Editor

Keeps airline, cruise ships, railroad, and terminal concessions management and purchasing departments up-to-date on all phases of passenger services.
Cost: $25.00
24 Pages
ISSN: 0892-4236
Founded in: 1968
Printed in 4 colors on glossy stock

9782 **Organic WORLD**
John Pappenheimer
3939 Leary Way NW
Seattle, WA 98107-5043

206-781-3347; *Fax:* 206-632-7055

Covers the news of organic gardening.
Cost: $15.00
Frequency: Quarterly

9783 **PMT Magazine**
Packaging Machinery Manufacturers Institute
11911 Freedom Drive
Suite 600
Reston, VA 20190

703-243-8555
888-275-7664; *Fax:* 703-243-8556
pmmi@pmmi.org; www.pmmi.org
Social Media: Facebook, Twitter, LinkedIn, YouTube

Chuck Yuska, President

The only publication dedicated to the packaging machinery end user. The magazine features articles on mechatronics, sustainability and the packaging professional. Regular features bring news about trends, automation solutions, processing and more.
500+ Members

9784 Pacific Farmer-Stockman
999 West Riverside Avenue
PO Box 2160
Spokane, WA 99201-1006
509-595-5385
800-624-6618; *Fax:* 509-459-3929;
www.nmv.pointshop.com
Barry Roach, Ad Director
Shaun Higgins, President
Colleen Striegel, Operations Manager
Mike Craigen, Marketing Executive
Offers farming news and information for farmers and herdsmen located in the Pacific states.
Cost: $29.95
Frequency: Monthly

9785 Packer
Vance Publishing
400 Knightsbridge Parkway
Lincolnshire, IL 60069
847-634-2600; *Fax:* 847-634-4379
info@vancepublishing.com;
www.vancepublishing.com
William C Vance, Chairman
Peggy Walker, President
Leading source of news and information on fresh fruit and vegetable marketing.
Frequency: Weekly
Circulation: 12434
Founded in: 1937
Printed in on glossy stock

9786 Peanut Farmer
Specialized Agricultural Publications
5808 Faringdon Place
Suite 200
Raleigh, NC 27609
919-872-5040; *Fax:* 919-876-6531;
www.peanutfarmer.com
Dayton H Matlick, President
Mary Evans, Publisher
Mary Cornwall, Chief Copy Editor
Jeanne Sherman, Director of Circulation
Offers peanut farmers profitable methods of raising, marketing and promoting peanuts, plus key related issues.
Cost: $15.00
24 Pages
Frequency: Monthly
Circulation: 18500
Founded in: 1965
Printed in 4 colors on glossy stock

9787 Peanut Grower
Vance Publishing
38 Peace Drive
Bronson, FL 32621
352-486-7006; *Fax:* 352-486-7009
ahuber@svic.net; www.peanutgrower.com
Amanda Huber, Editor
Lia Guthrie, Sales
Written for the largest 24,000 US peanut farmers. Covers disease, weed and insect control, legislation, farm equipment, marketing and new research.
Founded in: 1937

9788 Peanut Science
American Peanut Research and Education Society
Oklahoma State University
376 Ag Hall
Stillwater, OK 74078-6025
405-372-3052; *Fax:* 405-624-6718;
www.peanutscience.com
Dr J Ronald Sholar, Executive Officer
A professional journal with current research results.
Cost: $9.00
Frequency: Bi-Annual
Founded in: 1979

9789 Pig International
WATT Publishing Company
303 N Main Street
Suite 500
Rockford, IL 61101
815-966-5400; *Fax:* 815-966-6416;
www.wattnet.com
James Watt, Chairman/CEO
Greg Watt, President/COO
Roger Abbott, Editor
Covers nutrition, animal health issues, feed procurement, and how producers can be profitable in the world pork market.
Cost: $50.00
Frequency: Monthly
Circulation: 17642
ISSN: 0191-8834
Founded in: 1971
Printed in 4 colors on glossy stock

9790 Pizza Today
National Association of Pizzeria Operators
908 S 8th Street
Suite 200
Louisville, KY 40203
502-736-9500
800-489-8324; *Fax:* 502-736-9502
plachapelle@pizzatoday.com;
www.pizzatoday.com
Social Media: Facebook, Twitter
Pete Lachapelle, Publisher/President
Jeremy White, Editor-in-Chief
Mandy Detwiler, Managing Editor
Pat Cravens, Editorial Coordinator
Up-to-date information on pizza restaurant management, pizza equipment for sale, a vendor directory and more.
130 Pages
Frequency: Monthly
Circulation: 47,000
Founded in: 1983
Printed in 4 colors on glossy stock

9791 Pork
10901 W 84th Ter
Suite 200
Lenexa, KS 66214-1631
913-438-8700
800-255-5113; *Fax:* 913-438-0695
info@vancepublishing.com;
www.vancepublishing.com
Cliff Becker, Publisher
Jane Messenger, Chief Financial Officer
Lori Eppel, Chief Financial Officer
Bill Raufer, Contributing Editor
A magazine specifically designed for the professional pork producer.
Cost: $59.88
Frequency: Monthly
Circulation: 21,464
Founded in: 1981
Mailing list available for rent

9792 Potato Country
Columbia Publishing
8405 Ahtanum Rd
Yakima, WA 98903-9432
509-248-2452
800-900-2452; *Fax:* 509-248-4056;
www.potatocountry.com
Brent Clement, Editor/Publisher
Mike Stoker, Publisher
Edited for potato growers and allied industry people throughout the Western fall-production states. Editorial material covers production, seed, disease forecast, equipment, fertilizer, irrigation, pest/weed management, crop reports and annual buyers guide.
Cost: $18.00
32 Pages
Circulation: 6300
ISSN: 0886-4780
Founded in: 1975
Printed in 4 colors on glossy stock

9793 Potato Grower
Harris Publishing Company
360 B Street
Idaho Falls, ID 83402
208-524-4217; *Fax:* 208-522-5241;
www.potatogrower.com
Jason Harris, Publisher
Gary Rawlings, Editor
Nancy Butler, Staff Writer
Rob Erickson, Marketing
Eula Endecott, Circulation
Current news on growing potatoes, market trends, technology.
Cost: $20.95
48 Pages
Frequency: Monthly
ISBN: m-ountai-n -w
Founded in: 1965
Printed in 4 colors on glossy stock

9794 Poultry
Marketing and Technology Group
1415 N Dayton St
Suite 115
Chicago, IL 60642-7033
312-266-3311; *Fax:* 312-266-3363
webinars@meatingplace.com;
www.meatingplace.com
Mark Lefens, Owner
Tom Cosgrove, Editor
Serves companies who deal with poultry slaughter, rendering or processing.
Frequency: Monthly
Circulation: 20,000
Founded in: 1993
Printed in 4 colors on glossy stock

9795 Poultry Digest
WATT Publishing Company
122 S Wesley Ave
Mt Morris, IL 61054-1451
815-734-7937; *Fax:* 815-734-4201
olentine@wattmm.com; www.wattnet.com
James W Watt, President
Charles G Olentine Jr, PhD, Publisher
A magazine serving the production side of the entire poultry industry.
Founded in: 1917

9796 Poultry International
WATT Publishing Company
303 N Main Street
Suite 500
Rockford, IL 61101
815-966-5400; *Fax:* 815-966-6416
mclements@wattnet.net; www.wattnet.com
James Watt, Chairman/CEO
Greg Watt, President/COO
Mark Clements, Editor

Viewed by commercial poultry integrators as the leading international source of news, data and information for their businesses. Serves commercial broiler, turkey, duck and egg producers.
Cost: $63.00
68 Pages
Frequency: Monthly
Circulation: 20000
ISSN: 0032-5767
Founded in: 1962
Printed in 4 colors

9797 Poultry Times
Poultry & Egg News
PO Box 1338
Gainesville, GA 30503-1338

770-536-2476; *Fax:* 770-532-4894;
www.poultrytimes.net
Social Media: Facebook

Cindy Wellborn, Manager
Chris Hill, CEO
Barbara L Olejnik, Associate Editor
Kyle Hatcher, National Sales Representative

The only newspaper in the poultry industry. Provides the most up to date news for the poultry industry.
Cost: $12.00
Frequency: 26 X a year
Circulation: 13000
ISSN: 0885-3371
Founded in: 1954
Printed in on glossy stock

9798 Poultry USA
WATT Publishing Company
303 N Main Street
Suite 500
Rockford, IL 61101

815-966-5400; *Fax:* 815-966-6416;
www.wattnet.com

James Watt, Chairman/CEO
Greg Watt, President/COO
Jeff Swanson, Publishing Director

Poultry USA serves individuals and firms engaged in the production, processing and marketing of broilers.
60 Pages
Frequency: Monthly
Circulation: 15,092
ISSN: 0007-2176
Founded in: 1917
Printed in 4 colors on glossy stock

9799 Practical Winery & Vineyard
58 Paul Dr
Suite D
San Rafael, CA 94903-2054

415-479-5819; *Fax:* 415-492-9325
Office@practicalwinery.com;
www.practicalwinery.com

Don Neel, Owner
Tina L Vierra, Associate Publisher

Journal of grape grown and wine production in North America.
Cost: $33.86
Frequency: 6 issues per ye
Circulation: 7,500
Founded in: 1985

9800 Prepared Foods
Business News Publishing
2401 W Big Beaver Rd
Suite 700
Troy, MI 48084-3333

248-362-3700; *Fax:* 248-362-0317;
www.bnpmedia.com

Mitchell Henderson, CEO
Kathy Travis, Art Director

About 600 food and beverage companies.
Cost: $95.00
109 Pages
Circulation: 70100
Founded in: 1926
Printed in 4 colors on glossy stock

9801 Private Label Buyer
Stagnito Communications
155 Pfingsten Road
Suite 205
Deerfield, IL 60015

847-205-5660; *Fax:* 847-205-5680;
www.stagnito.com

Steven T Lichtenstein, Publisher
Jill Bruss, Editor

Serves the private label industry, including retailers, voluntaries, wholesalers, manufacturers and others allied to the field.
Frequency: Monthly
Circulation: 30021
Founded in: 1986

9802 Process Cooling & Equipment
BNP Publications
1050 IL Route 83
Suite 200
Bensenville, IL 60106-1096

630-377-5909; *Fax:* 630-694-4002;
www.process-cooling.com

Katie Rotella, Manager
Doug Glenn, Publishing Director

Written for manufacturing engineers who use cooling equipment, components, materials and supplies. refrigerated engineers and technicians assoc

9803 Prograzier
Meat & Livestock Australia
1401 K Street NW
Suite 602
Washington, DC 20005

202-521-2551; *Fax:* 202-521-2699
info@mla.com.au; www.mla.com.au
Social Media: Facebook, Twitter, YouTube

Don Heatley, Chairman
David Palmer, Managing Director
Bernie Bindon, Director
Chris Hudson, Director

Companion publication to feedback magazine. Highlights how individual producers have succesfully introduced best management practices into their farming enterprise and the benefits that have been achieved.
30000 Members
Frequency: Quarterly
Founded in: 1998

9804 Progressive Farmer
2100 Lakeshore Drive
Birmingham, AL 35209-6721

205-877-6333
800-357-4466; *Fax:* 205-877-6860
ProgressiveFarmer@timeinc.com;
www.progressivefarmer.com

Ed Dickinsen, Publisher
Jack Odle, Editor

Farming news with regional focus on the midwest, midsouth and southwest.
Cost: $84.00
106 Pages
Frequency: Monthly
Circulation: 610000
ISSN: 0033-0760

9805 Progressive Grocer's Marketing Guidebook
Trade Dimensions
770 Broadway
New York, NY 10003

847-763-9050; *Fax:* 203-563-3131;
www.progressivegrocer.com

Jenny McTaggart, Senior Editor
Olivia Wilson, Publisher

Over 800 retailer chains and wholesalers in the US and Canada. Also includes over 20,000 key executives. Plus, over 1,700 speciality distributors including C-Store and smaller food store wholesalers, food brokers, and candy, tobacco, and media distributors.
Cost: $380.00
Founded in: 1970

9806 QSR Magazine
101 Europa Drive
Suite 150
Chapel Hill, NC 27517

919-945-0705; *Fax:* 919-945-0701;
www.qsrmagazine.com

Sam Oches, Editor
Eugene Drezner, National Sales Director
Webb Howell, President
Frequency: Monthly
Founded in: 1997

9807 RCI Magazine
Retail Confectioners International
2053 S Waverly Ave
Suite 204
Springfield, MO 65804-2414

417-883-2775
800-545-5381; *Fax:* 847-724-2719
info@retailconfectioners.org;
www.retailconfectioners.org

Evans Billington, Executive Director
Covers the retail confection industry.
Frequency: Monthly
Circulation: 800
Founded in: 1917

9808 RF Design
131 E Main Street
Bellevue, OH 44811-1449

419- 48- 741; *Fax:* 419-483-3617;
www.rfdesign.com/

David Morrison, Editor
Pete May, President

Comprehensive source of rural agricultural news and information for farmers and the general public.
Frequency: Monthly
Founded in: 2000

9809 Reciprocation
American Meat Science Association
2441 Village Green Pl
Champaign, IL 61822-7676

800-517-AMSA; *Fax:* 888-205-5834; *Fax:* 217-356-5370
information@meatscience.org;
www.meatscience.org

William Mikel, President
Scott J. Eilert, President Elect
Casey B. Frye, Treasurer

Published twice a year for all AMSA members, this magazine features articles on current meat science issues facing the industry.

9810 Refrigerated & Frozen Foods
Stagnito Communications

155 Pfingsten Road
Suite 205
Deerfield, IL 60015

847-205-5660; *Fax:* 847-205-5680;
www.refrigeratedfrozenfood.com

Jeff Plaster, Publisher
Geneine Esquibel, Marketing Manager
Katie Gutierrez, Marketing Manager

Features on leading refrigerated and frozen food processors. Current and future trends in processing, packaging, new product development, food safety and logistics. Serves the dairy, meat, vegetable, fruit, bakery, deli, ingredient, snack, ethnic and other food industry related organizations. Free to qualified subscribers.
Cost: $65.00
64 Pages
Frequency: Monthly
Circulation: 20500
ISSN: 1061-6152
Founded in: 1919
Printed in 4 colors on glossy stock

9811 Render
National Renderers Association
801 N Fairfax St
Suite 205
Alexandria, VA 22314-1776

703-683-0155; *Fax:* 703-683-2626;
www.nationalrenderers.org

Thomas M Cook, President

Keeping members abreast of advancements and trends taking place within the industry.
Frequency: Monthly

9812 Restaurant Business
National Council of Chain Restaurants
325 7th St NW
Suite 1100
Washington, DC 20004

202-783-7971
800-673-4692; *Fax:* 202-737-2849
info@nrf.com; www.nccr.net

Mike Starnes, Chairman
Rob Green, Executive Director
Scott Vinson, Vice President
Chip Kunde, Treasurer
Mary Schell, Secretary

The only publication that is all about and only about the restaurant entrepreneur, serving regional and emerging chains, multi-concept operators and high-volume independents with ideas to innovate and grow. Features include growth strategies, innovations, the restaurant life, and more.
Frequency: Monthly
Founded in: 1965

9813 Restaurant Digest
Panagos Publishing
7913 Westpark Drive
Suite 305
McLean, VA 22102

703-917-6420; *Fax:* 703-917-6408;
www.restaurantdigest.com

Bruce Panagos, Publisher

Developments and news of interest to owners, managers, and operators of dining and entertainment establishments in the region.

9814 Restaurant Hospitality
Penton Media
1300 E 9th St
Suite 316
Cleveland, OH 44114-1503

216-696-7000; *Fax:* 216-696-6662
information@penton.com; www.penton.com

Jane Cooper, Marketing
Mike Sanson, Editor-in-Chief

A national trade publication that covers the full-service restaurant industry. It offers cover story features, an extensive food section with recipes, a multi-page news section and a variety of one page profiles on rising stars, equipment, food safety, beverages, design and more.
Cost: $70.00
130 Pages
Frequency: Monthly
Circulation: 117,721
ISSN: 0147-9989
Founded in: 1892
*Mailing list available for rent*at $165 per M
Printed in 4 colors on glossy stock

9815 Restaurant Marketing
Oxford Publishing
Ste 1
1903b University Ave
Oxford, MS 38655-4150

662-236-5510
800-247-3881; *Fax:* 662-236-5541
ed@oxpub.com; www.nightclub.com

Ed Meek, Publisher
Taylor Rau, Editor
Jennifer Parsons, Marketing Director
Amy Dierks, VP Advertising
Michael Harrelson, Executive Editor

A trade magazine providing marketing information and promotional ideas for restaurant owners, hotel and casino operators and caterers.
Cost: $30.00
Frequency: Monthly
Circulation: 30000
Founded in: 1985

9816 Restaurant Wine
Wine Profits
PO Box 222
Napa, CA 94559-222

707-224-4777; *Fax:* 707-224-6740;
www.restaurantwine.com

Zelma Long, President
Ronn R Wiegand, Publisher
Sandy Flanders, Director of Marketing
Paul Grieco, Co-Owner

Information on the marketing of wine in restaurants, hotels and clubs, wine and food pairing ideas and review of wines.
Cost: $99.00
Circulation: 3000
ISSN: 1040-7030
Printed in 2 colors on matte stock

9817 Restaurants & Institutions
Reed Business Information
2000 Clearwater Dr
Oak Brook, IL 60523-8809

630-574-0825
800-446-6551; *Fax:* 630-288-8781;
www.rimag.com

Jeff Greisch, President
Scott Hume, Managing Editor

For restaurant professionals faced with fast-paced consumer demands, government regulations, health concerns and evolving food trends in a variety of market segments.
Frequency: Monthly
Circulation: 154110
Founded in: 1937
Printed in 4 colors on glossy stock

9818 Restaurants USA
National Restaurant Association
1200 17th St Nw
Washington, DC 20036-3006

202-331-5900
800-424-5156; *Fax:* 202-331-2429;
www.restaurant.org

Dawn M Sweeney, CEO
Sarah Smith-Hamaker, Treasurer
Phil Hickey, Treasurer

A trade magazine offering information for restaurant owners and managers, including industry trends, operational pointers, management principles and association activities.
Cost: $125.00
48 Pages
Frequency: Monthly
Circulation: 44,000
Founded in: 1980
Printed in 4 colors

9819 Rice Farming
Vance Publishing
5050 Poplar Avenue
Suite 200
Memphis, TN 38157-2099

901-767-4020
800-888-9784; *Fax:* 901-767-4026
vlboyd@worldnet.att.net;
www.ricefarming.com

John Sowell, Publisher
Marci Deshores, Editor
Barbara Johnson, Manager

Profitable production strategies for commercial rice growers.
Founded in: 1937

9820 Rice Journal
Specialized Agricultural Publications
3000 Highwoods Boulevard
Suite 300
Raleigh, NC 27604-1029

919-878-0540; *Fax:* 919-876-6531;
www.ricejournal.com

Dayton H Matlick, President
Mary Evans, Publisher

Offers rice growers profitable methods of producing, marketing and promoting rice, plus key related issues.
Cost: $15.00
24 Pages
Frequency: Monthly January-July
Circulation: 11,600
Founded in: 1897
Printed in 4 colors on glossy stock

9821 Ristorante|
1010 Lake St
Suite 604
Oak Park, IL 60301-1136

708-848-3200; *Fax:* 708-445-9477;
www.ristorantemag.com

Joe Madden, Owner

9822 Rural Heritage
Allan Damerow
281 Dean Ridge Ln
Gainesboro, TN 38562-5039

931-268-0655; *Fax:* 931-268-5884
info@ruralheritage.com;
www.ruralheritage.com

Gail Damerow, Owner
Allan Damerow, Publisher

Publication for people who farm and log with horses and other draft animals.
Cost: $28.00
100 Pages
ISSN: 0889-2970
Founded in: 1976
Printed in 4 colors on glossy stock

9823 **Rural Living**
Michigan Farm Bureau
7373 W Saginaw Highway
PO Box 30960
Lansing, MI 48909-8460

517-237-7000
800-292-2680; *Fax:* 517-323-6793;
www.michiganfarmbureau.com

Dennis Rudat, Editor
Sue Snyder, President
Brigette Leach, Director
Earl Butz, Secretary

Editorial emphasis on consumer food news, travel information and issue analysis.
24 Pages
Frequency: Quarterly

9824 **S.O. Connected**
National Society on Healthcare Foodservice
455 S. 4th Street
Suite 650
Louisville, KY 40202

888-528-9552; *Fax:* 502-589-3602
info@healthcarefoodservice.org;
www.healthcarefoodservice.org
Social Media: Facebook, LinkedIn, YouTube

Patti Oliver, President
Beth Yesford, President-Elect
Laura Watson, Secretary
Randy Sparrow, Treasurer
Robert Darrah, Treasurer-Elect

An important resource for news and recognition.

9825 **School Foodservice & Nutrition**
School Nutrition Association
120 Waterfront St
Suite 300
Oxon Hill, MD 20745-1142

301-749-1481
800-877-8822; *Fax:* 301-739-3915
servicecenter@schoolnutrition.org;
www.schoolnutrition.org

Mary Hill, Director
Dora Rivas SNS, President-Elect
Nancy Rice SNS, VP

This is the official publication of the School Nutrition Association which contains the latest information on a host of items that affect the successful operation of a school foodservice program.
Cost: $75.00
Frequency: Monthly
Circulation: 57,000

9826 **School Nutrition Magazine**
School Nutrition Association
120 Waterfront St
Suite 300
National Harbor, MD 20745-1142

301-686-3100
800-877-8822; *Fax:* 301-686-3115
servicecenter@schoolnutrition.org;
www.schoolnutrition.org

Helen Phillips, President
Sandy Ford, President-Elect
Leah Schmidt, Vice President
Beth Taylor, Secretary/Treasurer

The latest information on a host of items that affect the successful operation of a school foodservice program.
55000 Members
Frequency: Monthly
Founded in: 1946

9827 **Science Matters**
Natural Products Association
2112 E 4th St
Suite 200
Santa Ana, CA 92705-3816

714-460-7732
800-966-6632; *Fax:* 714-460-7444;
www.npainfo.org
Social Media: Facebook, Twitter, LinkedIn

John F. Gay, Executive Director & CEO
Jeffrey Wright, President

Dedicated to providing timely information and advancing the understanding of natural products from a scientific perspective.
1900+ Members
Frequency: Monthly
Founded in: 1936

9828 **Seafood Business**
Diversified Business Communications
121 Free Street
PO Box 7437
Portland, ME 04112-7437

207-842-5500; *Fax:* 207-842-5503
bspringer@divcom.com;
www.seafoodbusiness.com

Fiona Robinson, Editor
Bill Springer, Publisher
Nancy Hasselback, CEO
Linda Skinner, Managing Editor
Wendy Jalbert, Production Director

Current, comprehensive news on the rapidly expanding seafood industry.
Frequency: Monthly
Circulation: 15,000
Founded in: 1949

9829 **Sheep!**
145 Industrial Drive
Medford, WI 54451

715-785-7979
800-551-5691; *Fax:* 715-785-7414
sheepmag@tds.net; www.sheepmagazine.com

Dave Belanger, Publisher
Nathan Griffith, Editor

Explores a wide range of sheep-related topics of interest to sheep growers and sheep product marketers at all levels of experience.
Cost: $21.00
Frequency: 6x Yearly

9830 **Shorthorn Country**
Durham Management Company
5830 S 142nd St
Suite A
Omaha, NE 68137-2894

402-827-8003; *Fax:* 402-827-8006;
www.durhamstaffingsolutions.com

Machael Durham, President
Pat Cloutier, Production Manager

Magazine published for cattle producers who breed and sell registered Shorthorn and Polled Shorthorn cattle.
Cost: $24.00
Frequency: 11 per year
Circulation: 3,000
ISSN: 0149-9319

9831 **Simply Seafood**
Sea Fare Group
2360 W Commodore Way
Suite 210
Seattle, WA 98199

206-829-2323; *Fax:* 206-789-0504
peter@seafare.com; www.simplyseafood.com

Peter Redmayne, Editor

Articles on today's seafood, with cooking ideas, tips & techniques and recipes for healthy meal. Editor's Letter provides all the latest news and insights on seafood products and consumer issues as well as a Market Report with each seasons best buys.
Frequency: Quarterly
Circulation: 131,257

9832 **Sizzle**
American Culinary Federation
180 Center Place Way
St Augustine, FL 32095-8859

904-824-4468
800-624-9458; *Fax:* 904-825-4758
acf@acfchefs.net; www.acfchefs.org
Social Media: Facebook, Twitter

Michael Ty, President
Thomas J. Macrina, Secretary
James Taylor, Treasurer

The American Culinary Federation quarterly for students of cooking. The only magazine in the United States exclusively targeting culinary, baking, and pastry students. Includes articles on emerging job markets, mentoring, continuing education, culinary trends and product application, as well as scholarship information and culinary/pastry techniques. Digital publication.
19000 Members
Founded in: 1929

9833 **Snack Food & Wholesale Bakery**
Stagnito Communications
155 Pfingster Road
Suite 205
Deerfield, IL 60015

847-205-5660; *Fax:* 847-205-5680;
www.stagnito.com

Ron Bean, Publisher
Harry Stagnito, Publishing Director
Dan Malovany, Editor
Bernard Pacyniak, Editorial Director
Andy Hanacek, Managing Editor

Covers topics and products in the snack and wholesale bakery market
Cost: $85.00
Frequency: Monthly
Circulation: 14,854
Founded in: 1912
Printed in 4 colors on glossy stock

9834 **Snack World**
Snack Food Association
1233 Janesville Avenue
Fort Atkinson, WI 53538-2738

703-836-4500
800-547-7377; *Fax:* 920-563-1702

Gloria Cosby, Publisher
Tracey McMahon, Editor

The official international publication of the Snack Food Association covering trends in the snack food industry, including new products and services, industry news and supplier services.
Frequency: 10 per year
Circulation: 14,000

9835 **Southeastern Peanut Farmer**
Southern Peanut Farmer's Federation
110 E 4th Street
PO Box 706
Tifton, GA 31794

229-386-3470; *Fax:* 229-386-3501
info@gapeanuts.com; www.gapeanuts.com/

Joy Carter, Editor

Offers information to peanut farmers.
Cost: $25.00
20 Pages
Frequency: 5x/Year
Circulation: 9000
ISSN: 0038-3694
Founded in: 1961
Printed in 4 colors on glossy stock

9836 **Southern Beverage Journal**
14337 Sw 119th Ave
Miami, FL 33186-6006
305-233-7230; *Fax:* 305-252-2580
info@bevmedia.com; www.bevmedia.com
Sharon Mijares, Manager
William Slone, Publisher
A magazine for the alcoholic beverage industry.
Cost: $35.00
Frequency: Monthly
Circulation: 10000

9837 **Soybean Digest**
Primedia Business
7900 International Dr
Suite 300
Minneapolis, MN 55425-2562
952-851-9329
800-722-5334; *Fax:* 952-851-4601
CorporateCustomerService@penton.com;
www.penton.com
Robert Moraczewski, Executive VP
Ron Sorensen, Chairman
Kelly Conlin Conlin, President/CEO
Leading publication in the soybean market. Offers in-depth coverage for wise management decisions dealing with production of soybeans, corn, wheat, sorghum and cotton.
Cost: $25.00
Frequency: Monthly
Circulation: 147000
Founded in: 1940

9838 **Soybean South**
6263 Poplar Avenue
Suite 540
Memphis, TN 38119-4736
901-385-0595; *Fax:* 901-767-4026
John Sowell, Publisher
Jeff Kehl, Circulation Director
Profitable prediction strategies for soybean farmers.
Frequency: 5 per year
Printed in 4 colors on glossy stock

9839 **Specialty Food Magazine**
National Association for the Specialty Food Trade
120 Wall St
27th Floor
New York, NY 10005-4011
212-482-6440; *Fax:* 212-482-6459;
www.fancyfoodshows.com
Ann Daw, President
Provides comprehensive planning information for each Show and aggressive on-site bonus distribution, as well as the industry's most in-depth pre-Show, on-site, and post-Show coverage.
Cost: $30.00
Frequency: Monthly
Circulation: 30100
Founded in: 1952

9840 **Spudman Magazine**
75 Applewood Drive
Sparta, MI 49435
616-887-9008; *Fax:* 616-887-2666;
www.spudman.com
Matt McCallum, Publisher
Greg Brown, Managing Editor
Erica Bernard, Circulation Manager
Marnie Draper, Advertising Manager
Jill Peck, Creative Director
Information for potato farming and marketing.
Frequency: 9 issues per ye
Circulation: 15500
Founded in: 1964

9841 **StateWays**
The Beverage Information Group
17 High St
2nd Floor
Norwalk, CT 06851
203-855-8499
lzimmerman@m2media360.com;
www.bevinfogroup.com
Liza Zimmerman, Editor-in-Chief
Jeremy Nedelka, Managing Editor
Written for commissioners, board members, headquarters personnel, and retail store managers responsible for buying beverage alcohol in the eighteen control states. Covered editorial product knowledge, market trends, store operations, merchandising, warehousing, comoputerization, administration, training and other topics.
Cost: $20.00
Frequency: Bi-Monthly
Circulation: 8500

9842 **Stores Magazine**
National Council of Chain Restaurants
325 7th St NW
Suite 1100
Washington, DC 20004
202-783-7971
800-673-4692; *Fax:* 202-737-2849
info@nrf.com; www.nccr.net
Mike Starnes, Chairman
Rob Green, Executive Director
Scott Vinson, Vice President
Chip Kunde, Treasurer
Mary Schell, Secretary
Offers an insider's view of the entire retail industry by featuring the latest trends, hottest ideas, current technologies and consumer attitudes.
Frequency: Monthly
Founded in: 1965

9843 **Sugar: The Sugar Producer Magazine**
Idaho Golf Harris Publishing
520 Park Avenue
Idaho Falls, ID 83402
208-523-1500
800-638-0135; *Fax:* 208-522-5241
customerservice@harrispublishing.com;
www.sugarproducer.com
Jason Harris, Publisher
David FairBourn, Editor
Eula Endecott, Circulation Manager
Rob Erickson, Marketing Manager
Sugar beet industry information.
Cost: $15.95
Frequency: Monthly
Circulation: 16000
Founded in: 1975

9844 **Sunbelt Food Service**
Shelby Publishing Company
517 Green St Nw
Gainesville, GA 30501-3300
770-534-8380; *Fax:* 770-535-0110;
www.shelbypublishing.com
Ron Johnston, President
Penny Smith, Account Manager
Sales and promotion of products and services sold through food service establishments across the sunbelt.
Cost: $36.00
Frequency: Monthly
Circulation: 30090
Founded in: 1965
Printed in on newsprint stock

9845 **Sunflower Magazine**
National Sunflower Association
Ste 206
2401 46th Ave SE
Mandan, ND 58554-4829
701-328-5100
888-718-7033; *Fax:* 701-328-5101;
www.sunflowernsa.com
Larry Kleingartner, Executive Director
John Sanbakken, Marketing Director
Magazine geared to sunflower products.
Cost: $9.00
Frequency: Monthly
Circulation: 29,300
Founded in: 1981
Printed in 4 colors

9846 **Sunflower and Grain Marketing Magazine**
Sunflower World Publishers
3307 Northland Drive
Suite 130
Austin, TX 78731-4964
512-407-3434; *Fax:* 512-323-5118
Ed Randall Allen
Offers news and information on the sunflower and grain industries.
Circulation: 15,000

9847 **Supermarket News: Center Store**
Penton Media Inc
249 W 17th St
Suite 6
New York, NY 10011-5390
212-204-4200; *Fax:* 212-206-3622
julie.gallagher@penton.com; www.penton.com
Sharon Rowlands, CEO
Jerry Rymont, Publisher
A nationally circulated weekly trade magazine for the food distribution industry.

9848 **Supermarket News: Retail/Financial**
Penton Media Inc
249 W 17th St
Suite 6
New York, NY 10011-5390
212-204-4200; *Fax:* 212-206-3622
mark.hamstra@penton.com; www.penton.com
Sharon Rowlands, CEO
A nationally circulated weekly trade magazine for the food distribution industry
Frequency: Monthly
Circulation: 36346
ISSN: 0039-5803
Founded in: 1892

9849 **Supermarket News: Technology & Logistics**
Penton Media Inc
249 W 17th St
Suite 6
New York, NY 10011-5390
212-204-4200; *Fax:* 212-206-3622
michael.garry@penton.com; www.penton.com
Sharon Rowlands, CEO
A nationally circulated weekly trade magazine for the food distribution industry
Cost: $45.00
ISSN: 0039-5803
Founded in: 1892

9850 **Swine Practitioner**
Vance Publishing
10901 W 84th Terrace
3 Pine Ridge Plaza
Lenexa, KS 66214-1649
913-438-8700
800-255-5113; *Fax:* 913-438-0695

cbecker@vancepublishing.com;
www.vancepublishing.com

Jim Carlton, Editor
Cliff Becker, Group Publisher
William C Vance, Chairman

Offers technical information, primarily on swine health and related production areas, to veterinarians and related industry professionals.
Founded in: 1937
Mailing list available for rent

9851 **THE SUNFLOWER**
National Sunflower Association
2401 46th Avenue SE
Suite 206
Mandan, ND 58554-4829

701-328-5100
888-718-7033; *Fax:* 701-328-5101
larryk@sunflowernsa.com;
www.sunflowernsa.com
Social Media: Facebook, YouTube

Larry Kleingartner, Executive Director

Contains fresh, current and important articles on production strategies, ongoing research and market information.
Frequency: 6x Yearly
Founded in: 1981

9852 **Tea & Coffee Trade Journal**
Lockwood Publications
26 Broadway
Floor 9M
New York, NY 10004-1704

212-391-2060
845-267-3489; *Fax:* 212-391-2060;
www.lockwoodpublications.com

Robert Lockwood Sr, President

Premiere magazine for tea and coffee industry.
Cost: $49.00
Frequency: Monthly
Circulation: 12
Founded in: 1901
Printed in 4 colors on glossy stock

9853 **The County Agent**
National Association of County Agricultural Agents
6584 W Duroc Road
Maroa, IL 61756

217-794-3700; *Fax:* 217-794-5901
exec-dir@nacaa.com; www.nacaa.com

Rick Gibson, President

Members receive professional improvement, news of association activities, shared education efforts from other states and reports from NACAA leadership and member states.
Frequency: Monthly
Circulation: 5000
Founded in: 1916

9854 **The New Brewer**
Brewers Association
736 Pearl Street
Boulder, CO 80302

303-447-0816
888-822-6273; *Fax:* 303-447-2825
webmaster@brewersassociation.org;
www.beertown.org
Social Media: Facebook, Twitter

Chris P. Frey, Chair
Jake Keeler, Vice Chair
Roxanne Westendorf, Secretary

Offers practical insights and advice for breweries of all sizes. Features on topics like brewing technology and problem solving, pub and restaurant management, and packaged beer sales and distribution. Also important industry news, sales charts and market share performance. The annual Industry Review tallies production for every craft brewery in America, producing both regional and national lists of the biggest players in every sector.
1900 Members
Founded in: 1978

9855 **TheConsultant**
Food Service Consultants Society International
144 Parkedge Street
Rockwood, ON, Canada N0B 2K0

519-856-0783; *Fax:* 519-856-0648
liz@fcsi.org; www.fcsi.org

Liz Campbell, Editor

Professional publication for FCSI members and the food service industry.
Cost: $40.00
150 Pages
Frequency: Quarterly
Circulation: 4500
Printed in 4 colors on glossy stock

9856 **Today's Grocers**
Florida Grocer Publications
PO Box 430760
S Miami, FL 33246

305-661-0792
800-440-3067; *Fax:* 305-661-6720

Jack Nobles, Publisher
Dennis Kane, Editor

Provides the latest food industry news and trends to Florida, Georgia, Alabama, Louisiana, Mississippi and the Carolinas.
Cost: $29.00
24 Pages
Frequency: Monthly
Circulation: 19,000
ISSN: 1529-4420
Founded in: 1956
Printed in on newsprint stock

9857 **Tomato Country**
Columbia Publishing
8405 Ahtanum Rd
Yakima, WA 98903-9432

509-248-2452
800-900-2452; *Fax:* 509-248-4056;
www.tomatomagazine.com

Brent Clement, Editor/Publisher
Mike Stoker, Publisher

Includes information on tomato production and marketing, grower and shipper feature stories, tomato research, from herbicide and pesticide studies to new varieties, market reports, feedback from major tomato meetings and conventions, along with other key issues and points of interest for US and Canada tomato growers.
Cost: $12.00
Frequency: Annually
Founded in: 1993

9858 **Trading Rules**
National Oilseed Processors Association
1300 L St NW
Suite 1020
Washington, DC 20005-4168

202-842-0463; *Fax:* 202-842-9126
nopa@nopa.org; www.nopa.org

Kathy Pennington, Manager
David J Hovermale, Executive VP
Karri L Moore, Project Manager
Julia Kinnaird, Manager
Cost: $50.00
Founded in: 1929

9859 **Transactions of the American Fisheries Society**
American Fisheries Society
5410 Grosvenor Ln
Suite 110
Bethesda, MD 20814-2199

301-897-8616; *Fax:* 301-897-8096;
www.fisheries.org

Gus Rassam, Executive Director
Myra Merritt, Office Administrator

The Society's highly regarded international journal of fisheries science features results of basic and applied research in genetics, physiology, biology, ecology, population dynamics, economics, health, culture, and other topics germane to marine and freshwater finfish and shellfish and their respective fisheries and environments
Cost: $43.00
Frequency: Bi-Monthly
ISSN: 0002-8487
Founded in: 1872

9860 **Tree Fruit**
Western Agricultural Publishing Company
4969 E Clinton Way
#104
Fresno, CA 93727-1546

559-252-7000
888-382-9772; *Fax:* 559-252-7387

Paul Baltimore, Publisher
Randy Bailey, Editor
Robert Fujimoto, Assistant Editor

For tree fruit growers in California.

9861 **Truth About Organic Foods**
Henderson Communications LLC
1422 Elbridge Payne Rd
Suite 250
Chesterfield, MO 63017-8544

636-728-1428; *Fax:* 636-777-4178
info@agrimarketing.com;
www.agrimarketing.com

Lynn Henderson, Owner

This 231-page book provides a fair and balanced look from a scientific standpoint about the heritage, production and nutritive value of organic foods.

9862 **US Beer Market: Impact Databank Review and Forecast**
M Shanken Communications
387 Park Ave S
8th Floor
New York, NY 10016-8872

212-684-4224; *Fax:* 212-684-5424
impact@mshanken.com;
www.cigaraficionado.com

Marvin Shanken, Publisher
Cost: $895.00
Frequency: Annual+
Founded in: 1972

9863 **US Fast Food and Multi-Unit Restaurants**
Business Trend Analysts/Industry Reports
2171 Jericho Tpke
Suite 200
Commack, NY 11725-2937

631-462-5454
800-866-4648; *Fax:* 631-462-1842;
www.businesstrendanalysts.com

Charles J Ritchie, Executive VP
Donna Priani, General Manager

This survey offers information on the fast food industry, including chains and franchises.
Cost: $1995.00
Founded in: 1986

9864 **US Liquor Industry**
Business Trend Analysts/Industry Reports

2171 Jericho Tpke
Suite 200
Commack, NY 11725-2937

631-462-5454; *Fax:* 631-462-1842;
www.businesstrendanalysts.com

Charles J Ritchie, Executive VP
Donna Priani, Marketing Director

A survey summarizing the past, current and future markets and trends in the liquor industry.
Cost: $1495.00
Founded in: 1999

9865 **US Market for Bakery Products**
Business Trend Analysts/Industry Reports
2171 Jericho Tpke
Suite 200
Commack, NY 11725-2937

631-462-5454
800-866-4648; *Fax:* 631-462-1842;
www.businesstrendanalysts.com/

Charles J Ritchie, Executive VP
Donna Priani, General Manager

Profiles markets for bread, rolls, cakes, pies, cookies, crackers, other sweets and pretzels; provides information on consumption patterns, distribution trends, pricing, new products, and advertising strategies.
Cost: $1495.00
Frequency: Annual+
Founded in: 1978

9866 **Valley Potato Grower**
Ola Highway 2 E
East Grand Forks, MN 56721

218-773-7783; *Fax:* 218-773-6227
communication@nppga.org;
www.rrvpotatoes.org

Duane W Maatz, President
Ted Kreis, Marketing

Information on potato farming.
Cost: $17.95
Frequency: Monthly
Founded in: 1946

9867 **Vegetable**
US Department of Agriculture
PO Box 1258
Sacramento, CA 95812-1258

www.usda.gov

Chris Smith, Chief Information Officer
Matt Paul, Director of Communications
Ramona Romero, General Counsel

Historic information relating to various types of vegetable crops.

9868 **Vegetable Growers News**
Great American Publishing
75 Applewood Drive Suite A
PO Box 128
Sparta, MI 49345-1531

616-887-9008; *Fax:* 616-887-2666;
www.vegetablegrowersnews.com

Kimberly Warren, Managing Editor
Matt McCallum, Executive Publisher
Erica Bernard, Circulation Manager
Jill Peck, Creative Director
Greg Ryan, Graphic Designer

Market and marketing news.
Cost: $12.00
Frequency: Monthly
Circulation: 14000
Founded in: 1970

9869 **Vegetables**
Western Agricultural Publishing Company
4969 E Clinton Way
#104
Fresno, CA 93727-1549

559-252-7000
888-382-9772; *Fax:* 559-252-7387

Paul Baltimore, Publisher
Randy Bailey, Editor
Robert Fujimoto, Assistant Editor

The definitive source for information on all aspects of western vegetable production.

9870 **Vegetarian Journal**
Vegetarian Resource Group
PO Box 1463
Baltimore, MD 21203

410-366-8343; *Fax:* 410-366-8804
vrg@vrg.org; www.vrg.org

Debra Wasserman, Director

The practical magazine for those interested in Vegetarian Health, Ecology, and Ethics.
Frequency: Quarterly
Circulation: 15000
Mailing list available for rent

9871 **Veggie Life Magazine**
EGW
4075 Papazian Way
Suite 204
Fremont, CA 94538-4372

510-668-0268; *Fax:* 510-668-0280
info@egw.com; www.veggielife.com

Chris Slaughter, VP
Shanna Masters, Editor

The modem voice on seasonal vegetarian cooking, optimum nutrition, and natural healing for today's health-conscious consumer features vaulable tips techniques, recipes, and remedies from dieticians, herbalists, doctors and other health experts on new ways to prpare creative plant-based cuisine, implement diet programs, and use natural remedies for an improved and vibrant lifestyle.
Cost: $19.96
68 Pages
Frequency: Quarterly
Circulation: 80000
Founded in: 1980

9872 **Vending Times**
Vending Times
1375 Broadway
6th Floor
New York, NY 10018

516-442-1850; *Fax:* 516-442-1849
subscriptions@vendingtimes.net;
www.vendingtimes.com

Alicia Lavay-Kertes, President/Publisher
Nick Montano, VP/Executive Editor
Tim Sanford, Editor-in-Chief

Vending Times serves the automatic merchandising and coffee service industries. This includes music and game operations, vending operations, mobile catering operations, consultants and associations.
Cost: $40.00
Frequency: Monthly
Circulation: 16,000
Founded in: 1962

9873 **Vineyard and Winery Management**
Vineyard & Winery Management
421 E Street
P.O. Box 14459
Santa Rosa, CA 95404

707-577-7700
800-535-5670; *Fax:* 707-577-7705;
www.vwmmedia.com

Robert Merletti, CEO/Publisher
Jason Thomas, Business Manager
Tina Caputo, Editor-in-Chief
Ethan Simon, Director of Sales
Suzanne Webb, Marketing Director

Leading independent and award-winning wine trade magazine serving all of North America.
Cost: $37.00
100 Pages
Frequency: Bi-monthly
Circulation: 6900
ISSN: 1047-4951
Founded in: 1975
Printed in 4 colors on glossy stock

9874 **WATT Poultry Magazine**
WATT Poultry USA
122 S Wesley Ave
Mt Morris, IL 61054-1451

815-734-7937; *Fax:* 815-734-4201;
www.wattnet.com

James Watt, President
Charles Olentine, Publisher
Gary Thornton, Editor

Dedicated to supporting every phase of the turkey industry by providing information for decision-makers on breeding, production, management, processing and marketing.

9875 **Wallaces Farmer**
Farm Progress Companies
255 38th Avenue
Suite P
St Charles, IL 60174-5410

630-462-2224
800-441-1410
rswoboda@farmprogress.com;
www.farmprogress.com

Rod Swoboda, Editor
Willie Vogt, Corporate Editorial Director
Frank Holdmeyer, Executive Editor

Serves Iowa farmers and ranchers with information to help them maximize their productivity and profitability. Each issue is packed with information, ideas, news and analysis.
Cost: $26.95
Frequency: Monthly
Founded in: 1855

9876 **Western Dairy Business**
DairyBusiness Communications
6437 Collamer Road
East Syracuse, NY 13057-1031

315-703-7979
866-520-2880; *Fax:* 315-703-7988
circ@dairybusiness.com;
www.dairybusiness.com

Ron Goble, Associate Publisher
Cecilia Parsons, Associate Editor
Scott A Smith, CEO

Business resource for successful milk producers. Covers 13 Western states. Provides information and news that is helpful in the daily operations of dairymen.
Cost: $38.95
67 Pages
Frequency: Monthly
Circulation: 14000
ISSN: 1528-4360
Founded in: 1904
Printed in 4 colors on glossy stock

9877 **Western Farm Press**
Primedia
2104 Harvell Circle
Bellevue, NE 68005

913-341-1300
866-505-7173; *Fax:* 913-967-1898
wfcs@pbsub.com; www.westernfarmpress.com
Social Media: Facebook, Twitter

Robert Fraser, Managing Editor
Harry Cline, Editor
Greg Frey, Publisher
Darrah Parker, Marketing Director

Timely reliable information for western agriculture.
Circulation: 16,000
Founded in: 1989

9878 Western Fruit Grower
Meister Media Worldwide
37733 Euclid Ave
Willoughby, OH 44094-5992
440-942-2000
800-572-7740; *Fax:* 440-975-3447;
www.meisternet.com
Gary Fitzgerald, President
Brian Sparks, Editor
Terry Doak, Circulation Manager
Edited for commercial growers of deciduous crops and citrus fruit, nut grape crops in the Western US.
Cost: $20.00
66 Pages
Frequency: Monthly
Circulation: 36,000

9879 Western Grocery News
80 Willow Road
Menlo Park, CA 94025-3661
650-321-3600
800-227-7346; *Fax:* 650-327-7537
Frequency: Bi-Monthly
Circulation: 9,187

9880 Western Growers & Shippers
Western Growers Association
PO Box 2130
Newport Beach, CA 92658-8944
949-863-1000; *Fax:* 949-863-9028;
www.wga.com
Tom Nassif, President
Tim Linden, Editor
Listing over 3,000 growers, shippers, packers, brokers and distributors of fruits and vegetables in California and Arizona.
32 Pages
Frequency: Monthly
Circulation: 5000
ISSN: 0043-3799
Founded in: 1926
Printed in 4 colors on glossy stock

9881 Western Livestock Journal
Crow Publications
7355 E Orchard Road
Suite 300
Greenwood Village, CO 80111
303-722-7600
800-850-2769; *Fax:* 303-722-0155
editorial@wlj.net; www.wlj.net
Pete Crow, Publisher
Offers its readers the best coverage of timely, necessary news and information that affects the livestock industry, particularly cattle.
Cost: $45.00
Frequency: Weekly
Founded in: 1922

9882 Whole Foods Magazine
WFC
4041g Hadley Rd
Suite 101
South Plainfiel, NJ 07080-1120
908-769-1160; *Fax:* 908-769-1171
info@wfcinc.com; www.wfcinc.com
Social Media: Facebook, Twitter, LinkedIn
Howard Wainer, President
Kaylynn Ebner, Editor
Ronda Collins, Circulation Manager
Tim Person, Assistant Editor
Serves the natural/health products industry.
Cost: $70.00
Frequency: Monthly
Founded in: 1979
Printed in on glossy stock

9883 Wine Advocate
Robert M Parker Jr
PO Box 311
Monkton, MD 21111
410-329-6477; *Fax:* 410-357-4504
wineadvocate@erobertparker.com;
www.erobertparker.com
Robert M Parker Jr, Editor/CEO
Daniel Thomases, Partner
An independent magazine covering reviews of wine.
Cost: $60.00
64 Pages
Frequency: Bi-monthly
Circulation: 40000
Founded in: 1978

9884 Wine World
Wine World Publishing
6433 Topanga Canyon Boulevard
#412
Canoga Park, CA 91303-2621
Dee Snidt, Editor
For the wine consumer and industry.
Cost: $16.00
48 Pages
Frequency: Monthly
Founded in: 1971

9885 Wines & Vines
1800 Lincoln Ave
San Rafael, CA 94901-1298
415-453-9700; *Fax:* 415-453-2517
info@winesandvines.com;
www.winesandvines.com
Chet Klingensmith, Publisher
Kendra Campbell, Director of Sales and Marketing
Tina Caputo, Editor
Jacques Brix, Vice President
Voice of the grape and wine industry.
Cost: $32.50
Frequency: Monthly
Circulation: 3200
Founded in: 1919
Printed in 4 colors on matte stock

9886 Yankee Food Service
201 Oak Street
Suite A
Pembroke, MA 02359
781-829-4700
866-677-4700; *Fax:* 781-829-0134
info@griffinpublishing.net;
www.griffinpublishing.net
Stephen M Griffin, President
Jack Walsh, Vice President
Karen Harty, Vice President
Julie Mignosa, Office Manager
Reports news and happenings of the food service industry in New England.
Cost: $47.00
48 Pages
Frequency: Monthly
Circulation: 22,111
Founded in: 1970

Trade Shows

9887 A Year of Enchantment
Int'l Council on Hotel, Restaurant Institute Edu.
1200 17th Street NW
Washington, DC 20036-3006
202-467-6300
publications@chrie.org; www.chrie.org
Susan Gould, Manager
Joseph Bradley, Treasurer
Containing over 70 booths and over 50 exhibits.
750 Attendees
Frequency: August
Founded in: 1946

9888 AACC International Annual Meeting
3340 Pilot Knob Road
St. Paul, MN 55121-2055
651-454-7250
800-328-7560; *Fax:* 651-454-0766
aacc@scisoc.org; www.aaccnet.org
Social Media: Facebook, Twitter, LinkedIn
Robert L. Cracknell, President
Lydia Tooker Midness, Chair
Laura M. Hansen, President-Elect
Dave L. Braun, Treasurer
Formerly the American Asociation of Cereal Chemists, the AACC meeting offers the chance to come together, network with peers, discuss critical issues in the science and discover the methods of others.
Frequency: Annual/October

9889 AACT Technical Conference
American Association of Candy Technologists
711 W. Water St.
PO Box 266
Princeton, WI 54968
920-295-6969; *Fax:* 920-295-6843
aactinfo@gomc.com; www.aactcandy.org
Bob Huzinec, President
Bill Dyer, First VP
Approximately 20 papers are presented to an audience of technologists in the sweet goods industry. These talks range from basics to innovations, provising the industry with practical information to help in understanding processes and ingredients used by their companies.
300 Attendees
Frequency: Annual/October

9890 AAEA Annual Meeting
American Agricultural Economics Association
1110 Buckeye Avenue
Ames, IA 50010-8063
515-233-9087; *Fax:* 575-233-3101
Nancy Knight, Manager Meetings
Annual meeting and trade show of 25 exhibitors.
1700 Attendees

9891 AAW Annual Convention
American Agri-Women
2103 Zeandale Road
Manhattan, KS 66502
785-537-6171; *Fax:* 785-537-9727
info@americanagriwomen.org;
www.americanagriwomen.org
Marcie Williams, President
Tradeshow consisting of products of interest to women in agriculture.
350 Attendees
Frequency: Annual/November

9892 ABI/ADPI Joint Annual Meeting
American Butter Institute

2101 Wilson Boulevard
Suite 400
Arlington, VA 22201

703-243-6111; *Fax:* 703-841-9328
AMiner@nmpf.org; www.butterinstitute.org

Jerome J Kozak, Executive Director
Chris Galen, Communications VP

This event is co-sponsored by The American Dairy Products Institute for manufacturers, marketers and suppliers of manufactured dairy products. 35 exhibitors.
700 Attendees
Frequency: Annual

9893 **ACF National Convention**
American Culinary Federation
180 Center Place Way
St Augustine, FL 32095-8859

904-824-4468
800-624-9458; *Fax:* 904-825-4758
acf@acfchefs.net; www.acfchefs.org
Social Media: Facebook, Twitter

Michael Ty, President
Thomas J. Macrina, Secretary
James Taylor, Treasurer

Learn the latest culinary trends during educational seminars and demonstrations and enjoy spectacular meal events. Competitions, exhibits and more.
19000 Members
Founded in: 1929

9894 **ACF National Convention & Trade Show**
American Culinary Federation
180 Center Place Way
Saint Augustine, FL 32095

904-824-4468
800-624-9458; *Fax:* 904-825-4758
acf@acfchefs.net; www.acfchefs.org
Social Media: Facebook, Twitter, Flickr

Kevin Brune, Director, Events & Operations Mgmt
Jennifer Keith, Event & Sales Specialist
Claudia More, Events Management Coordinator

Two-hundred booths of products and foodstuffs for the food service industry. Seminars, workshops, cooking demos, more.
2000 Attendees
Frequency: Annual/July

9895 **ACF Regional Conference**
American Culinary Federation
180 Center Place Way
St Augustine, FL 32095-8859

904-824-4468
800-624-9458; *Fax:* 904-825-4758
acf@acfchefs.net; www.acfchefs.org
Social Media: Facebook, Twitter

Michael Ty, President
Thomas J. Macrina, Secretary
James Taylor, Treasurer

Catch up on the latest culinary trends and watch cooking demonstrations from expert chefs. This events series is a great way to earn continuing education hours and meet other professionals in the culinary industry.
19000 Members
Founded in: 1929

9896 **ACS Annual Conference and Competition**
American Cheese Society
304 W Liberty Street
Suite 201
Louisville, KY 40202

502-583-3783; *Fax:* 502-589-3602
mwilson@hqtrs.com; www.cheesesociety.org

Marci Wilson, Executive Director
Carlos Scrivener, Manager

This Conference and Competition offers a unique opportunity to learn the latest about cheese in America and indulge your cheese fantasies by tasting more than 700 American artisan and specialty cheeses.
Frequency: Associate Fee

9897 **ADPI/ABI Annual Conference**
American Dairy Products Institute
126 N Addison St
Elmhurst, IL 60126

630-530-8700; *Fax:* 630-530-8707
info@adpi.org; www.adpi.org

Dale Kleber, CEO

Held in Chicago, this event attracts programs, the annual meeting, and the exhibition hall. Fifty exhibits of equipment and supplies for condensed milk, dry and evaporated milk and whey products, plus conference, seminar, workshop and banquet.
650 Attendees
Frequency: Annual/April

9898 **AEA National Convention**
American Emu Association
PO Box 2502
San Angelo, TX 76902

541-332-0675
info@aea-emu.org; www.aea-emu.org

Charles Ramey, President
Martha Hendricks, VP

This convention provides a chance for the AEA Board of Directors (AEA-BOD) to meet, face to face, during the week prior to the actual convention. It is a place for members to gather to learn the latest information and research about the emu industry, see the latest new products and network with other emu growers from across the U.S. and around the world.
Frequency: July/Non-Member $230

9899 **AFFI Frozen Food Convention**
American Frozen Food Institute
2000 Corporate Ridge, Blvd.
Suite 1000
McLean, VA 22102-7862

703-821-0770; *Fax:* 703-821-1350
info@affi.com; www.affi.com

Kraig R Naasz, President/CEO
Thomas Bradshaw, Manager Legislative Affairs
Corey Henry, VP Communications
Robert L Garfield, SVP Public Policy/Intl Affairs

Learn more about the frozen food industry, network with peers, see new research, and get higher education.
500 Members
Founded in: 1942

9900 **AFFI-Con**
American Frozen Food Institute
2000 Corporate Ridge Blvd
Suite 1000
McLean, VA 22102

703-821-0770; *Fax:* 703-821-1350
info@affi.com; www.affi.com

Mary Becton, Conference Director

Helping you make connections and helping you be better informed about industry issues.
1500 Attendees
Frequency: Annual/February

9901 **AFS Annual Meeting**
American Fisheries Society
5410 Grosvenor Lane
Bethesda, MD 20814

301-897-8616; *Fax:* 301-897-8096;
www.fisheries.org
Social Media: Facebook, Twitter, Flickr

Gus Rassa,, Executive Director
Myra Merritt, Office Administrator

Held in conjunction with American Institute of Fishery Research Biologists. Explore the interrelation between fish, aquatic habitats and man; highlight challenges facing aquatic resource professionals and the methods that have been employed to resolve conflicts between those that use or have an interest in our aquatic resources.
Frequency: Annual/September

9902 **AMI International Meat, Poultry & Seafood Convention and Exposition**
Convention Mangement Group
10472 Armstrong Street
Fairfax, VA 22031

703-934-4700; *Fax:* 703-934-4899;
www.amiexpo.com
Social Media: Facebook, Twitter, LinkedIn

Anne Halal, Convention/Member Services VP
Anne Nuttall, Convention/Members Director
Katie Brannan, Convention/Members Sr. Manager

Sponsored by the American Meat Institute it features exhibits featuring the latest innovations in processing and packaging equipment, business and processing software systems, supplies, services and formulations.
25000 Attendees
Frequency: Annual/April

9903 **AMSA Reciprocal Meat Conference**
American Meat Science Association
2441 Village Green Place
Champaign, IL 61822

217-356-5370
800-517-AMSA; *Fax:* 888-205-5834; *Fax:* 217-356-5370
information@meatscience.org;
www.meatscience.org\rmc

Thomas Powell, Executive Director
Diedrea Mabry, Program Director
Kathy Ruff, Meetings & Member Svcs Director

RMC is the annual meeting for AMSA, featuring an interactive program tailored to bring attendees the very best and inspiring educational experience. Attendees are professionals in academia, government and industry, as well as students in the meat, food and animal science fields.
Frequency: Annual

9904 **AOCS Annual Meeting & Exposition**
American Oil Chemists' Society
2710 S Boulder
Urbana, IL 61802-6996

217-359-2344; *Fax:* 217-359-8091
meetings@aocs.org; www.aocs.org

Nurhan Dunford, General Chairperson
Mindy Cain, Meetings Specialist

The premier global science and business forum on fats, oils, surfactants, lipids, and related materials. Includes oral and poster presentations, short courses, and exhibit, and networking with more than 1,600 colleagues from 60 countries.
2000 Attendees
Frequency: Annual/April

9905 **APA Annual Meeting**
Apple Processors Association
1701 K Street NW
Suite 650
Washington, DC 20006

202-785-6715; *Fax:* 202-331-4212
pweller@agriwashington.org;

www.appleprocessors.org
Social Media: Facebook

Andrea Ball, President
Paul S. Weller, Jr., EVP, Communications
Elizabeth Johnson, VP, Food & Nutrition Policy
Jacquie Ball, Director, Administration

A three-day meeting which brings top industry and consumer experts together for a dialogue on timely issues. These include marketing tips, packaging trends, consumer research, and media reports and reaction to industry initiatives.
Frequency: Annual/June

9906 **APS/CPS/MSA Annual Joint Meeting**
American Phytopathological Society
3340 Pilot Knob Road
Saint Paul, MN 55121-2097

651-454-7250
800-328-7560; *Fax:* 651-454-0766
aps@scisoc.org; www.apsnet.org
Social Media: Facebook, Twitter, LinkedIn, YouTube

Betty Ford, Director of Meetings

Featuring over 18 state-of-the-art education sessions daily, over 700 poster presentations, one-of-a-kind preconvention tours and workshops and exhibits from leading suppliers.
Frequency: Annual/Summer

9907 **ASA/CSSA/SSSA International Annual Meeting**
American Society of Agronomy
677 S Segoe Road
Madison, WI 53711

608-273-8080; *Fax:* 608-273-2021;
www.agronomy.org

Keith R Schlesinger, Meetings/Convention Director
Stacey Phelps, Exhibit/Meetings Assistant
Linda Nelson, Meetings Specialist
Ellen Bergfeld, Executive Vice President

Co-sponsored with Crop Science Society of America and with the Soil Science Society of America. This event is a unique convergence of the leading agronomy, crops, soils and environmental sciences professionals from around the world. A blend of technical sessions, poster sessions, social functions, career networking and exhibits draw a growing number of prominent professionals and students.
3,500 Attendees
Frequency: November
Founded in: 1907

9908 **ASABE Annual International Meeting**
American Society of Agricultural & Biological Eng.
950 S Cherry Street
Suite 508
Denver, CO 80246-2664

303-759-5091; *Fax:* 303-758-0190
chesser@asabe.org; www.asabe.org

Michael Chesser, Meetings/Conference Director
Sharon McKnight, Meetings Support Staff

100 and more diverse technical sessions, 11 continuing professional development sessions, 5 technical tours, an industry exhibit hall and a keynote address from Dr. Lowell B. Catlett; this year's meeting is full of must attend events.
Frequency: July

9909 **ASBC Annual Meeting**
American Society of Brewing Chemists
3340 Pilot Knob Road
Saint Paul, MN 55121-2055

651-454-7250; *Fax:* 651-454-0766
bford@scisoc.org; www.meeting.asbcnet.org

Betty Ford, Meetings Director
Sue Casey, Meetings Coordinator
Steven Nelson, VP

Network with peers and learn about the latest technologies available to brewers.
300 Attendees
Frequency: Annual/June

9910 **ASHS Annual Conference**
American Society for Horticultural Science
1018 Duke Street
Alexandria, VA 22314

703-836-4606; *Fax:* 703-836-2024;
www.ashs.org
Social Media: Facebook, Twitter, LinkedIn

Michael W. Neff, Executive Director
Negar Mahdavian, Conference Manager

A place to meet with colleagues, talk with exhibitors and view over 400 posters.
Cost: $560.00
Frequency: Annual

9911 **ASME Business Forum & Expo**
Associaton of Sales and Marketing Companies
2100 Reston Parkway
Suite 400
Reston, VA 20191

703-758-7790; *Fax:* 703-758-7787
info@asmc.org; www.ama.org

Julie Casson, Sales Manager

Seminar and 75 exhibits of food manufacturers, computer equipment and services, food product services, foreign trade, incentive displays, shelf space management and related information.
7000 Attendees
Frequency: Annual
Founded in: 1985

9912 **ASTA/CSTA Joint Annual Convention**
American Seed Trade Association
225 Reinekers Lane
Suite 650
Alexandria, VA 22314-2875

703-837-8140; *Fax:* 703-837-9365;
www.amseed.com

Jennifer Lord, Meetings Director
Jason Laney, Meetings Associate Director

Includes meetings of all divisions of ASTA and CSTA and several joint meetings of both organizations, exhibits, prominent keynote speakers relevant to both associations, sessions that include representatives discussing how seed moves through the pipelines of our industry to the end user and those whose roles affect the regulation and administration of the framework.
800 Attendees
Frequency: July/Fee $129-$799

9913 **AWMA Real Deal Expo**
American Wholesale Marketers Association
2750 Prosperity Avenue
Suite 530
Fairfax, VA 22031

703-208-3358; *Fax:* 703-573-5738
info@awmanet.org; www.cdaweb.net

Marcia Barker, Public Affairs Manager
Nate Wills, Exhibit Information

The only trade show geared to convenience distributors. Exhibitors include purveyors of tobacco products, candy, beverages, snacks, foodservice, health and beauty care items, general merchandise, warehouse equipment, computer systems and much more.
2,500 Attendees
Frequency: Annual/February

9914 **AWS National Conference**
American Wine Society
P.O. Box 889
Scranton, PA 18501

888-297-9070; www.americanwinesociety.org

David Falchuk, Executive Director
Kristin Casler Kraft, President

The annual conference brings professional, serious amateurs and novices together to discover what is new in wine. Seminars and lectures on all aspects of wine appreciation, wine production, grape growing and cuisine. Attendees must be a member of the society.
Frequency: Annual/November
Founded in: 1967

9915 **Ag Progress Days**
Penn State University Agricultural Sciences
420 Agricultural Administration Building
University Park, PA 16802

814-865-2081; *Fax:* 814-865-1677;
www.apd.cas.psu.edu

Bob Oberheim, Manager

Agricultural trade show focusing on the innovations and progress made in the agricultural industry.
50M Attendees
Frequency: Annual/August

9916 **Agri News Farm Show**
Agri News
18 1st Avenue SE
Rochester, MN 55904-3722

507-857-7707
800-633-1727; *Fax:* 507-281-7474
rallen@agrinews.com; www.agrinews.com

Rosie Allen, Advertising Manager
John Losness, President
Todd Heroff, Manager

Annual show of 160 exhibitors of farming equipment, supplies and services.
8000 Attendees
Frequency: March

9917 **Agri-Marketing Conference**
National Agri-Marketing Association
11020 King Street
Suite 205
Overland Park, KS 66210-1201

913-491-6500; *Fax:* 913-491-6502
agrimktg@nama.org; www.nama.org
Social Media: Facebook, Twitter, LinkedIn, YouTube, Flickr

Vicki Henrickson, President
Beth Burgy, President Elect
Paul Redhage, Secretary/Treasurer

Learn more about customer behaviors, market shares, and other top industry tips.
3500 Members
Frequency: Annual/April
Founded in: 1957

9918 **Agricultural Retailers Association Convention and Expo**
Agricultural Retailers Association
1156 15th Street
Suite 500
Washington, DC 20005

202-457-0825
800-844-4900; *Fax:* 314-567-6888;
www.aradc.org

Daren Coppock, President/CEO
Richard Gupton, Sr. VP., Public Policy
Michelle Hummel, VP Marketing/Communications

Annual show of 120 manufacturers, suppliers and distributors of agricultural chemicals and fertilizers. Seminar, conference and banquet.
1200 Attendees
Frequency: December, St. Louis

9919 Agro-International Trade Fair for Agricultural Machinery & Equipment
Glahe International
PO Box 2460
Germantown, MD 20875-2460
301-515-0012; *Fax:* 301-515-0016
Biennial show of agricultural machinery and equipment.

9920 All Candy Expo
National Confectioners Association
110 30th Street NW
Suite 200
Washington, DC 20007
202-534-1440
AllCandyExpo@CandyUSA.com
allcandyexpo.com
Theresa Delaney, Expo/Membership Director
Daria Moore, Exhibits Manager
A trade show offering exhibits of confectionery industry supplies.
5000+ Attendees
Frequency: Annual/June

9921 All Things Organic Conference and Trade Show
Organic Trade Association
28 Vernon St.
Suite 413
Brattleboro, VT 05301
802-275-3800; *Fax:* 802-275-3801
info@ota.com; www.ota.com
Christine Bushway, Executive Director
Linda Lutz, Membership Manager
Laura Batcha, Marketing/Public Relations Director
Join OTA members, Board and staff for association business, member meetings, and social and networking events.
Frequency: Annual/June

9922 America's Supermarket Showcase
National Grocer's Association
1825 Samuel Morse Drive
Reston, VA 20190
703-437-5300; *Fax:* 703-437-7768
Dan Rudt
350 exhibits of food and non food consumer goods and services, fixtures and equipment for supermarket operations. Workshop, conference, banquet, luncheon and tours.
5000 Attendees
Frequency: Annual
Founded in: 1983

9923 American Bakery Expo
5 Executive Court
Suite 2
South Barrington, IL 60010
610-667-9600; *Fax:* 610-667-1475;
www.americanbakers.org
Social Media: Facebook, Twitter
Mark Gedris, Membership Manager
Sponsored by Retail Bakers of America and New York/New Jersey Bakers Association. A trade show, creative decorating competition, bakery arts and cakes display, industry chats, tips and trends demonstrations and seminars.
8000 Attendees
Frequency: Annual/October

9924 American Beverage Licensees Annual Convention & Trade Show
American Beverage Licensees
5101 River Road
Suite 108
Bethesda, MD 20816-1560
301-656-1494; *Fax:* 301-656-7539;
www.ablusa.org
Harry Wiles, Executive Director
Susan Day Pirieda, Office Manager
Annual show of 75 manufacturers, suppliers and distributors of alcoholic beverages.
700 Attendees
Frequency: March

9925 American Butter Institute Annual Conference
American Butter Institute
2101 Wilson Boulevard
Suite 400
Arlington, VA 22201
703-243-5630; *Fax:* 703-841-9328
AMiner@nmpf.org; www.butterinstitute.org
The annual conference and meeting is a joint project between the American Butter Institute and the American Diary Products Institute. Over 600 manufacturers, marketers and suppliers of butter and dairy products are represented at the convention which offers the opportunity to network with industry professionals.
Frequency: Annual/November

9926 American Convention of Meat Processors
American Association of Meat Processors
One Meating Place
Elizabethtown, PA 17022
717-367-1168; *Fax:* 717-367-9096
aamp@aamp.com; www.aamp.com
Tom K Inboden, President
Jon Frohling, First VP
Daniel T Weber, Second VP
Features a serious educational program for operators, sparkling entertainment, fun and fellowship...plus exhibits and displays by leading industry manufacturers and suppliers.
Frequency: Annual

9927 American Convention of Meat Processors & Suppliers' Exhibition
American Association of Meat Processors
One Meating Place
Elizabethtown, PA 17022
717-367-1168; *Fax:* 717-367-9096
aamp@aamp.com; www.aamp.com
Jon Frohling, President
Tim J. Haen, 1st Vice President
Kevin Western, 2nd Vice President
Gary Bardine, 3rd Vice President
Michael D. Sloan, Treasurer
Geared toward U.S., Canadian, and Foreign operators of small and very small firms in the meat, poultry & food business: packers, processors, wholesalers, HRI, retailers, caterers, deli operators, home food service dealers, and catalog marketers. Both members and non-members of the Association attend this event looking for a vast array of ideas, supplies, and services.
1400 Members
Founded in: 1939

9928 American Correctional Food Service Association Conference
ACFSA
4248 Park Glen Road
Minneapolis, MN 55416-4758
952-928-4658; *Fax:* 952-929-1318
webmaster@acfsa.org; www.acfsa.org
Karen Wesloh, Executive Director
Hope Cook, Assistant Director Exhibits
Gloria Grove, Assistant Director Atendees
Annual exhibit of 200 exhibitors of food products, kitchen equipment, food processing equipment, dining facility equipment, tableware and related food service equipment.
450 Attendees
Frequency: August
Founded in: 1999

9929 American Craft Beer Week
Brewers Association
736 Pearl Street
Boulder, CO 80302
303-447-0816
888-822-6273; *Fax:* 303-447-2825
webmaster@brewersassociation.org;
www.beertown.org
Social Media: Facebook, Twitter
Chris P. Frey, Chair
Jake Keeler, Vice Chair
Roxanne Westendorf, Secretary
Celebrates craft brewers and craft beer culture in the US.
1900 Members
Founded in: 1978

9930 American Cured Meat Championships, Cured Meat Competition
American Association of Meat Processors
One Meating Place
Elizabethtown, PA 17022
717-367-1168; *Fax:* 717-367-9096
aamp@aamp.com; www.aamp.com
Jon Frohling, President
Tim J. Haen, 1st Vice President
Kevin Western, 2nd Vice President
Gary Bardine, 3rd Vice President
Michael D. Sloan, Treasurer
This competition is the only national event of its kind in North America. Meat processors enter their products for evaluation by judges who are meat scientists and specialists in the meat industry. This evaluation provides information for product enhancement that could result in greater sales and business opportunities.
1400 Members
Founded in: 1939

9931 American Farm Bureau Federation Annual Convention
600 Maryland Avenue SW
Suite 1000
Washington, DC 20024
202-406-3600; *Fax:* 202-406-3602
bstallman@fb.org; www.fb.org
Bob Stallman, President
Kathleen Early, Director
Julie Anna Potts, Secretary
Exhibits of farm equipment, chemical fertilizers and agricultural equipment and supplies.
6M Attendees
Frequency: Annual/January

9932 American Mushroom Institute
North American Mushroom Conference
1 Massachusetts Avenue, Suite 800
Washington, DC 20001
202-842-4344; *Fax:* 202-408-7763
Laura Phelps, President

9933 American Peanut Research and Education Society Annual Meeting
American Peanut Research and Education Society
Oklahoma State University
376 Ag Hall
Stillwater, OK 74078

405-372-3052; *Fax:* 405-624-6718;
www.apresinc.com/meetings/annual-meeting/

Ron Sholar, Executive Officer

Annual meetings of the Society are held for the presentation of papers and/or discussion, and for the transaction of business. At least one general business session will be held during regular annual meetings at which reports from the executive officer and all standing committees will be given to such other matters as the Board of Directors may determine.
Frequency: Annual/July

9934 American Society for Enology and Vinticulture Annual Meeting
American Society for Enology and Vinticulture
PO Box 1855
Davis, CA 95617

530-753-3142; *Fax:* 530-753-3318
society@asev.org; www.asev.org

Bill Mead, Event/Tradeshow Coordinator

With technical sessions, research forums, symposia and a supplier shocasw.
Frequency: June
Founded in: 1951
Mailing list available for rent

9935 American Spice Trade Association Annual Meeting
2025 M Street NW
Washington, DC 20036

202-367-1127; *Fax:* 202-367-2127
info@astaspice.org; www.astaspice.org

Cheryl Deem, Executive Director

9936 American Sugarbeet Growers Asscociation Annual Meeting
American SugarBeet
1156 15th Street NW
Suite 101
Washington, DC 20005-1704

202-833-2398; *Fax:* 202-833-2962
RGeib@americansugarbeet.org;
www.americansugarbeet.org

Ruthann Geib, Meetings Director/VP
Luther Markwart, Executive VP
James Creek, Executive Assistant
Pam Alther, Office/Financial Manager

Attendees are primarily the officers and board members of these local associations and their spouses, as well as representatives of seed, chemical, and other supplier companies. The purpose of the Annual Meeting is to bring members up-to-date on legislative and international issues that affect the domestic sugar industry, and to determine future policy and strategies.
350 Attendees
Frequency: July/November
Founded in: 1983

9937 Animal Transportation Association
PO Box 797095
Dallas, TX 75379-7095

Fax: 214-769-2867

Cherie Derouin, Administrator
Sherry Lynne Boone, Administrative Assistant

An international association promoting the humane handling and transportation of animals. 10-15 booths.
150 Attendees
Frequency: Spring

9938 Annual Chicken Marketing Seminar
National Poultry & Food Distributors
2014 Osborne Road
Saint Marys, GA 31558

770-535-9901; *Fax:* 770-535-7385
kkm@npfda.org; www.npfda.org

Chris Sharp, President
Al Acunto, Vice President
Marc Miro, Treasurer
Kristin McWhorter, Executive Director

Features a very informative program, great networking opportunities, and golf. Learn new techniques for greater marketing success.
Frequency: Annual/July
Founded in: 1967

9939 Annual Conference of the Food Distribution Research Society
Food Distribution Research Society
PO Box 441110
Fort Washington, MD 20749

301-292-1970; *Fax:* 301-292-1787
Jonathan_baros@ncsu.edu
fdrs.tamu.edu

John Park, President
Ron Rainey, President-Elect
Kellie Raper, Secretary/ Treasurer
Jennifer Dennis, Director
Stan Ernst, Director

Meeting the quality demands of food buyers. Discuss how the industry is meeting these specific aspects of quality demands, and how these factors impact trade success, how members of the food chain are incorporating them in food production and handling, and how sensory examination is incorporated into food quality assurance, design and product development.
Frequency: Annual/October

9940 Annual Food Manufacturing & Packaging Expo and Conference
The Foodservice Group, Inc
PO Box 681864
Marietta, GA 30068-0032

770-971-8116; *Fax:* 770-971-1094;
www.fsgroup.com

Chris Bresler, President
Brad Johnson, Vice President
Bob Sheridan, Secretary
Bryan Lewis, Treasurer

This event attracts a diverse range of professionals including CEO's, plant managers, puchasing managers, production and quality assurance managers, engineers, and sales/marketing managers as well as mechanics on the production floor. See and experience the latest technology, systems and related information to improve business operations.
Frequency: Annual/January

9941 Annual Hotel, Motel and Restaurant Supply Show of the Southeast
Leisure Time Unlimited
PO Box 332
Myrtle Beach, SC 29577

843-448-9483
800-261-5991; *Fax:* 843-626-1513
hmrss@sc.rr.com; www.hmrsss.com
Social Media: Facebook, Twitter

Trade show for the hospitality industry.
23000 Attendees
Frequency: Annual/January

9942 Annual Meat Conference
American Meat Institute
1150 Connecticut Ave NW
12th Floor
Washington, DC 20036-4126

202-587-4200; *Fax:* 202-587-4300;
www.meatami.com
Social Media: Facebook, Twitter

Dennis Vignieri, Chairman
Larry Odom, Vice Chairman
Nick Meriggioli, Treasurer
Greg Benedict, Secretary
J. Patrick Boyle, President & CEO

The educational format of this conference includes a variety of ways to explore the latest developments in meat retailing today. Gain tools, insights, inspiration and new ideas to differentiate unique products and services, fortify marketing ROI, increase sales, and build customer loyalty.
300 Members
Frequency: Membership Fees Vary
Founded in: 1906

9943 Annual Sugar Outlook
1300 L Street NW
Suite 1001
Washington, DC 20005

202-785-1122; *Fax:* 202-785-5019
sugar@sugar.org; www.sugar.org
Social Media: Facebook, Twitter

Andrew Briscoe, President/CEO
Charles W Baker, Executive VP/Chief Science Officer
Melanie Miller, VP Public Relations
Cheryl Digges, VP Public Publicy & Education

To discuss sugar consumption and demand issues and initiatives.
Frequency: Annual/April

9944 Asia Food Processing & Packaging Technology Exhibition
Reed Exhibition Companies
383 Main Avenue
PO Box 6059
Norwalk, CT 06851

203-840-4800; *Fax:* 203-840-9628

One hundred and seventy four exhibitors for an audience of manufacturers, packaging design and development professionals.
Frequency: Biennial

9945 Associated Food Dealers Annual Trade Show
Associated Food Dealers of Michigan
18470 W Ten Mile
Southfield, MI 48075

248-557-9600; *Fax:* 248-557-9610;
www.afpdonline.org

Ginny Bennett, Show Manager
Frequency: September

9946 Association for Dressing and Sauces Annual Meeting
1100 Johnson Ferry Road
Atlanta, GA 30342

404-252-3663; *Fax:* 404-252-0774
ads@kellencompany.com;
www.dressings-sauces.org
Social Media: Facebook

Pam Chumley, President
Jeannie Milewski, Executive Director
Jacque Knight, Membership/Administration Manager

Learn about the most up-to-date technologies and guidelines for packaging, food safety, emulsions and quality.
Frequency: Annual/October

9947 **Association of College Unions International Conference**
One City Centre, 120 W. 7th St.
Suite 200
Bloomington, IN 47404
812-245-2284; *Fax:* 812-245-6710
acui@acui.org; www.acui.org
Rich Steele, President
Marsha Herman-Betzen, Executive Director
Andrea Langeveld, Marketing
International conference with 100 exhibits of graphic supplies, recreation equipment, computer hardware & software, furnishings, entertainment and speaker bureau information, food service equipment, and more related information and supplies.
1000 Attendees
Frequency: Annual

9948 **Atlantic Bakery Expo**
Retail Bakers of America
202 Village Circle
Suite 1
Slidell, LA 70458
985-643-6504
800-638-0924; *Fax:* 985-643-6929
Info@RBAnet.com; www.rbanet.com
Social Media: Facebook
Felix Sherman, Sr., President
Kenneth Downey, Sr., 1st Vice President
Marlene Goetzeler, 2nd Vice President
Dale A. Biles, Treasurer
Susan Nicolais, CAE, Secretary
A complete educational program with demonstrations, seminars and hands-on classes to go along with a trade show floor packed with all the exhibitors.
2000 Members
Frequency: Annual
Founded in: 1918

9949 **Atlantic Coast Exposition: Showcasing the Vending and Food Service Industry**
InfoMarketing
2501 Aerial Center Parkway
Suite 103
Morrisville, NC 27560
919-459-2070; *Fax:* 919-459-2075;
www.atlanticcoastexpo.com
Social Media: Facebook
Sarah Gillian, Executive Director
This convention offers exhibits of vending machines, office coffee service products, commissary equipment, food and beverage products for the institututional market, as well as accountability systems and security devices.
3M Attendees
Frequency: Annual/May

9950 **B&CMA Convention**
Biscuit & Cracker Manufacturer's Association
6325 Woodside Court
Suite 125
Columbia, MD 21046
443-545-1645; *Fax:* 410-290-8585;
www.thebcma.org
Stacey Sharpless, President
Kerry Kurowski, Education/Meetings Manager
Provides members an invaluable opportunity to network with fellow executives.
Founded in: 1901

9951 **BIF Annual Meeting and Research Symposium**
Red Angus Association of America
4201 N Interstate 35
Denton, TX 76207-3415
940-387-3502; *Fax:* 888-829-5573
info@redangus.org; www.redangus.org
Social Media: Facebook
Joe Mushrush, President
Greg Comstock, CEO
Seedstock and commercial cow-calf producers, university specialists and breed association leaders will gather to explore innovative technologies and management practices to improve beef production for the benefit of seedstock and commercial producers.
2000 Members
Founded in: 1954

9952 **BakingTech**
American Society of Baking
PO Box 336
Swedesboro, NJ 08085
800-713-0462; *Fax:* 888-315-2612
info@asbe.org; www.asbe.org
Technical sessions, receptions, luncheons, meetings, speakers, and ceremonies with industry experts sharing their knowledge, ideas and experience.
Frequency: Annual/March

9953 **Beer, Wine & Spirits Industry Trade Show**
Indiana Association of Beverage
200 S Meridian Street
Suite 350
Indianapolis, IN 46225
317-684-7580; *Fax:* 317-673-4210
Teresa Koch, Show Manager
Annual show of 125 exhibitors of alcohol beverage distillers brewers that are recognized primary sources in the state of Indiana as supplies for retailers.
2500 Attendees

9954 **Beltwide Cotton Conference**
National Cotton Council of America
7193 Goodlett Farms Parkway
Cordova, TN 38016
901-274-9030; *Fax:* 901-725-0510;
www.cotton.org/beltwide/
Mark Lange, President/CEO
A. John Maguire, Senior Vice President
Offers a forum for agricultural professionals.
Frequency: Annual/January

9955 **Big Iron Farm Show and Exhibition**
Red River Valley Fair Association
PO Box 797
West Fargo, ND 58058-0797
701-282-2200
800-456-6408; *Fax:* 701-282-6909
bryan@redrivervalleyfair.com;
www.bigironfarmshow.com
Bryan Schulz, Manager
Connects agricultural exhibitors and attendees who all come together for one purpose, to advance agriculture.
80M Attendees
Frequency: Annual/September

9956 **Branding ID: Strategies to Drive Sales**
Association of Sales & Marketing Companies
1010 Wisconsin Avenue NW #900
Washington, DC 20007
202-337-9351; *Fax:* 202-337-4508
info@asmc.org
Mark Baum, President
Karen Connell, Executive VP
Rick Abraham, VP/COO Foodservice
Jamie DeSimone, Director Marketing/Member Services
Frequency: March

9957 **CFESA Conference**
Commercial Food Equipment Service Association
2216 W Meadowview Road
Suite 100
Greensboro, NC 27407
336-346-4700; *Fax:* 336-346-4745
asidders@cfesa.com; www.cfesa.com
Social Media: Facebook, LinkedIn, MySpace, YouTube
Scott Hester, President
Held twice yearly, members benefit from networking within the foodservice industry, viewing high quality presentations and speeches, visiting interactive workshops, and learning from group meetings to create awareness of new development.
450 Members
Frequency: Bi-Annual
Founded in: 1963

9958 **CMAA's World Conference on Club Management & Club Business Expo**
Club Managers Association of America
1733 King Street
Alexandria, VA 22314
703-739-9500; *Fax:* 703-739-0124
cmaa@cmaa.org; www.cmaa.org
Guy Doria, Show Manager
Jim Singerling, Executive VP
Provides a variety of unique education opportunities that reflect the latest trends in the club industry.
5000 Attendees
Frequency: Annual/February

9959 **California League of Food Processors Expo & Showcase of Processed Foods**
980 Ninth Street
Sacremento, CA 95814
916-444-9260; *Fax:* 916-444-2746;
www.clfp.com
Robert Graf, President/CEO
Ed Yates, Senior VP
Nora Basrai, Meetings/Members Services
Rob Neenan, Senior Vice President
Amy Alcorn, Marketing Manager
Information, networking and displays of processed food from apricots to zucchini in every package type imaginable.
Frequency: January
Founded in: 1905

9960 **Candy Hall of Fame**
National Confectionery Sales Association
Spitfire House
3135 Berea Road
Cleveland, OH 44111
216-631-8200; *Fax:* 216-631-8210
info@candyhalloffame.org;
www.candyhalloffame.com/NCSA
Social Media: Facebook, Twitter
Michael F. Gilmore, Chairman
Alastair Northway, President
Mark Antonucci, 1st Vice President
Joe Muck, 2nd Vice President
Morton B. Gleit, Treasurer
Recognizes the achievements of industry leaders drawn from across the world. Inductees are selected from numerous nominations of candy brokers, sales personnel, manufacturers, retail buyers, wholesalers, industry suppliers, retail confectioners and others allied to the industry.
375 Members
Founded in: 1899

9961 CaterSource
PO Box 14776
Chicago, IL 60614

773-525-6800
800-932-3632; *Fax:* 800-387-4744
info@catersource.com; www.catersource.com

Micheal Roman, President
Jean Blackmer, Creative Director
Laurie Scheel, Advertising Director

9962 Cattle Industry Convention
Red Angus Association of America
4201 N Interstate 35
Denton, TX 76207-3415

940-387-3502; *Fax:* 888-829-5573
info@redangus.org; www.redangus.org
Social Media: Facebook

Joe Mushrush, President
Greg Comstock, CEO

The oldest and largest convention for the cattle business. The convention and trade show create a unique, fun environment for cattle industry members to come together to network, create policy for the industry and to have some fun.
2000 Members
Founded in: 1954

9963 Chicken Marketing Seminar
National Chicken Council
1015 15th Street NW
Suite 930
Washington, DC 20005-2622

202-296-2622; *Fax:* 202-293-4005
ncc@chickenusa.org;
www.nationalchickencouncil.org
Social Media: Facebook

Michael J. Brown, President
William P. Roenigk, Senior Vice President
Mary M. Colville, VP of Government Affairs
Dr. Ashley Peterson, VP of Science & Technology

Brings together poultry marketing and sales managers, distributors, supermarket and foodservice buyers, further processors, traders and brokers, and other executives working in the chicken industry. Informative general sessions, social networking events, and recreational opportunities.
Frequency: Annual/July
Founded in: 1954

9964 Commodity Classic
American Soybean Association
12125 Woodcrest Executive Drive
Suite 100
Saint Louis, MO 63141-5009

314-576-1770
800-688-7692; *Fax:* 314-576-2786
registration@commodityclassic.com;
www.commodityclassic.com

Meeting and exhibits of soybean industry related equipment and information.
4000 Attendees
Frequency: Annual/March

9965 Conference on New Food & Beverage Concepts Innovators
NorthStar Conferences
1211 Avenue of the Americas
New York, NY 10036

212-596-6006; *Fax:* 212-596-6092;
www.northstarconferences.com

Cheryl Callahan, Marketing Director

9966 Council of Food Processors Association Annual Convention
1401 New York Avenue NW
Suite 400
Washington, DC 20005-2124

202-471-1835; *Fax:* 202-639-5932

John Cady, President
Barbara Arnwine, Executive Director

9967 Craft Brewers Conference and Brew Expo America
Brewers Association
736 Pearl Street
Boulder, CO 80302

303-447-0816
888-822-6273; *Fax:* 303-447-2825;
www.craftbrewersconference.com

Charlie Papazian, President
Bob Pease, VP
Cindy Jones, Sales/Marketing Director

For professional brewers, CBC is the number one environment in North America for concentrated, affordable brewing education and idea sharing to improve brewery quality and performance.
2600 Attendees
Frequency: Annual/May

9968 Crop Life America & RISE Spring Conference
Crop Life America
1156 15th St NW
Washington, DC 20005-1752

202-296-1585; *Fax:* 202-463-0474
webmaster@croplifeamerica.org;
www.croplifeamerica.org
Social Media: Facebook, Twitter, LinkedIn, YouTube
Jay Vroom, President
Rich Nolan, VP

Discuss the most up-to-date science and regulatory issues impacting the crop protection and specialty pesticide industries.
Frequency: Annual/April

9969 Crop Science Society of America Meeting and Exhibits
Crop Science Society of America
677 S Segoe Road
Madison, WI 53711-1048

608-273-8086; *Fax:* 608-273-2021
tmoeller@agronomy.org; www.crops.org

John Nicholiadis, Managing Editor
David M Kral, Associate Executive VP
Ellen Bergfeld, Executive VP

Annual exhibits of agricultural equipment, supplies and services.
Frequency: October

9970 Dairy-Deli-Bake Seminar & Expo
International Dairy-Deli-Bakery Association
636 Science Drive
Madison, WI 53711-1073

608-310-5000; *Fax:* 608-238-6330
iddba@iddba.org; www.iddba.org

Judy Valaskey, Membership Coordinator

The largest show in the world serving these categories. Also the most focused show because it only targets the serious buyers, merchandisers, and executives who have a shared passion for food.
7000 Attendees
Frequency: Annual/June

9971 Distribution Solutions Conference
International Foodservice Distributors Association
1410 Spring Hill Road
Suite 210
McLean, VA 22102-3035

703-532-9400; *Fax:* 703-538-4673;
www.ifdaonline.org

Mark Allen, President & CEO
Jonathan Eisen, Senior VP/ Government Relations

Includes a robust operations agenda that incorporates warehouse and transportation issues, plus a powerful executive track, people issues in an HR track, and special sessions on convenience distribution and supply chain issues.
Frequency: Annual/October

9972 Dixie Classic Fair
City of Winston-Salem
PO Box 7525
Winston-Salem, NC 27109

336-727-2236; *Fax:* 336-727-2236

David Sparks, Executive Director

9973 EMDA Industry Showcase
Equipment Marketing & Distribution Association
PO Box 1347
Iowa City, IA 52244

319-354-5156; *Fax:* 319-354-5157
pat@emda.net; www.emda.net

Patricia A Collins, Executive VP

Annual convention and 130 exhibits of equipments, supplies and services for wholesaler-distributor and independent manufacturer's representatives of shortline and specialty farm equipment, light industrial, lawn and garden, turf care equipment, eestate and park maintenance equipment.
600 Attendees
Frequency: Annual/November

9974 EastPack
Cannon Communications
11444 W Olympic Boulevard
Los Angeles, CA 90064-1549

323-755-7646; *Fax:* 310-996-9499;
www.eastpackshow.com

9975 Eastern Perishable Products Association Trade Show
Eastern Perishable Products Association
17 Park Street
Wanaque, NJ 07465

973-831-4100; *Fax:* 973-831-8100;
www.eppainc.org

Barry Kahn, President
Steve Migliara, Administrative Vice President

For the perishable food industry, including dairy, deli, bakery, seafood, food service, meat ect. Exhibitors are manufacturers and services of perishable food products. Attendees are buyers, executives, managers and supervisors of supermarket chains, independents and specialty stores. 400 Booths
8M Attendees
Frequency: April
Founded in: 1971

9976 El Foro
WATT Publishing Company
122 S Wesley Avenue
Mount Morris, IL 61054-1497

815-734-4171; *Fax:* 815-734-7727
olentine@wattmm.com; www.wattnet.com

James Watt, Owner

A trade show and technical symposium for the Latin American poultry, pig and feed industries. Containing 50 booths and 150 exhibits.
275 Attendees
Frequency: July

9977 **Executive Conference**
Association of Sales & Marketing Companies
1010 Wisconsin Avenue NW
#900
Washington, DC 20007
202-337-9351; *Fax:* 202-337-4508
info@asmc.org
Mark Baum, President
Karen Connell, Executive VP
Rick Abraham, VP/COO Foodservice
Jamie DeSimone, Director Marketing/Member Services
Frequency: July

9978 **Executive Leadership Forum**
Snack Food Association
1600 Wilson Blvd
Suite 650
Arlington, VA 22209-2510
703-836-4500
800-628-1334; *Fax:* 703-836-8262
sfa@sfa.org; www.sfa.org
James A McCarthy, President/CEO
An invitation only event for CEO's and senior level executives in the international snack food industry.
800 Members
Frequency: Annual/September
Founded in: 1937

9979 **Expo Carnes**
Consejo Mexicano de la Carne
Ave. Parque Fundidora
#505 Loc. 88, P.N. Col. Obrera
Monterrey N.L. Mexico
52(81)8369 6660; *Fax:* 52(81)8369 6732
lsierra@apex.org.mx; www.expocarnes.com
The every other year Meat Industry International Exposition and Convention that brings together meat suppliers, meat packers and other sectors of the meat industry, facilitating meat specialists from around the world to do business in Latin America. This event takes place in February 2011.
150 Members

9980 **Expo of the Americas**
EJ Krause & Associates
6550 Rock Spring Drive
Suite 500
Bethesda, MD 20817-1126
301-493-5500; *Fax:* 301-493-5705;
www.ejkrause.com
Ned Krause, President
Annual show and exhibits of hotel and restaurant food and beverages.

9981 **FEMA Annual Convention**
FEMA
1620 I Street NW
Suite 925
Washington, DC 20006
202-293-5800; *Fax:* 202-462-8998;
www.femaflavor.org
Social Media: YouTube
Ed R. Hays, Ph.D., President
George C. Robinson, III, President Elect
Mark Scott, Treasurer
Arthur Schick, VP & Secretary
John Cox, Executive Director
FEMA is comprised of flavor manufacturers, flavor users, flavor ingredient suppliers and others with an interest in the U.S. flavor industry.
Founded in: 1909

9982 **FEMA Winter Committee Meetings**
FEMA
1620 I Street NW
Suite 925
Washington, DC 20006
202-293-5800; *Fax:* 202-462-8998;
www.femaflavor.org
Social Media: YouTube
Ed R. Hays, Ph.D., President
George C. Robinson, III, President Elect
Mark Scott, Treasurer
Arthur Schick, VP & Secretary
John Cox, Executive Director
FEMA is comprised of flavor manufacturers, flavor users, flavor ingredient suppliers and others with an interest in the U.S. flavor industry.
Founded in: 1909

9983 **FFA National Agricultural Career Show**
5632 Mount Vernon Memorial Highway
Alexandria, VA 22309-1502
888-332-2668; *Fax:* 800-366-6556
jack-pitzer@ffa.org; www.ffa.org
Jack Pitzer, Show Manager
Eight hundred and fifty booths encouraging high school youth to select careers in the agricultural industry.
45M Attendees
Frequency: November

9984 **FIAE Annual Convention**
Food Industry Association Executives
5657 W. 10770 North
Highland, UT 84003-2711
801-599-1095; *Fax:* 815-550-1731;
www.fiae.net
Jim Olsen, President
Format of the convention continues to provide valuable information and networking opportunities.
125 Members
Frequency: Annual/November
Founded in: 1927

9985 **FMI/AMI Annual Meat Conference**
American Meat Institute
1150 Connecticut Avenue NW
Washington, DC 20036
202-587-4200; *Fax:* 202-587-4223;
www.meatconference.com
Eric Zito, Manager, Convention & Member Svcs
400 booths for equipment, supplies and services to the meat-packaging industry.
12M Attendees
Frequency: Annual/Spring

9986 **FPSA Annual Conference**
Food Processing Suppliers Association
1451 Dolley Madison Blvd
Suite 101
Mc Lean, VA 22101-3850
703-761-2600; *Fax:* 703-761-4334
info@fpsa.org; www.fpsa.org
Social Media: Facebook, Twitter, LinkedIn
David Seckman, President
George Melnykovich, Senior Advisor
Robyn Roche, CFO
Where suppliers to the food and beverage industry connet and network. Ample opportunity is given to network with peers as participants expand their industry knowledge through educational business sessions and research roundtables.
510 Members
Frequency: Annual/November
Founded in: 2005

9987 **Farm Progress Show**
Farm Progress Companies
255 38th Avenue
Suite P
St Charles, IL 60174-5410
630-462-2224
800-441-1410
drovner@farmprogress.com;
www.farmprogressshow.com
Social Media: Facebook, Twitter
Matt Jungmann, National Shows Manager
Annual farm show of 400 exhibitors representing various types of agricultural products and services for farmers and agribusiness, including small operations to top producers.
Frequency: Annual/August

9988 **Farm Science Review**
Ohio State University
590 Woody Hayes Drive
Agricultural Engr. Building- Rm 232
Columbus, OH 43210
614-292-3671
800-644-6377; *Fax:* 614-292-9448
fendrick.1@osu.edu
fsr.osu.edu
Social Media: Facebook, Twitter, YouTube, Flickr
Craig Fendrick, Manager
Annual show of 625 exhibitors of agricultural equipment, supplies and services.
140M Attendees
Frequency: Annual/September

9989 **Farmfest**
Farm Fairs
PO Box 731
Lake Crystal, MN 56055-0731
507-726-6863
800-347-5863; *Fax:* 507-726-6750
Annual show of 450 manufacturers, suppliers and distributors of farm equipment and machinery, computers and software products, chemicals, seeds and crops, and techniques of planting, tillage and harvesting.
50M Attendees

9990 **Fertilizer Outlook and Technology Conference**
Fertilizer Institute
425 Third Street, SW
Suite 950
Washington, DC 20024
202-962-0490; *Fax:* 202-962-0577
information@tfi.org; www.tfi.org
Social Media: Facebook, Twitter, LinkedIn
Ford West, President
Geared towards industry members, financial analysts, business consultants, trade press representatives, agricultural retailers, agronomists, engineers and government economists. Key topics of discussion include new technology and issues that impact plant nutrition.
Frequency: Annual/November

9991 **Fish Expo Workboat Northwest**
National Fisherman Magazine
121 Free Street
PO Box 7437
Portland, ME 04112
207-842-5608; *Fax:* 207-842-5509
cmmarketing@divcom.com;
www.pacificmarineexpo.com
Jane Bogual, Director
West Coast trade show attracting thousands of visitors from the fields of commercial fishing, workboat, port/harbor, boatbuilding, seafood processing, and other marine industries.
6,000 Attendees
Frequency: November

9992 Food & Nutrition Conference & Expo
American Dietetic Association
120 South Riverside Plaza
Suite 2000
Chicago, IL 60606

312-899-0040
800-877-1600
info@eatright.org; www.eatright.org
Social Media: Facebook, Twitter

Katie Roski, Exhibits Manager

The premiere event for food and nutrition professionals. Features the latest nutrition science information, foodservice trends and access to the top experts.
Frequency: Annual/October

9993 Food Marketing Institute Conferences
2345 Crystal Drive
Suite 800
Arlington, VA 22202

202-452-8444; *Fax:* 202-429-4519
fmi@fmi.org; www.fmi.org

Laurel Kelly, Manager Education
Beth Watt, Contact
Tim Hammonds, CEO

Hosts shows that cover a number of different topics.

9994 Food Processing Suppliers Association Annual Conference
1451 Dolley Madison Boulevard
Suite 101
McLean, VA 22101

703-761-2600; *Fax:* 703-761-4334
info@fpsa.org; www.fpsa.org

George Melnykovich, President/CEO
Andrew Drennan, VP

Gain insights into the business of food processing and production.
Frequency: Annual/ March

9995 Food Product Design
Virgo Publishing LLC
3300 N Central Avenue
Suite 300
Phoenix, AZ 85012

480-990-1101; *Fax:* 480-675-8154
peggyj@vpico.com;
www.foodproductdesign.com

Peggy Jackson, Publishing Director

Publication distributed to product development professionals and corporate management executives at food and beverage manufacturing and foodservice companies.

9996 Food Safety Summit
ASI Food Safety Consultants
7625 Page Boulevard
St. Louis, MO 63133

314-725-2555
800-477-0778; *Fax:* 314-727-2563
kristah@asifood.com; www.asifood.com
Social Media: Facebook, Twitter, LinkedIn

Dr. W. Ernest McCullough, Vice President of Operations
Tom Huge, President, Food Safety Consultant
Gary Huge, VP, Food Safety Consultants

Provides useful food safety information and solutions to those responsible for assuring food safety across the food supply chain thereby keeping the food safety platform current and relevant for today and tomorrow.
Founded in: 1930

9997 Food Safety Summit: Chicago
Eaton Hall Exhibitions
256 Columbia Turnpike
Florham Park, NJ 07932

973-514-5900
800-746-9646; *Fax:* 973-514-5977
sgoldman@eatonhall.com;
www.foodsafetysummit.com

Scott Goldman, President
Michael Pesick, Exhibits/Sponsors
Amy Reimer, Registration

Food safety, quality assurance, microbiology and plant sanitation.
1500 Attendees
Frequency: October

9998 Food Safety Summit: Washington
Eaton Hall Exhibitions
256 Columbia Turnpike
Florham Park, NJ 07932

973-514-5900
800-746-9646; *Fax:* 973-514-5977
sgoldman@eatonhall.com;
www.foodsafetysummit.com

Scott Goldman, President
Michael Pesick, Exhibits/Sponsors
Amy Reimer, Registration

Held in Washington DC. Food safety, quality assurance, microbiology and plant sanitation.
1500 Attendees
Frequency: March

9999 Food System Summit: Food Choices, Challenges and Realities
Crop Life America
1156 15th St NW
Washington, DC 20005-1752

202-296-1585; *Fax:* 202-463-0474
webmaster@croplifeamerica.org;
www.croplifeamerica.org
Social Media: Facebook, Twitter, LinkedIn, YouTube

Jay Vroom, President
Rich Nolan, VP

Hosts speakers sharing a wide range of perspectives on key food and health issues focusing on four significant topic areas: food animal well-being, nutrition and health, food safety, and technology and innovation.
Frequency: Annual/October

10000 Food Tech
Glahe International
PO Box 6009
Sun City Center, FL 33571

813-633-6335; *Fax:* 813-633-6355

Iye Boyd, President

Annual exhibits of food technology.

10001 Fresh Summit International Convention & Exposition
Produce Marketing Association
1500 Casho Mill Road
PO Box 6036
Newark, DE 19711

302-738-7100; *Fax:* 302-731-2409
solutionctr@pma.com; www.pma.com
Social Media: Twitter, Flickr, YouTube, Xchange

Bryan Silbermann, President & CEO
Lorna D. Christie, Vice President & COO
Duane Eaton, Senior VP, Administration
Yvonne Bull, CFO

Where participants throughout the global fresh produce and floral supply chains come together as a community to learn, network, build relationships and do business.
18500 Attendees
Frequency: Annual/October

10002 Global Minor Use Summit
Crop Life America
1156 15th St NW
Washington, DC 20005-1752

202-296-1585; *Fax:* 202-463-0474
webmaster@croplifeamerica.org;
www.croplifeamerica.org
Social Media: Facebook, Twitter, LinkedIn, YouTube

Jay Vroom, President
Rich Nolan, VP

Brings regulators, growers, and representatives of the crop protection industry from around the world together to explore options and incentives for improving the availability of crop protection tools for production of minor crops.
Frequency: Annual/December

10003 Gourmet Products Show
George Little Management
577 Airport Boulevard
Suite 440
Burlingame, CA 94010

650-344-5171
800-272-SHOW; *Fax:* 650-344-5270;
www.thegourmetshow.com

Susan Corwin, VP

Cookware, tabletop, gadgets, cutlery, specialtry electric appliances, home textiles, contemporary lifestyle, furnishings, garden and travel accessories, home storage items, personal care, coffee and teas and specialty foods. Contains 950 exhibitors. 2700 booths
9000 Attendees
Frequency: April

10004 Government Action Summit
American Frozen Food Institute
2000 Corporate Ridge Blvd.
Suite 1000
McLean, VA 22102-7844
703-821-0770; *Fax:* 703-821-1350
info@affi.com; www.affi.com

Kraig R. Naasz, President & CEO

National trade association representing the interests of the frozen food industry for more than 60 years. Its 540 corporate members account for more than 90 percent of the frozen food production in the US.
Frequency: Annual/September

10005 Government Affairs Conference
USA Rice Federation
4301 N Fairfax Drive
Suite 425
Arlington, VA 22203
703-226-2300; *Fax:* 703-236-2301
riceinfo@usarice.com; www.usarice.com

Jamie Warshaw, Chairman

Discuss issues and activities for the U.S. rice industry, legislation, training, and seminars.
Frequency: Annual

10006 Grape Grower Magazine Farm Show
Western Agricultural Publishing Company
4974 E Clinton Way
Suite 123
Fresno, CA 93727-1520

559-261-0396; *Fax:* 559-252-7387

Phill Rhoads, Manager

Seminars, exhibits and prizes for grape growers. Contianing 80 booths and exhibits.

10007 Great American Beer Festival
Brewers Association
736 Pearl Street
Boulder, CO 80302

303-447-0816
888-822-6273; *Fax:* 303-447-2825;

www.greatamericanbeerfestival.com
Social Media: Facebook, Twitter

Charlie Papazian, President
Bob Pease, VP
Cindy Jones, Sales/Marketing Director

Don't miss the largest gathering of beer enthusiasts.
Frequency: Annual/September

10008 GrowerExpo
Ball Publishing
PO Box 9
Batavia, IL 60510-0009

630-208-9080
800-456-5380; *Fax:* 630-456-0132

John Martens, President

A trade show devoted to horticulture and floriculture production and marketing. 175 booths.
2M Attendees
Frequency: January

10009 HMAA Food & New Products Show
Pacific Expositions
1580 Makaola Street
Suite 1200
Honolulu, HI 92814

808-945-3594; *Fax:* 808-946-6399

Pat Shine, General Sales Manager
Kimalar K Carroll, Show Director/Coordinator

This popular event, featuring the Food Show in the arena and New Products Show in the exhibition hall, is the original new products expo. Local and mainland exhibitors gather each year to present electronic, household, recreational and food products and service— often unvailed for the first time in Hawaii.
96000 Attendees

10010 Hawkeye Farm Show
Midwest Shows
PO Box 737
Austin, MN 55912

507-437-7969; *Fax:* 507-437-7752;
www.farmshowsusa.com

Penny Swank, Show Manager
18000 Attendees
Frequency: March

10011 Health & Nutrition Product Development Start to Finish
New Hope Natural Media
1401 Pearl Street
Suite 200
Boulder, CO 80302

303-998-9399
rdebarros@newhope.com

Rob DeBarros, Marketing Manager
Frequency: March, Anaheim

10012 Heart of America Hospitality Expo
Bartle Hall Convention & Entertainment Center
301 W 13th Street, Suite 100
Kansas City, MO 64105

816-513-5000
800-821-7060; *Fax:* 816-513-5001;
www.kcconvention.com

Charles Hart II, President
Pat Bergaur, Regional Director

10013 Home Baking Association Annual Conference
10841 S Crossroads Drive
Suite 105
Parker, CO 80135

303-840-8787; *Fax:* 303-840-6877;
www.homebaking.org

Sharon Davis, Show Manager

Learn the newest techniques and technologies available to the home bakers of America!
Frequency: Annual

10014 Hospitality Food Service Expo
Reed Business Information
275 Washington Street
Boston, MA 02458

617-261-1166; *Fax:* 630-288-8686;
www.reedbusiness.com

Patrick Paleno, Show Manager
Barry Reed Jr, CFO
Stuart Whayman, CFO

Four hundred booths featuring educational seminars, culinary salon, and exhibits of products and services.
12M Attendees
Frequency: October

10015 Hydroponic Society of America
PO Box 6067
Concord, CA 94524-1067

Fax: 510-232-2323

Gene Brisbon, Executive Director

Thirty five booths featuring the latest in hydroponic equipment.
500 Attendees
Frequency: April

10016 IACP Annual Conference
International Association of Culinary Professional
1221 Avenue of the Americas
42nd Floor
New York, NY 10020

646-358-4957
866-358-4951; *Fax:* 866-358-2524
info@iacp.com; www.iacp.com
Social Media: Facebook, Twitter, Flickr

Martha Holmberg, Cheif Executive Officer
Shani Phelan, Member Programs And Ops Manager
Glenn Mack, Chair
Margaret Crable, Communications & Marketing Manager

Go behind the scenes with key industry players, getting access to the style-makers, tasting the latest culinary trends.
3000+ Members
Frequency: Annual/March
Founded in: 1978

10017 IAOM Conferences and Expos
International Association of Operative Millers
10100 West 87th Street
Suite 306
Overland Park, KS 66212

913-338-3377; *Fax:* 913-338-3553
info@iaom.info; www.iaom.info
Social Media: Facebook, LinkedIn

Bart Hahlweg, President
Joe Woodard, Executive VP
Aaron Black, Treasurer

Premier educational events for grain milling and seed processing professionals. The annual events gather milling and allied trade professionals from around the world for several days of education, networking and fellowship.
Frequency: Annual/May
Founded in: 1896

10018 IBA Messe Duesseldorf North America
150 N Michigan Avenue
Suite 2920
Chicago, IL 60601

312-621-5800; *Fax:* 312-781-5188
info@mdna.com; www.mdna.com

Frank Thorwirth, President
Pyon Klemon, Vice President
Eva Rowe, Vice President
Justin Kesselring, Project Manager
100 T Attendees
Frequency: October

10019 IBIE Bakery Expo
BEMA: Baking Industry Suppliers Association
7101 College Boulevard
Suite 1505
Overland Park, KS 66210

913-338-1300; *Fax:* 913-338-1327
info@bema.org; www.ibie2007.org

Matt Zielsdorf, Convention Chairman

Co-sponsored with the American Bakers Association. event that offers complete equipment, ingredient and supply solutions to serious baking professionals. Directors and managers from every segment of the grain-based food industry count on IBIE for the new technology, products, strategies and information they need to stay competitive in all aspects of their operation.
20000 Attendees
Frequency: October

10020 IBWA Convention & Trade Show International Bottled Water Assn
International Bottled Water Association
1700 Diagonal Road
Suite 650
Alexandria, VA 22314

703-683-5213
800-WAT-ER11; *Fax:* 703-683-4074
ibwainfo@bottledwater.org;
www.bottledwater.org

Trade association representing the bottled water industry. IBWA's member companies produce and distribute 80 percent of the bottled water sold in the US. Our membership includes US and international bottlers, distributors and suppliers.
3250 Attendees
Frequency: Annual/October

10021 IFDA Sales & Marketing Conference
International Foodservice Distributors Association
1410 Spring Hill Road
Suite 210
McLean, VA 22102-3035

703-532-9400; *Fax:* 703-538-4673;
www.ifdaonline.org

Mark Allen, President & CEO
Jonathan Eisen, Senior VP/ Government Relations

Newest technologies and marketing ideas for the foodservice distributors industry.
Frequency: Annual/July

10022 IFDA Supply Chain Connect
International Foodservice Distributors Association
1410 Spring Hill Road
Suite 210
McLean, VA 22102-3035

703-532-9400; *Fax:* 703-538-4673;
www.ifdaonline.org

Mark Allen, President & CEO
Jonathan Eisen, Senior VP/ Government Relations

Designed to connect distributor and manufacturer counterparts involved in distributor inbound to help drive efficiencies.
Frequency: Annual/July

10023 IFEC Annual Conference
International Food Service Editorial Council
7 Point Place
PO Box 491
Hyde Park, NY 12538-491

845-229-6973; *Fax:* 845-229-6973
ifec@ifeconline.com; www.ifeconline.com
Social Media: Facebook, Twitter

Megan McKenna, President
Jeffrey Yarbrough, Vice President
Amelia Levin, Secretary
John Scroggins, Treasurer

Sessions with government and industry leaders, top chefs, and food tour hosts, gain new insights into the complex role that government plays in shaping America's diet, the growing impact that food environmentalism is having on foodservice, and the confluence of the two.
Frequency: Annual/November

10024 IFT Annual Meeting & Food Expo
Institute of Food Technologists
525 W Van Buren St
Suite 1000
Chicago, IL 60607-3842

312-782-8424; *Fax:* 312-782-8348;
www.ift.org

Barbara Byrd Keenan, EVP
Marianne Gillette, President

Brings together the most repected food professionals in industry, government and academia.
20000 Attendees
Frequency: June

10025 IHA Educational Conference & Meeting of Members
International Herb Association
PO Box 5667
Jacksonville, FL 32247-5667

904-399-3241; *Fax:* 904-396-9467;
www.iherb.org

Nancy Momsen, President
Kathryn Clayton, Vice President
Karen O'Brien, Secretary
Marge Powell, Treasurer

Conference offers tours, herb information and recipes, as well as leading industry news.
Frequency: Annual/July
Founded in: 1986

10026 IMPA Convention & Trade Show
Iowa Meat Processors Association
PO Box 334
Clarence, IA 52216-0334

563-452-3329; *Fax:* 563-452-2141
execdirector@iowameatprocessors.org;
www.iowameatprocessors.org

David L. Walter, President
Kent Stricker, 1st Vice President
Kevin Hastings, 2nd Vice President
Andy Thesing, 3rd Vice President

IMPA, leading the way in innovations, marketing, profits and adaptations. Also featuring a cured meat competition and product show.

10027 IS/LD Conference
1350 I Street NW
Suite 300
Washington, DC 20005

202-639-5900; *Fax:* 202-639-5932
info@gmaonline.org; www.gmabrands.com

Cindy Baker, Meetings/Conference Sr. Manager

A place where senior logistics and information technology executives from CPG manufacturers and leading retailers come together to study and seek solutions to the pressing issues affecting today's global supply chain.
Frequency: Annual/April

10028 IWLA Convention & Expo
International Warehouse Logistics Association
2800 S River Rd
Suite 260
Des Plaines, IL 60018-6003

847-813-4699; *Fax:* 847-813-0115
email@iwla.com; www.iwla.com

Joel Anderson, President & CEO
Linda Hothem, Chairman
Paul Verst, Treasurer
Tom Herche, Secretary

Promoting professional development and expose attendees to newer and better ways of doing business.
Founded in: 1891

10029 Independent Bakers Association Annual Convention
Independent Bakers Association
Georgetown Station
PO Box 3731
Washington, DC 20027-0231

202-333-8190; *Fax:* 202-337-3809
independentbaker@yahoo.com;
www.independentbaker.net

Enables bakers and allied industry representatives to tackle vital issues and develop strategies to enhance industry interests.
Frequency: Annual/June

10030 Institute of Food Technologists Annual Meeting & Food Expo
Institute of Food Technologists
525 W Van Buren
Suite 1000
Chicago, IL 60607-3814

312-782-8424; *Fax:* 312-782-8348
info@ift.org; www.ift.org

Roger Clemens, President
John Ruff, President-Elect
Bruce Stillings, Treasurer
Barbara Byrd Keenan, Executive VP

Technical exposition directed to the $302 billion food industry. Offering person-to-person marketplace and technical forum for suppliers of food ingredients. 2,400 booths.
24M Attendees
Frequency: Annual/June

10031 International Air Conditioning, Heating & Refrigerating Expo
ASHRAE
1791 Tullie Circle NE
Atlanta, GA 30329

404-636-8400
800-527-4723; *Fax:* 404-321-5478
ashrae@ashrae.org; www.ashrae.org

William A Harrison, President
Jeff H Littleton, Executive VP

The largest HVAC&R event in America featuring over 1,600 exhibiting companies. Held in conjunction with the ASHRAE Winter Meeting
30000 Attendees
Frequency: Annual/January

10032 International Assoc of Operative Millers Technical Conference/Trade Show
International Association of Operative Millers
10100 W 87th Street
Suite 306
Overland Park, KS 66212

913-338-3377; *Fax:* 913-338-3553
info@iaom.info; www.iaom.info
Social Media: Facebook, LinkedIn

Joe Woodard, President
Aaron Black, Vice President
Joel Hoffa, Treasurer
Melinda Farris, Executive VP

Conference, banquet and over 100 exhibits of cereal milling equipment, ancillary equipment, supplies and information.
Frequency: Annual/May

10033 International Baking Industry Exposition
Retail Bakers of America
202 Village Circle
Suite 1
Slidell, LA 70458
985-643-6504
800-638-0924; *Fax:* 985-643-6929
Info@RBAnet.com; www.rbanet.com
Social Media: Facebook

Felix Sherman, Sr., President
Kenneth Downey, Sr., 1st Vice President
Marlene Goetzeler, 2nd Vice President
Dale A. Biles, Treasurer
Susan Nicolais, CAE, Secretary

Thousands of industry professionals unite for the world's largest, most comprehensive Baking Expo of the year. More than 700 exhibiting companies will showcase cutting-edge technologies, equipment and new products to help attendees from the grain-based foods industry strengthen their competitive position, uncover new opportunities and maximize profits.
2000 Members
Frequency: Annual/September
Founded in: 1918

10034 International Beverage Industry Exposition
1101 16th Street NW
Washington, DC 20036-4803

202-857-4722

Lisa Feldman, Show Manager
450 booths.
16M Attendees
Frequency: October

10035 International Boston Seafood Show
National Fishermans Expositions
PO Box 7437
Portland, ME 04112-7437

207-842-5500; *Fax:* 207-842-5505

Diane Vassar, Promotions Director
David Lowell, President

Nine hundred and seventy booths. Annual trade show for the seafood industry.
20M Attendees
Frequency: March

10036 International Dairy Foods Show
International Dairy Foods Association
1250 H St NW
Suite 900
Washington, DC 20005-5902

202-737-4332; *Fax:* 202-331-7820
membership@idfa.org; www.idfa.org

Constance Tipton, President
Neil Moran, Sr. VP, Finance/Tradeshow/Admin.
Peggy Armstrong, VP, Communications
Diana Carmenates, VP, Meetings & Educational Services
Cindy Cavallo, Director, Membership

The International Dairy Foods Association, the Milk Industry Foundation and the International

Ice Cream Association work to represent the best interests of manufacturers, distributors and marketers of ice cream, frozen yogurt, frozen desserts, fluid milk, cultured dairy products, dips and other milk products.
Frequency: Annual

10037 International Exposition for Food Processors
Food Processing Machinery Association
1451 Dolly Madison Boulevard
Suite 200
McLean, VA 22101
703-761-2600
800-331-8816; *Fax:* 703-548-6563;
www.ippexpo.com
Nancy Janssen, Show Manager
Show with more than 1,600 exhibitors, up-to-the-minute technology, fast-track educational sessions. Great source for solutions and networking with industry peers. Colocated with Pack Expo International. McCormick Place, Chicago, IL.
50M Attendees
Frequency: Annual/September

10038 International Food Processors Association Expo
200 Daingerfield Road
Suite 100
Alexandria, VA 22314-2884
703-299-5001; *Fax:* 703-299-5100
George Melnykozich, Show Manager
Four hundred and twenty five booths of food processing and supplies.
16M Attendees
Frequency: January

10039 International Food Service Exposition
Florida Restaurant Association
230 S Adams Street
Tallahassee, FL 32301
850-224-2250; *Fax:* 850-224-9213;
www.flra.com
Hosting the third largest food service show in the country with over 1,200 booths and over 23,000 qualified buyers and attendees.
22000 Attendees

10040 International Foodservice Distributors: Productivity Convention & Expo
201 Park Washington Court
Falls Church, VA 22046-4521
703-532-9400; *Fax:* 703-538-4673;
www.ifdaonline.org
Mark Allen, President/CEO
Jonathan Eisen, Senior VP Of Government Relations
Workshops, assemblies, facility tours and an exposition are featured. Educational programming features many practitioners who sahre knowledge to be applied to various operations. Practical information for transportation, information technology, human resources and more.
Frequency: October
Founded in: 2003

10041 International Fundraising Conference
Association of Fundraising Professionals
4300 Wilson Blvd.
Suite 300
Arlington, VA 22203
703-684-0410
800-666-3863; *Fax:* 703-684-0540
afpfc.com
Social Media: Facebook, Twitter, LinkedIn, Instagram, YouTube
Andrew Watt, President & CEO
Terry Rauh, Chief Operating Officer
Skills building and thought leaders in international fundraising and philanthropy.
Founded in: 2006

10042 International Institute of Foods and Family Living Annual Meeting
225 W Ohio Street
Chicago, IL 60610-4198
312-527-3860; *Fax:* 312-670-0824
Phyllis Favelman, President

10043 International Marketing Conference & Annual Membership Meeting
US Grains Council
1400 K St NW
Suite 1200
Washington, DC 20005-2449
202-789-0789; *Fax:* 202-898-0522
grains@grains.org; www.grains.org
Thomas C. Dorr, President/CEO
Wendell Shauman, Chairman
Don Fast, Vice Chairman
Julius Schaaf, Treasurer
Ron Gray, Secretary
Join Council members and guests to kick off this special meeting with a welcome reception. Great opportunity to network with industry colleagues, get acquainted with new Council members and talk with the Council's international directors and staff.
Frequency: Annual/February
Founded in: 1960

10044 International Pizza Expo
MacFadden Protech
137 E Market Street
New Albany, IN 47150
812-949-0909
800-489-8324; *Fax:* 812-949-1867
boakley@pizzatoday.com;
www.pizzaexpo.com
William T Oakley, Senior VP Expositions
Linda Keith, Manager
Patty Crone, Manager
One thousand booths featuring exhibits of equipment for pizza industry and restaurants.
6000 Attendees
Frequency: February/March

10045 International Poultry Expo
US Poultry & Egg Association/American Feed Assoc.
1530 Cooledge Road
Tucker, GA 30084-7303
770-493-9401; *Fax:* 770-493-9257;
www.internationalpoultryexposition.com
Social Media: Facebook, Twitter, LinkedIn
Charles Olentine, Executive VP
Pennie Stathes, Logistics Manager
A world large trade show for the poultry and feed sectors.
15000 Attendees
Frequency: January

10046 International Whey Conference
American Dairy Products Institute
126 N Addison St
Elmhurst, IL 60126
630-530-8700; *Fax:* 630-530-8707;
www.internationalwheyconference.org
Dale Kleber, CEO
Offers an unparalleled opportunity to learn about the latest research, cutting-edge product innovations, technical developments and marketing strategies relating to this intriguing, value-added ingredient.
500 Attendees
Frequency: September

10047 Interpack
150 N Michigan Avenue
Suite 2920
Chicago, IL 60601
312-781-5180; *Fax:* 312-781-5188
info@mdna.com; www.mdna.com
Ryan Klemm, Senior Project Manager
Eva Rowe, Vice President
Justin Kesselring, Project Manager
Frequency: April

10048 JPA Annual Meeting
Juice Products Association
750 National Press Building
529 14th Street NW
Washington, DC 20045
202-785-3232; *Fax:* 202-223-9741
jpa@kellencompany.com;
www.juiceproducts.org
Richard E Cristol, President
Carol Freysinger, Executive Director
Includes presentations of current interest, such as crop estimates and conditions, transportation and export problems, packaging and marketing concepts, advertising trends and government and regulatory reporting.
Frequency: Annual/Spring

10049 KFYR Radio Agri International Stock & Trade Show
KFYR Radio
PO Box 1658
Bismarck, ND 58502-1738
701-224-9393
800-472-2170; *Fax:* 701-255-8155
mwall@clearchannel.com; www.kfyr.com
Syd Stewart, General Manager
Michelle J Wall, Manager
Jim Lowe, Manager
Annual show of 250 exhibitors of agricultural equipment, supplies, livestock and services.
15000 Attendees
Frequency: February

10050 Keystone Farm Show
Lee Publications
PO Box 121
Palatine Bridge, NY 13428-0121
518-673-2269; *Fax:* 518-673-2699
info@leepub.com; www.leepub.com
Ken Maning, Show Manager
Tom Mahoney, Sales Manager

10051 MEATXPO
National Meat Association
1970 Broadway
Suite 825
Oakland, CA 94612
510-763-1533; *Fax:* 510-763-6186;
www.meatxpo.org
Barry Carpenter, CEO
Jen Kempis, Operations Manager
Biennial suppliers' exposition that brings together consultants, equipment manufacturers and other professionals in the industry, to give a first-hand view of the newest industry equipment, packaging and related services.
Frequency: Annual/February
Founded in: 1948

10052 MWR Expo
American Logistics Association

1133 15th Street NW
Suite 640
Washington, DC 20005-2708

202-466-2520; *Fax:* 202-296-4419
membership@ala-national.org;
www.ala-national.org

Cologne Hunter, Meetings/Expo Director
Maurice Branch, Operations VP

A gathering of MWR professionals and brings together the many components of the Morale, Welfare and Recreation industry. The event features products and services that are sold to military and government agencies for use in community support activities on military installations throughout the world.
Frequency: Biennial/August
Founded in: 1972

10053 Maraschino Cherry and Glace Fruit Processors Annual Convention
5 Ravine Drive
#776
Matawan, NJ 07747-3106

Fax: 732-583-0798

Richard Sullivan, Executive VP
Frequency: April/May

10054 Marketechnics
Food Marketing Institute
800 Connecticut Avenue NW
Washington, DC 20006

202-220-0600; *Fax:* 202-429-4519

Beth Watt, Contact
6000 Attendees

10055 Meat Industry Research Conference
American Meat Science Association
2441 Village Green Pl
Champaign, IL 61822-7676

800-517-AMSA; *Fax:* 888-205-5834; *Fax:* 217-356-5370
information@meatscience.org;
www.meatscience.org

William Mikel, President
Scott J. Eilert, President Elect
Casey B. Frye, Treasurer

Cosponsored by the American Meat Institute Foundation and the American Meat Science Association. A forum for presenting the latest research in terms of direct application for the meat industry.

10056 Mid-America Farm Show
Salina Area Chamber of Commerce
120 W Ash Street
PO Box 586
Salina, KS 67401

785-827-9301; *Fax:* 785-827-9758;
www.salinakansas.org

Don Weiser, Show Manager

Annual show of 325 exhibitors of agricultural equipment, supplies and services, including irrigation equipment, fertilizer, farm implements, hybrid seed, agricultural chemicals, tractors, feed, farrowing crates and equipment, silos and bins, storage equipment and farm buildings.
13M Attendees
Frequency: Annual/March

10057 Mid-America Horticultural Trade Show
1000 N Rand Road
Suite 214
Wauconda, IL 60084-1188

847-526-2010; *Fax:* 847-526-3993
mail@midam.org; www.midam.org

Rand A Baldwin CAE, Managing Director
Suzanne Spohr, President
Jim Melka, Secretary

Mid-Am is the premier event featuring more than 650 leading suppliers offering countless products, equipment, and services for the horticulture industry. Mid-Am also offers a variety of educational seminars featuring the best and the brightest in the horticultural and business communities to help keep you informed of the latest trends.
Frequency: January

10058 Mid-America Resturant, Soft Serve & Pizza Exposition
Exhibition Productions
PO Box 81845
Wellesley, MA 02481

800-909-7469; *Fax:* 617-431-2662

17000 Attendees

10059 Mid-Atlantic Food, Beverage & Lodging Expo
Restaurant Association of Maryland
6301 Hillside Court
Columbia, MD 21046

410-290-6800
800-874-1313; *Fax:* 410-290-7898
dimbessi@marylandrestaurants.com;
www.midatlanticexpo.com

Dennis Imbessi, Director Expo/Membership Sales
Licia Spinelli, Director Marketing/Special Events
Valerie Maione, Owner

Annual Mid-Atlantic regional trade show of products and services for the restaurant and hospitality industry. Exhibitors include food manufacturers, equipment, beverages and services providers. Open to food service professionals, taking place annually during the month of September with 500 exhibitors and 600 booths.
15M Attendees
Frequency: Annual/October

10060 Midway USA Food Service and Hospitality Exposition
Kansas Restaurant and Hospitality Association
359 S Hydraulic Street
Wichita, KS 67211-1908

316-267-8383; *Fax:* 316-267-8400

Dennis Carpenter, CEO

Annual show of 35 food service, beverage, suppliers.
6000 Attendees

10061 Midwest Expo: IL
Illinois Fertilizer & Chemical Association
130 W Dixie Highway
PO Box 186
Saint Anne, IL 60964-0186
815-939-1566
800-892-7122; *Fax:* 815-427-6573

Jean Trobec, President

Annual show of 130 manufacturers, suppliers and distributors of agricultural chemical and fertilizer application equipment, supplies and services.
2500 Attendees
Frequency: August, Danville

10062 Midwest Farm Show
North Country Enterprises
5322 250th Street
Cadott, WI 54727

715-289-4632
nceinfo@yahoo.com;
www.northcountryenterprises.com

Steve Henry, President

Top farm show exhibiting dairy and Wisconsin's tillage equipment, feed and seed. 20 booths.
11M+ Attendees
Frequency: January
Founded in: 1975

10063 Midwest Food Processors Association Convention/Trade Show
4600 American Pkwy
Suite 110
Madison, WI 53718-8334

608-255-9946; *Fax:* 608-255-9838
info@mwfpa.org; www.mwfpa.org

Nick George, President
Robin Fanshaw, Office Manager/Event Planner
Brian Elliott, Director of Communications
Bruce Jacobson, Chair

Processing industry members come together at the convention to learn, network and gain insight to improve their company's course.
1M Attendees
Frequency: Annual/November
Founded in: 1905

10064 Midwest Gourmet Exposition
Fairchild Urban Expositions
1395 S Marietta Parkway
Building 400, Suite 210
Marietta, GA 30067

678-901-1700; *Fax:* 770-956-9644

Robert Collins, President

10065 Midwest Leadership Conference
Indiana Retail Grocers Association
115 W Washington Street
Suite 1364
Indianapolis, IN 46204

317-220-0033; *Fax:* 317-231-7858

10066 Midwest Regional Grape & Wine Conference
Missouri Grape and Wine Board
1616 Missouri Boulevard
Jefferson City, MO 65109-0630

573-751-3374
800-392-WINE; *Fax:* 573-751-2868
sue.berendzen@mda.mo.gov;
www.missouriwine.org
Social Media: Facebook, Twitter, YouTube, Flickr

Jim Anderson, Executive Director
Denise Kottwitz, Assistant

A major national conference for hundreds of vintners, growers and wine industry executives throughout the US Conference includes speakers, trade show, workshops and wine dinners. Over 45 booths.
400+ Attendees
Frequency: Annual/February
Founded in: 1985

10067 Midwestern Food Service and Equipment Exposition
Missouri Restaurant Association
9233 Ward Parkway
Suite 123
Kansas City, MO 64114

816-753-5222; *Fax:* 816-753-6993;
www.morestaurants.org

Chad Treaster, President

Annual show of 200 suppliers of food service and hospitality industries equipment, supplies and services.
12M Attendees

10068 NAAB Annual Convention
National Association of Animal Breeders

PO Box 1033
Columbia, MO 65205

573-445-4406; *Fax:* 573-446-2279
naab-css@naab-css.org; www.naab-css.org

Gordon Doak, President
Jere Mitchell, Technical Director

A welcomer reception, election of directors, consideration of Bylaw Amendments, resolutions and other association business and a award recognitions presentation.
Frequency: Annual/September

10069 NAAE Annual Convention
National Association of Agricultural Educators
University of Kentucky
300 Garrigus Building
Lexington, KY 40546-215
859-257-2224
800-509-0204; *Fax:* 859-323-3919
JJackman.NAAE@uky.edu; www.naae.org

Wm Jay Jackman, Executive Director
Samantha Alvis, Associate Executive Director

Featuring a meet and greet, professional development workshops, meetings, tours and a career tech expo.
Frequency: Nov/Fees Vary
Founded in: 1948
Mailing list available for rent

10070 NABCA Annual Conference
National Alcohol Beverage Control Association
4401 Ford Avenue
Suite 700
Alexandria, VA 22302

703-784-4200; *Fax:* 703-820-3551
jsgueo@nabca.org; www.nabca.org
Social Media: Facebook, Twitter

James M Sgueo, President/CEO

An event to provides its members opportunities to interact and conduct business. Featuring nationally known speakers, informative seminars, interact workshops and suppliers and vendors demonstrating their products.
Frequency: Annual

10071 NABR Tasting & Display Event Annual Convention
American Beverage Licensees
5101 River Road
Suite 108
Bethesda, MD 20816-1560

301-656-1494; *Fax:* 301-656-7539;
www.ablusa.org

Harry Wiles, Executive Director
Shawn Ross, Office Manager

Offers exhibits on spirits, beer and wine industry supplies, equipment, bar accessories and computers. The NABR Annual Convention is a gathering of alcohol beverage retailers and proprietors for networking and educational opportunities. An exclusive trade display and tasting event is held to promote brands and services of use to retailers and proprietors. There are 25-75 booths.
500+ Attendees
Frequency: March

10072 NAC Annual Convention & Trade Show
35 E Wacker Drive
Suite 1816
Chicago, IL 60601-2103

312-236-3858; *Fax:* 312-236-7809;
www.naconline.org
Social Media: Facebook, LinkedIn

John Evans Jr., President
Ron Krueger II, Board Chairman
Jeff Scudillo, President-Elect
Andrew Cretors, Treasurer

Bringing together the top food and beverage concession leaders in the recreation and leisure-time industry at this annual event.
3M Attendees
Frequency: Annual/August
Founded in: 1982

10073 NACD Annual Meeting
National Association of Conservation Districts
509 Capitol Court NE
Washington, DC 20002-4937

202-547-6223; *Fax:* 202-547-6450;
www.nacdnet.org
Social Media: Facebook, Flickr

Krysta Harden, CEO
Bob Cordova, Second Vice President

Discussions with agency leaders on priorities for the coming years, training sessions, key leaders in agricultural, conservation and wildlife discussing their perspectives on the future Farm Bill, highlighted challenges and addressing areas of common interest.
Frequency: Annual/February
Founded in: 1946

10074 NACS Show
National Association of Convenience Stores
1600 Duke Street
Alexandria, VA 22314

703-684-3600; *Fax:* 703-836-4564
sromello@nacsonline.com;
www.nacsshow.com
Social Media: Facebook, Twitter, LinkedIn, YouTube

Sherri Romello, Conventions/Meeting Director
Bob Hughes, Expo/Advertising Director

Access thousands of new profit centers on the expo floor, discover insights on issues facing convenience and petroleum retailers in educational sessions and network with industry peers.
24M Attendees
Frequency: Annual/October

10075 NAFEM Annual Meeting & Management Workshop
NAFEM
161 N Clark Street
Suite 2020
Chicago, IL 60601

312-821-0201; *Fax:* 312-821-0202
info@nafem.org; www.nafem.org

Steven R. Follett, President
Thomas R. Campion, President-Elect
Michael L. Whiteley, Secretary/Treasurer
Deirdre Flynn, Executive Vice President

Workshop geared toward CEOs, CFOs, COOs and directors of member companies. Education is offered on a wide range of topics designed to inspire you personally and professionally. Plenty of networking time with industry peers is built in to encourage the exchange of ideas and expertise.
625 Members
Frequency: Biennial/February

10076 NAFEM Show
North American Assoc of Food Equipment Manufacture
161 N Clark Street
Suite 2020
Chicago, IL 60601
312-245-1054; *Fax:* 312-821-0202
info@nafem.org; www.nafem.org

Deirdre Flynn, Executive VP

Attracts approximately 20,000 foodservice professionals and features 500+ exhibitors displaying products for food preparation, cooking, storage and table service.
Frequency: Biennial/February

10077 NAG Conference
National Convenience Store Advisory Group
3331 Street Road
Suite 410
Bensalem, PA 19020

215-245-4555; *Fax:* 215-245-4060
jhowton@nag-net.com; www.nag-net.com

Joseph Howton, Executive VP/COO

Promoting relationships, networking, and executable ideas and takeaways.
Frequency: Annual/September

10078 NAMA National Expo
National Automatic Merchandising Association
20 N Wacker Drive
Suite 3500
Chicago, IL 60606-3102

312-346-0370
800-331-8816; *Fax:* 312-704-4140
dmathews@vending.org; www.vending.org
Social Media: Facebook, Twitter, YouTube

Brad Ellis, Chairman
Mark Dieffenbach, Chairman-Elect
Pete Tullio, Vice Chairman
Dennis Hogan, Secretary/Treasurer

This event features an impressive array of the industry's newest products and hottest technology, educational sessions and unmatched networking opportunities.
5000+ Attendees
Frequency: Annual/October

10079 NAMP PROCESS EXPO
NAMP
1910 Association Drive
Reston, VA 20191-1545

703-758-1900
800-368-3043; *Fax:* 703-758-8001
smoore@namp.com; www.myprocessexpo.com

Sabrina Moore, Accounting/Meeting Manager
Philip Kimball, Executive Director

Delivering the most valuable tradeshow experience to food industry suppliers and processors at the lowest possible cost.
250 Attendees
Frequency: Annual/November

10080 NAPO International Pizza Expo
National Association of Pizzeria Operators
908 S 8th Street
Suite 200
Louisville, KY 40203

502-736-9500
800-489-8324; *Fax:* 502-736-9501
bmacintosh@pizzatoday.com;
www.pizzatoday.com

Bobbie MacIntosh, Booth/Sponsorship Sales Director

The trade show for the pizza industry that includes; pizzeria owners, operators, managers, distributors and food brokers. Workshops, seminars and exhibits.
5400 Attendees
Frequency: March

10081 NASFT Fancy Food Shows
National Association for the Specialty Food Trade

136 Madison Avenue
12th Floor
New York, NY 10016

212-482-6440; *Fax:* 212-482-6459;
www.fancyfoodshows.com
Social Media: Facebook

Dennis Deschaine, Chairman
Mike Silver, Vice Chairman
Shawn McBride, Treasurer
Becky Renfro Borbolla, Secretary

Held three times a year; winter, spring and summer time. Over 350 domestic exhibitors from around the country, presentations of exotic new specialty foods from all over the world, tastings, seminars and workshops. These shows are a chance to learn about each product first-hand and do business directly with the decision makers onsite.
30M Attendees
Frequency: 3x Yearly

10082 NBBQA Annual Convention
National Barbecue Association
455 S. 4th Street
Suite 650
Louisville, KY 40202

888-909-2121; *Fax:* 502-589-3602
nbbqa@hqtrs.com; www.nbbqa.org

Kell Phelps, President
Roy Slicker, President-Elect
Marc Farris, Treasurer
Bonnie Gomez, Secretary

Learn and network with a group of BBQ folks on how to better prepare and utilize grills, smokers, fuels, sauces, marinades, rubs and all the necessary utensils. Barbeque presentations, programming, demonstrations, contests, sampling and contacts and leads.
Frequency: Annual/February

10083 NBVA Annual Convention
National Bulk Vendors Association
1202 East Maryland Avenue
Suite 1K
Phoenix, AZ 85014

888-628-2872; www.nbva.org
Social Media: Facebook

Bernie Schwarzli, President
Lauri Logue, Vice President
Steve Schnecher, Secretary
Andy Belsky, Treasurer & CPA

Each spring the leading manufacturers and suppliers of bulk vending machines and products display their merchandise. Featuring workshops and seminars to discuss current industry problems and interchange ideas.
530 Attendees
Frequency: Annual/Spring

10084 NBVA Conference
National Bulk Vendors Association
1202 East Maryland Avenue
Suite 1k
Phoenix, AZ 85014

888-628-2872; www.nbva.org
Social Media: Facebook

Bernie Schwarzli, President
Lauri Logue, Vice President
Steve Schnecher, Secretary
Andy Belsky, Treasurer & CPA

Brings together suppliers, manufacturers, distributors and operators to see the newest products and innovations. Seminars are created to familiarize attendees with the latest bulk vending innovations and legal issues.
Frequency: Annual/April
Founded in: 1950

10085 NBWA Annual Convention
National Beer Wholesalers Association
1101 King Street
Suite 600
Alexandria, VA 22314

703-683-4300; *Fax:* 703-683-8965
info@nbwa.org; www.nbwa.org
Social Media: Facebook, Twitter

Craig A Purser, President & CEO
Michael Johnson, EVP/Chief Advisory Officer
Rebecca Spicer, VP Public Affairs/Chief
Paul Pisano, SVP Industry Affairs & Gen. Counsel

Designed to provide valuable education programs and important networking opportunities for the beer industry. Featuring speakers and seminars on a number of topics of importance to beer distributors.
2500 Attendees
Frequency: Annual/Fall

10086 NBWA Legislative Conference
National Beer Wholesalers Association
1101 King Street
Suite 600
Alexandria, VA 22314-2944

703-683-4300; *Fax:* 703-683-8965
info@nbwa.org; www.nbwa.org
Social Media: Facebook, Twitter, YouTube, Flickr

Craig A Purser, President & CEO

Industry leaders meet in Washington, D.C. to discuss the industry's legislative goals and priorities with members of Congress and their staffs.
Frequency: Annual/April
Founded in: 1938

10087 NBWA Trade Show
National Beer Wholesalers Association
1101 King Street
Suite 600
Alexandria, VA 22314-2944

703-683-4300; *Fax:* 703-683-8965
info@nbwa.org; www.nbwa.org
Social Media: Facebook, Twitter, YouTube, Flickr

Craig A Purser, President & CEO

Gives beer distributors an opportunity to interact with brewers and vendors and make valuable contacts for future business needs. Introduces distributors to new brewers as well as new products, innovative technologies and vendors who supply the materials needed to run their operations.
Frequency: Biennial
Founded in: 1938

10088 NCA Annual Convention
National Coffee Association
45 Broadway
Suite 1140
New York, NY 10006

212-766-4007; *Fax:* 212-766-5815
info@ncausa.org; www.ncausa.org
Social Media: Facebook, Twitter, LinkedIn

Dub Hay, Chairman
John E. Boyle, Vice Chairman
Richard Emanuele, Secretary
Robert F. Nelson, President & CEO

Meet a worldwide mix of leadership in the industry in one location, get educational as well as social interaction that cannot be matched at any other convention.
Frequency: Annual/March

10089 NCA Coffee Summit
National Coffee Association
45 Broadway
Suite 1140
New York, NY 10006

212-766-4007; *Fax:* 212-766-5815
info@ncausa.org; www.ncausa.org
Social Media: Facebook, Twitter, LinkedIn

Dub Hay, Chairman
John E. Boyle, Vice Chairman
Richard Emanuele, Secretary
Robert F. Nelson, President & CEO

Bringing together industry knowledge and expertise, for the best available education, networking and product knowledge.
Frequency: Annual/March

10090 NCBA Annual Convention & Trade Show
National Cattlemen's Beef Association
9110 E Nichols Avenue
Suite 300
Centennial, CO 80112

303-694-0305; *Fax:* 303-694-2851
dkaylor@beef.org; www.beefusa.org
Social Media: Facebook, Twitter

Debbie Kaylor, Convention/Meetings Executive Dir.
Valerie Proni, Registration Manager
Kristin Torres, Trade Show Coordinator
Forest Roberts, CEO

The meeting features joint and individual meetings by five industry organizations. Over 250 companies will offer attendees a chance to see the latest products and services while networking with other cattle producers.
28000 Members
6000 Attendees
Frequency: Annual
Founded in: 1898

10091 NCC's Annual Conference
National Chicken Council
1015 15th Street NW
Suite 930
Washington, DC 20005-2622

202-296-2622; *Fax:* 202-293-4005
ncc@chickenusa.org;
www.nationalchickencouncil.org
Social Media: Facebook

Michael J. Brown, President
William P. Roenigk, Senior Vice President
Mary M. Colville, VP of Government Affairs
Dr. Ashley Peterson, VP of Science & Technology

Brings together senior executives from US chicken processing companies and allied industries to address current agricultural, public affiars, legislative, regulatory, political, economic, and world trade issues affecting the chicken industry.
Frequency: Annual/October
Founded in: 1954

10092 NCIMS Conference
National Conference on Interstate Milk Shipments
585 County Farm Road
Monticello, IL 61856

217-762-2656
ncims.bordson@gmail.com; www.ncims.org

Leon Townsend, Executive Secretary

Bringing together the people in the dairy industry to discuss laws that directly involve the dairy industry.
Frequency: Biennially/May
Founded in: 1950

10093 NCPA's Annual Convention
National Cottonseed Products Association

866 Willow Tree Circle
Cordova, TN 38018-6376

901-682-0800; *Fax:* 901-682-2856
info@cottonseed.com; www.cottonseed.com
Social Media: Twitter, Flickr, YouTube

Ben Morgan, Executive VP & Secretary
Sandi Stine, Treasurer

Featuring a board of directors meeting, committee meeting, luncheons, and discussion on the latest trends in the industry.
Founded in: 1897

10094 NCSLA Annual Conference
National Conference of State Liquor Administrators
C/O Massachusetts ABCC
239 Causeway Street, 1st Floor
Boston, MA 02114

617-727-3040; *Fax:* 617-727-1510
cmarshall@tre.state.ma.us; www.ncsla.org

Cheryl Marshall, Conference Coordinator

Provide opportunities for state-licensed administrators to meet and exchange ideas and information and to formulate uniform regulations, statue and laws affecting the sales of alcholic beverages.
Frequency: June/Fee Varies

10095 NICRA Annual Meeting
National Ice Cream Retailers Association
1028 W Devon Avenue
Elk Grove Village, IL 60007

847-301-7500
866-303-6960; *Fax:* 847-301-8402
info@nicra.org; www.nicra.org

Offers educational seminars, exhibits, networking and social opportunities
325 Attendees
Frequency: Annual/November
Founded in: 1933

10096 NPFDA Annual Convention
National Poultry & Food Distributors
2014 Osborne Road
Saint Marys, GA 31558

770-535-9901; *Fax:* 770-535-7385
kkm@npfda.org; www.npfda.org

Chris Sharp, President
Al Acunto, Vice President
Marc Miro, Treasurer
Kristin McWhorter, Executive Director

Features the Poultry Suppliers Showcase and many opportunities to network with other industry representatives. Participating in this convention provides access to the latest industry trends, presents ways to improve business operations, and increases number of industry contacts.
Frequency: Annual/January
Founded in: 1967

10097 NW Food Manufacturing & Packaging Expo
Northwest Food Processors Association
9700 SW Capitol Highway
Suuite 250
Portland, OR 97219

503-327-2200; *Fax:* 503-327-2201
nwfpa@nwfpa.org; www.nwfpa.org

Teonna Embelton, Events Coordinator
Stephanie Kennedy, Events Consultant

Provides comprehensive programs encompassing topics ranging from food sciences and technologies to energy efficiencies.
Frequency: Jan Oregon

10098 NW Food Manufacturing and Packaging Expo
8338 NE. Alderwood Road
Suite 160
Portland, OR 97220

503-327-2200; *Fax:* 503-327-2201
nwfpa@nwfpa.org; www.nwfpa.org
Social Media: Facebook, Twitter, LinkedIn

David Zepponi, President
David C Klick, Cluster Outreach Executive
Craig Smith, VP
Connie Kirby, Scientific & Technical Director
Pam Barrow, Energy Affairs Manager

NWFPA is an advocate for members interests and a resource for enhancing the food processing industry in Oregon, Washington and Idaho.
350 Members
4000 Attendees
Founded in: 1914

10099 NWA Annual Education and Networking Conference & Exhibits
National WIC Association
2001 S St NW
Suite 580
Washington, DC 20009-1165

202-232-5492; *Fax:* 202-387-5281;
www.nwica.org
Social Media: Facebook, Twitter

Douglas Greenaway, President & CEO

Offers a terrific opportunity to learn new skills and to network with more than 1200 colleagues and peers, public health professionals, technical experts and nationally recognized speakers from a variety of fields who will engage participants during plenary and concurrent sessions.
900 Members
Frequency: Annual/May
Founded in: 1983

10100 NWA Technology Conference
National WIC Association
2001 S St NW
Suite 580
Washington, DC 20009-1165

202-232-5492; *Fax:* 202-387-5281;
www.nwica.org
Social Media: Facebook, Twitter

Douglas Greenaway, President & CEO

The future is now! Learn about the latest technologies available and used in all the WIC programs.
900 Members
Frequency: Annual/September
Founded in: 1983

10101 NWA Washington Leadership Conference
National WIC Association
2001 S St NW
Suite 580
Washington, DC 20009-1165

202-232-5492; *Fax:* 202-387-5281;
www.nwica.org
Social Media: Facebook, Twitter

Douglas Greenaway, President & CEO

The conference will provide a forum to discuss Federal initiatives affecting the health and nutritional wellbeing of WIC mothers and young children, WIC's role as a preventative public health nutrition program, as well as service delivery and the effective management of the Program.
900 Members
Frequency: Annual/March
Founded in: 1983

10102 National Agri-Marketing Association Conference
National Agri-Marketing Association
11020 King Street
Suite 205
Overland Park, KS 66210-1201

913-491-6500; *Fax:* 913-492-6502
agrimktg@nama.org; www.nama.org
Social Media: Facebook, Twitter, LinkedIn, YouTube, Flickr

Stephanie Gable, National President
Vicki Henrickson, Vice President

Annual show of 60 exhibitors of marketing and communication suppliers, including trade publications, radio and television broadcast sales organizations, premium/incentive manufacturers, printers, marketing research firms and photographers.
1100 Attendees
Frequency: Annual

10103 National Agricultural Plastics Congress
American Society for Plasticulture
526 Brittany Drive
State College, PA 16803-1420
814-238-7045; *Fax:* 814-238-7051
contact@plasticulture.org;
www.plasticulture.org

Patricia Heuser, Executive Director

Congress of research presentations, with exhibit area of equipment, supplies and services relating to greenhouse production and mulch film production of agricultural and horticultural crops.
225 Attendees
Frequency: September

10104 National Association Extension 4-H Agents Convention
University of Georgia
Hoke Smith Annex
Athens, GA 30602

706-542-3000; *Fax:* 706-542-2115

Peggy Adkins, Show Manager

Fifty booths for young people, youth staff and volunteers involved in 4-H.
1.2M Attendees
Frequency: November

10105 National Association of College and University Food Services Convention
Michigan State University-Manly Miles Building
1405 S Harrison Road
Suite 305
East Lansing, MI 48823-5245

517-332-2494; *Fax:* 517-332-8144
jspina@nacufs.org; www.nacufs.org/nacufs

Joseph Spina, Executive Director
Donna Addy, Administrative Assistant
Nancy Lane, Director

Annual convention and exhibits of equipment, supplies and services for food preparation and service on college and university campuses.

10106 National Association of County Agricultural Agents Conference
National Association of County Agricultural Agents
Courthouse-Room 217
5th & Main Street
Ellensburg, WA 98926
Fax: 509-627-74

Annual conference and exhibits for county agricultural agents and extension workers.

10107 National Association of Fruits, Flavors and Syrups Annual Convention
5 Ravine Drive
#776
Matawan, NJ 07747-3106
732-988-4800; *Fax:* 732-583-0798
Bob Bauer, Director
Frequency: September

10108 National Chicken Council Conference
1015 15th Street NW
Suite 930
Washington, DC 20005-2622
202-296-2622; *Fax:* 202-293-4005;
www.nationalchickencouncil.org
Michael J. Brown, President
William P. Roenigk, Senior VP
NCC's Annual Conference brings together senior executives from U.S. chicken processing companies and allied industries to address current agricultural, public affairs, legislative, regulatory, political, economic, and world trade issues affecting the chicken industry.
Frequency: Annual
Founded in: 1954

10109 National Confectioners Association Education Exposition
National Confectioners Association
7900 Westpar Drive
Suite A-320
McLean, VA 22102
703-790-5750; *Fax:* 730-790-5752
Linda Jamie, Finance Executive
600 Attendees

10110 National Confectioners Association Expo
8320 Old Courthouse Road
Suite 300
Vienna, VA 22182
703-790-5750; *Fax:* 703-790-5752
info@candyusa.org; www.allcandyexpo.com
Larry Graham, President
Libby Taylor, VP
Confectionery trade show featuring more chocolate, candy and gum than one can imagine. Held annually in June at Chicago's McCormick Place.
1200 booths.
15 M Attendees
Frequency: June

10111 National Conservation Association District Annual Convention
9150 W Jewell Avenue
Suite 113
Lakewood, CO 80232-6469
303-839-1852
Robert Raschke, Regional Representative
Eighty booths including companies who manufacture, service or who are otherwise involved with equipment used in agricultural production.
2M Attendees
Frequency: February

10112 National Convenience Store Advisory Group Convention
2063 Oak Street
Jacksonville, FL 32204
904-845-5989; *Fax:* 904-387-3362;
www.nag-net.com
Joseph Howton, Executive VP/COO
One-hundred booths.
500 Attendees
Frequency: January

10113 National Corn Growers Association
1000 Executive Parkway Drive
Suite 105
Creve Cocur, MO 63141-6397
314-275-9915; *Fax:* 314-275-7061
Peggy Findley, Director of Conventions
Five hundred and fifty booths of equipment, seed and chemicals.
4000 Attendees
Frequency: February

10114 National Country Ham Association Annual Meeting
PO Box 948
Conover, NC 28613
828-466-2760
800-820-4426; *Fax:* 828-466-2770
eatham@countryham.org;
www.countryham.org
Candace Cansler, Executive Director
Providing an array of speakers, discussion topics and activities.
Frequency: Non-Members:$300

10115 National Farm Machinery Show and Championship Tractor Pull
Kentucky Fair and Exposition Center
PO Box 37130
Louisville, KY 40233
502-367-5000; *Fax:* 502-367-5299;
www.farmmachineryshow.org
Harold Workman, Show Manager
Annual show of 800 plus exhibitors of agricultural products, equipment, supplies and services.
280M Attendees
Frequency: February

10116 National Food Processors Association Convention
National Food Processors Association
1350 I Street NW
Suite 300
Washington, DC 20005-3377
202-930-0890; *Fax:* 202-639-5932
John Cady, President
Lisa Weddig, Executive Director
Annual convention and exhibits of equipment, supplies and services for food processing quality control measures, spoilage prevention, frozen food technology, sanitation techniques and waste treatment techniques.

10117 National Frozen and Refrigerated Foods Convention
National Frozen & Refrigerated Foods Association
4755 Linglestown Road Suite 300
PO Box 6069
Harrisburg, PA 17112
717-657-8601; *Fax:* 717-657-9862
info@nfraweb.org; www.nfraweb.org
Dayna Jackson, Admin Asst, Meetings/Member Service
The National Frozen and Refrigerated Foods Convention is an opportunity for you to meet with hundreds of frozen and refrigerated food decision-makers. This premier business event brings representatives from all segments of our industry together to conduct business and build relationships. it is structured around one-on-one business appointments, with ample opportunity to network.
1,200 Attendees
Frequency: Annual/October

10118 National Grange Annual Meeting
1616 H Street NW
Washington, DC 20006
202-628-3507
888-447-2643; *Fax:* 503-622-0343
info@nationalgrange.org;
www.nationalgrange.org
William Steel, President
Jennifer Dugent, Secretary
Phil Prelli, Secretary
Judy Sherrod, National Secretary
Agricultural forum.
3M Attendees
Frequency: November

10119 National Grocers Association Annual Convenience & Supermarket Showcase
National Grocers Association
1825 Samuel Morse Drive
Reston, VA 22090
703-437-5300; *Fax:* 703-437-7768
2800 Attendees

10120 National Homebrewers Conference and National Homebrew Competition
Brewers Association
736 Pearl Street
Boulder, CO 80302
303-447-0816
888-822-6273; *Fax:* 303-447-2825
webmaster@brewersassociation.org;
www.beertown.org
Social Media: Facebook, Twitter
Chris P. Frey, Chair
Jake Keeler, Vice Chair
Roxanne Westendorf, Secretary
Education and fun combine for a great experience at the national conference for amateur brewers.
1900 Members
Founded in: 1978

10121 National Ice Cream Retailers Association Annual Convention
1028 West Devon Avenue
Elk Grove Village, IL 60007
847-301-7500
866-303-6960; *Fax:* 847-301-8402
info@nicra.org; www.nicra.org
Dan Messer, President
David Zimmerman, President-Elect
Nanette Frey, Vice President
Carl Chaney, Secretary/Treasurer
Lynda Utterback, Executive Director
A major national convention for those in the retail ice ceam and frozen dessert business. Attendees are mostly independent operators/owners and vendors that sell to the retail/wholesale trade.
Thirty-five to forty booths.
Frequency: Annual/November

10122 National Nutritional Foods Association
1773 T Street, NW
Washington, DC 20009
202-223-0101
800-966-6632; *Fax:* 202-223-0250
natural@NPAinfo.org; www.npainfo.org
Social Media: Facebook, Twitter, LinkedIn
John F. Gay, Executive Director & CEO
Jeffrey Wright, President
Six hundred booths including educational seminars and exhibits of health and natural foods.
7.5M Attendees
Frequency: Annual/June

10123 National Orange Show
PO Box 5749
San Bernardino, CA 92412-5749
909-888-6788; *Fax:* 909-889-7666
Esther Armstrong, Executive Director
Brad Randall, Manager
Agricultural forum.
262M Attendees
Frequency: May

10124 National Pest Management Association Annual Eastern Conference
10460 North Street
Fairfax, VA 22030
703-352-6762
800-678-6722; *Fax:* 703-352-3031;
www.npmapestworld.org
Social Media: Facebook, Twitter
Robert Lederer, Executive VP
Two hundred forty booths.
7000 Members
3500 Attendees
Frequency: Annual/October
Founded in: 1933

10125 National Policy Conference
Crop Life America
1156 15th St NW
Washington, DC 20005-1752
202-296-1585; *Fax:* 202-463-0474
webmaster@croplifeamerica.org;
www.croplifeamerica.org
Social Media: Facebook, Twitter, LinkedIn, YouTube
Jay Vroom, President
Rich Nolan, VP
Brings together leading experts, academics and politicos to engage in a debate on the development of the Farm Bill. How does Congress design a Farm Bill that addresses human, social, economic, research and environmental needs while taking into account farmers, consumers and the natural systems that give us the food and fiber we need to live?
Frequency: Annual/May

10126 National Potato Council's Annual Meeting
National Potato Council
5690 Dtc Boulevard
Greenwood Village, CO 80111-3232
303-773-9295; *Fax:* 303-773-9296;
www.npcspod.com
Annual meeting and exhibits of potato growing equipment, supplies and services.

10127 National ProStart Invitational
NRAEF
175 W Jackson Boulevard
Suite 1500
Chicago, IL 60604-2814
312-715-1010
800-765-2122; *Fax:* 312-583-9767;
www.nraef.org
Culinary and management competition attracts top high school ProStart students from around the country. Winning teams secure scholarships from the NRAEF and The Coca-Cola Company, along with colleges and universities.
Frequency: Annual/April
Founded in: 1987

10128 National Restaurant Association Convention
National Restaurant Association
150 N Michigan Avenue
Suite 2000
Chicago, IL 60601
312-853-2525; *Fax:* 312-853-2548
Mary Heftman, Senior VP
80000 Attendees
Frequency: May

10129 National Soft Drink Association Show
1101 16th Street NW
Suite 700
Washington, DC 20036-4877
202-463-6732; *Fax:* 202-463-8178
Susan K Neely, President
Patricia M Vaughan, Secretary
Jim L Turner, Treasurer
Annual show of 300 members of soft drink makers and their suppliers.
25M Attendees
Frequency: Annual Fall
Founded in: 1919

10130 National Turkey Federation Annual Meeting
National Turkey Federation
1225 New York Avenue NW
Suite 400
Washington, DC 20005-6404
202-898-0100; *Fax:* 202-898-0203
info@turkeyfed.org; www.eatturkey.com
Social Media: Facebook, Twitter, YouTube
Joel Brandenberger, President
Jennifer Zukowski, Meetings & Membership
Advocates for all segments of the US turkey industry, providing services and conducting activities that increase demand for its members' products. The federation also protects and enhances its members' ability to effectively and profitably provide wholesome, high quality, nutritious turkey products.
Frequency: Annual

10131 National Watermelon Association
Annual Meeting
406 Railroad Street
Morven, GA 31638
229-775-2130; *Fax:* 229-775-2344
Nacy Childers, Contact

10132 National Wheat Growers Association Convention
415 2nd Street NE
Suite 300
Washington, DC 20002-4900
202-547-7800; *Fax:* 202-546-2638
wheatworld@wheatworld.org;
www.wheatworld.org
Social Media: Facebook, Twitter, YouTube
Brett Blankenship, President
Jim Palmer, Chief Executive Officer
Major agri business exhibits including farm equipment and services. 100 booths.
Frequency: Annual/January

10133 Natural Products Exposition East
New Hope Natural Media
1301 Spruce Street
Boulder, CO 80302
303-939-8440; *Fax:* 303-939-9559
20000 Attendees

10134 Natural Products Exposition West
New Hope Communications
1301 Spruce Street
Boulder, CO 80302
303-939-8440; *Fax:* 303-939-9559
31000 Attendees

10135 New England Equipment Dealers Association
PO Box 895
Concord, NH 03302-0895
603-225-5510; *Fax:* 603-225-5510
George M Becker, Managing Director
Annual convention and trade show held the first weekend in December for farm, industrial and outdoor equipment dealers in the six New England states. 95 booths.
300 Attendees
Frequency: December

10136 Nightclub & Bar Beverage Retailer Beverage & Food Convention and Trade Show
Oxford Publishing
307 West Jackson Avenue
Oxford, MS 38655
662-236-5510
888-966-2727; *Fax:* 662-513-3990
registration@oxpub.com; www.nightclub.com

10137 Nightclub & Bar/Beverage Retailer Food & Beverage Trade Show
Oxford Publishing
307 W Jackson Avenue
Oxford, MS 38655-2154
662-236-5510
888-966-2727; *Fax:* 662-513-3990
jrobinson@oxpub.com; www.nightclub.com
Jennifer Robinson, Show Manager
Adam Alson, Founder
Yosi Benvenisti, Owner
Fastest growing food, beverage and hospitality show in the US. This show is for both on-premise and off-premise.
20M Attendees
Frequency: March/July/November

10138 Nightclub and Bar/Beverage Retailer Convention and Trade Show
National Bar and Restaurant Association
307 Jackson Avenue W
Oxford, MS 38655
662-236-5510
800-247-3881; *Fax:* 662-236-5541;
www.bevindustry.com
Jennifer Robinson, Senior VP
Hollis Green, Trade Show Director
Kaytee Hazlewood, VP Marketing
The industry's first national conference and trade show devoted to business basics, promotions and marketing for liquor stores, nightclubs and bars. More than 2,500 exhibits.
38800 Attendees
Frequency: March

10139 North American Deer Farmers Association Annual Conference & Exhibit
North American Deer Farmers Association
104 S Lakeshore Drive
Lake City, MN 55041-1266
651-345-5600; *Fax:* 651-345-5603
info@nadefa.org; www.nadefa.org
Social Media: Facebook
Carolyn Laughlin, President
R.Ray Burdette, First VP
Will Ainsworth, Second VP
Bill Pittenger, Third VP
Dr. Hank Dimuzio, Treasurer
Annual show of more than 30 exhibitors of deer farming equipment, supplies and services.
550+ Attendees
Frequency: Annual/Summer
Founded in: 1984

10140 North American Farm and Power Show
Tradexpos
811 W Oakland Avenue
PO Box 1067
Austin, MN 55912
507-437-4697
800-949-3976; *Fax:* 507-437-8917
steve@tradexpos.com; www.tradexpos.com
Steve Guenthner, Show Director
Agri-business farm show for the 5-state region. Free admission and parking.
32M Attendees
Frequency: Annual/March

10141 North American Fertilizer Transportation Conference
Fertilizer Institute
425 Third Street, SW
Suite 950
Washington, DC 20024
202-962-0490; *Fax:* 202-962-0577
information@tfi.org; www.tfi.org
Social Media: Facebook, Twitter, LinkedIn
Ford West, President
Provides an opportunity for shippers and carriers to discuss issues of concern and work to reach mutually-beneficial solutions to logistical problems.
Frequency: Annual/October

10142 North American Olive Oil Association Mid- Year Meeting
North American Olive Oil Association
3301 Route 66
Suite 205, Building C
Neptune, NJ 07753
732-922-0500; *Fax:* 732-922-3590;
www.aboutoliveoil.org
Bob Bauer, President
Olive growers and oil processors group for legislative advocacy and trade networking.

10143 North American Specialty Coffee Retailers' Expo
PO Box 14827
Portland, OR 97293
503-236-2587
800-548-0551; *Fax:* 503-236-3165;
www.nascore.net
Jan Weigel, Director
Founded in: 1995

10144 Northeast Food Service and Lodging Expo and Conference
Reed Exhibition Companies
383 Main Avenue
Norwalk, CT 06851
203-840-4800; *Fax:* 203-840-4824
Linda Karpowich, Customer Service Manager
Annual show of 600 exhibitors of food services, operating equipment and services for the hospitality and institutional foodservice industry.
29000 Attendees

10145 Northeast Pizza Expo
MacFadden Protech
137 E Market Street
New Albany, IN 47150
812-949-0909
800-489-8324; *Fax:* 812-949-1867
lkeith@pizzatoday.com; www.pizzaexpo.com
William T Oakley, Senior VP Expositions
Linda F Keith, Manager
Patty Crone, Manager
Manufacturers, food purveyors and service representatives from pizza or related industries.

10146 Northwest Agricultural Congress
4991 Drift Creek Rd SE
Sublimity, OR 97385-9764
503-769-8940; *Fax:* 503-769-8946;
www.nwagshow.com
Jim Heater, Show Manager
Second largest agricultural show on the west coast. Show is produced by the Northwest Horticultural Congress which is a partnership between Oregon Horticultural Society, the Oregon Association of Nurseries and Northwest Nut Growers Association. Show held in conjunction with annual meetings and seminars by all three of the horticultural groups.
21000 Members

10147 Northwest Food Manufacturing & Packaging Association
Northwest Food Processors Association
6950 SW Hampton Street
Suite 340
Portland, OR 98223-8332
503-639-7676; *Fax:* 503-639-7007;
www.nwpfa@nwpfa.org
Stephanie Green, Show Manager
Mindy Todd, Marketing Coordinator
Containing 450 booths.
3000 Attendees
Frequency: Janurary

10148 Nut Grower Magazine Farm Show
Western Agricultural Publishing Company
4974 E Clinton Way
Suite 123
Fresno, CA 93727-1520
559-261-0396; *Fax:* 559-252-7387
Phill Rhoads, Manager
Productions seminars, guest speakers, prizes and exhibits for nut growers. Containing 80 booths and exhibits.

10149 OFPA Annual Convention and Exposition
Ozark Food Processors Association
2650 N Young Avenue
Fayetteville, AR 72704
479-575-4607; *Fax:* 479-575-2165
ofpa@uark.edu
ofpa.uark.edu
Cindy Stricklaw, President
Roure Threfall, Director
OFPA members and registered guests learn about new trends in the food industry during technical sessions and the exposition. The location for the 2012 meeting is Springfield, AR.
500 Attendees
Frequency: Annual/ April
Founded in: 1906

10150 Oklahoma Restaurant Convention & Expo
Oklahoma Restaurant Association
3800 N Portland Avenue
Oklahoma City, OK 73112-2948
405-942-8181
800-375-8181; *Fax:* 405-942-0541;
www.okrestaurants.com
Lori Culver, Convention Manager
Annual show of 450 manufacturers, suppliers and distributors. Exhibits of providers of food service and hospitality products, services and equipment. Held at the Myriad Convention Center in Oklahoma City, Oklahoma.
9M Attendees
Frequency: April
Founded in: 1938

10151 PACK International Expo
Packaging Machinery Manufacturers Institute
4350 N Fairfax Drive
Suite 600
Arlington, VA 22203
703-243-8555; *Fax:* 703-243-8556
expo@pmmi.org; www.pei2006.packexpo.com
Jim Pittas, Trade Show VP
Dinah Sprouse, Trade Show Operations Director
Kim Beaulieu, Exhibitor Services Manager
Browse more than 2,000 packaging and processing exhibitors covering virtually the entire packaging supply chain. Network with others in the industry, attend specialized education sessions led by industry experts and evaluate the latest advances while experiencing hands on demonstrations of the latest technologies in the industry.
1600 Attendees
Frequency: Oct-Nov

10152 PACex International
Packaging, Food Process and Logistics Exhibition
2255 Sheppard Avenue E
Suite E330
Toronto Ontario M2J-4YI
416-490-7860; *Fax:* 416-490-7844;
www.pacexinternational.com
Maria Tavares, Expositions Manager
15000 Attendees
Frequency: September-October

10153 PLMA Trade Show
Private Label Manufacturers Association
630 Third Avenue
New York, NY 10017-6506
212-972-3131; *Fax:* 212-983-1382
info@plma.com; www.plma.com
Brian Sharoff, President
Myra Rosen, VP
Tom Prendergast, Director, Research Services
The best place for private label networking.
3200+ Members
10000 Attendees
Frequency: Annual/November
Founded in: 1979

10154 PMA Foodservice Conference & Exposition
Produce Marketing Association
1500 Casho Mill Road
Newark, DE 19711-3547
302-738-7100; *Fax:* 302-731-2409
showmanagement@pma.com; www.pma.com
Social Media: Twitter, YouTube, Flickr
Jamie Hillegas, Show Manager
Susan Eller, Trade Show Planner
Join the who's-who of chefs, menu developers, restaurant operators, grower-shippers, distributors and foodservice suppliers to see and sample the newest products and services, learn about the latest consumer trends and tastes, see old colleagues or make new contacts.
Frequency: Annual/July
Founded in: 1981

10155 PMA Fresh Summit International Convention & Exposition
Produce Marketing Association
1500 Casho Mill Road
PO Box 6036
Newark, DE 19711-3547
302-387-7100; *Fax:* 302-731-2409
showmanagement@pma.com;
www.pma.com/freshsummit
Social Media: Facebook, Twitter, YouTube
Don Harris, Summit Chairman
Jamie Hillegas, Show Manager

Susan Eller, Trade Show Planner
Sheli Parlier, Exhibits Sales Manager
Bryan Silbermann, President

An event that attracts buyers and suppliers from the produce and floral industries; from the retail and foodservice channels and from more than 70 counties.
17M Attendees
Frequency: Annual/October

10156 PTNPA Annual Convention
Peanut & Tree Nut Processors Association
PO Box 2660
Alexandria, VA 22301

301-365-2521; *Fax:* 301-365-7705
ptnpa.org
Social Media: Twitter

General meeting sessions, keynote speakers, exhibitors from the industry.
400 Attendees
Frequency: Annual/January

10157 Pan-American International Livestock Exposition
State Fair of Texas
PO Box 150009
Dallas, TX 75315-0009

214-565-9931; *Fax:* 214-421-8792
livestock@greatstatefair.com; www.bigtex.com

Benny Clark, Director
Elvis Presley, Vice President

Annual show and exhibits of livestock, livestock equipment, agricultural technology and consumer products.
3.5M Attendees
Frequency: September/October

10158 Pickle Packers International Pickle Fair
1620 i St Nw
Suite 925
Washington, DC 20006-4035

202-312-2859; *Fax:* 630-584-0759

Richard Hentschell, Executive VP

Fifty booths, seminars and programs held in odd numbered years.
300+ Attendees
Frequency: October

10159 Poultry Supplier Showcase
National Poultry & Food Distributors
2014 Osborne Rd
Saint Marys, GA 31558

770-535-9901
877-845-1545; *Fax:* 770-535-7385
info@npfda.org; www.npfda.org

Chris Sharp, President
Al Acunto, Vice President
Marc Miro, Treasurer
Kristin McWhorter, Executive Director

Annual convention and poultry suppliers showcase. Three day convention and trade show.
900 Attendees
Frequency: Annual/January
Founded in: 1967

10160 Pre-Harvest Food Safety Conference
North American Meat Processors Association
1910 Association Drive
Reston, VA 20191-1500

703-758-1900
800-368-3043; *Fax:* 703-758-8001;
www.namp.com

Philip Kimball, Executive Director
Sabrina Moore, Accounting/Meetings Manager
Ann Wells, Director Scientific Affairs
Jane Jacobs, Communications Director

Brings regulators and researchers together with experts from the poultry industry, and the allied industries that serve them, to discuss the known and unknown issues associated with the control of food borne pathogens in pre-harvest operations. Conference will be one of the most thorough explorations into the poultry pre-harvest arena that has ever been conducted.
Frequency: Annual/January

10161 Presidents Conference
International Foodservice Distributors Association
1410 Spring Hill Road
Suite 210
McLean, VA 22102-3035

703-532-9400; *Fax:* 703-538-4673;
www.ifdaonline.org

Mark Allen, President & CEO
Jonathan Eisen, Senior VP/ Government Relations

Gain breakthrough insights and take away high value solutions. Collaborate with fellow leaders in an information rich learning environment with plenty of networking opportunities. All-industry forum addressing issues impacting the foodservice supply chain.
Frequency: Annual/October

10162 Private Label Manufacturers Association Trade Show
630 Third Avenue
New York, NY 10017

212-972-3131; *Fax:* 212-983-1382
info@plma.com; www.plma.com

Brian Sharoff, President
Myra Rosen, Vice President

A private label trade show.
3200+ Members
Frequency: Annual/November
Founded in: 1979

10163 ProMat
Material Handling Industry of America
8720 Red Oak Boulevard
Suite 201
Charlotte, NC 28217-3992

704-676-1190; *Fax:* 704-676-1199
gbaer@mhia.org; www.mhia.org

Greg Baer, Senior Sales Associate
Jennifer Breadling, Manager Of Communications

The premier showcase of material handling and logistics solutions in North America. The show is designed to offer productivity solutions and information by showcasing the products and services of over 700 leading material handling and logistics providers.
Frequency: Annual

10164 Process Expo
Food Processing Suppliers Association
1451 Dolley Madison Blvd
Suite 101
Mc Lean, VA 22101-3850

703-761-2600; *Fax:* 703-761-4334
info@fpsa.org; www.fpsa.org
Social Media: Facebook, Twitter, LinkedIn

David Seckman, President
George Melnykovich, Senior Advisor
Robyn Roche, CFO

Tradeshow where qualified buyers representing every market of the food industry meet face to face with suppliers showcasing the newest developments in processing technology. Exhibitors are able to demonstrate state-of-the-art food processing equipment in baking, beverage, dairy, fruit and vegetable, and meat/poultry industries.
510 Members
Frequency: Annual/November
Founded in: 2005

10165 Produce Marketing Association
1500 Casho Mill Road
PO Box 6036
Newark, DE 19711-3547

302-738-7100; *Fax:* 302-731-2409;
www.pma.com

Bryan Silbermann, President
Dan Henderaon, Marketing

Largest convention and exposition for the fresh fruit, vegetable and floral industries. More than 12,000 people and 1,500 booths.
12M Attendees
Frequency: October

10166 Productivity Conference and Distribution/ Transportation Exposition
Food Distributors International
1410 Spring Hill Road
Suite 210
McLean, VA 22102

703-532-9400; *Fax:* 703-538-4673;
www.ifdaonline.org

Mark S. Allen, President/CEO
Malcolm Sullivan, Jr., Chairman
Thomas Zatina, Vice Chairman
James Crawford, Treasurer

A conference exhibiting services and supplies geared toward the grocery industry. Containing 200 booths and 200 exhibits.
2400 Attendees
Frequency: Annual/October

10167 R&DA Annual Spring & Fall Meeting and Exhibition
R&D Associates
16607 Blanco Road
Suite 305
San Antonio, TX 78232-1940

210-682-4302; *Fax:* 830-493-8036
jfagan@militaryfood.org

Jim Fagan, Meeting Coordinator

Hear presentations by key officials, network with decision makers, get updates on key issues and gain a competitive edge within the industry.
300 Attendees
Frequency: Apr/Oct/Non-Members:$1099

10168 RFA Annual Conference
Refrigerated Foods Association
1640 Powers Ferry Road
Bldg. 2, Suite 200A
Marietta, GA 30067

770-303-9905; *Fax:* 770-303-9906
info@refrigeratedfoods.org;
www.refrigeratedfoods.org

Brian Edmonds, President
George Bradford, Vice President
Steve Loehndorf, Secretary
Wes Thaller, Treasurer

The RFA Conference is a great way to network and gain important new information affecting the industry, including technical innovations, sales and marketing tips, consumer trends, distribution solutions, new product and package development, and food safety issues.
200+ Members
Frequency: Annual/February
Founded in: 1980

10169 RFA Annual Conference & Exhibition
Refrigerated Foods Association

2971 Flowers Road S
Suite 266
Atlanta, GA 30341-5403

770-452-0660; *Fax:* 770-455-3879
info@refrigeratedfoods.org;
www.refrigeratedfoods.org

Brian Edmonds, President
George Bradford, Vice President
Steve Loehndorf, Secretary
Wes Thaller, Treasurer

Suppliers displaying the latest offerings in equipment, packaging, ingredients and services for the industry. A great way to network and gain important new information affecting the industry, including technical innovations, sales and marketing tips, consumer trends, distribution solutions, new product and packaging development and food safety issues.
Frequency: Annual/April

10170 Restaurants Rock
NRAEF
175 W Jackson Boulevard
Suite 1500
Chicago, IL 60604-2814

312-715-1010
800-765-2122; *Fax:* 312-583-9767;
www.nraef.org

The only official party of the NRA Show, Restaurants Rock brings together the restaurant and hospitality industry in a night of networking and celebration.
Frequency: Annual/May
Founded in: 1987

10171 Retail Confectioners International Annual Convention and Exposition
Retail Confectioners International
1807 Glenview Road
Suite 204
Glenview, IL 60025-2968

847-724-6120; *Fax:* 847-724-2719

Van Billington, Director
Michelle May, Contact

Annual exhibition offering exhibits of confectionery equipment, supplies, finished products and packaging materials.
1.5M Attendees
Frequency: Annual

10172 SANA/USB Annual Soy Symposium
Soyfoods Association of North America
1001 Connecticut Avenue NW
Suite 1120
Washington, DC 20036

202-659-3520
info@soyfoods.org; www.soyfoods.org

Nancy Chapman, Executive Director
Anne Chambers, Membership Coordinator

Co-sponsored with United Soybean Board, see the latest innovative designs and products from industry representatives.
Frequency: Apr/Non-Members:$995
Founded in: 1978

10173 SAVOR, An American Craft Beer & Food Experience
Brewers Association
736 Pearl Street
Boulder, CO 80302

303-447-0816
888-822-6273; *Fax:* 303-447-2825
webmaster@brewersassociation.org;
www.beertown.org
Social Media: Facebook, Twitter

Chris P. Frey, Chair
Jake Keeler, Vice Chair
Roxanne Westendorf, Secretary

The main beer and food pairing event in the US. Where beer enthusiasts and foodies can interact directly with some of the greatest brewers and brewery owners in the world.
1900 Members
Founded in: 1978

10174 SBS Annual Conference & Exhibition
Society for Biomolecular Sciences
36 Tamarack Avenue
Suite 348
Danbury, CT 06811

203-788-8828; *Fax:* 203-748-7557
email@sbsonline.org; www.sbsonline.org

Agnes Amos, Exhibitions/Meetings Director
Marietta Manoni, Exhibitions/Meetings Manager

This event brings together leaders in the pharmaceutical, biotech and agrochemical industries from around the world. Highlighting the impact of screening and technology applications on drug discovery.
Frequency: Sept/Non-Members $1,445
Founded in: 1995

10175 SCAA Annual Conference & Exhibition
Specialty Coffee Association of America
330 Golden Shore
Suite 50
Long Beach, CA 90802

562-624-4100; *Fax:* 562-624-4101
coffee@scaa.org; www.scaa.org

Ted Lingle, Executive Director
Scott Welker, Administrative Director

The country's premier coffee event, attracting coffee professionals from more than 40 countries. Attendees include coffee producers, exporters and importers, roasters, manufacturers, brew masters, and consumer enthusiasts.
8000 Attendees
Frequency: April/Non-Members:$585
Founded in: 1982

10176 SCAA Annual Exposition
Specialty Coffee Association of America
330 Golden Shore
Suite 50
Long Beach, CA 90802-4246

562-624-4100; *Fax:* 562-624-4101
info@scaa.org; www.scaa.org
Social Media: Facebook, Twitter, YouTube

Ric Rhinehart, Executive Director
Tracy Ging, Deputy Executive Director
Ted Lingle, Senior Advisor

Roasters & retailers attend and have the opportunity to exhibit products on the show floor, network with industry's decision makers, and further their professional careers by participating in the SCAA's numerous lectures, labs or certification programs.
2500+ Members
Frequency: Annual/April
Founded in: 1982

10177 SCST Annual Meeting
Society of Commerical Seed Technologists
101 E State Street
Suite 214
Ithaca, NY 14850

607-256-3313; *Fax:* 607-256-3313
scst@twcny.rr.com; www.seedtechnology.net

Anita Hall, Executive Director

A joint meeting with the Association of Official Seed Analysts and the Association of Official Seed Certifying Agencies. Workshops, Exhibits, speakers and more regarding the seed industry.
Frequency: June
Founded in: 1922

10178 SEAFWA Annual Convention
Southeast Association of Fish & Wildlife Agencies
8005 Freshwater Farms Road
Tallahassee, FL 32309-9009

850-893-1204; *Fax:* 850-893-6204;
www.seafwa2006.org/www.seafwa.org

Robert M Brantly, Executive Secretary
Dianne Waller, Conference Coordinator

Providing a forum for presentation of information and exchange of ideas regarding the management and protection of fish and wildlife resources throughout the nation but emphasis on the southeast.
Frequency: Oct/Nov
Founded in: 1947

10179 SFA's Legislative Summit
Snack Food Association
1600 Wilson Blvd
Suite 650
Arlington, VA 22209-2510

703-836-4500
800-628-1334; *Fax:* 703-836-8262
sfa@sfa.org; www.sfa.org

James A McCarthy, President/CEO

Discuss many of the most important legislative issues which will impact the snack food industry.
800 Members
Frequency: Annual/May
Founded in: 1937

10180 SNAXPO
Snack Food Association
1600 Wilson Blvd
Suite 650
Arlington, VA 22209-2510

703-836-4500
800-628-1334; *Fax:* 703-836-8262
sfa@sfa.org; www.sfa.org

James A McCarthy, President/CEO

The world's largest, most comprehensive trade show devoted exclusively to the international snack food industry. Owners, executives and buyers from every segment of the industry around the globe come together for this premier event.
800 Members
Frequency: Annual/March
Founded in: 1937

10181 SNAXPO: Snack Food Association
1600 Wilson Boulevard
Suite 650
Arlington, VA 22209-2510

703-836-4500
800-628-1334; *Fax:* 703-836-8262;
www.sfa.org

Judi Barth, VP Marketing
Ann Wilkes, VP Communications
2000 Attendees
Frequency: February/March
Founded in: 1938

10182 School Nutrition Association Annual National Conference
School Nutrition Association
120 Waterfront Street
Suite 300
National Harbor, MD 20745

301-686-3100
800-877-8822; *Fax:* 301-686-3115
servicecenter@schoolnutrition.org;
www.schoolnutrition.org

Helen Phillips, President
Sandy Ford, President-Elect
Leah Schmidt, VP
Beth Taylor, Secretary/Treasurer

Learn, grow and exchange ideas with others committed to the healthful feeding of our children. With over 400 exhibitors and more than 90 quality education sessions, ANC gives you the opportunity to learn about the top trends and issues in school nutrition.
Frequency: Annual/July

10183 Southern Convenience Store & Petroleum Show
GA Ass'n of Convenience Stores/Petroleum Retailers
168 North Johnston Street
Suite 209
Dallas, GA 30132-4744

770-736-9723
877-294-1885; *Fax:* 770-736-9725
jtudor@aol.com; www.gacs.com
Social Media: Facebook

Jim Tudor, President
Angela Holland, Vice President

Targeted to reach key individuals in the convenience store and petroleum industry from throughout the South. Attendees will include board members and key representatives from the Georgia Association of Convenience Stores and will be open to retailers from throughout the southern US.
2000 Attendees
Frequency: Annual/October

10184 Southwest Foodservice Exposition
Texas Restaurant Association
PO Box 1429
Austin, TX 78767

512-472-8990; *Fax:* 512-472-2777

31000 Attendees

10185 Special Event
Special Event Corporation
PO Box 8987
Malibu, CA 90265-8987

310-317-4522; *Fax:* 310-317-9644

4300 Attendees

10186 Sunbelt Agricultural Exposition
PO Box 28
Tifton, GA 31793-0028

229-985-1968; *Fax:* 229-387-7503

Dr. Edward White, Director

The latest agricultural technology in products and equipment plus harvesting and tillage demonstrations in the field. Largest farm show in North America. 4,000 booths.
Frequency: October

10187 Supermarket Industry Convention and Educational Exposition
Food Marketing Institute
2345 Crystal Drive
Suite 800
Arlington, VA 22202

202-452-8444; *Fax:* 202-429-4519;
www.fmi.org
Social Media: Facebook, Twitter, LinkedIn, YouTube

Brian Tully, Show Manager
Matt Olmsted, Consumer Goods Exhibiting
Allyson Samuel, Technolgy and Packaging Exhibits
Carrie Anderson, Attending

Features over 1,500 exhibitors, over 30 educational workshops and unique pavilions as well as the presentation of the Food Marketing Institute's annual state of the industry research. Attended by a worldwide audience of professionals with an interest in the food distribution industry from CEOs through store level management.
36000 Attendees
Frequency: Annual/May

10188 SupplySide East
Virgo Publishing LLC
3300 N Central Avenue
Suite 300
Phoenix, AZ 85012

480-990-1101; *Fax:* 480-675-8154
peggyj@vpico.com; www.supplysideshow.com
Social Media: Facebook, Twitter, LinkedIn

Tradeshow that brings global dietary supplement, food and personal care companies together with healthy and innovative ingredient suppliers. Meadowlands Exposition Center, Secaucus New Jersey. More than 340 booths.
Frequency: Annual/May

10189 SupplySide West
Virgo Publishing LLC
3300 N Central Avenue
Suite 300
Phoenix, AZ 85012

480-990-1101; *Fax:* 480-675-8154
peggyj@vpico.com; www.supplysideshow.com

Tradeshow that brings global dietary supplement, food and personal care companies together with healthy and innovative ingredient supplier. More than 1100 booths.
Frequency: Annual/October

10190 TFI Fertilizer Marketing & Business Meeting
Fertilizer Institute
425 Third Street, SW
Suite 950
Washington, DC 20024

202-962-0490; *Fax:* 202-962-0577
information@tfi.org; www.tfi.org
Social Media: Facebook, Twitter, LinkedIn

Ford West, President

Brings together members from each sector of the fertilizer industry for two days of networking and conducting business leading up the the spring planting season.
Frequency: Annual/February

10191 TFI World Fertilizer Conference
Fertilizer Institute
425 Third Street, SW
Suite 950
Washington, DC 20024

202-962-0490; *Fax:* 202-962-0577
information@tfi.org; www.tfi.org
Social Media: Facebook, Twitter, LinkedIn

Ford West, President

Providing two days of networking and conducting business with industry leaders. Agenda includes two breakfast sessions with high profile speakers focusing on the global challenges facing the fertilizer industry.
Frequency: Annual/September

10192 The NAFEM Show
NAFEM
161 N Clark Street
Suite 2020
Chicago, IL 60601

312-821-0201; *Fax:* 312-821-0202
info@nafem.org; www.nafem.org

Steven R. Follett, President
Thomas R. Campion, President-Elect
Michael L. Whiteley, Secretary/Treasurer
Deirdre Flynn, Executive Vice President

Attracts foodservice professionals and features exhibitors displaying products for food preparation, cooking, storage and table service. Connecting buyers and sellers of foodservice equipment and supplies, The NAFEM Show provides a showcase for the hottest and coolest products available and features education sessions and social events with big-name entertainment.
625 Members
Frequency: Biennial/February

10193 The NGA Show
National Grocers Association
1005 N Glebe Rd
Suite 250
Arlington, VA 22201-5758

703-516-0700; *Fax:* 703-516-0115
info@nationalgrocers.org;
www.nationalgrocers.org
Social Media: Facebook, Twitter, LinkedIn, YouTube

Peter J. Larkin, President & CEO
Charlie Bray, Executive VP & COO
Tom Wenning, Executive VP & General Counsel

Providing an unparalleled opportunity to network, learn, and advance business. Guaranted a convention experience that is informational, motivational, and enjoyable.
Frequency: Annual/February

10194 Top-to-Top Conference
Association of Sales & Marketing Companies
1010 Wisconsin Avenue NW
#900
Washington, DC 20007

202-337-9351; *Fax:* 202-337-4508
info@asmc.org

Mark Baum, President
Karen Connell, Executive VP
Rick Abraham, VP/COO Foodservice
Jamie DeSimone, Director Marketing/Member Services
Frequency: February

10195 Top2Top
Grocery Manufactures Association
1801-J York Road
Suite 384
Lutherville, MD 21093

410-715-4084
800-617-1170; *Fax:* 888-668-7496
info@fsmaonline.com; www.fsmaonline.com
Social Media: Facebook

Rick Abraham, President & CEO
Sharon Boyle, Vice President
Jessica Muffoletto, Manager, Membership & Meetings

Learn, share, and be inspired. Network with industry peers and hear from extraordinary speakers.
250 Members
Founded in: 1995

10196 Tortilla Industry Annual Convention and Trade Exposition
Tortilla Industry Association
1600 Wilson Blvd
Suite 650
Arlington, VA 22209

800-944-6099; *Fax:* 800-944-6177
info@tortilla-info.com; www.tortilla-info.com

Nathan W. Fisher, Chairman
Joseph F. Riley, Chairman-Elect
Nick Scheurer, 2nd Vice President
Sam Tamayo, Treasurer

A growing event for tortilla producers and suppliers that provides the only annual trade show featuring materials, equipment, and services exclusively for the Tortilla industry, plus business lectures to assist in improving your business and personal knowledge.
900 Attendees
Frequency: Annual/September

10197 Tree Fruit Expo
Western Agricultural Publishing Company

4974 E Clinton Way
Suite 123
Fresno, CA 93727-1520

559-261-0396; *Fax:* 559-252-7387

Phill Rhoads, Manager

Productions seminars, dessert contest, guest speakers, prizes and exhibits for tree fruit growers. Containing 80 booths and exhibits.

10198 **US Apple Association Annual Apple Crop Outlook & Marketing Conference**
8233 Old Courthouse Road
Suite 200
Vienna, VA 22182

703-442-8850; *Fax:* 703-790-0845
info@usapple.org; www.usapple.org
Social Media: Facebook, Twitter, YouTube

Provides up to the minute apple market analysis and premier networking opportunities.
300+ Attendees
Frequency: Annual/April

10199 **US Meat Export Federation**
1050 17th Street
Suite 2200
Denver, CO 80265-2077

303-623-6328; *Fax:* 303-623-0297;
www.usmef.org

Jackie Boubin, Director of Services
Phil Seng, President

A convention of meat packers, grain, cattle and hog producers, trade officials and agribusiness and a trade show offering exhibits of beef, pork, veal, lamb products and more for foreign buyers. Trade show in May, convention in November.
300 Attendees

10200 **USA Rice Millers' Association Convention**
USA Rice Millers Association/Federation
4301 N Fairfax Drive
Suite 425
Arlington, VA 22203-1616

703-226-2300; *Fax:* 703-236-2301
riceinfo@usarice.com;
www.usarice.com/industry/meetings/hotel_annual.html
Social Media: Facebook, Twitter, YouTube

Jeanette Davis, Convention Coordinator
Betsy Ward, President/CEO
Linda Sieh, Vice President Finance
Johnny Broussard, Legislative Affairs Director
Lauren Echols, Government Affairs Coordinator

Exhibits, seminars on the advances in products, technologies and services, keynote speakers from the industry. The convention is recognized as the annual gathering for the U.S. rice milling industry. It is an opportunity to strengthen business ties and make new connections.
Frequency: Annual/June
Founded in: 1900

10201 **Unified Wine and Grape Symposium**
PO Box 1855
Davis, CA 95617-1855

530-753-3142; *Fax:* 530-753-3318
info@unifiedsymposium.org
unifiedsymposium.org

Bill Mead, Event/Tradeshow Coordinator

One of the industry's premier gatherings, presents a vital platform to focus on the issues shaping today, while interfacing the topics and trends shaping the future of grapegrowing and winemaking.
Frequency: Annual/January

10202 **Unipro Food Service Companies Association**
Unipro Food Service
PO Box 724945
Atlanta, GA 31139-1945

770-952-0871; *Fax:* 770-952-0872

Donna Campbell, Show Manager
Roger Toomey, CEO

250 tables.
1.3M Attendees

10203 **United Produce Show**
United Fresh Fruit & Vegetable Association
1901 Pennsylvania Avenue NW
Suite 1100
Washington, DC 20006

202-303-3400; *Fax:* 202-303-3433
united@unitedfresh.org; www.uffva.org
Social Media: Facebook, Twitter, YouTube

Access to the best and newest products from the entire retail supply continuum, make new contacts, learn what your competition is bringing to the table and much more.
30M Attendees
Frequency: Annual/May

10204 **Upper Midwest Hospitality Restaurant & Lodging Show**
Corcoran Expositions
100 W. Monroe
Suite 1001
Chicago, IL 60603

312-541-0567; *Fax:* 312-541-0573;
www.corcexpo.com

Tom Corcoran, President
33000 Attendees
Founded in: 1990

10205 **Vinegar Institute Annual Meeting**
1100 Johnson Ferry Road
Suite 300
Atlanta, GA 30342

404-252-3663; *Fax:* 404-252-0774
vi@kellencompany.com;
www.versatilevinegar.org

Pamela A Chumley, President
Jeannie Milewski, Executive Director

Presentations regarding possible health claims for vinegar, an economic update and a world wine and grape supply update. Other topics include from green to greenwashing; how food companies are succeeding (and failing) at market sustainability and best practices in energy & carbon management. Also numerous networking opportunities available for all attendees.
Frequency: Annual/March

10206 **WFLO/IARW Annual Convention & Trade Show**
World Food Logistics Organization
1500 King Street
Suite 201
Alexandria, VA 22314

703-373-4300; *Fax:* 707-373-4301
mkalaski@iarw.org; www.wflo.org

Megan Kalaski, Trade Show Coordinator
Lorien Onderdonk, Member Services Coordinator

offers a singular opportunity to present product and service information to the largest concentration of public refrigerated warehouse executives in the world.
Frequency: Annual/April

10207 **WSWA Annual Convention**
Wine and Spirits Wholesalers of America
805 15th Street NW
Suite 430
Washington, DC 20005

202-719-9792; *Fax:* 202-789-2405
Kari.Mazanec@wswa.org; www.wswa.org

Rae Ann Bevington, Convention Manager
Kari Mazanec, Exhibit Manager
Juanita Duggan, CEO

Get the latest information for wholesale wine distributors, exhibits and speakers from the industry.
Frequency: April-May
Founded in: 1943

10208 **WSWA Convention & Exposition**
Wine and Spirits Wholesalers of America
805 15th Street NW
Suite 430
Washington, DC 20005

202-371-9792; *Fax:* 202-789-2405;
www.wswa.org

Robert Harmelin, Chairman
Charles Merinoff, Vice Chairman
Douglas Hertz, Senior Vice President
Alan Dreeben, Vice President
Brien Fox, Secretary

Where distributors seek out new and exciting beverage products for US consumers, meet with existing portfolio partners and look for services to enhance internal operations. Providing the opportunities needed to introduce new products or grow brands, products, or services in the US marketplace.
450 Members
Frequency: Annual/April
Founded in: 1943

10209 **WSWA Executive Committee Meeting**
Wine and Spirits Wholesalers of America
805 15th Street NW
Suite 430
Washington, DC 20005

202-371-9792; *Fax:* 202-789-2405;
www.wswa.org

Robert Harmelin, Chairman
Charles Merinoff, Vice Chairman
Douglas Hertz, Senior Vice President
Alan Dreeben, Vice President
Brien Fox, Secretary

The Executive Committee, Committee Chairs and Vice Chairs and past chairmen are invited to attend.
450 Members
Frequency: Annual/January
Founded in: 1943

10210 **Waldbaum International Food Nutrition Show**
80 Town Line Road
Rocky Hill, CT 06067-1249

860-529-1416; *Fax:* 860-721-6258

John Masterson, Manager

A wide variety of new and existing food products and services. 225 booths.
25M Attendees
Frequency: March

10211 **Walnut Council Annual Meeting**
Walnut Council
Wright Forestry Center
1011 N 725 West
West Lafayette, IN 47906-9431
765-583-3501; *Fax:* 765-583-3512
walnutcouncil@walnutcouncil.org;
www.walnutcouncil.org

Liz Jackson, Exhibits Coordinator

Exhibits of equipment, supplies and services for walnut growing.
Frequency: Annual/July

10212 **Washington Insight & Advocacy Conference**
International Foodservice Distributors Association
1410 Spring Hill Road
Suite 210
McLean, VA 22102-3035

703-532-9400; *Fax:* 703-538-4673;
www.ifdaonline.org

Mark Allen, President & CEO
Jonathan Eisen, Senior VP/ Government Relations

IFDA members from coast-to-coast converge on the capitol to gain insight from congressional leaders and federal regulators and let them know how their decisions affect the foodservice distribution idustry.
Frequency: Annual/April

10213 **West Coast Seafood Show**
Diversified Expositions
121 Free Street
Portland, ME 04112

207-842-5500; *Fax:* 207-842-5505
food@divcom.com;
www.westcoastseafood.com

Karen Butland, Show Manager
Brian Perkins, Executive Director
Frequency: November

10214 **Western Farm Show**
Southwestern Association
638 W 39th Street
Kansas City, MO 64111

816-561-5323
800-728-2272; *Fax:* 816-561-1991

Annual show of 700 manufacturers, suppliers and distributors of equipment, supplies and services relating to the agricultural industry.
35M Attendees
Frequency: February

10215 **Western Food Industry Exposition**
555 Capitol Mall
Suite 235
Sacramento, CA 95814-4557

Fax: 703-876-0904

Keith Biersner, Account Executive

Retailers from 13 western states and suppliers from around the world. Relevant education sessions, vibrant exhibits and excellent social events are all designed to create the best form to enhance your companies bottom line. 400 booths.
3500 Attendees
Frequency: October
Founded in: 1998

10216 **Western Food Service and Hospitality Expo**
California Restaurant Association
383 Main Avenue
PO Box 6059
Norwalk, CT 06851

203-840-5612
800-840-5612; *Fax:* 203-840-9612;
www.westernfoodexpo.com

Chris Tatulli, Sales Manager
Steve Kalman, Industry VP

Showcases food products, food service equipment and allied services for the restaurant, food service and hospitality industries, as well as gourmet and prepared foods. Located on the West Coast, the show alternates annually between the Moscone Center in San Francisco and the LA Convention Center.
20M Attendees
Frequency: August

10217 **Western Restaurant Show**
California Restaurant Association
1011 10th St
Sacramento, CA 95814-3501

916-447-5793; *Fax:* 213-384-1723

A trade show of food service equipment, supplies and services. 2,000 booths.
35M Attendees
Frequency: August

10218 **Wine and Spirits Wholesalers of America**
805 15th Street NW
Suite 430
Washington, DC 20005

202-371-9792; *Fax:* 202-789-2405
wswa@wswa.org; www.wswa.org

Craig Wolf, President/CEO
Megan McIntire, Director Convention/Meetings
Karen Gravois, VP Public Relations/Communications

Suppliers of alcoholic beverages from around the world. 300 booths plus educational sessions.
3M Attendees
Frequency: April

10219 **Wineries Unlimited**
Vineyard & Winery Management
3883 Airway Drive
Suite 250
Santa Rosa, CA 95403

707-577-7700; *Fax:* 707-577-7705;
www.wineriesunlimited.com
Social Media: Facebook, Twitter

The largest, longest running, and most powerful wine industry event in the eastern US.
2000 Attendees
Frequency: Annual/February

10220 **Winter State Policy Conference**
Wine and Spirits Wholesalers of America
805 15th Street NW
Suite 430
Washington, DC 20005

202-371-9792; *Fax:* 202-789-2405;
www.wswa.org

Robert Harmelin, Chairman
Charles Merinoff, Vice Chairman
Douglas Hertz, Senior Vice President
Alan Dreeben, Vice President
Brien Fox, Secretary

Provides an opportunity for wholesaler state association leaders to discuss the political and legal issues facing wholesalers across the country.
450 Members
Frequency: Annual/December
Founded in: 1943

10221 **Wisconsin Restaurant Expo**
Wisconsin Restaurant Association
2801 Fish Hatchery Road
Madison, WI 53703-3197

608-270-9950
800-589-3211; *Fax:* 608-270-9960
dfaris@wirestaurant.org;
www.wirestaurant.org

Dawn Renz-Faris, Exposition Director
Carrie Douglas, Executive Assistant
Gail Parr, Executive Vice President

Comprehensive foodservice trade show featuring hundreds of exhibits, free educational seminars and exciting floor show events.
10000 Attendees
Frequency: March
Founded in: 1933
Mailing list available for rent

10222 **World Conference & Exhibition on Oil Seed and Vegetable Oil Utilization**
American Oil Chemists Society
2710 S. Boulder
Urbana, IL 61802-6996

217-359-2344; *Fax:* 217-351-8091
general@aocs.org; www.aocs.org
Social Media: Facebook, Twitter

Sevim Erhan, Committee Chairperson

Attendees are interested in learning the latest information on currint and emerging technologies from all areas in oilseed and vegetable oil utilization.
Frequency: Annual/August

10223 **World Dairy Expo**
3310 Latham
Madison, WI 53713

608-224-6455; *Fax:* 608-224-0300
wde@wdexpo.com; www.worlddairyexpo.com

Tom McKittrick, Manager
Lisa Behnke, Marketing Manager
65M Attendees
Frequency: October, Annually
Founded in: 1966

10224 **World Pork Exposition**
National Pork Producers Council
PO Box 10383
Des Moines, IA 50306-9960

515-788-8012; *Fax:* 847-838-1941
wrigleyj@nppc.org; www.worldpork.org

John Wrigley, General Manager
Alice Vinsand, Trade Show Manager

More than 450 companies show the newest technology, information, products and services for pork producers. Activities include breed shows and sales, business district, environmental education center, pork product showcase, big grill, pork 101, educational seminars and activities.
40000 Attendees
Frequency: June

10225 **World Wine Market**
775 E Blithedale Avenue
#370
Mill Valley, CA 94941

415-383-1226; *Fax:* 415-383-0858
sclarke@world-wine-market.com;
www.world-wine-market.com

Stephanie Clarke, VP Sales/Marketing

10226 **World of Food and Fuel EXPO**
Tennessee Grocers Association
1838 Elm Hill Pike
Suite 136
Nashville, TN 37210-3726

615-889-0136
800-238-8742; *Fax:* 615-889-2877;
www.tngrocer.org

Jarron Springer, President
Cyndi Randle, Chairman
John Wampler, Treasurer
8000 Attendees
Frequency: April

10227 **Worldwide Food Expo**
Dairy and Food Industries Supply Association
1451 Dolley Madison Boulevard
Suite 101
McLean, VA 22101

703-761-2600; *Fax:* 703-761-4334;
www.worldwidefoodexpo.com

Trade show and education forum for the food, dairy, beverage and technologically related industries, featuring equipment, services and ingredients that highlight new development and

technologies in processing and packaging. 350,000 square feet.
Frequency: Annual/October

Directories & Databases

10228 ACFSA Directory
American Correctional Food Service Affiliates
210 N Glenoaks Blvd
Suite C
Burbank, CA 91502

818-843-6608; *Fax:* 818-843-7423;
www.acfsa.org

Jon Nichols, Executive Director

Directory of ACFSA members and the services provided by vender members.
Cost: $5.00
235 Pages
Frequency: Annually
Circulation: 1,500
Printed in 4 colors on glossy stock

10229 AGRICOLA
US National Agricultural Library
10301 Baltimore Ave
Room 13
Beltsville, MD 20705-2351

301-504-5755; *Fax:* 301-504-5675;
www.nal.usda.gov

Gary K McCone, Associate Director

A database containing more than 3.2 million citations to journal literature, government reports, proceedings, books, periodicals, theses, patents, audiovisuals, electronic information, and other materials related to agriculture and its allied sciences.

10230 ARI Network
330 E Kilbourn Ave
Suite 565
Milwaukee, WI 53202-3144

414-220-9100
800-558-9044; *Fax:* 414-283-4357;
www.aris-corporation.com

Lawrence Shindell, Owner
John Kermath, Director

Offers current information on agricultural business, financial and weather information as well as statistical information for farmers.

10231 Ag Ed Network
ARI Network Services
330 E Kilbourn Ave
Suite 565
Milwaukee, WI 53202-3144

414-220-9100
800-558-9044; *Fax:* 414-283-4357;
www.aris-corporation.com

Lawrence Shindell, Owner
John Kermath, Director

Offers access to more than 1,500 educational agriculture lessons covering farm business management and farm production.
Frequency: Full-text

10232 AgriMarketing Services Guide
Henderson Communications LLC
1422 Elbridge Payne Rd
Suite 250
Chesterfield, MO 63017-8544

636-728-1428; *Fax:* 636-777-4178;
www.agrimarketing.com

Lynn Henderson, Owner

AgriMarketing Services Guide is published each December and is commonly referred to as the Who's Who in the North American ag industry sector.
Frequency: Annual

10233 Agribusiness Worldwide International Buyer's Guide Issue
Keller International Publishing Corporation
150 Great Neck Rd
Great Neck, NY 11021-3309

516-829-9722; *Fax:* 516-829-9306;
www.supplychainbrain.com

Jerry Keller, President
Mary Chavez, Director of Sales

A list of companies that supply, manufacture or distribute agricultural products and services.
Cost: $42.00
Frequency: Annual

10234 Agricultural Research Institute: Membership Directory
Agricultural Research Institute
9650 Rockville Pike
Bethesda, MD 20814-3998

301-530-7122; *Fax:* 301-530-7007

Richard A Herrett, Executive Director

One hundred and twenty-five member institutions; also lists study panels and committees interested in environmental issues, pest control, agricultural meteorology, biotechnology, food irradiation, agricultural policy, research and development, food safety, technology transfer and remote sensing.
Cost: $50.00
Frequency: Annual

10235 Airline, Ship & Catering: Onboard Service Buyer's Guide & Directory
International Publishing Company of America
664 La Villa Dr
Miami Springs, FL 33166-6030

305-887-1700; *Fax:* 305-885-1923

Alexander Morton, Owner

Offers information on over 6,000 airlines, railroads, ship lines and terminal restaurants.
Cost: $125.00
Frequency: Annual
Circulation: 6,000

10236 Almanac of Food Regulations and Statistical Information
Edward E Judge & Sons
PO Box 866
Westminster, MD 21158-0866

410-876-2052
800-729-5517; *Fax:* 410-848-2034;
www.eejudge.com

Includes labeling law and FDA regulations, HACCP requirements for seafood, FDA current good manufacturing practice regulations, USDA canning regulations, frozen food handling code, FDA standards of identity, quality and fill of container, USDA quality grade standards, frozen fruit and vegetable pack statistics, agricultural statistics, and census of manufacturing.
Cost: $71.00
824 Pages
Frequency: Annual
Circulation: 3,000
ISBN: 1-880821-19-2
Founded in: 1916

10237 American Butter Institute: Membership Directory
American Butter Institute
2101 Wilson Boulevard
Suite 400
Arlington, VA 22201

703-243-5630; *Fax:* 703-841-9328;
www.butterinstitute.org

Cindy Cazallo, Editor

This directory offers a comprehensive list of over 35 processors, distributors and packagers of butter in the US and suppliers to the industry. Members only.
Cost: $250.00
25 Pages
Frequency: Annual

10238 American Fruit Grower
Meister Media Worldwide
37733 Euclid Ave
Willoughby, OH 44094-5992

440-942-2000
800-572-7740; *Fax:* 440-975-3447
jwmonahan@meistermedia.com;
www.meisternet.com

Gary Fitzgerald, President
Sue Stearns, Assistant Circulation Manager
JoAnne Mauer, Sales Assistant

Offers a list of manufacturers and distributors of equipment and supplies for the commercial fruit growing industry.
Cost: $19.95
66 Pages
Frequency: 10x
Circulation: 35,849
Founded in: 1880

10239 American Meat Science Association Directory of Members
American Meat Science Association
2441 Village Green Pl
Champaign, IL 61822-7676

217-356-5370
800-517-AMSA; *Fax:* 888-205-5834; *Fax:* 217-356-5370
information@meatscience.org;
www.meatscience.org

Thomas Powell, Executive Director
Randy Huffman, President-Elect
Kathy Ruff, Meetings & Member Services Director

Directory for American Meat Science members only.
Cost: $20.00
230 Pages
Frequency: Biennial

10240 American Red Angus: Breeders Directory
Red Angus Association of America
4201 N Interstate 35
Denton, TX 76207-3415

940-387-3502; *Fax:* 940-383-4036
info@redangus.org; www.redangus.org
Social Media: Facebook

Judy Edwards, Manager
Betty Grimshaw, Association Admin Director
Clint Berry, Commercial Marketing Director

This directory is a list of over 1,800 breeders of Red Angus cattle.
Frequency: Annual
Circulation: 8,000

10241 American Society of Consulting Arborists: Membership Directory
American Society of Consulting Arborists
15245 Shady Grove Road
Rockville, MD 20850-3222

301-947-0483

Beth Palys, Executive Director
Steven Geist, President

About 270 persons specializing in the growth and care of urban shade and ornamental trees; includes expert witnesses and monetary appraisals.
Frequency: Annual March

10242 American Spice Trade Association Membership Roster
American Spice Trade Association
2025 M St NW
Suite 800
Washington, DC 20036-2422
202-367-1127; *Fax:* 202-367-2127;
www.iamss.org
Cheryl Deem, Executive Director
Frequency: Annual

10243 Automatic Merchandiser Blue Book Buyer's Guide Issue
Cygnus Publishing
PO Box 803
Fort Atkinson, WI 53538-0803
920-000-1111
800-547-7377; *Fax:* 920-563-1699;
www.cygnusb2b.com
John French, CEO
Kathy Scott, Director of Public Relations
Paul Bonaiuto, CFO
Thousands of suppliers are profiled that offer products, services and equipment to the merchandise vending, food service and office coffee service industries.
Cost: $35.00
Frequency: Annual

10244 BEMA Equipment & Suppliers Datebase
BEMA
10740 Nall Avenue
Suite 230
Overland Park, KS 66211
913-338-1300; *Fax:* 913-338-1327
info@bema.org; www.bema.org
Find the baking industry's leading suppliers.
220 Pages
Founded in: 1918

10245 Bakery Materials and Methods
Elsevier Science
655 Avenue of the Americas
New York, NY 10010-5107
212-633-3800; *Fax:* 212-633-3850;
www.elsevier.com
Young Suk Chi, Chairman
Bill Godfrey, Chief Information Officer
David Clark, Senior Vice President
Cost: $41.50
Founded in: 1978

10246 Bakery Production and Marketing Buyers Guide Issue
Delta Communications
11617 W Bluemound Road
Wauwatosa, WI 53226
414-774-7270; *Fax:* 414-777-7277
delta@deltacommunications.com
Pat Reynolds, Editor
This publication offers a list of over 1,800 manufacturers of equipment, ingredients, and supplies for bakeries. Enteries offer company names, addresses, phones, faxes and name and title of contract.

10247 Bakery Production and Marketing Red Book Issue
Delta Communications
Ste 300
20900 Swenson Dr
Waukesha, WI 53186-4050
262-542-9111; *Fax:* 262-542-8820
delta@deltacommunications.com;
www.deltairaq.net
Offers a list of over 2,500 wholesale, multi-unit retail, grocery chain and co-op bakery companies and plants in the US and Canada that manufacture bread, cakes, cookies, crackers, pretzels, snack foods, and frozen bakery products.
Cost: $255.00
Frequency: Annual

10248 Baking & Snack Directory and Buyers Guide
Sosland Publishing Company
4800 Main St
Suite 100
Kansas City, MO 64112-2513
816-756-1000; *Fax:* 816-756-0494;
www.sosland.com
Wholesalers of bread and baked goods, as well as snacks and frozen dough are listed in this directory.
Cost: $205.00
Frequency: Annual
Circulation: 8,000

10249 Beef Sire Directory
American Breeders Service/Customer Service
PO Box 459
De Forest, WI 53532-0459
608-846-3721; *Fax:* 608-846-6392
custserv_dept@absglobal.com;
www.absglobal.com
Ian Biggs, CEO
A directory listing beef cattle associations in the US and Canada.
Frequency: Annual

10250 Beverage Digest Fact Book
Beverage Digest
PO Box 621
Bedford Hills, NY 10507-0621
914-244-0700; *Fax:* 914-244-0774
order@beverage-digest.com;
www.beverage-digest.com
John Sicher, Owner
This book is a complete portrait of the global non-alcoholic beverage business.

10251 Beverage Digest Soft Drink Atlas
Beverage Digest
PO Box 621
Bedford Hills, NY 10507-0621
914-244-0700; *Fax:* 914-244-0774
order@beverage-digest.com;
www.beverage-digest.com
John Sicher, Owner
Book of US maps related to soft drink bottler territories. This book offers a geographic portrait of the US carbonated beverage bottling business.

10252 Beverage Marketing Directory
Beverage Marketing Corporation
2670 Commercial Ave
Mingo Junction, OH 43938-1613
740-598-4133
800-332-6222; *Fax:* 740-598-3977;
www.beveragemarketing.com
Andrew Standardi III, Director of Operations
Kathy Smurthwaite, Editor
Publication is available in Print Copy (Price-$1,465), PDF Format (Price-$1,465), CD-ROM Format (For pricing, call number listed for details or visit website), and Online.
1196 Pages

10253 Biological & Agricultural Index
HW Wilson Company
950 Dr Martin L King Jr Blvd
Bronx, NY 10452-4297
718-588-8405
800-367-6770; *Fax:* 718-590-1617;
www.hwwilson.com
Harold Regan, CEO
Kathleen McEvoy, Director of Public Relations
Provides fast access to core literature. In addition to citations to research and feature articles, users finding indexing of reports of symposia and conferences, and citations to current book reviews. Available on Web and disc.

10254 Blue Book Buyer's Guide
Food Processing Machinery Association
1451 Dolley Madison Blvd
Suite 101
McLean, VA 22101-3850
703-761-2600; *Fax:* 703-761-4334
info@fpsa.org; www.fpsa.org
A buyers guide offering information on over 500 member food and beverage industry firms. Entries are cross-referenced with both a product and commodity locator.
Cost: $50.00
200 Pages
Circulation: 30,000

10255 Blue Book: Fruit and Vegetable Credit and Marketing Service
Produce Reporter Company
845 E Geneva Rd
Carol Stream, IL 60188-3520
630-668-3500; *Fax:* 630-668-0303;
www.bluebookprco.com
C James Carr, President
A directory offering information on over 15,000 produce growers, wholesalers, shippers and retailers in the US.
Cost: $575.00
1275 Pages
Frequency: Semiannual
Founded in: 1901

10256 Bottled Water Market
MarketResearch.com
641 Avenue of the Americas
3rd Floor
New York, NY 10011
212-807-2629
800-298-6699; *Fax:* 212-807-2676
The report provides descriptions and coverage of market size and growth, market comppsition, leading marketers, the competitive situation, new product trends, advertising and promotion, and more.
Cost: $2750.00
139 Pages

10257 Brand Directory
Vance Publishing
10901 W 84th Ter
Suite 200
Lenexa, KS 66214-1631
913-438-5721
800-255-5113; *Fax:* 913-438-0697
info@vancepublishing.com;
www.vancepublishing.com
Cliff Becker, Vice President, Director
Dan Woods, Chief Financial Officer
Lori Eppel, Chief Financial Officer
A composite of major fresh fruit and vegetable brands and suppliers. It is divided into three sections and contains 66 commodities.
Cost: $10.00

10258 Brewers Digest: Buyers Guide and Brewery Directory
Ammark Publishing
4049 W Peterson Avenue
Chicago, IL 60646-6001

Lists all breweries in the Western Hemisphere, suppliers, associations and importers.
Cost: $30.00
Frequency: Annual
Circulation: 3,000

10259 Brewers Resource Directory
Brewers Association
736 Pearl Street
Boulder, CO 80302

303-447-0816
888-822-6273; *Fax:* 303-447-2825;
www.beertown.org
Social Media: Facebook, Twitter

Various categories of listees are included that have a direct relation to the beer and liquor industry.
Mailing list available for rent

10260 Brown Swiss Cattle Breeders' Association Directory
Brown Swiss Cattle Breeders' Association
800 Pleasant St
Beloit, WI 53511-5456

608-365-4474; *Fax:* 608-365-5577
info@brownswissusa.com;
www.brownswissusa.com

Roger Neitzel, Manager
David Kendall, Secretary

10261 CID Service
US Department of Agriculture
200 Independence Ave SW
Washington, DC 20201-0007

202-690-7650

This database contains 467 categories of information prepared by the US Department of Agriculture and its agencies.
Frequency: Full-text

10262 CRC Press
2000 NW Corporate Boulevard
Boca Raton, FL 33431

561-994-0555
800-272-7737; *Fax:* 561-998-0876
techsupport@crcpress.com; www.crcpress.com

Eleanor Riemer, Publisher
Emmett Dages, CEO

Publisher in science, medicine, environmental science, forensic, engineering, business, technology, mathematics, and statistics. Our food science and nutrition books and our journal, Critical Reviews in Food and Nutrition, are well established and respected publications in the food science industry.

10263 CRIS/USDA Database
Current Research Information System
1400 Independence Avenue SW
Suite 2270
Washington, DC 20250

202-690-0119; *Fax:* 202-690-0634
cris@csrees.usda.gov
cris.csrees.usda.gov

Ellen A Terpstra, CEO
Don Tilmon, Director

Offers over 35,000 ongoing and recently completed agricultural, food and nutrition and forestry research projects sponsored by the US Department of Agriculture.

10264 California League of Food Processors Annual Directory of Members
980 Ninth Street
Sacremento, CA 95814

916-444-9260; *Fax:* 916-444-2746;
www.clfp.com

Robert Graf, President/CEO
Ed Yates, Senior VP
Nora Basrai, Meetings/Members Services
Rob Neenan, Senior Vice President
Amy Alcorn, Marketing Manager

Contains listings of all members, including plant locations and products produced. Over 800 industry leaders are listed.
200 Pages
Founded in: 1905

10265 Candy Marketer: Candy, Snack and Tobacco Buyers' Guide
Stagnito Communications
155 Pfingster Road
Suite 205
Deerfield, IL 60015

847-205-5660; *Fax:* 847-205-5680

Linda Stagnito, President

A publication that includes a list of suppliers to the confectionery, snack and tobacco products industries. Entries include company names, addresses, key personnel, warehouse locations and firms represented.
Cost: $25.00
Frequency: Annual

10266 Chain Restaurant Operators Directory
Chain Store Guide
3922 Coconut Palm Dr
Suite 300
Tampa, FL 33619-1389

813-627-6700
800-972-9202; *Fax:* 813-627-7094
info@csgis.com; www.csgis.com

Mike Jarvis, Publisher
Chris Leedy, Advertising Sales

Discover more than 5,600 listings and more than 26,000 unique personnel within the Restaurant Chain, Foodservice Management, and Hotel/Motel Operator markets in the U.S. and Canada. Each company must have at least $1 million in annual sales either system wide or industry and have two or more units/accounts.
Cost: $335.00
Frequency: Annual

10267 Cheese Market News: Annual
Quarne Publishing
PO 628254
Middleton, WI 53562

608-831-6002; *Fax:* 608-831-1004
squarne@cheesemarketnews.com;
www.cheesemarketnews.com

Susan Quarne, Publisher

Comprehensive listings include the companies that manufacture the latest styles and varieties of cheese as well as the industry's key suppliers of cheese equipment, packaging equipment, materials and supplies and services.
Cost: $30.00
Frequency: Annual
Circulation: 3,000

10268 Citrus & Vegetable Magazine: Farm Equipment Directory Issue
Vance Publishing
10901 W 84th Ter
Suite 200
Lenexa, KS 66214-1631

913-438-5721; *Fax:* 913-438-0697
info@vancepublishing.com;
www.vancepublishing.com

Cliff Becker, Vice President, Director
Lori Eppel, Chief Financial Officer

Offers information on a list of manufacturers of produce and citrus growing, handling, picking and packaging equipment.
Cost: $25.00
48 Pages
Frequency: Annual
Circulation: 12,000
ISSN: 0009-7586
Founded in: 1938

10269 Coffee Anyone???
9616 Thunderbird Drive
Suite 215
San Ramon, CA 94583

925-829-4022
800-347-9687; *Fax:* 925-829-4025
coffee@coffee-anyone.com
http://www.coffeeanyone.com

This database contains descriptions of gourmet, regular, decaffenated and flavored coffees, including a chart summarizing the strength and taste of each coffee.

10270 Coffee, Sugar and Cocoa Exchange Guide
Commerce Clearing House
2700 Lake Cook Rd
Riverwoods, IL 60015-3867

847-940-4600; *Fax:* 847-779-1535
mediahelp@cch.com; www.cch.com

Mike Sabbatis, President

Offers information on member and member organizations of the Exchange.
Cost: $240.00
170 Pages
Frequency: Monthly

10271 Commercial Food Equipment Service Association Directory
Commercial Food Equipment Service Association
2216 W Meadowview Road
Suite 100
Greensboro, NC 27407

336-346-4700; *Fax:* 336-346-4745
cstrickland@cfesa.com; www.cfesa.com

Carla Strickland, Executive Director
Lauri Smith, Treasurer
Wayne Stoutner, Treasurer
David Hahn, Secretary

Independent food service companies that repair commercial food equipment.
Frequency: Annual

10272 Complete Directory of Concessions & Equipment
Sutton Family Communications & Publishing Company
920 State Route 54 East
Elmitch, KY 42343

270-276-9500
jlsutton@apex.net

Theresa Sutton, Editor
Lee Sutton, General Manager

Printout from database of wholesalers, manufacturers, distributors, importers and close-out houses; updated daily to guarantee the most current and up-to-date sources available.
Cost: $27.90
100+ Pages

10273 Complete Directory of Food Products
Sutton Family Communications & Publishing Company
920 State Route 54 East
Elmitch, KY 42343
270-276-9500
jlsutton@apex.net
Theresa Sutton, Editor
Lee Sutton, General Manager
Printout from database of wholesalers, manufacturers, distributors, importers and close-out houses. Database is updated daily to guarantee the most current and up-to-date sources available.
Cost: $27.90
100+ Pages

10274 Consumer's Guide to Fruits & Vegetables & Other Farm Fresh Products
Missouri Cooperative Extension Service
PO Box 29
Jefferson City, MO 65102-0029
573-681-5301; *Fax:* 573-635-2314
David N Sasseville, Editor
A directory covering over 400 fruit and vegetable farm markets in Missouri.
124 Pages
Frequency: Annual

10275 Contemporary World Issues: Agricultural Crisis in America
ABC-CLIO
PO Box 1911
Santa Barbara, CA 93116-1911
805-705-9339
800-422-2546; *Fax:* 805-685-9685
Barbara McEwan, Editor
List of agencies and organizations in the US concerned with agricultural issues.
Cost: $39.50

10276 Convenience Store Decisions Sales Tracking Study
Harbor Communications
19111 Detroit Road
Suite 201
Rocky River, OH 44116
440-250-1583; *Fax:* 440-333-1892;
www.csdecisions.com
Joseph Howton, Executive VP/COO
Survey of convenience store chain buyers that tracks the effectiveness of supplier promotional programs. It reports on how manufacturers call on retail chains and how those chains are responding to suppliers' merchandising efforts.
Frequency: Annual

10277 Cookies Market
MarketResearch.com
641 Avenue of the Americas
3rd Floor
New York, NY 10011
212-807-2629
800-298-6699; *Fax:* 212-807-2676
This report uncovers trends in its in-depth investigation of US retail sales of packaged and fresh-baked cookies. The analysis covers packaged cookie retail sales by distribution channel, marketer, and product line. The leading marketers are profiled in order to review growth-and-profit-oriented strategies. The data information is analyzed in order for users to uncover growing product lines, target key demographics, pinpoint distribution channel sales opportunities, and profitable strategies.
Cost: $2250.00
169 Pages

10278 Corn Annual
Corn Refiners Association
1701 Pennsylvania Ave NW
Suite 950
Washington, DC 20006-5806
202-331-1634; *Fax:* 202-331-2054;
www.corn.org
Report featuring articles on the state of the industry. Includes statistical report on corn shipments, supply and consumption in the US and abroad.
Frequency: Annually
Circulation: 8,000

10279 Crop Protection Reference
C&P Press
565 5th Ave
5th Floor
New York, NY 10017-2413
212-587-8620; *Fax:* 646-733-6010;
www.pharmpress.com
A single comprehensive source of up-to-date label information of crop protection products marketed in the US by basic manufacturers and formulators. Extensive product indexing helps to locate products by brand name, manufacturer, crop site, mode of action, disease, insect, week, product category, common name and tank mix.
Cost: $170.00
Frequency: Annual

10280 Culinary Collection Directory
International Association/Culinary Professionals
304 W Liberty Street
Suite 201
Louisville, KY 40202
502-587-7953
800-928-4227; *Fax:* 502-589-3602
info@iacp.com; www.iacp.com
Kerry Edwards, Sr Member Services Representative
Trina Gribbins, Manager
Teachers, cooking school owners, caterers, writers, chefs, media cooking personalities, editors, publishers, food stylists, food photographers, restauranteurs, leaders of major food corporations and vintners. Literally a who's who of the food world.

10281 Dairy Foods Market Guide
Delta Communications
455 N Cityfront Plaza Drive
Chicago, IL 60611-5503
312-836-2000; *Fax:* 312-222-2026
A guide including a list of 1,600 manufacturers of dairy processing equipment and over 900 distributors of dairy processing equipment.
Cost: $99.00
Frequency: Annual

10282 Developing Successful New Products for Foodservice Markets
International Food Service Manufacturers
180 North Stetson Avenue
Suite 4400
Chicago, IL 60601-6766
312-540-4400; *Fax:* 312-540-4401
ifma@ifmaworld.com; www.ifmaworld.com
Social Media: Facebook, LinkedIn, YouTube
Larry Oberkfell, President & CEO
Jennifer Tarulis, CFO
Michael Hickey, Chairman
Mark Bendix, 1st Vice Chairman
Loren Kimura, Treasurer
Handbook on new product development offers sound advice on the critical success factors confronting new product managers. Up-to-date information on new products and practices and an expanded section on market research.
Cost: $ 495.00
Frequency: Annual

10283 Directory & Products Guide
Vineyard & Winery Services
PO Box 2358
Windsor, CA 95492
707-836-6820
800-535-5670; *Fax:* 707-836-6825
vwm-online.com
Jennifer Merietti, Sales/Marketing Manager
Dennis Black, General Manager
Suzanne Webb, Marketing Director
A must have reference book that belongs on the desk of every wine professional. Whether it's tracking down a particular vendor, shopping for the best deal on oak barrels or searching for out-of-state winery contacts, the DPG is a powerhouse of information. Over 2,300 supplier listings and 2,700 winery/vineyard listings, it is a reliable resource that saves time and money.
Cost: $95.00
450+ Pages
Frequency: Annually

10284 Directory of AFFI Member Companies
American Frozen Food Institute
2000 Corporate Ridge
Suite 1000
McLean, VA 22102-7862
703-821-0770; *Fax:* 703-821-1350
info@affi.com; www.knowitsyogurt.com
Robert L Garfield, President
Jason Bassett, Director Legislative Affairs
Chuck Fuqua, VP Communications
Cost: $100.00
Frequency: Annual
Circulation: 5000

10285 Directory of American Agriculture
Agricultural Resources & Communications
301 Broadway
Belvue, KS 66407
785-456-9705; *Fax:* 785-456-1654
chris@agresources.com; www.agresources.com
Christina Wilson, President
This directory lists over 7,000 state and national associations involved in providing products and services related to food and fiber industries, in 27 categories. There are categorical indexes as well. Includes guide to Washington, DC offices, USDA listings, and guide to ag commodity commissions. Available on CD for $99.
Cost: $64.95
350 Pages
ISSN: 0897-1919
Founded in: 1988
Printed in on matte stock

10286 Directory of Convenience Stores
Trade Dimensions
45 Danbury Rd
Wilton, CT 06897-4445
203-563-3000; *Fax:* 860-563-3131;
www.tradedimensions.com
Jennifer Gillbert, Editor
Lynda Guticulez, Managing Editor
The directory comprises nearly 1,500 detailed profiles on the companies you need to do business with. Extensive dependable information on the grocery industry's most volatile segment.
Cost: $245.00
Frequency: Annual

10287 Directory of Custom Food Processors and Formulators
Delphi Marketing Services

400 E 89th Street
Apartment 2J
New York, NY 10128-6728

Covers formulators and processors of custom food products.
Cost: $260.00
Frequency: Annual

10288 **Directory of State Departments of Agriculture**
US Department of Agriculture
200 Independence Ave SW
Room 3964
Washington, DC 20201-0007

202-690-7650; www.usda.gov

Chris Smith, Chief Information Officer
Matt Paul, Director of Communications
Ramona Romero, General Counsel

Offer valuable information on all the state departments of agriculture, including their officials.
73 Pages
Frequency: Biennial

10289 **Directory of the Canning, Freezing, Preserving Industries**
Edward E Judge & Sons
PO Box 866
Westminster, MD 21158-0866

410-876-2052; *Fax:* 410-848-2034; www.eejudge.com

Daniel P Judge, Publisher

This directory offers extensive company profiles including over 10,000 managers, over 3,000 North American Food plants that are involved in canning, freezing and preserving fruits, vegetables, dinners, specialties and more. Published in standard edition, 768 pages, and special deluxe edition 1,408 pages.
Cost: $175.00
768 Pages
Frequency: Biennial
ISBN: 1-880821-20-6
Founded in: 1966

10290 **Diversified Business Communications**
PO Box 7437
Portland, ME 04112-7437

207-842-5600; *Fax:* 207-842-5503; www.divbusiness.com

Nancy Hasselback, CEO
Nancy Gelette, VP Operations

A producer of international trade expositions for the seafood and commercial marine industries.

10291 **EMDA Membership Directory**
Equipment Marketing & Distribution Association
PO Box 1347
Iowa City, IA 52244-1347

319-354-5156; *Fax:* 319-354-5157
pat@emda.net; www.emda.net

Patricia A Collins, Executive VP

Annual directory of Association members, includes address, phone, fax, web, e-mail, territory covered (with map) product descriptions, key personnel and a descriptive paragraph.
Cost: $50.00

10292 **Electronic Pesticide Reference: EPR II**
C&P Press
New York, NY 10001

212-326-6760; *Fax:* 646-733-6010; www.pharmpress.com

Complete electronic reference to our 1,500 crop protection products; a full range of product information: full text labels and supplemental labels, full text MSDS's, product summaries, list of labeled tank mixes, worker protection information, DOT shipping information, SARA Title III reporting information. Search by brand name, manufacturer, common name crop, plant, site, weed, disease, insect plus much more. All versions of EPR II are provided on CD-ROM for windows.

10293 **Essential Rendering**
National Renderers Association
801 N Fairfax St
Suite 205
Alexandria, VA 22314-1776

703-683-0155; *Fax:* 703-683-2626; www.nationalrenderers.org

Thomas M Cook, President

An in-depth guide that covers the various aspects of rendering.
Frequency: Monthly

10294 **Feed Additive Compendium**
The Miller Publishing Company
12400 Whitewater Dr
Suite 160
Hopkins, MN 55343-4590

952-931-0211; *Fax:* 952-938-1832; www.feedcompendium.com

Sarah Muirhead, Publisher

Provides the latest information on which medicated additives can be used at what inclusion levels for what puposes. Also provides information on regulation, compliance and quality control, product specimen labels, and a directory of state and FDA contacts.
Cost: $52.00
Frequency: Weekly
Founded in: 1931

10295 **Food & Beverage Marketplace Directory**
Grey House Publishing
4919 Route 22
PO Box 56
Amenia, NY 12501

518-789-8700
800-562-2139; *Fax:* 845-373-6390
books@greyhouse.com; www.greyhouse.com
Social Media: Facebook, Twitter

Richard Gottlieb, President
Leslie Mackenzie, Publisher

A three-volume set that is the most comprehensive resource in the food and beverage industry. Available in print, a subscription-based online database, as well as a mailing list and database formats.
Cost: $595.00
2000 Pages
Frequency: Annual

10296 **Food & Beverage Marketplace: Online Database**
Grey House Publishing
4919 Route 22
PO Box 56
Amenia, NY 12501

518-789-8700
800-562-2139; *Fax:* 845-373-6390
gold@greyhouse.com
http://gold.greyhouse.com
Social Media: Facebook, Twitter

Richard Gottlieb, President
Leslie Mackenzie, Publisher

This complete updated Food & Beverage Market Place: Online Database is the go-to source for the food and beverage industry. Anyone involved in the food and beverage industry needs this 'industry bible' and the important contacts to develop critical research data that can make for successful business growth.
Frequency: Annual
Founded in: 1981

10297 **Food Businesses: Snack Shops, Specialty Food Restaurants & Other Ideas**
Prosperity & Profits Unlimited
PO Box 416
Denver, CO 80201

303-573-5564

A Doyle, Editor

Ideas and possibilities for food businesses, snack shops, restaurants.
Cost: $29.95
82 Pages
Circulation: 8000
ISBN: 0-911569-69-3
Founded in: 1990
Printed in on matte stock

10298 **Food Channel Database**
Noble Communications
500 N Michigan Avenue
Chicago, IL 60611-3764

312-670-4470; *Fax:* 312-670-7410

This database reports industry news and developments of interest to decision-makers in food processing, grocery, and c-store retailing distribution.

10299 **Food Engineering Directory**
Business News Publishing
3817 Timothy Lane
Bethlehem, PA 18020

610-317-6180; *Fax:* 610-317-0378

George Misko

Hardbound reference book listing of all food and beverage companies with 20 or more employees throughout the US.
Cost: $395.00

10300 **Food Master**
BNP Media
45 Beacon St
Sommerville, MA 02143

617-660-1322; www.foodmasterinc.com

Bob Iannaccone, Manager
Founded in: 1947

10301 **Food Processing Guide & Directory**
555 W Pierce Road
Suite 301
Itasca, IL 60143

773-252-7891; *Fax:* 630-467-1108

Lily Modjeski, Sales Manager

Presents advertising opportunities that will generate quality sales leads, incerase market share, identify market opportunities and increase exposure through our website.
Frequency: Annual

10302 **Food Production Management: Advertisers Buyers Guide Issue**
CTI Publications
2823 Benson Mill Rd
Sparks Glencoe, MD 21152-9575
410-308-2080; *Fax:* 410-308-2079; www.ctipubs.com

W Randall Gerstmyer, Publisher
Cost: $15.00
48 Pages
Frequency: Annual
Circulation: 5,000
ISSN: 0191-6181
Founded in: 1878

10303 **Food Service Industry**
MarketResearch.com
641 Avenue of the Americas
3rd Floor
New York, NY 10011

212-807-2629
800-298-6699; *Fax:* 212-807-2676

The report analyzes sales and profit trends of full-service restaurants, limited-service restaurants, cafeterias, snack bars, in-plant contractors, caterers, mobile food services and drinking places.
Cost: $2250.00
240 Pages

10304 **Food and Agricultural Export Directory**
US Department of Agriculture
PO Box 2022
Washington, DC 20250-0001

202-690-7650; *Fax:* 202-512-2250;
www.access.gpo.gov

Offers valuable information on federal and state agencies, trade associations and others willing to assist the US firms that wish to export food and agricultural products overseas.
100 Pages
Frequency: Annual

10305 **Food, Beverages & Tobacco in US Industrial Outlook**
Superintendent of Documents
US Government Printing Office
Washington, DC 20402-0001

Fax: 202-512-2250

Contains industry reviews and forecasts; coverage includes bakery products.
Cost: $34.00
Frequency: Annual

10306 **Food, Hunger, Agribusiness: A Directory of Resources**
Third World Resources
218 E 21st Street
Oakland, CA 94606

510-533-7583; *Fax:* 510-533-0923

Offers information on organizations and publishers of books and other materials on food, hunger and agribusiness overseas.
Cost: $12.95
160 Pages

10307 **FoodService Distributors Database**
Chain Store Guide
3922 Coconut Palm Dr
Suite 300
Tampa, FL 33619-1389

813-627-6700
800-778-9794; *Fax:* 813-627-7094
info@csgis.com; www.csgis.com

Mike Jarvis, Publisher
Shami Choon, Manager

Over 4,900 distributors of food, equipment and supplies to restaurants and institutions are reviewed in this directory for the food service industry. The names of more than 23,000 key executives are included, along with each company's distribution centers.
Cost: $335.00
800 Pages

10308 **Foods ADLIBRA**
Foods ADLIBRA Publications
9000 Plymouth Avenue N
Minneapolis, MN 55427-3870

763-764-4759; *Fax:* 763-764-3166

Judith O'Connell, Editor

This database offers over 287,000 citations, with abstracts to journal literature on research and development in food technology and packaging. Seafood, food service, snacks and beverage monthly current awareness are also available.
Cost: $200.00
ISSN: 0146-9304

10309 **Foodservice Yearbook International/Global Foodservice**
150 Great Neck Road
Great Neck, NY 11021

516-829-9210; *Fax:* 516-829-5414

10310 **Foreign Countries and Plants Certified to Export Meat and Poultry to the US**
US Department of Agriculture
Food Safety & Inspection Services
Washington, DC 20250-0001

202-690-7650
800-535-4555

A comprehensive list of over 1,000 meat and poultry plants in foreign countries.
150 Pages
Frequency: Annual

10311 **Fortified Foods Market**
MarketResearch.com
641 Avenue of the Americas
3rd Floor
New York, NY 10011

212-807-2629
800-298-6699; *Fax:* 212-807-2676

This new study examines the regulatory environment, analyzes the growth and product trends shaping the fortified foods market and inspects the changing retail picture. It also unveils the marketing and promotional strategies of major players such as Kellogg's, General Mills, PepsiCo, Coca-Cola, Novartis, Heinz and many others. Finally, the study takes a look at differences and commonalities among consumers of fortified cereals, breads, juice drinks, baby foods and snacks.
Cost: $2750.00
234 Pages

10312 **Frozen Dinners and Entrees**
Leading Edge Reports/Industry Reports
2171 Jericho Turnpike
Suite 200
Commack, NY 11725-2937

631-462-5454; *Fax:* 631-462-1842
bta@li.net; www.businesstrendanalysts.com

Charles J Ritchie, Executive VP
Donna Priani, Marketing Director
Linda Sherman, Production Manager
Jennifer Wichert, Research Director

A product-by-product analysis of the markets for frozen dinners and entrees, including traditional as well as low-calorie and health oriented products.
Cost: $1995.00
170 Pages
Founded in: 1996

10313 **Getaways for Gourmets in the Northeast**
Wood Pond Press
365 Ridgewood Rd
West Hartford, CT 06107-3517

860-521-0389; *Fax:* 860-313-0185;
www.green-cuisine.com

Richard M Woodworth, Owner

Directory of services and supplies to the industry.
Cost: $14.95
514 Pages

10314 **Gold Book: AAMP**
American Association of Meat Processors
1 Meating Pl
Elizabethtown, PA 17022-2883

717-367-1168; *Fax:* 717-367-9096
aamp@aamp.com; www.aamp.com

Jay Wenther, Executive Director
Daniel W Flier, First VP
Jon Frohling, Second VP

Consists of AAMP members, including: honorary members, associates, operators/wholesalers, home food service companies, suppliers, distributors, allied and affiliated state/regional/provincial associations. A powerful source for meat business buyers seeking products/services.
Cost: $300.00
170 Pages
Frequency: Every 2 Years
Circulation: 2,000

10315 **Grain & Milling Annual**
Sosland Publishing Company
4801 Main St
Suite 100
Kansas City, MO 64112-2513

816-756-1000; *Fax:* 816-756-0494;
www.sosland.com

Offers a list of milling companies, mills, grain companies and cooperatives.
Cost: $100.00
Frequency: Annual
Circulation: 6,000

10316 **Grain Journal**
Country Journal Publishing Company
2490 N Water Street
Decatur, IL 62526-4251

217-877-9660
800-728-7511; *Fax:* 217-877-6647
webmaster@grainnet.com; www.grainnet.com

Mark Avery, Publisher
Ed Zdrojewski, Editor
Deb Coontz, Advertising Sales
Jeff Miller, Advertising Sales

Provides a list of over 700 equipment manufacturers, suppliers and system designers, as well as offering useful information on governmental agencies relevant to the grain industry.
Cost: $40.00
254 Pages
Frequency: Bi-Monthly
Circulation: 13,000
ISSN: 0274-7138
Founded in: 1972
Mailing list available for rent: 10,000 names at $600 per M
Printed in 4 colors on glossy stock

10317 **Great Lakes Vegetable Growers News**
PO Box 128
Sparta, MI 49345-0128

616-887-9008; *Fax:* 616-887-2666

Barry Brand, Editor

10318 **Guernsey Breeders' Journal: Convention Directory Issue**
Purebred Publishing Inc
7616 Slate Ridge Blvd
Reynoldsburg, OH 43068-3126

614-575-4620; *Fax:* 614-864-5614
sjohnson@usguernsey.com;
www.usguernsey.com

Seth Johnson, Manager
Dale Jensen, President
Tom Ripley, VP

A convention directory offering a list of officers and national members of the American Guernsey Cattle Association.
Cost: $15.00
Frequency: Annual

10319 Guide to Poultry Associations
Poultry & Egg News
PO Box 1338
Gainesville, GA 30503-1338

770-536-2476; *Fax:* 770-532-4894

Randall Smalladod, Publisher
Chris Hill, Editor

This directory offers information on national, regional and state poultry associations.
Cost: $25.00
24 Pages
Frequency: Annual
Circulation: 11,500

10320 Health and Natural Foods Market
MarketResearch.com
641 Avenue of the Americas
3rd Floor
New York, NY 10011

212-807-2629
800-298-6699; *Fax:* 212-807-2676

The report covers six product categories: packaged groceries, bulk groceries, frozen, refrigerated, produce and other/miscellaneous. The major players in the market are profiled, including Gardenburger, Hain Food Group, Horizon Organic Dairy, Small Planet Foods and others. The report details which types of new products have been recently introduced and reports on consumer attitudes and behavior.
Cost: $2750.00
289 Pages

10321 Health and Natural Foods Market: Past Performance, Current Trends & More
Business Trend Analysts/Industry Reports
2171 Jericho Tpke
Suite 200
Commack, NY 11725-2937

631-462-5454; *Fax:* 631-462-1842;
www.businesstrendanalysts.com

Charles J Ritchie, Executive VP
Vincent Seeno, Editor
Donna Priani, General Manager
Linda Holm, Production Manager

A statistical summary and analysis offering historical, current and projected sales data for the natural foods market.
Cost: $2195.00
335 Pages
Founded in: 1986

10322 Herbal Green Pages
Herb Growing and Marketing Network
PO Box 245
Silver Spring, PA 17575-0245

Fax: 717-393-9261
herbworld@aol.com; www.herbnet.com

Maureen Rogers, Editor

This annual guide offers information on 5,000 companies involved in herbal marketing and growing.
Cost: $25.00
Frequency: Annual
Printed in one color on matte stock

10323 High Volume Independent Restaurants Database
Chain Store Guide
3922 Coconut Palm Dr
Suite 300
Tampa, FL 33619-1389

813-627-6700
800-778-9794; *Fax:* 813-627-7094
info@csgis.com; www.csgis.com

Mike Jarvis, Publisher
Shami Choon, Manager

Covers this growing niche through its nearly 5,900 listings featuring casual dining, family restaurants and fine dining establishments. Plus, access to over 15,000 key personnel names puts you in contact with key decision makers.
Cost: $335.00
1,000 Pages
Frequency: Annual

10324 Hort Expo Northwest
Mt Adams Publishing and Design
14161 Fort Road
White Swan, WA 98552-9786

509-948-2706
800-554-0860; *Fax:* 509-848-3896;
www.hortexponw.com

Vee Graves, Editor
Julie LaForge, Advertising Manager

Besides being mailed to it's family of subscribers it is also available complimentary at horticulture shows in the Northwest.
32 Pages
Frequency: Annually
Circulation: 11,000
Founded in: 1989
Printed in 4 colors on glossy stock

10325 IGWB Buyer's Guide
BNP Media
PO Box 1080
Skokie, IL 60076-9785

847-763-9534; *Fax:* 847-763-9538
igwb@halldata.com; www.igwb.com

James Rutherford, Editor
Lynn Davidson, Marketing
Nikki Smith, Director

A comprehensive resource listing over 1000 gaming products and services suppliers.
Frequency: Annual
ISSN: 0 -

10326 Ice Cream and Frozen Desserts
Business Trend Analysts/Industry Reports
2171 Jericho Tpke
Commack, NY 11725-2937

631-462-5454; *Fax:* 631-462-1842
bta@li.net; www.businesstrendanalysts.com

Charles J Ritchie, Executive VP
Donna Priani, Marketing Director
Linda Sherman, Production Manager
Jennifer Wichert, Research Director

A survey of the ice cream and frozen dessert market, including low-calorie, low-fat and gourmet ice creams and frozen desserts.
Cost: $1295.00
Founded in: 2000

10327 Illinois Beverage Guide
Indiana Beverage Life, Inc
7379 Fox Hollow Ridge
PO Box 5067
Zionsville, IN 46077

317-733-0527; *Fax:* 317-733-0528
ibjzstew@indy.rr.com

Stewart Baxter, Publisher/Editor

10328 Impact International Directory: Leading Spirits, Wine and Beer Companies
M Shanken Communications
387 Park Ave S
8th Floor
New York, NY 10016-8872
212-684-4224; *Fax:* 212-684-5424;
www.cigaraficionado.com

Marvin Shanken, Publisher

A directory offering information on the major players of the alcoholic beverage industry.
Cost: $295.00

10329 Impact Yearbook: Directory of the US Wine, Spirits & Beer Industry
M Shanken Communications
387 Park Ave S
8th Floor
New York, NY 10016-8872

212-684-4224; *Fax:* 212-684-5424;
www.cigaraficionado.com

Marvin Shanken, Publisher

A directory offering information on the top 40 American distributors and profiles of companies.
Cost: $170.00
Frequency: Annual

10330 International Association of Food Industry Suppliers
1451 Dolley Madison Boulevard
Suite 101
McLean, VA 22101

703-761-2600; *Fax:* 703-761-4334
info@fpsa.org; www.fpsa.org

George Melnykovich, President/CEO

A directory offering information on member manufacturers and suppliers of equipment, ingredients and services to the food and dairy industry.
700 Pages
Founded in: 1911

10331 International Dairy Foods Association: IDFA Membership Directory
IDFA Membership Directory
1250 H St NW
Suite 900
Washington, DC 20005-5902

202-737-4332; *Fax:* 202-331-7820
membership@idfa.org; www.idfa.org

Constance Tipton, President
Miriam Brown, Advisory Committee

The directory provides a complete listing of IDFA's members— over 500 companies— representing approximately 83 percent of all dairy foods processed in the US, as well as the industry's leading supplier companies. Information about locations, products and contacts is included.
Cost: $495.00
250 Pages

10332 International Directory of Refrigerated Warehouse & Distribution Centers
Int'l Association of Refrigerated Warehouses
1500 King Street
Suite 201
Alexandria, VA 22314

301-652-5674; *Fax:* 703-373-4301
email@iarw.org; www.iarw.org

Corey Rosenbusch, Vice President
Nikki Duncan, Programs Manager
Margot Dersal, Controller

A complete listing of public refrigerated warehouses available to the food industry.
Cost: $18.00

10333 International Green Front Report
Friends of the Trees
PO Box 1064
Tonasket, WA 98855-1064

Fax: 509-485-2705
michael@friendsofthetrees.net

Michael Pilarski, Editor

Organizations and periodicals concerned with sustainable forestry and agriculture and related

fields.
Cost: $7.00
Frequency: Irregular

10334 International Soil Tillage Research Organization
International Soil Tillage Research
1680 Madison Avenue
Wooster, OH 44691-4114
330-263-3700; *Fax:* 330-263-3658
More than 750 individuals and institutions in 72 countries involved in the research or application of soil tilage and related subjects.
Cost: $100.00
Frequency: Semiannual

10335 Kosher Directory: Directory of Kosher Products & Services
Union of Orthodox Jewish Congregations of America
333 7th Avenue
18th Floor
New York, NY 10001-5004
212-563-4122; *Fax:* 212-564-9058
Shelly Sharf, Editor
A directory covering over 10,000 consumer, institutional and industrial products and services.

10336 Landscape & Irrigation: Product Source Guide
Adams Business Media
Suite J
Cathedral City, CA 92234
760-322-9878; *Fax:* 312-846-4638;
www.americanbusinessmedia.com
Leslee Adams, Owner
Offers information on suppliers, distributors and manufacturers serving the professional agriculture and landscaping community.
Cost: $6.00
Circulation: 37,000

10337 LifeWise Ingredients
350 Telser Rd
Lake Zurich, IL 60047-6701
847-550-8270; *Fax:* 847-550-8272
info@lifewise1.com; www.lifewise1.com
Millie Galey, Manager
Carol Bender, Manager
Richard Share, Owner
Manufacture industrial food ingredients.

10338 MISA Buyer's Guide on CD
Meat Industry Suppliers Alliance
1451 Dolly Madison Boulevard
McLean, VA 22101
703-761-2600
800-331-8816; *Fax:* 703-548-6563
info@fpsa.org;
www.foodprocessingmachinery.com
George O Melnkovich, PhD, President
Cheryl Clark, Director Member Services
Frequency: Annual

10339 Manufacturing Confectioner: Directory of Ingredients, Equipment & Packaging
Manufacturing Confectioner Publishing Company
P.O.Box 2249
New Preston Marble Dale, CT 06777-0249
201-652-2655; *Fax:* 201-652-3419
mcinfo@gomc.com; www.gomc.com
Kate Allured, Editor
Publication offers suppliers of machinery, equipment, raw materials, and supplies to the confectionery industry.
Cost: $25.00
Frequency: Annual

10340 Market for Nutraceutical Foods & Beverages
Frost & Sullivan Market Intelligence
2525 Charleston Road
Mountain View, CA 94043-1626
650-961-1000; *Fax:* 650-961-5042
Analyzes the nutraceutical market and offers information on ongoing laboratory research and forecasts for this particular industry.
Cost: $1850.00

10341 Material Safety Data Sheet Reference
C&P Press
565 5th Ave
5th Floor
New York, NY 10017-2413
212-587-8620; *Fax:* 646-733-6010;
www.pharmpress.com
Regulatory and product safety requirements. Contains full text MSDS's for products listed in the 1999 15th Edition Crop Protection Reference plus additional safety information such as DOT shipping information, SARA Title III regulations, Hazardous Chemical inventory reporting information plus much more.

10342 Meat Buyer's Guide
North American Meat Processors Association
1920 Association Dr
Suite 400
Reston, VA 20191-1500
703-758-8001
800-368-3043; *Fax:* 703-758-8001;
www.namp.com
Sabrina Moore, Accounting/Meeting Manager
Philip Kimball, Executive Director
A pictorial directory depicting the food service cuts of beef, lamb, pork, and veal, along with their corresponding IMPS numbers (Institutional Meat Purchase Specification) numbers, instituted by USDA. The Guide is used by chefs, meat processors, and purveyors, food service personnel in institutions, hotels and restaurants.

10343 Meat Price Book
Urner Barry Publications
PO Box 389
Toms River, NJ 08754-0389
732-240-5330
800-932-0617; *Fax:* 732-341-0891
help@urnerbarry.com; www.urnerbarry.com
Paul B Brown Jr, President
Sheila M Deane, Marketing Manager
Seven year price history of selected beef, lamb and veal cuts as quoted in Urner Barry's Yellow Sheet.
Cost: $95.00
Frequency: Annual
Circulation: 400

10344 Meat and Poultry Inspection Directory
US Department of Agriculture
Administration Building
Room 344
Washington, DC 20250-0001
202-690-7650; *Fax:* 202-512-2250;
www.access.gpo.gov
Offers valuable information on all meat and poultry plants that ship meat interstate and therefore come under the US Department of Agriculture inspection.
Cost: $16.00
600 Pages
Frequency: Semiannual

10345 Membership Directory of the Retail Confectioners International
1807 Glenview Rd
Suite 104
Glenview, IL 60025-2961
847-657-7400; *Fax:* 847-724-2719;
www.retailconfectioners.org
Frequency: Annual

10346 Mid-Atlantic Retail Food Industry Buyers' Guide
Mid-Atlantic Food Dealers Services
19 Hamill Rd # E
Baltimore, MD 21210-1754
410-522-6924; *Fax:* 410-377-7137
Robert Mead, Executive Director
Offers extensive coverage of retail food stores and suppliers to the food industry in the states of Delaware, Maryland, New Jersey, Virginia and Washington, DC.
Cost: $15.00
130 Pages
Frequency: Annual
Circulation: 5,000

10347 Missouri Grocers Association Annual Convention & Food Trade Show
Missouri Grocers Association
PO Box 10223
Springfield, MO 65808
417-831-6667; *Fax:* 417-831-3907
http://www.missourigrocers.com
1300 Pages

10348 NAMA Directory of Members
National Automatic Merchandising Association
20 N Wacker Dr
Suite 3500
Chicago, IL 60606-3102
312-346-0370
800-331-8816; *Fax:* 312-704-4140
dmathews@vending.org; www.vending.org
Richard Geerdes, President
Craig Hesch NCE, Senior Vice Chairman
Brad Ellis NCE, Vice Chairman
Listings of over 2,200 vending, coffee service and foodservice management firms that are NAMA members, including independent firms and branches of national operating companies. Listed by state and city, identifies products vending by each firm and other services provided. Includes listing of machine manufacturer and product supplier firms that are members as well as brokers and distributors and sustaining.
Cost: $25.00
Frequency: Annual
Founded in: 1936

10349 NASDA Directory
National Association of State Dept of Agriculture
1156 15th St NW
Suite 1020
Washington, DC 20005-1711
202-296-9680; *Fax:* 202-296-9686;
www.nasda.org
Stephen Haterius, Executive Director
Top agricultural officials in 50 states and four territories.
Cost: $100.00
Frequency: Annual

10350 National Agri-Marketing Association Directory
11020 King St
Suite 205
Overland Park, KS 66210-1201
913-491-6500; *Fax:* 913-491-6502
agrimktg@nama.org; www.nama.org
Jennifer Pickett, CEO
Vicki Henrickson, Vice President
Cost: $150.00
2500 Pages
Frequency: Annual Spring
Founded in: 1956

10351 National Association of Specialty Food and Confection Brokers
11004 Wood Elves Way
Columbia, MD 21044-1085
410-969-3663; *Fax:* 410-740-2958
Judi Epstein, Secretary
Lists members by state of residence and by states covered. Code of ethics and articles describing the function of a 'specialty' food broker in the marketplace.
86 Pages

10352 National Coffee Service Association: Membership Directory
8201 Greensboro Drive
Suite 300
McLean, VA 22102-3814
703-610-9000
800-221-3196; *Fax:* 703-273-9011
A directory covering over 800 member operators and suppliers of office coffee service products.
Frequency: Annual

10353 National Meat Association: Membership Directory
1970 Broadway
Suite 825
Oakland, CA 94612-2299
510-763-1533; *Fax:* 510-763-6186
staff@nmaonline.org; www.nmaonline.org
Barry Carpenter, CEO
Jen Kempis, Associate Director
This annual guide offers information on over 250 meat packers, processors and jobbers in 19 western states.
100 Pages
Frequency: Annual

10354 National Organic Directory
Community Alliance with Family Farmers
PO Box 464
Davis, CA 95617-0464
916-786-5155
800-852-3832; *Fax:* 530-756-7857
Annual directory offering information on over 1,000 growers and wholesalers of organically grown produce and organic products. The new edition includes information on regulations and resources for the industry.
Cost: $34.95
288 Pages
Frequency: Annual
Circulation: 2,500

10355 New Product News
Avtex
N6w23673 Bluemound Rd
Waukesha, WI 53188-1741
262-542-9111; *Fax:* 262-542-8820
info@avtex.com; www.avtex.com
Spencer Thomason, President
Martin Friedman, Editor
Diane McBride, Circulation Manager
Chris Kumsher, Chief Financial Officer
Offers food and drug manufacturers up-to-date information on products sold in supermarkets, drug stores, gourmet stores and natural food stores. Includes in-depth analysis of new product trends.
Cost: $359.00
65 Pages
Frequency: Monthly
*Mailing list available for rent*at $300 per M
Printed in one color on matte stock

10356 Organic Food Mail Order Suppliers
Center for Science in the Public Interest
1875 Connecticut Avenue NW
Suite 300
Washington, DC 20009-5736
202-332-9110; *Fax:* 202-265-4954;
www.cspinet.org
Michael Jacobson, Executive Director
Jamie Jonker, Director Regulatory Affairs
A directory of organic-food growers and suppliers who make their products available by mail-order.
Founded in: 1992

10357 Organic Pages Online
Organic Trade Association
60 Wells Street
PO Box 547
Greenfield, MA 01302
413-774-7511; *Fax:* 413-774-6432;
www.theorganicpages.com
Christine Bushway, Executive Director/CEO
Linda Lutz, Membership Manager
Laura Batcha, Marketing/Public Relations Manager
Online searchable directory
Founded in: 1984

10358 PMMI Packaging Machinery Directory
Packaging Machinery Manufacturers Institute (PMMI)
4350 Fairfax Dr
Suite 600
Arlington, VA 22203-1632
703-243-8555; *Fax:* 703-243-8556
maria@pmmi.org; www.pmmi.org
Chuck Yuska, President
Alaina Sacramo, Services Coordinator
Contains information on all 500+ member companies, who are committed to producing quality products and providing world class service to their customers.
Cost: $5.00
Frequency: Non-Members Fee

10359 Packer: Produce Availability and Merchandising Guide
Vance Publishing
10901 W 84th Ter
Suite 200
Lenexa, KS 66214-1631
913-438-5721
800-255-5113; *Fax:* 913-438-0697
info@vancepublishing.com;
www.vancepublishing.com
Cliff Becker, Vice President, Director
Ben Wood, Editor
Lance Jungmeyer, Managing Editor
Leanne Ball, Manager
Lori Eppel, Chief Financial Officer
Publication of about 6,000 fruit and vegetable suppliers and sales agents.
Cost: $35.00
Frequency: Annual

10360 Parity Corp
11812 N Creek Pkwy N
Suite 204
Bothell, WA 98011-8202
425-487-0997; *Fax:* 425-487-2317
info@paritycorp.com; www.paritycorp.com
Arvid Tellevik, Owner
Integrated business information system and services designed specifically for the food industry.
Founded in: 1985

10361 Pasta Industry Directory
National Pasta Association
1156 15th St NW
Suite 900
Washington, DC 20005-1717
202-367-1861; *Fax:* 202-367-1865
info@ilovepasta.org; www.civilwar.org
Jim Lighthizer, President
Lists by category pasta manufacturers and industry suppliers, including contact names.
Cost: $25.00
Frequency: Annual
Circulation: 1,000

10362 Pickle Packers International Directory
1620 Eye St NW
Suite 925
Washington, DC 20006-4076
202-293-5800; *Fax:* 202-463-8998;
www.hazmatshippers.org
Glenn Roberts, President
Frequency: Annual

10363 Pioneers of the Hospitality Industry
CHRIE
2810 N Parham Road
Suite 230
Richmond, VA 23294
804-346-4800; *Fax:* 804-346-5009
info@chrie.org; www.chrie.org
Social Media: Facebook, Twitter, LinkedIn
Susan Fournier, President
Josette Katz, Vice President
Chris Roberts, Secretary
John Drysdale, Treasurer
Kathy McCarty, CEO
Lessons from Leaders, Innovators and Visionaries. A tribute to those dedicated individuals who have shaped the hospitality industry through their colorful lives, their foresight, and their leadership. These profiles offer readers the opportunity to analyze successful leadership and entrepreneurial characteristics, and to evaluate the significance of their contributions.
Cost: $45.00

10364 Pizza Today: Pizza Industry Buyer's Guide
National Association of Pizzeria Operators (NAPO)
908 S 8th Street
Suite 200
Louisville, KY 40203
502-736-9530
800-489-8324; *Fax:* 502-736-9531;
www.pizzatoday.com
Pete Lachapelle, Publisher
Joe Straughan, Association Executive Director
A directory listing over 3,000 manufacturers and suppliers of products, equipment and services to the pizza industry.
Cost: $25.00
Frequency: Annual
Circulation: 40000
Founded in: 1984

10365 Pork Guide to Hero Health Issue
Vance Publishing
10901 W 84th Ter
Suite 200
Lenexa, KS 66214-1631

913-438-5721; *Fax:* 913-438-0697
info@vancepublishing.com;
www.vancepublishing.com

Cliff Becker, Vice President, Director
Lori Eppel, Chief Financial Officer

This comprehensive directory offers a list of manufacturers of swine health products.
Cost: $25.00
Frequency: Annual
Circulation: 77,000

10366 Poultry Digest: Buyer's Guide Issue
WATT Publishing Company
122 S Wesley Ave
Mt Morris, IL 61054-1451

815-734-7937; *Fax:* 815-734-4201
olentine@wattmm.com; www.wattnet.com

Charles Perry, Editor
James Watt, Owner

A list of suppliers to the poultry industry of the US and Canada are listed.
Cost: $6.00
Frequency: Annual
Circulation: 20,000

10367 Poultry International: Who's Who International
WATT Publishing Company
303 N Main Street
Suite 500
Rockford, IL 61101

815-966-5400; *Fax:* 815-966-6416;
www.wattnet.com

James Watt, Chairman/CEO
Greg Watt, President/COO
Jeff Swanson, Publishing Director

A guide offering information on over 2,500 manufacturers and suppliers of poultry equipment, services and products.
Cost: $15.00
Frequency: Annual
Circulation: 20,000
ISSN: 0032-5767

10368 Poultry Price Book
Urner Barry Publications
PO Box 389
Toms River, NJ 08754-0389

732-240-5330
800-932-0617; *Fax:* 732-341-0891
help@urnerbarry.com; www.urnerbarry.com

Paul B Brown Jr, President
Sheila M Deane, Marketing Manager

Seven year price history of selected turkey and chicken items as quoted in Urner Barry's Price—Current.
Cost: $55.00
Frequency: Annual
Circulation: 400

10369 Poultry Processing: Buyer's Guide Issue
WATT Publishing Company
122 S Wesley Ave
Mt Morris, IL 61054-1451

815-734-7937; *Fax:* 815-734-4201;
www.wattnet.com

Virginia Lazar, Editor
James Watt, Owner

Annual reference offering information on over 800 manufacturers and suppliers of equipment, machinery and raw materials for the poultry packing industry.

10370 Prepared Foods
Delta Communications
455 N Cityfront Plaza Drive
Chicago, IL 60611-5503

312-836-2000; *Fax:* 312-222-2026

This database offers information of interest to the processed food industry.
Frequency: Full-text

10371 Proceedings
Flavor & Extract Manufacturers Assn of the US
1620 Eye St NW
Suite 925
Washington, DC 20006-4076

202-293-5800; *Fax:* 202-463-8998;
www.hazmatshippers.org

Glenn Roberts, President
Kim Earle, Contact

Updates and reports on the proceedings of the association.
Frequency: Annual

10372 Produce Marketing Association Membership Directory & Buyer's Guide
Produce Marketing Association
1500 Casho Mill Road
PO Box 6036
Newark, DE 19711-3547

302-738-7100; *Fax:* 302-731-2409

Kathy Means, VP Membership
Dan Henderson, Marketing
Bryan Silbermann, President

A directory offering information on over 2,000 members involved in retail grocery and food service marketing.
Cost: $70.00
280 Pages
Frequency: Annual

10373 Produce Services Sourcebook
Vance Publishing
10901 W 84th Ter
Suite 200
Lenexa, KS 66214-1631

913-438-5721
800-255-5113; *Fax:* 913-438-0697
info@vancepublishing.com;
www.vancepublishing.com

Cliff Becker, Vice President, Director
Lori Eppel, Chief Financial Officer

The produce industry's directory of allied services and products. Content is a balance between practical reference information, allied trends and supplier or source listings.
Cost: $20.00

10374 Professional Workers in State Agricultural Experiment Stations
US Department of Agriculture
PO Box 2022
Washington, DC 20250-0001

202-690-7650; *Fax:* 202-512-2250;
www.access.gpo.gov

This directory offers information on academic and research personnel in all agricultural, forestry, aquaculture and home economics industries.
Cost: $15.00
289 Pages
Frequency: Annual

10375 Purebred Picture: Breeders Directory Issue
American Berkshire Association
PO Box 2346
W Lafayette, IN 47996-2346

765-497-3618; *Fax:* 765-497-2959

Lois Wall, Managing Editor

Annual guide offering information on cattle and hog breeders in the US.
Cost: $12.00
Frequency: Annual
Circulation: 4,000

10376 Quick Frozen Foods Annual Processors Directory & Buyer's Guide
Frozen Food Digest, Saul Beck Publications
271 Madison Ave
Suite 1402a
New York, NY 10016-1014

212-557-8600; *Fax:* 212-986-9868

Saul Beck, Owner
Audrey Beck, General Manager

A buyer's guide listing over 10,000 frozen food processors, associations, equipment manufacturers and suppliers, and public refrigerated warehouses, transportation, freezing & refrigerated equipment, manufacturers, packagers and railroad lines, brokers, etc.
Cost: $140.00
400 Pages
Frequency: Annual
Circulation: 5,000

10377 RIFM/FEMA Fragrance and Flavor Database
Flavor & Extract Manufacturers Association
1620 I Street NW
Suite 925
Washington, DC 20006

202-293-5800; *Fax:* 202-462-8998;
www.femaflavor.org
Social Media: YouTube, RSS Feed

Ed R. Hays, Ph.D., President
George C. Robinson, III, President Elect
Mark Scott, Treasurer
Arthur Schick, VP & Secretary
John Cox, Executive Director

The Database currently contains over 50,000 references and more than 103,000 human health and environmental studies.
Frequency: Annual
Founded in: 1909

10378 Refrigerated Transporter: Warehouse Directory Issue
Penton
PO Box 66010
Houston, TX 77266

713-523-8124
800-880-0368; *Fax:* 713-523-8384
refrigeratedtransporter.com

Ray Anderson, Publisher

Listing of approximately 265 refrigerated warehouses in the US and Canada.

10379 Restaurant Hospitality: Hospitality 500 Issue
Penton Media
1300 E 9th St
Suite 316
Cleveland, OH 44114-1503

216-696-7000; *Fax:* 216-696-6662
information@penton.com; www.penton.com

Jane Cooper, Marketing

500 independent restaurants selected on basis of sales.
Cost: $25.00
Frequency: Annual June
Circulation: 123,000

10380 **Restaurant TrendMapper**
National Restaurant Association
1200 17th St Nw
Washington, DC 20036-3006

202-331-5900
800-424-5156; *Fax:* 202-331-2429;
www.restaurant.org
Social Media: Facebook, Twitter, LinkedIn, YouTube, Flickr

Sally Smith, Chair
Rosalyn Mallet, Vice Chair
Phil Hickey, Treasurer
Dawn Sweeney, President & CEO

Contains detailed analysis of the economic trends that impact the restaurant industry, as well as forecasts of key industry indicators on the national and state levels.
60000 Members
Founded in: 1919

10381 **Restaurants and Institutions: Annual Issue**
Reed Business Information
1350 E Touhy Avenue
Suite 200E
Des Plaines, IL 60018-3358

847-962-2200; *Fax:* 630-288-8686;
www.reedbusiness.com

Roland Dietz, CEO
Stuart Whayman, CFO
Cost: $25.00
Frequency: Annual
Circulation: 16,000

10382 **Santa Gertrudis Breeders International Membership Directory**
PO Box 1257
Kingsville, TX 78364-1257

361-592-9357; *Fax:* 361-592-8572
http://www.santagertrudis.com

Ervin Kaatz, Executive Director

Annual guide offering information on over 4,5000 producers of Santa Gertrudis beef and cattle throughout the world.

10383 **Santa Gertrudis USA**
Santa Gertrudis Breeders International
PO Box 1257
Kingsville, TX 78364-1257

361-592-9357; *Fax:* 361-592-8572
http://www.santagertrudis.com

Ervin Kaatz, Executive Director

Monthly publication offering information on over 1,000 producers of Santa Gertrudis beef cattle throughout the United States.
Cost: $30.00
125 Pages
Frequency: Monthly
Circulation: 2,500
Founded in: 1998
Printed in on glossy stock

10384 **Sauces and Gravies**
MarketResearch.com
641 Avenue of the Americas
3rd Floor
New York, NY 10011

212-807-2629
800-298-6699; *Fax:* 212-807-2676

This market profile analyzes US shipments, retail sales, consumer demographics, and food service and food processor purchases for 22 product lines. Also analyzes the sauce and gravy product line, retail sales, brand share, and customer demographics for 16 major marketers.
Cost: $2250.00
250 Pages

10385 **Seafood Buyer's Handbook**
Diversified Business Communications
PO Box 7438
Portland, ME 04112-7438

207-842-5500; *Fax:* 207-842-5505;
www.divbusiness.com

Nancy Gelette, VP Operations

This comprehensive directory lists about 1,200 North American fish and shellfish suppliers, distributors and suppliers of related services and equipment to the seafood industry.
Cost: $18.00
250 Pages
Frequency: Annual
Circulation: 15,000

10386 **Seafood Price Book**
Urner Barry Publications
PO Box 389
Toms River, NJ 08754-0389

732-240-5330
800-932-0617; *Fax:* 732-341-0891
help@urnerbarry.com; www.urnerbarry.com

Paul B Brown Jr, President
Sheila M Deane, Marketing Manager

Seven year price history of selected fresh/frozen seafood items as quoted in Urner Barry's Seafood Price— Current.
Cost: $95.00
Frequency: Annual
Circulation: 400

10387 **Seafood Shippers' Guide**
American Seafood Institute
25 Fairway Circle
Hope Valley, RI 02832

401-491-9017; *Fax:* 401-491-9024;
www.americanseafood.org

Trucking, freight and cold storage companies that directly affect the seafood packing and shipping industry.
Cost: $29.95
100 Pages
Circulation: 2,000

10388 **Seed Technologist Training Manual**
Society of Commercial Seed Technologists
101 E State Street
Suite 214
Ithaca, NY 14850

607-256-3313; *Fax:* 607-256-3313;
www.seedtechnology.net

Anita Hall, Executive Director
Dr Wayne Guerke, Editor

This manual represents the most comprehensive treatment of seed testing technology anywhere.
Cost: $175.00
450 Pages
Frequency: Bi-Annually
Circulation: 500
Founded in: 1922

10389 **Single Unit Supermarkets Operators Directory**
Chain Store Guide
3922 Coconut Palm Dr
Suite 300
Tampa, FL 33619-1389

813-627-6700
800-778-9794; *Fax:* 813-627-7094
info@csgis.com; www.csgis.com

Mike Jarvis, Publisher
Shami Choon, Manager

Discover more than 7,100 single-unit supermarkets with annual sales topping $500,000 dollars. This comprehensive desktop reference makes it easy to reach our compiled list of 21,000 key executives and buyers, plus their primary wholesalers.
Cost: $335.00
725 Pages
Frequency: Annual

10390 **Soya & Oilseed Bluebook**
Soyatech Inc
P.O.Box 1307
Southwest Harbor, ME 04679-1307

207-288-4969
800-424-7692; *Fax:* 207-288-5264
subscribe@soyatech.com; www.soyatech.com

Provides the world with information on the processing industry that supports development and value creation along each step of the supply chain.

10391 **Supermarket News Distribution Study of Grocery Store Sales**
Fairchild Publications
7 W 34th St
3rd Floor
New York, NY 10001-8100

212-630-3880; *Fax:* 212-630-3868

Directory of services and supplies to the industry.
Cost: $75.00
Frequency: Annual

10392 **Supermarket News Retailers & Wholesalers Directory**
Fairchild Publications
7 W 34th St
New York, NY 10001-8100

212-630-3880
800-360-1700; *Fax:* 212-630-3868

Over 2,200 US and Canadian retailers, including supermarkets, discount department stores, membership clubs, drug stores, plus voluntary, cooperative and nonsponsoring wholesalers.

10393 **Supermarket, Grocery & Convenience Store Chains**
Lebhar-Friedman
425 Park Ave
New York, NY 10022-3526

212-756-5088; *Fax:* 212-838-9487
info@lf.com; www.nrn.com

Heather Martin, Manager

Directory of US and Canadian supermarket chains.
Cost: $335.00

10394 **Supermarket, Grocery & Convenience Stores**
Chain Store Guide
3922 Coconut Palm Dr
Suite 300
Tampa, FL 33619-1389

813-627-6700
800-778-9794; *Fax:* 813-627-7094
info@csgis.com; www.csgis.com

Mike Jarvis, Publisher
Shami Choon, Manager

Contains information on close to 3,400 U.S. and Canadian supermarket chains, each with at least $2 million in annual sales - one of the most profitable segments in this sector of the economy. The companies in this database operate over 41,000 individual supermarket, superstore, club store, gourmet supermarkets and combo-store units. A special convenience store section profiles 1,700 convenience store chains operating over 85,000 stores.
Cost: $335.00
Frequency: Annual

10395 **Technomic Top 500 Chain Restaurant Report**
International Food Service Manufacturers

180 North Stetson Avenue
Suite 4400
Chicago, IL 60601-6766
312-540-4400; *Fax:* 312-540-4401
ifma@ifmaworld.com; www.ifmaworld.com
Social Media: Facebook, LinkedIn, YouTube

Larry Oberkfell, President & CEO
Jennifer Tarulis, CFO
Michael Hickey, Chairman
Mark Bendix, 1st Vice Chairman
Loren Kimura, Treasurer

Provides a comprehensive ranking, analysis and overview of the US chain resaurant industry, helping readers develop sales and marketing strategies, identify growth opportunities, and monitor performance. All data is compiled for US operations and adjusted to calendar-year basis, making it an accurate and easy-to-use resource.
Cost: $850.00
Frequency: Annual

10396 Top 100 Fast Casual Chain Restaurant Report
International Food Service Manufacturers
180 North Stetson Avenue
Suite 4400
Chicago, IL 60601-6766
312-540-4400; *Fax:* 312-540-4401
ifma@ifmaworld.com; www.ifmaworld.com
Social Media: Facebook, LinkedIn, YouTube

Larry Oberkfell, President & CEO
Jennifer Tarulis, CFO
Michael Hickey, Chairman
Mark Bendix, 1st Vice Chairman
Loren Kimura, Treasurer

Provides rankings, analysis and profiles of the leading Fast Casual chain restaurants and gives manufacturers a handle on the evolving trends. Also featuring an in-depth industry overview, a segment performance review and update on emerging chains, performance report, key trends, and individual profiles and sales rankings.
Cost: $850.00
Frequency: Annual

10397 Trade Dimensions
45 Danbury Rd
Wilton, CT 06897-4445
203-563-3000; *Fax:* 203-563-3131;
www.tradedimensions.com

Hal Clark, Owner

Trade Dimensions has over 30 years of experience and innovation in developing some of the most sophisticated, reliable and widely used directories and retail site data bases available.

10398 US Agriculture
WEFA Group
800 Baldwin Tower Boulevard
Eddystone, PA 19022-1368
610-490-4000; *Fax:* 610-490-2770
info@wefa.com; www.wefa.com

Harry Baurnes

This large database offers information on US macroeconomic farm crop and related agricultural data.

10399 US Alcohol Beverage Industry Category CD
Beverage Marketing Corporation
2670 Commercial Ave
Mingo Junction, OH 43938-1613
740-598-4133
800-332-6222; *Fax:* 740-598-3977;
www.beveragemarketing.com

Andrew Standardi III, Director of Operations
Kathy Smurthwaite, Editor

Contains information on approximately 3,030 companies including breweries, microbreweries, wineries, distilleries, wholesalers and importers.
Cost: $3010.00
Frequency: Annual

10400 US Bagel Industry
Leading Edge Reports/Industry Reports
2171 Jericho Turnpike
Suite 200
Commack, NY 11725-2937
631-462-5454; *Fax:* 631-462-1842
bta@li.net; www.businesstrendanalysts.com

Charles J Ritchie, Executive VP
Donna Priani, Marketing Director
Linda Sherman, Production Manager
Vincent Seeno, Research Director

A comprehensive investigation of the dynamics of the US Bagel Industry. Both historical and current market data is presented.
Cost: $1995.00
150 Pages
Founded in: 2000

10401 US Beer Industry Category CD
Beverage Marketing Corporation
2670 Commercial Ave
Mingo Junction, OH 43938-1613
740-598-4133
800-332-6222; *Fax:* 740-598-3977;
www.beveragemarketing.com

Andrew Standardi III, Director of Operations
Kathy Smurthwaite, Editor

Contains information on approximately 2,084 companies including breweries, microbreweries, beer wholesalers and beer importers.
Cost: $2070.00
Frequency: Annual

10402 US Beverage Distribution Landscape Category CD
Beverage Marketing Corporation
2670 Commercial Ave
Mingo Junction, OH 43938-1613
740-598-4133
800-332-6222; *Fax:* 740-598-3977;
www.beveragemarketing.com

Andrew Standardi III, Director of Operations
Kathy Smurthwaite, Editor

Contains information on approximately 3,340 companies distributing soft drinks, bottled water, beer, wine and spirits.
Cost: $3320.00
Frequency: Annual

10403 US Beverage Manufacturers and Filling Locations Category CD
Beverage Marketing Corporation
2670 Commercial Ave
Mingo Junction, OH 43938-1613
740-598-4133
800-332-6222; *Fax:* 740-598-3977;
www.beveragemarketing.com

Andrew Standardi III, Director of Operations
Kathy Smurthwaite, Editor

Contains information on approximately 2,402 companies including breweries, microbreweries, wineries, distilleries, soft drink fillers and franchise companies, bottled water fillers, juice, sports beverages and energy drinks, soy, coffee, tea, and milk manufacturers.
Cost: $2390.00
Frequency: Annual

10404 US Bottled Water Industry
Business Trend Analysts/Industry Reports
2171 Jericho Tpke
Suite 200
Commack, NY 11725-2937
631-462-5454; *Fax:* 631-462-1842
bta@li.net; www.businesstrendanalysts.com

Charles J Ritchie, Executive VP
Donna Priani, Marketing Director
Linda Sherman, Production Manager
Vincent Seeno, Research Director

BTA continues its pioneering coverage of the bottled water industry with this updated and dramatically expanded edition.
Cost: $1550.00
Founded in: 1997

10405 US Bottled Water Operations Category CD
Beverage Marketing Corporation
2670 Commercial Ave
Mingo Junction, OH 43938-1613
740-598-4133
800-332-6222; *Fax:* 740-598-3977;
www.beveragemarketing.com

Andrew Standardi III, Director of Operations
Kathy Smurthwaite, Editor

Contains information on approximately 3,010 companies including bottled water fillers and distributors.
Cost: $2995.00
Frequency: Annual

10406 US Bread Market
MarketResearch.com
641 Avenue of the Americas
3rd Floor
New York, NY 10011
212-807-2629
800-298-6699; *Fax:* 212-807-2676

This study covers packaged, fresh and frozen bread products, including a growing number of specialty bread products. Major marketing, retailing and demographic trends are all explored in-depth. Special attention is given to the in-store bakery phenomenon.
Cost: $2750.00
197 Pages

10407 US Candy and Gum Market
MarketResearch.com
641 Avenue of the Americas
3rd Floor
New York, NY 10011
212-807-2629
800-298-6699; *Fax:* 212-807-2676

This report dissects the 23.5 billion market for chocolate candy, hard candy, soft candy, mints and gum, covering both the mass-market and gourmet levels. Market size, growth and composition are tabulated, with sales projections through 2004. Competition at the retail level as a major impetus to market growth is covered in full, as are consumer demographics by product type, brand and usage levels.
Cost: $2750.00
351 Pages

10408 US Carbonated Soft Drink Operations Category CD
Beverage Marketing Corporation
2670 Commercial Ave
Mingo Junction, OH 43938-1613
740-598-4133
800-332-6222; *Fax:* 740-598-3977;
www.beveragemarketing.com

Andrew Standardi III, Director of Operations
Kathy Smurthwaite, Editor

Contains information on approximately 2,713 companies including CSD bottlers, canners,

franchise companies and distributors.
Cost: $2700.00
Frequency: Annual

10409 US Cheese Market
Business Trend Analysts/Industry Reports
2171 Jericho Tpke
Suite 200
Commack, NY 11725-2937

631-462-5454
800-866-4648; *Fax:* 631-462-1842;
www.bta-ler.com

Charles J Ritchie, Executive VP
Donna Priani, Marketing Director
Linda Holm, Production Manager
Jennifer Wichert, Research Director

Survey offering the size and growth of markets for natural, process, cottage and substitute cheeses.
Cost: $1395.00
480 Pages
Founded in: 2001

10410 US Confectionary Market
Business Trend Analysts/Industry Reports
2171 Jericho Tpke
Suite 200
Commack, NY 11725-2937

631-462-5454; *Fax:* 631-462-1842
bta@li.net; www.businesstrendanalysts.com

Charles J Ritchie, Executive VP
Donna Priani, Marketing Director
Linda Sherman, Production Manager
Vincent Seeno, Research Director

Profiles markets for chocolate and nonchocolate candies, gum, snack nuts, and seeds, as well as providing information on distribution, trends and future opportunities.
Cost: $1250.00
760 Pages
Founded in: 1996

10411 US Date Code Directory for Product Labeling
Danis Research
1 Gothic Plaza
Fairfield, NJ 07004-2411

973-575-3509; *Fax:* 973-575-5366

Over 500 companies using date code labeling on their food products; over 500 quality control managers and consumer affairs managers from companies that produce snack foods, baked goods, confectioneries and other food products.
Cost: $295.00

10412 US Ethnic Foods Market
Business Trend Analysts/Industry Reports
2171 Jericho Tpke
Suite 200
Commack, NY 11725-2937

631-462-5454; *Fax:* 631-462-1842
bta@li.net; www.businesstrendanalysts.com

Charles J Ritchie, Executive VP
Donna Priani, Marketing Director
Linda Sherman, Production Manager
Vincent Seeno, Research Director

A detailed analysis of the expanding US markets for Italian, Hispanic/Mexican, Oriental, Indian and Kosher foods.
Cost: $995.00
Founded in: 1995

10413 US Hot Beverage Market
Business Trend Analysts/Industry Reports
2171 Jericho Tpke
Suite 200
Commack, NY 11725-2937

631-462-5454; *Fax:* 631-462-1842
bta@li.net; www.businesstrendanalysts.com

Charles J Ritchie, Executive VP
Donna Priani, Marketing Director
Linda Sherman, Production Manager
Vincent Seeno, Research Director

A survey offering profiles of the coffee, tea and cocoa products market.
Cost: $1995.00
330 Pages
Founded in: 1998

10414 US Market for Cereal & Other Breakfast Foods
Business Trend Analysts/Industry Reports
2171 Jericho Tpke
Suite 200
Commack, NY 11725-2937

631-462-5454
800-866-4648; *Fax:* 631-462-1842;
www.businesstrendanalysts.com

Charles J Ritchie, Executive VP
Donna Praini, General Manager
Linda Sherman, Production Manager
Jennifer Wichert, Research Director

Provides up-to-date information on consumer attitudes and buying patterns, new product development, marketing strategies and current and projected sales trends for all types of hot and cold cereals, baked breakfast foods and frozen breakfast products.
Cost: $1495.00
396 Pages
Founded in: 1986

10415 US Market for Fats & Oils
Business Trend Analysts/Industry Reports
2171 Jericho Tpke
Suite 200
Commack, NY 11725-2937

631-462-5454; *Fax:* 631-462-1842
bta@li.net; www.businesstrendanalysts.com

Charles J Ritchie, Executive VP
Donna Priani, Marketing Director
Linda Sherman, Production Manager
Vincent Seeno, Research Director

Analyzes the markets for different oils (corn, soybean, peanut, canola, linseed, cottonseed, fish and others), edible and inedible tallow, grease and lard.
Cost: $1295.00
540 Pages
Founded in: 1998

10416 US Market for Fruit and Vegetable Based Beverages
MarketResearch.com
641 Avenue of the Americas
3rd Floor
New York, NY 10011

212-807-2629
800-298-6699; *Fax:* 212-807-2676

This new study covers refrigerated juices and juice drinks, aseptic juices, frozen and unfrozen concentrates, shelf-stable juices and juice drinks in bottles and cans. It provides the latest available sales and volume by category and retail outlet, as well as detailed marketer/brand shares. The report unveils the competitive strategies, advertising and promotional campaigns and new product launches of major players; tracks trends in packaging, flavor-blending, health drinks, and other niches.
Cost: $2750.00
258 Pages

10417 US Market for Juices, Aides & Noncarbonated Drinks
Business Trend Analysts/Industry Reports
2171 Jericho Tpke
Suite 200
Commack, NY 11725-2937

631-462-5454; *Fax:* 631-462-1842
bta@li.net; www.businesstrendanalysts.com

Charles J Ritchie, Executive VP
Donna Priani, Marketing Director
Linda Sherman, Production Manager
Vincent Seeno, Research Director

A comprehensive market analysis covering all types of fresh and frozen fruit juices, fruit drinks, vegetable juices and canned ades.
Cost: $1195.00
810 Pages
Founded in: 1998

10418 US Market for Pizza
Leading Edge Reports/Industry Reports
2171 Jericho Turnpike
Suite 200
Commack, NY 11725-2937

631-462-5454; *Fax:* 631-462-1842
bta@li.net; www.businesstrendanalysts.com

Charles J Ritchie, Executive VP
Donna Priani, Marketing Director
Linda Sherman, Production Manager
Vincent Seeno, Research Director

This report examines the size and growth of the US Pizza market through all channels.
Cost: $1995.00
225 Pages
Founded in: 1999

10419 US Market for Salted Snacks
MarketResearch.com
641 Avenue of the Americas
3rd Floor
New York, NY 10011

212-807-2629
800-298-6699; *Fax:* 212-807-2676

This new study provides a coherent view of the market as well as its individual segments: potato chips, tortilla chips, corn chips, pretzels, popcorn, snack nuts and extruded snacks. It explains not only what the industry does, but how it works: how shelf life shapes the entire industry; how hundreds of smaller companies manage to thrive in a market dominated by Frito-Lay. This study profiles the giant companies and regional players.
Cost: $2750.00
263 Pages

10420 US Non-Alcoholic Beverage Industry Category CD
Beverage Marketing Corporation
2670 Commercial Ave
Mingo Junction, OH 43938-1613

740-598-4133
800-332-6222; *Fax:* 740-598-3977;
www.beveragemarketing.com

Andrew Standardi III, Director of Operations
Kathy Smurthwaite, Editor

Contains information on approximately 4,206 companies including CSD and bottled water operations, sports beverages and energy drinks, juice, soy, coffee, tea, and milk manufacturers.
Cost: $4185.00
Frequency: Annual

10421 US Organic Food Market
MarketResearch.com

641 Avenue of the Americas
3rd Floor
New York, NY 10011

212-807-2629
800-298-6699; *Fax:* 212-807-2676

This report covers the booming organic market as it expands into mainstream and gains increased public awareness. The report covers the market size and composition, important trends, and projections for future growth. The information contained in this report will help players in the organic arena make informed decisions to complete successfully in this exciting market.
Cost: $2750.00
275 Pages

10422 US Pasta Market
Business Trend Analysts/Industry Reports
2171 Jericho Tpke
Suite 200
Commack, NY 11725-2937

631-462-5454; *Fax:* 631-462-1842
bta@li.net; www.businesstrendanalysts.com

Charles J Ritchie, Executive VP
Donna Priani, Marketing Director
Linda Sherman, Production Manager
Vincent Seeno, Research Director

Quantifies historial, current and projected sales trends in the ever-expanding market for pasta products. Covers all typed of dry, canned, frozen and fresh pasta, as well as shelf-stable noodle dishes and pasta meals.
Cost: $ 1395.00
380 Pages
Founded in: 2000

10423 US Poultry and Small Game Market
Business Trend Analysts/Industry Reports
2171 Jericho Tpke
Suite 200
Commack, NY 11725-2937

631-462-5454; *Fax:* 631-462-1842
bta@li.net; www.businesstrendanalysts.com

Charles J Ritchie, Executive VP
Donna Priani, Marketing Director
Linda Sherman, Production Manager
Vincent Seeno, Research Director

Profiles market for poultry and small game products and provides information on pricing, foreign trade, and advertising and promotion.
Cost: $1995.00
280 Pages
Founded in: 1999

10424 US Processed Fruits & Vegetables Market
Business Trend Analysts/Industry Reports
2171 Jericho Tpke
Suite 200
Commack, NY 11725-2937

631-462-5454; *Fax:* 631-462-1842
bta@li.net; www.businesstrendanalysts.com

Charles J Ritchie, Executive VP
Donna Priani, Marketing Director
Linda Sherman, Production Manager
Vincent Seeno, Research Director

A comprehensive marketing, economic and financial analysis of the processed fruits and vegetables industry, covering all types of canned, frozen, dried and dehydrated fruits and vegetables.
Cost: $1195.00
815 Pages
Founded in: 1997

10425 US Processed Meat Market
Business Trend Analysts/Industry Reports
2171 Jericho Tpke
Suite 200
Commack, NY 11725-2937

631-462-5454; *Fax:* 631-462-1842
bta@li.net; www.businesstrendanalysts.com

Charles J Ritchie, Executive VP
Donna Priani, Marketing Director
Linda Sherman, Production Manager
Vincent Seeno, Research Director

Profiles markets for processed meat products, including sausage, processed pork products, canned meats, and meat snacks.
Cost: $1295.00
800 Pages
Founded in: 2000

10426 US Snack Food Market
Business Trend Analysts/Industry Reports
2171 Jericho Tpke
Suite 200
Commack, NY 11725-2937

631-462-5454; *Fax:* 631-462-1842;
www.businesstrendanalysts.com

Charles J Ritchie, Executive VP
Donna Priani, Marketing Director
Linda Sherman, Production Manager
Vincent Seeno, Research Director

A product-by-product analysis of the intensely competitive US snack food industry.
Cost: $1495.00
860 Pages
Founded in: 1999

10427 US Soyfoods Market
MarketResearch.com
641 Avenue of the Americas
3rd Floor
New York, NY 10011

212-807-2629
800-298-6699; *Fax:* 212-807-2676

This report covers five product categories: meat alternatives, dairy alternatives, snacks, cereals, breads, bulk soybeans, meal replacements/protein powders and other soyfoods including soy sauce and miso. It profiles leading soyfoods producers such as Kellog's, White Wave and Lightlife Foods. The report projects sales trends through 2005 and provides insight into the factors shaping this market. Distributor trends and consumer attitudes and behaviors are also covered in detail.
Cost: $2750.00
150 Pages

10428 US Sweeteners Market
Business Trend Analysts/Industry Reports
2171 Jericho Tpke
Suite 200
Commack, NY 11725-2937

631-462-5454; *Fax:* 631-462-1842
bta@li.net; www.businesstrendanalysts.com

Charles J Ritchie, Executive VP
Donna Priani, Marketing Director
Linda Sherman, Production Manager
Vincent Seeno, Research Director

In-depth coverage of the continually evolving sweetener industry, providing up-to-date information on the latest product developments.
Cost: $1995.00
375 Pages
Founded in: 1998

10429 US Vitamins & Nutrients Market
Business Trend Analysts/Industry Reports
2171 Jericho Tpke
Suite 200
Commack, NY 11725-2937

631-462-5454; *Fax:* 631-462-1842
bta@li.net; www.businesstrendanalysts.com

Charles J Ritchie, Executive VP
Donna Priani, Marketing Director
Linda Sherman, Production Manager
Vincent Seeno, Research Director

Statistical report on the vitamin and health food industries.
Cost: $1995.00
410 Pages
Founded in: 1999

10430 US Wine & Spirits Industry Category CD
Beverage Marketing Corporation
2670 Commercial Ave
Mingo Junction, OH 43938-1613

740-598-4133
800-332-6222; *Fax:* 740-598-3977;
www.beveragemarketing.com

Andrew Standardi III, Director of Operations
Kathy Smurthwaite, Editor

Contains information on approximately 1,484 companies including wineries, distilleries, wine & spirit wholesalers, and wine & spirit importers.
Cost: $1475.00
Frequency: Annual

10431 US Wine Market
Business Trend Analysts/Industry Reports
2171 Jericho Tpke
Suite 200
Commack, NY 11725-2937

631-462-5454; *Fax:* 631-462-1842;
www.businesstrendanalysts.com

Charles J Ritchie, Executive VP
Donna Priani, Marketing Director
Linda Sherman, Production Manager
Jennifer Wichert, Research Director

An analysis of the wine industry, domestic and imported.
Cost: $1295.00
470 Pages
Founded in: 1996

10432 Uker's International Tea and Coffee Buyer's Guide & Directory
Lockwood Trade Journal
26 Broadway
Suite 1050
New York, NY 10004-1777

212-269-7053; *Fax:* 212-827-0945
teacof@aol.com;
www.lockwoodpublications.com

Robert Lockwood, CEO
Jane McCabe, Editor

A directory covering firms that are involved in importing and exporting coffee and tea; manufacturers, suppliers and retailers to the industry; and specialty roasters and their suppliers.
Cost: $48.00
Frequency: Annual
Printed in 4 colors on glossy stock

10433 Urner Barry's Meat & Poultry Directory
Urner Barry Publications
PO Box 389
Toms River, NJ 08754-0389

732-240-5330
800-932-0617; *Fax:* 732-341-0891
help@urnerbarry.com; www.urnerbarry.com

Paul B Brown Jr, President
Karen Mick, Circulation Director

National business directory of traders in the meat and poultry industry.
Cost: $95.00
760 Pages
Frequency: Annual
Circulation: 2,000
ISSN: 0738-6745

10434 Vinegar Institute Directory
1100 Johnson Ferry Road
Suite 300
Atlanta, GA 30342

404-252-3663; *Fax:* 404-252-0774
vi@kellencompany.com;
www.versatilevinegar.org

Pamela A Chumley, President
Jeannie Milewski, Executive Director

Online membership directory for members only

10435 Vinegar Institute: Basic Reference Manual
Vinegar Institute
1100 Johnson Ferry Road
Suite 300
Atlanta, GA 30342

404-252-3663; *Fax:* 404-252-0774
vi@kellencompany.com;
www.verstailevinegar.org

Looseleaf service guide to vinegar products for technical personnel such as shop foremen and production managers.
Cost: $250.00

10436 Vineyard & Winery Management Magazine
Vineyard & Winery Services
PO Box 2358
Windsor, CA 95492

707-836-6820
800-535-5670; *Fax:* 707-836-6825
vwm-online.com

Robert Merletti, President
Jennifer Merletti, Sales/Marketing Manager

A leading technical trade publication serving the North American Wine Industry and designed for today's serious wine business professional.
Founded in: 1975

10437 Warehouses Licensed Under US Warehouse Act
Farm Service Agency-US Dept. of Agriculture
PO Box 2415
Washington, DC 20013-2415

Fax: 202-690-0014

Agricultural warehouses voluntarily licensed under the US Warehouse Act governing public storage facilities.
Frequency: Annual

10438 Western Fruit Grower: Source Book Issue Agriculture
Meister Publishing Company
37733 Euclid Ave
Willoughby, OH 44094-5992

440-942-2000
800-572-7740; *Fax:* 440-975-3447;
www.meisternet.com

Gary Fitzgerald, President

This annual resource offers information on manufacturers and distributors of suppliers and supplies for the fruit growing industry.
Cost: $5.00
Frequency: Annual
Circulation: 57,000

10439 Western Growers Export Dirctory
Western Growers Association
PO Box 2130
Newport Beach, CA 92658-8944

949-863-1000; *Fax:* 949-863-9028;
www.wga.com

Heather Flower, Editor

A directory offering information on shippers of fresh produce and fruit in the states of California and Arizona.
32 Pages
Frequency: Annual

10440 Who is Who: A Directory of Agricultural Engineers Available for Work
American Society of Agricultural Engineers
2950 Niles Rd
St Joseph, MI 49085-8607

269-429-0300
800-371-2723; *Fax:* 269-429-3852;
www.asabe.org

Mark D Zielke, CEO
Donna Hukk, Publication Director

This directory pertains to the availability of agricultural engineers to work in developing countries. The directory lists over 650 individuals from 60 countries, primarily engineers, available for work in land or water management, farm structures and other aspects of the field.
Cost: $27.50
210 Pages

10441 Who's Who International
WATT Publishing Company
303 N Main Street
Suite 500
Rockford, IL 61101

815-966-5400; *Fax:* 815-966-6416;
www.wattnet.com

James Watt, Chairman/CEO
Greg Watt, President/COO
Jeff Swanson, Publishing Director
Founded in: 1917

10442 Who's Who in Beer Wholesaling Directory
National Beer Wholesalers Association
1101 King Street
Suite 600
Alexandria, VA 22314-8965

703-683-4300; *Fax:* 703-683-8965
info@nbwa.org; www.nbwa.org
Social Media: Facebook, Twitter

Craig A Purser, President & CEO
Michael Johnson, EVP/Chief Advisory Officer
Rebecca Spicer, VP Public Affairs/Chief
Paul Pisano, SVP Industry Affairs & Gen. Counsel

A listing of more than 3,000 beer distributors and suppliers in the industry.
Cost: $50.00

10443 Who's Who in the Egg & Poultry Industries in the USA & Canada
WATT Publishing Company
303 N Main Street
Suite 500
Rockford, IL 61101

815-966-5400; *Fax:* 815-966-6416;
www.wattnet.com

James Watt, Chairman/CEO
Greg Watt, President/COO
Jeff Swanson, Publishing Director

Annual directory offering information on producers, processors, and distributors of poultry meat and eggs in the US and Canada.
Cost: $75.00
170 Pages
Frequency: Annual
Circulation: 10,000

10444 Who's Who in the Egg & Poultry Industry
WATT Publishing Company
303 N Main Street
Suite 500
Rockford, IL 61101

815-966-5400; *Fax:* 815-966-6416;
www.wattnet.com

James Watt, Chairman/CEO
Greg Watt, President/COO
Jeff Swanson, Publishing Director

10445 Who's Who in the Fish Industry
Urner Barry Publications
PO Box 389
Toms River, NJ 08754-0389

732-240-5330
800-932-0617; *Fax:* 732-341-0891
help@urnerbarry.com; www.urnerbarry.com

Paul B Brown Jr, President
Sheila M Deane, Marketing Manager

A business directory of Canadian traders in the seafood industry.
Cost: $125.00
Frequency: Annual
Circulation: 2,000

10446 Whole Foods Annual Source Book
Wainer Finest Communications
3000 Hadley Road
2nd Floor
South Plainfield, NJ 07080-1183

908-769-1160; *Fax:* 908-769-1171
info@wfcinc.com; www.wfcinc.com

Howard Wainer, Publisher
Alan Richman, Editor
Heather Wainer, Associate Publisher
Cost: $75.00
135 Pages
Frequency: Monthly
Circulation: 16,000
Founded in: 1979
Mailing list available for rent: 16000 names at $125 per M

10447 Wholesale Beer Association Executives of America Directory
Wholesale Beer Association Executives of America
2805 E Washington Avenue
Madison, WI 53704-5165

608-255-6464; *Fax:* 608-255-6466

7 Pages
Frequency: Annual

10448 Wholesale Grocers Directory
Chain Store Guide
3922 Coconut Palm Dr
Suite 300
Tampa, FL 33619-1389

813-627-6700
800-972-0292; *Fax:* 813-627-7094
info@csgis.com; www.csgis.com

Mike Jarvis, Publisher
Shami Choon, Manager

We have uncovered the facts on more than 1,900 grocery suppliers in the U.S. and Canada in this database. This targeted database allows you to reach food wholesalers, cooperatives and voluntary group wholesalers, non-sponsoring wholesalers, and cash and carry operators who serve grocery, convenience, discount and drug stores. You will also find information regarding company headquarters, divisions, branches, and over 11,000 key executives and buyers.
Cost: $335.00
Frequency: Annual

10449 Wine & Spirits Industry Marketing
Jobson Publishing Corporation

100 Avenue of the Americas
9th Floor
New York, NY 10013-1678

212-274-7000; *Fax:* 212-431-0500

Michael J Tansey, CEO

List of about 300 wine and liquor firms including wineries, producers, distillers and importers.
Cost: $150.00
Frequency: Annual April

10450 Wines and Vines Directory of the Wine Industry in North America Issue
Hiaring Company
1800 Lincoln Avenue
San Rafael, CA 94901-1221

415-453-9700; *Fax:* 415-453-2517
info@winesandvines.com;
www.winesandvines.com

Dorthy Kubota-Cordery, Editor
Phil Hiaring, Publisher
Debbie Hennessy, Editor
Renee Skiadas, Circulation Director
Chet Klingensmith, Owner

Annual guide offering listings of wineries and wine industry suppliers in the US, Canada and Mexico.
Cost: $85.00
505 Pages
Frequency: Annual
Circulation: 5000

10451 Yogurt Market
MarketResearch.com
641 Avenue of the Americas
3rd Floor
New York, NY 10011
212-807-2629
800-298-6699; *Fax:* 212-807-2676

Brand share and brand consumer profiles are supplemented with profiles of major US manufacturers and new product information in order to provide the reader with competitor intelligence.
Cost: $2250.00
140 Pages

10452 Zagat.Com Restaurant Guides
Zagat Survey
4 Columbus Cir
3rd Floor
New York, NY 10019-1180

212-977-6000; *Fax:* 212-977-9760
customerservice@zagat.com; www.zagat.com

Tim Zagat, CEO

Zagat.com was launched in May of 1999 and contains the most trusted and authoritive dining information online for over 20,000 restaurants in dozens of cities worldwide. Based in New York City, the Zagat survey was founded in 1979 by Tim and Nina Zagat.

Industry Web Sites

10453 http://gold.greyhouse.com
G.O.L.D Grey House OnLine Databases

Grey House Publishing's online database platform, GOLD, offers Quick Search, Keyword Search and Expert Search for most business sectors including food, beverage and agriculture markets. The GOLD platform makes finding the information you need quick and easy - whether you're a novice searcher or an experienced database user. All of Grey House's directory products are available for subscription on the GOLD platform.

10454 www.aaccnet.org
American Association of Cereal Chemists

Non profit international organization of nearly 4,000 members who are specialists in the use of cereal grains in foods. AACC has been an innovative leader in gathering and disseminating scientific and technical information to professionals in the grain-based foods indusrty wordwide for over 85 years. We know it's hard to keep up with the latest technology, that's why AACC is here to help you. We're a tool unlike any other in your lab or office. Industry leaders turn to and trust AACC.

10455 www.aaea.org
American Agricultural Economics Association

The professional association for agricultural economists and related fields.

10456 www.aaicc.org
National Alliance of Independent Crop Consultants

Represents individual crop consultants and contract researchers.

10457 www.aaminc.org
American Agriculture Movement

An umbrella organization composed of state organizations representing family farm producers.

10458 www.aamp.com
American Association of Meat Processors

Membership consists of small to medium sized meat, poultry and food businesses including: packers, processors, wholesalers, home food service businesses, retailers, deli and catering operators and suppliers to the industry. AAMP is also affiliated with 34 states, regional and provincial organizations which represent meat and poultry businesses.

10459 www.aanc.net
American Association of Nutritional Consultants

An association combating public ignorance and adverse legislation.

10460 www.aapausa.org
American Alfalfa Processors Association

Information for the processors and suppliers in the alfalfa industry.

10461 www.abfnet.org
American Beekeeping Federation

For honey producers, packers, suppliers and shippers of honey products.

10462 www.aceweb.org
Agricultural Communicators in Education

For writers, editors, broadcasters and communicators who are involved in the dissemination of agricultural, food sciences and natural resource information in land-grant colleges, federal and state agencies, international agencies and other private communications work.

10463 www.acfsa.org
American Correctional Food Service Affiliates

International, professional association created to serve the needs and interests of food service personnel in the correctional environments. The association brings together highly skilled food service workers and their vendors who are interested in the common goal of providing nutritious, cost-efficient meal service for confined populations.

10464 www.acsh.org
American Council on Science and Health

A nonprofit, consumer education organization concerned with issues related to food, nutrition, chemicals, pharmaceuticals, lifestyles, the environment and health.

10465 www.adpi.org
American Dairy Products Institute

An association for manufactured dairy products, including dry milks, whey, lactose, evaporated and condensed milk. ADPI's main purpose is to effectively communicate the many positive attributes and benefits of our members' products. Additionally, we serve our membership by offering the most current industry information available and by collaborating with dairy associations to represent members' interests before state and federal regulatory agencies.

10466 www.adsa.uiuc.edu
American Dairy Science Association

Publications, information, etc.

10467 www.aeb.org
American Egg Board

Facts, recipes, industry and nutrition information.

10468 www.afco.org
Association of American Feed Control Officials

Officials of government agencies at the state and federal levels engaged in the regulation and distribution of products, animal feeds and livestock remedies.

10469 www.affi.com
American Frozen Food Institute

News and events, facts, tips, and recipes, etc.

10470 www.afia.org
Animal Industry Foundation

Works to improve animal production practices in the US, to dispel misconceptions that a diet containing meat, milk and eggs is unhealthy and that animals raised for foods in the US are mistreated.

10471 www.afius.org
Association of Food Industries

The association is a trade association serving the food import trade.

10472 www.ag.ohio-state.edu/~farmshow
North American Farm Show Council

Agriculture trade shows and suppliers of services to these shows. Strives to improve education, communication and evaluation and provide the best possible marketing showcase for exhibitors and related products to the farmer/rancher/producer customer.

10473 www.agnic.org/

Access to experts in various fields of agriculture as well as links to agricultural databases. Find out about conferences, meetings and seminars in your area.

10474 www.agribsuiness.com
National Agri-Marketing Association

Industry information, member directory and links to member sites.

10475 www.agriwashington.org
Apple Processors Association

Organization consisting of processors and suppliers which provides a forum for discussion regarding legislation, regulations and new technology.

10476 www.agriwashington.org/aagiwa.html
American Association of Grain Inspection

Established to provide a liaison between the Federal Grain Inspection Service and designated agencies.

10477 www.agview.com/

All aspects of agriculture: Usenet groups, Web resources, archives, mailing lists, etc.

10478 www.ahpa.org
American Herbal Products Association

For manufacturers, importers and distributors of herbs and herbal products. AHPA seeks self-regulation, establishment of standards and rules of ethical conduct, member enrichment and public outreach.

10479 www.aibonline.org
American Institute of Baking Technical Bulletin

This organization provides research, education, training and consulting for the baking and food industries worldwide.

10480 www.aiccbox.org
International Corrugated Packaging Foundation

Videos, promotional materials, demonstrating support of the corrugated packaging industry worldwide. Place corrugated equipment into universities and technical colleges to provide students with corrugated industry skills.

10481 www.aicr.org
American Institute for Cancer Research

Third largest cancer charity in the US, focusing exclusively on research and education in regard to diet and cancer.

10482 www.aiwf.org
American Institute of Wine & Food

A non-profit educational organization devoted to improving the appreciation, understanding and accessibility of food and drink.

10483 www.ala-national.org
American Logistics Association

A nonprofit trade organization supporting the Military Resale and Morale, Welfare & Recreation industry.

10484 www.alaskaseafood.org
Alaska Seafood Marketing Institute

Organization of private industry and government fishing. Markets only Alaskan seafood. This association also offers educational and promotional materials on fresh and frozen seafood.

10485 www.allied-purchasing.com
Allied Purchasing

A group of ice cream plants, soft drink bottlers, dairies, brewries and water companies collaborating to obtain group purchasing rates on equipment, services, ingredients and supplies.

10486 www.almond-growers.com
California Independent Almond Growers

Association for almond growers, processors, packers and shippers

10487 www.almondsarein.com
Almond Board of California

This association provides production research, mandatory inspection and marketing promotion statistics for the almond/nut industry.

10488 www.americanbakers.org
American Bakers Association

Association comprised of wholesale bakers.

10489 www.americanberkshire.com
American Berkshire Association

Association for cattle and hog breeders in the US.

10490 www.americandairyproducts.com
American Dairy Products Institute

A national trade association representing the processed dairy products industry.

10491 www.americanhoneyproducers.org
American Honey Producers Association

Represents the interests of major USA honey producers and pollinators.

10492 www.americanwineries.org
American Vintners Association

10493 www.amif.org
American Meat Institute Foundation

10494 www.amseed.com
American Seed Trade Association

Producers of seeds for planting purposes.

10495 www.amsey.org
American Soybean Association

To improve US soybean farmer profitability. Publishes a monthly newsletter

10496 www.angus.org
American Angus Association

Industry and member links, information, etc.

10497 www.animalagriculture.org
National Institute for Animal Agriculture

10498 www.aob.org
Association of Brewers

Membership, publications, news, events, etc.

10499 www.aomillers.org
International Association of Operative Millers

An international organization, comprised of flour millers, cereal grain and seed processors and allied trades representatives and companies devoted to the advancement of technology in the flour milling and cereal grain processing industries.

10500 www.apics.org
APICS Association for Operations Management

The primary purpose of this specific industry group is to educate food and beverage manufacturers on effective marketing strategies, market trends and material management.

10501 www.applejuice.org
Processed Apples Institute

Producers of processed apple products; suppliers of equipment, packaging or ingredients to the industry and brokers and concentrate manufacturers.

10502 www.appleprocessors.org
Apple Processors Association

A national association of companies that manufacture quality apple products from whole apples. Members are either apple grower/processor cooperatives, or proprietary firms.

10503 www.appleproducts.org
Processed Apples Institute

Links to related industry sites.

10504 www.apricotproducers.com
Apricot Producers of California

10505 www.ari.org/crm
Commercial Refrigerator Manufacturers Division

Provides information, instruction, education to members in technical and business areas; also specializes in solving common problems and stimulating growth within the industry.

10506 www.asac.org
American Society of Agricultural Consultants

For agricultural consultants acting as an information base for members.

10507 www.asae.org
American Society of Agricultural Engineers

Information on agricultural engineering, biological engineering and food process engineering.

10508 www.asas.org
American Society of Animal Society

For professional researchers, publishes journals and holds seminars in the Animal Science field.

10509 www.asbe.org
American Society of Baking

Research and development of machinery for baking applications.

10510 www.asfsa.org
American School Food Service Association

An association focused on good nutrition for all children.

10511 www.ashrae.org
American Society of Heating, Refrigerating and
Air Conditioning

An international membership organization of engineers who create the worlds we live in.

10512 www.asifood.com
ASI Food Safety Consultants

ASI Food Safety Consultants is a full service provider of food safety audits, seminars and HACCP programs.

10513 www.asmc.org
Association of Sales & Marketing Companies

Members are representatives for producers of food, packaged goods, and other consumer products.

10514 www.astaspice.org
American Spice Trade Association

United States based organization whose worldwide membership is comprised of the leading firms in the spice industry.

10515 www.atsea.org
AT-SEA Processors Association

The At-sea Association represents US flag catcher/processor vessels that participate in the healthy and abundant ground fish fisheries of the Bering Sea.

10516 www.australian-beef.com
Meat & Livestock Australia

Promotes comsumption of Australian beef, lamb, mutton and goat in Canada, US and Mexico. The company is funded by Australian producers. They key focus is to increase access for Australian meat producers to the North American market and to raise awareness of its nutritional value, quality and safety.

10517 www.australian-lamb.com
Meat & Livestock Australia

Promotes comsumption of Australian beef, lamb, mutton and goat in Canada, US and Mexico. The company is funded by Australian producers. They key focus is to increase access for Australian meat producers to the North American market and to raise awareness of its nutritional value, quality and safety.

10518 www.australianmeatsafety.com
Meat & Livestock Australia

Promotes comsumption of Australian beef, lamb, mutton and goat in Canada, US and Mexico. The company is funded by Australian producers. They key focus is to increase access for Australian meat producers to the North American market and to raise awareness of its nutritional value, quality and safety.

10519 **www.avocado.org**
California Avacado Commission
A resource for the California avocado industry.

10520 **www.awmanet.org**
American Wholesale Marketers Association
An international trade organization working on behalf of convenience distributors in the United States.

10521 **www.awwpa.com**
American White Wheat Producers Association
Organization of white wheat producers promoting and introducing new white wheat products.

10522 **www.bakeryonline.com**
Bakery Online
A database for bakers, food scientists, food engineers, process engineers, plant managers, business managers, executives and other professionals involved in the bakery industry. Features a comprehensive buyer's guide, interactive discussion forums and daily news updates and reports on business, regulatory and technology trends vital to the industry.

10523 **www.bbga.org**
Bread Bakers Guild of America
Links to member sites.

10524 **www.beef.org**
National Cattlemen's Beef Association
Related industry information.

10525 **www.beerinstitute.org**
Beer Institute
National trade association for the malt beverage industry. Represents the diversity of brewers and suppliers.

10526 **www.beertown.org**
American Homebrewers Association
Devoted to the education of home-brewed beer. Publishes magazine devoted exclusively to education, art and science of homebrewing. Services include: Beer Judge Certification Program, Sanctioned Competitions, World's Largest Homebrew Competition.

10527 **www.bema.org**
Bakery Equipment Manufacturers Association
An international nonprofit association representing leading bakery and food equipment manufacturers and suppliers whose combined efforts in research and development have led to the continual improvement of the baking and food industries.

10528 **www.bestapples.com**
Washington Apple Commission
Marketing professionals promote apples through retail marketing, advertising, public relations, health and food communications.

10529 **www.beverageonline.com**
Beverage Online
A database for beverage chemists, food scientists, food technologists, process engineers, plant managers, business managers, executives and other professionals involved in the beverage processing industry.

10530 **www.biodynamics.com**
Bio-Dynamic Farming and Gardening Association
Supporting biodynamic growers and processors in North America and acts to safeguard and promote the biodynamic method of agriculture.

10531 **www.bisoncentral.com**
National Bison Association
The National Bison Association was formed to promote the production, marketing and preservation of bison.

10532 **www.bissc.org**
Baking Industry Sanitation Standards Committee
Develops and promotes sanitation standards for the design and construction of bakery equipment. Offers self certification and third party certification programs for member companies whose equipment conforms to the BISSC standards.

10533 **www.blueberry.org**
North American Blueberry Council
History, crop information, products, international markets and berry sites.

10534 **www.bottledwater.org**
Bottled Water Association

10535 **www.brownswissusa.com**
Brown Swiss Cattle Breeders Associ of the USA

10536 **www.bsdf-assbt.org**
Beet Sugar Development Foundation
Association specializing in beet sugar research and the advertisement of seed companies.

10537 **www.butterinstitute.org**
American Butter Institute
Represents butter manufacturers and conducts research.

10538 **www.ca-seafood.org**
California Seafood Council

10539 **www.caa-aqua.org**
California Aquaculture Association

10540 **www.cacheeseandbutter.org**
California Cheese & Butter Association
Membership directory along with links.

10541 **www.calbeef.org**
California Beef Council

10542 **www.californiadates.org**
California Date Commission

10543 **www.californiafigs.com**
California Fig Advisory Board
History and facts, nutritional information, recipes and contests.

10544 **www.calolive.org**
California Olive Committee

10545 **www.caloriecontrol.org**
Calorie Control Council

10546 **www.calpear.com**
California Pear Association
Consumer information, research reports, marketing and promo information.

10547 **www.calstrawberry.com**
California Strawberry Commission
Health and nutrition, contests, recipes, news, etc.

10548 **www.cancentral.com**
Can Manufacturers Institute
Serves can manufacturers and can industry suppliers

10549 **www.candyhalloffame.com**
National Confectionery Sales Association
Association of salespersons, brokers, sales managers, wholesalers and manufacturers in the confectionery industry.

10550 **www.candyusa.org**
National Confectioners Association
Association news, candy stats, health information, and candy history.

10551 **www.cannedveggies.org**
Canned Vegetable Council
An educational and promotional organization of vegetable canners whose goals are to raise the awareness of consumer and food service buyers regarding canned vegetables.

10552 **www.canonline.org**
Composite Can & Tube Institute
Serving the composite cans and tube industry.

10553 **www.cast-science.org**
Council for Agricultural Science and Technology
Identifies food, fiber, environmental and other agricultural issues for all stake holders.

10554 **www.cawineclub.com**
California Wine Club
A wine of the month club that features only California's small boutique wineries. Each month members receive two bottles of award-winning wine.

10555 **www.ccpgab.com**
California Cling Peach Advisory Board

10556 **www.cdfa.ca.gov**
North American Agricultural Marketing
For state and provincial officials responsible for agricultural products marketing programs in the US, Canada and ultimately Mexico.

10557 **www.cemanet.org**
Conveyor Equipment Manufacturers Association

10558 **www.cheesesociety.org**
American Cheese Society
Promotes cheese industry. Holds cheese tasting and workshops on cheesemaking. Sponsors competition.

10559 **www.chicagomidwestmeatasso.com**
Chicago-Midwest Meat Association
The CMMA conducts its activities as a not-for-profit trade association for meat companies in the midwest. Its purpose is to support and promote the meat industry

10560 **www.chocolateandcocoa.org**
American Cocoa Research Institute

10561 **www.choosecherries.org**
Cherry Marketing Institute
Association representing the cherry industry. Provides promotional material to food service operators, brokers, retailers and manufacturers.

10562 **www.chowbaby.com**
This web site is a search engine for restaurants. Provides help in finding the perfect eatery close to your home or travel destination. Online reservations, maps, menus and more. Can be searched by International Location, US Location, US Map or Cuisine type.

10563 **www.chrie.org**
Int'l Council on Hotel, Restaurant Institute Edu.
To enhance professionalism at all levels of the hospitality and tourism industry through education and training.

10564 **www.christree.org**
National Christmas Tree Association
Provides industry leaders a chance to work directly with their suppliers and distributors.

10565 www.ciachef.edu
Culinary Institute of America

10566 www.clm1.org
Council of Logistics Management

10567 www.coffeeindustry.org
Specialty Coffee Association of America
Association offering business, professional, promotional and educational assistance in the areas of cultivation, processing, and marketing of specialty coffees. The association also hosts the largest event in the world dedicated to coffee, the SCAA Annual Conference and exhibition.

10568 www.colborne.com/apc/home.htm
American Pie Council
Membership, recipes, coupons, etc.

10569 www.corn.org
Corn Refiners Association
Stats, career opportunities, publications and newsbriefs.

10570 www.cosmos.com.mx:80
Index of Food
Manufacturers indexed by industry, company name, products and brands.

10571 www.cottonseed.com
National Cottonseed Products Association
National association of cottonseed products.

10572 www.countryham.org
National Country Ham Association
The NCHA encourages promotion, development, and improvement at the businesses of country ham carvers and encourages the use of country carved meats through cooperative methods of production, promotion, education and advertisement.

10573 www.cpif.org
California Poultry Industry Federation
Links to other associations.

10574 www.cpma.ca
Canadian Produce Marketing Association
Profile and services, links, technical resources, etc.

10575 www.cranberries.org
Cranberry Institute
Association which gathers and disseminates information about cranberry growing, horticultural and environmental issues to cranberry growers and handlers in the US and Canada.

10576 www.crnusa.org
Council for Responsible Nutrition
Vitamin manufacturers.

10577 www.cropinsurance.org
Crop Insurance Research Bureau
Crop insurance trade organization.

10578 www.croplifeamerica.org
CropLife America
Information on protecting crops and environmentally fragile agriculture.

10579 www.crops.org
Crop Science Society of America
Seeks to advance research, extension and teaching of all basic and applied phases of the crop sciences.

10580 www.csce.com
Coffee, Sugar and Cocoa Exchange
Acts as a financial exchange where futures and options are traded, the CSCE provides hedging and investing, opportunities in the coffee, sugar, cocoa and dairy markets.

10581 www.css.orst.edu/weeds/iwss
International Weed Science Society
For institutions and individuals concerned with the study of weeds and their control.

10582 www.culinary.com
Louisiana Sweet Potato Commission
Links to member sites.

10583 www.dairyinfo.com
Dairy Management
Links to related associations.

10584 www.dairynetwork.com
Dairy Network
Searchable database of food industry related items.

10585 www.delianet.com
Deli Associates
Association for manufacturers or suppliers of confectionary, candy and bakery products.

10586 www.delicouncil.com
Dairy, Deli-Bakery Council of Southern California

10587 www.dhia.org
National Dairy Herd Improvement Association
Sets policies, holds meetings and offers seminars for dairymen.

10588 www.diamondwalnut.com
Diamond Walnut Growers

10589 www.doitwithdairy.com
Dairy Management — American Dairy Association, National Dairy Council, US Dairy Export Council

10590 www.dressings-sauces.org
Association for Dressings and Sauces
This association is comprised of manufacturers of mayonnaise, salad dressings and condiment sauces, as well as industry suppliers.

10591 www.drink-milk.com
American Dairy Association Mideast
We represent dairy farmers and serve as the local affiliate for the American Dairy Association and the National Dairy Council. We work closely with Dairy Management Inc. and the Milk Processors Education Program to extend national dairy promotion programs to the local level.

10592 www.duckling.org
Duckling Council
Consortium of duckling producers located coast-to-coast, whose goal is to increase consumption of duckling nationwide and increase awareness of duckling's nutritionally improved profile.

10593 www.eatchicken.com
National Broiler Council
Recipes, industry information and statistics.

10594 www.eatright.org
American Dietetic Association
Nutrition resources, hot topics, FAQ's.

10595 www.eatturkey.com
National Turkey Federation
Advocate for all segments of the US turkey industry, providing services and conducting activities that increase demand for its members' products. The federation also protects and enhances its members' ability to effectively and profitably provide wholesome, high quality, nutritious turkey products.

10596 www.eddal.com
Eastern Dairy Deli Bakery Association
This association encourages growth and education regarding dairy, deli and bakery industries. It promotes the sales of Dairy, Deli and Bakery products through supermarkets and specialty stores and acts as a resource and information center for the industry.

10597 www.eggs.org
Egg Clearing House
Links to related members and associations.

10598 www.ejkrause.com
EJ Krause & Associates
Association for suppliers of hotel and restaurant food and beverages.

10599 www.elettric80.com
Electric 80
Supports automated material handling systems, robotic palletizers and laser-guided vehicles.

10600 www.eppainc.org
Eastern Dairy Perishable Products Association
This association encourages growth and education regarding perishable products. It promotes the sales of perishable products through supermarkets and specialty stores and acts as a resource and information center for the industry.

10601 www.fancyfoodshows.com
Nat'l Association for the Specialty Food Trade
Members are manufacturers, importers, distributors and retailers of specialty gourmet and fancy foods. Has an annual budget of approximately $15 million.

10602 www.fb.com
American Farm Bureau Federation
For state Farm Bureaus in the 50 states and Puerto Rico.

10603 www.fbminet.ca/agnews.htm
Agricultural news releases.

10604 www.fcsi.org
Food Service Consultants Society International
Membership, publications, industry links etc.

10605 www.fda.gov
Food and Drug Administration
The official website of FDA.

10606 www.fdi.org
Food Service Distributors International

10607 www.fdrs.ag.utk.edu/
Food Distribution Research Society
Investigates how food is distributed and traded.

10608 www.feda.com
Food Service Equipment Distributors Association
Dealers and distributors of foodservice equipment and supplies.

10609 www.femaflavor.org
Flavor & Extract Manufacturers Assn of the US
1620 I Street NW
Suite 925
Washington, DC 210006
202-293-5800; *Fax:* 202-463-8998
Ed R. Hayes, President
George C. Robinson III, President Elect

Mark Scott, Treasurer
Arthur Schick, Vice President & Secretary
FEMA is comprised of flavor manufacturers, flavor users, flavor ingredient suppliers, and others with an interest in the U.S. flavor industry. FEMA workds with legislators and regulators to assure that the needs of members and consumers are continuously addressed and is committed to assuring a substantial supply of safe flavoring substances.

10610 www.fewa.org
Farm Equipment Wholesalers Association
For wholesale/distributors of ag equipment and related products.

10611 www.ffane.org
Frozen Food Association of New England
Promotes the frozen food industry.

10612 www.fiae.com
Food Industry Association Executives

10613 www.fightbac.org
Fight Bac
Sound advice for better food safety.

10614 www.fl-citrus-mutual.com
Florida Citrus Mutual
History and mission, member information.

10615 www.foodallergy.org
Food Allergy & Anaphylaxis Network
The only nonprofit organization in the US devoted solely to patient education for food allergies. Mission is to create public awareness about food allergies and anaphylaxis to provide education, and to advance research on behalf of all those affected by food allergy.

10616 www.foodcontact.com
Food Contact
Searchable directory of food and beverage processors and exporters.

10617 www.foodexplorer.com
Food Explorer
Database of industry related materials.

10618 www.foodfront.com
Internet Foodfront
Searchable database of food industry related items and resources.

10619 www.foodindustry.com
Industry Guides.net
Link directory for related industry.

10620 www.foodingredientsonline.com
Food Ingredients Online
International forum where buyers and sellers connect. Highly targeted and focused site offers original material, daily news updates, a product showcase, projects for bid, employment opportunities, downloadbale software, and a free interactive buyers guide which produces instant leads.

10621 www.foodinstitute.com
American Institute of Food Distribution
Serves as a central information service for food trades. Issues, reports, studies and statistical data and maintains a library. Member companies throughout the US and over 40 foreign countries.

10622 www.foodnet.gr
FoodNet
Searchable database of food industry related items and resources.

10623 www.foodonline.com
Food Online
Searchable database of food industry related items.

10624 www.foodproductdesign.com
Food product design magazine

10625 www.foodprotection.org
International Association for Food Protection
The International Association for Food Protection, founded in 1911, is a nonprofit educational association with a mission to provide food safety professional worldwide with a forum to exchange information on protecting the food supply. The Association is comprised of over 3,000 members from 50 nations. Affiliate chapters are located in the US, Canada, Mexico and South Korea.

10626 www.foodservice.com/doorway.htm
Foodservice.com
Database of information and resources for food industry buyers and sellers.

10627 www.foodserviceworld.com
Food Service World
Food associations, suppliers and events.

10628 www.foodshow.com
Foodshow
Electronic food show with booths for manufacturers.

10629 www.foodweb.com
Foodweb
Links to suppliers of food and equipment, distributors, unions, etc.

10630 www.foodwine.com/digest
Netfood Directory (The BLUE Directory)
List of relevant food and food service internet sites.

10631 www.fourhcouncil.edu
National 4-H Council
Focuses on diverse groups of young people in a variety of urban and suburban locales while continuing to serve youth in rural areas. Helps provide hands-on co-educational programs and activities to young people nationwide.

10632 www.fpaota.org
Fresh Produce Association of the Americas
Trade association for Mexican produce. Formerly known as West Mexico Vegetable Distributors Association.

10633 www.fpfc.org
Fresh Produce and Floral Council
Promotes through communication and education, fresh fruit, vegetable and floral products.

10634 www.fpi.org
Food Service & Packaging Institute
A national association comprised of manufacturers and suppliers of disposables for the food service industry.

10635 www.fpmsa.org (or www.iefp.org)
Food Processing Machinery Association
List of exhibitors from IEFP (links included).

10636 www.fresh-cuts.org
International Fresh-Cut Produce Association
IFPA advances the fresh-cut produce industry by supporting members with technical information, representation, and knowledge to provide convenient safe and wholesome food. Members are processor companies, suppliers and researchers.

10637 www.freshcut.com
Columbia Publishing
Information on carrot production, growers and shippers.

10638 www.frozenfoodcouncil.com
Frozen Food Council of Northern California
Coupons, promotions, contests, member information and events.

10639 www.fsgroup.com
Food Service Group
This organization is comprised of food service brokerage companies meeting the needs and offering a national exchange of ideas and information of food service sales professionals.

10640 www.fspronet.com
Food Service Professionals Network
Database of food industry related items including directories, etc.

10641 www.georgiapecans.org
Georgia Pecan Commission

10642 www.gmabrands.com
Grocery Manufacturers of America
Government affairs, industry regulations, news, etc.

10643 www.gpi.org
Glass Packaging Institute
Serves the glass container suppliers for the beer, juice, RTD tea, liquor, wine and dairy businesses.

10644 www.grains.org
US Feed Grains Council
For grain sorghum, barley and corn producer associations and representatives of the agricultural community. Provides commodity export market development.

10645 www.greyhouse.com
Grey House Publishing
Authoritative reference directories for most business sectors including food, beverage and agriculture markets. Users can search the online databases with varied search criteria allowing for custom searches by product category, geographic area, sales volume, keyword, subject and more. Full Grey House catalog and online ordering also available.

10646 www.hazelnut.com
Hazelnut Growers of Oregon
Recipes, health and ingredient information, etc.

10647 www.hazelnutcouncil.org
Hazelnut Council
Promotion to commercial information exhibiting ingredient users and recipies, formulas and food service

10648 www.healthfinder.gov
Association of Food and Drug Officials
Promotes the enforcement of laws and regulations at all levels of government. Fosters understanding and cooperation between industry and regulators. Develops model laws and regulations and seeks their adoption.

10649 www.herbnet.com/, www.herbworld.com
Herb Growing and Marketing Network
Trade association information services for herb related businesses. Hosts national conference for those in the herb industry with seminars covering commercial production, medicinal herbs and general business topics.

10650 www.herbs.org
Herb Research Foundation
Provides scientific-based and traditional information about use and safety of herbs for health.

Fee-based hotline, information packs and literature are available to members.

10651 www.herbsociety.org
Herb Society of America
Educates its members and the public on the cultivation of herbs, as well as the history and uses of herbs.

10652 www.hereford.org
American Hereford Association
For people in the Hereford cattle industry.

10653 www.holsteinusa.com
Holstein Association
For people with strong interests in breeding, raising and milking Holstein cattle.

10654 www.iacp.com
International Association of Culinary Professional
A not-for-profit organization whose members represent virtually every profession in the culinary universe: teachers, cooking school owners, caterers, writers, chefs, media cooking personalities, editors, publishers, food stylists, food photographers, restauranteurs, leaders of major food corporations and vintners. Literally a who's who of the food world. Founded in 1978.

10655 www.iacsc.org
International Association of Cold Storage

10656 www.iafenet.org
International Association of Fairs & Expositions
Membership consists of individual agricultural fairs and regional associations of agricultural fairs.

10657 www.iaff.ttu.edu/aals
Association for Arid Land Studies

10658 www.iafis.org
Int'l Association of Food Industry Suppliers
Serves the dairy food and beverage industries, and related sanitary processing industries addressing the marketing and business information needs of the food supply channel.

10659 www.iaicv.org
International Association of Ice Cream Vendors
Members are manufacturers and distributors of ice cream novelties and street vendors.

10660 www.iarw.org
International Association of Refrigerated
Trade association of public refrigerated warehouse storing of all types of perishable products.

10661 www.ibdea.org
International Beverage Dispensing Equipment
Serves independent purveyors of equipment, service and products for the food and beverage industry.

10662 www.iddanet.org
International Dairy-Deli-Bakery Association
Newsletter, training information, publications, member list and FQA's.

10663 www.iddba.org
International Dairy-Deli-Bakery Association
Furthers relationship between manufacturing, production, marketing used in delivery of goods to marketplace. Presents awards and maintains a hall of fame.

10664 www.idfa.org
International Dairy Foods Association
IDFA represents the best interests of the U.S. dairy processing and manufacturing industry, as well as its supplier members and industry's leading suppliers companies.

10665 www.ifas.ufl.edu
Agricultural Communicators of Tomorrow
For college students professionally interested in communications related to agriculture, food, natural resources and allied fields.

10666 www.ific.org
International Food Information Council
Food safety and nutritional information, press releases and publications.

10667 www.ifmaworld.com
International Foodservice Manufacturers
Trade association for food, beverage, equipment and supply manufacturers and ancillary service companies serving the food service industry.

10668 www.ifse.tamu.edu/sma.html
Southwest Meat Association
Newsletter, member information and links.

10669 www.ifsea.org
International Food Service Executives
Provides education and community service to the foodservice industry.

10670 www.ift.org
Institute of Food Technologists
Member information, publications, calender of expos and meetings.

10671 www.iherb.org
International Herb Association
Supports the herb businesses and educates the public.

10672 www.iiar.org
International Institute of Ammonia Refrigeration
Promotes the safe use of ammonia as a refrigerant. Offers educational, promotional and standards development programs and legislative/regulatory support to manufacturers, contractors, consulting engineers, wholesalers and end users.

10673 www.ilovepasta.org
National Pasta Association
List of members, FAQ's, pasta nutrition and recipes.

10674 www.ilovepickles.org
Pickle Packers International
Addresses the concerns of pickle packers, shippers and manufacturers.

10675 www.ilsi.org
International Life Sciences Institute
Scientific institution that supports research on nutrition, food safety and toxicology.

10676 www.independentbaker.org
Independent Bakers Association
Organization of member bakers.

10677 www.insca.org
International Natural Sausage Casing Association

10678 www.iopp.org
Institute of Packaging Professionals

10679 www.ipmwww.ncsu.edu/cernag/
All aspects of agriculture: Usenet groups, Web resources, archives, mailing lists, etc.

10680 www.irrigation.org
Irrigation Association
Irrigation industry information.

10681 www.iseo.org
Institute of Shortening & Edible Oils

10682 www.jps.net/ahaherb
American Herb Association
Membership is comprised of professional herablists and herbal enthusiasts. The goal is to increase knowledge and offer updated scientific information on herbs.

10683 www.juanvaldez.com
National Federation of Coffee Growers of Colombia
This organization is comprised of coffee growers from Colombia whose goal is to promote Colombian coffee in the US.

10684 www.kab.org
Keep America Beautiful
National nonprofit education organization whose corporate members include packagers, retailers, bottlers, and makers of chemical, steel, glass, paper and aluminum products.

10685 www.kiwifruit.org
California Kiwifruit Commission
News, recipes, export information, etc.

10686 www.kla.org
Kansas Livestock Association

10687 www.lambchef.com
American Lamb Council

10688 www.larw.org
Refrigeration Research and Education Foundation
Sponsors graduate-level scientific research on the refrigeration of perishable commodities. Offers annual training institute for public refrigerated warehouse personnel.

10689 www.leafy-greens.org
Leafy Greens Council
Made up of growers and shippers. This association promotes the consumption of leafy greens and vegetables for battling diseases like cancer.

10690 www.ilovepecans.org
National Pecan Shellers Association
An association aimed at promoting the pecan shelling and processing industry.

10691 www.mainelobsterpromo.com
Maine Lobster Promotion Council

10692 www.mainpotatoes.com
Maine Potato Board

10693 www.meatami.com
American Meat Institute
A leading trade association for the meat processing industry.

10694 www.meatandpoultryonline.com
Meat and Poultry Online
Searchable database of food industry related items.

10695 www.meatnz.co.nz
Meat New Zealnd

10696 www.meatpoultry.com
Meat and poultry magazine

10697 www.mhia.org
Material Handling Industry

10698 www.micausa.org
Meat Importers Council of America

10699 **www.michiganapples.dcom**
Michigan Apple Committee

10700 **www.militaryfood.org**
Research and Development Associates for Military
Founded as a forum for the interchange of technical data on food products, feeding systems, food and feeding equipment and food packaging between industry and professors of Food Science and Technology and the US Armed Forces and Government.

10701 **www.mindspring.com/~independentbaker**
Independent Bakers Association
Links, issue papers, etc.

10702 **www.msgfacts.com**
Glutamate Association— US
Members are manufacturers, distributors and processed food users of glutamate, glutamate acid and its salts in the food industry.

10703 **www.mtgplace.com**
Source of information for food product developers

10704 **www.mushroomcouncil.com**
Mushroom Council

10705 **www.mwfpa.org**
Midwest Food Processors Association
This association offers member companies information on legislation and industry matters.

10706 **www.naab-css.org**
National Association of Animal Breeders
For farmer co-ops and others interested in livestock improvement.

10707 **www.nabi-inc.gpg.com**
National Association of Beverage Importers
Members hold a Federal Basic Importer's permit.

10708 **www.nabronline.org**
National Association of Beverage Retailers
Represents over 15,000 off-premise licensees in the 'open' or 'license' states and on-premise proprietors in markets across the nation. Offers members information on legislation and industry matters.

10709 **www.nacaa.com**
National Association County Agricultural Agents
For agents focusing on educational programs for the youth of the community.

10710 **www.naconline.org**
National Association of Concessionaires
This association works to professionalize the concession industry by providing information services and training programs for concession managers and employees. Holds conventions, seminars, trade shows, and certification programs for the leisure time food and beverage industry. Produces newsletters and magazines for its international membership.

10711 **www.nacufs.org**
National Assn of College & University Food Service
Educational programs, conferences, publications, etc.

10712 **www.nadefa.org**
North American Deer Farmers Association
A nonprofit organization that offers representation of US and Canadian breeders and producers of venison. Velvet and trophy stock.

10713 **www.nafem.org**
Food Equipment Manufacturers Association
A trade association of foodservice equipment and supplies manufacturers, that provide products for food preparation, cooking, storage and table service.

10714 **www.naffs.org**
National Association of Fruits, Flavors & Syrups
Industry information, member directory and links to member sites.

10715 **www.nama.org**
National Agri-Marketing Association
Marketing and communication suppliers, including trade publications, radio and television broadcast sales organizations, premium/incentive manufacturers, printers, marketing research firms, photographers and related professionals.

10716 **www.namamillers.org**
North American Millers' Association

10717 **www.namp.com**
North American Meat Processors Association
Represents processors and distributors of meat, poultry, seafood and game to the food service industry.

10718 **www.nanca.org**
North American Natural Casing Association
The NANCA responds to issues and service needs that are unique to the North American segment of the industry.

10719 **www.nas.edu**
National Research Council/National Academy

10720 **www.nasda-hq.org**
National Association of State Departments of
Agriculture

10721 **www.nationalgrange.org**
National Grange
Promotes general welfare and agriculture through local organizations. Presides over the advancement and promotion of the farming and agriculture industry.

10722 **www.nationalgrocers.org**
National Grocers of America
This association services as the information network to the National Grocers Association. Purposes of this organization: handling government affairs regarding the operation of retail groceries; developing educational programs and literature regarding the industry; and supports women in the retail distribution industry.

10723 **www.navigator.tufts.edu**
Tufts University Nutrition Navigator
A rating guide for more than 300 nutrition websites.

10724 **www.nbva.org**
National Bulk Vendors Association
An organization comprised of manufacturers, distributors and operators of bulk vending merchandise and equipment.

10725 **www.nbwa.org**
National Beer Wholesalers Association
Research and development, quality control and ingredients.

10726 **www.nca-cna.org**
National Confectioners Association
Manufacturers of confectionary products and services.

10727 **www.ncausa.org and www.coffeescience.org**
National Coffee Association of USA
This association promotes business relations among members of the trade. Also collects and publishes information on the coffee industry, maintaining a library of 1000 science and medical books and literature about coffee and caffeine.

10728 **www.ncga.com**
National Corn Growers Association

10729 **www.neffa.com**
Northeast Fresh Foods Alliance

10730 **www.nfdffa.org**
National Frozen Dessert and Fast Food Association
This association is made up of small, independent owners and operators of ice cream and fast food establishments.

10731 **www.nffa.org**
National Frozen Food Association
Training, research, networking services, etc.

10732 **www.nfi.org**
National Aquaculture Council
For farmers, food processors and food distributors with an interest in aquaculture.

10733 **www.nfo.org**
National Farmers Union
Promotes educational, cooperative and legislative activities of farm families in 44 states.

10734 **www.nfpa-food.org**
National Food Processors Association
A leading food industry trade association.

10735 **www.nfraweb.org**
National Frozen & Refrigerated Foods Association
Nonprofit trade association comprised of 650 member companies representing all segments of the frozen and refrigerated food industry. NFRA has been serving the frozen food industry since 1945 and just recently in 2001 began serving the refrigerated foods industry. The mission of NFRA is to promote the sales and consumption of frozen and refrigerated foods through: educations, training, research, sales planning and menu development and providing a forum for industry dialogue.

10736 **www.nhb.org**
National Honey Board
This organization offers information and support to members in the honey producing industry.

10737 **www.nicra.org**
National Ice Cream Retailers Association
A trade organization whose members are in the retail ice cream; frozen custard; gelato; frozen yogurt and water ice business. Members are located all across the United States, Canada and several other countries.

10738 **www.nims.com**
Network of Ingredient Marketing Specialists
This organization has established a network of ingredient manufacturers' representatives that offers ingredient manufacturers the most cost effective access to US, Canadian and European markets.

10739 **www.njpa.com**
National Juice Products Association

10740 **www.nmaonline.org**
National Meat Association

Provides it members unique one-on-one assistance resolving regulatory issues. Mission is to be proactive and responsive in serving members both individually and collectively.

10741 www.nmpf.org
National Milk Producers Federation

10742 www.noble.net
Noble & Associates
Advertising agency for food industry professionals.

10743 www.nopa.org
National Oilseed Processors Association

10744 www.npcspud.com
National Potato Council
Represents US potato growers on federal legislative and regulatory issues.

10745 www.nppc.org
National Pork Producers Council
Nutrition information, educational resources and research results.

10746 www.nsda.org
National Soft Drink Association
Industry, product and recycling information, issues and events.

10747 www.nwcherries.com
Northwest Cherry Growers

10748 www.nwfpa.com
Northwest Food Processors Association
Conventions and exhibits, member listings and links.

10749 www.nwfpa.org
Northwest Food Processors Association
An organization that aims to develop and promote the food processing industry located in Oregon, Idaho, and Washington.

10750 www.nyapplecounty.com
New York Apple/New York Cherry Growers

10751 www.oamp.org
Ohio Association of Meat Processors

10752 www.ocia.org
Organic Crop Improvement Association
For farmers, processors, manufacturers and traders of organic crops.

10753 www.oilseeds.org
American Soybean Association
Consumption statistics, related associations.

10754 www.onions-usa.org
National Onion Association
Recipes, member information and allied industry and export information.

10755 www.opensecrets.org
Cheese Association of America
The Center for Responsive Politics is a nonpartisan, nonprofit research group based in Washington, DC that tracks money in politics, and its effect on campaign finance issues for the news media, academics, activists and the public at large.

10756 www.oregon-berries.com
Oregon Rasberry & Blackberry Commission
Supports the rasberries, blackberries, marionberries and boysenberries industries.

10757 www.oregonhazelnuts.org
Hazelnut Marketing Board
This organization was established to promote and provide for the Oregon hazelnut industry.

10758 www.organic.org
Organic Alliance

10759 www.ostriches.org
American Ostrich Association
Organization that provides leadership for the ostrich industry and its future through the promotion of ostrich products.

10760 www.osu.orst.edu/dept/iifet
International Institute of Fisheries Economics
Promotes discussion, research projects and sponsors educational courses. Publications available.

10761 www.ota.org
Organic Trade Association
For businesses involved in the organic agriculture and products industry. Seeks to promote the industry and establish production and marketing standards.

10762 www.ou.org
Orthodox Union

10763 www.pabeef.org
Pennsylvania Cattlemen's Association

10764 www.packagingeducation.org
Packaging Education Forum
A membership organization through which industry guides the development of, establishes quality standards for, and provides financial assistance to packaging education programs, curricula and students at the university.

10765 www.packagingnetwork.com
Packaging Network
Searchable database of food industry related items.

10766 www.packexpo.com
Packging Machinery Manufacturers Institute
Members are manufacturers of packaging and packaging related coconverting machinery in the US and Canada. PMMI offers meetings, an inquiry service, statistics and surveys and a business to business service on it's website. PMMI also sponsors several Pack Expos (packaging related tradeshows).

10767 www.packinfo-world.com
World Packaging Organization
Information regarding the packaging industry internationally.

10768 www.packinfo-world.org
Contract Packaging and Manufacturing Association
Information on major packaging associations.

10769 www.peanutbutterlovers.com
Peanut Advisory Board
This organization conducts the marketing and promotion of peanut and peanut butter products.

10770 www.peanutsusa.com
American Peanut Council
Association members include growers and manufacturers of peanuts and peanut products.

10771 www.pigglywiggly.com
National Piggly Wiggly Operators Association
An association of independent grocers operating under Piggly Wiggly franchises in 24 states. Includes both small operators of one to five supermarkets as well as multiple store organizations of as many as 90 or more supermarkets.

10772 www.pistachios.org
California Pistachio Commission
Commodity board representing California pistachio growers.

10773 www.pizzatoday.com
National Association of Pizza Operators
The membership of this organization is independent and franchised pizza operators, manufacturers and suppliers of pizza equipment.

10774 www.plma.com
Private Label Manufacturers Association (PLMA)
Trade Association promoting the private label industry.

10775 www.pma.com
Produce Marketing Association
For those who market fresh fruits, vegetables, and floral products worldwide; involved in the production, distribution, retail, and food service sectors of the industry.

10776 www.popcorn.org
Popcorn Institute
A trade association representing the popcorn industry. Institute activites include projects to improve popcorn growing and processing technology, serving as a liasion with several government regulatory agencies and a generic marketing program to promote product awareness and consumption.

10777 www.poultryegg.org
US Poultry & Egg Association

10778 www.ppws.vt.edu/newss/society.htm
Northeastern Weed Science Society

10779 www.processfood.com
Food Processing Machinery & Supplies Association

10780 www.prunes.org
California Prune Board

10781 www.ptnpa.org
Peanut and Tree Nut Processors Association

10782 www.qba.com
Quality Bakers of America Cooperative
Members are independent wholesale bakeries and their suppliers.

10783 www.qchekd.com
Quality Checked Dairies
A cooperative of Dairy foods processors who use the Quality Checked trademark on their products and engage in group purchasing of ingredients and supplies.

10784 www.raisins.org
California Raisin Marketing Food Tech. Program

10785 www.rbanet.com
Retail Bakers Association
Links to other associations.

10786 www.realbutter.com
American Dairy Association
Recipes, media information, celebrity chefs and industry news.

10787 www.redangus1.org
Red Angus Association of America
Association for breeders of Red Angus cattle.

10788 www.redraspberry.com
Washington Red Raspberry Commisson

10789 www.refrigeratedfoods.com
Refrigerated Foods Association

Formerly called the Salad Manufacturers Association, the Refrigerated Foods Association is an international organization comprised of manufacturers and suppliers of prepared, refrigerated, ready-to-eat food products.

10790 **www.register.com/food**
Food Institute
Member and industry links.

10791 **www.renderers.org**
National Renderers Association
Members recycle animal by-products only, also provide services to renderers.

10792 **www.restaurant.org**
National Restaurant Association
Trends, government affairs, training, research, dining guides and links.

10793 **www.reta.com**
Refrigerating Engineers & Technicians Association

10794 **www.retailconfectioners.org**
Retail Confectioners International
Provides education, promotion and legislative services. Holds courses and bestows awards.

10795 **www.saltinstitute.org**
Salt Institute
Industry information and member businesses.

10796 **www.sbsonline.org**
Society for Biomolecular Screening
Supports research and discovery in pharmaceutical biotechnology and the agrichemical industry that utilize biomolecular screening procedures.

10797 **www.scaa.com**
Specialty Coffee Association of America
Training programs, newsletter, member websites, etc.

10798 **www.scisoc.org/asbc**
American Society of Brewing Chemists
Annual scientific meeting for professionals in the brewing industry.

10799 **www.seafwa.org**
Southeastern Association of Fish and Wildlife
The Southeastern Association of Fish and Wildlife Agencies is an organization whose members are the state agencies with primary responsibility for management and protection of the fish and wildlife resources in 16 states, Puerto Rico and the US Virgin Islands.

10800 **www.seedtechnology.net**
Society of Commercial Seed Technologists
Professionals involved in the testing and analysis of seeds, including research, production and handling based on botanical and agricultural sciences.

10801 **www.sheepusa.org**
American Sheep Industry Association
For state associations dedicated to the welfare and profitability of the sheep industry.

10802 **www.shellfish.org**
National Shellfisheries Association
Organization comprised of scientists, public health workers, shellfish producers and fishery administrators. To promote and advance shellfisheries research and the application of results to the shellfish industry

10803 **www.snax.com**
Snack Food Association
Facts, stats and trivia about snack food industry.

10804 **www.southeastdairy.org**
Southeast United Dairy Industry Association
Promotes milk and milk products in the southeastern states.

10805 **www.southerncottonginners.org**
Southern Cotton Ginners Association
Operates in a five state area as an information center covering safety and governmental regulations.

10806 **www.soyfoods.com**
US Soy Food Directory
Searchable database of soy food processors, suppliers, and industry information.

10807 **www.soyfoods.org**
Soyfoods Association of North America
Sponsors April as soy foods month. Conducts annual seminar on soy foods in fall.

10808 **www.spcouncil.org**
Soy Protein Council
Members of this association include persons, firms and corporations regularly engaged within the US in the processing and sale of vegetable proteins or vegetable protein products derived from agricultural services.

10809 **www.specialityfoods.org**
Speciality Food Distributors & Manufacturers

10810 **www.state.id.us/bean**
Idaho Bean Commission
Directory of dealers, recipes, nutritional values and research.

10811 **www.steel.org**
American Iron and Steel Institute
Develops and implements market development programs for appropriate food and beverage packaging applications.

10812 **www.suebeehoney.com**
Sioux Honey Association

10813 **www.sugar.org**
Sugar Association
Represents processors and refiners of beet and cane sugar in nutrition and health matters.

10814 **www.sugaralliance.org**
American Sugar Alliance
For domestic producers, processors, suppliers and labor organizations in the sugar and sugarcane industry.

10815 **www.sunflowernsa.com**
National Sunflower Association
For companies associated with sunflower products.

10816 **www.sunmaid.com**
Sun-Maid Growers of California

10817 **www.susta.org**
Southern US Trade Association
A non-profit agricultural export trade development association comprised of the Departments of Agriculture of the 15 southern states and the Commonwealth of Puerto Rico.

10818 **www.teausa.com**
Tea Council of the USA
International companies and governments interested in cultivating and expanding the demand for the sale and consumption of tea in the US.

10819 **www.teleport.com/~hazelnut**
Hazelnut Marketing Board
This organization was established to promote and provide for the Oregon hazelnut industry.

10820 **www.tfi.org**
Fertilizer Institute
For brokers, producers, importers, dealers and manufacturers of fertilizer and fertilizer-related equipment.

10821 **www.theamericancenter.org**
American Center for Wine, Food & the Arts

10822 **www.thebcma.org**
Biscuit & Cracker Manufacturers Association
An organization that represents and promotes the cookie and cracker manufacturing industry.

10823 **www.therestaurantfinder.com**
This search engine help to find restaurants by type or location.

10824 **www.tianet.org**
Transportation Intermediaries Association
Education and policy organization for North American transportation intermediaries representing the interests of all third party transportation service providers. Members include logistics management firms, property brokers, perishable commodities brokers, freight forwarders, intermodal marketers, ocean and air forwarders, and NVOCC's.

10825 **www.tortilla-info.com**
Tortilla Industry Association
News, trade information, 'where to buy' and recipes.

10826 **www.turkeyfed.org**
National Turkey Federation
Member site links and industry information.

10827 **www.txbeef.com**
Texas Beef Council
Recipes, ranching information, tips and links.

10828 **www.uark.edu/depts/ifse/ofpa**
Ozark Food Processors Association
This association is comprised of regional food processors and national suppliers for the food service industry. Hosts an annual convention in the spring which includes at attendence of over 700 and over 100 exhibitors.

10829 **www.uffva.org**
United Fresh Fruit & Vegetable Association
Equipment, supplies, cartons, packaging machinery, computers, sorting and sizing equipment, harvesting equipment, film wrap manufacturing and commodity organizations.

10830 **www.usapears.com**
Pear Bureau Northwest
Promotes fresh pears grown in the Pacific Northwest area.

10831 **www.usapple.org**
US Apple Association
Members are US and foreign firms, other than retailers, that handle apples.

10832 **www.usarice.com**
USA Rice Federation

10833 **www.usda.gov**
US Department of Agriculture
The official website of USDA.

10834 **www.usda.gov/fcs/fcs.html**
Food & Nutrition Service

10835 **www.usguernsey.com**
American Guernsey Association

Register and deliver guernsey cattle throughout the US.

10836 **www.usmef.org**
US Meat Export Federation

10837 **www.uspastry.org**
US Pastry Alliance

10838 **www.uspotatoes.com**
National Potato Promotion Board

Also known as the potato board. Organized to operate a national promotion plan to position potatoes as low calorie, nutritious vegetables and to facilitate market expansion into domestic and export sales.

10839 **www.vealfarm.com**
American Veal Association

For veal producers and processors.

10840 **www.vending.org**
National Automatic Merchandising Association

Serves merchandising, vending, contract foodservice management and office coffee service industries.

10841 **www.versatilevinegar.org**
Vinegar Institute

Manufacturers and bottlers of vinegar and suppliers to the industry are the members of this association. Publications available only to members.

10842 **www.vrg.org**
Vegetarian Resource Group

10843 **www.vtcheese.com**
Vermont Cheese Council

10844 **www.walnut.org**
Walnut Marketing Board

History, statistics, supplier listings, etc.

10845 **www.warehouselogistics.org**
American Warehouse Association

10846 **www.watermelon.org**
National Watermelon Promotional Board

10847 **www.wawgg.org**
Washington Association of Wine Grape Growers

Guidance in research and education, and maintaining leadership in local, state and national wine grape issues.

10848 **www.wdairycouncil.com**
Western Dairyfarmers' Promotion Association

Promotes dairy products for the dairy farmer.

10849 **www.westernassn.com**
Western Retail Implement and Hardware Association

For manufacturers, suppliers and distributors of equipment, supplies and services relating to the agricultural industry.

10850 **www.wflo.com**
World Food Logistics Organization

The activities of the WFLO include improving the application of refrigeration technology for the preservation and distribution of food and other commodities, stimulating and supporting research in the science of food refrigeration through grants, training and educating industry personnel, growing its bank of scientific information on the storage and distribution of perishable goods, and developing and supporting national associations.

10851 **www.wga.com**
Western Growers Association

Links and news, safety and legal information.

10852 **www.wheatfoods.org**
Wheat Foods Council

Links, nutrition and product information, news and tips.

10853 **www.wheatworld.org**
National Association of Wheat Growers

Member information, government agencies, research information, etc.

10854 **www.whybiotech.com**
Council for Biotechnology Information

Our vision and mission is to improve understanding and acceptance of biotechnology by collecting balanced, credible and science based information, then communicating this information through a variety of channels. Plant biotechnology has the potential to provide more and better food for a growing world population while helping steward the environment.

10855 **www.wicdirectors.org**
National Association of WIC Directors

Members are geographic state, Native American state and local agency directors of the special supplement nutrition program for women, infants and children.

10856 **www.wildblueberries.com**
Wild Blueberry Association of North America

Sources, recipes, news and product ideas.

10857 **www.wineinstitute.org**
Wine Institute

Organization that represents the wine and spirit industry to state and federal lawmaking bodies.

10858 **www.wislink.org**
Wisconsin Milk Marketing Board

10859 **www.worldfoodnet.com**

Source of information for food product developers

10860 **www.wssa.com**
Wine and Spirits Shippers Association

Provides members, importers and exporters with efficient and economical ocean transportation and other logistic services.

10861 **www.wusata.org**
Western US Agricultural Trade Association

This organization offers information and support to increase exports of US agricultural products.

Associations

10862 American Apparel & Footwear Association
1601 N Kent Street
Suite 1200
Arlington, VA 22209
703-524-1864
800-520-2262; *Fax:* 703-522-6741
nherman@wewear.org;
www.apparelandfootwear.org
Social Media: Facebook, Twitter, LinkedIn, YouTube
Aaron M. Albert, President
Thomas Glaser, Treasurer
Katherine Gold, Secretary
Rick Helfenbein, Chairman
Rob DeMartini, Vice Chairman
The national trade association representing apparel, footwear and other swen products companies and their suppliers which compete in the global market.
400 Members
Founded in: 1960

10863 Association of Footwear Distributors
1319 F St Nw
Suite 700
Washington, DC 20004
202-737-5660; *Fax:* 202-645-0789
info@fdra.org
fdra.org
Social Media: Facebook, Twitter, LinkedIn, Flickr, Instagram
Matt Priest, President
Andy Polk, Vice President
Thomas Crockett, Director of Gov. & Reg. Affairs
Christie Horan, Marketing & Comm. Coordinator
Sue Myrick, Strategic Policy Advisor
Major distributors of footwear.
130+ Members
Founded in: 1944

10864 Fashion Footwear Association of New York
274 Madison Avenue
Suite 1701
New York, NY 10016
212-751-6422; *Fax:* 212-751-6404
info@ffany.org; www.ffany.org
Social Media: Facebook, Twitter, Pinterest, Youtube
Ronald Fromm, President
Diane Sullivan, Secretary
Debbie King, Vice Chairman
Jim Issler, Chairman
Wayne Kulkin, Treasurer
4 International Trade Shows per year.
300 Members
Founded in: 1980

10865 Footwear Distributors and Retailers of America
1319 F St Nw
Suite 700
Washington, DC 20004
202-737-5660; *Fax:* 202-645-0789
info@fdra.org; www.fdra.org
Social Media: Facebook, Twitter, LinkedIn, Flickr, Instagram
Andy Polk, Vice President
Rick Muskat, Chairman
Edward Rosenfeld, Vice Chair
Mike Jeppesen, Treasurer
Matt Priest, President
Trade association for footwear distributors and volume retailers.
130+ Members
Founded in: 1944

10866 Pedorthic Footwear Association
1610 East Forsyth Street
Suite D
Americus, GA 31709
229-389-3440; *Fax:* 888-563-0945
pedorthicsusa@gmail.com;
www.pedorthics.org
Social Media: Facebook, Twitter, LinkedIn, Google+, Pinterest
Matt Almeida, Secretary
Jay Zaffater, Past President
Robert Sobel, President
Dean Mason, Vice President
Christopher J. Costantini, Treasurer
Membership organization for individuals and companies involved in the design, manufacture, modification and fit of therapeutic footwear. Provides educational programs, publications, legislative monitoring, marketing materials, professional liason and business operations services.
Cost: $55.00
2000 Members
Founded in: 1958

10867 Sports and Fitness Industry Association
8505 Fenton Street
Suite 211
Silver Spring, MD 20910
301-495-6321; *Fax:* 301-495-6322
info@sfia.com; www.sfia.org
Social Media: Facebook, Twitter, LinkedIn
Tom Cove, President & CEO
Cameron Jacobs, Manager,Business Operations
Chip Baldwin, CFO
Bill Sells, VP of Government Relations
Lauren Wallace, Director
Our purpose is to support our member companies and promote a healthy environment for the sporting goods industry. SGMA enhances industry vitality and fosters sports, fitness and active lifestyle participation.
1000 Members
Founded in: 1906

10868 Two Ten Footwear Foundation
1466 Main St
Waltham, MA 02451
800-346-3210; *Fax:* 781-736-1555
info@twoten.org; www.twoten.org
Social Media: Facebook, Twitter, LinkedIn, Flickr, YouTube
Michael Atmore, Editorial Director
Robert McHugh, Treasurer
Blake Krueger, Chairman
Diane Sullivan, Vice Chair
Lawrence Siff, Secretary
Mission is to take action and create change for those in need. Built upon a foundation of caring, serving our community through social services and educational programs.
Founded in: 1939

10869 United Shoe Retailers Association
PO Box 4931
West Hills, CA 91308
818-703-6062; *Fax:* 866-929-6068
usraonline.org
Linda Hauss, Executive Director
The Association helps independent shoe retailers be profitable.
Founded in: 1977

Newsletters

10870 Footwear News
Fairchild Publications
750 3rd Ave
Suite 7
New York, NY 10017-2700
212-630-4320
800-360-1700; www.wwd.com/footwear-news
Jay Spaleta, Publisher
Katie Abel, Editor
Weekly publication covering the international footwear industry's fashion trends, news developments, finances and market data.
Cost: $72.00
Frequency: Weekly
Circulation: 17892
Founded in: 1892

10871 WSA Today
Show Dailies International
460 Richmond Street West
Suite 701
Toronto, ON 90049-5103
416-730-8488
800-360-3234; *Fax:* 416-730-1878;
www.ingle-international.com
Rich DiGiacomo, Publisher
Robin Ingle, Chairman/CEO
Features products and industry news, conference information and interviews. Published daily during the semiannual Western Shoe Show.
Founded in: 1946

Magazines & Journals

10872 Current Pedorthics
Pedorthic Footwear Association
7150 Columbia Gateway Drive
Suite G
Columbia, MD 21046-1151
410-381-8282
800-673-8447; *Fax:* 410-381-1167
info@pedothrics.org; www.pedorthics.org
Ed Habre, Board Chairman
Chuck Schuyler, President
Tanya Allain, Communicaton Coordinator
Covers pedorthics; the design, manufacture, modification and fit of shoes and foot orthoses to alleviate foot problems caused by disease, overuse or injury.
Cost: $35.00
44 Pages
Frequency: Quarterly
Circulation: 5000
Founded in: 1958

10873 Footwear Market Guide
307 West 38th Street
Suite 1005
New York, NY 10018
212-398-5505; *Fax:* 212-398-5504
customercare@infomat.com;
www.infomat.com
Social Media: Facebook, Twitter, LinkedIn
Provides a broad industry overview, including key press, manufacturing and sales contacts in one superb, value-prived package.
Cost: $165.00

10874 **National Shoe Retailers Magazine**
7150 Columbia Gateway Drive
Suite G
Columbia, MD 21046-1151

410-381-8282
800-673-8446; *Fax:* 410-381-1167
info@nsra.org; www.nsra.org

Nancy Hultquist, Director Communications
Bill Boettge, President

Provides businesses information such as credit-card processing and shipping at special features for the industry.
36 Pages
Founded in: 1912
Printed in 2 colors on glossy stock

10875 **Pedorthic Footwear Magazine**
7150 Columbia Gateway Drive
Suite G
Columbia, MD 21046-1151

410-381-7278
800-673-8447; *Fax:* 410-381-1167
info@pedorthics.org; www.pedorthics.org

Nancy Hultquist, Director Communications
Brian Lagana, Executive Director
Kalin Wilburn, Sales Coordinator
Mike Forgrave, Publisher
Amy Bloom, Membership Manager

Provides educational articles, marketing materials and professional information.
Cost: $55.00
44 Pages
Circulation: 5000
Founded in: 1958
Printed in 2 colors on glossy stock

10876 **Runner's World**
Runner's World Magazine Company
135 N 6th Street
Emmaus, PA 18098

610-967-5171
800-845-8050; *Fax:* 610-967-8883
rwforums@rodale.com;
www.runnersworld.com

Andrew R Hersam, Publisher
David Willey, Editor
Steven Pleshette Murphy, CEO/President
Charles DeLana, Marketing
Richard Alleger, Vice President of Finance

A magazine dedicated to the lifestyle fitness activity of running. Aims to inform, advise, educate and motivate runners of all ages and abilities.
Cost: $21.00
Frequency: Monthly
Circulation: 530511
Founded in: 1966
Mailing list available for rent: 370,000 names
Printed in on glossy stock

10877 **Shoe Retailing Today**
National Shoe Retailers Association
7150 Columbia Gateway Drive
Suite G
Columbia, MD 21046-1151

410-381-8282
800-673-8446; *Fax:* 410-381-1167
info@nsra.org; www.nsra.org

Bill Boettge, Managing Director
Nancy Hultquist, Editor

Offers information to independent shoe retailers across the country.
Cost: $35.00
Circulation: 4000
Founded in: 1912

10878 **Shoestats**
Footwear Industries of America
1420 K St NW
Suite 600
Washington, DC 20005-2506

202-962-0380; *Fax:* 202-789-7257
shoes@shoeinfonet.com;
www.shoeinfonet.com

Maria L Abrantes, President
Ivo Geidl, office Manager

Complete statistical coverage of the footwear industry.
Cost: $40.00
210 Pages
Frequency: Bi-annually

Trade Shows

10879 **Annual Symposium**
Pedorthic Footwear Association
7150 Columbia Gateway Drive
Columbia, MD 21046-2972
800-673-8447; *Fax:* 410-381-1167
info@pedorthics.org; www.pedorthics.org

Jeanne Williams, Manager
Brian Lagana, Executive Director

The Annual Symposium is a combination education event and trade show expo. Containing 100+ booths and exhibits.
600+ Attendees
Frequency: November
Founded in: 1958

10880 **Global Leather**
American Apparel & Footwear Association
1601 N Kent Street
Suite 1200
Arlington, VA 22205

703-524-1864
800-520-2262; *Fax:* 847-522-6741;
www.apparelandfootwear.org

Kevin M Burke, President
Stephen E Lamar, VP
Scott Elmore, Marketing

Showcases the best in new leather materials and components for the footwear leather, needle and allied trades of North America. Brings together hundreds of exhibitors from the major sourcing cities around the world, showcasing thousands of products.
400 Members
1500 Attendees
Frequency: February/August
Founded in: 2000

10881 **Metropolitan Shoe Show New York**
50 W 34th Street
Apartment 8A6
New York, NY 10001-3057

212-564-1069

Mary Stanton, Show Manager

225 booths.
2M Attendees
Frequency: March/September

10882 **Northwest Show Travelers Buying Show Market**
2720 W 43rd Street
Minneapolis, MN 55410-1643

612-920-5005

Dona Merchant, Show Manager

100 booths of shoe retailers and specialty store personnel from Minnesota, Iowa, North Dakota, Maryland and South Dakota.
1.5M Attendees
Frequency: January

10883 **PFA Annual Symposium & Exhibition**
Pedorthic Footwear Association
1610 E Forsyth St.
Suite D
Americus, GA 31709

229-389-3440; *Fax:* 888-563-0945
pedorthicsusa@gmail.com;
www.pedorthics.org

Jeanne Williams, Show Manager
Brian Lagana, Executive Director
Nancy Hultquist, Director Communications

One hundred fifty booths plus educational sessions regarding the design, manufacture or modification and fit of shoes and foot orthoses to alleviate foot problems caused by disease, congenital condition, overuse or injury.
1000 Attendees
Frequency: November

10884 **University of Shoe Retailing Conference**
National Shoe Retailers Association
7386 N. La Cholla Blvd
Tucson
Arizona 85741

520-209-1710
800-673-8446; www.nsra.org

Rob Kaufman, Conference Chairman
Tricia Keane, Conference Co-Chair
Chuck Schuyler, President
Mark Denkler, Chair
Frequency: July, Las Vegas

10885 **World Shoe Associates: Shoe Show**
15821 Ventura Boulevard
Suite 415
Encino, CA 91436-2974

818-799-9400; *Fax:* 949-851-8523;
www.wsashow.com

Chris Aiken, Show Manager

One million square feet of exhibition space. Features thousands of footwear styles, accesories, handbags and foot care products.
12M Attendees
Frequency: August/February

Directories & Databases

10886 **American Shoemaking**
Shoe Trades Publishing Company
61 Massachusetts Avenue
PO Box 1530
East Arlington, MA 02174-8160

781-648-8160; *Fax:* 781-646-9832;
www.shoetrades.com

John J Moynihan, Publisher

Brings the shoe manufacturer the news he needs to know.
Cost: $55.00
30 Pages
Frequency: Monthly

10887 **Business Performance Report**
National Shoe Retailers Association
7387 N. La Cholla Blvd
Tucson
Arizona 85741

520-209-1711
800-673-8446
info@nsra.org; www.nsra.org

Rob Kaufman, Conference Chairman
Tricia Keane, Conference Co-Chair
Chuck Schuyler, President
Mark Denkler, Chair

Comprehensive, in-depth, financial account of retail shoe stores. Benchmark for retailers to compare their own operations.

10888 Complete Directory of Socks & Shoes
Sutton Family Communications & Publishing Company
155 Sutton Lane
Fordsville, KY 42343
270-740-0870
jlsutton@apex.net; www.suttoncompliance.com
Theresa Sutton, Editor
Lee Sutton, General Manager
Print-out from database of wholesalers, manufacturers, distributors, importers and close-out houses. Database is updated daily to guarantee the most current and up-to-date sources available.
Cost: $44.50
100+ Pages

10889 Directory of Mail Order Catalogs
Grey House Publishing
4919 Route 22
PO Box 56
Amenia, NY 12501
518-789-8700
800-562-2139; *Fax:* 845-373-6390
books@greyhouse.com; www.greyhouse.com
Social Media: Facebook, Twitter
Leslie Mackenzie, Publisher
Richard Gottlieb, Editor
The premier source of information on the mail order catalog industry. Covers over 13,000 consumer and business catalog companies with 44 different product chapters from Animals to Toys and Games.
Cost: $395.00
1900 Pages
Frequency: Annual
ISBN: 1-592373-96-8
Founded in: 1981

10890 Directory of Mail Order Catalogs - Online Database
Grey House Publishing
4919 Route 22
PO Box 56
Amenia, NY 12501
518-789-8700
800-562-2139; *Fax:* 845-373-6390
gold@greyhouse.com
http://gold.greyhouse.com
Social Media: Facebook, Twitter
Leslie Mackenzie, Publisher
Richard Gottlieb, Editor
Reach over 10,000 consumer catalog companies in one easy-to-use source with The Directory of Mail Order Catalogs - Online Database. Filled with business-building detail, each company profile gives you the information you need to access that organization quickly and easily. Listings provide key contacts, sales volume, employee size, printing information, circulation, list data, product descriptions and much more.
Frequency: Annual
Founded in: 1981

10891 Financial Performance Profile of Public Consumer Products Manufacturers
Kurt Salmon Associates
1355 Peachtree St NE
Suite 900
Atlanta, GA 30309-3257
404-892-0321; *Fax:* 404-898-9590
services@kurtsalmon.com; www.kurtsalmon.com
William B Pace, CEO
About 23 publicly held footwear manufacturers.
Frequency: Annual June

10892 Footwear Distributors and Retailers of America: Membership Directory
Footwear Distributors and Retailers of America
1319 F Street NW
Washington, DC 20004-1106
202-628-1838; *Fax:* 202-638-2615
http://www.fdra.org
Peter Mangione, President
About 65 American footwear importers and retailers.

10893 Shoe Factory Buyer's Guide
Shoe Trades Publishing Company
323 Cornelia Street
Suite 274
Plattsburgh, NY 12901
514-457-8787; *Fax:* 514-457-5832
sfbg@shoetrades.com; www.shoetrades.com
George McLeash, Publisher
Over 750 suppliers and their representatives to the shoe manufacturing industries in the US and Canada.
Cost: $59.00
Frequency: Annual
Circulation: 1,000

Industry Web Sites

10894 http://gold.greyhouse.com
G.O.L.D Grey House OnLine Databases
Grey House Publishing's online database platform, GOLD, offers Quick Search, Keyword Search and Expert Search for most business sectors including shoe and accessory markets. The GOLD platform makes finding the information you need quick and easy - whether you're a novice searcher or an experienced database user. All of Grey House's directory products are available for subscription on the GOLD platform.

10895 www.apparelandfootwear.org
American Apparel & Footwear Association
National trade association representing apparel, footwear and other sewn products companies and their suppliers. Our mission is to promote and enhance our members competitiveness, productivity and profitability in the global market.

10896 www.greyhouse.com
Grey House Publishing
Authoritative reference directories for most business sectors including shoe and accessory makrets. Users can search the online databases with varied search criteria allowing for custom searches by product category, geographic area, sales volume, keyword, subject and more. Full Grey House catalog and online ordering also available.

10897 www.sgma.com
Sporting Goods Manufacturers Association
For manufacturers, producers, and distributers of sports apparel, athletic footwear, fitness,and sporting goods equipment.

10898 www.ssia.info
Shoe Service Institute of America
Shop to shop chat room, links and listings of manufacturers and wholesalers plus shoe care tips.

Associations

10899 A Philanthropic Partnership for Black Communities
333 Seventh Avenue
14th Floor
New York, NY 10001

646-230-0306; *Fax:* 646-230-0310
info@abfe.org; www.abfe.org
Social Media: Facebook

Gary Cunningham, Chair
Samuel Cargile, PH.D., Vice Chair
Kenneth Jones, Treasurer
Towalame Austin, Secretary
Susan TAYLOR BATTEN, President

Encourages blacks in the grantmaking field and helps members improve their job effectiveness.
Founded in: 1971

10900 American Society of Association Executives
1575 I St NW
Washington, DC 20005

202-371-0940
888-950-2723; *Fax:* 202-371-8315
service@asaenet.org; www.asaecenter.org
Social Media: Facebook, Twitter, LinkedIn

Abe Eshkenazi, Chairman
Scott D. Wiley, Chairman-Elect
Matthew R. Shay, Secretary-Treasurer
Francine Alestock, Executive Coordinator
Dana Anaman , CAE, Marketing Manager

ASAE is the premier source of learning, knowledge and future-oriented research for the association and nonprofit profession, and provides resources, education, ideas and advocacy to enhance the power and performance of the association and nonprofit community.
21M Members
Founded in: 1920

10901 Arthritis Foundation
1330 W Peachtree St.
Suite 100
Atlanta, GA 30309

404-872-7100; www.arthritis.org
Social Media: Facebook, Twitter, LinkedIn, Instagram

Ann M. Palmer, President & CEO
Michael V. Ortman, Chair

The Arthritis Foundation is the voice of the arthritis community.

10902 Association for Healthcare Philanthropy
313 Park Avenue
Suite 400
Falls Church, VA 22046

703-532-6243; *Fax:* 703-532-7170
ahp@ahp.org; www.ahp.org
Social Media: Facebook, LinkedIn

David L. Flood, Chair
Jory Pritchard-Kerr, Vice Chair
Steven W. Churchill, MNA, President & CEO
Randy A. Varju, Secretary/Treasurer
Norman Flores, Finance Director

Represents health care fundraising professionals through education and eventually bestows the credentials upon them.
4100 Members
Founded in: 1967

10903 Association of Fund-Raising Professionals
4300 Wilson Blvd.
Suite 300
Arlington, VA 22203

703-684-0410
800-666-3863; *Fax:* 703-684-0540
mbrship@afpnet.org; www.afpnet.org
Social Media: Facebook, Twitter, LinkedIn, YouTube, Pinterest, Instagram

Patrick J. Feeley, Chair
Ann M. Hale, Chair-Elect
Susan Earl Hosback, Vice Chair,Resource Dev.
Joshua R. Newton, Secretary
Joseph Goepfrich, Treasurer

Supports all involved in the fundraising profession. Publishes monthly newsletter.
26000 Members
Founded in: 1965

10904 Association of Fundraising Professionals
4300 Wilson Blvd.
Suite 300
Arlington, VA 22203

703-684-0410
800-666-3863; *Fax:* 703-684-0540;
www.afpnet.org

Andrew Watt, President & CEO
Terry Rauh, Chief Operating Officer

The Association promotes the professional development of fundraising professionals and advocates for high ethical standards in the industry.
30000 Members
Founded in: 1960

10905 Association of Small Foundations/ASF
1720 N St NW
Washington, DC 20036

202-580-6560
888-212-9922; *Fax:* 202-580-6579
info@exponentphilanthropy.org;
www.exponentphilanthropy.org
Social Media: Twitter

Christopher Petermann, Chair
Jean Buckley, Vice Chair
Shirish Dayal, Officer-at-Large
Megan McTiernan, Secretary
Janis A. Reischmann, Treasurer

ASF enhances the power of small foundation giving by providing the donors, trustees, and staff of member foundations with peer learning opportunities, targeted tools and resources, and a collective voice in and beyond the philanthropic community.
3000 Members

10906 BoardSource
750 9th Street, NW
Suite 650
Washington, DC 20001-4793

202-349-2500
877-892-6873; *Fax:* 202-349-2599
mail@boardsource.org; www.boardsource.org

John Griswold, Chair
Philip Henderson, Vice Chair
Anne Wallestad, President & CEO
Sharon Rossmark, Treasurer
Kimberly Roberson, Secretary

Formerly the National Center for Nonprofit Boards, is the premier resource for practical information, tools and best practices, training, and leadership development for board members of nonprofit organizations worldwide.
7000 Members
Founded in: 1988

10907 Bond Market Foundation
360 Madison Avenue
New York, NY 10017-7111

646-637-9200; *Fax:* 646-637-9120
kedmundson@bondmarkets.com;
www.bondmarkets.org

Michael D McCarthy, Chairman
Kathryn L Edmundon, Executive Director
Robert E Foran, Vice Chairman
Hugh Moore, Treasurer
Brian Macwilliams, Assistant Secretary

The Bond Market Foundation is a charitable and educational not for profit (501-c-3) association. The Foundation develops and enhances the public's access to quality saving and investor education in addition to providing credible non-proprietary research capacity and expert discussion on public issues relevant to the bond markets. The Bond Market Foundation is partner to the Securities Industry and Financial Markets Association (SIFMA).

10908 Center for Effective Philanthropy
675 Massachusetts Avenue
7th Floor
Cambridge, MA 02139

617-492-0800; *Fax:* 617-492-0888
addya@effectivephilanthropy.org;
www.effectivephilanthropy.org
Social Media: Facebook, Twitter, LinkedIn, Youtube, Flickr

Phil Buchanan, President
Latia King, Executive Assistant to President
Ellie Beteau, Vice President, Research
Kevin Bolduc, Vice President, Assessment Tools
Grant Oliphant, Chair

To provide management and governance tools to define, assess, and improve overall foundation performance
Mailing list available for rent

10909 Council for Advancement & Support of Education
1307 New York Ave NW
Suite 1000
Washington, DC 20005

202-328-2273; *Fax:* 202-387-4973
memberservicecenter@case.org; www.case.org
Social Media: Facebook, Twitter, LinkedIn, Blog

Sue Cunningham, President/CEO
Brett Chambers, Executive Director of Volunteers
Donald Falkenstein, VP business and finance
Ron Mattocks, VP marketing, membership
Norma Walker, VP advancement programs

Supports all those involved in campus fund raising, public relations,and alumni administration. Publishes monthly magazine.
Founded in: 1974

10910 Council on Foundations
2121 Crystal Drive
Suite 700
Arlington, VA 22202

800-673-9036
MEMBERSHIP@COF.ORG; www.cof.org
Social Media: Facebook, Twitter

Sherry P. Magill, Chair
JAVIER SOTO, Vice Chair
Vikki Spruill, President & CEO
SHERRY ELISE RISTAU, Secretary
EUGENE W. COCHRANE JR., Treasurer

Supports all those involved in the foundation business. Publishes monthly magazine. We provide leadership expertise, legal services and networking opportunities among other services to our members and to the general public.
2000 Members
Founded in: 1949

10911 **Foundation Center**
32 Old Slip
24th Floor
New York, NY 10005

212-620-4230
800-424-9836; *Fax:* 212-807-3677
feedback@foundationcenter.org;
www.foundationcenter.org
Social Media: Facebook, Twitter, YouTube, Flickr,Googleplus, Fo

Bradford K. Smith, President
Lisa Philip, VP for Strategic Philantropy
Lawrence T. McGill, VP for Research
Jeffery Falkenstein, VP for Data Architecture
R. Nancy Albilal, VP Development

A national association for those interested in fund raising related to government agencies. The leading source on philanthropy worldwide.
Founded in: 1956

10912 **Giving Institute**
225 W. Wacker Drive
Chicago, IL 60606-3396

312-981-6794
800-462-2372; *Fax:* 312-265-2908
info@givinginstitute.org;
www.givinginstitute.org
Social Media: Facebook, Twitter

Jeffrey D. Byrne, Chair
Rachel Hutchison, 1st Vice Chair
Sarah J. Howard, 2nd Vice Chair
Derek Alley, Secretary
Peter J. Fissinger, Treasurer

Formerly the American Association of Fundraising Counsel (AAFRC). Mission is to educate and engage members in the ethical delivery of counsel and related services to non-profits through research, advocacy, and best practices.
Founded in: 1935
Mailing list available for rent

10913 **Independent Sector**
1602 L St NW
Suite 900
Washington, DC 20036

202-467-6100
888-860-8118; *Fax:* 202-467-6101
info@independentsector.org;
www.independentsector.org
Social Media: Facebook, Twitter

Stephen B. Heintz, Chair
Ralph B. Everett, Vice Chair
Diana Aviv, President & CEO
Lorie A. Slutsky, Treasurer
Kelvin H. Taketa, Secretary

The leadership forum for charities, foundations, and corporate giving programs committed to advancing the common good in America and around the world.
700 Members
Founded in: 1980

10914 **MacArthur Foundation**
140 S Dearborn Street
Chicago, IL 60603-5285

312-726-8000; *Fax:* 312-920-6258
4answers@macfound.org;
www.macfound.org/site/htm
Social Media: Facebook, Twitter, YouTube, RSS

Majorie M. Scardino, Chair
Julia M. Stasch, President
Marc P. Yanchura, Vice President & CFO
Elizabeth Kane, Secretary
Angela Abbott, Communications Assistant

Private, independent grant-making institution dedicated to helping groups and individuals foster lasting improvement in the human condition. Through the support it provides, the Foundation fosters the development of knowledge, nurtures individual creativity, strengthens institutions, helps improve public policy, and provides information to the public, primarily through support for public interest media.
Founded in: 1978

10915 **Music Performance Trust Fund**
1501 Broadway
Suite 600
New York, NY 10036

212-391-3950; *Fax:* 212-221-2604
sramos@musicpf.org; www.musicpf.org
Social Media: Facebook

Dan Beck, Trustee
Vidrey Blackburn, Contact
Al Elvin, Director of Finance
Samantha Ramos, Contact

Foundation allocates money for the promotion of live music for the general public. The concerts must be free of charge and have no admittance restrictions.
Founded in: 1948

10916 **National Catholic Development Conference Inc.**
734 15th St NW
Suite 700
Washington, DC 20005-1013

202-637-0470
888-879-6232; *Fax:* 202-637-0471
glehmuth@ncdcusa.org; www.ncdc.org
Social Media: Facebook, Twitter, LinkedIn

Chad McEachern, Chair
Greg Griffin, Vice-Chair
Georgette Lehmuth, President & CEO
Daniel McCormack, Treasurer
Dolly Sokol, Ph.D., Secretary

Members include development officers and key fund raisers of charitable institutions and agencies.
400 Members
Founded in: 1968
Mailing list available for rent

10917 **National Committee for Responsive Philanthropy**
1331 H Street NW
Suite 200
Washington, DC 20005

202-387-9177; *Fax:* 202-332-5084
info@ncrp.org; www.ncrp.org
Social Media: Facebook, Twitter, RSS

Sherece Y. West-Scantlebury, Chair
Gara LaMarche, Vice Chair
Judy Hatcher, Treasurer
Priscilla Hung, Secretary
Aaron Dorfman, Executive Director

Supports all those involved in the philanthropy field. Publishes quarterly newsletter.
Founded in: 1976

10918 **National Council of Nonprofits**
1001 G St. NW
Suite 700E
Washington, DC 20001

202-962-0322; *Fax:* 202-962-0321;
www.councilofnonprofits.org

Tim Delaney, President & CEO
Kyle Caldwell, Chair

The Council is a resource for the nation's nonprofits, identifying trends, sharing best practices and promoting solutions.

10919 **National School Foundation Association (NSFA)**
509 Aurora Ave
Ste 406
Naperville, IL 60540

516-971-2324
866-824-8513; *Fax:* 813-280-4820
bill@billhoffmanandassociates.com;
www.schoolfoundations.org
Social Media: Facebook, Twitter

Bill Hoffman, Board Chair
Nina Menis, Executive Director
David Else, Vice Chair
Shanon Solava, Membership Director
Jennifer Nihart, Accounting & Website Updates

The mission of the National School Foundation Association is to encourage K-12 school and school foundation personnel in the very rewarding and important process of establishing, developing and maintaining school foundations.
Founded in: 2001

10920 **Northwest Development Officers Association**
2150 N 107th Street
Suite 205
Seattle, WA 98133-9009

206-971-3605; *Fax:* 206-367-8777
office@afpadvancementnw.org; www.ndoa.org
Social Media: Facebook, Twitter, LinkedIn

Anne Marie MacPherson, Co President
Jodie Miner, Co President
Ray Li, President Elect
Kirk Laughlin, Secretary
Linda Hunt, Treasurer

To provide its members and other fundraising professionals with collegial peer support, networking, and comprehensive training opportunities to advance philanthropy and strengthen community. Provides fellowship,. targeted training, and a sounding board for development officers, volunteers, board members, students, nonprofit managers and others who are committed to fundraising and philanthropy.
800+ Members
Founded in: 1978

10921 **Partnership for Philanthropic Planning**
233 S McCrea St
Suite 300
Indianapolis, IN 46225

317-269-6274; *Fax:* 317-269-6268
info@pppnet.org;
www.charitablegiftplanners.org
Social Media: Facebook, Twitter, LinkedIn, YouTube, Flickr,Googleplus

Gregory Sharkey, Chair
Melanie J. Norton, Chair Elect
Michael Kenyon, President & CEO
Alexandra Brovey, Treasurer
Thomas Armstrong, Secretary

Serving people and organizations that work together to make charitable giving most meaningful.
112 Members
Founded in: 1988

10922 **Society for Non-Profits**
P.O.Box 510354
Livonia, MI 48151

734-451-3582; *Fax:* 734-451-5935
submit@feedbackform; www.snpo.org
Social Media: Facebook, Twitter, LinkedIn, Yahoo

Katie Burnham Laverty, President

Provides busy nonprofit leaders with concise and practical articles whose advice can be easily implemented .
Cost: $69.00
6000 Members
Frequency: Bi-Monthly
Circulation: 7000
ISSN: 8755-7614
Founded in: 1983

10923 Society for Nonprofit Organizations
PO Box 510354
Livonia, MI 48151

734-451-3582; *Fax:* 734-451-5935;
www.snpo.org
Social Media: Facebook, Twitter, LinkedIn, Yahoo

Katie Burnham Laverty, President

Dedicated to bringing together those who serve in the nonprofit world in order to build a strong network of professionals throughout the country. Publishes Nonprofit World Magazine and has an on-line certificate in Nonprofit Management in partnership with Michigan State University.
6000 Members
Founded in: 1983

10924 The Association of Fund-Raising Distributors & Suppliers
1100 Johnson Ferry Rd
Suite 300
Atlanta, GA 30342

404-252-3663; *Fax:* 404-252-0774
afrds@kellencompany.com; www.afrds.org
Social Media: Facebook

Kurt Koehler, President
Russ Colombo, Vice President Distributor Affairs
Mark Van Wyk, Vice President Supplier Affairs
Paul Mahler, Treasurer
Lisa Dieltz, Secretary

Association for manufacturers or suppliers of fundraising products, supplies and services. Its members manufacturer, supply or distribute products that are resold by not-for-profit organizations for fundraising purposes.
700+ Members

10925 The Grantsmanship Center
350 South Bixel St., Suite 110
PO Box 17220
Los Angeles, CA 90017

213-482-9860
800-421-9512; *Fax:* 213-482-9863
info@tgci.com; www.tgci.com
Social Media: Facebook, Twitter, YouTube,Pinterest,Googleplus

Cathleen Kiritz, President & Publisher
Barbara Floersch, Director
Susan Andres, Editor
Mariano Diaz, VP Strategic Innovation
Gail Brauner, Training Program Coordinator

Provides training and publications about obtaining funidng for nonprofit and government agencies. Free e-magazine, Centerd, offers a digest of useful articles for grant proposal writers, as well as expert advice from The Grantsmanship Center's trainers.
Founded in: 1972

Newsletters

10926 AFP eWire
Association of Fund-Raising Professionals
4300 Wilson Blvd.
Suite 300
Arlington, VA 22203

703-684-0410
800-666-3863; *Fax:* 703-684-0540
mbrship@afpnet.org; www.afpnet.org
Social Media: Facebook, Twitter, LinkedIn, YouTube

Andrew Watt, President & CEO
Tom Clark, COO
Rebecca A. Knight, Director
Mike Eason, CFO

Delivers the latest fundraising news and information.
26000 Members
Frequency: Weekly
Founded in: 1965

10927 AHP E-Connect
Association for Healthcare Philanthropy
313 Park Avenue
Suite 400
Falls Church, VA 22046

703-532-6243; *Fax:* 703-532-7170
ahp@ahp.org; www.ahp.org
Social Media: Facebook, LinkedIn

Susan J. Doliner, Chair
William S. Littlejohn, Chair Elect
Merv D. Webb, Secretary/Treasurer

Provides updates on industry news and research, educational and professional opportunities, book reviews and articles related to health care philanthropy.
Cost: $60.00
4100 Members
Frequency: 8x Yearly
Founded in: 1967

10928 AID for Education
CD Publications
8204 Fenton St
Silver Spring, MD 20910-4571

301-588-6380
800-666-6380; *Fax:* 301-588-6385
info@cdpublications.com;
www.cdpublications.com

Michael Gerecht, President
Frank Kalimko, Editor

Private and federal funding opportunities and news for all levels of education including grants for bilingual education, special education, literacy, minorities and more.
Cost: $419.00
18 Pages
Founded in: 1991
Mailing list available for rent: 2,000 names at $160 per M

10929 Board Source
Board Source
1828 L St Nw
Suite 900
Washington, DC 20036-5114

202-452-6262
800-883-6262; *Fax:* 202-452-6299
mail@boardsource.org; www.boardsource.org

Linda Crompton, CEO
Betsy Rosenblatt, Senior Editor

National newsletter for board members and staff leaders of nonprofit organizations includes strategies for building effective nonprofit boards. Comentaries from nonprofit leaders, case studies, and nonprofit governance news.
Cost: $139.00
Founded in: 1988

10930 BoardSource E-Newsletter
BoardSource
750 9th Street, NW
Suite 650
Washington, DC 20001-4590

202-349-2500
877-892-6873; *Fax:* 202-349-2599
mail@boardsource.org; www.boardsource.org

Linda C. Crompton, President & CEO
Fred Sherman, CFO
Anne Wallestad, COO
David J. Nygren, Ph.D, Chair
Roxanne Spillett, Vice Chair

Members-only benefit, offering timely news and information on nonprofit governance issues and trends affecting nonprofit boards.
7000 Members
Frequency: Monthly
Founded in: 1988

10931 CEO Connection
Association for Healthcare Philanthropy
313 Park Avenue
Suite 400
Falls Church, VA 22046

703-532-6243; *Fax:* 703-532-7170
ahp@ahp.org; www.ahp.org
Social Media: Facebook, LinkedIn

Susan J. Doliner, Chair
William S. Littlejohn, Chair Elect
Merv D. Webb, Secretary/Treasurer

From AHP President to health care organization CEOs discussing issues affecting health care philanthropy.
4100 Members
Frequency: Quarterly
Founded in: 1967

10932 Centered
The Grantsmanship Center
1125 W 6th Street 5th Floor
PO Box 17220
Los Angeles, CA 90017

213-482-9860
800-421-9512; *Fax:* 213-482-9863
centered@tgci.com; www.tgci.com

Susan Andres, Editor
Cathleen Kiritz, Publisher

Provides a digest of useful articles for grantseekers and proposal writers, as well as expert advice from The Grantsmanship Center's trainers. Our goal is to deliver practical information that will help you sharpen your grant research, proposal-writing, evaluation, and team-building skills.
Frequency: Monthly
Circulation: 35000

10933 Chronicle of Philanthropy
1255 23rd St Nw
Suite 700
Washington, DC 20037-1146

202-466-1200
800-728-2819; *Fax:* 202-452-1033
press@philanthropy.com;
www.philanthropy.com

Robin Ross, Publisher
Phil Semas, Editor
Michael Solomon, Manager of External Communications

A newspaper providing news and information for executives of nonprofit, tax-exempt organizations in health, education, religion, the arts, social services and other fields, as well as fund raisers, professional employees of foundation, and corporate grant makers. Features news, lists of grants, fundraising ideas and techniques, statistics, updates on regulations, reports on tax and court rulings, book summaries, calendar of events.
Cost: $72.00
Frequency: Fortnightly
Circulation: 100000
Founded in: 1997

10934 Community Health Funding Report
CD Publications
8204 Fenton St
Silver Spring, MD 20910-4571

301-588-6380
800-666-6380; *Fax:* 301-588-6385

info@cdpublications.com;
www.cdpublications.com

Michael Gerecht, President
Amy Bernstein, Editor
Jessica Cha, Owner

Highlights sources of funding for healthcare ranging from AIDS education to teen pregnancy to minority health care. Plus national and local community health news.
Cost: $339.00
Mailing list available for rent: 2,000 names at $160 per M

10935 Connections
Foundation Center
79 5th Ave
New York, NY 10003-3076

212-620-4230
800-424-9836; *Fax:* 212-807-3677
feedback@foundationcenter.org;
www.foundationcenter.org
Social Media: Facebook, Twitter, YouTube, Flickr

Melissa Berman, President & CEO

The best philanthropy-related content the Web has to offer.
Frequency: Bi-Weekly
Founded in: 1956

10936 Contributions
Contributions
28 Park St
Suite A
Medfield, MA 02052-2518

508-359-0019; *Fax:* 508-359-2703
kbrennan@contributionsmagazine.com;
www.contributionsmagazine.com

Jerry Cianciolo, Editor
Kathleen Brennan, Director of Communications
Robert Riordan, Director of Communications

Offers full coverage of fund raising campaigns.
Cost: $40.00
Circulation: 22,000
Founded in: 1987

10937 Corporate Giving Directory
Information Today Inc
143 Old Marlton Pike
Medford, NJ 08055-8750

609-654-6266; *Fax:* 609-654-4309
custserv@infotoday.com; www.infotoday.com

Thomas H Hogan, President

Delivers the latest information on program priorities, giving preferences, evaluation criteria, corporate and foundation officers and directors, and all the other data you need to help your nonprofit organization gain a crucial edge as corporate philanthropy budgets tighten.

10938 Corporate Philanthropy Report
LRP Publications
PO Box 24668
West Palm Beach, FL 33416-4668

561-622-6520; *Fax:* 561-622-0757
webmaster@lrp.com; www.lrp.com

Kenneth Kahn, President
Eileen Banashek, Editor

A report for both the corporate and nonprofit communities, spotlighting a different field or industry in each issue.
Cost: $235.00
Frequency: Monthly
Founded in: 1977

10939 Development and Alumni Relations Report
LRP Publications
747 Dresher Road Suite 500
PO Box 980
Horsham, PA 19044-980

215-784-0912
800-341-7874; *Fax:* 215-784-9639
webmaster@lrp.com; www.lrp.com

Anne Checkosky, Editor
Dionne Ellis, Marketing

Gives innovative ideas for improving annual giving, endowment and capital campaigns, planned giving, and alumni relations. Offers suggestions on new ways to spur participation and increase total contributions from alumni, corporate donors and foundations.
Cost: $185.00
Frequency: Monthly
Founded in: 1977

10940 Dimensions
National Catholic Development Conference
86 Front St
Hempstead, NY 11550-3667

516-481-6000
888-879-6232; *Fax:* 516-489-9287
glehmuth@ncdcusa.org; www.ncdc.org

Rachel Donofrio, Editor
Richard Reale, Director Membership
Georgette Lehmuth, CEO
Patricia Newman, Manager

Offers information on development and fund raising including direct mail, planned giving and major gifts and capitol campaigns.
Cost: $1000.00
16 Pages
Circulation: 550
Founded in: 1968
Printed in 2 colors on matte stock

10941 Disability Funding News
CD Publications
8204 Fenton St
Silver Spring, MD 20910-4571

301-588-6380
800-666-6380; *Fax:* 301-588-6385
info@cdpublications.com;
www.cdpublications.com

Michael Gerecht, President
Martha McPartlin, Editor

Alerts the reader to funding for programs for the disabled, including housing, transportation, rehabilitation, research and special education. Plus advice on successful grantseeking and news updated on national and local developments.
Cost: $419.00
Founded in: 1993
Mailing list available for rent: 2,000 names at $160 per M

10942 E-ssentials
National Catholic Development Conference
86 Front St
Hempstead, NY 11550-3667

516-481-6000
888-879-6232; *Fax:* 516-489-9287
glehmuth@ncdcusa.org; www.ncdc.org

Mark Melia, Chair
Curtis Yarlott, Vice-Chair
Keith Zekind, Treasurer

Connects NCDC members together by providing news about upcoming NCDC events, workshops, and webinars; membership committee news; member success stories; award notifications; fundraising white papers and quick tips; and CFRE exam information.
400 Members
Frequency: Weekly
Founded in: 1968

10943 Funding Alert Newsletter
Society for Nonprofit Organizations
PO Box 510354
Livonia, MI 48151

734-451-3582; *Fax:* 734-451-5935;
www.snpo.org
Social Media: Facebook, Twitter, LinkedIn

Katherine Burnham Leverty, Co-Founder/President/CEO

The leading e-newsletter for current grant and funding opportunities.
7000 Members
Founded in: 1983

10944 Giving USA Update
American Association of Fund-Raising Counsel
4700 W Lake Avenue
Glenview, IL 60025

847-375-4709
800-462-2372; *Fax:* 866-263-2491
info@aafrc.org; www.aafrc.org

Ann Kaplan, Publisher
John J Glier, Chair

Contains analysis, data and comments on charitable giving.
Cost: $125.00
Frequency: Quarterly
Founded in: 1935

10945 Health Grants Funding Alert
Health Resources Publishing
1913 Atlantic Ave
Suite 200
Manasquan, NJ 08736-1067

732-292-1100
888-843-6242; *Fax:* 732-292-1111
info@healthresourcesonline.com;
www.hin.com/ehealthcare

Robert K Jenkins, Publisher
Barbara Brown, Regional Director
Brett Powell, Regional Director
Alice Burron, Director

Monthly report sharing news of critical federal and foundation funding opportunities and trends, read by development directors and grants officers.
Cost: $495.00
8 Pages
Frequency: Monthly
ISSN: 0193-7928
Founded in: 1978

10946 Kaleidoscope
Association of Fund-Raising Professionals
4300 Wilson Blvd.
Suite 300
Arlington, VA 22203

703-684-0410
800-666-3863; *Fax:* 703-684-0540
mbrship@afpnet.org; www.afpnet.org
Social Media: Facebook, Twitter, LinkedIn, YouTube

Andrew Watt, President & CEO
Tom Clark, COO
Rebecca A. Knight, Director
Mike Eason, CFO

Supports AFP's strategic goal of connecting communities around the world by promoting diversity to donors, boards and fundraisers.
26000 Members
Frequency: Quarterly
Founded in: 1965

10947 National Center for Nonprofit Boards: Board Member Newsletter
1828 L Street NW
Washington, DC 20036
202-452-6262
800-883-6262; *Fax:* 202-452-6299;
www.ncnb.org
Monthly newsletter for board members and staff leaders of nonprofit organizations includes news updates, case studies, checklists, interviews and opinion pieces to increase the effectiveness of nonprofit boards.
Cost: $99.00
Frequency: Monthly
Circulation: 6800
Printed in 2 colors on matte stock

10948 Philanthropy News Digest
Foundation Center
79 5th Ave
New York, NY 10003-3076
212-620-4230
800-424-9836; *Fax:* 212-807-3677
feedback@foundationcenter.org;
www.foundationcenter.org
Social Media: Facebook, Twitter, YouTube, Flickr
Melissa Berman, President & CEO
Long-running, award-winning news digest of the Foundation Center.
Frequency: Weekly
Founded in: 1956

10949 RFP Bulletin
Foundation Center
79 5th Ave
New York, NY 10003-3076
212-620-4230
800-424-9836; *Fax:* 212-807-3677
feedback@foundationcenter.org;
www.foundationcenter.org
Social Media: Facebook, Twitter, YouTube, Flickr
Melissa Berman, President & CEO
A roundup of recently announced Requests for Proposals (RFPs) from private, corporate, and government funding sources.
Frequency: Weekly
Founded in: 1956

10950 Responsive Philanthropy
National Committee for Responsive Philanthropy
2001 S St Nw
Suite 620
Washington, DC 20009-1165
202-387-9177; *Fax:* 202-332-5084
info@ncrp.org; www.ncrp.org
Aaron Dorfman, Executive Director
Naomi Tacuyan, Editor
With news and feature articles about philanthropy, fund raising and social justice, covering issues often unreported in mainstream philanthropic publications.
Cost: $25.00
16 Pages
Frequency: Quarterly
Circulation: 5000
Founded in: 1976
Mailing list available for rent: 10000 names
Printed in 2 colors on matte stock

10951 Smith Funding Report
SFR
20 O'Neill Circle
Monroe, NY 10950-3210
914-774-4449
Melanie Smith, President
Quarterly guide to private foundation research/project grant opportunities for education and health institutions.
Cost: $195.00
40 Pages
Frequency: Quarterly
Printed in one color on matte stock

10952 Substance Abuse Funding News
CD Publications
8204 Fenton St
Silver Spring, MD 20910-4571
301-588-6380
800-666-6380; *Fax:* 301-588-6385
info@cdpublications.com;
www.cdpublications.com
Michael Gerecht, President
Joseph Smith, Editor
Detailed coverage of private and federal funding opportunities nationwide for alcohol and substance abuse programs. Advice on successful grantmaking strategies and roundup of national news.
Cost: $419.00
Founded in: 1992
Mailing list available for rent: 2,000 names at $160 per M

10953 Te Informa
Association of Fund-Raising Professionals
4300 Wilson Blvd.
Suite 300
Arlington, VA 22203
703-684-0410
800-666-3863; *Fax:* 703-684-0540
mbrship@afpnet.org; www.afpnet.org
Social Media: Facebook, Twitter, LinkedIn, YouTube
Andrew Watt, President & CEO
Tom Clark, COO
Rebecca A. Knight, Director
Mike Eason, CFO
AFP's Spanish-language e-newsletter covering issues of fundraising pertinent to Mexico and other Latin American countries.
26000 Members
Frequency: Quarterly
Founded in: 1965

Magazines & Journals

10954 Advancing Philanthropy
Association of Fund-Raising Professionals
4300 Wilson Blvd.
Suite 300
Arlington, VA 22203
703-684-0410
800-666-3863; *Fax:* 703-684-0540
mbrship@afpnet.org; www.afpnet.org
Social Media: Facebook, Twitter, LinkedIn, YouTube
Andrew Watt, President & CEO
Tom Clark, COO
Rebecca A. Knight, Director
Mike Eason, CFO
Provides practical information, useful tools and other resources to help members succeed and advance.
26000 Members
Frequency: Bi-Monthly
Founded in: 1965

10955 Association Management
American Society of Association Executives
1575 I St NW
Washington, DC 20005-1103
202-626-2700; *Fax:* 202-408-9635
publicpolicy@asaenet.org; www.asaenet.org
Keith C Skillman, Editor
Karl Ely, Publisher
Association Management strives to provide timely, practical information to help association executives succeed in their dual role as manager and visionary.
Cost: $50.00
106 Pages
Frequency: Monthly
Circulation: 24678
ISSN: 0004-5578
Founded in: 1920
Printed in 4 colors on glossy stock

10956 Association for Healthcare Philanthropy
313 Park Avenue
Suite 400
Falls Church, VA 22046-3303
703-532-6243; *Fax:* 703-532-7170
ahp@ahp.org; www.ahp.org
Kathy Renzetti, Marketing Manager/Editor
William C McGinly, CEO/President
Yvette Banks, Membership Manager
Alison Shaffer, Administrative Assistant
Written for development professionals, fundraisers, trustees, public relations professionals and executives in health care fundraising. Provides timely information on fundraising, career enhancement, planned giving, donor relations, organizational strategies and the effect of health care reform on philanthropy.
Founded in: 1967
Mailing list available for rent: 3000 names at $200 per M

10957 BBB Wise Giving Guide
BBB Wise Giving Alliance
4200 Wilson Boulevard
Suite 800
Arlington, VA 22203-1838
703-276-0100; *Fax:* 703-525-8277;
www.bbb.org
Margery Heitbrink, Editor
Includes a summary of the latest results of the Alliance's national charity evaluations along with a cover story about giving tips and or charity accountability issues.
Frequency: 3x Yearly
Circulation: 35000

10958 Centered
The Grantsmanship Center
350 South Bixel St., Suite 110
PO Box 17220
Los Angeles, CA 90017
213-482-9860
800-421-9512; *Fax:* 213-482-9863
info@tgci.com; www.tgci.com
Social Media: Facebook, Twitter, MySpace
Cathleen Kiritz, President
Barbara Floersch, Director
Susan Andres, Editor
Cathleen Kiritz, Publisher
Provides a digest of useful articles for grantseekers and proposal writers, as well as expert advice from the Center's trainers.
Frequency: Monthly
Founded in: 1972

10959 Currents
Council for Advancement & Support of Education

1307 New York Ave NW
Suite 1000
Washington, DC 20005-4726

202-393-1301; *Fax:* 202-387-4973
memberservicecenter@case.org; www.case.org

John Lippincott, President
Deborah Bangiorno, Editor-in-Chief
Andrea Gabrick, Senior Editor
Toni Lewis-Bennett, Director of Membership
Anne Brown, Executive Director

Offers information on campus fund raising, public relations,and alumni administration.
Cost: $115.00
Circulation: 15,000
Founded in: 1994

10960 **Essentials**
Association of Small Foundations/ASF
1720 N St NW
Washington, DC 20036-2907

202-580-6560
888-212-9922; *Fax:* 202-580-6579
asf@smallfoundations.org;
www.smallfoundations.org
Social Media: Twitter

Henry L. Berman, CEO
Floyd S. Keene, Chair

Provides practical articles on a range of information in one easy read.
3000 Members
Frequency: Quarterly

10961 **Foundation News & Commentary**
Council on Foundations
2121 Crystal Drive
Suite 700
Arlington, VA 22202

8006739036; www.foundationnews.org

Offers news and information for foundations, legislation news and fundraising campaign reviews.
Cost: $24.00
Frequency: Monthly

10962 **Fundraising EDGE**
Association of Fund-Raising Distributors
1100 Johnson Ferry Rd
Suite 300
Atlanta, GA 30342-1733

404-252-3663; *Fax:* 404-252-0774
afrds@kellencompany.com; www.afrds.org
Social Media: Facebook

Kurt Koehler, President
Leslie Lawrence, Secretary
Steve Wienkers, Treasurer

Published by the Association of Fund-Raising distributors and suppliers, offers the latest information about product fundraising.
700+ Members

10963 **Fundraising: Hands on Tactics for Nonprofit Groups**
McGraw-Hill Trade
2 Penn Plz
New York, NY 10121-0101

212-904-4450
877-833-5524; *Fax:* 212-904-2348
Philip_Ruppel@mcgraw-hill.com;
www.aviationdaily.com

L Peter Edles, Editor
Philip Ruppel, VP & Group Publisher
Jeffrey Krames, Publisher & Editor-in-Chief
William Garvey, Managing Editor
Iain Blackhall, Managing Director

This hands-on operations manual remedies the funding crisis by showing nonprofit professionals and volunteers how to design and run successful fundraising campaigns for their organizations. Combines sound, cost-effective strategies for building better organizational, management, sales, and marketing practices.
Cost: $19.95
288 Pages
ISBN: 0-070189-28-5
Founded in: 1992

10964 **Giving USA**
American Association of Fund-Raising Counsel
4700 W Lake Avenue
Glenview, IL 60025-7406

847-375-4709
800-462-2372; *Fax:* 866-263-2491
info@aafrc.org; www.aafrc.org/

Ann Kaplan, Editor

An annual report on charitable giving in the United States, tracking total charitable giving from four categories of sources to seven kinds of organizations.
Cost: $125.00
Frequency: Quarterly
Circulation: 9000
Founded in: 1935

10965 **Grant Funding for Elderly Health Services**
Health Resources Publishing
1913 Atlantic Ave
Suite 200
Manasquan, NJ 08736-1067

732-292-1100
888-843-6242; *Fax:* 732-292-1111
info@healthresourcesonline.com;
www.hin.com/ehealthcare

Robert K Jenkins, Publisher
Lisa Mansfield, Marketing Assistant
Caroline Pense, Editor
Brett Powell, Regional Director
Alice Burron, Director

This report will give insight into which proposals will get funds for which organization. Lists the organizations that will recieve the most funds from grantmakers during this decade and beyond. Also studies different case histories of successful grant proposals.
Cost: $95.00
Frequency: Monthly
ISBN: 1-882364-46-5
Founded in: 1978

10966 **Grants Magazine**
Plenum Publishing Corporation
233 Spring St
New York, NY 10013-1522

212-242-1490; *Fax:* 212-463-0742
info@plenum.com; www.plenum.com

Ricot Paillent, Manager

A magazine listing sources for grants, offering legislative news for the fundraising community, and foundation listings.
Founded in: 1946

10967 **Healthcare Philanthropy**
Association for Healthcare Philanthropy
313 Park Avenue
Suite 400
Falls Church, VA 22046

703-532-6243; *Fax:* 703-532-7170
ahp@ahp.org; www.ahp.org
Social Media: Facebook, LinkedIn

Susan J. Doliner, Chair
William S. Littlejohn, Chair Elect
Merv D. Webb, Secretary/Treasurer

Previously called the AHP Journal. Contains articles on health care fundraising and development, including ideas and methods for creating successful development programs, analyses of the current health care environment and projections of future trends.
Cost: $50.00
4100 Members
Frequency: Bi-Annually
Founded in: 1967

10968 **International Journal of Educational Advancement**
Association of Fundraising Professionals
Henry Stewart Publications
PO Box 10812
Birmingham, AL 35202-0812

205-995-1567
800-633-4931; *Fax:* 205-995-1588
brenda@hspublications.co.uk; www.afpnet.org / www.henrystewart.com

Joyce O'Brien, VP of Communications & Marketing
Brenda Rouse, Publisher

Features new ideas, shares examples of best practices and develops a body of knowledge in educational advancement.
Cost: $250.00
Frequency: 4x/year

10969 **Journal of Gift Planning**
National Committee on Planned Giving
233 S McCrea St
Suite 400
Indianapolis, IN 46225-1068

317-269-6274; *Fax:* 317-269-6276;
www.ncpg.org

Tanya Howe Johnson, President

Provides in-depth analysis of issues of daily concern to both nonprofit planners and for-profit donor advisors. Each issue provides an orientation to national issues and trends affecting the profession, such as the release of major research related to planned gift fundraising or the debate over professional certification for gift planners.
Cost: $45.00
Frequency: Quarterly

10970 **Nonprofit World**
Society for Nonprofit Organizations
PO Box 510354
Livonia, MI 48151

734-451-3582; *Fax:* 734-451-5935
info@snpo.org; www.snpo.org
Social Media: Facebook, Twitter, LinkedIn

Katherine Burnham Laverty, President
Jason Chmura, Membership Director
Jill Muehrcke, Editor

Contains original articles and departments on all aspects of running an effective nonprofit organization. Accepts advertising. Now includes the Directory of Service and Product Providers and the Resource Center Catalog with discounted resources for nonprofit organizations.
Cost: $79.00
40 Pages
Frequency: Bi-Monthly
Circulation: 4000
ISSN: 8755-7614
Founded in: 1983
Printed in 2 colors

10971 **Philanthropy Monthly**
Non-Profit Report
PO Box 989
New Milford, CT 06776

860-354-7132
860-354-7132; *Fax:* 860-354-7132

Henry Suhrke, Publisher

Editorial range covers concerns of nonprofits; legislative, economic, fund raising, nonprofit accounting, litigation, etc.
Cost: $84.00
Circulation: 6208

10972 **Responsive Philanthropy**
National Committee for Responsive Philanthropy
1331 H Street NW
Suite 200
Washington, DC 20005

202-387-9177; *Fax:* 202-332-5084
info@ncrp.org; www.ncrp.org
Social Media: Facebook, Twitter

Diane Feeney, Chair
Dave Beckwith, Vice Chair
Cynthia Guyer, Secretary
Robert Edgar, Treasurer

Looks at ending homelessness, funding direct services, supporting re0enfranchisement efforts and more.
Frequency: Quarterly
Founded in: 1976

Trade Shows

10973 **AFP International Conference on Fundraising**
Association of Fundraising Professionals
1101 King Street
Suite 700
Alexandria, VA 22314-2944

703-684-0410
800-666-3863; *Fax:* 703-684-0540
webmaster@afpnet.org; www.afpnet.org

Shannon Watson, Director Meetings & Expositions
Myrlin Young, Conferences Coordinator
Paulette Maehara, President
Michael Nilsen, senior Director public affairs

The largest gathering of fundraisers in the profession. The Conference has become the premier resource for fundraisers to network, learn, and discover new products and services.
Frequency: April
Founded in: 1962

10974 **ASF Annual National Conference**
Association of Small Foundations/ASF
1720 N St NW
Washington, DC 20036-2907

202-580-6560
888-212-9922; *Fax:* 202-580-6579
asf@smallfoundations.org;
www.smallfoundations.org
Social Media: Twitter

Henry L. Berman, CEO
Floyd S. Keene, Chair

Dozens of educational sessions, preconference workshops, networking opportunities, and inspiring site visits and service projects.
3000 Members
Frequency: Biennial

10975 **Annual AFRDS Convention & Trade Show**
Association of Fund-Raising Distributors
1100 Johnson Ferry Rd
Suite 300
Atlanta, GA 30342-1733

404-252-3663; *Fax:* 404-252-0774
afrds@kellencompany.com; www.afrds.org
Social Media: Facebook

Kurt Koehler, President
Leslie Lawrence, Secretary
Steve Wienkers, Treasurer

The biggest event in product fundraising.
700+ Members
1000+ Attendees
Frequency: Annual/January

10976 **Annual NCDC Conference and Exposition**
National Catholic Development Conference
86 Front St
Hempstead, NY 11550-3667

516-481-6000
888-879-6232; *Fax:* 516-489-9287;
www.ncdc.org

Mark Melia, Chair
Curtis Yarlott, Vice-Chair
Keith Zekind, Treasurer

Network, learn and be inspired by the amazing community gathered in the spirit of the ministry of fundraising.
400 Members
Frequency: Weekly
Founded in: 1968

10977 **Annual Winter & Spring Conferences**
Northwest Development Officers Association
2150 N 107th Street
Suite 205
Seattle, WA 98133

206-367-8704; *Fax:* 206-367-8777;
www.ndoa.org

Lara Littlefield, President
Louise S. Miller, Executive Director
Jenny Poast, Secretary

Educational meetings focusing on fundraising issues, skills, and best practices. 30 exhibitiors.
400 Attendees
Frequency: Annual Winter & Spring

10978 **CEP Bi-Annual Conference**
Center for Effective Philanthropy
675 Massachusetts Avenue
7th Floor
Cambridge, MA 02139

617-492-0800; *Fax:* 617-492-0888
addya@effectivephilanthropy.org;
www.effectivephilanthropy.org

Phil Buchanan, President

To provide management and governance tools to define, assess, and improve overall foundation performance.
Frequency: Bi-Annual

10979 **Council on Foundations Annual Conference**
Council on Foundations
1828 L Street NW
Washington, DC 20036-5104

202-466-6512; *Fax:* 202-785-3926
jonee@cof.org; www.cof.org

Edward Jones, Program Director
Heidi Lyn Capati, Conference Logistics
Michelle Dunston, Registration
Dorothy Ridings, President

Annual conference and exhibits relating to trends and legislation in the field of philanthropy.
Frequency: April

10980 **Fall Conference for Community Foundations**
Council on Foundations
2121 Crystal Drive
Suite 700
Arlington, VA 22202

800-673-9036
info@cof.org; www.cof.org
Social Media: Facebook, Twitter

Carol Larson, Chair
Kevin Murphy, Vice Chair
Sherece West, Secretary
Will Ginsberg, Treasurer

Three days of bold steps, original ideas, and new solutions for community foundations.
2000 Members
Frequency: Annual/September

10981 **Independent Sector Annual Conference**
Independent Sector
1602 L Street NW
Suite 900
Washington, DC 20036

202-467-6100
888-860-8118; *Fax:* 202-467-6101
info@independentsector.org;
www.independentsector.org
Social Media: Facebook, Twitter

Stephen B. Heintz, Chair
Ralph B. Everett, Vice Chair
Kelvin H. Taketa, Treasurer
Lorie A. Slutsky

The conference focuses on the social compact of the charitable community's role.
1000 Attendees
Frequency: Annual/November

10982 **National Conference on Planned Giving**
National Committee on Planned Giving
233 McCrea Street
Suite 400
Indianapolis, IN 46225-1030

317-269-6274; *Fax:* 317-269-6276;
www.ncpg.org

Shana McMahon, Meetings Manager
Kathryn J Ramsey, Meetings Director
Tanya Howe Johnson, President

Annual conference and exhibits of fundraising equipment, supplies and services.
Frequency: September-October

10983 **Rural Philanthropy Conference**
Council on Foundations
2121 Crystal Drive
Suite 700
Arlington, VA 22202

800-673-9036
info@cof.org; www.cof.org
Social Media: Facebook, Twitter

Carol Larson, Chair
Kevin Murphy, Vice Chair
Sherece West, Secretary
Will Ginsberg, Treasurer

Each session encourages defining rural philanthropy's role, focusing on successful case studies, providing the tools needed to replicate them in the communities.
2000 Members
Frequency: Annual/July

10984 **Windows Annual Conference**
Council on Foundations
2121 Crystal Drive
Suite 700
Arlington, VA 22202

800-673-9036
info@cof.org; www.cof.org
Social Media: Facebook, Twitter

Carol Larson, Chair
Kevin Murphy, Vice Chair
Sherece West, Secretary
Will Ginsberg, Treasurer

Features three days of transparency, honesty, and candor in the field of philanthropy.
2000 Members
Frequency: Annual/April

Directories & Databases

10985 Annual Register of Grant Support: A Directory of Funding Services
Information Today
143 Old Marlton Pike
Medford, NJ 08055-8750

609-654-6266
800-300-9868; *Fax:* 609-654-4309
custserv@infotoday.com; www.infotoday.com

Beverley McDonough, Editor
Daniel Bazikian, Editor

Contains more that 3,500 grant giving organziations. IS also the definitive resource for researching and uncovering a full range of available grant sources.Also directs you to traditional corporate, private, and public funding programs, it also shows you the way to little known, nontraditional grant sources such as educational associations and unions.
Cost: $240.00
1476 Pages
Frequency: Annual
ISBN: 1-573872-04-0

10986 Charitable Trust Directory
Office of the Secretary of State
Charitable Trust Program
801 Capitol Way South
Olympia, WA 98504-0234

360-753-0863
800-332-GIVE; www.secstate.wa.gov/charities

Sam Reed, Chairman/Secretary of State
Linda Vallegos Bremer, Director of General Administration

Directory of charitable trusts regulations in the State of Washington.
Cost: $27.00
290 Pages
Frequency: CD-ROM Available

10987 Corporate Giving Directory
Information Today Inc
143 Old Marlton Pike
Medford, NJ 08055-8750

609-654-6266; *Fax:* 609-654-4309
custserv@infotoday.com; www.infotoday.com

Thomas H Hogan, President

Delivers the latest information on program priorities, giving preferences, evaluation criteria, corporate and foundation officers and directors, and all the other data you need to help your nonprofit organization gain a crucial edge as corporate philanthropy budgets tighten.
1610 Pages
Frequency: Biennial
ISBN: 1-573872-93-5

10988 Directory of Research Grants
Greenwood Publishing Group
130 Cremona Drive
PO Box 1911
Santa Barbara, CA 93117

800-368-6868; *Fax:* 866-270-3856
CustomerService@abc-clio.com;
www.abc-clio.com

Directory containing information for more than 5,100 programs being offered through 1,880 sponsors. Includes contact info for grants and examples of past grants awarded, all of which is divided by subject, program, location, and sponsoring organization.
Cost: $151.95
1208 Pages
ISBN: 9-780897-74-9

10989 Environmental Grantmaking Foundations Directory
Resources for Global Sustainability
PO Box 3665
Cary North, NC 27519-3665

800-724-1857; *Fax:* 919-363-9841;
www.environmentalgrants.com

Corrine Szymko, President

Over 900 private foundations, community foundations and corporate giving programs that provide funding for environmental interests.
Cost: $115.00
Frequency: Annual
ISBN: 0-976788-00-4

10990 Financial Aid for African Americans
Reference Service Press
5000 Windplay Dr
Suite 4
El Dorado Hills, CA 95762-9319

916-939-9620; *Fax:* 916-939-9626
info@rspfunding.com; www.rspfunding.com

Gail Schlachter, Editor
Martin Sklar, Manager

This directory describes nearly 1,450 scholarships, fellowships, loans, grants, awards and internships for African Americans
Cost: $40.00
522 Pages
Frequency: Biennial
ISBN: 1-588410-68-5
Founded in: 1997

10991 Financial Aid for Asian Americans
Reference Service Press
5000 Windplay Dr
Suite4
El Dorado Hills, CA 95762-9319

916-939-9620; *Fax:* 916-939-9626
info@rspfunding.com; www.rspfunding.com

Gail Schlachter, Editor
Martin Sklar, Manager

Use this source to find funding for Americans of Chinese, Japanese, Korean, Vietnamese, Filipino, or other Asian origins. Nearly 1,000 funding opportunities are described.
Cost: $37.50
346 Pages
Frequency: Biennial
ISBN: 1-588410-69-2
Founded in: 1997
Printed in on matte stock

10992 Financial Aid for Hispanic Americans
Reference Service Press
5000 Windplay Dr
Suite 4
El Dorado Hills, CA 95762-9319

916-939-9620; *Fax:* 916-939-9626
info@rspfunding.com; www.rspfunding.com

Gail Schlachter, Editor
Martin Sklar, Manager

This directory describes nearly 1,300 funding opportunities open to Americans of Mexican, Puerto Rican, Central American, or other Latin American heritage.
Cost: $30.00
402 Pages
Frequency: Biennial
ISBN: 1-588410-70-6
Founded in: 1997
Printed in on matte stock

10993 Financial Aid for Native Americans
Reference Service Press
5000 Windplay Dr
Suite 4
El Dorado Hills, CA 95762-9319

916-939-9620; *Fax:* 916-939-9626
info@rspfunding.com; www.rspfunding.com

Gail Schlachter, Editor
Martin Sklar, Manager

In this directory you will find 1,500 funding opportunities set aside just for American Indians, Native Alaskans, and Native Pacific Islanders.
Cost: $40.00
546 Pages
ISBN: 1-588410-71-4
Founded in: 1997

10994 Financial Aid for Veterans, Military Personnel and their Dependents
Reference Service Press
5000 Windplay Dr
Suite 4
El Dorado Hills, CA 95762-9319

916-939-9620; *Fax:* 916-939-9626
info@rspfunding.com; www.rspfunding.com

Gail Schlachter, Editor
Martin Sklar, Manager

This one-stop directory identifies 1,200 scholarships, fellowships, loans, awards, grants and internships.
Cost: $40.00
418 Pages
Frequency: Biennial
ISBN: 1-588410-97-8
Founded in: 1988
Printed in on matte stock

10995 Financial Aid for the Disabled and their Families
Reference Service Press
5000 Windplay Dr
Suite 4
El Dorado Hills, CA 95762-9319

916-939-9620; *Fax:* 916-939-9626
info@rspfunding.com; www.rspfunding.com

Gail Schlachter, Editor
Martin Sklar, Manager

A comprehensive directory identifies 1,200 scholarships, fellowships, loans, internships, awards, and grants for these groups.
Cost: $40.00
502 Pages
Frequency: Biennial
ISBN: 0-918276-65-9

10996 Foundation Directory
Foundation Center
79 5th Ave
New York, NY 10003-3076

212-620-4230
800-424-9836; *Fax:* 212-807-3677
feedback@foundationcenter.org;
www.foundationcenter.org

Bradford K Smith, President
Laura Cascio, Chief Information Officer
Patrick Collins, Chief Information Officer
Nancy Kami, Executive Director

Key facts on the nation's top 10,000 foundations by total giving. And, with over 46,000 descriptions of selected grants, the Directory provides fundraisers with unique insight into foundation giving priorities.
Cost: $215.00
2,533 Pages
ISBN: 1-595420-18-5

10997 Foundation Directory Online Database
Foundation Center

79 5th Ave
New York, NY 10003-3076
212-620-4230
800-424-9836; *Fax:* 212-807-3677
feedback@foundationcenter.org;
www.foundationcenter.org
Bradford K Smith, President
Laura Cascio, Chief Information Officer
Patrick Collins, Chief Information Officer
Nancy Kami, Executive Director

Search our databases online to get detailed information on up to nearly 80,000 foundations, links to current foundation 990-PF returns, crucial facts on more than half a million grants, including the purpose of grants.
Cost: $ 19.95
Frequency: Monthly

10998 **Foundation Directory Supplement**
Foundation Center
79 5th Ave
New York, NY 10003-3076
212-620-4230
800-424-9836; *Fax:* 212-807-3677
feedback@foundationcenter.org;
www.foundationcenter.org
Bradford K Smith, President
Laura Cascio, Chief Information Officer
Patrick Collins, Chief Information Officer
Nancy Kami, Executive Director

Provides revised entries for hundreds of foundations in The Foundation Directory and The Foundation Directory Part 2. Any alterations in giving interests, or updates on staff, financial data, contact information, and more, will be reflected in the Supplement.
Cost: $125.00
1000 Pages
ISBN: 1-931923-89-2

10999 **Foundation Grants Index**
Foundation Center
79 5th Ave
New York, NY 10003-3076
212-620-4230
800-424-9836; *Fax:* 212-807-3677
feedback@foundationcenter.org;
www.foundationcenter.org
Bradford K Smith, President
Laura Cascio, Fulfillment Manager
Michael Seltver, President
Patrick Collins, Chief Information Officer
Nancy Kami, Executive Director

Covers the grants of over 1,000 of the largest independent, corporate, and community foundations in the U.S. and features approximately 125,000 grant descriptions in all.
Cost: $175.00
Frequency: CD-ROM
ISBN: 1-595420-09-6

11000 **Foundation Grants to Individuals**
Foundation Center
79 5th Ave
New York, NY 10003-3076
212-620-4230
800-424-9836; *Fax:* 212-807-3677
feedback@foundationcenter.org;
www.foundationcenter.org
Bradford K Smith, President
Laura Cascio, Fulfillment Manager
Michael Seltver, President
Patrick Collins, Chief Information Officer
Nancy Kami, Executive Director

Featuring over 6,200 entries packed with current information for individual grantseekers.
Cost: $65.00
1,117 Pages
Frequency: Biennial
ISBN: 1-595420-42-8

11001 **Foundation Operations and Management Report**
Association of Small Foundations/ASF
1720 N St NW
Washington, DC 20036-2907
202-580-6560
888-212-9922; *Fax:* 202-580-6579
asf@smallfoundations.org;
www.smallfoundations.org
Social Media: Twitter
Henry L. Berman, CEO
Floyd S. Keene, Chair

The tool for small foundation benchmarking. Easy-to-read data and commentary on small foundation administration, boards, grantmaking and investments.
3000 Members
50+ Pages
Frequency: Annual

11002 **Foundation Salary & Benefits Report**
Association of Small Foundations/ASF
1720 N St NW
Washington, DC 20036-2907
202-580-6560
888-212-9922; *Fax:* 202-580-6579
asf@smallfoundations.org;
www.smallfoundations.org
Social Media: Twitter
Henry L. Berman, CEO
Floyd S. Keene, Chair

Small foundations use this annual report to benchmark base salaries by region, gender, experience, asset size, and more. Data includes information on health insurance premiums, retirement contributions, paid leave, and more.
3000 Members
50+ Pages
Frequency: Annual

11003 **Funding for Persons with Visual Impairments**
Reference Service Press
5000 Windplay Dr
Suite 4
El Dorado Hills, CA 95762-9319
916-939-9620; *Fax:* 916-939-9626
info@rspfunding.com; www.rspfunding.com
Gail Schlachter, Editor
Martin Sklar, Manager

For low-vision readers, we have prepared a large-print listing of the scholarships, fellowships, loans, grants-in-aid, awards, and internships that are set aside just for persons with visual impairments (from high school seniors through professionals and others). Nearly 270 funding opportunities are described in detail here.
Cost: $30.00
274 Pages
Frequency: Annual
ISBN: 1-588411-29-X
Founded in: 1997

11004 **Grants for Foreign and International Programs**
Foundation Center
79 5th Ave
New York, NY 10003-3076
212-620-4230
800-424-9836; *Fax:* 212-807-3677
feedback@foundationcenter.org;
www.foundationcenter.org
Bradford K Smith, President
Michael Seltver, Chief Information Officer
Patrick Collins, Chief Information Officer
Nancy Kami, Executive Director

A customized list of thousands of recent grants of $10,000 or more that have been awarded to organizations in foreign countries and to domestic recipients for international activities in such areas as: development and relief, peace and security, arms control, human rights, conferences and research, and more.
Cost: $75.00
436 Pages
ISBN: 1-595420-23-1

11005 **Guide to Funding for International and Foreign Programs**
Foundation Center
79 5th Ave
New York, NY 10003-3076
212-620-4230
800-424-9836; *Fax:* 212-807-3677
feedback@foundationcenter.org;
www.foundationcenter.org
Bradford K Smith, President
Patrick Collins, Chief Information Officer
Nancy Kami, Executive Director

Includes up-to-date information on over 1,000 foundations and corporate givers that have supported a wide range of projects with an international focus both in the U.S. and in foreign countries.
Cost: $125.00
358 Pages
ISBN: 1-931923-95-7

11006 **Guide to US Foundations, Their Trustees, Officers and Donors**
Foundation Center
79 5th Ave
New York, NY 10003-3076
212-620-4230
800-424-9836; *Fax:* 212-807-3677
feedback@foundationcenter.org;
www.foundationcenter.org
Bradford K Smith, President
Patrick Collins, Chief Information Officer
Nancy Kami, Executive Director

The only published source of data on all active grantmaking foundations and the individuals who run them, provides current information on over 68,000 foundations. Featuring a master list of the decision-makers who direct America's foundations, the Guide is a powerful fundraising reference tool.
Cost: $350.00
4,235 Pages
Frequency: Annual
ISBN: 1-595420-35-5

11007 **Matching Gift Details**
Council for Advancement & Support of Education
1307 New York Ave NW
Suite 1000
Washington, DC 20005-4726
202-393-1301; *Fax:* 202-387-4973
memberservicecenter@case.org; www.case.org
Silvia France, Matching Gifts Coordinator

Compiled and maintained by the Matching Gifts Clearinghouse, a comprehensive annual directory of more than 8,600 companies that match employee charitable gifts.
Cost: $100.00
286 Pages
ISBN: 0-899643-83-3

11008 **National Directory of Corporate Giving**
Foundation Center
79 5th Ave
New York, NY 10003-3076
212-620-4230
800-424-9836; *Fax:* 212-807-3677;
www.foundationcenter.org
Bradford K Smith, President
Patrick Collins, Chief Information Officer
Nancy Kami, Executive Director

This comprehensive directory features up-to-date information that helps fundraisers tap into their share of grant money earmarked by companies for nonprofit support. Detailed portraits of close to 2,500 corporate foundations and some 1,400 direct giving programs feature essential information.
Cost: $195.00
1,165 Pages
Frequency: Annual
ISBN: 1-595420-04-5

11009 **New Foundation Guidebook**
Association of Small Foundation
4905 Del Ray Avenue
Suite 200
Bethesda, MD 20814
301-073-3337
888-212-9922; *Fax:* 301-907-0980
asf@smallfoundations.org;
www.smallfoundations.org
Carmen Wong, Director of Communications
Deborah Brody Hamilton, CEO
Hanh Le, Director Member Services
Kathryn Petrillo-Smith, Managing Director
Contains articles and advice from over 40 foundation respresentatives and experts included in the Association of Small Foundations' newsletters and publications.
Cost: $40.00
86 Pages

11010 **New Nonprofit Almanac & Desk Reference**
Independent Sector
1602 L St NW
Suite 900
Washington, DC 20036-5682
202-467-6100
888-860-8118; *Fax:* 202-467-6101
info@independentsector.org;
www.independentsector.org
Provides managers, researchers, volunteers, and the press with the essential facts and figures needed to understand the size, scope, and nature of the nonprofit sector and its contributions to American society.
Cost: $42.00
288 Pages
ISBN: 9-780787-95-7

11011 **The Complete Guide to Grantmaking Basics: A Field Guide for Funders**
Council on Foundations
2121 Crystal Drive
Suite 700
Arlington, VA 22202
800-673-9036
info@cof.org; www.cof.org
Social Media: Facebook, Twitter
Carol Larson, Chair
Kevin Murphy, Vice Chair
Sherece West, Secretary
Will Ginsberg, Treasurer
A practical guide to honing your grantmaking effectiveness and adapting to the changing nonprofit world.
Cost: $65.00
2000 Members

11012 **The Foundation Guidebook**
Association of Small Foundations/ASF
1720 N St NW
Washington, DC 20036-2907
202-580-6560
888-212-9922; *Fax:* 202-580-6579
asf@smallfoundations.org;
www.smallfoundations.org
Social Media: Twitter
Henry L. Berman, CEO
Floyd S. Keene, Chair
Gain the baseline knowledge to operate your foundation smoothly and effectively.
Cost: $69.00
3000 Members

Industry Web Sites

11013 **http://gold.greyhouse.com**
G.O.L.D Grey House OnLine Databases
Grey House Publishing's online database platform, GOLD, offers Quick Search, Keyword Search and Expert Search for most business sectors including foundation and fund raising markets. The GOLD platform makes finding the information you need quick and easy - whether you're a novice searcher or an experienced database user. All of Grey House's directory products are available for subscription on the GOLD platform.

11014 **www.aafrc.org**
American Association of Fund-Raising Counsel
To promote ethical practice and professional standards in the fund-raising consultant field.

11015 **www.ahp.org**
Association for Healthcare Philanthropy
Represents health care fundraising professionals through education and eventually bestows the credentials upon them.

11016 **www.boardsource.org**
BoardSource
Formerly the National Center for Nonprofit Boards, is the premier resource for practical information, tools and best practices, training, and leadership development for board members of nonprofit organizations worldwide.

11017 **www.cof.org**
Council on Foundations
Supports all those involved in the foundation business. Publishes monthly magazine. We provide leadership expertise, legal services and networking opportunities among other services to our members and to the general public.

11018 **www.grantsmart.org**
Grantsmart
An online resource database that contains 96,337 private foundations and charitable trusts.

11019 **www.greyhouse.com**
Grey House Publishing
Authoritative reference directories for most business sectors including foundation and fund raising markets. Users can search the online databases with varied search criteria allowing for custom searches by product category, geographic area, sales volume, keyword, subject and more. Full Grey House catalog and online ordering also available.

11020 **www.guidestar.org**
GuideStar
A database of more than 1 million nonprofit organizations in the United States. It's the world's most comprehensive source of information about American nonprofit organizations.

11021 **www.idealist.org**
Action Without Borders
Over 45,000 nonprofit and community organizations in 165 countries, which you can search or browse by name, location or mission.

11022 **www.independentsector.org**
Independent Sector
The leadership forum for charities, foundations, and corporate giving programs committed to advancing the common good in America and around the world.

11023 **www.naspl.org**
North American Assn of State & Provincial Lottery
Represents 47 lottery organizations throughout North America. Provides information and benefits of state and provincial lottery organizations.

11024 **www.ncdcusa.org**
National Catholic Development Conference
Members include development officers and key fund raisers of charitable institutions and agencies.

11025 **www.philathropy.org**
A Philanthropic Partnership for Black Communities
Providing information on innovative vehicles for the black communities.

11026 **www.snpo.orgorg/snpo**
Society for Nonprofit Organizations
Dedicated to bringing together those who serve in the nonprofit world in order to build a strong network of professional throughout the country.

11027 **www.tgci.com**
The Grantsmanship Center
Launched the world's first training program for grantseekers in 1972 and continues to set the standard in the field.

11028 **www.uwex.edu/li**
Learning Institute
The Center provides you with a number of resources on the web that could provide you with assistance in a variety of nonprofit management and leadership issues. In the nonprofit web sites section you will find a number of useful annotated resources organized by topic.

Associations

11029 **Adhesive and Sealant Council**
7101 Wisconsin Avenue
Suite 990
Bethesda, MD 20814

301-986-9700; *Fax:* 301-986-9795
data@ascouncil.org; www.ascouncil.org
Social Media: Twitter, LinkedIn

Traci Jensen, Chair
William Allmond, President
Charles R. Williams, Jr., Treasurer
Steve Duren, Senior Director, Member Services
Malinda Armstrong, Director, Meetings & Expositions

ASC is a North American trade association dedicated to representing the adhesive and sealant industry. ASC is bound by the collective efforts of its members, and strives to improve the industry operating environment and strengthen its member companies.

11030 **American Chemistry Council**
700 Second St, NE
Washington, DC 20002

202-249-7000; *Fax:* 202-249-6100
plastics.americanchemistry.com/pfpg
Social Media: Facebook, Twitter

Calvin M. Dooley, President
Raymond J. O Bryan, CFO & Chief Administrative Officer
Rudy Underwood, Vice President, State Affairs
Bryan Zumwalt, Vice President of Federal Affairs
Anne Womack Kolton, Vice President of Communications

Promotes effective use of recycling of polystyrene. Works to provide effective information about waste disposal and offers technical assistance.
Founded in: 1988

11031 **American Trucking Association**
950 North Glebe Road
Suite 210
Arlington, VA 22203-4181

703-838-1700
nafc@trucking.org; www.trucking.org

Pat Thomas, Chairman
Bill Graves, President & CEO
Kevin Burch, First Vice Chairman
Karla Hulett, Secretary
G. Tommy Hodges, Treasurer

Largest national trade association for the trucking industry.
1000 Members
Founded in: 1933

11032 **Composite Can and Tube Institute**
50 S Pickett Street
Suite 110
Alexandria, VA 22304-7206

703-823-7234; *Fax:* 703-823-7237
ccti@cctiwdc.org; www.cctiwdc.org

Kristine Garland, Executive Vice President
Janine Marczak, Associate Manager, Events
Wayne Vance, Association Counsel

CCTI is an international nonprofit trade association representing the interests of manufacturers of composite paperboard cans, containers, canisters, tubes, cores, edgeboard and related or similar composite products and suppliers to those manufacturers of such items as paper, machinery, adhesives, labels and other services and materials.
Founded in: 1934

11033 **Containerization & Intermodal Institute**
960 Holmdel Road
Bldg 2, Suite 201
Holmdel, NJ 07733

732-817-9131; *Fax:* 732-817-9133
connie@containerization.org;
www.containerization.org
Social Media: LinkedIn

Brendan McCahill, Sr., Chairman
Allen Clifford, Vice Chairman
Michael DiVirgilio, President
Steven Blust, Vice President
Sue Coffey, Treasurer

Provides educational opportunities through existing programs and initiatives, including educational outreach, scholarships, and award programs.
Founded in: 1960

11034 **Contract Packaging Association**
One Parkview Plaza
Suite 800
Oakbrook Terrace, IL 60181
630-544-5053; *Fax:* 630-544-5055
info@contractpackaging.org;
www.contractpackaging.org
Social Media: Twitter, LinkedIn

Vicky Smitley, President
Tim Koers, Vice President
Mark O'Malley, Treasurer
Chris Nutley, Past-President
John Mazelin, Executive Director

A national, not-for-profit trade association that includes dynamic and growing companies offering contract packaging services.
155 Members
Founded in: 1992

11035 **Corrugated Packaging Alliance**
25 Northwest Point Blvd
Suite 510
Elk Grove Village, IL 60007

847-364-9600; *Fax:* 847-364-9739
inquiries@corrugated.org; www.corrugated.org
Social Media: LinkedIn

Rachel K Kenyon, Vice President
Dennis Colley, Executive Director

Develops and coordinates industry-wide programs to address corrugated packaging issues. The Council's mission is to inform consumers, manufacturers, retailers and government officials of corrugated packaging's performance and environmental attributes.
Founded in: 1994

11036 **EPS Industry Alliance (EPS-IA)**
1298 Cronson Blvd.
Suite 201
Crofton, MD 21114

800-607-3772
info@epscentral.org; www.epspackaging.org
Social Media: Facebook, Twitter

EPS-IA is a union of 60 companies dedicated to the sustainability of the expanded polystyrene (EPS) industry and environmental protection.
Founded in: 2012

11037 **Envelope Manufacturers Association**
500 Montgomery St.
Suite 550
Alexandria, VA 22314
703-739-2200; *Fax:* 703-739-2209;
www.envelope.org

Maynard H. Benjamin, President & CEO

Association representing the interests of the envelope manufacturing industry.
Founded in: 1933

11038 **Express Carriers Association**
9532 Liberia Avenue
Suite 752
Manassas, VA 20110
703-361-1058
866-322-7447; *Fax:* 703-361-5274
eca@expresscarriers.org;
www.expresscarriers.org

Paul Steffes, President
Jim Luciani, 1st Vice President
Mike Coyle, 2nd Vice President
Jim King, Treasurer
Jim Bernecker, Secretary

Trade association representing regional carriers. Presents annual marketplace to bring together carriers and shippers

11039 **Fibre Box Association**
25 Northwest Point Blvd
Suite 510
Elk Grove Village, IL 60007

847-364-9600; *Fax:* 847-364-9639
fba@fibrebox.org; www.fibrebox.org
Social Media: LinkedIn

John Davis, Chairman
Mike Waite, First Vice Chairman
Bill Hoel, Second Vice Chairman
Dennis Colley, President
Rachel Kenyon, Vice President1

Represents 90 percent of the US corrugated paper board, packaging, manufacturing industry.
141 Members
Founded in: 1940

11040 **Flexible Intermediate Bulk Container Association**
PO Box 241894
Saint Paul, MN 55124-7019

952-412-8867; *Fax:* 661-339-0023
info@fibca.com; www.fibca.com
Social Media: Facebook, Twitter, LinkedIn, Youtube, Googleplus, blogspot

Lewis Anderson, Executive Director

Works to develop minimum standards of testing and performance for FIBC. Acts as a forum through seminars and other programs and serves as an advocate for the industry.
50 Members
Founded in: 1983

11041 **Flexible Packaging Association**
185 Admiral Cochrane Drive
Suite 105
Annapolis, MD 21401

410-694-0800; *Fax:* 410-694-0900
fpa@flexpack.org; www.flexpack.org

Marla Donahue, President

One of the leading trade associations for converters of flexible packaging and suppliers to the industry. Also provides a wealth of information to its members through focused services and benefits of membership.

11042 **Foodservice & Packaging Institute**
7700 Leesburg Pike
Suite 421
Falls Church, VA 22043

703-592-9889; *Fax:* 703-592-9864
fpi@fpi.org; www.fpi.org
Social Media: Facebook, Twitter, LinkedIn

Lynn Dyer, President
Natha Freiburg, Vice President
Rob Kittredge, Chair
Michael Evans, 1st Vice Chair
Tracy Pearson, 2nd Vice Chair

Manufacturers, suppliers and distributors of one-time use products used for food service, as

well as packaging products made from paper, plastic, aluminum and other materials.
37 Members
Founded in: 1933

11043 **Gemini Shippers Group**
137 West 25th Street
3rd Floor
New York, NY 10001

212-947-3424; *Fax:* 212-629-0361
info@geminishippers.com;
www.geminishippers.com

Sara L. Mayes, CEO and President
Kenneth O'Brien, Chief Operating Officer
Nicole Uchrin, Managing Director
Rich Moore, Sales Director
Arlene L. Blocker, Membership Director

Shippers association with global contracts for all commodities.
200 Members
Founded in: 1916

11044 **Glass Packaging Institute**
1220 North Fillmore Street
Suite 400
Arlington, VA 22201

703-684-6359; *Fax:* 703-546-0588
info@gpi.org; www.gpi.org
Social Media: Facebook, Twitter

Andres Lopez, Chairman
Lynn M. Bragg, President
John Riordan, Board Member
Sanjay Gandhi, Board Member
John Gallo, Board Member

Develops and evaluates testing procedures and equipment, conducts advertising campaigns for generic products.
Founded in: 1945

11045 **Healthcare Compliance Packaging Council**
2711 Buford Road
#268
Bon Air, VA 23235-2423

804-338-5778; *Fax:* 888-812-4272;
www.hcpconline.org
Social Media: Facebook, LinkedIn

Walt Berghahn, Executive Director

Promotes the many benefits of unit dose blister and strip packaging, especially its ability to be designed in compliance, promoting formats that help people take their medications properly.
Founded in: 1990

11046 **Institute of International Container Lessors**
1120 Connecticut Avenue
Suite 440
Washington, DC 20036-3946

202-223-9800; *Fax:* 202-223-9810
info@iicl.org; www.iicl.org

Philip Brewer, Chairman
Steven Blust, President & Secretary
Simon Vernon, 1st Vice President
Keith Lovetro, 2nd Vice President
George Elkas, Treasurer

Represents international container and chassis leasing industry in technical, governmental and legal matters. Publishes leading worldwide manuals on inspection and repair of containers and inspector and maintenance of chassis. Sponsors container and chassis inspection examination once a year in over 40 countries and chassis examination in North America.
Founded in: 1971

11047 **Institute of Packaging Professionals**
One Parkview Plaza
Suite 800
Oakbrook Terrace, IL 60181

630-544-5050; *Fax:* 630-544-5055
info@iopp.org; www.iopp.org
Social Media: Facebook, Twitter, LinkedIn, YouTube

Jane Chase, Chair
Dan Alexander, Vice Chair
Dana Alexander, Executive VP- Finance & Operations
Robert Meisner, Executive VP- Education
Suzanne Simmons, Executive VP- Membership

Dedicated to creating networking and educational opportunities that help packaging professionals succeed.

11048 **International Air Transport Association**
800 Place Victoria
PO Box 113
Montreal, CA H4Z 1M1

514-874-0202; *Fax:* 514-874-9632;
www.iata.org/
Social Media: Twitter, LinkedIn, YouTube

Tony Tyler, Director General & CEO

Seeks to improve understanding of the industry among decision makers and increase awareness of the benefits that aviation brings to national and global economies. It fights for the interests of airlines across the globe, challenging unreasonable rules and charges, holding regulators and governments to account, and strivign for sensible regulation.
240+ Members
Founded in: 1945

11049 **International Molded Fiber Association**
355 Lexington Avenue
Floor 15
New York, NY 10017

212-297-2150; *Fax:* 262-241-3766
Alan@IMFA.org; www.imfa.org
Social Media: Facebook, Twitter, LinkedIn

Cassandra Niesing, Asst. Director
Joseph Grygny, Chairman

Acts as an information center for the molded fiber industry with worldwide membership of users and manufacturers of molded fiber producs. Promotes use of natural and recycled fibers.
Founded in: 1997

11050 **Keep America Beautiful**
1010 Washington Blvd
Stamford, CT 06901

203-659-3000; *Fax:* 203-659-3001
info@kab.org; www.kab.org
Social Media: Facebook, Twitter, Youtube

Howard Ungerleider, Chairman
Jennifer M. Jehn, President and CEO
Steve Navedo, VP Development
Mike Rogers, Chief Development Officer
Becky Lyons, Chief Operating Officer

National, nonprofit, education organization whose corporate members include packagers, retailers, bottlers, and makers of chemical, steel, glass, paper and aluminum products.
Founded in: 1953

11051 **Lake Carriers Association**
20325 Center Ridge Road
Suite 720
Rocky River, OH 44116

440-333-4444; *Fax:* 440-333-9993
info@lcaships.com; www.lcaships.com

James H I Weakley, President
Glen Nekvasil, Vice President
Harold W. Henderson, General Counsel
Katie Gumeny, Administrative Assistant
Katherine A. Gumeny, Secretary/Treasurer

Members are US-Flag Great Lakes vessel operators engaged in transporting iron ore, coal, grain, limestone, cement and petroleum products.
Founded in: 1880

11052 **National Customs Brokers and Forwarders Association of America, Inc.**
1200 18th St NW
Suite 901
Washington, DC 20036

202-466-0222; *Fax:* 202-466-0226
staff@ncbfaa.org; www.ncbfaa.org

Darrell Sekin, Jr., Chairman
Geoffrey Powell, President
Amy Magnus, Vice President
Scott E. Larson, Treasurer
William S. App. Jr., Secretary

Learn about new business leads, stay on top of Customs Service and other agency regulations that will impact your operations and provide invaluable professional development resources for your employees.
600+ Members
Founded in: 1897

11053 **National Institute of Packaging, Handling, and Logistics Engineers**
5903 Ridgeway Drive
Grand Prairie, TX 75052

817-466-7490
866-464-7490
admin@niphle.com; www.niphle.com
Social Media: Facebook, Twitter, LinkedIn

Sean Kernis, President
Anna Boulware, Board Member
Michael Werneke, Board Member
Sher Paul Singh, Board Member
Brian Ramsey, Board Member

An assemblage of professionals whose interest in the complex and diverse practice of distribution and logistics is a common bond.
600 Members
Founded in: 1956

11054 **Paperboard Packaging Council**
1350 Main Street
Suite 1508
Springfield, MA 01103-1670

413-686-9191; *Fax:* 413-747-7777
paperboardpackaging@ppcnet.org;
www.ppcnet.org
Social Media: Facebook, Twitter, LinkedIn, Youtube

Kyle Eldred, Chair
Charles Johnson, Vice Chair
Marc Anderson, Director at large
Michael Ukropina, Director at large
Steven Levkoff, Treasurer

The leading industry association serving suppliers and converters of all forms of paperboard packaging, works to grow, promote, and protect the paperboard packaging industry while providing its members with resources and tools to compete effectively and successfully in the marketplace.
Founded in: 1967

11055 **Petroleum Packaging Council**
ATD Management Inc.
1519 Via Tulipan
San Clemente, CA 92673

949-369-7102; *Fax:* 949-366-1057
PPC@ATDmanagement.com;

www.ppcouncil.org
Social Media: LinkedIn

John Whittenhall, President
Elizabeth Wagg, Vice President
Sam Merenda, Secretary/ Treasurer
Darren Booth, Assistant Treasurer
Carolyn Booms, Director

Provides technical leadership and education to the petroleum packaging industry.
400 Members
Founded in: 1950

11056 Pressure Sensitive Tape Council
One Parkview Plaza
Suite 800
Oakbrook Terrace, IL 60181

630-544-5048; *Fax:* 630-544-5055
info@pstc.org; www.pstc.org
Social Media: Twitter, LinkedIn, Flickr

Michael Merkx, President
Curt Rutsky, Vice President
Charlie McKenna, Treasurer
Brad Boelkins, Directors
Tom Boyle, Directors

Trade association for tape manufacturers and affiliate suppliers, dedicated to helping the industry produce quality pressure sensitive adhesive tape products in the global marketplace. PSTC provides education and training, works with ASTM and global trade organizations to harmonize test methods and monitors legislative and regulatory activities.
Founded in: 1953

11057 Recycled Paperboard Technical Association
P.O. Box 5774
Elgin, IL 60121-5774

847-622-2544; *Fax:* 847-622-2546
rpta@rpta.org; www.rpta.org

David Briere, President
Mark Sklar, Vice President
Peter Traeger, Treasurer
Amy E. Schaffer, Ex-Officio
Tim Hagenbuch, Chair

An association of US, Canadian and overseas companies interested in cooperative research and development in the industry.
33 Members
Founded in: 1953

11058 Retail Packaging Association
105 Eastern Avenue
Suite 104
Annapolis, MD 21403

410-940-6459; *Fax:* 410-263-1659
info@retailpackaging.org;
www.retailpackaging.org

Tony Van Belkom, President
Jatin Patel, Treasurer
Denise Cabrera, Secretary
Don Smith, Executive Director
Amy Luckado, Membership Director

Serves its members and the entire retail packaging industry. Also organizes the largest trade show and conference of its kind in the US. A self-governed not-for-profit organization comprised of professionals involved in all facets of production and distribution of retail packaging products.
Founded in: 1989
Mailing list available for rent

11059 Reusable Industrial Packaging Association
51 Monroe Street
Suite 812
Rockville, MD 20850

301-577-3786; *Fax:* 301-577-6476
prankin@ripaus.com;
www.reusablepackaging.org
Social Media: Facebook, Twitter

Ricky Buckner, Chair
Jerry Butler, Vice Chair
Paul W. Rankin, President
Dan Burek, Treasurer
Tim O'Bryan, Secretary

Founded in: 1942

11060 Technical Association of the Pulp & Paper Industry
15 Technology Parkway South
Suite 115
Peachtree Corners, GA 30092

770-446-1400
800-322-8686; *Fax:* 770-446-6947
webmaster@tappi.org; www.tappi.org
Social Media: Facebook, Twitter, LinkedIn

Chris Luettgen, Chair
Paul R. Durocher, Vice Chair
Larry N. Montague, President & CEO
Peter R. Augustine, Director
Medwick V. Byrd, Director

To engage the people and resources of our association in providing technically sound solutions to the workplace problems and opportunities that challenge our current and future members.
12000 Members
Founded in: 1915

11061 The Independent Packaging Association Converters
113 S. West Street
3rd Floor
Alexandria, VA 22314

703-836-2422
877-836-2422; *Fax:* 703-836-2795
info@aiccbox.org; www.aiccbox.org
Social Media: Facebook, Twitter, LinkedIn, YouTube

Mark Williams, Chairman
Tony Schleich, First Vice Chairman
Joseph M. Palmeri, Vice Chairman
Jeff Pallini, Associate Vice Chairman
John Forrey, Director at Large

Provides a forum for discussion of problems and offers educational programs and seminars.
1100 Members
Founded in: 1974

11062 Transportation Intermediaries Association
1625 Prince St
Suite 200
Alexandria, VA 22314-2883

703-299-5700; *Fax:* 703-836-0123
info@tianet.org; www.tianet.org

Robert Voltmann, President
Jeff Tucker, Chair
Jason Beardall, Vice Chair
Michael Riccio, Treasurer
Barcy Vidt, Secretary

Education and policy organization for North American transportation intermediaries. The only national association representing the interests of all third party transportation service providers. Members include logistics management firms, property brokers, perishable commodities brokers, freight forwarders, intermodal marketers and ocean and air forwarders.
700 Members
Founded in: 1977

11063 Transportation Marketing Communications Association (TMCA)
9382 Oak Avenue
Waconia, MN 55387

952-442-5638; *Fax:* 952-442-3941
brian07@tmcatoday.org; www.tmcatoday.org

John Ferguson, President
Tom Nightingale, VP
Tracy Robinson, Treasurer
Edward Moritz, Secretary
Brian Everett, Executive Director

The only association serving transportation marketing, sales and communications pros in all modes and market segments of the North American transportation industry.
225 Members
Founded in: 1924

Newsletters

11064 Air Cargo Report
Phillips Publishing
1201 Seven Locks Road
Potomac, MD 20854-2931

301-541-1400; *Fax:* 301-424-2098
info@accessintel.com; www.accessintel.com

Richard Koulbanis, Publisher
Donald Pazour, CEO/President

Reports on emerging trends and business strategies for airline cargo, integrator, freight forwarding and all-cargo carrier operations.
Circulation: 1430

11065 CanTube Bulletin
Composite Can and Tube Institute
50 S Pickett Street
Suite 110
Alexandria, VA 22304-7206

703-823-7234; *Fax:* 703-823-7237
ccti@cctiwdc.org; www.cctiwdc.org

Excellent source of information about issues affecting this industry, as well as updates on CCTI activities.
Frequency: Bi-Monthly
Circulation: 800+

11066 E-Catalyst Industry Update
Adhesive & Sealant Council
7101 Wisconsin Avenue
Suite 990
Bethesda, MD 20814

301-986-9700; *Fax:* 301-986-9795
data@ascouncil.org; www.ascouncil.org

Traci Jensen, Chair
Charles R. Williams, Jr., Treasurer
William Allmond, President

Delivers the latest ASC news, industry information and end-user trends.
Frequency: Monthly

11067 Mail Center Management Report
Institute of Management and Administration
3 Bethesda Metro Center
Suite 250
Bethesda, MD 20814-5377

800-372-1033; *Fax:* 800-253-0332;
www.ioma.com

Shows you how to improve mail center productivity, reduce costs, and get you the recognition you deserve through buying and leasing new equipment, negotiating rates with carriers, and much more. Shows proven techniques to improve relations with the USPS and other service vendors. You'll find tactics for improving your dealing with senior management, purchasing, marketing and logistics.

11068 Packaging Strategies
Packaging Strategies
600 Willowbrook Lane
Suite 610
West Chester, PA 19382
610-436-4220
800-524-7225; *Fax:* 610-436-6277
packinfo@packstrat.com; www.packstrat.com
Social Media: Facebook, Twitter, LinkedIn

Joe Pryweller, Editor/Conference Director
Janet Martinelli, Conference/Study Support Manager
Randy Green, Publisher
Karen Vaillancourt, Sales Manager
Karen Close, Senior Events Manager

A subscription newsletter focusing on news and analysis of technology and business issues in the packaging industry. Also producer of 4 conferences per year: structural packagingsummit, food packaging technologies summit, global pouch firum, sustainable packaging forum and multi-client industry studies.
Cost: $497.00
8 Pages
ISSN: 8755-6189
Founded in: 1983
Printed in 2 colors on matte stock

11069 Transportation Intermediaries Update
Transportation Intermediaries Association
1625 Prince St
Suite 200
Alexandria, VA 22314-2883

703-299-5700; *Fax:* 703-836-0123
voltmann@tianet.org; www.tianet.org

Robert Voltmann, President

Education and policy organization for North American transportation intermediaries. TIA is the only national association representing the interests of all third party transportation service providers. The members of TIA include logistics management firms, property brokers, perishable commodities brokers, freight forwarders, intermodal marketers, ocean and air forwarders, and NVOCC's.
700 Pages
Frequency: Monthly

Magazines & Journals

11070 Advanced Packaging
PennWell Publishing Company
98 Spit Brook Rd
Suite L11
Nashua, NH 03062-5737
603-891-0123; *Fax:* 603-891-9294
lwilliam@pennwell.com; www.pennwell.com

Christine Shaw, VP
Gail Flower, Editor

Focuses on materials, assembly, design and reliability issues facing the global packaging community.
Cost: $88.00
Frequency: Monthly
Circulation: 22,000
Founded in: 1910

11071 Air Cargo Focus
Cargo Network Services Corporation
703 Waterford Way
Suite 680
Miami, FL 33126-4677

786-413-1000; *Fax:* 786-413-1005
cns@cnsc.us; www.cnsc.net

Fernando Garcia, VP
Anthony P Calabrese, President

A forum for professionals involved in the sale , marketing, services and movement of air cargo.
Frequency: Quarterly
Circulation: 8000
Founded in: 1986

11072 Air Cargo News
PO Box 98
Portage, MI 49081-98

718-479-0716; *Fax:* 718-740-0761
judy@aircargonews.com;
www.aircargonews.com

Geoffrey Arend, Publisher

CAB regulations, and other news of interest to those in the air cargo industry.
Cost: $39.95
Frequency: Monthly
Circulation: 100,000
Founded in: 1975

11073 American Shipper
Howard Publications
300 W Adams Street Suite 600
PO Box 4728
Jacksonville, FL 32201-4728

904-355-2601
800-874-6422; *Fax:* 904-791-8836;
www.americanshipper.com
Hayes H Howard, Publisher
Gary G. Burrows, Managing Editor

Provides those involved in domestic and global supply chain management with news and information of a strategic nature, useful in the formation of logistics polices and partnerships.
Cost: $30.00
100 Pages
Frequency: Monthly
Circulation: 13487
ISSN: 1074-8350
Founded in: 1951
Printed in 4 colors on glossy stock

11074 Cargo Facts
Air Cargo Managment Group
520 Pike St
Suite 1010
Seattle, WA 98101-4058

206-587-6537; *Fax:* 206-587-6540;
www.cargofacts.com

Edwin Laird, Manager
David Harris, Editor
Jackie Edinger, Circulation Manager

Includes fiscal reports, freighter aircraft transactions, short segments, international perspectives, and industry updates.
Cost: $395.00
24 Pages
Frequency: Monthly
Circulation: 7500
ISSN: 0278-0801
Founded in: 1980

11075 Cosmetic Personal Care Packaging
O&B Communications
11444 W Olympic Boulevard
Los Angeles, CA 90064-1303

310-445-4200; *Fax:* 310-445-4299
info@cpcpkg.com; www.cpcpkg.com

Patricia Spinner, Publisher
John Bethune, Editorial Director
Jennifer Kwok, Managing Editor

Provides information on new packaging containers, materials, equipment and services that are involved with the cosmetic industry.
Cost: $60.00
Frequency: Monthly
Circulation: 12,500
Founded in: 1996

11076 Courier Times
Courier Times
27-16 168th Street
Flushing, NY 11358-1130

718-291-1253; *Fax:* 718-359-1959;
www.couriertimes.com

Bill Goodman, Editor
C Tsamis, Owner

New products vital to the industry, discusses insurance and technology updates, also offers customer service guidelines.
Cost: $39.00
Frequency: Monthly
Circulation: 1100

11077 Electronic Packaging & Production
Reed Business Information
360 Park Ave S
New York, NY 10010-1737

646-746-6400; *Fax:* 646-756-7583
corporatecommunications@reedbusiness.com;
www.reedbusiness.com

John Poulin, CEO
Michael Sweeney, Editorial Director
James Reed, Owner

Edited for engineers and managers who are involved in packaging design, printed circuit board fabrication and assembly, and production testing of electronic circuits, systems, products and equipment.
Founded in: 1960

11078 Flexible Packaging
Flexible Packaging Association
971 Corporate Blvd
Suite 403
Linthicum, MD 21090-2253

410-694-0800; *Fax:* 410-694-0900
fpa@flexpack.org; www.flexpack.org

Marla Donahue, President

Offering subscribers up-to-the-minute information on industry news and trends, material and substrate developments, innovations in equipment, and the latest in business management. The only magazine in the market that dedicates 100 percent of its editorial content and circulation to flexible packaging converters.
Frequency: Monthly

11079 Food & Beverage Packaging
155 Pfingsten Road
Suite 205
Deerfield, IL 60015

847-405-4000; *Fax:* 847-405-4100;
www.foodandbeveragepackaging.com

Randy Green, Publisher

Identifies and analyzes the market trends and packaging solutions that matter to food and beverage processors.
Frequency: Monthly
Circulation: 75140
Founded in: 1959

11080 Harbour & Shipping
Progress Publishing Company, Ltd
1489 Marine Drive
Suite 510
West Vancouver, BC V7 T1

604-922-6717; *Fax:* 604-922-1739

Allison Smith, Editor
Murray McLellan, Publisher/Marketing

Serves the deep sea and coastal shipping, and ship building, repair and supply industries of Canada and worldwide. Accepts advertising.
Cost: $60.00
Frequency: Monthly
Circulation: 2200
ISSN: 0017-7637
Printed in 4 colors on glossy stock

11081 International Paper Board Industry
Brunton Publications & NV Public

43 Main Street
Avon By The Sea, NJ 07717-1051

732-502-0500; *Fax:* 732-502-9606
jcurley@NVPublications.com
nvpublications.com

Mike Brunton, Publisher
Jim Curley, Editor
Tom Vilardi, President

Information on corrugated paper and converting industry, encompassing news and production worldwide.
Cost: $60.00
Frequency: Monthly
Circulation: 6500

11082 Journal of HazMat Transportation
Packaging Research International
404 Price St
West Chester, PA 19382-3531

610-436-8292
877-429-7447; *Fax:* 610-436-9422;
www.hazmatship.com

Vincent A Vitollo, Owner

A professionally prepared technical reporting system, focused exlusively on explaining changes to the hazardous materials transportation regulations. Thoroughly covers and provides technical reviews of the US 49CFR, International Civil Aviation Organization Technical Instructions, the International Maritime Dangerous Goods Code, and the European Road and Rail Regulations.
Cost: $209.00
Circulation: 1000
Founded in: 1990
Printed in 4 colors on matte stock

11083 MAIL: The Journal of Communication Distribution
1 Elmcoft Road
Stamford, CT 06926-700

203-356-5000
800-672-6937; *Fax:* 203-739-3488;
www.pb.com

Meg Reiley, President
Ina Steiner, Publisher

Manages change and positions customers for both tactical and long-term success with innovative, cost-effective, end-to-end messaging solutions.

11084 Modern Bulk Transporter
Tunnell Publications
PO Box 66010
Houston, TX 77266

713-523-8124; *Fax:* 713-523-8384;
www.bulktransporter.com/
Social Media: Facebook, Twitter

Charles Wilson, Editor
Martine Ewing, Advertising Director
Mary Davis, Associate Editor

Serves the truck industry that transports petroleum and petroleum products. Accepts advertising.
Frequency: Monthly
Circulation: 15000

11085 PARCEL
RB Publishing
2901 International Lane
Madison, WI 53704-3102

608-778-8785
800-536-1992; *Fax:* 608-241-8666;
www.parcelindustry.com
Social Media: LinkedIn

Marll Thiede, CEO
Chad Griepentrog, President
Mike Beacom, Editor

Brings the insights needed to improve parcel operations and keep costs under control. PARCEL gives you access to experts who look at the entire process, from order entry to the shipping dock to customer delivery, to give you information you can use.
Circulation: 30000
Founded in: 1988

11086 Packaging Digest Magazine
UBM Canon
1200 Jorie Blvd.
Suite 230
Oak Brook, IL 60523-2260

630-990-2371; *Fax:* 630-990-8894
packagingdigest@ubm.com;
www.packagingdigest.com

John Kalkowski, Editorial Director
Lisa McTigue Pierce, Editor
Jenni Spinner, Senior Editor

Serves the manufacturing, wholesale and service industries.
Cost: $75.00
Frequency: Monthly
Founded in: 1963

11087 Packaging Technology & Engineering
North American Publishing Company
1500 Spring Garden St
12th Floor
Philadelphia, PA 19130-4094

215-238-5300
800-777-8074; *Fax:* 215-238-5342
customerservice@napco.com; www.napco.com

Ned S Borowsky, CEO
Richard Soloway, CEO/President
Glen Reynolds, Circulation Manager
Nolle Skodzinski, Editor

Reports on evironmental concerns, legislation and regulation, product design, material availability, and economic trends.
Cost: $69.00
Frequency: Monthly
Circulation: 20271
Founded in: 1958

11088 Packaging World
Summit Publishing Company
330 N Wabash Ave
Suite 2401
Chicago, IL 60611-7618

312-222-1010; *Fax:* 312-222-1310
reynolds@packworld.com;
www.packworld.com

Lloyd Ferguson, Owner
Joseph Angel, Vice President
Patrick Reynolds, VP/Editor
Timothy Hammack, Circulation Director
Jim George, Marketing & Design Editor

Serves the manufacturing, wholesaling, and service industries.
Frequency: Monthly
Circulation: 92547
ISSN: 1073-7367
Founded in: 1994
Printed in 4 colors on matte stock

11089 Paperboard Packaging
2835 North Sheffield Avenue
Suite 226
Chicago, IL 60657

773-880-2234; *Fax:* 773-880-2244;
www.packaging-online.com
Social Media: Facebook, Twitter

Marisa Palmieri, Editor

Publication edited for management and other key personnel involved in the manufacturing and marketing segments of the paperboard packaging industry.
Cost: $39.00
Frequency: Monthly
ISSN: 0031-1227

11090 Pharmaceutical & Medical Packaging News
Canon Communications
11444 W Olympic Blvd
Suite 900
Los Angeles, CA 90064-1555

310-445-4200; *Fax:* 310-445-4299;
www.devicelink.com

Charlie Mc Curdy, President
Daphne Allen, Managing Editor
Bob Michaels, Managing Editor
Nicole Welter, Account Executive

Information and news on events, new technology, industry trends, regulatory matters, and health care trade associations for professionals involved in the pharmaceutical and medical product packaging industry.
Cost: $150.00
Frequency: Monthly
Circulation: 20000
ISSN: 1081-5481
Founded in: 1978

11091 Refrigerated Transporter
Penton
PO Box 66010
Houston, TX 77266

713-523-8124
800-880-0368; *Fax:* 713-523-8384
refrigeratedtransporter.com

Ray Anderson, Publisher

The information source for those involved in the transportation and distribution of refrigerated products ranging from food to pharmaceuticals, from film and cosmetics to chemicals. Provides practical information derived from the experience of businesses in the field as well as up-to-the-minute news on developments and equipment for the industry.
Frequency: Monthly
Circulation: 15023
Founded in: 1905

11092 TAPPI Journal
Technical Association of the Pulp & Paper Industry
15 Technology Parkway South
Norcross, GA 30092

770-446-1400
800-322-8686; *Fax:* 770-446-6947
webmaster@tappi.org; www.tappi.org

Larry N. Montague, President & CEO

Serves domestic and international pulp, paper, paperboard, packaging and converting industries; manufacturers and suppliers of machinery, equipment, chemicals and other material.
Cost: $350.00
130 Pages
Frequency: Monthly
Circulation: 5300
ISSN: 0734-1415
Founded in: 1949
Printed in 4 colors on glossy stock

11093 Trucker's Connection
Megan Cullingford
5960 Crooked Creek Road
Suite 15
Norcross, GA 30092

770-416-0927; *Fax:* 770-416-1734;
www.truckersconnection.com

Megan Cullingford, General Manager
Dan Barnhill, Editor
Reid Ramsay, Production Manager

Published for the use of long haul, over-the-road truck drivers, owner operators, small trucking

company fleet owners, safety and recruiting of personnel for trucking companies in the US and Canada.
Frequency: Monthly
Circulation: 165000
Founded in: 1986
Printed in 4 colors on glossy stock

11094 World Wide Shipping (WWS)
World Wide Shipping Guide
16302 Byrnwyck Ln
Odessa, FL 33556-2807

813-920-4788; *Fax:* 813-920-8268
info@wwship.com; www.wwship.com

Lee Di Paci, Publisher
Barbara Edwards, Marketing Manager
Bob Susor, Marketing Manager

Dedicated to the interests of North American exporters, importers, distributors, freight forwarders, NVOCC's and customs brokers requiring freight tranportation services and equipment.
Cost: $32.00
32 Pages
Frequency: Fortnightly
Circulation: 9000
ISSN: 1060-7900
Founded in: 1919
Printed in 4 colors on glossy stock

Trade Shows

11095 International Molded Fiber Packaging Seminar
International Molded Fiber Association
1425 W Mequon Rd
Suite C
Mequon, WI 53092-3262

262-241-0522; *Fax:* 262-241-3766
info@imfa.org; www.imfa.org
Social Media: Facebook, Twitter, LinkedIn

Cassandra Niesing, Asst. Director
Joseph Grygny, Chairman

Opportunity to network, learn, and grow in the molded fiber industry.
Founded in: 1996

11096 LabelExpo
Tarsus Group
9501 W Devon Avenue
Rosemont, IL 60018-4811

847-292-3700; *Fax:* 847-318-1506;
www.tarsus.com

Steve Krogulski, Manager

The largest event for the lable, web printing, product decoration, converting and packaging industry in the Americas.
13700 Attendees
Frequency: Annual/September

11097 Outlook & Strategies Conference
Paperboard Packaging Council
1350 Main Street
Suite 1508
Springfield, MA 01103-1670

413-686-9191; *Fax:* 413-747-7777;
www.ppcnet.org

Ben Markens, President
Lou Kornet, Vice President/Chief of Staff

Industry leaders specializing in sustainability, the economy, and education will come together to impart their knowledge, experience, and business predictions.
325 Attendees
Frequency: Annual/March

11098 PROPAK Asia
Reed Exhibition Companies
383 Main Avenue
PO Box 6059
Norwalk, CT 06851

203-840-4800; *Fax:* 203-840-9628

One hundred and seventy four exhibitors for an audience of manufacturers, packaging design and development professionals. International food processing and packaging technology exhibition.
Frequency: Annual

11099 Shipper/Carrier Marketplace
Express Carriers Association
9532 Liberia Ave
Suite 752
Manassas, VA 20110-1719

703-361-1058
866-322-7447; *Fax:* 703-361-5274;
www.expresscarriers.org

Stuart Hyden, President
Lance Adams, First VP
Fiona Morgan, Executive Director

Brings about 500 representatives from regional and national companies together to explore business relationships through face-to-face interviews
500 Attendees
Frequency: Annual

11100 Transportation Intermediaries Annual Convention & Trade Show
Transportation Intermediaries Association
1625 Prince Street
Suite 200
Alexandria, VA 22314

703-299-5700; *Fax:* 703-836-0123
voltmann@tianet.org; www.tianet.org
Social Media: Facebook, Twitter, LinkedIn

Robert Voltmann, President/CEO

The only meeting for third-party logistics providers. A once a year opportunity to interact with representatives from throughout North America and abroad. Key decision makers with buying authority attend this meeting.
700 Attendees
Frequency: Annual/March
Founded in: 1978

11101 World Packaging Conference
Reed Business Information
2000 Clearwater Drive
Oak Brook, IL 60523

630-740-0825; *Fax:* 630-288-8686;
www.reedbusiness.com

Jay Singh, Conference Chair
Bruce Harte, Consultant

One thousand three hundred and fourteen booths.
500 Attendees
Frequency: Annual/June

Directories & Databases

11102 ABS International Directory of Offices
American Bureau of Shipping
16855 Northchase Dr
Houston, TX 77060-6006

281-673-2800; *Fax:* 281-877-5801;
www.abs-group.com

Tony Nassif, CEO

Over 175 operations offices of the bureau worldwide are listed.
122 Pages
Frequency: Semiannual

11103 Air Freight Directory
Air Cargo
1819 Bay Ridge Avenue
Suite 1
Annapolis, MD 21403-2899

410-805-5578
800-747-6505; *Fax:* 410-268-3154

Debbi Mayes

Gives contact details for 35,000 global air cargo companies including 24,000 freight forwarders and 1700 airports. Track and trace shipments, locate airfreight personnel, or just follow the latest air cargo industry news.
Cost: $84.00
Frequency: Bi-Monthly

11104 American Drop-Shippers Directory
World Wide Trade Service
PO Box 283
Medina, WA 98039-0283

206-236-4795

Over 200 firms are listed that are willing to drop ship single item orders at wholesale prices for mail order and other direct marketers.
Cost: $15.00
36 Pages
Frequency: Biennial
Circulation: 5,000

11105 Commercial Carrier Journal: Buyers' Guide Issue
Reed Business Information
1 Chilton Way
Wayne, PA 19089-0002

646-746-6400; *Fax:* 646-746-7433;
www.reedbusiness.com
Social Media: Facebook, Twitter, LinkedIn

Gerald F Standley, Editor
Stuart Whayman, CFO

List of vehicles, components and accessories suppliers for the truck and bus fleet markets.
Cost: $10.00
Frequency: Annual/October
Circulation: 85,000

11106 Commercial Carrier Journal: Top 100 Issue
Reed Business Information
360 Park Avenue
New York, NY 10010

212-450-0067; *Fax:* 646-746-7433;
www.ccjdigital.com

List of top 100 for-hire motor carriers, ranked by gross revenues; also the next 200 carriers in gross revenue.
Cost: $10.00
Frequency: Annual/August
Circulation: 85,000

11107 Directory of Contract Packagers and their Facilities
Institute of Packaging Professionals
Ste 123
1833 Centre Point Cir
Naperville, IL 60563-4848

630-544-5050
800-432-4085; *Fax:* 630-544-5055
info@iopp.org; www.iopp.org

Edwin Landon, Executive Director
Patrick Farrey, General Manager

More than 400 contract packagers in the US and abroad.
Frequency: Biennial

11108 Directory of Corrugated Plants
Fibre Box Association

25 Northwest Point Blvd
Suite 510
Elk Grove Village, IL 60007

847-364-9600; *Fax:* 847-364-9639
fba@fibrebox.org; www.fibrebox.org
Social Media: LinkedIn

Over 1,600 manufacturing facilities in the North American corrugated and solid fibre industry. Distributed in microsoft excel spreadsheet.
Cost: $200.00

11109 Directory of Freight Forwarders and Custom House Brokers
International Wealth Success
PO Box 186
Merrick, NY 11566-0186

516-766-5850
800-323-0548; *Fax:* 516-766-5919
admin@iwsmoney.com; www.iwsmoney.com
Social Media: Facebook, LinkedIn

Tyler G Hicks, President

Lists hundreds of these firms throughout the U.S. who help in the export/import business.
Cost: $20.00
106 Pages
Frequency: Annual
ISBN: 1-561503-46-0
Founded in: 1980

11110 Directory of Packaging Consultants
Institute of Packaging Professionals
Ste 123
1833 Centre Point Cir
Naperville, IL 60563-4848

630-544-5050
800-432-4085; *Fax:* 630-544-5055
info@iopp.org; www.iopp.org
Social Media: Facebook, Twitter, LinkedIn

Edwin Landon, Executive Director
Patrick Farrey, General Manager

Packaging consultants in the US.
Cost: $25.00
Frequency: Annual

11111 Directory of US Flexographic Packaging Sources
JPC Directories
PO Box 488
Plainview, NY 11803-0488

516-822-6861

Joel J Shulman, Editor

Offers information on narrow web and wide web printer/converters and suppliers to the printing industry.
125 Pages
Frequency: Annual
Circulation: 50,000

11112 Flexible Packaging Association Membership Directory
Flexible Packaging Association
971 Corporate Boulevard
Suite 403
Linthicum, MD 21090-4769

410-694-0800; *Fax:* 410-694-0900
fpa@flexpack.org

Over 200 member companies that manufacture flexible packaging and supplies used in this industry are profiled.
Frequency: Annual
Circulation: 20,000

11113 Food & Beverage Market Place
Grey House Publishing
4919 Route 22
PO Box 56
Amenia, NY 12501

518-789-8700
800-562-2139; *Fax:* 845-373-6390
books@greyhouse.com; www.greyhouse.com
Social Media: Facebook, Twitter

Leslie Mackenzie, Publisher
Richard Gottlieb, Editor

This information packed three-volume set is the most powerful buying and marketing guide for the US food and beverage industry. Includes thousands of industry and transportation listings. Contains a significant chapter on food and beverage transportation.
Cost: $595.00
2000 Pages
Frequency: Annual
ISBN: 1-592373-61-5
Founded in: 1981

11114 Food & Beverage Marketplace: Online Database
Grey House Publishing
4919 Route 22
PO Box 56
Amenia, NY 12501

518-789-8700
800-562-2139; *Fax:* 845-373-6390
gold@greyhouse.com
http://gold.greyhouse.com
Social Media: Facebook, Twitter

Richard Gottlieb, President
Leslie Mackenzie, Publisher

This complete updated Food & Beverage Market Place: Online Database is the go-to source for the food and beverage industry. Anyone involved in the food and beverage industry needs this 'industry bible' and the important contacts to develop critical research data that can make for successful business growth.
Frequency: Annual
Founded in: 1981

11115 Modern Bulk Transporter: Buyers Guide
Tunnell Publications
PO Box 66010
Houston, TX 77266

713-523-8124; *Fax:* 713-523-8384

Charles Wilson, Editor

Directory of suppliers of products or services for companies operating tank trucks.
Frequency: Annual/October
Circulation: 16,000

11116 NCBFAA Membership Directory
National Customs Brokers & Forwarders Association
1200 18th St NW
Suite 901
Washington, DC 20036-2572

202-466-0222; *Fax:* 202-466-0226
staff@ncbfaa.org; www.ncbfaa.org

About 600 customs brokers, international air cargo agents, and freight forwarders in the United States.
Cost: $24.00
Frequency: Annual

11117 National Motor Carrier Directory and Additional Products
Transportation Technical Services
500 Lafayette Boulevard
Fredericksburg, VA 22401-6070

540-899-9872
888-665-9887; *Fax:* 540-899-1948
truckinfo@ttstrucks.com;
www.ttstrucks.com/www.fleetseek.com

Ronald D Roth, Executive VP

Over 46,000 motor carriers with revenues of $100,000 or more.
Cost: $495.00
1781 Pages
Frequency: Annual/November
Founded in: 1989

11118 Official Container Directory
Advanstar Communications
641 Lexington Ave
8th Floor
New York, NY 10022-4503

212-951-6600; *Fax:* 212-951-6793
info@advanstar.com; www.advanstar.com

Joseph Loggia, CEO

Directory of services and supplies to the industry.
200 Pages
Circulation: 5,000

11119 Official Freight Shippers Guide
Official Motor Freight Guides
1700 W Cortland Street
Chicago, IL 60622-1121

773-342-1000
800-621-4650; *Fax:* 773-489-0482

E Koch, Editor
Eric J Robison, Editor

Major air, rail, water and motor carriers published in three local editions covering Chicago, New York and St. Louis.
Cost: $55.00
516 Pages
Frequency: Annual

11120 Official Motor Carrier Directory
Official Motor Freight Guides
1700 W Cortland Street
Chicago, IL 60622-1121

773-342-1000
800-621-4650; *Fax:* 773-489-0482

Edward K Koch, Editor

Approximately 2,100 general and specialized motor carriers and air cargo carriers; federal and state agencies concerned with the trucking industry; tariff publishing bureaus, US and Canadian port authorities; state associations.
Cost: $59.50
Frequency: SemiAnnual
Circulation: 6,000

11121 Official Motor Freight Guide
C&C Publishing Company
1700 W Cortland Street
Chicago, IL 60622-1121

773-536-2050

This directory is published in over 21 regional editions that list air and water freight transportation, motor carriers and warehouse facilities for the metropolitan areas of Baltimore, Boston, Chicago, Cincinnati, Cleveland, Denver, Detroit, Evansville, Ft. Wayne, Indianapolis, Kansas City, Philadelphia, Pittsburgh, Quad Cities and Toledo.
Cost: $45.00
500 Pages
Frequency: Semiannual

11122 PMMI Packaging Machinery Directory
Packaging Machinery Manufacturers Institute (PMMI)
4350 Fairfax Dr
Suite 600
Arlington, VA 22203-1632

703-243-8555; *Fax:* 703-243-8556
pmmiwebhelp@pmmi.org; www.pmmi.org

Chuck Yuska, President
Sara Kryder, Manager Communications

Contains information on all 500+ member companies, who are committed to producing quality products and providing world class service to their customers.

11123 **Packaging Digest: Machinery Materials Guide Issue**
Delta Communications
Ste 300
20900 Swenson Dr
Waukesha, WI 53186-4050
262-429-9111; *Fax:* 262-546-8820
delta@deltacommunications.com;
www.deltacommunicatons.com
Barbara McDonough, Editor
List of more than 3,100 manufacturers of machinery and materials for the packaging industry, and about 260 contract packagers.
Frequency: Annual

11124 **Rauch Guide to the US Packaging Industry**
Impact Marketing Consultants
PO Box 1226
Manchester Center, VT 05255
802-362-2325
802-362-3693; www.impactmarket.com
Donald R Dykes, Editor
C Verbanic, Editor
Analyzes the US packaging industry, with data on industry economics, raw materials, major products, and unique profiles of 50% producers.
Cost: $495.00
Frequency: Triennial

11125 **Transportation Telephone Tickler**
Commonwealth Business Media
50 Millstone Rd
Building 400, Suite 200
East Windsor, NJ 08520-1418
609-371-7700
800-215-6084; *Fax:* 609-371-7879;
www.cbizmedia.com
Alan Glass, CEO
Edith Chaudoin-Stahlberger, Editor
Provides vital contact information for 24,000 suppliers of 160 types of transportation services in the US, Canada, Caribbean and parts of Latin America.
Cost: $124.95
2425 Pages
Frequency: Annual
Founded in: 1949

11126 **Who's Who & What's What in Packaging**
481 Carlisle Drive
Herndon, VA 20170-4830
703-471-8922
Offers information on members of the Institute of Packaging Professionals, including placement firms, colleges that offer packaging curricula, and related organizations.
Cost: $125.00
240 Pages
Frequency: Annual

Industry Web Sites

11127 **http://gold.greyhouse.com**
G.O.L.D Grey House OnLine Databases
Grey House Publishing's online database platform, GOLD, offers Quick Search, Keyword Search and Expert Search for most business sectors including freight, packaging and transportation markets. The GOLD platform makes finding the information you need quick and easy - whether you're a novice searcher or an experienced database user. All of Grey House's directory products are available for subscription on the GOLD platform.

11128 **plastics.americanchemistry.com**
Polystyrene Packaging Council
Links to other associations.

11129 **www.adhesives.org**
Adhesive and Sealant Council
Association for the packaging industry.

11130 **www.aiccbox.org**
Association of Independent Corrugated Converters
Provides a forum for discussion of problems and offers educational programs and seminars.

11131 **www.corrugated.org**
Corrugated Packaging Council
Develops and coordinates industry-wide programs to address corrugated packaging issues. The Council's mission is to inform consumers, manufacturers, retailers and government officials of corrugated packaging's performance and environmental attributes.

11132 **www.fibca.com**
Flexible Intermediate Bulk Container Association

Social Media: Facebook, Twitter

11133 **www.fibrebox.org**
Fibre Box Association
Represents 90 percent of the US corrugated paper board, packaging, manufacturing industry.

11134 **www.flexpack.org**
Flexible Packaging Association
Trade association of manufacturers, converters and suppliers of paper, metal foil and plastic or cellulose film.

11135 **www.fpi.org**
Foodservice & Packaging Institute
Sanitation and environmental information, plus programs and services.

11136 **www.ftd.com**
Florists' Transworld Delivery Association
Has an annual budget of approximately $140 million.

11137 **www.geminishippers.com**
Gemini Shippers Group
Shippers association with global contracts for all commodities.

11138 **www.graysonassociates.com**
Grayson Associates
Association for those interested in marketing analysis of the package goods industry.

11139 **www.greyhouse.com**
Grey House Publishing
Authoritative reference directories for most business sectors including freight, packaging, and transportation markets. Users can search the online databases with varied search criteria allowing for custom searches by product category, geographic area, sales volume, keyword, subject and more. Full Grey House catalog and online ordering also available.

11140 **www.homefair.com**
Offers comprehensive content and services for people moving to a new home or relocating to another community.

11141 **www.iicl.org**
Institute of International Container Lessors
Represents international container and chassis leasing industry in technical, governmental and legal matters. Publishes leading worldwide manuals on inspection and repair of containers and inspector and maintenance of chassis. Sponsors container and chassis inspection examination once a year in over 40 countries and chassis examination in North America.

11142 **www.lcaships.com**
Lake Carriers Association
Members are US- Flag Great Lakes vessel operators engaged in transporting iron ore, coal, grain, limestone, cement and petroleum products.

11143 **www.mfsanet.org/**
Mailing & Fulfillment Service Association
For over 80 years, this national trade association has been serving the mailing and fulfillment services industry by providing opportunities for learning and professional development of the managers of these companies.

11144 **www.niphle.com**
National Institute of Packaging, Handling and
Logistics
Originally the DC chapter of the Society of Packaging and Handling engineers, the Institute became independent in an effort to give more emphasis on the governmental responsibilities of its members.

11145 **www.nmaonline.org**
National Meat Association
Association for meat packers, processors and jobbers through out the USA.

11146 **www.packagingnetwork.com**
Packaging Network
Searchable database of food industry related items.

11147 **www.palletcentral.com**
National Wooden Pallet & Container Association
Membership roster, tech talk, publications and industry watch.

11148 **www.pmmi.org**
Packaging Machinery Manufacturers Institute (PMMI)
For manufacturers of packaging and packaging-related converting equipment.

11149 **www.polysort.com**
Polysort LLC
Links to related companies.

11150 **www.ppcnet.org**
Paperboard Packaging Council
Represents industry before legislative and regulatory bodies. Conducts technical seminars on sales, marketing, costs and management methods. Publishes a quarterly newsletter

11151 **www.ppcouncil.org**
Petroleum Packaging Council
Provides technical leadership and education to the petroleum packaging industry.

11152 **www.tianet.org**
Transportation Intermediaries Association
Education and policy organization for North American transportation intermediaries. TIA is the only national association representing the interests of all third party transportation service providers. The members of TIA include logistics management firms, property brokers, perishable commodities brokers, freight forwarders, intermodal marketers, ocean and air forwarders, and NVOCC's.

11153 **www.unitdose.org**
Healthcare Compliance Packaging Council
A not-for-profit trade association that was established in 1990 to promote the many benefits of unit dose blister and ship packaging - especially its ability to be designed in compliance-promoting formats that help people take their medications properly.

11154 **www.unitedfresh.org**
United Fresh Fruit & Vegetable Association
Equipment, supplies, cartons, packaging machinery, computers, sorting and sizing equipment, harvesting equipment, film wrap manufacturing and commodity organizations.

Associations

11155 American Innerspring Manufacturers Association
1918 N Parkway
Memphis, TN 38112
901-749-9030
800-882-5604
aimy@aiminfo.org;
www.sleepproducts.org/ispa/industry-links
Members make and sell innerspring units and box springs to mattress manufacturers. Also conducts year round public relations program directed at consumers, encouraging purchase of innerspring mattresses.
Founded in: 1966

11156 American Society of Furniture Designers
PO Box 5445
4136 Coachmans Court
High Point, NC 27262-5445
336-307-0999; *Fax:* 910-576-1573
info@asfd.com; www.asfd.com
Jason Phillips, President
John Conrad, Executive Director
Jena Hall, Editor-in-Chief
Rick Schroeder, Chairman
Tim O'Hare, Vice President
An international non-profit professional organization dedicated to advancing, improving, and supporting the profession of furniture design and its positive impact in the marketplace.
Founded in: 1981

11157 Association of Progressive Rental Organizations
1504 Robin Hood Trail
Austin, TX 78703
800-204-2776; *Fax:* 512-794-0097
cferguson@rtohq.org; www.rtohq.org
Social Media: Facebook, Twitter, Youtube, Flickr
Gary Ferriman, President
Gopal Reddy, 1st Vice President
Mark Connelly, 2nd Vice President
Jonathan Rose, Secretary
Ernie Lewallen, Treasurer
Members include television, appliance and furniture dealers who rent merchandise with an option to purchase.
2000 Members
Founded in: 1980
Mailing list available for rent

11158 Authentic Home Furnishings Association
PO Box 520
Spofford, NH 03462
518-832-7939
800-487-8321; *Fax:* 518-824-5719;
www.unfinishedfurniture.org
Fred Moriarty, Executive Director
Tim Case, President
Lara Lindner, Secretary
Steve Cavanaugh, Treasurer
Anthony Sabatino, Vice President
Our mission is to promote the common business interests of the unfinished furniture industry, encourage the most efficient and professional organization and administration of firms in the unfinished furniture industry; and to conduct meetings and educational programs, and to collect and publish information about the unfinished furniture industry.
600 Members
Founded in: 1990

11159 Business and Institutional Furniture Manufacturers Association
678 Front Avenue NW
Suite 150
Grand Rapids, MI 49504-5368
616-285-3963; *Fax:* 616-285-3765
email@bifma.org; www.bifma.org
Social Media: Twitter, LinkedIn
Tom Reardon, Executive Director
Melissa Hubbel, Finance & Administration
Sylvain Garneau, President
Don Van Winkle, Vice President
Franco Bianchi, Treasurer
BIFMA is a not-for-profit trade association of furniture manufacturers and suppliers, addressing issues of common concern.
245+ Members
Founded in: 1973

11160 Futon Association International
PO Box 593730
Orlando, FL 32859
800-327-3262
Members are retailers, manufacturers, distributors, associates, sales representatives of their country in the industry.
400 Members
Founded in: 1984

11161 Illuminating Engineering Society of North America
120 Wall St
Floor 17
New York, NY 10005-4001
212-248-5000; *Fax:* 212-248-5017
ies@ies.org; www.ies.org
Social Media: Facebook, Twitter, LinkedIn
Daniel Salinas, President
Paul Mercier, President-Elect
William Hanley, Executive Vice President
Nick Bleeker, Treasurer
Nicole DeGirolamo, Executive Assistant
To advance knowledge and disseminate information for the improvement of the lighted environment to the benefit of society. Publishes a monthly magazine.

11162 International Furniture Rental Association
5008 Pine Creek Drive
#6
Westerville, OH 43081-4848
614-755-3910
800-367-7368
A non-profit trade organization devoted exclusively to furniture rental and leasing.
Founded in: 1967

11163 International Furniture Transportation and Logistics Council
PO Box 889
Gardner, MA 01440-0889
978-632-1913; *Fax:* 978-630-2917
jsears@iftlc.org; www.iftlc.org
Raynard F Bohman Jr, Managing Director
Members are furniture manufacturers, retailers, carriers, wholesalers and warehouses of allied products.
150 Members

11164 International Home Furnishings Representatives Association
PO Box 670
High Point, NC 27261
336-889-3920; *Fax:* 336-802-1959
ihfra@ihfra.org; www.ihfra.org
Matthew Keepers, Chairman
Kathy Parks, Executive Director
Association for the professional development of home furnishings representatives and the improvement of the home furnishings industry as a whole.

11165 International Home Furnishings Center
210 E Commerce Ave
High Point, NC 27260
336-888-3700
336-801-6102; *Fax:* 336-882-1873;
www.imchighpointmarket.com
Nonprofit trade association of wholesale distributors, importers and manufacturers of finished goods. Supports furniture retailers by continuous improvement of the industry through advocacy, research and the exchange of ideas. Membership is open to any legitimate furniture wholesaler, importer, manufacturer, agent or any other firm operating within the supply chain of finished goods.
150 Members
Founded in: 1928

11166 International Housewares Association
6400 Shafer Ct
Suite 650
Rosemont, IL 60018
847-292-4200; *Fax:* 847-292-4211
pbrandl@housewares.org;
www.housewares.org
Social Media: Facebook, Twitter, LinkedIn, YouTube
Gary Seehoff, Chairman
Gregory C. Cairo, Vice Chairman
Philip J. Brandl, President/CEO
Brett Bradshaw, Treasurer
Dean Kurtis, Vice President, Finance
A full-service trade association dedicated to promoting the sales and marketing of housewares.
Founded in: 1938

11167 International Sleep Products Association
501 Wythe Street
Alexandria, VA 22314-1917
703-683-8371; *Fax:* 703-683-4503
info@sleepproducts.org;
www.sleepproducts.org
Social Media: Facebook, Twitter, LinkedIn, Googleplus,Pinterest,Youtube
Ryan Trainer, President
Maintains a strong organization to influence government actions, inform and educate the membership and act on industry issues to enhance the growth, profitability and stature of the sleep products industry. Provides members with information and services to manage their business more effectively and efficiently. Publishes a magazine devoted exclusively to the mattress industry, BEDtimes covers a broad range of issue and news important to the industry.
Cost: $65.00
650 Members
Frequency: Monthly
Circulation: 3,500
Founded in: 1915

11168 Juvenile Products Manufacturers Association
15000 Commerce Parkway
Suite C
Mt. Laurel, NJ 08054
856-638-0420; *Fax:* 856-439-0525
jpma@jpma.org; www.jpma.org/
Social Media: Facebook, Twitter, LinkedIn
Mark Messner, Chairman
Andy Newmark, Vice Chairman
Michael Dwyer-CAE, President
Rob Conley, Treasurer
Kelly Mariotti, Executive Director

The Juvenile Products Manufacturers Association exists to advance the interests, growth and well-being of the juvenile products industry through advocacy,public relations, information sharing and business devrlopment opportunities.
Founded in: 1962

11169 **National Association of Display Industries**
4651 Sheridan Street
Suite 200
Hollywood, FL 33021

954-893-7300; *Fax:* 954-893-7500
nadi@nadi-global.com; www.nadi-global.com

Klein Merriman, Executive Director
Tracy Dillon, Director Communications

Sponsors seminars and annual contests. Conducts research programs and maintains placement services.
400 Members
Founded in: 1937

11170 **National Cotton Batting Institute**
4322 Bloombury St
Southaven, MS 38672

901-218-2393; *Fax:* 662-449-0046
info@natbat.com; www.natbat.com

Weston Arnall, President
Greg Windsperger, VP
Fred Middleton, Executive Secretary-Treasurer

NCBI represents U.S. companies that manufacture and sell batting for use in mattresses, futons, home furnishing, and upholstered products. It provides a range of services to assist its members in expanding markets, monitoring and contributing to legislative and regulatory decisions that affect the industry, and conducting consumer education and information programs.
27 Members
Founded in: 1954

11171 **National Unfinished Furniture Institute**
1850 Oak Street
Northfield, IL 60093-3042

847-784-1225; *Fax:* 847-446-3523

Ray Passis, Executive Director

Provides publicity and insurance for industry, offers educational seminars and bestows awards.
1.2M Members
Founded in: 1979

11172 **National Waterbed Retailers Association**
2 Greentree Center
Suit 225
Marlton, NJ 08053-3102

312-236-6662
800-832-3553; *Fax:* 312-236-1140

Promotes industry through educational seminars, sells educational materials on waterbeds, health care and conducts surveys.
500 Members
Founded in: 1972

11173 **North America Home Furnishings Association**
2050 N Stemmons Fwy
Suite 292
Dallas, TX 75207

800-422-3778; *Fax:* 916-784-7697
info@hfia.com; www.nahfa.org
Social Media: Facebook, Twitter, LinkedIn

Richard Howard, Chairman
Marty Cramer, President
Jeff Child, President-Elect
Sharron Bradley, CEO
Steve Kidder, Vice President

Committed to strengthening the home furnishing industry trhough collective support, services, and leadership.
Founded in: 1923

11174 **Paint & Decorating Retailers Association**
1401 Triad Center Dr
St Peters, MO 63376

636-326-2636; *Fax:* 636-326-1823
info@pdra.org; www.pdra.org
Social Media: Facebook, Twitter, LinkedIn

Phil Merlo, President
Bahia Taylor, Executive Vice President
Craig Bond, Treasurer
Jeff Baggaley, Past-President
Robert Mueller, Director at Large

Provides members with the tools they need and prosper such as information, sales training, and business operations programs.
1500 Members
Founded in: 1947

11175 **Quarters Furniture Manufacturers Association**
1211 Popes Head Drive
Fairfax, VA 22030

240-215-9700; *Fax:* 276-632-7894
matt.yanson@cma-gsa.com; www.qfma.net

Michael Gittinger, President
Chris Arndt, Vice President
Malcolm Wilson, Secretary
Allyn Richert, Treasurer
Tom Chapman, Board Member

Represents companies who produce furniture for military markets. Monitors federal procurement policy as it relates to prison industries.
20 Members
Founded in: 1995

11176 **Society of Glass & Ceramic Decorated Products**
PO Box 2489
Zanesville, OH 43702

740-588-9882; *Fax:* 740-588-0245
info@sgcd.org; www.sgcd.org

Chad Yaw, President
Jan Weyrich, Vice President
Mike Gervais, Treasurer
David Stanton, Secretary
Myra Warne, Executive Director

Provides designers, decorators and marketers of glass, ceramic and related products with resources for maximizing profitability, technical applications and regulatory compliance.
525 Members

11177 **Summer and Casual Furniture Manufacturers Association**
1912 Eastchester Drive
Suite 100
High Point, NC 27265

336-884-5000; *Fax:* 336-884-5303
jlogan@ahfa.us; www.ahfa.us
Social Media: Facebook, LinkedIn

Ken Burrows, Chairman
George Revington, Immediate Past Chairman
KEVIN O'CONNOR, 1st Vice President
RICHARD MAGNUSSEN, 2nd Vice President
ROGER BLAND, Board Member

Sponsors the International Casual Furniture and Accessories Market in Chicago, the Apollo Awards, recognizing excellence in casual furniture retailing and the Casual Furniture Design Excellence Awards.
500+ Members
Founded in: 1959

11178 **The American Home Furnishings Alliance**
1912 Eastchester Drive
Suite 100
High Point, NC 27265

336-884-5000; *Fax:* 336-884-5303
pbowling@ahfa.us; www.ahfa.us
Social Media: Facebook, LinkedIn

Ken Burrows, Chairman
George Revington, Immediate Past Chairman
KEVIN O'CONNOR, 1st Vice President
RICHARD MAGNUSSEN, 2nd Vice President
ROGER BLAND, Board Member

The world's largest and most influential trade organization serving the home furnishings industry. AHFA is dedicated to fostering the growth and global well being of its member companies.
450 Members
Founded in: 1905

11179 **The Association of Woodworking & Furnishings Suppliers**
2400 E Katella Ave
Suite 340
Anaheim, CA 92806

323-838-9440
800-946-2937; *Fax:* 323-838-9443;
www.awfs.org
Social Media: Facebook, Twitter, LinkedIn

Wade Gregory, President
Archie Thompson, Vice President
Philip Martin, Secretary/Treasurer
Joan Kemp, IMMEDIATE PAST PRESIDENT
Daniel Hershberger, TRADE SHOW CHAIR

The largest national trade association in the US representing the interests of the broad array of companies that supply the home and commercial furnishings industry. Members include manufacturers and distributors of machinery, hardware, lumber, upholstery materials, bedding components, wood products and other supplies to furnishings and wood products manufacturers.
Founded in: 1979

11180 **Upholstered Furniture Action Council**
PO Box 2436
High Point, NC 27261

336-885-5065; *Fax:* 336-885-5072
info@ufac.org; www.ufac.org

Joseph Ziolkowski, Executive Director

Conducts research and disseminates information about adoption of guidelines for cigarette-resistant furniture. Educates public about safe use of smoking materials.
Founded in: 1972

11181 **World Floor Covering Association**
2211 E Howell Ave
Anaheim, CA 92806

714-978-6440
800-624-6880; *Fax:* 714-978-6066
wfca@wfca.org; www.wfca.org
Social Media: Facebook, Twitter

Scott Humphrey, CEO
Terry Hearne, Director of Operations
Cammie Weitzel, Director of Finance/Administration
Donna Archambault, Membership Operations Manager

Shapes and defines public policy through agressive, national legislative advocacy on behalf of our members. Provides continuing professional educational programming through educational forums and the Regional Installation and Training Education (RITE) program.
45 Members
Founded in: 1973

Newsletters

11182 AWFS Suppliers' Edge
Association of Woodworking & Furnishings Suppliers
500 Citadel Drive
Suite 200
Commerce, CA 90040
323-838-9440
800-946-2937; *Fax:* 323-838-9443;
www.awfs.org
Social Media: Facebook, Twitter, LinkedIn
Joan Kemp, President
Wade Gregory, Vice President
Archie Thompson, Secretary/Treasurer
Industry events, manufacturing news, AWFS Fair news, member news and more.
Frequency: Tri-Annually
Founded in: 1979

11183 At The Table
American Home Furnishings Alliance
317 High Avenue
10th Floor
High Point, NC 27260
336-884-5000; *Fax:* 336-884-5303
pbowling@ahfa.us; www.ahfa.us
Social Media: Facebook, LinkedIn
Andy Counts, CEO
News from legislative and regulatory forums where AHRA is at the table, serving as the voice of the home furnishings industry.
450 Members
Frequency: Quarterly
Founded in: 1905

11184 Focus on Benefits
American Furniture Manufacturers Association
PO Box Hp7
High Point, NC 27261
336-884-5000; *Fax:* 336-884-5303
pbowling@ahfa.us; www.ahfa.us
Patricia Bowling, VP Communications
Adresses timely benefits subjects along with developing trends.
Frequency: Quarterly

11185 Furniture Executive
American Furniture Manufacturers Association
PO Box Hp7
High Point, NC 27261
336-884-5000; *Fax:* 336-884-5303
pbowling@ahfa.us; www.ahfa.us
Patricia Bowling, VP Communications
Includes news on all upcoming programs and events, a message from the AHFA President, news from Washington, updates on the AHFA public relations program, and updates on AHFA member benefits and programs.
Frequency: Monthly

11186 Human Resources Close-Up
American Home Furnishings Alliance
317 High Avenue
10th Floor
High Point, NC 27260
336-884-5000; *Fax:* 336-884-5303
pbowling@ahfa.us; www.ahfa.us
Social Media: Facebook, LinkedIn
Andy Counts, CEO
Online newsletter, addresses pertinent legal subjects in the employment/labor relations arena, along with relevant court and National Labor Relations Board cases.
450 Members
Frequency: Monthly
Founded in: 1905

11187 National Association of Display Industries Newsletter
4651 Sheridan Street
Suite 470
Hollywood, FL 33021
954-893-7300; *Fax:* 954-893-7500
nadi@nadi-global.com; www.nadi-global.com
Klein Merriman, Executive Director
Tracy Dillon, Director Communications
Accepts advertising.
Cost: $45.00
16 Pages
Circulation: 8000
Founded in: 1956

11188 Square Yard
American Floorcovering Association
2211 E Howell Avenue
Anaheim, CA 92806-6009
714-572-8370; *Fax:* 714-780-0488
Edward Korczak, Publisher
Offers full coverage of interior design in association with floor coverings, carpets and rug manufacturers.
8 Pages
Frequency: Monthly

11189 Suppliers on Demand
American Home Furnishings Alliance
317 High Avenue
10th Floor
High Point, NC 27260
336-884-5000; *Fax:* 336-884-5303
pbowling@ahfa.us; www.ahfa.us
Social Media: Facebook, LinkedIn
Andy Counts, CEO
Online newsletter designed to help manufacturer members find the product and service suppliers they need, when they need them.
450 Members
Frequency: Quarterly
Founded in: 1905

Magazines & Journals

11190 Architectural Lighting
One Thomas Circle, NW
Suite 600
Washington, DC 20005
202-452-0800; *Fax:* 202-785-1974
Social Media: Twitter
Ned Cramer, Editor-in-Chief
Elizabeth Donoff, Editor
Covers design specifications and application of electrical lighting and daylighting systems.
Frequency: Monthly
Circulation: 54,000

11191 BEDtimes Magazine
International Sleep Products Association
501 Wythe Street
Alexandria, VA 22314-1917
703-683-8371; *Fax:* 703-683-4503
info@sleepproducts.org;
www.sleepproducts.org
Julie Palm, Editor
Kerri Bellias, Administrative Assistant
Dana Jackson, Administrative Assistant
Mary Best, Managing Editor
A magazine covering the bedding industry. Target audience as mattress suppliers and manufacturers.
Cost: $50.00
Frequency: Monthly
Circulation: 3000
ISSN: 0893-5556
Founded in: 1915
Printed in 4 colors on glossy stock

11192 Designer
HDC Publications
429 Montague Ave
Caro, MI 48723-1921
989-673-4121
800-843-6394; *Fax:* 989-673-2031
info@hdc-caro.org; www.hdc-caro.org
Maryann Vandemark, Executive Director
A magazine offering information on interior design.
Frequency: Monthly

11193 Draperies and Window Coverings
840 US Highway One
Suite 330
North Palm Beach, FL 33408
561-627-3393
847-548-3900; *Fax:* 561-694-6578;
www.dwcdesignet.com
Carolyn Silberman, Publisher
Howard Shingle, Editor
Sarah Christy, Associate Editor
Covers trends and specific industry topics.
Cost: $33.00
160 Pages
Frequency: Monthly
Circulation: 28,000
Founded in: 1981

11194 Eastern Floors Magazine
Specialist Publications
22801 Ventura Boulevard
Suite 115
Woodland Hills, CA 91364-1230
818-224-8035
800-835-4398; *Fax:* 818-224-8042;
www.icsmag.com
Social Media: Facebook, Twitter
Howard Olansky, Editor
Phil Johnson, Group Publisher
Evan Kessler, Publisher
Amy Levin, Production Manager
Serving the floor covering and tile industry.
Cost: $140.00
Frequency: Monthly
Founded in: 1990

11195 Furniture Today
Reed Business Information
PO Box 2754
High Point, NC 27261-2754
336-605-1000
800-395-2329; *Fax:* 336-605-1143;
www.reedbusiness.com
Social Media: Facebook, Twitter
Kevin Castellani, President
Ray Allegeeza, Editor-in-Chief
Helene Checinski, Circulation Manager
Kim Bashford, Production Manager
Delaney Rudd, Ower
Business and fashion newspaper of the furniture industry, edited for retail furniture executives in furniture stores, department stores, mass merchants, furniture specialty stores and catalog showrooms, as well as manufacturing executives at all levels. Focus is on the business and fashion news that these executives need at key decision times in their merchandising and marketing cycles.
Cost: $159.97
Frequency: Weekly
Circulation: 21212

Founded in: 1976
Printed in on glossy stock

11196 Home Accents Today
Reed Business Information
360 Park Ave S
New York, NY 10010-1737

646-746-6400; *Fax:* 646-756-7583;
www.homeaccentstoday.com
Social Media: Facebook, Twitter

John Poulin, CEO
Marion Kelly, Publisher
Gerard Van de Aast, CEO
Becky Boswell Smith, Editor-in-Chief
James Reed, Owner

Enables home furnishing retailers to develop merchandising programs, define new style statements, make buying decisions, and create retail strategies. Editorially covers the broad fashion mix of home accent products.
Cost: $24.94
Frequency: Monthly
Circulation: 21300

11197 Home Furnishing Retailer
National Home Furnishings Association
3910 Tinsley Drive
Suite 101
Highpoint, NC 27265-3610

336-886-6100
800-888-9590; *Fax:* 336-801-6102
info@nhfa.org; www.nhfa.org
Social Media: Facebook, Twitter, LinkedIn, YouTube

Provides the latest information specifically for industry retailers; current trends and strategies to keep business profitable.
Cost: $70.00
Frequency: Monthly
Circulation: 10000
ISSN: 1073-5585

11198 Home Lighting & Accessories
Doctorow Communications
1011 Clifton Ave
Suite 1
Clifton, NJ 07013-3518

973-779-1600; *Fax:* 973-779-3242
email@homelighting.com;
www.homelighting.com

Jeffrey Doctorow, President
Jon Doctorow, Circulation Director

Home Lighting & Accessories is a magazine of lamps, lighting fixtures, shades and decorative home accessories. Articles cover marketing and retailing aspects applied to portable lamps, lamps shades, residential lighting fixtures and decorative home accessories - customer relations, sales training, trends, lighting showroom laycut, design and operations. Plus industry and company news, new promotions, appointments, literature, patents
Cost: $15.00
Founded in: 1953

11199 ICS Cleaning Specialist
Business News Publishing Company
22801 Ventura Blvd
Suite 115
Woodland Hills, CA 91364-1230

818-224-8035
800-835-4398; *Fax:* 818-224-8042;
www.bnpmedia.com

Phil Johnson, Publisher
Evan Kessler, Publisher
Jeffrey Stouffer, Editor
Amy Levin, Production Manager

For carpet cleaning, restoration and floor care service providers.
68 Pages
Frequency: Monthly
Circulation: 24250
ISSN: 1522-4708
Founded in: 1963
Printed in 4 colors on glossy stock

11200 Journal of Family & Consumer Sciences
American Association of Family & Consumer Sciences
400 N Columbus St
Suite 202
Alexandria, VA 22314-2264

703-706-4600
800-424-8080; *Fax:* 703-706-4663
pr@aafcs.org; www.aafcs.org
Social Media: Facebook, Twitter, LinkedIn, Flickr

Carolyn Jackson, Executive Director

Contains scholarly peer-reviewed articles, practical information geared toward family and consumer sciences professionals, and news and information about AAFCS.
Frequency: Quarterly

11201 Metropolis
Bellerophon Publications
61 W 23rd St
Floor 4
New York, NY 10010-4246

212-627-9977; *Fax:* 212-627-9988
edit@metropolismag.com;
www.metropolismag.com

Horace Havemeyer, Publisher
Susan Szenasy, Editor in Chief
Julie Taraska, Editor
Denise Csaky, Marketing Director

The only magazine that covers all facets of design: architecture, interiors, furniture, preservation, urban design, graphics and crafts.
Cost: $27.95
Circulation: 51000
Founded in: 1981

11202 NHFA Trade Show
National Home Furnishings Association
3910 Tinsley Drive
Suite 101
Highpoint, NC 27265-3610

336-886-6100
800-888-9590; *Fax:* 336-801-6102
info@nhfa.org; www.nhfa.org

Steve DeHaan, Executive VP
Karin Mayfield, Senior Director for Membership
Frequency: Annual

11203 Panel World
Hatton-Brown Publishers
PO Box 2268
Montgomery, AL 36102-2268

334-834-1170
800-669-5613; *Fax:* 334-834-4525
mail@hattonbrown.com;
www.hattonbrown.com/

D K Knight, Editor-in-chief
Rich Donnell, Editor
David Ramsey, President
Rhonda Thomas, Marketing

A magazine covering the interior design community.
Cost: $40.00
Frequency: Monthly
Circulation: 12000
Printed in 4 colors on matte stock

11204 RTOHQ: The Magazine
Association of Progressive Rental Merchandise
1540 Robinhood Trail
Austin, TX 78703-2624

512-794-0095
800-204-APRO; *Fax:* 512-794-0097
cferguson@rtohq.org; www.rtohq.org

Bill Keese, Executive Director
John C Cleek, President
Bill Kelly, Secretary

Emphasis on larger issues facing it players in the rent-to-own industry. Readers are rent-to-own dealers, owners, managers, employees, manufacturers and suppliers to the industry.
Frequency: Bi-Monthly
Circulation: 11000

Trade Shows

11205 AAFCS Annual Conference & Exposition
American Association of Family & Consumer Sciences
400 N Columbus Street
Suite 202
Alexandria, VA 22314

703-706-4600; *Fax:* 703-706-4663
connect@aafcs.org; www.aafcs.org
Social Media: Facebook, Twitter, LinkedIn, Flickr

Johnny Reynolds, Project Manager
Roxana Ayona, Manager

Informative speakers, cutting-edge workshops, and a panel discussion.
Frequency: Annual/June

11206 APRO Rent-To-Own Convention & Trade Show
Association of Progressive Rental Organizations
1504 Robin Hood Trail
Austin, TX 78703

512-794-0095
800-204-APRO; *Fax:* 512-794-0097;
www.rtohq.org

Shannon Strunkec, President
John C Cleek, First VP
Jeannie Hutchison, Program Coordinator
Bill Keese, Manager

Seminar, reception and tours, plus 280 exhibits of products and services of interest to rent to own dealers: stereos, televisions, furniture, fabric protection and more.
1400 Attendees
Frequency: Annual

11207 Association of College Unions International Conference
120 W. Seventh St.
Suite 200
Bloomington, IN 47404

812-245-2284; *Fax:* 812-245-6710;
www.acui.org

Rich Steele, President
Marsha Herman-Betzen, Executive Director
Andrea Langeveld, Marketing

One hundred exhibits of graphic supplies, recreation equipment, computer hardware and software, furnishings, entertainment and speaker bureau information, food service equipment, and more related information and supplies.
1000 Attendees
Frequency: Annual

11208 Canyon County Home & Garden Show
Spectra Productions

837 E State Street
PO Box 333
Eagle, ID 83616

208-939-6426; *Fax:* 208-939-6437
david@spectraproductions.com;
www.spectraproductions.com

David Beale, Show Manager

Features exhibitors displaying building materials, contractors, decorators, doors and windows, pools and spas, heating and cooling systems and much more.
150 Attendees
Frequency: April

11209 **Denver Home Show**
Industrial Expositions
PO Box 480084
Denver, CO 80248-0084

303-892-6800
800-457-2434; *Fax:* 303-892-6322
info@iei-expos.com;
www.bigasalloutdoors.com

Formerly the Spring Home & Patio Show.
23000 Attendees
Frequency: Annual/March

11210 **Evergreen Home Show**
Westlake Promotions
6020 Seaview Avenue NW
Seattle, WA 98107

206-783-5957; *Fax:* 206-782-6250;
www.westlakepromo.com

Bill Bradley, VP

See what's new and what you can do for your home. Fresh ideas and practical advice from our remodeling and construction specialists. See demonstrations on how to make dramatic improvements to your home.
7500 Attendees

11211 **Fall Home and Garden Expo**
Mid-America Expositions, Inc
7015 Spring Street
Omaha, NE 68106

402-346-8003
800-475-7469; *Fax:* 402-346-5412
info@showofficeonline.com;
www.showofficeonline.com

Robert P Mancuso, CEO
Mike Mancuso, VP/Manager

Displays on everything for the home including kitchens, room additions, bathrooms, interior decorating, fireplaces, outdoor equipment, heating and air conditioning, remodeling contractors, security, siding, appliances, windows, doors, fencing, roofing, fitness equipment, spas and much more.
Frequency: Annual/October

11212 **Furniture Expo**
Glahe International
PO Box 2460
Germantown, MD 20875-2460

301-515-0012; *Fax:* 301-515-0016

Annual show and exhibits of furniture making.

11213 **Glass & Ceramic Decorators Annual Seminar & Exposition**
Society of Glass & Ceramic Decorators
47 N 4th Street
PO Box 2489
Zanesville, OH 43702

202-298-8660; *Fax:* 740-588-0245;
www.sgcd.org

Myra Warne, Exhibit

The SGCD show attracts major suppliers to the decorating industry, including several firms from overseas. With a full seminar program and first step program that attracts attendees on their own merits.
525 Attendees

11214 **Great Northeast Home Show**
Osborne/Jenks Productions
936 Silas Deane Highway
Wethersfield, CT 06109-4273

860-563-2111
800-955-7469; *Fax:* 860-563-3472

Two hundred and fifty booths.
25M Attendees
Frequency: Annual/February

11215 **Home and Outdoor Living Expo**
Tower Show Productions
800 Roosevelt Road
Building A, Suite 109
Glen Ellyn, IL 60137

630-469-4611
800-946-4611; *Fax:* 630-469-4811;
www.towershow.com

J Lake, VP Home Shows

The largest and longest running home improvement show.
15000 Attendees
Frequency: January
Founded in: 1977

11216 **ICFF International Contemporary Furniture**
George Little Management
10 Bank Street
White Plains, NY 10606-1933

914-486-6070
800-272-7469; *Fax:* 914-948-6180
info@icff.com; www.icff.com
Social Media: Facebook, Twitter

Troy Hansen, Show Manager
Alex Cabat, Show Coordinator
George Little II, President
Tony Orlando, Operations Manager

More than 500 exhibitors will display contemporary furniture, seating, lighting, carpet and flooring, wall coverings, textiles, accessories, kitchen and bath, outdoor furniture, and materials for residential and commercial interiors. The combination of domestic and international exhibitors provides easy access to the best and hippest home and contract products.
12000 Attendees
Frequency: Annual/December

11217 **International Bedding Exposition**
International Sleep Products Association
501 Wythe Street
Alexandria, VA 22314-1917

703-683-8371; *Fax:* 703-683-4503
info@sleepproducts.org;
www.sleepproducts.org

Susan Perry, Executive VP, Business Development
Dana Jackson, Administrative Assistant
Mary Best, Managing Editor

200 booths, net 120,000 square feet with 200 exhibitors participating.
4M Attendees
Frequency: Annual/March

11218 **International Home Furnishings Market**
International Home Furnishings Market Authority
101 S Main Street
High Point, NC 27262

336-691-1000; *Fax:* 336-889-6999;
www.highpointmarket.org

Judy Mendenhall, President
Jan Wellmon, Executive Assistant
Shannon Kennedy, Director of Marketing

Large home furnishings trade show with a variety of new opportunities to make your visit easy, cost effective and productive. Ten million square seet of exhibition space with 2,500 manufacturers represented.
75000 Attendees
Frequency: Bi-Annual
Founded in: 1921

11219 **International Housewares Show**
National Housewares Manufacturers Association
6400 Shafer Court
Suite 650
Rosemont, IL 60018

708-292-4200; *Fax:* 847-292-4211;
www.housewares.org

Mia Rampersad, VP Trade Show & Meetings

See first-hand consumer lifestyle and product trends for all areas of the home, both inside and out, under one roof.
60000 Attendees

11220 **International Woodworking Machinery and Furniture Supply Fair: USA**
Reed Exhibition Companies
1350 E Touhy Avenue
Des Plaines, IL 60018-3303

847-294-0300; *Fax:* 847-635-1571

Paul Pajor, National Marketing Manager

The largest woodworking machinery and furniture supply manufacturing exposition held in the Western Hemisphere. Exhibitors interface with North American furniture, cabinet, and woodworking manufacturers. One thousand booths.
37M Attendees
Frequency: Biennial/August

11221 **Juvenile Products Manufacturers Association Trade Show**
PO Box 955
Marlton, NJ 08053-0955

856-231-8500; *Fax:* 856-985-2878

William Macmillan, Show Manager

Home accessories and products for children's rooms.
2.5M Attendees
Frequency: Annual/October

11222 **Kitchen & Bath Industry Show**
National Kitchen & Bath Association
687 Willow Grove Street
Hackettstown, NJ 07840

908-520-0033
800-843-6522; *Fax:* 908-852-1695;
www.kbis.com

Lee Hershberg, Sales Manager
Grayson Lutz, Operations Manager

Targeting dealers, designers, distributors, retailers, consumers, home centers and many other high-quality kitchen and bath professionals. Showcasing the latest products and cutting-edge design ideas of the kitchen and bath industry.
40000 Attendees
Frequency: Annual/April

11223 **Kitchen/Bath Industry Show & Multi-Housing World Conference**
VNU Expositions
1145 Sanctuary Parkway
Suite 355
Alpharetta, GA 30004

770-691-1540
800-933-8735; *Fax:* 770-777-8700

Lee Hershberg, Sales Manager

The latest products and technologies, industry and consumer trends, design and business tools and more to stay ahead of your competitors.
35000 Attendees

11224 LightFair
AMC
120 Wall Street
17th Floor
New York, NY 10005
212-843-8358; *Fax:* 212-248-5017;
www.iesna.org
Pamela R Weess, Circulation Director
Nini Schwenk, Manager
A major lighting trade show in North America featuring architectural lighting products from all spectrons of the industry. Containing 600 booths and 400 exhibits.
17M Attendees
Frequency: June
Mailing list available for rent: 10M names at $100 per M
Printed in 4 colors on glossy stock

11225 Mid-Atlantic Industrial Woodworking Expo Supply Show
Trade Shows
PO Box 2000
Claremont, NC 28610-2000
828-459-9894; *Fax:* 828-459-1312
tsi@tsishows.com; www.tsishows.com
Keith Eidson, Show Manager
Annual show of 300 manufacturers of woodworking and furniture industry equipment, supplies and services.
4500 Attendees
Frequency: Annual/April

11226 National City Home & Garden Show
Expositions
PO Box 550
Edgewater Branch
Cleveland, OH 44107-0550
216-529-1300; *Fax:* 216-529-0311
showinfo@expoinc.com; www.expoinc.com
Featuring showcases on how to make your dream home a reality. Create the garden oasis, backyard retreat or a relaxing sanctuary.
35000 Attendees
Frequency: Annual/February

11227 National Hardware Show
Reed Exhibition Companies
383 Main Avenue
Norwalk, CT 06851
203-840-4800; *Fax:* 203-840-4824
The prime time and place for face to face sourcing, trading and learning for the US home improvement and DIY markets.
70000 Attendees

11228 Old House New House Home Show
Kennedy Productions
1208 Lisle Place
Lisle, IL 60532-2262
630-515-1160; *Fax:* 630-515-1165;
www.kennedyproductions.com
Laura McNamara, Event Producer
Over 300 home improvement exhibitors displaying cutting-edge home enhancements for kitchens, baths, home and garden including landscape, interior remodeling, pools, spas, floors, doors and more.
8000 Attendees
Frequency: Biannual
Founded in: 1984

11229 PDRA Paint & Decorating Show
Paint & Decorating Retailers Association
403 Axminister Drive
Fenton, MO 63026
636-326-2636
800-737-0107; *Fax:* 636-326-1823
tina@pdra.org; www.pdra.org
Dan Simon, Executive Vice President
Retailers from the paint and decorating products industry to discuss a variety of business topics. Gain insight from retailers who face the same problems that you do everyday.
1000 Attendees
Frequency: Annual/May

11230 Remodeling and Decorating Expo
893 N Jan Mar Ct
Olathe, KS 66061-3693
913-768-8148; *Fax:* 785-780-4777
Tom Reno, VP
Mary Jo Doherty, Executive Director
Four hundred booths of the latest products and services related to remodeling and decorating. Also a presentation of How-To stage presentations on remodeling, decorating and home repair.
40M Attendees
Frequency: Annual/February

11231 Southern Home & Garden Show
Home Builders Association
702 E McBee Avenue
Greensville, SC 29601
864-229-7722; *Fax:* 864-232-3541
Exhibitors include professional landscapers, nurseryment, interior designers and home and garden experts.
40000 Attendees
Frequency: Biannual

11232 Spring Home Show
Osborne/Jenks Productions
936 Silas Deane Highway
Wethersfield, CT 06109
860-563-2111; *Fax:* 860-563-3472
Exhibitors include remodelers, homebuilders, custom cabinets, kitchens & baths, chimneys, wood stoves, sunrooms, awnings & decks, duct & vent maintenance, storage buildings, heating & cooling services, windows, doors & siding, water treatment systems, banks & mortgage companies, home theatre systems, security systems, financial planners, building supplies, insulation, energy management companies and so much more.
Frequency: Annual/March

11233 Surfaces Conference
World Floor Covering Association
2211 E Howell Avenue
Anaheim, CA 92806
714-978-6440
800-624-6880; *Fax:* 714-978-6066
wfca@wfca.org; www.wfca.org
Casey Voorhees, Executive Director
Tina Krulich, Administrative Assistant
The event for the floor covering industry with the latest trends to keep your business competitive, proven strategies to increase sales and profitability and all the critical industry information you need to make the right decisions.
40000 Attendees
Frequency: Annual/January

11234 West Week
Pacific Design Center
8687 Melrose Avenue
West Hollywood, CA 90069
310-652-6992; *Fax:* 310-652-9576
Show featuring the top interior designers and decorators.
Frequency: Annual/March

11235 Woodworking and Furniture Expo
Glahe International
PO Box 2460
Germantown, MD 20875-2460
301-515-0012; *Fax:* 301-515-0016
Annual show and exhibits of woodworking and furniture making.

Directories & Databases

11236 AHFA's Industry Resource Guide
American Home Furnishing Alliance
PO Box HP-7
High Point, NC 27261
336-884-5000; *Fax:* 336-884-5303;
www.ahfa.us
Andy Counts, Executive VP
A who's who in the furniture industry, supplying information on over 500 furniture manufacturers and their suppliers.
80 Pages
Founded in: 1966

11237 Casual Living: Casual Outdoor Furniture and Accessory Directory Issue
Reed Business Information
360 Park Ave S
New York, NY 10010-1737
646-746-6400; *Fax:* 646-756-7583;
www.reedbusiness.com
John Poulin, CEO
Toni Agpar, Editor
List of manufacturers, manufacturers' trepresentatives, and suppliers of outdoor furniture, wicker and rattan furniture, and backyard accessories such as barbecue grills, picnic accessories, outdoor lighting cushions, pads, patio umbrellas, vinyl refinishing, and maintenance, products.
Cost: $10.00
Frequency: Annual
Circulation: 13,000

11238 Complete Directory of Discount & Catalog Merchandisers
Sutton Family Communications & Publishing Company
920 State Route 54 East
Elmitch, KY 42343
270-276-9500
jlsutton@apex.net
Theresa Sutton, Publisher
Lee Sutton, Editor
Print-out from database of wholesalers, manufacturers, distributors, importers and close-out houses. Database is updated daily to guarantee the most current and up-to-date sources available.
Cost: $125.00
100 Pages

11239 Complete Directory of Home Furnishings
Sutton Family Communications & Publishing Company
920 State Route 54 East
Elmitch, KY 42343
270-276-9500
jlsutton@apex.net
Theresa Sutton, Publisher
Lee Sutton, Editor
Print-out from database of wholesalers, manufacturers, distributors, importers and close-out houses. Database is updated daily to guarantee the most current and up-to-date sources avail-

able.
Cost: $44.50
100 Pages

11240 Complete Directory of Kitchen Accessories
Sutton Family Communications & Publishing Company
920 State Route 54 East
Elmitch, KY 42343
270-276-9500
jlsutton@apex.net
Theresa Sutton, Editor
Lee Sutton, General Manager
Print-out from database of wholesalers, manufacturers, distributors, importers and close-out houses. Database is updated daily to guarantee the most current and up-to-date sources available.
Cost: $49.50
100+ Pages

11241 Complete Directory of Lamps, Lamp Shades & Lamp Parts
Sutton Family Communications & Publishing Company
955 Sutton Lane
20 State Route 54 East
Elmitch, KY 42343
270-276-9500
jlsutton@apex.net
Theresa Sutton, Editor
Lee Sutton, General Manager
Print-out from database of wholesalers, manufacturers, distributors, importers and close-out houses. Database is updated daily to guarantee the most current and up-to-date sources available.
Cost: $39.50
100+ Pages

11242 Complete Directory of Serving Ware
Sutton Family Communications & Publishing Company
920 State Route 54 East
Elmitch, KY 42343
270-276-9500
jlsutton@apex.net
Theresa Sutton, Editor
Lee Sutton, General Manager
Print-out from database of wholesalers, manufacturers, distributors, importers and close-out houses. Database is updated daily to guarantee the most current and up-to-date sources available.
Cost: $39.50
100+ Pages

11243 Complete Directory of Showroom Fixtures and Equipment
Sutton Family Communications & Publishing Company
920 State Route 54 East
Elmitch, KY 42343
270-276-9500
jlsutton@apex.net
Theresa Sutton, Publisher
Lee Sutton, Editor
Print-out from database of wholesalers, manufacturers, distributors, importers and close-out houses. Database is updated daily to guarantee the most current and up-to-date sources available.
Cost: $39.50
100 Pages

11244 Complete Directory of Small Furniture
Sutton Family Communications & Publishing Company
920 State Route 54 East
Elmitch, KY 42343
270-276-9500
jlsutton@apex.net
Theresa Sutton, Publisher
Lee Sutton, Editor
Print-out from database of wholesalers, manufacturers, distributors, importers and close-out houses. Database is updated daily to guarantee the most current and up-to-date sources available.
Cost: $39.50
100 Pages

11245 Complete Directory of Upholstery Materials Supplies and Equipment
Sutton Family Communications & Publishing Company
920 State Route 54 East
Elmitch, KY 42343
270-276-9500
jlsutton@apex.net
Theresa Sutton, Publisher
Lee Sutton, Editor
Print-out from database of wholesalers, manufacturers, distributors, importers and close-out houses. Database is updated daily to guarantee the most current and up-to-date sources available. Over 600 American wholesale direct supplies in 3-ring binder.
Cost: $67.50
100 Pages

11246 Furniture Retailer Resource Guide
Pace Communications
PO Box 13607
Suite 100
Greensboro, NC 27415-3607
336-378-6065; *Fax:* 336-275-2864;
www.pacecommunications.com
Bonnie McElveen, CEO
Directory of services and supplies to the industry.
Cost: $20.00
Frequency: Annual;
Circulation: 16,000

11247 Hearth & Home: Furnishings Issue
Village West Publishing
PO Box 1288
Laconia, NH 03247-2008
603-528-4285
800-258-3772; *Fax:* 603-524-0643
avignone@villagewest.com
Richard Wright, Publisher/Editor
Jackie Avignone, Advertising Director
Karen Dipietro, Owner
Trade journal for hearth, barbecue and patio retailing. July issue is Buyer's Guide for the three industries, available separately for $15.
Cost: $6.00
Frequency: Annual
Circulation: 17,000
ISSN: 0273-5695

11248 Home Furnishing Retailers
Chain Store Guide
3922 Coconut Palm Dr
Suite 300
Tampa, FL 33619-1389
813-627-6700
800-972-0292; *Fax:* 813-627-7094
info@csgis.com; www.csgis.com
Mike Jarvis, Publisher
Shami Choon, Manager
This database features detailed information on over 2700 companies in the U.S. and Canada, with contact information for over 8600 key executives and buyers.
Cost: $275.00
Frequency: Annual

11249 IFRA Member Directory
International Furniture Rental Association
5008 Pine Creek Drive
#6
Westerville, OH 43081-4848
614-755-3910
800-367-7368; www.ifra.org
About 100 member furniture rental companies.

11250 Market Resource Guide
International Home Furnishings Center
PO Box 828
High Point, NC 27261-0828
336-888-3700; *Fax:* 336-882-1873
marketing@ihfc.com; www.ihfc.com
Bruce Miller, CEO
Two-volume directory offers over 1,500 manufacturers and distributors in the furniture industry with exhibits at the International Home Furnishings Market.
Cost: $25.00
624 Pages
Frequency: Semiannual
Founded in: 1974
Printed in 4 colors on glossy stock

11251 Specialized Furniture Carriers Directory
National Furniture Traffic Conference
PO Box 889
Gardner, MA 01440-0889
978-632-1913; *Fax:* 978-630-2917
Ray Bohman, Editor
Nearly 200 trucking firms specializing in transportation of new furniture, not including household moving firms.
Cost: $39.95

Industry Web Sites

11252 http://gold.greyhouse.com
G.O.L.D Grey House OnLine Databases
Grey House Publishing's online database platform, GOLD, offers Quick Search, Keyword Search and Expert Search for most business sectors including furnishing, fixture and decorating markets. The GOLD platform makes finding the information you need quick and easy - whether you're a novice searcher or an experienced database user. All of Grey House's directory products are available for subscription on the GOLD platform.

11253 www.ahfa.us
American Home Furnishings Alliance
The largest and most influential trade organization serving the home furnishings industry. Dedicated to fostering the growth and global well being of its member companies.

11254 www.ahfa.us/divisions/scfma.asp
Summer & Casual Furniture Manufacturers Assn
Sponsors the International Casual Furniture and Accessories Market in Chicago, the Apollo Awards recognizing excellence in casual furniture retailing and the Casual Furniture Design Excellence Awards.

11255 www.awfs.org
Association of Woodworking & Furnishings Suppliers
Organization for furniture and accessories manufacturers and suppliers that are covered in this comprehensive journal.

11256 **www.bifma.org**
Business and Institutional Furniture Manufacturers

The voice of the office furniture industry, BIFMA members are manufacturers and suppliers of goods and services to the industry.

11257 **www.greyhouse.com**
Grey House Publishing

Authoritative reference directories for most business sectors including furnishings, fixtures and decorating marekts. Users can search the online databases with varied search criteria allowing for custom searches by product category, geographic area, sales volume, keyword, subject and more. Full Grey House catalog and online ordering also available.

11258 **www.hfia.com/**
Home Furnishings International Association

Product categories include residential casegoods, upholstery, gift and decorative accessories, lighting and area floor coverings and beddings.

11259 **www.natbat.com**
National Cotton Batting Institute

Association representing members of the cotton batting industry.

11260 **www.nhfa.org**
National Home Furnishings Association

Trade association of furniture retailers which works to improve retailer's business opportunities and management practices.

11261 **www.ofdanet.org**
Office Furniture Dealers Association

Explores the effect of office environment on productivity and uses contract sales staff to anticipate changes in market.

11262 **www.rtohq.org/**
Association of Progressive Rental Organizations

Members include television, appliance and furniture dealers who rent merchandise with an option to purchase.

11263 **www.unfinishedfurniture.org**
Unfinished Furniture Association

Associations

11264 American Herbal Products Association
8630 Fenton St
Suite 918
Silver Spring, MD 20910
301-588-1171; *Fax:* 301-588-1174
ahpa@ahpa.com; www.ahpa.org
Graham Rigby, Chair
Steven Dentali, Vice Chair
Michael McGuffin, President
Steven Yeager, Secretary
Mitch Coven, Treasurer
A organization that only focuses on herbs and herbal products.
200 Members
Founded in: 1982

11265 American Horticultural Society
7931 E Boulevard Dr
Alexandria, VA 22308
703-768-5700
800-777-7931; *Fax:* 703-768-8700
dhundley@ahs.org; www.ahs.org
Social Media: Facebook, Twitter, Flickr
Amy Bolton, Chair
Jane Diamantis, 1st Vice Chair
Mary Pat Matheson, 2nd Vice Chair
Nancy Hargroves, Secretary
J. Landon Reeve, Treasurer
Educates and inspires people of all ages to become successful and environmentally responsible gardeners by advancing the art and science of hoticulture. It is an education, nonprofit, 501 organization that recognizes and promotes best practices in American horticulture. AHS is known for its educational programs and the dissemination of horticultural information.
27M Members
Founded in: 1922
Mailing list available for rent

11266 American Horticultural Therapy Association
610 Freedom Business Centre
#110
King of Prussia, PA 19406
610-992-0020
800-634-1603; *Fax:* 610-225-2364;
www.ahta.org
Social Media: Facebook, Twitter, LinkedIn, Youtube, Pinterest
MaryAnne McMillan, President
Leigh Anne Starling, Vice President
Todd Schappell, Treasurer
Patricia Cassidy, Secretary
Advancing the practice of horticulture as therapy to improve human well-being.
Founded in: 1973

11267 American Institute of Floral Designers
720 Light Street
Baltimore, MD 21230
410-752-3318; *Fax:* 410-752-8295
aifd@assnhqtrs.com; www.aifd.org
Social Media: Facebook, Twitter, LinkedIn, YouTube
Joyce Mason-Monheim, President
Anthony Vigliotta, President-Elect
Kim Oldis, Vice President
Frank Feysa, Secretary
Tom Simmons, Treasurer
Nonprofit association to support the floral design industry.
1300 Members
Founded in: 1962

11268 American Nursery & Landscape Association
1200 G Street NW
Suite 800
Washington, DC 20005
202-789-2900; *Fax:* 202-789-1893
info@anla.org; www.anla.org
Social Media: Facebook
Bob Terry, President
Dale Deppe, President Elect
Michael V. Geary, Executive Vice President
The American Nursery and Landscape Association serves firms who grow, sell or use plants. ANLA advocates the industry's interests before government and provides its members with unique business knowledge essential to long-term growth and profitability.
2000 Members
Founded in: 1876

11269 American Rose Society
8877 Jefferson Paige Road
PO Box 30000
Shreveport, LA 71130
318-938-5402
800-637-6534; *Fax:* 318-938-5405
ars@ars-hq.org; www.rose.org
Social Media: Facebook, Twitter, Flickr,Pinterest,Youtube
Steve Jones, President
Jeff Wycoff, VP
Laura Seabaugh, Executive Director
Carol Spiers, Assistant to Executive Director
Peggy Spivey, Administrative Assistant
Striving to provide educational services to encourage the greater use of our national flower in private and public gardens throughout the country.
24000 Members
ISSN: 1078-5833
Founded in: 1892

11270 American Society for Horticultural Science
1018 Duke Street
Alexandria, VA 22314
703-836-4606; *Fax:* 703-836-2024
webmaster@ashs.org; www.ashs.org
Social Media: Facebook, Twitter, LinkedIn, Pinterest
Curt Rom, Chair
John Dole, President
Michael W. Neff, Executive Director
A cornerstone of research and education in horticulture and an agent for active promotion of horticultural science.
1200 Members
Founded in: 1903

11271 American Society of Consulting Arborists
9707 Key West Avenue
Suite 100
Rockville, MD 20850-3222
301-947-0483; *Fax:* 301-990-9771
asca@mgmtsol.com; www.asca-consultants.org
Social Media: Facebook, Twitter, LinkedIn, Pinterest
Chris D. Ahlum, President
Beth W. Palys, Executive Director
Shannon Sperati, Senior Member Services Manager
Julie Hill, Marketing Director
The industry's premier professional association focusing solely on arboricultural consulting. Consulting Arborists are authoritative experts on trees, consulting property owners, municipalitites, attorneys, insurance professionals and others on tree disease, placement, preservation and dispute resolution in addition to providing consulting and experto testimony in the legal, insurance and environmental arenas.
Founded in: 1967

11272 American Society of Irrigation Consultants
4700 S. Hagadorn
Suite 195D
East Lansing, MI 48823
508-763-8140
866-828-5174; *Fax:* 508-763-8102
info@asic.org; www.asic.org
Carol Colein, Executive Director
Ivy Munion, President
Corbin Schneider, Vice President
Stacy Gardner, Secretary
Michael Krones, Treasurer
Provides a forum wherein irrigation design professionals can meet to exchange information and advance skills and techniques in irrigation design, installation and product application.

11273 American Society of Landscape Architects
636 Eye Street, NW
Washington, DC 20001-3736
202-898-2444
800-787-2752; *Fax:* 202-898-1185
info@asla.org; www.asla.org
Social Media: Facebook, Twitter, LinkedIn, Pinterest, Instagram, RSS
Thomas R Tavella, President
Mark A Focht, President Elect
Mark H Hough, VP, Communications
David L Lycke, VP, Finance
K Richard Zweifel, VP, Education
Residential and commercial real estate developers, federal and state agencies, city planning commissions and individual property owners are all among the thousands of people and organizations in America and Canada that will retain the services of landscape architect this year.
13500 Members
Founded in: 1899

11274 Association of Specialty Cut Flower Growers
17 1/2 W. College St.
MPO Box 268
Oberlin, OH 44074
440-774-2887; *Fax:* 440-774-2435
mail@ascfg.org; www.ascfg.org
Social Media: Facebook
John Dole, Executive Advisor
Frank Arnosky, President
Mike Hutchison, Vice-President
Josie Crowson, Treasurer
Barb Lamborne, Secretary
Trade association that provides cultural and marketing information to specialty cut flower growers.
700 Members
Founded in: 1988

11275 Floral Trade Council
101 N Main Street
Ovid, MI 48866
989-341-1322; *Fax:* 517-339-1393
Will Carlson, Executive Director
Association of US fresh cut flower growers.
70 Members
Founded in: 1988

11276 Garden Centers of America
2873 Saber Dr.
Clearwater, FL 33759
800-721-0024;
www.gardencentersofamerica.org
Kris Shepard, President

National association focused on the needs of retail nurseries.

11277 Garden Writers Association of America
7809 FM 179
Shallowater, TX 79363

806-832-1870; *Fax:* 806-832-5244
webtech@gardenwriters.org; www.gwaa.org
Social Media: Facebook, Twitter

Kirk Brown, President
Becky Health, Vice President
Jo Ellen Meyers Sharp, Treasurer
Maria Zampini, Secretary
Robert LaGasse, Executive Director

A organization with materials of interest to garden writers and news on members of the Association.
1800 Members

11278 Illinois Landscape Contractors Association
Illinois Landscape Contractors Association
2625 Butterfield Road
Suite 204W
Oak Brook, IL 60523

630-472-2851; *Fax:* 630-472-3150
information@ilca.net; www.ilca.net

Kevin Vancina, President
Michael Schmechtig, Secretary/Treasurer
Rusty Maulding, Vice President
Charlie Keppel, Immediate Past President
Scott Grams, Executive Director

ILCA's mission is to enhance the professionalism and capabilities of members by providing leadership, education and valued services while promoting environmental awareness within the landscape industry. Sponsor or Mid-Am Horticulture Trade Show.
Founded in: 1959

11279 International Society of Arboriculture
1400 W Anthony Drive
PO Box 3129
Champaign, IL 61826

217-355-9411
888-472-8733; *Fax:* 217-355-9516
isa@isa-arbor.com; www.isa-arbor.com
Social Media: Facebook, Twitter, LinkedIn, YouTube, RSS

Jim Skiera, Executive Director
Karin Phelps, Executive Assistant
Mark Bluhm, Director, Finance & Operations
Keely Roy, Director, Marketing
Sharon Lilly, Director, Educational Goods

A worldwide professional organization dedicated to fostering a greater appreciation for trees and to promoting research, technology, and the professional practice of arboriculture.

11280 Los Angeles Community Garden Council
4470 W Sunset Blvd
#381
Los Angeles, CA 90027
847-864-5781; *Fax:* 847-448-8805;
www.lagardencouncil.org
Social Media: Facebook

Glen Dake, President
Ada Berman, Treasurer
Eileen Zwiers, Secretary
David De La Torre, Contact
Francesca de la Rosa, Contact

Connect people with community garden space in their neighborhoods.

11281 Mailorder Gardening Association
PO Box 429
LaGrange, GA 30241

706-298-0022; *Fax:* 706-883-8215
satkinson@asginfo.net;
www.directgardeningassociation.com
Social Media: Facebook, Twitter, LinkedIn

Noel Valdes, President
Polly Welch, 1st VP
Ken Oakes, 2nd VP
Matt Bollinger, Secretary
Alisa Meggison, Treasurer

Mail-order suppliers of gardening and nursery stock and supplies.
210 Members
Founded in: 1934

11282 National Council of Commercial Plant Breeders
1701 Duke Street
Suite 275
Alexandria, VA 22314

703-299-6633
ajorss@amseed.org; www.nccpb.org

Stephen Smith, President
Andrew LaVigne, Executive Vice President
Tom Koch, 1st Vice President
Marcelo Queijo, 2nd Vice President
Ann Jorss, Secretary/Treasurer

A non-profit organization to promote the achievement and interest of American plant breeders both in the United States and abroad.

11283 National Gardening Association
237 Commerce St.
Suite 101
Williston, VT 05495

802-863-5251; *Fax:* 802-864-6889
assoc.garden.org

Nichole Rothaupt, Chief Operating Officer
Jennifer Tedeschi, Executive Director

A nonprofit promoting garden-based education.
Founded in: 1982

11284 National Pest Management Association
10460 North Street
Fairfax, VA 22030

703-352-6762
800-678-6722; *Fax:* 703-352-3031;
www.npmapestworld.org
Social Media: Facebook, Twitter, Flickr

Gary McKenzie, CFO
Bob Rosenberg, EVP
Jean Baum, Executive Assistant
Gene Harrington, VP, Govt. Affairs
Alexis Wirtz, VP, Conventions & Professional Dev

Represents the interests of its members and the structural pest control industry.
7000 Members
3500 Attendees
Founded in: 1933

11285 North American Horticultural Supply Association
100 North 20th Street
Suite 400
Philadelphia, PA 19103-3572

215-320-3877; *Fax:* 215-564-2175
nahsa@fernley.com; www.nahsa.org

Neal Farnham, President
Richard Smith, Vice President
Charles Germano, Treasurer

Promotes full service distributors in the greenhouse and nursery hard good supply market.
120 Members
Founded in: 1988

11286 Professional Grounds Management Society
720 Light St
Baltimore, MD 21230-3850

410-223-2861
800-609-7467; *Fax:* 410-752-8295
pgms@assnhqtrs.com; www.pgms.org
Social Media: Facebook, Twitter, LinkedIn, YouTube, RSS

John Burns, President
Marion Bolick, President-Elect
Gerald Landby, Vice President
Jeff McManus, Treasurer/Secretary
John Burns, Past President

Members are professionals involved in the care and maintenance of public and private sites.
1400 Members
Founded in: 1911

11287 Professional Landcare Network
950 Herndon Parkway
Suite 450
Herndona, GA 20170

703-736-9666
800-395-2522; *Fax:* 703-736-9668
webmaster@landcarenetwork.org;
www.landscapeprofessionals.org
Social Media: Facebook, Twitter, LinkedIn, YouTube

Scott Jamieson, President
Brett Lemcke, President-Elect
Jason Becker, Directors at Large
Sabeena Hickman, CEO
Scott Lindley, VP Sales

PLANET emerged from the joining of the PLCAA and the ALCA in 2005. It is an educational, professional resource for landcare, exterior maintenance and interiorscape professionals and the lawn and landscape industry.
1200 Members
Founded in: 1979

11288 Society of American Florists
1601 Duke St
Alexandria, VA 22314-3406

703-836-8700
800-336-4743; *Fax:* 703-836-8705
info@safnow.org; www.safnow.org
Social Media: Facebook, Twitter, LinkedIn

Robert Williams, Chairman
Shirley Lyons, President
Martin Meskers, President-Elect
Dwight Larimer, Treasurer
Peter J Moran, EVP/CEO

Represents all segments of the U.S. floral industry.
12K Members
Founded in: 1884

11289 The United States Lawn Mower Racing Association
PO Box 628
Northbrook, IL 60065

www.letsmow.com
Social Media: Facebook, Twitter, Instagram, YouTube

An association run for racing enthusiasts who love to tinker and compete.
Founded in: 1992

11290 Turf Grass Producers International
2 East Main Street
East Dundee, IL 60118

847-649-5555
800-405-8873; *Fax:* 847-649-5678
info@turfgrasssod.org; www.turfgrasssod.org
Social Media: Facebook

Den Gardner, Editor
Lynn Grooms, Managing Editor
Veronica Iwanski, Membership & Marketing

Manager
Jim Novak, Public Relations Manager
Geri Hannah, Accounting & Office Manager

An organization featuring business news and updates on legislation and agronomics concerning the turf industry.
1000 Members
Founded in: 1967

Newsletters

11291 Bulletin
Garden Club of America
590 Madison Ave
Suite 19
New York, NY 10022-2544
212-872-1000; *Fax:* 212-872-1002;
www.akingump.com
Daniel H Golden, Partner
GCA's oldest publication, articles include news from GCA member clubs around the country, with reports from national committees, zones, and GCA conferences and meetings.
Cost: $8.00
Frequency: Bi-Monthly

11292 Front Page News
Professional Landcare Network, Inc
950 Herndon Parkway
Suite 450
Herndon, VA 20170
703-736-9666
800-395-2522; *Fax:* 703-736-9668;
www.landscapeprofessionals.org
Dan Foley, Publisher
E-newsletter with timely association and industry news and topics.
16 Pages
Frequency: Monthly

11293 Landscape Architect and Specifier News
George Schmok
14771 Plaza Dr
Suite M
Tustin, CA 92780-8012
714-979-5276; *Fax:* 714-979-3543
webmaster@landscapeonline.com;
www.landscapeonline.com
George Schmok, Publisher
Jim Lipot, Circulation Manager
Leslie McGuire, Managing Editor
A photographically oriented professional journal featuring topics of concern and state of the art projects designed or influenced by registered landscape architects worldwide.
Frequency: Monthly
Circulation: 29162
Printed in 4 colors on glossy stock

11294 PLANET News Magazine
Professional Landcare Network, Inc
950 Herndon Parkway
Suite 450
Herndon, VA 20170
703-736-9666
800-395-2522; *Fax:* 703-736-9668
info@actionletter.com;
www.landscapeprofessionals.org
News and information of the gardening and landscaping industries.
Frequency: Monthly

11295 Quill and Trowel
Garden Writers Association of America
10210 Leatherleaf Ct
Manassas, VA 20111-4245
703-257-1032; *Fax:* 703-257-0213
webmaster@gardenwriters.org; www.gwaa.org
Robert C La Gasse, Executive Director
Ann Marie Van Nest, Vice President
Seymour Jordan, Publisher
Material of interest to garden writers and news of members of the Association.
12 Pages
Frequency: Monthly
Circulation: 1800
Founded in: 1848

11296 The Cut Flower Quarterly
Association of Specialty Cut Flower Growers
17 1/2 W. College St.
MPO Box 268
Oberlin, OH 44074
440-774-2887; *Fax:* 440-774-2435
ascfg@oberlin.net; www.ascfg.org
Newsletter
Cost: $175.00
Frequency: Quarterly
Circulation: 1200
ISSN: 1068-8013

11297 The Dirt
American Society of Landscape Architects
636 Eye Street, NW
Washington, DC 20001-3736
202-898-2444
800-787-2752; *Fax:* 202-898-1185
info@asla.org; www.dirt.asla.org
Covers the latest news on the build and natural environments and features stories on landscape architecture.
13500 Members
Frequency: Weekly
Founded in: 1899

Magazines & Journals

11298 American Nurseryman
American Nurseryman Publishing Company
223 W Jackson Blvd
Suite 500
Chicago, IL 60606-6911
312-427-7318
800-621-5727; *Fax:* 312-427-7346
editors@amerinursery.com;
www.amerinursery.com
Social Media: Facebook, Twitter
Allen Seidel, President
Sally Benson, Editor
Focuses on topics relevant to professional growers, landscapers and retail garden center operators.
Cost: $48.00
100 Pages
Frequency: Fortnightly
Circulation: 16000
ISSN: 0003-0198
Founded in: 1904
Printed in 4 colors on glossy stock

11299 American Rose Magazine
American Rose Society
PO Box 30000
Shreveport, LA 71130
318-221-5026
800-637-6534; *Fax:* 318-938-5405;
www.ars.org
Mike Kromer, Executive Director
Beth Smiley, Editor
Benny Ellerbe, Executive Director
Marny Fife, Marketing Director
Publication focusing on rose growing, culture and enjoyment. Accepts advertising.
Cost: $37.00
Frequency: Monthly
Circulation: 21000
ISSN: 1078-5833
Founded in: 1894

11300 Casual Living
Reed Business Information
PO Box 2754
Suite 200
High Point, NC 27261-2754
336-605-1000
800-652-2948; *Fax:* 336-605-1143;
www.reedbusiness.com
Kevin Castellani, President
Becky B Smith, Editor-in-Chief
Delaney Rudd, Owner
Stuart Whayman, CFO
Content includes industry lifestyle features, business analysis and product trend information.
Frequency: Monthly
Circulation: 10000
Founded in: 1958

11301 Fine Gardening
Taunton Press
63 South Main St
PO Box 5506
Newtown, CT 06470-5506
203-706-6206
800-888-8286; *Fax:* 203-426-3434
fg@taunton.com; www.taunton.com
LeeAnne White, Editor
Cathy Austermann, Advertising Manager
Todd Meier, Publisher
John Lagan, National Account Manager
Landscaping and ornamental gardening are the magazine's primary editorial focus. Step-by-step in-depth information for the country. Articles written by gardening experts and enthusiasts.
Cost: $29.95
83 Pages
Circulation: 202163
Founded in: 1988

11302 Florists' Review
WildFlower Media Inc.
3300 SW Van Buren
Topeka, KS 66611
785-266-0888
800-367-4708; *Fax:* 785-266-0333
mail@floristsreview.com;
www.floristsreview.com
Social Media: Facebook, Twitter
Travis Rigby, President / Publisher
David L Coake, Editorial Director
Brenda Wettengel, Circulation Coordinator
Lisa Strydom, Advertising Sales Director
Teresa Salts, Account Executive
For wholesalers and retailers and desingers of fresh and dried flowers.
Cost: $42.00
Frequency: Monthly
Circulation: 28000
Founded in: 1897

11303 Flowers&
Richard Salvaggio
11444 W Olympic Boulevard
Los Angeles, CA 90064-1549
310-966-3518
800-321-2665; *Fax:* 310-966-3610;
www.flowersandmagazine.com
Bruce Wright, Editor
Jill Fox, Circulation Manager
Richard Salvaggio, Publisher

Business information and tips for the retail florist.
Cost: $54.00
Frequency: Monthly
Circulation: 30,000
Founded in: 1985
Printed in 4 colors on glossy stock

11304 Garden Center Magazine
GIE Media
801 Cherry St.
Suite 960 Unit 2
Fort Worth, TX 76102

817-882-4110
800-456-0707; *Fax:* 817-882-4121;
www.gardencentermagazine.com
Social Media: Facebook

Yale Youngblood, Publisher
Sarah Martinez, Managing Editor

Garden Center magazine has made the business decision to be the voice to serve the total market with the content to serve common needs; the business of buying, merchandising and selling of trees, ornamentals, bedding plants and related garden materials and accessories to homeowner consumers.
Cost: $90.00
Frequency: Monthly
Circulation: 16249

11305 Garden Center Merchandising & Management
Branch-Smith Publishing
120 St. Louis Avenue
PO Box 1868
Fort Worth, TX 76101

817-882-4120
800-433-5612; *Fax:* 817-882-4121;
www.gardencentermag.com

Carol Miller, Editor
Patricia Kuhl, Publisher
Tiffany O'Kelley, Media Manager
Mike Branch, President
Frequency: Monthly

11306 Green Industry PRO
Cygnus Publishing
1233 Janesville Avenue
Fort Atkinson, WI 53538-0803

920-000-1111
800-547-7377; *Fax:* 920-563-1699
Grant.Dunham@cygnuspub.com;
www.cygnusb2b.com

Rick Monogue, Publisher
Gregg Wartgow, Associate Publisher
Lisa Danes, Associate Editor

A national trade publication providing the critical business information landscape contractors need for success. Readership includes the leaders of companies performing landscape management, installation, lawn care, irrigation and maintenance. Covers how to topics such as surviving and thriving through the pinch-points of growth, maximizing productivity, matching the right tools and equipment to the appliation at ahnd, and taking innovative approaches to the marketplace.
Frequency: Monthly
Circulation: 55000
Founded in: 1937

11307 Greenhouse Management
GIE Media
4020 Kinross Lakes Pkwy
Richfield, OH 44286

800-456-0707;
www.greenhousemanagementonline.com

Richard Foster, Publisher
Todd Davis, Editorial Director
Kristy O'Hara, Editor
Kelli Rodda, Managing Editor

National magazine for commercial greenhouse growers. Accepts advertising.
Frequency: Monthly

11308 Grounds Maintenance
Penton Media
249 W. 17th Street
New York, NY 10011

212-204-4200; www.grounds-mag.com

Keeping readers informed on the latest techniques and products for gounds care. The most popular source of information for grounds maintenance professionals. Readership includes golf course superintendants, corporate/municipal groundskeepers and landscape professionals, providing them with content they trust and creating a deep source of reference and how-to information.
Frequency: Monthly
Circulation: 70000
Founded in: 1966

11309 Hearth & Home
Village West Publishing
PO Box 1288
Laconia, NH 03247

603-284-4285
800-258-3772; *Fax:* 603-524-0643

Richard Wright, Editor
Jackie Avignone, Advertising Director

Magazine for retailers, including specialty, hardware, patio and barbecue.
Frequency: Monthly
Circulation: 17,000
Founded in: 1980

11310 HortScience
American Society for Horticultural Science
1018 Duke Street
Alexandria, VA 22314-2851

703-836-4606; *Fax:* 703-836-2024
webmaster@ashs.org; www.ashs.org
Social Media: Facebook

Michael W. Neff, Executive Director

Journal of interest to a broad array of horticultural scientists and others interested in horticulture. Goals are to provide information on significant research, education, extension findings and methods, and developments and trends that affect the profession.
Frequency: Monthly
ISSN: 0018-5345
Founded in: 1903

11311 HortTechnology
American Society for Horticultural Science
1018 Duke Street
Alexandria, VA 22314-2851

703-836-4606; *Fax:* 703-836-2024
webmaster@ashs.org; www.ashs.org
Social Media: Facebook

Michael W. Neff, Executive Director
Ruth Gaumond, Managing Editor
Tecola Forbes, Publications Coordinator

Brings reliable, current, peer-reviewed technical information to help solve problems and deal with current challenges in production, education, and extension.
Frequency: Bi-Monthly
Founded in: 1903

11312 Horticulture Magazine
F+W Media
10151 Carver Road
Suite 200
Cincinnati, OH 45242

513-531-2690; *Fax:* 513-891-7153;
www.hortmag.com
Social Media: Facebook, Twitter

Dedicated to celebrating the passion of avid gardeners, who take delight not just in gardens but in garden-making. Our informative, engaging writing and brilliant photography enables gardeners to create spaces that make them proud, beautify their hometowns and provide a gathering place for family and friends.
Frequency: Monthly

11313 Journal of Arboriculture
International Society of Arboriculture
1400 W Anthony Drive
PO Box 3129
Champaign, IL 61826

217-355-9411
888-472-8733; *Fax:* 217-355-9516
isa@isa-arbor.com; www.isa-arbor.com

Jim Skiera, Executive Director
Jerri Moorman, Executive Assistant

Refereed journal devoted to the dissemination of knowledge in the science and art of planting and caring for trees in the urban environment. Published by the International Society of Arboriculture, whose mission is to foster a greater appreciation for trees and to promote the research, technology, and practice of professional arboriculture.
Cost: $105.00
Frequency: Bi-Monthly
Circulation: 17000
ISSN: 0278-5226
Founded in: 1924

11314 Journal of the American Society for Horticultural Science
American Society for Horticultural Science
113 S West St
Suite 200
Alexandria, VA 22314-2851

703-836-4606; *Fax:* 703-836-2024
journal@ashs.org
journal.ashspublications.org/

Neal D. De Vos, Editor in Chief
Michael W. Neff, Publisher
Ruth Gaumond, Managing Editor

Publishes papers on the results of original research on horticultural plants and their products or directly related research areas. Its prime function is to communicate mission-oriented, fundamental research to other researchers. The journal includes detailed reports of original research results on various aspects of horticultural science and directly related subjects.
Frequency: Bi-Monthly
ISSN: 0003-1062
Founded in: 1903
Mailing list available for rent: 2500 names at $100 per M

11315 Landscape & Irrigation
Adams Business Media
111 W Jackson Blvd
7th Floor
Chicago, IL 60604-3589

312-846-4600; *Fax:* 312-977-1042;
www.adamsbusinessmedia.com

John Kmitta, Editor
Steve Brackett, VP/Group Publisher
Joanne Juda, Circulation Manager

Targets decision-makers throughout the landscape industry, from residential contractors to commercial grounds managers, to public works professionals and irrigation and water management professionals. Information includes advice from industry professionals, coverage of specific

projects, details on the latest products and innovations, and news from around the world.
Cost: $57.50
Frequency: 9x Yearly
ISSN: 0745-3795

11316 Landscape Illinois
Illinois Landscape Contractors Association
2625 Butterfield Road
Suite 204W
Oak Brook, IL 60523

630-472-2851; *Fax:* 630-472-3150
information@ilca.net; www.ilca.net

Scott Grams, Executive Director

An annual publication geared toward homeowners, business owners and consumers
36 Pages
Frequency: Monthly
Circulation: 40,000
Printed in 4 colors on glossy stock

11317 Landscape Management
Advanstar Communications
7500 Old Oak Blvd
Cleveland, OH 44130-3343

440-243-8100
800-225-4569; *Fax:* 440-891-2740;
www.ubmamericas.com
Social Media: Facebook, Twitter

Tony D Avino, General Manager
Kevin Stoltman, Publisher
Michael Harris, Sales Manager
Stephanie Ricca, Managing Editor
Ron Hall, Editor In Chief

Covers news, market trends, business and operations management, technical information on horticulture and agronomy for 51,000 professional landscape contractors, lawncare operators and inhouse grounds managers.
Cost: $46.00
Frequency: Monthly
Circulation: 60,000
Founded in: 1965
Printed in 4 colors on glossy stock

11318 Lawn & Landscape
Gie Publishing
4012 Bridge Avenue
Cleveland, OH 44113

216-961-4130
800-456-0707; *Fax:* 216-961-0364;
www.gie.net

Ron Lowy, Publisher
Dan Moreland, Executive Vice President

National trade magazine for the landscape professional. Accepts advertising.
120 Pages
Frequency: Monthly
Circulation: 73000
Founded in: 1980

11319 Nursery Management
GIE Media
4020 Kinross Lakes Pkwy
Richfield, OH 44286

800-456-0707;
www.nurserymanagementonline.com

Todd Davis, Publisher
Kelli Rodda, Editor

Nurserymen, landscapers and garden centers. Accepts advertising.
Cost: $24.00
136 Pages
Frequency: Monthly
Founded in: 1910

11320 Nursery Retailer
Brentwood Publications
3023 Eastland Boulevard
Clearwater, FL 33761-4106

727-724-0200; *Fax:* 727-724-0021;
www.nurseryretailer.com

Jeff Morey, President & Publisher
Cheryl Morey, Vice President & Publisher

News of retail growers.
Cost: $15.00
Frequency: Bi-Monthly
Founded in: 1955

11321 Power Equipment Trade
Hatton-Brown Publishers
225 Hanrick Street
PO Box 2268
Montgomery, AL 36102-2268

334-834-1170
800-669-5613; *Fax:* 334-834-4525
rich@hattonbrown.com; www.poweret.com

David H Ramsey, Co-Publisher
DK Knight, CEO
Rich Donnell, Editor

Leading publication in the power equipment community. Articles include profiles on successful power equipment retailers (dealers) and manufacturers and accounts pertaining to technology, market trends and timely issues.
Frequency: 10x Yearly
Circulation: 21788
ISSN: 0163-0414
Founded in: 1952

11322 Southern Nursery Digest
Betrock Information Systems
7770 Davie Road Ext
Hollywood, FL 33024-2516

954-810-0300; *Fax:* 954-438-2632

Irv Betrock, Editor
Sean Patrick, Manager

This comprehensive magazine covers the gardening and nursery business in the south.
Frequency: Monthly

11323 The American Gardener
Amerian Horticultural Society
7931 E Boulevard Dr
Alexandria, VA 22308-1300
703-768-5700
800-777-7931; *Fax:* 703-768-8700
dhundley@ahs.org; www.ahs.org

Tom Underwood, Executive Director
Harry Rissetto, Chair
Mary Pat Matheson, 1st Vice Chair
Leslie Ariail, Secretary
J. Landon Reeve, Treasurer

Features inspiring color photographs and in-depth articles on new and native plants, influetial garden personalities, garden history, and earth friendly gardening techniques and products. Also regular departments on design, children's gardening, conservation issues, and reviews of the latest gardening books, as well as a calendar of gardening events nationwide.
27M Members
Founded in: 1922

11324 The Cut Flower Quarterly
Association of Specialty Cut Flower Growers
17 1/2 W. College St.
MPO Box 268
Oberlin, OH 44074

440-774-2887; *Fax:* 440-774-2435
ascfg@oberlin.net; www.ascfg.org

Judy Laushman, Executive Director
Vicki Stamback, President
Leah Cook, Vice-President
Andrea Gagnon, Treasurer
Carolyn Tschetter, Secretary

The only regular publication dedicated to information about the production, postharvest care and marketing of cut flowers.
700 Members
Frequency: Quarterly
Founded in: 1988

11325 The Landscape Contractor
Illinois Landscape Contractors Association
2625 Butterfield Road
Suite 204W
Oak Brook, IL 60523

630-472-2851; *Fax:* 630-472-3150
information@ilca.net; www.ilca.net

Scott Grams, Executive Director

Providing readers with news and developments in the industry with emphasis on regional concerns. Read by ILCA members and nonmembers who own, manage or supervise exterior and interior design/guild and maintenance firms, nurseries and garden centers, landscape architectural firms, as well as the staffs of parks and recreation districts and landscape industry professionals throughout the Midwest.
Cost: $75.00
Frequency: Monthly
Founded in: 1959

11326 Tomato Country
Columbia Publishing
8405 Ahtanum Rd
Yakima, WA 98903-9432

509-248-2452
800-900-2452; *Fax:* 509-248-4056;
www.tomatomagazine.com

Brent Clement, Editor/Publisher
Mike Stoker, Publisher

Includes information on tomato production and marketing, grower and shipper feature stories, tomato research, from herbicide and pesticide studies to new varieties, market reports, feedback from major tomato meetings and conventions, along with other key issues and points of interest for USA and Canada tomato growers.
Cost: $12.00

11327 Turf News
Turf Grass Producers International
2 East Main Street
East Dundee, IL 60118

847-649-5555
800-405-8873; *Fax:* 847-649-5678
info@turfgrasssod.org; www.turfgrasssod.org

Kirk T Hunter, Executive Director

The only magazine devoted exclusively to turfgrass sod production. focuses on the business of turfgrass by targeting farm owners and managers. A valuable tool for suppliers and manufacturers, featuring industry trends, product news, technical information, marketing, research, government issues, human resources, seed & planting stock, equipment/machinery, farm profiles, as well as vital industry and association news.
Frequency: Bi-Monthly
Circulation: 1600
Founded in: 1977

11328 Yard and Garden
Cygnus Publishing
PO Box 803
Fort Atkinson, WI 53538-0803

920-000-1111
800-547-7377; *Fax:* 920-563-1699
noel.brown@cygnuspub.com;
www.cygnusb2b.com

John French, CEO
Dan Newman, Director of Public Relations
Kathy Scott, Director of Public Relations
Paul Bonaiuto, CFO

A national trade publication providing the critical business information independent outdoor

power equipment servicing dealers need for success. Readership includes the owners and managers of full-service outdoor power equipment dealerships serving both commercial and residential customers. Focuses on retail trends, management strategies, dealer best practices, supplier news, and the latest products and services to hit the lawn and garden marketplace.
Frequency: 8x Yearl
Circulation: 17504
Founded in: 1977

Trade Shows

11329 ASCA Annual Conference
American Society of Consulting Arborists
9707 Key West Avenue
Suite 100
Rockville, MD 20850-3222

301-947-0483; *Fax:* 301-990-9771
asca@mgmtsol.com; www.asca-consultants.org

Chris D. Ahlum, President
Beth W. Palys, Executive Director
Shannon Sperati, Senior Member Services Manager
Barbara Bienkowski, Exhibits & Sponsorship Manager

Recognized as a high quality, in-depth conference with cutting edge speakers. Combining the best forum for discussion of current and relevant arboricultural issues, as well as consulting practice management issues and key consulting topics such as the role of the expert witness, risk assessment and tree appraisal.
Founded in: 1967

11330 ASHS Annual Conference
American Society for Horticultural Science
1018 Duke Street
Alexandria, VA 22314-2851
703-836-4606; *Fax:* 703-836-2024
webmaster@ashs.org; www.ashs.org
Social Media: Facebook, Twitter, LinkedIn

Curt Rom, Chair
John Dole, President
Michael W. Neff, Executive Director
Negar Mahdavian, Conference Manager

Attracts US and international horticulturists who attend to learn about research and new developments in horticulture.
Cost: $560.00
Frequency: Annual

11331 American Nursery & Landscape Association Convention
American Nursery & Landscape Association
1200 G Street NW
Suite 800
Washington, DC 20005

202-789-2900; *Fax:* 202-789-1893;
www.anla.org
Social Media: Facebook

Robert S. Lyons, President
Robert Terry, President-Elect

Serves firms who grow, sell or use plants. ANLA advocates the industry's interests before government and provides its members with unique business knowledge essential to long-term growth and profitability.
Frequency: Annual/July

11332 American Society of Irrigation Consultants Conference
PO Box 426
Byron, CA 94514-0426

925-516-1124; *Fax:* 925-516-1301

Wanda M Sarsfield, Secretary

Addressing major industry issues and learn from each other and leading experts in irrigation, water management and related fields. Member participate in the conference to showcase the latest in irrigation solution technology and services.
Frequency: Annual
Founded in: 1970

11333 American Society of Landscape Architects Annual Meeting & Educational Expo
636 Eye Street NW
Washington, DC 20001-3736

202-898-2444
800-787-2752; *Fax:* 202-898-1185
info@asla.org; www.asla.org

Nancy Somerville, Executive Vice President
Gerald Beaulieu, CFO/Director Business Operations

Landscape architect ecucational session and workshop plus 500 exibits of outdoor lighting, playground and park equipment, landscape maintanence equipment, computer hardware and software and much more.
4700 Attendees

11334 Annual Convention of the International Lilac Society
9500 Sperry Road
Kirtland, OH 44094

440-946-4400; *Fax:* 216-256-1655

Exhibits on lilacs, including innovative cultivation and the use of lilacs in public and private landscaping.
Frequency: Annual
Founded in: 1974

11335 Annual Fort Worth Home & Garden Show
International Exhibitions
1635 W Alabama
Houston, TX 77006

713-295-5366; *Fax:* 713-529-0936

The place to experience what's new in home, gardening, remodeling, home decor, and much more. Meet over 400 experts and experience thousands of products and services.
40000 Attendees

11336 Annual Gulf Coast Home & Garden Expo
Exposition Enterprises of Alabama
PO Box 430
Pinson, AL 35126

205-680-0234; *Fax:* 205-680-0615

Like a well tended garden, the show keeps growing and growing.
12000 Attendees

11337 Central Environmental Nursery Trade Show (CENTS)
Ohio Nursery & Landscape Association
72 Dorchester Square
Westerville, OH 43081-3350

614-991-1195
800-825-5062; *Fax:* 614-899-9489
info@onla.org; www.onla.org/cents
Social Media: Facebook, LinkedIn

Jay Daley, President
Andy Harding, President-Elect
Kevin Thompson, Executive Director
Tracie Zody, Trade Show/Even Manager

Innovations and ideas in an expanded market.
Frequency: Annual/January

11338 Farwest
2780 SE Harrison Street
Suite 102
Milwaukie, OR 97222-7574

Fax: 503-653-1528

Clayton Hannon, Executive Director

775 booths promoting the sale and exchange of nursery/landscape products and services.
13M Attendees
Frequency: August

11339 GIE+EXPO - Green Industry & Equipment Expo
Professional Lawncare Network, Inc
222 Pearl Street
Suite 300
New Albany, IN 47150

812-949-9200
800-558-8767; *Fax:* 812-949-9600
info@gie-expo.com; www.gie-expo.com

Anna Demoret, Trade Show Coordinator

Annual show of 400 manufacturers, suppliers and distributors of lawn care equipment, supplies and services, including fertilizers, weed control materials, insurance information and power equipment. Take advantage of the education sessions and presentations and demos, as well as six-hundred and fifty booths.
Frequency: Annual

11340 Green Industry Conference - GIC
Professional Lawncare Network, Inc (PLANET)
950 Herndon Parkway
Suite 450
Herndon, VA 20170

703-736-9666
800-395-2522; *Fax:* 703-736-9668
info@gie-expo.com;
www.landscapeprofessionals.org

Keep current as a green industry professional. Stay tuned in to the new technology, products and services hitting the market every year. Hone your skills with applicable education that you can practice immediately. Green industry firms in all market segments including landscape management, lawn care, design, build and installation, irrigation and water management should attend.
Frequency: Annual

11341 Green Industry Great Escape
Professional Landcare Network
950 Herndon Parkway
Suite 450
Herndona, GA 20170

703-736-9666
800-395-2522; *Fax:* 703-736-9668
webmaster@landcarenetwork.org;
www.landscapeprofessionals.org
Social Media: Facebook, Twitter, LinkedIn, YouTube

Gerald J. Grossi, President
Norman Goldenberg, President-Elect

An annual destination meeting for upper-level management, owners, and key personnel.
1200 Members
Founded in: 1979

11342 Green Profit's Retail Experience
Green Profit Magazine
335 N River Street
Batavia, IL 60510

630-208-9080
888-888-0013; *Fax:* 630-208-9350
info@ballpublishing.com;
www.ballpublishing.com/conferences

Michelle Mazza, Show Manager

Educational event and tradeshow dedicated exclusively to garden center retailing. Covers top-

ics from store layout and design to merchandising strategies and business management. 20 booths
300 Attendees
Frequency: Annual/September
Founded in: 2006

11343 Interior Plantscape Symopsium
Professional Landcare Network
950 Herndon Parkway
Suite 450
Herndon, VA 20170

703-736-9666
800-395-2522; *Fax:* 703-736-9668
webmaster@landcarenetwork.org;
www.plcaa.org/conference
Social Media: Facebook, Twitter, LinkedIn, YouTube

Education will offer practical training for the front line with opportunities to earn CEUs toward Landscape Industry Certified Technician recertification as well as pesticide credits. Attendees will walk away with knowledge on how to run their businesses more effectively and keep customers happy. Technicians will learn cutting-edge techniques to make their jobs easier.
Frequency: Annual/April

11344 International Floriculture Expo
207-842-5508; *Fax:* 207-842-5509;
www.floriexpo.com

Where buyers and suppliers from each stage of the floriculture production cycle come together to network, teach and learn from one another. With the live products, equipment, technology and education necessary for cultivating and retailing, find the ideas, new products, suppliers, trends and tools to flourish in the US market. Open to all buyers within the floriculture industry.
Frequency: Annual

11345 International Floriculture Trade Fair (IFTF)
Trade Show Bookings
PO Box 499
Fresh Meadows, NY 11365-0499
George Birne, Show Manager

The industry wide event serving all segments of the floriculture chain, from breeders, propagators, growers to the fresh flower trade.
40M Attendees
Frequency: Annual/November

11346 International Lawn Garden & Power Equipment Expo
Andry Montgomery and Associates
550 S 4th Avenue
#200
Louisville, KY 40202-2504

Fax: 502-473-1999

Warren Sellers, Show Manager

The dream trade show for those interested in the concept of more power. The show is filled with outdoor lawn equipment that could do more faster, more quietly, more efficiently, and with the least amount of emissions.
25M Attendees
Frequency: Annual/July

11347 International Symposium on Orchids and Ornamental Plants

www.orchidsociety.com

There are 75 booths and 50 exhibits that include bonsai trees, pots, tools and supplies, orchids, live plants and supplies for orchids and more.
Frequency: Annual/January

11348 Lawn & Garden Marketing & Distribution Summit Conference
2105 Laurel Bush Road
Suite 200
Bel Air, MD 21015

443-640-1080; *Fax:* 443-640-1031;
www.lgmda.org

Steven T King, Executive VP
Marci L Hickey, Director Meetings/Member Services
Amy Chetelat, Financial Manager

Lawn and garden products. 120 booths.
500 Attendees
Frequency: Bi-Annual

11349 Lawn, Flower and Patio Show
Mid-America Expositions, Inc
7015 Spring Street
Omaha, NE 68106-3518

402-346-8003
800-475-7469; *Fax:* 402-346-5412
info@showofficeonline.com;
www.showofficeonline.com

Robert P Mancuso, CEO
Mike Mancuso, VP/Manager

Annual show and exhibits of equipment, supplies and services for the lawn, flower and patio.
Frequency: Annual/February

11350 Mid Atlantic Nursery Trade Show
PO Box 11739
Baltimore, MD 21206-0339

410-882-5300

Carville Akehurst, Executive VP

Landscaping materials and horticultural tools. 750 booths, nursery stock, garden center and greenhouse supplies. 750 booths.
7.1M Attendees
Frequency: Annual/January

11351 Mid-Atlantic Nursery Trade Show
Mid Atlantic Nurserymen's Trade Shows
PO Box 818
Brooklandville, MD 21022

800-431-0066; *Fax:* 410-296-8288

Widely known as the masterpiece of trade shows.
11M Attendees
Founded in: 1970

11352 Midwest Herb and Garden Show
PO Box 3434
Omaha, NE 68103-0434
Jane Booth, Show Manager

With vendors from throughout the midwest and nationally known speakers, this event is geared for everyone from the novice to master gardeners. Exhibitors display a variety of items including fresh herbs, herbs for culinary, medicinal, and decorative use, bulbs, seeds, books on birds, herbs and gardening, plans, herbal cookbooks, gardening magazines, bird feeders, houses and baths, antiques, china, spices, trellises, gourds, orchids, fudge, and much more.
15M Attendees
Frequency: Annual/February

11353 National City Home & Garden Show
Expositions
PO Box 550
Edgewater Branch
Cleveland, OH 44107-0550

216-529-1300; *Fax:* 216-529-0311
showinfo@expoinc.com; www.expoinc.com

Featuring showcases on how to make your dream home a reality. Create the garden oasis, backyard retreat or a relaxing sanctuary.
35000 Attendees
Frequency: Annual/February

11354 National Lawn & Garden Trade Show
Great American Exhibitions
112 Main Street
Norwalk, CT 06851

203-498-8735; *Fax:* 203-845-9183

Ronald Gratt, Manager

Sole mission has been to provide an affordable, efficient, alternative to traditional tradeshows which assures buyer/vendor introductions in pre-set scheduled appointments.
5000 Attendees
Frequency: Annual

11355 National Lawn and Garden Show
Controlled Marketing Conferences
PO Box 1771
Monument, CO 80132

719-488-0226
888-316-0226; *Fax:* 719-488-8168;
www.nlgshow.com
Social Media: Facebook, Twitter, LinkedIn

Bob Mikulas, President

This is the lawn and gardens premier headlines event and features both a pre-set scheduled appointment division and a traditional booth division.
300 Attendees
Frequency: June
Founded in: 1995

11356 National Pest Management Association Annual Eastern Conference
10460 North Street
Fairfax, VA 22030

703-352-6762; *Fax:* 703-352-3031
info@pestworld.com; www.npmapestworld.org
Social Media: Facebook, Twitter

Robert Lederer, Executive VP
7000 Members
3500 Attendees
Frequency: January
Founded in: 1933

11357 Novi Expo Backyard, Pool and Spa Show
Show Span
1400 28th Street SW
Grand Rapids, MI 48509

616-530-1919
800-328-6550; *Fax:* 616-530-2122
events@showspan.com; www.showspan.com

Melissa Moore
Mike Wilbraham, President
Adam Starr, Manager
Molly Harrison, Administrative Assistant

Held at the Novi Expo Center in Novi, Michigan.

11358 Nursery/Landscape Expo
Texas Nursery & Landscape Association
7730 S IH-35
Austin, TX 78745-6698

512-280-5182
800-880-0343; *Fax:* 512-280-3012;
www.txnla.org

Ed Edmonson, Show Manager
Amy Prenger, President
Nancy Sollohub, Executive Assistant
Darlene Lanham, Communications Manager

Learn about industry trends, experience the breadth and depth of the green industry all under one roof, network, hear about industry best practices from peers and industry experts, and find the best deals from the best dealers in the southwest and beyond.
11M Attendees
Frequency: Annual/August

11359 **Old House New House Home Show**
Kennedy Productions
1208 Lisle Place
Lisle, IL 60532

630-515-1160; *Fax:* 630-515-1165
info@kennedyproductions.com;
www.kennedyproductions.com
Social Media: Facebook

Laura McNamara, Event Producer

Over 300 home improvement exhibitors displaying cutting-edge home enhancements for kitchens, baths, home and garden including landscape, interior remodeling, pools, spas, floors, doors and more.
8000 Attendees
Frequency: Bi-Annual
Founded in: 1984

11360 **Perennial Production Conference**
335 N River Street
Batavia, IL 60510

630-208-9080
888-888-0013; *Fax:* 630-208-9350
perennialplantconference.org

Michelle Mazza, Show Manager

Perennial producers of all levels are urged to attend this unique event, which offers an educational and networking experience focused 100 percent on perennials. Learn everything about perennial production and retailing through workshops, seminars, tours, and a trade show.
600 Attendees
Frequency: Annual/September
Founded in: 2003

11361 **Tropical Plant Industry Exhibition**
Florida Nursery Growers Landscape Association
1533 Park Center Drive
Orlando, FL 32835

407-295-7994
800-375-3642; *Fax:* 407-295-1619
info@fngla.org; www.fngla.org/tpie/
Social Media: Facebook, Twitter, LinkedIn

Linda Adams, Show Manager
Sabrina Haines, Trade Show Coordinator

The trade event showcasing the latest trends in foliage, floral and tropicals. More than an exhibit area, it's 200,000 square feet of living and vibrant plants creating a virtual indoor garden of showstopping displays.
8,000 Attendees
Frequency: Annual/January

Directories & Databases

11362 **Complete Directory of Home Gardening Products**
Sutton Family Communications & Publishing Company
920 State Route 54 East
Elmitch, KY 42343

270-276-9500
jlsutton@apex.net

Theresa Sutton, Editor
Lee Sutton, General Manager

Print-out from database of wholesalers, manufacturers, distributors, importers and close-out houses. Database is updated daily to guarantee the most current and up-to-date sources available.
Cost: $39.50
100+ Pages

11363 **Complete Directory of Horticulture**
Sutton Family Communications & Publishing Company
920 State Route 54 East
Elmitch, KY 42343

270-276-9500
jlsutton@apex.net

Theresa Sutton, Editor
Lee Sutton, General Manager

Print-out from database of wholesalers, manufacturers, distributors, importers and close-out houses. Database is updated daily to guarantee the most current and up-to-date sources available.
Cost: $39.50
100+ Pages

11364 **DGA Membership Directory**
Mailorder Gardening Association
5836 Rockburn Woods Way
Elkridge, MD 21075-7302

410-540-9830; *Fax:* 410-540-9827;
www.mailordergardening.com

Camille Cimino, Executive Director

Member catalogers who sell gardening and nursery stock and supplies to consumers.
Cost: $2.00
Frequency: Annual

Industry Web Sites

11365 **KidsGardening.org**
National Gardening Association
237 Commerce St.
Suite 101
Williston, VT 05495

800-538-7476; *Fax:* 802-864-6889;
www.kidsgardening.org

Jennifer Tedeschi, Executive Director
Sarah Pounders, Youth Education Specialist

Educational resources and garden grants for youth.

11366 **http://gold.greyhouse.com**
G.O.L.D Grey House OnLine Databases

Grey House Publishing's online database platform, GOLD, offers Quick Search, Keyword Search and Expert Search for most business sectors including garden and lawncare markets. The GOLD platform makes finding the information you need quick and easy - whether you're a novice searcher or an experienced database user. All of Grey House's directory products are available for subscription on the GOLD platform.

11367 **www.ahs.org**
American Horticultural Society

Individuals, institutions and businesses interested in a wide range of horticultural concerns.

11368 **www.ahta.org**
American Horticultural Therapy Association

Professional therapists, rehabilitation specialists and others using horticulture as a medium of rehabilitation.

11369 **www.aifd.org**
American Institute of Floral Designers

Non-profit association to support the floral design industry.

11370 **www.anla.org**
American Nursery & Landscape Association

The American Nursery and Landscape Association serves firms who grow, sell or use plants. ANLA advocates the industry's interests before government and provides its members with unique business knowledge essential to long-term growth and profitability.

11371 **www.ascfg.org**
Association of Specialty Cut Flower Growers

Trade association that provides cultural and marketing information to specialty cut flower growers.

11372 **www.asla.org**
American Society of Landscape Architects

Landscape architects.

11373 **www.emda.net**
Farm Equipment Wholesalers Association

International trade association of wholesale/distributors of ag equipment and related products.

11374 **www.gardenwriters.org**
Garden Writers Association of America

A organization with materials of interest to garden writers and news on members of the Association.

11375 **www.greyhouse.com**
Grey House Publishing

Authoritative reference directories for most business sectors including garden and lawncare markets. Users can search the online databases with varied search criteria allowing for custom searches by product category, geographic area, sales volume, keyword, subject and more. Full Grey House catalog and online ordering also available.

11376 **www.landcarenetwork.org**
Professional Landcare Network

Lawn care companies, manufacturers/suppliers, ground managers and university personnel comprise membership of PLCAA. PLCAA is an educational, professional resource for the lawn and landscape industry.

11377 **www.mailordergardening.com**
Mailorder Gardening Association

Mail-order suppliers of gardening and nursery stock and supplies.

11378 **www.nahsa.org**
North American Horticultural Supply Association

Promotes full service distributors in the greenhouse and nursery hard good supply market.

11379 **www.pgms.org/**
Professional Grounds Management Society

Members are professionals involved in the care and maintenance of public and private sites.

11380 **www.safnow.org**
Society of American Florists

Represents all segments of the U.S. floral industry.

11381 **www.turfgrassod.org**
Turf Grass Producers International

An organization featuring business news and updates on legislation and agronomics concerning the turf industry.

11382 **www.turfzone.com**
Turf Zone

Includes, commerical lawn care, consumer lawn care, irrigation equipment, fertilizer and other turf products.

11383 **www2.gcamerica.org**
Garden Club of America

Bestows awards, maintains a library and more.

Associations

11384 American Craft Council
1224 Marshall St. NW
Suite 200
Minneapolis, MN 55413
612-206-3100
800-836-3470; *Fax:* 612-355-2330
council@craftcouncil.org;
www.craftcouncil.org
Social Media: Facebook, Twitter, Flickr, YouTube, RSS
Chris Amundsen, Executive Director
Alanna Nissen, Office Coordinator
Greg Allen, Director, Finance & Administration
Claudia Cackler, Director, Development
Pamela Diamond, Director, Marketing & Communication
The American Craft Council is a national, non-profit educational organization to champion craft.
Founded in: 1943

11385 Gift & Home Trade Association
2550 Sandy Plains Road
Suite 225, PO Box 214
Marietta, GA 30066
877-600-4872
info@giftandhome.org; www.giftandhome.org
Social Media: Facebook, Twitter, LinkedIn
Todd Litzman, Chairman
Bob Ricciardi, President
Joe Harris, Vice President
Fred Schmidt, Treasurer
Allison Barrows, Secretary
The association was designed to help and encourage vendors, sales agencies, industry affiliates and retailers to work together, improving relationships and making business better by providing members with the opportunity to exchange ideas and network with industry leaders.
Founded in: 2000

11386 Gift Association of America
115 Rolling Hills Road
Johnstown, PA 15905-5225
814-288-3893
Michael Russo, President
Gift association comprised of retailers and wholesalers in the gift industry.
Founded in: 1592

11387 Greeting Card Association
1444 I St. NW
Suite 700
Washington, DC 20005
202-216-9627; *Fax:* 202-216-9646;
www.greetingcard.org
Peter Doherty, Executive Director
Trade association representing American and international publishers - large and small - and production and distribution providers.
Founded in: 1941

11388 Museum Store Association
3773 E Cherry Creek North Drive
#755
Denver, CO 80246-3055
303-504-9223; *Fax:* 303-504-9585
info@museumstoreassociation.org;
www.museumstoreassociation.org
Social Media: Facebook, Twitter, LinkedIn, Pinterest
Jama Rice, CEO/Executive Director
Andrea Miller, Manager Of Learning
Kathy Cisar, Communications Manager
Jennifer Anderson, Meetings & Conference Manager
David Duddy, President
Providing member representatives with the professional opportunities and educational resources they need to operate effectively and ethically.
2500 Members
Founded in: 1955

11389 National Gift Organization
332 Hurst Mill N
Bremen, GA 30110
505-798-0375
800-446-2533; www.naled.org
Ken Shirley, President
Trade association for the gift and collectibles industry. Offers once yearly expositions, a newsletter, software, low cost credit card processing, telephone service discounts and more to help you run your business profitably.
350 Members

11390 National Specialty Gift Association
PO Box 843
Norman, OK 73070
405-329-7847
Joni Damico, Executive Director
Specialty gift resource center for retailers, wholesale vendors and related professionals.
Cost: $29.95
400 Members
Founded in: 1998

11391 Organization of Associated Salespeople in the Southwest/OASIS
15591 W Yucatan Drive
Surprise, AZ 85379
602-952-2050
800-424-9519; *Fax:* 602-952-2244
information@oasis.org; www.oasis.org
Social Media: Facebook
Kristi Thomas, Media Relations
A gift trade association which represents the manufacturing, sales and distribution side of the giftware industry. OASIS exhibitors offer trend setting general merchandise, world imports, home d,cor, jewelry, Native American art and crafts, western flair and southwestern gifts.
Founded in: 1976

Magazines & Journals

11392 American Craft Magazine
American Craft Council
1224 Marshall St. NW
Suite 200
Minneapolis, MN 55413
612-206-3100
800-836-3470; *Fax:* 612-355-2330
council@craftcouncil.org;
www.craftcouncil.org
Chris Amundsen, Executive Director
Alanna Nissen, Office Coordinator
Greg Allen, Director, Finance & Administration
Claudia Cackler, Director, Development
Pamela Diamond, Director, Marketing & Communication
Official magazine of the American Craft Council containing contemporary craft art and happenings of the Council.
Cost: $25.00
Frequency: 6x/Year
Founded in: 1943

11393 Gift Basket Review
Festivities Publications
815 Haines Street
Jacksonville, FL 32206-6025
904-634-1902
800-729-6338; *Fax:* 904-633-8764;
www.festivities-pub.com
Debra Paulk, Publisher
Kathy Horak, Managing Editor
Magazine devoted to issues relating to the gift basket and gift packing industries.
Cost: $29.94
Frequency: Monthly
Circulation: 15000
Founded in: 1990

11394 Gifts & Decorative Accessories
Reed Business Information
360 Park Ave S
4th Floor
New York, NY 10010-1737
646-805-0234; *Fax:* 646-756-7583
corporatecommunications@reedbusiness.com;
www.giftsanddec.com
Caroline Kennedy, Editor in Chief
Kathy Krassner, Editor at Large
Pamela Brill, Editor at Large
Serves retailers of stationery, greeting cards, collectibles, china, glass, lamps, and accessories.
Cost: $49.95
Frequency: Monthly
Circulation: 23737
ISSN: 0016-9889
Founded in: 1946
Printed in 4 colors on glossy stock

11395 Giftware News
Talcott Communications Corporation
20 W Kinzie St
12th Floor
Chicago, IL 60654-5827
312-849-2220
800-229-1967; *Fax:* 312-849-2174;
www.talcott.com
Social Media: Twitter
Daniel Von Rabenau, Executive Director
Claire Weingarden, Associate Editor
John Saxtan, Editor in Chief
Edited for gift, stationery and department stores.
Cost: $39.00
Frequency: 18x Yearly
Circulation: 60000
Founded in: 1982

11396 Museum Store
Museum Store Association
4100 E Mississippi Ave
Suite 800
Denver, CO 80246-3055
303-504-9223; *Fax:* 303-504-9585
info@museumstoreassociation.org;
www.museumstoreassociation.org
Social Media: Facebook, Twitter, LinkedIn
Beverly J Barsook, Executive Director
Valerie Troyansky, President
Beth Ricker, 1st Vice President
Stacey Stachow, 2nd Vice President
Providing ideas, tips, insights and unique product sources for nonprofit retailers.
2500 Members
Frequency: Quarterly
Founded in: 1955

11397 Souvenirs, Gifts & Novelties Magazine
Kane Communications

7000 Terminal Square
Suite 210
Upper Darby, PA 19082-2330

610-734-2420; *Fax:* 610-734-2423;
www.souvmag.com

Scott Borowsky, President
Mary Anne Peacocti, Director Circulation
Caroline Burns, Managing Editor
Larry White, VP Marketing

Serves the general gift and trend marketplace with a core readership in the tourism and resorts gift and apparel stores.
Cost: $30.00
140 Pages
Frequency: 8x Yearly
Circulation: 43085
Founded in: 1962
Printed in 4 colors on glossy stock

Trade Shows

11398 **ASD/AMD National Trade Show**
ASD/AMD Merchandise Group
2950 31st Street
Suite 100
Santa Monica, CA 90405

310-255-4633; *Fax:* 310-396-8476

The nation's largest, most comprehensive merchandise trade show. Featuring thousands of exhibitors, carrying products in more than 100 catebories, from jewelry and home decor to fashion accessories and general discount merchandise items.
10000 Attendees
Frequency: Annual/March

11399 **ASD/AMD's Gift Expo**
ASD/AMD Merchandise Group
2950 31st Street
Suite 100
Santa Monica, CA 90405

310-396-6006
800-421-4511; *Fax:* 310-399-2662;
www.merchandisegroup.com

Julie Ichiba, Show Director

A general merchandise event which attracts over 50,000 buyers to Las Vegas. Tens of thousands of unique products in hundreds of popular consumer product categories are on display at this event.
55000 Attendees
Frequency: Bi-Annual

11400 **Accent on Design**
George Little Management
10 Bank Street
Suite 1200
White Plains, NY 10606-1954

914-486-6070
800-272-7469; *Fax:* 914-948-2867;
www.nyigf.com

Elizabeth Murphy, Manager
George Little II, President

370 booths of the latest and most innovative gift lines such as decorative accessories and home furnishings.
50M Attendees
Frequency: Annual/August
Founded in: 1999

11401 **American Craft Council Show**
American Craft Council
1224 Marshall St. NW
Suite 200
Minneapolis, MN 55413

612-206-3100
800-836-3470; *Fax:* 612-355-2330
council@craftcouncil.org;
www.craftcouncil.org

Chris Amundsen, Executive Director
Alanna Nissen, Office Coordinator
Greg Allen, Director, Finance & Administration
Claudia Cackler, Director, Development
Pamela Diamond, Director, Marketing & Communication

The American Craft Council Show presents outstanding works by America's leading craftspeople for purchase by the public and to the trade
Founded in: 1943

11402 **Annual Dickens Christmas Show and Festival**
Leisure Time Unlimited
2101 N. Oak Street
Myrtle Beach, SC 29577

843-448-9483
800-261-5991; *Fax:* 843-626-1513
dickensshow@sc.rr.com;
www.dickenschristmasshow.com
Social Media: Facebook, Twitter

Linda Cremer, Show Director

Victorian craft and gift show.
28000 Attendees
Frequency: Annual/November
Founded in: 1981

11403 **Annual Spring New Products Show**
Pacific Expositions
1580 Makaola Street
Suite 1200
Honnolulu, HI 96814-3801

808-945-3594; *Fax:* 808-946-6399

Pat Shine, General Sales Manager
Kimalar K Carrol, Show Director/Coordinator

Over 200 New Products Booth Displays featuring for the entire family. All categories of consumer products and service are presented: roofing, siding, jewelry, cosmetics, cars, boats, home improvement products. Over 75 Food & Crafts displays, Sportscards & memorabilia displays.
18000 Attendees
Frequency: Annual/April
Founded in: 1974

11404 **GHTA Annual Conference**
Gift & Home Trade Association
4380 Brockton Drive SE
Suite 1
Grand Rapids, MI 49512

877-600-4872
info@giftandhome.org; www.giftandhome.org

Marc Rice, Chairman of the Board
Julie Dix, President
John Keiser, Vice President
Todd Litzman, Treasurer
Denny King, Secretary

GHTA has partnered with the Gift Associates Interchange Network, Inc. (GAIN) to form a new credit reporting interchange. The interchange will give GHTA members access to retailer payment experiences, flash notices, predictive payment scoring, educational resources and more.
Frequency: Annual
Founded in: 2000

11405 **General Gifts: A Division of the New York International Gift Fair**
George Little Management
10 Bank Street
White Plains, NY 10606-1954

914-486-6070
800-272-7469; *Fax:* 914-948-6180;
www.nyigf.com

George Little II, President

Featuring stationary, collectibles, ceramic giftware, toys, pet items, party lines, trend merchandise, premiums, trim-a-tree, souvenirs and novelties, specialty foods, home office, floral & garden accessories, Judaica, and general items.
Frequency: Biennial

11406 **Grand Strand Gift and Resort Merchandise Show**
Fairchild Urban Expositions
5500 Interstate N Parkway
Suite 520
Atlanta, GA 30328

770-952-6444; *Fax:* 770-956-9644
Social Media: Facebook

Bringing the nation's retailers an unrivaled selection of themed merchandise, resort apparel, gifts and souvenirs.
300 Attendees
Frequency: Annual/December

11407 **Gulf Coast Gift Show**
Fairchild Urban Expositions
5500 Interstate N Parkway
Suite 520
Atlanta, GA

770-952-6444; *Fax:* 770-956-9644;
www.urban-expo.com
Social Media: Facebook

Offering retailers from the Florida Panhandle and surrounding Gulf Coast areas to New Orleans an opportunigy to buy last minute holiday merchandise and get a jump on their spring/summer resort buying.
4000 Attendees
Frequency: Annual/October

11408 **Holiday Market**
Gilmore Enterprises
3514 Drawbridge Pkwy
Suite A
Greensboro, NC 27410-8584

336-282-5550; *Fax:* 336-282-0555
contact@gilmoreshows.com;
www.gilmoreshows.com
Social Media: Facebook

Tami Gilmore, Show Manager
Clyde Gilmore, Executive Director
Jan Donovon, Marketing Manager

There are two Holiday Market Shows, one in Greensboro, NC and the others in N. Cahrleston, SC. celebrate the season at Holiday Market. Children visit with santa and you will come away with ideas, recipes, samples, beauty makeovers and treats and holiday gifts.
35000 Attendees
Frequency: Annual/November
Founded in: 1989

11409 **Immediate Delivery Show: Fall**
AMC Trade Shows/DMC Expositions
240 Peachtree Street NW
Suite 2200
Atlanta, GA 30303

404-220-3000; *Fax:* 404-220-3030

Mary Ellen Jackson, Show Manger

A trade show that allows you to move discontinued merchandise, overstocked inventory, samples and one of a kind items.
9000 Attendees
Frequency: Annual/November

11410 **Indoor/Outdoor Home Show**
True Value
PO Box 17
Bethel Park, PA 15102

412-276-6292; *Fax:* 412-851-6975;
www.pitthomeshow.com

Plenty of exhibits and vendors, and the ultimate displays for the home office, garage, backyard

and patio, dream windows, home flooring, and bathroom.
61000 Attendees
Frequency: Annual/January

11411 International Jewelry Fair/General Merchandise Show
Helen Brett Enterprises
5111 Academy Drive
Lisle, IL 60532

630-241-9865
800-541-8171; *Fax:* 630-241-9870
dharrington@helenbrett.com;
www.gift2jewelry.com

Dave Harrington, Show Manager

Containing 1500 booths during the fall show and 800 booths during the spring show. Tradeshow open to wholesale buyers only (credentials required to attend).
44000 Attendees
Frequency: Bi-Annual

11412 Licensing International Expo

310-857-7544
888-644-2022; www.licensingexpo.com

Talia Loggia, Marketing Manager

Annual show of 220 exhibitors of logos, corporate trademarks, characters, designs and other advertising techniques that require licensing.
7000 Attendees
Frequency: Annual/July

11413 Memphis Gift & Jewelry Show-Fall
Helen Brett Enterprises
5111 Academy Drive
Lisle, IL 60532

630-241-9865
800-541-8171; *Fax:* 630-241-9870
dharrington@helenbrett.com;
www.gift2jewelry.com

Dave Harrington, Show Manager

Containing over 350 booths during the fall show and 350 booths during the spring show. Tradeshow open to wholesale buyers only (credentials required to attend).
9000 Attendees
Frequency: Annual/August

11414 Memphis Gift & Jewelry Show-Spring
Helen Brett Enterprises
5111 Academy Drive
Lisle, IL 60532

630-241-9865
800-541-8171; *Fax:* 630-241-9870
dharrington@helenbrett.com;
www.gift2jewelry.com

Dave Harrington, Show Manager

Containing over 350 booths during the spring show and 350 booths during the fall show. Tradeshow open to wholesale buyers only (credentials required to attend).
9000 Attendees
Frequency: Annual/February

11415 Mid-South Jewelry & Accessories Fair -Spring
Helen Brett Enterprises
5111 Academy Drive
Lisle, IL 60532

630-241-9865
800-541-8171; *Fax:* 630-241-9870
dharrington@helenbrett.com;
www.gift2jewelry.com

Dave Harrington, Show Manager

Containing over 300 booths during the spring show and 500 booths during the fall show. Tradeshow open to wholesale buyers only (credentials required to attend).
8500 Attendees
Frequency: Annual/May

11416 Mid-South Jewelry & Accessories Fair-Fall
Helen Brett Enterprises
5111 Academy Drive
Lisle, IL 60532

630-241-9865
800-541-8171; *Fax:* 630-241-9870
dharrington@helenbrett.com;
www.gift2jewelry.com

Dave Harrington, Show Manager

Containing 500 booths during the fall show and over 300 booths during the spring show. Tradeshow open to wholesale buyers only (credentials required to attend).
16000 Attendees
Frequency: Annual/November

11417 Motivation Show
Hall-Erickson
98 E Naperville Road
Westmont, IL 60559

630-963-9185
800-752-6312; *Fax:* 630-434-1216
moti@heiexpo.com; www.motivationshow.com

Nancy A Petitti, Show Director

Connecting engagement, loyalty, and financial results, learn from professional seminars on the latest trends, topics and best practices from some of America's leading organizations.
24000 Attendees
Frequency: Annual/September
Founded in: 1929

11418 Museum Source
George Little Management
10 Bank Street
Suite 1200
White Plains, NY 10606-2867

914-486-6070
800-272-7469; *Fax:* 914-948-6180
customer_relations@glmshows.com;
www.glmshows.com/nyigf

Chelsea A Weinert, Divisional Manager
George Little II, President

Semi-annual show devoted to manufacturers, importers and publishers whose products are appropriate for museum gift shops, bookshores, specialty shops, zoos, aquariums and galleries. Items displayed include calendars, novelties, ethnic and craft items, historical interpretational products, art objects, children's educational items and posters.
Frequency: SemiAnnual

11419 Museum Source: West
George Little Management
10 Bank Street
Suite 1200
White Plains, NY 10606-1954

914-486-6070
800-272-7469; *Fax:* 914-948-6180
customer_relations@glmshows.com;
www.glmshows.com/sfig

Elizabeth Murphy, Division Manager
George Little II, President

Semi-annual show devoted to manufacturers, importers and publishers whose products are appropriate for museum gift shops, bookshores, specialty shops, zoos, aquariums and galleries. Items displayed include calendars, novelties, ethnic and craft items, historical interpretational products, art objects, children's educational items and posters.
Frequency: SemiAnnual

11420 Museum Store Association Trade Show
Museum Store Association
4100 E Mississippi Avenue
Suite 800
Denver, CO 80246

303-504-9223; *Fax:* 303-504-8585;
www.museumdistrict.com

Beverly Barsook, Executive Director
Stacey Woldt, Assistant Director Programs

Identify new sales leads, enhance your image and visibility in this niche market, reach your target audience, personally meet your customers, introduce a new product or service, generate sales, and network.
2500 Attendees
Frequency: Annual/April
Founded in: 1955

11421 National Halloween Convention
Transworld Exhibits
1850 Oak Street
Northfield, IL 60093

847-784-6905
800-323-5462; *Fax:* 847-446-3523;
www.nationalhalloweenconvention.com

This once a year event is where over 10,000 attendees will converge on Chicago from all across the US and over 50 foreign countries to see what over 700 manufacturers and distributors are showcasing as new and exciting for parties, shops and haunted houses. Free educational seminars and workshops.
Frequency: Annual/May

11422 National Stationery Show
Gerorge Little Management
10 Bank Street
Suite 1200
White Plains, NY 10606

741-421-3200
800-272-7469; *Fax:* 914-948-2918
nationalstationeryshow@gmshows.com;
www.nationalstationeryshow.com

Lori Robinson, Show Manager

The National Stationery Show is the premiere market for stationery resources in the Unite States. The National Stationery Show presents more than 1,400 exhibitors and product in five distinctive sections; Presents, Celebrate, Take Note, HomeWork, and Indulgences. The show draws 15,000 domestic and international retailers representing department, chain and specialty stores, museum shops, galler and craft retailers, boutiques, stationery, greeting card and gift shops, bookstores, bridal shops
15000 Attendees
Frequency: Annual/May

11423 New Orleans Gift & Jewelry Show-Fall
Helen Brett Enterprises
5111 Academy Drive
Lisle, IL 60532

630-241-9865
800-541-8171; *Fax:* 630-241-9870
dharrington@helenbrett.com;
www.gift2jewelry.com
Social Media: Facebook

Dave Harrington, Show Manager

Containing 850 booths during the fall show and 750 booths during the spring show. Tradeshow open to wholesale buyers only (credentials required to attend).
27000 Attendees
Frequency: Annual/August

11424 New Orleans Gift & Jewelry Show-Spring
Helen Brett Enterprises

5111 Academy Drive
Lisle, IL 60532

630-241-9865
800-541-8171; *Fax:* 630-241-9870
dharrington@helenbrett.com;
www.gift2jewelry.com

Dave Harrington, Show Manager

Containing 750 booths during the spring show and 850 booths during the fall show. Tradeshow open to wholesale buyers only (credentials required to attend).
20000 Attendees
Frequency: Annual/January

11425 New Yorks Newest: A Division of the New York International Gift Fair
George Little Management
10 Bank Street
White Plains, NY 10606-1954

914-486-6070
800-272-7469; *Fax:* 914-948-6180;
www.nyigf.com

George Little II, President

Showcasing 250 exhibitors new to the NYIGF spanning all categories and featuring fresh and innovative lines.
Frequency: SemiAnnual

11426 OASIS Gift Show
Organization of Assn Salespeople in the Southwest
1250 E Missouri Avenue
Phoenix, AZ 85014

602-952-2050
800-424-9519; *Fax:* 602-952-2244
information@oasis.org; www.oasis.org

Brings success, opportunity, and convenience to buyers and exhibitors. Each show features an expansive product selection on the main floor, the jury-chosen artisans' showcase, and the gifts 2 go cash and carry area. Exhibitors offer trend setting general merchandise, world imports, home decor, jewelry, native american arts and crafts, western flair and southwestern gifts. OASIS is dedicated to providing a wholesale gift marketplace.
6000+ Attendees
Frequency: Annual/January

11427 Offinger's Handcrafted Martketplace
Offinger Management Company
1100-H Brandywine Boulevard
Zanesville, OH 43701-7303

888-878-4438; *Fax:* 740-452-2552
gift@offinger.com;
www.offingershandcrafted.com

Providing safe, convenient and inexpensive trade shows with rich collections of handmades, limited-production creations, traditional crafts and gifts, home furnishings, furniture and home accents. Meet the country's top producers of folk art, rustic primitives, museum quality replicas, handmade country collectibles, as well as one-of-a-kind, contemporary works of art.
3300 Attendees
Frequency: Triannual

11428 San Francisco International Gift Fair
San Francisco, CA
sfigf.com

Top name manufacturers, innovative newcomers, and cutting edge designs.
2500 Attendees

11429 Smoky Mountain Gift Show: Fall
Smoky Mountain Gift Show
PO Box 50
Gatlinburg, TN 37738

865-436-4418
800-441-7889; *Fax:* 865-436-2878;
www.smokymountaingiftshow.com

Eva Havlicek, Owner

The most beloved, most popular trade shows for the souvenir, resort and gift industry. Brings the top-name product selection, buyer base, service levels, and spirit of fun and hospitality that defined the show at its prime.
3000 Attendees
Frequency: Annual/November
Founded in: 1966

11430 Smoky Mountain Gift Show: Spring
Smoky Mountain Gift Show
PO Box 50
Gatlinburg, TN 37738

865-436-4418
800-441-7889; *Fax:* 865-436-2878;
www.smokymountaingiftshow.com

Eva Havlicek, Owner

Geared to the gift and souvenier market. Wholesale trade show open only to buyers in the retail industry. Buyers must present credentials upon registration.
12000 Attendees
Frequency: Annual/March

11431 Southern Christmas Show
Southern Shows
PO Box 36859
Charlotte, NC 28236

704-566-1898; *Fax:* 703-376-6345

Check out the holiday trees, mantels and doors, stroll the Christmas Village, munch on tasty treats and sway with yuletide entertainment.
13200 Attendees

11432 Southern Ideal Home Show: Fall
Southern Shows
PO Box 36859
Charlotte, NC 28236

704-566-1898
800-849-0248; *Fax:* 704-676-6345
dzimmerman@southernshows.com;
www.southershows.com

David Zimmerman, Show Manager
Brenda Crofts, Assistant Show Manager

Gardens, designer rooms, seminars, exhibitors, and experts on remodeling, decorating, home improvement and landscaping
20000 Attendees
Frequency: Annual/September

11433 Toy Fair
Toy Industry Association
1115 Broadway
Suite 400
New York, NY 10010

212-675-1141; *Fax:* 212-645-3246
toyfairs@toy-tia.org; www.toy-tia.org

Thomas Conley, President
Diane Cardinale, Public Information Manager

Products include: games, toys, puzzles, dolls, science and hobby craft kits, books, bicycles and ride-ons, computer and video games and software, playground and sporting equipment, costumes and holiday decorations.
22000 Attendees
Frequency: Annual/February

11434 Variety Merchandise Show
Miller Freeman Publications
One Penn Plaza
PO Box 2549
New York, NY 10116

212-714-1300; *Fax:* 212-714-1313

An emphasis on customer service, community building forums and practical business education seminars.
20000 Attendees

11435 Western States Toy and Hobby Show
Western Toy and Hobby Representative Association
9397 Reserve Drive
Corona, CA 92883

951-771-1598; *Fax:* 909-277-1599;
www.wthra.com

Phylis St. John, Manager

The biggest assortment of toys, games, hobbies and educational fun.
3000 Attendees
Frequency: March

Directories & Databases

11436 AR100 Award Show Guide
Black Book Marketing Group
10 Aston Place
6th Floor
New York, NY 10003

212-956-1425; *Fax:* 212-539-9801

H Huntington Stehli, President/Publisher

Lists of winners at the AR100 Award Show, which recognizes excellence in the field of annual reports; includes photographers, design firms, illustrators, printers and paper companies; includes listings and ads for winners of past shows.
Cost: $60.00
Frequency: Annual
Circulation: 10,000

11437 Complete Directory of Giftware Items
Sutton Family Communications & Publishing Company
920 State Route 54 East
Elmitch, KY 42343

270-276-9500
jlsutton@apex.net

Theresa Sutton, Publisher
Lee Sutton, Editor

Print-out from database of wholesalers, manufacturers, distributors, importers and close-out houses. Database is updated daily to guarantee the most current and up-to-date sources available. Approximately 1,500 American direct wholesale sources in a three-ring binder.
Cost: $107.50
100 Pages

11438 Complete Directory of Tabletop Items
Sutton Family Communications & Publishing Company
920 State Route 54 East
Elmitch, KY 42343

270-276-9500
jlsutton@apex.net

Theresa Sutton, Editor
Lee Sutton, General Manager

Print-out from database of wholesalers, manufacturers, distributors, importers and close-out houses. Database is updated daily to guarantee the most current and up-to-date sources available.
Cost: $54.50
100+ Pages

11439 **Gift Associates Interchange Database**
1100 Main Street
Buffalo, NY 14209

716-885-4444; *Fax:* 716-878-2866

J Warren Wright, Secretary

An online credit interchange database.
240 Pages
Founded in: 1974

11440 **Gift Associates Interchange Network**

716-887-9508
800-746-9428; www.gaingroup.com

Donna Mosteller, Director, Member Group Services
Rosanne Battaglia, Member, Development Representative

GAIN is an online credit interchange database designed by and for credit managers in giftware, greeting card, silk floral, and related industries.
200 Members

11441 **Giftware Manufacturers Credit Interchange**
1100 Main Street
Buffalo, NY 14209-2356

716-885-4444; *Fax:* 716-878-2866;
www.gaingroup.com

J Warren Wright, Executive Secretary

Manufacturers and importers of giftware and china.
60 Pages

Industry Web Sites

11442 **http://gold.greyhouse.com**
G.O.L.D Grey House OnLine Databases

Grey House Publishing's online database platform, GOLD, offers Quick Search, Keyword Search and Expert Search for most business sectors including home and corporate gift markets. The GOLD platform makes finding the information you need quick and easy - whether you're a novice searcher or an experienced database user. All of Grey House's directory products are available for subscription on the GOLD platform.

11443 **www.greyhouse.com**
Grey House Publishing

Authoritative reference directories for most business sectors including home and corporate gift markets. Users can search the online databases with varied search criteria allowing for custom searches by product category, geographic area, sales volume, keyword, subject and more. Full Grey House catalog and online ordering also available.

11444 **www.museumstoreassociation.org**
Museum Store Association

Providing member representatives with the professional opportunities and educational resources they need to operate effectively and ethically.

11445 **www.naled.org**
National Gift Organization

Trade association for the gift and collectibles industry. Offers once yearly expositions, a newsletter, software, low cost credit card processing, telephone service discounts and more to help you run your business profitably.
350 Pages

11446 **www.oasis.org**
Organization of Associated Salespeople Southwest

A gift trade association which represents the manufacturing, sales and distribution side of the giftware industry.

11447 **www.shop.com**
Altura International

CatalogCity.com is a powerful and flexible e-commerce technology. This site includes recognized brand names such as Blair, Bombay, Chef's Catalog, Fisher-Price, Gump's by Mail, Hammacher Schlemmer, Ross-Simmons, The Sharper Image, and many more.

Associations

11448 ASM International Everything Material
Materials Information Society
9639 Kinsman Rd
Materials Park, OH 44073-0002

440-338-5151
800-336-5152; *Fax:* 440-338-4634
memberservicecenter@asminternational.org;
www.asminternational.org

Jon D. Tirpak, President-Elect
Dr. William E. Frazier, Vice President-Elect
Craig D. Clauser, Treasurer-Elect
Ellen K. Cerreta, Trustee-Elect
Ryan M. Deacon, Trustee-Elect

The society for materials engineers and scientists, a worldwide network dedicated to advancing industry, technology and applications of metals and materials.
35000 Members
Founded in: 1913

11449 American Art Pottery Association
aapa.info
Social Media: Facebook, Pinterest

Arnie Small, President

Association of dealers and collectors of American Art Pottery.
Founded in: 1983

11450 American Ceramic Society
600 N. Cleveland Ave.
Suite 210
Westerville, OH 43082

240-646-7054
866-721-3322; *Fax:* 301-206-9789
customerservice@ceramics.org;
www.ceramics.org
Social Media: Facebook, Twitter, LinkedIn, RSS

Charles Spahr, Executive Director
10000 Members
Founded in: 1898

11451 American Cut Glass Association
PO Box 482
Ramona, CA 92065

760-789-2715; *Fax:* 760-789-7112
acgakathy@aol.com; www.cutglass.org
Social Media: Facebook, YouTube

Kathy Emmerson, Executive Secretary
Judy Northrop, President

A non-profit organization devoted to the study and research of American Brilliant Cut Glass.
1500 Members
Founded in: 1978

11452 American Flint Glass Workers Union
1440 S Byrne Road
Toledo, OH 43614-2363

419-385-6687; *Fax:* 419-385-8839
ljs@primenet.com

Timothy Tuttle, President

Organized as the United Flint Glass Workers.
21.7M Members
Founded in: 1878

11453 American Scientific Glassblowers Society
PO Box 453
Machias, NY 14101

716-353-8062; *Fax:* 716-353-4259
natl-office@asgs-glass.org;
www.asgs-glass.org
Social Media: Facebook

Skip Huckaby, President
Joe Gregar, President-Elect
Philip Legge, Secretary
Victor Mathews, Treasurer
Jerry Cloninger, Executive Secretary

A not for profit organization that is dedicated to sharing the knowedge,techniques, and skills of scientific glassblowing to its worldwide membership.
650 Members
Founded in: 1952

11454 Art Glass Association
5610 Pleasant View Dr.
Nashport, OH 43830

740-450-6547
866-301-2421; *Fax:* 661-264-5277;
www.artglassassociation.com

Steve Shupper, Chairman
Jennifer Urbaniak, Vice Chair
Bill Bird, Treasurer
Craig Bradley, Secretary
Vickie Gillespie, Membership

International, nonprofit organization whose purpose is to create awareness, knowledge and involvement for the growth and prosperity of the art glass industry. Programs include an annual conference, group health insurance, marchant listings on our website and more.
Founded in: 1986

11455 Ceramic Tile Distributors Association
800 Roosevelt Rd
Building C, Suite 312
Glen Ellyn, IL 60137-5899

630-545-9415
800-938-2832; *Fax:* 630-790-3095
info@ctdahome.org; www.ctdahome.org

Tom Kotel, President
Heidi Martin, VP
Robert DeAngelis, Treasurer
Bill Ives, Legal Counsel
Rick Church, Executive Director

An international association of distributors, manufacturers and allied professionals of ceramic tile and related products. Mission is to provide educational and networking opportunities for distributors of ceramic tile and their suppliers to further the consumption of ceramic tile.
500 Members
Founded in: 1978

11456 Ceramic Tile Institute of America
12061 Jefferson Blvd.
Culver City, CA 90230-6219

310-574-7800; *Fax:* 310-821-4655
ctioa@earthlink.net; www.ctioa.org

Thomas Brady, Board Member
Michael J, Nisenbaum, Board Member
Thomas Domenici, Board Member
Lindell Lummer, Board Member
Bill Klaser, Board Member

Promoting excellence in tile installation and encouraging greater consumption of tile through education, public relations and liaison with all facets of the construction industry as well as the general public.
Founded in: 1992

11457 China Clay Producers Association-CCPA
113 Arkwright Landing
Macon, GA 31210

478-757-1211; *Fax:* 478-757-1949
info@georgiamining.org; www.kaolin.com/

Lee Lemke, Executive VP

Organized to advance and encourage the development and production of kaolin-based products, and to work together with the people of Georgia in the communities where the mineral is mined and products manufactured.
Founded in: 1978

11458 Glass Art Society
6512 23rd Ave. NW
Suite 329
Seattle, WA 98117

206-382-1305; *Fax:* 206-382-2630
info@glassart.org; www.glassart.org
Social Media: Facebook, Twitter, LinkedIn, Pinterest

Cassandra Straubing, President
Kim Harty, Vice President
Natali Rodrigues, VP
Roger MacPherson, Treasurer
Kelly Conway, Director

International nonprofit organization encouraging excellence, advancing education, promoting appreciation and development of the glass arts, and supporting the worldwide community of artists who work with glass. Members are artists, students, educators, collectors, gallery and museum personnel, writers and critics.
3100 Members
Founded in: 1971

11459 Glass Association of North America
800 SW Jackson St.
Suite 1500
Topeka, KS 66612-1200

785-271-0208; *Fax:* 785-271-0166
gana@glasswebsite.com;
www.glasswebsite.com

William M Yanek, Executive VP
Ashley M Charest, Account Executive
Urmilla Sowell, Technical Director
Sara Neiswanger, Technical Coordinator
Erin Roberts, Director of Marketing

Offers education on blueprint reading, labor and glass estimating and analysis; manuals on glazing guidelines, sealant compatibility and labor hours and a quarterly newsletter. Serves distributors, installers and fabricators of glass for use in the construction automotive and industrial industries.
250 Members
Founded in: 1994

11460 Insulating Glass Certification Council
PO Box 730
Sackets Harbor, NY 13685

315-646-2234; *Fax:* 315-646-2297
erin@amscert.com; www.igcc.org

Erin Ackley, Administrative Staff
John G Kent, Administrative Staff
Don Boutelle, President
Bruce Kaskel, Vice President
Brian Burnet, Secretary

IGCC sponsors and directs an independent, true third-party certification program. Periodic accelerated laboratory tests, per American Society for Testing and Materials specifications, and unannounced plant quality audits and inspections assure the quality and performance of sealed insulating glass products.
48 Members
Founded in: 1977

11461 National Glass Association
1945 Old Gallows Rd
Suite 750
Vienna, VA 22182

703-442-4890
866-342-5642; *Fax:* 703-442-0630
nga@glass.org; www.glass.org
Social Media: Facebook, Twitter, LinkedIn

Philip J. James, President & CEO
Nicole Harris, Vice President & Publisher
Denise M Sheehan, VP, Industry Events

James Gandorf, VP, Association Services
Pamela S Paroline, Director, Administration & Finance

The National Glass Association is the largest trade association representing the flat (architectural and automotive) glass industy. Member companies and locations reflect the entire vertical flat glass market. To support this ever changing industry, NGA produces products and services specifically for the industry.
4900 Members
Founded in: 1948

11462 National Industrial Sand Association
2011 Pennsylvania Avenue, NW
Suite 301
Washington, DC 20006

202-457-0200; *Fax:* 202-457-0287
info@sand.org; www.sand.org

Mark Ellis, President
Darrell K. Smith, Ph.D, Executive Vice President
Chris Greissing, VP Government Affairs
Paige Huggins, Financial Assistant

Trade association representing major manufacturers of industrial sand in North America. Committed to the safe use of industrial sand products and to advancing research and maintaining a dialogue with industry, legislators, regulatory agencies and the scientific community in support of the safety of empoyees and customers.
Founded in: 1936

11463 Porcelain Enamel Institute
PO Box 920220
Norcross, GA 30010

770-676-9366; *Fax:* 770-409-7280
penamel@aol.com; www.porcelainenamel.com
Social Media: Twitter, LinkedIn, RSS

Cullen Hackler, Executive Director
Kevin Coursin, Chairman
Glenn Pfendt, President
Phil Flasher, Treasurer
Cullen Hackler, Executive VP and Secretary

Dedicated to advancing the common interests of porcelain enameling plants and suppliers of porcelain enameling materials and equipment.
85 Members
Founded in: 1930

11464 Refractory Ceramic Fiber Coalition
1200 Seventeenth Street, NW
Room 07-54
Washington, DC 20036-3006

202-663-9188; *Fax:* 202-354-4982;
www.htiwcoalition.org

An association of the leading US producers of refractory ceramic fibers(RCFs). The RCF Coalition develops and promotes proper work practices and standards for the RCF industry, conducts RCF health research and disseminates information on the proper handling and use of refractory ceramic fiber.
Founded in: 1992

11465 Safety Glazing Certification Council
100 West Main Street
PO Box 730
Sackets Harbor, NY 13685

315-646-2234; *Fax:* 315-646-2297
staff@amscert.com; www.sgcc.org

Bill Nugent, President
Bernie Herron, Vice President
June Willcott, Secretary
Elaine S. Rodman, Treasurer

A nonprofit corporation that provides for the certification of safety glazing materials. Comprised of safety glazing manufacturers and other parties concerned with public safety.
105 Members
Founded in: 1971

11466 Society of Glass and Ceramic Decorated Products (SGCDpro)
47 N 4th Street
PO Box 2489
Zanesville, OH 43702

740-588-9882; *Fax:* 740-588-0245
info@sgcd.org; www.sgcd.org

Ed Weiner, President

Membership gives decorators and marketers of glass, ceramic and related products the confidence that they are part of a network of professionals who have shared knowledge and resources for nearly 50 years. Helps industry professionals identify new and profitable technology, keeps members abreast of the latest regulatory mandates and works with government and industry to provide reasonable solutions to regulatory compliance.
525 Members

11467 Stained Glass Association of America
9313 East 63rd Street
Raytown, MO 64133

816-737-2090
800-438-9581; *Fax:* 816-737-2801
headquarters@sgaaonline.com;
www.stainedglass.org
Social Media: Facebook, Twitter

Membership consists of the finest architectural stained and decorative art glass artists and studios in the US and around the world. Actively works for the betterment of the craft of stained glass and architectural art glass through various programs that are designed to benefit the members of the SGAA and the clients whom we serve.
Founded in: 1903

11468 Technical Ceramics Manufacturers Association
25 N Broadway
Tarrytown, NY 10591-3221

914-332-0040; *Fax:* 914-332-1541

A organization of manufacturers of custom and standard technical ceramic products for use in commercial, residential or industrial applications.

11469 The American Ceramic Society
600 N Cleveland Ave.
Suite 210
Westerville, OH 43082

240-646-7054
866-721-3322; *Fax:* 240-396-5637
customerservice@ceramics.org
ceramics.org
Social Media: Facebook, Twitter, LinkedIn, Google+, YouTube

Charlie Spahr, Executive Director

The National Institute of Ceramic Engineers, the Ceramic Manufacturing Council and the Ceramic Education Council are affiliated groups. All are leading organizations dedicated to the advancement of ceramics.
10000 Members
Founded in: 1898

11470 United States Advanced Ceramics Association
1020 19th St NW
Suite 375
Washington, DC 20036-6118

202-467-5459; *Fax:* 202-467-5469
usaca@strategicmi.com;
www.advancedceramics.org

Todd E Steyer, Chairman
Steve Johnson, Vice Chair
Tom Foltz, Treasurer
Kent W Buesking, Secretary
Glen Mandigo, Executive Director

The premier association that champions the common business interests of the advanced ceramic producer and end user industries.
Founded in: 1985

11471 Wedgwood Society of Boston

E-Mail: wedgwoodboston@gmail.com
wedgwoodsociety.org

Jeremy Hagger, 1st Vice President
Lorraine C. Horn, Corporate Secretary
Edward C. McCabe, Recording Secretary
Ronald F. Frazier, Treasurer

Organization for those who appreciate the work of the potter Josiah Wedgwood and related decorative arts.
Founded in: 1969

11472 Wedgwood Society of New York
7 Palatine Ct.
Syosset, NY 11791-1105

E-Mail: info@wsny.org; www.wsny.org

Organization for collectors of Wedgwood. Holds auctions and publishes a widely read newsletter.
Founded in: 1957

Newsletters

11473 American Ceramic Society Bulletin
The American Ceramic Society
600 N. Cleveland Ave.
Suite 210
Westerville, OH 43082

866-720-3322; *Fax:* 301-206-9789
customerservice@ceramics.org;
www.ceramics.org

L David Pye, President
Scott Steen, Executive Director

The undisputed authority on news and new developments in the Ceramics and Glass industries, focuses on five end-use industries: transportation, electronics, defense, energy and construction.
Cost: $75.00
Frequency: 9x Yearly
Circulation: 10,000
ISSN: 0002-7812
Founded in: 1898
Printed in 4 colors on glossy stock

11474 The Hobstar
American Cut Glass Association
PO Box 482
Ramona, CA 92065

760-789-2715; *Fax:* 760-789-7112
acgakathy@aol.com; www.cutglass.org

ACGA's highly educational journal.
Frequency: 10x Yearly
Founded in: 1876
Printed in 2 colors on glossy stock

11475 WDweekly
National Glass Association
1945 Old Gallows Rd
Suite 750
Vienna, VA 22182

703-442-4890
866-342-5642; *Fax:* 703-442-0630
nga@glass.org; www.glass.org
Social Media: Facebook, Twitter, LinkedIn

Philip J. James, President & CEO
Nicole Harris, Vice President & Publisher
John Swanson, Editor & Associate Publisher

E-newsletter for manufacturers, distributors and dealers. The most thorough, convenient source for the latest industry news and insights on market, design, technology and economic trends.
4900 Members
Frequency: Weekly

Circulation: 30000
Founded in: 1948

Magazines & Journals

11476 **AGRR Magazine**
Key Communications
PO Box 569
Garrisonville, VA 22463

540-577-7174; *Fax:* 540-720-5687
info@agrrmag.com; www.agrrmag.com
Social Media: Facebook, Twitter, LinkedIn

Debra Levy, Publisher
Megan Headley, President

Source of unbiased, accurate information about auto glass repair and replacement industry.
Cost: $49.95
Frequency: 6x Yearly
Circulation: 10000+
Founded in: 1993

11477 **Advanced Materials & Processes**
ASM International
9639 Kinsman Rd
Materials Park, OH 44073

440-338-5151
800-336-5152; *Fax:* 440-338-4634;
www.asminternational.org

Joseph M Zion, Publisher
Joanne Miller, Managing Editor
Margaret Hunt, Editor-in-Chief

Covers the latest developments in materials technology.
Frequency: Monthly
Circulation: 32M
Founded in: 1977

11478 **American Flint Magazine**
American Flint Glass Workers Union
1440 S Byrne Road
Toledo, OH 43614-2363

419-385-6687; *Fax:* 419-385-8839

Timothy Tuttle, President

Union news and information for the glass industry.
Frequency: Monthly

11479 **Ceramic Bulletin**
American Ceramic Society
600 N. Cleveland Avenue
Suite 210
Westerville, OH 43082

240-646-7054
866-721-3322; *Fax:* 240-396-5637
customerservice@ceramics.org;
www.ceramics.org

L David Pye, President
Scott Steen, Executive Director

Written for ceramic and materials engineers and production management teams involved in industrial ceramics manufacturing. Topics covered include government relations, environmental issues, developing technology, industry statistics, cutting-edge manufacturing processes and technology.
Cost: $75.00
Frequency: Monthly
Circulation: 50000
ISSN: 0027-812
Founded in: 1953
Printed in 4 colors on glossy stock

11480 **Ceramic Industry**
Business News Publishing Company
6075 B Glick Rd
Powell, OH 43065

281-550-5855; *Fax:* 248-244-6439
ci@halldata.com; www.ceramicindustry.com

Amy Vallance, Publisher
Susan Sutton, Editor in Chief/Integrated Media
Teresa Mcpherson, Managing Editor
Cory Emery, Art Director
Karen Telan, Production Manager

Serves manufacturers of advanced ceramics, glass, whitewares, refractories and other ceramic businesses. CI's offerings include practical, real-world solutions to manufacturing problems, information on the latest technological advancements, and up-to-date coverage of news, issues and trends.
Frequency: Monthly
Circulation: 10000
Founded in: 1926

11481 **Ceramics Monthly**
American Ceramic Society
735 Ceramic Pl
Suite 100
Westerville, OH 43081-8728

614-895-4213; *Fax:* 614-891-8960
editorial@ceramicsmonthly.org;
www.ceramicsmonthly.org

Sherman Hall, Editor
Rich Guerrein, Publisher
Jennifer Poellot, Assistant editor
Susan Enderle, Marketing Manager
Erin Pfeifer, Advertising Manager

An internationally distributed magazine covering ceramic arts and crafts. Includes lists of conferences, exhibitions, festivals, fairs, sales and workshops for crafts people.
Cost: $32.00
Frequency: Monthly
Circulation: 35000
ISSN: 0009-0328
Founded in: 1953
Printed in on glossy stock

11482 **Fired Arts and Crafts**
Jones Publishing
N7450 Aanstad Road
PO Box 5000
Iola, WI 54945-5000

715-445-5000
800-331-0038; *Fax:* 715-445-4053
jonespub@jonespublishing.com;
www.jonespublishing.com

Joe Jones, CEO/President
Mick Harbridge, Editor
Branden Hardy, Marketing

Features on projects and patterns, celebrity clips, new products, show listings, industry news and book reviews.
Cost: $32.95
Frequency: Monthly
Circulation: 15000

11483 **Fusion**
American Scientific Glassblowers Society
PO Box 778
Madison, NC 27025

336-427-2406; *Fax:* 336-427-2496
natl-office@asgs-glass.org;
www.asgs-glass.org

Marylin Brown, Editor

Contains technical articles, references and abstracts from other publications, book reviews, new product information, local section reports and announcements, committee reports, and information about health and safety concerns. An excellent source for vendor information with ads of goods and services.
Cost: $40.00
Frequency: Quarterly
Circulation: 850
Founded in: 1954

11484 **Glass Craftsman**
Arts & Media
10 Canal Street
Suite 300
Bristol, PA 19007

215-826-1799; *Fax:* 215-826-1788
webmaster@artglassworld.com;
www.artglassworld.com

Joe Porcelli, Publisher

Providing the best professionally produced, technical, aesthetic and practical information to its readers and a strong, committed audience of glass enthusiasts and professionals to its family of advertisers.
Cost: $25.00
Circulation: 12000
ISSN: 1079-199X

11485 **Glass Magazine**
National Glass Association
1945 Old Gallows Rd
Suite 750
Vienna, VA 22182

703-448-1319; *Fax:* 703-442-0630;
www.glassmagazine.com

Nicole Harris, VP
Nancy Davis, Editor-in-Chief

Provides subscribers informative coverage of glass industry news, trends and analysis, product introductions, and best business practices, in addition to glass industry statistics and supplier resource guides.
Cost: $34.95
Frequency: 11x Yearly
Circulation: 27098
Founded in: 1948

11486 **Journal of Materials Engineering and Performance**
ASM International
9639 Kinsman Road
Materials Park, OH 44073-0002

440-338-5151
800-336-5152; *Fax:* 440-338-4634;
www.asminternational.org

Jeffrey A. Hawk, Editor
Rajiv Asthana, Associate Editor
Narandra Dahotre, Associate Editor
Omar S. Es-Said, Associate Editor

Covers all aspects of materials selection, design, processing, characterization and evaluation, including how to improve materials properties through processes and process control of casting, forming, heat treating, surface modification and coating, and fabrication.
Cost: $1965.00
Frequency: Bimonthly
Circulation: 305
Founded in: 1992

11487 **Journal of Phase Equilibria and Diffusion**
ASM International
9639 Kinsman Rd
Materials Park, OH 44072

440-338-5151
800-336-5152; *Fax:* 440-338-4634;
www.asminternational.org

J.F. Smith, Editor
John Morral, Deputy Editor
H. Okamoto, Supplemental Lit. Review Editor

Covers the significance of diagrams as well as new research techniques, equipment, data evaluation, nomenclature, presentation and other as-

pects of phase diagram preparation and use. Content includes information on phenomena such as kinetic control of equilibrium, coherency effects, impurity effects, and thermodynamic and crystallographic characteristics.
Frequency: Bimonthly
Circulation: 305

11488 Journal of the American Ceramic Society
American Ceramic Society
735 Ceramic Pl
Suite 100
Westerville, OH 43081

866-721-3322; *Fax:* 301-206-9789
customerservice@ceramics.org;
www.ceramics.org

David J. Green, Associate Editor
David W. Johnson, Jr., Associate Editor
Lisa Klein, Associate Editor
John Halloran, Associate Editor

Contains records of original research that provide or lead to fundamental principles in the science of ceramics and ceramic-based composites. These papers include reports of the discovery of new phases, phase relationships, processing approaches and microstructures that relate to ceramic materials and processes.
Cost: $1190.00
Frequency: Monthly
ISSN: 0002-7820
Founded in: 1905

11489 Pottery Making Illustrated
Ceramic Publications Company
735 Ceramic Pl
Suite 100
Westerville, OH 43081

866-721-3322; *Fax:* 301-206-9789
customerservice@ceramics.org;
www.ceramics.org

Charlie Spahr, Publisher
Bill Jones, Editor
Mona Thiel, Advertising Manager
Steve Hecker, Marketing Manager
Erin Pfeifer, Editorial Assistant

Provides intermediate to advanced potters with practical techniques, tips and information for the studio in a well-illustrated format. With articles on throwing, handbuilding, sculpture, decorating and firing, PMI covers every aspect of the studio ceramic process. In addition, PMI provides up-to-date information on tools, supplies and materials for the ceramic studio.
Cost: $22.00
Frequency: Bi-Monthly
Circulation: 20000
Founded in: 1905

11490 Stained Glass
Stained Glass Association of America
9313 East 63rd Street
Raytown, MO 64133

816-737-2090
800-438-9581; *Fax:* 816-737-2801
headquarters@sgaaonline.com;
www.stainedglass.org
Social Media: Facebook, Twitter

Features articles about historical and contemporary installations that will show you what others in the field are doing.
Frequency: Quarterly
Founded in: 1903

11491 The Hobstar
American Cut Glass Association
PO Box 482
Ramona, CA 92065

760-789-2715; *Fax:* 760-789-7112
acgakathy@aol.com; www.cutglass.org
Social Media: Facebook, YouTube

Kathy Emmerson, Executive Secretary
Karen Parker, President

ACGA's highly educational journal.
1500 Members
Frequency: 10x Yearly
Founded in: 1978

11492 US Glass, Metal & Glazing
Key Communications
PO Box 569
Garrisonville, VA 22463

540-577-7174; *Fax:* 540-720-5687
scarpenter@glass.com; www.usglassmag.com
Social Media: Facebook, Twitter, LinkedIn

Penny Stacey, Advertising Coordinator
Ellen Giard Chilcoat, Editor
Debra Levy, President

Serves manufactures/fabricators, contract glaziers, distributors and wholesalers, retailors/dealers of glass/metal and/or glass/metal products and others allied to the field.
Frequency: Monthly
Circulation: 25572
ISSN: 0041-7661
Founded in: 1965
Printed in 4 colors on glossy stock

11493 Window & Door
National Glass Association
1945 Old Gallows Rd
Suite 750
Vienna, VA 22182

703-442-4890
866-342-5642; *Fax:* 703-442-0630
nga@glass.org; www.glass.org
Social Media: Facebook, Twitter, LinkedIn

Philip J. James, President & CEO
Nicole Harris, Vice President & Publisher
John Swanson, Editor & Associate Publisher

Serves the entire fenestration industry, including manufacturers, distributors, and dealers. Offers readers focused news coverage, insightful articles on market and design trends, regular columns on codes, legal issues, and marketing ideas, full coverage of new products, expert articles on operations and technology, and much more.
4900 Members
Frequency: 8x Yearly
Founded in: 1948

Trade Shows

11494 ACGA Annual Convention
PO Box 482
Ramona, CA 92065-0482

760-789-2715; *Fax:* 760-789-7112
acgakathy@aol.com; www.cutglass.org

Kathy Emmerson, Executive Secretary
Karen Parker, President

Opportunity to learn about cut glass.
Frequency: Annual/July

11495 ASM Heat Treating Society Conference & Exposition
ASM International
9639 Kinsman Road
Materials Park, OH 44073-0002

440-338-5151
800-336-5152; *Fax:* 440-338-4634
pamela.kleinman@asminternational.org;
www.asminternational.org

Pamela Kleinma, Senior Manager, Events
Kellye Thomas, Exposition Account Manager

The ASM Heat Treating Society and the American Gear Manufacturers Association partner to create a mix of education, technology, networking and exposition opportunities.
3500 Attendees
Frequency: Bi-Annual
Founded in: 1974

11496 AeroMat Conference and Exposition
ASM International
9639 Kinsman Road
Materials Park, OH 44073-0002

440-338-5151
800-336-5152; *Fax:* 440-338-4634;
www.asminternational.org

Kim Schaefer, Event Manager
Kelly Thomas, Exposition Account Manager

Brings together hundreds of delegates and exhibiting companies to discuss and display the latest advances in materials and processes for aerospace applications. AeroMat is the world's leading aerospace conference devoted entirely to materials and processes used in the fabrication of flight vehicles. Learn the latest technologies in aerospace materials, research and processes.
1500 Attendees
Frequency: Annual/June
Founded in: 1984

11497 American Ceramic Society Annual Meeting and Expo
600 N. Cleveland Ave.
Suite 210
Westerville, OH 43082

866-721-3322; *Fax:* 240-396-5637
customerservice@ceramics.org;
www.ceramics.org

George Wicks, President
Richard Brow, President-Elect
Ted Day, Treasurer
Charlie Spahr, Executive Director

Three-hundred booths of ceramic materials, products manufacturing, testing, processing, research, components and software. Technical conference on ceramic materials research and development with over 1000 papers presented in more than 25 topical areas.
2,500 Attendees
Frequency: Annual/April

11498 American Scientific Glassblowers Exhibition
American Scientific Glassblowers Society
PO Box 453
Machias, NY 14101

716-353-8062; *Fax:* 716-353-4259
natl-office@asgs-glass.org;
www.asgs-glass.org

Patrick DeFlorio, President
Frank Meints, President-Elect
Steven Moder, Secretary
Victor Mathews, Treasurer
Jerry Cloninger, Executive Secretary

Great opportunity to expand glassblowing knowledge through seminars, demonstrations, technical papers and posters.
650 Members
Frequency: Annual/June
Founded in: 1952

11499 BEC Conference
Glass Association of North America

800 SW Jackson St.
Suite 1500
Topeka, KS 66612-1200

785-271-0208; *Fax:* 785-271-0166;
www.glasswebsite.com

William M Yanek, Executive VP
Ashley M Charest, Account Executive
Urmilla Sowell, Technical Director

Features educational seminars for glazing contractors and executives in contracting companies.
Frequency: Annual/March

11500 **DECO**
Society of Glass & Ceramic Decorators
4340 E West Highway
Suite 200
Bethesda, MD 20814

301-986-9800; *Fax:* 301-951-3801;
www.sgcd.org

Focusing on technical and regulatory issues affecting glass and ceramic decorators.

11501 **Dealers Show of the American Cut Glass Association**
American Cut Glass Association
PO Box 482
Ramona, CA 92065-0482

760-789-2715; *Fax:* 760-789-7112
acgakathy@aol.com; www.cutglass.org

Kathy Emmerson, Executive Secretary

Annual show and exhibits of American brilliant period cut glass and related articles.

11502 **Electronic Materials and Applications**
American Ceramic Society
600 N. Cleveland Ave.
Suite 210
Westerville, OH 43082

240-646-7054
866-721-3322; *Fax:* 301-206-9789
customerservice@ceramics.org;
www.ceramics.org

Charles Spahr, Executive Director

Focuses on electronic materials for energy generation, conversion and storage applications.
10000 Members
Frequency: Annual/January
Founded in: 1898

11503 **GANA Annual Conference**
Glass Association of North America
800 SW Jackson St.
Suite 1500
Topeka, KS 66612-1200

785-271-0208; *Fax:* 785-271-0166;
www.glasswebsite.com

William M Yanek, Executive VP
Ashley M Charest, Account Executive
Urmilla Sowell, Technical Director

Seven Divisions of GANA have meetings planned at this event, along with the non-Division Committees including Fire-Rated Glazing, Glazing Industry Code Committee, Marketing, and Protective Glazing.
250 Members
Founded in: 1994

11504 **Glass & Optical Materials Division Annual Meeting**
American Ceramic Society
600 N. Cleveland Ave.
Suite 210
Westerville, OH 43082

240-646-7054
866-721-3322; *Fax:* 301-206-9789
customerservice@ceramics.org;
www.ceramics.org

Charles Spahr, Executive Director

Involving the physical properties and technological processes important to glasses, amorphous solids and optical materials.
10000 Members
Frequency: Annual/May
Founded in: 1898

11505 **Glass Art Society Conference**
Glass Art Society
6512 23rd Ave. NW
Suite 329
Seattle, WA 98117

206-382-1305; *Fax:* 206-382-2630
info@glassart.org; www.glassart.org

Jeremy Lepisto, President
Jutta-Annette Page, Vice-President
Caroline Madden, Secretary
Lance Friedman, Treasurer

Annual conference and exhibits for those who make, collect, exhibit and appreciate objects made with glass.
2000 Attendees
Frequency: Annual/June

11506 **Glass Craft Exposition**
Las Vegas Management
2408 Chapman Drive
Las Vegas, NV 89104

702-734-0070
800-217-4527; *Fax:* 702-734-0636;
www.glasscraftexpo.com

Shirley Harvey, Director

Learn new techniques and create new things.
3500 Attendees
Frequency: Annual/March

11507 **Glass Expo Midwest**
US Glass Magazine
PO Box 569
Garrisonville, VA 22463

540-720-5584; *Fax:* 540-720-5687
expos@glass.com; www.glassexpos.com/

Patrick Smith, Marketing Manager

Annual show and exhibits of flat, container, heavy insulated and tempered glass, architectural sealants and hardware, mirror products and windows and doors.
800 Attendees
Frequency: Annual/August

11508 **Glass TEXpo**
Key Communications, Inc.
PO Box 569
Garrisonville, VA 22463-0569

540-720-5584; *Fax:* 540-720-5687
expos@glass.com; www.glassexpos.com

Patrick Smith, Marketing Manager

Annual show and exhibits of flat, container, heavy insulated and tempered glass, architectural sealants and hardware, mirror products and windows and doors. Hosted in Dallas, TX.
700 Attendees
Frequency: Annual/October

11509 **International Conference and Expo on Advanced Ceramics and Composites**
American Ceramic Society
600 N. Cleveland Ave.
Suite 210
Westerville, OH 43082

240-646-7054
866-721-3322; *Fax:* 301-206-9789
customerservice@ceramics.org;
www.ceramics.org

George Wicks, President
Richard Brow, President-Elect
Ted Day, Treasurer
Charlie Spahr, Executive Director

Showcases cutting-edge research and product developments in advanced ceramics, armor ceramics, solid oxide fuel cells, ceramic coating, bioceramics and more.
Frequency: Annual/January

11510 **International Conference and Exposition on Advanced Ceramics & Composites**
American Ceramic Society
600 N. Cleveland Ave.
Suite 210
Westerville, OH 43082

240-646-7054
866-721-3322; *Fax:* 301-206-9789
customerservice@ceramics.org;
www.ceramics.org

Charles Spahr, Executive Director

Showcases cutting-edge research and product developments in advanced ceramics, armor ceramics, solid oxide fuel cells, ceramic coatings, bioceramics and more.
10000 Members
Frequency: Annual/January
Founded in: 1898

11511 **International Glass Show**
Dame Associates
100 Lincoln Street
Boston, MA 02135

617-783-4777
800-843-3263; *Fax:* 617-783-4787;
www.dameassoc.com

Annual show of 115 manufacturers and suppliers of windows, doors, sun enclosures, windshields and mirrors, glass, machinery, hardware and insulating units, sealants, adhesives, mastic, security glazing and thermal barriers, aluminum, curtain wall computers and trucks.
2500 Attendees
Frequency: Annual/May

11512 **International Symposium for Testing and Failure Analysis**
ASM International
9639 Kinsman Road
Materials Park, OH 44073-0002

440-338-5151
800-336-5152; *Fax:* 440-338-4634
pamela.kleinman@asminternational.org;
www.asminternational.org

Pamela Kleinman, Senior Manager, Events
Kelly Thomas, Exposition Account Manager

Annual event focusing on testing, analysis, characterization and research of materials such as engineered materials, high performance metals, powdered metals, metal forming, surface modification, welding and joining.
4,000 Attendees
Frequency: Annual/October
Founded in: 2005

11513 **International Thermal Spray Conference & Exposition**
ASM International
9639 Kinsman Road
Materials Park, OH 44073

440-338-5151
800-336-5152; *Fax:* 440-338-4634
natalie.nemec@asminternational.org;
www.asminternational.org

Natalie Neme, Event Manager
Kelly Thomas, Exposition Account Manager

Global annual event attracting professional interested in thermal spray technology focusing on advances in HVOF, plasma and detonation gun, flame spray and wire arc spray processes, performance of coatings, and future trends. 150 exhibitors.
1000 Attendees
Frequency: Annual/May

11514 **International Window Film Conference and Expo**
Window Film Magazine
PO Box 569
Garrisonville, VA 22463-0569

540-720-5584; *Fax:* 540-720-5687
expos@glass.com; www.glassexpos.com

Patrick Smith, Marketing Manager

Numerous opportunities to network, socialize, and learn from others in the window film industry.
Frequency: Annual/March

11515 **MCARE: Materials Challenges in Alternative & Renewable Energy**
American Ceramic Society
600 N. Cleveland Ave.
Suite 210
Westerville, OH 43082

240-646-7054
866-721-3322; *Fax:* 301-206-9789
customerservice@ceramics.org;
www.ceramics.org

Charles Spahr, Executive Director

Facilitates information sharing on the latest developments involving materials for alternative and renewable energy systems. Emphasis will be on materials challenges and innovations in areas of solar energy, wind power, hydro, geothermal, biomass, nuclear, hydrogen, electric grid, materials availability, nanocomposites/manomaterials, and battery and energy storage.
10000 Members
Frequency: Annual/February
Founded in: 1898

11516 **Porcelain Enamel Institute Technical Forum & Suppliers Mart**
4004 Hillsboro Pike
Suite B224
Nashville, TN 37215-2722

615-385-5357; *Fax:* 615-385-5463
penamel@aol.com; www.porcelainenamel.com

Cullen Hackler, Executive VP
Patricia Melton, Executive Secretary

Members include suppliers and makers of porcelain enamel products and raw materials. Attendees of the PEI conference and workshops attend this show. There will be 20 booths.
250 Attendees
Frequency: Annual/May
Founded in: 1989

11517 **Seattle Gift Show**
George Little Management
10 Bank Street
Suite 1200
White Plains, NY 10606

914-486-6070
800-272-7469; *Fax:* 914-948-2918;
www.washingtongiftshow.com

Louise Seeber, Show Manager
Laura Scott, Exhibit Sales Manager
George Little II, President

See new products and proven bestsellers that cater to the eclectic tastes of the discerning Pacific Northwest consumer.
6000 Attendees
Frequency: Annual/January

Directories & Databases

11518 **Ceramic Abstracts**
American Ceramic Society
600 N. Cleveland Ave.
Suite 210
Westerville, OH 43081

240-646-7054
866-721-3322; *Fax:* 240-396-5637
customerservice@ceramics.org;
www.ceramics.org

Charles Spahr, Executive Director

Abstracting/indexing publication covering ceramic materials-related literature. 15,000 entries published annually.
Frequency: Bi-Monthly
Circulation: 2,500

11519 **CeramicSOURCE**
American Ceramic Society
735 Ceramic Pl
Suite 100
Westerville, OH 43081-8728

614-904-4700; *Fax:* 614-794-5892;
www.ceramicsource.org

Patricia Janeway, Editor
Marc Bailey, Director Global Marketing

Annual buyer's guide/directory of equipment and materials' suppliers to the industrial ceramic manufacturing market.
Cost: $25.00
Frequency: 1 issue
Circulation: 14,500
ISSN: 0002-7812
Founded in: 1985
Printed in 4 colors on glossy stock

11520 **Complete Directory of Glassware & Glass Items**
Sutton Family Communications & Publishing Company
920 State Route 54 East
Elmitch, KY 42343

270-276-9500
jlsutton@apex.net

Theresa Sutton, Publisher
Lee Sutton, Editor

Print-out from database of wholesalers, manufacturers, distributors, importers and close-out houses. Database is updated daily to guarantee the most current and up-to-date sources available. Over 800 American firms which sell direct to small retailers, in three-ring binder format.
Cost: $94.50
100 Pages

11521 **Complete Guide: US Advanced Ceramic Industry**
Business Communications Company
49 Walnut Park
Building 2
Wellesley, MA 02481-1713

866-285-7215; *Fax:* 781-489-7308
sales@bccresearch.com; www.bccresearch.com

David Nydam, President
Kevin R. Fitzgerald, Editorial Director
Andrew Hunt, Marketing Director

Approximately 450 companies and institutions involved in the advanced ceramic industry in the US.

11522 **Data Book and Buyers' Guide**
Ceramic Industry
2540 Billingsley Road
Business News Publishing Company
Columbus, OH 43235-1990

Fax: 440-498-9121

List of over 1300 suppliers of equipment and materials for the advanced and traditional ceramics and heavy clay products.
Cost: $25.00
Frequency: Biennially

11523 **Glass Factory Directory of North America**
Glass News
Box 2267
Hempstead, NY 11551-2267

516-481-2188; www.glassfactorydir.com

Liz Scott, Editor

Over 600 glass manufacturers and plants in the US, Canada and Mexico.
Cost: $25.00
Frequency: Annually
Circulation: 1,500

11524 **Porcelain Enamel Institute Source List**
4004 Hillsboro Pike
Suite B224
Nashville, TN 37215-2722

615-385-5357; *Fax:* 615-385-5463
penamel@aol.com; www.porcelainenamel.com

Tom Sanford, Executive VP
Patricia Melton, Executive Secretary
Frequency: Annual/Fall
Founded in: 1930

11525 **Society of Glass & Ceramic Decorating Products Directory**
Society of Glass & Ceramic Decorating Products
PO Box 2489
Zanesville, OH 43702

740-588-9882; *Fax:* 740-588-0245
info@sgcd.org; www.sgcd.org

Directory of more than 700 member manufacturers, suppliers, decorators and designers of glass and ceramics; international coverage indexed by product type and decorating technology.
Cost: $250.00
172 Pages
Frequency: Annual
Circulation: 800
Founded in: 1964

11526 **US Glass, Metal & Glazing: Buyers Guide**
Key Communications
PO Box 569
Garrisonville, VA 22463-0569

540-577-7174; *Fax:* 540-720-5687;
www.usglass.com

Debra A Levy, Publisher

About 3,000 suppliers of glass and glazing supplies for the glass, metal and glazing industry.
Cost: $20.00
Frequency: Annual
Circulation: 21,000

Industry Web Sites

11527 **Ceramic Arts Daily**
Ceramic Publications Company

600 N Cleveland Ave.
Suite 210
Westerville, OH 43082

614-794-5843; *Fax:* 614-794-5842
ceramicartsdaily.org

The online community of potters and ceramic artists provides a daily newsletter promoting related products and services as well as tools for learning.

11528 http://gold.greyhouse.com
G.O.L.D Grey House OnLine Databases

Grey House Publishing's online database platform, GOLD, offers Quick Search, Keyword Search and Expert Search for most business sectors including glass and ceramic markets. The GOLD platform makes finding the information you need quick and easy - whether you're a novice searcher or an experienced database user. All of Grey House's directory products are available for subscription on the GOLD platform.

11529 www.acers.org
American Ceramic Society

The National Institute of Ceramic Engineers, the Ceramic Manufacturing Council and the Ceramic Education Council are affiliated classes.

11530 www.advancedceramics.org
United States Advanced Ceramics Association

Promotes the use of advanced ceramic materials in industrial applications.

11531 www.asgs-glass.org
American Scientific Glassblowers Society

Encourages the free exchange of knowledge and the broadening of scientific glassblowing skills to assist scientists, educators and the industry by designing and constructing glass components and scientific apparatus.

11532 www.ceramics.org
American Ceramic Society

The National Institute of Ceramic Engineers, the Ceramic Manufacturing Council and the Ceramic Education Council are affiliated groups.

11533 www.ctdahome.org
Ceramic Tile Distributors Association

Promotes the sales of ceramic tile and similar products.

11534 www.ctioa.org
Ceramic Tile Institute of America

This organization has over 500 member manufacturers of ceramic tile in the western United States.

11535 www.cutglass.org
American Cut Glass Association

A non-profit organization devoted to the study and research of Americal Brilliant Cut Glass.

11536 www.dameassoc.com
Dame Associates

An organization with a biennial show w/250 manufacturers and suppliers of windows, doors, sun enclosures, windshields, mirrors, glass machinery, hardware, insulating units, sealants, adhesives, mastic, security glazing, thermal barriers, aluminum, curtain wall computers and trucks.

11537 www.glass.org
National Glass Association

An organization with an annual show of 325 manufacturers, suppliers and distributors of glass and glass-related products, supplies, equipment, tools and machinery, automotive glazing, equipment/machinery, curtain wall, store front systems, doors/hardware, windows, mirrors, shower/tub enclosures and tools.

11538 www.glasswebsite.com
Glass Association of North America

Offers educational on blueprint reading, labor, and glass estimating and analysis; manuals on glazing guidelines, sealant compatibility and labor hours; and a quarterly newsletter. Serves distributors, installers, fabricators of glass for use in the construction automotive and industrial industries.

11539 www.glasswebsite.com/gicc
Glazing Industry Code Committee

Protects the glass and glazing interests by monitoring, testifying and developing code proposals at the model building and energy codes.

11540 www.greyhouse.com
Grey House Publishing

Authoritative reference directories for most business sectors including glass and ceramic markets. Users can search the online databases with varied search criteria allowing for custom searches by product category, geographic area, sales volume, keyword, subject and more. Full Grey House catalog and online ordering also available.

11541 www.igcc.org
Insulating Glass Certification Council

Sponsors and directs a program of laboratory testing and unannounced plant inspection to ensure continuing product information.

11542 www.igmaonline.org
Insulating Glass Manufacturers Alliance

11543 www.porcelainenamel.com
Porcelain Enamel Institute

Members include suppliers and makers of porcelain enamel products and raw materials.

11544 www.sgcc.org
Safety Glazing Certification Council

Information center for this nonprofit corporation that provides for the certification of safety glazing materials.

Associations

11545 Academy for State and Local Government
444 N Capitol St NW
Washington, DC 20001-1512
202-434-4850; *Fax:* 202-434-4851
The policy center for the national organizations for the chief elected and appointed officials for state and local governments, functioning as their joint technical assistance, training and research organization. Its mission is to promote cooperation among federal, state and local governments.

11546 American Association of State Highway and Transportation Officials
444 N Capitol St NW
Suite 249
Washington, DC 20001-1539
202-624-5800; *Fax:* 202-624-5806
info@aashto.org; www.transportation.org
Social Media: Facebook, Twitter
Mike Hancock, President
John Cox, Vice-President
Carlos Braceras, Secretary/ Treasurer
Bud Wright, Executive Director
Selim Amah, Accounts Payable Specialist
Membership is composed of highway and transportation departments in the 50 states, the District of Columbia, and Puerto Rico.
52 Members

11547 American Conference of Governmental Industrial Hygienists (NCGIH)
1330 Kemper Meadow Drive
Cincinnati, OH 45240
513-742-2020; *Fax:* 513-742-3355
mail@acgih.org; www.acgih.org
Social Media: Facebook, Twitter, LinkedIn, Google+
J Torey Nalbone, Chair
John S. Morawetz, ScM, Treasurer
Jeff Washington, Deputy Executive Director
A Anthony Rizzuto, Executive Director
India Vargas, Administrative Assistant
A professional society of government and university employees engaged in a full program of industrial hygiene.
Founded in: 1938

11548 American Correctional Association
206 N Washington St
Alexandria, VA 22314-2528
703-224-0000
800-222-5646; *Fax:* 703-224-0179
jeffw@aca.org; www.aca.org
Social Media: Facebook, Twitter
Jeff Washington, Deputy Executive Director
James Gondles Jr, Executive Director
Debbi Seeger, Director of the Executive Office
Hok Gao, Director of Finance
Larry Strother, Director of Management
For individuals involved in the correctional field.
20000 Members
Founded in: 1870

11549 American Federation of Government Employees
80 F St NW
Washington, DC 20001-1528
202-737-8700; *Fax:* 202-639-6490
comments@afge.org; www.afge.com
Social Media: Facebook, Twitter, Youtube, Flickr, RSS
J David Cox Sr., President
Eugene Hudson, Secretary/Treasurer
Augusta Thomas, VP for Women's & Fair Practices
The largest federal employee union representing workers nationwide and overseas. Workers in virtually all functions of government at every federal agency depend upon AFGE for legal representation, legislative advocacy, technical expertise and informational services.
600K Members
Founded in: 1932

11550 American Federation of State, County & Municipal Employees
1625 L Street NW
Washington, DC 20036-5687
202-429-1000; *Fax:* 202-429-1293
afsa@afsaadmin.org; www.afscme.org
Social Media: Facebook, Twitter, YouTube, RSS
Lee Saunders, President
Laura Reyes, Secretary/ Treasurer
With members in hundreds of different occupations, AFSCME advocates for fairness in the workplace, excellence in public services and prosperity and opportunity for all working families.

11551 American Foreign Service Association
2101 E St Nw
Washington, DC 20037-2990
202-338-4045; *Fax:* 202-338-6820
member@afsa.org; www.afsa.org
Social Media: Facebook, Twitter, Youtube, RSS
Hon. Barbara Stephenson, President
Hon. Charles A Ford, Treasurer
William Haugh, Secretary
Steve Morrison, FCS Vice President
Mark Petry, FAS Vice President
Missions are to enhance the effectiveness of the Foreign Service, to protect the professional interests of its members, to ensure the maintenance of high professional standards for both career diplomats and political appointeese, and to promote understanding of the critical role of the Foreign service in promoting America's national security and economic prosperity.
11M Members
Founded in: 1924

11552 American Judges Association
300 Newport Ave
Williamsburg, VA 23185-4147
757-259-1841; *Fax:* 757-259-1520
aia@ncsc.dni.us
aja.ncsc.dni.us
Judge Brian MacKenzie, President
Judge John E Conery, President-Elect
Justice Russell Otter, Vice President
Judge Catherine Shaffer, Secretary
Jugde Kevin S Burke, Treasurer
The objective and purpose of the Association is: to promote and improve the effective administration of justice; to maintain the status and independance of the judiciary; to provide a forum for the continuing education of its members and the general public; and for the exchange of new ideas among all judges.
2500 Members
Founded in: 1959

11553 American League of Lobbyists
300 North Washington Street
Suite 205
Alexandria, VA 22314
703-960-3011
888-712-1357
grprofessionals.org
Social Media: Facebook, Twitter, LinkedIn
Monte Ward, President
James Hickey, 1st Vice President
Paul T Kelly, 2nd Vice President
Wright Andrews, Secretary
Paul Kangas, Treasurer
National association dedicated to serving government relations and public affairs professionals. Provides programs and conferences of interest to lobbyists.
600+ Members
Founded in: 1979

11554 American Logistics Association
1101 Vermont Ave NW
Suite 1002
Washington, DC 20005-2710
202-466-7636; *Fax:* 202-296-4419
membership@ala-national.org;
www.ala-national.org
Patrick B Nixon, President
Russ Moffett, VP, Member Relations
Maurice Branch, VP, Operations
Tracey Durand, Director, Meetings & Expositions
Joseph Campagna, Chair
Organization that represents the private industry to promote food sales to commissaries on military bases.
Cost: $828.00
400 Members
Frequency: Membership Dues Vary
Founded in: 1972

11555 American National Standards Institute
1889 L Street NW
11th Floor
Washington, DC 20036-3864
202-293-8020; *Fax:* 202-293-9287
info@ansi.org; www.ansi.org
Social Media: Facebook, Twitter, LinkedIn, Youtube, Google+
James T Pauley, Chairman
Joe Bhatia, President & CEO
Kemi Allston, Program Administrator
Promotes the knowledge for approved standards for industry, engineering and safety design.
1000 Members
Founded in: 1918

11556 American Public Human Services Association
1133 19th Street NW
Suite 400
Washington, DC 20036-3623
202-682-0100; *Fax:* 202-289-6555;
www.aphsa.org
Social Media: Facebook, Twitter, LinkedIn
Reggie Bicha, President
Uma Ahluwalia, Treasurer
Tracy Wareing, Secretary
APHSA pusues excellence in health and human services by supporting state and local agencies, informing policymakers, and working with partners to drive innovative, integrated and efficient solutions in policy and practice.
Founded in: 1930

11557 American Society for Public Administration
1301 Pennsylvania Avenue NW
Suite 700
Washington, DC 20004
202-393-7878; *Fax:* 202-638-4952
info@aspanet.org; www.aspanet.org
Social Media: Facebook, Twitter, LinkedIn
Maria Aristigueta, President
Susan T. Gooden, President Elect
William P. Shields Jr., Executive Director
Lisa Sidletsky, Chief of Program Operations
Janice Lachance, Vice President

Offers a wide range of services and membership options for individuals in public administration careers. Sponsors 127 local chapters and 16 sections on specific areas of governments, such as the Section of Natural Resources and Environmental Administration and the Section on Human Resource Administration.
15M Members
Founded in: 1939

11558 American Society of Access Professionals
1444 I(Eye) St. NW
Suite 700
Washington, DC 20005-6542
202-712-9054; *Fax:* 202-216-9646
asap@bostrom.com; www.accesspro.org
Social Media: Facebook, Twitter
Amy Bennett, President
Cindy Allard, Vice President
Amy McNulty, Treasurer
Ginger McCall, Secretary
Jonathan Cantor, Director
Members are government employees, lawyers, journalists and others concerned with access to government data under current personal privacy and public informaiton statues.
Founded in: 1980

11559 Americans for Democratic Action
1629 K Street NW
Suite 300
Washington, DC 20006-1611
202-785-5980; *Fax:* 202-204-8637
info@adaction.org; www.adaction.org
Social Media: Facebook, Twitter, Flickr, YouTube
Lynn Woolsey, President
David Card, Treasurer
Mary Von Euler, Secretary
Elijah Cummings, VP
James K. Galbraith, VP
Liberal lobbying group.

11560 Association for Federal Information Resources Management
400 North Washington St.
Suite 300
Alexandria, VA 22314
703-778-4646; *Fax:* 703-683-5480
info@affirm.org; www.affirm.org
Social Media: Facebook, Twitter, LinkedIn, Flickr
Robert Foster, President
Richard Young, Vice President
Deirdre Murray, VP, Industry
Christopher Hamm, VP
James Maas, VP
A non-profit, volunteer, educational organization whose overall purpose is to improve the management of information, and related systems and resources, within the Federal government. Members include information resource management professionals from the Federal, academic, and industry sectors.
350 Members
Founded in: 1979

11561 Association for Postal Commerce
1800 Diagonal Rd.
Suite 320
Alexandria, VA 22314-2862
703-524-0096; *Fax:* 703-997-2414;
www.postcom.org
Social Media: Facebook
National organization representing those who use, or who support, the use of mail as a medium for communication and commerce. Publishes a weekly newsletter covering postal policy and operational issues.
Founded in: 1947

11562 Association of Boards of Certification
2805 SW Snyder Blvd.
Suite 535
Ankeny, IA 50023
515-232-3623; *Fax:* 515-965-6827
abc@abccert.org; www.abccert.org
Ray Olson, President
Mike Gosselin, President-Elect
Michael Bolt, Vice President
Brian Thorburn, Immediate Past-President
Paul D. Bishop, CAE, Ex-Officio
The Association of Boards of Certification is dedicated to protecting public health and the environment by advancing the quality and integrity of environmental certification programs through innovative technical support services, effective information exchange, professional and cost-effective examination services, and other progressive services for certifying members.
Founded in: 1972

11563 Association of Civilian Technicians (ACT)
12620 Lake Ridge Dr
Lake Ridge, VA 22192-2335
703-494-4845; *Fax:* 703-494-0961
actnational@actnat.com; www.actnat.com
Social Media: Facebook
Terry Garnett, President
Raul Toro, Treasurer
Labor organization of civilian employees of Air Force, Army, National Guard and Reserves.
12M Members

11564 Association of Fish and Wildlife Agencies
1100 First Street, NE
Suite 825
Washington, DC 20002
202-838-3474; *Fax:* 202-350-9869
info@fishwildlife.org; www.fishwildlife.org
Social Media: Facebook, Twitter, Blogger
Ron Regan, Executive Director
Carol Bambery, Association Counsel
Kathy Boydston, Wildlife & Energy Liasion
John Bloom, Accounting Manager
Arpita Choudhury, Science & Research Liasion
The organization that represents all of North America's fish and wildlife agencies that promotes sound management and conservation, and speaks with a unified voice on important fish and wildlife issues.
Founded in: 1902

11565 Association of Food and Drug Officials
2550 Kingston Rd
Suite 311
York, PA 17402-3734
717-757-2888; *Fax:* 717-650-3650
afdo@afdo.org; www.afdo.org
Social Media: Twitter
Joseph Korby, Executive Director
Krystal Reed, Association Manager
Pat Smith, Support Staff
Randy Young, IT Administrator
Patty Fitzgerald, Admin/Special Projects Assistant
Promotes the enforcement of laws and regulations at all levels of government. Fosters understanding and cooperation between industry and regulators. Develops model laws and regulations and seeks their adoption.
800 Members
Founded in: 1986

11566 Association of Former Agents of the US Secret Service
6919 Vista Drive West
Des Moines, IA 50266
515-282-8192; *Fax:* 515-282-9117;
www.oldstar.org
Founded to bring together former and current employees of the Secret Service for comradeship, friendship and support in time of need. Members include Special Agents, Technical Specialists and other support personnel who carried out the investigative and protective responsibilities of the United States Secret Service.
950 Members
Founded in: 1971

11567 Association of Labor Relations Agencies
38 Wolcott Hill Road
Wethersfield, CT 06109
860-263-6860; *Fax:* 860-263-6875;
www.alra.org
Pat Sims, President
Ginette Brazeau, President-Elect
Sylvie Guilbert, VP, Administration
Scot Beckenbaugh, VP, Finance
Jennifer Abruzzo, Board Member
An association of impartial government agencies in the US and Canada responsible for administering labor-management relations laws or services. Promotes cooperation among these agencies, high professional standards, public interest in labor relations, improved employer-employee relationships, peaceful resolution of employment and labor disputes, and the exchange of information regarding the administration and improvement of agency services.

11568 Center for Neighborhood Enterprise
1625 K. Street NW
Suite 1200
Washington, DC 20006
202-518-6500; *Fax:* 202-588-0314
info@cneonline.org; www.cneonline.org
Social Media: Facebook, Twitter, YouTube, Flickr
Robert L Woodson Sr, President
Clifford Ehrlich, Chair
Founded to help the residents of low-income neighborhoods address the problems of their communities. Mission is to transform lives, schools, and troubled neighborhoods, from the inside out. Current programs are the Violence-Free Zone youth violence reduction program; Training and Technical Assistance for Community-Based Organizations; and Adult Financial Literacy.
Founded in: 1981

11569 Center for the Study of the Presidency and Congress (CSPC)
601 Thirteenth St, NW
Suite 1050N
Washington, DC 20005
202-872-9800; *Fax:* 202-872-9811
email@thepresidency.org;
www.thepresidency.org
Social Media: Facebook, Twitter, YouTube
David M Abshire, Vice Chair
Maxmillian Angerholzer III, President/CEO
Dan Mahaffee, Director, Policy & Board Relations
Jonathan Murphy, Director, External Affairs
Elizabeth Perch, COO & CFO
CSPC strives to: promote leadership in the Presidency and Congress to generate innovative solutions to current national challenges; preserve the historic memory of the Presidency by identifying lessons from successes and failures of such leadership; draw on a wide range of talent to offer

ways to better organize an increasingly compartmentalized Federal Government; educate and inspire the next generation of America's leaders to incorporate civility, inclusiveness, and character into their lives.

11570 Citizens Against Government Waste
1301 Pennsylvania Ave
Suite 1075
Washington, DC 20004

202-467-5300; *Fax:* 202-467-4253
membership@cagw.org; www.cagw.org
Social Media: Facebook, Twitter, Youtube

Thomas A Schatz, President
Ariane E Sweeney, VP, Membership & Development
Leslie K Paige, VP Policy & Communications
Robert J Tedeschi, Treasurer/CFO
William M. Christian, Director of Government Affairs

Public advocacy, non-partisan organization committed to eliminate government waste, fraud, abuse, mismanagement and inefficiency.
1MM+ Members
Founded in: 1984
Mailing list available for rent

11571 Citizens for Global Solutions
420 7th St SE
Washington, DC 20003-2707

202-546-3950; *Fax:* 202-546-3749
info@globalsolutions.org;
www.globalsolutions.org
Social Media: Facebook, Twitter, YouTube

Marvin Perry, CEO
Jordan Bankhead, MS, Chairman
Scott Paul,, Vice-Chair
Shirley Lee Davis, Secretary
Evan Freund, Treasurer

Nonprofit, tax deductible membership organization of 50 chapters and groups throughout the United States. We work to educate policy-makers and the American public on issues of global governance, international law and grassroots activism.
11000 Members
Founded in: 1978

11572 Coalition for Government Procurement
1990 M St NW
Suite 450
Washington, DC 20036-3466

202-331-0975; *Fax:* 202-822-9788
info@thecgp.org; www.thecgp.org
Social Media: Facebook, Twitter, LinkedIn, Flickr, RSS

Roger Waldron, President
Carolyn Alston, EVP & General Counsel
Robert Rendely, CFO
Denise Meliski, Director, Business Development
Matt Cahill, VP, Membership & Marketing

Representing commercial contractors in the Federal market. Advocating for common sense policies that improve the acquisition environment for government, industry and ultimately the American taxpayer. Focusing outreach efforts on the General Services Administration, Department of Veterans Affairs, Office of Management and Budget, Department of Defense, and Capitol Hill.
350 Members
Founded in: 1979

11573 Commissioned Officers Association of the United States Public Health Service
8201 Corporate Dr
Suite 200
Landover, MD 20785-2230

301-731-9080
866-366-9593; *Fax:* 301-731-9084
gfarrell@coausphs.org; www.coausphs.org
Social Media: Facebook

Jim Currie, Executive Director
John McElligott, Deputy Executive Director
Teresa Hayden Foley, Chief Financial Officer
Judith Rensberger, Government Relations Director
Erica Robinson, Administrative Assistant

Protects the interests of the Commissioned Corps officers of the US Public Health Service, who are leaders in the realms of public and global health. Dedicated to improving and protecting the public health of the US by addressing unmet health needs and providing support.
7M Members

11574 Community Leadership Association
1240 S Lumpkin Street
Athens, GA 30602

706-542-0301; *Fax:* 706-542-7007
sheena@claweb.org; www.claweb.org

Gene A Honn, Executive Director

Organization dedicated to nurturing leadership in communities throughout the US and internationally. Members include hundreds of diverse community leadership organizations at local, state and national levels, thousands of individual graduates of these organizations and others interested in community leadership development.
2M Members
Founded in: 1979

11575 Conference of Minority Public Administrators
PO Box 1552
Norfolk, VA 23510

301-333-5282; *Fax:* 202-638-4952;
www.compaspanet.com
Social Media: Facebook

Stanley Skinner, President
Linda A. Harmon, President-Elect
Pamela Alexxander, Treasurer
Tiffany L. Smith, Recording Secretary
Lynn Cherry-Miller, Corresponding Secretary

COMPA is one of America's leading national organizations committed to excellence in public service and public administration in city, county, state and federal government.
500 Members
Founded in: 1977

11576 Contract Services Association of America
1000 Wilson Boulevard
Suite 1800
Arlington, VA 22209-3920

703-243-2020; *Fax:* 703-243-3601

Christopher Jahn, President

Represents the government services contracting industry. Membership ranges from small businesses and corporations servicing federal and state government in numerous capacities. CSA acts to foster the effective implementation of the government's policy of reliance on the private sector for support services.
650 Members
Founded in: 1965

11577 Council of Chief State School Officers
One Massachusetts Ave. NW
Suite 700
Washington, DC 20001-1431

202-336-7000; *Fax:* 202-408-8072
communications@ccsso.org; www.ccsso.org
Social Media: Facebook, Twitter, LinkedIn

Chris Minnich, Executive Director
Bruce Buterbaugh, Chief Financial Officer

Nationwide, nonprofit organization is a voice for elementary and secondary school heads of departments to government and the public.

11578 Council of State Community Development Agencies
1825 K St NW
Suite 515
Washington, DC 20006-1261

202-293-5820; *Fax:* 202-293-2820;
www.coscda.org

Steve Charleston, President
Keith Heaton, VP
Alison George, Secretary
Leslie Leager, Treasurer
Dianne E Taylor, Executive DIrector

The premier national association advocating and enhancing the leadership role of states in community development through innovative policy development and implementation, customer-driven technical assistance, education, and collaborative efforts.
Founded in: 1974

11579 Council of State Governments
2760 Research Park Drive
PO Box 11910
Lexington, KY 40578-1910

859-244-8000
800-800-1910; *Fax:* 859-244-8001;
www.csg.org
Social Media: Facebook, Twitter, YouTube, RSS

David Adkins, Executive Director & CEO
Brian Sandoval, President
Luis Fortuno, President-Elect
Sen. Carl Marcellino, Chair
Sen. Beau McCoy, Chair-Elect

Members include every elected and appointed state and territorial official in the US. A nonpartisan organization that brings state leaders together to share capitol ideas, providing them the chance to learn valuable lessons from each other. Also foster innovation in state government and shine a spotlight on examples of how ingenuity and leadership are transforming the way state government serves residents of the states and territories.
Founded in: 1933

11580 Council of State Housing Agencies
Hall of States
444 N Capitol St NW
Suite 438
Washington, DC 20001-1505

202-624-7710; *Fax:* 202-624-5899
bthompson@ncsha.org; www.ncsha.org
Social Media: Facebook, Twitter

Brian A Hudson, President
Thomas R Gleason, Vice President
Grant S Whitaker, Secretary/Treasurer
Barbara J. Thompson, Executive Director
Cary D Knox, Executive Office Admin

A nonprofit, nonpartisan organization created to represent members in Washingtong before Congress, the Administration, and the several federal agencies concerned with housing, including the Department of Housing and Urban Development, the Department of Agriculture, and the Treasury, and with other advocates for affordable housing.

11581 Council on Licensure, Enforcement and Regulation
403 Marquis Ave
Suite 200
Lexington, KY 40502-2104

859-269-1289; *Fax:* 859-231-1943
jhorne@clearhq.org; www.clearhq.org
Social Media: Facebook, Twitter, LinkedIn

Robin Jenkins, President
Steve Hart, President-Elect
Adam Parfitt, Executive Director
Janet Horne, Office Manager
Rosa Brown, Administrative Associate

Members include occupational and professional licensing boards and agencies and private interests in the 50 states, territories and Canada.
380 Members
Founded in: 1980

11582 Digital Government Institute
1934 Old Gallows Road
Suite 350
Vienna, VA 22182

703-752-6243; *Fax:* 703-752-6201
info@digitalgovernment.com;
www.digitalgovernment.com
Social Media: Facebook, Twitter, LinkedIn, Flickr

Specializes in the design and production of leading edge educational programs on emerging trends and technologies for government IT management professionals. A trusted source for education, networking and results.
Founded in: 1998

11583 Energy Bar Association
2000 M Street, N.W.,
Suite 715
Washington, DC 20036-3429

202-223-5625; *Fax:* 202-833-5596
admin@eba-net.org; www.eba-net.org
Social Media: Facebook

Richard Meyer, President
Emma Hand, President-Elect
Robert A. Weishaar, JR, Vice President
Caileen N. Gamache, Secretary
Noha Sidhom, Treasurer

An international, nonprofit association of attorneys and non-attorney professionals active in all areas of energy law. EBA's voluntary membership is comprised of government, corporate and private attorneys, as well as non-attorney professionals from across the globe, and includes law students interested in energy law.
2600 Members
Founded in: 1946

11584 Federal Bar Association
1220 North Fillmore St.
Suite 444
Arlington, VA 22201

571-481-9100; *Fax:* 571-481-9090
fba@fedbar.org; www.fedbar.org
Social Media: Facebook, Twitter, LinkedIn

Karen Silberman, Executive Director
Stacy King, Executive Deputy Director
Heather Gaskins, Director, Development
Monique Dennis, Membership Coordinator
Maria Conticelli, Sections and Divisions Manager

Members are attorneys in the Federal Government or who have interest in federal law.
16000 Members
Founded in: 1920

11585 Federal Criminal Investigators Association
5868 Mapledale Plaza
Suite 104
Woodbridge, VA 22193

630-969-8537
800-403-3374
info@fedcia.org; www.fedcia.org

Mission of FCIA is to ensure that Federal Law Enforcement Professionals have the tools and the support network to meet the challenges of future criminal investigations while becoming more community oriented.
1500 Members
Founded in: 1953

11586 Federal Facilities Council
500 Fifth St. NW
Washington, DC 20001

202-334-3374; *Fax:* 202-334-3370
coskvig@nas.edu
sites.nationalacademies.org/DEPS/FFC/
Social Media: Facebook, Twitter

James Rispoli, Chair
Carmelo Melendez, Vice Chair

Operating under the auspices of the BICE, the FFC's mission is to identify and advance technologies, processes, and management practices that improve the performance of federal facilities over their entire life-cycle, from planning to disposal.
130 Members
Founded in: 1953

11587 Federal Managers Association
1641 Prince St
Alexandria, VA 22314-2818

703-683-8700; *Fax:* 703-683-8707
info@fedmanagers.org; www.fedmanagers.org

Patricia A Niehaus, President
Dora L. Quinlan, VP
Christine C. Parker, Secretary
Katie L Smith, Treasurer
Todd V Wells, Executive Director

Advocates excellence in public service through effective management and professionalism, as well as the active representation of its members' interests and concerns.
15M Members
Founded in: 1913

11588 Federal Physicians Association
12427 Hedges Run Drive
Suite 104
Lake Ridge, VA 22192

703-426-8400
877-333-7497; *Fax:* 703-426-8400
info@fedphy.org; www.fedphy.org

Brian J Ribiero, MD, President
Indira Jevaji, MD, VP
Michael Nesemann, MD, Treasurer
Michael Borecky, MD, Secretary

Represents and advocates for Physicians employed by the Federal Government.
400 Members
Founded in: 1979

11589 Federation of Tax Administrators
444 N Capitol St NW
Suite 348
Washington, DC 20001-1538

202-624-5890; *Fax:* 202-624-7888;
www.taxadmin.org

Gale Garriott, Executive Director
Michael Reissig, President
Dawn Cash, First Vice President
Julie Magee, Second Vice President
Kevin Sullivan, Secretary

Members are the tax agencies of the 50 state governments, the District of Columbia & New York City.
53 Members

11590 Fund for Constitutional Government
122 Maryland Ave NE
Washington, DC 20002-5610

202-546-3799; *Fax:* 202-543-3156
info@fcgonline.org; www.fcgonline.org

Anne B. Zill, President
John Cavanagh, Chairperson
Conrad Martin, Executive Director
Kat Saunders, Secretary
Steven Aftergood, Board Member

Seeks to expose and correct illegal activities, corruption, and lack of accountability in the federal government.
Founded in: 1974

11591 Government Finance Officers Association
203 N La Salle St
Suite 2700
Chicago, IL 60601-1210

312-977-9700; *Fax:* 312-977-4806
inquiry@gfoa.org; www.gfoa.org

Heather A. Johnston, President
Marc Gonzales, President Elect
Jeffrey Esser, Executive Director, CEO
Robert Bishop, Finance Director
Frank C. Gambosi, Finance Director

The purpose of the Government Finance Officers Association is to enhance and promote the professional management of governments for the public benefit by identifying and developing financial policies and practices and promoting them through education, training and leadership.
17300 Members
Founded in: 1906

11592 Hispanic Elected Local Officials
National League of Cities
1301 Pennsylvania Ave NW
Suite 550
Washington, DC 20004-1747

202-626-3169; *Fax:* 202-626-3103;
www.nlc.org/build-skills-and-networks/networks/constituency-group
Social Media: Facebook, Twitter, LinkedIn, Youtube, RSS, Google+

Oscar Trevino, President
Joel Navarro, 1st Vice President
Lydia N. Martinez, 2nd Vice President
Clarence E Anthony, Executive Director

Serves as a forum for communication and exchange among Hispanic local government officials within the framework of the National League of Cities.
100+ Members
Founded in: 1976

11593 Housing Assistance Council
1025 Vermont Ave NW
Suite 606
Washington, DC 20005-3516

202-842-8600; *Fax:* 202-347-3441
hac@ruralhome.org; www.ruralhome.org
Social Media: Facebook, Twitter, LinkedIn

Moises Loza, Executive Director
Joe Belden, Senior Policy Analyst
Lilla Sutton, Executive Coordinator
Leslie Strauss, Senior Policy Analyst
Stephen Sugg, Government Relations

Expands the pool of decent housing available to the rural poor. Creates and sustains interest and action from all levels of government concerning rural housing for low-income people and helps

rural housing organizations become more productive and professional.
30 Members
Founded in: 1971

11594 **Industry Coalition on Technology Transfer**
1400 L St NW
Suite 800
Washington, DC 20005-3502
202-371-5994; *Fax:* 202-371-5950
Coalition of major high technology trade associations concerned with the US Government export controls. Monitors and addresses federal regulations on technology transfer.
4 Members
Founded in: 1983

11595 **International Association of Correctional Training Personnel**
PO Box 81826
Lincoln, NE 68501
312-341-6340; www.iactp.org
Pete Norris, President
Tracy Reveal, President Elect
Mary O'Connor, Secretary
Terry Satterfield, Conference Coordinator
Joe Bouchard, Higher Education
Correctional officers and juvenile administrators.
9.5M Members
Founded in: 1974

11596 **International Association of Fire Chiefs**
4025 Fair Ridge Drive
Suite 300
Fairfax, VA 22033-2868
703-273-0911; *Fax:* 703-273-9363
thicks@iafc.org; www.iafc.org
Social Media: Facebook, Twitter
Mark Light, Executive Director & CEO
Karin Soyster Fitzgerald, Chief Operations Officer
Chief John Sinclair, President & Chairman
Chief Thomas Jenkins, First Vice President
Chief Gary Curmode, Second Vice President
Represents the leadership of firefighters and emergency responders worldwide; members are the world's leading experts in firefighting, emergency medical services, terrorism response, hazardous materials spills, natural disasters, search and rescue, and public safety policy.
12000 Members
Founded in: 1873

11597 **International Association of Official Human Rights Agencies**
444 N Capitol Street NW
Suite 536
Washington, DC 20001
202-624-5410; *Fax:* 202-624-8185
iaohra@sso.org; www.iaohra.org
Jean Kelleher Niebauer, President
Alisa Warren, 2nd Vice President
Paula Haley, Secretary
Merrill Smith, Jr., Treasurer
Robin S. Toma, First Vice-President
Private non-profit corporation consisting of human rights agencies in the US and Canada. Provides opportunities and forums for the exchange of ideas and information among human rights advocates. Also provides training opportunities for members and other concerned groups and organizations.
200 Members
Founded in: 1968

11598 **International City/County Management Association (ICMA)**
777 North Capitol St. NE
Suite 500
Washington, DC 20002-4201
202-289-4262
800-745-8780; *Fax:* 202-962-3500
icma.org
Social Media: Facebook, Twitter, LinkedIn, YouTube, Pinterest, Flickr
Robert J. O'Neill, Executive Director
A worldwide organization for the advancement of professional local government.
Founded in: 1914

11599 **International Code Council**
500 New Jersey Ave NW
6th Floor
Washington, DC 20001-2005
888-422-7233; *Fax:* 202-783-2348
webmaster@iccsafe.org; www.iccsafe.org
Social Media: Facebook
Alex Olszowy III, President
Dwayne Garriss, Vice President
Jay Elbettar, Secretary/Treasurer
A nonprofit membership association dedicated to preserving the public health, safety and welfare in the built environment through the promulgation of model codes suitable for adoption by governmental entities and assisting code enforcement officials, design professionals, builders, manufacturers and others involved in the design, construction and regulatory processes.
16M Members
Founded in: 1915

11600 **International Downtown Association**
1025 Thomas Jefferson Street, NW
Suite 500W
Washington, DC 20007
202-393-6801; *Fax:* 202-393-6869
customerservice@ida-downtown.org;
www.ida-downtown.org
Social Media: Facebook, Twitter, LinkedIn
David Downey, President & CEO
Kevin Moran, Communications & IT Manager
Rebecca Bishophall, Manager, Membership Services
Tracie Clemmer, Development & Exhibits Director
Patricia Stephenson, Director, Finance & Administration
The International Downtown Association has member organizations worldwide in North America, Europe, Asia and Africa. Through a network of committed individuals, a rich body of knowledge and unique capacity to nurture community-building partnerships, IDA is a guiding force in creating healthy and dynamic centers that anchor the well being of towns, cities and regions of the world.
650+ Members
Founded in: 1954

11601 **International Economic Development Council**
734 15th Street NW
Suite 900
Washington, DC 20005
202-223-7800; *Fax:* 202-223-4745;
www.iedconline.org/
Social Media: Facebook, Twitter, LinkedIn
Dyan Lingle Brasington, CEc, Chair
Jeff Finkle, CEcD, President/CEO
Katelyn Palomo, Executive Assistant
Swati Ghosh, Director, Research
Carrie Mulcaire, Director, Federal Grants
Nonprofit membership organization dedicated to helping economic developers do their job more effectively and raising the profile of the profession. Members create more high-quality jobs, develop more vibrant communities, and generally improve the quality of life in their regions.
1.8M Members
Founded in: 1967

11602 **Interstate Council on Water Policy**
505 North Ivy Street
Arlington, VA 22220-1707
703-243-7383; *Fax:* 301-984-5841;
www.icwp.org
Social Media: Facebook, Twitter
Dru Buntin, 2nd Vice-Chairman
Ryan Mueller, Executive Director
Andrew Dehoff, Secretary & Treasurer
Jerry Schulte, 1st Vice Chairman
The ICWP is the national organization of state and regional water resources management agencies. It provides a means for members to exchange information, ideas and experience to work with federal agencies which share water management responsibilities.
70 Members
Founded in: 1959

11603 **Interstate Oil and Gas Compact Commission**
900 NE 23rd Street
Oklahoma City, OK 73105
405-525-3556
800-822-4015; *Fax:* 405-525-3592
communications@iogcc.ok.gov;
www.iogcc.state.ok.us
Mike Smith, Executive Director
Gerry Baker, Associate Executive Director
Hannah Barton, Member Services Coordinator
Amy Childers, Federal Projects Manager
Carol Booth, CommunicationsManager
A multi-state government agency that champions the conservation and efficient recovery of domestic oil and natural gas resources.
700 Members
Founded in: 1935

11604 **National Academy of Public Administration**
1600 K Street, NW
Suite 400
Washington, DC 20006
202-347-3190; *Fax:* 202-223-0823
feedback@napawash.org; www.napawash.org
Social Media: Facebook, Twitter, LinkedIn, Vimeo
Robert J. Shea, Chair
Nancy R. Kingsbury, Vice Chair
Dan G. Blair, President and CEO
Tom Reidy, Chief Financial Officer
Lisa Trahan, Director of Fellow Relations
Through its trusted and experienced leaders, the Academy improves the quality, performance, and accountability of governments in the nation and the world.
500 Members
Founded in: 1967

11605 **National Affordable Housing Management Association**
400 N Columbus Street
Suite 203
Alexandria, VA 22314
703-683-8630; *Fax:* 703-683-8634;
www.nahma.org
Kris Cook, Executive Director
Larry Keys, Jr., Director, Government Affairs
Rajni Agarwal, Director, Finance
Brenda Moser, Director, Meetings & Membership

Scott McMillen, Coordinator, Government Affairs

The leading voice for affordable housing, advocating on behalf of multifamily property managers and owners whose mission is to provide quality affordable housing. Membership includes the industry's most distinguished multifamily managers, owners, and industry stakeholders.
3000 Members
Founded in: 1990

11606 National Alliance of State and Territorial AIDS Directors
444 N Capitol St NW
Suite 339
Washington, DC 20001

202-434-8090; *Fax:* 202-434-8092
nastad@nastad.org; www.nastad.org
Social Media: Facebook, Twitter, LinkedIn, Blogger, Youtube

Julie Scofield, Executive Director
Addis Tilahun, Senior Manager Finance & Accounting
Anna Carroll, Manager Global Program
Anne Redmond Sites, Manager Global Program
Brent Parker, Senior Director

NASTAD strengthens state and territory-based leadership, expertise, and advocacy and brings them to bear in reducing the incidence of HIV and viral hepatitis infections and on providing care and support to all who live with HIV/AIDS and viral hepatitis. NASTAD's vision is a world free of HIV/AIDS and viral hepatitis.
59 Members
Founded in: 1992

11607 National Assembly of State Arts Agencies
1200 18th Street NW
Suite 1100
Washington, DC 20036

202-347-6352; *Fax:* 202-737-0526
nasaa@nasaa-arts.org; www.nasaa-arts.org
Social Media: Facebook

Pam Breaux, Chief Executive Officer
Kelly J. Barsdate, Chief Program and Planning Officer
Laura S. Smith, CFRE, Chief Advancement Officer
Sharon Gee, Director of Meetings and Events

Unites, represents and serves the nation's state and jurisdictional arts agencies. Representing state arts agencies by empowering their work through knowledge, and advance the arts as an essential public benefit.
56 Members
Founded in: 1968

11608 National Association for County Community and Economic Development
2025 M St NW
Suite 800
Washington, DC 20036-3309

202-367-1149; *Fax:* 202-367-2149;
www.nacced.org

John Murphy, Executive Director
Tony Agliata, President
Jim Vazquez, Vice President
Chuck Robbins, Secretary/Treasurer
Bill J. Lake, Director

Purpose is to develop the technical capacity of county government practitioners to professionally administer federally-funded affordable housing, community development, and economic development programs that benefit their low- and moderate-income households.
120+ Members
Founded in: 1989

11609 National Association for Search and Rescue
PO Box 232020
Centreville, VA 20120-2020

703-222-6277
877-893-0702; *Fax:* 703-222-6277
meganr@nasar.org; www.nasar.org

Monty Bell, President
Christopher Boyer, Executive Director
Ross Robinson, Chief Financial Officer
Ellen Wingerd, Customer Care Manager
Mike Vorachek, Secretary

A not-for-profit membership association dedicated to advancing professional, literary, and scientific knowledge in fields related to search and rescue.
3M Members

11610 National Association of Clean Air Agencies
444 N Capitol Street NW
Suite 307
Washington, DC 20001-1506

202-624-7864; *Fax:* 202-624-7863
4cleanair@4cleanair.org; www.4cleanair.org

Stu A Clark, Co-President
Merlyn Hough, Co-President
Bill Becker, Executive Director
Nancy Kruger, Deputy Director
Dave Klemp, Co-Vice President

Represents state and local air pollution control officers from over 150 major metropolitan areas and 53 states and territories.

11611 National Association of Conservation Districts (NACD)
509 Capitol Court, NE
Washington, DC 20002-4937

202-547-6223; *Fax:* 202-547-6450;
www.nacdnet.org
Social Media: Facebook, Twitter, LinkedIn, Vimeo, Google Plus, Flickr

Earl Garber, President
Lee McDaniel, First Vice President
Brent Van Dyke, Second Vice President
John Larson, Chief Executive Officer
Laura Wood Peterson, Director of Government Affairs

NACD develops national conservation policies, influences lawmakers and builds partnerships with other agencies and organizations. NACD also provides services to its districts to help them share ideas in order to better serve their local communities.
17000 Members
Founded in: 1946

11612 National Association of Counties
25 Massachusetts Ave NW
Suite 500
Washington, DC 20001-1450

202-393-6226
888-407-6226; *Fax:* 202-393-2630
nacomeetings@naco.org; www.naco.org/
Social Media: Facebook, Twitter, LinkedIn, YouTube

Linda Langston, President
Riki Hokama, 1st Vice President
Sallie Clark, 2nd Vice President
Matthew D. Chase, Executive Director
Karen McRunnel, Executive Assistant to the CEO

The National Association of Counties (NACo) is an organization that represents county governments in the United States. NACo advances issues with a unified voice before the federal government, improves the public's understanding of county government, and assists counties in finding and sharing innovative solutions through education and research. NACo's membership totals more than 2,000 counties, representing over 80 percent of the nation's population.
Founded in: 1935

11613 National Association of County Engineers
25 Mass. Ave, NW
Suite 580
Washington, DC 20001-1454

202-393-5041; *Fax:* 202-393-2630
nace@naco.org; www.countyengineers.org

Brian C Roberts, Executive Director
Rebecca Page, Director of Marketing & Membership
Constantine Connie Radoulovitch, Office Manager
Duane J. Ratermann, President
Brian D. Stacy, President Elect

Members are county engineering professionals or road management authorities.
1900 Members
Founded in: 1956

11614 National Association of Development Organizations (NADO)
400 N Capitol St NW
Suite 390
Washington, DC 20001-6505

202-624-7806; *Fax:* 202-624-8813
info@nado.org; www.nado.org
Social Media: Facebook, Twitter, RSS

Terry Bobrowski, President
Vicki Glass, Director of Meetings and Membership
Susan Howard, Director of Government Relations
Brian Kelsey, Director of Economic Development
Carrie Kissel, Associate Director

The National Association of Development Organizations (NADO) serves as the national voice for regional development organizations. NADO helps its members achieve their goals by providing effective advocacy and lobbying services at the federal level, producing timely information and research, and offering opportunities for professional and organizational growth.

11615 National Association of Government Archives & Records Administrators
444 N. Capitol Street, NW
Suite 237
Washington, DC 20001-6505

202-508-3800; *Fax:* 202-508-3801
nagara@caphill.com; www.nagara.org
Social Media: LinkedIn

Pari Swift, President
Patty Davis, Vice President
Jannette Goodall, Secretary
Galen R. Wilson, Treasurer
Steve Grandin, Membership Services & Publications

Professional association dedicated to the improvement of federal, state, and local government records and information management and the professional development of government records administrators and archivists. Members include county, municipal, and special district governments, state agencies, the National Archives and Records Administration; individual federal employees; the General Archives of Puerto Rico; and a number of provincial and institutional programs.
Founded in: 1974

11616 **National Association of Housing and Redevelopment Officials**
630 Eye Street, NW
Washington, DC 20001-3736
202-289-3500
877-866-2476; *Fax:* 202-289-8181
nahro@nahro.org; www.nahro.org
Saul Ramirez, Executive Director
Donald J Cameron, Senior VP
Joseph E Gray Jr, VP
Elizabeth C Morris, VP Housing
Saul Ramirez, Manager
A professional membership association representing local housing authorities, community development agencies and individual professionals in the housing, community development and redevelopment fields.
700 Members
Founded in: 1933

11617 **National Association of Local Housing Finance Agencies**
2025 M St NW
Suite 800
Washington, DC 20036-2422
202-367-1197; *Fax:* 202-367-2197
info@nalhfa.org; www.nalhfa.org
Ron Williams, President
W. D. Morris, Vice President
Vivian Benjamin, Treasurer
Tom Cummings, Secretary
The national association of professionals working to finance affordable housing in the broader community development context at the local level. Nonprofit association working as an advocate before Congress and federal agencies on legislative and regulatory issues affecting affordable housing and provides technical assistance and educational opportunities to its members and the public.
Founded in: 1982

11618 **National Association of Neighborhoods**
1300 Pennsylvania Ave NW
Suite 700
Washington, DC 20004-3024
202-332-7766; *Fax:* 202-588-5881
info@nanworld.org; www.nanworld.org
Sam Thompson Jr., Board Member
Debra K. Powell, Board Member
Mission is to improve the quality of life in the nation's most important communities- its neighborhoods. Remains an organization of neighborhood coalitions, block clubs, community councils, and individuals, united by a love of neighborhoods and a strong determination to make them better.
2500+ Members
Founded in: 1975

11619 **National Association of Postmasters of the United States**
8 Herbert St
Alexandria, VA 22305-2600
703-683-9027; *Fax:* 703-683-6820;
www.napus.org
Robert J. Rapoza, President
Michael E. Quinn, Secretary/ Treasurer
Mission is to represent, promote, and protect postmasters. To foster a favorable image of public service and to assure users of the mail the best possible service. To be an advocate with the Congress of the United States. And to work closely with the United States Postal Service in the development of strategies for the enhancement of Postmasters and the Postal Service.
41M Members
Founded in: 1898

11620 **National Association of Regional Councils**
777 North Caoitol Street NE
Suite 305
Washington, DC 20002
202-618-5696; *Fax:* 202-986-1038
lindsey@narc.org; www.narc.org
Social Media: Twitter
Joanna Turner,, Executive Director
Lindsey Riley, Deputy of Communications
Leslie Wollack,, Deputy Executive Director
Mia Colson,, Grants Manager
State of regional repositories of instructional materials or services.
250 Members
Founded in: 1965

11621 **National Association of Regulatory Utility Commissioners (NARUC)**
1101 Vermont Ave NW
Suite 200
Washington, DC 20005-3553
202-898-2200; *Fax:* 202-898-2213
admin@naruc.org; www.naruc.org
Lisa Polak Edgar, President
Travis Kavulla, 1st Vice President
Robert F Powellson, 2nd Vice President
Charles D. Gray, Executive Director
David E. Ziegner, Treasurer
Representing the State Public Service Commissioners who regulate essential utility services, including energy, telecommunications, and water. Members are responsible for assuring reliable utility service at fair, just, and reasonable rates. The Association is an invaluable resource for members and the regulatory community, providing a venue to set and influence public policy, share best practices, and foster innovative solutions to improve regulation.
Founded in: 1889

11622 **National Association of State Development**
12884 Harbor Drive
Woodbridge, VA 22192
703-490-6777; *Fax:* 703-880-0509
Miles Friedman, President/CEO
Sally Pope, Director Finance
Pofen Salem, Project Manager
Established to provide a forum for directors of state economic development agencies to exchange information, compare programs, and establish an organizational base to approach the Federal Government on issues of mutual interest.
250 Members
Founded in: 1946

11623 **National Association of State Facilities**
2760 Research Park Drive
PO Box 11910
Lexington, KY 40578-1910
859-244-8000
800-800-1910; *Fax:* 859-244-8001
membership@csg.org; www.csg.org
Social Media: Facebook, Twitter, YouTube, RSS
Carl Marcellino, Chair
Gov. Brian Sandoval, President
Sen. Kelvin Atkinson, Vice Chair
Sen. Beau McCoy, Chair-Elect
David Adkins, Executive Director/CEO
Brings state leaders together to share capitol ideas, providing them the chance to learn valuable lessons from each other. Fosters innovation in state government and shining a spotlight on examples of how ingenuity and leaderhsip are transforming the way state government serves residents of the states and territories.
Founded in: 1933

11624 **National Association of Towns and Townships**
1130 Connecticut Ave NW
Suite 300
Washington, DC 20036-3981
202-454-3950
866-830-0008; *Fax:* 202-331-1598;
www.natat.org
Larry Merrill, President
Matthew DeTemple, Vice President
Jennifer Imo, Federal Director
Bill Hanka, Deputy Federal Director
Mark Limbaugh, Senior Advisor
Seeks flexible and alternative approaches to federal policies to ensure that small communities can meet federal requirements. Advocates for fair share funding, technical assistance, and other affirmative steps to address the inherent disadvantages that small governments face in our present intergovernmental system.
13M Members

11625 **National Border Patrol Council**
2445 Fifth Ave.
Suite 350
San Diego, CA 92101
520-219-5152
800-620-1613; *Fax:* 520-219-5154;
www.nbpc1613.org
Social Media: Facebook
James Harlan, President
Dan Mais, 1st Vice President
Terence Shigg, 2nd Vice President
Robert Lopez, 3rd Vice President
Victor Cantu, Treasurer
Exclusive representative for non-supervisory Border Patrol Agents and support personnel assigned to the San Diego Sector of the United States Border Parol.
69000 Members
Founded in: 1965

11626 **National Community Development Association**
522 21st St NW
#120
Washington, DC 20006-5012
202-293-7587; *Fax:* 202-887-5546;
www.ncdaonline.org
Social Media: LinkedIn
Cardell Cooper, Executive Director
Vicki Watson, Assistant Director
Karen Parker, Operations Manager
National nonprofit organization at the forefront in securing effective and responsive housing and community development programs for local governments. Provides timely, direct information and technical support to its members on federal housing and community development programs.
550+ Members

11627 **National Conference of State Legislatures**
National Conference of State Legislatures
7700 E 1st Pl
Denver, CO 80230-7143
303-364-7700; *Fax:* 303-364-7800;
www.ncsl.org
Social Media: Facebook, Twitter, LinkedIn, Youtube
Terie Norelli, President
Jean Cantrell, Vice President
Patsy Spaw, Secretary/Treasurer
A bipartisan organization that serves the legislators and staffs of the nation's 50 states, its commonwealths and territories.
Cost: $49.00
15000 Members
Circulation: 18000
ISSN: 0147-0644

Founded in: 1975
Printed in 4 colors

11628 National Council of State EMS Training Coordinators
201 Park Washington Court
Falls Church, VA 22046

888-240-4696; *Fax:* 703-241-5603;
www.nscemstc.org

Members are supervisors or coordinators of state EMS training programs, and limited to three from each state.

11629 National Council of State Housing Agencies
Hall of States
444 N Capitol St NW
Suite 438
Washington, DC 20001-1505

202-624-7710; *Fax:* 202-624-5899
bthompson@ncsha.org; www.ncsha.org
Social Media: Facebook, Twitter,

Thomas R. Gleason, President
Grant S. Whitaker, Vice President
Barbara J. Thompson, Executive Director
Maury L. Edwards, Director of Meetings
Kevin B. Burke, CPA, Director of Finance and Operations

NCSHA represents its members in Washington before Congress, the Administration, and the several federal agencies concerned with housing, including the Department of Housing and Urban Development, the Department of Agriculture, and the Treasury, and with other advocates for affordable housing.
350 Members
Founded in: 1974

11630 National District Attorneys Association
99 Canal Center Plaza
Suite 330
Alexandria, VA 22314-1548

703-549-9222; *Fax:* 703-836-3195;
www.ndaa.org
Social Media: Facebook

Kay Chopard Cohen, Executive Director
Rick Hasey, CFO
Richard Hanes, Chief of Staff
Duane Kokesch, Director, Traffic Program
Allie Phillips, Deputy Director

Serves as a nationwide, interdisciplinary resource center for training, research, technical assistance, and publications reflecting the highest standards and cutting-edge practices of the prosecutorial profession.
7000 Members
Founded in: 1950

11631 National Emergency Management Association
2760 Research Park Drive
Lexington, KY 40578

859-244-8000; *Fax:* 859-244-8239
nemaadmin@csg.org; www.nemaweb.org
Social Media: Facebook

Bryan Koon, President
Wendy Smith-Reeve, Vice President
Trina R. Sheets, NEMA Executive Director
Beverly Bell, Senior Policy Analyst
Karen Cobuluis, Meeting & Marketing Coordinator

A nonpartisan, nonprofit association dedicated to enhancing public safety by improving the nation's ability to prepare for, respond to, and recover from all emergencies, disasters, and threats to our nation's security. Provides national leadership and expertise in comprehensive emergency management, serves as a vital emergency management information and assistance resource, and advances continuous improvement in emergency management.
263 Members
Founded in: 1970

11632 National Forum for Black Public Administrators
777 N Capitol St NE
Suite 807
Washington, DC 20002-4291

202-408-9300; *Fax:* 202-408-8558
webmaster@nfbpa.org; www.nfbpa.org
Social Media: Facebook, YouTube

Verdenia C. Baker, President
Bruce T. Moore, 1st Vice President
Regina V. K. Williams, Interim Executive Director
Malick Diagne, Fiscal Director
Yvette Harris, Membership Coordinator

Committed to strengthening the position of Blacks within the field of public administration; increasing the number of Blacks appointed to executive positions in public service organizations; and, to groom and prepare younger, aspiring administrators for senior public management posts in the years ahead.
2.8M Members
Founded in: 1983

11633 National Governors' Association
Hall of States
444 N Capitol St
Suite 267
Washington, DC 20001-1512

202-624-5300; *Fax:* 202-624-5313
webmaster@nga.org; www.nga.org
Social Media: Facebook, Twitter

Governor Mary Fallin, Chair
Governor John Hickenlooper, Vice Chair
Dan Crippen, Executive Director
Barry Anderson, Deputy Director
David Quam, Deputy Director, Policy

Coordinates the formulation of state policies by governors, and works to ensure consideration of these positions in the development of national policies and programs. The governors belong to seven standing committees: agriculture; community and economic development; justice and public protection; energy and environment; human resources; international trade; and foreign relations.
Founded in: 1908

11634 National Housing Law Project
703 Market Street
Suite 2000
San Francisco, CA 94103

415-546-7000; *Fax:* 415-546-7007
nhlp@nhlp.org; www.nhlp.org

Robert C. Pearman, Jr., Chairperson
John Relman, Vice Chair
Gideon Anders, Senior Staff Attorney
Catherine M. Bishop, Senior Staff Attorney
James R. Grow, Deputy Director

A nonprofit corporation that provides assistance on public and private housing and community development matters to Legal Services attorneys and housing specialists throughout the country. The project's goals are to produce, maintain and conserve low and moderate income housing and protect and expand the rights of lower income persons to decent and affordable housing.
Founded in: 1968

11635 National Institute of Governmental Purchasing/NIGP
2411 Dulles Corner Park
Suite 350
Herndon, VA 20170-5223

703-736-8900
800-367-6447; *Fax:* 703-736-9639
grante@co.cape-may.nj.us; www.nigp.org
Social Media: Facebook, Twitter, LinkedIn

Marcheta E. Gillespie, CPPO, CPPB,, President
Rick Grimm, CPPO, CPPB, Chief Executive Officer
Brent Maas, Executive Director, Business
Catherine Patin, Communications Manager
Carol Hodes, CAE, Executive Director

An international not-for-profit educational and technical organization of public purchasing agencies. NIGP develops, supports and promotes the public procurement profession through premier educational and research programs, professional support, and advocacy initiatives that benefit members and constituents.
2600+ Members
Founded in: 1944

11636 National League of Cities
1301 Pennsylvania Ave NW
Suite 550
Washington, DC 20004-1747

202-626-3180
877-827-2385; *Fax:* 202-626-3043
info@nlc.org; www.nlc.org
Social Media: Facebook, Twitter, LinkedIn, RSS, Youtube, Google Plus

Ralph Becker, President
Melodee Colbert Kean, 1st Vice President
Matt Zone, 2nd Vice President
Clarence Anthony, Executive Director
David DeLorenzo, Chief Digital Officer

Dedicated to helping city leaders build better communities. The NLC advocates for cities and towns, provides programs and services, provides opportunities for involvement and networking, keeps leaders informed, strengthens leadership skills, recognizes municipal achievements, partners with state leagues, and promotes cities and towns.
1700 Members
Founded in: 1924

11637 National Public Employer Labor Relations Association
1012 South Coast Highway
Suite M
Oceanside, CA 92054

760-433-1686
877-673-5721; *Fax:* 760-433-1687
mike@npelra.org; www.npelra.org
Social Media: Facebook, Twitter, LinkedIn

Michael T. Kolb, Executive Director
Yvonne Gillengerten, Operations Manager
Janessa Stephens, Association Specialist
Allison Wittwer, Administrative Assistant
Stephanie Biggs, Administrative Assistant

Provides Professional Development, Networking, and Advocacy Services to Labor Relations & Human Resources professionals, so that public sector employers may deliver the most efficient and effective services to citizens & taxpayers.
2000+ Members
Founded in: 1971

11638 National Rural Housing Coalition
1331 G St NW
10th FL
Washington, DC 20002

202-393-5229; *Fax:* 202-393-3034;
www.nrhcweb.org
Social Media: Facebook, Twitter

Karen Speakman, President
Marty Miller, 1st Vice President
Kathleen Tyler, 2nd Vice President
Hope Cupit, Secretary
Lee Beaulac, Treasurer

Works to focus policy makers on the needs of rural areas by direct advocacy and by coordinating a network of rural housing advocates around the nation. National Rural Housing Coalition is sup-

ported entirely by donations, contributions and subscriptions.
300 Members
Founded in: 1969

11639 National Urban League
120 Wall St.
New York, NY 10005
212-558-5300; *Fax:* 212-344-5332
nul.iamempowered.com
Social Media: Facebook, Twitter, LinkedIn, YouTube
Marc H. Morial, President & CEO
Paul Wycisk, SVP & Chief Financial Officer
Nicolaine M. Lazare, SVP & General Counsel
Historic civil rights organization focused on improving quality of life in underserved urban communities.
Founded in: 1911

11640 National WIC Association
2001 S Street NW
Suite 580
Washington, DC 20009-1165
202-232-5492; *Fax:* 202-387-5281
crichardson@nwica.org; www.nwica.org
Social Media: Facebook, Twitter, Pinterest
Jacqueline Marlette-Boras, Chair
Douglas Greenaway, President & CEO
Cecilia Richardson, Staff/Nutrition Programs Director
Robert A. Lee, Membership Coordinator
Samantha Lee, Communications, Media and Marketing
NWA is the proactive voice supporting, inspiring and empowering the WIC Community through creativity, teamwork and leadership to serve America's low-income, high-risk women, infants and children.
900 Members
Founded in: 1979

11641 North American Gaming Regulators Association
1000 Westgate Drive
Suite 252
St Paul, MN 55114-8612
651-203-7244; *Fax:* 651-290-2266
info@nagra.org; www.nagra.org
Lisa M. Christiansen, President
Dave Jeseritz, Vice President
Tracy L. Bigelow, Treasurer
Craig Durbin, Secretary
A nonprofit professional association of gaming regulators throughout North America. The organization brings together agencies that regulate gaming activities and provides them a forum for the mutual exchange of regulatory information and techniques. Collecting and disseminating regulatory and enforcement information, procedures, and experiences from all jurisdictions provides on-going gaming education and training for all members.
120 Members
Founded in: 1984

11642 North American Securities Administrators Association, Inc.
750 First Street NE
Suite 1140
Washington, DC 20002-8034
202-737-0900; *Fax:* 202-783-3571;
www.nasaa.org
Social Media: Facebook, RSS
Judith Shaw, President
Russ Iuculano, Executive Director
John H. Lynch, Deputy Executive Director
Joseph Brady, General Counsel
Michael Canning, Director of Policy
NASAA is the international organization representing securities administrators from all 50 states, the District of Columbia, Canada, Mexico and Puerto Rico, and is responsible for investor protection and education. NASAA recommends national policies in the securities industry and provides model legislation for state securities agencies to adopt affecting the regulation of broker/dealers and investment advisers. Consumers can contact NASAA to get phone numbers of state securities regulators.
66 Members
Founded in: 1919

11643 Patent and Trademark Office Society
PO Box 2089
Arlington, VA 22202-0089
703-305-8340; www.ptos.org
Matthew Troutman, President
Brandon Rosati, Vice President
David Sosnowski, Secretary
Fred Guillermety, Administrator
Tsung-Yin Tsai, Treasurer
Internationally recognized for its activities in the patent and trademark fields. The Society has actively influenced the patent and trademark systems- promoting the systems' growth and well-being.
1800 Members
Founded in: 1917
Mailing list available for rent

11644 Procurement Round Table
1464 Nieman Road
Shady Side, MD 20764
301-261-9918;
www.procurementroundtable.org
Allan V. Burman, Chairman
Bill Gormley, Vice Chair
Kenneth J. Oscar, Treasurer
Chartered by former federal acquisition officials concerned about the economy, efficiency and effectiveness of the federal acquisition system. Its Directors and Officers are private citizens who serve pro bono with the objective of advising and assisting the government in making improvements in federal acquisition.
40 Members
Founded in: 1984

11645 Public Employees Roundtable
PO Box 75248
Washington, DC 20013-5248
202-927-4926; *Fax:* 202-927-4920;
www.theroundtable.org
Committed to helping future public servants reach their goals. Supporting young people planning careers in public service through the scholarship, fellowship and internship programs of its members.

11646 Public Housing Authorities Directors Association
511 Capitol Court NE
Washington, DC 20002-4947
202-546-5445; *Fax:* 202-546-2280;
www.phada.org
Timothy Kaiser, Executive Director
Ted Van Dyke, Director of Government Affairs
Yaniv Goury, Director of Communications
Jim Armstrong, Policy Analyst
Kathleen Whalen, Policy Analyst
Represents and serves the needs of executive directors of housing authorities of all sizes, in all regions of the nation. In pursuing the Association's goal of improving assisted housing, the corporation works with Congress and federal agencies as well as with all interested groups to improve the nation's housing programs.
1.6M Members
Founded in: 1979

11647 Republican Communications Association
Longworth House Office Building
1317 Longworth
PO Box 550
Washington, DC 20515-0001
E-Mail: RCA@mail.house.gov;
www.rcaweb.org
Neal Patel, President
Tom Wilbur, Vice-President
Shea Snider, Treasurer
Michael Marinaccio, Digital Director
John Cummins, Professional Development Director
Sponsors professional development and networking programs. Conducts seminars, briefings, and tours.
165 Members
Founded in: 1970

11648 Society of Government Economists
PO Box 77082
Washington, DC 20013
202-643-1743
sge@sge-econ.org; www.sge-econ.org
Robert Lerman, President
Julia Lane, Vice-President
Marvin Ward, Executive Director
Andrew Felton, Website Director
Brian Sloboda, Outreach Director and Event Planner
Supports the professional development of government economists, and those who are interested in public policy economics, by providing them with research, publications, and professional communication opportunities.
500 Members
Founded in: 1970

11649 State Government Affairs Council
108 North Columbus Street
2nd Floor
Alexandria, VA 22314
571-312-3426
eloudy@sgac.org; www.sgac.org
Social Media: Facebook, Twitter, LinkedIn
Donna Gehlhaart, President
Elizabeth A. Loudy, Executive Director
Jon Burton, Vice President
Crislyn Lumia, Director, Education & Training
Katherine Kilgore, Manager, Communications
The premier national association for multi-state government affairs professionals, providing opportunities for networking and professional development.
200 Members
Founded in: 1975

11650 State Higher Education Executive Officers Association
3035 Center Green Drive
Suite 100
Boulder, CO 80301-2205
303-541-1600; *Fax:* 303-541-1639
sheeo@sheeo.org; www.sheeo.org
Social Media: Twitter
Peter A. Blake, Chair
George Pernsteiner, President
Julie Carnahan, Senior Associate
Glady Kerns, Director of Administration
Eileen I. Klein, Treasurer
A nonprofit, nationwide association of the chief executive officers serving statewide coordinating boards and governing boards of postsecondary education.
56 Members
Founded in: 1954

11651 **The National Association for State Community Services Programs**
111 K Street NE
Suite 300
Washington, DC 20002

202-624-5866; *Fax:* 202-624-8472
nascsp@nascsp.org; www.nascsp.org
Social Media: Facebook, Twitter

Jenae Bjelland, Executive Director
Joan Harris, Director
Brad Penney, General Counsel
Gretchen Knowlton, Policy Director
Tabitha Beck, Research Director

The premier national association charged with advocating and enhancing the leadership role of states in preventing and reducing poverty.
100 Members
Founded in: 1968

11652 **Trust for Public Land**
101 Montgomery Street
Suite 900
San Francisco, CA 94104

415-495-4014; *Fax:* 415-495-4103
info@tpl.org; www.tpl.org
Social Media: Facebook, Twitter, Youtube

William Rogers, President & CEO
Brian Beitner, Chief Investment Officer
Sean Connolly, Chief Marketing Officer
Ernest Cook, Senior Vice President
Kathy DeCoster, Vice President

A nonprofit land acquisition and conservation organization, working with community groups, landowners, public land management agencies and rural groups to preserve open space lands and to pioneer methods of community ownership of land. Through its Investment Lands Program, the Trust for Public Land also acquires underutilized properties by gift or bargain sales.
Founded in: 1972

11653 **U.S. Chamber of Commerce**
1615 H St Nw
Washington, DC 20062-2000

202-659-6000
800-638-6582; *Fax:* 202-463-5836
press@uschamber.com; www.uschamber.org
Social Media: Facebook, Twitter

Thomas J Donohue, President & CEO
David C. Chavern, Executive Vice President
Myron Brilliant, Executive Vice President
Lily Fu Claffee, Senior Vice President
Shannon DiBari, Senior Vice President

The mission of the Chamber of Commerce is to advance human progress through an economic, political and social system based on individual freedom, incentive, initiative, opportunity, and responsibility. The Chamber of Commerce provides a voice of experience and influence in Washington, D.C., and around the globe, fighting for business and free enterprise before Congress, the White House, regulatory agencies, and the courts.

11654 **United States Conference of Mayors**
1620 Eye Street, NW
Washington, DC 20006-4033

202-293-7330; *Fax:* 202-293-2352
info@usmayors.org; www.usmayors.org
Social Media: Facebook, Twitter

Mayor Scott Smith, President
Mayor Kevin Johnson, Vice President
Mayor Stephanie Rawlings-Blake, 2nd Vice President
Tom Cochran, CEO and Executive Director

Primary roles are to promote development of policies, strengthen federal-city relationships, ensure federal policy meets urban needs, provide mayors with leadership and management tools, and create a forum in which mayors can share ideas and information.
30000 Members
Founded in: 1987

11655 **United States Interagency Council on Homelessness**
Federal Center SW
409 Third St. SW Suite 310
Washington, DC 20024

202-708-4663; *Fax:* 202-708-1216
usich@usich.gov; www.ich.gov
Social Media: Facebook, Twitter

Barbara Poppe, Executive Director

Mission is to coordinate the federal response to homelessness and to create a national partnership at every level of government and with the private sector to reduce and end homelessness in the nation while maximizing the effectiveness of the Federal Government in contributing to the end of homelessness.
Founded in: 1987

11656 **Urban Land Institute**
1025 Thomas Jefferson St NW
Suite 500 West
Washington, DC 20007-5230

202-624-7000; *Fax:* 202-624-7140
ulifoundation@uli.org; www.uli.org
Social Media: Facebook, Twitter, LinkedIn, YouTube, Flickr, Google Plus

Randall Rowe, Chairman
Patrick L. Phillips, Chief Executive Officer
Michael Terseck, CFO
Kathleen B. Carey, Chief Content Officer
Jason Ray, Chief Technology Officer

Founded to provide a land-use information resource for both the professionals and the public. ULI conducts seminars, workshops, semiannual meetings, research programs and publishes books on all aspects of land use and development issues. ULI offers an advisory service, and gives annual Awards for Excellence.
14M Members
Founded in: 1936

11657 **Urban and Regional Information Systems Association**
701 Lee Street
Suite 680
Des Plaines, IL 60016-4508

847-824-6300; *Fax:* 847-824-6363
info@urisa.org; www.urisa.org
Social Media: Facebook, Twitter, LinkedIn

Rebecca Somers, President
Wendy Nelson, Executive Director
Keri Brennan, GISP, Education Manager
Patricia Francis, Meeting Coordinator
Verlanda McBride, Registrar & Database Manager

Concerned with the effective use of information systems technology at the state, regional and local levels. Members informed of current developments in the information systems field. Its goal is to stimulate and encourage the advancement of an interdisciplinary professional approach to planning, designing and operating information systems.
3000 Members
Founded in: 1963

11658 **Western Governor's Association**
1600 Broadway
Suite 1700
Denver, CO 80202

303-623-9378; *Fax:* 303-534-7309;
www.westgov.org
Social Media: Facebook, Twitter, LinkedIn, Google+, Pinterest

James Ogbury, Executive Director
Holly Propst, Deputy Executive Director

Association for policy development, information exchange and collective action by the Governors of 19 Western states and 3 US-flag Pacific islands.
Founded in: 1984

Newsletters

11659 **ADA Today**
Americans for Democratic Action
1625 K St NW
Suite 102
Washington, DC 20006-1611

202-785-5980; *Fax:* 202-785-5969
info@adaction.org; www.adaction.org

David Card, Editor

The nation's oldest liberal lobbying group. This newsletter describes national and local chapter activities and updates federal legislative action.
Cost: $20.00
Frequency: Quarterly
Circulation: 65000
Mailing list available for rent: 65000 names
Printed in 2 colors on matte stock

11660 **ADAction News and Notes**
Americans for Democratic Action
1625 K St NW
Suite 210
Washington, DC 20006-1611

202-785-5980; *Fax:* 202-785-5969
info@adaction.org; www.adaction.org

Allen Kukovich, Executive Committee Chair
Jim McDermott, CEO
Don Kufler, Circulation Manager

Offers information on legislative issues and lobbying.
Cost: $20.00
Frequency: Weekly
Circulation: 3000
Founded in: 1948
Mailing list available for rent: 3000 names
Printed in one color on matte stock

11661 **AJA Benchmark**
American Judges Association
300 Newport Ave
Williamsburg, VA 23185-4147

757-259-1841; *Fax:* 757-259-1520
aja.ncsc.dni.us

Judge Kevin S. Burke, President
Judge Toni Manning Higginbotham, President-Elect
Judge Elliott L. Zide, Vice President
Judge Brian MacKenzie, Secretary
Judge Harold V. Froehlich, Treasurer

Latest news from the American Judges Association.
2500 Members
Frequency: Quarterly
Founded in: 1959

11662 **ANSI Congressional Standards Update**
American National Standards Institute
1819 L St NW
11th Floor
Washington, DC 20036-3864

202-293-8020; *Fax:* 202-293-9287
info@ansi.org; www.ansi.org

Arthur E. Cote, Chairman
Joe Bhatia, President & CEO

Designed to provide members of Congress and their staff with timely information on key standards and conformity assessment issues that im-

pact the global competitiveness of US business and the US quality of life.
1000 Members
Frequency: Monthly
Founded in: 1918

11663 ASAP Newsletter
American Society of Access Professionals
1444 I St Nw
Suite 700
Washington, DC 20005-6542
202-712-9054; *Fax:* 202-216-9646
asap@bostrom.com; www.accesspro.org
Claire Shanley, Executive Director
Provides information about upcoming and recent ASAP events, insights, and information about changes in the laws, and court decisions.
Frequency: Yearly

11664 Advocate
PHADA
511 Capitol Court NE
Washington, DC 20002-4947
202-546-5445; *Fax:* 202-546-2280;
www.phada.org
Timothy Kaiser, Executive Director
Provides members with insights into HUD and Congressional actions, funding opportunities, job vacancies, and major developments in the public housing field.
1.6M Members
Frequency: Bi-Weekly
Founded in: 1979

11665 American Planning Association
American Planning Association
1030 15th St.
Suite 750 W
Washington, DC 20005
202-872-0611; *Fax:* 202-872-0643
CustomerService@planning.org;
www.planning.org/
Social Media: Facebook, Twitter, LinkedIn
Paul Farmer, CEO
Ann Simms, CFO/EOO
The American Planning Association(APA) brings together thousands of people- practicing planners, citizens, elected officials-committed to making great communities.
Cost: $645.00
40000 Members
Frequency: Monthly
Founded in: 1917

11666 Assisted Housing Accounts & Audits Insider
Brownstone Publishers
149 5th Ave
16th Floor
New York, NY 10010-6832
212-473-8200
800-643-8095; *Fax:* 212-473-8786
info@vendomegrp.com;
www.vendomegrp.com
David B Klein, Editor
John M Striker, Publisher
Explains how to comply with regulatory STET requirements for accounting and auditing for HUD-assisted housing. Includes accounting control policies, audit preparation checklists, model accounting book entries, forms, staff memos and model letters.
Cost: $195.00
Frequency: Monthly
Founded in: 1980
Printed in 2 colors on matte stock

11667 Assisted Housing Management Insider
Brownstone Publishers
149 5th Ave
16th Floor
New York, NY 10010-6832
212-473-8200
800-643-8095; *Fax:* 212-473-8786
info@hcmarketplace.com;
www.hcmarketplace.com
John Striker, Publisher
Explains HUD regulatory requirements for federally-assisted housing, and gives advice on how to stay in compliance. Includes sample copies of model leases, clauses, letters, eviction notices, authorization forms, checklists and signs.
Printed in 2 colors on matte stock

11668 BNA's Eastern Europe Reporter
Bureau of National Affairs
1801 S Bell St
Arlington, VA 22202-4501
703-341-3000
800-372-1033; *Fax:* 800-253-0332
customercare@bna.com; www.bnabooks.com
Paul N Wojcik, CEO
William A. Beltz
This is just one of many biweekly notification services covering legislative, regulatory and legal developments affecting business, trade and investment in Eastern Europe and the former Soviet Union.
Cost: $1750.00
Frequency: Bi-annually

11669 CQ Congressional Quarterly
Congressional Quarterly
1414 22nd Street NW
Washington, DC 20037-1003
202-887-8500
Offers information on House and Senate committee hearings scheduled for up to two months from publication date.
Cost: $1299.00

11670 CQ Schedules
Congressional Quarterly
77 K Street NE
Washington, DC 20002-4681
202-650-6500
800-432-2250
customerservice@cqrollcall.com; www.cq.com
Susan Benkelman, Executive Editor
Randy Wynn, Deputy Executive Editor
Anne Q Hoy, Managing Editor, Spec. Publications
Caitlin Hendel, Managing Editor, CQ Today
Melanie Starkey, Editor, Daily News
A daily guide to what's happening in Washington.

11671 CQ Today
Congressional Quarterly
77 K Street NE
Washington, DC 20002-4681
202-650-6500
800-432-2250
customerservice@cqrollcall.com; www.cq.com
Susan Benkelman, Executive Editor
Randy Wynn, Deputy Executive Editor
Anne Q Hoy, Managing Editor, Spec. Publications
Caitlin Hendel, Managing Editor, CQ Today
Melanie Starkey, Editor, Daily News
CQ Today, available in print and online, delivers unparalleled coverage and analysis from the floor, committee markups, hearings and more. Subscribers receive updates throughout the day as news breaks on Capitol Hill.

11672 Census and You
Census Bureau
4700 Silver Hill Rd
Washington, DC 20233-0001
301-763-3030; *Fax:* 301-457-3670
NPC.Call.Center.Info@census.gov;
www.census.gov
Thomas E Zebelsky, Plant Manager
Highlights data products and program of the US Census Bureau. Shows which reports, CD-ROMs, tapes, etc. to choose and also highlights releases on the Internet.
Cost: $21.00
12 Pages
Frequency: Monthly
Circulation: 11000
Founded in: 1790
Printed in 2 colors on matte stock

11673 Civil Rights: From the State Capitals
Wakeman Walworth
PO Box 7376
Alexandria, VA 22307-7376
703-768-9600; *Fax:* 703-768-9690;
www.statecapitals.com/civilrights.html
Keyes Walworth, Publisher
Covers ethnic, race and gender discrimination; including hate crime legislation, racial profiling, the current battle over affirmative action plus gay rights, domestic partner issues, rights of the disabled, rights of minors, women in the workforce, Hispanic issues. Includes legislation, judicial and administrative decisions across the country, as well as federal actions that affect the states.
Cost: $245.00
4 Pages
Frequency: Weekly
Founded in: 1962
Printed in one color on matte stock

11674 Clearinghouse
NAGARA
1450 Western Avenue
Suite 101
Albany, NY 12203
518-694-8472; *Fax:* 518-463-8656
nagara@caphill.com; www.nagara.org
Paul R. Bergeron, President
Daphne DeLeon, Vice President
Caryn Wojcik, Secretary
Nancy Fortna, Treasurer
Illustrated newsletter of NAGARA. Features lively articles, informative announcements, a wide variety of news, and a column by the Archivist of the United States. Provides a forum for archivists to share information and learn from each other. Electronic publication only.
Frequency: Quarterly

11675 Connections
National Public Employer Labor Relations Assoc
1012 South Coast Highway
Suite M
Oceanside, CA 92054
760-433-1686
877-673-5721; *Fax:* 760-433-1687
mike@npelra.org; www.npelra.org
The outstanding monthly e-newsletter, your connection to national, regional and local developments. For members only
Frequency: Monthly
Circulation: 2000

11676 Cooperative Housing Bulletin
National Association of Housing Cooperatives

1444 I St Nw
Suite 700
Washington, DC 20005-6542

202-737-0797; *Fax:* 202-216-9646
info@nahc.coop; www.coophousing.org

Provides up-to-date information on issues of interest to the cooperative housing community. Accepts advertising.
Frequency: Monthly
Circulation: 2500
Printed in 2 colors on matte stock

11677 Divisions Digest
Federal Bar Association
1220 North Fillmore St.
Suite 444
Arlington, VA 22201

571-481-9100; *Fax:* 571-481-9090
fba@fedbar.org; www.fedbar.org
Social Media: Facebook, Twitter, LinkedIn

Fern C. Bomchill, President
Robert J. DeSousa, President-Elect
Hon. Gustavo Gelpi, Jr., Treasurer

Serves the Corporate and Association Counsel, Federal Career Service, Senior Lawyers, and the Younger Lawyers Divisions of the FBA.
16000 Members
Frequency: Bi-Annually
Founded in: 1920

11678 Downtown Idea Exchange
Alexander Communications Group
1916 Park Ave
8th Floor
New York, NY 10037-3733

212-281-6099
800-232-4317; *Fax:* 212-283-7269
info@downtowndevelopment.com;
www.downtowndevelopment.com

Laurence Alexander, Owner
Nadine Harris, Marketing Manager

News of downtown revitalization for downtown leaders and officials in local and state government.
Cost: $167.00
8 Pages
Frequency: Monthly
ISSN: 0012-5822

11679 Downtown Promotion Reporter
Alexander Communications Group
1916 Park Ave
8th Floor
New York, NY 10037-3733

212-281-6099
800-232-4317; *Fax:* 212-283-7269
info@downtowndevelopment.com;
www.downtowndevelopment.com

Romauld Alexander, Owner
Laurence Alexander, CEO
Sarah Benardos, Production Manager
Paul Felt, Editor

Proven promotion ideas and methods to bring shoppers to downtown stores.
Cost: $189.00
12 Pages
Frequency: Monthly
Circulation: 1000
ISSN: 0363-2830
Founded in: 1954

11680 EBA UPDATE
Energy Bar Association
1990 M St NW
Suite 350
Washington, DC 20036-3429

202-223-5625; *Fax:* 202-833-5596
admin@eba-net.org; www.eba-net.org
Social Media: Facebook

Derek A. Dyson, President
Susan A. Olenchuk, President-Elect
Jason F. Leif, Vice President
Emma F. Hand, Secretary
Hugh E. Hilliard, Treasurer

Providing members with the latest news regarding the energy industry.
2600 Members
Frequency: Quarterly
Founded in: 1946

11681 EENR Pursuits
Federal Bar Association
1220 North Fillmore St.
Suite 444
Arlington, VA 22201

571-481-9100; *Fax:* 571-481-9090
fba@fedbar.org; www.fedbar.org
Social Media: Facebook, Twitter, LinkedIn

Fern C. Bomchill, President
Robert J. DeSousa, President-Elect
Hon. Gustavo Gelpi, Jr., Treasurer

EENR Section newsletter.
16000 Members
Frequency: Bi-Annually
Founded in: 1920

11682 Economic Development Now
International Economic Development Council
734 15th Street NW
Suite 900
Washington, DC 20005

202-223-7800; *Fax:* 202-223-4745;
www.iedc.org

Jeff Finkle, President & CEO
Dennis G. Coleman, Chair
Jay C. Moon, Vice Chair
Paul Krutko, Secretary/ Treasurer

Member publication providing a survey of current economic development news, original reports examining best practices, and updates concerning federal funding and activity.
1.8M Members
Frequency: Bi-Monthly
Founded in: 1967

11683 Economic Development: From the State Capitals
Wakeman Walworth
PO BOX 7376
Alexandria, VA 22307-7376

703-768-9600; *Fax:* 703-768-9690;
www.statecapitals.com/

Keyes Walworth, Publisher

Covers environmental requirements, land use regulation, mass transportation, highway construction plans, utility rates, changes in labor laws, tax policies, enterprise zones, parkland development, taxes, licensing and fees. Includes vital urban development programs: growth control legislation, state construction programs involving airports, stadiums, and building codes.
Cost: $245.00
8 Pages
Frequency: Weekly
Founded in: 1963
Printed in one color on Y stock

11684 Employee Policy for the Public and Private Sector: From the State Capitals
Wakeman Walworth
PO Box 7376
Alexandria, VA 22307-7376

703-768-9600; *Fax:* 703-549-1372;
www.statecapitals.com/employeepolicy.html

Keyes Walworth, Publisher

Provides a nationwide perspective on employee health insurance programs, sexual harassment policies, unemployment and workers' compensation, retirement policies, family medical leave, new ergonomic rules, pay equity programs, collective bargaining, dismissal practices, minimum wages, drug testing, background checks, day care centers, domestic partner rules.
Cost: $245.00
4 Pages
Frequency: Weekly
Printed in one color on matte stock

11685 EuroWatch
WorldTrade Executive
PO Box 761
Concord, MA 01742

978-287-0301; *Fax:* 978-287-0302
info@wtexec.com; www.wtexec.com

Alison French, Production Manager

Analyzes the most recent EU judicial and legislative developments. Covers EU trade issues, labor issues, single market and currency issues, EU and individual country business law, trademark issues.
Cost: $797.00

11686 Federal Action Affecting the States: From the State Capitals
Wakeman Walworth
PO Box 7376
Alexandria, VA 22307-7376

703-768-9600; *Fax:* 703-768-9690;
www.statecapitals.com/fedaction.html

Keyes Walworth, Publisher

Gives a state perspective on Federal court rulings, overseer programs, changes in state jurisdiction, federal funds for state programs, highway, drug abuse control, disaster, environmental and other programs that involve both the states and the Feds.
Cost: $245.00
4 Pages
Frequency: Weekly
Founded in: 1955
Printed in one color on matte stock

11687 Federal Assistance Monitor
CD Publications
8204 Fenton St
Silver Spring, MD 20910-4571

301-588-6380
800-666-6380; *Fax:* 301-588-6385;
www.cdpublications.com

Michael Gerecht, President
Dave Kittross, Editor

Comprehensive review of federal funding announcements, private grants, rule changes and legislative actions affecting the community programs.
Cost: $419.00
Frequency: Monthly
Founded in: 1961
Mailing list available for rent: 2,000 names at $160 per M

11688 Federal Employees News Digest
1850 Centennial Park Drive
Suite 520
Reston, VA 20191

703-648-9551
800-989-3363; *Fax:* 703-648-0265

Publishes weekly newsletter and self-help books for federal and postal employees on retirement and pay, as well as other benefit-related topics.

Accepts advertising.
Cost: $49.00
4 Pages
Frequency: 5x Yearly
Founded in: 1951

11689 **Federal Times**
6883 Commercial Dr
Springfield, VA 22159
800-368-5718
armylet@atpco.com; www.defensenews.com
Mark Winans, VP
Elaine Howard, President/CEO
Alex Neill, Managing Editor
Jim Tice, Senior Writer
David Smith, Marketing
Timely news and information on the rapid changes impacting today's federal managers, managing staff, the latest technology, and financial and career decisions.
Cost: $55.00
Frequency: Weekly
Circulation: 1MM

11690 **Friday Flash**
Coalition for Government Procurement
1990 M St Nw
Suite 450
Washington, DC 20036-3466
202-331-0975; *Fax:* 202-822-9788
info@thecgp.org; www.thecgp.org
A weekly newsletter published by the Coalition for Government Procurement.
38387 Pages
Frequency: Weekly
Circulation: 1200
Founded in: 1979

11691 **From the State Capitals**
Wakeman Walworth
PO BOX 7376
Alexandria, VA 22307-7376
703-768-9600; *Fax:* 703-768-9690
thecapitolcollection.com
Keyes Walworth, Publisher
Keeps readers informed of national trends in domestic lawmaking. Issues dealing with taxes, the environment, economic development, drug abuse, abortion and education.
Founded in: 1955

11692 **GovManagement Daily**
American Society for Public Administration
1301 Pennsylvania Avenue NW
Suite 700
Washington, DC 20004
202-393-7878; *Fax:* 202-638-4952
info@aspanet.org; www.aspanet.org
Social Media: Facebook, Twitter, LinkedIn
Erik O. Bergrud, President
Stephen E. Condrey, Vice-President
Kuotsai Tom Liou, President-Elect
Presenting headlines and brief summaries of news and other information and analysis on public-sector management at all levels of government.
15M Members
Frequency: Daily
Founded in: 1939

11693 **Government Employee Relations Report**
Bureau of National Affairs
1801 S Bell St
Arlington, VA 22202-4501
703-341-3000
800-372-1033; *Fax:* 800-253-0332
customercare@bna.com; www.bnabooks.com
Paul N Wojcik, CEO
A notification service that covers federal, state and municipal government employee relations.
Cost: $1479.00
Frequency: Weekly

11694 **Government PROcurement**
Penton Media
1300 E 9th St
Suite 316
Cleveland, OH 44114-1503
216-696-7000; *Fax:* 216-696-6662;
www.govpro.com
Jane Cooper, Marketing
Kristin M Atwater, Managing Editor
Kay Ross Baker, Publisher
Specifically for the public sector purchasing professional.
58 Pages
Circulation: 20000
ISSN: 1078-0769
Founded in: 1892
Printed in 4 colors on glossy stock

11695 **Government Waste Watch Newspaper**
Citizens Against Government Waste
1301 Pennsylvania Ave NW
Suite 1075
Washington, DC 20004-1707
202-467-5300; *Fax:* 202-467-4253
membership@cagw.org; www.cagw.org
Thomas A. Schatz, President
Robert J. Tedeschi, Treasurer & CFO
A quarterly newspaper published by Citizens Against Government Waste.
Cost: $25.00
Frequency: Quarterly
Circulation: 108000
Founded in: 1984
Mailing list available for rent

11696 **HAC News**
Housing Assistance Council
1025 Vermont Ave NW
Suite 606
Washington, DC 20005-3516
202-842-8600; *Fax:* 202-347-3441
hac@ruralhome.org; www.ruralhome.org
Moises Loza, Executive Director
Janice Clark, Editor
Newsletter publishing issues of rural and low-income housing. Free.
ISSN: 1093-8036

11697 **HOTLINE**
National Journal
The Watergate
600 New Hampshire Ave., NW
Washington, DC 20037
202-739-8400
800-207-8001; *Fax:* 202-833-8069
webmaster@asahq.org;
www.nationaljournal.com
Julie Abramson, Associate Production Editor
Tim Alberta, Sr Editor, National Journal Hotline
Ronald Brownstein, Editorial Director
Online daily newsletter offers information on US national, state and local political campaigns and issues.
Frequency: Weekly
Founded in: 1987

11698 **Health Officer News**
US Conference of Local Health Officers
1620 I Street NW
Washington, DC 20006-4005
202-887-6120; *Fax:* 202-293-2352
Alan Campbell, Publisher
Stephen Horn, Editor
The official publication of the US conference of local health officers. Accepts advertising.
Cost: $35.00
12 Pages
Frequency: BiWeekly

11699 **Housing Law Bulletin**
National Housing Law Project
703 Market Street
Suite 2000
San Francisco, CA 94103
415-546-7000; *Fax:* 415-546-7007
nhlp@nhlp.org; www.nhlp.org
Marcia Rosen, Executive Director
James Grow, Deputy Director
Susan Stern, Deputy Director, Administration
Updates in housing law information for use by legal services organizations.
Cost: $175.00
Frequency: Monthly
Circulation: 400

11700 **ICBA NewsWatch Today**
Independent Community Bankers of America
1615 L Street NW
Suite 900
Washington, DC 20036
800-422-8439; *Fax:* 202-659-3604
info@icba.org; www.icba.org
Salvatore Marranca, Chairman
Jeffrey L. Gerhart, Chairman-Elect
William A. Loving, Jr., Vice Chairman
Steven R. Gardner, Secretary
Jack Hartings, Treasurer
Free electronic news bulletin highlighting breaking industry news and information.
Frequency: Daily

11701 **In Hot Pursuit**
Federal Bar Association
1220 North Fillmore St.
Suite 444
Arlington, VA 22201
571-481-9100; *Fax:* 571-481-9090
fba@fedbar.org; www.fedbar.org
Social Media: Facebook, Twitter, LinkedIn
Fern C. Bomchill, President
Robert J. DeSousa, President-Elect
Hon. Gustavo Gelpi, Jr., Treasurer
Criminal Law Section newsletter.
16000 Members
Frequency: Bi-Annually
Founded in: 1920

11702 **Inside Energy**
Platts, McGraw Hill Companies
1221 Avenue of the Americas
New York, NY 10020-1001
212-512-2000; *Fax:* 212-512-3840
support@platts.com; www.mcgraw-hill.com
Glenn S Goldberg, President
Georgia Safos, Circulation Director
Covers the Department of Energy including energy, science/technology, and environmental management programs as well as energy programs at the Interior Department.
Cost: $1395.00
16 Pages
Frequency: Weekly
Founded in: 1884

11703 **International Association of Emergency Managers**
201 Park Washington Court
Falls Church, VA 22046-4513
703-538-1795; *Fax:* 703-241-5603
info@iaem.com; www.iaem.com
Elizabeth B Armstrong, Executive Director
Sharon L Kelly, Member Director

Elizabeth B Armstrong, CEO
Karen Thompson, Editor
Dawn Shiley, Communication Manager

Representatives of city and county government departments responsible for emergency management and disaster preparedness.
Cost: $160.00
20 Pages
Frequency: Monthly
Circulation: 2700
Founded in: 1952
Printed in 2 colors on matte stock

11704 **Lottery, Parimutuel & Casino Regulation: From the State Capitals**
Wakeman Walworth
PO BOX 7376
Alexandria, VA 22307-7376

703-768-9600; *Fax:* 703-768-9690;
www.statecapitals.com/lotterypari.html

Keyes Walworth, Publisher

Covers regulation, or attempts to regulate every form of gambling from internet gambling to cockfighting. It covers state lottery prize structures, ticket marketing policies, distribution of revenues, new games and equipment; Indian gaming, gambling compacts with tribes and revenue sharing; regulation and taxation of casinos, pari-mutuel wagering operations plus horse racing, dog racing, jai alai, riverboat gambling, bingo and other forms of gaming.
Cost: $345.00
4 Pages
Frequency: Weekly
Founded in: 1962
Printed in one color on matte stock

11705 **Managing Today's Federal Employees**
LRP Publications
PO Box 980
Horsham, PA 19044-0980

215-784-0912
800-341-7874; *Fax:* 215-784-9639
webmaster@lrp.com; www.lrp.com

Todd Lutz, CFO
Patrick Byrne, Editor
Chris Donohue, Legal Editor

Keeping supervisors informed of their personnel management responsibilities has always been one of the most difficult tasks facing federal agency personnel officers. This newsletter is a working resource as well as a comprehensive training tool. Gives sensible solutions to common management challenges and covers controversial issues such as sexual harassment, contracting out of federal jobs, alternative dispute resolutions and more.
Cost: $155.00
8 Pages
Frequency: Monthly
Founded in: 1977
Printed in 2 colors on matte stock

11706 **Mediaite**
584 Broadway
Suite 510
New York, NY 10012

E-Mail: info@mediaite.com;
www.mediaite.com

Dan Abrams, Founder
Jon Nicosia, Senior Editor & Video Director
Nando Di Fino, Senior Editor & TV Reporter
Tommy Christopher, Political Editor & WH Correspondent
Colby Hall, Editor at Large

Mediaite is the site for news, information and smart opinions about print, online and broadcast media, offering original and immediate assessments of the latest news as it breaks.

11707 **Motor Vehicle Regulation: From the State Capitals**
Wakeman Walworth
PO Box 7376
Alexandria, VA 22307-7376

703-768-9600; *Fax:* 703-768-9690;
www.statecapitals.com/motorreg.html

Keyes Walworth, Publisher

Covers all fifty states regarding inspections, tags, fees and taxes, emissions standards, drunken driving laws, motorist licensing, insurance and education . We report on helmet , seat belt, and child restraint seat laws; regulation of all motor vehicles including autos, trucks, motorcycles, school buses, electric vehicles, watercraft. We also cover motor vehicle department administrative changes.
Cost: $245.00
4 Pages
Frequency: Weekly
Founded in: 1962
Printed in one color on matte stock

11708 **NACCED Alerts**
Nat'l Assoc. for County & Economic Development
2025 M St NW
Suite 800
Washington, DC 20036-3309

202-367-1163; *Fax:* 202-367-2149;
www.nacced.org

John Murphy, Executive Director
Brian Paulson, President
Jack Exler, Vice President
Tony Agliata, Secretary/Treasurer
Bill J. Lake, Director

Analyze federal legislation and regulations, highlight innovative county activities, report on current developments in the field, and provide updates on association activities.
120+ Members
Frequency: Bi-Weekly
Founded in: 1989

11709 **NADC News**
National Association of Development Companies
6764 Old McLean Village Dr
Mc Lean, VA 22101-3906

703-748-2575; *Fax:* 703-748-2582;
www.nadco.org

Chris Crawford, President

Provides long-term fixed asset financing to small businesses. Publishes newsletter.
Frequency: Monthly
Circulation: 244
Founded in: 1981

11710 **NAHMA News**
National Affordable Housing Management Association
400 N Columbus Street
Suite 203
Alexandria, VA 22314

703-683-8630; *Fax:* 703-683-8634;
www.nahma.org

Trade association for professional property managers of federally assisted housing. Publishes a newsletter.
Cost: $95.00
Frequency: Bimonthly
Circulation: 3000

11711 **NASAA Insight**
NA Securities Administrators Association
750 First Street NE
Suite 1140
Washington, DC 20002-8034

202-737-0900; *Fax:* 202-783-3571;
www.nasaa.org
Social Media: Facebook

Jack Herstein, President
Preston DuFauchard, President-Elect
Rick Hancox, Secretary
Fred J. Joseph, Treasurer

Designed to keep readers informed of recent NASAA activities.
Frequency: Quarterly
Founded in: 1919

11712 **NASCSP Newsletter**
Nat'l Assoc. for State Community Service Programs
444 N Capitol St NW
Suite 846
Washington, DC 20001-1556

202-624-5866; *Fax:* 202-624-7745
nascsp@nascsp.org; www.nascsp.org
Social Media: Facebook, Twitter

Steve Payne, President
William Brand, Vice President
Jennifer Sexson, Treasurer
Ditzah Wooden-Wade, Secretary

Updates the Community Action Network on pertinent legislation, best practices, CSBG and WAP program highlights, and the latest events.
100 Members
Founded in: 1968

11713 **NASFA News**
Natl' Assoc. of State Facilities Administrators
2760 Research Park Drive
PO Box 11910
Lexington, KY 40578-1910

859-311-1877
800-800-1910; *Fax:* 859-244-8001
nasfa@nasfa.net; www.nasfa.net/

Marcia Stone, Executive Director

State administrators of facilities and property. A newsletter is published for members.
Cost: $1800.00
Frequency: Quarterly
Circulation: 2000
Founded in: 1987

11714 **NATAT's Reporter**
National Association of Towns and Townships
444 N Capitol St Nw
Suite 397
Washington, DC 20001-1512

202-624-8195; *Fax:* 202-624-3554
natat@sso.org; www.natat.org

Kelly Aylward, Manager
Larry Merrill, Vice President
Matthew DeTemple, Secretary, Treasurer

Covers federal legislation and regulation that pertain to local governments, with emphasis on compact or small towns (under 50,000; many under 1,000); also includes case studies of exemplary, creative local government, programs and association news from the National Association of Towns & Townships.
Cost: $36.00
24 Pages
Frequency: BiWeekly
Circulation: 15,200
Mailing list available for rent: 11700 names at $85 per M
Printed in 2 colors on newsprint stock

11715 **NCDA News**
National Community Development Association

522 21st St NW
Suite 120
Washington, DC 20006-5012

202-293-7587; *Fax:* 202-887-5546;
www.ncdaonline.org

Shandra Western, Editor

A national nonprofit membership organization representing local governments that implement community development programs. The members administer federally supported community development, housing and human services programs. NCDA provides counsel at the federal level on new program design and current program implementation and advocates on behalf of responsive community development.
13 Pages

11716 Nation's Cities Weekly
National League of Cities
1301 Pennsylvania Ave NwW
Suite 550
Washington, DC 20004-1747

202-626-3180; *Fax:* 202-626-3043
info@nlc.org; www.nlc.org

Donald J Borut, Executive Director

News for and about cities.
Cost: $96.00
Frequency: Weekly
Circulation: 30000
ISSN: 0164-5935

11717 National Association of Conservation Districts
NACD
509 Capitol Court, NE
Washington, DC 20002-4937

202-547-6223; *Fax:* 202-547-6450;
www.nacdnet.org

John Larson, CEO

Highlights forestry issues of importance to districts and to showcase district-related forestry projects and success stories.
17000 Members
Frequency: Monthly
Founded in: 1946

11718 National Association of Regional Councils
National Association of Regional Councils
1666 Connecticut Ave NW
Suite 305
Washington, DC 20002

202-986-1032; *Fax:* 202-986-1038
lindsey@narc.org; www.narc.org

Fred Abousleman, Executive Director
Lindsey Riley, Deputy of Communications
Frequency: Weekly
Circulation: 2000

11719 Navy Times
Gannett Government Media
6883 Commercial Drive
Springfield, VA 22159-500

703-750-7400
800-368-5718; *Fax:* 703-750-8622
tnaegele@atpco.com; www.navytimes.com

Elaine Howard, President
Judy McCoy, Associate Publisher
David Smith, VP Marketing/Business Dev
Dick Howlett, AVP Circulation Operations
Tobias Naegele, Executive Editor

The trusted, independent source for news and information of the Navy community. Breaking news, personal finance information, healthcare, recreational resources, exclusive videos and photos, Guard and Reserve information, and an expanded community area connecting service members, military families and veterans.
Cost: $143.00
Frequency: Weekly

11720 Outlook: From the State Capitals
Wakeman Walworth
PO Box 7376
Alexandria, VA 22307-7376

703-768-9600; *Fax:* 703-549-1372;
www.statecapitals.com/theoutlook.html

Keyes Walworth, Publisher

Gives an excellent perspective of trend- setting topics in state lawmaking: internet taxes, school choice, economic development, abortion, environmental issues, gambling laws. Each week is devoted to a different subject. In addition, a special feature called In the Works Around The Nation provides current highlights from other State Capitals newsletters.
Cost: $245.00
4 Pages
Frequency: Weekly
Printed in one color on matte stock

11721 PA TIMES
American Society for Public Administration
1301 Pennsylvania Avenue NW
Suite 700
Washington, DC 20004

202-393-7878; *Fax:* 202-638-4952
info@aspanet.org; www.aspanet.org
Social Media: Facebook, Twitter, LinkedIn

Erik O. Bergrud, President
Stephen E. Condrey, Vice-President
Kuotsai Tom Liou, President-Elect

ASPA's newspaper covering developments in the professional field of public administration. Article topics include successful local state and federal government programs, PA trends and new PA methods. Focuses on the issues that face public managers today. Also highlights best practices in the field and updates members on how ASPA plays a role in the support of the public sector.
15M Members
Frequency: Monthly
Founded in: 1939

11722 Politico
Capitol News Company
1100 Wilson Blvd
Suite 610
Arlington, VA 22209

703-647-7999
newsrelease@politico.com; www.politico.com

Robert L Allbritton, Publisher
Frederick J Ryan Jr, President & CEO
Kim Kingsley, Chief Operating Officer
John F Harris, Editor-In-Chief
Jim VandeHei, Executive Editor

Provides insider-like access to Washington and the latest from the world of politics.

11723 Public Health: From the State Capitals
Wakeman Walworth
PO Box 7376
Alexandria, VA 22307-7376

703-768-9600; *Fax:* 703-768-9690;
www.statecapitals.com

Keyes Walworth, Publisher

Reports on a wide range of health care legislation such as AIDS disclosure and testing, drug programs, abortion rulings, cancer prevention including smoking restrictions in public places, mental health and disability programs, disease control, regulation of hospitals and nursing homes, clinics, food inspection policies, organ donor management and Medicare. It covers such current issues as mail order through pharmacies on the internet.
Cost: $245.00
4 Pages
Frequency: Weekly
Printed in one color on matte stock

11724 Public Safety and Justice Policies: From the State Capitals
Wakeman Walworth
PO Box 7376
Alexandria, VA 22307-7376

703-768-9600; *Fax:* 703-768-9690;
www.statecapitals.com/publicsafety.html

Keyes Walworth, Publisher

Covers gun control on school grounds, buy-back programs, gunmaker lawsuits, law enforcement, arrest procedures, drug law enforcement and penalties; financing and administration of substance-abuse counseling, school violence , police administration, truth in sentencing , prison administration, prisoner drug testing and AIDS testing, new evidence such as DNA, inmate work programs, gender bias in the courtroom, family and juvenile justice, victim compensation laws, inmate living conditions
Cost: $245.00
4 Pages
Frequency: Weekly
Printed in one color on matte stock

11725 Roads and Bridges
Scranton Gillette Communications
3030 W Salt Creek Lane
Suite 201
Arlington Heights, IL 60005-5025

847-391-1000; *Fax:* 847-390-0408
bwilson@sgcmail.com;
www.scrantongillette.com/roadsandbridges

Bill Wildon, Editorial Director
Allen Zeyher, Managing Editor
Rick Schwer, Publisher

Provides engineers, contractors and government officials with the latest advancements in the road and bridge industry, timely news coverage and important information on products beneficial to the job site of office.
Cost: $40.00
92 Pages
Frequency: Monthly
Circulation: 70000
ISSN: 8750-9229
Founded in: 1905

11726 SideBAR
Federal Bar Association
1220 North Fillmore St.
Suite 444
Arlington, VA 22201

571-481-9100; *Fax:* 571-481-9090
fba@fedbar.org; www.fedbar.org
Social Media: Facebook, Twitter, LinkedIn

Fern C. Bomchill, President
Robert J. DeSousa, President-Elect
Hon. Gustavo Gelpi, Jr., Treasurer

Federal Litigation Section Newsletter
16000 Members
Frequency: Quarterly
Founded in: 1920

11727 Standards Action
American National Standards Institute
1819 L St NW
11th Floor
Washington, DC 20036-3864

202-293-8020; *Fax:* 202-293-9287
info@ansi.org; www.ansi.org

Arthur E. Cote, Chairman
Joe Bhatia, President & CEO

Published to assure a complete consensus of ANSI members and the general public by facilitating review of proposed standards. Also in-

cluded is information on draft American National Standards, governmental and other foreign standards and conformity assessment activities.
1000 Members
Frequency: Weekly
Founded in: 1918

11728 Tax Administrators News
Federation of Tax Administrators
444 N Capitol St NW
Suite 348
Washington, DC 20001-1538

202-624-5890; *Fax:* 202-624-7888;
www.taxadmin.org

Harley Duncan, Executive Director
Rian Turruss, Editor

Covers state and federal legislation, US Supreme Court and state court cases, and developments relating to state tax administration.
Cost: $40.00
12 Pages
Frequency: Monthly
Circulation: 2000
Founded in: 1930
Printed in one color on matte stock

11729 Taxes-Property: From State Capitals
Wakeman Walworth
PO Box 7376
Alexandria, VA 22307-7376

703-689-9600; *Fax:* 703-768-9690;
www.statecapitals.com/taxprop.html

Keyes Walworth, Publisher

Covers new property tax legislation, initiatives, referenda, property assessment programs, tax exemptions, tax incentives, and tax collection methods. This newsletter emphasizes the use of property taxes for school financing including state aid formulas, alternative school financing methods, budget issues related to teacher pay and class sizes.
Cost: $345.00
4 Pages
Frequency: Weekly
Printed in one color on matte stock

11730 The Certifier
Association of Boards of Certification
2805 SW Snyder Blvd.
Suite 535
Ankeny, IA 50023

515-232-3623; *Fax:* 515-965-6827
abc@abccert.org; www.abccert.org

Paul Bishop, Executive Director
Bob Hoyt, Vice President
Cheryl Bergener, President
Kathy Cook, VP

The newsletter for environmental certification authorities, filled with news and updates on the latest in certification and focuses on state and provincial certification programs, certification issues, and association events.
Frequency: Monthly
Founded in: 1972

11731 The Government Standard
American Federation of Government Employees
80 F St NW
Washington, DC 20001-1528

202-737-8700; *Fax:* 202-639-6490
comments@afge.org; www.afge.com

John Gage, President
J. David Cox, Secretary/Treasurer
Augusta Thomas, VP for Women's & Fair Practices

AFGE's official membership publication keeping members up to date on what their local government is up to.
Frequency: Quarterly
Founded in: 1932

11732 The Resolver
Federal Bar Association
1220 North Fillmore St.
Suite 444
Arlington, VA 22201

571-481-9100; *Fax:* 571-481-9090
fba@fedbar.org; www.fedbar.org
Social Media: Facebook, Twitter, LinkedIn

Fern C. Bomchill, President
Robert J. DeSousa, President-Elect
Hon. Gustavo Gelpi, Jr., Treasurer

Turning conflict into resolution, Alternative Dispute Resolution Section newsletter.
16000 Members
Frequency: Bi-Annually
Founded in: 1920

11733 The Resource
National Association of Conservation Districts
509 Capitol Ct. NE
Washington, DC 20002-4937

202-547-6223; *Fax:* 202-547-6450;
www.nacdnet.org

Krysta Harden, CEO
Bob Cordova, Second Vice President

NACD's print publication provides in depth coverage of the association's recent activities and features columns by the NACD CEO and President, in addition to guest and partnership columns.
Cost: $35.00
12 Pages
Frequency: Monthly
Circulation: 25000
Founded in: 1937

11734 This Week in Washington
American Public Human Services Association
1133 19th Street NW
Suite 400
Washington, DC 20036-3623

202-682-0100; *Fax:* 202-289-6555;
www.aphsa.org

Tracy Wareing, Executive Director

Gives readers concise updates on initiatives of the administration, legislative action in human service programs, the latest information on federal regulations, and state agency personnel changes- everything the human service administrator needs to know from the nation's capital.
Frequency: Weekly
Founded in: 1930

11735 URISA Newsletter
Association for GIS Professionals
701 Lee St.
Suite 680
Des Plaines, IL 60016-4508

847-824-6300; *Fax:* 847-824-6363
info@urisa.org; www.urisa.org

Susan Johnson, President
Wendy Nelson, Executive Director

Effective use of information systems technology at the state, regional and local levels Newsletter is published.
Frequency: Monthly
Founded in: 1963

11736 US Mayor
US Conference of Mayors
1620 I St Nw
Suite 40
Washington, DC 20006-4034

202-464-0790; *Fax:* 202-293-2352
info@usmayors.org; www.usmayors.org

Don Plusquellic, President
Tom Cochan, Editor
Guy Smith, Managing Editor
Michael Guido, Chair Advisory Board
J Thomas Cochran, CEO

Federal government and congressional activities.
Cost: $35.00
16 Pages
Circulation: 6000
Founded in: 1933

11737 USNC News and Notes
American National Standards Institute
1819 L St NW
11th Floor
Washington, DC 20036-3864

202-293-8020; *Fax:* 202-293-9287
info@ansi.org; www.ansi.org

Arthur E. Cote, Chairman
Joe Bhatia, President & CEO

For the electrotechnology community summarizing activities, events, and items of interest for the US National Committee of the International Electrotechnical Commission, keeping US stakeholders informed about the latest standards and conformity assessment updates in the domestic, regional and global arenas.
1000 Members
Frequency: Quarterly
Founded in: 1918

11738 United Nations Jobs Newsletter
Thomas F Burola & Associates
6477 Telephone Road
Suite 7R
Ventura, CA 93003-4459

805- 64- 725; *Fax:* 805-654-1708

Thomas F Burola, Publisher

Focus of this newsletter is employment conditions within the United Nations System and vacancy notices.
Cost: $145.00
Circulation: 3,500
Founded in: 1994
Printed in 2 colors on matte stock

11739 United States Conference of Mayors News
United States Conference of Mayors
1620 Eye Street, NW
Washington, DC 20006-4005

202-293-7330; *Fax:* 202-293-2352
info@usmayors.org; www.usmayors.org/uscm/

J Thomas Cochran, President
William Fay, CEO

City government officials. Newsletter is available for members.
Circulation: 30000
Founded in: 1932

11740 Washington Report
Federal Managers Association
1641 Prince St
Alexandria, VA 22314-2818

703-683-8700; *Fax:* 703-683-8707
info@fedmanagers.org; www.fedmanagers.org

Todd Wells, Manager
Darryl A Perkinson, President

News bulletin detailing the latest developments on Capitol Hill and in the nation's capital.
15M Members
Frequency: Quarterly
Founded in: 1913

11741 **Washington Spectator**
Public Concern Foundation
PO Box 20065
New York, NY 10011

212-741-2365
subscriptions@washingtonspectator.com; www.washingtonspectator.com/

Kevin Walter, Publisher
Ben A Franklin, Editor
Lisa Vandepaer, Associate Editor
Marvin Shanken, Owner
Ruth Shikes, Co-Founder

News, comment and analysis on current national and international affairs; politics, economics, environment and social issues.
Cost: $15.00
4 Pages
Circulation: 60,000
Founded in: 1974
Mailing list available for rent: 60000 names at $75 per M
Printed in one color on matte stock

11742 **Washington Trade Daily**
Trade Reports International Group
PO Box 1802
Wheaton, MD 20915-1802

301-946-0817; *Fax:* 301-946-2631
trigtrig@aol.com; www.washingtontradedaily.com/
Social Media: Twitter

Jim Berger, CEO
D Kanth, Editor

The only faxed daily newsletters of its kind that covers the goings-on in the nation's Capital related to imports, exports and foreign investment. It reports daily to readers on the Executive Branch - including the US Trade Representative's office and the Commerce Department - as well as Congress. Readers can gain insight every morning on what are likely to be new laws and regulations governing international business tomorrow.
Cost: $650.00
16 Pages
Frequency: Daily
Founded in: 1991
Printed in one color

11743 **What's New?**
American National Standards Institute
1819 L St NW
11th Floor
Washington, DC 20036-3864

202-293-8020; *Fax:* 202-293-9287
info@ansi.org; www.ansi.org

Arthur E. Cote, Chairman
Joe Bhatia, President & CEO

Electronic newsletter distributed to members and constituents free of charge. Includes synopses and links to the most recent news, events and publications available from ANSI Online.
1000 Members
Frequency: Weekly
Founded in: 1918

11744 **Worldwide Government Report**
Worldwide Government Directories
7979 Old Georgetown Road
Suite 900
Bethesda, MD 20814-2429

301-258-2677
800-332-3535; *Fax:* 301-718-8494

Jonathan Hixon, Publisher

Each issue provides detailed reports of elections, government and military turnover. Events covered include ousted heads of state, reshuffled governments, changes in ruling majorities, analyses of recent elections, outlooks for upcoming elections, and senior military appointments.
Cost: $247.00
Frequency: Monthly

11745 **eNotes**
National Association of Conservation Districts
509 Capitol Ct. NE
Washington, DC 20002-4937

202-547-6223; *Fax:* 202-547-6450; www.nacdnet.org

Krysta Harden, CEO
Bob Cordova, Second Vice President

NACD's weekly news briefs.
Cost: $35.00
12 Pages
Frequency: Monthly
Circulation: 25000
Founded in: 1937

Magazines & Journals

11746 **AASHTO Daily Transportation Update**
Amer. Assoc. of State Highway & Trans. Officials
444 N Capitol St NW
Suite 249
Washington, DC 20001-1539

202-624-5800; *Fax:* 202-624-5806
info@aashto.org; www.transportation.org
Social Media: Facebook, Twitter

Kirk T. Steudle, President
Michael P. Lewis, Vice-President
Carlos Braceras, Secretary/ Treasurer
John Horsley, Executive Director

To help members and other transportation professionals stay informed about critical industry happenings and events.
52 Members
Frequency: Daily

11747 **AASHTO Journal**
Amer. Assoc. of State Highway & Trans. Officials
444 N Capitol St NW
Suite 249
Washington, DC 20001-1539

202-624-5800; *Fax:* 202-624-5806
info@aashto.org; www.transportation.org
Social Media: Facebook, Twitter

Kirk T. Steudle, President
Michael P. Lewis, Vice-President
Carlos Braceras, Secretary/ Treasurer
John Horsley, Executive Director

Electronic journal to help members and other transportation professionals stay informed about critical industry happenings and events.
52 Members

11748 **ANSI's Annual Report**
American National Standards Institute
1819 L St NW
11th Floor
Washington, DC 20036-3864

202-293-8020; *Fax:* 202-293-9287
info@ansi.org; www.ansi.org

Arthur E. Cote, Chairman
Joe Bhatia, President & CEO

Designed to inform members of the standards community of the Institute's accomplishments and financial activities of the past year, while also laying out goals for the future as presented by the chairman and president.
1000 Members
Frequency: Annually
Founded in: 1918

11749 **APWA Reporter**
American Public Works Association
1275 K Street NW
Suite 750
Washington, DC 20005

202-408-9541
800-848-2792; *Fax:* 202-408-9542
ddancy@apwa.net; www.apwa.net

Peter King, Executive Director
David Dancy, Director Of Marketing
Connie Hartline, Publisher

Prime communication link uniting the community of public works professionals that make up APWA.
Cost: $100.00
Frequency: Monthly
Circulation: 25000
ISSN: 0092-4873
Founded in: 1937
Mailing list available for rent

11750 **Armed Forces Journal**
6883 Commercial Dr
Springfield, VA 22159

800-368-5718
armylet@atpco.com; www.defensenews.com

Mark Winans, VP
Elaine Howard, President/CEO
Alex Neill, Managing Editor
Jim Tice, Senior Writer
David Smith, Marketing

The leading joint service monthly magazine for officers and leaders in the US military community. AFJ has been providing essential review and analysis on key defense issues for more than 140 years. Offers in-depth coverage of military technology, procurement, logistics, strategy, doctrine and tactics. Also covers special operations, US Coast Guard and US National Guard developments.
Cost: $55.00
Frequency: Monthly
Circulation: 1MM

11751 **Army Magazine**
2425 Wison Boulevard
Arlington, VA 22201-3326

703-841-4300
800-336-4570; *Fax:* 703-525-9039
membersupport@ausa.org; www.ausa.org

Gen. Gordon Sullivan, President
Mary Blake French, Editor
Millie Hurlbut, Director of Marketing
Founded in: 1950

11752 **Army Times**
Army Times Publishing Company
6883 Commercial Dr
Springfield, VA 22151-4202

703-750-9000
800-368-5718; *Fax:* 703-750-8622
jmccoy@atpco.com; www.armytimes.com

Elaine Howard, CEO
Judy McCoy, Associate Publisher
Tobias Naegele, Executive Editor
David Smith, Marketing Manager

Magazine soldiers and their families rely on as trusted, independent sources for news and information on the most important issues affecting their careers and personal lives. A single source for breaking news; personal finance information; healthcare; recreational resources; exclusive videos and photos; Guard and Reserve information; and an expanded community area connecting service members, military families and veterans.
Cost: $52.00
Frequency: Weekly

11753 **C41SR Journal**
Defense News

6883 Commercial Dr
Springfield, VA 22159

800-368-5718
armylet@atpco.com; www.defensenews.com

Mark Winans, VP
Elaine Howard, President/CEO
Alex Neill, Managing Editor
Jim Tice, Senior Writer
David Smith, Marketing

Dedicated to the rapidly advancing, high-tech realm of military intelligence, surveillance and reconnaissance. It was the first major periodical to specifically serve this key area of military growth and development, and has a strong following in the world's network-centric warfare community.
Cost: $55.00
Frequency: Monthly
Circulation: 1MM

11754 CQ Weekly
Congressional Quarterly
77 K Street NE
Washington, DC 20002-4681

202-650-6500
800-432-2250
customerservice@cqrollcall.com; www.cq.com

Susan Benkelman, Executive Editor
Randy Wynn, Deputy Executive Editor
Anne Q Hoy, Managing Editor, Spec. Publications
Caitlin Hendel, Managing Editor, CQ Today
Melanie Starkey, Editor, Daily News

This award-winning publication provides a clear perspective on how legislation is shaped, who is shaping it and how the process could affect your interests.

11755 Capitol Ideas
National Association of State Facilities
2760 Research Park Drive
PO Box 11910
Lexington, KY 40578-1910

859-244-8000
800-800-1910; *Fax:* 859-244-8001;
www.csg.org
Social Media: Facebook, Twitter, YouTube

Gov. Brian Schweitzer, President
Gov. Luis Fortuno, President-Elect
Bob Godfrey, Chair
Jay Emler, Chair-Elect
Gary Stevens, Vice Chair

Includes member-driven content, including a targeted focus for each issue, news from each region and association news, focusing on what is going on in the states that might be of interest to other states.

11756 Code Official
International Code Council
4051 Flossmoor Rd
Country Club Hl, IL 60478-5771

708-799-2300
800-214-4321
202-783-2348; *Fax:* 708-799-4981;
www.bocai.org

Paul K Myers, CEO
Margaret M Leddin, Managing Editor

Serves a wide-ranging readership of professionals who are interested in the development, maintenance and enforcement of progressive and reponsive building regulations.
Cost: $30.00
Frequency: Monthly
Circulation: 16000
Founded in: 1994
Printed in on glossy stock

11757 Congressional Digest
Congressional Digest Corporation
4416 East-West Highway
Suite 400
Bethesda, DC 20814-3389

301-634-3113
800-638-8380; *Fax:* 301-634-3189;
www.congressionaldigest.com

Griff Thomas, President
Page Robinson, Publisher
Kathy Thorne, Circulation Manager
Sarah Orrick, Editor

The only publication about Congress that concentrates each month on a single legislative issue in a unique Pro and Con format. It is an indispensable education tool for students of national and world affairs.
Cost: $62.00
36 Pages
ISSN: 0010-5899
Founded in: 1921
Printed in 2 colors on glossy stock

11758 Contract Management
National Contract Management Association
8260 Greensboro Drive
Suite 200
McLean, VA 22102-3728

571-382-0082
800-344-8096; *Fax:* 703-448-0939
cm@ncmahq.org; www.ncmahq.org

Neal J Couture, Executive Director
Kathryn Mullan, Assistant Editor

It covers the myriad aspects of government and commercial contract management. News and features provide information on such topics as procurement policy, on-the-job techniques, regulations, case law, ethics, contract administration, electronic commerce, international and small business matters, education and career development.
Cost: $178.00
80 Pages
Frequency: Monthly
Circulation: 22000
Founded in: 1959
Printed in 4 colors on glossy stock

11759 Cooperative Housing Bulletin
National Association of Housing Cooperatives
1444 I Street, NW
Suite 700
Washington, DC 20005-6542

202-737-0797; *Fax:* 202-216-9646
info@nahc.coop; www.coophousing.org

Member benefit conatining articles for co-op board members and professionals, up-to-date news on legislative issues that NAHC is monitoring, and practical information on issues facing housing cooperatives.
Frequency: Quarterly
Printed in 2 colors on matte stock

11760 Correctional Health Today
American Correctional Association
206 N Washington St
Suite 200
Alexandria, VA 22314-2528

703-224-0000
800-222-5646; *Fax:* 703-224-0179
jeffw@aca.org; www.aca.org

Jeff Washington, Deputy Executive Director
James Gondles Jr, Executive Director

An interdisciplinary, peer-reviewed, academic publication devoted to examining all areas of health care within corrections. Available in print and electronically.
20000 Members
Frequency: Monthly
Founded in: 1870

11761 Corrections Compendium
American Correctional Association
206 N Washington St
Suite 200
Alexandria, VA 22314-2528

703-224-0000
800-222-5646; *Fax:* 703-224-0179
jeffw@aca.org; www.aca.org

Jeff Washington, Deputy Executive Director
James Gondles Jr, Executive Director

The peer-reviewed, research-based journal of the American Correctional Association. Presents research findings and trends and examines events in corrections and criminal justice.
20000 Members
Frequency: Quarterly
Founded in: 1870

11762 Corrections Today
American Correctional Association
206 N Washington St
Suite 200
Alexandria, VA 22314-2528

703-224-0000; *Fax:* 703-224-0179
execoffice@aca.org; www.aca.org
Social Media: Facebook, Twitter

James Gondles, Executive Director

The professional membership publication of the ACA. Its international readership includes individuals involved in every sector of the corrections and criminal justice fields.
Frequency: 6x Yearly

11763 Court Review
American Judges Association
300 Newport Ave
Williamsburg, VA 23185-4147

757-259-1841; *Fax:* 757-259-1520
aja.ncsc.dni.us

Judge Kevin S. Burke, President
Judge Toni Manning Higginbotham, President-Elect
Judge Elliott L. Zide, Vice President
Judge Brian MacKenzie, Secretary
Judge Harold V. Froehlich, Treasurer

Court technology, managing your staff, controlling your docket-a bench's eye view of information you won't find anywhere else.
2500 Members
Frequency: Quarterly
Founded in: 1959

11764 Defense News
6883 Commercial Dr
Springfield, VA 22151-4202

703-750-9000
800-424-9335; *Fax:* 703-658-8412
armylet@atpco.com; www.defensenews.com

Mark Winans, VP
Elaine Howard, President/CEO
Alex Neill, Managing Editor
Jim Tice, Senior Writer
David Smith, Marketing

Provides the global defense community with the latest news and analysis on defense programs, policy, business and technology. With bureaus and reporters around the world, Defense News sets the standard for accuracy, credibility and timeliness in defense reporting. Circulates to top leaders and decisionmakers in North America and in Europe, Asia and the Middle East.
Cost: $55.00
Frequency: Weekly
Circulation: 1MM

11765 Democratic Communique
Union for Democratic Communications

777 Glades Rd
Boca Raton, FL 33431

www.democraticcommunications.net

Janet Wasko, Publisher

News of Democratic and grassroots communications projects, issues and publications.
Cost: $20.00
12 Pages
Frequency: BiWeekly

11766 **Economic Development Journal**
International Economic Development Council
734 15th Street NW
Suite 900
Washington, DC 20005

202-223-7800; *Fax:* 202-223-4745;
www.iedc.org

Jeff Finkle, President & CEO
Dennis G. Coleman, Chair
Jay C. Moon, Vice Chair
Paul Krutko, Secretary/ Treasurer

Premier publication of IEDC's diverse and dynamic discipline, featuring in-depth accounts of important programs, projects, and trends from the US and around the world.
1.8M Members
Frequency: Quarterly
Founded in: 1967

11767 **Energy Law Journal**
Energy Bar Association
1990 M St NW
Suite 350
Washington, DC 20036-3429

202-223-5625; *Fax:* 202-833-5596
admin@eba-net.org; www.eba-net.org
Social Media: Facebook

Derek A. Dyson, President
Susan A. Olenchuk, President-Elect
Jason F. Leif, Vice President
Emma F. Hand, Secretary
Hugh E. Hilliard, Treasurer

Providing members with the latest news regarding the energy industry.
2600 Members
Frequency: Bi-Annually
Founded in: 1946

11768 **Federal Criminal Investigator**
P.O. Box 23400
Washington, DC 20026

800-403-3374
630-969-8537; *Fax:* 800-528-3492
fcianat@aol.com; www.fedcia.org

Richard Zehme, President
William Paulin, Vice President
Rich Ahern, National Treasurer/Secretary

This comprehensive publication covers legislation and federal information for the police official and officer.
Frequency: Quarterly
Founded in: 1956

11769 **Federal Manager**
Federal Managers Association
1641 Prince St
Alexandria, VA 22314-2818

703-683-8700; *Fax:* 703-683-8707
info@fedmanagers.org; www.fedmanagers.org

Todd Wells, Manager
Darryl A Perkinson, President

Magazine focusing on current management issues.
15M Members
Frequency: Quarterly
Founded in: 1913

11770 **Foreign Service Journal**
American Foreign Service Association
2101 E St NW
Washington, DC 20037-2990

202-338-4045
800-704-2572; *Fax:* 202-338-6820
member@afsa.org; www.afsa.org

Susan R. Johnson, President
Andrew Winter, Treasurer

Each issue covers foreign affairs from an insider's perspective, providing thoughtful articles on international issues, the practice of diplomacy and the US Foreign Service.
Cost: $40.00
68 Pages
Frequency: Monthly
Circulation: 12500
ISSN: 0146-3543
Founded in: 1924
Printed in on glossy stock

11771 **Government Executive**
National Journal
600 New Hampshire Ave NW
Suite 4
Washington, DC 20037-2403

202-739-8400; *Fax:* 202-833-8069
webmaster@govexec.com; www.govexec.com
Social Media: Facebook, Twitter

John Fox Sullivan, President
Shane Harris, Editor

Serving senior executives and managers in the federal government's departments and agencies. Subscribers are high-ranking civilian and military officials who are responsible for defending the nation and carrying out the many laws that define the government's role in our economy and society. Covers the business of the federal government and its huge departments and agencies.
Cost: $48.00
72 Pages
Frequency: Monthly
Circulation: 75,000
Founded in: 1970

11772 **Government Product News**
Penton Media
1300 E 9th St
Suite 316
Cleveland, OH 44114-1503

216-696-7000; *Fax:* 216-696-6662;
www.penton.com

Jane Cooper, Marketing
Kristin M Atwater, Managing Editor
Vaughn Rockhold, Group Publisher
Kay Ross-Baker, Publisher
Sarah Arnold, Marketing Director

Serves officials in the executive, legislative, administrative, engineering, purchasing, financial and other operational departments, within government agencies.
40 Pages
Frequency: Monthly
Circulation: 85000
ISSN: 0017-2642
Founded in: 1962
Printed in 4 colors on glossy stock

11773 **Government Recreation & Fitness**
Executive Business Media
825 Old Country Road
PO Box 1500
Westbury, NY 11590

516-334-3030; *Fax:* 516-334-3059
mail@ebmpubs.com; www.ebmpubs.com

Murry Greenwald, Publisher
Paul Ragnoz, Managing Editor

Government Recreation and Fitness reaches recreation and fitness professionals in every department and agency of the federal government, goes directly to the people who purchase your products, with deep market penetration, and covers both appropriated and nonappropriated fund budgets.
Cost: $35.00
42 Pages
Frequency: 10x Yearly
Circulation: 8521
ISSN: 1086-7899
Founded in: 1996
Printed in 4 colors on glossy stock

11774 **Government Technology**
GT Publications
150 Almaden Blvd
Suite 600
San Jose, CA 95113-2016

408-275-9000; *Fax:* 408-275-0582;
www.grantthornton.com
Social Media: Facebook

Jeffrey S Pera, Managing Partner
Sherese Graves, Advertising Director
Dennis McKenna, Publisher
Micki Gerardi, Manager

Covering information technology's role in state and local governments. Through in-depth coverage of IT case studies, emerging technologies, and the implications of digital technology on the policies and management of public sector organizations, Government Technology chronicles the dynamics of governing in the information age. Readers include managers, elected officials, CIOs and technology staff at all levels of government.
56 Pages
Frequency: Monthly

11775 **ICBA Independent Banker**
Independent Community Bankers of America
1615 L Street NW
Suite 900
Washington, DC 20036

800-422-8439; *Fax:* 202-659-3604
info@icba.org; www.independentbanker.org

Salvatore Marranca, Chairman
Jeffrey L. Gerhart, Chairman-Elect
William A. Loving, Jr., Vice Chairman
Steven R. Gardner, Secretary
Jack Hartings, Treasurer

Covers the news topics and trends that are important to the nation's community bank senior executives. Keeping members informed about and connected with their national association and its activities; and providing them with timely, relevant information on developments to growth their business franchise within the rapidly evolving financial services industry.
Frequency: Monthly

11776 **International Debates**
Congressional Digest Corporation
4416 E West Hwy
Suite 400
Bethesda, MD 20814-4568

301-634-3113
800-637-9915; *Fax:* 301-634-3189
info@congressionaldigest.com;
www.pro-and-con.org/

Griff Thomas, President
Page Robinson, Publisher

Independent journal featuring controversies before the United Nations and other international forums. Each issue covers an important and timely international issue and includes in-depth background information, key documents, and diverse global perspectives.
Frequency: 9x Yearly
Founded in: 1921

11777 **Journal of Food Protection**
International Association for Food Protection

6200 Aurora Ave
Suite 200W
Urbandale, IA 50322-2864

515-276-3344
800-369-6337; *Fax:* 515-276-8655
info@foodprotection.org;
www.foodprotection.org
Social Media: Facebook, Twitter, LinkedIn

Lisa Hovey, Managing Editor
Didi Loynachan, Administrative Editor

Internationally recognized as the leading publication in the field of food microbiology, each issue contains scientific research and authoritative review articles reporting on a variety of topics in food science pertaining to food safety and quality.
Cost: $335.00
Frequency: Monthly
Circulation: 11000+
ISBN: 0-362028-X -
Founded in: 1911
Mailing list available for rent: 3000+ names at $150 per M
Printed in 4 colors on glossy stock

11778 Journal of Housing Economics
630 Eye St NW
Washington, DC 20001-3736

202-289-3500
877-866-2476; *Fax:* 202-289-8181;
www.journals.elsevier.com

Saul Ramirez, Executive Director
Donald J Cameron, CEO

Provides a focal point for the publication of economic research related to housing and encourages papers that bring to bear careful analytical technique on important housing-related questions. The journal covers the broad spectrum of topics and approaches that constitute housing economics, including analysis of important public policy issues.
Cost: $33.00
Founded in: 1933

11779 Journal of Medical Regulation
Federation of State Medical Boards
400 Fuller Wiser Rd
Suite 300
Euless, TX 76039-3856

817-868-4043; *Fax:* 817-868-4099
dcarlson@fsmb.org; www.fsmb.org

Rhonda Olsobrook, Manager

Peer-reviewed scholarly publication that helps raise awareness of important trends and challenging issues in the regulatory community.
Frequency: Monthly

11780 Journal of Occupational and Environmental Hygiene (JOEH)
ACGIH
1330 Kemper Meadow Drive
Cincinnati, OH 45240

513-742-2020; *Fax:* 513-742-3355
mail@acgih.org; www.acgih.org
Social Media: Facebook, Twitter, LinkedIn

Stephen J. Reynolds, President
Mark Nicas, Editor-in-Chief

Focuses on publishing information that practicing professionals can apply in their day-to-day activities. A joint publication of AIHA and ACGIH.
Frequency: Monthly
Founded in: 1938

11781 Journal of the Association of Food and Drug Officials
2550 Kingston Road
Suite 311
York, PA 17402

717-757-2888; *Fax:* 717-755-8089
afdo@afdo.org; www.afdo.org

News and the latest legislation for the Food and Drug Association.
Cost: $80.00
Frequency: Quarterly
Founded in: 1896

11782 Legislative Update
1250 Eye St NW
Suite 902
Washington, DC 20005-3947

202-393-5225; *Fax:* 202-393-3034;
www.nrhcweb.org

Robert A Rapoza, Publisher/Executive Director

Published by the National Rural Housing Coalition.
Cost: $250.00
Frequency: 25x Yearly
Circulation: 300
Founded in: 1969

11783 McGraw-Hill's Federal Technology Report
McGraw Hill
1200 G St Nw
Suite 900
Washington, DC 20005-3821

202-383-2377
800-223-6180; *Fax:* 202-383-2438;
www.aviationweek.com

Jennifer Michels, Manager
Georgia Safos, Circulation Director

Brings readers inside those areas of the federal government where federal technology policy and legislation is made; also identifies commercial opportunities at federal labs.
Cost: $1015.00
16 Pages
Frequency: Weekly

11784 NCOA Journal
Todays NCOA
10635 N 35th
San Antonio, TX 78233-6627
210-653-6161
800-662-2620; *Fax:* 210-637-3337
membsvc@ncoausa.org; www.uag-inc.com

Gene Overstreet, President/CEO
Cathy John, Advertising Manager

The official magazine for the Non Commissioned Officers Association.
Frequency: Quarterly
Circulation: 60000
Founded in: 1960

11785 NIST Tech Beat
National Institute of Standards & Technology
Public & Business Affairs
100 Bureau Drive, Stop 1070
Gaithersburg, MD 20899-1070

800-877-8339; *Fax:* 301-926-1630
media@nist.gov; www.nist.gov
Social Media: Facebook, Twitter, YouTube, Flickr

Michael Baum, Segments Editor
Ben Stein, Segments Editor
Michael E Newman, Segments Editor
Evelyn Brown, Segments Editor
Laura Ost, Segments Editor

A biweekly lay-language newsletter of recent research results and other news from the National Institute of Standards and Technology. NIST is the nation's physical sciences and engineering measurement laboratory. Archives available online.
Frequency: Biweekly

11786 Nation's Cities Weekly
National League of Cities
1301 Pennsylvania Ave NW
6th Floor, Suite 550
Washington, DC 20004-1747

202-626-3180; *Fax:* 202-626-3043
memberservices@nlc.org; www.nlc.org

Donald J Borut, Executive Director
Cyndy Hogan, Managing Editor

Delivers top stories about advocacy activities, successful and innovative city programs, new research and networking opportunities for local elected officials and city employees.
Cost: $96.00
12 Pages
Frequency: Weekly
Circulation: 27000
Founded in: 1978

11787 National Journal
National Journal
600 New Hampshire Ave NW
Suite 4
Washington, DC 20037-2403

202-739-8400
800-207-8001; *Fax:* 202-833-8069
nationaljournal.com
Social Media: Facebook, Twitter

John Fox Sullivan, President

Delivers highly engaged consumers with all of the information and insights that they need to know to conduct business successfully in Washington. Trusted professional resource for Members of Congress and their senior staffs, the Executive branch, federal agency executives, government affairs professionals, corporate and association leaders, and the political news media.
Cost: $1799.00
Founded in: 1969

11788 Navy News and Undersea Technology
Pasha Publications
1616 N Fort Myer Drive
Suite 1000
Arlington, VA 22209-3107

703-528-1244
800-424-2908; *Fax:* 703-528-1253

Harry Baisden, Group Publisher
Thomas Jandl, Editor
Tod Sedgwick, Publisher

This report on the Navy, as well as the Marine Corps and naval developments overseas. Frequently cited by experts in the field as the source for breaking developments in submarine and anti-submarine warfare technology, this newsletter sets the standard for Navy reporting.
Cost: $545.00
Frequency: Weekly

11789 Off the Shelf
Coalition for Government Procurement
1990 M St NW
Suite 450
Washington, DC 20036-3466

202-331-0975; *Fax:* 202-822-9788
info@thecgp.org; www.thecgp.org

Larry Allen, Executive VP

Providing vital updates on rules, regulations, and GSA Schedule developments that may impact your business.
Frequency: Monthly
Founded in: 1979

11790 Parameters
US Army War College

122 Forbes Ave
Suite C34
Carlisle, PA 17013-5220

717-245-3131; *Fax:* 717-245-3323;
www.strategicinstitute.army.mil/pubs/parameters

Robert J Ivany, Manager

Refereed journal of ideas and issues. Provides a forum for mature thought on the art and science of land warfare, joint and combined matters, national and international security affairs, military strategy, military leadership and management, military history, ethics, and other topics of significant and current interest to the US Army and the Department of Defense.
Cost: $26.00
Frequency: Quarterly
Circulation: 1300

11791 Policy & Practice

American Public Human Services Association
1133 19th Street NW
Suite 400
Washington, DC 20036-3623

202-682-0100; *Fax:* 202-289-6555;
www.aphsa.org

Tracy Wareing, Executive Director

Presents a lively and comprehensive look at key human service issues. Its aim is to highlight the experiences of those who administer public assistance programs and services; to examine cutting-edge public human service research and demonstration projects; and to provide readers with a variety of resources to guide them in their challenging roles in the human service arena.
Frequency: Bi-Monthly
Founded in: 1930

11792 Presidential Studies Quarterly

Center for the Study of the Presidency & Congress
1020 19th St NW
Suite 250
Washington, DC 20036-6120

202-872-9800; *Fax:* 202-872-9811;
www.thepresidency.org
Social Media: Facebook, Twitter, YouTube

George C Edwards III, Editor

Available in print and online, PSQ is widely viewed by scholars and professionals as an indispensable resource for understanding the Presidency. The only scholarly journal that focuses on the most powerful political figure in the world - the President of the United States. Offers articles, features, review essays, and book reviews covering Presidential decision making, the operations of the White House, and much more.
Frequency: Quarterly
Circulation: 6000
ISSN: 0360-4918

11793 Prosecutor

National District Attorneys Association
44 Canal Center Plaza
Suite 110
Alexandria, VA 22314-1548

703-549-9222; *Fax:* 703-836-3195;
www.ndaa.org

Jean Hemphill, Publications Director/Editor

Fascinating articles, names in the news, upcoming conferences, capital perspective, profiles, course announcements, message from the President, message from the Executive Director, and much more.
Frequency: Quarterly
Circulation: 7000

11794 Public Administration Review (PAR)

American Society for Public Administration
1301 Pennsylvania Avenue NW
Suite 700
Washington, DC 20004

202-393-7878; *Fax:* 202-638-4952
info@aspanet.org; www.aspanet.org
Social Media: Facebook, Twitter, LinkedIn

Erik O. Bergrud, President
Stephen E. Condrey, Vice-President
Kuotsai Tom Liou, President-Elect

The preeminent journal in the field of public administration research and theory.
15M Members
Frequency: Bi-Monthly
Founded in: 1939

11795 Public Integrity

American Society for Public Administration
1301 Pennsylvania Avenue NW
Suite 700
Washington, DC 20004

202-393-7878; *Fax:* 202-638-4952
info@aspanet.org; www.aspanet.org
Social Media: Facebook, Twitter, LinkedIn

Erik O. Bergrud, President
Stephen E. Condrey, Vice-President
Kuotsai Tom Liou, President-Elect

Furthering the understanding of ethics in government by publishing articles of interest to practitioners and scholars.
15M Members
Frequency: Monthly
Founded in: 1939

11796 Public Risk

Public Risk Management Association
500 Montgomery St
Suite 750
Alexandria, VA 22314-1565
703-647-6244; *Fax:* 703-739-0200
info@primacentral.org; www.primacentral.org
Social Media: Facebook, LinkedIn

Jim Hirt, Executive Director
Jon Ruzan, Manager
Kerry Langley, Manager

Provides risk managers in the public sector with timely, focused information in an easy-to-read format. Features articles from risk management practitioners as well as industry experts.
Frequency: 10x Yearly
Circulation: 8000+
Founded in: 1978

11797 Pull Together

1306 Dahlgren Avenue SE
Washington Navy Yard, DC 20374-5055

202-678-4333; *Fax:* 202-889-3565
nhfwny@navyhistory.org;
www.navyhistory.org

Captain Charles Creekman, Executive Director
Robert F Dunn, President
Cost: $25.00
Founded in: 1926

11798 Rural Housing Reporter

1250 Eye St NW
Suite 902
Washington, DC 20005-3947

202-393-5225; *Fax:* 202-393-3034;
www.nrhcweb.org

Robert A Rapoza, Publisher/Executive Director

Published by the National Rural Housing Coalition.
Cost: $250.00
Frequency: Monthly
Founded in: 1969

11799 Rural Voices

Housing Assistance Council
1025 Vermont Ave NW
Suite 606
Washington, DC 20005-3516

202-842-8600; *Fax:* 202-347-3441
hac@ruralhome.org; www.ruralhome.org
Social Media: Twitter, LinkedIn

Moises Loza, Executive Director

Written in non-technical language for a general audience.
Frequency: Quarterly
Founded in: 1971

11800 Society of Cost Estimating and Analysis Journal

Society of Cost Estimating and Analysis
527 Maple Ave E
Suite 301
Vienna, VA 22180-4753

703-938-5090; *Fax:* 703-938-5091
scea@sceaonline.org; www.sceaonline.net

Elmer Cleg, Executive Director
Joseph Dean, National VP

Subscribers are professionals engaged primarily in the field of government contract estimating and pricing.
Cost: $40.00
Frequency: Annual+
Circulation: 4500
ISSN: 0882-3871
Founded in: 1984

11801 State Legislatures

National Conference of State Legislatures
7700 E 1st Pl
Denver, CO 80230-7143

303-364-7700; *Fax:* 303-364-7800
pubs-info@ncsl.org; www.ncsl.org
Social Media: Twitter, LinkedIn

William Pound, Executive Director
Edward Smith, Managing Editor
LeAnn Hoff, Director, Revenue & Sales

The national magazine of state government and policy.
Cost: $49.00
15000 Members
Circulation: 18000
ISSN: 0147-0644
Founded in: 1975
Printed in 4 colors

11802 Supreme Court Debates

Congressional Digest Corporation
4416 E West Hwy
Suite 400
Bethesda, MD 20814-4568

301-634-3113
800-637-9915; *Fax:* 301-634-3189
info@congressionaldigest.com;
www.pro-and-con.org/

Griff Thomas, President
Page Robinson, Publisher

Independent journal featuring controversies before the US Supreme Court. Each issue covers a current prominent case, along with in-depth historical and legal background and excerpts from lawyers' arguments before the Court. Each issue also lists cases expected to be considered by the High Court during the current term.
Frequency: 9x Yearly
Founded in: 1921

11803 The Federal Lawyer

Federal Bar Association

1220 North Fillmore St.
Suite 444
Arlington, VA 22201

571-481-9100; *Fax:* 571-481-9090
fba@fedbar.org; www.fedbar.org
Social Media: Facebook, Twitter, LinkedIn

Fern C. Bomchill, President
Robert J. DeSousa, President-Elect
Hon. Gustavo Gelpi, Jr., Treasurer

The only magazine written and edited for lawyers who practice in federal courts or have an interest in federal law as well as judges who sit on the federal bench. Editorial content covers immigration, Indian, antitrust, labor and employment, bankruptcy, criminal, intellectual property, environmental, and other types of law that fall within federal jurisdiction.
Cost: $35.00
16000 Members
Frequency: Monthly
Founded in: 1920

11804 **The Forum**
National Forum for Black Public Administrators
777 N Capitol St NE
Suite 807
Washington, DC 20002-4291

202-408-9300; *Fax:* 202-408-8558
webmaster@nfbpa.org; www.nfbpa.org
Social Media: Facebook, YouTube

Aretha R. Ferrell-Benavides, President
Verdenia C. Baker, 1st Vice President
Bruce T. Moore, 2nd Vice President
Jelynne LeBlanc Burley, Secretary/Treasurer
John E. Saunders, III, Executive Director

Has been used as a means of polishing and honing the skills of capable and experienced administrators by providing practical advice on professional development and insight on social and economic concerns impacting the Black community. Strives to present timely, factual, and comprehensive information on subjects of critical importance to its readers who share a common commitment to excellence in public service.
2.8M Members
Frequency: Quarterly
Founded in: 1983

11805 **Training & Simulation Journal**
6883 Commercial Dr
Springfield, VA 22159

800-368-5718
armylet@atpco.com; www.defensenews.com

Mark Winans, VP
Elaine Howard, President/CEO
Alex Neill, Managing Editor
Jim Tice, Senior Writer
David Smith, Marketing

About trends in the global military training and simulation market, and a forum for market leaders to obtain and exchange information on emerging issues, new technologies, and new products.
Cost: $55.00
Frequency: Bi-Monthly
Circulation: 1MM

11806 **Translog**
200 Stovall Street
Hoffman Building Room 11N57
Alexandria, VA 22332-5000

703-428-3207; *Fax:* 703-428-3312

An authorized online publication for members of the Department of Defense, published under supervision of the SDDC Director of Command Affairs to provide timely, relevant information concerning SDDC people, missions, policies, operations, technical developments, trends, and ideas of and about SDDC and the US Army.

11807 **Urban Land**
Urban Land Institute
1025 Thomas Jefferson St NW
Suite 500 West
Washington, DC 20007-5230

202-624-7000; *Fax:* 202-624-7140
ulifoundation@uli.org; www.uli.org
Social Media: Facebook, Twitter, LinkedIn, YouTube

Patrick Phillips, CEO
Richard Rosan, President
Michael Terseck, CFO

Focuses on the information needs of land use and development professionals worldwide, providing them with timely, objective, practical, and accessible articles on a wide variety of subjects related to their professional interests.
14M Members
Frequency: Monthly
Founded in: 1936

11808 **Washington Law & Politics**
100 W Harrison St
Suite 340
Seattle, WA 98119-4196

206-282-9527; *Fax:* 206-282-9601;
www.superlawyers.com

Keith Goben, Publisher
Beth Taylor, Editor
Paul Englund, Circulation Manager
Tina Justison, Production Manager

A magazine for those who care about, or have a stake in, the public policy debate that is the basis of our editorial. Readers consist of those in positions of power in media, government, politics, law and business. Attracts a curious blend of readers ranging from corporate CEOs to political junkies.
48 Pages
Frequency: 6x Yearly
Circulation: 18000
Founded in: 1977
Printed in 4 colors on glossy stock

11809 **Washington Remote Sensing Letter**
Dr. Murray Felsher
1057B National Press Building
Washington, DC 20045-2001

202-393-3640

Dr. Murray Felsher, Publisher
Murray Felsher, Editor
Dr. Murray Felsher, Publisher
Dr. Murray Felsher, Marketing
Dr. Murray Felsher, Circulation Manager

The recognized leader in reporting and analysis of US and international news dealing with all phases and applications of satellite remote sensing of the earth and global analyses research, including imagery, photography, surveillance and monitoring the Earth from space.
Cost: $1100.00
4 Pages
ISSN: 0739-6538
Founded in: 1980
Printed in 2 colors on matte stock

11810 **Western City Magazine**
League of California Cities
1400 K St
4th Floor
Sacramento, CA 95814-3971

916-658-8200
800-262-1801; *Fax:* 916-658-8289
info@westerncity.com; www.cacities.org
Social Media: Facebook

Pam Blodgett, Ad Manager
Eva Spiegel, Managing Editor
Chris McKenzie, Executive Director

The magazine of the League of California Cities.
Cost: $39.00
Frequency: Monthly
Circulation: 10500
Founded in: 1924
Printed in 4 colors on glossy stock

Trade Shows

11811 **ACAP National Training Conference**
American Society of Access Professionals
1444 I(Eye) St. NW
Suite 700
Washington, DC 20005-6542

202-712-9054; *Fax:* 202-216-9646
asap@bostrom.com; www.accesspro.org

Anne Weismann, President
Will Kammer, Vice President
Karen Finnegan, Treasurer
Carmen L. Mallon, Secretary

Created to bring educational opportunities beyond the Washington, D.C. area. Combines training topics with the thought-provoking and practical issues associated with FOIA and Privacy Act processing and requesting.
Frequency: Annual/March
Founded in: 1980

11812 **ASPA Annual Conference**
American Society for Public Administration
1301 Pennsylvania Avenue NW
Suite 840
Washington, DC 20004

202-393-7878; *Fax:* 202-638-4952
info@aspanet.org; www.aspanet.org

Antoinette Samuel, Executive Director
Lyric Jonze, Administration Assistant

Offers cutting-edge educational programming at this year's conference. There are over 150 educational options to choose from - Panel Sessions, Best Practice Workshops, and Roundtable Discussions.
550 Attendees
Frequency: Annual/May

11813 **AURP International Conference**
Association of University Research Parks
6262 N. Swan Road
Suite 100
Tucson, AZ 85718-8936

520-529-2521; *Fax:* 520-529-2499
info@aurp.net; www.aurp.net
Social Media: Facebook, Twitter

Eileen Walker, CEO
Victoria Palmer, Events Manager
Chelsea Simpson, Membership & Marketing Manager

Bringing together the world's leaders in high-tech economic development, this conference features professional development for university research park professionals.
Frequency: Annual/September

11814 **America's Town Meeting**
National Association of Towns and Townships
1130 Connecticut Ave NW
Suite 300
Washington, DC 20036-3981

202-454-3954
866-830-0008; *Fax:* 202-331-1598;
www.natat.org

NATaT's national conference is the largest national conference for grassroots government leaders. Educational workshops and legislative workshops help officials be more effective representatives for the citizens they serve. The conference provides a time for attendees to lobby

members of Congress on issues important to their towns.
13M Members
Frequency: Annual

11815 American Association of Port Authorities Annual Convention
1010 Duke Street
Alexandria, VA 22314-3589

703-684-5700; *Fax:* 703-684-6321
info@aapa-ports.org; www.aapa-ports.org

Kurt Nagle, President/CEO

AAPA's largest membership meeting of the year. It includes technical and policy committee meetings, business sessions and social networking opportunities for port professionals and others in the marine transportation industry.
700 Attendees
Frequency: Annual/September
Founded in: 1912

11816 American Political Science Association Annual Meeting
1527 New Hampshire Avenue NW
Washington, DC 20036-1206

202-483-2512; *Fax:* 202-483-2657
apsa@apsanet.org; www.apsanet.org

G. Bingham Powell, Jr., President
Jane Mansbridge, President-Elect
Jonathan Benjamin-Alvarado, Treasurer
Lisa L. Martin, Secretary
Michael A. Brintnall, Executive Director

Workshop, luncheon and 150 plus exhibits of publications and software relating to political science.
6500 Attendees
Frequency: Annual
Founded in: 1903

11817 CLEAR Annual Educational Conference
Council on Legislative Enforcement & Regulation
403 Marquis Ave
Suite 200
Lexington, KY 40502-2104

859-269-1289; *Fax:* 859-231-1943
jhorne@clearhq.org; www.clearhq.org
Social Media: Facebook

Bruce Matthews, President
Michelle Pedersen, President-Elect

Conference content focuses on compliance and discipline, credentialing and licensing, examination issues, and legislative and policy issues/reulatory administration.
380 Members
400+ Attendees
Frequency: Annual/September
Founded in: 1980

11818 CSG National Conference & North American Summit
Council of State Governments
2760 Research Park Drive
PO Box 11910
Lexington, KY 40578-1910

859-244-8000
800-800-1910; *Fax:* 859-244-8001;
www.csg.org
Social Media: Facebook, Twitter

Key officials that shape and make today's economic decisions.
1000+ Attendees
Frequency: Annual/October

11819 Congress of Cities & Exposition
National League of Cities
1301 Pennsylvania Avenue NW
Suite 550
Washington, DC 20004

202-626-3100
800-564-4220; *Fax:* 202-626-3043;
www.nlc.org

Ted Ellis, President
Marie Lopez Rogers, 1st Vice President
Chris Coleman, 2nd Vice President
Don Borut, Executive Director

Provides educational content on the most pressing challenges facing city leaders. Conference attendees hear from prominent speakers and issue experts, participate in leadership training sessions, attend issue-specific workshops, visit best practices keynote speakers, issue workshops, mobile workshops, and leadership training sessions.
4200 Attendees
Frequency: Annual/December
Founded in: 1924

11820 EANGUS National Conference
Exhibit Promotions Plus
11620 Vixens Path
Ellicott City, MD 21042

301-596-3028; *Fax:* 410-997-0764;
www.eangus.org

Kevin Horowitz, Exhibit Mgmt.

General conference and exhibition for the Enlisted Association of the National Guard of the United States. All attendees are either National Guard members, retirees or their families.
2000+ Attendees
Frequency: Annual/August
Founded in: 1971

11821 Energy - Exhibit Promotions Plus
US Dept. of Energy/US Dept. of Defense/GSA
11620 Vixens Path
Ellicott City, MD 21042

301-596-3028; *Fax:* 410-997-0764;
www.epponline.com

Harve Horowitz, President
Kevin Horowitz, Senior Association Manager

Energy is an exclusive Federal Grant sponsored annual educational forum and exhibition.
1000+ Attendees
Frequency: Annual/August

11822 FOSE
Contingency Planning & Management Conference
3141 Fairview Park Drive
Suite 777
Falls Church, VA 22042

703-876-5100
800-638-8510; www.fose.com
Social Media: Facebook, Twitter, LinkedIn

Sylvia Griffiths, Customer Supervisor

Vendors in different marketplaces & pavilions, providing the opportunity to source effective & actionable IT solutions, in-depth conferences, workshops, camps, keynote & theater education designed to help achieve sucess with government IT mandates & initiatives. Association meetings, CIO Summits and peer networking opportunities, bringing the government IT community together.
80M Attendees
Frequency: April

11823 Government Finance Officers Association Annual Conference
203 N LaSalle Street
Suite 2700
Chicago, IL 60601-1210

312-977-9700; *Fax:* 312-977-4806
inquiry@gfoa.org; www.gfoa.org

Jeffrey Esser, Executive Director/CEO
Barbara Mollo, Director Operations & Marketing
Anne Spray Kinney, Director Research & Consulting
John Jurkash, CFO/Financial Administration
Barrie Tabin Berger, Federal Liaison Coordinator

The Government Finance Officers Association's Annual Conference provides training and networking opportunities for public sector finance professionals from across the United States and Canada. 250 booths with 200 exhibitors.
4000 Attendees
Frequency: June

11824 HFA Institute
National Council of State Housing Agencies
444 N Capitol St NW
Suite 438
Washington, DC 20001-1505

202-624-7710; *Fax:* 202-624-5899
bthompson@ncsha.org; www.ncsha.org
Social Media: Facebook, Twitter

Gerald M. Hunter, President
Brian A. Hudson, Vice President
Thomas R. Gleason, Secretary/ Treasurer
Barbara J. Thompson, Executive Director

Premier training event providing an unprecedented chance to network with peers and receive top-notch education and invaluable advice from key federal officials, leading trainers and consultants, noted industry professionals, and experienced HFA practitioners.
350 Members
Frequency: Annual/December
Founded in: 1974

11825 Housing Credit Conference & Marketplace
National Council of State Housing Agencies
444 N Capitol St NW
Suite 438
Washington, DC 20001-1505

202-624-7710; *Fax:* 202-624-5899
bthompson@ncsha.org; www.ncsha.org
Social Media: Facebook, Twitter

Gerald M. Hunter, President
Brian A. Hudson, Vice President
Thomas R. Gleason, Secretary/ Treasurer
Barbara J. Thompson, Executive Director

The industry event of the year. Only NCSHA brings leaders and top development and compliance staff from the state Housing Credit allocating agencies together with government officials, developmers, lenders syndicators, investors, attorneys, accountants, property managers, compliance experts, owners, and nonprofits.
350 Members
Frequency: Annual/June
Founded in: 1974

11826 IAEM Annual Conference
International Association of Emergency Managers
201 Park Washington Court
Falls Church, VA 22046

703-538-1795; *Fax:* 703-241-5603
info@iaem.com; www.iaem.com

Provides a forum for current trends and topics, information about the latest tools and technology in emergency management and homeland security, and advances IAEM-USA committee work.

Sessions encourage stakeholders at all levels of government, the private sector, public health and related professions to exchange ideas on collaborating to protect lives and property from disaster.
1000 Attendees
Frequency: Annual/November

11827 ICMA Annual Conference
International City/County Management Association
777 N Capitol Street NE
Suite 500
Washington, DC 20002

202-624-4600
800-745-8780; *Fax:* 202-962-3500
amahoney@icma.org; www.icma.org

Robert J. O'Neill, Executive Director
David Ellis, Conference Committee Co-Chair
Maria A. Hurtado, Conference Committee Co-Chair

The largest annual event in the world for local government managers and staff.
3814 Attendees
Frequency: Annual/September
Founded in: 1914

11828 ICMA Regional Summit
International City/County Management Association
777 N Capitol Street NE
Suite 500
Washington, DC 20002-4239

202-289-4262
800-745-8780; *Fax:* 202-962-3500
customerservices@icma.org; www.icma.org
Social Media: Facebook, Twitter, LinkedIn, YouTube, Flickr

Barry Sacks, Show Manager
Robert J. O'Neill, Executive Director

A networking and professional development opportunity for members and state officers in the four regions.
3.5M Attendees
Frequency: Annual/September

11829 Legislative Conference
National Council of State Housing Agencies
444 N Capitol St NW
Suite 438
Washington, DC 20001-1505

202-624-7710; *Fax:* 202-624-5899
bthompson@ncsha.org; www.ncsha.org
Social Media: Facebook, Twitter

Gerald M. Hunter, President
Brian A. Hudson, Vice President
Thomas R. Gleason, Secretary/ Treasurer
Barbara J. Thompson, Executive Director

Join HFA leaders and their board members and stakeholders in Washington to learn about NCSHA's legislative priorities and strategize the best way to communicate our message to Congress with one unified voice. Hear from key Congressional staff and industry leaders about the issues of the day.
350 Members
Frequency: Annual/March
Founded in: 1974

11830 MMA Annual Meeting and Trade Show
Massachusetts Municipal Association
One Winthrop Square
Boston, MA 02110

617-426-7272; *Fax:* 617-695-1314;
www.mma.org

The largest regular gathering of Massachusetts local government officials. Features educational workshops, nationally recognized speakers, awards programs, a large trade show, and an opportunity to network with municipal officials from across the state.
1000 Attendees
Frequency: Annual/January

11831 Marine West Military Expo
Nielsen Business Media, USA
1145 Sanctuary Parkway
Suite 355
Alpharetta

703-488-2762
Ron Bates, Event Organizer

This event is fully dedicated to the defense industry. The event will showcase the latest products and equipments used for marine and related industry at one place. The visitors will be the military professionals, equipment buyers, decision makers and the other people related to the field of defense.
Frequency: Annual/February

11832 NACE Annual Conference
National Association County Engineers
25 Mass. Avenue NW
Suite 580
Washington, DC 20001

202-393-5041; *Fax:* 202-393-2630
nace@naco.org; www.countyengineers.org

Mark A. Craft, President
Richie Beyer, President-Elect
Mark K. Servi, Secretary/ Treasurer

Attendees will have many opportunities to meet road and bridge professionals and their counterparts from other counties around the country, to exchange ideas and have some fun. The exhibit show offers a friendly environment for delegates to learn about the latest products and services.
450 Attendees
Frequency: Annual/April

11833 NACo Annual Conference and Exposition
National Association of Counties
25 Massachusetts Avenue, NW
Suite 500
Washington, DC 20001

202-393-6226
888-407-6226; *Fax:* 202-393-2630
nacomeetings@naco.org
admin.naco.org

Larry E. Naake, Executive Director

Provides an opportunity for all county leaders and staff to learn, network and guide the direction of the association. Provides county officials with a great opportunity to vote on NACo's policies related to federal legislation and regulation; elect officers; network with colleagues; learn about innovative county programs; find out about issues impacting counties across the country; and view products and services from participating companies and exhibitors.
Frequency: Annual/July

11834 NACo's Annual Conference and Exposition
National Association of Counties
440 1st Street NW
Washington, DC 20001-2028

202-393-6226; *Fax:* 202-393-2630
webmaster@naco.org; www.naco.org

Amanda Clark, Conference & Meetings Associate
Kim Struble, Conference & Meetings Director
Larry Naake, CEO

The place for elected and appointed county officials to network, attend educational sessions and meet with companies that sell products to counties. It includes a variety of activities designed to meet the needs of all delegates. In addition to strong educational sessions, the conference includes affiliate, steering and subcommittee meetings, state association meetings and social events.
4000 Attendees
Frequency: Annual

11835 NAHRO National Conference
Nat'l Assn of Housing & Redevelopment Officials
630 Eye Street NW
Washington, DC 20001-3736

202-289-3500
877-866-2476; *Fax:* 202-289-8181
nahro@nahro.org; www.nahro.org

A wide array of products and services needed by the housing and community development field.
3M Attendees
Frequency: Annual/October

11836 NARC Conference and Exhibition
National Association of Regional Councils
1666 Connecticut Ave NW
Suite 305
Washington, DC 20002

202-986-1032; *Fax:* 202-986-1038;
www.narc.org

Fred Abousleman, Executive Director
Lindsey Riley, Deputy of Communications
500+ Attendees
Frequency: Annual/June

11837 NASTAD Annual Conference
Nat'l Alliance of State/Territoral AIDS Directors
444 N Capitol St NW
Suite 339
Washington, DC 20001

202-434-8090; *Fax:* 202-434-8092
nastad@nastad.org; www.nastad.org

Julie Scofield, Executive Director

Apprenticeship directors from around the nation come together to problem solve, share innovative ideas to the Registered Apprenticeship model as well as to bring the association up to date on each state's activities.
Frequency: Annual/May

11838 NCBM Annual Convention
National Conference of Black Mayors
191 Peachtree Street, NE
Suite 849
Atlanta, GA 30303

404-765-6444; *Fax:* 404-765-6430
info@ncbm.org; www.ncbm.org

Vanessa R. Williams, Executive Director
Robert L. Bowser, President
Jamie Mayo, Treasurer
Johnny L. DuPree, Ph.D, Secretary
John White, Sergeant-at-Arms

Serving as a catalyst for bringing together mayors and municipal leaders, including several international delegations, state and federal officials, as well as leaders in the public and private sectors for the purpose of networking and obtaining information on the latest policies and strategies for enhancing municipal government.
542 Members
Founded in: 1974

11839 NCSHA Housing Credit Conference & Marketplace
444 N Capitol Street NW
Suite 438
Washington, DC 20001-1512

202-624-7710; *Fax:* 202-624-5899;
www.ncsha.org

Louise Moors, Membership Coordinator
William Pound, Executive Director

Brings leaders and top development and compliance staff from the state Housing Credit allocat-

ing agencies together with government officials, developers, lenders, syndicators, investors, attorneys, accountants, property managers, compliance experts, owners, and nonprofits. Heavy hitters of the industry and their partners will deliver the latest news on how to make the housing Credit work in these unprecedented times.
700 Attendees
Frequency: Annual/June

11840 NCSL Fall Forum
National Conference of State Legislatures
7700 East First Place
Denver, CO 80230

303-364-7700; *Fax:* 303-364-7800;
www.ncsi.org

Peg Coniglio, Manager
Deana Blackwood, Circulation Director
Focuses on how best to advance the States' Agenda and tackle the difficult policy issues of our time, including budget gaps, health care coverage, education affordability, transportation funding, energy costs and many others.
6700 Attendees
Frequency: Annual/November

11841 NCSL Legislative Summit
National Conference of State Legislatures
444 North Capitol Street NW
Suite 515
Washington, DC 20001

202-624-5400; *Fax:* 202-737-1069
deana.blackwood@ncsl.org; www.ncsl.org

William T Pound, Executive Director
Leticia Van de Putte, President
Steven Rauschenberger, VP
Max Arinder, Staff Chair
Four days of 150 policy sessions on the most pressing issues facing state legislatures. Some of the topics include budget conditions, education reform, health care implementation and renewable energy.
13M+ Members
4800+ Attendees
Frequency: Annual/August
Founded in: 1975

11842 NCWM Annual Meeting
National Conference on Weights and Measures
1135 M Street
Suite 110
Lincoln, NE 68508

402-434-4880; *Fax:* 402-434-4878
info@ncwm.net; www.ncwm.net

Don Onwiler, Executive Director
Technical presentations are a way to stay on the cutting edge of new developments in the weights and measures community. Complete the business of the conference through open hearings and voting on national standards.

11843 NEMA Mid-Year Conference
National Emergency Management Association
PO Box 11910
Lexington, KY 40578

859-244-8000; *Fax:* 859-244-8239
nemaadmin@csg.org; www.nemaweb.org

Jim Mullen, President
John Madden, Vice President
Charley English, Treasurer
Tom Sands, Secretary
Brenda Bergeron, Legal Counsel
Gives the opportunity to discuss important issues in the field of emergency management and homeland security. Also hear from respected leaders working on many of these issues. Opportunities to meet and network with peers are invaluable in these times of rapid change and economic challenges.
Frequency: Annual/March

11844 NFBPA FORUM
National Forum for Black Public Administrators
777 N Capitol Street NE
Suite 807
Washington, DC 20002-4239

202-289-5851
800-745-8780; *Fax:* 202-962-3500
webmaster@nfbpa.org; www.nfbpa.org

Aretha R. Ferrell-Benavides, President
Verdenia C. Baker, 1st Vice President
Bruce T. Moore, 2nd Vice President
Jelynn LeBlanc Burley, Secretary/ Treasurer
Waves of change, oceans of opportunity repositioning our communities for the future. Plenary sessions and luncheons, public policy forum, workshops, banquet and brunch, corporate exhibit, vendor showcase, artist's gallery and more.
1.4M Attendees
Frequency: Annual/April

11845 NPELRA Annual Training Conference
National Public Employer Labor Relations Assoc.
1620 I Street NW
4th Floor
Washington, DC 20006-4005

202-591-1190; *Fax:* 202-293-2352;
www.npelra.org
Social Media: Facebook, Twitter, LinkedIn

Sam Penrod, President
Michael S. Bates, Executive Vice President
Christa Ballowe, Vice President
Walt Pellegrini, Vice President
Joel Kuhl, Secretary/ Treasurer
Attend the best training available for public sector Labor Relations & Human Resources professionals with over 30 program sessions; in addition the conference provides credit hours for CLE and HRCI recertification. Interact with colleagues representing public sector labor relations professionals from across the country.
350 Attendees
Frequency: Annual

11846 NPELRA Training Conference
National Public Employer Labor Relations Assoc
1012 South Coast Highway
Suite M
Oceanside, CA 92054

760-433-1686
877-673-5721; *Fax:* 760-433-1687;
www.npelra.org
Social Media: Facebook, Twitter, LinkedIn

Michael T Kolb, Executive Director
Janessa Stephens, Association Specialist
Yvonne Gillengerten, Operation Manager
Stephanie Biggs, Administrative Assistant
Allison Wittwer, Administrative Assistant
Attend the best training available for public sector Labor Relations and Human Resources professionals with over 30 program sessions; in addition the conference provides credit hours for CLE and HRCI recertification. Interact wth colleagues representing public sector labor relations professionals from across the country.
Frequency: Annual

11847 NSCL Legislative Summit
National Conference of State Legislatures
7700 E 1st Pl
Denver, CO 80230-7143

303-364-7700; *Fax:* 303-364-7800
pubs-info@ncsl.org; www.ncsl.org
Social Media: Twitter, LinkedIn

William Pound, Executive Director
Edward Smith, Managing Editor
LeAnn Hoff, Director, Revenue & Sales
A bipartisan organization that serves the legislators and staffs of the nation's 50 states, its commonwealths and territories.
15000 Members
5500 Attendees
Founded in: 1975

11848 National Association Regional Councils
1666 Conneticut Ave NW
Suite 305
Washington, DC 20002

202-986-1032; *Fax:* 202-986-1038;
www.narc.org

Shawn Sample, Show Manager
80 booths.
1.2M Attendees
Frequency: June
Founded in: 1965

11849 National Council of State Housing Agencies Conference
444 N Capitol St NW
Suite 438
Washington, DC 20001-1505

202-624-7710; *Fax:* 202-624-5899
bthompson@ncsha.org; www.ncsha.org
Social Media: Facebook, Twitter

Gerald M. Hunter, President
Brian A. Hudson, Vice President
Thomas R. Gleason, Secretary/ Treasurer
Barbara J. Thompson, Executive Director
The premier gathering of state HFAs and NCSHA affiliate members. It is the main networking event of the year for HFAs and the partners who work with them to increase housing opportunities through the financing, developemnt, and preservation of affordable housing.
350 Members
Frequency: Annual/October
Founded in: 1974

11850 National Electricity Forum
NARUC
1101 Vermont Ave NW
Suite 200
Washington, DC 20005-3553

202-898-2200; *Fax:* 202-898-2213
admin@naruc.org; www.naruc.org

David A. Wright, Chairman & President
Philip B. Jones, 1st Vice President
Colette D. Honorable, 2nd Vice President
David E. Ziegner, Treasurer
Charles D. Gray, Executive Director
Addressing cutting-edge issues and discuss how collaboration can successfully modernize the nation's electricity infrastructure. The forum will feature national thought leaders from all sectors of the electric power industry, academia, policymakers, equipment manufacturers, consumers, and other affected parties.
Frequency: Annual/February
Founded in: 1889

11851 National League of Postmasters Annual National Convention
National League of Postmasters

5904 Richmond Highway
Suite 500
Alexandria, VA 22303-1864

703-329-4550; *Fax:* 703-329-0466
exhibit@epponline.com; www.epponline.com

Mark W. Strong, President

Extensive training and educational opportunities.
1400 Attendees
Frequency: Annual/August
Founded in: 1903

11852 National Postal Forum
3998 Fair Ridge Drive
Suite 300
Fairfax, VA 22033

703-218-5015; *Fax:* 703-218-5020
info@npf.org; www.npf.org
Social Media: Facebook, Twitter, LinkedIn, Flickr

Mary Guthrie, Director, Marketing & Exhibits
Laurie Woodhams, Exhibits Assistant

The premier educational event and tradeshow available to mail professionals today. Attend the National Postal Forum to get a complete education in the Business of Mail.
Frequency: Annual/April

11853 Norfolk NATO Festival
440 Bank Street
Norfolk, VA 23510

757-282-2800; *Fax:* 757-282-2787;
www.azaleafestival.org

Kelly Harlan, General Manager

A salute to the NATO's Allied Command Atlantic forces in order to create new friendships, provide a basis for cultural exchange, recognize the military's role in maintaining peace in the world and pursue new lines of trade between Norfolk and the world.
5M Attendees
Frequency: Canada
Founded in: 1953

11854 PHADA Annual Convention and Exhibition
Public Housing Authorities Directors Association
511 Capitol Court NE
Washington, DC 20002-4937

202-546-5445; *Fax:* 202-546-2280;
www.phada.org

Timothy G. Kaiser, Executive Director
Stephanie White, Director of Meetings

Provides the latest information and tools housing authorities need to run their agencies in these changing times. Also, many exciting housing suppliers and vendors will be on-hand to showcase their services. There are many sessions to provide attendees with important information emanating from Congress and HUD headquarters.
800 Attendees
Frequency: Annual/May

11855 SGAC Annual National Summit
State Government Affairs Council
108 North Columbus Street
2nd Floor
Alexandria, VA 22314

571-312-3426
eloudy@sgac.org; www.sgac.org

Donna Gehlhaart, President
Elizabeth A. Loudy, Executive Director
Jon Burton, Vice President
Holly Johnson, Operations Associate
Katherine Kilgore, Manager, Communications

Professional development and networking opportunity for SGAC members.
200 Members
Frequency: Annual
Founded in: 1975

11856 Transforming Local Government Conference
Mid-America Regional Council
6604 Harney Road, Suite L
PO Box 16645
Tampa, FL 33687-6645

813-622-8484; *Fax:* 813-664-0051;
www.tlgconference.org
Social Media: Facebook, Twitter, Flickr, YouTube

Mary Laird, Executive Assistant
David Warm, Executive Director

Through innovative case study sessions, conference attendees will take an in-depth look at the ingenuity and creativity of successful government programs. TLG attracts participation from local governments that are deliberately seeking new and innovative ways to connect people, information and ideas that support their efforts to be the best communities in which to live, work, and prosper.
800 Attendees
Frequency: Annual
Printed in one color on matte stock

11857 UDT: Undersea Defense Technology Conference and Exhibition
Reed Exhibition Companies
255 Washington Street
Newton, MA 02458-1637

617-584-4900; *Fax:* 617-630-2222
Social Media: Facebook, Twitter, LinkedIn

Elizabeth Hitchcock, International Sales

The world's leading exhibition and conference for undersea defence and security. Gain access to the latest technologies, connect with existing suppliers and create new business relationships. Gives the invaluable opportunity to network across the global maritime community. Suppliers exhibiting; UUVs and components, acoustic technologies, maritime surveillance solutions, harbour and port security products, mine detection systems, and submarine hardware and electronics.
Frequency: Annual/May

11858 UNA-USA Annual Meeting
United Nations Association of the USA
1800 Massachusetts Avenue NW
Suite 400
Washington, DC 20036

202-887-9040; *Fax:* 202-887-9021;
www.unausa.org

Patrick Madden, Executive Director

Brings together UNA-USA's constituencies for a variety of skills trainings, issue briefings, networking opportunities and capacity-building.
400 Attendees
Frequency: Annual/November

11859 Western Legislative Conference
1107 9th Street
Suite 730
Sacramento, CA 95814

916-553-4423; *Fax:* 916-446-5760
csgw@csg.org; www.csgwest.org

Rosie Berger, Chair
Kelvin Atkinson, Chair-Elect
Craig Johnson, Vice Chair

Brings together legislators from western states to learn from each other and collaborate on issues of regional concern such as water, public lands, energy and transportation. Also offers training and professional development opportunities for all legislators.
500 Attendees
Frequency: Annual/July
Founded in: 1933

Directories & Databases

11860 Almanac of American Politics
National Journal
1730 M St NW
Suite 800
Washington, DC 20036-4551

202-828-0300; *Fax:* 202-457-5160

Marcia Coyle, Manager

The definitive guide to understanding the forces that shape American politics. Has been established as a Washington institution in its own right and an indespensable resource for anyone involved or interested in the American political scene.
Cost: $59.95
1500 Pages
Frequency: Biennial

11861 Almanac of the Federal Judiciary
Prentice Hall Law & Business
270 Sylvan Avenue
Englewood Cliffs, NJ 07632-2521

201-569-0006

Providing balanced, responsible judicial profiles of every federal judge and all the key bankruptcy judges and magistrate judges- profiles that include reliable inside information based on interviews with lawyers who have argued cases before the federal judiciary.
Cost: $1715.00
2130 Pages
Frequency: Annual
ISBN: 9-780735-56-8

11862 American Bench
Forster-Long
3280 Ramos Cir
Sacramento, CA 95827-2513

916-362-3276
800-328-5091; *Fax:* 916-362-5643;
www.forster-long.com

Jay Long, Vice President, Marketing

Over 19,000 judges who sit in local, state and federal courts are profiled. The definitive biographical reference to the American judiciary.
Cost: $595.00
Frequency: Daily
Founded in: 1977

11863 BRB Publications
BRB Publications
PO Box 27869
Tempe, AZ 85285-7869

480-829-7475
800-929-3811; *Fax:* 800-929-4981
brb@brbpublications.com;
www.brbpublications.com
Social Media: Facebook, LinkedIn

Mike Sankey, President

Comprehensive listing of government agencies that have placed public records online, both free and fee based.
Founded in: 1988

11864 Billcast Archive
George Mason University, Public Choice Center
4400 University Dr
Fairfax, VA 22030-4444

703-993-1120

Clayton Austin, Manager

This database contains information on public bills introduced in the US House of Representatives and Senate during the preceding session of Congress.

11865 **Book of the States**
Council of State Governments
2760 Research Park Drive
PO Box 11910
Lexington, KY 40578-1910

859-244-8000
800-800-1910; *Fax:* 859-244-8001
research@csg.org; www.csg.org

Jodi Rell, President
Carol Juett, Director of Development
Roger Werholtz, Secretary

A reference tool of choice and includes comparative information on everything from highway miles to state government employment and everything in between.
Cost: $99.00
Frequency: Annually
Founded in: 1935

11866 **CSG State Directories**
Council of State Governments
2760 Research Park Drive
PO Box 11910
Lexington, KY 40578-1910

859-244-8000
800-800-1910; *Fax:* 859-244-8001
research@csg.org; www.csg.org

Jodi Rell, President
Carol Juett, Director of Development
Roger Werholtz, Secretary

Includes the names and contact information for key state government officials.
Frequency: Annually

11867 **Canadian Almanac & Directory**
Grey House Publishing Canada
555 Richmond Street West
Suite 301
Toronto, ON M5V 3B1

416-644-6479
866-433-4739; *Fax:* 416-644-1904
info@greyhouse.ca; www.greyhouse.ca
Social Media: Facebook, Twitter, LinkedIn

Richard Gottlieb, President
Leslie Mackenzie, Publisher

A combination of textual material, charts, colour photographs and directory listings, the Canadian Almanac & Directory provides the most comprehensive picture of Canada, from physical attributes to economic and business summaries to leisure and recreation.
Cost: $360.00
1936 Pages
Frequency: Annual
ISBN: 1-592377-69-5

11868 **Canadian Parliamentary Guide**
Grey House Publishing Canada
555 Richmond Street West
Suite 301
Toronto, ON M5V 3B1

416-644-6479
866-433-4739; *Fax:* 416-644-1904
info@greyhouse.ca; www.greyhouse.ca
Social Media: Facebook, Twitter, LinkedIn

Richard Gottlieb, President
Leslie Mackenzie, Publisher

Canadian Parliamentary Guide provides the most complete and comprehensive information on elected and appointed members in federal and provincial government.
Cost: $229.00
1152 Pages
Frequency: Annual
ISBN: 1-592377-65-7

11869 **Capital Source**
National Journal
600 New Hampshire Ave NW
Suite 4
Washington, DC 20037-2403

202-739-8400; *Fax:* 202-833-8069

John Fox Sullivan, President

Directory brimming with key information on the most important players and institutions Inside-the-Beltway, The Capital Source is the place for essential and current contact information all year round. A must-have resource for anyone in the business of politics, policy, government relations or the media.
Cost: $29.95
160 Pages
Frequency: Monthly

11870 **Carroll's County Directory**
Carroll Publishing
4701 Sangamore Rd
Suite S-155
Bethesda, MD 20816-2532

301-263-9800
800-336-4240; *Fax:* 301-263-9805
customersvc@carrollpub.com;
www.carrollpub.com
Social Media: Twitter, LinkedIn

Bill Wade, President/COO
Kathleen Undegraff, VP Marketing
Cost: $350.00
Founded in: 1973

11871 **Carroll's Federal Directory**
Carroll Publishing
4701 Sangamore Rd
Suite 155S
Bethesda, MD 20816-2532

301-263-9800
800-336-4240; *Fax:* 301-263-9805
info@carrollpub.com; www.carrollpub.com

Tom Carroll, President

Offers complete coverage of the headquarter offices of the Executive, Legislative, and Judicial branches of government. Includes over 38,000 positions offering direct contact information for all Executive departments, independent agencies, Congressional Agencies and US Federal Courts.
Cost: $500.00
450 Pages
Frequency: Annual

11872 **Carroll's Federal Regional Directory**
Carroll Publishing
4701 Sangamore Rd
Suite 155S
Bethesda, MD 20816-2532

301-263-9800
800-336-4240; *Fax:* 301-263-9805
info@carrollpub.com; www.carrollpub.com

Tom Carroll, President

The one regional resource that has it all. Covering regional and field offices of Federal government departments, home-state offices for members of Congress, federal district courts and more. Reach over 32,000 government people located outside of Washington.
Cost: $170.00
370 Pages
Frequency: Bi-Annually

11873 **Carroll's Municipal Directory**
Carroll Publishing
4701 Sangamore Rd
Suite 155S
Bethesda, MD 20816-2532

301-263-9800
800-336-4240; *Fax:* 301-263-9805
info@carrollpub.com; www.carrollpub.com

Tom Carroll, President

The most comprehensive municipal directory available anywhere. It includes more than 60,000 appointed officials, career officials and local authorities across the US. Covering more cities than any other source, this has nearly 8,000 cities, towns and villages.
Cost: $170.00
550 Pages
Frequency: Bi-Annually

11874 **Carroll's State Directory**
Carroll Publishing
4701 Sangamore Rd
Suite 155S
Bethesda, MD 20816-2532

301-263-9800
800-336-4240; *Fax:* 301-263-9805;
www.carrollpub.com
Social Media: Twitter, LinkedIn

Bill Wade, President/COO
Kathleen Updegraff, VP Marketing

Provides complete contact information for over 68,000 key officials in all 50 states, plus the District of Columbia, Puerto Rico and the American Territories.
Cost: $210.00
530 Pages
Frequency: TriAnnual

11875 **Congress at Your Fingertips: Congressional Directory**
Capitol Advantage
1255 22nd St NW
Washington, DC 20037-1217

703-899-9636
800-659-8708; *Fax:* 703-289-4678
sales@capitoladvantage.com;
www.capitoladvantage.com

Dr. John Hansan, Production Manager

Comprehensive directory lists members of the US Senate and House of Representatives, complete with color photos and a fold-out map of Capitol Hill.
Cost: $13.95
Frequency: Annual

11876 **Congressional Staff Directory**
Leadership Directories, Inc.
1167 K Street NW
Suite 801
Washington, DC 20006

202-628-7757; *Fax:* 202-628-3430;
www.leadershipdirectories.com

Gretchen Teichgraeber, CEO
William Cressey, Chairman

Locate key decision-makers and support staff that work behind the scenes on important legislative issues. Pinpoint key contacts on committees who work day-to-day on legislation that's most important.
Cost: $69.00
1200 Pages
Frequency: SemiAnnual

11877 **Daily Defense News Capsules**
United Communications Group
11300 Rockville Pike
Suite 1100
Rockville, MD 20852-3030

301-816-8950; *Fax:* 301-816-8945
Greg Beaudoin, Editor

This database offers the complete text of Periscope - Daily Defense News Capsules, that provide abstracts of international press coverage of military and defense news.

11878 Defense Industry Charts
Carroll Publishing
4701 Sangamore Rd
Suite 155S
Bethesda, MD 20816-2532
301-263-9800
800-336-4240; *Fax:* 301-263-9805
info@carrollpub.com; www.carrollpub.com
Tom Carroll, President
19000 key personnel in top US defense contractors, including major aerospace, electronic, military hardware, information technology and systems integration companies. Serves as a road map to the critical players in this important industry.
Cost: $2050.00
Frequency: Quarterly

11879 Defense Programs
Carroll Publishing
4701 Sangamore Rd
Suite 155S
Bethesda, MD 20816-2532
301-263-9800
800-336-4240; *Fax:* 301-263-9805
info@carrollpub.com; www.carrollpub.com
Tom Carroll, President
Detailed description of more than 2,000 military research, development, test and evaluation programs and projects.
Cost: $1060.00
Frequency: Quarterly

11880 Defense and Foreign Affairs Handbook
International Strategic Studies Association
PO Box 19289
Alexandria, VA 22320-0289
703-548-1070; *Fax:* 703-684-7476
dfa@strategicstudies.org;
www.strategicstudies.org
Gregory Copley, Editor
Important global reference encyclopedia for most world leaders .Comprehensive chapters on 238 countries and territories worldwide, with each chapter giving full cabinet and leadership listings, history, recent developments, demographics, economic statistics, political and constitutional data, news media,defense overview, defense structure.
Cost: $297.00
2500 Pages
Frequency: Monthly
Circulation: 4,000
ISBN: 1-892998-06-8
Founded in: 1976

11881 Directory of Congressional Voting Scores and Interest Group Ratings
1414 22nd Street NW
Washington, DC 20037-1003
202-887-8500
800-432-2250; *Fax:* 800-380-3810;
www.cqpress.com
Complete compilation of CQ voting studies and interest group rating data for every legislator who has served in Congress since 1947. This resource is perfect for quick or in-depth research and provides the easiest, most accurate way to gauge the political orientation of members of Congress over time. This is the best source for understanding the political preferences of US senators and representatives, and what it means about their choices on future votes.
Cost: $450.00
1700 Pages
Frequency: Triennial

11882 Encyclopedia of Governmental Advisory Organizations
Gale/Cengage Learning
PO Box 6904
Florence, KY 41022-6904
800-354-9706; *Fax:* 800-487-8488
gale.galeord@cengage.com; www.gale.com
Patrick C Sommers, President
Contains entries which describe the activities and personnel of groups and committees that function to advise the President of the United States and various departments and bureaus of the federal government, as well as detailed information about historically significant committees.
Frequency: Annual

11883 Federal Benefits for Veterans, Dependents and Survivors
US Department of Veterans Affairs
810 Vermont Ave NW
Washington, DC 20420-0002
202-273-5400; *Fax:* 202-273-4880
John R Gingirch, CEO
Health care benefits, disability benefits, pensions, home loan, insurance, and much more.
Cost: $3.25
Frequency: Annual

11884 Federal Buyers Guide
Gold Crest
650 Ward Dr # A
Santa Barbara, CA 93111-2395
805-683-9000
800-922-3233; *Fax:* 805-683-7661;
www.goldcrestresourcesplc.com
Roger Edgar, CEO
Gunnar Sundstrom, OPS Manager
Companies that serve or wish to serve as vendors to the federal government. Reading specialty lights, giftware, manufacturer, distributor, Mighty Bright brand.
170 Pages
Frequency: Quarterly
ISSN: 1043-7568
Founded in: 1979

11885 Federal Directory of Contract Administration Services Components
Contract Mgmt. Command/Defense Logistics Agency
Caremon Station
Alexandria, VA 22304
703-781-9807
Lists the names and telephone numbers of those DCMA and other agency offices that offer contract administration services within designated geographic areas and at specified contractor plants.
110 Pages
Frequency: Annually

11886 Federal Government Certification Programs
US National Institute of Standards & Technology
Administration Building
Room 629
Gaithersburg, MD 20899-0001
301-975-2281; *Fax:* 301-963-2871
A directory available certification programs.
Cost: $18.95
229 Pages

11887 Federal Staff Direcotry
1414 22nd Street NW
Washington, DC 20037-1003
202-887-8500
800-432-2250; *Fax:* 800-380-3810;
www.cqpress.com
Penny Perry, Editor
Pinpoint senior officials and top aides working directly with the President and Vice President using the most well-researched information available. Find all the information needed to locate high-ranking policy-makers, their deputies, bureau chiefs, and division heads. Connect with top-level officials at agencies ranging from the American Red Cross to the Environmental Protection Agency.
Cost: $450.00
1700 Pages
Frequency: Monthly

11888 Federal Technology Source
Government Executive- National Journal Group
600 New Hampshire Ave NW
Suite 4
Washington, DC 20037-2403
202-739-8500
800-356-4838; *Fax:* 202-739-8511
webmaster@govexec.com; www.govexec.com
Matt Dunie, President
Sue Fourney, Managing Editor
A directory of most important people and organizations in the federal technology community.
Cost: $9.95
168 Pages
Frequency: Annual
Circulation: 73,500
ISSN: 0017-2626
Printed in 4 colors on glossy stock

11889 Foreign Consular Offices in the United States
Bureau of Public Affairs/US Department of State
2201 C Street NW
Washington, DC 20520-0001
202-647-6141
A complete and official listing of the foreign consular offices in the US, and recognized consular officers. Compiled by the US Department of State, with the full cooperation of the foreign missions in Washington, it is offered as a convenience to organizations and persons who must deal with consular government agencies, state tax officials, international trade organizations, chamber of commerce, and judicial authorities.
Cost: $4.00
290 Pages
Frequency: Annual

11890 Getting Started in Federal Contracting: A Guide Through the Federal Maze
Panoptic Enterprises
PO Box 11220
Burke, VA 22009-1220
703-451-5953
800-594-4766; *Fax:* 703-451-5953;
www.fedgovcontracts.com
Vivina Mcvay, President
Barry L McVay, Editor
Information is given on over 65 government procurement offices, Department of Labor offices, General Services Administration business services and Small Business Administration regional and branch offices.
Cost: $39.95
395 Pages
ISBN: 0-912481-24-2
Founded in: 1984

11891 **Government Assistance Almanac: Guide to all Federal Financial Programs**
Omnigraphics
615 Griswold
Detroit, MI 48226
313-961-1340
800-234-1340; *Fax:* 313-961-1383
editorial@omnigraphics.com;
www.omnigraphics.com
Robert Dumouchel, Editor
Provides updated information on all 1,613 federal domestic assistance programs available. These programs represent $1.675 trillion worth of federal assistance earmarked for distribution to consumers, children, parents, veterans, senior citizens, students, businesses, civic groups, state and local agencies, and others.
Cost: $240.00
1,000 Pages
Frequency: Annual
ISBN: 0-780807-00-6

11892 **Government Phone Book USA**
Omnigraphics
615 Griswold Street
Detroit, MI 48226
313-961-1340
800-234-1340; *Fax:* 313-961-1383
editorial@omnigraphics.com;
www.omnigraphics.com
David Bianco, Marketing Director
Key federal, state and local government offices in the US are profiled. More than 270,000 listings with complete contact data.
Cost: $275.00
2,700 Pages
Frequency: Annual
ISBN: 0-780806-93-X
Founded in: 1992

11893 **Government Research Directory**
Gale/Cengage Learning
PO Box 09187
Detroit, MI 48209-0187
248-699-4253
800-877-4253; *Fax:* 248-699-8049
gale.galeord@cengage.com; www.gale.com
Patrick C Sommers, President
In this vital resource you'll find research facilities and programs of the US and Canadian federal governments. Listings include e-mail addresses, information on patents available for licensing and expanded coverage of key personal contact.
ISBN: 1-414420-23-4

11894 **Governments Canada**
Grey House Publishing Canada
555 Richmond Street West
Suite 301
Toronto, ON M5V 3B1
416-644-6479
866-433-4739; *Fax:* 416-644-1904
info@greyhouse.ca; www.greyhouse.ca
Social Media: Facebook, Twitter, LinkedIn
Richard Gottlieb, President
Leslie Mackenzie, Publisher
Governments Canada is the most complete and comprehensive tool for locating people and programs in Canada. It provides regularly updated listings on federal, provincial and territorial government departments, offices and agencies across Canada. Branch and regional offices are also included, along with all associated agencies, boards, commissions and crown corporations. Listings include contact names, full address, telephone and fax numbers, as well as e-mail addresses.
Cost: $299.00
600 Pages
Frequency: 2x/Year
ISBN: 1-592379-85-9

11895 **Grey House Safety & Security Directory**
Grey House Publishing
4919 Route 22
PO Box 56
Amenia, NY 12501
518-789-8700
800-562-2139; *Fax:* 845-373-6390
books@greyhouse.com; www.greyhouse.com
Social Media: Facebook, Twitter
Leslie Mackenzie, Publisher
Richard Gottlieb, Editor
Comprehensive guide to the safety and security industry, including articles, checklists, OSHA regulations and product listings. Focuses on creating and maintaining a safe and secure enviroment, and dealing specifically with hazardous materials, noise and vibration, workplace preparation and maintenance, electrical and lighting safety, fire and rescue and more.
Cost: $165.00
1600 Pages
ISBN: 1-592373-75-5
Founded in: 1981

11896 **Guide to Management Improvement Projects in Local Government**
ICMA Publications
777 N Capitol St NE
Suite 600
Washington, DC 20002-4240
202-216-9408
800-745-8780; *Fax:* 202-962-3500;
www.icma.org
Joan Mc Callen, President
Projects conducted by municipal governments that have resulted in improvements in efficiency or cost reductions are listed.
Cost: $65.00
50 Pages
Frequency: Quarterly

11897 **Hudson's Washington News Media Contacts Directory**
Grey House Publishing
4919 Route 22
PO Box 56
Amenia, NY 12501
518-789-8700
800-562-2139; *Fax:* 845-373-6390
books@greyhouse.com; www.greyhouse.com
Social Media: Facebook, Twitter
Leslie Mackenzie, Publisher
Richard Gottlieb, President
A comprehensive guide to the entire Washington, D.C. press corps, broken down into categories.
Cost: $289.00
350 Pages
ISBN: 1-592378-53-6
Printed in one color on matte stock

11898 **Hudson's Washington News Media Contacts - Online Database**
Grey House Publishing
4919 Route 22
PO Box 56
Amenia, NY 12501
518-789-8700
800-562-2139; *Fax:* 845-373-6390
gold@greyhouse.com
http://gold.greyhouse.com
Social Media: Facebook, Twitter
Leslie Mackenzie, Publisher
Richard Gottlieb, President
With 100% verification of data, Hudson's is the most accurate, most up-to-date source for media contacts in our nation's capital. With the largest concentration of news media in the world, having access to Washington's news media will get your message heard by these key media outlets.

11899 **IAEM Directory**
International Association of Emergency Managers
111 Park Pl
Falls Church, VA 22046-4513
703-538-1795; *Fax:* 703-241-5603
info@iaem.com; www.iaem.com
Shan Coffin, Editor
Sharon L Kelly, Circulation Director
Cost: $100.00
Circulation: 8,000

11900 **Immediate Need Resource Directory**
Gold Crest
650 Ward Dr
Suite A
Santa Barbara, CA 93111-2395
805-683-9000
800-922-3233; *Fax:* 805-683-7661;
www.goldcrestresourceplc.com
Roger Edgar, CEO
Gunnar Sundstrom, OPS Manager
A directory catering to the immediate needs of Federal government purchasing agents. Reading and speciality lights, giftware, manufacturer, distributor, Mighty Bright brand.
Cost: $20.00
50 Pages
Frequency: Monthly
Founded in: 1990

11901 **Judicial Yellow Book**
Leadership Directories
104 5th Ave
New York, NY 10011-6901
212-627-4140; *Fax:* 212-645-0931
judicial@leadershipdirectories.com;
www.leadershipdirectories.com
David Hurvitz, CEO
James M Petrie, Associate Publisher
Contact information for over 3,250 federal and state judges in federal and state appellate courts, including staff and law clerks, and the law schools they attended.
Cost: $245.00
1,100 Pages
Frequency: SemiAnnual
ISSN: 1082-3298
Founded in: 1995
Mailing list available for rent: 13,000 names at $125 per M

11902 **Kaleidoscope: Current World Data**
ABC-CLIO
PO Box 1911
Santa Barbara, CA 93102-1911
805-968-1911; *Fax:* 805-685-9685
CustomerService@abc-clio.com;
www.abc-clio.com
Ron Boehm, CEO
This comprehensive database takes a look at all aspects of the American culture. Listings of information include statistics and factual information on the population, culture, economy, military forces, government, and political systems of countries around the world, the US States and Canadian provinces.
Frequency: Full-text

11903 Leadership Directories
104 5th Ave
New York, NY 10011-6901
212-627-4140; *Fax:* 212-645-0931
info@leadershipdirectories.com;
www.leadershipdirectories.com
David Hurvitz, CEO
Barry Graubart, Executive VP/CMO
The mission of Leadership Directories is to compile, produce and offer subscribers, in all media and in easily usable form, the most current and accurate directories of leaders in the major categories of American activity, including government, business, the professions, and the nonprofits.
Founded in: 1969

11904 Leadership Library in Print
Leadership Directories
104 5th Ave
New York, NY 10011-6901
212-627-4140; *Fax:* 212-645-0931
info@leadershipdirectories.com;
www.leadershipdirectories.com
David Hurvitz, CEO
Complete set of all 14 leadership directories. Provides subscribers with complete contact information for the 400,000 individuals who constitute the institutional leadership of the US.
Cost: $2300.00
Frequency: Semiannually
Founded in: 1996

11905 Leadership Library on Internet and CD-ROM
Leadership Directories
104 5th Ave
New York, NY 10011-6901
212-627-4140; *Fax:* 212-645-0931
info@leadershipdirectories.com;
www.leadershipdirectories.com
David Hurvitz, CEO
Makes all 14 leadership directories available over the Internet and on CD-ROM in one integrated directory. They provide subscribers with complete contact information, in one database. Subscription includes Internet access and four CD-ROM editions quarterly.
Cost: $3065.00
Frequency: Updated Daily
ISSN: 1075-3869
Founded in: 1999
Mailing list available for rent
Printed in A colors on B stock

11906 Member Data Disk
CQ Staff Directories
815 Slaters Lane
Alexandria, VA 22314-1219
800-252-1722; *Fax:* 703-739-0234
Bruce B Brownson, Editor
Covers all members of the US Congress and their key staff members in Washington, DC and principal district offices.
Cost: $395.00
Frequency: Quarterly

11907 Military Biographical Profiles
CTB/McGraw Hill
20 Ryan Ranch Rd
Monterey, CA 93940-5770
831-393-0700
800-538-9547; *Fax:* 831-393-6528
CTBTechnicalSupport@CTB.com;
www.ctb.com
Ellen Haley, President
Sandor Nagy, Chief Operating Officer
Offers valuable information on US military officers and Department of Defense officials.
Frequency: Full-text

11908 Municipal Year Book
ICMA Publications
777 N Capitol St NE
Suite 600
Washington, DC 20002-4240
202-216-9408
800-745-8780; *Fax:* 202-962-3500
cpmmail@icma.org; www.icma.org
Joan Mc Callen, President
Gary Huff, Founder
Directory of services and supplies to the industry.
Cost: $79.95
416 Pages
Frequency: Annual

11909 Municipal Yellow Book
Leadership Directories
104 5th Ave
New York, NY 10011-6901
212-627-4140; *Fax:* 212-645-0931
municipal@leadershipdirectories.com;
www.leadershipdirectories.com
David Hurvitz, CEO
James M Petrie, Associate Publisher
Contact information for over 33,000 elected and administrative officials of US cities, counties, and local authorities.
Cost: $245.00
1,200 Pages
Frequency: SemiAnnual
ISSN: 1054-4062
Founded in: 1991
Mailing list available for rent: 30,000 names at $125 per M

11910 National Directory of Corporate Public Affairs
Columbia Books
PO Box 251
Annapolis Junction, MD 20701-0251
888-265-0600; *Fax:* 240-646-7020
info@columbiabooks.com;
www.columbiabooks.com
J Valerie Steele, Senior Editor
Tracks the public/government affairs programs of about 1,900 major US corporations and lists the 14,00 people who run them, Also lists: Washington area offices, corporate PACs, federal and state lobbyists, outside contract lobbyists. Indexed by subject and geographic area. Includes membership directory of the Public Affairs Council.
Cost: $109.00
Frequency: Annual January

11911 National Directory of Women Elected Officials
National Women's Political Caucus
1630 Connecticut Avenue NW
Suite 201
Washington, DC 20009
202-785-1100; *Fax:* 202-785-3605
info@nwpc.org; www.nwpc.org
Directory of services and supplies to the industry.
230 Pages
Frequency: Biennial

11912 National and Federal Employment Report
Federal Reports
1010 Vermont Ave NW
Suite 408
Washington, DC 20005-4945
202-393-1552; *Fax:* 202-393-1553;
www.attorneyjobs.com
Richard L Hermann, Owner
Over 600 current attorney and law-related job opportunities with the US government are listed.
Cost: $111.20
Frequency: Monthly

11913 New York State Directory
Grey House Publishing
4919 Route 22
PO Box 56
Amenia, NY 12501
518-789-8700
800-562-2139; *Fax:* 845-373-6390
books@greyhouse.com; www.greyhouse.com
Social Media: Facebook, Twitter
Leslie Mackenzie, Publisher
Richard Gottlieb, Editor
A comprehensive and easy-to-use guide to accessing public officials and private sector organizations and individuals who influence public policy in the state of New York. Includes important information on all New York state legislators and congressional representatives, including biographies and key committee assignments.
Cost: $145.00
800 Pages
ISBN: 1-592373-58-5
Founded in: 1981

11914 New York State Directory - Online Database
Grey House Publishing
4919 Route 22
PO Box 56
Amenia, NY 12501
518-789-8700
800-562-2139; *Fax:* 845-373-6390
gold@greyhouse.com
http://gold.greyhouse.com
Social Media: Facebook, Twitter
Leslie Mackenzie, Publisher
Richard Gottlieb, Editor
A comprehensive and easy-to-use guide to accessing public officials and private sector organizations and individuals who influence public policy in the state of New York. Includes important information on all New York state legislators and congressional representatives, including biographies and key committee assignments. With a subscription to the online database, you'll have immediate access to this wealth of contact information.
Founded in: 1981

11915 Organization Charts
Carroll Publishing
4701 Sangamore Rd
Suite 155S
Bethesda, MD 20816-2532
301-263-9800
800-336-4240; *Fax:* 301-263-9805;
www.carrollpub.com
Tom Carroll, President
Provide a unique graphic visualization of the personnel relationships in Federal, Defense and Defense Industry organizations. Traditionally used to display report relationships between individuals, these charts are the #1 authoritative source for getting an up-to-date picture of the hierarchy within government, defense and defense contractors, including major aerospace, military hardware and IT companies.
Cost: $1160.00
185 Pages
Frequency: 8x Yearly

11916 PRRN Directory (Public Record Retriever Network)
BRB Publications

PO Box 27869
Tempe, AZ 85285

480-829-7475
800-929-3811; *Fax:* 800-929-4981
brb@brbpublications.com; www.brbpub.com
Social Media: Facebook, LinkedIn

Mike Sankey, President

Offers listings for professional on-site researchers possessing skills in searching court dockets, local recorded documents, and obtaining court information.
Cost: $9.95
256 Pages
Frequency: Annual
ISBN: 0-988563-66-7

11917 Politics in America
Congressional Digest
4416 East West Highway
Suite 400
Bethesda, MD 20814-4568

301-634-3113
800-637-9915; *Fax:* 301-634-3189;
www.pro-and-con.org

Offers information on United States senators and representatives.
Cost: $89.95
1700 Pages
Frequency: Biennial

11918 Profiles of Worldwide Government Leaders
Worldwide Government Directories
7979 Old Georgetown Road
Suite 900
Bethesda, MD 20814-2429

301-258-2677
800-332-3535; *Fax:* 301-718-8494

Jonathan Hixon, Publisher

Spanning 195 countries, includes comprehensive biographical snapshots of as many as 30 or more ministers from each country. The material is obtained from primary and secondary sources including embassies, government ministries, offices of the United States government and proprietary global network of correspondents.
Cost: $297.00
850+ Pages
Frequency: Annual

11919 Public Human Services Directory
American Public Human Services Association
1133 19th Street NW
Suite 400
Washington, DC 20036-3623

202-682-0100; *Fax:* 202-289-6555;
www.aphsa.org

Tracy Wareing, Executive Director

State-by-state guide to people, programs and a must-have for all human service professionals.
Frequency: Annual
Founded in: 1930

11920 Public Risk Management Association Membership Directory
500 Montgomery Street
Suite 750
Alexandria, VA 22314

703-528-7701; *Fax:* 703-739-0200
info@primacentral.org; www.primacentral.org

Jim Hirt, Executive Director
Jon Ruzan, Manager
Kerry Langley, Manager

Lists all members alphabetically; by state/country; by category; government; private; associate. Yellow pages give vender and service provider 50-wind thumbnail descriptions. Advertising sold.
Circulation: 2,000

11921 US Congress Handbook
8120 Woodmont Ave.
Suite 110
Bethesda, MD 20814

E-Mail: info@uscongresshandbook.com;
www.uscongresshandbook.com
Social Media: Facebook, Twitter

Washington's most trusted source for information on Congressional offices and their staff. The most comprehensive Congressional directory available.
Frequency: Annually
Founded in: 1974

11922 United States Government Manual
Office of the Federal Register
National Archives Administration
Washington, DC 20408-0001

202-564-2480; *Fax:* 202-501-0599

The official handbook of the United States government; includes descriptions and lists of principal personnel of agencies and government bodies.
Cost: $30.00
935 Pages
Frequency: Annual

11923 Washington Information Directory
Congressional Quarterly
1414 22nd Street NW
Washington, DC 20037-1003

202-887-8500; *Fax:* 202-822-6583

Paul McClure, Editor
Will Gardner, Associate Editor

5,000 governmental agencies, congressional committees and non-governmental associations considered competent sources of specialized information.
Cost: $105.00
Frequency: Annual June

11924 Washington: Comprehensive Directory of the Key Institutions and Leaders
Columbia Books
1212 New York Avenue NW
Suite 330
Washington, DC 20005-3969

202-641-1662
888-265-0600; *Fax:* 202-898-0775
info@columbiabooks.com;
www.columbiabooks.com

Buck Downs, Senior Editor

Over 5,000 federal and district government offices, businesses, associations, publications, radio and television stations, labor organizations, religious and cultural institutions, health care facilities and community organizations in the District of Columbia area.
Cost: $75.00
Frequency: Annual May

11925 Worldwide Directory of Defense Attorneys
Worldwide Government Directories
7979 Old Georgetown Road
Suite 900
Bethesda, MD 20814-2429

301-258-2677
800-332-3535; *Fax:* 301-718-8494

Jonathan Hixon, Publisher

One-of-a-kind resource covering military and civilian defense and national security agencies from the ministry of defense down to service branches in 195 countries worldwide.
Cost: $647.00
1,100 Pages
Frequency: Annual

11926 Worldwide Government Directory
Worldwide Government Directories
7979 Old Georgetown Road
Suite 900
Bethesda, MD 20814-2429

301-258-2677
800-332-3535; *Fax:* 301-718-8494

Jonathan Hixon, Publisher

Offers valuable information on every senior government official in the executive, legislative, and judicial branches as well as the diplomatic and defense communities of 195 countries worldwide. Plus senior officials in over 100 international organizations. Each entry includes name, address, title, telephone, telex, facsimile number, and more. Also included are current state agencies and corporations, official forms of address, international dialing codes and central bank information.
Cost: $347.00
1,400 Pages
Frequency: Annual

11927 Worldwide Government Directory with International Organizations
1414 22nd Street NW
Washington, DC 20037-1003

202-887-8500
800-432-2250; *Fax:* 800-380-3810;
www.cqpress.com

Linda Dziobek, Editor

Coverage includes over 1800 pages of executive, legislative and political branches; heads of state, ministers, deputies, secretaries and spokespersons as well as state agencies, diplomats and senior level defense officials. Also covers the leadership of more than 100 international organizations.
Cost: $450.00
1700 Pages
Frequency: Annually

Industry Web Sites

11928 http://gold.greyhouse.com
G.O.L.D Grey House OnLine Databases

Grey House Publishing's online database platform, GOLD, offers Quick Search, Keyword Search and Expert Search for most business sectors including government markets. The GOLD platform makes finding the information you need quick and easy - whether you're a novice searcher or an experienced database user. All of Grey House's directory products are available for subscription on the GOLD platform.

11929 www.aashto.org
American Association of State Highway and Transportation

Membership is composed of highway and transportation departments in the 50 states, the District of Columbia, and Puerto Rico.

11930 www.abccert.org
Association of Boards of Certification

The Association of Boards of Certification is dedicated to protecting public health and the environment by advancing the quality and integrity of environmental certification programs through innovative technical support services, effective information exchange, professional and cost-effective examination services, and other progressive services for certifying members.

11931 **www.access.digex.net/fedbar**
Federal Bar Association
Members are attorneys in the Federal Government or who have interest in federal law.

11932 **www.accesspro.org**
American Society of Access Professionals
Members are government employees, lawyers, journalists and others concerned with access to government data under current personal privacy and public information statutes.

11933 **www.acsp.uic.edu/iaco**
International Association of Correctional Officers
Correctional officers and juvenile administrators.

11934 **www.actnat.com**
Association of Civilian Technicians
Union of civilian employees of the Army and National Guard and Air Reserve.

11935 **www.admin.org**
American Federation of School Administrators
Established in 1971 as the school administrators and supervisors organizing committee. Information of interest to those in public education.

11936 **www.affirm.org**
Associ for Federal Information Resources Mngt
Seeks to improve the management of information systems and resources of the Federal Government.

11937 **www.afge.org**
American Federation of Government Employees
The largest federal employee union representing 700,000 workers nationwide and overseas.

11938 **www.afscase.org**
American Federation of State, County and Municipal Employees
Sponsors their own Political Action Committee.

11939 **www.aglf.org/**
Association for Governmental Leasing and Finance
Provides an exchange of information among tax-exempt issuers, investment banking firms and party lease brokers.

11940 **www.aja.ncsc.dni.cs**
American Judges Association
An independent organization of judges in all jurisdictions in Canada, Mexico and the United States.

11941 **www.alexandriagroup.com**
National Association of Government Communicators
A merger of Federal Editors Association, the Government Information Organization, and the Armed Forces Writers League.

11942 **www.alldc.org**
American League of Lobbyists
National association dedicated to serving government relations and public affairs professionals. Provides programs and conferences of interest to lobbyists.

11943 **www.ansi.org**
American National Standards Institute
Promotes the knowledge for approved standards for industry, engineering and safety design.

11944 **www.aphf.org**
American Federation of Police & Concerned Citizens
Operates the American Police Academy as its educational arm. Maintains the American Police Hall of Fame & Museum in Miami, Florida.

11945 **www.aspanet.org**
American Society for Public Administration
Offers a wide range of services and membership options for individuals in public administration careers. Sponsors 127 local chapters and 16 sections on specific areas of governments, such as the Section of Natural Resources and Environmental Administration and the Section on Human Resource Administration.

11946 **www.aspehhs.gov**
Interagency Council on the Homeless
Seeks to evaluate and monitor federal activities for the homeless, collect information, study problems related to homelessness and disseminate information. Provides technical and professional assistance to the State and local governments and other public and private organizations to maximize resources and develop innovative programs to help the homeless.

11947 **www.brbpub.com**
BRB Publications
Public Records Directory and Records search.

11948 **www.brbpublications.com**
BRB Publications
Key resource providing publications, manuals, and databases on finding information from public record sources.

11949 **www.cagw.com**
Citizens Against Government Waste
Public advocacy, non-partisan organization committed to eliminate government waste, fraud, abuse, mismanagement and inefficiency.

11950 **www.clearhq.org**
Council on Licensure, Enforcement and Regulation
Members include occupational and professional licensing boards and agencies and private interests in the 50 states, territories and Canada.

11951 **www.communityleadership.org**
Community Leadership Association
Founded by 40 community leadership organizations.

11952 **www.coscda.org**
Council for State Community Development Agencies
Employees of state community affairs agencies.

11953 **www.csa-dc.org**
Contract Services Association of America
Represents the government services contracting industry in Washington, DC. Members range from small businesses to large corporations servicing federal and state government in numerous capacities. CSA acts to foster effective implementation of the government's policy of reliance on the private sector for support services.

11954 **www.cued.org**
National Council for Urban Economic Development
National membership organization serving public and private participants in economic development across the United States and in international settings. CUED provides information to its members who build local economies through the tools used for job creation, attraction and retention. Members include public economic development directors, chamber of commerce staff, utility executives and academicians, plus the many other professionals who help design and implement development programs.

11955 **www.eba-net.org**
Energy Bar Association
Lawyers engaged in promoting proper administration of federal laws relating to the production, development and economic regulation of energy.

11956 **www.epic.org**
Fund for Constitutional Government
Seeks to expose and correct illegal activities, corruption, and lack of accountability in the federal government.

11957 **www.fbi.gov**
Federal Investigators Association
Formerly the United States Treasury Agents.

11958 **www.fedphy.org**
Federal Physicians Association
The purpose of the Federal Physicians Association is to improve the practice of medicine within the federal government; and to improve the working conditions and benefits of Federal Civil Service Physicians.

11959 **www.foodprotection.org**
International Association for Food Protection
The International Association for Food Protection founded in 1911, is a nonprofit educational association with a mission to provide food safety professionals worldwide with a forum to exchange information on protecting the food supply. The Association is comprised of a cross-section of over 3,000 members from 50 nations. Affiliate chapters are located in the United States, Canada and South Korea.

11960 **www.ginniemae.gov/about/contract.htm**
Government National Mortgage Association
Ginnie Mae
Supports government housing objectives by establishing secondary markets for residential mortgages. Through its mortgage-backed securities programs, Ginnie Mae creates a vehicle for channeling funds from the securities markets into the mortgage market and helps to increase the supply of credit available for housing.

11961 **www.govexec.com**
National Journal
The website of Government Executive Magazine.

11962 **www.greyhouse.com**
Grey House Publishing
Authoritative reference directories for most business sectors including government markets. Users can search the online databases with varied search criteria allowing for custom searches by product category, geographic area, sales volume, keyword, subject and more. Full Grey House catalog and online ordering also available.

11963 **www.healthfinder.gov**
Association of Food and Drug Officials
Promotes the enforcement of laws and regulations at all levels of government. Fosters understanding and cooperation between industry and regulators. Develops model laws and regulations and seeks their adoption.

11964 **www.ida-downtown.org**
International Downtown Association
Represents organizations and individuals involved in downtown development. Members include city center redevelopment organizations and local officials, businesses, property owners, financiers, planners, university and foundation

representatives, and legal and accounting professionals. Offers conferences, technical assistance, consulting services and extensive information services.

11965 **www.ihs.com**
International Code Council
Nonprofit membership association with more than 16,000 members who span the building community, from code enforcement officials to materials manufacturers. Dedicated to preserving the public health, safety and welfare in the built environment through the effective use and enforcement of model codes.

11966 **www.imsasafety.org**
International Municipal Signal Association
International resource for information, education and certification for public safety.

11967 **www.iogcc.state.ok.us**
Interstate Oil and Gas Compact Commission
Represents the governors of 37 states that produce virtually all the domestic oil and natural gas in the United States.

11968 **www.leadershipdirectories.com**
Leadership Directories
Offers free online directory of Presidential Transition Team, free online roster of newly elected congressman and subscription information.

11969 **www.liberty.uc.wlu.edu**
Journalism Resources
Lists of newspapers, film resources, jobs and internships and political advocacy groups.

11970 **www.nacced.org**
National Association for County Community and Economic Development
Members are directors and staff members of county, community and economic development agencies.

11971 **www.naco.org**
Nat'l Assn of County Information Technology Admin

11972 **www.nagra.org**
North American Gaming Regulators Association
Members are government entities involved in local, state, federal and provincial regulation of gambling activities.

11973 **www.nahma.org**
National Affordable Housing Management Association
Trade association representing companies and individuals involved in the management of affordable multifamily housing.

11974 **www.nahro.org**
Ntl Assoc of Housing & Redevelopment Officials
A professional membership association representing local housing authorities, community development agencies, and individual professionals in the housing, community development, and redevelopment fields.

11975 **www.nalhfa.org**
National Assn. of Local Housing Finance Agencies
County and city agencies which finance affordable housing using tax-exempt annual tools such as the low income housing tax credit and private activity bonds.

11976 **www.napawash.org**
National Academy of Public Administration
An independent, non-profit organization chartered by Congress to improve governance at all levels- local, regional, state, national and international.

11977 **www.napus.org**
National Association of Postmasters of the US
Sponsors and supports the Political Education for Postmasters Political Action Committee.

11978 **www.narc.org**
National Association of Regional Councils
State of regional repositories of instructional materials or services.

11979 **www.nasaa-arts.org**
National Assembly of State Arts Agencies
NASAA's mission is to advance and promote a meaningful role for the arts in the lives of individuals, families and communities throughout the United States. We empower state art agencies through strategic assistance that fosters leadership, enhances planning and decision making, and increases resources. TTD 202-347-5948.

11980 **www.nasaa.org**
North American Securities Administrators Assoc
NASAA is the international organization representing 66 securities administrators from all 50 states, the District of Columbia, Canada, Mexico and Puerto Rico, and is responsible for investor protection and education. NASAA recommends national policies in the securities industry and provides model legislation for state securities agencies to adopt affecting the regulation of broker/dealers and investment advisers. Consumers can contact NASAA to get phone numbers of state securities regulators.

11981 **www.nasar.org**
National Association for Search and Rescue
Members belong to various emergency medical, fire or survival rescue services.

11982 **www.nasda.com**
National Association of State Development Agencies
Established to provide a forum for directors of state economic development agencies to exchange information, compare programs, and establish an organizational base to approach the Federal Government on issues of mutual interest.

11983 **www.nast.net**
Ntl Assoc of State Facilities Administrators
State administrators of facilities and property.

11984 **www.nastad.org**
Nat'l Alliance of State/Territorial AIDS Directors
NASTAD strengthens state and territory-based leadership, expertise, and advocacy and brings them to bear in reducing the incidence of HIV and viral hepatitis infections and on providing care and support to all who live with HIV/AIDS and viral hepatitis. NASTAD's vision is a world free of HIV/AIDS and viral hepatitis.

11985 **www.natat.org**
National Association of Towns and Townships
A nonprofit membership organization offering technical assistance, educational services and public policy support to local officials from more than 13,000 town and township governments across the country. The purpose is to strengthen the effectiveness of town and township governments and promote their interests in the public and private sectors.

11986 **www.nbpc.net**
National Border Patrol Council
A labor union representing employees of the US border patrol.

11987 **www.ncne.com**
National Center for Neighborhood Enterprise
A research demonstration and development organization providing support and technical assistance to grassroots organizations who are working toward revitalization of urban communities. The Center accomplishes this goal by promoting, and explaining alternative approaches to community development; identifies successful transferable program principles, strategies and techniques; and encouraging policy recommendations to assist neighborhood revitalization.

11988 **www.ncsha.org**
National Council of State Housing Agencies
Represents the views of state housing finance agencies in 48 states. A high priority for the Council is promoting the views of state housing agencies on the issue of delivery of housing financing for low and moderate income people. Other priorities include increasing the stock of affordable rental units and generating innovative approaches to providing public housing acceptable to residents and communities.

11989 **www.ncsl.org**
National Conference of State Legislatures
A bipartisan organization dedicated to serving the lawmakers and staffs of the nations 50 states, its commonwealths and territories.

11990 **www.ndaa.org**
National District Attorneys Association
Voice of America's prosecutors and to support their efforts to protect the rights and safety of the people.

11991 **www.nedaonline.org**
National Community Development Association
A national nonprofit membership organization representing local governments that implement community development programs. The members administer federally supported community development, housing and human services programs. NCDA provides counsel at the federal level on new program design and current program implementation and advocates on behalf of responsive community development.

11992 **www.nemaweb.org**
National Emergency Management Association
Members include federal agencies, local emergency management representatives and interested individuals, associations and corporations.

11993 **www.nfbpa.org**
National Forum for Black Public Administrators
An association for public administrators.

11994 **www.nhlp.org**
National Housing Law Project
A nonprofit corporation that provides assistance on public and private housing and community development matters to Legal Services attorneys and housing specialists throughout the country. The project's goals are to produce, maintain and conserve low and moderate income housing and protect and expand the rights of lower income persons to decent and affordable housing.

11995 **www.nlc.org**
National League of Cities

Advocates on behalf of cities and regularly monitors all three branches of the federal government. Promotes the National Municipal Policy developed and adopted by member cities at the annual Congress of Cities.

11996 www.npelra.org
National Labor Relations Board of Professionals
Represents members in contract negotiations and grievance laws.

11997 www.nrhcweb.org
National Rural Housing Coalition
A national membership organization that advocates improved housing for low-income rural families and works to increase public awareness of rural housing problems. The Coalition works with a network of state coalitions and nonprofit organizations to promote federal housing policy that benefits both rural housing and community development programs.

11998 www.patriot.net/users/permail
Public Employees Roundtable
Demonstrates the value of government employees. Develop an 'espirit de corps' among public service employees and encourages public service careers.

11999 www.phada.org
Public Housing Authorities Directors Association
Represents and serves the needs of executive directors of housing authorities of all sizes, in all regions of the nation. In pursuing the Association's goal of improving assisted housing, the corporation works with Congress and federal agencies as well as with all interested groups to improve the nation's housing programs.

12000 www.postcom.org
Association for Postal Commerce
National organization representing those who use, or support the use, of mail as a medium for communication and commerce. Postcom publishes a weekly newsletter covering postal policy and operational issues.

12001 www.ptos.org
Patent and Trademark Office Society
Members are examiners in the US Patent & Trademark Office, registered patent attorneys and agents, agencies, judges and other patent professionals.

12002 www.ruralhome.org
Housing Assistance Council
Expands the pool of decent housing available to the rural poor. Creates and sustains interest and action from all levels of government concerning rural housing for low-income people and helps rural housing organizatins become more productive and professional.

12003 www.sgac.org
State Government Affairs Council
Seeks to improve the state legislative process through interaction with major state governmental conferences. Conducts educational programs on public policies to further understanding between private sector businesses and state legislations.

12004 www.sge-econ.org
Society of Government Economists
Membership benefits economists employed in the public sector or who are interested in the economic aspects of government policies.

12005 www.sheeo.org
State Higher Education Executive Officers
Members are the full-time chief executive officers serving statewide coordinating or governing boards of postsecondary education.

12006 www.sso.org
Intl Assoc of Official Human Rights Agencies
Members are state and local government human rights and human relations agencies.

12007 www.sso.org/iafwa
Intl Assoc of Fish and Wildlife Agencies
Established as the National Association of Game Commissioners.

12008 www.statenews.org
Council of State Governments
Research and service agency for state governments and state officials.

12009 www.theiacp.org
International Association of Chiefs of Police
Has an annual budget of approximately $7 million.

12010 www.urisa.org
Urban & Regional Information Systems Association
Concerned with the effective use of information systems technology at the state, regional and local levels. Members informed of current developments in the information systems field. Its goal is to stimulate and encourage the advancement of an interdisciplinary professional approach to planning, designing and operating information systems.

12011 www.usmayors.org/uscm/
United States Conference of Mayors
An organization of city government officials.

12012 www.water.dnr.state.sc.us/water/icwp
Interstate Council on Water Policy
Members are state and regional agencies concerned with conservation and environmental issues.

12013 www.wicdirectors.org
National Association of WIC Directors
Members are geographic state, Native American state and local agency directors of the Special Supplement nutrition program for woman,infants and children.

International Trade Resources

12014 Embassy of Bosnia and Herzegovina
2109 East Street NW
Washington, DC 20037
202-337-1500; *Fax:* 202-337-1502
info@bhembassy.org; www.bhembassy.org
Social Media: Facebook
Haris Hrle, Ambassador
Milenko Misic, Minister Counselor
Sanja Juric, First Secretary
Denita Lelo, 1st Consular Officer
10 Members

Associations

12015 **ACM SIGGRAPH**
Association for Computing Machinery
www.siggraph.org
Social Media: Facebook, Twitter, LinkedIn, YouTube, Google Plus, RSS
Jeff Jortner, President
Paul Debevec, VP
Tony Baylis, Treasurer
The Association for Computing Machinery's Special Interest Group on Computer Graphics and Interactive Techniques promotes the generation and dissemination of information on computer graphics and interactive techniques. Fostering a membership community whose core values help them to catalyze the innovation and application of computer graphics and interactive techniques.
8300+ Members
Founded in: 1974

12016 **American Institute of Graphic Arts**
164 Fifth Avenue
New York, NY 10010-5989
212-807-1990; *Fax:* 212-807-1799;
www.aiga.org
Social Media: Facebook, Twitter, LinkedIn
Richard Grefe, Executive Director
Katie Baker, Director of chapter development
Jennifer Bender, Director of Communications
Elaine Bowen, Director of strategic partnerships
Kathleen Bundy, Program director
To further excellence in design as a broadly defined discipline, strategic tool for business and cultural force. A professional association committed to stimulating thinking about design through the exchange of ideas and information, the encouragement of critical analysis and research and the advancement of education and ethical practice.
18575 Members
Founded in: 1922

12017 **Association of Graphic Communications**
330 7th Ave
9th Floor
New York, NY 10001-5010
212-279-2100; *Fax:* 212-279-5381;
www.aiga.org
Serves as a provider of graphic arts education and training, a network for industry information and idea exchange, an advocate for legislative and regulatory/environmental issues, and a vehicle for industry promotion.
560 Members
Founded in: 1865

12018 **Design Management Institute**
38 Chauncy St.
Suite 800
Boston, MA 02111
617-338-6380; www.dmi.org
Social Media: Facebook, Twitter, LinkedIn, YouTube, Flickr
International nonprofit seeking to improve organizations through design management.
Founded in: 1975

12019 **Graphic Artists Guild**
32 Broadway
Suite 1114
New York, NY 10004-1612
212-791-3400; *Fax:* 212-791-0333
admin@graphicartistsguild.org;
www.graphicartistsguild.org
Social Media: Facebook, Twitter, LinkedIn, Google Plus
Haydn Adams, President
Chuck Schultz, Vice President
Lauren Rabinowitz, Treasurer
Lara Kisielewska, Secretary
Patricia McKiernan, Executive Director
Promotes and protects the economic interests of member artists and is committed to improving conditions for all ceators of graphic arts and raising standards for the enitre industry.
1400 Members
Founded in: 1967

12020 **Graphic Arts Association**
1210 Northbrook Dr
Suite 200
Trevose, PA 19053-8406
215-396-2300; *Fax:* 215-396-9890
gaa@gaaonline.org;
www.graphicartsassociation.org
Social Media: Facebook, Twitter
Melissa Jones, President
Bill Scotese, Director of Credit and Collections
Stephen Stankavage, Environmental, Health
Rita Donlan, Bookkeeper/Office Manager
Patti Rose, Administrative Assistant
Mission is to be the leading resource for the printing and graphic communications industry in advocacy, education, and information to enhance the strength and profitability of its members.
400 Members
Founded in: 1886

12021 **Guild of Natural Science Illustrators**
Guild of Natural Science Illustrators
P.O. Box 42410
Ben Franklin Station
Washington, DC 20015
301-309-1514; *Fax:* 301-309-1514
gnsihome@his.com; www.gnsi.org
Amelia Janes, President
Britt Griswold, Vice President
Gail Guth, Membership Secretary
Ikumi Kayama, Secretary
Marjorie Leggitt, Treasurer
A nonprofit organization of persons employed or genuinely interested in the field of natural science illustration. It maintains and encourages high standards of competence and professional ethics by increasing communication among its members. Provides opportunities for professional and scholarly development, and seeks to promote better understanding of the profession among the general public and potential clients requiring the services of natural science illustrators.
1.1M Members
Founded in: 1968

12022 **International Digital Enterprise Alliance**
1600 Duke Street
Suite 420
Alexandria, VA 22314-2805
703-837-1070; *Fax:* 703-837-1072
dsteinhardt@idealliance.org;
www.idealliance.org
Social Media: Facebook, Twitter, LinkedIn
Laura C Reid, Board Chair
David J Steinhardt, President & CEO
Joe Duncan, Board Vice Chair
Debbie Cooper, Treasurer
Penny Sullivan, Secretary
A global community of content and media creators, and their service providers, material suppliers, and technology partners. Association identifies best practices for efficient end-to-end digital media workflows, from content creation through distribution. Providing members the forum for the exchange of information that results in the creation of the industry's most valued standards.
300+ Members
Founded in: 1966

12023 **National Association for Printing Leadership (NAPL)**
One Meadowlands Plaza
Suite 1511
East Rutherford, NJ 07073
201-634-9600
800-642-6275; *Fax:* 201-634-0324
webmaster@napl.org; www.napl.org
Social Media: Facebook, Twitter, LinkedIn, YouTube, Google Plus, Pinteres
Nigel Worme, Chairman
Niels Winther, Vice Chairman
Joseph P. Truncale, Ph.D., CAE,, President & CEO
Mike Philie, Senior Vice President
Mark R. Hahn, Senior Vice President
A not-for-profit national trade association serving companies in the $100 billion+ graphic communications industry. NAPL offers a comprehensive slate of business and building solutions that provides company leaders with the strategies, insights, and guidance they can use to make informed business decisions, minimize risk, anticipate change, and profitably grow their business.
2000 Members
Founded in: 1933

12024 **Pacific Printing & Imaging Association**
6825 SW Sandburg Street
Portland, OR 97223
877-762-7742; *Fax:* 503-221-5691
info@ppiassociation.org;
www.ppiassociation.org
Social Media: Facebook, Twitter, LinkedIn, YouTube
Jules Van Sant, Executive Director
Dedicated to promoting members and their industries while providing a variety of benefits and money saving programs to Visual & Graphic Communications Companies and individuals in six states. Purpose is to deliver what it takes to help members become more successful and profitable in their businesses.
200 Members
Founded in: 1948

12025 **Printing Industries of America**
200 Deer Run Rd
Sewickley, PA 15143-2600
412-741-6860
800-910-4283; *Fax:* 412-741-2311
info@printing.org; www.printing.org
Social Media: Facebook, Twitter, LinkedIn, Pinterest
Michael F. Makin, President & CEO
Mary Garnett, Executive Vice President
Nicholas Stratigos, CFO
Ronnie Davis Senior, Vice President & Chief Economist
Lisbeth Lyons, Vice President, Government Affairs
A graphic arts trade association representing our members in this industry. Printing Industries of America, along with its affiliates, delivers products and services that enhance the growth, efficiency and profitability of its members and the industry through advocacy, education, research and technical information
10000 Members
Founded in: 1887

12026 **Society for Environmental Graphic Design**
1900 L Street NW
Suite 710
Washington, DC 20036
202-638-5555; *Fax:* 202-478-2286
segd@segd.org; www.segd.org
Social Media: Facebook, Twitter, LinkedIn, RSS

Clive Roux, CEO
Ann Makowski, COO

Members work in the planning, design, fabrication, and implementation of communications in the built environment. SEGD is the global community of people working at the intersection of communication design and the built environment.
1600+ Members
Founded in: 1974

12027 **Society of Publication Designers**
27 Union Square West
Suite 207
New York, NY 10003
212-223-3332; *Fax:* 212-223-5880
mail@spd.org; www.spd.org
Social Media: Twitter, RSS

Tim Leong, President
David Curcurito, Vice President
Allyson Torrisi, Vice President
Leah Bailey, Secretary
Courtney Murphy, Treasurer

The only organication specifically addressing the visual concerns of print and online editorial professionals. Activities promote the role of members as journalists and partners in the editorial process, as well as fostering new generations of publication designers through educational outreach and scholarship opportunities.
550 Members
Founded in: 1965

12028 **Technical Association of the Graphic Arts**
200 Deer Run Road
Sewickley, PA 15143
412-259-1706
800-910-4283; *Fax:* 412-741-2311;
www.printing.org/taga
Social Media: Facebook, Twitter, LinkedIn, Pinterest, Google Plus

Michael F. Makin, President & CEO
Mary Garnett, Executive Vice President
Nicholas Stratigos, CFO
Ronnie Davis Senior, Vice President & Chief Economist
Lisbeth Lyons, Vice President, Government Affairs

Provides a worldwide forum for sharing and disseminating theoretical,functional and practical information on current and emerging technologies for Graphic Arts print production and related processes
900+ Members
Founded in: 1948

Newsletters

12029 **Graphic News**
Printing Industry of Minnesota
2829 University Avenue SE
Suite 750
Minneappolis, MN 55414-3222
612-379-3360
800-448-756; *Fax:* 618-379-6030
davidr@pimn.org; www.pimn.org

David Radziej, President
Arlene Roth, Director Public Relations
John Connelly, Director of Membership
Carla Steuck, Director of Education Services
Patricia Barnum, CFO

For the printing and graphic arts industries.
16 Pages
Frequency: Bi-Monthly
Circulation: 12000
Founded in: 1955

12030 **Graphics Update**
Printing Association of Florida
6095 NW 167 Street
Suite D-7
Miami, FL 33015
305-558-4855
800-331-0461; *Fax:* 305-823-8965;
www.flprint.org
Social Media: Facebook, Twitter, LinkedIn, Flickr, YouTube

Gene Strul, Editor
Michael H Streibig, Staff Executive
Ron Davis, Chief Economist

A monthly newsletter to the members of the Printing Association of Florida. Full color publication with attractive advertising purchases and a focused buying circulation.
Cost: $200.00
Frequency: Monthly

12031 **Guild News**
Graphic Artists Guild
32 Broadway
Suite 1114
New York, NY 10004-1612
212-791-3400; *Fax:* 212-791-0333;
www.graphicartistsguild.org

Patricia McKiernan, Executive Director
Haydn Adams, President
Chuck Schultz, Vice President
Lauren Rabinowitz, Treasurer
Lara Kisielewska, Secretary

Designed to keep individuals abreast of what's going on with the Guild, the industry, and in the area.
Frequency: Bimonthly

12032 **Holography News**
Reconnaissance International Consulting
PO Box 40976
Denver, CO 80204
303-628-5568; *Fax:* 303-628-5594;
www.reconnaissance-intl.com

Ian Lancaster, Director
Jon Senft, VP
Lewis Kontnik, Publisher

Leading global source of business intelligence on holography and authentication for document security, personal identification and brand protection. Unique knowledge and experience of these highly-specialized and rapidly-changing industries, this newsletter is offering invaluable insight into and authoritative information on markets, strategic management and technical issues through reports, newsleters, conferences, executive briefings and consultancy.
Cost: $774.00
Frequency: Monthly
Founded in: 1987

12033 **Messages**
Society of Environmental Graphic Designers
1000 Vermont Ave Nw
Suite 400
Washington, DC 20005-4903
202-638-0891; *Fax:* 202-638-0891
segd@segd.org; www.segd.org
Social Media: Facebook, Twitter, LinkedIn

Be the first to hear about new SEGD initiatives, events, and educational resources. Also learn about new contracts, new products, personnel changes, and other news from SEGD member companies. Messages is also the conduit for special SEGD publications and resources such as the ADA White Papers, the SEGD Green Paper, and other valuable educational materials.
Frequency: Monthly

Magazines & Journals

12034 **Animation Magazine**
Animation Magazine
30941 Agoura Rd
suite 102
Westlake Villag, CA 91361-4637
818-991-2884; *Fax:* 818-991-3773
info@animationmagazine.net;
www.animationmagazine.net

Jean Thoren, President

Covers the animation industry trends, technology, new products, historical perspectives coverage of current animated programming and features, and general news.
Cost: $65.07
Frequency: Monthly
Founded in: 1985
Printed in 4 colors on glossy stock

12035 **Before & After: How to Design Cool Stuff**
Pagelab
323 Lincoln Street
Roseville, CA 95678-2229
956-78 -229
800-266-5783; *Fax:* 916-784-3995
contact@bamagazine.com;
www.bamagazine.com
Social Media: Facebook, Twitter, YouTube

John McWade, Publisher
Gaye McWade, Editor

Practical approach to graphic design. Dedicated to making graphic design understandable, useful and even fun for everyone.
Cost: $36.00
Circulation: 26000
Founded in: 1990

12036 **Bulletin Magazine**
International Digital Enterprise Alliance
1421 Prince St
Suite 230
Alexandria, VA 22314-2805
703-837-1070; *Fax:* 703-837-1072;
www.idealliance.org
Social Media: Facebook, Twitter, LinkedIn

David Steinhardt, President & CEO
Lisa Bos, Chair
Chip Harding, Vice Chair
Paul Clancy, Treasurer
Jim Mikol, Secretary

The voice of IDEAlliance+IPA, keeping members abreast of business challenges and opportunities, assuring workflows are state-of-the-art, speeding information across the end-to-end digital media supply chain, from content creation through delivery. Since its founding, the Bulletin has played a significant role in the dissemination of information for the graphic communications industry.
300+ Members
Frequency: Bi-Monthly
Founded in: 1966

12037 **Cadalyst**
Longitude Media
www.cadalyst.com
Social Media: Facebook, Twitter

Nancy Spurling Johnson, Editor-in-Chief
Cyrena Respini-Irwin, Senior Editor

The most complete source of essential information about computer-aided design and related software and hardware technologies for the fields of AEC, manufacturing, and GIS. Delivers timely, objective, and practical product reviews and updates, tips, tutorials, insight, and advice to help CAD managers and users make informed decisions about technology, get productive, and get the job done.
Cost: $39.95
100 Pages
Frequency: Monthly
Circulation: 90000
ISSN: 0360-3520
Founded in: 1987
Printed in 4 colors

12038 Communication Arts
Coyne & Blanchard
110 Constitution Dr
Menlo Park, CA 94025-1107

650-326-6040; *Fax:* 650-326-1648
editorial@commarts.com; www.commarts.com

Patrick Coyne, Publisher
Ernie Schenck, Creative Director
Mike Krigel, Marketing Executive

Features profile individuals, studios and agencies with examples of their work. Includes reviews of software, books and products, as well as discussing the latest in digital and broadcast design.
Cost: $53.00
Frequency: 8 issues per ye
Circulation: 71927
ISSN: 0010-3519
Founded in: 1959
Printed in 4 colors

12039 Computer Graphics World
COP Communications, Inc.
620 W. Elk Ave
Glendale, CA 91204

603-432-7568
karen@cgw.com; www.cgw.com

Karen Moltenbrey, Chief Editor
William R. Rittwage, Publisher, President & CEO
Kelly Ryan, Marketing Coordinator
Michael Viggiano, Art Director

Covers specific applications of computer graphics, written by users and vendors of equipment and services to the industry. The magazine of 3D computer graphics for engineering and animation professionals.
Cost: $55.00
Frequency: Monthly
Circulation: 40597
Founded in: 1977
Printed in 4 colors on glossy stock

12040 Critique
Neumeier Design Team
120 Hawthorne Avenue
#102
Palo Alto, CA 94301-1000

650-326-4396; *Fax:* 650-323-3298;
www.critiquemag.com

Marty Neumeier, Editor

Features include methods and products to increase the creativity and technological advance of graphic artwork.
Cost: $60.00
Frequency: Quarterly
Circulation: 10000

12041 Desktop Publishers Journal
Desktop Publishing Institute
462 Boston Street
Topsfield, MA 01983-1200
Fax: 978-887-9245

Thomas Tetreault, Publisher
Barry Harrigan, Editor

Desktop publishing topics and issues and association information.
Frequency: Weekly
Circulation: 60000

12042 Digital Imaging
Cygnus Publishing
3 Huntington Quadrangle
Suite 301N
Melville, NY 11747

631-845-2700
800-308-6397; *Fax:* 631-845-2798;
www.cygnuspub.com

Laureen Delaney, Associate Publisher
Kathy Schneider, Group Publisher
Andrew Darlow, Editorial Director
Liz Vickers, Advertising Sales Manager
Paul Bonaiuto, CFO

For the imaging professional. Dedicated to bridging the digital imaging gap between graphics and photography while providing in-depth solutions.
Circulation: 30,000
Founded in: 1966

12043 Dynamic Graphics
Dynamic Graphics
6000 N Forest Park Drive
Peoria, IL 61614-3592

309-888-8851
888-698-8542; *Fax:* 800-488-3492;
www.dynamicgraphics.com

Alan Meckler, President, JupiterMedia
David Moffly, President/CEO
Marcy Slane, Managing Editor

Encourages users to take their electronic tools to the next level of productivity and creativity. Emphasizes practical and real-world solutions.
Cost: $36.00
72 Pages
Frequency: 6
Circulation: 66143
ISSN: 1094-2548
Founded in: 1964
Printed in on glossy stock

12044 GATFWORLD Magazine
Graphic Arts Technical Foundation Association
200 Deer Run Road
Sewickley, PA 15143-2324

412-741-6860
800-910-4283; *Fax:* 412-741-2311
gain@piagatf.org; www.gain.net

George Ryan, Executive VP/COO
Michael Makin, President/CEO
Deanna Gentile, Editor

A bi-monthly magazine for GATF members and subscribers that reports on research and technical trends in the graphic arts (printing) industry, environmental and safety news, developments in graphic communications education and news of emerging products, programs and services.
Cost: $75.00
Circulation: 18000
Founded in: 1924

12045 Gasp Report
GASP Engineering
234 Benjamin W Avenue
Swarthmore, PA 19081-1421

610-543-5194
800-256-4282; *Fax:* 610-328-1358;
www.gaspnet.com

Steve Hannaford, Publisher

Covers new technology, financing, marketing and other business concerns of the printing, graphics and publishing industries. In-depth articles highlight strategies for industry professionals.
Cost: $195.00
Frequency: Monthly
Circulation: 400

12046 Graphic Arts Monthly
360 Park Avenue S
New York, NY 10010

212-636-6834
800-217-7874; *Fax:* 646-746-7422;
www.worldleadersinprint.com

Phil Saran, Publisher
Roger Ynostroza, Editorial Director

The magazine of the printing industry including commercial, in-plant and related operations, such as color separations, composition, binding and pre-press service bureaus.
Frequency: Monthly
Circulation: 75,000

12047 Graphic Design: USA
Kaye Publishing Corporation
641 Lexington Ave
Suite 1202
New York, NY 10022-4503

212-259-0400; *Fax:* 212-489-4736
gkaye@gdusa.com; www.gdusa.com

M Kaye, Owner
Maria Mohamed, Circualtion Manager
Gordon D. Kaye, Publisher

A publication for the graphic designer, offering information and news of the industry.
Cost: $60.00
120 Pages
Frequency: Monthly
ISSN: 0274-7499
Founded in: 1965

12048 Graphics Pro
Graphic Products Association
4709 N El Capitan Avenue
Suite 103
Fresno, CA 93722

559-276-8494
800-276-8428; *Fax:* 559-276-8496;
www.gpionline.org

Michael R Neer, Publisher
Steven V Neer, Associate Publisher
Damara Torres, Owner

A bi-monthly journal published by the Graphic Products Association.
Cost: $55.00
Circulation: 7500
Founded in: 1994
Printed in on glossy stock

12049 Graphis
Graphis Press
307 5th Ave
10th Floor
New York, NY 10016-6517

212-532-9387
866-648-2915; *Fax:* 212-213-3229
info@graphis.com; www.graphis.com

Martin Pederson, Owner
Walter Herdeg, Editor

Graphis is an international journal of design and visual communication, covering graphic arts, design, photography, architecture and related topics. The targeted readership includes professionals in these disciplines as well as all creative visual communicators.
Cost: $90.00
Circulation: 22000
Founded in: 1944

12050 HOW Magazine
F&W Publications
4700 E Galbraith Rd
Cincinnati, OH 45236-2726

513-531-2690; *Fax:* 513-531-1843
editorial@howdesign.com;
www.fwpublications.com

David Nussbaum, CEO
Bryn Mooth, Editor
William R. Reed, President
Jim Ogle, Chief Financial Officer
Kate Rados, Marketing Director

Business and creative resource for graphic designers. Latest business, technological and creative information.
Cost: $49.00
194 Pages
Circulation: 39946
ISSN: 0886-0483
Founded in: 1900
Printed in 4 colors on glossy stock

12051 ID Magazine
38 East 29th Street
Floor 3
New York, NY 10016

212-447-1400
800-258-929; *Fax:* 212-447-5231;
www.id-mag.com

Kelly N Kofron, Executive Editor
Dave Richmond, Executive Editor

Leading critical magazine covering the art, business and culture of design.
Frequency: 8 per year

12052 PC Graphics & Video
Advanstar Communications
Ste 300
17770 Cartwright Rd
Irvine, CA 92614-5815

714-513-8400; *Fax:* 714-513-8481
info@advanstar.com; www.advanstar.com

Michael Forcillo, Publisher
Gene Smarte, Chief Executive Officer

Covers graphics and video for personal computers.
Cost: $5.00
Circulation: 10,699

12053 Print Magazine
RC Publications
38 E 29th Street
3rd Floor
New York, NY 10016

212-447-1400; *Fax:* 212-447-5231
info@printmag.com; www.printmag.com

Joyce Rutter Kay, Editor in Chief
Joel Toner, Publisher
Stephany Skirvin, Art Director
Steven Kent, CEO
William Reed, President

News and information for the graphic design industry.
Cost: $53.00
160 Pages
Circulation: 45000
ISSN: 0032-8510
Founded in: 1940
Printed in 4 colors on glossy stock

12054 Printer's Northwest Trader
Eagle Newspapers
650 N 1st Street
PO Box 96
Woodburn, OR 97071-450

503-981-3441; *Fax:* 503-981-1253;
www.eaglenewspapers.com

Rod Stollery, Publisher
Sandy Hubbard, Founder
Elmo Smith, Founder

Reviews new equipment and techniques and highlights industry leaders of note. Serves the northwestern portion of the United States.
Cost: $10.00
Frequency: Monthly
Circulation: 16000
Founded in: 1933

12055 Publication Design Annual #39
Society of Publication Designers
17 East 47th Street
6th Floor
New York, NY 10017

212-223-3332; *Fax:* 212-223-5880
mail@spd.org; wwww.spd.org

Bruce Ramsay, President
Amid Capeci, Treasurer
Gail Bichler, Treasurer
Nancy Stamatopoulos, Secretary

A compendium of the best designed magazine/trade and consumer newspapers. Annual reports of the year as judged by a panel. Also includes web and interactive design sites and annual reports.
Cost: $195.00
Frequency: Monthly
Circulation: 15000
ISBN: 1-564966-21-6
Founded in: 1969
Printed in 4 colors on matte stock

12056 Publish How-to Magazine
MacWorld Communications
501 2nd St
Suite 310
San Francisco, CA 94107-1496

415-243-0505; *Fax:* 415-442-0766

Mike Kisseberth, CEO
Susan Gubemat, Editor

The definitive source on how to use personal computers to integrate text and graphics into printed communication.
Cost: $4.00
Circulation: 98,819

12057 Sign & Digital Graphics
National Business Media
PO Box 1416
Broomfield, CO 80038-1416

303-469-0424
800-669-0424; *Fax:* 303-465-3424;
www.sdgmag.com

Mary Tohill, Publisher
Ken Mergentime, Executive Editor
Matt Dixon, Managing Editor
James Kochevar, Associate Publisher
Sara Siauw, Production Coordinator

The most widely read industry trade publication covering the business of visual communications and offering a broad range of in-depth reporting for sign industry and wide-format digital graphics professionals. This distinguished and unique magazine provides comprehensive professional coverage on all aspects of commercial signage, commercial graphics production, electric LED-based signage and letter systems, architectural signage, electronic digital displays, vehicle wraps, and much more.
Frequency: Monthly

12058 Southern Graphics
PTN Publishing Company
445 Broadhollow Road
Suite 21
Melville, NY 11747-3601

Fax: 631-845-7109

Rob Schweiger, Publisher
KJ Moran, Editor

Edited for those in the graphic arts industry throughout the southeastern US and the Caribbean.
Cost: $5.00
Circulation: 21,000

12059 TAGA Journal of Graphic Technology
Technical Association of the Graphic Arts
200 Deer Run Road
Sewickley, PA 15143

412-259-1706; *Fax:* 412-741-2311;
www.taga.org

Mark Bohan, Managing Director

A peer-reviewed journal designed to meet the needs of the global professional graphic applications industries and to bring together the multi-disciplinary community in further development of printing as a manufacturing process. Embraces the fundamental science and technology, application and technology transfer and the genergic problems and experience associated with the management and implementation of graphic applications.
900+ Members
Frequency: Bi-Annually
Founded in: 1948

12060 Trade Show Times
Fichera Communications
441 S State Road
Suite 14
Margate, FL 33063

954-971-4360
800-327-8999; *Fax:* 954-971-4362;
www.tradeshowtimes.com

Orazio Fichera, Publisher
Rick Kelly, Contact

Hand distributed to attendees at major graphic arts trade shows. Accepts advertising.
32 Pages
Frequency: Monthly
Founded in: 1974

12061 Visual Communications Journal
Graphic Arts Technical Foundation Association
200 Deer Run Road
Sewickley, PA 15143-2324

412-741-6860
800-910-4283; *Fax:* 412-741-2311
gain@piagatf.org; www.gain.net

George Ryan, Executive VP/COO
Michael Makin, President/CEO
Peter Oresick, VP Publishing

Educational guide and news for scholars and students studying the graphic arts industry.

12062 segdDESIGN
Society for Environmental Graphic Design
1000 Vermont Ave NW
Suite 400
Washington, DC 20005-4921

202-638-5555; *Fax:* 202-638-0891
pat@segd.org; www.segd.org

Ann Makowski, Manager

The magazine of choice for creative professionals working at the intersection of communication design and the built environment. A rich source of information on the key people, research, technologies, materials, and resources that influence communications in the built environment. International Journal of Environmental Graphic Design
Frequency: Quarterly

Trade Shows

12063 3D Design & Animation Conference & Expo
Miller Freeman Publications

525 Market Street
Suite 500
San Francisco, CA 94110

415-955-5533; *Fax:* 415-278-5341;
www.mfi.com

For animators and digital content creators, exibits include equipment supplies and services for the 3D design and animation industry. Conferences, reception and publications. Space rental available.
Frequency: Annual

12064 Annual Automated Imaging Associates Business Conference
Appliance Manufacturer
5900 Harper Road
Suite 105
Solon, OH 44139-1935

440-349-3060; *Fax:* 440-498-9121
jburnstein@robotics.org;
www.machinevisiononline.org

Jeff Burnstein, Executive Director

The industry's leading conference and networking event. This conference gathers over 150 top industry executives to do business with their peers and hear presentations on issues affecting the global economy in general and the machine vision industry specifically.
Frequency: Annual,February

12065 Grafix
Conference Management Corporation
200 Connecticut Avenue
Norwalk, CT 06854-1940

800-342-3238; *Fax:* 203-831-8446

Annual show of 200 exhibitors of computer hardware and software for graphic design and computer publishing, paper supplies, typesetting equipment and services, stock photography, clip art service and related equipment, supplies and services.
4000 Attendees

12066 Graph Expo
Graphic Arts Show Company
1189 Preston White Drive
Reston, VA 20191-5435

703-264-7200; *Fax:* 703-620-9187;
www.graphexpo.com

Where top executives come to learn, network and make informed intelligent purchasing decisions. Leading manufacturers and suppliers will be exhibiting at the show and many of them will be showcasing newly released products, technologies and services. The year's largest and most exciting display of live running equipment in the Americas.
40000 Attendees
Frequency: Annual/September

12067 Graph Expo West
Graphic Arts Show Company
1899 Preston White Drive
Reston, VA 20191

703-264-7200; *Fax:* 703-620-9187
info@gasc.org; www.gasc.org

Lilly Kinney, Conference Manager
Chris Theil, Administrative Assistant
Erin Omwake, Administrative Assistant
Deborah Vieder, Director of Communications

Two hundred booths for the graphics industry.
13M Attendees
Frequency: November
Founded in: 1982

12068 Graphics Trade Show Expo Southwest
910 W Mockingbird Lane
Dallas, TX 75247-5182
Jim Weinstein, Show Manager

Six hundred and fifty booths.
13M Attendees
Frequency: June

12069 Graphics of the Americas
Printing Association of Florida
6275 Hazeltine National Drive
Orlando, FL 32822

407-240-8009; *Fax:* 407-240-8333;
www.flprint.org

Holly Price, Booth Sales & Marketing
Michelle Torres, Attendee Info.

Largest annual international graphic commincations education and exhibit showplace. Over 450 exhibitors in 500,000 square feet.
22000 Attendees
Frequency: February

12070 Gutenberg & Digital Outlook
Graphic Arts Show Company
1189 Preston White Drive
Reston, VA 22091

703-264-7200; *Fax:* 703-620-9187
info@gasc.org; www.gasc.org

Chris Thiel, VP
Kelly Kilga, Administrative Assistant
Erin Omwake, Administrative Assistant
Deborah Vieder, Director of Communications

Largest graphic design, digital prepress, printing, publishing, and converting trade show in the Westen United States. Over 100 exhibitors with the widest selection of vendors.
8000 Attendees
Frequency: Annual,June

12071 IMPA Annual Conference
In-Plant Printing and Mailing Association
125 S. Jefferson
Suite B-4
Kearney, MO 64060

816-903-4762; *Fax:* 816-902-4766;
www.ipma.org

John Sarantakos, Administrator
Larry Wright, Treasurer

Annual educational conference and vending show.

12072 Printing Expo Conference Mid America
Graphics Arts Show Company
1899 Preston White Drive
Reston, VA 20191
703-264-7200; *Fax:* 703-620-9187
info@gasc.org; www.gasc.org

Paul Kaplan, Show Manager
Erin Omwake, Administrative Assistant
Deborah Vieder, Director of Communications

Exhibits by manufacturers and dealers of the latest graphics equipment and services.
3000 Attendees
Frequency: June
Founded in: 1982

12073 Sunbelt Computer and Graphics
Printing Industry Association of Georgia
5020 Highlands Parkway
Smyrna, GA 30082
770-433-3050
800-288-1894; *Fax:* 770-433-3062;
www.sunbeltshow.org

Dianne McPherson, Trade Show Director
Denise Holland, VP Communications

Two hundred and fifty exhibitors of current printing technology.
18M Attendees

Directories & Databases

12074 365: AIGA Year In Design
American Institute of Graphic Arts
164 Fifth Avenue
New York, NY 10010-5989

212-807-1990; www.aiga.org
Social Media: Facebook, Twitter, LinkedIn

Doug Powell, President
Zia Khan, Secretary/ Treasurer
Richard Grefe, Executive Director

About 500 works of graphic designers that have been cited for outstanding design by the American Institute of Graphic Arts.
Cost: $45.00
Frequency: Annual

12075 Graphic Artist's Guide to Marketing and Self-Promotion
North Light Books
1557 Dana Avenue
Cincinnati, OH 45207-1005

Fax: 513-531-4082

A list of publishers of resources about marketing for the graphic artist.
Cost: $19.95

12076 Graphic Arts Blue Book
AF Lewis & Company
360 Lexington Ave
Suite 21
New York, NY 10017-6529

212-682-8448; *Fax:* 212-682-2442;
www.d-net.com/graphartsbb

Andrew Lewis, Owner
Timothy Lewis, Editor

Offers information on printing plants, bookbinders, imagesetters, platemakers, paper merchants, paper manufacturers, printing machinery manufacturers and dealers and others serving the graphic arts industry.
Cost: $85.00
Frequency: 8 Annual Editions
Circulation: 51500

12077 Graphic Arts Monthly Sourcebook
Reed Business Information
2000 Clearwater Dr
Oak Brook, IL 60523-8809

630-574-0825; *Fax:* 630-288-8781;
www.reedbusiness.com

Jeff Greisch, President
Bill Esler, Editor-in_Chief
Roger Ynostroza, Editorial Director

About 1,400 manufacturers and distributors of graphic arts equipment, supplies and services, as well as over 700 graphic arts dealers.
Cost: $50.00
Frequency: Annual March
Circulation: 85,000

12078 Graphic Communications Association Bar Code Reporter
International Digital Enterprise Alliance
1421 Prince St
Suite 230
Alexandria, VA 22314-2805

703-837-1060; *Fax:* 703-548-2867;
www.idealliance.org

David Steinhardt, CEO

The authoritative quarterly journal of bar codes, electronic data interchange, and related electronic commerce technologies in the publishing,

printing, and paper industries.
Cost: $95.00
Frequency: Quarterly
Circulation: 150

12079 **Publication Design Annual**
Society of Publication Designers
27 Union Square West
Suite 207
New York, NY 10003
212-223-3332; *Fax:* 212-223-5880
mail@spd.org; www.spd.org
Social Media: Twitter

Josh Klenert, President
Andrea Dunham, Vice President
Jennifer Pastore, Vice President
Nancy Stamatopoulos, Secretary
Gail Bichler, Treasurer

Celebrates the journalists, editorial directors, photographers, and other talented individuals who brought the year with all its triumphs and disasters to light. Featuring work published in a wide range of mediums and created by journalistic, design, and publishing talent from around the world.
Cost: $14.49
ISBN: 1-592531-81-4
Founded in: 1965

12080 **RSVP: Directory of Illustration and Design**
RSVP
PO Box 050314
Brooklyn, NY 11205
718-857-9267
info@rsvpdirectory.com;
www.rsvpdirectory.com

Kathleen Creighton, Co-Publisher/Co-Editor
Richard Lebenson, Co-Publisher/Co-Editor

Fully illustrated resource book for the graphic arts/media industry. Showcases work of illustrators and designers, nationwide.
Circulation: 18,000

Industry Web Sites

12081 **Creative Business**
38 Indian Rd.
Suite 200
Marshfield, MA 02050
617-451-0041
mail@creativebusiness.com;
www.creativebusiness.com
Social Media: Facebook, LinkedIn, YouTube

Cameron S. Foote, Editor

Business resources - forms, articles, books - for creative services organizations and freelancers.

12082 **http://gold.greyhouse.com**
G.O.L.D Grey House OnLine Databases
Grey House Publishing's online database platform, GOLD, offers Quick Search, Keyword Search and Expert Search for most business sectors including graphic design markets. The GOLD platform makes finding the information you need quick and easy - whether you're a novice searcher or an experienced database user. All of Grey House's directory products are available for subscription on the GOLD platform.

12083 **www.agcomm.org**
Association of Graphic Communications
Promtes the interest of graphic communication professionals.

12084 **www.aiga.org**
American Institute of Graphic Arts
The purpose of the AIGA is to further excellence in a communication design as a broadly defined discipline, as a strategic tool for business and as a cultural force. The AIGA is the place design professionals turn first to exchange ideas and information, participate in critical analysis and research and advance education and ethical practice.

12085 **www.gaa1900.com**
Graphic Arts Association
Promotes the interests of graphic art professionals. Members consist of suppliers and distributors of graphic arts equipment.

12086 **www.gatf.org**
Graphic Arts Technical Foundation Association
To serve the graphic comunications community as the leading source for the technical information and services through research and education.

12087 **www.graphicartistsguild.org**
Graphic Artists Guild
Promotes and protects the economic interests of member artists and is committed to improving conditions for all ceators of graphic arts and raising standards for the enitre industry.

12088 **www.greyhouse.com**
Grey House Publishing
Authoritative reference directories for most business sectors including graphic design markets. Users can search the online databases with varied search criteria allowing for custom searches by product category, geographic area, sales volume, keyword, subject and more. Full Grey House catalog and online ordering also available.

12089 **www.idealliance.org**
International Digital Enterprise Alliance
Provides the opportunity for those who create, produce, manage, and deliver content to interface with those who develop the software tools to facilitate these functions.

12090 **www.myfonts.com**
MyFonts.com
Allows a user to find fonts with simple keywords. The user can test a font. The site also offers a MyFonts forum, where users can ask the experts

12091 **www.nagasa.org**
North American Graphic Arts Suppliers Association
The association for the channel that distributes printing and imaging technologies.

12092 **www.napl.org**
National Association for Printing Leadership
NAPL publishes industry specific books and periodicals for the graphic arts community. Topics cover management in the areas of sales, marketing, human resources, finance and operations technology.

12093 **www.ppi-assoc.org**
Pacific Printing & Imaging Association
To provide programs, offer services, and promote an environment, which assists members to see and adapt to the future, while continuing to improve and profit in the present.

12094 **www.recouncil.org**
Research and Engineering Council of the National
Association for Printing Leadership
A technical trade association established to identify graphic arts industry problems, coordinate graphic arts technical activities and develop industry associated technical/education programs, conference and seminars.

12095 **www.siggraph.org**
Special Interest Group on Computer Graphics
A forum for the promotion and distribution of current computer graphics research and technology.

12096 **www.taga.org**
Technical Association of the Graphic Arts
Organized to advance the science and technology of graphic arts. Disseminates graphic arts research internationally via annual technical conference and proceedings.

Associations

12097 American Hardware Manufacturers Association
801 N Plaza Drive
Schaumburg, IL 60173-4977
847-605-1025; *Fax:* 847-605-1030
info@ahma.org; www.ahma.org
Social Media: Twitter, LinkedIn
A leading industry trade association providing a wide range of programs and services for member firms as well as the entire industry, including industry conferences, events and workshops; legislative representation in Washington; domestic and international marketing support; technology initiatives; cost-saving programs; targeted publications; networking opportunities; and many other industry-directed services.
Founded in: 1901

12098 Associated Locksmiths of America
3500 Easy St
Dallas, TX 75247
214-819-9733
800-532-2562; *Fax:* 214-819-9736
webmaster@aloa.org; www.aloa.org
Social Media: Facebook
International professional organization of highly qualified security professionals engaged in consulting,sales,installation and maintenance of locks,keys,safes,premises security,access controls,alarms, and other secutriy relates endeavors.
10000 Members

12099 Builders Hardware Manufacturers Association
355 Lexington Avenue
15th Floor
New York, NY 10017
212-297-2122; *Fax:* 212-370-9047;
www.buildershardware.com
Social Media: LinkedIn
Scott James, President
Dan Picard, 1st Vice President
Patricia Yulkowkski, 2nd Vice President
John Cringole, 3rd Vice President
The trade association for North American manufacturers of commercial builders hardware. Nationally recognized for its leadership role in ensuring the quality and performance of builders hardware. Any organization that manufactures and sells builders hardware in the United States is eligible for Association membership.
Founded in: 1925

12100 Builders' Hardware Manufacturers
355 Lexington Avenue
15th Floor
New York, NY 10017
212-297-2122; *Fax:* 212-370-9047;
www.buildershardware.com
Social Media: LinkedIn
Sandy Johnson, President
Scott James, 1st Vice President
Dan Picard, 2nd Vice President
Ed Pruitt, 3rd Vice President
Founded in: 1925

12101 Door and Hardware Institute
14150 Newbrook Drive
Chantilly, VA 20151-2232
703-222-2010; *Fax:* 703-222-2410
info@dhi.org; www.dhi.org
Social Media: Facebook, Twitter, LinkedIn
Jerry Heppes, Sr, CAE, Chief Executive Officer
Stephen R Hildebrand, FDHI, Executive Vice President
Sharon Newport, Director of Operations
Kathleen Fite, CPA, Director of Finance
Julie Walter, Director of Events
Represents the architectural openings industry. Membership consists of individuals and consultants involved in the architectural openings industry, representing distributors, manufacturers and sales representatives/agency firms, as well as architects, specifiers and contractors who rely on such professionals. Advancing the safety and security of the built environment.
5000 Members
Founded in: 1975

12102 Hand Tools Institute
25 North Broadway
Tarrytown, NY 10591-3221
914-332-0040; *Fax:* 914-332-1541
info@hti.org; www.hti.org
Trade association of North American manufacturers of non-powered hand tools and tool boxes. The objectives of the Institute are to promote and further the interests of its members relative to manufacturing, safety, standardization, international trade and government relations.
Founded in: 1935

12103 International Door Association
PO Box 246
West Milton, OH 45383-0246
937-698-8042
800-355-4432; *Fax:* 937-698-6153
info@longmgt.com; www.doors.org
Social Media: Facebook, Twitter, LinkedIn, YouTube
Chris Long, Managing Director
Roe Long-Wagner, Meetings/Exposition Manager
Dawn Jennings, Accounting Manager
Jane Treiber, Membership Manager
Shawn Hicks, Marketing Manager
Supports all those in the door and door operator industry, especially garage doors, installation hardware, roller shades and garage door openers. Publishes bimonthly magazine.
Founded in: 1996

12104 Midwest Hardware Association
2301 Country Club Dr.
Suite A
Stevens Point, WI 54481
E-Mail: johnh@midwesthardware.com;
www.midwesthardware.com
John Haka, Managing Director
Nonprofit supporting independent hardware, lumber and building supply retailers.
Founded in: 1896

12105 National Lumber & Building Material Dealers Association (NLBMDA)
2025 M Street, NW
Suite 800
Washington, DC 20036-3309
202-367-1169; *Fax:* 202-367-2169
info@dealer.org; www.dealer.org
Social Media: Facebook, Twitter, LinkedIn
JD Saunders, Chair
Jonathan M Paine, President
Ben Gann, Director of Legislative Affairs
Frank Moore, Regulatory Counsel
Promoting the industry and educating legislators and public policy personnel, assising legislative, regulatory, standard-setting and other government or private bodies in the development of laws, regulations and policies affecting lumber and building material dealers, its customers and suppliers.
6M Members
Founded in: 1917

12106 North American Retail Hardware Association
6325 Digital Way
#300
Indianapolis, IN 46278-1679
317-275-9400
800-772-4424; *Fax:* 317-275-9403
nrha40@nrha.org; www.nrha.org
Social Media: Facebook, Twitter, YouTube
Serving the needs of independent hardware retailers in the United States and Canada. Purpose is to help independent home improvement retailers become better and more profitable merchants. Providing members with a wide array of educational and training programs, financial management resources and human resource tools that are all available online with unlimited access.
Founded in: 1805

12107 Pacific Northwest Association
PO Box 17819
Salem, OR 97305
503-375-9024
800-933-7437; *Fax:* 888-686-6271;
www.pnwassoc.com
Ronald F. Moore, President
Newell Weatherly, Vice President
Serving as a bureau of information for its members, offering health and other insurance coverage. Membership is available to any person, firm or corporation regularly engaged in the retail hardware, home center, lumber, farm equipment, outdoor power and industrial equipment industry.
Founded in: 1899

Newsletters

12108 American Hardware Manufacturers Association Newsletter
American Hardware Manufacturers Association
801 N Plaza Dr
Schaumburg, IL 60173-4977
847-605-1025; *Fax:* 847-605-1030
info@ahma.org; www.ahma.org
Timothy Farrell, CEO
Industry association news.
36 Pages
Frequency: Monthly
Founded in: 1900

12109 MLA LINE
Mid-America Lumbermens Association
638 W 39th St
Kansas City, MO 64111
816-561-5323
800-747-6529; *Fax:* 816-561-1249
mail@themla.com; www.themla.com
Olivia Holcombe, Executive Vice President
Lumber Industry News Express is the e-newsletter of the MLA.
Frequency: Monthly

Magazines & Journals

12110 Asian Sources Hardwares
Asian Sources
PO Box 2118
Santa Fe Springs, CA 90670
562-945-4612; *Fax:* 562-906-2420;
www.globalsources.com
Dianna Corriero, US Circulation Manager
The leading publication providing the latest product and market information on home cen-

ter/DIY, lighting, security and safety, auto parts and accessories, and machinery and industrial supplies from around the world for volume buyers worldwide.
Frequency: Monthly
Founded in: 1976

12111 Brushware
Centaur Company
5515 Dundee Rd
Huddleston, VA 24104

540-297-1517; *Fax:* 540-297-1519

Carl Wurzer, Owner
Tom Goldberg, Editor

Accepts advertising.
Cost: $35.00
88 Pages
Circulation: 1200

12112 Hardware Retailing
National Retail Hardware Association
6325 Digital Way
#300
Indianapolis, IN 46278-1787

317-290-0338
800-772-4424; *Fax:* 317-328-4354;
www.nrha.org

The hardware and home improvement industry's leading trade publication. Covers hard hitting issues many retailers in the industry face. Content includes practical profitability advice and up-and-coming new products from the industry's leading manufacturers.
Cost: $50.00
Frequency: Monthly
Circulation: 36000
Founded in: 1901

12113 Hearth & Home
Village West Publishing
PO Box 2008
Laconia, NH 03247

800-258-3772; *Fax:* 603-524-0643

Richard Wright, Editor

Magazine for retailers, including specialty, hardware, patio and barbecue.

12114 Home Channel News
Lebhar-Friedman
425 Park Ave
6th Floor
New York, NY 10022-3526

212-756-5088; *Fax:* 212-838-9487
info@lf.com; www.nrn.com

Heather Martin, Manager
Terry Evans, Editor
J.Roger Friedman, CEO

Merchandising, marketing, management, and product trends that are important to owners, managers, and buyers.
Cost: $120.00
Frequency: 50 issues per y
Circulation: 50,000
Founded in: 1925

12115 International Door & Operator Industry
International Door Association
PO Box 246
West Milton, OH 45383-0246

800-355-4432; *Fax:* 937-698-6153;
www.doors.org

Art Komorowksi, Publications Manager
Shawn Hicks, Marketing Manager

The first magazine published specifically for the door and access systems industry. Informing the industry about new products, new services, and the latest industry news. In addition, the publication features articles directed to help both door and access systems dealers and those who provide them products and services.
Circulation: 14000
Founded in: 1996

12116 Keynotes
Associated Locksmiths of America
3003 Live Oak Street
Dallas, TX 75204-6189

214-827-1701
800-532-2562; *Fax:* 214-827-1810;
www.aloa.org

Betty Handerson, Editor
Charles Gibson, CEO

Technical magazine for locksmiths.
Frequency: Monthly
Circulation: 8000
Founded in: 1956

12117 Modern Paint & Coatings
2 Grand Central Tower
140 East 45th Street 40th Floor
New York, NY 10017

212-884-9528; *Fax:* 212-884-9514
jmennella@chemweek.com;
www.chemweek.com

Joe Mennella, Global Sales Director
Lyn Tattum, Vice President/ Publisher

Keep up with the latest trends in the paint/decorating industry. Read about hot topics, successful business practices, industry performance & compliance. Covers topics relating to everything from sales and marketing to business and finance to wholesale and retail trade.
Cost: $59.00
Frequency: Monthly

12118 Outdoor Power Equipment
Adams Business Media
111 W Jackson Blvd
7th Floor
Chicago, IL 60604-3589

312-846-4600; *Fax:* 312-846-4634;
www.adamsbusinessmedia.com

Joanne Juda, Circulation Manager
Steve Brackett, VP/Group Publisher
Steve Noe, Editor

Serves retailers and distributors who sell and service outdoor power equipment products, including retailers, lawn and garden supply retailers, farm supply retailers, hardware store retailers, home centers, and building supply retailers.

12119 Power Equipment Trade
Hatton-Brown Publishers
PO Box 2268
Montgomery, AL 36102-2268

334-834-1170; *Fax:* 334-834-4525
petnet@powerequipmenttrade.com;
www.powerequipmenttrade.com

David Knight, Co-Owner/Editor-in-Chief
Dan Shell, Managing Editor
Rich Donnell, Editor
Dianne Sullivan, General Manager
Dave Ramsey, Co-Owner Advertising Sales Manager

Service-oriented and technical articles, product evaluations, industry news, dealer surveys and business management information.
Cost: $55.00
Circulation: 21441
ISSN: 0163-0414
Founded in: 1952
Printed in on glossy stock

Trade Shows

12120 Ace Hardware Fall Convention and Exhibit
Ace Hardware Corporation
2200 Kensington Court
Oak Brook, IL 60521

630-990-6600; *Fax:* 708-990-0278

Over 950 exhibitors with hardware related products for Ace Hardware dealers. Seminar and dinner are part of the event.
17000 Attendees
Frequency: Annual/October

12121 Ace Hardware Spring Convention and Exhibit
Ace Hardware Corporation
2200 Kensington Court
Oak Brook, IL 60521

630-990-6600; *Fax:* 708-990-0278

David Myer, Senior VP

Over 900 exhibitors with hardware related products for Ace Hardware dealers.
8000 Attendees
Frequency: Annual

12122 Door & Hardware Exposition & Convention
Door & Hardware Institute
14170 Newbrook Drive
Suite 200
Chantilly, VA 20151

703-222-2010; *Fax:* 703-222-2410
info@dhi.org; www.dhi.org

Stephen R Hildebrand, Director Business Development
Garld Heppes Sr, Executive Assistant
Cathy Jones, Executive Assistant

Over 150 exhibitors bringing the latest in industry trends, education and developments to safely secure the built environment.
4200 Attendees
Frequency: Annual

12123 Equipment Leasing Association Annual Meeting
1825 K Street NW
Suite 900
Washington, DC 20006

202-238-3400; *Fax:* 202-238-3401
rscoggins@elfaonline.org; www.elfaonline.org

Sally Maloney, Meeting Manager
Michael Fleming, President

25 booths.
1,200 Attendees
Frequency: October

12124 Florida Building Products and Design Show
Florida Lumber & Building Material Dealers
1303 Limit Avenue
Mount Dora, FL 32757

352-383-0366; *Fax:* 352-383-8756;
www.fbma.org

Bill Tucker, President
Kair Hebrank, VP Government Relations
Betty Askew, Director of Operations

A place for members of the Building Supply Industry to gather. It provides an affordable opportunity to learn about new and innovative equipment and products.
3000 Attendees
Frequency: Annual
Founded in: 1920

12125 Gemstate Industrial and Construction Show
Trade Shows West
360 S Fort Ln
Suite 2C
Layton, UT 84041-5708
801-485-0176
800-794-3706; *Fax:* 801-485-0241
jeffwfredericks@hotmail.com;
www.facetofacemarketing.net
Exhibit focusing on the needs of the industrial, construction, and plant maintenance industries.
6049 Attendees
Frequency: Annual/November

12126 Hardware Wholesalers: Merchandise Mart
Hardware Wholesalers
Nelson Road
Box 868
Ft.Wayne, IN 46801
260-748-5300; *Fax:* 260-496-1245
11500 Attendees

12127 International Hardware Week
American Hardware Manufacturers Association
801 N Plaza Drive
Schaumburg, IL 60173-4977
847-605-1025; *Fax:* 847-605-1030
info@ahma.org; www.ahma.org
William Farrell, Vice Chairman Of The Board
Timothy Farrell, President/CEO
3,000 exhibitors.
62.5M Attendees
Frequency: August
Founded in: 2001

12128 Iowa Lumber Convention
Northwestern Lumber Association
5905 Golden Valley Road
Suite 110
Minneapolis, MN 55422-4535
763-544-6822
888-544-6822; *Fax:* 763-595-4060;
www.nlassn.org
Jodie Fleck, Director of Conventions
Hosts educational seminars and trade show.
Frequency: Annual/March

12129 Lumber and Hardware Show Mid-America
PO Box 1828
Columbus, OH 43216
614-460-6000; *Fax:* 614-833-6983
Joe Bailey, Show Manager
300 booths for retail lumber yard stores.
7M Attendees
Frequency: February

12130 National Building Products Exposition & Conference
American Hardware Manufacturers Association
801 N Plaza Drive
Schaumburg, IL 60173-4977
847-605-1025; *Fax:* 847-605-1030
info@ahma.org; www.ahma.org
William Farrell, Vice Chairman Of The Board
Timothy Farrell, President/CEO
70000 Attendees

12131 National Hardware Show
Association Expositions & Services
383 Main Avenue
Norwalk, CT 06851
203-840-5622
888-425-9377; *Fax:* 203-840-4824
inquiry@hardware.reedexpo.com;
www.nationalhardwareshow.com
Timothy Farrell, Executive VP
Martin O'Rourke, Membership Manager
Held in conjunction with International Hardware Week, this is the industry's leading hardware/home improvement event, with products from over 2,000 manufacturers from around the world. Includes hardware and allied lines, plumbing, paint and home decorating, lawn and garden, building products and housewares. Also international pavilions.
70000 Attendees
Frequency: August
Founded in: 1945

12132 National Hardware Show/National Building Products Exposition & Conference
Reed Exhibition Companies
383 Main Avenue
Norwalk, CT 06851
203-840-4800; *Fax:* 203-840-4801
inquiry@reedexpo.com; www.reedexpo.com

12133 Service Specialists Association Annual Convention
Service Specialists Association
4015 Marks Road
Suite 2B
Medina, OH 44256-8316
330-725-7160
800-763-5717; *Fax:* 330-722-5638
trucksvc@aol.com; www.truckservice.org
Cara R Giebner, Manager
Containing 70 booths and 70 exhibits.
400 Attendees

12134 Servistar Corporation Lumber & Home Center: Fall
Servistar Corporation
PO Box 1510
Butler, PA 16001
773-695-5000; *Fax:* 773-695-5172
1500 Attendees

12135 Servistar Corporation Lumber & Home Center : Spring
Servistar Corporation
8600 W Bryn Mawr Avenue
Chicago, IL 60631-3505
773-695-5000; *Fax:* 773-695-5172
1500 Attendees

12136 Servistar Market
Truserv Corporation
8600 W Bryn Mawr Avenue
Chicago, IL 60631-3505
773-695-5000; *Fax:* 773-695-5172
Johnathan Mills, Show Manager
Hardware manufacturers, suppliers and distributors.
5M Attendees
Frequency: September

Directories & Databases

12137 Complete Directory of Hardware Items
Sutton Family Communications & Publishing Company
920 State Route 54 East
Elmitch, KY 42343
270-276-9500
jlsutton@apex.net
Theresa Sutton, Editor
Lee Sutton, General Manager
Print-out from database of wholesale distributors,importers,manufacturers,close-out houses, and liquidators. Database is updated daily to guarantee the most current and up-to-date sources available.
Cost: $109.00
100+ Pages

12138 Complete Directory of Household Items
Sutton Family Communications & Publishing Company
920 State Route 54 East
Elmitch, KY 42343
270-276-9500
jlsutton@apex.net
Theresa Sutton, Editor
Lee Sutton, General Manager
Print-out from database of wholesalers, manufacturers, distributors, importers and close-out houses. Database is updated daily to guarantee the most current and up-to-date sources available.
Cost: $109.00
100+ Pages

12139 Directory and Buyer's Guide of the Door and Hardware Institute
Door and Hardware Institute
14150 Newbrook Dr
Suite 200
Chantilly, VA 20151-2232
703-222-2010; *Fax:* 703-222-2410
info@dhi.org; www.dhi.org
Gerald S Heppes Sr, Executive Director
Cathy Jones, Executive Assistant
More than 700 firms which supply doors, hinges, locks, cabinets and closet hardware, door motors, smoke clothing and detection devices.
Frequency: Annual

12140 Door and Hardware Institute: Membership Directory
Door and Hardware Institute
14150 Newbrook Dr
Suite 200
Chantilly, VA 20151-2232
703-222-2010; *Fax:* 703-222-2410
info@dhi.org; www.dhi.org
Gerald S Heppes Sr, Executive Director
Cathy Jones, Executive Assistant
Includes names and addresses of more than 5,000 members, including 700 manufacturing firms. Excellent resource for networking and staying in touch with your colleagues. Advertising is available.
Frequency: Annually
Founded in: 1999

12141 Home Center Operators & Hardware Chains
Chain Store Guide
3922 Coconut Palm Dr
Suite 300
Tampa, FL 33619-1389
813-627-6700
800-927-9292; *Fax:* 813-627-7094
info@csgis.com; www.csgis.com
Mike Jarvis, Publisher
Arthur Rosenberg, Editor
Shami Choon, Manager
The facts on more than 4,600 company headquarters and subsidiaries operating almost 23,500

units in the vast Home Improvement Building Material Industry. Also included are 19 major buying/marketing groups and coops that contribute approximately $30 billion and serve 103,243 accounts.
Cost: $30.00
Frequency: Annual, Paperback

12142 **MLA Buyer's Guide & Dealer Directory**
Mid-America Lumbermens Association
638 W 39th St
Kansas City, MO 64111
816-561-5323
800-747-6529; *Fax:* 816-561-1249
mail@themla.com; www.themla.com
Olivia Holcombe, Executive Vice President

Industry Web Sites

12143 **http://gold.greyhouse.com**
G.O.L.D Grey House OnLine Databases
Grey House Publishing's online database platform, GOLD, offers Quick Search, Keyword Search and Expert Search for most business sectors including hardware markets. The GOLD platform makes finding the information you need quick and easy - whether you're a novice searcher or an experienced database user. All of Grey House's directory products are available for subscription on the GOLD platform.

12144 **www.ahma.org**
American Hardware Manufacturers Association
Over 280 manufacturer representatives in the hardware industry.

12145 **www.aloa.org**
Associated Locksmiths of America
Strives to educate and provide information to industry. Maintains referral service and offers insurance and bonding programs. Holds technical training.

12146 **www.americanladderinstitute.org**
American Ladder Institute
Members include manufacturers of wood, metal and fiberglass ladders. Represents US companies engaged in the research, development, manufacture and safety ladders.

12147 **www.greyhouse.com**
Grey House Publishing
Authoritative reference directories for most business sectors including hardware markets. Users can search the online databases with varied search criteria allowing for custom searches by product category, geographic area, sales volume, keyword, subject and more. Full Grey House catalog and online ordering also available.

12148 **www.hti.org**
Hand Tools Institute
Provides safety education and concerned with product standards.

12149 **www.nrha.org**
National Retail Hardware Association
An organization which features news and information for hardware retailers.

Associations

12150 ALS Association
1275 K Street NW
Suite 250
Washington, DC 20005

202-407-8580; *Fax:* 202-289-6801;
www.alsa.org
Social Media: Facebook, Twitter, LinkedIn, YouTube

Barbara Newhouse, President, CEO
Gregory L. Mitchell, Chief Financial Officer
Carrie Martin Munk, Chief Comm. & Marketing Officer
Lucie Bruijn, PhD, Chief Scientist
Steve Gibson, Chief Public Policy Officer

National nonprofit organization fighting Lou Gehrig's Disease—leads the way in research, care services, public education, and public policy.
Founded in: 1869

12151 ARMA International
11880 College Blvd
Suite 450
Overland Park, KS 66210

913-341-3808
800-422-2762; *Fax:* 913-341-3742
headquarters@armaintl.org; www.arma.org
Social Media: Twitter

Komal Gulich, CRM, Chairman
Julie J. Colgan, CRM, President
Brenda Prowse, CRM, Treasurer
Nicholas De Laurentis, Chair

ARMA is a not-for-profit professional association and the authority on managing records and information. Members include records managers, archivists, corporate librarians, imaging specialists, legal professionals, IT managers, consultants, and educators, all of whom work in a wide variety of industries, including government, legal, healthcare, financial services, and petroleum.
11M Members
Founded in: 1955

12152 ASET - The Neurodiagnostic Society
402 East Bannister Road
Suite A
Kansas City, MO 64131-3019

816-931-1120; *Fax:* 816-931-1145
info@aset.org; www.aset.org
Social Media: Facebook, Twitter

Arlen Reimritz, Executive Director
Cheryl Plummer, President
Susan Agostini, President-Elect
Cherie Young, Secretary-Treasurer
Kathy Wolf, Membership Manager

Professional association dedicated to the promotion and advocacy of best practices in the study of electrical activity in the brain and nervous system., with a focus on bettering the quality of patient care.
5600 Members
Founded in: 1959

12153 Academy of Dental Materials
21 Grouse Terrace
Lake Oswego, OR 97035

503-636-0861; *Fax:* 503-675-2738;
www.academydentalmaterials.org

Objectives of the Academy are; to provide a forum for the exchange of information on all aspects of dental materials, to enhance communication between industry, researchers and practicing dentists, to encourage dental materials research and its applications and to promote dental materials through its activities.
Founded in: 1941

12154 Academy of General Dentistry
560 W. Lake Street
Sixth Floor
Chicago, IL 60611-6600

888-243-3368; *Fax:* 312-440-0559
abgd@agd.org; www.agd.org

Linda J Edgar, DDS, MEd, MAGD, President
W. Mark Donald, DMD, MAGD, Vice-President
Manuel A Cordero, DDS, MAGD, Secretary
Maria A Smith, DMD, MAGD, Treasurer
W. Carter Brown, DMD, FAGD, President-Elect

Mission is to serve the needs and represent the interest of general dentists, to promote the oral health of the public, and to foster continued proficiency of general dentists through quality continuing dental education in order to better serve the public.
37M Members
Founded in: 1952

12155 Academy of Nutrition and Dietetics
120 South Riverside Plaza
Suite 2000
Chicago, IL 60606

312-899-0040
800-877-1600
info@eatright.org; www.eatright.org
Social Media: Facebook, Twitter, Google Plus, Youtube

Striving to improve the nation's health and advance the profession of dietetics through research, education, and advocacy.
70M Members
Founded in: 1917

12156 Academy of Osseointegration
85 W Algonquin Rd
Suite 550
Arlington Hts, IL 60005-4460

847-439-1919
800-656-7736; *Fax:* 847-439-1569
academy@osseo.org; www.osseo.org

Russell D. Nishimura DDS, President
Michael R. Norton,, Vice President
Kevin P. Smith, MA, MBA, Executive Director
Jean Lynch, Director of Exhibits
Gina Seegers, Director of Meeting Services

Established to provide a focus for the rapidly advancing biotechnology involving the natural bond between bone and certain alloplastic reconstructive materials.
5200 Members
Founded in: 1987

12157 Acoustic Neuroma Association
600 Peachtree Pkwy
Suite 108
Cumming, GA 30041-6899

770-205-8211
877-200-8211; *Fax:* 770-205-0239; *Fax:* 877-202-0239
info@anausa.org; www.anausa.org
Social Media: Facebook, Twitter, YouTube

Alan Goldberg, President
Karla Jacobus, Vice President
John Gigliello, Treasurer
David Puzzo, Secretary
Jeffrey D. Barr, Immediate Past President

A patient organization that provides education and support to thosediagnosed with an acoustic neuroma.
Founded in: 1981

12158 Adult Congenital Heart Association
6757 Greene Street,
Suite 335
Philadelphia, PA 19119-3508

215-849-1260
888-921-ACHA; *Fax:* 215-849-1261
info@achaheart.org; www.achaheart.org
Social Media: Facebook, Twitter

John C. Fernie, Chair
Cindy Huie, Vice Chair
Kevin Gordon, Treasurer
Denise Garvy, Secretary
Curt J. Daniels, MD, Medical Advisory Board Chair

Information, resources, and support for adults with congenital heart disease.
Founded in: 1998

12159 Advanced Medical Technology Association
701 Pennsylvania Ave, NW
Suite 800
Washington, DC 20004-2654

202-783-8700; *Fax:* 202-783-8750
info@advamed.org; www.advamed.org
Social Media: Facebook, Twitter, LinkedIn, Youtube

David C. Dvorak, Chairman of the Board
Stephen J. Ubl, President &Chief Executive Officer
David H. Nexon, Senior Executive Vice President
JC Scott, Senior Executive Vice President
Kenneth Mendez, Senior Executive VP

Advocates for a legal, regulatory and economic environment that advances global health care by assuring worldwide patient access to the benefits of medical technology. Promoting policies that foster the highest ethical standards, rapid product approvals, appropriate reimbursement, and access to international markets.
1100 Members
Founded in: 1980

12160 Aerospace Medical Association
320 S Henry St
Alexandria, VA 22314-3579

703-739-2240; *Fax:* 703-739-9652
rrayman@asma.org; www.asma.org

Jeffrey C. Sventek, MS, CAsP, Executive Director
Gisselle Vargas, Operations Manager
Gloria Carter, Director, Member Services
Sheryl Kildall, Subscriptions Manager
Frederick Bonato, PhD, Editor-in-Chief

Organized exclusively for charitable, educational, and scientific purposes. It is the largest, most-representative professional membership organization in the fields of aviation, space, and environmental medicine.
3200 Members
Founded in: 1929
Mailing list available for rent

12161 Alexander Graham Bell Association for the Deaf and Hard of Hearing
3417 Volta Place, NW
Washington, DC 20007

202-337-5220; *Fax:* 202-337-8314
info@agbell.org;
www.listeningandspokenlanguage.org
Social Media: Facebook, Twitter, YouTube, Pinterest

Emilio Alonso-Mendoza, Chief Executive Officer
Lisa Chutjian, Chief Development Officer
Susan Boswell, Director of Communications
Robin Bailey, Programs Specialist
Judy Harrison, Director of Programs

A resource, support network and advocate for listening, learning, talking, and living independently with hearing loss.
Founded in: 2005

12162 **Alzheimer's Association**
225 N. Michigan Ave.
Floor 17
Chicago, IL 60601-7633

312-335-8700; *Fax:* 866-699-1246
advocate@alz.org; www.alz.org/
Social Media: Facebook, Twitter, YouTube

Michelle Helton, Vice President, Financial Operation
Christine Foh, Vice President, Legal
Beth Kallmyer, Vice President, Constituent Service
Maria Carrillo, Chief Science Officer
Richard Hovland, Chief Operations Officer

Information on Alzheimer's disease and dementia symptoms, diagnosis, stages, treatment, care and support resources.

12163 **Ambulatory Surgery Center Association**
1012 Cameron Street
Alexandria, VA 22314-2427

703-836-8808; *Fax:* 703-549-0976
asc@ascassociation.org;
www.ascassociation.org
Social Media: Facebook, Twitter, LinkedIn

Nap Gary, President
Michael A. Guarino, Vice President
David S. George, MD, Secretary

Membership and advocacy organization that provides member benefits and services, combats legislative, regulatory and other challenges at the federal and state level, assists state ASC association, enhances ASC representation at the state and federal level, and has established a political action committee.

12164 **America's Health Insurance Plans (AHIP)**
601 Pennsylvania Avenue
NW South Building, Suite 500
Washington, DC 20004

202-778-3200; *Fax:* 202-331-7487
ahip@ahip.org; www.ahip.org/

The national trade association representing the health insurance industry. Members provide health and supplemental benefits to more than 200 million Americans through employer-sponsored coverage, the individual insurance market, and public programs such as Medicare and Medicaid. Advocates for public policies that expand access to affordable health care coverage to all Americans through a competitive marketplace that fosters choice, quality and innovation.

12165 **American Academy for Cerebral Palsy and Developmental Medicine**
555 East Wells
Suite 1100
Milwaukee, WI 53202-3800

414-918-3014; *Fax:* 414-276-2146
info@aacpdm.org; www.aacpdm.org
Social Media: Facebook, Twitter

Richard Stevenson, MD, President
Darcy Fehlings, MD MSc FRCPC, First Vice President
Eileen Fowler, PhD PT, Second Vice President
Johanna Darrah, PhD PT, Secretary
Joshua Hyman, MD, Treasurer

Mission is to provide multidisciplinary scientific education for health professionals and promote excellence in research and services for the benefit of people with cerebral palsy and childhood-onset disabilities. A global leader in the multidisciplinary scientific education of health professionals and researchers.
1100 Members
Founded in: 1947

12166 **American Academy of Allergy, Asthma and Immunology**
555 E Wells St
Suite 1100
Milwaukee, WI 53202-3823

414-272-6071
info@aaaai.org; www.aaaai.org
Social Media: Facebook

The largest professional medical specialty organization in the United States, representing allergists, asthma specialists, clinical immunologists, allied health professionals, and others with a special interest in the research and treatment of allergic disease.
6M Members
Founded in: 1943

12167 **American Academy of Child and Adolescent Psychiatry**
3615 Wisconsin Ave NW
Washington, DC 20016-3007

202-966-7300; *Fax:* 202-966-2891
cme@aacap.org; www.aacap.org
Social Media: Facebook, Twitter

Martin J. Drell, President
Paramjit T. Joshi, President-Elect
David R. DeMaso, Secretary
Steven P. Cuffe, Treasurer

Membership based organization, composed of child and adolescent psychiatrists and other interested physicians. Members actively research, evaluate, diagnose, and treat psychiatric disorders and pride themselves on giving direction to and responding quickly to new developments in addressing the health care needs of children and their families.
7500 Members
Founded in: 1953

12168 **American Academy of Dermatology**
930 E. Woodfield Road
Schaumburg, IL 60173

847-240-1280
866-503-7546; *Fax:* 847-240-1859
jbarnes@aad.org; www.aad.org
Social Media: Facebook, Twitter, Pinterest, Youtube

Dirk M Elston, MD, President
Lisa A Garner, MD, Vice President
Suzanne M Olbricht, MD, Secretary-Treasurer
Brett M Coldiron, MD, President-Elect
Elise A Olsen, MD, Vice President-Elect

The largest, most influential and most representative dermatology group in the United States. Represents virtually all practicing dermatologists in the US, as well as a growing number of international dermatologists.
13700 Members
Founded in: 1938

12169 **American Academy of Family Physicians**
11400 Tomahawk Creek Pkwy.
Leawood, KS 66211-2680

913-906-6205; *Fax:* 913-906-6086
contactcenter@aafp.org; www.aafp.org
Social Media: Facebook, Twitter

Douglas E. Henley, EVP & CEO
Todd C. Dicus, Dep. EVP & COO

The national association of family doctors.
Founded in: 1947

12170 **American Academy of Fixed Prosthodontics**
6661 Merwin Road
Columbus, OH 43235

614-761-1927; *Fax:* 614-292-0941
aafpsec@gmail.com;
www.fixedprosthodontics.org
Social Media: Twitter

Steven Morgagno, D.M.D., President
David Burns, Vice President
Stephen F Rosenstiel, Secretary
Richard D Jordan, Treasurer
Gerry Santulli, President-Elect

Mission is to foster excellence in the field of prosthodontics, implants and esthetic dentistry through mutual study, participation, and cooperation.
Founded in: 1950

12171 **American Academy of Forensic Sciences**
410 North 21st Street
Colorado Springs, CO 80904-2712

719-636-1100; *Fax:* 719-636-1993
awarren@aafs.org; www.aafs.org
Social Media: Facebook, RSS, YouTube

Victor W. Weedn, MD, JD, President
Norm Sauer, PhD, Vice President
Susan M. Ballou, MS, Secretary
Betty Layne DesPortes, JD, Treasurer
John E. Gerns, MFS, President-Elect

Committed to the promotion of education and the elevation of accuracy, precision, and specificity in the forensic sciences. Membership consists of physicians, attorneys, dentists, toxicologists, physical anthropologists, document examiners, digital evidence experts, and others.
5M Members
Founded in: 1948

12172 **American Academy of Home Care Medicine**
8735 W. Higgins Road
Suite 300
Chicago, IL 60631

847-375-4719; *Fax:* 847-375-6395
info@aahcm.org; www.aahcm.org
Social Media: Facebook, Twitter, LinkedIn, YouTube

Bruce Leff, President
Thomas Cornwell, President-Elect
Kathy A. Kemle, Secretary
Brent T. Feorene, Treasurer

Organization working towards the goal of improving healthcare services for those who receive homecare. Offers news, information, and resources to home care physicians, nurses, social workers, and other industry professionals.
Founded in: 1988

12173 **American Academy of Implant Dentistry**
211 East Chicago Avenue
Suite 750
Chicago, IL 60611

312-335-1550
877-335-2243; *Fax:* 312-335-9090
info@aaid.com; www.aaid.com
Social Media: Facebook, Twitter, LinkedIn, YouTube, Google Plus

John Da Silva, President
Shankar Iyer, DDS, Vice President
David G. Hochberg, DDS, Treasurer
Natalie Wong, DDS, Secretary
Richard Mercurio, DDS, President-Elect

AAID offers a rigorous implant dentistry credentialing program which requires at least 300 hours of post-docroal or continuing education instruction in implant dentistry, passing a comprehensive exam, and presenting successful cases of different types of implants to a group of examiners. It is one of the most comprehensive credentialing programs in dentistry.
4000 Members
Founded in: 1951

12174 American Academy of Medical Administrators
330 N Wabash Avenue
Suite 2000
Chicago, IL 60611
312-321-6815; *Fax:* 312-673-6705
info@aameda.org
aama.socious.com
John Garrity, MHA, CFAAMA, Chairman
Jennifer Smith, Vice Chair
Thomas Draper, Treasurer
David Schmahl, Executive Director
Bruce Hammond, CRA, CFAAMA, Appointed Director
To advance excellence in healthcare leadership through individual relationships, multi-disciplinary interaction, practical business tools and active engagement.
Founded in: 1957

12175 American Academy of Neurology
201 Chicago Avenue
Minneapolis, MN 55415
612-928-6000
800-879-1960; *Fax:* 612-454-2746
memberservices@aan.com; www.aan.com
Social Media: Facebook, Twitter, LinkedIn, YouTube, Pinterest, Google+
Bruce Sigsbee, President
Timothy A. Pedley, President Elect
Lisa M. DeAngelis, Vice President
Terrence L. Cascino, Treasurer
Lisa M. Shulman, Secretary
An international professional association of neurologists and neuroscience professionals dedicated to promoting the highest quality patient-centered neurologic care. The AAN is strongly committed to its mission and focuses its efforts on ensuring the reality of the principles and standards set forth in AAN mission statement.
18000 Members
Founded in: 1948

12176 American Academy of Ophthalmology
655 Beach Street
San Francisco, CA 94109
415-561-8500; *Fax:* 415-561-8533
customer_service@aao.org; www.aao.org
Social Media: Facebook, Twitter, LinkedIn, YouTube, RSS, Google+
Richard L. Abbott, Chair
Mission is to advance the lifelong learning and professional interests of opthalmologists to ensure that the public can obtain the best possible eye care.
80000 Members
Founded in: 1979

12177 American Academy of Optometry
2909 Fairgreen Street
Orlando, FL 32803
321-710-3937
800-969-4226; *Fax:* 407-893-9890
aaoptom@aaoptom.org; www.aaopt.org
Social Media: Facebook, Twitter, LinkedIn, Youtube
Brett G. Bence, OD, FAAO, President
Lois Schoenbrun, CAE, FAAO, Executive Director
Barbara Caffery, OD, PhD, FAAO, Secretary-Treasurer
Joseph P. Shovlin, OD, FAAO, President-Elect
Richard Jones, CPA, Senior Director, Finance
A philanthropic organization that develops and provides financial support for optometric research and education in vision and eye health.
5000 Members
Founded in: 1922

12178 American Academy of Oral and Maxillofacial Surgeons
9700 West Bryn Mawr Avenue
Rosemont, IL 60018-5701
847-678-6200
800-822-6637; *Fax:* 847-678-6286
inquiries@aaoms.org; www.aaoms.org
Social Media: Facebook, Twitter, LinkedIn, YouTube, Vimeo, Instagram
Douglas W. Fain, DDS, MD, FACS, President
Brett L. Ferguson, DDS, FACS, President-Elect
J. David Johnson, Jr., DMD, Treasurer
Scott C. Farrell, MBA, CPA, Secretary/Executive Director
The professional organization representing oral and maxillofacial surgeons in the US, supporting its members' ability to practice their specialty through education, research, and advocacy. Members comply with rigorous continuing education requirements and submit to periodic office examinations, ensuring the public that all office procedures and personnel meet stringent national standards.
11359 Members
Founded in: 1946

12179 American Academy of Orofacial Pain
174 S. New York Ave
PO Box 478
Oceanville, NJ 08231
609-504-1311; *Fax:* 609-573-5064;
www.aaop.org
Social Media: Facebook, Twitter
Steven D. Bender, President
Gary D Klasser, President-Elect
Maureen Lang, Council Chair
Barry Rozenberg, Treasurer
Kenneth S Cleveland, Executive Director
Dedicated to alleviating pain and suffering through the promotion of excellence in education, research and patient care in the field of orofacial pain and associated disorders.
Founded in: 1975

12180 American Academy of Orthopaedic Surgeons
9400 West Higgins Rd.
Rosemont, IL 60018
847-823-7186; *Fax:* 847-823-8125;
www.aaos.org
Social Media: Facebook, Twitter
David Teuscher, President
Karen L. Hackett, Chief Executive Officer
Provider of medical education to orthopaedic surgeons.
Founded in: 1933

12181 American Academy of Osteopathy
3500 DePauw Boulevard
Suite 1100
Indianapolis, IN 46268-1136
317-879-1881
800-875-6360; *Fax:* 317-879-0563
info@academyofosteopathy.org;
www.academyofosteopathy.org/
Social Media: Facebook, Twitter, LinkedIn, YouTube
Doris B. Newman, DO, FAAO, President
Laura E. Griffin, DO, FAAO, President-Elect
Judith A. O'Connell, DO, FAAO, Treasurer, Secretary
Kenneth J. Lossing, DO, Immediate Past President
Michael E. Fitzgerald, Executive Director
Mission is to teach, advocate, and research the science, art and philosophy of osteopathic medicine, emphasizing the integration of osteopathic principles, practices and manipulative treatment in patient care.
Founded in: 1937

12182 American Academy of Otolaryngology-Head and Neck Surgery
1650 Diagonal Road
Alexandria, VA 22314-2857
703-836-4444
membership@entnet.org; www.entnet.org
Social Media: Facebook, Twitter, LinkedIn, YouTube
Gregory W. Randolph, MD, President
Gavin Setzen, MD, President -Elect
James C. Denneny, MD, Executive Vice President and CEO
Scott P. Stringer, MD, Secretary/Treasurer
The world's largest organization representing specialists who treat the ear, nose, throat, and related structures of the head and neck. Represents otolaryngologist- head and neck surgeons who diagnose and treat disorders of those areas.
12M Members
Founded in: 1896

12183 American Academy of Pain Medicine
8735 W. Higgins Rd.
Suite 300
Chicago, IL 60631-2738
847-375-4731; *Fax:* 847-375-6477
info@painmed.org; www.painmed.org
Social Media: LinkedIn
Perry Fine, President
Martin Grabois, President-Elect
Lynn Webster, Treasurer
Zahid H. Bajwa, Secretary
Has evolved as the primary organization for physicians practicing the specialty of Pain Medicine in the US. Purpose is to optimize the health of patients in pain and eliminate the major public health problem of pain by advancing the practice and the specialty of pain medicine.
Founded in: 1983

12184 American Academy of Pediatric Dentistry
211 East Chicago Avenue
Suite 1600
Chicago, IL 60611-2637
312-337-2169; *Fax:* 312-337-6329
info@aapd.org; www.aapd.org
Social Media: Facebook, Twitter
Robert L. Delarosa, D.D.S., President
Robert L Delarosa, D.D.S, Vice President
Jade Miller, D.D.S., Secretary-Treasurer
Edward J. Moody, President-Elect
Mission is to advocate policies, guidelines, and programs that promote optimal oral health and oral health care for infants and children through adolescence, including those with special health care needs. Serves and represents its membership in the areas of professional development and governmental and legislative activities. It is a liaison to other health care groups and the public.
8M Members
Founded in: 1948

12185 American Academy of Periodontology
737 N. Michigan Avenue
Suite 800
Chicago, IL 60611-6660
312-787-5518; *Fax:* 312-787-3670
staff@abperio.org; www.perio.org
Social Media: Facebook, Twitter, YouTube, Google Plus
Joan Otomo-Corgel, President
Terrence J. Griffin, Vice President
Steven R. Daniel, Secretary/ Treasurer
Wayne A. Aldredge, President-Elect
Stuart J. Froum, Immediate Past President
Purpose is to advance the periodontal and general health of the public and promote excellence in the practice of periodontics. Membership includes

periodontists and general dentists from all 50 states as well as around the world.
8,400 Members
Founded in: 1914

12186 American Academy of Physical Medicine and Rehabilitation (AAPMR)
9700 West Bryn Mawr Avenue
Suite 200
Rosemont, IL 60018-5701
847-737-6000
877-227-6799; *Fax:* 847-754-4368
info@aapmr.org; www.aapmr.org
Social Media: Facebook, Twitter
Kurt M Hoppe, MD, President
Thomas E Stautzenbach, CAE, Executive Director
Gregory M Worsowicz, MD, MBA, Vice President
Darryl L Kaelin, MD, Secretary
David G. Welch, MD, Treasurer
Exclusively serving the needs of today's physical medicine and rehabilitation physician.
9000+ Members
Founded in: 1938

12187 American Academy of Physician Assistants
2318 Mill Road
Suite 1300
Alexandria, VA 22314
703-836-2272; *Fax:* 703-684-1924
aapa@aapa.org; www.aapa.org
Social Media: Facebook, Twitter, LinkedIn, Youtube, Huddle
Jeffrey A. Katz, PA-C, DFAAPA, President and Chair
John G. McGinnity, President Elect
L Gail Curtis, Vice President/Speaker of the House
Tillie Fowler, SVP, Advocacy
Jennifer L Dorn, Chief Executive Officer
Advocates and educates on behalf of the profession and the patients PAs serve. AAPA works to ensure the professional growth, personal excellence and recognition of physician assistants. It also works to enhance their ability to improve the quality, accessibility and cost-effectiveness of patient-centered health care.
81M Members
Founded in: 1968

12188 American Academy of Professional Coders
2233 S Presidents Dr.
Salt Lake City, UT 84120
801-236-2200
800-626-2633; *Fax:* 801-236-2258
info@aapc.com; www.aapc.com
Social Media: Facebook, Twitter, LinkedIn
Jaci Johnson Kipreos, President
Ann M. Bina, CPC, COC, CPC-I, Secretary
Michael D. Miscoe, President-elect
Angela Clements, Member Relations Officer
Founded to provide education and professional certification to physician-based medical coders and to elevate the standards of medical coding by providing student training, certification, ongoing education, networking, and job opportunities.
111M Members
Founded in: 1988

12189 American Alliance for Health, Physical Education, Recreation and Dance
1900 Association Drive
Reston, VA 20191-1598
703-476-3400
800-213-7193; *Fax:* 703-476-9527;
www.shapeamerica.org
Social Media: Facebook, Twitter, Instagram
Steven Jefferies, President
E. Paul Roetert, Chief Executive Officer
Dolly D Lambdin, President-Elect
Mission is to promote and support leadership, research, education, and best practices in the professions that support creative, healthy, and active lifestyles. AAHPERD envisions a society in which all individuals enjoy an optimal quality of life through appreciation of and participation in an active and creative, health-promoting lifestyle.
25M Members
Founded in: 1885

12190 American Art Therapy Association
4875 Eisenhower Avenue
Suite 240
Alexandria, VA 22304
703-548-5860
888-290-0878; *Fax:* 703-783-8468
info@arttherapy.org; www.arttherapy.org
Social Media: Facebook, Twitter, LinkedIn, RSS
Donna Betts, PhD, ATR-BC, President
Christianne Strang, PHD, ATR-BC, President Elect
Stephanie Wise, Treasurer
Cynthia Woodruff, Executive Director
Michelle Dean, Secretary
A U.S. national professional association of over 5,000 practicing art therapy professionals, including students, educators, and related practitioners in the field art therapy.

12191 American Association for Cancer Research
615 Chestnut St.
17th Fl.
Philadelphia, PA 19106-4404
215-440-9300
866-423-3965; *Fax:* 215-440-9313
aacr@aacr.org; www.aacr.org
Social Media: Facebook, Twitter, LinkedIn, YouTube
Margaret Foti, Chief Executive Officer
Jos, Baselga, President
The AACR is the oldest and largest cancer research organization in the world.
Founded in: 1907

12192 American Association for Clinical Chemistry
900 Seventh Street, NW
Suite 400
Washington, DC 20001
202-857-0717
800-892-1400; *Fax:* 202-887-5093
custserv@aacc.org; www.aacc.org
Social Media: Facebook, Twitter, LinkedIn, YouTube, Google+
David D. Koch, PhD, DABCC, FACB, President
Patricia M. Jones, PhD, President-Elect
David G. Grenache, Secretary
Michael J. Bennett, Treasurer
Steven Wong, PhD, DABCC, FACB, Past President
An international scientific/ medical society of clinical laboratory professionals, physicians, research scientists and other individuals involved with clinical chemistry and related disciplines. Vision is to provide leadership in advancing the practice and profession of clinical laboratory science and its application to health care.
10M Members
Founded in: 1948

12193 American Association for Continuity of Care
342 N. Main Street
West Hartford, CT 06117-2500
860-586-7525
info@continuityofcare.org;
www.continuityofcare.org
Social Media: Facebook, LinkedIn, RSS
A national nonprofit multidisciplinary professional organization dedicated to providing leadership and supporting excellence in practice among those involved in continuity of care within the health care system through education and pationt focused advocacy.
Founded in: 1982

12194 American Association for Geriatric Psychiatry
6728 Old McLean Village Drive
McLean, VA 22101
703-556-9222; *Fax:* 703-556-8729
main@aagponline.org; www.aagponline.org
Social Media: Facebook, Twitter, LinkedIn
Gary W. Small, MD, President
Dan Sewell, MD, President Elect
Susan K. Schultz, MD, Past President
Amita Patel, Secretary/Treasurer
Christopher N. Wood, Executive Director
National association that has products, activities, and publications which focus exclusively on the challenges of geriatric psychiatry.
Founded in: 1978

12195 American Association for Hand Surgery
500 Cummings Center
Suite 4550
Beverly, MA 1915
978-927-8330; *Fax:* 978-524-8890;
www.handsurgery.org
Social Media: LinkedIn
Michael W Neumeister, M.D., President
William C Pederson, M.D., Vice President
John D. Lubahn, M.D., Treasurer
Robert Spinner, M.D., Secretary
Peter M. Murray, M.D., President Elect
Resource for hand surgeons and patients.

12196 American Association for Laboratory Animal Science
9190 Crestwyn Hills Drive
Memphis, TN 38125-8538
901-754-8620; *Fax:* 901-753-0046
info@aalas.org; www.aalas.org
Social Media: Facebook, Twitter, LinkedIn, YouTube
Scott Mischler, Past President
An association of professionals that advances responsible laboratory animal care and use to benefit people and animals. Dedicated to the humane care and treatment of laboratory animals and the quality research that leads to scientific gains that benefit people and animals.
11M+ Members
Founded in: 1950

12197 American Association for Marriage and Family Therapy
112 South Alfred Street
Alexandria, VA 22314-3061
703-838-9808; *Fax:* 703-838-9805
central@aamft.org; www.aamft.org

Social Media: Facebook, Twitter, LinkedIn, Youtube

Marvarene Oliver, EdD, President
Christopher Habben, PhD, President-Elect
Michael Chafin, MEd, Past President
Thomas Smith, PhD, Secretary
Mike Fitzpatrick, MSW, Treasurer

The professional association for the field of marriage and family therapy. Representing the professional interests of marriage and family therapists throughout the US, Canada, and abroad. The Association facilitates research, theory development and education.
25M Members
Founded in: 1942

12198 American Association for Pediatric Ophthalmology and Strabismus

655 Beach Street
San Francisco, CA 94109-1336

415-561-8505; *Fax:* 415-561-8531
aapos@aao.org; www.aapos.org
Social Media: Facebook, Twitter, Google+

M. Edward Wilson, MD, President
Robert E. Wiggins, Jr, MD, Vice President
Derek T. Sprunger, MD, Vice President Elect
Sherwin J. Isenberg, MD, Past President
Christie L. Morse MD, Executive Vice President

An academic association of pediatric ophthalmologists and strabismus surgeons.

12199 American Association for Respiratory Care

9425 N MacArthur Blvd
Suite 100
Irving, TX 75063-4706

972-243-2272; *Fax:* 972-484-2720
info@aarc.org; www.aarc.org

Tom Kallstrom, Executive Director/CEO
Doug Laher, Associate Executive Director
Sherry Milligan, Associate Executive Director
Tim Myers, Associate Executive Director
Steve Nelson, Associate Executive Director

Leading the respiratory care profession in science, education and research. Its members are committed to providing exemplary respiratory care and improving lung health worldwide.
38M Members
Founded in: 1947

12200 American Association for Thoracic Surgery

500 Cummings Center
Suite 4550
Beverly, MA 01915

978-927-8330; *Fax:* 978-524-0498
aats@prri.com; www.aats.org
Social Media: Facebook, Youtube

Joseph S. Coselli, President
Thoralf M. Sundt, III, President-Elect
Marc R. Moon, Secretary
Shaf Keshavjee, Treasurer
Duke E. Cameron, Vice President

The promotion and fostering of education and research in the field of cardiothoracic surgery, membership consists of the world's foremost cardiothoracic surgeons representing 35 countries. Surgeons must have a proven record of distinction within the cardiothoracic surgical field and have made meritorious contributions to the extant knowledge base about cardiothoracic disease and its surgical treatment to be considered for membership.
1231 Members
Founded in: 1917

12201 American Association for the Advancement of Science

1200 New York Ave NW
Washington, DC

202-326-6400; www.aaas.org
Social Media: Facebook, Twitter, Google+, YouTube

Gerald Fink, Chair
Geraldine Richmond, President
Barbara A. Schaal, President-Elect
David Evans Shaw, Treasurer
Rush D. Holt, Chief Executive Officer

A nonprofit organization that has research news, issue papers, educational programs, etc.
Founded in: 1848

12202 American Association for the Study of Liver Disease

1001 North Fairfax Street
Suite 400
Alexandria, VA 22314

703-299-9766; *Fax:* 703-299-9622
aasld@aasld.org; www.aasld.org
Social Media: Facebook, Twitter, LinkedIn, Instagram, YouTube

Gyongyi Szabo, MD, PhD, FAASLD, President
Keith D. Lindor, MD, FAASLD, President Elect
Adrian M. Di Bisceglie, Past President
W. Ray Kim, Treasurer
Gary L. Davis, MD, FAASLD, Secretary

Organization of scientists and health care professionals committed to preventing and curing liver disease.
Founded in: 1950

12203 American Association of Bioanalysts

906 Olive Street
Suite 1200
Saint Louis, MO 63101-1448

314-241-1445; *Fax:* 314-241-1449
aab@aab.org; www.aab.org

Mark S Birenbaum PhD, Administrator

Professional Association representing clinical laboratory directors, owners, managers and supervisors, medical technologistsm medical laboratory technicians,and physical office laboratory technicians. AAB provides a broad range of services, including representation before federal and state legislative and regulatory agencies, educational programs, and publications.
Founded in: 1956

12204 American Association of Blood Banks

8101 Glenbrook Road
Bethesda, MD 20814-2749

301-907-6977; *Fax:* 301-907-6895
aabb@aabb.org; www.aabb.org
Social Media: Facebook, Twitter, LinkedIn, YouTube

Lynne Uhl, MD, President
Graham Sher, MD, PhD, Past President
Zbigniew M. Szczepiorkowski, Vice President
Donald Berglund, MHA, FACHE, Treasurer
Lynne Uhl, MD, President-Elect

Advances the practice and standards of transfusion medicine and cellular therapies to optimize patient and donor care and safety. AABB vision is to be the pre-eminent knowledge-based organization focused on improving health through advancing the science and practice of transfusion medicine and cellular therapies.
Founded in: 1947

12205 American Association of Cardiovascular & Pulmonary Rehabilitation

330 N. WabashAvenue
Suite 2000
Chicago, IL 60611

312-321-5146; *Fax:* 312-673-6924
aacvpr@aacvpr.org; www.aacvpr.org
Social Media: Facebook

Adam T. deJong, President
Thomas A. Draper, MBA, FAACVPR, President Elect
Todd Brown, MD, MSPH, Secretary
Zack Klint, MS, CES, Treasurer
Megan Cohen, Executive Director

Mission is to reduce morbidity, mortality, and disability from cardiovascular and pulmonary diseases through education, prevention, rehabilitation, research, and disease management.
Founded in: 1985

12206 American Association of Clinical Endocrinologists

245 Riverside Avenue
Suite 200
Jacksonville, FL 32202-4933

904-353-7878; *Fax:* 904-353-8185
info@aace.com; www.aace.com
Social Media: Facebook, Twitter, LinkedIn

George Grunberger, President
Donald C Jones, Chief Executive Officer
Dan Kelsey, MS,MBA,CAE, Deputy CEO
Michael Avallone, CPA, Chief Financial Officer
Pauline M. Camacho, MD, FACE, President-Elect

Professional medical organization devoted to the enhancement of the practice of clinical endocrinology. Maintains high standards in a society of qualified medical, pediatric, reproductive and surgical endocrinologists to futher the practice through advocacy and education.
6200 Members
Founded in: 1991

12207 American Association of Colleges of Nursing

One Dupont Circle, NW
Suite 530
Washington, DC 20036

202-463-6930; *Fax:* 202-785-8320
info@aacn.nche.edu; www.aacn.nche.edu
Social Media: Facebook, Twitter, LinkedIn

Eileen Breslin, PhD, RN, FAAN, President
Juliann Sebastian, President-Elect
Teri Murray, PhD, RN, FAAN, Treasurer
Judy Beal, DNSc, RN, FAAN, Secretary
Jennifer Ahearn, COO

Education, research, federal advocacy, data collection, publications, and special programs for nursing education.
765 Members
Founded in: 1969

12208 American Association of Critical-Care Nurses

101 Columbia
Aliso Viejo, CA 92656-4109

949-362-2000
800-899-2226; *Fax:* 949-362-2020
info@aacn.org; www.aacn.org
Social Media: Facebook, Twitter, RSS

Karen McQuillan, President
Clareen Wiencek, President-Elect
Deborah Klein, Secretary
Paula S. McCauley, Treasurer
Teri Lynn Kiss, Immediate Past President

The largest specialty nursing organization in the world, representing the interests of nurses who are charged with the responsibility of caring for acutely and critically ill patients. The Associa-

tion is dedicated to providing members with the knowledge and resources necessary to provide optimal care to critically ill patients.
Founded in: 1969

12209 American Association of Diabetes Educators
200 W Madison Street
Suite 800
Chicago, IL 60606

800-338-3633
info@diabeteseducator.org;
www.diabeteseducator.org
Social Media: Facebook, Twitter, LinkedIn, Google+, Pinterest

Tami Ross, RD, LD, CDE, President
Charles Macfarlane, FACHE, CAE, Chief Executive Officer
Laura Downes, CAE, Chief Operating Officer
Ruth Lipman, PhD, Chief Science and Practice Officer
Ken Widelka, CAE, CPA, Chief Financial Officer

A multidisciplinary association of healthcare professionals dedicated to integrating self-management as a key outcome in the care of people with diabetes and related chronic conditions.
10M Members
Founded in: 1973

12210 American Association of Healthcare Administrative Management
11240 Waples Mill Road
Suite 200
Fairfax, VA 22030-6078

703-281-4043; *Fax:* 703-359-7562
info@aaham.org; www.aaham.org
Social Media: Facebook, Twitter, LinkedIn, YouTube, Google+, Pinterest

Victoria Di Tomaso, CRCE-I, President
Christine Stottlemyer, CRCE-I, Chair of the Board
John Currier, CRCE-I, National First Vice President
Lori Sickelbaugh, National Second Vice President
Amy Mitchell, CRCE-I, National Treasurer

The premier professional organization in healthcare administrative management. Actively represents the interests of healthcare administrative management professionals through a comprehensive program of legislative and regulatory monitoring and its participation in industry goups such as ANSI, DISA, and NUBC. AAHAM is a major force in shaping the future of health care administrative management.
Founded in: 1968

12211 American Association of Hip and Knee Surgeons
9400 W. Higgins Rd.
Suite 230
Rosemont, IL 60018-4976

847-698-1200; *Fax:* 847-698-0704;
www.aahks.org
Social Media: Facebook, Twitter, LinkedIn

Jay R. Lieberman, MD, President
William A. Jiranek, MD, First Vice President
David A. Halsey, MD, Second Vice President
Mark I. Froimson, MD, Third Vice President
C. Lowry Barnes, MD, Treasurer

Specialty society for orthopedic surgeons who specialize in hip andknee replacements.
Founded in: 1991

12212 American Association of Immunologists
9650 Rockville Pike
Bethesda, MD 20814

301-634-7178; *Fax:* 301-634-7887
infoaai@aai.org; www.aai.org
Social Media: Facebook

Marc K Jenkins, Ph.D., President
Linda A Sherman, Ph.D., Vice President
Mitchell Kronenberg, Ph.D., Secretary-Treasurer
M. Michele Hogan, Ph.D., Executive Director
David G. Jackson, CPA, MBA, Director of Finance

An association of professionally trained scientists from all over the world dedicated to advancing the knowledge of immunology and its related disciplines, fostering the interchange of ideas and information among investigators, and addressing the potential integration of immunologic principles into clinical practice.
Founded in: 1913

12213 American Association of Integrated Healthcare Delivery Systems
4435 Waterfront Drive
Suite 101
Glen Allen, VA 23060

804-747-5823; *Fax:* 804-747-5316;
www.aaihds.org
Social Media: Facebook, Twitter, LinkedIn, Google+

A nonprofit organization dedicated to the educational advancement of provider-based managed care professionals involved in integrated healthcare delivery. Mission is to provide managed healthcare professionals in IPAs, PHOs, health systems, hospitals and other integrated delivery systems with the tools, education, skills and resources to be successful in the marketplace.
1000 Members
Founded in: 1993

12214 American Association of Managed Care Nurses
4435 Waterfront Drive
Suite 101
Glen Allen, VA 23060-3393

804-747-9698; *Fax:* 804-747-5316
keads@aamcn.org; www.aamcn.org
Social Media: Facebook, Twitter, LinkedIn, Google+

Jacquelyn Smith, President
Gloria J. Hayman, RN, CMCN, Board of Director
LaNita Knoke RN, BS, CMCN, Board of Director
Veronica Sheffield, CMCN, Board of Director
Joyce Thiem, RN, BSN, CCM, Board of Director

Nonprofit organization representing Registered Nurses, Nurse Practitioners and Licensed Practical Nurses. AAMCN seeks to offer those nurses the opportunity to become more successful, both in their workplace and their community, through interactive membership services, quality educational resources and unparalleled networking with other managed care nurses throughout the industry.
Founded in: 1994

12215 American Association of Medical Assistants
20 N Wacker Dr
Suite 1575
Chicago, IL 60606-2963

312-899-1500
800-228-2262; *Fax:* 312-899-1259;
www.aama-ntl.org
Social Media: Facebook, YouTube, WordPress

Ann Naegele, President
Chris Hollander, Vice President
Charlene Couch, Secretary/ Treasurer

Mission is to provide the medical assistant professional with education, certification, credential acknowledgment, networking opportunities, scope-of-practice protection, and advocacy for quality patient-centered health care.
Founded in: 1955

12216 American Association of Naturopathic Physicians
818 18th Street, NW
Suite 250
Washington, DC 20006

202-237-8150
866-538-2267; *Fax:* 202-237-8152
member.services@naturopathic.org;
www.naturopathic.org
Social Media: Facebook, Twitter, LinkedIn, Google+

Kasra Pournadeali, ND, President
Jaclyn Chasse, ND, President-Elect
Michelle Simon, ND, PhD, AANP Treasurer
Michael Cronin, ND, Board of Director
Laura Farr, Board of Director

Vision is to transform the healthcare system from a disease management system to a comprehensive health program incorporating the principles of naturopathic medicine.
1800 Members
Founded in: 1985

12217 American Association of Neurological Surgeons
5550 Meadowbrook Drive
Rolling Meadows, IL 60008-3852

847-378-0500
888-566-2267; *Fax:* 847-378-0600
info@aans.org; www.aans.org
Social Media: Facebook, Twitter, LinkedIn, Youtube, iTunesU

H. Hunt Batjer, President
Deborah L. Benzil, Vice President
Frederick A. Boop,MD, FAANS, FACS, President-Elect
Alex B. Valadka, Treasurer
Christopher I. Shaffrey,MD, FAANS, Secretary

The organization that speaks for all of neurosurgery. The AANS is dedicated to advancing the specialty of neurological surgery in order to promote the highest quality of patient care.
6500+ Members
Founded in: 1931

12218 American Association of Neuromuscular and Electrodiagnostic Medicine
2621 Superior Drive NW
Rochester, MN 55901

507-288-0100; *Fax:* 507-288-1225
aanem@aanem.org; www.aanem.org
Social Media: Facebook, Twitter, LinkedIn, YouTube

Vincent J. Tranchitella, MD, President
Vern C. Juel, MD, President Elect
Francis O. Walker, MD, Past President
Shirlyn A. Adkins, JD, Executive Director
Anthony E. Chiodo, MD, Secretary-Treasurer

A nonprofit membership association dedicated to the advancement of neuromuscular, musculoskeletal medicine.
Founded in: 1953

12219 **American Association of Neuromuscular and Electrodiagnostic Medicine**
2621 Superior Drive NW
Rochester, MN 55901-8350

507-288-0100; *Fax:* 507-288-1225
aanem@aanem.org; www.aanem.org
Social Media: Facebook, Twitter, LinkedIn, Youtube

Vincent J. Tranchitella, MD, President
Vern C. Juel, MD, President Elect
Francis O. Walker, MD, Past President
Shirlyn A. Adkins, JD, Executive Director
Anthony E. Chiodo, MD, Secretary-Treasurer

Dedicated to the advancement of neuromuscular, musculoskeletal, and electrodiagnostic medicine. Physician members- primarily neurologists and physiatrists- now are joined by allied health professionals and PhD Researchers working to improve the quality of medical care provided to patients with muscle and nerve disorders.
5200 Members
Founded in: 1953

12220 **American Association of Neuroscience Nurses**
8735 W. Higgins Road
Suite 300
Chicago, IL 60631

847-375-4733
888-557-2266; *Fax:* 847-375-6430; *Fax:* 732-460-7313
info@aann.org; www.aann.org

Jan Hinkle, RN PhD CNRN, President
Cindy M. Sullivan, President Elect
Sandra J. Brettler, MSN RN CNRN, Secretary/Treasurer
Megan Keiser, RN DNP CNRN, Immediate Past President
Joan Kram, MBA RN FACHE, Executive Director

The leading authority in neuroscience nursing, inspires passion in nurses and creates the future for the specialty. AANN is committed to the advancement of neuroscience nursing as a specialty through the development and support of nurses to promote excellence in patient care.
3000 Members
Founded in: 1968

12221 **American Association of Nurse Anesthetists**
222 South Prospect Avenue
Park Ridge, IL 60068-4001

847-692-7050
855-526-2262; *Fax:* 847-692-6968
info@aana.com; www.aana.com
Social Media: Facebook, Twitter, LinkedIn, Youtube

Juan F. Quintana, President
Bruce A. Weiner, MS, CRNA, Vice President
Kathryn L. Jansky, CRNA, ARNP, Treasurer
Cheryl L. Nimmo, CRNA, DNP, President-Elect
Robert Gauvin, CRNA, MS, Director, Region 1

The AANA promulgates education and practice standards and guidelines, and affords consultation to both private and governmental entities regarding nurse anesthetists and their practice.
Founded in: 1931

12222 **American Association of Occupational Health Nurses**
7794 Grow Drive
Pensacola, FL 32514

850-474-6963
800-241-8014; *Fax:* 850-484-8762
AAOHN@aaohn.org; www.aaohn.org/
Social Media: Facebook, Twitter, LinkedIn

Jeannie Tomlinson, MSN, RN, President
Ronda Weiss, MS, MPH, MBA, Secretary
Mary Gene Ryan, President-Elect
Phyllis Berryman, Director
David Allcott, Director

Dedicated to advancing and maximizing the health, safety and prductivity of domestic and global workforces by providing education, research, public policy and practice resources for occupational and environmental health nurses. Mission is to advance the profession of occupational and environmental health nursing.

12223 **American Association of Orthodontists**
401 North Lindbergh Boulevard
St. Louis, MO 63141-7816

314-993-1700
800-424-2841; *Fax:* 314-997-1745
info@aaortho.org; www.aaoinfo.org
Social Media: Facebook, Twitter, LinkedIn

Jill Nowak, Director Of Finance & Admin
Linda Gladden, Director Of Comm. & Marketing
Sarah Dvorak, Meetings Coordinator
Sherry Nappier, Member Coordinator
Mike Nappier, Shipping And Receiving Coordinator

Official organization for board qualified and board certified orthodontists.
Founded in: 1900

12224 **American Association of Physician Specialists Inc.**
5550 West Executive Drive
Suite 400
Tampa, FL 33609

813-433-2277; *Fax:* 813-830-6599
wcarbone@aapsus.org; www.aapsus.com

Martin E. Thornton, D.O., FAAEP, President
Surinder K. Kad, M.D., FAAIM, Secretary/Treasurer
Craig S. Smith, M.D., President-Elect
Mark DeSantis, D.O., Membership Officer
Kenneth A. Wallace, III, M.D., Vice President

AAPS was founded to fill a professional need among physicians practicing in medical specialities. Distinct from other medical societies, the AAPS accepts qualified physicians into membership who have either an allopathic (MD) or osteopathic (DO) degree.
Founded in: 1950

12225 **American Association of Poison Control Centers**
515 King St.
Suite 510
Alexandria, VA 22314

703-894-1858
800-222-1222
info@aapcc.org; www.aapcc.org
Social Media: Facebook, Twitter, RSS, WordPress

Jay L. Schauben, PharmD, President
William Banner, MD, PhD, President Elect
Marsha Ford, MD, FACMT, Past President
Stuart Heard, PharmD, FCSHP, Treasurer
Julie Weber, RPh, CSPI, Secretary

National voluntary health organization that supports poison centersto prevent poisonings, provide education, conduct scientific research and treat individuals exposed to poisoning.

12226 **American Association of Public Health Physicians**
1605 Pebble Beach Blvd.
Green Cove Springs, FL 32043-8077

888-447-7281; *Fax:* 202-333-5016
membership@aaphp.org; www.aaphp.org

Ryung Suh, President

The AAPHP speaks on behalf of all public health physicians on major issues affecting public health.
Founded in: 1954

12227 **American Association of Retired Persons**
601 E Street NW
Washington, DC 20049-0003

202-434-3525
888-687-2277; *Fax:* 202-434-7599
member@aarp.org; www.aarp.org
Social Media: Facebook, Twitter, YouTube

Jo Ann Jenkins, CEO
Lawrence Flanagan, President, AARP Services
Scott Frisch, Chief Operating Officer
Nancy Smith, Corporate Secretary
Martha M. Boudreau, Chief Comm. & Marketing Officer

A nonprofit, nonpartisan membership organization for people age 50 and over. AARP is dedicated to enhancing quality of life for all.
21 Members
Founded in: 1958

12228 **American Association of Sexuality Educators, Counselors & Therapists**
1444 I Street NW
Suite 700
Washington, DC 20005

202-449-1099; *Fax:* 202-216-9646
info@aasect.org; www.aasect.org

Konnie McCaffree, President
Debby Herbenick, President Elect
Douglas Braun-Harvey, LMFT, Treasurer
Chris F. Fariello, PhD, MA, Secretary
Michael Chan, Executive Director

A not-for-profit, interdisciplinary professional organization that is devoted to the promotion of sexual health by the development and advancement of the fields of sexual therapy, counseling and education.
Founded in: 1967

12229 **American Association of Suicidology**
5221 Wisconsin Avenue, NW
Washington, DC 20015

202-237-2280
800-273-TALK; *Fax:* 202-237-2282;
www.suicidology.org
Social Media: Facebook, Twitter, YouTube

David Miller, PhD, President
Julie Cerel, PhD, President Elect
Amy Boland, CPA, Treasurer
Marnin J. Heisel, Secretary
Michelle Cornette, PhD, Executive Director

A membership organization for those involved in suicide prevention and intervention, or touched by suicide.

12230 **American Association on Intellectual and Developmental Disabilities**
501 3rd Street, NW
Suite 200
Washington, DC 20001

202-387-1968; *Fax:* 202-387-2193;
www.aaidd.org/
Social Media: Facebook, Twitter, LinkedIn, YouTube

Susan B. Palmer, PhD, President
William Gaventa, MDiv, President Elect
Susan Havercamp, PhD, VP
Patti N. Martin, MEd, Secretary-Treasurer
Amy S. Hewitt, PhD, Immediate Past President

An American nonprofit professional organization concerned with intellectual disability and related developmental disabilities.
Founded in: 1876

12231 **American Autoimmune Related Diseases Association**
22100 Gratiot Ave.
Eastpointe, MI 48021

586-776-3900; *Fax:* 586-776-3903;
www.aarda.org
Social Media: Facebook, Twitter, YouTube, RSS

Betty Diamond, M.D., Chairperson
Noel R. Rose, M.D., Ph.D., Chairman Emeritus
Edward K. Christian, Advisor
Stephanie P. Hales, Advisor
Virginia T. Ladd, President and Executive Director

Includes patient information about autoimmunity and autoimmune related diseases.

12232 **American Behcet's Disease Association**
PO Box 80576
Rochester, MN 48308

631-656-0537
800-723-4238; *Fax:* 480-247-5377
info@behcets.com; www.behcets.com

Deb Kleber, President
Mary Burke, VP
Belinda Rivas, Treasurer
Marcia Wise, Executive Secretary
Mirta Avila Santos, MD, Executive Dir. & Comm Coordinator

Provides information and support for patients with Behcet's Diseaseand for their family members and caretakers.

12233 **American Brain Tumor Association**
8550 W. Bryn Mawr Ave.
Suite 550
Chicago, IL 60631
773-577-8750
800-886-2282; *Fax:* 773-577-8738
info@abta.org; www.abta.org
Social Media: Facebook, Twitter, YouTube

Jeff Fougerousse, Chair
Brian Olson, Vice Chair
Carla Varner, Treasurer
James Reilly, Secretary
Elizabeth M. Wilson, MNA, President and CEO

National nonprofit organization dedicated to providing support services and programs to brain tumor patients and their families, as well as the funding of brain tumor research.
Founded in: 1973

12234 **American Burn Association**
311 S. Wacker Drive
Suite 4150
Chicago, IL 60606

312-642-9260; *Fax:* 312-642-9130;
www.ameriburn.org
Social Media: Facebook, Twitter

Edward E. Tredget, MD, MSc, President
Michael D. Peck, MD, ScD, FACS, President Elect
Linwood R. Haith, MD, FACS, First Vice President
Ernest J. Grant, RN, BSN, MSN, Second Vice President
William L. Hickerson, MD, FACS, Treasurer

Involved in research in the methods of treating burn injuries and fostering prevention efforts.
3500+ Members

12235 **American Chronic Pain Association**
PO Box 850
Rocklin, CA 95677

800-533-3231; *Fax:* 916-632-3208
ACPA@theacpa.org
theacpa.org
Social Media: Facebook, Twitter, YouTube, Pinterest

Penney Cowan, Founder& CEO
Mary Jane Bent, Board of Director
Chris Duncan, Board of Director
Daniel Galia, Board of Director
Steve Feinberg, MD, Board of Director

Information is provided concerning services, conditions, and pain management issues.
Founded in: 1980

12236 **American College Health Association**
1362 Mellon Road
Suite 180
Hanover, MD 21076

410-859-1500; *Fax:* 410-859-1510
contact@acha.org; www.acha.org
Social Media: Facebook, Twitter, YouTube

Jake Baggott, MLS, 1SG, President
Jamie Davidson, PhD, President Elect
Stephanie Hanenberg, RN, MSN, Vice President
Beverly Kloeppel, MD, MBA, Treasurer
Sarah Van Orman, MD, MMM, FA, Immediate Past President

The American College Health Association (ACHA) is the principal advocate and leadership organization for college and university health. The association provides advocacy, education, communications, products, and services, as well as promoting research and culturally competent practices to enhance its members' ability to advance the health of all students and the campus community.
2600 Members
Founded in: 1920

12237 **American College of Allergy, Asthma and Immunology**
85 West Algonquin Road
Suite 550
Arlington Heights, IL 60005-4460

847-427-1200; *Fax:* 847-427-1294
mail@acaai.org; www.acaai.org
Social Media: Facebook, Twitter, LinkedIn, YouTube, Pinterest

Michael B Foggs, MD, President
Bryan L Martin, MD*, Vice President
Bradley E Chipps, MD, FACAAI*, Treasurer
James L Sublett, MD, FACAAI*, President-Elect
Bob Q Lanier, MD, Executive Medical Director

Information and news service for patients, parents of patients, members, the news media, and purchasers of health care programs.
5200 Members
Founded in: 1942

12238 **American College of Cardiology**
Heart House
2400 N Street NW
Washington, DC 20037-1153

202-375-6000
800-253-4636; *Fax:* 202-375-7000
resource@acc.org; www.acc.org
Social Media: Facebook, Twitter, LinkedIn, YouTube

Robert A. Shor, MD, FACC, Chair
Matthew Phillips, MD, FACC, Chair-Elect
Michael Mansour, MD, FACC, Immediate Past Chair
Kim Allan Williams, President
Richard A. Chazal, MD, FACC, President-Elect

The mission is to advocate for quality cardiovascular care-through education, research promotion, development and application of standards and guidelines-and to influence health care policy.
39M Members
Founded in: 1949

12239 **American College of Cardiovascular Administrators (ACCA)**
American Academy of Medical Administrators
701 Lee Street
Suite 600
Des Plaines, IL 60016-4516

847-759-8601; *Fax:* 312-673-6705
info@aameda.org; www.acc.org

Renee L. Mazeroll, President
Kathy A. Miller, President-Elect

Mission is to advance ACCA members and the field of cardiovascular management and promote excellence and integrity in cardiovascular leadership.

12240 **American College of Emergency Physicians**
1125 Executive Circle
Irving, TX 75038-2522

972-550-0911
800-798-1822; *Fax:* 972-580-2816
membership@acep.org; www.acep.org
Social Media: Facebook

Rebecca B. Parker, MD, FACEP, Chair
Michael J. Gerardi, President
Paul D. Kivela, MD, FACEP, VP
Jay A. Kaplan, MD, FACEP, President-Elect
John J. Rogers, MD, FACEP, Secretary-Treasurer

Promoting the highest quality emergency care, ACEP is the leading advocate for emergency physicians and their patients.
28M Members
Founded in: 1968

12241 **American College of Healthcare Executives**
One North Franklin Street
Suite 1700
Chicago, IL 60606-3529

312-424-2800; *Fax:* 312-424-0023
contact@ache.org; www.ache.org
Social Media: Facebook, Twitter, LinkedIn, Youtube

Edward H. Lamb, Chairman
Charles D. Stokes, Chairman-Elect
Deborah J. Bowen, FACHE, President & CEO
Thomas C. Dolan, PhD, President & CEO
Richard J. Stull, Executive Vice President

An international professional society of healthcare executives who lead hospitals, healthcare systems and other healthcare organizations.
40M Members
Founded in: 1933

12242 **American College of Healthcare Information Administrators (ACHIA)**
701 Lee Street
Suite 600
Des Plaines, IL 60016-4516
847-759-8601; *Fax:* 847-759-8602
info@aameda.org;
www.aameda.org/Colleges/ACHIA/healthcareinformation.html

Charles D. Chapdelaine, President

Develops innovative concepts in the field of healthcare information and promotes the advancement of its members in knowledge, professional standing, and personal achievements through continuing education and research in healthcare information administration. ACHIA focuses on providing education, support and opportunity for information technology leaders in the healthcare industry.
300 Members
Founded in: 1991

12243 **American College of Medical Practice**
104 Inverness Terrace East
Englewood, CO 80112-5306

303-799-1111
877-275-6462
support@mgma.org; www.mgma.com
Social Media: Facebook, Twitter, LinkedIn, Google+

Stephen A. Dickens, JD, FACMPE, F, Board Chair
Debra J. Wiggs, FACMPE, Vice Chair
Susan L. Turney, MD, MS, FACP,, President and CEO
Ronald W. Holder, Jr., MHA, FACM, Finance/Audit Chair

Delivering networking, professional education and resources and political advocacy for medical practice management.
3000 Members
Founded in: 1926

12244 **American College of Medical Quality**
5272 River Road
Suite 630
Bethesda, MD 20816

301-718-6516; *Fax:* 301-656-0989;
www.acmq.org
Social Media: Facebook, Twitter, LinkedIn

Prathibha Varkey, President
Mark Lyles, MD, MBA, FACMQ, President Elect
Donald E. Casey, Jr MD, MPH, Vice President
John Vigorita, Secretary
Henry C. L. Johnson, Jr., MD, MPH, Treasurer

The mission of the American College of Medical Quality is to provide leadership and education in healthcare quality management.
Founded in: 1973

12245 **American College of Oncology Administrators**
701 Lee Street
Suite 600
Des Plaines, IL 60016-4516

847-759-8601; *Fax:* 847-759-8602
info@aameda.org;
www.aameda.org/Colleges/ACOA/oncology.html

Margaret A. O'Grady, President
Bonnie J. Miller, President-Elect

Focuses on providing support and opportunity for oncology administrators and managers in all types of healthcare institutions.
300 Members
Founded in: 1991

12246 **American College of Oral and Maxillofacial Surgeons**
2025 M Street NW
Suite 800
Washington, DC 20036

202-367-1182
800-522-6676; *Fax:* 202-367-2182
admin@acoms.org; www.acoms.org
Social Media: Facebook, Twitter, LinkedIn, RSS

Pedro F. Franco, President
R. Bryan Bell, President-Elect
Steven C. Kemp, Executive Director
Jeffrey Bennett, Treasurer
Kevin L. Rieck, Secretary

The diplomates have joined together in the College for the purpose of enhancing the level of patient care. This enhancement of surgical care through the furthering of research and education in OMS surgery is achieved by the College's sponsoring of educational programs, research activities, and fellowships as a service to not only the members of the College, but to the profession at large.
2M+ Members
Founded in: 1975

12247 **American College of Osteopathic Family Physicians**
330 E. Algonquin Road
Suite 1
Arlington Heights, IL 60005-4665

800-323-0794; *Fax:* 847-228-9755
membership@acofp.org; www.acofp.org
Social Media: Facebook, Twitter, LinkedIn, Youtube

Kevin D. de Regnier, DO, FACOFP, President
Peter L Schmelzer, CAE, Executive Director
Rodney M. Wiseman, DO, FACOFP, Vice President
Duane G. Koehler, DO, FACOFP, Secretary/Treasurer
Annie DeVries, Sr. Administrative Assistant

Works to promote excellence in osteopathic family medicine through quality education, visionary leadership and responsible advocacy.
20M Members
Founded in: 1950

12248 **American College of Osteopathic Surgeons**
123 North Henry Street
Alexandria, VA 22314-2903

703-684-0416
800-888-1312; *Fax:* 703-684-3280
info@facos.org; www.facos.org
Social Media: Facebook, Twitter, LinkedIn, YouTube

Linda Ayers, MHCM, CAE, CEO
Don Kaveny, Director of Postdoctoral Training
Sonjya Johnson, Director of Membership Recruitment
Brandon Roberts, Director of Finance
Allison Hamrick, Manager, Marketing & Communication

Committed to assuring excellence in osteopathic surgical care through education, advocacy, leadership, development and the fostering of professional and personal relationship.
2147 Members
Founded in: 1927

12249 **American College of Physician Executives**
400 North Ashley Drive
Suite 400
Tampa, FL 33602

813-287-2000
800-562-8088; *Fax:* 813-287-8993
acpe@acpe.org; www.acpe.org
Social Media: Facebook, Twitter, LinkedIn, YouTube

Peter B. Angood, CEO

The nation's largest health care organization for physician executives who want to boost their leadership skills while adding weight to their CVs. The primary focus of the College is to provide superior leadership and management skills to physicians and encouraging them to assume more active roles in the leadership and management of their organizations.
10M Members
Founded in: 1975

12250 **American College of Physicians**
190 North Independence Mall West
Philadelphia, PA 19106-1572

215-351-2400
800-523-1546; *Fax:* 215-351-2759
archives@acponline.org; www.acponline.org
Social Media: Facebook, Twitter, LinkedIn, RSS

Tanveer P. Mir, MD, MACP, Chair, Board of Regents
Wayne J. Riley, President
Steven E. Weinberger, EVP/CEO
Robert A Gluckman, MD, FACP, Treasurer
David A. Fleming, MD, MA, FACP, Immediate Past President

Mission is to enhance the quality and effectiveness of health care by fostering excellence and professionalism in the practice of medicine.
Founded in: 1915

12251 **American College of Rheumatology**
2200 Lake Boulevard NE
Atlanta, GA 30319

404-633-3777; *Fax:* 404-633-1870
acr@rheumatology.org;
www.rheumatology.org/
Social Media: Facebook, Twitter, LinkedIn, YouTube

E. William St.Clair, MD, President
Joan Von Feldt, MD, MSEd, President Elect
Mark Andrejeski, Executive Director
Steve Echard, CAE, IOM,, Foundation Executive Director
David I. Daikh, MD, PhD, Foundation Secretary

Mission is advancing rheumatology. The organization is for physicians, health professionals, and scientists that meets the mission through programs of education, research, advocacy and practice support.
Founded in: 1934

12252 **American College of Sports Medicine**
401 West Michigan Street
Indianapolis, IN 46202-3233

317-637-9200; *Fax:* 317-634-7817;
www.acsm.org
Social Media: Facebook, Twitter, YouTube, Pinterest, Instagram

Lawrence E. Armstrong, President
NiCole Keith, Ph.D., FACSM, First Vice President
Walter Thompson, Ph.D., FACSM, First Vice President
Craig Harms, Ph.D., FACSM, Second Vice President
Kathryn Schmitz, Ph.D., FACSM, Second Vice President

From academicians to students and from personal trainers to physicians, the association of sports medicine, exercise science, and health and fitness professionals is dedicated to helping people worldwide live longer, healthier lives.
50,00 Members
Founded in: 1954

12253 **American College of Surgeons**
633 N Saint Clair Street
Chicago, IL 60611-3211

312-202-5000
800-621-4111; *Fax:* 312-202-5001
postmaster@facs.org; www.facs.org
Social Media: Facebook, Twitter, LinkedIn, Youtube

Fabrizio Michelassi, MD, FACS, Chair, Board of Governors
Diana Farmer, MD, FACS, Vice-Chair, Board of Governors
Steven Stain, MD, FACS, Secretary, Board of Governors
David B. Hoyt, MD, FACS, Executive Director
Felix Niespodziewanski, Convention and Meetings Director

Dedicated to improving the care of the surgical patient and to safeguarding standards of care in an optimal and ethical practice environment.
Founded in: 1913

12254 American Congress of Obstetricians and Gynecologists
409 12th Street SW
PO Box 70620
Washington, DC 20024-2188
202-638-5577
800-673-8444
sales@acog.org; www.acog.org
Social Media: Facebook, Twitter, Youtube, RSS
Mark S. DeFrancesco, MD, MBA, President
Dr. Hal C Lawrence III, EVP, CEO
Richard C Bailey, CPA, MBA, CFO, VP - Finance
Thomas M. Gellhaus, MD, President Elect
Dr Sandra Ann Carson, MD, Vice President, Education
Serving as a strong advocate for quality health care for women, maintaining the highest standards of clinical practice and continuing education for its members, promoting patient education and stimulating patient understanding of and involvement in medical care, and increasing awareness among its members and the public of the changing issues facing women's health care.
45M Members
Founded in: 1951

12255 American Congress of Rehabilitation Medicine
11654 Plaza America Drive
Suite 535
Reston, VA 20190-4700
703-435-5335; *Fax:* 866-692-1619
info@ACRM.org; www.acrm.org
Social Media: Facebook, Twitter, LinkedIn, Google+
Sue Ann Sisto, PT, MA, PhD, President
Jon W Lindberg, MBA, CAE, Chief Executive Officer
Douglas Katz, MD, FACRM, FAAN, Vice President
Wayne A. Gordon, PhD ABPP-CN, Treasurer
Cindy Harrison-Felix, Secretary
An organization of rehabilitation professionals dedicated to serving people with disabling conditions by supporting research that; promotes health, independence, productivity, and quality of life, and meets the needs of rehabilitatio clinicians and people with disabilities.
Founded in: 1923

12256 American Council of Academic Plastic Surgeons
500 Cummings Center
Suite 4550
Beverly, MA 01915
978-927-8330; *Fax:* 978-524-0498;
www.acaplasticsurgeons.org/
W. John Kitzmiller, M.D., President
C. Scott Hultman, M.D., President-Elect
Michael L. Bentz, M.D., VP Finance and Communication
Donald R. Mackay, MD, FACS, VP Academic Administration
Anthony A Smith, M.D., Vice President of Education
Goal is to provide leadership and support for educational programs for plastic surgery residents.

12257 American Counseling Association (ACA)
6101 Stevenson Ave
Suite 600
Alexandria, VA 22304-3302
703-823-9800
800-347-6647; *Fax:* 703-823-0252
membership@counseling.org;
www.counseling.org
Social Media: Facebook, Twitter, LinkedIn
Thelma Duffey, Ph.D., President
Catherine Roland, President-Elect
Elias Zambrano, Treasurer
Richard Yep, CEO
Robert L. Smith, Past President
Dedicated to the growth and development of the counseling profession and those who are served.
45M Members
Founded in: 1952

12258 American Dance Therapy Association
10632 Little Patuxent Parkway
Suite 108
Columbia, MD 21044
410-997-4040; *Fax:* 410-997-4048;
www.adta.org
Social Media: Facebook, LinkedIn, YouTube, Pinterest
Jody Wager, MS, BC-DMT, President
Margaret Migliorati, R-DMT, VP
Meghan Dempsey, MS, BC-DMT, Treasurer
Gail Wood,MA, BC-DMT, NCC, Secretary
Susan D. Imus, Board of Director
Establishes and maintains standards of professional education in the field of dance/movement therapy.
Founded in: 1966

12259 American Dental Association
211 East Chicago Avenue
Chicago, IL 60611-2678
312-440-2500; *Fax:* 312-440-2800
affiliates@ada.org; www.ada.org
Social Media: Facebook, Twitter, LinkedIn, YouTube
Dr. Maxine Feinberg, President
Dr. Carol Gomez Summerhays, President Elect
Dr. Kathleen T. T. O'Loughlin, Executive Director
The oldest and largest national dental society in the world. Becoming the leading source of oral health related information for dentists and their patients. The professional association of dentists that fosters the success of a diverse membership and advances the oral health of the public.
156M Members
Founded in: 1859

12260 American Dental Education Association
655 K Street, NW
Suite 800
Washington, DC 20001
202-289-7201; *Fax:* 202-289-7204
membership@adea.org; www.adea.org
Social Media: Facebook, Twitter, YouTube
Huw F. Thomas, Chair of the Board
Cecile A. Feldman, Chair-elect of the Board
Lily T Garcia, Immediate Past Chair of the Board
David M. Shafer, D.M.D., Board Director for Hospitals
Richard W. Valachovic, President and CEO
The voice of dental education. Members include all US and Canadian dental schools and many allied and postdoctoral dental education programs, corporations, faculty, and students. Mission is to lead individuals and institutions of the dental education community to address contemporary issures influencing education, research, and the delivery of oral health care for the health of the public.
21,00 Members
Founded in: 1983

12261 American Dental Hygenists Association
444 North Michigan Avenue
Suite 3400
Chicago, IL 60611-3980
312-440-8900; *Fax:* 312-440-8929
member.services@adha.net; www.adha.org
Social Media: Facebook, Twitter, LinkedIn, YouTube, Instagram
Jill Rethman, RDH, BA, President
Betty Kabel, RDH, BS, President Elect
Tammy Filipiak, RDH, MS, VP
Donnella Miller, RDH, BS, MPS, Treasurer
Kelli Swanson Jaecks, Immediate Past President
Mission is to advance the art and science of dental hygiene, and to promote the highest standards of education and practice in the profession.
Founded in: 1993

12262 American Dental Society of Anesthesiology
211 E Chicago Ave
Suite 780
Chicago, IL 60611-6983
312-664-8270
877-255-3742; *Fax:* 312-224-8624
adsahome@mac.com; www.adsahome.org
Social Media: Facebook, Twitter, Vimeo, Instagram
Kenneth L. Reed, DMD, President
Edward C. Adlesic, DMD, Board of Director
Michael Rollert, DDS, President-Elect
Morton B. Rosenberg, DMD, Treasurer
Daniel S. Sarasin, DDS, VP
Mission is to provide a forum for education, research, and recognition of achievement in order to promote safe and effective patient care for all dentists who have an interest in anesthesiology, sedation and the control of anxiety and pain.
5000 Members
Founded in: 1953

12263 American Diabetes Association
C/o Center for Information
2451 Crystal Drive
Arlington, VA 22202
703-549-1500
800-342-2383; *Fax:* 703-549-6995
askada@diabetes.org; www.diabetes.org
Social Media: Facebook, Twitter, Vimeo, Instagram, Pinterest
Robin Richardson, Chair
Margaret Powers, President, Health Care & Education
Desmond Schatz, President, Medicine & Science
Lorrie W. Liang, Secretary/Treasurer
Kevin L. Hagan, Chief Executive Officer
Leading the fight against the deadly consequences of diabetes and fight for those affected. Funding research to prevent, cure and manage diabetes. Delivering services to hundreds of communitites. Providing objective and credible information. Giving a voice to those denied their rights because of diabetes.
Founded in: 1940

12264 American Gastroenterological Association
4930 Del Ray Avenue
Bethesda, MD 20814
301-654-2055; *Fax:* 301-654-5920
member@gastro.org; www.gastro.org
Social Media: Facebook, Twitter, LinkedIn, YouTube
Michael Camilleri, MD, AGAF, President
Sheila E. Crowe, MD, AGAF, Vice President
Francis M. Giardiello, MD, AGAF, Secretary/Treasurer
Timothy C. Wang, MD, AGAF, President-Elect
Martin Brotman, MD, AGAF, Foundation Chair

Advancing the science and practice of gastroenterology.
16000 Members
Founded in: 1897

12265 **American Head and Neck Society**
11300 W Olympic Boulevard
Suite 600
Los Angeles, CA 90064
310-437-0559; *Fax:* 310-437-0585
admin@ahns.info;
www.headandneckcancer.org
Social Media: Facebook, Twitter, YouTube

Dennis Kraus, MD, President
Jonathan Irish, MD, Vice President
Brian B Burkey, MD MEd, Secretary
Ehab Hanna, MD, Treasurer
Jeffery Myers, MD, President-Elect

The single largest organization in North American for the advancement of research and education in head and neck oncology.
Founded in: 1998

12266 **American Headache Society**
19 Mantua Road
Mount Royal, NJ 08061
856-423-0043; *Fax:* 856-423-0082
achehq@talley.com;
www.americanheadachesociety.org
Social Media: Facebook, Twitter

Paul Winner, DO, Chair

Professional society of health care providers dedicated to the study and treatment of headache and face pain. Members collaborate in producing educational programs and materials, coordinating the support groups, and undertaking public awareness initiatives all aimed at improving care for headache sufferers.
1500 Members
Founded in: 1990

12267 **American Health Care Association**
1201 L Street, N.W.
Washington, DC 20005-4046
202-842-4444; *Fax:* 202-842-3860
webmaster@ahca.org; www.ahcancal.org
Social Media: Facebook, Twitter, YouTube, Flickr, Blogspot

Represents the long term care community to the nation at large- to government, business leaders, and the general public. Serves as a force for change, providing information, education, and administrative tools that enhance quality at every level.
12M Members
Founded in: 1949

12268 **American Health Information Management Association**
233 N. Michigan Avenue
21st Floor
Chicago, IL 60601-5809
312-233-1100
800-335-5535; *Fax:* 312-233-1090;
www.ahima.org
Social Media: Facebook, Twitter, LinkedIn, RSS, YouTube

Cassi Birnbaum, President/Chair
Melissa M. Martin, President/Chair-elect
Laura Pait, RHIA, CDIP, CCS, Speaker of The HoD
Lynne Thomas Gordon, CEO
Susan W. Carey, RHIT, PMP, Treasurer

Professional organization for the field of effective management of health data and medical record needed to deliver quality healthcare to the public management.
71,00 Members
Founded in: 1928

12269 **American Health Information Management Association**
233 N. Michigan Avenue
21st Floor
Chicago, IL 60601-5809
312-233-1100
800-335-5535; *Fax:* 312-233-1090
info@ahima.org; www.ahima.org
Social Media: Facebook, Twitter, LinkedIn, RSS, YouTube

Cassi Birnbaum, President/ Chair
Melissa M. Martin, President/ Chair-Elect
Laura Pait, RHIA, CDIP, CCS, Speaker of The HoD
Lynne Thomas Gordon, CEO
Susan W. Carey, RHIT, PMP, Treasurer

Mission is to be the professional community that improves healthcare by advocating best practices and standards for health information management and the trusted source for education, reasearch, and professional credentialing.
46M Members
Founded in: 1928

12270 **American Health Quality Association**
7918 Jones Branch Drive
Suite 300
McLean, VA 22102
202-331-5790; *Fax:* 202-331-9334
info@ahqa.org; www.ahqa.org

Dawn FitzGerald, MS, MBA, President
Jane Brock, MD, MSPH, President Elect
Kathleen D. Merrill, Immediate Past President
Rick Potter, Treasurer
Colleen Delaney Eubanks, CAE, Executive Director

Represents Quality Improvement Organizations and professionals working to improve the quality of health care in communities across America. QIOs share information about best practices with physicians, hospitals, nursing homes, home health agencies, and others. Working together with health care providers, QIOs identify opportunities and provide assistance for improvement.

12271 **American Heart Association**
7272 Greenville Ave
Dallas, TX 75231-4596
214-373-6300
800-242-8721; *Fax:* 214-570-5930
Review.personal.info@heart.org;
www.americanheart.org
Social Media: Facebook, Twitter, YouTube, Google Plus

Bernie Dennis, Chairman
Mariell Jessup, President
Nancy Brown, CEO
Sunder Joshi, Chief Administrative Officer
Suzie Upton, Chief Development Officer

A nonprofit organization funding research and providing information on the diagnosis, treatment, and prevention of heart diseases and stroke. Mission is to build healthier lives, free of cardiovascular diseases and stroke.
Founded in: 1924

12272 **American Horticultural Therapy Association (AHTA)**
610 Freedom Business Center
Suite 110
King of Prussia, PA 19406
610-992-0020; *Fax:* 610-225-2364
martha@ahta.org; www.ahta.org
Social Media: Facebook, Twitter, LinkedIn, Pinterest, Youtube, RSS

MaryAnne McMillan, HTR, President
Leigh Anne Starling, MS, CRC, Vice President
Todd Schappell, OTR/L, Treasurer
Patricia Cassidy, HTR, Secretary
Gabriela Harvey, HTR, Immediate Past President

A champion of barrier-free, therapeutic gardens that enable everyone to work, learn, and relax in the garden. Horticultural therapists are skilled at creating garden spaces that accommodate people with a wide range of abilities.
Founded in: 1973

12273 **American Hospital Association**
155 N. Wacker Dr.
Chicago, IL 60606
312-422-3000
800-424-4301; *Fax:* 312-422-4500
ddavidson@aha.org; www.aha.org
Social Media: Facebook, Twitter, YouTube

Benjamin K Chu, M.D., Chairman
Richard J Pollack, President and CEO
John Evans, CFO, SVP
Alicia Mitchell, SVP, Communications
Richard Umbdenstock, Past President, CEO

Represents and serves all types of hospitals, health care networks, and their patients and communities. Provides education for health care leaders and is a source of information on health care issues and trends.
43,00 Members
Founded in: 1898

12274 **American Industrial Hygiene Association**
3141 Fairview Park Drive
Suite 777
Falls Church, VA 22042
703-849-8888; *Fax:* 703-207-3561
infonet@aiha.org; www.aiha.org
Social Media: Facebook, Twitter, LinkedIn, RSS, YouTube

Steven E. Lacey, PhD, CIH, CSP, President
Cynthia A. Ostrowski, CIH, Vice President
J. Lindsay Cook, CIH, CSP, Treasurer
Kathleen S. Murphy, CIH, Secretary
Deborah Imel Nelson, PhD, CIH, President-Elect

Organization of professionals in the science of occupational and environmental health and safety. Devoted to achieving and maintaining the highest professional standards for members. Promoting certification of industrial hygienists.
10000 Members
Founded in: 1939

12275 **American Institute of Ultrasound in Medicine**
14750 Sweitzer Lane
Suite 100
Laurel, MD 20707-5906
301-498-4100
800-638-5352; *Fax:* 301-498-4450
cvalente@aium.org; www.aium.org
Social Media: Facebook, Twitter, LinkedIn, YouTube, Instagram

Beryl R. Benacerraf, MD, President
Joseph R Wax, MD, First Vice President
Charlotte G. Henningsen, Second Vice President
Michael Blaivas, MD, Third Vice President
Brian D. Coley, MD, President-Elect

A multidisciplinary association dedicated to advancing the safe and effective use of ultrasound in medicine through professional and public education, research, development of guidelines, and accreditation.
85M Members
Founded in: 1952

12276 **American Institute of Ultrasound in Medici ne**
14750 Sweitzer Lane
Suite 100
Laurel, MD 20707-5906
301-498-4100
800-638-5352; *Fax:* 301-498-4450
cvalente@aium.org; www.aium.org

Social Media: Facebook, Twitter, LinkedIn, YouTube, Instagram

Beryl R. Benacerraf, MD, President
Joseph R Wax, MD, First Vice President
Charlotte G. Henningsen, Second Vice President
Michael Blaivas, MD, Third Vice President
Brian D. Coley, MD, President-Elect

A multidisciplinary association dedicated to advancing the safe and effective use of ultrasound in medicine through professional and public education, research, development of guidelines, and accreditation.
9.8M Members
Founded in: 1952

12277 American Lung Association
1301 Pennsylvania Ave. NW
Suite 800
Washington, DC 20004

202-785-3355; *Fax:* 202-452-1805
info@lungusa.org; www.lung.org
Social Media: Facebook, Twitter, YouTube, Google Plus, RSS

Albert A. Rizzo, Chair
Ross P. Lanzafame, Esq., Chair-Elect
Christine L. Bryant, Secretary/ Treasurer

Dedicated to the prevention, cure, and control of lung diseases such as asthma, emphysema, tuberculosis, and lung cancer. The Association offers community service, public health education, advocacy, and research.
Founded in: 1904

12278 American Massage Therapy Association
500 Davis Street
Suite 900
Evanston, IL 60201

847-864-0123
877-905-0577; *Fax:* 847-864-5196
info@amtamassage.org;
www.amtamassage.org/
Social Media: Facebook, Twitter, LinkedIn, RSS, YouTube

Jeff Smoot, President
Nathan J. Nordstrom, President Elect
Nancy M. Porambo, Immediate Past President
Glyn Desmond, Board of Director
Maureen P. Hoock, Board of Director

Nonprofit, professional association serving massage therapists, massage students and massage schools.

12279 American Medical Association
330 N. Wabash Avenue
Chicago, IL 60611-5885

800-621-8335
robin_rusell@ama-assn.org;
www.ama-assn.org
Social Media: Facebook, Twitter, LinkedIn, Google+

James L. Madara, MD, CEO, EVP
Bernard L. Hengesbaugh, Chief Operating Officer
Denise M Hagerty, SVP, CFO
Robert W Davis, SVP, HR & Corporate Services
Kenneth J. Sharigian, SVP, Chief Strategy Officer

Mission is to promote the art and science of medicine and the betterment of public health. The American Medical Association helps doctors help patients by uniting physicians nationwide to work on the most important professional and public health issues.
Founded in: 1847

12280 American Medical Directors Association
11000 Broken Land Parkway
Suite 400
Columbia, MD 21044

410-740-9743
800-876-2632; *Fax:* 410-740-4572
info@amda.com; www.amda.com
Social Media: Facebook, Twitter, LinkedIn

Naushira Pandya, MD, FACP, CMD, President
Heidi K. White, Vice President
Daniel Haimowitz, Secretary
Arif Nazir, MD, FACP, CMD, Treasurer
Susan M. Levy, MD, CMD, AGSF, President-Elect

Professional association of medical directors, attending physicians, and others practicing in the long term care continuum, is dedicated to excellence in patient care and provides education, advocacy, information, and professional development to promote the delivery of quality long term care medicine.
Founded in: 1978

12281 American Medical Group Association
One Prince Street
Alexandria, VA 22314-3318

703-838-0033; *Fax:* 703-548-1890
dfisher@amga.org; www.amga.org
Social Media: Facebook, Twitter, LinkedIn, YouTube, Flickr

Don L. Wreden, M.D., Chair
Donald W Fisher, Ph.D., CAE, President and CEO
Donn E. Sorensen, Chair Elect
Barbara A. Walters, D.O., M.B.A., Treasurer
Clyde L. Morris, C.P.A., CFO

Represents medical groups and organized systems of care, including some of the nation's largest, most prestigious integrated healthcare delivery systems. Mission is to improve health care for patients by supporting multispecialty medical groups and other organized systems of care.
113M Members
Founded in: 1950

12282 American Medical Informatics Association
4720 Montgomery Lane
Suite 500
Bethesda, MD 20814

301-657-1291; *Fax:* 301-657-1296
mail@amia.org; www.amia.org
Social Media: Facebook, Twitter, LinkedIn, YouTube

Blackford Middleton, Chair
Thomas H. Payne, MD, FACMI, Chair Elect
Douglas B. Fridsma, President, CEO
Karen Greenwood, Executive Vice President, COO
Steven Labkoff, Treasurer

Aims to lead the way in transforming health care through trusted science, education, and the practice of informatics. Connecting a broad community of professionals and students interested in informatics, AMIA is the bridge for knowledge and collaboration across a continuum, from basic and applied research to the consumer and public health arenas.
3200 Members
Founded in: 1990

12283 American Medical Student Association
45610 Woodland Road
Suite 300
Sterling, VA 20166

703-620-6600
800-767-2266; *Fax:* 703-620-6445
members@amsa.org; www.amsa.org
Social Media: Facebook, Twitter, Inex, Youtube

Deborah Vozzella Hall, MD, National President
Kelly Thibert, President Elect
Joshua Weinstock, VP for Internal Affairs
Rinku Skaria, VP for Membership
Perry Tsai, VP for Program Development

The oldest and largest independent association of physicians-in-training in the United States. Committed to improving the lives of medical students.
40M Members
Founded in: 1950

12284 American Medical Technologists
10700 West Higgins Road
Suite 150
Rosemont, IL 60018-3722

847-823-5169
800-275-1268; *Fax:* 847-823-0458
mail@americanmedtech.org;
www.americanmedtech.org
Social Media: Facebook, Twitter, LinkedIn, Youtube

Everett Bloodworth, President
Jeffrey Lavender, Vice President
Heather Herring, Secretary
Jeannette Hobson, Treasurer
Edna Anderson, Executive Councillor

Mission is to manage, promote, expand upon and continuously improve their certification programs for allied health professionals who work in a variety of disciplines and settings, to administer certification examinations in accordance with the highest standards of accreditation, and to provide continuing education, information, advocacy services and other benefits to members.
Founded in: 1939

12285 American Medical Women's Association
1100 E Woodfield Rd.
Suite 350
Schaumburg, IL 60173

847-517-2801
866-564-2483; *Fax:* 847-517-7229
associatedirector@amwa-doc.org;
www.amwa-doc.org
Social Media: Facebook, Twitter, LinkedIn, Flickr

Kimberly Templeton, MD, President
Eliza Lo Chin, MD, MPH, Executive Director
Sharon Batista, MD, Treasurer
Laura McCann, MD, Secretary

An organization of women physicians, medical students and other persons dedicated to serving as the unique voice for women's health and the advancement of women in medicine.
Founded in: 1915

12286 American Music Therapy Association (AMTA)
8455 Colesville Road
Suite 1000
Silver Spring, MD 20910-3392

301-589-3300; *Fax:* 301-589-5175
info@musictherapy.org;
www.musictherapy.org
Social Media: Facebook, Twitter, YouTube

Andrea Farbman, Executive Director
Mary Ellen Wylei, AMTA President

AMTA's purpose is the progressive development of the therapeutic use of music in rehabilitation, special education, and community settings. AMTA is committed to the advancement of education, training, professional standards, credentials, and research in support of the music therapy profession.
3800 Members
Founded in: 1998

12287 **American Nephrology Nurses Association**
East Holly Avenue
Box 56
Pitman, NJ 08071-0056
856-256-2320; *Fax:* 856-589-7463
anna@annanurse.org; www.annanurse.org
Social Media: Facebook, Twitter, RSS
Cindy A. Richards, BSN RN CNN, President
Sheila J. Doss-McQuitty, President-Elect
Sharon M. Longton, Immediate Past President
Susan Cary, MN APRN NP CNN, Treasurer
Lynda K. Ball, MSN RN CNN, Secretary
Mission is to promote excellence by advancing nephrology nursing practice and positively influence outcomes for individuals with kidney disease.
Founded in: 1969

12288 **American Nurses Association**
8515 Georgia Avenue
Suite 400
Silver Spring, MD 20910-3492
800-274-4ANA; *Fax:* 301-628-5001
anf@ana.org; www.nursingworld.org
Social Media: Facebook, Twitter, LinkedIn, YouTube
Pamela F. Cipriano, PhD, RN, President
Cindy R. Balkstra, MS, RN, Vice President
Gingy Harshey-Meade, MSN, Treasurer
Patricia Travis, PhD, RN, CCRP, Secretary
Andrea C. Gregg, PhD, RN, Director at Large
Advances the nursing profession by fostering high standards of nursing practice, promoting the rights of nurses in the workplace, projecting a positive and realistic view of nursing, and by lobbying the Congress and regulatory agencies on health care issues affecting nurses and the public.

12289 **American Occupational Therapy Association**
4720 Montgomery Lane
Ste 200
Bethesda, MD 20814-3449
301-652-6611
800-729-2682; *Fax:* 301-652-7711;
www.aota.org
Social Media: Facebook, Twitter, LinkedIn, RSS
Florence Clark, President
Ginny Stoffel, Vice President
Paul A. Fontana, Secretary
Saburi Imara, Treasurer
Representing the interests and concerns of occupational therapy practitioners and students of occupational therapy and to improve the quality of occupational therapy services.
42M Members
Founded in: 1917

12290 **American Optometric Association**
243 N Lindbergh Blvd
Flr. 1
St Louis, MO 63141-7881
314-991-4100
800-365-2219; *Fax:* 314-991-4101;
www.aoa.org
Social Media: Facebook, Twitter, LinkedIn, RSS, Youtube
Mitchell T. Munson, O.D, President
Steven A. Loomis, O.D., Vice President
Andrea P. Thau, O.D., Secretary/ Treasurer
National organization of optometrists, evaluates ophthalmic products and sponsors continuing education programs.
36M Members
Founded in: 1898

12291 **American Optometric Student Association**
243 N Lindbergh Blvd
Suite 311
St Louis, MO 63141-7881
314-983-4231
rfoster@theaosa.org; www.theaosa.org/
Robert Foster, Executive Director
Alan Wegener, Vice President
Vicky Wong, Secretary
Elizabeth Turnage, Treasurer
Committed to promoting the optometric profession, enhancing the education and welfare of optometry students, as well as enhancing the vision and ocular health of the public.
6M Members

12292 **American Orthopaedic Foot & Ankle Society**
9400 West Higgins Road
Suite 220
Rosemont, IL 60018-4263
847-698-4654
800-235-4855; *Fax:* 847-823-8125;
www.aofas.org
Social Media: Facebook, Twitter, LinkedIn
Mark E. Easley, MD, President
Jeffrey E. Johnson, MD, President-Elect
ThomasH. Lee, MD, Vice President
J. Chris Coetzee, MD, Treasurer
Bruce J. Sangeorzan, MD, Immediate Past President
Mission is to promote quality, ethical and cost effective patient care through education, research and training of orthopaedic surgeons and other health care providers, create public awareness for the prevention and treatment of foot and ankle disorders, provide leadership, and serve as a resource for government, industry and the national and international health care community.
35000 Members
Founded in: 1969

12293 **American Orthopaedic Foot and Ankle Society**
9400 West Higgins Road
Suite 220
Rosemont, IL 60018-4975
847-698-4654
800-235-4855; *Fax:* 847-692-3315
aofasinfo@aofas.org; www.aofas.org/
Social Media: Facebook, Twitter, LinkedIn
Mark E. Easley, MD, President
Jeffrey E. Johnson, MD, President-Elect
ThomasH. Lee, MD, Vice President
J. Chris Coetzee, MD, Treasurer
Bruce J. Sangeorzan, MD, Immediate Past President
Specialty society for orthopedic surgeons with training and interest in the prevention and treatment of foot and ankle conditions.
Founded in: 1969

12294 **American Orthopaedic Society for Sports Medicine**
9400 W. Higgins Road
Suite 300
Rosemont, IL 60018
847-292-4900
877-321-3500; *Fax:* 847-292-4905;
www.sportsmed.org
Social Media: Facebook, Twitter
Irvin E. Bomberger, Executive Director
Camille Petrick, Managing Director
Heather Hodge, Education Director
Kevin M. Boyer, MPH, Director of Research
Lisa Weisenberger, Director of Communications
Promotes sports medicine education, research, communication, and fellowship and includes national and international orthopaedic sports medicine leaders.

12295 **American Orthopsychiatric Association**
C/o Clemson University, IFNL
225 S. Pleasantburg Dr.
Suite B-11
Greenville, SC 29607
864-250-4622; *Fax:* 864-250-4633
orthocontact@aoatoday.com;
www.bhjustice.org
Andres J. Pumariega, President
Donald Wertlieb, President-Elect
Jan L. Culbertson, Secretary
William Reay, Treasurer
Robin Kimbrough-Melton, Executive Officer
Provides a common ground for collaborative study, research, and knowledge exchange among individuals from a variety of disciplines engaged in preventive, treatment, and advocacy approaches to mental health.
Founded in: 1923

12296 **American Orthotic & Prosthetic Association**
330 John Carlyle Street
Suite 200
Alexandria, VA 22314
571-431-0876; *Fax:* 571-431-0899
info@aopanet.org; www.aopanet.org
Social Media: Facebook, Twitter, LinkedIn, Youtube
Michael Oros, President
Chris Nolan, Vice President
Jim Weber, President Elect
Jeff Collins, Treasurer
Tom Fise, Executive Director
A national trade association committed to providing high quality, unprecedented business services and products to O&P professionals.
Founded in: 1917

12297 **American Osteopathic Association**
142 E Ontario St
Chicago, IL 60611-2864
312-202-8000
800-621-1773; *Fax:* 312-202-8200
info@osteotech.org; www.osteopathic.org
Social Media: Facebook, Twitter, LinkedIn, Youtube, Pinterest
John W. Becher, DO, President
Adrienne White-Faines, MPA, CEO
Geraldine O'Shea, DO, Second Vice President
Frank M. Tursi, DO, Third Vice President
Boyd R. Buser, DO, President-Elect
Promotes public health, encourages scientific research, and is the accrediting agency for all osteopathic medical schools and health care facilities.
52M Members
Founded in: 1897

12298 **American Osteopathic College of Dermatology**
2902 North Baltimore Street
P.O. Box 7525
Kirksville, MI 63501
660-665-2184
800-449-2623; *Fax:* 660-627-2623;
www.aocd.org
Social Media: Facebook, Twitter, Tumblr
Marsha Wise, Executive Director
John Grogan, Resident Coordinator
Shelley Wood, Grants Coordinator
Alpesh Desai, President
Specialty college that promotes the practice of osteopathic dermatology.
Founded in: 1958

12299 American Pain Society
8735 W. Higgins Road
Suite 300
Chicago, IL 60631

847-375-4715; *Fax:* 847-375-6479; *Fax:* 732-460-7318
info@americanpainsociety.org; www.americanpainsociety.org/
Social Media: Facebook, Twitter, LinkedIn, Youtube

Roger Fillingim, PhD, President
Catherine H Underwood, MBA CAE, Executive Director
David A. Williams, PhD, Treasurer
Kathleen Sluka, PT PhD, Secretary
Gregory W Terman, MD PhD, President-Elect

The American Pain Society is a multidisciplinary community that brings together a diverse group of scientists, clinicians and other professionals to increase the knowledge of pain and transform public policy and clinical practice to reduce pain-related suffering.
Founded in: 1977

12300 American Pediatric Society/Society for Pediatric Research
3400 Research Forest Drive
Suite B7
The Woodlands, TX 77381

281-419-0052; *Fax:* 281-419-0082
info@aps-spr.org; www.aps-spr.org
Social Media: Facebook, Twitter, Instagram

Eileen G. Fenton, Executive Director
Belinda Thomas, PAS Education Program Director
Stephanie Dean, Managing Editor, Pediatric Research
Antonio Moreno, Information Technology Director
Belinda Thomas, Information Services Manager

Coordinates meetings, research and further education of health professionals. Features policies, publications and details of research programs.
Founded in: 1888

12301 American Pediatric Surgical Association
One Parkview Plaza
Suite 800
Oakbrook Terrace, IL 60181

847-686-2237; *Fax:* 847-686-2253
eapsa@eapsa.org; www.eapsa.org/
Social Media: Twitter

Mary Fallat, President
Diana Farmer, President-Elect
Michael D. Klein, Immediate Past President
Daniel Von Allmen, Treasurer
John H.T. Waldhausen, Secretary

Pediatric surgical care of patients and their families.

12302 American Pharmacists Association (APhA)
2215 Constitution Avenue NW
Suite 400
Washington, DC 20037-2985

202-628-4410
800-237-2742; *Fax:* 202-783-2351;
www.pharmacist.com
Social Media: Facebook, Twitter, LinkedIn, RSS, Youtube

Stacie Maass, SVP, Pharmacy Practice
Thomas E. Menighan, BSPharm, MBA, Chief Executive Officer
Jule Miller, SVP, Human Resources
Joseph J. Janela, Chief Financial Officer
Elizabeth K. Keyes, Chief Operating Officer

The American Pharmacists Association (APhA) is an organization whose members are recognized in society as essential in all patient care settings for optimal medication use that improves health, wellness, and quality of life. Through information, education, and advocacy, APhA empowers its members to improve medication use and advance patient care.
60000 Members
Founded in: 1852

12303 American Physical Therapy Association
1111 North Fairfax Street
Alexandria, VA 22314-1488

703-683-6748
800-999-2782; *Fax:* 703-684-7343
memberservices@apta.org; www.apta.org
Social Media: Facebook, Twitter, LinkedIn, Youtube

Sharon L. Dunn, PT, PhD, OCS, President
Lisa K. Saladin, Vice President
J. Michael Bowers, CEO
Rob Batarla, MBA, CPA, CAE, EVP, Financial and Business Affairs
Elmer Platz, PT, Treasurer

The principal membership organization representing and promoting the profession of physical therapy, is to furhter the profession's role in the prevention, diagnosis, and treatment of movement dysfunctions and the enhancement of the physical health and functional abilities of members of the public.
74000 Members

12304 American Physiological Society
9650 Rockville Pike
Bethesda, MD 20814-3991

301-634-7164; *Fax:* 301-634-7241
webmaster@the-aps.org; www.the-aps.org
Social Media: Facebook, Twitter, LinkedIn, YouTube

Patricia Molina, M.D., Ph.D., President
David M. PollockPh.D, Past President
Jane Reckelhoff, Ph.D., President Elect
Martin Frank, PhD, Executive Director
Robert Price, Director of Finance

A nonprofit devoted to fostering education scientific research and dissemination of information in the physiological sciences. A member of the Federation of American Societies for Experimental Biology (FASEB) a coalition of 18 independent societies that plays an active role in lobbying for the interests of biomedical scientists.
10,50 Members
Founded in: 1887

12305 American Podiatric Medical Association
9312 Old Georgetown Road
Bethesda, MD 20814-1621

301-581-9200; *Fax:* 301-530-2752
mskulick@apma.org; www.apma.org
Social Media: Facebook, Twitter, LinkedIn, YouTube

Matthew G. Garoufalis, DPM, President
Phillip E. Ward, DPM, Vice President
R. Daniel Davis, DPM, Treasurer
Glenn B. Gastwirth, DPM, Secretary

An association of podiatrists providing services and information on foot problems and foot health.
11000 Members
Founded in: 1912

12306 American Porphyria Foundation
4900 Woodway
Suite 780
Houston, TX 77056-1837

713-266-9617
866-APF-3635; *Fax:* 713-840-9552
porphyrus@porphyriafoundation.com; www.porphyriafoundation.com

James V. Young, Chairman, Board of Trustee
Desiree H. Lyon, Executive Director
Dr. William McCutchen, Board Member
Warren Hudson, Board Member
Andrew Turell, Board Member

Dedicated to improving the health and well-being of individuals andfamilies affected by Porphyria. Also advocates for public, private, and government agencies interested in funding research and educational programs.
Founded in: 1982

12307 American Psychiatric Association
1000 Wilson Boulevard
Suite 1825
Arlington, VA 22209-3901

703-907-7300
888-357-7924; *Fax:* 703-907-1085
apa@psych.org; www.psychiatry.org
Social Media: Facebook, Twitter, LinkedIn

Saul M. Levin, M.D., M.P.A., CEO, Medical Director
Maria A. Oquendo, President

Association for manufacturers, suppliers, distributors, publishers, state/federal agencies and psychiatric facilities.
Founded in: 1844

12308 American Psychological Association
750 First St. NE
Washington, DC 20002-4242

202-336-5500
800-374-2721; *Fax:* 202-336-5518;
www.apa.org
Social Media: Facebook, Twitter, LinkedIn, YouTube, Google+, RSS

Barry S. Anton, PhD, President
Norman B. Anderson, PhD, Chief Executive Officer, EVP
Susan McDaniel, PhD, President Elect
Nadine J. Kaslow, PhD, Past President
Bonnie Markham, PhD, PsyD, Treasurer

The largest scientific and professional organization representing psychology in the United States and the largest association of psychologists in the world, dedicated to advancing psychology as a science and as a means of promoting health, education, and human welfare.
12250 Members
Founded in: 1892

12309 American Public Health Association
800 I Street, NW
Washington, DC 20001

202-777-2742; *Fax:* 202-777-2534;
www.apha.org
Social Media: Facebook, Twitter

Pamela Aaltonen, PhD, RN, Chair
Jose Ramon Fernandez-Pena, Vice Chair
Joyce R. Gaufin, BS, Immediate Past President
Shiriki Kumanyika, PhD, MPH, President
Richard J. Cohen, PhD, FACHE, Treasurer

Professional association dedicated to improving the public's healththrough education.
24 Members

12310 American Public Human Services Association
1133 19th Street, NW
Suite 400
Washington, DC 20036-3623

202-682-0100; *Fax:* 202-289-6555;
www.aphsa.org
Social Media: Facebook, Twitter, LinkedIn

Reggie Bicha, President
Tracy Wareing, Executive Director
Nicole Lobban, Human Resources Director

Raymond Washington III, Director of Finance
Anita Light, Senior Deputy Executive Director
Pursues excellence in health and human services by supporting state and local agencies, informing policymakers, and working wtih our partners to drive innovative, integrated and efficient solutions in policy and practice.
Founded in: 1930

12311 American Rhinologic Society
PO Box 495
Warwick, NY 10990
845-988-1631; *Fax:* 845-986-1527;
www.american-rhinologic.org/
Roy Casiano, MD, President
Joseph Jacobs, MD, Executive Vice President
Peter Hwang, MD, President-elect
John DelGaudio, MD, 1st Vice President
Richard Orlandi, MD, 2nd Vice President
Physician organization whose focus is upon the medical and surgicaltreatment of patients with diseases of the nose and paranasal sinuses.

12312 American School Health Association
7918 Jones Branch Drive
Suite 300
McLean, VA 22102
703-506-7675; *Fax:* 703-503-3266
info@ashaweb.org; www.ashaweb.org
Social Media: Facebook, Twitter, LinkedIn, YouTube
Linda Morse, RN, MA, CHES, President
Ty Oehrtman, VP
Sharon Murray, MHSE, FASHA, Treasurer
Sharon Miller, Secretary
Sandy Klarenbeek, Chair of Advocacy
Concerned with all health factors that are necessary for students to be ready to learn, including optimum nutrition, physical fitness, emotional well-being, and a safe and clean environment.
2000 Members
Founded in: 1927

12313 American Sleep Apnea Association
1717 Pennsylvania Avenue, NW
Suite 1025
Washington, DC 20006
888-293-3650; *Fax:* 888-293-3650;
www.sleepapnea.org/
Social Media: Facebook, Twitter, Google+, YouTube, Vimeo
Will Headapohl, Chair
Adam Amdur, COO
Addison Closson, Treasurer
Nancy Rothstein, Secretary
Tracy R. Nasca, Executive Director
A nonprofit organization that promotes education, awareness and research into sleep apnea.
Founded in: 1990

12314 American Society for Aesthetic Plastic Surgery
36 W 44th Street
New York, NY 10036
212-921-0500; *Fax:* 212-921-0011
media@surgery.org; www.surgery.org
Social Media: Facebook, Twitter, LinkedIn
Jack Fisher, MD, President
James C. Grotting, MD, Vice President
Daniel C. Mills, II, MD, Treasurer
Clyde H. Ishii, MD, Secretary
Organization of plastic surgeons certified by the American Board of Plastic Surgery who specialize in cosmetic surgery of the face and body.

12315 American Society for Cell Biology
8120 Woodmont Avenue
Suite 750
Bethesda, MD 20814-2762
301-347-9300; *Fax:* 301-347-9310
ascbinfo@ascb.org; www.ascb.org
Social Media: Facebook, Twitter, LinkedIn, Vimeo
Shirley M. Tilghman, President
Stefano Bertuzzi, PhD, Executive Director
Thea Clarke, Director of Comm. & Education
John Fleischman, Senior Science Writer
Christina Szalinski, Science Writer/Program Coordinator
A nonprofit membership organization of biologists studying the cell, the fundamental unit of life. Membership is open to all research scientists, students, educators, and technicians who have education or research experience in cell biology or an allied field.
10M Members
Founded in: 1960

12316 American Society for Dermatologic Surgery
5550 Meadowbrook Drive
Suite 120
Rolling Meadows, IL 60008
847-956-0900; *Fax:* 847-956-0999
info@asds.net; www.asds.net
Social Media: Facebook, Twitter, LinkedIn, YouTube
Naomi Lawrence, MD, President
Lisa M. Donofrio, MD, Vice President
Katherine J. Duerdoth, CAE, Executive Director
Thomas Rohrer, MD, President Elect
Mathew M. Avram, MD, JD, Treasurer
To promote optimal quality care for patients as well as support and develop investigative knowledge in the field of dermatologic surgery.
5,800 Members
Founded in: 1973

12317 American Society for Histocompatability and Immunogenetics
1120 Route 73
Suite 200
Mt. Laurel, NJ 08054
856-638-0428; *Fax:* 856-439-0525
info@ashi-hla.org; www.ashi-hla.org
Social Media: Facebook, Twitter, LinkedIn
Kathy Miranda, Executive Director
Deb Dupnik, Assistant Executive Director
Melissa Weeks, Accreditation Manager
Caitlin O'Brien, Meeting Manager
Cecilia Blair, Director of Operations
Dedicated to advancing the practice and science of inherited aspects of immunity, and its impact on the quality of human life.
Founded in: 1972

12318 American Society for Laser Medicine and Surgery, Inc.
2100 Stewart Avenue
Suite 240
Wausau, WI 54401-1709
715-845-9283
877-258-6028; *Fax:* 715-848-2493
information@aslms.org; www.aslms.org
Social Media: Facebook, Twitter, LinkedIn, Google+, YouTube, Pinterest
Dianne Dalsky, Executive Director
Corri Marschall, Conference Specialist
Paula Deffner, Accounting Specialist
Diane Dodds, Member and Customer Service
Andrea Alstad, Marketing & Communications Mgr.
Promotes excellence in patient care by advancing biomedical application of lasers and other related technologies worldwide.
Founded in: 1980

12319 American Society for Microbiology
1752 N Street, N.W.
Washington, DC 20036-2904
202-737-3600; *Fax:* 202-942-9341
service@asmusa.org; www.asm.org
Social Media: Facebook, Twitter, LinkedIn, Instagram, Youtube
Jeffery Miller, President
Joseph M. Campos, Secretary
The world's largest scientific society of individuals interested in the microbiological sciences.
39,00 Members

12320 American Society for Nutrition
9650 Rockville Pike
Bethesda, MD 20814
301-634-7050; *Fax:* 301-634-7894;
www.nutrition.org
Social Media: Facebook, LinkedIn, Youtube, RSS
Patrick J. Stover, PhD, President
Marian Neuhouser, PhD, RD, Vice-President
Simin Nikbin Meydani, Past President
Barbara Lyle, PhD, Treasurer
Susan Percival, PhD, Secretary
A non-profit organization dedicated to bringing together the world's top researchers, clinical nutritionists and industry to advance our knowledge and application of nutrition for the sake of humans and animals.
Founded in: 1928

12321 American Society for Pharmacology and Experimental Therapeutics
9650 Rockville Pike
Bethesda, MD 20814-3995
301-634-7060; *Fax:* 301-634-7061
info@aspet.org; www.aspet.org
Social Media: Facebook, Twitter, LinkedIn, Flickr
Judith A. Siuciak, Ph.D., Executive Director
Matthew Hilliker, Chief Financial Officer
Suzie Thompson, Director of Marketing
Richard Dodenhoff, Director of Journals
Cecilia Fox, Meetings and Admin. Coordinator
Members research efforts help develop new medicines and therapeutic agents to fight existing and emerging diseases.
5,000 Members
Founded in: 1909

12322 American Society for Surgery of the Hand
822 W. Washington Boulevard
Suite 600
Chicago, IL 60607
312-880-1900; *Fax:* 847-384-1435
info@assh.org; www.assh.org
Social Media: Facebook, Twitter, LinkedIn
Mark C. Anderson, FASAE, CAE, EVP, CEO
Pamela Schroeder, CAE, Deputy EVP
Angie Legaspi, CMP, VP, Professional Development
Bill Chandler, Director of Finance
Tara Spiess, Director of Publishing, Marketing
The oldest medical specialty society in the United States devoted entirely to continuing medical education related to hand surgery.
3,500 Members
Founded in: 1946

12323 **American Society for Therapeutic Radiology And Oncology**
8280 Willow Oaks Corporate Drive
Suite 500
Fairfax, VA 22031

703-502-1550
800-962-7876; *Fax:* 703-502-7852
meetings@astro.org; www.astro.org
Social Media: Facebook, Twitter, LinkedIn, YouTube

Bruce D. Minsky, MD, FASTRO, Chairman
David C. Beyer, MD, FASTRO, President
Jeff M. Michalski, Secretary/Treasurer
Brian Kavanagh, President-elect
Bruce G. Haffty, MD, FASTRO, Immediate Past Chair

Provides members with the continuing medical education, health policy analysis, patient information resources and advocacy that they need to succeed in today's ever-changing health care delivery system.
10M Members
Founded in: 1958

12324 **American Society of Addiction Medicine**
4601 North Park Ave.
Upper Arcade, Suite 101
Chevy Chase, MD 20815-4520

301-656-3920; *Fax:* 301-656-3815
email@asam.org; www.asam.org
Social Media: Facebook, Twitter, LinkedIn

Penny S. Mills, Executive Vice President
Carolyn C. Lanham, Chief Operating Officer

ASAM represents professionals in the addiction field. It promotes research and prevention, education for physicians and the public and improving access to, and quality of, treatment.
3600+ Members
Founded in: 1954

12325 **American Society of Anesthesiologists**
1061 American Lane
Schaumburg, IL 60173-4973

847-825-5586; *Fax:* 847-825-1692
info@asahq.org; www.asahq.org
Social Media: Facebook, Twitter, LinkedIn, YouTube

J.P. Abenstein, President
Daniel J. Cole, MD, President Elect
Jane C. K. Fitch, M.D., Immediate Past President
Jeffrey Plagenhoef, M.D., First Vice President
James D. Grant, MD, Treasurer

An educational, research and scientific association of physicians organized to raise and maintain the standards of the medical practice of anesthesiology and improve the care of the patient.
39M Members
Founded in: 1905
Mailing list available for rent

12326 **American Society of Angiology**
708 Glen Cove Ave
Glen Head, NY 11545

516-671-1975; *Fax:* 516-759-5524
anngailius@amsocang.org;
www.amsocang.org/

David K Jackson, MD, President
Ann Gailius, Director, Membership

Striving to incorporate a variety of disciplines to encourage education and interaction in our common fields of endeavor.

12327 **American Society of Bariatric Physicians**
2821 S Parker Rd
Suite 625
Aurora, CO 80014-2735

303-770-2526
877-266-6834; *Fax:* 303-779-4834
info@asbp.org; www.asbp.org
Social Media: Facebook, Twitter, LinkedIn, Youtube, RSS

David Bryman, D.O., F.A.S.B., Chairman
Eric C. Westman, M.D., M.H.S., President
Wendy Scinta, M.D., M.S., Vice President
Laurie Traetow, CAE, CPA, Executive Director
Heidi Gordon, Director of Marketing

ASBP is a nonprofit international professional medical association headquartered in Aurora, Colorado. The ASBP was awarded a seat in the House of Delegates of American Medical Association. The American Society of Bariatric Physicians has members worldwide.
Founded in: 1950

12328 **American Society of Cataract & Refractive Surgery**
4000 Legato Rd
Suite 700
Fairfax, VA 22033-4055

703-591-2220
800-451-1339; *Fax:* 703-591-0614
ascrs@ascrs.org; www.ascrs.org
Social Media: Facebook, Twitter, YouTube, Flickr

Robert J. Cionni, MD, President
Kerry D. Solomon, MD, Vice President/President Elect
Richard A. Lewis, MD, Immediate Past President
Bonnie An Henderson, MD, Treasurer
Thomas W. Samuelson, MD, Secretary

The mission of the American Society of Cataract and Refractive Surgery is to advance the art and science of ophthalmic surgety and the knowledge and skills of ophthalmic surgeons. It does so by providing clinical and practice management education and by working with patients, government, and the medical community to promote the delivery of quality eye care.
9,000 Members
Founded in: 1974

12329 **American Society of Clinical Oncology**
2318 Mill Road
Suite 800
Alexandria, VA 22314

571-483-1300; *Fax:* 703-299-1044
abstracts@asco.org; www.asco.org
Social Media: Facebook, Twitter, LinkedIn, Youtube

Julie M. Vose, MD, MBA, FASCO, President
Craig R. Nichols, MD, Treasurer
Daniel F. Hayes, MD, FASCO, President-Elect
Peter Paul Yu, Past-President
Richard L. Schilsky, Chief Medical Officer

Goal is to improve cancer care and prevention. Members include physicians and health-care professionals in all levels of the practice of oncology.
30M Members
Founded in: 1964
Mailing list available for rent

12330 **American Society of Clinical Pathologists**
33 West Monroe Street
Suite 1600
Chicago, IL 60603

312-541-4999; *Fax:* 312-541-4998
info@ascp.org; www.ascp.org
Social Media: Facebook, Twitter, LinkedIn, Youtube

William G. Finn, MD, FASCP, President
William E. Schreiber, MD, FASCP, Vice President
Melissa Perry Upton, MD, FASCP, Secretary
Gregory N. Sossaman, MD, FASCP, Treasurer
David N.B. Lewin, MD, FASCP, President Elect

Mission is to provide excellence in education, certification and advocacy on behalf of patients, pathologists and laboratory professionals across the globe.
100M+ Members

12331 **American Society of Colon and Rectal Surgeons**
85 West Algonquin Road
Suite 550
Arlington Heights, IL 60005

847-290-9184
800-791-0001; *Fax:* 847-290-9203
ascrs@fascrs.org; www.fascrs.org
Social Media: Facebook, Twitter, LinkedIn

Charles Littlejohn, MD, President
Patricia L. Roberts, MD, President-Elect
Terry C. Hicks, MD, Past President
Guy R. Orangio, MD, Vice President
Neil H. Hyman, MD, Treasurer

The premier society for colon and rectal surgeons and other surgeons dedicated to advancing and promoting the science and practice of the treatment of patients with diseases and disorders affecting the colon, rectum and anus.
3,300 Members
Founded in: 1899

12332 **American Society of Cytopathology**
100 West 10th Street
Suite 605
Wilmington, DE 19801-6604

302-543-6583; *Fax:* 302-543-6597
asc@cytopathology.org;
www.cytopathology.org
Social Media: Facebook, Twitter, LinkedIn, YouTube

Michael R. Henry, MD, President
Eva M. Wojcik, MD, MIAC, President Elect
Edmund S. Cibas, MD, Vice President
Daniel F. I. Kurtycz, MD, Treasurer
Elizabeth Jenkins, Executive Director

A professional organization dedicated to the science and study of cells. Membership includes physicians, cytotechnologists and scientists who practice the cytologic method of diagnostic pathology. Committed to education, research, and advocacy on behalf of its membership, with the ultimate goal of improving the standards and quality of patient care.
3,000 Members
Founded in: 1951

12333 **American Society of ExtraCorporeal Technology**
2209 Dickens Road
Richmond, VA 23230-2005

804-565-6363; *Fax:* 804-282-0090
stewart@amsect.org; www.amsect.org
Social Media: Facebook, Twitter, LinkedIn, YouTube

Jeffrey B. Riley MHPE CCT CCP, President
Kenny Shann CCP, President-Elect
Robert C. Groom MS CCP, Treasurer
Susan J. Englert RN CCP CPBMT, Secretary
Stewart Hinckley, Executive Director

Enhancing the quality of extracorporeal (involving heart and lung machines) technology rendered to the public by engaging in the programmatic activities that will further the

knowledge, skills, abilities and general proficiency of practitioners.
2000 Members
Founded in: 1964

12334 American Society of Forensic Odontology
4414 82nd Street
Suite 212
Lubbock, TX 79424
www.asfo.org
Social Media: Facebook, Twitter

Dr. Roger Metcalf, President
Dr. Bruce Schrader, Executive Director
Dr.Jacqueline Reid, Secretary
Dr. Eric Wilson, Treasurer
Dr.David Senn, President Elect

ASFO is one of the largest organizations representing all of those interested in forensic dentistry worldwide. Mission and goal to encourage and stimulate investigation and research in forensic odontology and related disciplines.
Founded in: 1970

12335 American Society of Health-System Pharmacists
7272 Wisconsin Avenue
Bethesda, MD 20814-4861

301-657-3000
866-279-0681; *Fax:* 301-664-8877
custserv@ashp.org
connect.ashp.org
Social Media: Facebook, Twitter, LinkedIn, YouTube, RSS

John A. Armitstead, President
Philip J. Schneider, Treasurer
Lisa M. Gersema, President-Elect
Paul W. Abramowitz, CEO
Christene M. Jolowsky, Immediate Past President

ASHP is a national professional association that represents pharmacists who practice in hospitals, health maintenance organizations, long-term care facilities, home care, and other compnents of health care systems.
30K Members
Founded in: 1936

12336 American Society of Hematology
2021 L Street NW
Suite 900
Washington, DC 20036-3508

202-776-0544; *Fax:* 202-776-0545
ash@hematology.org; www.hematology.org
Social Media: Facebook, Twitter, LinkedIn, Youtube

David A. Williams, MD, President
Charles S. Abrams, MD, President-Elect
Kenneth C. Anderson, MD, Vice President
Stephanie J. Lee, MD, MPH, Secretary
Susan B. Shurin, MD, Treasurer

Mission is to further the understanding, diagnosis, treatment, and prevention of disorders affecting the blood, bone marrow, and the immunologic, hemostatic and vascular systems, by promoting research, clinical care, education, training, and advocacy in hematology.
15,00 Members
Founded in: 1958

12337 American Society of Human Genetics, Inc.
9650 Rockville Pike
Bethesda, MD 20814-3998

301-634-7300
866-HUM-GENE; *Fax:* 301-634-7079
society@ashg.org; www.ashg.org
Social Media: Facebook, Twitter, LinkedIn, YouTube, RSS

Neil J. Risch, PhD, President
Cynthia C. Morton, PhD, Past President
Harry C. Dietz, MD, President-Elect
Geoffrey M. Duyk, MD PhD, Treasurer
Brendan Lee, MD PhD, Secretary

The primary professional membership organization for human genetics worldwide. Members include researchers, academicians, clinicians, laboratory practice professionals, genetic counselors, nurses and others involved in or with special interest in human genetics.
8000 Members
Founded in: 1948

12338 American Society of Nephrology
1510 H Street, NW
Suite 800
Washington, DC 20005

202-640-4660; *Fax:* 202-637-9793
email@asn-online.org; www.asn-online.org
Social Media: Facebook, Twitter, LinkedIn, YouTube, Google+, Flickr, RSS

Jonathan Himmelfarb, MD, FASN, President
Sharon M. Moe, MD, FASN, Past President
Raymond C. Harris, MD, FASN, President-Elect
John R. Sedor, MD, FASN, Secretary-Treasurer
Tod Ibrahim, Executive Director

Leads the fight against kidney disease by educating health professionals, sharing new knowledge, advancing research, and advocating the highest quality care for patients.

12339 American Society of Neuroradiology
800 Enterprise Dr.
Suite 205
Oak Brook, IL 60523

630-574-0220; *Fax:* 630-574-0661
ltannehill@asnr.org; www.asnr.org
Social Media: RSS

Laurie A. Loevner, MD, President
Howard A. Rowley, MD, President-Elect
Joshua A. Hirsch, MD, Treasurer
Tina Y. Poussaint, MD, Secretary
James B. Gantenberg, FACHE, Executive Director

Active members must devote approximately one half or more of their professional practice to nueroradiology. Publishes a monthly journal and holds an annual meeting.
3000 Members
Founded in: 1962

12340 American Society of Ophthalmic Administrators
4000 Legato Road
Suite 700
Fairfax, VA 22033

703-788-5777
800-451-1339; *Fax:* 703-547-8827
asoa@asoa.org; www.asoa.org
Social Media: Facebook, Twitter

John S. Bell, MBA, COE, CMPE, President
William T. Koch, COE, COA, CPC, Vice President
Daniel Chambers, MBA, COE, President-Elect
Sondra Soffman, COE, CPC, Immediate Past President
Laureen Rowland, CAE, Executive Director

The premier organization for the business side of the ophalmic practice.
Founded in: 1986

12341 American Society of Plastic Surgeons
444 E Algonquin Road
Arlington Heights, IL 60005

847-228-9900
888-475-2784; *Fax:* 847-228-9131
webmaster@plasticsurgery.org;
www.plasticsurgery.org
Social Media: Facebook, Twitter, YouTube, Google+, Instagram, P

Scot Bradley Glasberg, MD, President
Michael D. Costelloe, JD, Executive Vice President
Keith M. Hume, Staff Vice President
Carol L. Lazier, Staff Vice President
Mark Espinosa, Staff Vice President

Promotes the specialty of plastic surgery and supports the highest quality patient care, professionalism and ethical standards through our role as patient and physician advocates.
Founded in: 1931

12342 American Speech-Language-Hearing Association
2200 Research Boulevard
Rockville, MD 20850-3289

301-897-5700
800-638-8255; *Fax:* 301-296-8580
actioncenter@asha.org; www.asha.org
Social Media: Facebook, Twitter, LinkedIn, YouTube, Instagram, Pinterest

Patricia A. Prelock, PhD, CCC-SLP, President
Donna Fisher Smiley, PhD, CCC-A, Vice President for Audiology
Howard Goldstein, PhD, CCC-SL, Vice President for Science
Carolyn W. Higdon, EdD, CCC-SLP, Vice President for Finance
Barbara J. Moore, EDD, CCC-SLP, Vice President for Planning

Represents the interests of medical specialists in speech, language, and hearing science and advocates for people with communication-related disorders.
Founded in: 1925

12343 American Stroke Association (ASA)
7272 Greenville Ave
Dallas, TX 75231-5129

214-706-1556
888-478-7653; *Fax:* 214-570-5930;
www.strokeassociation.org
Social Media: Facebook, Twitter, YouTube, RSS

Lee Schwamm, Chairman

The American Stroke Association (ASA) is the division of the American Heart Association that's solely focused on reducing disability and death from stroke through research, education, fundraising and advocacy. The ASA offers a wide array of programs, products and services, from patient education materials to scientific statements.

12344 American Tinnitus Association
522 SW Fifth Avenue
Suite 825
Portland, OR 97204-2143

503-248-9985
800-634-8978; *Fax:* 503-248-0024
tinnitus@ata.org; www.ata.org/
Social Media: Facebook, Twitter, YouTube

Melanie F. West, Chair
Scott C. Mitchell, J.D., C.P.A., Vice Chair
Gary P. Reul, Ed.D., Treasurer
David M. Sykes, Secretary
Paul F. Morris, CFRE, Development Director

The American Tinnitus Association (ATA) exists to cure tinnitus through the development of resources that advance tinnitus research. ATA board and staff work with researchers, tinnitus sufferers, donors, legislators and other concerned individuals to support vital tinnitus research.
Founded in: 1971

12345 **American Urological Association**
1000 Corporate Boulevard
Linthicum, MD 21090-2260

410-689-3700
866-746-4282; *Fax:* 410-689-3800
aua@AUAnet.org; www.auanet.org
Social Media: Facebook, Twitter, LinkedIn, YouTube

William F. Gee, MD, FACS, President
Richard K. Babayan, MD, President-Elect
William W. Bohnert, MD, FACS, Immediate Past President
Manoj Monga, MD, FACS, Secretary
Steven M. Schlossberg, MD, MBA, Treasurer

The premier professional association for the advancement or urologic patient care, and works to ensure that its members are current on the latest research and practices in urology.

12346 **Arthroscopy Association of North America**
9400 W. Higgins Road
Suite 200
Rosemont, IL 60018

847-292-2262; *Fax:* 847-292-2268
info@aana.org; www.aana.org

Jeffrey S. Abrams, MD, President
John C. Richmond, MD, First Vice-President
Robert E. Hunter, MD, Second Vice-President
Louis F. McIntyre, MD, Treasurer
Larry D. Field, MD, Secretary

Goal is to promote, encourage, support and foster through continuing medical education functions, the development and dissemination of knowledge in the discipline of arthroscopic surgery.

12347 **Association for Gerontology in Higher Education**
1220 L Street NW
Suite 901
Washington, DC 20005-4018

202-289-9806; *Fax:* 202-289-9824
aghe@aghe.org; www.aghe.org
Social Media: Facebook, Twitter, LinkedIn, YouTube, Google+

Donna L. Wagner, President
Christine A. Fruhauf, Treasurer
Lydia Manning, Secretary
Nina M. Silverstein, President-Elect
M Angela Baker, Director

A membership organization devoted primarily to gerontological education, the Association for Gerontology in Higher Education (AGHE) strives to develop and sponsor education and training initiatives and to involve students, educators, researchers, and officials from across the country in providing resources for older adults and for those who serve them.
Founded in: 1974

12348 **Association for Healthcare Documentation Integrity**
4120 Dale Road
Suite J8-233
Modesto, CA 95356

209-527-9620
800-982-2182; *Fax:* 209-527-9633
ahdi@ahdionline.org; www.ahdionline.org
Social Media: Facebook, Twitter, LinkedIn, Pinterest

Jay Vance, President
Sheila Guston, CHDS, AHDI-F, President-Elect
Sheryl Williams, CHDS, AHDI-F, Treasurer
Diane Warth, CHDS, RHIT, CPC, Secretary
Susan Dooley, Immediate Past President

AHDI works tirelessly to give thousands of medical transcriptionists a voice before legislative and regulatory agencies and to ensure MTs are recognized for their contributions to patient safety and risk management.
7000 Members
Founded in: 1978

12349 **Association for Medical Imaging Management**
490B Boston Post Rd
Suite 200
Sudbury, MA 01776-3367

978-443-7591
800-334-2472; *Fax:* 978-443-8046
memberservices@ahraonline.org; www.ahraonline.org
Social Media: Facebook, Twitter, LinkedIn, YouTube

Ernie Cerdena, CRA, FAHRA, President
Chris Tomlinson, CRA, FAHRA, Finance Director
Edward J Cronin, Jr., Chief Executive Officer
Kerri Hart-Morris, Associate Editor
Jason Newmark, CRA, FAHRA, President Elect

Professional association of radiology administrators from the US, Canada and several other countries. AHRA is a resource and catalyst for the development of professional leaders in imaging sciences and other health care disciplines.
5,000 Members
Founded in: 1973

12350 **Association for Professionals in Infection Control and Epidemiology, Inc.**
1275 K St NW
Suite 1000
Washington, DC 20005-4006

202-789-1890; *Fax:* 202-789-1899
info@apic.org; www.apic.org
Social Media: Facebook, Twitter, LinkedIn, Youtube

Mary Lou Manning, President
Marc Oliver Wright, MT, MS, Treasurer
Connie Steed, RN, MSN, CIC, Secretary
Susan A. Dolan, RN, MS, CIC, President-Elect
Katrina Crist, MBA, CEO

Mission is to improve health and patient safety by reducing risks of infection. APIC advances its mission through education, research, collaboration, practice guidance, public policy, and credentialing.
15,00 Members
Founded in: 1972

12351 **Association for the Advancement of Medical Instrumentation**
4301 N. Fairfax Drive
Suite 301
Arlington, VA 22203-1633

703-525-4890; *Fax:* 703-276-0793
customerservice@aami.org; www.aami.org
Social Media: Facebook, Twitter, LinkedIn, Youtube

Michael Scholla, PhD, Chair
Mary Logan, JD, CAE, President
Eamonn V. Hoxey, PhD BPharm, Treasurer/Secretary
C. Phillip Cogdill, Chair Elect
Ray Laxton, Immediate Past Chair

Mission is to increase the understanding and beneficial use of medical instrumentation through effective standards, educational programs, and publications.
Founded in: 1967

12352 **Association of Air Medical Services**
909 N. Washington Street
Suite 410
Alexandria, VA 22314-3143

703-836-8732; *Fax:* 703-836-8920
information@aams.org; www.aams.org/
Social Media: RSS

Martin F. Arkus, CMTE, Chair
Dave Evans, EMT-P, CMTE, Vice Chair
Rick Sherlock, President, CEO (ex-officio)
Christopher Hall, BS, FP-C, CMTE, Treasurer
Douglas A. Garretson, Secretary

Voluntary, nonprofit organization, encourages and supports its members in maintaining a standard of performance reflecting safe operations and efficient, high quality patient care. Built on the idea that representation from a variety of medical transport services and businesses can be brought together to share information, collectively resolve problems and provide leadership in the medical transport community.
Founded in: 1980

12353 **Association of American Physicians and Surgeons**
1601 N Tucson Boulevard
Suite 9
Tucson, AZ 85716-3450

800-635-1196; *Fax:* 520-325-4230
aaps@aapsonline.org; www.aapsonline.org
Social Media: Facebook, Twitter

Tom Kendall, Sr., M.D., President, Executive Director
David Stumph

AAPS is a nonpartisan professional association of physicans in all types of practices and specialties across the country.
Founded in: 1943

12354 **Association of Applied Psychophysiology and Biofeedback**
10200 West 44th Avenue
Suite 304
Wheat Ridge, CO 80033-2837

303-422-8436
800-477-8892; *Fax:* 303-422-8894
info@aapb.org; www.aapb.org
Social Media: Facebook, Twitter

Richard Harvey, PhD, President
Thomas Collura, PhD, President-Elect
Stuart C. Donaldson, PhD, Past-President
Fred B. Shaffer, PhD, Treasurer
David Stumph, CAE, AAPB, Executive Director

Goals of the association are to promote a new understanding of biofeedback and advance the methods used in this practice. Mission is to advance the development, dissemination and utilization of knowledge about applied psychophysiology and biofeedback to improve health and the quality of life through research, education and practice.
Founded in: 1969

12355 **Association of Family Medicine Administration**
11400 Tomahawk Creek Parkway
Leawood, KS 66211-2672

800-274-2237; *Fax:* 913-906-6084
cestes@aafp.org; www.afmaonline.org/

Star Andrews, C-TAGME, President
Eileen Morroni, C-TAGME, President-Elect
Debbie Blackburn, C-TAGME, Immediate Past President
Gina Silvey, C-TAGME, Co-Treasurer
Bobbi Kruse, AA, Edu. Comm.-RAD Workshop, Chair

Promotes professionalism in family practice administration. Serves as a network for sharing information and fellowship among members. Provides technical assistance to members, functions as a liaison to related professional organizations.

12356 **Association of Family Medicine Residency Directors**
11400 Tomahawk Creek Parkway
Suite 670
Leawood, KS 66211-2672

913-906-6000
800-274-2237; *Fax:* 913-906-6105
afmrd@aafp.org;
www.afmrd.org/i4a/pages/index.cfm?pageid=1

Michael Mazzone, MD, President
Todd D. Shaffer, MD, MBA,, Immediate Past President
Lisa Maxwell, MD, President Elect
Karen Mitchell, MD, Treasurer
Katy Kirk, MD, MPH, Resident Representative

Inspires and empowers family medicine residency program directors to achieve excellence in family medicine residency training.
410 Members
Founded in: 1990

12357 **Association of Healthcare Internal Auditors**
10200 W 44th Avenue
Suite 304
Wheat Ridge, CO 80033

303-327-7546
888-275-2442; *Fax:* 720-881-6101
info@ahia.org; www.ahia.org
Social Media: LinkedIn, Youtube

Cavell Alexander, Chair
David Richstone, Vice Chair
Bryon Neaman, CPA, CIA, Secretary/Treasurer
Heidi Crosby, CPA, CIA, CHFP, Immediate Past Chair
David Stumph, Executive Director

Promotes cost containment and increased productivity in health care institutions through internal auditing. Serves as a forum for the exchange of experience, ideas, and information among members, provides continuing professional education courses and informs members of developments in health care internal auditing. Offers employment clearinghouse services.
1000 Members
Founded in: 1981

12358 **Association of Otolaryngology Administrators**
2400 Ardmore Boulevard
Suite 302
Pittsburgh, PA 15221

412-243-5156; *Fax:* 412-243-5160;
www.oto-online.org
Social Media: Facebook, LinkedIn

Jo Ann LoForti, President
Jeff Dudley, President-Elect
James Benson, Secretary-Treasurer
Robin L. Wagner, Executive Director

Seeks to promote the concept of professional management in otolaryngology, provide a forum for interaction and exchange of information between otolaryngological managers and present educational programs. Maintains data exchange service for members researching specific topics.
1000 Members
Founded in: 1983

12359 **Association of Pediatric Hematology/ Oncology Nurses**
8735 W. Higgins Rd
Ste 300
Chicago, IL 60631

847-375-4724; *Fax:* 847-375-6478
info@aphon.org; www.aphon.org

Jami Gattuso, MSN RN CPON, President
Dave Bergeson, PhD CAE, Executive Director
Nicole Wallace, Senior Operations Manager
Jennifer Schap, Education Manager
Stephanie Sayen, Marketing Manager

Members are dedicated to promoting optimal nursing care for children, adolescents, and young adults with cancer and blood disorders, and their families. APHON provides the leadership and expertise to pediatric hematology/oncology nurses by defining and promoting the highest standards of practice and care to the pediatric, adolescent, and young adult communities.
3,000 Members
Founded in: 1973

12360 **Association of Perioperative Registered Nurses**
2170 South Parker Rd
Suite 400
Denver, CO 80231-5711

303-755-6300
800-755-2676; *Fax:* 800-847-0045
custserv@aorn.org; www.aorn.org
Social Media: Facebook, Twitter, LinkedIn, Slideshare, Pinterest, Youtube

Renae Battie, MN, RN, CNOR, President
Martha Stratton, President-Elect
Nathalie Walker, MBA, RN, CNOR, Secretary
Stephanie S. Davis, MSHA, RN, CNOR, Treasurer
Callie Craig, VP

A nonprofit membership association that represents the interests of perioperative nurses by providing nursing education, standards, and clinical practice resources.
41,00 Members
Founded in: 1954

12361 **Case Management Society of America**
6301 Ranch Drive
Little Rock, AR 72223

501-225-2229; *Fax:* 501-221-9068
cmsa@cmsa.org; www.cmsa.org
Social Media: Facebook, Twitter, LinkedIn

Kathy Fraser, President
Rebecca Perez, RN, BSN, CCM, Secretary
Catherine Campbell, RN, MSN, MBA, Treasurer
Cheri A Lattimer, RN, BSN, Executive Director
Mary McLaughlin-Davis, President-Elect

The leading memberhsip association providing professional collaboration across the health care continuum to advocate for patients' wellbeing and improved health outcomes.
Founded in: 1990

12362 **Catholic Health Association**
4455 Woodson Road
St Louis, MO 63134-3797

314-427-2500; *Fax:* 314-427-0029
khewitt@chausa.org; www.chausa.org
Social Media: Facebook, Twitter, LinkedIn, YouTube

Carol Keehan, DC, President
Adele Gianino, Director, Meetings & Travel
Ana Hilton, Government Relations Coordinator
Betsy Taylor, Associate Editor, Catholic Health
Betty Crosby, Executive Assistant

Led by dedicated women and men, both religious and lay, who combine advanced technology and innovative treatment with caring tradidtion. As provider, employer, and advocate, Catholic health care is committed to improving the health status of communities and creating quality and compassionate health care that works for everyone, especially the vulnerable.
2000+ Members
ISSN: 0882-1577
Founded in: 1915

12363 **Christopher & Dana Reeve Paralysis Resource Center**
636 Morris Turnpike
Suite 3A
Short Hills, NJ 07078-2608

973-467-8270
800-225-0292; *Fax:* 973-912-9433;
www.christopherreeve.org
Social Media: Facebook, Twitter, LinkedIn, YouTube, Google+, Pinterest, F

John M. Hughes, Chairman
John E. McConnell, Vice Chairman
Peter T. Wilderotter, President and CEO
Susan Howley, Executive Vice President, Research
Maggie Goldberg, Vice President, Policy and Programs

The Christopher & Dana Reeve Paralysis Resource Center (PRC) promotes the health and well-being of people living with paralysis and their families by providing comprehensive information resources and referral services.
Founded in: 2001
Mailing list available for rent

12364 **Clinical Laboratory Management Association**
330 N. Wabash Avenue
Suite 2000
Chicago, IL 60611

312-321-5111; *Fax:* 610-995-9568
info@clma.org; www.clma.org
Social Media: Facebook, Twitter, LinkedIn, YouTube

Patty Eschliman, President
Jane M Hermansen, President Elect
Rodney W Forsman, Treasurer
Paul L. Epner, Past-President
Deborah Wells, Board Member
Founded in: 1976

12365 **Consumer Healthcare Products Association**
1625 Eye Street, NW
Suite 600
Washington, DC 20006-2105

202-429-9260; *Fax:* 202-223-6835
eassey@chpa-info.org; www.chpa.org
Social Media: Twitter, YouTube, Pinterest

Scott Melville, President and CEO
Brian Green, Vice President, Finance, CFO
John F Gay, Vice President, Government Affairs
Barbara A Kochanowski, Ph.D, Vice President, Regulatory Affairs
Theodore L Peterson, Vice President, Corporate Dev

Promotes industry growth through consumer understanding, appreciation, and acceptance of responsible self-care in America's health care system by developing and sustaining a climate that provides consumers with convenient access to safe and effective nonprescription medicines and other self-care products marketed without undue restrictions.
Founded in: 1881

12366 **Cremation Association of North America**
499 Northgate Parkway
Wheeling, IL 60090-2646

312-245-1077; *Fax:* 312-321-4098
info@cremationassociation.org;
www.cremationassociation.org
Social Media: Facebook, Twitter, LinkedIn, Youtube

Sheri Stahl, President
Michael Sheedy, First Vice President
Mitch Rose, Second Vice President
Timothy R. Borden, President-Elect (Treasurer)
Robert M Boetticher, Jr., Past President

Founded in: 1913, the Cremation Association of North America is an international association of over 3,300 members comprised of funeral homes, cemeteries, crematories, consultants and suppliers. CANA members believe that cremation is prepareation for memorialization.

12367 Dental Group Management Association

North Point Dental Group
2525 E Arizona Biltmore Circle
Suite 127
Phoenix, AZ 85016

602-381-8980; *Fax:* 602-381-1093;
www.dgma.org

Vincent Cardillo, President
Jill Nesbtt, Vice President

The DGMA is a national organization which recognizes the importance of professional management in group dental practices. The purpose of the Association is to advance dental group management and practice administration.
200 Members
Founded in: 1951

12368 Digital Phenom

700 Princess Street
Suite 2M
Alexandria, VA 22314

202-393-0000
800-432-3247; *Fax:* 202-737-8406
staff@digitalphenom.com;
www.digitalphenom.com

Atilla Kocsis, President
Ismaila Togola, Sr. Developer - Content Management
James Patterson, Project Management
Siaka Togola, Junior Dev. -Content Management

A non-profit educational foundation with a membership of companies engaged in the manufacture, preparation, compounding or processing of aspirin and aspirin products. AFA serves as a central source of information on the health benefits of aspirin and aspirin products, when used as directed.
Founded in: 1995

12369 Emergency Nurses Association

915 Lee Street
Des Plaines, IL 60016-6569

847-460-4100
800-900-9659; *Fax:* 847-698-9406
membership@ena.org; www.ena.org
Social Media: Facebook, Twitter, Google Plus

JoAnn Lazarus, MSN, RN, CEN, President
Susan M. Hohenhaus, LPD,RN, CE, Executive Director
Matthew F Powers, MS, BSN, RN, M, Secretary/Treasurer
Deena Brecher,MSN, RN, APRN, President-Elect
Founded in: 1968

12370 Federation of American Health Systems

750 9th Street, NW
Suite 600
Washington, DC 20001-4524

202-624-1500; *Fax:* 202-737-6462
info@fah.org; www.fah.org
Social Media: Facebook, Twitter, LinkedIn, RSS

Chip Kahn, President and CEO
Keith Pitts, Vice Chairman
Matthew D. Klein, Treasurer
William F. Carpenter III, Secretary
Michael D. Bromberg, Vice Chair of the Board
Founded in: 1966

12371 Gerontological Society of America

1220 L Street NW
Suite 901
Washington, DC 20005

202-842-1275; *Fax:* 202-842-1150
geron@geron.org; www.geron.org
Social Media: Facebook, Twitter, LinkedIn, YouTube, Google+

Rita Effros, President
Nancy Morrow, President Elect
Rosemary Blieszner, Past President
Suzanne Kunkel, Treasurer
Tamara Baker, Secretary
800+ Members
Founded in: 1945

12372 Health Industry Distributors Association

310 Montgomery Street
Alexandria, VA 22314-1516

703-549-4432; *Fax:* 703-549-6495
rowan@hida.org; www.hida.org

Matthew Rowan, President and CEO
Jennifer Gilbertson, Director, Marketing
Ian Fardy, ExecutiveVice President
Elizabeth Hilla, Sr. Vice President, Education
Linda Rouse O'Neill, Vice President, Government Affairs

The trade association representing medical products distributors. Provides leadership in the healthcare distribution industry.
Founded in: 1902

12373 Health Industry Manufacturers Association

1200 G Street NW
Washington, DC 20005-3814

Fax: 202-783-8750

Established as the Wholesale Surgical Trade Association. Represents manufacturers of health care technology, including medical devices, diagnostic products, and health care information systems.

12374 Healthcare Compliance Packaging Council

2711 Buford Road
#268
Bon Air, VA 23235-2423

804-338-5778; *Fax:* 888-812-4272
pgmayberry@aol.com; www.hcpconline.org
Social Media: Facebook, LinkedIn

Peter G Mayberry, Executive Director
Kathleen Hemming, Staff Consultant

Nonprofit trade association promoting the benefits of unit dose blister and strip packaging — especially its ability to be designed in compliance prompting formats that help people take their medications properly.
Founded in: 1990

12375 Healthcare Convention & Exhibitors Association

1100 Johnson Ferry Rd.
Suite 300
Atlanta, GA 30342-1733

678-298-1183; *Fax:* 404-836-5595
hcea@kellencompany.com; www.hcea.org
Social Media: Facebook, Twitter, LinkedIn

Christine Farmer, President
Kyle Wood, Vice President
Sue Huff, Secretary/Treasurer
Don Schmid, MBA, CME/H, President-Elect
Diane Benson, CTSM, Immediate Past President

Trade association of organizations involved in health care exhibiting or providing services to health care conventions, exhibitions and/or meetings.
600 Members
Founded in: 1930

12376 Healthcare Distribution Management Association

901 North Glebe Road
Suite 1000
Arlington, VA 22203-1853

703-787-0000; *Fax:* 703-812-5282;
www.healthcaredistribution.org
Social Media: Twitter, LinkedIn

Ted Scherr, Chairman and President/CEO
Jon Giacomin, Vice Chairman & CEO
Peri L Fri, Senior Vice President
Patrick M Kelly, Senior Vice President, Government
Karen J Ribler, Executive Vice President

An organization representing all major constituents of healthcare product distribution management.
Founded in: 1876

12377 Healthcare Financial Management Association

3 Westbrook Corporate Center
Suite 600
Westchester, IL 60154-5723

708-531-9600
800-252-4362; *Fax:* 708-531-0032
jfifer@hfma.org; www.hfma.org
Social Media: Facebook, Twitter, LinkedIn, YouTube

Joseph J Fifer, FHFMA, CPA, CEO & President
Edwin P Czopek, FHFMA, CPA, Executive Vice President & CFO
Susan Brenkus, Vice President, Human Resources
Richard L Gundling, FHFMA, CMA, Vice President, Healthcare
Todd Nelson, Vice President, Education

Brings perspective and clarity to the industry's complex issues for the purpose of preparing our members to succeed. Through our programs, publications and partnerships we enhance the capabilities that strengthen not only individual careers, but also the organizations from which our members come.
34000 Members
Founded in: 1946

12378 Healthcare Marketing & Communications Council

1525 Valley Center Parkway
Bethlehem, PA 18017

610-868-8299; *Fax:* 610-868-8387;
www.hmc-council.org

Janis Cohen, President/CEO
Gary J Gyss, Founder

Enhancing the professional development of its members by providing continuing education and career development opportunities. The council also works toward a better understanding of the role of marketing, education, and communications in health care.

12379 Home Medical Equipment and Services Association of New England

515 Kempton St
New Bedford, MA 02740-3852

508-993-0700; *Fax:* 508-993-0797
info@homesne.org; www.homesne.org

Karyn Estrella, Executive Director
Brian Simonds, President
Jim Greatorex, VP
Rebecca Godley, Secretary
Paula Finamore, Treasurer

Works together supporting the common goals and interests of the home medical equipment, re-

spiratory, and rehab/assistive techology and home infusion therapy industry.
15 Members
Founded in: 1988

12380 Infectious Diseases Society of America
1300 Wilson Blvd.
Suite 300
Arlington, VA 22209

703-299-0200; *Fax:* 703-299-0204;
www.idsociety.org
Social Media: Facebook, Twitter, Flickr

Johan S. Bakken, President

The IDSA represents health care professionals specializing in infectious diseases.

12381 Infusion Nurses Society
315 Norwood Park South
Norwood, MA 02062-4694

781-440-9408
800-694-0298; *Fax:* 781-440-9409
ins@ins1.org; www.ins1.org
Social Media: Facebook, Twitter, LinkedIn, Youtube

Cheryl Dumont, PhD, RN, CRNI, President
Mary Alexander, MA, RN, Chief Executive Officer
Christopher Hunt, Executive Vice President
Lisa Bruce, BSN, RN, CRNI, Secretary/Treasurer
Richelle Hamblin, MSN, RN, CRNI, President-Elect

The INS is committed to bringing innovative new resources and opportunities to a wide range of healthcare professionals who are involved with the specialty practice of infusion therapy.
6000 Members
Founded in: 1973

12382 International Anesthesia Research Society
44 Montgomery Street
Suite 1605
San Francisco, CA 94104-4703

415-296-6900; *Fax:* 415-296-6901
info@iars.org; www.iars.org

Alex Evers, MD, Chair
Thomas A Cooper, Executive Director
Davy C H Cheng, MD, Treasurer
Makoto Ozaki, MD, PhD, Secretary
Laura J Kuhar, Education Director
Founded in: 1922

12383 International Association For Healthcare Security & Safety
PO Box 5038
Glendale Heights, IL 60139

630-529-3913
888-353-0990; *Fax:* 630-529-4139
info@iahss.org; www.iahss.org
Social Media: Facebook, Twitter, LinkedIn

David LaRose, CHPA, CPP, President
Dana Frentz,CHPA, Vice-President/Treasurer
Ben Scaglione, CHPA, CPP, Vice-President/Secretary
Jeff A. Young, CHPA, CPP, President-Elect
Colleen Kucera, Executive Director

The International Association for Healthcare Security and Safety, (IAHSS) is an organization dedicated to professionals involved in managing and directing security and safety programs in healthcare institutions. Its members have joined together to develop educational and credentialing programs and create a body of knowledge that meets the needs of today's fast paced and ever changing environment.
2000 Members
Founded in: 1968

12384 International Association for Worksite Health Promotion
401 West Michigan Street
Indianapolis, IN 46202

317-637-9200
iawhp@acsm.org; www.acsm-iawhp.org/
Social Media: Facebook, LinkedIn

George Pfeiffer, MSE, President
Stephen Cherniak, MS, MBA, Secretary/Treasurer
Charlie Estey, MS, President Elect
Wolf Kirsten, MS, Past President
Kristine Holbrook, MEd, Board of Director

Mission is to advance the global community of worksite health promotion practitioners through high-quality information, services, educational activities, personal and professional development and networking opportunities.

12385 International Association of Healthcare Central Service Material Management
213 W Institute Place
Suite 307
Chicago, IL 60610-3195

312-440-0078
800-962-8274; *Fax:* 312-440-9474
mailbox@iahcsmm.com; www.iahcsmm.com

Sharon Greene-Golden, CRCST,, President
Susan Adams, Executive Director
Marilyn T Conde, CRCST, MAOM, FC, Secretary/Treasurer
Nick Baker, Certification Manager
Elizabeth Berrios, Member Services Coordinator

Membership consists of persons serving in a technical, supervisory or management capacity in hospital central service departments responsible for the sterilization management and distribution of supplies.
9000 Members
Founded in: 1958
Mailing list available for rent: 13000 names

12386 International Bone and Mineral Society
330 N Wabash
Suite 1900
Chicago, IL 60611

312-321-5113; *Fax:* 312-673-6934;
www.ibmsonline.org
Social Media: Twitter

John Eisman, President
Theresa Guise, Immediate Past President
Anna Teti, Vice President
Richard Eastell, Treasurer Secretary
David Schmahl, Executive Director
3600 Members
Founded in: 1960

12387 International Oxygen Manufacturers Association
1025 Thomas Jefferson Street, NW
Suite 500 East
Washington, DC 20007

202-521-9300; *Fax:* 202-833-3636
ioma@iomaweb.org; www.iomaweb.org

The International Oxygen Manufacturers Association is the truly worldwide trade association of companies in the industrial and medical gas business
190 Members
Founded in: 1943

12388 International Sleep Products Association
501 Wythe Street
Alexandria, VA 22314-1917

703-683-8371; *Fax:* 703-683-4503
info@sleepproducts.org;
www.sleepproducts.org
Social Media: Facebook, Twitter, LinkedIn, Youtube, Flickr, Google Plus,

Debi Sutton, VP, Marketing & Member Services

Maintains a strong organization to influence government actions, inform and educate the membership and act on industry issues to enhance the growth, profitability and stature of the sleep products industry. Provides members with information and services to manage their business more effectively and efficiently. Publishes a magazine devoted exclusively to the mattress industry, BEDtimes covers a broad range of issue and news important to the industry.
Cost: $65.00
650 Members
Frequency: Monthly
Circulation: 3,500
Founded in: 1915

12389 International Society for Quality-of-Life Studies
2056 Pamplin
Virginia Tech
Blacksburg, VA 24061-0236

540-231-5110; *Fax:* 540-231-3076
sirgy@vt.edu; www.isqols.org
Social Media: RSS

Rhonda Phillips, President
Mariano Rojas, President Elect
Denis Huschka, Executive Director/Treasurer
Peter Krause, VP-Programs
Don Rahtz, VP-Publications

Was founded to stimulate interdisciplincary research in quality-of-life studies and closer cooperation among scholars. Members are academic and government social/behavioral science researchers drawn from such fields as marketing, management, applied psychology, applies sociology, political science, economics, public administration, educational administration family/child development leisure/recreation studies and technology development.
Founded in: 1995

12390 Interstate Postgraduate Medical Association
PO Box 5474
Madison, WI 53705

608-231-9045
866-446-3424; *Fax:* 877-292-4489
cmehelp@ipmameded.org;
www.ipmameded.org
Social Media: Facebook

Carolyn C. Lopez, MD, Board Chair
Robert A. Lee, MD, Vice Chair
William E. Kobler, MD, Board Treasurer
Don Klitgaard, MD, Board of Trustee
Rodney A. Erickson, MD, Board of Trustee

Dedicated to sponsoring clinically relevant education for primary care clinicians.
Founded in: 1916

12391 Leading Age
2519 Connecticut Avenue NW
Washington, DC 20008-1520

202-783-2242; *Fax:* 202-783-2255
info@leadingage.org; www.leadingage.org
Social Media: Facebook, Twitter, LinkedIn, Google+, RSS

William L. Minnix, Jr., President & CEO
Katrinka Smith Sloan, COO & Sr. Vice President
Robyn I. Stone, Senior Vice President of Research
Cheryl Phillips, Senior Vice President
Majd Alwan, Senior Vice President of Technology

Focused on advocacy, leadership development, and applied research and promotion of effective services, home health, hospice, community services, senior housing, assisted living residences,

continuing care communities, nursing homes, as well as technology solutions, to seniors, children, and others with special needs.
6M Members
Founded in: 1961

12392 **Leukemia & Lymphoma Society**
1311 Mamaroneck Ave.
Suite 310
White Plains, NY 10605
914-949-5213; *Fax:* 914-949-6691;
www.lls.org
Social Media: Facebook, Twitter, LinkedIn, Instagram, Pinterest, YouTube
Louis J. DeGennaro, President & CEO
Rosemarie Loffredo, CAO & CFO
Mark Roithmayr, Chief Development Officer
Volunteer organization dedicated to funding blood cancer research and ensuring access to treatment.
Founded in: 1949

12393 **Medical Group Management Association**
104 Inverness Terrace East
Englewood, CO 80112-5306
303-799-1111
877-275-6462; *Fax:* 303-643-9599
support@mgma.org; www.mgma.com
Social Media: Facebook, Twitter, LinkedIn, Google+
William Jessee, CEO
Nicholas H Kupferle, Board Chair
Jyl D Bradley, Chair
Warren C White Jr, Chair
Nicholas H Kupferle III, Chair
The mission of the MGMA is to continually improve the performance of medical group practice professionals and the organizations they represent.
19000 Members
Founded in: 1926

12394 **Medical Library Association**
65 East Wacker Place
Suite 1900
Chicago, IL 60601-7246
312-419-9094; *Fax:* 312-419-8950
info@mlahq.org; www.mlanet.org
Social Media: Facebook, Twitter, LinkedIn, Youtube
Michelle Kraft, AHIP, President
Kevin Baliozian, Executive Director
Teresa L. Knott, AHIP, President-Elect
Linda Walton, AHIP, Immediate Past President
Chris Shaffer, AHIP, Treasurer
A nonprofit, educational organization that is a leading advocate for health sciences information professionals worldwide. Through it's programs and services, we provide lifelong educational opportunities, supports a knowledgebase of health information research and works with a global network of partners to promote the importance of quality information for improved health to the health care community and the public.
4500 Members
Founded in: 1898
Mailing list available for rent

12395 **Medical Marketing Association**
10293 N Meridian Street
Suite 175
Indianapolis, IN 46290
317-816-1640; *Fax:* 317-816-1633;
www.medicalmarketingassociation.org/
Social Media: Facebook, Twitter, Google+, RSS
Michael L Boner, President
Steve Hamburger, Treasurer
Stewart Marsden, Secretary
Builds diagnostic industry leadership by providing market education, professional development and a forum for fellowship and the exchange of ideas.

12396 **National Association Medical Staff Services**
2025 M Street NW
Suite 800
Washington, DC 20036-2422
202-367-1196; *Fax:* 202-367-2196
info@namss.org; www.namss.org
Social Media: Facebook, LinkedIn, YouTube, Flickr, RSS
Sharon Kimbrough, CPCS, CPMSM, President
Lynn Boyd, Executive Director
Tiffany Boykin, Operations Manager
Andrew Miller, Member Services Coordinator
Chris Murphy Peck, Education & Learning Services
NAMSS' vision is to advance a healthcare environment that maximizes the patient experience through the delivery of quality services.
4000 Members
Founded in: 1978

12397 **National Association for Healthcare Recruitment**
18000 W. 105th St.
Suite 103
Olathe, KS 66061-7543
913-895-4627; *Fax:* 913-895-4652;
www.nahcr.com
Social Media: Facebook, Twitter, LinkedIn, Blogger, youtube
Jude Hill, President
Sheila O'Neal, Executive Director
Christie Ross, CAE, Education Director
Candice Miller, Administrative Assistant
Debbie Jennings, Meeting Planner
Individuals employed directly by hospitals and other health care organizations which are involved in the practice of professional health care recruitment. Promotes sound principles of professionals health care recruitment. Provides financial assistance to aid members in planning and implementing regional educational programs. Offers technical assistance and consultation services. Compiles statistics.
800 Members
Founded in: 1975

12398 **National Association for Home Care and Hospice**
228 Seventh Street, SE
Washington, DC 20003-4306
202-547-7424; *Fax:* 202-547-3540
ads@nahc.org; www.nahc.org
Social Media: Facebook, Twitter, Pinterest
Denise Schrader, Chairman
Lucy Andrews, Vice Chair
Val J. Halamandaris, President
Walter W. Borginis, Treasurer
Karen Marshall Thompson, Secretary

12399 **National Association for Medical Direction of Repiratory Care (NAMDRC)**
8618 Westwood Center Drive
Suite 210
Vienna, VA 22182-2222
703-752-4359; *Fax:* 703-752-4360
ExecOffice@namdrc.org; www.namdrc.org
Timothy A. Morris, MD, President
Phillip Porte, Executive Director
Vickie Parshall, Director Member Services
Charles W. Atwood, MD, President-Elect
Karen Lui, RN, Associate Executive Director
The National Association for Medical Direction of Respiratory Care, our mission is to improve access to quality care for patients with respiratory disease by removing regulatory and legislative barriers to appropriate treatment. It advises on coding issues and federal reimbursement policies; provides economic and regulatory updates; and offers unique educational opportunities.
700 Members
Founded in: 1977

12400 **National Association of County & City Health Officials**
1100 17th Street NW
Seventh Floor
Washington, DC 20036-4619
202-783-5550; *Fax:* 202-783-1583
info@naccho.org; www.naccho.org
Social Media: Facebook, Twitter
Paul Yeghiayan, President, NACCHO Foundation
Mark Jorritsma, COO
John Mericsko, Chief Financial Officer
LaMar Hasbrouck, Executive Director
William Barnes, Chief Program Officer
Administrators of freestanding and hospital-based long-term care facilities owned and operated by county governments or city-county consolidations; elected local officials. Promotes interests of county long-term care facilities; offers guidance in relevant legislative and regulatory areas. Provides technical assistance; conducts training workshops. Compiles statistics on public policy changes, such as changes in the Medicaid program, which affect long-term care facilities.
250 Members
Founded in: 1977

12401 **National Association of School Nurses**
1100 Wayne Avenue
Suite 925
Silver Spring, MD 20910
240-821-1130
866-627-6767; *Fax:* 301-585-1791
nasn@nasn.org; www.nasn.org
Beth Mattey, MSN, RN, NCSN, President
Susan Zacharski, Vice President
Donna J. Mazyck, RN, MS, NCSN, Executive Director
Catherine Davis, BSN, RN, NCSN, Secretary/Treasurer
Nina Fekaris, President Elect
15500 Members
Founded in: 1968

12402 **National Athletic Trainers Association**
1620 Valwood Parkway
Suite 115
Carrollton, TX 75006
214-637-6282
860-437-5700; *Fax:* 214-637-2206
webmaster@nata.org; www.nata.org
Scott Sailor, EdD, ATC, President
MaryBeth Horodyski, Vice President
Kathy Dieringer, Secretary/Treasurer
Dave Saddler, Executive Director
Rachael Oats, Associate Executive Director
35,00 Members
Founded in: 1950

12403 **National Cancer Institute**
9609 Medical Center Drive
Bethesda, MD 20892-9760
800-422-6237
cancergovstaff@mail.nih.gov; www.cancer.gov
Social Media: Facebook, Twitter, LinkedIn, Google+, YouTube, Instagram, R
Douglas R. Lowy, M.D., Acting Director
Lynn Austin, PhD, Deputy Director for Management
Jeffrey S. Abrams, MD, Acting Director, Clinical

Research
Stephen J. Chanock, MD, Director
Peter Greenwald, MD, Associate Director, Prevention

Conducts and supports research, training, health information dissemination and other programs with respect to the cause, diagnosis, prevention and treatment of cancer, rehabilition from cancer and the continuing care of cancer patients.

12404 National Council for Behavioral Health

1701 K Street NW
Suite 400
Washington, DC 20005

202-684-7457; *Fax:* 202-386-9391
communications@thenationalcouncil.org;
www.TheNationalCouncil.org
Social Media: Facebook, Twitter, LinkedIn, YouTube, Pinterest, Google+

Susan Blue, Chair
Donald Miskowiec, Vice Chair
Jeff Richardson, Second Vice Chair
Linda Rosenberg, President & CEO
Jeannie Campbell, Executive Vice President and COO

Advocates for public policies in mental and behavioral health that ensure that people who are ill can access comprehensive healthcare services.
2,500 Members

12405 National Council on the Aging

251 18th Street South
Suite 500
Arlington, VA 22202

571-527-3900; *Fax:* 202-479-0735
info@ncoa.org; www.ncoa.org
Social Media: Facebook, Twitter, LinkedIn, Youtube, RSS

Carol Zernial, Chair
James Firman, EdD, President and CEO
Richard Browdie, Immediate Past-Chair
Donna Whitt, SVP, CFO
Wendy Zecker, SVP, Public/Private Programs
Founded in: 1950

12406 National Environmental Health Association

720 S Colorado Blvd
Suite 1000-N
Denver, CO 80246-1926

303-756-9090
866-956-2258; *Fax:* 303-691-9490
staff@neha.org; www.neha.org
Social Media: Facebook, Twitter, LinkedIn

Bob Custard REHS, CP-FS, President
David Riggs, President Elect
Adam London MPA, RS, First VP
Vince Radke, 2nd VP
David T. Dyjack Dr.PH, CIH, Executive Director

NEHA offers a variety of programs that are all in keeping with the association's mission which is as relevant today as it was when the organization was founded. The mission of NEHA is to advance the environmental health and protection professional for the purpose of providing a healthful environment for all.
5000 Members
Founded in: 1937

12407 National Managed Health Care Congress

71 2nd Avenue
3rd Floor
Waltham, MA 02154

888-882-2500; *Fax:* 941-365-0157;
www.nmhcc.org

12408 National Medical Association

8403 Colesville Road
Suite 820
Silver Spring, MD 20910

202-347-1895
800-257-8290; *Fax:* 202-347-0722
cme@nmanet.org; www.nmanet.org
Social Media: Facebook, Twitter, LinkedIn, YouTube

Garfield Clunie, M.D, Chair of the Board
Edith P. Mitchell, M.D., President
Lawrence Sanders, Immediate Past President
Richard Allen Williams, M.D., President-Elect
Traci C. Burgess, M.D., M.P.H., Secretary

The mission of the NMA is to advance the art and science of medicine for people of African descent through education, advocacy, and health policy to promote health and wellness, eliminate health disparities, and sustain physician viability.
Founded in: 1895

12409 National Renal Administrators Association

100 North 20th Street
Suite 400
Philadelphia, PA 19103-1462

215-320-4655; *Fax:* 215-564-2175
nraa@nraa.org; www.nraa.org/index.php
Social Media: Facebook, Twitter, LinkedIn

Helen Currier, President
Karen Kelley, MHA, BSN, CNN, President-Elect
Anthony Messana, Secretary
Rob Bomstad,RN, BSBA, MS, Treasurer
Deb Cote, Past-President

Administrative personnel involved with dialysis programs for patients suffering from kidney failure. Provides a vehicle for the development of educational and informational services for members. Maintains contact with health care facilities and government agencies. Operates placement serve; compiles statistics; conducts political action committee.
475 Members
Founded in: 1977

12410 National Rural Health Association

4501 College Blvd
#225
Leawood, KS 66211-1921

816-756-3140; *Fax:* 816-756-3144
mail@NRHArural.org;
www.ruralhealthweb.org
Social Media: Facebook, Twitter, LinkedIn

Jodi Schmidt, President
Lisa Kilawee, President-Elect
Dave Pearson, Treasurer
Tommy Barnhart, Secretary
Raymond G. hristensen, MD, Past-President

A national membership organization, whose mission is to improve the health care of rural Americans and to provide leadership on rural issues through advocacy, communications, education and research.
20,00 Members

12411 National Society Of Certified Healthcare Business Consultants

12100 Sunset Hills Road
Suite 130
Reston, VA 20190-3233

703-234-4099; *Fax:* 703-435-4390
info@nschbc.org; www.nschbc.org
Social Media: Facebook, Twitter, LinkedIn, Pineterst, Youtube

H. Christopher Zaenger, CHBC, President
Michael J. Dejno, CHBC, CPA, President-Elect
Robert C. Scroggins, Secretary/Treasurer
Reed Tinsley, Immediate Past-President
Carol Wynne, Executive Director

Maintains code of ethics, rules of professional conducts, and certification program; administers exams and conduct certification course. Membership by successful completion of certification examination only.
350 Members
Founded in: 1975

12412 National Society for Histotechnology

8850 Stanford Boulevard
Suite 2900
Columbia, MD 21045

443-535-4060; *Fax:* 443-535-4055
histo@nsh.org; www.nsh.org
Social Media: Facebook, Twitter, LinkedIn

Elizabeth Sheppard, President
Sharon Kneebone, Executive Director
Jerry Santiago, Vice President
Diane Sterchi, Secretary
Monty Hyten, Treasurer

A non-profit organization, committed to the advacement of histotechnology, its practitioners and quality standards of practice through leadership, education and advocacy.
Founded in: 1974

12413 National Strength and Conditioning Association

1885 Bob Johnson Drive
Colorado Spring, CO 80906-4000

719-632-6722
800-815-6826; *Fax:* 719-632-6367
nsca@nsca.com; www.nsca.com/Home/

G. Gregory Haff, President
Colin Wilborn, PhD, ATC, VP
Joel T. Cramer, PhD, CSCS, Treasurer
Lee Madden, Sr. Director of Admin. Services
Wayde Rivinius, Sr. Director of Technology

Develops and presents the most advanced information regarding strength training and conditioning practices, injury prevention, and research findings.
30000 Members
Founded in: 1978

12414 Northwest Urological Society

914 164th St. SE
Suite 145
Mill Creek, WA 98012

866-800-3118; *Fax:* 800-808-4749
support@nwurologicalsociety.org;
www.nwurologicalsociety.org/

William Ellis, MD, President
John Corman, MD, VP
Stan Myers, MD, VP
John Corman, MD, Secretary-Treasurer
Michael Conlin, MD, Immediate Past President

12415 OMA: Optical Industry Association
6055A Arlington Boulevard
Falls Church, VA 22044-2721
703-237-8433; *Fax:* 703-237-0643
Members are makers and importers of spectacle frames, and related products.
57 Members
Founded in: 1916

12416 Optical Society of America
2010 Massachusetts Ave, NW
Washington, DC 20036-1023
202-223-8130; *Fax:* 202-223-1096
info@osa.org; www.osa.org
Social Media: Facebook, Twitter, LinkedIn, YouTube, Blog
Philip Russell, President
Elizabeth A. Rogan, Chief Executive Officer
Sean Bagshaw, COO, Chief Information Officer
Melissa Russell, Chief Industry Relations Officer
Tracy Schario, Chief External Relations Officer
OSA was organized to increase and diffuse the knowledge of optics, pure and applied; to promote the common interests of investigators of optical problems, of designers and of users of optical apparatus of all kinds; and to encourage cooperation among them.
Founded in: 1916

12417 Orthopedic Surgical Manufacturers Association
BioMet
7302 Texas Heights Ave
Kalamazoo, MI 49009
269-303-3831; *Fax:* 574-372-1790
secretary@osma.net; www.osma.net/
Sharon Starowicz, President
Lynnette Jackson, Vice President
Lori Burns, Secretary
Ed Chin, Treasurer
Susan Krasny, Past President
Members are manufacturers of orthopedic surgical items. Sponsors research, information and ethics programs.
25 Members
Founded in: 1954

12418 Pacific Dermatological Association
575 Market Street
Suite 2125
San Francisco, CA 94105
415-927-5729
888-388-8815; *Fax:* 415-764-4915;
www.pacificderm.org
Janellen Smith, MD, President
Tina Suneja, MD, President Elect
Keith Duffy, MD, Vice President
Hege Grande Sarpa, MD, Secretary-Treasurer
Catherine Ramsay, MD, Immediate Past President
Provides opportunitites for exchange of information and advancement of knowledge of dermatology among physicians within the membership area. Execlusively for education, scientific and charitable purposes.
Founded in: 1948

12419 Pacific Northwest Radiological Society
2001 6th Ave
Ste 2700
Seattle, WA 98121
206-956-3650
800-552-0612; *Fax:* 206-441-5863
lmk@wsma.org; www.pnwrs.org
Tess Chapman, MD, President
Greg Kicska, MD, First Vice President
Debra Alderman, Association Director
Jonathan Helwig, MD, Secretary/Treasurer
Shane Greek, MD, Immediate Past President

12420 Professional Association of Health Care Office Management
1576 Bella Cruz Drive
Suite 360
Lady Lake, FL 32159
847-375-4717
800-451-9311; *Fax:* 407-386-7006
info@pahcom.com; www.pahcom.com
Social Media: Facebook, Twitter, LinkedIn, Youtube
Richard Blanchette, MS, Founder
Daniel Labelle, CISSP CEH, Chief Technology Officer
Karen Blanchette, MBA, Association Director
Darlene Born, CMM, HITCM-PP, Business Development
Aaron Miller, Web Developer
A national organization dedicated to promoting professionalism in physician office practice by providing professional development opportunities, continuing education in health care office management principles and practice, and certification for health care office managers.
Founded in: 1988

12421 Radiological Society of North America
820 Jorie Blvd
Oak Brook, IL 60523-2251
630-571-2670
800-381-6660; *Fax:* 630-571-7837;
www.rsna.org
Social Media: Facebook, Twitter, LinkedIn, Flickr, Youtube
Richard L. Ehman, MD, Chairman
Ronald L. Arenson, MD, President
Richard L. Baron, MD, President-Elect/Secretary-Treasurer
William P. Dillon, MD, First Vice-President
William G. Bradley Jr, MD, PhD, Second Vice-President
The mission is to promote and develop the highest standards of radiology and related sciences through education and research. The society seeks to provide radiologists and allied health scientists with educational programs and materials of the highest quality and to constantly improve the content and value of these educational activities.
54,00 Members

12422 Radiology Business Management Association
10300 Eaton Place
Suite 460
Fairfax, VA 22030
703-621-3355
888-224-7262; *Fax:* 703-621-3356
info@rbma.org; www.rbma.org
Social Media: Facebook, Twitter, LinkedIn
Suzanne Taylor, BS, FRMBA, President
Keith E. Chew, MHA, CMPE, Immediate Past President
Jim Hamilton, President Elect
Thomas C. Dickerson, Treasurer, MidWestern Director
Michael R. Mabry, Executive Director
The only radiology-specific business organization in existence today. Dedicated to providing managers with information, resources, educatio and networking to run a successful radiology business.
2200 Members
Founded in: 1968

12423 Sisters Network: National Headquarters
2922 Rosedale Street
Houston, TX 77004
713-781-0255
866-781-1808; *Fax:* 713-780-8998
infonet@sistersnetworkinc.org;
www.sistersnetworkinc.org
Social Media: Facebook, Twitter, Youtube
Karen Eubanks Jackson, Founder & CEO
Bettie Eubanks, Vice Chair
Dr John Green, Treasurer
Erie E. Calloway, Executive Director
Monica Jones, Administrative Assistant
Committed to increasing local and national attention to the devastating impact that breast cancer has in the African American community.
3000 Members
Founded in: 1994

12424 Society for Healthcare Strategy and Market Development
155 North Wacker Drive
Chicago, IL 60606-3421
312-422-3888; *Fax:* 312-278-0883
shsmd@aha.org; www.shsmd.org/
Social Media: Facebook, Twitter, LinkedIn
Christine Gallery, President
Lawrence Margolis, President Elect
Mark Parrington, Immediate Past President
Diane Weber, RN, Executive Director
Lisa Hinkle, Education Manager
The society of choice for thousands of healthcare marketing, public relations, strategic planning, communications and business development professionals.
4,000 Members
Founded in: 1996

12425 Society for Imaging Informatics In Medicine
19440 Golf Vista Plaza
Suite 330
Leesburg, VA 20176-8264
703-723-0432; *Fax:* 703-723-0415
info@siim.org; www.siim.org
Social Media: Facebook, Twitter, LinkedIn, Google+, YouTube, Instagram
David E. Brown, CIIP, Chair
William W Boonn, MD, Secretary
Rasu B. Shrestha, MD, MBA, Treasurer
Paul G. Nagy, PhD, FSIIM, CIIP, Chair-Elect
Anna Marie Mason, MS,CAE, Executive Director
Devoted to advance informatics and information technology in medical imaging through education and research. Provides an open environment for imaging information professionals to access expert and cutting edge resources in a collegial and practical atmosphere.
2200 Members
Founded in: 1980

12426 Society of Critical Care Medicine
500 Midway Drive
Mount Prospect, IL 60056-5811
847-827-6869; *Fax:* 847-827-6886
info@sccm.org; www.sccm.org
Social Media: Facebook, Twitter, Google+
Carol Thompson, President
David Julian Martin, CAE, CEO, EVP
Brian Schramm, CAE, Director Business Affairs
James Flanigan, CAE, Director, Marketing
Pamela S. Dallstream, CMP, CMM, Director of Education
Professional organization devoted exclusively to the advancement of multidisciplinary, multiprofessional intensive care through excel-

lence in patient care, education, research, and advocacy.
11000 Members
Founded in: 1972

12427 **Society of Medical-Dental Management**
125 Strafford Avenue
Suite 300
Wayne, PA 19087-3318

800-826-2264; *Fax:* 610-687-7702
patricia01@aol.com; www.smdmc.org

Joseph Cobo, President
Richard G Bock, Regional Director/Coordinator
Rex Stanley, Secretary/Treasurer

Professional medical and/or dental management consultants associated for educational and information sharing purposes. Objectives are to: advance the profession; share management techniques; improve individual skills; provide clients with competent and capable business management. Provides information on insurance and income tax. Conducts surveys; compiles statistics.
60+ Members
Founded in: 1968

12428 **Society of NeuroInterventional Surgery**
3975 Fair Ridge Drive
Suite 200 North
Fairfax, VA 22033

703-691-2272; *Fax:* 703-537-0650
info@snisonline.org; www.snisonline.org
Social Media: Facebook, Twitter

Donald F. Frei, MD, President
Blaise W. Baxter, MD, Vice President
Charles J. Prestigiacomo, MD, President Elect
Richard P. Klucznik, MD, Treasurer
Adam S. Arthur, MD, Secretary

Formerly the American Society of Interventional and Therapeutic Neuroradiology, mission is to promote excellence in patient care, provide education, support research, influence health care policy, and foster the growth of the specialty.
3000 Members
Founded in: 1992

12429 **Society of Nuclear Medicine & Molecular Imaging**
1850 Samuel Morse Dr
Reston, VA 20190-5316
703-708-9000; *Fax:* 703-708-9015
volunteer@snmmi.org; www.snm.org
Social Media: Facebook, Twitter, LinkedIn, Youtube

Hossein Jadvar, MD,PhD,MPH,MBA, President
Sally W. Schwarz, MS, RPh, BCNP, President-Elect
Bennett S. Greenspan, Vice President-Elect
Michael L. Middleton, MD, FACNM, Secretary/Treasurer
Peter Herscovitch, Immediate Past President

International scientific and professional organization that promotes the science, technology and practical applications of nuclear medicine.
18,00 Members
Founded in: 1954

12430 **Southern Medical Association**
35 W. Lakeshore Drive
Suite 201
Birmingham, AL 35209-7254

205-945-8903
800-423-4992; *Fax:* 205-945-1840
CustomerService@sma.org; www.sma.org
Social Media: Facebook, Twitter, Youtube

Mark S. Williams, President
Benjamin M. Carmichael, President-Elect
Ajoy Kumar, President-Elect
Stuart J. Goodman, Immediate Past President
William L. Hartsfield FLMI, Executive Director

Physician's choice for education and support to enhance practice and performance and career development.
88 Members
Founded in: 1906

12431 **TLPA Annual Convention & Trade Show**
Taxicab, Limousine & Paratransit Association
3200 Tower Oaks Boulevard
Suite 220
Rockville, MD 20852

301-984-5700; *Fax:* 301-984-5703
info@tlpa.com; www.tlpa.org

James Campolongo, PA, President
Alfred LaGasse, MD, Chief Executive Officer
Carl Ward, KY, Treasurer
Robert McBride, CO, Vice President
Harold Morgan, MD, Secretary

Shares information vital to owners or taxicab, limousine, airport shuttle, paratransit and nonemergency medical transportation fleets. 100 supplier exhibits of the newest products available to the industry.
1000 Attendees
Frequency: Annual
Founded in: 1917

12432 **The American Association of Tissue Banks**
8200 Greensboro Drive
Suite 320
McLean, VA 22102

703-827-9582; *Fax:* 703-356-2198;
www.aatb.org
Social Media: Facebook, Twitter, LinkedIn

Daniel Schultz, MD, Chairman
Frank Wilton, President & Chief Executive Officer
Louis Barnes III, Chairman-Elect
Kevin Cmunt, Immediate Past Chairman
Diana Buck, Secretary/Treasurer

Transplant trade organization dedicated to ensuring that human tissues intended for transplantation are safe and free of infectious disease and available in quantities sufficient to meet national needs.
Founded in: 1976

12433 **The American Board of Surgery**
1617 John F. Kennedy Blvd.
Suite 860
Philadelphia, PA 19103

215-568-4000; *Fax:* 215-563-5718;
www.absurgery.org
Social Media: Facebook, Twitter

Stephen R. T. Evans, Chair
Frank R. Lewis Jr., Executive Director

Independent, nonprofit organization promoting excellence in surgical practice.
Founded in: 1937

12434 **The American Chiropractic Association**
1701 Clarendon Boulevard
Suite 200
Arlington, VA 22209

703-276-8800; *Fax:* 703-243-2593
memberinfo@acatoday.org; www.acatoday.org
Social Media: Facebook, Twitter, LinkedIn, RSS, YouTube, Instagram

John Falardeau, SVP, Public Policy and Advocacy
Janet Ridgely, Deputy Executive Vice President
Kim Hodes, Senior Director, Finance
Felicity Clancy, SVP, Communications
Dean Millard, Vice President, Information Systems

Professional organization representing chiropractors.

12435 **The American Geriatrics Society**
40 Fulton St.
New York, NY 10038
212-308-1414; *Fax:* 212-832-8646
info.amger@americangeriatrics.org;
www.americangeriatrics.org
Social Media: Facebook, Twitter, LinkedIn, Instagram, Pinterest

Nancy E. Lundebjerg, Chief Executive Officer
Steven Counsell, President

AGS is a nonprofit dedicated to improving the lives of the elderly.
6000 Members

Newsletters

12436 **AAB Bulletin**
American Association of Bioanalysts
906 Olive Street
Suite 1200
Saint Louis, MO 63101-1448

314-241-1445; *Fax:* 314-241-1449
aab@aab.org; www.aab.org

Mark S Biernbaum PhD, Administrator

Newsletter that provides the latest information on meetings, conferences, legislative and regulatoryy issues and developments.
Frequency: Quarterly
Founded in: 1956

12437 **AABB News**
American Association of Blood Banks
8101 Glenbrook Rd
Suite 2
Bethesda, MD 20814-2747
301-907-6977; *Fax:* 301-907-6895
aabb@aabb.org; www.aabb.org

Karen Lipton, CEO
Frequency: Monthly

12438 **AAMI News**
Assoc for the Advancement of Medical Instrumentat
4301 N. Fairfax Drive
Suite 301
Arlington, VA 22203-1633

703-525-4890; *Fax:* 703-276-0793
publications@aami.org; www.aami.org

Sean Loughlin, Publications Director
Robert King, Editor

Keeps individuals up-to-date with timely and relevant infustry news, breaking information about new standards activities and AAMI benefits, and guidance from experts in the field.
Cost: $160.00
Frequency: Monthly
Circulation: 6000

12439 **AAMI News Extra!**
Assoc for the Advancement of Medical Instrumentat
4301 N. Fairfax Drive
Suite 301
Arlington, VA 22203-1633

703-525-4890; *Fax:* 703-276-0793
publications@aami.org; www.aami.org

Sean Loughlin, Publications Director

Online newsletter that includes the top stories of the month; an up-to-date listing of career opportunities in the field; and updates on AAMI's standards, benefits, and services.
Frequency: Monthly

12440 **ACOG Clinical Review**
American College of Obstetricians/Gynecologists
409 12th Street SW
PO Box 96920
Washington, DC 20090-6920
202-638-5577; *Fax:* 202-484-5107
resources@acog.org; www.acog.org
Kathleen Harrison, Advertising
Frequency: 6 X

12441 **ACOS News**
American College of Osteopathic Surgeons
123 N Henry Street
Alexandria, VA 22314-2903
703-684-0416; *Fax:* 703-684-3280
info@facos.org; www.facos.org
Guy Beaumont, Executive Director
Judith T Mangum, Director Finance
Frequency: Monthly

12442 **ACOS Review**
American College of Osteopathic Surgeons
330 E Algonquin Rd
Suite 1
Arlington Hts, IL 60005-4665
847-228-6090
800-323-0794; *Fax:* 847-228-9755;
www.acofp.org
Peter Schmelzer, Executive Director
Frequency: Monthly

12443 **AMGA's Advocacy ENewS**
American Medical Group Association
One Prince Street
Alexandria, VA 22314-3318
703-838-0033; *Fax:* 703-548-1890;
www.amga.org
Don Fisher, CEO
Ryan O'Connor, VP, Membership/Marketing
Timely analysis on the latest issues that affect medical groups on the federal legislative and regulatory front.
375 Members

12444 **AOA News**
American Optometric Association
243 N Lindbergh Blvd
Suite 1
St Louis, MO 63141-7881
314-991-4100; *Fax:* 314-991-4101
info@iacconline.org; www.aoa.org
Barry Barresi, Executive Director
Tom Cappucci, First Vice President
Michael Jones, CEO
Official newspaper of the American Optometric Association
Cost: $93.50
Circulation: 30000
ISSN: 0094-9620
Founded in: 1896
Mailing list available for rent: 22,500 names at $70 per M
Printed in 4 colors on glossy stock

12445 **AOPA in Advance SmartBrief**
American Orthotic & Prosthetic Association
330 John Carlyle Street
Suite 200
Alexandria, VA 22314
571-431-0876; *Fax:* 571-431-0899
info@aopanet.org; www.aopanet.org
Social Media: Facebook, Twitter, LinkedIn
Tom Fise, Executive Director
Michael Oros, President
Lauren Anderson, Manager, Communications
Don DeBolt, Chief Operating Officer
Provides updates and information to the O&P community.
Frequency: Twice-Weekly

12446 **ASET News**
American Society of Electroneurodiagnostic Tech
402 East Bannister Road
Suite A
Kansas City, MO 64131-3019
816-931-1120; *Fax:* 816-931-1145
info@aset.org; www.aset.org
Arlen Reimnitz, Executive Director
Anne Bonner, Director, Publications
Newsletter detailing society updates, news briefings, and other information of interest to neurodiagnostic technologists.
Frequency: Quarterly

12447 **ASHI Quarterly**
American Society for Histocompatability
1120 Route 73
Suite 200
Mt. Laurel, NJ 08054
856-638-0428; *Fax:* 856-439-0525
info@ashi-hla.org; www.ashi-hla.org
Kathy Miranda, Executive Director
Sarah Black, Managing Editor
Latest updates and news on society activities as well as scholarly insights.
Frequency: Quarterly

12448 **Adult Day Services Letter**
Health Resources Publishing
1913 Atlantic Ave
Suite 200
Manasquan, NJ 08736-1067
732-292-1100; *Fax:* 732-292-1111
info@healthresourcesonline.com;
www.hin.com/ehealthcare
Robert K Jenkins, Publisher
Brett Powell, Regional Director
Alice Burron, Director
A monthly newsletter that contains management information, reports on trends and new developments and information about other adult day care programs across the country.
Cost: $147.00
38574 Pages
Frequency: Monthly
ISSN: 0885-4572
Founded in: 1985

12449 **BNA's Health Law Reporter**
Bureau of National Affairs
1801 S Bell St
Arlington, VA 22202-4501
703-341-3000
800-372-1033; *Fax:* 800-253-0332
customercare@bna.com; www.bnabooks.com
Paul N Wojcik, CEO
Of many newsletters from BNA, this contains information on health care policy, bankruptcy, antitrust, insurance and state developments, employment issues as well as a congressional and a regulatory calendar.
Cost: $1782.00
Frequency: Weekly

12450 **Biomedical Market Newsletter**
Biomedical Market
3237 Idaho Pl
Costa Mesa, CA 92626-2207
714-434-9500
800-875-8181; *Fax:* 714-434-9755
info@biomedical-market-news.com;
www.biomedical-market-news.com
David G Anast, President
Steve Baker, Director of Marketing/Sales
Richard Guiss, Senior Editor
George Anast, CFO
New business development, FDA, regulatory, financial, and marketing NL on medical equipment, device, diagnostic test and instrument industries worldwide.
Cost: $199.00
Frequency: Monthly
ISSN: 1064-4180
Founded in: 1991
Printed in 4 colors on matte stock

12451 **Bulletin on Long-Term Care Law**
Health Resources Publishing
1913 Atlantic Ave
Suite 200
Manasquan, NJ 08736-1067
732-292-1100; *Fax:* 732-292-1111
info@healthresourcesonline.com;
www.hin.com/ehealthcare
Robert K Jenkins, Publisher
Lisa Mansfield, Regional Director
Brett Powell, Regional Director
Alice Burron, Director
A newsletter that covers compliance problems, Medicaid and Medicare overhauls, charges of abuse, fraud, negligence, needless litigation and other concerns of those involved in long-term health care.
Cost: $227.00
Frequency: Monthly
ISSN: 1093-6939
Founded in: 1978

12452 **Communique**
213 W Institute Place
Suite 307
Chicago, IL 60610-3195
312-440-0078
800-962-8274; *Fax:* 312-440-9474
mailbox@iahcsmm.com; www.iahcsmm.com
Betty Hanna, Executive Director
Marilyn Corida, Secretary/Treasurer
Lisa Huber, President
Bi-monthly publication separates supervisors/directors from technicians.
Cost: $40.00
Frequency: 6/Annual
Circulation: 15M
ISBN: 1-605309-30-9
Mailing list available for rent: 13000 names

12453 **Diagnostic Testing & Technology Report**
Institute of Management and Administration
1 Washington Park
Suite 1300
Newark, NJ 07102
212-244-0360; *Fax:* 973-622-0595;
www.ioma.com
Contains up-to-the minute information and unique perspectives on where diagnostic testing is headed, covering every innovation, new product, manufacturer, market and end-user applications.
Cost: $549.00
Frequency: Monthly

12454 **Directions: Looking Ahead in Healthcare**
Health Resources Publishing
1913 Atlantic Ave
Suite 200
Manasquan, NJ 08736-1067
732-292-1100
888-843-6242; *Fax:* 732-292-1111
info@healthresourcesonline.com;
www.hin.com/ehealthcare
Robert K Jenkins, Publisher
Lisa Mansfield, Marketing Assistant
Carolin Pense, Publisher

Brett Powell, Regional Director
Alice Burron, Director

Provides management news on such topics as alerts, trends, forecasts, profitable innovations, facts and statistics.
Cost: $127.00
Frequency: Monthly
ISSN: 1093-6920
Founded in: 1978

12455 Dispatch & Division Newsletters

Taxicab, Limousine & Paratransit Association
3200 Tower Oaks Blvd
Suite 220
Rockville, MD 20852

301-984-5700; *Fax:* 301-984-5703
info@tlpa.org; www.tlpa.org

Alfred LaGasse, CEO
Victor Dizengoff, President

Dispatch features articles on industry business issues, provides advice on running a transportation company, and comes with division specific bi-monthly newsletters.
Frequency: Bimonthly
Circulation: 6000

12456 Elderly Health Services Letter

Health Resources Publishing
1913 Atlantic Ave
Suite 200
Manasquan, NJ 08736-1067

732-292-1100
888-843-6242; *Fax:* 732-292-1111
info@themcic.com; www.hin.com/ehealthcare

Robert K Jenkins, Publisher
Lisa Mansfield, Regional Director
Brett Powell, Regional Director
Alice Burron, Director

A newsletter on projections and trends for health services provided for the elderly. Subjects include inpatient care, long-term care, outpatient, home care, primary care, ambulatory care, day care, health promotion, disease prevention, support groups, health education and residental care.
Cost: $227.00
Frequency: Monthly
ISSN: 0891-9275

12457 Emergency Department Law

Business Publishers
8737 Colesville Road
Suite 1100
Silver Spring, MD 20910-3928

301-876-6300
800-274-6737; *Fax:* 301-589-8493
custserv@bpinews.com; www.bpinews.com

Leonard A Eiserer, Publisher
James Lawlor, Editor

Devoted entirely to legal issues pertinent to emergency medicine, and covers monthly the latest case law, legal trends, risk management, tort reform and explains how they could impact your emergency care facility.
Cost: $357.00
Frequency: Monthly

12458 Employee Assistance Program Management Letter

Health Resources Publishing
1913 Atlantic Ave
Suite 200
Manasquan, NJ 08736-1067

732-292-1100
888-843-6242; *Fax:* 732-292-1111
info@themcic.com;
www.healthresourcesonline.com

Robert K Jenkins, Publisher
Lisa Mansfield, Regional Director
Brett Powell, Regional Director
Alice Burron, Director

A briefing published monthly on the range of influences surrounding your employee assistance program.
Cost: $237.00
Frequency: Monthly
ISSN: 0896-0941
Founded in: 1978

12459 Executive Report on Integrated Care & Capitation

Managed Care Information Center
1913 Atlantic Ave
Suite 200
Manasquan, NJ 08736-1067

732-292-1100
888-843-6242; *Fax:* 732-292-1111
info@themcic.com; www.themcic.com

Robert K Jenkins, Publisher
Joseph Schmidt, Editor

A newsletter published twice a month to keep readers informed of the competitive market. Gives facts on strategic issues, mergers and acquisitions, market facts, economics, network alliances and plan affiliations.
Cost: $447.00
Frequency: Monthly
ISSN: 1085-3103

12460 Executive Report on Managed Care

Managed Care Information Center
1913 Atlantic Ave
Suite 200
Manasquan, NJ 08736-1067
732-292-1100
888-843-6242; *Fax:* 732-292-1111
info@themcic.com; www.themcic.com

Robert K Jenkins, Publisher

A monthly report that gives news of how major employers are implementing their managed care programs. The report also aids companies in preparing to evaluate and monitor different managed care proposals to determine cost effectiveness, quality and liability to the employer.
Cost: $437.00
ISSN: 0898-9753

12461 Executive Report on Physician Organizations

Managed Care Information Center
1913 Atlantic Ave
Suite 200
Manasquan, NJ 08736-1067
732-292-1100
888-843-6242; *Fax:* 732-292-1111
info@themcic.com; www.themcic.com

Robert K Jenkins, Publisher

The newsletter covers mergers, acquisitions, practice management agreements and strategic planes implemented in the physician marketplace. Also provides information about the ways that managed care and goverment regulations affect the physician marketplace.
Cost: $257.00
8-10 Pages
Frequency: 12 per year
ISSN: 1097-7309
Founded in: 1998

12462 Eye-Mail Monthly

American Academy of Optometry
6110 Executive Blvd
Suite 506
Rockville, MD 20852-3929

301-984-1441; *Fax:* 301-984-4737
aaoptom@aaoptom.org; www.aaopt.org

Lois Schoenbrun, Executive Director
Frequency: Monthly

12463 G-2 Compliance Report

Institute of Management and Administration
1 Washington Park
Suite 1300
Newark, NJ 07102

212-244-0360; *Fax:* 973-622-0595;
www.ioma.com

Designed to guide hospital, lab, and pathology professionals in developing, implementing and revising compliance programs to meet federal standards.
Cost: $469.00

12464 HCEA Edge

Healthcare Convention & Exhibitors Association
5775 Peachtree Dnwdy Rd
Building G, Suite 500
Atlanta, GA 30342-1556

404-252-3663; *Fax:* 404-252-0774
hcea@kellencompany.com; www.hcea.org

Eric Allen, Executive Vice President
Nancy Hoppe, President

News and events of the trade association of over 600 organizations involved in healthcare exhibiting or providing services to healthcare conventions, exhibitions and/or meetings.
Frequency: Monthly, Members Only

12465 HFMA's The Business of Caring

Healthcare Financial Management Association
Two Westbrook Corporate Center
Suite 700
Westchester, IL 60154-5700

708-319-9600
800-252-4362; *Fax:* 708-531-0032;
www.hfma.org/boc

Robert Fromberg, Editor-in-Chief
Maggie Van Dyke, Product Manager & Editor
Chris Burke, Advertising Manager
Kurt Belisle, Sponsorhip Manager

Helps nurse managers navigate the business side of health care to become successful hospital leaders. Topics discussed include: budgeting, workforce management, cost containment, and IT implementation. Available Free Online.
Frequency: Quarterly

12466 HMFA Healthcare Cost Containment Newsletter

Healthcare Finance Management Association
3 Westbrook Corporate Center
Suite 600
Westchester, IL 60154

708-531-9600; *Fax:* 708-531-0032;
www.hfma.org/publications/healthcarecost

Issues illustrate how to implement strategic cost management that will reduce labor and supply expenses, enhance operational efficiency, satisfy your patients, and improve your competitive position.
Cost: $125.00
Frequency: Quarterly
Mailing list available for rent

12467 HMFA Revenue Cycle Stragetist Newsletter

Healthcare Finance Management Association
3 Westbrook Corporate Center
Suite 600
Westchester, IL 60154

708-531-9600; *Fax:* 708-531-0032;
www.hfma.org/publications/

Improve your organization's bottom line while maintaining regulatory compliance.
Cost: $165.00
Frequency: Quarterly
Mailing list available for rent

12468 Health Care Reimbursement Monitor
Health Resources Publishing
1913 Atlantic Ave
Suite 200
Manasquan, NJ 08736-1067

732-292-1100
888-843-6242; *Fax:* 732-292-1111
info@themcic.com;
www.healthresourcesonline.com

Robert K Jenkins, Publisher
Lisa Mansfield, Regional Director
Brett Powell, Regional Director
Alice Burron, Director

A monthly newsletter that covers the latest details of actions taken or proposals in Washington concerning changes to the BBA; updates on Medicaid and Medicare budget and reimbursement issues; reimbursement news for hospital operations executives as well as top financial management. Reimbursement briefings cover hospitals, home health care, long-term care, hospice, ambulatory care and physician payment.
Cost: $257.00
Frequency: Monthly

12469 Health Product Marketing
PRS Group
6320 Fly Rd
Suite 102
East Syracuse, NY 13057-9792

315-431-0511; *Fax:* 315-431-0200
custserv@prsgroup.com; www.prsgroup.com

Mary Lou Walsh, President
Ben McTernan, Managing Editor
Patti Davis, Circulation Manager
Patty Redhead, Production Manager

Provides current information, analysis and ideas for strategic planning in the health industry.
ISSN: 1520-3271
Founded in: 1979

12470 Healthcare Market Reporter
Managed Care Information Center
1913 Atlantic Ave
Suite 200
Manasquan, NJ 08736-1067

732-292-1100
888-843-6242; *Fax:* 732-292-1111
info@themcic.com; www.themcic.com

Robert K Jenkins, Publisher

Twice-a-month newsletter to help you abreast of the fiercely competitive market. Get the facts and details you'll need on strategies issues, market facts, mergers and acquisitions, economics, network alliances and plan affiliations.
Cost: $457.00
10 Pages
ISSN: 1073-6816

12471 Healthcare Marketers Executive Briefing
Health Resources Publishing
1913 Atlantic Ave
Suite 200
Manasquan, NJ 08736-1067

732-292-1100; *Fax:* 732-292-1111
info@healthresourcesonline.com;
www.healthresourcesonline.com

Robert K Jenkins, Publisher
Lisa Mansfield, Regional Director
Brett Powell, Regional Director
Alice Burron, Director

Helps managers stay informed of the latest innovations and changes in the health care field. Gives contact information for other community relations, publication practioners, administrators and marketing and advertising professionals.
Cost: $237.00
Frequency: Monthly
ISSN: 0894-9980

12472 Healthcare PR & Marketing News
Phillips Business Information
1201 Seven Locks Road
Potomac, MD 20854-2931

301-354-1400
888-707-5814; *Fax:* 301-309-3847;
www.prandmarketing.com

Matthew Schwartz, Editor
Diane Schwartz, Publisher
Amy Urban, Marketing Manager

Issues faced by health care executives in PR firms and hospitals. Regular features include industry surveys, case studies and executive profiles.
Cost: $397.00
Founded in: 1944

12473 Healthcare e-Business Manager
Managed Care Information Center
1913 Atlantic Ave
Suite 200
Manasquan, NJ 08736-1067

732-292-1100
888-843-5242; *Fax:* 732-292-1111
info@themcic.com; www.themcic.com

Robert K Jenkins, Publisher

Monthly executive briefing on the latest developments in the proliferation of electronic commerce among healthcare and managed care organization. Focuses on the internet marketplace, reports on trends in the industry and predictions of where the market seems to be heading.
Cost: $477.00
10 Pages
ISSN: 1526-6052

12474 Hospice Letter
Health Resources Publishing
1913 Atlantic Ave
Suite 200
Manasquan, NJ 08736-1067

732-292-1100
888-843-6242; *Fax:* 732-292-1111
info@themcic.com;
www.healthresourcesonline.com

Robert K Jenkins, Publisher
Lisa Mansfield, Regional Director
Brett Powell, Regional Director
Alice Burron, Director

Monthly newsletter reporting the latest development in the rapidly hospice concept of caring for the terminally ill. Ready by administrators and directors who follow Medicare reimbursement and hospice accreditation. How hospices are raising money and staging community events; new legislation and regulations and the latest on nursing care, volunteers and counseling programs. Delivery options: via mail or e-mail (indicate PDF or HTML format)
Cost: $227.00
10 Pages
Frequency: Monthly
ISSN: 0913-6816
Founded in: 1978

12475 Integrated Healthcare News
American Association of Integrated Healthcare
4435 Waterfront Drive
Suite 101
Glen Allen, VA 23060

804-747-5823; *Fax:* 804-747-5316;
www.aaihds.org

Jerry Williams, Editorial
Mark Abernathy, Managing Director
Dalal Haldeman, PhD, MBA, Director, Marketing Operations

12476 Journal of the American Association of Forensic Dentists
1000 N Avenue
Waukegan, IL 60085

847-244-0292
info@andent.net; www.andent.net

Quarterly journal that brings forensic dental knowledge not only to dentists and their staff, but also to anthropologists, attorneys and law enforcement personnel.
3000 Pages
Founded in: 1978

12477 Legislative Alert
Taxicab, Limousine & Paratransit Association
3200 Tower Oaks Blvd
Suite 220
Rockville, MD 20852

301-984-5700; *Fax:* 301-984-5703
info@tlpa.org; www.tlpa.org

Alfred LaGasse, CEO
William Rouse, President
Harold Morgan, Executive Vice President
Michelle A. Hariston, CMP, Manager of Meetings
Leah New, Manager of Communications

TLPA's members-only bulletin of early alerts to critical changes in the industry, announcing threats and opportunities on issues that are before Congress and federal agencies. Organizes operators to take action, and provides knowledge and awareness.
Circulation: 6000
Founded in: 1917
Mailing list available for rent

12478 Medical Group Management Update
Medical Group Management Association
104 Inverness Ter E
Englewood, CO 80112-5313

303-799-1111; *Fax:* 303-643-9599
infocenter@mgma.com; www.mgma.com

William Jessee, CEO
Eileen Barker, senior Vice President
Anders Gilberg, senior Vice President
Natalie Jamieson, Administrative Assistant

Monthly association newspaper offering up-to-the-minute articles on current legislation, practical management, health care trends, association activities and other timely subjects.
Frequency: Monthly

12479 National Intelligence Report
Institute of Management and Administration
1 Washington Park
Suite 1300
Newark, NJ 07102-3130

212-244-0360; *Fax:* 973-622-0595
customercare@bna.com; www.ioma.com

Provides concise, independent coverage and analysis of fast-breaking lab, pathology, blood banking, imaging and diagnostic radiology news from the Nation's Capital.
Cost: $489.00
Frequency: Biweekly

12480 Nephrology News and Issues
Nephrology News and Issues
17797 N Perimeter Dr
Suite 109
Scottsdale, AZ 85255-5455

480-443-4635; *Fax:* 480-443-4528;
www.nephronline.com

Melissa Laudenschlager, Publisher
Mark Neumann, Editor

Marcia Coutts, Circulation Manager
Cost: $55.00
Frequency: Monthly
Circulation: 22000
Founded in: 1986

12481 **News Now**
American Physical Therapy Association
1111 N Fairfax St
Alexandria, VA 22314-1488

703-684-2782; *Fax:* 703-706-8536
memberservices@apta.org; www.apta.org
Social Media: Facebook, Twitter, LinkedIn

Maryann DiGiacomo, Editor
John D. Barnes, Chief Executive Officer
Janet Bezner, VP, Education, Governance
Rob Batarla, VP, Finance & Business Development
Felicity Clancy, VP, Communications & Marketing
Reports timely legislative, health care, and Association news to APTA members and subscribers.
80000 Members
Frequency: Weekly
Mailing list available for rent

12482 **Nurses' Notes**
American Association of Managed Care Nurses
4435 Waterfront Dr
Suite 101
Glen Allen, VA 23060-3393

804-747-9698; *Fax:* 804-747-5316
keads@aamcn.org; www.aamcn.org

Bill Williams, President
A quarterly newsletter published by the American Association of Managed Care Nurses. Available to members only.
Circulation: 2000

12483 **Nursing News Update**
American Association of Managed Care Nurses
4435 Waterfront Dr
Suite 101
Glen Allen, VA 23060-3393

804-747-9698; *Fax:* 804-747-5316
keads@aamcn.org; www.aamcn.org

Bill Williams, President
Laura Givens, Executive Admin
A weekly electronic newsletter published by the American Association of Managed Care Nurses. Available to members only.
Circulation: 2000

12484 **Physician's News Digest**
Physician's New Digest
230 Windsor Ave
Suite 216
Narberth, PA 19072-2217

610-668-1040
800-220-6109; *Fax:* 610-668-9177
info@physiciansnews.com;
www.physiciansnews.com

Jeffery Barg, CEO/President
Christopher Gaudagnino, Business Manager
Ben Birenbaum, Business Manager
Cost: $35.00
Frequency: Monthly
Circulation: 40000
ISSN: 1079-6312
Founded in: 1987
Printed in 4 colors on newsprint stock

12485 **Public Health**
State Capitals Newsletters
PO Box 7376
Alexandria, VA 22307-7376

703-768-9600; *Fax:* 703-768-9690
thecapitolcollection.com
Cost: $245.00
Frequency: Weekly

12486 **Sisters Network/National Newsletter**
Sisters Network
2922 Rosedale St
Suite 4206
Houston, TX 77004-6188

713-781-0255
866-781-1808; *Fax:* 713-780-8998
infonet@sistersnetworkinc.org;
www.sistersnetworkinc.org

Erie Calloway, Executive Director
Karen E. Jackson, CEO
Caleen Burtonalleen, Public Relations Manager
Cherlyn K Latham, Project Director
Kelly P. Hodges, National Program Director
Publication of the group committed to awareness of the impact that breast cancer has on the African American community, with the latest information, medical research and news about events taking place within the Sisters National Network of affiliate chapters.
Frequency: Monthly
Founded in: 1994

12487 **Today's School Psychologist**
LRP Publications
747 Dresher Road
PO Box 980
Horsham, PA 19044-2247

215-784-0912
800-341-7874; *Fax:* 215-784-9639
webmaster@lrp.com; www.lrp.com

Caroline Miller, Editor
In-depth guide to a school psychologists job, offering proactive strategies and tips for handling day-to-day tasks and responsibilities, encouraging change and improving professional standing and performance.
Cost: $135.00
Frequency: Monthly

12488 **US Medicine Newsletter**
US Medicine
39 York Street
Suite 400
Lambertville, NJ 08530

609-397-5522; *Fax:* 609-397-4237
usmedicine@usmedicine.com;
www.usmedicine.com

James F Breuning, Publisher
Brenda L. Mooney, Editorial Director
Stephen Spotswood, Correspondent
Beth Scholz, Account Manager
Anita Crandall, Production Manager
US Medicine is an organization that supports physicians and healthcare workers with medical and legal information. Publishes a newspaper. Founded in 1964.
9 Members
Founded in: 1964

12489 **Walking Tomorrow**
Christopher Reeve Paralysis Foundation
500 Morris Ave
Springfield, NJ 07081-1027

973-467-5915
800-225-0292; *Fax:* 973-912-9433;
www.christopherreeve.org/

Julie Kwon, Director of Marketing
Kathy Lewis, Controller
Ed Jobst, Controller
Newsletter of the Christopher Reeve Paralysis Foundation.
Frequency: Monthly
Founded in: 1982

12490 **Wellness Program Management Advisor**
Health Resources Publishing
1913 Atlantic Ave
Suite 200
Manasquan, NJ 08736-1067

732-292-1100
888-843-6242; *Fax:* 732-292-1111
info@themcic.com;
www.healthresourcesonline.com

Robert K Jenkins, Publisher
Lisa Mansfield, Regional Director
Brett Powell, Regional Director
Alice Burron, Director
A newsletter that is designed to help professionals manage their organization's health promotion and wellness programs. Gives information about how other wellness programs are doing in such areas as strategies adopted, expenses and return on investments. Also included are in depth profiles of wellness programs around the country that list the problems that they encountered and the steps that they took to alter them.
Cost: $247.00
Frequency: Monthly
ISSN: 1085-7125

Magazines & Journals

12491 **24 X 7**
HealthTech Publishing Company
6100 Center Drive
Suite 1000
Los Angeles, CA 90045

310-642-4400; *Fax:* 310-641-4444;
www.24x7mag.com

Tony Ramos, Publisher
Kelly Stephens, Editor
Jennifer Bezahler, Circulation Manager
News and business magazine for the healthcare service support and technology management industry.
Frequency: Monthly
Circulation: 15000
ISSN: 1091-1626
Founded in: 1996
Printed in 4 colors on glossy stock

12492 **AAMA Executive**
American Academy of Medical Administrators
701 Lee St
Suite 600
Des Plaines, IL 60016-4516

847-759-8601
800-621-6902; *Fax:* 847-759-8602
info@aameda.org; www.aameda.org

Renee Schleichar, CEO
Nancy L Anderson, Director of Education
Guy Snyder, Director of Education
Rhonda Guptill, Chief Financial Officer
Cost: $90.00
Frequency: Quarterly
Founded in: 1957

12493 **AAPS Newsmagazine**
American Association of Pharmaceutical Scientists

2107 Wilson Blvd
Suite 700
Arlington, VA 22201-3042

703-243-2800; *Fax:* 703-243-9054
aaps@aaps.org; www.aaps.org

John Lisack, Executive Director
Joy Metcalf, Managing Editor
Janelle Kihlstrom, Editorial Assistant
Ken Corch, Executive Assistant

Exclusive to AAPS members. Features expanded coverage of the industry, complete with expert information on marketplace trends, regulatory matters, and career opportunities.
Mailing list available for rent

12494 **AAPS PharmSciTech Journal**
American Association of Pharmaceutical Scientists
2107 Wilson Blvd
Suite 700
Arlington, VA 22201-3042

703-243-2800; *Fax:* 703-243-9054
aaps@aaps.org; www.aaps.org

John Lisack, Executive Director
Joy Metcalf, Managing Editor
James Greif, Communications Specialist
Ken Corch, Executive Assistant

An online-only journal published and owned by the American Association of Pharmaceutical Scientists. The journal's mission is to disseminate scientific and technical information on drug product design, development, evaluation and processing to the global pharmaceutical research community, taking full advantage of web-based publishing by presenting innovative text with 3-D graphics, interactive figures and databases, video and audio files.
ISSN: 1530-9932
Mailing list available for rent

12495 **AARP The Magazine**
American Association of Retired Persons
601 E St NW
Washington, DC 20049-0003

202-434-2277
888-687-2277
202-434-3525; *Fax:* 202-434-7599
member@aarp.org; www.aarp.org

Hop Backus, Executive Vice President
Steve Cone, Executive Vice President
Joann Jenkins, Foundation President
A. Barry Rand, Chief Executive Officer
Cindy Lewin, General Counsel

AARP is a nonprofit, nonpartisan organization with a membership that helps people age 50 and over have independence, choice and control in ways that are beneficial and affordable to them and society as a whole, ways that help people 50 and over improve their lives. Founded through support from staffed offices in all 50 states.
Frequency: Monthly
Founded in: 1958
Mailing list available for rent

12496 **ACSM's Health & Fitness Journal**
Lippincott Williams & Wilkins
351 W Camden St
Baltimore, MD 21201-2436

410-949-8000
800-222-3790; *Fax:* 410-528-4414;
www.lww.com

J Arnold Anthony, Operations
Michael Hargrett, Publisher
Edward Howley, Editor-in-Chief

The Journal strives to help health and fitness practitioners improve their knowledge and experience through reports and recommendations from experts, CEC offerings, opportunities to question the experts, listings of job openings and more.
Cost: $40.00
Frequency: Fortnightly
Circulation: 11144
ISSN: 1091-5397
Founded in: 1997
Printed in 4 colors on matte stock

12497 **ADA Courier**
American Dietetic Association
120 South Riverside Plaza
Suite 2000
Chicago, IL 60606-6995

312-990-0040
800-877-1600; *Fax:* 312-899-4757
affiliate@eatright.org; www.eatright.org

Susan H Laramee, President
Ronald S Moen, CEO
Patricia M. Babjak, Executive VP
Jennifer Herendeen, Editorial Director
Jason Switt, Editor

Readers look to the Courier for current association activities, membership news, updates on continuing education opportunities, ADA policies and coverage of the Associations' lobbying efforts in Washington.
Cost: $315.00
10 Pages
Frequency: Monthly
Circulation: 80000
ISSN: 1050-7434
Founded in: 1917
Printed in 4 colors on glossy stock

12498 **ADA News**
American Dental Association
211 E Chicago Ave
Chicago, IL 60611-2678

312-440-2897; *Fax:* 312-440-3538;
www.ada.org

Judy Jakush, Editor
Jill Philbein, Circulation Manager
James Bramson, CEO
Cost: $64.00
Founded in: 1859

12499 **AHA News**
AHA
1 N Franklin St
Suite 700
Chicago, IL 60606-4425

312-895-2500
800-242-2626; *Fax:* 312-895-2501
storeservice@aha.org; www.aha.org

Anthony Burke, CEO
Cliff Lehman, Director Membership Services

Provides extensive coverage of regulatory, judicial and legislative developments while also providing news and information from the AHA.
Cost: $45.00
Frequency: Weekly
Circulation: 40000
Founded in: 1917

12500 **AMA Alliance Today**
AMA
515 N State St
Chicago, IL 60654-9104

312-464-4470; *Fax:* 312-464-5020
amaa@ama-assn.org; www.ama-assn.org

Jo Posselt, Executive Director
Megan Pellegrini, General Counsel
Jon Ekdahl, General Counsel
Bernard Hengesbaugh, Chief Operating Officer
Jacqueline Drake, Secretary
Circulation: 30,000
Founded in: 1922

12501 **AdvaMed SmartBrief**
Advanced Medical Technology Association
1200 G St NW
Suite 400
Washington, DC 20005-3832

202-408-9788; *Fax:* 202-408-9793
info@advamed.org; www.avamed.org

Andrea Levre, President

12502 **Advance for Health Information Executives**
Advance Newsmagazines/Merion Publications
2900 Horizon Dr
King of Prussia, PA 19406-2651

610-265-8249
800-355-5627; *Fax:* 610-962-0639;
www.advanceforhie.com

Frank Irving, Editor
Maryann Kurkowski, Circulation Manager

Coverage of emerging e-health and computer-based patient record technologies.
Frequency: Monthly
Founded in: 1997

12503 **Aesthetic Plastic Surgery**
6277 Sea Harbor Drive
Orlando Florida
Orlando, Fl 32887-7703

407-345-4000
800-364-2147; *Fax:* 407-363-9661
elspcs@elsevier.com; www.surgery.org/

Elizabeth Sadati, Executive Editor
Paul Bernstein, Scientific Forum Editor
Stanley A Klatsky, Managing Director
Cost: $196.00
Frequency: Monthly
Founded in: 1996

12504 **Air Medical Journal**
Mosby
11830 Westline Industrial Drive
Saint Louis, MO 63146-3318

314-453-4307
800-325-4307; *Fax:* 314-872-9164
elspcs@elsevier.com;
www.mosby.com/airmedj

David Dries, Editor
Liz Bennett-Bailey, Publisher
Eric Ferguson, Issue Manager
Cost: $85.00
Frequency: bi-monthly
Founded in: 1986

12505 **American Family Physician**
American Academy of Family Physicians
11400 Tomahawk Creek Pkwy.
Leawood, KS 66211-2672

913-906-6205; *Fax:* 913-906-6086
afpjournal@aafp.org;
www.aafp.org/journals/afp.html
Social Media: Facebook, Twitter, YouTube

Jay Siwek, Editor

Peer-reviewed clinical journal of the American Academy of Family Physicians.
Cost: $240.00
Frequency: Monthly
ISSN: 0002-838X
Founded in: 1947

12506 **American Health Line**
600 New Hampshire Avenue NW
Washington, DC 20037

202-295-5381
800-717-3245; *Fax:* 202-266-5700
ahl@advisory.com;
www.americanhealthline.com

Joshua Perin, Editor-in-Chief
Josh Kotzman, Editors
Frequency: Weekly
Founded in: 1992

12507 **American Imago: Studies In Psychoanalysis and Culture**
Johns Hopkins University Press
2715 N Charles St
Baltimore, MD 21218-4319
410-516-6900
800-548-1784; *Fax:* 410-516-6998
webmaster@jhupress.jhu.edu;
www.press.jhu.edu/journals
William Brody, President
Kathleen Keane, Director
William M. Breichner, Publisher
Founded in: 1878

12508 **American Journal of Clinical Medicine**
American Association of Physician Specialists, Inc
5550 West Executive Drive
Suite 400
Tampa, FL 33609
813-433-2277; *Fax:* 813-830-6599
wcarbone@aapsus.org; www.aapsus.com
Nadine Simone, Executive Administrative Assistant
Debi Colmorgen, Communications Coordinator
William Carbone, Chief Executive Officer
Anthony Durante, Director of Finance & Operations
Sandy Martin, Finance & Operations Coordinator
The official peer-reviewed journal of the AAPS, an organization dedicated to promoting the highest intellectual, moral, and ethical standards of its members.
1000 Attendees

12509 **American Journal of Cosmetic Surgery**
737 N Michigan Ave
Suite 2100
Chicago, IL 60611-5641
312-981-6760; *Fax:* 312-981-6787
info@cosmeticsurgery.org;
www.cosmeticsurgery.org
Jeffrey Knezovich, Executive VP
Charlie Baase, Marketing Manager

12510 **American Journal of Health Education (AJHE)**
1900 Association Dr
Reston, VA 20191-1502
703-476-3400
800-213-7193; *Fax:* 703-476-9527;
www.aahperd.org
Social Media: Facebook, Twitter, YouTube
Monica Mize, President
Judith C Young, VP
Paula Kun, Marketing
Covers today's health education and health promotion issues head on with timely, substantive, and thought provoking articles for professionals working in medical care facilities, professional preparation, colleges and universities, community and public health agencies, schools, and businesses.
25000 Members
Founded in: 1885

12511 **American Journal of Human Genetics**
American Society of Human Genetics
9650 Rockville Pike
Bethesda, MD 20814-3998
301-634-7300
866-HUM-GENE; *Fax:* 301-634-7079
society@ashg.org; www.ashg.org
Social Media: Facebook, Twitter, LinkedIn
Joann Boughman, PhD, Executive VP
Chuck Windle, Director of Finance/Administration
Karen Goodman, Executive Assistant
Pauline Minhinnett, Dir. of Meetings/Exhibit Management
Mary Shih, Membership Manager
ASHG is the primary professional membership organization for human genetics specialists worldwide.
8000 Members
Frequency: Monthly
Circulation: 7,199
ISSN: 0002-9297
Founded in: 1948
Mailing list available for rent

12512 **American Journal of Hypertension**
148 Madison Ave
Fifth Floor
New York, NY 10016-6700
212-532-0537; *Fax:* 212-696-0711
journal@ash-us.org; www.ash-us.org
John H Laragh, Editor In Chief
Ellen Twyne, President
Cost: $246.00
Frequency: Monthly
Founded in: 1985

12513 **American Journal of Managed Care**
American Medical Publishing
241 Forsgate Drive
Jamesburg, NJ 08831
732-656-1006; *Fax:* 732-656-0818
info@ajmc.com; www.ajmc.com
Jim King, Publisher
Lyn Beamesderfer, Editor
The American Journal of Managed Care is an independent, peer-reviewed forum for the publication of clinical research and opinion related to quality, value, and policy in health care delivery. The Journal delivers original research on patient outcomes, clinical effectiveness, cost effectiveness, quality management, and health policy to managed care decision makers.
Frequency: Monthly
Circulation: 53000
ISSN: 1088-0224
Founded in: 1995

12514 **American Journal of Neuroradiology**
2210 Midwest Rd
Suite 207
Oak Brook, IL 60523-8205
630-574-1487
800-783-4903; *Fax:* 630-786-6251;
www.ajnr.org
Karen Halm, Managing Editor
Victor M Haughton MD, VP
Relays news and schedules of events for members.
Cost: $235.00
Circulation: 7000
Founded in: 1937

12515 **American Journal of Roetgenology**
American Roentgen Ray Society
1891 Preston White Dr
Reston, VA 20191-4326
703-729-3353
800-438-2777; *Fax:* 703-729-4839
info@arrs.org; www.arrs.org
Susan Brown, Executive Director
Connie Wolfe, Publications Assistant
Fran Schuweiler, Managing Editor
Charles Kahn, Vice President
Melissa Rosado, Secretary
A monthly journal published by the American Roentgen Ray Society.
Cost: $275.00
Frequency: Monthly
Circulation: 25,000
Founded in: 1900
Mailing list available for rent: 10000 names at $160 per M

12516 **American Medical News**
American Medical Association
515 N State St
9th Floor
Chicago, IL 60654-9104
312-464-4429
800-621-8335; *Fax:* 312-464-4445
ben_mindell@ama-assn.org;
www.ama-assn.org
Ben Mindell, Vice President
John Nelson, CEO/President
Kathryn Trombatore, Manager
Jon Ekdahl, General Counsel
Bernard Hengesbaugh, Chief Operating Officer
Intended to serve as an impartial forum for information affecting physicians and their practices. The views expressed in AMNews are not necessarily endorsed by the American Medical Association.
Cost: $95.00
Frequency: Weekly
Circulation: 230,000
Founded in: 1847

12517 **American Nurse Today**
American Nurses Association
600 Maryland Avenue SW
Washington, DC 20024-2571
202-651-7000; *Fax:* 202-651-7003;
www.NursingWorld.org
Pamela Cipriano PhD RN FAAN, Editor-in-Chief
Serves registered nurses in North America.
Frequency: 6 per year
Printed in 4 colors on glossy stock

12518 **Anesthesiology News**
545 W 45th St
8th Floor
New York, NY 10036-3409
212-957-5300; *Fax:* 212-957-7230
marsap@mcmahonmed.com;
www.anesthesiologynews.com
Adam Marcus, Managing Editor
Raymond E. McMahon, CEO/Publisher
Marsha Radebaugh, Circulation Coordinator
Cost: $65.00
Frequency: Monthly
Circulation: 39720
Founded in: 1975

12519 **Annals of Allergy, Asthma & Immunology**
85 W Algonquin Road
Suite 550
Arlington Heights, IL 60005-4460
847-427-1200; *Fax:* 847-427-1294
mail@acaai.org; www.acaai.org
Social Media: Facebook, Twitter, LinkedIn, YouTube
Dana Wallace, MD, President
Stanley Fineman, MD, MBA, President-Elect
Information and news service for patients, parents of patients, members, the news media, and purchasers of health care programs.
5200 Members
Frequency: Monthly
Circulation: 5100
ISSN: 1081-1206
Founded in: 1942

12520 **Annals of Emergency Medicine**
Elsevier Publishing

1125 Executive Circle
P.O. Box 619911
Irving, TX 75038-2522

972-550-0911
800-798-1822; *Fax:* 972-580-2816
customerservice@acep.org; www.acep.org

Nancy B Medina, CAE, Editorial Director
Tracy Napper, Managing Editor
Michael L Callaham, MD, Editor-in-Chief
Dean Wilkerson, Executive Director
Marco Coppola, Council Speaker

An international, peer-reviewed journal dedicated to improving the quality of care by publishing the highest quality science for emergency medicine and related medical specialties.
Frequency: Monthly
Circulation: 30000
ISSN: 0196-0644
Mailing list available for rent

12521 Annals of Opthalmology
Am. Society of Cont. Medicine, Surgery & Opth.
North Cisero Avenue
Suite 208
Chicago, IL 60712

847-677-9093
800-621-4002; *Fax:* 847-677-9094
iaos@aol.com;
www.medlit.ru/medeng/vof5.htm

Mikhail Krasnov, Editor-in-Chief
Randall Bellows MD, CEO/President

Exclusive articles written and peer-reviewed by doctors.
Frequency: bi-monthly
Founded in: 1884

12522 Annals of Periodontology
737 N Michigan Ave
Suite 800
Chicago, IL 60611-2690

312-787-5518; *Fax:* 312-787-3670
member.services@perio.org; www.perio.org

Alice Deforest, Executive Director
Julie Daw, Managing Editor
Vincent J. Iacono, President
Sarah Schneider, Administrative Assistant
Cost: $365.00
Frequency: Monthly

12523 Annals of Plastic Surgery
530 Walnut St
Philadelphia, PA 19106-3603

215-521-8300; *Fax:* 215-521-8411;
www.lww.com

Melissa Ricks, Manager
Cost: $375.00
Frequency: Monthly

12524 Applied Clinical Trials
Advanstar Communications
6200 Canoga Avenue
2nd Floor
Woodland Hills, CA 91367

818-593-5000; *Fax:* 818-593-5020;
www.appliedclinicaltrialsonline.com
Social Media: Facebook, Twitter, LinkedIn

Joseph Loggia, President
Chris DeMoulin, VP
Susannah George, Marketing Director

Practical information for clinical research professionals in industry and academia who develop, execute and manage clinical trials worldwide. Regular topics include regulatory affairs, protocol development, data management and harmonization updates.
Frequency: Monthly
Circulation: 16255
ISSN: 1064-8542

Founded in: 1987
Mailing list available for rent

12525 Archives of Physical Medicine and Rehabilitation
American Congress of Rehabilitation Medicine
11654 Plaza America Drive
Suite 535
Reston, VA 20190

703-435-5335; *Fax:* 866-692-1619;
www.acrm.org

Jon W. Lindberg, Executive Director
Dinara Suleymanova, Director of Operations
Judy Reuter, Publications & Web Development
Cindy Robinson, Marketing Coordinator
Margo Holen, Chief Meetings Officer

Available with membership to American Congress of Rehabilitation Medicine.
Frequency: Monthly
Circulation: 900
Founded in: 1923

12526 Arthritis Hotline
2824 Swift Avenue
Dallas, TX 75204

972-286-6664; *Fax:* 214-363-2817

12527 Aviation, Space and Environmental Medicine
Aerospace Medical Association
320 S Henry St
Alexandria, VA 22314-3579

703-739-2240; *Fax:* 703-739-9652
asemjournal@att.net; www.asma.org

Gisselle Vargas, Manager
Jeffrey C. Sventek, Executive Director
Gisselle Vargas, Operations Manager
Gloria Carter, Director, Member Services
Sheryl Kildall, Subscriptions Manager

Provides contact with physicians, life scientists, bioengineers and medical specialists working in both basic medical research and in its clinical applications.
Frequency: Monthly
Mailing list available for rent

12528 BNA's Health Care Policy Report
3 Bethesda Metro Center
Suite 250
Bethesda, MD 20814

202-452-4107
800-372-1033; *Fax:* 202-452-4084
edcontactslitigation@bna.com; www.bna.com

Greg McCaffey, President, Bloomburg BNA
Frequency: Weekly
Founded in: 1929

12529 Behavioral Health Management
MEDQUEST Communications
3800 Lakeside Ave E
Suite 201
Cleveland, OH 44114-3857

216-391-9100; *Fax:* 216-391-9200;
www.behavioral.net

Mark Goodman, Manager
Monica E Oss, Editor-in-Chief

Largest publication reporting on the cutting edge trends and management practices in the behavioral health field.
Cost: $94.00
52 Pages
Circulation: 21615
ISSN: 1075-6701
Printed in 4 colors on glossy stock

12530 Behavioral Neuroscience
750 1st St NE
Washington, DC 20002-4242

202-336-5500
800-374-2721; *Fax:* 202-336-5549
journals@apa.org;
www.apa.org/pubs/journals/bne/index.aspx

Rebecca Burwell, Editor
Cost: $235.00
Circulation: 200,000
Founded in: 1988

12531 Biomedical Instrumentation & Technology
Assoc for the Advancement of Medical Instrumentat
4301 N. Fairfax Drive
Suite 301
Arlington, VA 22203-1633

703-525-4890; *Fax:* 703-276-0793
publications@aami.org; www.aami.org

Sean Loughlin, Managing Editor

Filled with practical guidance and regular features on troubleshooting, certification, career trends, management issues, sterilization, quality assurance, and more.
Cost: $182.00
Frequency: Bimonthly
Circulation: 6000
Mailing list available for rent

12532 Biomedical Safety & Standards
Aspen Publishers
280 Orchard Ridge Drive
Suite 200
Gaithersburg, MD 20878-1978

301-417-7591

Jack Bruggeman, Publisher

12533 Birth-Issues in Perinatal Care
350 Main Street
6th Floor
Malden, MA 02148-5023

781-388-8200
800-759-6102; *Fax:* 781-388-8210;
www.blackwellpublishing.com

Diony Young, Editor
Gordon Tibbitts III, President
Robert Campbell, Publisher
Ginny Foley, Manager
Cost: $36.00
Frequency: Quarterly
Circulation: 1709
Founded in: 1897

12534 Body Positive
19 Fulton Street
Suite 308 B
New York, NY 10038-2100

212-566-7333
800-566-6599; *Fax:* 212-566-4539;
www.bodypos.org/

Raymond A Smith, Editor
Eric Rodriguez, Executive Director
Cost: $40.00
Frequency: Quarterly
Circulation: 10000
Founded in: 1987

12535 Bulletin
1650 Diagonal Road
Alexandria, VA 22314-3357

703-836-4444; *Fax:* 703-683-5100
membership@entnet.org; www.entnet.org
Social Media: Facebook, Twitter

Marty Stewart, Sr Manager, Media/Public Relations
James L. Netterville, President
J. Gavin Setzen, Secretary/Treasurer

David R. Nielsen, Executive Vice President and CEO
Paul T. Fass, Director - Private Practice

Features articles written by member otolaryngologists and Academy staff, as well as regular segments on political advocacy, the grassroots member network, practice management, and the latest specialty news and information.
Frequency: Monthly
Circulation: 12,000
ISSN: 0731-8359
Mailing list available for rent

12536 Business and Health
Medical Economics Publishing
131 West First Street
Duluth, Mi 55802-2065

218-723-9200
888-346-0085; *Fax:* 218-723-9437
info@advanstar.com; www.advanstar.com

Tracey Walker, Senior Editor
Julie Miller, Managing Editor
Daniel Corcoran, Publisher
Joseph Loggia, Chief Executive Officer
Thomas Ehardt, Chief Administrator

Provides the business and industry fields with information on manufacturing, wholesale, retail and financial, insurance companies, law/accounting firms, hospitals, HMO/PPOs, labor unions, consulting firms, and Medicare/Medicade.
Cost: $64.00
Frequency: Monthly
Circulation: 39736
Founded in: 1987
Printed in 4 colors on glossy stock

12537 CA: A Cancer Journal for Clinicians
1599 Clifton Road NE
Atlanta, GA 30329-4251

404-929-6902; *Fax:* 404-325-9341
journals@cancer.org
caonline.amcancersoc.org

Harmon J Eyre, Editor
Vickie Thaw, Publisher
John R. Seffrin, CEO
Circulation: 90,000
Founded in: 1913

12538 CVS InStep with Healthy Living
Drug Store News Consumer Health Publications
425 Park Ave
New York, NY 10022-3526

212-756-5220
845-426-7612; *Fax:* 212-756-5250
jtanzola@lf.com; www.drugstorenews.com

Lebhar Friedman, Publisher
John Tanzola, National Sales Manager

Helps educate and inform over 25 millions 45+ shoppers that visit CVS every month. Topics include health, nutrition, fitness, lifestyle, travel, coupons and CVS programs and events.
Frequency: Quarterly
Circulation: 950000
Founded in: 2002

12539 Case Manager
Mosby
10801 Executive Center Drive
Suite 509
Little Rock, AR 72211

501-223-5165; *Fax:* 501-220-0519;
www.mosby.com

Catherine Mullahy, Editor
Tom Strickland, Editor-in-Chief
Cheri Lattimer, Executive Director

Exclusively for the case management profession.
Cost: $52.00
80 Pages
Frequency: Bi-Monthly
Circulation: 20M
Founded in: 1990
Printed in 4 colors on glossy stock

12540 Circulation Research
PO Box 1620
Suite 230
Hagerstown, MD 21741

301-223-2300
800-638-3030; *Fax:* 301-223-2400
educsales@lww.com; www.lww.com

Eduardo Marb n, Editor
Cost: $377.00
Founded in: 1792

12541 CleanRooms Magazine
PennWell Publishing Company
98 Spit Brook Rd
Nashua, NH 03062-5737

603-891-0123; *Fax:* 603-891-9294
georgem@pennwell.com; www.pennwell.com

Christine Shaw, VP
John Haystead, Editor
James Enos, Publisher
Adam Japko, President
Heidi Barnes, Circulation Manager

Serves the contamination control and ultrapure materials and process industries. Written for readers in the microelectronics, pharmaceutical, biotech, health care, food processing and other user industries. Provides technology and business news and new product listings.
Circulation: 34019
Founded in: 1910

12542 Clinical Chemistry
American Association for Clinical Chemistry
1850 K St NW
Suite 625
Washington, DC 20006-2215

202-857-0717
800-892-1400; *Fax:* 202-887-5093
custserv@aacc.org; www.aacc.org

Richard Flaherty, VP
8,000 Members
Mailing list available for rent

12543 Clinical Lab Products
MWC Allied Healthcare Group
6100 Center Drive
Suite 1000
Los Angeles, CA 90045

310-642-4400; *Fax:* 310-641-4444;
www.clpmag.com

Scott Anderson, Publisher
Carol Andrews, Editor
Sharon Marsee, Production Manager
Tony Ramos, President
Jennifer Bezahler, Circulation Director

CLP is the leading monthly product news magazine on key decision makers in the clinical diagnostic laboratory. New product annoucements and editorial features assist lab professionals in providing cost effective timely and accurate patient diagnostic information.
Cost: $125.00
Frequency: Monthly
Circulation: 45000
Founded in: 1976
Printed in 4 colors on glossy stock

12544 Clinical Pulmonary Medicine
530 Walnut St
Philadelphia, PA 19106-3603

215-521-8300
800-638-6423; *Fax:* 215-521-8411;
www.lww.com

Barry Morrill, Publisher
Michael S Niederman MD, Editor-in-Chief
Jay Lippincott, President

Provides a forum for the discussion of important new knowledge in the field of pulmonary medicine that is of interest and relevance to the practitioner.

12545 Computers and Biomedical Research
525 B Street
Suite 1900
San Diego, CA 92101-4401

619-231-6616
800-321-5068; *Fax:* 619-699-6422;
www.elsevier.com

Gilbert Laporte, Editor
Bill Godfrey, Chief Information Officer
David Clark, Senior Vice President
Frequency: Monthly
Founded in: 1974

12546 Computers, Informatics, Nursing
Lippincott Williams & Wilkins
10 A Beech Street
Suite 2
Portland, ME 04101

207-553-7750; *Fax:* 207-553-7751
CustomerService@NursingCenter.com;
www.nursingcenter.com

Leslie H. Nicoll, Editor
Lippin Cott, Publisher/President

Computer and informatics applications and product selection in nursing and education for nurse managers, patient care executives, nurses in direct patient care, nurse educators and researchers.
Cost: $63.00
Circulation: 4112
Founded in: 1985

12547 Contemporary Urology
Medical Economics Publishing
5 Paragon Dr
Montvale, NJ 07645-1791

973-944-7777
888-581-8052; *Fax:* 973-944-7778;
www.contemporaryurology.com

Curtis Allen, President
Culley C Carson MD, Editor-in-Chief
Matthew J Holland, Publisher
Don Berman, Director Business Development

Comtemporary Urology serves medical and osteopathic physicians specializing in urology.
Cost: $120.00
Frequency: Monthly
Circulation: 4276
ISSN: 1042-2250
Founded in: 1992
Printed in 4 colors on glossy stock

12548 Contingency Planning & Management
Witter Publishing Corporation
20 Commerce Street
Flemington, NJ 08822

908-788-0343; *Fax:* 908-788-3782;
www.witterpublishing.com

Bob Joudanin, Publisher
Paul Kirvan, Editor-in-Chief
Mike Viscel, Production Manager
Andrew Witter, President

Serves the fields of financial/banking, manufacturing industrial, transportation, utilities, telecommunications, health care, government, insurance and other allied fields.
Cost: $195.00
Frequency: Monthly
Founded in: 1987

12549 Continuing Care
Stevens Publishing Corporation

5151 Belt Line Rd
10th Floor
Dallas, TX 75254-7507

972-687-6700; *Fax:* 972-687-6767;
www.stevenspublishing.com

Craig S Stevens, President/CEO
Mike Valenti, Executive Vice President
Angela Neville, Editor

To provide case management and discharge planning professions with practical and professional information to ensure quality patient services at a cost-effective price.
Cost: $119.00
Founded in: 1925

12550 Coping with Allergies and Asthma
Media America
PO Box 682268
Franklin, TN 37068-2268

615-790-2400; *Fax:* 615-794-0179
info@copingmag.com; www.copingmag.com

Michael D Holt, Publisher
Julie McKenna, Editor
Michael D Holt, CEO

Information, tips and news for sufferers of allergies or asthma.
Cost: $13.95
36 Pages
Circulation: 30,000
Founded in: 1998

12551 Coping with Cancer
Media America
PO Box 682268
Franklin, TN 37068-2268

615-790-2400; *Fax:* 615-794-0179
info@copingmag.com; www.copingmag.com

Michael D Holt, Publisher
Julie McKenna, Editor

A magazine for people whose lives have been touched by cancer. Provides knowledge, hope and inspiration to its readers including cancer patients (survivors) and their families, caregivers, healthcare teams and support group leaders.
Cost: $19.00
Circulation: 572,000
Founded in: 1987

12552 Cosmetic Surgery Times
Advanstar Communications
7500 Old Oak Blvd
Cleveland, OH 44130-3343

440-243-8100
888-527-7008; *Fax:* 440-891-2740
info@advanstar.com; www.advanstar.com

Claudia Shayne-Ferguson, Group Publisher
Maureen Hrehocik, Editor-in-Chief
Michelle Tackla, Senior Editor
Ray Lender, General Manager
Carol Bessick, Manager

Provides cosmetic surgeons with the most current clinical news available. Covers latest surgical techniques, medicolegal issues, updates on new technologies, and suggestions for practice management.
Cost: $95.00
Frequency: 10x/yr
Circulation: 10,003
ISSN: 1094-6810
Founded in: 1987

12553 Cost Reengineering Report
National Health Information
PO Box 15429
Atlanta, GA 30333-0429

404-607-9500
800-597-6300; *Fax:* 404-607-0095;
www.nhionline.com

David Schwartz, President

Contains strategies for reengineering clinical and operational functions, and cutting costs while maintaining or improving quality.
Cost: $299.00
Frequency: Monthly

12554 Counseling Today
5999 Stevenson Ave
Alexandria, VA 22304-3302

703-823-9800
800-347-6647; *Fax:* 703-823-0252
membership@counseling.org;
www.counseling.org
Social Media: Facebook, Twitter

Marvin D. Kuehn, Executive Director
Tom Evenson, President

The mission of the American Counseling Association (ACA) is to enhance the quality of life in society by promoting the development of professional counselors, advancing the counseling profession, and using the profession and practice of counseling to promote respect for human dignity and diversity. ACA is a not-for-profit, professional and educational organization.
Frequency: Monthly
Circulation: 50000
Founded in: 1952
Mailing list available for rent: 60M names

12555 Critical Strategies: Psychotherapy in Managed Care
Bill Cohen
10 Alice Street
Binghamton, NY 13904-1580

607-722-5857
800-342-9678; *Fax:* 607-722-6362
getinfo@haworthpressinc.com;
www.haworthpressinc.com

Frank DePiano, Editor
Sandra J Sickels, Marketing VP
William Cohen, Owner

Resource for innovative and effective approaches to clinical practice in relation to managed care.
Cost: $35.00
Frequency: 2 per year

12556 Data Strategies & Benchmarks
National Health Information
PO Box 15429
Atlanta, GA 30333-429

404-607-9500
800-597-6300; *Fax:* 404-607-0095;
www.nhionline.net

David Schwartz, Publisher
Steve Larose, Editor
David Schwartz, CEO
Edgardo Rivera, Director

Provides insightful guidance and how-to advice to help them meet all the key challenges faced under managed care.
Cost: $339.00
Frequency: Monthly
Founded in: 1994

12557 Dental Economics
PennWell Publishing Company
1421 S Sheridan Rd
Tulsa, OK 74112-6619

918-831-9421
800-331-4463; *Fax:* 918-831-9476
joeb@pennwell.com; www.pennwell.com

Robert Biolchini, President
Lyle Hoyt, Publisher
Cost: $105.76
Frequency: Monthly
Founded in: 1910

12558 Dental Lab Products
MEDEC Dental Communications
2 Northfield Plaza
Suite 300
Northfield, IL 60093-1219

847-441-3700
800-225-4569; *Fax:* 847-441-3702;
www.dentalproducts.net

Bob Kehoe, Editorial Director
Gail Weisman, Editor
Fran Martin, Managing Editor
Richard Fischer, Publisher
Tom Delaney, National Sales Manager

Serves the dental profession and the dental industry, list rentals, classifieds and other services to complete your marketing plan.$35 subscription per year
35 Pages
Circulation: 19,000
ISSN: 0146-9738
Founded in: 1967
Printed in 4 colors on glossy stock

12559 Dental Materials
Academy of Dental Materials
21 Grouse Terrace
PO Box 980566
Lake Oswego, OR 97035

503-636-0861; *Fax:* 503-675-2738;
www.academydentalmaterials.org

David C Watts PhD FADM, Editor-in-Chief
Dr. Lorenzo Breschi, President
J. Robert Kelly, Vice President
Paulo F. Cesar, Secretary
Tom Hilton, Treasurer

12560 Dental Practice
MEDEC Dental Communications
2 Northfield Plaza
Suite 300
Northfield, IL 60093-1219

847-441-3700
800-225-4569; *Fax:* 440-826-2865;
www.dentalproducts.net

Richard Fischer, Publisher
Bob Kehoe, Editorial Director
Steven Diogo, Editor
Daniel McCann, Senior Editor
Tom Delaney, National Sales Manager

Serves the dental industry. Subscription
75 Pages
Circulation: 120,000
ISSN: 1078-1250
Printed in 4 colors on glossy stock

12561 Dental Products Report
MEDEC Dental Communications
2 Northfield Plaza
Suite 300
Northfield, IL 60093-1219

847-441-3700; *Fax:* 847-441-3702;
www.dentalproducts.net

Dolph Sharp, Publisher
Gail Weisman, Editor
Matthew LaFleur, Illustrator

Serves the dental profession and the dental industry. $120 subscription per year
141 Pages
Frequency: 12 per year
ISSN: 0011-8737
Founded in: 1967
Printed in 4 colors on glossy stock

12562 Dental Products Report Europe
MEDEC Dental Communications
Two Northfield Plaza
Suite 300
Northfield, IL 60093-1219

847-441-3700; *Fax:* 847-441-3702;
www.dentalproducts.net

Richard Fisher, Publisher
Pam Johnson, Editor

Keith Easty, Circulation Director
Dennis Spaeth, Editor
Bob Kehoe, Editorial Director

Designed to inform dentists in Europe and selected Middle Eastern and North African countries and dental distributors and depot personnel worldwide of new developments and ongoing trends in the dental market.
Cost: $40.00
Circulation: 50000
Founded in: 1987

12563 **Dentistry Today**
100 Passaic Ave
Fairfield, NJ 07004-3508

973-882-4700; *Fax:* 973-783-7112
admin@dentistrytoday.com;
www.dentistrytoday.com/

Paul Radcliffe, Owner
Phillip Bonner, Editor
Susan Oettinger, Treasurer, Manager
Jan Nigro, Production Manager
Janice Yawdoszyn, Director

The nation's leading clinical news magazine for dentists
Cost: $65.00
122 Pages
Frequency: Monthly
Circulation: 150,000
ISSN: 8750-2186
Founded in: 1981
Printed in 4 colors on glossy stock

12564 **Devices and Diagnostics Letter**
300 N Washington Street
Suite 200
Falls Church, VA 22046-3431

703-538-7600
888-838-5578; *Fax:* 703-538-7676
customerservice@fdanews.com;
www.fdanews.com

Robert Barton, Editorial Director
Matt Salt, Publisher
Maritza Lizama, Marketing Director
Cynthia Carter, President
Cost: $987.00
Frequency: Weekly
Circulation: 3300
Mailing list available for rent

12565 **Diabetes Care**
1701 N Beauregard St
Alexandria, VA 22311-1742

703-549-1500
800-342-2383; *Fax:* 703-739-0290
askada@diabetes.org; www.diabetes.org

Donna Lucas, Human Resources
Joseph Scheffer, Editor
Peter Banks, Publisher
Joe Herget, Marketing Manager
Cost: $314.00
Frequency: Monthly
Circulation: 13637
Founded in: 1940

12566 **Diabetes Digest Family**
Drug Store News Consumer Health Publications
425 Park Ave
New York, NY 10022-3526

212-756-5220; *Fax:* 212-756-5250;
www.drugstorenews.com

Lebhar Friedman, Publisher

Contains health news of importance to those with diabetes.
Frequency: Annual
Circulation: 6.8mm

12567 **Diabetes Educator**
American Association of Diabetes Educators
100 W Monroe Street
Suite 400
Chicago, IL 60603

312-424-2426
800-338-3633; *Fax:* 312-424-2427
aade@aadenet.org; www.diabeteseducator.org

James Sain, Editor
Chris Laxton, CEO
Michael Warner, Marketing Director
Tami Ross, Vice President

Published by the American Association of Diabetes Educators.
Founded in: 1973
Mailing list available for rent: 10000 names at $160 per M

12568 **Diabetes Interview**
6 School St
Suite 160
Fairfax, CA 94930-1655

415-258-2828
800-234-1218; *Fax:* 415-258-2822
webmaster@diabeteshealth.com;
www.diabeteshealth.com

Nadia Al-Samarrie, Publisher
Scott King, Editorial
Daniel Trecroci, Managing Editor
Dick Young, Production
Susan Art, Director
Cost: $12.00
Frequency: Monthly
Circulation: 120,000
Founded in: 1989

12569 **Diagnostic Imaging**
Miller Freeman Publications
600 Harrison Street
San Francisco, CA 94107

415-947-6478; *Fax:* 415-947-6099;
www.diagnosticimaging.com

John C. Hayes, Editor
Gary Marshall, President
Suzanne Johnston, Publisher
Kathy Mischak, Associate Publisher

The news magazine of imaging innovation and economics.
Cost: $113.00
90 Pages
Frequency: Monthly
Circulation: 31240
ISSN: 0194-2514
Founded in: 1984
Printed in 4 colors on glossy stock

12570 **Diagnostic Imaging America Latina**
Miller Freeman Publications
600 Harrison Street
San Francisco, CA 94107

415-947-6478; *Fax:* 415-947-6099;
www.diagnosticimaging.com

Suzanne Johnston, Editor/Publisher
John Hayes, Editorial
Buckley Dement, Circulation
Heidi Torpey, Marketing
Cost: $113.00
Frequency: Monthly
Founded in: 1996

12571 **Diagnostic Imaging Asia Pacific**
Miller Freeman Publications
600 Harrison Street
San Francisco, CA 94107

415-947-6491; *Fax:* 415-947-6099;
www.diagnosticimaging.com

Philip Ward, Editor
David E Lese, Publisher

A newsmagazine aimed at radiologists and allied medical professionals involved in the practice of diagnostic imaging, and provides timely articles on new diagnostic and technical developments in the field mixed with extensive coverage of important political, commercial and economic trends in the specialty.
Cost: $120.00
42 Pages
Frequency: Quarterly
Circulation: 10,000
Printed in 4 colors on glossy stock

12572 **Diagnostic Imaging Europe**
Miller Freeman Publications
600 Harrison Street
San Francisco, CA 94107

415-947-6478; *Fax:* 415-947-6099;
www.diagnosticimaging.com

Philip Ward, Editor
Suzanne Johnston, Publisher
Jose Joaquin, Circulation
Kim Spinoso, National Sales Manager

A newsmagazine aimed at radiologists and allied medical professionals involved in the practice of diagnostic imaging. Provides a balanced mix of timely articles on new diagnostic and technical developments in the field mixed with extensive coverage of important political, commercial and economic trends in the specialty.
Cost: $125.00
58 Pages
Circulation: 10062
Founded in: 1996
Printed in 4 colors on glossy stock

12573 **Dialysis and Transplantation**
Creative Age Publications
7628 Densmore Ave
Van Nuys, CA 91406-2042

818-782-7560
800-442-5667; *Fax:* 818-782-7450;
www.creativeage.com

Deborah Carver, Publisher/CEO
Joseph G Herman, Executive Editor
Carlos Benskin, Circulation Manager
Gail Edwards, Accounting Manager
Diane Jones, Advertising Director

Serves the renal care community. Subscription: $17.50.
Cost: $35.00
Frequency: Monthly
Founded in: 1975
Printed in 4 colors on glossy stock

12574 **Director**
National Funeral Director Association
13625 Bishops Dr
Brookfield, WI 53005-6607

262-789-1880
800-228-6332; *Fax:* 262-789-6977
nfda@nfda.org; www.nfda.org

Coverage concentrates on funeral service education and licensure, community service and public relations as well as public health concerns and legal, ethical and moral issues.
Cost: $45.00
84 Pages
Frequency: Monthly
Circulation: 13906
ISSN: 0199-3186
Founded in: 1882
Printed in 4 colors on glossy stock

12575 **Diseases of the Colon & Rectum**
American Society of Colon & Rectal Surgeons
85 W Algonquin Road
Suite 550
Arlington Heights, IL 60005

847-290-9184
800-791-0001; *Fax:* 847-290-9203

ascrs@fascrs.org; www.fascrs.org
Social Media: Facebook

Pat Oldenburg, Managing Editor
Rick Slawny, Executive Director
Stella Zedalis, Associate Executive Director
Julie Weldon, Assistant Director
John Nocera, Chief Financial Officer
2800 Members
Mailing list available for rent

12576 Drug Store News
Lebhar-Friedman
425 Park Ave
New York, NY 10022-3526

212-756-5088
800-216-7117; *Fax:* 212-838-9487
info@lf.com; www.nrn.com

Heather Martin, Manager
Tony Lisanti, Editor/Associate Publisher
Terry Nicosia, Senior Production Manager
K Dement, Circulation Manager
Wayne Bennett, Advertising Manager

Publication consists of merchandising trends and pharmacy developments. Provides extensive coverage of every major segment of chain drug retailing and combination stores.
Frequency: Monthly
Circulation: 44372
Founded in: 1925

12577 Emergency Medicine
7 Century Dr
Suite 302
Parsippany, NJ 07054-4609

973-206-3434; *Fax:* 973-206-9378;
www.quadranthealth.com

Susan Alburtus, Manager
Michael Pepper, Publisher
Martin Dicarlantonio, Editor
Donna Sickles, Circulation Manager
Kathleen Corbett, Advertising Coordinator
Cost: $90.00
Frequency: Monthly
Circulation: 158000
Founded in: 1967

12578 Emerging Trends
Trends Analysis Group
1 N Franklin
29th Floor
Chicago, IL 60606-3421

312-422-3990; *Fax:* 312-422-4569

Marcia Foley, Editor

Published as a community hospital trends which focuses on financial performance, personnel, utilization and facilities.
Cost: $135.00
Frequency: Quarterly
Circulation: 1,700

12579 EndoNurse
Virgo Publishing LLC
3300 N Central Ave
Suite 300
Phoenix, AZ 85012-2532

480-990-1101; *Fax:* 480-990-0819
jsiefert@vpico.com; www.vpico.com

Jenny Bolton, President
John Siefert, CEO
Jennifer Janos, Controller
Kelly Ridley, Executive VP, CFO, Copado

EndoNurse provides the practical information and updated protocol for those practicing in hospitals and freestanding facilities.
Mailing list available for rent: 13000+ names at $var per M

12580 Endocrine
505 NW 185th Avenue
Beaverton, OR 97006-3448

503-690-5350; *Fax:* 503-690-5245;
www.bioscience.org

P Michael Conn, Editor-in-Chief
Peter O Kohler, President
Cost: $365.00
Founded in: 1867

12581 Endocrine Practice
American Association of Clinical Endocrinologists
245 Riverside Avenue
Suite 200
Jacksonville, FL 32202

904-353-7878; *Fax:* 904-353-8185
info@aace.com; www.aace.com

Donald Jones, CEO
Donna Beasley, CPA, Finance Manager
Michael Avallone, CPA, Chief Financial Officer
Lynn Blanco, Executive Assistant
Lucille Killgore, Director of College Activities

To enhance the health care of patients with endocrine diseases through continuing education of practicing endocrinologists
Cost: $350.00
Frequency: Bi-Monthly
Circulation: 5000
Mailing list available for rent

12582 Endocrine Reviews
The Endocrine Society
8401 Connecticut Ave
Suite 900
Chevy Chase, MD 20815-5817

301-941-0200
888-363-6274; *Fax:* 301-941-0259
societyservices@endo-society.org;
www.endo-society.org

Scott Hunt, Executive Director
Anthony R. Means, Secretary
John Marshall, Secretary
Cost: $252.00
Circulation: 5907
Founded in: 1916

12583 European Medical Device Manufacturer
Canon Communications
11444 W Olympic Blvd
Los Angeles, CA 90064-1555

310-445-4200; *Fax:* 310-445-4299;
www.cancom.com

Charlie Mc Curdy, President
Cost: $150.00
Circulation: 15,048
Founded in: 1978

12584 Exercise and Sport Sicence Reviews
Lippincott Williams & Wilkins
530 Walnut St
Philadelphia, PA 19106-3604

215-521-8300; *Fax:* 215-521-8902
support@ovid.com; www.lww.com

Gordon Macomber, CEO
Lori A Tish, Editorial Assistant
Michael A. Hargrett, Associate Publisher

This Journal provides premier reviews of the most contemporary scientific, medical and research-based topics emerging in the field of sports medicine and exercise science, targeted to students, professors, clinicians, scientists and professionals for practical and research applications.
192 Pages
Frequency: Quarterly
ISSN: 0091-6331
Founded in: 1998
Printed in 4 colors on matte stock

12585 Extended Care Product News
HMP Communications
83 General Warren Blvd
Suite 100
Malvern, PA 19355-1252
610-560-0500
800-237-7285; *Fax:* 610-560-0502
pnorris@hmpcommunications.com;
www.hmpcommunications.com

Christine Franey, VP
Elizabeth Klumpp, Executive Editor
Peter Treaill, CEO/President
Bonnie Shannon, Manager
Michelle Koch, Circulation Manager

Serves purchasing professionals in acute, long term, and home care, offering product information, reimbursement updates, legislative news, industry trends, and a health care business focus.
24 Pages
Circulation: 100000
ISSN: 0895-2906
Founded in: 1989
Printed in 4 colors on glossy stock

12586 Family Medicine
11400 Tomahawk Creek Parkway
Leawood, KS 66211

913-906-6000
800-274-2237; *Fax:* 913-906-6096
fmjournal@stfm.org; www.stfm.org

Traci Nolte, Publisher
John Saultz, President/Editor
Stacy Brungardt, Executive Director
Circulation: 6000
Founded in: 1967

12587 Family Therapy Magazine
American Assoc for Marriage and Family Therapy
112 S Alfred Street
Alexandria, VA 22314-3061

703-838-9808; *Fax:* 703-838-9805
central@aamft.org; www.aamft.org
Social Media: Facebook, Twitter, LinkedIn

Linda S. Metcalf, PhD, President
Michael L. Chafin, President-Elect
Michael Bowers, Executive Director
Robin Stillwell, MA, Secretary
Silvia M. Kaminsky, MsED,, Treasurer

AAMFT Association has been involved with the problems, needs and changing patterns of couples and family relationships. The assocation leads the way to increasing understanding, research and education in the field of marriage and family therapy, and ensuring that the public's needs are met by trained practitioners. The AAMFT provides individuals with the tools and resources they need to succeed as marriage and family therapists.
25000 Members
Frequency: Bi-Monthly
Circulation: 25,000
Founded in: 1942

12588 First Messenger
American Association of Clinical Endocrinologists
245 Riverside Avenue
Suite 200
Jacksonville, FL 32202

904-353-7878; *Fax:* 904-353-8185
info@aace.com; www.aace.com

Donald Jones, CEO
Donna Beasley, CPA, Finance Manager
Michael Avallone, CPA, Chief Financial Officer
Lynn Blanco, Executive Assistant
Lucille Killgore, Director of College Activities

Serves as a fast track communications tool for AACE members. AACE members utilize The First Messenger to remain in touch with the latest news that may impact their practices, including

legislative and socioeconomic issues, cutting edge educational programs, practice management issues and new coding changes.
Frequency: Bi-Monthly
Circulation: 5000
Mailing list available for rent

12589 **Frontiers of Health Services Management**
American College of Healthcare Executives
One North Franklin Street
Suite 1700
Chicago, IL 60606-3529
312-424-2800; *Fax:* 312-424-0023
contact@ache.org; www.ache.org
Trudy Land, FACHE, Editorial
Frequency: Quarterly

12590 **General Dentistry**
211 E Chicago Ave
Suite 900
Chicago, IL 60611-2637
312-440-4300
888-243-3368; *Fax:* 312-440-0559
executiveoffice@agd.org; www.agd.org
John Maher, Manager
Mark Heiss, AGD Member
Jay Donohue, Executive Director
Circulation: 37,000
Founded in: 1951

12591 **General Surgery News**
545 W 45th St
8th Floor
New York, NY 10036-3409
212-957-5300; *Fax:* 212-957-7230
cdahnke@mcmahonmed.com; www.mcmahonmed.com
Raymond E Mc Mahon, CEO
Van Velle, Director
James Prudden, Director
Megan Roloff, Managing Editor
Cost: $60.00
Frequency: Monthly
Circulation: 37,268
Founded in: 1974

12592 **Grant Funding for Elderly Health Services**
Health Resources Publishing
1913 Atlantic Ave
Suite F4
Manasquan, NJ 08736-1067
732-292-1100
888-843-6242; *Fax:* 732-292-1111
info@healthresourcesonline.com; www.healthresourcesonline.com
Robert K Jenkins, Publisher
Lisa Mansfield, Marketing Assistant
Robert Jenkins, Editor
Brett Powell, Regional Director
Alice Burron, Director
This report will give insight into which proposals will get funds for which organization. Lists the organizations that will recieve the most funds from grantmakers during this decade and beyond. Also studies different case histories of successful grant proposals.
Cost: $147.00
Frequency: Monthly
ISBN: 1-882364-46-5
Founded in: 1969

12593 **Group Practice Data Management**
SourceMedia
550 W Van Buren
Suite 1100
Chicago, IL 60607-6680
312-913-1334; *Fax:* 312-913-1959;
www.sourcemedia.com
Howard Anderson, Publisher/Editor
Melissa Sefic, Director of Sales
Analyses of trends, insights on technology and practice advice from automation pioneers for executive and physician administrators of medical groups in charge of making decisions about information technology investments. Profiles on practices, new software development updates, and ideas on plans for implementing information technology.
Frequency: Semiannual
Circulation: 15M

12594 **Harvard Mental Health Letter**
Harvard Health Publcations
10 Shattuck Street
Boston, MA 02115
617-432-1485
877-649-9457; *Fax:* 617-432-1506
mental_health@hms.harvard.edu; www.health.harvard.edu/mental
Michael Craig Miller, Editor in Chief
Edward Coburn, Publishing Director
Cost: $59.00
Frequency: Monthly
Circulation: 50000
Founded in: 1985

12595 **Harvard Public Health Review**
Harvard School of Public Health
665 Huntington Ave
Boston, MA 02115-6018
617-495-1000; *Fax:* 617-384-8989
fphelps@hsph.harvard.edu; www.hsph.harvard.edu/review
Martha Cassin, Manager
Barry R. Bloom, Dean of the School
Martha Cassin, Manager
Flagship magazine of the Harvard School of Public Health.
60 Pages
Frequency: Bi-annually
Circulation: 10000
Founded in: 1922
Printed in 4 colors on glossy stock

12596 **Health Data Management**
SourceMedia
550 W Van Buren
Suite 1100
Chicago, IL 60607-6680
312-913-1334; *Fax:* 312-913-1959;
www.healthdatamanagement.com/
Howard J Anderson, Publisher
Bill Siwicki, Editorial Director
Greg Gillespie, Managing Editor
Bill Briggs, Senior Editor
Jim Siebert, Sales/Marketing Manager
Reporting on important information technology issues in health care with emphasis on computerization trends that improve health care efficiency.
Frequency: Monthly
Circulation: 41116
Founded in: 1994

12597 **Health Facilities Management**
American Hospital Publishing
1 N Franklin St
29th Floor
Chicago, IL 60606-3530
312-893-6800
800-821-2039; *Fax:* 312-422-4500
hfcustsvc@healthforum.com; www.hfmmagazine.com
Mary Grayson, Publisher
Mike Hrickiewicz, Managing Editor
Gary A. Mecklenburg, Chairman
Neil J. Jesuele, Director
Reflects their highly specialized needs such as changes in codes and standards, industry news, new products and technical developments of suppliers.
Cost: $30.00
Frequency: Monthly
Circulation: 28160
Founded in: 1998

12598 **Health Management Technology**
Nelson Publishing
2500 Tamiami Trl N
Nokomis, FL 34275-3476
941-966-9521; *Fax:* 941-966-2590;
www.healthmgttech.com
Social Media: Facebook, Twitter
A Verner Nelson, Owner
Robin Blair, Editor
Serves the health care industry including hospitals/multi-hospital systems, managed care organizations and others allied to the field.
Cost: $60.00
66 Pages
Frequency: Monthly
Circulation: 45751
ISSN: 0745-1075
Founded in: 1965
Printed in 4 colors on glossy stock

12599 **Health Progress**
Catholic Health Association
4455 Woodson Rd
St Louis, MO 63134-3797
314-427-2500; *Fax:* 314-427-0029
rmueller@chausa.org; www.chausa.org
Rhonda Mueller, Senior Vice President of Operations
Monica Heaton, Editor
Martha Slover, Circulation Manager
Focuses on management concepts, ethical issues, legislative trends, and theological issues.
Cost: $50.00
Frequency: Monthly
Circulation: 12000
Founded in: 1914

12600 **Healthcare Executive**
American College of Healthcare Executives
One North Franklin Street
Suite 1700
Chicago, IL 60606-3529
312-424-2800; *Fax:* 312-424-0023
contact@ache.org; www.ache.org
Social Media: Facebook, Twitter, LinkedIn
Edward H. Lamb, Chairman
Charles D. Stokes, Chairman-Elect
Deborah J. Bowen, FACHE, President & CEO
Thomas C. Dolan. PhD, President & CEO
Richard J. Stull, Executive Vice President
Serves members of the American College of Health care executives, whose primary business/industries include hospitals, managed care organizations, long-term care facilities and others allied to the field.
Cost: $110.00
Frequency: Bi-Monthly
ISSN: 0883-5381
Mailing list available for rent
Printed in 4 colors on glossy stock

12601 Healthcare Financial Management
2 Westbrook Corporate Ctr
Westchester, IL 60154-5723
708-531-9614; *Fax:* 708-531-0032;
www.hfma.org
Richard L Clarke, President

12602 Healthcare Foodservice Magazine
International Publishing Company of America
664 La Villa Dr
Miami Springs, FL 33166-6030
305-887-1700
800-525-2015; *Fax:* 305-885-1923;
www.healthcarefoodservice.org
Alexander Morton, Owner
Melora Grattan, Assistant Editor
Devoted to foodservice topics for foodservice directors, foodservice managers, dieticians, foodservice supervisors, chefs, purchasing managers, purchasing agents, administrators and others.
Cost: $25.00
24 Pages
Frequency: Quarterly
Printed in 4 colors on glossy stock

12603 Healthcare Informatics
McGraw Hill
4530 W 77th St
Suite 350
Edina, MN 55435-5018
952-832-7887; *Fax:* 952-832-7908
Jim Dougherty, Publisher

12604 Healthcare Purchasing News
Nelson Publishing
7650 S Tamiami Trail N
Suite 10
Sarasota, FL 34275
941-927-9345; *Fax:* 941-927-9588;
www.hpnonline.com
Rick Dana Barlow, Senior Editor
Jeannie Akridge, New Products Editor
Kristine Russell, Publisher
Julie Williamson, Features Editor
Susan Cantrell, Infection Control Editor
Serves the field of hospital materials management, purchasing, central services and administration.
Cost: $63.00
27 Pages
Frequency: Monthly
Circulation: 33000
ISSN: 0279-4799
Founded in: 1965
Printed in 4 colors on glossy stock

12605 Healthplan
American Association of Health Plans
601 Pennsylvania Ave NW
Suite 500
Washington, DC 20004-2601
202-778-3200; *Fax:* 202-955-4394
ahip@ahip.org; www.ahip.org
Kevin New, Editor
A magazine of trends, insights and best practices.
Cost: $60.00
Circulation: 19000
Founded in: 2004

12606 Home Health Products
Stevens Publishing Corporation
5151 Belt Line Rd
Dallas, TX 75254-7507
972-687-6700; *Fax:* 972-687-6767;
www.stevenspublishing.com
Craig S Stevens, President
Mike Valenti, Executive Vice President
Randy Dye, Publisher
Sandra Bienkowski, Editor
Cost: $119.00
Circulation: 20000
Founded in: 1925

12607 Home Medical Equipment News
United Publications
106 Lafayette Street
PO Box 998
Yarmouth, ME 04096
207-846-0600; *Fax:* 207-846-0657;
www.hmenews.com
Rick Rector, Publisher
Brook Taliaferro, Editorial Director
Brenda Boothby, Circulation Director
James G. Taliaferro, President
Jim Sullivan, Editor
Serves home medical equipment providers.
Cost: $84.00
Frequency: Monthly
Circulation: 17100
Founded in: 1995

12608 HomeCare
Penton Media Inc
249 W 17th St
New York, NY 10011-5390
212-204-4200; *Fax:* 212-206-3622;
www.penton.com
Sharon Rowlands, CEO
Gail Walker, Editor
David Kieselstein, Chief Executive Officer
Kurt Nelson, Vice President, Human Resources
Andrew Schmolka, Senior Vice President
For business leaders in home medical equipment
Frequency: Monthly
Founded in: 1989
Mailing list available for rent

12609 Hospital Law Manual
Publishers
111 Eighth Avenue
7th Floor
New York, NY 10011-1978
212-771-0600
800-234-1660; *Fax:* 212-771-0885
customer.service@aspenpubl.com;
www.aspenlawschool.com
Robert Becker, CEO
Stacey Caywood, Publisher
Richard H Kravitz, VP
Hospital law.
Cost: $1325.00
Frequency: Quarterly
Founded in: 1965

12610 Hospital Outlook
801 Pennsylvania Ave NW
Suite 245
Washington, DC 20004-2697
202-624-1500
202-624-1500; *Fax:* 202-737-6462
info@fah.org; www.fah.org
Charles Kahn, President
LaQuanda Washington, Editor Asst.
Richard P Coorsh, Publisher
Letitia Faison-Mahoney, Controller
Founded in: 1966

12611 Hypertension
1516 Jefferson Highway
BH 514
New Orleans, LA 70121
504-842-3700; *Fax:* 504-842-3258

12612 Immediate Care Business
Virgo Publishing LLC
3300 N Central Ave
Suite 300
Phoenix, AZ 85012-2532
480-990-1101; *Fax:* 480-990-0819
jsiefert@vpico.com; www.vpico.com
Jenny Bolton, President
John Siefert, CEO
Jennifer Janos, Controller
Kelly Ridley, Executive VP, CFO, Copado
Immediate Care Business provides practical business solutions to professionals who own, operate or are planning to open an urgent care/immediate care facility.
Mailing list available for rent

12613 Infection Control Today
Virgo Publishing LLC
3300 N Central Ave
Suite 300
Phoenix, AZ 85012-2532
480-990-1101; *Fax:* 480-990-0819
jsiefert@vpico.com; www.vpico.com
Jenny Bolton, President
John Siefert, CEO
Jennifer Janos, Controller
Kelly Ridley, Executive VP, CFO, Copado
Infection Control Today provides science based articles for the general ward, operating room, sterile processing and environmental services departments of healthcare facilities as well as for the public health community.
Mailing list available for rent: 30000+ names at $var per M

12614 Information Management Magazine
ARMA International
11880 College Blvd
Suite 450
Overland Park, KS 66210
913-341-3808
800-422-2762; *Fax:* 913-341-3742
hq@arma.org; www.arma.org
Marilyn Bier, Executive Director
Jody Becker, Associate Editor
Kerrianne Aulet, Education Program Administrator
Michael Avery, Chief Operating Officer
Paula Banes, Sales Project Manager
The leading source of information on topics and issues central to the management of records and information worldwide. Each issue features insightful articles written by experts in the management of records and information.
Cost: $115.00
10,00 Members
Frequency: Bi-monthly
Circulation: 11000
ISSN: 1535-2897
Founded in: 1955
Mailing list available for rent: 9000 names
Printed in 4 colors on glossy stock

12615 International Journal of Trauma Nursing
Mosby/Professional Opportunities
11830 Westline Industrial Drive
St Louis, MO 63146-3318
314-453-4338
800-237-9851; *Fax:* 314-872-9164
c.kilzer@elsevier.com;
www.mosby.com/trauma
Judith Stoner Halpern, Editor
Sarah Papke Kalamazoo, EDITORIAL ASSISTANT
Carol Kilzer, Advertising Sales Service
Reaches today's trauma nurses, coordinators,and managers who direct the nursing aspects of patient care. The journal's multidisciplinary and collaborative approach to the unique needs of the trauma patient represents the vision and clinical expertise of each nursing specialty. These profes-

sionals influence the purchase of supplies and equipment for use in emergency and trauma departments.
Cost: $42.00
Frequency: Quarterly
Circulation: 1298
Founded in: 1995

12616 Internet Healthcare Strategies
Dean Anderson
PO Box 50507
Santa Barbara, CA 93150
805-564-2177; *Fax:* 805-564-2146;
www.corhealth.com

12617 JAAPA
Medical Economics Publishing
131 W 1st Street
Duluth, MN 55802-2065
877-922-2022; *Fax:* 218-723-9437
aapa@aapa.org; www.jaapa.com
Leslie A Kole, Editor-in-Chief
Tanya Gregory, Editor
Dominic Barone, Publisher
Miguel Van Brakle, Circulation manager
Lee Maniscalco, CEO
Official journal of the American Academy of Physican Assistants.
92 Pages
Frequency: Monthly
Circulation: 52500
ISSN: 0893-7400

12618 Journal Of Oncology Management
Alliance Communications Group
810 E 10th St
Lawrence, KS 66044-3018
785-843-1235
800-627-0932; *Fax:* 785-843-1274;
www.acgpublishing.com
Gerald Lillian, CEO
Jorgene Hallett, Chief Financial Officer
Rob Chestnut, Chief Financial Officer
Barbara Buzzi, Manager
Bi-monthly, peer-reviewed journal. Includes original research, case studies and other features pertinent to improving performance of oncology administrators.
Cost: $87.00
32 Pages
Circulation: 10000
ISSN: 1061-9364
Founded in: 1935
Printed in 4 colors on glossy stock

12619 Journal Watch
860 Winter Street
Waltham, MA 02154
781-893-3800
800-843-6356; *Fax:* 781-893-3914
jwatch@mms.org; www.jwatch.org
Allan S Brett, Editor In Chief
Alberta L Fitzpatrick, Publisher
Founded in: 1987

12620 Journal of Allergy and Clinical Immunology
American Academy of Allergy, Asthma and Immunology
555 E Wells St
Suite 1100
Milwaukee, WI 53202-3800
414-272-6071
info@aaaai.org; www.aaaai.org
Thomas B. Casale, MD, Executive VP
Kay A. Whalen, Executive Director
Roberta Silvensky, Associate Executive Director
Amy Flanders, Director of Grants & Development
Rachel McCormick, Executive Assistant
The official scientific journal of the American Academy of Allergy, Asthma and Immunology and the premiere journal in the field. Each issue features the very latest and best research in the allergy/immunology specialty.
6000+ Members
Frequency: Monthly
Founded in: 1943

12621 Journal of American Dietetic Association
American Dietetic Association
120 South Riverside Plaza
Suite 2000
Chicago, IL 60606-6995
312-990-0040
800-877-1600; *Fax:* 312-899-4757
elspcs@elsevier.com; www.adajournal.org
Linda Van Horn, Editor-in-Chief
Jason T Switt, Editors:
The Journal of American Dietetic Association serves the dietetic field.
Cost: $220.00
Frequency: Monthly
Circulation: 65000
ISSN: 0002-8223
Founded in: 1925
Printed in 4 colors on glossy stock

12622 Journal of Cardiovascular Management
Alliance Communications Group
810 E 10th St
Lawrence, KS 66044-3018
785-843-1235
800-627-0932; *Fax:* 785-843-1274
info@aameda.org; www.acgpublishing.com
Gerald Lillian, CEO
Jorgene Hallett, Publishing Manager
Renee S Schleicher, CEO/President
Rob Chestnut, Chief Financial Officer
Bi-monthly, peer-reviewed journal of articles pertinent to cardiovascular administration.
Cost: $87.00
32 Pages
Circulation: 12,500
ISSN: 1053-5330
Founded in: 1957
Mailing list available for rent: 400 names at $350 per M
Printed in 4 colors on glossy stock

12623 Journal of Clinical Epidemiology
Elsevier Publishing
PO Box 28430
St Louis, MO 63146-0930
314-872-8370
800-545-2522; *Fax:* 314-432-1380;
www.elsevier.com
Erik Engstrom, CEO
Bill Godfrey, Chief Information Officer
David Clark, Senior Vice President

12624 Journal of Clinical Investigation
11830 Westline Industrial Drive
St Louis, MO 63146
314-453-7010
800-460-3110; *Fax:* 314-453-7095;
www.elsevier.com
A Knottnerus, Editor
P Tugwell, Editor
Laurence Zipson, Group Advertisement Manag
Karlyn Messinger, Communications Manager
Cost: $274.00
Frequency: Monthly
Founded in: 1955

12625 Journal of Craniofacial Surgery
Lippencott Williams & Wilkins
16522 Hunters Green Pkwy
Hagerstown, MD 21740-2116
301-223-2300
800-638-3030; *Fax:* 301-223-2398
service@lww.com;
www.nursingdrugguide.com
Mutaz B Habal MD, Editor
Jay Lippioctt, CEO
An international journal dedicated to the art and science essential to the practice of craniofacial surgery. Online version available.
Cost: $586.00
ISSN: 1049-2275
Founded in: 1998

12626 Journal of Digital Imaging
Society for Imaging Informatics in Medicine
19440 Golf Vista Plaza
Suite 330
Leesburg, VA 20176-8264
703-723-0432; *Fax:* 703-723-0415
info@siimweb.org; www.siimweb.org
Janice Honeyman-Buck PhD, Editor-in-Chief
Goal is to enhance the exchange of knowledge encompassed by the general topic of Imaging Informatics in Medicine such as research and practice in clinical, engineering, information technologies and techniques in all medical imaging environments. JDI topics are of interest to researchers, developers, educators, physicians, and imaging informatics professionals.
Frequency: Bi-Monthly

12627 Journal of Emergency Nursing
Mosby/Professional Opportunities
PO Box 1510
Clearwater, FL 33757-1510
727-443-3047
800-237-9851; *Fax:* 727-445-9380;
www.mosby.com/trauma
Presents original, peer-reviewed clinical articles as well as the annual ENA Scientific Assembly program.
Circulation: 27240

12628 Journal of ExtraCorporeal Technology
American Society of ExtraCorporeal Technology
2209 Dickens Road
Richmond, VA 23230-2005
804-565-6363; *Fax:* 804-282-0090
judyr@amsect.org; www.amsect.org
Stewart Hinckley, Executive Director
Donna Pendarvis, Associate Manager
Michael Troike, Government Relations Chairman
Kimberly Robertson, CPA, Controller
Greg Leasure, Membership Services
Cost: $225.00
2,000 Members
Frequency: Quarterly
Circulation: 2000
ISSN: 0022-1058
Founded in: 1964

12629 Journal of Forensic Psychology Practice
Bill Cohen
10 Alice Street
Binghamton, NY 13904-1580
607-225-5857
607-722-5857; *Fax:* 607-771-0012
getinfo@haworthpress.com;
www.haworthpressinc.com
Bill Cohen, President/Publisher
Jim Hom, Editor
Provides the forensic psychology practicioner and professional with timely information and regional research that examines the impact of new

knowledge in the field as it relates to their practice.
Cost: $60.00
Frequency: Quarterly
Circulation: 700
Founded in: 1978

12630 Journal of Hand Surgery
American Society for Surgery of the Hand
822 W. Washington Boulevard
Suite 600
Chicago, IL 60607

312-880-1900; *Fax:* 847-384-1435
info@assh.org; www.assh.org

Roy A Meals, Editor-in-Chief

Publishes original, peer-reviewed articles related to the diagnosis, treatment, and pathophysiology of diseases and conditions of the upper extremity; these include both clinical and basic science studies, along with case reports.
Frequency: Monthly
Mailing list available for rent

12631 Journal of Healthcare Management
American College of Healthcare Executives
One North Franklin Street
Suite 1700
Chicago, IL 60606-3529

312-424-2800; *Fax:* 312-424-0023
contact@ache.org; www.ache.org
Social Media: Facebook, Twitter, LinkedIn

Deborah J. Bowen, FACHE, President & CEO
Thomas C. Dolan, PhD, President & CEO
Founded in: 1933

12632 Journal of Healthcare Quality
National Association for Healthcare Quality
4700 W Lake Ave
Glenview, IL 60025-1468

847-375-4732
800-966-9392; *Fax:* 888-576-4349
info@nahq.org; www.nahq.org

Sheila Lee, Manager
John D Hartley, President

Professional forum that advances quality in a diverse and changing health care environment. Health care professionals worldwide depend upon the Journal for its creative solutions and scientific konwledge in the pursuit of quality.
Cost: $115.00
54 Pages
ISSN: 1062-2551
Founded in: 1976
Printed in 4 colors on glossy stock

12633 Journal of Magnetic Resonance
525 B Street
Suite 1900
San Diego, CA 92101-4401

619-231-6616
800-321-5068; *Fax:* 619-699-6280;
www.elsevier.com/

S.J. Opella, Editor
JJH Ackerman, Associate Editor
L Frydman, Associate Editor
W.S. Brey, Founding Editor
Founded in: 1880

12634 Journal of Managed Care Medicine
American Assoc of Integrated Healthcare Delivery
4435 Waterfront Drive
Suite 101
Glen Allen, VA 23060

804-747-5823; *Fax:* 804-747-5316
phulcher@aaihds.org; www.aaihds.org

Bill Edwards, Managing Editor
Jeremy Williams, Communications Director
Mark Abernathy, Managing Director
David Tyler, Manager
Steven M. Abramson, Senior Manager

12635 Journal of Marriage & Family Therapy
American Assoc for Marriage and Family Therapy
112 S Alfred Street
Alexandria, VA 22314-3061

703-838-9808; *Fax:* 703-838-9805
central@aamft.org; www.aamft.org
Social Media: Facebook, Twitter, LinkedIn

Linda S. Metcalf, PhD, President
Michael Chafin, President-Elect
Michael Bowers, Executive Director
Robin K. Stillwell, MA, Secretary
Silvia M. Kaminsky, MSEd, Treasurer

The AAMFT has been involved with the problems, needs and changing patterns of couples and family relationships. The association leads the way to increasing understanding, research and education in the field of marriage and family therapy, ensuring that the public's needs are met by trained practitioners.
25000 Members
Frequency: Quarterly
Circulation: 25,000
Founded in: 1942

12636 Journal of Midwifery & Women's Health
American College of Nurse-Midwives
8403 Colesville Road,Suite 1550
Silver Spring, MD 20910

240-485-1815; *Fax:* 240-485-1817
jmwh@acnm.org; www.jmwh.org/

tekoa king, Editor
Tekoa King, President, Chief Executive Officer
Kalpana Raina, Managing Partner
Cost: $130.00
Circulation: 8000

12637 Journal of Music Therapy
8455 Colesville Rd
Suite 1000
Silver Spring, MD 20910-3392

301-589-3300; *Fax:* 301-589-5175
info@musictherapy.org;
www.musictherapy.org
Social Media: Facebook, Twitter

Andrea Farbman, Executive Director
Mary Ellen Wylei, AMTA President

Founded in: 1998, AMTA's purpose is the progressive development of the therapeutic use of music in rehabilitation, special education, and community settings. AMTA is committed to the advancement of education, training, professional standards, credentials, and research in support of the music therapy profession.
3800 Members
Frequency: 4 Issues Per Year
Founded in: 1998

12638 Journal of Neurotherapy
Taylor & Francis Group LLC
325 Chestnut Street
Suite 800
Philadelphia, PA 19106

215-625-8900
800-354-1420; *Fax:* 215-625-2940
haworthorders@taylorandfrancis.com;
www.haworthpressinc.com

Timothy Tinius PhD, Editor
David Kaiser PhD, Editor

Provides an integrated multidisciplinary perspective on clinically relevant research, treatment and public policy for neurotherapy. The journal reviews important findings in clinical neurotherapy and electroencephalography for use in assessing baselines and outcomes of various procedures.
Frequency: Monthly

12639 Journal of Nuclear Medicine
Society of Nuclear Medicine
1850 Samuel Morse Dr
Reston, VA 20190-5316

703-708-9000; *Fax:* 703-708-9015
volunteer@snm.org; www.snm.org

Virginia Pappas, Executive Director
Vincent Pistilli, Chief Financial Officer
Matt Dickens, Director, Information Services
Judy Brazel, Director, Meeting Services
Joanna Spahr, Director, Marketing

12640 Journal of Occupational and Environmental Hygiene (JOEH)
American Industrial Hygiene Association
3141 Fairview Park Drive
Suite 777
Falls Church, VA 22042

703-849-8888; *Fax:* 703-207-3561
infonet@aiha.org; www.aiha.org
Social Media: Facebook, Twitter, LinkedIn, RSS, YouTube

Stephen J. Reynolds, President
Mark Nicas, Editor-in-Chief

A joint publication of AIHA and ACGIH that is published to enhance the knowledge and practice of occupational and environmental hygiene and safety.
Frequency: Monthly
Founded in: 1939

12641 Journal of Oral Implantology
American Academy of Implant Dentistry
211 E Chicago Avenue
Suie 750
Chicago, IL 60611

312-335-1550
877-335-2243; *Fax:* 312-335-9090;
www.aaid.org
Social Media: Facebook, Twitter, LinkedIn

James Rutkowski, Editor-in-Chief
Sheldon Winkler, Senior Editor

Dedicated to providing valuable information to general dentists, oral surgeons, prosthodontists, periodontists, scientists, clinicians, laboratory owners and technicians, manufacturers, and educators
Cost: $140.00
Frequency: Bimonthly
Circulation: 4200
ISSN: 0160-6972

12642 Journal of Prosthetics and Orthotics
351 W Camden St
Baltimore, MD 21201-7912

410-528-4000
800-638-6423; *Fax:* 410-528-4452
webmaster@lww.com; www.lww.com

Jeffrey A Nemeth, Editor
Cost: $91.00
Frequency: Quarterly
Founded in: 1792

12643 Journal of School Nursing (JOSN)
Sage Publications
2455 Teller Rd
Newbury Park, CA 91320-2234

805-499-9774
800-818-7243; *Fax:* 805-499-0871
info@sagepub.com; www.sagepub.com

Blaise R Simqu, CEO
Janice Denehy, Executive Editor

A forum for advancing the specialty of school nursing, promoting professional growth of school nurses, and improving the health of children in school. Published bi-monthly, this is the

official journal of the National Association of School Nurses.
Cost: $164.00
Frequency: bi-Monthly
Mailing list available for rent

12644 Journal of Social Behavior & Personality
Drawer 37
Corte Madera, CA 94976
415-209-9838; *Fax:* 415-209-6719; www.sbp-journal.com
Rick Crandall, CEO/President
Rick Crandall, Editor
Cost: $70.00
Frequency: Quarterly
Founded in: 1985

12645 Journal of Thoracic and Cardiovascular Surgery
American Association for Thoracic Surgery
500 Cummings Center
Suite 4550
Beverly, MA 01915
978-927-8330; *Fax:* 978-524-8890
aats@prri.com; www.aats.org
Social Media: Facebook
G Alexander Patterson, President
Elizabeth Dooley Crane, Executive Director
Cost: $354.00
Frequency: Monthly
Circulation: 6000
Founded in: 1917
Mailing list available for rent

12646 Journal of Trauma & Dissociation
Taylor & Francis Group LLC
325 Chestnut Street
Suite 800
Philadelphia, PA 19106
215-625-8900
800-354-1420; *Fax:* 215-625-2940
haworthorders@taylorandfrancis.com; www.haworthpressinc.com
Jennifer J Freyd PhD, Editor
Dedicated to publishing peer reviewed scientific literature on psychological trauma, dissociation, and traumatic memory in children and adults. The journal addresses issues ranging from controlled management of traumatic memories and successful interventions to the ethical and philosophical issues entailed by trauma.
Frequency: Quarterly

12647 Journal of Ultrasound in Medicine
American Institute of Ultrasound in Medicine
14750 Sweitzer Ln
Suite 100
Laurel, MD 20707-5906
301-498-4392
800-638-5352; *Fax:* 301-498-4450
admin@aium.org; www.aium.org
Dr Beryl R Benacenraf, Editor-in-Chief
Bruce Totaro, Director of Publications
Thomas R. Nelson, Deputy Editor
Dedicated to the rapid, accurate publication of original articles dealing with all aspects of diagnostic ultrasound, particularly its direct application to patient care, but also relevant basic science, advances in instrumentation and biologic effects. Research papers, case reports, review articles, technical notes and letters to the editor are published.
Cost: $265.00
Frequency: Monthly
Circulation: 8200
ISSN: 0278-4297
Founded in: 1952
Mailing list available for rent
Printed in 4 colors on glossy stock

12648 Journal of the American Academy of Child and Adult Psychiatry
American Academy of Child and Adult Psychiatry
3615 Wisconsin Ave NW
Washington, DC 20016-3007
202-966-7300; *Fax:* 202-966-2891
communications@aacap.org; www.aacap.org
Social Media: Facebook, Twitter
Eva Brown, Manager
Martin J. Drell, President
Virginia Anthony, Executive Director
Founded in: 1953
Mailing list available for rent

12649 Journal of the American Academy of Child & Adolescent Psychiatry
Lippincott Williams & Wilkins
351 W Camden St
Baltimore, MD 21201-2436
410-949-8000; *Fax:* 410-528-4414; www.lww.com
Social Media: Facebook, Twitter
J Arnold Anthony, Operations
AndrSs Martin, MD/MPH, Editor-Elect
Rebecca Jensen, Managing Editor
The official journal of the American Academy of Child & adolescent Psychiatry, the journal is recognized as the major journal exclusivley on todays psychiatric research and treatment of the child and adolescent.
Frequency: Monthly
ISSN: 0890-8567

12650 Journal of the American College of Surgeons
633 N St. Clair Street
Chicago, IL 60611
312-202-5136
800-440-5227; *Fax:* 312-202-5027

12651 Journal of the American Dental Association
American Dental Association
211 E Chicago Ave
Chicago, IL 60611-2678
312-440-2897; *Fax:* 312-440-2800; www.ada.org
Lawrence H Meskin, Editor
Daniel M Castagna, Editorial Board
Serves the dental profession and dental industry.
Cost: $95.00
Frequency: Monthly
Circulation: 135361
ISSN: 0002-8177
Founded in: 1859
Printed in 4 colors on glossy stock

12652 Journal of the American Health Information Management Association
American Health Information Management Association
633 N St. Clair Street
Chicago, IL 60611-3211
312-202-5000
800-621-4111; *Fax:* 312-202-5001
postmaster@facs.org; www.facs.org/
Barry M. Manuel, Editor-in-chief
Paul F. Nora, Editor
Provides information in the field of health information and medical record management in all health care settings. Subscription: non-members $72,
Cost: $25.00
Frequency: Monthly
Founded in: 1913
Printed in 4 colors on glossy stock

12653 Journal of the Medical Library Association
Medical Library Association
65 E Wacker Drive
Suite 1900
Chicago, IL 60601-7246
312-419-9094; *Fax:* 312-419-8950
info@mlahq.org; www.mlanet.org
Elizabeth Lund, Director Publication
Carla J Funk, Executive Officer
Susan Talmage, Editorial Assistant
Scott Plutchak, Editor
Cost: $163.00
Frequency: Quarterly
Circulation: 5000
Founded in: 1898
Mailing list available for rent

12654 Journal of the National Medical Association
4930 Del Ray Avenue
Bethesda, MD 20814
301-654-2055; *Fax:* 301-654-5920
member@gastro.org; www.gastro.org
Robert Greenberg, Executive Vp
Michael Stolar, Senior Vp

12655 Journals of the American Osteopathic College of Dermatology
American Osteopathic College of Dermatology
2902 North Baltimore Street
Kirksville, MO 63501
660-665-2184
800-449-2623; *Fax:* 660-627-2623
journalaocd@gmail.com; www.aocd.org
Karthik Krishnamurthy, Co-Editor-in-Chief
Derrick Adams, Co-Editor-in-Chief
Offers scholarly research and education for members.
Founded in: 1958

12656 MS Connection
Lippincott Williams & Wilkins
351 W Camden St
Baltimore, MD 21201-2436
410-949-8000
800-787-8981; *Fax:* 410-528-4414; www.lww.com
J Arnold Anthony, Operations
Michael Levin-Epstein, Managing Editor
Michele Swain, Marketing Manager

12657 Managed Healthcare
Advanstar Communications
7500 Old Oak Blvd
Cleveland, OH 44130-3343
440-243-8100; *Fax:* 440-891-2740
info@advanstar.com
Daniel J. Corcoran, Publisher
Michael T. McCue, Editor-In-Chief
Craig Roth, Group Publisher
Tracey L. Walker, Senior Editor
Julie Miller, Managing Editor
Valuable resource for managers charged with controlling health care costs and quality.
Cost: $64.00
Frequency: Monthly
Circulation: 40000
ISSN: 1060-1392
Founded in: 1987

12658 McKnight's Long-Term Care News
McKnight Medical Communications

1 Northfield Plz
Suite 300
Northfield, IL 60093-1216

847-784-8706
800-558-1703; *Fax:* 847-784-9346;
www.mcknightsonline.com

William Pecover, CEO
Lee Maniscalco, Executive VP
Jim Berklan, Editor
Jeff Hartford, Circulation Director

Serves the field of long term care including nursing homes, senior housing centers, assisted living facilities, hospitals with LTC units, continuing care retirement communities, nursing home chains and other allied organizations in the field.
35 Pages
Frequency: Weekly
Circulation: 46000
ISSN: 1048-3314
Printed in 4 colors on glossy stock

12659 Medical Economics
Advanstar Communications
5 Paragon Dr
Montvale, NJ 07645-1791

973-944-7777; *Fax:* 973-944-7778

Curtis Allen, President
Marianne Dekker Mattera, Editor-in-Chief
Mike Graziani, Publisher
Sean Keating, Managing Editor
Laura Wagner, VP Operations

Medical Economics guides physicians in the business of practicing by giving advice about malpractice, third-party reimbursement, managed care, tax strategies, legal information and counseling, fraud, abuse and anti-trust strategies. It helps them manage their practice more efficiently so they can be more effective in delivering patient care.
Cost: $109.00
Frequency: Monthly
Circulation: 154897
Founded in: 1987

12660 Medical Reference Services Quarterly
Taylor & Francis Group LLC
325 Chestnut Street
Suite 800
Philadelphia, PA 19106

215-625-8900
215-625-8900; *Fax:* 215-625-2940
haworthorders@taylorandfrancis.com;
www.haworthpress.com

M Sandra Wood, Editor

Covers topics of current interest and practical value in the areas of reference in medicine and related specialties, the biomedical sciences, nursing and allied health.
Cost: $60.00
Frequency: Quarterly
ISSN: 0276-3869
Founded in: 1978

12661 Medical Research Funding Bulletin
PO Box 7507
New York, NY 10150-7507

212-371-3398; *Fax:* 801-761-4200

John Connolly, CEO
Carroll Gordon, Circulation Manager
Cost: $75.00
Frequency: Fortnightly
Circulation: 4500
Founded in: 1972

12662 Modern Healthcare
Crain Communications
360 N Michigan Ave
Chicago, IL 60601-3800

312-649-5200; *Fax:* 312-649-7937
info@crain.com; www.crain.com

Keith Crain, CEO

Examines and reports on the issues that have a direct impact on the business decisions healthcare professionals make every day.
Frequency: Weekly
Circulation: 70180

12663 Molecular Endocrinology
Molecular Society Journals
8401 Connecticut Avenue
Suite 900
Chevy Chase, MD 20815-4410

301-941-0200
888-363-6274; *Fax:* 301-941-0259
societyservices@endo-society.org;
www.endo-society.org

John A Cidlowski, Editor-in-chief
Scott Hunt, Executive Director
Maggie Haworth, Managing Editor
Jessica Peterson, Marketing Manager
John Marshall, Secretary
Cost: $376.00
Frequency: Weekly
Circulation: 11000
Founded in: 1916

12664 NASN Newsletter
National Association of School Nurses
163 US Route 1
PO Box 1300
Scarborough, ME 04074-9060

207-883-2117
877-627-6476; *Fax:* 207-883-2683
nasn@nasn.org; www.nasn.org

Devin Dinkel, Editor
Wanda Miller, Executive Director
Donna Mazyck, President
Gloria Durgin, Administrator/Sponsorship
Kenny Lull, Communications Manager
Cost: $2.00
Founded in: 1968

12665 New England Journal of Medicine
Massachusetts Medical Society
10 Shattuck St
Boston, MA 02115-6094

617-734-9800; *Fax:* 617-739-9864
comments@nejm.org; www.nejm.org

Debra Weinstein, Chair
Jeffrey M Drazen, Editor-in-Chief
Gregory Curfman, Executive Editor

General medicine journal that publishes new medical research findings, review articles, and editorial opinion on a wide variety of topics of importance to biomedical science and clinical practice. Published with an emphasis on internal medicine and specialty areas including allergy/immunology, cardiology, endocrinology, gastroenterology, hematology, kidney disease, oncology, pulmonary disease, rheumatology, HIV, and infectous diseases.
Cost: $149.00
Frequency: Weekly

12666 Nursing
Ambler Office of Lippincott Williams and Wilkins
323 Norristown Rd
Suite 200
Ambler, PA 19002-2758

215-646-8700
800-346-7844; *Fax:* 215-654-1328;
www.lww.com

Mary Gill, Human Resources
Cheryl Mee, Publisher & Editor
Keith Sollweiler, Marketing
Cost: $34.00
Frequency: Monthly
Circulation: 300000
Founded in: 1971

12667 Nursing News
48 W Street
Concord, NH 03301-3595

603-225-3783; *Fax:* 603-228-6672;
www.nhnurses.org

Bob Desc, CEO
Susan Fetzer, President
Cost: $26.00
Frequency: Quarterly
Circulation: 18000
Founded in: 1906

12668 Nursing Outlook
1111 Middle Drive
Indiana, IN 46202

317-274-1486; *Fax:* 317-278-1842
mbroome@iupui.edu; www.nursiniupui.edu

Marion Broome, Editor
Adam Herberg, President, Circulation Manager

12669 Nutrition Business Journal
4452 Park Boulevard
Suite 306
San Diego, CA 92116

619-295-7685; *Fax:* 619-295-5743
info@nutritionbusiness.com;
www.nutritionbusiness.com

David Nussbaum, CEO
Preston Vice, CFO
Cost: $995.00
Frequency: Monthly
Founded in: 1892

12670 O&P Almanac
American Orthotic & Prosthetic Association
330 John Carlyle Street
Suite 200
Alexandria, VA 22314

571-431-0876; *Fax:* 571-431-0899
info@aopanet.org; www.aopanet.org
Social Media: Facebook, Twitter, LinkedIn

Tom Fise, Executive Director
Michael Oros, President
Josephine Rossi, Editor, O&P Almanac
Bob Heiman, Advertising Sales Director
84 Pages
Frequency: Monthly
Circulation: 13000
Founded in: 1951
Mailing list available for rent
Printed in 4 colors on glossy stock

12671 Occupational Health & Safety
Stevens Publishing Corporation
5151 Belt Line Rd
10th Floor
Dallas, TX 75254-7507

972-687-6700; *Fax:* 972-687-6767
jlaws@stevenspublishing.com;
www.stevenspublishing.com

Craig S Stevens, President
Jerry Laws, Executive Vice President
Mike Valenti, Executive Vice President
Craig Stevens, CEO
Margaret Perry, Circulation Director

Practical advice on workplace safety and compliance with laws and regulations. Feature articles and product information.
Frequency: Monthly
Circulation: 84000
Founded in: 1925

12672 Oncology Times
333 7th Ave
19th Floor
New York, NY 10001-5015
646-674-6544
800-933-6525; *Fax:* 646-674-6500
ot@lww.com; www.lww.com
Serena Stockwell, Manager
Ken Senerth, Publisher
Frank Cox, Advertising Manager
Larry Klein, Director
Cost: $189.00
Circulation: 45000
Founded in: 1972

12673 Optometry: Journal of the American Optometric Association
American Optometric Association
243 N Lindbergh Blvd
St Louis, MO 63141-7881
314-991-4100; *Fax:* 314-991-4101
journalsonlinesupport-usa@elsevier.com;
www.optometryjaoa.com
Paul B. Freeman, OD, Editor-in-Chief
Most widely circulated scholarly optometry journal, provides a forum for research that advances the art and science of the practice of primary care optometry.
Cost: $95.00
68 Pages
Frequency: Monthly
Circulation: 34000
ISSN: 1529-1839
Founded in: 1898
Printed in 4 colors on glossy stock

12674 Ostomy Wound Management
HMP Communications
83 General Warren Blvd
Suite 100
Malvern, PA 19355-1252
610-560-0500
800-237-7285; *Fax:* 610-560-0502
subscriptions@hmpcommunications.com;
www.hmpcommunications.com
Social Media: Facebook, Twitter, LinkedIn
Jeff Hennessy, CEO
Barbara Zeiger, Editor
Jeremy Bowden, Publisher
Bonnie Shannon, Circulation Manager
Information on the disciplines of ostomy care, wound care, incontinence care, and related skin and nutritional issues.
Cost: $39.95
Frequency: Monthly
Circulation: 230000
ISSN: 0889-5099
Founded in: 1980
Printed in 4 colors on glossy stock

12675 PT in Motion
American Physical Therapy Association
1111 N Fairfax St
Alexandria, VA 22314-1488
703-684-2782; *Fax:* 703-706-8536
memberservices@apta.org; www.apta.org
Social Media: Facebook, Twitter, LinkedIn
Don Tepper, Editor
John D. Barnes, Chief Executive Officer
Janet Bezner, VP, Education, Governance
Rob Batarla, VP, Finance & Business Development
Felicity Clancy, VP, Communications & Marketing
Formerly PT Magazine, published to meet the needs and interests of APTA members and to promote physical therapy as a vital professional career, PT provides legislative, health care, human interest, and Association news and serves as a forum for discussion of professional issues and ideas in physical therapy practice.
80000 Members
Mailing list available for rent

12676 Patient Care
Medical Economics Publishing
5 Paragon Dr
Montvale, NJ 07645-1791
973-944-7777; *Fax:* 973-944-7778;
www.patientcareonline.com
Curtis Allen, President
Stuart Williams, Publisher
Christine Shappell, Circulation Manager
Don Berman, Director Business Development
Patient care serves selected medical and osteopathic physicians.
Cost: $51.50
Frequency: Monthly
Founded in: 1967
Printed in 4 colors

12677 Physicians & Computers
Moorhead Publications
810 S Waukegan Road
#200
Lake Forest, IL 60045-2672
847-615-8333; *Fax:* 847-615-8345;
www.physicians-computers.com
Tom Moorhead, Publisher
Provides physicians with information on computer advances helpful in the private practice of medicine. Practice management, current medical and non-medical software, computer diagnostics, etc.
Cost: $40.00
Frequency: Monthly
Circulation: 90M

12678 Pneumogram
1961 Main Street
#246
Sacremento, CA 95076
916-441-2222
888-730-2772; *Fax:* 916-442-4182
arosenberg@csrc.org; www.csrc.org/
Janyth Bolden, President
Abbie Rosenberg, Secretary
Sherry Blansfield, Secretary
Frequency: Quarterly
Founded in: 1968

12679 Psychoanalytic Psychology
211 E 70th Street
Suite 17-H
New York, NY 10021
212-633-9162; *Fax:* 212-628-8453
Lori Sloan, Executive Director

12680 Psychology of Addictive Behaviors
University of South Florida
BEH 339
Department of Psychology
Tampa, FL 33620
813-974-4826
800-374-2721; *Fax:* 202-336-5568;
www.apa.org
Social Media: Facebook, Twitter
Stephen A. Maisto, Editor
Norman B. Anderson, Chief Executive Officer
L. Michael Honaker, Chief Operating Officer
Cynthia D. Belar, Executive Director
Tony Habash, Chief Information Officer
Mailing list available for rent

12681 Public Health Nursing
350 Main Street
6th Floor
Malden, MA 02148
781-388-8200; *Fax:* 781-388-8210;
www.blackwellpublishing.com/
Sarah E Abrams, Editor
Judith C Hays, Editor
Otis Dean, Publisher
Alice Meadows, Senior Manager, Circulation
Paige Larkin, Sr. Marketing Manager
Cost: $149.00
Founded in: 1922

12682 Quality Matters
385 Highland Colony Parkway
Suite 120
Ridgeland, MS 39157
601-957-1575
800-844-0500; *Fax:* 601-956-1713

12683 RDH
PennWell Publishing Company
1421 S Sheridan Rd
Tulsa, OK 74112-6619
918-831-9421; *Fax:* 918-831-9476;
www.pennwell.com
Robert Biolchini, President
Mark Hartley, Editor
National magazine for dental hygiene professionals.
Cost: $48.00
60 Pages
Frequency: Monthly
Founded in: 1910

12684 RN Magazine
Medical Economics Publishing
5 Paragon Dr
Montvale, NJ 07645-1791
973-944-7777
888-581-8052; *Fax:* 973-944-7778;
www.rnweb.com
Curtis Allen, President
Wendy Raupers, Associate Publisher
Joy Puzzo, Marketing/Circulation Manager
Don Berman, Director Business Development
Published to serve professional nurses in hospitals, physician's offices, extended care facilities, schools of nursing, occupational and community health agencies and other professional nurses.
Cost: $35.00
Frequency: Monthly
Circulation: 2500
ISSN: 0033-7021
Founded in: 1937

12685 Radiology
820 Jorie Boulevard
Oak Brook, IL 60523-2251
630-571-2670
800-381-6660; *Fax:* 630-571-7837
reginfo@rsna.org; www.rsna.org
Anthony V. Proto, Editor
Michael Ulezlo, Senior Marketing Manager
Cost: $250.00
Frequency: Monthly
Circulation: 35000
Founded in: 1915

12686 Radiology Management
American Healthcare Radiology Administrators
490B Boston Post Rd
Suite 200
Sudbury, MA 01776-3367
978-443-7591
800-334-2472; *Fax:* 978-443-8046

info@ahraonline.org; www.ahraonline.org
Social Media: Facebook, Twitter, LinkedIn

Edward Cronin, Jr., CEO
Sarah Murray, Executive Assistant
Emily Ryan, Membership Coordinator
Debra Murphy, Publications Director

A peer reviewed journal with an editorial review board of AHRA members.
Cost: $65.00
64 Pages
Circulation: 4,000
ISSN: 0198-7097
Founded in: 1978
Printed in 4 colors on glossy stock

12687 Remington Report
Remington Report
30100 Town Center Drive
Suite 421
Laguna Niguel, CA 92677

800-247-4781
800-247-4781; *Fax:* 949-715-1797
remrptedit@aol.com;
www.remingtonreport.com

Lisa Remington, Publisher
Cost: $44.50
Founded in: 1993

12688 Renal Business Today
Virgo Publishing LLC
3300 N Central Ave
Suite 300
Phoenix, AZ 85012-2532

480-990-1101; *Fax:* 480-990-0819
jsiefert@vpico.com; www.vpico.com

Jenny Bolton, President
John Siefert, CEO
Jennifer Janos, Controller
Kelly Ridley, Executive VP, CFO, Copado

Renal Business Today delivers editorials for practice management professionals. Editorials include the latest business and technology trends in renal care, expert advice, strategic business solutions written by industry leaders and human interest articles.
Mailing list available for rent

12689 Research Quarterly for Exercise and Sport
AAHPERD
1900 Association Dr
Reston, VA 20191-1598

703-476-3400
800-213-7193; *Fax:* 703-476-9527;
www.aahperd.org

E. Paul Roetert, CEO
Judith C Young, VP
Paula Kun, Marketing

RQES is a professional journal providing members with numerous articles and research on subjects that focus on the art and science of human movement studies.
Cost: $295.00
128 Pages
Frequency: Quarterly
Circulation: 6000
ISSN: 0270-1367
Mailing list available for rent
Printed in one color on glossy stock

12690 Respiratory Care
9425 N Macarthur Blvd
Suite 100
Irving, TX 75063-4725

972-243-2272; *Fax:* 972-484-2720
info@aarc.org; www.aarc.org

Sam Giordano, CEO

Journal for the professional respiratory care therapist. Member publication of the American Association for Respiratory Care.
Cost: $89.95
Frequency: Monthly
Founded in: 1947

12691 Review of Optometry
11 Campus Boulevard
Newton Square, PA 19073

610-492-1000; *Fax:* 610-492-1039
reviewofoptometry@jobson.com;
www.revoptom.com

Amy Hellem, Editor-in-Chief
Jeffrey S Eisenberg, Director
Paul Karpecki, Director
Frequency: Monthly

12692 Risk Management Handbook
NACHA: The Electronic Payments Association
13450 Sunrise Valley Drive
Suite 100
Herndon, VA 20171

703-561-1100; *Fax:* 703-787-0996
info@nacha.org; www.nacha.org

Janet O Estep, CEO
Marcie Haitema, Chairperson

A comprehensive guide to ACH Risk Issues and Control Procedures. Explains the types of ACH payments risk, assesses the operational implications, and provides best practices for developing an effective risk management program.
Cost: $65.00
Frequency: Monthly
Founded in: 1991

12693 Rite Aid Be Healthy & Beatiful
Drug Store News Consumer Health Publications
425 Park Ave
New York, NY 10022-3526

212-756-5220; *Fax:* 212-756-5250
jtanzola@lf.com; www.drugstorenews.com

Lebhar Friedman, Publisher

Provides health and beauty tips to millions of women who visit Rite Aid stores.
Frequency: Quarterly
Circulation: 950,000
Founded in: 2002

12694 Scrip Magazine
270 Madison Ave
New York, NY 10016-0601

212-262-8230; *Fax:* 212-262-8234;
www.pjbpubs.com

Ken May, Executive Director
Alice Dunmore, Circulation Manager
Jenefer Trevena, Marketing Manager
Phillip Every, Worldwide Advertising Sales

An in-depth view of the issues and challenges facing all sectors of the pharmaceutical industry worldwide. Analytical features are written by pharmaceutical experts and opinion leaders as well as specialist journalists.
Cost: $ 1190.00

12695 Sports Medicine Digest
351 W Camden St
Baltimore, MD 21201-7912

410-528-4000
800-787-8981; *Fax:* 410-528-4452;
www.lww.com

Daniel Schwartz, Publisher
Michael Levin-Epstein, Managing Editor
Cost: $125.00
12 Pages
Frequency: Monthly
ISSN: 0731-9770
Founded in: 1978
Printed in one color on matte stock

12696 SurgiStrategies
Virgo Publishing LLC
3300 N Central Ave
Suite 300
Phoenix, AZ 85012-2532

480-990-1101; *Fax:* 480-990-0819
jsiefert@vpico.com; www.vpico.com

Jenny Bolton, President
John Siefert, CEO
Jennifer Janos, Controller
Kelly Ridley, Executive VP, CFO, Copado

SurgiStrategies identifies and analyzes the high level trends impacting physician and corporation owned outpatient healthcare facilities with relevant, timely, ahead of the curve content.
Mailing list available for rent: 22000+ names at $var per M

12697 Surgical Products
Reed Business Information
100 Enterprise Drive
Suite 600
Rockaway, NJ 07866-912

973-920-7000; *Fax:* 630-288-8686
rritsma@reedbusiness.com;
www.surgprodmag.com/

Noreen Costelloe, Group VP/Publisher
Richard Ritsma, Editor-in-Chief
James Reed, Owner
Sabrina Crow, Managing Director
Steve Koppelman, Circulation Manager

Surgical products provides surgeons, OR supervisors and OR materials managers working in hospitals and surgi-centers with new product technology and equipment.
Frequency: Monthly
Circulation: 71000
Founded in: 1946

12698 The Consultant Pharmacist
American Society of Consultant Pharmacists
1321 Duke St
Alexandria, VA 22314-3563

703-739-1300
800-355-2727; *Fax:* 703-739-1321
info@ascp.com; www.ascp.com

Frank Grosso, RPh, Executive Director & CEO
Kelly Jennings, Chief Financial Officer
Marlene Bloom, Editor
Debbie Furman, Circulation

Official peer reviewed journal of the American Society of Consultant Pharmacists. Editorial deals with geriatric pharmacotherapy.
76 Pages
Frequency: Monthly
Circulation: 11000
Founded in: 1969
Mailing list available for rent
Printed in 4 colors on glossy stock

12699 The Neurodiagnostic Journal
American Society of Electroneurodiagnostic Tech
402 East Bannister Road
Suite A
Kansas City, MO 64131-3019

816-931-1120; *Fax:* 816-931-1145
info@aset.org; www.aset.org

Arlen Reimritz, Executive Director
Anna M. Bonner, Managing Editor

Peer-reviewed journal that contains research articles, case studies, technical articles and book reviews.
Frequency: Quarterly
Circulation: 5000
ISSN: 2164-6821
Founded in: 1961

12700 **Transplantation**
351 W Camden St
Baltimore, MD 21201-7912

410-528-4000
800-222-3790; *Fax:* 410-528-4452;
www.lww.com

Sherry Reed, Manager
Mark A Hardy, Editor
Jim Mulligan, Publisher
Taron Buttler, National Sales Manager
Jeff Hargrove, Manager
Cost: $657.00
Circulation: 2556

12701 **Transportation Leader**
Taxicab, Limousine & Paratransit Association
3200 Tower Oaks Blvd
Suite 220
Rockville, MD 20852

301-984-5700; *Fax:* 301-984-5703
info@tlpa.org; www.tlpa.org

Alfred LaGasse, CEO
William Rouse, President
Harold Morgan, Executive Vice President
Michelle A. Hariston, CMP, Manager of Meetings
Leah New, Manager of Communications

Leading resource for news and information on issues, trends, and people in the private, for-hire passenger transportation industry. Provides readers with an array of features, articles, and columns that include information on managing a transportation company, industry trends, driver's tips, an industry calendar of events, coverage of TLPA events, and advertisements from the industry's leading suppliers.
Cost: $4.00
48 Pages
Frequency: Quarterly
Circulation: 6000
Founded in: 1917
Mailing list available for rent: 6,000 names at $100 per M
Printed in 4 colors on glossy stock

12702 **Urologic Nursing**
Society of Urologic Nurses and Associates
East Holly Avenue
PO Box 56
Pitman, NJ 08071

856-256-2300; *Fax:* 856-589-7463
uronsg@ajj.com; www.suna.org

Nancy Mueller, President
Robert McIlvaine, Circulation Manager
Mike Cunningham, Marketing
Jane Hokanson Hawks, Editor
Anthony Jannetti, Executive Director
Cost: $40.00
Circulation: 4500
Founded in: 1981
Printed in 4 colors on glossy stock

12703 **Virology**
125 Park Avenue
23rd Floor
New York, NY 10017

212-309-5498
800-821-5068; *Fax:* 212-309-5480
d.weerd@elsevier.com;
www.reed-elsevier.com/

A Pinczuk, Editor-in-Chief
Karlyn Messinger, Communications Manager
Cost: $139.00
Frequency: Monthly
Circulation: 280
Founded in: 1993

12704 **Volunteer**
119 W 24th Street
9th Floor
New York, NY 10011-1913

212-870-4940; *Fax:* 212-367-1236

Esperanza Jorge-Garcia, Executive Director

12705 **Walgreens Diabetes & You**
Drug Store News Consumer Health Publications
425 Park Ave
New York, NY 10022-3526

212-756-5220; *Fax:* 212-756-5250;
www.drugstorenews.com

Lebhar Friedman, Publisher
Edward H King, Director

Contains health news of importance to those with diabetes.

12706 **World Disease Weekly**
2900 Paces Ferry Road
Bldg D 2nd Floor
Atlanta, GA 30339

770-507-7777
800-726-4550; *Fax:* 770-435-6800
subscribe@newsrx.com
Cost: $2329.00
Frequency: Weekly
Founded in: 1984

Trade Shows

12707 **AAAAI Annual Conference and Exhibition**
American Academy Allergy, Asthma, and Immunology
555 E Wells Street
Suite 100
Milwaukee, WI 53202-3823

414-272-6071
800-822-2762; *Fax:* 414-272-6070
info@aaaai.org; www.aaaai.org

Katie Ferguson, Sr. Meetings Manager

Exhibits, pharmaceuticals, medical supplies and books.
7000 Attendees
Frequency: Annual
Founded in: 1943

12708 **AAAAI Annual Meeting**
American Academy of Allergy, Asthma and Immunology (AAAAI)
555 E. Wells Street, Suite 1100
Milwaukee, WI 53202-3823

414-272-6071
info@aaaai.org; www.aaaai.org

Thomas B. Casale, MD, Executive Vice President
Kay A. Whalen, Executive Director
Roberta Slivensky, Associate Executive Director
Amy Flanders, Director of Grants & Development
Rachel McCormick, Executive Assistant

Annual gathering of immunology and allergy experts. Those attending the annual meeting include academicians, allied health professionals and clinicians.
6000+ Members
Founded in: 1943

12709 **AAB Annual Meeting and Educational Conference**
American Association of Bioanalysts
906 Olive Street
Suite 1200
Saint Louis, MO 63101-1448

314-241-1445; *Fax:* 314-241-1449
aab@aab.org; www.aab.org

Mark S Biernbaum PhD, Administrator

Educational programs, abstract presentations, poster presentations and exhibits.
Founded in: 1956

12710 **AACAP Annual Meeting**
American Academy of Child & Adolescent Psychiatry
3615 Wisconsin Avenue NW
Washington, DC 20016-3007

202-966-7300; *Fax:* 202-966-2891
communications@aacap.org; www.aacap.org
Social Media: Facebook, Twitter

Thomas F Anders, MD, President
Virginia Anthony, Executive Director
Martin J. Drell, President
Founded in: 1953
Mailing list available for rent

12711 **AAHP Institute & Display Forum**
American Association of Health Plans
1129 20th Street NW
Washington, DC 20036

202-778-3200; *Fax:* 202-778-8506

12712 **AAID Annual Meeting**
American Academy of Implant Dentistry
211 E Chicago Avenue
Suite 750
Chicago, IL 60611

312-335-1550
877-335-2243; *Fax:* 312-335-9090
info@aaid.com; www.aaid.com
Social Media: Facebook, Twitter, LinkedIn

Sharon Bennett, Executive Director
Max Moses, Director Communications

The 2012 meeting will be in Washington, DC.
1500 Attendees
Frequency: October 3-6, 2012

12713 **AAMFT Conference**
American Assoc for Marriage and Family Therapy
112 S Alfred Street
Alexandria, VA 22314-3061

703-838-9808; *Fax:* 703-838-9805
central@aamft.org; www.aamft.org
Social Media: Facebook, Twitter, LinkedIn

Linda S. Metcalf, PhD, President
Michael L. Chafin, President-Elect
Michael Bowers, Executive Director
Robin K. Stillwell, MA, Secretary
Silvia M. Kaminsky, MSEd, Treasurer

AAMFT represents the professional interests of more than 25,000 marriage and family therapists throughout the United States, Canada and abroad.
25000 Members
1500 Attendees
Frequency: Annual
Founded in: 1942

12714 **AAMI Conference & Expo**
Assoc for the Advancement of Medical Instrumenta
4301 N. Fairfax Drive
Suite 301
Arlington, VA 22203-1633

703-525-4890; *Fax:* 703-276-0793
customerservice@aami.org; www.aami.org

Michael Miller, President
Ed Leonardo, Meetings/Expositions Director

Offers educational, networking, and personal-development opportunities that wil lenable

you to expand your expertise, increasr your productivity, develop lasting relationships with peers, and ultimately advance your career.
Frequency: Annual

12715 AANEM Annual Meeting
American Assoc of Neuromuscular & Electro Medicine
2621 Superior Drive NW
Rochester, MN 55902-3018

507-288-0100; *Fax:* 507-288-1225
aanem@aanem.org; www.aanem.org

Shirlyn A Adkins, Executive Director
Patrick D Aldrich, Finance Director
Emily Spaulding, Executive Assistant
Loretta Bronson, Senior Director of Operations
Catherine French, Director of Health Policy

Forty exhibits of electromyographic and electrodiagnosis equipment and accessories. Seminar, workshop and breakfast.
1000 Attendees
Mailing list available for rent

12716 AAO-HNSF Annual Meeting & OTO Experience
American Academy of Otolaryngology-Head & Neck
1650 Diagonal Road
Alexandria, VA 22314

703-836-4444; www.etannualmeeting.org
Social Media: Facebook, Twitter, LinkedIn, YouTube

Gregory W. Randolph, MD, President
James C. Denneny, MD, Executive Vice President & CEO

Over 300 exhibits of otolaryngology, diseases of the ear, nose and throat, head and neck surgery equipment, supplies and services plus seminar.
9000+ Attendees
Frequency: Annual
Founded in: 1896

12717 AAOMS Scientific Meeting
American Assn. of Oral & Maxillofacial Surgeons
9700 W Bryn Mawr Avenue
Rosemont, IL 60018-5701

847-678-6200
800-822-6637; *Fax:* 847-678-6286
inquiries@aaoms.org; www.aaoms.org
Social Media: Facebook, Twitter, LinkedIn

J. David Johnson, Treasurer
A. Thomas Indresano, Vice President

Educational session, reception, tours. Over 275 exhibits relating to the profession.
4000 Attendees
Frequency: Annual
Founded in: 1918

12718 AAOS Annual Meeting
American Academy of Orthopaedic Surgeons
9400 West Higgins Rd.
Rosemont, IL 60018

847-823-7186; *Fax:* 847-823-8125;
www.aaos.org

David Teuscher, President
Karen L. Hackett, Chief Executive Officer

Three hundred and fifty-five exhibits of surgical equipment, supplies and services used by the orthopedic professional.
28000 Attendees
Frequency: Annual
Founded in: 1933

12719 AAPS Annual Scientific Meeting
American Association of Physician Specialists, Inc
5550 West Executive Drive
Suite 400
Tampa, FL 33609-1035

813-433-2277; *Fax:* 813-830-6599
wcarbone@aapsus.org; www.aapsus.com

Esther Berg, Director of CME/Meetings/Membership
Keely Clarke, Membership/CME Coordinator
William Carbone, Chief Executive Officer

The American Association of Physician Specialists, Inc.(AAPS) annual meeting is used to educate medical professionals on relevant medical topics that include continuing medical education(CME) credits. The association also holdsbusiness meetings at this time.
1000 Attendees

12720 AARC International Respiratory Congress
American Association for Respiratory Care
9425 N MacArthur Boulevard
Suite 100
Irving, TX 75063-4706

972-243-2272; *Fax:* 972-484-2720
info@aarc.org; www.aarc.org

Sam P Giordano, Executive Director/Executive VP
Beth Binkley, Communication Coordinator
Steve Bowden, Web developer
Kathy Blackmon, Convention and Meetings Manager
Asha Desai, Customer Service Manager

Largest respiratory care meeting in the world. Offers the latest information in all aspects of respiratory care. The congress offers you an opportunity to earn all the continuing education hours required for your state license annually.
7000 Attendees
Frequency: December
Founded in: 1947
Mailing list available for rent

12721 ACA Annual Conference & Expo
Journal of Counseling and Development
5999 Stevenson Ave
Alexandria, VA 22304-3302

703-823-9800; *Fax:* 703-823-0252
membership@counseling.org;
www.counseling.org
Social Media: Facebook, Twitter

Marvin D. Kuehn, Executive Director
Tom Evenson, President

The mission of the American Counseling Association (ACA) is to enhance the quality of life in society by promoting the development of professional counselors, advancing the counseling profession, and using the profession and practice of counseling to promote respect for human dignity and diversity. ACA is a not-for-profit, professional and educational organization. The annual expo features over 100 exhibitors.
4000 Attendees
Frequency: Annual
Founded in: 1952
Mailing list available for rent

12722 ACOFP Convention & Scientific Seminar
American College of Osteopathic Family Physicians
330 E Algonquin Road
Arlington Heights, IL 60005

847-228-6090; *Fax:* 800-323-0794

2500 Attendees

12723 ACOMS Annual Scientific Conference and Exhibition
American College of Oral & Maxillofacial Surgeons
2025 M Street Nw
Suite 800
Washington, DC 20036

202-367-1182
800-522-6676; *Fax:* 202-367-2182
admin@acoms.org; www.acoms.org
Social Media: Facebook, Twitter, LinkedIn

Pedro F. Franco, President
R. Bryan Bell, President-Elect
Steven C. Kemp, Executive Director
Jeffrey Bennett, Treasurer
Kevin L. Rieck, Secretary
Frequency: Annual

12724 AHRA Annual Meeting and Exposition
Association for Medical Imaging Management
490B Boston Post Road
Suite 200
Sudbury, MA 01776

978-443-7591
800-334-2472; *Fax:* 978-443-8046
info@ahraonline.org; www.ahraonline.org
Social Media: Facebook, Twitter, LinkedIn

Edward Cronin, Jr., CEO
Sarah Murray, Executive Assistant
Emily Ryan, Membership Coordinator
Debra Murphy, Publications Director

Educational event for Radiology Administration. Topics that are covered include human resources, finance, operations and communication.
3000 Attendees
Frequency: Annual

12725 AMGA's Annual Conference
American Medical Group Association
One Prince Street
Alexandria, VA 22314-3318

703-838-0033; *Fax:* 703-548-1890;
www.amga.org
Social Media: Facebook, Twitter, LinkedIn

Donald W Fisher PhD, CAE, President/CEO
Ryan O'Connor, VP Membership/Marketing
April Noland, Assistant to the President/CEO
Clyde L. Morris, C.P.A., CFO
Nanette Lewis, Administrative Asst/Office Manager

Brings together physician and nonphysician executives from the nation's leading health care organizations, medical groups and physician owned and operated IPAs. It offers both an interactive exhibit area and a relaxed environment for meeting one-on-one with management from the nation's leading health care organizations. National conference dedicated to leadership development in multispecialty medical groups.
375 Members
1100+ Attendees
Frequency: March, Arizona
Founded in: 1949
Mailing list available for rent: 600 names

12726 AORN Congress
Association of PeriOperative Registered Nurses
2170 S Parker Road
Suite 300
Denver, CO 80231-5711

303-755-6300
800-755-2676; *Fax:* 303-755-4511
sales@aorn.org; www.aorn.org

Garth Jordan, VP Marketing/Business
Lori Ropa, Manager

Surgical tradeshow featuring medical devices and supplies for the operating room and facilities recruiting for open OR nursing positions.
7000 Attendees
Frequency: Annual
Founded in: 1954

12727 AORN World Conference of Perioperative Nurses
Association of PeriOperative Registered Nurses
2170 S Parker Road
Suite 300
Denver, CO 80231-5711
303-755-6300; *Fax:* 303-755-5411
sales@aorn.org; www.aorn.org
Christine Lindmark, Exhibits Director
Lori Ropa, Manager
Seminar and 82 equipment & supplies displays used in operating room suites, and pre-surgical areas.
2500 Attendees
Frequency: Biennial
Founded in: 1978

12728 APTA Annual Conference & Exposition
American Physical Therapy Association
1111 N Fairfax Street
Alexandria, VA 22314
703-684-2782; *Fax:* 703-706-3396
memberservices@apta.org; www.apta.org
R Scott Ward, President
John Barnes, CEO
The national event for physical therapy.
Frequency: June

12729 ARMA International Conference & Expo
ARMA International
11880 College Blvd
Suite 450
Overland Park, KS 66210
913-341-3808
800-422-2762; *Fax:* 913-341-3742
hq@arma.org; www.arma.org/conference
Social Media: Facebook, Twitter, LinkedIn
Carol Jorgenson, Meetings/Education Coordinator
Wanda Wilson, Senior Manager, Conferences
Elizabeth Zlitni, Exposition Manager
Conference, seminar, workshop, banquet, award ceremony and 175 exhibits of micrographics, optical disk, automated document storage and retrieval systems and more technology of interest to information professionals.
3500 Attendees
Frequency: Annual
Founded in: 1956
Mailing list available for rent

12730 ARVO
FASEB/OSMC
9650 Rockville Pike
Bethesda, MD 20814
301-634-7100; *Fax:* 301-634-7014
info@faseb.org; www.faseb.org/meetings
Jacquelyn Roberts, Marketing Manager
David Craven, Executive Director

12731 ASC Association Annual Conference
Ambulatory Surgery Center Association
1012 Cameron Street
Alexandria, VA 22314-2427
703-836-8808; *Fax:* 703-549-0976
asc@ascassociation.org;
www.ascassociation.org
Social Media: Facebook, Twitter, LinkedIn
Kathy Bryant, President
Sarah Silberstein, Executive Director
71000 Attendees
Frequency: April
Founded in: 1970

12732 ASCRS Annual Meeting
American Society of Colon & Rectal Surgeons
85 W Algonquin Road
Suite 550
Arlington Heights, IL 60005
847-290-9184
800-791-0001; *Fax:* 847-290-9203
ascrs@fascrs.org; www.fascrs.org
Social Media: Facebook
James W J Felshman MD, President
John H Pemberton MD, VP
Alan G Thorson MD, Treasurer
Rick Slawny, Executive Director
Stella Zedalis, Associate Executive Director
2800 Members
Mailing list available for rent

12733 ASCRS Symposium & ASOA Congress
American Society of Cataract & Refractive Surgery
American Society of Opthalmic Administrators
4000 Legato Road, # 850
Fairfax, VA 22033-4003
703-912-2220
800-451-1339; *Fax:* 703-591-0614
ascrs@ascrs.org; www.ascrs.org
Jane Krause, Show Manager
Seminar and 700 exhibits of opthalmic related intruments of interest to opthalmologists, administrators, nurses and technicians.
7000 Attendees
Frequency: June
Founded in: 1986

12734 ASET Annual Conference
American Society of Electroneurodiagnostic Tech
402 East Bannister Rd
Suite A
Kansas City, MO 64131-3019
816-931-1120; *Fax:* 816-931-1145
info@aset.org; www.aset.org
Social Media: Facebook, Twitter
Arlen Reimnitz, Executive Director
Sarah Dolezilek, Marketing/Communications Manager
The premier education and exposition opportunity for the Neurodiagnostic technologists in the country. A must attend event for all neurodiagnostic professionals whether you are a technologist, laboratory manager, physician or representing a supplier.
500+ Attendees
Frequency: Annual

12735 ASHCSP Annual Conference: American Society for Heathcare Central Servi
American Hospital Association
One N Franklin
Chicago, IL 60601
312-422-2000; *Fax:* 312-422-4572
Conference and exhibition of health care administration supplies and services.

12736 ASHHRA'S Annual Conference & Exposition
American Society of Healthcare & Human Resources
155 North Wacker
Suite 400
Chicago, IL 60606
312-422-3720; *Fax:* 312-422-4577
ricky@corcexpo.com; www.ashhra.org
Social Media: Facebook, Twitter, LinkedIn
Ricky Iovino, Exhibit Manager
ASHHRA's Annual Conference & Exposition is the opportunity to connect face-to-face with the top human resource executives and decision-makers in the healthcare field. The attendees come from hospital, hospital system, ambulatory care, long-term care and hospice organizations. Attendee job titles include: Chief Human Resource Officer; Vice President/Director of Human Resources; Director/Manager of Recruitment, Compensation, Benefits, Organizational Development or Employee Relations
500 Attendees
Frequency: September, Disneyland
Mailing list available for rent

12737 ASHP Midyear Clinical Meeting
American Society of Health-System Pharmacists
7272 Wisconsin Avenue
Bethesda, MD 20814-4836
301-657-3000
866-279-0681; *Fax:* 301-657-1641;
www.ashp.org
Social Media: Facebook, Twitter, LinkedIn
Kathryn R. Schultz, President
Paul W. Abramowitz, Chief Executive Officer
Philip J. Schneider, Treasurer
Gerald Meyer, Vice-Chairman
Containing 1,160 booths and 320 exhibits.
Mailing list available for rent

12738 ASNP Convention & Exhibition
American Association of Naturopathic Physicians
4435 Wisconsin Avenue NW
Suite 403
Washington, DC 20016
202-237-8150
866-538-2267; *Fax:* 202-237-8152
member.services@naturopathic.org;
www.naturopathic.org
Karen Howard, Executive Director
Michael Cronin, ND, President
Joe Pizzorno, ND, Treasurer
Shelly Nichols, Executive Administrator
Stephanie Geller, Membership Associate
900 Attendees
Frequency: Annual/August
Mailing list available for rent

12739 ASPET Annual Meeting
ASPET
9650 Rockville Pike
Bethesda, MD 20814
301-347-7060; *Fax:* 301-634-7061
info@aspet.org; www.aspet.org
Jean Lash, Exhibit Manager
Christine Carrico, Secretary, Treasurer
Paul Czoty, Secretary, Treasurer
The American Society for Pharmacology & Experimental Therapeutics annual meeting consisting of four-hundred exhibits of pharmacology and toxicology equipment, supplies and services.
13000 Attendees
Frequency: April

12740 ASPRS/PSEF/ASMS Annual Scientific Meeting
American Society of Plastic Surgeons
444 E Algonquin Road
Arlington Heights, IL 60005
847-228-9900
888-475-2784; *Fax:* 847-228-9131
webmaster@plasticsurgery.org;
www.plasticsurgery.org
Bonnie Burkoth, Exhibit Manager

Close to four hundred exhibits of plastic surgery products, patient education and software to assist plastic surgeons, nurses and paramedical staff.
4000 Attendees
Frequency: October
*Mailing list available for rent*at $750 per M

12741 **ASSH Annual Meeting**
American Society for Surgery of the Hand
822 W. Washington Boulevard
Suite 600
Chicago, IL 60607

312-880-1900; *Fax:* 847-384-1435
info@assh.org; www.assh.org

Mark Anderson, CEO
Daniel Nagle, President
W P Andrew Lee, Secretary/VP
3500 Members
Frequency: September
Mailing list available for rent

12742 **Academy of General Dentistry Annual Meeting**
Academy of General Dentistry
211 E Chicago Avenue
Suite 900
Chicago, IL 60611

312-440-4300
888-243-3368; *Fax:* 312-440-0559
executiveoffice@agd.org; www.agd.org

Heather Nash CMP, Director Meetings
Jay Donohue, Executive Director

Educational session and over 225 dental manufacturers and supplier exhibits. Attended by dentists and the general public.
5000 Attendees
Frequency: Annual
Founded in: 1954

12743 **Academy of Osseointegration Convention**
Smith, Bucklin and Associates
401 N Michigan Avenue
Chicago, IL 60611-4267

312-644-6610; *Fax:* 312-245-1082
info@smithbucklin.com;
www.smithbucklin.com

Henry S. Givray, President & CEO
C. Albert Koob, Executive Vice President
Carolyn Dolezal, Executive Vice President
Michael L. Payne, Executive Vice President
Cele Fogarty, Vice President - Event Services

Osseointegration medical exhibition.
Founded in: 1949

12744 **Adult Day Services Exposition**
VNU Expositions
Dulles International Airport
PO Box 17413
Washington, DC 20041

703-318-0300
800-765-7616; *Fax:* 703-318-8833;
www.vnuexpo.com

Luellen Hoffman, Show Director

Adult/geriatric health care professionals gather to see exhibits of equipment, supplies, services and consulting for those who represent senior centers, adult day centers, nursing homes, hospitals and other health care markets.
300 Attendees
Frequency: Annual

12745 **Air Medical Transport Conference**
Association of Air Medical Services
526 King Street
Sutie 415
Alexandria, VA 22314-3143

703-836-8732; *Fax:* 703-836-8920
information@aams.org; www.aams.org

Johanna VanArsdall, Education/Meetings Manager
Blair Marie Kelly, Commuications/Marketing Director
Andy Papovie, Member Serives Coordinator
John Fiegel, Director

Annual exhibit of air medical transport equipment, supplies and services.
1500 Attendees
Frequency: November

12746 **AmSECT International Conference**
American Society of ExtraCorporeal Technology
2209 Dickens Road
Richmond, VA 23230-2005

804-565-6363; *Fax:* 804-282-0090
judyr@amsect.org; www.amsect.org

Stewart Hinckley, Executive Director
Donna Pendarvis, Associate Manager
Michael Troike, Government Relations Chairman
Kimberly Robertson, CPA, Controller
Greg Leasure, Membership Services
2000 Members
600 Attendees
Frequency: Annual
Founded in: 1964
Mailing list available for rent

12747 **American Academy for Cerebral Palsy and Developmental Medicine Meeting**
Amer. Academy for Cerebral Palsy/Dev. Medicine
555 E Wells St
Suite 1100
Milwaukee, WI 53202-3800

414-918-3014; *Fax:* 414-276-2146
info@aacpdm.org; www.aacpdm.org

Maureen O'Donnell, President
Scott Hoffinger, Treasurer
Richard Stevenson, First Vice President
Darcy Fehlings, Second Vice President
Annette Majnemer, Secretary

Provides dissemination of current and emerging information in the basic sciences, prevention, diagnosis, treatment and technical advances as applied to persons with cerebral palsy and developmental disabilities.
800 Attendees
Frequency: Yearly
Founded in: 1940

12748 **American Academy of Dermatology Annual Meeting**
American Academy of Dermatology
930 N Meacham Road
PO Box 4014
Shaumburg, IL 60168-4014

708-330-1090; *Fax:* 708-330-1090

Seven hundred exhibits from 300 technical companies relating to skin care, professional and scientific organizations.
Frequency: Annual
Founded in: 1940

12749 **American Academy of Environmental Medicine Conference**
American Academy of Environmental Medicine
7701 E Kellog
Suite 625
Wichita, KS 67207-1705

316-684-5500; *Fax:* 316-684-5709
centraloffice@aaem.com; www.aaem.com

D E Rodgers, Executive Director

Environmental medicine equipment, supplies and services of interest to physicans.
175 Attendees
Frequency: October
Mailing list available for rent

12750 **American Academy of Family Physicians Scientific Assembly**
American Academy of Family Physicians
11400 Tomahawk Creek Parkway
Leawood, KS 66211-2680

913-906-6000
800-274-2237; *Fax:* 913-906-6082;
www.aafp.org

Sondra Biggs CMP, Meetings/Convention Director
20000 Attendees
Frequency: Annual

12751 **American Academy of Fixed Prosthodontics Scientific Session**
American Academy of Fixed Prosthodontics
6661 Merwin Road
Columbus, OH 43235

614-761-1927
800-860-5633; *Fax:* 614-292-0941
aafpsec@gmail.com;
www.fixedprosthodontics.org
Social Media: Facebook, Twitter

Stephen F. Rosenstiel, Secretary
Richard D. Jordan, Treasurer
Carl F. Driscoll, President
Jack Lipkin, VP

Thirty-two exhibits of prosthodontics equipment, supplies and services. Luncheon and meeting.
800 Attendees
Frequency: Annual Feb.
Founded in: 1951

12752 **American Academy of Forensic Sciences Annual Meeting**
American Academy of Forensic Sciences
410 N 21st St
Colorado Springs, CO 80904-2712

719-636-1100; *Fax:* 719-636-1993
awarren@aafs.org; www.aafs.org

Anne Warren, Executive Director
Nancy Jackson, Director Development

Professionals in the forensic science field attend meeting and see 120 exhibits of scientific instruments.
2300 Attendees
Frequency: Annual

12753 **American Academy of Implant Dentistry Annual Meeting**
American Academy of Implant Dentistry
211 E Chicago Avenue
Chicago, IL 60611

312-335-1550
877-335-2243; *Fax:* 312-335-9090;
www.aaid.org
Social Media: Facebook, Twitter, LinkedIn

Sharon Bennett, Executive Director
Joyce Sigmon, Director Administrative Activities
Max Moses, Director Communications
1500 Attendees
Frequency: Annual

12754 **American Academy of Neurology: Annual Meeting**
American Academy of Neurology
1080 Montreal Avenue
Suite 335
Saint Paul, MN 55116-2325
651-951-1940
800-879-1960; *Fax:* 651-695-2791
aan@aan.com; www.aanos.org
Judy Larson
One hundred and seventy-four publishers, pharmaceutical companies, and related suppliers have exhibits, along with the seminar, workshop, banquet and reception.
6500 Attendees
Frequency: Annual, August

12755 **American Academy of Ophthalmology Annual Meeting**
American Academy of Ophthalmology
655 Beach Street
P.O. Box 7424
San Francisco, CA 94109
415-618-8500; *Fax:* 415-561-8533
meetings@aao.org; www.aao.org
Karen Cristello, Promotions Coordinator
Dunbar Hoskins, Executive VP
25000 Attendees
Frequency: November
Founded in: 1896
Mailing list available for rent

12756 **American Academy of Optometry Annual Meeting**
American Academy of Optometry
2909 Fairgreen Street
Suite 506
Orlando, FL 32803
301-984-1441; *Fax:* 407-893-9890
aaoptom@aaoptom.org; www.aaopt.org
Bernard J. Dolan, President
Lois Schoenbrun, Executive Director
Jenny Brown, Program Manager, Membership
Randy Consola, Office Manager
Dana Edwards, MLIS, Database Administrator
Two hundred exhibits focusing on the latest patient treatment and research. Workshop and banquet.
4000 Attendees
Frequency: Annual

12757 **American Academy of Oral and Maxillofacial Radiology Annual Session**
American Academy of Oral & Maxillofacial Radiology
PO Box 55722
Jackson, MS 39296
601-984-6060; *Fax:* 601-984-6086;
www.aaomr.org
Dr. Sanjay Mallya, President
Dr. Debra Gander, President-Elect
Dr. Robert Cederberg, Executive Director
Professor Gail Williamson, Associate Executive Director
Over 20 exhibits relating to dental radiology, equipment, software and accessories.
120 Attendees
Frequency: November
Founded in: 1949

12758 **American Academy of Orofacial Pain Annual Scientific Meeting**
American Academy of Orofacial Pain
19 Mantua Road
Mount Royal, NJ 00861
856-233-3629; *Fax:* 856-423-3420
Donna Blackmore, Manager Meetings
Bob Talley, President
Ten exhibits relating to orofacial pain and temporomandibular disorders. Medical and dental doctors attend meeting, luncheon, tours and a reception.
350 Attendees
Frequency: Annual

12759 **American Academy of Pain Medicine Annual Conference and Review Course**
American Academy of Pain Medicine
4700 Lake Avenue
Glenview, IL 60025
847-375-4731; *Fax:* 847-375-4777
info@painmed.org; www.painmed.org
Samuel Hassenbusch, President
Frederick Burgess, Treasurer
Meeting and exhibits relating to pain medicine, particularly related socioeconomic and governmental issues.
Frequency: Annual

12760 **American Academy of Pediatric Dentistry Annual Meeting**
American Academy of Pet Owners
830 Taylor Street
Suite 1700
Ft. Worth, TX 76102
312-337-2169
800-992-8044; *Fax:* 312-337-6329;
www.aapd.org
Social Media: Facebook, Twitter
Keith Morley, President
William Berlocher, Vice President
John Rutkauskas, Executive Director
Seventy-five to 100 displays of dental products and publications.
2500 Attendees
Frequency: May
Founded in: 1948

12761 **American Academy of Pediatrics Annual Meeting**
American Academy of Pediatrics
141 NW Point Boulevard
Elk Grove Village, IL 60009
847-434-4000; *Fax:* 847-434-8000
kidsdocs@aap.org; www.aap.org
E Stephen Edwards MD FAAP, President
Joe M Sanders Jr, MD FAAP, Executive Director
Joann Barbour, Manager
Three hundred and fifty exhibits relating to prescription and over the counter drugs, infant formulas medical equipment and publications. Reception, tours and meeting.
10000 Attendees
Frequency: Annual

12762 **American Academy of Periodontology Annual Meeting & Exhibition**
American Academy of Periodontology
737 N Michigan Avenue
Suite 800
Chicago, IL 60611
312-787-5518; *Fax:* 312-573-3225
member.services@perio.org; www.perio.org
Melody Anderson, Meetings Manager
Alice Deforest, Administrative Assistant
Sarah Schneider, Administrative Assistant
Two hundred and seventy-five exhibits of products and services relating to periodontics, including dental instruments, literature, X-ray equipment, furniture, software and more.
5800 Attendees
Frequency: Annual
Founded in: 1914

12763 **American Academy of Physical Medicine and Rehabilitation Annual Assembly**
330 N Wabash Avenue
Suite 2500
Chicago, IL 60611-7617
312-464-9700; *Fax:* 312-464-0227;
www.aapmr.org/assembly.htm
Steve M Gnatz MD/MHA, President
Thomas E Stautzenbach CAE, Executive Director
Joanne Constantine, Assembly Press Releases/Media
Elsa Lightfoot, Assembly Registration Coordinator
Linda Griffin, Assembly Technical Information
One hundred twenty-five exhibitors representing pharmceutical companies, diagnostics, rehabilitation equipment manufacturers and more.
2500 Attendees
Frequency: Annual/November
Founded in: 1938

12764 **American Academy of Professional Coders National Conferences**
2480 South 3850 West
Suite B
Salt Lake City, UT 84120
801-236-2200
800-626-2633; *Fax:* 801-236-2258
info@aapc.com; www.aapc.com
Reed Pew, CEO
Sandra Nestman, Conference Coordinator
Amy Pistorius, Conference Coordinator
Kira Golding, Conference Coordinator
Raemarie Jimenez, Conference Coordinator
Provides the opportunity to meet the National Advisory Board, members, staff and management. Mingle with local chapters from all over the country. Get education on the most popular and needed subject matter taught by industry experts.
Frequency: January and June
Founded in: 1988
Mailing list available for rent

12765 **American Alliance for Health, Physical Education, Recreation & Dance Expo**
AAHPERD
1900 Association Drive
Reston, VA 20191
703-476-3400
800-213-7193; *Fax:* 703-476-9527;
www.aahperd.org
E. Paul Roetert, CEO
Judith C Young, VP
Paula Kun, Marketing
National convention and exposition that features many exhibits focusing on products, services and equipment within the fields of health, physical education, recreation and dance.
5000 Attendees
Frequency: Annual
Mailing list available for rent

12766 **American Ambulance Association Annual Conference & Trade Show**
Executive Management Services
1255 23rd Street NWrd
Suite 200
Washington, DC 20037
202-213-3999
800-523-4447; *Fax:* 202-452-0005;
www.the-aaa.org
David Saunders, Executive Director
Maria Bianchi, Executive Vice President
6100 Attendees
Frequency: Annual, October

12767 **American Association for Continuity of Care Annual Conference**
American Association for Continuity of Care
638 Prospect Avenue
Hartford, CT 06105-4250
860-867-7525; *Fax:* 203-586-7550
Seminar, reception and 35 exhibits of suppliers of health care delivery resources, products and services.
Frequency: Annual
Founded in: 1982

12768 **American Association for Laboratory Animal Science National Meeting**
American Association for Laboratory Animal Science
9190 Crestwyn Hills Drive
Memphis, TN 38125
901-754-8620; *Fax:* 901-753-0046
info@aalas.org; www.aalas.org
Ann Turner, Executive Director
Two-hundred and seventy exhibits of pharmaceuticals and laboratory animal supplies.
4,500 Attendees
Frequency: October

12769 **American Association for Medical Transcription Annual Meeting**
PO Box 576187
Modesto, CA 95357-6187
209-551-0883
800-982-2182; *Fax:* 209-551-9317;
www.aamt.org
Daryl Ochs, Director Marketing
Terri White, Operations Manager
Exhibitors are medical transcription businesses, hardware, software, publishers and services.
750 Attendees
Frequency: Annual
Founded in: 1978

12770 **American Association for Thoracic Surgery Annual Meeting**
American Association for Thoracic Surgery
500 Cummings Center
Suite 4550
Beverly, MA 01915
978-927-8330; *Fax:* 978-524-8890
aats@prri.com; www.aats.org
Social Media: Facebook
G Alexander Patterson, President
Elizabeth Dooley Crane, Executive Director
4700 Attendees
Frequency: Annual
Founded in: 1917
Mailing list available for rent

12771 **American Association for the Study of Headache Meeting**
19 Mantua Road
Mount Royal, NJ 08061
856-423-0043; *Fax:* 856-423-0082
ahshq@talley.com;
www.americanheadachesociety.org
Paul Winner, President
David Dodick, Treasurer
Twenty-five exhibits of research equipment supplies, and services related to headache study.
650 Attendees
Frequency: Annual
Founded in: 1958

12772 **American Association of Nurse Anesthetists Midyear Assembly**
222 S Prospect Avenue
Park Ridge, IL 60068-4001
847-927-7055; *Fax:* 847-692-6968
info@aana.org; www.aana.com
Wanda Wilson, President
Daniel Vigness, Vice President
Exhibits relating to nurse anesthetists.
350 Attendees

12773 **American Association of Blood Banks Annual Meeting**
American Association of Blood Banks
8101 Glenbrook Road
Bethesda, MD 20814-2749
301-907-6977; *Fax:* 301-907-6895
aabb@aabb.org; www.aabb.org
Daniel Connor, President
Jacquelyn Fredrick, VP
Four hundred and eighty-nine exhibits relating to blood banking and transfusion medicine, gloves, donor coaches, chairs and equipment. Seminar, workshop and banquet.
7500 Attendees
Frequency: November
Founded in: 1947
Mailing list available for rent

12774 **American Association of Cardiovascular & Pulmonary Rehabilitation Conf.**
American Assoc of Cardiovascular & Pulmonary Rehab
7611 Elmwood Avenue
Suite 201
Middleton, WI 53562
608-316-6989; *Fax:* 608-831-5122
aacvpr@tmahq.com; www.aacvpr.org
Sheil Kirshbaum, Director Meetings
Seminar and workshop, plus 70 exhibits of cardiovascular and pulmonary rehabilitation equipment, supplies and services.
1800 Attendees
Frequency: Annual
Founded in: 1985

12775 **American Association of Diabetes Educators Annual Meeting & Educational Prog.**
American Association of Diabetes Educators
100 W Monroe
Chicago, IL 60603
312-424-2426
800-338-3633; *Fax:* 312-424-2427;
www.diabeteseducator.org
Christopher Laxton, Executive Director
Tami Ross, Vice President
Six hundred exhibits of dietary food and beverages, testing and screening tools, educational programs and publications. Banquet and reception available.
Mailing list available for rent: 10000 names at $160 per M

12776 **American Association of Homes and Services for the Aging Convention**
American Association of Homes and Services/Aging
901 E Street NW
Suite 500
Washington, DC 20004-2037
202-661-5700; *Fax:* 202-783-2255
mraynor@aahsa.org; www.leadingage.org
Daniel Smith, VP
Mary-Louise Raynor, Secretary
Bonnie Gauthier, Secretary
Douglas Struyk, Treasurer
One thousand eight hundred exhibitors of equipment, supplies and services for housing and long term care facilities for the aged, conference and tours.
4000 Attendees
Frequency: Annual
Founded in: 1980

12777 **American Association of Immunologists Annual Meeting**
American Association of Immunologists
9650 Rockville Pike
Bethesda, MD 20814
301-634-7178; *Fax:* 301-634-7887
infoaai@aai.org; www.aai.org
Social Media: Facebook
M Michele Hogan PhD, Executive Director
Gail A. Bishop, President
Exhibits related to immunological research, equipment and supplies.
7,600 Members
10000 Attendees
Frequency: May
Founded in: 1913

12778 **American Association of Managed Care Nurses Annual Conference**
American Association of Managed Care Nurses
4435 Waterfront Drive
Suite 101
Glen Allen, VA 23060
804-747-9698; *Fax:* 804-747-5316
keads@aamcn.org; www.aamcn.org
Sloane Reed, VP Sales
Laura Givens, Executive Admin
The AAMCN Annual Conference is designed to provide registered nurses, licensed practical nurses, advanced practice, executive nurses and other healthcare professionals with current information they can use to influence their marketplace.

12779 **American Association of Medical Assistants National Convention**
American Association of Medical Assistants
20 N Wacker Drive
Suite 1575
Chicago, IL 60606-2963
312-899-1500
800-228-2262; *Fax:* 312-899-1259
info@aama-ntl.org; www.aama-ntl.org
David Balasa, Executive Director
Kathy Langley, Director Of Board Services
Main exhibits, data processing equipment, pharmaceuticals, publications, insurance services, text books, coding system reference guides, health care services and more.
500 Attendees
Frequency: Annual

12780 **American Association of Naturopathic Physicians Convention**
American Association of Naturopathic Physicians
4435 Wisconsin Avenue NW
Suite 403
Washington, DC 20016
202-237-8150; *Fax:* 202-237-8152;
www.naturopathic.org
Karen Howard, Executive Director
Michael Cronin, ND, President
Joe Pizzorno, ND, Treasurer
Shelly Nichols, Executive Administrator
Stephanie Geller, Membership Associate
One hundred and twenty exhibits of Naturopathic medicine, supplies and services plus conference and banquet.
750 Attendees
Frequency: Annual

Founded in: 1986
Mailing list available for rent

12781 American Association of Neurological Surgeons Annual Meeting
American Association of Neurologists
5550 Meadowbrook Drive
Rolling Meadows, IL 60008
847-378-0500
888-566-2267; *Fax:* 847-378-0600
info@aans.org; www.aans.org
John Robertson, President
Troy Tippett, Vice President
Griffith R. Harsh, Chairperson
Two hundred manufacturers and suppliers have 500 booths of equipment, publications and supplies.
2400 Attendees
Frequency: Annual
Mailing list available for rent

12782 American Association of Neuroscience Nurses Convention
224 N Des Plaines
#601
Chicago, IL 60661
312-258-1200
800-477-2266; *Fax:* 312-993-0362
info@aann.org; www.aann.org
Thomas O'Dowd, Manager Meetings
Sixty exhibits of nuerological and neurosurgical supplies, services and industry related recruiters.
900 Attendees
Frequency: Annual
Founded in: 1968

12783 American Association of Nurse Anesthetists Annual Meeting
222 S Prospect Avenue
Park Ridge, IL 60068-4001
847-985-5400; *Fax:* 847-692-6968
meetings@aana.com; www.aana.com
Cindy Wood, Director Programs
325 exhibits of equipment, supplies, publications and recruiters. Seminar and workshop, as well as a banquet.
3500 Attendees

12784 American Association of Nurse Anesthetists Assembly of School Faculty
222 S Prospect Avenue
Park Ridge, IL 60068-4001
847-927-7055; *Fax:* 847-692-6968
info@aana.com; www.aana.com
Wanda Wilson, President
Daniel Vigness, Vice President
Nurse anesthetist related exhibits
250 Attendees
Frequency: Annual

12785 American Association of Office Nurses Annual Meeting & Convention
52 Park Avenue
Suite B4
Park Ridge, NJ 07656
201-391-2600
800-457-7504; *Fax:* 201-573-8543;
www.aaacn.org
Michelle Aronowitz, Managing Director
Sherry Levy, Associate Managing Director
American Association of Office Nurses annual meeting and convention at the Eden Roc Hotel in Miami Beach, Florida.
150 Attendees
Frequency: Sept
Founded in: 1988

12786 American Association of Orthodontists Trade Show and Scientific Session
401 N Lindbergh Boulevard
Saint Louis, MO 63141-7816
314-993-1700; *Fax:* 314-997-1745
info@aaortho.org; www.aaortho.org
Chris Varanas, Manager
Five hundred and fifty exhibits of orthodontic equipment, publications, supplies and services.
9000 Attendees
Frequency: Annual

12787 American Association of Suicidology Conference
4201 Connecticut Avenue NW
Suite 408
Washington, DC 20008
202-237-2280; *Fax:* 202-237-2282;
www.suicidology.org
Alan Berman PhD, Executive Director
Exhibits relating to the advancement of studies to prevent suicide and life threatening behavior.
Frequency: Annual
Founded in: 1969

12788 American Association of Tissue Banks Meeting
1320 Old Chain Bridge Road
Suite 450
Mc Lean, VA 22101
703-827-9582; *Fax:* 703-356-2198
aatb@aatb.org; www.aatb.org
Robert Rigney, CEO
Scott Brubaker, Chief Policy Officer
Exhibits for the revival, preservation, storage, and distribution of tissues for transplantation.

12789 American Association on Mental Retardation Annual Meeting
444 N Capitol Street
Suite 846
Washington, DC 20001-1512
202-387-1968
800-424-3688; *Fax:* 202-387-2193
dcroser@aamr.org; www.aamr.org
Doreen Croser, Executive Director
Paul Aitken, Director Of Finance Administration
2000 Attendees
Founded in: 1876

12790 American Chiropractic Association Annual Convention and Exhibition
1701 Clarendon Boulevard
Arlington, VA 22209
703-276-8800
800-986-4636; *Fax:* 703-243-2593
http://www.acatoday.org
Kevin Corcoran, VP
Fifty displays of chiropractic tables and products, mattress companies, nutritional supplements, computer software, services and supplies.
500 Attendees
Frequency: Annual
Founded in: 1963

12791 American Cleft Palate Craniofacial Association Annual Meeting
104 S Estes Drive
Suite 204
Chapel Hill, NC 27514
919-933-9044; *Fax:* 919-933-9604
meetings@acpa-cpf.org; www.acpa-cpf.org
Kathy Bogie, Manager Meetings
Nancy Smythe, Administrative Assistant
Hillary Jones, Administrative Assistant
Scientific meeting.
600 Attendees
Frequency: March
Founded in: 1943

12792 American Clinical Neurophysiology Society Convention
1 Regency Drive
PO Box 30
Bloomfield, CT 06002
860-447-9408; *Fax:* 860-286-0787
info@acns.org; www.acns.org
Mark Ross, President
Alan Legatt, First Vice President
Over 40 exhibits of electroencephalographic and neurophysiology equipment, seminar, workshop and conference.
400 Attendees
Frequency: Annual
Founded in: 1946

12793 American College Health Association Annual Meeting
American College Health Association
1362 Mellon Road
Suite 180
Hanover, MD 21076
410-859-1500; *Fax:* 410-859-1510
contact@acha.org; www.acha.org
Social Media: Facebook, Twitter
Jenny Haubenreiser, President
Pat Ketcham, President-Elect
Doyle Randall, Executive Director
The largest conference for college professionals. This year we honor the spirit of service and compassion that college health professionals have shown in their dedication to serving college students and their campus communities.
1800 Attendees
Frequency: Annual
Founded in: 1922

12794 American College of Allergy, Asthma and Immunology Annual Meeting
85 W Algonquin Road
Suite 550
Arlington Heights, IL 60005-4460
847-427-1200; *Fax:* 847-427-1294
mail@acaai.org; www.acaai.org
Richard G Gowes MD, President
Sami L Bahna MD, President-Elect
2006 Annual Meeting will be held November 9-15 in Philadelpia, Pennsylvania
Frequency: November
Founded in: 1942
Mailing list available for rent: 4500 names at $100 per M

12795 American College of Angiology Conference
295 Northern Boulevard
Suite 104
Great Neck, NY 11021-4701
516-466-4055; *Fax:* 516-466-4099;
www.intlcollegeofangiology.org
Joan Shaffer, Executive Director
CME Seminars and 50 exhibits from commercial and scientific suppliers.
300 Attendees
Frequency: October
Founded in: 1954

12796 American College of Cardiology Annual Scientific Session
American College of Cardiology

2400 N Street, NW
Washington, DC 20037-1699

202-375-6000
800-253-4636; *Fax:* 202-375-7000
resource@acc.org; www.acc.org

Christine McEntee, CEO
Julie Miller, Assistant Professor of Medicine

Seminar, workshop, dinner and 385 exhibits of products, supplies and services related to cardiovascular medicine.
30000 Attendees
Founded in: 1949

12797 **American College of Cardiovascular Administrator Leadership Conference**
American Academy of Medical Administrators
701 Lee Street
Suite 600
Des Plaines, IL 60016

847-759-8601; *Fax:* 847-759-8602
info@aameda.org; www.acc.org

Holly Estal Ed M, Director Education
Gen Hedland, Manager of Exhibits
S. Patrick Alford, Chairman
Linda R. Larin, Treasurer
Tina R. Brinton, Vice Chairman

Featuring keynote and concurrent sessions on human relations, finance and business developments, CV program development technology plus exhibitors that include the latest technological and innovative systems and products in cardiovascular health care. There are 30-40 booths.
300 Attendees
Frequency: March
Mailing list available for rent: 3,000 names at $150 per M

12798 **American College of Emergency Physicians Scientific Assembly**
American College of Emergency Physicians
PO Box 619911
Dallas, TX 75261-9911

972-550-0911
800-798-1822; *Fax:* 972-580-2816
publicaffairs@acep.org; www.acep.org

Dana Bellantone, Manager Meetings

Five hundred and twenty-five exhibits of products and services related to emergency medicine.
4400 Attendees
Frequency: Annual
Founded in: 1972

12799 **American College of Medical Quality Annual Meeting**
4334 Montgomerey Avenue
2nd Floor
Bethesda, MD 20814-4402

301-913-9149
800-924-2149; *Fax:* 301-656-0989
acmq@aol.com; www.acmq.org

Louis H. Diamond MB, ChB, President
Alan Krumholz, MD, Vice President

Seminar, reception and exhibits of computer hardware and software, publications, phamaceuticals and supplies. Medical professionals and others involved in quality assurance and utilization review and risk management attend.
150 Attendees
Founded in: 1973
Mailing list available for rent

12800 **American College of Nurse Practitioners**
J Spargo & Associates
11208 Waples Mill Road
Suite 112
Fairfax, VA 22030

703-631-6200
800-564-4220; *Fax:* 703-654-6931;
www.afcea.org
Social Media: Facebook, Twitter, LinkedIn

June LaMountain, Exhibit Sales Account Manager
Kent Schneider, President and CEO
Pat Miorin, Chief Financial Officer
Al Grasso, Chairman

The premier educational offering for nurse practitioners. It offers the opportunity to earn a full scope of continuing education contact hours at sessions led by top clinical experts in many areas.
1200 Attendees
Frequency: October
Mailing list available for rent

12801 **American College of Obstetricians and Gynecologists Clinical Meeting/Expo**
American College of Obstetricians
409 12th Street SW
Washington, DC 20024

202-857-3288; *Fax:* 202-484-3933
http://www.acog.org

Professionally related exhibits.

12802 **American College of Physicians Annual Convention**
American College of Physicians
Independence Mall W
6th Street & Race
Philadelphia, PA 19106

215-351-2400
http://www.acponline.org

John Tooker, CEO

Five hundred exhibits of medical supplies and services, as well as a seminar.
8000 Attendees

12803 **American College of Rheumatology Scientific Meeting**
Slack
4930 Del Ray Avenue
Bethesda, MD 20814

301-654-2055; *Fax:* 301-654-5920
member@gastro.org; www.gastro.org

Robert Greenberg, Executive Vp
Michael Stolar, Senior Vp

Two hundred and ten exhibits of diagnostic testing kits, pharmaceuticals, equipment and supplies, of interest to professionals in Rheumatology.
4500 Attendees
Frequency: Annual
Founded in: 1934

12804 **American College of Surgeons Annual Clinical Congress**
American College of Surgeons
633 N Saint Clair Street
Chicago, IL 60611

312-202-5000; *Fax:* 312-440-7143
postmaster@facs.org; www.facs.org

Felix P Niespodziewanski, Conventions Manager
Thomas Russell, Chairman
Andrew Warshaw, Treasurer
Courtney Townsend, Secretary

One thousand one hundred exhibits of medical and patient care products, equipment and supplies. Conference, seminar and workshop, as well as luncheon and tours.
10000 Attendees
Frequency: Annual
Founded in: 1914

12805 **American Congress of Rehabilitation Medicine Annual Meeting**
6801 Lake Plaza Drive
Suite B- 205
Indianapolis, IN 46220

317-915-2250; *Fax:* 317-915-2245
crobinson@acrm.org; www.acrm.org

Richard D Morgan, Executive Director

Seminar, workshop and conference with 20 exhibits of rehabilitation supplies and equipment.
250 Attendees
Frequency: September/October
Founded in: 1923
Mailing list available for rent: 750 names at $275 per M

12806 **American Dental Association Annual Session & Technical Exhibition**
211 E Chicago Avenue
Suite 200
Chicago, IL 60611-2678

312-440-2500; *Fax:* 312-440-2707
donovanj@ada.org; www.ada.org

James P Donovan, Exhibit Manager
Patricia A Johnson, Manager Program Development
Vicki Guinta, Director
James Bramson, CEO

The annual session scientific program consists of over 180 programs, including science of dentistry, practice of dentistry, dental technology and general insterest programs as well as participation workshops. The leading suppliers will showcase their products and services. Dental professionals can compare products, see demonstrations, and make decisions about applying the latest technology. Attendees visiting the Technical Exhibition can also look for the ADA Seal which has long been recognizd
30000 Attendees
Frequency: October

12807 **American Dental Education Association Annual Session and Exposition**
1400 K Street NW
Suite 1100
Washington, DC 20005

202-289-7201; *Fax:* 202-289-7204;
www.adea.org

Rhonda Buford, Meetings Manager
Renee Latimer, Meeting Manager
Simone Smith, Meetings Manager
Novella Abrams, Senior Administrative Associate
Cassandra Allen, Program Associate

One hundred commercial and educational exhibits of supplies, video equipment, publications and more.
3000 Attendees
Frequency: Annual
Founded in: 1983

12808 **American Dental Hygienists Association Conference**
444 N Michigan Avenue
Suite 3400
Chicago, IL 60611

312-440-8900; *Fax:* 312-440-8929;
www.adha.org

Ann Battrell, Executive Director
Kathy Madryk, Marketing Manager
Katie Powell, Director, Members Service
Ann Lynch, Director, Governmental Affairs
Isaac Carpenter, Director, Finance and MIS

Educational session and 120 exhibits of dental products.
1500 Attendees
Frequency: Annual

Founded in: 1993
Mailing list available for rent

12809 American Dental Society of Anesthesiology Scientific Meeting
211 E Chicago Avenue
Suite 948
Chicago, IL 60611

312-664-8270
800-722-7788; *Fax:* 312-642-9713

R Knight Charlton, Executive Director

Meeting and over 15 exhibits of anesthetics and monitoring equipment.
200 Attendees
Frequency: Annual
Founded in: 1954

12810 American Diabetes Association Annual Scientific Sessions
American Diabetes Association
2451 Crystal Drive
Suite 900
Arlington, VA 22202

703-549-1500
800-342-2383; *Fax:* 703-549-6995
meetings@diabetes.org; www.diabetes.org
Social Media: Facebook, Twitter, YouTube

Robin Richardson, Chair
Kevin L. Hagan, Chief Executive Officer

Three hundred and fifty exhibits of medical and dietary products and services, seminar and workshop.
Frequency: June
Founded in: 1940

12811 American Health Care Association Annual Convention and Exhibition
1201 L Street NW
Washington, DC 20005

202-842-4444; *Fax:* 202-842-3860
webmaster@ahca.org; www.ahcancal.org
Social Media: Facebook, Twitter, LinkedIn

Dave Kyllo, VP

Three hundred and fifty exhibits of supplies and information for the long term health care industry, banquet, luncheon and tours.
5000 Attendees
Frequency: Annual
Mailing list available for rent

12812 American Health Information Management Association National Convention
American Health Information Management Association
233 N Michigan Avenue
21st Floor
Chicago, IL 60601-5809

312-233-1100; *Fax:* 312-233-1090
info@ahima.org; www.ahima.org
Social Media: Facebook, Twitter, LinkedIn

Erin Toth, Exhibition Manager
Linda Kloss, Executive Director
Patty Thierry Sheridan, President
Lynne Thomas Gordon, Chief Executive Officer
Beth Kost-Woodrow, Treasurer

Five hundred exhibits of interest to health information management professionals, reception.
3500 Attendees
Frequency: Annual
Founded in: 1928
Mailing list available for rent

12813 American Health Quality Association Annual Session
1140 Connecticut Avenue NW
Washington, DC 20036

202-331-5790
info@ahqa.org; www.ahqa.org

David Thomas MD, President
David Adler, Public Affairs Associate

Quality Improvement Organizations (QIOs) and professionals working to improve the quality of health care in communities across America gather for educational sessions and networking.
Frequency: March

12814 American Heart Association Scientific Sessions
American Heart Association
7272 Greenville Avenue
Dallas, TX 75231

214-736-6300; *Fax:* 214-373-3406;
www.amhrt.org

M Cass Wheeler, CEO

Conference, seminar and tours, plus 325 exhibits relating to exercise, equipment, pharmceuticals and services related to cardiovascular health care.
29000 Attendees

12815 American Hospital Association Convention
155 N. Wacker Dr.
Chicago, IL 60606

312-422-3000
800-424-4301; *Fax:* 312-422-4500
ddavidson@aha.org; www.aha.org
Social Media: Twitter, YouTube

Richard Umbdenstock, President & CEO
Richard Pollack, VP, Advocacy
Neil Jesuelo, SVP Business Development

Exhibits of equipment, supplies and services for the medical and hopsital industry.

12816 American Industrial Hygiene Conference & Exposition (AIHce)
American Industrial Hygiene Association
3141 Fairview Park Drive
Suite 777
Falls Church, VA 22042

703-849-8888; *Fax:* 703-207-3561
infonet@aiha.org; www.aiha.org
Social Media: Facebook, Twitter, LinkedIn

Bethany Chirico, Director, Global Meeting & Expos
Alison Daniels, Manager , Exposition
Laura Cilano Garcia, Program Director

Attracts OEHS professionals that are industrial hygienists, EHS specialists, safety professionals, risk management professionals and other who are esponsible for safety, health and the environment at their organization.
Frequency: Annual
Founded in: 1939

12817 American Lung Association/American Thoracic Society Int Conference
1740 Broadway
New York, NY 10019-4374

212-315-8700; *Fax:* 212-265-5642

John Kirkwood, CEO

Two hundred and fifty exhibits of pharmaceuticals, equipment and books.
8500 Attendees
Frequency: Annual
Founded in: 1904

12818 American Medical Directors Association Annual Symposium
American Medical Directors Association
11000 Broken Land Parkway, Suite 400
Suite 760
Columbia, MD 21044

410-740-9743
800-876-2632; *Fax:* 410-740-4572
info@amda.com; www.amda.com

Megan Brey, Director Meetings
Lorraine Tarnove, Manager

Exhibits relating to geriatrics, pharmaceuticals and medical administration of long term care facilities. Long term health care physicians and professionals attend educational sessions, receptions and special events. Spouse/guest program offered.
1400 Attendees
Frequency: April
Founded in: 1978

12819 American Medical Informatics Association Fall Symposium
American Medical Informatics Association
4915 Saint Elmo
Suite 401
Bethesda, MD 20814

301-657-1291; *Fax:* 301-657-1296

Megan Brey, Meeting Coordinator
Karen Greenwood, Manager

One hundred ten commercial and scientific medical informatics software and hardware, supplies and service dealers. Attended by medical professionals and the general public.
2500 Attendees
Frequency: Annual
Founded in: 1977

12820 American Medical Student Association Convention
American Medical Student Association
1902 Association Drive
Reston, VA 20191

703-620-6600
800-767-2266; *Fax:* 703-620-5873
amsa@amsa.org; www.amsa.org

One hundred exhibits relating to medical supplies and equipment, residency programs, physician recruitment and professional associations.
1500 Attendees

12821 American Medical Technologists Convention
American Medical Technologists
10700 West Higgins Road
Rosemont, IL 60018

847-823-5169
800-275-1268; *Fax:* 847-823-0458
dianepowell.amt@juno.com; www.amtc.com

Diane Powell, Show Manager

Forty eight exhibits of clinical laboratory books, supplies and equipment, seminar, workshop, banquet and tours.
600 Attendees
Frequency: Annual
Founded in: 1991

12822 American Medical Women's Association Annual Meeting
12100 Sunset Hills Road, Suite 130
4th Floor
Reston, VA 20190

703-234-4069
866-564-2483; *Fax:* 215-564-2175;
www.amwa-doc.org

Gayatri Devi, President
Beatrice S Desper MD, President-Elect
Ana Maria Lopez, Secretary
Mary Fitzsimmons MD, Treasurer

Seminar, banquet, tours and 60 exhibits of medical equipment, supplies and services.
1000 Attendees
Frequency: Annual
Founded in: 1915
Mailing list available for rent

12823 American Nephrology Nurses Association Symposium
Society of Urologic Nurses and Associates
E Holly Avenue
Box 56
Pittman, NJ 08071

856-256-2350; *Fax:* 856-589-7463

Mike Cunningham, Manager

One hundred fifteen companies have exhibits of equipment, supplies, pharmaceuticals and services for nephrology.
2000 Attendees
Frequency: Annual
Founded in: 1970

12824 American Nurses Association Convention
600 Maryland Avenue SW
Suite 100
Washington, DC 20024-2571

202-651-7000; *Fax:* 301-628-5001
exhibits@ana.org; www.nursingworld.org

Exhibits of nursing professional equipment, supplies and services.
Frequency: Annual

12825 American Occupational Health Conference & Exhibits
Slack
4930 Del Ray Avenue
Bethesda, MD 20814

301-654-2055; *Fax:* 301-654-5920
member@gastro.org; www.gastro.org
Social Media: Facebook, Twitter, LinkedIn

Robert Greenberg, Executive Vp
Michael Stolar, Senior Vp
Derek Randolph, Director of Building Services
Arceli Bacsinila, Senior Director of Finance
Hillina Fetehawoke, Staff Accountant

Four hundred exhibits of pharmaceuticals, equipment, software and supplies for health professionals, offices and labs.
4500 Attendees
Mailing list available for rent

12826 American Occupational Therapy Association Annual Conference
American Occupation Therapy Association
4720 Montgomery Lane
PO Box 31220
Bethesda, MD 20824-1220

301-652-2682; *Fax:* 301-652-7711;
www.aota.org

M Carolyn Baum, President
Lizette Rosales, Manager
7000 Attendees
Frequency: May
Founded in: 1919

12827 American Optometric Student Association Annual Meeting
243 N Lindbergh Boulevard
Saint Louis, MO 63141

314-993-8575; *Fax:* 314-993-8919
info@iacconline.org;
www.iaccnorthamerica.org
Social Media: Facebook, Twitter, LinkedIn

James Mahon, Director Marketing
Tom Cappucci, First Vice President

Optometry equipment, supplies and services.
Frequency: Annual

12828 American Organization of Nurse Executives Meeting and Exposition
American Hospital Association
1 N Franklin
Suite 27
Chicago, IL 60606

312-222-2000
312-422-4519
aone@aha.org; www.aha.org

Pamela Thompson, CEO
Cliff Lehman, Director Membership Services

One hundred fifty exhibits of patient care equipment and supplies, computer hardware and software, communications systems and information for the professional in health care.
Frequency: Annual

12829 American Orthopsychiatric Association Annual Meeting
330 7th Avenue
18th Floor
New York, NY 10001

212-564-5930; *Fax:* 212-564-6180

Rachel L MacAulay, Program Associate

Meeting and exhibits by social service agencies, publications, computer software companies and more.
1928 Members
700 Attendees
Frequency: Annual
Founded in: 1923

12830 American Orthotic & Prosthetic Association National Assembly
American Orthotic & Prosthetic Association
330 John Carlyle Street
Suite 200
Alexandria, VA 22314

571-431-0876; *Fax:* 571-431-0899
info@aopanet.org; www.aopanet.org

Michael Oros, President
Tom Fise, Executive Director
Don DeBolt, Chief Operating Officer
Betty Leppin, Manager, Membership & Operations

AOPA's goal is to advocate for policies that improve patient care.
2200 Attendees
Frequency: Annual
Founded in: 1917

12831 American Osteopathic Association Meeting & Exhibits
American Osteopathic Hospital Association
142 E Ontario Street
Chicago, IL 60611

312-587-3709; *Fax:* 312-202-8212

John Crosby, Executive Director

Over 25 exhibits of products and services relating to the osteopathic health care industry, including building and finacing, marketing and operations.
500 Attendees
Founded in: 1983

12832 American Pain Society Scientific Meeting
4700 W Lake Avenue
Glenview, IL 60025

847-375-4715; *Fax:* 877-734-8758
info@ampainsoc.org; www.ampainsoc.org

Judith A Paice, President
Catherine Underwood, Executive Director
Marilyn Rutkowski, Marketing Manager
Kathryn Checea, Director of Sales
Deborah Pinkston, Managing Editor

Designed for a diverse group of pain clinicians, scientists and other professionals, the Annual Scientific Meeting features a prominent faculty presenting basic, translational, and clinical research advancements. Seminar, banquet, luncheon, breakfast and 150 exhibits of pharmceutical and medical instruments, medical equipment, products, supplies, services, and alternative delivery systems.
Frequency: Annual
Founded in: 1977

12833 American Physical Therapy Association Annual Conference
American Physical Therapy Association
1111 N Fairfax Street
Alexandria, VA 22314

703-684-2782
800-999-2782; *Fax:* 703-706-8575
webmaster@apta.org; www.apta.org

Kelly Glascoe, Director/Exposition
Frank Mallon, CEO

450 exhibits of physical therapy equipment, supplies and services.
4000 Attendees
Frequency: Annual

12834 American Physical Therapy Association: Private Practice Session
1111 N Fairfax Street
Alexandria, VA 22314

703-684-2782
800-999-2782; *Fax:* 703-706-8575
http://www.apta.org

Frank Mallon, CEO

Seminar, workshop, dinner and 120 exhibits of physical therapy and rehabilitation equipment, supplies and services.
1200 Attendees
Frequency: Annual
Founded in: 1983

12835 American Podiatric Medical Association Annual Meeting
9312 Old Georgetown Road
Bethesda, MD 20814

301-581-9200; *Fax:* 301-530-2752
Social Media: Facebook, Twitter, LinkedIn

Anne Martinez CMP, Meetings Administrator

One-hundred and fifty exhibits of medical and laser equipment, supplies and podiatric services.
1,500 Attendees
Frequency: August

12836 American Psychiatric Association Annual Meeting
American Psychiatric Association
1000 Wilson Boulevard
Suite 1825
Arlington, VA 22209-3901

703-907-7300
888-357-7924; *Fax:* 703-907-1085
apa@psych.org; www.psychiatry.org
Social Media: Facebook, Twitter, LinkedIn

Saul M. Levin, M.D., M.P.A, CEO & Medical Director
Maria A. Oquendo, President

Conference, seminar, workshop and 850 exhibits of computer online service and software, media products, criminal justice, dianostic tools and much more.
18000 Attendees
Frequency: Annual
Founded in: 1844

12837 American Psychological Association Annual Convention
American Psychological Association

750 1st Street NE
Washington, DC 20002-4242

202-336-5500
800-374-2721; *Fax:* 202-336-5568;
www.apa.org

James H Bray PhD, President
Norman Anderson PhD, Executive VP/CEO
Paul L Craig PhD, Treasurer
12000 Attendees
Frequency: Annual, August

12838 American Public Health Association Annual Exhibition
American Public Health Association
800 I Street NW
Washington, DC 20001
202-777-2742; *Fax:* 202-777-2534
lynn.schoen@apha.org; www.apha.org

Lynn Schoen, Exhibition Manager
Georges Benjamin, Executive Director
Five-hundred seventy exhibits of medical interest, pharmaceuticals, publishers, educational, governmental, software, helth promotion products and more. Scientific Sessions available.
13000 Attendees
Frequency: November

12839 American Roentgen Ray Society Meeting
American Roentgen Ray Society
44211 Slatestone Court
Leesburg, VA 20176
703-729-3353
800-438-2777; *Fax:* 703-729-4839
info@arrs.org; www.arrs.org

Maureen Robertson, Show Manager
Noel Montesa, Vice President
Charles Kahn, Vice President
Melissa Rosado, Secretary
Forty-one and a half hours of Category ICME credits available; Categorical course on Body CT; 30 commercial exhibits; 300 scientific exhibits; scientific paper presentations.
2,500 Attendees
Frequency: April-May

12840 American School Health's Annual School Health Conference
American School Health Association
4340 East West Highway
Suite 403
Bethesda, MD 20814

301-652-8072
800-445-2742; *Fax:* 301-652-8077
info@ashaweb.org; www.ashaweb.org
Social Media: Facebook, Twitter, LinkedIn

Mary Bamer Ramsier, Meeting Planner
Thomas Reed, Manager
Stephen Conley, Executive Director
Julie Greenfield, Marketing and Conferences Director
Lori Lawrence, Membership/Database Manager
Join school health professionals who will come together to learn, share perspectives and resources, and network during the more than 120 educational sessions and workshops. General Sessions, multiple break-outs, and exhibits.
800 Attendees
Frequency: Annual
Founded in: 1927
Mailing list available for rent: 650 names

12841 American Society for Aesthetic Plastic Surgery Conference
American Society for Aesthetic Plastic Surgery
36 W 44th Street
Suite 630
New York, NY 10036

212-921-0500; *Fax:* 212-921-0011
media@surgery.org; www.surgery.org

Educational sessions and displays of the latest prdoducts and developments.
2500 Attendees
Frequency: May

12842 American Society for Artificial Internal Organs Meeting and Exhibits
PO Box C
Boca Raton, FL 33429-8589

561-391-8589; *Fax:* 561-368-9153;
www.asaio.com

Workshop, and over 30 exhibits of interest to physicians, nurses, engineers, perfusionists and technicians.
1000 Attendees
Frequency: Annual
Founded in: 1954

12843 American Society for Bone and Mineral Research Congress
1200 19th Street NW
Suite 300
Washington, DC 20036

202-289-5900; *Fax:* 202-857-1880;
www.asbmr.org

Joan Goldberg, Executive Director
Exhibits for the research of bone and mineral diseases.
Frequency: Annual
Founded in: 1977

12844 American Society for Cell Biology Annual Meeting
9650 Rockville Pike
Bethesda, MD 20814

301-530-7153; *Fax:* 301-530-7139
enewman@ascb.org; www.ascb.org/ascb

Edward Newman, Director Marketing
Joan Goldberg, Manager
Jean Schwarzbauer, Secretary
Conference and 425 exhibits of interest to biomedical researchers, scientists, and related trade professionals.
8000 Attendees
Frequency: Annual
Founded in: 1961

12845 American Society for Dermatologic Surgery Annual Meeting
American Society for Dermatologic Surgery
5550 Meadowbrook Drive
Suite 120
Rolling Meadows, IL 60008
847-956-0900; *Fax:* 847-956-0999;
www.asds.net

Alastair Carruthers, President
Kimberly Butterwick, Board of Directors
Educational session, banquet and tours plus 80 exhibits of surgical instruments, dressings, closure materials and dermatologic pharmceuticals.
800 Attendees
Founded in: 1973

12846 American Society for Health Care Human Resources Administration Meeting
American Hospital Association
1 N Franklin
Chicago, IL 60606

312-222-2000; *Fax:* 312-422-4519;
www.aha.org

Human resources administration in health care exhibition.

12847 American Society for Healthcare Management Convention
Corcoran Expositions
100 W Monroe Street
Suite 1001
Chicago, IL 60603

312-541-0567; *Fax:* 312-541-0573

12848 American Society for Histocompatability and Immunogenetics
PO Box 15804
Lexana, KS 66285-5804
913-541-0009; *Fax:* 913-541-0156

Michael P Flanigan CAE, Executive Director
Fifty exhibits from medical suppliers relating to tissue typing.
1000 Attendees
Frequency: Annual
Founded in: 1974

12849 American Society for Laser Medicine and Surgery Conference
2100 Stewart Avenue
Suite 240
Wausau, WI 54401-1709
715-845-9283; *Fax:* 715-848-2493
information@aslms.org; www.aslms.org

Richard O Gregory MD, Board Secretary
Dianne Dalsky, Executive Director
Seventy five exhibits of laser medicine and supplies of interest to physicians, physicists, nurses, veterinarians, dentists, podiatrists and technicians.
Frequency: Annual
Founded in: 1980

12850 American Society for Microbiology: General Meeting
1325 Massachusetts Anvenue NW
Washington, DC 20005

202-942-9252; *Fax:* 202-942-9340
Professionally related exhibits.

12851 American Society for Nutrition Annual Meeting
9650 Rockville Pike
Bethesda, MD 20814-3998

301-634-7050; *Fax:* 301-634-7892;
www.nutrition.org

Teresa A. Davis, President
John E Courtney PhD, Executive Officer
Gordon L. Jensen, VP
Cheryl Rock, Treasurer
Catherine Field, Secretary
Exhibits relating to clinical nutrition of interest to physicians and scientists.
Frequency: Annual
Mailing list available for rent

12852 American Society for Surgery of the Hand Annual Meeting
American Society for Surgery of the Hand
6300 N River Road
Suite 600
Rosemont, IL 60018

847-384-8300; *Fax:* 847-384-1435
info@assh.org; www.assh.org

Carissa Wehrman, Meetings/Exhibits Coordinator
Mark Anderson, Executive Director
Meeting plus exhibits of microsurgical instruments, finger splinting devices, surgical telescopes, trauma products, external fixation systems and more.
2,000 Attendees
Frequency: September

12853 American Society for Therapeutic Radiology and Oncology Annual Meeting
American Society for Therapeutic Radiology & Onc.
12500 Fairlakes Circle
Suite 375
Fairfax, VA 22033

703-502-1550
800-962-7876; *Fax:* 703-502-7852
meetings@astro.org; www.astro.org

Laura Mulay, ASTRO Meetings Manager

Eight-hundred exhibits of products, supplies and services for the treatment of cancer.
10000 Attendees
Frequency: October

12854 American Society of Aesthetic Plastic Surgery Meeting
11081 Winners Circle
Suite 200
Los Alamitos, CA 90720-2813

562-799-2356; *Fax:* 310-427-2234

Robert Stanton, Manager

Meeting and 100 exhibits of plastic surgery medical instruments and equipment.
Frequency: Annual

12855 American Society of Anesthesiologists Annual Meeting
American Society of Anesthesiologists
520 N Northwest Highway
Park Ridge, IL 60068-2573

847-825-5586; *Fax:* 847-825-1692
mail@asahq.org; www.asahq.org

Ronald Bruns, Executive Director
18000 Attendees
Frequency: Annual, October

12856 American Society of Clinical Oncology Annual Convention
J Spargo & Associates
11208 Waples Mill Road
Suite 112
Fairfax, VA 22030

703-631-6200
800-564-4220; *Fax:* 703-299-1044;
www.jspargo.com

John Spargo, President

Three hundred exhibits of medical equipment, supplies and services used in the practice of clinical oncology.
20000 Attendees
Frequency: Annual
Founded in: 1964

12857 American Society of Clinical Pathologists and College of American Pathologist
American Society of Clinical Pathologists
2100 W Harrison Street
Chicago, IL 60612

312-738-1336; *Fax:* 312-738-1619

John Ball, Executive VP
4500 Attendees

12858 American Society of Cytopathology Annual Scientific Meeting
100 West 10th Street
Suite 605
Wilmington, DE 19801

302-543-6583; *Fax:* 302-543-6597
asc@cytopathology.org;
www.cytopathology.org
Social Media: Facebook, Twitter, LinkedIn

Christy Myers, Meetings Manager
Elizabeth Jenkins, Manager
Andrew Renshaw, President

Premier event in the field of cytopathology. The objectives of the Annual Meeting are to update cytologists on the current practice of cytopathology, foster research in early diagnosis and effective treatment of human disease and provide a forum for advocacy on behalf of cytologists and their patients.
850 Attendees
Frequency: November
Founded in: 1951

12859 American Society of Directors of Volunteer Services Leadership Training Conf
1 N Franklin
Chicago, IL 60606

312-223-3937; *Fax:* 312-442-4575

Audrey Harris, Executive Director

Workshop, banquet, luncheon and 55 exhibits of health care administration equipment, supplies and services.
700 Attendees
Frequency: Annual
Founded in: 1964

12860 American Society of Extra-Corporeal Tech. International Conference
503 Carlisle Drive
Suite 125
Herndon, VA 20170-4838

703-435-8556; *Fax:* 703-435-0056
webmaster@amsect.org; www.amsect.org

Judy Luther, Deputy Executive Director

Seminar, workshop, conference and 75 exhibits relating to the practice of extra-corporeal technology (involving heart and lung machines).
Frequency: Annual

12861 American Society of Hand Therapists Convention
Smith, Bucklin and Associates
401 N Michigan Avenue
Chicago, IL 60611-4267

312-644-6610; *Fax:* 312-245-1082
info@smithbucklin.com;
www.smithbucklin.com

Henry S. Givray, President & CEO
C. Albert Koob, Executive Vice President
Carolyn Dolezal, Executive Vice President
Michael L. Payne, Executive Vice President
Cele Fogarty, Vice President - Event Services

Workshop and 40 - 60 exhibits of books, and hand therapy equipment.
800 Attendees
Frequency: Annual
Founded in: 1949

12862 American Society of Health Care Marketing & Public Relations
1 N Franklin Street
31st Floor
Chicago, IL 60606-3421

773-327-1064; *Fax:* 312-422-4579

Lauren Barnett, Executive Director

Sixty booths of communications, printing, computer equipment, public relations and fund raising consultants in the health care profession.
600 Attendees
Frequency: September

12863 American Society of Hematology Annual Meeting & Exposition
1200 19th Street NW
Suite 300
Washington, DC 24226

202-857-1118; *Fax:* 202-847-1164

Gail Sparks

Four hundred fifty exhibits of equipment and supplies of interest to hematologists and related professionals.
15000 Attendees
Founded in: 1958

12864 American Society of Human Genetics Annual Meeting
American Society of Human Genetics
9650 Rockville Pike
Bethesda, MD 20814-3998

301-634-7300; *Fax:* 301-634-7079
society@ashg.org; www.ashg.org
Social Media: Facebook, Twitter, LinkedIn

Joann Boughman, PhD, Executive VP
Chuck Windle, Director of Finance/Administration
Karen Goodman, Executive Assistant
Pauline Minhinnett, Dir. of Meetings/Exhibit Management
Mary Shih, Membership Manager

A meeting of researchers, clinicians, trainees and others who share the most recent research findings in human genetics. Includes invited speaker sessions and about 3000 contributed abstracts; 266 to platform and the remainder to poster presentations.
8000 Members
6,000 Attendees
Founded in: 1948

12865 American Society of Nephrology
American Society of Nephrology
1200 19th Street NW
Suite 300
Washington, DC 20036

202-857-1190; *Fax:* 202-429-5112

13000 Attendees

12866 American Society of PeriAnesthesia Nurses
American Gastroenterological Association
4930 Del Ray Avenue
Bethesda, MD 20814

301-654-2055; *Fax:* 301-654-5920
member@gastro.org; www.gastro.org

12867 American Society of Post Anesthesia Nurses Meeting
Slack
4930 Del Ray Avenue
Bethesda, MD 20814

301-654-2055; *Fax:* 301-654-5920
member@gastro.org; www.gastro.org

Robert Greenberg, Executive Vp
Michael Stolar, Senior Vp

One hundred seventy exhibits of pharmaceuticals and recovery room supplies.
1700 Attendees
Frequency: Annual
Founded in: 1981

12868 American Society of Psychoprophylaxis in Obstetrics/Lamaze Conference
Smith, Bucklin and Associates
1200 19th Street NW
Suite 300
Washington, DC 20036-2412

202-861-6416; *Fax:* 202-429-5112

Leigh McMillan, Senior Convention Director

One hundred exhibitors of educational materials for Lamaze method of prepared childbirth, obstetric equipment and supplies, infant products, breast pumps and more.
500 Attendees
Frequency: Annual
Founded in: 1960

12869 **American Society of Transplant Physicians Scientific Meeting**
Slack
4930 Del Ray Avenue
Bethesda, MD 20814
301-654-2055; *Fax:* 301-654-5920
member@gastro.org; www.gastro.org
Robert Greenberg, Executive Vp
Michael Stolar, Senior Vp
Fifty exhibits of medical supplies and services of interest to physicans and others actively involved with transplantaion.
800 Attendees
Frequency: Annual
Founded in: 1981

12870 **American Society of Transplant Surgeons Annual Meeting**
Wright Organization
716 Lee Street
Des Plaines, IL 60016-4515
847-245-5700; *Fax:* 708-824-0394
Sixty exhibitors of medical equipment, supplies and services relating to renal and cardiac transplants.
750 Attendees
Founded in: 1974

12871 **American Society of Tropical Medicine and Hygiene Annual Scientific Meeting**
60 Revere Drive
Suite 500
Northbrook, IL 60062
847-480-9592; *Fax:* 847-480-9282
info@astmh.org; www.astmh.org
Madhuri Carson, Conference Administrator
Judy DeAcetis, Director
Karen Goraleski, Executive Director
Reception and over 20 exhibits related to tropical medicine and hygiene, including the areas of arboviology, entomology, medicine, nursing and parasitology.
1500 Attendees
Frequency: November
Founded in: 1951

12872 **American Speech-Language-Hearing Association Annual Convention**
American Speech- Language Hearing Association
10801 Rockville Pike
Rockville, MD 20852
301-897-5700
800-498-2071; *Fax:* 301-296-8580
productsales@asha.org; www.asha.org
Mary Harding, Exhibition Manager
Arlene Pietranton, Associate Director
Amy Hasselkus, Associate Director
Four hundred exhibits of medical, educational and testing equipment, plus publications.
12000 Attendees

12873 **American Urological Association Convention**
1000 Corporate Boulevard
Linthicum, MD 21090
410-689-3700; *Fax:* 410-689-3800
convention@auanet.org; www.auanet.org/
Jane Conway, Advertising & Exhibit Sales
Sarah Hardy, Exhibitor Customer Service
Andrew Niles, Exhibit Operations
Michael T Sheppard, Executive Director
Paul F Schellhammer, Board of Directors President
At the American Urological Association (AUA)'s Annual Meeting there are more than 10,000 urologists and health care professionals in attendance and over 300 exhibitors showcasing their urological products or services-there is no better place to learn about the latest advances in urology.
10000 Attendees
Frequency: Annual

12874 **Annual Clinical Assembly of Osteopathic Specialists**
American College of Osteopathic Surgeons
123 N Henry Street
Alexandria, VA 22314
703-684-0416; *Fax:* 703-684-3280
info@facos.org; www.facos.org
Social Media: Facebook, Twitter, LinkedIn
Guy Beaumont, Executive Director
Judith T Mangum, Director Finance
Jennifer B. Colwell, Director of Continuing Education
Sonjya Johnson, Director of Membership Recruitment
Brandon Roberts, Director of Finance
700 Members
Frequency: Annual
Mailing list available for rent

12875 **Annual Conference on Healthcare Marketing**
Alliance for Healthcare Strategy & Marketing
11 S LaSalle Street
Suite 2300
Chicago, IL 60603
312-704-9700; *Fax:* 312-704-9709;
www.shsmd.org
Workshop and social events plus 50 exhibits of marketing communications, health care information lines, strategic planning and more.
600 Attendees
Frequency: Annual
Founded in: 1984

12876 **Annual Contact Lens and Primary Care Seminar, MOA**
Michigan Optometric Association
530 W Ionia Street
Suite A
Lansing, MI 48933-1062
517-482-0616; *Fax:* 517-482-1611;
www.themoa.org
William D Dansby CAE, Executive VP
Mark Margolies, Treasurer
Continuing education program and trade show for optometrists and optometric technicians/assistants.
1100 Attendees
Frequency: October, Annually
Founded in: 1968

12877 **Annual Convention of American Institute of Ultrasound in Medicine**
American Institute of Ultrasound in Medicine
14750 Sweitzer Lane
Suite 100
Laurel, MD 20707
301-498-4392
800-638-5352; *Fax:* 301-498-4450
conv_edu@aium.org; www.aium.org
Jenny Clark, Director of Development
Brenda Kinney, Meeting Coordinator
Lisa Shendan, Sales Manager
Frequency: June

12878 **Annual Convention of the American College of Osteopathic Obstetricians**
American College Of Osteopathic Obstetricians
900 Auburn Road
Pontiac, MI 48342
248-332-6360
800-875-6360; *Fax:* 248-332-4607;
www.acoog.com
Jaki Britton, Administrator
Workshop, reception and banquet as well as exhibits relating to women's health, medical equipment and supplies.
350 Attendees
Frequency: Annual
Founded in: 1934

12879 **Annual Critical Care Update**
National Professional Education Institute
2525 Ossen Fort Road
PO Box 118
Glencoe, MO 63068-1107
636-735-5570
800-575-5575; *Fax:* 561-743-9596
JJMcDaid@aol.com; www.npeinursing.com
Judie McDaid, Exhibitor Relations Manager
Leslie Brock, Registration Manager
The Annual Critical Care Update and Nurse Managers Conference/EXPO provides a fully integrated program dedicated to the continuing education of critical care nurses, nurse managers and other healthcare professionals. Exhibitors showcase their latest healthcare products, pharmaceuticals, services, research and facilities. Knowledge gained in the informative, entertaining EXPO Hall, will influence these nurses' purchasing decisions throughout the year.
1500 Attendees
Frequency: Annual, April
Founded in: 1973

12880 **Annual Disease Management Congress: Innnovative Strategies**
National Managed Health Care Congress
71 2nd Avenue
3rd Floor
Waltham, MA 02154
888-882-2500; *Fax:* 941-365-0157;
www.nmhcc.org
Frances Pratt, Director/Marketing
One hundred exhibits of targeted disease management and services.
1700 Attendees
Frequency: Annual
Founded in: 1996

12881 **Annual Educational Conference and Exhibits**
Society for Healthcare Strategy & Market Dev.
One N Franklin
Chicago, IL 60606
312-422-3840; *Fax:* 312-422-4579
stratsoc@aha.org; www.stratsociety.org
Frequency: September

12882 **Annual Meeting & Clinical Lab Exposition**
American Association for Clinical Chemistry
1850 K St NW
Suite 625
Washington, DC 20006-2215
202-857-0717
800-892-1400; *Fax:* 202-887-5093
custserv@aacc.org; www.aacc.org
Jean Rhame, Director Professional Affairs

Six hundred exhibitors of clincal laboratory equipment, supplies and services for lab automation, information, robotics and OEM products. Seminar, worhshop and conference.
20000 Attendees
Frequency: Annual
Mailing list available for rent: 11000 names at $150 per M

12883 Annual Meeting & Homecare Expo
National Association for Home Care and Hospice
228 7th Street SE
Washington, DC 20003

202-547-7424; *Fax:* 202-547-3540
webmaster@nahc.org; www.nahc.org

Gathering of Home Care and Hospice professionals.
4000 Attendees
Frequency: October

12884 Annual Meeting & OTO Expo
American Academy of Otolaryngology-Head & Neck
1650 Diagonal Road
Alexandria, VA 22314-3357

703-836-4444; *Fax:* 703-683-5100
membership@entnet.org; www.entnet.org

Marty Stewart, Sr Manager, Media/Public Relations
James L. Netterville, President
J. Gavin Setzen, Secretary/Treasurer
David R. Nielsen, Executive Vice President and CEO
Paul T. Fass, Director - Private Practice
Frequency: September
Mailing list available for rent

12885 Annual Meeting of the American Association on Mental Retardation
American Association on Mental Retardation
444 N Capitol Street NW
Suite 846
Washington, DC 20001-1512

202-387-1968
800-424-3688; *Fax:* 202-387-2193
dcroser@aamr.org; www.aamr.org

Doreen Croser, Executive Director
Paul Aitken, Director Of Finance Administration
2000 Attendees
Frequency: Annual, May

12886 Annual Meeting of the Microscopy Society of America
Bostrom Corporation
230 E Ohio
Suite 400
Chicago, IL 60611-3265

312-644-1527
800-538-3672; *Fax:* 312-644-8557;
www.msa.microscopy.com

Judy Janes, Manager

Microscopes and related supplies of interest to medical, biological, metalurgical, and polymer research scientists, technicians and physicists interested in instrument design and improvement.
Frequency: Annual, August

12887 Annual National Managed Health Care Congress
71 2nd Avenue
3rd Floor
Waltham, MA 02154

888-882-2500; *Fax:* 941-365-0157;
www.nmhcc.org

Seminar, workshop, conference, and 600 exhibits of services and products dedicated to improving the quality of health care.
10000 Attendees
Frequency: Annual
Founded in: 1989

12888 Annual PPO Forum
American Assn of Preferred Provider Organizations
222 South First Street
Suite 303
Louisville, KY 40202

502-403-1122; *Fax:* 502-403-1129
mcox@aappo.org; www.aappo.org

Melissa Cox, Event Coordinator
Michael Taddeo, Chairperson
Keith Vangeison, Vice-Chairman
Kenneth Hamm, Treasurer
William Ross, Secretary
Frequency: San Diego
Founded in: 1983

12889 Annual Scientific & Clinical Congress
American Association of Clinical Endocrinologists
245 Riverside Avenue
Suite 200
Jacksonville, FL 32202

904-353-7878; *Fax:* 904-353-8185
info@aace.com; www.aace.com

Donald Jones, CEO
Jeffrey Garber, President

Clinical endocrinologists and endocrine surgeons gather for meeting and exhibits of equipment, supplies and services.
2000 Attendees
Frequency: April

12890 Annual Scientific Meeting
Aerospace Medical Association
320 S Henry Street
Alexandria, VA 22314-3579

703-739-2240; *Fax:* 703-739-9652;
www.asma.org

Sheryl Kildall, Subscriptions Manager
Warren Silberman DO, VP
Jeffrey C. Sventek, Executive Director
Gisselle Vargas, Operations Manager
Gloria Carter, Director, Member Services

Provides a multi-faceted forum for all aerospace medical disciplines and concurrently provides continuing education credits for those attending the meeting.
3000 Attendees
Frequency: Annual/May
Mailing list available for rent

12891 Annual Scientific Meeting of the Gerontological Society of America
Gerontological Society of America
1030 15th Street NW
Suite 250
Washington, DC 20005

202-842-1275; *Fax:* 202-842-1150;
www.geron.org

Carol Schutz, Executive Director

12892 Applied Ergonomics Conference
Institute of Industrial Engineers
3597 Parkway Lane
Suite 200
Norcross, GA 30097

770-449-0461
800-494-0460; *Fax:* 770-263-8532
webmaster@iienet.org; www.iienet.org/annual

Carol LeBlanc, Conference Manager

An exclusive event for ergonomists, engineers, and safety professionals. The conference focuses on how companies have successfully implemented programs that provide excellent return on their ergonomics investment.
800 Attendees
Frequency: March
Founded in: 1998

12893 Arthroscopy Association of North America Annual Meeting
6300 N River Road
#104
Rosemont, IL 60018

847-292-2262; *Fax:* 847-292-2268
holly@aana.org; www.aana.org

Holly Albert, Meetings Manager
Edward Goss, Executive Director

Seminar, reception and 100 exhibits of video and arthroscopy equipment, braces, books and more.
1000 Attendees

12894 Assisted Living Expo
VNU Expositions
Dulles International Airport
PO Box 17413
Washington, DC 20041

703-318-0300
800-765-7616; *Fax:* 703-318-8833;
www.vnuexpo.com

Displays of assisted living information and equipment.

12895 Association for Applied Psychophysiology & Biofeedback Annual Meeting
Association for Applied Psychophysiology
10200 W 44th Avenue
Suite 304
Wheat Ridge, CO 80033

303-228-8436
800-477-8892; *Fax:* 303-422-8894
info@aapb.org; www.aapb.org

Tina Watkins, Meetings Manager
Francine Butler, Treasurer
Fred Schaffer, Treasurer

Exhibits of biofeedback equipment, supplies, and training programs, medical supplies and software, as well as annual meeting.
500 Attendees
Frequency: March
Founded in: 1969

12896 Association for Healthcare Philanthropy Annual Int'l Educational Conference
Association for Healthcare Philanthropy
313 Park Avenue
Suite 400
Falls Church, VA 22046

703-532-6243; *Fax:* 703-532-7170
ahp@ahp.org; www.ahp.org

Conference and 120 exhibits with information about equipment and services for the fundraising and helatcare development community, including computer software, recognition gifts, direct mail companies, executive recriuters, special events and more.
900 Attendees
Frequency: September

12897 Association for Professionals in Infection Control & Epidemiology
Association for Professionals in Infection Control
1275 K Street NW
Suite 1000
Washington, DC 20005-4006

202-789-1890
800-650-9570; *Fax:* 202-789-1899
apicinfo@apic.org; www.apic.org

Christine J Nutty, President
Carolyn E Jackson, Secretary
Katrina Crist, CEO
Jacqueline Manson, Accounting
Sara Haywood, Education

Workshop, banquet, reception and 150 exhibits of infection control products, pharmaceuticals, disinfectants, soaps, dataprocessing software, housekeeping equipment and supplies.
2700 Attendees
Frequency: Annual
Founded in: 1974

12898 Association for Worksite Health Promotion Annual International Conference
60 Revere Drive
Suite 500
Northbrook, IL 60062-1577

847-480-9574; *Fax:* 847-480-9282;
www.awhp.org

Liz Freyn, Conference Manager

One hundred twenty two booths of information and supplies to promote and develop quality programs of health and fitness in business and industry. Seminar, workshop, conference, tours and luncheon.
950 Attendees
Founded in: 1974

12899 Association of Behavioral Healthcare Management Convention
60 Revere Drive
Suite 500
Northbrook, IL 60062

847-480-9626; *Fax:* 847-480-9282

Exhibits related to the administation of services for the emotionally disturbed, mentally ill, mentally retarded, developmentally disabled, and those with substance abuse problems.
Frequency: Annual

12900 Association of Healthcare Internal Auditors Conference
PO Box 449
Onstead, MI 49265-0449

517-467-7729; *Fax:* 517-467-6104
ahia@ahia.org; www.ahia.org

Thomas Monahan, Executive Director
Michelle Cunningham, Account Executive
Robert Michalski, Secretary, Treasurer

Exhibits concerning cost containment and increased productivity in health care institutions through internal auditing.
1000 Attendees
Founded in: 1981

12901 Association of Pediatric Oncology Nurses Annual Conference
Association of Pediatric Nurses
4700 W Lake Avenue
Glenview, IL 60025-1485

847-375-4724; *Fax:* 847-375-4777
info@apon.org; www.apon.org

Pamela Asfahani, Product Manager
Elizabeth Sherman, senior marketing Manager

Exhibits on caring for children who have cancer.

12902 Association of Rehabilitation Nurses Annual Educational Conference
4700 W Lake Avenue
Glenview, IL 60025-1485

847-375-4710
800-229-7530; *Fax:* 847-375-4777

Conference, educational session, workshop and 225 exhibits of rehabilitational aids and supplies, medical equipment, hospitals and rehbilitation facilities and publications of interest to rehabilitation nurses.
2300 Attendees
Founded in: 1974

12903 Benefits Health Care New York Show
Flagg Management
353 Lexington Avenue
New York, NY 10016

212-286-0333; *Fax:* 212-286-0086
flaggmgmnt@msn.com; www.flaggmgmt.com

Russell Flagg, President

Sponsored by Employee Benefit News, the conference will focus on the recent health care reform, as well as coping with the economic downturn. Human resources, personnel, administration and training marketplace. HRMS, systems and services 250 exhibits. $295.
Frequency: Annual
Mailing list available for rent

12904 Building Bridges VII
American Association of Health Plans
1129 20th Street NW
Washington, DC 20036

202-778-3200; *Fax:* 202-778-8506

12905 CHPA Annual Executive Conference
Consumer Health Care Products Association
900 19th St NW
Suite 700
Washington, DC 20006-2105

202-429-9260; *Fax:* 202-223-6835
eassey@chpa-info.org; www.chpa-info.org

Paul L. Sturman, Chair

Join top healthcare executives from across the nation and participate in high-level education sessions focused on the industry's rapidly shifting environment.

12906 Center for School Mental Health Assistance National Convention
Exhibit Promotions Plus
11620 Vixens Path
Ellicott City, MD 21042

301-596-3028; *Fax:* 410-997-0764

Harve C Horowitz, President

Supports school health, mental health professionals by offering ongoing consutation to address administrative, clinical and systems issues relevant to school health services.
Frequency: October

12907 Clinical Laboratory Expo
AACC; c/o Scherago International
11 Penn Plaza
Suite 1003
New York, NY 10001

212-643-1750; *Fax:* 212-643-1758
tonym@scherago.com;
www.scherago.com/AACC

Tony Maiorino, Vice President
20000 Attendees
Frequency: July-August

12908 Clinical Laboratory Management Association Annual Conference & Exhibition
Clinical Laboratory Management Association
989 Old Eagle School Road
Suite 815
Wayne, PA 19087

610-995-9580; *Fax:* 610-995-9568
info@clma.org; www.clma.org

Dana Procsal, VP
Ruth Nelson, Director of Operations

CLMA-ASCP have combined forces to offer the largest, most comprehensive laboratory conference and exhibition ever, specifically designed for laboratory professionals at all levels.
4800 Attendees
Frequency: June

12909 Clinical and Scientific Congress of the Int'l Anesthesia Research Society
International Anesthesia Research Society
2 Summit Park Drive
Suite 140
Cleveland, OH 44131

216-642-1124; *Fax:* 216-642-1127
info@iars.org; www.iars.org

Donald S Prough, Chair
Hugo Van Aken, Chairman
1200 Attendees
Frequency: March

12910 Congress on Invitro Biology
Society for Invitro Biology
9315 Lango Drive W
Suite 255
Lango, MD 20774

301-324-5054
800-741-7476; *Fax:* 301-324-5057
sivb@sivb.org; www.sivb.org

Marietta Ellis, Managing Director
Richard Heller, Treasurer

Focus on issues pertinent to the Vertebrate, Invertebrate, and Cellular Toxicology Sections and will give participants a unique learning experience on animal cell culture and biotechnology.
1,000 Attendees
Frequency: June

12911 Consumer Directed Health Care Conference
Po Box 448, East Cary Street
Suite 102
Richmond, VA 23219

804-266-7422; *Fax:* 804-225-7458;
www.galen.org

Carlotta Farmer, Director of Programming
Frequency: December, Washington

12912 Digestive Disease Week Meeting & Exhibition
American Gastroenterological Association
4930 Del Ray Avenue
Bethesda, MD 20814

301-654-2055; *Fax:* 301-652-3890
member@gastro.org; www.gastro.org

14000 Attendees
Frequency: March

12913 Distribution Management Conference & Expo
Healthcare Distribution Management Association
900 N Glebe Road
Suite 1000
Arlington, VA 22203

703-787-0000; *Fax:* 703-935-3200;
www.healthcaredistribution.org

Lori Burke, Director Meetings/Conferences
Denise Woodson, Managing Director
Laurel Todd, Managing Director

Provides the latest information on the most important topics affecting healthcare distribution.
Frequency: June

12914 **Drug Discovery Technology**
Hynes Convention Center
900 Boylston Street
Boston, MA 02115
617-954-2000
800-845-8800; *Fax:* 617-954-2125
info@mccahome.com; www.mccahome.com
2000 Attendees
Frequency: August

12915 **Emergency Nurses Association Scientific Assembly & Exhibits**
Emergency Nurses Association
915 Lee Street
Des Plaines, IL 60016-6569
847-460-4100
800-900-9659; *Fax:* 847-460-4001
webmaster@ena.org; www.ena.org
David Westman, CEO
Anita Dorr, Co-Founder
Kathy Szumanski, Director
3500 Attendees
Frequency: Annual, September

12916 **Endocrine Society Annual Meeting**
Scherago International
11 Penn Plaza
Suite 1003
New York, NY 10001
212-643-1750; *Fax:* 212-643-1758
6500 Attendees

12917 **Experimental Biology**
FASEB/OSMC
9650 Rockville Pike
Bethesda, MD 20814
301-634-7100; *Fax:* 301-634-7014
info@faseb.org; www.faseb.org/meetings
Pauline Minhinnett, Meeting Manager
Jean Lash, Marketing Manager
Jacquelyn Roberts, Marketing Manager
David Craven, Executive Director
12M Attendees
Frequency: April

12918 **FASEB Conference Federation for American Societies for Experimental Biology**
FASEB/OSMC
9650 Rockville Pike
Bethesda, MD 20814
301-634-7100; *Fax:* 301-634-7014
info@faseb.org; www.faseb.org/meetings
Jean Lash, Exhibit Manager
Marcella Jackson, Marketing Manager
Jacquelyn Roberts, Marketing Manager
David Craven, Executive Director
900 Attendees
Frequency: March

12919 **Fall Symposium**
American College of Emergency Physicians
PO Box 619911
Dallas, TX 75261
972-550-0911; *Fax:* 972-580-2816
325 Attendees

12920 **Federation of Hospitals Public Policy Conference & Business Exposition**
Federation of American Health Systems
801 Pennsylvania Avenue NW
Suite 245
Washington, DC 20004-2604
202-624-1500; *Fax:* 202-737-6462
info@fah.org; www.fah.org
Bonnie Moneypenny, Senior VP Administrative Services
Letitia Faison-Mahoney, Controller
The conference brings together hospital executives and leading policymakers each Spring for important discussions. It also affords an important opportunity for suppliers to meet face-to-face with hospital managers and buyers.
Frequency: Annual, March
Founded in: 1966

12921 **Fire-Rescue International**
International Association of Fire Chiefs
4025 Fair Ridge Drive
Suite 300
Fairfax, VA 22033
703-273-0911; *Fax:* 703-273-9363
lyonkers@iafc.org; www.iafc.org
Mark Light, Executive Director & CEO
Lisa Yonkers, Director, Conference & Education
Jason Nauman, Education & Learning Manager
Leanne Shroeder, Conference Manager
Conference and exposition of the fire service industry.
Frequency: Annual

12922 **Food & Nutrition Conference & Expo**
American Dietetic Association
120 South Riverside Plaza
Suite 2000
Chicago, IL 60606
312-899-0040
800-877-1600; *Fax:* 312-899-0008
gandruch@eatright.org; www.eatright.org
Social Media: Facebook, Twitter
Greg Andruch, Exhibits Manager
Allison MacMunn, Public Relations Manager
Donna Wickstrom, Manager
Karen Didriksen, Purchasing Manager
More than 8,000 professionals come to the Food & Nutrition Conference & Expo for the latest technological and nutritional advancements. This is the premier selling opportunity in the fields of nutrition and food service management. The event continues to expand-attracting a wider audience of professionals, including hotel and restarurant managers, sports, health and nutrition professionals and executive chefs.
8000 Attendees
Frequency: September, Pennsylvania
Circulation: 65000

12923 **HCEA Annual Meeting**
Healthcare Convention & Exhibitors Association
1100 Johnson Ferry Rd NE
Suite 300
Atlanta, GA 30342-1733
404-252-3663; *Fax:* 404-252-0774
hcea@kellencompany.com; www.hcea.org
Eric Allen, Executive Vice President
Jackie Beaulieu, Associate Director
Michelle Hall, Staff Associate
Carol Wilson, Meetings Director
Frank Skinner, Executive Director
Cost varies; approximately 50 booths; 800 attendees.
200 Attendees
Frequency: Annual
Founded in: 1930
Mailing list available for rent: 1400 names

12924 **HCEA Marketing Summit**
Healthcare Convention & Exhibitors Association
1100 Johnson Ferry Rd NE
Suite 300
Atlanta, GA 30342-1733
404-252-3663; *Fax:* 404-252-0774
hcea@kellencompany.com; www.hcea.org
Eric Allen, Executive Vice President
Jackie Beaulieu, Associate Director
Michelle Hall, Staff Associate
Carol Wilson, Meetings Director
Frank Skinner, Executive Director
Cost varies; no exhibits; 200-250 attendees.
200 Attendees
Frequency: Annual
Founded in: 1930
Mailing list available for rent: 1400 names

12925 **HDMA Annual Meeting**
Healthcare Distribution Management Association
900 N Glebe Road
Suite 1000
Arlington, VA 22203
703-787-0000; *Fax:* 703-935-3200;
www.healthcaredistribution.org
Lori Burke, Director Meetings/Conferences
Denise Woodson, Managing Director
Laurel Todd, Managing Director
Provides a unique opportunity for senior-level retailer and supplier member executives to interact and discuss strategic issues.
Frequency: October

12926 **HIDA Conference & Expo**
Health Industry Distributors Association
310 Montgomery Street
Alexandria, VA 22314-1516
703-549-4432; *Fax:* 703-549-4695
rowan@hida.org; www.hida.org
Matt Rowan, CEO
Includes education sessions, training rotation, and the best-attended trade showin the industry.
8000 Attendees
Frequency: October

12927 **HMFA's ANI: The Healthcare Finance Conference**
Healthcare Finance Management Association
3 Westbrook Corporate Center
Suite 600
Westchester, IL 60154
708-531-9600; *Fax:* 708-531-0032;
www.hfma.org/events/ani
Access to education programs, speaker sessions and hundreds of vendors, as well as networking and best practices sharing opportunities.
Mailing list available for rent

12928 **HMFA's Virtual Healthcare Finance Conference & Career Fair**
Healthcare Finance Management Association
3 Westbrook Corporate Center
Suite 600
Westchester, IL 60154
708-531-9600
800-252-4362; *Fax:* 708-531-0032
virtualhcfc@hfma.org; www.hfma.org
Social Media: Facebook, Twitter, LinkedIn
Access live education programs and on-demand sessions from your office. Keynote speakers and presenters, and a virtual exhibit hall and career fair.
39000 Members
Founded in: 1991
Mailing list available for rent

12929 Healthcare Information and Management Systems Society
HIMSS/Healthcare Information and Management
230 E Ohio
Suite 500
Chicago, IL 60611
312-664-4467; *Fax:* 312-664-6143

12930 IAHCSMM Annual Conference
213 W Institute Place
Suite 307
Chicago, IL 60610-3195
312-440-0078
800-962-8274; *Fax:* 312-440-9474
mailbox@iahcsmm.com; www.iahcsmm.com
Betty Hanna, Executive Director
Marilyn T. Conde, Secretary/Treasurer
Bruce T. Bird, President
David Jagrosse, Executive Board Member
David Narance, Executive Board Member
Internationational Association of Healthcare Central Service Material Management - 125 EXHIBITORSlication separates supervisors/directors from technicians.
600+ Attendees
Frequency: Annual

12931 IAHSS Annual General Meeting
International Association for Healthcare Security
PO Box 5038
Glendale Heights, IL 60139
888-353-0990
888-353-0990; *Fax:* 630-529-4139
info@iahss.org; www.iahss.org
Bryan Warren, President
Evelyn Meserve, Executive Director
Jim Stankevich, President-Elect
Lisa Pryse, VP/Treasurer
Bryan Warren, VP/Secretary
Non-profit organization of healthcare security and safety executives from around the world. The association works to improve and professionalize security and safety in healthcare facilities through the exchange of information and experiences among members.
1700 Members
Founded in: 1968

12932 INTERPHEX - The World's Forum for the Pharmaceutical Industry
Reed Exhibition Companies
383 Main Avenue
Norwalk, CT 06851
203-840-4800; *Fax:* 203-840-4804
Chet Burchett, President
11000 Attendees

12933 Infusion Nurses Society
Infusion Nurses Society
315 Norwood Park South
Norwood, MA 02062
781-440-9408
800-694-0298; *Fax:* 781-440-9409
ins@ins1.org; www.ins1.org
Social Media: Facebook, Twitter, LinkedIn
Britt Meyer, President
Mary Alexander, CEO
Chris Hunt, Executive VP
Michaelle Frost, Accounting Manager
Chelsea McCue, Accounting Coordinator
7000 Members
1000 Attendees
Frequency: Annual
Founded in: 1973
*Mailing list available for rent*at $200 per M

12934 Infusion Nurses Society Annual Meeting
Infusion Nurses Society
315 Norwood Park South
Norwood, MA 02062
781-440-9408
800-694-0298; *Fax:* 781-440-9409
ins@ins1.org; www.ins1.org
Social Media: Facebook, Twitter, LinkedIn
Cora Vizcarra, President
Mary Alexander, CEO
Chris Hunt, Executive VP
Michaelle Frost, Accounting Manager
Chelsea McCue, Accounting Coordinator
Mailing list available for rentat $200 per M

12935 International Conference on Head and Neck Cancer
American Head and Neck Society
1805 Ardmore Boulevard
Pittsburgh, PA 15221
412-243-5156; *Fax:* 412-243-5160
rwagnercme@aol.com;
www.headandneckcancer.org
Robin Wagner, Show Manager
Sixty exhibits of equipment and supplies, conference, luncheon and reception.
2,500 Attendees
Frequency: August

12936 International Congress on Ambulatory Surgery Conference
Hynes Convention Center
900 Boylston Street
Boston, MA 02115
617-954-2000; *Fax:* 617-954-2125
info@mccahome.com; www.mccahome.com
1500 Attendees
Frequency: May

12937 International Society for Magnetic Resonance in Medicine
International Society for Magnetic Resonance
2118 Milvia Street
Suite 201
Berkeley, CA 94704
510-841-1899; *Fax:* 510-841-2340
info@ismrm.org; www.ismrm.org
Frequency: May

12938 International Vision Exposition & Conference
Association Expositions & Services
383 Main Avenue
Norwalk, CT 06851
203-840-4820
800-811-7151; *Fax:* 203-840-4824
visionexpo.com
Eileen Baird
Ed Gallo, Sales Manager
Tracy Flacherty, Marketing Director
As the most comprehensive vision care show and conference in the US, International Vision Expo is where today's eye care professionals meet, learn and conduct business. International vision expo draws optical professionals from all career path including: Ophthalmologist, Optometrist, Opticians, Lab Personnel, Practice managers, Ophthalmic Medical Personnel, Retailers, Manufacturing Executives, Import Export buyers, Ophthalmic Assistants, Optical Interns and more.
15000 Attendees
Frequency: March/September

12939 Managed Care Institute & Display Forum
American Association of Health Plans
601 Pennsylvania Avenue, NW
South Building, Suite 500
Washington, DC 20004
202-778-3200; *Fax:* 202-331-7487
ahip@ahip.org; www.aahp.org
Social Media: Twitter
Michael Abbott, President
William Cameron, Chairman
Two hundred exhibits by suppliers to the managed health care industry, conference and reception.
2000 Attendees
Frequency: Annual
Founded in: 1986

12940 Managed Care Law Conference
American Association of Health Plans
1129 20th Street NW
Washington, DC 20036
202-778-3200; *Fax:* 202-778-8506

12941 Medical Design & Manufacturing Conference & Exhibition West
Canon Communications
11444 W Olympic Boulevard
Los Angeles, CA 90064
310-445-4200; *Fax:* 310-996-9499;
www.cancom.com
Diane O'Conner, Trade Show Director
Dan Cutrone, Show Marketing Manager
Devoted to the design, development, and manufacture of medical products. Visitors can preview the latest advances in medical-grade materials, assembly components, machinery, electronics, systems, software, services and more. Held at the Anaheim Convention Center in Anaheim, California.
8,500 Attendees
Frequency: January

12942 Medical Design and Manufacturing Minneapolis Conference
Canon Communications
11444 W Olympic Boulevard
Los Angeles, CA 90064
310-445-4200; *Fax:* 310-996-9499;
www.mdm-minneapolis.com
Diane O'Connor, Trade Show Director
Dan Cutrone, Show Marketing Manager
Four hundred thirty three exhibitors in 52,500 square feet of the Minneapolis Convention Center. Medical supplies and information promotional opportunities in show directory, web site advertising, conference program, sponsorships and product previews.
3374 Attendees
Frequency: October
Founded in: 1994

12943 Medical Equipment Design & Technology Exhibition & Conference
Canon Communications
11444 W Olympic Boulevard
Los Angeles, CA 90064-1549
310-445-4200; *Fax:* 310-445-4299;
www.medtecshow.com
Diane O'Conner, Trade Show Director
Dan Cutrone, Show Marketing Manager
Devoted to the design, development and manufacture of medical products. Visitors can preview the latest advances in medical-grade materials, assembly components, electronics, machinery, software, systems, services and more. Held at the RAI International Exhibition and Congress Center in Amsterdam, Netherlands.
2231 Attendees
Frequency: October

12944 Medical Group Management Association
Medical Group Management Association
104 Inverness Terrace E
Englewood, CO 80112-5306
303-991-1111
800-275-6462; *Fax:* 877-329-6462
infocenter@mgma.com; www.mgma.com
William Jessee, President, Chief Executive Officer
Anders Gilberg, senior Vice President
Natalie Jamieson, Administrative Assistant
3800 Attendees
Frequency: Annual, October

12945 Medical Meetings
Penton Media Inc
249 W. 17th St., third floor
New York, NY 10011
847-763-9504
866-505-7173
shatch@meetingsnet.com;
www.meetingsnet.com
Susan Hatch, Editor
Betsy Bair, Director, Content and Media
Melissa Fromento, Group Publisher
Regina McGee, Religious Conference Manager
Susan Hatch, Executive Editor
International guide for health care and meeting planners.
Cost: $57.00
106 Pages
Circulation: 12000
Founded in: 1989
Printed in 4 colors on glossy stock

12946 Medicare and Medicaid Conference
American Association of Health Plans
1129 20th Street NW
Washington, DC 20036
202-778-3200; *Fax:* 202-778-8506

12947 Medtrade West
VNU Expositions
Dallas International Airport
PO Box 17413
Washington, DC 20041
703-318-0300; *Fax:* 703-318-8833

12948 Medtrade/Comtrade
VNU Communications
1130 Hightower Trail
Atlanta, GA 30350
770-569-1540; *Fax:* 703-318-8833

12949 NCPA Rx Exposition
NCPA
100 Daingerfield Road
Alexandria, VA 22314
703-683-8200
800-544-7447; *Fax:* 703-683-3619;
www.ncpanet.org
Donnie Calhoun, President
B. Douglas Hoey, Chief Executive Officer
2000 Attendees
Frequency: Annual, October
Mailing list available for rent

12950 National Athletic Trainers Association
National Athletic Trainers
2952 Stemmons Freeway
#200
Dallas, TX 75247
214-637-6282; *Fax:* 214-637-2206
webmaster@nata.org; www.nata.org
Charles Kimmel, President
Charles Rozanski, VP
Mailing list available for rent

12951 National Convention: Opticians Association of America
Opticians Association of America
10341 Democracy Lane
Fairfax, VA 22030
703-916-8856; *Fax:* 703-691-8929

12952 National Council on the Aging Annual Conference
National Council on the Aging
1901 L Street Nw
4th Fl
Washington, DC 20036
202-479-1200; *Fax:* 202-479-0735
info@ncoa.org; www.ncoa.org
Social Media: Facebook, Twitter
James Firman, President/CEO
Richard Browdie, Chair
Andrew Greene, Treasurer
Jay Greenberg, Senior Vice President
Donna Whitt, Senior Vice President
Mailing list available for rent

12953 National Managed Healthcare Congress
Po Box 3685
Boston, MA 02441-3685
888-670-8200; *Fax:* 941-365-2507;
www.nmhcc.com
Frequency: March Atlanta

12954 National Medical Association Annual Convention & Scientific Assembly
National Medical Association
8403 Colesville Road
Suite 920
Silver Spring, MD 20910
703-631-6200
800-564-4220; *Fax:* 703-654-6931;
www.nmanet.org
Social Media: Facebook, Twitter
June LaMountain, Exhibit Sales Account Manager
Rahn K. Bailey, President
C. Freeman, Treasurer
Darryl R. Matthews, Executive Director
Promotes the collective interests of physicians and patients of African descent. NMA carries out this mission by serving the collective voice of physicians of African descent and a leading force for purity in medicine, elimination of health disparities and optimal health.
3000 Attendees
Frequency: August
Founded in: 1895

12955 National Safety Council Congress Expo
National Safety Council
1121 Spring Lake Drive
Itasca, IL 60143
630-775-2213
800-621-7619; *Fax:* 630-285-0798
customerservice@nsc.org;
www.congress.nsc.org
Nancy Gavin, Expo Manager
Bill Steinbach, Exhibit Sales
Janet Froetscher, CEO
Annual event for safety, health and the environment.
16000 Attendees
Frequency: September

12956 National Society for Histotechnology Symposium/Convention
National Society for Histotechnology
8850 Stanford Blvd
Suite 2900
Columbia, MD 21045
443-535-4060; *Fax:* 443-535-4055
histo@nsh.org; www.nsh.org
Aubrey M J Wanner, Meeting Manager
Carrie Diamond, Executive Director
Kerry Crabb, President
Kristin Ramseur, Administrative Assistant
Beth Wise, Administrative Assistant
National gathering for all chapters, advancing professional growth through educational sessions and the exchange of ideas.
1500 Attendees
Frequency: October
Founded in: 1964

12957 Neocon South
Designfest/NeoCon South
200 World Trade Center Chicago
Chicago, IL 60654
312-527-7999; *Fax:* 312-527-7782
http://www.neocon.com
Chris Kennedy, President

12958 Neocon West
Designfest/Neocon South
200 World Trade Center
Chicago, IL 60654
312-527-7999; *Fax:* 312-527-7782
http://www.neocon.com
Chris Kennedy, President

12959 Neocon's World Trade Fair
Design/Neocon South
200 World Trade Center
Chicago, IL 60654
312-527-7999; *Fax:* 312-527-7782
Chris Kennedy, President

12960 New England Grows
Hynes Convention Center
900 Boylston
Boston, MA 07115
617-954-2000; *Fax:* 617-954-2125
info@mccahome.com; www.mccahome.com
1500 Attendees
Frequency: February

12961 Northwest Urological Society
Northwest Urological Society
914 164th Street Se
Suite B-12 #145
Mill Creek, WA 98012
866-800-3118; *Fax:* 800-808-4749;
www.nwus.org
S Larry Goldenberg, President
Martin Gleave, VP
180 Attendees

12962 Nurse Managers Update
National Professional Education Institute
2525 Ossen Fort Road
PO Box 118
Glencoe, MO 63068-1107
636-735-5570
800-575-5575; *Fax:* 561-743-9596
JJMcDaid@aol.com; www.npeinursing.com
Judie McDaid, Exhibitor Relations Manager
Leslie Brock, Registration Manager
The Nurse Managers Update and Critical Care Conference/EXPO provides a fully integrated program dedicated to the continuing education of critical care nurses, nurse managers and other healthcare professionals. Exhibitors showcase their latest healthcare products, pharmaceuticals, services, research and facilities. Knowledge gained in the informative, entertaining EXPO

Hall, will influence these nurses' purchasing decisions throughout the year.
1500 Attendees
Frequency: Annual, April
Founded in: 1989

12963 Obesity and Associated Conditions Symposium
American Society of Bariatric Physicians/ASBP
5453 E Evans Place
Denver, CO 80222

303-794-4833; *Fax:* 303-779-4834
info@asbp.org; www.asbp.org

Cathy Suski, Communications
Stacy Schmidt, Director

Learn about the latest research in obesity treatment and how to use it in your practice.
500 Attendees
Frequency: Annual

12964 Optometry's Meeting
American Optometric Association
243 N Lindbergh Boulevard
Saint Louis, MO 63141

314-993-8575; *Fax:* 314-993-8919
info@iacconline.org;
www.iaccnorthamerica.org

Tom Bolman, Executive VP
Jerry White, Director of Education

Main exhibits: optometric equipment, supplies and services.
8000 Attendees
Frequency: June

12965 Osteopathic Physicians & Surgeons Annual Convention
Osteopathic Physicians & Surgeons of California
455 Capitol Mall
Suite 230
Sacramento, CA 95814

916-561-0724

Kathleen Creason, Executive Director

12966 Pacific Dermatological Association
Pacific Dermatological Association
575 Market Street
Suite 2125
San Francisco, CA 94105

415-927-5729
888-388-8815; *Fax:* 415-764-4915;
www.pacificderm.org

Edgar F. Fincher, President
Catherine Ramsay, VP
Anita Gilliam, Secretary/Treasurer
Kent Lindeman, Executive Director
Ben Hsu, Executive Committee

Exclusively for education, scientific and charitable purposes. Provides opportunities for exchange of information and advancement of knowledge of dermatology among physicians within the membership area.
Frequency: August
Founded in: 1948
Mailing list available for rent

12967 Pacific Northwest Radiological Society
Pacific Northwest Radiological Society
2033 6th Avenue
Suite 1100
Seattle, WA 98121

206-441-9762
800-552-0612; *Fax:* 206-441-5863
lmk@wsma.org; www.pnwrs.org

Gautham Reddy, President
Eric Stern, VP
Pauline Proulx, Association Executive
Jason Clement, Secretary/Treasurer

12968 Pediatric Academic Societies Annual Meeting
American Pediatric Society & Society for Pediatric
3400 Research Forest Drive
Suite B7
The Woodlands, TX 77381

281-419-0052; *Fax:* 281-419-0082
info@aps-spr.org; www.aps-spr.org

Debbie Anagnostelis, Executive Director
Kathy Cannon, Associate Executive Director
Belinda Thomas, Information Services Director
Kate Culliton, Accounting Manager
Rachael Vogler, Executive Assistant
4500 Attendees
Frequency: May

12969 Pediatric Perfusion
American Society of ExtraCorporeal Technology
2209 Dickens Road
Richmond, VA 23230-2005

804-565-6310; *Fax:* 804-282-0090
judyr@amsect.org; www.amsect.org

Stewart Hinckley, Executive Director
Donna Pandarvis, Manager
Michael Troike, Government Relations Chairman
Kimberly Robertson, CPA, Controller
Greg Leasure, Membership Services
2000 Members
100 Attendees
Frequency: Bi-Annual
Founded in: 1964
Mailing list available for rent

12970 Perfusion Safety & Best Practices in Perfusion
American Society of ExtraCorporeal Technology
2209 Dickens Road
Richmond, VA 23230-2005

804-532-2323; *Fax:* 804-282-0090
judyr@amsect.org; www.amsect.org

Stewart Hinckley, Executive Director
Donna Pandarvis, Manager
Michael Troike, Government Relations Chairman
Kimberly Robertson, CPA, Controller
Greg Leasure, Membership Services
2000 Members
150 Attendees
Frequency: Annual/October
Founded in: 1964
Mailing list available for rent

12971 Policy Conference
American Association of Health Plans
1129 20th Street NW
Washington, DC 20036

202-778-3200; *Fax:* 202-778-8506

12972 Postgraduate Assembly in Anesthesiology
New York State Society of Anesthesiologists
85 5th Avenue
8th Floor
New York, NY 10003

212-867-7140; *Fax:* 212-867-7153;
www.nyssa-pga.org

Kurt G Becker, Executive Director
David Wlody, Director

Annual conference for anesthesia professionals, held each December in New York City.
7000 Attendees
Frequency: December

12973 Primary Care Update
Interstate Postgraduate Medical Association
PO Box 5474
Madison, WI 53705

608-231-9045
866-446-3424; *Fax:* 877-292-4489
cmehelp@ipmameded.org;
www.ipmameded.org

Designed to enhance your practice and improve the patient's health.
Frequency: November

12974 Radiological Society of North America's Scientific Assembly
Radiological Society of North America
2021 Spring Road
Suite 600
Oak Brook, IL 60521

630-571-5424
62000 Attendees

12975 SCCM Educational & Scientific Symposium
Society of Critical Care Medicine
8101 E Kaiser Blouevard
Anaheim, CA 92808

714-282-6000

2500 Attendees

12976 SIIM Annual Meeting & Conference
Society for Imaging Informatics in Medicine
19440 Golf Vista Plaza
Suite 330
Leesburg, VA 20176-8264

703-723-0432; *Fax:* 703-723-0415
info@siimweb.org; www.siimweb.org
Social Media: Facebook, Twitter, LinkedIn

Andrea Saris, Meetings Director

Provides a vibrant community and collegial forum for learning and networking with peers and thought leaders in the imaging informatics field. This is where physicians, health care IT decision-makers, PACS administrators, and vendors from around the world come together to explore the emerging field of informatics.
2000 Members
1800 Attendees
Frequency: June
Founded in: 1980

12977 Society for Disability Studies Annual Meeting
Exhibit Promotions Plus
11630 Vixens Path
Ellicott City, MD 21042

301-596-3028; *Fax:* 410-997-0764;
www.epponline.com

Harve C Horowitz, President
Frequency: June

12978 Society for Neuroscience
Herlitz Company
1890 Palmer Avenue
Suite 202 A
Larchmont, NY 10538

914-833-1979; *Fax:* 914-833-0920

Bruce Herlitz, President

12979 Society of Nuclear Medicine Annual Meeting
Society of Nuclear Medicine
1850 Samuel Morse Drive
Reston, VA 20190

703-708-9000; *Fax:* 703-708-9015
volunteer@snm.org; www.snm.org

Rebecca Maxey, Director
Vincent Pistilli, Chief Financial Officer
Matt Dickens, Director, Information Services

Judy Brazel, Director, Meeting Services
Joanna Spahr, Director, Marketing
7000 Attendees

12980 Society of Thoracic Surgeons Annual Meeting
Society of Thoracic Surgeons
633 N Saint Clair Street
Suite 2320
Chicago, IL 60611

312-202-5800; *Fax:* 312-202-5801
sts@sts.org; www.sts.org
Social Media: Facebook, Twitter

Robert A Wynbrandt, Executive Director
Cheryl D. Wilson, Administrative Manager & Executive
Natalie Boden, Director of Marketing
Phillip A. Bongiorno, Director of Government Relations
Courtney Donovan, Director of Meetings
4200 Attendees
Mailing list available for rent

12981 Society of Toxicology Annual Meeting
Society of Toxicology
1821 Michael Faraday Drive
Suite 300
Reston, VA 20190

703-438-3115; *Fax:* 703-438-3113
sothq@toxicology.org; www.toxicology.org

Shawn Lamb, Executive Director
Clarissa Russell Wilson, Contact

Professional and scholarly organization meeting of scientists from academic institutions, government and industry representing the great variety of scientists who practice toxicology in the US and abroad.
5000 Attendees
Frequency: March

12982 Southeastern Surgical Congress Annual Assembly
South Med. Associates
PO Box 330
Pelham, AL 35124

205-991-3552; *Fax:* 205-991-6771

12983 Southern Association for Primary Care
Southern Medical Association
35 Lake Shore Drive
Birmingham, AL 35209

205-945-1840
800-423-4992; *Fax:* 205-945-1830;
www.sma.org
Social Media: Facebook, Twitter, LinkedIn

Michael C. Gosney, President
Ed Waldron, Administration
G. Richard Holt, Editor-in-Chief

12984 Southern Medical Association Meeting
Southern Medical Association
PO Box 190088
Birmingham, AL 35219

205-451-1840
800-423-4992; *Fax:* 205-945-1830

Ed Waldron, CEO
2500 Attendees

12985 Symposium of the Protein Society
FASEB
9650 Rockville Pike
Bethesda, MD 20814

301-634-7100; *Fax:* 301-530-7001
info@faseb.org; www.faseb.org

David Craven, Executive Director
Jacquelyn Roberts, Marketing Manager
Richard Dunn, Director

12986 Symposium on New Advances in Blood Management
American Society of ExtraCorporeal Technology
2209 Dickens Road
Richmond, VA 23230-2005

804-532-2323; *Fax:* 804-282-0090
judyr@amsect.org; www.amsect.org

Stewart Hinckley, Executive Director
Donna Pandarvis, Manager
Michael Troike, Government Relations Chairman
Kimberly Robertson, CPA, Controller
Greg Leasure, Membership Services
2000 Members
150 Attendees
Frequency: Annual/August
Founded in: 1964
Mailing list available for rent

12987 TLPA Annual Convention & Trade Show
Taxicab, Limousine & Paratransit Association
3200 Tower Oaks Boulevard
Suite 220
Rockville, MD 20852

301-984-5700; *Fax:* 301-984-5703
info@tlpa.com; www.tlpa.org

Alfred LaGasse, CEO
William Rouse, President
Harold Morgan, Executive Vice President
Michelle A. Hariston, CMP, Manager of Meetings
Leah New, Manager of Communications

Shares information vital to owners or taxicab, limousine, airport shuttle, paratransit and nonemergency medical transportation fleets. 100 suppliers and exhibitors of the newest products available to the industry.
1000 Attendees
Frequency: Annual
Founded in: 1917
Mailing list available for rent

12988 The Synergist
American Industrial Hygiene Association
3141 Fairview Park Drive
Suite 777
Falls Church, VA 22042

703-849-8888; *Fax:* 703-207-3561
infonet@aiha.org; www.aiha.org

Steven E. Lacey, PhD, CIH, CSP, President
Cynthia A. Ostrowski, CIH, Vice President

AIHA's official magazine, offering information and resources on health and safety for occupational environments.
Frequency: Monthly

12989 Today's Surgicenter Conference
Virgo Publishing LLC
3300 N Central Avenue
Suite 300
Phoenix, AZ 85012

480-675-8177; *Fax:* 602-567-6841
mikes@vpico.com; www.xchangemag.com
Social Media: Facebook, Twitter, LinkedIn

Mike Saxby, Group Publisher
Craig Galbraith, Senior Online Managing Editor
Buffy Naylor, Managing Editor
Khali Henderson, Contributing Editor
Melissa Budwig, Online Advertising

Offers owners and operators of ambulatory surgery centers high-caliber instructive seminars by leading industry veterans, exhibits, and networking opportunities. Decision makers attend to learn more about construction and design, technology, equipment, legal and regulatory issues, marketing and finance and development. Approximately 50 booths.
200+ Attendees
Frequency: September
Founded in: 2004
Mailing list available for rent: 15000+ names

12990 United States and Canadian Academy of Pathology
Herlitz Company
1890 Palmer Avenue
Suite 202A
Larchmont, NY 10538

914-833-1979; *Fax:* 914-833-0929
kris@herlitz.com; www.herlitz.com

Kris Herlitz, Show Manager
3000 Attendees
Frequency: March

12991 Vision New England
Hynes Convention Center
900 Boylston Street
Boston, MA 07115

617-954-2000; *Fax:* 617-954-2125
info@mccahome.com; www.mccahome.com

24000 Attendees
Frequency: January

12992 World Congress on Pediatric & Intensive Care
Hynes Convention Center
900 Boylston Street
Boston, MA 02115

617-954-2000
800-845-8800; *Fax:* 617-954-2125
info@mccahome.com; www.mccahome.com

2500 Attendees
Frequency: June

12993 Yankee Dental Congress
Hynes Convention Center
900 Boylston Street
Boston, MA 07115

617-954-2000; *Fax:* 617-954-2125
info@mccahome.com; www.mccahome.com
2400 Attendees
Frequency: January

Directories & Databases

12994 ARMA International's Buyers Guide
ARMA International
11880 College Blvd
Suite 450
Overland Park, KS 66210

913-341-3808
800-422-2762; *Fax:* 913-341-3742
hq@arma.org; www.arma.org/conference

Marilyn Bier, Executive Director
Jody Becker, Associate Editor
Kerrianne Aulet, Education Program Administrator
Michael Avery, Chief Operating Officer
Paula Banes, Sales Project Manager

75-100 companies listed. Free.
10,00 Members
Founded in: 1955
Mailing list available for rent

12995 American Academy of Forensic Sciences Membership Directory
410 N 21st St
Colorado Spring, CO 80904-2712

719-636-1100; *Fax:* 719-636-1993
awarren@aafs.org; www.aafs.org

Anne Warren, Executive Director
Nancy Jackson, Director Development

Offers valuable information on over 5,000 persons qualified in forensic sciences including law, anthropology and psychiatry.
Cost: $50.00
250 Pages
Frequency: Annual

12996 **Antimicrobial Therapy in Otolaryngology Head and Neck Surgery**
American Academy of Otolaryngology
1650 Diagonal Road
Alexandria, VA 22314-3357

703-836-4444; *Fax:* 703-683-5100
membership@entnet.org; www.entnet.org

Richard Carson, Senior Manager, Board of Govenors
Paul T. Fass, Director - Private Practice
J. Gavin Setzen, Secretary/Treasurer
David R. Nielsen, Executive Vice President and CEO
James L. Netterville, President
Frequency: Yearly
Mailing list available for rent

12997 **Catalog of Professional Testing Resources**
Psychological Assessment Resources
PO Box 998
Odessa, FL 33556

800-331-8378; *Fax:* 800-727-9329;
www.parinc.com

12998 **Comparative Guide to American Hospitals**
Grey House Publishing
4919 Route 22
PO Box 56
Amenia, NY 12501

518-789-8700
800-562-2139; *Fax:* 845-373-6390
books@greyhouse.com; www.greyhouse.com
Social Media: Facebook, Twitter

Leslie Mackenzie, Publisher
Richard Gottlieb, Editor

This new edition compares all of the nation's hospitals by 24 measures of quality in the treatment of heart attack, heart failure, pneumonia, and, new to this edition, surgical procedures and pregnancy care. Plus, this edition is now available in regional volumes, to make locating information about hospitals in your area quicker and easier than ever before.
Cost: $350.00
2000 Pages
ISBN: 1-532371-82-5
Founded in: 1981

12999 **Complete Directory for Pediatric Disorders**
Grey House Publishing
4919 Route 22
PO Box 56
Amenia, NY 12501

518-789-8700
800-562-2139; *Fax:* 845-373-6390
books@greyhouse.com; www.greyhouse.com
Social Media: Facebook, Twitter

Leslie Mackenzie, Publisher
Richard Gottlieb, Editor

Provides parents and caregivers with information about pediatric conditions, disorders, diseases and disabilities. Contains understandable descriptions of major bodily systems, descriptions of more than 200 disorders and a resource section.
Cost: $165.00
1200 Pages
ISBN: 1-592371-50-7
Founded in: 1981

13000 **Complete Directory for People with Disabilities**
Grey House Publishing
4919 Route 22
PO Box 56
Amenia, NY 12501

518-789-8700
800-562-2139; *Fax:* 845-373-6390
books@greyhouse.com; www.greyhouse.com
Social Media: Facebook, Twitter

Leslie Mackenzie, Publisher
Richard Gottlieb, Editor

Comprehensive resource for people with disabilities, detailing independent living centers, rehabilitation facilities, state and federal agencies, associations and support groups. This one-stop resource also provides immediate access to the latest products and services for people with disabilities, such as periodicals and books, assistive devices, employment and education programs and travel groups.
Cost: $165.00
1200 Pages
ISBN: 1-592373-67-4
Founded in: 1981

13001 **Complete Directory for People with Chronic Illness**
Grey House Publishing
4919 Route 22
PO Box 56
Amenia, NY 12501

518-789-8700
800-562-2139; *Fax:* 845-373-6390
books@greyhouse.com; www.greyhouse.com
Social Media: Facebook, Twitter

Leslie Mackenzie, Publisher
Richard Gottlieb, Editor

This directory provides a comprehensive overview of the support services and information resources available for people diagnosed with a chronic illness. It details the wide range of organizations, educational materials, books, newsletters, web sites, periodicals and databases that address 88 specific chronic illness.
Cost: $165.00
1200 Pages
ISBN: 1-952371-83-3
Founded in: 1981

13002 **Complete Learning Disabilities Directory**
Grey House Publishing
4919 Route 22
PO Box 56
Amenia, NY 12501

518-789-8700
800-562-2139; *Fax:* 845-373-6390
books@greyhouse.com; www.greyhouse.com
Social Media: Facebook, Twitter

Leslie Mackenzie, Publisher
Richard Gottlieb, Editor

The most comprehensive database of programs, services, curriculum materials, professional meetings and resources, camps, newsletters and support groups for teachers, students and families concerned with learning disabilities. Includes information about associations and organizations, schools, colleges and testing materials, government agencies, legal resources and more.
Cost: $145.00
800 Pages
ISBN: 1-592373-68-2
Founded in: 1981

13003 **Complete Learning Disabilities Directory - Online Database**
Grey House Publishing
4919 Route 22
PO Box 56
Amenia, NY 12501-0056

518-789-8700
800-562-2139; *Fax:* 518-789-0556
gold@greyhouse.com;
www.gold.greyhouse.com
Social Media: Facebook, Twitter

Leslie Mackenzie, Publisher
Richard Gottlieb, President

The most comprehensive database of important learning disability resources, details associations and organizations, national and state programs, schools, colleges and learning centers, publishers, publications and periodicals, classroom resources, testing materials, exchange programs, and more. Locating learning disability resources has never been easier - it's only a click away.
Founded in: 1981

13004 **Complete Mental Health Directory**
Grey House Publishing
4919 Route 22
PO Box 56
Amenia, NY 12501

518-789-8700
800-562-2139; *Fax:* 845-373-6390
books@greyhouse.com; www.greyhouse.com
Social Media: Facebook, Twitter

Leslie Mackenzie, Publisher
Richard Gottlieb, Editor

Comprehensive information covering the field of behavioral health, with critical information for both the layman and mental health professional. Provides the layman with understandable descriptions of 25 mental health disorders, as well as detailed information on associations, media, support groups and mental health facilities. Offers the professional critical and comprehensive information on managed care organizations, information systems, government agencies and provider organizations.
Cost: $165.00
800 Pages
ISBN: 1-592372-85-6
Founded in: 1981

13005 **Complete Mental Health Directory - Online Database**
Grey House Publishing
4919 Route 22
PO Box 56
Amenia, NY 12501-0056

518-789-8700
800-562-2139; *Fax:* 518-789-0556
gold@greyhouse.com;
www.gold.greyhouse.com
Social Media: Facebook, Twitter

Leslie Mackenzie, Publisher
Richard Gottlieb, President

This award-winning directory, now available in a quick-to-search, easy-to-use, online database provides the most comprehensive compilation of mental health resources available anywhere, with data for both layman and mental health professionals.
Founded in: 1981

13006 **Detwiler's Directory of Health and Medical Resources**
Information Today
143 Old Marlton Pike
Medford, NJ 08055-8750

609-654-6266
800-300-9868; *Fax:* 609-654-4309
custserv@infotoday.com; www.infotoday.com

Thomas H Hogan, President
Roger R Bilboul, Chairman Of The Board
Joe Menendez, Marketing Manager
John Brokenshire, Chief Financial Officer
Michael V. Zarrello, Advertising Director

A comprehensive guide to over 2,000 health and medical corporations,associations, state and federal agencies, helathcare market research firms, foundations, institutes, and more.
Cost: $195.00
ISBN: 1-573871-55-9

13007 **Directory for Pediatric Disorders - Online Database**
Grey House Publishing
4919 Route 22
PO Box 56
Amenia, NY 12501-0056

518-789-8700
800-562-2139; *Fax:* 518-789-0556
gold@greyhouse.com;
www.gold.greyhouse.com
Social Media: Facebook, Twitter

Leslie Mackenzie, Publisher
Richard Gottlieb, President

The Complete Directory for Pediatric Disorders - Online Database is an important reference tool that provides parents and caregivers with information about common pediatric and adolescent conditions, disorders, diseases, and disabilities. This comprehensive, informative database is designed to meet the growing consumer demands for current, understandable medical information on pediatric disorders.
Founded in: 1981

13008 **Directory for People with Chronic Illness - Online Database**
Grey House Publishing
4919 Route 22
PO Box 56
Amenia, NY 12501-0056

518-789-8700
800-562-2139; *Fax:* 518-789-0556
gold@greyhouse.com;
www.gold.greyhouse.com
Social Media: Facebook, Twitter

Leslie Mackenzie, Publisher
Richard Gottlieb, President

This important database is structured around the 80 most prevalent chronic illnesses and provides a comprehensive overview of the support services and information resources available for people diagnosed with a chronic illness. With a subscription to the Complete Directory for People with Chronic Illness - Online Database, your organization will have immediate access to a wealth of resources available for people diagnosed with a chronic illness, their families and support systems.
Founded in: 1981

13009 **Directory for People with Disabilities - Online Database**
Grey House Publishing
4919 Route 22
PO Box 56
Amenia, NY 12501-0056

518-789-8700
800-562-2139; *Fax:* 518-789-0556
gold@greyhouse.com;
www.gold.greyhouse.com
Social Media: Facebook, Twitter

Leslie Mackenzie, Publisher
Richard Gottlieb, President

Comprehensive resource for people with disabilities, detailing independent living centers, rehabilitation facilities, state and federal agencies, associations and support groups. This one-stop resource also provides immediate access to the latest products and services for people with disabilities, such as periodicals and books, assistive devices, and more. With a subscription to the online databse, your organization will have immediate access to a wealth of resources available.
Founded in: 1981

13010 **Directory of Health Care Group Purchasing Organizations**
Grey House Publishing
4919 Route 22
PO Box 56
Amenia, NY 12501

518-789-8700
800-562-2139; *Fax:* 845-373-6390
books@greyhouse.com; www.greyhouse.com
Social Media: Facebook, Twitter

Leslie Mackenzie, Publisher
Richard Gottlieb, Editor

This comprehensive directory profiles over 800 Purchasing Organizations that negotiate more than 65% of all health care products purchased by hospitals and related facilities, and the institutions they represent.
Cost: $465.00
800 Pages
ISBN: 1-592372-87-2
Founded in: 1981

13011 **Directory of Health Care Group Purchasing Organizations - Online Database**
Grey House Publishing
4919 Route 22
PO Box 56
Amenia, NY 12501-0056

518-789-8700
800-562-2139; *Fax:* 518-789-0556
gold@greyhouse.com;
www.gold.greyhouse.com
Social Media: Facebook, Twitter

Leslie Mackenzie, Publisher
Richard Gottlieb, President

This interactive online database offers immediate access to detailed information about over 800 GPOs, over 3,000 key contacts and 16,000 member hospitals and institutions they represent. These 800+ organizations represent billions of dollars in purchasing power for the medical and device supplies industry. This data is so critical for market research, sales plans and market development.
Founded in: 1981

13012 **Directory of Hospital Personnel**
Grey House Publishing
4919 Route 22
PO Box 56
Amenia, NY 12501

518-789-8700
800-562-2139; *Fax:* 845-373-6390
books@greyhouse.com; www.greyhouse.com
Social Media: Facebook, Twitter

Leslie Mackenzie, Publisher
Richard Gottlieb, Editor

A Who's Who of the hospital universe, The Directory of Hospital Personnel puts you in touch with over 100,000 key decision makers. This comprehensive directory contains listings of over 6,000 hospitals within the US, arranged alphabetically by city within state.
Cost: $325.00
2300 Pages
ISBN: 1-592372-86-4
Founded in: 1981

13013 **Directory of Hospital Personnel - Online Database**
Grey House Publishing
4919 Route 22
PO Box 56
Amenia, NY 12501-0056

518-789-8700
800-562-2139; *Fax:* 518-789-0556
gold@greyhouse.com;
www.gold.greyhouse.com
Social Media: Facebook, Twitter

Richard Gottlieb, President
Leslie Mackenzie, Publisher

The DHP Online Database is the best resource you can have at your fingertips when researching or marketing a product or service to the hospital market. A 'Who's Who' of the hospital universe, this database puts you in touch with over 140,000 key decision-makers at 5,800 hospitals nationwide.
Founded in: 1981

13014 **Employee Assistance Program Management Yearbook**
Health Resources Publishing
1913 Atlantic Ave
Suite 200
Manasquan, NJ 08736-1067

732-292-1100
888-843-6242; *Fax:* 732-292-1111
info@themcic.com;
www.healthresourcesonline.com

Robert K Jenkins, Publisher
Lisa Mansfield, Regional Director
Brett Powell, Regional Director
Alice Burron, Director

Explore major areas of involvement for EAPS. Investigate tools for effectively managing your EAP. Learn how screening tools for mental illness can help EAPS manage care. Learn how to help families deal with workplace changes. Learn how to identify potentially violent situations in the workplace and much more.
Cost: $149.00
ISBN: 1-882364-25-2

13015 **HCEA Directory of Healthcare Meetings and Conventions**
Healthcare Convention & Exhibitors Association
1100 Johnson Ferry Rd NE
Suite 300
Atlanta, GA 30342-1556

404-252-3663; *Fax:* 404-252-0774
hcea@kellencompany.com; www.hcea.org

Susan Huff, President
Carol Wilson, Meetings Director
Michelle Hall, Staff Associate
Jackie Beaulieu, Associate Director
Frank Skinner, Executive Director

Information on 6,000 health care meetings, available to members only.
500 Pages
Founded in: 1930
Mailing list available for rent: 1400 names

13016 **HMO/PPO Directory**
Grey House Publishing
4919 Route 22
PO Box 56
Amenia, NY 12501

518-789-8700
800-562-2139; *Fax:* 845-373-6390
books@greyhouse.com; www.greyhouse.com
Social Media: Facebook, Twitter

Leslie Mackenzie, Publisher
Richard Gottlieb, Editor

The HMO/PPO Directory is a comprehensive source that provides detailed information about Health Maintenance Organizations and Preferred Provider Organizations nationwide. Within the HMO/PPO Profiles, over 1,300 HMOs, PPOs and affiliated companies are listed, arranged alphabetically by state.
Cost: $325.00
600 Pages
ISBN: 1-592373-69-0
Founded in: 1981

13017 HMO/PPO Directory - Online Database
Grey House Publishing
4919 Route 22
PO Box 56
Amenia, NY 12501-0056
518-789-8700
800-562-2139; *Fax:* 518-789-0556
gold@greyhouse.com;
www.gold.greyhouse.com
Social Media: Facebook, Twitter
Leslie Mackenzie, Publisher
Richard Gottlieb, President
The HMO/PPO Directory - Online Database is your in-depth searchable guide to health plans nationwide - their contact information, key executives, plan information and more. The online database is a necessary tool when researching or marketing a product or service to this important industry.
Founded in: 1981

13018 Health Funds Grants Resources Yearbook
Health Resources Publishing
1913 Atlantic Ave
Suite 200
Manasquan, NJ 08736-1067
732-292-1100
888-843-6242; *Fax:* 732-292-1111
info@themcic.com;
www.healthresourcesonline.com
Robert K Jenkins, Publisher
Judy Granholm, Regional Director
Brett Powell, Regional Director
Alice Burron, Director
A resource book that gives dollar amounts, descriptions of previous grant recipients and programs that attract funding and details of future funding trends.
Cost: $165.00
ISBN: 1-882364-30-9

13019 Managed Care Yearbook
Health Resources Publishing
1913 Atlantic Ave
Suite 200
Manasquan, NJ 08736-1067
732-292-1100
888-843-6242; *Fax:* 732-292-1111
info@themcic.com;
www.healthresourcesonline.com
Robert K Jenkins, Publisher
Judy Granholm, Regional Director
Brett Powell, Regional Director
Alice Burron, Director
Resource book that includes critical facts, statistics cost, analysis, comparisions, enrollment and trends studies on managed care. Topics also include member retention, international markets and disease management.
Cost: $29.00
608 Pages
ISBN: 1-882364-26-0

13020 Medical Abbreviations: 24,000
Niel M Davis Associates
2049 Stout Dr
B-3
Warminster, PA 18974-3861
215-442-7430; *Fax:* 888-333-4915
med@neilmdavis.com; www.neilmdavis.com
Neil M Davis, Owner
This current edition paperback pocket book contains 16,000 medical related abbreviations and 24,000 of their possible meanings. It is current, comprehensive, and formatted so that it is easy to use. It also contains a cross-referenced listing of 3,300 generic and trade drug names.
Cost: $24.95
Frequency: Monthly
ISBN: 0-931431-09-3
Founded in: 1981

13021 Medical Device Register
Grey House Publishing
4919 Route 22
PO Box 56
Amenia, NY 12501
518-789-8700
800-562-2139; *Fax:* 845-373-6390
books@greyhouse.com; www.greyhouse.com
Social Media: Facebook, Twitter
Leslie Mackenzie, Publisher
Richard Gottlieb, Editor
The only one-stop resource of every medical supplier licensed to sell products in the US. This edition offers fast access to over 13,000 companies - and more than 65,000 products. This comprehensive resource saves you hours of time and trouble when searching for the equipment and supplies you want and the manufacturers who provide them.
Cost: $350.00
3000 Pages
ISBN: 1-592373-73-9
Founded in: 1981

13022 National Directory of Integrated Healthcare Delivery Systems
Health Resources Publishing
1913 Atlantic Ave
Suite 200
Manasquan, NJ 08736-1067
732-292-1100
888-843-6242; *Fax:* 732-292-1111
info@themcic.com;
www.healthresourcesonline.com
Robert K Jenkins, Publisher
Lisa Mansfield, Regional Director
Brett Powell, Regional Director
Alice Burron, Director
Gives facts and stastics on more than 850 health care delivery systems and affiliations. Includes profiles of IHDSs by state and by alphabetical order. Also includes a directory of health care associations, a ranking of systems by revenues and an analysis of IHDSs growth projections.
Cost: $995.00
ISBN: 1-882364-31-7

13023 National Directory of Managed Care Organzatons
Health Resources Publishing
1913 Atlantic Ave
Suite 200
Manasquan, NJ 08736-1067
732-292-1100
888-843-6242; *Fax:* 732-292-1111
info@themcic.com;
www.healthresourcesonline.com
Robert K Jenkins, Publisher
Lisa Mansfield, Regional Director
Brett Powell, Regional Director
Alice Burron, Director
Published by Health Resources Publishing. Available in print ($325), database ($1695) or CD-Rom ($695).
Cost: $325.00
ISSN: 0898-9753

13024 National Directory of Physician Organizations Database On Cd-Rom
Health Resources Publishing
1913 Atlantic Ave
Suite 200
Manasquan, NJ 08736-1067
732-292-1100
888-843-6242; *Fax:* 732-292-1111
info@themcic.com;
www.healthresourcesonline.com
Robert K Jenkins, Publisher
Judy Granholm, Regional Director
Brett Powell, Regional Director
Alice Burron, Director
Detailed profiles on over 1,800 physician organizations. Listings include physician hospitals organizations (PHOs), independent practice associations, management services organizations and physician practice management companies. Key elements of the data profile include: executive officers; year founded; profits status, statue of incorporation; numbers of associates physician; market area; market analysis; affiliated/participating hospital; management service organizations used.
Cost: $995.00
ISBN: 1-882364-18-X

13025 Older Americans Information Directory
Grey House Publishing
4919 Route 22
PO Box 56
Amenia, NY 12501
518-789-8700
800-562-2139; *Fax:* 845-373-6390
books@greyhouse.com; www.greyhouse.com
Social Media: Facebook, Twitter
Leslie Mackenzie, Publisher
Richard Gottlieb, Editor
Important resources for older americans, including national, regional, state and local organizations, government agencies, research centers, legal resources, discount travel information, continuing education programs, disability aids and assistive devices, health, print media and electronic media.
Cost: $165.00
1200 Pages
ISBN: 1-592373-57-7
Founded in: 1981

13026 Older Americans Information Directory - Online Database
Grey House Publishing
4919 Route 22
PO Box 56
Amenia, NY 12501-0056
518-789-8700
800-562-2139; *Fax:* 518-789-0556
gold@greyhouse.com;
www.gold.greyhouse.com
Social Media: Facebook, Twitter
Leslie Mackenzie, Publisher
Richard Gottlieb, President
The Older Americans Information Directory is an easy to use source that offers up-to-date information on the prevalent social, health and financial issues facing older Americans in the 21st century, as well as recreational and educational opportunities to enrich their lives. With a subscription to the online database, you'll have immediate access to over 8,000 resources including national, regional, state and local organziations, government agencies, health facilities and more.
Founded in: 1981

13027 Wellness Program Management Yearbook
Health Resources Publishing
1913 Atlantic Ave
Suite 200
Manasquan, NJ 08736-1067
732-292-1100
888-843-6242; *Fax:* 732-292-1111
info@themcic.com;
www.healthresourcesonline.com
Robert K Jenkins, Publisher
Lisa Mansfield, Regional Director

Brett Powell, Regional Director
Alice Burron, Director

This yearbook highlights such issues as obtaining senior management support, encouraging employment participation in programs, finding, funding and developing different programs. Also helps in planning initiatives by providing details of the components that will be important to include about the programs that will help you to meet your goals.
Cost: $155.00
ISBN: 1-882364-39-2

Industry Web Sites

13028 http://gold.greyhouse.com
G.O.L.D Grey House OnLine Databases

Grey House Publishing's online database platform, GOLD, offers Quick Search, Keyword Search and Expert Search for most business sectors including healthcare markets. The GOLD platform makes finding the information you need quick and easy - whether you're a novice searcher or an experienced database user. All of Grey House's directory products are available for subscription on the GOLD platform.

13029 www.aaaai.org
American Academy of Allergy, Asthma And Immunology

The largest professional medical specialty organization in the United States, representing allergists, asthma specialists, clinical immunologists, allied health professionals, and others with the special interest in the research and treatment of allergic disease.

13030 www.aaham.org
American Association of Healthcare Administrative
Management

Business offices, credit and collection managers, and admitting officers for hospitals, clincis and other health care organizaitons. To educate members, exchange information and techniques, and keep members abreast of new regulations relating to their field. Seeks proper recognition for the financial aspect of hospital and clinic managememnt.

13031 www.aahperd.org
American Alliance for Hlth, Phys. Edu. Rec. Dance
Recreation & Dance

13032 www.aaid.org
American Academy of Implant Dentistry

Offers a rigorous implant dentistry credentialing program which requires at least 300 hours of post-docroal or continuing education instruction in implant dentistry, passing a comprehensive exam, and presenting successful cases of different types of implants to a group of examiners. It is one of the most comprehensive credentialing programs in dentistry.

13033 www.aaihds.org
American Association of Integrated Healthcare
Delivery Systems

Physicians, hospital executives and board members, health plan executives, and other key entities and professionals employed by all forms of IDDSs including PHOS, IPA POSOS, and MSOS. Seeks to provide advocacy for issues related to integrated health care through research, education, and communication. Conducts educational and research programs; maintains speakers' bureau and information clearinghouse.

13034 www.aameda.org
American Academy of Medical Administrators

Individuals involved in medical administration at the executive- or midele-management levels. Promotes educational courses for the training of persons in medical administration. Conducts research. Offers placement service.

13035 www.aamft.org
American Assoc for Marriage and Family Therapy

AAMFT represents the professional interests of more than 25,000 marriage and family therapists in the United States, Canada and abroad.

13036 www.aami.org
Assoc for the Advancement of Medical Instrumentati

The Association for the Advancement of Medical Instrumentation (AAMI), founded in 1967, is a unique alliance of over 6,000 members united by the coommon goal of increasing the understanding and use of medical instrumentation. AAMI is the primary source of consensus and timely information on medical instrumentation and technology for the industry, professionals, and the government for national and intemational standrards.

13037 www.aaos.org
American Academy for Cerebral Palsy and Developmental Medicine

13038 www.aap.org
American Academy of Pediatrics

13039 www.academydentalmaterials.org
Academy of Dental Materials

Formerly known as American Academy for Plastics Research in Dentistry.

13040 www.ache.org
American College of Healthcare Executives

International professional society of more than 30,000 healthcare executives. Credentialing and educational programs, Congress on Healthcare Management. ACHE's publishing division, Health Administration Press, is one of the largest publishers of books.

13041 www.acpe.org
American College of Physician Executives

Physicians whose primary professional responsibility is the management of health care organizations. Provides for continuing education and certification of the physician executive and the profession. Offers specialized career planning, counseling, recruitment and placement services, and research and information data on physican managers.

13042 www.acrm.org
American Congress of Rehabilitation Medicine

13043 www.acsm.org
American College of Sports Medicine

The ACSM promotes and integrates scientific research, education, and practical applications of sports medicine and exercise science to maintain and enhance physical performance, fitness, health, and quality of life.

13044 www.afprd.org
Association of Family Practice Residency Directors

Provides representation for residency directors at a national level and provides a political voice for them to approprite arenas. Promotes cooperation and communication between residency programs and different branches of the family practice specialty. Dedicated to improving of education of family physicians. Provides a network for mutual assistance among FP, residency directors.

13045 www.aha.org
American Hospital Association

13046 www.ahia.org
Association of Healthcare Internal Auditors

Promotes cost containment and increased productivity in health care institutions through internal auditing. Serves as a forum for the exchange of experience, ideas, and information among members; provides continuing professional education courses and informs members of developments in health care internal auditing. Offers employment clearinghouse services.

13047 www.ahqa.org
American Health Quality Association

Central news area for the group that represents quality improvement organizations and professionals working to improve the quality of health care in communities across America.

13048 www.ahraonline.org
Association for Medical Imaging Management

For radiology administrators from the US, Canada, and several other countries.

13049 www.ama-assn.org
American Medical Association

A partnership of physicians and their professional associations dedicated to promoting the art and science of medicine and the betterment of the public health. To serve physicians and their patients by establishing and promoting ethical, educational, and clinical standards for the medical profession and by advocating for the highest principle of all - the integrity of the physician/patient relationship.

13050 www.amga.org
American Medical Group Association

13051 www.apta.org
American Physical Therapy Association

The principal membership organization representing and promoting the profession of physical therapy, is to furhter the profession's role in the prevention, diagnosis, and treatment of movement dysfunctions and the enhancement of the physical health and functional abilities of members of the public.

13052 www.arrs.org
American Roentgen Ray Society

102 years strong radiological association for all subspecialties.

13053 www.ascrs.org
American Society of Ophthalmic Administrators

A division of the American Society of Cataract and Retractive Surgery. Persons involved with the administration of an ophthalmic office or clinic. Facilitates the exchange of idease and information in order to improve management practices and working conditions. Offers placement services.

13054 www.asma.org
Aerospace Medical Association

Our mission is to apply and advance scientific knowledge to promote and enhance the health, safety and performance of those involved in aerospace and related activities.

13055 www.asnr.org
American Society of Neuroradiology

13056 www.asrm.org
American Society for Reproductive Medicine

Organization devoted to advancing knowledge and expertise in reproductive medicine and biology. Members of this voluntary nonprofit organization must demonstrate the high ethical principals of the medical profession, evince an interest in reproductive medicine and biotechnology, and adhere to the objectives of the Society.

13057 **www.assh.org**
American Society for Surgery of the Hand
The oldest medical specialty society in the United States devoted entirely to continuing medical education related to hand surgery.

13058 **www.awhp.org**
Association for Worksite Health Promotion
Exists to advance the profession of worksite health promotion and the career development of its practitioners and to improve the performance of the programs they administer. Represents a variety of disciplines and worksites, for decision-makers in the areas of health promotion/disease prevention and health-care cost management.

13059 **www.cdc.gov**
Centers for Disease Control and Prevention
The official website of CDC, the government's public health agency.

13060 **www.chpa-info.org**
Consumer Healthcare Products Association
Members are producers of nonprescription medicines and dietary supplements for self-care. Has an annual budget of approximately $10 million.

13061 **www.claims.org**
Alliance of Claims Assistance Professionals
Professionals dedicated to the effective management of health insurance claims. Our members are claims assistance professionals who work for patients.

13062 **www.cleftline.org**
American Cleft Palate Craniofacial Association
Organization of plastic surgeons, dentists, orthodontists, speech pathologists, geneticists, social workers and others.

13063 **www.cmsa.org**
Case Management Society of America
Exclusively for the case management profession.

13064 **www.crnusa.com**
Council for Responsible Nutrition
Government relations, scientific and regulatory affairs, publications.

13065 **www.docinfo.org**
A national data bank of disciplinary histories on US licensed physicians from the Federation of State Medical Boards; charges $9.95 per report

13066 **www.entnet.org**
American Academy of Otolarygngology-Head & Neck

13067 **www.fascrw.org**
American Society of Colon & Rectal Surgeons

13068 **www.foodallergy.org**
Food Allergy & Anaphylaxis Network
Facts, common questions, resources and news.

13069 **www.gretmar.com/webdoctor/**
General medical information.

13070 **www.greyhouse.com**
Grey House Publishing
Authoritative reference directories for most business sectors including healthcare markets. Users can search the online databases with varied search criteria allowing for custom searches by product category, geographic area, sales volume, keyword, subject and more. Full Grey House catalog and online ordering also available.

13071 **www.hcea.org**
Healthcare Convention & Exhibitors Association
Trade association of over 650 organizations involved in health care exhibiting or providing services to health care conventions, exhibitions and/or meetings.

13072 **www.healthfinder.gov**
A comprehensive guide to resources for health information from the federal government and related agencies

13073 **www.hfma.org**
Healthcare Financial Management Association
Brings perspective and clarity to the industry's complex issues for the purpose of preparing our members to succeed. Through our programs, publications and partnerships, we enhance the capabilities that strengthen not only individuals careers, but also the organizations from which our members come.

13074 **www.hida.org**
Health Industry Distributors Association
The trade association representing medical products distributors. Provides leadership in the healthcare distribution industry.

13075 **www.iahss.org**
International Association for Healthcare Security
Non-profit professional organization of healthcare security and safety executives from around the world.

13076 **www.ichbc.org**
Institute of Healthcare Business Consultants
Maintains code of ethics, rules of professional conducts, and certification program, administers examination and conducts certification course. Membership by successful completion of certification examination only.

13077 **www.jamesbeard.org**
James Beard Foundation
Not-for-profit organization dedicated to preserving the country's culinary heritage and fostering the appreciation and development of gastronomy by recognizing and promoting excellence in all aspects of the culinary arts.

13078 **www.managedcaremarketplace.com**
Managed Care Information Center
An online yellow pages for companies providing services to MCOs, hospitals and physicians groups. There are more than three dozen targeted categories, offering information on vendors from claims processing to transportation services to health care compliance.

13079 **www.medicaid.apwa.org**
National Association of Medicaid Directors
Promotes effective Medicaid policy and program administration; works with the federal government on issues through technical advisory groups. Conducts forums on policy and technical issues.

13080 **www.mgma.com**
American College of Medical Practice Executives
Professional credentialing organization. Works to encourage medical group practice administrators to improve and maintain their proficiency and to provide appropriate recognition; to establish a program with uniform standards of admission, advancement, certification and fellowship in order to achieve the highest possible standards in the profession of medical group practice administration; to participate in the development of educational and research programs.

13081 **www.mwsearch.com/**
Medical world search.

13082 **www.mywebmd.com**
The largest commercial health site, offers easy - to read information on health and wellness issues and latest medical news

13083 **www.naher.com**
National Association for Healthcare Recruitment
Individuals employed directly by hospitals and other health care organizations which are involved in the practice of professional health care recruitment. Promotes sound principles of professionals health care recruitment. Provides financial assistance to aid members in planning and implementing regional educational programs. Offers technical assistance and consultation services. Compiles statistics.

13084 **www.namdrc.org**
National Association of Medical Directors for
Respiratory Care
Works to provide educational opportunities to fit the needs of medical directors of respiratory care and represents the interests of members to regulatory agencies to ensure that the needs of respiratory patients are not overlooked. Offers educational programs; maintains speakers' bureau.

13085 **www.namss.org**
National Association Medical Staff Service
Individuals involved in the management and administration of health care provider services. Seeks to enhance the knowledge and experience of medical staff services professionals and promote the certification of those involved in the profession.

13086 **www.nerf.org**
National Eye Research Center
Improving your vision through eyecare, education and research.

13087 **www.nlm.nih.gov/databases/medline.html**
Vast bibliographic database maintained by the US National Library of Medicine. Medline contains citations and abstracts from several thousand biomedical journals, covering medicine, nursing, dentistry, vetinary medicine and other fields.

13088 **www.nraa.org/renal/**
National Renal Administrators Association
Administrative personnel involved with dialysis programs for patients suffering from kidney failure. Provides a vehicle for the development of educational and informational services for members. Maintains contact with health care facilities and government agencies. Operates placement serve; compiles statistics; conducts political action committee.

13089 **www.oncolink.com**
Founded by specialist at the University of Pennsylvania, provides information on wide range of childhood and adult cancers

13090 **www.pahcom.com**
Professional Association of Health Care Office

Management

Office managers of small group and solo medical practices. Operates certification program for health care office managers.

13091 www.paralysis.org
Christopher Reeve Paralysis Foundation

Our mission is to raise money to help fing spinal cord injury research.

13092 www.quackwatch.com

A nonprofit corporation whose purpose is to combat health - related frauds, myths, fads, and fallacies and investigate phony medical news

13093 www.rbma.org
Radiology Business Management Association

Business managers for private radiology groups; corporate members include: vendors of equipment, services, or supplies. Purposes are to improve business administration of radiologists' practices to better serve patients and the medical profession; and to provide opportunities for professional development and recognition. Offers extensive educational and networking opportunities and informal placement service. Maintains information services emphasizing those aspects unique to the business.

13094 www.siim.org
Society for Imaging Informatics in Medicine

Devoted to advance informatics and information technology in medical imaging through education and research. Provides an open environment for imaging information professionals to access expert and cutting edge resources in a collegial and practical atmosphere.

13095 www.sleepproducts.org
International Sleep Products Association

Maintains a strong organization to influence government actions, inform and educate the membership and act on industry issues to enhance the growth,profitability and stature of the sleep products industry. Provides members with information and services to manage their business more effectively and efficiently. Publishes a magazine devoted exclusively to the mattress industry, BEDtimes covers a broad range of issue and news important to the industry.

13096 www.smamc.org
Society of Medical-Dental Management Consultants

Professionals medical and/or dental management consultants associated for educational and information sharing purposes. Objectives are to: advance the profession; share management techniques; improve individual skills; provide clients with competent and capable business management. Provides information on insurance and income tax. Conducts surveys; compiles statistics.

13097 www.themcic.com
Healthcare IS/IT Yearbook

The Health care IS/IT Market Yearbook is a unique and valuable sales and marketing reference tool for IT companies selling into the health and managed care industries. Great for sales and marketing research; developing reports or preparing presentations. Now, it's easy to identify what hospitals are contracting for, get information on hundreds of millions of dollars in healthcare. IT contract deals, discover what other companies are doing.

13098 www.toxicology.org
Society Of Toxicology

Members are scientists concerned with the effects of chemicals on man and the environment. Promotes the aquisition and utilization of knowledge in toxicology, aids in the protection of public health and facilitates disiplines. The society has a strong commitment to education in toxicology and to the recruitment of students and new members into the profession.

13099 www.uams.edu/afpa/
Association of Family Practice Administrators

Promotes professionalism in family practice administration. Serves as a network for sharing of information and fellowship among network for sharing of information and fellowship among members. Provides technical assistance to members; functions as a liaison to related professional organizations.

Associations

13100 **ASHRAE**
1791 Tullie Circle, N.E.
Atlanta, GA 30329-2398

404-636-8400
800-527-4723; *Fax:* 404-321-5478
ashrae@ashrae.org; www.ashrae.org
Social Media: Facebook, Twitter

T. David Underwood, P.Eng., President
Timothy G. Wentz, P.E., President-Elect
Walid Chakroun, Ph.D., P.E., VP
Patricia T. Graef, P.E., VP
James K. Vallort, VP

An international organization that fulfills its mission of advancing heating, ventilation, air conditioning and refrigeration to serve humanity and promote a sustainable world through research, standards writing, publishing and continuing education.
55000 Members
Founded in: 1894
Mailing list available for rent

13101 **Air Conditioning Contractors of America**
2800 S Shirlington Rd
Suite 300
Arlington, VA 22206-3607

703-575-4477
888-290-2220
info@acca.org; www.acca.org
Social Media: Facebook, Twitter, LinkedIn, YouTube

Paul T. Stalknecht, President/CEO
Don Langston, Secretary/Treasurer
Kevin W. Holland, SVP, Business Operations
Glenn Hourahan, SVP, Research & Technology
Charlie McCrudden, SVP, Government Relations

Represents HVAC contractors and holds annual meetings and exhibits for heating, air conditioning and refrigeration equipment, supplies and services.

13102 **Air Diffusion Council**
1901 North Roselle Road
Suite 800
Schaumburg, IL 60195

847-706-6750; *Fax:* 847-706-6751
info@flexibleduct.org; www.flexibleduct.org

Jack Lagershausen, President

The purpose of the Air Diffusion Council is to promote and further the interests of the manufacturers of air distribution equipment, more specifically, flexible air ducts and related products, and the interests of the general public in the areas of safety, quality, efficiency and energy conservation. Also, to develop programs approved and supported by the membership that legally promote and further these interests.
40 Members
Founded in: 1961

13103 **Air Movement and Control Association International, Inc.**
30 West University Dr.
Arlington Heights, IL 60004

847-394-0150; www.amca.org
Social Media: Facebook, Twitter, LinkedIn

Dr. Geoff Sheard, Chairman
Patrick Cockrum, President
Mark Stevens, Executive Director

AMCA represents manufacturers of air movement devices from 34 countries.
330 Members
Founded in: 1917

13104 **Air-Conditioning, Heating, Refrigeration**
2111 Wilson Boulevard
Suite 500
Arlington, VA 22201

703-524-8800; *Fax:* 703-562-1942;
www.ahrinet.org
Social Media: Facebook, Twitter, RSS

Stephen Yurek, President and CEO
Amanda M Donahue, Executive Assistant
Stephanie Murphy, CFO
Cade Clark, Vice President, Government Affairs
Henry Hwong, Senior Vice President
300+ Members
Founded in: 1953

13105 **Air-Conditioning, Heating, and Refrigeration Institute (AHRI)**
2111 Wilson Blvd.
Suite 500
Arlington, VA 22201

703-524-8800; www.ahrinet.org
Social Media: Facebook, Twitter, YouTube

Stephen Yurek, President & CEO
Stephanie Murphy, Chief Financial Officer

Institute members manufacture 90 percent of the residential and commercial HVAC equipment in North America.

13106 **American Boiler Manufacturers Association**
8221 Old Courthouse Road
Suite 380
Vienna, VA 22015

703-356-7172; *Fax:* 703-356-4543
info@abma.com; www.abma.com
Social Media: Facebook, Twitter, LinkedIn

Robert Stemen, Chairman of the Board
Robert Forslund, Vice Chairman
Scott Lynch, President/Chief Executive Officer
Thomas Giaier, Secretary/ Treasurer
Kevin Hoey, Immediate Past Chair

Manufacturers' trade association representing companies involved in utility, industrial and commercial steam generation. Includes associate memberships for companies who sell to or work with these companies and those who own boilers. Holds technical and production conferences and publishes technical guideline publications.
Founded in: 1888

13107 **American Supply Association**
1200 North Arlington Heights Road
Suite 150
Itasca, IL 60143

630-467-0000; *Fax:* 630-467-0001
info@asa.net; www.asa.net
Social Media: Facebook, Twitter, LinkedIn

John Strong, Chairman
Rick Fantham, President
Tim Milford, President Elect
Steve Cook, Treasurer
Brian Tuohey, VP

The national association of full-service plumbing, heating, cooling, and piping products for wholesalers, manufacturers, and distributors.
4000 Members
Founded in: 1969

13108 **Association of Professional Energy**
3916 W Oak Street
Suite D
Burbank, CA 91505

818-972-2159; *Fax:* 818-972-2863;
www.apem.org

John Sykes, Communications
Mark Martinez, Chair/Chapter Development
Bernell Loveridge, Chair/Treasurer
Lynne Eichner Kelley, Chair/Membership

Members include individuals responsible for energy production, consumption or management decisions.
1.5M Members
Founded in: 1982

13109 **Cooling Technology Institute**
PO Box 681807
Houston, TX 77268

281-583-4087; *Fax:* 281-537-1721
vmanser@cti.org; www.cti.org

Jack Bland, President
Frank Michell, Vice-President
Steven Chaloupka, Treasurer
Thomas Toth, Secretary
Helene Troncin, Director

Seeks to improve technology, design and performance of water conservation apparatus. Provides inspection services and conducts research.
400 Members
Founded in: 1950

13110 **Heating, Air Conditioning & Refrigeration Distributors International**
3455 Mill Run Drive
Suite 820
Columbus, OH 43026

614-345-4328
888-253-2128; *Fax:* 614-345-9161
hardimail@hardinet.org; www.hardinet.org
Social Media: Facebook, Twitter, LinkedIn, Flickr, Youtube, Instagram

William Bergamini, President
Tom Roberts, Vice President
Troy Meachum, Secretary / Treasurer
Michael Meier, President-Elect
Royce Henderson, Immediate Past President

Nonprofit organization dedicated to advancing the science of wholesale distribution in the HVACR industry.
1200 Members
Founded in: 1947

13111 **International Microwave Power Institute**
PO Box 1140
Mechanicsville, VA 23111-5007

804-559-6667; *Fax:* 804-559-4087
info@impi.org; www.impi.org
Social Media: Facebook, Twitter, LinkedIn

Bob Schifmann, President
Ben Wilson, VP
Dorin Boldor, Secretary
Amy Lawson, Treasurer
Molly Poisant, Executive Director

To be the global organization that provides a forum for the exchange of information on all aspects of microwave and RF heating technologies.
Founded in: 1966

13112 **Masonry Heater Association of North America**
2180 S Flying Q Lane
Tuscon, AZ 85731

520-883-0191; *Fax:* 480-371-1139
execdir@mha-net.org; www.mha-net.org

Richard Smith, Executive Director
Tim Seaton, VP
Rod Zander, Treasurer
Beverly Marois, Administrator

Promotes use of masonry heaters, increases public awareness and encourages reasonable governmental regulation.
115 Members
Founded in: 1989

13113 **Mechanical Contractors Association of America**
1385 Piccard Drive
Rockville, MD 20850-4329

301-869-5800; *Fax:* 301-990-9690;
www.mcaa.org

John Gentille, Executive VP

Represents heating, piping and air conditioning professionals.
1.4M Members

13114 **Mobile Air Conditioning Society Worldwide**
225 South Broad Street
PO Box 88
Lansdale, PA 19446

215-631-7020; *Fax:* 215-631-7017
info@macsw.org; www.macsw.org
Social Media: Facebook, Twitter, LinkedIn, Youtube, WordPress, Google+, T

Elvis L. Hoffpauir, President, Chief Operating Officer
Marion J. Posen, VP Marketing & Member Relations
Pam Smith, Events Manager
Maria Whitworth, Director of Operations
Laina Casey, Manager of Graphics and Design

Non-profit organization provides technical training, information and communication for the professionals in the automotive air-conditioning industry.
1700 Members
Founded in: 1981

13115 **National Air Duct Cleaners Association**
1120 Route 73
Suite 200
Mt Laurel, NJ 08054

856-380-6810
855-GON-ADCA; *Fax:* 856-439-0525
info@nadca.com; www.nadca.com
Social Media: Facebook, Twitter, LinkedIn, Youtube

Michael Vinick,ASCS, President
Jodi Araujo, CEM, Executive Director
Mike Dwyer, CAE, Chief Relationship Officer
Richard Lantz,ASCS, 1st Vice President
Rick MacDonald, ASCS, 2nd Vice President

The trade association of the HVAC/Heating-Ventilation-Air Conditioning industry.
1000 Members
Founded in: 1989

13116 **National Association of Plumbing, Heating and Cooling Contractors Association**
180 S Washington Street
Suite 100
Falls Church, VA 22046

703-237-8100
800-533-7694; *Fax:* 703-237-7442
naphcc@naphcc.org; www.phccweb.org
Social Media: Facebook, Twitter, LinkedIn

Dawn Dalton, Administrative Coordinator
Katie Gilbert, Membership Coordinator
Merry Beth Hall, Director, Apprentice and Journeyman
Don Hawkins, Accounts Receivable Clerk
Patrice L Jackson, Coordinator, QSC Member Services

National organization designed for suppliers of equipment, supplies and services for the plumbing, heating and cooling industries.
3700 Members
Founded in: 1883

13117 **National Association of Power Engineers**
One Springfield Street
Chicopee, MA 01013-2672

413-592-6273; *Fax:* 413-592-1998
nape@powerengineers.com;
www.powerengineers.com
Social Media: Facebook, Twitter, LinkedIn

Michael Morin, National President
Shawn Fitzpatrick, National Vice President
William Love, National Treasurer/Secretary

Members include power plant operators and maintenance personnel who supply the industry with process power and related building and plant services.

13118 **National Environmental Balancing Bureau**
8575 Grovemont Circle
Gaithersburg, MD 20877-4121

301-977-3698
866-497-4447; *Fax:* 301-977-9589
glenn@nebb.org; www.nebb.org

Jean Paul Le Blanc, President
Donald E. Hill, Vice President
Jim Kelleher, President Elect
Jim Whorton, Treasurer
James Huber, Past President

NEBB is an international certification association for firms that deliver high performance building systems. Members perform testing, adjusting and balancing (TAB) of heating, ventilating and air-conditioning systems, commission and retro-commission building systems commissioning, execute sound and vibration testing, and test and certify lab fume hoods and electronic and bio clean rooms. NEBB holds the highest standards in certification.
Founded in: 1971

13119 **Wholesalers Association of the Northeast**
1200 N. Arlington Heights Rd.
Suite 150
Itasca, IL 60143

630-467-0000; *Fax:* 508-923-1044
wane5@asa.net; www.wane5.org

Chris Murin, Executive Director

Presently comprised of the leading wholesale distributors of pluming, heating, cooling and industrial pipe supplies, located throughout the northeast states.
Founded in: 1932

Newsletters

13120 **HVACR News**
Trade News International
4444 Riverside Drive
Suite 202
Burbank, CA 91505

818-848-6397; *Fax:* 818-848-1306;
www.hvacrnews.com

Gary McCarty, Editor-in -Chief
Mark Deitch, Publisher
Jordan Tolila, Associate Publisher
Barb Kerr, Executive Assistant

A monthly national trade newspaper serving contractors, technicians, mechanical engineers, manufactures, manufacturer representatives, wholesalers, distributors, trade associations, government representatives, schools, students and other in the heating, ventilating, air conditioning, refrigerating, hydronics, sheet metals, solar, and allied trades.
Frequency: Monthly
Circulation: 50000

Founded in: 1981
Printed in 4 colors on n stock

13121 **Heating/Combustion and Equipment News**
Business Communications Company
1 Penn Plz
Suite 42
New York, NY 10119-4200

212-273-7100
800-685-4488; *Fax:* 212-244-3721;
www.firstalbany.com

Equipment, materials and supplies for the heating and air conditioning industry.
Cost: $12.00
Frequency: Monthly

13122 **Impact Compressor/Turbines News And Patents**
Impact Publishers
PO Box 3113
Ketchum, ID 83340-3113

208-726-2332; *Fax:* 208-726-2115

Mary Jo Helmeke, Publisher

Regular features include new product announcements, patent information and up-to-date industry news and information on current books, brochures, software, seminars and meetings.
Cost: $60.00
30 Pages
Frequency: Annual

13123 **Impact Pump News and Patents**
Impact Publishers
PO Box 3113
Ketchum, ID 83340-3113

208-720-4876; *Fax:* 208-726-2115

Mary Jo Helmeke, Publisher

Regular features include new product announcements, patent information and up-to-date industry news and information on current books, brochures software, seminars and meetings.
Cost: $100.00
25 Pages

13124 **Indoor Air Quality Update**
Cutter Information Corporation
37 Broadway
Suite 1
Arlington, MA 02474-5500

718-648-8700; *Fax:* 718-648-8707;
www.cutter.com
Social Media: Facebook, Twitter

Karen Coburn, President and CEO
Paul Bergeron, CFO and COO
Israel Gat, Director, Agile Practice
Anne Mullaney, VP, Prodct Development
Cuitlahuac Osorio, Director, Cutter Latin America

Practical control of indoor air problems.
Cost: $287.00
Frequency: Monthly

13125 **MACS Action!**
Mobile Air Conditioning Society Worldwide
225 S Broad Street
PO Box 88
Lansdale, PA 19446

215-631-7020; *Fax:* 215-631-7017
info@macsw.org; www.macsw.org

Elvis Hoffpauir, President/COO
Marion Posen, VP Marketing/Sales

Industry informational newsletter of Mobile Air Conditioning Society Worldwide.
Cost: $5.00
Frequency: 8x Yearly
Circulation: 13000
ISSN: 1949-3436

13126 **MACS Service Reports**
Mobile Air Conditioning Society Worldwide
PO Box 100
East Greenville, PA 18041
215-679-2220; *Fax:* 215-541-4635
elvis@macsw.org; www.macsw.org
Elvis Hoffpauir, Editor
Paul DeGuiseppi, Manager of Training
Amy Anderson, Production Designer
Pam Smith, Manager
Maria Whitworth, Director of Operations
Technical newsletter for mobile air conditioning industry.
Frequency: Monthly
Circulation: 1600
Founded in: 1981

13127 **Residential Heat Recovery Ventilators Directory**
Cutter Information Corporation
37 Broadway
Suite 1
Arlington, MA 02474-5500
781-648-1950; *Fax:* 781-648-1950;
www.cutter.com
Verna Allee, Senior Consultant
A comprehensive comparative guide and product directory to heat exchangers and ventilators.
Cost: $75.00

13128 **Superinsulated House Design and Construction Workbook**
Cutter Information Corporation
37 Broadway
Suite 1
Arlington, MA 02474-5500
781-648-1950; *Fax:* 781-648-1950;
www.cutter.com
Verna Allee, Senior Consultant
Detailed, graphic information to design and build superior houses.
Cost: $85.00

Magazines & Journals

13129 **AHRI Trends Magazine**
Air Conditioning & Refrigeration Institute
2111 Wilson Boulevard
Suite 500
Arlington, VA 22201
703-524-8800; *Fax:* 703-528-3816
ahri@ahri.net; www.ahrinet.org
Social Media: Facebook
Stephen Yurek, President & CEO
A resource for HVAC contractors and technicians.
300+ Members
Frequency: Monthly

13130 **ASHRAE Journal**
1791 Tullie Circle NE
Atlanta, GA 30329
404-636-8400
800-527-4723; *Fax:* 404-321-5478
ashrae@ashrae.org; www.ashrae.org
Social Media: Facebook
Ronald Jarnagin, President
Thomas Watson, President-Elect
William Bahnfleth, Tresurer
Constantinos A Balaras, VP
Ross D Montgomery, VP
Explores topical technical issues, such as: indoor air quality, energy management, thermal storage, alternative refrigerants, fire and life safety and more.
Printed in 4 colors on matte stock

13131 **Air Conditioning Today**
PO Box 311776
New Braunfels, TX 78131
830-627-0605
877-669-4228; *Fax:* 830-627-0614
info@ac-today.com
ac-today.com
Joe Eaton, Editor
Updates readers on the latest products, materials and technologies available.
Frequency: Monthly
Circulation: 19000
Founded in: 1986

13132 **Air Conditioning, Heating & Refrigeration News**
Business News Publishing Company
1050 IL Route 83
Suite 200
Bensenville, IL 60106-1096
630-377-5909; www.bnpmedia.com
Katie Rotella, Manager
Timely information to contractors, wholesalers, distributors, manufacturers, owner/operators and consulting engineers. Features technical, marketing, design, engineering, installation, management, governmental and labor aspects of the heating and cooling industry. Regular columns highlight new products and literature, legal rulings, manufacturer announcements, industry events and the latest HVAC/r patents.
Cost: $49.00
Frequency: Weekly
Circulation: 32854
Founded in: 1926
Mailing list available for rent: 35M names
Printed in 4 colors on glossy stock

13133 **American Supply Association News**
222 Merchandise Mart Plaza
Suite 1400
Chicago, IL 60654-1203
312-464-0090; *Fax:* 312-464-0091
info@asa.net; www.asa.net
Joel Becker, President
Bob Christian, Vice President
Kevin Neupert, Marketing
Joel Becker, Editor
Articles on plumbing, heating, cooling, and piping products.
50 Pages
Frequency: Monthly
Circulation: 2500
Founded in: 1969
Mailing list available for rent: 4,000 names
Printed in 4 colors on matte stock

13134 **Automotive Cooling Journal**
National Automotive Radiator Service Association
3000 Villiage Run Rd
Suite 103, #221
Wexford, PA 15090-6315
412-847-5747
800-551-3232; *Fax:* 724-934-1036
info@narsa.org; www.narsa.org
Jim Holowka, National President
Chuck Braswell, National Chairman-Past President
Rick Fuller, National 1st VP
Maarten Taal, National 2nd VP
Angelo Miozza, National Treasurer
Auto cooling system service data. Free to members.
Cost: $30.00
60 Pages
Frequency: Monthly
Circulation: 10,000
Founded in: 1954

13135 **Boiler Systems Engineering Magazine**
HPAC Engineering
1300 E 9th Street
Cleveland, OH 44144
216-696-7000; *Fax:* 216-696-3432
hpac@penton.com; www.hpac.com
Social Media: Facebook, Twitter
Mike Well, Editorial Director
Scott Arnold, Executive Editor
Ron Rajecki, Senior Editor
The official publication of the American Boiler Manufacturers Association, assists consulting engineers, in-house engineers, and building managers with the design, installation, operations, maintenance and commissioning of steam and hot water systems for institutional, commercial and industrial buildings.

13136 **Contracting Business**
Penton Media
249 W 17th St
New York, NY 10011
212-204-4200; *Fax:* 216-696-6662
information@penton.com; www.penton.com
Jane Cooper, Marketing
Michael S Weil, Editor-in-Chief
Gwen Hostnik, Marketing Manager
Directed to the residential, commercial and industrial mechanical systems contracting marketplace. HVAC mechanical systems and Design/Build/Maintain contractors, wholesalers and commercial/industrial in-house service organizations.
Cost: $75.00
120 Pages
Frequency: Monthly
Circulation: 49,001
Founded in: 1944
Printed in 4 colors on glossy stock

13137 **Contractor Magazine**
Penton Media
1300 E 9th St
Cleveland, OH 44114-1503
216-696-7000; *Fax:* 216-696-6662
information@penton.com;
www.contractormag.com
Social Media: Facebook, Twitter
Jane Cooper, Marketing
Bob Mader, Managing Editor
David B. Nussbaum, CEO
For contractors who sell, install, service air conditioning, heating, piping, plumbing, air handling, heat transfer and fluid controls equipment. Accepts advertising.
70 Pages
Frequency: Monthly
Circulation: 50000
Founded in: 1892

13138 **District Energy**
International District Enery Association (IDEA)
24 Lyman Streetad
Suite 230
Westborough, MA 01581
508-366-9339; *Fax:* 508-366-0019
idea@districtenergy.org;
www.districtenergy.org
Peter Myers, Editor
Rob Thornton, President
Journal of district heating and cooling industry, congeneration, physical plants and energy efficiency. Accepts advertising.
Cost: $40.00
Frequency: Quarterly

13139 **Energy Engineering**
Association of Energy Engineers

4025 Pleasantdale Rd
Suite 420
Atlanta, GA 30340-4264

770-447-5083; *Fax:* 770-446-3969
info@aeecenter.org; www.aeecenter.org
Social Media: Facebook, Twitter, LinkedIn, YouTube

Jennifer Venola, Controller
Ruth Whitlock, Executive Admin
Albert Thumann, Executive Director
Kate Feltgen, Executive Director's Assistant

Engineering solutions to cost efficiency problems and mechanical contractors who design, specify, install, maintain, and purchase non-residential heating, ventilating, air conditioning and refrigeration equipment and components.
Cost: $40.00
Circulation: 8000

13140 **Engineered Systems**
Business News Publishing Company
1050 IL Route 83
Suite 200
Bensenville, IL 60106-1096

630-377-5909; www.esmagazine.com

Katie Rotella, Manager
Peter E Moran, Publisher

Research conducted by us shows that end users, consulting engineers, and contractors work together closely on the specification and selection of engineered HVAC/r systems and components. We give this receptive audience solid editorial information about real-world solutions to the everyday situations faced in the industry.
72 Pages
Frequency: Monthly
Circulation: 57515
Founded in: 1985
Mailing list available for rent: 57.5M names
Printed in 4 colors on glossy stock

13141 **Fuel Oil News**
Hunter Publishing Limited
3100 S King Dr
7th Floor
Chicago, IL 60616-3483

312-567-9981; *Fax:* 312-846-4632;
www.fueloilnews.com

Luke Hunter, Partner
Joanne Juda, Circulation Director
Kate Kenny, Publisher
Chris Traczek, Editor-in-Chief
Patricia McCartney, Associate Editor

For home heating oil retailers.
Cost: $28.00
70 Pages
Frequency: Monthly
Circulation: 15200
Founded in: 1935
Printed in 4 colors on glossy stock

13142 **HVAC Insider**
Retailing Newspapers
PO Box 81489
Conveyors, GA 30013

770-787-0115; *Fax:* 770-787-1213;
www.mindspring.com/~insider/insider

Jerry M Lawson, Publisher
Robert Scott, Chief Information Officer

Up to date information on technical tips, product reviews, commercial and industrial industry new, a job bulletin, new businesses and promotions, and a calendar of events. Retailing Newspapers issues a monthly publication for the Appliance and Electronics trade. Insiders Newspapers issues a quarterly national and 14 monthly regionals for the HVAC trade and a monthly regional publication for the plumbing trade.
Frequency: Monthly
Circulation: 118740

Founded in: 1969
Printed in 4 colors on newsprint stock

13143 **HVAC/R Distribution Today**
HARDI
3455 Mill Run Dr
Suite 820
Columbus, OH 43026-7578

614-345-4328
888-253-2128; *Fax:* 614-345-9161
HARDImail@Hardinet.org; www.hardinet.org

Talbot H Gee, Executive VP & COO
Donald L Frendberg, Chairman
Susan Little, Director of Marketing
Mary Gustafson, Director of Operations
Alan Beaulieu, Chief Economist

Official publication of Heating, Air Conditioning and Refrigeration International. Uniting world class distribution.
Frequency: Quarterly
Founded in: 1960

13144 **HVACR & Plumbing Distribution**
Penton Media
1300 E 9th St
Cleveland, OH 44114-1503

216-696-7000; *Fax:* 216-696-6662
information@penton.com; www.penton.com

Jane Cooper, Marketing
Perry Clark, Publisher

Exclusively for plumbing and heating equipment distributors.
Circulation: 10,000
Founded in: 1890

13145 **Hearth & Home**
Village West Publishing
PO Box 1288
Laconia, NH 03246

603-528-4285
800-258-3772; *Fax:* 603-524-0643
info@hearthnhome.com
villagewest.com

Richard Wright, Editor
Susan Salls, Publisher

Magazine for retailers, including specialty, hardware, patio and barbecue.
Cost: $36.00
Frequency: Monthly
Circulation: 18000

13146 **Industrial Heating**
Business News Publishing Company
1910 Cochran Road
Manor Oak One, Suite 450
Pittsburgh, PA 15220

412-531-3370; *Fax:* 412-531-3375;
www.industrialheating.com
Social Media: Facebook, Twitter

Ed Kubel, Editor
Beth McClelland, Production Manager
Doug Glenn, Publisher
Kathy Pisano, Advertising Director
Patrick Connolly, Sales Representative

We have been applying the latest advances in thermal technology to practical use since 1931. With over 22,000 BPA audited circulation comprised of mostly thermal processing engineers, technical articles cover heat treatments, brazing, sintering, melting, process control, instrumentation, refractories, burners, heating elements, and other thermal processes typically in excess of 1000 degrees.
Cost: $55.00
70 Pages
Circulation: 22100
ISSN: 0019-8374
Founded in: 1931
Printed in 4 colors on glossy stock

13147 **PM Engineer**
Business News Publishing Company
1050 IL Route 83
Suite 200
Bensenville, IL 60106-1096

630-377-5909; www.pmengineer.com
Social Media: Facebook, Twitter

Bob Miodonski, Group Publisher & Editor
Mike Miazga, Senior Editor
Julius Ballanco, Editorial Director
Suzette Rubio, Online Editor
John Siegenthaler, Hydronics Editor

Provides technical sheets, manufacturer product brochures, news features and analysis of useful industry information on the engineering and design of plumbing, piping, hydronics, cooling/heating, and fire protection/sprinkler systems. Free to trade engineers.
Cost: $64.00
80 Pages
Frequency: Monthly
Circulation: 25000
Founded in: 1926
Printed in 4 colors on glossy stock

13148 **RSES Journal**
Refrigeration Service Engineers Society
1666 Rand Rd
Des Plaines, IL 60016-3552

847-297-6464
800-297-5660; *Fax:* 847-297-5038
general@rses.org; www.rses.org
Social Media: Facebook, Twitter, LinkedIn

John Iwanski, Publishing Director
Lori A Kasallis, Editor

Providing quality technical content in digital and printed forms that can be applied on the job site.
Frequency: Monthly
Circulation: 15231

13149 **Reeves Journal**
23421 S Pointe Drive
Suite 280
Laguna Hills, CA 92654

949-830-0881; *Fax:* 949-859-7845;
www.reevesjournal.com

Ellyn Fishman, Publisher
John Fultz, Editor
Tagg Henderson, CEO

An invaluable tool for Western plumbing contractors and industry professionals for more than 80 years.
Frequency: Monthly
Circulation: 13545
Founded in: 1926

13150 **Refrigeration**
John W Yopp Publications
73 Sen Island Parkway Suite 21
PO Box 1147
Beaufort, SC 29901-1147

843-521-0239
800-849-9667; *Fax:* 843-521-1398
cgraffo@jwyopp.com;
www.refrigeration-magazine.com

John W Yopp, Chairman
Joe Cronley, Publisher
Mary Yopp Cronley, Associate Publsiher
Cheryl Graffo, Editor

About the plants and processes used in ice manufacture, marketing and merchandising information, news of associations, meetings and new products available.
Cost: $20.00
Frequency: Monthly
Circulation: 3200
Founded in: 1919
Printed in 4 colors on glossy stock

13151 **Snips**
Business News Publishing Company
2401 W. Big Beaver Road
Suite 700
Troy, MI 48084
248-362-3700; *Fax:* 248-362-0317
snips@halldata.com; www.snipsmag.com
Katie Rotella, Manager
Sally Fraser, Advertising Sales
Karen Koppins, Advertising Productions
Ann Kalb, Customer Service
Michael McConnel, Editorial Director
Magazine directed to the heating, air conditioning, sheet metal and ventilation industry. Accepts advertising.
Cost: $18.00
120 Pages
Frequency: Monthly
Circulation: 22000
Founded in: 1926
Printed in 4 colors on glossy stock

13152 **Tab Journal**
Associated Air Balance Council
1518 K Street NW
Washington, DC 20005-1203
202-737-0202; *Fax:* 202-638-4833;
www.aabchq.com/
Kenneth M Sufka, Publisher
Mike Young, President
Case studies, industry updates, as well as other news of importance to engineers.
Cost: $24.00
Frequency: Quarterly
Circulation: 12000
Founded in: 1965

13153 **Todays A/C and Refrigeration News**
Todays Trade Publications
PO Box 521247
130 W Pine Ave
Longwood, FL 32750-1247
407-332-4959
866-320-2773; *Fax:* 407-332-5319;
www.todays-ac.com
Thomas Fatchell, Editor
Covers industry legislation, building codes, licensing requirements and continuing educations. New product reviews and personnel changes are also included.
Frequency: Monthly
Circulation: 20000
Founded in: 1988

Trade Shows

13154 **ABMA Annual Meeting**
American Boiler Manufacturers Association
8221 Old Courthouse Road
Suite 207
Vienna, VA 22182-3839
703-356-7172; *Fax:* 703-356-4543;
www.abma.com
W Randall Rawson, President/CEO
Diana McClung, Executive Assistant
Cheryl Jamall, Director of Meetings
Geoffrey Halley, Director of Technical Affairs
Hugh K Webster, Association General Counsel
The association's premier membership networking events. In casual and relaxed settings, members have the opportunity to not only learn about developments and trends, both inside and outside their industry, that are likely to influence their business, members are also afforded the opportunity, through committee and product/market group meetings to focus on issues and concerns of specific relevance to their product and market segments.
Frequency: Bi-Annual
Founded in: 1888

13155 **ABMA Manufacturers Conference**
American Boiler Manufacturers Association
8221 Old Courthouse Road
Suite 207
Vienna, VA 22182-3839
703-356-7172; *Fax:* 703-356-4543;
www.abma.com
W Randall Rawson, President/CEO
Diana McClung, Executive Assistant
Cheryl Jamall, Director of Meetings
Geoffrey Halley, Director of Technical Affairs
Hugh K Webster, Association General Counsel
Designed to bring together manufacturing plant, office and others concerned with the design, fabrication, sales and distribution of ABMA'products and services to network, discuss trends and developments, and problem solve with others in the industry and with outside experts.
Frequency: Annual/October
Founded in: 1888

13156 **AMCA Annual Meeting**
Air Movement and Control Assoc. Intl., Inc.
30 West University Dr.
Arlington Heights, IL 60004
847-394-0150; www.amca.org
Social Media: Facebook, Twitter, LinkedIn
Dr. Geoff Sheard, Chairman
Patrick Cockrum, President
Mark Stevens, Executive Director

13157 **ASA Convention and ISH North America Trade Show**
American Supply Association
222 Merchandise Mart Plaza
Suite 1400
Chicago, IL 60654
312-640-0090; *Fax:* 312-464-0091
info@asa.net; www.asa.net or www.ish-na.com
Ruth Mitchell, Manager/Convention Director
Bob Jarvie, Show Manager
Annual conference for wholesalers, distributors and manufacturers of plumbing and heating pipes, valves and fittings.
1800 Attendees
Frequency: Annual/September

13158 **Air Conditioning Contractors of America Annual Conference**
Air Conditioning Contractors of America
1712 New Hampshire Avenue NW
Washington, DC 20009-2502
202-518-3236; *Fax:* 202-332-5293;
www.acca.org
Christopher Holelzel, Director Marketing
Rosemary Graeme, Executive Assistant
Annual meeting and exhibits of heating, air conditioning and refrigeration equipment, supplies and services. Over 140 exhibitors, plus seminar, workshop and banquet.
1000 Attendees

13159 **Air Conditioning Heating & Refrigeration Expo Mexico - AHR**
Industrial Shows of America
164 Lake Front Drive
Hunt Valley, MD 21030-2215
410-771-1445
800-638-6396; *Fax:* 410-771-1158;
www.isoa.com
Bryan Mayes, President
Phillip McKay, Managing Director
300 exhibitors with air conditioning, heating and refrigerating equipment, supplies and information. Attended by professionals.
5000 Attendees
Frequency: Annual

13160 **Annual Campus Energy Conference**
International District Energy Association
24 Lyman Street
Suite 230
Westborough, MA 01581
508-366-9339; *Fax:* 508-366-0019
idea@districtenergy.org;
www.districtenergy.org
Robert Thornton, President
Vincent Bedeli, Chair
Leonard Phillips, Director of Business Development
IDEA fosters the success of its members as leaders in providing reliable, economical, and environmentally sound district energy services.
600 Attendees
Frequency: Annual/June
Founded in: 1909

13161 **Hearth Products Association**
1555 Wilson Boulevard
Suite 300
Arlington, VA 22209-2405
703-522-0086; *Fax:* 703-812-8875
Social Media: Facebook, Twitter
Joan Letch Worth, Show Manager
900 booths of products related to the residential alternative fuel heating industry.
8M Attendees
Frequency: Annual/March

13162 **Heating, Air Conditioning & Refrigeration Distributors International**
3455 Mill Run Drive
Suite 820
Columbus, OH 43026
614-345-4328
888-253-2128; *Fax:* 614-345-9161;
www.hardinet.org
Talbot H Gee, Executive VP & COO
Donald L Frendberg, Chairman
Susan Little, Director of Marketing
Mary Gustafson, Director of Operations
Alan Beaulieu, Chief Economist
Annual show of 200 exhibitors of heating and air conditioning equipment, supplies and services.
1200 Attendees
Founded in: 2003

13163 **International Air Conditioning, Heating & Refrigerating Expo**
International Exposition Company
15 Franklin Street
Westport, CT 06880
203-221-9232; *Fax:* 203-221-9260
info@ahrexpo.com; www.ahrexpo.com
Mark Stevens, Vice President
Jeff Stevens, Sales Vice President
Co-sponsored by American Society of Heating, Refrigeration and Air Conditioning Engineers and the Air Conditioning and Refrigeration Institute, this expo features exhibits that include equipment and services of industrial, commercial and residential heating, refrigeration, air conditioning and ventilation.
37292 Attendees
Frequency: Annual/January
Founded in: 1930

13164 **International Air Conditioning, Heating, & Refrigerating Expo**
ASHRAE

1791 Tullie Circle NW
Atlanta, GA 30329

404-636-8400
800-527-4723; *Fax:* 404-321-5478
ashrae@ashrae.org; www.ashrae.org

William A Harrison, President
Jeff H Littleton, Executive VP

The largest HVAC&R event in America featuring over 1,600 exhibiting companies. Held every year in conjunction with the ASHRAE Winter Meeting.
30000 Attendees
Frequency: Annual/January
Founded in: 1894

13165 International District Energy Association (IDEA) Show
1200 19th Street NW
Suite 300
Washington, DC 20036-2428

202-429-5131; *Fax:* 202-429-5113;
www.districtenergy.org

John L Fiegel, Editor
Tammie Jackson, Advertising Manager

Show of the district heating and cooling industry, cogeneration, physical plants, energy efficiency.
40 booths.
450 Attendees
Frequency: Annual/June

13166 International Institute of Ammonia Refrigeration Annual Conference
1001 N Fairfax St
suite 503
Alexandria, VA 22314

703-312-4200; *Fax:* 202-857-1104
iiar_request@iiar.org

Adolfo Blasquez, Chair
Robert Port Jr, Vice Chair
Joe Mandato, Chair Elect
Marcos Braz, Treasurer
Bruce Badger, President

Show of the district heating and cooling industry, cogeneration, physical plants, energy efficiency.
40 booths.
750 Attendees
Frequency: Annual/March

13167 International Thermal Spray Conference & Exposition
ASM International
9639 Kinsman Road
Materials Park, OH 44073-0002

440-338-5151
800-336-5152; *Fax:* 440-338-4634
natalie.nemec@asminternational.org;
www.asminternational.org

Carole Chesla, Administrator, Awards
Thom Passek, Associate Managing Director
Leslie Taylor, Executive Office Manager
Stanley Theobald, Managing Director

Global annual event attracting professional interested in thermal spray technology focusing on advances in HVOF, plasma and detonation gun, flame spray and wire arc spray processes, performance of coatings, and future trends. 150 exhibitors.
1000 Attendees
Frequency: Annual/May

13168 MACS Convention & Trade Show
Mobile Air Conditioning Society Worldwide
225 S Broad Street
PO Box 88
Lansdale, PA 19446

215-631-7020; *Fax:* 215-631-7017
info@macsw.org; www.macsw.org

Pam Smith, Events Manager
2000 Attendees
Frequency: Annual

13169 Midwest Contractors Expo
Kansas Assn of Plumbing, Heating & Cooling Contr
320 Laura Street
Wichita, KS 67211-1517

316-262-8860; *Fax:* 316-262-2782

Ray Katzenmeier, Owner

Annual show and exhibits of plumbing, heating and cooling equipment, supplies and services.

13170 National Plumbing, Heating, Cooling and Piping Products Exposition
Nat'l Assn of Plumbing-Heating-Cooling Contractors
180 S Washington Street
PO Box 6808
Falls Church, VA 22046
703-237-8100
800-533-7694; *Fax:* 703-237-7442;
www.phccweb.org
Social Media: Facebook, LinkedIn

Elicia Magruder, VP of Member Services
Cynthia A Sheridan, Foundation Chief Operating Officer
Charlotte R Perham, Senior Director of Communications

Annual show of 500 manufacturers and suppliers of equipment, supplies and services for the plumbing, heating and cooling industries.
15M Attendees
Frequency: Annual/October

13171 North American Thermal Analysis Society
Complete Conference
1540 River Park Drive
Suite 111
Sacramento, CA 95815-4608

916-922-7032; *Fax:* 916-922-7379

Marilyn Hauck, President

30 booths.
300 Attendees
Frequency: Annual/September

13172 Oil Heat Business and Industry Expo
20 Summer Street
#9137
Watertown, MA 02472-3468

Fax: 781-924-1022

Bernard A Smith, Executive VP
Nancy Spinney, Expo Manager

This show provides a marketplace for prime purchasers of heating oil; oil heating, and air conditioning, as well as accessory equipment; fuel oil distribution equipment, trucks, transports, service and salesmen's vehicles; computers, office equipment; insurance programs and more.
8.5M Attendees
Frequency: Annual/June

13173 RSES Annual Conference and HVAC Technology Expo
Refrigeration Service Engineers Society
1666 Rand Road
Des Plaines, IL 60016-3552

847-297-6464
800-297-5660
general@rses.org; www.rses.org
Social Media: Facebook, Twitter, LinkedIn

Mark Lowry, Executive Vice President
Josh Flaim, Operations Manager
Jean Birch, Conference & Seminar Manager

80 booths consisting primarily of products and services.

13174 Sheet Metal Air Conditioning Contractors National Association Show
4201 Lafayette Center Drive
Chantilly, VA 20151-1209
703-032-2980
http://www.smacna.org

Mary Lou Taylor, Convention Director
John Sroka, Executive VP

250 booths.
2.3M Attendees
Frequency: Annual/October

13175 Southwestern Ice Association Show
823 Congress Avenue
1300
Austin, TX 78701

512-479-0425; *Fax:* 512-495-9031

Andrea Barnard, Executive Director

30 booths.
200 Attendees
Frequency: Annual/February
Founded in: 1891

Directories & Databases

13176 Air Conditioning, Heating & Refrigeration News Directory Issue
The Air-Conditioning, Heating & Refrigeration New
2401 W. Big Beaver Road
Suite 700
Troy, MI 48084
248-362-3700; www.achrnews.com

John Conrad, Publisher
Mike Murphy, Editor-in-Chief
Kyle Gargaro, Managing Editor
Greg Mazurkiewicz, Web Editor
Barbary Checket-Hanks, Service & Maintenance Editor

This issue offers a list of over 2,000 manufacturers, 5,000 wholesalers and factory outlets. Over 10,000 HVAC/R products, exporters and related trade organizations are also covered.
Cost: $35.00
618 Pages
Frequency: Annual
Circulation: 38,000
Printed in 4 colors on glossy stock

13177 Annual Member Directory
Air Conditioning & Heating Contractors of America
1712 New Hampshire Avenue NW
Washington, DC 20009-2502

202-483-9370; *Fax:* 202-234-4721

Rae Dorsey, Production Manager

A publication for the members of the Air Conditioning and Heating Contractors of America.
Circulation: 5,000

13178 Directory of Certified Applied Air-Conditioning Products
Air-Conditioning & Refrigeration Institute

4301 Fairfax Drive
Suite 425
Arlington, VA 22203-1634

703-248-8800

A list of 50 manufacturers of air conditioning and heating products.
Cost: $8.50
Frequency: Bi-Annual

13179 **Directory of Certified Unitary Air-Conditioners & Heat Pumps**
Air-Conditioning & Refrigeration Institute
4301 Fairfax Drive
Suite 425
Arlington, VA 22203-1634

703-248-8800

Air and coil heating and cooling units and air-to-air heat pumps manufacturers are profiled.
Cost: $13.00
Frequency: Bi-Annual

13180 **HPAC Engineering Information**
Penton Media
1300 E 9th St
Cleveland, OH 44114-1501

216-696-7000; *Fax:* 216-696-1752
information@penton.com; www.penton.com

Jane Cooper, Marketing
Cost: $30.00
300 Pages
Frequency: Annual
Circulation: 56,000
ISSN: 1527-4055
Printed in 4 colors on glossy stock

13181 **Industrial Heating Buyers Guide and Reference Handbook**
Business News Publishing
1050 IL Route 83
Suite 200
Bensenville, IL 60106-1096

630-377-5909; www.industrialheating.com
Social Media: Facebook, Twitter, LinkedIn

Katie Rotella, Manager

Companies are profiled that have over 1,200 heating products, and heat treating, and other services in the worldwide industrial heating market.
Cost: $25.00
250 Pages
Circulation: 20,000

13182 **LP/Gas: Industry Buying Guide Issue**
Advanstar Communications
131 W 1st St
Duluth, MN 55802-2065

218-740-7200
800-346-0085; *Fax:* 218-723-9122
info@advanstar.com; www.advanstar.com

Kent Akervik, Manager

List of about 1,000 liquid propane gas equipment manufacturers and suppliers; list of about 700 distributors of gas appliances and equipment.
Cost: $50.00
Frequency: Annual
Circulation: 16,000
Printed in 4 colors on glossy stock

13183 **PM Directory & Reference Issue**
Business News Publishing
1050 IL Route 83
Suite 200
Bensenville, IL 60106-1096

630-377-5909; www.bnpmedia.com

Katie Rotella, Manager

Manufacturers, wholesalers, exporters, associations, products, consultants and manufacturers' representatives in the industries of plumbing, piping and hydronic heating.
Cost: $30.00
Frequency: Annual/December
Circulation: 42,000

13184 **Refrigeration: Ice Industry's Buyer's Guide Issue**
John W Yopp Publications
PO Box 1147
Beaufort, SC 29901-1147

843-521-0239
800-849-9677; *Fax:* 800-849-8418

Joe Cronley

Directory of services and supplies to the industry.
Cost: $3.00
Frequency: Annual
Circulation: 3,000

Industry Web Sites

13185 **http://gold.greyhouse.com**
G.O.L.D Grey House OnLine Databases

Grey House Publishing's online database platform, GOLD, offers Quick Search, Keyword Search and Expert Search for most business sectors including heating and air conditioning markets. The GOLD platform makes finding the information you need quick and easy - whether you're a novice searcher or an experienced database user. All of Grey House's directory products are available for subscription on the GOLD platform.

13186 **www.abma.com**
American Boiler Manufacturers Association

Manufacturers trade association representing companies involved in utility, industrial and commercial steam generation. Includes associate memberships for companies who sell to or work with these companies and those who own boilers. Holds technical and production conferences, and publishes technical guideline publications.

13187 **www.achrnews.com**
BNP Media

News, tips and a calendar of events for the heating & cooling industry.

13188 **www.aga.com**
American Gas Association

Events, publications, information, etc.

13189 **www.ari.org**
Air Conditioning & Refrigeration Institute

Trade association representing manufacturers of more than 90% of North American produced air-conditioning and commercial refrigeration equipment.

13190 **www.asa.net**
American Supply Association

The National association of full-service plumbing, heating, cooling, and piping products for wholesalers, manufacturers, and distributors.

13191 **www.ashrae.org**
American Society of Heating, Refrigeration, AC

Research, activities, education and publications.

13192 **www.construction.com**

McGraw-Hill Construction (MHC), part of The McGraw-Hill Companies, connects people and projects across the design and construction industry, serving owners, architects, engineers, general contractors, subcontractors, building product manufacturers, suppliers, dealers, distributors and adjacent markets.

13193 **www.districtenergy.org**
International District Energy Association

Journal of district heating and cooling industry, congeneration, physical plants and energy efficiency. Accepts advertising.

13194 **www.gamanet.org**
Gas Appliance Manufacturers Association

Represents manufacturers of residential, commercial and industrial gas and oil fired appliances, associated controls and accessories, as well as equipment used in the production, transmission and distribution of fuel gases.

13195 **www.greyhouse.com**
Grey House Publishing

Authoritative reference directories for most business sectors including heating and air conditioning markets. Users can search the online databases with varied search criteria allowing for custom searches by product category, geographic area, sales volume, keyword, subject and more. Full Grey House catalog and online ordering also available.

13196 **www.impi.org**
International Microwave Power Institute

IMPI's members include scientists, researchers, lab technicians, product developers, marketing managers and a variety of other professionals in the microwave industry. The Institute serves the information needs of all specialists working with dielectric (microwave and RF) heating sytems, and was expanded in 1977 to meet the information needs relating to consumer microwave ovens and related products.

13197 **www.macsw.org**
Mobile Air Conditioning Society Worldwide

Information on technical training for professionals in the automotive air-conditioning industry.

13198 **www.mha-net.org**
Masonry Heater Association of North America

Promotes use of masonry heaters, increases public awareness and encourages reasonable governmental regulation.

13199 **www.sweets.construction.com**
McGraw Hill Construction

In depth product information that lets you find, compare, select, specify and make purchase decisions in the industrial product marketplace.

Associations

13200 **American Camping Association**
5000 State Road 67 North
Martinsville, IN 46151-7902
765-342-8456
800-428-2267; *Fax:* 765-342-2065
shallway@aca-camps.org; www.acacamps.org
Social Media: Facebook, Twitter, LinkedIn, YouTube, Pinterest, Google+
Tisha Bolger, Chair
Rue Mapp, Vice Chair
Craig Whiting, Treasurer
Tom Holland, CEO
Steve Baskin, Board Member
6600+ Members
Founded in: 1910
Mailing list available for rent

13201 **American Craft Council**
1224 Marshall Street NE.
Suite 200
Minneapolis, MN 55413
612-206-3100
800-836-3470; *Fax:* 612-355-2330
council@craftcouncil.org; www.craftcouncil.org
Social Media: Facebook, Twitter, LinkedIn, YouTube, Pinterest, Google+, I
Stuart Kestenbaum, Board Chair
Gariel Ofiesh, Board Vice Chair
Libba Evans, Board Secretary
Kevin Buchi, Board Treasurer
Barbara Berlin, Board of Trustee Member
National nonprofit, educational organization dedicated to promotion, understanding and appreciation of contemporary American craft. Sponsors annual wholesale and retail shows, a magazine, a library and seminars.
Founded in: 1943
Mailing list available for rent

13202 **American Home Sewing and Craft Association**
PO Box 369
Monroeville, PA 15146
412-372-5950; *Fax:* 212-714-1655
info@sewing.org; www.sewing.org

13203 **American Philatelic Society**
100 Match Factory Place
Bellefonte, PA 16823-1367
814-933-3803; *Fax:* 814-933-6128
apsinfo@stamps.org; www.stamps.org
Social Media: Facebook, Twitter, LinkedIn, YouTube, Pinterest
Mick Zais, President
Scott English, Executive Director
Ken Martin, Chief Operating Officer
Judy Johnson, Membership Administration Manager
Mercer Bristow, Director, Expertizing
National organization for postage stamp collectors.
30000 Members
Founded in: 1886

13204 **American Quilt Study Group**
American Quilt Study Group
1610 L Street
Lincoln, NE 68508-2509
402-477-1181; *Fax:* 402-477-1181
aqsg2@americanquiltstudygroup.org; www.americanquiltstudygroup.org
Lisa Erlandson, President
Lenna DeMarco, Vice President
Kathy Moore, Vice President
Judy J. Brott Buss, Ph.D., Executive Director
Anne E. Schuff, Member Services Coordinator
Establishes, sustains, and promotes the highest standards for quilt-related studies. We stimulate, nurture, and affirm engagement in quilt studies and provide opportunities for its dissemination.
1000 Members
Founded in: 1980
Mailing list available for rent

13205 **American Specialty Toy Retailing Association**
432 N. Clark St.
Suite 305
Chicago, IL 60654
312-222-0984
800-591-0490; *Fax:* 312-222-0986
info@astratoy.org; www.astratoy.org
Social Media: Facebook, Twitter
Dean May, Chair
Michael Levins, Past Chair
Ann Kienzle, Chair Elect
Tim Holliday, Treasurer
Erik Quam, Secretary
Providing a unified voice for the specialty toy industry, and opportunities to exchange information and ideas with counterparts. Membership benefits include workshops and seminars, vendor representative roundtables, membership directory and annual convention.
1000 Members
Founded in: 1992

13206 **American Stamp Dealers Association**
PO Box 858
Suite 205
Morris Plains, NJ 07950
973-267-1644
800-369-8207; *Fax:* 800-369-8207
asda@americanstampdealer.com; www.asdaonline.com
Mark Reasoner, President
Stanley Piller, Vice President
Richard A. Friedberg, Secretary
James F. Bardo, Treasurer
Robert Prager, Director
800 Members
Founded in: 1914

13207 **Archery Trade Association**
PO Box 70
101 N German St
New Ulm, MN 56073-0070
507-233-8130
866-266-2776; *Fax:* 507-233-8140
jaymcaninch@archerytrade.org; www.archerytrade.org
Social Media: Facebook, Twitter
Jay McAninch, President/CEO
Kurt Weber, Director of Marketing
Patrick Durkin, Contributing Editor and Writer
Mitch King, Director of Government Relations
John Nelson, Director of Finance and Operations
Provides core funding and direction for two new foundations critical to the future of archery and bowhunting: Arrow Sport and the Bowhunting Preservation Alliance. In addition the ATA continues to direct the industry's annual archery and bowhunting trade show.
Founded in: 1953
Mailing list available for rent

13208 **Association of Traditional Hooking Artists**
600 1/2 Maple Street
Endicott, NY 13760
E-Mail: jcahill29@aol.com; www.rughookersnetwork.com
Social Media: Facebook
Joan Cahill, Membership Chairperson
Karen Balon, Guild Secretary
Mary Henck, President
Provides educational material about rug hooking, free patterns, supplies information, chapter/rug camp meetings and teacher information that is not available through any other source. Membership includes all 50 states, England, Japan and Australia.
Founded in: 1996

13209 **Embroidery Trade Association**
PO Box 793967
Dallas, TX 75379-3967
972-247-0415
888-628-2545; *Fax:* 972-755-2561
info@embroiderytrade.org; www.mesadist.com/trade_associations
John Swinburn, Executive Director
Dolores Cheek, Director of Membership
Keith Amen, VP
An organization with the objective to continually strengthen the commercial embriodery business.
1200 Members
Founded in: 1990

13210 **Entertainment Consumers Association**
www.theeca.com
Hal Halpin, Founder & President
Non-profit representing the interests of consumers of digital entertainment in the US and Canada.

13211 **Game Manufacturers Association**
240 N. Fifth St.
Suite 340
Columbus, OH 43215
614-255-4500; *Fax:* 614-255-4499
president@gama.org; www.gama.org
Social Media: Facebook
Justin Ziran, President
Jamie Chambers, Vice President
Aaron Witten, Treasurer
Brian Dalrymple, Secretary
John Ward, Executive Director
A non-profit trade association dedicated to the advancement of the hobby game business.
Founded in: 1977
Mailing list available for rent

13212 **Hobby Industry Association**
319 E 54th Street
Elmwood Park, NJ 07407-2712
201-835-1200; *Fax:* 201-797-0657
info@craftandhobby.org; www.craftandhobby.org
Social Media: Facebook, Twitter, LinkedIn, Pinterest, Youtube
David Murray, Chair
Mark Hill, Interim President, CEO
Chuck McGonigle, Vice Chair
Natalie Cohn, Vice President, Finance & Admin.
Maureen Walsh, Vice President, Marketing
Trade association in the craft and hobby market. The group produces an international trade show open to qualified professionals and is the industry's only market research show.
4000 Members
Founded in: 1940
Mailing list available for rent

13213 **Hobby Manufacturers Association**
1410 East Erie Avenue
Philadelphia, PA 07405-0315
267-341-1604; *Fax:* 215-744-4699
heather.stoltzfus@hmahobby.org; www.hmahobby.org
Richard Janyszek, President
Bill Jeric, Vice President
Fred Hill, Treasurer
Abby Robey, Secretary
Mike MacDowell, Board of Director

The mission of the Hobby Manufacturers Association is to stimulate the growth of the model hobby industry.
292 Members
Founded in: 2005

13214 **International Council of Toy Industries**
ICTI Secretariat, c/o Toy Industry Association
1115 Broadway, Suite 400
New York, NY 10010

212-675-1141; www.toy-icti.org

May Liang, President

Association of toy brands from 20 countries acting on issues of importance to the toy industry.
Founded in: 1975

13215 **Major League Gaming**

www.majorleaguegaming.com
Social Media: Facebook, Twitter, YouTube

Sundance DiGiovanni, Co-Founder & CEO
Greg Chisholm, Chief Financial Officer

A professional eSports organization. MLG.tv, its free video streaming eSports showcase, attracts 27 million users per month.
Founded in: 2002

13216 **Museum Store Association**
3773 E. Cherry Creek North Drive
Suite 755
Denver, CO 80209-3804

303-504-9223; *Fax:* 303-504-9585
info@museumstoreassociation.org;
www.museumdistrict.com
Social Media: Facebook, Twitter, LinkedIn, Pinterest

David Duddy, President
Jama Rice, MBA, CAE, Executive Director/CEO
Stuart Hata, 1st Vice President
Julie Steiner, 2nd Vice President
Alice McAuliffe, Treasurer

Providing member representatives with the professional opportunities and educational resources they need to operate effectively and ethically.
2500 Members
Founded in: 1955

13217 **National School Supply Equipment Association**
8380 Colesville Rd
Suite 250
Silver Spring, MD 20910-6225

301-495-0240
800-395-5550; *Fax:* 301-495-3330
memberservices@nssea.org; www.nssea.org
Social Media: Facebook, Twitter, LinkedIn, Youtube

Jim McGarry, President/CEO
Bill Duffy, Vice President - Operations
Adrienne Dayton, Vice President - Marketing
Joe Tucker, CEM, CMP, Director of Meetings & Experiences
Michael Nercesian, Exhibits Manager

Trade Association for the educational products industry.
1400+ Members
Founded in: 1916

13218 **Toy Industry Association**
1115 Broadway
Suite 400
New York, NY 10010-3466

212-675-1141; *Fax:* 212-633-1429
info@toyassociation.org;
www.toyassociation.org/
Social Media: Facebook, Twitter, LinkedIn, Youtube

John Gessert, Chairman
David Hargreaves, Vice Chairman
Steve Pasierb, President and CEO
Bob Wann, Secretary-Treasurer
Shirley Price, Member of the Executive Committee

National organization with toy, game and holiday decoration manufacturers and their representatives, as well as toy designers, testing laboratories, licensors, sales representatives and trade magazines.
400+ Members
Founded in: 1916

13219 **Western Toy & Hobby Representatives Association**
PO Box 2250
Pomona, CA 91786

909-899-3753; *Fax:* 909-697-2014
toyshow@wthra.com; www.wthra.com

Phylis St John, Show Director

A nonprofit association organization. Produces and promotes the Western States Toy & Hobby Show.
Founded in: 1961

Newsletters

13220 **American Stamp Dealers Association Newsletter**
American Stamp Dealers Association
3 School St
Suite 205
Glen Cove, NY 11542-2548

516-759-7000; *Fax:* 800-369-8207;
www.asdaonline.com

Joseph Savarese, Executive VP
Elizabeth Pope, Secretary
Kim Kellermann, Secretary
Thomas Jacks, Treasurer

Association news.
Frequency: Monthly
Circulation: 810
Founded in: 1914
Printed in on matte stock

13221 **Bill Nelson Newsletter**
Nelson Newsletter Publishing Corporation
PO Box 90890
Tucson, AZ 85752-0890

520-297-8240
800-368-8434; *Fax:* 520-629-0387;
www.billnelsonnewsletter.com/

James Lee, President

Features news on the pin collecting hobby.
Cost: $20.00
8 Pages
Frequency: Monthly
Printed in one color on matte stock

13222 **Guild of Natural Science Illustration**
Guild of Natural Science Illustrators
PO Box 652
Ben Franklin Station
Washington, DC 20044-652

301-309-1514; *Fax:* 301-309-1514
gnsihome@his.com; www.gnsi.org

Gretchen Kai Halpert, President
Erica Beade, Vice President

Non-profit organization for those interested in the field of natural science illustrations. Newsletter is published 10 times a year.
Cost: $75.00
Frequency: 10x Yearly
Circulation: 1000
Founded in: 1968

13223 **This Time**
Homeworkers Organized for More Employment
PO Box 10
Orland, ME 04472

207-469-7961; *Fax:* 207-469-1023
info@homecoop.net; www.homecoop.net/

Lucy Toulin, President
J Ralph, Editor
F Eldridge, Volunteer Coordinator

Home community newsletter, part of the world Emmaus movement, offering information on craft store items and antiques. Member of rural coalition , Washington D.C..
Cost: $5.00
16 Pages
Frequency: Quarterly
Circulation: 300
Founded in: 1970

Magazines & Journals

13224 **ABCs of Retailing**
Hobby Industry Association
319 E 54th St
Suite 348
Elmwood Park, NJ 07407-2712

201-794-1133; *Fax:* 201-797-0657;
www.craftandhobby.org

Steve Berger, CEO

Guide to opening and maintaining a craft/hobby retail store.
20 Pages
Founded in: 1940

13225 **American Craft Magazine**
72 Spring St
New York, NY 10012-4090

212-274-0630; *Fax:* 212-274-0650
council@craftcouncil.org;
www.craftcouncil.org

Andrew Wagner, Manager
John Gourlay, Publisher
Lois Moran, Editor-in-Chief

Celebrates the excellence of contemporary craft, focusing on masterful achievements in the craft media — clay, fiber, metal, glass, wood and other materials — with the goal to create intellectual and visual interest for the reader on today's craft.
Cost: $40.00
Founded in: 1943

13226 **American Philatelist**
American Philatelic Society
100 Match Factory Place
Bellefonte, PA 16823-1367

814-237-3803; *Fax:* 814-933-6128
apsinfo@stamps.org; www.stamps.org
Social Media: Facebook, Twitter, LinkedIn, YouTube, Pinterest

Jay Bigalke, Editor
Jeff Stage, Editorial Associate
Doris Wilson, Editorial Associate
Helen Bruno, Advertising Manager
Scott English, Executive Director

Monthly magazine for stamp collectors, including articles, society news, and calendar of events.
Cost: $80.00
30000 Members
100 Pages
Frequency: Monthly
Circulation: 37500
ISSN: 0003-0473
Founded in: 1886

13227 **Antiques and Collecting Hobbies**
Lightner Publishing Corporation

1006 S Michigan Ave
Chicago, IL 60605-2216

312-939-4767; *Fax:* 312-939-0053

Antiques and collectible news articles.
Cost: $32.00
88 Pages
Frequency: Monthly
Circulation: 18,000
Founded in: 1931

13228 Bank Note Reporter
F+W Media
38 E. 29th Street
New York, NY 10016

212-447-1400; *Fax:* 212-447-5231
contact_us@fwmedia.com;
www.fwpublications.com
Social Media: Facebook, Twitter, LinkedIn

Bill Bright, General Manager
Dave Harper, Editor
Buddy Redling, Manager
Chad Phelps, Chief Digital Officer
Stacie Berger, Communications Director

Recognized as the finest publication for paper money collectors available. Contains news on market values, 'Bank Note Clinic' (a collector Q&A), an up-to-date foreign exchange chart, 'Fun Notes' (interesting, odd & unusual notes), a price guide, a world currency section, historical features on paper money worldwide (emphasizing US issues), & hundreds of display & classified ads offering to buy, sell, & trade bank notes of all kinds. Contributors include some of the top experts in the field.
Cost: $21.98
84 Pages
Frequency: Monthly
Circulation: 8072
Founded in: 1952
Mailing list available for rent

13229 Blade
F+W Media
38 E. 29th Street
New York, NY 10016

212-447-1400; *Fax:* 212-447-5231
contact_us@fwmedia.com;
www.fwpublications.com
Social Media: Facebook, Twitter, LinkedIn

David Nussbaum, CEO/Chairman
Steve Shackleford, Editor
Jim Ogle, Chief Financial Officer
Chad Phelps, Chief Digital Officer
Stacie Berger, Communications Director

Provides knifemakers, collectors, and knife enthusiasts with information concerning new knife-making techniques and processes, field tests, and the latest news and features on knives and their makers. Also includes a Q&A section, letters to the editor, features about individual knifemakers, an extensive listing of upcoming knife shows, and a reader feature entitled, 'The Knife I Carry.'
Cost: $25.98
140 Pages
Frequency: Monthly
Circulation: 38068
ISSN: 1064-5853
Founded in: 1973
Mailing list available for rent

13230 Cast On Magazine
The Knitting Guild Association (TKGA)
1100-H Brandywine Blvd.
Zanesville, OH 43701-7303

740-452-4541
tkga@tkga.com; www.tkga.com
Social Media: Facebook, Twitter, LinkedIn

Penny Sitler, Executive Director

Educational journal for knitters.
10000 Members
Frequency: Quarterly
Circulation: 11,000
Mailing list available for rent

13231 Coin Prices
F+W Media
38 E. 29th Street
New York, NY 10016

212-447-1400; *Fax:* 212-447-5231
contact_us@fwmedia.com;
www.fwpublications.com
Social Media: Facebook, Twitter, LinkedIn

Bill Bright, General Manager
Bob Van Ryzin, Editor
Jim Ogle, Chief Financial Officer
Chad Phelps, Chief Digital Officer
Stacie Berger, Communications Director

Coin Prices is a complete guide to retail values for collectible US coins. A market update section (value guide) by market editor Joel Edler beings each issue. Rotating special sections provide values for Canadian and Mexican coins, Colonial coins, territorial coins, errors and varieties and selected issues of US paper money. Regular departments include a guide to grading US coins.
Cost: $18.98
96 Pages
Circulation: 56611
Founded in: 1952
Mailing list available for rent

13232 Coins
F+W Media
38 E. 29th Street
New York, NY 10016

212-447-1400; *Fax:* 212-447-5231
contact_us@fwmedia.com;
www.fwpublications.com
Social Media: Facebook, Twitter, LinkedIn

Bill Bright, General Manager
Bob Van Ryzin, Editor
Jim Ogle, Chief Financial Officer
Chad Phelps, Chief Digital Officer
Stacie Berger, Communications Director

Covers market trends, buying tips, and historical perspectives on all aspects of numismatics. The news section, 'Bits and Pieces,' wraps up the latest happenings in numismatics. Regular columns and departments include 'Basics& Beyond,' 'Budget Buyer,' 'Coin Clinic' (Q&A), the editor's column, coin finds, a calendar of upcoming shows nationwide, 'Coin Values Guide' and 'Market Watch.'
Cost: $20.98
120 Pages
Frequency: Monthly
Circulation: 52660
Founded in: 1955
Mailing list available for rent

13233 Comics & Games Retailer
F+W Media
38 E. 29th Street
New York, NY 10016

212-447-1400; *Fax:* 212-447-5231
contact_us@fwmedia.com;
www.fwpublications.com
Social Media: Facebook, Twitter, LinkedIn

Mark Williams, Publisher
John Miller, Editor
Norma Jean Fochs, Ad Manager

Provides information to retailers about marketing, industry news, and practical how-to tips on selling comics and games at the retail level. Regular columns include 'Suggested for Mature Retailers,' 'Small Store Strategy,' 'Trade Show Calendar,' 'Retailer News,' and 'Distributor News.' Special issue focus on the comic book industry, trade shows, trading cards, gaming, display racks, and other retail store supplies. 'Market Beat' gives a national overview of the comics market.
Cost: $29.95
72 Pages
Frequency: Monthly
Circulation: 5,201
Founded in: 1971
Mailing list available for rent

13234 Comics Buyer's Guide
F+W Media
38 E. 29th Street
New York, NY 10016

212-447-1400; *Fax:* 212-447-5231
contact_us@fwmedia.com;
www.fwpublications.com
Social Media: Facebook, Twitter, LinkedIn

David Nussbaum, CEO/Chairman
Maggie Thompson, Editor
Jim Ogle, Chief Financial Officer
Chad Phelps, Chief Digital Officer
Stacie Berger, Communications Director

The longest-running magazine about comic books. Each 200+ page monthly issue features new comic reviews, nostalgic retroviews, interviews and the largest monthly price guide. Aslo included is the latest convention news, opinion pieces from celebrity columnists and expanded coverage of anime, manga and other comics-related auctions.
Cost: $38.95
244 Pages
Frequency: Monthly
Circulation: 30,000
ISSN: 1064-5853
Founded in: 1952
Mailing list available for rent

13235 Craftrends
Primedia Enthusiast Group Publishing
741 Corporate Circle
Suite A
Golden, CO 80401

303-278-1010
800-881-6634; *Fax:* 303-277-0370;
www.enthusiastnetwork.com

Bill Gardner, Editorial Director
Beth Hess, Managing Editor
Dave O'Neil, VP Group Publishing
Kelly P. Conlin, President/CEO

Includes new products, coverage of industry trade shows, merchandising and promotion ideas. Also has timely information to operate a craft business and stay on top of a rapidly changing retail environment.
Cost: $26.00
Frequency: Monthly
Circulation: 22000
Founded in: 1989

13236 Crafts Magazine
Primedia Enthusiast Group Publishing
PO Box 420494
Palm Coast, FL 32142-9524

800-727-2387; *Fax:* 386-447-2321
papercrafts@palmcoastd.com;
www.craftcouncil.org

Valerie Pingree, Editor-in-Chief
Mike Irish, Associate Publisher
Kelly P Conlin, CEO/President

Monthly craft consumer magazine reaching the crafting enthusiast.
Cost: $15.97
112 Pages
Circulation: 300272
ISSN: 0148-9127
Founded in: 1989
Printed in 4 colors on glossy stock

13237 Crafts Report
Crafts Reports Publishing

100 Rogers Road
Wilmington, DE 19801

302-656-2209
800-777-7098; *Fax:* 302-656-4894
theeditor@craftsreport.com;
www.craftsreport.com

Lammot Copeland Jr, Publisher
Heather Skelly, Editor
Stewart Abowitz, Marketing Director
Deborah Copeland, Co-Publisher

Monthly business magazine for the crafts professional, providing information on marketing, growing your craft business, time management, studio safety, retail relationships, artist/retailer profiles, show listings and more.
Cost: $29.00
Frequency: Monthly
Circulation: 30000
ISSN: 0160-7650
Founded in: 1975
Printed in 4 colors on glossy stock

13238 Creative Knitting
House of White Birches
306 E Parr Rd
Berne, IN 46711-1100

260-589-8741
800-829-5865; *Fax:* 260-589-8093
customer_service@drgbooks.com;
www.whitebirches.com

David J McKee, CEO
John Boggs, Advertising Sales Director
Carl Musselman, Editor
David J McKee, Publishing Director
Greg Deily, Marketing Director

Serves the knitting industry.
Cost: $13.00
64 Pages
Frequency: Monthly
Founded in: 1947

13239 Doll Artisan
Jones Publishing
N7 450 Aanstad Road
PO Box 5000
Iola, WI 54945-5000

715-445-5000; *Fax:* 715-445-4053
joejones@jonespublishing.com;
www.dollsbeautiful.com

Edited to entertain, fascinate and educate the doll maker in reproduction of antique porcelain dolls. Encourages and promotes efforts to make porcelain doll making easier, safer and more accessible to a growing number of enthusiasts.
Cost: $5.95
Frequency: Bi-Monthly

13240 Doll World
Jones Publishing
N7 450 Aanstad Road
PO Box 5000
Iola, WI 54945-5000

715-445-5000
800-331-0038; *Fax:* 715-445-4053
jonespub@jonespublishing.com;
www.jonespublishing.com

Joe Jones, President
Nayda Rondon, Editor
Trina Laube, Assistant Editor
Virginia Adams, Marketing
Brandan Hardie, Circulation Manager
Cost: $32.95
Frequency: Monthly

13241 Dollmaking
Jones Publishing
N7 450 Aanstad Road
PO Box 5000
Iola, WI 54945-5000

715-445-5000; *Fax:* 715-445-4053
jonespub@jonespublishing.com;
www.Dollmaking/Artisan.com

Resource for makers of porcelain and sculpted modern dolls, is edited for the serious costume and doll maker.
Cost: $4.95
Frequency: Bi-Monthly

13242 Essentials Magazine
National School Supply Equipment
8300 Colesville Rd
Suite 250
Silver Spring, MD 20910-6225

301-495-0240
800-395-5550; *Fax:* 301-495-3330
customerservice@nssea.org; www.nssea.org
Social Media: Facebook, Twitter, LinkedIn

Jim McGarry, President/CEO
Rashad Cheeks, Meetings Coordinator
Tamara Davis, Bookkeeper/Office Manager
Karen Prince, Director of Membership
Bill Duffy, Vice President - Operations

13243 Family Tree
B&W Publications
1507 Dana Avenue
Cincinnati, OH 45207-1056

513-943-9464; *Fax:* 513-531-1843

Ideas and advice for discovering, preserving and celebrating family history.

13244 Family Tree Magazine
F+W Media
38 E. 29th Street
New York, NY 10016

212-447-1400; *Fax:* 212-447-5231
contact_us@fwmedia.com;
www.fwpublications.com
Social Media: Facebook, Twitter, LinkedIn

David Nussbaum, CEO/Chairman
Allison Stacy, Editor
Kelly Klener, Marketing
Chad Phelps, Chief Digital Officer
Stacie Berger, Communications Director

America's most popular family history magazine. It covers all areas of potential interest to family history enthusiasts, reaching beyond strict genealogy research to include ethnic heritage, family reunions, memoirs, oral history, scrapbooking, historical travel and other ways that families connect with their pasts. Each issue features the latest tools, how-to tips and expert advice to guide readers through the journey of discovering, preserving and celebrating their roots.
Cost: $27.00
84 Pages
Circulation: 80050
Founded in: 1952
Mailing list available for rent

13245 Fine Woodworking
Taunton Press
63 S Main Street
PO Box 5506
Newtown, CT 06470-5506

203-270-6206
800-926-8776; *Fax:* 203-426-3434
fw@taunton.com; www.taunton.com

David Grey, Publisher
Linda Abbett, Advertising Manager
Anatole Burkin, Editor
John Lagan, National Account Manager

Published since 1975, written by woodworkers for woodworkers regularly shows the finest work in wood being done today.
Cost: $34.95
120 Pages
Circulation: 295000
Founded in: 1975
Mailing list available for rent: 185M names
Printed in 4 colors on glossy stock

13246 Gun Digest
F+W Media
38 E. 29th Street
New York, NY 10016

212-447-1400; *Fax:* 212-447-5231
contact_us@fwmedia.com;
www.fwpublications.com
Social Media: Facebook, Twitter, LinkedIn

David Nussbaum, CEO/Chairman
Steve Hudziak, Marketing
Jim Ogle, Chief Financial Officer
Chad Phelps, Chief Digital Officer
Stacie Berger, Communications Director

An all-advertising, nationwide marketplace for buyers and sellers of new, used and antique firearms. Display advertising from the nation's top dealers, manufacturers, distributors, and suppliers is found in each bi-weekly issue, along with thousands of classified word ads, organized alphabetically, from collectors all over the world. The nation's leading indexed firearms paper. Hundreds of gun show listings and knife show listings are included to help readers schedule their show attendance.
Cost: $37.98
136 Pages
Circulation: 81120
Founded in: 1952
Mailing list available for rent

13247 HIA Craft/Hobby Consumer Study
Hobby Industry Association
319 E 54th St
Elmwood Park, NJ 07407-2712

201-794-1133; *Fax:* 201-797-0657
info@craftandhobby.org;
www.craftandhobby.org

Steve Berger, CEO

An extensive study of consumer behavior and buying habits relevant to the hobby/craft/creative industry. Executive summary is available on-line.
Cost: $400.00
Circulation: 5000
Founded in: 2004

13248 Hobby Merchandiser
Hobby Publications
207 Commercial Court
PO Box 102
Morganville, NJ 07751-102

732-536-5160
800-969-7176; *Fax:* 732-536-5761
info@hobbymerchandiser.com;
www.hobbymerchandiser.com/

Robert Gherman, Publisher
Jeff Troy, Editor
Patrick Sarver, Associate Publisher

Trade magazine for the model hobby industry, available to professionals only.
Cost: $20.00
96 Pages
Frequency: Monthly
Circulation: 7000
ISSN: 0744-1738
Founded in: 1947
Mailing list available for rent: 8,300 names at $241 per M
Printed in 4 colors on glossy stock

13249 Hobby Rocketry
California Rocketry Publishing

PO Box 1242
Claremont, CA 91711-1242

760-389-2233; *Fax:* 661-824-0868
info@v-serv.com; www.v-serv.com/crp

Jerry Irvine, Publisher

Covers consumer rocket products which are available in hobby, toy and retail outlets. Product reviews, manufacturers notes, consumer feedback and more. Back issues available.
Cost: $16.00
16 Pages
Frequency: Quarterly
Circulation: 8M
Founded in: 1992
Printed in on newsprint stock

13250 Horizons
Hobby Industry Association
319 E 54th St
Elmwood Park, NJ 07407-2712

201-794-1133; *Fax:* 201-797-0657;
www.craftandhobby.org

Steve Berger, CEO

Available only to members of the Hobby Association of America. This magazine offers information and updates on what is happening in the industry.
6 Pages
Frequency: Quarterly

13251 Master Embroidery Manual
Embroidery Trade Association
P.O. Box 794534
Suite 414
Dallas, TX 75379-4534

972-247-0415
888-628-2545; *Fax:* 972-755-2561;
www.mesadist.com/trade_associations
Social Media: Twitter, LinkedIn

John Swinburn, Executive Director
Dolores Cheek, Director Of Membership
Keith Amen, VP

Developed and published by ETA, this manual is an embroiderer's encyclopedia, especially for those new to the embroidery industry. Chapters include hooping & framing, backings & toppings, common goods and fabrics, and much more.
1200 Members
Founded in: 1990

13252 Model Retailer
Kalmbach Publishing Company
21027 Crossroads Circle
PO Box 1612
Waukesha, WI 53187

262-796-8776
800-533-6644; *Fax:* 262-796-8776
hmiller@modelretailer.com;
www.modelretailer.com

Kevin Keefe, Publisher
Hal Miller, Editor
Rick Albers, Advertising Sales Manager
Jim Meinhardt, Circulation Manager

The business of hobbies, from financial and shop management issues to industry news and trends, as well as the latest in product releases. Provides hobby shop entreprenuers with the information, ideas and examples they need in order to be successful retailers.
Frequency: Monthly
Circulation: 6350
Founded in: 1934

13253 Needlework Retailer
Yarn Tree Designs
117 Alexander Avenue
PO Box 2438
Ames, IA 50010-2438

515-232-3121
800-247-3952; *Fax:* 515-232-0789
info@needleworkretailer.com;
www.needleworkretailer.com

Larry Johnson, VP
Megan Chriswisser, Editor

Highlights a variety of new products and designs in needlework. Includes information on upcoming needlework trade shows and association news.
Cost: $12.00
Circulation: 11000

13254 Numismatic News
F+W Media
38 E. 29th Street
New York, NY 10016

212-447-1400; *Fax:* 212-447-5231
contact_us@fwmedia.com;
www.fwpublications.com
Social Media: Facebook, Twitter, LinkedIn

Bill Bright, General Manager
Dave Harper, Editor
Jim Ogle, Chief Financial Officer
Chad Phelps, Chief Digital Officer
Stacie Berger, Communications Director

Provides timely reports on market happenings and news concerning collectible coins. 'Coin Clinic' is a very popular weekly Q&A column that gives readers a chance to learn all about numismatics. The 'Coin Market' section provides comprehensive pricing monthly. Each issue also includes columns with practical how-to advice and historical features by some of the top experts in the field including 'Making the Grade' and 'Facts about Fakes.' Sponsors the annual Mid-America Coin Convention.
Cost: $35.99
72 Pages
Frequency: Weekly
Circulation: 34392
Founded in: 1952
Mailing list available for rent

13255 Play Meter
Skybird Publishing Company
PO Box 337
Metairie, LA 70004-0337

504-488-7003
888-473-2376; *Fax:* 504-488-7083
news@playmeter.com; www.playmeter.com
Social Media: Facebook, Twitter, LinkedIn

Bonnie Theard, Editor
Carol P. Lally, Publisher
Carol Ann Lally, President
Bonnie Theard, Managing Editor
Courtney McDuff, Assistant Editor

Trade publication that provides members with information on the coin-operated entertainment industry, including upcoming trade shows, new products, ongoing trends and more.
Cost: $60.00
Frequency: Monthly
Circulation: 60000
Founded in: 1974

13256 Playthings
Reed Business Information
360 Park Ave S
4th Floor
New York, NY 10010-1737

646-746-6400
800-309-3332; *Fax:* 646-756-7583
mlaporte@reedbusiness.com;
www.reedbusiness.com
Social Media: Twitter, LinkedIn

John Poulin, CEO
Larry Oliver, VP/Group Publisher
Micki LaPorte, Circulation Director
James Reed, Owner
Andrew Rak, Senior Vice President

Emphasizes a merchandising approach for improving sales and promotional techniques. Features include new product listings, market reports, licensing updates and general industry trends.
Cost: $33.95
80 Pages
Frequency: Monthly
Founded in: 1903
Printed in 4 colors on glossy stock

13257 SCRYE
F+W Media
38 E. 29th Street
New York, NY 10016

212-447-1400; *Fax:* 212-447-5231
contact_us@fwmedia.com;
www.fwpublications.com
Social Media: Facebook, Twitter, LinkedIn

Mark Williams, Publisher
Joyce Greenholdt, Editor
Jim Ogle, Chief Financial Officer
Chad Phelps, Chief Digital Officer
Stacie Berger, Communications Director

The most respected price guide in the industry for collectible card games and collectible miniatures. SCRYE also provides collectors and players the latest news, checklists, player strategies, deck building tips and tricks for collectible card games. The latest collectible card games are reviewed in each issue in addition to related role-playing and board games.
Cost: $29.98
160 Pages
Frequency: Monthly
Circulation: 47000
Founded in: 1994
Mailing list available for rent

13258 Snapshot Memories
PRIMEDIA Consumer Magazine & Internet Group
2 News Plaza
PO Box 1790
Peoria, IL 61656-1790

309-682-6626; *Fax:* 309-679-5057

Mike Irish, Associate Publisher
Miram Olson, Editor-in-Chief

Scrapbook page idea magazine.
Cost: $16.98
92 Pages
Frequency: Quarterly
Circulation: 90,000
Founded in: 1998
Printed in 4 colors on glossy stock

13259 Sports Collectors Digest
F+W Media
38 E. 29th Street
New York, NY 10016

212-447-1400; *Fax:* 212-447-5231
contact_us@fwmedia.com;
www.fwpublications.com
Social Media: Facebook, Twitter, LinkedIn

Dean Listle, Publisher
TS O'Connell, Editor
Jim Ogle, Chief Financial Officer
Chad Phelps, Chief Digital Officer
Stacie Berger, Communications Director

The Bible of Hobby covers every aspect of modern sports collecting, including cards, memorabilia, equipment, lithographs, figurines, and autographed material. Online collecting, graded cards, memorabilia and auction news are covered each week in specially designed sections that complement columns from some of the most respected experts in the hobby and up-to-date card pricing checklisting data from expert analysts, along with display advertisements from all the

major dealers in the country.
Cost: $49.95
96 Pages
Frequency: Weekly
Circulation: 23356
Founded in: 1973
Mailing list available for rent

13260 **Stamp Collector**
F+W Media
38 E. 29th Street
New York, NY 10016
212-447-1400; *Fax:* 212-447-5231
contact_us@fwmedia.com;
www.fwpublications.com
Social Media: Facebook, Twitter, LinkedIn
Wayne Youngblood, Publisher
Jill Ruesch, Ad Manager
Jim Ogle, Chief Financial Officer
Chad Phelps, Chief Digital Officer
Stacie Berger, Communications Director
Covers a wide variety of US & foreign stamp news. Sepcial inserts cover topicals, errors, postal history, and many others. Regular columns and features include 'Decoding the Catalog,' 'Q&A,' 'Meet the Designer,' 'Postal History,' 'New Stamps of the World,' 'Stamp Values Today,' an auction guide and the most extensive stamp show calendar in the hobby. The first issue each month cotains Stamp Wholesaler - stamp dealer info that is used as a 'philatelic phone book' by the entire industry.
Cost: $32.98
60 Pages
Circulation: 13251
Founded in: 1931
Mailing list available for rent

13261 **Tole World**
EGW.com
4075 Papazian Way
Suite 208
Fremont, CA 94538-4372
510-668-0268; *Fax:* 510-668-0280;
www.toleworld.com
Chris Slaughter, VP
Rickie Wilson, Advertisement Manager
Serving crafters in the decorative painting field; each issue features 10 to 12 projects complete with full color photographs, step-by-step instructions and line art patterns. Project designs come from the nation's leading decorative artists, many of whom are also teachers in the field.
Cost: $35.94
84 Pages
Frequency: Quarterly
Circulation: 85956
Founded in: 1977

13262 **Toy Book**
Adventure Publishing Group
1107 Broadway
Suite 1204
New York, NY 10010
212-575-4510; *Fax:* 212-575-4521;
www.adventurepub.com
Owen Shorts, Owner
Nelson Lombardi, Editor
A Schwartz, Marketing
Anthony Guardiola, Production Manager
Keeps readers abreast of new products and marketing information related to the industry.
Cost: $48.00
Frequency: Monthly
Circulation: 18000
Founded in: 1980

13263 **Toy Shop**
F+W Media
38 E. 29th Street
New York, NY 10016
212-447-1400; *Fax:* 212-447-5231
contact_us@fwmedia.com;
www.fwpublications.com
Social Media: Facebook, Twitter, LinkedIn
Mark Williams, Publisher
Tom Bartsch, Editor
David Nussbaum, CEO/Chairman
Chad Phelps, Chief Digital Officer
Stacie Berger, Communications Director
A complete marketplace for buyers and sellers of toys, action figures, Barbie, Hot Wheels, character toys, and more. Offers thousands of easy-to-read, categorized classified ads, display ads, and a complete editorial package covering baby-boomer toys, vintage collectibles, TV toys, action figures, and many helpful Q&A columns. Also contains up-to-date market trends as well as thorough auction updates and reports from toy shows nationwide.
Cost: $33.98
76 Pages
Circulation: 11577
Founded in: 1988
Mailing list available for rent

13264 **Trapper & Predator**
F+W Media
38 E. 29th Street
New York, NY 10016
212-447-1400; *Fax:* 212-447-5231
contact_us@fwmedia.com;
www.fwpublications.com
Social Media: Facebook, Twitter, LinkedIn
Hugh McAloon, Publisher
Paul Wait, Editor
Jim Ogle, Chief Financial Officer
Chad Phelps, Chief Digital Officer
Stacie Berger, Communications Director
Contains news, in-depth features, and how-to tips on trapping, the art of predator calling, and animal damage control. Contributors include the top names in the business. Regular columns and departments include 'The Fure Shed,' 'Let's Swap Ideas,' 'Q&A,' and news from state trapping associations nationwide.
Cost: $18.95
80 Pages
Circulation: 38260
Founded in: 1975
Mailing list available for rent

13265 **Tuff Stuff**
F+W Media
38 E. 29th Street
New York, NY 10016
212-447-1400; *Fax:* 212-447-5231
contact_us@fwmedia.com;
www.fwpublications.com
Social Media: Facebook, Twitter, LinkedIn
Dean Listle, Publisher
Rocky Landsverk, Editor
Jim Ogle, Chief Financial Officer
Chad Phelps, Chief Digital Officer
Stacie Berger, Communications Director
A guide to the sports card and collectibles hobby. Coverage of sports cards includes the latest prices on baseball, football, basketball, hockey, racing, and more. Each issue lists pricing information on Hall of Fame baseball and football memorabilia, autographed items, and commentary on the sports card industry. Columns and opinion pieces include a Q&A section, directories to professional teams, geographical and product directories, and hobby dealer listings for the US and Canada.
Cost: $29.95
Frequency: Monthly
Circulation: 175,682
Founded in: 1983
Mailing list available for rent

13266 **Turkey & Turkey Hunting**
F+W Media
38 E. 29th Street
New York, NY 10016
212-447-1400; *Fax:* 212-447-5231
contact_us@fwmedia.com;
www.fwpublications.com
Social Media: Facebook, Twitter, LinkedIn
David Nussbaum, CEO/Chairman
James Schlender, Editor
Jim Ogle, Chief Financial Officer
Chad Phelps, Chief Digital Officer
Stacie Berger, Communications Director
Edited for serious, technical, year-round, gun and bow turkey hunters. Features emphasize success and enjoyment of the sport. Articles focus on hunting, scouting, turkey behavior and biology, hunting ethics, new equipment, methodologies, turkey management, and current research. Columns include 'Tree Call,' 'Mail Pouch,' 'Turkey Biology,' a Q&A column, 'Hunter's Library,' 'Turkey Gear,' and 'Last Call.'
Cost: $15.95
72 Pages
Circulation: 68962
Founded in: 1975
Mailing list available for rent

13267 **Weekend Woodcrafts**
EGW.com
1041 Shary Circle
Concord, CA 94518-2407
925-671-9852; *Fax:* 925-671-0692
info@egw.com; www.weekendwoodcrafts.com
Chris Slaughter, Circulation Director
Rickie Wilson, Advertising
Wide selection of easy-to-finish wood projects ranging from craft fair novelties and decorative home-accents to useful housewares and wooden toys.
Cost: $35.94
68 Pages
Frequency: Monthly
Founded in: 1980

13268 **Wood Strokes**
EGW.com
1041 Shary Circle
Concord, CA 94518-2407
925-671-9852; *Fax:* 925-671-0692;
www.egw.com
Chris Slaughter, Circulation Manager
Wide selection of easy-to-finish decorative wood painting projects ranging from craft fair novelties and decorative home accents to useful housewares and wooden toys.
Cost: $5.99
76 Pages
Circulation: 110437

13269 **World Coin News**
F+W Media
38 E. 29th Street
New York, NY 10016
212-447-1400; *Fax:* 212-447-5231
contact_us@fwmedia.com;
www.fwpublications.com
Social Media: Facebook, Twitter, LinkedIn
Bill Bright, General Manager
Dave Harper, Editor
Jim Ogle, Chief Financial Officer
Chad Phelps, Chief Digital Officer
Stacie Berger, Communications Director
Recognized as the leading authority on world coins. It regularly reports on new issues, auctions and other coin news from around the world. Features by some of the top experts in the field provide in-depth historical information on coins and the countries that issue them. Regular features include World Coin Clinic (Q&A), World Coin

Roundup (newly issued coins), Rule Britannia, Nautical Numismatics, Mexican Potpourri, and Coin Critters. Each issue provides a calendar of shows.
Cost: $30.99
84 Pages
Frequency: Monthly
Circulation: 8729
Founded in: 1952
Mailing list available for rent

Trade Shows

13270 **ACC Craft Show**
American Craft Council
21 S Eltings Corner Road
Highland, NY 12528
845-883-6100
800-836-3670; *Fax:* 845-883-6130
shows@craftcouncil.org; www.craftcouncil.org
Craft fair.
Frequency: Annual

13271 **APS AmeriStamp Expo**
American Philatelic Society
100 Match Factory Place
Bellafonte, PA 16823-1367
814-933-3803; *Fax:* 814-933-6128
stampshow@stamps.org; www.stamps.org
Scott English, Executive Director
Megan Orient, Manager, Shows & Exhibitions
Kathleen Edwards, Shows & Exhibitions Assistant
Annual event for postage stamp collectors, featuring 75 dealers, 50 meetings and services, auction, 5,000 pages of exhibits and beginner actions.
Frequency: Annual/February-March
Founded in: 1957

13272 **APS Stampshow**
American Philatelic Society
100 Match Factory Place
Bellefonte, PA 16823-1367
814-933-3803; *Fax:* 814-933-6128
stampshow@stamps.org; www.stamps.org
Scott English, Executive Director
Megan Orient, Manager, Shows & Exhibitions
Kathleen Edwards, Shows & Exhibitions Assistant
Annual show for postage stamp collectors. Includes 150 dealers buying and selling material, more than 100 seminars, and 10,000 pages of stamps in collection.
Frequency: Annual/August

13273 **AQSG Conference and Annual Meeting**
American Quilt Study Group
1610 L St
Lincoln, NE 68508-2509
402-477-1181; *Fax:* 402-477-1183
aqsg2@americanquiltstudygroup.org; www.americanquiltstudygroup.org
Social Media: Twitter, LinkedIn
Lisa Erlandsonn, President
Lenna DeMarco, VP
Flavin Glover, VP
Judy J. Brott Buss, Ph.D., Executive Director
Anne E. Schuff, Member Services Coordinator
For members. Research presentations and quilt and textile study
200 Attendees
Frequency: Annual
Mailing list available for rent

13274 **ASD/AMD Group**
Flectcher
2950 31st Street
Suite 100
Santa Monica, CA 90405
310-255-4633; *Fax:* 310-396-8476
15000 Attendees

13275 **American Camping Association Conference & Exhibits**
5000 State Road 67 N
Martinsville, IN 46151-7902
765-342-8456
800-428-2267; *Fax:* 765-342-2065
bwilliems@aca-camps.org
http://www.acacamps.org
Peg Smith, CEO
Bill Willems, Director Business
One hundred fifty booths of arts and crafts, computer software, sporting goods, waterfront equipment and more plus a seminar and workshop.
1,200 Attendees
Frequency: Annual
Founded in: 1943

13276 **American Craft Council Fairs**
ACC
21 S Elting Corners Road
Highland, NY 12528-2805
845-883-6100
800-836-3470; *Fax:* 612-355-2330
shows@craftcouncil.org; www.craftcouncil.org
Nine fairs nationwide each year. Each show incorporates crafts from the ceramics, wood, metal, mixed media, fiber, glass, jewelry, accessories and related industries. Most fairs include retail portion (public sales); some fairs also have wholesale (trade) component.

13277 **American International Toy Fair**
Toy Industry Association
1115 Broadway
Suite 400
New York, NY 10010
212-675-1141; *Fax:* 212-675-3246; www.toy-tia.org
Laura Green, VP Trade Shows/Meetings
Diane Cardinale, Public Information Manager
1,800-2,000 booths for producers of all types of toys and games, party and holiday items, models, hobby products, as well as collectibles, dolls, plush and miniatures. Attendees are retail buyers and trade professionals. Seminar and program.
20000 Attendees
Frequency: Annual
Founded in: 1903

13278 **American Needlepoint Guild Show**
3410 Valley Creek Circle
Middleton, WI 53562-1990
608-831-3328; *Fax:* 608-831-0651
seminars@needlepoint.org; www.needlepoint.org
Estelle Kelley, Seminars Director
Two hundred exhibits of needlework pieces, banquet and luncheon.
830 Attendees
Frequency: Annual
Founded in: 1972

13279 **American Numismatic Association Trade Show**
8181 N Cascade Avenue
Colorado Springs, CO 80903
719-632-2646
webmaster@money.org; www.money.org
Brenda Bishop, Show Manager
Nancy Green, Manager
Four hundred twenty five booths of coins, medals and paper money.
15M Attendees
Frequency: August

13280 **American Quilt Study Group**
American Quilt Study Group
1610 L St
Lincoln, NE 68508-2509
402-477-1181; *Fax:* 402-477-1181
aqsg2@americanquiltstudygroup.org; www.americanquiltstudygroup.org
Social Media: Twitter, LinkedIn
Lisa Erlandsonn, President
Lenna DeMarco, Vice President
Kathy Moore, VP
Judy J. Brott Buss, Ph.D., Executive Director
Anne E. Schuff, Member Services Coordinator
Annual Seminar, Annual Journal member organization
Frequency: October, Kansas
Founded in: 1980
Mailing list available for rent

13281 **American Stamp Dealers Association Stamp Shows**
3 School Street
Suite 201
Glen Cove, NY 11542-2548
516-759-7000; *Fax:* 800-369-8207
Joseph Savarese, Show Manager/Executive VP
Two hundred booths.
12.5M Attendees

13282 **Americover**
American First Day Cover Society
PO Box 1335
Maplewood, NJ 07040
973-762-2012; *Fax:* 973-762-7916
webmaster@afdcs.org; www.afdcs.org
Steve Ripley, Show Manager
US and international first day postal covers, USPS first day ceremonies at most shows, 50 stamp dealers, cover dealers, cachetmalchers philatelic suppliers.
1500 Attendees
Frequency: Annual

13283 **Annual Spring-Easter Arts & Crafts Show & Sale**
Finger Lakes Craftsmen Shows
1 Freshour Road
Shortsville, NY 14548
585-289-9439; *Fax:* 585-289-9440
Ronald L Johnson, President
Annual show of 150 exhibitirs of arts and crafts manufacturers. Exhibits include handcrafted arts and crafts, including photos and prints.
9000 Attendees
Frequency: March
Founded in: 1999

13284 **Antique Arms Show**
P.O. Box 2917
Cathedral City, CA 92234
760- 20- 448; *Fax:* 760-202-4793; www.antiquearmsshow.com
Wallace Beinfield
Public show with 850 booths of antiques and collectibles.
4M Attendees
Frequency: January

13285 **Association of Crafts and Creative Industries Show: ACCI Show**
Offinger Management Company

1100-H Brandywine Boulevard
PO Box 3388
Zanesville, OH 43702

740-452-4541
888-360-2224; *Fax:* 740-452-2552
accishow@offinger.com; www.accicrafts.org
Social Media: Facebook, Twitter, LinkedIn

Marrijane Jones, Executive Director
Erica McKenzie, ACCI Communications Manager

The ACCI Show is sponsored by the Association of Crafts and Creative Industries. Over 1,300 booths are represented, featuring general crafts, softcrafts, art materials and framing, scrapbooking materials and floral, home and garden items.
8000+ Attendees
Frequency: Annual

13286 Christmas Gift & Hobby Show
HSI Show Productions
PO Box 502797
Indianapolis, IN 46250

317-576-9933
800-215-1700; *Fax:* 317-576-9955
info@hsishows.com; www.hsishows.com

Donell Hebererwalton, Sales Director
Todd Jameson, Show Manager
45000 Attendees

13287 Christmas Gift and Hobby Show
HSI Show Productions
PO Box 502797
Indianapolis, IN 46250-7797

317-576-9933
800-215-1700; *Fax:* 317-576-9955
info@hsishows.com; www.hsishows.com

Donell Hebererwalton, Sales Director
Todd Jameson, Show Manager

Annual show of 360 exhibitors of arts, crafts and giftware.
70M Attendees

13288 Coin and Stamp Exposition: San Francisco
Bick International
PO Box 854
Van Nuys, CA 91408

818-997-6496; *Fax:* 818-988-4337
iibick@sbcglobal.net;
www.bickinternational.com

Israel I Bick, Managing Director
5000 Attendees
Frequency: June/September, Annually

13289 Doll, Teddy Bear & Toy Show & Sale
Jones Publishing
9572 Forest Hills Lodge & Route 13
Rockford, IL 54945-5000

715-445-5000

JoAnn Reynolds, Contact

Great assortment of toys featuring teddy bears of all kinds.

13290 Eastern States Doll, Toy, and Teddy Bear Show and Sale
Maven Company
PO Box 937
Plandome, NY 11030

914-248-4646; *Fax:* 914-248-0800;
www.mavencompany.com

N Chittenden, VP

Wide variety of dolls, toys and teddy bears. Largest show of its kind in the northeast.
5000 Attendees
Frequency: November/April
Founded in: 1982

13291 Ed Expo
National School Supply & Equipment Association
8380 Colesville Road
Suite 250
Silver Spring, MD 20910

301-495-0240
800-395-5550; *Fax:* 301-495-3330
nssea@nssea.org; www.nssea.org

Bill Duffy, VP Operations
Adrienne Dayton, VP Marketing

The world's premier back-to-school purchasing event, specifically geared toward helping the educational products/parent-teacher retailer, cataloger and full-line distributor find the best teaching tools and resources for the classrooms of today, tomorrow and the future.
3000 Attendees
Frequency: Annual/April

13292 Evolution Championship Series

evo.shoryuken.com
Social Media: Facebook, Twitter

Annual open eSports tournament focused on fighting games.
Frequency: Annual
Founded in: 1996

13293 HIA: Hobby Industries of America Trade Show
Hobby Industries of America
319 E 54th Street
PO Box 348
Elmwood Park, NJ 07407

201-794-1133; *Fax:* 201-798-0657
sberger@craftandhobby.org; www.hobby.org

Steve Berger, Executive Director

International trade show open to qualified professionals and is the industry's only market research show.
10000 Attendees

13294 Halloween Costume and Party Show
TransWorld Exhibits
1850 Oak Street
Northfield, IL 60093
847-784-6905
800-323-5462; *Fax:* 847-446-3523;
www.transworldexhibits.com

Don Olstinske, Manager
Stephanie Geitner, Operations Director

13295 International Coin + Stamp Collection Society
Bick International
PO Box 854
Van Nuys, CA 91408

818-997-6496; *Fax:* 818-988-4337
iibick@sbcglobal.net;
www.bickinternational.com

Israel I Bick, Managing Director
5000 Attendees
Frequency: Annual/December/May, NV

13296 International Gift and Collectible Expo
F+W Media
38 E. 29th Streett
New York, NY 10016

212-447-1400; *Fax:* 212-447-5231
contact_us@fwmedia.com;
www.fwpublications.com
Social Media: Twitter, LinkedIn

Claude Chmiel, Show Producer
John Swinburn, Executive Director
17000 Attendees
Frequency: June

13297 International JPMA Show
Juvenile Products Manufacturers Association
15000 Commerce Parkway
Suite C
Mt Laurel, NJ 08054

856-439-0500; *Fax:* 856-439-0525;
www.jpma.org

Linda Still, Director of Trade Show

Items of interest to retailers of children's apparel and toys.
3000 Attendees
Frequency: Annual

13298 International Miniature Collectibles Trade Show
10 Estes Street
Ipswich, MA 1938

978-356-6500
800-653-2726; *Fax:* 978-356-6565;
www.miniatures.org/showlist
Social Media: Facebook, Twitter, LinkedIn

Frequency: August

13299 Just Kidstuff & The Museum Source
George Little Management
10 Bank Street
Suite 1200
White Plains, NY 10606

914-486-6070
800-272-7469; *Fax:* 914-948-2918
George Little II, President
45000 Attendees

13300 Knitting Guild Association Conference
The Knitting Guild Association (TKGA)
1100-H Brandwine Blvd.
Zanesville, OH 43701-7303

740-452-4541; *Fax:* 740-452-2552
tkga@tkga.com; www.tkga.com
Social Media: Facebook, Twitter, LinkedIn

Penny Sitler, Executive Director

The TKGA conference is held twice each year and offers items such as fiber, stitching tools, patterns, books, finishing accessories and more.
10000 Members
Mailing list available for rent

13301 National Dollhouse & Miniatures Trade Show & Convention
Miniatures Association of America
10 Estes Street
Ipswich, MA 1938

978-356-6500
800-653-2726; *Fax:* 978-356-6565
miniatures.org/ShowList
Social Media: Facebook, Twitter, LinkedIn

1400 Attendees

13302 National Merchandise Show
Miller Freeman Publications
One Penn Plaza
PO Box 2549
New York, NY 10119

212-714-1300; *Fax:* 212-714-1313

16000 Attendees

13303 National NeedleArts Association Trade Show
National Needlework Association
PO Box 3388
Zanesville, OH 43702-3388

740-452-4541
800-889-8662; *Fax:* 740-452-2552
tnna.info@offinger.com; www.tnna.org

Joel Woodcock, VP
Frequency: January

13304 **National Sewing Show: Home Sewing Association**
American Home Sewing and Craft Association
1350 Broadway
Suite 1601
New York, NY 10018

212-714-1633; *Fax:* 212-714-1655
info@sewing.org; www.sewing.org

Pat Kobishyn, Show Manager

Two hundred exhibits of fabric, notions, patterns, sewing and trimmings. Attended by professionals from major chain stores, independent retailers, wholesalers and manufacturers.
3000 Attendees
Frequency: Annual

13305 **SHOPA**
SHOPA
3131 Elbee Road
Dayton, OH 45439-1900
937-297-2250
800-854-7467; *Fax:* 937-297-2254;
www.shopa.org

Steven Jacober, President
Doris Condron, Director of Communications
7500 Attendees
Frequency: November

13306 **School Equipment Show**
National School Supply & Equipment Association
8380 Colesville Rd
Suite 250
Silver Spring, MD 20910-6225

301-495-0240
800-395-5550; *Fax:* 301-495-3330
customerservice@nssea.org; www.nssea.org
Social Media: Facebook, Twitter, LinkedIn

Jim McGarry, President/CEO
Rashad Cheeks, Meetings Coordinator
Tamara Davis, Bookkeeper/Office Manager
Karen Prince, Director of Membership
Bill Duffy, Vice President - Operations

Source new products, engage in industry discussion, hear perspectives on current issues, and network with existing and potential new suppliers, distributors and purchasing influencers.
Frequency: Annual/November

13307 **Souvenirs Gifts & Novelties Trade Association**
Kane Communications
7000 Terminal Square
Suite 210
Upper Darby, PA 19082-2330

610-734-2420; *Fax:* 610-734-2423;
www.souvmag.com

Al Barry, Show Manager
Larry White, VP Marketing

Trade show serving amusements, museums, zoos, entertainment, bowling, and retailers. Seminars and networking party.
5000 Attendees
Frequency: July

13308 **Variety Merchandise Show**
Miller Freeman Publications
One Penn Plaza
PO Box 2549
New York, NY 10119

212-714-1300; *Fax:* 212-714-1313

20000 Attendees

13309 **Western States Toy and Hobby Show**
Western Toy and Hobby Representative Association
9397 Reserve Drive
Corona, CA 92883

951-771-1598; *Fax:* 909-277-1599;
www.wthra.com

Phylis St. John, Contact

If it's for kids, it's here. Show is for trade members only, not open to the public.
3000 Attendees
Frequency: March

13310 **iHobby Expo**
Hobby Manufacturers Association
PO Box 315
Butter, NJ 07405-0315

973-283-9088; *Fax:* 973-838-7124
pat.koziol@hmahobby.org;
www.hmahobby.org
Social Media: Twitter, LinkedIn

Patricia S. Koziol, Executive Director
Jodi Araujo, Expositions and Events Manager

Models, trains, rc, cars, boats, planes and more
Frequency: October

Directories & Databases

13311 **American International Toy Fair Official Directory of Showrooms & Exhibits**
Toy Industry Association
1115 Broadway
Suite 400
New York, NY 10010-3466

212-675-1142; *Fax:* 212-633-1429;
www.toy-tia.org

Thomas Conley, President
Diane Cardinale, Public Information Manager

Over 1,500 toy, game and hobby decoration manufacturers and their representatives are profiled.
Cost: $50.00
400 Pages
Frequency: Annual
Circulation: 12,000

13312 **Complete Directory of Collectibles**
Sutton Family Communications & Publishing Company
920 State Route 54 East
Elmitch, KY 42343

270-276-9500
jlsutton@apex.net

Theresa Sutton, Publisher
Lee Sutton, Editor

Print-out from database of wholesalers, manufacturers, distributors, importers and close-out houses. Database is updated daily to guarantee the most current and up-to-date sources available.
Cost: $67.50
100 Pages

13313 **Complete Directory of Crafts and Hobbies**
Sutton Family Communications & Publishing Company
920 State Route 54 East
Elmitch, KY 42343

270-276-9500
jlsutton@apex.net

Theresa Sutton, Editor
Lee Sutton, General Manager

Print-out from database of wholesalers, manufacturers, distributors, importers and close-out houses. Database is updated daily to guarantee the most current and up-to-date sources available.
Cost: $54.50
100+ Pages

13314 **Complete Directory of Figurines**
Sutton Family Communications & Publishing Company
920 State Route 54 East
Elmitch, KY 42343

270-276-9500
jlsutton@apex.net

Theresa Sutton, Publisher
Lee Sutton, Editor

Print-out from database of wholesalers, manufacturers, distributors, importers and close-out houses. Database is updated daily to guarantee the most current and up-to-date sources available.
Cost: $44.50
100 Pages

13315 **Complete Directory of Games**
Sutton Family Communications & Publishing Company
920 State Route 54 East
Elmitch, KY 42343

270-276-9500
jlsutton@apex.net

Theresa Sutton, Publisher
Lee Sutton, Editor

Print-out from database of wholesalers, manufacturers, distributors, importers and close-out houses. Database is updated daily to guarantee the most current and up-to-date sources available.
Cost: $39.50
100 Pages

13316 **Complete Directory of Novelties**
Sutton Family Communications & Publishing Company
920 State Route 54 East
Elmitch, KY 42343

270-276-9500
jlsutton@apex.net

Theresa Sutton, Publisher
Lee Sutton, Editor

Print-out from database of wholesalers, manufacturers, distributors, importers and close-out houses. Database is updated daily to guarantee the most current and up-to-date sources available.
Cost: $79.50
100 Pages

13317 **Complete Directory of Pewter Items**
Sutton Family Communications & Publishing Company
920 State Route 54 East
Elmitch, KY 42343

270-276-9500
jlsutton@apex.net

Theresa Sutton, Publisher
Lee Sutton, Editor

Print-out from database of wholesalers, manufacturers, distributors, importers and close-out houses. Database is updated daily to guarantee the most current and up-to-date sources available.
Cost: $39.50
100 Pages

13318 **Complete Directory of Plush and Stuffed Toys and Dolls**
Sutton Family Communications & Publishing Company
920 State Route 54 East
Elmitch, KY 42343

270-276-9500
jlsutton@apex.net

Theresa Sutton, Editor
Lee Sutton, General Manager

Print-out from database of wholesalers, manufacturers, distributors, importers and close-out houses. Database is updated daily to guarantee the most current and up-to-date sources available.
Cost: $39.50
100+ Pages

13319 **Complete Directory of Posters, Buttons and Novelties**
Sutton Family Communications & Publishing Company
920 State Route 54 East
Elmitch, KY 42343
270-276-9500
jlsutton@apex.net
Theresa Sutton, Editor
Lee Sutton, General Manager
Print-out from database of wholesalers, manufacturers, distributors, importers and close-out houses. Database is updated daily to guarantee the most current and up-to-date sources available.
Cost: $39.50
100+ Pages

13320 **Complete Directory of Toys and Games**
Sutton Family Communications & Publishing Company
920 State Route 54 East
Elmitch, KY 42343
270-276-9500
jlsutton@apex.net
Theresa Sutton, Editor
Lee Sutton, General Manager
Print-out from database of wholesalers, manufacturers, distributors, importers and close-out houses. Database is updated daily to guarantee the most current and up-to-date sources available.
Cost: $44.50
100+ Pages

13321 **Directory of Manufacturer Representatives Service Suppliers**
Hobby Industry Association
319 E 54th St
Elmwood Park, NJ 07407-2712
201-794-1133; *Fax:* 201-797-0657
sberger@craftandhobby.org;
www.craftandhobby.org
Steve Berger, CEO
Two hundred manufacturers representatives and 105 trade show booth demonstrators working in the hobby equipment industry.
Cost: $25.00
Frequency: Biennial

13322 **Game Manufacturers Association Membership Directory**
Game Manufacturers Association
240 N. Fifth St.
Suite 340
Columbus, OH 43215
614-255-4500; *Fax:* 614-255-4499;
www.gama.org
Social Media: Twitter, LinkedIn
Justin Ziran, President
Jamie Chambers, Vice President
Aaron Witten, Treasurer
Brian Dalrymple, Secretary
Approximately 350 member manufacturers and distributors of adventure games.
Frequency: Annual
Founded in: 1977
Mailing list available for rent

13323 **Games and Entertainment on CD-ROM**
Mecklermedia Corporation
20 Ketchum Street
Westport, CT 06880-5908
203-341-2806; *Fax:* 203-454-5840
Over 1,300 multimedia encyclopedias, children's educational software and interactive 'board games'.
Cost: $29.95

13324 **Hobby Industries of America Trade Show Program and Buyers Guide**
Hobby Industry Association
319 E 54th St
Elmwood Park, NJ 07407-2712
201-794-1133; *Fax:* 201-797-0657
hia@ihobby.org; www.craftandhobby.org
Steve Berger, CEO
Over 1000 manufacturers are listed that exhibit at the HIA trade show.
Cost: $25.00
170 Pages
Frequency: Annual
Founded in: 1940

13325 **Hobby Merchandiser Annual Trade Directory**
Hobby Publications
207 Commercial Ct
Morganville, NJ 07751-1099
732-536-5160; *Fax:* 732-536-5761;
www.hobbypub.com
David Gherman, President
Jeff Troy, Editor
Ellen Gherman, Circulation Director
Tracey Decesure, Production Manager
Offers valuable information on manufacturers, wholesalers, industry suppliers and publishers of books and periodicals in the hobby trade industry.
Cost: $35.00
140 Pages
Frequency: Annual
Circulation: 7,000
Founded in: 1945
Mailing list available for rent: 8M names
Printed in 4 colors on glossy stock

13326 **Hobby RoundTable**
GE Information Services
401 N Washington Street
Rockville, MD 20850-1707
301-388-8284
Cathy Ge, Owner
This database offers a forum enabling participants to share information on hobby-related topics, the hobby industry and hobby-related software.
Frequency: Bulletin Board

13327 **Radio Control Hobby Membership Directory**
Radio Control Hobby Trade Association
31632 N Ellis Avenue
Unit 111
Volo, IL 60073
847-740-1111; *Fax:* 847-740-1111;
www.rchta.org
Members and manufacturers of radio control products.
Founded in: 1983

Industry Web Sites

13328 **http://gold.greyhouse.com**
G.O.L.D Grey House OnLine Databases
Grey House Publishing's online database platform, GOLD, offers Quick Search, Keyword Search and Expert Search for most business sectors including hobby and game markets. The GOLD platform makes finding the information you need quick and easy - whether you're a novice searcher or an experienced database user. All of Grey House's directory products are available for subscription on the GOLD platform.

13329 **www.amo-archery.org**
Archery Manufacturers & Merchants Organization
Members are producers and sellers to the archery consumer.

13330 **www.asdaonline.com**
American Stamp Dealers Association
Holds annual International Philatelic Exhibition Interpex. Sponsors the annual International Dealers course. Postage stamp mega event twice a year (spring and fall).

13331 **www.craftdesigners.org**
Society of Craft Designers
The Society of Craft Designers (SCD), founded in 1975, is a professional organization for those who believe that quality craft design is the basis of a strong and viable craft industry. It is the only membership organization exclusively serving those who design for the consumer craft industry.

13332 **www.greyhouse.com**
Grey House Publishing
Authoritative reference directories for most business sectors including hobby and game markets. Users can search the online databases with varied search criteria allowing for custom searches by product category, geographic area, sales volume, keyword, subject and more. Full Grey House catalog and online ordering also available.

13333 **www.hobby.org**
Hobby Industry Association
The world's largest trade association in the craft and hobby market. The group produces an International Trade Show open to qualified professionals and is the industrys only market research show.

13334 **www.hubcityhobby.com**
5182 Old Highway 11
Suite 3
Hattiesburg, MS 39402
601-264-1040; www.hubcityhobby.com
Social Media: Facebook, Twitter
Links to clubs, events, races and shows of interest to hobbyists.

13335 **www.mria.org**
Model Railroad Industry Association
Works to publicize the hobby and to keep members informed on the industry. Assists clubs and retailers in their shows.

13336 **www.nssea.org**
Naitonal School Supplu Equipment
Trade Association for the educational products industry.

13337 **www.rchta.org**
Radio Control Hobby Trade Association
For manufacturers and distributors of model hobby kits and hobby equipment, supplies and services and products associated with retail hobby stores.

13338 **www.stamps.org**
American Philatelic Society
National organization for stamp collectors, offering services including a lending library; insurance for philatelic materials; sales division,

seminars and annual conventions open to the public.

13339 www.tkga.com
The Knitting Guild Association (TKGA)
Membership organization for knitters with focus on knitting education and enhancing knitter's skills

13340 www.tnna.org
National Needlework Association
For maufacturers, suppliers and distributers of needlework and related equipment, supplies and services.

13341 www.toyassociation.org
Toy Industry Association
National organization for U.S. producers and importers of toys, games and children's entertainment products. Represents more than 500 member companies including designers, safety consultants, testing laboratories, licensors, communication professionals and inventors.

13342 www.wccwis.gr.jp/home.html
World Craft Council
A national organization for Handicraft

Associations

13343 African American Association of Innkeepers International
877-422-5777
africanamericaninns@yahoo.com; www.africanamericaninns.com
Association dedicated to increasing awareness of African American-owned inns.

13344 American Hotel & Lodging Association
1250 I Street, N.W.
Suite 1100
Washington, DC 20005-3931
202-289-3100; *Fax:* 202-289-3199
membership@ahla.com; www.ahla.com
Social Media: Facebook, Twitter, LinkedIn
Jim Abrahamson, CHA, CEO, Chair of the Board
Mark Carrier, CHA, Vice-Chair
Katherine Lugar, President/CEO
Geoff Ballotti, Secretary/ Treasurer
Kimberly Miles, CMP, Senior Vice President, Operations
Supports all those involved in managing or franchising properties worldwide. Publishes annual directory.
10000 Members
Founded in: 1910

13345 American Hotel & Lodging Educational Institute
800 N. Magnolia Avenue
Suite 300
Orlando, FL 32803
407-999-8100
800-344-4381; *Fax:* 407-236-7848
info@ahlei.org; www.ahlei.org/
Social Media: Facebook, Twitter, LinkedIn, Google Plus, Youtube, Instagra
Minaz Abji, Board Chairman
S. Kirk Kinsell, Vice Chairman
Paul Kirwin, Secretary/Treasurer
Joori Jeon, Chief Executive Officer
Brenda Moons, CMHS, Senior Vice President, Sales
Fosters education, research programming, and information regarding operating techniques in the lodging industry.
11000 Members
Founded in: 1953

13346 Asian American Hotel Owners Association
1100 Abernathy Road
Suite 1100
Atlanta, GA 30328-6707
404-816-5759; *Fax:* 404-816-6260
info@aahoa.com; www.aahoa.com
Social Media: Facebook, Twitter, LinkedIn, YouTube, Instagram
Bharat (Bruce) Patel, CHO, Chairman
Bhavesh B. Patel, CHO, Vice Chairman
Chip Rogers, President & CEO
Hitesh Patel, CHO, Treasurer
Jagruti Panwala, CHO, Secretary
Supports Asian/American hotel and motel owners and operators.
16600 Members
Founded in: 1989

13347 Associated Luxury Hotels International
1667 K Street, NW
Suite 610
Washington, DC 20006
202-887-7020; *Fax:* 202-887-0085
midatlantic@alhi.com; www.alhi.com
Social Media: Facebook, Twitter, YouTube
Jim Schultenover, President
David Gabri, Chief Executive Officer
Chris Riccardi, Division VP
Mike Coutu, Executive VP & CFO
Ashly Balding, Division VP - East
Provided a National Sales Network to associations and corporations in America for the distinguished hotels and resorts now in 26 states, Canada, Mexico, and the Caribbean.
Founded in: 1986

13348 Bed and Breakfast League
PO Box 9490
Washington, DC 20016-9490
202-363-7767; *Fax:* 202-363-8396
Millie Groobey, Director
A reservation service for bed and breakfasts in Washington, DC, that welcome selected travelers into their homes.
Founded in: 1976

13349 Educational Institute of the American Hotel & Lodging Association
2113 N High St
Lansing, MI 48906-4221
517-372-8800
800-752-4567; *Fax:* 517-372-5141
info@ei-ahla.org; www.ahlei.org
Social Media: Facebook, Twitter
George Glazer, VP
Anthony Farris, Chairman
Thomas J. Corcoran Jr., Vice Chair
Brenda Moons, Senior Vice President of Sales
K.V. Simon, Regional Vice President
A nonprofit educational foundation of the American Hotel & Lodging Association and the world's largest provider of hospitality education training resources, videos, books, workbooks, seminars, management courses, complete training systems and professional certification programs.
120 Members
Founded in: 1953

13350 Green Hotels Association
PO Box 420212
Houston, TX 77242-0212
713-789-8889; *Fax:* 713-789-9786
green@greenhotels.com; www.greenhotels.com
Social Media: Facebook, Twitter
Patricia Griffin, President
Association of hoteliers for environmentally-friendly properties.
Founded in: 1993

13351 Hospitality Financial & Technology Professionals
11709 Boulder Lane
Suite 110
Austin, TX 78726-1832
512-249-5333
800-646-4387; *Fax:* 512-249-1533
membership@hftp.org; www.hftp.org
Social Media: Facebook, Twitter, LinkedIn
Daniel N. Conti, Jr., CHAE, CAM, President
Arlene Ramirez, Vice President
Lyle Worthington, CHTP, Treasurer
Jerry M. Trieber, Immediate Past President
Connie Hong, Executive Services Administrator
Professional society for those in the financial segment of the hospitality industry.
4,700 Members
Founded in: 1952
Mailing list available for rent

13352 Hotel Employees and Restaurant Employees
275 7th Avenue
16th Floor
New York, NY 10001-6708
212-265-7000
ccarrera@unitehere.org; www.unitehere.org
Social Media: Facebook, Twitter, Google Plus
D. Taylor, General President
Jo Marie Agriesti, General VP
Sherri Chiesa, Secretary-Treasurer
Maria Elena Durazo, General VP for Immigration
Peter Ward, Recording Secretary
Hosts a diverse membership, comprised largely of immigrants and including high percentages of African-American, Latino, and Asia-American workers. The majority of members are women.
850m Members
Founded in: 1891

13353 International Council on Hotel, Restaurant and Institutional Education
2810 North Parham Road
Suite 230
Richmond, VA 23294
804-346-4800; *Fax:* 804-346-5009
webmaster@chrie.org; www.chrie.org
Social Media: Facebook, Twitter, LinkedIn
Maureen Brookes, President
Martin O'Neill, Immediate Past President
Margaret Steiskal, VicePresident
Wanda Costen, Secretary
Stephanie Hein, Treasurer
A nonprofit professional association which provides programs and services to continually improve the quality of global education, research, service, and business operations in the hospitality and tourism industry.
Founded in: 1946

13354 International Executive Housekeepers Association
1001 Eastwind Drive
Suite 301
Westerville, OH 43081-3361
614-895-7166
800-200-6342; *Fax:* 614-895-1248
excel@ieha.org; www.ieha.org
Social Media: Facebook, Twitter, LinkedIn
Michael Patterson, President
Wayne Bledy, Director at Large
Wanda Joyce, Secretary/Treasurer
Lorrie Tripp, President-Elect
Sarah Larsen Miller, Convention Manager
An organization for persons working in the housekeeping area of the lodging industry.
3,500 Members
Founded in: 1930

13355 International Facility Management Association
800 Gessner Rd
Suite 900
Houston, TX 77024-4257
713-623-4362; *Fax:* 713-623-6124
ifma@ifma.org; www.ifma.org
Social Media: Facebook, Twitter, LinkedIn, Flickr, Youtube, RSS
Michael D. Feldman, FMP, CM, Chair
Tony Keane, CAE, President and CEO
Maureen Ehrenberg, FRICS, CRE, First Vice Chair

William M. O'Neill, CFM, Second Vice Chair
John Perry, Chief Operating Officer

Certifies facility managers, conducts research, provides educational programs, recognizes facility management degree and certificate programs and produces World Workplace, the world's largest facility management conference and exposition.
24,00 Members
Founded in: 1980
Mailing list available for rent

13356 NEWH: The Hospitality Industry Network
PO Box 322
Shawano, WI 54166

800-593-6394; *Fax:* 800-693-6394
newh.org
Social Media: Facebook, Twitter, LinkedIn

Shelia Lohmiller, Executive Director
Jena Seibel, Deputy Director

The Network of Executive Women in Hospitality promotes the professional development of women in hospitality and related industries.
Founded in: 1984

13357 National Bed & Breakfast Association
1011 W Fifth Street
Suite 300
Austin, TX 78703

512-322-2710; *Fax:* 512-320-0883
Sales@BedandBreakfast.com;
www.bedandbreakfast.com
Social Media: Facebook, Twitter, Pinterest, Google Plus

John Banczac, Vice President
Denis Kashkin, Sr. Directory of Technology
Eric Goldreyer, Founder & President

An organization of services and supplies to the industry offering a list of the best in bed and breakfast accommodations in the USA, Canada and the Caribbean.
Founded in: 1981
Mailing list available for rent

13358 Preferred Hotels and Resorts Worldwide
311 S Wacker Dr
Suite 1900
Chicago, IL 60606-6676

312-913-0400
866-990-9491; *Fax:* 312-913-5124
info@preferredhotels.com;
www.preferredhotels.com
Social Media: Facebook, Twitter, Pinterest, Instagram

John Ubberoth, CEO
Nora Gainer, Director Marketing

Independently owned luxury hotels and resorts. Each provides the highest standards of quality and extraordinary service.
120 Members
Founded in: 1968

13359 Professional Association of Innkeepers International
295 Seven Farms Drive
Suite 236-C
Charleston, SC 29492

856-310-1102
800-468-7244; *Fax:* 856-895-0432
questions@paii.org; www.paii.org
Social Media: Facebook, Twitter, Pinterest, Google+

Jay Karen, CEO
Isabel Abreu, Membership Sales Manager
Brook Patterson, Director of Vendor Services
Ingrid Thorson, Marketing & Communications Manager
Kris Ullmer, Executive Director

Serving bed and breakfast/country inn owners, aspiring innkeepers, inn sitters, vendors with educational and consultative services. International conference.
3000 Members
Founded in: 1988

13360 Select Registry
295 Seven Farms Drive
Suite C-279
Charleston, SC 29492

269-789-0393
800-344-5244; *Fax:* 269-789-0970
maincontact@selectregistry.com;
www.selectregistry.com/
Social Media: Facebook, Twitter

Emily Cisewski, Content Manager
Carol Riggs, Director of Membership Services
Renee Flowers, Director of Marketing
Susan Galvin, Director of Membership Development
Susan Butler, Operations Manager

Represents the finest country inns, B&Bs, and unique small hotels from California to Nova-Scotia. The very best the travel industry has to offer.
400 Members
Founded in: 1968
Mailing list available for rent

13361 Small Luxury Hotels
370 Lexington Avenue
Suite 1506
New York, NY 10017

212-953-2064
800-608-0273
reservation@slh.com; www.slh.com
Social Media: Facebook, Twitter, LinkedIn, Pinterest, Instagram, Google+,

Members are independent owners and managers of deluxe hotels with fewer than 200 rooms.
233 Members
Founded in: 1991

13362 Small Luxury Hotels of the World
370 Lexington Avenue
Suite 1506
New York, NY 10017

212-953-2064
800-608-0273; *Fax:* 212-953-0576
reservation@slh.com; www.slh.com
Social Media: Facebook, Twitter, LinkedIn, Pinterest, Instagram, Google+,

Lanny Grossman, Marketing
Johnathan Slater, Chairman
Ed Donaldson, Manager

Collection of independently owned exclusive hotels in more than 50 countries. Selected for style and comfort, properties include spas, country houses, golf resorts, island retreats, city sanctuaries, game and wilderness lodges. Publishes directory.
300 Members
Founded in: 1991

13363 Textile Rental Services Association
1800 Diagonal Road
Suite 200
Alexandria, VA 22314-2842

703-519-0029
877-770-9274; *Fax:* 703-519-0026
trsa@trsa.org; www.trsa.org
Social Media: Facebook, Twitter, LinkedIn, RSS, YouTube

Roger Cocivera, President
George F. Ferencza, VP

Develops new programs and services to help textile rental operators meet today's challenges.
1400 Members
Founded in: 1913

Newsletters

13364 AHA Hotline Newsletter
American Hospitality Association
603 S Pulaski
PO Box 3866
Little Rock, AR 72201

501-376-2323
800-472-5022; *Fax:* 501-376-6517;
www.arhospitality.org
Social Media: Facebook, Twitter, LinkedIn

Montine McNulty, Executive Director
Rita Walker, Executive Assistant
Amanda Glover, Education Coordinator
Holly Heer, Director of Membership
Kristen Smith, Director of Finance

For members, focuses on trends in the hospitality industry, upcoming events, training and education opportunities and more.
Frequency: Monthly

13365 AHF Developments
American Hotel & Lodging Association
1201 New York Ave Nw
Suite 600
Washington, DC 20005-3931

202-289-3100; *Fax:* 202-289-3199
webmaster@ahla.com; www.ahla.com

Joseph Mc Inerney, President
Pam Inman, Executive Vice President & COO
Joori Jeon, Executive Vice President & CFO
Marlene M. Colucci, Executive Vice President
Lisa Costello, Vice President, Gov Affairs

AHF Developments is published three times a year with circulation to donors, scholarship recipients and members of the American Hotel and Motel association.
Frequency: Quarterly
Founded in: 1910

13366 Cameron's Foodservice Marketing Reporter
Cameron's Publications
5423 Sheridan Drive
PO Box 676
Williamsville, NY 14231

519-586-8785; *Fax:* 519-586-8816;
www.cameronpub.com

Bob McClelland, CEO
Nina Cameron, Editor

Successful promotion and advertising case histories for the restaurant and hotel industry.

13367 Epicurean Revue
PO Box 35128
Sarasota, FL 34242-5128

Fax: 941-349-4370

Jean-Noel Prade, Publisher
Georgia Brown, Editor
JN Prade, Circulation Manager

The publication for the jetsetters exclusive recommendations on top class hotels and restaurants. Total analysis of the various issues of the Michelin Guide and results of the wine auctions.
Cost: $79.00
8 Pages
Frequency: Monthly
Circulation: 5,000
Printed in one color on matte stock

13368 Hospitality Law
LRP Publications

PO Box 24668
West Palm Beach, FL 33416-4668

561-622-6520
800-341-7874; *Fax:* 561-622-0757
webmaster@lrp.com; www.lrp.com

Kenneth Kahn, President
Dave Light, Editor

Details and analyzes significant cases in the hospitality industry so you can learn from the mistakes that landed other properties in court. You receive summaries of the latest court cases - without legalese - involving hotels, inns, resorts and restaurants.
Cost: $229.00
12 Pages
Frequency: Monthly
Circulation: 1400

13369 **Hotel Technology Newsletter**
Chervenak, Keane and Company
307 E 44th Street
New York, NY 10017

212-986-8230; *Fax:* 212-983-5275;
www.hospitalityleaderonline.com

J Christmas, Publisher
L Chervenak, Editor

Covers hotel information processing, telecommunications, security, fire safety, energy and audio-visual systems.
Cost: $180.00
Frequency: Annual

13370 **Hotel and Casino Law Letter**
William F Harrah College of Hotel Administration
4505 Maryland Parkway
Box 456013
Las Vegas, NV 89154-6013

702-895-3161; *Fax:* 702-895-4109
hotel.unlv.edu/

Annette Kannenberg, Business Manager
Stuart H Mann, Dean
Alice Baker, Administrative Assistant
Pat Merl, Management Assistant
Sherri Theriault, Director

Legislative news for executive level management of hotels and motels.

13371 **Hyatt Overseas**
Hyatt International Corporation
71 S Wacker Dr
Chicago, IL 60606-4637

312-701-7063; *Fax:* 312-750-8578

Thomas Pritzker, CEO

A summary of news, packages and events happening at Hyatt Hotels.
2 Pages

13372 **Inn Side Issues**
Hotel and Motel Brokers of America
10220 N Executive Boulevard
Suite 610
Kansas City, MO 64153

816-891-8776; *Fax:* 816-891-7071

Robert Kralicek, Editor

News of hotel owners and investors with articles about hospitality real estate.

Magazines & Journals

13373 **Bottomline**
Hospitality Financial & Technology Professionals
11709 Boulder Lane
Suite 110
Austin, TX 78726-1832

512-249-5333
800-646-4387; *Fax:* 512-249-1533
Sales@hftp.org; www.hftp.org

Jen Gonzales, Communications Manager
Theresa Pulley, Advertising Director

Official publication of the international association for individuals employed as controllers and financial officers in the hospitality industry. Articles include topics such as technology, personnel management, financial analysis, ethics and financial controls.
Cost: $200.00
Circulation: 4300
Founded in: 1952
Printed in on glossy stock

13374 **Cameron's Worldwide Hospitality Marketing Reporter**
53256 Sheridan Drive
Williamsville, NY 14221-3503

416-636-5666; *Fax:* 416-636-5026

13375 **Cheers**
257 Park Avenue S
3rd Floor, Suite 303
New York, NY 10010

212-967-1551; *Fax:* 646-654-2099

John Eastman, Owner

Every issue is designed to help on-premise operators enhance the profitability of their beverage operations.

13376 **Club Management Magazine**
Finan Publishing Company
107 W Pacific
Saint Louis, MO 63119-3776

314-961-6644; *Fax:* 314-961-4809;
www.cmaa.org

Thomas J Finan, IV, Managing Editor
Dee Kaplan, Publisher
Dianne Dierkes, Circulation Manager

The resource for successful club operations.
Cost: $26.95
150 Pages
Founded in: 1921
Mailing list available for rent: 21,000 names
Printed in 4 colors on glossy stock

13377 **Consortium of Hospitality Research Information Services**
Quanta Press
1313 5th St SE
Suite 223A
Minneapolis, MN 55414-4513

612-379-3618

Nancy J Hall, Owner

Consists of academic and industry groups which together have produced a comprehensive index of hospitality literature in CD-ROM format. Over 47,000 bibliographic records with abstracts from over 50 journals serving the hospitality industry.

13378 **Cornell Hotel & Restaurant Administration Quarterly**
Elsevier Science Publishing Company
415 Horsham Road
Horsham, PA 19044

212-633-3730
888-437-4636; *Fax:* 212-633-3680;
www.hotelschool.cornell.edu/

Glenn Withiam, Executive Editor
Dr. Michael Sturman, Editor
Thomas Cullen, Associate Professor

A journal devoted to the development and exchange of management ideas for the hospitality industry.
Cost: $113.00
Frequency: Quarterly
Circulation: 4500
Founded in: 1960

13379 **Developments Magazine**
American Resort Development Association
1201 15th St NW
Suite 400
Washington, DC 20005-2842

202-371-6700; *Fax:* 202-289-8544
customerservice@arda.org;
www.ardafoundation.org

Howard Nusbaum, President/CEO
Lou Ann Burney, Vice President of Marketing
Robert Craycraft, Vice President of Industry Relation
Rob Dunn, Vice President of Finance
Jason C. Gamel, Vice President of State Governments

13380 **Executive Housekeeping Today (EHT)**
International Executive Housekeepers Association
1001 Eastwind Dr
Suite 301
Westerville, OH 43081-3361

614-895-7166
800-200-6342; *Fax:* 614-895-1248
excel@ieha.org; www.ieha.org
Social Media: Facebook, Twitter, LinkedIn

Beth Risinger, CEO
Laura DiGiulio, Advertising/Sales/Ed

Magazine for management personnel in the institutional housekeeping industry. Highlighting products, services, association news and industry trends.
Cost: $40.00
3500 Members
30 Pages
Frequency: Monthly
Circulation: 4130
ISSN: 0738-6583
Founded in: 1930

13381 **Foodservice Equipment & Supplies Specialist**
Reed Business Information
2000 Clearwater Dr
Oak Brook, IL 60523-8809

630-574-0825; *Fax:* 630-288-8781
411_webmaster@reedbusiness.com;
www.reedbusiness.com

Jeff Greisch, President
Maureen Slocum, Publisher
Paulette Cortopassi, Managing Editor
Victoria Jones, Production Manager
Andrew Rak, Senior Vice President

Magazine for professionals who specify, sell and distribute foodservice equipment, supplies and furnishings.
Frequency: Monthly
Circulation: 22719
Founded in: 1948
Printed in 4 colors on glossy stock

13382 **Hospitality News**
PO Box 11960
Prescott, AZ 86304-1960

206-686-7378
800-685-1932; *Fax:* 206-463-0090;
www.hospnews.com

Linda Sanders, Publisher
Miles Small, Editor-in-Chief

Serves restaurants, lodges, health care facilities, schools, clubs, casino's, caterers, and culinary and beverage marketplaces.
Circulation: 105000
ISSN: 1084-2551
Founded in: 1988

13383 Hospitality Product News
Advanstar Communications
2501 Colorado Avenue
Suite 280
Santa Monica, CA 90404
310-857-7500
888-527-7008; *Fax:* 310-857-7510
info@advanstar.com; www.advanstar.com/
Doug Ferguson, Group Publisher
Helen Gardner, General Manager
Georgiann Decenzo, Director of Corporate mar
Joseph Loggia, CEO
Thomas Ehardt, Chief Administrator
Contains ADA compliance, maintenance and cleaning, fitness, leisure and entertainment, food and beverage, foodservice equipment and supplies, furnishings and fixtures, guest amenities, tabletop, technology, uniforms, and bedding and linens.
Cost: $35.00
Circulation: 30019
Founded in: 1987

13384 Hospitality Technology
Edgell Communications
4 Middlebury Boulevard
Randolph, NJ 07869
973-252-0100; *Fax:* 973-252-9020;
www.htmagazine.com
Lenore O'Meara, Associate Publisher
Reid Paul, Editor
Gerald Ryerson, President
Jan Miciak, Production Manager
Leah Segarra, Account Executive
Aimed at owners/operators, franchise and chain executives, and managers in operations, finance, sales/marketing and information systems. Emphasis on applications, new products, industry news and trade show highlights.
Circulation: 16000
Founded in: 1984
Printed in 4 colors on glossy stock

13385 Hotel & Motel Management
Advanstar Communications
757 3rd Avenue
New York, NY 10017-2013
212-951-6600; *Fax:* 212-951-6793
info@advanstar.com; www.advanstar.com
Scott E Pierce, President
Mike Malley, Publisher
Jeff Higley, Editor-in-Chief
Mary M. Malloy, National Sales Manager
Publication reaching more than 57,000 management personnel in hotels, motels, motor inns and other related businesses.
Circulation: 53058
ISSN: 0018-6082
Founded in: 1875

13386 Hotels
Reed Business Information
2000 Clearwater Dr
Oak Brook, IL 60523-8809
605-3 8-09; *Fax:* 630-288-8781
hotels_webmaster@reedbusiness.com;
www.reedbusiness.com
Jeff Greisch, President
Andrew Rak, Senior Vice President
Jeff Weinstein, Editor
The magazine for the worldwide hotel industry
Cost: $125.90
Frequency: Monthly
Circulation: 62000
ISSN: 1047-2975
Printed in 4 colors on glossy stock

13387 Infoline
Hospitality Financial & Technology Professionals
11709 Boulder Lane
Suite 110
Austin, TX 78726-1832
512-249-5333
800-646-4387; *Fax:* 512-249-1533
eliza.selig@hftp.org; www.hftp.org
Eliza Selig, Editor
Lance Peterson, Director Marketing
Frank Wolfe, Executive ViP
Chapter and officer activities.
Frequency: Monthly
Circulation: 4000
Founded in: 1952

13388 Journal of Quality Assurance in Hospitality & Tourism
Bill Cohen
10 Alice Street
Binghamton, NY 13904-1580
607-722-5857
800-342-9678; *Fax:* 607-722-6362;
www.haworthpressinc.com
Timothy R Hinkin, Editor
Pyo Sungsoo, Editor
William Cohen, Owner
Serves as a medium to share and disseminate information coming from new research findings and superior practices in tourisim and hospitality; covers planning, development, management and marketing.
Cost: $50.00
Frequency: Quarterly
Founded in: 1978

13389 Journal of Teaching in Travel & Tourism
Bill Cohen
10 Alice Street
Binghamton, NY 13904-1580
607-722-5857
800-342-9678; *Fax:* 607-722-6362
getinfo@haworthpress.com;
www.haworthpressinc.com
Timothy R Hinkin, Editor
Pyo Sungsoo, Editor
Cathy HC Hsu, Editor
William Cohen, Owner
Serves as an international interdisiplinary forum and reference source for travel and tourisim education at professional schools and universities.
Founded in: 1978

13390 Lodging Hospitality
Penton Media
1300 E 9th St
Cleveland, OH 44114-1503
216-696-7000; *Fax:* 216-696-6662
ewatkins@penton.com; www.penton.com
Jane Cooper, Marketing
Edward Watkins, Editor
David Kieselstein, CEO
Preston L. Vice, Chief Financial Officer
Andrew Schmolka, Senior Vice President
Serving the US hotel, motel and resort industry. Published 16 times per year, LH provides owners and operators with the latest trends and information on the development, operations and marketing of lodging properties
Frequency: Monthly
Circulation: 50,976
ISSN: 0148-0766
Founded in: 1892
Mailing list available for rent
Printed in 4 colors on glossy stock

13391 Market Watch
M Shanken Communications
387 Park Ave S
Floor 8
New York, NY 10016-8872
212-684-4224; *Fax:* 212-684-5424;
www.cigaraficionado.com
Marvin Shanken, Publisher
Felicia Bedoya, President
Up-to-date information for individuals and businesses working in the beverage and alcohol industry.
Cost: $75.42
200 Pages
Circulation: 65000
Founded in: 1981
Printed in 4 colors

13392 Nation's Restaurant News
Lebhar-Friedman Publications
425 Park Ave
New York, NY 10022-3526
212-756-5220; *Fax:* 212-756-5250
info@lf.com
Lebhar Friedman, Publisher
Michael Cardillo, VP Sales
Ellen Koteff, Editor
Serves commercial and onsite food service and lodging establishments including restaurants, schools, universities, hospitals, nursing homes and other health and welfare facilities, hotels and motels with food service, government installations, clubs and other related firms.
Cost: $44.95
Circulation: 85,999
Founded in: 1925
Mailing list available for rent: 100,000 names at $100 per M
Printed in 4 colors on matte stock

13393 National Culinary Review
American Culinary Federation
180 Center Place Way
St Augustine, FL 32095-8859
904-824-4468
800-624-9458; *Fax:* 904-825-4758
acf@acfchefs.net; www.acfchefs.org
Heidi Cramb, Executive Director
Kay Orde, Editor
Edward Leonard, Presient
Michael Feierstein, Administrative Assistant
Bryan Hunt, Graphic Designer
Accepts advertising.
Cost: $50.00
Frequency: Monthly
Circulation: 20000
Founded in: 1929

13394 Restaurant Hospitality
Penton Media
1300 E 9th St
Cleveland, OH 44114-1503
216-696-7000; *Fax:* 216-696-6662
information@penton.com; www.penton.com
Jane Cooper, Marketing
Jennifer Daugherty, Communications Manager
David Kieselstein, Chief Executive Officer
Kurt Nelson, Vice President, Human Resources
Andrew Schmolka, Senior Vice President
A national trade publication that covers the full-service restaurant industry. If offers cover story features, an extensive food section with recipes, a multi-page news section and a variety of one page profiles on rising stars, equipment, food safety, beverages, design and more.
130 Pages
Frequency: Monthly
Circulation: 117721
ISSN: 0147-9989
Founded in: 1892

Mailing list available for rent
Printed in 4 colors on glossy stock

13395 Restaurants & Institutions
Reed Business Information
2000 Clearwater Dr
Oak Brook, IL 60523-8809

605-3 8-09; *Fax:* 630-288-8781
privacymanager@reedbusiness.com;
www.reedbusiness.com

Patricia B Dailey, Editor-in-Chief
Scott Hume, Managing Editor
Jim Casella, CEO
Brion Palmer, Publisher
Andrew Rak, Senior Vice President

Commercial and noncommercial foodservice establishments including restaurant, hotels, motels, fast-food chains,coffee shops, food stores with foodservice
Cost: $477.00
Frequency: Monthly
Circulation: 154,110
Founded in: 1937
Printed in 4 colors on glossy stock

13396 Ski Area Management
Beardsley Publishing Corporation
PO Box 644
Woodbury, CT 06798-644

203-263-0888; *Fax:* 203-266-0452;
www.saminfo.com

Jennifer Rowan, Publisher
Rick Kahl, Editor
Donna Jacobs, Production Manager

Content includes technologies of skilifts, snowmaking and slope grooming, at year-round resort operations. Other features include product and supplier directories, resort architecture and design, new products, marketing, real estate and rental.
Cost: $42.00
Frequency: Monthly
Circulation: 3100
Printed in 4 colors on glossy stock

13397 Textile Rental Magazine
Textile Rental Services Association
1800 Diagonal Rd
Suite 200
Alexandria, VA 22314-2842

703-519-0029
877-770-9274; *Fax:* 703-519-0026
trsa@trsa.org; www.trsa.org
Social Media: Facebook, Twitter, LinkedIn

Roger Cocivera, President/CEO
Jack Morgan, Editor

Packed with valuable tips and ideas.
Frequency: Monthly
Founded in: 1912

Trade Shows

13398 AAHOA Annual Convention and Trade Show
Asian American Hotel Owners Association
1100 Abernathy Road
Suite 1100
Atlanta, GA 30328-6707

404-816-5759; *Fax:* 404-816-6260
info@aahoa.com; www.aahoa.com
Social Media: Facebook, Twitter, LinkedIn, YouTube, Instagram

Chip Rogers, President & CEO
Bharat Patel, CHO, Chairman
Bhavesh B. Patel, CHO, Vice Chairman
Hitesh Patel, CHA, CHO, Treasurer
Jagruti Panwala, CHO, Secretary

Bringing together experts and professionals in the hotel and motel businesses to discuss and share industry tips, insights, and trends among Asian American owners.
16600 Members
Founded in: 1989

13399 American Hotel & Motel Association Annual Conference/Leadership Forum
1201 New York Avenue NW
Suite 600
Washington, DC 20005-3931

202-289-3100; *Fax:* 202-289-3158
webmaster@ahla.com; www.ahlef.org

Gerald Petitt, Chairman
Joseph A. McInerney, President/Ceo
Pam Inman, Executive Vice President & COO
Joori Jeon, Executive Vice President & CFO
Marlene M. Colucci, Executive Vice President

189 exhibits of hotel supplies, equipment and information, conference and workshop.
1500 Attendees
Frequency: Annual
Founded in: 1910

13400 American Hotel & Motel Association Annual Convention
1201 New York Avenue NW
Suite 600
Washington, DC 20005-3931

202-289-3100; *Fax:* 202-289-3199
webmaster@ahla.com; www.ahlef.org

Gerald Petitt, Chairman
Joseph A. McInerney, President/Coo
Pam Inman, Executive Vice President & COO
Joori Jeon, Executive Vice President & CFO
Marlene M. Colucci, Executive Vice President

125 booths consisting of telecommunication systems, supplies and equipment for the hotel and motel industry.
1.5M Attendees
Frequency: April

13401 American Resort Development Association Convention
1201 15th Street NW
Suite 400
Washington, DC 20005-2842

202-371-6700; *Fax:* 202-289-8544
customerservice@arda.org; www.arda.org

Howard C Nusbaum, President/CEO
Lou Ann Burney, Vice President of Marketing
Robert Craycraft, Vice President of Industry Relation
Rob Dunn, Vice President of Finance
Jason C. Gamel, Vice President of State Government

One hundred fifty booths.
3600 Attendees
Frequency: April

13402 Annual Council on Hotel, Restaurant and Institutional Education Conference
Int'l Council on Hotel & Restaurant Education
2810 North Parham Roaf
Suite 230
Richmond, VA 23294

804-346-4800; *Fax:* 804-346-5009
publications@chrie.org; www.chrie.org

Kathy McCarty, Executive VP/CEO
Bill Shoemaker, Treasurer
Joseph Bradley, Treasurer

Terrific opportunity to gain knowledge, exchange ideas, and enjoy the camaraderie and fellowship of colleagues in the hospitality industry
6MM Attendees
Frequency: July

13403 Annual Hotel, Motel and Restaurant Supply Show of the Southeast
Leisure Time Unlimited
708 Main Street
PO Box 332
Myrtle Beach, SC 29577

843-448-9483
800-261-5991; *Fax:* 843-626-1513
hmrss@sc.rr.com; www.hmrsss.com

Brooke P Baker, Show Director

Trade show for the hospitality industry.
23000 Attendees
Frequency: January
Founded in: 1975

13404 Fall Conference for Hospitality Supply Management
Institute for Supply Management
Po Box 22160
Tempe, AZ 85285-2160
480-752-6276
800-888-6276; *Fax:* 480-752-7890;
www.ism.ws
Social Media: Facebook, Twitter, LinkedIn

Sidney Johnson, Chairman
Thomas W. Derry, Chief Executive Officer
Debbie Webber, Senior VP/Corporate Treasurer
Holly LaCroix Johnson, Senior VP/Corporate Secretary
Nora Neibergall, CPM, Senior VP
Frequency: Oct, Dallas, TX
Mailing list available for rent

13405 Great Southwest Lodging & Restaurant Show
Arizona Hotel and Lodging Association
1240 East Missouri Avenue
Phoenix, AZ 85014

602-604-0729
800-788-2462; *Fax:* 520-604-0769
info@southwestshow.com;
www.southwestshow.com

Britt Kimball, Show Manager

Seminars, workshops and 450+ exhibits of food service and lodging equipment, marketing, decorations, berverage services (alcoholic and non), cleaning services and pest control, furnishings, lighting, insurance, transportation and more.
5000 Attendees
Frequency: Annual
Founded in: 1970

13406 IEHA's Association Convention/in Conjunction with ISSA Interclean
International Executive Housekeepers Association
1001 Eastwind Drive
Suite 301
Westerville, OH 43081-3361

614-895-7166
800-200-6342; *Fax:* 614-895-1248
excel@ieha.org; www.ieha.org
Social Media: Facebook, Twitter, LinkedIn

Beth Risinger, CEO

Educational seminars and exhibits by firms engaged in manufacturing, marketing and distribution of cleaning and maintenance suppliers. Containing 750 exhibits.
3500 Members
15M Attendees
Frequency: Oct 23-26 Orlando Florida

13407 Innkeeping
PAII
Box 97010
Santa Barbara, CA 93190

805-965-4525

JoAnn Bell, Publisher

Offers a forum for innkeepers, hotel and motel managers, owners and operators.
500 Attendees
Frequency: March/April

13408 **International Hotel/Motel & Restaurant Show**
George Little Management
10 Bank Street
Suite 1200
White Plains, NY 10606-1954
914-486-6070
800-272-7469; *Fax:* 914-948-6180;
www.ihmrs.com
Christian Falkemberg, Show Manager
George Little II, President
Products and services for lodging and food service properties organized in 12 categories: Technology; Uniforms, Linens and Bedding; Tabletop; Guest amenities and services; Food and Beverage; Cleaning and Maintenance; Food Service Equipment and Supplies; Franchise, Finance and Management; Furnishings and Fixturtes; Fitness, Leisure and Entertainment; The Environment; Advertising and Promotion
45000 Attendees
Frequency: Early November

13409 **Marine Hotel Catering Duty Free Conference**
PO Box 1659
Sausalito, CA 94966
415-332-1903; *Fax:* 415-332-9457
mha@mhaweb.org; www.mhaweb.org
Caroline Prichard, Administrator
100 booths.
700 Attendees
Frequency: April

13410 **National Restaurant Association: Restaurant, Hotel-Motel Show**
Convention Office
150 North Michigan Avenue
Suite 2000
Chicago, IL 60601
312-853-2525; www.restaurant.org
Mary Pat Heftman, Sr VP Conventions
Jamie Schaefer, Treasurer
Phil Hickey, Treasurer
1,800 booths.
Frequency: Annual,May

13411 **Pacific Hospitality Expo Convention Center**
1801 Kalakaua Avenue
Honolulu, HI 96815-2558
808-973-9790
Joanie Gribbin, Director
220 booths.
2.5M Attendees
Frequency: June

13412 **Rocky Mountain Hospitality Convention and Expo**
899 Logan Street
Suite 300
Denver, CO 80203-3155
303-792-9621
Bruce Whiticker, Convention Director
413 booths.
7M Attendees
Frequency: June

Directories & Databases

13413 **All Suite Hotel Guide**
Ten Speed Press
PO Box 7123
Berkeley, CA 94707-0123
510-559-1600
800-841-2665; *Fax:* 510-559-1629;
www.tenspeedpress.com
Phil Wood, President
Over 1,600 hotels are offered which have suites available consisting of two or more rooms for rent.
Cost: $14.95
336 Pages
Frequency: Annual
ISBN: 1-580080-91-

13414 **America's Wonderful Little Hotels & Inns**
St. Martin's Press
175 5th Ave
4th Floor
New York, NY 10010-7703
212-674-5151; *Fax:* 212-674-3179
John Sargent, CEO
A directory listing hotels and inns that are located throughout the United States and Canada in various volumes. Prices vary per region, per volume.
ISBN: 0-312081-30-8
Founded in: 1952

13415 **Bed & Breakfast Home Directory: Homes Away from Home, West Coast**
Knighttime Publications
890 Calabasas Road
Watsonville, CA 95076-0418
Diane Knight, Author
Suzy Blackaby, Author
Kevin McElvain, Author
Over 250 bed and breakfast homes are listed that are located in the areas of California, Oregon, Washington and British Columbia, Canada.
Cost: $12.95
203 Pages
Frequency: Biennial
ISBN: 0-942902-03-3

13416 **Bed and Breakfast Guest Houses and Inns of America**
PO Box 38066
Germantown, TN 38183-0066
901-946-1902; *Fax:* 901-758-0816
Directory of services and supplies to the industry.
Cost: $45.00
350 Pages
Frequency: Annual
ISSN: 1056-8069

13417 **Cabin Guide to Wilderness Lodging**
Hammond Publishing
1500 E Tropicana Ave
Suite 110
Las Vegas, NV 89119-6515
702-878-2008; www.prosofrealty.com
Jim Smith, Manager
Information is given on over 500 cabins in national and state forests, preserves and other wildlife areas.
Cost: $14.95
250 Pages
Frequency: Annual

13418 **Complete Guide to Bed & Breakfasts, Inns and Guesthouses in US & Canada**
Lanier Publishing International
963 Transport Way
Petaluma, CA 94954-8011
707-763-0271; *Fax:* 707-763-5762
lanier@travelguides.com;
www.travelguides.com
Pamela Lanier, Owner
Directory of services and supplies to the industry.
Cost: $16.95
536 Pages
Frequency: Annual

13419 **Country Inns and Back Roads, North America**
HarperCollins
10 E 53rd St
Cellar 1 Floor
New York, NY 10022-5299
212-207-7000; *Fax:* 212-207-6964
feedback2@harpercollins.com;
www.harpercollins.com
Brian Murray, CEO
Over 200 country inns in the United States and Canada are listed.
Cost: $13.00
450 Pages
Frequency: Annual

13420 **Directory of Hotel & Lodging Companies**
American Hotel & Lodging Association
1201 New York Ave NW
Suite 600
Washington, DC 20005-3931
202-289-3100; *Fax:* 202-289-3199
webmaster@ahla.com; www.ahla.com
Joseph McInerney, President
Joori Jeon, Executive Vice President & CFO
Pam Inman, Executive Vice President & COO
Marlene M. Colucci, Executive Vice President
Lisa Costello, Vice President, Government Affairs
Lists over 1,000 companies that own, manage or franchise properties worldwide. Also lists, in 7 sections: companies by type, company/brand web site, company listings, geographical, company rankings, hotel brokers, and vendors.
Cost: $100.00
Frequency: Annual
Founded in: 1931

13421 **Hotel Development Guide**
Hospitality Media
17950 Preston Rd
Suite 710
Dallas, TX 75252-5637
972-934-2040; *Fax:* 972-934-2070
Info@hospitalitymgt.com;
www.hospitalitymgt.com
Leo Spriggs, CEO
John Connor, Director of Operations
Bill Sullivan, Chief Financial Officer
Offers a list of suppliers of equipment, fixtures and services needed for new motels.
Cost: $100.00

13422 **Hotel and Travel Index**
Reed Travel Group
904 Haddonfield Rd
Subscription Department
Cherry Hill, NJ 08002-2745
856-665-4455
800-442-0900; *Fax:* 856-488-4867
Over 45,000 hotels worldwide are profiled in this travel directory.
Cost: $125.00
2000 Pages
Frequency: Quarterly
Circulation: 60,000

13423 **Inspected, Rated and Approved Bed and Breakfast Country Inns**
American Bed & Breakfast Association

10800 Midlothian Tpke
Suite 254
Richmond, VA 23235-4700

www.abba.com

Beth Burgreen Stuhlman, Editor

Information on over 500 overnight accommodations in North American bed and breakfast locations are listed.
Cost: $17.95
350 Pages
ISBN: 0-934473-27-7
Founded in: 1996

13424 **National Directory of Budget Motels**
Pilot Books
127 Sterling Avenue
#2102
Greenport, NY 11944-1439

631-477-0978
800-79 -ILOT; *Fax:* 631-477-0978

Guide to the best in economy-priced chain motel accommodations in the United States and Canada.
Cost: $12.95
346 Pages
Frequency: Annual

13425 **National Trust Guide to Historic Bed & Breakfasts, Inns & Small Hotels**
Preservation Press
1785 Massachusetts Ave NW
Washington, DC 20036-2117

202-588-6083; *Fax:* 202-588-6172

James Schwartz, Manager

Directory of services and supplies to the industry.
Cost: $13.95
416 Pages
Frequency: Biennial

13426 **Official Bed and Breakfast Guide**
National Bed & Breakfast Association
148 E Rocks Road
Norwalk, CT 06851

203-847-6196; *Fax:* 203-847-0469;
www.nbba.com

Phyllis Featherston, President

A who's who directory of services and supplies to the industry offering a list of the best in bed and breakfast accommodations in USA, Canada and the Carribbean.
Cost: $17.95
560 Pages

13427 **Official Hotel Guide**
Reed Hotel Directories Network
500 Plaza Drive
Secaucus, NJ 07094-3619

201-902-1960; *Fax:* 201-319-1628

Wilma Goldenberg, Editor

3 volumes of 25,000 hotels, motels and resorts worldwide.
Cost: $385.00
Frequency: Annual
Circulation: 20,000

13428 **Pelican's Select Guide to American Bed and Breakfast**
Pelican Publishing Company
1000 Burmaster St
Gretna, LA 70053-2246

504-368-1175; *Fax:* 504-368-1195
sales@pelicanpub.com; www.pelicanpub.com

Milburn Calhoun, Publisher
Joseph Billingsley, Sales Manager

Independent guest houses, inns and bed and breakfast accommodations are profiled.
Cost: $14.95
216 Pages
ISBN: 1-589800-61-8
Printed in 2 colors on matte stock

13429 **Preferred Hotels Directory**
Preferred Hotels & Resorts Worldwide
311 S Wacker Dr
Suite 1900
Chicago, IL 60606-6676

312-913-0400
800-323-7500; *Fax:* 312-913-5124;
www.preferredhotels.com

John Ubberoth, CEO
Casey Ueberroth, Managing Director
80 Pages
Frequency: Annual
Circulation: 25,000

13430 **Recommended Country Inns**
Globe Pequot Press
246 Goose Lane
PO Box 480
Guilford, CT 06437

203-458-4500
888-249-7586; *Fax:* 800-820-2329;
www.globepequot.com

Elizabeth Squier
Elenor Berman

This series of directories offers information on country inns located in certain parts of the United States.
Cost: $18.95
416 Pages
Frequency: Biennial
ISBN: 0-762728-48-5

13431 **Where to Stay USA**
Prentice Hall Law & Business
1 Lake St
Upper Saddle Rv, NJ 07458-1828

201-236-7000; *Fax:* 201-236-3381

Information is given on over 1,200 places to stay and eat from $4 to $35 a night.
Cost: $16.00
350 Pages
Frequency: Biennial

Industry Web Sites

13432 **http://gold.greyhouse.com**
G.O.L.D Grey House OnLine Databases

Grey House Publishing's online database platform, GOLD, offers Quick Search, Keyword Search and Expert Search for most business sectors including hotel, motel and hospitality markets. The GOLD platform makes finding the information you need quick and easy - whether you're a novice searcher or an experienced database user. All of Grey House's directory products are available for subscription on the GOLD platform.

13433 **www.abba.com**
American Bed & Breakfast Association

National organization with information on over 500 overnight accomodations in North American bed and breakfast locations.

13434 **www.ahma.com**
American Hotel & Lodging Foundation

Trade association covering news, issues and activities of related industry groups.

13435 **www.biztravel.com**
Biztravel.com

Internet travel service offering discounts on flights, hotels, car rentals, packages and cruises.

13436 **www.chrie.org**
Int'l Council on Hotel & Restaurant Education

To enhance professionalism at all levels of the hospitality and tourism industry through education and training.

13437 **www.ei-ahla.org**
American Hotel&Lodging Educational Foundation

A non-profit educational foundation of the American Hotel & Lodging Association and the world's largest provider of hospitality education training resources, videos, books, workbooks, seminars, management courses, complete training systems and professional certification programs.

13438 **www.expedia.com**
Expedia.com

Internet travel service offers access to airlines, hotels, car rentals, vacation packages, cruises and corporate travel.

13439 **www.goworldnet.com/cgi-bin**
Worldnet USA

A database of states with hotels, theaters and museums.

13440 **www.greyhouse.com**
Grey House Publishing

Authoritative reference directories for most business sectors including hotel, motel and hospitality markets. Users can search the online databases with varied search criteria allowing for custom searches by product category, geographic area, sales volume, keyword, subject and more. Full Grey House catalog and online ordering also available.

13441 **www.hanyc.org**
Hotel Association of New York City

One of the oldest professional trade associations in the nation.

13442 **www.hotels.com**
Hotels.com

Provides discount accommodations worldwide.

13443 **www.hotwire.com**
Hotwire.com

Internet travel service offering discounts on flights, hotels, car rentals, packages and cruises.

13444 **www.ieha.org**
International Executive Housekeepers Association

An organization for persons working in the housekeeping area of the lodging industry.

13445 **www.innbook.com**
Bed and Breakfast Inns & Small Luxury Hotels

Includes the finest inns, B&Bs, and getaway retreats in Canada and the Us, carefully chosen and inspected to maintain the highest standards.

13446 **www.masslodging.com**
Massachusetts Lodging Association

A trade association representing and promoting the lodging industryin Massachusetts.

13447 **www.nmhotels.com**
New Mexico Lodging Association

New Mexico's trade association representing the lodging industry.

13448 **www.orbitz.com**
Orbitz.com

Internet travel service offering discounts on flights, hotels, car rentals, packages and cruises.

13449 **www.paii.org**
Professional Association of Innkeepers International
Serving bed and breakfast/country inn owners, aspiring innkeepers, inn sitters, vendors with educational and consultative services. International conference.

13450 **www.preferredhotels.com**
The Luxury Hotels of Preferred Hotels & Resorts Worldwide
An exclusive group of independent luxury hotels in the United States.

13451 **www.travel.lycos.com**
Lycos.com
Internet travel service offering discounts on flights, hotels, car rentals, packages and cruises.

13452 **www.travel.yahoo.com**
Yahoo.com
Internet travel service providing access to flights, hotels, car rentals, vacation packages and cruises.

13453 **www.travelocity.com**
Sabre Holdings
Travel service offering consumers access to hundreds of airlines and thousands of hotels, as well as cruises, last-minute and vacation packages and best-in-class car rental companies.

13454 **www.travelweb.com**
Travelweb.com
Internet provider of hotel accommodations.

Associations

13455 **ASM International**
9639 Kinsman Road
Materials Park, OH 44073-0002
440-338-5151
800-336-5152; *Fax:* 440-338-4634
memberservices@asminternational.org;
www.asminternational.org
Social Media: Facebook, Twitter, LinkedIn
Stanley Theobald, Senior Director, Business
Tom Passek, Managing Director
Nichol Campana, Director of Development
Skip Wolfe, Membership Product Manager
Norina Columbaro, Senior Manager, Education
The society for materials engineers and scientists, a worldwide network dedicated to advancing industry, technology and applications of metals and materials.
35000 Members
Founded in: 1913

13456 **American Coatings Association**
1500 Rhode Island Ave., NW
Washington, DC 20005
202-462-6272; *Fax:* 202-462-8549
members@paint.org; www.coatingstech.org
Social Media: Facebook, Twitter, LinkedIn, Reddit, Digg, MySpace, Stumble
J. Andrew Doyle, President & CEO
Thomas J. Graves, Vice President, General Counsel
Allen Irish, Counsel / Director
Alison Keane, Vice President, Government Affairs
Robin Eastman Caldwell, Senior Gov. Affairs Specialist
Provides technical education and professional development to its members and to the global industry through its multinational Constituent Societies and collectively as a Federation
Founded in: 1922

13457 **American Composites Manufacturers Association**
3033 Wilson Blvd.
Suite 420
Arlington, VA 22201-4749
703-525-0511; *Fax:* 703-525-0743
info@acmanet.org; www.acmanet.org
Social Media: Facebook, Twitter, LinkedIn, RSS
Jeff Craney, Chairman
Leon Garoufalis, Vice Chairman
Tom Dobbins, CAE, President
John Schweitzer, Vice President, Government Affairs
Heather Rhoderick, CMP, CAE, SVP, Events & Information
A trade association serving the composites industry.
1100 Members
Founded in: 1979

13458 **American Electroplaters and Surface Finishers Society (AESF)**
1155 15th Street NW
Suite 500
Washington, DC 20005
202-457-8401; *Fax:* 202-530-0659
info@aesf.org; www.aesf.org
Social Media: Facebook, Twitter, LinkedIn, Google+, RSS
John Flatley, Executive Director
Courtney Mariette, Bookstore/Education
Holly Wills, Membership
Carrie Hoffman, Deputy Executive Director
Cheryl Clark, Director of Events
AESF is an international society that advances the science of surface finishing to benefit industry and society through education, information and social involvement, as well as those who provide services, supplies and support to the industry.
5000 Members
Founded in: 1909

13459 **American Society of Industrial Security**
1625 Prince Street
Alexandria, VA 22314-2882
703-519-6200; *Fax:* 703-519-6299
asis@asisonline.org; www.asisonline.org
Social Media: Facebook, Twitter, LinkedIn, YouTube
Richard E. Widup, Jr., CPP, Chairman
Dave N. Tyson, CPP, President
Michael J. Stack, ASIS Chief Executive Officer
Thomas J. Langer, CPP, Treasurer
Richard E. Chase, CPP, PCI, PSP, Secretary
The largest international organization for professionals who are responsible for security, including managers and directors of security.
38000 Members
Founded in: 1955
Mailing list available for rent

13460 **Asphalt Recycling and Reclaiming Associates**
15 Harold Court
Suite 250
Bayshore, NY 11706
631-231-8400; *Fax:* 631-434-1116
sales@arra.com; www.arra.com
Mike Krissoff, Executive Director
Promotes the interest of owners and manufacturers of recycling equipment, engineers, suppliers and businesses involved in the asphalt recycling industry. Newsletter published quarterly.
200 Members
Founded in: 1957
Mailing list available for rent

13461 **Associated Equipment Distributors**
600 22nd Street
Suite 220
Oak Brook, IL 60523-8807
630-574-0650
800-388-0650; *Fax:* 630-574-0132
info@aednet.org; www.aednet.org
Social Media: Facebook, Twitter, YouTube, Google+
Don Shilling, Chairman
Whit Perryman, Vice Chairman
Brian P. McGuire, President, CEO
Bob Henderson, Executive VP & COO
Jason Blake, Senior VP & CFO
Membership organization of independent distributors, manufacturers and other organizations involved in the distribution of construction equipment and related products and services in North America and throughout the world.
1200 Members
Founded in: 1919
Mailing list available for rent

13462 **Association for Manufacturing Excellence**
3701 Algonquin Rd.
Suite 225
Rolling Meadows, IL 60008-3150
224-232-5980; *Fax:* 224-232-5981
info@ame.org; www.ame.org
Social Media: Facebook, Twitter, LinkedIn, YouTube
Jerry Wright, Chairman
Greg Williams, Vice Chairman
Organization promoting personal and enterprise improvement in the manufacturing industry.
4000 Members
Founded in: 1985

13463 **Association of Equipment Manufacturers**
6737 West Washington Street
Suite 2400
Milwaukee, WI 53214-5647
414-272-0943
866-236-0943; *Fax:* 414-272-1170
aem@aem.org; www.aem.org
Social Media: Twitter
John Patterson, Chair
Leif J. Magnusson, Vice Chair
Goran Lindgren, Treasurer
Dennis J Slater, Secretary
Judy Gaus, Vice President, Human Resources
The trade and business development resource for companies that manufacture equipment, products and services used worldwide in the construction, agricultural, mining, forestry, and utility fields.
Founded in: 2002
Mailing list available for rent

13464 **Association of Machinery and Equipment Appraisers**
315 South Patrick Street
Alexandria, VA 22314-3532
703-836-7900
800-537-8629; *Fax:* 703-836-9303
amea@amea.org; www.amea.org
Social Media: LinkedIn, YouTube
Jack Mendenhall, CEA, President
Randy Koster, CEA, 1st Vice President
Don Bentley, 2nd Vice President
Dave Troutman, Treasurer
James Zvonar, CEA, Immediate Past President
Certifies and accredits the most qualified capital equipment appraisers in the appraisal industry through promotion of standards of professional practice, ethical conduct, and marketing based experience.
300 Members
Founded in: 1983
Mailing list available for rent

13465 **Athletic Equipment Managers Association**
207 E. Bodman
Bement, IL 13068-9643
217-678-1004; *Fax:* 217-678-1005
aema@frontiernet.nen;
www.equipmentmanagers.org
Dan Siermine E.M., C., President
Mike Royster, Executive Director
Matthew Althoff E.M.,C., Associate Executive Director
Meli Resendiz E.M.,C, Vice President
Clifton Perry, Vice President
The purpose of the AEMA is to promote, advance, and improve the Equipment Managers Profession in all of its many phases
700 Members
Founded in: 1974

13466 **Casting Industry Suppliers Association**
14175 West Indian School Road
Suite B4-504
Goodyear, AZ 85395
623-547-0920; *Fax:* 623-536-1486;
www.cisa.org
Social Media: RSS
Lew Fish, President
Roger A Hayes, Executive Director
Lew Fish, 2nd Vice President
Mike Bartol, 1st Vice President

Fosters better trade practices. Serves as industry representative before the government and public. Encourages member research into new processes and methods of foundry operation. Association of suppliers to the worldwide metal casting industry.
70 Members
Founded in: 1919
Mailing list available for rent

13467 Composite Can and Tube Institute
50 South Pickett Street
Suite 110
Alexandria, VA 22304-7206

703-823-7234; *Fax:* 703-823-7237
ccti@cctiwdc.org; www.cctiwdc.org

Kristine Garland, Executive Vice President
Wayne Vance, Association Councel
Janine Marczak, Associate Manager, Events

CCTI is an international nonprofit trade association representing the interests of manufacturers of composite paperboard cans, containers, canisters, tubes, cores, edgeboard and related or similar composite products and suppliers to those manufacturers of such items as paper, machinery, adhesives, labels and other services and materials.
Founded in: 1933

13468 Conveyor Equipment Manufacturers Association
5672 Strand Ct.
Suite 2
Naples, FL 34110

239-514-3441; *Fax:* 239-514-3470
phil@cemanet.org; www.cemanet.org
Social Media: Facebook, Twitter, LinkedIn

Jerry Heathman, President
Garry Abraham, VP
Robert Reinfried, Executive VP
E.A. (Ned) Thompson, Treasurer
Paul Ross, Secretary

Involved in writing industry standards, the CEMA seeks to promote among its members and the industry standardization of design manufacture and application on a voluntary basis and in such manner as will not impede development of conveying machinery and component parts or lessen competition. CEMA sponsors an annual Engineering Conference that allows Member Company Engineers to meet and develop or improve CEMA Consensus Industry Standards and National Standards that affect the conveyor industry.
96 Members
Founded in: 1933

13469 Equipment Leasing and Finance Association
1825 K Street NW
Suite 900
Washington, DC 20006

202-238-3400; *Fax:* 202-238-3401
jbenson@elfaonline.org; www.elfaonline.org
Social Media: Facebook, Twitter, LinkedIn, RSS, YouTube

William G. Sutton, CAE, President and CEO
Amy Vogt, Vice President of Communications
Paul Stilp, Vice President of Finance
Lesley Sterling, Vice President-Business
Andy Fishburn, VP, Federal Government Relations

Represents companies involved in the dynamic equipment leasing and finance industry to the business community, government and media.
700+ Members
Founded in: 1961
Mailing list available for rent

13470 Fluid Controls Institute
1300 Sumner Avenue
Cleveland, OH 44115-2851

216-241-7333; *Fax:* 216-241-0105;
www.fluidcontrolsinstitute.org

Manufacturers of equipment for fluid (liquid or gas) control and conditioning. This institute is organized into product specific sections which address issues that are relevant to particular products and or/or technologies.
Founded in: 1921

13471 Fluid Sealing Association
994 Old Eagle School Rd
Suite 1019
Wayne, PA 19087-1802

610-971-4850; *Fax:* 610-971-4859
info@fluidsealing.com; www.fluidsealing.com

Robert Ecker, Executive Director
Hope Silverman, Administrative Director

Influence and support the development of related standards and to provide education in the fluid sealing area.
57 Members
Founded in: 1933
Mailing list available for rent

13472 Hoist Manufacturers Institute
8720 Red Oak Boulevard
Suite 201
Charlotte, NC 28217-3996

704-676-1190; *Fax:* 704-676-1199
cmiller@mhi.org; www.mhi.org
Social Media: Facebook, Twitter, LinkedIn

E Larry Strayhorn, Last Retiring Executive Chairman
Dave Young, Executive Vice Chairman
John Paxton, President
Gregg E. Goodner, VP
Carol Miller, VP, Marketing

An affiliate of Material Handling Industry, also a trade association of maufacturers of overhead handling hoists. The products of member companies include hand chain hoists, ratchet lever hoists, trolleys, air chain and air rope hoists, and electric chain and electric wire rope hoists.
800 Members
Founded in: 1945
Mailing list available for rent

13473 Independent Lubricant Manufacturers Association
400 N. Columbus Street
Suite 201
Alexandria, VA 22314-2264

703-684-5574; *Fax:* 703-836-8503
tmack@ilma.org; www.ilma.org
Social Media: Facebook, Twitter

Barbara A. Bellanti, President
Frank H. Hamilton III, VP
Beth Ann Jones, Treasurer
Lon Fanning, Immediate Past President
Dave Croghan, Secretary

Independent blenders and compounders of lubricants.
320 Members
Founded in: 2004
Mailing list available for rent: 2000 names at $750 per M

13474 Industrial & Municipal Cleaning Association
906 Olive Street
Suite 1200
Saint Louis, MO 63101-1448

314-241-1445; *Fax:* 314-241-1449
wjta-imca@wjta.org; www.wjta.org

Bill Gaff, Chairman
George Savanick, Ph.D., President
Bill McClister, VP
Larry Loper, Treasurer
Kathy Krupp, Secretary

International association of professionals involved in high/ultra-high waterjet technology and industrial cleaning. Members are contractors, end users, job shops, manufacturers, researchers, and academicians.
Founded in: 1983

13475 Industrial Diamond Association of America
PO Box 29460
Columbus, OH 43229

614-797-2265; *Fax:* 614-797-2264
tkane-ida@insight.rr.com;
www.superabrasives.org

Mike Mustin, President
Terry M Kane, Executive Director
Troy Heuermann, Vice President
Keith Reckling, Secretary/Treasurer

Trade association for those in the superabrasives industry. Products and services provided and used in most manufacturing and constuction industries such as: stone processing, glass, construction, woodworking, electronics, medical, etc.
Founded in: 1946

13476 Industrial Heating Equipment Association
5040 Old Taylor Mill Rd., PMB 13
Taylor Mill, KY 41015

859-356-1575; *Fax:* 859-356-0908
ihea@ihea.org; www.ihea.org
Social Media: Facebook

Anne Goyer, Executive Vice President
Amanda Goyer, Marketing
Mark Gentry, Membership Director
Kelly LeCount, Conference Manager
Leslie Muck, Webmaster and Database Management

A voluntary national trade association representing the major segments of the industrial heat processing equipment industry. Provides services to member companies that will enhance member company capabilities to serve end users in the industrial heat processing industry and improve the member company's business performance as well.
Founded in: 1929
Mailing list available for rent

13477 Industrial Supply Association
100 North 20th Street
Suite 400
Philadelphia, PA 19103

215-320-3862
866-460-2360; *Fax:* 215-564-2175; *Fax:* 877-460-2365
info@isapartners.org; www.isapartners.org
Social Media: Facebook, Twitter, LinkedIn, RSS, YouTube

Craig Vogel, Chairman
John Wiborg, Vice Chairman
Derek Yurgaitis, Treasurer
William Henricks, Secretary
Tommy Thompson, Immediate Past Chairman

ISA goal is to help members increase sales, reduce expenses and improve profitability.
600 Members
Founded in: 1988

13478 Institute for Supply Management
2055 E. Centennial Circle
Tempe, AZ 85284-1802

480-752-6276
800-888-6276; *Fax:* 480-752-7890
custsvc@instituteforsupplymanagement.org;
www.ism.ws

Social Media: Facebook, Twitter, LinkedIn, Youtube, Google Plus

Thomas Derry, CEO
Nora Neibergall, CPSM CPO
Cindy Urbaytis, Managing Director
Mary Lue Peck, Managing Director

The mission of ISM is to enhance the value and performance of procurement and supply chain management practitioners and their organizations worldwide.
45000 Members
Founded in: 1915
Mailing list available for rent

13479 Institute of Industrial Engineers
3577 Parkway Lane
Suite 200
Norcross, GA 30092

770-449-0460
800-494-0460; *Fax:* 770-441-3295
cs@iienet.org; www.iienet.org
Social Media: Facebook, Twitter, LinkedIn, Google+, YouTube

Don Greene, P.E., C.A.E., Chief Executive Officer
Donna Calvert, Chief Operating Officer
Hope Teaque, Dir. - Multimedia Advertising Sales
Nancy LaJoice, Director of Membership
Monica Elliott, Director of Communications

Supports all industrial engineers with training, education, publications, conferences, etc.
15000 Members
Founded in: 1948
Mailing list available for rent

13480 International Staple, Nail and Tool
8735 W. Higgins Road
Suite 300
Chicago, IL 60631

847-375-6454; *Fax:* 847-375-6455
info@isanta.org; www.isanta.org

John Kurtz, Executive VP
David Rapp, Codes/Technical Services

An international organization of premier power fastening companies involved in the design, and manufacturing, and sales of power fastening tools and the fasteners they drive.
22 Members
Founded in: 1966

13481 Machinery Dealers National Association
315 S. Patrick Street
Alexandria, VA 22314-3532

703-836-9300
800-872-7807; *Fax:* 703-836-9303
office@mdna.org; www.mdna.org
Social Media: Facebook, Twitter, LinkedIn, Youtube

Kim Khoury, CEA, President
Joe Lundvick, CEA, First Vice President
John Greene, CEA, Second Vice President
Terry Yoder, Treasurer
Mark Robinson, Executive Vice President

An international, non-profit trade association dedicated to the promotion of the used machinery industry.
400+ Members
Founded in: 1941

13482 NIBA - The Belting Association
6737 W Washington St
Suite 1300
Milwaukee, WI 53214-5648

414-389-8606
800-488-4845; *Fax:* 414-276-7704
staff@niba.org; www.niba.org
Social Media: Facebook, Twitter, LinkedIn

John Shelton, President
Tom Pientok, First Vice President
Vernon Smith, Second Vice President
Bill Hornsby, Second Vice President
Jennifer Rzepka, Executive Director

A voluntary association of individuals and organizations who have joined together to further the interests of all fabricators, distriubtors and manufacturers of belting and related products. Promtes common business interests of all distributors/fabricators and manufacturers of conveyor and flat power transmission belting and material that enhances/changes belt.
Founded in: 1927
Mailing list available for rent

13483 National Corrugated Steel Pipe Association
14070 Proton Road
Suite 100 LB9
Dallas, TX 75244

972-850-1907; *Fax:* 972-490-4219
info@ncspa.org; www.ncspa.org
Social Media: Twitter, LinkedIn, Youtube, RSS

Mike Mihelick, President
Dan Kadrmas, First Vice President
Roger Loding, Treasurer
Wallace Johnson, Immediate Past President
Pat Loney, Secretary

Seeks to promote sound public policy relating to the use of corrugated steel drainage structures in private and public construction.
60 Members
Founded in: 1956

13484 National Spray Equipment Manufacturers
PO Box 2147
Skokie, IL 60076

440-366-6808; *Fax:* 847-763-9538
ipp@halldata.com; www.ippmagazine.com

Bruce Bryan, Advertising Director
Ted Klaiber, Sales Manager

Serves as a technical forum for safety and environmental matters pertaining to the spray finishing industry.
16 Members
Founded in: 1922

13485 New England Equipment Dealers Association
PO Box 895
Concord, NH 03302-0895

603-225-5510; *Fax:* 603-225-5510

George M Becker, Managing Director

The New England Equipment Association serve equipment manufacturing companies who provide products and services to the food and beverage industry.

13486 North American Equipment Dealers Association
1195 Smizer Mill Road
Fenton, MO 63026-3480

636-349-5000; *Fax:* 636-349-5443
naeda@naeda.com; www.naeda.com
Social Media: Facebook, Twitter, LinkedIn

Blaine Bingham, Chairman
Brian Carpenter, First Vice Chairman & Treasurer
Mark Foster, Second Vice Chairman & Secretary
Tom Nobbe, Immediate Past Chairman
Richard Lawhun, President and CEO

NAEDA and its affiliates provides a variety of educational, financial, legislative and legal services to equipment dealers in the United States and Canada.
5000 Members
Founded in: 1900

13487 North American Sawing Association
1300 Sumner Avenue
Cleveland, OH 44115-2851

216-241-7333; *Fax:* 216-241-0105;
www.sawingassociation.com

Charles M Stockinger, Secretary/Treasurer

The purpose of this association is to improve the band sawing and power tool accessoried industries.
8 Members
Founded in: 1959

13488 Society of Tribologists & Lubrication Engineers
840 Busse Hwy
Park Ridge, IL 60068-2302

847-825-5536; *Fax:* 847-825-1456
information@stle.org; www.stle.org
Social Media: Facebook, Twitter, LinkedIn, Youtube

Dr. Martin N. Webster, President
Dr. Ali Erdemir, Vice President
Mr. Michael Anderson, Secretary
Greg Croce, Treasurer
Dr. Maureen E. Hunter, Past President

Purpose is to advance the science of tribology and the practice of lubrication engineering in order to foster innovation, improve the performance of equipment and products, conserve resources and protect the environment.
4000 Members
Founded in: 1944
Mailing list available for rent

13489 The National Council for Advanced Manufacturing (NACFAM)
2025 M St. NW
Suite 800
Washington, DC 20036

202-367-1178; www.nacfam.org

Robert (Rusty) Patterson, Chairman & CEO
Fred Wentzel, Executive Vice President

The non-partisan Council advocates for federal policies that will spur innovation in U.S. manufacturing and make it more competitive globally.

13490 ToolBase Services
NAHB Research Center
400 Prince George's Boulevard
Upper Marlboro, MD 20774

301-494-4000
800-898-2842
toolbase@nahbrc.org; www.toolbase.org

The housing industry's resource for technical information on building products, materials, new technologies, business management, and housing systems.
Mailing list available for rent

13491 Unified Abrasive Manufacturers' Association
30200 Detroit Road
Cleveland, OH 44145-1967

440-899-0010; *Fax:* 440-892-1404
contact@uama.org; www.uama.org

Jeff Wherry, Executive Director

The purpose is to undertake those activties that can be pursued more effectively by an association than individual companies in order to enable the industry to freely create and market safe, productive abrasive products throughout the world.
30 Members
Founded in: 1999

13492 **WaterJet Technology Association Industrial & Municipal Cleaning Association**
906 Olive Street
Suite 1200
Saint Louis, MO 63101-1448

314-241-1445; *Fax:* 314-241-1449
wjta-imca@wjta.org; www.wjta.org

Bill Gaff, Chairman
George Savanick, Ph.D., President
Bill McClister, VP
Larry Loper, Treasurer
Kathy Krupp, Secretary

A professional association of high pressure waterjet and industrial vacuum equipment users, manufacturers, distributors, researchers, regulators and consultants.
Founded in: 1983

13493 **Web Sling & Tiedown Association**
9 Newport Drive
Suite 200
Forest Hill, MD 21050

443-640-1070; *Fax:* 443-640-1031
wstda@stringfellowgroup.net; www.wstda.com
Social Media: LinkedIn

Jeff Iden, President
Greg Pilgrim, Vice-President
Jim Bailey, Secretary/Treasurer
Kathleen A. DeMarco, CAE, Executive Director
Amy Chetelat, CAE, Director of Finance

Manufacturers of web slings which are used as hoists in various industrial lifting operations.
79 Members
Founded in: 1973

Newsletters

13494 **Asphalt Recycling and Reclaiming Association**
Asphalt Recycling and Reclaiming Association
3 Church Cir
PMB Box 250
Annapolis, MD 21401-1933

410-267-0023; *Fax:* 410-267-7546;
www.arra.com

Mike Krissoff, Executive Director

Promotes the interest of owners and manufacturers of recycling equipment, engineers suppliers and businesses involved in the asphalt recycling industry.
Frequency: Quarterly
Circulation: 1200
Founded in: 1976
Mailing list available for rent

13495 **Can Tube Bulletin**
Composite Can & Tube Institute
50 S Pickett Street
Suite 110
Alexandria, VA 22304-7206

703-823-7234; *Fax:* 703-823-7237
ccti@cctiwdc.org; www.cctiwdc.org

Kristine Garland, Executive VP
Wayne Vance, Association Counsel
Janine Marczak, Associate Manager, Events
Frequency: Bi-monthly
Circulation: 800+

13496 **Fastener Industry News**
Business Information Services
5028 Dumont Place
Woodland Hills, CA 91364-2407

818-248-5023
800-929-5586; *Fax:* 818-249-1169
info@biscomputer.com;
www.biscomputer.com

Richard Callahan, Publisher
John Wolz, Editor
Miro Macho, CEO/President

Publication written for executives and administrators in the fastener industry. Focuses on providing readers with business and financial news from within the industry. Includes personnel notices, management ideas and related materials.
Cost: $200.00
8 Pages
Frequency: Monthly
Founded in: 1971
Mailing list available for rent
Printed in 2 colors on matte stock

13497 **Instrumentation and Automation News**
Chilton Company
201 King of Prussia Rd
Radnor, PA 19087-5147

610-964-4762
800-274-2207; *Fax:* 610-964-1888

Matt DeJulio, Publisher

The control technology/instrumentation market's only product news tabloid.

13498 **Journal of the National Spray Equipment Manufacturers Association**
550 Randall Road
Elyria, OH 44035-2974

440-366-6808; *Fax:* 440-892-2018

Don R Scarbrough, Executive Secretary

Includes editorial on safety and environmental matters pertaining to the spray finishing industry. Regular monthly features.
16 Pages
Founded in: 1922

13499 **Manufacturing Automation**
Vital Information Publications
754 Caravel Lane
Foster City, CA 94404-1712

650-345-7018; www.sensauto.com

Peter Adrian, Owner
Gary Kuba, Marketing Director

Provides market research data and vital information about key products, applications, and technologies for a wide range of industrial automation segments, such as CAD/CAM, supply chain management, e-Commerce solutions, enterprise resource planning, automation software, manufacturing technology, industrial controls, and manufacturing systems.

13500 **Sensor Business Digest**
Vital Information Publications
754 Caravel Lane
Foster City, CA 94404-1712

650-345-7018; www.sensauto.com

Peter Adrian, Owner
Gary Kuba, Marketing Director

A widely recognized as a major source of information about the sensors industry-provides unique information about vital sensor markets, products, and applications, sensor technology, as well as in-depth company profiles
Frequency: Monthly

13501 **Sensor Technology**
John Wiley & Sons
111 River St
Hoboken, NJ 07030-5774

201-748-6000
800-825-7550; *Fax:* 201-748-6088
info@wiley.com; www.wiley.com

William J Pesce, CEO

Written for companies and enterprises involved in a broad range of industrial disciplines. Publication follows advances in sensor technologies and their applications, along with opportunities for their use in the industrial marketplace.
Cost: $565.00
10 Pages
Frequency: Daily
Founded in: 1807
Mailing list available for rent: 25000 names at $180 per M
Printed in 2 colors on newsprint stock

13502 **Waterjet Technology Association-Industrial and Municipal Cleaning Association**
906 Olive Street
Suite 1200
Saint Louis, MO 63101-1448

314-241-1445; *Fax:* 314-241-1449
wjta-imca@wjta.org; www.wjta.org

George A Savanick PhD, President, Jet News Editor
Kenneth C Carroll, Association Manager

A professional association of high pressure waterjet and industrial cleaning equipment users, manufacturers, distributors, researchers, regulators, consultants and academicians.
Founded in: 1983

Magazines & Journals

13503 **Advanced Materials & Processes**
ASM International
9639 Kinsman Rd
Materials Park, OH 44073-0002

440-338-5151
800-336-5152; *Fax:* 440-338-4634
memberservices@asminternational.org;
www.asminternational.org

Joseph M Zion, Publisher
Joanne Miller, Managing Editor
Margaret Hunt, Editor-in-Chief
Gernant E. Maurer, President
Thomas S. Passek, Managing Director

AM&P, the monthly technical magazine from ASM International, is designed to keep readers aware of leading-edge developments and trends in engineering materials - metals and alloys, engineering polymers, advanced ceramics, and composites - and the methods used to select, process, fabricate, test, and characterize them.
Frequency: Monthly
Circulation: 32M
Founded in: 1977

13504 **American Industry**
Publications for Industry
21 Russell Woods Road
Great Neck, NY 11021-4644

516-487-0990; *Fax:* 516-487-0809;
www.publicationsforindustry.com

Jack S Panes, Publisher

Created for those executives responsible for overall plant operations and maintenance. Editorial focus is on new products and related services.
Cost: $25.00
Circulation: 300000
Founded in: 1946
Printed in 4 colors on newsprint stock

13505 **American Tool, Die & Stamping News**
Eagle Publications
42400 Grand River Ave
Suite 103
Novi, MI 48375-2572

248-347-3487
800-783-3491; *Fax:* 248-347-3492

info@ameritooldie.com;
www.ameritooldie.com

Applications, techniques, equipment and accessories of metal stamping, moldmaking, electric discharge machining; and new product information relating to the tool and die industry. Accepts advertising.
70 Pages
Frequency: Monthly
Circulation: 30000
ISSN: 0192-5709
Founded in: 1971
Printed in 5 colors on glossy stock

13506 Asian Industrial Report
Keller International Publishing Corporation
150 Great Neck Rd
Great Neck, NY 11021-3309
516-829-9722; *Fax:* 516-829-9306

Gerald E Keller, President
Bryan DeLuca, Editorial Director
Terry Beirne, Publisher
Bob Herlihy, Sales manager

English language tabloid presenting new products, equipment and services.
36 Pages
Circulation: 37107
ISSN: 1076-8351
Founded in: 1882
Printed in 4 colors on glossy stock

13507 Business & Industry
Business Magazines
1720 28th Street
Suite B
West Des Moines, IA 50266-1400
515-225-2545; *Fax:* 515-225-2318;
www.locu.com

James V Snyder, Publisher
RJ Balch, Editor

Industrial news publication
Cost: $24.00
56 Pages
Frequency: Monthly
Circulation: 14M
ISSN: 0021-0463
Founded in: 1946
Printed in 4 colors on glossy stock

13508 Cleaner
COLE Publishing
1720 Maple Lake Dam Road
PO Box 220
Three Lakes, WI 54562-0220

715-546-3346
800-257-7222; *Fax:* 715-546-3786
info@cleaner.com; www.cleaner.com
Social Media: Facebook, Twitter

Jeff Bruss, President
Winnie May, Advertising Sales/Subscriptions
Ted Rulseh, Editor
Bob Kendall, Co-founder

The latest tools and equipment promoting safety and efficiency, employment and enviromental concerns, as well as industry profiles.
Cost: $15.50
Frequency: Monthly
Circulation: 22780
Founded in: 1979

13509 Composites Manufacturers Magazine
American Composites Manufacturers Association
1010 N Glebe Rd
Suite 450
Arlington, VA 22201-5761

703-525-0511; *Fax:* 703-525-0743
info@acmanet.org; www.acmanet.org

Tom Dobbins, Chief Staff Executive
Patti Washburn, Deputy Chief Staff Executive
Frequency: Monthly

13510 Crane & Hoist Canada
Capamara Communications
815 1st Ave
#301
Seattle, WA 98104

250-474-3982
800-936-2266; *Fax:* 250-478-3979
jeremy@capamara.com; www.naqua.com

Peter Chetteburgh, Editor-in-Chief
Jeremy Thain, Sales Manager
James Lewis, Production Department

Only magazine focused exclusively on Canada's crane and hoist sectors. Provides essential news and information that Canadian crane and hoist professionals need in order to operate successfully and profitably. Articles on company profiles, practical crane & rigging information, new product news, industry trends, policy & regulations, safety/training/certification, and risk management.
Cost: $27.95
Frequency: Bi-monthly
Circulation: 3,500
Founded in: 1985

13511 Filtration News
Eagle Publishers
42400 Grand River Ave
Suite 103
Novi, MI 48375-2572

248-347-3487; *Fax:* 248-347-3492
info@filtnews.com

Arthur Brown, Editor
Antoinette DeWaal, Associate Publisher/VP
Ken Norberg, Editor-in-Chief

New products and events on the special aspects of filtraion ranging from new equipment applications to new trends in the filtraion industry.
Cost: $65.00
Frequency: Bi-Monthly
Founded in: 1981

13512 Finer Points Magazine
Industrial Diamond Association of America
PO Box 29460
Columbus, OH 43229
614-797-2265; *Fax:* 614-797-2264
tkane-ida@insight.rr.com;
www.superabrasives.org

Terry Kane, Publisher/Editor
Joe Tabling, President

Information for people who are involved in superabrasives or superabrasive products in some way.
Cost: $35.00
Frequency: Quarterly
Circulation: 7,500
Founded in: 1946

13513 Flow Control
Grand View Media Group
200 Croft Street
Suite 1
Birmingham, AL 35242

888-431-2877; *Fax:* 205-408-3799
flowcontrol@grandviewmedia.com;
www.flowcontrolnetwork.com
Social Media: Facebook, Twitter, LinkedIn

John P Harris, Publisher
Matt Migliore, Editor
Matt Migliore, Executive Director of Content
Amy W. Richardson, Managing Editor
Mary Beth Timmerman, Marketing Manager

Technology information and new products for fluid handling engineers

13514 Hauler
Hauler Magazine
166 S Main Street
PO Box 508
New Hope, PA 18938

800-220-6029
800-220-6029; *Fax:* 215-862-3455
mag@thehauler.com; www.thehauler.com

Thomas N Smith, Publisher/Editor
Barbara Gibney, Circulation Manager
Leslie T Smith, Marketing Director

Dedicated to the refuse and solid waste industry. It is the acknowledged leader in the new and used refuse truck and equipment marketplace, and now lists hundreds of new and used trash trucks, trailers, containers, services, plus parts and accessories from the best suppliers in the industry.
Cost: $12.00
Frequency: Monthly
Circulation: 18630
Founded in: 1978

13515 High Performance Composites
Ray Publishing
P.O.Box 992
Morrison, CO 80465-0992

303-467-1776; *Fax:* 303-467-1777
info@raypubs.com; www.compositeworld.com

Approach is technical, offering cutting-edge design, engineering, prototyping, and manufacturing solutions for aerospace and other traditional and emerging structural applications for advanced composites.

13516 I&CS-Instrumentation & Control Systems
PennWell Publishing Company
1421 S Sheridan Rd
Tulsa, OK 74112-6619

918-831-9421
800-331-4463; *Fax:* 918-831-9476
headquarters@pennwell.com;
www.pennwell.com

Robert Biolchini, President

Regular issue features include new systems analyses, new products listings, application ideas, and tutorial technology features.
Cost: $65.00
Frequency: Monthly
Circulation: 92,618
Founded in: 1910

13517 ICS Cleaning Specialist
BNP Media
22801 Ventura Boulevard
#115
Woodland Hills, CA 91364

818-224-8035
800-835-4398; *Fax:* 818-224-8042;
www.icsmag.com
Social Media: Facebook, Twitter, LinkedIn

Phil Johnson, Group Publisher
Evan Kessler, Publisher
Jeffrey Stouffer, Editor

Dedicated to providing cleaning and restoration/remediation professionals with the most current and relevant information available to the industry.
Frequency: Annual+
Circulation: 25000
Mailing list available for rent

13518 Industrial Distribution
199 East Badger Road
Suite 201
Madison, WI 53713

781-734-8000; *Fax:* 781-734-8070;
www.manufacturing.net/ind
Social Media: Facebook, Twitter

Eric Wixom, Publisher
Jeff Reinke, Editorial Director

Joel Hans, Managing Editor
Mary Ann Gajewski, Production Manager

Provides current, comprehensive, issues-oriented editorial unique to the distribution industry including news, product updates, profitable product selection, management techniques, features on distribution-manufacturer relationships, legal issues and sales improvement.
Cost: $89.90
Frequency: Monthly
Circulation: 38000+
Mailing list available for rent

13519 **Industrial Equipment News**
Thomas Publishing Company
5 Penn Plaza
Manhattan, NY 10001

212-695-0500
800-733-1127; *Fax:* 212-290-7206;
www.ien.com

Mark Maskin, Editorial Director
Deborah Maskin, Managing Editor
Ciro Buttacavoli, Publisher
Marie Urbanowicz, Marketing Director

Serves the industrial field including manufacturing, mining, utilities, construction, transportation,governmental establishments, and educational services.
Frequency: Monthly
Circulation: 205,000+
ISSN: 0019-8258
Founded in: 1898

13520 **Industrial Laser Solutions**
PennWell Publishing Company
1421 S Sheridan Rd
Tulsa, OK 74112-6619

918-831-9421; *Fax:* 918-831-9476;
www.pennwell.com

Robert Biolchini, President
Laureen Belleville, Associate Publisher/Senior Editor

Devoted exclusively to global coverage of industrial laser applications, technology, and the people and companies who participate in this, the largest commerical portion of the global laser market.
45 Pages
Frequency: Monthly
Circulation: 10000
ISSN: 1523-4266
Founded in: 1910

13521 **Industrial Literature Review**
Thomas Publishing Company
5 Penn Plz
12th Floor
New York, NY 10001-1860

212-695-0500; *Fax:* 212-290-7362
businesslists@thomaspublishing.com;
www.thomaspublishing.com

Carl Holst-Knudsen, CEO

Created to provide the dissemination of manufacturer catalogs and literature and mailed to buyers and specifies at plants with more than twenty employees.
Founded in: 1976

13522 **Industrial Maintenance & Plant Operation**
Advantage Business Media
199 E Badger Road
Suite 201
Madison, WI 53713

973-920-7787; *Fax:* 973-607-5599;
www.impomag.com

Tom Lynch, Group Publisher
Eric Wixom, Associate Publisher
Anna Wells, Editor
Jeff Reinke, Editorial Director

provides timely, relevant coverage of manufacturing news, technology breakthrough, and in-plant advancements for plant managers and engineers looking to increase productivity, operate more efficiently and improve competitiveness.
Frequency: Monthly
Founded in: 1940

13523 **Industrial Management**
Institute of Industrial Engineers
3577 Parkway Lane
Suite 200
Norcross, GA 30092

770-449-0460
800-494-0460; *Fax:* 770-441-3295
cs@iienet.org; www.iienet.org

Elaine Fuerst, Marketing Director
Don Greene, Chief Executive Officer
Donna Calvert, Chief Operating Officer
Heather Bradley, Director of Membership
Monica Elliott, Director of Communications

Directed to the full range of management issues including adapting and evaluating new technologies, improving productivity and quality, and motivating employees.
Cost: $35.00
Frequency: Monthly
Circulation: 8500
Founded in: 1948
Mailing list available for rent

13524 **Industrial Market Place**
Wineberg Publications
7842 Lincoln Avenue
Skokie, IL 60077

847-676-1900
800-323-1818; *Fax:* 847-676-0063
info@industrialmktpl.com;
www.industrialmktpl.com

Joel Wineberg, President
Jakie Bitensky, Editor

Has advertisements on machinery, industrial and plant equipment, services and industrial auctions in each issue.
Cost: $175.00
Frequency: Bi-Weekly
Circulation: 14,000
Founded in: 1951
Mailing list available for rent: 120 names at $70 per M
Printed in 4 colors on glossy stock

13525 **Industrial Purchasing Agent**
Publications for Industry
21 Russell Woods Road
Great Neck, NY 11021-4644

516-487-0990; *Fax:* 516-487-0809;
www.PublicationsforIndustry.com

Jack Panes, Publisher
Pearl Shaine, Editor

New products publication for industrial purchasing agent executives in largest plants in the United States. Contains new releases on products, brochures, materials handling, etc.
Cost: $25.00
Frequency: Monthly
Circulation: 27000
Founded in: 1958
Printed in 4 colors on newsprint stock

13526 **International Journal of Purchasing & Materials Management**
National Association of Purchasing Management
2055 E Centennial Circle
PO Box 22160
Tempe, AZ 85285-2160

480-752-2277; *Fax:* 480-491-7885;
www.capsresearch.com
Social Media: Twitter

Phillip L Carter, CEO/President
Richard A. Boyle, Director of Corporate
Kristina Cahill, Research Specialist
Phillip L. Carter, Executive Director
Kim Dixon-Williams, Executive Programs Manager

Publishes articles dealing with concepts from business, economics, operations management, information systems, the behavioral sciences, and other disciplines which contribute to the advancement of knowledge in the various areas of purchasing, materials management, and related fields.
Cost: $59.00
Frequency: Quarterly
Circulation: 2800
Founded in: 1986

13527 **Journal of Coatings Technology**
Federation of Societies for Coatings Technology
1500 Rhode Island Ave., NW
Suite 415
Washington, DC 20005

202-462-6272; *Fax:* 202-462-8549;
www.coatingstech.org

J. Andrew Doyle, President & CEO
Thomas J. Graves, VP, General Counsel
Allen Irish, Counsel / Director, Industry Affair
Alison Keane, Vice President, Government Affairs
Robin Eastman Caldwell, Senior Government Affairs

Includes practical articles, Q&A features, and roundtable discussions with coatings professionals related to industry segments, manufacturing processes, business operations, environmental concerns, and other pertinent topics.
Frequency: 11x/Year

13528 **Journal of Materials Engineering and Performance**
ASM International
9639 Kinsman Road
Materials Park, OH 44073-0002

440-338-5151
800-336-5152; *Fax:* 440-338-4634
memberservice@asminternational.org;
www.asminternational.org

Gernant E. Maurer, President
Thomas S. Passek, Managing Director

Peer-reviewed journal that publishes contributions on all aspects of materials selection, design, characterization, processing and performance testing. The journal for solving day-to-day engineering challenges - especially those involving components for larger systems.
Cost: $1965.00
Frequency: Bimonthly
Circulation: 305
Founded in: 1992

13529 **Journal of Phase Equilibria**
ASM International
9639 Kinsman Rd
Materials Park, OH 44073-0002

440-338-5151
800-336-5152; *Fax:* 440-338-4634
memberservices@asminternational.org;
www.asminternational.org

Gernant E. Maurer, President
Thomas S. Passek, Managing Director

Peer-reviewed journal that contains basic and applied research results, evaluated phase diagrams, a survey of current literature, and comments or

other material pertinent to the previous three areas. The aim is to provide a broad spectrum of information concerning phase equilibria for the materials community.
Cost: $1965.00
Frequency: Bimonthly
Circulation: 305

13530 Journal of Protective Coatings & Linings
Technology Publishing Company
2100 Wharton St
Suite 310
Pittsburgh, PA 15203-1951

412-431-8300
800-837-8303; *Fax:* 412-431-5428
webmaster@paintsquare.com;
www.paintsquare.com
Social Media: Facebook, Twitter

Harold Hower, Owner
Karen Kapsanis, Editor
Milissa Bogats, Production Director
Pam Simmons, Director of Marketing
Julie Birch, Marketing Manager

Focuses on good practice in the use of protective coatings for steel and concrete surfaces. Features articles on such topics as coatings selection for specific service environments, surface preparation, coating application, quality control, cost-effectiveness in maintenance programs, safety issues, and environmental regulations.
Cost: $80.00
Frequency: Monthly
Circulation: 15000
Mailing list available for rent

13531 Journal of Thermal Spray Technology
ASM International
9639 Kinsman Rd
Novelty, OH 44073-0002

440-338-5151
800-336-5152; *Fax:* 440-338-4634
Cust-Srv@asminternational.org;
www.asminternational.org

Gernant E. Maurer, President
Thomas S. Passek, Managing Director

Peer-reviewed journal which publishes contributions on all aspects, fundamental and practical, of thermal spray science, including processes, feedstock manufacture, testing and characterization. As the primary vehicle for thermal spray information transfer, its mission is to synergize the rapidly advancing thermal spray industry and related industries by presenting research and development efforts leading to advancements in implementable engineering applications of the technology.
Cost: $1577.00
Frequency: Bimonthly
Circulation: 680
Founded in: 1952

13532 Lift Equipment
Group III Communications
204 W Kansas Street
Suite 103
Independence, MO 64050
816-254-8735; *Fax:* 816-254-2128

Terry Ford, President
Michael Scheibach, Publisher
Tracy L Bennett, Editor/Associate Publisher

The buyer's source for equipment, technology and trends. Free to qualified subscribers.
Cost: $24.00
80 Pages
Frequency: 10 per year
Circulation: 18,000
ISSN: 1056-0149
Printed in 4 colors on glossy stock

13533 Lubes-N-Greases
LNG Publishing Company
6105 Arlington Blvd
Suite G
Falls Church, VA 22044-2708

703-536-0800; *Fax:* 703-536-0803
info@LNGpublishing.com;
www.lngpublishing.com

Gloria Stienberg, Owner
Tim Sullivan, Managing Editor
Sheryl Unangst, Circulation Manager
Michele Persaud, Senior Editor
Richard Beercheck, Senior Editor

Features and informed opinions covering automotive and industrial lubricants, metalworking fluids, greases, base stocks, additives, packaging, biodegradable and synthetic products, companies, people, issues and trends affecting the industry.
Frequency: Monthly
Circulation: 16000
ISSN: 1080-9449
Founded in: 1995
Printed in 4 colors

13534 Lubricating Engineering
Society of Tribologists & Lubrication Engineers
840 Busse Hwy
Park Ridge, IL 60068-2376

847-825-5536; *Fax:* 847-825-1456
information@stle.org; www.stle.org

Ed Salek, Executive Director
Karl Phipps, Associate Managing Editor
Tracy Nicholas, National Sales Manager

Technical papers and news articles with up to date developments in the lubrication industry.
Frequency: Monthly
Circulation: 6000

13535 MRO Today
Pfingsten Publishing
730 Madison Avenue
Fort Atkinson, WI 53538-606
920-563-5225
800-932-7732; *Fax:* 920-563-4269;
www.mrotoday.com

Todd Rank, VP
Tom Hammel, Associate Publisher/Editorial Dir
John Mansavage, Circulation and Research
Jill Sheppard, Marketing Manager

Provides best practices for industrial maintanence, production, MRO purchasing, quality and safety personnel. MRO Today helps these pros do their jobs cheaper, better, faster and smarter.
Circulation: 120,000
ISSN: 1091-0638
Founded in: 1996
Printed in on glossy stock

13536 Maintenance Technology
Applied Technology Publications
1300 S Grove Ave
Suite 105
Barrington, IL 60010-5246

847-382-8100; *Fax:* 847-304-8603;
www.mt-online.com

Arthur Rice, President/CEO
Bill Kiesel, Vice President/Publisher
Jane Alexander, Editor-In-Chief
Rick Carter, Executive Editor
Randy Buttstadt, Director of Creative Services

Maintenance Technology magazine serves the business and technical information needs of managers and engineers responsible for assuring availability of plant equipment and systems. It provides readers with articles on advanced technologies, strategies, tools, and services for the life-cycle management of capital assets.
Frequency: Monthly
Circulation: 50,827
Mailing list available for rent: 35,263 names at $$15 per M

13537 Measurements & Control
100 Wallace Avenue
Suite 100
Sarasota, FL 34237
941-954-8405
800-883-8894; *Fax:* 941-366-5743

13538 Modern Paint & Coatings
Cygnus Publishing
445 Broad Hollow Road
Melville, NY 11747-3601

631-845-2700; *Fax:* 631-845-2723;
www.cygnuspub.com

Esther D'Amico, Editor
Paul Bonaiuto, CFO
Kathy Scott, Director of Public Relations

The latest technology and news including chemical innovations, new production equipment,new trends and coverage of regulatory affairs.
Cost: $45.00
Frequency: Monthly
Circulation: 14,000

13539 NAEDA Equipment Dealer
North American Equipment Dealers Association
1195 Smizer Mill Rd
Fenton, MO 63026-3480

636-349-5000; *Fax:* 636-349-5443
naeda@naeda.com; www.naeda.com
Social Media: Twitter, LinkedIn

Paul Kindinger, President/CEO
Michael Williams, VP, Government Relations/Treasurer
Terry Leath, Executive Assistant
Roger Gjellstad, First Vice Chair
Lester Killebrew, Chairman

A monthly management and merchandising magazine features articles about successful dealers, new products, new technology, industry news, insurance loss control solutions, and top management tips.
Cost: $45.00
5000 Members
32 Pages
Frequency: Monthly
ISSN: 1074-5017
Founded in: 1959
Printed in 4 colors on glossy stock

13540 New Equipment Digest
Penton Media
1300 E 9th St
Cleveland, OH 44114-1503

216-696-7000; *Fax:* 216-696-6662
information@penton.com; www.penton.com

Jane Cooper, Marketing
Diane Madzelonka, Production Manager
David Kieselstein, Chief Executive Officer
Kurt Nelson, Vice President, Human Resources
Andrew Schmolka, Senior Vice President

Serves the general industrial field which includes manufacturing, processing, engineering services, construction, transportation, mining, public utilities, wholesale distributors, educational services, libraries, and governmental establishments.
Frequency: Monthly
Circulation: 206154
Founded in: 1936
Mailing list available for rent

13541 OEM Off-Highway
1233 Janesville Avenue
PO Box 803
Fort Atkinson, WI 53538-803

920-563-6388
800-547-7377; *Fax:* 920-328-9029

Leslie.Shalabi@cygnuspub.com;
www.oemoffhighway.com

Richard Reiff, Executive VP
Leslie Shalabi, Publisher/Editor
Paul Mackler, President/CEO
Barb Hesse, Circulation Manager

Offers information on off-road machinery and farm equipment.
Founded in: 1965

13542 **Purchasing Magazine's Buying Strategy Forecast**
Reed Business Information
275 Washington St
Newton, MA 02458-1611

617-964-3030; *Fax:* 617-558-4327
kbecker@reedbusiness.com

Kathy Doyle, Publisher
Paul Teague, Chief Editor
Kathy Becker, Publisher's Assistant

Provides insight and forecasts of numerous industrial and commercial raw materials products.
Circulation: 95,095
Founded in: 1960

13543 **Rental Product News**
Cygnus Business Media
3 Huntington Quadrangle
Suite 301N
Melville, NY 11747

631-845-2700
800-308-6397; *Fax:* 631-845-2741
info@cygnus.com; www.cygnusb2b.com

Dave Davel, VP Publishing
Kris Flitcroft, Group Publisher
Carrier Grall, Publisher
Paul Bonaiuto, Chief Financial Officer
John French, Chief Executive Officer

Provides professional rental operators with the latest insights on equipment asset management so they can make their businesses more productive and competitive. Also provides insight on how leaders in the equipment rental field are getting the best return from their assets through better equipment selection, application, maintenance and safety techniques.
Circulation: 20000
Founded in: 1966

13544 **Robotics World**
Douglas Publications
2807 N Parham Road
Suite 200
Richmond, VA 23294

804-762-9600
800-791-8699
570-567-1982; *Fax:* 570-320-2079;
www.douglaspublications.com

Jack Browne, Editor
Andrew Dwyer, Publisher

Covers key developments in the field of flexible automation and intelligent machines for an audience of management level automation professionals.
Frequency: Monthly
Circulation: 87000
Founded in: 1985

13545 **Twin Plant News**
5400 Suncrest
Suite D-5
El Paso, TX 79912

915-532-1567; *Fax:* 915-544-7556;
www.twinplantnews.com

Michele Lee, President
Rosa Ma Nibbe, Executive Publisher
Mike Patten, Managing Editor

Focuses on the operations of major companies in the United States and the maquiladoras in Mexico. Includes articles about changes affecting the automotive, electronics, plastics and metal industries, as well as information about customs regulations on both sides of the border and other relevant topics.
Frequency: Monthly
Founded in: 1985

13546 **World Industrial Reporter**
Keller International Publishing Corporation
150 Great Neck Rd
Great Neck, NY 11021-3309

516-829-9722; *Fax:* 516-829-9306;
www.supplychainbrain.com

Bryan DeLuca, Editor
Terry Beirne, Publisher
Jerry Keller, President
Mary Chavez, Director of Sales

New equipment, machinery and techniques for the industry.
34 Pages
Circulation: 37,107
Founded in: 1882

Trade Shows

13547 **AMSE Internation Manufacturing Science & Engineering Conference**
American Society of Mechanical Engineers
Three Park Avenue
New York, NY 10016-5990

973-882-1170
800-843-2763
infocentral@asme.org; www.asme.org

David Walsh, Editor
Chitra Sethi, Managing Editor
John Kosowatz, Senior Editor

The MSEC highlights cutting edge manufacturing research in technical paper, poster and panel sessions.
3200 Attendees
Frequency: Annual/Fall
Founded in: 1880
*Mailing list available for rent*at $125 per M

13548 **ASIS Annual Conference and Exhibits**
American Society of Industrial Security
1625 Prince Street
Alexandria, VA 22314-2818

703-519-6200
703-519-6299; *Fax:* 703-519-6299
asis@asisonline.org; www.asisonline.org

Eduard J. Emde, President
Michael J Stack, CEO

The most comprehensive educational and networking event in the security industry that offers high-quality and insightful educational sessions on every aspect of security; exhibits featuring the latest security technology and innovations and providing a forum for 900 companies to demonstrate the cutting-edge security products and services that are shaping the security industry.
38000 Members
14M Attendees
Frequency: September
Founded in: 1955
Mailing list available for rent

13549 **ASM Heat Treating Society Conference & Exposition**
Materials Information Society
9639 Kinsman Road
Materials Park, OH 44073-0002

440-385-5151
800-336-5152; *Fax:* 440-338-4634
pamela.kleinman@asminternational.org;
www.asminternational.org

Pamela Kleinma, Senior Manager, Events
Kellye Thomas, Exposition Account Manager
Gernant E. Maurer, President
Thomas S. Passek, Managing Director

Conference and exhibits of heat treating equipment and supplies plus information of interest to metallurgists, manufacturing, research and design technical professionals. 300 exhibitors.
3500 Attendees
Frequency: September, Bi-Annual
Founded in: 1974

13550 **ASM Materials Science & Technology (MS&T)**
Materials Information Society
9639 Kinsman Road
Materials Park, OH 44073-0002

440-338-5151
800-336-5152; *Fax:* 440-338-4634
pamela.kleinman@asminternational.org;
www.asminternational.org

Pamela Kleinman, Senior Manager, Events
Kelly Thomas, Exposition Account Manager
Gernant E. Maurer, President
Thomas S. Passek, Managing Director

Annual event focusing on testing, analysis, characterization and research of materials such as engineered materials, high performance metals, powdered metals, metal forming, surface modification, welding and joining. 350 exhibitors.
4,000 Attendees
Frequency: Annual/October
Founded in: 2005

13551 **ASME Annual Meeting**
American Society of Mechanical Engineers
Three Park Avenue
New York, NY 10016

973-882-1170
800-843-2763; *Fax:* 212-591-7856
infocentral@asme.org; www.asme.org

Melissa Torres, Meetings Manager
Mary Jakubowski, Meetings Manager
David Walsh, Editor
Chitra Sethi, Managing Editor
John Kosowatz, Senior Editor
Frequency: Annual/June
Founded in: 1880
Mailing list available for rent

13552 **ASME Gas Turbine Users Symposium (GTUS)**
American Society of Mechanical Engineers/IGTI
6525 The Corners Pkwy
Ste. 115
Norcross, GA 30092

404-847-0072; *Fax:* 404-847-0151
igti@asme.org; www.asme.org/igti

Stephanie Searsr, Coordinator, IGTI Conferences
Judy Osborn, Manager, IGTI Conferences & Expos
Michael Ireland, Managing Director
Charity Golden, Operations Director
Shirley Barton, Manager, Professional Development

A show focused on the role gas turbines will play in meeting the nation's future energy demands, provides the information related to gas turbine operations, maintenance, advances, and design.
2000 Attendees
Frequency: Annual
Mailing list available for rent

13553 **AeroMat Conference and Exposition**
ASM International

9639 Kinsman Road
Materials Park, OH 44073-0002

440-385-5151
800-336-5152; *Fax:* 440-338-4634
kim.schaefer@asminternational.org;
www.asminternational.org

Kim Schaefer, Event Manager
Kelly Thomas, Exposition Account Manager
Gernant E. Maurer, President
Thomas S. Passek, Managing Director

Conference for Aerospace Meterials Engineers, Structural Engineers and Designers. The annual event focuses on affordable structures and low-cost manufacturing, titanium alloy technology, advanced intermetallics and refractory metal alloys, materials and processes for space applications, aging systems, high strength steel, NDT evaluation, light alloy technology, welding and joining, and engineering technology. 150 exhibitors.
1500 Attendees
Frequency: Annual/June
Founded in: 1984

13554 **Association of Machinery and Equipment Appraisers Annual Conference**
315 S Patrick Street
Alexandria, VA 22314-3501

703-836-7900
800-537-8629; *Fax:* 703-836-9303
amea@amea.org; www.amea.org

Lorna Lindsey, Manager
Charles J. Winternitz, President
Pamela Reid, Director, Member Services

Exhibits of interest to machinery and equipment appraisers.
300 Members
Founded in: 1983
Mailing list available for rent

13555 **CCTI Annual Meeting**
Composite Can & Tube Institute
50 S Pickett Street
Suite 110
Alexandria, VA 22304-7206

703-823-7234; *Fax:* 703-823-7237
ccti@cctiwdc.org; www.cctiwdc.org

Kristine Garland, Executive VP
Wayne Vance, Association Counsel
Janine Marczak, Associate Manager, Events
Frequency: May

13556 **Capital Industrial Show**
Industiral Shows of America
1794 The Alameda
San Jose, CA 95126-1729

408-947-0233; *Fax:* 408-286-8836

Annual show and exhibits of industrial equipment, supplies and services.
4000 Attendees

13557 **Dynamic Positioning Conference**
Marine Technology Society
1100 H St., Nw
Suite LL-100
Washington, DC 20005

202-717-8705; *Fax:* 202-347-4302
membership@mtsociety.org;
www.mtsociety.org
Social Media: Facebook, Twitter, LinkedIn

Jerry Boatman, President
Drew Michel, President-Elect
Jerry Wilson, VP of Industry and Technology
Jill Zande, VP of Education and Research
Justin Manley, VP of Gov. & Public Affairs

Recognized as the leading symposium covering developments and technology associated with Dynamic Positioning. Industry leaders discuss DP-related vessel design, and operations, and DP manufacturers and service companies exhibit their products and services to a highly targeted and focused audience.
2M Members
Founded in: 1963

13558 **FABFORM**
Industrial Shows of America
164 Lake Front Drive
Hunt Valley, MD 21030-2215

410-771-1445
800-638-6396; *Fax:* 410-771-1158

This is the most effective way to reach forming, fabricating and welding equipment buyers in the Northern California area.
3000 Attendees
Frequency: April

13559 **Federation of Societies for Coatings Technology**
Federation of Societies for Coatings Technology
492 Norristown Road
Blue Bell, PA 19422-2350

610-940-0777; *Fax:* 610-940-0292;
www.coatingstech.com

Robert Ziegler, Publisher
Patricia D Ziegler, Semior Editor
Ray Dickie, Editor

Provides a major service to the coatings industry, serves as a link between users and supplies of raw materials, production equipment, coatings, adhesives, inks, sealants, testing equipment, containers and laboratory apparatus.International Coating Expo November, Georgia World Congress Center in Atlanta, Georgia.

13560 **Great Lakes Industrial Show**
North American Expositions Company
33 Rutherford Avenue
Boston, MA 02129

617-242-6092
800-225-1577; *Fax:* 617-242-1817;
www.greatlakesindustrialcontrols.com

Denise Novack, Contact

With over 300 companies exhibiting, showcases the latest technology, products, services and solutions for your manufacturing needs.
14319 Attendees
Frequency: November
Founded in: 1972

13561 **ISMA/IDA Spring & Fall Conventions**
Industrial Distribution Association
100 N 20th Street
Suite 400
Philadelphia, PA 19103

215-320-3862
866-460-2360; *Fax:* 215-963-9785
info@isapartners.org; www.isapartners.org
Social Media: Facebook, Twitter, LinkedIn

John Duffy, Director
Ed Gerber, President
Michael Carr, Vice President
Tommy Thompson, Treasurer

Semi-annual conventions for distributors and manufacturers of industrial (MROP) supplies.

13562 **Industrial Marketing Expo**
Lobos Services
16016 Perkins Road
Baton Rouge, LA 70810

225-751-5626

Debbie Balough, Show Manager

250 booths.
6M Attendees
Frequency: April

13563 **Industrial Products Expo and Conference**
Key Productions
94 Murphy Road
Hartford, CT 06114-2121

860-247-8363
880-753-9776; *Fax:* 860-947-6900
webadmin@keypro.com; www.keypro.com

Maura Lewis, Show Manager

This show features exhibits and/or services used in manufacturing, management and warehousing.
6M Attendees
Frequency: September

13564 **Industrial Show Pacific Coast**
Industrial Shows of America
164 Lake Front Drive
Hunt Valley, MD 21030-2215

410-771-1445
800-638-6396; *Fax:* 410-771-1158

James K Donahue, President

Four hundred booths.
11M Attendees
Frequency: November

13565 **International Fastener and Precision Formed Parts Manufacturing Expo**
Pemco
383 Main Avenue
Norwalk, CT 06851-1543

203-840-7700
800-323-5155; *Fax:* 630-260-0395

Biennial show and exhibits of cold headers and header tooling, tools and dies, forming machines, parts feeding and handling equipment and test equipment for the industrial fastener and precision formed parts manufacturing industry.

13566 **International Off-Highway and Power Plant Meeting and Exposition**
Society of Automotive Engineers
400 Commonwealth Drive
Warrendale, PA 15096-0001

724-776-4841; *Fax:* 724-776-4026;
www.sae.org

Diane Rogne, Show Manager
Sam Barill, Treasurer
Andrew Brown, Treasurer

Annual show of 270 suppliers of parts, components, materials and systems utilized in farm and industrial machinery and off-road and recreational vehicles.
5000 Attendees
Circulation: 84,000

13567 **International Symposium for Testing & Failure Analysis**
ASM International
9639 Kinsman Road
Materials Park, OH 44073-0002

440-338-5151
800-336-5152; *Fax:* 440-338-4634
kim.schaefer@asminternational.org;
www.asminternational.org

Kim Schaefer, Event Manager
Kelly Thomas, Exposition Account Manager
Gernant E. Maurer, President
Thomas S. Passek, Managing Director

Annual event focusing on microelectronic and elcetronic device failure analysis, techniques, EOS/ESD testing and descretes aimed at failure analysis engineers and managers, technisians and new failure analysis engineers. 200 exhibitors.
1100 Attendees
Frequency: Annual/November

13568 Mid South Industrial, Material Handling and Distribution Expo
Industrial Shows of America
164 Lake Front Drive
Hunt Valley, MD 21030-2215

410-771-1445
800-638-6396; *Fax:* 410-771-1158

James K Donahue, President

300 booths of industrial and business related products and services.
8M Attendees
Frequency: June

13569 National Association of Industrial Technology Convention
National Association of Industrial Technology
3300 Washtenaw Avenue
Suite 220
Ann Arbor, MI 48104-4294

734-677-0720; *Fax:* 734-677-2407
nait@nait.org; www.nait.org

Dr. Alvin Thadisill, Show Manager
Dave Monporan, Exhibit Manager
Rick Coscarelli, Executive Director

Annual convention of National Association of Industrial Technology, professional association of two and four year Industrial Technology program, faculty, standards and professionals in industry. Exhibitors desired in textbooks, training manuals, software and video; testing and training equipment, computer hardware and software, ISP's and distance learning hosts; CAD/CAM; Rapid Protyping; PC's. There are 25 booths. Next show is in Pittsburgh, Pennsylvania.
500 Attendees
Frequency: November

13570 Pacific Coast Industrial and Machine Tool Show
ISOA
1794 The Alameda
San Jose, CA 95126-1729

408-947-0233
800-286-2882; *Fax:* 408-286-8836

Annual show of 260 exhibitors of industrial equipment, machine tools, business services, hand tools and related equipment, supplies and services.
12M Attendees
Frequency: November, Santa Clara

13571 Rocky Mountain Industrial and Machine Tool Show
Trade Shows West
360 S Fort Ln
Suite 2C
Layton, UT 84041-5708

801-485-0176; *Fax:* 801-485-0241;
www.facetofacemarketing.net

A three day exhibit focusing on the needs of the industrial, manufacturing and plant maintenance industries.
8463 Attendees
Frequency: Annual/May

13572 Salt Lake Machine Tool & Manufacturing Exposition
Trade Shows West
2880 S Main Street
Suite 110
Salt Lake City, UT 84115

801-485-0176; *Fax:* 801-485-0241
jeffwfredericks@hotmail.com;
www.facetofacemarketing.net

13573 Tidewater Industrial & Manufacturing Technology Show
Industrial Shows of America
164 Lake Front Drive
Hunt Valley, MD 21030-2215

410-771-1445
800-638-6396; *Fax:* 410-771-1158;
www.isoa.com

Annual show of 250 suppliers and distributors of industrial and marine equipment, machine and hand tools, business services and related equipment, supplies and services.
Frequency: September, VA Beach

13574 Tri-State Industrial & Machine Tools Show
Industrial Shows of America
164 Lake Front Drive
Hunt Valley, MD 21030-2215

410-771-1445
800-638-6396; *Fax:* 410-771-1158

This show will bring together exhibitors and customers to preview products and discuss new technologies for the metalworking and manufacturing industries. The show will feature machine tools, metalworking equipment, services for manufacturing industrial products and supplies. Thousands of qualified decision-makers involved in management, engineering, purchasing and manufacturing will attend.
Frequency: April

13575 USA/Mexico Industrial Expo
Industrial Shows of America
164 Lake Front Drive
Hunt Valley, MD 21030-2215

410-771-1445
800-638-6396; *Fax:* 410-771-1158

This event draws attendees from avariety of manufacturing and assembly companies. Product categories include material handling, safety equipment, compressors, maintenance equipment, industrial water products, hydraulic/pneumatics, tools and many more. On average, attendees spend over $100,000 per year obn these products.
9000 Attendees
Frequency: June

Directories & Databases

13576 Capital Cities Regional Industrial Buying Guide
Thomas Publishing Company
5 Penn Plaza
New York, NY 10001-1810

212-950-0500

A who's who directory of supplies to the industry.
Cost: $65.00
1200 Pages
Frequency: Annual

13577 Directory of the Association of Machinery and Equipment Appraisers
Association of Machinery and Equipment Appraisers
315 S Patrick St
Alexandria, VA 22314-3532

703-836-7900
800-537-8629; *Fax:* 703-836-9303
amea@amea.org; www.amea.org

Pamela Reid, Director, Member Services
Lorna Lindsey, Manager
Charles J. Winternitz, President

Nearly 300 member certified machinery appraisers.
300 Members
Frequency: Annual January
Founded in: 1983
Mailing list available for rent

13578 IGWB Buyer's Guide
BNP Media
PO Box 1080
Skokie, IL 60076-9785

847-763-9534; *Fax:* 847-763-9538
igwb@halldata.com; www.igwb.com

James Rutherford, Editor
Lynn Davidson, Marketing
Nikki Smith, Director

A comprehensive resource listing over 1000 gaming products and services suppliers.
Frequency: Annual

13579 Industrial Machinery Digest
Cygnus Interactive
262 Yeager Parkway
Suite C
Pelham am, AL 35124

866-833-5346; *Fax:* 866-826-5918
william.strickland@cygnusb2b.com;
www.indmacdig.com
Social Media: Facebook, Twitter, LinkedIn

William Strickland, Publisher
Adrienne Gallender, Associate Publisher
Lisa Hanschu, Sales Consultant
Amy Boelk, Art Director / Print Product
Susan Hopkins, Accounting

A leader among industrial trade publications distributed to machine shops, job shops, fabricating shops, gear manufacturers, industrial warehouses & distribution centers, large industrial facilities & manufacturing plants, material handling, retro & rebuilding machine maintenance, pipe & tube manufacturers and manchinery dealers and wholesalers.

13580 SBC Industrial Purchasing Guide
100 E Big Beaver Rd
Suite 700E
Troy, MI 48083-1248

248-524-4800
800-331-1385; *Fax:* 248-524-4849;
www.smartpages.com

Susan Wright, Industrial Operations Manager
Nicole Howard-Combs, Director

Providers of industrial products and services; seperate regional editions cover Illinois, Wisconsin, Indiana, Michigan, and Ohio.

13581 Sweets Directory
Grey House Publishing/McGraw Hill Construction
1221 Avenue of the Americas
New York, NY 10020-1095

212-512-2000
800-442-2258; *Fax:* 212-512-3840
webmaster@mcgraw-hill.com;
www.mcgraw-hill.com
Social Media: Facebook, Twitter

Harold W McGraw III, CEO

The leading desktop reference and preliminary research guide, featuring more than 10,000 building product manufacturers and their products.
Cost: $145.00
950 Pages
Frequency: Annual
ISBN: 1-592378-50-1
Founded in: 1906

13582 ThomasNet
Thomas Publishing Company, LLC
User Services Department
5 Penn Plaza
New York, NY 10001

212-695-0500
800-699-9822; *Fax:* 212-290-7362
contact@thomaspublishing.com;

www.thomasnet.com
Social Media: Facebook, Twitter, LinkedIn

Carl Holst-Knudsen, President
Robert Anderson, VP, Planning
Mitchell Peipert, VP, Finance
Ivy Molofsky, VP, Human Resources

A way to reach qualified businesses that list their company information on ThomasNet.com. Detailed profiles promote their products, services, capabilities and brands carried. The ThomasNet.com web site is the most up-to-date compilation of 650,000 North American manufacturers, distributors, and service companies in 67,000 industrial categories.
Founded in: 1898
Mailing list available for rent

13583 World Industrial Reporter: Directory of Distributors Issue
Keller International Publishing Corporation
150 Great Neck Rd
Great Neck, NY 11021-3309

516-829-9722; *Fax:* 516-829-9306;
www.supplychainbrain.com

Jerry Keller, President
Mary Chavez, Director of Sales

A list of over 3,000 international advertisers and their distributors with product line related to the industrial supplies and equipment industry.
Cost: $45.00
Frequency: Annual

13584 World Industrial Reporter: International Buyer's Guide Issue
Keller International Publishing Corporation
150 Great Neck Rd
Great Neck, NY 11021-3309

516-829-9722; *Fax:* 516-829-9306;
www.supplychainbrain.com

Jerry Keller, President
Mary Chavez, Director of Sales

Over 275 international advertisers are listed that offer industrial supplies and equipment for export.
Cost: $5.00
Frequency: Annual
Circulation: 40,000

Industry Web Sites

13585 http://gold.greyhouse.com
G.O.L.D Grey House OnLine Databases

Grey House Publishing's online database platform, GOLD, offers Quick Search, Keyword Search and Expert Search for most business sectors including industrial equipment markets. The GOLD platform makes finding the information you need quick and easy - whether you're a novice searcher or an experienced database user. All of Grey House's directory products are available for subscription on the GOLD platform.

13586 www.amea.org
Association of Machinery and Equipment Appraisers

The premier international association of appraisers who specialize in appraising machinery and equipment.

13587 www.arra.org
Asphalt Recycling and Reclaiming Association

Promotes the interest of owners and manufacturers of recycling equipment, engineers suppliers and businesses involved in the asphalt recycling industry.

13588 www.atmae.org
Assoc of Tech, Management, and Applied Engineering

Faculty, students and industry professionals dedicated to solving complex technological probelms and developing the competitive technologist and applied engineering workforce.

13589 www.greyhouse.com
Grey House Publishing

Authoritative reference directories for most business sectors including industrial equipment markets. Users can search the online databases with varied search criteria allowing for custom searches by product category, geographic area, sales volume, keyword, subject and more. Full Grey House catalog and online ordering also available.

13590 www.ida-assoc.org
Industrial Supply Association

To help members increase sales, reduce expenses and improve profiyability

13591 www.mdna.org
Machinery Dealers National Association

Represents dealers of used industrial equipment.

13592 www.mt-online.com
Applied Technology Publications

MT-online.com is the premier source of capacity assurance and best practice solutions for manufacturing, process and service operations worldwide. Online home of Maintenance Technology magazie, the dynamic MT-online.com portal serves the critical technical, business and professional-development needs of engineers, managers and technicians from across all industrial, institutional and commercial sectors.

13593 www.polysort.com
Polysort.com

A portal for the plastics and rubber industry, providing news, information about plastics and rubber industry trade shows, company links, as well as plastics and rubber classified advertising

13594 www.sweets.construction.com
McGraw Hill Construction

In depth product information that lets you find, compare, select, specify and make purchase decisions in the industrial product marketplace.

13595 www.thomasregister.com Thomas Register
Thomas Register

Comprehensive online resource for defining companies and products manufactured in North America. Use it for placing orders, downloading computer-aided design drawings, and viewing thousands of online company catalogs and websites.

Associations

13596 **Alliance of Claims Assistance Professionals**
9600 Escarpment
Suite 745-65
Austin, TX 78749

512-394-0008
888-394-5163
capinfo@claims.org; www.claims.org
Social Media: Twitter

Rebecca Stephenson, Co-President
Katalin Goencz, Co-President

Professionals dedicated to the effective management of health insurance claims. Our members are claims assistance professionals who work for patients.
50 Members
Founded in: 1991

13597 **America's Health Insurance Plans**
601 Pennsylvania Ave., NW
South Building, Suite 500
Washington, DC 20004-2601

202-778-3200; *Fax:* 202-331-7487
ahip@ahip.org; www.ahip.org
Social Media: Twitter

Karen M Ignagni, President/CEO

Mission is to be an effective advocate for a workable legislative and regulatory environment at the federal and state levels in which our members can advance their vision of a health care system that meets the needs of consumers, employers and public purchasers.
1300 Members
Founded in: 2003
Mailing list available for rent

13598 **American Academy of Actuaries**
1850 M Street NW
Suite 300
Washington, DC 20036

202-223-8196; *Fax:* 202-872-1948
webmaster@actuary.org; www.actuary.org
Social Media: Facebook, Twitter, LinkedIn, Youtube

Mary D. Miller, President
Tom Wildsmith, President-Elect
Tom Terry, Immediate Past President
Art Panighetti, Treasurer
John Moore, Secretary

AAA is a public policy organization for actuaries within the US. The Academy acts as the public information organization for the profession. Assisting public policy process through the presentation of clear actuarial analysis, the Academy regularly prepares testimony for Congress, provides information to federal elected officials, regulators and congressional staff, comments on proposed federal regulations, and works closely with state officials on issues related to insurance.
18,00 Members
Founded in: 1965
Mailing list available for rent

13599 **American Agents Alliance**
1231 I Street
Suite 201
Sacramento, CA 95814

916-283-9473
866-497-9222; *Fax:* 916-283-9479
info@agentsalliance.com;
www.agentsalliance.com
Social Media: Facebook, Twitter, LinkedIn, Google Plus

Ken May, President
Brady Harrigan, Vice President
Charlie Garrison, Chief Financial Officer
Mike D'Arelli, Executive Director
Toni Damberger, Secretary

We're a national insurance association dedicated to serving the professional needs of independent insurance agents & brokers.
Founded in: 1962

13600 **American Association for Long Term Care Insurance**
3835 E. Thousand Oaks Blvd.
Suite 336
Westlake Village, CA 91362

818-597-3227; *Fax:* 818-597-3206
info@aaltci.org; www.aaltci.org

Jesse Slome, Media Inquiries
Joseph Howard, Board of Advisor
Don Hansen, Board of Advisor
Tom Hebrank, Board of Advisor
Larry Thomas, Board of Advisor

National trade organization for the long term care insurance industry in the United States.
Founded in: 1998

13601 **American Association of Crop Insurers**
1 Massachusetts Ave NW
Suite 800
Washington, DC 20001-1401

202-789-4100; *Fax:* 202-408-7763
aaci@mwmlaw.com; www.cropinsurers.com

Mike McLeod, Executive Director
David Graves, Manager/Secretary

A organization that represents companies involved with the Federal crop insurance program.
25 Members
Founded in: 1980

13602 **American Association of Dental Consultants**
10032 Wind Hill Drive
Greenville, IN 47124

812-923-2600
800-896-0707; *Fax:* 812-923-2900;
www.aadc.org

Dr.Michael D. Weisenfeld, President
Dr. Marc K. Zweig, President-Elect
Dr. Lawrence M Hoffman, Secretary-Treasurer
Dr. Kay D. Eckroth, PastPresident
Judith K. Salisbury, Executive Director

Members are dentists, insurance consultants, benefits programs administrators and other dental professionals.
350 Members
Founded in: 1979

13603 **American Association of Insurance Management Consultants**
Eaglemark Consulting Group
PO Box 20
Lemoyne, PA 17043

717-763-7717; *Fax:* 717-763-7989
lesley.Perkins@aaimco.com; www.aaimco.com

Lee M Hoffman, President
Mary LaPorte, Membership Director
Lesley Perkins, Executive Director
Kevin Hromas, Membership Inquiries
Van Hedges, General Inquiries

THe premier association of consultants to the insurance industry: insurance companies, agents, brokers, and their consumers. Also dedicated to helping the insurance industry operate more efficiently and more profitably, thus enabling improved service to the buying public.
35 Members
Founded in: 1979

13604 **American Association of Insurance Services**
701 Warrenville Road
Lisle, IL 60532

630-681-8347
800-564-AAIS; *Fax:* 630-681-8356;
www.aaisonline.com
Social Media: Facebook, LinkedIn

Edmund J. Kelly, President, CEO
Joan Zerkovich, SVP, Operations
Robin Westcott, VP, Govt. Affairs
John Kadous, CPCU, CPM, VP, Personal Lines
Bill Bickerton, VP, Data Analytics

A member-owned, nonprofit national insurance advisory organization that provides specialized services to property/casualty insurers.

13605 **American Association of Managing General Agents**
610 Freedom Business Center
Suite 110
King of Prussia, PA 19406-2832

610-992-0022; *Fax:* 610-992-0021
bernie@aamga.org; www.aamga.org
Social Media: Facebook, Twitter, LinkedIn

Roger Ware, Jr., ARM, President
Ed Dickerson, III, CIC, Senior Vice President
Corinne Jones, CPCU, Senior Vice President
Edward Levy, CIW, President Elect
Mark Maucere, CIW, Vice President

A trade association of the premier wholesale property and casualty agents and companies in the insurance industry, committed to fostering the business partnerships, networking, professionalism, trusted expertise and exchange of knowledge among its members.
Founded in: 1926
Mailing list available for rent

13606 **American Association of Retired Persons (AARP)**
American Association of Retired Persons
601 E Street NW
Suite A1-200
Washington, DC 20049-0003

202-434-2277
888-687-2277
202-434-3525; *Fax:* 202-434-7599
member@aarp.org; www.aarp.org
Social Media: Facebook, Twitter, RSS

Gail E. Aldrich, Board Chair
Josh Collett, VP, International Affairs
Jeffrey Gullo, Policy Analyst
Holly Schulz, Editorial Manager
Bradley Schurman, Senior Advisor

AARP is a nonprofit membership organization of persons 50 and older dedicated to addressing their needs and interests. Services include: informing members and the public on issues important to this age group; advocating on legislative, consumer and legal issues; promoting community service, and offering a wide range of special products and services to members. There are 39+ million members within the United States.
Founded in: 1958
Mailing list available for rent

13607 **American Association of State Compensation Insurance Funds**
P.O. Box 20073
Towson, MD 21284

877-494-3237; *Fax:* 800-925-9420
dgarfield@wcf.com; www.aascif.org/
Social Media: Facebook

Ray Pickup, President and CEO
Tom Phelan, Past President
Kristin Walls, Vice President
Gerard Adams, Vice President
Dennis Lloyd, Treasurer/Secretary

An association of workers' compensation insurance companies from 27different states, plus 11 workers' compensation boards in Canada.

13608 American Cargo War Risk Reinsurance
30 Broad Street
7th floor
New York, NY 10004
212-405-2835; *Fax:* 212-344-1664;
www.ahtins.org
TD Montgomery, Chairman
RJ Decker, Vice Chairman
TA Haig Dick, Secretary/Director
Warren C Dietz, Treasurer
Reinsurance pool of member companies.
Founded in: 1939

13609 American Council of Life Insurance
101 Constitution Avenue, NW
Suite 700
Washington, DC 20001-2133
202-624-2000; *Fax:* 202-624-2115
contact@acli.com; www.acli.com
Social Media: Facebook, Twitter, YouTube, RSS
Dirk Kempthorne, President & Chief Executive Officer
Brian Waidmann, Chief of Staff
Gary E. Hughes, EVP, General Counsel
J. Bruce Ferguson, SVP, State Relations
Don Walker, SVP, Administration & CFO
Works to advance the interests of the life insurance industry and to provide effective government relations. Conducts investment and social research programs.
631 Members
Founded in: 1976
Mailing list available for rent

13610 American Fraternal Alliance
1301 West 22nd Street
Suite 700
Oak Brook, IL 60523-6022
630-522-6322; *Fax:* 630-522-6326
info@fraternalalliance.org;
www.fraternalalliance.org
Social Media: Facebook, Twitter
Harald Borrmann, Chair
Patrick Dees, Vice Chair
Joseph J. Annotti, President, CEO
Allison Koppel, Executive Vice President
Melanie Hinds, Director, Advocacy
The trade association of America's fraternal benefit societies.
69 Members
Founded in: 1886

13611 American Institute of Marine Underwriters
14 Wall Street
Suite 820
New York, NY 10005-2145
212-233-0550; *Fax:* 212-227-5102
aimu@aimu.org; www.aimu.org
Frank Costa, Chairman of the Board
Drew Feldman, Vice Chairman
John A Miklus, President
Michael McKenna, Director of Finances
Eileen Monreale, Education/Training Specialist
Provides information of interest to marine underwriters and promotes their interests.

13612 American Insurance Association
2101 L Street, NW
Suite 400
Washington, DC 20037-1542
202-828-7100; *Fax:* 202-293-1219
info@aiadc.org; www.aiadc.org
Social Media: Facebook, Twitter, Youtube
Leigh Ann Pusey, President & CEO
J. Stephen Zielezienski, Senior Vice President
Joseph Digiovanni, Senior VP, State Affairs
Peter R Foley, Vice President, Claims Admin.
Eric M Goldberg, Vice President, State Govt Affairs
The leading property and casualty insurance trade organization. Member companies offer all types of property and casualty insurance, as well as personal and commercial auto insurance, commercial property and liability coverage for small businesses, worker's compensation, homeowners' insurance, medical malpractice coverage, and product liability insurance.
Founded in: 1886

13613 American Insurance Marketing & Sales Society
PO Box 35718
Richmond, VA 23235
804-674-6466
877-674-2742; *Fax:* 703-579-8896
info@aimssociety.org; www.aimssociety.org
Social Media: Facebook, Twitter, LinkedIn, RSS
Craig Most, CPIA, CIC, President
Jim Mansfield, CPIA, Vice President
Donna Gray, Executive Director
Carlos Vargas, CPIA, Secretary
Bob Klinger, CPIA LUTCF, Treasurer
A sales training organization that is managed by agents for agents; makes an active effort to ensure that its sales training material is current and takes into consideration today's agency sales approaches.
Founded in: 1968

13614 American Nuclear Insurers
95 Glastonbury Boulevard
Suite 300
Glastonbury, CT 06033-4453
860-682-1301; *Fax:* 860-659-0002;
www.amnucins.com
Social Media: Facebook, Twitter
George Turner, President/CEO
John Quatrocchi, Senior VP
A joint underwriting association, and and organization created by some of the largest stock insurance companies in the United States. The purpose is to pool the financial assets pledged by these member companies to provide significant amount of property and liability insurance we make available to nuclear power plants and related facilities throughout the world.
60 Members
Founded in: 1957

13615 American Risk and Insurance Association ARIA
716 Providence Road
Malvern, PA 19355-3402
610-640-1997; *Fax:* 610-725-1007
aria@TheInstitutes.org; www.aria.org
Andreas Richter, President
Richard Phillips, Vice President
Paul Thistle, President-Elect
Patricia Born, Immediate Past President
Anthony Biacchi, Executive Director
ARIA is the premier academic organization devoted to the study and promotion of knowledge about risk management and insurance.
500 Members
Founded in: 1932

13616 American Society for Healthcare Risk Management
155 N. Wacker Drive
Suite 400
Chicago, IL 60606-4425
312-422-3980; *Fax:* 312-422-4580
ashrm@aha.org; www.ashrm.org
Social Media: Facebook, Twitter, LinkedIn, YouTube
Ellen Grady Venditti, President
Ann Gaffey, President Elect
Jacque Mitchell, Past-President
Kimberly Hoarle, MBA, CAE, Executive Director
Virginia Petrancosta, CAE, Director, Marketing & Comm.
National organization for the health care industry risk management equipment, supplies and services.
4400+ Members
Founded in: 1980
Mailing list available for rent

13617 American Society of Appraisers
11107 Sunset Hills Rd
Suite 310
Reston, VA 20190
703-478-2228
800-272-8258; *Fax:* 703-742-8471
asainfo@appraisers.org; www.appraisers.org
Social Media: Facebook, Twitter, LinkedIn, YouTube
Jim Hirt, CEO
Bonny Price, Chief Operations Officer
Joseph Noselli, MBA, CPA, Chief Financial Officer
Todd Paradis, Dir., Marketing & Comm.
Susan Fischer, Governance Operations Manager
Organization provides education and accreditation for appraisers, plus an appraiser locator service.

13618 American Society of Pension Professionals and Actuaries
4245 N. Fairfax Drive
Suite 750
Arlington, VA 22203
703-516-9300; *Fax:* 703-516-9308
customercare@asppa.org; www.asppa.org
Social Media: Facebook, LinkedIn, RSS, YouTube
Kyla M. Keck, CPC, QPA, QKA, President
Joseph A. Nichols, MSPA, President-Elect
Richard A. Hochman, APM, VP
David M. Lipkin, MSPA, Immediate Past President
Brian H. Graff, Esq., APM, Executive Director
(ASPPA) is a national organization for career retirement plan professionals. The membership consists of the many disciplines supporting retirement income management and benefits policy. Its members are part of the diversified, technical, and highly regulated benefits industry.

ASPPA represents those who have made a career of retirement plan and pension policy work.
7,000 Members
Founded in: 1966

13619 American Society of Safety Engineers
520 N. Northwest Hwy
Park Ridge, IL 60068
847-699-2929; *Fax:* 847-768-3434
customerservice@asse.org; www.asse.org
Social Media: Facebook, Twitter, LinkedIn, Instagram, Blog
Michael Belcher, CSP, President
Thomas F. Cecich, CSP, CIH, President Elect
James D. Smith, CSP, M.S., Senior Vice President
Stephanie A. Helgerman, CSP, Vice President, Finance
Fred J. Fortman, Jr., LL.M., Secretary & Executive Director
The oldest and largest professional safety organization. Its members manage, supervise and consult on safety, health, and environmental issues in industry, insurance, government and education.
30000 Members
Founded in: 1911

13620 Appraisers Association of America
212 West 35th Street
11th Floor South
New York, NY 10001
212-889-5404; *Fax:* 212-889-5503
aaa@appraisersassoc.org;
www.appraisersassoc.org
Social Media: Facebook, Twitter, LinkedIn
Deborah G. Spaniermann, AAA, President
Cynthia D. Herbert, AAA, First Vice President
Edward Yee, AAA, Second Vice President
Sharon Chrust, AAA, Recording Secretary
Erica Hartman, AAA, Treasurer
The oldest non-profit professional association of personal property appraisers. The mission and primary purpose of the association is to develop and promote standards of excellence in the profession of appraising through education and the application of the highest form of professionals practice, which results in enhancing the visibility and standing of appraisers within the private and professional communities in which they serve.
900 Members
Founded in: 1949
Mailing list available for rent

13621 Arbitration Forums
3820 Northdale Boulevard
Suite 200A
Tampa, FL 33624
813-915-2263
866-977-3434; *Fax:* 813-915-4153
status@arbfile.org; www.arbfile.org
Russ Smith, President & CEO
Jay Arcila, CFO/Secretary Treasurer
John Shedd, Director of Information Technology
Geoff Engert, Director of Mktg, Corp Compliance
Ken Butler, Director, Human Resource
Arbitration Forums is a not-for-profit provider of intercompany insurance dispute resolution services. More than 2,000 insurers and self-insurers participate in AF's programs. AF resolves over 250,000 disputes with a claim value approaching one billion dollars.
Founded in: 1943

13622 Associated Risk Managers International
Two Pierce Place
20th Floor
Itasca, IL 60143-3141
630-285-4324; *Fax:* 630-285-3590
Scott.Spangler@armiweb.com;
www.armiweb.com
Social Media: Facebook, LinkedIn
Priscilla Hottle, Chairman
Greg Easley, Vice Chairman
Brenda Case, Immediate Past President
Richard Simmons, Treasurer
Mary Pursell, Secretary
Develops specialized insurance/risk management services for trade associations, professional groups and other industry organizations. Conducts seminars and sponsors competitions.
505 Members
Founded in: 1969

13623 Association of Advanced Life Underwriters
11921 Freedom Drive
Suite 1100
Reston, VA 20190
703-641-9400
888-275-0092; *Fax:* 703-641-9885
stertzer@aalu.org; www.aalu.org
Mark B. Murphy, President
Richard A. DeVita, Vice President & Treasurer
David J Stertzer, Chief Executive officer
David F. Byers Jr., Secretary
Chris Foster, President - Elect
Offers services in complex fields of estate analysis, business, insurance, pension planning, employee benefit plans.
1.4M Members
Founded in: 1957

13624 Association of Average Adjusters of the United States and Canada
126 Midwood Avenue
Farmingdale, NJ 11735
973-597-0824
averageadjusters@aol.com;
www.averageadjustersusca.org/
Phil Gran, Chair
Richard P Carney, Executive Chairman
Eileen M Fellin
Marine insurance and general average adjusters, ship and cargo surveyors and admiralty lawyers. Has no paid staff. Membership principally in New York area.
700+ Members
Founded in: 2011

13625 Association of Finance and Insurance Professionals
4104 Felps Drive
Suite H
Colleyville, TX 76034
817-428-2434; *Fax:* 817-428-2534
info@afip.com; www.afip.com
Social Media: Facebook, Twitter, LinkedIn
David N Robertson, Executive Director
Tarrah Lett, Sr VP
Heather M Barnett, Communications Director
A nonprofit educational foundation that serves the needs of in-dealership finance and insurance personnel for the automobile, RV, commercial truck and equipment, motorcycle, and motorized sports industries while assisting the lenders, vendors, and independent general agents who support the F&I function.
Cost: $95.00
3500 Members
Frequency: $2,500 for Company's
Founded in: 1989
Mailing list available for rent

13626 Association of Financial Guaranty Insurers
139 Lancaster Street
Albany, NY 12210-1903
518-449-4698; *Fax:* 212-391-6920
tcasey@mackinco.com; www.afgi.org
Bruce E. Stern, AFGI Chairman
Teresa M. Casey, Executive Director
Margaret Towers, Contact Person
A trade association of the insurers and reinsurers of municipal bonds and asset-backed securities.
10 Members
Founded in: 1986

13627 Association of Home Office Underwriters
1155 15th Street, Nw
Suite 500
Washington, DC 20005
202-962-0167; *Fax:* 202-530-0659
memberservices@ahou.org; www.ahou.org
Social Media: Facebook, Twitter, LinkedIn
Cheryl Johns, FALU, CLU, FLMI, President
Traci Davis, AALU, ACS, FLMI, Executive Vice President
Jean Pfundtner, RN, BSN, VP, Publications & Secretary
Tim Ranfranz, Vice President, Treasurer
Bob Cicchi, Vice President, Program Development
Founded when the Home Office Life Underwriters Association and Institute of Homes Office Underwriters joined forces to provide one unified underwriting voice. The mission is to advance the knowledge of sound underwriting of life and disability insurance risks, toward which end it holds meetings, publishes papers and discussions, and promotes educational programs.
Cost: $100.00
1,400 Members
Frequency: Membership Fee
Founded in: 2002
Mailing list available for rent

13628 Association of Insurance Compliance Professionals
12100 Sunset Hills Road
Suite 130
Reston, VA 20190
703-437-4377; *Fax:* 703-435-4390
aicp@aicp.net; www.aicp.net
Sue Eckler-Kerns, President
Roger Osgood, AINS, BA, MBA, Vice President
Karen L. Pollitt, AIRC, CCP, Secretary
Jim Morgan, Treasurer
Elaine Douglas, Past President
Formerly the Society of State Filers. AICP represents individuals involved or interested in statutes, state filing methods, and/or regulatory requirements. Associate members are consultants, attorneys, association managers, education/service organizations and other interested individuals.
Cost: $175.00
1200 Members
Frequency: Membership Fee
Founded in: 1985

13629 Association of Life Insurance Counsel
17 South High Street
Suite 200
Columbus, OH 43215
614-221-1900; *Fax:* 614-221-1989
kate@assnofficers.com; www.alic.cc/
Raymond J. Manista, President
Carl Wilkerson, President-Elect
Jason Walters, Secretary-Treasurer
Association for life insurance counsel.
Founded in: 1913

13630 Association of Professional Insurance Women
990 Cedar Bridge Avenue
suite B7 PMB210
Brick, NJ 08723-4157

973-941-6024; *Fax:* 732-920-1260
scb@thebeaumontgroup.com; www.apiw.org
Social Media: LinkedIn

Cheryl Vollweiler, President
Susan Zdroik, CPCU, ARe, First Vice President
Bina Dagar, Senior Vice President
Lucy Mendieta, Treasurer
Kathryn Turck-Rose, Corporate Secretary

Provides women in the insurance insudtry with opportunities for professional development and assistance in advancing their careers. Our membership consists of professional insurance women, highly regarded, decision makers with primary insurers, reinsurers, insurance brokers, risk management, professional services firms and other industry related organizations.
135 Members
Founded in: 1976

13631 Association of Professional Insurance Agen ts
400 North Washington Street
Alexandria, VA 22314

703-836-9340; *Fax:* 703-836-1279
web@pianet.org; www.pianet.com
Social Media: Facebook, Twitter, LinkedIn, RSS

Richard A. Clements, President
Robert W Hansen, President-Elect
Gareth W Blackwell, Jr., Vice President/Treasurer
John G. Lee, Past President
Mike Becker, Executive Vice President & CEO

Represents professional independent insurance agents in all 50 states, Puerto Rico and the District of Columbia. Our members are local Main Street Agents who serve their communities throughout America
Founded in: 1931
Mailing list available for rent

13632 Automobile Insurance Plans Service Office
302 Central Ave
Johnston, RI 02919-4995

401-275-1000; *Fax:* 401-528-1350;
www.aipso.com

David Kohlhammer, President

AIPSO's mission is to provide high quality services for the insurance residual market at the lowest possible cost.

13633 Aviation Insurance Association
7200 W. 75th Street
Overland Park, KS 66204

913-627-9632; *Fax:* 913-381-2515
mandie@aiaweb.org; www.aiaweb.org
Social Media: Facebook, Blog

David Sales, President
Paul Herbers, Vice President
James Gardner, Secretary
Christopher R. Zanette, Treasurer
Amanda Bannwarth, Executive Director

A not-for-profit association dedicated to expanding the knowledge of and promoting the general welfare of the aviation insurance industry through numerous educational programs and events.
900 Members
Founded in: 1976

13634 Blue Cross and Blue Shield Association
225 North Michigan Avenue
Chicago, IL 60601-6026

312-540-0460; *Fax:* 312-297-6609
bcbswebmaster@bcbsa.com; www.bcbs.com
Social Media: Facebook, Twitter, RSS, YouTube

Scott P Serota, President& Chief Executive Officer
William A. Breskin, VP, Govt. Programs
Bhaskar Bulusu, VP, Enterprise Information
Kathy Didawick, VP, Congressional Relations
John T. Ericksen, VP, Federal Relations

Formerly Blue Cross Association and National Association of Blue Shield Plans. Members must be medical and/or hospital plans and operate according to established standards. Offers information, consulting, representation and operation services to members. Member plans represent over 68.1 million health care consumers.
55 Members
Founded in: 1946
Mailing list available for rent

13635 Captive Insurance Companies Association
4248 Park Glen Road
Minneapolis, MN 55416

952-928-4655; *Fax:* 952-929-1318
info@cicaworld.com; www.cicaworld.com
Social Media: Facebook, Twitter, LinkedIn

Scott Beckman, Board Chair
Michael Bemi, Board Vice Chair
Joel Chansky, Secretary/Treasurer
Dennis P. Harwick, President
Amy Sellheim, CICA Staff

An organization dedicated to networking, educating, and promoting the captive insurance industry. Its mission is to be the first and best source of unbiased information, knowledge, and leadership for captive insurance decision makers.
Founded in: 1972

13636 Casualty Actuarial Society
4350 N. Fairfax Drive
Suite 250
Arlington, VA 22203-1620

703-276-3100; *Fax:* 703-276-3108
office@casact.org; www.casact.org
Social Media: Facebook, Twitter, LinkedIn, RSS, YouTube, Flickr

Robert S. Miccolis, President
Stephen P. Lowe, President Elect
G. Chris Nyce, Vice President- Administration
Steven D. Armstrong, Vice President-Admissions
Jeff Courchene, Vice President- Internation

The purpose is to advance the body of knowledge of actuarial science applied to property, casualty and similar risk exposures, to establish and maintain standards of qualification for membership, to promote and maintain highstandards of conduct and competence for the members, and to increase the awareness of actuarial science.
6,300 Members
Founded in: 1914
Mailing list available for rent

13637 Certified Claims Professional Accreditation Council
PO Box 550922
Jacksonville, FL 32255-0922

301-292-1988; *Fax:* 301-292-1787
animag@lattmag.com; www.ccpac.com

Dave Nordt, CCP, President
Judy R. Johnson, CCP, Vice President - Certifications
Deborah Baker, CCP, Vice President - Membership
Brenda Baker, CCP, Secretary
Jean Zimmerman, CCP, Treasurer

A nonprofit organization that seeks to raise the professional standards of individuals who specialize in the administration and negotiation of freight claims. Specifically it seeks to give recognition to those who have acquired the necessary degree of experience, education, and expertise in domestic and international freight claims to warrant acknowledgment of their professional stature.
Founded in: 1981

13638 Chartered Property Casualty Underwriters
720 Providence Road
Suite 100
Malvern, PA 19355-3446

610-251-2733
800-932-2728; *Fax:* 610-725-5969
MemberResources@theinstitutes.org;
www.cpcusociety.org
Social Media: Facebook, Twitter, LinkedIn

Jane M. Wahl, President and Chairman
Kevin H Brown, Esq., CPCU, CAE, SVP, Executive Director
Brian P. Savko, CPCU, CLU, ChFC, President Elect
Stanley W. Plappert, Secretary/Treasurer
Cynthia A. Baroway, CPCU, M.Ed., Immediate Past President, Chairman

A community of credentialed property and casualty insurance professionals who promote excellence through ethical behavior and continuing education. Mission is to meet the career development needs of a diverse membership pf professionals who have earned the CPCU designation, so that they may serve others in a competent and ethical manner
22,00 Members
Founded in: 1944

13639 Coalition Against Insurance Fraud
1012 14th St. NW
Suite 200
Washington, DC 20005

202-393-7330
info@insurancefraud.org;
www.insurancefraud.org
Social Media: Facebook, Twitter

Frank Sztuk, Co-Chair
Don Rounds, Co-Chair

The Coalition fights insurance fraud on behalf of consumers, insurance companies and government.
Founded in: 1993

13640 Conference of Consulting Actuaries
3880 Salem Lake Drive
Suite H
Long Grove, IL 60047-5292

847-719-6500; *Fax:* 847-719-6506
conference@ccactuaries.org;
www.ccactuaries.org
Social Media: Twitter, LinkedIn

Philip A. Merdinger, President
Donald E. Fuerst, President-Elect
Donald J. Segal, President-Elect
Edward M. Pudlowski, Treasurer
John H. Lowell, Secretary

The Conference advances the quality of consulting practice, supports the needs of consulting actuaries, and represents their interests.
1200+ Members
Founded in: 1950

13641 Consumer Credit Industry Association
6300 Powers Ferry Road
Suite 600-286
Atlanta, GA 30339

678-858-4001
webmaster@cciaonline.com;
www.cciaonline.com

Dick Williams, Chair
Jim Pangburn, President
Rebecca Smart, VP
Tom Keepers, EVP
Stephanie Neal, Director of Member Services

Preserves, promotes and enhances the availability, utility and integrity of insurance and related products and services delivered in connection with financial transactions.
140+ Members
Founded in: 1951

13642 Council on Employee Benefits
1501 M Street, N.W
Suite 620
Washington, DC 20005

202-861-6025; *Fax:* 202-861-6027
info@ceb.org; www.ceb.org
Social Media: LinkedIn

Donna A Sexton, President
Shane Canfield, Executive Director
Karen M Welch, Vice President
John R. Collins, Treasurer
Julie R Sheehy, Secretary

Composed of major corporations having a common interest in the management of employee benefits. Stimulates the development and improves the adminstration of sound, progressive employee benefit plan among its members. Also provides an excellent medium for the exchange of ideas, thought and information on the design, operation and financing of such plans.
Founded in: 1946

13643 Crop Insurance and Reinsurance Bureau
440 First St NW
Suite 500
Washington, DC 20001

202-544-0067; *Fax:* 202-330-5255
mtorrey@cropinsurance.org;
www.cropinsurance.org

Sheri Bane, Chairwoman
Ron Rutledge, Vice Chairman
Zane Vaughn, Treasurer
Greg Mills, Immediate Past Chairman
Mike Torrey, Executive Vice President

National trade association made up of insurance providers and related organization who provide a variety of insurance products for our Nation's Farmers.
Founded in: 1964

13644 Eastern Claims Conference
PO Box 863902
Ridgewood, NY 11386

732-922-7037; *Fax:* 212-615-7345
easternclaimsconference@gmail.com;
www.easternclaimsconference.com

Jennifer Cobb, Conference Chair
Christine Prutting, Program
Melissa J Thomas, Marketing
Ann Healy, Ad Journal/Publications
Arlene Walsh, Ad Journal/Publications

Provides education and training to examiners, managers, and officers who review medical and disability claims. Holds seminars for life, health and disability clinics.
Founded in: 1977

13645 Employee Benefit Research Institute
1100 13th St NW
Suite 878
Washington, DC 20005-4051

202-659-0670; *Fax:* 202-775-6312
info@ebri.org; www.ebri.org

Dallas L Salisbury, President
Stephen Blakely, Communications Director
Martha Bobbino, Director, Library Resources
Marcene Pugh, Director of Finance and Admin.
Jack VanDerhei, Director of Research

Mission is to contribute to, to encourage, and to enhance the development of sound employee benefit programs and sound public policy through objective research and education.
Founded in: 1978
Mailing list available for rent

13646 Federal Insurance Administration
500 C Street SW
Washington, DC 20472-2110

202-646-3535; *Fax:* 202-646-4320

Bud Schaurte, Administrator

Administers the federal flood insurance and crime insurance programs.

13647 Federation of Defense & Corporate Counsel
11812 North 56th Street
Tampa, FL 33617-1528

813-983-0022; *Fax:* 813-988-5837
mstreeper@thefederation.org;
www.thefederation.org
Social Media: Facebook, Twitter, LinkedIn

Victoria H. Roberts, Board Chair
Steven E. Farrar, President
J. Scott Kreamer, Secretary-Treasurer
H. Mills Gallivan, President-Elect
Walter Dukes, Senior Director

The Federation is an organization of recognized leaders in the legal community dedicated to representation of insurers and corporations.
1400+ Members
Founded in: 1936

13648 Financial & Insurance Conference Planners
330 N. Wabash Avenue
Suite 2000
Chicago, IL 60611

312-245-1023; *Fax:* 312-321-5150
info@icpanet.com; www.ficpnet.com
Social Media: Facebook, Twitter, LinkedIn, YouTube, Flickr

Shelia R. Cleary, Chair
Caryn Taylor Lucia, Chair Elect and Treasurer
Marla Hannigan, CMP, Chair Elect and Treasurer
Sherri Lindenberg, CLU, Chair Elect and Treasurer
Kathy Roche, Chair Elect and Treasurer

An association of insurance and financial services industry meeting planners who exchange proven meeting management techniques and explore trends and new ideas that may enhance the value of conferences.
Founded in: 1957

13649 Financial Planning Association
7535 E. Hampden Ave.
Suite 600
Denver, CO 80231

303-759-4900
800-322-4237; *Fax:* 303-759-0749
info@onefpa.org; www.fpanet.org
Social Media: Facebook, Twitter, LinkedIn

Mary Tuttle, CEO
Maureen Peck, Executive Communications Manager
Lauren Schadle, Assoc Exec Dir, COO
Curt Niepoth, Assoc Exec Dir, CFO
Ian MacKenzie, Managing Dir Bus Dev, CMO

Members include accountants, financial planners, lawyers, bankers, stockbrokers, insurance professionals and others who provide financial advice and services to individuals.
15M Members
Founded in: 2000
Mailing list available for rent

13650 Fraternal Field Managers' Association
Concordia Mutual Life
3020 Woodcreek Drive
Downers Grove, IL 60515

630-971-8000; *Fax:* 630-971-9332;
www.ffma.co

William J. Murray, President
Jay Schenk, VP

FFMA is dedicated to the promotion of higher ethical standards and the professional development of the fraternal field force, fostering harmony, unity of purpose and the exchange of ideas among the member societies.
70 Members
Founded in: 1935

13651 GAMA International
2901 Telestar Ct
Suite 140
Falls Church, VA 22042-1205

703-770-8184
800-345-2687; *Fax:* 571-499-4302
membership@gamaweb.com;
www.gamaweb.com
Social Media: Facebook, Twitter, LinkedIn

Bonnie Godsman, Chief Executive Officer
Debra Grommons, Chief of Staff / EVP
John Behn, Executive Vice President
Steven Mandurano, Sr. Director, Media & Marketing
Kathryn Kellam, CEO, GAMA Foundation

The only association dedicated to promoting the professional development needs of managers in the insurance and financial services industry. Also the only volunteer organization that focuses on the agency building tasks and skills of successful career agenices and firms.
Cost: $300.00
5500 Members
Frequency: Membership Fee
Mailing list available for rent

13652 General Agents and Managers Conference of NALU
2901 Telestar Ct
Suite 140
Falls Church, VA 22042-1205

703-770-8184
800-345-2687; *Fax:* 571-499-4302
membership@gamaweb.com;
www.gamaweb.com
Social Media: Facebook, Twitter, LinkedIn

Bonnie Godsman, Chief Executive Officer
Debra Grommons, Chief of Staff / EVP
John Behn, Executive Vice President
Steven Mandurano, Sr. Director, Media & Marketing
Kathryn Kellam, CEO, GAMA Foundation

Seeks to improve quality of management and life insurance selling through educational programs, code of ethical practices, and research programs.
7.2M Members
Founded in: 1951
Mailing list available for rent

13653 Great American Insurance Group Tower
301 E Fourth Street
Cincinnati, OH 45202
513-369-5000
800-545-4269; *Fax:* 212-885-1535
service@fcia.com;
www.greatamericaninsurancegroup.com
Social Media: Facebook, LinkedIn, YouTube

Lindley M Franklin, CEO

To provide credit insurance covering teh risk of non-payment on foreign and,in certain cases, domestic receivables.
Founded in: 1961

13654 Group Underwriters Association of America
P.O. Box 735
Northbrook, IL 60065-0735
205-427-2638; *Fax:* 205-981-2901
info@guaa.com; www.guaa.com/

Libby Corcillo, President
Shawn R. Dutremble, Vice President
Steve Ginsburg, Treasurer
Patty Marshall, Secretary
Jennifer Kyle, Past President

Comprised of industry professionals that promote the study, analysis, and discussion of all matters relating to the underwriting of group products.

13655 Health Insurance Association of America
601 Pennsylvania Avenue, NW South Building
Suite 500
Washington, DC 20004
202-778-3200; *Fax:* 202-331-7487
ahip@ahip.org; www.ahip.org

A national political advocacy and trade association with about 1,300 member companies that sell health insurance coverage to Americans.

13656 Highway Loss Data Institute
1005 N. Glebe Road
Suite 800
Arlington, VA 22201-5759
703-247-1500; *Fax:* 703-247-1588
rrader@iihs.org; www.iihs.org
Social Media: Twitter, YouTube, RSS

Adrian Lund, President
Russ Rader, Senior Vice President
Shelley M. Shelton, CAP, Senior Legal & Admin. Associate
Brenda O'Donnell, Vice President, Insurer Relations
Andrew Hauff, Communications Specialist

Provides the public with insurance industry data concerning human and economic loss resulting from crashes.
12 Members
Founded in: 1959
Mailing list available for rent

13657 Home Office Life Underwriters Association
Minnesota Mutual Life
400 Robert Street N
Suite A
Saint Paul, MN 55101-2098
651-665-3500; *Fax:* 651-665-4488

Lynn Patterson, President
Jane Hall, Executive Vice President

Offers educational programs through the Academy Life Underwriting designed for professional home office underwriters.
560 Members
Founded in: 1930

13658 I-Car
5125 Trillium Blvd
Hoffman Estates, IL 60192-3600
847-590-1198
800-422-7872; *Fax:* 800-590-1215
tom.mcgee@i-car.com; www.i-car.com
Social Media: LinkedIn, Google+, YouTube

William Brower, Chair
John S. Van Alstyne, CEO & President
Rollie Benjamin, Vice Chair
Dustin Womble, Secretary
Bob Keith, Treasurer

Formed by the collision industry, an international not-for-profit training organization. Develops and delivers technical training programs to professionals in all areas of the collision industry. Also provides a communication forum for anyone interested in proper collision repair.
100 Members
Founded in: 1979

13659 IMCA Annual Meeting
Insurance Marketing Communications Association
4248 Park Glen Road
Minneapolis, MN 55416
206-219-9811; *Fax:* 866-210-2481
tseibert@imcanet.com; www.imcanet.com
Social Media: Facebook, Twitter, LinkedIn

Rob Martin, President
Gloria Grove, Executive Director
Mark Friedlander, Executive Vice President
Anna Hargis, Treasurer

To promote education and development of its members.
Cost: $795.00
Frequency: Registration Fee
Mailing list available for rent

13660 Independent Automotive Damage Appraisers Association
PO Box 12291
Columbus, GA 31917-2291
800-369-IADA; *Fax:* 888-423-2669
admin@iada.org; www.iada.org

Mark Nathan, President
Bill Ambrosino, First Vice President
John Williams, Executive Vice President
Michael M. Sellman, Secretary/Treasurer
Mike Wilson, Regional Vice President

A nationwide network of appraiser specialists with the knowledge and experience to assess vehicle damage and to make unbiased repair decisions based on the manufacturer's specifications, accepted industry procedures, and safety concerns.
731 Members
Founded in: 1947

13661 Independent Insurance Agents & Brokers of America
127 S Peyton Street
Alexandria, VA 22314-2803
703-683-4422
800-221-7917; *Fax:* 703-683-7556
info@iiaa.org; www.independentagent.com/
Social Media: Facebook, Twitter, LinkedIn, Vimeo

Robert A Rusbuldt, CEO
Ronald Tubertini, Chairman

A national alliance of business owners and their employees who offer all types of insurance and financial services products. IIABA agents and brokers not only advise clients about insurance, they recommend loss-prevention ideas that can cut costs.
300M+ Members
Founded in: 1896
Mailing list available for rent

13662 Information, Incorporated
2025 M Street NW
Washington, DC 20036
301-215-4688
800-497-5636; *Fax:* 301-215-4600
acarr@mail.infoinc.com; www.infoinc.com

Alain Carr, Manager

Organization offers evaluations of companies on their claims-paying ability. Association news services.
Founded in: 1979
Mailing list available for rent

13663 Inland Marine Underwriters Association
14 Wall Street
8th Floor
New York, NY 10005
212-233-0550; *Fax:* 212-227-5102
lcolson@imua.org; www.imua.org
Social Media: Facebook, Twitter, LinkedIn

Michelle Hoehn, Chair
Kevin O'Brien, President & CEO
William Rosa, Deputy Chair
Lloyd J. Stoik, Vice Chair
Lillian L. Colson, Vice President & Secretary

Serves as the collective voice of the U.S. inland marine insurance industry. Also provides its members with education, research and communications services that support the inland marine underwriting discipline.
Cost: $1750.00
400+ Members
Frequency: Membership Fee
Founded in: 1930
Mailing list available for rent

13664 Institute of Home Office Underwriters
General American Life Insurance Company
1155 15th Street, Nw
Suite 500
Washington, DC 20005
202-962-0167; *Fax:* 202-530-0659
memberservices@ahou.org; www.ahou.org
Social Media: Facebook, Twitter, LinkedIn

Cheryl Johns, FALU, CLU, FLMI, President
Traci Davis, AALU, ACS, FLMI, Executive Vice President
Jean Pfundtner, RN, BSN, VP, Publications & Secretary
Tim Ranfranz, Vice President, Treasurer
Bob Cicchi, Vice President, Program Development

Goals are to increase underwriting knowledge of members through educational programs. Prepares program and examinations leading to Fellowship in Academy of Life Underwriting.
1,400 Members
Founded in: 1937
Mailing list available for rent

13665 Insurance Accounting Systems Association
3511 Shannon Rd, Suite 160
PO Box 51340
Durham, NC 27707-6330
919-489-0991; *Fax:* 919-489-1994
info@iasa.org; www.iasa.org
Social Media: Facebook, Twitter, LinkedIn, YouTube

Forrest Mills, Jr., Board Chair
Tim Morgan, President
Joseph Pomilia, Executive Director
Margaret McKeon, VP-Conference
Kim Morris, Director-Exhibits

Membership includes insurance companies of all types, as well as companies that serve the insurance industry, regulators and also organizations more broadly representative of the financial ser-

vices industry, including banks and investment brokerage firms.
1.7M Members
Founded in: 1928
Mailing list available for rent

13666 Insurance Accounting and Systems Association
3511 Shannon Road, Suite 160
PO Box 51340
Durham, NC 27707
919-489-0991; *Fax:* 919-489-1994
info@iasa.org; www.iasa.org/
Social Media: Facebook, Twitter, LinkedIn, YouTube
Forrest Mills, Jr., Chairman of the Board
Tim Morgan, President
Rod Travers, President-Elect
Tom Ewbank, CFO
Joe Pomilia, Executive Director
A nonprofit education association that strives to enhance the knowledge of insurance professionals and participants from similar organizations closely allied with the insurance industry.

13667 Insurance Committee for Arson Control
3601 Vincennes Road
Indianapolis, IN 46268
317-575-5601; *Fax:* 317-879-8408
info@arsoncontrol.org; www.arsoncontrol.org
Social Media: Facebook, Twitter, LinkedIn, Google+
Jerry Mulhearn, Chairman
Scott Sanderson, Vice Chairman
Rick Hammond, Executive Director
Don Hancock, Technical Director
Larry Baile, Event Director
Serves as a national resource, education and communications organization. ICAC works to increase public awareness of the arson problem, what can be done and how the industry is responding on both the national and local levels.
Founded in: 1978
Mailing list available for rent

13668 Insurance Consumer Affairs Exchange
PO Box 746
Lake Zurich, IL 60047
847-991-8454
nbrebner@icae.com; www.icae.com
Kendra Franklin, President
Kristi Colbert, Secretary
Erica Hiemstra, Treasurer
Joan Holson, VP
Nancy Brebner, Executive Director
A not-for-profit organization that promotes professionalism and shapes the standards of behavior in relationships between insurance organizations, regulators and customers through proactive dialogue, research, communication and education.
110 Members
Founded in: 1976

13669 Insurance Cost Containment Service
330 S Wells
Chicago, IL 60606-4701
312-427-2520; *Fax:* 312-368-8336
Robert Kissane, President
Assists insurance companies with property claims adjustment and arson and fraud claims investigation.

13670 Insurance Information Institute
110 William Street
New York, NY 10038-3908
212-346-5500
800-942-4242; *Fax:* 212-732-1916
members@iii.org; www.iii.org
Social Media: Facebook, Twitter, LinkedIn, Google+, YouTube, Flickr
Andrea C. Basora, Executive Vice President
Jeanne M Salvatore, SVP, Public Affairs
Michael Barry, VP, Media Relations
Loretta Worters, Vice President, Communications
James P. Ballot, Director, Digital Communications
A factfinding communication and media organization for all lines of insurance except life and health insurance. Affiliated with Western Insurance Information Services offering consumer information services to 10 western states. Also offers a national insurance consumer helpline.
250 Members
Founded in: 1959

13671 Insurance Loss Control Association
PO Box 346
Morton, IL 61550
309-696-2551; *Fax:* 317-879-8408
president@insurancelosscontrol.org; www.insurancelosscontrol.org
Ron Huber, CSP, ALCM, President
Robert J. Cruse, CSP, ARM, ALCM, First Vice President
Daniel Finn, ALCM, CFPS, AIM, Second Vice President
Mark Bates, CSP, Secretary
Stig T Ruxlow, CSP, Financial Secretary
Supports loss control professionals. Publishes quarterly newsletter.
Founded in: 1931

13672 Insurance Marketing Communications Association
4248 Park Glen Road
Minneapolis, MN 55416
206-219-9811; *Fax:* 866-210-2481
tseibert@imcanet.com; www.imcanet.com
Social Media: Facebook, Twitter, LinkedIn, Youtube
Rob Martin, President
Gloria Grove, Executive Director
Mark Friedlander, Executive Vice President
Anna Hargis, Treasurer
An international organization of insurance communications professionals who specialize in marketing, marketing communications, advertising, sales promotion, and public relations.
Cost: $500.00
180 Members
Frequency: Annual Membership Fee
Founded in: 1923
Mailing list available for rent

13673 Insurance Premium Finance Association
2890 Niagara Falls Boulevard
PO Box 726
Amherst, NY 14226
716-695-8757; *Fax:* 716-695-8758
Eric Bouskill, Contact
Firms licensed by New York State to finance property and casualty insurance premiums.
16 Members
Founded in: 1961

13674 Insurance Research Council
718 Providence Road
Malvern, PA 19355-0725
610-644-2212; *Fax:* 610-640-5388
irc@theinstitutes.org; www.ircweb.org
Social Media: Facebook, Twitter, LinkedIn, Pinterest, Google+
Victoria McCarthy, Chairperson
Elizabeth A. Sprinkel, SVP
David Corum, Vice President
Victoria Kilgore, Director of Research
Patrick Schmid, PhD, Director of Research
Non profit division of the American Institute for Chartered Property Casualty Underwriters and the Insurance Institute of America. Addresses subjects relating to all lines of property-casualty insurance, including coverages of automobiles, homes, businesses, municipalities, and professionals.
Founded in: 1977

13675 Insurance Value Added Network Services
1455 E Putnam Avenue
Old Greenwich, CT 06870-1307
203-698-1900
800-548-2675; *Fax:* 203-698-7299
ivans.info@ivans.com; www.ivans.com
Social Media: Twitter, LinkedIn
Clare DeNicola, President/CEO
Jeffery K Dobish, Sr VP/CFO
Linda Welsh, CAO
Industry-sponsored organization offering value added data communications network linking agencies, companies and healthcare providers to the insurance industry.
Founded in: 1983

13676 Insured Retirement Institute
1100 Vermont Avenue, NW
10th Floor
Washington, DC 20005
202-469-3000; *Fax:* 202-469-3030;
www.irionline.org
Social Media: Twitter, LinkedIn, YouTube, RSS
Nick Lane, Chairman
William Benjamin, Vice Chairman
Catherine J Weatherford, President, CEO
Lee Covington, SVP, General Counsel
Danielle Holland, SVP, Communications, Marketing
An association for the retirement income industry.

13677 Intermediaries and Reinsurance Underwriters Association
3626 East Tremont Avenue
Suite 203
Throggs Neck, NY 10465
718-89- 022; *Fax:* 908-203-0213
mcs@irua.com; www.irua.com
Mike Sowa, President
Amy Barra, Executive Director
A not-for-profit corporation, organized for the purposes of reinsurance education and research and the dissemination of information relevant to the reinsurance industry.
60 Members
Founded in: 1967

13678 International Association for Insurance Law: United States Chapter
Chase Communications
PO Box 3028
Malvern, PA 19355-0728
Fax: 914-966-3264
Stephen C Acunto, VP
Members are attorneys, professors, regulators and others who are interested in international or comparative aspects of insurance law.
700 Members
Founded in: 1963

13679 **International Association of Accident Reconstruction Specialists**
1036 Gretchen Lane
Grand Ledge, MI 48837-1873
517-622-3135; www.iaars.org
Fred Rice, President
Eino Butch Thompson, Vice President
Composed of members and associates from 38 states, as well as abroad. Membership comprised of law enforcement officers and civilian personnel.
152 Members
Founded in: 1980

13680 **International Association of Arson Investigators**
2111 Baldwin Avenue
Suite 203
Crofton, MD 21114
410-451-3473
800-468-4224; *Fax:* 410-451-9049
iaai@firearson.com; www.firearson.com
Social Media: Facebook, Twitter, LinkedIn, Youtube
Daniel Heenan, President
George Codding, First Vice President
Scott Bennett, Second Vice President
Peter Mansi, IAAI-CFI, MIAAI, Immediate Past President
Deborah Keeler, Executive Director
Dedicated to improving the professional development of fire and explosion investigators by being the global resource for fire investigation, technology and research.
7500 Members
Founded in: 1949

13681 **International Association of Defense Counsel**
303 West Madison
Suite 925
Chicago, IL 60606-3300
312-368-1494; *Fax:* 312-368-1854
info@iadclaw.org; www.iadclaw.org
Social Media: Facebook, Twitter, LinkedIn
Joseph E. O'Neil, President
John T. Lay, Jr., President Elect
Tripp Haston, Immediate Past President
Albert C. Hilber, Vice President of Insurance
Alfred R. Paliani, Vice President of Corporate
Formerly the International Association of Insurance Counsel. Members are defense attorneys and insurance and corporate counsels, by invitation only.
Cost: $650.00
2400 Members
Frequency: Membership Fee
Founded in: 1920

13682 **International Association of Industrial Accident Boards and Commissions**
5610 Medical Circle
Suite 24
Madison, WI 53719
608-663-6355; *Fax:* 608-663-1546
webmaster@iaiabc.org; www.iaiabc.org
Social Media: Facebook, Twitter, LinkedIn
R.D. Maynard, President
Dave Threedy, President Elect
Dwight Lovan, Immediate Past President
Matt Carey, Secretary/Treasurer
Jennifer Wolf Horejsh, Executive Director
A not for profit trade association representing government agencies charged with the administration of workers' compensation systems throughout most of the United States and Canada, and other nations and territories.
300+ Members
Founded in: 1914

13683 **International Association of Insurance Receivers**
610 Freedom Business Center
Suite 110
King of Prussia, PA 19406
610-992-0017; *Fax:* 610-992-0021
nancy@iair.org; www.iair.org
Bart Boles, President
Alan Gamse, Esq., First Vice President
Bruce Gilbert, Second Vice President
Donna Wilson, CIR-ML, Treasurer
James Kennedy, Esq., Corporate Secretary
Founded to provide an association to individuals involved with insurance receiverships in order to receive education, promote information exchange, and enhance the standards followed those who work in this position.
Founded in: 1991

13684 **International Association of Insurance Pro fessionals Corporate Centre**
3525 Piedmont Road
Building Five, Suite 300
Atlanta, GA 30305
404-789-3153
800-766-6249; *Fax:* 404-240-0998
joinnaiw@naiw.org;
www.internationalinsuranceprofessionals.org
Social Media: Facebook, Twitter, LinkedIn
Rebecca Clusserath, Education
Beth Chitnis, CAE, Management
John C McColloch, Membership
Michael North, Accounting
Betsey Blimline, Marketing
Serves its members by providing professional education, an environment in which to build business alliances and the opportunity to make connections with people of differing career paths and levels of experience within the insurance industry.
2000 Members
Founded in: 1940
Mailing list available for rent

13685 **International Association of Special Investigation Units (IASIU)**
N83 W13410 Leon Road
Menomonee Falls, WI 53051
414-375-2992; *Fax:* 414-359-1671
info@iasiu.org; www.iasiu.org
Social Media: Facebook, LinkedIn
Wade Wickre, CIFI, FCLA, President
J. Michael Skiba, Vice President
Ellen Withers, Secretary
John D. Kloc, FCLS, Treasurer
Bill Elliott, Executive Director
An association of more than 870 insurance company SIU professionals representing 130 of the largest property and casualty companies in the country.
4000 Members
Founded in: 1984

13686 **International Claim Association**
1155 15th Street NW
Suite 500
Washington, DC 20005
202-452-0143; *Fax:* 202-530-0659
cmurphy@claim.org; www.claim.org
Social Media: Facebook
Emily E. Sudermann, Chairperson
David W. Grannan, CFE, President
Erin M. Worthington, President Elect
Rebecca L. Huerta, Secretary
Lester L. Bohnert, ALHC, FLMI, Treasurer
Provides a forum for information exchange and a program of education tailored to the needs of its member life and health insurance companies, reinsurers, managed care companies, TPAs, and Blue Cross and Blue Shield organizations worldwide
Founded in: 1909
Mailing list available for rent

13687 **International Claim Association Newsletter**
International Claim Association
1155 15th Street NW
Suite 500
Washington, DC 20005
202-452-0143; *Fax:* 202-530-0659
cmurphy@claim.org; www.claim.org
Social Media: Facebook
Emily E. Sudermann, Chairperson
David W. Grannan, CFE, President
Erin M. Worthington, President Elect
Rebecca L. Huerta, Secretary
Lester L. Bohnert, ALHC, FLMI, Treasurer
Frequency: Quarterly
Founded in: 1909
Mailing list available for rent

13688 **International Cooperative and Mutual Insurance Federation**
8400 Westpark Drive
Second Floor
McLean, VA 22102-5116
703-245-8077; *Fax:* 703-610-0211
ww.icmif.org
Edward L Potter, CAE, Executive Director
Formerly the North American Association of the International Cooperative Insurance Federation.

13689 **International Foundation of Employee Benefit Plans**
18700 W. Bluemound Rd
P.O. Box 69
Brookfield, WI 53045
262-786-6700
888-334-3327; *Fax:* 262-786-8780
pr@ifebp.org; www.ifebp.org
Social Media: Facebook, Twitter, LinkedIn, Youtube
Thomas T. Holsman, President and Chair of the Board
Michael Wilson, Chief Executive Officer
Thomas W. Stiede, Treasurer
Regina C Reardon, President-Elect
Kenneth R Boyd, Immediate Past President
The largest educational association serving the employees and compensation industry.
Cost: $295.00
35000 Members
Frequency: $575/Organization Fee
Founded in: 1954

13690 **International Insurance Society**
101 Astor Place
Suite 202
New York, NY 10003
212-277-5171; *Fax:* 212-277-5172
ej@iisonline.org; www.iisonline.org
Social Media: Facebook, Twitter, LinkedIn
Greig Woodring, Chairman
Michael Morrissey, President & Chief Executive Officer
Takeo Inokuchi, Vice Chairman
Chang Jae Shin, Vice Chairman
Yassir Albaharna, Board Member
Provides a world forum for leading insurance executives, academicians and others interested in insurance to share interests and ideas on timely global issues.
1000 Members
Founded in: 1965

13691 **International Risk Management Institute**
12222 Merit Drive
Suite 1600
Dallas, TX 75251-3297

972-996-0800
800-827-5991; *Fax:* 972-371-5128;
www.zeroriskhr.com
Social Media: Facebook, Twitter, LinkedIn, Google+

Jack P Gibson, Chairman
Mike Poskey, President
Dr. Robert Kinsel Smith, Senior Adviser/Consultant
Heath Hilliard, National Sales Manager
Michelle Lima, Operations Manager

Provides important risk and insurance information to business, legal, risk management, and insurance professionals
Founded in: 1978

13692 **International Society of Appraisers**
225 West Wacker Drive
Suite 650
Chicago, IL 60606

312-981-6778; *Fax:* 312-265-2908
isa@isa-appraisers.org;
www.isa-appraisers.org/
Social Media: Facebook, Twitter, LinkedIn, RSS

Christine Guernsey, ISA CAPP, President
Perri Guthrie, ISA CAPP, Vice President
Steven R. Roach, JD, ISA CAPP, Treasurer
Karen S. Rabe, ISA CAPP, Secretary
Hughene D. Acheson, ISA AM, Director

A nonprofit, professional personal property appraisal association representing appraisers in the United States and Canada.
Founded in: 1979

13693 **International Tax and Investment Center**
1800 K St NW
Suite 718
Washington, DC 20006-2202

202-530-9799; *Fax:* 202-530-7987
Washington@iticnet.org; www.iticnet.org
Social Media: Facebook, Twitter, RSS

Daniel A. Witt, President
Blake Marshall, Vice President
Irene Savitsky, Vice President
Brian Mandel, Program Manager
Diana McKelvey, Communications Manager

A trade association that advances the use of structured settlements as a means of using periodic payments to resolve personal injury claims, workers compensation, and other types of claims.
600+ Members
Founded in: 1993

13694 **Intersure Ltd**
3 Hotel St
Warrenton, VA 20186-3221

540-349-0969; *Fax:* 540-349-0971;
www.intersure.com
Social Media: Vimeo

Millie Curtis, Executive Officer

Formerly the Association of International Insurance Agents. Founded to promote the principles of a free exchange of ideas and mutual cooperation based on the highest standards of intergrity, confidentiality and trust.
45 Members
Founded in: 1965

13695 **LIMRA International**
300 Day Hill Road
Windsor, CT 6095

860-688-3358
800-235-4672; *Fax:* 860-298-9555
customer.service@limra.com; www.limra.com
Social Media: Facebook, Twitter, LinkedIn, Google+, RSS, YouTube

Tim Stonehocker, Chair
Deanna Strable, Vice Chair
Robert A. Kerzner, CLU, ChFC, President
Alison Salka, Ph.D., SVP, Director - Research
Sean F. O'Donnell, Vice President, Member Relations
800 Members
Founded in: 1916
Mailing list available for rent

13696 **LOMA: Life Office Management Association**
6190 Powers Ferry Road
Suite 600
Atlanta, GA 30339

770-951-1770
800-275-5662; *Fax:* 770-984-0441
askloma@loma.org; www.loma.org
Social Media: Facebook, Twitter, LinkedIn, YouTube

Robert A Kerzner, CLU, ChFC, President and CEO
Jeffrey Hasty, FLMI, ACS, SVP, Corporate Secretary
Michele LaBouff, SVP, Human Resources
Kathy Milligan, FLMI, ACS, Senior Vice President, Education
Ian J Watts, SVP, Managing Director

Insurance worldwide association of insurance companies specializing in research and education.
1200+ Members
Founded in: 1924
Mailing list available for rent

13697 **Life Insurance Marketing & Research Association (LIMRA)**
300 Day Hill Rd.
Windsor, CT 06095

860-688-3358; *Fax:* 860-285-7792
customer.service@limra.com; www.limra.com
Social Media: Facebook, Twitter, LinkedIn, Google+, YouTube

Catherine Theroux, Director, Public Relations

We offer our clients insight in the form of cooperative research and value added marketing and distribution expertise. Insight that helps you identify trends, evaluate options and implement solutions. All of which leads to one clear outcome; the growth of your company.
800 Members
Founded in: 1916
Mailing list available for rent

13698 **Life Insurance Settlement Association**
225 South Eola Drive
Orlando, FL 32801

407-894-3797; www.lisa.org/
Social Media: Facebook, Twitter, LinkedIn, Google+, RSS, YouTube

Cynthia Poveda, Chairman
Michael Freedman, Vice Chairman
Phil Loy, Treasurer
James W. Maxson, Secretary
Alan Buerger, Board Member

Promotes the development, integrity, and reputation of the life settlement industry and promotes a competitive market for the people it serves.
85+ Members
Founded in: 1994

13699 **Life Insurers Council**
2300 Windy Ridge Parkway
Suite 600
Atlanta, GA 30339

770-984-3724
800-275-5662; *Fax:* 770-984-3780
askloma@loma.org; www.loma.org/lic/

Robert A Kerzner, CLU, ChFC, President and CEO
Jeffrey Hasty, FLMI, ACS, Senior Vice President, Assessment
Michele LaBouff, Senior Vice President
Kathy Milligan, FLMI, ACS, A, Senior Vice President, Education
Ian J Watts, Senior Vice President

In 1997, the LIC merged with (LOMA) Life Office Management Association which added extensive benefits for all LIC members. Serving the basic insurance needs of the general public, including the underserved market, through various distribution methods.
62 Members
Founded in: 1910
Mailing list available for rent

13700 **Lightning Protection Institute**
25475 Magnolia Drive
PO Box 99
Maryville, MO 64468

804-314-8955
800-488-6864; *Fax:* 660-582-0430
lpi@lightning.org; www.lightning.org
Social Media: Facebook, Twitter

Harold VanSickle III, Executive Director
Kim Loehr, Communications Director

A not-for-profit organization whose members are dedicated to insuring that today's lightning protection systems are the best possible quality in design, materials and installation, so that precious live and property can be protected from the damaging and costly effects of one of nature's most exciting phenomenons, lightning.
100 Members
Founded in: 1955

13701 **Loss Executives Association**
Industrial Risk Insurers
P.O. Box 37
Tenafly, NJ 07670
201-569-3346
info@lossexecutives.com;
www.lossexecutives.com

Edward J. Ryan, President
Jean L. Broderick, Vice President
Paul Aviles, Treasurer
Raymond Mattia, Secretary
Harris E. Berenson, Esq., Board Member

A professional association of property loss executives providing education to the industry.

13702 **Mass Marketing Insurance Institute**
3007 Tilden Street, NW
Suite 7M-103
Washington, DC 20008

816-221-7575; *Fax:* 816-772-7765
gregc@robstan.com; www.mi2.org
Social Media: Facebook, Twitter, LinkedIn, Google Plus, Youtube, Pinteres

Mark Smith, Director
Laurie Weber, Associate Director
Jim Barrett, First VP
Mary Walsh, VP Membership
Jennifer Branfort, Associate Director

The oldest not-for-profit membership organization that promotes the voluntary benefits industry by providing a forum for education, business development and fellowship.
300 Members
Frequency: Annual Meeting (Spring)
Founded in: 1970

13703 Massachusetts Association of Insurance Agents
91 Cedar Street
Milford, MA 01757

508-634-2900
800-972-9312; *Fax:* 508-634-2929
info@massagent.com; www.massagent.com
Social Media: Facebook, LinkedIn, Google+

Raymond Sirois, AAI, Chairman
G. L. Gaudette, III, CPCU, Chairman Elect
Glen E. Davis, CIC, CRM, LIA, Vice Chairman
Ely Kaplansky, Secretary-Treasurer
Raymond D. Gallant, National Director

Trade show for everyday use in the insurance agency office.
1800 Members
Frequency: November
Mailing list available for rent

13704 Million Dollar Round Table
325 West Touhy Ave
Park Ridge, IL 60068-4265

847-692-6378; *Fax:* 847-518-8921
info@mdrt.org; www.mdrt.org
Social Media: Facebook, Twitter, LinkedIn, Pinterest

Brian Heckert, CLU, ChFC, President
Caroline Banks, FPFS, Immediate Past President
Mark Hanna, CLU, ChFC, First Vice President
James Douglas Pittman, Second VP
Ross Vanderwolf, CFP, Secretary

Provides its members with resources to improve their technical knowledge, sales and client service while maintaining a culture of high ethical standards. Mission is to be a valued, member-driven international network of leading insurance and investment financial services professionals/advisors who serve their clients by exemplary performance and the highest standards of ethics, knowledge, service and productivity.
35000 Members
Founded in: 1927
Mailing list available for rent

13705 Mortgage Bankers Association of America
1919 M Street NW
5th Floor
Washington, DC 20036

202-557-2700
800-793-6222; www.mortgagebankers.org
Social Media: Facebook, Twitter, LinkedIn, YouTube

Thomas Dennard, Chairman
Kurt Pfotenhauer, Vice Chairman
David H. Stevens, President, Chief Executive Officer
Bill Killmer, SVP, Legislative & Pol. Affairs
Marcia Davies, Chief Operating Officer

United States national association representing all facets of the real estate finance industry.
2200 Members

13706 Mortgage Insurance Companies of America
1425 K St Nw
Suite 210
Washington, DC 20005-3590

202-682-2683; *Fax:* 202-842-9252;
www.privatemi.com

Suzanne Hutchinson, Executive VP

Representing the private mortgage insurance industry.
4 Members
Founded in: 1973

13707 National African American Insurance Association
1718 M Street, NW
Box #1110
Washington, DC 20036

866-56 -AAIA; *Fax:* 513-563-9743
info@naaia.org; www.naaia.org
Social Media: Facebook, Twitter, LinkedIn

Leslie L. Skinner-Leslie, Chairman
Jerald L. Tillman,LUTCF, Founder
Quincy Branch, Vice Chair
Cherie Coffey, Treasurer
Henry Pippins, Secretary

Helps create a network among minorities who are employed by insurance companies or self-employed in the insurance industry.
Founded in: 1997

13708 National Alliance for Insurance Education & Research
3630 North Hills Drive
PO Box 27027
Austin, TX 78755-2027

512-457-7932
800-633-2165; *Fax:* 512-349-6194
alliance@scic.com; www.scic.com/
Social Media: Facebook, Twitter, LinkedIn, Google Plus, RSS

William T Hold, Ph.D, CIC, CPCU, President and CEO
Skyla Badger, Assistant Vice President, Marketing
Theresa Bucek, CISR, Assistant Vice President
Paula Cook, CISR, SVP, Program Administration
Bettie Duff, SVP, Customer Care

National education providers offering programs for all insurance and risk management professionals in property, liability and life insurance, with a continuing education requirement upon designation.
75000 Members
Founded in: 1969

13709 National Association of Professional Agents
8430 Enterprise Circle
Suite 200
Lakewood Ranch, FL 34202

800-593-7657; *Fax:* 800-411-4771;
www.napa-benefits.org/
Social Media: Facebook, Twitter, LinkedIn

Offers insurance agents direct access to insurance benefits and professional services.
Founded in: 1989

13710 National Association of Bar-Related Title Insurers
1430 Lee Street
Des Plaines, IL 60018

847-298-8300; *Fax:* 847-298-8388
joanne@elliottlaw.com; www.nabrti.com

Joanne P Elliott, Executive Vice President
Kathleen Waters, Secretary/Treasurer

Members are bar-related title insurance companies registered with the US Patent Office.
10 Members
Founded in: 1965

13711 National Association of Casualty and Surety Agents
316 Pennsylvania Avenue SE
Suite 400
Washington, DC 20003-1172

202-543-7500; *Fax:* 202-293-1219

Lawrence Zippin, Executive Director

A trade organization of insurance agentswho represent and sell for stock insurers. Its purpose is to foster the growth of its members through cooperation with the insurers its members represent.

13712 National Association of Catastrophe Adjusters
P.O. Box 499
Alvord, TX 76225

817-498-3466; *Fax:* 817-498-0480
naca@nacatadj.org; www.nacatadj.org
Social Media: Facebook, Twitter, LinkedIn

Chris Hatcher, President
Jon Joyce, Vice President
Jimmy Clark, Secretary/Treasurer

Provides a professional organization focused on excellence in catastrophe insurance adjusting for members through education, shared resources, and technology.
347 Members
Founded in: 1976

13713 National Association of Dental Plans
12700 Park Central Drive
Ste. 400
Dallas, TX 75251

972-458-6998; *Fax:* 972-458-2258
info@nadp.org; www.nadp.org
Social Media: Facebook, Twitter, LinkedIn, Youtube

Chris Swanker, FSA, MAAA, Chair
Theresa McConeghey, Vice Chair
Dr Gene Sherman, Secretary
Kirk Andrews, Treasurer
Evelyn F. Ireland, CAE, Executive Director

Non profit trade association representing the entire dental benefits industry; dental HMOs, dental PPOs, discount dental plans and dental indemnity products. Members include major commercial carriers, regional and single state companies, as well as companies organized as Delta and Blue Cross Blue Shield plans.
80 Members
Founded in: 1989

13714 National Association of Disability Evaluating Professionals
13801 Village Mill Drive
Midlothian, VA 23113

804-378-7275; www.nadep.com

Virgil Robert May III, Executive Director

Members are lawyers, medical doctors and other professionals involved in the evaluation and rehabilitation of persons with disabilities resulting from work or personal injuries.
Cost: $150.00
1000 Members
Frequency: Membership Fee
Founded in: 1984

13715 National Association of Fire Investigators , International
857 Tallevast Road
Sarasota, FL 34243

941-359-2800
877-506-6234; *Fax:* 941-351-5849
info@nafi.org; www.nafi.org
Social Media: Facebook, Twitter, LinkedIn

Heather Perkins, Executive Director
Kathryn Smith, Vice Chairman

Primary purpose of this association is to increase the knowledge and improve the skills of persons engaged in the investigation and analysis of fires, explosions, or in the litigation that ensues from such investigations. The Association also originated and implemented the National Certification Board.
7000 Members
Founded in: 1961

13716 **National Association of Fraternal Insurance Counselors**
211 Canal Road
Waterloo, WI 53594

920-478-4901
866-478-3880; *Fax:* 920-478-9586
office@nafic.org; www.nafic.org
Social Media: Facebook

James Dietrich, FIC, AFA, President
Joy Collins, FICF, Vice President
Rick Kremel, CLU, LUTCF, Secretary/Treasurer
Robert Cooper, FICF, Immediate Past President
Anna Maenner, Executive Director

Promotes and educates the sales force in fraternal life insurance. Bestows quality service award and production awards annually.
3.1M Members
Founded in: 1950

13717 **National Association of Health Underwriters**
1212 New York Avenue NW
Suite 1100
Washington, DC 20005

202-552-5060; *Fax:* 202-747-6820
info@nahu.org; www.nahu.org
Social Media: Facebook, Twitter, LinkedIn, Youtube, RSS, B2B

Janet Trautwein, Executive Vice President & CEO
Jennifer B Murphy, CFO, COO
Illana Maze, Senior Vice President of Technology
Brooke Willson, Vice President of Leadership
Melanie Gibson, VP, Member & Corporate Relations

The mission is to improve its members' ability to meet the health, financial and retirement security needs of all Americans through education, advocacy and professional development.
18000 Members
Founded in: 1930
Mailing list available for rent: 18000 names at $350 per M

13718 **National Association of Independent Insurance Adjusters (NAIIA)**
1880 Radcliff Ct.
Suite 117-C&B
Tracy, CA 95376

209-832-6962; *Fax:* 209-832-6964
admin@naiia.com; www.naiia.com

Matt Ouellette, President
Peter Crosa, President Elect
Susan Daniels, Secretary/Treasurer
James Hunt, Immediate Past President
Brenda Reisinger, Executive Director

Members are companies and individuals adjusting claims for insurance companies on a fee basis.
300 Members
Founded in: 1937

13719 **National Association of Independent Insura nce Adjusters (NAIIA)**
1880 Radcliff Ct.
Suite 117-C & B
Tracy, CA 95376

209-832-6962; *Fax:* 209-832-6964
admin@naiia.com; www.naiia.com

Matt Ouellette, President
Peter Crosa, President Elect
Susan Daniels, Secretary/Treasurer
James Hunt, Immediate Past President
Brenda Reisinger, Executive Director

Membership consists of property-liability companies Supports the National Association of Independent Insurers Political Action Committee.

13720 **National Association of Independent Life Brokerage Agencies**
11325 Random Hills Road
Suite 110
Fairfax, VA 22030

703-383-3081; *Fax:* 703-383-6942
jnormandy@nailba.org; www.nailba.org
Social Media: Facebook, Twitter, LinkedIn, RSS

David Long, Chairman
Jack Chiasson, CAE, Chief Executive Officer
George C. Van Dusen IV, Chair Elect
James Sorebo, Secretary/Treasurer
Susan D. Haning, CEM, CMP, Director, Business Development

Influencing the independent life and health brokerage community.
300+ Members
Founded in: 1981

13721 **National Association of Insurance Commissioners**
1100 Walnut Street
Suite 1500
Kansas City, MO 64106-2197

816-842-3600; *Fax:* 816-783-8175
news@naic.org; www.naic.org
Social Media: Facebook, Twitter, LinkedIn, YouTube, RSS

Monica J. Lindeen, NAIC President, Commissioner
Sharon P. Clark, NAIC Vice President Commissioner
John M. Huff, NAIC President Elect Director
Sen. Ben Nelson, NAIC Chief Executive Officer
Ted Nickel, NAIC Secretary-Treasurer

Assists state insurance regulators, individually and collectively, in serving the public interest and achieving the following fundamental insurance regulatorygoals in a responsive, efficient and cost effective manner, consistent with the wishes of its members.
Founded in: 1871
Mailing list available for rent

13722 **National Association of Insurance and Financial Advisors**
2901 Telestar Court
PO Box 12012
Falls Church, VA 22042-1205

877-866-2432
877-866-2432; *Fax:* 703-770-8201
membersupport@naifa.org; www.naifa.org
Social Media: Facebook, Twitter, LinkedIn, Youtube

Jules O. Gaudreau, President
Kevin M. Mayeux, CAE, Chief Executive Officer
Paul R. Dougherty, President Elect
Matthew S. Tassey, Treasurer
Keith M. Gillies, Secretary

Mission is to advocate for a positive legislative and regulatory environment, enhance business and professional skills, and promote the ethical conduct of our members.
Founded in: 1890

13723 **National Association of Mutual Insurance Companies**
3601 Vincennes Road
Indianapolis, IN 46268-0700

317-875-5250; *Fax:* 317-879-8408;
www.namic.org
Social Media: Facebook, Twitter, LinkedIn, YouTube, RSS

Charles M Chamness, President/CEO
Neil Alldredge, SVP, State & Policy Affairs
Gregg Dykstra, COO, General Counsel
Michael Ulmer, VP, Business Development
Pam Keeney, Vice President - Underwriting

A full service nationaltrade association with more than 1,400 member companies that underwrite 43 percent of the property/casualty insurance premium in the United States.
1400 Members
Founded in: 1985
Mailing list available for rent

13724 **National Association of Professional Surplus Lines Offices, Ltd.**
4131 N. Mulberry Drive
Suite 200
Kansas City, MO 64116
816-741-3910; *Fax:* 816-741-5409
info@napslo.org; www.napslo.org
Social Media: Facebook, Twitter, LinkedIn

Gilbert C. Hine, Jr., CPCU, CFP, President
David E. Leonard, CPCU, Are, Vice President
Hank Haldeman, Immediate Past President
Jacqueline M. Schaendorf, CPCU, Treasurer
James C. Drinkwater, Secretary

A national trade association representing the surplus lines industry and the wholesale insurance marketing system. Acting as a source of information, spends a great deal of time identifying and explaining to regulatory, other segments of the insurance industry, the media and the public the vital role surplus lines in the insurance industry.
Founded in: 1975
Mailing list available for rent

13725 **National Association of Professional Insur ance Agents**
400 North Washington Street
Alexandria, VA 22314

703-836-9340; *Fax:* 703-836-1279
web@pianet.org; www.pianet.org/
Social Media: Facebook, Twitter, LinkedIn, RSS

Mike Becker, Executive Vice President & CEO
Ted Besesparis, SVP, Comm./Public Relations
Patricia A. Borowski, CPIW, SVP, Government/Industry Affairs
Alexi Papandon, CAE, SVP, Products & Services
Jon Gentile, Director of Federal Affairs

Voluntary, membership based, trade association representing professional independent insurance agents throughout the United States.
Founded in: 1931

13726 **National Association of Public Insurance Adjusters**
21165 Whitfield Place
Suite 105
Potomac Falls, VA 20165

703-433-9217; *Fax:* 703-433-0369
info@napia.com; www.napia.com

Scott deLuise, SPPA, President
Diane Swerling, SPPA, First Vice President
Jeff Gould, CPA, Second Vice President
Damon Faunce, Third VP
Greg Raab, Fourth VP

Experts on property loss adjustment who are retained by policy holders to assist in preparing, filing and adjusting insurance claims. NAPIA members have joined together for the purpose of professional education, certification, and promotion of a code of professional conduct.
Founded in: 1951
Mailing list available for rent

13727 **National Association of State Comprehensive Health Insurance**

580-512-1488; www.naschip.org/

Tanya Case, Chair
Vic Kensler, Chair-Elect/Vice President
Cecil Bykerk, Treasurer
Vernita McMurtrey, Secretary
Michele Eberle, Board Member

Provides educational opportunities and information for state high risk health insurance pools that have been, or are yet to be, established by state governments to serve the medically "uninsurable" population.

13728 National Association of Surety Bond Producers
1140 19th Street
Suite 800
Washington, DC 20036-5104

202-686-3700; *Fax:* 202-686-3656
info@nasbp.org; www.nasbp.org
Social Media: Facebook, Twitter, LinkedIn

Susan Hecker, President
Lynne Cook, First Vice President
Howard Cowan, Second VP
Robert Shaw, Third VP
Mark McCallum, CEO

International organization of professional surety bond producers and brokers.
500+ Members
Founded in: 1942

13729 National Cargo Bureau
17 Battery Place
Suite 1232
New York, NY 10004-1110

212-785-8300; *Fax:* 212-785-8333
ncbnyc@natcargo.org; www.natcargo.org

Ian J. Lennard, President
Kristian Wiede, Corporate Secretary
Philip Anderson, Chief, Technical Department
Capt. Thomas Sheridan, Deputy Chief Surveyor
Capt. Peter Ho, Deputy Chief Surveyor

The Bureau was created to render assistance to the United States Coast Guard in discharging its responsibilities under the 1948 International Convention for Safety of Life at Sea and for other purposes closely related thereto.
Founded in: 1952

13730 National Conference of Insurance Legislators
385 Jordan Road
Troy, NY 12180

518-687-0178; *Fax:* 518-687-0401
info@ncoil.org; www.ncoil.org
Social Media: Facebook, Twitter

Sen. Neil Breslin, President
Sen. Travis Holdman, IN, Vice President
Rep. Steve Riggs, Secretary
Sen. Jason Rapert, Treasurer

NCOIL is an organization of state legislators whose main area of public policy concern is insurance legislation and regulation. Many legislators active in NCOIL either chair or are members of the committees reponsible for insurance legislation in their respective state houses across the country.
Founded in: 1969

13731 National Conference of Insurance Legislato rs (NCOIL)
1100 13th Street NW
Suite 1000
Washington, DC 20005

202-955-3500; *Fax:* 202-955-3599
customersupport@ncqa.org; www.ncqa.org
Social Media: Facebook, Twitter, LinkedIn, YouTube, Google+, Pinterest

David Chin, MD, Chair
Margaret E. O'Kane, President
Michael S. Barr, MD, MBA, FACP, EVP, Quality Measurement
Tom Fluegel, Chief Operating Officer
Patricia Barrett, VP, Product Design and Support

Independent, non profit organization dedicated to improving healthcare quality.
Founded in: 1990
Mailing list available for rent

13732 National Council of Self-Insurers
P.O. Box 98248
Des Moines, WA 98198

206-409-6995; *Fax:* 206-212-9488
dave.kaplan@natcouncil.com; www.natcouncil.com

Dave Kaplan, Executive Director
Robin R Obetz, VP

The Council believes that the workers' compensation system, properly administered by the states, is a vital part of the economic and social fabric of the United States. The Council aime to preserve it and protect it as the most effective means of resolving claims for industrial injuries and occupational diseases between employers and employees.
3500 Members
Founded in: 1946

13733 National Council on Compensation Insurance
901 Pennisula Corporate Circle
Boca Raton, FL 33487-1362

561-893-1000; *Fax:* 561-893-1191
robert_pierson@ncci.com; www.ncci.com

Cheryl Budd, Chief Communications Officer
Robert Pierson, Affiliate Services Executive
Jennie Dennison, Account Manager
Gregory Quinn, Media Relations Director
Judy Joffe, Community Relations Director

Manages the nation's largest database of workers' compensation insurance information. They analyze industry trends, prepares workers compensation insurance rate recommendations, determines the cost of propsed legislation, and provides a variety of services and tools to maintain a healthy workers compensation system.
Founded in: 1922

13734 National Independent Statistical Service
3601 Vincennes Road
PO Box 68950
Indianapolis, IN 46268-0950

317-876-6200; *Fax:* 317-876-6210
questions@niss-stat.org; www.niss-stat.org

Theresa Szwast, President

A unique resource for the property/casualty insurance industry. Collect and report timely, quality insurance data, and perform other related functions, at a reasonable cost.
Founded in: 1966

13735 National Insurance Association
1133 Desert Shale Avenue
Las Vegas, NV 89120

702-269-2445; *Fax:* 702-269-2446

Josephine King, Executive Director

Organization of about 14 insurance companies owned or controlled by African Americans.
14 Members
Founded in: 1921

13736 National Insurance Crime Bureau
1111 E Touhy Ave
Suite 400
Des Plaines, IL 60018-5804

847-544-7000
800-447-6282; *Fax:* 847-544-7100
rjones@nicb.org; www.nicb.org
Social Media: Facebook, Twitter, LinkedIn, Youtube

Joseph H Wehrle, Jr, President
James K Schweitzer, SVP, COO
Daniel G Abbott, SVP, Chief Information Officer
Robert Jachnicki, SVP, CFO
Andrew J Sosnowski, SVP, General Counsel

Not for profit organization that receives support from property/casualty insurance companies. Partners with insurers and law enforcement agencies to facilitate the identification, detection and prosecution of insurance criminals. Formed from the merging of the National Automobile Theft Bureau and the Insurance Crime Prevention Institute.
1000 Members
Founded in: 1992

13737 National Organization of Life and Health Insurance Guaranty Associations
13873 Park Center Road
Suite 329
Herndon, VA 20171

703-481-5206; *Fax:* 703-481-5209
info@nolhga.com; www.nolhga.com/

Deborah J. Long, Esq., Chair
Lee Douglass, Vice Chair
Deborah Bello, Treasurer
Margaret M . Parker, Secretary
Melody R. J. Jensen, Esq., Immediate Past Chair

A voluntary, U.S. association made up of the life and health insurance guaranty associations of all 50 states and the District of Columbia.
Founded in: 1983

13738 National Risk Retention Association
16133 Ventura Blvd.
Suite 1055
Encino, CA 91436

818-995-3274
800-928-5809; *Fax:* 818-995-6496; *Fax:* 800-421-5981
joe@riskretention.org; www.nrra-usa.org

Dan Labrie, Chair
Michael J. Schroeder, Chair Elect/Vice Chair
Sanford Elsass, Immediate Past Chair
Jon Harkavy, Secretary
Nancy Gray, Treasurer

Promotes Risk Retention Act-authorized group insurance programs as a practical, economical, efficient and financially sound option for distributing the liability risks of member insuerds.
Founded in: 1987

13739 National Underwriter Company
5081 Olympic Blvd
Erlanger, KY 41018-3164

859-692-2100
800-543-0874; *Fax:* 859-692-2295
webmistress@nuco.com; www.nationalunderwriter.com

Charlie Smith, CEO

Organization with listings which include companies, brokers and agents in each area handling all lines of insurance.

13740 National Viatical Association
1030 15th Street NW
Washington, DC 20005

202-347-7361
800-741-9465; *Fax:* 202-393-0336

Charles C Reely, Executive Director

NVA is dedicated to financially assisting and effectively promotingthe needs of people coping with terminal illnesses in a compassionate, professional and ethical manner. The National Viatical Association is further dedicated to educating and informing the public on the viatical settlement processs.
60 Members
Founded in: 1993

13741 New England Professional Insurance Agents Association
1 Ash Street
Hopkinton, MA 01748-1822
508-497-2590
Stella Di Camilo, Manager
Supports all those in professional agents in the insurance industry in the New England region. Hosts annual trade show.

13742 Nonprofit Risk Management Center
204 South King Street
Leesburg, VA 20175
202-785-3891; *Fax:* 703-443-1990
info@nonprofitrisk.org; www.nonprofitrisk.org
Social Media: Twitter
Peter Andrew, President
Lisa Prinz, Treasurer
Carolyn Hayes-Gulston, Secretary
Melanie Lockwood Herman, Executive Director
Kay Nakamura, Director of Client Solutions
Provides assistance and resources for community serving organizations.
Founded in: 1990
Mailing list available for rent

13743 North American Pet Health Insurance Association
200 - 692 Osborne Street
Winnipeg, MB R3L 2B9
877-962-7442
info@naphia.org; www.naphia.org
Social Media: Facebook, Twitter, LinkedIn, YouTube
Dennis Rushovich, President and Past Treasurer
Laura Bennett, Past President
Steve Popovich, Treasurer
Tim Graff, Secretary
Randy Valpy, Board Member
Represents experienced and reputable pet health insurance companiesand pet health professionals.

13744 Physician Insurers Association of America
2275 Research Blvd
Suite 250
Rockville, MD 20850-6213
301-947-9000; *Fax:* 301-947-9090
membership@piaa.us; www.piaa.us
Social Media: Twitter
Gloria H. Everett, Chair
Paul C. McNabb, II, MD, Vice Chair
Richard E. Anderson, MD, Secretary
Brian Atchinson, President & CEO
Eric Anderson, VP of Marketing & Communications
An organization of healthcare liability insurance entities which share the common values of its founders to advocate on behalf of physicians, dentists, and other healthcare providers in the areas of legislation, education, risk management and research.
1000 Members
Founded in: 1977

13745 Professional Insurance Communicators of America
3601 Vincennes Road
Po Box 60700
Indianapolis, IN 46268-0700
317-875-5250; *Fax:* 317-879-8408;
www.pica.informe.com
Social Media: Twitter, LinkedIn
Janet EH Wright, Secretary/Treasurer
Members are editors of insurance company newsletters.
90 Members
Founded in: 1955

13746 Professional Insurance Marketing Association
35 E. Wacker Dr.
Suite 850
Chicago, IL 60601-2106
817-569-7462; *Fax:* 312-644-8557
mona@pima-assn.org; www.pima-assn.org
Social Media: Twitter, LinkedIn
Michael Mercer, President
Mark Kelsey, President-Elect
Daniel O'Brien, CLU, Imm. Past President
William Suneson, Treasurer
Mona Buckley, CEO (ex-officio)
The leading national membership association of third-party administrators, insurance carriers and allied business partners involved in the direct marketing of insurance products. Also provides educational conferences, legislative updates, networking opportunities, publications and manuals to all those whose primary business is insurance marketing.
117 Members
Founded in: 1974

13747 Professional Liability Underwriting Society
5353 Wayzata Blvd
Suite 600
Minneapolis, MN 55416-1335
952-746-2580
800-845-0778; *Fax:* 952-746-2599
info@plusweb.org; www.plusweb.org
Social Media: Twitter, LinkedIn, RSS
James Skarzynski, President
Heather Fox, President-Elect
Peter Herron, Imm. Past President
Debbie Schaffel, RPLU, Secretary-Treasurer
Robbie Thompson, Executive Director
Enhances the professionalism of its members through education and other activities and to responsibly address issues related to professional liability.
7000 Members
Founded in: 1986

13748 Property Casualty Insurers Association of America
8700 West Bryn Mawr Avenue
Suite 1200S
Chicago, IL 60631-3512
847-297-7800; *Fax:* 847-297-5064
pcinet@pciaa.net; www.pciaa.net
Social Media: Facebook, Twitter, YouTube
David A. Sampson, President
Paul C. Blume, Senior Vice President
Nathaniel Wienecke, Senior Vice President
Randi Cigelnik, Senior Vice President
Joanne M. Orfanos, Senior Vice President
Established by the Merger of the Alliance of American Insurers and the National Association Association of Independent Insurers. Provides a responsible and effective voice on public policy questions affecting insurance products and services, fosters a competitive insurance marketplace for the benefit of insurers and consumers, and provides members with the highest quality products, information and services at a reasonable cost.
1000 Members
Founded in: 2004

13749 Property Insurance Loss Register
700 New Brunswick Avenue
Rahway, NJ 07065-3819
732-388-0332; *Fax:* 732-388-0537
Lawrence Zippin, President
A voluntary nonprofit organization administered by the American Insurance Services Group; maintains a computerized registry of property loss claims which can be used by its subscribers to fight insurance fraud, and provides data for nonactuarial/statistical research.

13750 Property Loss Research Bureau (PLRB/LIRB)
3025 Highland Parkway
Suite 800
Downers Grove, IL 60515-1291
630-724-2200
888-711-7572; *Fax:* 630-724-2260;
www.plrb.org
Social Media: Facebook, Twitter, Instagram
Tom Mallin, President
Paul C Despensa, VP/General Counsel
PLRB/LIRB provides legal research, consulting and educational services in auto liablility and CGL lines, in addition to promoting education and new, beneficial developments within the property and casualty insurance industry. Members are stock and mutual insurance companies.
252 Members
Founded in: 1990
Mailing list available for rent

13751 Public Agency Risk Managers Association
PO Box 6810
San Jose, CA 95150
888-907-2762; *Fax:* 888-412-5913
Info@parma.com; www.parma.com
Social Media: Facebook, Twitter, LinkedIn, Vimeo, Instagram
Jim Thyden, President
Kim Hunt, Vice President
Susan Eldridge, Secretary Treasurer
Coni Hernandez, Alliance of Schools
Jeff J Rush, Senior Claims Administrator
A forum promoting, developing and advancing education and leadership in public agency risk management. PARMA is dedicated to facilitating the exchange of ideas and innovative solutions toward risk management in government.
600+ Members
Founded in: 1974

13752 Registered Mail Insurance Association
100 William Street
New York, NY 10038-4512
212-612-4000
800-969-7462; *Fax:* 212-425-2539
Cheryl Martinez, Assistant VP
Insurance companies providing insurance for shipments of currency, securities and other valuables. LSTD Instrument Bonds are provided to facilitate the reproduction of lost documents.
3 Members
Founded in: 1921

13753 Reinsurance Association of America
1445 New York Ave
7th Floor
Washington, DC 20005
202-638-3690; *Fax:* 202-638-0936
infobox@reinsurance.org;
www.reinsurance.org
Social Media: Facebook, Twitter, LinkedIn
Franklin W Nutter, President
Dennis C Burke, Vice President, State Relations
Marsha A Cohen, SVP, Director of Education
Tracey W Laws, SVP, General Counsel
Karalee C Morell, VP, Assistant General Counsel
Non profit association committed to an activist agenda that represents the interests of reinsurance professionals across the United States.
Founded in: 1968

13754 **Risk and Insurance Management Society**
5 Bryant Park
13th Floor
New York, NY 10018-0713
212-286-9292; *Fax:* 212-986-9716;
www.rims.org
Social Media: Facebook, Twitter, LinkedIn
Mary Roth, Executive Director
Deborah Flam, Human Resoures Manager
Lynn Chambers, CFO
Stephanie Orange, Chief Marketing Officer
Valerie Cammiso, Membership/Chapter Services
Dedicated to advancing the practice of risk management, a professinal discipline that protects physical, financial and human resources.
3900 Members
Founded in: 1950
Mailing list available for rent

13755 **SNL Financial**
212 7th Street NE
One SNL Plaza
Charlottesvle, VA 22902
434-977-1600; *Fax:* 434-977-4466
customerservice@snl.com; www.snl.com
Social Media: Facebook, Twitter, LinkedIn, YouTube, Google+
Michael Chinn, President
Reid Nagle, CEO
Bjorn Turnquist, Director Product Management
This organization offers the most up-to-date information available in the insurance industry featuring the latest news releases, filings and important events. Provides current data on top-performing stocks, insider trades, ownership filings, company news and events and legislative issues.
Founded in: 1987
Mailing list available for rent

13756 **Securities Industry and Financial Markets Association (SIFMA)**
1101 New York Avenue, NW
8th Floor
Washington, DC 20005-4279
202-962-7300; *Fax:* 202-962-7305;
www.sifma.org
Social Media: Facebook, Twitter, LinkedIn
William A. Johnstone, Chair
John F. W. Rogers, Chair Elect
Timothy C. Scheve, Vice Chair
Kenneth E. Bentsen, Jr., President, CEO
Gerard McGraw, Treasurer
SIFMA's mission is to champion policies and practices that benefit investors and issuers, expand and perfect global capital markets, and foster the development of new products and services. SIFMA provides an enhanced member network of access and forward-looking services, as well as premiere educational resources for the professionals within the industry and the investors whom they serve.
Mailing list available for rent

13757 **Self Insurance Institute of America**
PO Box 1237
Simpsonville, SC 29681
800-851-7789; *Fax:* 864-962-2483
administration@siia.org; www.siia.org
Social Media: Facebook, Twitter
Donald K. Drelich, Chairman of the Board
Steven J. Link, Chairman Elect
Ronald K. Dewsnup, Treasurer/Corporate Secretary
Mike Ferguson, President, CEO
Erica Massey, EVP
Dedicated to protecting and promoting the self insurance and alternative risk transfer industry.
1500 Members
Founded in: 1981

13758 **Shipowners Claims Bureau**
1 Battery Park Plaza
31st Floor
New York, NY 10004-1487
212-847-4500; *Fax:* 212-847-4599
info@american-club.com;
www.american-club.com
J. Arnold Witte, Chairman
Markos K. Marinakis, Deputy Chairman
Arpad A. Kadi, Senior Vice President - Treasurer
Donald R. Moore, Senior Vice President
Members are claim managers and adjusters for shipping lines and protection and indemnity clubs.
31 Members
Founded in: 1917
Mailing list available for rent

13759 **Society of Actuaries**
475 North Martingale Rd.
Suite 600
Schaumburg, IL 60173-2252
847-706-3500
888-697-3900; *Fax:* 847-706-3599
customerservice@soa.org; www.soa.org
Social Media: Twitter, LinkedIn, YouTube
Craig W. Reynolds, President
Jeremy J. Brown, President-Elect
Joan C. Barrett, Vice-President
Susan E. Pantely, Vice-President
Susan R. Sames, Vice-President
An educational, research and professional organization dedicated to serving the public and Society members. The vision is for actuaries to be recognized as the leading professionals in the modeling and management of finanacial risk and contingent events.
17000 Members
Founded in: 1949

13760 **Society of Certified Insurance Counselors**
3630 North Hills Drive
Austin, TX 78731-3028
512-457-7932
800-633-2165; *Fax:* 512-349-6194
alliance@scic.com; www.scic.com
Social Media: Facebook, Twitter, LinkedIn, Google+, RSS
William Hold, Ph.D, CIC, CPCU, President/CEO
Skyla Badger, Assistant Vice President, Marketing
Theresa Bucek, CISR, Assistant Vice President
Paula Cook, CISR, SVP, Program Administration
Bettie Duff, SVP, Customer Care
National education program in property, liability and life insurance, with a continuing education requirement upon designation.

13761 **Society of Financial Examiners**
12100 Sunset Hills Rd
Suite 130
Reston, VA 20190-3221
703-234-4140
800-787-7633; *Fax:* 888-436-8686
sofe@sofe.org; www.sofe.org
Social Media: Facebook, LinkedIn
Annette Knief, CFE, President
Richard Nelson, CFE, VP
Susan Bernard, CFE, AES, VP
James Kattman, CFE, Treasurer
Mark Murphy, CFE, Secretary
The one organization where financial examiners of inusurance companies, banks, savings and loans, credit unions come together for training and to share exchange information on a formal and informal level.
1600 Members
Founded in: 1973

13762 **Society of Financial Service Professionals**
3803 West Chester Pike
Suite 225
Newtown Square, PA 19073-3230
610-526-2500; *Fax:* 610-359-8115
info@societyoffsp.org; www.financialpro.org
Social Media: Facebook, Twitter, LinkedIn, Flickr, RSS
Joseph E. Frack, Chief Executive Officer
Anthony R. Bartlett, President
James S. Aussem, President Elect
Elvin D. Turner, Secretary
Members are dedicated to the highest standards of competence and service in insurance and financial services.
9000 Members
Founded in: 1928
Mailing list available for rent

13763 **Society of Insurance Research**
631 Eastpoint Drive
Shelbyville, IN 46176-2291
317-398-3684; *Fax:* 317-642-0535
sir.mail@comcast.net; www.sirnet.org
Sharon Markovsky, President
Tom Forristell, CPA, Vice President - Controller
Karen Imbrogno, Vice President - Annual Conference
Michael Warner, VP Marketing
Carol Smith, Vice President - Membership
Provides a forum for the free exchange of ideas in all areas of insurance research. The Society includes representation from many different organizations such as insurance and non-insurance companies, government agencies, institutions of higher education, and trade associations.
350 Members
Founded in: 1970
Mailing list available for rent

13764 **Society of Insurance Trainers and Educators**
1821 University Ave W
Ste S256
St. Paul, MN 55104
651-999-5354; *Fax:* 651-917-1835
ed@insurancetrainers.org;
www.insurancetrainers.org
Social Media: Facebook, Twitter, LinkedIn, Instagram
Deborah Davenport, CIC, ITP, President
Brad Gutcher, Immediate Past President
Elise Quadrozzi, CPCU, AIC,, VP Annual Conference
Treg Camper, VP Membership Services
Heather Hubbard, MSHRM, Vice President - Marketing
Professional organization of trainers and educators in insurance.
600 Members
Founded in: 1953

13765 **Society of Professional Benefit Administrators**
2 Wisconsin Circle
Suite 670
Chevy Chase, MD 20815
301-718-7722; *Fax:* 301-718-9440
info@spbatpa.org; www.spbatpa.org
Social Media: Twitter
Anne C Lennan, President
National Association of Third Party Administrators (TPAs) of employee benefit health and pen-

sion plans. SPBA represents TPAs who offer comprehensive services.
300 Members
Founded in: 1975

13766 Society of Risk Management Consultants
621 North Sherman Avenue
Madison, WI 53704

800-765-SRMC; *Fax:* 212-572-6499
webmaster@srmcsociety.org;
www.srmcsociety.org

Susan Kaufman, Public Relations
Mark R. Forsythe, CPCU, President
Robert Harder, ARM, Secretary
Michael Norek, Treasurer
Joy M. Gander, CPCU, ARM, President Elect

The mission is to advance these professions to benefit the consultants themselves, their clients and the public through research, education, the exchange of information, anf the promotion of professional and ethical guidlines.
150 Members
Founded in: 1984

13767 Sun States Professional Insurance Agents Association
13416 N 32nd Street
Suite 106
Phoenix, AZ 85032-6000

602-482-3333

Maryls M Graser, Executive VP

Supports all those professional insurance agents who serve the southern region of the country. Hosts annual trade show.

13768 Teachers Insurance and Annuity Association
730 Third Avenue
New York, NY 10017

800-842-2252; *Fax:* 800-842-2252;
www.tiaa-cref.org
Social Media: Facebook, Twitter, LinkedIn, YouTube, Google+

Roger Ferguson, President, CEO
Gina Wilson, EVP, CFO
Connie Weaver, EVP, Chief Marketing Officer
Ron Pressman, EVP, Chief Operating Officer
Annabelle Bexiga, EVP, Chief Information Officer

Financial services organization that is a retirement provider for people who work in the academic, research, medical and cultural fields.

13769 The American Council of Life Insurers
101 Constitution Avenue, NW
Suite 700
Washington, DC 20001-2133

202-624-2000; *Fax:* 202-624-2115
contact@acli.com; www.acli.com
Social Media: Facebook, Twitter, RSS, YouTube

Dirk Kempthorne, President, CEO
Brian Waidmann, Chief of Staff
Gary E. Hughes, EVP, General Counsel
J. Bruce Ferguson, SVP, State Relations
Don Walker, SVP, Administration & CFO

A Washinton, D.C.-based lobbying and trade group for the life insurance industry.
300 Members
Founded in: 1976

13770 The American Society of Law, Medicine & Ethics
765 Commonwealth Avenue
Suite 1634
Boston, MA 02215-1401

617-262-4990; *Fax:* 617-437-7596
info@aslme.org; www.aslme.org
Social Media: Facebook, Twitter, LinkedIn

Ted Hutchinson, Executive Director
Margo Smith, Membership Department
Katie Kenney Johnson, Conference Director
Courtney McClellan, Assistant Editor
Arthur R. Derse, MD, JD, FACEP, Board of Director

Provides high-quality scholarship, debate, and critical thought to the community of professionals at the nexus of law, medicine, and ethics.
Founded in: 1972
Mailing list available for rent

13771 The Blue Cross and Blue Shield Association
225 North Michigan Avenue
Chicago, IL 60601

E-Mail: bcbswebmaster@bcbsa.com;
www.bcbs.com/
Social Media: Facebook, Twitter, YouTube, RSS

Scott P. Serota, President, CEO
William A. Breskin, VP, Government Programs
Doug Porter, SVP, Operations, CIO
Maureen E. Sullivan, SVP, Strategic Services
Robert Kolodgy, SVP, Financial Services, CFO

Trade association for the independent, locally operated Blue Cross and Blue Shield plans in the USA.

13772 The Council of Insurance Agents & Brokers
701 Pennsylvania Avenue NW
Suite 750
Washington, DC 20004-2661

202-783-4400; *Fax:* 202-783-4410
ciab@ciab.com; www.ciab.com
Social Media: Facebook, Twitter, LinkedIn

Bill D. Henry, Chairman
Ken A Crerar, President/CEO
Robert Cohen, Vice Chairman
David L. Eslick, Treasurer
Martin P. Hughes, Secretary

Formerly the National Association of Casualty and Surety agents. The council represents the nation's largest commercial property and casualty insurance agencies and brokerage firms. Council members annually place some 80% of the commercial property/casualty insurance premiums in the United States. Council members who operate both nationally and internationally, specialize in a wide range of insurance products and risk management services for business, industry, government and the public.
300 Members
Founded in: 1913

13773 The Griffith Insurance Education Foundation
720 Providence Rd
Suite 100
Malvern, PA 19355

855-288-7743; *Fax:* 610-725-5967
info@griffithfoundation.org;
www.griffithfoundation.org
Social Media: Facebook, Twitter

Susan Krieger, Chair
James Jones, MBA, CPCU, ARM, Vice Chair
Dana Rudmose, CPA, Treasurer
Janice M. Abraham, Immediate Past Chairman
Kevin Brown, Esq., CAE, Executive Director

Nonprofit, nonadvocacy, educational organization that provides riskmanagement and insurance education for students and public policymakers.
Founded in: 1960

13774 The Institutes
720 Providence Road
Suite 100
Malvern, PA 19355-3433

610-644-2101
800-644-2101
610-644-2100; *Fax:* 610-640-9576
cserv@cpcuiia.org; www.theinstitutes.org
Social Media: Facebook, Twitter, LinkedIn

Peter L. Miller, CPCU, President
Anita Z. Bourke, CPCU, AINS, EVP
Kevin H. Brown, Esq., CPCU, CAE, SVP, General Counsel, Exe. Dir.
Jeffrey Scheidt, SVP
Elizabeth A. Sprinkel, CPCU, SVP

An independent, nonprofit organization offering educational programs and professional certification to people in all segments of the property and liability insurance business. More than 150,000 insurance practitioners around the world are involved in Institute programs.
Mailing list available for rent

13775 The National Association for Fixed Annuities
1155 F Street NW
Suite 1050
Washington, DC 20004

414-332-9306; *Fax:* 415-946-3532
bailey@nafa.com; www.nafa.com
Social Media: Facebook, Twitter, LinkedIn

S. Christopher Johnson, NAFA Chair
Nathan Zuidema, NAFA Vice Chair
Dominic Cursio, NAFA Treasurer
Brian D. Mann, Secretary
Chip Anderson, Executive Director

Trade association dedicated to promoting fixed annuities.

13776 The National Association of Independent Insurance Adjusters
1880 Radcliff Ct.
Tracy, CA 95376

209-832-6962; *Fax:* 209-832-6964
admin@naiia.com; www.naiia.com

Matt Ouellette, President
Peter Crosa, President Elect
Susan Daniels, Secretary/Treasurer
James Hunt, Immediate Past President
Brenda Reisinger, Executive Director

Trade group of property and casualty claims companies.

13777 The National Association of Mutual Insurance Companies
122 C Street N.W.
Suite 540
Washington, DC 20001

202-628-1558; *Fax:* 202-628-1601;
www.namic.org
Social Media: Facebook, Twitter, LinkedIn, RSS, YouTube

Paul G. Stueven, PFMM, Chairman
Paul A. Ehlert, J.D., Vice Chairman
Stuart Henderson, J.D., CPCU, Immediate Past Chairman
Charles Chamness, President, CEO
Steve Linkous, Chairman Elect

National trade association of mutual property and casualty insurance companies.

13778 **The Society of Chartered Property and Casualty Underwriters (CPCU)**
720 Providence Road
Malvern, PA 19355
800-932-2728; *Fax:* 610-725-5969
MemberResources@theinstitutes.org;
www.cpcusociety.org/
Social Media: Facebook, Twitter, LinkedIn
Jane M. Wahl, CPCU, CSSBB, President, Chair
Brian P. Savko, CPCU, CLU, ChFC, President-Elect
Stanley W. Plappert, JD, CPCU, Treasurer, Secretary
Cynthia A. Baroway, CPCU, M.Ed., Immediate Past President, Chairman
Kevin H. Brown, Esq., CPCU, CAE, SVP, Executive Director
A community of credentialed property and casualty insurance professionals.
22,00 Members

13779 **Think Believe Act**
220 West 42nd Street
10th Floor
New York, NY 10036
646-445-7000; *Fax:* 646-445-7001
losangeles@tbaglobal.com;
www.tbaglobal.com
Social Media: Facebook, Twitter, LinkedIn, Instagram
Robert Geddes, CEO
TBA is a privately-held company that is now one of the world's leading producers and marketers of brand events and experiences for Fortune 1000 companies

13780 **Transportation & Logistics Council**
120 Main Street
Huntington, NY 11743
631-549-8988; *Fax:* 631-549-8962
tlc@transportlaw.com; www.tlcouncil.org
Reed Tepper, Chairman
Nadia Martin, CCP, President
Curtis Hart, VP
Phillip Lamb, Secretary/Treasurer
George CarlPezold, Executive Director
Formerly the Transportation Consumer Protection Council, a not for profit trade association dedicated to the education of shippers, carriers and others involved in the transportation of goods, the prevention of transit loss and damage, the promulgation of reasonable practices, laws and regulations, and the equitable resolution of disputes invloving frieght claims, freight charges and related maters.
250 Members
Founded in: 1974

13781 **US Travel Insurance Association**
2080 Western Avenue
Guilderland, NY 12084
800-224-6164
president@ustia.org; www.ustia.org
Bruce Kirby, President
Mark Carney, Vice President
Linda Finkle, Treasurer
Mike Kelly, Past President
Henry Carpenter, Secretary
National association of insurance carriers, third-party administrators, insurance agencies and related businesses involved in the development, administration and marketing of travel insurance and travel assistance products.
Founded in: 2004

13782 **Underwriters Laboratories**
333 Pfingsten Road
Northbrook, IL 60062-2096
847-272-8800
877-854-3577; *Fax:* 847-272-8129
CustomerExperienceCenter@ul.com;
www.ul.com
Social Media: Facebook, Twitter, LinkedIn, YouTube, Google+, Pinterest
Keith E Williams, President/CEO
Michael Saltzman, SVP & CFO
Christian Anschuetz, Senior VP and CIO
Adrian Groom, Senior Vice President
Terry Brady, SVP & Chief Legal Officer
An independent, not for profit product safety testing and certification organization. They have also tested products for public safety for more than a century.
Founded in: 1894
Mailing list available for rent

13783 **Women In Insurance and Financial Services**
136 Everett Road
Albany, NY 12205
518-694-5506
866-264-9437; *Fax:* 518-935-9232
office@wifsnational.org; www.w-wifs.org
Social Media: Facebook, Twitter, LinkedIn
Susan L. Combs, PPACA, President
Susan Glass, LUTC, President-Elect
Evelyn Gellar, LUTCF, Secretary
Lisa Pilgrim, Deputy Treasurer
Angelia Z. Shay, Immediate Past President
Vision is to provide a strong network of women helping each other develop the success that lies within each of us.
1.5M Members
Founded in: 1987

13784 **Women in Insurance and Financial Services**
136 Everett Road
Albany, NY 12205
518-694-5506
866-264-9437; *Fax:* 518-935-9232
office@wifsnational.org;
www.wifsnational.org
Social Media: Facebook, Twitter, LinkedIn
Susan L. Combs, PPACA, President
Susan Glass, LUTC, President-Elect
Evelyn Gellar, LUTCF, Secretary
Lisa Pilgrim, Deputy Treasurer
Angelia Z. Shay, Immediate Past President
National organization devoted to the success of women in the insurance and financial services fields.

13785 **Workers Compensation Reinsurance Bureau**
2 Hudson Place
Hoboken, NJ 07030-5515
201-798-6312; *Fax:* 201-792-4441
Alfred O Weller, President
An association of insurance companies which pool their workers compensation excess losses as an alternative to purchasing reinsurance.
Founded in: 1912

13786 **Workers Compensation Research Institute**
955 Massachusetts Ave.
Cambridge, MA 02139
617-661-9274; *Fax:* 617-661-9284
wcri@wcrinet.org; www.wcrinet.org
Vincent Armentano, Chair
Richard A. Victor, President & CEO
WCRI conducts research into public policy issues surrounding workers' compensation systems.

Newsletters

13787 **ARIA Newsletter**
American Risk and Insurance Association
716 Providence Road
Malvern 19355-3402
610-640-1997; *Fax:* 610-725-1007
diana.lee@pciaa.net; www.aria.org
Frequency: 2x/Year

13788 **AWCP Newsletter**
Association of Workers' Compensation Professionals
PO Box 760
Rancho Cordova, CA 95741-0760
916-290-8017; *Fax:* 916-914-1706
info@awcp.org; www.awcp.org
Debra Real, President
Connie Conley, Executive Director
An educational newsletter with information about our constantly changing industry, how to contact our sponsors as well as announcing our upcoming events.
Frequency: Monthly

13789 **Actuarial Studies in Non-Life Insurance**
Astin Bulletin
B641 Locust Walk
Philadelphia, PA 19104-6218
215-898-2741
Jean Lemaire, Chairman
Promotes actuarial research and study and publishes the ASTIN Bulletin.
2.2M Pages
Founded in: 1957

13790 **Advanced Underwriting Services**
Dearborn Financial Publishing
155 N Wacker Drive
Floor 1
Chicago, IL 60606-6819
312-836-4400; *Fax:* 312-836-1146
Georgia Mann, Publisher
Information on the law.
Cost: $395.00
Frequency: Monthly

13791 **Best's Agents Guide to Life Insurance Companies**
AM Best Company
Ambest Rd
Oldwick, NJ 08858
908-439-2200
800-544-2378; *Fax:* 908-439-3296
webmaster@ambest.com; www.ambest.com
Arthur Snyder, CEO
Offers information on over 1,400 life and health insurance companies nationwide.
Cost: $150.00
Frequency: Monthly
Founded in: 1899

13792 **Compensation & Benefits for Law Offices**
Institute of Management and Administration
1 Washington Park
Suite 1300
Newark, NY 07102-3130
212-244-0360; *Fax:* 973-622-0595
customercare@bna.com; www.ioma.com
An indespensible reference for law firm recruitment, training, compensation, benefits, and HR managers who want and need to keep pace with what it takes to successfully, recruit, retain, train,

reward, recognize, and compensatetop legal talent.
Cost: $449.00

13793 **Crittenden Insurance Markets Newsletter**
Crittenden Publishing
45 Leveroni Court
Suite 204
Novato, CA 94949-5721
415-475-1522
800-421-3483; *Fax:* 619-923-3518
ins@crittendenonline.com;
www.crittendenonline.com
Social Media: Twitter
Offers readers a behind-the-scenes look at everything going on in the commercial insurance market. Provides all the coverage necessary for agents to be successful in the board field of commercial insurance
Frequency: Weekly
Founded in: 1972

13794 **Disability Eval and Rehab Review**
National Association of Disability Evaluating
13801 Village Mill Drive
Midlothian, VA 23113
804-378-7275; www.nadep.com
This periodical is peer reviewed and addresses issues which are impacting the field of medicine and rehabilitation and which specifically address impairment rating, disability determination, functional capacity evaluation, vocational evaluation and current trends in reimbursement and how the Americans with Disabilities Act of 1990 has changed the practice of medicine and rehabilitation.
Frequency: Quarterly

13795 **HELP Newsletter**
Insurance Loss Control Association
PO Box 346
Morton, IL 61550
309-696-2551; *Fax:* 317-879-8408
ccarson@namic.org;
www.insurancelosscontrol.org
Brock Bell, President
Daniel Finn, VP
Stig Ruxlow, Financial Secretary
Association news and activities.
Frequency: Quarterly
Circulation: 325
Founded in: 1931
Printed in 2 colors on matte stock

13796 **Highlights**
American Association of Retired Persons
601 E St Nw
Washington, DC 20049-0003
202-434-2277; *Fax:* 202-434-7599
PCMNationalOffice@aarp.org; www.aarp.org
A Barry Rand, CEO
Ethel Andrus, Founder
Offers information and updates on the association, tax information and legal statistics.
4 Pages
Frequency: BiWeekly

13797 **IOMA's Report on Hourly Compensation**
Institute of Management and Administration
1 Washington Park
Suite 1300
Newark, NJ 07102-3130
212-244-0360; *Fax:* 973-622-0595
customercare@bna.com; www.ioma.com
RHC is a sister publication for IOMA's Report on Salary Surveys and takes compensation and salary dates from major surveys produced by firms like Watson Wyatt Data Services, the Big Six Accounting firms and local HR groups to show benefits and compensation managers the going rate for hourly workers in a variety of positions.

13798 **Insurance Daily**
SNL Financial
One SNL Plaza
PO Box 2124
Charlottesville, VA 22902
434-977-1600; *Fax:* 434-293-0407;
www.snl.com
Social Media: Facebook, Twitter, LinkedIn
Akash Sinha, Editor
Tom Mason, Editor
The most comprehensive news source on the insurance sector. The news desk researches filings and investor presentations, conducts exclusive interviews with industry executives and analysts for the stories that impact the insurance market
Cost: $995.00
Frequency: Daily
Mailing list available for rent

13799 **Insurance Finance & Investment**
Institutional Investor
488 Madison Ave
New York, NY 10022-5701
212-303-3100
800-715-9195; *Fax:* 212-224-3491
iieditor@institutionalinvestor.com;
www.institutionalinvestor.com
Erik Kolk, Publisher
Chris Brown, CEO/President
Stuard Wise, Senior Editor
Nick Ferris, Marketing Director
Provides reviews of investment performance, financing strategies, overviews of ratings, and highlights of new issues.
Cost: $1495.00
Frequency: Monthly
Founded in: 1905

13800 **Insurance Forum**
Insurance Forum
PO Box 245
Ellettsville, IN 47429
812-876-6502; *Fax:* 812-876-6572;
www.theinsuranceforum.com
Joseph M Belth, Editor
Ann I Belth, Business Manager
Jeffrey E Belth, Circulation Manager
Provides objective information and incisive analysis of important insurance topics.
Cost: $120.00
Frequency: Monthly
Founded in: 1974

13801 **Insurance Performance Graph**
SNL Financial
PO Box 2124
Charlottesvle, VA 22902-2124
434-977-1600; *Fax:* 434-977-4466
isales@snl.com; www.snl.com
Mike Deane, Editor
Matt Mueller, Chief Operating Officer
Nick Cafferillo, Chief Operating Officer
Adam Hall, Managing Director
For publicly traded insurance companies and law, accounting and consulting firms. Compares the investment performance of an insurance company to a specific SNL index or to a selected peer group and the appropriate broad multi-industry index. Covers a 5-year period or the period beginning with the IPO date.
Cost: $399.00
Frequency: Monthly
Founded in: 1987

13802 **Insurance Regulation**
Wakeman Walworth Inc
PO Box 7376
Alexandria, VA 22307-7376
703-768-9600; *Fax:* 703-768-9690
statecapitals.com
Keyes Walworth, Publisher
The best way to track day-to-day changes and innovations at the state level ☐ covers health insurance including HMOs, CHIP programs and the battle to increase health insurance benefits. It also covers life, automobile, homeowner, unemployment insurance, workers compensation and malpractice. It reports on tort reform, licensing, self-insurance, plus new approaches such as lifestyle considerations.
Cost: $245.00
Frequency: Weekly

13803 **Insurance Weekly: Life & Health**
SNL Financial
One SNL Plaza
PO Box 2124
Charlottesville, VA 22902-2124
434-977-1600; *Fax:* 434-977-4466
subscriptions@snlnet.com; www.snl.com
Social Media: Facebook, Twitter, LinkedIn
Akash Sinha, Editor
Tom Mason, Editor
Super-focused coverage of the dynamic life and health, managed care and insurance agency sectors
Cost: $396.00
Frequency: Weekly
ISSN: 1098-8149
Mailing list available for rent

13804 **Insurance Weekly: Property & Casualty**
SNL Financial
One SNL Plaza
PO Box 2124
Charlottesville, VA 22902-2124
434-977-1600; *Fax:* 434-977-4466;
www.snl.com
Social Media: Facebook, Twitter, LinkedIn
Akash Sinha, Editor
Tom Mason, Editor
Complete, current coverage of the property and casualty, title, financial and mortgage guaranty and insurance agency sectors
Cost: $396.00
Frequency: Weekly
ISSN: 1098-8130
Mailing list available for rent

13805 **Journal for Insurance Compliance Professionals Newsletter**
Association of Insurance Compliance Professionals
12100 Sunset Hills Road
Suite 130
Reston, VA 20190
703-234-4074; *Fax:* 703-435-4390
aicp@aicp.net; www.aicp.net
Doug Simino, President
Darrell Turner, Editor
Elaine Douglas, Vice President
Dawn Murphy, Secretary
Doug Geraci, Treasurer
Includes topical information for members, covering regulatory and industry issues, along with the latest techniques in filings nad news from each Association Region and Chapter
Frequency: Quarterly
Founded in: 1998

13806 **LIC Newsletter**
Life Insurers Council

2300 Windy Ridge Pkwy SE
Suite 600
Atlanta, GA 30339-5665
770-951-1770
800-275-5662; *Fax:* 770-984-0441
askloma@loma.org; www.loma.org

Jeff Shaw, Executive Director
Rose Hoyt, Administrative Assistant

Includes news and analysis about issues of concern to executives and those involved in operations, plus information on upcoming events and company activities
Frequency: Monthly
Mailing list available for rent

13807 Mealey's Catastrophic Loss
LexisNexis Mealey's
555 W 5th Avenue
Los Angeles, CA 90013
213-627-1130
800-253-4182
mealeyinfo@lexisnexis.com;
www.lexisnexis.com/mealeys
Social Media: Facebook, Twitter, LinkedIn, RSS, Youtube

Tom Hagy, CEO
Maureen McGuire, Editorial Director
Gina Cappello, Editor
Mike Wash, Chief Executive Officer, Legal
Lisa Agona, Chief Marketing Officer

This report focuses on business interruption insurance claims in the aftermath of the Hurricane Katrina, September 11th, and other catastrophic loss tragedies. Additionally, the report will go beyond these claims and will offer important business interruption insurance coverage news related to computer viruses, computer failures, and natural disasters.
Cost: $1075.00
100 Pages
Frequency: Monthly
Founded in: 2001
Mailing list available for rent

13808 Mealey's Emerging Insurance Disputes
LexisNexis Mealey's
555 W 5th Avenue
Los Angeles, CA 90013
213-627-1130
800-253-4182
mealeyinfo@lexisnexis.com;
www.lexisnexis.com/mealeys
Social Media: Facebook, Twitter, LinkedIn, RSS, Youtube

Tom Hagy, CEO
Maureen McGuire, Editorial Director
Gina Cappello, Editor
Mike Wash, Chief Executive Officer, Legal
Lisa Agona, Chief Marketing Officer

The report tracks new areas of coverage liability, novel policy applications, and conflicting policy language interpretations as they arise in insurance litigation. Some areas of coverage featured are: sexual harassment and discrimination, assault and battery, professional liability, patent and trademark infringement, construction defects, directors and officers claims, emotional distress, intentional acts, technology, and insurance business practices.
Cost: $ 1229.00
100 Pages
Frequency: Semi-Monthly
Founded in: 1996
Mailing list available for rent

13809 Mealey's Litigation Report: Asbestos
LexisNexis Mealey's
555 W 5th Avenue
Los Angeles, CA 90013
213-627-1130
800-253-4182
mealeyinfo@lexisnexis.com;
www.lexisnexis.com/mealeys
Social Media: Facebook, Twitter, LinkedIn, RSS, Youtube

Tom Hagy, CEO
Maureen McGuire, Editorial Director
Bryan Redding, Editor
Mike Wash, Chief Executive Officer, Legal
Lisa Agona, Chief Marketing Officer

The report offers unsurpassed coverage of litigation arising from asbestos-related injury and death. Key issues include: massive class action settlements involving present and future claimants, state and federal verdicts, litigation experts, medical monitoring claims, suits against the tobacco industry, discovery battles, discovery rule decisions, insurance coverage rulings, and asbestos property decisions.
Cost: $1789.00
100 Pages
Frequency: Semi-Monthly
Founded in: 1984
Mailing list available for rent

13810 Mealey's Litigation Report: California Insurance
LexisNexis Mealey's
555 W 5th Avenue
Los Angeles, CA 90013
213-627-1130
800-253-4182
mealeyinfo@lexisnexis.com;
www.lexisnexis.com/mealeys
Social Media: Facebook, Twitter, LinkedIn, RSS, Youtube

Tom Hagy, CEO
Maureen McGuire, Editorial Director
Jennifer Hans, Editor
Mike Wash, Chief Executive Officer, Legal
Lisa Agona, Chief Marketing Officer

The Report focuses on ever-changing California and federal Ninth Circuit insurance coverage disputes and developments. Topics include California developments in bad faith litigation, earthquake damage coverage, disability insurance, products liability coverage, environmental insurance coverage, mold coverage, asbestos coverage, aviation litigation coverage, entertainment law and more.
Cost: $949.00
100 Pages
Frequency: Monthly
Founded in: 2001
Mailing list available for rent

13811 Mealey's Litigation Report: Disability Insurance
LexisNexis Mealey's
555 W 5th Avenue
Los Angeles, CA 90013
213-627-1130
800-253-4182
mealeyinfo@lexisnexis.com;
www.lexisnexis.com/mealeys
Social Media: Facebook, Twitter, LinkedIn, RSS, Youtube
Tom Hagy, CEO
Maureen McGuire, Editorial Director
Karen Miehle, Editor
Mike Wash, Chief Executive Officer, Legal
Lisa Agona, Chief Marketing Officer

This report tracks the burgeoning number of disputes involving complex disability coverage claims. Topics covered include: claims for chronic fatigue, chronic pain, stress, psychiatric disabilities, chemical dependency and risk of relapse, plus key issues like total disability, own occupation, bad faith, ERSA, class actions and much more.
Cost: $849.00
100 Pages
Frequency: Monthly
Founded in: 2000
Mailing list available for rent

13812 Mealey's Litigation Report: Insurance
LexisNexis Mealey's
555 W 5th Avenue
Los Angeles, CA 90013
213-627-1130
800-253-4182
mealeyinfo@lexisnexis.com;
www.lexisnexis.com/mealeys
Social Media: Facebook, Twitter, LinkedIn, RSS, Youtube

Tom Hagy, CEO
Maureen McGuire, Editorial Director
Vivi Gorman, Editor
Shawn Rice, Co-Editor
Mike Wash, Chief Executive Officer, Legal

The report tracks declaratory judgment actions regarding coverage for litigation arising from long-tail claims, including environmental contamination and latent damage and injury allegedly caused by asbestos, tox chemicals and fumes, lead, breast implants, medical devices, construction defects, and more. Key issues: allocation, occurrence, policy exclusion, choice of law, discovery, duty to defend, notice, trigger of coverage and known loss.
Cost: $2115.00
100 Pages
Frequency: Weekly
Founded in: 1984
Mailing list available for rent

13813 NACA NEWS
National Association of Catastrophe Adjusters
P.O. Box 499
Alvord, TX 76225
817-498-3466; *Fax:* 817-498-0480
naca@nacatadj.org; www.nacatadj.org
Social Media: Facebook, Twitter, LinkedIn

Lori Ringo, Executive Administrator
Chris Hatcher, President
Jon Joyce, Vice President

Contains information of interest and benefit to the members of NACA and the president of the association provides his insights for the quarter.
Frequency: Quarterly
Circulation: 2500
Founded in: 1976

13814 NAPIA Newsletter
National Association of Public Insurance Adjusters
21165 Whitfield Place
Suite 105
Potomac Falls, VA 20165
703-433-9217; *Fax:* 703-433-0369
info@napia.com; www.napia.com

David W Barrack, Executive Director
Ronald R. Reitz, President
Frequency: Quarterly
Circulation: 600
Mailing list available for rent

13815 NCOILetter
National Conference of Insurance Legislators
385 Jordan Road
Troy, NY 12180
518-687-0178; *Fax:* 518-687-0401
info@ncoil.org; www.ncoil.org

Susan F. Nolan, Executive Director
Candace Thorson, Deputy Executive Director
Simone Smith, Director, Operations/Administration

Mike Humphreys, Director,State-Federal Relations
Jordan Estey, Dir, Legislative Affairs/Education

NCOIL is an organization of state legislators whose main area of public policy concern is insurance legislation and regulation. Many legislators active in NCOIL either chair or are members of the committees responsible for insurance legislation in their respective state houses across the country.
Frequency: Monthly
Circulation: 2500
Founded in: 1969

13816 NFPA Journal Update
National Fire Protection Association
1 Batterymarch Park
Quincy, MA 02169-7471

617-770-3000
800-344-3555; *Fax:* 617-770-0700
publicaffairs@nfpa.org; www.nfpa.org

James M. Shannon, President/CEO
Peg O'Brien, Administrator - Public Affairs
Sharon Gamache, Executive Director
Bruce Mullen, CFO
Paul Crossman, VP, Marketing

Member newsletter that contains the latest articles, features, and special online exclusives from NFPA Journal , as well as quick access to the information and resources on NFPA's codes and standards-making process, research, training, safety information, and more.
75000 Members
Frequency: Monthly
Founded in: 1896

13817 PIA Connection
Association of Professional Insurance Agents
400 N Washington Street
Alexandria, VA 22314-2312

703-836-9340; *Fax:* 703-836-1279
web@pianet.org; www.pianet.com
Social Media: Facebook, Twitter, LinkedIn

Andrew C. Harris, President
John G. Lee, President-elect
Richard A. Clements, Vice President, Treasurer
Robert W. Hansen, Secretary/Assistant Treasurer

Contains current insurance industry news that is particularly relevant to independent insurance agents
Cost: $24.00
Frequency: 10x/Year
Mailing list available for rent

13818 Report on Property/Casualty Rates & Ratings
Institute of Management and Administration
1 Washington Park
Suite 1300
Newark, NJ 07102-3130

212-244-0360; *Fax:* 973-622-0595
customercare@bna.com; www.ioma.com

Helps agents and brokers get competitive premium rates for their clients.
Cost: $389.00
16 Pages
Frequency: Monthly
Founded in: 1755

13819 Risk Management Essentials
Nonprofit Risk Management Center
15 N King Street
Suite 203
Leesburg, VA 20176

202-785-3891; *Fax:* 703-443-1990
info@nonprofitrisk.org; www.nonprofitrisk.org

Melanie Herman, Executive Director
Erin Gloeckner, Project Manager
Sue Weir Jones, Office Manager
Jennifer Walther, Director of Client Solutions

Each issue covers a selection of issues, showcases the Center's training and workshops, and/or highlights new publications offering risk management advice from a nonprofit perspective
16 Pages
Frequency: 3 times a year
Mailing list available for rent

13820 Riskwatch
Public Risk Management Association
700 S. Washington St.
Suite 218
Alexandria, VA 22314-1565

703-528-7701; *Fax:* 703-739-0200
info@primacentral.org; www.primacentral.org
Social Media: Facebook, Twitter, LinkedIn

Marshall Davies, Executive Director
Jennifer Ackerman, Deputy Executive Director
Bles Dones, Manager, Member Services
Jennifer W. Morris, Manager, Meetings and Conferences
Paulette Washington, Office Administrator

E-news service that delivers handpicked, high-quality news articles relating to the public risk management industry. Provides PRIMA members with valuable association-related news. Keeps you on top of the latest news and trends in the public sector risk management field.
Frequency: Weekly
Mailing list available for rent

13821 SFFA Newsletter
Surety & Fidelity Association of America
1101 Connecticut Avenue NW
Suite 800
Washington, DC 20036

202-463-0600; *Fax:* 202-463-0606
information@surety.org; www.surety.org
Social Media: Facebook, Twitter

Lynn Schubert, President
Mailing list available for rent

13822 Surety Association of America
Surety Association of America
1101 Connecticut Ave Nw
Suite 800
Washington, DC 20036-4347

202-463-0600; *Fax:* 202-463-0606
information@surety.org; www.surety.org

Lynn Schubert, President

13823 UPDATE
Insurance Marketing Communications Association
PO Box 473054
Charlotte, NC 28247

704-755-5551; *Fax:* 704-543-6345;
www.imcanet.com

September J Seibert, Executive Director

Contains reviews and previews of meetings, articles on communications issues and techniques, and news of IMCA members.
Frequency: For Members Only

Magazines & Journals

13824 AHIP Solutions Directory Resource Directory of Health Plans
America's Health Insurance Plans
601 Pennsylvania Ave NW
South Building, Suite 500
Washington, DC 20004-2601
202-778-3200
877-291-2247; *Fax:* 202-331-7487
ahip@ahip.org; www.ahip.org
Social Media: Twitter

Karen M Ignagni, President/CEO
Susan Pisano, VP Communications

More than 3,400 key executives listed, types of products offered such as HMO, PPO, POS, etc., company contact information, national enrollment by type of products, and national and state level enrollment data by company. There is also a CD-ROM availablie for $1,495.00
Cost: $492.00
Mailing list available for rent

13825 ASPPA Journal
American Society of Pension Professionals & Act
4245 Fairfax Dr
Suite 750
Arlington, VA 22203-1648

703-516-0512; *Fax:* 703-516-9308
asppa@asppa.org; www.asppa.org

Thomas Finnegan, President

A technical publication providing critical insight into legislative and regulatory developments. Also features technical analysis of benefit plan matters as well as information regarding ASPPA's programs.
Frequency: Quarterly
Circulation: 7500

13826 Actuarial Digest
Actuarial Digest Publishing Company
PO Box 1127
Ponte Vedra, FL 32004-1127

904-273-1245; www.theactuarialdigest.com

Gene Hubbard, Editor

Covers fields such as life, group, health, reinsurance, pension/employee benefits, government regulations and educational institutions.
Founded in: 1982

13827 Actuarial Studies in Non-Life Insurance
Peeters
1600 Arch St
Philadelphia, PA 19103-2032

215-567-0097; *Fax:* 215-567-0107
webmaster@actuaries.org; www.actuaries.org

Lucy Peters, Owner
Andrew Cairns, Editor
David G Hartman, Chairman
Carla Melvin, Executive Assistant
Katy Martin, Project Manager

Promotes actuarial research and study and publishes the ASTIN Bulletin.
Cost: $65.00
500 Pages
Frequency: Quarterly
Circulation: 3000
Founded in: 1957

13828 Advisor Today
Natl Assoc of Insurance and Financial Advisors
2901 Telestar Court
Falls Church, VA 22042

703-770-8100
877-866-2432
membersupport@naifa.org;
www.advisortoday.com
Social Media: Facebook, Twitter, LinkedIn

Ayo Mseka, Editor-In-Chief
Julie Britt, Senior Editor
Preeti Vasishtha, Editor
Tara Heuser, Publication and Circulation

Provides practical information, sales idas resources and business strategies to hel pinsurance and financial advisors succeed.
Founded in: 1906
Mailing list available for rent

13829 American Journal of Law & Medicine
American Society of Law, Medicine and Ethics

765 Commonwealth Ave
Suite 1634
Boston, MA 02215-1401

617-262-4990; *Fax:* 617-437-7596
info@aslme.org; www.aslme.org
Social Media: Facebook, Twitter, LinkedIn

Ted Hutchinson, Executive Director
Courtney McClellan, Assistant Editor
Katie Kenney Johnson, Conference Director
Margo Buege, Membership Department
Courtney McClellan, Assistant Editor

A law review fulfilling the need to improve communication between leagal and medical professionals. Contains professional articles and case notes on themes in health law and policy, and on the legal, ethical, and economic aspects of medical practice, research, and education-and health law court decisions and book reviews.
Cost: $150.00
Frequency: Quarterly
Mailing list available for rent

13830 Annuity Shopper
Annuity Shopper
28 Harrison Ave.
D209
Englishtown, NJ 07726

732-521-5110
877-206-8141; *Fax:* 732-521-5113;
www.annuityshopper.com

Hersh Stern, Owner
Laura Stern, Editor

Helps consumers purchase the safest and most reliable lifetime income annuities for their retirement.
Frequency: Semi-annually
ISSN: 1071-4510
Founded in: 1986
Mailing list available for rent

13831 Beacon
American Association of Dental Consultants
10032 Wind Hill Dr
Greenville, IN 47124-9673

812-923-2600
800-896-0707; *Fax:* 812-923-2900;
www.aadc.org

Judith Salisburty, Executive Director
Dr Larry Hoffman, Secretary/Treasurer

Informs members about the latest issues affecting dentistry and dental benefits.
Frequency: Twice/Year
Circulation: 350

13832 Benefits Magazine
International Foundation of Employee Benefit Plans
18700 W Bluemound Road
Brookfield, WI 53045

262-786-6700
888-334-3327; *Fax:* 262-786-8670
pr@ifebp.org; www.ifebp.org
Social Media: Facebook, Twitter, LinkedIn

Michael Wilson, CEO
Terry Davidson, VP, Business Development
Beth Harwood, VP, Educ Program/Content Management

Covers issues such as healthcare, retirement and related trends. Authors are experienced professionals in the field.
Cost: $175.00
35000 Members
Frequency: Monthly
Circulation: 28336
ISSN: 2157-6157
Founded in: 1954

13833 Benefits Quarterly
Int'l Society of Certified Employee Benfit Special
18700 W Bluemound Road
PO Box 209
Brookfield, WI 53008-0209

262-786-8771; *Fax:* 262-786-8650
iscebs@iscebs.org; www.iscebs.org
Social Media: Facebook, Twitter, LinkedIn

Daniel W Graham, CEBS, Executive Director
Sandra L. Becker, Director
Jennifer Mathe, Manager Member Services
Kathy Frank, Administrative Assistant
Julie Dickow, Department Assistant

Offers comprehensive coverage of the latest trends and innovations in benefits and compensation. Features articles on health care, retirement and total compensation, each issue includes a section focused on a topic of special interest.
Cost: $125.00
Frequency: Quarterly
Circulation: 15000
Founded in: 1981
Mailing list available for rent

13834 Best's Review
AM Best Company
Ambest Rd
Oldwick, NJ 08858

908-439-2200
800-424-2378; *Fax:* 908-439-3296
editor_br@bestreview.com; www.ambest.com

Arthur Snyder, Chairman & President
Paul Tinnirello, CIO
Larry Mayewski, Chief Rating Officer

Best's Review, the insurance industry's premier news magazine, contains insightful, award-winning coverage of the worldwide insurance industry, giving you the information you need to make informed decisions about your business and career.
Cost: $60.00
Frequency: Monthly
ISSN: 1527-5914
Founded in: 1900

13835 BestWeek
AM Best Company
Ambest Rd
Oldwick, NJ 08858

908-439-2200; *Fax:* 908-439-3296
bestweek@ambest.com; www.ambest.com

Arthur Snyder, Chairman and President
Paul Tinnirello, CIO
Larry Mayewski, Chief Rating Officer

BestWeek, the cornerstone of a Best's Insurance News & Analysis subscription, now provides even more ratings information and A.M. Best-generated analytical content in three region-focused editions.
Frequency: Weekly
ISSN: 1945-4139
Founded in: 1953

13836 Broker World
Insurance Publications
9404 Reeds Road
PO Box 11310
Overland Park, KS 66207-1010

913-383-9191
800-762-3387; *Fax:* 913-383-1247
info@brokerworldmag.com;
www.brokerworldmag.com

Rita S Reeves, Sales Manager
Sharon A Chace, Editor
Stephen P Howard, Publisher
Betsy Masters, Production Manager
Patty L Godfrey, Director of Circulation

The first and only national insurance magazine founded, focused and edited to specifically address the unique informational needs of independent like and health producers.
Frequency: Monthly
Circulation: 28600
Founded in: 1980

13837 Business Insurance
Crain Communications
711 3rd Ave
New York, NY 10017-4014

212-210-0785; *Fax:* 212-210-0200
info@crain.com; www.businessinsurance.com

Norm Feldman, Manager
Charmain Benton, Assistant Managing Editor
Paul Bomberger, Managing Editor
Roberto Ceniceros, Senior Editor
Matt Dunning, Associate Editor

Reports on risk management, risk financing, employee benefits management and workers compensation. Our audience also includes insurance brokers, agents, consultants, insurers, reinsurers, and others concerned with corporate insurance, risk management, alternative risk financing, employee benefits, workers compensation and reinsurance.
Frequency: Weekly
Circulation: 44639
*Mailing list available for rent*at $89y per M

13838 CICA International Conference
Captive Insurance Companies Association
4248 Park Glen Road
Minneapolis, MN 55416

952-928-4655; *Fax:* 952-929-1318
info@cicaworld.com; www.cicaworld.com

Dennis Harwick, President

2012 International Conference is located in Scottsdale, AZ during March 11-13.
500 Attendees
Frequency: Annual

13839 CPCU Journal
Chartered Property Casualty Underwriters
720 Providence Rd
Malvern, PA 19355-3446

610-251-2733; *Fax:* 610-251-2761;
www.cpcusociety.org

Steve McElhiney, President
Cynthia Barouex, Vice President

13840 CPCU e-Journal
Chartered Property Casualty Underwriter Society
720 Providence Road
Suite 100
Malvern, PA 19355

610-512-2728
800-932-2728; *Fax:* 610-725-5969
membercenter@cpcusociety.org;
www.cpcusociety.org
Social Media: Facebook, Twitter, LinkedIn

James R Marks, CEO
David C Marlett, Editor
Mark A. Robinson, President and Treasurer

Provides information on practical and timely issues of interest to financial services and property and casualty insurance professionals.
Frequency: Monthly

13841 Contingencies
American Academy of Actuaries
1850 M Street NW
Suite 300
Washington, DC 20036

202-223-8196; *Fax:* 202-872-1948
webmaster@actuary.org; www.actuary.org

Linda Mallon, Editor
Cindy Johns, Marketing/Publications Production

Magazine of the actuarial profession, available in print and digital editions; its circulation includes legislators, regulators, CEOs, and all Academy members
Cost: $24.00
Frequency: Bi-Monthly
ISSN: 1048-9851
Founded in: 1965
Printed in 4 colors on glossy stock

13842 Contingency Planning & Management
Witter Publishing Corporation
20 Commerce Street
Flemington, NJ 08822
908-788-0343; *Fax:* 908-788-3782;
www.witterpublishing.com
Bob Joudanin, Publisher
Paul Kirvan, Editor-in-Chief
Mike Viscel, Production Manager
Courtney Witter, Circulation Manager
Andrew Witter, President
Serves the fields of financial/banking, manufacturing industrial, transportation, utilities, telecommunications, health care, government, insurance and other allied fields.
Cost: $275.00
Frequency: Monthly
Circulation: 62000
Founded in: 1987

13843 Crittenden Excess & Surplus Insider
Crittenden Publishing
250 Bel Marin Keys Boulevard
PO Box 1150, #A
Novato, CA 94948-1150
415-382-2400; *Fax:* 415-382-2476
ins@crittendenonline.com;
www.crittendenonline.com
Robert Fink, Publisher
Focuses on new products, trade literature, industry news, and personnel changes.
Cost: $411.00
Frequency: Weekly
Circulation: 20,000

13844 EXAMINER Magazine
Society of Financial Examiners
174 Grace Blvd
Altamonte Spgs, FL 32714-3210
407-682-4930
800-787-7633; *Fax:* 407-682-3175;
www.sofe.org
Social Media: Facebook, LinkedIn
L. Brackett, Executive Director
Stephen J Szypula, Financial Administrator
Judy Estus, Administrator
Ryan Havick, President
Eric Dercher, Treasurer
A quarterly magazine offering association news and information.
Cost: $65.00
Frequency: Quarterly
Circulation: 2500
Founded in: 1973
Printed in 2 colors on glossy stock

13845 GAMA International Journal
GAMA International
2901 Telestar Ct
Suite 140
Falls Church, VA 22042-1261
703-770-8184
800-345-2687; *Fax:* 703-770-8182;
www.gamaweb.com
Social Media: Facebook, Twitter, LinkedIn
Mary Barnes, Director of Communications / Editor
Jeff Hughes, CEO
Miriam Hankins, Marketing Director
Stephanie Beattie, Membership and Awards Coordinator
Jen D'Alessio, Program Manager
Devoted to the professional development of leaders in the insurance and financial services industry.
Cost: $300.00
56 Pages
Circulation: 5000
ISSN: 1095-7367
Founded in: 1951
Mailing list available for rent
Printed in 4 colors on glossy stock

13846 Health Insurance Underwriters
National Association of Health Underwriters
1212 New York Avenue NW
Suite 1100
Washington, DC 20005
202-552-5060; *Fax:* 202-747-6820
editor@nahu.org; www.nahu.org
Social Media: Facebook, Twitter, LinkedIn
Martin Carr, Publisher/Editor
Covers technology, legislation and product news-everything that affects how health insurance professionals do business
Cost: $40.00
Frequency: Monthly
Circulation: 30,000
ISSN: 0017-9019
Founded in: 1930
Mailing list available for rent: 19000 names at $350 per M
Printed in 4 colors on glossy stock

13847 IAIABC Journal
Int'l Assoc of Industrial Accident Boards/Commis.
5610 Medical Circle
Suite 24
Madison, WI 53719
608-663-6355; *Fax:* 608-663-1546
hlore@iaiabc.org; www.iaiabc.org
Robert Aurbach, Editor
Jennifer Wolf Horejsh, Executive Director
Faith Howe, Manager
Christina Klein, Events and Office Administrator
Heather Lore, Manager of Membership and Marketing
Advances the understanding and management of workers' compensation system administration through the availability of data, research, policy analysis, and thoughtful opinion.
Frequency: 2x/Year
Mailing list available for rent

13848 Independent Agent Magazine
Independent Insurance Agents & Brokers of America
127 S Peyton St
Alexandria, VA 22314-2803
703-683-4422
800-221-7917; *Fax:* 703-683-7556
info@iiaba.net; www.iiaba.net
Social Media: Facebook, Twitter
Robert A Rusbuldt, CEO
Ronald Tubertini, Chairman
Regular issue features include agency management and automation, insurance products and markets, legislative issues, and analysis of industry trends.
Cost: $24.00
Frequency: Monthly
Circulation: 57,814
Mailing list available for rent

13849 Inquiry
Excellus Health Plan
1807 Glenview Rd
Suite 100
Glenview, IL 60025-2944
847-724-9280; *Fax:* 847-729-2199
inquiry@hartleydata.com;
www.inquiryjournal.org
Howard J Berman, Publisher
Kevin P Kane, Editor-In-Chief
Alan Monheit, Editor
Ronny G. Frishman, Managing Editor
Seeks to contribute to the continued improvement of the nation's health care system by providing a thoughtful forum for the communication and discussion of relevant public policy issues, innovative concepts, and original research and demonstrations in the areas of health care organization, provision and financing
Cost: $1.00
Frequency: Quarterly
ISSN: 0046-9580

13850 Insurance & Financial Meetings Managment
Coastal Communications Corporation
2700 N Military Trail
Suite 120
Boca Raton, FL 33431
561-989-0600; *Fax:* 561-989-9509
ccceditor@att.net;
www.themeetingmagazines.com
Harvey Grotsky, Publisher/Editor-In-Chief
Susan Wyckoff Fell, Managing Editor
Susan Gregg, Managing Editor
The executive source for planning meetings and incentives for the financial and insurance sectors. With regular features and special focus on site selection, destinations, industry-related studies and activities, motivational and incentive programs, program and event planning.
Frequency: Monthly
Circulation: 40,000
Founded in: 1983

13851 Insurance & Technology
TechWeb
240 West 35th Street
New York, NY 10011
212-600-3000; *Fax:* 212-600-3060;
www.insurancetech.com
Katherine Burger, Editorial Director
Anthony O'Donnell, Executive Editor
Nathan Golia, Associate Editor
Cara Latham, Online Managing Editor
Information on how technology can help life, health, property and casualty and multi-line insurance companies perform more productively, profitably, and competitively.
Frequency: Monthly
ISSN: 1054-0733
Mailing list available for rent

13852 Insurance Advocate
PO Box 14367
Cincinatti, OH 45250-0367
908-859-0893
cluke@nuco.com;
www.nationaunderwriter.com
Chris Luke, Publisher
Phil Gusman, Editor
Eric V Gilkey, Assistant Editor
Steve Acunto, Associate Publisher
Covers the people and issues affecting the insurance industry in New York, New Jersey, Connecticut and beyond. Also the source for new markets and coverages, financial trends, legislative isssues, M&A, insurance law and industry developments.
Cost: $59.00
Frequency: Weekly
Circulation: 7200

Founded in: 1889
Printed in 4 colors on glossy stock

13853 Insurance Conference Planner
Penton Media Inc
249 W. 17th St., third floor
New York, NY 10011

847-763-9504
866-505-7173
shatch@meetingsnet.com;
www.meetingsnet.com

Susan Hatch, Editor
Betsy Bair, Director, Content and Media
Melissa Fromento, Group Publisher
Regina McGee, Religious Conference Manager
Susan Hatch, Executive Editor

Meeting and incentive strategies for the financial services industry.
Cost: $57.00
148 Pages
Circulation: 9000
Founded in: 1989
Printed in 4 colors on glossy stock

13854 Insurance Insight
Professional Independent Insurance Agents of IL
4360 Wabash Ave
Springfield, IL 62711-7009

217-793-6660
800-628-6436; *Fax:* 217-793-6744
info@IIAofIllinois.org; www.iiaofillinois.org

Sandy Cuffle, Manager
Dennis Garrett, VP Marketing/Membership
Mark Kuchar, CPA, CFO
Mike Tate, CAE, Chief Operating Officer
Peter Gulatto, Marketing Representative

Features articles that are relevant to the Illinois insurance industry, and includes topics such as industry news, technology, markets and coverages, financial planning, sales and marketing, state and federal issues, agency management, The Middleton Letter, and education.
Cost: $65.00
68 Pages
Frequency: Monthly
Circulation: 2500
Founded in: 1993
Mailing list available for rent

13855 Insurance Journal West
3570 Camino Del Rio N
Suite 200
San Diego, CA 92108-1747

619-584-1100
800-897-9965; *Fax:* 619-584-5889
info@insurancejournal.com;
www.insurancejournal.com
Social Media: Facebook, Twitter, LinkedIn

Mark Wells, Publisher
Mitch Dunford, Chief Operating Officer
Katie Robley, Circulation Manager
Suzie Song, Marketing Manager
Andrea Ortega-Wells, Editor-In-Chief

Insurance Journal is written for the independent agent and broker. Insurance Journal West covers California and the western states, while Insurance Journal Texas/South Central covers Texas, Arkansas, Oklahoma & Louisiana. We cover legal issues, people, markets, regulations and legistation, the very things that affect our readers.
Cost: $58.00
Circulation: 40000
Founded in: 1923
Printed in 4 colors on matte stock

13856 Insurance Networking News
SourceMedia
550 W. Van Buren St.
Suite 1110
Chicago, IL 60607

847-933-5183; *Fax:* 312-566-0656;
www.insurancenetworking.com
Social Media: Facebook, Twitter

Carrie Burns, Editor-In-Chief

A trusted source for information on how technology is being implemented to support insurers' strategic business objectives, providing insightful analysis of-and case studies on-how technology is being innovatively utilized to automate critical processes.
Frequency: Monthly
Founded in: 1997
Mailing list available for rent

13857 Journal of Healthcare Risk Management
American Society for Healthcare Risk Management
1 N Franklin St
Chicago, IL 60606-4425

312-422-3840; *Fax:* 312-422-4573;
www.aha.org

Deborah Sprindzunas, Executive Director
Cliff Lehman, Director Membership Services
Cost: $80.00
Circulation: 4500
Mailing list available for rent: 4400 names

13858 Journal of Law, Medicine & Ethics
American Society of Law, Medicine and Ethics
765 Commonwealth Ave
Suite 1634
Boston, MA 02215-1401

617-262-4990; *Fax:* 617-437-7596
info@aslme.org; www.aslme.org
Social Media: Facebook, Twitter, LinkedIn

Ted Hutchinson, Executive Director
Ted Hutchinson, Publications Director
Katie Kenney Johnson, Conference Director
Margo Buege, Membership Department
Courtney McClellan, Assistant Editor

Provides articles on such timely topics as health care quality and access, managed care, pain relief, genetics, child/maternal health, reproductive health, informed consent, assisted dying, ethics committees, HIV/AIDS, and public health. Issues review significant policy developments, health law court decisions, and books.
Cost: $140.00
Frequency: Quarterly
Circulation: 4,500+
Mailing list available for rent

13859 Journal of Reinsurance
Intermediaries and Reinsurance Underwriters Assoc
971 Rte 202 North
Branchburg, NJ 08876

908-203-0211; *Fax:* 908-203-0213
info@irua.com; www.irua.com

Paul Walther, Editor

To encourage an exchange of ideas and to disseminiate educational information for the benefit and betterment of the Intermediaries & Reinsurance Underwriters Association membership and the reinsurance community.
Cost: $195.00
Frequency: Quarterly

13860 Journal of Risk and Insurance
Wiley-Blackwell Publishing
111 River Street
Hoboken, NJ 07030-5774

201-748-6000; *Fax:* 201-748-6088
info@wiley.com; www.wiley.com

Georges Dionne, Editor

The flagship journal for the American Risk and Insurance Association. The JRI is the most well recognized academic risk management and insurance journal in the world and is currently indexed by the American Economic Association's Economic Literature Index, the Finance Literature Index, RePEc, the Social Sciences Citation Index, ABI/Inform, Business and Company ASAP, Lexis-Nexis, Dow Jones Interactive, and others.
Frequency: Quarterly
ISSN: 0022-4367

13861 LIMRA's MarketFacts Quarterly
LIMRA
300 Day Hill Rd.
Windsor, CT 06095

860-688-3358; *Fax:* 860-285-7792
bragaglia@limra.com; www.limra.com

Wendy Weston, Contact

Features in-depth, timeless articles devoted to the critical issues of the day, including such topics as distribution, technology, marketing strategies, retirement, globalization, demographics, financial integration and products and services.
Cost: $500.00
Frequency: Quarterly
Circulation: 7500

13862 Leader's Edge Magazine
Council of Insurance Agents & Brokers
701 Pennsylvania Ave NW
Suite 750
Washington, DC 20004-2661

202-783-4400; *Fax:* 202-783-4410
webmaster@ciab.com; www.ciab.com

Ken A Crerar, President
Pat Wade, Director of Communications
Brianne Mallaghan, Director of Communications
Scott Sinder, General Counsel

Comprised of vital information and news for the industry of insurance agents and brokers.
Cost: $100.00
Frequency: Bi-Monthly

13863 Liability & Insurance Week
JR Publishing
PO Box 6654
McLean, VA 22106-6654

703-532-2235; *Fax:* 703-532-2236

John Reistrup, Publisher

Reports on political, legislative and regulatory actions affecting the insurance and legal industries.

13864 Life & Health Advisor
JonHope Communications
71 Emerson Road
PO Box 613
Walpole, MA 02081

508-668-8025
888-578-8025; *Fax:* 508-668-8056
pkelley@lifehealth.com; www.lifehealth.com
Social Media: Facebook, Twitter, LinkedIn

Sally O'Connell, Publisher/Ad Sales Manager
Peter Kelley, Editor

Access, exposure & market visibility for financial services, investment and retirement income plannigo.
Frequency: Monthly
Founded in: 1995
Mailing list available for rent

13865 Life Insurance Selling
Summit Buisness Media

5081 Olympic Blvd.
Suite 550
Erlanger, KY 41018

859-692-2100; *Fax:* 859-692-2000;
www.lifeinsuranceselling.com
Social Media: Facebook, Twitter, LinkedIn, RSS

Dave O'Neil, Group Publisher
John K Moore, Publisher
Brian Anderson, Editor
Tashawna Rodwell, Publisher
Bill Coffin, Group Editorial Director

The leading sales publication for life, health and financial planning professionals.

13866 Life and Health Insurance Sales Magazines
Rough Notes Company
11690 Technology Drive
Carmel, IN 46032-5600

317-582-1600
800-321-1909; *Fax:* 317-816-1000
rnc@roughnotes.com; www.roughnotes.com

Walter Gdowski, Owner
Nancy Doucette, Senior Editor
Elisabeth Boone, CPCU, Associate Editor
Dennis Pillsbury, Associate Editor

For life and health agents, general agents, managers and brokers with prospects to culivate and clients to serve. Accepts advertising.
48 Pages
Frequency: Monthly
Founded in: 1878
Mailing list available for rent

13867 Long-Term Care Insurance Sales Strategies
Sales Creators
3835 E Thousand Oaks Boulevard
Suite 336
Westlake Village, CA 91362

818-597-3205
888-599-5997; *Fax:* 818-597-3206
jslome@ltcsales.com; www.ltcsales.com

Jesse Sloame, Publisher/President
Mindy Hartman, Ad Director

Content covers successful sales approaches, new and unexplored marekts, industry trends, and upcoming training seminars.
Cost: $24.00
Frequency: Quarterly
Circulation: 7500
Founded in: 1998

13868 Momentum
Metropolitan Life Insurance Company
1 Madison Ave
New York, NY 10010-3603

212-867-2165; *Fax:* 212-685-8042;
www.metlife.com

Robert H Benmosche, CEO

Magazine covering the Metropolitan Life Insurance Company.
Frequency: Monthly
Founded in: 1970

13869 NRRA News
National Risk Retention Association
4248 Park Glen Road
Minneapolis, MN 55416-4758

952-284-4643
800-999-4505; *Fax:* 952-929-1318;
www.captive.com

Judith Harrington, Editor
Cost: $195.00
Frequency: Quarterly
Circulation: 250,000

13870 National Underwriter Life & Health Financial Services Edition
33-41 Newark Street
2nd Floor
Hoboken, NJ 07030

201-526-1230; *Fax:* 201-526-1260
spiontek@nuco.com
cms.nationalunderwriter.com

Stephen Piontek, Editor-In-Chief
Jim Connolly, Senior Editor

Uniquely positioned to provider producers, brokers, marketers and company executives with timely, insightful information. Each week, identifies, analyzes and comments on the latest trends and developments for their significance to the market-giving our readers the information they need to make critical business decisions.
Frequency: Weekly

13871 National Underwriter: Life & Health Insurance Edition
National Underwriter Company
5081 Olympic Blvd
Erlanger, KY 41018-3164

859-692-2100
800-543-0874; *Fax:* 859-692-2295;
www.nationalunderwriter.com

Charlie Smith, CEO

Offers features on agent activities, stocks and marketing, brokers and financial planners, trade meetings, business trends and outside developments in the industry.
Cost: $75.00
Frequency: Weekly
Circulation: 48,5070

13872 National Underwriter: Property & Casualty Risk & Benefits Management
National Underwriter Company
5081 Olympic Blvd
Erlanger, KY 41018-3164

859-692-2100
800-543-0874; *Fax:* 859-692-2295;
www.nationalunderwriter.com

Charlie Smith, CEO

Covers industry trends, risk management, state and federal legislation, and judicial affairs.
Cost: $149.00
Frequency: Weekly
Circulation: 485070
Founded in: 1897

13873 POA Bulletin/Merritt Risk Management News and Review
POA Publishing
1625 Prince Street
Alexandria, VA 22314-2818

703-519-6200
877-663-4890; *Fax:* 703-519-6299
asis@asisonline.org; www.asisonline.org

Michael E. Knoke, Managing Editor
Sherry Harowitz, Editor-In-Chief
Denny White, Director/Publishing

Editorial content is designed to keep security managers and risk managers abreast of legal, legislative and insurance issues, and contains features that identify security and risk management trends and present analysis of insurance coverage and needs.
Cost: $690.00
Frequency: Quarterly
Circulation: 3400
Founded in: 1955

13874 Proceedings
Conference of Consulting Actuaries
3880 Salem Lake Drive
Suite H
Long Grove, IL 60047-5292

847-719-6500; *Fax:* 847-719-6506
conference@ccactuaries.org;
www.ccactuaries.org

Rita K DeGraaf, Executive Director
Keith G Stewart, Director of Operations
Patricia D Johnson, Project Manager
Matthew D Noncek, Member Services Manager

The professional journal of the Conference of Consulting Actuaries. Promotes the interchange of information among actuaries and the various actuarial organizations, and to keep its publics informed of the viewpoints and activities of the professional consulting actuary.
Cost: $95.00
500 Pages
Circulation: 1,200
Founded in: 1950

13875 Professional Agent
Association of Professional Insurance Agents
400 N Washington Street
Alexandria, VA 22314-2312

703-836-9340; *Fax:* 703-836-1279
piainfo@pianet.org; www.pianet.com

Magazine for the insurance professional.
Cost: $24.00
65 Pages
Frequency: Monthly
Circulation: 35000
Founded in: 1931

13876 Property/Casualty Insurance
National Association of Mutual Insurance Companies
3601 Vincennes Road
PO Box 68700
Indianapolis, IN 46268

317-875-5250; *Fax:* 317-879-8408
webmaster@namic.org; www.namic.org

Bart Anderson, Publisher
Laura Biddle-Bruckman, Managing Editor
Matt Keating, Editor
Kristen Eichhorn, Program Director

Highlights insurance industry news, personnel announcements, industry events, and new products in the field.
Cost: $20.00
Frequency: Monthly
Circulation: 2500
Founded in: 1895

13877 Public Risk
Public Risk Management Association
700 S. Washington St.
Suite 218
Alexandria, VA 22314-1565

703-528-7701; *Fax:* 703-739-0200
info@primacentral.org; www.primacentral.org
Social Media: Facebook, Twitter, LinkedIn

Marshall Davies, Executive Director
Jon Ruzan, Editor
Jennifer Ackerman, Deputy Executive Director
Bles Dones, Manager, Member Services
Paulette Washington, Office Administrator

Magazine exclusively targeting risk management practitioners in the public sector: state and local governments.
Cost: $130.00
Frequency: 1 Year 10 Issue
Circulation: 8250
ISSN: 0891-7183
Founded in: 1978
Mailing list available for rent

13878 Resource Magazine
Life Office Management Association

2300 Windy Ridge Pkwy SE
Suite 600
Atlanta, GA 30339-5665

770-951-1770
800-275-5662; *Fax:* 770-984-0441
resource@loma.org; www.loma.org

Thomas P Donaldson, President/CEO
Jerry Woo, Director
Robert Lai, Managing Director

Covers every topic of interest to management of insurance and financial services companies.
Frequency: Monthly

13879 Risk & Insurance
LRP Publications
PO Box 980
Horsham, PA 19044-0980

215-784-0912
800-341-7874; *Fax:* 215-784-9639
custserv@lrp.com; www.lrp.com

Todd Lutz, CFO
Jack Roberts, Editor-in-Chief
Cyril Tuohy, Managing Editor

Provides business executives and insurance professionals with the insight, information and strategies they need to mitigate challenging business risks. Published monthly and semi-monthly in April when publish two special editions focusing on the Risk and Insurance Management Society's annual RIMS conference.
Frequency: Monthly
Circulation: 51541
Founded in: 1977

13880 Risk Management
Risk Management Society Publishing
1065 Avenue of the Americas
13th Floor
New York, NY 10018-5637

212-286-9292; *Fax:* 212-986-9716
tdonovan@rims.org; www.rims.org
Social Media: Facebook, Twitter, LinkedIn

Ted Donovan, Publisher
Bill Coffin, Editor-In-Chief
Morgan O'Rouke, Managing Editor
Jared Wade, Editor
Callie Nelson, Circulation Manager

The premier source of analysis, insight and news for corporate risk managers. RM strives to explore existing and emerging techniques and concepts that address the needs of those who are tasked with protecting the physical, financial, human and intellectual assets of their companies.
Cost: $64.00
Frequency: Monthly
Circulation: 17000
Founded in: 1950
Mailing list available for rent

13881 Risk Management and Insurance Review
Wiley Publications
111 River Street
Hoboken, NJ 07030-5774

201-748-6000; *Fax:* 201-748-6088
info@wiley.com; www.wiley.com

Mary A Weiss, Editor

Publishes respected, accessible, and high-quality applied research, and well-reasoned opinion and discussion in the field of risk and insurance. The Review's Feature Articles section includes original research involving applications and applied techniques. The Perspectives section contains articles providing new insights on the research literature, business practice, and public policy.
Frequency: Bi-Annual
ISSN: 1098-1616

13882 Risk Report
International Risk Management Institute
12222 Merit Dr
Suite 1450
Dallas, TX 75251-3297

972-996-0800
800-827-5991; *Fax:* 972-371-5128;
www.zeroriskhr.com
Social Media: Facebook, Twitter, LinkedIn

Mike Poskey, Vice President
Jack P Gibson, President
Paul D Murray, VP Marketing/Sales
Robert Kinsel Smith, Senior Adviser/Consultant
Mike Wojcik, Information Technology Director

Helps risk and insurance professionals in both of these areas with analysis and interpretation of the latest innovations in insurance
Cost: $219.00
Frequency: Monthly
Founded in: 1987

13883 Rough Notes
Rough Notes Company
PO Box 1990
Carmel, IN 46082-1990

317-582-1600
800-428-4384; *Fax:* 317-816-1000
rnc@roughnotes.com; www.roughnotes.com

Monthly sales and management magazine for property and casualty insurance agents.
Cost: $357.00
120 Pages
Frequency: Monthly
Founded in: 1878
Printed in 4 colors on glossy stock

13884 Round the Table Magazine
Million Dollar Round Table
325 W Touhy Ave
Park Ridge, IL 60068-4265

847-692-6378; *Fax:* 847-518-8921
editor@mdrt.org; www.mdrt.org

Guy E Baker, President
Kathyrn F Keuneke, Associate Editor
John Prast, Executive VP
Scott Brennan, Secretary

Productivity ideas, reaching your clients, professional knowledge, motivational stories, all this to share with clients and to help you make the sale.
Cost: $14.00
Frequency: Bi-Monthly

13885 Standard
Standard Publishing Corporation
155 Federal St
13th Floor
Boston, MA 02110-1752

617-457-0600; *Fax:* 617-457-0608
e.ayers@spcpub.com; www.standardpub.com

John Cross, President/Publisher

Content focuses on all aspects involving legislative and regulatory developments at the state and federal levels, court decisions, trade association positions and more. Coverage includes news, feature articles and opinion pieces, with an emphasis on property/casualty insurance.
Cost: $80.00
Frequency: Weekly
Circulation: 5000
Founded in: 1870

13886 The Brief (Tort & Insurance Practice Section)
American Bar Association
321 N Clark St
Chicago, IL 60654-7598

312-988-5000
800-285-2221; *Fax:* 312-988-6281
askaba@abanet.org; www.abanet.org
Social Media: Facebook, Twitter

Jane Harper-Alport, Staff Editor
John Warren May, Editor
Janet Jackson, Director
Bill Pritchard, Assistant to the Director

The Brief explores all aspects of tort and insurance law, including the many facets of trial practice essential to the profession.
Cost: $50.00
400,0 Members
60 Pages
Frequency: Quarterly
Circulation: 30000
ISSN: 0273-0995
Founded in: 1878
Printed in 4 colors

13887 Today's Insurance Woman
National Association of Insurance Women
1847 E 15th Street
PO Box 4410
Tulsa, OK 74159-0410

918-744-5195; *Fax:* 918-743-1968

Melissa Carlson, Editor

Focus is on business careers, legislation, leadership, management and social issues facing women in the industry.
Cost: $15.00
Frequency: Bi-Monthly
Circulation: 12,887

13888 Underwriters' Report
National Underwriters Company
5081 Olympic Boulevard
Erlanger, KY 41018

859-922-2100
800-543-0874; *Fax:* 800-874-1916;
www.nationalunderwriter.com

Charlie Smith, CEO

Offering complete information on fire, casualty and life insurance every week.
Cost: $45.00
40 Pages
Frequency: Weekly
Circulation: 5000

13889 Worker's Compensation Monitor
LRP Publications
PO Box 24668
West Palm Beach, FL 33416-4668

561-622-6520; *Fax:* 561-622-0757
webmaster@lrp.com; www.lrp.com

Kenneth Kahn, President
Leslie Lake, Managing Editor
Josh Clifton, Editor

Information on worker's compensation laws.
Cost: $210.00
Frequency: Monthly
Founded in: 1977

Trade Shows

13890 AADC Annual Spring Workshop
American Association of Dental Consultants
10032 Wind Hill Drive
Greenville, IN 47124

812-923-2600
800-896-0707; *Fax:* 812-923-2900;
www.aadc.org

Dr George Koumaras, President
Dr Larry Hoffman, Secretary/Treasurer
Judith K. Salisbury, Executive Director

These meetings provide a forum to discuss topical subjects involving the Dental Benefit Industry and Clinical Dentistry as a whole. AADC presenters and lectures are recognized as leaders in the Dental Industry. 10 exhibitors.
300 Attendees
Frequency: Annual/May
Founded in: 1979

13891 AHIP Annual Meeting
America's Health Insurance Plans
601 Pennsylvania Avenue NW
South Building, Suite 500
Washington, DC 20004

202-778-3200
877-291-2247; *Fax:* 202-331-7487
ahip@ahip.org; www.ahip.org

Karen M Ignagni, President/CEO
Susan Pisano, VP Communications

This meeting continues to be the nation's leading health care conference where all segments of the health insurance industry convene to share perspectives on, and analysis of, the most recent developments in health care.
300 Attendees

13892 AHOU Annual Conference
Association of Home Office Underwriters
22300 Windy Ridge Parkway
Suite 600
Atlanta, GA 30339-8443

770-984-3715; *Fax:* 770-984-6418
ahou@loma.org; www.ahou.org

Jennifer Richards, Convention VP
Lee Janecek, Convention Assistant VP

Providing career development, underwriting solutions, the latest medical issues and valuable insight to keep you prepared.
Frequency: Annual/October
Founded in: 2001

13893 AIA Annual Conference
Aviation Insurance Association
400 Admiral Blvd
Suite 200
Kansas City, MO 64106-1508

816-221-8488; *Fax:* 816-472-7765
mandie@robstan.com; www.aiaweb.org
Social Media: Facebook

Paul Leonard, President
Todd McCredie, Vice President
Patrick Bailey, Secretary
Mary D'Alauro, Treasurer
Mandie Bannwarth, Executive Director

Provides a forum for the biggest names and best minds in the aviaiton insurance industry. Offers top-notch speakers, continuing education classes, time with vendors and opportunities to network and develop relationships that last a lifetime.
900 Members
Frequency: April/May
Founded in: 1976

13894 AICP Annual Conference
Association of Insurance Compliance Professionals
12100 Sunset Hills Road
Suite 130
Reston, VA 20190

703-234-4074; *Fax:* 703-435-4390
aicp@aicp.net; www.aicp.net

Richard A Guggolz, Executive Director
Elaine Bailey, Conference Chair

Learning opportunities for a broad range of compliance professionals, sessions for beginners and seasoned professionals and networking opportunities with colleagues, peers and state regulators.
680 Attendees
Frequency: Annual/Sept-Oct

13895 ASPPA Annual Conference
American Society of Pension Professionals & Act
4245 N Fairfax Drive
Suite 750
Arlington, VA 22203

703-160-0512; *Fax:* 703-516-9308
asppa@asppa.org; www.asppa.org

Tom Finnegan, President

Attendees of this conference share quality time with representatives from every aspect of the retirement plan industry. Offers 20 hours of ASPPA continuing education credits and provides Joint Board for the Enrollemnt of Actuaries credit hours for enrolled actuaries.
1600 Attendees

13896 ASSE Annual Conference & Exposition
American Society of Safety Engineers
1800 E Oakton Street
Des Plaines, IL 60018

847-699-2929; *Fax:* 847-768-3434
customerservice@asse.org; www.asse.org
Social Media: Facebook, Twitter, LinkedIn, Blogger, Pinterest, Tumblr

Fred Fortman, Executive Director
Jim Drzewiecki, Finance/Controller Director
Diane Hurns, Manager Public Relations Department
Richard A. Pollock, President
Stephanie A. Helgerman, Vice President, Finance

Featuring more than 200 sessions, an exposition with 300 exhibitors, special pre- and post-conference seminars, conference proceedings on CD, numerous networking events and more! Learn the latest strategies to expand your knowledge base and network with other safety, health and environmental professionals
3500 Attendees
Frequency: Annual/June
Mailing list available for rent

13897 Advanced Life Underwriting Association
1922 F Street NW
Washington, DC 20006-4302

202-331-6099; *Fax:* 202-331-2164

Karen G Keating, Director

22 booths.
1.1M Attendees
Frequency: February

13898 Alliance of Insurance Agents and Brokers Convention & Expo
1029 J. Street
Suite 120
Sacramento, CA 95814

916-283-9473
866-497-9222; *Fax:* 916-283-9479
info@agentsalliance.com;
www.agentsalliance.com
Social Media: Facebook, Twitter

Joe Jimenez, President
David Nelson, Executive Direcetor
Mike D'Arelli, Executive Vice President
Yolanda Olquin, Sales/Marketing Manager

The largest insurance industry trade show in the western U.S. Offers the perfect blend of business networking opportunities, education seminars, and fun and laughs with old and new friends.
Frequency: Annual
Founded in: 1962

13899 American Association of Managing General Agents Annual Meeting
American Association of Managing General Agents
9140 Ward Parkway
Kansas City, MO 64114-3306

816-444-3500; *Fax:* 816-444-0330

Jeanne Corlew-Knox, Director Meetings

Annual meeting and exhibits for managing general agents of insurance companies.
1000 Attendees
Frequency: Annual

13900 American Fraternal Alliance Annual Meeting
American Fraternal Alliance
1301 W 22nd St
Suite 700
Oak Brook, IL 60523-6022

630-522-6322; *Fax:* 630-522-6326
info@fraternalalliance.org;
www.fraternalalliance.org
Social Media: Facebook, Twitter

Joseph Annotti, President & CEO
Linda McLaughlin, Admin Services Manager
Melanie Hinds, Director, Advocacy
Allison Koppel, Executive Vice President
Andrea Litewski, Executive Administrator

Keeps members abreast of industry trends, to promote the spirit of fraternalism and to resolve mutual concerns.
Frequency: September

13901 American Society for Healthcare Risk Management Convention
American Society for Healthcare Risk Management
American Hospital Association
1 N Franklin
Chicago, IL 60606

312-422-3840; *Fax:* 312-422-4580;
www.aha.org

Deborah Sprindzunas, Executive Director
Cliff Lehman, Director Membership Services

Annual convention and exhibits of health care industry risk management equipment, supplies and services.
Frequency: Annual

13902 American Society of CLU and CHFC Annual Conference
American Society of CLU and CHFC
270 S Bryn Mawr Avenue
Suite 2
Bryn Mawr, PA 19010-2195

215-726-3160; *Fax:* 610-527-1400

Annual conference and exhibits for insurance agents and financial services professionals who hold Chartered Life Underwriter or Chartered Financial Consultant designations.
Frequency: October, San Diego

13903 Annual Conference for Public Agencies
Public Risk Management Association
1815 Fort Myer Drive
Suite 1020
Arlington, VA 22209-1805

703-527-5546; *Fax:* 703-528-7966
info@primacentral.org; www.primacentral.org

James F Coyle, Executive Director
Tony D'Alba, Manager
Kerry Langley, Manager

Largest conference in North America for state and local government risk managers who purchase insurance, safety and training products, computer software, TPA and consultant services.
150 booths.
2000 Attendees
Frequency: June
Founded in: 1979
Mailing list available for rent: 2000 names

13904 Annual National Association of Insurance Women International
1847 E 15th
PO Box 4410
Tulsa, OK 74159
918-744-5195
800-766-6249; *Fax:* 918-743-1968;
www.naiw.org
Mark Adams, Executive Vice-President
Equipment, information and supplies for women in the insurance industry.
900 Attendees
Frequency: Annual

13905 Appraisers Association of America National Conference
386 Park Avenue S
Suite 2000
New York, NY 10016-8804
212-889-5404; *Fax:* 212-889-5503;
www.appraisersassoc.org
Aleya Lehmann, Executive Director
A unique opportunity to connect with fellow appraisers as well as with allied professionals in insurance companies, law firms, government agencies, auction houses, galleries, museums, and libraries to debate and discuss the latest issues impacting the appraisal profession. We'll offer panels, specialist sessions, roundtable discussions, networking, and behind-the-scenes tours.

13906 Association for Advanced Life Underwriting
2901 Telester Court
Falls Church, VA 22042
703-641-9400
888-275-0092
Karen Keating, Communications Director
David Stertzer, Executive VP
Twenty two booths.
1M Attendees
Frequency: March

13907 CEB Spring Conference
Council on Employee Benefits
1311 King Street
Alexandria, VA 22314
703-549-6025; *Fax:* 703-549-6027
scanfiled@ceb.org; www.ceb.org
Shane Canfield, Executive Director
Robert B. Arthur, President
John R. Collins, Treasurer
Donna A. Sexton, Vice President
Charles A. Jordan, Secretary
For members only and affords a great opportunity to exchange ideas in an interactive workshop format.
Frequency: April

13908 CIRB Annual Meeting
Crop Insurance Research Bureau
201 Massachusetts Avenue, NE
Suite C5
Washington, DC 20002
202-544-0067; *Fax:* 202-330-5255
mtorrey@cropinsurance.org;
www.cropinsurance.org
Mike Torrey, Executive VP/Federal Affairs Rep
Naomi Watson, Operations Manager
W. Kurt Henke, Legal Counsel
The annual meeting brings together crop industry leaders to learn from expert speakers and newtwork with others in their industry.
Frequency: Annual/January-February

13909 CPCU Annual Meeting & Seminar
Chartered Property Casualty Underwriter Society
720 Providence Road
PO Box 3009
Malvern, PA 19355-0709
610-251-2728
800-932-2728; *Fax:* 610-251-2780
lrizzo@cpcusociety.org; www.cpcusociety.org
Liliana Rizzo, CMP, Meeting Services Director
Join your fellow society members, new designees and industry leaders for the best in education, networking and leadership the property and casualty insurance industry has to offer.
2600 Attendees
Frequency: Annual/October
Founded in: 1944

13910 CPCU Conferment Ceremony
American Institute for CPCU
720 Providence Road
PO Box 3016
Malvern, PA 19355
610-251-2733
800-644-2101; *Fax:* 610-640-9576
cserv@cpcuiia.org; www.aicpcu.org
Karen Burger CPCU CPIW, Public Relations
Roch Parayre, Senior Partner
Annual graduation ceremony for people who have earned the Chartered Property Casualty Underwriter - CPCU - designation.
Frequency: October

13911 Captive Insurance Companies Association Conference
Captive Insurance Companies Association
4248 Park Glen Road
Minneapolis, MN 55416
952-928-4655; *Fax:* 952-928-1318;
www.cicaworld.com
Annual conference and exhibits of captive insurance equipment, supplies and services.

13912 Chartered Property Casualty Underwriters Society Fall Seminar
Chartered Property Casualty Underwriter Society
720 Providence Road
Malvern, PA 19355-3402
610-512-2728
http://www.cpcusociety.org
Joseph Wisniewski, VP Finance
Jim Marks, Executive Director
Offers a forum for the exchange of ideas between insurance representatives.
3M Attendees
Frequency: October

13913 Employee Benefits Annual Conference
International Foundation of Employee Benefit Plans
18700 W Bluemound Road
Brookfield, WI 53045
262-786-6700
888-334-3327; *Fax:* 262-786-8780
pr@ifebp.org; www.ifebp.org
Social Media: Facebook, Twitter, LinkedIn
Michael Wilson, CEO
Terry Davidson, VP, Business Development
Beth Harwood, VP, Educ Program/Content Management
This conference is designed to meet the specific needs of multiemployer and public sector plan trustees and administrators, attorneys, accountants, actuaries, investment managers and others who provide services or who are involved in the overall management and administration of benefit trust funds. The 2011 conference will be in New Orleans, LA.
35000 Members
4500 Attendees
Frequency: Annual/Nov 4-7

13914 FICP Conference
Financial & Insurance Conference Planners
330 N. Wabash Avenue
Suite 2000
Chicago, IL 60611
312-245-1023; *Fax:* 312-321-5150;
www.ficpnet.com
James Schultze, CMP, Conference Manager
Laura Vanderbur, Conference Associate
Steve Bova, CAE, Executive Director
Mark Swets, Membership Manager
Ellie Hurley, Events Senior Manager
Exhibits, education and networking activities.
Frequency: Annual/November

13915 Financial Service Forum
Society of Financial Service Professionals
3803 West Chester Pike
Suite 225
Newtown Square, PA 19073-3230
610-526-2500
800-392-6900; *Fax:* 610-359-8115
info@societyoffsp.org; www.financialpro.org
Social Media: Facebook, Twitter, LinkedIn
Joseph E. Frack, Chief Executive Officer
Anthony R. Bartlett, President
Composed of motivational speakers, break-out educational session with continuing education for insurance, CFP, PACE, CLE, CPE, ICB, and EA. Exhibithall includes demo theaters.
3000+ Attendees
Frequency: October

13916 General Agents and Managers Life Agency Management Program
1922 F Street NW
Washington, DC 20006-4302
202-331-6099; *Fax:* 202-785-5612
Jo Anne Kohler, Show Manager
80 booths including publishers, computer software and hardware manufacturers and office management services.
2.7M Attendees
Frequency: March

13917 Health Law Professors Conference
American Society of Law, Medicine and Ethics
765 Commonwealth Avenue
16th Floor
Boston, MA 02215
617-262-4990; *Fax:* 617-437-7596
conferences@aslme.org; www.aslme.org
Social Media: Facebook, Twitter, LinkedIn
Ted Hutchinson, Executive Director
Katie Kenney Johnson, Conference Director
Margo Buege, Membership Department
Courtney McClellan, Assistant Editor
Frequency: June
Mailing list available for rent

13918 I-Car International Annual Meeting
3701 W Algonquin Road
Suite 400
Rolling Meadows, IL 60008
925-961-0393
800-422-7872; *Fax:* 800-590-1215
webmaster@i-car.com; www.i-car.com
Pat Perren, Meetings Manager
Matt Forpanek, Customer Care Manager
A important event that brings together collision industry leaders from across the United States, Canada and New Zealand to address current trends and issues in the industry. Attendees will

have the opportunity to learn about new products and technologies and share ideas with other industry leaders.
Frequency: Annual/July

13919 IAAI Annual Conference and General Meeting
International Association of Arson Investigators
12770 Boenker Road
Bridgeton, MO 63044

314-739-4224; *Fax:* 314-739-4219
orders@firearson.com; www.firearson.com

Marsha Sipes, Conference/Meeting Services
Dolores Nelson, Executive Director
Dave Allen, Executive Director

Provides the means to stay abreast of the latest techniques and theories in the investigation of the crime of arson.
Frequency: Annual/April

13920 IADC Annual Meeting
International Association of Defense Counsel
303 West Madison
Suite 925
Chicago, IL 60606

312-368-1494; *Fax:* 312-368-1854
info@iadclaw.org; www.iadclaw.org
Social Media: Facebook, Twitter, LinkedIn

Mary Beth Kurzak, Executive Director
Mathew Hornberger, Director Membership/Administration
Liz Anderson, Administrative Assistant
Carmela Balice, Senior Manager, Member Services
Ashley Fitzgerald, Communications Coordinator

Offering interests CLE and excellent networking opportunities in family friendly environment.
Frequency: Annual/July

13921 IAIABC Annual Convention
Int'l Assoc of Industrail Accident Boards/Commissi
5610 Medical Circle
Suite 24
Madison, WI 53719

608-663-6355; *Fax:* 608-663-1546
hlore@iaiabc.org; www.iaiabc.org

Jennifer Wolf Horejsh, Executive Director
Faith Howe, EDI Manager
Christina Klein, Events/Education Coordinator
Christina Klein, Events and Office Administrator
Heather Lore, Manager of Membership and Marketing

Brings together regulators and administrators of workers' compensation agencies and private sector professionals to discuss the industry's most common and pressing problems.
Frequency: August
Mailing list available for rent

13922 IAIR Roundtable and Meetings
International Association of Insurance Receivers
174 Grace Boulevard
Altamonte Springs, FL 32714

407-682-4513; *Fax:* 407-682-3175
info@iair.org; www.iair.org

Daniel A Orth III, Meetings VP
Mary Cannon Veed, Vice President
Douglas Hartz, Vice President

Quarterly meetings that provides an opportunity to share information about important industry issues and topics in insurance and reinsurance as they relate specifically to insurance receiverships.
Frequency: June, Sept, December

13923 IASA Annual Conference
Insurance, Accounting & Systems Association
3511 Shannon Road
Suite 160
Durham, NC 27707

919-489-0991; *Fax:* 919-489-1994
info@iasa.org; www.iasa.org

Thom Hoffman, Exhibit Manager
R Iovino, Account Manager

Providing the most comprehensive education program and business show targeted for financial and technology professionals in the industry.
1800 Attendees
Frequency: June

13924 ICAE's Annual Exchange
Insurance Consumer Affairs Exchange
PO Box 746
Lake Zurich, IL 60047

847-997-8454
nbrebner@icae.com; www.icae.com

Mike Hammond, President
Kendra Franklin, VP
Nancy Brebner, Executive Director
Chad Batterson, Executive Committee
Gail Cleary, Secretary

A not-for-profit organization that promotes professionalism and shapes the standards of behavior in relationships between insurance organizations, regulators and customers through proactive dialogue, research, communication and education.
110 Members
Frequency: Annual/October
Founded in: 1976

13925 IRU Spring Conference
Intermediaries and Reinsurance Underwriters Assoc
971 Rte 202 North
Branchburg, NJ 08876

908-203-0211; *Fax:* 908-203-0213
info@irua.com; www.irua.com

Amy Barra, Executive Director
Frequency: Annual, March

13926 Insurance and Financial Communications Association Annual Conference
1037 N 3rd Ave
Tucson, AZ 85705

602-350-0717
info@ifcaonline.com; www.ifcaonline.com
Social Media: Facebook, Twitter, LinkedIn, YouTube

Susan o'Neill, President
Ralph Chaump, VP
Kim Schultz, Secretary
Kim Schultz, Secretary

An international organization dedicated to the ongoing professional development of its members in life insurance and related financial services communications.
700 Members
Founded in: 1933

13927 International Claim Association Conference
International Claim Association
1155 15th Street NW
Suite 500
Washington, DC 20005

202-452-0143; *Fax:* 202-530-0659
cmurphy@claim.org; www.claim.org

Marlon Nettleton, President
Christopher Murphy, Executive Director
Lisa Phillips, Secretary
400 Attendees
Frequency: Annual
Founded in: 1909
Mailing list available for rent

13928 LAMP Annual Meeting
GAMA International
2901 Telestar Court
Suite 140
Falls Church, VA 22042-1205

703-770-8184; *Fax:* 703-770-8182
gamamail@gamaweb.com;
www.gamaweb.com

Nicole Travers, Meetings/Products Administrator
Delaine Everett, Meetings/Conference Director

The event for field leaders in the insurance and financial services industry. Featuring top-notch main platform speaker presentations, more than 30 leading practices concurrent sessions, resource center with more than 50 exhibitors that will be offering valuable products and services and networking opportunities with your peers.
Frequency: Annual/March
ISSN: 1095-7367
Printed in 4 colors on glossy stock

13929 LIC Annual Meeting
Life Insurers Council
2300 Windy Ridge Parkway
Suite 600
Atlanta, GA 30339-8443

770-984-3724
800-275-5662; *Fax:* 770-984-3780
askloma@loma.org;
www.loma.org/IndexPage-LIC.asp

Michael H Siris, Executive Director
Rose Hoyt, Administrative Assistant

Designed to educate members about critical issues for competing in today's regulatory, legislative and business climates.
Frequency: Annual/May
Mailing list available for rent

13930 MDRT Annual Meeting
Million Dollar Round Table
325 W Touhy Avenue
Park Ridge, IL 60068-4265

847-926-6378; *Fax:* 847-518-8921
meetings@mdrt.org; www.mdrt.org

Ray Kopcinski, Meeting Services Director
Jody Egel, Meeting Coordinator
Kathyrn H Pagura, Meeting Coordinator
John Prast, Executive Vice President
Scott Brennan, Secretary

Known throughout the industry as the premier meeting for financial professionals. Motivational stories, educational sessions, experienced colleagues, networking opportunities come together at these annual meetings.
Frequency: Annual/June

13931 NACA Convention
National Association of Catastrophe Adjusters
P.O. Box 499
Alvord, TX 76225

817-498-3466; *Fax:* 817-498-0480
naca@nacatadj.org; www.nacatadj.org
Social Media: Facebook, Twitter, LinkedIn

Chris Hatcher, President
Jon Joyce, Vice President

Rebecca Wheeling, Communications Committee Chair

Annual convention and business meeting offering continuing education credits for some states; also a vendor show. Convention is held in Las Vegas, NV.
200 Attendees
Frequency: January
Founded in: 1976

13932 NADP Annual Conference

National Association of Dental Plans
8111 LBJ Freeway
Suite 935
Dallas, TX 75251-1347

972-458-6998; *Fax:* 972-458-2258
info@nadp.org; www.nadp.org

Evelyn F Ireland, CAE, Executive Director
Tim Brown, Executive Assistant
Jeremy May, Executive Assistant

Get the greater industry insight, re-energized creativity and influential contacts.
Frequency: Annual/September

13933 NAFIC Annual Convention

National Association of Fraternal Insurance Counselors
211 Canal Road
Waterloo, WI 53594
920-478-4901
866-478-3880; *Fax:* 920-478-9586
office@nafic.org; www.nafic.org
Social Media: Facebook

James Dietrich, President
Joy Collins, Vice President
Anna Maenner, Executive Director
Frequency: Annual

13934 NAIFA Convention and Career Conference

Ntl Association of Insurance & Financial Advisors
2901 Telestar Court
PO Box 12012
Falls Church, VA 22042-1205

703-770-8100
877-866-2432; *Fax:* 703-770-8201
membersupport@naifa.org; www.naifa.org

Robert O. Smith, President
Matthew S. Tassey, Treasurer
Juli McNeely, Secretary
Susan B. Waters, CEO
Susan B Waters, Deputy Chief Executive Officer

Features educational workshops from more than a dozen prominent speakers and the NAIFA Expo, one of the largest exhibits of financial services and products in the nation.
2000 Attendees
Frequency: Annual/September
Founded in: 1890

13935 NAIIA Annual Conference

National Association of Independent Insurance Adj.
825 W State Street
Suite 117-C&B
Geneva, IL 60134

630-397-5012; *Fax:* 630-397-5013
assist@naiia.com; www.naiia.com

David F Mehren, Executive Director
Brenda Reisenger, President
Mark Nixon, Secretary, Treasurer

Attendance is open to claims handling professionals.
Frequency: Annual

13936 NAPIA Annual Meeting

National Association of Public Insurance Adjusters
21165 Whitfield Place
Suite 105
Potomac Falls, VA 20165

703-433-9217; *Fax:* 703-433-0369
info@napia.com; www.napia.com

David W Barrack, Executive Director
Ronald R. Reitz, President

Education sessions, networking and social events and exhibits by industry suppliers.
Frequency: Annual/June
Mailing list available for rent

13937 National Association of Independent Life Brokerage Agencies Conference

National Assn of Independent Life Brokerage Agents
8201 Greensboro Drive
Suite 300
Mc Lean, VA 22102-3814

703-610-9011; *Fax:* 703-524-2303

Annual conference and exhibits of equipment, supplies and services for licensed independent life brokerage agencies that represent at least 3 insurance companies, but are not controlled or owned by an underwriting company.
Frequency: November, San Diego

13938 National Association of Life Underwriters Conference

1922 F Street NW
Washington, DC 20006-4394

202-331-6099; *Fax:* 202-331-2179

William V Regan III, Executive VP
Teresa Bonnema, Advertising Account

Sales professionals in life and health insurance and other financial services. 110 booths.
3.5M Attendees
Frequency: September

13939 National Association of Mutual Insurance Companies Annual Convention & Expo

National Association of Mutual Insurance Companies
3601 Vincennes Road
#68700
Indianapolis, IN 46268-1154

317-875-5250; *Fax:* 317-879-8408
bnastally@namic.org; www.namic.org

Charles Chamness, President
Barbara Nastally, Program Director
Kristen Eichhorn, Program Director
Gregg Dykstra, COO

Convention and exhibit show for property/casualty insurance executives. Four day event.
1700 Attendees
Frequency: Fall
Founded in: 1895

13940 New England Professional Insurance Agents Association Conference

1 Ash Street
Hopkinton, MA 01748-1822
508-497-2590

Stella Di Camilo, Show Manager

100 booths of insurance-related products.
1.5M Attendees
Frequency: November

13941 PIA Annual Convention and Trade Fair

Professional Insurance Agents Association of VA & DC
8751 Park Central Dr., Suite 140
Richmond, VA 23227

804-264-2582; *Fax:* 804-266-1075
pia@piavadc.com; www.piavadc.com
Social Media: Facebook, Twitter

Dennis Yooom, Executive VP
Lori Lohr, Education Manager
Carol Throokmorton, Accounting Manager
Founded in: 1936

13942 PLRB/LIRB Claims Conference & Insurance Expo

PLRB/LIRB-Property Loss Research Bureau
3025 Highland Parkway
Suite 800
Downers Grove, IL 60515-1291

630-242-2250
888-711-7572; *Fax:* 630-724-2260
pdispensa@lirb.org; www.lirb.org

Tom Mallin, President
Paul C Despensa, VP/General Counsel

Concept sessions that feature a thorough presentation of a topic by expert panelists. A forum of experts/panels that will discuss controversial topics in response to questions and comments from participants on a range of subjects outlined in the agenda for that forum. Participants form a small discussion group to reach consensus on hypothetical problems. Each table debates and defends its conclusions with other groups.
Frequency: April
Mailing list available for rent

13943 PRIMA Annual Conference Trade Show

700 S. Washington St.
Suite 218
Alexandria, VA 22314
703-528-7701; *Fax:* 703-739-0200
info@primacentral.org; www.primacentral.org
Social Media: Facebook, Twitter, LinkedIn

Marshall Davies, Executive Director
Jon Ruzan, Editor
Jennifer Ackerman, Deputy Executive Director
Bles Dones, Manager, Member Services
Paulette Washington, Office Administrator

Containing 150 exhibits concerning insuring the public.
2,200 Attendees
Frequency: June
Founded in: 1976
Mailing list available for rent

13944 Physician Insurers Association of America Annual Conference

Physician Insurers Association of America
2275 Research Boulevard
Rockville, MD 20850-3268

301-947-9000; *Fax:* 301-947-9090

Annual exhibits related to physician liability insurance.

13945 Professional Insurance Agents National Annual Conference & Exhibition

National Association of Prof. Insurance Agents
400 N Washington Street
Alexandria, VA 22314-2312

703-836-9340; *Fax:* 703-836-1279
http://www.pianet.com

Ted Besesparis, VP

Annual conference and exhibits of equipment, supplies and services for independent property and casualty agents.

13946 **Public Agency Risk Managers Association Convention**
Public Agency Risk Managers Association
PO Box 6810
San Jose, CA 95150-6810
Annual convention and exhibits of risk management equipment, supplies and services.

13947 **Risk Insurance Management Society**
1065 Avenue of Americas
13th Floor
New York, NY 10018
212-286-9292
chapterservices@RIMS.org; www.rims.org
Brian Stevenson, Show Manager
Mary Roth, Manager
Fran Jordan, Manager
500 booths of premier insurance companies and associated service companies.
5M Attendees

13948 **Securities Industry and Financial Markets Association (SIFMA) Annual Meeting**
1101 New York Avenue Nw
8th Floor
Washington, DC 20005
202-962-7300; *Fax:* 202-962-7305;
www.sifma.org
Social Media: Facebook, Twitter, LinkedIn
T Timothy Ryan Jr, President/CEO
Randy Snook, Senior Managing Director/EVP
Cheryl Crispen, Executive VP, Communications
Ira D. Hammerman, Senior Managing Director
David Krasner, Chief Financial Officer
The Securities Industry and Financial Markets Association/SIFMA Annual Meeting and Conference program addresses a variety of topics that may include competitiveness of the U.S. capital markets, global exchange consolidation, regulatory and legal initiatives, and trends in the fixed-income and capital markets.
Mailing list available for rent

13949 **Society of Insurance Trainers and Educators Conference**
2120 Market Street
Suite 108
San Francisco, CA 94114
415-621-2830; *Fax:* 415-621-0889
ed@insurancetrainers.org;
www.insurancetrainers.org
Lois A Markovich, Executive Director
Forty booths. A major conference for those involved with training and education in the insurance industry.
200 Attendees
Frequency: June-July
Founded in: 1953

13950 **Sun States Professional Insurance Agents Association**
13416 N 32nd Street
Suite 106
Phoenix, AZ 85032-6000
602-482-3333
Social Media: Facebook, Twitter, LinkedIn
Maryls M Graser, Executive VP
50 booths.
300 Attendees
Frequency: May

13951 **Vermont Captive Insurance Association**
Vermont Captive Insurance Association
180 Battery Street
Suite 200
Burlington, VT 05401-5212
802-658-8242; *Fax:* 802-658-9365
vcia@vcia.com; www.vcia.com
Richard Smith, President
Diane Leach, Education/Program Planning Director
Janice Valgoi, Membership/Development Director
Elizabeth Halpern, Communications Director
Peggy Companion, Director of Finance
Frequency: August
Founded in: 1985

13952 **WCRI Annual Issues & Research Conference**
Workers Compensation Research Institute
955 Massachusetts Ave.
Cambridge, MA 02139
617-661-9274; *Fax:* 617-661-9284
wcri@wcrinet.org;
www.wcrinet.org/conference.html
Vincent Armentano, Chair
Richard A. Victor, President & CEO

13953 **Women Life Underwriters Confederation**
1126 S 70th Street
Suite S-106
Milwaukee, WI 53214-3151
800-776-3008; *Fax:* 414-475-2585
Ann Wells, Managing Director
For women insurance agents, their managers and their companies. 20 booths.
100 Attendees
Frequency: September

Directories & Databases

13954 **ADP Parts Exchange New**
ADP Claims Services Group
2010 Crow Canyon Place
San Ramon, CA 94583
925-866-1100; www.adpclaims.com
Provides an electronic link from your ADP estimating system to comprehensive database of new replacement parts. Data on over three and a half million parts facilitates the writing of complete, cost-effective damage reports.

13955 **Adjusters Reference Guide**
Bar List Publishing Company
425 Huehl Road
Building 6B
Northbrook, IL 60062-2323
847-498-6133
800-726-1007; *Fax:* 847-498-6695
info@barlist.com; www.barlist.com
Bruce Rodgers, President
Leslie Rodgers, Production Manager
A professional service for anyone who handles insurance claims. It contains a complete set of ISO Policy and Forms and is divided into two major categories; Personal Lines and Commercial Lines.
Frequency: Annual

13956 **Best's Directory of Recommended Insurance Attorneys and Adjusters**
AM Best Company
Ambest Rd
Oldwick, NJ 08858
908-439-2200; *Fax:* 908-439-3296
webmaster@ambest.com; www.ambest.com
Arthur Snyder, CEO
Includes over 5,300 insurance defense law firms and over 1,200 insurance adjusters companies recommended by the insurance industry. Includes a section on expert services providers, insurance company groups or fleets, legal and claims services, officials and a digest of insurance laws.
Cost: $1205.00
5100 Pages
Frequency: Annual
Circulation: 19,000
Founded in: 1928

13957 **Best's Insurance News & Analysis**
AM Best Company
Ambest Rd
Oldwick, NJ 08858
908-439-2200
800-424-2378; *Fax:* 908-439-3296;
www.ambest.com
Arthur Snyder, Chairman & President
Paul Tinnirello, CIO
Larry Mayewski, Chief Rating Officer
Best's Insurance News & Analysis makes it easy to take advantage of A.M. Best's extensive insurance news and industry research. A Best's Insurance News & Analysis subscription grants you access to a full range of news products as well as unique statistical studies and special reports - all of which are accessible from one convenient online location. Allows access to receive BestDay, BestWeek, Best's Review, and Best's Special Reports.

13958 **Best's Insurance Reports**
AM Best Company
Ambest Rd
Oldwick, NJ 08858
908-439-2200; *Fax:* 908-439-3296
webmaster@ambest.com; www.ambest.com
Arthur Snyder, CEO
Published in two editions - life-health insurance and property-casualty insurance, United States and Canada.
Cost: $570.00
Frequency: Annual

13959 **Best's Insurance Reports: International Edition**
AM Best Company
Ambest Rd
Oldwick, NJ 08858
908-439-2200; *Fax:* 908-439-3296
webmaster@ambest.com; www.ambest.com
Arthur Snyder, CEO
Offers information on over 800 insurance companies in Canada, Europe, Asia, Africa, Australia, and South America that offer life/health and property/casulaty insurance policies.
Cost: $495.00
1200 Pages
Frequency: Annual

13960 **Best's Key Rating Guide**
AM Best Company
Ambest Rd
Oldwick, NJ 08858
908-439-2200; *Fax:* 908-439-3296
webmaster@ambest.com; www.ambest.com
Arthur Snyder, CEO
Larry Mayewski, Editor
Financial and operating characteristics on over 2,600 major property/casualty insurance companies, over 1,750 major life and health insurance companies.
Cost: $95.00
Frequency: Annual August

13961 **Best's Market Guide**
AM Best Company

Ambest Rd
Oldwick, NJ 08858

908-439-2200; *Fax:* 908-439-3296
webmaster@ambest.com; www.ambest.com

Arthur Snyder, CEO

In each volume, separate volumes for corporate stocks, corporate bonds, and municipal bonds, a list of insurance company investment officers are offered.
Cost: $1425.00
Frequency: 3-Volume Set

13962 Business Insurance Directory of Reinsurance Intermediaries
Crain Communications
360 N Michigan Ave
Chicago, IL 60601-3800

312-649-5200
800-678-9595; *Fax:* 312-649-7937;
www.crain.com

Keith Crain, CEO
Sandra L Budde, Editor

Lists nearly 100 reinsurance intermediaries in the United States and Bermuda.
Cost: $4.00
Frequency: Annual
Circulation: 53,000

13963 Captive Insurance Company Directory
Tillinghast/Towers Perrin Company
263 Tresser Boulevard
Stamford, CT 06901-3236

203-631-1900; *Fax:* 203-326-5498

Corinne Ramming, Editor

Lists over 3,000 captive insurance companies and their parent or sponsor companies; management companies and insurance subsidiary investment advisors.
Cost: $210.00
270 Pages
Frequency: Annual

13964 Certified Claims Professional Accreditation Council
PO Box 441110
Fort Washington, MD 20749-1110

301-292-1988; *Fax:* 301-292-1787;
www.lattmag.com

Dale L Anderson, Editor

Offers a variety of information on members of the CCPAC and certified claims professionals.
76 Pages
Circulation: 350

13965 Claim Service Guide
Bar List Publishing Company
425 Huehl Road
Building 6B
Northbrook, IL 60062-2323

847-498-6133
800-726-1007; *Fax:* 847-498-6695
info@barlist.com; www.barlist.com

Bruce Rodgers, President
Edna MacMillan, Editor

National Directory of Independent Insurance Adjusters, Appraisers, Expert Consultants and Property Specialists. Distributed to every home and branch office insurance company claims manager.
Cost: $80.00
Frequency: Annual
Circulation: 13,000

13966 Corporate Yellow Book
Leadership Directories
104 5th Ave
New York, NY 10011-6901

212-627-4140; *Fax:* 212-645-0931
corporate@leadershipdirectories.com;
www.leadershipdirectories.com
Social Media: Facebook, Twitter

David Hurvitz, CEO

Contact information for over 48,000 executives at over 1,000 companies and more than 9,000 board members and their outside affiliations.
Cost: $360.00
1,400 Pages
Frequency: Quarterly
ISSN: 1058-2098
Founded in: 1969

13967 Custom Publishing & News Services Information
7707 Old Georgetown Rd
Suite 700
Bethesda, MD 20814

301-215-4688; *Fax:* 301-215-4600;
www.infoinc.com

Alain Carr, Owner

Offers evaluations of companies on their claims-paying ability.

13968 Directory of Corporate Buyers
Crain Communications Inc
360 N Michigan Ave
Chicago, IL 60601-3800

312-649-5200; *Fax:* 312-649-7937;
www.crain.com

Keith Crain, CEO

Provides complete contact information for more that 3,200 top level corporate executives from Fortune 500 companies involved in risk management and employee benefits.
Frequency: Annual

13969 Directory of Employee Assistance Program Providers
Crain Communications Inc
360 N Michigan Ave
Chicago, IL 60601-3800

312-649-5200; *Fax:* 312-649-7937;
www.crain.com

Keith Crain, CEO

Lists organizations that provide a variety of EAP services to employers on a direct, stand alone basis.
Frequency: Annual
Circulation: 50,000

13970 Directory of Property Loss Control Consultants
Crain Communications
360 N Michigan Ave
Chicago, IL 60601-3800

312-649-5200; *Fax:* 312-649-7937;
www.crain.com

Keith Crain, CEO

Lists companies that provide loss control services on a direct, unbundled basis. Consultants that provide loss control assistance only in conjunction with other services such as brokering insurance are not listed.
Frequency: Annual
Circulation: 53,000

13971 Directory of Specialty Markets Issue
Insurance Journal
9191 Towne Centre Drive
Suite 550
San Diego, CA 92122-1231

619-584-1100; *Fax:* 619-584-1200

Mark Wells, Editor

Lists about 200 insurance companies and surplus lines brokers offering specialty lines to insurance agents and brokers in California, Arizona, Alaska, Oregon, Hawaii and Washington.
Cost: $10.00
Frequency: SemiAnnual
Circulation: 10,400

13972 HMO/PPO Directory
Grey House Publishing
4919 Route 22
PO Box 56
Amenia, NY 12501

518-789-8700
800-562-2139; *Fax:* 845-373-6390
books@greyhouse.com; www.greyhouse.com
Social Media: Facebook, Twitter

Leslie Mackenzie, Publisher
Richard Gottlieb, Editor

The HMO/PPO Directory is a comprehensive source that provides detailed information about Health Maintenance Organizations and Preferred Provider Organizations nationwide. Within the HMO/PPO Profiles, over 1,300 HMOs, PPOs and affiliated companies are listed, arranged alphabetically by state.
Cost: $325.00
600 Pages
ISBN: 1-592373-69-0
Founded in: 1981

13973 HMO/PPO Directory - Online Database
Grey House Publishing
4919 Route 22
PO Box 56
Amenia, NY 12501-0056

518-789-8700
800-562-2139; *Fax:* 518-789-0556
gold@greyhouse.com;
www.gold.greyhouse.com
Social Media: Facebook, Twitter

Leslie Mackenzie, Publisher
Richard Gottlieb, President

The HMO/PPO Directory - Online Database is your in-depth searchable guide to health plans nationwide - their contact information, key executives, plan information and more. The online database is a necessary tool when researching or marketing a product or service to this important industry.
Founded in: 1981

13974 III Data Base Search
Insurance Information Institute
110 William St
New York, NY 10038-3908

212-346-5500; *Fax:* 212-732-1916;
www.iii.org

Gary Johnson, Manager
Cary Schneider, Executive Vice President

Provides citations and abstracts of insurance-related literature appearing in magazines, newspapers and trade publications and books.

13975 III Insurance Daily
Insurance Information Institute
110 William St
New York, NY 10038-3908

212-346-5500; *Fax:* 212-732-1916;
www.iii.org

Gary Johnson, Manager
Cary Schneider, Executive Vice President

This insurance database provides summaries of news and articles relating to the property and casualty insurance industry.
Frequency: Full-text

13976 IRU Members +
Intermediaries and Reinsurance Underwriters Assoc

971 Rte 202 North
Branchburg, NJ 08876

908-203-0211; *Fax:* 908-203-0213
info@irua.com; www.irua.com

Jim Brost, President

List of all member companies and contacts; conference and attendee list provided to attendees only.
Founded in: 1967

13977 **Independent Insurance**
Independent Insurance Agents of America
127 S Peyton St
Alexandria, VA 22314-2803

703-683-4422
800-221-7917; *Fax:* 703-683-7556
info@iiaba.net; www.independentagent.com
Social Media: Facebook, Twitter

Robert A Rusbuldt, CEO
Alex Soto, President

This web site contains information for consumers on property and casualty insurance including homeowner, renter, landlord, and automobile insurance.
Frequency: Full-text
Founded in: 1896
Mailing list available for rent

13978 **Insurance Almanac**
Underwriter Printing & Publishing Company
244 North Main St.
P.O. Box 622
New City, NY 10956

845-634-2720; *Fax:* 845-634-2989
jgcrothers@criterionpub.com;
www.criterioninsurancedirectory.com

Over 3,000 insurance companies that write fire, casualty, accident, health and life insurance policies.
650 Pages
Frequency: Annual
Circulation: 10,000

13979 **Insurance Bar Directory**
Bar List Publishing Company
425 Huehl Road
Building 6B
Northbrook, IL 60062-2323

847-498-6133
800-726-1007; *Fax:* 847-498-6695
info@barlist.com; www.barlist.com

Bruce Rodgers, President
Edna MacMillin, Editor
Leslie Rodgers, Production Manager

National Directory of Insurance Defense Attorneys that is distributed to all insurance company home office and branch office company executives and claims personnel.
Cost: $80.00
Frequency: Annual
Circulation: 40,000

13980 **Insurance Companies' Directory List of Mortgage Directors**
Communication Network International
3918 Avenue T
Brooklyn, NY 11234-5028

718-396-6245

Listing of 210 mortgage offices of major insurance companies that make real estate mortgages and related investments.
Cost: $75.00
Founded in: 1993

13981 **Kelly Casualty Insurance Claims Directory**
Francis B Kelley & Associates
123 Veteran Avenue
Los Angeles, CA 90024-1900

800-328-4144; *Fax:* 310-472-1290;
www.fbka.com

Francis B Kelley, Editor

Lists only casualty insurance claims payment offices. Workers' Compensation and Auto Insurance can pay health care providers for their services. Directory covers Casualty Insurance Companies, Independent Claims Companies, Insurance Commissioners with their Web sites.
Cost: $150.00
280 Pages
Frequency: Annual

13982 **LEXIS Insurance Law Library**
Mead Data Central
9443 Springboro Pike
Dayton, OH 45401

888-223-6337; *Fax:* 518-487-3584;
www.lexis-nexis.com

Andrew Prozes, CEO
Rebecca Schmitt, Chief Financial Officer

This full database contains the complete text of the insurance statutes for 50 states, the District of Columbia and Puerto Rico.
Frequency: Full-text

13983 **LOMA's Information Center Database**
Life Office Management Association
2300 Windy Ridge Pkwy SE
Suite 600
Atlanta, GA 30339-5665

770-951-1770
800-275-5662; *Fax:* 770-984-0441
infoctr@loma.org; www.loma.org

Thomas P Donaldson, President/CEO
Jerry Woo, Director
Robert Lai, Managing Director

A team of experienced researchers provide current data utilizing our comprehensive database. More than 10,000 documents are maintained and updated. A comprehensive list of Industry Research Links can also be found in this area.
Frequency: Available to Members

13984 **Life Insurance Selling: Sources Issue**
Commerce Publishing Company
330 N 4th Street
Suite 200
Saint Louis, MO 63102-2041

314-421-5445; *Fax:* 314-421-1070

Larry Albright, Editor

Lists life insurance companies, publishers of software used in the insurance field and financial planning corporations.
Cost: $7.00
Frequency: 45000

13985 **Life Office Management Association Directory**
5770 Powers Ferry Road NW
Atlanta, GA 30327-4350

770-953-6872; *Fax:* 770-984-0441

Philippa Griffith, Editor

Offers information on life insurance and financial service companies.
190 Pages
Frequency: Annual

13986 **Morningstar**
Morningstar
225 W Washington Street
Chicago, IL 60602

312-384-4000; *Fax:* 312-696-6001
productinfo@morningstar.com;
www.morningstar.com

Joe Mansueto, Chairman & CEO
Chris Boruff, President, Software Division
Peng Chen, President, Global Investment Div.
Bevin Desmond, President, International Operations
Scott Cooley, Chief Financial Officer

Morningstar provides data on approximately 330,000 investment offerings, including stocks, mutual funds, and similar vehicles, along with real-time global market data on more than 5 million equities, indexes, futures, options, commodities, and precious metals, in addition to foreign exchange and Treasury markets. Morningstar also offers investment management services and has more than $167 billion in assets under advisement and management.

13987 **NAIC Database**
National Association of Insurance Commissioners
1100 Walnut Street
Suite 1500
Kansas City, MO 64106-2197

816-842-3600; *Fax:* 816-783-8175;
www.naic.org

Sandy Praeger, President
Andrew Beal, CEO
Kevin M. McCarty, President
James J. Donelon, President-Elect
Monica J. Lindeen, Secretary-Treasurer
Mailing list available for rent

13988 **National Association of Catastrophe Adjusters Membership Directory**
National Association of Catastrophe Adjusters
P.O. Box 499
Alvord, TX 76225

817-498-3466; *Fax:* 817-498-0480
naca@nacatadj.org; www.nacatadj.org

Chris Hatcher, President
Jon Joyce, Vice President
Jimmy Clark, Secretary/Treasurer
Founded in: 1976

13989 **National Insurance Law Service/Insource Insurance**
NILS Publishing Company
PO Box 2507
Chatsworth, CA 91313-2507

818-998-8830
800-423-5910; *Fax:* 818-718-8482;
www.nils.com

Jon Fish, Circulation Director
Karen G Beaudoin, VP Marketing
Jonathon K Fish, Production Manager

This insurance database contains the complete text of insurance codes, related laws, regulations, bulletins and selected attorney general opinions for all 50 states and the federal government. Available on CD-ROm and in looseleaf print. The CD-ROM service 'Insource Insurance' is accessible for licensed users on the NILS Publishing Website.
Cost: $520.00
Frequency: Monthly Updates
Circulation: 5,000

13990 **National Underwriter Kirschner's Insurance Directories (Red Book)**
National Underwriter Company

5081 Olympic Blvd
Erlanger, KY 41018-3164

859-692-2100; *Fax:* 859-692-2295;
www.nationalunderwriter.com

Charlie Smith, CEO
Charlie Smith, Chief Executive Officer

This series of 24 directories are published by state or region. Listings include companies, brokers and agents and services for each state handling property and casualty.
Cost: $19.95
150+ Pages
Frequency: Semi-Annual/Annual
Printed in on matte stock

13991 Profiles: Health Insurance Edition
National Underwriter Company
5081 Olympic Blvd
Erlanger, KY 41018-3164

859-692-2100
800-543-0874; *Fax:* 859-692-2295;
www.nationalunderwriter.com

Charlie Smith, CEO

Your reliable resource for up-to-date news and information in the life & health insurance/financial services industry.
Cost: $39.95
300 Pages
Frequency: Annual

13992 Profiles: Property and Casualty Insurance Edition
National Underwriter Company
505 Gest Street
Cincinnati, OH 45203-1716

513-723-0012

Edward A Lyon, Editor

Offers information on more than 1,500 property and liability insurance companies.
Cost: $39.95
852 Pages
Frequency: Annual

13993 Register of North American Insurance Companies
American Preeminent Registry
PO Box 622
Old Bridge, NJ 08857-0622

732-225-5533

Brian Axelrod, Publisher

Directory of services and supplies to the industry.
Cost: $125.00
450 Pages
Frequency: Annual

13994 Risk Retention Group Directory and Guide
Insurance Communications
PO Box 50147
Pasadena, CA 91115-0147

626-796-4972; *Fax:* 626-796-4972
http://www.rrr.com

Karen Cutts, Editor

Offers information on over 80 risk retention groups formed under the 1986 Risk Retention Act or the 1981 Product Liability Risk Retention Act through 1990.
Cost: $165.00
144 Pages
Frequency: Annual

13995 Shortcut 2: Insurance Markets Tracking Systems
National Underwriter Company
505 Gest Street
Cincinnati, OH 45203-1716

513-723-0012

Directory of services and supplies to the industry.
Cost: $300.00

13996 Society of Professional Benefit Administrators
Society of Professional Benefit Administrators
2 Wisconsin Circle
Suite 670
Chevy Chase, MD 20815

301-718-7722; *Fax:* 301-718-9440
info@spbatpa.org; www.spbatpa.org

Anne Lennan, President

For members only. Discusses and analyzes government compliance requirements of administration and plan design and industry and market trends
300 Members
350 Attendees
Frequency: 2x/Year
Founded in: 1975

13997 Statistics of Fraternal Benefit Societies
1240 Iroquois Avenue
Suite 300
Naperville, IL 60563-8476
630-355-6633; *Fax:* 630-355-0042;
www.nfcanet.org

Anthony Snyder, Communications Director

NFCA membership is currently made up of 82 fraternal benefit societies in the United States and Canada. Each of these societies pay annual membership dues to belong to the organization and it is their executives, employees and grassroots members who serve on the NFCA Board of Directors and various NFCA committees and sections.
Cost: $11.00

13998 TPA Directory
Society of Professional Benefit Administrators
2 Wisconsin Circle
Suite 670
Chevy Chase, MD 20815

301-718-7722; *Fax:* 301-718-9440
info@spbatpa.org; www.spbatpa.org

Frederick D Hunt Jr, President
Anne C Lennan, President-Elect

Detailed description of contact information and types of plans and services and size of each firm in an easy-to-cross-reference and compare format.
Cost: $495.00
Mailing list available for rent

13999 WESTLAW Insurance Library
West Publishing Company
610 Opperman Drive
Eagan, MN 55123-1340
651-687-7327; www.westgroup.com

This database offers information on US state laws relating to the insurance industry.
Frequency: Full-text

14000 Weiss Ratings Consumer Box Set
Grey House Publishing
4919 Route 22
PO Box 56
Amenia, NY 12501

518-789-8700
800-562-2139; *Fax:* 845-373-6390
books@greyhouse.com; www.greyhouse.com
Social Media: Facebook, Twitter

Leslie Mackenzie, Publisher
Richard Gottlieb, Editor

Each guide in the Weiss Ratings Consumer Box Set is packed with accurate, unbiased information, including helpful, step-by-step Worksheets & Planners. The set consists of Consumer Guides to Variable Annuities, Elder Care Choices, Medicare Supplement Insurance, Medicare Prescription Drug Coverage, Homeowners Insurance, Automobile Insurance, Long-Term Care Insurance, and Term Life Insurance.
Cost: $249.00
600 Pages
Frequency: Quarterly
Founded in: 1981

14001 Weiss Ratings Guide to Health Insurers
Grey House Publishing
4919 Route 22
PO Box 56
Amenia, NY 12501

518-789-8700
800-562-2139; *Fax:* 845-373-6390
books@greyhouse.com; www.greyhouse.com
Social Media: Facebook, Twitter

Leslie Mackenzie, Publisher
Richard Gottlieb, Editor

Weiss Ratings Guide to Health Insurers is the first and only source to cover the financial stability of the nation's health care system, rating the financial safety of more than 6,000 health maintenance organizations (HMOs) and all of the Blue Cross Blue Shield plans - updated quarterly to ensure the most accurate, up-to-date informations.
Cost: $249.00
600 Pages
Frequency: Quarterly
Founded in: 1981

14002 Weiss Ratings Guide to Life & Annuity Insurers
Grey House Publishing
4919 Route 22
PO Box 56
Amenia, NY 12501

518-789-8700
800-562-2139; *Fax:* 845-373-6390
books@greyhouse.com; www.greyhouse.com
Social Media: Facebook, Twitter

Leslie Mackenzie, Publisher
Richard Gottlieb, Edtior

Each easy-to-use edition provides independent, unbiased ratings on the financial strength of 1,000 life and annuity insurers, including companies providing life insurance, annuities, guaranteed investment contracts (GICs) and other pension products.
Cost: $249.00
600 Pages
Frequency: Quarterly
Founded in: 1981

14003 Weiss Ratings Guide to Property & Casualty Insurers
Grey House Publishing
4919 Route 22
PO Box 56
Amenia, NY 12501

518-789-8700
800-562-2139; *Fax:* 845-373-6390
books@greyhouse.com; www.greyhouse.com
Social Media: Facebook, Twitter

Leslie Mackenzie, Publisher
Richard Gottlieb, Editor

Updated quarterly, this publication is the only resource that provides independent, unbiased ratings and analyses on the 2,400 insurers offering

auto & homeowners, business, worker's compensation, product liability, medical malpractice and other professional liability insurance in the United States.
Cost: $249.00
600 Pages
Frequency: Quarterly
Founded in: 1981

14004 **Yearbook of the Insurance Industry**
American Association of Managing General Agents
150 S Warner Rd
Suite 156
King of Prussia, PA 19406-2832

610-225-1999; *Fax:* 610-225-1996;
www.aamga.org

Bernie Heinz, Executive Director
250 managing general agents of insurance companies and more than 500 branch offices; coverage includes Canada.
Frequency: Annual Spring

Industry Web Sites

14005 **http://gold.greyhouse.com**
G.O.L.D Grey House OnLine Databases
Grey House Publishing's online database platform, GOLD, offers Quick Search, Keyword Search and Expert Search for most business sectors including insurance markets. The GOLD platform makes finding the information you need quick and easy - whether you're a novice searcher or an experienced database user. All of Grey House's directory products are available for subscription on the GOLD platform.

14006 **www.aaimco.com**
American Association of Insurance Management
Consultants
Supports the insurance management industry.

14007 **www.aaimedicine.org**
American Academy of Insurance Medicine
This organization offers information and legislative updates for people in the medical insurance field.

14008 **www.actuary.org**
American Academy of Actuaries
The AAA is a public policy organization for actuaries within the US The Academy acts as the public information organization for the profession. Assisting public policy process through the presentation of clear actuarial analysis, the Academy regularly prepares testimony for Congress, provides information to federal elected officials, regulators and congressional staff, comments on proposed federal regulations, and works closely with state officials on issues related to insurance.

14009 **www.aha.org**
American Society for Healthcare Risk Management
National organization for the health care industry risk management equipment, supplies and services.

14010 **www.aicpcu.org**
Insurance Institute of America
Sponsors programs for property and casualty insurance firms, conducts exams and award certificates. Maintains a library.

14011 **www.aicpeu.org**
American Institute for CPCU
An independent, nonprofit educational organization that confers the Chartered Property Casualty Underwriter professional designation on those individuals who meet its education and ethics requirements.

14012 **www.allianceai.org**
Alliance of American Insurers
Trade association of property and casualty insurers providing educational, legislative and safety services to its members.

14013 **www.apiw.org**
Association of Professional Insurance Women
Promotes cooperation and understanding among members. Maintains high professional standards and provides a network of professional contacts. Encourages women in industry.

14014 **www.arbifile.org**
Arbitration Forums
Arbitration Forums is a not-for-profit provider of intercompany insurance dispute resolution services. More than 2,000 insurers and self-insurers participate in AF's programs. AF resolves over 250,000 disputes with a claim value approaching 1 billion dollars.

14015 **www.arminet.com**
Associated Risk Managers International
Develops specialized insurance/risk management services for trade associations, professional groups and other industry organizations. Conducts seminars and sponsors competitions.

14016 **www.asppa.org**
American Society of Pension Professionals & Act
(ASPPA) is a national organization for career retirement paln professionals. The membership consists of the many disciplines supporting retirement income management and benefits policy. Its members are part of the diversified, technical, and highly regulated benefits industry. ASPPA represents those who have made a career of retirement plan and pension policy work.

14017 **www.awpc.org**
Association of Workers' Compensation Professionals
A nonprofit organization for those engaged in the field of workers' compensation, providing members with training and certification.

14018 **www.ccactuaries.org**
Conference of Consulting Actuaries
Full-time consulting actuaries.

14019 **www.easternclaimsconference.com**
Eastern Claims Conference
Provides education and training to examiners, managers, and officers who review medical and disability claims. Holds seminars for life, health and disability clinics.

14020 **www.financialpro.org**
Society of Financial Service Professionals
Members are dedicated to the highest standards of competence and service in insurance and financial services.

14021 **www.financialratingsseries.com**
Grey House Publishing
Financial Ratings Series Online combines the strength of Weiss Ratings and TheStreet Ratings to offer the library community with a single source for financial strength ratings and financial planning tools covering Banks, Insurers, Mutual Funds and Stocks. This powerful database will provide the accurate, independent information consumers need to make informed decisions about their financial planning.

14022 **www.fraternalalliance.org**
American Fraternal Alliance
The trade association of America's fraternal benefit societies.

14023 **www.greyhouse.com**
Grey House Publishing
Authoritative reference directories for most business sectors including insurance markets. Users can search the online databases with varied search criteria allowing for custom searches by product category, geographic area, sales volume, keyword, subject and more. Full Grey House catalog and online ordering also available.

14024 **www.highwaysafety.org**
Insurance Institute for Highway Safety
Traffic and motor vehicle safety organization supported by auto insurers.

14025 **www.hwsafety.org**
Highway Loss Data Institute
Provides the public with insurance industry data concerning human and economic loss resulting from crashes.

14026 **www.iasa.org**
Insurance Accounting Systems Association
Facilitates the exchange of ideas among insurance industry professionals and their industry-related associates.

14027 **www.icae.com**
Insurance Consumer Affairs Exchange
Promotes professionalism and shapes the standards of behavior in relationships between insurance organizations, regulators and customers through proactive dialogue, research, communication and education.

14028 **www.insuranceallnations.com**
Allnations Insurance
Provides financial and technical assistance to new and developing cooperative insurance facilities. Promotes and develops all types of cooperative insurance organizations.

14029 **www.irua.org**
Intermediaries & Reinsurance Underwriters Assoc
A not-for-profit corporation, organized for the purposes of reinsurance education and research and the dissemination of information relevant to the reinsurance industry.

14030 **www.ivans.com**
Insurance Value Added Network Services
Industry-sponsored organization offering value added data communications network linking agencies, companies and providers of data to the insurance industry.

14031 **www.nacatadj.org**
National Association of Catastrophe Adjusters
Association of Catstrophe Insurance Adjusters and independent adjustment companies.

14032 **www.nafi.org**
National Association of Fire Investigators
Primary purpose of this association is to increase the knowledge and improve the skills of persons engaged in the investigation and analysis of fires, explosions, or in the litigation that ensues from such investigations. The Association also originated and implemented the National Certification Board.

14033 **www.nahu.org**
National Association of Health Underwriters
Sponsors advanced health insurance underwriting and research seminars. Testifies before federal and state committees on pending health insurance legislation. Presents numerous awards.

14034 **www.naiw.org**
National Association of Insurance Women
Professional membership association for employees in all facets of the insurance industry. The association exists to promote continuing education and networking for the professional advancement of its members, and offers education programs, meetings, publications, services and leadership opportunities for its members' benefits.

14035 **www.ncci.com**
National Council on Compensation Insurance
Develops and administers rating plans and systems for workers compensation insurance.

14036 **www.ncoil.org**
National Conference of Insurance Legislators
NCOIL is an organization of state legislators whose main area of public policy concern is insurance legislation and regulation. Many legislators active in NCOIL either chair or are members of the committees responsible for insurance legislation in their respective state houses across the country.

14037 **www.nonprofitrisk.org**
Nonprofit Risk Management Center
Publishes materials and delivers workshops and conferences on risk management, liability and insurance issues of special concern to nonprofit organizations.

14038 **www.ontherisk.org/houla/**
Home Office Life Underwriters Association
Offers educational programs through the Academy Life Underwriting designed for professional home office underwriters.

14039 **www.plrb.org**
Property Loss Research Bureau
Provides access to legal and technical databases, legal research on property and inland marine coverage issues countrywide, claims education, and daily catastrophe information for a membership of 570 property/casualty insurance companies.

14040 **www.sirnet.org**
Society of Insurance Research
Members are individuals actively engaged in some form of insurance research.

14041 **www.snl.com**
SNL Securities
News articles on banks and thrifts, insurance and other financial services. Also features vital company information.

14042 **www.snlnet.com**
SNL Securities
This organization offers the most up-to-date information available in the insurance industry featuring the latest news releases, filings and important events. Provides current data on top-performing stocks, insider trades, ownership filings, company news and events and legislative issues.

14043 **www.soa.org**
Society of Actuaries
Nonprofit professional society of 17,000 members involved in the modeling and management of financial risk and contingent events. The mission of the SOA is to advance actuarial knowledge and to enhance the ability of actuaries to provide expert advice and relevant solutions for financial, business and societal problems involving uncertain future events.

14044 **www.spbatpa.org**
Society of Professional Benefit Administrators
National Association of Third Party Administrators (TPAs) of employee benefit health and pension plans. SPBA represents TPAs who offer comprehensive services.

14045 **www.thefederation.org**
Federation of Insurance and Corporate Counsel
For members of the bar who are actively engaged in the legal aspects of the insurance business, executives of insurance companies and associations and corporate counsel engaged in the defense of claims.

14046 **www.thepiaa.org**
Physician Insurers Association
Represents domestic and international medical malpractice insurance companies which are practioner-owned or controlled.

14047 **www.transportlaw.com**
Transportation Consumer Protection Council
Dedicated to the reduction of transit losses and the improvement of freight claim and freight charge payment procedures in domestic and international commerce.

14048 **www.users.erols.com/spba**
Society of Professional Benefit Administrators
Third-party contract administration (TPA) administers employee benefit plans for client employers and unions. It is estimated that 66 percent of US workers with employee benefits are in plans administered by TPA.

Associations

14049 **American Floorcovering Alliance**
210 West Cuyler Street
Dalton, GA 30720

706-278-4101
800-288-4101; *Fax:* 706-278-5323
afa@americanfloor.org;
www.americanfloor.org
Social Media: Facebook, RSS

Wanda J. Ellis, Executive Director

Promotes the industry's products and services to the world, and educates the members and others through seminars, press releases, and trade shows.
Founded in: 1979

14050 **American Lighting Association**
2050 N Stemmons Freeway
Ste 10046
Dallas, TX 75207

214-698-9898
800-605-4448;
www.americanlightingassoc.com
Social Media: Facebook, YouTube

Ray S. Angelo, Chair
Eric Jacobson, CAE, President/CEO
W. Lawrence Lauck, Vice President, Communications
Michael Weems, Vice President, Government Affairs
Beth Bentley, CMP, LA, Director of Confrences

A trade association uniting lighting; component manufacturers, showrooms/distributors, manufacturer representatives; industry related companies dedicated to providing quality residential illumination in the U.S., Canada and the Caribbean.
700 Members
Founded in: 1945

14051 **American Society of Interior Designers**
608 Massachusetts Avenue NE
Washington, DC 20002-6006

202-546-3480; *Fax:* 202-546-3240;
www.asid.org
Social Media: Facebook, Twitter, LinkedIn, Stagram

Thom Banks, COO
Randy Fiser, EVP/ CEO
Kevin Mulavaney, Marketing/Communications
Don Davis, Government/Public Affairs
Rick Peluso, CFO

The American Society of Interior Designers (ASID) is a community of people-designers, industry representatives, educators and students committed to interior design. Through education, knowledge sharing, advocacy, community building and outreach, the Society strives to advance the interior design profession and, in the process, to demonstrate and celebrate the power of design to positively change people's lives.
34500 Members
Founded in: 1975

14052 **Association of University Interior Design**
1652 Cross Center Drive
Norman, OK 73019-5050

Fax: 405-325-4164; www.auid.org

Debra Barresse, President
Sara Powell, First VP
Debi Miller, Second VP
Susan Carlyle, Secretary
Lisa Kring, Treasurer

Provides a network for individuals who work within institutions of higher education and to promote activities designed to benefit its members through education, research, and communication.
Founded in: 1979

14053 **Association of the Wall and Ceiling Industry**
513 West Broad Street
Suite 210
Falls Church, VA 22046

703-538-1600; *Fax:* 703-534-8307
info@awci.org; www.awci.org
Social Media: Facebook, Twitter, LinkedIn, YouTube

Scott Casabona, President
John Hinson, VP
Mike Taylor, Treasurer
Ed Sellers, Secretary
Steven A. Etkin, Executive Vice President/CEO

Represents acoustic systems, ceiling systems, drywall systems, exterior insulation and finishing systms, fireproofing, flooring systems, insulation, and stucco contractors, suppliers and manufacturers and those in allied trades.
2400 Members
Founded in: 1918
Mailing list available for rent

14054 **Carpet Cushion Council**
5103 Brandywine Drive
Eagleville, PA 19043

484-687-5170; *Fax:* 610-885-5131;
www.carpetcushion.org

Chris Bradley, President
Gary Lanser, Vice President
Bob Ambrose, Secretary
Mark Vitale, Treasurer
G. William Haines, Executive Director

Encourages distribution and use of seperate carpet cushions. Works with regulatory agencies at the national, state and local levels.
33 Members
Founded in: 1976

14055 **Carpet and Rug Institute**
100 South Hamilton Street
P.O. Box 2048
Dalton, GA 30720

706-278-3176; *Fax:* 706-278-8835;
www.carpet-rug.org
Social Media: Facebook, Twitter, LinkedIn, YouTube, Google+

Jim Jolly, CEO
Georgina Sikorski, Executive Director
Werner Braun, President

CRI is a nonprofit trade association representing the manufacturers of more than 95 percent of all carpet made in the United States, as well as service providers and their suppliers.To help increase consumers' satisfaction with carpet and to show them how carpet creates a better environment, they coordinate with other segments of the industry, such as installers, distributors, and retailers.
115 Members
Founded in: 1969

14056 **Certified Interior Decorators International, Inc.**
649 SE Central Pkwy.
Stuart, FL 34994

772-287-1855
800-624-0093; *Fax:* 772-287-0398;
www.cidinternational.org
Social Media: Facebook, Twitter, LinkedIn

Ron Renner, President

Worldwide certifying body and professional association for interior decorators.

14057 **Council for Interior Design Accreditation**
206 Grandville Avenue
Suite 350
Grand Rapids, MI 49503-4014

616-458-0400; *Fax:* 616-458-0460
info@accredit-id.org; www.accredit-id.org
Social Media: Facebook

Pamela K. Evans, Ph.D., FIDEC, Chair
Jan Johnson, FIIDA, Industry Rep.
Secretary-Treasurer
Holly Mattson, Executive Director
Laura Hozeska, Office Manager
Stacy I. Peck, Director of Public Relations

Leads the interior design profession to excellence by setting standards and accrediting academic programs.
135 Members
Founded in: 1970

14058 **Custom Electronic Design & Installation Association**
7150 Winton Drive
Suite 300
Indianapolis, IN 46268

317-328-4336
800-669-5329; *Fax:* 317-735-4012
info@cedia.org; www.cedia.net
Social Media: Facebook, Twitter, RSS

Larry Pexton, Chairman
Dennis Erskine, Chairman Elect
David Humphries, Treasurer
Richard Millson, Secretary
Vin Bruno, CEO

The Custom Electronic Design & Installation Association (CEDIA) is an international trade association of companies that specialize in planning and installing electronic systems for the home. CEDIA provides educational conferences, industry professional training, and certification focused on the installation and integration of residential electronic systems that consumers use to enhance their lifestyles.
3,500 Members
Mailing list available for rent

14059 **Designer Society of America**

866-721-7857
support@dsasociety.org; www.dsasociety.org

The Society offers networking and showcasing opportunities for practicing designers.

14060 **Foundation for Design Integrity**
1950 N Main Street
Suite 139
Salinas, CA 93906

650-326-1867; *Fax:* 408-449-7040;
www.ffdi.org

Justin Binnix, President
Eleanor McKay, Chairman
Susan E. Farley, Esquire

Promotes original design and to fight the unethical and illegal practice of manufacturing knockoffs. Honors those who conceive, design, engineer and develop innovative new products for the Interior and Architectural Design Community and their clients.
150+ Members
Founded in: 1994

14061 **Home Fashion Products Association**
355 Lexington Ave.
Suite 1500
New York, NY 10017

212-297-2122;
www.homefashionproducts.com

Association for the promotion of manufacturers of bedding, window, floor and wall coverings,

kitchen textiles and allied home fashion products.
Founded in: 1996

14062 Illuminating Engineering Society
120 Wall St
17th Floor
New York, NY 10005-4001

212-248-5000; *Fax:* 212-248-5017
ies@ies.org; www.iesna.org

Daniel Salinas, President
Clayton Gordon, Marketing Manager
William Hanley, Executive Vice President
Calyton Gordon, Marketing Manager
Nick Bleeker, Treasurer

To advance knowledge and disseminate information for the improvement of the lighted environment to the benefit of society. Publishes a monthly magazine.
8500 Members
Founded in: 1906

14063 Institute of Inspection Cleaning and Restoration Certification
4317 NE Thurston Way
Ste 200
Vancouver, WA 98662

360-693-5675
800-835-4624; *Fax:* 360-693-4858
info@iicrc.org; www.iicrc.org
Social Media: Facebook, Twitter, LinkedIn, Google+

Patrick Winters, President & CEO
Hank Unck, 1st Vice President
Pete Duncanson, 2nd Vice President
Norm Maia, Treasurer
Kevin Pearson, Secretary

Sets standards of skill and ethics in fabric restoration industry. Works with regulatory bodies to develop proficiency standards and issues certification.
1.6M Members
Founded in: 1972

14064 Interior Design Educators Council
One Parkview Plaza
Suite 800
Oakbrook Terrace, IL 60181

630-544-5057; *Fax:* 317-280-8527
info@idec.org; www.idec.org
Social Media: Facebook, Twitter, LinkedIn, YouTube, Google+, Yahoo, Flick

Cynthia Mohr, President
Katherine Ankerson, Past President
Migette Kaup, President Elect
Cindy Martimo, Secretary/Treasurer
Jill Pable, IDEC Director

Dedicated to the advancement of education and research in interior design. IDEC fosters exchange of information, improvement of educational standards, and development of the body of knowledge relative to the quality of life and human performance in the interior environment.
Founded in: 1963

14065 Interior Design Society
164 S. Main St.
Suite 404
High Point, NC 27260

336-884-4437; *Fax:* 336-885-3291
info@interiordesignsociety.org;
www.interiordesignsociety.org
Social Media: Facebook, Twitter, LinkedIn, YouTube, Blogspot, Instagram,

Bruce Knott, President
Anna Mavrakis, Past President
Jan Cregier, Vice President
Kimberly Joi McDonald, Treasurer/Secretary
Snoa Garrigan, Executive Director

The largest design organization exclusively dedicated to serving the residential interior design industry. Promote retail interior design, emphasizing education and skills improvement.
2500 Members
Founded in: 1973

14066 International Feng Shui Guild
705-B SE Melody Ln.
Suite 106
Lees Summit, MO 64063

816-246-1898
office@ifsguild.org
ifsguild.org

Mia Staysko, Chair
Bridget Saraka, Chief Executive Officer

Professional organization for Feng Shui consultants of all perspectives.

14067 International Furnishings and Design Association
610 Freedom Business Center
Suite 110
King of Prussia, PA 19406

610-992-0011; *Fax:* 610-992-0021
info@ifda.com; www.ifda.com
Social Media: Facebook, Twitter, LinkedIn

Diane Nicolson, FIFDA, President
Linda Kulla, FIFDA, Treasurer
Jennifer Jones, MPA, Executive Director
Diane Fairburn, Immediate Past President
Athena Charis, Immediate Past Treasurer

The only all-industry association whose members provide services and products to the furnishings and design industry. IFDA is the driving force, through its programs and services, to enhance the professionalism and strature of the industry worlwide.
1400 Members
Founded in: 1947

14068 National Association of Decorative Fabric Distributors
One Windsor Cove
Suite 305
Columbia, SC 29223

800-445-8629; *Fax:* 803-765-0860
info@nadfd.com; www.nadfd.com

Ted Sargetakis, President
Debbye Lustig, Vice President, Membership Chair
Frank Governal, 1st Vice Presiden
Dee Duncan, Director
Kathy Gowdy, Secreatry-Treasurer

Comprised of the leading fabric distributors who reach the reupholsterers, made to order drapery and home decorator markets, and more than fifty of their major suppliers, fabric mills, fabric finishers, manufacturers of upholstery and drapery supplies.
75 Members
Founded in: 1968

14069 National Council for Interior Design Qualification, Inc.
1602 L Street, NW
Suite 200
Washington, DC 20036-5681

202-721-0220; *Fax:* 202-721-0221
inquiries@ncidqexam.org; www.ncidq.org
Social Media: Facebook, Twitter, LinkedIn, Pinterest

Laurie McRae, President
David Hanson, President Elect
Victoria Horobin, Past President
Carol Williams-Nickelson, Executive Director
Lola Liao, Director of Finance & Admin.

Serves to identify to the public those interior designers who have met the minimum standards for professional practice by passing the NCIDQ examination in addition to protecting the public by identifying those individuals who are competent to practice interior design.
10000 Members
Founded in: 1974

14070 National Guild of Professional Paperhangers, Inc.
136 S Keowee Street
Dayton, OH 45402

937-222-6477
800-254-6477; *Fax:* 937-222-5794
ngpp@ngpp.org; www.ngpp.org
Social Media: Facebook, Twitter, LinkedIn

Kimberly Fantaci, Executive Director
Bob Banker, Secretary
Cyndi Green, President
Carl Bergaman, Treasurer
Vincent LaRusso, Vice President

Promotes products, upgrades skills of paperhangers and encourages good business ethics. Holds workshops and seminars.
650 Members
Founded in: 1974

14071 National Home Furnishings Association
3910 Tinsley Drive
Suite 101
High Point, NC 27265-3610

336-886-6100
800-422-3778; *Fax:* 916-784-7697
info@nhfa.org; www.nhfa.org
Social Media: Facebook, Twitter, LinkedIn, YouTube

Rick Howard, Chairman
Marty Cramer, President
Jeff Child, President Elect
Steve Kidder, Vice President
Jim Fee, Secretary/Treasurer

The nation's largest organization devoted specifically to the needs and interests of home furnishings retailers. Also to provide members with the information, education, products and services they need to remain successful.
2800 Members
Founded in: 2013

14072 North American Association of Floor Covering Distributors
330 N. Wabash Ave.
Suite 2000
Chicago, IL 60611-4267

312-321-6836
800-383-3091; *Fax:* 312-673-6962
info@nafcd.org; www.nafcd.org
Social Media: LinkedIn, YouTube

Rosana Chaidez, President
Heidi Cronin Mandell, Vice President
Geoff Work, Treasurer
Torrey Jaeckle, President Elect
Craig Folven, Immediate Past President

Organized to foster trade and commerce for those having a business, financial, or professional interest as wholesale distributors or manufacturers of floor coverings and allied products.
557 Members
Founded in: 1971

14073 Paint and Decorating Retailers Association
1401 Triad Center Drive
St Peters, MO 63376

636-326-2636
800-737-0107; *Fax:* 636-229-4750
info@pdra.org; www.pdra.org
Social Media: Facebook, Twitter, LinkedIn

Phil Merlo, President
Bahia Taylor, VP
Craig Bond, Treasurer

Jeff Baggaley, Past President
Dan Simon, Executive Vice President/Publisher

PDRA serves the independent dealer through education, membership benefits and trade shows. The Board of Director's initiative to bring top-quality, efficient education to all independent dealers has resulted in development of a new online seminar. The PDRA Coatings Specialist course eliminates the time and expense of traveling to a seminar site. This new course can be taken right in the store, during slow times or at the dealer's convenience.
1500 Members
Founded in: 1947

14074 Painting and Decorating Contractors of America
2316 Millpark Drive
Maryland Heights, MO 63043

314-514-7322
800-332-7322; *Fax:* 314-890-2068
bhoran@pdca.org; www.pdca.org
Social Media: Facebook, Twitter, LinkedIn, YouTube

Dave Ryker, BOD Chair
Tony Severino, BOD Vice Chair
Mark Adams, BOD Treasurer
Richard Bright, National Sales Director
Chris Shank, Education Manager

PDCA exists to lead the industry by providing quality products, programs, services, and opportunities essential to the success of our members.
5M Members
Founded in: 1884
Mailing list available for rent

14075 Professional Picture Framers Association
2282 Springport Road
Suite F
Jackson, MI 49202

517-788-8100
800-762-9287; *Fax:* 517-788-8371
info@ppfa.com; www.ppfa.com
Social Media: Facebook, Twitter, LinkedIn

John Pruitt, President
Elaine Truman, Administrative
Jeff Frazine, Trade Exhibit Sales
Nick Shaver, Membership
Sheila Pursglove, FMO

An international trade association for the art and framing industry. Supporting a membership of custom picture framers, art galleries, manufacturers, and distibutors.
3000+ Members
Founded in: 1971

14076 Society of Glass & Ceramic Decorated Products
PO Box 2489
Zanesville, OH 43702

740-588-9882; *Fax:* 740-588-0245
sgcd@sgcd.org; www.sgcd.org

Mark Kelly, President
Walter Lumley, VP
Nancy Klinefelter, Secretary/Treasurer

Provides decorating professionals with a competitive edge in business by providing opporotunities for networking to learn about new decorating technologies and techniques.
525 Members

14077 Window Coverings Association of America
P.O. Box 731
Wake Forest, NC 27588

919-263-9850
888-298-9222; *Fax:* 919-426-2047
solutions@wcaa.org; www.wcaa.org
Social Media: Facebook, LinkedIn, YouTube, Google+

Michele Williams, President
Julie A. Wood, VP
Sandra VanSickle, Treasurer
Ronica VanGelder, Secretary
Linda Principe, Past President

The only national non-profit trade association dedicated to the retail window covering industry and to the dealers, decorators, and workrooms that are our members.
1200 Members
Founded in: 1987

Newsletters

14078 Architectural Lighting
1515 Broadway
34th Floor
New York, NY 10036-8901

212-360-0660
847-763-9050; *Fax:* 646-654-4484
archl@halldata.com; www.archlighting.com

Gary Gyss, Group Publisher
Emilie Worth Sommerhoff, Editor-in-Chief
Elizabeth Donoff, Managing Editor
Carolyn Cunningham, Brand Manager
Cliff Smith, Sales Manager

Showcases the application of lighting in architectural and interior design applications.
Circulation: 25,000
Founded in: 1964

14079 Installer
National Guild of Professional Paperhangers
136 S Keowee Street
Dayton, OH 45402

937-222-6477
800-254-6477; *Fax:* 937-222-5794
ngpp@ngpp.org; www.ngpp.org

Elsie Kaptetna CP, President
Phil Curtis CP, First VP
Vincent Larusso CP, Second VP

Promotes products, upgrades skills of paperhangers and encourages good business ethics.
Frequency: Bimonthly
Circulation: 900

14080 Mirror News
Market Power
103 2nd Street N
Hopkins, MN 55343-9276

E-Mail: feedback@mirror.co.uk; www.mirror.co.uk

Wil Tiller, Publisher
Paul Hodd, Head of Digital

Offers interior design news and developments for professionals in the industry.
Cost: $16.00
24 Pages
Frequency: Monthly

14081 National Guild of Professional Paperhangers
136 S Keowee Street
Dayton, OH 45402

937-222-6477
800-254-6477; *Fax:* 937-222-5794
ngpp@ngpp.org; www.ngpp.org

Kim Fantaci, Executive VP
Joseph Parker, President

Accepts advertising.
16 Pages
Founded in: 1974

14082 NewsFash
American Society of Interior Designers
608 Massachusetts Avenue NE
Washington, DC 20002-6006

202-546-3480; *Fax:* 202-546-3240
asid@asid.org;
www.asid.org/designer/ASID+Member+Benefits.htm

Julie Warren, Editor
Jennifer Lipner, Associate Editor
Rick McCosh, Director of Chapter Services
Thom Banks, COO
Rick Peluso, CFO

Bi-weekly newsletter published by the American Society of Interior Designers (ASID) that provides need-to-know design and Society news delivered biweekly. Through education, knowledge sharing, advocacy, community building and outreach, the Society strives to advance the interior design profession and, in the process, to demonstrate and celebrate the power of design to positively chang
Frequency: Bi-Weekly
Founded in: 1975
Mailing list available for rent

Magazines & Journals

14083 ASID ICON
American Society of Interior Designers
608 Massachusetts Avenue NE
Washington, DC 20002-6006

202-546-3480; *Fax:* 202-546-3240
asid@asid.org;
www.asid.org/designer/ASID+Member+Benefits.htm

Julie Warren, Editor
Jennifer Lipner, Associate Editor
Rick McCosh, Director of Chapter Services
Thom Banks, COO
Rick Peluso, CFO

ASID ICON, the magazine of the American Society of Interior Designers/ASID, provides readers with success strategies bi-monthly. ASID is a community of people-designers, industry representatives, educators and students committed to interior design. Through education, knowledge sharing, advocacy, community building and outreach, the Society strives to advance the interior design profession and, in the process, to demonstrate and celebrate the power of design to positively change people's lives.
Frequency: Monthly
Circulation: 40,000
Founded in: 1975
Mailing list available for rent

14084 Better Homes and Gardens
Meredith Corporation
1716 Locust St
Des Moines, IA 50309-3023

515-284-3000
800-678-8091; *Fax:* 515-284-3371
shareholderhelp@meredith.com;
www.meredith.com

Stephen M Lacy, CEO
Daniel M. Lagani, V.P./Publisher
Karol DeWulf Nickell, Editor in Chief

Ideas and how-to information on both new and remodeled kitchen and bath.
Cost: $11.00
Frequency: Monthly
Circulation: 7.6 mill
Founded in: 1902

14085 Country Home Product Guide
Meredith Corporation

1716 Locust St
Des Moines, IA 50309-3023

515-284-2015; *Fax:* 515-284-3684
shareholderhelp@meredith.com;
www.meredith.com

David Kahn, Publisher

Offers information on residential projects focusing on innovative design work for homes with a country motif.
Frequency: Monthly

14086 Decor
Pfingsten Publishing
330 N 5th Street
Saint Louis, MO 63102-2036

314-421-5445
800-867-9285; *Fax:* 314-421-1070;
www.decormagazine.com

Gary S Goldman, Publisher
Alice C Gibson, Editor

In the business of furnishing helpful information, education, and marketing services that will assist art and framing retailers, distributors, and wholesalers in the manufacture and sale of their products and services, and in the successful management of their business. Every article of Decor must give art and framing retailers helpful information that they can use to make their business stronger.
Cost: $20.00
Frequency: 13 per year
Circulation: 27,000

14087 Design Solutions Magazine
Architectural Woodwork Institute
46179 Westlake Drive
Suite 120
Potomac Falls, VA 20165-5874

571-323-3636; *Fax:* 571-323-3630
awiweb@vt.edu; www.awinet.org

David Ritchey, Editor
Judith Durham, Executive VP
Matthew Lundahl, President
Randy Jensen, Vice President
Bruce Spitz, Treasurer

Covers new commercial construction, as well as renovation. Updates on doors, paneling, laminatem plywood, architectural hardware and finishes.
Cost: $25.00
Frequency: Quarterly
Circulation: 25000
Mailing list available for rent

14088 Designers West
Designers World Corporation
8914 Santa Monica Boulevard
Los Angeles, CA 90069-4902

213-748-8291; *Fax:* 213-748-0039

Carol Soucek King, Editor
Rafael Nadal, President

For interior designers, architects and other design professionals involved in residential, office and hospitality projects. Accepts advertising.
Cost: $30.00
120 Pages
Frequency: Monthly
Founded in: 1953

14089 Designing with Tile and Stone
Tile & Stone
20 Beekman Pl
20th Floor
New York, NY 10022-8043

212-929-0500; *Fax:* 212-376-7723;
www.ashlee.com

Michelle Tillou, Owner

Articles on design, selection, installation and maintenance.
Frequency: Quarterly
Circulation: 12000

14090 Donna Dewberry's One-Day Decorating
F+W Media
38 E. 29th Street
New York, NY 10016

212-447-1400; *Fax:* 212-447-5231
contact_us@fwmedia.com;
www.fwpublications.com
Social Media: Facebook, Twitter, LinkedIn

Colleen Cannon, Publisher
David Nussbaum, CEO
Jim Ogle, Chief Financial Officer
Chad Phelps, Chief Digital Officer
Stacie Berger, Communications Director

A how-to magazine for decorative painters, crafters, and do-it-yourself home decorators. Its goal is to inspire anyone interested in embellishing their home, and it features easy-to-complete, step-by-step project ideas using decorative painting, stamping, faux finishing, stenciling, and other crafting techniques.
Cost: $27.00
76 Pages
Frequency: Monthly
Circulation: 100000
Founded in: 1945
Mailing list available for rent

14091 Eye on Design
American Society of Interior Designers
608 Massachusetts Avenue NE
Washington, DC 20002-6006

202-546-3480; *Fax:* 202-546-3240
asid@asid.org;
www.asid.org/designer/ASID+Member+Benefits.htm

Julie Warren, Editor
Jennifer Lipner, Associate Editor
Rick McCosh, Director of Chapter Services
Thom Banks, COO
Rick Peluso, CFO

Eye on Design, provided by the American Society of Interior Designers\ASID, focuses on industry news and developments and is delivered electronically on a weekly basis. Through education, knowledge sharing, advocacy, community building and outreach, the Society strives to advance the interior design profession and, in the process, to demonstrate and celebrate the power of design to positively change people's lives.
Founded in: 1975
Mailing list available for rent

14092 Facilities Design & Management
1515 Broadway
34th Floor
New York, NY 10036-8901

212-840-0595
800-950-1314; *Fax:* 212-302-6273

Anne Fallucchi, Editor-in-Chief

Covers all aspects of the planning, design and management of facilities for corporate offices and related facilities, health care, government, hospitality and education.
Frequency: Monthly

14093 Floor Care Professional
Vacuum Dealers Trade Association
2724 2nd Ave
Des Moines, IA 50313-4933

515-282-9101
800-367-5651; *Fax:* 515-282-4483
mail@vdta.com; www.vdta.com

Charles Dunham, Owner
Beth Vitiritto, Managing Editor
Rob Heater, Managing Editor
Sherry Graham, Administrative Assistant
Judy Patterson, Vice President

Offers news and information for the distributers and dealers of vacuum and sewing machines.
Cost: $100.00
Frequency: Monthly
Circulation: 18000
Founded in: 1981
Printed in 4 colors on glossy stock

14094 Flora-Line
Berry Hill Press
7336 Berry Hill Drive
Palos Verdes Estates, CA 90275-4404

310-377-7040

Dody Lyness, Editor

Targeted to the home-based business person engaged in dried floral design. Its format keeps readers abreast of the floral trends in herbal growing and the most modern techniques for drying and designing with flowering herbs. Accepts advertising.
Cost: $16.95
20 Pages
Frequency: Quarterly
Circulation: 1,000
Founded in: 1981

14095 Furniture Style
400 Knightsbridge Parkway
Lincolnshire, IL 60069-3613

847-634-4339
800-621-2845; *Fax:* 847-634-4379
info@vancepublishing.com;
www.vancepublishing.com

Michael R Reckling, Publisher
Judy Riggs, Director
Steve Chair, Marketing Manager
Douglas A. Riemer, Circulation Manager
William C Vance, Chairman
Cost: $49.95
Frequency: Monthly
Circulation: 25000
Founded in: 1937

14096 HOW Design Ideas at Work
F&W Publications
4700 E Galbraith Rd
Cincinnati, OH 45236-2726

513-531-2690
800-333-1115; *Fax:* 513-531-1843
editorial@howdesign.com;
www.fwpublications.com

David Nussbaum, CEO
Bryn Mooth, Chief Financial Officer
Jim Ogle, Chief Financial Officer
Kate Rados, Marketing Director
Stacie Berger, Communications Director

HOW reaches visual communicators, including art directors, graphic designers, type designers, typographers, illustrators, advertising and sales promotion managers, and other design-minded executives; also manufacturers and suppliers of graphic arts products and services.
Cost: $29.96
194 Pages
Frequency: Monthly
Circulation: 39946
ISSN: 0886-0483
Founded in: 1990
Printed in 4 colors on glossy stock

14097 Home Furnishings Executive
305 W High Ave
Suite 400
High Point, NC 27260-4950

336-885-6981
800-888-9590; *Fax:* 336-885-4424

14098 Home Lighting & Accessories
Doctorow Communications

1011 Clifton Ave
Clifton, NJ 07013-3518

973-779-1600; *Fax:* 973-779-3242;
www.homelighting.com

Jeffrey Doctorow, President
Cost: $15.00
Frequency: Monthly
Founded in: 1953

14099 Homeworld Business
45 Research Way
Suite 106
East Setauket, NY 11733

631-246-9300; *Fax:* 631-246-9496;
www.homeworldbusiness.com

Ian Gittlitz, Publisher/Editor-in-Chief
Peter Giannetti, Editor
Bill McLoughlin, Executive Editor
Peter Chamberlin, Circulation Manager
Hope Rosenzweig, Classified Advertising
Cost: $185.00

14100 House Beautiful
959 8th Ave
New York, NY 10019-3737

212-649-2098; *Fax:* 212-765-3528;
www.housebeautiful.com

Kate Kelly Smith, Publisher
Victor F Ganzi, CEO
Bruce Paisner, VP
Michael A Hurley, Marketing Director
Cost: $19.97
Frequency: Monthly
Circulation: 854627
Founded in: 1887

14101 Interior Design
Reed Business Information
360 Park Avenue South
17th floor
New York, NY 10010

212-772-8300; *Fax:* 630-288-8686
custserv@espcomp.com;
www.reedbusiness.com
Social Media: Facebook, Twitter, LinkedIn, RSS

Lawrence S Reed
Woody Goldfien, Owner
Jim Casella, CEO

Offers information on quality residential and contract design work. Recent issues include corporate offices, remodeling/restoration, kitchen and bath design, health care and hospitality.
Cost: $64.95
250 Pages
Frequency: Monthly
Circulation: 59,000
Founded in: 1932
Printed in 4 colors on glossy stock

14102 Interiors and Sources
840 US Highway 1
Suite 330
North Pal Beach, FL 33408

561-627-3393; *Fax:* 561-694-6578;
www.isdesignet.com

Robert Nieminen, Editor
Guy De Silva, Publisher
Charlotte Vann, Circulation Manager
Adam Moore, Managing Editor

Offers national commercial and residential design work articles. Emphasizes design solutions and focuses on challenges encountered by designers.
Cost: $27.00
Frequency: Monthly
Circulation: 28,000
Founded in: 1990

14103 Kitchen & Bath Design News
Cygnus Publishing
PO Box 803
Fort Atkinson, WI 53538-0803

920-000-1111; *Fax:* 920-563-1699;
www.cygnusb2b.com

John French, CEO
Eliot Sefrin, Director of Public Relations
Kathy Scott, Director of Public Relations
Paul Bonaiuto, CFO

Offers articles for kitchen and bath dealers, interior designers and architects.
Frequency: Monthly
Circulation: 50000
Founded in: 1966

14104 Laminating Design & Technology
Cygnus Publishing
PO Box 803
Fort Atkinson, WI 53538-0803

920-000-1111; *Fax:* 920-563-1699;
www.cygnusb2b.com

John French, CEO
Rich Reiff, Director of Public Relations
Kathy Scott, Director of Public Relations
Paul Bonaiuto, CFO

Global design and color trends, as well as surfacing solutions for furniture architecture and interior design. Focuses on surface design, performance and application.
Cost: $30.00
44 Pages
Frequency: Monthly
Circulation: 40006
Founded in: 1937

14105 Lighting Dimensions
Primedia
PO Box 12901
Shawnee Mission, KS 66282-2901

913-341-1300; *Fax:* 913-514-6895

Eric Jacobson, Senior VP
David Barbour, Editorial Director
Cost: $34.97
Frequency: Monthly

14106 Metropolis
Bellerophon Publications
61 W 23rd St
23rd Street
New York, NY 10010-4246

212-627-9977
800-344-3046; *Fax:* 212-627-9988
info@metropolismag.com;
www.metropolismag.com

Horace Havemeyer, Publisher
Susan S Szenasy, Editor-in-Chief
Denise Csaky, Marketing Director
Tamara Costa, Advertising Manager
Peter Sangiorgio, Circulation Controller

The only magazine that covers all facets of design: architecture, interiors, furniture, preservation, urban design, graphics and crafts.
Cost: $32.95
Circulation: 54000
Founded in: 1980

14107 Michaels Create!
F+W Media
38 E. 29th Streett
New York, NY 10016

212-447-1400; *Fax:* 212-447-5231
contact_us@fwmedia.com;
www.fwpublications.com

Debbie Knauer, Publisher
Jane Beard, Editor

Features contemporary designs reflecting the latest trends with clear instructions. The home decorating, fashion, and gift ideas will inspire experienced crafters as well as seasonal crafters to explore new possibilities. Step-by-step instructions, tips, and techniques will engage crafters of all ages - including kids - with the creative skills of crafting to be enjoyed as a year-round activity.
Cost: $21.97
116 Pages
Frequency: Monthly
Circulation: 24991
Founded in: 1952

14108 Midwest Retailer
8528 Columbus Ave S
Bloomington, MN 55420-2460

952-854-7610; *Fax:* 952-854-6460

Joan Thomasberg, Owner
Cost: $10.00
38588 Pages
Circulation: 5000
Founded in: 1972
Printed in 2 colors on newsprint stock

14109 NHFA Trade Show
National Home Furnishings Association
3910 Tinsley Drive
Suite 101
Highpoint, NC 27265-3610

336-886-6100
800-888-9590; *Fax:* 336-801-6102
info@nhfa.org; www.nhfa.org

Steve DeHaan, Executive VP
Karin Mayfield, Senior Director for Membership
Frequency: Annual

14110 National Floor Trends
Business News Publishing Company
22801 Ventura Blvd
Suite 113
Woodland Hills, CA 91364-1230

818-224-8035; *Fax:* 818-224-8042
privacy@BNPMedia.com; www.bnpmedia.com

Phil Johnson, Publisher
Rick Arvidson, Director

For interior designers.
Frequency: Monthly
Founded in: 1952

14111 Paint & Decorating Retailer Magazine
Paint and Decorating Retailers Association
1401 Triad Center Dr
St. Peters, MO 63376-7353

636-326-2636
800-737-0107; *Fax:* 636-229-4750
info@pdra.org; www.pdra.org

Dan Simon, Executive VP/Publisher
Tina Sullivan, Dir Membership/Education/Tradeshows
Diane Capuano, Managing Editor
Renee Nolte, Director, Finance/Human Resources
Tony Sarantakis, Account Executive

Monthly trade magazine dedicated to the informational needs of paint and decorating store owners, managers and employees.
1500 Members
Frequency: Annual May
Circulation: 26,000+
Founded in: 1947

14112 Panel World
Hatton-Brown Publishers
225 Hanrick Street
PO Box 2268
Montgomery, AL 36102

334-834-1170; *Fax:* 334-834-4525
rich@hattonbrown.com;
www.hattonbrown.com

Rich Donnell, Editor
David Knight, Co-Owner

Rhonda Thomas, Circulation Director
Dianne Sullivan, Chief Operating Officer
Phil Grissett, Operations Manager
Cost: $30.00
Frequency: Monthly
Circulation: 12754
ISSN: 1048-826X
Founded in: 1948
Printed in on glossy stock

14113 Perspective
13-500 Merchandise Mart
Chicago, IL 60654-1104

312-467-1950
888-799-4432; *Fax:* 312-467-0779;
www.iida.org

John Lijewski, President
Cheryl Durst, Executive Vice President
Jocelyn Pysarchuk, Managing Director, Communications
Suzanne Murphy, Director, Membership & Chapter
Robert Friedman, Editor
International magazine of IIDA.
Cost: $30.00
Frequency: Monthly
Circulation: 10000
Founded in: 1994
Mailing list available for rent: 10000 names
Printed in on matte stock

14114 Picture Framing Magazine
Hobby Publications
225 Gordon's Corner Road
PO Box 420
Manalapan, NJ 07726

732-446-4900
800-969-7176; *Fax:* 732-446-5488
gcoughlin@hobbypub.com;
www.pictureframingmagazine.com

Bruce Gherman, Executive Publisher
Anne Vazquez, Editor
Deborah Salmon, Circulation Director
Alan Pegler, Production Manager of Advertising
News and trends in the picture framing trade, marketing strategies, and economic developments.
Cost: $20.00
Frequency: Monthly
Circulation: 23000
ISSN: 1052-9977
Founded in: 1995

14115 Progressive Architecture
Progressive Scale
382 S Beach Avenue
Old Greenwich, CT 06870-2223

203-792-2854; *Fax:* 203-748-2456

Valerie Kanter Sisca, Managing Editor
This magazine has been covering the fields of architecture and interiors for more than 60 years and publishes projects that illustrate both current trends and innovative design solutions.
Cost: $48.00
Frequency: Monthly
Circulation: 65,000

14116 Upholstery Journal
Industrial Fabrics Association International
1801 County Road B W
Roseville, MN 55113-4061

651-222-2508
800-225-4324; *Fax:* 651-631-9334
generalinfo@ifai.com; www.ifai.com

Stephen Warner, CEO
JoAnne Farris, Marketing Director
Serves as the industry resource for after-market furniture, marine and automotive upholstery. Provides education for both the craft and business of upholstery.
Frequency: Bimonthly
Circulation: 5,000

14117 Wall Paper
Waldman Publishers
570 Fashion Ave
New York, NY 10018-1603

212-730-9590; *Fax:* 212-391-6610

Edited for wallcovering retailers and the wallcovering industry. Accepts advertising.
Cost: $25.00
40 Pages
Frequency: Monthly
Circulation: 18,000
Founded in: 1980

14118 Wallcoverings, Windows and Interior Fashion
Cygnus Publishing
445 Broad Hollow Road
Melville, NY 11747-3669

631-845-2700; *Fax:* 631-845-2723;
www.cygnuspub.com

Paul Bonaiuto, CFO
Kathy Scott, Director of Public Relations

14119 Walls & Ceilings
Business News Publishing Company
2401 W. Big Beaver Rd
Suite 700
Troy, MI 48084

248-362-3700; www.bnpmedia.com
Social Media: Facebook, Twitter, LinkedIn

Katie Rotella, Manager
Information regarding management, building methods, technology, government regulations, consumer trends, and product information for the contractor involved in exterior finishes, waterproofing, insulation, metal framing, drywall, fireproofing, partitions, stucco and plaster.
Cost: $49.00
140 Pages
Frequency: Monthly
Circulation: 32800
Founded in: 1939
Printed in 4 colors

Trade Shows

14120 Accent on Design
George Little Management
10 Bank Street
Suite 1200
White Plains, NY 10606-1954

914-486-6070
800-272-7469; *Fax:* 914-948-2867;
www.nyigf.com

George Little II, President
Elizabeth Murphy, Show Manager
370 booths of the latest and most innovative gift lines such as decorative accessories and home furnishings.
50M Attendees
Frequency: August
Founded in: 1984

14121 Aidex: Asian International Interior Design Exposition
Reed Exhibition Companies
383 Main Avenue
PO Box 6059
Norwalk, CT 06851

203-840-4800; *Fax:* 203-840-9628

Audio visual systems, bathroom equipment, supplies and services, plus interior decorations. More than 22 exhibitors, for trade professionals.
Frequency: Annual

14122 American Society of Interior Designers National Conference
American Society of Interior Designers
608 Massachusetts Avenue NE
Washington, DC 20002-6006

202-546-3480; *Fax:* 202-546-3240
asid@asid.org; www.asid.org

Randy Fiser, Executive Vice President/CEO
Thom Banks, COO
Rick Peluso, CFO
Deanna Waldron, Government/Public Affairs
Willie Pugh, Information Technology
Workshop and annual conference with 100 manufacturers and suppliers. Exhibits include interior design merchandise, wall coverings, laminates, lighting fixtures, plumbing fixtures, carpets, furniture, office systems and fabrics.
3000 Attendees
Frequency: Annual
Founded in: 1975
Mailing list available for rent

14123 Dickens Christmas Show & Festival
Leisure Time Unlimited
708 Main Street
Myrtle Beach, SC 29577

843-448-9483; *Fax:* 843-362-6153
dickensshow@sc.rr.com;
www.dickenschristmasshow.com

Offers a unique blend of craft and gift exhibits presented in a 19th century setting
25000 Attendees
Frequency: Annual November

14124 Evergreen Home Show
Westlake Promotions
8740 Golden Gardens Dr. NW
Seattle, WA 98117

206-783-5957; *Fax:* 206-708-7406;
www.westlakepromo.com
Social Media: Facebook, Twitter

Bill Bradley, VP
Sam Scott, Marketing Director, Operations
Michael R. Scott, President
See what's new and what you can do for your home. Fresh ideas and practical advice from our remodeling and construction specialists. See demonstrations on how to make dramatic improvements to your home.
7500 Attendees

14125 Fall Decor
Paint & Decorating Retailers Association
403 Axminister Drive
Fenton, MO 63026

636-326-2636; *Fax:* 314-991-5039
info@pdra.org; www.pdra.org

Tina Sullivan, Show Coordinator
Kathy Witmeyer, Director of Trade Shows
Annual show of 350 manufacturers, suppliers and distributors of decorating and office products and related equipment, supplies and services.
4000 Attendees
Frequency: October

14126 Galeria
Decor Magazine

330 N 4th Street
Saint Louis, MO 63102

314-421-5445; *Fax:* 314-421-1070

12000 Attendees

14127 **Holiday Fair**
Textile Hall Corporation
25 Woodslake Road
Greenville, SC 29607

864-331-2277; *Fax:* 864-293-0619
http://www.holidayfairgreenville.com

25000 Attendees

14128 **Home Furnishings Summer Market**
1355 Market Street
San Francisco, CA 94103-1324

415-934-1380

Donald Preiser, Show Manager
600 booths.
30M Attendees

14129 **Home and Garden Show**
Reed Exhibition Companies
255 Washington Street
Newton, MA 02458-1637

617-584-4900; *Fax:* 617-630-2222

Elizabeth Hitchcock, International Sales

Home products and services.
75M Attendees
Frequency: March

14130 **IDS National Conference**
Interior Design Society
164 S Main Street
Suite 404
High Point, NC 27260

336-884-4437
888-884-4469; *Fax:* 336-885-3291
info@interiordesignsociety.org;
www.interiordesignsociety.org
Social Media: Facebook, Twitter, Youtube, Blogger

Domnick Minella, President
Snoa Garrigan, Executive Director
Dennis Novosel, Treasurer
Anna Mavrakis, VP

IDS is the largest design organization exclusively dedicated to serving the residential interior design industry. Promotes retail interior design, emphasizing education and skills improvement.
3000 Members
Founded in: 1973

14131 **IFAI Annual Expo**
Industrial Fabrics Association International
1801 County Road BW
Roseville, MN 55113-4061

651-222-2508
800-225-4324; *Fax:* 651-631-9334
generalinfo@ifai.com; www.ifai.com
Social Media: Facebook, Twitter, LinkedIn, Youtube

Beth Wistrcill, Conference Manager
Mary J. Hennessy, President and CEO
Pam Egan-Blahna, Director of Human Resources
Todd V. Lindemann, Vice President
Susan R. Niemi, Publisher

Trade event in the American for the technical textiles and specialty fabrics industry.
Frequency: Annual/September

14132 **International Home Furnishings Market**
International Home Furnishings Market Authority
POBox 5243
High Point, NC 27262

336-888-3794
800-874-6492; *Fax:* 336-889-6999;
www.highpointmarket.org

Judy Mendenhall, President
G Bruce Miller, CEO
Tammy Covington, Director Operations
Jan Wellmon, Executive Assistant
Shannon Kennedy, Director of Marketing

Large home furnishings trade show with a variety of new opportunities to make your visit easy, cost effective and productive. Ten million square feet of exhibition space with 2,500 manufacturers represented.
80000 Attendees
Frequency: April & October
Founded in: 1921

14133 **International Silk Flower Accessories Exhibition**
Dallas Market Center
2000 N Stemmons Freeway
Dallas, TX 75207

214-655-6100
800-325-6587; *Fax:* 214-655-6238

8000 Attendees

14134 **LightFair**
AMC
120 Wall Street
17th Floor
New York, NY 10005

212-843-8358; *Fax:* 212-248-5017;
www.iesna.org

Pamela R Weess, Circulation Director
Nini Schwenk, Manager

A major lighting trade show in North America featuring architectural lighting products from all spectrons of the industry. Containing 600 booths and 400 exhibits.
17M Attendees
Frequency: June
Mailing list available for rent: 10M names at $100 per M
Printed in 4 colors on glossy stock

14135 **Museum Store Association**
4100 E Mississippi Avenue
Suite 800
Denver, CO 80246-3055

303-504-9223; *Fax:* 303-504-9585
expo@msaweb.org; www.museumdistrict.com

Beverly Barsook, Executive Director
Stacey Woldt, Assistant Director Programs
Eric Curtis, Conference & Expo Manager
2500 Attendees
Frequency: April, Annually
Founded in: 1955

14136 **NGPP National Convention & Trade Show**
National Guild of Professional Paperhangers
136 S Keowee Street
Dayton, OH 45402

937-222-6477
800-254-6477; *Fax:* 937-222-5794
ngpp@ngpp.org; www.ngpp.org

Elsie Kaptetna CP, President
Phil Curtis CP, First VP
Vincent Larusso CP, Second VP

Promotes products, upgrades skills of paperhangers and encourages good business ethics. Workshops and product launches with over 130 vendors.
Frequency: Annual

14137 **National Decorating Product Show**
Paint & Decorating Retailers Association
403 Axminister Drive
Fenton, MO 63026-2941

636-326-2636; *Fax:* 314-991-5039

James B Savens III, Executive Director

430 booths for home supplies, equipment and services.
10M Attendees
Frequency: November

14138 **National Decorating Products Association: Western Show**
1050 N Lindbergh Boulevard
Saint Louis, MO 63132-2912

314-432-6001; *Fax:* 314-991-5039

Ruth Williams, Convention Manager

230 booths of decorating products such as paint, furniture and more.
2.5M Attendees
Frequency: March

14139 **National Decorating Products Southern Show**
Paint & Decorating Retailers Association
403 Axminster Drive
Fenton, MO 63026-2941

636-326-2636; *Fax:* 314-991-5039

Ruth Williams, Convention Manager

850 display booths of floor coverings, paint, furniture and various interior decorating products.
4M Attendees
Frequency: February

14140 **Needlework Markets**
Needlework Markets
PO Box 533
Pine Mountain, GA 31822

706-663-0140; *Fax:* 706-663-0202;
www.stitching.com

Emily Castleberry, Owner
Frequency: February

14141 **Old House New House Home Show**
Kennedy Productions
1208 Lisle Place
Lisle, IL 60532-2262

630-515-1160; *Fax:* 630-515-1165
info@kennedyproductions.com;
www.kennedyproductions.com

Laura McNamara, Event Producer
Joanne Kennedy, President

Over 300 home improvement exhibitors displaying cutting-edge home enhancements for kitchens, baths, home and garden including landscape, interior remodeling, pools, spas, floors, doors and more.
8000 Attendees
Frequency: Feb/Sept
Founded in: 1977

14142 **PDCA Painting & Decorating Expo**
Paint and Decorating Retailers Association
1401 Triad Center Dr
St. Peters, MO 63376-7353

636-326-2636
800-737-0107; *Fax:* 636-229-4750
info@pdra.org; www.pdra.org

Dan Simon, Executive VP/Publisher
Tina Sullivan, Dir Membership/Education/Tradeshows
Diane Capuano, Managing Editor
Renee Nolte, Director, Finance/Human Resources
Tony Sarantakis, Account Executive

Over thiry education sessions, multiple special networking events and the latest in products and services to support the trade.
2000 Members
Frequency: May
Founded in: 1947

14143 Paint Industries Show
492 Norristown Road
Blue Bell, PA 19422-2355
610-940-0777; *Fax:* 215-840-0292
Robert F Ziegler, Show Manager
Exhibits of raw materials, production equipment, instrumentation and testing apparatus for the coatings, inks and adhesives manufacturing industries. 920 booths.
3.5M Attendees
Frequency: October

14144 Painting and Decorating Contractors of America National Convention
3913 Old Lee Highway
Suite 301
Fairfax, VA 22030-2433
703-359-0826; *Fax:* 703-359-2976
Mary S DePersig, Director Meetings
200 booths of painting, wallcoverings, coatings and sundries.
1.2M Attendees
Frequency: March

14145 Surtex
George Little Management
10 Bank Street
Suite 1200
White Plains, NY 10606-1954
914-486-6070
800-272-7469; *Fax:* 914-948-6180;
www.SURTEX.com
Gina DeLuca, Show Coordinator
Rita Malek, Show Manager
George Little II, President
Annual show of 350 exhibitors featuring prints and patterns for all applications-decorative fabrics, linens, and domestics, apparel and contract textiles, wall and floor coverings, greeting cards, giftwrap and other paper products, tabletop, ceramics and packaging. Available for sale and/or license.
5000 Attendees
Frequency: May

14146 TEXBO
Reed Exhibition Companies
255 Washington Street
Newton, MA 02458-1637
617-584-4900; *Fax:* 617-630-2222
Elizabeth Hitchcock, International Sales
International trade fair for the interior design industry.
7M Attendees
Frequency: January

14147 Tabletop Market
George Little Management
577 Airport Boulevard
Burlingame, CA 94010-2020
650-548-1200
800-272-SHOW; *Fax:* 650-344-5270;
www.glmshows.com/table
Susan Corwin, VP
Annual show of 90 exhibitors featuring tableware, table linens, better housewares and decorative accessories.
1500 Attendees
Frequency: October

14148 West Coast Art and Frame
Art Trends/Picture Framing/Digital Fine Arts
PO Box 594
Lynbrook, NY 11563
516-596-3937; *Fax:* 516-596-3941
3500 Attendees

Directories & Databases

14149 Carpet & Rug Industry Buyers Guide Issue
Rodman Publishing
17 S Franklin Tpke
Ramsey, NJ 07446-2522
201-252-2552
More than 300 suppliers of machinery, equipment and colors and dyes used in the making of carpets and rugs.
Cost: $7.00
Frequency: Annual
Circulation: 5,500

14150 Carpet Cleaners Institute of the Northwest Membership Roster
Carpet Cleaners Institute of the Northwest
PMB #40 2421 South Union Avenue
Suite L-1
Tacoma, WA 98405
253-759-5762
877-692-2469; *Fax:* 253-761-9134
info@ccinw.org; www.ccinw.org
Lyle Neville, President
Matt O'Haleck, Treasurer
Jim Thomas, Secretary
Mike Elias, Director of Education
Over 330 member companies involved in the carpet cleaning industry in Washington, Oregon, and Montana, USA and Alberta and British Columbia, Canada.
Frequency: Annual

14151 Decor-Sources Issue
Commerce Publishing Company
330 N 4th Street
Suite 200
Saint Louis, MO 63102-2041
314-421-5445
Over 1,200 wholesale suppliers of pictures, frames, interior accessories and mirrors to art galleries and home accessories retailers are profiled.
Cost: $5.00
Frequency: Annual
Circulation: 35,000

14152 Decorating Registry
Paint and Decorating Retailers Association
1401 Triad Center Dr
St. Peters, MO 63376-7353
636-326-2636
800-737-0107; *Fax:* 636-229-4750
info@pdra.org; www.pdra.org
Dan Simon, Executive VP/Publisher
Tina Sullivan, Dir Membership/Education/Tradeshows
Diane Capuano, Managing Editor
Renee Nolte, Director, Finance/Human Resources
Tony Sarantakis, Account Executive
A searchable industry database listing paint and decorating companies, products, trademarks, distributors and manufacturer reps.
Cost: $15.00
1500 Members
200 Pages
Frequency: Annual, Magazine
Founded in: 1947
Printed in on glossy stock

14153 Decorating Retailer's Decorating Registry
National Decorating Products Association
1050 N Lindbergh Boulevard
Saint Louis, MO 63132-2912
314-432-6001
800-737-0107; *Fax:* 314-991-5039
Ernest Stewart, Executive VP
Cindy Nusbaum, Directories Editor
Trademark and brand name directory covering paint, wallcovering, window covering, floor covering and related sundries.
Cost: $9.00
Frequency: Annual
Circulation: 30,000
Mailing list available for rent: 30,000+ names
Printed in 4 colors on glossy stock

14154 Decorating Retailer: Directory of the Wallcoverings Industry Issue
National Decorating Products Association
1050 N Lindbergh Boulevard
Saint Louis, MO 63132-2912
314-432-6001
800-737-0107; *Fax:* 314-991-5039
Ernest Stewart, Publisher
Cindy Nusbaum, Editor
Over 1,000 manufacturers and distributors of wallcoverings and related products are listed.
Cost: $25.00
Frequency: Annual
Circulation: 5,000
Printed in 4 colors

14155 DesignSource: Official Specifying and Buying Directory
PO Box 5059
Hoboken, NJ 07030-1501
201-963-9000
More than 10,000 companies that manufacture or supply products or services for interior designers.
Cost: $25.00
Frequency: Annual
Circulation: 40,000

14156 Directory of African American Design Firms
San Francisco Redevelopment Agency
770 Golden Gate Avenue
San Francisco, CA 94102
415-749-2400; *Fax:* 415-749-2526
Over 100 architectural, engineering, planning and landscape design firms.
Frequency: Annual December

14157 Draperies & Window Coverings: Directory and Buyer's Guide Issue
LC Clark Publishing Company
840 US Highway 1
Suite 330
North Palm Beac, FL 33408-3878
561-627-3393; *Fax:* 561-694-6578
John Clark, Owner
Sarah Christy, Associate Editor
Katie Sosnowchik, Senior Editor
Over 2,000 manufacturers and distributors of window coverings and other products used in the window coverings and interior fashions industry.
Cost: $15.00
Frequency: Annual

14158 ENR Directory of Design Firms
McGraw Hill

PO Box 182604
Columbus, OH 43272

877-833-5524; *Fax:* 614-759-3749
customer.service@mcgraw-hill.com;
www.mcgraw-hill.com
Social Media: Facebook, Twitter, LinkedIn, Blog, Youtube, Social

Paul Hermannsfeldt, Editor
Harold McGraw III, Chairman, President
Jack F. Callahan, Executive Vice President
John Berisford, Executive Vice President
Mary Jo Vittor, Executive Vice President

Profiles of 88 architects, architectural engineers, consultants and other design firms; limited to advertisers.
Cost: $95.00
Frequency: Biennial
Mailing list available for rent

14159 ENR: Top 500 Design Firms Issue
McGraw Hill
1221 Avenue of the Americas
Suite C3A
New York, NY 10020-1095

212-512-2000; *Fax:* 212-512-3840
webmaster@mcgraw-hill.com;
www.mcgraw-hill.com

Harold W McGraw III, CEO

List of 500 leading architectural, engineering and specialty design firms selected on basis of annual billings.
Cost: $35.00
Frequency: Annual April
Circulation: 71,000

14160 Flooring: Buying and Resource Guide Issue
Leo Douglas
9609 Gayton Road
Suite 100
Richmond, VA 23233-4904

Lists various manufacturers, workrooms, manufacturers' representatives and distributors of floor, and other interior surfacing products and equipment.
Cost: $38.50
Frequency: Annual
Circulation: 24,000

14161 Home Lighting & Accessories Suppliers Directory
Doctorow Communications
1011 Clifton Ave
Clifton, NJ 07013-3518

973-779-1600; *Fax:* 973-779-3242
info@homelighting.com;
www.homelighting.com

Jeffrey Doctorow, President
Linda Longo, Editor-in-Chief
Susan Grisham, Managing Editor
Dina Tamburro, Associate Publisher

A list of over 1,000 suppliers of lighting fixtures and other products for use in the retail lighting industry are provided.
Cost: $6.00
Frequency: Semi-Annual
Circulation: 9,690

14162 Interior Decorators Handbook
EW Williams Publications
370 Lexington Ave
Suite 1409
New York, NY 10017-6583

212-661-1516; *Fax:* 212-661-1713;
www.williamspublications.com

Philippa Hochschild, Publisher
Phillip Russo, Publishing Director
Lynne Lancaster, Advertising Sales Director

Designers resource guide with over 600 product/service categories. 3,000 suppliers are listed with their headquarters, showrooms. Addresses, phone numbers, fax numbers and e-mail.
Cost: $36.00
230 Pages
Frequency: Bi-annual
Circulation: 25,000
Founded in: 1922
Printed in 4 colors on glossy stock

14163 LDB Interior Textiles Annual Buyers' Guide
EW Williams Publications
370 Lexington Ave
Room 1409
New York, NY 10017-6583

212-661-1516; *Fax:* 212-661-1713;
www.williamspublications.com

Philippa Hochschild, Publisher

Over 2,000 manufacturers and importers of home accessories and interior design products are listed.
Cost: $40.00
Frequency: Monthly
Circulation: 14000
Founded in: 1927

14164 Market Resource Guide
International Home Furnishings Center
PO Box 828
High Point, NC 27261-0828

336-888-3700; *Fax:* 336-882-1873
marketing@ihfc.com; www.ihfc.com

Bruce Miller, CEO

Two-volume directory offers over 1,500 manufacturers and distributors in the furniture industry with exhibits at the International Home Furnishings Market.
Cost: $25.00
624 Pages
Frequency: Semiannual
Founded in: 1974
Printed in 4 colors on glossy stock

14165 Painting and Wallcovering Contractor
Painting and Decorating Contractors of America
2316 Millpark Drive
Suite 220
Maryland Heights, MO 63043

314-514-7322
800-332-7322; *Fax:* 314-514-9417;
www.pdca.org
Social Media: Facebook

Beth Horan, VP Operations
David Ayala, Chairman
David Ryker, Vice Chairman
Darylene Dennon, Treasurer

Offers a list of over 3,300 member contractors engaged in painting, decorating and special coatings applications.
Frequency: Annual
Circulation: 3,500
Mailing list available for rent

14166 Rauch Guide to the US Paint Industry
Grey House Publishing
4919 Route 22
PO Box 56
Amenia, NY 12501

518-789-8700
800-562-2139; *Fax:* 845-373-6390
books@greyhouse.com; www.greyhouse.com
Social Media: Facebook, Twitter

Leslie Mackenzie, Publisher
Richard Gottlieb, Editor

Provides industry structure and current market information about this $16.6 billion industry. The report is divided into five major chapters with 100+ tables and 20 figures in its 500 pages. Unique to the Guide is a profile over 800 industry manufacturers, with sales estimates, products, mergers and acquisitions, divestitures and other information for the 400 largest companies.
Cost: $595.00
500 Pages
ISBN: 1-592371-27-2
Founded in: 1981

14167 Specifiers' Guide and Directory of Contract Wallcoverings
Wall Publications
570 Fashion Ave
New York, NY 10018-1603
212-730-9590

Anne Gober, Owner

A who's who directory of services and supplies to the industry.
Cost: $15.95
Frequency: Annual
Circulation: 15,000

14168 Tile & Decorative Surfaces
18 E 41st Street
New York, NY 10017-6222

212-376-7722; *Fax:* 212-376-7723;
www.ashlee.com/tile

Jordan M Wright, President/Publisher

The Tile industry including ceramic, natural stone, terrazzo, agglomerated, cement glasstiles and others allied to the field. Architects, designers, importers, retail floor covering dealers, distributors, installers and contractors. Also, firms involved with renovation and restoration of tile. Accepts advertising.
Cost: $25.00
Frequency: Monthly
Circulation: 24,000
ISSN: 0192-9550
Founded in: 1950

14169 Wallcovering Pattern Guide and Source Directory
Home Fashion Information Network
557 S Duncan Avenue
Clearwater, FL 33756-6255

A list of wallcovering manufacturers and distributors are offered in this comprehensive directory aimed at the interior design community.
Cost: $78.00
Frequency: Semiannual
Circulation: 10,000

14170 Western Floors: Buyers Guide & Directory
Specialist Publications
17835 Ventura Boulevard
Suite 312
Encino, CA 91316-3634

818-709-1437

A list of firms which manufacture, import or distribute floor coverings.
Cost: $15.00
Frequency: Annual
Circulation: 17,000

14171 Who's Who in Floor Covering Distribution
National Association of Floor Covering Distributor
122 S. Michigan Avenue
Suite 1040
Chicago, IL 60603

312-461-9600; *Fax:* 312-461-0777
info@nafed.org; www.nafed.org

Jack Lidenschmidt, President
Danny Harris, Executive Director/CEO
Norbert Makowka, Vice President, Technical
Tamara Matthews, Communications

Coordinator
Socorro Garcia, Office Manager

Offers information on over 400 member distributors and suppliers of floor coverings.
40 Pages
Frequency: Annual
Mailing list available for rent

Industry Web Sites

14172 http://gold.greyhouse.com
G.O.L.D Grey House OnLine Databases

Grey House Publishing's online database platform, GOLD, offers Quick Search, Keyword Search and Expert Search for most business sectors including interior design, decorating and lighting markets. The GOLD platform makes finding the information you need quick and easy - whether you're a novice searcher or an experienced database user. All of Grey House's directory products are available for subscription on the GOLD platform.

14173 www.carpet-rug.com
Carpet and Rug Institute

National association of carpet and rug manufacturers. Source for product information.

14174 www.fider.org
Foundation for Interior Design Education Research

Promotes excellence in interior design education through research and the accreditation of academic programs.

14175 www.greyhouse.com
Grey House Publishing

Authoritative reference directories for most business sectors including interior design, decorating and lighting markets. Users can search the online databases with varied search criteria allowing for custom searches by product category, geographic area, sales volume, keyword, subject and more. Full Grey House catalog and online ordering also available.

14176 www.homeshows.net
Home Show Management

Organizes three annual south Flordia home design and remodeling shows in Coconut Grove, Ft. Lauderdale and Miami Beach convention centers. Open to the trade and public.

14177 www.i-d-d.com
Interior Design Directory

Sources and links for the interior designer.

14178 www.iesna.org
Illuminating Engineering Society of North America

To advance knowledge and disseminate information for the improvement of the lighted environment to the benefit of society. Publishes a monthly magazine.

14179 www.iida.org
International Interior Design Association

Members are professionals from various facets of the interior design trade.

14180 www.interiordesignsociety.org
Interior Design Society

The largest design organization exclusively dedicated to serving the residential interior design industry. Promotes retail interior design, emphasizing education and skills improvement.

14181 www.nadfd.com
National Assn of Decorative Fabric Distributors

Promotes the textile and home furnishings manufacturers and distributors.

14182 www.nafcd.org
National Assn of Floor Covering Distributors

This organization offers information on over 500 member distributors and suppliers of floor coverings. Publications available to members.

14183 www.ncidq.org
National Council for Interior Design Qualification

Serves to identify to the public those interior designers who have met the minimum standards for professional practice by passing the NCIDQ examination.

14184 www.ngpp.org
National Guild of Professional Paperhangers

Promotes products, upgrades skills of paperhangers and encourages good business ethics. Holds workshops and seminars.

14185 www.nhfa.org
National Home Furnishings Association

A federation of local home furnishings representatives association.

14186 www.oikos.com
Oikos

Devoted to serving professionals whose work promotes sustainable design and construction. Oikos is a Greek word meaning house. Oikos serves as the root for two English words: ecology and economy. That may seem contradictory at first, but it makes perfect sense. Ecology is the science of interactions in natural communities. It examines the web of life where plants, animals, rocks and gases all affect one another. Healthy communities, healthy ecosystems exist ina dynamic equilibrium.

14187 www.pdra.org
Paint and Decorating Retailers Association

This organization lists 1,500 manufacturers, manufacturers' representatives, distributors, and suppliers of decorating merchandise.

14188 www.resources.com
Resources

Organized into easy point and click directories under a highly interactive database.

Associations

14189 Academy of International Business
The Eli Broad College of Businesss, Eppley Cent
645 N. Shaw Ln Rm 7
East Lansing, MI 48824
517-432-1452; *Fax:* 517-432-1009
webmaster@aib.msu.edu
aib.msu.edu
Social Media: Facebook, Twitter, LinkedIn
Rosalie Tung, President
Masaaki Kotabe, President-Elect
Nakiye Boyacigiller, Past President
Charles Dhanaraj, Vice President Program
Jeremy VP, Administration, VP, Administration
Leading association of scholars and specialists in the field of international business. Members include academics, consultants, researchers, and NGO representatives. AIB has chapters worldwide to facilitate networking and information exchange at a local level.
3,089 Members
Founded in: 1959
Mailing list available for rent: 3000 names at $250 per M

14190 American Association of Exporters and Importers
1717 K Street, NW
Suite 1120
Washington, DC 20006
202-857-8009; *Fax:* 202-857-7843
hg@aaei.org; www.aaei.org
Social Media: Facebook, Twitter, LinkedIn, Google+
Phyliss Wigginton, Chair
Karen Kelly, Vice Chair
Lori Goldberg, Vice Chair
Theresa Walker, Secretary/Treasurer
Marianne Rowden, President, CEO
Supports those involved in trade development with other countries and conducting business in the United States, as well as developments affecting trade originating from Treasury, Customs, US Courts, Commerce Department, International Trade Commission, Federal Maritime Commission and other regulatory agencies. Hosts annual trade show.
Founded in: 1921

14191 American Foreign Service Association
2101 E Street NW
Washington, DC 20037
202-338-4045; *Fax:* 202-338-6820;
www.afsa.org
Social Media: Facebook, Twitter, YouTube, Flickr
Barbara Stephenson, President
Sharon Wayne, Vice President
Angie Bryan, State Vice President
Hon. Charles A. Ford, Treasurer
Ian Houston, Executive Director
Organization dedicated specifically to preserving and enhancing theintegrity of the U.S. Foreign Service.
31000 Members
Founded in: 1924

14192 American League for Exports and Security Assistance
122 C St NW
Suite 740
Washington, DC 20001-2109
202-393-3903; *Fax:* 202-737-4727
David Lewis, President
Encourages and supports the sale of American defense products abroad in agreement with foreign policy, security and economic goals of the nation.
38 Members
Founded in: 1976

14193 Assist International
90 John Street
Room 505
New York, NY 10038
212-244-2074; *Fax:* 831-439-9602
info@assist-intl.com; www.assist-intl.com
International trade promotion and consulting firm: mailing lists, seminars, conferences, international business expo.

14194 Association Of American Chambers of Commerce in Latin America
1615 H. Street, NW
Washington, DC 20062-2000
202-463-5485
info@aaccla.org; www.aaccla.org
Nicholas Galt, Chair
Thomas H. Kenna, Vice Chair
Aldo Defilippi, VP for Executive Management
Neil Herrington, Executive Vice President
Reuben Smith-Vaughan, Executive Director
Promotes trade and investment between the United States and the countries of the region through free trade, free markets, and free enterprise.
20000 Members

14195 CalChamber Council for International Trade
1215 K Street
Suite 1400
Sacramento, CA 95814
916-444-6670
800-649-4921; *Fax:* 916-325-1272;
www.calchamber.com
Social Media: Facebook, Twitter, LinkedIn
Allan Zaremberg, President/CEO
Ann Amioka, VP, Communications
Drew Savage, VP, Corporate Relations
Karen Olson, VP, Marketing
Denise Davis, Vice President, Media Relations
Formed by the merging of California Council for International Trade and California Chamber of Commerce International Trade Committee. The foundation is dedicated to preserving and strengthening the California business climate and private enterprise through accurate, impartial research and education on public policy issues of interest to the California business and public policy communities.
15000 Members
Founded in: 1890
Mailing list available for rent

14196 Customs and International Trade Bar Association
www.citba.org
Joseph W. Dorn, President
Lawrence M. Friedman, Vice President
Melvin S. Schwechter, Chair, Export Committee
Kathleen W. Cannon, Secretary
William Sjoberg, Treasurer
Members represent importers, exporters, and domestic producers in matters involving U.S. customs laws, antidumping and countervailing duty laws, safeguards, export licensing, and other federal laws and regulations that affect imported or exported merchandise or international commerce.
Founded in: 1917

14197 FSC/DISC Tax Association
Council for International Tax Education
PO Box 1012
White Plains, NY 10602
914-328-5656
800-207-4432; *Fax:* 914-328-5757;
www.citeusa.org
Robert Ross, Owner
The only organization operating on a national level devoted to educational interests of companies that have set up a foreign sales corporation.
300 Members
Founded in: 1984
Mailing list available for rent

14198 Foreign Trade Association
437 S. Cataract Avenue
Suite #4B
San Dimas, CA 91773
888-223-6459; *Fax:* 310-220-4474
info@foreigntradeassociation.com;
www.foreigntradeassociation.com
Social Media: Facebook, Twitter, LinkedIn
Keith Sanchez, Chairman
Tom Gould, President
Adonna Martin, 1st VP
Cameron Roberts, 2nd VP
Glenn Patton, Treasurer
Business association of European and International commerce that promotes the values of free trade.

14199 Forum for International Trade Training
116 Lisgar Street
Suite 100
Ottawa, ON K2P 0C2
613-230-3553
800-561-3488; *Fax:* 613-230-6808
info@fitt.ca; www.fitt.ca
Social Media: Facebook, Twitter, LinkedIn, Google+
Bill Walsh, Chair
Leslie Meingast, Vice Chair
Paloma Healey, Board Member
Scott Forbes, Board Member
Carl Burlock, Treasurer
Nonprofit organization that develops international business programs, sets competency standards, designs the certification and accreditation programs for the Certified International Trade Professional (CITP) designation, and generally ensures continuing professional development in the practice of international trade.
Founded in: 1992

14200 Futures Industry Association
2001 Pennsylvania Avenue NW
Suite 600
Washington, DC 20006-1823
202-466-5460; *Fax:* 202-296-3184
info@fia.org; www.futuresindustry.org/
Social Media: Facebook, Twitter, LinkedIn, Flickr
Gerald Corcoran, Chair
Walter L. Lukken, President & CEO
Mary Ann Burns, EVP & COO
M. Clark Hutchison, Treasurer
Emily Portney, Secretary
Trade association in the United States composed of futures commission merchants.
Founded in: 1955

14201 Gemini Shippers Group National Fashion Accessories Assoc
137 West 25th Street
3rd Floor
New York, NY 10001
212-947-3424; *Fax:* 212-629-0361
info@geminishippers.com;
www.geminishippers.com

Social Media: Facebook, Twitter, LinkedIn, Google+

Sara L. Mayes, President
Kenneth O'Brien, Chief Operating Officer
Nicole Uchrin, Managing Director
Rich Moore, SalesDirector
Arlene L. Blocker, Membership Director

Offers membership to importers and exporters of various products.
200 Members
Founded in: 1916

14202 **Hong Kong Association of New York**
115 East 54th Street
New York, NY 10022-4563

646-770-1676
contact@hkany.org; www.hkany.org
Social Media: Facebook, LinkedIn, Instagram

Mary Wadsworth Darby, Chairman
Sylvia S. Ng, Vice Chairman
Amy Shang, Vice Chairman
Sebastien J. Granier, Treasurer
Raymond H. Wong, Secretary

Nonprofit organization that promotes global co-operation, communication exchange and synergy among the Hong Kong business associations worldwide.
1100 Members
Founded in: 1987

14203 **Hong Kong Trade Development Council**
219 East 46th Street
New York, NY 10017-2951

212-838-8688; *Fax:* 212-838-8941
new.york.office@hktdc.org; www.hktdc.com
Social Media: Facebook, Twitter, LinkedIn, Google+, YouTube, RSS, Weibo

Margaret Fong, Executive Director
Benjamin Chau, Deputy Executive Director
Raymond Yip, Deputy Executive Director
Ralph Chow, Regional Director, America

Promotes trade between the United States and Hong Kong.
Founded in: 1966
Mailing list available for rent

14204 **International Chamber of Commerce (ICC)**
33-43 Ave. du President Wilson
Paris, Fr 75116

33- 0 -1 49; *Fax:* 3- 0- 1 4
icc@iccwbo.org; www.iccwbo.org
Social Media: Facebook, Twitter, LinkedIn, Google+, YouTube

Harold McGraw III, Chairman
Sunil Bharti Mittal, Vice Chairman
Frederico Fleury Curado, Vice Chairman
Dennis M. Nally, Vice Chairman
Gerard Worms, Honorary Chairman
Founded in: 1919
Mailing list available for rent

14205 **International Reciprocal Trade Association**
524 Middle Street
Portsmouth, VA 23704

Fax: 757-257-4014; www.irta.com
Social Media: Facebook, LinkedIn, Google+, YouTube

Annette Riggs, President
Scott Whitmer, Vice President
Ron Whitney, Executive Director
Chong Kee Tan, Secretary
Mary Ellen Rosinski, Treasurer

A nonprofit organization committed to promoting just and equitable standards of practice and operation within the Modern Trade and Barter and otherAlternative Capital Systems Industry.
Founded in: 1979

14206 **International Trade Administration**
U.S. Department of Commerce
1401 Constitution Ave NW
Washington, DC 20230

800-USA-TRAD
trade.gov
Social Media: Facebook, Twitter, LinkedIn, Blog

Tim Rosado, CFO & CAO
Arthur Paiva, Chief Information Officer
Stefan M. Selig, Under Secretary
Kenneth E. Hyatt, Deputy Under Secretary
Arun Venkataraman, Policy Director

An agency in the United States Department of Commerce that promotesUnited States exports of nonagricultural U.S. services and goods.

14207 **International Trade and Finance Association**
PO Box 2145
Kingsville, TX 78363

E-Mail: itfaconf@ymail.com;
www.itfaconference.org

Khosrow Fatemi, President
Janina Witkowska, VP of Membership
Alfred Eckes, EVP
Scheherazade Rehman, President Elect
Pompeo Della Posta, Board Member

A multidisciplinary association for academics and professionals interested in studying international trade and finance and in promoting a general awareness of these fields and related global economic issues.
Founded in: 1988

14208 **International Trademark Association**
655 Third Avenue
10th Floor
New York, NY 10017

212-642-1700; *Fax:* 212-768-7796
memberservices@inta.org; www.inta.org
Social Media: Facebook, Twitter, LinkedIn

J. Scott Evans, President
Joseph Ferretti, Vice President
Ronald Van Tuijl, President Elect
Tish Berard, VP
Etienne Sanz de Acedo, CEO

A global association of trademark owners and professionals dedicated to supporting trademarks and related intellectual property in order to protectconsumers and to promote fair and effective commerce.
6400 Members
Founded in: 1878

14209 **International Warehouse Logistics Association**
2800 S. River Road
Suite 260
Des Plaines, IL 60018

847-813-4699; *Fax:* 847-813-0115
mail@iwla.com; www.iwla.com
Social Media: Facebook, Twitter, LinkedIn, YouTube

Steve DeHaan, President/CEO
Jay Strother, Vice President
John Levi, Executive Director
Jennifer Rezny, Membership Director
Ben Fairbank, Senior Coordinator, Strategic Data

The unified voice of the global logistics outsourcing industry, representing third party warehousing, transportation and logistics service providers. Our member companies provide the most timely and cost-effective global logistics solutions for their customers and are committed to protecting the free flow of products across international borders.
500 Members
Founded in: 1891
Mailing list available for rent

14210 **Italian Trade Agency**
33 East 67th Street
New York, NY 10065-5949

212-980-1500; *Fax:* 212-758-1050
newyork@ice.it; www.italtrade.com

Maurizio Forte, Trade Commissioner & Executive Dir.
Gemma Di Gangi, Executive Secretary
Gioia Gatti, Food and Wine section
Marc Littell, Graphic Design
Alessandro Greco, Fashion and Start Up

Trade promotion section of the Italian Consulate.

14211 **Latin American Studies Association**
University of Pittsburgh
416 Bellefield Hall
University of Pittsburgh
Pittsburgh, PA 15260

412-648-7929; *Fax:* 412-624-7145
lasa@pitt.edu
lasa.international.pitt.edu/
Social Media: Facebook, Twitter, LinkedIn

Gilbert Joseph, President
Joanne Rappaport, Vice President-President Elect
Timothy J. Power, Treasurer
Debra Castillo, Past President
Milagros Pereyra-Rojas, Executive Director

To foster intellectual discussion, research, and teaching on Latin America, the Caribbean, and its people throughout the Americas, promote the interests of its diverse membership, and encourage civic engagement through network building and public debate.
5000+ Members
Mailing list available for rent

14212 **MIQ Logistics, LLC**
11501 Outlook Street
Suite 500
Overland Park, KS 66211
913-696-7100
877-246-4909; *Fax:* 913-696-7501
contact_us@miq.com; www.meridianiq.com
Social Media: Facebook, Twitter, LinkedIn, Google+, RSS Feed

John E. Carr, President/CEO
Dan Bentzinger, Senior VP Transportation Services
Brenda Stasiulis, Chief Financial Officer
Reid Schultz, General Counsel & CAO
Clint Dvorak, Managing Director

Plans and coordinates the movement of goods throughout the world.

14213 **NEXCO, Inc.**
Grand Central Station
PO Box 3949
New York, NY 10163

877-291-4901; *Fax:* 646-349-9628
director@nexco.org; www.nexco.org
Social Media: Facebook, Twitter, LinkedIn, YouTube

Barney Lehrer, President
David Reiff, Secretary
Susan T. Gilligan, B.O.D.
Henry Lapidos, Director
Neil Lenok, B.O.D.

Members are import and export trading and import and export management companies, international trade service vendors and other international trade companies.
300 Members
Founded in: 1963

14214 National Association of College Stores
500 E. Lorain Street
Oberlin, OH 44074

800-622-7498; *Fax:* 440-775-4769
nacs.org

Brian Cartier, CEO
Tony Ellis, VP, Industry Advancement
Jenny Febbo, VP, Strategic Communications
Rich Hershman, VP, Government Relations
Cindy Thompson, Director, Assocation Relations

14215 National Council on International Trade Development
1901 Pennsylvania Ave. NW
Suite 804
Washington, DC 20006

202-872-9280; *Fax:* 202-293-0495
cu@ncitd.org; www.ncitd.org

Mary Fromyer, Executive Director
David Joy, Senior Counsel
Cathleen Ryan, Asst. Dir. Of Enforcement
kevin J. Wolf, Asst. Secretary of Commerce
Gerard Horner, Head of Economic Analysis Program

Non-profit membership organization dedicated to providing direct expertise on a wide range of international trade topics. Our mission is to identify impediments to all aspects of international commerce and to provide solutions to faciliting the global process.
Founded in: 1967

14216 National Foreign Trade Council
1625 K Street, NW
Suite 200
Washington, DC 20006

202-887-0278; *Fax:* 202-452-8160
nftcinformation@nftc.org; www.nftc.org
Social Media: Facebook, Twitter

William A. Reinsch, President & CEO
J. Daniel O'Flaherty, Vice President
Marshall Lane, Sr Director of Operations
Andrew Watrous, Program Manager
Catherine Schultz, VP, Tax Policy

Business organization advocating a rules-based world economy.
300 Members
Founded in: 1914

14217 PromaxBDA
5700 Wilshire Blvd
Suite 275
Los Angeles, CA 90036

310-788-7600; *Fax:* 310-788-7616
steve.kazanjian@promaxbda.org; www.promaxbda.org
Social Media: Facebook, Twitter, LinkedIn, RSS

Steve Kazanjian, President/CEO
Randy Smith, SVP & CFO
Stacy La Cotera, General Manager and Vice President
Lucian Cojescu, CIO
Stephen Earley, VP, Strategic Partnerships

International association of promotion and marketing, professionals in electronic media. Promotes the effectiveness of promotion and marketing within the industry and the academic community.
2400 Members
Founded in: 1952

14218 Russian Trade Development Association
Palms & Company
6421 Lake Washington Boulevard North East
Penthouse Suite 408
Kirkland, WA 98033-6876

425-828-6774; *Fax:* 425-821-9101
Palms@PeterPalms.com; www.peterpalms.com

Variety of industrial trade shows by SIC code occuring in the Russian Federation throughout the year. Export services from USA to purchasing agent services in Russia for buyers worldwide.
25000 Members
Founded in: 1934

14219 Small Business Exporters Association
800-345-6728
info@sbea.org; www.sbea.org

Jody Milanese, Government Affairs
Patrick Post, Membership
Molly Day, Media/ Press Inquires

Association for small and mid-sized exporters and serves as the international trade arm of the National Small Business Association (NSBA), the nation's first small-business advocacy organization with more than 65,000 members across the country.
65000 Members

14220 The Association of Women in International Trade
4070 52nd Street NW
Washington, DC 20016

202-293-2948
info@wiit.org; www.wiit.org
Social Media: Twitter, LinkedIn

Stefanie Holland, President
Rowan M. Dougherty, VP of Programming
Jennifer Shore, VP of Communications
Dana Watts, VP of Professional Development
Peggy A. Clarke, Secretary

Provides educational and networking opportunities to professional women involved in international trade and business.
Founded in: 1987

14221 The Federation of International Trade Associations
172 Fifth Avenue
#118
Brooklyn, NY 11217

888-491-8833
info@fita.org; www.fita.org

Kimberly Park, President & CEO

Provides resources, benefits and services to the international trade community.
45000 Members
Founded in: 1984

14222 The Women in International Trade Charitable Trust
www.wiittrust.org

Nicole Bivens Collinson, Chair
Amy Breeman-Rhodes, Treasurer
Emily Ruger-Beline, Advisory Committee
Amanda DeBusk, Advisory Committee
Cami Mazard, Advisory Committee

Funds charitable, scientific, and educational activities in international trade.
Founded in: 2001

14223 US China Business Council
1818 N Street, NW
Suite 200
Washington, DC 20036

202-429-0340; *Fax:* 202-775-2476
info@uschina.org; www.uschina.org
Social Media: Facebook, Twitter, LinkedIn, Google+

Mark Fields, Chair
Robert A. Iger, Vice Chair
Paul D. Conway, Vice Chair
Indra K. Nooyi, Vice Chair
John Frisbie, President

Membership association for US companies doing business with the People's Republic of China. Provides representation, practical assistance, and up-to-date information to members.
240 Members
Founded in: 1973
Mailing list available for rent

14224 US Council for International Business
1212 Avenue of the Americas
New York, NY 10036

212-354-4480; *Fax:* 212-575-0327
info@uscib.org; www.uscib.org
Social Media: Facebook, Twitter, LinkedIn, RSS, Flickr, YouTube

Harold McGraw III, Chair
Dennis Nally, Vice Chair
Thomas M. T. Niles, Vice Chair
Donald Monks, Treasurer
Peter M. Robinson, President, CEO

Addresses a broad range of policy issues with the objective of promoting an open system of world trade, finance and investment in which business can flourish and contribute to economic growth, human welfareand protection of the environment.
300 Members
Founded in: 1945

14225 US International Trade Association
1401 Constitution Ave Nw
U.S. Department of Commerce
Washington, DC 20230

202-482-2867
800-USA-TRAD; *Fax:* 202-482-2867; www.trade.gov
Social Media: Facebook, Twitter, LinkedIn, Blog, YouTube

Tim Rosado, CFO & CAO
Arthur Paiva, Chief Information Officer
Stefan M. Selig, Under Secretary
Kenneth E. Hyatt, Deputy Under Secretary
Arun Venkataraman, Policy Director

Association for those interested in export opportunities for United States businesses.

14226 US Russia Business Council
1110 Vermont Avenue, NW
Suite 350
Washington, DC 20005

202-739-9180; *Fax:* 202-659-5920
info@usrbc.org; www.usrbc.org
Social Media: LinkedIn

Klaus Kleinfield, Chairman of the Board
Daniel A. Russell, President, CEO
Randi Levinas, EVP, Chief Operating Officer
Jeff Barnett, Senior Director of Policy
Marc Luet, Board Member

A Washington-based trade association that provides significant business developme, dispute resolution, government relations, and market intelligence services to its American and Russian member companies.

14227 United States Council for International Business
1212 Avenue of the Americas
New York, NY 10036

212-354-4480; *Fax:* 212-575-0327
info@uscib.org; www.uscib.org
Social Media: RSS, Flickr, YouTube

Harold McGraw III, Chair
Dennis Nally, Vice Chair
Thomas M. T. Niles, Vice Chair
Donald Monks, Treasurer
Peter M. Robinson, President, CEO

Promotes open markets, competitiveness and innovation, sustainable development and corpo-

rate responsibility, supported by international engagement and regulatory coherence.
300 Members
Founded in: 1945

14228 WESTCONN International Trade Association
www.westconn.org
Social Media: Facebook, Twitter, LinkedIn
George Woods, President
Edward Carey, Vice President
Sam Fischel, Treasurer
Mark Bishop, Co-Secretary
Susan Leavitt, Co-Secretary
Promotes industrial and academic awareness of the importance of international trade to our national economy.
Founded in: 1972

14229 Women's International Shipping & Trading Association
www.wista.net
Social Media: Facebook, Twitter
Karin Orsel, President
Rachel Lawton, Treasurer
Despina Panayiotou Theodosiou, Secretary
Katerina Stathopoulou, Board Member
Sanjam Gupta, Board Member
An international organization for women in management positions involved in the maritime transportation business and related trades worldwide.
2,100 Members
Founded in: 1997

Newsletters

14230 AAMA News
Asian American Manufacturers Association
3300 Zanker Road
Maildrop Sj2f8
San Jose, CA 95134
408-955-4505; *Fax:* 408-955-4516
Robert M Lee, Executive Director
Cost: $30.00
Frequency: Monthly
Circulation: 1000

14231 AIB Newsletter
Academy of International Business
Michigan State University
7 Eppley Center
East Lansing, MI 48824-1121
517-432-1452; *Fax:* 517-432-1009
aib@aib.msu.edu
aib.msu.edu
G Tomas M Hult, Executive Director
Tunga Kiyak, Managing Director
Irem Kiyak, Treasurer
Provides feature reports and news articles. Information on upcoming events such as conference announcements, calls for papers, and publishing opportunities are also featured.
Frequency: Quarterly
ISSN: 1520-6262

14232 Asahi Shimbun Satellite Edition
Japan Access
757 3rd Avenue
Front 3
New York, NY 10017-2013
212-869-7018; *Fax:* 212-317-3025
Mo Matsuchita, Publisher
Cost: $3.00
Circulation: 12,000

14233 Asian Economic News
Kyodo News International
50 Rockefeller Plz
Room 803
New York, NY 10020-1605
212-603-6600; *Fax:* 212-397-3721
kni@kyodonews.com; www.kyodonews.com
Economic business news of Asian countries and regions.

14234 Buisness IP Services in Brazil
Probe Research
3 Wing Drive
Suite 240
Cedar Knolls, NJ 07927-1000
973-285-1500; *Fax:* 973-285-1519;
www.proberesearch.com
Provides an overview of the business IP services market in Brazil; one of the most active IP markets in South America. Breakdown of Brazil companies. IT investment in B2B and networking applications. We discuss cable and ADSL broadband services and the e-government project. Profile of over 15 service providers.

14235 Business Russia
Economist Intelligence Unit
111 W 57th Street
New York, NY 10019-2211
212-586-1115
800-938-4685; *Fax:* 212-586-1181;
www.eiu.com
Hyunkyu Lee, Owner
Monthly newsletter providing financial and market information as well as current business statistics, economic forecasts and political risk analysis for Russia.
Cost: $865.00
12 Pages
Frequency: Monthly
ISSN: 1357-0293

14236 Business Africa
Economist Intelligence Unit
111 W 57th Street
New York, NY 10019-2211
212-861-1115
800-938-4685; *Fax:* 212-586-1181;
www.eiu.com
Daniel Franklin, Editorial Director
Richard Epstein, Director
Ingersoll Rand, Managing Director
Jane Morley, Senior Editor
Fortnightly newsletter identifying key business issues across Africa; forecasting future developments and trends and analysing their implications on Africa's business environment.
Cost: $1095.00
12 Pages
ISSN: 0968-4468
Founded in: 1946

14237 Business Asia
Economist Intelligence Unit
111 W 57th Street
New York, NY 10019-2211
212-861-1115
800-938-4685; *Fax:* 212-586-1181;
www.eiu.com
Daniel Franklin, Editorial Director
David Butter, Editor
Euan Rellie, Executive Director
Fortnightly newsletter focusing on operating issues and analyzing current political, business and economic developments across Asia.
Cost: $1055.00
12 Pages
Frequency: Fortnightly
ISSN: 0572-7545
Founded in: 1946

14238 Business China
Economist Intelligence Unit
111 W 57th Street
New York, NY 10019-2211
212-586-1115
800-938-4685; *Fax:* 212-586-1181;
www.eiu.com
Daniel Franklin, Editorial Director
Richard Epstein, Advertising Manager
Fortnightly newsletter alerting business executives to the political economic and legal changes that will affect corporate interests. Provides corporate case studies. Analysis financial issues in, and affecting, China. Offers practical, detailed advice.
Cost: $895.00
12 Pages
Frequency: 50 issues per y
ISSN: 1016-9766
Founded in: 1946

14239 Business Eastern Europe
Economist Intelligence Unit
111 W 57th Street
New York, NY 10019-2211
212-861-1115
800-938-4685; *Fax:* 212-586-1181;
www.eiu.com
Daniel Franklin, Editorial Director
Richard Epstein, Advertising Manager
Fortnightly newsletter providing information for business planning on the latest political and economic developments in Eastern Europe on a country-by-country basis.
Cost: $1395.00
12 Pages
Frequency: Weekly
ISSN: 1351-8763
Founded in: 1946

14240 Business Europe
Economist Intelligence Unit
111 W 57th Street
New York, NY 10019-2211
212-861-1115
800-938-4685; *Fax:* 212-586-1181;
www.eiu.com/
Lou Hencken, CEO/President
Paul Lewis, Editor
Nina Andrikian, Marketing
Fortnightly newsletter providing hard facts about changes in the EU's business environment; identifying opportunities for growth and analysing the impact of current issues on business in Europe.
Cost: $1435.00
12 Pages
Frequency: 44 issues per y
ISSN: 1351-8755
Founded in: 1946

14241 Business India Intelligence
Economist Intelligence Unit
111 W 57th Street
New York, NY 10019-2211
212-586-1115
800-938-4685; *Fax:* 212-586-1181;
www.eiu.com
Helen Alexander, CEO
Lou Kelly, Marketing Manager
Louis Ceil, VP
Monthly newsletter tracking the issues and trends in India's business environment; providing information on infrastructure and industries, tariffs, taxes and economic policy and consumer markets.
Cost: $660.00
16 Pages
Frequency: Monthly
ISSN: 1352-8335
Founded in: 1946

14242 Business Latin America
Economist Intelligence Unit
111 W 57th Street
New York, NY 10019-2211
212-861-1115
800-938-4685; *Fax:* 212-586-1181;
www.eiu.com
Daniel Franklin, Editorial Director
Richard Epstein, Director, Business Development
Weekly newsletter covering vital issues affecting business in Latin America, identifying the opportunities, and forecasting the risks to help executives make competetive corporate decisions.
Cost: $1370.00
12 Pages
Founded in: 1946

14243 Caribbean Update
52 Maple Avenue
Maplewood, NJ 07040-2626
973-762-1565; *Fax:* 973-762-9585
mexcarib@cs.com; www.caribbeanupdate.org
Kal Wagenheim, Editor/Publisher
Monthly newsletter focusing on trade and investment opportunities in the Caribbean and Central America.
Cost: $267.00
24 Pages
Frequency: Monthly
Founded in: 1985
Mailing list available for rent: 2500 names
Printed in one color on newsprint stock

14244 Country Finance
Economist Intelligence Unit
111 W 57th Street
New York, NY 10019-2211
212-861-1115
800-938-4685; *Fax:* 212-586-1181;
www.eiu.com
Daniel Franklin, Editorial Director
Richard Epstein, Director, Business Development
Covering 47 countries, this service is a comprehensive overview of global financial issues and conditions. Provides case studies and resources to help companies find and manage finances in countries around the globe. A weekly alert service highlights changes as they happen.
Cost: $445.00
Frequency: 41 issues per y
Founded in: 1946

14245 Country Forecasts
Economist Intelligence Unit
111 W 57th Street
New York, NY 10019-2211
212-861-1115
800-938-4685; *Fax:* 212-586-1181;
www.eiu.com
Daniel Franklin, Editorial Director
Five-year forecasts of political, economic and business trends in 60 countries. Each quarterly updated forecast focuses on the key factors affecting a country's political and economic outlook and its business environment over the next five years.
Cost: $845.00
36 Pages
Frequency: Quarterly

14246 Country Monitor
Economist Intelligence Unit
111 W 57th Street
New York, NY 10019-2211
212-861-1115
800-938-4685; *Fax:* 212-586-1181;
www.eiu.com
Daniel Franklin, Editorial Director
Richard Epstein, Director, Business Development
Weekly newsletter analysing the latest global economic and political events; providing risk assessment in emerging markets and facts on global trends and markets.
Cost: $895.00
12 Pages
Frequency: Weekly
Founded in: 1946

14247 Country Reports
Economist Intelligence Unit
111 W 57th Street
New York, NY 10019-2211
212-861-1115
800-938-4685; *Fax:* 212-586-0248;
www.eiu.com
Daniel Franklin, Editorial Director
Emily Morris, Senior Editor
Quarterly updates on the situation in over 180 countries. Each report includes and analysis of a country's current political and economic climate as well as 12-18 month economic projection.
Cost: $425.00
Founded in: 1946

14248 Country Risk Service
Economist Intelligence Unit
111 W 57th Street
New York, NY 10019-2211
212-861-1115
800-938-4685; *Fax:* 212-586-1181;
www.eiu.com
Daniel Franklin, Editorial Director
Information to assist financial risk management in emerging countries. Country Risk Service is an exclusive two-year forecasting service, assessing the solvency of 100 indebted countries. Each report includes projections of GDP, the budget deficit, trade and current account balances, financing requirements and debt-service ratio.
Cost: $760.00
60 Pages
Frequency: Quarterly
Founded in: 1946

14249 East Asian Business Intelligence
International Executive Reports
717 D St Nw
Suite 300
Washington, DC 20004-2815
202-737-6366; *Fax:* 202-628-6618
execrep@aol.com
William Hearn, Publisher
Twice-a-month newsletter containing business leads and market studies on Far East business.
Cost: $345.00
8 Pages
Frequency: 22 per year
Circulation: 300
ISSN: 0888-058X
Founded in: 1986
Printed in on matte stock

14250 East/West Executive Guide
WorldTrade Executive
PO Box 761
Concord, MA 01742
978-287-0301; *Fax:* 978-287-0302
info@wtexec.com; www.wtexec.com
Alison French, Production Manager
Provides detailed information on how to do business in Russia, the CIS, and East/Central Europe. Focuses on key mechanical issues such as accounting and tax matters, local sourcing, the due diligence process, labor, finance, permits, environmental issues etc.
Cost: $656.00
Frequency: Monthly

14251 European Community
US Council for International Business
1212 Ave of the Americas
Suite 1800
New York, NY 10036-1689
212-354-4480; *Fax:* 212-575-0327;
www.uscib.org
Peter Robinson, President
Newssheet on developments in the European community affecting business on council activities.
Circulation: 2,800

14252 Export Update
Trade Communications
733 15th Street NW
Suite 1100
Washington, DC 20005-2112
202-737-1060; *Fax:* 202-783-5966
Stephen Pfeiderer, Publisher
Includes significant buying trends, specific sales leads, in-depth country market profiles, latest figures on trade activity, schedules for trade affairs and missions and insight on the affects of international news.

14253 Hong Kong Means Business
Hong Kong Trade Development Council
219 East 46th Street
New York, NY 10017-2951
212-838-8688; *Fax:* 212-838-8941
new.york.office@hktdc.org; www.hktdc.com
Social Media: Facebook, Twitter, LinkedIn, Google+, YouTube, RSS, Weibo
Margaret Fong, Executive Director
Loretta Wan, Director, Publications & E-Commerce
Frequency: Weekly

14254 Hong Kong Trade Development Council Newsletter
Hong Kong Trade Development Council
219 East 46th Street
New York, NY 10017-2951
212-838-8688; *Fax:* 212-838-8941
new.york.office@hktdc.org; www.hktdc.com
Social Media: Facebook, Twitter, LinkedIn, Google+, YouTube, RSS, Weibo
Loretta Wan, Director, Publications & E-Commerce
Margaret Fong, Executive Director
Promotes trade between United States and Hong Kong.
Frequency: Weekly
Founded in: 1966

14255 Indonesia Letter
Asia Letter Group
12508 Whitley Street
Whittier, CA 90601-2729
Fax: 852-526-2950

14256 International Finance & Treasury
WorldTrade Executive
PO Box 761
Concord, MA 01742
978-287-0301; *Fax:* 978-287-0302
info@wtexec.com; www.wtexec.com
Alison French, CEO

Focus on techniques used by leading firms to manage worldwide financial resources. Topics covered include: tax, accounting and regulatory changes, currency and interest rate risk, cash management techniques, risk management strategies, regional treasury alerts.
Cost: $1245.00
Frequency: Weekly

14257 International Observer
PO Box 5997
Washington, DC 20016-1597

202-244-7050; *Fax:* 202-244-5410

J Wagner, Publisher

Informs on world developments in political, diplomatic, government, security, and economic origins.
Cost: $240.00
10 Pages
Frequency: Monthly
Printed in one color

14258 International Securitization & Structured Finance
WorldTrade Executive
PO Box 761
Concord, MA 01742

978-287-0301; *Fax:* 978-287-0302
info@wtexec.com; www.wtexec.com

Jill McKenna, Production Manager
George Veoger, Editor
Pierre Brown, Publisher
Alleesa Aughas, Marketing Manager

A twice monthly report devoted exclusively to asset-backed securities in international markets. Covers all aspects of international asset-backed securitization, including innovative product trends, issuer considerations, regulatory matters, and tax and accounting considerations. Examines what is working in emerging markets and spotlights unique US transactions.
Cost: $1296.00
Frequency: Bi-monthly
Founded in: 1996

14259 International Trade Alert
American Association of Importers and Exporters
1200 G Street NW
Suite 800
Washington, DC 20005

212-944-2230; *Fax:* 202-661-2185;
www.aaei.org

Mathew Mermigousis, Production Manager
Stuart Iserber, Director of Events
Michelle Measel, Director of Events

Reports on current trade developments and advance notices of changes in rules for conducting business in the United States, as well as developments affecting trade originating from Treasury, Customs, US Courts, Commerce Department, International Trade Commission, Federal Maritime Commission and other regulatory agencies.
10 Pages
Frequency: Monthly
Circulation: 2,200

14260 International Trade Reporter Current Reports
Bureau of National Affairs
1801 S Bell St
Arlington, VA 22202-4501

703-341-3000
800-372-1033; *Fax:* 800-253-0332
customercare@bna.com; www.bnabooks.com
Social Media: Facebook, Twitter, LinkedIn

Paul N Wojcik, Chairman
Gregory C. McCaffery, President and CEO
John Camp, Vice President
Lisa A. Fitzpatrick, Vice President
Audrey Hipkins, Vice President

A comprehensive source that reports and analyzes legislative and regulatory developments as well as private sector activities affecting international trade (both export and import).
Cost: $1744.00
Frequency: Weekly
Founded in: 1929

14261 International Trade Reporter Decisions
Bureau of National Affairs
1801 S Bell St
Arlington, VA 22202-4501

703-341-3000
800-372-1033; *Fax:* 800-253-0332
customercare@bna.com; www.bnabooks.com
Social Media: Facebook, Twitter, LinkedIn

Paul N Wojcik, Chairman
Gregory C. McCaffery, President and CEO
John Camp, Vice President
Lisa A. Fitzpatrick, Vice President
Audrey Hipkins, Vice President

Only available source of digested, classified and indexed judicial and administrative decisions dealing with legal issues arising from US trade law (mostly import cases).
Cost: $2265.00
ISSN: 0748-0709

14262 International Trade Reporter Import Reference Manual
Bureau of National Affairs
1801 S Bell St
Arlington, VA 22202-4501

703-341-3000
800-372-1033; *Fax:* 800-253-0332
customercare@bna.com; www.bnabooks.com
Social Media: Facebook, Twitter, LinkedIn

Paul N Wojcik, Chairman
Gregory C. McCaffery, President and CEO
John Camp, Vice President
Lisa A. Fitzpatrick, Vice President
Audrey Hipkins, Vice President

A complete guide to the entire import process with analysis and full text of statutes, regulations, and executive orders on subjects such as customhouse brokers, dumping, countervailing duties, escape clauses, and presidential retaliation.
Cost: $1781.00

14263 Investing, Licensing & Trading
Economist Intelligence Unit
111 W 57th Street
New York, NY 10019-2211

212-586-1115
800-938-4685; *Fax:* 212-586-1181;
www.eiu.com

Updated twice a year, ILT outlines business requirements for operating successfully in the world's major markets. This reference service, shows how the laws work in practice, with case studies of how leading multinationals obtain government approvals, set up local companies, calculate corporate and personal taxes and overcome restrictions and other legal hurdles in 60 countries and the European Union.
Cost: $345.00

14264 Managing Imports and Exports
Institute of Management and Administration
1 Washington Park
Suite 1300
Newark, NJ 07102-3130
212-244-0360; *Fax:* 973-622-0595
customercare@bna.com; www.ioma.com

The source of information on customs policies and procedures, BIS rules and regulations, and how to best enhance the compliance programs.
Cost: $437.00

14265 Market Europe
PRS Group
6320 Fly Rd
Suite 102
East Syracuse, NY 13057-9792

315-431-0511; *Fax:* 315-431-0200
custserv@prsgroup.com; www.prsgroup.com

Mary Lou Walsh, President
Doris Walsh, Chairman

Demographic and lifestyle information about consumers in Europe to help businesses do a better job marketing to those consumers.
Cost: $397.00
Frequency: Monthly
Circulation: 325
Founded in: 1985
Printed in one color on matte stock

14266 Mexican Forecast
WorldTrade Executive
2250 Main St
Suite 100
Concord, MA 01742-3838

978-287-0301; *Fax:* 978-287-0302
info@wtexec.com; www.wtexecutive.com

Gary Brown, President
Jay Stanley, Sales Manager

Provides up-to-date information and forecasts on Mexican business. Includes coverage of foreign trade, currency, major industry sectors, market trends and investment climates.
Cost: $535.00

14267 Middle East Business Intelligence
International Executive Reports
717 D St Nw
Suite 300
Washington, DC 20004-2815

202-737-6366; *Fax:* 202-628-6618
execrep@aol.com

William Hearn, Publisher

Twice-a-month newsletter containing business leads and market studies on Middle East business.
Cost: $345.00
8 Pages
Circulation: 400
ISSN: 0731-5305
Printed in one color on matte stock

14268 Middle East Trade Letter
PO Box 472986
Charlotte, NC 28247-2986

704-536-9847; *Fax:* 704-543-6161

Leslie B Cohen, Publisher

Business in the Middle East.
Cost: $139.00
4 Pages
Frequency: Quarterly
Circulation: 500
Printed in one color on newsprint stock

14269 Nielsen's International Investment Letter
Nielsen & Nielsen
1901 South Bay Rd Ne
Olympia, WA 98506-3532

360-352-7485; *Fax:* 360-352-7485;
www.nelsonfurnitureworks.com

Paul Nelson, President

Tracks domestic and international stock markets and economics, precious metals and other commodities, USA and foreign bonds, interest rates, foreign currencies and real estate; offers clients specific buy and sell recommendations on domestic and international investments for both

traders and investors.
Cost: $360.00
10 Pages
Frequency: Monthly
Printed in on matte stock

14270 North American Free Trade & Investment
WorldTrade Executive
PO Box 761
Concord, MA 01742
978-287-0301; *Fax:* 978-287-0302
info@wtexec.com; www.wtexec.com
Alison French, Production Manager
Gary Brown, CEO/President
Gary Brown, Editor
Dana Pierce, Marketing Manager
Dana Pierce, Circulation Manager
Covers NAFTA trade and investment developments. Key topics include rules of origin, tariff phaseouts, intellectual property protection, compliance and planning options, and business opportunities.
Cost: $734.00
Frequency: Annual+
Circulation: 100
Founded in: 1992

14271 Practical Latin American Tax Strategies
WorldTrade Executive
PO Box 761
Concord, MA 01742
978-287-0301; *Fax:* 978-287-0302
info@wtexec.com; www.wtexec.com
Alison French, Production Manager
A monthly report on how leading companies are reacting to changes and developments in Latin American tax practice. Includes commentary from senior practitioners at major law and accounting firms and case studies from major corporations.
Cost: $645.00
Frequency: Monthly

14272 Practical US/International Tax Strategies
WorldTrade Executive
PO Box 761
Concord, MA 01742-761
978-287-0301; *Fax:* 978-287-0302
info@wtexec.com; www.wtexec.com
Dana Pierce, Production Manager
Gary Brown, CEO/Publisher
David Cooper, Editor
John Nartel, Marketing Manager
Jay Stanley, Sales Manager
Analyzes how leading companies are reacting to changes in US-international tax practice. Leading experts provide practical guidance covering every area of international transactions.
Cost: $614.00
Frequency: Fortnightly
Circulation: 200
Founded in: 1992

14273 Russian Far East Update
Russian Far East Update
PO Box 22126
Seattle, WA 98122-0126
206-447-2668; *Fax:* 206-628-0979;
www.russianfareast.com
Trade and economic information plus news analysis of Russia's far east.
Cost: $20.00
Circulation: 1,300

14274 Vietnam Business Info Track
Vietnam Access
PO Box 1210
Port Hueneme, CA 93044-1210
Fax: 805-985-0839
Kahn Le, Editor
Comprehensive coverage of Vietnam market. Focuses on trade, investment and sector reports. Gives you an immediate advantage in evaluating the potential of doing business in Vietnam and operating in a timely and cost effective matter.

14275 Vietnam Market Watch
Vietnam Market Resources
375 Lexington Avenue
New York, NY 10017
212-499-2000; *Fax:* 203-256-9790
mail@inc.com; www.inc.com/
Khoung Ho, Publisher
Aaron Goldstein, Chief Operating Officer
Caroline Basquez, Owner
For companies and professionals doing business in Vietnam.
Cost: $295.00
Frequency: Monthly
Circulation: 500
Founded in: 2004

14276 Weekly International Market Alert
International Business Communications
114 E 32nd Street
#602
New York, NY 10016
212-686-1460
Johnathan Block, Publisher
International trade news.
Frequency: Monthly

14277 World Trade
Taipan Press
4199 Campus Drive
Suite 230
Irvine, CA 92612-4684
949-410-0980; *Fax:* 949-725-0306
Will Swaim, Publisher
Articles aim to help companies expand international opportunities. Accepts advertising.
Cost: $24.00
96 Pages
Frequency: Monthly

Magazines & Journals

14278 AIB Insights
Academy of International Business
Michigan State University
7 Eppley Center
East Lansing, MI 48824-1121
517-432-1452; *Fax:* 517-432-1009
aib@aib.msu.edu
aib.msu.edu
Ilan Alon, Editor
Provides an outlet for short, interesting, topical, current, and thought provoking articles. Articles can discuss theoretical, empirical, practical or pedagogical issues affecting the international business community.
Frequency: Quarterly
ISSN: 1938-9590

14279 Aaonline
Africa-America Institute
420 Lexington Ave
Suite 1706
New York, NY 10170-0007
212-949-5666; *Fax:* 212-682-6174
aainy@aaionline.org; www.aaionline.org
Amber Jones, Executive Assistant
Mora McLean, Vice President
Joy Phumaphi, Vice President
Frequency: Quarterly
Circulation: 3000
Founded in: 1953

14280 American Business in China
Caravel
23545 Crenshaw Blvd
Suite 101E
Torrance, CA 90505-5201
310-325-0100; *Fax:* 310-325-2583
info@china4us.com; www.china4us.com
Directory of US firms operating in China and Hong Kong; Hong Kong: a special administrative region; exporting to China - best US exporting prospects; China's major cities for foreign investments; marketing, advertising and exhibiting in China.
Cost: $99.00
288 Pages
Circulation: 10,000
ISBN: 0-964432-29-3
Founded in: 1993
Mailing list available for rent: 2,000 names at $95 per M

14281 Asian Finance
Asian Finance Publications
14 Davis Drive
Armonk, NY 10504-3005
Focuses on international banking and finance.
Circulation: 13147

14282 Asian Industrial Report
Keller International Publishing Corporation
150 Great Neck Rd
Great Neck, NY 11021-3309
516-829-9722; *Fax:* 516-829-9306
Robert Herihly, Publisher
Brian Deluca, Editor
Jerry Keller, President
New machinery and equipment.
Cost: $85.00
36 Pages
Frequency: Monthly
Circulation: 20000
Founded in: 1882
Printed in 4 colors on matte stock

14283 Business America: the Magazine of International Trade
US Department of Commerce
200 Constitution Ave NW
Washington, DC 20210-0001
202-693-5000; *Fax:* 202-219-8822;
www.dol.gov
Social Media: Facebook, Twitter, LinkedIn, Pinterest, Blogger, Tumblr
Hilda L Solis, CEO
Designed to help American exporters penetrate overseas markets by providing them with timely information on opportunities for trade and methods of doing business in foreign countries.
Cost: $2.00
Circulation: 13,000
Mailing list available for rent

14284 Cross Border
Economist Intelligence Unit
111 W 57th Street
New York, NY 10019-2211
212-586-1115; *Fax:* 212-586-1181
Debrah Langley, Publisher

Focuses on multinational management issues faced by managers of international businesses.
Circulation: 55,000

14285 **East Asian Executive Report**
International Executive Reports
717 D St NW
Suite 300
Washington, DC 20004-2815

202-737-6366; *Fax:* 202-628-6618
execrep@aol.com

William Hearn, Publisher

Monthly magazine covering the legal and practical requirements of doing business in Far Eastern countries.
Cost: $455.00
28 Pages
Frequency: Monthly
Circulation: 600
ISSN: 0272-1589
Founded in: 1979
Printed in on matte stock

14286 **Economist**
PO Box 58524
Boulder, CO 80322-8524

303-945-1917
800-456-6086; *Fax:* 303-604-7455
ukpressoffice@economist.com;
www.economist.com

Helen Alexander, CEO
Kate Cooke, Group Communications Manager
David Hanger, Publisher
James Wilson, Founder

The Economist is a news and business publication written for top business decision-makers and opinion leaders who need a wide range of information and views on world events. It explores the close links between domestic and international issues, business, finance, current affairs, science and technology.
160 Pages
Frequency: Weekly
Circulation: 1009759
ISSN: 0013-0613
Founded in: 1843
Printed in 4 colors on glossy stock

14287 **Export**
Adams/Hunter Publishing
2101 S Arlington Heights Road
Suite 150
Arlington Heights, IL 60005-4142

Fax: 847-427-2006

David Thayer, Publisher

Covers all aspects of international trade for distributors of consumer durables in 183 countries.

14288 **Foreign Affairs**
Foreign Affairs
58 E 68th St
New York, NY 10065-5953

212-434-9522
800-829-5539; *Fax:* 212-861-2759
order@wshein.com; www.foreignaffairs.org

David Kellogg, Publisher
Gideon Rose, Editor
Michael Pasuit, Marketing Coordinator
Eugnia Chang, Circulation Director

Reviews on events, news, people, and foreign relations.
Cost: $44.00
Founded in: 1921

14289 **Global Trade**
North American Publishing Company
1500 Spring Garden St
Suite 1200
Philadelphia, PA 19130-4094

215-238-5300; *Fax:* 215-238-5342;
www.napco.com

Ned S Borowsky, President and CEO
Bennett Zucker, Publisher

Assists international cargo decision makers in planning, financing and documenting goods and commodities in international trade. Accepts advertising.
Cost: $45.00
Frequency: Monthly
Founded in: 1958

14290 **IGT Magazine**
World Trade Winds
610 Old Campbell Rd
Suite 108
Richardson, TX 75080-3379

972-994-9816
877-861-1188; *Fax:* 972-699-1189;
www.asiatrademart.com

Offers information for exporters to find international buyers.
ISSN: 0259-9880
Founded in: 1975

14291 **Journal of International Business Studies**
Academy of International Business
Michigan State University
7 Eppley Center
East Lansing, MI 48824-1121

517-432-1452; *Fax:* 517-432-1009
managing-editor@jibs.net; www.aib.msu.edu

Lorraine Eden, Editor

The leading peer-reviewed, scholarly journal that publishes research across the entire range of topics encompassing the domain of international business studies.
Frequency: 9x/Year
ISSN: 0047-2506

14292 **LASA Forum**
Latin American Studies Association
946 William Pitt Union
University of Pittsburgh
Pittsburgh, PA 15260

412-648-7929; *Fax:* 412-624-7145
lasa@pitt.edu
lasa.international.pitt.edu/

Hane Horowitz, Exhibit Management Head
Arturo Arias, Associate Editor
Sonia E Alvarez, President/Editor
Charles R Hale, VP
Milagros Pereyra-Rojas, Managing Editor

Published by the Latin American Studies Association.
Cost: $30.00
Frequency: Quarterly
Founded in: 1969
Mailing list available for rent

14293 **Latin Trade Magazine**
Freedom Latin America
1001 Brickell Bay Drive
Suite 2700
Miami, FL 33131

305-749-0880; *Fax:* 786-513-2407
info@latintrade.com; www.latintrade.com
Social Media: Facebook, Twitter, LinkedIn, RSS

Rosemary Winters, Chief Executive Officer
Maria Lourdes Gallo, Executive Director & Publisher
Santiago Gutierrez, Executive Editor
Elida Bustos, Managing Editor
Manny Melo, Art & Production Director

Comprehensive news coverage and analysis of business issues in Latin America and the Caribbean. Available in English or Spanish
Cost: $64.00
Frequency: Monthly
Circulation: 92,319
Founded in: 1993

14294 **Middle East Executive Reports**
International Executive Reports
717 D St NW
Suite 300
Washington, DC 20004-2815

202-737-6366; *Fax:* 202-628-6618
execrep@aol.com

William Hearn, Publisher

Monthly magazine covering the legal and practical requirements of doing business in the Middle East.
Cost: $455.00
28 Pages
Frequency: Monthly
Circulation: 1,000
ISSN: 0271-0498
Founded in: 1978
Printed in 2 colors on matte stock

14295 **Showcase USA**
Bobit Publishing Company
23210 Crenshaw Blvd
Torrance, CA 90505-3181

310-539-1969; *Fax:* 310-539-4329;
www.bobit.com

John Bebout, Owner

International marketing vehicle for American manufacturing.
Cost: $12.00
165 Pages
Founded in: 1979

14296 **Trade and Culture Magazine**
Key Communications
PO Box 569
Garrisonville, VA 22463-0569

540-657-7174
800-544-5684; *Fax:* 540-720-5687;
www.key-com.com

Debra Levy, Owner
Kim White, Managing Editor
Penny Stacey, Advertising Coordinator

Published to help executives make their companies competitive worldwide, featuring 22 trade zone presentations in each issue covering every country. Trade and Culture blends cultural insight with practical how-to business information.
Cost: $39.95
96 Pages
Frequency: Quarterly
Circulation: 45000
Founded in: 1993

14297 **US Council for International Business**
1212 Avenue of the Americas
Suite 1805
New York, NY 10036-1689

212-354-4480; *Fax:* 212-575-0327
info@uscib.org; www.uscib.org

Peter Robinson, President
Davis Hodge, Marketing & Advertising

Monthly newsletter that supports those involved in the developments in the European community affecting business on council activities.
Frequency: Monthly
Founded in: 1945

14298 **US-China Business Council**
US China Business Council

1818 N St NW
Suite 200
Washington, DC 20036-2470

202-429-0340; *Fax:* 202-775-2476
info@uschina.org; www.uschina.org

John Frisbie, President
Erin Ennis, VP
Ryan Ong, Director/Business Advisory Services

Covers all aspects of doing business with China and Hong Kong.
Cost: $100.00
240+ Members
Circulation: 6000
ISSN: 0163-7169
Founded in: 1973
Printed in on glossy stock

14299 Vietnam Business Journal
VIAM Communications Group
535 W 114th Street
New York, NY 10027

212-854-2271; *Fax:* 212-854-9099

Kenneth Felderbaum, Publisher

Research and experience based articles and graphics produces by journalists.

14300 World Trade
Freedom Magazine
2401 W. Big Beaver Rd
Suite 700
Troy, MI 48084

248-362-3700; www.bnpmedia.com
Social Media: Facebook, Twitter, LinkedIn

Steve Beyer, Director

Articles are aimed at helping companies to expand their international opportunities.
Frequency: Monthly
Circulation: 70590
Founded in: 1987

Trade Shows

14301 AIB Annual Meeting
Academy of International Business
645 N. Shaw Ln
Rm 7
East Lansing, MI 48824-1121

517-432-1452; *Fax:* 517-432-1009
aib@aib.msu.edu; www.aib.msu.edu

G Tomas M Hult, Executive Director
Tunga Kiyak, Managing Director
Irem Kiyak, Treasurer
Robert Grosse, President
Elizabeth Rose, Vice President Administration

Features a combination of plenaries, panels, and papers.
Frequency: June-July

14302 American-Turkish Council Annual Meeting
Ideea
6233 Nelway Drive
McLean, VA 22101

703-760-0762; *Fax:* 703-760-0764
qwhiteree@ideea.com; www.ideea.com

Quentin C Whiteeree, President

High level military and government officials and businessmen from Turkey and the United States. Seminar and over 25 exhibits of trade, defense, banking, investments and tourism.
1000 Attendees
Frequency: Annual
Founded in: 1983

14303 Annual Convention and Trade Show
American Association of Exporters and Importers
1050 17th Street NW
Suite 810
Washington, DC 20036

202-857-8009; *Fax:* 202-857-7843
hq@aaei.org; www.aaei.org
Social Media: Facebook, Twitter

Kathy Corrigan, Director Meetings/Events
Marianne Rowden, President and CEO
Terri A Lankford, Director Membership & Marketing
David A Potts, Manager Office Administration
Megan Montgomery, Director of Government Affairs

Reports on current trade developments and advance notices of changes in rules for conducting business in the United States, as well as developments affecting trade originating from Treasury, Customs, US Courts, Commerce Department, International Trade Commission, Federal Maritime Commission and other regulatory agencies. 50 exhibitors with 50 booths.
550 Attendees
Frequency: May
Founded in: 1921

14304 International Business Expo
Assist International
90 John Street
Room 505
New York, NY 10038

212-442-2074; *Fax:* 212-725-3312;
www.assist-intl.com

Peter Robinson, Director

This expo has 170 exhibitors with 170 booths.
1800 Attendees
Frequency: April
Founded in: 1999

14305 Showcase USA Trade Show
Bobit Publishing Company
3520 Challenger Street
Torrance, CA 90503

310-533-2400; *Fax:* 310-533-2500
webmaster@bobit.com; www.bobit.com

Mike Spivak, Editor
Ty Bobit, CEO

International marketing vehicle for American manufacturing.
165 Attendees
Founded in: 1979

14306 USRBC Annual Meeting
US Russia Business Council
1701 Pennsylvania Avenue NW
Suite 520
Washington, DC 20006

202-739-9180; *Fax:* 202-659-5920
lawson@usrbc.org; www.usrbc.org

Eugene K Lawson, President

Highlights the opportunities and risks that are emerging in the Russian market as it enters a new stage of development.

Directories & Databases

14307 A Basic Guide to Exporting
World Trade Press
1450 Grant Avenue
Suite 204
Novato, CA 94945

415-549-9934
800-833-8586; *Fax:* 415-898-1080;
www.worldtradepress.com

Alexandra Woznick

Includes significant new information on export regulations, customs benefit, and tax incentives. There are also hundreds of new sources of assistance available with updated addresses and telephone numbers.
188 Pages
ISBN: 1-885073-83-6
Founded in: 1999

14308 American Business in China
Caravel
23545 Crenshaw Blvd
Sutie 101E
Torrance, CA 90505-5201

310-325-0100; *Fax:* 310-325-2583
info@china4us.com; www.china4us.com

Davisson Chang, Owner
Sheryl Chang, Production Manager
Betty Yao, Marketing Manager

Directory of US firms operating in China and Hong Kong; Hong Kong as a special administrative region; exporting to China - best US exporting prospects; China's major cities for foreign investments; marketing, advertising and exhibiting in China. Also contains 1,000+ US contacts and 1,800+ China & Hong Kong contacts
Cost: $99.00
288 Pages
Frequency: Annual
ISBN: 0-964432-29-3
Founded in: 1995
Mailing list available for rent: 2,000 names at $95 per M

14309 Arthur Andersen North American Business Sourcebook
Triumph Books
601 S La Salle St
Suite 500
Chicago, IL 60605-1725

312-939-3330; *Fax:* 312-663-3557;
www.triumphbooks.com

Mitch Rogatz, President/Publisher
Tom Bast, Editorial Director
Blythe Hurley, Managing Editor
Kelley Thornton, Associate Editor

Government and trade agencies and trade-related databases in the United States, Canada and Mexico are profiled.
Cost: $150.00
Founded in: 1994

14310 AtoZ World Business
World Trade Press
800 Lindberg Lane
Suite 190
Petaluma, CA 94952

707-778-1124
800-833-8586; *Fax:* 707-778-1329
egh@worldtradepress.com;
www.worldtradepress.com

Edward Hinkelman, Publisher

The world's most comprehensive country-by-country resource for success in international business and trade. Consists of 100 Country Business Guides and 76 World Trade Resources. Offers entrepreneurs, business professionals and researchers access to vetted international business and trade intelligence, compiled into a single, reliable source.
Founded in: 1993

14311 Brazil Tax, Law, & Business Briefing
WorldTrade Executive
2250 Main St
Suite 100
Concord, MA 01742-3838

978-287-0301; *Fax:* 978-287-0302
info@wtexec.com; www.wtexecutive.com

Gary Brown, Owner
Jay Stanley, Sales Manager

Coverage includes economic analysis and risk assessment, new transfer pricing rules, foreign direct investment, labor regulation, environ-

ment, privatization, accessing the Mercosur market, litigation, arbitration, and debt collection in Brazil, antitrust concerns for foreign acquisition, securitizing infrastructure projects, foreign investor access to the telecommunications market, and choices in creating Brazilian subsidiaries.
Cost: $297.00
340 Pages
ISBN: 1-893323-57-9

14312 CSI Market Statistics
Commodity Systems
200 W Palmetto Park Rd
Suite 200
Boca Raton, FL 33432-3788

561-392-1556
800-274-4727; *Fax:* 561-392-7761
info@csidata.com; www.csidata.com

Bob Pelletier, President

Offers information on daily, weekly and monthly time series of price and trading data for commodity markets worldwide, cash, futures options, index options, US stocks and mutual funds and government instruments.

14313 Chinese Business in America
Caravel
23545 Crenshaw Blvd
Suite 101E
Torrance, CA 90505-5201

310-325-0100; *Fax:* 310-325-2583
info@china4us.com; www.china4us.com

Davisson Chang, Owner
Sheryl Chang, CEO

Directory of ethnic Chinese importers and exporters in the US; marketing, sourcing and establishing a business in the US; US business laws and immigration regulations; money saving tips and business bargains.
Cost: $88.00
288 Pages
Frequency: Annual
Circulation: 5,000
ISBN: 0-964432-26-9
Founded in: 1997

14314 DACA Directory
Distributors & Consolidators of America
2240 Bernays Drive
York, PA 17404

888-519-9195; *Fax:* 717-764-6531
daca@comcast.net; www.dacacarriers.com

Mike Wichert, Chairman
Mike Oliver, President
Steve Hubbard, VP
Andy Delaney, Secretary
Rich Eberhart, Treasurer

Firms and individuals active in the shipping, warehousing, receiving, distribution or consolidation of freight shipments.

14315 DRI Europe
DRI/McGraw-Hill
24 Hartwell Ave
Lexington, MA 02421-3103

781-860-6060; *Fax:* 781-860-6002
support@construction.com;
www.construction.com

Walt Arvin, President

Subjects covered in this database include macroeconomic, microeconomic, and financial indicators for the European countries.

14316 DRI Middle East and African Forecast
DRI/McGraw-Hill
24 Hartwell Ave
Lexington, MA 02421-3103

781-860-6060; *Fax:* 781-860-6002
support@construction.com;
www.construction.com

Walt Arvin, President

This large database offers more than 500 annual historical and forecast time series for 10 Middle Eastern and African economies.

14317 DRI/TBS World Sea Trade Forecast
DRI/McGraw-Hill
24 Hartwell Ave
Lexington, MA 02421-3103

781-860-6060; *Fax:* 781-860-6002
support@construction.com;
www.construction.com

Walt Arvin, President

This comprehensive database covers cargo movements over major water trade routes worldwide.

14318 DRI/TBS World Trade Forecast
DRI/McGraw-Hill
24 Hartwell Ave
Lexington, MA 02421-3103

781-860-6060; *Fax:* 781-860-6002
support@construction.com;
www.construction.com

Walt Arvin, President

Offers over 82,000 annual historical and forecast time series on import and export volumes, and prices in current US dollars.

14319 Dictionary of International Trade
World Trade Press
1450 Grant Avenue
Suite 190
Petaluma, CA 94952

707-778-1124
800-833-8586; *Fax:* 707-778-1329
egh@worldtradepress.com;
www.worldtradepress.com

Edward G Hinkelman

The most respected and largest-selling dictionary of trade in the world. It is in use in more than 100 countries by importers, exporters, bankers, shippers, logistics professionals, attorneys, economists, and government officials.
Cost: $55.00
688 Pages
ISBN: 1-885073-72-0
Founded in: 2004

14320 Directory of US Exporters
Journal of Commerce
33 Washington Street
Floor 13
Newark, NJ 07102

973-848-7000
amiddlebrook@cbizmedia.com;
www.cbizmedia.com

Amy Middlebrook, Group Publisher

Provides logistics professionals with active confirmed leads for over 60,000 US companies involved in world trade.
Cost: $450.00
Frequency: Annual

14321 Directory of US Importers
Journal of Commerce
33 Washington Street
13 Floor
Newark, NJ 07102

973-848-7000; www.cbizmedia.com

Amy Middlebrook, Group Publisher

Provides logistics professionals with active confirmed leads for over 60,000 US companies involved in world trade.
Cost: $450.00

14322 Export Yellow Pages
US West Marketing Resources Group
1101 30th Street NW
Suite 200
Washington, DC 20007-3769

202-934-4584
800-228-2582; *Fax:* 202-944-4680

David Lee, President

Approximately 16,000 US suppliers distributed worldwide through US commerce department channels.

14323 Foreign Exchange Forecast Data Base
Global Insight
800 Baldwin Tower
Eddystone, PA 19022

610-490-4000; *Fax:* 610-490-2770
info@wefa.com; www.wefa.com

Ben G Hackett, International Trade/Transportation

This large database covers over 130 monthly and 60 quarterly time series of historical and forecast data for foreign exchange rates.

14324 Foreign Representatives in the US Yellow Book
Leadership Directories
104 5th Ave
New York, NY 10011-6901

212-627-4140; *Fax:* 212-645-0931
info@leadershipdirectories.com;
www.leadershipdirectories.com
Social Media: Facebook, Twitter

David Hurvitz, CEO
James M Petrie, Associate Publisher

Contact information for foreign representatives of over 187 nations at embassies, consulates, and intergovernmental organizations in the US, US executives of over 1,100 foreign corporations, over 275 foreign financial institutions with offices in the US, and over 300 international media outlets with bureaus in the US.
Cost: $245.00
850+ Pages
Frequency: SemiAnnual
ISSN: 1089-5833
Founded in: 1969
Mailing list available for rent: 12,000 names at $125 per M

14325 GIN International Database
Global Information Network
146 W 29th St
Suite 7E
New York, NY 10001-5303

212-244-3123; www.g-i-n.net/home

Lisa Vives, Owner

This large database offers all sorts of information on developing countries, ranging from economics and finance to health and social trends.
Frequency: Full-text

14326 GLOBAL Vantage
Standard & Poor's Corporation
55 Water St
New York, NY 10041-0003
212-438-1000
800-525-8640; *Fax:* 212-438-0299

Deven Sharma, President

This database provides corporate financial data covering more than 2,500 US companies and over 1,500 companies in 23 other countries.

14327 Global Report
Citicorp

800 3rd Ave
New York, NY 10022-7669

212-688-1308; www.citibank.com

One of the most comprehensive databases in the world offering information on foreign exchange, country reports, money markets, bonds, companies, industries and news.
Frequency: Full-text

14328 Importers Manual USA
World Trade Press
800 Lindberg Lane
Suite 190
Petaluma, CA 94952

707-778-1124
800-833-8586; *Fax:* 707-777-1329
egh@worldtradepress.com;
www.worldtradepress.com

Edward Hinkelman, Publisher
James Nolan, Editor
Karla Shippey, Editor

Lists of trade fairs, embassies, chambers of commerce, banks, and other sources of information on various aspects of international trade.
Cost: $145.00
960 Pages
Frequency: 2-3 per year
Circulation: 3,000
ISBN: 1-885073-93-3
Founded in: 1993

14329 International Directory of Importers
1741 Kekamek NW
Poulsbo, WA 98730

360-779-1511
800-818-0140; *Fax:* 360-697-4696;
www.export-leads.com

Esther Camacho, Circulation

Publishes reference guides for worldwide importers, wholesalers, agents, and distributors.
Cost: $250.00
5000 Pages
Frequency: Annual
Founded in: 1978

14330 Japan Economic Daily
Kyodo News International
747 3rd Ave
Suite 1803
New York, NY 10017-2803

212-935-4440; *Fax:* 212-508-5441
kni@kyodonews.com; www.kyodonews.com

This full coverage database contains news on Japanese business, industry, economics and finance developments.
Frequency: Full-text

14331 LEXIS International Trade Library
Mead Data Central
9443 Springboro Pike
Dayton, OH 45401

888-223-6337; *Fax:* 518-487-3584;
www.lexis-nexis.com

Andrew Prozes, CEO
Rebecca Schmitt, Chief Financial Officer

This database contains information on international trade regulation decisions handed down from the Supreme Court and other legislative bodies.
Frequency: Full-text

14332 Local Chambers of Commerce Which Maintain Foreign Trade Services
US Chamber of Commerce-International Division
1615 H St NW
Washington, DC 20062-0002

202-659-6000; *Fax:* 202-463-5836;
www.uschamber.org

Thomas J Donohue, CEO
Jean Hunt, Administrative Assistant
Cost: $15.00

14333 Mexico Tax, Law,& Business Briefing
WorldTrade Executive
2250 Main St
Suite 100
Concord, MA 01742-3838

978-287-0301; *Fax:* 978-287-0302
info@wtexec.com; www.wtexecutive.com

Gary Brown, Owner
Jay Stanley, Sales Manager

A single volume special report that provides guidance on tax and legal issues investors should consider when evaluating a possible company aquisition, starting a business or entering into a joint venture or strategic alliance in Mexico. Also featuring important guidance prepared by major accounting and law firms.
Cost: $297.00
291 Pages
ISBN: 1-893323-67-6

14334 North American Export Pages
US West Marketing Resources Group
1101 30th Street NW
Suite 200
Washington, DC 20007-3769

202-934-4584
800-288-2582; *Fax:* 202-944-4680

David Lee, President

Approximately 50,000 suppliers from the United States, Canada, and Mexico wishing to export products worldwide.
Cost: $39.95

14335 Official Export Guide
North American Publishing Company
1500 Spring Garden St
Suite 1200
Philadelphia, PA 19130-4094

215-238-5300; *Fax:* 215-238-5342;
www.napco.com

Ned S Borowsky, President and CEO

Offers information on customs officials, port authorities, embassies and consulates, chambers of commerce and other organizations involved in international trade.
Cost: $399.00
1800 Pages
Frequency: Annual
Founded in: 1958

14336 Political Handbook of the World
McGraw Hill
PO Box 182604
Columbus, OH 43272

614-866-5769; *Fax:* 614-759-3759
webmaster@mcgraw-hill.com;
www.mcgraw-hill.com

Arthur S Banks, Editor
Thomas C Muller, Editor

Annual reference book containing separate sections on every country in the world and more than 100 intergovernment organizations. Each edition completely updates political developments over the past year while retaining the extensive background information necessary for researchers to place current events in a comprehensive historical perspective.
1400 Pages
Founded in: 1979

14337 Practical Guide: Doing Business in Ukraine
WorldTrade Executive
PO Box 761
Concord, MA 01742-0761

978-287-0301; *Fax:* 978-287-0302
info@wtexec.com; www.wtexec.com

Alison French, Production Manager

Topics covered include: common business structures, registration procedures, real property transactions, tax and foreign investment legislation, currency reforms and regulations, privatization programs, intellectual property.
Cost: $145.00

14338 Protecting Intellectual Property in Latin America
WorldTrade Executive
PO Box 761
Concord, MA 01742-0761

978-287-0301; *Fax:* 978-287-0302
info@wtexec.com; www.wtexec.com

Alison French, Production Manager

A complete guide to the protection of intellectual property in Latin America, including in-depth coverage of copyright law, patents and trademarks, software, pharmaceuticals, etc. Also deals with issues of enforcement and prosecution.
Cost: $235.00

14339 Russian Far East: A Business Reference Guide
Russian Far East Advisory Group
PO Box 22126
Seattle, WA 98122-0126

206-447-2668; *Fax:* 206-628-0979;
www.russianfareast.com

Elisa Miller, Editor
Alexander Karp, Editor

Sourcebook for business people, travelers, and researchers focusing on trends and economic developments in the Russian Far East. Includes reviews of each of the ten administrative regions and 27 maps
Cost: $79.00
270 Pages
ISBN: 0-964128-63-2

14340 Selling Successfully in Mexico
WorldTrade Executive
PO Box 761
Concord, MA 01742-0761

978-287-0301; *Fax:* 978-287-0302
info@wtexec.com; www.wtexec.com

Alison French, Production Manager

A detailed guide to market research, advertising, direct marketing, and trade show exhibition in Mexico, written by marketing professionals and supplemented by extensive data and key contracts.
Cost: $129.00

14341 Showcase USA: American Export-Buyers Guide and Membership
Bobit Publishing Company
3623 Artesia Boulevard
Redondo Beach, CA 90278

Fax: 310-376-9043

List of member companies and organizations of Sell Overseas America.

14342 Trade Opportunity
US International Trade Association

1401 Constitution Ave NW
Washington, DC 20230-0001

202-482-2867
800-872-8723; *Fax:* 202-482-2867;
www.ita.doc.gov

David L Aaron, Manager
Renee Macklin, Chief Information Officer

Leads to export opportunities for United States businesses.

14343 Trade Shows Worldwide
Gale/Cengage Learning
PO Box 09187
Detroit, MI 48209-0187

248-699-4253
800-877-4253; *Fax:* 248-699-8049
gale.galeord@cengage.com; www.gale.com
Social Media: Facebook, Twitter, Google+, Youtube

Patrick C Sommers, President

Each edition of this resource includes listings for more than 10,000 trade shows; approximately 6,000 trade show sponsoring organizations and more than 5,900 facilities, services and information sources on trade shows and exhibitions held in the United States and around the globe.
Frequency: Annual
ISBN: 1-414435-24-X

14344 US Custom House Guide
U.S. Custom House Guide

609-371-7825
888-215-6084; *Fax:* 609-371-7885;
www.uscustomhouseguide.com

Monica McCarthy, Associate Editor
Amy Middlebrook, Vice President, Directories
Dennis Ferrere, Advertising Sales Rep

List of ports having customs facilities, customs officials, port authorities, chambers of commerce, embassies and consulates, foreign trade zones and other organizations; related trade services.
Cost: $399.00
Frequency: Annual January

14345 World Trade Almanac
World Trade Press
1450 Grant Avenue
Suite 204
Novato, CA 94945

415-454-9934
415-898-1124; www.worldtradepress.com

Gayle Madison
Peter Jones

Industry Web Sites

14346 Www.hktdc.com
Hong Kong Trade Development Council

Promotes trade between United States and Hong Kong.

14347 http://gold.greyhouse.com
G.O.L.D Grey House OnLine Databases

Grey House Publishing's online database platform, GOLD, offers Quick Search, Keyword Search and Expert Search for most business sectors including international trade markets. The GOLD platform makes finding the information you need quick and easy - whether you're a novice searcher or an experienced database user. All of Grey House's directory products are available for subscription on the GOLD platform.

14348 www.aib.msu.edu/
Academy of International Business

Members are executives and teachers in the international business field.

14349 www.fancyfoodshows.com
National Association for the Specialty Food Trade

Members are manufacturers, importers, distributors and retailers of specialty gourmet and fancy foods. Has an annual budget of approximately $15 million. Publications available to members.

14350 www.geminishippers.com
Gemini Shippers Group

Shippers association with global contracts for all commodities.

14351 www.greyhouse.com
Grey House Publishing

Authoritative reference directories for most business sectors including international trade markets. Users can search the online databases with varied search criteria allowing for custom searches by product category, geographic area, sales volume, keyword, subject and more. Full Grey House catalog and online ordering also available.

14352 www.iwla.com
International Warehouse Logistics Association

14353 www.ncitd.org
National Council on Int'l Trade Development

For exporters and importers and other professionals serving the international commerce industry.

14354 www.uschina.org
US China Business Council

Membership association for US companies doing business with the People's Republic of China. Provides representation, practical assistance, and up-to-date information to members.

14355 www.vita.com
VMEbus International Trade Association (VITA)

Association for manufacturers of microcomputer boards, hardware, software, military products, controllers, bus interfaces and other accessories compatible with VMEbus architecture.

International Trade Resources

14356 Albania to the United Nations
320 E 79th Street
New York, NY 10075

212-249-2059; *Fax:* 212-535-2917
albania.un@albania-un.org;
www.albania-un.org
Social Media: Facebook, Twitter, LinkedIn, RSS Feed, Google+

Ferit Hoxha, Ambassador
Petrik Jorgji, Minister Counselor
Olisa Cifligu, Second Secretary
Ermal Frasheri, Adviser, legal Issues
Admira Jorgji, Counselor

14357 Antigua and Barbuda Department of Tourism and Trade
25 S.E. 2nd Avenue
Suite 300
Miami, FL 33131

305-381-6762; *Fax:* 305-381-7908
cganuear@bellsouth.net;
www.antigua-barbuda.org

Byron Spencer, Manager

14358 Austrian Trade Commission
120 West 45th Street
9th Floor
New York, NY 10036

212-421-5250; *Fax:* 212-421-5251
newyork@advantageaustria.org;
www.advantageaustria.org/us
Social Media: Facebook, Twitter, RSS Feed

Peter Athanasiadis, Manager
Sabine Miller, Project Manager
Walter HAfle, Director

14359 Azerbaijan - Permanent Mission to the United Nations
866 United Nations Plaza, Ste 560
48 str. & 1 Avenue
New York, NY 10017

212-371-2559; *Fax:* 212-371-2784;
www.un.int/azerbaijan/

Eldar Kouliev, Manager

14360 Bahamas Consulate General
231 E 46th Street
New York, NY 10017

212-421-6420; *Fax:* 212-688-5926
consulate@bahamasny.com;
www.un.it/bahamas

Hon Eldred E Bethel, Contact
Forrester J. Carroll, JP, Consul General
Sandra N. McLaughlin, Vice Consul
Clemmy Eneas-varence, Sr. Information Clerk
Carolyn Young-Miller, Administrative Asst.

14361 Bulgarian General Consulate
121 E 62nd Street
New York, NY 10021

212-935-4646; *Fax:* 212-319-5955
consulate.newyork@mfa.bg;
www.consulbulgaria-ny.org

14362 Business Council for the United Nations
801 2nd Avenue
Ste 900
New York, NY 10017

212-697-3315; *Fax:* 212-682-9185
unahq@unausa.org; www.unfoundation.org
Social Media: Facebook, Twitter, YouTube, RSS Feed

Allison B MacEachron, Executive Director
Kathy Calvin, President & CEO
Richard S. Parnell, COO
Walter Cortes, CFO
Aaron Sherinian, VP, Communications

14363 Chile Trade Commission
866 United Nations Plaza
Suite 603
New York, NY 10017

212-207-3266; *Fax:* 212-207-3649

Alejandro Cerda, Trade Commissioner

14364 Consulate General of Bahrain
866 2nd Avenue
14th Floor
New York, NY 10017

212-223-6200; *Fax:* 212-319-0687;
www.un.int/bahrain/consulate.html

Jassim Buallay, Manager

14365 Consulate General of Belgium in New York
1065 Avenue of Americas
22nd Floor
New York, NY 10018

212-586-5110
212-586-7472; *Fax:* 212-582-9657

NewYork@diplobel.fed.be;
www.diplomatie.be/newyork/

Piet Morisse, Manager
Marc Calcoen, Consul General
Leon Cortens, Deputy Consul General

14366 Consulate General of Brazil
220 E. 42nd St.
26th Floor
New York, NY 10017

917-777-7777; *Fax:* 212-827-0225
cg.novayork@itamaraty.gov.br
http://novayork.utamaraty.gov.br/en-us/

Julio Cesar Gomes Dos Sant, Manager

14367 Consulate General of Costa Rica
14 Penn Plaza, #1202
225 West 34th Street
New York, NY 10122

212-509-3066
212-509-3066; *Fax:* 212-509-3068; *Fax:* 212-509-3068; www.costaricaembassy.com

Otto Barcas, Manager

14368 Consulate General of Germany
871 United Nations Plaza
New York, NY 10017

212-610-9700; *Fax:* 212-940-0402

Bernhard Von Der Planit, Manager

14369 Consulate General of Haiti
815 2nd Ave.
6th Floor
New York, NY 10017

212-697-9767; *Fax:* 212-681-6991;
www.haitianconsulate-nyc.org

Marie Therese, Manager
Charles A. Forbin, Consul General

14370 Consulate General of Honduras
255 West 36th Street
First Level
New York, NY 10018

212-714-9451; *Fax:* 212-714-9453;
www.hondurasemb.org
Social Media: Facebook, Twitter

14371 Consulate General of India
3 E 64th Street
New York, NY 10065

212-774-0600; *Fax:* 212-861-3788;
www.indiacgny.org

Ambassador Prabhu Dayal, Consul General
Mr. P.K. Bajaj, Consul (Head of Chancery)
Shambhu Amitabh, Vice Consul (Passport & Consular)
Ajay Purswani, Consul (Visa)
Dhirendra Singh, Counsel

14372 Consulate General of Indonesia
5 E 68th Street
New York, NY 10021

212-879-0600

14373 Consulate General of Israel in New York
800 Second Avenue
New York, NY 10017

212-499-5000
info@newyork.mfa.gov.il; www.israelfm.org
Social Media: Facebook, Twitter, YouTube, flickr

Ido Aharoni, Consul General
Founded in: 1948

14374 Consulate General of Kenya
866 UN Plaza
Suite 4016
New York, NY 10017

212-421-4741; *Fax:* 212-486-1985
kenyahighcommission.ca

Rolando Visconti, Manager

14375 Consulate General of Lebanon in New York
9 E 76th Street
New York, NY 10021

212-744-7905; *Fax:* 212-794-1510
lebconsny@aol.com; www.lebconsny.org

Hassan Saad, Manager

14376 Consulate General of Lithuania
420 5th Avenue
3rd Floor
New York, NY 10018

212-354-7840; *Fax:* 212-354-7911
kons.niujorkas@urm.lt
ny.mfa.lt

Rimantas Morkvenas, Manager
Valdemaras Sarapinas, Consul General

14377 Consulate General of Malta
249 E 35th Street
New York, NY 10016

212-725-2345; *Fax:* 212-779-7097

14378 Consulate General of Morocco
10 East 40th Street
New York, NY 10016

212-758-2625; *Fax:* 646-395-8077
info@moroccanconsulate.com;
www.moroccanconsulate.com

Ramon Xilotl, Manager
Mohammed Benabdeljalil, Consul general
Sidi Mohammed El Bakkari, Deputy Consul

14379 Consulate General of Nigeria
828 2nd Avenue
New York, NY 10017

212-808-0301; *Fax:* 212-687-1476
cgnny@nigeriahouse.com;
www.nigeriahouse.com

14380 Consulate General of Paraguay
801 2nd . Ave.
Suite 600
New York, NY 10017

212-682-9441
212-682-9442; *Fax:* 212-682-9443
info@consulparny.com;
www.consulparny.com/ingles/html/visas.html

Juan Baiardi, Manager

14381 Consulate General of Peru
241 East 49th St.
New York, NY 10017

646-735-3828; *Fax:* 646-735-3866
consulado@conperny.org;
www.consuladoperu.com

Fortunato Ricar Quesada Seminario, Consul General

14382 Consulate General of Qatar
2555 M St NW
Washington, DC 20037-1305

202-274-1600; *Fax:* 202-237-9880
info@qatarembassy.net;
www.qatarembassy.net

Mohammad Al-Madadi, Consul

14383 Consulate General of Saudi Arabia
866 United Nations Plaza
Suite 480
New York, NY 10017

212-752-2740

Abdulrahman Gdaia, Execellency

14384 Consulate General of Slovenia
120 East 56th Street
Suite 320
New York, NY 10022

212-370-3006; *Fax:* 212-421-1532
nky@gov.si

Reimo Pettai, Manager

14385 Consulate General of South Africa
333 E 38th Street
9th Floor
New York, NY 10016

212-213-4880; *Fax:* 212-213-0102
consulate.ny@foreign.gov.za;
www.southafrica-newyork.net

Fikile Magubane, Consul-General
Thami Sono, Consul
Leon Naidoo, Consul
George Monyemangene, Consul General

14386 Consulate General of St. Lucia
2005 Massachusetts Ave., NW
Washington, DC 20036-1030

202-558-2216
800-345-6541
202-364-6795; *Fax:* 202-318-0771
info@visahq.com
saint-lucia.visahq.com

Julian Hunte, Manager

14387 Consulate General of Switzerland
633 3rd Avenue
30th Floor
New York, NY 10017-6706

212-599-5700; *Fax:* 212-599-4266;
www.eda.admin.ch

Raymond Loretan, Excellency

14388 Consulate General of Trinidad & Tobago
125 Maidan Lane
4th Floor
New York, NY 10038

212-682-7272; *Fax:* 212-232-0368
consulate@ttcgny.com; www.ttcgnewyork.com
Social Media: Facebook, Twitter, YouTube, RSS Feed

Hon Harold Robertson, Contact
Rudrawatee Nan Ramgoolam, Consul General

14389 Consulate General of Ukraine
240 E 49th Street
New York, NY 10017

212-371-5690; *Fax:* 212-371-5547
gc_usn@mfa.gov.ua
ny.mfa.gov.ua

Serhii Pohoreltsev, Consul General

14390 Consulate General of Uruguay
420 Madison Street
6th Floor
New York, NY 10017

212-753-8581
212-753-8192; *Fax:* 212-753-1603
consulado@consuladouruguaynewyork.com;
www.consuladouruguaynewyork.com

Basil Bryan, Manager
Carlos Orlando, Consul General

14391 Consulate General of Venezuela
7 East 51st Street
New York, NY 10022

212-826-1660; *Fax:* 212-644-7471
ven.newyork@gmail.com
nuevayork.consulado.gob.ve

Carol Delgado Arria, Consul General
Ayerim Flores Rivas, Consul General of the Second

14392 Consulate General of the Dominican Republic
1715 22nd Street, NW
Washington, DC 20008

202-332-6280
202-332-7670; *Fax:* 202-265-8057;
www.domrep.org
Social Media: Facebook, Blogspot

Jose Luis Dominguez, Minister Counselor
Felipe Herrera, Cunselor
Morela Baez, Commercial Affairs
Alejandra Hernandez, Minister Counselor
Ligia Reid Bonetti, Minister Counselor

14393 Consulate General of the Netherlands
666 Third Avenue
19th floor
New York, NY 10017

877-388-2443; *Fax:* 212-333-3603
nyc@minbuza.nl
ny.the-netherlands.org
Social Media: Facebook, Twitter, YouTube, RSS Feed

Wanda Fleck, Manager

14394 Consulate General of the Principality of Monaco
565 5th Avenue
23rd Floor
New York, NY 10017

212-286-0500; *Fax:* 212-286-1574
info@monaco-consulate.com;
www.monaco-consulate.com
Social Media: Facebook, Twitter

Maguy Maccario-Doyle, Consul General, Minister Cousellor

14395 Consulate General of the Republic of Belarus
708 3rd Avenue
20th Floor
New York, NY 10017

212-682-5392; *Fax:* 212-682-5491;
www.belarusconsul.org
Social Media: RSS Feed

Sergei Kolos, Manager

14396 Consulate General of the Russian Federation
2343 Massachusettes Ave, NW
Washington, DC 20008-2803

202-588-5899; *Fax:* 202-588-8937;
www.croatiaemb.org

14397 Consulate of Guyana
370 7th Avenue
New York, NY 10017

212-947-5110; *Fax:* 212-573-6225;
www.guyana.org
Social Media: Facebook, Twitter, Gmail, StumbleUpon,Pinterest,G

Samuel Insanally, Ambassador, Permanent Rep
Edwin Carrington, Secretary
Mohammed A. O. Ishmael, Managing Director
Amral Khan, Administrator & Editor

14398 Consulate of the Republic of Uzbekistan in New York City
801 Second Ave
20th Floor
New York, NY 10017

212-754-7403; *Fax:* 212-838-9812
info@uzbekconsulny.org;
www.uzbekconsulny.org

14399 Croatia Consulate, United States
369 Lexington Avenue
11th Floor
New York, NY 10017

212-599-3066; *Fax:* 212-599-3106
croatian.consulate@gte.net
us.mvep.hr/en

Abdul Seraj, Manager

14400 Ecuadorian Consulate
2535 15th Street NW
Washington, DC 20009

202-234-7200
866-ECU-DOR; *Fax:* 202-667-3482
consuladodc@ecuador.org; www.ecuador.us

Pablo Yanez, Consul General

14401 Egyptian Consulate Economic & Commercial Office
3521 International Ct. NW
Washingotn, DC 20008

202-895-5400; *Fax:* 202-244-5131
embassy@egyptembassy.net;
www.egyptembassy.net
Social Media: Facebook

Ayden Nour, Executive Director
Mohamed M. Tawfik, Ambassador

14402 Embassy of Australia
1601 Massachusetts Avenue NW
Washington, DC 20036

202-797-3000; *Fax:* 202-797-3168;
www.usa.embassy.gov.au
Social Media: Facebook, Twitter

Kim Beazley, Ambassador

14403 Embassy of Benin
2124 Kalorama Road NW
Washington, DC 20008

202-232-6656; *Fax:* 202-232-2611
info@beninembassy.us; www.beninembassy.us

Boni T. Yayi, President
Cyrille S. Oguin, Ambassador

14404 Embassy of Bosnia and Herzegovina
2109 East Street NW
Washington, DC 20037

202-337-1500; *Fax:* 202-337-1502
info@bhembassy.org; www.bhembassy.org
Social Media: Facebook

Haris Hrle, Ambassador
Milenko Misic, Minister Counselor
Sanja Juric, First Secretary
Denita Lelo, 1st Consular Officer
10 Members

14405 Embassy of Cambodia
4530 16th Street NW
Washington, DC 20011

202-726-7742
202-726-7824; *Fax:* 202-726-8381
camemb.usa@mfa.gov.kh;
www.embassyofcambodia.org
Social Media: Facebook

Hem Heng, Ambassador
Mouth Keo Thida, Commercial Counselor
Koeut navuth, Defense Attache
Neang Chanthou, Finance Attache

14406 Embassy of Estonia
2131 Massachusetts Avenue NW
Washington, DC 20008

202-588-0101; *Fax:* 202-588-0108
embassy.washington@mfa.ee;
www.estemb.org
Social Media: Facebook, Twitter, Flickr

Marina Kaljurand, Ambassador

14407 Embassy of Ethiopia
3506 International Drive NW
Washington, DC 20008

202-364-1200; *Fax:* 202-587-0195
ethiopia@ethiopianembassy.org;
www.ethiopianenmbassy.org

Girma Birru, Ambassador
Tsegab Kebebew, Minister Counselor
Kidist Yakob, Counselor (Politcal Affairs)
Wahide Belay, Minister Counselor
Yohannes Getahun, Minster Counselor

14408 Embassy of Finland
3301 Massachusetts Avenue NW
Washington, DC 20008

202-298-5800; *Fax:* 202-298-6030
sanomat.was@formin.fi; www.finland.org
Social Media: Facebook, Twitter

Ritva Koukku-Ronde, Ambassador

14409 Embassy of Georgia
2209 Massachusettes Avenue, NW
Washington, DC 20008

202-387-2390; *Fax:* 202-387-0864
embgeo.usa@mfa.gov.ge;
www.embassy.mfa.gov.ge

Temur Yakobashvili, Ambassador
David Rakviashvili, Envoy
Mikheil Darchiashvili, Minister
Thea Kentchadze, Sr. Counselor
Mariam Lebanidze, Counselor

14410 Embassy of Grenada
1701 New Hampshire Ave, NW
Washington, DC 20009-2501

202-265-2561; *Fax:* 292-265-2468
gdaembassydc@gmail.com;
www.grenadaembassyusa.org
Social Media: Facebook, Twitter, Google+

E. Angus Friday, Ambassador
Patricia D.M. Clarke, Counsellor
Dianne C. Perrotte, Adminstrative Asst
Lucia Amedee, Receptionist/ Clerical Asst.

14411 Embassy of Jamaica (JAMPRO)
1520 New Hampshire Ave, NW
Washington, DC 20036

202-452-0660; *Fax:* 202-452-0036
firstsec@jamaicaembassy.org;
www.embassyofjamaica.org

Audrey P. Marks, Ambassador

14412 Embassy of Jordan
3504 International Drive NW
Washington, DC 20008

202-966-2664; *Fax:* 202-966-3110
HKJEmbassyDC@jordanembassyus.org;
www.jordanembassyus.org
Social Media: Facebook, Twitter, YouTube, RSS Feed, Pinterest,

Alia Hatoung Bouran, Ambassador
Amjad Hatem Al-Mbideen, Consul
Fawaz Bilbesi, Deputy Chief of Mission
Aishabint Al hussein, Military Attache
Qais Biltaji, Fist Secretary

14413 Embassy of Mali
2130 R Street NW
Washington, DC 20008

202-332-2249; *Fax:* 202-332-6603
info@maliembassy.us; www.maliembassy.us

Al Maamoun Baba Lamine Kehta, Ambassador
Muhamed Ouzouna Maiga, 1st Counselor
Ahmadou Barazi Maiga, 2nd Counselor
Colonel Bourama Sangare, Defence Attache
Mahama Dicko, Financial Attache

14414 Embassy of Mongolia
2833 M Street NW
Washington, DC 20007

202-333-7117; *Fax:* 202-298-9227
dc@mongolianembassy.us;
www.mongolianembassy.us

Khasbazaryn Bekhbat, Ambassador

14415 Embassy of Panama
2862 McGill Terrace NW
Washington, DC 20008

202-483-1407
202-483-1407; *Fax:* 202-483-8413
info@embassyofpanama.org;
www.embassyofpanama.org
Social Media: Facebook

Mario E. Jaramillo, Ambassador

14416 Embassy of Tanzania
1232 22nd St, NW
Washington, DC 20037

202-884-1080
202-939-6125, 202-; *Fax:* 202-797-7408
ubalozi@tanzaniaembassy-us.org;
www.tanzaniaembassy-us.org
Social Media: Facebook, Twitter

Liberata Mulamula, Ambassador
Lily Munanka, Minister/ Head of Chancery
Paul Mwafongo, Minister, Economic Affairs
B.G. Emmanuel Maganga, Defense Attache
Edward Masanja, Finacial Attache

14417 Embassy of Tunisia
1515 Massachusetts Avenue NW
Washington, DC 20005

202-862-1850; *Fax:* 202-862-1858;
www.tunconsusa.org/

Gordon Gray, Ambassador

14418 Embassy of Uganda
5911 16th Street NW
Washington, DC 20011

202-726-7100; *Fax:* 202-726-1727
info@ugandaembassyus.org;
www.ugandaemb.org

Oliver Wonekha, Ambassador
Alfred Nnam, Deputy Chief of Commission
Dickson Ogwang, Minister Counselor
Patrick Muganda Guma, Counselor
Sam Bhoi Omara, 1st Secretary

14419 Embassy of Vietnam
1233 20th Street NW
Suite 400
Washington, DC 20036

202-861-0737; *Fax:* 202-861-0917;
www.vietnamembassy-usa.org

Nguyen Quoc Cuong, Ambassador

14420 Embassy of Zimbabwe
1608 New Hampshire Avenue NW
Washington, DC 20009

202-332-7100; *Fax:* 202-483-9326
info33@zimbabwe-embassy.us;
www.zimbabwe-embassy.us

Dr. Machivenyik Mapuranga, Ambassador
Richard T. Chibuwe, Minister Counselor & Deputy Chief
Whatmore Goora, Counselor (Political)
R. Matsika, Counselor
Lt. Col. George Chinoingira, Defence Attache

14421 Embassy of the Lao People's Democratic Republic
2222 S Street NW
Washington, DC 20008

202-332-6416
202-667-0076; *Fax:* 202-332-4923
embasslao@gmail.com; www.laoembassy.com

H.E. Seng Soukhathivong, Ambassador
Thongmoon Phongphailath, 1st Secretary
Somxai Kittanouvong, 2nd Secretary (Consular)
Kerlor Yangko, 3rd Secretary (Economy And Culture)
Sounthone Duangxaty, Attache (Economic & Culture)

14422 Embassy of the People's Republic of China
3505 International Place NW
Washington, DC 20008

202-495-2266; *Fax:* 202-495-2138
chinaembpress_us@mfa.gov.cn;
www.china-embassy.org

Cui Tiankai, Ambassador
Lu Kang, Minister

14423 Embassy of the Republic of Angola
2100-2108 16th Street, NW
Washington, DC 20009

202-785-1156; *Fax:* 202-822-9049
angola@angola.org; www.angola.org

Alberto do Carmo Bento Ribeiro, Ambassador
Sofia Pegado da Silva, Minster Counselor
Manuel Fransisco Lourenco, 1st Secretary
Ismael Filipe, 2nd secretary- Political Affairs
Gil Cardoso, Financial Attache

14424 Embassy of the Republic of Botswana and GlobeScope, Inc.
1531-1533 New Hampshire Avenue NW
Washington, DC 20036

202-244-4990
smautle@botswanaembassy.org;
www.botswanaembassy.org

H.E. Dr.Tebelel Mazile Seretse, Ambassador
Ms. Sophie Heide Mautle, Deputy Head of Mission
Innocent Matengu, Counselor (Politcal Affairs)
Dineo Mpuchane, 1st Secretary (Administration)
Mighty Mohurutshe, Administrative Attache
Founded in: 1965

14425 Embassy of the Republic of Fiji
2000 M Street,NW
Suite 710
Washington, DC 20036

202-466-8320; *Fax:* 202-466-8325
info@fijiembassydc.com;
www.fijiembassydc.com

Winston Thompson, Ambassador
Akuila Vuira, 1st Secretary
Teresita R. Sauler-Cooke, Executive Asst.
Lathanzuala Phillips, Chauffer

14426 Embassy of the Republic of Latvia
2306 Massachusettes Ave, NW
Washington, DC 20008

202-328-2840; *Fax:* 202-328-2860
embassy.usa@mfa.gov.lv;
www.mfa.gov.lv/en/usa

Andrejs Pildegovics, Ambassador

14427 Embassy of the Republic of Yemen
2319 Wyoming Ave, NW
Washington, DC 20008

202-965-4760; *Fax:* 202-337-2017
ambassador@yemenembassy.org;
www.yemenembassy.org

Abdulwahab Abdulla Al-Hajjri, Ambassador
Nadia Fhashem, Asst to the Ambassador

14428 Embassy of the Republic of the Marshall Islands
2433 Massachusetts Avenue NW
Washington, DC 20008

202-234-5414; *Fax:* 202-232-3236
info@rmiembassyus.org;
www.rmiembassyus.org

Charles R. Paul, Ambassador
Dixie Lomae, 1st Secretary
Donna Dizon, Office Manager

14429 Export-Import Bank of the United States
800-565-3946; www.exim.gov
Social Media: Twitter, LinkedIn, YouTube

Fred P. Hochberg, Chairman & President

An agency of the Executive Branch of the U.S. Government, EXIM is the official export credit agency of the United States.

14430 Export.gov

www.export.gov

Export.gov is managed by the U.S. Department of Commerce's International Trade Administration. It connects businesses with U.S. Government resources that will assist them in their international sales efforts.

14431 Fair Trading Commission
Good Hope, Green Hill
St. Michael, Ba BB12003

246-424-0260; *Fax:* 246-424-0300
info@ftc.gov.bb; www.ftc.gov.bb

Peggy Griffith, CEO
Sir Neville Nicholls, Chairman
Andrew Downes, Deputy chairman
Monique Taitt, Commissioner
Kendrid Sargeant, Commissioner

14432 French Trade Commission
200 N Colombus Dr.
Chicago, IL 60601

312-565-8000; *Fax:* 312-856-1032;
www.firmafrance.com
Social Media: Facebook, Twitter, LinkedIn, RSS Feed, Google +

14433 Gambia Mission to the United Nations
800 2nd Avenue
Suite 400 F
New York, NY 10017

212-949-6640; *Fax:* 212-856-9820
gambia@un.int;
www.un.int/wcm/content/site/gambia

Tamsir Jallow, Ambassador

14434 General Consulate of Luxembourg
17 Beekman Place
New York, NY 10022

212-888-6664; *Fax:* 212-888-6116
newyork.cg@mae.etat.lu/;
www.newyork-cg.mae.lu/

Jean-Claude Knebelar, Consul General
Saba Amroun-Forbes, Consular Officer

14435 Gibraltar Information Bureau
1156 15th Street NW
Suite 1100
Washington, DC 20005

202-452-1108; *Fax:* 202-452-1109

Perry Stieglitz, Executive Director

14436 Greek Trade Commission
150 E 58th Street
17th Floor
New York, NY 10155

212-751-2404; *Fax:* 212-593-2278

Yannis Papadimitriou, Manager

14437 Hungarian Trade Commission
425 Bloor Street, East
Suite 501
Toronto-Ontario M4W 3R4

416-923-3596; *Fax:* 416-923-2097
itdtoronto@hungariantrade.org

Gyula Cseko, Trade Commissioner

14438 Icelandic Consulate General
800 3rd Avenue
36th Floor
New York, NY 10022

646-282-9360; *Fax:* 646-282-9369
icecon.ny@mfa.is; www.iceland.is/us/nyc

Hlynur Gudjonsson, Consul & Trade Commissioner

14439 International Chamber of Commerce (ICC)
1212 Avenue of the Americas
New York, NY 10036-1689

212-703-5065; *Fax:* 212-575-0327;
www.iccwbo.org
Social Media: Facebook, Twitter, LinkedIn, Google+, YouTube

Sunil Bharti Mittal, Vice-Chairman
Harold McGraw III, Chairman
Gerard Worms, Honorary Chairman
Jean-Guy Carrier, Secretary General
Founded in: 1919
Mailing list available for rent

14440 Irish Trade Board
345 Park Avenue
17th Floor
New York, NY 10154

212-180-0800

Jean McCluskey, Marketing Executive

14441 Japanese External Trade Organization
1221 Avenue of the Americas
McGraw Hill Building, 42nd Floor
New York, NY 10020

212-997-0400; *Fax:* 212-997-0464
jetrony@jetro.go.jp; www.jetro.org
Social Media: Facebook, Twitter

Hiroyuki Ishige, Chairman
Masaki Fujihara, Dir., Business Development
Daiki Nakajima, ICT/ Environment

14442 Kazakhstan Mission to the United Nations
305 East 47th Street
3rd Floor
New York, NY 10017

212-230-1900; *Fax:* 212-230-1172
kazakhstan@un.int; www.kazakhstanun.org

Byrganym Aitimova, Ambassador
Akan Rakhmetulin, Deputy Permanent Rep
Israil Tilegen, Minister Counsellor
Ruslan Bultrikov, Counsellor
Col. Alexander Kabentayev, Counsellor Military Adviser

14443 Korea Trade Promotion Center (KOTRA)
460 Park Avenue
14th Floor
New York, NY 10022

212-826-0900; *Fax:* 212-888-4930
kotrany@hotmail.com; www.kotrana.org

Sungpil Um, Presiden/North America
Il Hoon Ko, Deputy Director

14444 Kyrgyzstan Mission to the United Nations
866 United Nations Plaza
Room 477
New York, NY 10017

212-486-4214; *Fax:* 212-486-5259;
www.un.int/wcm/content/site/kyrgyzstan

Talaibek Kydyrov, Ambassador
Nuran Niyazaliev, Counsellor/DPR
Nurbek Kasymov, 1st secretary
Asel Davydova, Chief Administrative Specialist
Salamat Supataev, Administrative Officer

14445 Malaysia Mission to the United Nations
313 E 43rd Street
3rd Floor
New York, NY 10017

212-986-6310; *Fax:* 212-490-8576
malnyun@kln.gov.my; www.kln.gov.my
Social Media: RSS Feed

Hussein Haniff, Ambassador

14446 Mexico Trade Commission
757 3rd Ave
Suite 2400
New York, NY 10017-2042

212-826-2978; *Fax:* 212-826-2979;
www.mexconnect.com
Social Media: Facebook, Twitter

14447 Moldova Mission to the United Nations
35 East 29th Street
New York, NY 10016

212-447-1867; *Fax:* 212-447-4067
unmoldova@aol.com;
www.un.int/wcm/content/site/moldova

Vlad Lupan, Ambassador
Larisa Miculet, Counsellor, Deputy Permanent Rep
Carolina Podoroghin, 3rd Secretary
Tatiana Dudnicenco, CFO,Head of Chancery
Litvac Sergiu, Administrator

14448 New Zealand Trade Development Board
222 East 41st Street
New York, NY 10017-6739

212-497-0200

14449 Norwegian Trade Council
2720 34th Street NW
Washington, DC 20008

202-333-6000; *Fax:* 202-469-3990
emb.washington@mfa.no; www.norway.org
Social Media: Facebook, Twitter, Flickr, Instagram

Kare A. Aas, Ambassador
Berit Enge, Minister Counselor
Beate Anderson Varrecchia, Officer for Administrative
Harald W. Storen, Counselor
Olav Heian-Engdal, 1st Secretary

14450 Pakistan Trade Commission
12 E 65th Street
4th Floor
New York, NY 10021

212-879-5800

Abbas Zaidi, Manager

14451 Permanent Mission of Armenia to the United Nations
119 E 36th Street
New York, NY 10016

212-686-9079; *Fax:* 212-686-3934;
www.un.mfa.am/
Social Media: RSS

Andrezej Towpik, Manager
Garen Nazarian, Permanent Representative to the UN
Tigran Samvelian, Counsell, Deputy Permanent Rep
Nikolay Sahakov, 1st Secretary
Sahak Sargsyan, 2nd Secretary

14452 Permanent Mission of Bangladesh to the United Nations
820 East 2nd Avenue, Diplomat Centre
4th Floor
New York, NY 10017

212-867-3434; *Fax:* 212-972-4038
bangladesh@un.int;
www.un.int/wcm/content/site/bangladesh

Sheikh Hasina, Prime Minister

14453 Permanent Mission of Belize to the United Nations
675 Third Avenue
Suite 1911
New York, NY 10017

212-986-1240; *Fax:* 212-593-0932
belize@un.int; www.belizemission.com
Social Media: Facebook, Twitter

Mohamed Latheef, Manager
Paulette Erlington, Counselor
Han Dean Barrow, Prime Minister
Lois M. Young, Ambassador
Janine felson, Deputy Permanent Representative

14454 Permanent Mission of Ghana to the United Nations
19 E 47th Street
New York, NY 10017

212-832-1300; *Fax:* 212-751-6743
ghanaperm@aol.com; www.un.int/ghana

Ken Kanda, Ambassador
William A. Awinador-Kanyirige, Minister
Henry Tachie-Menson, Minister-Counsellor
N.A. Abayena, Counsellor
A. Ayebi Arthur, 1st Secretary

14455 Permanent Mission of Myanmar (Formerly Burma)
10 E 77th Street
New York, NY 10075

212-744-1271; *Fax:* 212-744-1290;
www.myanmarmissionny.org

Janis Priedkalns, Manager
U Han Thu, Deputy Permanent Representative
U Aung Kyaw Zan, Minister Counsellor
U kyaw Tin, Permanent representative
U Ko Ko Shein, Minister Counselor

14456 Permanent Mission of Saint Vincent & the Grenadines
800 2nd Avenue
Suite 400-G
New York, NY 10017

212-599-0950; *Fax:* 212-599-1020;
www.suv-un.org
Social Media: Facebook, Twitter, YouTube

Camillo M. Gonsalves, Ambassador
Nedra Miguel, Minister Counsellor
Mozart Carr, Attache
Maglyn Carrington, Secretary/ Accountant
N. Pepper Alexander, Security Officer/ Aide de Camp

14457 Permanent Mission of Slovakia to the United Nations
801 2nd Ave.
New York, NY 10017

212-286-8880
un.newyork@mzv.sk; www.mzv.sk/unnewyork

Founded in: 1993

14458 Permanent Mission of Tajikistan to the United Nations
216 East 49th St.
4th Floor
New York, NY 10017

212-207-3315; *Fax:* 212-207-3855;
www.un.int/

Khamrokhon Zaripov, President
Sirodjidin Aslov, Ambassador

14459 Permanent Mission of the Czech Republic to the United Nations
1109-1111 Madison Avenue
New York, NY 10028

646-981-4000; *Fax:* 646-981-4099
un.newyork@embassy.mzv.cz;
www.mzv.cz/un.newyork
Social Media: RSS

Edita Hrda, Ambassador
David Cervenka, Minister Counsellor
Peter Urbanek, Counsellor
Ladislav Steinhubel, 1st Secretary
Petra Benesova, 3rd Secretary

14460 Permanent Mission of the Kingdom of Bhutan to the United Nations
343 East 43rd Street
New York, NY 10017

212-682-2268; *Fax:* 212-661-0551
bhutan@un.int;
www.un.int/wcm/content/site/bhutan

Lhatu Wangchuk, Ambassador

14461 Permanent Mission of the Republic of Sudan to the United Nations
305 East 47th Street
3 Dag Hammarskjold Plaza, 4th Floor
New York, NY 10017

212-573-6033; *Fax:* 212-573-6160
sudan@sudanmission.org;
www.un.int/wcm/content/site/sudan

Jenine Selson, Manager

14462 Permanent Mission of the Solomon Islands to the United Nations
800 2nd Avenue
Suite 400
New York, NY 10017-4709

212-599-6192; *Fax:* 212-661-8925
simun@foreignaffairs-solomons.org;
www.un.int/wcm/content/site/solomonislands/cache/offonce/pid/4707

B Jagne, Manager

14463 Philippines Commercial Office
556 5th Avenue
New York, NY 10036

212-764-1330

14464 Poland Trade Commission
675 3rd Avenue
19th Floor
New York, NY 10017

212-351-1713

Phyllis Poland, Owner

14465 Portuguese Trade Commission
590 5th Avenue
3rd Floor
New York, NY 10036

212-354-4627; *Fax:* 212-575-4737

Soto Moura, Manager

14466 Romanian Consulate General
11766 Wilshire Blvd
Suite 560
Los Angeles, CA 90025

310-444-0043; *Fax:* 310-445-0043
http://www.romanian.com
Social Media: RSS

Corina Suteu, Manager
Eugen Chivu, Consul General

14467 Singapore Trade Commission
55 E 59th Street
Suite 21-B
New York, NY 10022

212-421-2200

Kc Yeoh, Executive Director

14468 Swedish Trade Council
150 N Michigan Avenue
Chicago, IL 60601

312-781-6222

Stefam Bergstrom, Manager

14469 Syrian Arab Republic Embassy
2215 Wyoming Avenue NW
Washington, DC 20008

202-232-6316; *Fax:* 202-265-4585;
www.syrianembassy.us/

14470 Taiwan Trade Center
1 Penn Plaza
Suite 2025
New York, NY 10119

212-904-1677; *Fax:* 212-904-1678
newyork@taitra.org.tw
http://newyork.taiwantrade.com.tw/

Kevin K. H. Wei, Director

14471 Thailand Trade Center-Consulate General of Thailand
401 N Michigan Avenue
Suite 544
Chicago, IL 60611

312-467-0044; *Fax:* 312-467-1690
ttcc@wwa.com

14472 Trade Commission of Denmark
3565 Piedimont Rd
NE #1-400
Atlanta, GA 30305

404-588-1588; *Fax:* 404-835-0799
atlhkt@um.dk
/www.dtcatlanta.um.dk

Henrik Bronner, Manager

14473 Trade Commission of Spain
500 N Michigan Avenue
Suite 1500
Chicago, IL 60611

312-644-1154

14474 Turkish Trade Commission
821 United Nations Plaza
4th Floor
New York, NY 10017

212-687-1530

14475 Turkmenistan Mission to the United Nations
866 United Nations Plaza
Suite 424
New York, NY 10017

212-486-8908; *Fax:* 212-486-2521

Aksoltan Ataeva, Manager

14476 UK Trade & Investment
1 Victoria St.
London, UK SW1H OET

212-745-0495
uktiusa@ukti.gsi.gov.uk; www.ukti.gov.uk
Social Media: Twitter, LinkedIn, Youtube, Flickr, Open to Expor

Nick Baird, CEO
Sandra Rogers, Managing Dir., Marketing
Jon Harding, COO
Charu Gorasia, Dir., Finance & IT
Michael W. Boyd, MD, Strategic Investments

14477 United Nations Mission to El Salvador
46 Park Avenue
New York, NY 10016

212-679-1616; *Fax:* 212-725-3467
elsalvador@un.int;
www.un.int/wcm/content/site/elsalvador

Antonio Montiero, Manager
Mauricio Fiunes, President

Associations

14478 American Gem Society Laboratories
8917 W Sahara Ave
Las Vegas, NV 89117-5826
702-233-6120; *Fax:* 702-233-6125
support@agslab.com; www.agslab.com
Social Media: Facebook, Twitter, RSS, Youtube, Tumblr, Blogger,
Frank Delahan, CEO
Donna Jolly, Marketing Executive
Seeks to build consumer confidence in the retail jeweler by promoting ethical business standards and professional excellence.
4.4M Members
Founded in: 1996

14479 American Gem Trade Association
3030 LBJ Freeway
Ste 840
Dallas, TX 75342-643
214-742-4367
800-972-1162; *Fax:* 214-742-7334
info@agta.org; www.agta.org
Social Media: Facebook, Twitter, YouTube
Ruben Bindra, Board President
Jeffrey Bilgore, Board VP
Gerry Manning, Board VP
Douglas K. Hucker, CEO
Joan Allen, Chief Financial Officer
Trade association for the colored gemstone industry in North America. Operates a gemological testing laboratory in New York.
750+ Members
Founded in: 1981
Mailing list available for rent

14480 American Jewelry Design Council
P.O. Box 1149
Hermitage, PA 16148
724-979-4992
800-376-3609
info@ajdc.org; www.ajdc.org
Social Media: Facebook, RSS
Barbara Heinrich, President
Alishan Halebian, VP
Jane Bohan, Secretary
Mark Schneider, Treasurer
Pascal Lacroix, Board Member
The American Jewelry Design Council is a non-profit educational corporation that recognizes and promotes the understanding of original jewelry designs as art.
Founded in: 1988

14481 American Watch Association
1201 Pennsylvania Avenue NW
PO Box 464
Washington, DC 20044
434-963-7773; *Fax:* 434-963-7776
egcollado@earthlink.net;
www.americanwatchassociation.com
David Periman, Chairman
Timothy Michno, First Vice President
Mark Goldberg, Second Vice President
Michael Kaplan, Treasurer
Steven Kaiser, Secretary
Trade association for communication among professionals and legislative advocacy.
45 Members
Founded in: 1933

14482 American Watchmakers-Clockmakers Institute
701 Enterprise Drive
Harrison, OH 45030-1696
513-367-9800
866-367-2924; *Fax:* 513-367-1414
awci@awci.com; www.awci.com
Social Media: Facebook, RSS, Instagram
Fred White, President
Drew Zimmerman, VP
Manuel Yazijian, Treasurer
Chris Carey, Secretary
Paul Wadsworth, Immediate Past President
Examines and certifies master watchmakers and clockmakers. Maintains a placement service. Conducts home study courses.
2500 Members
Founded in: 1892
Mailing list available for rent

14483 Appraisers Association of America
212 West 35th Street
11th Floor South
New York, NY 10001
212-889-5404; *Fax:* 212-889-5503;
www.appraisersassoc.org
Social Media: Facebook, Twitter, LinkedIn
Deborah G. Spanierman, AAA, President
Cynthia D. Herbert, AAA, First Vice President
Edward Yee, AAA, Second Vice President
Erica Hartman, AAA, Treasurer
Sharon Chrust, AAA, Recording Secretary
The oldest non-profit professional association of personal property appraisers. The mission and primary purpose of the association is to develop and promote standards of excellence in the profession of appraising through education and the application of the highest form of professional practice, which results on enhancing the visibility and standing of appraisers within the private and professional communities in which they serve.
900 Members
Founded in: 1949

14484 Brotherhood of Traveling Jewelers
Leys, Christie & Company
342 Madison Avenue
Suite #1530
New York, NY 10013
212-869-9162
Represents traveling jewelers.
300 Members

14485 Cultured Pearl Information Center
331 E 53rd Street
New York, NY 10022-4923
212-688-5580; *Fax:* 212-688-5857;
www.pearlinfo.com
Devin MacNow, Executive Director
Conference information and buying guide for pearls.

14486 Diamond Council of America
3212 West End Ave
Suite 400
Nashville, TN 37203
615-385-5301
877-283-5669; *Fax:* 615-385-4955;
www.diamondcouncil.org
Social Media: Facebook
Peter Engel, Chairman
Terry Chandler, President/CEO
Provides courses in diamontology and gemology to retail jewelers and their employees who are DCA members. Sixty-six retailers representing 1,800 locations.
70 Members
Founded in: 1944

14487 Diamond Dealers Club
580 Fifth Avenue
Floor 10
New York, NY 10036
212-790-3600; *Fax:* 212-869-5164
mhochbaum@nyddc.com; www.nyddc.com
Social Media: Facebook, Twitter, LinkedIn
Reuven Kaufman, President
Israel Ashkenazy, VP
Abraham Einhorn, Treasurer
Elliot Krischer, Secretary
William Lerner, General Counsel
Seeks to foster the interest of the diamond industry, promote equitable trade principles and eliminate abuses and unfair trading practices.
Founded in: 1931

14488 Diamond Manufacturers and Importers Association of America
580 Fifth Avenue
Suite 2000
New York, NY 10036
212-944-2066
800-223-2244; *Fax:* 212-202-7525
info@dmia.net; www.dmia.net
Ronald VanderLinden, President
Stuart Samuels, Secretary
Parag Shah, Treasurer
Eli Haas, VP
Steve Eisen, Director, Board Member
Represents and promotes manufacturers and importers of diamonds and rare gems.
150 Members
Founded in: 1931

14489 Diamond Peacock Club Kebadjian Brothers
Kebadjian Brothers
333 Washington Street
Suite 638
Boston, MA 02108-5111
617-523-5565; *Fax:* 617-523-7193
info@kebadjian.com; www.kebadjian.com
Claude Kebadjian, Founder And Designer
Seta Kebadjian, Designing
Michael Kebadjian, Jewelry Design
Founded in: 1957

14490 Diamond Promotion Service
466 Lexington Avenue
New York, NY 10017-9998
800-370-6789; *Fax:* 877-276-1224
newyorkdps@jwt.com;
www.diamondpromotions.com
Social Media: Facebook, Twitter
Resource for the tools and strategies to sell more diamonds. Buy marketing materials, train your staff, find the suppliers of advertised jewelry and more.

14491 Estate Jewelry Association of America
209 Post Street
Suite 718
San Francisco, CA 94108-5209
415-834-0718
800-584-5522; *Fax:* 212-840-1644
jaa@aol.com

14492 Fashion Jewelry Association of America
3 Davol Sq
Unit 135
Providence, RI 02903-4710
401-273-1515
Nick Macris, President
150 Members
Founded in: 1985

14493 Gem & Lapidary Dealers Association
120 Derwood Circle
Rockville, MD 20850

301-294-1640; *Fax:* 301-294-0034
info@glda.com; www.glda.com
Social Media: Facebook, Twitter, Google+, Pinterest

Arnold Duke, President
Brandy Swanson, Customer Service
Jennifer Guillot, Exhibit Sales/Services
Monique Anderson, PR/ Marketing & New Media
Don Wyatt, PR/ Marketing & New Media

G.L.D.A. is a firmly established, successful wholesale gem & jewelry show promotion company. For the past 30 years, our Tucson show has enjoyed a booming success growth rate. Our show has included 400 exhibit booths which is the maximum that this facility would accomodate.

14494 Gold Prospectors Association of America
43445 Business Park Drive
Suite #113
Temecula, CA 92590

951-699-4749
800-551-9707; *Fax:* 951-699-4062
info@goldprospectors.org;
www.goldprospectors.org
Social Media: Facebook, Twitter, LinkedIn, YouTube

Thomas Massie, CEO

GPAA is the largest recreational gold prospecting club. Owner of The Outdoor Channel, a cable TV channel featuring real outdoors for real people.
35M Members
Founded in: 1985
Mailing list available for rent

14495 Independent Jewelers Organization
136 Old Post Road
Southport, CT 06890-1302

203-846-4215
800-624-9252; *Fax:* 203-254-7429
ijo@ijo.com; www.ijo.com
Social Media: Facebook, Twitter, LinkedIn

Penny Palmer, Member Services Director

Jewelry buying group and service organization for retail jewelers.
850 Members
Founded in: 1972

14496 Indian Arts & Crafts Association
4010 Carlisle NE
Suite C
Albuquerque, NM 87107

505-265-9149; *Fax:* 505-265-8251
info@iaca.com; www.iaca.com
Social Media: Facebook, Twitter

Jacque Foutz, President
Joseph P. Zeller, President
Kathi Ouellet, Treasurer
Georgia Fischel, Secretary
Beth Hale, Membership Director

Nonprofit trade association whose mission is to promote, protect and preserve Indian arts.
700 Members
Founded in: 1974
Mailing list available for rent

14497 Industrial Diamond Association of America
PO Box 29460
Columbus, OH 43229

614-797-2265; *Fax:* 614-797-2264
tkane-ida@insight.rr.com;
www.superabrasives.org

Terry M. Kane, Executive Director
Mike Mustin, President
Keith Reckling, Secretary/Treasurer
Troy Heuermann, Vice President
Edward E. Galen, Executive Director

Association of industrial diamond, cvd diamond and polycrystalling supplies, toolmakers. Products and services provided and used in most manufacturing and constuction industries such as: stone processing, glass construction, electronics, medical, woodworking, etc.
190 Members
Founded in: 1946

14498 International Colored Gemstone Association
30 West 47th Street
Suite 201
New York, NY 10036

212-352-8814; *Fax:* 212-352-9054
claudiu@gemstone.org; www.gemstone.org
Social Media: RSS Feed

Benjamin Hackman, President
Damien Cody, VP
Santpal Sinchawla, Vice-President
Marcelo Ribeiro Fernandes, Treasurer
Ehud Harel, Secretary

Nonprofit association representing the international gemstone industry. Works to increase the understanding, appreciation and sales of colored gemstones worldwide.
Founded in: 1984

14499 International Fine Jewelers Guild
257 Adams Lane
Hewlett, NY 11557

516-295-2516; *Fax:* 516-374-5060
Info@InternationalFineJewelersGuild.com;
www.iwjg.com

Bertram Kalisher, Chairman
Olivia Cornell, President
Berge Abajian, Jewelry Industry Advisory Board
Kari Allen, Jewelry Industry Advisory Board
Zoltan David, Jewelry Industry Advisory Board

14500 International Precious Metals Institute
5101 North 12th Avenue
Suite C
Pensacola, FL 32504

850-476-1156; *Fax:* 850-476-1548
mail@ipmi.org; www.ipmi.org
Social Media: Facebook, LinkedIn, YouTube

Robert Bullen Smith, Chairman
Jon Potts, Vice Chairman
Sascha Biehl, Treasurer
Bodo Albrecht, Secretary
Chris Jones, Immediate Past Chairman

International association of producers, refiners, fabricators, scientists, users, financial institutions, merchants, private and public sector groups and the general precious metals community created to provide a forum for the exchange of information and technology.
Founded in: 1976

14501 International Society of Appraisers
225 West Wacker Drive
Suite 650
Chicago, IL 60606

312-981-6778; *Fax:* 312-265-2908
isa@isa-appraisers.org; www.isa-appraisers.org
Social Media: Facebook, Twitter, LinkedIn

Christine Guernsey, ISA CAPP, President
Perri Guthrie, ISA CAPP, Vice President
Steven R. Roach, JD, ISA CAPP, Treasurer
Karen S. Rabe, ISA CAPP, Secretary
Hughene D. Acheson, ISA AM, Director

Nonprofit professional association of personal property appraisers. ISA provides education and organizational support to its members, to serve the public by producing highly qualified and ethical appraisers who are recognized authorities in personal property appraising.
1400+ Members
Founded in: 1979
Mailing list available for rent

14502 Jewelers Board of Trade
95 Jefferson Boulevard
Warwick, RI 02888

401-467-0055; *Fax:* 401-467-6070
jbtinfo@jewelersboard.com;
www.jewelersboard.com
Social Media: Twitter

Dione Kenyen, President

Trade Association: credit and collection for the jewelry industry.
3300 Members
Founded in: 1884

14503 Jewelers Vigilance Committee
801 2nd Avenue
Suite 303
New York, NY 10017

212-997-2002; *Fax:* 212-997-9148
clg@jvclegal.org; www.jvclegal.org
Social Media: Facebook, LinkedIn

Beryl Raff, Chairman
Steven P. Kaiser, 1st Vice President
Scott Berg, 2nd Vice President
Mark Goldberg, Treasurer
Cecilia L. Gardner, President, CEO, General Counsel

The sole legal compliance association in the jewelry industry. Educates the trade to understand complex rules governing the manufacture, sale and marketing of fine jewelry.
1300 Members
Founded in: 1917

14504 Jewelers of America
120 Broadway
Suite 2820
New York, NY 10271

646-658-0246
800-223-0673; *Fax:* 646-658-0256
info@jewelers.org; www.jewelers.org
Social Media: Facebook, Twitter, LinkedIn

Ryan Berg, Chairman
David J. Bonaparte, President and CEO
John Henne, Chair Elect
Mark Light, Vice Chair
Coleman Clark, Treasurer

Center of knowledge for the jeweler and an advocate for professionalism and high social, ethical and environmental standards in the jewelry trade. Our mission is to assist all members in improving their business skills and profitability. JA will provide acess to meaningful educational programs and services, leadership in public and industry affairs, and encourage members with common interests to act in the industry's best interest.
Founded in: 1906
Mailing list available for rent

14505 Jewelry Industry Distributors Association
701 Enterprise Drive
Harrison, OH 45030
513-367-2357; *Fax:* 513-367-1414;
www.jida.info
Bill Nagle, President
Harvey Cobrin, First VP
Rick Foster, Secretary/Treasurer
Sets standards of service and facilitates the exchange of information of all types among members in order to improve business, maximize opportunities, and minimize risks.
150 Members
Founded in: 1946

14506 Jewelry Information Center
120 Broadway
Suite 2820
New York, NY 10271
646-658-0246
800-223-0673; *Fax:* 646-658-0256
info@jewelers.org; www.jic.org
Social Media: Facebook, Twitter, RSS
Matthews Runzi, President and CEO
Robert Headley, Vice President & COO
Carlon Alexandr, Administrative Assistant
Carey Miller, Membership Manager
Identifies deceptive trade practices and misleading advertising. Provides advice on marketing and assists in prosecution of violations. The media side of the Jewelers Vigilance Committee.
1000 Members
Founded in: 1946
Mailing list available for rent

14507 Jewelry Manufacturers Guild
PO Box 46099
Los Angeles, CA 90046
909-769-1820
800-359-0340; *Fax:* 909-769-1920
Paula Glick Hill, Operations Manager
Promotes and improves conditions in the fine jewelry manufacturing industry.
400 Members

14508 Leading Jewelers Guild
PO Box 64609
Los Angeles, CA 90064
310-820-3386; *Fax:* 310-820-3530;
www.love-story.com
Social Media: Facebook, Twitter, Google+, Pinterest
James West, President
Mailing list available for rent

14509 Manufacturing Jewelers & Suppliers of America
8 Hayward St.
Attleboro, MA 2703
508-316-2132
800-444-6572; *Fax:* 508-316-1429
info@mjsa.org; www.mjsa.org
Social Media: Facebook, Twitter, LinkedIn, Pinterest
Ann Arnold, Chair
Darrell Warren, Vice Chair
Steven A. Cipolla, Vice Chair
David W. Cochran, President, CEO
James K. McCarty, Chief Operating Officer & CFO
National trade association for the manufacturing jewelers and silversmiths. Sponsors trade shows, expositions and social events.
1.8M Members
Founded in: 1903

14510 Manufacturing Jewelers and Silversmiths
8 Hayward St.
Attleboro, MA 2703
508-316-2132
800-444-6572; *Fax:* 508-316-1429
info@mjsa.org; www.mjsa.org
Social Media: Facebook, Twitter, LinkedIn
Ann Arnold, Chair
Darrell Warren, Vice Chair
Steven A. Cipolla, Vice Chair
David W. Cochran, President, CEO
James K. McCarty, Chief Operating Officer & CFO
The trade association for all segments of the American jewelry manufacturing and supply industry.
Founded in: 1903

14511 National Association of Jewelry Appraisers
P.O. Box 18
Rego Park, NY 11374-0018
718-896-1536; *Fax:* 718-997-9057
office@NAJAAppraisers.com;
www.najaappraisers.com
Social Media: Facebook
Gail Brett Levine, Executive Director
Purpose is to maintain professional standards and education in the field of jewelry appraising and provide members benefits at lower cost than can be attained individually.
720 Members
Founded in: 1981

14512 Platinum Guild International USA
620 Newport Center Dr
Suite 800
Newport Beach, CA 92660-6420
212-404-1600
800-207-PLAT; *Fax:* 949-760-8780;
www.preciousplatinum.com
Social Media: Facebook, Twitter, Google+, Pinterest
Laurie A Hudson, President
Organization promoting platinum jewelry. Maintains a website where the press and the public can find helpful information.
Founded in: 1975

14513 Plumb Club
157 Engle Street
Englewood, NJ 07631
201-816-8881; *Fax:* 201-816-8882;
www.plumbclub.com
Jonathan Goodman Cohen, President
Michael Lerche, VP
Michael Langhammer, Treasurer
Roger Forman, Secretary
Jeffrey Cohen, Director
Exclusive social organization within the jewelry industry holding black tie events for members and their clients and exhibitor shows.

14514 Schneider National
3101 S Packerland Drive
Po Box 2545
Green Bay, WI 54306-2545
920-592-2000
800-558-6767; www.schneider.com
Social Media: RSS
Don Schneider, Chairman
Christopher Lofgren PhD, President & CEO
A leading provider of transportation and logistics services with a comprehensive reach across North America and a growing presence in Europe and Asia.
Founded in: 1935

14515 Silver Institute
1400 I Street, NW
Suite #550
Washington, DC 20005
202-835-0185; *Fax:* 202-835-0155
info@silverinstitute.org;
www.silverinstitute.org
Fernando Alanis, President
Michael DiRienzo, Executive Director and Secretary
Mitchell Krebs, Vice President
Thomas Angelos, Treasurer
Mark Spurbeck, Assistant Treasurer
International association of miners, refiners, fabricators and wholesalers of silver and silver products.
Founded in: 1971

14516 Silver Users Association
3930 Walnut Street
Suite 210
Fairfax, VA 22030
703-930-7790
800-245-6999; *Fax:* 703-359-7562
pmiller@mwcapitol.com;
www.silverusersassociation.org
Bill LeRoy, President
Mike Huber, VP
Jack Gannon, Immediate Past President
Bill Hamelin, Treasurer
John King, Secretary
Represents manufacturers and distributors of products in which silver is an essential element, such as photographic materials, medical and dental supplies, batteries and electronic and electrical equipment, silverware, mirrors, commemorative art and jewelry.
27 Members
Founded in: 1947

14517 Society of American Silversmiths
P.O.Box 786
West Warwick, RI 02893
401-461-6840; *Fax:* 401-828-0162
sas@silversmithing.com;
www.silversmithing.com
Jeffrey Herman, Founder/Executive Director
Organization devoted to the preservation and promotion of the silversmithing art and craft.
240 Members
Founded in: 1989
Mailing list available for rent

14518 Society of North American Goldsmiths
PO Box 1355
Eugene, OR 97440
541-345-5689; *Fax:* 541-345-1123
info@snagmetalsmith.org;
www.snagmetalsmith.org
Social Media: Facebook, Twitter, LinkedIn, Pinterest, Flickr, RSS, YouTub
Renee Zettle-Sterling, President
Anne Havel, Treasurer
Gwynne Rukenbrod, Executive Dir.
Tara Jecklin, Operations Manager
John Garbett, Advertising & Production Director
Promotes a favorable and enriching environment in which contemporary metalsmiths practice their art. One aspect of this process is educating the public about the quality and rich diversity within the field of metalsmithing. Exhibitions, public forums, lectures, and published documents are our primary methods of reaching out to the public. SNAG sponsors workshops, seminars, audio-visual services and an annual conference.
Founded in: 1968

14519 The Fashion Jewelry & Accessories Trade Association (FJATA)
25 Sea Grass Way
North Kingstown, RI 02852

401-667-0520; *Fax:* 401-267-9096
bcleaveland@fjata.org; www.fjata.org
Social Media: Twitter

Brent Cleaveland, Executive Director

The voice of jewelry and accessories manufacturers, suppliers and retailers to regulatory agencies.
225 Members

14520 Women's Jewelry Association
80 Washington Street
Suite 205
Poughkeepsie, NY 12601

845-473-7323; *Fax:* 646-355-0219
info@womensjewelryassociation.com;
www.womensjewelryassociation.com

Andrea Hansen, President
Brandee Dallow, President Elect
Tryna Kochanek, Immediate Past President
Kristie Nicolosi, Treasurer
Bernadette Mack, Executive Director

To empower women to achieve their highest goals in the international jewelry, watch and related businesses.
Founded in: 1983

14521 World Gold Council
685 Third Avenue
27th Floor
New York, NY 10017

212-317-3800; *Fax:* 212-688-0410
info@gold.org; www.gold.org
Social Media: Facebook, Twitter, LinkedIn, YouTube Flickr, RSS Feed, Goog

Aram Shishmanian, CEO
Brenda Bates, Managing Director, Corporate Comm.
Natalie Dempster, Managing Director, Central Banks
Roland Wang, Managing Director, China
William Rhind, Managing Director, Investment

Organization formed and funded by the world's leading gold mining companies with the aim of stimulating and maximizing the demand for, and holding of gold by consumers, investors, industry and the official sector.
23 Members
Founded in: 1987

Newsletters

14522 Benchmark
Manufacturing Jewelers & Suppliers of America
57 John L Dietsch Sq
Attleboro Falls, MA 02763-1027

401-274-3840
800-444-6572; *Fax:* 401-274-0265
info@mjsa.org; www.mjsa.org

James McCarthy, COO
Bruce Coltin, Operations Manager
Kristin Kopaz, Operations Manager
Corrie Berry, Sales Manager

Offers details of association activities and industry events for members.
4 Pages
Frequency: Bi-Monthly

14523 Costume Jewelry Review
Retail Reporting Bureau
302 5th Ave
11th Floor
New York, NY 10001-3604

212-279-7000

Offers news and information on the costume jewelry industry, suppliers and manufacturers.
Cost: $108.00
Frequency: Monthly

14524 Diamond Insight
Tryon Mercantile
790 Madison Avenue
New York, NY 10021-6124

212-288-9011; *Fax:* 212-772-1286;
www.newsletteraccess.com

Guido Giovannini-Torelli, Editor

Penetrates the multifaceted world of diamonds, giving intelligence on the world's important stones, future price indicators, key individuals behind the trends, jewelry auctions and DeBeers/CSO Activities.
Cost: $325.00
12 Pages
Frequency: Monthly
Circulation: 250
Printed in one color on glossy stock

14525 Diamond Registry Bulletin
Diamond Registry
580 5th Avenue
New York, NY 10036-4701

212-575-0444
800-223-7955; *Fax:* 212-575-0722
info@diamondregistry.com;
www.diamondregistry.com
Social Media: Facebook

Joseph Schlussel, Founder
Nissan Perla, President & CEO

Monthly newsletter offering the latest trends, prices and forecasts concerning diamonds, diamond jewelry and diamond mining.
Frequency: Monthly
ISSN: 0199-9753
Founded in: 1961

14526 Jewelers' Security Alliance Newsletter
Jewelers' Security Alliance
6 E 45th St
Suite 1305
New York, NY 10017-2469

212-687-0328
800-537-0067; *Fax:* 212-808-9168
jsa2@jewelerssecurity.org;
www.jewelerssecurity.org

John J Kennedy, President
Robert W. Frank, Vice President
Helen M. Buck, Manager of Membership Services

Principal activity is providing education and information to jewelers so they can guard against loss through crimes, including burglary, robbery and theft.
Cost: $375.00
Frequency: Annual+
Founded in: 1883

14527 Jewelers' Security Bulletin
Jewelers' Security Alliance
6 E 45th St
Suite 1305
New York, NY 10017-2469

212-687-0328
800-537-0067; *Fax:* 212-808-9168
jsa2@jewelerssecurity.org;
www.jewelerssecurity.org

John J Kennedy, President
Robert W. Frank, Vice President
Helen M. Buck, Manager of Membership Services

Principal activity is providing education and information to jewelers so they can guard against loss through crimes, including burglary, robbery and theft.
19500 Members
Founded in: 1883
Mailing list available for rent

14528 Jewelry Newsletter International
Newsletters International
7710 T Cherry Park Drive
#421
Houston, TX 77095

888-972-4662; www.jewellerybusiness.com

Len Fox, Editor

Informs manufacturers, wholesalers, suppliers, and retailers of jewelry how to stimulate sales, increase profits, and cut costs.
Cost: $250.00
4-8 Pages
Frequency: Monthly
Founded in: 1975
Printed in on matte stock

14529 Precious Metals News
International Precious Metals Institute
5101 N 12th Avenue
Suite C
Pensacola, FL 32504

850-476-1156; *Fax:* 850-476-1548
mail@ipmi.org; www.ipmi.org

Robert Ianniello, President
Frequency: Quarterly
Circulation: 1000

14530 Spectra
American Gem Society
8917 W Sahara Ave
Las Vegas, NV 89117-5826

702-233-6120; *Fax:* 702-233-6125
support@agslab.com; www.agslab.com

Frank Delahan, CEO

Society news covering all aspects of the jewelry world.
12 Pages
Frequency: Quarterly
Founded in: 1934

Magazines & Journals

14531 AJM Magazine: The Authority on Jewelry Manufacturing
Manufacturing Jewelers & Suppliers of America
57 John L Dietsch Sq
Attleboro Falls, MA 02763-1027

401-274-3840
800-444-6572; *Fax:* 401-274-0265
info@mjsa.org; www.mjsa.org

James McCarthy, COO
Corrie Silvia Berry, Director of Sales & Business
David W. Cochran, President & CEO
Kristin Kopaz, Operations Manager
Dawn Britland, Assistant Controller

This is the only magazine dedicated solely to jewelry manufacturers. It delivers the three T's of jewelry manufacturing: trends, technology and techniques.
Cost: $47.00
Frequency: Monthly
Founded in: 1903
Printed in 4 colors on glossy stock

14532 Accent Magazine
Larkin Group

485 Fashion Ave
Suite 1400
New York, NY 10018-6804

212-594-1439; *Fax:* 212-594-8556

AJ Larkin, Publisher

Provides trend analysis and market forecasts for buyers and designers, for accessories, clothing, and footwear. Also covers convention and tradeshow news, and new product launches.
Cost: $24.00
Frequency: Monthly
Circulation: 13,000

14533 Adornment: Newsletter of Jewelry and Related Arts
1333A N Avenue
New Rochelle, NY 10804

914-636-3784
ekarlin@usa.net

Elyse Karlin, Publisher/Editor/CEO
Cost: $60.00
Frequency: Quarterly
Circulation: 800
Founded in: 1999

14534 Chronos
Golden Bell Press
2403 Champa St
Denver, CO 80205-2621

303-296-1600; *Fax:* 303-295-2159
print@goldenbellpress.com;
www.goldenbellpress.com

Editorial material looks at timepieces of the past, present and future, bringing you the latest, the best and the most intriguing creation from the leading international watch and clock makers. The history of timepiece manufacturers and their significant milestones are also reported as well as armchair tours of the world's most prestigious horological museums.
Cost: $2250.00
Frequency: Quarterly
Circulation: 20000
Founded in: 1933

14535 Colored Stone
PRIMEDIA
60 Chestnut Avenue
Suite 201
Devon, PA 19333-1312

610-964-6300
610-232-5700; *Fax:* 610-293-1717;
www.colored-stone.com

Joseph Breck, Publisher
Morgan Beard, Editor-in-Chief

Contains news and information on the gem and gemstone jewelry industry.
Cost: $29.95
64 Pages
Circulation: 10000
Founded in: 1986

14536 Couture International Jeweler
Miller Freeman Publications
770 Broadway
5th Floor
New York, NY 10003-9595

212-780-0400; *Fax:* 847-763-9037
ijmag@halldata.com; www.couturejeweler.com

Debra De Roo Ballard, Publisher
Lynda Roguso, Operations Director
Karen Stewart, Operations Director

Publication features information on hot trends in fine jewelry and fashion.
Cost: $60.00
Circulation: 20000
Founded in: 1964

14537 GZ (European Jeweler)
JCK International Publishing Group
360 Park Ave S
New York, NY 10010-1710

646-746-6400; *Fax:* 646-746-7131;
www.jckgroup.com

Ted Smith, CEO
Donna Borrelli, Associate Publisher
Hedda Schupak, Editor-in-Chief
Tracey Peden, Marketing Manager
Nancy Walsh, Senior Vice President
Cost: $49.95
Frequency: Monthly
Founded in: 1874

14538 High-Volume Jeweler
Reed Business Information
201 King of Prussia Road
Radnor, PA 19087-5114

610-889-9577; *Fax:* 630-288-8686;
www.reedbusiness.com

Shawn Mery, Publisher
Lisa Reed, CFO
Stuart Whayman, CFO

Provides original market research and in-depth analysis of current news and industry trends affecting this segment of the jewelry and watch market. Features operational strategies and new technological developments that can make and save money for retailers and vendors.
Cost: $60.00
Frequency: Bi-Monthly
Circulation: 5,000

14539 Horological Times
American Watchmakers-Clockmakers Institute
701 Enterprise Drive
Harrison, OH 45030-1696

513-367-9800
866-367-2924; *Fax:* 513-367-1414;
www.awci.com
Social Media: Facebook, RSS

James Lubic, Executive Director
Tom Pack, Operations Director
Jennifer Bilodeau, Assistant Editor
Elizabeth Janszen, Membership Coordinator

Contains articles dealing with the techniques of servicing and repairing watches and clockes; the uses of shop tool and equipment; the functional characteristics of mechanical, electronic, and antique timepieces.
Frequency: Monthly
Founded in: 1892
Mailing list available for rent

14540 International Wristwatch Magazine USA
International Publishing Corporation
979 Summer Street
PO Box 110204
Stamford, CT 06905

203-259-8100; *Fax:* 203-295-0847;
www.iwmagazine.com

Gary George, Editor-in-Chief
Patricia Russo, General Manager

Editorial content provides a consumer-oriented focus on new, vintage, and collectable watches.
Cost: $7.95
150 Pages
Frequency: Bi-Monthly
Circulation: 30,000
ISBN: 0-744706-22-2
Founded in: 1989
Printed in 4 colors on glossy stock

14541 JCK Magazine
JCK International Publishing Group
1018 W Ninth Avenue
King of Prussia, PA 19406-1

610-205-1100
800-305-7759; *Fax:* 610-205-1139;
www.jckgroup.com

Nancy Walsh, Senior VP
Fran Pennella, Marketing Director
Mark Smelzer, Publisher
Hedda Schupak, Editor-in-chief
Jay Jackson, Chief Operating Officer

Serves retailers, manufacturers, and vendors of fine jewelry and selected upscale gift categories, providing valuable market and design trend information and how-to information about gemology, financial management, employee relations, marketing, advertising, and visual merchandising, e-commerce, and other topics.
Cost: $49.95
Frequency: Monthly
Founded in: 1869

14542 JQ Limited Edition
JQ Publishing
585 5th Street W
Sonoma, CA 95476-6831

707-938-1082; *Fax:* 707-935-6585;
www.retailmerchandising.net

Audrey Bromstad, Publisher
Cynthia Unninayar, Editor
Deborah Rittenberg, Marketing Manager

Issues contain articles presented with illustrations on precious colored gems and diamonds, creative jewelry designs, designers, and luxury watches.
Frequency: Monthly
Circulation: 300000
Founded in: 1985

14543 Jewelers' Circular: Keystone
Reed Business Information
360 Park Ave S
New York, NY 10010-1737

646-746-6400; *Fax:* 646-756-7583
hschupak@reedbusiness.com;
www.reedbusiness.com
Social Media: Twitter, LinkedIn

John Poulin, CEO
Hedda Schupak, Editor
Victoria Jones, Production Manager
James Reed, Owner
Andrew Rak, Senior Vice President

Discusses news of interest mainly to the jewelry shop owner and manager. Covers such topics as; product notices, manufacturer news and tips on operating a successful business.
Cost: $49.95
Frequency: Monthly
Circulation: 25000
Founded in: 1874
Printed in on glossy stock

14544 Jewelry Appraiser
National Association of Jewelry Appraisers
P. O. Box 18
Rego Park, NY 11374-0018

718-896-1536; *Fax:* 718-997-9057
office@najaappraisers.com;
www.najaappraisers.com

Gail Brett Levine, Executive Director

An important source for all jewelry appraisers.
Frequency: Quarterly
Founded in: 1981

14545 Lapidary Journal
300 Chesterfield Parkway
Suite 100
Malvern, PA 19355-937

610-232-5700
800-676-4336; *Fax:* 610-232-5754;
www.lapidaryjournal.com

Merle White, Editor
Karen Nuckols, Sales Director
Joe Breck, Publisher

This publication focuses fundamentally on the all aspects of the jewelry industry.
Cost: $29.95
Frequency: Monthly
Circulation: 45000
Founded in: 1947

14546 Link
National Cuff Link Society
PO Box 5970
Vernon Hills, IL 60061-5970

847-816-0035; *Fax:* 847-816-0035;
www.cufflink.com

Gena Klompus, President
Founded in: 1990

14547 Lustre
Cygnus Publishing
19 W 44th St
Suite 1405
New York, NY 10036-6101

212-921-1091; *Fax:* 212-921-5539
lorraine.depasque@cygnuspub.com;
www.cygnusb2b.com

Tim Murphy, Publisher
Roy Kim, Sales Director
Lorraine DePasque, Editor In Chief
Barb Hesse, Circulation Manager
Paul Mackler, President/CEO
Circulation: 4000
Founded in: 1966

14548 Modern Jeweler
3 Huntington Quadrangle
Suite 301N
Melville, NY 11747-3602

631-845-2700
800-255-5113; *Fax:* 631-845-7109
tim.murphy@cygnuspub.com;
www.modernjeweler.com

Matthew Kramer, Managing Editor
Timothy Murphy, Publisher
Cheryl Kremkow, Editor in Chief
Barb Hesse, Circulation Manager
Jeff Prine, Executive Editor

A trade publication serving retail jewelers, wholesalers and manufacturers of jewelry, watches and related items. Accepts advertising.
Cost: $66.00
90 Pages
Frequency: Monthly
Circulation: 30000

14549 Monroe Originals
Karen Monroe
14014 Moorpark Street
Apartment 122
Sherman Oaks, CA 91423-3492

Fax: 818-783-5009

Handmade wholesale jewelry designs magazine.
Cost: $2.00
50 Pages
Frequency: Monthly

14550 Ornament Magazine
PO Box 2349
San Marcos, CA 92079-9806

760-599-0222
800-888-8950; *Fax:* 760-599-0228
ornament@sbcglobal.net
ornamentmagazine.com

Robert Liu, Co-Editor
Carolin Denish, Co-Editor

Offers information on contemporary, ethnic, ancient jewelry and costumes.
Cost: $26.00
Frequency: Quarterly
Circulation: 38,000
Founded in: 1976

14551 Professional Jeweler
Bond Communications
1500 Walnut Street
Suite 1200
Philadelphia, PA 19102-3523

215-670-0727
888-557-0727; *Fax:* 215-545-9629
askus@professionaljeweler.com;
www.professionaljeweler.com

Lee Lawrence, Publisher/President
Peggy Jo Donahue, Editor-in-Chief
Peter James, Manager
Carole Masciantonio, Marketing Coordinator
Lisa Pastore, Advertising Manager

Editorial content provides these professionals with the information they need to meet business objectives and ensure success. Regular departments offer the latest news, trends, technical and practical information on all aspects of the jewelry industry.
Cost: $49.95
105 Pages
Frequency: Monthly
Circulation: 24000
ISSN: 1097-5314
Founded in: 1998
Printed in 4 colors on glossy stock

14552 Southern Jewelry News
Mullen Publications
9629 Old Nations Ford Rd
Charlotte, NC 28273-5719

704-527-5111
800-738-5111; *Fax:* 704-527-5114;
www.mullenpublications.com

Chip Smith, Publisher
Bill Newnam, Production Manager
Robert Cutshaw, Production Manager
Elesa Dillon, Sales Manager

Dedicated to the southern jewelry industry and contains industry news, local and regional events, personnel announcements, and pricing information.
Frequency: Monthly
Circulation: 13,431
Founded in: 1945

14553 Watch and Clock Review
Golden Bell Press
2403 Champa St
Denver, CO 80205-2621

303-296-1600; *Fax:* 303-295-2159
print@goldenbellpress.com;
www.goldenbellpress.com

Offers news and information on fashion accessories and jewelry.
Cost: $19.50
48 Pages
ISSN: 1082-2453
Founded in: 1935

Trade Shows

14554 ASD/AMD Las Vegas Variety Merchandise Show
ASD/AMD Merchandise Group
Las Vegas Convention Center
3150 Paradise Road
Las Vegas, NV 89109

702-892-0711; *Fax:* 702-892-2933;
www.lvcva.com

Features tens of thousands of unique products in hundres of popular categories.
10000 Attendees
Frequency: March

14555 Accent on Design
George Little Management
10 Bank Street
Suite 1200
White Plains, NY 10606-1954

914-486-6070
800-272-7469; *Fax:* 914-948-2867;
www.nyigf.com

Elizabeth Murphy, Show Manager
George Little II, President

Three hundred and seventy booths of the latest and most innovative gift lines such as decorative accessories and home furnishings.
50M Attendees
Frequency: August
Founded in: 1984

14556 American Gem Society Conclave
8881 W Sahara Avenue
Las Vegas, NV 89117

702-255-6500; *Fax:* 702-255-7420;
www.ags.org

Glory Wade, Show Manager

One hundred and sixty booths. Conference and exhibitors.
1M Attendees
Frequency: April

14557 American Gem Trade Association Expo
3030 LBJ Freeway
Suite 840
Dallas, TX 75234

214-742-4367
800-972-1162; *Fax:* 214-742-7334
info@agta.org; www.agta.org

Elizabeth Ross, Marketing Manager
Rick Krementz, President

Two booths featuring exhibits of loose colored gemstones and diamonds.
10.3M Attendees
Frequency: February

14558 Annual Spring New Products Show
Pacific Expositions
1600 Kapiolani Boulevard
Suite 1660
Honnolulu, HI 96814

808-945-3594; *Fax:* 808-946-6399

48000 Attendees
Frequency: Annual

14559 Bead and Button Show
Kalmbach Publishing Company
21027 Crossroads Circle
PO Box 1612
Waukesha, WI 53187-1612

262-796-8776
800-553-6644
262-796-8776; *Fax:* 262-796-1615;
www.beadandbuttonshow.com
Social Media: Facebook, Pinterest

3500 Attendees

14560 Best Bead Show
Crystal Myths

PO Box 3243
Albuquerque, NM 87190

505-883-9295; *Fax:* 505-889-9553

14561 Business to Business Gem Trade Show
Gem & Lapidary Wholesalers
Holiday Inn Palo Verde/Holidome
Tucson, AZ

601-879-8832; *Fax:* 601-879-3282
info@glwshows.com; www.glwshows.com

Frequency: February

14562 Catalog in Motion
Bell Group
Tucson E Hilton
Tucson, AZ

505-839-3249; *Fax:* 505-839-3248;
www.riogrande.com

Frequency: February

14563 Fashion Accessories Expo
Business Journals
50 Day Street
Norwalk, CT 06854

203-853-6015; *Fax:* 203-852-8175;
www.busjour.com

Britton Jones, President
Lizette Chin, Show Director Market
14000 Attendees

14564 Fashion Accessories Expo Accessories to Go
Business Journals
50 Day Street
Norwalk, CT 06854

203-853-6015; *Fax:* 203-852-8175;
www.busjour.com

Britton Jones, President
Lorrie Frost, Accessories Publisher
14000 Attendees

14565 GJX Gem and Jewelry Show
198 S Granada Avenue
Tucson, AZ

520-824-4200; *Fax:* 520-882-4203;
www.gjxusa.com

Allan Norville, President
Frequency: February

14566 GLDA Gem and Jewelry Show
Gem & Lapidary Dealers Association
PO Box 2391
Tucson, AZ 85702

520-792-9431; *Fax:* 520-882-2836
info@glda.com; www.glda.com

Paul Page, Director Marketing

Qualified buyers receive free admission. Buyers are jewerly retailers, manufacturers, wholesalers, gem dealers.
16000 Attendees
Frequency: February

14567 Gem & Jewelry Show
International Gem & Jewelry Show
120 Derwood Circle
Rockville, MD 20850-1264

301-294-1640; *Fax:* 301-294-0034

Herb Duke, Owner

Annual show and exhibits of jewelry and gemstones and related equipment, supplies and services.
Frequency: October, Denver

14568 Gem, Jewelry & Mineral Show
Trade Shows International
PO Box 8862
Tucson, AZ 85738

520-791-2210; *Fax:* 520-825-9115

14569 IJO Trade Show & Seminars
Independent Jewelers Organization
25 Seir Hill Rd
Norwalk, CT 06850-1322

203-846-4215
800-624-9252; *Fax:* 203-846-8571;
www.ijo.com

Penny Palmer, Member Services Director

For members only
3500 Attendees
Frequency: Semi-Annual

14570 IPMI Conference
International Precious Metals Institute
5101 N 12th Avenue
Suite C
Pensacola, FL 32504

850-476-1156; *Fax:* 850-476-1548
mail@ipmi.org; www.ipmi.org

Robert Ianniello, President
Frequency: Annual

14571 International Gem & Jewelry Show
120 Derwood Circle
Rockville, MD 20850

301-294-1640; *Fax:* 301-294-0034;
www.intergem.net

Herb Duke, Owner

Jewelry, gemstones and related equipment, supplies and services.

14572 International Gift Show: The Jewelry & Accessories Expo
Business Journals
50 Day Street
Norwalk, CT 06854

203-853-6015; *Fax:* 203-852-8175
14000 Attendees

14573 International Jewelry Fair/General Merchandise Show-Spring
Helen Brett Enterprises
5111 Academy Drive
Lisle, IL 60532-2171

630-241-9865
800-541-8171; *Fax:* 630-241-9870
dharrington@helenbrett.com;
www.gift2jewelry.com
Social Media: Facebook

Dave Harrington, Show Manager

Containing 800 booths during the spring show and 1500 booths during the fall show. Tradeshow open to wholesale buyers only (credentials required to attend).
24000 Attendees
Frequency: May
Founded in: 1946
Mailing list available for rent

14574 International Watch and Jewelry Show
Burley and Olg Bullock
5901-Z Westheimer Road
Houston, TX 77057

713-783-8188
800-554-4992; *Fax:* 281-589-8987
info@iwjg.com; www.iwjg.com

JJ Gilbreath
Christina LeDoux
Frequency: June-Nov./January-March

14575 JA International Jewelry Show
Jewelers of America
52 Vanderbuilt Avenue
19th Floor
New York, NY 10017

646-580-0255; *Fax:* 212-768-8087
info@jewelers.org; www.jewelers.org

Matthew Runci, President
Donald Jackson, Controller
Timothy Haake, Founder
Lauren Thompson, Communications Manager

Showcase of fine jewelry open to the trade only.
11000 Attendees
Frequency: Febuary/July

14576 JCK Orlando International Jewelry Show
Reed Exhibition Companies
383 Manin Avenue
Norwalk, CT 06850

203-404-4800; *Fax:* 203-840-5830;
www.jckgroup.com

Jay Jackson, Chief Operating Officer
Matthew Stuller, Founder
John Bachman, Secretary

Conference and exhibition.
2000 Attendees
Frequency: February

14577 Jewelers International Showcase (JIS)
6421 Congress Avenue
Suite 105
Boca Raton, FL 33487-2858

561-998-0205; *Fax:* 561-998-0209
jisshow@aol.com; www.jisshow.com

Michael G Breslow CEM, President
Jordan Tuchband, Sales Director
Vito J. Miceli, Sales Manager
Cindy Corrente, Financial Coordinator
Michele Carter, Show Director

Worldwide manufacturers and wholesalers of jewelry exhibit to trade buyers from Florida, Caribbean, Central and South America, plus other USA states. Exhibits of 1000 suppliers of fine jewelry, fashion jewelry and related products and services. The leading and largest independent Jewelery Trade-Only Show in the Western Hemisphere.
12000 Attendees
Frequency: October, January, April
Founded in: 1979

14578 Merchandise Mart Gift/Jewelry/ Resort Show
Denver Merchandise Mart
451 E 58th Avenue #470
Suite 4270
Denver, CO 80216

303-292-6278
800-289-6278; *Fax:* 303-298-8473
bridget@denvermart.com;
www.denvermart.com

Bridget Oakes, Gift Show Exhibit Manager

A wholesale market for retail store buyers for resorts, theme parksand national parks, specialty gift stores and interior designers. Semi - Annual Show.
7000 Attendees
Frequency: February/August

14579 Mid-South Jewelry & Accessories Fair -Spring
Helen Brett Enterprises
5111 Academy Drive
Lisle, IL 60532-2171

630-241-9865
800-541-8171; *Fax:* 630-241-9870
dharrington@helenbrett.com;
www.gift2jewelry.com
Social Media: Facebook

Dave Harrington, Show Manager

Containing over 300 booths during the spring show and 500 booths during the fall show. Tradeshow open to wholesale buyers only (credentials required to attend).
8500 Attendees
Frequency: May
Founded in: 1946
Mailing list available for rent

14580 **Mid-South Jewelry & Accessories Fair-Fall**
Helen Brett Enterprises
5111 Academy Drive
Lisle, IL 60532-2171
630-241-9865
800-541-8171; *Fax:* 630-241-9870
dharrington@helenbrett.com;
www.gift2jewelry.com
Social Media: Facebook
Dave Harrington, Show Manager
Containing 500 booths during the fall show and over 300 booths during the spring show. Tradeshow open to wholesale buyers only (credentials required to attend).
16000 Attendees
Frequency: November
Founded in: 1946
Mailing list available for rent

14581 **Midwest Jewelry Expo**
Wisconsin Jewelry Assocation
1 East Main Street
Suite 305
Madison, WI 53703
608-257-3541; *Fax:* 608-257-8755;
www.midwestjewelryexpo.com
Mary Kaja, Executive Director
The next jewelry trade show exposition is scheduled for March 24th to March 25th in 2007.
3000 Attendees
Frequency: March

14582 **National Accessory Maintenance Exposition**
240 Peachtree Street NW
Suite 2200
Atlanta, GA 30303-1327
404-203-3000; *Fax:* 404-607-8682
Jeff Portman, CEO
Charles Sydney, Manager
Offers a forum for the exchange of ideas between manufacturers and suppliers of fashion accessories.
10M Attendees
Frequency: January

14583 **Pacific Jewelry Show**
California Jewelers Association
911 Wilshire Boulevard
Suite 1740
Los Angeles, CA 90017-3446
213-235-5722; *Fax:* 213-623-5742
Richard Trujillo, Owner
Alberta E Hultman, Manager
Annual show of 250 exhibitors of jewelry and related items.
3000 Attendees
Frequency: August
Founded in: 1999

14584 **Stylemax**
Merchandise Mart Properties Inc
222 Merchandise Mart Plaza
Suite 470
Chicago, IL 60654
312-527-4141
800-677-6278
sglick@mmart.com; www.mmart.com
Social Media: Facebook
Susan Glick, VP
A women's apparel and accessory trade show with over 4,000 exhibitors.
5000 Attendees
Founded in: 1920
Mailing list available for rent

14585 **The Whole Bead Show**
PO Box 1100
Nevade City, CA 95959
530-652-2725
800-292-2577; *Fax:* 530-265-2776
info@wholebead.com; www.wholebead.com
Social Media: Facebook
Ava Motherwell, Owner
An international bread trade show that occurs thirteen times per year. Contemporary pieces made from glass, stone, metal, pearl, amber and porcelain. Offering antique beads, handmade, findings, buttons, charms and beaded jewelry. Access merchants, bead makers and importers who are direct suppliers of many professional and novice jewelry makers.
N/A Attendees
Frequency: Jan/Feb/Mar/Apr
Founded in: 1993
Mailing list available for rent

14586 **Trade Show for Jewelry Making**
Manufacturing Jewelers & Suppliers of America
57 John L Dietsch Sq
Attleboro Falls, MA 02763-1027
401-274-3840
800-444-6572; *Fax:* 401-274-0265
info@mjsa.org; www.mjsa.org
James McCarthy, COO
Corrie Silvia Berry, Director of Sales & Business
David W. Cochran, President & CEO
Kristin Kopaz, Operations Manager
Dawn Britland, Assistant Controller
New regional trade show designed to service jewelry makers and manufacturers of all sizes throughout New England and surrounding areas. Providing a full range of products that industry professionals need to make their jewelry and operate their business.
1000 Attendees
Frequency: September
Founded in: 1903

14587 **Transworld's Jewelry, Fashion & Accessories Show**
Transworld Exhibits
1850 Oak Street
Northfield, IL 60093
847-446-8434
800-323-5462; *Fax:* 847-446-3523;
www.tweshows.com/jfa
Don Olstinske, Show Manager
Yianna Manokas, Creative Director
Donna Connolly, Customer Service Rep
Ron Carlson, Logistics Manager
Hundreds of the country's finest exhibitors. Thousands of the best buyers nationwide. The perfect venue for the latest jewelry collections, the most current fashion ideas and new accessories.
25000 Attendees
Frequency: July/October/December

14588 **Tucson Gem and Mineral Show (tm)**
Tucson Gem and Mineral Society
PO Box 42588
Tucson, AZ 85733
520-322-5773; *Fax:* 520-322-6031
tgms@tgms.org; www.tgms.org
Sponsored by the Tucson Gem and Mineral Society. Retail show open to the public at the Tucson Convention Center every February for four days. Over 200 dealers, over 100 exhibitors, children's activities.
25000 Attendees
Frequency: February
Founded in: 1946

Directories & Databases

14589 **AJM Technology Sourcebook**
Manufacturing Jewelers & Suppliers of America
57 John L Dietsch Sq
Attleboro Falls, MA 02763-1027
401-274-3840
800-444-6572; *Fax:* 401-274-0265
info@mjsa.org; www.mjsa.org
James McCarthy, COO
Corrie Silvia Berry, Director of Sales & Business
David W. Cochran, President & CEO
Kristin Kopaz, Operations Manager
Dawn Britland, Assistant Controller
This publication provides listings and specs on machinery, equipment, raw materials, and software specifically geared to jewelry manufacturing.
Cost: $4.50
Frequency: Annual
Circulation: 5,000
Founded in: 1903
Printed in 4 colors on glossy stock

14590 **Accent Source Book**
Larkin Group
100 Wells Avenue
Newton, MA 02459-3210
617-326-6525
800-869-7469; *Fax:* 617-964-2752
Lauren Parker, Editor
Michael Corkin, Owner
Information on over 1,500 manufacturers of jewelry, watches and accessories is available in this comprehensive directory aimed at the gemology and related industries.
Cost: $25.00
200 Pages
Frequency: Annual
Circulation: 15,000
ISSN: 0192-7507

14591 **Accessories Resource Directory**
Business Journals
50 Day Street
Norwalk, CT 06854-3100
203-853-6015; *Fax:* 203-852-8175;
www.busjour.com
Britton Jones, President
Over 1,500 manufacturers, importers and sales representatives that produce accessories are profiled.
Frequency: Annual
Circulation: 10,000

14592 **Complete Directory of Cubic Zirconia Jewelry**
Sutton Family Communications & Publishing Company

920 State Route 54 East
Elmitch, KY 42343

270-276-9500
jlsutton@apex.net

Theresa Sutton, Editor
Lee Sutton, General Manager

Print-out from database of wholesalers, manufacturers, distributors, importers and close-out houses. Database is updated daily to guarantee the most current and up-to-date sources available.
Cost: $39.50
100+ Pages

14593 Complete Directory of Earrings & Necklaces
Sutton Family Communications & Publishing Company
920 State Route 54 East
Elmitch, KY 42343

270-276-9500
jlsutton@apex.net

Theresa Sutton, Editor
Lee Sutton, General Manager

Print-out from database of wholesalers, manufacturers, distributors, importers and close-out houses. Database is updated daily to guarantee the most current and up-to-date sources available.
Cost: $37.00
100+ Pages

14594 Complete Directory of Jewelry Close-Outs
Sutton Family Communications & Publishing Company
920 State Route 54 East
Elmitch, KY 42343

270-276-9500
jlsutton@apex.net

Theresa Sutton, Editor
Lee Sutton, General Manager

Print-out from database of wholesalers, manufacturers, distributors, importers and close-out houses. Database is updated daily to guarantee the most current and up-to-date sources available.
Cost: $34.50
100+ Pages

14595 Complete Directory of Jewelry: General
Sutton Family Communications & Publishing Company
920 State Route 54 East
Elmitch, KY 42343

270-276-9500
jlsutton@apex.net

Theresa Sutton, Editor
Lee Sutton, General Manager

Print-out from database of wholesalers, manufacturers, distributors, importers and close-out houses. Database is updated daily to guarantee the most current and up-to-date sources available.
Cost: $54.50
100+ Pages

14596 Complete Directory of Low-Price Jewelry & Souvenirs
Sutton Family Communications & Publishing Company
920 State Route 54 East
Elmitch, KY 42343

270-276-9500
jlsutton@apex.net

Theresa Sutton, Editor
Lee Sutton, General Manager

Print-out from database of wholesalers, manufacturers, distributors, importers and close-out houses. Database is updated daily to guarantee the most current and up-to-date sources available.
Cost: $39.50
100+ Pages

14597 Complete Directory of Watches and Watch Bands
Sutton Family Communications & Publishing Company
920 State Route 54 East
Elmitch, KY 42343

270-276-9500
jlsutton@apex.net

Theresa Sutton, Editor
Lee Sutton, General Manager

Print-out from database of wholesalers, manufacturers, distributors, importers and close-out houses. Database is updated daily to guarantee the most current and up-to-date sources available.
Cost: $39.50
100+ Pages

14598 Diamond Report
Rapaport Diamond Corporation
15 W 47th Street
Suite 600
New York, NY 10036-3305

212-540-0575; *Fax:* 212-840-0243
rap@diamonds.net; www.diamond.net

Amber Michelle, Editor
Eillene Furrel, Advertising Manager

This large directory database offers background information and current prices for more than 100,000 stores.
Cost: $185.00
Frequency: Annual

14599 International Society of Appraisers
International Society of Appraisers
Ste 400
230 E Ohio St
Chicago, IL 60611-3646

206-241-0359; *Fax:* 312-265-2908
isa@isa-appraisers.org; www.isa-appraisers.org

Nan B Shelton, President
Connie Davenport, Vice President
Charles Pharr, Treasurer
Philip Hawkins, Secretary

Be Certain of its Value - A Consumer's Guide To Hiring a Competent Personal Property Appraiser is available complimentary to the public. Alphabetical list of appraisers with specialty areas plus indexes: area of expertise, zip code, state and city, company, and related services.
Cost: $15.00
305 Pages
Frequency: Annual
Circulation: 1500
Founded in: 1979
Printed in 2 colors

14600 Jewelers Board of Trade: Confidential Reference Book
Jewelers Board of Trade
95 Jefferson Blvd
Warwick, RI 02888-1046

401-467-0055; *Fax:* 401-467-1199
jbtinfo@jewelersboard.com;
www.jewelersboard.com

Dione Kenyen, President

Importers, distributors and retailers, close to 45,000, are profiled that are directly related to the jewelry industry.
Frequency: Semiannual
Circulation: 3,400

14601 Jewelers' Circular/Keystone: Brand Name and Trademark Guide
Chilton Company
1 Chilton Way
Wayne, PA 19089-0002

610-964-4243
800-866-0206; *Fax:* 610-964-4481

L Roberts, Editor

Over 5,000 manufacturers of jewelry store products.
Cost: $49.95

14602 Jewelers' Circular/Keystone: Jewelers' Directory Issue
Chilton Company
PO Box 2045
Radnor, PA 19089

610-964-4000; *Fax:* 610-964-4512

Kathleen Ellis, Editor

About 10,000 manufacturers, importers and wholesale jewelers providing merchandise and supplies to the jewelry retailing industry and related trade organizations.
Cost: $32.00
Frequency: Monthyly
Circulation: 30,000

14603 Lapidary Journal: Annual Buyers' Directory Issue
Lapidary Journal
60 Chestnut Avenue
Suite 201
Devon, PA 19333-1312

610-325-5700
800-676-GEMS; *Fax:* 610-293-1717

Michele Erazo, Marketing Executive

List of 4,000 suppliers and retailers of gem-cutting and jewelry making and mineral collecting equipment, beads, fossils, minerals and gems, gem and mineral clubs, bead societies, museums, schools and shops.
Cost: $6.50
Frequency: Annual May
Circulation: 67,000

14604 MJSA Buyers' Guide
Manufacturing Jewelers & Suppliers of America
57 John L Dietsch Sq
Attleboro Falls, MA 02763-1027

401-274-3840
800-444-6572; *Fax:* 401-274-0265
info@mjsa.org; www.mjsa.org

James McCarthy, Coo
Bruce Coltin, Operations Manager
Kristin Kopaz, Operations Manager
Corrie Berry, Sales Manager

Contains finished jewelry as well as equipment, supplies, and components necessary for jewelry manufacturing.
Cost: $45.00
Frequency: BiAnnual
Circulation: 5,000

14605 National Jeweler: Industry Yellow Pages
Miller Freeman Publications
28 East 28th Street
12th Floor
New York, NY 10016

212-378-0400; *Fax:* 212-378-0470
sedorusa@optonline.net;
www.governmentvideo.com
Social Media: RSS

Gary Rhodes, International Sales Manager

Approximately 5,000 companies providing products and services in the jewelry and watch

industries.
Cost: $10.00
Frequency: Annual December
Circulation: 36,000

Industry Web Sites

14606 **Gemological Institute of America**
The Robert Mouawad Campus
5345 Armada Dr.
Carlsbad, CA 92008

760-603-4000
800-421-7250; *Fax:* 760-603-4080;
www.gia.edu
Social Media: Facebook, Twitter, LinkedIn, Google+, YouTube

John A. Green, Chair
Susan M. Jacques, President & CEO

The jewellery industry's source for knowledge, standards and education since 1931.
Founded in: 1931

14607 **http://gold.greyhouse.com**
G.O.L.D Grey House OnLine Databases

Grey House Publishing's online database platform, GOLD, offers Quick Search, Keyword Search and Expert Search for most business sectors including jewelry and watch markets. The GOLD platform makes finding the information you need quick and easy - whether you're a novice searcher or an experienced database user. All of Grey House's directory products are available for subscription on the GOLD platform.

14608 **www.agta.org**
American Gem Trade Association

A trade association for the colored gemstone industry in North Africa. Operates gemological testing in New York.

14609 **www.awi-net.org**
American Watchmakers Institute

Examines and certifies master watchmakers and clockmakers. Maintains a placement service. Conducts home study courses.

14610 **www.cufflink.com**
National Cuff Link Society

For cuff link wearers and collectors.

14611 **www.glda.com**
Gem & Lapidary Dealers Association

14612 **www.goldinstitue.org**
Gold Institute

14613 **www.greyhouse.com**
Grey House Publishing

Authoritative reference directories for most business sectors including jewelry and watch markets. Users can search the online databases with varied search criteria allowing for custom searches by product category, geographic area, sales volume, keyword, subject and more. Full Grey House catalog and online ordering also available.

14614 **www.iaca.com**
Indian Arts & Crafts Association

Not for profit trade association. Our mission is to promote, protect and preserve Indian arts.

14615 **www.independentjewelers.com**
Independent Jewelers

Works to aid independent jewelers in competing in local markets through advertising, promotion, and buyers assistance.

14616 **www.ipmi.org**
International Precious Metals Institute

International association of producers, refiners, fabricators, scientists, users, financial institutions, merchants, private and public sector groups and the general precious metals community created to provide a forum for the exchange of information and technology.

14617 **www.isa-appraisers.org**
International Society of Appraisers

A not-for-profit professional association of personal property appraisers. ISA provides education and organizational support to its members, to serve the public by producing highley qualified and ethical appraisers who are recognized authorities in personal property appraising.

14618 **www.jewelers.org**
Jewelers of America

14619 **www.jewelersboard.com**

Trade association providing credit reporting, collections and marketing services to the US and overseas jewelry industries. Our members are wholesalers, manufacturers and service providers to the jewelry industry.

14620 **www.jewelerssecurity.org**
Jewelers' Security Alliance

Principal activity is providing education and information to jewelers so they can guard against loss through crimes, including burglary, robbery and theft.

14621 **www.jewelryinfo.org**
Jewelery Information Center

Identifies deceptive trade practices and misleading advertising. Provides advice on marketing and assists in prosecution of violations. The media side of the Jewelers Vigilance Committee.

14622 **www.jvclegal.org**
Jewelers Vigilance Committee

Identifies deceptive trade practices and misleading advertising. Provides advice on marketing and assists in prosecution of violations.

14623 **www.love-story.com**
Leading Jewelers Guild

14624 **www.silverinstitute.org**
Silver Institute

14625 **www.silversmithing.com**
Society of American Silversmiths

14626 **www.silverusersassociation.org**
Silver Users Association

Represents manufacturers and distributors of products in which silver is an essential element, such as photographic materials, medical and dental supplies, batteries and electronic and electrical equipment, silverware, mirrors, commemorative art and jewelry.

14627 **www.superabrasives.org**
Industrial Diamond Association of America

14628 **www.womensjewelry.org**
Women's Jewelry Association

For jewelry industry professionals.

Associations

14629 National Academy of Television Journalists
PO Box 289
Salisbury, MD 21803

410-251-2511; *Fax:* 410-543-0658;
www.angelfire.com/md/NATJ/

Dr Catherine North, Executive Director
Dr Cathy Roche, Director

Works with newly graduated journalist school students to assist them as they enter in the world of television news. Honors those in the industrry for excellence in their field of endeaver.
Founded in: 1985

14630 Accrediting Council on Education in Journalism and Mass Communications
1435 Jayhawk Blvd
Lawrence, KS 66045-7575

785-864-3973; *Fax:* 785-864-5225;
www2.ku.edu/~acejmc/

Christopher Callahan, Chair
Marie Hardin, Vice Chair
David Boardman, President
Doug Anderson, Vice President
Cindy Reinardy, Assistant to the Executive Dir.

ACEJMC members are journalism and media departments, education associations and professional organizations.
113 Members
Founded in: 1945

14631 American Agricultural Editors' Association
120 Main Street W
PO Box 156
New Prague, MN 56071

952-758-6502; *Fax:* 952-758-5813
aaea@gandgcomm.com; www.ageditors.com
Social Media: Facebook, Twitter, LinkedIn

Elaine Shein, President
Kurt Lawton, Immediate Past President
Mike Wilson, President Elect
Den Gardner, Executive Director
Doug Rich, Board Member

National professional development member association for agricultural communicators.
Founded in: 1921

14632 American Association of Sunday & Feature Editors
1921 Gallows Road
Suite 600
Vienna, VA 22182-3900

703-902-1639; *Fax:* 703-620-4557
contact@aasfe.org; www.aasfe.org

Chris Beringer, President
Gina Seay, VP
Denise Joyce, VP
Kim Marcum, Secretary-Treasurer

An organization of editors from the United States and Canada dedicated to the quality of features in newspapers and the craft of feature writing.

14633 American Copy Editors Society
155 E. Algonquin Road
Arlington Heights, IL 60005-4617

E-Mail: info@copydesk.org;
www.copydesk.org
Social Media: Facebook, Twitter, LinkedIn, RSS

Teresa Schmedding, President
David Sullivan, Vice President
Sara Ziegler, Treasurer
Brady Jones, Secretary
Christine Steele, Director of Membership

A professional nonprofit association for copy editors at U.S. newspapers, magazines, websites, and corporations.
Founded in: 1997

14634 American Copy Editors Society (ACES)
7 Avenida Vista Grande
Suite B7 #467
Santa Fe, NM 87508

E-Mail: info@copydesk.org;
www.copydesk.org
Social Media: Facebook, Twitter, LinkedIn, RSS

Teresa Schmedding, President
Lisa McLendon, Vice President Conferences
Sara Ziegler, Treasurer
Rudy Bahr, Executive Director
David F. Sullivan, Secretary

ACES is a professional organization working toward the advancement of editors. Their aim is to provide opportunities through training, discussion and advocacy that promote the editing profession.
Founded in: 1997

14635 American Medical Writers' Association
30 W Gude Dr
Suite 525
Rockville, MD 20850-4347

240-238-0940; *Fax:* 301-294-9006
amwa@amwa.org; www.amwa.org
Social Media: Facebook, Twitter, LinkedIn

Susan Krug, CAE, Executive Director
Ann Silveira, Membership Manager & Database Coor
Shari Rager, CAE, Deputy Director
Julia Shedlin, Membership Program Assistant
Josie Zeman, Education Program Assistant

Concerned with the advancement and improvement of medical communications.
5000+ Members
Founded in: 1940
Mailing list available for rent

14636 American Newspaper Representatives
2075 W Big Beaver Rd
Suite 310
Troy, MI 48084-3439

248-643-9910
800-550-7557; *Fax:* 248-643-9914
accountsales@gotoanr.com
gotoanr.com

Hilary Howe, President
Robert Sontag, Executive VP/COO
John Jepsen, Controller
Melanie Cox, Regional Sales Manager

Supports those newspaper representatives and distributors in the United States. Hosts annual trade show.
Founded in: 1943

14637 American Press Institute
4401 Wilson Boulevard
Suite 900
Arlington, VA 22203

571-366-1200
hello@pressinstitute.org;
www.americanpressinstitute.org/
Social Media: Facebook, Twitter, YouTube, RSS

Robert J. Weil, Chair
Michael G. Abernathy, Vice Chair
Tom Rosenstiel, Executive Director
Jeff Sonderman, Deputy Director
Jane Elizabeth, Senior Research Project Manager

Conducts research, training, convenes thought leaders and creates tools to help chart a path ahead for journalism in the 21st century.
Founded in: 1946

14638 American Press Institute (API)
4401 Wilson Blvd.
Ste 900
Arlington, VA 22203

571-366-1200; *Fax:* 571-366-1195
hello@pressinstitute.org;
www.americanpressinstitute.org
Social Media: Facebook, Twitter, RSS, YouTube

Robert J. Weil, Chair
Michael G. Abernathy, Vice Chair
Tom Rosenstiel, Executive Director
Jeff Sonderman, Deputy Director
Jane Elizabeth, Senior Research Project Manager

API is the trusted source for career leadership development for the newsmedia industry in North America and around the world. They help companies innovate and leaders realize their full potential.
Founded in: 1946

14639 American Society of Business Press Editors
214 North Hale Street
Wheaton, IL 60187

630-510-4588; *Fax:* 630-510-4501
info@asbpe.org; www.asbpe.org
Social Media: Facebook, Twitter, LinkedIn, RSS

Jessica Zemler, President
Dominick Yanchunas, Vice President
Janet Svazas, Executive Director
Steve Ross, Treasurer
Robin Sherman, Associate Dir. & Newsletter Editor

ASBPE is the professional association for full-time and freelance editors and writers employed in the business, trade, and specialty press. It is widely known for its annual Awards of Excellence competition, which recognizes the best editorial, design, and online achievement.
Founded in: 1964
Mailing list available for rent

14640 American Society of Business Publication Editors
214 North Hale St.
Wheaton, IL 60187

630-510-4588; *Fax:* 630-510-4501
info@asbpe.org; www.asbpe.org
Social Media: Facebook, Twitter, LinkedIn, YouTube

Jessica Zemler, President
Dominick Yanchunas, Vice President
Janet Svazas, Executive Director
Steve Ross, Treasurer

Professional association for full-time and freelance editors and writers employed in the business, trade, and specialty press.
Founded in: 1964

14641 American Society of Journalists and Authors
355 Lexington Avenue
15th Floor
New York, NY 10017-6603

212-997-0947; *Fax:* 212-937-2315
webeditor@asja.org; www.asja.org

Social Media: Facebook, Twitter, LinkedIn, Google+, Instagram

Randy Dotinga, President
Sherry Beck Paprocki, Vice President
Alexandra Cantor Owens, Executive Director
Meredith Taylor, General Manager
Neil O'Hara, Treasurer

For freelance nonfiction writers whose bylines appear in periodicals and in books.

1000+ Members
Founded in: 1948

14642 American Society of Magazine Editors

757 Third Avenue
11th Floor
New York, NY 10017

212-872-3700
mpa@magazine.org; www.magazine.org/
Social Media: Facebook, Twitter, LinkedIn, YouTube, Google+

Mary G. Berner, President, CEO
Nancy Telliho, Interim CEO
Sid Holt, Chief Executive
Eric John, SVP, Digital Strategy & Initiatives
Rita Cohen, SVP/ Legislative & Reg Policy

An industry trade group for editors of magazines published in the United States.

Founded in: 1919

14643 American Society of Media Photographers (ASMP)

150 North 2nd Street
Philadelphia, PA 19106

215-451-2767; *Fax:* 215-451-0880
info@asmp.org
asmp.org
Social Media: Facebook, Twitter, LinkedIn

Tom Kennedy, Executive Director
Victor Perlman, General Counsel
Elena Goertz, General Manager
Chris Chandler, Bookkeeper
Ellen Khlystova, IT Specialist

ASMP is the premier trade association for the world's most respectd photograhers. ASMP is the leader in promoting photographers' rights, providing education in better business practices, producing business publications for photographers, and helping to connect purchasers with professional photographers.

7000 Members
Founded in: 1944

14644 American Society of News Editors (ASNE)

209 Reynolds Journalism Institute
Mission School of Journalism
Columbia, MO 65211

573-884-2405; *Fax:* 573-884-3824
asne@asne.org; www.asne.org
Social Media: Facebook, Twitter, Storify

Pam Fine, President
Mizell Stewart III, Vice President
Teri Hayt, Executive Director
Arnie Robbins, Senior Adviser
Cindy L. Roe, Finance Director

ASNE is a membership organization for editors, producers or directors in charge of journalistic organizations or departments, deans or faculty at university journalism schools, and leaders and faculty of media-related foundations and training organizations.

Founded in: 1922

14645 Asian American Journalists Association (AAJA)

5 Third Street
Suite 1108
San Francisco, CA 94103

415-346-2051; *Fax:* 415-346-6343
national@aaja.org; www.aaja.org
Social Media: Facebook, Twitter, LinkedIn

Paul Cheung, President
Kathy Chow, Executive Director
Glenn E. K. Sugihara, Accounting Consultant
Karen A. Sugihara, Accounting Consultant
Derric Jones, Event Manager Consultant

AAJA provides support among Asian American and Pacific Islander journalists. It provides encouragement, information, advice and scholarship assistance to Asian American and Pacific Islander students who aspire to professional journalism careers.

Founded in: 1981

14646 Associated Press

1825 K Street NW
Suite 800
Washington, DC 20006-1202

212-621-1500; *Fax:* 202-736-1107
info@ap.org; www.ap.org
Social Media: Facebook, Twitter, LinkedIn, Google+, Youtube

Mary Junck, Chairman
Gary Pruitt, President and CEO
Jessica Bruce, SVP, Director of Human Resources
Ken Dale, Senior Vice President and CFO
Ellen Hale, SVP, Director of Corporate Comm.

Seeks to advance journalism through radio and television, and cooperates with the AP to promote accurate and impartial news.

5.9m Members
Founded in: 1846

14647 Associated Press Media Editors

450 West 33rd Street
New York, NY 10001

212-621-7007
sjacobsen@ap.org; www.apme.com
Social Media: Facebook, Twitter, Blog

Bill Church, President
Jim Simon, Vice President
Angie Muhs, Secretary
Dennis Anderson, Treasurer

Members are managing editors or executives of Associated Press News Executives.

Founded in: 1930

14648 Associated Press Sports Editors

9000 N. Broadway
Oklahoma City, OK 73114

405-475-3164; *Fax:* 405-475-3315
apsportseditors.com
Social Media: Facebook, Twitter, RSS

Mike Sherman, Chairman
Mary Byrne Byrne, President
Tommy Deas, First Vice President
John Bednarowski, Third VP
Jack Berninger, Executive Director

A national organization that strives to improve professional standards of sports departments.

14649 Association for Education in Journalism and Mass Communication

234 Outlet Pointe Boulevard
Suite A
Columbia, SC 29210-5667

803-798-0271; *Fax:* 803-772-3509
aejmchq@aol.com; www.aejmc.org/
Social Media: Facebook, Twitter, LinkedIn, Friendfeed, YouTube, RSS

Lori Bergen, President
Jennifer McGill, Executive Director
Kathy Bailey, Association Business Manager
Felicia G. Brown, Desktop Publisher
Lillian Coleman, Newsletter Editor/Project Manager

AEJMC promotes the highest possible standards for education in journalism and mass communication, encouraging the widest possible range of communication research and the implementation of a multi-cultural society in the classroom and curriculum, defending and maintaining the freedom of expression in day-to-day living.

Founded in: 1912

14650 Association for Women in Communications

3337 Duke Street
Alexandria, VA 22314

703-370-7436; *Fax:* 703-342-4311;
www.womcom.org
Social Media: Facebook, Twitter, LinkedIn, Google+, YouTube

Mitzie Zerr, Chair
Missy Kruse, Vice Chair
Pat Meads, Treasurer
Hannah Schmuckler, AWC Membership & Comm. Coordinator
Pamela Valenzuela, AWC Executive Director

Supports all those professional women in the fields of journalism online media, public relations, advertising, marketing, educational communications, graphic and web design, photography and film. Hosts bi-annual conference.

Founded in: 1909

14651 Association for Women in Sports Media

7742 Spalding Dr.
#377
Norcross, GA 30092

E-Mail: info@awsmonline.org;
www.awsmonline.org
Social Media: Facebook, Twitter, LinkedIn, Instagram

Lydia Craver, Chair of the Board
Jennifer Overman, President
Rachel Whittaker, VP, Administration
Jill Ann Bouffard, VP, Convention
Allison Creekmore, VP, Digital

Nonprofit organization founded as a support network and advocacy group for women who work in sports writing, editing, broadcast and production, andpublic and media relations.

14652 Association of Alternative Newsmedia

116 Cass Street
Traverse City, MI 49684

703-470-2996; *Fax:* 866-619-9755
web@aan.org; www.altweeklies.com/
Social Media: Facebook, Twitter, RSS, Google+

Blair Barna, President
Chuck Strouse, Vice President
Ellen Meany, Treasurer
Tiffany Shackelford, Executive Director
Jason Zaragoza, Deputy Director

Trade association of alternative weekly newspapers in North America.

Founded in: 1978

14653 **Association of American Editorial Cartoonists**
PO Box 460673
Fort Lauderdale, FL 33346
717-703-3003; *Fax:* 717-703-3008;
www.editorialcartoonists.com
Social Media: Twitter
Jack Ohman, President
Jen Sorensen Sorensen, Vice President
R.C. Harvey, Secretary-Treasurer

14654 **Association of Food Journalists**
www.afjonline.com
Social Media: Facebook
Debbie Moose, President
Bob Batz, Jr., Vice President
Jennifer Palcher-Silliman, Executive Director
Nancy Stohs, Secretary
Patricia West-Barker, Treasurer
Founded in: 1974

14655 **Association of Health Care Journalists**
Missouri School of Journalism
10 Neff Hall
Columbia, MO 65211
573-884-5606; *Fax:* 573-884-5609;
www.healthjournalism.org
Social Media: Facebook, Twitter
Karl Stark, President
Ivan Oransky, M.D., Vice President
Len Bruzzese, Executive Director
Jeff Porter, Special Projects Director
Pia Christensen, Managing Editor/Online Services
1,400 Members
Founded in: 1997

14656 **Association of Magazine Media**
757 Third Avenue
11th Floor
New York, NY 10017
212-872-3700; *Fax:* 212-906-0128
mpa@magazine.org; www.magazine.org
Social Media: Facebook, Twitter, LinkedIn, Youtube, Pinterst
Mr. Stephen M. Lacy, Chairman
Ms. Nancy Telliho, Interim President and CEO
Sid Holt, Chief Executive
Nina Fortuna, Director, ASME
Julie Ryu, Marketing and Events Coordinator
ASME is the principal organization for magazine journalists in the United States. ASME works to defend the First Amendment, protect editorial independence and support the development of journalism.
700 Members
Founded in: 1919

14657 **Association of Opinion Journalists**
2301 Vanderbilt Place
VU Station B 351669
Nashville, TN 37233-1699
E-Mail: opinionjournalists@gmail.com;
www.opinionjournalists.org/
Social Media: Facebook, Twitter
David D. Haynes, President
Jennifer Hemmingsen, Secretary
Dan Morain, Treasurer
Founded in: 1947

14658 **Baptist Communicators Association**
1519 Menlo Drive
Kennesaw, GA 30152
770-425-3728; www.baptistcommunicators.org
Social Media: Facebook, RSS
Brian Hobbs, Program Chair
Eric Yarbrough, Awards Chairman
Ian Richardson, President
Neisha Fuson Roberts, Membership Vice President
Brooke Zimny, Communications Vice President
PR and journalism profesionals.
300 Members
Founded in: 1953

14659 **Center for Investigative Reporting**
1400 65th St.
Suite 200
Emeryville, CA 94608
510-809-3160; *Fax:* 510-849-6141
jalvarado@cironline.org; www.revealnews.org
Social Media: Facebook, Twitter, Tumblr, RSS
Phil Bronstein, Executive Chair
Joaquin Alvarado, CEO
Laurel Leichter, Human Resources Consultant
Robert J. Rosenthal, Executive Director
Christa Scharfenberg, Head of Studio
Founded in: 1977

14660 **Center for Media Literacy**
22837 Pacific Coast Highway
#472
Malibu, CA 90265
310-804-3985
cml@medialit.com; www.medialit.org
Social Media: YouTube
Elizabeth Thoman CHM, Founder
Tessa Jolls, President, CEO
Beth Thornton, Communications
Founded in: 1977

14661 **Collegiate Press Association**
330 21st Avenue S
Minneapolis, MN 55455-0480
612-625-3500; *Fax:* 612-626-0720
Tom Rolnicki, Manager
Supports all those involved in the development and betterment of collegiate press. Hosts annual trade show.

14662 **Committee of Concerned Journalists**
Administrative Offices
Suite 300
Columbia, MO 65211
573-884-9121; *Fax:* 573-884-3824
rji@rjionline.org; www.rjionline.org
Social Media: Facebook, Twitter, LinkedIn, Google+, YouTube
Randy Picht, Executive Director
Roger Gafke, Director of Program Development
Edward McCain, Digital Curator of Journalism
Brian Steffens, Director, Communications
Esther Thorson, Director, Research
Founded in: 2004

14663 **Committee to Protect Journalists**
330 7th Avenue
11th Floor
New York, NY 10001
212-465-1004; *Fax:* 212-465-9568
info@cpj.org; www.cpj.org/
Social Media: Facebook, Twitter, YouTube, Tumblr, RSS
Joel Simon, Executive Director
Robert Mahoney, Deputy Director
John Weis, Development & Outreach Director
Sue Marcoux, Director, Finance & Admin.
Kavita Menon, Senior Program Officer
Founded in: 1981

14664 **Dart Center for Journalism & Trauma**
Columbia University
Graduate School of Journalism, 2950
New York, NY 10027
212-854-8056
bruce.shapiro@dartcenter.org;
www.dartcenter.org
Social Media: Facebook, Twitter
Bruce Shapiro, Executive Director
Kate Black, Associate Director
Kelly Boyce, Administrative Coordinator
Ariel Ritchin, Website Editor

14665 **Education Writers Association**
3516 Connecticut Avenue NW
Washington, DC 20008
202-452-9830; *Fax:* 202-452-9837;
www.ewa.org
Social Media: Facebook, Twitter, LinkedIn, Google+
Scott Elliott, President
Greg Toppo, Vice President (Journalists)
Christine Tebben, Vice President (Community Members)
Caroline W. Hendrie, Executive Director
George Dieter, Chief Operating Officer
The Education Writers Association is the national professional organization of education reporters and intent of improving education reporting to the public.

14666 **First Amendment Center**
555 Pennsylvania Ave. N.W.
Washington, DC 20001
202-292-6288; *Fax:* 202-292-6295
kcatone@newseum.org;
www.firstamendmentcenter.org
Social Media: Facebook, Twitter, RSS
Ken Paulson, President and CEO
Gene Policinski, SVP and Executive Director
John Seigenthaler, Founder
Karen Catone, Director
Ashlie Hampton, Event Coordinator

14667 **Football Writers Association of America**
18652 Vista del Sol
Dallas, TX 75287
972-713-6198
webmaster@sportswriters.net;
www.sportswriters.net
Social Media: Twitter
Kirk Bohls, President
Steve Richardson, Executive Director
Lee Barfknecht, 1st VP
Mark Anderson, Second VP
1,000 Members
Founded in: 1941

14668 **Garden Writers Association of America**
7809 FM 179
Shallowater, TX 79363
806-832-1870; *Fax:* 806-832-5244
webtech@gardenwriters.org;
www.gardenwriters.org/
Social Media: Facebook, Twitter, LinkedIn, Pinterest, Google+
Kirk Brown, President
Becky Heath, Vice President
Jo Ellen Meyers Sharp, Treasurer
Robert LaGasse, Executive Director
Debra Prinzing, Past President

14669 **Gay and Lesbian Press Association**
PO Box 8185
Universal City, CA 91618-8185
Fax: 818-902-9576
Supports those gay and lesbian professionals in the field of journalism. Publishes quarterly newsletter.

14670 Hollywood Foreign Press Association
646 N Robertson Blvd
West Hollywood, CA 90069

310-657-1731; *Fax:* 310-939-9034
info@hfpa.org; www.hfpa.org
Social Media: Facebook, Twitter, Youtube, RSS

Lorenzo Soria, President
Meher Tatna, VP
Serge Rakhlin, Executive Secretary
Jorge Camara, Treasurer
Meher Tatna, Treasurer

Foreign correspondents covering Hollywood and the entertainment industry.
Mailing list available for rent

14671 Inland Press Association
701 Lee Street
Suite 925
Des Plaines, IL 60016

847-795-0380; *Fax:* 847-795-0385
inland@inlandpress.org; www.inlandpress.org/
Social Media: Facebook, Twitter, LinkedIn

Tom Slaughter, Executive Director
Patty Slusher, Director, Membership & Programming
Tim Mather, Financial Studies Manager
Mark Fitzgerald, Publications Editor
Maria Choronzuk, Graphic Designer
Founded in: 1885

14672 Inter American Press Association
Jules Dubois Building
1801 Sw 3rd Ave
Miami, FL 33129

305-634-2465; *Fax:* 305-635-2272
info@sipiapa.org; www.sipiapa.org
Social Media: Facebook, Twitter, Blogger, Youtube

Ricardo Trotti, Executive Director
Martha Estrada, Assistant Executive Director
Melba Jimenez, Assistant Press Freedom Committee
Carlos Fernandez, Financial counselor
Ana Maria Perez, Accounting

Supports all those involved in the media and journalism industry. Hosts annual trade show.
Founded in: 1926

14673 International Center for Journalists
2000 M St. NW
Suite 250
Washington, DC 20036

202-737-3700; *Fax:* 202-737-0530;
www.icfj.org
Social Media: Facebook, Twitter, LinkedIn, YouTube, Instagram, Google+

Michael Golden, Chairman
James F. Hoge, Jr., Vice Chair
Pamela Howard, Vice Chair
Matthew Winkler, Vice Chair
Joyce Barnathan, President

14674 International Communications Association
1500 21st St Nw
Washington, DC 20036

202-955-1444; *Fax:* 202-955-1448
icahdq@icahdq.org; www.icahdq.org
Social Media: Facebook, Twitter, LinkedIn, Google+, Tumblr, Reddit

Michael L. Haley, Executive Director
Francois Heinderyckx, President
John Paul Gutierrez, Communication Director
Jennifer Le, Executive Assistant
Michael J. West, Publications Manager

Supports all students and professionals in the international communications industry. Publishes bi-monthly newsletter.
3400 Members
Founded in: 1950
Mailing list available for rent

14675 International Food, Wine and Travel Writers Association
39252 Winchester Rd.
Ste 107 #418
Murrieta, CA 92563

877-439-8929
951-970-8326; *Fax:* 909-396-0014
admin@ifwtwa.org; www.ifwtwa.org
Social Media: Facebook, Twitter, LinkedIn, RSS, Youtube, Instagram

Linda Kissam, President, Officer, Chair Marketing
Allen Cox, VP, Officer, Chair Excellence Award
Elizabeth Willoughby, Secretary
Michelle M. Winner, Director
Andrew M. Harris, Director, Culinary Advisor

Staff and/or freelance writers in the food, wine and travel field. Also includes other media professionals and industry associate members in 28 countries worldwide.
300 Members
Founded in: 1956

14676 International Food, Wine and Travel Writer
39252 Winchester Rd
Ste 107 #418
Murrieta, CA 92563

877-439-8929
951-970-8326; *Fax:* 877-439-8929
admin@ifwtwa.org; www.ifwtwa.org/
Social Media: Facebook, Twitter, LinkedIn, YouTube, RSS, Instagram

Linda Kissam, President, Officer, Chair Marketing
Allen Cox, VP, Officer, Chair Excellence Award
Elizabeth Willoughby, Secretary
Michelle M. Winner, Director
Andrew M. Harris, Director, Culinary Advisor

14677 International News Media Association
PO Box 740186
Dallas, TX 75374

214-373-9111
972-991-3151; *Fax:* 214-373-9112
inma@inma.org; www.inma.org
Social Media: Facebook, Twitter, LinkedIn, RSS

Ross McPherson, Executive Chairman
Mark Challinor, President
Yasmin Namini, Senior VP, Chief Consumer Officer
Earl J. Wilkinson, Executive Director/CEO
Brie Logsdon, Social Media Editor

Individuals in marketing, circulation, research and public relations of newspapers.
1100 Members
Founded in: 1930
Mailing list available for rent

14678 Investigative Reporters and Editors
141 Neff Annex
Missouri School of Journalism
Columbia, MO 65211

573-882-2042; *Fax:* 573-882-5431
info@ire.org; www.ire.org

Sarah Cohen, Board President
Matt Goldberg, Vice President
Andrew Donohue, Treasurer
Mark Horvit, Executive Director
Jaimi Dowdell, Senior Training Director

For individuals involved in investigative journalism.
Founded in: 1975

14679 Journalism Center on Children and Families
Knight Hall, Room 1100
College Park, MD 20742

301-405-8808
info@journalismcenter.org;
www.journalismcenter.org
Social Media: Facebook, Twitter, LinkedIn

Julie Drizin, Director
Aysha Khan, Editorial Intern
Zoe King, Editorial Intern
Fatimah Waseem, Editorial Intern
Founded in: 1993

14680 Magazine Publishers of America
757 Third Avenue
11th Floor
New York, NY 10017

212-872-3700
mpa@magazine.org; www.magazine.org
Social Media: Facebook, Twitter, LinkedIn, YouTube, Google+

Mr. Stephen M. Lacy, Chairman
Ms. Nancy Telliho, Interim President and CEO
Sid Holt, Chief Executive
Eric John, SVP
Rita Cohen, SVP / Legislative & Reg Policy
Founded in: 1919

14681 Media Financial Management Association
550 W. Frontage Road
Ste. 3600
Northfield, IL 60093

847-716-7000; *Fax:* 847-716-7004
info@mediafinance.org; www.infe.org

Ralph Bender, Chairman
Mary M. Collins, President & CEO
Jamie L. Grande, Director of Operations
Arcelia Pimentel, Director of Sales
Caitlin Hahne, Membership Coordinator

Focuses on newspaper financial management, with members representing most North American newpaper companies, as well as many offshore. INFE's activities include publishing, conferences, workshops, industry surveys and studies, and offers members networking opportunities.
1200 Members
Founded in: 1961

14682 National Association of Black Journalists
1100 Knight Hall
Suite 3100
College Park, MD 20742

301-405-0248; *Fax:* 301-314-1714;
www.nabj.org
Social Media: Facebook, Twitter

Sarah Glover, President
Dorothy Tucker, Vice President/Broadcast
Marlon A. Walker, Vice President/Print
Ben,t Wilson, Vice President/Digital
Sherlon Christie, Secretary

An organization of journalists, students and media-related professionals that provides quality programs and services and advocates on behalf of black journalists worldwide.
Founded in: 1975

14683 National Association of Broadcast Employees & Technicians
501 3rd St Nw
Washington, DC 20001

202-434-1254; *Fax:* 202-434-1426
guild@cwa-union.org; www.nabetcwa.org
Social Media: Facebook, Youtube, RSS, Flickr

Charles G. Braico, Sector President
Lou Marinaro, Sector Vice President

William Murray, Staff Representative
Eric Seggi, Staff Representative
Jodi Fabrizio-Clontz, Assistant to the President

Organization covering the newspaper industry, its employment practices, press freedom and labor movement.
Founded in: 1934

14684 National Association of Hispanic Journalists
1050 Connecticut Avenue NW
10th Floor
Washington, DC 20036

202-662-7145; *Fax:* 202-662-7144
nahj@nahj.org; www.nahj.org
Social Media: Facebook, Twitter, LinkedIn, YouTube

Mekahlo Medina, President
Rebecca Aguilar, VP, Online
Barbara Rodriguez, VP Print
Francisco Cortes, Financial Officer
Sid Garcia, Secretary

NAHJ is dedicated to the recognition and professional advancement of Hispanics in the news industry. NAHJ created a national voice and unified vision for all Hispanic journalists.
2300 Members
Founded in: 1984

14685 National Association of Hispanic Journalis ts
1050 Connecticut Avenue NW
10th Floor
Washington, DC 20036

202-662-7145
NAHJ@nahj.org; www. nahj.org/
Social Media: Facebook, Twitter, LinkedIn, YouTube

Mekahlo Medina, President
Rebecca Aguilar, VP, Online
Barbara Rodriguez, VP, Print
Francisco Cortes, Financial Officer
Sid Garcia, Secretary
Founded in: 1984

14686 National Association of Science Writers
P.O. Box 7905
Berkeley, CA 94707

510-647-9500; www.nasw.org
Social Media: Facebook, Twitter, LinkedIn, Google+

Robin Marantz Henig, President
Laura Helmuth, Vice President
Jill Adams, Treasurer
Deborah Franklin, Secretary
Tinsley Davis, Executive Director
Founded in: 1934

14687 National Book Critics Circle
160 Varick Street
11th Floor
New York, NY 10013

E-Mail: info@bookcritics.org;
www.bookcritics.org
Social Media: Twitter

Tom Beer, President
Jane Ciabattari, VP, Online
Rigoberto Gonzalez, VP/Awards
Michael Miller, VP/Treasurer
Karen Long, VP/Secretary
Founded in: 1974

14688 National Federation of Press Women
200 Little Falls Street
Ste.405
Falls Church, VA 22046

703-237-9804
800-780-2715; *Fax:* 703-237-9808
presswomen@aol.com; www.nfpw.org
Social Media: Facebook, Twitter, LinkedIn, RSS, Flickr, Youtube

Teri Ehresman, President
Marsha Hoffman, 1st VP
Marianne Wolf, 2nd VP (Membership Adviser)
Gay Porter DeNileon, Secretary
Ellen Crawford, Treasurer (Financial Advisor)

Members are writers, editors and other communication professionals for newspapers, magazines, wire services, agencies and freelance.
2000 Members
Founded in: 1937
Mailing list available for rent: 1700 names at $40 per M

14689 National Journalism Center
11480 Commerce Park Dr.
Suite 600
Reston, VA 20191

800-872-1776; *Fax:* 703-318-9122;
www.yaf.org/NationalJournalismCenter.aspx

Journalism training with a conservative edge.
Founded in: 1977

14690 National Lesbian & Gay Journalists Association
2120 L St, NW
Suite 850
Washington, DC 20037

202-588-9888
info@nlgja.org; www.nlgja.org/
Social Media: Facebook, Twitter, LinkedIn

Jen Christensen, President
Sarah Blazucki, Vice President of Print & Online
Ken Miguel, Vice President of Broadcast
Sharif Durhams, Treasurer
Rick Stuckey, Secretary
Founded in: 1990

14691 National Lesbian and Gay Journalists Association (NLGJA)
2120 L Street NW
Suite 850
Washington, DC 20037

202-588-9888
info@nlgja.org; www.nlgja.org
Social Media: Facebook, Twitter

Jen Christensen, President
Sarah Blazucki, Vice President of Print & Online
Ken Miguel, Vice President of Broadcast
Sharif Durhams, Treasurer
Rick Stuckey, Secretary

NLGJA is an organization of journalists, media professionals, educators and students working within the news industry to foster fair and accurate coverage of LGBT issues. NLGJA opposes all forms of workplace bias and provides professional development to its members.
220 Members
Founded in: 1990
Mailing list available for rent

14692 National Newspaper Association
900 Community Drive
Springfield, IL 62703

217-241-1400; *Fax:* 217-241-1301
membership@nna.org; www.nnaweb.org
Social Media: Facebook, Twitter, RSS Feeds

Matthew Paxton, President
Susan Rowell, Vice President
Tonda Rush, Director, Public Policy
Dennis DeRossett, Chief Operating Officer
Lynne Lance, Director, Membership Services

To protect, promote and enhance America's community newspapers.
2100 Members
Founded in: 1885

14693 National Press Club
529 14th St NW
13th Floor
Washington, DC 20045

202-662-7500; *Fax:* 202-662-7512
press.org/
Social Media: Facebook, Twitter, Google+, RSS

angela Greiling Keane, President
Myron Belkind, Vice President
Joel Whitaker, Secretary
John Hughes, Treasurer
Marc Wojno, Membership Secretary

A private organization composed of professional journalists who are directly related to the media. Persons must qualify to be admitted.
4.6M Members
Founded in: 1921

14694 National Press Foundation
1211 Connecticut Ave NW
Suite 310
Washington, DC 20036

202-663-7280; *Fax:* 202-662-1232
maha@nationalpress.org;
www.nationalpress.org
Social Media: Facebook, Twitter, Flickr, Youtube, Google+, Scri

Sandy Johnson, President/COO
Amun Nadeem, Program Manager
Linda Topping Streitfeld, Director of Training and Content
Jenny Ash-Maher, Director of Operations
Reyna Abigale Levine, Digital Media Manager

Supports all those involved with national press and the media. Publishes bi-weekly newsletter.
Founded in: 1976

14695 National Scholastic Press Association
2221 University Ave SE
Suite 121
Minneapolis, MN 55414

612-625-8335; *Fax:* 612-605-0072
info@studentpress.org; www.studentpress.org
Social Media: Facebook, Twitter, Flickr, RSS

Diana mitsu Klos, Executive Director
Paul Schwarzkopf, Dir. Of Communications & Technology
Lindasy Grome, Dir. Of Community Engagement
Albert R. Tims, President
Christopher J. Ison, Treasurer

Supports all those involved in yearbook printing and photographic services, college journalism departments and video yearbook production services. Hosts annual trade show.
Founded in: 1921
Mailing list available for rent

14696 Native American Journalists Association (NAJA)
OU Gaylord College
395 W. Lindsey St.
Norman, OK 73019-4201

405-325-1649; *Fax:* 405-325-6945;
www.naja.com/
Social Media: Facebook, Twitter, RSS

Jason Begay, President
Bryan Pollard, Vice President
Tristan Ahtone, Treasurer
Shannon Shaw-Duty, Secretary

NAJA serves and empowers Native journalists through programs and actions designed to enrich journalism and promote Native cultures. NAJA educates and unifies its membership through journalism programs that promote diversity and defends challenges to free press.
Founded in: 1983

14697 New England Newspaper and Press Association
370 Common Street, Barletta Hall
3rd Floor, Suite 319
Dedham, MA 02026
781-320-8050; *Fax:* 781-320-8055;
www.nenpa.org
Social Media: Facebook, Twitter

Peter Haggerty, President
Mark S. Murphy, VP
Linda Conway, Executive Director
Megan Sherman, PR and Events Manager
Robin LaPolla, Business Manager

This organization offers a publication about the newspaper industry specifically focusing on New England newspapers and the issues that affect them, which goes to every newspaper in New England.
460 Members
Founded in: 1950

14698 New Jersey Press Association
810 Bear Tavern Rd
Suite 307
West Trenton, NJ 08628-1022
609-406-0600; *Fax:* 609-406-0300;
www.njpa.org

Stanley M. Ellis, Chairman
Thomas M. Donovan, President
Brett Ainsworth, 1st Vice President
Michael Lawson, 2nd Vice President
George H. White, Executive Director/ Secretary

Supports all those involved in the development and betterment of collegiate press. Hosts annual trade show.
49 Members
Founded in: 1857

14699 Newspaper Association Managers
New England Press Association
32 Dunham Rd.
Beverly, MA 01929
978-338-2555; *Fax:* 978-744-0333
mlpiper52@comcast.net;
www.nammanagers.com

Lisa Hills, President
Layne Bruce, VP
Tom Newton, Director
Michelle Rea, Director
George H. White, Secretary

Executives of state, regional, national and international newspaper associations.
65 Members
Founded in: 1923

14700 Newspaper Association of America
4401 Wilson Blvd
Suite 900
Arlington, VA 22203
571-366-1000; *Fax:* 571-366-1195
joan.mills@naa.org; www.naa.org
Social Media: Facebook, Twitter, LinkedIn, RSS, Youtube, Google+

Donna Barrett, Chairman
Stephen P. Hills, Vice Chairman
Tony W. Hunter, Secretary
Michael J. Klingensmith, Treasurer
Robert M. Nutting, Chairan

Newspaper Association of America maintains close, cooperative relations with other newspaper and journalism organizations.
2000 Members
Founded in: 1992

14701 Overseas Press Club of America
40 W 45th St
New York, NY 10036
212-626-9220; *Fax:* 212-626-9210
sonya@opcofamerica.org;
www.opcofamerica.org
Social Media: Facebook, Twitter, LinkedIn, Yahoo, Stumbleupon, Google, Di

Marcus Mabry, President
Calvin Sims, First Vice-President
Abigail Pesta, Second Vice-President
Pancho Bernasconi, Third Vice-President
Tim Ferguson, Treasurer

OPC is a private non-profit membership organization of journalists engaged in international news.
600 Members
Founded in: 1939

14702 Pulic Radio News Directors Incorporated
PO Box 838
Sturgis, SD 57785
605-490-3033; *Fax:* 605-490-3085
info@prndi.org; www.prndi.org
Social Media: Facebook, Twitter, RSS

George Bodarky, President
Rachel Osier Lindley, Treasurer
Teresa Collier, Large Station Rep
Catherine Welch, Medium Station Rep
Christine Paige Diers, Business Manager

A non-profit professional association that exists to improve local news and information programming by serving public radio journalists.
Founded in: 1985

14703 Society for Features Journalism
www.featuresjournalism.org
Social Media: Facebook, Twitter, RSS
Lisa Glowinski, President
Kathy Lu, First Vice-President
Jim Haag, Second Vice-President
Margaret Myers, Secretary-Treasurer
Andrew Nynka, Executive Director
Founded in: 1947

14704 Society for News Design
424 E. Central Blvd.
Suite 406
Orlando, FL 32801
407-420-7748; *Fax:* 407-420-7697
snd@snd.org; www.snd.org
Social Media: Facebook, Twitter, LinkedIn, RSS, Pinterest

Lee Steele, President
Sara Quinn, Vice President
Douglas Okasaki, Secretary/Treasurer
Stephen Komives, Executive Director
Jonathon Berlin, Immediate Past President

An international professional organization that encourage high standards of journalism through design. An international forum and resource for all those interested in news design, SND works to recognize excellence and strengthen visual journalism as a profession.
1500 Members
Founded in: 1979
Mailing list available for rent

14705 Society of American Business Editors and Writers
ASU, Walter Cronkite School of Journalism & Mas
555 North Central Ave, Suite 302
Phoenix, AZ 85004-1248
602-496-7862; *Fax:* 602-496-7041
sabew@sabew.org; www.sabew.org
Social Media: Facebook, Twitter, RSS

Joanna Ossinger, President
Cory Schouten, VP
Kathleen Graham, Executive Director
Spring Eselgroth, Web/ Membership Director
Liisa Straub, Fiscal Manager

Members are financial and economic news writers and editors for print and broadcast outlets.
3200 Members
Founded in: 1964

14706 Society of American Travel Writers
One Parkview Plaza
Suite 800
Oakbrook Terrace, IL 60181
414-359-1625; *Fax:* 414-359-1671
info@satw.org; www.satw.org
Social Media: Facebook, Twitter, LinkedIn

Paul Lasley, President
Barbara Orr, Vice President, Membership
Marla Schrager, Executive Director
John Kingzette, Membership Coordinator
Cindy Lemek, Executive Director

Photographers and 35 associate member representatives of airlines, hotels, resorts, tourist agencies and public relations firms.
Founded in: 1955

14707 Society of Professional Journalists
3909 N Meridian Street
Indianapolis, IN 46208
317-927-8000; *Fax:* 317-920-4789
webmaster@spj.org; www.spj.org
Social Media: Facebook, Twitter, LinkedIn, RSS, Pinterest, Flickr, Storif

Paul Fletcher, President
Rebecca Baker, Secretary/Treasurer
Joe Skeel, Executive Director
Chris Vachon, Associate Executive Director
Linda Hall, Director of Membership

Broad-based journalism organization, dedicated to encouraging the free practice of journalism and stimulating high standards of ethical behavior.
7500 Members
Founded in: 1909
Mailing list available for rent

14708 The American Society of Journalists and Authors
355 Lexington Avenue
15th Floor
New York, NY 10017-6603
212-997-0947; www.asja.org/
Social Media: Facebook, Twitter, LinkedIn, Instagram, Google+

Randy Dotinga, President
Sherry Beck Paprocki, Vice President
Neil O'Hara, Treasurer
Alexandra Cantor Owens, Executive Director
Meredith Taylor, General Manager
Founded in: 1948

14709 The Fund for Investigative Journalism
529 14th Street NW
13th Floor
Washington, DC 20045
202-662-7564
fundfij@gmail.com; www.fij.org/
Social Media: Facebook, Twitter, RSS

Ricardo Sandoval Palos, President
Marcia Bullard, Vice President
Clarence Page, Treasurer
Founded in: 1969

14710 The Gridiron Club
Prestigious organization of Washington, D.C. journalists. Membership is by invitation only. The Club is best known for its annual dinner featuring skits and speeches by politicians of both parties.
Founded in: 1885

14711 **The Poynter Institute for Media Studies**
801 Third St. S
St. Petersburg, FL 33701
727-821-9494; www.poynter.org
Social Media: Facebook, Twitter
Tim Franklin, President
Non-profit journalism school begun by Nelson Poynter, owner of the St. Petersburg Times (now the Tampa Bay Times).
Founded in: 1975

14712 **The Society of Environmental Journalists**
PO Box 2492
Jenkintown, PA 19046
215-884-8174; *Fax:* 215-884-8175
sej@sej.org; www.sej.org
Social Media: Facebook, Twitter, RSS
Jeff Burnside, President
Beth Parke, Executive Director
Jennifer Bogo, First Vice Pres. & Programs Chair
Kate Sheppard, SVP/Membership Chair
Gloria Gonzalez, Treasurer & Finance Chair
Mission is to strengthen the quality. reach and viability of journalism across all media to advance public understanding of environmental issues.
Founded in: 1990
Mailing list available for rent

14713 **UNITY Journalists for Diversity, Inc.**
PO Box 511783
Milwaukee, WI 53203
414-335-1478
info@unityjournalists.org
unityjournalists.org
Social Media: Facebook, Twitter, LinkedIn, Google+, Tumblr
Alliance of Asian American Journalists Association, National Lesbian and Gay Journalists Association and the Native American Journalists Association. Advocates fair and accurate coverage of diversity issues.
Founded in: 1994

Newsletters

14714 **AEJMC News Association for Education in Journa**
234 Outlet Pointe Boulevard
Columbia, SC 29210-5667
803-798-0271; *Fax:* 803-772-3509
meirick@ou.edu; www.aejmc.org
Jenniffer Mcgrill, CEO
Kyshra Brown, Executive Director
Jennifer McGill, Executive Director
Supports all those scholars and educators of journalism and mass communications.
Frequency: Monthly
Circulation: 3425
Founded in: 1912

14715 **AGENDA**
National Federation of Press Women
PO Box 34798
Alexandria, VA 22334-0798
800-780-2715; *Fax:* 703-812-4555
jane@janeleecomm.com; www.nfpw.org
Social Media: Facebook, Twitter, LinkedIn, RSS, Flickr, Youtube
Lori Potter, President
A quarterly newletter published by the National Federation of Press Women.
Cost: $51.50
4 Pages
Frequency: Quarterly
Circulation: 2000
Founded in: 1937
Mailing list available for rent: 1700 names at $40 per M

14716 **APME Update**
Associated Media Press Editors
450 West 33rd Street
New York, NY 10001
212-621-7007
sjacobsen@ap.org; www.apme.com
Social Media: Facebook, Twitter
Bill Church, President
Jim Simon, Vice President
Kathleen Carroll, AP SVP & Executive Editor
Brian Carovillano, AP Managing Editor
Mark Baldwin, Program Chair
APME is an association of U.S. and Canadian editors, broadcasters and educators whose entitites are members of The Associated Press.
Founded in: 1933

14717 **ASBPE News**
American Society of Business Publication Editors
214 North Hale Street
Wheaton, IL 60187
630-510-4588; *Fax:* 630-510-4501
info@asbpe.org; www.asbpe.org
Social Media: Facebook, Twitter, LinkedIn, RSS
Amy Florence Fischbach, President
Erin Erickson, Vice President
Tina Grady Barbaccia, Secretary/Treasurer
Janet Svazas, Executive Director
Robin Sherman, Associate Dir. & Newsletter Editor
ASBPE is the professional association for full-time and freelance editors and writers employed in the business, trade, and specialty press. It is widely known for its annual Awards of Excellence competition, which recognizes the best editorial, design, and online achievement.
Founded in: 1964
Mailing list available for rent

14718 **ASJA Newsletter**
American Society of Journalists and Authors
1501 Broadway
Suite 403
New York, NY 10036-5505
212-997-0947; *Fax:* 212-937-2315
staff@asja.org; www.asja.org
Social Media: Facebook, Twitter, LinkedIn, Goggle+
Alexandra Cantor Owens, Executive Director
Minda Zetlin, President
Barbara DeMarco- Barrett, Newsletter Editor
Dave Mosso, Art Director
Confidential news for journalists and authors, available only to members of the Society.
Frequency: Monthly
Founded in: 1948
Mailing list available for rent

14719 **ASMP Bulletin**
American Society of Media Photographers
150 North 2nd Street
Philadelphia, PA 19106
215-451-2767
info@asmp.org; www.asmp.org
Social Media: Facebook, Twitter, LinkedIn, Pinterest, Blogger, Tumblr
Peter Dyson, Director of Communications
Victor Perlman, General Counsel
Eugene Mopsik, Executive Director
Elena Goertz, General Manager
Khaisha Allford, Member Services Coordinator
ASMP is the premier trade association for the world's most respectd photograhers. The ASMP Bulletin is a newsletter benefit for members.
Founded in: 1944
Mailing list available for rent

14720 **Bulldog Reporter**
James Sinkinson/InfoCom Group
124 Linden Street
Suite L
Oakland, CA 94607
510-596-9300
800-959-1059; www.bulldogreporter.com
Social Media: Facebook, Twitter, RSS, Pinterest, Google+
James Sinkson, President
Jacques Guatreaux, Vice President
Journalist contact updates and intelligence on how to successfully place stories with the most influential business media and journalists in the US.
Cost: $449.00
Frequency: 24 issues per y
Founded in: 1980
Mailing list available for rent

14721 **Clio Among the Media**
Association for Education in Journalism
234 Outlet Pointe Blvd
Suite A
Columbia, SC 29210-5667
803-798-0271; *Fax:* 803-772-3509
aejmc@aejmc.org; www.asjmc.org
Georgia NeSmith, Assistant Editor
Jennifer McGill, Executive Director
This newsletter is aimed directly at scholars and educators of Journalism and Mass Communications.
Cost: $107.50
24 Pages
Frequency: Quarterly
Circulation: 450
Founded in: 1966

14722 **Communicator**
American Institute of Parliamentarians
550m Ritchie Highway #271
Severna Park, MD 21146
888-664-0428; *Fax:* 410-544-4640
aip@aipparl.org; www.aipparl.org
Rob James, Vice President
Alison Wallis, President
Mary Remson, Treasurer
Jim Jones, CPP-T, Accrediting Director
Jeanette Williams, CP-T, Education Director
Quarterly newsletter listing AIP's board of directors, committees, parliamentary activities, chapter news and activities.
Founded in: 1958

14723 **GP Reporter**
Star Reporter Publishing Company
PO Box 60193
Staten Island, NY 10306-0193
718-981-5700; *Fax:* 718-981-5713
RA Lindberg, Publisher
Covers journalism for educational purposes.
Cost: $9.00
20 Pages

14724 **Guild Reporter**
Newspaper Guild: CWA
501 3rd St Nw
6th Floor
Washington, DC 20001-2760
202-434-1254; *Fax:* 202-434-1426
guild@cwa-union.org; www.nabetcwa.org
Social Media: Facebook, Youtube, RSS, Flickr
John Clark, President
Carol D Rothman, Secretary/Treasurer

Andy Zipser, Guild Reporter
Charles G. Braico, Sector Vice President

Covers the newspaper industry, its employment practices, press freedom and labor movement.
Cost: $20.00
6 Pages
Frequency: Monthly
Founded in: 1933

14725 ICA Newsletter
International Communications Association
1500 21st St Nw
Washington, DC 20036-1000

202-955-1444; *Fax:* 202-530-9851
icahdq@icahdq.org; www.icahdq.org
Social Media: Facebook, Twitter, LinkedIn, Google+

Michael L. Haley, Executive Director
Sam Luna, Member Services Director
John Paul Gutierrez, Communication Director
Jennifer Le, Executive Assistant
Michael J. West, Publications Manager

Trade association publication for scholars in the field of communication.
Cost: $20.00
Frequency: 10 times a year
Founded in: 1950
Mailing list available for rent
Printed in on matte stock

14726 Journalist and Financial Reporting
TJFR Publishing Company
82 Wall Street
Suite 1105
New York, NY 10005-3600

212-422-2456; *Fax:* 212-663-3260

Dean Rotbart, Publisher

Financial and business news.
Cost: $549.00
12 Pages
Frequency: BiWeekly

14727 Media Reporter
Gay and Lesbian Press Association
PO Box 8185
Universal City, CA 91618-8185

Fax: 818-902-9576

RJ Curry, Publisher

Accepts advertising.
Cost: $40.00
16 Pages
Frequency: Quarterly

14728 N2 Newspaper Next:
American Press Institute
4401 Wilson Boulevard
Suite 900
Arlington, VA 22203

703-620-3611; *Fax:* 703-620-5814;
www.americanpressinstitute.org
Social Media: Facebook, Twitter, LinkedIn

Thomas A. Silvestri, Chairman
Peter Bhatia, Editor
Caroline H. Little, President and CEO
Margaret G. Vassilikos, Finance & Operations
Mary Peskin, Training Programs

N2 Newspaper Next: is the forward-thinking project undertaken by API - to identify and test new business models for newspaper companies. It has grown to include not just research, but two reports of the project's findings as well as cuountless seminars, worksops, tailored programs offerings and special events.
Founded in: 1946
Mailing list available for rent

14729 National Press Foundation Update
National Press Foundation
1211 Connecticut Ave Nw
Suite 310
Washington, DC 20036-2709

202-663-7280; *Fax:* 202-662-1232;
www.nationalpress.org
Social Media: Facebook, Twitter, RSS, Youtube, Google+, Scribd,

Bob Meyers, President/COO
Gerald Seib, Vice Chairman
Linda Topping Streitfeld, Director of Programs
Maha Masud, Programs Manager
Kerry Buker, Director of Operations

News.
4 Pages
Frequency: BiWeekly
Founded in: 1993

14730 New England Press Association Bulletin
New England Press Association
360 Huntington Avenue
428CP
Boston, MA 02115-5005

617-254-4880; *Fax:* 617-373-5615;
www.nepa.org

Brenda Need, Publisher
Linda Conway, Marketing Director
Thomas Guenette, Circulation Manager
Brenda Need, Editor

A monthly publication about the newspaper industry specifically focusing on New England newspapers and the issues that affect them.
Cost: $15.00
Frequency: Monthly
Circulation: 1500
Founded in: 1950
Printed in 4 colors on newsprint stock

14731 OCP Bulletin
Overseas Press Club of America
40 W 45th St
New York, NY 10036-4202
212-626-9220; *Fax:* 212-626-9210;
www.opcofamerica.org

Sonya Fry, Executive Director
David Andelman, President
Jacqueline Albert-Simon, Treasurer

Foreign correspondence news and features.
Frequency: Monthly

14732 Publisher's Auxiliary
National Newspaper Association
900 Community Drive
Springfield, IL 62703

217-241-1400; *Fax:* 217-241-1301
stan@nna.org; www.nnaweb.org
Social Media: Facebook, Twitter

Matthew Paxton, President
Tonda Rush, Director, Public Policy
Stan Schwartz, Managing Editor

The only national publication serving America's community newspapers. First published in 1865, Publishers' Auxiliary is also the oldest newspaper serving the newspaper industry.
Founded in: 1865

Magazines & Journals

14733 APME News Magazine
Associated Press Media Editors
450 W 33rd St
New York, NY 10001-2647

212-621-1849; *Fax:* 212-833-7574
info@ap.org; www.apme.com

Bill Church, President
Kathleen Carroll, AP SVP & Executive Editor
Brian Carovillano, AP Managing Editor

Frequency: Quarterly
Circulation: 7000
Founded in: 1848

14734 Alternative Press Review
P.O. Box 444
Columbia, MD 21045

E-Mail: alternativepressreview@comcast.net;
www.alternativepressreview.org

Jason McQuinn, Editor

Covers alternative press including humor, opinion and art.
Cost: $16.00
Frequency: Quarterly
Circulation: 7000

14735 American Editor
American Society of Newspaper Editors
11690B Sunrise Valley Drive
Reston, VA 20191-1409

703-453-1122; *Fax:* 703-453-1133;
www.asne.org

Arnie Robbins, Executive Director
Kathy Bates, Development Director
Cindy L. Roe, Finance Director
Diana Mitsu Klos, Senior Project Director
Megan Schumacher, Sr. Information Specialist

A magazine published by the American Society of Newspaper Editors.
30 Pages
Frequency: Daily
Founded in: 1922

14736 American Journalism Review
University of Maryland
1117 Journalism Building
College Park, MD 20742-1

301-405-8803
800-827-0771; *Fax:* 301-405-8323
editor@ajr.org; www.ajr.org

Tom Kunkel, President
Rem Rieder, Editor
Reese Cleghorn, Publisher
Kathy Darragh, Circulation Manager
Kevin Klose, Senior Vice President

Monthly magazine for media professionals.
Cost: $24.00
Circulation: 25000
Founded in: 1972

14737 American Prospect
5 Broad Street
Boston, MA 02109

617-570-8030; *Fax:* 617-570-8028
editors@prospect.org; www.prospect.org

Robin Hutson, Publisher
Tim Lysler, Associate Publisher
Robert Kuttner, President

Progressive liberal publication
Cost: $19.95
Frequency: Monthly
Circulation: 55000
Founded in: 1990
Printed in 4 colors on matte stock

14738 Brilliant Ideas for Publishers
Creative Brilliance Associates

Mathey Road
PO Box 32
Clam Lake, WI 94517

715-749-2186
800-975-5474; *Fax:* 715-749-2180

Naomi Shapiro, Editor

Edited and published for the newspaper industry.

14739 Catholic Journalist
3555 Veterans Memorial Highway
Unit O
Ronkonkoma, NY 11779

631-471-4730; *Fax:* 631-471-4804;
www.catholicpress.org

Penny Wiegert, President
Tim Walker, Executive Director
Cost: $12.00
Frequency: Quarterly

14740 Columbia Journalism Review
Columbia University
2960 Broadway
New York, NY 10027-6900

212-854-1754
888-425-7782; *Fax:* 212-749-0397
subscriptions@cjr.org; www.columbia.edu

Robert Kasdin, Executive VP
Evan Cornog, Publisher
Michael Hoyt, Executive Editor

Evaluates all of the media as well as establishes standards for the profession.
Cost: $19.95
72 Pages

14741 ESD Technology
Kelvin Publishing
22700 Wood Street
Saint Clair Shores, MI 48080-1762

586-777-0440; *Fax:* 586-774-3892

John Kelvin, Editor
Kevin Campbell, VP Marketing

Technical articles highlighting new applications and research.
Founded in: 1936

14742 Ideas
International Newspaper Marketing Association
10300 N Central Expressway
Suite 467
Dallas, TX 75231

214-373-9111; *Fax:* 214-373-9112
inma@inma.org; www.inma.org
Social Media: Facebook, Twitter, LinkedIn, RSS

Earl Wilkinson, Executive Director
Marise Trevino, Editor
Earl Wilkinson, CEO/President
Dawn McMullan, Editor
Ravi Dhariwal, President

Marketing and promotion ideas for newspaper executives.
32 Pages
Frequency: Monthly
Circulation: 1200
Founded in: 1930
Mailing list available for rent

14743 International Communications Association
1500 21st St NW
Washington, DC 20036-1000

202-955-1444; *Fax:* 202-955-1448
icahdq@icahdq.org; www.icahdq.org
Social Media: Facebook, Twitter, LinkedIn, Google+

Michael L. Haley, Executive Director
Sam Luna, Member Services Director
John Paul Gutierrez, Communication Director
Jennifer Le, Executive Assistant
Michael J. West, Publications Manager

Bi-monthly newsletter that supports all students and professionals in the international communications industry.
Mailing list available for rent
Printed in on matte stock

14744 Journalism & Mass Communication Quarterly (JMC)
234 Outlet Pointe Road
Columbia, SC 29210-5667

803-798-0271; *Fax:* 803-772-3509
aejmchq@aol.com; www.aejmc.org/
Social Media: Facebook, Twitter, LinkedIn, FriendFeed, Flickr, Youtube, R

Lillian Coleman, JMC Production Manager (AEJMC)
Dan Riffe, Editor (JMCQ Contact)
Jennifer McGill, Executive Director
Pamela Price, Membership/Subscription Coordinator
Kysh Anthony, Website Content Manager

Published by the Association for Education in Journalism and Mass Communication, the JMC Quarterly focuses on research in journalism and mass communication. Each issue features reports of original investigation, presenting the latest developments in theory and methodology of communication, international communication, journalism history, and social and legal problems. Also contains book reviews. Refereed. Four times per year. (est. 1924)
Cost: $80.00
Circulation: 4800
Mailing list available for rent

14745 Latinos in the US: A Resource Guide for Journalists
National Association of Hispanic Journalists
529 14th St Nw # 1240
Washington, DC 20045-2520

202-789-1157; *Fax:* 202-347-3444
rnutting@marketwatch.com;
www.marketwatch.com

Rex Nutting, Manager
Joseph Torres, Communications Director
Rex Nutting, Manager

Purposes are to increase educational and career opportunities in journalism for Hispanic Americans.
Cost: $8.50
Mailing list available for rentat $500 per M

14746 Magazine Media Factbook (ASME)
American Society of Magazine Editors
810 Seventh Avenue
24th Floor
New York, NY 10019

212-872-3700; *Fax:* 212-906-0128
info@magazine.org; www.magazine.org
Social Media: Facebook, Twitter, LinkedIn, Youtube, Pinterst

Mary Berner, President & CEO
Nina Fortuna, Program Coordinator
Larry Hackett, President
Peggy Northrop, Vice President
Lucy Danziger, Secretary

A comprehensive guide of magazine media facts for advertisers, advertising agencies, media planners and consumer magazine marketers.
700 Members
Founded in: 1963

14747 Newspaper Financial Executive Journal
Interactive & Newsmedia Financial Executives
550 W. Frontage Road
Ste. 3600
Northfield, IL 60093

847-716-7000; *Fax:* 703-421-4068;
www.infe.org

Mary M. Collins, President & CEO
Jamie L. Smith, Director of Operations
Arcelia Pimentel, MFM Membership Manager & Sales
Debi Borden, Administrative Manager
Cindy Laser, Sales Account Executive

Trade publication for financial management of newspapers. More than 800 members.
Frequency: Weekly
Circulation: 1000
Founded in: 1947
Mailing list available for rent

14748 Newspapers & Technology
Conley Magazines
1623 Blake Street
Suite 250
Denver, CO 80202

303-575-9595; *Fax:* 303-575-9555
letters@newsandtech.com;
www.newsandtech.com/

Mary Van Meter, Publisher
Chuck Moozakis, Editor-in-Chief
Tara McMeekin, Editor
Hays Goodman, Associate Editor/Webmaster
Jessica Shade, Creative Services Assistant

Newspapers & Technology is a monthly trade publication for newspaper publishers and department managers involved in applying and integrating technology. Written by industry experts, News & Tech provides regular coverage of the following departments: prepress, press, postpress and new media.
Circulation: 16,874
Mailing list available for rent

14749 Overseas Press Club of America Magazine
Overseas Press Club of America
40 W 45th St
New York, NY 10036-4202

212-626-9220; *Fax:* 212-626-9210;
www.opcofamerica.org
Social Media: Facebook, Twitter, LinkedIn

Sonya Fry, Executive Director
David Andelman, President
Jacqueline Albert-Simon, Treasurer
600 Members
Frequency: Annual
Circulation: 600
Founded in: 1939

14750 Parliamentary Journal
American Institute of Parliamentarians
550m Ritchie Highway #271
Severna Park, MD 21146

888-664-0428; *Fax:* 410-544-4640
aip@aipparl.org; www.aipparl.org

Rob James, Vice President
Alison Wallis, President
Mary Remson, Treasurer
Jim Jones, CPP-T, Accrediting Director
Jeanette Williams, CP-T, Education Director

Wide range of subjects for AIP members
Founded in: 1958

14751 Ways With Words
American Society of News Editors
11690B Sunrise Valley Drive
Reston, VA 20191-1409

703-453-1122
asne@asne.org; www.asne.org
Social Media: Facebook, Twitter, Storify

Cindy L. Roe, Finance Director
Arnie Robbins, Executive Director

Diana Mitsu Klos, Senior Project Director
Megan Schumacher, Sr. Information Specialist
Kevin Goldberg, Legal Counsel

Ways With Words is the result of unusual, perhaps unique, collaboration among a diverse group of people who care about newspapers and reading. It may well be a model for joint research and development by journalism scholars and practitioners into the future of newspaper journalism.
Cost: $1.00
Founded in: 1922

Trade Shows

14752 APME/ASNE/APPM Annual Conference
Associated Press Media Editors
450 West 33rd Street
New York, NY 10001

212-621-7007
sjacobsen@ap.org; www.apme.com
Social Media: Facebook, Twitter

Bill Church, President
Jim Simon, Vice President
Angie Muhs, Secretary
Mark Baldwin, Program Chair

APME is an association of U.S. and Canadian editors, broadcasters and educators whose entitites are members of The Associated Press.
Frequency: Annual
Founded in: 1933

14753 AWC National Conference
Association for Women in Communications
3337 Duke Street
Alexandria, VA 22314

703-370-7436; *Fax:* 703-342-4311
info@womcom.org; www.womcom.org
Social Media: Facebook, Twitter, LinkedIn, Youtube

Patricia Valenzuela, National Administrator
Judy Arent-Morency, Board Chair
Pamela Valenzuela, Executive Director
Liz Booth, Membership Coordinator
Beth Veney, Communications and Programs Manager

Annual conference and exhibits of journalism, public relations, advertising, marketing, educational communications and film.
Mailing list available for rent

14754 American Society of Journalists and Authors Conference
1501 Broadway
Suite 403
New York, NY 10036-5501

212-997-0947; *Fax:* 212-937-2315
director@ajsa.org; www.asja.org
Social Media: Facebook, Twitter, LinkedIn, Goggle+

Alexandra Cantor Owens, Executive Director
Minda Zetlin, President
Barbara DeMarco- Barrett, Newsletter Editor
Dave Mosso, Art Director
Bruce Miler, Web Master

A forum for the exchange of ideas between journalists.
700 Attendees
Frequency: May
Mailing list available for rent

14755 American Society of News Editors (ASNE) Convention
11690B Sunrise Valley Drive
2660 Woodley Road, NW
Reston, VA 20191-1409

703-453-1122
800-656-4622
registrar@naa.org; www.asne.org
Social Media: Facebook, Twitter

Cindy L. Roe, Finance Director
Arnie Robbins, Executive Director
Diana Mitsu Klos, Senior Project Director
Megan Schumacher, Sr. Information Specialist
Kevin Goldberg, Legal Counsel
ASNE's annual convention is the largest annual gathering of newsroom leaders from daily newspapers and other news organizations. Editors and leaders in the field of journalism education will gather to refresh their spirits and create a roadmap to transform their newsrooms and shape the future of professional journalism.
Frequency: April
Founded in: 1922

14756 Annual Multimedia Convention & Career Expo (NAHJ)
National Association of Hispanic Journalists
Disney's Coronado Spings Resort
1000 W Buena Vista Drive
Lake Buena Vista, FL 32830

866-257-5990; www.nahjconvention.org
Social Media: Facebook, Twitter, LinkedIn, YouTube

Michele Salcedo, President
Manuel De La Rosa, Vice President/Broadcast
Russell Contreras, VP Print/Financial Officer

NAHJ is dedicated to the recognition and professional advancement of Hispanics in the news industry. NAHJ created a national voice and unified vision for all Hispanic journalists.
2300 Members
Frequency: August
Founded in: 1984

14757 Association for Education in Journalism and Mass Communication Annual Show
234 Outlet Pointe Boulevard
Suite A
Columbia, SC 29210-5667

803-798-0271; *Fax:* 803-772-3509;
www.aejmc.org/

Fred Williams, Communications & Convention Manager
Richard Burke, Business Manager/Convention Manager
Jennifer McGill, Executive Director

Annual show of publishers and educational groups. Exhibits include publications, information retrieval services and special programs.
2000 Attendees
Frequency: August
Founded in: 1912

14758 Collegiate Press Association Trade Show
330 21st Avenue S
Minneapolis, MN 55455-0480

612-625-3500; *Fax:* 612-626-0720

Tom Rolnicki, Show Manager

20 booths including learning sessions and press conferences.
1.2M Attendees
Frequency: November

14759 Edward R. Murrow Forum on Issues in Journalism
Tufts University
95 Talbot Ave.
Medford, MA 02155

617-627-2155; *Fax:* 617-627-3449
fms@tufts.edu
ase.tufts.edu/cms/murrow.html

Annual interdisciplinary panel reflecting on contemporary issues in journalism.
Frequency: Annual
Founded in: 2006

14760 International American Press Association Trade Show
2911 NW 39th Street
Miami, FL 33142-5148

305-634-2465

Julio Munoz, Executive Director

12 booths.
500 Attendees
Frequency: September
Mailing list available for rent

14761 International Newspaper Marketing Association Central
World-Herald Square
Omaha, NE 68102

402-734-7632; *Fax:* 402-444-1370

Terry Ausenbaugh

20 booths.
100 Attendees
Frequency: October

14762 Magazine Media Factbook (ASME)
American Society of Magazine Editors
810 Seventh Avenue
24th Floor
New York, NY 10019

212-872-3700; *Fax:* 212-906-0128
info@magazine.org; www.magazine.org
Social Media: Facebook, Twitter, LinkedIn, Pinterest, Youtube
Sid Holt, Chief Executive
Nina Fortuna, Program Coordinator
Larry Hackett, President
Peggy Northrop, Vice President
Lucy Danziger, Secretary
A comprehensive guide of magazine media facts for advertisers, advertising agencies, media planners and consumer magazine marketers.
700 Members
Founded in: 1963

14763 National Conference of the American Copy Editors Society
Sheraton New Orleans Hotel
500 Canal Street
Nw Orleans, LA 70130

504-525-2500
866-716-8106; *Fax:* 504-595-5552;
www.sheratonneworleans.com
Social Media: Facebook, Twitter, LinkedIn

Teresa Schmedding, President
Lisa McLendon, Vice President Conferences
Sara Hendricks, Vice President Membership
Rudy Bahr, Executive Director
Gerri Berendzen, Content Editor

ACES is a professional organization working toward the advancement of editors. Their aim is to provide opportunities through training, discussion and advocacy that promote the editing profession.
Frequency: April
Founded in: 1997

14764 National Convention & Annual LGBT Media Summit
National Lesbian and Gay Journalists Association

2120 L Street NW
Suite 850
Washington, DC 20037
202-588-9888
info@nlgja.org; www.nlgja.org
Social Media: Facebook, Twitter

Bach Polakowski, National Office Administrator
Matthew Rose, Membership Coordinator
Michael Tune, Executive Director
David Steinberg, President
Jen Christensen, Vice President/Broadcast

NLGJA is an organization of journalists, media professionals, educators and students working within the news industry to foster fair and accurate coverage of LGBT issues. NLGJA opposes all forms of workplace bias and provides professional development to its members.
220 Members
Founded in: 1990
Mailing list available for rent

14765 National Editorial Conference
American Society of Business Publication Editors
The Gleacher Center
450 N. Cityfront Plaza Drive
Chicago, IL 60611
312-464-8787; *Fax:* 312-464-8683
info@gleachercenter.com; www.gleachercenter.com
Social Media: Facebook, Twitter, LinkedIn

Amy Florence Fischbach, President
Erin Erickson, Vice President
Tina Grady Barbaccia, Secretary/Treasurer
Janet Svazas, Executive Director
Robin Sherman, Associate Dir. & Newsletter Editor

The National Editorial Conference focuses on the skills and ideas you need to weather the down economy and thrive in the new B2B publishing landscape.
Frequency: August

14766 National Magazine Awards
American Society of Magazine Editors
810 Seventh Avenue
24th Floor
New York, NY 10019
212-872-3700; *Fax:* 212-906-0128; www.magazine.org
Social Media: Facebook, Twitter, LinkedIn, Pinterest, Youtube

Sid Holt, Chief Executive
Nina Fortuna, Program Coordinator
Larry Hackett, President
Peggy Northrop, Vice President
Lucy Danziger, Secretary

The National Magazine Awards honor magazines, published in print and on digital platforms, that consistently demonstrate superior execution of editirial objectives, innovative techniques, noteworthy journalistic enterprise and imaginative art direction.
Founded in: 1966

14767 National Scholastic Press Association Conference
National Scholastic Press Association
330 21st Avenue S
Suite 620
Minneapolis, MN 55455-0479
612-625-8335; *Fax:* 612-626-0720

Tom Rolnicki, Executive Director

Annual conference and exhibits of information on yearbook printing and photographic services, college journalism departments and video yearbook production services.
1800 Attendees

14768 Newspaper Association of America/ Circulation Managers International
1921 Gallows Road
Suite 600
Vienna, VA 22182-3995
703-902-1600; *Fax:* 703-902-1600

James Abbott, VP

Newspaper management forum.
1M Attendees

14769 SABEW Annual Conference
Society of American Business Editors & Writers
ASU, Walter Cronkite School of Journalism
555 North Central Ave, Suite 302
Phoenix, AZ 85004-1248
602-496-7862; *Fax:* 602-496-7041
sabew@sabew.org; www.sabew.org
Social Media: Facebook, Twitter, LinkedIn, RSS

Warren Watson, Executive Director
Lacey Clements, Marketing Director
Mark Scarp, Membership Director
Spring Eselgroth, Web/ Membership Coordinator

Defines and inspires excellence in business journalism.
Frequency: April

14770 West Coast Practicum
American Institute of Parliamentarians
550m Ritchie Highway #271
Severna Park, MD 21146
888-664-0428; *Fax:* 410-544-4640
aip@aipparl.org; www,aipparl.org

Rob James, Vice President
Alison Wallis, President
Mary Remson, Treasurer
Jim Jones, CPP-T, Accrediting Director
Jeanette Williams, CP-T, Education Director

Topics being covered are convention committees, boards and problems related to boards, reference committees and the parliamentarian's role in consulting with boards.
Founded in: 1958

Directories & Databases

14771 1,000 Worldwide Newspapers
Albertsen's
PO Box 339
Nevada City, CA 95959-0339

Over 500 English-language newspapers overseas and in the United States are listed.
Cost: $10.00
54 Pages
Frequency: Annual

14772 American Society of Journalists and Authors Directory
ASJA
1501 Broadway
Suite 403
New York, NY 10036-5505
212-997-0947; *Fax:* 212-937-2315; www.asja.org
Social Media: Facebook, Twitter, LinkedIn, Goggle+

Alexandra Cantor Owens, Executive Director
Minda Zetlin, President
Barbara DeMarco- Barrett, Newsletter Editor
Dave Mosso, Art Director

Lists over 800 member freelance nonfiction writers.
Cost: $75.00
90 Pages
Mailing list available for rent

14773 American Society of News Editors (ASNE) Database
11690B Sunrise Valley Drive
Reston, VA 20191-1409
703-453-1122
asne@asne.org; www.asne.org
Social Media: Facebook, Twitter, Storify

Cindy L. Roe, Finance Director
Arnie Robbins, Executive Director
Diana Mitsu Klos, Senior Project Director
Megan Schumacher, Sr. Information Specialist
Kevin Goldberg, Legal Counsel

Free access to ASNE's extensive online archive of reports and journalism studies, the gold standard in newsroom-related research.
Founded in: 1922

14774 Asian American Journalists Accountants Directory
1182 Market St
Suite 320
San Francisco, CA 94102-4919
415-346-2051; *Fax:* 415-346-6343; www.aaja.org

Ellen Endo, Executive Director
Luke Stangel, Co-Founder
Christine Choy, Director
Marcus Brauchli, Executive Editor

Student development, job referrals, fellowship and internship reports.
700 Pages
Founded in: 1981

14775 Bacon's Newspaper & Magazine Directories
Cision U.S., Inc.
322 South Michigan Avenue
Suite 900
Chicago, IL 60604
312-263-0070
866-639-5087
info.us@cision.com
us.cision.com

Joe Bernardo, President & CEO
Heidi Sullivan, VP & Publisher
Valerie Lopez, Research Director
Jessica White, Research Director
Rachel Farrell, Research Manager

Two volume set listing all daily and community newspapers, magazines and newsletters, news service and syndicates, syndicated columnists, complete editorial staff listings of each publication provided, covers U.S., Canada, Mexico, and Carribean.
Cost: $350.00
4,700 Pages
Frequency: Annual
ISSN: 1088-9639
Founded in: 1951
Printed in one color on matte stock

14776 Bacon's Radio/TV/Cable Directory
Cision U.S., Inc.
332 South Michigan Avenue
Suite 900
Chicago, IL 60604
312-263-0070
866-639-5087
info.us@cision.com; www.us.cision.com

Joe Bernardo, President & CEO
Heidi Sullivan, VP & Publisher
Valerie Lopez, Research Director
Jessica White, Research Director
Rachel Farrell, Research Manager

Includes comprehensive coverage for contact and programming information for more than 3,500 televsion networks, cable networks, television syndicators, television stations, and cable

systems in the United States and Canada.
Cost: $350.00
Frequency: Annual
ISSN: 1088-9639
Printed in one color on matte stock

14777 **Burrelle's Media Directory**
BurrellesLuce
75 E Northfield Rd
Livingston, NJ 07039-4532

973-992-6600
800-631-1160; *Fax:* 973-992-7675;
www.burrellesluce.com
Social Media: Facebook, Twitter, LinkedIn, RSS

Robert C Waggoner, CEO
Johna Burke, Senior Vice President, Marketing

Approximately 60,000 media listings in North America. Listings cover newspapers, magazines (trades and consumer), broadcast, and internet outlets.
Cost: $795.00
Frequency: Annual

14778 **Directory of Selected News Sources Issue**
American Journalism Review
8701 Adelphi Road
Suite 310
Adelphi, MD 20783-1716

800-827-0771; *Fax:* 301-405-8323

Rem Reider, Editor

List of about 400 companies, organizations and associations that provide information to newspapers and freelance reporters.
Cost: $2.95
Frequency: Annual
Circulation: 28,295

14779 **FYI Directory of News Sources and Information**
JSC Group
PO Box 868
Severna Park, MD 21146-0868

410-647-1013; *Fax:* 410-647-9557;
www.fyinews.com

Julia Stocks Corneal, Editor

About 400 associations, corporations, individuals and sources for background story gathering for journalists.
Cost: $19.95
Frequency: Annual
Circulation: 20,000

14780 **Find A Photographer Database**
American Society of Media Photographers
150 North 2nd Street
Philadelphia, PA 19106

215-451-2767
info@asmp.org; www.asmp.org;
Social Media: Facebook, Twitter, LinkedIn, Pinterest, Blogger, Tumblr

Peter Dyson, Director of Communications
Victor Perlman, General Counsel
Eugene Mopsik, Executive Director
Elena Goertz, General Manager
Khaisha Allford, Member Services Coordinator

Find a Photographer is a search engine to help ASMP members connect with the most respected photographers in the industry.
Founded in: 1944
Mailing list available for rent

14781 **Journalism Forum**
CompuServe Information Service
5000 Arlington Centre Blvd
Columbus, OH 43220-5439

614-326-1002
800-848-8199

This database provides information on all aspects of professional journalism.
Frequency: Full-text

14782 **National Directory of Community Newspapers**
American Newspaper Representatives
1000 Shelard Parkway
Suite 360
Minneapolis, MN 55426-4933

612-545-1116
800-752-6237; *Fax:* 612-545-1116

Hilary Howe, President

A directory of community and weekly newspapers in the United States offering rates, circulation, etc.
Cost: $85.00
550 Pages
Frequency: Annual
Circulation: 2,000

14783 **News Media Yellow Book**
Leadership Directories
104 5th Ave
New York, NY 10011-6901

212-627-4140; *Fax:* 212-645-0931
newsmedia@leadershipdirectories.com;
www.leadershipdirectories.com
Social Media: Facebook, Twitter

David Hurvitz, CEO
James M Petrie, Associate Publisher

Contact information for over 39,000 journalists at over 2,500 new services, networks, newspapers, television, radio stations, as well as independent journalists and syndicated columnists.
Cost: $325.00
1,200 Pages
Frequency: Quarterly
ISSN: 1071-8931
Founded in: 1969
Mailing list available for rent: 32,000 names at $125 per M

14784 **Newswire ASAP**
Information Access Company
362 Lakeside Drive
Foster City, CA 94404-1171

650-378-5200
800-227-8431

Provides citations and the complete text of more than 1 million news releases and wire stories from the international news wire agencies. Subjects covered include banking, commodities, companies, currency and economics.
Frequency: Full-text
Founded in: 1983

14785 **Overseas Press Club of America Directory**
Overseas Press Club of America
40 W 45th St
New York, NY 10036

212-626-9220; *Fax:* 212-626-9210
sonya@opcofamerica.org;
www.opcofamerica.org
Social Media: Facebook, Twitter, LinkedIn

Sonya Fry, Executive Director
David Andelman, President
Jacqueline Albert-Simon, Treasurer

OPC is a private non-profit membership organization of journalists engaged in international news.
600 Members
Founded in: 1939

Industry Web Sites

14786 **http://gold.greyhouse.com**
G.O.L.D Grey House OnLine Databases
Grey House Publishing's online database platform, GOLD, offers Quick Search, Keyword Search and Expert Search for most business sectors including communication, broadcast and journalism markets. The GOLD platform makes finding the information you need quick and easy - whether you're a novice searcher or an experienced database user. All of Grey House's directory products are available for subscription on the GOLD platform.

14787 **www.aarwba.org**
American Auto Racing Writers and Broadcasters
Association
Members are professional journalists who regularly cover auto racing and other related sports events.

14788 **www.ajr.newslink.org**
American Journalism Review
Provides links to sources, journalism organizations, search tools and media newsletters.

14789 **www.apme.com**
Associated Press Managing Editors
Members are executives of Associated Press News Executives.

14790 **www.asja.org**
American Society of Journalists and Authors
For freelance nonfiction writers whose bylines appear in periodicals and in books.

14791 **www.asne.org**
American Society of Newspaper Editors
Directing editors who determine editorial and news policy on daily newspapers and news gathering operations of daily newspapers.

14792 **www.cjr.org/resources**
Columbia Journalism Review
Contains resource guides and other journalism-related lists.

14793 **www.drudgereport.com**
Links to international news sources and columnists.

14794 **www.greyhouse.com**
Grey House Publishing
Authoritative reference directories for most business sectors including communication, broadcast and journalism markets. Users can search the online databases with varied search criteria allowing for custom searches by product category, geographic area, sales volume, keyword, subject and more. Full Grey House catalog and online ordering also available.

14795 **www.house.gov**
Association of House Democratic Press Assistants
Promotes education and professional standards of members through speakers, series, seminars and papers. Offers placement services.

14796 **www.infesecure.org**
International Newspaper Financial Executives
Controllers, chief accountants, auditors, business managers, treasurers, secretaries and related newspaper executives, educators and public accountants.

14797 **www.inma.org**
International Newspaper Marketing Association

Individuals in marketing, circulation, research and public relations of newspapers.

14798 **www.ire.org**
Investigative Reporters and Editors

For individuals involved in investigative journalism.

14799 **www.jour.missouri.edu/home.nsf/**
Resources at the University of Missouri's School of Journalism and beyond.

14800 **www.jrn.columbia.edu/ressources**
Columbia University School of Journalism

Access to Columbia University's Journalism School, the library's bibliographies and reference works, job listings and other associations.

14801 **www.kausfiles.com**
Site for journalists and media specialists.

14802 **www.liberty.uc.wlu.edu**
Journalism Resources

Lists of newspapers, film resources, jobs and internships and political advocacy groups.

14803 **www.naa.org**
Newspaper Association of America

Focuses on the major issues that affect today's newspaper industry public policy and legal matters, advertising revenue growth and audience development across the medium's broad portfolio of products and digital platforms.

14804 **www.nepa.org**
New England Press Association

This organizatiom offers a publication about the newspaper industry specifically focusing on New England newspapers and the issues that affect them, which goes to every newspaper in New England.

14805 **www.nnaweb.org**
National Newspaper Association

To protect, promote and enhance America's community newspapers.

14806 **www.opcfamerica.org**
Overseas Press Club of America

A media/journalist organization.

14807 **www.poynter.org**
Poynter Institute is dedicated to teaching and inspiring journalists and media leaders. Promotes excellence and integrity in the practice of craft and in the practical leadership of successful businesses.

14808 **www.press.org**
National Press Club

A private organization composed of professional journalists who are directly related to the media. Persons must qualify to be admitted.

14809 **www.ukans.edu/~acejmc/**
Accrediting Council on Education in Journalism
and Mass Communications

ACEJMC members are journalism and media departments, education associations and professional organizations.

Associations

14810 Academy of Criminal Justice Sciences

PO Box 960
Suite A
Greenbelt, MD 20768-0960

301-446-6300
800-757-2257; *Fax:* 301-446-2819
info@acjs.org; www.acjs.org

Lorenzo M. Boyd, President
Nicole Leeper Piquero, First Vice-President
Faith Lutze, Second Vice-President
Mary K. Stohr, Executive Director
Heather L. Pfeifer, Secretary

An international association established to foster professional and scholarly activities in the field of criminal justice.
2800 Members
Founded in: 1963

14811 Air Force Security Forces Association

818 Willow Creek Cir
San Marcos, TX 78666

512-396-5444
888-250-9876; *Fax:* 512-396-7328
afsfaonline.com

Scott Castillo, President
Jim Saulnier, Vice President
John Probst, Executive Director
Jerry Bullock, Executive Director Emeritus
Lucille Bullock, Executive Treasurer-Secretary

The mission is to bring together all those currently serving in the US Air Force as Security Forces members, past Air Police and Security Police members, as well as future Security forces members.
Founded in: 1947

14812 Airborne Law Enforcement Association

50 Carroll Creek Way
Suite 260
Frederick, MD 21701

301-631-2406; *Fax:* 301-631-2466
webmaster@alea.org; www.alea.org
Social Media: Facebook, Twitter, LinkedIn

Steve Roussell, Chair:Executive Committee
Daniel B. Schwarzbach, Executive Director/CEO
Benay Osborne, CEM, CMP, Operations Manager
Don Ruby, Training Program Manager
Bryan Smith, Safety Program Manager

Supports and encourages the use of aircraft in public safety and provides networking systems, educational seminars and product expositions.
3500 Members
Founded in: 1968

14813 American Academy of Forensic Sciences

410 N 21st St
Colorado Spring, CO 80904

719-636-1100; *Fax:* 719-636-1993
awarren@aafs.org; www.aafs.org
Social Media: Facebook, YouTube, RSS

Victor W. Weedn, President
Norm Sauer, PhD, Vice President
Zeno J. Geradts, PhD, Vice President
Anne Warren, Executive Director
Nancy Jackson, Director of Dev. & Accreditation

The need to identify forensic scientists unequivocally qualified to provide essential professional services for the Nation's judicial and executive branches of government has long been recognized. In response to this professional mandate, The American Board of Forensic Odontology was organized under the auspices of the National Institute of Justice.
Founded in: 1948
Mailing list available for rent

14814 American Association of Motor Vehicle Administrators

4401 Wilson Boulevard
Suite 700
Arlington, VA 22203

703-522-4200; *Fax:* 703-522-1553
info@aamva.org; www.aamva.org
Social Media: Facebook, Twitter, YouTube, Flickr

Neil D Schuster, President & CEO
Sandy Bloomfield, Executive Asst.
Philip Quinlan, VP, Business Solutions
Marc Saitta, Vice President & CFO
Kathy King, Director, Program Business Services

A nonprofit association that supports both state and provincial official members throughout North America who oversee the administration and enforcement of motor vehicle laws. Services include development and research in motor vehicle administration, law enforcement and highway safety as well as being an information clearinghouse.
Founded in: 1933
Mailing list available for rent

14815 American Association of Police Polygraphists

3223 Lake Ave
Unit 15c-168
Wilmette, IL 60091-1069

847-635-3980
888-743-5479; *Fax:* 937-488-1046
NOM@policepolygraph.org; www.policepolygraph.org
Social Media: Facebook

Karen Clark, Chairperson
James Wardwell, President
Tracey Hilton, Vice President
Robert C. Heard, Secretary
Gordon W. Moore, Treasurer

Promote and maintain the highest standards of ethics, integrity, honor and conduct in the polygraph profession; provide an opportunity and forum for the exchange of information regarding polygraph experiences, studies and research; cooperate with other national, regional and state polygraph associations and other professional organizations in matters of mutual interest and benefit to the profession.
900 Members
Founded in: 1977

14816 American Association of Police Officers

1109 W 6th St
Suite 205
Austin, TX 78703

800-961-9773; *Fax:* 800-227-1042
policeusa@gmail.com; www.policeusa.com
Social Media: Facebook

Phil LeConte, Executive Officer
David Dierks, Financial Officer
Suzanne D'Ambrose, Law Enforement Instructor
Dennis Haley, Veteran Homicide Investigator
Curt Schwake, General Counsel & Advisor

Dedicated to bringing the wisdom of America's law enforcement veterans to the next generation of police officers and citizens. AAPO has provided a national stage for veteran law enforcement officers to share their wisdom and experience. Guided by an advisory council of law enforcement veterans and distinguished citizens, AAPO is committed to tapping into this often overlooked resource - veteran law enforcers both active duty and retired - and putting this unique knowledge to a useful purpose.

14817 American Association of State Troopers

1949 Raymond Diehl Road
Tallahassee, FL 32308

800-765-5456
850-765-5456; *Fax:* 850-385-8697
joan@statetroopers.org; www.statetroopers.org
Social Media: Facebook

Keith Barbier, President
Jeffrey Lane, First Vice President
Lee Burch, Second Vice President
Noel Houze Jr., Secretary
Kenneth Musick, Treasurer
Founded in: 1989

14818 American Correctional Association

206 N Washington St
Alexandria, VA 22314

703-224-0000
800-222-5646; *Fax:* 703-224-0179
jeffw@aca.org; www.aca.org
Social Media: Facebook, Twitter, LinkedIn, YouTube

Mary L Livers, President
Michael Wade, Vice President
Gary C Mohr, Treasurer
James A Gondles, Jr., Secretary

For individuals involved in the correctional field.
20000 Members
Founded in: 1870
Mailing list available for rent

14819 American Criminal Justice Association

PO Box 601047
Sacramento, CA 95860-1047

916-484-6553; *Fax:* 916-488-2227
acjalae@aol.com; www.acjalae.org

Preston Koelling, President
Steve Atchley, VP
Jeanne Church-Elson, Region 1 President
Karen Campbell, Executive Secretary
David Redford, Region 2 President

Objectives are to improve criminal justice through educational activities, foster professionalism in law enforcement personnel and agencies, promote professional, academic and public awareness of criminal justice issues and promote high standards of ethical conduct, professional training and higher education within the criminal justice field.
7200 Members
Founded in: 1937

14820 American Jail Association

1135 Professional Ct
Hagerstown, MD 21740-5853

301-790-3930; *Fax:* 301-790-2941
rickn@aja.org; www.aja.org
Social Media: Facebook, Twitter, LinkedIn, YouTube, Instagram

Robert J. Kasabian, Executive Director
Steve Custer, Director of Communications
Patty Vermillion, Program Manager
Lauren Pirri, Marketing and Sales Coordinator
Nico Gentile, Dir. Of Business Development

Dedicated to supporting those who work in and operate our nations's jails. AJA is the only national association that focuses exclusively on issues specific to the operations of local correctional facilities.
5000 Members
Founded in: 1981

14821 **American Police Hall of Fame and Museum**
6350 Horizon Drive
Titusville, FL 32780

321-264-0911; *Fax:* 321-264-0033
policeinfo@aphf.org; www.aphf.org
Social Media: Facebook

Donna Shepherd, CEO
Barry Shepherd, Executive Director
Debra Chitwood, CFO
Jamie Maynard, Dir. Of Communications
Brent Shepherd, Director of Operations

Offers benefits and various types of awards to members, magazine, line of duty benefits, film and training library as well as support services, scholarships and financial assistance for police family survivors.
Founded in: 1960

14822 **American Police Hall of Fame and Museum**
6350 Horizon Drive
Titusville, FL 32780

321-264-0911; *Fax:* 321-264-0033
policeinfo@aphf.org; www.aphf.org
Social Media: Facebook

Donna Shepherd, CEO
Barry Shepherd, Executive Director
Debra Chitwood, Chief Financial Officer
Brent Shepherd, Director of Operations
Jamie Maynard, Director of Communications

The nation's first national police museum dedicated to law enforcement officers who have died in the line of duty.
104M Members
Founded in: 1960

14823 **American Polygraph Association**
PO Box 8037
Chattanooga, TN 37414-0037

423-892-3992
800-APA-8037; *Fax:* 423-894-5435
manager@polygraph.org; www.polygraph.org
Social Media: Facebook, Twitter, LinkedIn, Pinterest, Google+, Myspace

Ray Nelson, Chairman
Walt Goodson, President
Lisa Jacocks, Office Manager and Secretary
Mark Handler, Editor & Web Administer
Darry Starks, VP, Govt

Representing experienced polygraph examiners in private business, law enforcement and government. Professional APA polygraph examiners administer hundreds of thousands of polygraph exams each year worldwide. The APA establishes standards of ethical practices, techniques, instrumentation and research, as well as provides advanced training and continuing education programs.
3200 Members
Founded in: 1966
*Mailing list available for rent*at $125 per M

14824 **American Probation and Parole Association**
2760 Research Park Drive
Lexington, KY 40511-8482

859-244-8203; *Fax:* 859-244-8001
appa@csg.org; www.appa-net.org
Social Media: Facebook, Twitter, LinkedIn

Dee Bell, Executive Director
Diane Kincaid, Deputy Director/Info. Specialist
Tracy Mullins, Deputy Director
Adam Matz, Research Associate
John Higgins, Graphic Designer

An international association composed of members from the United States, Canada and other countries actively involved with probation, parole and community based corrections, inboth adult and juvenile sectors
2200 Members
Founded in: 1975

14825 **American Psychiatric Association**
1000 Wilson Blvd
Suite 1825
Arlington, VA 22209-3901

703-907-7300
888-35 -7792; *Fax:* 703-907-1085
apa@psych.org; www.psychiatry.org
Social Media: Facebook, Twitter, LinkedIn

Saul M. Levin, M.D., M.P.A, CEO & Medical Director
Maria A. Oquendo, President

U.S. and international member physicians work together to ensure humane care and effective treatment for all persons with mental disorder, including mental retardation and substance-related disorders. It is the voice and conscience of modern psychiatry. Its vision is a society that has available, accessible quality psychiatric diagnosis and treatment.

14826 **American Society of Crime Laboratory Directors**
139A Technology Drive
Garner, NC 27529

919-773-2044; *Fax:* 919-861-9930
asclddirector@gmail.com; www.ascld.org
Social Media: Twitter, LinkedIn, RSS

Jody Wolf, President
Jean Stover, Executive Director
Kris Deters, Training & Education Chair
Andrea Swiech, Treasurer
Cecilia Doyle, Secretary
Founded in: 1974

14827 **American Society of Criminology**
1314 Kinnear Rd
Suite 212
Columbus, OH 43212-1156

614-292-9207; *Fax:* 614-292-6767
asc@asc41.com; www.asc41.com
Social Media: Twitter, LinkedIn

Bonnie Fisher, Treasurer
Joanne Belknap, President-Elect
Christopher Uggen, Executive Secretary
Robert Agnew, President
Becky Block, VP

Objectives are to encourage the exchange, in a multidisciplinary setting, of those engaged in research, teaching, and practice so as to foster criminological scholarship, and to serve as a forum for the dissemination of criminological knowledge.
Founded in: 1941

14828 **American Speaker Association**
32 East Riverhead Drive
Houstan, TX 77042-2501

713-914-9444
800-636-2722; www.nsaspeaker.org
Social Media: Facebook, LinkedIn

Don Akers, Customer Service/Sales
Richard Alderman, Director of Consumer Law

Assists in proceedings involving legislation and arbitration.
37 Members
Founded in: 1979
Mailing list available for rent

14829 **American Traffic Safety Services Association**
15 Riverside Parkway
Suite 100
Fredericksburg, VA 22406-1022

540-368-1701
800-272-8772; *Fax:* 540-368-1717
foundation@atssa.com; www.atssa.com
Social Media: Facebook, Twitter, LinkedIn, Pinterest, Google+, YouTube

Sue Reiss, President
Kathleen Holst, Vice President
Chad England, Traffic Director
john Tobin, Director, Manufacturers & Suppliers
Juan Arvizu, At-Large Director

Promotes uniform use of lights, signs, pavement markings and barricades. Distributes technical information and sponsors training courses for worksite traffic supervisors.
1600 Members
Founded in: 1969

14830 **Americans for Effective Law Enforcement**
P.O. Box 75401
Chicago, IL 60675-5401

847-685-0700; *Fax:* 847-685-9700
info@aele.org; www.aele.org
Social Media: RSS

Daniel B. Hales, President
Wayne W. Schmidt, Esq., Executive Director
Bernard J. Farber, Editor/ Research Counsel
Helen Finkel, Staff Vice President
Missy Taki, Supervisor/Manager

Incorporated as a not for profit educational organization for the purpose of establishing an organized voice for the law-abiding citizens regarding this country's crime problem, and to lend support to professional law enforcement.
Founded in: 1966

14831 **Association of Firearm and Tool Mark Examiners**
525 Carter Hill Rd.
Montgomery, AL 36106

334-242-2938; *Fax:* 334-240-3284
kathy.richert@adfs.alabama.gov; www.afte.org

Brandon Giroux, President
Travis Spinder, 1st Vice President
Justine Kreso, Secretary
Alison Quereau, Membership Secretary
Melissa Oberg, Treasurer

14832 **Association of Paroling Authorities Inernational**
Sam Houston State University
Huntsville, TX 77341-2296

877-318-2724; *Fax:* 936-294-1671
keith@apaintl.org; www.apaintl.org

Cyndi Mausser, President
Tena Pate, Vice President
Keith Hardison, Chief Administrative Officer
David Blumberg, Treasurer
Dan Fetsco, Secretary
511 Members
Founded in: 1970

14833 **Association of Public-Safety Communication s Officials International (APCO)**
351 N Williamson Boulevard
Daytona Beach, FL 32114-1112

386-322-2500
888-272-6911; *Fax:* 386-322-2501
apco@apcointl.org; www.apcointl.org/
Social Media: Facebook, Twitter, LinkedIn

Brent Lee, President
Cheryl J. Greathouse, RPL, 1st Vice President
Martha K. Carter, ENP, 2nd Vice President
Doreen Geary, Accounting
Sarah Hill, Awards

International, nonprofit organization fostering the development and progress of the art of public safety communications by means of research, planning, training and education. Promotes cooperation between towns, cities, counties, states

and federal, public safety agencies in the area of communications.
15000 Members
Founded in: 1935

14834 Border Patrol Supervisors' Association
3755 Avocado
Blvd #404
La Mesa, CA 91941

www.bpsups.org

Richard Haynes, President
Richard Marzec, Vice President
Linwood Knowles, Secretary
Logan Snider, Treasurer
Mike Diaz, Sergeant at Arms
500 Members
Founded in: 1990

14835 Central Station Alarm Association
8150 Leesburg Pike
Suite 700
Vienna, VA 22182

703-242-4670; *Fax:* 703-242-4675
techadmin@csaaintl.org; www.csaaintl.org
Social Media: Facebook, Twitter, LinkedIn, RSS

Pamela Petrow, President
Joe Nuccio, First Vice President
Graham Westphal, Secretary
Ivan Spector, Treasurer
Peter Lowitt, Secretary

Represents companies offering security (alarm) monitoring systems through a central station. It also represents companies that provide services and products to the industry.
300+ Members
Founded in: 1950
Mailing list available for rent

14836 Commission on Accreditation for Law Enforcement Agencies, Inc.
13575 Heathcote Boulevard
Suite 320
Gainesville, VA 20155

703-352-4225
800-368-3757; *Fax:* 703-890-3126
calea@calea.org; www.calea.org
Social Media: RSS, Pinterest, Google+, Myspa

W. Craig Hartley, Jr., Executive Director
Travis Parrish, Dir, Client Services and Relations
Antonio T. Beatty, Administrative Services Manager
Margaret Giglio, Program Specialist
Wendi Jones, Contract Specialist

Established as an independent accrediting authority by the four major law enforcement membership associations: International Association of Chiefs of Police; National Organization of Black Law Enforcement Executives; National Sheriffs' Association; and Police Executive Research Forum.
21 Members
Founded in: 1979

14837 Concerns of Police Survivors
846 Old South 5
PO Box 3199
Camdenton, MO 65020

573-346-4911; *Fax:* 573-346-1414
cops@nationalcops.org; www.nationalcops.org
Social Media: Facebook, Twitter, Youtube

Brenda Donner, President
Dianne Bernhard, Executive Director
Sarah Slone, Director of Public Relations
Shelley Jones, Director of Operations
Lynn Kuse, Financial Manager

Resources are offered in the rebuilding of the lives of surviving families of law enforcement officers killed in the line of duty or determined by federal criteria. Futhermore, COPS provides training to law enforcement agencies on survivor victimizationa issues and educates the public of the need to support the law enforcement profession and its survivors.

14838 Congressional Fire Services Institute
900 2nd St NE
Suite 303
Washington, DC 20002-3557

202-371-1277; *Fax:* 202-682-3473
update@cfsi.org; www.cfsi.org
Social Media: Facebook

William Jenaway, President
Jim Estepp, Vice President
Bill Webb, Executive Director
Sean Carroll, Director of Government Affairs
Brian Goldfeder, Special Events Manager

Designed to educate members of Congress about the needs and challenges of our nation's fire and emergency services so that the federal government provides the types of training and funding needed by our first responders.
Founded in: 1989

14839 Cops Who Care
PO Box 20688
Wickenburg, AZ 85358

860-500-8926; www.copswhocare.org

Founded in: 1982

14840 Criminal Justice Center
Sam Houston State University
PO Box 2296
Huntsville, TX 77341

936-294-1635; *Fax:* 281-294-1653
icc_www@shsu.edu

Vincent Webb, Director/Dean
Kristi Kreier, Business Office Director

Established to provide an educational program for students seeking careers in law enforcement, cours and corrections and for the development of a continuing education program for professionals working in the field.

14841 D.A.R.E. America
PO Box 512090
Los Angeles, CA 90051-0090

310-215-0575
800-223-DARE; *Fax:* 310-215-0180
webmaster@dare.com; www.dare.com

Louis Miller, Chair
David M. Horn, Vice Chair
Francisco X Pegueros, President and CEO
Thomas Hazelton, President of Development
Anita Bryan, Deputy Director of Education

A police officer led series of classroom lessons that teaches children from kindergarten through 12th grad how to resist peer pressure and live productive drug and violence free lives.
Mailing list available for rent

14842 Dogs Against Drugs/Dogs Against Crime National Law Enforcement K9 Assn.
3320 Main St.
Suite G
Anderson, IN 46013

765-642-9447
888-323-3227; *Fax:* 765-642-4899
office@daddac.com
daddac.tripod.com
Social Media: Facebook

Darron Sparks, President/National Director

Dedicated to the betterment of law enforcement K9 operations and to educating the youth on the dangers of drug abuse. DAD/DAC provides grants to officers for purchasing highly trained special purpose dogs and related training equipment and supplies and to provide training for the officer and/or dog. Working/training seminars are offered for K9 officers on numerous topics related to police service dogs.

14843 Evidence Photographers International Council
229 Peachtree St. NE
Ste #2200
Atlanta, GA 30303

570-253-5450
866-868-3742; *Fax:* 404-614-6404
EPICheadquarters@verizon.net;
www.evidencephotographers.com
Social Media: Facebook

Robert F Jennings, Executive Director

Nonprofit scientific/educational organization with a primary purpose of advancement of forensic photography/videography in civil evidence and law enforcement.
Founded in: 1968

14844 FBI National Academy Associates
422 Garrisonville Road
Suite 103
Stafford, VA 22554

540-628-0834; *Fax:* 703-632-1993;
www.fbinaa.org

Barry Thomas, Association President
Steve Tidwell, Executive Director
Korri Roper, CFO/COO
Denise MacLane, Financial Accountant
Ashley Sutton, Communications Manager

A non-profit international organization of senior law enforcement professionals dedicated to providing the communities and profession with the highest degree of law enforcement expertise, training, education and information.
17000 Members
Founded in: 1935

14845 Federal Criminal Investigators Association
5868 Mapledale Plaza
Suite 104
Woodbridge, VA 22193

800-403-3374; www.fedcia.org

Founded in: 1991

14846 Federal Law Enforcement Officers Association
7945 MacArthur Blvd
Suite 201
Cabin John, MD 20818

202-870-5503
866-553-5362
fleoa@fleoa.org; www.fleoa.org
Social Media: Facebook, Twitter, Reddit, Pinterest

Jon Adler, National President
Nate Catura, Executive Vice President
Chris Schoppmeyer, Vice President - Agency Affairs
Frank Terreri, Vice President- Legislative Affairs
John Ramsey, Vice President - Membership Benefit
Founded in: 1977

14847 Fire Equipment Manufacturers' Association
1300 Sumner Avenue
Cleveland, OH 44115

216-241-7333; *Fax:* 216-241-0105
fema@femalifesafety.org;

www.femalifesafety.org
Social Media: YouTube, Wikipedia, Slideshare

The premier trade association representing leading brands, and spanning dozens of product categories, related to fire protection.
24 Members
Founded in: 1925

14848 Fire Suppression Systems Association
3601 East Joppa Road
Baltimore, MD 21234

410-931-8100; *Fax:* 410-931-8111
fssa@clemonsmgmt.com; www.fssa.net
Social Media: Facebook, Twitter, LinkedIn, Reddit, Pinterest, Blooger

Tim Carman, President
Ray Aldridge, Vice President
Helen Lowery, Secretary/Treasurer
Tim Carman, Secretary/Treasurer
Eric Burkland, VP

An organization of manufacturers, suppliers, and design-installers, dedicated to providing a higher level of fire protection. Members are specialists in protecting high value special hazardareas from fire.
Founded in: 1982

14849 Fire and Emergency Manufacturers and Services Association
P.O. Box 147
Lynnfield, MA 01940-0147

781-334-2771; *Fax:* 781-334-2771
info@femsa.org; www.femsa.org
Social Media: Twitter, LinkedIn

William Lawson, President
William Van Lent, Vice President

The leading trade association for the fire and emergency services industry whose members provide products and services to millions of fire and EMS professionals throughout the world. Works to strengthen its membership, planning for future development and directing programs that build industry opportunities.
150 Members
Founded in: 1966

14850 Flight Safety Foundation
801 N. Fairfax Street
Suite 400
Alexandria, VA 22314-1774

703-739-6700; *Fax:* 703-739-6708;
www.flightsafety.org
Social Media: Facebook, Twitter, LinkedIn

Ken Hylander, Chairman
Jon Beatty, President and CEO
David Barger, Treasurer
Kenneth P. Quinn, General Counsel & Secretary
David McMillan, Chairman

Independent, nonprofit, international organization engaged in research, auditing, education, advocacy and publishing to improve aviation safety.
Founded in: 1947

14851 Fraternal Order of Police
701 Marriott Dr
Nashville, TN 37214-5043

615-399-0900; *Fax:* 615-399-0400
webmaster@grandlodgefop.org; www.fop.net

Chuck Canterbury, National President
Ed Brannigan, National VP
Les Neri, National Second Vice President
Tom Penoza, National Treasurer
Patrick Yoes, National Secretary

This is the world's largest organization of sworn law enforcement officers, with more than 324,000 members in more than 2,100 lodges. It is the voice of those who dedicate their lives to protecting and serving our communities, and is committed to improving the working conditions of law enforcement officers and the safety of those served through education, legislation, information, community involvement,and employeee representation.
324M Members
Founded in: 1915
Mailing list available for rent

14852 Hispanic National Law Enforcement Association
PO Box 766
Cheltenham, MD 20623

240-244-9189; www.hnlea.com

Mike Rodriguez, President
Luis Rodriguez, Executive Director
Miguel I. Core, Vice President
Jose Perez, Treasurer
Adriane Clayton, Secretary

Non-profit organization of professionals involved in the administration of justice and dedicated to the advancement of Hispanic(Latino) and minority interests within the law enforcement profession.
Founded in: 1988

14853 Institute of Investigative Technology
AccuQuest
6950 Phillips Hwy, #46
Jacksonville, FL 32216-6087

904-296-0212; *Fax:* 904-296-7385;
www.aqonline.com/iitframeset.html

John Ramming, Director

Provides training for law enforcement and corporate clients. Programs can be designed from one-day to multiple week training courses.

14854 Institute of Police Technology and Management
University of North Florida
12000 Alumni Dr
Jacksonville, FL 32224-2678

904-620-4786; *Fax:* 904-620-2453
info@iptm.org; www.iptm.org
Social Media: Facebook

Teresa R. Dioquino, Management Section Coordinator
Cameron Pucci, Dictor
Tony Becker, Administration
Kenin Al Roop, Marketing
Harry Walters, Traffic Enforcement

Mission of the Institute is to provide the law enforcement community with the highest quality of training at competitive prices. By providing this service, IPTM continues to support law enforcement's efforts in building and maintaining safer communitites.
Founded in: 1980

14855 Insurance Institute for Highway Safety
1005 N Glebe Rd
Suite 800
Arlington, VA 22201

703-247-1500; *Fax:* 703-247-1588
rrader@iihs.org; www.iihs.org
Social Media: Twitter, RSS, YouTube

Adrian Loud, President
Russ Rader, Senior Vice President
Shelley Shelton, Executive Assistant, Legal Affairs
Brenda O'Donnell, Vice President, Insurer Relations
Chamelle Matthew, Communications Associate

Independent, nonprofit, scientific and educational organization dedicated to reducing the losses (deaths, injuries, and property damage) from crashes on the nation's highways.
Founded in: 1959
Mailing list available for rent

14856 International Association for Identification
2131 Hollywood Blvd.,
Suite 403
Hollywood, FL 33020

954-589-0628; *Fax:* 954-589-0657;
www.theiai.org
Social Media: Facebook

Bridget Lewis, President
Harold Ruslander, 1st Vice President
Ray Jorz, 2nd Vice President
Lisa Hudson, 3rd Vice President
Glen Calhoun, Chief Operations Officer
Founded in: 1915

14857 International Association for Property Evidence, Inc.
903 N San Fernando Boulevard
Suite 4
Burbank, CA 91504-4327

818-846-2926
800-449-4273; *Fax:* 818-846-4543
Mail@IAPE.org; www.iape.org
Social Media: Facebook

Joseph T. Latta, Executive Director/Lead Instructor
William Kiley, Board Member, Instructor
Steve Campbell, Secretary, Instructor
Suzanne Cox, Tresurer
Robin Lynn Trench, Founder

Established to further the education, training and professional growth of Law Enforcement Property and Evidence Personnel.
Founded in: 1993

14858 International Association of Arson Investigators
2111 Baldwin Avenue
Suite 203
Crofton, MD 21114

410-451-3473
800-468-4224; *Fax:* 410-451-9049
Dan.Heenan@firearson.com;
www.firearson.com
Social Media: Facebook, Twitter, LinkedIn, YouTube

Daniel Heenan, President
George Codding, 1st Vice President
Scott Bennett, 2nd Vice President
Deborah Keeler, Executive Director
Debra Miller, Accounting & Finanace Manager

Dedicated to improving the professional development of fire and explosion investigators by being the global resource for fire investigation, technology and research.
7500 Members
Founded in: 1949

14859 International Association of Auto Theft Investigators
PO Box 223
Clinton, NY 13323-0223

315-853-1913; *Fax:* 315-883-1310
jvabounader@iaati.org; www.iaati.org

Todd M. Blair, President
Robert C. Hasbrouck, Treasurer
John V Abounader, Executive Director
Heidi M. Jordan, 1st VP
Todd M. Blair, 3rd VP

Provides members who are auto theft investigators with resources to develop and maintain professional standards within the industry.
3604 Members
Founded in: 1952

14860 International Association of Bloodstain Pattern Analysts
www.iabpa.org
Pat Laturnus, President
Donald Schuessler, VP
Norman Reeves, Secretary/ Treasurer
Jeff Scozzafava, Sergeant at Arms
Stuart H James, Historian

14861 International Association of Bomb Technicians and Investigators
1120 International parkway
Fredricksburg, VA 22406
540-752-4533; *Fax:* 540-752-2796
admin@iabti.org; www.iabti.org
Social Media: Facebook, Twitter, LinkedIn
Ralph Way, Executive Director
An independent professional association formed for countering the criminal use of explosives. This is sought through the exchange of training, expertise and information among personnel employed in the fields of law enforcement, fire and emergency services, the military, forensic science and other related fields.
4000 Members
Founded in: 1973

14862 International Association of Campus Law Enforcement Administrators
342 N Main Street
West Hartford, CT 06117-2507
860-586-7517; *Fax:* 860-586-7550
info@iaclea.org; www.iaclea.org
Social Media: Facebook
William F. Taylor, President
Christopher Blake, CAE, Executive Director
Kendra Pheasant, CAE, Associate Director
Susan Koczka, Corporate Relations
Eva Storrs, Membership Services
Advances public safety for educational institutions by providing educational resources, advocacy and professional development.
Founded in: 1958
Mailing list available for rent

14863 International Association of Directors of Law Enforcement Standards/Training
1330 N. Manship Pl.
Meridian, ID 83642
208-288-5491; *Fax:* 517-857-3826;
www.iadlest.org
David Harvey, President
Brian Grisham, First Vice-President
Dan Zivkovich, Second Vice-President
Michael N. Becar, Executive Director
Mark Damitio, Secretary
An international organization of training managers and executives dedicated to the improvement of public safety personnel. The Association serves as the national forum of Peace Officer Standards and Training (POST) agencies, boards and commissions as well as statewide training academies throughout the United States.
Mailing list available for rent

14864 International Association of Law Enforcement Firearms Instructors
25 Country Club Road
Suite 707
Gilford, NH 03249
603-524-8787; *Fax:* 603-524-8856
info@ialefi.com; www.ialefi.com
R Steven Johnson, President
Robert D Bossey, Executive Director/Treasurer
Michial Dunlap, Secretary
John T. Meyer, 1st VP
Emanuel Kapelson, 2nd VP
An independent, non-profit association whose mission is to update and modernize the instruction and teaching techniques used to train the majority of law enforcement officers.
Founded in: 1981

14865 International Association of Undercover Officers
142 Banks Drive
Brunswick, GA 31523
800-876-5943; *Fax:* 800-876-5912
charlie@undercover.org; www.undercover.org
Brian Sallee, President
Brian Sallee, President
Steve Cook, First Vice-President
David Redemann, Second Vice-President
Frank Swirko, Treasurer
Established for the purpose of promoting safety and professionalism among undercover officers. The association continues to foster mutual cooperation, discussion and interests among its members. It provides vast international network of intelligence gathering means for today's undercover officer and sponsors high quality training programs for undercover officers.

14866 International Association of Women
1352 NE 47th Avenue
Portland, OR 97213
301-464-1402; *Fax:* 301-464-1402
carolpaterick@gmail.com; www.iawp.org
Social Media: Twitter
Margaret Shorter, President
Deborah Friedl, First Vice President
Andrea Humphrys, Executive Director
Michelle Lish, Foundation Treasurer
Julia Jaeger, Recording Secretary
Founded in: 1915

14867 International Association of Women Police
1352 NE 47th Avenue
Portland, OR 97213
301-464-1402; *Fax:* 301-464-1402
carolpaterick@gmail.com; www.iawp.org
Social Media: Twitter
Margaret Shorter, President
Deborah Friedl, First Vice President
Andrea Humphrys, Executive Director
Michele Lish, Foundation Treasurer
Julia Jaeger, Recording Secretary
To strengthen, unite, and raise the profile of women in criminal justice internationally.
24000 Members
Founded in: 1915

14868 International Board of Certification for Safety Managers
173 Tucker Road
Suite 202
Helena, AL 35080
205-664-8412; *Fax:* 205-663-9541
info@ibfcsm.org; www.ibfcsm.org
Social Media: Facebook
James Tweedy, Executive Director
A professional credentialing organization that promotes the application of managerial techniques to eliminate or control unsafe and unhealthy conditions, behavior and other factors detrimental to people and property. Offers credentials in safety, product safety, healthcare safety, patient safety, and healthcare emergency management.
2500 Members
Founded in: 1976

14869 International Crime Scene Investigator's Association
15774 S. LaGrange Road
Orland Park, IL 60462
708-460-8082; www.icsia.org
Hayden B Baldwin, Executive Director
Christopher Anderson, Caribbean Director
Paul Echols, Board of Directors
Chad Pitfield, Board of Directors
Steven W Hulsey, Board of Directors

14870 International Critical Incident Stress Foundation
3290 Pine Orchard Ln
Suite 106
Ellicott City, MD 21042
410-750-9600; *Fax:* 410-750-9601
info@icisf.org; www.icisf.org
Social Media: Facebook, Twitter
Dave Evans, CPA, Chairman
Lisa Joubert, Finance Director
Richard Barton, CEO
C. Kenneth Bohn, Director of Operations
Jeannie Gow, General Information Requests
A foundation dedicated to the prevention and mitigation of disabling stress through the provision of; Education, training and support services for all Emergency Services professions, continuing education and training in Emergency Mental Health Services for Psychologists, Psychiatrists, Social Workers and Licensed Professional Counselors and Consultation in the establishment of Crisis and Disaster Response Programs for varied organizations and communities worldwide.

14871 International Footprint Association
PO Box 1652
Walnut, CA 91788
323-981-1488
877-432-3668; *Fax:* 323-265-4657;
www.footprinter.org
Robert H. Hubbell, Grand President
Doug Partlow, First Grand Vice President
Michael Leary, Second Grand Vice President
Maura Mattson, Grand Secretary/Treasurer
Michael Leary, Assistant Grand Secretary/Treasurer
A non-profit association that promotes and encourages fellowship, respect, cooperation, and helpfulness between all arms of law enforcement and all others who are sympathetic with and understanding toward law enforcement and all of its agencies.
4000 Members
Founded in: 1929

14872 International Law Enforcement Educators & Trainers Association
4742 79 Street
Kenosha, WI 53142
262-767-1406; *Fax:* 262-767-1813
info@ILEETA.org; www.ileeta.org
Social Media: Facebook
Harvey Hedden, Executive Director
Brian Wills, Deputy Executive Dir.
Alexis Artwohl, Advisory Board Member
Massad Ayoob, Advisory Board Member
Steve Ashley, Advisory Board Member
An organization by, for and about instructors and training for the criminal justice professions. Committed to the reduction of law enforcement risk through the enhancement of training for criminal justice practitioners.
Founded in: 2003

14873 **International Narcotic Enforcement Officers Association**
112 State Street
Suite 1200
Albany, NY 12207-2079

518-463-6232; www.ineoa.org

John J Bellizer Jr, Executive Director
Michael Harris, President

Basic purpose is to promote and foster mutual interest in the problems of narcotic control; provide a medium for the exchange of ideas, conduct seminars, conferences and study groups and issue publications.

14874 **International Police Association**
PO Box 516
Greystone Station
Yonkers, NY 10703-0516

855-241-9998; www.ipa-usa.org
Social Media: Facebook, Twitter

Kevin Gordon, President
Calvin Chow, 1st VP
Cory Freadling, 2nd VP
Joe Johnson, 3rd VP
Viola Powrie, Treasurer
Founded in: 1950

14875 **International Union of Police Associations**
1549 Ringling Blvd.
Suite 600
Sarasota, FL 35236

800-247-4872; *Fax:* 941-487-2570
iupa@iupa.org
iupa.org
Social Media: Facebook, Twitter, LinkedIn, YouTube

Samuel A. Cabral, President

The voice of the law enforcement community within the organized labor movement.
Founded in: 1954

14876 **Law Enforcement & Emergency Services Video Association**
84 Briar Creek Road
Whitesboro, TX 76273

469-285-9435; *Fax:* 469-533-3659;
www.leva.org
Social Media: Facebook, Twitter, LinkedIn

Alan Salmon, Chairman of the Board
Tracy Peloquin, Vice Chairman
Juan Ruano, President
Scott Olar, Executive Vice President
Scott Sullivan, Forensic Training, Program Manager

Committed to improving the quality of video training and promoting the use of state-of-the-art, effective equipment in the law enforcement and emergency services community.
Mailing list available for rent

14877 **Law Enforcement Alliance of America**
12427 Hedges Run Drive
Suite 113
Lake Ridge, VA 22192-1715

202-706-9218; *Fax:* 703-556-6485
membership@leaa.org; www.leaa.org

Jim Fotis, Executive Director
Kevin Watson, Communications Director

Nation's largest nonprofit, non-partisan coalition of law enforcement professionals. Crime victims, and concerned citizens united for justice; with a major focus on public education, LEAA is dedicated to providing hard facts and real world insights into the world of law enforcement and the battle against violent crime. Fighting at every level of government for legislation that reduces violent crime while preserving the rights of honest citizens, particularly the right of self-defense.
Founded in: 1992

14878 **Law Enforcement Bloodhound Association**
PO Box 190442
Anchorage, AL 99519-0442

907-602-3542
leba@gci.net; www.npba.com

Gerry Nichols, President

LEBA is a professional nonprofit organization dedicated to the promotion of bloodhounds in law enforcement. Also provides beginning, continuing and advanced education to law enforcement professionals and thier bloodhound partners.
Founded in: 1998
Mailing list available for rent

14879 **Law Enforcement Executive Development Association, Inc.**
5 Great Valley Pkwy.
Suite 125
Malvern, PA 19355

484-321-7821
877-772-7712; *Fax:* 610-644-3193
info@fbileeda.org; www.fbileeda.org
Social Media: Facebook, Twitter, LinkedIn

Chief David Boggs, President
Paul Shastany, First Vice President
Thomas Alber, Second Vice President
Chief John Horsman, Third Vice President
Charles Robb, Executive Director

Purpose of the association is to advance the Science and Art of Police Management and Administration; to develop and disseminate improved administrative and technical practices; promote the exchange of information and training for executives of law enforcement.

14880 **Law Enforcement Legal Defense Fund**
1428 Duke Street
Alexandria, VA 703-807-18

E-Mail: info@leldf.org;
www.policedefense.org
Social Media: Facebook, Twitter, LinkedIn, YouTube

Alfred S Regnery, Chairman
John J Burke, Vice Chairman
Ron Hosko, President
Edwin Meese, Director
Daniel J DeSimone, Secretary-Treasurer
Founded in: 1995

14881 **Law Enforcement Standards Office**
100 Bureau Drive
MS 8102
Gaithersburg, MD 20899-8102

301-975-6478; *Fax:* 301-948-0978
inquiries@nist.gov; www.nist.gov/oles/

Patrick D. Gallagher, Director
Michael D. Herman, Executive Officer
Kevin Kimball, Chief of Staff
Henry N. Wixon, Chief Counsel
Mary Saunders, Associate Director

OLES's mission is to serve as the principal agent for standards development for the criminal justice and public safety communities. Helping criminal justice and public safety agencies acquire, on a cost-effective basis, the high quality resources they need to do their jobs.
Founded in: 1901

14882 **Major Cities Chiefs Police Association**
P.O. Box 8717
Salt Lake City, UT 84047

E-Mail: stephens@majorcitieschiefs.com;
www.majorcitieschiefs.com

J. Thomas Manger, President
Art Acevedo, 1st Vice President
George Turner, 2nd Vice President
Darrel W. Stephens, Executive Director

An organization bringing together Chiefs and Sheriffs from the largest cities of the United States, Canada, and the United Kingdom, with the intent of creating a forum for shared ideas and insights across international borders.
Founded in: 1949

14883 **Metropolitan Alliance of Police**
215 Remington Blvd.
Suite C
Bolingbrook, IL 60440

630-759-4925; *Fax:* 630-759-1902
mapunion@msn.com; www.mapunion.org

Joseph Andalina, President
Keith George, Vice President
Richard Tracy, Secretary
Joseph R. Mazzone, Chief Counsel
Richard J. Reimer, Co-Counsel

14884 **Narcotic Enforcement Officers Association**
29 N Plains Hwy
Suite 10
Wallingford, CT 06492

203-269-8940; *Fax:* 203-284-9103;
www.neoa.org

Michael R Rinaldi, President
Gabriel Lupo, VP
Richard Stook, Treasurer
Duane Tompkins, Secretary

A non-profit educational organization of more than a thousand law enforcement personnel and others in the criminal justicce system, includin state and local police, D.E.A., F.B.I. and customs.

14885 **National Asian Peace Officers' Association**
1776 I Street, NW,
Suite 900
Washington, DC 20006

646-632-5384; *Fax:* 202-756-1301;
www.napoablue.org

James Ng, President
Taerance Oh, 1st Vice President
Thomas Masters, 3rd Vice President
Rolland Ogawa, Secretary
Simone Bangphraxay, Treasurer

14886 **National Association School Resource Officers**
2020 Valleydale Road
Suite 207A
Hoover, AL 35244

205-739-6060
888-316-2776; *Fax:* 205-536-9255;
www.nasro.org
Social Media: Facebook, Twitter, RSS, Youtube

Joe Carter, President
Don Bridges, 1st Vice President
Bill West, 2nd Vice President
Jon Carrier, Secretary
Jennifer Thornton, Marketing Manager

A not-for-profit organization for school based law enforcement officers, school administrators, and school security/safety professionals working as partners to protect students, school faculty and staff and the schools they attend.

14887 **National Association of Attorneys General**
2030 M Street NW
8th Floor
Washington, DC 20036
202-326-6000; *Fax:* 202-331-1427
feedback@naag.org; www.naag.org
Social Media: Facebook, Twitter
Jim McPherson, Executive Director
Theresia Heller, Chief Financial Officer
Janet Fernandes, Accounting Manager
Al Lama, Chief of Staff
Marjorie Tharp, Director of Communications
Founded to help Attorneys General fulfill the responsibilities of their office and to assist in the delivery of high quality legal services to the states and territorial jurisdictions.
Founded in: 1907
Mailing list available for rent

14888 **National Association of Chiefs of Police**
6350 Horizon Drive
Titusville, FL 32780-8002
321-264-0911; *Fax:* 321-264-0033
policeinfo@aphf.org; www.aphf.org
Jamie Maynard, Director of Communications
Barry Shepherd, Executive Director
Debra Chitwood, Chief Financial Officer
Brent Shepherd, Director of Operations
The mission is to encourage through the leadership of persons who hold a command law enforcement or security position within the United States and her territories and possessions, educational activities and services to upgrade law enforcement and security on a professional level.
Founded in: 1967
Mailing list available for rent

14889 **National Association of Drug Court Professionals**
1029 N. Royal St
Suite 201
Alexandria, VA 22314
703-575-9400; *Fax:* 703-706-0577;
www.nadcp.org
Social Media: Facebook, Twitter, YouTube, Instagram
West Huddleston, CEO
Meghan Wheeler, Project Director
Seeks to reduce substance abuse, crime and recidivism by promoting and advocating for the establishment and funding of Drug Courts and providing for collection and dissemination of information, technical assistance, and mutual support to association members.
Founded in: 1997
Mailing list available for rent

14890 **National Association of Field Training Officers**
7942 W. Bell Rd.
Suite C5 #463
Glendale, AZ 85308
812-483-6588
info@nafto.org; www.nafto.org
Social Media: Facebook, Twitter, RSS
Lt. Bob Smith, President
Officer Jeff Crippen, First VP
Sgt. Daniel Greene, Second VP
Sgt. Jeff Chapman, Executive Director
An educational and professional association concerned with apprenticeship and advance ongoing training for law enforcement, communications, and corrections personnel. Educators, administrators and other criminal justice practitioners are also encouraged to participate.

14891 **National Association of Fleet Administrators**
125 Village Boulevard
Suite 200,Princeton Forrestal Villa
Princeton, NJ 08540
609-720-0882; *Fax:* 609-452-8004
info@nafa.org; www.nafa.org
Social Media: Facebook, Twitter, LinkedIn, Youtube, RSS
Charles A Gibbens, President
Gayle Pratt, Senior VP
Serving the needs of those managing fleets of automobiles, light duty trucks and/or vans for US and Canadian organizations. Offers statistical research, publications, including NAFA's Fleet Executive monthly magazine, regional meetings, government representation, conferences, trade shows and seminars.
2600+ Members
Mailing list available for rent

14892 **National Association of Police Organizations**
317 S Patrick St
Alexandria, VA 22314-3501
703-549-0775; *Fax:* 703-684-0515
info@napo.org; www.napo.org
Social Media: Facebook, Twitter
Mick McHale, President
John Flynn, Vice President
William J. Johnson, Executive Director
Craig Lally, Executive Secretary
Sean Smoot, Treasurer
A coalition of police unions and associations from across the United States that serves to advance the interests of America's law enforcement officers through legislative and legal advocacy, political action and education.
241k Members
Founded in: 1978
Mailing list available for rent

14893 **National Black Police Association**
3100 Main Street
#256
Dallas, TX 75226
855-879-6272; *Fax:* 202-986-0410
nationaloffice@blackpolice.org;
www.blackpolice.org
Malik Aziz, Chairperson
Rochelle Bilal, Vice Chairperson
Carlos Bratcher, Sergeant at Arms
Sherri V. Lockett, Secretary
Donna Ross, Fiscal Officer
Law enforcement association to improve the relationship between Police Departments as institutions and the minority.
35000 Members
Founded in: 1972

14894 **National Burglar & Fire Alarm Association**
2300 Valley View Lane
Suite 230
Irving, TX 75062-1733
214-260-5970
888-447-1689; *Fax:* 214-260-5979
MerlinG@alarm.org; www.alarm.org
Social Media: Facebook, Twitter, Youtube
Merlin Guilbeau, Executive Director
Georgia Calaway, Communications/PR Director
Representing, promoting and enhancing the growth and professional development of the electronic life safety, security, and integrated systems industry. In cooperation with a federation of state associations, NBFAA provides government advocacy and delivers timely information, professional development tools, products and services that members use to grow and prosper their businesses.
Founded in: 1948

14895 **National Constables Association (NCA)**
16 Stonybrook Drive
Levittown, PA 19055-2217
215-943-3110
800-292-1775; *Fax:* 215-943-0979;
www.angelfire.com/la/nationalconstable
Hal Lefcourt APR, Executive Director
John Sindt, President
Leo Bullock, Secretary
Helping to preserve and clearly define the significant role of the constable in the delivery of justice system in the United States; to train, educate and upgrade the quality of performance of the constable; to serve as a clearing house for all positive actions to give a continued rebirth to the dignity, respect, status and duties and responsibilities of the position of constable as the heritage of the law enforcement community.
Founded in: 1973

14896 **National Correctional Industries Association**
800 North Charles Street
Suite 550B
Baltimore, MD 21201
410-230-3972; *Fax:* 410-230-3981
memberservices@nationalcia.org;
www.nationalcia.org
Social Media: Facebook
Gina Honeycutt, Executive Director
Wil Heslop, Director of Operations
Karl Wiley, Accounting Manager
Rebekah Zinno, Sales and Marketing Manager
Farrah Marriott, Systems Coordinator
An affiliate body of the American Correctional Association, the Jail Industries Association and The Workman Fund. The mission is to promote excellence and credibility in correctional industries through professional development and innovative business solutions.
Founded in: 1941
Mailing list available for rent

14897 **National Crime Prevention Council**
1201 Connecticut Avenue, NW
Suite 200
Washington, DC 20036
202-466-6272; *Fax:* 202-296-1356
webmaster@ncpc.org; www.ncpc.org
David A. Dean, Chairman
Robert F. Diegelman, Vice Chairman
Ann M. Harnkins, President/CEO
John P. Box, Treasurer
Jean Adnopoz, Secretary
Aids people in keeping themselves, their families, and their communities safe from crime. NCPC produces tools that communities can use to learn crime prevention strategies, engage community members, and coordinate with local agencies.
136 Members
Founded in: 1982
Mailing list available for rent

14898 **National Crime and Punishment Learning Center**
300 S 25th Ave
Hattiesburg, MS 39401-7301
228-447-0285; *Fax:* 228-896-8696
ncplc@crimeandpunishment.net;
www.crimeandpunishment.net
William H Sanford, President/Founder
Provide free information on the most common crimes and their punishments in each state. The center is unique in its dedicated endeavor to ac-

complish this task by providing information to bridge the gap between the legal justice system and the American people.

14899 **National Criminal Justice Association**
720 7th St Nw
3rd Floor
Washington, DC 20001-3902
202-628-8550; *Fax:* 202-448-1723
info@ncja.org; www.ncja.org
Social Media: Facebook, Twitter, LinkedIn, RSS
Jeanne Smith, President
Karhlton Moore, Vice President
Cabell Cropper, Executive Director
David Fredenburgh, Director of Program Services
Bethany Broida, Director of Communications
A national voice in shaping and implementing criminal justice policy since its founding. As the representative of state, tribal and local criminal and juvenile justice practitioners, the NCJA works to promote a balanced approach to communities' complex public safety and criminal and juvenile justice system problems.
Founded in: 1971

14900 **National Criminal Justice Reference Service**
PO Box 6000
Rockville, MD 20849-6000
301-519-5500
800-851-3420
202-836-6998; *Fax:* 301-240-5830;
www.ncjrs.gov
Social Media: Facebook, Twitter, LinkedIn, RSS, Youtube, Google+, Vimeo,
Dolores Kozloski, Executive Director
A federally funded resource offering justice and substance abuse information to support research, policy, and program development worldwide.
Founded in: 1972
Mailing list available for rent

14901 **National District Attorneys Association**
99 Canal Center Plz
Suite 330
Alexandria, VA 22314-1548
703-549-9222; *Fax:* 703-836-3195
berryb@co.yamhill.or.us; www.ndaa.org
Social Media: Facebook, Twitter
William Fitzpatrick, President
Kay Chopard Cohen, Executive Director
Rick Hanes, Chief of Staff
Development resource for prosecutors at all levels of government. APRI has become a vital resource and national clearinghouse for information on the prosecutorial function. The Institute is committed to providing interdisciplinary responses to the complex problems of criminal justice. It is also committed to supporting the highest professional standards among officials entrusted with the crucial responsibility for public safety.
Founded in: 1950

14902 **National Drug Court Institute**
1029 N. Royal St
Suite 201
Alexandria, VA 22314
703-575-9400; *Fax:* 703-575-9402
webmaster@nadcp.org; www.ndci.org
Social Media: Facebook, Twitter, RSS, Youtube
Lars Levy, President
Milly Merrigan, President-Elect
Promote education, research and scholarship for drug court and other court-based intervention programs.

14903 **National Drug Enforcement Officers Association**
Drug Enforcement Administration
Office of Training/TRDS
FBI Academy, PO Box 1475
Quantico, VA 22134-1475
202-298-9653
paul.stevens@state.mn.us; www.ndeoa.org
Paul Stevens, President
Steve Peterson, First VP
NDEOA's purpose and objective is to promote the cooperation, education and exchange of information among all Law Enforcement Agencies involved in the enforcement of controlled substance laws.
Founded in: 1970

14904 **National Emergency Number Association**
1700 Diagonal Road
Suite 500
Alexandria, VA 22314
202-466-4911; *Fax:* 202-618-6370
rhixson@nena.org; www.nena.org
Social Media: Facebook, Twitter, YouTube
Christy Williams, President
Renee Hardwick, ENP, 1st Vice President
Rob McMullen, ENP, 2nd Vice President
Brian Fontes, Chief Executive Officer
Trey Forgety, Director of Government Affairs

14905 **National Fire Protection Association**
1 Batterymarch Park
Quincy, MA 02169-7471
617-770-3000
800-344-3555; *Fax:* 617-770-0700
custserv@nfpa.org; www.nfpa.org
Social Media: Facebook, Twitter, LinkedIn, Youtube, RSS, Google+, Flickr
Ernest J. Grant, RN, MSN, PhD, Chair
Randolph W. Tucker, First Vice Chair
Jim Pauley, President and CEO
Amy R. Acton, Secretary
Thomas A. Lawson, Treasurer
Mission is to reduce the worldwide burden of fire and other hazards on the quality of life by providing and advocating scientifically based concensus codes and standards, research, training, and education. Also serves as the world's leading advocate of fire prevention and is an authoritive source on public safety.
70000 Members
Founded in: 1896

14906 **National Gang Crime Research Center**
Research Center
PO Box 990
Peotone, IL 60468-0090
708-258-9111; *Fax:* 708-258-9546
gangcrime@aol.com; www.ngcrc.com
George W Knox, Director
Research on gangs and gang members, disseminate information through publications and reports, and provide training and consulting services.
Founded in: 1990

14907 **National Institute of Justice**
US Department Of Justice
810 7th Street NW
Washington, DC 20531
202-664-4000
800-851-3420; *Fax:* 202-307-6394
askncjrs@ncjrs.org; www.ojp.usdoj.gov
Social Media: Facebook, Twitter, RSS, YouTube
Leigh Benda, Chief Financial Officer
Karol Virginia Mason, Assistant Attorney General
Phillip Merkle, Director
Mary Lou Leary, Principal Deputy Assistant Attorney
James H. Burch, II, Deputy Assistant Attorney General
Research, development and evaluation agency of the US department of Justice. Supports all those in the justice industry with education and training, publications and trade shows.
Mailing list available for rent

14908 **National Insurance Crime Bureau**
1111 E Touhy Ave
Suite 400
Des Plaines, IL 60018-5804
847-544-7002
800-447-6282; *Fax:* 708-544-7100
rjones@nicb.org; www.nicb.org
Social Media: Facebook, Twitter, LinkedIn, Youtube
Joseph H. Wehrle, President/CEO
James K. Schweitzer, Senior Vice President
Daniel G. Abbott, Senior Vice President
Robert Jachnicki, Senior Vice President
Andrew J. Sosnowski, Senior Vice President
A not for profit organization that recieves support from approximately 1,000 property/casualty insurance companies. NICB partners with insurers and law enforcement agencies to facilitate the identification, detection and prosecution of insurance criminals.
1000 Members
Founded in: 1992

14909 **National Latino Peace Officers Association**
PO Box 23116
23116
Santa Ana, CA 92711
E-Mail: nlpoamgr@gmail.com;
www.nlpoa.com
Social Media: Facebook
Andrew P Peralta, National President
Alfredo Dean, Vice President
Maria B. Thomas, Secretary
Cindy Rodriguez, Treasurer
Vicente Calderon, Founder
Founded in: 1972

14910 **National Native American Law Enforcement Association**
PO Box 171
Washington, DC 20040
202-207-3065; *Fax:* 866-506-7631;
www.nnalea.org
Joseph Wicks, President
Mark Murtha, Vice President
Gary Edwards, CEO
Dave Nichols, CFO
Daryll Davis, Senior Director
NNALEA is a nonprofit organization that promotes and fosters mutual cooperation between American Indian Law Enforcement Officers/Agents/Personnel, their agencies, tribes, private industry and public.
Founded in: 1993

14911 **National Organization for Victim Assistance**
510 King St
Suite 424
Alexandria, VA 22314-3132
703-535-6682
800-879-6682; *Fax:* 703-535-5500;
www.trynova.org
Social Media: Facebook, Twitter, RSS
Will Marling, Executive Director
Claire Ponder Selib, Director of Education
James Gierke, Director of Victim Services

Deborah Baroch, Director of Finance and Operations
Barbara Kendall, Director of Training

A private, non-profit organization of victim and witness assistance programs and practitioners, criminal justice agencies and professionals, mental health professionals, researchers, former victims and survivors, and others committed to the recognition and implementation of victim rights and services.

14912 National Organization of Black Law Enforcement Executives

4609 Pinecrest Office Park Dr
Alexandria, VA 22312-1442

703-658-1529; *Fax:* 703-658-9479
jakers@noblenatl.org; www.noblenatl.org
Social Media: Facebook, Twitter, LinkedIn, Tumblr, Stumbleupon, Pinterest

Gregory Thomas, National President
Perry Tarrant, National First Vice President
Clarence Cox, National Second Vice President
Hubert Bell, Treasurer
Thomas Nelson, National Recording Secretary

Ensure equity in the administration of justice in the provision of public service to all communities, and to serve as the conscience of law enforcement by being committed to justice by action.
Founded in: 1976

14913 National Police Athletic/Activities League , Inc.

1662 N. US Highway 1
Suite C
Jupiter, FL 33469

561-745-5535; *Fax:* 561-745-3147
mdillhyon@nationalpal.org;
www.nationalpal.org
Social Media: Facebook, Twitter

Christopher Hill, President
Barbara Bonilla, 1st Vice President
Ronald Allen, 2nd Vice President
Donna Miller, 3rd Vice President
Frank Williams, Secretary

Exists to prevent juvenile crime and violence by providing civic, athletic, recreational, and educational opportunities and resources to PAL Chapters.
Founded in: 1940

14914 National Police Bloodhound Association

E-Mail: president@npba.com; www.npba.com
Social Media: Facebook

Doug Lowry, President
Roger G. Titus, Vice President
Kevin Osuch, Secretary
Coby Webb, Treasurer
Roger G. Titus, Training
Founded in: 1966

14915 National Police Institute

Central Missouri State University
200 Ming Street
Warrensburg, MO

660-543-4090; *Fax:* 660-543-4709;
www.theipti.org

Dr Mike Wiggins, Director

An internationally recognized police training center. Provides advanced police training in a number of areas as well as housing the Regional Police Academy.

14916 National Public Safety Information Bureau

PO Box 365
Stevens Point, WI 54481

715-345-2772
800-647-7579; *Fax:* 715-345-7288
info@safetysource.com;
www.safetyresource.com

Steve Cywinski, President/Publisher
Ronald Tippel, VP Information Services
Laura Gross, VP Data Procurement
Celia Piesik, Data Procurement Specialist
Christina Scott, Data Procurement Specialist

Working hand in hand with law enforcement, fire and emergency departments to develop the most accurate database in the public safety industry with over 70,000 contacts. The result is; the most current and comprehensive reference tools available.
Founded in: 1964

14917 National Public Safety Telecommunications Council

8191 Southpark Lane
Unit 205
Littleton, CO 80120-4641

407-836-9668
866-907-4755; *Fax:* 303-649-1844
support@npstc.org; www.npstc.org
Social Media: Facebook, Twitter, LinkedIn, YouTube, Blogger

Don Root, Committee Vice Chair
Stu Overby, Committee Vice Chair
Marilyn Ward, Ecexutive Director
Charles Bryson, Outreach News Editor
Mark Grubb, Participant Development Coordinator

NPSTC is a federation of associations representing public safety telecommunications. They follow up on the recommendations of the Public Safety Wireless Advisory Committee.
Founded in: 1997
Mailing list available for rent

14918 National Reserve Law Officers Association

PO Box 6505
San Antonio, TX 78209

210-805-8917; *Fax:* 210-653-9655
nrloa01@earthlink.net; www.nrlo.net

Capt. Chuck Mantkus, Director of Training

Provides members with training information and services plus the best, most extensive, and lowest cost in-line-of-duty accidental insurance coverage available.

14919 National Safety Council

1121 Spring Lake Dr
Itasca, IL 60143-3201

630-285-1121
800-621-7615; *Fax:* 630-285-1434;
www.nsc.org
Social Media: RSS

John P. Surma, Chairman
Deborah Hersman, President & CEO
Patrick Phelan, Chief Financial Officer
Shay Gallagher, Vice President, General Manager
Michael Pollock, VP, Relationship Management

Provides information sharing opportunities, continuing education and professional fellowship to people with environmental health and safety responsibilities in higher education.
936 Members
Founded in: 1912
Mailing list available for rent

14920 National Sheriffs' Association

1450 Duke St
Alexandria, VA 22314-3490

703-836-7827
800-424-7827; *Fax:* 703-683-5349
jthompson@sheriffs.org; www.sheriffs.org
Social Media: Facebook, Twitter, LinkedIn, Googe+

Aaron D. Kennard, Executive Director
John Thompson, Chief of Staff and Deputy Executive
Fred G. Wilson, Director of Operations
Ed Hutchison, Director of Traffic Safety & Triad
Greg J. MacDonald, Director of Homeland Security

Devoted to helping sheriffs and other law enforcers to execute their duties most effectively and professionally.
21M Members
Founded in: 1940
Mailing list available for rent: 3M names

14921 National Tactical Officers Association

PO Box 797
Doylestown, PA 18901

215-230-7552
800-279-9127; *Fax:* 215-230-7552
membership@ntoa.org; www.ntoa.org
Social Media: Facebook, Twitter

Deputy Chief Bo Chabali, Board Chairman
Mark Lomax, Executive Director
Rob Cartner, Director of Training
Corey Luby, Marketing Director
Marsha Martello, Membership Coordinator

Enhance the performance and professional status of law enforcement personnel by providing a credible and proven training resource, as well as a forum for the development of tactics and information exchange. The Association's ultimate goal is to improve public safety and domestic security through training, education, and tactical excellence.
32000 Members
Founded in: 1983

14922 National Technical Investigators Association (NATIS)

1069 West Broad Street
Box 757
Falls Church, VA 22046

703-237-9338
800-966-2842
770-485-1820; *Fax:* 703-832-2600
admin@natia.org; www.natia.org

Michael Woods, President

The purpose of NATIA is to further knowledge, develop skills and promote fellowship between those law enforcement and intelligence professionals who support their agencies' and departments' technical surveillance, tactical operations, and forensic activities.

14923 National United Law Enforcement Officers

256 E McLemore Avenue
Memphis, TN 38106-2833

901-774-1118; *Fax:* 901-774-1139

Clyde Venson, Executive Director
Samantha Macklin, Secretary

Protects the needs and interests of persons in the law enforcement industry.
5000 Members
Founded in: 1969

14924 National White Collar Crime Center

10900 Nuckols Rd
Suite 325
Glen Allen, VA 23060-9288

804-967-6200; www.nw3c.org
Social Media: Facebook, Twitter, Youtube

Don Brackman, Director
Ken Brooks, Deputy Director

Through a combination of training and critical support services, law enforcement agencies are

given the skills and resources they need to tackle emerging economic and cyber crime problems.
Mailing list available for rent

14925 Naval Criminal Investigative Services
27130 Telegraph Road
Suite 2000
Quantico, VA 22134
202-433-8800; *Fax:* 724-794-3293;
www.ncis.navy.mil
Andrew L. Traver, Director
John Beattie, Senior Intelligence Officer
Mark D. Ridley, Deputy Director
Rod Baldwin, Executive Assistant Director
Charlton Howard, Chief Intelligence Officer
Primary law enforcement and counterintelligence arm of the United States Department of the Navy. It works closely with other local, state, federal and foreign agencies to counter and investigate the most serious crimes.

14926 Organized Crime Task Force
The Capitol
Albany, NY 12224-0341
518-474-7330; *Fax:* 914-422-8795;
www.ag.ny.gov
John Amodeo, Assistant Attorney General
Colleen Glavin, Public Integrity Officer
A forum that brings government, law enforcement and a range of agencies together to set priorities for tackling organized crime.
Founded in: 1970

14927 Park Law Enforcement Association
www.myparkranger.org
Tom Wakolbinger, President
William Westerfield, Vice President
Dale Steele, Secretary
Capt. Carl Nielsen, Executive Director
Steve Newsom, Treasurer
Founded in: 1979

14928 Police & Firemen's Insurance Association
101 E 116th St
Carmel, IN 46032-5629
317-581-1913
800-221-7342; *Fax:* 317-571-5946;
www.pfia.net
Mark Kemp, President
Jeanie Williams, Operations VP
Mission of the association is to create and operate a Supreme Lodge and Subordinate Branches for the purpose of inculcating principles of friendship and brotherhood among police officers and fire fighters. Providing financial assistance to its members through disability certificates and pay final expenses for members with legal reserve life insurance policies.

14929 Police Executive Research Forum
1120 Connecticut Ave NW
Suite 930
Washington, DC 20036-3951
202-466-7820; *Fax:* 202-466-7826;
www.policeforum.org
Chief J. Scott Thomson, President
Chief Tom Manger, VP
Chief Robert White, Secretary
Chief Roberto Villase¤or, Treasurer
Shannon Branly, Deputy Chief of Staff
A national membership organization of progressive police executives from the largest city, county and state law enforcement agencies. Dedicated to improving policing and advancing professionalism through research and involvement in public policy debate.
100 Members
Founded in: 1976
Mailing list available for rent

14930 Police Foundation
1201 Connecticut Ave NW
Suite 200
Washington, DC 20036-2636
202-833-1460; *Fax:* 202-659-9149
info@policefoundation.org;
www.policefoundation.org
Social Media: Facebook, Twitter, RSS, Google+, YouTube
Weldon J. Rougeau, Chairman
Chief Jim Bueermann, President
Karen L. Amendola, PhD, Chief Behavioral Scientist
Tari Lewis, CPA, Chief Financial Officer
Blake Norton, VP/COO
A national, nonpartisan, nonprofit organization dedicated to supporting innovation and improvement in policing through its research and evaluation, technical assistance, training, technology, professional services, and communication programs.
Founded in: 1970
Mailing list available for rent

14931 Public Safety Diving Association
904-743-3025
psdahq@bellsouth.net;
www.publicsafetydivingassociation.com
David Scoggins, President
Mark Reese, Director
Founded in: 1972

14932 Public Services Health and Safety Association
4950 Yonge Street
Suite 902
Toronto, ON M2N 6K1
416-250-2131
877-250-7444; *Fax:* 416-250-7484
elearning@pshsa.ca; www.pshsa.ca
Michael Papadakis, Chair
Thomas Hayes, Vice Chair
Ron Kelusky, CEO
Joanne Clark, Director, Marketing and Comm.
Susan Sun, Director, Finance & Administration
Founded in: 2009

14933 Reserve Police Officers Association
89 Rockland Ave
Yonkers, NY 10705
800-326-9416
800-326-9416; *Fax:* 212-555-1234;
www.reservepolice.org
Brooke Webster, President
Dedicated to the support of law enforcement with an emphasis on the role of the reserve and auxiliary law enforcement officer.
Founded in: 1996

14934 Texas Department of Public Safety Officer's Association
5821 Airport Boulevard
Austin, TX 78752
512-451-0571
800-933-7762; *Fax:* 512-451-0709
info@dpsoa.com; www.dpsoa.com
Social Media: Facebook, Twitter, RSS, Google+, Tumblr
Sgt. Gary Chandler, President
Lt. Jimmy Jackson, VP
John M. Pike, Executive Director
Trooper Clay Taylor, Secretary/Treasurer
Patti Benson, Membership Services
Offers and executes programs that benefit Texas Troppers and the communitites around them. Also publishes DPSOA a quarterly magazine.
2650 Members
Founded in: 1974

14935 The Association of Certified Fraud Specialists
4600 Northgate Blvd.
Suite 105
Sacramento, CA 95834
916-419-6319; *Fax:* 916-419-6318
headquarters@acfsnet.org; www.acfsnet.org
Social Media: Facebook, LinkedIn
Bill Cramer, President
Mark Menz, National Vice President
Charles Raborn, Executive Director
Jeremy Krater, Information Technology Specialist
Brittany Cyrus, Graphic Designer
Founded in: 1993

14936 The Commission on Accreditation forLaw Enforcement Agencies
13575 Heathcote Boulevard
Suite 320
Gainesville, VI 20155
703-352-4225; *Fax:* 703-890-3126
jgregory@calea.org; www.calea.org
Social Media: Facebook, Twitter, LinkedIn, Reddit, Google+, Tumblr
J. Grayson Robinson, President
Craig Webre, Vice-President
W. Craig Hartley, Jr., Executive Director
Richard Myers, Secretary
Gary Margolis, Treasurer

14937 The Federal Law Enforcement Association
7945 MacArthur Blvd
Suite 201
Cabin John, MD 20818
202-870-5503
866-553-5362
fleoa@fleoa.org; www.fleoa.org
Social Media: Facebook, Twitter, Reddit, Google+, Tumblr
Jon Adler, National President
Nate Catura, Executive Vice President
Chris Schoppmeyer, Vice President - Agency Affairs
Frank Terreri, Vice President- Legislative Affairs
Enid Febus, National Secretary
Founded in: 1977

14938 The International Association of Chiefs of Police
44 Canal Center Plaza
Suite 200
Alexandria, VA 22314
703-836-6767
beckmann@theiacp.org; www.theiacp.org
Social Media: Facebook, Twitter, LinkedIn, YouTube
Richard Beary, President
Vincent Talucci, Executive Director/CEO
Gwen Boniface, Deputy Executive Director
John Firman, Director of Strategic Partnerships
Jacqueline Gooding, Director of Human Resources
Founded in: 1893

14939 The United Deputy Sheriffs' Association
319 S. Hydraulic St.,
Suite B
Wichita, KS 67211
316-263-2583
info@usdeputy.org; www.usdeputy.org
Social Media: Facebook
Mike Willis, Executive Director
David Hinners, Deputy Director

14940 TheAssociationofPublic-Safety Communications Officials
351 N. Williamson Blvd
Daytona Beach, FL 32114-1112

386-322-2500; *Fax:* 386-322-2501
apco@apcointl.org; www.apcointl.org
Social Media: Facebook, Twitter

Brent Lee, President
Cheryl J. Greathouse, RPL, First Vice President
Martha K. Carter, ENP, Second Vice President
Gigi Smith, Immediate Past President
Derek Poarch, Executive Director
Founded in: 1982

14941 Transportation Research Board National Research Council
500 Fifth Stret NW
Washington, DC 20001

202-334-2934; *Fax:* 202-334-2003;
www.trb.org
Social Media: Facebook, Twitter, LinkedIn, RSS, Blogger, Pinterest, Tumbl

Neil Pedersen, Executive Director
Rosa Allen, Administrative Coordinator
Stephen J. Andrle, Deputy Director
Javy Awan, Director, Publications
Terri M. Baker, Senior Program Assistant

A division of the National Research Council, which serves as an independent advisor to the federal government and others on scientific and technical questions of national importance.

14942 Transportation Technology Center
55500 DOT Rd.
Pueblo, CO 81001-0130

719-584-0750; *Fax:* 719-584-0711
ttci_marketing@ttci.aar.com; www.aar.com
Social Media: Facebook, Twitter, Youtube

Roy Allen, Manager
Michele Johnson, Administrative Assistant
Mark Nordling, Assistant Director Business
Ron Lang, Manager Business Development
Michele Johnson, Executive Assistant

A wholly owned subsidiary of the Association of American Railroads. TTCI is a world-class transportation research and testing organization, providing emerging technology solutions for the railway industry throughout North America and the world.

14943 U.S. First Responders Association
420 Kimbrel Avenue
Panama City, FL 32404

E-Mail: Corporate@usfra.org; www.usfra.org
Social Media: Facebook, Twitter, LinkedIn, RSS

14944 United States Conference of Mayors
1620 Eye St NW
Washington, DC 20006

202-293-7330; *Fax:* 202-293-2352
info@usmayors.org; www.usmayors.org
Social Media: Facebook, Twitter

Mayor Stephanie Rawlings-Blake, President
Mick Cornett, VP
Mitchell J. Landrieu, Second Vice President
Tom Cochran, CEO and Executive Director

An organization of city government officials whose primary roles are to promote the development of effective national urban/suburban policy; strengthen federal-city relationships; ensure that federal policy meets urban needs; provide mayors with leadership and management tools; and create a forum in which mayors can share ideas and information.
Founded in: 1932

14945 United States Deputy Sheriff's Association
319 S. Hydraulic St.
Suite B
Wichita, KS 67211

316-263-2583
877-800-8854; *Fax:* 281-578-0669
info@usdeputy.org; www.usdeputy.org

Mike Willis, Executive Director/Training
David Hinners, Deputy Director/National Trainer

Provides needed equipment, free of charge, to the mostly rural, underfunded county law enforcement agencies. All members are given an Emergency Disaster Relief of $2,000, if killed in the line of duty.
Founded in: 1995

14946 United States Deputy Sheriffs' Association
319 S. Hydraulic St.,
Suite B
Wichita, KS 67211

316-263-2583
info@usdeputy.org; www.usdeputy.org
Social Media: Facebook

Mike Willis, Executive Director
David Hinners, Deputy Director

Survival training for men and women in law enforcement.

14947 United States Police Canine Association
PO Box 80
Springboro, OH 45066

937-751-6469
800-531-1614
uspcadir@aol.com; www.uspcak9.com
Social Media: Facebook

Russ Hess, Executive Director
Kevin Johnson, President
Melinda Roupp, Secretary
James Matarese, Treasurer

Nonprofit organization striving for the establishment of minimum standards for Police K-9 dogs through proper methods of training. Police K-9 dogs, properly trained and handled, give Law Enforcement officers one of the finest non-lethal aids in the prevention and detection of crime.
Founded in: 1971

Newsletters

14948 CGAA Signals
Central Station Alarm Association
8150 Leesburg Pike
Suite 700
Vienna, VA 22182-2721

703-242-4670; *Fax:* 703-242-4675
communications@csaaul.org; www.csaaul.org
Social Media: Facebook, Twitter, LinkedIn

Stephen P Doyle, Executive VP/CEO
Celia Besore, VP Marketing & Programs
Robert R. Bean, President
Jay Hauhn, First Vice President
Peter Lowitt, Secretary
300+ Members
Frequency: Quarterly
Circulation: 1200
Founded in: 1950
Mailing list available for rent

14949 Correctional Education Bulletin
LRP Publications
747 Dresher Road Suite 500
PO Box 980
Horsham, PA 19044

215-784-0912
800-341-7874; *Fax:* 215-784-9639
webmaster@lrp.com; www.lrp.com

Kim Yablonski, Editor

Combines and analyzes corrections education issues and management topics. You'll learn how educators are coping with shrinking budgets and the growing number of youths being sentenced as adults. Expert analysis of current legal issues and the latest regulatory updates given.
Cost: $125.00
Frequency: Monthly
Founded in: 1977

14950 Corrections Professional
LRP Publications
PO Box 980
Horsham, PA 19044

215-840-0912
800-341-7874; *Fax:* 215-784-9639
webmaster@lrp.com; www.lrp.com

Debi Pelletier, Editor
Kenneth Kahn, President

Tracks innovative strategies, proven techniques and legal developments impacting correction facilities across the country. Gives profiles of other professionals and their institutions, giving an opportunity to learn from their experiences and avoid costly mistakes. Contains Q-A section that addresses difficult situations.
Cost: $210.00
Frequency: 104 issues per
Founded in: 1977

14951 Criminal Justice Newsletter
Pace Publications
443 Park Ave S
New York, NY 10016-7322

212-685-5450; *Fax:* 212-679-4701

Sid Goldstein, Publisher
Craig Fischer, Editor
Peter Kiers, Executive Director

Independent publication providing system-wide perspective of law enforcement.
Cost: $219.00
Frequency: BiWeekly

14952 Emergency Preparedness News
Business Publishers
2222 Sedwick Dr
Suite 101
Durham, NC 27713

800-223-8720; *Fax:* 800-508-2592
custserv@bpinews.com; www.bpinews.com

Dedicated solely to disaster management: from securing pre-disaster mitigation and counter terrorism funds, to staying prepared for hurricanes, terrorist threats, fires, floods and other natural disasters.
Cost: $327.00

14953 FEMSA News
Fire and Emergency Manufacturers and Services Asso
PO Box 147
Lynnfield, MA 01940-0147

781-334-2771; *Fax:* 781-334-2771
info@femsa.org; www.femsa.org
Social Media: Twitter, LinkedIn

William Lawson, President
William Van Lent, Vice President

Member newsletter
Frequency: 3x/Year

14954 FLEOA Newsletter
Federal Law Enforcement Officers Association

PO Box 326
Lewisberry, PA 17339-2900

717-938-2300; *Fax:* 717-932-2262
fleoa@fleoa.org; www.fleoa.org
Social Media: Facebook, Twitter

Jon Adler, National President
Nate Catura, National Executive VP

Federal newsletter offering information, legislative updates and news for law enforcement officers nationwide.
12 Pages
Circulation: 2400
Founded in: 1976

14955 Journal of the American Association of Forensic Dentists
1000 N Avenue
Waukegan, IL 60085

847-223-5077
info@andent.net; www.andent.net
Social Media: RSS

Quarterly journal that brings forensic dental knowledge not only to dentists and their staff, but also to anthropologists, attorneys and law enforcement personnel.
Cost: $8.00
Frequency: Quarterly
Founded in: 1978

14956 Keepers' Voice
International Association of Correctional Officers
PO Box 53
Chicago, IL 60690

312-996-5401; *Fax:* 312-413-0458

Jim Clark, Publisher
Jess Maghan, Editor

Of special interest to correctional officers because it focuses on current developments in the field, including practical, day-to-day training topics, current legislation, resources, conference notices and job openings.

14957 Law Enforcement Legal Publications
421 Ridgewood Avenue
Suite 100
Glen Ellyn, IL 60137-4900

630-858-6092; *Fax:* 630-858-6392
lelp@xnet.com; www.lelp.com

James Manak, Publisher/President

Publication for law enforcement, legal professional civil liability, personnel law, labor law, criminal law and law libraries.
ISSN: 1070-9967
Founded in: 1970
Printed in 3 colors on newsprint stock

14958 Law Enforcement Legal Review
Law Enforcement Legal Publications
421 Ridgewood Avenue
Suite 100
Glen Ellyn, IL 60137-4900

630-858-6392; *Fax:* 630-858-6392
lelp@xnet.com; www.lelp.com/

James Manak, Publisher
Glen Manak, VP Marketing

Case reporter for law enforcement, legal profession and law libraries, covering criminal law, civil liability and personnel law.
Cost: $98.00
16 Pages
Frequency: Bi-monthly
Circulation: 500
ISSN: 1070-9967
Founded in: 1975

14959 Legal Employment Weekly Law Bulletin Publishing Company
415 N State Street
Chicago, IL 60610-4674

312-644-7800; *Fax:* 312-644-1215
editor@lbpc.com; www.lawbulletin.com

Bernard Judge, Publisher
Stephen Brown, Managing Editor
Lanning Macfarland, Chairman

Legal employment opportunities.
Frequency: Weekly
Founded in: 1854
Printed in 2 colors on newsprint stock

14960 National Constables Association Newsletter
National Constables Association
PO Box 1172
Haverhill, MA 01831-1572

978-373-5234
800-272-1775; *Fax:* 978-373-1191
mike@constables.com; www.constables.com

Hal Lefcourt, Executive Director
John Sindt, President

A newsletter published for the members of National Constables Association.
4 Pages
Frequency: Quarterly
Printed in one color on glossy stock

14961 Police Executive Research Forum
1120 Connecticut Avenue NW
Suite 930
Washington, DC 20036

202-466-7820; *Fax:* 202-466-7826;
www.policeforum.org

Chuck Wexler, Executive Director
Chief John Timoney, VP
Daniel Woods, Research Associate
Jessica Toliver, Deputy Director
Raquel Rodriguez, Accounting Manager

Members are chief executives of city, county and state police agencies. Membership dues are general $300.00, subscribing $125.00.
Cost: $35.00
Frequency: Monthly
Circulation: 1000
Founded in: 1977
Mailing list available for rent

14962 Signal
American Traffic Safety Services Association
15 Riverside Parkway
Suite 100
Fredericksburg, VA 22406-1022

540-368-1701
800-272-8772; *Fax:* 540-368-1717;
www.atssa.com

James Baron, Communications Director
Douglas Danko, Chairman

Covers legislative updates, industry news and meeting information, as well as other items of interest to the roadway safety industry as is a full-color publication.
Frequency: Quarterly
Mailing list available for rent

14963 Women Police
International Association of Women Police
PO Box 690418
Tulsa, OK 74169

918-234-6445
jvanland@aol.com; www.iawp.org/

Mona Moore, Publisher
Kim Covert, Treasurer

Accepts advertising.
Cost: $25.00
50 Pages
Frequency: Quarterly

Magazines & Journals

14964 Air Beat Magazine
Airborne Law Enforcement Association
50 Carroll Creek Way
Suite 260
Frederick, MD 21701-4786

301-631-2406; *Fax:* 301-631-2466;
www.alea.org

Steven Ingley, Executive Director
Kevin R. Caffery, VP
Nicole Gentile, Operations Manager
Keith Johnson, Safety Program Director
Carrie Cosens, Membership Manager

Dedicated to Airborne Law Enforcement. The subscription also includes the annual Buyer's Guide and special Convention issue with membership.
Cost: $40.00
3500 Members
Frequency: Bi-Monthly
Circulation: 6500
Founded in: 1968

14965 Campus Safety Journal
Bricepac
12228 Venice Boulevard
PO Box 66515
Los Angeles, CA 90066

310-390-5277; *Fax:* 310-390-4777
tnelson@campusjournal.com;
www.capussafetymagazine.com

John Van Horn, Publisher
Tom Nelson, Managing Editor
Wendy Rackley, Production Manager

Provides a vehicle for communicating campus safety and security issues to all interested parties at the middle, secondary, college and university levels.
40 Pages
Frequency: Monthly
Circulation: 20100
Founded in: 1992
Printed in 4 colors on glossy stock

14966 Contingency Planning & Recovery Journal
Management Advisory Services & Publications
PO Box 81151
Wellesley Hills, MA 02481-0001

781-235-2895; *Fax:* 781-235-5446
info@masp.com; www.masp.com/

An independent, subscription supported to all issues of contingency planning, disaster recovery and business continuity. Includes tutorial extensive literature review on the fields of business continuity.
Cost: $75.00
Frequency: Quarterly
Founded in: 1972
Printed in on glossy stock

14967 Corrections Today
4380 Forbes Boulevard
Lanham, MD 20706

301-918-1800
800-222-5646; *Fax:* 301-918-1900
customerservice@corrections.com;
www.corrections.com/aca

Susan Clayton, Editor
Gwendolyn C Chunn, President
Harry Wilhelm, Marketing Manager

Alice Heiserman, Publications and Research Manager
Published by the American Correctional Association.
Cost: $25.00
200 Pages
Circulation: 20000
Founded in: 1870
Mailing list available for rent

14968 Credit Card Crime, Law Enforcement Kit
9770 S Military Trail
Suite 380
Boynton Beach, FL 33436-4011
561-737-8700; *Fax:* 561-737-5800
sales@fraudandtheftinfo.com; www.fraudandtheftinfo.com
Larry Schwartz, Editor
Ways to catch and punish the thieves, including corporate support of police, reverse sting operations, paying informants. Case histories, specific recommendations.
Cost: $59.95
ISBN: 0-914801-05-8
Founded in: 1982

14969 Crime & Delinquency
Sage Publications
2455 Teller Rd
Newbury Park, CA 91320-2234
805-499-9774
800-818-7243; *Fax:* 805-499-0871
info@sagepub.com; www.sagepub.com
Blaise R Simqu, CEO
Janice Denehy, Executive Editor
Offers information to probation and parole executives as well as criminologists and lawyers.
Cost: $105.00
Frequency: Quarterly
Circulation: 3250
Founded in: 1965
Mailing list available for rent

14970 Justice Quarterly
Academy of Criminal Justice Sciences
7339 Hanover Parkway
Suite A
Greenbelt, MD 20770
301-446-6300
800-757-2257; *Fax:* 401-446-2819
info@acjs.org; www.acjs.org
Dr. Cassia Spohn, Editor
The official ACJS journal offering articles of professional insight and industry news on crime and criminal justice.
Frequency: 6 times a year
ISSN: 0741-8825

14971 Law Enforcement Legal Review
Law Enforcement Legal Publications
421 Ridgewood Avenue
Suite 100
Glen Ellyn, IL 60137-4900
630-858-6392; *Fax:* 630-858-6392
lelp@xnet.com
home.xnet.com/~lelp
James Manak, President
Glen P Manak, VP Marketing
Civil liability, driminal law and personnel law case reporter for law enforcement, legal professional and law libraries.
Cost: $98.00
Circulation: 1000
ISSN: 1070-9967
Founded in: 1970
Printed in on n stock

14972 Law Enforcement Product News
100 Garfield Street
2nd Floor
Denver, CO 80206
303-322-6400
800-291-3911; *Fax:* 303-322-0627;
www.law-enforcement.com
Michael George, Publisher
Jeannine Heinecke, Editor
Paul Mackler, CEO
Chuck Cummings, Sales Manager
Circulation: 57000
Founded in: 1966

14973 Law Enforcement Technology
Cygnus Publishing
PO Box 803
Fort Atkinson, WI 53538-0803
920-000-1111; *Fax:* 920-563-1699
Patrick.Bernardo@cygnuspub.com;
www.cygnusb2b.com
John French, CEO
Scott Cravens, Circulation Director
Gordon Gavin, VP
Ronnie Garrett, Editor
Kathy Scott, Director of Public Relations
Covers the innovative products and technology available to the law enforcement manager. Accepts advertising.
64 Pages
Frequency: Monthly
Circulation: 30,000
Founded in: 1966

14974 Law and Order
Hendon
130 Waukegan Rd
Deerfield, IL 60015-4912
847-444-3300
800-843-9764; *Fax:* 847-444-3333
info@hendonpub.com
hendonpub.com
Henry Kingwill, Owner
Bruce Cameron, Editor
Pete Kingwill, National Director
Yesenia Salcedo, Managing Editor
Tim Davis, Graphic Designer
Tailored to the law enforcement officer, the magazine updates professionals on trends, covers new methods and incorporates articles with special focuses.
Cost: $24.00
100 Pages
Frequency: Monthly
Circulation: 32304
Founded in: 1953

14975 Materials Evaluation
American Society for Nondestructive Testing
PO box 28518
1711 Arlingate Lane
Columbus, OH 43228-518
614-274-6003
800-222-2768; *Fax:* 614-274-6899;
www.asnt.org
Paul McIntire, Publication Manager
Betsy Blazar, Marketing Manager
Wayne Holliday, Executive Director
Shelby Reeves, Owner
Research, reviews and information of nondestructive testing materials. Provides members and subscribers the latest news and technical information concerning this industry.
Frequency: Monthly
Circulation: 10200
Founded in: 1941

14976 National Fire Protection Association Newsletter
1 Batterymarch Park
Quincy, MA 02169-7471
617-770-3000
800-344-3555; *Fax:* 617-770-0700
custserv@nfpa.org; www.nfpa.org
James M. Shannon, President/CEO
Peg O'Brien, Administrator - Public Affairs
Lorraine VP - Communications, Executive Director
Bruce Mullen, CFO
Paul Crossman, VP, Marketing
Written for various fire safety professionals and covers major topics in fire protection and suppression. The Journal carries investigation reports written by NFPA specialists, special NFPA statistical studies on large-loss fires, multiple deaths, fire fighter deaths and injuries, and others annually. Articles on fire protection advances, public education and information of interest to NFPA members.
Cost: $135.00
70000 Members
Circulation: 85000
Founded in: 1896

14977 Peace Officer
Dale Corporation
22150 W 9 Mile Road
Southfield, MI 48034
248-204-2244; *Fax:* 248-204-2240;
www.salesdoctors.com
Dale Jabolonski, President
Covers areas of interest to law enforcement personnel.
Cost: $12.00
40 Pages
Founded in: 1958

14978 Perspectives Journal
American Probation and Parole Association
PO Box 11910
Lexington, KY 40578-1910
859-244-8203; *Fax:* 859-244-8001
appa@csg.org; www.appa-net.org
Social Media: Facebook, Twitter, LinkedIn
Carl Wicklund, Executive Director
Barbara Broderick, President
Diane Kincaid, Deputy Director
Carrie Abner, Research Associate
John Higgins, Graphic Designer
Mailing list includes mailing addresses only, no email
Frequency: Quarterly
Circulation: 2200
Mailing list available for rent: 2200 names

14979 Police
Bobit Publishing Company
3520 Challenger St
Torrance, CA 90503-1640
310-533-2400; *Fax:* 310-533-2500
webmaster@bobit.com; www.bobit.com
Edward J Bobit, CEO
The law officer's magazine. Accepts advertising.
Cost: $35.00
104 Pages
Frequency: Monthly
Circulation: 50000
Founded in: 1961

14980 Police Chief
International Association of Chiefs of Police
515 N Washington St
Alexandria, VA 22314-2340
703-836-6767
800-843-4227; *Fax:* 703-836-4543
information@theiacp.org; www.theiacp.org

Social Media: Facebook, Twitter, RSS, Youtube

Dan Rosenblatt, Executive Director
Mark L. Whitman, Chair Commissioner

A monthly magazine published by the International Association of Chiefs of Police.
Cost: $25.00
80 Pages
Frequency: Monthly
Circulation: 21300
Founded in: 1893
Mailing list available for rent

14981 Police Times
American Federation of Police & Concerned Citizens
6350 Horizon Drive
Titusville, FL 32780

321-264-0911; *Fax:* 321-573-9819
policeinfo@aphf.org; www.aphf.org
Social Media: Facebook

Barry Shepard, Executive Director
Deputy Dennis Wise, National President
Debra Chitwood, CEO
Brent Shephard, Director of Operations

Quarterly publication focusing on law enforcement, security and police survivors.
Circulation: 31,000
Founded in: 1978

14982 Public Safety Communications/APCO Bulletin
Assn of Public Safety Communication Officials
351 N Williamson Boulevard
Daytona Beach, FL 32114-1112

386-322-2500
888-272-6911; *Fax:* 386-322-2501
apco@apcointl.org
https://www.apcointl.org/about-apco/current-annual-report/past-re

Toni Edwards, Editor
George S Rice Jr, President
Susan Stowell, Member Services Director
Garry Mendez, Marketing/Communications Director
Robert Gurss Esq., Legal/Government Affairs Director

The world's oldest and largest professional organization dedicated to the enhancement of public safety communications and to serving its more than 15,000 members, the people who use public safety communications systems and services.
Cost: $12.00
Frequency: Monthly
Circulation: 13000
ISSN: 1526-1646
Founded in: 1935

14983 Public Safety Product News
Cygnus Publishing
PO Box 803
Fort Atkinson, WI 53538-0803

920-000-1111
800-547-7377; *Fax:* 920-563-1699
Patrick.Bernardo@cygnusB2B.com;
www.cygnusb2b.com

John French, CEO
Sharon Haberkorn, Development Manager
Ronnie Garrett, Editor-in-Chief
Kathy Scott, Director of Public Relations
Paul Bonaiuto, CFO
Frequency: Monthly

14984 Sheriff
National Sherriff's Association
1450 Duke St
Alexandria, VA 22314-3490

703-836-7827
800-424-7827; *Fax:* 703-836-6541
nsamail@sheriffs.org; www.sheriffs.org

Suzanne Kitts, Editor
Aaron Kennard, President
Thomas N Faust, Executive Director

Published for the law enforcement official.
Cost: $25.00
Circulation: 20,000
Founded in: 1948

14985 Tactical Edge
National Tactical Officers Association
PO Box 797
Doylestown, PA 18901

215-230-7616
800-279-9127; *Fax:* 215-230-7552
membership@ntoa.org; www.ntoa.org
Social Media: Facebook, Twitter, LinkedIn, Google+, Blogger, Bloggy, Pint

Phil Hansen, Board Chairman
Jim Torkar, Treasurer
Bob Chabali, Secretary
Mark Lomax, Executive Director
Rob Cartner, Director of Training
Cost: $40.00
Frequency: Quarterly
Circulation: 12000
Mailing list available for rent

14986 Today's Policeman
Towerhigh Productions
PO Box 875108
Los Angeles, CA 90087-208
Donald Mack, President

General philosophy of the police services.
Cost: $9.00
40 Pages
Founded in: 1961

Trade Shows

14987 ACFSA International Conference
American Correctional Food Service Affiliates
210 N Glenoaks Blvd
Suite C
Burbank, CA 91502

818-843-6608; *Fax:* 818-843-7423
jonnichols@acfsa.org; www.acfsa.org

Jon Nichols, Executive Director
150 Attendees
Frequency: Annual/August
Founded in: 1969

14988 APCO Annual Conference & Expo
351 N Williamson Boulevard
Daytona Beach, FL 32114-1112

386-322-2500
888-272-6911; *Fax:* 386-322-2501
apco@apcointl.org; www.apcointl.org/

Barbara Myers, Director Conference Services
Casey Epton Roush, Conference/Meeting Services Manager
Brigid Blaschak, Tradeshow Manager
Patricia Giannini, Senior Meeting Coordinator
Garry Mendez, Marketing/Communications Director

APCO's Annual Conference and Exposition brings together more than 300 vendors to provide hands-on demonstrations of new technologies you might use in your agency or call centers. The Conference also offers sessions on personal and professional development and a variety of technical skills. Banquet, breakfast and exhibitors of radio, computer, and supporting equipment companies.
6000 Attendees
Frequency: Annual
Founded in: 1935

14989 Academy of Criminal Justice Sciences Annual Meeting
Academy of Criminal Justice Sciences
7339 Hanover Parkway
Suite A
Greenbelt, MD 20770

301-446-6300
800-757-2257; *Fax:* 401-446-2819
info@acjs.org; www.acjs.org

Lorenzo M. Boyd, President
Nicole Leeper Piquero, First-Vice President
Faith Lutze, Second Vice-President
L. Edward Day, Treasurer

Criminal justice educators, researchers, practicioners, students and the general public visit 45 exhibits and seminars.
2000 Attendees
Frequency: Annual
Founded in: 1963

14990 Airborne Law Enforcement Annual Conference & Expo
Airborne Law Enforcement Association
50 Carroll Creek Way
Suite 260
Frederick, MD 21701-4786

301-631-2406; *Fax:* 301-631-2466;
www.alea.org

Steven Ingley, Executive Director
Kevin R. Caffery, VP
Nicole Gentile, Operations Manager
Keith Johnson, Safety Program Director
Carrie Cosens, Membership Manager

Containing 157 booths.
1100 Attendees
Frequency: July
Founded in: 1968

14991 American Academy of Forensic Sciences Annual Meeting
American Academy of Forensic Sciences
410 N 21st St
Colorado Springs, CO 80904-2712
719-636-1100; *Fax:* 719-636-1993
awarren@aafs.org; www.aafs.org

Nancy Jackson, Director Development
Anne Warren, Executive Director
Sondra Bynoe-Doolittle, Assistant Meetings Manager
Addie Arellano, Meetings/Exposition Assistant
Anne Warren, Executive Director

Professionals in the forensic science field attend meeting and see 120 exhibits of scientific instruments.
2300 Attendees
Frequency: Annual,February
Mailing list available for rent

14992 American Correctional Association Congress
206 N Washington St
Suite 200
Alexandria, VA 22314

703-224-0000
800-222-5646; *Fax:* 703-224-0179
pres@aca.org; www.aca.org

Daron Hall, President
James Gondles Jr, Executive Director
Jeff Washington, Deputy Executive Director

Five hundred booths featuring association whose membership is concerned with correctional services.
3900 Attendees
Mailing list available for rent

14993 **American Correctional Association Winter Conference**
206 N Washington St
Suite 200
Alexandria, VA 22314

703-224-0000
800-222-5646; *Fax:* 703-224-0179
pres@aca.org; www.aca.org

James Gondles Jr, Executive Director
Daron Hall, President
Jeff Washington, Deputy Executive Director

Three hundred and fifty booths.
3M Attendees
Frequency: January
Founded in: 1935
Mailing list available for rent

14994 **American Criminal Justice Association National Conference**
American Criminal Justice Association
PO Box 601047
Sacramento, CA 95860-1047

916-484-6553; *Fax:* 916-488-2227
acjalae@aol.com; www.acjalae.org

Joe Davenport, President
Karen Campbell, Executive Secretary
Abby Schofield, Region 1 President
Preston Koelling, Vice-President

Business meetings, awards, competitions, job fairs, physical agility competitions, safety meetings and crime scene competitions
7200 Members
Founded in: 1937

14995 **American Jail Association Training Conference & Jail Expo**
1135 Professional Court
Hagerstown, MD 21740

301-790-3930; *Fax:* 301-790-2941
dorothyd@aja.org; www.aja.org
Social Media: Facebook

Dorothy Drass, Marketing Director
Holly Nicarry, Assistant Marketing Director
Robert J. Kasabian, Executive Director
Patty Vermillion, Training Coordinator
Leslie Brozna, Marketing and Sales Coordinator

Brings together more than 2,200 participants from around the world and over 275 companies who provide products and services to jails.
2200 Attendees
Frequency: May
Founded in: 1981

14996 **American Society of Criminology Show**
1314 Kinnear Road
Columbus, OH 43212

614-292-9207; *Fax:* 614-292-6767
webmaster@asc41.com; www.asc41.com

Bonnie Fisher, Treasurer

Twenty-five tables.
1.5M Attendees
Frequency: October

14997 **Convention & Traffic Expo**
American Traffic Safety Services Association
15 Riverside Parkway
Suite 100
Fredericksburg, VA 22406-1022

540-368-1701
800-272-8772; *Fax:* 540-368-1717;
www.atssa.com

Douglas Danko, Chairman

The premier meeting place for roadway professionals around the world. The program and exhibits are dedicated to issues and products related to all aspects of temporary traffic control and roadway safety.
Frequency: Annual/February
Mailing list available for rent

14998 **FBINAA Conference**
FBI National Academy Associates
422 Garrisonville Road
Suite 103
Stafford, VA 22554

540-628-0834; *Fax:* 703-632-1993
info@fbinaa.org; www.fbinaa.org

Timothy D Overton, National President
Steve Tidwell, Executive Director
Rhonda Stites, Administrative Assistant
Becky Storm, Business Manager
Nell Cochran, Financial Manager
Frequency: July
Mailing list available for rent

14999 **FEMSA Annual Conference**
Fire and Emergency Manufacturers and Services Asso
PO Box 147
Lynnfield, MA 01940-0147

781-334-2771; *Fax:* 781-334-2771
info@femsa.org; www.femsa.org
Social Media: Twitter, LinkedIn

William Lawson, President
William Van Lent, Vice President

Works to strengthen its membership, planning for future development, and directing programs that build industry opportunities
100+ Attendees
Frequency: Fall

15000 **GovSec: The Govenment Security Conference & Expo**
1105 Media
9201 Oakdale Avenue
Suite 101
Chatsworth, CA 91311

818-734-5200; *Fax:* 818-734-1522
info@1105media.com; www.1105media.com

Jules Gagne, Exhibits & Sponsorships
Deborah Lovell, Conference Program
Brad Wills, Press & Media
Neal Vitale, President & Chief Executive Officer
Richard Vitale, Senior Vice President & CFO

GovSec is the premier government security conference & expo that has joined forces with the Contingency Planning & Management Network (Centric Security) and U.S. Law Enforcement Conferences, to strengthen its focus on critical infrastructure protection, cybercrime and cyberterrorism, counterterrorism and homeland security. Washington Convention Center, Washington, DC.
Frequency: Annual/April
Founded in: 2001

15001 **Int'l Assn of Campus Law Enforcement Administrators Annual Conference**
International Assn of Campus Law Enforcement Admin
342 North Main Street
West Hartford, CT 06117-2507

860-586-7522; *Fax:* 860-586-7550
info@iaclea.org; www.iaclea.org

Pamela Hayes, Exhibitor Contact
Peter Berry, Executive Director

Offers members an opportunity to attend informative programs to learn more about current issues and developments in campus public safety, network with peers, visit exhibitor booths, and enjoy special events.
Frequency: Annual

15002 **International Association of Chiefs of Police Annual Conference**
International Association of Chiefs of Police
515 N Washington Street
Alexandria, VA 22314-2357

703-836-6767
800-843-4227; *Fax:* 703-836-4543
information@theiacp.org; www.theiacp.org
Social Media: Facebook, Twitter, RSS, Youtube

Lia Muwwakkil, Exhibits & Conferences
Colleen Phalen, Exhibits & Sponsorships
Dan Rosenblatt, Executive Director

Enables professionals to examine the state of the police industry through highly rated seminars, forums, and technical workshops. Only open to IACP members and their guests.
Frequency: Annual,September
Mailing list available for rent

15003 **Major Cities Chiefs Conference**
Major Cities Chiefs Police Association
P.O. Box 8717
Salt Lake City, UT 84047

E-Mail: stephens@majorcitieschiefs.com;
www.majorcitieschiefs.com

J. Thomas Manger, President
Art Acevedo, 1st Vice President
George Turner, 2nd Vice President
Darrell W. Stephens, Executive Director

Association meetings held three times a year - winter, summer, and fall.
Founded in: 1949

15004 **National Education & Training Conference**
National Black Police Association
3100 Main Street
#256
Dallas, TX 75226

855-879-6272; *Fax:* 202-986-0410;
www.blackpolice.org

Ronald Hampton, Executive Director
Malik Aziz, Chairperson
Walter L Holloway, Vice Chairperson
Sherri Lockett, Secretary
Donna Ross, Fiscal Officer
400 Attendees
Frequency: Annual

15005 **National Forensic League**
125 Watson Street
PO Box 38
Ripon, WI 54971

920-748-6206; *Fax:* 920-748-9478
nflcustomerservice@nflonline.org;
www.nflonline.org

Diane Rasmussen, Associate Secretary
J Scott, Executive Director

Ten booths.
2.8M Attendees
Frequency: June

15006 **National Sheriff's Association**
1450 Duke Street
Alexandria, VA 22314-3490

703-836-7827
800-424-7827
kbright@sheriffs.org; www.sheriffs.org

Kimberly Bright, Director, Marketing & Exhibits
Thomas Faust, Executive Director

More than 500 exhibits.
3M Attendees
Frequency: June

15007 **Tactical Operations Conference**
National Tactical Officers Association

PO Box 797
Doylestown, PA 18901

215-230-7616
800-279-9127; *Fax:* 215-230-7552
membership@ntoa.org; www.ntoa.org
Social Media: Facebook, Twitter, LinkedIn, Google+, Blogger, Bloggy, Pint

Mark Lomax, Executive Director
Laura Gerhart, Conference Coordinator
Rob Cartner, Director of Training
Mary Heins, Editor
Michelle Griffin, Assistant Editor
1000 Attendees
Frequency: September
Mailing list available for rent

Directories & Databases

15008 American Academy of Forensic Sciences Membership Directory
410 N 21st St
Colorado Spring, CO 80904-2712

719-636-1100; *Fax:* 719-636-1993
awarren@aafs.org; www.aafs.org

Anne Warren, Executive Director

Offers valuable information on over 5,000 persons qualified in forensic sciences including law, anthropology and psychiatry.
Cost: $50.00
250 Pages
Frequency: Annual

15009 Directory of Law Enforcement and Criminal
Law Enforcement Standards Office
US National Institute of Standards
100 Bureau Drive M/S 8102
Gaithersburg, MD 20899-8102

301-975-2757; *Fax:* 301-948-0978

Marilyn Leach, Editor
Ruth Joel, Editor

More than 200 local, national and international organizations involved in the fields of law enforcement, corrections, forensic science and criminal justice in the US.

15010 Fire Chief: Equipment and Apparatus Directory Issue
Primedia
1300 E 9th St
Cleveland, OH 44114-1503

216-696-7000; *Fax:* 216-696-6662;
www.penton.com

Eric Jacobson, Senior VP
Jane Cooper, Marketing
David Kieselstein, Chief Executive Officer
Kurt Nelson, Vice President, Human Resources
Andrew Schmolka, Senior Vice President

List of approximately 1,000 suppliers of fire protection equipment, including ladder trucks, protective clothing, alarms, alternators and others.
Cost: $10.00
Frequency: Monthly
Circulation: 52901
Mailing list available for rent

15011 Grey House Homeland Security Directory
Grey House Publishing
4919 Route 22
PO Box 56
Amenia, NY 12501

518-789-8700
800-562-2139; *Fax:* 845-373-6390
books@greyhouse.com; www.greyhouse.com
Social Media: Facebook, Twitter

Leslie Mackenzie, Publisher
Richard Gottlieb, Editor

Features the latest contact information for government and private organizations involved with Homeland Security along with the latest product information. The directory provides detailed profiles of nearly 1,500 Federal & State Organizations & Agencies and over 3,000 Officials and Key Executives involved with Homeland Security.
Cost: $195.00
800 Pages
ISBN: 1-592370-75-6
Founded in: 1981

15012 Grey House Homeland Security Directory - Online Database
Grey House Publishing
4919 Route 22
PO Box 56
Amenia, NY 12501-0056

518-789-8700
800-562-2139; *Fax:* 518-789-0556
gold@greyhouse.com;
www.gold.greyhouse.com
Social Media: Facebook, Twitter

Leslie Mackenzie, Publisher
Richard Gottlieb, President

This comprehensive database presents a wide range of information that is scattered and hard to find elsewhere, providing subscribers with access to the most comprehensive, up-to-date and detailed information on the nation's homeland security contacts and services. This online database contains over 1,100 profiles of Federal and State agencies and companies along with the names of 11,000 key contacts.
Founded in: 1981

15013 Grey House Safety & Security Directory
Grey House Publishing
4919 Route 22
PO Box 56
Amenia, NY 12501

518-789-8700
800-562-2139; *Fax:* 845-373-6390
books@greyhouse.com; www.greyhouse.com
Social Media: Facebook, Twitter

Leslie Mackenzie, Publisher
Richard Gottlieb, Editor

Comprehensive resource guide to the safety and security industry, including articles, checklists, OSHA regulations and product listings. Focuses on creating and maintaining a safe and secure enviroment, and dealing specifically with hazardous materials, noise and vibration, workplace preparation and maintenance, electrical and lighting safety, fire and rescue and more.
Cost: $165.00
1600 Pages
ISBN: 1-592373-75-5
Founded in: 1981

15014 Law Enforcement Technology Directory
Hendon
130 Waukegan Rd
Deerfield, IL 60015-4912

847-444-3300
800-843-9764; *Fax:* 847-444-3333
info@hendonpub.com;
www.lawandordermag.com

Henry Kingwill, Owner

Directory of manufacturers and suppliers of one type of law enforcement equipment such as computers, weapons, training, surveillance, forensics and radio and communications equipment.
Cost: $60.00
Frequency: Annual December

15015 Law and Order Magazine: Police Management Buyer's Guide Issue
Hendon
130 Waukegan Rd
2nd Floor
Deerfield, IL 60015-4912

847-444-3300
800-843-9764; *Fax:* 847-444-3333
esanow@hendonpub.com;
www.hendonpub.com

Henry Kingwill, Owner
Jennifer Gavigan, Managing Editor
Yesenia Salcedo, Managing Editor
Tim Davis, Graphic Designer
Marilou Go, Office Manager

Monthly publication for police managers, covering all aspects of law enforcement including a list of manufacturers, dealers and distributors of products and services for police departments.
Cost: $15.00
Frequency: Annual February

15016 National Directory of Law Enforcement Administrators Correctional Inst
National Public Safety Information Bureau
PO Box 365
Stevens Point, WI 54481

715-345-2772
800-647-7579; *Fax:* 715-345-7288
info@safetysource.com;
www.safetysource.com

Steve Cywinski, Publisher
John Diser, Account Manager
Christina Scott, Business Development Manager

Listing of police departments, sheriffs, criminal prosecutors, state law enforcement, criminal investigation agencies, federal law enforcement and homeland security.
Cost: $129.00
924 Pages
Frequency: Annual, paperback
Circulation: 9,000
ISBN: 1-880245-22-1
ISSN: 1066-5595
Founded in: 1964

15017 National Employment Listing Service Bulletin
Criminal Justice Center
Sam Houston State University
1803 Avenue I
Huntsville, TX 77341

936-295-6371

Kay Billingsley, Editor

Job openings in police departments, sheriff's departments, courts and other law enforcement and security agencies.

15018 Police: Buyer's Guide Issue
Bobit Publishing Company
23210 Crenshaw Blvd
Torrance, CA 90505-3181

310-539-1969; *Fax:* 310-539-4329
police@bobit.com

John Bebout, Owner

List of suppliers of police products and services.
Cost: $10.00
Frequency: Annual August

15019 Transportation Security Directory & Handbook
Grey House Publishing

4919 Route 22
PO Box 56
Amenia, NY 12501

518-789-8700
800-562-2139; *Fax:* 845-373-6390
books@greyhouse.com; www.greyhouse.com
Social Media: Facebook, Twitter

Leslie Mackenzie, Publisher
Richard Gottlieb, Editor

Provides information on everything from Regulatory Authorities to Security Enforcement, this top-flight directory brings together the relevant information necessary for creating and maintaining a security plan for a wide range of transportation facilities.
Cost: $195.00
800 Pages
ISBN: 1-592370-75-6
Founded in: 1981

15020 Who's Who in Jail Management Jail Directory
American Jail Association
1135 Professional Ct
Hagerstown, MD 21740-5853

301-790-3930; *Fax:* 301-790-2941;
www.aja.org

Gwyn Smith-Ingley, Executive Director
Kelton Chapman, Manager
Sheryl Ebersole, Business Manager
Connie Lacy, Director

Offers the most current information available on local jails in the US. Also offers an up-to-date listing of all the jails in the US that is available for rent electronically and a valuable resource for sheriffs, jail administrators and vendors.
Cost: $85.00

Industry Web Sites

15021 http://gold.greyhouse.com
G.O.L.D Grey House OnLine Databases
Grey House Publishing's online database platform, GOLD, offers Quick Search, Keyword Search and Expert Search for most business sectors including law enforcement and public safety markets. The GOLD platform makes finding the information you need quick and easy - whether you're a novice searcher or an experienced database user. All of Grey House's directory products are available for subscription on the GOLD platform.

15022 www.aamva.org
American Assn. of Motor Vehicle Administrators
Nonprofit organization represents state and provincial officials in the US and Canada who administer and enforce motor vehicle laws. Strives to develop model programs in motor vehicle administration, police traffic services and highway safety.

15023 www.aca.org
American Correctional Association
This organization offers information on the correctional field.

15024 www.alea.org
Airborne Law Enforcement Association
Members are law enforcement officers who use both fixed and rotary wing air craft, in law enforcement, and equipment suppliers.

15025 www.apco911.org
Association of Public-Safety Communications Officials International
The world's oldest and largest professional organization dedicated to the enhancement of public safety communications and to serving its more than 15,000 members, the people who use public safety communications systems and services.

15026 www.aphf.org
American Police Hall of Fame
Offers benefits, and various types of awards to members, magazine, line of duty death benefits, film and training library as well as support services, scholarships and financial assistance for police family survivors.

15027 www.atssa.org
American Traffic Safety Services Association
Promotes uniform use of lights, signs, pavement markings and barricades. Distributes technical information and sponsors training courses for worksite traffic supervisors.

15028 www.blr.com
Business & Legal Reports
Provides essential tools for safety and environmental compliance and training needs

15029 www.corrections.com/
Corrections Professionals
Information about events, careers, news, legal happenings and newsletters.

15030 www.dpsoa.com
Texas Department of Public Safety Officer's Association

15031 www.fema.gov
Federal Emergency Management Agency.

15032 www.femsa.org
Fire and Emergency Manufacturers and Services Asso
The leading trade association for the fire and emergency services industry whose members provides products and services to millions of fire and EMS professionals throughout the world.

15033 www.footprinter.org
International Footprint Association

15034 www.fssa.net
Fire Suppression Systems Association
Designers, suppliers and installers of special hazard fire suppression equipment, gases and detectors.

15035 www.greyhouse.com
Grey House Publishing
Authoritative reference directories for most business sectors including law enforcement and public safety markets. Users can search the online databases with varied search criteria allowing for custom searches by product category, geographic area, sales volume, keyword, subject and more. Full Grey House catalog and online ordering also available.

15036 www.highwaysafety.org
Insurance Institute for Highway Safety
Traffic and motor vehicle safety organization supported by auto insurers.

15037 www.home.xnet.com/~lelp
Law Enforcement Legal Publications
Publication for law enforcement, legal professional and law libraries.

15038 www.iaati.org
International Association of Auto Theft Investigators
Provides members who are auto theft investigators with resources to develop and maintain professional standards within the industry.

15039 www.iawp.org
International Association of Women Police
To strengthen, unite and raise the profile of women in criminal justice internationally.

15040 www.ncpc.org
National Crime Prevention Council

15041 www.neoa.org
Narcotic Enforcement Officers Association
A non-profit educational organization of more than a thousand law enforcement personnel and others in the criminal justicce system, includin state and local police, D.E.A., F.B.I. and customs.

15042 www.nist.gov/oles/
Law Enforcement Standards Office

15043 www.ntoa.org
National Tactical Officers Association
Enhance the performance and professional status of law enforcement personnel by providing a credible and proven training resource as well as a forum for the development of tactics and information exchange.

15044 www.policeforum.org
Police Executive Research Forum
For chief executives of city, county and state police agencies.

15045 www.polygraph.org
American Polygraph Association
A merger of Academy of Scientific Interrogation, American Academy of Polygraph Examiners and National Board of Polygraph examiners.

15046 www.psa.com
Production Services Associates,Inc.
Dealers and dealer banks who underwrite and trade federal, state and local government securities and mortgage-backed securities.

15047 www.sheriffs.org
National Sherriff's Association
Devoted to helping sheriffs and other law enforcers to execute their duties most effectively and professionally.

15048 www.theiacp.org
International Association of Chiefs of Police
Organization that focuses on topics of interest to professional law enforcers.

15049 www.toxicology.org
Society of Toxicology
Members are scientists concerned with the effects of chemicals on man and the environment. Promotes the aquisition and utilization of knowledge in toxicology, aids in the protection of public health and facilitates disiplines. The society has a strong commitment to education in toxicology and to the recruitment of students and new members into the profession.

Associations

15050 American Leather Chemists Association
1314 50th Street
Suite 103
Lubbock, TX 79412
806-744-1798; *Fax:* 806-744-1785
alca@leatherchemists.org;
www.leatherchemists.org
Steve Lange, President
Sarah Drayna, Vice President
Robert F. White, JALCA Editor
Carol Adcock, Executive Secretary
Group of leather chemists who are interested in the development of methods that could be utilized to standardize both the supply and application of the tanning agents utilized by the industry.
500 Members
Founded in: 1903
Mailing list available for rent

15051 American Saddle Makers Association
12155 Donovan Lane
Black Forest, CO 80908
729-494-2848
info@saddlemakers.org;
www.saddlemakers.org
Cheryl Rifkin, President
Bob Brenner, Executive Director
Steve Bowen, Director of Membership
Representing manufacturers of Western and English saddles in the US.

15052 International Federation Leather Guild
2264 Logan Drive
New Palestine, IN 46163
317-691-0321
eddjanlucas@sbcglobal.net; www.ifolg.org
David Smith, Executive Director
Alex Madson, Assistant Director
Carol Higgins, Secretary
Monica Nibbes, Treasurer
Roger Bligan, Web Master
Supports all leather craftsmen via education, training, publications and trade shows.

15053 Leather Apparel Association
19 W 21st Street
Suite 403
New York, NY 10010
212-727-1210; *Fax:* 212-727-1218
info@leatherassociation.com;
www.leatherassociation.com
Morris Goldfarb, President
Richard Harrow, Executive Director
Represents the nation's leading leather retailers, manufacturers, cleaners and other businesses in promoting leather apparel in the US.
Founded in: 1990

15054 Leather Industries of America
3050 K St NW
Suite 400
Washington, DC 20007-5100
202-342-8497; *Fax:* 202-342-8583
info@leatherusa.com; www.leatherusa.com
John Wittenborn, President
John M. Pike, Executive Director
A trade association representing the leather industry: tanners; chemical suppliers; hide, skin and leather suppliers; and product manufacturers. Provides environmental, technical, educational, statistical, and marketing services.
Founded in: 1917

15055 Leathercraft Guild
9108 Garvey Ave
Rosemead, CA 91770
www.theleathercraftguild.com
Social Media: Facebook, Twitter, Myspace
Preserves and promotes the art of leather carving and stamping. Seeks to improve skills of members, raise standards of crafts and promote the product.
200 Members
Founded in: 1949

15056 National Shoe Retailers Association
7386 N. La Cholla Blvd.
Suite G
Tucson, AZ 85741
520-209-1710
800-673-8446; *Fax:* 410-381-1167
info@nsra.org; www.nsra.org
Social Media: Facebook, Twitter, LinkedIn, Pinterest, Google Plus
Rick Ravel, Board Chairman
Lenny Comeras, Vice Chairman
Jeff Greenberg, Vice Chairman
Chuck Schuyler, President
Tanja Towne, Membership Director
Membership association for independent shoe ratailers. Provides business services such as credit-card processing and shipping at special low members only prices. Also provides educational and training programs, consulting and other services.
63 Members
Founded in: 1912

15057 Pedorthic Footwear Association
1610 East Forsyth Street
Suite D
Americus, GA 31709
229-389-3440
703-995-4456; *Fax:* 888-563-0945
info@pedorthics.org; www.pedorthics.org
Social Media: Facebook, Twitter, LinkedIn, Google+, Blogger, Bloggy, Pint
Rob Sobel, C. Ped., President
Dean Mason, Vice President
Matt Almeida, Secretary
Christopher J. Costantini, C. Ped., Treasurer
Rebecca Fazzari, Meeting and Convention Manager
Membership organization for individuals and companies involved in the design, manufacture, modification and fit of therapeutic footwear. Provides educational programs, publications, legislative monitoring, marketing materials, professional liason and business operations services.
Cost: $55.00
2000 Members
Founded in: 1958

15058 Proleptic, Inc.
PO Box 17817
Asheville, NC 28816
828-505-8474; *Fax:* 828-505-8476
shoptalk@proleptic.net; www.proleptic.net
Social Media: Facebook
Daniel S Preston, PhD, Director
A Comprehensive Source for Sewing Machines, Leather working Equipment, Supplies, Tools, Horse Healthcare and Finished Products Repair Shops Retailers, Crafters, Collectors.
320 Members
Founded in: 1984

15059 Sponge and Chamois Institute
10024 Office Center Ave
Suite 203
Saint Louis, MO 63128
314-842-2230; *Fax:* 314-842-3999
scwaters@swbell.net;
www.chamoisinstitute.org
Members are suppliers and dealers of natural sponges and chamois leather.

15060 Travel Goods Association
301 North Harrison Street
#412
Princeton, NJ 08540-3512
609-720-1200; *Fax:* 877-842-1938
info@travel-goods.org; www.travel-goods.org
Social Media: Facebook, Twitter, LinkedIn, YouTube
Michele Marini Pittenger, President/CEO
Rob Holmes, Vice President/ CFO
Kim Wong, Creative Director
Kate Ryan, Media Relations
Nate Herman, Director, Government Relations
Trade association that represents manufacturers of luggage, business and computer cases,handbags and accessories. Formerly the Luggage and Leather Goods Association.
450 Members
Founded in: 1938
Mailing list available for rent

15061 Western-English Trade Association
451 East 58th Avenue
Suite 4323
Denver, CO 80216-8468
303-295-2001; *Fax:* 303-295-6108;
www.wetaonline.org
Glenda Chipps, Executive Director
Members are manufacturers and retailers of western and english style riding equipment and clothes.
158 Members
Founded in: 1963

Newsletters

15062 Leather Conservation News
Minnesota Historical Society
345 Kellogg Blvd W
St Paul, MN 55102-1906
651-259-3000; *Fax:* 651-296-1004
webmaster@mnhs.org; www.mnhs.org
Nina Archabal, Executive Director
Jackie Swanson, Secretary
Sue Leas, Executive Assistant
Research and advancements in the specialty of leather conservation and preservation; articles on materials science research and treatments; news of conferences and workshops.
Cost: $15.00
24 Pages
Frequency: 2 per year
Circulation: 250
ISSN: 0898-0128
Printed in on matte stock

15063 Leather Facts
US Hide, Skin & Leather Association
1700 N Moore Street
Suite 1600
Arlington, VA 22209
703-841-2400; *Fax:* 703-527-0938;
www.meatami.com
John Reddington, President
Association news covering the leather and hide industry.

15064 Leather International
www.leathermag.com

Carl Friedmann, Editor

In-depth coverage of every aspect of the international leather industry.

Magazines & Journals

15065 Journal of the American Leather Chemists Association (JALCA)
American Leather Chemists Association
1314 50th Street
Suite 103
Lubbock, TX 79412

806-744-1798; *Fax:* 806-744-1785
alca@leatherchemists.org;
www.leatherchemists.org

Carol Adcock, Executive Secretary
Robert F. White, Editor
Steven Gilberg, President
Steve Lange, Vice President
Cost: $175.00
Frequency: Monthly
Circulation: 500
Founded in: 1903
Mailing list available for rent

15066 Leather Crafters & Saddlers Journal
222 Blackburn St
Rhinelander, WI 54501

715-362-5393
888-289-6409; *Fax:* 715-362-5391
journal@newnorth.net;
www.leathercraftersjournal.com
Social Media: Facebook

Dot Reis, Editor

Publication for leather workers. Sponsors several trade shows throughout the year which attract vendors of leather, tools, equipment and supplies.
Cost: $32.00; *Frequency:* Bi-Monthly
Circulation: 6000; *ISSN:* 1082-4480

15067 Travel Goods Showcase
Travel Goods Association
301 North Harrison St.
Suite 412
Princeton, NJ 08540-3512

877-842-1938; *Fax:* 877-842-1938
travel-goods.org/travel-goods-showcase
Social Media: Facebook, Twitter, LinkedIn, YouTube

Michele Marini Pittenger, Editor-in-chief
Founded in: 1975

Trade Shows

15068 ALCA Annual Meeting
American Leather Chemists Association
1314 50th Street
Suite 103
Lubbock, TX 79412

806-744-1798; *Fax:* 806-744-1785;
www.leatherchemists.org

Carol Adcock, Executive Secretary
Robert F. White, Editor
Steven Gilberg, President
Steve Lange, Vice President
100 Attendees
Mailing list available for rent

15069 International Federation Leather Guild Trade Show
748 NW Wood Street
Burleson, TX 76028-2619

817-478-2335

Ernie Wayman, Executive Director

Open exhibition of leather craftsmen.
400 Attendees

15070 Leather Allied Trade Show
2214 S Brentwood Boulevard
Saint Louis, MO 63144-1804

314-961-2829

Virginia Breen, Secretary

Exhibition of leathers and components.
2.1M Attendees
Frequency: February

15071 PFA Annual Symposium & Exhibition
Pedorthic Footwear Association
1610 E Forsyth St.
Suite D
Americus, GA 31709

229-389-3440; *Fax:* 888-563-0945
pedorthicsusa@gmail.com;
www.pedorthics.org
Social Media: Facebook, Twitter, LinkedIn

Robert Sobel, President

One hundred fifty booths plus educational sessions regarding the design, manufacture or modification and fit of shoes and foot orthoses to alleviate foot problems caused by disease, congenital condition, overuse or injury.
1000 Attendees
Frequency: November

15072 The International Travel Goods Show
Travel Goods Association
301 North Harrison St.
Suite 412
Princeton, NJ 08540-3512
877-842-1938; *Fax:* 877-842-1938;
www.thetravelgoodsshow.org

Michele Marini Pittenger, President/CEO
Cathy Hays, VP/Trade Show

Directories & Databases

15073 Complete Directory of Leather Goods & Luggage
Sutton Family Communications & Publishing Company
920 State Route 54 East
Elmitch, KY 42343

270-276-9500; jlsutton@apex.net

Theresa Sutton, Publisher
Lee Sutton, Editor

Print-out from database of wholesalers, manufacturers, distributors, importers and close-out houses. Database is updated daily to guarantee the most current and up-to-date sources available.
Cost: $39.50
100 Pages

15074 LIA Member Directory & Buyer's Guide
Leather Industries of America
3050 K St. NW; Suite 400
Washington, DC 20007

202-342-8497; *Fax:* 202-342-8583
info@leatherusa.com; www.leatherusa.com

John Wittenborn, President
30 Pages
Frequency: Annual/March
Founded in: 1917

15075 Leather Manufacturer Directory
Shoe Trades Publishing Company
323 Cornelia; Suite 274
Plattsburg, NY 12901

514-457-8787
800-973-7463; *Fax:* 514-457-5832;
www.shoetrades.com

George McLeish, Group Publisher
Inta Huns, Managing Editor

Classified directory of major leather finishers, tanneries and hide processors in the United States and Canada, and their suppliers.
Cost: $61.00; 413 Pages
Frequency: Annual; *Circulation:* 1,200

15076 U.S. Leather Industry Statistics
Leather Industries of America
3050 K St. NW
Suite 400
Washington, DC 20007

202-342-8497; *Fax:* 202-342-8583
info@leatherusa.com; www.leatherusa.com

John Wittenborn, President

Statistical record of the U.S. leather industry for over 85 years.
Cost: $18.00; 10 Pages; *Frequency:* Annual
Founded in: 1917

Industry Web Sites

15077 http://gold.greyhouse.com
G.O.L.D Grey House OnLine Databases

Grey House Publishing's online database platform, GOLD, offers Quick Search, Keyword Search and Expert Search for most business sectors including leather markets. The GOLD platform makes finding the information you need quick and easy - whether you're a novice searcher or an experienced database user. All of Grey House's directory products are available for subscription on the GOLD platform.

15078 www.greyhouse.com
Grey House Publishing

Authoritative reference directories for most business sectors including leather markets. Users can search the online databases with varied search criteria allowing for custom searches by product category, geographic area, sales volume, keyword, subject and more. Full Grey House catalog and online ordering also available.

15079 www.hidenet.com
Hidenet

Furnishes detailed information on the daily hide market worldwide.

15080 www.leatherusa.com
Leather Industries of America

Works to promote the leather industry through collection of statistics, chemical and technical research and public relations.

15081 www.meatami.org
US Hide, Skin & Leather Association

15082 www.ssia.info
Shoe Service Institute of America

Shop to shop chat room, links and listings of manufacturers and wholesalers plus shoe care tips.

15083 www.travel-goods.org
Travel Goods Association

Manufacturers of luggage and other leather goods.

Associations

15084 ABA Young Lawyers Division
American Bar Association
321 N Clark St
Chicago, IL 60654-7598

312-988-5000
800-285-2221; *Fax:* 312-988-5280
yld@staff.abanet.org;
www.abanet.org/yld/home.html
Social Media: Facebook, Twitter, LinkedIn, Youtube

James R. Silkenat, President
Robert M. Carlson, Chair, House of Delegates
Jack L. Rives, Executive Director
Hon. Cara Lee T Neville, Secretary
Lucian T. Pera, Treasurer

The Division is committed to assuring it is best able to represent the newest members of the profession, ensuring that it reflects the society it serves, and providing young lawyers wth the tools and opportunities for professional and personal success.
150M Members
Founded in: 1878

15085 AILA's Immigration Lawyer Search
E-Mail: ils@aila.org; www.ailalawyer.com
12,00 Members

15086 Academy of Family Mediators
PO Box 51090
Eugene, OR 97405

541-345-1629
admin@mediate.com; www.mediate.com
Social Media: Facebook, Twitter, LinkedIn, Google+

Jim Melamed, CEO
Carol Knapp, CTO
Josh Remis, COO
John Blair, Business Advisor & Board Member
Byron Knapp, Systems Administrator

Produce conflict management specialists who can advance conflict resolution and engagement, as well as a functional approach to conflict within our communities and society.
2M Members
Founded in: 1981
Mailing list available for rent

15087 Adjutants General Association of the United States
One Massachusetts Ave, N.W.
Washington, DC 20001

504-278-8357; *Fax:* 302-326-7196
agausinfo@gmail.com; www.agaus.org

MG Glenn H. Curtis, President
MG Robert E. Livingston, Jr., VP Army
H. Michael Edwards, VP Air
MG Kenneth Reiner, Treasurer
MG Timothy A. Reisch, Secretary

Composed of the commander of the National Guard in each state.
55 Members

15088 Alliance for Justice
11 Dupont Cir NW
2nd Floor
Washington, DC 20036-1206

202-822-6070; *Fax:* 202-822-6068
alliance@afj.org; www.afj.org
Social Media: Facebook, Twitter, Youtube, Google Plus

Ken Grossinger, Chair
Nan Aron, President
Paulette Meyer, Vice-Chair
Elizabeth Posner, Director of Foundation Relations
Kyle Barry, Director of Justice Programs

Nonprofit association of public interest advocacy organization. Offers workshops, advocacy projects, legal guides, techinical assistance and public education. Publishes a directory of public interest law centers.
Founded in: 1979
Mailing list available for rent

15089 American Academy of Psychiatry and the Law
One Regency Drive
PO Box 30
Bloomfield, CT 06002-2310

860-242-5450
800-331-1389; *Fax:* 860-286-0787
office@aapl.org; www.aapl.org

Graham D. Glancy, MB, President
Christopher Thompson, MD, Vice President
Barry W. Wall, MD, Vice President
Susan Hatters Friedman, MD, Secretary
Douglass Mossman, MD, Treasurer

Members are psychiatrists who have a professional interest in psychiatry and the law.
1500 Members
Founded in: 1969

15090 American Alliance of Paralegals
4023 Kennett Pike
Suite 146
Wilmington, DE 19807-2018

E-Mail: info@aapipara.org; www.aapipara.org
Social Media: Facebook, Twitter, LinkedIn

Carolyn M. Saenz, AACP, President
Sandra M. Herdler, Vice President
Patricia S. Carr, AACP, Treasurer
Keelie J. Fike, Secretary
Leslie L. Adams, AACP, Director of Education
Founded in: 2003

15091 American Arbitration Association
1633 Broadway
Floor 10
New York, NY 10019-6707

212-716-5800; *Fax:* 877-304-8457
websitemail@adr.org; www.adr.org

William K Slate II, CEO
Debi Miller-Moore, VP

Available to resolve a wide range of disputes through mediation, arbitration, elections and other out-of-court settlement procedures.
Founded in: 1996

15092 American Association for Justice
777 6th Street, NW
Suite 200
Washington, DC 20001

202-965-3500
800-424-2725
membership@justice.org; www.justice.org
Social Media: Facebook, Twitter, LinkedIn

Burton LeBlanc, President
Larry Tawwater, Vice President
Charles Jeffress, Chief Operating Officer
Kathi Berge, Chief Financial Officer
Anjali Jesseramsing, Executive Vice President
56000 Members
Founded in: 1972
Mailing list available for rent

15093 American Association for Paralegal Education
222 S. Westmonte Drive
Suite 101
Altamonte Springs, FL 32714

407-774-7880; *Fax:* 407-774-6440
info@aafpe.org; www.aafpe.org
Social Media: Facebook, Twitter, LinkedIn

Julia Dunlap, President
Dave Wenhold, Executive Director
Christina Griffin, Exhibits & Meetings Manager
Marcy Delesandri, Secretary

National organization serving paralegal education and institutions which offer paralegal education programs.
Founded in: 1981

15094 American Association of Attorney-Certified Public Accountants
PO Box 706
Ste. 639
Warrendale, PA 15095

703-352-8064
888-288-9272; *Fax:* 703-352-8073
info@attorney-cpa.com;
www.attorney-cpa.com
Social Media: Facebook, Twitter, LinkedIn

John W. Pramberg, President
David M. Berger, President Elect/Vice President
Eric J. Rollinger, Treasurer
Jo Ann M. Koontz, Secretary
William B. Le Vay, Assistant Treasurer/Secretary

Seeks to safeguard the professional and legal rights of CPA attorneys.
1400 Members
Founded in: 1964

15095 American Association of Law Libraries
105 W Adams Street
Suite 3300
Chicago, IL 60603-6225

312-939-4764; *Fax:* 312-431-1097
aallhq@aall.org; www.aallnet.org
Social Media: Facebook, Twitter, LinkedIn, RSS

Kate Hagan, Executive Director
Emily Feltren, Director of Government Relations
Paula Davidson, Director of Finance and Admin
Cara Schillinger, Director
Ashley St. John, Director Marketing/Communications

Promotes and enhances the value of law libraries to the legal and public communities, fosters the profession of law librarianship and provides leadership in the field of legal information.
5000+ Members
Founded in: 1906

15096 American Bail Coalition
3857 Lewiston Place
Fairfax, VA 22030

877-385-9009; *Fax:* 703-385-1809;
www.americanbailcoalition.com
Social Media: Facebook, Twitter, LinkedIn, Youtube

William B Carmichael, President
Thomas Ritchey, Treasurer

Dedicated to the long term growth and continuation of the surety bail bond industry.
Founded in: 1992

15097 American Bar Association
321 N Clark St
Chicago, IL 60654-7598

312-988-5000
800-285-2221; *Fax:* 312-988-5280
askaba@abanet.org; www.abanet.org
Social Media: Facebook, Twitter, LinkedIn

Patricia Lee Refo, Chairman
Paulette Brown, President
Jack L. Rives, Executive Director
G. Nicholas Casey, Jr., Treasurer
Mary T. Torres, Secretary

The American Bar Association is the largest coluntary professional association in the world, with over 400,000 members. The ABA provides

law school accreditation, continuing legal education, information about the law, programs to assist lawyerd and judges in their work, and initiatives to improve the legal system for the public.
400M Members
Founded in: 1878
Mailing list available for rent

15098 American Bar Foundation
750 N Lake Shore Dr
Chicago, IL 60611-4403
312-988-6500; *Fax:* 312-988-6579
khannaford@abfn.org;
www.americanbarfoundation.org
David A. Collins, President
Ellen J. Flannery, Vice President
David S. Houghton, Secretary
George S. Frazza, Treasurer
Katharine Hannaford, Senior Writer & Grants Officer
Memberships are elected and limited to one third of one percent of the lawyers in the United States.
Founded in: 1955
Mailing list available for rent

15099 American Civil Liberties Union
125 Broad St
18th Floor
New York, NY 10004-2427
212-549-2500; *Fax:* 212-549-2646
membership@aclu.org; www.aclu.org
Social Media: Facebook, Twitter, RSS, Youtube
Susan N. Herman, President
Anthony D Romero, Executive Director
Steven Shapiro, Legal Director
Mark Wier, Chief Development Officer
Dorothy M. Ehrlich, Deputy Executive Director
Protection of civil liberties and constitutional rights through litigation, public education and legislative lobbying.
Founded in: 1920
Mailing list available for rent

15100 American College of Legal Medicine
9700 West Bryn Mawr Avenue
Suite 210
Rosemont, IL 60018
847-447-1713; *Fax:* 847-447-1150
info@aclm.org; www.aclm.org
Social Media: Facebook, Twitter
Laurie Krueger, Executive Director
Daniel L. Orr, President
C. William Hinnant, President-Elect
Veling Tsai, Secretary
David Donnersberger, Treasurer
Organization related to the field of health law, legal medicine or medical jurisprudence.
1400 Members
Founded in: 1960

15101 American Health Lawyers Association
1620 Eye Street, NW
6th Floor
Washington, DC 20006-4010
202-833-1100; *Fax:* 202-833-1105;
www.healthlawyers.org
Social Media: Facebook, Twitter, LinkedIn
Lois Dehls Cornell, President
Hon. Wiliam C. Koch, Jr., Executive Vice President
BG Malinda E. Dunn, Executive Director
David W. Akridge, CAE, Deputy Executive Director
Rita Denniston Zimmerman, Communications Coordinator
Health Lawyers offers numerous services for their members and most are freely available to nonmembers as well.
Mailing list available for rent

15102 American Immigration Lawyers Association
1331 G St NW
Suite 300
Washington, DC 20005-3142
202-507-7600; *Fax:* 202-783-7853
info@aila.org; www.aila.org
Social Media: Facebook, Twitter, LinkedIn, Youtube
Victor D. Nieblas Pradis, President
Annaluisa Padilla, First Vice President
Anastasia Tonello, Second Vice President
Marketa Lindt, Treasurer
Jennifer Minear, Secretary
Attorneys practicing in the field of immigration and naturalization law.
11200 Members
Founded in: 1946
Mailing list available for rent

15103 American Inns of Court
225 Reinekers Lane
Suite 770
Alexandria, VA 22314
703-684-3590; *Fax:* 703-684-3607
info@innsofcourt.org
home.innsofcourt.org
Social Media: Facebook, Twitter, LinkedIn, Pinterest, Tumblr, Blogger, St
Hon. Carl E. Stewart, President
Carl E. Stewart, Vice President
Malinda E. Dunn, Executive Director
Cindy Dennis, Awards & Scholarships Coordinator
Andrew Young, Director of Knowledge Resources
AIC is designed to improve skills, professionalism and ethics of the bench and bar. The American Inns of Court is an amalgam of judges, lawyers, and in some cases, law professors and law students.
Mailing list available for rent

15104 American Institute of Parliamentarians
618 Church Street
Suite 220
Nashville, TN 37219
888-664-0428; *Fax:* 615-248-9253
aip@aipparl.org; www.aipparl.org
Kay Allison Crews, CP, PRP, President
Daniel Ivey-Soto, CP-T, PRP, Vice President
Barbara J. Rosi, PRP, Treasurer
Lucy Hicks Anderson, Secretary
Jeanette Williams, CP-T, Education Director
Promotes the use of effective, democratic and parliamentary practices by teaching of parliamentary procedures; training and certification of parliamentarians; promoting the use of parliamentarians; and maintaining a representative, democratic organization.
1.4M Members
Founded in: 1958

15105 American Intellectual Property Law Association
241 18th Street, South
Suite 700
Arlington, VA 22202
703-415-0780; *Fax:* 703-415-0786
aipla@aipla.org; www.aipla.org
Social Media: Facebook, Twitter, LinkedIn, Pinterest, Tumblr, Blogger, St
Sharon A. Israel, President
Lisa Jorgenson, Executive Director
Meghan Donohoe, Chief Operating Officer
Cathleen Clime, Director of Meetings & Events
Meghan Donohoe, Chief Operating Officer
Lawyers whose specialty is trademark, patent or copyright laws.
Founded in: 1897
Mailing list available for rent

15106 American Judicature Society
Center Building, 2014 Broadway
Suite 100
Nashville, TN 37203
615-873-4675
800-626-4089; *Fax:* 615-873-4671
sandersen@ajs.org; www.ajshawaii.org
Social Media: Facebook, Twitter, Youtube
Martha Hill Jamison, President
Rebecca Lee Wiggs, Vice President
Jon Comstock, Vice President
James Alfini, Interim Executive Director
Cynthia Gray, Director, Center Judicial Ethics
Lawyers, judges and educators interested in the effective administration of justice.
5000 Members
Founded in: 1913

15107 American Law & Economics Association
PO Box 208245
New Haven, CT 06520-8245
203-432-7801; *Fax:* 203-432-7225
ALEA@yale.edu; www.amlecon.org
Kathryn Spier, President
Ian Ayres, Vice President
Keith N. Hylton, Secretary-Treasurer
Dedicated to the advancement of economic understanding of law and related areas of public policy and regulation.
Founded in: 1991

15108 American Law Institute
4025 Chestnut St
Suite 5
Philadelphia, PA 19104-3099
215-243-1600
800-253-6397; *Fax:* 215-243-1636
ali@ali.org; www.ali.org
Social Media: Facebook, Twitter, LinkedIn, Vimeo
Roberta Cooper Ramo, President
Douglas Laycock, 1st Vice President
Lee H. Rosenthal, 2nd Vice President
Julie Scribner, Chief Financial Officer
Stephanie A. Middleton, Deputy Director
A private, nonprofit organization that seeks to promote the clarification and simplification of the law through legal research and reform activities.
Founded in: 1923
Mailing list available for rent

15109 American Law Institute Continuing Legal Education Group (ALI CLE)
4025 Chestnut St
Suite 5
Philadelphia, PA 19104
215-243-1600
800-253-6397; *Fax:* 215-243-1664
ali@ali.org; www.ali-cle.org
Julie Scribner, CFO and Director
Nancy Mulloy-Bonn, Chief CLE Content Officer
Nancy Cline, Customer Service/MCLE Director
Diane Schnitzer, Director of Human Resources
Frank Paul Tomasello, Director
Provides continuing legal education courses, books, and periodicals for practicing attorneys and others in the legal profession. This organization is a collaborative effort of the ALI and the ABA.
Founded in: 2012

15110 American Lawyers Auxiliary
321 North Clark Street
Chicago, IL 60610-4714
312-988-6387; *Fax:* 312-988-5494
moisantj@staff.abanet.org;
www.americanlawyersauxiliary.org
Social Media: Facebook, RSS
Sue Patterson, President
Anne Santorelli, First Vice President
Marilyn McDowell, Second Vice President
Connie Meigs, Secretary
Sharon Chappelear, Treasurer
Acts as a clearinghouse for state and local groups throughout the country and suggests educational programs pertaining to the law. Encourages members to volunteer their services.
75M Members
Founded in: 1958

15111 American Lawyers Newspapers Group
1730 M Street NW
Washington, DC 20036-4513
202-457-0686
Supports all those involved in the reporting of legal issues. Publishes a weekly newsletter.
Founded in: 1977

15112 American Prepaid Legal Services Institute
321 N Clark Street
Chicago, IL 60654
312-988-5751; *Fax:* 312-932-6436
info@aplsi.org
glsaonline.org
Social Media: Facebook, Twitter, LinkedIn
Nicolle Schippers, President
Stephen Ginsberg, Treasurer
Jean Clauson, Secretary
Professional trade organization representing the legal services plan industry. The members include lawyers, sponsor representatives, administrators and marketers of legal service plans. These people have invested their time, money and organizational resources to build legal service plans into the premier mechanism for supplying affordable legal services.
Founded in: 1975

15113 American Society for Legal History
185 West Broadway
PO Box R
New York, NY 10013
574-631-6984; *Fax:* 574-631-3595
walter.f.pratt.1@nd.edu; www.aslh.net
Michael Grossberg, President
Sally Hadden, Secretary
Craig Evan Klafter, Treasurer
Rebecca J. Scott, President-Elect
Exhibits relating to legal history and its uses in formulating legal policy, decisions and actions; unearthing historical items; and preserving legal and legislative records.
1200 Members
Founded in: 1956
Mailing list available for rent

15114 American Society of Comparative Law
University of Baltimore
1420 N. Charles Street
Baltimore, MD 21201
410-837-4689; *Fax:* 410-837-4560
lschnitzer@ubalt.edu;
www.comparativelaw.org
David J. Gerber, President
Vivian Curran, Vice President
Franklin Gervurtz, Secretary
Mortimer Sellers, Treasurer
Helge Dedek, Editor
An organization of institutional and individual members devoted to study, research, and write on foreign and comparative law as well as private international law.
60 Members
Founded in: 1951
Mailing list available for rent

15115 American Society of International Law
2223 Massachusetts Ave Nw
Washington, DC 20008-2864
202-939-6000; *Fax:* 202-797-7133
services@asil.org; www.asil.org
Social Media: Facebook, Twitter, LinkedIn, Youtube
Lori Fisler Damrosch, President
Gabrielle Kirk McDonald, Honorary President
Mark Agrast, Executive Director
Matthew Gomez, Membership Manager
Michael Farley, Director of Development
Supports all those involved with overseas litigation. Publishes monthly newsletter.
4000 Members
Founded in: 1906
Mailing list available for rent

15116 American Society of Notaries
PO Box 5707
Tallahassee, FL 32314-5707
850-671-5164; *Fax:* 850-671-5165;
www.asnnotary.org
Kathleen Butler, Executive Director
Carly Hayes, Member Services Director
Helps to organize, improve and uphold high standards for notaries public.
21M Members
Founded in: 1965

15117 American Society of Trial Consultants
10534 York Road
Suite 102
Hunt Valley, MD 21030
410-560-7949; *Fax:* 410-560-2563
ASTCOffice@astcweb.org; www.astcweb.org
Richard Jenson, President
Ronald Matlon, Ph.D., Executive Director
Bill Grimes, Treasurer & Board Member
Carol Bauss, J.D., Secretary & Board Member
Members come from diverse professional fields: communication, psychology, theatre, marketing, linguistics, political science and law.
500+ Members
Founded in: 1982
Mailing list available for rent

15118 American Society of Trial Consultants Foun dation
10951 West Pico Blvd.
Suite 203
Los Angeles, CA 90064
424-832-3641
info@astcfoundation.org;
www.astcfoundation.org
Daniel Wolfe, J.D., Ph.D., Board of Director
Karen Ohnemus Lisko, Ph.D., Board of Director
Mark Modlin, M.S., N.C.C., Board of Director
Ken Broda-Bahm, Ph.D., Board of Director
Ted Donner, Esq., Board of Director
Founded in: 2004

15119 Association of American Law Schools
1614 20th Street, Northwest
Washington, DC 20009-1001
202-296-8851; *Fax:* 202-296-8869
aals@aals.org; www.aals.org
Social Media: Facebook, Twitter, LinkedIn, YouTube, RSS
Brian Harrison, Staff Accountant
Judith Areen, Executive Director/CEO
Pablo Molina, Chief Information Officer
Melinda Price, Communications Coordinator
Tim Bloomquist, Facilities Manager
An association of law schools that serves as the law teachers' learned society.
Founded in: 1900
Mailing list available for rent

15120 Association of Corporate Counsel
1025 Connecticut Ave NW
Suite 200
Washington, DC 20036-5425
202-293-4103; *Fax:* 202-293-4701
acc.chair@acc.com; www.acc.com
Social Media: Facebook, Twitter, LinkedIn, RSS
Sabine Chalmers, Chair
Iohann Le Frapper, Vice-Chair
William Mordan, Treasurer
Mary Kennard, Secretary
Jan Alonzo, Director
Lawyers who practice law in a corporation or other private sector entity and do not hold themselves out to the public to practice law.
15000 Members
Founded in: 1982
Mailing list available for rent

15121 Association of Family and Conciliation
6525 Grand Teton Plaza
Madison, WI 53719
608-664-3750; *Fax:* 608-664-3751
afcc@afccnet.org; www.afccnet.org
Social Media: Facebook, Twitter, LinkedIn, RSS
Hon. Peter Boshier, President
Annette T. Burns, JD, Vice President
Peter Salem, MA, Executive Director
Leslye Hunter, MA, LMFT, Associate Director
Carly Wieman, BA, Program Director
AFCC is an interdisciplinary, international association of professionals dedicated to improving the lives of children and families through the resolution of family conflict.
3700 Members
Founded in: 1963

15122 Association of Insolvency and Restructuring Advisors
221 Stewart Ave
Suite 207
Medford, OR 97501-3647
541-858-1665; *Fax:* 541-858-9187
aira@aira.org; www.aira.org
Social Media: Facebook, Twitter, LinkedIn
Matthew Schwartz, CIRA, Chairman
Thomas Morrow, CIRA, President
David Payne, CIRA, CDBV, Vice President - Conferences
Joel Waite, Vice President - Development
Grant Newton, Executive Director
Disseminates judicial and financial information relating to insolvency proceedings as well as offering methods to increase skills needed in these cases. Also administers the (CIRA) Certified Insolvency and Reorganization Account Program.
1250 Members
Founded in: 1984

15123 Association of Legal Administrators
8700 W. Bryn Mawr Ave.
Suite 110S
Chicago, IL 60631-3512

847-267-1252; *Fax:* 847-267-1329
publications@alanet.org; www.alanet.org
Social Media: Facebook, Twitter, LinkedIn

Paul Farnsworth, President
Oliver Yandle, JD, CAE, Executive Director
Renee Tibbetts, Director of Administration
Gwen Biasi, CAE, Director of Marketing
Michelle Goldberg, Sr. Director Marketing

Professional support for management of private law firms and other legal organizations worldwide.
10000 Members
Founded in: 1971

15124 Association of Professional Responsibility Lawyers (APRL)
20 South Clark Street
Suite 1050
Chicago, IL 60603

312-782-4396; *Fax:* 312-782-4725
admin@aprl.net
aprl.net

Arthur J Lachman, President
Charles Lundberg, President-Elect
Lynda C Shely, Secretary
Donald Campbell, Treasurer

An organization of lawyers who concentrate on professional responsibilities issues.
300 Members
Founded in: 1990

15125 Association of Prosecuting Attorneys
1615 L St. NW
Suite 1100
Washington, DC 20036

202-861-2480; *Fax:* 202-223-4688
info@apainc.org; www.apainc.org
Social Media: Facebook, Twitter

David LaBahn, President & CEO
Steven Jansen, VP & COO

Advocacy body and global forum focused on proactive and innovative prosecutorial practices.

15126 Biz Law Association
PO Box 247
Springdale, UT 84767-0247

Fax: 435-635-9817

Suppports all those involved in business law, especially business owners and managers. Publishes newsletter.

15127 Business & Legal Reports
100 Winners Circle
Suite 300
Brentwood, TN 37027

860-510-0100
800-727-5257; *Fax:* 860-510-7225
service@blr.com; www.blr.com
Social Media: Facebook, Twitter, LinkedIn

Robert L Brady, JD, Founder
Dan Oswald, Chief Executive Officer
Elizabeth Petersen, Vice President of Healthcare
Lawton Miller, Chief Financial Officer
Brad Forrister, VP, Training and Legal

Provides essential tools for safety and environmental compliance and training needs.
32 Members
Mailing list available for rent

15128 Center for Professional Responsibility
American Bar Association
321 North Clark Street
Chicago, IL 60654

312-988-5000
800-285-2221; *Fax:* 312-988-5491
cpr@staff.abanet.org; www.americanbar.org
Social Media: Facebook, Twitter, LinkedIn

James R. Silkenat, President
Jack L. Rives, Executive Director
Robert M. Carlson, Chair, House of Delegates
Lucian T. Pera, Treasurer
Cara Lee T. Neville, Secretary

Since 1978, the Center has provided national leadership and vision in developing and interpreting standards and scholarly resources in legal ethics, professional regulation, professionalism and client protection mechanisms.
Founded in: 1878
Mailing list available for rent

15129 Center on Children and the Law
American Bar Association Young Lawyers Division
1050 Connecticut Ave. N.W.
Suite 400
Washington, DC 20036

202-662-1000
800-285-2221; *Fax:* 202-662-1755
ctrchildlaw@abanet.org; www.americanbar.org
Social Media: Facebook, Twitter, LinkedIn

James R. Silkenat, President
Jack L. Rives, Executive Director
Robert M. Carlson, Chair, House of Delegates
Lucian T. Pera, Treasurer
Cara Lee T. Neville, Secretary

This is a program of the Young Lawyers Division that aims to improve children's lives through advances in law, justice, knowledge, practice and public policy. Areas of expertise include child abuse and neglect, child welfare and protective services system enhancement, foster care, family preservation, termination of parental rights, parental substance abuse, adolescent health, and domestic violence.
15 Members
Founded in: 1878

15130 Commercial Law League of America
1000 N. Rand Rd.
Suite 214
Wauconda, IL 60084

312-240-1400
800-978-2552; *Fax:* 847-526-3993
info@clla.org; www.clla.org
Social Media: Facebook, Twitter, LinkedIn, YouTube

Robert S. Bernstein, President
Jeff Henderson, Executive Vice President
Casey Henderson, Executive Assistant
Kate Friedman, Marketing Manager
Ann Scheible, Membership Services

Supports those involved in bankruptcy, collections, debt and insolvency legislation. Publishes quarterly magazine and weekly e-newsletter.
1500 Members
Founded in: 1895
Mailing list available for rent

15131 Commission on Mental & Physical Disability Law
American Bar Association
1050 Connecticut Ave. N.W.
Suite 400
Washington, DC 20036

202-662-1000
800-285-2221; *Fax:* 202-442-3439
cdr@americanbar.org; www.americanbar.org
Social Media: Facebook, Twitter, LinkedIn

Mark D. Agrast, Esq., Chair
Amy L. Allbright, Director
M. Tovah Miller, Program Specialist
Michael J. Stratton, Administrative Coordinator
Brandon M. Moore-Rhodes, Technology Associate

The Commission's mission is 'to promote the ABA's commitment to justice and the rule of law for persons with mental, physical, and sensory disabilities and to promote their full and equal participation in the legal profession.' The Commission consists of 15 members appointed by the ABA President-elect on an annual basis. It meets bi-annually at its headquarters in Washington, D.C., to map out future plans and to direct the current activities.
15 Members
Founded in: 1973
Mailing list available for rent

15132 Copyright Society of The USA
1 East 53rd Street
8th Floor
New York, NY 10022

www.csusa.org
Social Media: Facebook, Twitter, LinkedIn

Eric J. Schwartz, President
Nancy E. Wolff, Vice President
Michael Donaldson, Treasurer
Judith Finell, Secretary
Kaitland Kubat, Director of Operations
Founded in: 1953

15133 Council of State Governments
2760 Research Park Drive
PO Box 11910
Lexington, KY 40578-1910

859-244-8000
800-800-1910; *Fax:* 859-244-8001
press@csg.org; www.csg.org
Social Media: Facebook, Twitter, LinkedIn, YouTube, RSS

Sen. Carl Marcellino, Chair
Brian Sandoval, President
David Adkins, Executive Director/CEO
Carl Marcellino, Vice Chair
Mark Norris, Chair-Elect
Founded in: 1933
Mailing list available for rent

15134 Council on Legal Education Opportunity
1101 Mercantile Lane
Suite 294
Largo, MD 20774

240-582-8600
866-886-4343; *Fax:* 240-582-8605
cleo@cleoinc.org; www.cleoscholars.org
Social Media: Facebook, Twitter

Cassandra Sneed Ogden, Executive Director
Bernetta J Hayes, Admissions Administrator
Leigh R. Allen II, Mentoring & Development Director
Lynda Cevallos, Pre-Law Coordinator
Julie D Long, Project Research Assistant

Provides law school preparation assistance for minority and disadvantaged students. Program is six-week summer institute paid for by the program. Scholarship of approximately $16,000 for the three years of law study is granted to selected and certified students, after completion of the summer program.

15135 Council on Licensure, Enforcement and Regulation
403 Marquis Ave
Suite 200
Lexington, KY 40502-2104

859-269-1289; *Fax:* 859-231-1943
rbrown@clearhq.org; www.clearhq.org
Social Media: Facebook, Twitter, LinkedIn

Robin Jenkins, President
Adam Parfitt, Executive Director
Rosa Brown, Administrative Associate
Lisa Eads, Marketing & Communications
Jodie Markey, Senior Program Coordinator

Supports all those involved in occupational and professional testing and credentialing. Publishes bi-annual magazine.
Mailing list available for rent

15136 DRI-The Voice Of The Defense Bar
55 W. Monroe Street
Suite 2000
Chicago, IL 60603
312-951-1101; *Fax:* 312-795-0749
dri@dri.org; www.dri.org
Social Media: Facebook, Twitter, LinkedIn, Youtube
Laura E. Proctor, President
John F. Kuppens, First Vice President
Toyja E. Kelley, Second Vice President
Kathleen M. Guilfoyle, Secretary-Treasurer
John Parker Sweeney, President-Elect
Service organization to improve the administration of justice and defense lawyers' skills.
Founded in: 1960

15137 Education Law Association
2121 Euclid Avenue
LL 212
Cleveland, OH 44115-2214
216-523-7377; *Fax:* 216-687-5284
ela@educationlaw.org; www.educationlaw.org
Social Media: Facebook, Twitter, LinkedIn
Patrick D. Pauken, J.D., Ph.D., President
Lynn Rossi Scott, J.D, Vice President
Cate K. Smith, J.D., M.P.A, Executive Director
Pat Petrusky, Member Services Coordinator
Pamela Hardy, Publications Specialist
Brings together educational and legal scholars and practitioners to inform and advance educational policy and practice through knowledge of the law. Together, our professional community anticipates trends in educational law and supports scholarly research through the highest value print and electronic publications, conferences, seminars and professional forums.
1400 Members
Founded in: 1954

15138 Environmental Law Alliance Worldwide
1412 Pearl St.
Eugene, OR 97401
541-687-8454; *Fax:* 541-687-0535
elawus@elaw.org; www.elaw.org
Bern Johnson, Executive Director
Attorneys, scientists and others advocating for a healthy planet.

15139 Equal Justice Works
1730 M Street NW
Suite 1010
Washington, DC 20036-4511
202-466-3686; *Fax:* 202-429-9766
mail@equaljusticeworks.org;
www.equaljusticeworks.org
Social Media: Facebook, Twitter, LinkedIn, Youtube, Flickr
Kim Koopersmith, Chair
David Stern, Executive Director
Jeanne Van Vlandren, Chief Operating Officer
Tammy Sun, Senior Manager, Fellowships
Anne Bloom, Director of Public Programs
Founded by law students dedicated to surmounting barriers to equal justice that affect millions of low income individuals and families. Equal Justice organizes, trains and supports public service minded law students, and in creating summer and postgraduate public interest jobs.
Founded in: 1986
Mailing list available for rent

15140 Federal Bar Association
1220 North Fillmore St.
Suite 444
Arlington, VA 22201
571-481-9100; *Fax:* 571-481-9090
fba@fedbar.org; www.fedbar.org
Social Media: Facebook, Twitter, LinkedIn
Matthew B. Moreland, President
Mark K. Vincent, President Elect
Michael J. Newman, Treasurer
Karen Silberman, Executive Director
Heather Gaskins, Director of Development
Founded in: 1920

15141 Federal Circuit Bar Association
1620 Eye St NW
Suite 801
Washington, DC 20006-4035
202-466-3923; *Fax:* 202-833-1061
ehaugFCBA@FLHlaw.com;
www.fedcirbar.org
Edgar H. Haug, Esquire, President
James E. Brookshire, Executive Director
Marcia Foster, Office Operations
Jeremy Atkinson, IT/Administration
Darren Davis, Membership Coordinator
FCBA is a national organization of attorneys who practice before the United States Court of Appeals for the Federal Circuit.
Mailing list available for rent

15142 Federal Communications Bar Association
1020 19th St NW
Suite 325
Washington, DC 20036-6101
202-293-4000; *Fax:* 202-293-4317
fcba@fcba.org; www.fcba.org
Christopher J. Wright, President
Julie M. Kearney, Secretary
Natalie G. Roisman, Assistant Secretary
Erin L. Dozier, Treasurer
Lee G. Petro, Assistant Treasurer
A nonprofit organization of attorneys and other professionals involved in the development, interpretation, implementation and practice of communications law and policy.
3000 Members
Founded in: 1936
Mailing list available for rent

15143 Federal Mediation & Conciliation Service
2100 K St NW
Washington, DC 20427
202-606-8100; *Fax:* 202-606-4251
jpinto@fmcs.gov; www.fmcs.gov
John Pinto, Manager of Field Operations

15144 Federation of Defense & Corporate Counsel
11812 N 56th St
Tampa, FL 33617-1528
813-983-0022; *Fax:* 813-988-5837;
www.thefederation.org
Social Media: Facebook, Twitter, LinkedIn
Victoria H. Roberts, Board Chair
Smith Moore Leatherwood, President
Martha J. Streeper, FDCC Executive Director
Michael W. Streeper, FDCC Financial Director
Susan J. Coone, Executive Administration
The objective and purposes of this Federation are to establish and maintain an organization consisting of members of the bar who are actively engaged in the legal aspects of the insurance business, executives of insurance companies an associations and corporate counsel engaged in the defense of claims; to assist in establishing standards for providing competent, efficient and economical legal services; to encourage and provide for legal education of the members of this Federation.
Founded in: 1960

15145 First Amendment Lawyers Association
123 W. Madison St.
Suite 3100
Chicago, IL 60602
312-236-0606; *Fax:* 312-236-9264
wgiampietro@wpglawyers.com;
www.firstamendmentlawyers.org
Wayne Gianpetro, General Counsel
Lawyers concentrating on defending clients under the first amendment of the Constitution.
180 Members
Founded in: 1972

15146 Hispanic National Bar Association
1020 19th Street NW
Suite 505
Washington, DC 20036
202-223-4777; *Fax:* 202-223-2324
info@hnba.com; www.hnba.com
Social Media: Facebook, Twitter, RSS
Robert Maldonado, President
Alba Cruz-Hacker, HNBA COO & Executive Director
Anjanette Cabrera, VP of Membership
Jaime Areizaga-Soto, VP of Regions & Affiliates
Raquel Matas, VP of External Affairs
Supports all Latino attorneys and legal professionals with publications and educational conferences.
25000 Members
Founded in: 1972
Mailing list available for rent

15147 Institute of Management & Administration
3 Bethesda Metro Center
Suite 250
Bethesda, MD 20814-5377
703-341-3500
800-372-1033; *Fax:* 800-253-0332
customercare@bna.com; www.ioma.com
Social Media: Facebook, Twitter, LinkedIn, YouTube
Gregory C. McCaffery, CEO & President
Sue Martin, Chief Operating Officer
Jean Lockhart, Chief of Staff
Michael Newborn, VP/Chief Security Officer
Rich Thompson, Chief Technology Officer
An independent source of exclusive business management information for experienced senior and middle management professionals.

15148 Inter-American Bar Association
1889 F Street, NW
3rd. Floor, Suite 355
Washington, DC 20006
202-466-5944; *Fax:* 202-466-5946
iaba@iaba.org; www.iaba.org
Social Media: Facebook, Twitter, LinkedIn, YouTube
Alejandro Lapad£, President
Alejandro Solano, Vice President
Tina di Battista, Secretary
The main purposes of this association are to establish and maintain relations among organizations of lawyers, national and local, in the Americas; to provide a forum for the exchange of views; to advance the science of jurisprudence particularly in the study of comparative law; to promote uniformity of the law; to disseminate knowledge of the laws; to promote the Rule of

Law and the administration of justice; to preserve and defend human rights and liberties.
3M Members
Founded in: 1940

15149 International Association of Defense Counsel
303 West Madison
Suite 925
Chicago, IL 60606-3401
312-368-1494; *Fax:* 312-368-1854
info@iadclaw.org; www.iadclaw.org
Social Media: Facebook, Twitter, LinkedIn
Joseph E. O'Neil, President
Mary Beth Kurzak, Executive Director
Amy O'Maley, Esq., Director, Professional Development
Carmela Balice, Senior Manager, Member Services
Ashley Fitzgerald, Manager, Communications
Offers continuing legal education and conducts research projects.
Cost: $650.00
2.5M Members
Founded in: 1920

15150 International Bar Association
1667 K Street, NW
Suite 1230
Washington, DC 20006
202-827-3250; *Fax:* 202-733-5657
iba@int-bar.org; www.ibanet.org
Social Media: Facebook, Twitter, LinkedIn, YouTube
David W Rivkin, President
Martin Solc, Vice President
Horacio Bernardes-Neto, Secretary-General
Mark Ellis, Executive Director
Ele Dexter, Executive Assistant
Founded in: 1947

15151 International BarAssociation
1667 K Street, NW
Suite 1230
Washington, DC 20006
202-827-3250; *Fax:* 202-733-5657;
www.ibanet.org
Social Media: Facebook, Twitter, LinkedIn, YouTube
David W Rivkin, President
Martin Solc, Vice President
Horacio Bernardes-Neto, Secretary-General
Mark Ellis, Executive Director
Ele Dexter, Executive Assistant
Founded in: 1947

15152 International Paralegal Management Association
980 N. Michigan Ave
Suite 1400
Chicago, IL 60611
312-214-4991; *Fax:* 888-662-9155;
www.theipma.org
Social Media: Facebook, Twitter, LinkedIn
Victoria L. Snook, President
Gary L. Melhuish, Vice President - Membership
Lynda S. McNie, Secretary-Treasurer
Jennifer Karns, Vice President - Trends & Positions
Larry C. Smith, CAE, Executive Director
Founded in: 1984

15153 International Probate Research Association
c/o Josh Butler & Company
PO Box 27
Cuyahoga Falls, OH 44222-0027
330-506-6400
inforequest@joshbutler.com;
www.lostheir.com/ipa.htm
Josh Butler, President
IPRA members are probate research companies.
Founded in: 1989

15154 International Society of Barristers
210 Science Drive
802 Legal Research Building
Durham, NC 27708-0360
919-613-7085; *Fax:* 734-764-8309
reedj@umich.edu
isob.com
John W Reed, Administrative Secretary
Members are trial lawyers interested in encouraging advocacy under the adversary system and preserving trial by jury.
750 Members
Founded in: 1965

15155 Investigative Professionals, Inc.
PO Box 35
Hardyville, KY 42746
928-451-1598; *Fax:* 877-657-6691;
www.investigativeprofessionals.com
Social Media: Facebook, Twitter, Google+, Blogger
Larry Troxel
NALI was formed with its primary focus to conduct investigations related to litigation. Membership in NALI is open to all professional legal investigators who are actively engaged in negligence investigations for the plaintiff and/or criminal defense, and who are emplyoed by investigative firms, law firms or public defender agencies.
Founded in: 1996
Mailing list available for rent

15156 Japanese American Society for Legal Studies
University of WA Law School-1100 NE Cam.
Seattle, WA 98105
206-233-9292; *Fax:* 206-685-4469
John Haley, Editor
Association for those interested in Japanese law and legal issues.

15157 Law and Society Association
383 South University Street
Suite 205
Salt Lake City, UT 84112
801-581-3219; *Fax:* 888-292-5515
lsa@lawandsociety.org;
www.lawandsociety.org
Social Media: Facebook, Twitter, LinkedIn
Valerie Hans, President
Susan Olson, Executive Director
Kris Monty, Administrative and Events Manager
Megan Crowley, Communication Specialist
Susan Olson, Executive Director
Founded in: 1964

15158 Legal Education and Admissions to the Bar Association
321 N Clark Street
21st Floor
Chicago, IL 60611-4403
312-988-5000
800-285-2221; *Fax:* 312-988-5681;
www.abanet.org/legaled/resources
Social Media: Facebook, Twitter
Barry Currier, Managing Director
William E. Adams, Deputy Managing Director
Camille deJorna, Associate Consultant
Carl A. Brambrink, Director of Operations
Beverly Holmes, Program Associate
Association for state bar admission administrators in the United States and its territories.
10000 Members
Founded in: 1878
Mailing list available for rent

15159 Legal Marketing Association
330 North Wabash Ave.
Suite 2000
Chicago, IL 60611
312-321-6898; *Fax:* 312-673-6894
membersupport@legalmarketing.org;
www.legalmarketing.org
Social Media: Facebook, Twitter, LinkedIn, YouTube
Timothy B. Corcoran, President
Susan Lane, Director of Operations
Lisa Rottler, Membership Services Coordinator
Adrianne Stokes, Membership Services Associate
Betsi Roach, Executive Director
Founded in: 1985

15160 Maritime Law Association of the United States
400 Poydras Street
27th Floor Texaco Center
New Orleans, LA 70130-324
504-680-8433; *Fax:* 904-421-8437;
www.mlaus.org
Robert B. Parrish, President
Robert G. Clyne, First VP
Harold K. Watson, Second VP
William Robert Connor III, Treasurer
David J. Farrell, Secretary
To advance reforms in the Maritime Law of the United States, to facilitate justice in its administration to promote uniformity in its enactment and interpretation, to furnish a forum for the discussion and consideration of problems affecting the Maritime Law and its administration to participate as a constituent member of the Comite Maritime International and as an affiliated organization of the American Bar Association.
Founded in: 1899
Mailing list available for rent

15161 Mid-America Association of Law Libraries
E-Mail: jeri_hopkins@ca8.uscourts.gov;
www.aallnet.org/chapter/maall/
Cynthia Bassett, President
Jennifer Prilliman, Vice President/ President Elect
Erika Cohn, Secretary
Jenny Watson, Treasurer
Association for suppliers of law library equipment, supplies and services.
Founded in: 1973

15162 NALS/The Association For Legal Professionals
8159 East 41st Street
#210
Tulsa, OK 74145
918-582-5188; *Fax:* 918-582-5907
info@nals.org; www.nals.org
Social Media: Facebook, Twitter, LinkedIn, RSS, Youtube, Google+, Flickr
Carl H. Morrison, PP-SC, AACP, President
Tammy Hailey, CAE, Executive Director
April Collins, Meetings & Communications Manager

Saundra Bates, Membership Services Manager
Melissa Wells, Certification/Education

Supports all those involved with the technology of the legal profession and the education and training of the legal administrative staff. Publishes quarterly magazine. NALS is dedicated to enhancing the competencies and contributions of members in the legal field.
Founded in: 1929
Mailing list available for rent

15163 National Academy of Elder Law Attorneys
1577 Spring Hill Road
Suite 220
Vienna, VA 22182-2223

703-942-5711; *Fax:* 703-563-9504
naela@naela.org; www.naela.org

Shirley Berger Whitenack, President
Hyman G. Darling, CELA, CAP, Vice President
Peter G. Wacht, CAE, Executive Director
Ann Watkins, Operations Manager
Courtney White, Marketing Coordinator

Non-profit association for attorneys specializing in Elder Law and Special Needs Law.
4200 Members
Founded in: 1987

15164 National American Indian Court Clerks Association
National Association of Tribal Court Personnel
920 Spring Creek Circle
Green Bay, WI 54311
Robert Miller, President

Devoted to upgrading the integrity capabilities and management of tribal courts through training, testing and certification of court clerks and court administrators.
257 Members

15165 National American Indian Court Judges
1942 Broadway
Suite 215
Boulder, CO 80303

303-449-4112; *Fax:* 303-449-4038
info@naicja.org; www.naicja.org
Social Media: Facebook, Youtube

Hon. Jill E. Tompkins, President
Richard Blake, First VP
Kevin Briscoe, Second VP
Winona Tanner, Treasurer
Catherine Bryan, Associate Director

National voluntary association of tribal court judges. Primarily devoted to the support of the American Indian and Alaska Native justice systems through education, information sharing and advocacy.
256 Members
Founded in: 1969
Mailing list available for rent

15166 National Association for Community Mediation
PO Box 3376
STE 252
Cumming, GA 30028

602-633-4213; *Fax:* 202-545-8873
jordway@nafcm.org; www.nafcm.org
Social Media: Facebook, Twitter, LinkedIn, Youtube, Blogger, Google+

Joanne Galindo, Senior Director
Victoria Tobin, Executive Director
D.G. Mawn, Associate Executive Director
LaDessa Croucher, Secretary
Laura Jeffords, Treasurer

Supports the maintenance and growth of community-based mediation program and processes: presents a compelling voice in appropriate policy-making, legislative, professional, and other arenas; and encourages the development and sharing of resources for these efforts.
779 Members
Founded in: 1994
Mailing list available for rent

15167 National Association for Court Management
300 Newport Avenue
Williamsburg, VA 23185-4147

757-259-1841
800-616-6165; *Fax:* 757-259-1520
nacm@ncsc.org; www.nacmnet.org
Social Media: Facebook, Twitter, LinkedIn

David W. Slayton, President
Stephanie Hess, Vice President
Scott C. Griffith, Secretary/Treasurer

Members are clerks of court, court administration and others serving in a court management capacity.
1700 Members
Founded in: 1985
Mailing list available for rent

15168 National Association for Legal Career Professionals
1220 19th Street NW
Suite 401
Washington, DC 20036-2405

202-835-1001; *Fax:* 202-835-1112
info@nalp.org; www.nalp.org
Social Media: Facebook, Twitter, LinkedIn, YouTube

Jean A. Durling, President
Beth Moeller, Vice-President for Member Services
Christina Fox, Vice-President for Finance
James G. Leipold, Executive Director
Frederick E. Thrasher, Deputy Director

Deals with issues such as career planning, recruiting and ethics.
Founded in: 1971

15169 National Association of Attorneys General
2030 M Street Nw
8th Floor
Washington, DC 20036

202-326-6000; *Fax:* 202-331-1427
feedback@naag.org; www.naag.org
Social Media: Facebook, Twitter

Jim McPherson, NAAG Executive Director
Chris Toth, NAAG Deputy Executive Director
Al Lama, NAAG Chief of Staff
Jeffrey Hunter, NAAG Executive Assistant
Marjorie Tharp, NAAG Communications Director

Fosters interstate cooperation on legal and law enforcement issues, conducts policy research and analysis, provides advocacy.
56 Members
Founded in: 1907
Mailing list available for rent: 56 names

15170 National Association of Black Criminal
1801 Fayetteville Street 106
Whiting Criminal Justice Building
Durham, NC 27707

919-683-1801
866-846-2225; *Fax:* 919-683-1903
office@nabcj.org; www.nabcj.org
Social Media: Facebook, Twitter, RSS

Carlyle I. Holder, President
Terri Mcgee, Vice President
Vernise Robinson, Secretary
Charles Lockett, Treasurer
Andre Turner, Assistant Treasurer
Founded in: 1974

15171 National Association of Blacks in Criminal Justice
1801 Fayetteville St.
106 Whiting Criminal Justice Bldg.
Durham, NC 27707

919-683-1801
866-846-2225; *Fax:* 919-683-1903
office@nabcj.org; www.nabcj.org
Social Media: Facebook, Twitter, RSS

Carlyle Holder, President
Terrie McGee, Vice President
Vernise Robinson, Secretary
Charles Lockett, Treasurer

Supports all black persons who are involved in the criminal justice system. Hosts annual trade show.
Founded in: 1974

15172 National Association of College and University Attorneys
One Dupont Circle
Suite 620
Washington, DC 20036-1134

202-833-8390; *Fax:* 202-296-8379
nacua@nacua.org; www.nacua.org

Kathleen Curry, CEO
Jeanna L. Grimes, Manager of Membership and Marketing
John R. Bishop, Director of Information Services
Meredith L. McMillan, Meetings and Events Planner
Paul L. Parsons, Deputy CEO

Educates attorneys and administrative executives about campus legal issues.
Mailing list available for rent

15173 National Association of Consumer Advocates
1215 17th Street NW
5th Floor
Washington, DC 20036

202-452-1989; *Fax:* 202-452-0099
info@consumeradvocates.org;
www.consumeradvocates.org
Social Media: Facebook, Twitter

Stuart Rossman, Co-Chair
Kirsten Keefe, Co-Chair
Daniel Blinn, Treasurer
Leslie Bailey, Secretary
Ira Rheingold, Executive Director

15174 National Association of Counsel for Children
13123 E. 16th Avenue
B390
Aurora, CO 80045

303-864-5320
Advocate@NACCchildlaw.org;
www.naccchildlaw.org
Social Media: Facebook, LinkedIn, Blog

Gerard Glynn, MS, JD / LLM, President
H.D. Kirkpatrick, Vice President
Kendall Marlowe, Executive Director
Daniel Trujillo, Certification Director
Sara Whalen, Membership Director
Founded in: 1977

15175 National Association of County Civil Attorneys
1100 17th St NW
Second Floor
Washington, DC 20036-4619

202-783-5550; *Fax:* 202-783-1583
info@naccho.org; www.naccho.org
Social Media: Facebook, Twitter, LinkedIn, RSS, Blogger, Pinterest, Tumbl

Paul Yeghiayan, President
Mark Jorritsma, Chief Operating Officer
John Mericsko, Chief Financial Officer

LaMar Hasbrouck, Executive Director
Laura Hanen, Chief, Government & Public Affairs

An affiliate of the National Association of Counties.
240 Members
Founded in: 1994
Mailing list available for rent

15176 National Association of Criminal Defense Lawyers
1660 L St NW
12th Floor
Washington, DC 20036-5632

202-872-8600; *Fax:* 202-872-8690
assist@nacdl.org; www.nacdl.org
Social Media: Facebook, Twitter, LinkedIn, YouTube

E. G. Morris, President
Rick Jones, First Vice President
Drew Findling, Second Vice President
Chris Wellborn, Treasurer
Norman L. Reimer, Executive Director

America's preeminent voluntary nar association supporting the Criminal Defense profession.
10000 Members
Founded in: 1958

15177 National Association of Legal Assistants
7666 E. 61st Street
Suite 315
Tulsa, OK 74133

918-587-6828; *Fax:* 918-582-6772
nalanet@nala.org; www.nala.org

Kelly A. LaGrave, ACP, President
Cassandra Oliver, ACP, First Vice President
Jill Francisco, ACP, Second Vice President
Debra L. Overstreet, ACP, Treasurer
Marge Dover, CAE, Executive Director

15178 National Association of Legal Investigator s
235 N. Pine Street
Lansing, MI 48933

517-702-9835
866-520-NALI; *Fax:* 517-372-1501
info@nalionline.org; www.nalionline.org
Social Media: Facebook, LinkedIn

David W. Luther, CLI, National Director
Don C. Johnson, CLI, CII, Assistant National Director
Neeta McClintock, National Secretary
Julian Vail, LLC, Association Management
John Hoda, CLI, Regional Director, Northeast Region
Founded in: 1967

15179 National Association of Legal Vendors
Juris
5106 Maryland Way
Brentwood, TN 37027-7501

615-377-3740

Mel Goldenburg, Chairman

Trade association of organizations who sell products to the legal community.
100 Members

15180 National Association of Parliamentarians (NAP)
213 South Main Street
Independence, MO 64050-3808

816-833-3892
888-627-2929; *Fax:* 816-833-3893
hq@nap2.org; www.parliamentarians.org
Social Media: Facebook, Twitter, RSS

Mary Randolph, President
James Jones, VP
Cyndy Launchbaugh, Executive Director
Courtney Emery, Membership Marketing & Comm.
Stefanie Luttrell, Administrative Coordinator

An association for those interested in parliamentary law and procedure, NAP's primary objectives are teaching, promoting, and disseminating the philosophy and principles underlying the rules of deliberative assemblies.
3500 Members
Founded in: 1930

15181 National Association of Women Lawyers
321 North Clark Street
Chicago, IL 60654

312-988-6186; *Fax:* 312-932-6450
nawl@nawl.org; www.nawl.org

Marsha L. Anastasia, President
Angela Beranek Brandt, Vice President
Jennifer A. Waters, Executive Director
Caitlin Kepple, Marketing and Development Director
Karen M. Richardson, Program Director

Promotes the advancement and welfare of women in the legal profession. NAWL is a professional association of attorneys, judges and law students serving the educational, legal and practical interests of the organized bar and women generally. Founded in 1899, long before most local and national bar associations admitted women.
800 Members
Founded in: 1899

15182 National Bar Association
1225 11th St Nw
Washington, DC 20001-4217
202-842-3900; *Fax:* 202-289-6170
headquarters@nationalbar.org;
www.nationalbar.org
Social Media: Facebook, Twitter, LinkedIn, YouTube

Benjamin Crump, President
Keith Andrew Perry, Executive Director
Chris Tinker, CFO
Heidi Franklin, Director
Nanjiba Hlemi, Director of Membership and Programs

Represents the interests of minority attorneys, offers education and research programs.
18000 Members
Founded in: 1925
Mailing list available for rent

15183 National Center for State Courts
300 Newport Ave
Williamsburg, VA 23185-4147

757-259-1819
800-616-6164; *Fax:* 757-220-0449
mmcqueen@ncsc.org; www.ncsc.org
Social Media: Facebook, Twitter, LinkedIn, Google+, Flickr, Vimeo, Pinter

David Gilbertson, Chair
Patricia W. Griffin, Vice-Chair
Mary McQueen, President
Thomas Clarke, VP, Research and Technology
Daniel Hall, Vice President of Court Consulting

Provides a forum for the state courts.
Founded in: 1971
Mailing list available for rent

15184 National College of District Attorneys
99 Canal Center Plaza
Suite 330
Alexandria, VA 22314

703-549-9222; *Fax:* 703-836-3195;
www.ndaa.org
Social Media: Facebook, Yahoo

William Fitzpatrick, President
Rick Hasey, Chief Financial Officer
Rick Hanes, Chief of Staff
Kay Chopard Cohen, Executive Director
Ann Ratnayake, Staff Attorney

Provides continuing legal education and training for prosecuting attorneys and their investigators and office administrators through programs specifically tailored to meet their needs. Programs include resident courses held each summer at the University of Houston Law Center, short courses conducted in locations throughout the country, and courses presented cooperatively with state associations and local offices.
Founded in: 1950
Mailing list available for rent

15185 National Conference of Bar Examiners
302 South Bedford Street
Madison, WI 53703-3622

608-280-8550; *Fax:* 608-280-8552
contact@ncbex.org; www.ncbex.org

Erica Moeser, President

A non-profit organization offering tests and services to state boards of bar examiners.
Founded in: 1931

15186 National Conference of Bar Foundations
ABA Division For Bar Services
321 North Clark Street
Suite 2000
Chicago, IL 60654

312-988-5344; *Fax:* 312-988-5492
info@ncbf.org; www.ncbf.org

Leonard Pataki, President
Leslie Barineau, Secretary
Alison Belfrage, Treasurer
Lorrie Albert, Secretary

Serves bar foundations in the United States and Canada; conducts biannual conferences; maintains information clearinghouses.
Founded in: 1977
Mailing list available for rent

15187 National Conference of Bar Presidents
321 North Clark Street
Suite 2000
Chicago, IL 60654-7598

312-988-5344; *Fax:* 312-988-5492
bware@staff.abanet.org; www.ncbp.org
Social Media: Facebook, Twitter

Lanneau W. Lambert Jr., President
Christine H. Hickey, Treasurer
Jennifer L. Parent, Secretary

Provides a forum for the exchange of ideas and seeks to stimulate work in bar associations.
1M Members
Founded in: 1950

15188 National Conference of Commissioners on US Law
211 E Ontario St
Suite 1300
Chicago, IL 60611-3242

312-283-5200; *Fax:* 312-915-0187
nccusl@nccusl.org; www.uniformlaws.org

John A. Sebert, Executive Director
J. Elizabeth Cotton-Murphy, Chief Administrative Officer
Robert Stein, Secretary
Carl Lisman, Treasurer
Elizabeth Cotton, Manager

Designed to foster interstate cooperation in legal issues.
Founded in: 1892
Mailing list available for rent

15189 National Conference of Women's Bar Associations
PO Box 82366
Portland, OR 97282

503-775-4396
info@ncwba.org; www.ncwba.org
Social Media: Facebook, Twitter, LinkedIn

Katherine L. Brown, President
Barbara L. Harris Chiang, Vice President - Membership
Robin Bresky, VP, Fundraising & Strategic Part.
Monica Parham, Vice-President-Finance
Celia J. Collins, Secretary

To promote and assist the growth of local and statewide women's bar associations and ideas among women's bar associations and women's bar sections of local and statewide bar associations; to serve as a vehicle for the exchange and dissemination of information and ideas among women's bar associations and women's bar sections of local and statewide bar associations.

15190 National Conference of Womens' Bar Associations
PO Box 82366
Portland, OR 97282

503-775-4396; *Fax:* 503-657-3932
info@ncwba.org; www.ncwba.org
Social Media: Facebook, Twitter, LinkedIn

Katherine L. Brown, President
Barbara L. Harris Chiang, Vice President - Membership
Robin Bresky, VP, Fundraising & Strategic Part.
Monica Parham, Vice-President-Finance
Celia J. Collins, Secretary

Supports women who are involved in the legal community and provides a forum for the exchange of ideas, thus stimulating work in bar associations.
30000 Members
Founded in: 1981
Mailing list available for rent

15191 National Court Reporters Association
12030 Sunrise Valley Drive
Suite 400
Reston, VA 20191

703-556-6272
800-272-6272; *Fax:* 703-391-0629
msic@ncra.org; www.ncraonline.org
Social Media: Facebook, Twitter, LinkedIn, Youtube, RSS

Stephen A. Zinone, RPR, President
Christine J. Willette, Vice President
Doreen Sutton, RPR, Secretary-Treasurer
Stephen A. Zinone, RPR, Secretary/Treasurer
Toni O'Neill, FAPR, RPR, Director
18000 Members
Founded in: 1899

15192 National District Attorneys Association
99 Canal Center Plaza
Suite 330
Alexandria, VA 22314-1548

703-549-9222; *Fax:* 703-836-3195;
www.ndaa.org
Social Media: Facebook, Yahoo

William Fitzpatrick, President
Rick Hasey, Chief Financial Officer
Mary McQueen, President
Thomas Clarke, VP, Research and Technology
Daniel Hall, Vice President of Court Consulting

Supports district attorneys nationwide with education, publications, and regular conferences.
7000 Members
Founded in: 1950

15193 National Federation of Paralegal Associations, Inc.
23607 Highway 99
Suite 2-C
Edmonds, WA 98026

425-967-0045; *Fax:* 425-771-9588
info@paralegals.org; www.paralegals.org
Social Media: Facebook, LinkedIn

Lisa Vessels, RP, CP, FRP, President
Allen F. Mihecoby, CLAS, RP, VP/Director of Profession Dev
Lynne-Marie Reveliotis, VP/Director of Positions and Issues
Yvonne DeAntoneo, VP/Director of Membership
Nita Serrano, RP, VP/Director of Paralegal Cert.

Nonprofit, professional organization comprising state and local paralegal associations throughout the United States and Canada. NFPA affirms the paralegal profession as an independent, self-directed profession which supports increased quality, efficiency and accessibility in the delivery of legal services. NFPA promotes the growth, development and recognition of the profession as a integral partner in the delivery of legal services.
15000 Members
Founded in: 1974

15194 National Forensic Center
17 Temple Terrace
Lawrenceville, NJ 08648

609-883-0550
800-526-5177
jon@midi.com
expertindex.com

Association for those interested in the application of scientific knowledge in litigation.

15195 National Institute for Trial Advocacy
1685 38th Street
Suite 200
Boulder, CO 80301-2735

800-225-6482; *Fax:* 720-890-7069
support@nita.org; www.nita.org

Karen Lockwood, Executive Director
Michelle Rogness, Director of Programs
Katie Grosso, Program Specialist, Public Programs
Jennifer Schneider, Director of Publications
Daniel McHugh, Director of Sales & Marketing
60 Members
Founded in: 1971

15196 National Law Foundation
P. O. Box 218
Montchanin, DE 19710

302-656-4757; *Fax:* 302-764-8697;
www.nlfcle.com

15197 National Lawyers Association
PO Box 327
Suite 400
Lee's Summit, MO 64063

844-917-1787
info@nla.org; www.nla.org
Social Media: Facebook, Twitter, LinkedIn, Pinterest, Google+

Joshua McCaig, President
Paul Brodersen, Vice President
Lenny A. Best, CEO
Jeremiah Morgan, Board Member
Cynthia Dunbar, Board Member
Founded in: 1993

15198 National Lawyers Guild
132 Nassau St
Room 922
New York, NY 10038-2486

212-679-5100; *Fax:* 212-679-2811
nlgno@nlg.org; www.nlg.org
Social Media: Facebook, Twitter

Azadeh Shahshahani, President
Heidi Boghosian, Executive Director
Natasha Bannan, Executive Vice President
Bina Ahmad, National Vice President
Camilo Romero, National Vice President

Dedicated to seeking economic justice, social equality and the right to political dissent.
5000 Members
Founded in: 1937
Mailing list available for rent

15199 National Legal Aid and Defender Associatio n
1901 Pennsylvania Avenue NW
Suite 500
Washington, DC 20006

202-452-0620; *Fax:* 202-872-1031
info@nlada.org; www.nlada100years.org

John Mauldin, Chairperson
Rosita Stanley, Vice-Chairperson
Alex Gulotta, Vice-Chairperson
Jo-Ann Wallace, President & CEO
Helen Katz, Chief Development Officer

Private, nonprofit association that dedicates all its resources to ensuring the availability of high quality legal assistance for the poor.
3500 Members
Founded in: 1911
Mailing list available for rent

15200 National Notary Association
9350 De Soto Avenue
Chatsworth, CA 91311-4926

818-739-4000
800-876-6827; *Fax:* 818-700-1942
hotline@nationalnotary.org;
www.nationalnotary.org
Social Media: Facebook, Twitter, LinkedIn, Google+

Milton G Valera, Chairman
Thomas A. Heymann, President And CEO
Deborah M Thaw, Executive VP
Rob Clarke, Chief Financial Officer
Dave Stephenson, Vice President, CIO/CTO

Supports all those involved in identity fraud and electronic notarization. Publishes newlsetter.
200M Members
Founded in: 1957

15201 National Organizations of Bar Counsel
275 N. York Street
Ste 401
Elmhurst, IL 60126

630-617-5153
BloomL@dcobc.org; www.nobc.org
Social Media: Facebook, Twitter

Paul J. Burgoyne, President
Kathleen M. Uston, Treasurer
Melinda Bentley, Secretary

NOBC is a non-proft of legal professionals whose members enforce ethics rules that regulate the professional conduct of lawyers who practice in the U.S., Canada and Australia. Via the

website, locate your local member office for information.
Founded in: 1965

15202 National Paralegal Association
23607 Highway 99
Suite 2-C
Edmonds, WA 98026

425-967-0045; *Fax:* 425-771-9588
info@paralegals.org; www.paralegals.org
Social Media: Facebook, LinkedIn

Lisa Vessels, RP, CP, FRP, President
Allen F. Mihecoby, CLAS, RP, VP/Director of Profession Dev.
Lynne Marie Reveliotis, VP & Director of Positions
Yvonne DeAntoneo, VP, Director of Membership
Nita Serrano, RP, VP, Dir. of Paralegal Certification
Founded in: 1974

15203 Native American Rights Fund
1506 Broadway St
Boulder, CO 80302-6296

303-447-8760; *Fax:* 303-443-7776
webmaster@narf.org; www.narf.org
Social Media: Facebook

Moses K. N. Haia III, Chairman
Mark Macarro, Board Vice-Chairman
John E. Echohawk, Executive Director
Michael Kennedy, Chief Financial Officer
Eric Anderson, Legal Administrative Assistant

National legal defense fund. Provides legal services and technical assistance to Indian tribes, organizations and individuals in the areas of preservation of tribal existence, protection of tribal natural resources, promotion of human rights, accountability of governments and development of Indian law.
35000 Members
Founded in: 1971
Mailing list available for rent

15204 People Against Racist Terror
PO Box 70447
Oakland, CA 94612

510-893-4648; *Fax:* 818-848-2680
info@prisonactivist.org;
www.prisonactivist.org

Michael Novick, Publisher

Association for those interested in anti-racist activism, research and education covering neo-nazi and other racist violence, efforts at conflict resolution and social justic reforms.

15205 Practising Law Institute
1177 Avenue of the Americas
2nd Floor
New York, NY 10036

212-824-5700
800-260-4754; *Fax:* 212-581-4670
cfbook@loc.gov; www.pli.edu
Social Media: Facebook, Twitter, LinkedIn, YouTtube, Pinterest

John Y Cole, Director
Anne Boni, Program Specialist

Nonprofit continuing legal education organization chartered by the Regents of the University of the State of New York. Dedicated to providing the legal community and allied professionals with the most up-to-date, revelant information and techniques which are critical to the development of a professional, competitive edge.
Founded in: 1977
Mailing list available for rent

15206 RAND Institute for Civil Justice
1776 Main Street
Santa Monica, CA 90407-3208

310-393-0411; *Fax:* 310-393-4898
webmaster@monroecc.edu; www.rand.org/icj
Social Media: Facebook, Twitter, LinkedIn, Instagram, YouTube

John L. Bartolotta, Chair
Grace S. Tillinghast, Vice Chair
Anne M. Kress, Ph.D., President
Andrea C. Wade, Ph.D., Provost/VP, Academic Services
Lloyd A. Holmes, Ph.D., Vice President, Student Services

Nonprofit research organization within the RAND Corporation dedicated to interdisciplinary, empirical research to facilitate change in the civil justice system.
1.1M Members
Founded in: 1961

15207 Rocky Mountain Mineral Law Foundation
9191 Sheridan Blvd
Suite 203
Westminster, CO 80031-3011

303-321-8100; *Fax:* 303-321-7657
igor@dramaguild.com; www.rmmlf.org
Social Media: Facebook, Twitter, Flickr, Tumblr, Youtube

Stephen Schwartz, President
Ralph Sevush, Executive Director, Business
Gary Garrison, Executive Director
Joey Stocks, Director of Publications
Deborah Murad, Director of Business Affairs
6M+ Members
Founded in: 1920
Mailing list available for rent

15208 The Center for HIV Law & Policy
65 Broadway
Suite 832
New York, NY 10006

212-430-6733; *Fax:* 212-430-6734;
www.hivlawandpolicy.org
Social Media: Facebook, Twitter, LinkedIn, Instagram

Catherine Hanssens, Executive Director
Allison Nichol, Co-Director

Center works to reduce impact of HIV on vulnerable communities.

15209 The International Association for Conflict Management
E-Mail: office@the-efa.org;
www.iacm-conflict.org
Social Media: Facebook, Twitter, LinkedIn

Karen Williams, Secretary
Robin Martin, Chapter Development
Jennifer Maybin, Education
Sheila Buff, Job List
Cassie Tuttle, Membership
Founded in: 1970

15210 The Sports Lawyers Association
12100 Sunset Hills Road
Suite 130
Reston, VA 20190

703-437-4377; *Fax:* 703-435-4390
ewa@ewa.org; www.sportslaw.org

Scott Elliott, President
Caroline W. Hendrie, Executive Director
George Dieter, Chief Operating Officer
Tracee Eason, Administrative Coordinator
Kenneth Terrell, Project Director
800 Members
Founded in: 1947

15211 Trial Lawyers Marketing
1 Boston Place
Suite 1260
Boston, MA 02108-4471

617-720-5356; *Fax:* 617-742-5417

James Sokolve, President

Provides education and marketing information to personal injury attorneys.
300 Members
Founded in: 1986

Newsletters

15212 ABA Child Law Practice
ABA Center on Children and the Law
740 15th Street, NW
Washington, DC 20005

202-662-1000
800-285-2221; *Fax:* 202-662-1755
teaguec@staff.abanet.org; www.abanet.org
Social Media: Facebook, Twitter

Laurel Bellows, President
Jack L. Rives, Executive Director
Robert M. Carlson, Chairman
Lucian T. Pera, Treasurer
Cara Lee T. Neville, Secretary

An online periodical for lawyers who advocate for children and youth, judges handling child protection-related cases, and other professionals who want to keep abreast of cutting edge legal issues affecting children. Includes litigation strategies, analyses of new laws, policies and research, and how they apply to practice, expert interviews, advice from judges, and more.
Cost: $50.00
Frequency: Online
Founded in: 1878
Mailing list available for rent

15213 ABA Washington Letter
American Bar Association Government Affairs Office
321 N Clark St
Chicago, IL 60654-7598

312-988-5000
800-285-2221; *Fax:* 202-662-1762
mcmillionr@staff.abanet.org;
www.abanet.org/poladv/home.html
Social Media: Facebook, Twitter

Thomas M. Susman, Director, GAO
Denise A. Cardman, Deputy Director
Jared D. Hess, Legislative Coordinator
Laurel Bellows, President
Jack L. Rives, Executive Director

A monthly publication produced by the GAO to report and analyze congressional and executive branch action on legislation issues of interest to the ABA and the legal profession, highlighting ABA involvment in the federal legislative process.
Cost: $30.00
Frequency: Monthly
Founded in: 1957
Mailing list available for rent

15214 ACC Docket
American Corporate Counsel Association
1025 Connecticut Ave Nw
Suite 200
Washington, DC 20036-5425

202-293- 410; *Fax:* 202-293-4701
acc.chair@acc.com; www.acc.com

Tiffani Alexander, Managing Editor
Ken Lawrence, Director Publishing
Fred Krebs, President/CEO
Moustafa W. Abdel-Kader, Marketing Manager
David Barre, Director Communications
Frequency: Monthly
Mailing list available for rent

15215 ALA News
Association of Legal Administrators
75 Tri-State International
Suite 222
Lincolnshire, IL 60069-4435

847-267-1252; *Fax:* 847-267-1329
publications@alanet.org; www.alanet.org

Larry Smith, Executive Director
Debbie Thomas, Director, Accounting & Finance
Renee Mahovsky, Director, Administration/Operations
Bob Abramson, Director, Marketing & Communication
Jan Waugh, Director, Member Services

Member magazine focusing on association news and career improvements for administrators in the association.
Cost: $36.00
40 Pages
Circulation: 9000
Founded in: 1971
Mailing list available for rent
Printed in 4 colors on glossy stock

15216 ATLA Advocate
Association of Trial Lawyers of America
1050 31st Street NW
Washington, DC 20007

202-965-3500
800-424-2725; www.justice.org

Kathleen Flynn Peterson, President
Linda Lipsen, Chief Executive Officer
Charles Jeffress, Chief Operating Officer
Kathi Berge, Chief Financial Officer
Anjali Jesseramsing, Executive Vice President

Keeps association members abreast of association news. Not available by subscription. No advertising or announcements.
Cost: $5.00
Frequency: Monthly
Mailing list available for rent
Printed in 2 colors

15217 Administrative & Regulatory Law News
American Bar Association-Administrative/Regulatory
740 15th St NW
11th Floor
Washington, DC 20005-1022

202-662-1000
800-285-2221; *Fax:* 202-662-1592
knightk@staff.abanet.org; www.abanet.org
Social Media: Facebook, Twitter

Laurel Bellows, President
Jack L. Rives, Executive Director
Robert M. Carlson, Chairman
Lucian T. Pera, Treasurer
Cara Lee T. Neville, Secretary

Newsletter for Section members providing information about recent developments affecting clients and practices with features such as Supreme Court News, News From the Circuits, and more.
16 Pages
Frequency: Quarterly
Circulation: 6000
Founded in: 1878
Mailing list available for rent

15218 Admiralty Law Newsletter
American Bar Association - TIPS
Admiralty/Maritime
321 N Clark St
Chicago, IL 60654-7598

312-988-5000
800-285-2221; *Fax:* 312-988-5280
askaba@abanet.org; www.abanet.org
Social Media: Facebook, Twitter

Laurel Bellows, President
Jack L. Rives, Executive Director
Robert M. Carlson, Chairman
Lucian T. Pera, Treasurer
Cara Lee T. Neville, Secretary

Focuses on summaries of recent case law development, CLE programs in maritime law area, and information and articles on programs and projects.
Frequency: Quarterly
Founded in: 1878
Mailing list available for rent

15219 Allen's Trademark Digest
Congressional Digest Corporation
152413 29th Street NW
Washington, DC 20007-2756

202-333-7332
800-637-9915; *Fax:* 202-625-6670
ededitor@aol.com; www.trademarkdigest.com

Griff Thomas, President
Page Robinson, Publisher
Brooke Beyer, Editor

Monthly digest of citable and uncitable tradmark decisions issues by the US Patent and Trademark Office.
Cost: $695.00
Frequency: 12 per year
ISSN: 8990-191X
Founded in: 1989

15220 American Association of Visually Impaired Attorneys
American Blind Lawyers Association
c/o American Council of the Blind
2220 Wilson Blvd, Suite 650
Arlingtonn, VA 22201

202-467-5081
800-424-8666; *Fax:* 703-465-5085
info@acb.org; www.acb.org

Melanie Brunson, Executive Director
Eric Bridges, Executive Director
12000 Members
Frequency: Audio
Circulation: 150
Founded in: 1961

15221 American Corporate Counsel Association Newsletter
Americna Corporate Counsel Association
1025 Connecticut Ave NW
Suite 200
Washington, DC 20036-5425

202-293-8439; *Fax:* 202-331-7454
http://www.acc.com

Deneen Stambone, Editor

Association news.
16 Pages
Frequency: Bi-Monthly
Circulation: 9,700
Printed in 2 colors on matte stock

15222 American Foreign Law Association Newsletter
Forman Law School
140 W 62nd Street
New York, NY 10023

212-636-6844; *Fax:* 212-636-6899

James Maxelner, Publisher

Reports on programs sponsored by the Association of American Foreign Law.
Cost: $20.00
4 Pages
Frequency: Monthly

15223 American Lawyers Newspapers Group
American Lawyers Newspapers
1730 M St Nw
Suite 802
Washington, DC 20036-4550

202-296-1995; *Fax:* 202-457-0718

Ted Goldman, Manager

Supports all those involved in the reporting of legal issues.
Founded in: 1977

15224 American Notary
American Society of Notaries
PO Box 5707
Tallahassee, FL 32314

850-671-5164
800-522-3392; *Fax:* 850-671-5165;
www.notaries.org

Lisa K Fisher, Publisher
Joanna Lilly, Executive Director
Kathleen Butler, Executive Director

Legislation news.
Cost: $21.00
20 Pages
Frequency: Quarterly
Circulation: 21000
Printed in 4 colors on glossy stock

15225 American Society of International Law Newsletter
American Society of International Law
2223 Massachusetts Ave Nw
Washington, DC 20008-2864

202-939-6000; *Fax:* 202-797-7133
http://www.asil.org

Charlotte Ku, Executive Director

Association news and updates on overseas litigation.
6 Pages
Frequency: Monthly

15226 Antitrust and Trade Regulation Report
Bureau of National Affairs
1801 S Bell St
Arlington, VA 22202-4501

703-341-3000
800-372-1033; *Fax:* 800-253-0332
customercare@bna.com; www.bnabooks.com
Social Media: Facebook, Twitter, LinkedIn

Paul N Wojcik, Chairman
Gregory C. McCaffery, President and CEO
John Camp, Vice President and Chief Technology
Lisa A. Fitzpatrick, Vice President
Audrey Hipkins, Vice President

Weekly comprehensive coverage of significant competition and deceptive trade practice law developments on the federal, state and international levels.
Cost: $1894.00
Frequency: Weekly

15227 Attorneys Marketing Report
James Publishing
3505 Cadillac Avenue
Suite H
Costa Mesa, CA 92626

714-755-5450
800-440-4780; *Fax:* 714-751-2709
customer-service@jamespublishing.com;
www.jamespublishing.com

Jim Pawell, Founder/President
Linda Standke, Editor

The latest practice development tips and news for law firms from Yellow Pages advertising to referral management.
Founded in: 1981
Mailing list available for rent

15228 **BNA's Bankruptcy Law Reporter**
Bureau of National Affairs
1801 S Bell St
Arlington, VA 22202-4501

703-341-3000
800-372-1033; *Fax:* 800-253-0332
customercare@bna.com; www.bnabooks.com
Social Media: Facebook, Twitter, LinkedIn

Paul N Wojcik, Chairman
Gregory C. McCaffery, President and CEO
John Camp, Vice President and Chief Technology
Lisa A. Fitzpatrick, Vice President
Audrey Hipkins, Vice President

Weekly notification service covering various areas of bankruptcy law.
Cost: $1331.00
Frequency: Weekly

15229 **BNA's Corporate Counsel Weekly Corporate Practice Series**
Bureau of National Affairs
1801 S Bell St
Arlington, VA 22202-4501

703-341-3000
800-372-1033; *Fax:* 800-253-0332
customercare@bna.com; www.bnabooks.com
Social Media: Facebook, Twitter, LinkedIn

Paul N Wojcik, Chairman
Gregory C. McCaffery, President and CEO
John Camp, Vice President and Chief Technology
Lisa A. Fitzpatrick, Vice President
Audrey Hipkins, Vice President

A weekly roundup of the latest developments in law that affect business, including coverage of the courts, federal regulatory agencies, the executive branch, states and professional associations.
Cost: $722.00
8 Pages
Frequency: Weekly
Printed in one color on matte stock

15230 **BNA's Medicare Report**
Bureau of National Affairs
1801 S Bell St
Arlington, VA 22202-4501
703-341-3000
800-372-1033; *Fax:* 800-253-0332
customercare@bna.com; www.bnabooks.com
Social Media: Facebook, Twitter, LinkedIn

Paul N Wojcik, Chairman
Gregory C. McCaffery, President and CEO
John Camp, Vice President and Chief Technology
Lisa A. Fitzpatrick, Vice President
Audrey Hipkins, Vice President

Biweekly notification service covering legislative, regulatory and legal developments affecting or pertaining to the Medicare program; also provides information about relevant developments in the Medicaid program that could have implications for Medicare.
Cost: $1108.00
Frequency: Weekly

15231 **Bankruptcy Court Decisions**
LRP Publications
PO Box 980
Horsham, PA 19044-0980

215-784-0912
800-341-7874; *Fax:* 215-784-9639
webmaster@lrp.com; www.lrp.com

Todd Lutz, CFO
Kenneth Khan, CEO

Full-text loose leaf bankruptcy reporting service with an expanded and informative newsletter.
Cost: $900.00
Founded in: 1977
Mailing list available for rent
Printed in one color on matte stock

15232 **Bankruptcy Law Letter**
Thomson West Publishing
610 Opperman Dr
Eagan, MN 55123-1340

651-687-7000
800-344-5008; *Fax:* 651-687-5581;
www.west.thomson.com
Social Media: Facebook, Twitter, LinkedIn, Blogger, Pinterest, Tumblr, St

Charles B Cater, Executive VP
Laurie Zenner, VP

Highly specialized coverage of case developments in the bankruptcy field. No outside submissions accepted.
Cost: $621.00
Frequency: Monthly
Circulation: 3000

15233 **Biotechnology Law Report**
Mary Ann Liebert
2 Madison Ave
Larchmont, NY 10538-1947

914-834-4348
800-6 5-3 23; *Fax:* 914-834-3688
info@liebertpub.com; www.liebertpub.com/

Mary Ann Liebert, President
Gerry J Elman, Editor
Harry Matisco, Marketing

Legislative news for the world of biotechnology and science.
Cost: $1858.00
96 Pages
ISSN: 0730-031X
Founded in: 1980

15234 **Business Crime: Criminal Liability of the Business Community**
Matthew Bender and Company
11 Penn Plz
Suite 5101
New York, NY 10001-2006

212-000-1111; *Fax:* 212-244-3188

Eric Blood, Data Processing

The most complete guide to the many criminal questions that can arise in modern business practice.

15235 **Business Information Alert**
Alert Publications
401 W Fullerton Parkway
Suite 1403E
Chicago, IL 60614-2801

773-525-7594
866-492-5266; *Fax:* 773-525-7015
info@alertpub.com; www.alertpubs.com

Donna T Heroy, Publisher/Editor
Nina Wendt, Director Marketing

Newsletter for business and law librarians to help them make purchasing decisions for their companies. Includes product reviews and columns on industry news. Discounted price of $99 for non-profit organizations.
Cost: $167.00
12 Pages
ISSN: 1042-0746
Founded in: 1981

15236 **CLE Guidebook**
Law Bulletin Publishing Company
415 N State St
Suite 1
Chicago, IL 60654-8116

312-644-7800; *Fax:* 312-644-4255;
www.lawbulletin.com

Lanning Macfarland Jr, President
Bernard M Judge, Publisher
Michael Loquercio, Sales Manager

Lists hundreds of CLE courses by date, subject and provider.
Cost: $219.00
34 Pages
Printed in 4 colors on matte stock

15237 **Chapter 11 Update**
Federal Managers Association
1641 Prince St
Alexandria, VA 22314-2818

703-683-8700; *Fax:* 703-683-8707
info@fedmanagers.org; www.fedmanagers.org

Todd Wells, Executive Director
George J. Smith, National VP
Patricia J. Niehaus, National President
Richard J. Oppedisano, National Secretary
Katie L. Smith, National Treasurer

Management issues and concerns.
Frequency: Monthly
Mailing list available for rent

15238 **Civil RICO Report**
LRP Publications
PO Box 24668
West Palm Beach, FL 33416-4668

561-622-6520
800-341-7874; *Fax:* 561-622-0757
webmaster@lrp.com; www.lrp.com

Kenneth Kahn, President
Robert K Latzko, Editor

Weekly report and analysis of litigation under the civil provisions of the Racketeer Influenced and Corrupt Organizations Act as well as legislative developments and state little RICO laws.
Cost: $812.00
Printed in 2 colors on matte stock

15239 **Client Counseling Update**
American Bar Association
321 N Clark St
Chicago, IL 60654-7598

312-988-5000
800-285-2221; *Fax:* 312-988-5280
askaba@abanet.org; www.abanet.org
Social Media: Facebook, Twitter

Laurel Bellows, President
Jack L. Rives, Executive Director
Robert M. Carlson, Chairman
Richard J. Oppe Pera, Treasurer
Cara Lee T. Neville, Secretary

e-Newsletter contains summaries of publications and news articles concerning client counseling.
Founded in: 1878
Mailing list available for rent

15240 **Collective Bargaining Negotiations and Contracts**
Bureau of National Affairs
1801 S Bell St
Arlington, VA 22202-4501

703-341-3000
800-372-1033; *Fax:* 800-253-0332
customercare@bna.com; www.bnabooks.com
Social Media: Facebook, Twitter, LinkedIn

Paul N Wojcik, Chairman
Gregory C. McCaffery, President and CEO
John Camp, Vice President and Chief Technology
Lisa A. Fitzpatrick, Vice President
Audrey Hipkins, Vice President

A biweekly notificaiton and reference service containing information designed to help unions and management prepare, negotiate and administer contracts.
Cost: $1541.00
Frequency: Monthly
Founded in: 1929

15241 **Commercial Law Bulletin**
Commercial Law League of America
205 N. Michigan
Suite 2212
Chicago, IL 60601-5961
312-240-1400
800-978-2552; *Fax:* 312-240-1408
info@clla.org; www.clla.org
Oliver Yandle, VP
Charles R Johnson III, Treasurer
Provides news and information on bankruptcy, collections, debt and insolvency information, as well as reports from Washington DC and updates on resolutions.
Cost: $65.00
Circulation: 5000
Founded in: 1895

15242 **Commercial Laws of the World**
Foreign Tax Law
PO Box 2189
Ormond Beach, FL 32175-2189
386-341-7405; www.foreignlaw.com
Contains company laws, commercial codes, and related law for over 100 countries.
Cost: $100.00

15243 **Communications Lawyer**
American Bar Association Forum - Communication Law
321 N Clark St
Chicago, IL 60654-7598
312-988-5000
800-285-2221; *Fax:* 312-988-5280
askaba@abanet.org; www.abanet.org
Social Media: Facebook, Twitter
Laurel Bellows, President
Jack L. Rives, Executive Director
Robert M. Carlson, Chairman
Lucian T. Pera, Treasurer
Cara Lee T. Neville, Secretary
Newsletter reviews significant activities and developments in communications law and reports on Forum activities.
Cost: $45.00
30 Pages
Frequency: Quarterly
ISSN: 0737-7622
Founded in: 1878
Mailing list available for rent

15244 **Computer & Internet LAWCAST**
Vox Juris
PO Box 389
Pennington, NJ 08534
609-737-6543
800-LAW-CAST; *Fax:* 609-737-3860
INFO@lawcast.com; www.lawcast.com
Jason Meyer, Publisher
Groundbreaking law arising from life and commerce in the digital age...in licensing, torts, intellectual property securities, contracts, privacy, joint ventures, antitrust, content regulation and more. If your clients use email or the internet, have their own websites, produce hardware or software or provide on-line service, listen up here. 60 minute audio and outline twice monthly
Cost: $25.00

15245 **Computer Industry Litigation Reporter**
Andrews Publications
175 Strafford Avenue
Building 4 Suite 140
Wayne, PA 19087
610-225-0510
800-345-1101; *Fax:* 610-225-0501; www.andrewspub.com
Donna Higgins, Editor
Mary Ellen Fox, Publisher
Jodine Mayberry, Executive Editor
Covers litigation involving copyright, patent, trade secrets, employment, securities, trademark, contracts and other issues related to the computer industry.
Cost: $1226.00
Founded in: 1983

15246 **Construction Claims Monthly**
Business Publishers
2222 Sedwick Dr
Suite 101
Durham, NC 27713
800-223-8720; *Fax:* 800-508-2592
custserv@bpinews.com; www.bpinews.com
Contains summaries of important decisions from the federal and state courts, boards of contract appeals, and the Office of Comptroller General on such topics as change orders, design problems, inspection, delay, home office overhead, claims administration, termination, waivers, differing site conditions, subcontractors and insurance.
Cost: $244.00
8 Pages
Frequency: Monthly
Founded in: 1962

15247 **Construction Litigation Reporter**
McGraw Hill
1221 Avenue of the Americas
New York, NY 10020-1095
212-512-2000
800-352-3566; *Fax:* 212-512-3840
webmaster@mcgraw-hill.com; www.mcgraw-hill.com
Harold W McGraw III, CEO
Summaries of judicial and agency decisions.
Cost: $300.00
24 Pages
Frequency: Monthly

15248 **Consumer Financial Services Law Report**
LRP Publications
PO Box 980
Horsham, PA 19044-0980
215-784-0912
800-341-7874; *Fax:* 215-784-9639
webmaster@lrp.com; www.lrp.com
Todd Lutz, CFO
Kenneth Kahn, President
Keeps you up-to-date with the latest changes and developments in the area of consumer financial services litigation. Provides timely coverage of legal developments involving fair lending, debt collection, state UDAP laws and fraud, automobile lending and leasing, damage theories and class actions, and more.
Cost: $220.00
Founded in: 1977

15249 **Consumer Product Litigation Reporter**
Andrews Publications
175 Strafford Avenue
Building 4, Suite 140
Wayne, PA 19087-3331
610-225-0510
800-345-1101; *Fax:* 610-225-0501; www.andrewspub.com
Robert Maroldo, Publisher
Eileen Gonyeau, Editor
Covers areas such as strict liability, assumption of risk, insurance coverage, adequacy of warning merchantability, punitive damages, component liability, forseeability and more.
Cost: $46.00

15250 **Controlling Law Firm Costs**
Institute of Management and Administration
1 Washington Park
Suite 1300
Newark, NJ 07102-3130
212-244-0360; *Fax:* 973-622-0595
customercare@bna.com; www.ioma.com
Laurel Bellows, President
Shows law office administrators how to reduce overhead, improve the firm's profitability and efficiency, get more value for the firm's budget dollar, and improve their own professional standing. Includes strategies to control the costs of support staff, insurance, leases, taxes, computers and more.
Cost: $300.00
Frequency: Annual+

15251 **Corporate Counsel LAWCAST**
Vox Juris
PO Box 389
Pennington, NJ 08534
609-737-6543
800-LAW-CAST; *Fax:* 609-737-3860
INFO@lawcast.com; www.lawcast.com
Jason Meyer, Publisher
Everything for the in-house counsel in one lively and substantive program. In-house ethics and privileges, the law of the workplace, intellectual property, corporate governance, contracts, regulations, and more...close-ups on how top counsel meet the demands of the in-house practice. 75 minute audio and online, 15 times per year
Cost: $25.00

15252 **Corporate Legal Times**
Corporate Legal Times
656 West Randolph Street
Suite 500 East
Chicago, IL 60611
312-654-3500; *Fax:* 312-654-3525; www.cltmag.com
Nat Slavin, Publisher
Larry Lannon, CEO
Written for general counsel and other in house corporate attourneys to provide information relevant to strategic planning and day-to-day operation of legal departments including in-house counsel's relationships with outside law firms.
Cost: $10.00
Frequency: Monthly
Circulation: 40000
Founded in: 1991

15253 **Corporate Practice Series**
Bureau of National Affairs
1801 S Bell St
Arlington, VA 22202-4501
703-341-3000
800-372-1033; *Fax:* 800-253-0332
customercare@bna.com; www.bnabooks.com
Social Media: Facebook, Twitter, LinkedIn
Paul N Wojcik, Chairman
Gregory C. McCaffery, President and CEO
John Camp, Vice President and Chief Technology
Lisa A. Fitzpatrick, Vice President
Audrey Hipkins, Vice President
A corporate law reference service organized into a series of portfolios written by legal experts, with a weekly newsletter. Each portfolio covers a different legal subject with detailed analyses, working papers and a bibliography.
Cost: $2426.00
ISSN: 0162-5691

15254 Criminal Law Reporter
Bureau of National Affairs
1801 S Bell St
Arlington, VA 22202-4501

703-341-3000
800-372-1033; *Fax:* 800-253-0332
customercare@bna.com; www.bnabooks.com
Social Media: Facebook, Twitter, LinkedIn

Paul N Wojcik, Chairman
Gregory C. McCaffery, President and CEO
John Camp, Vice President and Chief Technology
Lisa A. Fitzpatrick, Vice President
Audrey Hipkins, VP

A weekly notification service providing coverage of court decisions, federal legislative activities and administrative developments in the field of criminal law. Fulltext of the cases highlighted in each issue are available free on CrL's web site. Subscribers can also recieve free email notification of Supreme Court decisions.
Cost: $1108.00
Frequency: Weekly
Founded in: 1929

15255 DataLaw Report
Clark Boardman Company
155 Pflingsten Road
Deerfield, IL 60015

847-374-0400; *Fax:* 847-948-7099

Amelia Boss, Editor

Analyzes the changing global legal environment for electronic information.

15256 Death Care Business Advisor
LRP Publications
747 Dresher Road
PO Box 980
Horsham, PA 19044-980

215-784-0912
800-341-7874; *Fax:* 215-784-9639
webmaster@lrp.com; www.lrp.com

Jay Kravetz, Editor
Dionne Ellis, Managing Editor

The only twice a month newsletter that offers you in-depth business coverage of memorialization and remembrance issues. You'll recieve news and tips on the latest trends and developments in funeral service, cemetery management and cremation and learn innovative strategies to capture the expanding preneed market and more.
Cost: $215.00
Founded in: 1977

15257 Digest of Environmental Law
Strafford Publications
PO Box 13729
Atlanta, GA 30324-0729

404-881-1141
800-926-7926; *Fax:* 404-881-0074
customerservice@straffordpub.com; www.straffordpub.com

Richard Ossoff, Presdient
Jennifer Vaughan, Managing Editor

Monthly digest of nationally significant litigation related to the full range of environmental issues, includes annual index.
Cost: $547.00
Frequency: Monthly
ISSN: 1073-9521
Founded in: 1984

15258 Disability Compliance for Higher Education
LRP Publications
747 Dresher Road
PO Box 980
Horsham, PA 19044-980

215-784-0912
800-341-7874; *Fax:* 561-622-2423
webmaster@lrp.com; www.lrp.com

Marsha Jaquays, Editor
Nancy Grover, Managing Editor

Helps colleges determine if they are complying with the Americans with Disabilities Act (ADA) and section 504 of the Rehabilitation Act. Readers find out how to fulfill legal obligations under the law and save their college from costly litigation.
Cost: $198.00
Frequency: Monthly
Founded in: 1977

15259 ELA Notes
Education Law Association
300 College Park Ave
Dayton, OH 45469-0001

937-229-3589; *Fax:* 937-229-3845
ela@educationlaw.org; www.educationlaw.org

Mandy Schrenk, Executive Director
Jody Thornburg, Publications Editor
Cate K Smith, Executive Director
Judy Pleiman, Member Services Coordinator
Jody Thornburg, Publications Manager

ELA is a nonprofit, nonadvocacy, member-based organization found in 1954 to provide an unbiased forum for the dissemination of information about current issues in education law. Membership is open to all individuals and organizations with a special interest in education law. ELA's mission is to bring together educational and legal scholars and practioners to inform and advance educational policy and practice through knowledge of the law.
Cost: $125.00
Frequency: Quarterly
Circulation: 1300
ISSN: 0047-8997
Founded in: 1954
Printed in 2 colors on matte stock

15260 Employee Benefits Cases
Bureau of National Affairs
1801 S Bell St
Arlington, VA 22202-4501

703-341-3000
800-372-1033; *Fax:* 800-253-0332
customercare@bna.com; www.bnabooks.com
Social Media: Facebook, Twitter, LinkedIn

Paul N Wojcik, Chairman
Gregory C. McCaffery, President and CEO
John Camp, Vice President and Chief Technology
Lisa A. Fitzpatrick, Vice President
Audrey Hipkins, VP

A weekly decisional service that reports the full text of federal and state court opinions and selected decisions of arbitrators and the NLRB on employee benefits issues.
Cost: $1582.00
54 Pages
Frequency: Weekly
Circulation: 6000+
ISSN: 0273-236X
Founded in: 1929
Printed in on matte stock

15261 Employment Law Report Strategist
Data Research
PO Box 490
Rosemount, MN 55068-0490

952-452-8694
800-365-4900; *Fax:* 952-452-8694

Covers the latest court cases and late-breaking legislation along with the most recent law review articles affecting employment.
Cost: $120.00
Frequency: Monthly
ISSN: 1058-1308

15262 Entertainment Law and Finance
345 Park Avenue S
New York, NY 10010-1707

212-779-6611
800-888-8300; *Fax:* 212-696-1848

Stan Soocher, Editor
Stuart M Wise, Production Manager
Kerry Kyle, Circulation Director

Laws and news in the entertainment field.
Cost: $195.00
8 Pages
Frequency: Monthly
ISSN: 0883-2455
Printed in 2 colors

15263 Entertainment and Sports Lawyer
American Bar Association
Forum-Entertainment/Sport
321 N Clark St
Chicago, IL 60654-7598

312-988-5000
800-285-2221; *Fax:* 312-988-5280
askaba@abanet.org; www.abanet.org
Social Media: Facebook, Twitter

Laurel Bellows, President
Vered Yakovee, Editor
Jack L. Rives, Executive Director
Robert M. Carlson, Chairman
Lucian T. Pera, Treasurer

Newsletter on recent developments in the sports and entertainment industries, public policy and scholarly viewpoints.
Cost: $60.00
40 Pages
Frequency: Quarterly
ISSN: 0732-1880
Founded in: 1878
Mailing list available for rent

15264 Estate Planner's Alert
Thomson Reuters
2395 Midway Rd
Suite 4
Carrollton, TX 75006

646-822-2000
800-231-1860; *Fax:* 646-822-2800
trta.lei-support@thomsonreuters.com; www.ria.thomsonreuters.com

Laurel Bellows, President
Thomas H Glocer, CEO & Director
Robert D Daleo, Chief Financial Officer
Kelli Crane, Senior Vice President & CIO

Offers complete coverage of estate planning and law.
Cost: $195.00
Frequency: Monthly
Founded in: 1935

15265 Exercise Standards and Malpractice Reporter
PRC Publishing
3976 Fulton Dr Nw
Canton, OH 44718-3043

330-492-6063
800-336-0083; *Fax:* 330-492-6176;
www.prcpublishingcorp.com

Molly Romig, VP
Dr. Doyice Cotton, Publisher
Mary Cotton, Publisher

Designed to cover topics of interest and concern to the exercise professionals.
Cost: $39.95
16 Pages
Circulation: 750
ISSN: 0891-0278

Founded in: 1997
Printed in 2 colors on matte stock

15266 FCBA Newsletter
Federal Communications Bar Association
1020 19th St Nw
Suite 325
Washington, DC 20036-6113
202-293-4000; *Fax:* 202-293-4317
fcba@fcba.org; www.fcba.org
Stanley Zenor, Executive Director
Kerry Loughney, Director of Membership Services
Diane J Cornell, Treasurer
Wendy Jo Parish, Administrative Assistant
Beth Phillips, Bookkeeper
A non-profit organization of attorneys and other professionals involved in the development, interpretation, implementation and practice of communications law and policy.
Frequency: Monthly
Founded in: 1936
Mailing list available for rent

15267 Family Law Reporter
Bureau of National Affairs
1801 S Bell St
Arlington, VA 22202-4501
703-341-3000
800-372-1033; *Fax:* 800-253-0332
customercare@bna.com; www.bnabooks.com
Social Media: Facebook, Twitter, LinkedIn
Paul N Wojcik, Chairman
Gregory C. McCaffery, President and CEO
John Camp, Vice President and Chief Technology
Lisa A. Fitzpatrick, Vice President
Audrey Hipkins, VP
A weekly notification and reference service dealing with all significant state and federal developments in the field of family law.
Cost: $974.00
Frequency: Weekly
Founded in: 1929

15268 Federal Contract Disputes
Business Publishers
2222 Sedwick Dr
Suite 101
Durham, NC 27713
800-223-8720; *Fax:* 800-508-2592
custserv@bpinews.com; www.bpinews.com
A monthly newsletter designed to help you avoid disputes, and successfully resolve those you can't avoid. Each issue brings you concise synopses of a dozen major decisions, from the courts, the Comptroller General, and the boards of contract appeals.
Cost: $285.00
Frequency: Monthly

15269 Federal Contracts Report
Bureau of National Affairs
1801 S Bell St
Arlington, VA 22202-4501
703-341-3000
800-372-1033; *Fax:* 800-253-0332
customercare@bna.com; www.bnabooks.com
Social Media: Facebook, Twitter, LinkedIn
Paul N Wojcik, Chairman
Gregory C. McCaffery, President and CEO
John Camp, Vice President and Chief Technology
Lisa A. Fitzpatrick, Vice President
Audrey Hipkins, VP
A weekly reporting service providing comprehensive coverage of the latest significant developments affecting federal contracts and grants.
Cost: $1887.00
Frequency: Weekly
Founded in: 1929

15270 Federal Discovery News
LRP Publications
747 Dresher Road
PO Box 980
Horsham, PA 19044-980
215-784-0912
800-341-7874; *Fax:* 215-784-9639
webmaster@lrp.com; www.lrp.com
John Massaro, Editor
Dionne Ellis, Managing Editor
Each issue covers the whole realm of pretrial case management and discovery, especially the impact of the new civil procedure rules on discovery in federal cases. Provides a timely review of how district developments pertain to your practice.
Cost: $275.00
Frequency: Monthly
Founded in: 1977

15271 Federal EEO Advisor
LRP Publications
747 Dresher Road
PO Box 980
Horsham, PA 19044-980
215-784-0912
800-341-7874; *Fax:* 215-784-9639
webmaster@lrp.com; www.lrp.com
Allison Uehling, Editor
Clarrisa Spasyk, Staff Writer
One-of-a-kind publication provides readers with essential tips, strategies and news about the constanly changing EEO profession. Each issue includes insightful coverage on topics such as: details on major developments and trends in federal EEO; tips on how to accomplish specific objectives within the EEO program; synopses of decisions by the EEOC and related courts, etc.
Cost: $220.00
Frequency: Monthly
Founded in: 1977

15272 Federal Human Resources Week
LRP Publications
747 Dresher Road Suite 500
PO Box 980
Horsham, PA 19044
215-840-0912
800-341-7874; *Fax:* 215-784-9639
custserve@lrp.com; www.feds.com
Daniel J Gephart, Editorial Director
Julie Davidson, Managing Editor
Kathleen Filipczyk, Staff Writer
Federal Human Resources Week helps you stay on top of changes affecting you and your workplace. This revolutionary resource enables you to experience each major development as it occurs.
Cost: $365.00
12 Pages
Frequency: Weekly
Founded in: 1977
Printed in 2 colors on matte stock

15273 Financial Management Newsletter
Association of Legal Administrators
75 Tri-State International
Suite 222
Lincolnshire, IL 60069-4435
847-267-1252; *Fax:* 847-267-1329
publications@alanet.org; www.alanet.org
Larry Smith, Executive Director
Debbie Thomas, Director, Accounting & Finance
Renee Mahovsky, Director, Administration/Operations
Bob Abramson, Director, Marketing & Communication
Jan Waugh, Director, Member Services
8 Pages
Frequency: Monthly
Founded in: 1971

15274 Forum
Federal Bar Association
1220 North Fillmore St.
Ste. 444
Arlington, VA 22201
571-481-9100; *Fax:* 571-481-9090
fba@fedbar.org; www.fedbar.org
Social Media: Facebook, Twitter, LinkedIn
Karen Silberman, Executive Director
Lori Beth Gorman, Executive Assistant
Stacy King, Deputy Executive Director
April Davis, Staff Accountant
Patty Richardson, Receptionist
A forum for the exchange of ideas, news, updates, and cases for lawyers.
Cost: $35.00
8 Pages
Frequency: Monthly
Founded in: 1920
Mailing list available for rent

15275 HRFocus
Institute of Management and Administration
1 Wasington Park
Suite 1300
Newark, NJ 07102-3130
212-244-0360; *Fax:* 973-622-0595
customercare@bna.com; www.ioma.com
Provides HR managers with timely information on a variety of topics, including talent management, HR legal and compliance issues, performance reviews, and workplace policies and standards.
Cost: $429.00
16 Pages
Frequency: Monthly
Printed in 4 colors

15276 Hastings Communications & Entertainment Law Journal
Hastings College of Law
200 McAllister St
2nd Floor, Room 213
San Francisco, CA 94102-4978
415-565-4600; *Fax:* 415-565-4854;
www.uchastings.edu
Nell Jessup Newton, Manager
Karen Gibbs, Editor
Specializing in a host of legal issues generally grouped under the rubric of communications and entertainment law. Focuses on, but is not limited to, telecommunications, broadcasting, cable and other non-broadcast video, and the print media.
Cost: $7.00
Frequency: Monthly
Circulation: 1300
Founded in: 1878

15277 Health Law Week
Strafford Publications
PO Box 13729
Atlanta, GA 30324-0729
404-881-1141
800-926-7926; *Fax:* 404-881-0074
customerservice@straffordpub.com;
www.straffordpub.com
Richard Ossoff, President
Case digest of judicial decision affecting all aspects of health care operations. Topics covered include AIPS abortion antitrust, drugs, ERISA, expert testimony, informed consent, amd much more.
Cost: $1397.00
Frequency: Weekly
ISSN: 1063-4061

Founded in: 1984
Mailing list available for rent: 25M names

15278 **Hospital Litigation Reporter**
Strafford Publications
PO Box 13729
Atlanta, GA 30324-0729

404-881-1141
800-926-7926; *Fax:* 404-881-0074
customerservice@straffordpub.com;
www.straffordpub.com

Richard Ossoff, President
Jennifer Vaughan, Editor

Monthly digest of judicial decisions that concern or affect the hospital environment. Cases are screened and selected to provide concise, comprehensive coverage of issues important to hospital attorneys and administrators.
Cost: $397.00
18 Pages
Frequency: Monthly
ISSN: 1048-5201
Founded in: 1984
Mailing list available for rent: 11M names
Printed in one color

15279 **Human Resources Report**
Bureau of National Affairs
1801 S Bell St
Arlington, VA 22202-4501

703-341-3000
800-372-1033; *Fax:* 800-253-0332
customercare@bna.com; www.bnabooks.com
Social Media: Facebook, Twitter, LinkedIn

Paul N Wojcik, Chairman
Gregory C. McCaffery, President and CEO
John Camp, Vice President and Chief Technology
Lisa A. Fitzpatrick, Vice President
Audrey Hipkins, VP

Covers current developments in every area of human resources; includes in-depth analysis of important events, developments or trends affecting human resource professionals.
Cost: $1140.00
28 Pages
Frequency: Weekly
ISSN: 1095-6239
Founded in: 1929
Printed in one color on matte stock

15280 **I-CBC Newsletter**
Institute of Certified Business Counselors
18831 Willamette Dr
West Linn, OR 97068-1711
503-751-1856
877-422-2674; *Fax:* 503-292-8237
inquiry@i-cbc.org; www.theicbc.org

Roger Murphy, Director, Newsletter

For counselors, brokers and attorneys qualified to act as advisors for persons with business problems. Regular editorial features.
Frequency: 6/Year
Mailing list available for rent

15281 **IOMA's Report on Controlling Law Firm Costs**
Institute of Management and Administration
1 Washington Park
Suite 1300
Newark, NJ 07102-3130

212-244-0360; *Fax:* 973-622-0595
customercare@bna.com; www.ioma.com

Information to control costs of law firms management.
Cost: $175.00
12 Pages
Frequency: Monthly

15282 **IRR News Report**
ABA Section - Individual Rights & Responsibilities
740 15th Stree, NW
10th Floor
Washington, DC 20005

202-662-1000
800-285-2221; *Fax:* 202-662-1031
askaba@abanet.org; www.abanet.org
Social Media: Facebook, Twitter

Laurel Bellows, President
Jack L. Rives, Executive Director
Robert M. Carlson, Chairman
Lucian T. Pera, Treasurer
Cara Lee T. Neville, Secretary

A quarterly newsletter including updates on Section events, news about members, a review of recent legislative events and decision by the Supreme Court.
Circulation: 6000
Founded in: 1878
Mailing list available for rent

15283 **Individual Employment Rights**
Bureau of National Affairs
1801 S Bell St
Arlington, VA 22202-4501

703-341-3000
800-372-1033; *Fax:* 800-253-0332
customercare@bna.com; www.bnabooks.com
Social Media: Facebook, Twitter, LinkedIn

Paul N Wojcik, Chairman
Gregory C. McCaffery, President and CEO
John Camp, Vice President and Chief Technology
Lisa A. Fitzpatrick, Vice President
Audrey Hipkins, VP

Case reference and notification on individual employment rights issues including employment at will, privacy, polygraph testing, and other employee rights issues outside the traditional labor-management relations context.
Cost: $1227.00
Frequency: Monthly
ISSN: 0148-7981
Founded in: 1929

15284 **Intellectual Property LAWCAST**
Vox Juris
PO Box 389
Pennington, NJ 08534-389

609-737-6543; *Fax:* 609-737-3860
INFO@lawcast.com; www.lawcast.com

Jason Meyer, Publisher

US legal news in patents, trademarks, copyrights, trade secrets, unfair trade, etc. including comprehensive coverage of PTO policies and a regular Listening Post on legal issues in the digital age. The buzz for thousands of IP lawyers, nationwide. 60 minute audio and online, twice monthly.
Cost: $488.00

15285 **Intellectual Property Law Review**
Clark Boardman Company
375 Hudson St
Room 201
New York, NY 10014-3658

585-546-5530
800-323-1336

David Doughty, Publisher

Compilation of the best law review articles.
Frequency: Monthly
Founded in: 1916

15286 **Intellectual Property Litigation Reporter**
Andrews Publications
175 Strafford Avenue
Building 4 Suite 140
Wayne, PA 19087-3331

610-225-0510
800-345-1101; *Fax:* 610-225-0501;
www.andrewspub.com

Robert Maroldo, Publisher
Jodine Mayberry, Editor

Covers litigation and regulation of intellectual property issues including patents, copyrights, and tradeworks.
Cost: $83.00

15287 **Intellectual Property Today**
Omega Communications
29 E Maryland Street
Indianapolis, IN 46204-7258

317-264-4010; *Fax:* 317-264-4020
planet@iptoday.com; www.omegac.com

Douglas Dean, Editor
Steve Barnes, Vice President
Laura Moore, Vice President

Emphasizes developments in leading edge technology, including multimedia, genetic engineering and computer software, and how they effect disciplines of law.
Cost: $96.00
Frequency: Monthly
Circulation: 20000
Founded in: 1971

15288 **Inter-American Bar Association Newsletter**
Inter-American Bar Association
1211 Connecticut Ave Nw
Suite 202
Washington, DC 20036-2712

202-466-5944; *Fax:* 202-466-5946
iaba@iaba.org; www.iaba.org
Social Media: Facebook

Marianne Cordier, Secretary General
Rafael Veloz, President
Cost: $60.00
Frequency: Quarterly

15289 **International Law News**
American Bar Association Internat'l Law & Practice
321 N Clark St
Chicago, IL 60654-7598

312-988-5000
800-285-2221; *Fax:* 312-988-5280
askaba@abanet.org; www.abanet.org
Social Media: Facebook, Twitter

Angela Gwizdala, Managing Editor
Laurel Bellows, President
Jack L. Rives, Executive Director
Robert M. Carlson, Chairman
Lucian T. Pera, Treasurer

Provides information concerning current, important developments pertaining to international law and practice, Section news, and other information of professional interest.
28 Pages
Frequency: Quarterly
Circulation: 15000
ISSN: 0047-0813
Founded in: 1878
Mailing list available for rent

15290 **Internet Lawyer**
GoAhead Productions
123 7th Avenue
#137
Brooklyn, NY 11215-1301

718-399-6136; *Fax:* 718-499-6039;
www.internetlawyer.com

Tatia L Gordon-Troy, Editor-in-Chief
Christopher Eddings, Publisher

Gives legal advice and examines how to use the Net for research, marketing and communications purposes. Includes book reviews as well as information on current law office technology.
Cost: $149.00
Frequency: Monthly

15291 Judicial Division Record
American Bar Association Judicial Division
321 N Clark St
Chicago, IL 60654-7598
312-988-5000
800-285-2221; *Fax:* 312-988-6281
askaba@abanet.org; www.abanet.org
Social Media: Facebook, Twitter
Laurel Bellows, President
Jack L. Rives, Executive Director
Robert M. Carlson, Chairman
Lucian T. Pera, Treasurer
Cara Lee T. Neville, Secretary
The Record is the only newsletter published by the Division, providing news about Division activites, products, publications and programs. It contains sections for each Division Conference, and an insert.
Cost: $25.00
Frequency: Free Online
Founded in: 1878
Mailing list available for rent

15292 Labor Arbitration and Dispute Settlements
Bureau of National Affairs
1801 S Bell St
Arlington, VA 22202-4501
703-341-3000
800-372-1033; *Fax:* 800-253-0332
customercare@bna.com; www.bnabooks.com
Social Media: Facebook, Twitter, LinkedIn
Paul N Wojcik, Chairman
Gregory C. McCaffery, President and CEO
John Camp, Vice President and Chief Technology
Lisa A. Fitzpatrick, Vice President
Audrey Hipkins, VP
Contains the full-text of arbitration cases, and digests of court decisions involving arbitration.
Cost: $1686.00
Frequency: Weekly
ISSN: 1043-5662
Founded in: 1929

15293 Labor Arbitration in Government
LRP Publications
PO Box 980
Horsham, PA 19044-0980
215-784-0912
800-341-7874; *Fax:* 215-784-9639
webmaster@lrp.com; www.lrp.com
Todd Lutz, CFO
Dionne Ellis, Marketing
Selected awards involving city, state, and federal employers (other than those employed by schools) are covered by this reporting service. Some of the issues arbitrated include: absenteeism, smoking policies, layoffs, and substance abuse.
Cost: $120.00
Frequency: Monthly
Founded in: 1977
Printed in 2 colors on glossy stock

15294 Labor Lawyer
American Bar Association - Labor & Employment Law
321 N Clark St
Chicago, IL 60654-7598
312-988-5000
800-285-2221; *Fax:* 312-988-5814
laboremplIaw@abanet.org; www.abanet.org
Social Media: Facebook, Twitter
Laurel Bellows, President
Jack L. Rives, Executive Director
Robert M. Carlson, Chairman
Lucian T. Pera, Treasurer
Cara Lee T. Neville, Secretary
Substantive articles on developments in labor and employment law.
Frequency: Quarterly
Circulation: 2300
Founded in: 1878
Mailing list available for rent

15295 Labor Relations Reporter
Bureau of National Affairs
1801 S Bell St
Arlington, VA 22202-4501
703-341-3000
800-372-1033; *Fax:* 800-253-0332
customercare@bna.com; www.bnabooks.com
Social Media: Facebook, Twitter, LinkedIn
Paul N Wojcik, Chairman
Gregory C. McCaffery, President and CEO
John Camp, Vice President and Chief Technology
Lisa A. Fitzpatrick, Vice President
Audrey Hipkins, VP
A multi-part notification and reference service covering labor-management relations, wages and hours, labor arbitration, fair employment practices, individual employment rights and more.
Cost: $6175.00
Frequency: Weekly
ISSN: 0148-7981
Founded in: 1929

15296 Labor Relations Week
Bureau of National Affairs
1801 S Bell St
Arlington, VA 22202-4501
703-341-3000
800-372-1033; *Fax:* 800-253-0332
customercare@bna.com; www.bnabooks.com
Social Media: Facebook, Twitter, LinkedIn
Paul N Wojcik, Chairman
Gregory C. McCaffery, President and CEO
John Camp, Vice President and Chief Technology
Lisa A. Fitzpatrick, Vice President
Audrey Hipkins, VP
A weekly reporting service that provides a comprehensive overview of developments influencing labor relations in the private sector.
Cost: $1472.00
Frequency: Weekly
ISSN: 0891-4141
Founded in: 1929

15297 Labor and Employment Law
American Bar Association - Labor & Employment Law
321 N Clark St
Chicago, IL 60654-7598
312-988-5000
800-285-2221; *Fax:* 312-988-6281
askaba@abanet.org; www.abanet.org
Social Media: Facebook, Twitter
Laurel Bellows, President
Jack L. Rives, Executive Director
Robert M. Carlson, Chairman
Lucian T. Pera, Treasurer
Cara Lee T. Neville, Secretary
Offers news items of interest to members and information on the latest developments in the labor field.
Cost: $5.00
16 Pages
Frequency: Quarterly
Circulation: 22000
ISSN: 0193-5739
Founded in: 1878
Mailing list available for rent

15298 Labor and Employment Law News
American Bar Association - Labor & Employment Law
321 N Clark St
Chicago, IL 60654-7598
312-988-5000
800-285-2221; *Fax:* 312-988-5280
service@abanet.org; www.abanet.org
Social Media: Facebook, Twitter
Laurel Bellows, President
Jack L. Rives, Executive Director
Robert M. Carlson, Chairman
Lucian T. Pera, Treasurer
Cara Lee T. Neville, Secretary
Legal issues and trends of interest to lawyers who represent employees, unions, and management.
Cost: $5.00
16 Pages
Frequency: Monthly
Circulation: 22000
ISSN: 0193-5739
Founded in: 1878
Mailing list available for rent
Printed in 4 colors

15299 Labor-Management Relations
Bureau of National Affairs
1801 S Bell St
Arlington, VA 22202-4501
703-341-3000
800-372-1033; *Fax:* 800-253-0332
customercare@bna.com; www.bnabooks.com
Social Media: Facebook, Twitter, LinkedIn
Paul N Wojcik, Chairman
Gregory C. McCaffery, President and CEO
John Camp, Vice President and Chief Technology
Lisa A. Fitzpatrick, Vice President
Audrey Hipkins, VP
Contains a table of cases, digest-summaries of all published NLRB decisions and full-text of opinions of the US Supreme Court, US Courts of Appeals and other courts, in one bound volume, issued several times a year.
Cost: $ 1776.00
Frequency: Monthly
ISSN: 1043-5506
Founded in: 1929

15300 Labor-Management Relations Analysis/News and Background Information
Bureau of National Affairs
1801 S Bell St
Arlington, VA 22202-4501
703-341-3000
800-372-1033; *Fax:* 800-253-0332
customercare@bna.com; www.bnabooks.com
Social Media: Facebook, Twitter, LinkedIn
Paul N Wojcik, Chairman
Gregory C. McCaffery, President and CEO
John Camp, Vice President and Chief Technology
Lisa A. Fitzpatrick, Vice President
Audrey Hipkins, VP
This weekly section of the Labor Relations Reporter summarizes developments and rulings in the field of labor law, covers major non-decisional developments and recent significant arbitration awards, and provides in-depth analysis and evaluation of the week's labor news.
Cost: $507.00
Frequency: Weekly
Founded in: 1929

15301 Land Use Law Report
Business Publishers

8737 Colesville Road
10th Floor
Silver Spring, MD 20910-3928
301-876-6300
800-274-6737; *Fax:* 301-589-8493
custserv@bpinews.com; www.bpinews.com/

Leonard Eiserer, Publisher
James Esq, Editor

Zoning and land use decisions at all levels of government; impact on business community and environment.
Cost: $397.00
Founded in: 1963

15302 Latin America Law and Business Report
WorldTrade Executive
2250 Main St
Suite 100
Concord, MA 01742-3838
978-287-0301; *Fax:* 978-287-0302
info@wtexec.com; www.wtexecutive.com

Gary Brown, President
Jay Stanley, Sales Manager

Provides practical, current information on how to do business in Latin America. Covers areas such as capital markets, accounting matters, labor issues, privatization, project finance techniques, joint venture regulation, local sourcing, export/import, taxation, intellectual property, environment.
Cost: $893.00
Frequency: Monthly

15303 Law Bulletin
Andrews Publications
175 Strafford Avenue
Building 4, Suite 140
Wayne, PA 19087-3331
610-225-0510
800-345-1101; *Fax:* 610-225-0501;
www.andrewspub.com

Donna Higgins, Editor
Rose MacDonald, Production Manager

Newsletter covering the legal issues raided by the Millenium. Bug along with insightful commentary from attorneys and other experts.
Cost: $25.00
Frequency: Monthly
Founded in: 1872

15304 Law Firm Profit Report
James Publishing
3505 Cadillac Avenue
Suite H
Costa Mesa, CA 92626
714-755-5450
800-440-4780; *Fax:* 714-751-2709
customer-service@jamespublishing.com;
www.jamespublishing.com

Jim Pawell, Founder/President
Lorraine Thinnes, Editor

How to manage a small to medium-sized law firm profitably, with tips on cost-cutting, managing automation, personnel and more.
Founded in: 1981
Mailing list available for rent

15305 Law Office Management & Administration Report
Institute of Management and Administration
1 Washington Park
Suite 1300
Newark, NJ 07102-3130
212-244-0360; *Fax:* 973-622-0595
customercare@bna.com; www.ioma.com

Covers the daily management concerns relevant for law firm administrators, office managers, and others.
Cost: $489.00
Frequency: Monthly
Founded in: 1983

15306 Law Practice Today
American Bar Association
321 N Clark St
Chicago, IL 60654-7598
312-988-5000
800-285-2221; *Fax:* 312-988-5280
askaba@abanet.org; www.abanet.org
Social Media: Facebook, Twitter

Laurel Bellows, President
Jack L. Rives, Executive Director
Robert M. Carlson, Chairman
Lucian T. Pera, Treasurer
Cara Lee T. Neville, Secretary

An e-newsletter focusing on how lawyers can improve their personal productivity in the hands-on practice of law.
Frequency: Monthly
Founded in: 1878
Mailing list available for rent

15307 Law and Society Association Newsletter
Denver College of Law
1900 Olive Street
Denver, CO 80220-1857
303-871-6306
Exec_Office@lawandsociety.org;
www.lawandsociety.org

Joyce Sterling, Publisher

Legal updates and information on the Society.
Frequency: Monthly

15308 LawPractice.news
American Bar Association - Law Practice Management
321 N Clark St
Chicago, IL 60654-7598
312-988-5000
800-285-2221; *Fax:* 312-988-5280
askaba@abanet.org;
www.abanet.org/lpm/home.shtml
Social Media: Facebook, Twitter, Youtube

Laurel Bellows, President
Jack L. Rives, Executive Director
Robert M. Carlson, Chairman
Lucian T. Pera, Treasurer
Cara Lee T. Neville, Secretary

A monthly e-newsletter for Law Practice Management Section members, keeping them abreast of Section events, publications, promotions and member news.
Frequency: Monthly
Founded in: 1974
Mailing list available for rent

15309 Lawyer's PC
West Group
1428 Dewey Ave
Rochester, NY 14613-1128
585-254-9585
800-327-2665; *Fax:* 585-258-3707
west.support@thomson.com;
www.west.thomson.com

Computer and electronics information aimed at the legal profession.
Cost: $299.00
16 Pages
Circulation: 4000
Founded in: 1872
Printed in one color

15310 Lawyering Tools and Techniques
American Bar Association
321 N Clark St
Chicago, IL 60654-7598
312-988-5000
800-285-2221; *Fax:* 312-988-5280
askaba@abanet.org; www.abanet.org
Social Media: Facebook, Twitter

Laurel Bellows, President
Jack L. Rives, Executive Director
Robert M. Carlson, Chairman
Lucian T. Pera, Treasurer
Cara Lee T. Neville, Secretary

Focuses on specific tools lawyers can use to improve the productivity of their work including electronic communications, laptops, desk publishing and resources.
Cost: $50.00
Frequency: Quarterly
Founded in: 1878
Mailing list available for rent

15311 Lawyers Tax Alert
Research Institute of America
90 5th Avenue
2nd Floor
New York, NY 10011-7696
212-367-6300

Peter Grean, Manager

Tax laws and news.
Frequency: Monthly

15312 Lawyers' Letter
American Bar Association
321 N Clark St
Chicago, IL 60654-7598
312-988-5000
800-285-2221; *Fax:* 312-988-5280
askaba@abanet.org; www.abanet.org
Social Media: Facebook, Twitter

Laurel Bellows, President
Jack L. Rives, Executive Director
Robert M. Carlson, Chairman
Lucian T. Pera, Treasurer
Cara Lee T. Neville, Secretary

Newsletter informing lawyers of new developments in court improvement and reports on Conference activities.
Founded in: 1878
Mailing list available for rent

15313 Legal Advisory
WPI Communications
55 Morris Ave
Suite 300
Springfield, NJ 07081-1422
973-467-8700
800-323-4995; *Fax:* 973-467-0368
info@wpicomm.com; www.wpicomm.com

Steve Klinghoffer, President
Marilyn Lang, Chairman

Offers updates, news and the latest legislation for lawyers.
Frequency: Monthly
Founded in: 1952

15314 Legal Assistant Today Magazine
James Publishing
3505 Cadillac Avenue
Suite H
Costa Mesa, CA 92626
714-755-5450
800-440-4780; *Fax:* 714-751-2709
customer-service@jamespublishing.com;
www.jamespublishing.com

Jim Pawell, Founder/President
Rod Hughes, Managing Editor

Written exclusively for paralegals and legal assistants. Each issue includes coverage if industry news and trends, how-to articles as well as colorful and informative pieces on unique areas and persons in the profession and sound advice for

becoming more efficient in the workplace., buy wisely and use their investments to maximize productivity and profitability.
Cost: $47.98
56 Pages
Circulation: 13000
ISSN: 1055-128X
Founded in: 1981

15315 Legal Review
Native American Rights Fund
1506 Broadway St
Boulder, CO 80302-6296

303-447-8760; *Fax:* 303-443-7776
webmaster@narf.org; www.narf.org
Social Media: Facebook

John E Echohawk, Executive Director
Carly Hare, Director Development
Rose Cuny, Office Manager
Katrina Mora, Office Services Assistant
Mireille Martinez, Development Projects Manager

A bi-annual case update published by the Native American Rights Fund.
Frequency: Bi-annually
Circulation: 30000
ISSN: 0739-862x
Mailing list available for rent
Printed in 4 colors on matte stock

15316 Litigation LAWCAST
Vox Juris
PO Box 389
Pennington, NJ 08534
609-737-6543
800-529-2278; *Fax:* 609-737-3860
info@lawcast.com; www.lawcast.com

Jason Meyer, Editor & Publisher
Linda Delp, General Manager

Analysis of legal departments and advanced strategic ideas for the most demanding litigators - whatever the subject of your litigation. Stay up to date on substance and tactics in evidence, discovery, advocacy, damages, client management and selection, settlement, ADR, and ethics, plus coverage of groudbreaking decisions affecting personal injury, commercial, and employment law.
60 min./monthly
Cost: $399.00
Frequency: Monthly
Founded in: 1994

15317 Litigation News
American Bar Association Section of Litigation
321 N Clark St
Chicago, IL 60654-7598
312-988-5000
800-285-2221; *Fax:* 312-988-5280
askaba@abanet.org; www.abanet.org
Social Media: Facebook, Twitter

Laurel Bellows, President
Jack L. Rives, Executive Director
Robert M. Carlson, Chairman
Lucian T. Pera, Treasurer
Cara Lee T. Neville, Secretary

Present articles on the latest developments in law, litigation trends, and topics of interest to litigators.
Frequency: Quarterly
Circulation: 60000
Founded in: 1878
Mailing list available for rent

15318 Marketing for Lawyers
Leader Publications
345 Park Avenue S
New York, NY 10010-1707

212-799-9200; *Fax:* 212-696-1848

Sam Adler, Editor
Kerry Kyle, Circulation Director

Helps lawyers expand their practice through marketing.
Cost: $17.50

15319 Mealey's Asbestos Bankruptcy Report
LexisNexis Mealey's
555 W 5th Avenue
Los Angeles, CA 90013

213-627-1130
800-253-4182
mealeyinfo@lexisnexis.com;
www.lexisnexis.com/mealeys
Social Media: Facebook, Twitter, LinkedIn, RSS, Youtube

Tom Hagy, CEO
Maureen McGuire, Editorial Director
Lisa Schaeffer, Editor
Mike Wash, Chief Executive Officer, Legal
Lisa Agona, Chief Marketing Officer

The report provides in-depth news and analysis of asbestos bankruptcy law and the progress of bankrupt asbestos companies through the ever-evolving Chapter 11 process. Topics include: insurance issues, impacts on settlements, how asbestos bankruptcies are affecting the landscape of the litigation and which companies may be forced to file for Chapter 11 protection in the future.
Cost: $475.00
100 Pages
Frequency: Quarterly
Founded in: 2000
Mailing list available for rent

15320 Mealey's California Section 17200 Report
LexisNexis Mealey's
555 5th Avenue
Los Angeles, CA 90013

213-627-1130
800-253-4182
mealeyinfo@lexisnexis.com;
www.lexisnexis.com/mealeys
Social Media: Facebook, Twitter, LinkedIn, RSS, Youtube

Tom Hagy, CEO
Maureen McGuire, Editorial Director
Bryan Redding, Editor
Mike Wash, Chief Executive Officer, Legal
Lisa Agona, Chief Marketing Officer

Monitors litigation and provides legislative updates on California's Unfair Competition Law. This monthly report will offer readers hard-to-find filings and briefs, new complaints, breaking news, concise case summaries, and trial updates. All major cases involving Section 17200 of the state's Business and Professions Code will be reported, including those dealings with insurance, employment, consumer law, the Internet, telecommunications, securities, fraud, product liability and many more.
Cost: $959.00
100 Pages
Frequency: Monthly
Founded in: 2002
Mailing list available for rent

15321 Mealey's Catastrophic Loss
LexisNexis Mealey's
555 W 5th Avenue
Los Angeles, CA 90013

213-627-1130
800-253-4182
mealeyinfo@lexisnexis.com;
www.lexisnexis.com/mealeys
Social Media: Facebook, Twitter, LinkedIn, RSS, Youtube

Tom Hagy, CEO
Maureen McGuire, Editorial Director
Gina Cappello, Editor
Mike Wash, Chief Executive Officer, Legal
Lisa Agona, Chief Marketing Officer

This report focuses on business interruption insurance claims in the aftermath of the Hurricane Katrina, September 11th, and other catastrophic loss tragedies. Additionally, the report will go beyond these claims and will offer important business interruption insurance coverage news related to computer viruses, computer failures, and natural disasters.
Cost: $1075.00
100 Pages
Frequency: Monthly
Founded in: 2001
Mailing list available for rent

15322 Mealey's Daubert Report
LexisNexis Mealey's
555 W 5th Avenue
Los Angeles, CA 90013

213-627-1130
800-253-4182
mealeyinfo@lexisnexis.com;
www.lexisnexis.com/mealeys
Social Media: Facebook, Twitter, LinkedIn, RSS, Youtube

Tom Hagy, CEO
Maureen McGuire, Editorial Director
Kristin Casler, Editor
Mike Wash, Chief Executive Officer, Legal
Lisa Agona, Chief Marketing Officer

This newsletter covers the interpretation, adoption and/or rejection of the Supreme Court's landmark expert admissibility ruling, Daubert v. Merrell Dow Pharmaceutical Inc. As the nation's jurisdictions grapple with so called junk science testimony, this monthly newsletter offers subscribers the latest key rulings in this contentious components of civil and criminal litigation.
Cost: $735.00
100 Pages
Frequency: Monthly
Founded in: 1997
Mailing list available for rent

15323 Mealey's Emerging Drugs & Devices
LexisNexis Mealey's
555 W 5th Avenue
Los Angeles, CA 90013

213-627-1130
800-253-4182
mealeyinfo@lexisnexis.com;
www.lexisnexis.com/mealeys
Social Media: Facebook, Twitter, LinkedIn, RSS, Youtube

Tom Hagy, CEO
Maureen McGuire, Editorial Director
Tom Moylan, Editor
Mike Wash, Chief Executive Officer, Legal
Lisa Agona, Chief Marketing Officer

The report covers cases involving a variety of prescription drug vaccines, implants and devices. Duract, Parlodel, Accutane, fen-phen, Rezulin, Propulsid, dietary supplements and blood products are among the topics tracked. Medical devices covered include heart catheters, breast implants, heart valves, intraocular lenses, jaw implants, joint replacements, latex gloves, pacemakers, pedicle screws, penile implants, and surgical lasers.
Cost: $1249.00
100 Pages
Frequency: Semi-Monthly
Founded in: 1996
Mailing list available for rent

15324 Mealey's Emerging Insurance Disputes
LexisNexis Mealey's
555 W 5th Avenue
Los Angeles, CA 90013
213-627-1130
800-253-4182; *Fax:* 610-768-0880
mealeyinfo@lexisnexis.com;

www.lexisnexis.com/mealeys
Social Media: Facebook, Twitter, LinkedIn, RSS, Youtube

Tom Hagy, CEO
Maureen McGuire, Editorial Director
Gina Cappello, Editor
Mike Wash, Chief Executive Officer, Legal
Lisa Agona, Chief Marketing Officer

The report tracks new areas of coverage liability, novel policy applications, and conflicting policy language interpretations as they arise in insurance litigation. Some areas of coverage featured are: sexual harassment and discrimination, assault and battery, professional liability, patent and trademark infringement, construction defects, directors and officers claims, emotional distress, intentional acts, technology, and insurance business practices.
Cost: $ 1229.00
100 Pages
Frequency: Semi-Monthly
Founded in: 1996
Mailing list available for rent

15325 **Mealey's Emerging Securities Litigation**
LexisNexis Mealey's
555 W 5th Avenue
Los Angeles, CA 90013

213-627-1130
800-253-4182; *Fax:* 610-768-0880
mealeyinfo@lexisnexis.com;
www.lexisnexis.com/mealeys
Social Media: Facebook, Twitter, LinkedIn, RSS, Youtube

Tom Hagy, CEO
Maureen McGuire, Editorial Director
Mike Lello, Editor
Mike Wash, Chief Executive Officer, Legal
Lisa Agona, Chief Marketing Officer

The report covers fiduciary duties to shareholders, 401k and pension implications, class actions, damage calculations, causation questions. Daubert issues, debt bondholder implications, bankruptcy issues and accountant liability in the securities law context.
Cost: $875.00
100 Pages
Frequency: Monthly
Founded in: 2002
Mailing list available for rent

15326 **Mealey's Emerging Toxic Torts**
LexisNexis Mealey's
555 W 5th Avenue
Los Angeles, CA 90013

213-627-1130
800-253-4182; *Fax:* 610-768-0880
mealeyinfo@lexisnexis.com;
www.lexisnexis.com/mealeys
Social Media: Facebook, Twitter, LinkedIn, RSS, Youtube

Tom Hagy, CEO
Maureen McGuire, Editorial Director
Bill Lowe, Editor
Mike Wash, Chief Executive Officer, Legal
Lisa Agona, Chief Marketing Officer

The report focuses on the hottest areas of toxic tort litigation including: chemical sensitivity; indoor air quality; groundwater, soil and air contamination; radiation; workplace exposure; pesticides; solvents; latex gloves; EMF's; MTBE; endocrine disruptors, and more. The report provides in-depth coverage of medical monitoring; fear of cancer/disease; stigma damages; expert admissibility; federal preemption; class actions; punitive damages and market share theory.
Cost: $1539.00
100 Pages
Frequency: Semi-Monthly
Founded in: 1992
Mailing list available for rent

15327 **Mealey's International Arbitration Quarterly Law Review**
LexisNexis Mealey's
555 W 5th Avenue
Los Angeles, CA 90013

213-627-1130
800-253-4182; *Fax:* 610-768-0880
mealeyinfo@lexisnexis.com;
www.lexisnexis.com/mealeys
Social Media: Facebook, Twitter, LinkedIn, RSS, Youtube

Tom Hagy, CEO
Maureen McGuire, Editorial Director
Edie Scott, Editor
Mike Wash, Chief Executive Officer, Legal
Lisa Agona, Chief Marketing Officer

The report provides thought-provoking commentary articles authored by aribitrators, scholars and attorneys with first-hand knowledge of the complex field of commercial dispute resolution. Each issue contains analytical discussions and practical insights on current case law, new treaties and statues, arbitration principles, dispute resolution techniques, and more from our prestigious international authors.
Cost: $475.00
100 Pages
Frequency: Quarterly
Founded in: 2000
Mailing list available for rent

15328 **Mealey's International Arbitration Report**
LexisNexis Mealey's
555 W 5th Avenue
Los Angeles, CA 90013

213-627-1130
800-253-4182; *Fax:* 610-768-0880
mealeyinfo@lexisnexis.com;
www.lexisnexis.com/mealeys
Social Media: Facebook, Twitter, LinkedIn, RSS, Youtube

Tom Hagy, CEO
Maureen McGuire, Editorial Director
Edie Scott, Editor
Mike Wash, Chief Executive Officer, Legal
Lisa Agona, Chief Marketing Officer

The report examines arbitration and related litigation in courts world-wide. Covers enforcement, jurisdictional disputes, forum selection, use of experts by arbitral parties, enforcement, judicial supervision, the Iran-US Claims Tribunal, the United Nations Compensation Commission, and events of interest at arbitration institutions around the globe.
Cost: $2049.00
100 Pages
Frequency: Monthly
Founded in: 1986
Mailing list available for rent

15329 **Mealey's International Asbestos Liability Report**
LexisNexis Mealey's
555 W 5th Avenue
Los Angeles, CA 90013

213-627-1130
800-253-4182; *Fax:* 610-768-0880
mealeyinfo@lexisnexis.com;
www.lexisnexis.com/mealeys
Social Media: Facebook, Twitter, LinkedIn, RSS, Youtube

Tom Hagy, CEO
Maureen McGuire, Editorial Director
Lisa Schaeffer, Editor
Mike Wash, Chief Executive Officer, Legal
Lisa Agona, Chief Marketing Officer

The report covers the latest litigation, regulatory, and medical news related to worldwide asbestos exposure - including the emerging issue of subsidiary liability and the question of US jurisdiction - with in-depth case summaries and news of medical findings, full-text court documents, and exclusive expert commentary articles.
Cost: $959.00
100 Pages
Frequency: Monthly
Founded in: 2003
Mailing list available for rent

15330 **Mealey's Litigation Report: Insurance Fraud**
LexisNexis Mealey's
555 W 5th Avenue
Los Angeles, CA 90013

213-627-1130
800-253-4182; *Fax:* 610-768-0880
mealeyinfo@lexisnexis.com;
www.lexisnexis.com/mealeys
Social Media: Facebook, Twitter, LinkedIn, RSS, Youtube

Tom Hagy, CEO
Maureen McGuire, Editorial Director
Teresa Kent Zink, Editor
Mike Wash, Chief Executive Officer, Legal
Lisa Agona, Chief Marketing Officer

The report reviews civil and criminal cases arising from efforts by policyholders and third parties to defraud insurance carriers. Topics include false and fraudulent claims, arson, reverse bad faith, restitution, RICO, incontestability clauses, material misrepresentation, rescission, qui tam actions and fraud rings. Readers receive reports on schemes involving property & casualty, health care, automobile, life, homeowners, and workers' compensation fraud.
Cost: $839.00
100 Pages
Frequency: Monthly
Founded in: 1994
Mailing list available for rent

15331 **Mealey's Litigation Report: Asbestos**
LexisNexis Mealey's
555 W 5th Avenue
Los Angeles, CA 90013

213-627-1130
800-253-4182; *Fax:* 610-768-0880
mealeyinfo@lexisnexis.com;
www.lexisnexis.com/mealeys
Social Media: Facebook, Twitter, LinkedIn, RSS, Youtube

Tom Hagy, CEO
Maureen McGuire, Editorial Director
Bryan Redding, Editor
Mike Wash, Chief Executive Officer, Legal
Lisa Agona, Chief Marketing Officer

The report offers unsurpassed coverage of litigation arising from asbestos-related injury and death. Key issues include: massive class action settlements involving present and future claimants, state and federal verdicts, litigation experts, medical monitoring claims, suits against the tobacco industry, discovery battles, discovery rule decisions, insurance coverage rulings, and asbestos property decisions.
Cost: $1789.00
100 Pages
Frequency: Semi-Monthly
Founded in: 1984
Mailing list available for rent

15332 **Mealey's Litigation Report: Baycol**
LexisNexis Mealey's
555 W 5th Avenue
Los Angeles, CA 90013

213-627-1130
800-253-4182; *Fax:* 610-768-0880
mealeyinfo@lexisnexis.com;

www.lexisnexis.com/mealeys
Social Media: Facebook, Twitter, LinkedIn, RSS, Youtube

Tom Hagy, CEO
Maureen McGuire, Editorial Director
Dylan McGuire, Editor
Mike Wash, Chief Executive Officer, Legal
Lisa Agona, Chief Marketing Officer

This report tracks the litigation surrounding Baycol and other statin-based anti-cholesterol drug cases. Since the voluntary withdrawl of Bayer's Baycol and Lipobay brand cerivastatin anti-cholesterol drugs, numerous complaints have been filed. The report will cover hard-to-find filings, new complaints, class actions, MDL developments, trial updates and more.
Cost: $950.00
100 Pages
Frequency: Monthly
Founded in: 2002
Mailing list available for rent

15333 Mealey's Litigation Report: California Insurance
LexisNexis Mealey's
1016 W Ninth Avenue
1st Floor
King of Prussia, PA 19406-1221

215-564-1788
800-448-1515; *Fax:* 610-768-0880
mealeyinfo@lexisnexis.com;
www.lexisnexis.com/mealeys
Social Media: Facebook, Twitter, LinkedIn, Itunes, Youtube

Kumsal Bayazit, Global Senior Vice President
Haywood Talcove, Chief Executive Officer, Government
Ian McDougall, Executive Vice President
Mike Walsh, CEO
Alex Watson, Executive Vice President

The Report focuses on ever-changing California and federal Ninth Circuit insurance coverage disputes and developments. Topics include California developments in bad faith litigation, earthquake damage coverage, disability insurance, products liability coverage, environmental insurance coverage, mold coverage, asbestos coverage, aviation litigation coverage, entertainment law and more.
Cost: $949.00
100 Pages
Frequency: Monthly
Founded in: 2001

15334 Mealey's Litigation Report: Class Actions
LexisNexis Mealey's
1016 W Ninth Avenue
1st Floor
King of Prussia, PA 19406-1221

215-564-1788
800-448-1515; *Fax:* 610-768-0880
mealeyinfo@lexisnexis.com;
www.lexisnexis.com/mealeys
Social Media: Facebook, Twitter, LinkedIn, Itunes, Youtube

Kumsal Bayazit, Global Senior Vice President
Haywood Talcove, Chief Executive Officer, Government
Ian McDougall, Executive Vice President
Mike Walsh, CEO
Alex Watson, Executive Vice President

This report will provide in-depth coverage of class action litigation involving mass torts and beyond - including consumer law, employment law, securities litigation and e-commerce disputes. Get the latest on: hard-to-find filings, notice plans, fairness hearings, class certification rulings, settlements, trial news and verdicts, attorney fee news, appeals, breaking news stories, new complaints, Supreme Court battles, and much more.
Cost: $1195.00
100 Pages
Frequency: Semi-Monthly
Founded in: 1997

15335 Mealey's Litigation Report: Construction Defects
LexisNexis Mealey's
1016 W Ninth Avenue
1st Floor
King of Prussia, PA 19406-1221

215-564-1788
800-448-1515; *Fax:* 610-768-0880
mealeyinfo@lexisnexis.com;
www.lexisnexis.com/mealeys
Social Media: Facebook, Twitter, LinkedIn, Itunes, Youtube

Kumsal Bayazit, Global Senior Vice President
Haywood Talcove, Chief Executive Officer, Government
Ian McDougall, Executive Vice President
Mike Walsh, CEO
Alex Watson, Executive Vice President

The Report tracks the growing area of construction defect litigation, including cases involving water intrusion, building settlement, concrete corrosion, mold and other defects. Topics covered include: recovery of damages, warranty issues, contractor liability, sub-contractor liability, developer liability, architect liability and related insurance cover actions.
Cost: $979.00
100 Pages
Frequency: Monthly
Founded in: 2000

15336 Mealey's Litigation Report: Copyright
LexisNexis Mealey's
1016 W Ninth Avenue
1st Floor
King of Prussia, PA 19406-1221

215-564-1788
800-448-1515; *Fax:* 610-768-0880
mealeyinfo@lexisnexis.com;
www.lexisnexis.com/mealeys
Social Media: Facebook, Twitter, LinkedIn, Itunes, Youtube

Kumsal Bayazit, Global Senior Vice President
Haywood Talcove, Chief Executive Officer, Government
Ian McDougall, Executive Vice President
Mike Walsh, CEO
Alex Watson, Executive Vice President

The report offers timely and practical analysis on the hot issues in the field. Also features in-depth reporting of copyright law, including court decisions, new suits, settlements, and trials, plus full-text court documents.
Cost: $849.00
100 Pages
Frequency: Monthly
Founded in: 2002

15337 Mealey's Litigation Report: Cyber Tech & E -Commerce
LexisNexis Mealey's
1016 W Ninth Avenue
1st Floor
King of Prussia, PA 19406-1221

215-564-1788
800-448-1515; *Fax:* 610-768-0880
mealeyinfo@lexisnexis.com;
www.lexisnexis.com/mealeys
Social Media: Facebook, Twitter, LinkedIn, Itunes, Youtube

Kumsal Bayazit, Global Senior Vice President
Haywood Talcove, Chief Executive Officer, Government
Ian McDougall, Executive Vice President
Mike Walsh, CEO
Alex Watson, Executive Vice President

The Report covers disputes arising from e-commerce. The report tracks emerging legal issues, including: Internet security, data destruction and/or alteration, defamation on the Web, software errors, hardware failure, electronic theft, e-mail trespass, online privacy, government action, shareholder lawsuits, Internet jurisdiction issues, file sharing (copyright) disputes and much more.
Cost: $999.00
100 Pages
Frequency: Monthly
Founded in: 1999

15338 Mealey's Litigation Report: Disability Insurance
LexisNexis Mealey's
1016 W Ninth Avenue
1st Floor
King of Prussia, PA 19406-1221

215-564-1788
800-448-1515; *Fax:* 610-768-0880
mealeyinfo@lexisnexis.com;
www.lexisnexis.com/mealeys
Social Media: Facebook, Twitter, LinkedIn, Itunes, Youtube

Kumsal Bayazit, Global Senior Vice President
Haywood Talcove, Chief Executive Officer, Government
Ian McDougall, Executive Vice President
Mike Walsh, CEO
Alex Watson, Executive Vice President

This report tracks the burgeoning number of disputes involving complex disability coverage claims. Topics covered include: claims for chronic fatigue, chronic pain, stress, psychiatric disabilities, chemical dependency and risk of relapse, plus key issues like total disability, own occupation, bad faith, ERSA, class actions and much more.
Cost: $849.00
100 Pages
Frequency: Monthly
Founded in: 2000

15339 Mealey's Litigation Report: Discovery
LexisNexis Mealey's
1016 W Ninth Avenue
1st Floor
King of Prussia, PA 19406-1221

215-564-1788
800-448-1515; *Fax:* 610-768-0880
mealeyinfo@lexisnexis.com;
www.lexisnexis.com/mealeys
Social Media: Facebook, Twitter, LinkedIn, Itunes, Youtube

Kumsal Bayazit, Global Senior Vice President
Haywood Talcove, Chief Executive Officer, Government
Ian McDougall, Executive Vice President
Mike Walsh, CEO
Alex Watson, Executive Vice President

This report covers all of the discovery litigation essentials, including how different districts and judges interpret federal discovery rules, procedural changes, the work product, attorney-client and common interest privileges, and discovery abuse.
Cost: $785.00
100 Pages
Frequency: Monthly
Founded in: 2003

15340 Mealey's Litigation Report: ERISA
LexisNexis Mealey's
1016 W Ninth Avenue
1st Floor
King of Prussia, PA 19406-1221

215-564-1788
800-448-1515; *Fax:* 610-768-0880

mealeyinfo@lexisnexis.com;
www.lexisnexis.com/mealeys
Social Media: Facebook, Twitter, LinkedIn, Itunes, Youtube

Kumsal Bayazit, Global Senior Vice President
Haywood Talcove, Chief Executive Officer, Government
Ian McDougall, Executive Vice President
Mike Walsh, CEO
Alex Watson, Executive Vice President

The report focuses on the hottest areas of ERISA litigation, including preemption, health plan actions, exhaustion of administrative remedies, contingent worker litigation, class actions 401k plans, attorney's fees, breach of fiduciary duty, what courts consider to be equitable relief, downsizing and benefit cutbacks, blackout periods and bad faith claims against disability insurers.
Cost: $875.00
100 Pages
Frequency: Monthly
Founded in: 2002

15341 **Mealey's Litigation Report: Ephedra/PPA**
LexisNexis Mealey's
1016 W Ninth Avenue
1st Floor
King of Prussia, PA 19406-1221

215-564-1788
800-448-1515; *Fax:* 610-768-0880
mealeyinfo@lexisnexis.com;
www.lexisnexis.com/mealeys
Social Media: Facebook, Twitter, LinkedIn, Itunes, Youtube

Kumsal Bayazit, Global Senior Vice President
Haywood Talcove, Chief Executive Officer, Government
Ian McDougall, Executive Vice President
Mike Walsh, CEO
Alex Watson, Executive Vice President

The report tracks every facet of the growing area of litigation resulting from injuries and deaths associated with over-the-counter decongestant and appetite suppressant, phenylpropanolamine (PPA), and the chemically similar weight-loss herb, ephedra. The report offers true litigation reporting of new complaints, answers, discovery motions, appeals, trials, verdicts, settlements, plus covers the latest regulatory news.
Cost: $995.00
100 Pages
Frequency: Monthly
Founded in: 2001

15342 **Mealey's Litigation Report: Fen-Phen/Redux**
LexisNexis Mealey's
1016 W Ninth Avenue
1st Floor
King of Prussia, PA 19406-1221

215-564-1788
800-448-1515; *Fax:* 610-768-0880
mealeyinfo@lexisnexis.com;
www.lexisnexis.com/mealeys
Social Media: Facebook, Twitter, LinkedIn, Itunes, Youtube

Kumsal Bayazit, Global Senior Vice President
Haywood Talcove, Chief Executive Officer, Government
Ian McDougall, Executive Vice President
Mike Walsh, CEO
Alex Watson, Executive Vice President

The report provides detailed coverage of the litigation surrounding fen-phen, Redux and other diet drugs. The report covers new filings, class actions, MDL proceedings, trials, settlements, rulings, medical studies, FDA activity and more.
Cost: $995.00
100 Pages
Frequency: Monthly
Founded in: 1997

15343 **Mealey's Litigation Report: Insurance**
LexisNexis Mealey's
1016 W Ninth Avenue
1st Floor
King of Prussia, PA 19406-1221

215-564-1788
800-448-1515; *Fax:* 610-768-0880
mealeyinfo@lexisnexis.com;
www.lexisnexis.com/mealeys
Social Media: Facebook, Twitter, LinkedIn, Itunes, Youtube

Kumsal Bayazit, Global Senior Vice President
Haywood Talcove, Chief Executive Officer, Government
Ian McDougall, Executive Vice President
Mike Walsh, CEO
Alex Watson, Executive Vice President

The report tracks declaratory judgment actions regarding coverage for litigation arising from long-tail claims, including environmental contamination and latent damage and injury allegedly caused by asbestos, tox chemicals and fumes, lead, breast implants, medical devices, construction defects, and more. Key issues: allocation, occurrence, policy exclusion, choice of law, discovery, duty to defend, notice, trigger of coverage and known loss.
Cost: $2115.00
100 Pages
Frequency: Weekly
Founded in: 1984

15344 **Mealey's Litigation Report: Insurance Bad Faith**
LexisNexis Mealey's
1016 W Ninth Avenue
1st Floor
King of Prussia, PA 19406-1221

215-564-1788
800-448-1515; *Fax:* 610-768-0880
mealeyinfo@lexisnexis.com;
www.lexisnexis.com/mealeys
Social Media: Facebook, LinkedIn, Itunes, Youtube

Kumsal Bayazit, Global Senior Vice President
Haywood Talcove, Chief Executive Officer, Government
Ian McDougall, Executive Vice President
Mike Walsh, CEO
Alex Watson, Executive Vice President

The report details insurance coverage disputes arising from alleged breaches of the implied covenant of good faith and fair dealing. The topics covered involve third-party and first-party actions, statutory suits, punitive damage claims, coverage denials and delays, the definition of bad faith, relevant legislation, verdicts, and discovery disputes.
Cost: $1325.00
100 Pages
Frequency: Semi-Monthly
Founded in: 1987

15345 **Medical Liability Advisory Service**
Business Publishers
8737 Colesville Road
10th Floor
Silver Spring, MD 20910-3928

301-876-6300
800-274-6737; *Fax:* 301-589-8493
custserv@bpinews.com; www.bpinews.com

Eric Easton, Publisher
Bonita Becker, Editor

Gives you practical information on just what triggers a lawsuit. Information you can pass on to your staff to claim-proof your procedures.
Founded in: 1963

15346 **Medical Malpractice Reports**
Matthew Bender and Company
11 Penn Plz
Suite 5101
New York, NY 10001-2006

212-000-1111; *Fax:* 212-244-3188

Eric Blood, Data Processing

All the facts, background information and expert analysis you need to keep on top of new legislation, new theories of liability, the impact of new medical technology and more.

15347 **Mental and Physical Disability Law Reporter: On-Line**
American Bar Association
740 15th Street NW
Washington, DC 20005-1019

202-662-1000; *Fax:* 202-442-3439
Social Media: Facebook, Twitter, LinkedIn

Stephen N. Zack, President
Katherine H. O'Neil, Commission Chair
John W. Parry, Commission Director
Jack L. Rives, Executive Director
Alice Richmond, Treasurer

A new online searchable database allows subscribers to research disability law cases and legislation by case name, federal or state legislation, subject area, jurisdiction, and year (beginning 2003). There are 22 subject areas that cover three main areas: civil mental disability law; criminal mental disability law; and disability discrimination law. The database, which is updated every two months, contains over 12,000 summaries of key cases and legislation.
Cost: $299.00
15 Members
Frequency: 6 X/Year
ISSN: 0883-7902
Founded in: 1973

15348 **Mergers & Acquisitions Litigation Reporter**
Thomson Reuters
610 Opperman Dr
St Paul, MN 55123-1340

651-687-7000
800-344-5008; *Fax:* 651-687-5581;
www.store.westlaw.com/default.aspx

Charles B Cater, Executive VP
Laurie Zenner, VP

Provides summaries and fulltext documents in key litigation concerning mergers and acquisitions. Offers general buyout and acquisition coverage as well as cases related to leveraged buyouts.
Cost: $1234.20
Frequency: Monthly
Mailing list available for rent

15349 **Money Laundering Alert**
Alert Global Media
80 SW 8th Street
Suite 2300
Miami, FL 33130-3031

305-530-0500
800-232-3652; *Fax:* 305-530-9434
customerservice@moneylaundering.com;
www.moneylaundering.com

Charles Intriago, President

Covers legal issues, including new laws, regulations and cases related to money laundering and the bank secrecy act in the US and worldwide. Provides practical guidance and analysis and serves as a training tool. Also full text on the internet.
Cost: $945.00
15 Pages
Frequency: Monthly
ISSN: 1046-3070
Founded in: 1989

15350 Municipal Litigation Reporter
Strafford Publications
PO Box 13729
Atlanta, GA 30324-0729

404-881-1141
800-926-7926; *Fax:* 404-881-0074
customerservice@straffordpub.com;
www.straffordpub.com

Richard Ossoff, President
Jennifer Vaughan, Managing Editor

Monthly digest of key court decisions on litigation involving local governments. Cases are screened and selected to provide concise, comprehensive coverage of issues important to municipal attorneys and others involved with the local government.
Cost: $497.00
16 Pages
ISSN: 0278-1301
Founded in: 1984
Mailing list available for rent: 7.4M names
Printed in one color

15351 NAELA News
National Academy of Elder Law Attorneys
1577 Spring Hill Road
Suite 220
Vienna, VA 22182-2223

703-942-5711; *Fax:* 703-563-9504
naela@naela.org; www.naela.org

Peter G Wacht, CAE, Executive Director
Nancy Sween, Director Publications
Kirsten Brown Simpson, Director, Membership & Marketing
Ann Watkins, Operations Manager
Roger Naoroji, Meetings & Education Coordinator

Communicates the activities, goals, and mission of its publisher, the National Academy of Elder Law Attorneys and seeks out and publishes information and diverse views related to Elder Law and Special Needs.
Frequency: 6x Year

15352 NCWBA Newsletter
National Conference of Women's Bar Associations
PO Box 82366
Portland, OR 97282

E-Mail: info@ncwba.org; www.ncwba.org

Jeanne Cezanne Collins, President
Pamela Berman, President-Elect
Diane Rynerson, Executive Director

To promote and assist the growth of local and statewide women's bar associations and ideas among women's bar associations and women's bar sections of local and statewide bar associations; to serve as a vehicle for the exchange and dissemination of information and ideas among women's bar associations and women's bar sections of local and statewide bar associations.
Frequency: Monthly

15353 National Bankruptcy Reporter
Andrews Communications
175 Stafford, Building 4
Suite 140
Wayne, PA 19087

610-225-0510
800-345-1101; *Fax:* 610-225-0501;
www.andrewspub.com

Robert Maroldo, Publisher

Commercial bankruptcy news.
Frequency: Monthly

15354 National Bar Bulletin
National Bar Association
1225 11th St Nw
Washington, DC 20001-4217

202-842-3900; *Fax:* 202-289-6170;
www.nationalbar.org

John Crump, Executive Director
Kim M Keenan, Manager
Teka Miller, Manager

Association news and activities, legislative updates and information for lawyers.
Cost: $20.00
8 Pages
Frequency: Monthly
Founded in: 1925

15355 National Financing Law Digest
Strafford Publications
PO Box 13729
Atlanta, GA 30324-0729

404-881-1141
800-926-7926; *Fax:* 404-881-0074
customerservice@straffordpub.com;
www.straffordpub.com

Richard Ossoff, President
Jennifer Vaughan, Managing Editor

Monthly digest of nationally significant litigation concerning secured and unsecured financing transactions, including bonds, bankruptcy collection, and lender liability.
Cost: $597.00
Frequency: Monthly
ISSN: 1073-953X
Founded in: 1984

15356 National Notary
National Notary Association
9350 DeSoto Avenue
PO Box 2402
Chatsworth, CA 91311-2402

818-394-4000
800-876-6827; *Fax:* 800-833-1211
publications@nationalnotary.org;
www.nationalnotary.org

Deborah Thaw, Executive VP
Armando Aguirre, Editor
Milton G. Valera, Chairman
Thomas A. Heymann, President /CEO
Deborah M. Thaw, Executive Vice President

Contents range from indentity fraud and electronic notarization, to legislation and practicing tips. Also includes human interest stories involving notaries.
Circulation: 250,000
ISSN: 0894-7872
Founded in: 1957
Printed in 4 colors on glossy stock

15357 National On-Campus Report
Magna Publications
2718 Dryden Drive
Madison, WI 53704-3086

608-246-3590
800-433-0499; *Fax:* 608-246-3597
support@magnapubs.com;
www.magnapubs.com

William Haight, President
Jody Glynn Patrick, VP
Therese Kattner, Editor
David Burns, Publisher
Debra Art, Director

The campus legal monthly.
Cost: $169.00
8 Pages
Founded in: 1972
Printed in 2 colors on matte stock

15358 National Paralegal Reporter
National Federation of Paralegal Associations
2815 Eastlake Ave E
Suite 160
Seattle, WA 98102-3278

206-285-1851; *Fax:* 206-284-3481
info@akpreparedness.com;
www.akproductions.com

Founded in: 1981

15359 National Property Law Digests
Strafford Publications
PO Box 13729
Atlanta, GA 30324-0729

404-881-1141
800-926-7926; *Fax:* 404-881-0074
customerservice@straffordpub.com;
www.straffordpub.com

Richard Ossoff, Presdient

Case digests of national significant court decisions affecting the acquisition, development, management, transfer and financing of real property.
Cost: $697.00
Frequency: Monthly
ISSN: 0363-8340
Founded in: 1984
Mailing list available for rent: 25M names

15360 National Report on Substance Abuse
National Retail Federation
325 7th St Nw
Suite 1000
Washington, DC 20004-2808

202-783-7971
800-673-4692; *Fax:* 202-737-2849;
www.nrf.com

Tracy Mullin, President
Terry Peters, Editor
Matthew Shay, President and CEO
Vicki Cantrell, Senior Vice President, Communities
Mallory Duncan, Senior Vice President

Biweekly review of federal and state laws, regulations and court cases involving alcohol and drug abuse, with an emphasis on workplace drug testing. Also covers treatment and prevention, EAPs, ADA, local laws and policies.
Cost: $377.00
Circulation: 36000
Founded in: 1981
Printed in 2 colors on matte stock

15361 National Report on Work & Family
Business Publishers
2222 Sedwick Dr
Suite 101
Durham, NC 27713

800-223-8720; *Fax:* 800-508-2592
custserv@bpinews.com; www.bpinews.com

Independent, authoritative resource covering the latest federal and state legislative, legal and regulatory developments concerning work/family issues. Includes case studies of organizations that have implemented family-friendly policies.
Cost: $497.00
Frequency: 25 per year

15362 National Security Law Report
American Bar Association-Law & National Security
740 15th St Nw
Suite 8
Washington, DC 20005-1022

202-662-1000; *Fax:* 202-662-1032
orders@abanet.org;
www.americanbar.org/aba.html
Social Media: Facebook, Twitter

Laurel G. Bellows, President

The Report includes reports of committee conferences, pertinent law and national security updates, recent cases, book reviews, pending

legislation, and other writing relevant to the field.
Frequency: Monthly
Circulation: 4000
Founded in: 1991

15363 Nolo News: Legal Self-Help Newspaper
Nolo Press
950 Parker St
Berkeley, CA 94710-2576

510-704-2248; *Fax:* 510-859-0027;
www.nolo.com

Maggie Wang, Manager
Mary Randolph, Editor

Self-help legal newspaper.
Cost: $39.99
Frequency: Weekly
Circulation: 120000
Founded in: 1971

15364 On the Line: Union Labor Reports Guide
Bureau of National Affairs
1801 S Bell St
Arlington, VA 22202-4501

703-341-3000
800-372-1033; *Fax:* 800-253-0332
customercare@bna.com; www.bnabooks.com
Social Media: Facebook, Twitter, LinkedIn

Paul N Wojcik, CEO

Reports on shopfloor issues affecting union stewards. Includes summaries of arbitration awards and court cases. $4.00 per year each subscription.
Cost: $4.00
ISSN: 1526-2863
Founded in: 1929

15365 Parascope
American Bar Association
321 N Clark St
Chicago, IL 60654-7598

312-988-5000
800-285-2221; *Fax:* 312-988-6281
askaba@abanet.org;
www.americanbar.org/aba.html
Social Media: Facebook, Twitter

Tommy H Wells Jr, President
Laurel G. Bellows, President

Newsletter for nation's appellate staff attorneys. Contains book reviews and articles on matters concerning appellate courts.
Cost: $19.00
Frequency: Quarterly

15366 Partner's Report for Law Firm Owners
Institute of Management and Administration
3 Bethesda Metro Center
Suite 250
Bethesda, MD 20814-5377

703-341-3500
800-372-1033; *Fax:* 800-253-0332;
www.ioma.com

Keeps partners up to date on salary guidelines and benefits, aw well as provide the reader with tips on increasing profit margins and exercising leadership skills.
Frequency: Monthly
Founded in: 1984

15367 Patent/Trade/Copyright Newsletter
American Bar Association
321 N Clark St
Chicago, IL 60654-7598

312-988-5000
800-285-2221; *Fax:* 312-988-6281;
www.americanbar.org/aba.html
Social Media: Facebook, Twitter

Tommy H Wells Jr, President
Laurel G. Bellows, President

Activities of the Section, recent developments in intellectual property law and calendar of events.
Frequency: Quarterly
Founded in: 1878

15368 People and Programs
American Bar Association
321 N Clark St
Chicago, IL 60654-7598

312-988-5000
800-285-2221; *Fax:* 312-988-6281
askaba@abanet.org;
www.americanbar.org/aba.html
Social Media: Facebook, Twitter

Tommy H Wells Jr, President
Laurel G. Bellows, President

A newsletter for donors and volunteers for the ABA fund for Justice and Education, which supports over 150 public service and law-related education programs.
Founded in: 1878

15369 People-to-People Newsletter
Association of Legal Administrators
75 Tri-State International
Suite 222
Lincolnshire, IL 60069-4435

847-267-1252; *Fax:* 847-267-1329
publications@alanet.org; www.alanet.org

Larry Smith, Executive Director
Debbie Thomas, Director, Accounting & Finance
Renee Mahovsky, Director, Administration/Operations
Bob Abramson, Director, Marketing & Communication
Jan Waugh, Director, Member Services

Offers the newest information and legislative updates for legal administrators.
Frequency: Monthly
Founded in: 1971

15370 Personal Injury Verdict Reviews
LRP Publications
PO Box 980
Horsham, PA 19044-0980

215-784-0912
800-341-7874; *Fax:* 215-784-9639
webmaster@lrp.com; www.lrp.com

Todd Lutz, CFO
David Light, Managing Editor
Brooke Doran, Research Associate

Each twice-monthly issue contains a statistically based feature article backed by nationwide personal injury case summaries. Each case summary includes description of the incident, names and locations of counsel and expert witnesses, verdict or settlement amount, amount of medical expense and wage loss and date and docket number.
Cost: $375.00
Founded in: 1977

15371 Personnel Legal Alert
Alexander Hamilton Institute
70 Hilltop Rd
Suite 2200
Ramsey, NJ 07446-2816

201-825-3377
800-879-2441; *Fax:* 201-825-8696
editorial@ahipubs.com; www.ahipubs.com

Schuyler T Jenks, President

Deals with legal aspects of personnel.
Cost: $97.00
4 Pages
Frequency: Fortnightly
Circulation: 4000
Founded in: 1989
Mailing list available for rent: 7,000 names at $125 per M
Printed in 2 colors on matte stock

15372 Personnel Manager's Legal Letter
Institute of Management and Administration
3 Bethesda Metro Center
Suite 250
Bethesda, MD 20814-5377

703-341-3500
800-372-1033; *Fax:* 800-253-0332;
www.ioma.com

PMLL regularly covers title VII, the Americans with Disabilities Act, ERISA, the Family and Medical Leave Act, and human resources legal issues around hiring, teminations, compensation and much more.

15373 Practical Law Books Reviews
Library Managemental Services
5914 Highland Hills Drive
Austin, TX 78731-4057

512-320-0320

Judith Helburn, Publisher

Reference book separated by field specification.

15374 Premises Liability Report
Strafford Publications
PO Box 13729
Atlanta, GA 30324-0729

404-881-1141
800-926-7926; *Fax:* 404-881-0074
customerservice@straffordpub.com;
www.straffordpub.com

Richard Ossoff, President
Jennifer Vaughan, Managing Editor

Digest of legal developments offering liability of property owners and managers. Warning system for potential lawsuits for injuries resulting from conditions on or near premises.
Cost: $287.00
Frequency: Monthly
ISSN: 1055-730X
Founded in: 1984

15375 Preservation Law Reporter
National Trust for Historic Preservation
1785 Massachusetts Ave Nw
Washington, DC 20036-2189

202-588-6000
800-944-6847; *Fax:* 202-588-6038
members@nthp.org; www.nationaltrust.org

Richard Moe, CEO
Andrew Carroll, Production Manager
Bob Barron, Publisher
Doug Loescher, Director

The definitive source on preservation law. It provides informative and reliable reports on recent court decisions, tax rulings, new publications and new legislation.
Cost: $95.00
Frequency: Monthly
Circulation: 400
Founded in: 1949

15376 Preview of US Supreme Court Cases
American Bar Association
321 N Clark St
Chicago, IL 60654-7598

312-988-5000
800-285-2221; *Fax:* 312-988-6281
askaba@abanet.org;
www.americanbar.org/aba.html
Social Media: Facebook, Twitter

Tommy H Wells Jr, President
Laurel G. Bellows, President

Previews cases coming before the US Supreme Court.
Cost: $130.00
Frequency: Annual

15377 Private Security Case Law Reporter
Strattford Publishers
590 Dutch Valley Road NE
Atlanta, GA 30324-729

404-881-1141
800-926-7926; *Fax:* 404-881-0074
customerservice@straffordpub.com;
www.straffordpub.com

Richard Ossoff, Publisher
Albert J Pucciarelli, VP

Monthly digest decisions on litigation involving private security operations; includes insights and trend analysis by nations leading security expert.
Cost: $347.00
Frequency: Monthly
Founded in: 1984

15378 Probate and Property
American Bar Association
321 N Clark St
Chicago, IL 60654-7598

312-988-5000
800-285-2221; *Fax:* 312-988-6281
askaba@abanet.org;
www.americanbar.org/aba.html
Social Media: Facebook, Twitter

Tommy H Wells Jr, President
Laurel G. Bellows, President

Aimed at lawyers who devote a large part of their practice to real estate law and laws dealing with wills, trusts and estates.
Cost: $60.00
Founded in: 1978

15379 Public Contract Newsletter
American Bar Association
321 N Clark St
Chicago, IL 60654-7598

312-988-5000
800-285-2221; *Fax:* 312-988-6281
askaba@abanet.org;
www.americanbar.org/aba.html
Social Media: Facebook, Twitter

Tommy H Wells Jr, President
Laurel G. Bellows, President

Contains informative articles on a wide range of timely topics including current developments in federal and grant law, recent developments in state and local public contract law, upcoming educational programs and legislative developments.
Cost: $60.00
Frequency: Quarterly

15380 Purchasing Law Report
Institute of Management and Administration
3 Bethesda Metro Center
Suite 250
Bethesda, MD 20814-5377

703-341-3500
800-372-1033; *Fax:* 800-253-0332;
www.ioma.com

Purchasing Law Report is the most practical, least expensive and quickest way to understand and apply new purchasing laws and regulations in your day-to-day operations without wasting time sorting through hundreds of legal documents.

15381 Report on Disability Programs
Business Publishers
8737 Colesville Road
Suite 1100
Silver Spring, MD 20910-3928

301-876-6300
800-274-6737; *Fax:* 301-589-8493
custserv@bpinews.com; www.bpinews.com

Leonard A Eiserer, Publisher

Follows legislation, regulations, legal actions and funding in areas import to all persons with disabilities including health care, employment, civil rights, housing, and transportation.
Cost: $227.00
8 Pages
Frequency: Monthly
Founded in: 1963
Printed in on matte stock

15382 School Law Reporter
Education Law Association
300 College Park Ave
Dayton, OH 45469-0001

937-229-3589; *Fax:* 937-229-3845
ela@educationlaw.org; www.educationlaw.org
Social Media: Facebook, Twitter, LinkedIn

W Brad Colwell, President
Mandy Schrank, Executive Director
Cate K. Smith, Executive Director
Judy Pleiman, Member Services Coordinator
Jody Thornburg, Publications Manager

Member association for those with an iunterest in school law issues, such as attorneys, law professors, education professors, school administrators, and teachers.
Frequency: Monthly
ISSN: 1059-4094
Founded in: 1954

15383 Search and Seizure Law Report
Clark Boardman Company
375 Hudson St
Room 201
New York, NY 10014-3658

585-546-5530
800-323-1336

Robert Bouchard, Publisher
Elizabeth Brooks, Editor

Provides detailed, current coverage of the law, procedure, trends, and developments evolving in search and seizure law.
Cost: $175.00
8 Pages
Frequency: Monthly
Circulation: 2,000
Printed in 2 colors on matte stock

15384 Section of Taxation Newsletter
American Bar Association
321 N Clark St
Chicago, IL 60654-7598

312-988-5000
800-285-2221; *Fax:* 312-988-6281
askaba@abanet.org;
www.americanbar.org/aba.html
Social Media: Facebook, Twitter

Tommy H Wells Jr, President
Laurel G. Bellows, President

Update on current tax developments, committee projects, meeting information and order forms.
Cost: $15.00
Frequency: Quarterly

15385 Security Law
Strafford Publications
PO Box 13729
Atlanta, GA 30324-0729

404-881-1141
800-926-7926; *Fax:* 404-881-0074
customerservice@straffordpub.com;
www.straffordpub.com

Richard Ossoff, President

Monthly updates on security law without all the legal jargon.
Cost: $297.00
Frequency: Monthly
ISSN: 0889-0625
Founded in: 1984
Mailing list available for rent: 31.6M names
Printed in one color

15386 Sexual Harassment Litigation Reporter
Andrews Publications
175 Strafford Avenue
Building 4 Suite 140
Wayne, PA 19087-3317

610-225-0510
800-345-1101; *Fax:* 610-225-0501;
www.andrewspub.com

Robert Maroldo, Publisher
Linda Coady, Editor
Cost: $49.00
Frequency: Monthly

15387 Small Firm Profit Report: Attorney Edition
Professional Newsletters
Atlanta, GA 30366-1143

770-819-4151

Robert Palmer, Publisher

Practice management and marketing help for small law firms and solo practitioners.

15388 Software Law Bulletin
Andrews Publications
1735 Market Street
Suite 1600
Wayne, PA 19087

610-225-0510
800-345-1101; *Fax:* 610-225-0501;
www.andrewspub.com

Donna Higgins, Editor

As pantenting becomes the predominant method of protecting software, and as cases involving technological copy protection measures wind through the court system, Andrews' Software Law Bulletin provides coverage of decisions and opinions in the key cases. Detailed articles put individual developments into the big picture of the changing law landscape.
Cost: $588.00
Frequency: Monthly
Founded in: 1972

15389 Special Court News
American Bar Association
321 N Clark St
Chicago, IL 60654-7598

312-988-5000
800-285-2221; *Fax:* 312-988-6281
askaba@abanet.org; www.abanet.org

Tommy H Wells Jr, President

Newsletter apprises members of the current activities and plans of the Conference. Also provides active, continual contact with members and solicits more active participation.
Cost: $11.00
Frequency: Quarterly

15390 Special Education Law Monthly
LRP Publications
747 Dresher Road Suite 500
PO Box 980
Horsham, PA 19044-980

215-784-0912
800-341-7874; *Fax:* 215-784-9639
webmaster@lrp.com; www.lrp.com

Jessyca Harrington, Editor
Dionne Ellis, Managing Editor

Covers court decisions and administrative rulings affecting the education of students with disabilities. Each issue begins with a brief overview of the case summaries covered allowing you to quickly focus on the decisions and hearings that affect you most.
Cost: $140.00
Frequency: Monthly
Founded in: 1977

15391 Sports & Entertainment Litigation Reporter
Andrews Publications
175 Strafford Avenue
Building 4 Suite 140
Wayne, PA 19087-3317

610-225-0510
800-345-1101; *Fax:* 610-225-0501;
www.andrewspub.com

Robert Maroldo, Publisher
Robert Sullivan, Editor

Covers the latest news in the fast-changing world of entertainment litigation.
Cost: $775.00
Frequency: Monthly
Founded in: 1960

15392 Sports Medicine Standards and Malpractice Reporter
PRC Publishing
3976 Fulton Dr Nw
Canton, OH 44718-3043

330-492-6063
800-336-0083; *Fax:* 330-492-6176;
www.prcpublishingcorp.com

Molly Romig, VP

Designed to keep sports medicine professionals informed about current trends in their challenging professions. Accepts advertising.
Cost: $29.95
16 Pages
Frequency: Quarterly
Circulation: 500
ISSN: 0141-696X
Founded in: 1984
Printed in 2 colors on matte stock

15393 Sports, Parks and Recreation Law Reporter
PRC Publishing
3976 Fulton Dr Nw
Canton, OH 44718-3043

330-492-6063
800-336-0083; *Fax:* 330-492-6176;
www.prcpublishingcorp.com

Molly Romig, VP

For those professionals in the sports, parks and recreational law. Accepts advertising.
Cost: $39.95
16 Pages
Frequency: Quarterly
Circulation: 500
ISSN: 0893-8210
Founded in: 1997
Printed in 2 colors on matte stock

15394 State Legislative Report
American Bar Association
1800 M Street NW
#450S
Washington, DC 20036-5802

202-662-1000; *Fax:* 202-331-2220

Patrick Sheehan, Publisher
Diane Gibson, Editor

A summary of key legislative developments of interest to attorneys.
Cost: $50.00
4 Pages
Circulation: 800

15395 State and Local Law News
American Bar Association
321 N Clark St
Chicago, IL 60654-7598

312-988-5000
800-285-2221; *Fax:* 312-988-6281
askaba@abanet.org;
www.americanbar.org/aba.html
Social Media: Facebook, Twitter

Tommy H Wells Jr, President
Laurel G. Bellows, President
Richard W. Bright, Staff Editor

Informs members regarding Section activities and important issues of law.
Cost: $40.00
Frequency: Quarterly
Circulation: 6000
Founded in: 1878

15396 Summary and Reports
American Bar Association
321 N Clark St
Chicago, IL 60654-7598

312-988-5000
800-285-2221; *Fax:* 312-988-6281
askaba@abanet.org;
www.americanbar.org/aba.html
Social Media: Facebook, Twitter

Tommy H Wells Jr, President
Laurel G. Bellows, President

Contains recommendations and informational reports to the ABA House of Delegates.

15397 Summary of Labor Arbitration Awards
LRP Publications
PO Box 980
Horsham, PA 19044-0980

215-784-0912
800-341-7874; *Fax:* 215-784-9639
webmaster@lrp.com; www.lrp.com

Todd Lutz, CFO
Ken Kahn, CEO
Dana Eynon, Marketing Director
Claude Werder, VP
Marcy Witt, Marketing Director

Since 1959, the summary has been providing digests of private-sector labor arbitration decisions, covering the latest topics in collective bargaining with non-governmental employers.
Cost: $120.00
16 Pages
Frequency: Monthly
Founded in: 1977
Printed in 2 colors on glossy stock

15398 Syllabus
American Bar Association
321 N Clark St
Chicago, IL 60654-7598

312-988-5000
800-285-2221; *Fax:* 312-988-6281
askaba@abanet.org;
www.americanbar.org/aba.html
Social Media: Facebook, Twitter

Tommy H Wells Jr, President
Laurel G. Bellows, President

Newspaper describing and commenting on developments in legal education.
Cost: $15.00
Frequency: Quarterly
Founded in: 1978

15399 Tax Laws of the World
Foreign Tax Law
PO Box 2189
Ormond Beach, FL 32175-2189

386-253-5785; *Fax:* 386-257-3003;
www.foreignlaw.com

Income, corporate and related tax laws for over 100 countries. Many full text translations.
Cost: $100.00

15400 Testifying Expert
LRP Publications
747 Dresher Road
PO Box 980
Horsham, PA 19044-2247

215-784-0912
800-341-7874; *Fax:* 215-784-9639
webmaster@lrp.com; www.lrp.com

Patrick Byrne, Editor
Gary Bagin, Circulation Manager

A newsletter designed to help experts develop a reputation or improve their present standing as an expert. Each monthly issue contains relevant decisions affecting the expert, book reviews and seminar listings.
Cost: $140.00
Frequency: Monthly
Founded in: 1977

15401 The ALI Reporter
American Law Institute-American Bar Association
Continuing Professional Education
4025 Chestnut Street, Suite 5
Philadelphia, PA 19104

215-243-1600; *Fax:* 215-243-1664
ali@ali.org; www.ali-aba.org
Social Media: Facebook, Twitter, LinkedIn

Julene Franki, Executive Director
Lawrence F. Meehan, Deputy Executive Director
Judith Cole, Executive Assistant
Bennett Boskey, Treasurer

This newsletter reports on the activities of the ALI and is primarily for its members.
Frequency: Quarterly
Founded in: 1947

15402 The Air and Space Lawyer
American Bar Association Forum on Air & Space Law
321 N Clark St
Chicago, IL 60654-7598

312-988-5000
800-285-2221; *Fax:* 312-988-6281
askaba@abanet.org;
www.americanbar.org/aba.html
Social Media: Facebook, Twitter

Kenneth P. Quinn, Editor-in-Chief
John Palmer, Staff Editor
Laurel G. Bellows, President

Newsletter of significant developments in the field of air and space law as well as reports of Forum Committee activities.
Cost: $40.00
24 Pages
Frequency: Quarterly
Circulation: 2000
ISSN: 0747-7449
Printed in 4 colors

15403 The Construction Lawyer
American Bar Association
321 N Clark St
Chicago, IL 60654-7598

312-988-5000
800-285-2221; *Fax:* 312-988-5280
askaba@abanet.org;
www.americanbar.org/aba.html
Social Media: Facebook, Twitter

Thomas J. Campbell, Staff Editor
John W. Ralls, Editor-in-Chief
Laurel G. Bellows, President

Newsletter containing articles on recent developments in the construction industry as well as announcements pertaining to the Forum Committee or to other organizations in the field.
Cost: $50.00
48 Pages
Frequency: Quarterly

15404 The Health Lawyer
American Bar Association Section on Health Law
321 N Clark St
Chicago, IL 60654-7598

312-988-5000
800-285-2221; *Fax:* 312-988-5280
askabanet@abanet.org;
www.americanbar.org/aba.html
Social Media: Facebook, Twitter

Laurel G. Bellows, President

Provides informative articles that focus on a wide range of areas in the health law field and offers incisice analysis of key issues.
Cost: $60.00
Frequency: Bi-monthly

15405 The National Notary
Po Box 2402
Chatsworth, CA 91313-2402

818-739-4000
800-876-6827; *Fax:* 818-700-1942
hotline@nationalnotary.org;
www.nationalnotary.org
Social Media: Facebook, Twitter, LinkedIn

Milton G Valera, President
Deborah M Thaw, Executive VP
Marc Reiser, CEO
Jane Eagle, Executive VP & CFO
Ron Johnson, VP Systems & Operations

The National Notary addresses pertinent cutting-edge notarial issues in depth, and also features helpful how-to articles on every phase of operating as a professional Notary Public in the venue of American law and commerce.
200M Members
Frequency: Bi-Monthly
Circulation: 200,000
Founded in: 1957

15406 The Procurement Lawyer
American Bar Association - Public Contract Law
321 N Clark St
Chicago, IL 60654-7598

312-988-5000
800-285-2221; *Fax:* 312-988-5280
pubcontract@abanet.org;
www.americanbar.org/aba.html
Social Media: Facebook, Twitter

John A. Burkholder, Editor-in-Chief
Laurel G. Bellows, President

Newsletter providing news on federal, state and local government procurement professionals.
Frequency: Quarterly

15407 The SciTech Lawyer
American Bar Association Science & Technology Law
321 N Clark St
Chicago, IL 60654-7598

312-988-5533
800-285-2221
sciencetech@abanet.org;
www.americanbar.org/aba.html
Social Media: Facebook, Twitter

Shawn T Kaminski, Section Director
Julie Fleming, Co-Editor-in-Chief
Eleanor Kellett, Co-Editor-in-Chief
Laurel G. Bellows, President

Quarterly practice specific magazine featuring cutting edge news.

15408 Tobacco Products Litigation Reporter
TPLR
PO Box 1162
Back Bay Annex
Boston, MA 02117-1162

617-373-2026; *Fax:* 617-373-3672;
www.tplr.com

Lissy Friedman, Publisher
Richard Daynard, Editor

Tobacco industry news.
Cost: $995.00
Founded in: 1975

15409 Transnational Bulletin
Lewis, D'Amato, Brisbois & Bisgaard
221 N Figueroa St
Suite 1200
Los Angeles, CA 90012-2663

213-250-1800; *Fax:* 213-250-7900

Legal information for the international business community written by lawyers of the firm.

15410 Trial Judges News
American Bar Association
321 N Clark St
Chicago, IL 60654-7598

312-988-5000
800-285-2221; *Fax:* 312-988-6281
askaba@abanet.org;
www.americanbar.org/aba.html
Social Media: Facebook, Twitter

Tommy H Wells Jr, President
Laurel G. Bellows, President

This newsletter informs membership of the National Conference of State Trial Judges of the activities and programs of that conference.
Frequency: Quarterly
Founded in: 1978

15411 Turning the Tide
People Against Racist Terror
PO Box 1990
Burbank, CA 91507-1990

Fax: 818-848-2680

Michael Novick, Publisher

Bimonthly newsletter of anti-racist activism, research and education covering neo-nazi and other racist violence, efforts at conflict resolution and social justic reforms.
Cost: $10.00
24 Pages
Frequency: BiWeekly
Circulation: 7,500
Printed in 2 colors on newsprint stock

15412 Urban Lawyer
American Bar Association
321 N Clark St
Chicago, IL 60654-7598

312-988-5000
800-285-2221; *Fax:* 312-988-6281
askaba@abanet.org;
www.americanbar.org/aba.html
Social Media: Facebook, Twitter

Tommy H Wells Jr, President
Laurel G. Bellows, President

Articles on various areas of urban, state and local government law.
Cost: $49.95
Frequency: Quarterly
Circulation: 6000
Founded in: 1879

15413 Utility Section Newsletter
American Bar Association
321 N Clark St
Chicago, IL 60654-7598

312-988-5000
800-285-2221; *Fax:* 312-988-6281;
www.americanbar.org/aba.html
Social Media: Facebook, Twitter

Tommy H Wells Jr, President
Laurel G. Bellows, President

Articles pertaining to the field of public utility law.
Frequency: Quarterly
Founded in: 1878

15414 Washington Employment Law Letter
M Lee Smith Publishers
PO Box 5094
Brentwood, TN 37219-2407

615-737-7517
800-274-6774; *Fax:* 615-256-6601;
www.mleesmith.com

M Lee Smith, Publisher
Michael Reynvaan, Editor

Reviews of employment laws.
Cost: $157.55
8 Pages
Frequency: Monthly
Circulation: 54,000
Founded in: 1975
Mailing list available for rent
Printed in 2 colors on matte stock

15415 Washington Summary
American Bar Association
740 15th St Nw
Suite 8
Washington, DC 20005-1022

202-662-1000; *Fax:* 202-662-1032
cmpdi@abanet.org;
www.americanbar.org/aba.html
Social Media: Facebook, Twitter

Stephanie A Marella, Editor
Laurel G. Bellows, President

Tracks legislation and federal regulations of interest to lawyers by abstracting the Congressional Record and Federal Register.
Cost: $55.00
Frequency: Daily
Founded in: 1878

15416 White-Collar Crime Reporter
Andrews Publications
175 Strafford Avenue
Building 4, Suite 140
Wayne, PA 19087-3317

610-225-0510
800-345-1101; *Fax:* 610-225-0501;
www.andrewspub.com

Robert Maroldo, Publisher
Edith McFail, Editor

Major articles guest written by practitioners in the area of white collar crame and covering such topics as sentencing guidelines, corporate liability, banking and securities fraud and government contract fraud.
Cost: $66.00
Frequency: Monthly
Founded in: 1872

15417 Word Progress
American Bar Association
321 N Clark St
Chicago, IL 60654-7598

312-988-5000
800-285-2221; *Fax:* 312-988-6281
askaba@abanet.org;
www.americanbar.org/aba.html
Social Media: Facebook, Twitter

Tommy H Wells Jr, President
Laurel G. Bellows, President

Newsletter of the Word Processing User Group, includes updates on more effective word processing in the law office.
Cost: $50.00
Frequency: Quarterly

15418 World Jurist
World Jurist Assn of the World Peace Through Law
1000 Connecticut Avenue NW
Suite 202
Washington, DC 20036

202-466-5428; *Fax:* 202-452-8540
wja@worldjurist.org
http://www.worldjurist.net

Sona Pancholy, Editor
M Henneberry, Executive VP

Research for international development as a basis for future world peace.
Cost: $80.00
Frequency: Fortnightly
Circulation: 6000
Founded in: 1963
Printed in on glossy stock

15419 Your School and the Law
LRP Publications
747 Dresher Road Suite 500
PO Box 980
Horsham, PA 19044-2247

215-840-0912
800-341-7874; *Fax:* 215-784-9639
webmaster@lrp.com; www.lrp.com

Stephen Bekiiacqwa, Editor

A monthly newsletter providing practical information on current judicial decisions affecting schools.
Cost: $190.00
Founded in: 1977
Mailing list available for rent
Printed in one color on matte stock

Magazines & Journals

15420 AALL Spectrum
American Association of Law Libraries
105 W Adams Street
Suite 3300
Chicago, IL 60603

312-939-4764; *Fax:* 312-431-1097
support@aall.org; www.aallnet.org
Social Media: Facebook, Twitter

Mark Estes, Editorial Director
Hillary Baker, Marketing and Communications
Kate Hagan, Executive Director
Kim Rundle,, Executive Assistant
Emily Feltren,, Director of Government Relations

Publishes substantive, well-written articles on topics of real interest to law librarians, as well as news about the American Association of Law Libraries, including its chapters, committees and Special Interest Sections
Cost: $ 75.00

15421 ABA Journal
American Bar Association
321 N Clark St
6th Floor
Chicago, IL 60654-7598

312-988-5000
800-285-2221; *Fax:* 312-988-6281
abajournal@abanet.org; www.abanet.org

Tommy H Wells Jr, President
Robert Brouwer, Associate Publisher
Elizabeth Sullivan, Marketing Manager

Its editorial materials include news of interest to members of the legal profession. Editorial highlights include reviews of general interest and legal books, a US Supreme Court Digest section, a section listing significant rulings of other courts and news from government agencies.
Cost: $75.00
Frequency: Monthly
Circulation: 389420
Founded in: 1878

15422 APA Magazine
American Polygraph Association
PO Box 8037
Chattanooga, TN 37414-0037

423-892-3992
800-272-8037; *Fax:* 423-894-5435
office@polygraph.org; www.polygraph.org

Robbie S Bennett, National Office Manager
Gordon L. Vaughan, General Counsel
Donald Krapohl, Editor
Robbie S. Bennett, National Office Manager
Barry Cushman, President
Cost: $125.00
Frequency: Bi-Monthly
Founded in: 1966

15423 Administrative Law Review
American University Washington College of Law
4801 Massachusetts Ave Nw
Suite 622
Washington, DC 20016-8180

202-274-4433; *Fax:* 202-274-4130
alr-editor-in-chief@wcl.american.edu;
www.wcl.american.edu/journal/alr/
Social Media: Facebook, LinkedIn

Stacey L.Z. Edwards, Editor-In-Chief
Keeley McCarty, Executive Editor
Brittany Ericksen, Managing Editor
Sharon Wolfe, Journal Coordinator

Scholarly legal journal on developments in the field of administrative law and regulatory practice.
Cost: $40.00
Frequency: Quarterly
Founded in: 1949

15424 Advance Sheet
150 Lincoln Street
Boston, MA 02111

617-695-3660; *Fax:* 617-695-3656

15425 AmLaw Tech
American Lawyer Media
345 Park Avenue S
New York, NY 10010

212-799-9434
800-888-8300; *Fax:* 212-972-6258
customersvc@amlaw.com;
www.americanlawyermedia.com

William L Pollak, President
Aric Press, Editorial Director
Kevin Vermeulen, Senior Vice President of Legal
Frequency: Annual+
Circulation: 16,500
Founded in: 1997

15426 American Bankruptcy Law Journal
American Bankruptcy Institute
235 Secret Cove
Lexington, SC 29072

803-576-6225; *Fax:* 703-739-1060
Support@abiworld.org; www.abiworld.org

Christine Molick, Executive Director
Marilyn Shea-Stonum, Editor-in-Chief
J Rich Leonard, Associate Editor

Offers information on bankruptcy, legislation and financial information.
Cost: $65.00
Frequency: Quarterly
Founded in: 1982

15427 American Lawyer
American Lawyer Corporation
Lbby L5
120 Broadway
New York, NY 10271-0096

917-562-2000
800-603-6571; *Fax:* 212-696-1845
lawcatalog@amlaw.com;
www.americanlawyermedia.com

Barbara Eskin, Circulation Director

Issues affecting lawyers and the legal profession, with an emphasis on the business aspect of law firms.
Cost: $349.00
102 Pages
Frequency: Monthly

15428 American Lawyers Quarterly
American Lawyers Company
853 Westpoint Pkwy
Suite 710
Cleveland, OH 44145-1546

440-871-8700
800-843-4000; *Fax:* 440-871-9997
alq@alqlist.com; www.alqlist.com

Thomas W Hamilton, Executive VP
Frequency: Quarterly
Founded in: 1899

15429 American University Business Law Review
American University Washington College of Law
4801 Massachusetts Ave Nw
Suite 615-A
Washington, DC 20016-8180

202-274-4433; *Fax:* 202-274-4130;
www.wcl.american.edu/blr/

Averell Sutton, Editor-In-Chief
Cameron Chong, Executive Editor
Sara Hill, Managing Editor
Sharon Wolfe, Journal Coordinator

Scholarly legal journal publishing articles providing cutting-edge legal analysis for the business law community, scholarly articles, case law analysis, and coverage of developing trends in a variety of areas to include financial regulation, international trade, antitrust, communications, healthcare and energy.
Cost: $40.00
Frequency: Quarterly
Founded in: 2011

15430 American University International Law Review
American University Washington College of Law
4801 Massachusetts Ave Nw
Suite 610
Washington, DC 20016-8180

202-274-4433; *Fax:* 202-274-4130;
www.auilr.org
Social Media: LinkedIn

Lauren R Dudley, Editor-In-Chief
Daniel F Martini, Executive Editor
Michelle Mora Rueda, Managing Editor
Sharon Wolfe, Journal Coordinator

Scholarly legal journal publishing articles, critical essays, comments, and casenotes on a wide variety of international law topics, including public and private international law, the law of international organizations, international trade law, international arbitration, and international human rights. AUILR also publishes pieces on topics of foreign and comparative law that are of particular interest to the international legal community.
Cost: $40.00
Frequency: Quarterly
Founded in: 1986

15431 **American University Journal of Gender, Social Policy & the Law**
American University Washington College of Law
4801 Massachusetts Ave Nw
Suite 632
Washington, DC 20016-8180
202-274-4433; *Fax:* 202-274-4130;
www.wcl.american.edu/journal/genderlaw/
Social Media: Facebook
Rafael Roberti, Editor-In-Chief
J. Peter Bodri, Executive Editor
Claire Griggs, Managing Editor
Sharon Wolfe, Journal Coordinator
Scholarly legal journal that publishes articles addressing social and political equality under the law.
Cost: $40.00
Frequency: Quarterly
Founded in: 1992

15432 **American University Law Review**
American University Washington College of Law
4801 Massachusetts Ave Nw
Suite 616
Washington, DC 20016-8180
202-274-4433; *Fax:* 202-274-4130
alr-editor-in-chief@wcl.american.edu;
www.wcl.american.edu/journal/alr/
Social Media: Facebook, Twitter, LinkedIn
Brian R Westley, Editor-In-Chief
Mary M Gardner, Executive Editor
Christopher J Walsh, Managing Editor
Sharon Wolfe, Journal Coordinator
Scholarly legal journal, which publishes articles from professors, judges, practicing lawyers, and renowned legal thinkers. It is the only jounal in the nation to publish an annual issue dedicated to decisions of the Court of Appeals for the Federal Circuit regarding patent law, international trade, government contracts, and trademark law.
Cost: $40.00
Frequency: Quarterly
Founded in: 1952

15433 **Animal Law Report**
American Bar Association
321 N Clark St
Chicago, IL 60654-7598
312-988-5000
800-285-2221; *Fax:* 312-988-6281
askaba@abanet.org;
www.americanbar.org/aba.html
Social Media: Facebook, Twitter
Tommy H Wells Jr, President
Laurel G. Bellows, President
Summarizes recent legislation, case decisions and literature.
Cost: $10.00
Frequency: SemiAnnual

15434 **AntiShyster**
AntiShyster
PO Box 540786
Dallas, TX 75354-786
Fax: 972-386-8604
Alfred Adask, Editor
Critical examination of the American legal system.
Circulation: 10000

15435 **Antitrust Law Journal**
American Bar Association
321 N Clark St
Chicago, IL 60654-7598
312-988-5000
800-285-2221; *Fax:* 312-988-6281
askaba@abanet.org;
www.americanbar.org/aba.html
Social Media: Facebook, Twitter
Tommy H Wells Jr, President
Laurel G. Bellows, President
MaryAnn Dadisman, Staff Editor
Covers proceedings of Section meetings, Section reports and positions on legislation, as well as content of National Institutes on antitrust law.
Cost: $120.00
Circulation: 10,000
Founded in: 1878

15436 **Arbitration Journal**
American Arbitration Association
1633 Broadway
Suite 2c1
New York, NY 10019-6707
212-716-5800
800-778-7879; *Fax:* 212-716-5905;
www.adr.org
William K Slate II, CEO
Christine Newhall, Senior Vice President
Harry Kaminsky, Vice President
Cost: $30.00
Frequency: Quarterly
Founded in: 1926

15437 **Association of Legal Administrators**
Association of Legal Administrators
75 Tri-State International
Suite 222
Lincolnshire, IL 60069-4435
847-267-1252; *Fax:* 847-267-1329
publications@alanet.org; www.alanet.org
Larry Smith, Executive Director
Debbie Thomas, Director, Accounting & Finance
Renee Mahovsky, Director, Administration/Operations
Bob Abramson, Director, Marketing & Communication
Jan Waugh, Director, Member Services
Professional support for management of private law firms and other legal organizations worldwide.
Cost: $10.00
9500 Members
Founded in: 1971
Printed in 4 colors on glossy stock

15438 **Attorney/CPA**
3921 Old Lee Highway
Suite71A
Fairfax, VA 22030-3926
703-352-8064; *Fax:* 703-352-8073;
www.attorney-cpa.com
Bernard Eizen, Publisher
Clark Mulligan, Executive Director
Promotes high ethical standards of dual licensed professionals.
Cost: $44.37
Founded in: 1964

15439 **BNA's Patent, Trademark and Copyright Journal**
Bureau of National Affairs
1801 S Bell St
Arlington, VA 22202-4501
703-341-3000
800-372-1033; *Fax:* 800-253-0332;
www.bnabooks.com
Social Media: Facebook, Twitter, LinkedIn
Paul N Wojcik, CEO
Provides an in-depth review of significant current developments in the intellectual property field. Covers congressional activity, court decisions, relevant conferences, professional associations, international developments, plus actions of the Patent and Trademark Office and the Copyright Office.
Cost: $1968.00
Frequency: Weekly

15440 **Barrister**
American Bar Association
321 N Clark St
Chicago, IL 60654-7598
312-988-5000
800-285-2221; *Fax:* 312-988-6281;
www.americanbar.org/aba.html
Social Media: Facebook, Twitter
Tommy H Wells Jr, President
Laurel G. Bellows, President
Magazine containing general articles about the profession, the law and society in general.
Cost: $19.95
Frequency: 5 per year

15441 **Broadcasting and the Law**
One SE 3rd Avenue
#1450
Miami, FL 33131-1714
305-530-1322; *Fax:* 305-539-0013
broadlaw@aol.com
Matthew L Leibowitz
Addresses legal issues within the broadcasting industry.
Frequency: Monthly
Circulation: 400

15442 **Business Law Today**
American Bar Association Section on Business Law
321 N Clark St
Chicago, IL 60654
312-988-5000
800-285-2221; *Fax:* 312-988-5280
askaba@abanet.org;
www.americanbar.org/aba.html
Social Media: Facebook, Twitter
John Palmer, Staff Editor
Arthur F. Ferguson, Editor
Laurel G. Bellows, President
The Business Law Section's magazine edited for busy professionals: no footnotes and lots of the latest in business law.
64 Pages
Frequency: Bimonthly
Circulation: 55000
ISSN: 1059-9436
Printed in 4 colors

15443 **Business Lawyer**
American Bar Association
321 N Clark St
Chicago, IL 60654-7598
312-988-5000
800-285-2221; *Fax:* 312-988-6281
askaba@abanet.org;
www.americanbar.org/aba.html
Tommy H Wells Jr, President
Journal of business and financial law, with articles on current legal topics and substantive section programs.
Cost: $20.00
Frequency: Quarterly
Circulation: 60000
Founded in: 1915

15444 **Business Lawyer's Computer News**
American Bar Association
321 N Clark St
Chicago, IL 60654-7598
312-988-5000
800-285-2221; *Fax:* 312-988-6281
askaba@abanet.org;
www.americanbar.org/aba.html
Tommy H Wells Jr, President

Information on new developments in technology for the business lawyer and news on how business lawyers are applying technology in their practices.
Cost: $50.00
Frequency: Quarterly

15445 Champion Magazine
National Association of Criminal Defense Lawyers
1660 L St Nw
Suite 1200
Washington, DC 20036-5632

202-872-8600; *Fax:* 202-872-8690
assist@nacdl.org; www.nacdl.org

Quintin Chatman, Editor

Offers timely, informative articles written for and by criminal defense lawyers, featuring the latest developments in search and seizure laws, DUI/DWI, grandy jury proceedings, habeas, the exclusionary rule, death penalty, RICO, federal sentencing guidelines, forfeiture, white-collar crime, and more
Cost: $70.00
Frequency: 10x/Year
Circulation: 13000

15446 Chinese Law and Government
ME Sharpe
80 Business Park Dr
Suite 202
Armonk, NY 10504-1715

914-273-1800
800-541-6563; *Fax:* 914-273-2106
info@mesharpe.com; www.mesharpe.com

Myron E Sharpe, President
James Tong, Executive Editor
George Lobell, Executive Editor

Translations of significant works and policy documents, primarily from the Peoples Republic of China.
Cost: $144.00
Frequency: 1 Year 6 Issues

15447 Clearinghouse Reference Guide
American Bar Association
1800 M Street NW
Washington, DC 20036-5802

202-662-1000; *Fax:* 202-331-2220

Patrick Sheehan, Editor
Diane Gibson, Publications Coordinator

A summary of key state legislative developments of interest to attorneys.
Frequency: Annual
Circulation: 800

15448 Columbia Law School Magazine
Columbia Law School
435 West 116 Street
Box A-2
New York, NY 10027

212-854-2640; *Fax:* 212-854-7801
webmaster@law.columbia.edu
http://web.law.columbia.edu
Social Media: Facebook, Twitter, LinkedIn

Matthew Malady, Editor
Joy Wang, Managing Editor

Features contributions that promotes ongoing discussion of social change and related issues.
Frequency: Biennial
Founded in: 1754

15449 Commercial Law Journal
Commercial Law League of America
205 N. Michigan
Suite 2212
Chicago, IL 60601

312-240-1400
800-978-2552; *Fax:* 312-240-1408
info@clla.org; www.clla.org
Social Media: Facebook, Twitter, LinkedIn

Oliver Yandle, VP
Charles R Johnson III, Treasurer

Law review journal covering such issues as credit, debt, insolvency, banking and the Uniform Commercial Code.
Frequency: Quarterly
Circulation: 6000
Founded in: 1895

15450 Communications and the Law
Fred B Rotham Company
10368 W Cenntenial Road
Littleton, CO 80127-4205

800-828-7971; *Fax:* 716-883-8100

Theodore Kupfeman, Publisher

Features articles and book reviews on communications law, new technologies and law.
Cost: $25.00
Circulation: 585

15451 Complete Lawyer
American Bar Association
321 N Clark St
Chicago, IL 60654-7598

312-988-5000
800-285-2221; *Fax:* 312-988-6281
askaba@abanet.org;
www.americanbar.org/aba.html

Tommy H Wells Jr, President

Magazine provides practical articles directed to general practitioners, on substantive areas of law, news of council and committee activities.
Cost: $23.00
Frequency: Quarterly
Circulation: 16743

15452 Computer Industry Litigation Reporter
Andrews Publications
175 Strafford Avenue
Building 4, Suite 140
Wayne, PA 19087-3331

610-225-0510
800-345-1101; *Fax:* 610-225-0501;
www.andrewspub.com

Robert Maroldo, Publisher

Legal issues as they relate to hardware, software electronic databaes and the computer industry in general.
Cost: $875.00

15453 Computer Law Strategist
Leader Publications
345 Park Avenue S
New York, NY 10010-1707

212-799-9200; *Fax:* 212-696-1848

Stuart Wise, Publisher

For lawyers operating in the area of computer law and intellectual property.
Frequency: Monthly

15454 Corporate Control Alert
The Deal, LLC.
14 Wall Street
New York, NY 10005

212-313-9200
888-667-3325; *Fax:* 212-481-8128
customerservice@thedeal.com;
www.thedeal.com
Social Media: Twitter

Mickey Hernandez, Advertising Sales
Elena Freed, Marketing
Frequency: Monthly
Founded in: 1999

15455 Corporate Counsel
American Lawyer Media
345 Park Avenue S
New York, NY 10010

212-779-9434
800-234-4256; *Fax:* 212-696-1845;
www.americanlawyermedia.com

15456 Court Review
American Judges Association
300 Newport Ave
Williamsburg, VA 23185-4147

757-259-1841; *Fax:* 757-259-1520
aja@ncsc.dni.us
aja.ncsc.dni.us

James McKay, President

Highlights court decicions and precedents through articles written by US jurists and legal scholars.
Cost: $35.00
Frequency: Quarterly
Circulation: 2000
ISSN: 0011-0647
Founded in: 1959

15457 Criminal Justice
American Bar Association
321 N Clark St
Chicago, IL 60654-7598

312-988-5000
800-285-2221; *Fax:* 312-988-6281
askaba@abanet.org;
www.americanbar.org/aba.html

Tommy H Wells Jr, President

Magazine providing practical treatment of aspects of the criminal law and reporting on legislative, policy-making and educational activities of the ABA Criminal Justice Section.
Cost: $38.00
Frequency: Quarterly
Circulation: 9000
Founded in: 1915

15458 Cyber Esq.
Daily Journal Corporation
PO Box 54026
Los Angeles, CA 90054-0026

213-229-5300; *Fax:* 213-229-5481;
www.dailyjournal.com

Gerald L Salzman, CEO

Cyber Esq. is a guide for lawyers who use technology and whose practices are affected by the impact on the latest hardware and software and analysis of cutting-edge legal issues.
52 Pages
Frequency: Quarterly
Printed in 4 colors on n stock

15459 Daily Journal
Daily Journal Corporation
PO Box 54026
Los Angeles, CA 90054-0026

213-229-5300; *Fax:* 213-229-5481;
www.dailyjournal.com

Gerald L Salzman, CEO
Ray Chagolla, Circulation Manager

The Daily Journal Corporation provides lawyers with concise, comprehensive and intelligent coverage of legal news throughout the city, state, and nation. Through our family of publications we are able to serve the nation's largest legal markets.
Cost: $628.00
28 Pages
Frequency: Daily
Circulation: 11000
ISSN: 1059-2636
Founded in: 1888
Printed in on n stock

15460 Decisions & Developments
PO Box 98
Bolton, MA 01740-0098
781-890-5678; *Fax:* 781-890-1150

15461 Dispute Resolution
American Bar Association Sec. Dispute Resolution
321 N Clark St
Chicago, IL 60654-7598
312-988-5000
800-285-2221; *Fax:* 312-988-5280
askaba@abanet.org;
www.americanbar.org/aba.html
Thomas J. Campbell, Staff Editor
Chip Stewart, Editor
A clearinghouse of information on programs related to the study of existing methods for prompt and effective resolution of disputes.
Cost: $45.00
32 Pages
Frequency: Quarterly
Founded in: 1978

15462 Dispute Resolution Journal
206 Hulston Hall
University of Missouri
Columbia, MO 65211
573-823-3645; *Fax:* 212-716-5906
umclawcdr@missouri.edu;
www.law.missouri.edu
Jonathan R Bunch, Editor-in-Chief
Cassandra A Rogers, Managing Editor
Leonard Riskin, Manager
Cost: $21.00
Founded in: 1984

15463 Docket
150 Lincoln Street
Boston, MA 02111
617-695-3660; *Fax:* 617-695-3656

15464 Duke Law Journal
Duke University School of Law
210 Science Drive
Box 90362
Durham, NC 27708
919-613-7006; *Fax:* 919-681-8460
dlj@law.duke.edu; www.law.duke.edu
Social Media: Facebook, Twitter, LinkedIn, Youtube
Sarah Boyce, Editor-in-Chief
Julia Wood, Managing Editor
Jennifer Brady, Executive Editor
Philip Alito, Research Editor
The journal's purpose is to publish legal writing of superior quality, to publish a collection of outstanding scholarship from established legal writers, up and coming authors, and student editors.
Frequency: 8x/year
Founded in: 1951

15465 EEOC Compliance Manual
Bureau of National Affairs
1801 S Bell St
Arlington, VA 22202-4501
703-341-3000
800-372-1033; *Fax:* 800-253-0332
customercare@bna.com; www.bnabooks.com
Social Media: Facebook, Twitter, LinkedIn
Paul N Wojcik, CEO
A two-binder monthly service containing the complete text of the EEOC Compliance Manual, as issued by the EEOC, with monthly notification to related developments.
Cost: $410.00

15466 Education Law Association
Education Law Association
300 College Park Ave
Dayton, OH 45469-0001
937-229-3589; *Fax:* 216-687-5284
ela@educationlaw.org; www.educationlaw.org
Social Media: Facebook, Twitter, LinkedIn
Mandy Schrenk, Executive Director
Cate K. Smith, Executive Director
Judy Pleiman, Member Services Coordinator
Jody Thornburg, Publications Manager
Brings together educational and legal scholars and practitioners to inform and advance educational policy and practice through knowledge of the law. Together, our professional community anticipates trends in educational law and supports scholarly research through the highest value print and electronic publications, conferences, seminars and professional forums.
Cost: $125.00
1400 Pages
Frequency: Monthly
Circulation: 1200
Founded in: 1954

15467 Energy Law Journal
Federal Energy Bar Association
1990 M St Nw
Suite 350
Washington, DC 20036-3429
202-223-5625; *Fax:* 202-833-5596
admin@eba-net.org; www.eba-net.org
Lorna Wilson, Administrator
Clinton A. Vince, Secretary, Treasurer
Michelle Grant, Secretary, Treasurer
Peter Trombley, Vice President
Lawyers and consultants engaged in energy and public utility law.
Cost: $35.00
Frequency: Monthly
Circulation: 2600
ISSN: 0270-9163
Founded in: 1946
Printed in 2 colors on matte stock

15468 Environmental Forum
Environmental Law Institute
2000 L St Nw
Suite 620
Washington, DC 20036-4919
202-939-3800
800-433-5120; *Fax:* 202-939-3868
law@eli.org; www.eli.org
John Cruden, President
Stephen R. Dujack, Editor
Linda Ellis, Manager Customer Service
Carolyn Fischer, Editorial Associate
Uses diverse points of view to stimulate the exchange of ideas and foster solutions for pressing environmental issues.
Cost: $115.00
60 Pages
Circulation: 2100
Founded in: 1985
Printed in 4 colors on matte stock

15469 Environmental Law Journal
State Bar of Texas
1515 S Capitol of Texas Highway
Suite 415
Austin, TX 78746-6544
512-322-5800; *Fax:* 512-478-7750
Jimmy Alan Hall, Editor-in-Chief
Charles Jordan, Chairman
Provides members with current legal activities, recent developments and information pertaining to environmental and natural resource law, as well as section activities and other events pertaining to this area of the law.
Cost: $ 10.00
68 Pages
Frequency: Monthly
Founded in: 1969

15470 Experience
American Bar Association
321 N Clark St
Chicago, IL 60654-7598
312-988-5000
800-285-2221; *Fax:* 312-988-6281
askaba@abanet.org;
www.americanbar.org/aba.html
Tommy H Wells Jr, President
News magazine for one of the fastest-growing sections in the ABA. Articles cover elderlaw, Council relationships, aspects of retirement including housing and health, and other topics of interest to lawyers pre- and post retirement.
Cost: $45.00
Frequency: Quarterly
Founded in: 1878

15471 Expert and the Law
National Forensic Center
17 Temple Terrace
Lawrenceville, NJ 08648-3254
800-562-5177
info@nfstc.org; www.nfstc.org/
Betty Lipscher, Publisher
David Epstein, Chief Operations Officer
Mike Berry, Program Manager
Appilcation of scientific, medical and technical knowledge to litigation.

15472 Fair Employment Practices/Labor Relations Reporter
Bureau of National Affairs
1801 S Bell St
Arlington, VA 22202-4501
703-341-3000
800-372-1033; *Fax:* 800-253-0332
customercare@bna.com; www.bnabooks.com
Social Media: Facebook, Twitter, LinkedIn
Paul N Wojcik, CEO
A guide to the regulation of fair employment practices, including federal laws, orders and regulations; policy guides and ground rules; and state and local fair employment practice laws.
Cost: $1576.00
Frequency: Weekly
Founded in: 1929

15473 Family Advocate
American Bar Association
321 N Clark St
Chicago, IL 60654-7598
312-988-5000
800-285-2221; *Fax:* 312-988-6281
askaba@abanet.com;
www.americanbar.org/aba.html
Social Media: Facebook, Twitter
Tommy H Wells Jr, President
Laurel G. Bellows, President
Amelia Stone, Marketer
Adrienne Cook, Development Editor
A practical journal in magazine format, containing information on divorce, mental health, juveniles, custody, support and problems of the aging as well as current trends, recent court decisions and new legislation.
Cost: $39.50
Frequency: Quarterly
Circulation: 11000
Founded in: 1984

15474 Family Law Quarterly
American Bar Association
321 N Clark St
Chicago, IL 60654-7598
312-988-5000
800-285-2221; *Fax:* 312-988-6281
askaba@abanet.org;

www.americanbar.org/aba.html
Social Media: Facebook, Twitter

Tommy H Wells Jr, President
Laurel G. Bellows, President

A scholarly journal, including regular coverage of judicial decisions, legislation, taxation, summaries of state and local bar association projects and book reviews.
Cost: $79.95
Frequency: Quarterly
Circulation: 11000
Founded in: 1998

15475 Federal Communications Law Journal
University of California-Los Angeles
Box 951476
Los Angeles, CA 90095-1476

310-825-7768; *Fax:* 310-206-6489
webmaster@law.ucla.edu; www.law.ucla.edu

John Alden, Editor in Chief
David Matheson, Advertising Director

Articles on legal issues relating to the communications industry.
Cost: $10.00
Circulation: 2500

15476 Federal Lawyer
Federal Bar Association
1220 North Fillmore St.
Ste. 444
Arlington, VA 22201

571-481-9100; *Fax:* 571-481-9090
fba@fedbar.org; www.fedbar.org
Social Media: Facebook, Twitter, LinkedIn

Jack D. Lockridge, Executive Director
Lori Beth Gorman, Executive Assistant
Lisa Sidletsky, Director Membership
Robert J. DeSousa, President
Hon. Gustavo Gelpi, Jr., President-Elect

Chronicles the news of the association and its members as well as providing practical coverage of issues affecting federal attorneys.
Cost: $35.00
Circulation: 15200
Founded in: 1931

15477 Fidelity and Surety News
American Bar Association
321 N Clark St
Chicago, IL 60654-7598

312-988-5000
800-285-2221; *Fax:* 312-988-6281
askaba@abanet.org;
www.americanbar.org/aba.html
Social Media: Facebook, Twitter

Tommy H Wells Jr, President
Laurel G. Bellows, President

Summarizes selected recent cases on fidelity and surety law for professionals and lawyers.
Cost: $165.00
Frequency: Quarterly
Circulation: 1000
Founded in: 1878

15478 Firestation Lawyer
Quinlan Publishing Company
23 Drydock Avenue
Boston, MA 02215-2336

617-542-0048; *Fax:* 617-345-9646;
www.quinlan.com

E Michael Quinlan, Publisher
Hoss Homaier, President, Chief Executive Officer

Case summaries of recent lawsuits involving fire departments. Discusses residency requirements of firefighters, worker's compensation, pensions, discrimination, and fire department rules and regulations.
Frequency: Monthly
Founded in: 1950

15479 Franchise Law Journal
American Bar Association
321 N Clark St
Chicago, IL 60654-7598

312-988-5000
800-285-2221; *Fax:* 312-988-6281;
www.americanbar.org/aba.html
Social Media: Facebook, Twitter

Tommy H Wells Jr, President
Laurel G. Bellows, President
Robert A Stein, Executive Director

Journal in newsletter format primarily on current legal trends in franchising; also reports on activities of the Forum.
Cost: $50.00
Frequency: Quarterly

15480 Health Law Litigation Reporter
Andrews Publications
175 Strafford Avenue
Building 4, Suite 140
Wayne, PA 19087-3331

610-225-0510
800-345-1101; *Fax:* 610-225-0501;
www.andrewspub.com/

John E Backe, Publisher

Focus on cases involving ERSA, experimental insurance coverage, patient dumping, Medicare and Medicaid, medical devices, and federal and state legislation.
Frequency: Monthly
Circulation: 4100

15481 Hospital Law Manual
Publishers
200 Orchard Ridge Drive
Gaithersburg, MD 20878-1978

301-417-7500
800-234-1660; *Fax:* 301-698-7931
customer.service@aspenpubl.com;
www.aspenlawschool.com

Patricia Younger, Director

Hospital law.
Cost: $1325.00
Frequency: Quarterly
Founded in: 1959

15482 Human Rights
American Bar Association
321 N Clark St
Chicago, IL 60654-7598

312-988-5000
800-285-2221; *Fax:* 312-988-6281
askaba@abanet.org;
www.americanbar.org/aba.html
Social Media: Facebook, Twitter

Tommy H Wells Jr, President
Laurel G. Bellows, President

Magazine containing news articles, features and commentary with relevance to human rights and individual rights and responsibilities.
Cost: $17.00
Frequency: Quarterly
Circulation: 6000
Founded in: 1878

15483 IP Worldwide
American Lawyer Media
345 Park Avenue S
New York, NY 10010

212-779-9434; *Fax:* 212-592-4900;
www.americanlawyermedia.com

Steve Pressman, Editor
William L Pollak, CEO/President
Kevin Vermeulen, Publisher
Frequency: Quarterly
Circulation: 8000
Founded in: 1997

15484 Institute of Management & Administration Newsletter
Institute of Management and Administration
3 Bethesda Metro Center
Suite 250
Bethesda, MD 20814-5377

703-341-3500
800-372-1033; *Fax:* 800-253-0332;
www.ioma.com

Monthly newsletter that supports law office administrators by offering training on how to reduce overhead, improve the firm's profitability and efficiency, get more value for the firm's budget dollar, and improve their own professional standing.
Frequency: Monthly

15485 International Commercial Litigation
Euromoney Publications
173 W 81st Street
New York, NY 10024-7227

212-874-4265; *Fax:* 212-501-8926

International litigation and dispute resolution news and developments in commercial law.

15486 International Lawyer
American Bar Association
321 N Clark St
Chicago, IL 60654-7598

312-988-5000
800-285-2221; *Fax:* 312-988-6281
askaba@abanet.org;
www.americanbar.org/aba.html
Social Media: Facebook, Twitter

Tommy H Wells Jr, President
Laurel G. Bellows, President

Practical issues facing lawyers engaged in an international practice.
Cost: $7.00
Circulation: 11000

15487 Journal of Court Reporting
National Court Reporters
8224 Old Courthouse Rd
Vienna, VA 22182-3808

703-556-6272
800-272-6272; *Fax:* 703-556-6291;
www.ncraonline.org
Social Media: Facebook, Twitter

Melanie Humphrey-Sonntag, President
Mark Golden, Executive Director & CEO
Tami Smith, VP
Bruce Matthews, Secretary/Treasurer

Covers information and views on matters related to the court recording and captioning professions.
20000 Members
Circulation: 34000
Founded in: 1905

15488 Journal of Internet Law
Apen Publishers

111 Eighth Avenue
7th Floor
New York, NY 10011

212-771-0600
800-638-8437; *Fax:* 212-771-0885;
www.aspenlawschool.com

Mark F Radcliffe, Editor-in-Chief
Stacey Caywood, VP/Publisher
Mark Radcliffe, Editor
Gerry Centrowitz, VP Marketing And Communication
Robert Becker, CEO

Discusses strategies utilized by top intellectual property, computer law and information technology industry experts.
Cost: $380.00
Frequency: Monthly

15489 **Journal of Legal Medicine**
American College of Legal Medicine
9700 West Brun Mawr Avenue
Suite 210
Rosemont, IL 60018

847-447-1713; *Fax:* 847-447-1150
info@aclm.org; www.aclm.org
Social Media: Facebook, Twitter

Laurie Krueger, Executive Director
Frequency: Quarterly
Founded in: 1960

15490 **Judges' Journal**
American Bar Association
321 N Clark St
Chicago, IL 60654-7598

312-988-5000
800-285-2221; *Fax:* 312-988-6281
askaba@abanet.org;
www.americanbar.org/aba.html
Social Media: Facebook, Twitter

Tommy H Wells Jr, President
Laurel G. Bellows, President

Created to help judges and lawyers improve the administration of justice.
Cost: $23.00
Frequency: Quarterly
Founded in: 1878

15491 **Judicature**
American Judicature Society
The Opperman Center at Drake University
2700 University Avenue
Des Moines, LA 50311

515-271-2281
800-626-4089; *Fax:* 515-279-3090;
www.ajs.org

Seth S. Andersen, Executive Director
Krista Maeder, Assistant to the Executive Director
Laury Lieurance, Accountant/Membership Coordinator
Danielle Mitchell, Program Manager
David Richert, Editor

A forum for fact and opinion relating to all aspects of the administration of justice and its improvement.
Cost: $60.00
Frequency: Bi-Monthly
ISSN: 0022-5800

15492 **Jurimetrics: Journal of Law, Science and Technology**
American Bar Association
321 N Clark St
Chicago, IL 60654-7598

312-988-5000
800-285-2221; *Fax:* 312-988-6281
askaba@abanet.org;
www.americanbar.org/aba.html
Social Media: Facebook, Twitter

Tommy H Wells Jr, President
Laurel G. Bellows, President

Covers a wide range of topics on legal issues in science and technology.
Cost: $29.00
Frequency: Quarterly

15493 **Juvenile and Child Welfare Law Reporter**
American Bar Association
321 N Clark St
Chicago, IL 60654-7598

312-988-5000
800-285-2221; *Fax:* 312-988-6281
askaba@abanet.org;
www.americanbar.org/aba.html
Social Media: Facebook, Twitter

Tommy H Wells Jr, President
Laurel G. Bellows, President

Contains abstracts of case law on juvenile delinquency, abuse and neglect, adoption, termination of parental rights and other topics on child welfare.
Cost: $145.00
Frequency: Monthly

15494 **Law**
National Association of Legal Professionals
314 E 3rd Street
Suite 210
Tulsa, OK 74120-2409

918-582-5188; *Fax:* 918-582-5907
moore@nals.org; www.nals.org

Jay Moore, Editor
Tammy Hailey, Publisher
Jay Moore, Communications Manager
Tammy Hailey, Executive Director
Cindy Rosser, Executive Assistant

Published content focuses on new products, technology and items of interest to the administrative staff within the legal profession.
Cost: $40.00
Frequency: Quarterly
Circulation: 7000
Founded in: 1929

15495 **Law Office Computing Magazine Services Section**
James Publishing
PO Box 25202
Santa Ana, CA 92799-5202

714-755-5450
800-440-4780; *Fax:* 714-751-2709
customer-service@jamespublishing.com;
www.jamespublishing.com

Jim Pawell, Founder/President
Tina Dhamija, Assistant Editor
Adrianne Choi, Production Manager

Focuses on law office automation. Issues contain independent reviews of legal software with side-by-side comparisons of the top programs, plus how-to articles and expert columns. Targeted editorial attracts legal technology buyers and helps them plan effectively for their purchases, buy wisely and use their investments to maximize productivity and profitability.
Cost: $49.00
96 Pages
Founded in: 1981

15496 **Law Practice Management**
American Bar Association
321 N Clark St
Chicago, IL 60654-7598

312-988-5000
800-285-2221; *Fax:* 312-988-6281
askaba@abanet.org;
www.americanbar.org/aba.html
Social Media: Facebook, Twitter

Tommy H Wells Jr, President
Laurel G. Bellows, President
Jody Thornburg, Publications Editor

The pre-eminent magazine on all phases of law office management. Includes feature articles, book reviews, reports on technical innovations and announcements of forthcoming events.
Cost: $40.00
Founded in: 1878

15497 **Law Reporter**
The American Association for Justice
777 6th Street, NW
Washington, DC 20001

202-965-3500
800-424-2725
membership@justice.org; www.justice.org/

Peter C Quinn, Editor-in-Chief
Linda Lipsen, Chief Executive Officer
Charles Jeffress, Chief Operating Officer
Kathi Berge, Chief Financial Officer
Anjali Jesseramsing, Executive Vice President

Covers civil law, including automobile ,civil rights, insurance, commercial, employment and family law, medical negligence, premises liability and products liability, and workplace safety.
Cost: $135.00
40 Pages
Circulation: 53000
ISSN: 1052-4649
Founded in: 1947
Printed in 2 colors

15498 **Law Technology News**
American Lawyer Media
345 Park Avenue S
New York, NY 10010

212-779-9434; *Fax:* 212-592-4900
subscribe@lawtechnews.com;
www.americanlawyermedia.com

Kevin Vermuellen, Publisher
Monica Bay, Editor
William L Pollak, President/CEO

Covers the use of technology in the law profession.
Cost: $99.00
Frequency: Monthly
Circulation: 40000
Founded in: 1997

15499 **Law and Social Inquiry: Journal of the American Bar Foundation**
American Bar Association
321 N Clark St
Chicago, IL 60654-7598

312-988-5000
800-285-2221; *Fax:* 312-988-6281
askaba@abanet.org;
www.americanbar.org/aba.html
Social Media: Facebook, Twitter

Tommy H Wells Jr, President
Laurel G. Bellows, President

An academic and legal journal containing a wide range of research reports relating to the law, the profession and legal institutions.
Frequency: Weekly
Circulation: 4,00,000
Founded in: 1878

15500 **Law in Japan**
Japanese American Society for Legal Studies
University of WA Law School-1100 NE Cam.
Seattle, WA 98105

206-233-9292; *Fax:* 206-685-4469

John Haley, Editor

Academic journal with translation, original articles, comments and case notes on Japanese law

and legal issues.
Cost: $13.00
Circulation: 1,400

15501 Lawyers Weekly USA
Lawyers Weekly Publications
10 Milk Street
Suite 1000
Boston, MA 02111-1203
617-451-7300
366-294-8963; *Fax:* 617-451-1466;
www.lawyersweeklyusa.com
Social Media: Facebook, Twitter, LinkedIn
Scott Murdock, CirculatIon Manager
Susan Bocamazo, Editor
Reni Germer, Managing Editor
Features profiles, practice tips, technology, marketing, management and other topics related to law practice.
Cost: $249.00
Frequency: Monthly
Circulation: 2500
Founded in: 1972

15502 Lawyers' Professional Liability Update
American Bar Association
321 N Clark St
Chicago, IL 60654-7598
312-988-5000
800-285-2221; *Fax:* 312-988-6281
askaba@abanet.org;
www.americanbar.org/aba.html
Social Media: Facebook, Twitter
Tommy H Wells Jr, President
Laurel G. Bellows, President
Current reports and articles on legal malpractice insurance marketplace and other aspects of legal malpractice.
Cost: $45.00
Circulation: 23,000

15503 Leadership and Management Directions
American Bar Association
321 N Clark St
Chicago, IL 60654-7598
312-988-5000
800-285-2221; *Fax:* 312-988-6281
askaba@abanet.org;
www.americanbar.org/aba.html
Social Media: Facebook, Twitter
Tommy H Wells Jr, President
Laurel G. Bellows, President
Focuses on trends, principles, and practices in law office management including financial matters, marketing, human resources, facilities and technology.
Cost: $50.00
Frequency: Quarterly

15504 Legal Management: Journal of the Association of Legal Administrators
Association of Legal Administrators
75 Tri-State International
Suite 222
Lincolnshire, IL 60069-4435
847-267-1252; *Fax:* 847-267-1329
publications@alanet.org; www.alanet.org
Larry Smith, Executive Director
Debbie Thomas, Director, Accounting & Finance
Renee Mahovsky, Director, Administration/Operations
Bob Abramson, Director, Marketing & Communication
Jan Waugh, Director, Member Services
Covers personnel management, finance, strategic planning, the legal industry, business software, technology. leadership, interpersonal communication, time and stress management, and disaster planning.
Circulation: 25000
Founded in: 1971

15505 Legal Tech
Leader Publications
345 Park Avenue S
New York, NY 10010-1707
212-799-9200
800-888-8300; *Fax:* 212-696-1848
Stuart Wise, Publisher
Frequency: Monthly

15506 Legal Times
American Lawyers Newspapers Group
1730 M St Nw
Suite 802
Washington, DC 20036-4550
202-296-1995; *Fax:* 202-457-0718;
www.legaltimes.com
Peter Scheer, Editor
Ann Pelham, Publisher
Eva Rodriguev, Editor-in-Chief
Gwen Jones, Circulation Manager
Rose Mahoney, Sales Manager
Covers law, lobbying and politics.
Cost: $349.00
36 Pages
Frequency: Weekly
Circulation: 6200
Founded in: 1977

15507 Lender Liability Litigation Reporter
Andrews Communications
175 Stafford Building 4
Suite 140
Wayne, PA 19087
610-225-0510
800-328-4880; *Fax:* 610-225-0501
Robert Maroldo, Publisher
Journal of record, of litigation proceedings involving lender liability issues.
Cost: $650.00
Frequency: Monthly

15508 License
1 Park Avenue
2nd Floor
New York, NY 10016
212-951-6600
888-527-7008; *Fax:* 212-951-6714
info@advanstar.com; www.licensemag.com
Joyceann Cooney, Editor-in-Chief
Lorri Freifeld, Managing Editor
Steven Ekstract, Publisher
Sharon Weisman, Sales Manager
Patents, trademarks and copyrights
Frequency: Monthly
Circulation: 25000
Founded in: 1987

15509 Litigation
American Bar Association
321 N Clark St
Chicago, IL 60654-7598
312-988-5000
800-285-2221; *Fax:* 312-988-6281
askaba@abanet.org;
www.americanbar.org/aba.html
Social Media: Facebook, Twitter
Tommy H Wells Jr, President
Laurel G. Bellows, President
A journal for trial lawyers and judges, each issue of which focuses on a particular topic involving trial practice.
Cost: $39.50
Frequency: Quarterly

15510 M and A Lawyer
Glasser LegalWorks
150 Clove Road
Little Falls, NJ 07424-2138
973-890-0008; *Fax:* 973-890-0042;
www.legalwks.com
Steven E Bochner, Editor
Stephen W Seemer, President
News affecting all types of mergers and acquisitions transactions, including securities law, state law, international, taxation, accounting and practice areas like intellectual property, employee benefits/compensation, antitrust and environmental.
Cost: $317.00
Circulation: 500
Founded in: 1995

15511 Mental & Physical Disability Law
American Bar Association
740 15th St Nw
Suite 8
Washington, DC 20005-1022
202-662-1000; *Fax:* 202-662-1032
cmpdi@abanet.org;
www.americanbar.org/aba.html
Social Media: Facebook, Twitter
William Neukom, President
Laurel G. Bellows, President
John Parry, Executive Director
A bi-monthly journal published by the Commission on Mental and Physical Disability Law, containing timely summaries of reported legal developments in 22 disability subject areas - over 1600 summaries annually.
Founded in: 1878

15512 Mental & Physical Disability Law Reporter
American Bar Association
740 15th Street NW
Washington, DC 20005-1019
202-662-1570; *Fax:* 202-442-3439
cmpdl@abanet.org; www.abanet.org/disability
Social Media: Facebook, Twitter, LinkedIn
Stephen N. Zack, President
Katherine H. O'Neil, Commission Chair
John W. Parry, Commission Director
Jack L. Rives, Executive Director
Alice Richmond, Treasurer
Published since 1976, the Reporter is the only periodical that comprehensively covers civil and criminal mental disability law and disability discrimination law. Organized by 22 subject areas, the Reporter allows you to target your research and save time. A perfect complement to your online legal research databases.
Cost: $325.00
15 Members
Frequency: 6 X/Year
Circulation: 300+
ISSN: 0883-7902
Founded in: 1973

15513 Mental Health Law Reporter
Business Publishers
2222 Sedwick Drive
Durham, NC 27713
800-223-8720; *Fax:* 800-508-2592
custserv@bpinews.com; www.bpinews.com
Sarah Terry, Managing Editor
Court decisions affecting mental health professionals.
Cost: $277.00
Frequency: Monthly
Founded in: 1963

15514 Midwest Alternative Dispute Resolution Guide
Law Bulletin Publishing Company

415 N State St
Suite 1
Chicago, IL 60654-8116

312-644-7800; *Fax:* 312-644-4255;
www.lawbulletin.com

Lanning Macfarland Jr, President

Profiles of midwest attorneys.
Cost: $219.00
156 Pages
Frequency: Monthly
Founded in: 1854

15515 Midwest Legal Staffing Guide
Law Bulletin Publishing Company
415 N State St
Suite 1
Chicago, IL 60654-8116

312-644-7800; *Fax:* 312-644-4255
editor@lbpc.com; www.lawbulletin.com

Lanning Macfarland Jr, President
Bernard Judge, Editor
Stephen E Brown, Publisher

Monthly magazine about law, people and opportunity.
Frequency: Daily
Founded in: 1854
Printed in 4 colors

15516 Midwest Legal Technology Guide
Law Bulletin Publishing Company
415 N State St
Suite 1
Chicago, IL 60654-8116

312-644-7800; *Fax:* 312-644-4255;
www.lawbulletin.com

Lanning Macfarland Jr, President

Supplement to the Chicago Daily Law Bulletin and Chicago Lawyer. Eliminates the confusion arising from the many new technological service and product providers.
60 Pages

15517 NAELA Journal
National Academy of Elder Law Attorneys
1577 Spring Hill Road
Suite 220
Vienna, VA 22182-2223

703-942-5711; *Fax:* 703-563-9504
naela@naela.org; www.naela.org

Peter G Wacht, CAE, Executive Director
Nancy Sween, Director, Comm. & Publications
Kirsten Brown Simpson, Director, Membership & Marketing
Ann Watkins, Operations Manager
Roger Naoroji, Meetings & Education Coordinator

Peer-reviewed, scholarly publication of substantive articles on Elder and Special Needs Law topics.
Frequency: 2x Year

15518 National Bar Association Magazine
National Bar Association
1225 11th St Nw
Washington, DC 20001-4217

202-842-3900; *Fax:* 202-289-6170
headquarters@nationalbar.org;
www.nationalbar.org
Social Media: Facebook, Twitter, LinkedIn

John Crump, Executive Director

Founded in: 1925, the National Bar Association (NBA) is the nation's oldest and largest association of African American lawyers and judges.
Cost: $32.00
Circulation: 25,000
Founded in: 1925

15519 National Jurist
PO Box 939039
Sandy, CA 92193

858-503-7786; *Fax:* 858-503-7588
jurist@clark.net; www.nationaljurist.com

Jack Crittenden, Editor-in-Chief
Keith Carter, Managing Editor
Rebecca Luczycki, Editor
Mike Wright, National Accounts Manager

Information, advice, news and entertainment for law and pre-law students to help them succeed in law school.
Cost: $30.00
Circulation: 100000
Founded in: 1996

15520 National Notary
National Notary Association
9350 Desoto Avenue
Post Office Box 2402
Chatsworth, CA 91313-2402

818-739-4000
800-876-6827; *Fax:* 800-833-1211;
www.nationalnotary.org

Deborah M. Thaw, Executive Vice President
Milton Valera, President
Mark Valera, Managing Director
Thomas Hayden, Director of Marketing

Focuses on the importance of notaries as public servants and updates readers on related news.
Founded in: 1957

15521 National Paralegal Reporter
National Federation of Paralegal Association
PO Box 2018
Edmonds, WA 98020

425-967-0045; *Fax:* 425-771-9588
info@paralegals.org; www.paralegals.org

Features in-depth articles on timely topics such as paralegal roles and choosing vendors; how-toarticles providing readers with practical information that can be directly applied to their careers; and provides legal updated providing information that affects the paralegal profession such as case law, legislation, and technology education.
Cost: $30.00
Frequency: Bi-Monthly
Circulation: 10,000

15522 Natural Resources and Environment
American Bar Association
740 15th St Nw
Suite 8
Washington, DC 20005-1022

202-662-1000
800-285-2221; *Fax:* 202-662-1032
service@abanet.org; www.abanet.org

Practical magazine on the latest developments in the field of natural resources law.
Cost: $60.00
Frequency: Quarterly
Circulation: 12000

15523 Negotiation Journal
Plenum Publishing Corporation
513 Pound Hall
Cambridge, MA 02138

617-495-1684; *Fax:* 617-495-7818;
www.pon.harvard.edu

Michael Wheeler, Editor
Nancy Waters, Managing Editor

Investigates theoretical and practical developments in the conflict resolution field.
Cost: $79.00
Frequency: Quarterly
Founded in: 1998

15524 Older Americans Report
Business Publishers
8737 Colesville Road
Suite 1100
Silver Spring, MD 20910-3928

301-876-6300
800-274-6737; *Fax:* 301-589-8493
custserv@bpinews.com; www.bpinews.com

Leonard A Eiserer, Publisher
Beth Early, Operations Director
Mark Sherman, Editor

Covers every issue and program that affects your decision-making: Older Americans Act, long term care, Social Security & SSI, nutrition, nursing home regulation, housing, retirement/pension issues, all block grants for the aged, and more.
Cost: $427.00
Frequency: Weekly
Founded in: 1963

15525 Payroll Administration Guide
Bureau of National Affairs
1801 S Bell St
Arlington, VA 22202-4501

703-341-3000
800-372-1033; *Fax:* 800-253-0332
customercare@bna.com; www.bnabooks.com
Social Media: Facebook, Twitter, LinkedIn

Paul N Wojcik, CEO

A notification and reference service for payroll professionals. Covers federal and state employment tax, wage-hour and wage-payment laws.
Cost: $896.00
Frequency: Bi-Weekly
Founded in: 1929

15526 Polygraph
American Polygraph Association
PO Box 8037
Chattanooga, TN 37414-0037

423-892-3992
800-272-8037; *Fax:* 423-894-5435
office@polygraph.org; www.polygraph.org

Robbie S Bennett, National Office Manager
Gordon L. Vaughan, General Counsel
Donald Krapohl, Editor
Robbie S. Bennett, National Office Manager
Barry Cushman, President

Features articles about the psychophysiological detection of deception, and related areas.
Cost: $125.00
Frequency: Quarterly
Founded in: 1966

15527 Preview of United States Supreme Court Cases
American Bar Association
321 N Clark St
Chicago, IL 60654-7598

312-988-5000
800-285-2221; *Fax:* 312-988-6281
askaba@abanet.org;
www.americanbar.org/aba.html
Social Media: Facebook, Twitter

Tommy H Wells Jr, President
Laurel G. Bellows, President

Advance analysis by legal experts of the issues, facts and significance of each case being argued before the Supreme Court, plus special summer issue with all court decisions.
Cost: $340.00
Frequency: 10-12 issues

15528 **Probate Lawyer**
3415 S Sepulveda Boulevard
Suite 460
Los Angeles, CA 90034-6014

310-478-4454

Offers legislative news for probate courts.
Frequency: Annual

15529 **Professional Lawyer**
American Bar Association
321 N Clark St
Chicago, IL 60654-7598

312-988-5000
800-285-2221; *Fax:* 312-988-6281
askaba@abanet.org;
www.americanbar.org/aba.html
Social Media: Facebook, Twitter

Tommy H Wells Jr, President
Laurel G. Bellows, President

A magazine providing a forum for exchange of views and ideas on professionalism issues for bar leaders, lawyers, law school education and others interested in professionalism.
Cost: $40.00
Founded in: 1878

15530 **Prosecutor**
National District Attorneys Association
44 Canal Center Plz
Suite 110
Alexandria, VA 22314-1548

703-549-4253; *Fax:* 703-836-3195;
www.ndaa.org

Thomas Charron, Executive Director
Paul F Walsh Jr, Manager
Bill Gibbs, Manager

Covers a variety of criminal justice topics including child abuse, telemarketing fraud, violence against women, vehicular crime, DNA, juvenile justice and community prosecution.
48 Pages
Circulation: 7000
ISSN: 0027-6383
Founded in: 1977
Mailing list available for rent: 6,500 names
Printed in 4 colors on glossy stock

15531 **Public Contract Law Journal**
American Bar Association
321 N Clark St
Chicago, IL 60654-7598

312-988-5000
800-285-2221; *Fax:* 312-988-6281
askaba@abanet.org;
www.americanbar.org/aba.html
Social Media: Facebook, Twitter

Tommy H Wells Jr, President
Laurel G. Bellows, President

Contains articles on all phases of federal, state and local procurement and grant law by leading authoritiies.
Cost: $60.00
Frequency: Annual+

15532 **Real Property, Property and Trust Journal**
American Bar Association
740 15th St Nw
Suite 8
Washington, DC 20005-1022

202-662-1000; *Fax:* 202-662-1032
collinsj@staff.abanet.org;
www.americanbar.org/aba.html
Social Media: Facebook, Twitter

William Neukom, President
Laurel G. Bellows, President
Jennifer Collins, Advertising Sales Coordinator

Scholarly articles in the fields of estate planning, trust law and real property law.
Cost: $60.00
Frequency: Quarterly

15533 **Review of Banking and Financial Services**
Standard & Poor's Corporation
55 Water St
New York, NY 10041-0003

212-438-1000; *Fax:* 212-438-0299
clientsupport@standardandpoors.com;
www.standardandpoors.com

Deven Sharma, President
Hendrik Kranenburg, Executive VP

Focuses on laws and regulations affecting the banking and related industries.
Founded in: 1941

15534 **Review of Securities & Commodities Regulation**
Standard & Poor's Corporation
55 Water St
44th Floor
New York, NY 10041-0003

212-438-1000; *Fax:* 212-438-0299

Deven Sharma, President

Information on the laws and regulations affecting the securities and future industries.
Cost: $8.55
Frequency: 22 per year
Printed in on newsprint stock

15535 **Right of Way**
International Right of Way
19750 S Vermont Ave
Suite 220
Torrance, CA 90502-1144

310-538-0233; *Fax:* 310-538-1471
info@irwaonline.org; www.irwa.net

Mark Rieck, Executive VP
Barbara Billitzer, Publisher
Cost: $425.00
Founded in: 1985

15536 **Specialization Update**
American Bar Association
321 N Clark St
Chicago, IL 60654-7598

312-988-5000
800-285-2221; *Fax:* 312-988-6281
askaba@abanet.org; www.abanet.org

Tommy H Wells Jr, President

A compilation of current news briefs and articles of interest on lawyer specialization and related topics.
Circulation: 4,00,000
Founded in: 1878

15537 **Student Lawyer**
American Bar Association
321 N Clark St
Chicago, IL 60654-7598

312-988-5000
800-285-2221; *Fax:* 312-988-6281
askaba@abanet.org;
www.americanbar.org/aba.html
Social Media: Facebook, Twitter

Tommy H Wells Jr, President
Laurel G. Bellows, President

Magazine for law students featuring articles on legal, political, social issues, law school and the profession.
Cost: $20.00
Frequency: Monthly
ISSN: 0039-274X
Founded in: 1972
Printed in 4 colors on glossy stock

15538 **Tax Lawyer**
American Bar Association
321 N Clark St
Chicago, IL 60654-7598

312-988-5000
800-285-2221; *Fax:* 312-988-6281
askaba@abanet.org;
www.americanbar.org/aba.html
Social Media: Facebook, Twitter

Tommy H Wells Jr, President
Laurel G. Bellows, President

Journal of scholarly articles written by highly respected attorneys in the field and a thought-provoking student notes and comments section.
Cost: $53.00
Frequency: Quarterly

15539 **Technology and Practice Guide**
ABA Publishing
321 N Clark St
Chicago, IL 60654-7598

312-988-5000
800-285-2221; *Fax:* 312-988-6281
askaba@abanet.org;
www.americanbar.org/aba.html
Social Media: Facebook, Twitter

Tommy H Wells Jr, President
Laurel G. Bellows, President

Helps law professionals of general practice in making decisions about legal information management and technology.
Cost: $18.00
Frequency: SemiAnnual
Circulation: 13,477

15540 **The Bar Examiner Magazine**
National Conference of Bar Examiners
302 South Bedford Street
Madison, WI 53703

608-280-8550; *Fax:* 608-280-8552
contact@ncbex.org; www.ncbex.org

Erica Moeser, President

Published by the NCBE as a servuce to courts, academia, bar admissions administrators, members of bar examining boards and character committees, and others with special interest in the bar admissions process. Views and opinions in the articles are not to be taken as official expressions of the NCBE's policy unless so stated.
Frequency: 4/Year
Founded in: 1931

15541 **The Paralegal Educator**
American Association for Paralegal Education
222 S Westmonte Drive
Suite 101
Altamonte Springs, FL 32714

407-774-7880; *Fax:* 407-774-6440
info@aafpe.org; www.aafpe.org

Ronald Goldfarb, President

A journal offering news, information, and scholarly articles pertaining to paralegal education.
Frequency: Annual

15542 **The Rules of the Game**
Alliance for Justice
11 Dupont Cir Nw
Suite 200
Washington, DC 20036-1206

202-822-6070; *Fax:* 202-822-6068
alliance@afj.org; www.afj.org

Nan Aron, President
Mailing list available for rent

15543 **Tort and Insurance Law Journal**
American Bar Association

740 15th St Nw
Suite 8
Washington, DC 20005-1022

202-662-1000; *Fax:* 202-662-1032
cmpdi@abanet.org;
www.americanbar.org/aba.html
Social Media: Facebook, Twitter

William Neukom, President
Laurel G. Bellows, President
Rick Paszkiet, Development Editor
Jennifer Collins, Advertising Sales Coordinator

Scholarly journal on current or emerging issues of national scope in the fields of tort and insurance law.
Cost: $23.00
Frequency: Quarterly

15544 Trial
The American Association for Justice
777 6th Street, NW
Washington, DC 20001

202-965-3500
800-424-2725
membership@justice.org; www.justice.org/

Kathleen Flynn Peterson, President
Linda Lipsen, Chief Executive Officer
Charles Jeffress, Chief Operating Officer
Kathi Berge, Chief Financial Officer
Anjali Jesseramsing, Executive Vice President

In depth articles by experts on socio-legal issues. Evaluates legal practices, points of law, civil law and recent developments in law.
Cost: $79.00
Frequency: Monthly
Circulation: 60000
Founded in: 1946

15545 Utilities Law Review
John Wiley & Sons
111 River St
Hoboken, NJ 07030-5790

201-748-6000
800-825-7550; *Fax:* 201-748-6088
info@wiley.com; www.wiley.com

William J Pesce, CEO

Edited by a team of specialist UK and European lawyers, it is the leading journal in this fast-changing field. Providing detailed coverage of electricity, gas, telecommunications, transport, water and broadcasting.
Founded in: 1807

15546 Verdicts & Settlement
Daily Journal Corporation
PO Box 54026
Los Angeles, CA 90054-0026

213-229-5300; *Fax:* 213-229-5481;
www.dailyjournal.com

Gerald L Salzman, CEO
Malisha Anderson, Editor
Ray Chagolla, Marketing Head
Ama Sanchev, Circulation Manager
Frequency: Weekly
Circulation: 11000
Founded in: 1888

15547 Women Lawyers Journal
National Association of Women Lawyers
American Bar Center 15.2
321 N Clark Street
Chicago, IL 60610-4403

312-988-6186; *Fax:* 312-988-5491
nawl@nawl.org;
www.abanet.org/nawl/journal/wlj.html

Janice Sperow, Editor
Peggy Golden, Managing Editor
Stephanie Scharf, President

Published since 1911 as a forum for the exchange of ideas and information of interest to women lawyers. Unsolicited articles and press releases about non members will not be published.
Cost: $45.00
Circulation: 1200
ISSN: 0043-7468
Founded in: 1899

15548 Young Lawyers Division Newsletter
Young Lawyers
104 Marietta St Nw
Suite 100
Atlanta, GA 30303-2743

404-527-8700
800-334-6865; *Fax:* 404-527-8717
webmaster@gabar.org; www.gabar.org

Cliff Brashier, Executive Director
Bryan Scott, Director
Natalie Kelly, Director
Frequency: Quarterly
Circulation: 21000
Founded in: 1978

Trade Shows

15549 ABA Annual Meeting
American Bar Association
740 15th Street NW
9th Floor
Washington, DC 20005

202-662-1570; *Fax:* 202-442-3439
cmpdl@abanet.org;
www.americanbar.org/aba.html
Social Media: Facebook, Twitter

Carolyn B Lamm, President
Alex J Hurder, Commission Chair
Laurel G. Bellows, President

The meeting includes a CLE event on incompetency and Miranda rights, and also a reception for lawyers with disabilities.

15550 AFCC Annual Conference
Association of Family and Conciliation Courts
6525 Grand Teton Plaza
Madison, WI 53719

608-664-3750; *Fax:* 608-664-3751
afcc@afccnet.org; www.afccnet.org

Peter Salem, Executive Director

Over 20 exhibits relating to family judicial issues, including child custody and marriage, family, and divorce counseling. Attended by judges, couselors, attorneys, court personnel, mediators, teachers and researchers.
Frequency: June

15551 AIRA Annual Bankruptcy & Restructuring Conference
Association of Insolvency & Restructuring Advisors
221 Stewart Avenue
Suite 207
Medford, OR 97501

541-858-1665; *Fax:* 541-858-9187
aira@airacira.org; www.airacira.org

Grant Newton, Executive Director

Exhibits for professionals involved in insolvency and restructuring.
Frequency: Annual/June
Founded in: 1984

15552 ALA Annual Educational Conference and Exposition
Association of Legal Administrators
75 Tri-State International
Suite 222
Lincolnshire, IL 60069-4435

847-267-1252; *Fax:* 847-267-1329
publications@alanet.org; www.alanet.org

Larry Smith, Exhibits Manager
Debbie Thomas, Director, Accounting & Finance
Renee Mahovsky, Director, Administration/Operations
Bob Abramson, Director, Marketing & Communication
Jan Waugh, Director, Member Services

Seminar, luncheon, tours and 200 exhibitors of information about computer hardware and software, facilities management, publications, printers, suppliers, litigation support, travel consultants and more.
2000 Attendees
Frequency: May

15553 APA Annual Meeting
American Polygraph Association
PO Box 8037
Chattanooga, TN 37414-0037

423-892-3992
800-272-8037; *Fax:* 423-894-5435
office@polygraph.org; www.polygraph.org

Robbie S Bennett, National Office Manager
Gordon L. Vaughan, General Counsel
Donald Krapohl, Editor
Robbie S. Bennett, National Office Manager
Barry Cushman, President
600 Attendees
Founded in: 1966

15554 Academy of Criminal Justice Sciences
Northern Kentucky University
402 Nunn Hall
Highland Heights, KY 41099

859-572-5100
800-757-ACJS; *Fax:* 859-572-6665

Patricia Delancey, Executive Director

Exhibits of publications pertaining to criminal justice and related areas. 45 booths.
1.8M Attendees
Frequency: March

15555 Academy of Legal Studies in Business Annual Meeting
School of Business-Forsyth
Western Carolina University
Cullowhee, NC 28723

Daniel Hebron, Executive Secretary

15 booths.
300 Attendees
Frequency: August

15556 Adjutants General Association of the United States Annual Meeting
1 Massachusetts Avenue NW
Washington, DC 20001-1401

302-326-7008; *Fax:* 302-326-7196;
www.agaus.org

Government legislation.
300 Attendees
Frequency: Spring

15557 American Association for Paralegal Education Conference
American Association for Paralegal Education
222 S Westmonte Drive
Suite 101
Altamonte Springs, FL 32714

407-774-7880; *Fax:* 407-774-6440
info@aafpe.org; www.aafpe.org

Dave Wenhold, Executive Director
Cristina Griffin, Exhibits & Meetings Manager

Annual conference of 20 exhibitors of computer hardware and software, paralegal publications and educational materials and related supplies.
Founded in: 1981

15558 **American Association of Attorney-Certified Public Accountants Convention**
American Association of Attorney-CPAs
3921 Old Lee Highway
Suite 71a
Fairfax, VA 22030

703-352-8064
888-288-9272; *Fax:* 703-352-8073
info@attorney-cpa.com;
www.attorney-cpa.com

Kenneth D Goodman, President
Susan Pollock, Membership Coordinator

Exhibits for persons licensed both as attorneys and CPAs.
Frequency: Annual

15559 **American Association of Law Libraries Meeting & Conference**
American Association of Law Libraries
105 W Adams Street
Suite 3300
Chicago, IL 60603

312-939-4764; *Fax:* 312-431-1097
support@aall.org; www.aallnet.org
Social Media: Facebook, Twitter

Paul Graller, Exhibits Manager
Susan Fox, Executive Director
Kate Hagan, Executive Director
Kim Rundle,, Executive Assistant
Emily Feltren,, Director of Government Relations

Annual show of 200 booths and 175 exhibitors of library equipment, supplies and services, including computer hardware and software/publishers of legal materials/information.
2000 Attendees
Frequency: July

15560 **American Bar Association Annual Meeting/ ABA Expo**
American Bar Association
321 N Clark Street
Chicago, IL 60610

312-988-5000
800-285-2221
askaba@abanet.org;
www.americanbar.org/aba.html
Social Media: Facebook, Twitter

William Neukom, President
Laurel G. Bellows, President

Annual meeting and 200 exhibits of legal technology, law books, computers, data processing equipment and other products and services related to the legal profession.
15000 Attendees
Frequency: August
Founded in: 1887

15561 **American College of Legal Medicine Annual Meeting**
American College of Legal Medicine
9700 West Bryn Mawr Avenue
Suite 210
Rosemont, IL 60018

847-447-1713; *Fax:* 847-447-1150
info@aclm.org; www.aclm.org
Social Media: Facebook, Twitter

Laurie Krueger, Executive Director
Daniel L. Orr, President

Annual conference and exhibits related to the field of legal medicine or health care related issues.

15562 **American Corporate Counsel Association Conference**
1025 Connecticut Avenue NW
Suite 200
Washington, DC 20036-5425

202-318-8327; *Fax:* 202-331-7454
http://www.acc.com

Frederick J Krebs, Executive Director

Corporate law.
600 Attendees
Frequency: November

15563 **American Immigration Lawyers Association Trade Show**
American Immigration Lawyers Association
1331 G Street NW
Suite 300
Washington, DC 20005-3142

202-507-7600; *Fax:* 202-783-7853
executive@aila.org; www.aila.org

Charles H Kuck, President
Bernard P Wolfadorf, President-Elect
David W Leopold, First VP
Gregory Chen, Director of Advocacy
Susan D. Quarles, Deputy Executive Director

628 booths.
600 Attendees
Frequency: June

15564 **American Society for Legal History Annual Meeting**
American Society for Legal History
Notre Dame Law School
PO Box R
Notre Dame, IN 46556-0780

574-631-6627; *Fax:* 574-631-3595;
www.aslh.net

Walter F Pratt Jr, Secretary/Treasurer

Annual meeting of scholarly presses. Exhibits relating to legal history and its uses in formulating legal policy, decisions and actions; unearthing historical items; and preserving legal and legislative records.
1200 Attendees
Frequency: Annual
Founded in: 1956

15565 **American Society of International Law Conference**
2223 Massachusetts Avenue NW
Washington, DC 20008-2847

202-939-6005; *Fax:* 202-797-7133
http://www.asil.org

Rosemarie Rauzino-Heller, Show Manager
Charlotte Ku, Executive Director

30 tables.
1M Attendees

15566 **Annual Education Conference & Resource Center Exhibition**
National Association for Law Placement
1666 Connecticut Avenue NW
Suite 1110
Washington, DC 20009

202-835-1001; *Fax:* 202-835-1112
info@nalp.org; www.nalp.org

Fred Thrasher, Deputy Director
Mark Weber, Senior Vice President
Pamela Malone, Senior Vice President

Annual conference and exhibits relating to recruitment and placement of lawyers.
800 Attendees
Frequency: Annual

15567 **Association of American Law Schools Annual Meeting**
Association of American Law Schools
1201 Connecticut Avenue NW
Suite 800
Washington, DC 20036-2605

202-296-8851; *Fax:* 202-296-8869
aals@aals.org; www.aals.org

Mary E Cullen, Director Meetings
Carl Monk, Executive Director

Annual meeting of 51 book publishers, suppliers and distributors, computer software suppliers.
4100 Attendees
Founded in: 1896

15568 **Association of Trial Lawyers Annual Summer Meeting**
The American Association for Justice
777 6th Street, NW
Washington, DC 20001

202-965-3500
800-424-2725
membership@justice.org; www.justice.org/

Kathleen Flynn Peterson, President
Linda Lipsen, Chief Executive Officer
Charles Jeffress, Chief Operating Officer
Kathi Berge, Chief Financial Officer
Anjali Jesseramsing, Executive Vice President

45 booths.
3M Attendees
Frequency: July/August

15569 **Association of Trial Lawyers Mid Winter Meeting**
The American Association for Justice
777 6th Street, NW
Washington, DC 20001

202-965-3500
800-424-2725
membership@justice.org; www.justice.org/

Kathleen Flynn Peterson, President
Linda Lipsen, Chief Executive Officer
Charles Jeffress, Chief Operating Officer
Kathi Berge, Chief Financial Officer
Anjali Jesseramsing, Executive Vice President

55 booths.
1.5M Attendees
Frequency: January/Febuary

15570 **Association of Trial Lawyers of America Convention/Exposition**
The American Association for Justice
777 6th Street, NW
Washington, DC 20001

202-965-3500
800-424-2725
membership@justice.org; www.justice.org/

Kathleen Flynn Peterson, President
Linda Lipsen, Chief Executive Officer
Charles Jeffress, Chief Operating Officer
Kathi Berge, Chief Financial Officer
Anjali Jesseramsing, Executive Vice President

Semi-annual convention and exhibits of 130 manufacturers, suppliers and distributors of legal products/service, including computer animation videos, computer software/hardware, demonstrative evidence products, expert witness services and marketing firms, as well as high end consumer gifts.
3000 Attendees
Frequency: July
Founded in: 1946

15571 **DRI- Annual Conference**
DRI-The Voice of the Defense Bar

55 W. Monroe Street
Suite 2000
Chicago, IL 60603

312-951-1101; *Fax:* 312-795-0749
dri@dri.org; www.dri.org
Social Media: Facebook, Twitter, LinkedIn

Mary Massaron Ross, President
J. Michael Weston, President-Elect
John Parker Sweeney, First Vice President
Laura E. Proctor, Second Vice President
John E. Cuttino, Secretary/Treasurer

DRI is an international organization of attorneys defending the interests of business and individuals in civil litigation. DRI provides numerous educational and informational resources to DRI members and offers many opportunities for liaison among defense trial lawyers.

15572 Education Law Association Annual Conference
Education Law Association
300 College Park Avenue
Dayton, OH 45469

937-229-3589; *Fax:* 216-687-5284
ela@educationlaw.org; www.educationlaw.org
Social Media: Facebook, Twitter, LinkedIn

Mandy Schrank, Executive Director
Cate K. Smith, Executive Director
Judy Pleiman, Member Services Coordinator
Jody Thornburg, Publications Manager

Annual conference with over 100 presenters giving presentations on current education law issues. Ten to twelve exhibitors of education law resources.
350 Attendees
Frequency: November

15573 Federal Bar Association Convention
Federal Bar Association
1220 North Fillmore St.
Ste. 444
Arlington, VA 22201

571-481-9100; *Fax:* 571-481-9090
fba@fedbar.org; www.fedbar.org
Social Media: Facebook, Twitter, LinkedIn

Jack D. Lockridge, Executive Director
Lori Beth Gorman, Executive Assistant
Robert J. DeSousa, President
Hon. Gustavo Gelpi, Jr., President-Elect

Annual convention and exhibits of legal publications, computer software and insurance information.
300 Attendees

15574 Federal Taxation Institute
11 W 42nd Street
New York, NY 10036-8002

212-921-2300

Lorrie Ann England, Show Manager

11 booths.
1M Attendees
Frequency: November

15575 Institute of Federal Taxation
USC Law Center
University Park
Suite 124
Los Angeles, CA 90089-0001

Fax: 213-740-9442

Karen Sprague, Director

10 booths.
1M Attendees
Frequency: January

15576 Law and Society Association Annual Meeting
University of Massachusetts
Hampshire House
Amherst, MA 01003

413-545-0111; *Fax:* 413-545-1640
Exec_Office@lawandsociety.org;
www.lawandsociety.org

Ronald Pipkin, Executive Officer
Lissa Ganter, Administrative Coord

The annual meeting brings together 800-1000 scholars from the US and around the world to present research in the field of socio-legal studies. This includes the place of law in relation to other social institutions, legal decision making, legal systems, and operations, and a variety of research methods and modes of analysis. 50 booths including publishers exhibit, mainly academic, in the fiels of legal studies, and social science.
Frequency: May

15577 Legal Administrators Association
Association of Legal Administrators
75 Tri-State International
Suite 222
Lincolnshire, IL 60069-4435

847-267-1252; *Fax:* 847-267-1329
publications@alanet.org; www.alanet.org

Larry Smith, Executive Director
Debbie Thomas, Director, Accounting & Finance
Renee Mahovsky, Director, Administration/Operations
Bob Abramson, Director, Marketing & Communication
Jan Waugh, Director, Member Services

350 booths of products and services related to the legal industry.
2M Attendees
Frequency: April
Founded in: 1971

15578 Mid-America Association of Law Libraries Convention
Mid-America Association of Law Libraries
105 W Adams Street
Suite 3300
Chicago, IL 60603

312-939-4764; *Fax:* 312-431-1097;
www.aallnet.org/chapter/maall/
Social Media: Facebook, Twitter

Annual show and exhibits of law library equipment, supplies and services.
Frequency: October, Omaha
Founded in: 1973
Mailing list available for rent

15579 NFPA Convention
National Federation of Paralegal Associations
23607 Highway 99
Suite 2-C
Edmonds, WA 98026

425-967-0045; *Fax:* 425-771-9588
info@paralegals.org; www.paralegals.org
Social Media: Facebook, LinkedIn

Dana Murphy-Love, Managing Director
Celeste Allen, Assistant Director
Rodney Dunham, Assistant Director

The premier annual event for legal professionals to gather for education seminars, dynamic speakers, knowledge sharing, networking, and of course product-shopping.
350 Attendees
Frequency: Annual

15580 National Association of Black Criminal Justice
1900 N Loop W
Suite 255
Houston, TX 77018-8116

713-681-3700; *Fax:* 713-956-8664

Keith Branch Esq, Chairman
Howard Thompson, Owner

60 booths.
700 Attendees
Frequency: July

15581 National Association of Parliamentarians (NAP) Conference
National Association of Parliamentarians
213 South Main Street
Independence, MO 64050-3850

816-833-3892
888-627-2929; *Fax:* 816-833-3893
hq@nap2.org; www.parliamentarians.org

Ronald R Stinson, President
Naurice S Henderson, VP
Sandra K Olson, Secretary

The NAP sponsors a conference and exhibit relating to parliamentary law and procedure on a biennial basis. In addition, the Association also holds a national event once each year, providing the opportunities for members, prospective members, and guests to learn more about effective meetings, how to help others learn the fundamentals of parliamentary procedure, and how to be an effective parliamentarian.

15582 National Bar Association Annual Convention
National Bar Association
1225 11th Street NW
Washington, DC 20001-4217

202-842-3900; *Fax:* 202-289-6170;
www.nationalbar.org
Social Media: Facebook, Twitter, LinkedIn

Maurice Foster, Director Special Projects
Reese Marshall, Coordinator Special Projects
John Crump, Executive Director

Annual convention and exhibits of computers and legal software, office products, accounting services, financial planners, temporary employment agencies, legal publications, travel agencies, luggage and leather goods, fine arts and jewelry. Containing 50 booths.
2500 Attendees
Frequency: July-August
Founded in: 1925

15583 National Court Reporters Association Annual Convention & Expo
National Court Reporters Association
8224 Old Courthouse Road
Vienna, VA 22182-3808

703-556-6272
800-272-6272; *Fax:* 703-556-6291
msic@ncra.org; www.ncra.org
Social Media: Facebook, Twitter, LinkedIn, Youtube

James M. Cudahy, Executive Director & CEO
18000 Members
1200 Attendees
Founded in: 1899

15584 National Federation Paralegal Associations
PO Box 33108
Kansas City, MO 64114

816-421-5989; *Fax:* 816-941-2725
info@paralegals.org; www.paralegals.org

Tena Nichols, Assistant Managing Director

Thirty-five booths.
300 Attendees
Frequency: April

15585 National Forensic Center Trade Show
National Forensic Center
17 Temple Ter
Lawrenceville, NJ 08648-3254

609-883-0550
800-526-5177; *Fax:* 609-883-7622
expertindex.com

Betty Lipschner, Director

Coverage of the application of scientific, medical and technical knowledge to litigation.
200 Attendees
Printed in one color on matte stock

15586 National Judges Association
P.O. Box 325
Glendale, OR 97442

Fax: 541-832-2674
njaoffice@yahoo.com;
www.nationaljudgesassociation.org

Whitney Sullivan, Executive Director
Charlene Hewitt, Secretary
Ralph Zeller, Vice President

10 booths.
150 Attendees
Frequency: May

15587 National Notary Association Annual National Conference
Po Box 2402
Chatsworth, CA 91313-2402

818-739-4000
800-876-6827; *Fax:* 818-700-1942
hotline@nationalnotary.org;
www.nationalnotary.org
Social Media: Facebook, Twitter, LinkedIn

Milton G Valera, President
Deborah M Thaw, Executive VP
Marc Reiser, CEO
Jane Eagle, Executive VP & CFO
Ron Johnson, VP Systems & Operations
200M Members
500+ Attendees
Frequency: Bi-Monthly
Circulation: 200,000
Founded in: 1957

Directories & Databases

15588 ABA Journal Directory of Legal Software and Hardware
American Bar Association
321 N Clark St
Chicago, IL 60654-7598

312-988-5000
800-285-2221; *Fax:* 312-988-6281
askaba@abanet.org;
www.americanbar.org/aba.html
Social Media: Facebook, Twitter

Tommy H Wells Jr, President
Laurel G. Bellows, President

Directory of supplies to the industry.
Cost: $7.00
Frequency: Annual
Circulation: 400,000

15589 Agricultural Law Update
American Agricultural Law Association
University of Arkansas Law Programs Building
Fayetteville, AR 72701

479-575-4671; *Fax:* 479-575-5830;
www.nationalaglawcentre.org/aglaw-reporter/ag-law-update

Susan Williams, Admininstrative Assistant
Linda McGormic, Editor

Monthly update of legal issues concerning the agricultural industry(members only)
Frequency: Biennial
Circulation: 1,500

15590 American Association of Attorney-Certified Public Accountants Directory
3291 Old Lee Highway
Suite 71a
Fairfax, VA 22030

703-352-8064
888-288-9272; *Fax:* 703-352-8073
info@attorney-cpa.com;
www.attorney-cpa.com

Kenneth D Goodman, President
Susan Pollock, Membership Coordinator

Offers names, addresses and biographical data on 1,400 individuals licensed as both attorneys and CPAs.
Cost: $175.00
100 Pages
Frequency: Annual

15591 American Bar Association Legal Education Database
American Bar Association
321 N Clark St
Chicago, IL 60654-7598

312-988-5000
800-285-2221; *Fax:* 312-988-6281
askaba@abanet.org;
www.americanbar.org/aba.html
Social Media: Facebook, Twitter

Tommy H Wells Jr, President
Laurel G. Bellows, President

Contains the complete text of the Third Tenative Draft of Law School Library Accreditation Standards.
Frequency: Full-text

15592 American College of Legal Medicine Member Directory
American College of Legal Medicine
9700 West Bryn Mawr
Suite 210
Rosemont, IL 60018

847-447-1713; *Fax:* 847-447-1150
info@aclm.org; www.aclm.org
Social Media: Facebook, Twitter

Laurie Krueger, Executive Director
Daniel L. Orr, President

Lists members alphabetically, specialty or area(s) of expertise, and geographic location.
Circulation: 1,425
Founded in: 1960

15593 American Law Reports Library
Lawyers Co-operative Publishing Company
50 Broad Street E
Rochester, NY 14694-0001

585-719-9760

A database, updated periodically, that contains the complete text of analyses of state and federal case law.
Frequency: Full-text

15594 BNA Criminal Practice Manual
Pike & Fischer
8505 Fenton St
Suite 1400
Silver Spring, MD 20910-4499

301-562-1530
800-255-8131; *Fax:* 301-562-1521
pike@pf.com; www.pf.com

Meg Hargreaves, President
David Heyman, Director Marketing
Karen James-Cody, Director of Communications
Kirk Swanson, Managing Editor

15595 BNA's Directory of State and Federal Courts, Judges and Clerks
BNA Books
1231 25th Street NW
Washington, DC 20037-1164

732-346-0089
800-960-1220; *Fax:* 732-346-1624
books@bna.com; www.bnabooks.com

Margaret Hullinger, Executive Editor
Lois Smith, Marketing Manager
Janie Meidhof, Media Specialist

Complete contact information including e-mail addresses on the nation's judges and clerks, as well as comprehensive details on the structure of federal, state, and territorial courts. Includes 2,201 state courts, 214 federal courts, 14,432 judges, and 5,303 clerks, list of nominations for federal judgeships, federal appellate court jurisdiction map and list, state court structure charts, reports of judicial decisions, directory of electronic public-access services, and personal name index.
714 Pages
Frequency: Annual
Circulation: 1,300
ISBN: 1-570184-11-9
ISSN: 1078-5582
Founded in: 1986

15596 Best Lawyers in America
Woodward/White
129 1st Ave Sw
Aiken, SC 29801-4862

803-648-0300; *Fax:* 803-641-4794
info@bestlawyers.com; www.bestlawyers.com

Steven Naifeh, President

Over 11,000 attorneys who are selected as the best in their specialities by a survey of over 150,000 lawyers are profiled.
Cost: $110.00
1000 Pages
Frequency: Biennial

15597 Business Litigation Database
Trans Union Credit Information Company
20 Constance Ct
Hauppauge, NY 11788-4200

631-582-2690; *Fax:* 516-582-2767

Over 8 million court records on companies from New York and New Jersey are included in this database.
Frequency: Directory

15598 CEMC/ENR Directory of Law Firms
Construction Education Management Corporation
8133 Leesburg Pike
Suite 700
Vienna, VA 22182-2706

703-734-2399; *Fax:* 703-734-2908

Over 70 construction-oriented law firms located nationwide and overseas are listed.
Cost: $75.00
Frequency: Annual

15599 Common Market Law Review
Kluwer Law and Taxation Publishers
101 Philip Drive
Assinippi Park
Norwell, MA 02061

781-871-6600
866-269-9527; *Fax:* 781-681-9045

Serves as a medium for the dissemination of legal thinking on community law matters, meeting the need of both the academic and the practitioner.

15600 Comprehensive Guide to Bar Admission Requirements
Legal Education and Admissions to the Bar

321 N Clark Street
21st Floor
Chicago, IL 60610

312-988-6738; *Fax:* 312-988-5681;
www.americanbar.org/aba.html
Social Media: Facebook, Twitter

Laurel G. Bellows, President

Offers a list of state bar admission administrators in the United States and its territories.
Cost: $5.00
Frequency: Annual

15601 Corporate Counsel's Law Library
LexisNexis Matthew Bender
1275 Broadway
Menands, NY 12204-2694

518-487-3385
888-223-1940; *Fax:* 518-487-3083
info.in@lexisnexis.com; www.lexisnexis.com

George Bearese, VP
Rebecca Schmitt, Chief Financial Officer

This database contains court decisions covering statutory and common law concepts related to the formation, maintenance and dissolution of corporations.
Cost: $2484.00

15602 Criminal Justice Information Exchange Directory
US National Criminal Justice Reference Service
P.O. Box 60769
Harrisburg, PA 17106-0769

717-232-7554; *Fax:* 717-232-2162;
www.pacounties.org

Carroll Penyak, Director
Lori Dabbondanza, Executive Secretary
Lucas Martsolf, Manager

Over 100 criminal justice-related organizations are listed.
95 Pages
Frequency: Annual

15603 Criminal Justice Periodical Index
University Microfilms International
125 Chapman Hall
1219 University of Oregon
Eugine, OR 97403-1219

541-346-5129; *Fax:* 541-346-2804

Mary Ann Gilbert, Editor

Offers information on more than 180,000 citations to articles in 145 magazines, journals, newsletters and law reporting periodicals on the administration of justice and law enforcement.
Cost: $315.00
Frequency: TriAnnual

15604 Current Index to Legal Periodicals
Marian Gould Gallagher Law Library-Univ. of Wash.
William H Gates Hall
Box 353025
Seattle, WA 98195-3025

206-543-4089; *Fax:* 206-685-2165
lib.law.washington.edu/clip/cilp.html

Susan M Sorensen, Editor
Muriel Quick, Information Specialist

List of publishers of titles indexed in the database.
Cost: $192.00
Frequency: 52 issues
Founded in: 1948
Printed in on matte stock

15605 Deskbook Encyclopedia of Employment Law
Data Research
PO Box 490
Rosemount, MN 55068-0490

952-452-8694
800-365-4900; *Fax:* 952-452-8694

An up-to-date compilation of summarized federal and state appellate court decisions which affect employment. The full legal citation is supplied for each case. A brief introductory note on the American judicial system is provided along with updated appendices of recent US Supreme Court cases and recently published law review articles. Also included are portions of the US Constitution which are most frequently cited in employment cases.
Cost: $85.75
500 Pages
Frequency: Annual
ISBN: 0-939675-55-2
Founded in: 1996

15606 Deskbook Encyclopedia of Public Employment Law
Data Research
PO Box 490
Rosemount, MN 55068-0490

952-452-8694
800-365-4900; *Fax:* 952-452-8694

An up-to-datre compilation of summarized federal and state appellate court decisions which affect public employment. The full legal citation is cupplied for each case. A brief introductory note on the American judicial system is provided along with updated appendices of recent US Supreme Court cases and recently published law review articles.
Cost: $987.54
531 Pages
Frequency: Annual
ISBN: 0-939675-56-0
Founded in: 1996

15607 Directory of Bar Associations
American Bar Association
321 N Clark St
Chicago, IL 60654-7598

312-988-5000
800-285-2221; *Fax:* 312-988-6281
askaba@abanet.org;
www.americanbar.org/aba.html
Social Media: Facebook, Twitter

Tommy H Wells Jr, President
Laurel G. Bellows, President

Offers information on more than 57 state bar associations, local bar associations and other local associations represented in the American Bar Association House of Delegates.
Cost: $95.00
40 Pages
Frequency: Annual

15608 Directory of Certified Business Counselors
Institute of Certified Business Counselors
18831 Willamette Dr
West Linn, OR 97068-1711

503-751-1856
877-422-2674; *Fax:* 503-292-8237;
www.i-cbc.org

David Finsterwald, President

120 member counselors, brokers and attorneys qualified to act as advisors for persons with business problems.

15609 Directory of Courthouses, Abstract and Title Companies of the USA
Harbors International
7020 S Yale Avenue
Suite 206
Tulsa, OK 74136-5744

918-496-3232; *Fax:* 918-496-8905

A who's who directory of counties, parishes and boroughs with a section on abstract and title companies.
Cost: $95.00
368 Pages
ISSN: 0896-7830

15610 Directory of Law-Related CD-ROMs
Infosource Publishing
140 Norma Road
Teaneck, NJ 07666-4234

201-836-7072

Arlene Eis, Editor

A who's who directory of supplies to the industry.
Cost: $64.00
200 Pages
Frequency: Annual

15611 Directory of Lawyer Disciplinary Agencies & Lawyers' Funds/Client Protection
Center for Professional Responsibility
321 North Clark Street
Chicago, IL 60610

312-988-5000; *Fax:* 312-988-6281;
www.americanbar.org/aba.html
Social Media: Facebook, Twitter

Laurel G. Bellows, President
35 Pages
Frequency: Annual

15612 Directory of Lawyer Referral Services
American Bar Association
321 N Clark St
Chicago, IL 60654-7598

312-988-5000
800-285-2221; *Fax:* 312-988-6281
askaba@abanet.org;
www.americanbar.org/aba.html
Social Media: Facebook, Twitter

Tommy H Wells Jr, President
Laurel G. Bellows, President

Names of services, sponsoring organizations, phones and names of the directors are listed for over 330 services.
Cost: $10.00
40 Pages
Frequency: Annual

15613 Directory of Legal Aid & Defender Offices in the United States & Territories
National Legal Aid and Defender Association
1140 Connecticut Ave NW
Suite 900
Washington, DC 20036-4019

202-452-0620; *Fax:* 202-872-1031
info@nlada.org; www.nlada100years.org

Jo Ann Wallace, President & CEO
Julie Clark, Secretary
Alex Gulotta, Treasurer
Cost: $70.00

15614 Directory of Opportunities in International Law
John Bassett Moore Society of International Law
School of Law: University of VA
Charlottesville, VA 22901

Offers hundreds of possible employers in international law.
Cost: $10.00
204 Pages

15615 Directory of Private Bar Involvement Programs
American Bar Association
321 N Clark St
Chicago, IL 60654-7598

312-988-5000
800-285-2221; *Fax:* 312-988-6281
askaba@abanet.org;
www.americanbar.org/aba.html
Social Media: Facebook, Twitter

Tommy H Wells Jr, President
Laurel G. Bellows, President

A list of over 900 programs that provide free or low-cost legal services.
Cost: $7.50
210 Pages
Frequency: Annual

15616 Directory of Public Interest Law Centers
Alliance for Justice
11 Dupont Cir NW
2nd Floor
Washington, DC 20036-1206

202-822-6070; *Fax:* 202-822-6068
alliance@afj.org; www.afj.org

Nan Aron, President

Nonprofit association of public interest advocacy organization. Offers workshops, advocacy projects, legal guides, techinical assistance and public education. Lists addresses, branch offices and directors of 200 public interest law centers around the country. Indexed by state and subject area.
Cost: $10.00
48 Pages
Founded in: 1996
Mailing list available for rent

15617 Directory of State Court Clerks & County Courthouses
WANT Publishing Company
420 Lexington Ave
Room 300
New York, NY 10170-0002

212-687-3774; *Fax:* 212-687-3779
rwant@msn.com; www.wantpublishing.com

Robert S Want, President

Allows easy access to vital information including court decisions, real estate records, UCC and tax liens, and other important documents maintained by State appellate and trial courts and county courthouses nationwide.
Cost: $ 75.00
380 Pages
Frequency: Annual
ISBN: 0-970122-91-8

15618 FCBA Directory
Federal Communications Bar Association
1020 19th St NW
Suite 325
Washington, DC 20036-6113

202-293-4000; *Fax:* 202-293-4317
fcba@fcba.org; www.fcba.org

Stanley Zenor, Executive Director
Kerry Loughney, Director Of Membership Services
Wendy Jo Parish, Administrative Assistant

A nonprofit organization of attorneys and other professionals involved in the development, interpretation, implementation and practice of communications law and policy.
Founded in: 1936

15619 Federal Careers for Attorneys
Federal Reports
1010 Vermont Ave NW
Suite 408
Washington, DC 20005-4945

202-393-1552; www.attorneyjobs.com

Richard L Hermann, Owner

United States government general counsel and other legal offices throughout the federal system.
Cost: $23.95
150 Pages

15620 Federal Law-Related Careers Directory
Federal Reports
1010 Vermont Ave NW
Suite 408
Washington, DC 20005-4945

202-393-1552
800-296-9611; *Fax:* 202-393-1553;
www.attorneyjobs.com

Richard L Hermann, Owner
Richard L Hermann, Editor

Listings of over 1,000 federal government recruiting offices.
Cost: $16.95

15621 General Bar Law Directory
General Bar
25000 Center Ridge Rd
Suite 3
Cleveland, OH 44145-4108

440-835-2000
800-533-2500; *Fax:* 440-835-3636
service@generalbar.com; www.generalbar.com

Charles Sonnhalter, Owner
700 Pages
Circulation: 10000
Founded in: 1941

15622 Insider's Guide to Law Firms
Mobius Press
PO Box 3339
Boulder, CO 80307

303-188-8205
800-529-5627; *Fax:* 303-499-5389

Directory of services and supplies to the industry.
Cost: $28.95
740 Pages
Frequency: Annual

15623 Judicial Yellow Book
Leadership Directories
104 5th Ave
New York, NY 10011-6901

212-627-4140; *Fax:* 212-645-0931
judicial@leadershipdirectories.com;
www.leadershipdirectories.com

David Hurvitz, CEO
James M Petrie, Associate Publisher

Contact information for over 3,250 federal and state judges in federal and state appellate courts, including staff and law clerks, and the law schools they attended.
Cost: $245.00
1,100 Pages
Frequency: SemiAnnual
ISSN: 1082-3298
Founded in: 1995
Mailing list available for rent: 13,000 names at $125 per M

15624 Latin American Labor Law Handbook
WorldTrade Executive
PO Box 761
Concord, MA 01742-0761

978-287-0301; *Fax:* 978-287-0302
info@wtexec.com; www.wtexec.com

Alison French, Production Manager

Designed to give firms doing business in Latin America some basic knowledge of labor and employment law in the region. Covers countries where US and foreign investment is particularly high: Argentina, Brazil, Venezuela, Colombia, Costa Rica and Chili - providing an overview of the complex network of laws, regulations, and customs affecting social security, wages, employment security, and labor organizing.
Cost: $185.00

15625 Law Books and Serials in Print
R R Bowker LLC
630 Central Ave
New Providence, NJ 07974-1506

908-286-0288
888-269-5372; *Fax:* 908-464-3553
info@bowker.com; www.bowker.com

R R Bowker
L Yuster-Freeman, Editor

Focusing on core legal and related titles, Law Books & Serials in Print includes descriptive annotations that provide expert guidance on selecting the right sources for every research need.
ISBN: 0-835249-42-3
Mailing list available for rent

15626 Law Books in Print
Glanville Publishers
75 Main St
Dobbs Ferry, NY 10522-1673

914-693-1320

Publishers of law books in English are listed.
Cost: $750.00
Frequency: Base Edition

15627 Law Firms Yellow Book
Leadership Directories
104 5th Ave
New York, NY 10011-6901

212-627-4140; *Fax:* 212-645-0931
lawfirms@leadershipdirectories.com;
www.leadershipdirectories.com

David Hurvitz, CEO
James M Petrie, Associate Publisher

Contact information for over 24,000 attorneys and administrators who make the business decisions and manage the practice areas in over 800 of the nation's leading law firms.
Cost: $245.00
1,100 Pages
Frequency: SemiAnnual
ISSN: 1054-4054
Founded in: 1991
Mailing list available for rent: 19,000 names at $125 per M

15628 Law Office Computing Directory
James Publishing
Po Box 25202
Suite E
Santa Ana, CA 92799-5202

714-755-5450; *Fax:* 714-751-2709;
www.jamespublishing.com

Jim Pawell, Owner

Approximately 25 computer products and services designed for use by the legal profession.
Cost: $49.95
Frequency: Bi-Monthly
Circulation: 9,000

15629 Law Office Economics & Management: Directory of Law Office Software
Clark Boardman Callaghan
155 Pfingsten Road
Deerfield, IL 60015

847-374-0400
800-323-1336; *Fax:* 847-948-9340

Paul S Hoffman, Editor

List of about 100 suppliers of data processing equipment and software.
Cost: $15.00
Frequency: Annual June

15630 Law and Legal Information Directory
Gale/Cengage Learning
27500 Drake Road
Farmington Hills, MI 48331-3535
248-699-4253
800-877-4253; *Fax:* 877-363-4253
gale.galeord@cengage.com;
www.gale.cengage.com
Social Media: Facebook, Twitter, Youtube

Patrick C Sommers, President
Jacqueline O'Brien, Editor

Provides descriptions and contact information for more than 21,000 institutions, services and facilities in the law and legal information industry.
Frequency: Annual
ISBN: 1-414421-26-5

15631 Lawyers Referral Directory
PO Box 40335
Cleveland, OH 44140-0335
440-899-8660
800-LAW-LIST; *Fax:* 440-899-1005
Support@LawListIL.com; www.lawlistil.com

Ted M McManamon, Editor
Richard T Ostovitz, Production Manager

Bonded reference guide to lawyers specializing in commercial law, creditors' rights and collection litigation. Free to users registering referrals sent.
700 Pages
Frequency: Annual

15632 Lawyers' List
Commercial Publishing Company
PO Box 2430
Easton, MD 21601-2430
410-820-4494
800-824-9911; *Fax:* 410-820-4474

DA Schwartz, President

A listing of law offices engaged in general, corporation and trial practice or patent, trademark and copyright practice.
1700 Pages
Frequency: Annual

15633 Legal Information Alert
Alert Publications
401 W Fullerton Parkway
Apartment 1403E
Chicago, IL 60614-2805
773-525-7594

Donna Tuke-Heroy, President

Publishers of books, databases, CD-ROM products and loose-leaf services for the legal profession are listed.
Cost: $149.00

15634 Legal Looseleafs in Print
Infosource Publishing
140 Norma Road
Teaneck, NJ 07666-4234
201-836-7072
aeis@carroll.com; www.infosourcespub.com

Over 230 publishers offering 3,600 looseleaf legal information services.
Cost: $106.00
400 Pages
Frequency: Annual March
Founded in: 1981

15635 Legal Newsletters in Print
Infosource Publishing
140 Norma Road
Teaneck, NJ 07666-4234
201-836-7072

Arlene Eis, Editor

Directory of services and supplies to the industry.
Cost: $90.00
400 Pages
Frequency: Annual

15636 Legal Researcher's Desk Reference
Infosource Publishing
140 Norma Road
Teaneck, NJ 07666-4234
201-836-7072

Arlene Eis, Editor

Information is provided on federal and state government officials and departments are listed, as well as publishers and law book dealers and much more.
Cost: $58.00
416 Pages
Frequency: Biennial

15637 Legal Resource Directory
McFarland & Company Publishers
PO Box 611
Jefferson, NC 28640-0611
336-246-4460; *Fax:* 336-246-5018
info@mcfarlandpub.com;
www.mcfarlandpub.com
Social Media: Facebook, Twitter, LinkedIn

Information is given on national, state and local organizations providing free or inexpensive legal advice to low-income families.
Cost: $30.95
148 Pages
Mailing list available for rent

15638 Legal Resources Index
Information Access Company
362 Lakeside Drive
Foster City, CA 94404-1171
650-378-5200
800-227-8431

This database contains more than 500,000 citations, with selected abstracts, to articles published in more than 800 key law journals, bar association publications and legal newspapers.

15639 Martindale-Hubbell Law Directory
Martindale-Hubbell/Reed Reference Publishing
121 Chanlon Rd
New Providence, NJ 07974-1544
908-464-6800
800-526-4902; *Fax:* 908-771-8704
info@martindale.com; www.martindale.com

Ralph Colistri, President

Directory of services and supplies to the industry.
Cost: $690.00
50000 Pages
Frequency: 26 Volumes

15640 NALP Directory of Legal Employers
National Association for Law Placement
1025 Connecticut Ave NW
Suite 1110
Washington, DC 20036-5413
202-835-1001; *Fax:* 202-835-1112
info@nalp.org; www.nalp.org

M Liepold, Executive Director
Fred Thrasher, Senior Vice President
Pamela Malone, Senior Vice President

Information on more than 1,700 employers nationwide and is an invaluable tool for job searchers, career counselors, and legal recruiters alike. Published both on-line and in print, this directory includes indexes by location and by practice area keyword.
Cost: $75.00
Frequency: Annual
Founded in: 1971
Mailing list available for rent: CBC names

15641 NLADA Directory of Legal Aid and Defender Offices in the US & Territories
National Legal Aid and Defender Association
1140 Connecticut Ave NW
Suite 900
Washington, DC 20036-4019
202-452-0620; *Fax:* 202-872-1031;
www.nlada100years.org

Jo Ann Wallace, President & CEO
Julie Clark, Secretary
Alex Gulotta, Treasurer

About 3,600 civil legal aid and indigent defense organizations in the US.
Cost: $70.00
Frequency: Biennial

15642 NSA Directory
National Sheriff's Association
1450 Duke St
Alexandria, VA 22314-3490
703-836-7827

Suzanne B Litts, Editor
David Strigel, Advertising Manager

Sheriffs of the US address phone and fax.
Cost: $50.00
94 Pages
Frequency: Annual

15643 National Directory of Corrections Construction
National Institute of Justice
PO Box 6000
Rockville, MD 20849-6000
301-251-5500

Offers valuable information on over 150 correctional institutions constructed since 1985.
Cost: $32.00
354 Pages

15644 National Directory of Courts of Law
Information Resources
1110 N Glebe Road
Suite 550
Arlington, VA 22201-5762
703-525-4750

Directory of services and supplies to the industry.
Cost: $95.00
888 Pages
Frequency: Biennial

15645 National Employment Listing Service Bulletin
Criminal Justice Center
Sam Houston State University
Huntsville, TX 77341
936-295-6371; *Fax:* 281-294-1653

Kay Billingsley, Editor

Job openings in police departments, sheriff's departments, courts and other law enforcement and security agencies.

15646 National Hispanic American Attorney Directory
Hispanic National Bar Association
100 Seaview Drive
Secaucus, NJ 07094-1800
201-348-4900; *Fax:* 201-348-6609

Carlos G Ortiz

National directory listing Hispanic American Attorneys.
Cost: $65.00
Circulation: 4,000

15647 **National Law Journal: Directory of Current Law & Law-Related Books**
New York Law Publishing Company
345 Park Avenue S
8th Floor
New York, NY 10010-1700

212-799-9434; *Fax:* 212-696-1875;
www.ljextra.com

Ben Gerson, Editor
Bill Pollak, General Counsel
Michael Holston, General Counsel
David Hechler, Executive Editor
Paula Martersteck, Managing Editor

Lists over 70 publishers of law and law-related books.
Cost: $124.00
Frequency: Annual January

15648 **National List**
PO Box 2486
Bismark, ND 58502-2486

701-237-7202
800-227-1675; *Fax:* 701-223-5634
info@nationallist.com; www.nationallist.com

Randy Nicola, VP
Gerry Cowgill, President
Kacey Rask, Account Executive
Leslie Herr, Director of Operations

A list of lawyers and law firms handling collections and general practice in the United States, Canada, and most foreign countries.
550 Pages
Frequency: Annual

15649 **National Trial and Deposition Directory**
321 W Franklin Street
Boise, ID 83702

208-344-3191; *Fax:* 208-345-8800
Cost: $39.95

490 Pages
Circulation: 2,000

15650 **National and Federal Legal Employment Report**
Federal Reports
1010 Vermont Ave NW
Suite 408
Washington, DC 20005-4945

202-393-1552
800-296-9611; *Fax:* 202-393-1553;
www.attorneyjobs.com

Richard L Hermann, Owner
Richard L Hermann, Editor

Listings of approximately 600 current attorney and law-related job opportunities with the US government and other public and private employers in Washington DC, nationwide and abroad.
Cost: $35.80
Frequency: Monthly

15651 **Nelson's Law Office Directory**
Nelson Company
53 West Jackson Blvd.
Chicago, IL 60604

877-464-6656; www.nelson.com

Richard Nelson, Owner
Michael Andrews, Chief Financial Officer

A directory of the top rated law firms in the United States. Rated on legal ability, integrity and diligence by the leading lawyers in each state.
Cost: $23.00
210 Pages
Frequency: Annual
Founded in: 1968

15652 **Now Hiring: Government Jobs for Lawyers**
American Bar Association
321 N Clark St
Chicago, IL 60654-7598

312-988-5000
800-285-2221; *Fax:* 312-988-6281
askaba@abanet.org;
www.americanbar.org/aba.html
Social Media: Facebook, Twitter

Tommy H Wells Jr, President
Laurel G. Bellows, President

Federal, quasi- and independent government agency jobs for lawyers.
Cost: $17.95
170 Pages

15653 **Parole and Probation Compact Administrator Association Mailing List**
Council of State Governments
2760 Research Park Drive
PO Box 11910
Lexington, KY 40578-1910

859-244-8000
800-800-1910; *Fax:* 859-244-8001;
www.csg.org

Jodi Rell, President

15654 **Preview of United States Supreme Court Cases**
American Bar Association
321 N Clark St
Chicago, IL 60654-7598

312-988-5000
800-285-2221; *Fax:* 312-988-6281
askaba@abanet.org;
www.americanbar.org/aba.html
Social Media: Facebook, Twitter

Tommy H Wells Jr, President
Laurel G. Bellows, President

This database contains full-text reviews of cases orally argued before the US Supreme Court.
Frequency: Full-text

15655 **Representative Offices in the Russian Federation**
WorldTrade Executive
PO Box 761
Concord, MA 01742-0761

978-287-0301; *Fax:* 978-287-0302
info@wtexec.com; www.wtexec.com

Alison French, Production Manager

Combines detailed information on the legal structure within which representative offices must operate, including tax and other requirements, with a user-friendly guide to the accreditation and registration process.
Cost: $135.00

15656 **Russell Law List**
Commercial Publishing Company
PO Box 2430
Easton, MD 21601-2430

410-820-4494
800-824-9911; *Fax:* 410-820-4474

DA Schwartz, President

A listing of law offices in general practice worldwide.
147 Pages
Frequency: Annual

15657 **Russia Business & Legal Briefing**
WorldTrade Executive
PO Box 761
Concord, MA 01742-0761

978-287-0301; *Fax:* 978-287-0302
info@wtexec.com; www.wtexec.com

Alison French, Production Manager

Topics include: economic analysis; hard currency regulations; investment legislation in St. Petersburg; enforcing foreign judgements in Russia; new laws on limited liability companies and bankruptcy; new commercial arbitration court in St. Petersburg; changes in tax legislation; managing the Russian tax burden.
Cost: $265.00

15658 **Sourcebook of Local Court and County Records Retrievers**
BRP Publications
200 E Eager Street
Baltimore, MD 21202-3704

202-312-6060
800-822-6338; *Fax:* - - 047

Offers information on firms that specialize in finding court and county records, including civil, criminal, probate and bankruptcy files.
Cost: $45.00
432 Pages

15659 **Summer Legal Employment Guide**
Federal Reports
1010 Vermont Ave NW
Suite 408
Washington, DC 20005-4945

202-393-1552; www.attorneyjobs.com

Richard L Hermann, Owner

Directory of services and supplies to the industry.
Cost: $170.00
36 Pages
Frequency: Annual

15660 **US Supreme Court Employment Cases**
Data Research
PO Box 490
Rosemount, MN 55068-0490

952-452-8694
800-365-4900; *Fax:* 952-452-8694

A compilation of summarized US Supreme Court decisions which affect employment. The full legal citation is supplied for each case.
Cost: $64.70
288 Pages
Frequency: Annual
ISBN: 0-939675-51-0
Founded in: 1995

15661 **United States Probation and Pretrial Services Officers Directory**
Probation Div./Admin. Office of US Courts
1 Columbus Circle NE
Suite 4-300
Washington, DC 20544-0001

Fax: 202-273-1603

Federal probation offices and pretrial services offices.
Frequency: Annual

15662 **WESTLAW International Law Library**
West Publishing Company
610 Opperman Drive
Eagan, MN 55123-1340

651-687-7327; www.westgroup.com

Database containing the complete information of international and US federal court decisions.
Frequency: Full-text

15663 WESTLAW Legal Services Library
West Publishing Company
610 Opperman Drive
Eagan, MN 55123-1340

651-687-7327; www.westgroup.com

This database offers the complete text of US federal and state court decisions, statutes and regulations.

15664 WESTLAW Litigation Library
West Publishing Company
610 Opperman Drive
Eagan, MN 55123-1340

651-687-7327; www.westgroup.com

Offers information on law reviews, bar association journals and law-related texts.
Frequency: Full-text

15665 Want's Federal-State Court Directory
WANT Publishing Company
420 Lexington Ave
Room 300
New York, NY 10170-0002

212-687-3774; *Fax:* 212-687-3779
rwant@msn.com; www.wantpublishing.com

Robert S Want, President

The nation's number one court reference source, offering comprehensive information on the nation's federal, state and county courts.
Cost: $35.00
235 Pages
Frequency: Softcover

Industry Web Sites

15666 http://gold.greyhouse.com
G.O.L.D Grey House OnLine Databases

Grey House Publishing's online database platform, GOLD, offers Quick Search, Keyword Search and Expert Search for most business sectors including legal markets. The GOLD platform makes finding the information you need quick and easy - whether you're a novice searcher or an experienced database user. All of Grey House's directory products are available for subscription on the GOLD platform.

15667 www.aallnet.org
American Association of Law Libraries

Membership consists of national law library professionals.

15668 www.abanet.org
American Bar Association

The largest organization serving lawyers and all professionals involved in the law enforcement and legal industries. Conducts research and educational activities, encourages professional improvement and provides public service.

15669 www.aclm.org
American College of Legal Medicine

Organization related to the field of health law, legal medicine or medical jurisprudence.

15670 www.aclu.org
American Civil Liberties Union

Protection of civil liberties and constitutional rights through litigation, public education and legislative lobbying.

15671 www.afccnet.org
Association of Family and Conciliation

AFCC is an interdisciplinary, international association of professionals dedicated to improving the lives of children and families through the resolution of family conflict.

15672 www.afj.org
Alliance for Justice

Nonprofit association of public interest advocacy organization. Offers workshops, advocacy projects, legal guides, techinical assistance and public education. Publishes a directory of public interest law centers.

15673 www.aipparl.org
American Institute of Parliamentarians

A not-for-profit educational organization for the advancement of the parliamentary procedure.

15674 www.ajs.org
American Judicature Society

Lawyers, judges and educators interested in the effective administration of justice.

15675 www.ali-aba.org
American Law Institute - American Bar Association

Provides continuing legal education courses, books, and periodicals for practicing attorneys and others in the legal profession.

15676 www.ascm.vicsc.dni.us
National Association for Court Management

Members are clerks of court, court administration and others serving in a court management capacity.

15677 www.atlanet.org
Association of Trial Lawyers of America

15678 www.attorney-cpa.com
American Association of Attorney-CPAs

Seeks to safeguard the professional and legal rights of CPA attorneys.

15679 www.blr.com
Business & Legal Reports

Provides essential tools for safety and environmental compliance and training needs

15680 www.educationlaw.org
Education Law Association

Association for manufacturers or suppliers of law education equipment, supplies and services.

15681 www.fala.org
First Amendment Lawyers Association

Lawyers concentrating on defending clients under the first amendment of the Constitution.

15682 www.fcba.org
Federal Communications Bar Association

A non-profit organization of attorneys and other professionals involved in the development, interpretation, implementation and practice of communications law and policy.

15683 www.findlaw.com

Online Legal Resources. Legal, Professionals, Students, Business, Legal News, etc.

15684 www.greyhouse.com
Grey House Publishing

Authoritative reference directories for most business sectors including legal markets. Users can search the online databases with varied search criteria allowing for custom searches by product category, geographic area, sales volume, keyword, subject and more. Full Grey House catalog and online ordering also available.

15685 www.honet.msu.edu/~law
American Society for Legal History

Exhibits relating to legal history and its uses in formulating legal policy, decisions and actions; unearthing historical items; and preserving legal and legislative records.

15686 www.lexis-nexis.com
Mead Data Central

Contains the Lexis-Nexis Source Locator, a powerful new tool for retrieving targeted information about the more 31,000 Lexi-Nexis sources.

15687 www.nacdl.org
National Association of Criminal Defense Lawyers

Supports all criminal defense lawyers with education, publications and trade shows.

15688 www.naela.org
National Academy of Elder Law Attorneys

Members are private attorneys, law professors and Title III interest in the provision of legal service to the elderly.

15689 www.narf.org
Native American Rights Fund

Provides legal services to Indian tribes, organizations and individuals in the areas of preservation of tribal existence, protection of tribal natural resources, promotion of human rights , accoutability of governments, development of Indian law.

15690 www.ncraonline.org
National Court Reporters Association

15691 www.ncwba.org
National Conference of Women's Bar Associations

To promote and assist the growth of local and statewide women's bar associations and ideas among women's bar associations and women's bar sections of local and statewide bar associations; to serve as a vehicle for the exchange and dissemination of information and ideas among women's bar associations and women's bar sections of local and statewide bar associations.

15692 www.paralegals.org
National Federation of Paralegal Association

For state and local paralegal associations throughout the United States and Canada.

15693 www.parliamentarians.org
National Association of Parliamentarians

An association for those interested in parliamentary law and procedure, NAP's primary objectives are teaching, promoting, and disseminating the philosophy and principles underlying the rules of deliberative assemblies.

15694 www.rand.org/icj
Institute for Civil Justice

Nonprofit research organization within the RAND Corporation dedicated to interdisciplinary empirical research to facilitate change in the civil justice system.

15695 www.rmmlf.org
Rocky Mountain Mineral Law Foundation

15696 www.romingerlegal.com

Is a Search Engine dedicated to Legal Links, Legal Research Page, Case Law and Professional Directories for Law, etc.

15697 www.searchcrawl.com/legal/justice.html
Searchcrawl

List of legal resources.

15698 www.usfca.edu/law/globaljustice

Web site for the Center for Law and Global Justice. Focus on legal education, judicial training, free and fair elections, and the protection of human rights. The Center is an integral part of the University of San Francisco School of Law.

15699 www.westlaw.com

Westlaw is the premier legal and business research tool on the Internet.

15700 www.worldjurist.org

World Jurist Association of the World Peace Through Law

Association for those interested in future world peace.

Associations

15701 Africana Librarians Council
African Studies Association
54 Joyce Kilmer Avenue
Piscataway, NJ 08854-8045

732-932-8173; *Fax:* 732-445-1366
kramer@tiac.net; www.africanstudies.org/

Eileen Kramer, President
Members consist of librarians, archivists or documentalists working with materials from and about Africa or scholars interested in the preseravtionof or access to Africana.
500 Members
Founded in: 1983

15702 American Association of Law Libraries
105 W Adams Street
Suite 3300
Chicago, IL 60603

312-939-4764; *Fax:* 312-431-1097
admin@ifwtwa.org; www.aallnet.org
Social Media: Facebook, Twitter, LinkedIn, Youtube, RSS, Instagram

Linda Kissam, President
Allen Cox, Vice President
Elizabeth Willoughby, Treasurer
Susan J Montgomery, Treasurer, Board Member
Marc d'Entremont, Director
Promotes and enhances the value of law libraries to the legal and public communities, fosters the profession of law librarianship and provides leadership in the field of legal information.
300 Members
Founded in: 1956

15703 American Association of School Librarians
American Library Association
50 E Huron Street
Chicago, IL 60611

312-944-6780
800-545-2433; *Fax:* 312-280-5276
ala@ala.org; www.ala.org/aasl/
Social Media: Facebook, Twitter, LinkedIn, Flickr, Pinterest, Google+, In

Sylvia Knight Norton, Executive Director
Jennifer Habley, Manager, Web Communications
Stephanie Book, Manager, Communications
Allison Cline, Deputy Executive Director
Meg Featheringham, Manager/Editor
Works to ensure that all members of the school library media field collaborate to provide leadership in the total education program, participate as active partners in the teaching and learning process, connect learners with ideas and information and prepare students for life long learning, informed decision making, a love of reading and the use of information technologies.
60000 Members

15704 American Indian Library Association
American Library Association
50 E Huron Street
Chicago, IL 60611

312-944-6780
800-545-2433; *Fax:* 312-664-7459
ala@ala.org; www.ala.org

Sari Feldman, President
Keith Michael Fiels, Executive Director
Sara Harris, Manager
Association for Native Americans and Native Alaskans libraries and librarians.
10000 Members
Founded in: 1949

15705 American Library Association
American Library Association
50 E Huron St
Chicago, IL 60611-2788

312-944-6780
800-545-2433
ala@ala.org; www.ala.org

Sari Feldman, President
Keith Michael Fiels, Executive Director
To provide leadership for the development, promotion, and improvement of library and information services and the profession of librarianship in order to enhance learning and ensure access to information for all.
65000 Members
Founded in: 1876

15706 American Society for Information Science
ASIS&T
8555 16th Street
Suite 850
Silver Spring, MD 20910

301-495-0900; *Fax:* 301-495-0810
mwa@mysterywriters.org; www.asis.org
Social Media: Facebook, Twitter, Instagram

Sara Paretsky, President
Donna Andrews, Executive Vice President
Elaine Viets, Secretary
Tona Perona, Treasurer
3000 Members
Founded in: 1945

15707 American Society of Indexing
American Society for Indexing
1628 E. Southern Avenue
Suite 9-223
Tempe, AZ 85282

480-245-6750; *Fax:* 303-422-8894
nahj@nahj.org; www.asindexing.org
Social Media: Facebook, Twitter, YouTube, RSS

Mekahlo Medina, President
Ivette Davila-Richards, Vice President/Broadcast
Rebecca Aguilar, Vice President, Online
Barbara Rodriguez, Vice President, Print
Francisco Cortes, Financial Officer
A national association with international membership and interests. A nonprofit charitable organization for indexers, librarians, abstractors, editors, publishers, database producers, and organizations concerned with indexing, seeking cooperation and membership of all persons, groups or institutions interested in indexing. Founded in 1968 to promote excellence in indexing and increase awareness of the value of well-written indexes.
2300 Members
Founded in: 1984

15708 American Theological Library Association
The American Theological Library Association
300 S Wacker Dr
Suite 2100
Chicago, IL 60606-6701

312-454-5100
888-665-2852; *Fax:* 312-454-5505
presswomen@aol.com; www.atla.com
Social Media: Facebook, Twitter, LinkedIn, Youtube, RSS, Flickr

Teri Ehresman, President
Marsha Hoffman, 1st Vice President
Marianne Wolf-Astrauskas, 2nd Vice President
Ellen Crawford, Treasurer (Financial Adviser)
Gay Porter DeNileon, Secretary
Provides indexing services in these formats: online database, CD-ROM versions, magnetic tape for OPAC tapeload and print publications. ATLA Religion indexes in print include Religious Index One: Periodicals, Religion Index Two: Multi-Author Works, Index to Book Reviews, Research in Ministry an Index to D. Min. Project Reports and Theses.
2000 Members
Founded in: 1937

15709 Americans For Libraries Council
Americans For Libraries Council
347 Congress Street
Boston, MA 02210

855-533-9335
800-542-1918; *Fax:* 646-336-6318
natlwritersassn@hotmail.com; www.lff.org

Sandy Whelchel, Executive Director
Americans for Libraries Council (ALC) is a national non-profit organization that advocates for libraries at the national level and develops and promotes programs aimed at realizing the potential of libraries in the 21st century.
2000 Members
Founded in: 1937

15710 Art Libraries Society of North America
Art Libraries Society of North America
7044 South 13th Street
Box 11
Oak Creek, WI 53154

403-247-3001
800-817-0621; *Fax:* 414-768-8001
info@owaa.org; www.arlisna.org
Social Media: Facebook, Twitter, LinkedIn, RSS Feeds

Lisa Ballard, President
Brett Prettyman, 1st Vice President
Phil Bloom, 2nd Vice President
Tom Sadler, Executive Director
Jessica Seitz, Membership & Conference Services
Membership organization for art libraries in the US and Canada.
2.4M Members
Founded in: 1927

15711 Asian/Pacific American Librarians
Asian/Pacific American Librarians
PO Box 677593
Orlando, FL 32867

415-422-5379; www.apalaweb.org

Alan Di Benedetto, President
Stan Cohen, Vice President / Online Director
Liz Kassler, Treasurer
Chris McDonough, Membership Director
George Kamper, Communications Director
Librarians and information specialists of Asian Pacific descent and those interested in APA librarianship.
Founded in: 1984

15712 Association for Library & Information Science Education
Association for Library & Information
2150 N 107th St
Suite 205
Seattle, WA 98133

206-209-5267; *Fax:* 206-367-8777
sabew@sabew.org; www.alise.org
Social Media: Facebook, Twitter, LinkedIn, RSS

Joanna Ossinger, President
Cory Schouten, VP
Kathleen Graham, Executive Director
Crystal Beasley, Membership
Renee McGivern, Director of conference sponsorship

Provides a forum for library educators to share ideas, discuss issues and seek solutions to common problems.
3200 Members
Founded in: 1964

15713 **Association for Library Collections & Technical Services**
American Library Association
50 E Huron Street
Chicago, IL 60611

312-944-6780
800-545-2433; *Fax:* 312-280-5033
ala@ala.org; www.ala.org/alcts

Norm Medeiros, President
Keri Cascio, Executive Director
Keri A Cascio, Director at Large
Norm Medeiros, Director at Large
Timothy T Strawn, Director at Large
Division of the American Library Association.
5M Members
Founded in: 1957

15714 **Association for Library Service to Children**
American Library Association
50 E Huron Street
Chicago, IL 60611

312-944-6780
800-545-2433; *Fax:* 312-944-7671
ala@ala.org; www.ala.org/alsc/

Andrew Medlar, President
Betsy Orsburn, Vice-President/President-Elect
Jenna Nemec-Loise, ALSC Division Councilor
Diane Foote, Fiscal Officer
Kristen Sutherland, Program Officer
A network of more than 4,000 children's and youth librarians, children's literature experts, publishers, education and library school faculty members, and other adults committed to improving and ensuring the future of the nation through exemplary library service to children, their families, and others who work with children.
3500 Members

15715 **Association for Population/Family Planning**
Family Health International Library
PO Box 13950
Research Triangle Park, NC 27709

919-447-7040; *Fax:* 215-898-2124
info@satw.org; www.aplici.org
Social Media: Facebook, Twitter, LinkedIn

Paul Lasley, President
Barbara Orr, Vice President, Membership
Marla Schrager, Executive Director
John Kingzette, Membership Coordinator
Peggy Bendel, Secretary
Global network of communication, information and resource professionals dedicated to providing assistance and support to members and to other population and reproductive health colleagues, especially in developing nations.
Founded in: 1955

15716 **Association for Recorded Sound Collections**
Association for Recorded Sound Collections
1299 University of Oregon
Eugene, OR 97403-1299

440-564-9340
scwg-jm@cfi.rr.com; www.arsc-audio.org
Social Media: Facebook, Twitter, LinkedIn, Google+

Scott Tilley, President
Kit Adams, VP
JP Osterman, Secretary
Peggy Insula, Treasurer
Bill Allen, Communications & Publicity
Persons in broadcasting and recording industries, librarians, sound archivists, curators, private collectors and reviewers.
Cost: $40.00
Frequency: 2 Per Year
Circulation: 1000
Founded in: 1982
Mailing list available for rent

15717 **Association of Christian Libraries**
PO Box 4
Cedarville, OH 45314

937-766-2255; *Fax:* 937-766-5499;
www.acl.org
Social Media: Facebook, Twitter, Youtube,RSS

Howard A. Rodman, President
David A. Goodman, Vice President
Aaron Mendelsohn, Secretary-Treasurer
Membership is composed of over 500 evangelical Christian librarians representing primarily evangelical institutions of higher education.
9500 Members
Founded in: 1912

15718 **Association of College and Research Libraries**
American Library Association
50 E Huron Street
Chicago, IL 60611

312-944-6780
800-545-2433; *Fax:* 312-280-2520
acrl@ala.org; www.ala.org/acrl/

Ann Campion Riley, President
Irene M. H. Herold, ACRL Vice-President
Margot Sutton Conahan, Manager of Professional Development
David Connolly, Classified Advertising Coordinator
Kathryn Deiss, Content Strategist
13M Members
ISSN: 0099-0086
Founded in: 1940

15719 **Association of Independent Information Professionals (AAIP)**
Association of Independent Information
8550 United Plaza Boulevard
Suite 1001
Baton Rouge, LA 70809

225-408-4400; *Fax:* 225-922-4611;
www.aiip.org

Lori Packwood, Director
Provides a forum for information professionals to meet and exchange views.
Founded in: 2000

15720 **Association of Jewish Libraries**
Association of Jewish Libraries
PO Box 1118
Teaneck, NJ 07666

201-371-3255
info@ablusa.org; www.jewishlibraries.org
Social Media: Facebook, Twitter, RSS

Warren Scheidt, President
John D Bodnovich, Executive Director
Susan Day Duffy, Director of Trade Relations
Jessica Anders, Manager, Comm. & Public Relations
Warren Scheidt, Vice President
Promotes the advancement of the interests of Jewish libraries and publications of Jewish biographical interest.
15000 Members
Founded in: 1933

15721 **Association of Mental Health Librarians**
Cedarcrest Regional Hospital, Medical Libary
One Beach Street
Suite 100
San Francisco, CA 94133

415-955-2157; *Fax:* 845-398-5551
society@asev.org; www.mhlib.org/
Social Media: Facebook, Twitter, LinkedIn, Picasa

Mark Greenspan, President
Dan Howard, Executive Director
Nichola Hall, First Vice President
James Harbertson, Second Vice President
Tom Collins, Secretary/Treasurer
Provides a forum for the introduction of new audiovisual and printed materials in the field of mental health.
2400+ Members
Founded in: 1950

15722 **Association of Moving Archivists**
1313 North Vine Street
Hollywood, CA 90028

323-463-1500; *Fax:* 323-463-1506
asbc@scisoc.org; www.amianet.org
Social Media: Facebook, Twitter, LinkedIn, Pinterest

Jeffery L Cornell, President
Christina Schoenberger, Vice President
Amy Hope, Executive Officer
Barbara Mock, Vice President of Finance
Kelly A Tretter, Secretary
A non-profit professional association established to advance the field of moving image archiving by fostering cooperation among individuals and organization concerned with the acquistion, description, preservation, exhibition and use of moving image materials.
750 Members
Founded in: 1934

15723 **Association of Research Libraries**
Association of Research Libraries
21 Dupont Circle NW
Suite 800
Washington, DC 20036

202-296-2296; *Fax:* 202-872-0884
info@beerinstitute.org; www.arl.org
Social Media: Facebook, Twitter, YouTtube

Joe McClain, President
Mary Jane Saunders, VP & General Counsel
Nonprofit organization striving to shape and influence forces affecting the future of research libraries in the process of scholarly communication.
100 Members
Founded in: 1986

15724 **Beta Phi Mu**
University of South Florida
PO Box 42139
Philadelphia, PA 19101

267-361-5018; *Fax:* - - 8
info@brewersassociation.org;
www.beta-phi-mu.org
Social Media: Facebook, Twitter, Youtube

Charlie Papazian, President
Bob Pease, Chief Operating Officer
Paul Gatza, Director
Erin Glass, Membership Coordinator
Katie Marisic, Federal Affairs Manager
Beta Phi Mu is an organization that recognizes and encourages scholastic achievement among library and information studies students.
1900 Members
Founded in: 1978

15725 **Black Caucus of ALA**
Gladys Smiley Bell

PO Box 5837
Lib. Med. Serv., Rm 161, Kent State
Chicago, IL 60680

330-672-3045; *Fax:* 330-672-3964;
www.bcala.org
Social Media: Facebook, Twitter

Peter H Cressy, President

Association that supports black librarians. Holds annual meeting in conjunction with the American Library Association conference.
32 Members
Founded in: 1973

15726 Catholic Library Association
Catholic Library Association
8550 United Plaza Blvd
Ste 1001
Baton Rouge, LA 70809

225-408-4417
855-739-1776; *Fax:* 312-739-1778;
www.cathla.org
Social Media: Facebook, Twitter, YouTube, flickr, RSS

Anthony Perrone, International President
William T. McDonough, Executive Vice President, UFCW
Patrick J. O'Neill, International Secretary-Treasurer
Stuart Appelbaum, Executive Vice President
Paul Meinema, Executive Vice President

International membership organization, providing its members professional development through educational and networking experiences, publications, scholarships and other services.
14M Members
Founded in: 1979

15727 Center for Children's Books
Center for Children's Books
501 E Daniel Street
Champaign, IL 61820

217-244-9331; *Fax:* 217-333-5603
ccb.lis.illinois.edu
Social Media: Facebook, Twitter, Youtube

Mark Alston, President
Steven Haynes, VP
Ray Ault, Secretary
Allison Babock, Treasurer
Dee Roberson, Executive Director

A crossroads for critical inquiry, professional training and educational outreach related to literature for youth from birth through adolescence. In partnership with The Bulletin of the Center for Children's Books, it aims to inspire and inform adults who connect young people with resources in person, in print, and online.
Founded in: 1976

15728 Center for Childrens Books
Center for Children's Books
501 E Daniel Street
Champaign, IL 61820
217-244-9331; *Fax:* 217-333-5603
newyork@ice.it
ccb.lis.illinois.edu

Michelle Jones, Editor
Robert Luongo, Executive Director

15729 Chief Officers of State Library Agencies
Chief Officers of State Library Agencies
201 E Main Street
Suite 1405
Lexington, KY 40507

859-514-9151; *Fax:* 859-514-9166
iwfi@aol.com; www.cosla.org

Lucio Caputo, President
Vincent Giampaoco, VP

Association for directors of state libraries.
Founded in: 1983

15730 Chinese-American Librarians Association
UCI Libraries
PO Box 19557
Irvine, CA 92623-9557

949-824-6836; *Fax:* 949-857-1988;
www.cala-web.org
Social Media: Facebook, Twitter, Youtube

Stephen Larson, Chairman
James M. Sgueo, President & CEO
Jerome J. Janicki, Sr. VP of Operations, COO
Patricia Kelly, Sr. VP of Administration, CFO
Steven L. Schmidt, SVP, Public Policy/Communications
175 Members
Founded in: 1938

15731 Church and Synagogue Library Association
10157 SW Barbur Boulevard
Suite 102C
Portland, OR 97219

503-244-6919
800-542-2752; *Fax:* 503-977-3734
info@nbwa.org; www.cslainfo.org
Social Media: Facebook, Twitter, Youtube, Flickr

Craig A. Purser, NBWA President & CEO
Kimberly McKinnish, CPA, Chief Financial Officer
Rebecca Spicer, SVP Comm. and Public Affairs
Paul Pisano, SVP Industry Affairs & Gen. Counsel
Patti Rouzie, VP, Membership and Meetings

Provides educational guidance in the establishment and maintenance of congregational libraries
Founded in: 1938

15732 Coalition for Networked Information
21 Dupont Circle
Suite 800
Washington, DC 20036-1109

202-296-5098; *Fax:* 202-872-0884;
www.cni.org

Robert P Koch, President / Chief Executive Officer
Nancy Light, Vice President, Communications
Steve Gross, Vice President, State Relations
Allison Jordan, VP, Environmental Affairs
Steve Hayes, VP, Finance and Administration

The Coalition for Networked Information is an organization dedicated to supporting the transformative promise of networked information technology for the advancement of scholarly communication and the enrichment of intellectual productivity.
80 Members
Founded in: 1934

15733 Council on Library and Information Resources
Council on Library and Information Resources
1707 L Street NW, Suite 650
Washington, DC 20036-2124

202-939-4750; *Fax:* 202-600-9628
info@wssa.com; www.clir.org
Social Media: Facebook, Twitter, LinkedIn, RSS

V. James Andretta, Jr., Chairman of the Board
Louis Healey, President
Howard Jacobs, Vice President
Heather Randolph, Director of Operations
Alison Leavitt, Managing Director

The mission of the Council on Library and Information Resources is to expand access to information, however recorded and preserved, as a public good.
460 Members
Founded in: 1976

15734 Council on Library/Media Technicians
PO Box 256
Oxon Hill, MD 20748

202-231-3836; *Fax:* 202-231-3838
Info@wswa.org
http://colt.ucr.edu/
Social Media: Facebook, Twitter, YouTube, RSS, Google+

Brien Fox, Chairman
Doug Epstein, Vice Chairman
Craig Wolf, President and CEO
Jim Rowland, VP, Government Affairs
Dawson Hobbs, Vice President, State Affairs

Supports library and media techicians by offering publications, training, networking and annual conference in conjunction with the American Library Association conference.
450 Members
Founded in: 1943

15735 Ethnic Employees of the Library of Congress
6100 Eastview Street
Bethesda, MD 20817-6004
George E Perry, President

Promotes and strengthens brotherhood among ethnic employees and ethnic members of society.
Founded in: 1973

15736 Federal Library and Information Network
Library of Congress
101 Independence Ave SE
Washington, DC 20540-4935

202-707-4800; *Fax:* 202-707-4818
help@apawood.org; www.loc.gov/flicc
Social Media: Facebook, Twitter

Tom Temple, Chairman
Don Grimm, Vice Chairman
Edward Elias, President
Marilyn Thompson, Director of Marketing and Comm.
Tom Kositzky, Director, Field Services Rep.

Representatives of departments and agencies of the federal government.
160 Members
Founded in: 1933
Mailing list available for rent

15737 Federal and Armed Forces Libraries Roundtable
American Library Association
50 E Huron Street
Chicago, IL 60611
312-944-6780
800-545-2433
ala@ala.org; www.ala.org

Amanda J. Wilson, President
Stephen V. Pomes, Vice President
Theresa Taylor, Armed Forces Director
Bianna E. Ine-Ryan, Armed Forces Director
Anne Harrison, Federal Director

Association for libraries and information services.

15738 Friends of Libraries (FOLUSA)
Association of Library Trustees, Advocates, Friend

50 E Huron Street
Chicago, IL 60611

312-944-6780
800-545-2433; *Fax:* 215-545-3821
jkalonick@ala.org; www.ala.org

Ed McBride, President
Sally Gardner Reed, Executive Director
Beth Nawalinski, Deputy Executive Director
Jillian Kalonick, Marketing/PR Specialist
Bette M Kozlowski, Treasurer

Encourages the development of excellent library service to all residents of the US. Aids in forming local and state, friends branches in academic and special libraries.
1.8M Members
Founded in: 1979

15739 Herbert Hoover Presidential Library Association
302 Park Side Drive
PO Box 696
West Branch, IA 52358

319-643-5327
800-828-0475; *Fax:* 319-643-2391
afa@fiberboard.org;
www.hooverassociation.org
Social Media: Twitter

Rina P. McGuire, President
Jim Pieczynski, VP
Louis E. Wagner, Executive Director
William C. Ives, Legal Counsel
Blair Ruzicka, Secretary/Treasurer
7 Members
Founded in: 1990

15740 Insurance Library Association of Boston
Insurance Library
156 State St
Boston, MA 02109-2584

617-227-2087; *Fax:* 617-723-8524
info@afandpa.org; www.insurancelibrary.org
Social Media: Facebook, Twitter, LinkedIn, Youtube

Mark R. Gardner, Chairman
Mark W. Kowlzan, President and CEO
Linda Massman, Second Vice Chairman
Samuel Kerns, VP, Administration and CFO
Chuck Fuqua, Executive Director, Strategic Comm.

Founded in: 1887, the Insurance Library Association of Boston is a resource for and provider of literature, information services, and quality professional education for the insurance industry and related interests. The Association offers a wide variety of research services and materials. The collection includes contemporary and historical versions of books, pamphlets, articles and reference materials in all areas of the insurance industry.
550 Members
Founded in: 1993
Mailing list available for rent

15741 Interagency Council on Information
American Nurses Association Library
8515 Georgia Avenue
Suite 400
Silver Spring, MD 20910-3492

301-628-5143; *Fax:* 301-628-5008
info@forestfoundation.org; www.icirn.org
Social Media: Facebook, Twitter

Kenneth Stewart, Chairman
Connie Best, Vice-Chair
Nathan Truitt, Vice President of Development
Scott Smiley, Vice President, Finance
Kathy McGlauflin, SVP, Project Learning Tree

To esablish an effective use of information resources available to the nursing community, and to advance the profession through the promotion and use of its literature.
120 Members

15742 International Association of Aquatic & Mar ine Science Libraries
The International Association of Aquatic and Marin
2030 S Marine Science Drive
Newport, OR 97365

772-460-9977
info@americanforests.org; www.iamslic.org
Social Media: Facebook, Twitter, YouTube

Ann Nichols, Chair
Scott Steen, President & CEO
Matthew Boyer, Vice President, Individual Giving
Peter Hutchins, VP/COO
Greg Meyer, VP, Corporate Partnerships

Encourages members to exchange scientific and technical information and explore issues of mutual concern. Conducts workshops about on line databases.
Founded in: 1990

15743 International Association of School Librarianship
65 E. Wacker Place
Suite 1900
Chicago, IL 60601-7246

814-474-1115; *Fax:* 312-419-8950;
www.iasl-online.org/

Michael Snow, Executive Director
An Di H Nguyen, Manager of International Programs
Stefani Brown, International Program Coordinator

IASL provides an international forum for those people interested in promoting effective school library media programs as viable instruments in the educational process.

15744 Library Binding Institute
4440 PGA Blvd.
Ste. 600
Palm Beach Gardens, FL 33410

561-745-6821; *Fax:* 561-472-8401
info@aitc-glulam.org; www.lbibinders.org

Don DeVisser P.E., Executive VP
Skeet Rominger, Director Quality Services
Mike Schoen, Controller
Robert A Horlacher, Senior District Manager, Eastern
John Zachariou, Senior District Manager, Western

Members are firms binding books for libraries and their suppliers.
Founded in: 1952

15745 Library Leadership and Management Association
American Library Association
50 E Huron Street
Chicago, IL 60611

312-944-6780
800-545-2433; *Fax:* 312-280-5033
lama@ala.org; www.ala.org/llama/

Jeff Steely, President
Kerry Ward, Executive Director
Fred Reuland, Program Officer
Jim Rettig, Treasurer

Works to improve and develop all aspects and levels of administration in all types of libraries.
5M Members
Founded in: 1957

15746 Library and Information Technology Association
American Library Association
50 E Huron Street
Chicago, IL 60611

312-944-6780
800-545-2433
lita@ala.org; www.ala.org/lita/

Thomas P. Dowling, President
Jenny Levine, Executive Director
Mark A. Beatty, Staff Liaison
Melissa Prentice, Program Planning and Marketing
Valerie A Edmonds, Program Coordinator

15747 Major Orchestra Librarians' Association
MOLA
1530 Locust Street
PMB 154
Philadelphia, PA 19102

E-Mail: alsc@alsc.org; www.mola-inc.org

Thomas D Searles, President, Chief Lumber Inspector

International organization whose objectives include: to improve communication among orchestra librarians; present a unified voice in publisher relations; and assist librarians in providing better service to their orchestras.
Founded in: 1924

15748 Medical Library Association
65 E Wacker Place
Suite 1900
Chicago, IL 60601-7246

312-419-9094; *Fax:* 312-419-8950
info@sportsbuilders.org; www.mlanet.org / www.marketing.mlanet.org
Social Media: Facebook, LinkedIn, Blog

Dan Wright, CFB, Chairman
Pete Smith, CTB, Tennis Division President
Troy Rudolph, Track Division President
Joe Covington, Jr, Indoor Division President
Jim Catella, CFB, CTB, Fields Division President

A nonprofit, educational organization that is a leading advocate for health sciences information professionals worldwide. Through it's programs and services, we provide lifelong educational opportunities, supports a knowledgebase of health information research and works with a global network of partners to promote the importance of quality information for improved health to the health care community and the public.
50 Members
Founded in: 1965

15749 Mid-America Association of Law Libraries
MidAmerican Energy Holdings Company
Po Box 657
Des Moines, IA 50306-0657

515-242-4300
800-358-6265; *Fax:* 515-242-4261
jackson@purdue.edu; www.midamerican.com

Brian Brookshire, Executive Director
Laura Brookshire, Comm. and Membership Manager
Beverly Heidbreder, Accountant

Association for suppliers of law library equipment, supplies and services.
8 Members
Founded in: 1912

15750 Middle East Librarians' Association
Middle East Librarians Association
Main Library
Santa Barbara, CA 93106

805-637-7749; www.mela.us
Social Media: Facebook, Twitter, LinkedIn, RSS

Kris J. Ormseth, Office Managing Partner

Interested in aspects of librarianship that support the study or dissemination of information about the Middle East. Publishes a bulletin (semi-annually) that is distributed to members and subscriber institutions in North America, Europe, the Middle East, Asia and Africa.
5 Members
Founded in: 1907

15751 Mountain Plains Library Association
14293 W. Center Drive
'
Lakewood, CO 80228
303-985-7795; *Fax:* 605-677-5488
email@awpa.com; www.mpla.us
Colin McCown, Executive Vice President
Purpose is to promote the development of librarians and libraries by providing significant educational and networking opportunities. The association meets annually in joint conferences with member stats on a rotational basis, and its governed by an elected board of representatives from each member state and a number of selections and roundtables representing interests and types of libraries. In addition to its board and officers, MPLA activities are carried out by a number of committees.
900 Members
Founded in: 1904

15752 Music Library Association
1600 Aspen Commons
Suite 100
Middleton, WI 53562
608-836-5825; *Fax:* 608-831-8200
tom@appalachianwood.org; www.musiclibraryassoc.org
Tom Inman, President
Dinah Farrington, Administrative Assistant
Promotes growth and establishment in the use of music libraries, musical instruments and musical literature.
154 Members
Founded in: 1926

15753 National Association of Media & Technology Centers
PO Box 9844
Cedar Rapids, IA 52409-9844
319-654-0608; *Fax:* 319-654-0609
info@awinet.org; www.namtc.org
Social Media: Facebook, Twitter, LinkedIn, YouTube, Flickr
Philip Duvic, Executive Vice President
Greg Heuer, Chief Learning Officer
Cassey Gibson, Chief Member Services Officer
Beth Holcomb, Meeting and Event Planner
Katie Allen, Project Manager
The National Association of Media & Technology Centers is an organization committed to promoting leadership among its membership through networking, advocacy, and support activities that will enhance the equitable access to media, technology, and information services to educational committees. Current membership is over 20 million students.
4000 Members
Founded in: 1954

15754 National Church Library Association
National Church Library Association
275 3rd St S
Suite 101A
Stillwater, MN 55082-5094
651-430-0770
Mail@WorldMillworkAlliance.com; www.churchlibraries.org
Social Media: Twitter, LinkedIn
Joe Bayer, President
Dave Ondrasek, First Vice President
Timothy Lyons, Second Vice President
Rosalie Leone, Chief Executive Officer
Brian Welsh, Membership & Marketing Director
Non-profit support organization that endeavours to further the gospel through church libraries. New resources and support programs are always under development to serve the ever changing needs of the church librarian. Membership is open to individuals, churches or libraries of any denomination or size.
1200 Members
Founded in: 1935

15755 National Information Standards Organization
3600 Clipper Mill Road
Suite 302
Baltimore, MD 21211
301-654-2512; *Fax:* 410-685-5278; www.niso.org
Social Media: Facebook, Twitter, LinkedIn
Wade Gregory, President
Archie Thompson, VP
Angelo Gangone, Executive Vice President
Amy Bartz, Fair Sales Director
Nancy Fister, Education & Conference Director
A non-profit association accredited by the American National Standards Institute, identifies, develops, maintains, and publishes technical standards to manage information in our changing and ever-more digital environment.
425 Members
Founded in: 1979

15756 National Library Service for the Blind
Library of Congress
1291 Taylor Street, NW
Washington, DC 20542
202-707-5100
800-424-8567; *Fax:* 202-707-0712
info@capital-lumber.com; www.loc.gov/nls
Social Media: Facebook, Twitter, LinkedIn, Pinterest
Dan Merrill, Division Manager
Bill Bieker, Sales Manager
ISSN: 0363-3805
Founded in: 1948
Mailing list available for rent

15757 National Media Market
National Media Market
PO Box 87410
Tucson, AZ 85754-7410
520-743-7735; *Fax:* 800-952-0442
info@capital-lumber.com; www.nmm.net
Social Media: Facebook, Twitter, LinkedIn, Pinterest
Matt Yates, Branch Manager
Darren Henderson, Operations Manager
Bill Butner, Sales Manager
Cindy DeLand, Office Manager
Phillip Floyd, Account Manager
Presents an exceptional opportunity for media professionals who purchase for public libraries, universities, media/technology centers and educational broadcasting to screen the newst and best quality motion medis from fifty-five prominent producers and distributors.
Founded in: 1999

15758 New England Library Association
New England Library Association
55 North Main Street, Unit 49
Belchertown, MA 01007
413-813-5254; *Fax:* 978-282-1304
info@cedarbureau.com; www.nelib.org
Social Media: Facebook, Twitter
Kent Gibson, Chairman
Ed Watkins, Vice-chairman
Terry Kost, Secretary-Treasurer
Lynne Christensen, MBA, CAE, Director of Operations
Barbara Enns, Accountant
Promotes excellence in library services to the people of New England and advances the leadership role of it's members. Holds an annual conference.
350 Members
Founded in: 1915

15759 Public Library Association
Public Library Association
50 E Huron Street
Chicago, IL 60611-5295
312-280-5752
800-545-2433; *Fax:* 312-280-5029
pla@ala.org; www.ala.org/pla
Social Media: Facebook
Vailey Oehlke, President
Barb Macikas, Executive Director
Julianna Kloeppel, Program Director
Melissa Faubel Johnson, CMP, Meeting & Special Events Planner
Mary Hirsh, Project Manager
Exists to provide a diverse program of communications and programming for its members and others interested in the advancment of public libaries.
Founded in: 1944

15760 Reference and User Services Association
American Library Association
50 E Huron St
Chicago, IL 60611-2729
312-280-4395
800-545-2433; *Fax:* 312-944-8085
rusa@ala.org; www.ala.org/RUSA
Susan Hornung, Executive Director
Andrea Hill, Manager, Web Services
Leighann Wood, Membership Assistant
Marianne Braverman, Marketing & Programs Manager
Reference and User Services Association is responsible for stimulating and supporting excellence in the delivery of general library services and materials to adults, and the provision of reference and information services, collection development, and resource sharing for all ages, in every type of library.
5000 Members
Founded in: 1876

15761 Society of American Archivists
17 North State Street
Suite 1425
Chicago, IL 60602
312-606-0722
866-722-7858; *Fax:* 312-606-0728
admin@decorativesurfaces.org; www2.archivists.org/
Jackson Morrill, President
Donald Bisson, VP, Gov. and Industry Affairs
Jeannie Ervin, VP, Membership and Administration
Gary Heroux, Vice President, Product Acceptance
Allyson O'Sullivan, Director of Marketing
Association for those interested in archival theory and practice in North America.
232 Members
Founded in: 1960

15762 Southeastern Library Association
P.O. Box 950
Rex, GA 30273
678-466-4334; *Fax:* 678-466-4349; www.selaonline.org/
James Mathers, President
Larry R Frye, Executive Director

For over 60 years, the Association has been a unifying force strong enough to influence legislation and to attract foundation and federal funds for regional library projects. The accomplishments of the Association include 2 regional library surveys; the adoption of school library standards; the establishment of state library agencies and the position of state school library supervisor; the founding of library schools; the sponsoring of a variety of informative workshops.
15 Members
Founded in: 1933

15763 Special Libraries Association
331 S Patrick St
Alexandria, VA 22314-3501

703-647-4900; *Fax:* 703-647-4901
license@landmobile.com; www.sla.org
Social Media: Facebook, Twitter

Kevin Mc Carthy, President

International association of information professionals who work in special libraries serving business, research, government and institutions that produce specialized information.
600 Members
Founded in: 1947

15764 State University of New York Librarians Association
Office of Library & Information Services
SUNY Plaza
Albany, NY 12246

518-443-5577; *Fax:* 518-443-5358
info@forestlandowners.com; www.sunyla.org
Social Media: Facebook, Twitter

Joe Hopkins, President
Scott P. Jones, Chief Executive Officer
Susan Johnson Klco, Director of Administration
Kent Sole, Director of Development
Katelin Baker, Marketing Coordinator

Statewide professional librarian organization.
10500 Members
Founded in: 1941

15765 Substance Abuse Librarians and Information
Substance Abuse Librarians & Information Specialis
PO Box 9513
Berkeley, CA 94709-0513

510-865-6225; *Fax:* 510-865-2467
info@forestprod.org; www.salis.org
Social Media: Facebook, Twitter, LinkedIn

Maureen Puettman, President
David DeVallance, Vice President
Stefan A. Bergmann, Executive Vice President

Provides professional development and exchange of information and concerns about access to and dissemination of information on substance abuse.
Founded in: 1947

15766 Theatre Library Association
40 Lincoln Center Plaza
New York, NY 10023

E-Mail: friendsofthetrees@yahoo.com;
www.tla-online.org

Michael Pilarski, Founder and Director

Supports librarians and archivists affiliated with theatre, dance, performance studies, popluar entertainment, motion picture and broadcasting collections. Promotes professional best practices in acquistion, organization, access and preservation of performing arts resources in libraries, archives, museums, private collections, and the digital environment.
Founded in: 1978

15767 Urban Libraries Council
1333 H Street, NW
Suite 1000 West
Washington, DC 20005

202-750-8650; *Fax:* 312-676-0950
jackhillman@woodtank.com;
www.urbanlibraries.org

Jack Hillman, Company Contact

Works to strengthen public libraries as an essential part of urban life. Serves as a forum for research widely recognized and used by public and prrivate sector leaders.
Founded in: 1854

Newsletters

15768 AASL Presidential Hotline
American Library Association
50 E Huron St
Chicago, IL 60611-2788

312-280-2518
800-545-2433
kfiels@ala.org; www.ala.org

Keith Michael Fiels, Executive Director

School library media association news.
Frequency: Monthly
Founded in: 1951

15769 Corporate Library Update
Reed Business Information
30 Technology Parkway South
Suite 100
Norcross, GA 30092

646-746-6400
800-424-3996; *Fax:* 646-756-7583
webmaster@reedbusiness.com;
www.reedbusiness.com

John Poulin, CEO
Lynn Blumenstein, Senior Editor
Susan DiMattia, Editor
Cost: $69.95
Frequency: Fortnightly
Circulation: 2500

15770 Libraries Alive
National Church Library Association
275 3rd St S
Suite 101A
Stillwater, MN 55082-5094

651-430-0770
info@churchlibraries.org;
www.churchlibraries.org
Social Media: Facebook

Sue Benish, Executive Director
Chuck Mann, President Board of Directors

Features informative articles, reviews of books and other media, a sharing of ideas, Internet resources, chapter news, news of authors and upcoming regional and national workshops.
Frequency: Quarterly

15771 Library Hotline
Library Journal/School Library Journal
360 Park Ave S
New York, NY 10010-1710

646-746-6819
800-446-6551; *Fax:* 646-746-6734;
www.libraryjournal.com

Ron Shank, Publisher
Justin Torres, Production Manager
Lynn Blumenstein, Senior Editor
Carol Batt, COO
Patty Braden, Director
Cost: $115.00
Frequency: Weekly
Founded in: 1876

15772 MLA News
Medical Library Association
65 E Wacker Place
Suite 1900
Chicago, IL 60601-7298

312-419-9094; *Fax:* 312-419-8950
info@mlahq.org; www.mlanet.org

Lynanne Fielen, Director Publications
Carla Funk, Editor
Lynanne Fielen, Circulation Manager
Elizabeth Rodriguez, Graphic Designer

Covers MLA programs and services as well as the medical librarian profession in general.
Cost: $58.00
Frequency: Monthly
Founded in: 1898
Mailing list available for rent

15773 Marcato
MOLA/Editor
1530 Locust Street
PMB 154
Philadelphia, PA 19102

202-416-8131; *Fax:* 202-416-8132
sfriedman@kennedy-center.org;
www.mola-inc.org

Shelley Friedman, Editor
Gordon Rowley, Treasurer
Elena Lence Talley, President

Newsletter of Major Orchestra Librarians' Association.
Cost: $20.00
Frequency: Quarterly

15774 Marketing Treasures
Chris Olson & Associates
857 Twin Harbor Drive
Arnold, MD 21012-1027

410-647-6708; *Fax:* 410-647-0415;
www.chrisolson.com

Christine Olson, Publisher

Provinding creative ideas, helpful hints and insights on how libraries can promote thier services
6 Pages
Frequency: Monthly
Circulation: 1000
Founded in: 1987
Printed in 2 colors on matte stock

15775 Report on Literacy Programs
Business Publishers
8737 Colesville Road
Suite 1100
Silver Spring, MD 20910-3928

301-876-6300
800-274-6737; *Fax:* 301-589-8493
custserv@bpinews.com; www.bpinews.com

Dave Speights, Editor
Leonard A Eiserer, Publisher
Beth Early, Operations Director

Covers all aspects of literacy including legislation, funding, training programs, important conferences, job skills and much more.
Cost: $317.00
Founded in: 1963

15776 Research Library Issues
Association of Research Libraries
21 Dupont Circle NW
Suite 800
Washington, DC 20036

202-296-2296; *Fax:* 202-872-0884;
www.arl.org
Social Media: Facebook, Twitter, LinkedIn, Flickr,YouTube

Charles B Lowry, Executive Director
Prudence S. Adler, Associate Executive Director
Sue Baughman, Deputy Executive Director
Julia Blixrud, Assistant Executive Director
Mary Jane Brooks, Assistant Executive Director

Member representatives
Frequency: Bi-Monthly
ISSN: 1947-4911

15777 State University of New York Librarians Association
Office of Library & Information Services
SUNY Plaza
Albany, NY 12246
518-443-5577; *Fax:* 518-443-5358
drewwe@morrisville.edu; www.sunyla.org
Social Media: Facebook, Twitter
Wilfred Drew, President
John Schumacher, Electronic Resources Coordinator
Provides news, notes and information from SUNY campus libraries.
Frequency: 2-3/Year

15778 Technicalities
Westport Publishing
802 Broadway Street
Kansas City, MO 64105
816-842-0641
Brian Alley, Editor
A professional journal presenting discussion, opinions, and reviews on library-management topics. Typical issues include articles ranging from computer applications, on-line public access catalogs, library budgets, collection building, book reviews, automation, software, library marketplace trends, and the Library of Congress. Articles are indexed in Library Literature and LISA: Library Information Science Abstracts and are available on microfilm from UMI.
Cost: $ 47.00
16 Pages
Frequency: Monthly
Circulation: 700
Mailing list available for rent
Printed in one color on matte stock

15779 Urban Libraries Council Exchange Letter
1603 Orrington Avenue
Suite 1080
Evanston, IL 60201
847-866-9999; *Fax:* 847-866-9989
info@urbanlibraries.org; www.urbanlibraries.org/
Eleanor Rodger, President/CEO
Linda Crismond, Editor
Newsletter for public libraries in cities with over 100,000 people. Free to members, also available without membership.
Cost: $50.00
150 Pages
Circulation: 6000
Founded in: 1971

Magazines & Journals

15780 AALL Spectrum
American Association of Law Libraries
105 W Adams Street
Suite 3300
Chicago, IL 60603
312-939-4764; *Fax:* 312-431-1097
support@aall.org; www.aallnet.org
Social Media: Facebook, Twitter
Mark Estes, Editorial Director
Hillary Baker, Marketing and Communications
Kate Hagan, Executive Director
Kim Rundle,, Executive Assistant
Emily Feltren,, Director of Government Relations
Publishes substantive, well-written articles on topics of real interest to law librarians, as well as news about the American Association of Law Libraries, including its chapters, committees and Special Interest Sections
Cost: $ 75.00

15781 Advanced Technology/Libraries
GK Hall & Company
1239 Broadway
Suite 1601
New York, NY 10001-4327
212-685-0602; *Fax:* 212-654-4751
sales@gkimport.com; www.gkimport.com
Dina Groudan, President
Audrey Ismal, Owner
Concise, practical information on the advances in development, implementation and use of library automation. Articles cover new products, new services, legislation and grant information.
Cost: $95.00
Frequency: Monthly

15782 American Archivist
Society of American Archivists
527 S Wells Street
5th Floor
Chicago, IL 60607-3922
312-922-0140; *Fax:* 312-347-1452; www.archivists.org
Susan Fox, Executive Director
Philip B Eppard, Editor
Teresa Brinati, Director of Publications
Offers information and essays on archival theory and practice in North America.
Cost: $85.00
Circulation: 4800+
Founded in: 1936

15783 American Libraries
American Library Association
50 E Huron St
Chicago, IL 60611-2788
312-280-2518
800-545-2433
customerservice@ala.org; www.ala.org
Claire Knowles, Manager
Carla D Hayden, President
Library development news.
Cost: $60.00
Frequency: Monthly
Founded in: 1876

15784 Book Report: Magazine for Secondary School Librarians
Linworth Publishing
480 East Wilson Bridge Road
Suite L
Worthington, OH 43085
614-436-7107
800-786-5017; *Fax:* 614-436-9490
linworth@linworthpublishing.com; www.linworth.com
Marlene Woo-Lun, Publisher
Amy Robinson, Marketing Manager
In-depth articles, helpful hints, and reviews on books, software, videos, and CD-Roms for secondary school librarians.
Cost: $49.00
105 Pages
Circulation: 15000
Founded in: 1981
Printed in 4 colors on glossy stock

15785 Booklist
American Library Association
50 E Huron St
Chicago, IL 60611-2788
312-280-2518
800-545-2433
customerservice@ala.org; www.ala.org
Claire Knowles, Manager
To provide a guide to current library materials in many formats appropriate for use in public libraries and school library media centers.
Cost: $89.95
Circulation: 25000
Founded in: 1876

15786 Bulletin of Bibliography
Greenwood Publishing Group
88 Post Road W
P O Box 5007
Westport, CT 06881-5007
203-226-3571
800-225-5800; *Fax:* 203-226-6009; www.greenwood.com
Bernard McTigue, Editor-in-Chief
Gerry Katz, Executive Editor
Naomi Caldwell Wood, Author
Offers bibliographies in humanities and social sciences.
Cost: $125.00
100 Pages
Frequency: Quarterly
Circulation: 1000
ISSN: 0190-745X
Printed in 2 colors on matte stock

15787 Bulletin of the Center for Children's Books
501 E Daniel Street
MC-493
Champaign, IL 61820
217-244-0324; *Fax:* 217-244-3302
alexia.lis.uiuc.edu
Deborah Stevenson, Editor
Marlow Welshon, Dean
Reviews of children's books for librarians, teachers, booksellers and parents.
Cost: $50.00
34 Pages
Frequency: Monthly
Circulation: 6500
Founded in: 1893

15788 CD-ROM Librarian
Mecklermedia Corporation
11 Ferry Lane W
Westport, CT 06880-5808
Fax: 203-454-5840
Alan Meckler, Editor
A periodical intended for the library professional.
Cost: $80.00
Frequency: Monthly
Founded in: 1986

15789 Catholic Library World
Catholic Library Association
205 W Monroe St, Ste 314
Pittsfield, MA 01201-5178
413-443-2252; *Fax:* 413-442-2252
cla@cathla.org; www.cathla.org
Social Media: Facebook
Nancy K Schmidtmann, President
Malachy R McCarthy, VP
Jean R Bostley SSJ, Executive Director
Articles and news of interest to the library profession. Extensive section of book and media reviews
Frequency: Quarterly
ISSN: 0008-820X

15790 Choice
Association of College and Research Libraries

575 Main Street
Suite 300
Middletown, CT 06457

800-545-2433
acrl@ala.org; www.ala.org/acrl/choice

Lori Goetsch, President
Irving Rockwood, Publisher
Francine Graf, Editorial Director
Lisa Gross, Information/Production Manager
Rita Balasco, Choice Reviews

Publishes reviews of books, internet sites, and microcomputer software suitable for college and university libraries.
Cost: $280.00
Frequency: Monthly
Circulation: 5000
Founded in: 1938

15791 Congregational Libraries Today
Church and Synagogue Library Association
10157 SW Barbur Boulevard
Suite 102C
Portland, OR 97219-4055

503-244-6919
800-542-2752; *Fax:* 503-977-3734
csla@worldacessnet.com; www.cslainfo.org
Social Media: Facebook, Twitter

Sue Poss, Publications Editor
Marcia Trauernicht, President

Contains news about CSLA and its chapters, feature stories about congregational libraries and librarians, promotion ideas, information on using computers and the internet in the library, and reviews of books, videos, CDs, and audiotapes for adults and children.
Cost: $40.00
800 Members
28 Pages
Frequency: Quarterly
Founded in: 1967

15792 Information Retrieval & Library Automation
Lomond Publications
PO Box 88
Mount Airy, MD 21771-0088

202-362-1361; *Fax:* 202-362-6156

Thomas Hattery, Publisher

New technology, products and equipment that improve information systems and library services, for science, social, social science, law, medicine, academic institutions and the public.
Cost: $75.00
Frequency: Monthly

15793 Journal of the Medical Library Association
Medical Library Association
65 E Wacker Drive
Suite 1900
Chicago, IL 60601-7298

312-419-9094
800-462-6420; *Fax:* 312-419-8950
info@mlahq.org; www.mlanet.org

Lynanne Feilen, Director Publication
Carla J Funk, Executive Director
Susan C Talmage, Editorial Assistant
Bleu caldwell, Production Assistant
Barbara Redmond, Advertising Coordinator
Cost: $163.00
Frequency: Quarterly
Mailing list available for rent

15794 Knowledge Quest
American Library Association
50 E Huron St
Chicago, IL 60611-2788

312-280-2518
800-545-2433
kfiels@ala.org; www.ala.org

Keith Michael Fiels, Executive Director
Andria Parker, Marketing
Vickie William, Circulation Manager

Articles on teaching, learning process, ideas and information to prepare students for life long learning.
Cost: $40.00
Circulation: 5000
ISSN: 1094-9046
Founded in: 1879
Printed in 4 colors on matte stock

15795 Library Bookseller
PO Box 9544
Berkeley, CA 94709-544
Scott Saifer, Publisher
Gail Russin, Editor

A journal focusing on suppliers to libraries.
Cost: $100.00
36 Pages

15796 Library Journal
Media Source
160 Varick Street
11th Floor
New York, NY 10013

646-380-0700; *Fax:* 646-380-0756
ljinfo@mediasourceinc.com;
www.libraryjournal.com

Ron Shank, Publisher
Francine Fialkoff, Editor-in-Chief
Brian Kenney, Editorial Director
Bette-Lee Fox, Managing Editor
Rebecca Miller, Executive Editor

Provides groundbreaking features and analytical news reports covering technology, management, policy and other professional concerns to public, academic and institutional libraries. Evaluates 8000 reviews annually of books, ebooks, audiobooks, videos/DVDs, databases, systems and websites.
Cost: $141.00
Circulation: 17936
Founded in: 1876
Printed in 4 colors on glossy stock

15797 Library Resources & Technical Services
American Library Association
50 E Huron St
Chicago, IL 60611-2788

312-280-2518
800-545-2433
kfiels@ala.org; www.ala.org

Keith Michael Fiels, Executive Director
Steven L Hofman, Circulation Manager
Andrea Parker Parker, Marketing Head

Offers articles to technical service librarians on acquisitions, cataloging and classification.
Cost: $30.00
Frequency: Bi-annually
Circulation: 60000
Founded in: 1951

15798 Library Software Review
Sage Publications
Vanderbilt University
419 21st Avenue S
Nashville, TN 37240-0001

615-343-6094; *Fax:* 615-343-8834
info@sagepub.com; www.sagepub.com

Marshall Breeding, Editor

Provides the library professional with information necessary to make intelligent software evaluation, procurement, integration and installation decisions. Issues review software and software books and periodicals.
Cost: $52.00
Frequency: Quarterly
Circulation: 1M

15799 Library Talk: Magazine for Elementary School Librarians
Linworth Publishing
480 E Wilson Bridge Road
Suite L
Worthington, OH 43085-2372

614-436-7107
800-786-5017; *Fax:* 614-436-9490
linworth@linworthpublishing.com;
www.linworth.com

Marlene Woo-Lun, Publisher
Amy Robinson, Marketing Manager
Carol Simpson, Consulting Editor

In-depth articles, helpful hints, and reviews on books, software, and CD-ROMS for elementary school library media and technology specialist.
Cost: $49.00
68 Pages
Circulation: 10000
Founded in: 1988
Printed in 4 colors on glossy stock

15800 Library Trends
University of Illinois Press
1325 S Oak St
Champaign, IL 61820-6975

217-333-0950
866-244-0626; *Fax:* 217-244-8082
journals@uillinois.edu;
www.press.uillinois.edu

Willis Regier, Director
Ann Lowry, Journals Manager
Cheryl Jestis, Manager
Pat Hoefling, Marketing and Sales Director

A journal which offers a medium for current thought and information in the library field.
Cost: $75.00
Frequency: Quarterly
Circulation: 2600
ISBN: 0-252725-23-9
Founded in: 1918

15801 Medical Reference Services Quarterly
Taylor & Francis
325 Chestnut Street
Suite 800
Philadelphia, PA 19106

800-354-1420; *Fax:* 215-625-2940;
www.tandf.co.uk

M Sandra Wood, Editor

An essential working tool for medical and health sciences librarians. Covers topics of current interest and practical value in the areas of reference in medicine and related specialities, the biomedical sciences, nursing and allied health.
Cost: $110.00
Frequency: Quarterly
ISSN: 0276-3869
Founded in: 1975

15802 Reference and User Services Quarterly (RUSQ)
American Library Association
50 E Huron St
Chicago, IL 60611-2788

312-280-2518
800-545-2433; *Fax:* 312-664-7459
customerservice@ala.org; www.ala.org

Keith Michael Fiels, Executive Director
Andrea Parker, Marketing Specialist
Steven L Hofmann, Manager, Communications
Connie Van Fleet, Editor in Chief

News of interest to reference and adult services librarians.
Cost: $60.00
Frequency: Quarterly
Circulation: 6,246
Founded in: 1951

15803 School Library Journal
Media Source
160 Varick Street
11th Floor
New York, NY 10013
646-380-0700; *Fax:* 646-380-0756
sljinfo@mediasourceinc.com; www.schoollibraryjournal.com
Ron Shank, Publisher
Francine Fialkoff, Editor-in-Chief
Brian Kenney, Editorial Director
Bette-Lee Fox, Managing Editor
Rebecca Miller, Executive Editor
Provides groundbreaking features and analytical news reports covering technology, management, policy and other concerns to school libraries. Evaluates 8000 reviews annually of books, ebooks, audiobooks, videos/DVDs, databases, systems and websites.
Frequency: Monthly
Circulation: 100000
Founded in: 1954
Printed in 4 colors on glossy stock

15804 School Library Media Research
American Library Association
50 E Huron St
Chicago, IL 60611-2788
312-280-2518
800-545-2433
kfiels@ala.org; www.ala.org
Keith Michael Fiels, Executive Director
Available online only. Current developments in the media and library field. Evaluates the most currently available print and nonprint materials for library media centers.

15805 Science and Technology Libraries
Taylor & Francis
325 Chestnut Street
Suite 800
Philadelphia, PA 19106
800-354-1420; *Fax:* 215-625-2940; www.tandf.co.uk
Tony Stankus, Editor-in-Chief
A peer-reviewed, scholarly journal covering all ascpects of the profession as librarians serving science, engineering, clinical investigation, and agriculture.
Cost: $110.00
Frequency: Quarterly
ISSN: 0194-262X
Founded in: 1978

15806 Today's Librarian
Virgo Publishing LLC
3300 N Central Ave
Suite 300
Phoenix, AZ 85012-2532
480-990-1101; *Fax:* 480-990-0819
mikes@vpico.com; www.vpico.com
Jenny Bolton, President
John Siefert, CEO
Kelly Ridley, Executive VP, CFO
Heather Wood, VP, Human Resources
Jon Benninger, VP, Health & Nutrition Network
Of interest to librarians and media professionals.

15807 Video Librarian
Video Librarian
3435 NE Nine Boulder Drive
Poulsbo, WA 98370
360-626-1259; *Fax:* 360-626-1260
vidlib@videolibrarian.com; www.videolibrarian.com
Randy Pitman, Publisher
Anne Williams, Graphic Designer
Carol Kaufman, Graphic Designer
Offers video reviews and news for public, school, academic and special libraries.
Cost: $64.00
56 Pages
Circulation: 2000
ISSN: 0887-6851
Founded in: 1986
Printed in 4 colors on glossy stock

Trade Shows

15808 ACL Conference
Association of Christian Librarians
PO Box 4
Cedarville, OH 45314
937-766-2255; *Fax:* 937-766-5499
info@acl.org; www.acl.org
Social Media: Facebook, Twitter, Delicious
Jo Ann Rhodes, President
Alice Ruleman, VP
Janelle Mazelin, Executive Director
Sheila O. Carlblom, Treasurer
Carrie Beth Lowe, Secretary
The purpose of the conference is to provide professional information, promote Christian philosophy and ethic of librarianship, provide an opportunity for exchange of ideas and promote service to the academic community worldwide
550 Members
Founded in: 1954

15809 ALA National Conference on Asian Pacific American Librarians
American Library Association
50 E Huron Street
Chicago, IL 60611
800-545-2433
customerservice@ala.org; www.ala.org

15810 American Association of School Librarians National Conference & Exhibition
50 E Huron Street
Chicago, IL 60611-5295
312-280-4386
800-545-2433; *Fax:* 312-664-7459
customerservice@ala.org; www.ala.org/aasl
Judy King, Director Program Development
Lissa Salvatierra, Meeting Planner
Biennial continuing education conference and 300-500 exhibits of equipment, supplies and services for school library media centers, including print and nonprint materials and other equipment.
3500 Attendees
Frequency: October
Founded in: 1876

15811 American Indian Library Association Conference
American Indian Library Assn Univ. of Pittsburgh
207 Hillman Library
Pittsburgh, PA 15260
412-621-4470; *Fax:* 412-648-1245
http://www.ailanet.org
Lisa A Mitten
Annual conference and exhibits relating to the development, maintenance and cultural information services on reservations and in communities of Native Americans and Native Alaskans.
Founded in: 1979

15812 American Library Association Annual Conference
American Library Association
50 E Huron Street
Chicago, IL 60611
800-545-2433
customerservice@ala.org; www.ala.org
Loriene Roy, President
Keith Michael Fiels, Executive Director
Annual meeting and exhibits of books, periodicals, reference works, audio visual equipment, films, data processing services, computer hardware and software, library equipment and supplies.

15813 American Library Association Midwinter Meeting
American Library Association
50 E Huron Street
Chicago, IL 60611
800-545-2433
customerservice@ala.org; www.ala.org
Loriene Roy, President
Keith Michael Fiels, Executive Director
Annual meeting and 418 exhibits of books, periodicals, reference works, audio visual equipment, films, data processing services, computer hardware and software, library equipment and supplies.

15814 Art Libraries Society of North America Annual Conference
Art Libraries Society of North America
4101 Lake Boone Trail
Suite 201
Raleigh, NC 27607-7506
919-518-1919
800-892-7547; *Fax:* 919-787-4916
arlisna@mercury.interpath.com
Annual conference and show of publishers, book dealers, library suppliers and visual resources suppliers.
500 Attendees
Founded in: 1977

15815 Association for Library & Information Science Education Annual Conference
11250 Roger Bacon Drive
Suite 8
Reston, VA 20190-5202
703-360-0500; *Fax:* 703-435-4390; www.alise.org/index.shtml
John Budd, President
Deborah York, Executive Director
Frequency: January

15816 Association for Population/Family Planning Libraries & Information Centers
Assn for Population Family Planning Libraries
Surgical Contraception-79 Madison
New York, NY 10016
212-780-2687; *Fax:* 212-779-9439
William Record
Annual conference and exhibits for effective documentation, information systems and services in the field of population/family planning.

15817 Association of College and Research Libraries
American Library Association

50 E Huron Street
Chicago, IL 60611-5295

312-280-2511
800-545-2433; *Fax:* 312-280-2520
customerservice@ala.org; www.ala.org/acrl

Mary Ellen Davis, Executive Director

Two hundred exhibitors with computers and web products, audiovisual products, furniture and library equipment.
3000 Attendees
Frequency: Biennial
ISSN: 0099-0086
Founded in: 1978
Mailing list available for rent

15818 **CSLA Conference**
Church and Synagogue Library Association
10157 SW Barbur Boulevard
Suite 102C
Portland, OR 97219-4055

503-244-6919
800-542-2752; *Fax:* 503-977-3734
csla@worldaccessnet.com; www.cslainfo.org
Social Media: Facebook, Twitter

Judith Janzen, Administrator
Marcia Trauernicht, President
Frequency: Annual/July

15819 **Culture Keepers: Making Global Connections**
Black Caucus of the American Library Association
Newark Public Library
5 Washington Street
Newark, NJ 07101

973-961-2540; *Fax:* 973-522-4827

Dr. Alex Boyd

Biennial show and exhibits of books, journals and library products.

15820 **Federal and Armed Forces Libraries Roundtable Conference**
American Library Association
50 E Huron St
Chicago, IL 60611-2729

312-944-6780
800-545-2433; *Fax:* 312-944-8085
ala@ala.org; www.ala.org/faflrt/front

Emily Sheketoff, Executive Director

Annual conference and exhibits of equipment, supplies and services for libraries and information services.

15821 **International Association of Aquatic & Marine Science Libraries Conference**
Harbor Branch Oceanographic Institution
5600 US 1 N
Fort Pierce, FL 34946

800-333-4264; *Fax:* 772-465-2446

Annual conference and exhibits of equipment, supplies and services for marine-related libraries and information centers.
Frequency: October, Charleston

15822 **Mid-Atlantic Regional Library Federation**
South Maryland Regional Library
37 606 New Market Road
Charlotte Hall, MD 20622

301-884-0436

Katharine Hurrey, President

Offers exhibits by vendors who provide services and products useful to libraries and information brokers.
1M Attendees
Frequency: March

15823 **Mountain Plains Library Association Annual Conference**
Mountain Plains Library Association
University of SD-I D Weeks Library
Vermillion, SD 57069

Fax: 605-677-5488

Annual conference and exhibits of publications and library equipment, supplies and services.
600 Attendees

15824 **New England Library Association Annual Conference**
New England Library Association
14 Main Street
Gloucester, MA 03031

978-820-0787; *Fax:* 978-282-1304;
www.nelib.org

Mary Ann Rupert, Technology Manager
Barry Blaisdell, Manager

Annual show of publishers, distributors and suppliers of books, media, supplies, furniture, equipment, hardware, software and services used by libraries. Containing 160 booths and 130 exhibits.
1,000 Attendees
Frequency: October

15825 **Public Library Association National Conference**
Public Library Association
50 E Huron Street
Chicago, IL 60611-5295

312-280-5752
800-545-2433; *Fax:* 312-280-5029
pla@ala.org

Barb Macikas, Show Manager

Biennial show of 200 exhibitors of books and other equipment, supplies and services for libraries.
3500 Attendees
Frequency: March

15826 **Southeastern Library Association**
Combined Book Exhibit
P.O. Box 950
Rex, GA 30273

678-466-4334; *Fax:* 678-466-4349
http://selaonline.org/

This biennial conference, offers attendees from over 12 states. The convention offers exhibits, meetings and an open reception in the exhibit hall. The three biggest states, Georgia, North Carolina and South Carolina spend twice as much of expenditures on CD-ROM and 8% more on books than the national average, which makes this the perfect exhibition for sellers.
2.1M+ Attendees
Frequency: Fall

15827 **Special Libraries Association**
331 South Patrick St
Alexandria, VA 22314-3501

703-647-4900; *Fax:* 703-647-4901
janice@sla.org
http://www.sla.org/content/SLA/contactus/index.cfm

James Mears, Conference Manager
Janice Lschance, CEO

An international professional association of people working in special libraries serving institutions and organizations that use or produce specialized information.
6M Attendees
Frequency: June

Directories & Databases

15828 **Address List, Regional and Subregional Libraries for the Handicapped**
Library of Congress
101 Independence Avenue SE
Washington, DC 20540

202-707-4800
888-657-7323; *Fax:* 202-707-0712
nls@loc.gov; www.loc.gov/nls
Social Media: Facebook, Twitter, LinkedIn

Kurt Cykle, Director
25 Pages
Frequency: Semi-Annual
ISSN: 0363-3805
Mailing list available for rent

15829 **American Library Association Handbook**
American Library Association
50 E Huron St
Chicago, IL 60611-2788

312-280-2518
800-545-2433
customerservice@ala.org; www.ala.org

Claire Knowles, Manager

Offers 56 regional groups comprised of libraries, trustees, librarians and others interested in the responsibilities of libraries in the educational and cultural needs of society.

15830 **American Library Directory**
Information Today
143 Old Marlton Pike
Medford, NJ 08055-8750

609-654-6266
800-300-9868; *Fax:* 609-654-4309
custserv@infotoday.com; www.infotoday.com

Thomas H Hogan, President
Roger R Bilboul, Chariman Of The Board

Detailed profiles for more than 35,000 public, academic, special, and government libraries and library related organizations in the US and Canada. These include addresses, phone and fax numbers, e-mail addresses, network participation, expenditures, holdings and special collections, key personnel, special services and more than 40 categories of library information in all. A two volume set.
Cost: $299.00
4000 Pages
ISBN: 1-573872-04-0
Mailing list available for rent

15831 **Association of Jewish Libraries Membership List**
Ramaz Upper School Library
60 E 78th St
New York, NY 10075-1838

212-517-2103

Ira Miller, Principal
Cost: $100.00
100 Pages
Frequency: Annual

15832 **BookQuest**
ABACIS
135 Village Queen Drive
Owings Mills, MD 21117-4470

Fax: 410-581-0398

This database offers descriptions of book dealers' offerings and books being sought by libraries, dealers and collectors.
Frequency: Full-text

15833 **Chief Officers of State Library Agencies Directory**
Chief Officers of State Library Agencies
201 E Main St
Suite 1405
Lexington, KY 40507-2004
859-514-9151; *Fax:* 859-514-9166;
www.cosla.org
Tracy Tucker, Executive Director
Directors, staff and consultants of state libraries.
Cost: $25.00
Frequency: Annual April

15834 **Computers in Libraries: Buyer's Guide & Consultants Directory Issue**
Mecklermedia Corporation
11 Ferry Lane W
Westport, CT 06880-5808
This comprehensive directory offers a list of suppliers of computer products and services for use in libraries.
Cost: $30.00
Frequency: Annual

15835 **DataLinx**
Faxon Company
1001 W Pines Road
Oregon, IL 61061-9507
815-732-9001
800-732-9001; *Fax:* 815-732-2132;
www.faxon.com
This online system was established to provide technical support to libraries for serials acquisition and control.

15836 **Directory of Special Libraries and Information Centers**
Gale Research
27500 Drake Road
Farmington Hills, MI 48331-3535
248-699-4253
800-877-4253; *Fax:* 877-363-4253
gale.galeord@cengage.com;
www.gale.cengage.com
Social Media: Facebook, Twitter, Youtube
Patrick C Sommers, President
Provides detailed contact and descriptive information on subject-specific resource collections maintained by various government agencies, businesses, publishers, educational and non-profit organizations, and associations around the world.
3600 Pages
Frequency: Annual
ISBN: 1-414433-49-2

15837 **Directory of US Government: Depository Libraries**
Joint Committee on Printing, US Congress
1309 Longworth
Washington, DC 20515
202-225-8281; *Fax:* 202-225-9957
Directory of federal depository libraries, regional and select throughout the United States. Includes list of GPO bookstores.
91pp Pages
Frequency: Annual

15838 **EBSCONET**
EBSCO Publishing
Po Box 682
Ipswich, MA 01938-0682
978-356-1372
800-653-2726; *Fax:* 978-356-6565
http://www.ebsco.com
Timothy S Collins, President
This database provides technical support to libraries, information centers and purchasing departments for serials acquisitions and control.

15839 **Employment Sources in the Library and Information Professions**
National Center for Information Media & Technology
University of Hertfordshire, College Lane
Chicago, IL 60611
773-846-7300
customerservice@ala.org; www.ala.org
Directory of services to the industry.
140 Pages
Frequency: Annual

15840 **Gale Directory of Databases**
Gale/Cengage Learning
27500 Drake Road
Farmington Hills, MI 48331-3535
248-699-4253
800-877-4253; *Fax:* 877-363-4253
gale.galeord@cengage.com;
www.gale.cengage.com
Social Media: Facebook, Twitter, Youtube
Patrick C Sommers, President
Bob Romanick, Editor
Profiles thousands of databases available worldwide in a variety of formats. Entries include producer name and contact information, description, cost and more.
ISBN: 1-414420-79-X

15841 **Interlibrary Loan Policies Directory**
Neal-Schuman Publishers
100 William St
New York, NY 10038-5017
212-925-8650
800-584-2414; *Fax:* 212-219-8916
info@neal-schuman.com;
www.neal-schuman.com
Patricia Schuman, Owner
A brand new edition of the standard source of current information about the policies of over 1,425 academic, public and other libraries that offer books through interlibrary loans in the United States, Canada and Puerto Rico. Updated to include all the members of the Association of Research Libraries, Internet addresses, Ariel addresses and libraries that loan periodicals, government documents, microfilms, software, newspapers, media and foreign countries.
Cost: $119.95
800 Pages

15842 **Librarian's Yellow Pages**
Garance
7823 Stratford Road
Bethesda, MD 20814
240-354-1281; www.lyponline.com
A database offering information on products and services intended for use by libraries and information centers in the United States.

15843 **Library Fax/Ariel Directory**
CBR Consulting Services
PO Box 22421
Kansas City, MO 64113-0421
Over 10,500 libraries with telefacsimile services in the United States and Canada and worldwide.
Cost: $49.50
475 Pages
Frequency: Annual

15844 **Library Literature & Information Science**
HW Wilson Company
950 Dr Martin L King Jr Blvd
Bronx, NY 10452-4297
718-588-8405; *Fax:* 718-590-1617;
www.hwwilson.com
Harold Regan, CEO
Kathleen McEvoy, Director of Public Relations
Comprehensive listings are offered in this database on more than 25,000 citations to articles and reviews of books, periodicals and audiovisual materials in the library and information science areas.

15845 **Library Periodicals: An Annual Guide for Subscribers, Authors and Publicists**
Periodical Guides Publishing
1633 Pearl Street
Alameda, CA 94501-3065
510-865-7439
Over 150 journals and newsletters in the United States and Canada of national or international scope devoted to library science.
Cost: $18.00
55 Pages
Frequency: Annual

15846 **One Hundred and One Software Packages to Use in Your Library**
American Library Association
50 E Huron St
Chicago, IL 60611-2788
312-280-2518
800-545-2433
customerservice@ala.org; www.ala.org
Claire Knowles, Manager
Directory of services and supplies to the industry.

15847 **Subject Directory of Special Libraries & Information Centers**
Gale/Cengage Learning
27500 Drake Road
Farmington Hills, MI 48331-3535
248-699-4253
800-877-4253; *Fax:* 877-363-4253
gale.galeord@cengage.com;
www.gale.cengage.com
Social Media: Facebook, Twitter, Youtube
Patrick C Sommers, President
Presents entries culled from the Directory of Special Libraries and Information Centers in three volumes arranged by subject matter. This rearrangement is especially important for all users who frame their searches in a subject context. In addition to expanded international coverage, users will also find fax numbers, E-mail addresses, Web and Internet addresses and increased reporting of online services
Frequency: Annual/Set
ISBN: 1-414434-59-6

15848 **Univ. of Missouri School of Journalism: Freedom of Information Center**
University of Missouri
133 Neff Annex
Columbia, MO 65210-0012
573-882-7539; *Fax:* 573-884-6204;
www.missouri.edu/~foiwww
Charles N Davis, Executive Director
Kathleen M Edwards, Center Manager
Reference and research library serving the public and media regarding access to government information. The center has a collection of over a million articles and documents concerning access to information at state, federal and local levels and offers a wide variety of online documents through its webpage.

15849 **Who's Who in Special Libraries**
Special Libraries Association

1700 18th St Nw
Washington, DC 20009-2508
202-234-4700; *Fax:* 202-265-9317
Directory of services and supplies to the industry.
Cost: $50.00
364 Pages
Frequency: Annual

Industry Web Sites

15850 http://gold.greyhouse.com
G.O.L.D Grey House OnLine Databases
Grey House Publishing's online database platform, GOLD, offers Quick Search, Keyword Search and Expert Search for most business sectors including library markets. The GOLD platform makes finding the information you need quick and easy - whether you're a novice searcher or an experienced database user. All of Grey House's directory products are available for subscription on the GOLD platform.

15851 www.aallnet.org
American Association of Law Libraries

15852 www.acl.org
Association of Christian Librarians
Membership is composed of over 500 evangelical Christian librarians representing primarily evangelical institutions of higher education.

15853 www.aiip.org
Association Independent Information Professionals

15854 www.akla.org
Alaska Library Association

15855 www.ala.org
American Library Association
Association for librarians, libraries, trustees, students and academics, encompassing all aspects of librarianship.

15856 www.ala.org./alcts
Assn for Library Collections & Technical Services
A division of the American Library Association.

15857 www.ala.org/aasl
American Association of School Librarians
Works to ensure that all members of the school library media field collaborate to: provide leadership in the total eduction program; participate as active partners in the teaching/learning process; connect learners with ideas and information; and prepare students for life-long learning. The American Association of School Librarians is a division of the American Library Association.

15858 www.ala.org/acrl
Association of College and Research Libraries
A division of the American Library Association. Represents academic and research librarians.

15859 www.ala.org/alsc
Association for Library Service to Children
A division of the American Library Association. For persons interested in the improvement and extension of library services to children.

15860 www.ala.org/lama
Library Administrative Management Association
Works to improve and develop all aspects and levels of administration in all types of libraries. The Library Administrative Management Association is a division of the Young Adult Library Services Association, which is part of the American Library Association.

15861 www.ala.org/yalsa
The Young Adult Library Services Association
Responsible for the evaluation and selection of books and nonbook materials and the interpretation and use of materials for teenagers and young adults. The Young Adult Library Services Association is a division of the American Library Association.

15862 www.alise.org/index.shtml
Association for Library & Information Science
Education

15863 www.allanet.org
Alabama Library Association

15864 www.amianet.org
Association of Moving Image Archivists

15865 www.arl.org
Association of Research Libraries
Non profit organization striving to shape and influence forces affecting the future of research libraries in the process of scholarly communication.

15866 www.arlib.org
Arkansas Library Association
Includes constitution and bylaws, conference information, publication, membership, and links to the Arkansas State Library.

15867 www.arlisna.org
Art Libraries Society of North America
Membership organization for art libraries in the US and Canada.

15868 www.arma.org
Assoc. for Information Management Professionals

15869 www.arsc-audio.org
Association for Recorded Sound Collections
Persons in broadcasting and recording industries, librarians, sound archivists, curators, private collectors and reviewers.

15870 www.asindexing.org
American Society of Indexers
A national association with international membership and interests. A nonprofit charitable organization for indexers, librarians, abstractors, editors, publishers, database producers, and organizations concerned with indexing, seeking cooperation and membership of all persons, groups or institutions interested in indexing. Founded in 1968 to promote excellence in indexing and increase awareness of the value of well-written indexes.

15871 www.atla.com/home.html
American Theological Library Association
Provides indexing services in these formats: online database, CD-ROM versions, magnetic tape for OPAC tapeload and print publications. ATLA Religion indexes in print include Religious Index One: Periodicals, Religion Index Two: Multi-Author Works, Index to Book Reviews, Research in Ministry: an Index to D. Min. Project Reports and Theses. ETHICS Index, a new ATLA interdisciplinary index on CD-ROM, contains indexing from polygraphs, articles, journals and newspapers.

15872 www.azla.org
Arizona Library Association

15873 www.bcala.org
Black Caucus of the American Library Association
Meets annually in conjunction with the American Library Association in August.

15874 www.beta-phi-mu-org
Beta Phi Mu

15875 www.cal-webs.org/aboutus.html
Colorado Association Of Libraries

15876 www.cala-web.org
Chinese-American Librarians Association

15877 www.cla-net.org
California Library Association

15878 www.clir.org
Council on Library & Information Resources

15879 www.cni.org
Coalition for Networked Information

15880 www.csla.org
Church and Synagogue Library Association
Provides educational guidance in the establishment and maintenance of congregational libraries

15881 www.ctlibraryassociation.org
Connecticut Library Association
Professional organization of librarians, library staff, friends, and trustees working together: to improve library service to Connecticut, to advance the interests of librarians, library staff, and librarianship, and to increase public awareness of libraries and library services.

15882 www.dla.lib.de.us
Delaware Library Association

15883 www.flalib.org
Florida Library Association

15884 www.floridamedia.org
Florida Library Association

15885 www.folgers.edu
Independent Research Libraries Association
Seeks to provide consultation to members concerning mutual problems.

15886 www.folusa.com
Friends of Libraries (FOLUSA)
Encourages the development of excellent library service to all residents of the US Aids in forming local and state friends branches in academic and special libraries.

15887 www.glma-inc.org/
Georgia Media Library Association

15888 www.greyhouse.com
Grey House Publishing
Authoritative reference directories for most business sectors including library markets. Users can search the online databases with varied search criteria allowing for custom searches by product category, geographic area, sales volume, keyword, subject and more. Full Grey House catalog and online ordering also available.

15889 www.hlaweb.org
Hawaii Library Association

15890 www.hooverassociation.org
Herbert Hoover Presidential Library Association
Foster the collection, interpretation and preservation of historical resources relating to the life, ideas, values, and times of Herbert Hoover, thirty-first President of the United States; we will promote public education about and appreciation for Herbert Hoover, support the Hoover Presidential Library-Museum and the National Historic Site at West Branch, Iowa, effectively garner and prudently manage Association resources, and serve Association members.

15891 **www.idaholibaries.org**
Idaho Library Association

15892 **www.idaholibraries.org**
Idaho Library Association

15893 **www.ifla.org**
International Federation of Library Associations

15894 **www.ila.org**
Illinois Library Association

15895 **www.ilfonline.org**
Indiana Library Federation

15896 **www.iowalibraryassociation.org**
Iowa Library Association

15897 **www.kylibasn.org**
Kentucky Library Association

15898 **www.lff.org**
Americans for Libraries Council

15899 **www.library.ucr.edu/COLT**
Council on Library/Media Technicians
Meets annually in conjunction with the American Library Association in August.

15900 **www.lita.org**
Library and Information Technology Association
Concerned with information dissemination in the areas of library information technology and automation. The Library and Information Technology Association is a division of the American Library Association.

15901 **www.llaonline.org**
Louisiana Library Association

15902 **www.mainelibraries.org**
Maine Library Association

15903 **www.masslib.org**
Massachusetts Library Association

15904 **www.mdlib.org**
Maryland Library Association

15905 **www.misslib.org**
Mississippi Library Association

15906 **www.mla.lib.mi.us**
Michigan Library Association

15907 **www.mlanet.org**
Medical Library Association
MLA is dedicated to the dissemination of quality health sciences information for use in education, research, and patient care.

15908 **www.mnlibraryassociation.org**
Minnesota Library Association

15909 **www.molib.org**
Missouri Library Association

15910 **www.mtlib.org**
Montana Library Association
The mission of the Montana Library Association is to develop, promote, and improve library and information services and the profession of librarianship in order to enhance learning and ensure accesss to information to all.

15911 **www.musiclibraryassoc.org**
Music Library Association
Promotes growth and establishment in the use of music libraries, musical instruments and musical literature.

15912 **www.namtc.org**
National Association of Media & Technology Centers

15913 **www.nativeculture.com/lisamitten/aila.html**
American Indian Library Association
Association for Native Americans and Native Alaskans libraries and librarians.

15914 **www.nclaonline.org**
North Carolina Library Association

15915 **www.nclis.gov**
U.S. National Commission On Libraries & Information Science

15916 **www.ndsl.lib.state.nd.usndla**
North Dakota Library Association

15917 **www.nelib.org**
New England Library Association

15918 **www.nevadalibraries.org**
Nevada Library Association

15919 **www.niso.org**
National Information Standards Organization

15920 **www.njla.org**
New Jersey Library Association

15921 **www.nmla.org**
New Mexico Library Association

15922 **www.nmm.net**
National Media Market

15923 **www.nol.org/home/nla**
Nebraska Library Association

15924 **www.nursingworld.org/icirn/indate.htm**
Library American Journal of Nursing Compliance
Comprised of representatives from agencies and organizations concerned with library needs of nurses.

15925 **www.nyla.org**
New York Library Association

15926 **www.oelma.org**
Ohio Educational Library Media Association

15927 **www.oema.net**
Oregon Educational Media Association

15928 **www.oklibs.org**
Oklahoma Library Association

15929 **www.olaweb.org**
Oregon Library Association

15930 **www.olc.org**
Ohio Library Council

15931 **www.palibraries.org**
Pennsylvania Library Association

15932 **www.pla.org**
Public Library Association
Plans programs on current public library issues and concerns, develops publications for public librarians and disseminates statistics on public libraries. The Public Library Association is a division of the American Library Association.

15933 **www.pnla.org**
Pacific Northwest Library Association

15934 **www.rig.org**
Research Libraries Group

15935 **www.rusa.org**
Reference & User Services Association

15936 **www.salis.org**
Substance Abuse Librarians & Info. Specialists
Provides professional development and exchange of information and concerns about access to and dissemination of information on substance abuse.

15937 **www.scla.org**
South Carolina Library Association

15938 **www.seflin.org/seflin/aboutsef.cfm**
Southeast Florida Library Information Network

15939 **www.skyways.lib.ks.us/kla**
Kansas Library Association

15940 **www.sla.org**
Special Libraries Association
International association of information professionals who work in special libraries serving business, research, government and institutions that produce specialized information.

15941 **www.state.nh.us/nhla**
New Hampshire Library Association

15942 **www.taet.org**
Texas Association for Educational Technology

15943 **www.tla.library.unt.edu/default.asp**
Theatre Library Association

15944 **www.tnla.org/**
Tennessee Library Association

15945 **www.txla.org**
Texas Library Association

15946 **www.ublib.buffalo.edu/libraries/units/cts**
University of North Florida, Carpenter Library
For catalogers of audiovisual materials and electronic resources. Provides information exchange, continuing education, and works toward a common understanding of practices and standards.

15947 **www.uic.edu/depts/lib/projects/resources**
Asian/Pacific American Librarians Association
Librarians and information specialists of Asian Pacific descent working in the United States.

15948 **www.ula.org**
Utah Library Assocation

15949 **www.urbanlibraries.org**
Urban Libraries Council
Works to strengthen public libraries as an essential part of urban life. Serves as a forum for research widely recognized and used by public and private sector leaders.

15950 **www.uri.edu/library/rila/rila.html**
Rhode Island Library Association

15951 **www.usd.edu/mpla**
Mountain Plains Library Association

15952 **www.usd.edu/sdla**
South Dakota Library Association

15953 **www.vermontlibraries.org**
Vermont Library Association

15954 **www.vla.org**
Virginia Library Association

15955 **www.wla.lib.wi.us**
Wisconsin Library Association

15956 **www.wla.org**
Washington Library Association

15957 **www.worldaccessnet.com/nesla**
Church and Synagogue Library Association
Religious groups interested in promoting church or synagogue libraries comprise the membership. This association also offers a bi-monthly newsletter to all its members.

15958 **www.worldaccessnet.com/netsa**
Church and Synagogue Library Association
Religious groups interested in promoting church or synagogue libraries comprise the membership. This association also offers a bi-monthly newsletter to all its members.

15959 **www.wvla.org**
West Virginia Library Association

15960 **www.wyla.org**
Wyoming Library Association

Associations

15961 American Agricultural Editors' Association
American Agricultural Editors' Association
120 Main Street W
PO Box 156
New Prague, MN 56071

952-758-6502; *Fax:* 952-758-5813
ljovanovich@hardwood.org;
www.ageditors.com
Social Media: Facebook, Twitter, Youtube, Pinterest

Susan M Regan, Executive VP

National professional development member association for agricultural communicators.
55 Members

15962 American Independent Writers
1001 Connecticut Ave Nw
Suite 701
Washington, DC 20036-5547

202-775-5150; *Fax:* 202-775-5810
hpva@hpva.org; www.amerindywriters.org/

Kip Howlett, HPVA President
Eva Mentel, Office Manager
Ketti Tyree, Membership and Conventions Manager
Matthew Windt, Marketing Manager

An association that seeks to create an open and inclusive community of authors, journalists and other writers.
73 Members
Founded in: 1921

15963 American Medical Writers' Association
American Medical Writers' Association
30 W Gude Dr
Suite 525
Rockville, MD 20850-4347

240-238-0940; *Fax:* 301-294-9006
paraman@vt.edu; www.amwa.org

Philip Araman, President

Concerned with the advancement and improvement of medical communications.

15964 American Society of Journalists and Authors
American Society of Journalists and Authors
355 Lexington Avenue
15th Floor
New York, NY 10017-6603

212-997-0947; *Fax:* 212-937-2315;
www.asja.org
Social Media: Facebook, Twitter

Jack Goldman, President & CEO
David E. Woodbury, Jr., Director - Finance & Operations
Debbie Scerbo, Office Manager
Ryan Carroll, Director - Government Affairs
John Crouch, Director - Public Affairs

Association for journalists and authors.
2600 Members
Founded in: 1980

15965 American Translators Association
225 Reinekers Lane
Suite 590
Alexandria, VA 22314

703-683-6100; *Fax:* 703-683-6122
ata@atanet.org; www.atanet.org
Social Media: Facebook, Twitter, LinkedIn

David Rumsey, President
Walter W. Bacak, Executive Director
Jane Maier, Secretary
Ted R. Wozniak, Treasurer

ATA membership is open to anyone with an interest in translation and interpreting as a profession or as a scholarly pursuit.
10500 Members
Founded in: 1959

15966 Association of American Collegiate Literary Societies
Philomathean Society
College Hall
Box G
Philadelphia, PA 19104
Andrew Smith, Governor

Works with literary societies in the United States to promote the creation of new societies, existing societies and reviving old societies.
400 Members
Founded in: 1978

15967 Association of Authors' Representatives, Inc.
302A W 12th St.
#112
New York, NY 10014

E-Mail: administrator@aaronline.org
aaronline.org

Gail Hochman, President

Professional organization whose members represent book authors and playwrights.
400+ Members

15968 Association of Professional Writing
Professional Writers Association
P.O. Box 7474
Daytona Beach, FL 32116

386-265-4279
info@iwpawood.org; www.prowriters.org
Social Media: Facebook, Twitter, LinkedIn

Craig Forester, President
Bronson Newburger, Vice President
JoAnn Gillebaard Keller, Treasurer
Cindy L Squires, Esq., Executive Director
Joseph L. O'Donnell, Manager

Organization founded to establish standards for writing consultants. Other goals are to draw new members into the writing consulting field. Also offers a referral system for companies looking for writing consultants.
220 Members
Founded in: 1956

15969 Association of Writers & Writing Programs
George Mason University
4400 University Dr., MSN 1E3
Fairfax, VA 22030

703-993-4301; *Fax:* 703-993-4302;
www.awpwriter.org
Social Media: Facebook, Twitter, Pinterest

David W. Fenza, Executive Director

Support, resources and advocacy for writers and creative writing programs, conferences and centers.
Founded in: 1967

15970 Before Columbus Foundation
The Raymond House
655 13th Street
Suite 302
Oakland, CA 94612

510-268-9775
infor@lma.org;
www.beforecolumbusfoundation.com
Social Media: Facebook, Twitter

Honorable Carro Breaux, President
Ronnie C Harris, Executive Director
Kerry Landry, Chief Financial Officer
Cliff Palmer, LaMATS Executive Director
Nikki Samrow, Events Coordinator

Participants are individuals interested in promoting contemporary American multicultural literature.
Founded in: 1926

15971 Center for the Book
Library of Congress
101 Independence Avenue SE
Washington, DC 20540

202-707-5000; *Fax:* 202-707-0269;
www.loc.gov/loc/cfbook

Steven Smith, President/Director
Elliott Smith, VP
Richard J Arde, Secretary/Treasurer

This organization strives to stimulate consumer interest in books and reading.
Founded in: 1876
Mailing list available for rent

15972 Children's Literature Association (ChLA)
1301 W 22nd St.
Suite 202
Oak Brook, IL 60523

630-571-4520; *Fax:* 708-876-5598
info@childlitassn.org; www.childlitassn.org
Social Media: Facebook, Twitter

Annette Wannamaker, President

ChLA is a nonprofit dedicated to promoting the study of children's literature.

15973 Council of Biology Editors
1000 East Henrietta Road
Rochester, NY 14623

585-292-2000
info@msrlumber.org; www.monroecc.edu

Dan Uskoski, President
Stacy Tiefenbach, Secretary/Treasurer
Sean Shields, Business Manager

Represents those members in life sciences who write for journals, medical science publications, and textbooks.
Founded in: 1987

15974 Council on National Literatures
Council on National Literatures
68-02 Metropolitan Avenue
Middle Village, NY 11379

718-821-3916
mfma@maplefloor.org;
www.annehenrypaolucci.homestead.com
Social Media: Facebook, Twitter, Pinterest

Daniel F. Heney, Executive Director
Heather Currier, Marketing Communications Director
Daniel J. Krupa, Technical Director
Madhuri Carson, Conference Manager
Amber Montgomery, Order Processing Specialist

Provides a forum for scholars concerned with comparative study of literature.
175 Members
Founded in: 1897

15975 Dramatists Guild of America
1501 Broadway
Suite 701
New York, NY 10036-5505

212-398-9366; *Fax:* 212-944-0420
info@nari.org; www.dramatistsguild.com/
Social Media: Facebook, Twitter, Pinterest, Houzz, YouTube

Kevin Anundson, MCR, CKBR, Chairman
Judy Mozen, CR, GCP, President
Tom Miller, Treasurer
Elsie Iturralde, CAE, Chief Operations Officer
Fred Ulreich, Chief Executive Officer

Protects the rights of its international membership of playwrights, composers and lyricists.

Supports fair royalty, maintenance of subsidiary rights, artistic control and ownership of copyright.
Founded in: 1983

15976 Editorial Freelancers Association
Editorial Freelancers Association
71 W 23rd St
4th Fl
New York, NY 10010-4102
212-929-5400
866-929-5425; *Fax:* 212-929-5439
info@nofma.org; www.the-efa.org
Social Media: Facebook, Twitter, LinkedIn
Michael Martin, President & CEO
Bree Urech-Boyle, CFO
Anita Howard, COO
Adam Williams, Marketing Manager
Laura Boyle, Marketing Production Coordinator
National nonprofit, professional organization of self-employed workers in the publishing and communications industries.
27 Members
Founded in: 1908

15977 Education Writers Association
Education Writers Association
3516 Connecticut Avenue NW
Suite 201
Washington, DC 20008
202-452-9830; *Fax:* 202-452-9837
info@nfba.org; www.ewa.org
Social Media: Facebook, RSS
Ken Gieseke, Chair
Todd Carlson, Secretary-Treasurer
Mike Dunipace, Director
Dan Nyberg, Director
Terry Burrow, Director
The Education Writers Association is the national professional organization of education reporters and intent of improving education reporting to the public.
Founded in: 1969

15978 Freelance Editorial Association
PO Box 380835
Cambridge, MA 02238-0835
617-643-8626
membership@nhla.com;
www.freelancepubs.com
Social Media: Facebook, Twitter, LinkedIn, RSS
Pem Jenkins, President
Brent Stief, 1st Vice President
Mark Barford, Chief Executive Officer
Kristina Bran, Digital Media Manager
Trisha Clariana, Office Manager
Offers editorial services that include editing, writing, proofreading, graphic design, desktop publishing, and project managemant.
1600 Members
Founded in: 1898
Mailing list available for rent

15979 International Food, Wine and Travel Writers Association
39252 Winchester Rd
Ste 107 #418
Murrieta, CA 92563
877-439-8929
909-860-6914
951-970-8326; *Fax:* 877-439-8929;
www.ifwtwa.org
Social Media: Facebook, Twitter, LinkedIn
JD Saunders, Chair
Jonathan M. Paine, President/CEO
Laura DeMaria, Membership Services Manager
Ben Gann, VP, Legislative & Political Affairs
Frank Moore, Regulatory Counsel
Staff and/or freelance writers in the food, wine and travel field. Also includes other media professionals and industry associate members in 28 countries worldwide.
6000 Members
Founded in: 1916

15980 Mystery Writers of America
1140 Broadway
Suite 1507
New York, NY 10001
212-888-8171; *Fax:* 212-888-8107
info@nwfa.org; www.mysterywriters.org
Social Media: Facebook, Twitter, LinkedIn
Michael Martin, President & CEO
Anita Howard, COO
Bree Urech-Boyle, CFO
Debbie Edgar, Human Resources Manager
Laura Boyle, Marketing Production Coordinator
Professional writers of crime and mystery stories and novels. Unpublished writers are affiliate members. MWA annually gives the Edgar Awards for excellence in the mystery genre.
3000 Members
Founded in: 1985

15981 National Association of Hispanic Journalists
1050 Connecticut Avenue NW
Washington, DC 20036
202-662-7145; *Fax:* 202-662-7144
membersupport@wdma.com; www.nahj.org
Social Media: Facebook, Twitter, LinkedIn, RSS Feeds
Al Babiuk, Chairman
Michael O'Brien, CAE, President & CEO
John McFee, Vice President, Certification
Jeff Lowinski, Vice President, Technical Services
Jeffrey Inks, VP, Code & Regulatory Affairs
NAHJ is dedicated to the recognition and professional advancement of Hispanics in the news industry. NAHJ created a national voice and unified vision for all Hispanic journalists.
140 Members
Founded in: 1926

15982 National Federation of Press Women
National Federation of Press Women
200 Little Falls Street
Suite 405
Falls Church, VA 22046
703-237-9804
800-780-2715; *Fax:* 703-237-9808
pjsherry@nepapallet.com; www.nfpw.org
Social Media: Facebook, Twitter, LinkedIn, YouTube
Brent J. McClendon, CAE, President/CEO
Isabel Sullivan, VP, Operations and Events
Brad Gething, PhD, Technical and PDS Manager
John A. McLeod III, Director
Annette Ferri, Comm. & Education Director
Members are writers, editors and other communication professionals for newspapers, magazines, wire services, agencies and freelance.
700+ Members
Founded in: 1947
Mailing list available for rent: 1700 names at $40 per M

15983 National Writers Association
10940 S Parker Rd
Suite 508
Parker, CO 80134-7440
303-841-0246; *Fax:* 303-841-2607
sales@kiln-direct.com;
www.nationalwriters.com
William Smith, Executive Director
Exists to enhance the future of writers by fostering continuing education through award winning scholarships and providing no or low cost workshops and seminars. A non-profit organization, we provide education and an ethical resource for writers at all levels of experience.
650 Members
Founded in: 1951

15984 Newspaper Features Council
22 Byfield Lane
Greenwich, CT 06830
203-661-3386; *Fax:* 203-661-7337
A forum for editors, writers, columnists, cartoonists and syndicates to exchange views and improve the content of newspapers.
130 Members
Founded in: 1955

15985 Outdoor Writers Association of America
615 Oak St
Suite 201
Missoula, MT 59801-1896
406-728-7434
800-692-2477; *Fax:* 406-728-7445
info@nawla.org; www.owaa.org
Social Media: Facebook, Twitter, LinkedIn
Scott Elston, Chairman
Jim McGinnis, First Vice Chairman
Bill Adams, Second Vice Chairman
Marc Saracco, Executive Director
Ben Barclay, Manager
Nonprofit, international organization representing over 2,000 professional outdoor communicators who report on diverse interests in the outdoors.
600+ Members
Founded in: 1893

15986 Self-Employed Writers and Artists Network
PO Box 175
Towaco, NJ 07082
E-Mail: nela@northernlogger.com;
www.njcreatives.org
Joseph E. Phaneuf, Executive Director
Eric A Johnson, Executive Editor
Mona Lincoln, Coordinator of Training and Safety
Debbie Haehl, Advertising Manager
Nancy E. Petrie, Circulation Manager
For more then 2 decades, companies and agencies alike have relied on the NJ Creatives Network organization as a cost-efficient, reliable source for freelance talent-from writers and artists to designers and photographers, plus film and video producers, and more.
2000 Members
Founded in: 1952

15987 Society of American Business Editors and Writers
ASU, Walter Cronkite School of Journalism
555 North Central Ave, Suite 416
Phoenix, AZ 85004-1248
602-496-7862; *Fax:* 602-496-7041;
www.sabew.org
Tom Partin, President
Members are financial and economic news writers and editors for print and broadcast outlets.
70 Members
Founded in: 1987

15988 Society of American Travel Writers
One Parkview Plaza
Suite 800
Oakbrook Terrace, IL 60181
414-359-1625; *Fax:* 414-359-1671
info@nlassn.org; www.satw.org
Social Media: Facebook
William Wood, Chairman of the Board
Cody Nuernberg, President
Abbie Diekmann, Membership & Financial

Assistant
Jodie Fleck, Director of Conventions & Tours
Melanie Hultman, Communications Coordinator

Photographers and 35 associate member representatives of airlines, hotels, resorts, tourist agencies and public relations firms.
1.5M Members
Founded in: 1890

15989 **Space Coast Writers Guild**
PO Box 262
Melbourne, FL 32902

E-Mail: osbguide@tecotested.com;
www.scwg.org

Nonprofit, tax-exempt organization of writers of all genres.
Cost: $35.00
Frequency: Annual
Founded in: 1978

15990 **Writers Alliance**
12 Skylark Lane
Stony Brook, NY 11790-3121
516-751-7080

Writers' organization.

15991 **Writers Guild of America: West**
Writers Guild of America
7000 W 3rd St
Los Angeles, CA 90048-4329

323-951-4000
800-548-4532; *Fax:* 323-782-4800
rikki@pacificloggingcongress.com;
www.wga.org
Social Media: Facebook, Twitter

Rikki Wellman, Executive Director
Craig Olson, President
Ron Simon, Treasurer

An independent labor union representing writers in motion pictures, television and radio in the west.
550 Members
Founded in: 1909

15992 **Writers Research Group LLC**
Po Box 891568
Oklahoma City, OK 73189-1568

405-682-2589; *Fax:* 405-685-3390
info@lumber-exporters.org;
www.writersresearchgroup.com
Social Media: Facebook, Twitter, LinkedIn, Google+

David Stallcop, President
Chip Setzer, Vice-President
Mark Rodakowski, Secretary
Chris Knowles, Treasurer

Writers Research Group is a professional writing and research firm. Our knowledgeable employees gather, examine, edit, and compile data to your company's specifications. Our services include research, writing, directory listing updates and new entries, indexing, copyediting, proofreading, data entry, document markup and permissions negotiations.
Founded in: 1923

Newsletters

15993 **AGENDA**
National Federation of Press Women
PO Box 34798
Alexandria, VA 22334-0798

800-780-2715; *Fax:* 703-237-9808;
www.nfpw.org
Social Media: Facebook, Twitter, LinkedIn, Youtube

A quarterly newletter published by the National Federation of Press Women.
Cost: $51.50
4 Pages
Frequency: Quarterly
Circulation: 2000
Founded in: 1937
Mailing list available for rent: 1700 names at $40 per M

15994 **ASJA Newsletter**
American Society of Journalists and Authors
1501 Broadway
Suite 302
New York, NY 10036-5505

212-997-0947; *Fax:* 212-937-2315
staff@asja.org; www.asja.org
Social Media: Facebook, Twitter, LinkedIn

Alexandra Owens, Executive Director
Lisa Collier Coloradool, President
Barbara Barrett, Newsletter Editor

Confidential news for journalists and authors, available only to members of the Society.
Frequency: Monthly
Founded in: 1948

15995 **American Writer**
American Independent Writers
1001 Connecticut Ave Nw
Suite 701
Washington, DC 20036-5547
202-775-5150; *Fax:* 202-775-5810
info@aiwriters.org; www.amerindywriters.org/

Donald Graul, Executive Director

News and information for freelance writers.
Cost: $160.00
8 Pages
Frequency: Monthly
Founded in: 1975

15996 **Copy Editor**
McMurry
1010 E Missouri Ave
Phoenix, AZ 85014-2602

602-395-5850
888-626-8779; *Fax:* 602-395-5853;
www.mcmurry.com

Chris McMurry, CEO
Barbara Wallraff, Editor

Helps editors stay up-to-date with the changing language. Articles discuss new words, changes in usage and reference books. Each issue contains interviews with copy editors.
Cost: $69.00
8 Pages
Circulation: 2000
Founded in: 1990
Printed in one color

15997 **EFA Newsletter**
Editorial Freelancers Association
71 W 23rd St
Suite 1910
New York, NY 10010-4181
212-929-5400
866-929-5400; *Fax:* 212-929-5439
office@the-efa.org; www.the-efa.org

Judi Greenstein, Office Manager
J P Partland, Co-Executive
Mary Ratcliffe, Editor
Martha Schuenman, Executive Director
Pat Molholt, Secretary

Book reviews, news, features and reports on matters of interest to writers, indexers and editors.
Cost: $20.00
Frequency: 6 issues/year
Founded in: 1970

15998 **Editorial Eye**
Editorial Experts
66 Canal Center Plz
Suite 200
Alexandria, VA 22314-5507

703-683-0683
800-683-8380; *Fax:* 703-683-4915
info@eeicommunications.com;
www.eeicom.com

Jim De Graffenreid, President
Candee Wilson, Director
Robin Cormier, VP Publications
Linda B Jorgensen, Editor
Keith C. Ivey, Technical Editor

Professional standards and practices for editors, writers and publication managers.
Cost: $139.00
12 Pages
Frequency: Monthly
Circulation: 3,000
Founded in: 1972

15999 **Freelance Writer's Report**
CNW Publishing
PO Box A
North Stratford, NH 03590

603-922-8338
800-351-9278; *Fax:* 603-922-8339
info@writers-editors.com;
www.writers-editors.com

Dana K Cassell, Executive Director

News and marketing information for freelance writers.
Cost: $39.00
Frequency: Monthly
Circulation: 1200

16000 **IDEAS Unlimited for Editors**
Omniprint
9700 Philadelphia Ct
Lanham, MD 20706-4405

301-731-7000
800-774-6809; *Fax:* 301-731-7001;
www.omniprint.net

Ken Kaufman, President
Stephen Brownan, VP

Editorial ideas and graphics for editors of in-house, corporate newsletters. Provides 16 pages of fresh, ready-to-use items and ideas editors can use to fill out their publications.
Cost: $5.00
16 Pages
Frequency: Monthly
Circulation: 6310
Founded in: 1973
Printed in one color on matte stock

16001 **KEYSTROKES**
Writers Alliance
12 Skylark Lane
Stony Brook, NY 11790-3121

516-751-7080

Kiel Stuart, Publisher
Howard Austerlitz, Editor
Charles Spataro, Circulation Manager

A writers newsletter containing marketing, how-to and computer information.
Cost: $10.00
16 Pages
Frequency: TriAnnual
Circulation: 250
Mailing list available for rent: 250 names
Printed in one color on matte stock

16002 **Linington Lineup**
1223 Glen Ter
Glassboro, NJ 08028-1315

856-589-1571

Rinehart S Potts, Editor

Editing, publishing, police procedural.
Cost: $12.00
16 Pages
Frequency: Bi-Monthly
Circulation: 400
Founded in: 1984
Printed in one color on matte stock

16003 NWA Newsletter
National Writers Association
10940 S Parker Rd
Suite 508
Parker, CO 80134-7440

303-841-0246; *Fax:* 303-841-2607
natlwritersassn@hotmail.com;
www.nationalwriters.com

Sandy Whelchel, Executive Director

A monthly e-mail newsletter that includes information on upcoming contests and conferences, announcements and job opportunities
2000 Members
Frequency: Monthly
Founded in: 1938

16004 Speechwriter's Newsletter
Ragan Communications
316 N Michigan Ave
Suite 400
Chicago, IL 60601-3773

312-960-4100
800-493-4867; *Fax:* 312-960-4106
cservice@ragan.com; www.ragan.com

Jim Ylisela, Publisher
David Murray, Editor
Rebecca Anderson, Managing Editor

Offers speechwriting tips, examples and criticism.
Cost: $307.00
4 Pages
Frequency: Monthly
Founded in: 1980

16005 Story Bag: National Storytelling Newsletter
5361 Javier St
San Diego, CA 92117-3215

858-569-9399; *Fax:* 858-569-0205
storybag@juno.com

Professional storytellers, whether freelance or working for a school or library, will find this newsletter stuffed full of tips on techniques, suggestions for handling the business, reviews of storytelling books and tapes, listings of events nationwide, bibliographies of suggested materials, and discussion of issues such as censorship. Note: Above phone is used on e-mail, if busy try again.
Cost: $15.00
8 Pages
Frequency: Bi-Monthly
Circulation: 300
Printed in one color on matte stock

16006 Strategic Employee Publications
Lawrence Ragan Communications
316 N Michigan Ave
Suite 400
Chicago, IL 60601-3773

312-960-4100
800-878-5331; *Fax:* 312-960-4106
cservice@ragan.com; www.ragan.com

Jim Ylisela, Publisher
David Murray, Editor
Diane Tillman, Marketing Manager

Designed to help organizational editors produce their company publications.
Cost: $139.00
8 Pages
Frequency: Monthly
Circulation: 2500
Founded in: 1970
Printed in 2 colors on matte stock

16007 Writers Connection
Writers Connection
1826 Crossover Roade
PMB 108
Fayetteville, AR 72703

www.thewritersconnection.com

Provides how-to information for writers, plus listings of markets, contests and events. Accepts advertising.
Cost: $45.00
16 Pages
Frequency: Monthly

Magazines & Journals

16008 ATA Chronicle
American Translators Association
225 Reinekers Lane
Suite 590
Alexandria, VA 22314

703-683-6100; *Fax:* 703-683-6122
ata@atanet.org; www.atanet.org
Social Media: Facebook, Twitter, LinkedIn

David Rumsey, President
Walter W. Bacak, Executive Director
Jane Maier, Secretary
Ted R. Wozniak, Treasurer

Contains feature articles, announcements, reviews, and association news.
Cost: $65.00
Frequency: Monthly
Circulation: 11,100

16009 Latinos in the US: A Resource Guide for Journalists
National Association of Hispanic Journalists
529 14th St Nw # 1240
Washington, DC 20045-2520

202-789-1157; *Fax:* 202-347-3444
rnutting@marketwatch.com;
www.marketwatch.com

Rex Nutting, Manager
Joseph Torres, Communications Director
Rex Nutting, Manager

Purposes are to increase educational and career opportunities in journalism for Hispanic Americans.
Cost: $8.50
Mailing list available for rentat $500 per M

16010 Modernism/Modernity
2715 N Charles Street
Baltimore, MD 21218-4319

410-516-6900
800-548-1784; *Fax:* 410-516-6968;
www.press.ghu.edu/journals

Jeffrey T Schnapp, Editor
Becky Brasington Clark, Marketing Director
Tom Lovett, Circulation Manager
Ken Sabol, Production Manager

Focuses systematically on the methodological, archival, and theoretical exigencies particular to modermist studies. It encourages and interdisciplinary approach linking music, architecture, the visual arts, literature, and social and intellectual history.
Cost: $40.00
Frequency: Quarterly
Founded in: 1994

Trade Shows

16011 ATA Annual Conference
American Translators Association
225 Reinekers Lane
Suite 590
Alexandria, VA 22314

703-683-6100; *Fax:* 703-683-6122
ata@atanet.org; www.atanet.org
Social Media: Facebook, Twitter

David Rumsey, President
Walter W. Bacak, Executive Director
Jane Maier, Secretary
Ted R. Wozniak, Treasurer
Frequency: Annual/October

16012 AWP Conference & Bookfair
Association of Writers & Writing Programs
George Mason University
4400 University Dr., MSN 1E3
Fairfax, VA 22030

703-993-4301; *Fax:* 703-993-4302
registration@awpwriter.org;
www.awpwriter.org/awp_conference/overview
Social Media: Facebook, Twitter, Pinterest

The largest literary conference in North America.
12K+ Attendees
Frequency: Annual

16013 Agricultural Publications Summit
American Agricultural Editors' Association
120 Main Street W
PO Box 156
New Prague, MN 56071

952-758-6502; *Fax:* 952-758-5813
aaea@gardnerandgardnercommunications.com;
www.ageditors.com

Den Gardner, Executive Director
Holly Martin, President
Kenna Rathai, Associate Executive Director
Frequency: July

16014 American Society of Journalists and Authors Conference
American Society of Journalists and Authors
1501 Broadway
Suite 302
New York, NY 10036-5501

212-997-0947; *Fax:* 212-937-2315;
www.asja.org
Social Media: Facebook, Twitter, LinkedIn

Alexandra Owens, Executive Director
Salley Shannon, President
Barbara DeMarco- Barrett, Newsletter Editor
Stephen Morril, Web Editor
Bruce Miler, Web Master

A forum for the exchange of ideas between journalists.
700 Attendees
Frequency: May

16015 Annual Multimedia Convention & Career Expo (NAHJ)
National Association of Hispanic Journalists
Disney's Coronado Spings Resort
1000 W Buena Vista Drive
Lake Buena Vista, FL 32830

866-257-5990; www.nahjconvention.org
Social Media: Facebook, Twitter, LinkedIn, YouTube

Michele Salcedo, President
Manuel De La Rosa, Vice President/Broadcast
Russell Contreras, VP Print/Financial Officer

NAHJ is dedicated to the recognition and professional advancement of Hispanics in the news industry. NAHJ created a national voice and unified vision for all Hispanic journalists.
2300 Members
Frequency: August
Founded in: 1984

16016 ChLA Conference
1301 W 22nd St.
Suite 202
Oak Brook, IL 60523

630-571-4520; *Fax:* 708-876-5598;
www.childlitassn.org/annual-conference

Roberta Seelinger Trites, Chair, Conf. Planning Committee
Jackie Stallcup, Committee Member
Annette Wannamaker, Committee Member
Eric Tribunella, Committee Member
Jennifer Miskec, Committee Member

Academic conference focused on the scholarly study of children's and adolescent literature.
Frequency: Annual/June
Founded in: 1973

16017 SABEW Annual Conference
Society of American Business Editors & Writers
ASU, Walter Cronkite School of Journalism
555 North Central Ave, Suite 416
Phoenix, AZ 85004-1248

602-496-7862; *Fax:* 602-496-7041
sabew@sabew.org; www.sabew.org
Social Media: Facebook, Twitter, LinkedIn

Carrie Paden, Executive Director
Rex Seline, VP
Jon Lansner, Secretary/Treasurer
Brant Houston, Executive Director
Frequency: April

Directories & Databases

16018 AWP Official Guide to Writing Programs
Association of Writers & Writing Programs
Mail Stop 1E3
Fairfax, VA 22030

703-993-4301; *Fax:* 703-993-4302
awp@awpwriter.org

Supriya Bhatngar, Director of Publications

About 300 colleges and universities offering workshops and degree programs in creative writing; approximately 100 writers' conferences, colonies and centers; coverage includes Canada and the United Kingdom.
Cost: $24.95
400 Pages
Frequency: Biennial

16019 American Directory of Writer's Guidelines
Dustbooks
PO Box 100
Paradise, CA 95967-0100

530-877-6110
800-477-6110; *Fax:* 530-877-0222
directories@dustbooks.com;
www.dustbooks.com

Brigitte M Phillips, Editor
Susan D Klassen, Editor
Doris Hall, Editor

These guidelines help writers target their submissions to the exact needs of the individual publisher. A compilation of information for freelancers from more than 1,500 magazine editors and book publishers.
Cost: $29.95
752 Pages
ISBN: 1-884956-40-8

16020 American Library Directory
Information Today
143 Old Marlton Pike
Medford, NJ 08055-8750

609-654-6266
800-300-9868; *Fax:* 609-654-4309
custserv@infotoday.com; www.infotoday.com

Thomas H Hogan, President
Roger R Bilboul, Chariman Of The Board

Detailed profiles for more than 35,000 public, academic, special, and government libraries and library related organizations in the US and Canada. These include addresses, phone and fax numbers, e-mail addresses, network participation, expenditures, holdings and special collections, key personnel, special services and more than 40 categories of library information in all. A two volume set.
Cost: $299.00
4000 Pages
ISBN: 1-573872-04-0
Mailing list available for rent

16021 American Society of Journalists and Authors Directory
American Society of Journalists and Authors
1501 Broadway
Suite 302
New York, NY 10036-5505

212-997-0947; *Fax:* 212-937-2315;
www.asja.org
Social Media: Facebook, Twitter, LinkedIn

Alexandra Owens, Executive Director

Lists over 800 member freelance nonfiction writers.
Cost: $75.00
90 Pages

16022 Applied Science & Technology Index
HW Wilson Company
950 Dr Martin L King Jr Blvd
Bronx, NY 10452-4297

718-588-8405
800-367-6770; *Fax:* 718-590-1617;
www.hwwilson.com

Harold Regan, CEO
Kathleen McEvoy, Director of Public Relations

Fast, convenient access to the cover-to-cover content of leading trade and industrial publications, journals issued by professional and technical societies, specialized subject periodicals, as well as buyers' guides, directories, and conference proceedings.
Frequency: Monthly on WlisonDisc

16023 Association of Professional Writing Consultants Membership Directory
Northwestern University
2315 Sheridan Rd
Evanston, IL 60201-2920

847-491-5500

Henry Bienen, President
Cost: $75.00
Frequency: Annual

16024 Authors and Artists for Young Adults
Gale/Cengage Learning
27500 Drake Road
Farmington Hills, MI 48331-3535
248-699-4253
800-877-4253; *Fax:* 877-363-4253
gale.galeord@cengage.com;
www.gale.cengage.com
Social Media: Facebook, Twitter, Youtube

Patrick C Sommers, President

A a source where teens can discover fascinating and entertaining facts about the writers, artists, film directors, graphic novelists and other creative personalities that most interest them.
ISBN: 0-787677-96-5

16025 Children's Writer's and Illustrator's Market
Writer's Market
1507 Dana Avenue
Cincinnati, OH 45207-1005

513-396-6160
800-289-0963; *Fax:* 513-531-4082

Offers valuable information about book and magazine publishers that publish works by authors and illustrators for young audiences.
Cost: $22.99
256 Pages
Frequency: Annual

16026 Complete Guide to Self-Publishing
Writer's Market
1507 Dana Avenue
Cincinnati, OH 45207-1005

513-396-6160
800-289-0963; *Fax:* 513-531-4082

Offers, in appendixes, a list of contacts and companies that help see to publication of a book at the author's expense.
Cost: $18.95

16027 Contemporary Authors
Gale/Cengage Learning
27500 Drake Road
Farmington Hills, MI 48331-3535

248-699-4253
800-877-4253; *Fax:* 877-363-4253
gale.galeord@cengage.com;
www.gale.cengage.com
Social Media: Facebook, Twitter, Youtube

Patrick C Sommers, President

Find biographical information on more than 130,000 modern novelists, poets, playwrights, nonfiction writers, journalists and scriptwriters. Sketches typically include personal information, contact information, career history, writings, biographical and critical sources, authors' comments and informative essays about their lives and work.
ISBN: 0-810319-11-X

16028 Directory of Literary Magazines
Council of Literary Magazines and Presses
154 Christopher St
Suite 3C
New York, NY 10014-2840

212-741-9110; *Fax:* 212-741-9112
info@clmp.org; www.clmp.org

Contains names, addresses and phone numbers of nearly 600 magazines in the US and abroad that publish poetry, fiction, essays, literary reviews and more.
Cost: $17.00
Frequency: Annual

16029 Directory of Poetry Publishers
Dustbooks
PO Box 100
Paradise, CA 95967-0100

530-877-6110
800-477-6110; *Fax:* 530-877-0222
directories@dustbooks.com;
www.dustbooks.com

Len Fulton, Editor

Over 2,100 magazines, small and commercial presses and university presses that accept poetry for publication.
Cost: $25.95
300 Pages
Frequency: Annual
Circulation: 2,000
ISBN: 0-916685-47-0

16030 Directory of Small Magazines Press Magazine Editors & Publishers
Dustbooks

PO Box 100
Paradise, CA 95967-0100

530-877-6110
800-477-6110; *Fax:* 530-877-0222
directories@dustbooks.com;
www.dustbooks.com

Len Fulton, Editor

This directory contains more than 7,500 listings of editors and publishers in alphabetical order, along with their associated publishing companies, their addresses, phones, e-mail addresses and Web pages. Includes self publishers.
Cost: $25.95
460 Pages
Frequency: Annual
Circulation: 1,000
ISBN: 0-913218-28-6
Founded in: 1967
Mailing list available for rent

16031 Editor & Publisher International Year Book
Editor & Publisher Company
17782 Cowan
Suite C
Irvine, CA 92614

929-660-6150
888-732-7323; *Fax:* 949-660-6172
circulation@editorandpublisher.com;
www.editorandpublisher.com

Duncan McIntosh, President/Publisher
Jeff Fleming, Editor-In-Chief
Kristina Ackermann, Managing Editor
Ralph Bayless, Sales Manager

It's the encyclopedia of the newspaper industry with listings for all dailies worldwide and all community and special interest U.S. and Canadian weeklies. Tabbed sections make it easy to find information from U.S. & Canadian dailies to foreign newspapers. Tables profile newspaper ad trends, circulation size by population groups, rankings by circulation size and more.
Cost: $125.00
600 Pages
Frequency: Annual
Founded in: 1884

16032 Editor & Publisher: Directory of Syndicated Services Issue
Editor & Publisher Company
11 W 19th Street
10th Floor
New York, NY 10011-4209
212-929-1259

Michael Parker, President

A directory of several hundred syndicates serving newspapers in the United States and abroad with news, features and comic strips.
Cost: $7.00
Frequency: Annual

16033 Editorial Freelancers Association: Membership Directory
Editorial Freelancers Association
71 W 23rd St
4th Fl
New York, NY 10010-4181

212-929-5400
866-929-5425; *Fax:* 212-929-5439
office@the-efa.org; www.the-efa.org
Social Media: Facebook, Twitter, LinkedIn

Jp Partland, Co-Executive
Judi Greenstein, Office Manager

1,100 member editorial freelancers.
Cost: $25.00
Frequency: Annual Spring

16034 Guide to Literary Agents
Writer's Market
1507 Dana Avenue
Cincinnati, OH 45207-1005

513-396-6160
800-289-0963; *Fax:* 513-531-4082;
www.writersmarket.com

Agents and representatives for professional writers.
Cost: $18.95
240 Pages
Frequency: Annual

16035 Guide to Writers Conferences & Workshops
Shaw Guides
PO Box 231295
New York, NY 10023

212-799-6464; *Fax:* 212-724-9287
info@shawguides.com; www.shawguides.com

Conferences, workshops, and seminars for amateur and professional writers.
Cost: $19.95
272 Pages

16036 Key Guide to Electronic Resources: Language and Literature
Information Today
143 Old Marlton Pike
Medford, NJ 08055-8750
609-654-6266
800-300-9868; *Fax:* 609-654-4309
custserv@infotoday.com; www.infotoday.com

Thomas H Hogan, President
Roger R Bilboul, Chairman Of The Board

Part of the ongoing topic related series of reference guides is an evaluative directory of electronic reference sources in the fields of language and literature.
Cost: $39.50
120 Pages
ISBN: 1-573870-20-x
Mailing list available for rent

16037 Literary Agents of North America
Author Aid/Research Associates International
340 E 52nd St
New York, NY 10022-6728
212-758-4213

Arthur Orrmont, Editor

More than 1,00 US and Canadian literary agencies.
Cost: $33.00

16038 Literary Forum
CompuServe Information Service
5000 Arlington Centre Blvd
Columbus, OH 43220-5439

614-326-1002
800-848-8199

This database covers literature, including books and poetry, writing, stage and screen, journalism and comic books.
Frequency: Bulletin Board

16039 Market Guide for Young Writers: Where and How to Sell What You Write
Writer's Market
1507 Dana Avenue
Cincinnati, OH 45207-1005

513-396-6160
800-289-0963; *Fax:* 513-531-4082;
www.writersmarket.com

A list of over 150 magazines and writers contests are profiles that all accept work from young writers for publishing purposes.
Cost: $16.95

16040 Mystery Writer's Market Place and Sourcebook
Writer's Market
1507 Dana Avenue
Cincinnati, OH 45207-1005

513-396-6160
800-289-0963; *Fax:* 513-531-4082;
www.writersmarket.com

Offers various profiles of about 50 publishers of mystery and crime books.
Cost: $17.95

16041 Novel & Short Story Writer's Market
Writer's Market
1507 Dana Avenue
Cincinnati, OH 45207-1005

513-396-6160
800-289-0963; *Fax:* 513-531-4082;
www.writersmarket.com

More than 2,000 literary magazines, publishers, agents and writer's organizations are profiled.
Cost: $19.95
Frequency: Annual

16042 Poet's Market
Writer's Market
1507 Dana Avenue
Cincinnati, OH 45207-1005
513-396-6160
800-289-0963; *Fax:* 513-531-4082;
www.writersmarket.com

Over 1,500 publishers, periodicals and other markets that accept poetry for publication are profiled.
Cost: $22.99
528 Pages
Frequency: Annual
ISSN: 0883-5470

16043 Professional Freelance Writers Directory
National Writers Club
314 Peoria
Suite 290
Aurora, CO 80014
303-841-0246

Over 200 professional members selected from the total membership on the basis of significant articles books or movies published.
Cost: $12.50
75 Pages
Frequency: Annual

16044 Science Fiction and Fantasy Writers of America Membership Directory
PO Box 877
Chestertown, MD 21620

E-Mail: exedir@sfwa.org; www.sfwa.org

Mary Kowal, Vice-President
Robert Howe, Secretary
Amy Casil, Treasurer

Directory of services and supplies to the industry.
Cost: $60.00
40 Pages
Frequency: Annual

16045 Self-Employed Writers and Artists Network Directory
Po Box 175
Towacos, NJ 07653-0440

www.swan-net.com
Social Media: Facebook, Twitter

Phil Cantor, President
Wayne Rousck, VP Marketing

Over 140 freelance writers and graphic designers, as well as illustrators, photographers and

more in northern New Jersey and Metropolitan New York City are profiled.
20 Pages
Frequency: Annual

16046 **Self-Publishing Manual: How to Write, Print and Sell Your Own Book**
Para Publishing
PO Box 8206
Santa Barbara, CA 93118-8206

805-968-7277
800-727-2782; *Fax:* 805-968-1379;
www.parapublishing.com

Dan Poynter, Publisher

A list of wholesalers, reviewers and exporters, etc, are profiled.
Cost: $19.95
900 Pages
Frequency: Biennial
ISBN: 1-568600-73-9
Founded in: 1979
Printed in one color on matte stock

16047 **Space Coast Writers Guild: Organization, Activities and Membership**
PO Box 262
Melbourne, FL 32902

www.scwg.org
Social Media: Facebook, Twitter, LinkedIn

Judy Mammay, President
Bill Allen, VP
Donna Chesher, President
Andy Vazquez, Vice-President
Carol Didier, Secretary

A who's who directory of professional writing services and training to the media industry.
25 Pages
Frequency: Annual

16048 **Who's Who in Writers, Editors and Poets: US and Canada**
December Press
Apt 406
2800 N Roadrunner Pkwy
Las Cruces, NM 88011-0859

847-940-4122

Curt Johnson, President

Directory of writers and editors.
Cost: $99.00
700 Pages
Frequency: Biennial

16049 **Writer's Digest: Writers Conference Issue**
F&W Publications
1507 Dana Avenue
Cincinnati, OH 45207-1005

513-531-2222; *Fax:* 513-531-1843

Directory of services and supplies to the industry.
Cost: $2.95
Frequency: Annual
Circulation: 225,000

16050 **Writer's Guide to Book Editors, Publishers and Literary Agents**
Prima Publishing
3000 Lava Ridge Ct
Roseville, CA 95661-2802

916-787-7000
800-632-8676; *Fax:* 916-787-7004;
www.primagames.com

Julie Asbury, Publisher

Offers information on more than 200 publishing houses and their editors.
Cost: $19.95
370 Pages
Frequency: Annual

16051 **Writer's Handbook**
Kalmbach Publishing Company
21027 Crossroads Circle
PO Box 1612
Waukesha, WI 53186-1612

262-796-8776
800-533-6644; *Fax:* 262-796-1615;
www.writermag.com

A list of more than 3,000 markets for the sale of manuscripts, ads and awards.
Cost: $29.95
Frequency: Annual

16052 **Writer's Market: Where and How to Sell What You Write**
Writer's Market
1507 Dana Avenue
Cincinnati, OH 45207-1056

513-396-6160; *Fax:* 513-531-4082

Directory of services and supplies to the industry.
Cost: $29.95
1000 Pages
Frequency: Annual
ISSN: 0084-2729

16053 **Writer's Northwest Handbook**
Media Weavers, Blue Heron Publishing
4140 S.E. 37
#10
Portland, OR 97202

www.mediaweavers.net

Over 3,000 markets for writers, including newspapers, magazines and book publishers in Northwestern United States and British Columbia, Canada.
Cost: $18.95
232 Pages
Frequency: Biennial

16054 **Writers Conferences**
Poets & Writers
150 Broadway
New York, NY 10038-4381

212-566-2424; *Fax:* 212-587-9673
mpettus@pettuswilliams.com;
www.pettuswilliams.com

Marvin K Pettus
Cost: $7.50
50 Pages
Frequency: Annual

16055 **Writers Directory**
St. James Press/Gale
27500 Drake Road
Farmington Hills, MI 48331-3535

248-699-4253
800-877-4253; *Fax:* 877-363-4253
gale.galeord@cengage.com;
www.gale.cengage.com
Social Media: Facebook, Twitter, Youtube

Patrick C Sommers, President

This comprehensive resource features uptodate bibliographical, biographical and contact information for approximately 20,000 living authors worldwide who have at least one English publication.
ISBN: 1-558626-20-4

16056 **Writers Guild Directory**
Writers Guild of America, West
8455 Beverly Blvd
Los Angeles, CA 90048-3445

323-651-2600; *Fax:* 323-782-4802

Bob Waters, Owner

Directory of services and supplies to the industry.
Cost: $17.50
450 Pages
Frequency: Annual

Industry Web Sites

16057 **http://gold.greyhouse.com**
G.O.L.D Grey House OnLine Databases

Grey House Publishing's online database platform, GOLD, offers Quick Search, Keyword Search and Expert Search for most business sectors including literary markets. The GOLD platform makes finding the information you need quick and easy - whether you're a novice searcher or an experienced database user. All of Grey House's directory products are available for subscription on the GOLD platform.

16058 **www.asja.org**
American Society of Journalists and Authors

Association for journalists and authors.

16059 **www.dramaguild.com**
Dramatists Guild

Protects the rights of its international membership of playwrights, composers and lyricists. Supports fair royalty, maintenance of subsidiary rights, artistic control and ownership of copyright.

16060 **www.freelancepubs.com**
Freelance Editorial Association

Self-employed contractors, or consultants with expertise in editorial functions such as copyediting, researching, indexing and proofreading, writing, illustrating, editing, project managing, desktop publishing, and translating.

16061 **www.greyhouse.com**
Grey House Publishing

Authoritative reference directories for most business sectors including literary markets. Users can search the online databases with varied search criteria allowing for custom searches by product category, geographic area, sales volume, keyword, subject and more. Full Grey House catalog and online ordering also available.

16062 **www.ifwtwa.org**
International Food, Wine and Travel Writers Association

Staff and/or freelance writers in the food, wine and travel field. Also includes other media professionals and industry associate members in 28 countries worldwide.

16063 **www.loc.gov/loc/cfbook/**
Library of Congress

This organization strives to stimulate the consumer interest in books and reading.

16064 **www.mysterywriters.org**
Mystery Writers of America

Professional writers of crime and mystery stories and novels. Unpublished writers are affiliate members. MWA annually gives the Edagar Awards for excellence in the mystery geare.

16065 **www.nationalwriters.com**

Membership organization for writers.

16066 **www.nfc.council.com**
Newspaper Features Council

A forum for editors, writers, columnists, cartoonists and syndicates to exchange views and improve the content of newspapers.

16067 **www.nfpw.org**
National Federation of Press Women

Members are writers, editors and other communication professionals for newspapers, magazines, wire services, agencies and freelance.

16068 www.owaa.org
Outdoor Writers Association of America

A nonprofit, international organization representing over 2,000 professional outdoor communicators who report on diverse interests in the outdoors.

16069 www.the-efa.org
Editorial Freelancers Association

National nonprofit, professional organization of self-employed workers in the publishing and communications industries.

16070 www.wga.org
Writers Guild of America, West

An independent labor union representing writers in motion pictures, television and radio in the west.

16071 www.writersresearchgroup.com
Writers Research Group

Associations

16072 American Fiberboard Association
2118 Plum Grove Rd.
#283
Rolling Meadows, IL 60008
847-934-8394
richard@westernforestry.org; www.fiberboard.org
Richard Zabel, Executive Director
The national trade organization of manufacturers of cellulose fiberboard products used for residential and commercial construction.
125 Members
Founded in: 1909

16073 American Forest & Paper Association
AF&PA
1101 K Street, NW
Suite 700
Washington, DC 20005
202-463-2700
800-878-8878; *Fax:* 202-463-2785
wrcla@wrcla.org; www.afandpa.org
Social Media: Facebook, Twitter, Youtube, Pinterest
Peter Lang, General Manager
Edward Burke, Eastern Field Representative
Represents member companies and related trade associations which grow, harvest and process wood and wood fiber, manufacture pulp, paper and paperboard products from both virgin and recovered fiber and produce solid wood products.
Founded in: 1954

16074 American Forest Foundation
2000 M Street, NW
Suite 550
Washington, DC 20036
202-765-3660; *Fax:* 202-827-7924
info@wwpa.org; www.forestfoundation.org
Michael O'Halloran, President
Tom Hanneman, VP/Director
Robert Bernhardt Jr, Director Information Services
Kevin CK Cheung, Director Technical Services
Kevin Binam, Director Economic Services
Committed to creating a future where North American forests are sustained by the public that understand and values the social, economic, and environmental benefits they provide to our communities, our nation, and the world.
135 Members
Founded in: 1964
Mailing list available for rent

16075 American Forest Resource Council
5100 SW Macadam
Suite 350
Portland, OR 97239
503-222-9505; *Fax:* 503-222-3255
info@amforest.org; www.amforest.org
Social Media: Facebook, Twitter
Tom Partin, President
Manufacturers and forest products companies working for responsible forestry.

16076 American Forests
1220 L Street NW
Suite 750
Washington, DC 20005
202-737-1944
membersupport@wdma.com; www.americanforests.org
Social Media: Facebook, Twitter, LinkedIn, RSS
Michael O'Brien, CAE, President & CEO
Jeff Lowinski, Vice President, Technical Services
Jeffrey Inks, Vice President, Code & Regulatory
John McFee, VP, Certification Programs
Jonathan Paine, VP, Membership & Operations
Restoring watersheds to help provide clean drinking water and replanting forests destroyed by human action and by natural disasters.
Founded in: 1927
Mailing list available for rent

16077 American Hardwood Export Council
American Hardwood Export Council
1825 Michael Faraday Dr
Reston, VA 20190
703-435-2900; *Fax:* 703-435-2537
wcma@wcma.com; www.ahec.org
Paul Dow, President
Sid Anderson, III, Vice President
Keith Malmstadt, Treasurer
AHEC provides the global hardwood industry with promotional assistance, technical information and sources of supply for American hardwoods from its international offices.
Founded in: 1929

16078 American Institute of Timber Construction
American Institute of Timber Construction
7012 S Revere Parkway
Suite 140
Centennial, CO 80112
503-639-0651; *Fax:* 503-684-8928
info@wmma.org; www.aitc-glulam.org
Social Media: Facebook, Twitter, LinkedIn
Jamison J. Scott, President
Chris Hacker, Vice President
Fred Stringfellow, Executive Director
Diane Schafer, Director of Meetings
Amy Chetelat, Director of Finance
The national trade association of the structural glued laminiated (glulam) timber industry.
Founded in: 1899

16079 American Lumber Standard Committee
American Lumber Standard Committee
PO Box 210
Germantown, MD 20875-0210
301-972-1700; *Fax:* 301-540-8004
info@wmmpa.com; www.alsc.org
Social Media: Facebook
Kellie Schroeder, CMP, CAE, CEO / Exec. VP
Clark Malak, Legal Counsel
Sadie Dickinson, Member Services
Scott Biesecker, Finance
Ric Morrison, Technical Advisor
Comprised of manufacturers, distributors, users, and consumers of lumber, serves as the standing committee for the American Softwood Lumber Standard

16080 American Sports Builders Association
American Sports Builders Association
9 Newport Drive
Suite 200
Forest Hill, MD 21050
410-730-9595
888-501-2722; *Fax:* 410-730-8833
info@wmia.org; www.sportsbuilders.org
Social Media: Facebook, Twitter
Scott Mueller, President
Dave Rakauskas, Vice President
Jim Besonen, Secretary/Treasurer
Liza Wentworth, Program Administrator
Dave Rakauskas, Secretary/Treasurer
Wood flooring manufacturers and distributors.
Founded in: 1977

16081 American Walnut Manufacturers Association
American Walnut Manufacturers Association
505 East State Street
Jefferson City, MO 65101
573-635-7877; *Fax:* 573-636-2591
memberservices@asminternational.org; www.walnutassociation.org
Social Media: Facebook, Twitter, LinkedIn
Dr. Sunniva R. Collins, FASM, President
Jon D. Tirpak, P.E., FASM, Vice President
Craig D. Clauser, P.E., Treasurer
Terry F. Mosier, Managing Director
Virginia Shirk, Foundation Executive Assistant
A national trade group representing manufacturers of walnut lumber, veneer, gunstock and dimensions.
35000 Members
Founded in: 1913

16082 American Wood Chip Export Association
Stoel Rives
101 South Capitol Boulevard
Suite 1900
Boise, ID 83702
208-389-9000; *Fax:* 208-389-9040; www.stoel.com
Social Media: Facebook, Wordpress
Chris Felix, President
Holly Hampton, Vice President
John Schultz, Executive Vice President
Ashley Davis, Administrative Assistant
Tina Schwart, Business & Finance Manager
Researches and compiles data on the wood chip export association.
Founded in: 1981

16083 American Wood Council
222 Catoctin Circle SE
Suite 201
Leesburg, VA 20175
202-463-2766; *Fax:* 202-463-2791; www.awc.org
Social Media: Twitter, LinkedIn, YouTube
Robert Glowinski, President & CEO
The wood products division of the American Forest & Paper Association promotes the use and manufacture of structural wood products.

16084 American Wood Protection Association
100 Chase Park S
Suite 116
Birmingham, AL 35244-1851
205-733-4077; *Fax:* 205-733-4075
webmaster@agma.org; www.awpa.com
Social Media: Facebook, Twitter
Dean Burrows, Chairman
Joe T Franklin Jr, President
Amir Aboutaleb, Vice President, Technical Division
Jan Alfieri, Director, Education
Mary Ellen Doran, Web Communications Manager
A non-profit organization which is responsible for promulgating voluntary wood preservation standards.
400 Members
Founded in: 1916

16085 Appalachian Hardwood Manufacturers
Appalachian Hardwood Manufacturers

PO Box 427
Suite 202
High Point, NC 27272

336-885-8315; *Fax:* 336-886-8865
info@amba.org; www.appalachianwood.org/

Todd Finley, President
Troy Nix, Executive Director
Kym Conis, Managing Director

Promotes the use of Appalachian hardwoods. Provides education and research programs.
400 Members
Founded in: 1973

16086 Architectural Woodwork Institute
Architectural Woodwork Institute
46179 Westlake Drive
Suite 120
Potomac Falls, VA 20165-5874

571-323-3636; *Fax:* 571-323-3630
CustomerCare@asme.org; www.awinet.org
Social Media: Facebook, Twitter, LinkedIn

Julio Guerrero, President
David Soukup, Managing Director, Governance
James W. Coaker, Secretary/Treasurer
John Delli Venneri, Assistant Secretary
William Garofalo, Assistant Treasurer

Members consist of architectural woodworkers, suppliers, design professionals and students from around the world.
12000 Members
Founded in: 1880

16087 Association of Equipment Manufacturers
Association of Equipment Manufacturers
6737 W Washington St
Suite 2400
Milwaukee, WI 53214-5647

414-272-0943; *Fax:* 414-272-1170
aem@aem.org; www.aem.org
Social Media: Twitter

John Patterson, Chairman
Leif J. Magnusson, Vice Chair
Renee Peters, Chief Financial Officer
Megan Tanel, VP, Exhibitions & Events
Luke, Anne Forristall, VP, Political & Public Affairs

Representing manufacturers of architectural, construction, forestry, materials handling and liabilty equipment.

16088 Association of Millwork Distributors
10047 Robert Trent Jones Pkwy
New Port Richey, FL 34655-4649

727-372-3665
800-786-7274; *Fax:* 727-372-2879
info@atmanet.org; www.amdweb.com

Will Motchar, Chairman
Clay D Tyeryar, President/Assistant Treasurer
Harry W. Buzzerd, Jr., ATMA Management Counsel
Susan A. Denston, ATMA SVP/Secretary
Carlos F. J. Moore, Consultant

Provides leadership, certification, education, promotion, networking and advocacy to, and for, the millwork distribution industry.
Founded in: 1933

16089 Association of Woodworking & Furnishings Suppliers
Association of Woodworking & Furnishings
2400 E Katella Ave
Suite 340
Anaheim, CA 92806

323-838-9440
800-946-2937; *Fax:* 323-838-9443
info@aednet.org; www.awfs.org
Social Media: Facebook, Twitter, Google+, YouTube

Don Shilling, Chair
Whit Perryman, Vice Chair
Brian P. McGuire, President & CEO
Bob Henderson, Executive Vice President / COO
Jason Blake, SVP/ CFO

Trade association for suppliers to the woodworking and furnishings industry. Services include three trade shows: Woodworking; Machinery and Supply Fair; Home and Commercial Furnishings.
500 Members

16090 Capital Lumber Company: Boise
Capital Lumber Company
5110 North 40th Street
Ste 242
Phoenix, AZ 85018

602-381-0709; *Fax:* 602-955-6191
info@AFE.org; www.capital-lumber.com
Social Media: Facebook, Twitter, LinkedIn

Dennis M. Hydrick, CPMM, President & Chairman
Wayne P. Saya, CPE, CPMM, Executive Director
Fred King, Vice Chair of Finance
Virginia N Gibson, Vice Chair of Membership
Wayne P. Saya Sr., CPE, Executive Director

Serves Idaho with a 10,000 square foot warehouse on a five acre site.
Founded in: 1915

16091 Capital Lumber Company: Tacoma
Capital Lumber Company
230 East F. Street
Ste 242
Tacoma, WA 98421

602-381-0709
877-479-5077; *Fax:* 602-955-6191;
www.capital-lumber.com
Social Media: Twitter, LinkedIn

Serves Western Washington, Alaska and Western Oregon through a seven acre asphalt covered yard and a 100,000 square foot fully enclosed warehouse.
Founded in: 1991

16092 Cedar Shake and Shingle Bureau
Cedar Shake & Shingle Bureau
PO Box 1178
Sumas, WA 98295-1178

604-820-7700; *Fax:* 604-820-0266
amt@amtonline.org; www.cedarbureau.org
Social Media: Facebook, Twitter, LinkedIn, Youtube

Douglas K Woods, President
Amber L Thomas, Vice President - Advocacy
JefferyH Traver, Vice President - Business
PeterR. Eelman, Vice President - Exhibitions
Rebecca Stahl, Chief Financial Officer

Nonprofit trade association representing manufacturer's, distributors, approved installers and service suppliers of Certilabel™ cedar shakes and shingles.
400 Members
Founded in: 1925

16093 Composite Panel Association
19465 Deerfield Avenue
Suite 306
Leesburg, VA 20176

703-724-1128; *Fax:* 703-724-1588
acmhelp@acm.org; www.compositepanel.org
Social Media: Facebook, Twitter, LinkedIn, Google+, YouTube

Alexander L Wolf, President
Vicki Hanson, Vice President
Erik R Altman, Secretary/Treasurer
Vicki Hanson, Vice President
Erik AR. Altman, Secretary/ Treasurer

Represents Northern American Particle Board and Manufacturers' sister association, Composite Wood Council. Represents manufacturers and suppliers of Composite Wood Council.
Founded in: 1947

16094 Fine Hardwood Veneer Association
American Walnut Manufacturers Association
260 S 1st Street
Suite 2
Zionsville, IN 46077

317-873-8780; *Fax:* 317-873-8788
amea@amea.org; www.hpva.org
Social Media: LinkedIn, YouTube

Jack Mendenhall, CEA, President
Randy Koster, CEA, 1st Vice President
Don Bentley, Second VP
Dave Troutman, Treasurer

Represents the decorative veneer industry. Members are face veneer manufacturers, dealers, veneer custom cutters, rotary face and crossband manufacturers, hardwood industry suppliers, veneer salesman and veneer face plants.
284 Members
Founded in: 1983

16095 Forest Industries Telecommunications
1565 Oak St
Eugene, OR 97401-4008

541-485-8441; *Fax:* 541-485-7556
avemexecsec@avem.org;
www.landmobile.com

David Dedman, Chairman
Ken Harrison, Vice Chairman
Dawn M. Shiley, Executive Director
Clay Tyeryar, MAM, CAE, Assistant Treasurer
Kim Fay, Data Analyst

Organized to assist the forest industry in radio matters before the FCC.
49 Members
Founded in: 1969

16096 Forest Landowners Association
900 Circle 75 Pkwy SE
Suite 205
Atlanta, GA 30339-3075

404-325-2954
800-325-2954; *Fax:* 404-325-2955
inquiries@clinicalrobotics.com;
www.forestlandowners.com

Gyu-Seog Choi, President
Mark Dylewski, Vice President
Rajan Sudan, Vice President
Chung Ngai Tang, Secretary
Joseph Colella, Treasurer

Proactive, progressive, grassroots organization of timberland owners - large and small - who operate more than 47 million acres of timberland in 17 southern and eastern states.
Mailing list available for rent

16097 Forest Products Society
15 Technology Parkway South
Ste. 115
Peachtree Corners, GA 30092

855-475-0291; *Fax:* 608-231-2152;
www.forestprod.org

John Addington, Manager

An international non-profit technical association founded to provide an information network for all segments of the forest products industry.
Founded in: 1915

16098 Forest Products Trucking Council
1025 Vermont Avenue NW
Suite 1020
Washington, DC 20005-3516

202-149-9250
Douglas Domenech, Secretary

An affiliate of the American Pulpwood Association.
50 Members

16099 **Friends of the Trees**
PO Box 165
Hot Springs, MT 59845

406-741-5809
info@csda.org; www.friendsofthetrees.net
Social Media: Facebook, LinkedIn, YouTube, Instagram

Kevin Baron, President
Jack Sondergard, Vice President
Pat O'Brien, Executive Director
Mike Orzechowski, Secretary/ Treasurer
500 Members
Founded in: 1971
Mailing list available for rent

16100 **Great Lakes Timber Professionals Association**
3243 Golf Course Road
PO Box 1278
Rhinelander, WI 54501-1278

715-282-5828; *Fax:* 715-282-4941
aimcal@aimcal.org; www.timberpa.com
Social Media: Facebook, Twitter, LinkedIn, YouTube, Instagram

Craig Sheppard, Executive Director
Tracey Ingram, Operations Manager
Melissa Crandall, Administrative Assistant
Ashley Wood, Event Planner
Colin Rupp, Web Designer

A nonprofit organization that is committed to leading the Forest Products industry in sustainable forest management through advocacy, professionalism, service to members, education and training.
Founded in: 1984

16101 **Hall-Woolford Tank Company, Inc.**
5500 N. Water Street
PO Box 2755
Philadelphia, PA 19120

215-329-9022; *Fax:* 215-329-1177
kim@cemanet.org; www.woodtank.com
Social Media: Facebook, Twitter, LinkedIn

Jerry Heathman, President
Garry Abraham, Vice President
Paul Ross, Secretary
Robert Reinfried, Executive Vice President of CEMA
E.A. Thompson, Treasurer

To promote the use and to guide the proper construction methods for wooden tanks as per NWTI S-82.
96 Members
Founded in: 1933

16102 **Hardwood Manufacturers Association**
Hardwood Manufacturers Association
665 Rodi Road
Suite 305
Pittsburgh, PA 15235

412-244-0440; *Fax:* 412-244-9090
info@farmequip.org; www.hardwoodinfo.com
Social Media: Twitter

Vernon Schmidt, Executive Vice President
Elaina Jackson, Membership Services
Tricia Kidd, Accounting and Meeting Services
Kristi Ruggles, Publications and Communications
Hannah Hamontree, Communications Director

Over 100 companies with over 150 locations in the US.
340 Members

16103 **Hardwood Plywood and Veneer Association**
1825 Michael Faraday Dr
Reston, VA 20190-5350

703-435-2900; *Fax:* 703-435-2537
fema@femalifesafety.org; www.hpva.org
Social Media: LinkedIn, Youtube

Provides public relations, advertising, marketing, and technical services to manufacturers and distributors of hardwood plywood, veneers and engineered hardwood flooring and suppliers who sell to these industries.
24 Members
Founded in: 1925

16104 **Hardwood Utilization Consortium**
USDA Forest Service
Southern Research Station
Blacksburg, VA 24061-0503
540-231-5341; *Fax:* 540-231-8868
info@fluidpowersafety.com;
www.consortium.forprod.vt.edu

Rory S. McLaren, Founder & Director

The role is to improve hardwood resource viability through better utilization, technology, markets, cooperative extension and education in the eastern United States.

16105 **Hearth, Patio & Barbecue Association**
1901 N Moore St
Suite 600
Arlington, VA 22209-1708

703-522-0086; *Fax:* 703-522-0548
Askus@ifps.org; www.hpba.org

Marti Wendel, CFPE, CFPS, CF, President & Chairperson
Donna Pollander, ACA, Executive Director
Jeff Morrow, Business Development Manager
Adele Kayser, Website/Communications Manager
Sue Dyson, Client Data Manager
2600 Members
Founded in: 1960

16106 **Intermountain Forest Association**
2218 Jackson Blvd
#10
Rapid City, SD 57702

605-341-0875; *Fax:* 605-341-8651
info@fpsa.org; www.intforest.org
Social Media: Facebook, Twitter, LinkedIn, Google+

Gil Williams, Chairman
David Seckman, President & CEO
Robyn Roche, CFO
Andy Drennan, Senior VP, International Market
Adam Finney, VP of Membership and Communications

Seeks to provide a unified voice for the industry. Promotes a sustained timber yield. Monitors federal legislation.
350+ Members
Founded in: 2005

16107 **International Wood Products Association**
4214 King St
Alexandria, VA 22302-1555

703-820-6696; *Fax:* 703-820-8550;
www.iwpawood.org

John H Addington, Secretary-Treasurer
Craig H Addington, Account Executive

International trade association for the North American imported wood products industry, representing companies and trade organizations engaged in the import of hardwoods and softwoods from sustainably managed forests in more than 30 nations across the globe.
19 Members
Founded in: 1933

16108 **Laminating Materials Association**
Louisiana Municipal Association
700 North 10th street
Baton Rouge, LA 70802

225-344-5001
800-234-8274; *Fax:* 225-344-3057
info@isapartners.org; www.lma.org

John Duffy, Director
Ed Gerber, Director

Nonprofit trade group representing all decorative overlays and edgebanding in North America. These products are applied to a composite wood substrate and used in the production of furniture, store fixtures, kitchen cabinets and more.
650 Members
Founded in: 1988

16109 **Lumbermen's Credit Association**
20 N Wacker Dr
Suite 1800
Chicago, IL 60606-2905

312-553-0943; *Fax:* 312-553-2149
staff@iadd.org; www.lumbermenscredit.com
Social Media: Facebook, Twitter, LinkedIn

Jeremy T. Guest, President
Mauro Tomelleri, VP, International Activities
Ian Young, Vice President, Media & Content
Jennifer Thoroe, Vice President, Membership
Eric B. Anderson, Vice President, Sales & Marketing

Assist credit managers and salesmen by providing listings and credit ratings of companies which deal in lumber and wood products. Also publishes a directory.

16110 **MSR Lumber Producers Council**
MSR Lumber Producers Council
6300 Enterprise Lane
Madison, WI 53719

888-848-5339; *Fax:* 888-212-5110
websteward@iamaw.org; www.msrlumber.org
Social Media: Facebook, Twitter, RSS, Ucubed

R Thomas Buffenbarger, CEO
Robert Martinez, Jr., General VP
Robert Roach, Jr., General Secretary-Treasurer
Diane Babineaux, Executive Assistant

Represents the interest of Machine Stress Rated Lumber Producers in the manufacturing, marketing, promotion, utilization and technical aspects of machine stress rated lumber.
Founded in: 1888

16111 **Maple Flooring Manufacturers Association**
Maple Flooring Manufacturers Association
One Parkview Plaza
Suite 800
Oakbrook Terrace, IL 60181
847-480-9138
888-480-9138; *Fax:* 847-686-2251;
www.maplefloor.org

International non-profit trade organization representing manufacturers of northern hard maple solid strip flooring along with flooring contractors, distributors and providers of instalation-related products and services. Maintains technical standards for product quality, grading, shipping and packaging, and quality central.
Founded in: 1954

16112 **National Association of the Remodeling Industry**
P.O. Box 4250
Des Plaines, IL 60016

847-298-9200
800-611-6274; *Fax:* 847-298-9225
office@mdna.org; www.nari.org
Social Media: Facebook, Twitter, LinkedIn, Youtube

Kim Shuster, AEA, President
Joe Lundvick, CEA, Vice President
John Greene, CEA, Second Vice President
Terry Yoder, Treasurer
Jennifer Gray, Director

Purpose is to establish and maintain a firm commitment to developing and sustaining programs that expand and unite the remodeling industry; to ensure the industry's growth and security; to encourage ethical conduct, sound business practices and professionalism in the remodeling industry; and to present NARI as the recognized authority in the remodeling industry.
383 Members
Founded in: 1941

16113 **National Food Flooring Association**
111 Chesterfield Industrial Boulevard
Suite B
Chesterfield, MO 63005

636-519-9663
800-422-4556
636-519-9663; *Fax:* 636-519-9664;
www.nofma.org
Social Media: Facebook, Twitter, LinkedIn, Youtube, RSS

Carlos M. Cardoso, Chairman
John M. Stropki, Vice Chairman
Stephen V. Gold, President
Cameron L. Mackey, Vice President, Sales and Marketing
Daniel J. Meckstroth, Vice President and Chief Economist

It's warmer with wood. Genuine hardwoods, plus one-of-a-kind beauty. You never get tired of solid hardware floors - provides the perfect setting.
500+ Members
Founded in: 1933

16114 **National Frame Builders Association**
8735 W Higgins Road
Suite 300
Chicago, IL 60631

785-843-2444
800-557-6957; *Fax:* 847-375-6495
jnofsinger@mhia.org; www.nfba.org
Social Media: Facebook, Twitter, LinkedIn, Youtube, Blooger, RSS

Dave Young, Executive Chairman
John Paxton, President
Gregg E. Goodner, Vice President
Cathy Moose, Executive Assistant
Victoria Wheeler, Director Member Services

Building contractors, suppliers, design and code professionals and academic personnel specializing in the post frame construction industry.
22 Members
Founded in: 1945

16115 **National Hardwood Lumber Association**
National Hardwood Lumber Association
PO Box 34518
Memphis, TN 38184

901-377-1818
800-933-0318
bob@mpta.org; www.nhla.com
Social Media: Youtube

Robert Reinfried, Executive VP

Founded to establish a uniform system of grading rules for the measurement and inspection of hardwood lumber
23 Members
Founded in: 1933

16116 **National Lumber and Building Material Dealers Association**
2025 M St NW
Suite 800
Washington, DC 20036-3309

202-367-1169
800-634-8645; *Fax:* 202-367-2169
nfpa@nfpa.com; www.dealer.org
Social Media: Facebook, Twitter, LinkedIn, Google+

Jeff Stuart, Chairman of the Board
Eric Lanke, Chief Executive Officer
Denise Rockhill, OEM Marketing Manager
Pete Alles, Director of Membership & Comm.
Sue Chase, Director of Finance & HR

To advance the national agenda for America's building material suppliers.
Founded in: 1955

16117 **National Wood Flooring Association**
111 Chesterfield Industrial
Suite B
Chesterfield, MO 63005-1219

636-519-9663
800-422-4556; *Fax:* 636-519-9664
info@ntma.org; www.nwfa.org
Social Media: Twitter, LinkedIn

Rob Akers, CEO
Rich Basalla, Membership Officer
Tiffany Bryson, Sales/Sponsorship Manager
John Capka, Chief Financial Officer

A not-for-profit trade association serving the wood flooring industry
2800 Members
Founded in: 1943

16118 **National Wood Window and Door Association**
330 N. Wabash Avenue
Suite 2000
Chicago, IL 60611-4267

312-321-6802; *Fax:* 847-299-1286
naeda@naeda.com; www.wdma.com
Social Media: Facebook, Twitter, LinkedIn

Blaine Bingham, Chairman
Richard Lawhun, President/CEO
Joseph Dykes, VP Industry Relations
Michael Williams, VP Operations
Doug Kreienkamp, Coordinator Operations

Members are makers of standard building products such as doors, windows and frames.
5000 Members
Founded in: 1900

16119 **National Wooden Pallet & Container Association**
1421 Prince Street
Suite 340
Alexandria, VA 22314-2805

703-519-6104; *Fax:* 703-519-4720
info@opeesa.com; www.palletcentral.com
Social Media: Twitter, LinkedIn

Jeff Plotka, President and Director
Nancy Cueroni, Executive Director
David Dollard, Director
Robert Smith, Director
Mark DeShetler, Director

An advocacy organization communicating regularly with key lawmakers and regulators, collaborating with a broad network of business groups and wood product organizations.

16120 **New England Kiln Drying Association**
SUNY
200A Progress Drive Ext,
Burgaw, NC 28425

910-259-9794; *Fax:* 910-259-1625
pmmiwebhelp@pmmi.org;
www.kiln-direct.com
Social Media: Facebook, Twitter, LinkedIn, Youtube

Charles D. Yuska, President and CEO
Tom Egan, Vice President, Industry Services
Maria Ferrante, VP, Education & Workforce Dev.
Patti Fee, Vice President Meetings And Events
Jim Pittas, Senior Vice President

Disseminates information on the dying of wood to the wood-using industry.
Founded in: 1933

16121 **North American Wholesale Lumber Association**
330 N. Wabash
Suite 2000
Chicago, IL 60611

312-321-5133
800-527-8258; *Fax:* 312-673-6838
info@patmi.org; www.nawla.org

Supports the wholesale lumber industry. Publishes monthly NAWLA Bulletin that includes industry and association news, and produces the NAWLA Traders Market, an annual trade show bringing together over 1500 manufacturers and wholesale lumber traders at the premier event in the forest products industry. NAWLA also produces a variety of educational programs designed to enhance professionalism in the lumber industry.
7 Members
Founded in: 1951

16122 **Northeastern Loggers Association**
3311 State Route 28
PO Box 69
Old Forge, NY 13420-0069

315-369-3078
800-318-7561; *Fax:* 315-369-3736;
www.northernlogger.com

Susan Young, Manager

Works to improve the industry in the Northeast and educate the public about policies and products of the industry.
Founded in: 1968

16123 **Northern Woods Logging Association**
PO Box 270
Jackman, ME 04945-0270

Provides members with a workers compensation protection program. Conducts on-site inspections and offers a first aid course and safety training program.
213 Members
Founded in: 1974

16124 **Northwest Forestry Association**
1500 SW 1st Ave
Suite 700
Portland, OR 97201-5837

503-222-9505; *Fax:* 503-222-3255
ptrahq@ptra.org; www.nwtrees.org

Doug Landgraf, President
Bill Taylor, First Vice President
Curt Benson, CPMR, Second Vice President
Susan Crolla, Executive Director
Walt Brooks, Treasurer

Promotes forestry throughout the region to assure a permanent industry and stable economy. Works to keep informed on current changes affecting forest products.
Founded in: 1972

16125 **Northwestern Lumber Association**
Northwestern Lumber Association

5905 Golden Valley Road
Suite 110
Minneapolis, MN 55422-4535

763-544-6822
888-544-6822; *Fax:* 763-595-4060
info@pmpa.org; www.nlassn.org
Social Media: Facebook, Twitter, LinkedIn, YouTube, Flickr, RSS

Tom Bernstein, Jr., President
Harry S Eighmy, First Vice President
Douglas R. Coster, Second Vice President
Bernard Nagle, Executive Director
Miles K. Free, Director, Industry Research & Tech.

Retail lumber dealer in Iowa, Minnesota, North Dakota, and South Dakota.
Mailing list available for rent

16126 OSBGuide
Structural Board Association
25 Valleywood Drive
Unit 27
Markham, L3R 5L9, ON

905-475-1100; *Fax:* 905-475-1101
ria@robotics.org
osbguide.tecotested.com
Social Media: Facebook, Twitter, LinkedIn, YouTube, Google+

Jeff Burnstein, Executive Director

Members are manufacturers of structural panels.
Founded in: 1974

16127 Pacific Logging Congress
Pacific Logging Congress
PO Box 1281
Maple Valley, WA 98038

425-413-2808; *Fax:* 425-413-1359
rbrothers@wade-partners.com;
www.pacificloggingcongress.com

Matt Thompson, President
Sean Ryan, Vice-President
Bill Wade, Executive Director
Toni Nastali, Treasurer
Randy Brothers, Manager

Logging firms.
140 Members
Founded in: 1981

16128 Pacific Lumber Exporters Association
720 NE Flanders
Suite 207
Portland, OR 97232

503-701-6510; *Fax:* 503-467-5273
advertising@sme.org;
www.lumber-exporters.org
Social Media: Facebook, Twitter, LinkedIn, Youtube, RSS

Wayne F. Frost, CMfgE, President/Interim CEO
Jeffrey M. Krause, Chief Executive Officer
Dean L. Bartles, PhD, FSME, Secretary/Treasurer
Debbie Holton, Managing Director
Jeannine Kunz, Managing Director

Provide forum to discuss trade issues and problems; promote member companies through governmental and other trade association channels.
7000 Members
Founded in: 1932

16129 Pacific Lumber Inspection Bureau
Pacific Lumber Inspection Bureau
909 S. 336th St.
Ste 203
Federal Way, WA 98003

253-835-3344; *Fax:* 253-835-3371
srs@wjweiser.com; www.plib.org
Social Media: Facebook

Accredited for grading and grade stamping of softwood lumber. Issues certificates on domestic and export lumber shipments.

16130 Pennsylvania Forest Products Association
301 Chestnut Street
Suite 102
Harrisburg, PA 17101

717-901-0420
800-232-4562; *Fax:* 717-901-0360
pmmiwebhelp@pmmi.org;
www.paforestproducts.org
Social Media: Facebook, Twitter

Charles D. Yuska, President and CEO
Tom Egan, Vice President, Industry Services
Maria Ferrante, VP, Education & Workforce Dev.
Patti Fee, Vice President Meetings And Events
Jim Pittas, Senior Vice President

Created to provide members with a unified voice on state legislative and regulatory issues.
650 Members
Founded in: 1933

16131 Railway Tie Association
Railway Tie Association
115 Commerce Dr
Suite C
Fayetteville, GA 30214-7335

770-460-5553; *Fax:* 770-460-5573
info@fpda.org; www.rta.org

Tim Gillig, President & Chairman
Patricia A. Lilly, Executive Director
Beth Hiltabidle, Marketing Specialist
Joseph M. Thompson, General Manager
Donald Smith, Accounting Manager

Members include crosstie producers, sawmill owners, chemical manufacturers, wood preservation companies, railroad maintenance engineers, purchasing officials and others.
180 Members
Founded in: 1974

16132 Redwood Inspection Service
818 Grayson Road
Suite 201
Pleasant Hill, CA 94523

925-935-1499
888-225-7339; *Fax:* 925-935-1496
contact@uama.org; www.calredwood.org

Authorized by Department of Commerce to develop and supervise redwood lumber grading.
Founded in: 1999

16133 Society of American Foresters
5400 Grosvenor Lane
Bethesda, MD 20814-2198

301-897-8720
866-897-8720; *Fax:* 301-897-3690
wsandler@vma.org; www.safnet.org

Greg Rogowski, Chairman
Bob Kemple, Vice Chairman
William S. Sandler, President
Marc Pasternak, VP/ VRC Executive Director
Malena Malone-Blevins, Meetings Manager

Provides access to information and networking opportunities to prepare members for the challenges and the changes that face natural resource professionals.
100 Members
Founded in: 1938

16134 Society of Wood Science & Technology
PO Box 6155
Monona, WI 53716-6155

608-577-1342; *Fax:* 608-467-8979
information@vi-institute.org; www.swst.org
Social Media: Facebook, Twitter, LinkedIn

Dave Corelli, President
Tom Spettel, Executive Vice President
Robin Ginner, Executive Director
Ellie Murphy, Finance Associate
Ronald L. Eshleman, Ph.D., Technical Director

Promotes policies and procedures which assure the wise use of wood and wood-based products; assures high standards for professional performance of wood scientists and technologists; fosters educational programs at all levels of wood science and technology and further the quality of such programs; represents the profession in public policy development.
3000 Members
Founded in: 1972

16135 Southeastern Lumber Manufacturers Association, Inc.
Southeastern Lumber Manufacturers
200 Greencastle Road
Tyrone, GA 30290

770-631-6701; *Fax:* 770-631-6720;
www.slma.org
Social Media: Facebook, Twitter, LinkedIn, RSS, Google+

Victor J Rubino, President
Sandra R. Geller, Executive Vice President
William C. Cubberley, Vice President of Publishing
Anita C. Shapiro, Vice President of Programs
Donald F. Berbary, Chief Sales & Marketing Officer

Represents membership in local, regional, and national problems that affect southeastern lumber industry. Conducts marketing and promotional activity.
Founded in: 1933

16136 Southern Cypress Manufacturers Association
Southern Cypress Manufacturers Association
400 Penn Center Boulevard
Suite 530
Pittsburgh, PA 15235

877-607-7262
zakaras@rand.org; www.cypressinfo.org
Social Media: Facebook, Twitter

Michael D Rich, President/CEO
Richard Fallon, SVP and Chief Financial Officer
Andrew R Hoehn, SVP, Research and Analysis
Allison Elder, Vice President, Human Resources
Naveena Ponnusamy, Executive Director, Development

Administrative support provided by the Hardwood Manufacturers Association.
Founded in: 1948
Mailing list available for rent

16137 Southern Forest Products Association
6660 Riverside Dr.
Suite 212
Metairie, LA 70003

504-443-4464; *Fax:* 504-443-6612
info@rmmlf.org; www.sfpa.org
Social Media: Facebook, Twitter, LinkedIn

David Phillips, Executive Director
Mark Holland, Associate Director
Catherine J. Boggs, President
Robert B. Keiter, Vice President
Gregory R. Danielson, Secretary

The Association and its members are committed to quality, and believe that Southern Pine forest products provide a smart, environmentally friendly way to meet our world's needs for a wide range of building and industrial products.
2000 Members
Founded in: 1955

16138 Southern Pine Inspection Bureau
Southern Pine Inspection Bureau

Po Box 10915
Pensacola, FL 32524-0915

850-434-2611; *Fax:* 850-434-1290;
www.spib.org

Anne Lytle, President

Develops grading standards for Southern pine lumber and provides an inspection service and grade marking systems.

Founded in: 1984
Mailing list available for rent

16139 Temperate Forest Foundation
528 Hennepin Avenue
Suite 703
Minneapolis, MN 55403

612-333-0430; *Fax:* 612-333-0432
sla@sportslaw.org; www.forestinfo.org
Social Media: Facebook, Twitter, LinkedIn

Matthew J. Mitten, President
Richard A. Guggolz, Executive Director
Ash Narayan, Treasurer
Vered Yakovee, Secretary
William M. Drohan, CAE, Deputy Executive Director

A tax-exempt, non-profit, public charity. Provides leadership by articulating the current realities, and a positive inspiring vision of the future. Helps people move toward the positive vision of living sustainably.

16140 Timber Products Manufacturers Association (TPM)
951 E 3rd Avenue
Spokane, WA 99202-2287

509-535-4646; *Fax:* 509-534-6106
secretariat@africanstudies.org;
www.timberassociation.com
Social Media: Facebook, Twitter, LinkedIn, Flickr

Toyin Samatar, President
Dorothy Hodgson, Vice President
Suzanne Moyer Baazet, Executive Director
Kathryn Salucka, Program Manager
Kathryn Salucka, Executive Assistant

Association of companies in the Timber and Wood products industry of the pacific northwest. TPM provides human resource and safety consulting, Training and employee benefits.

Founded in: 1957

16141 Tree Care Industry Association
Tree Care Industry Association
136 Harvey Road
Suite 101
Londonderry, NH 03053

603-314-5380
800-733-2622; *Fax:* 603-314-5386
aallhq@aall.org; www.tcia.org/
Social Media: Facebook, Twitter, LinkedIn, Flickr

Kate Hagan, Executive Director
Kim Rundle, Executive Assistant
Emily Feltren, Director Government Relations
Julia O'Donnell, Director Membership Marketing
Ashley St. John, Director Marketing/Communications

Supports all those involved with trees and tree care by offering education and training, community events, and publications.
5000+ Members
Founded in: 1906
Mailing list available for rent

16142 Truss Plate Institute
218 North Lee Street
Suite 312
Alexandria, VA 22314-2800

703-683-1010; *Fax:* 866-501-4012
asis@asis.org; www.tpinst.org
Social Media: Facebook, Twitter, LinkedIn

Dr. Sandra G. Hirsh, President
Richard Hill, Executive Director
Jan Hatzakos, Director of Finance & Admin
Vanessa Foss, Director of Meetings and Membership
Sandra Holder, Receptionist, Office Assistant

The Truss Plate Institute's mission is '...to maintain the truss industry on a sound engineering basis..'. To accomplish its mission, TPI establishes methods of design and construction for trusses in accordance with the American National Standards Institute's accredited consensus procedures for coordination and development of American National Standards in addition to providing a Quality Assurance Inspection program and by contributing its expertise in other technical areas.
4000 Members
Founded in: 1937

16143 West Coast Lumber Inspection Bureau
PO Box 23145
Portland, OR 97281-3145

503-639-0651; *Fax:* 503-684-8928
info@asindexing.org; www.wclib.org

Fred Leise, President
Diana Witt, Vice President and President-Elect
Gwen Henson, Executive Director
Janet Perlman, Treasurer
Judi Gibbs, Secretary

Supervises manufacturing practices, grade stamping, and inspecting.
1M Members
Founded in: 1957

16144 Western Building Material Association
Western Building Material Association
909 Lakeridge Dr. SW
PO Box 1699
Olympia, WA 98502

360-943-3054
888-551-9262; *Fax:* 360-943-1219
sales@atla.com; www.wbma.org
Social Media: Facebook

Kelly Campbell, President
Timothy D. Lincoln, Vice President
Brenda Bailey-Hainer, Executive Director
Gillian Harrison Cain, Director of Member Programs
Jim Butler, Director of Information Systems

Regional trade association derving building material dealers throughout the states of Alaska, Idaho, Montana, Oregon and Washington and a federated association of the National Lumber and Building Material Dealers Association.
800 Members
Founded in: 1991

16145 Western Forestry and Conservation Association
4033 SW Canyon Rd
Portland, OR 97221

503-226-4562
888-722-9416; *Fax:* 503-226-2515
info@lff.org; www.westernforestry.org

Diantha Dow Schull, President
Bruce Astrein, Executive Director
Nina Sonenberg, VP Communications
Sabrina Waldron, Program Manager
William Zeisel, Operations Director

Offers high-quality continuing education workshops and seminars for professional foresters throughout Oregon, Washington, Idaho, Montana, Northern California and British Columbia.
Mailing list available for rent

16146 Western Red Cedar Lumber Association
Western Red Cedar Lumber Association
1501-700 West Pender Street
Pender Place 1, Business Building
Vancouver, BC V6C 1G8

604-891-1262
800-266-1910; *Fax:* 604-687-4930
ww.realcedar.com
Social Media: Facebook, Twitter, LinkedIn

Kristen Regina, President
Heather Gendron, Vice-President/President Elect
Jamie Lausch Vander Broek, Secretary
Mark Pompelia, Treasurer
Carol Graney, Editorial Director

Mission is to produce quality Western Red Cedar lumber products and support them with technical education and promotion.
Founded in: 1972

16147 Western Wood Products Association
1500 SW First Ave.
Suite 870
Portland, OR 97201

503-224-3930; *Fax:* 503-224-3935
webmaster@apalaweb.org; www2.wwpa.org
Social Media: Facebook, Twitter, LinkedIn, Flickr

Buenaventura Ven Basco, Executive Director

Represents lumber manufacturers in 12 Western states and Alaska. Provides lumber quality control, technical support, and business information to supporting mills.
310 Members
Founded in: 1980

16148 Window & Door Manufacturers Association
Window & Door Manufacturers Association
330 N. Wabash Avenue
Suite 2000
Chicago, IL 60611-4267

312-321-6802
800-223-2301; *Fax:* 847-299-1286
office@alise.org; www.wdma.com
Social Media: Facebook, Twitter, LinkedIn

John Budd, President
Connie Van Fleet, VP/President-Elect
Deborah York, Executive Director
Jeremy Uthank, Information Management

A trade association representing approximately 145 U.S. and Canadian manufacturers and suppliers of windows and doors for the domestic and export markiets.
Founded in: 1915

16149 Wood Component Manufacturers Association
Wood Component Manufacturers Association
PO Box 662 Lindstrom
Ste 350
Minneapolis, MN 55045

651-332-6332; *Fax:* 651-400-3502
info@aplici.org; www.woodcomponents.org
Social Media: Twitter

Allison Burns, President
Debbie Dickson, Vice President
Liz Nugent, Recording Secretary
Joann Donatiello, Acting Treasurer

Represents manufacturers of wood component products for furniture, cabinetry, building products, and decorative wood products.
Founded in: 1968

16150 Wood Machinery Manufacturers of America
9 Newport Dr.
Suite 200
Forest Hill, MD 21050

443-640-1052; *Fax:* 443-640-1031
info@wmma.org; www.wmma.org
Social Media: Facebook, Twitter, LinkedIn

Jamison Scott, President
Chris Hacker, Vice President
Fred Stringfellow, Executive Director

WMMA has worked to increase the productivity and profitability of U.S. machinery and tooling manufacturers and the businesses that support them.
Founded in: 1899

16151 Wood Machinery Maufacturers of America
Wood Machinery Maufacturers of America
9 Newport Drive
Suite 200
Forest Hill, MD 21050

443-640-1052; *Fax:* 443-640-1031
execdir@arsc-audio.org; www.wmma.org
Social Media: Facebook, LinkedIn, YouTube

Sam Brylawski, President
David Seubert, VP
Louise Spear, Second VP/Program Chair
Esther Gillie, Secretary/Editor
1000 Members
Founded in: 1966

16152 Wood Moulding and Millwork Producers Association
MMPA
507 1st St
Woodland, CA 95695-4025

530-661-9591
800-550-7889; *Fax:* 530-661-9586
info@acl.org; www.wmmpa.com
Social Media: Facebook, Twitter

Frank Quinn, President
Janelle Mazelin, Executive Director
Rodney Birch, Vice President
Sheila O Carlblom, Treasurer
Denise Nelson, Secretary

Promote quality products produced by its members, to develop sources of supply, to promote optimum use of raw materials to standardize products, and to increase the domestic and foreign usage of moulding and millwork products.
574 Members
Founded in: 1956

16153 Wood Products Manufacturers Association
PO Box 761
Westminster, MA 01473-0761

978-874-5445; *Fax:* 978-874-9946
woodprod@wpma.org; www.wpma.org
Social Media: Facebook, LinkedIn

Philip Bibeau, Executive Director

Information and services to support businesses in the industry.
Founded in: 1929

16154 Woodworking Machinery Industry Association
225 Reinekers Lane
Suite 410
Alexandria, VA 22314

860-350-9642; *Fax:* 860-354-0677
info@aiip.org; www.wmia.org
Social Media: Facebook, Twitter, LinkedIn, YouTube, Instagram

June Boyle, President
Shelly Azar, Secretary
Marilyn Harmacek, Treasurer
Michelle Rawl, Director - Membership
Jennifer Burke, Director - Marketing - Content

Providing the North American wood products industry with technologically advanced woodworking systems available in the global market. A wide range of special programs provide industry awards, safety publications, scholarships and a host of other methods to support industry initiatives and address industry issues.
700 Members
Founded in: 1987

Newsletters

16155 AFRC News
American Forest Resource Council
5100 SW Macadam
Suite 350
Portland, OR 97239

503-222-9505; *Fax:* 503-222-3255
info@amforest.org; www.amforest.org

Tom Partin, President

Newsletter of the American Forest Resource Council.
Frequency: Monthly

16156 American Wood Protection Association Newsletter
American Wood Protection Association
100 Chase Park South
Suite 116
Birmingham, AL 35244-1851

205-733-4077; *Fax:* 205-733-4075
info@awpa.com; www.awpa.com

John Hall, Publisher

Reports on governmental issues and environmental news.
Cost: $7.50
12 Pages
Frequency: Monthly
Founded in: 1921

16157 Association of Millwork Distributors Newsletter
Association Of Millwork Distributors
10047 Robert Trent Jones Pkwy
Trinity, FL 34655-4649

727-372-3665
800-786-7274; *Fax:* 727-372-2879
marketing@amdweb.com; www.amdweb.com/

Rosalie Leone, CEO
Kim Cotterman, Director of Membership

Updates for wholesale millwork distribution companies.
Frequency: Monthly
Circulation: 1500
Founded in: 1964
Printed in 2 colors on glossy stock

16158 Building Products CONNECTION
Northwestern Lumber Association
5905 Golden Valley Road
Suite 110
Minneapolis, MN 55422-4535

763-544-6822
888-544-6822; *Fax:* 763-595-4060
info@nlassn.org; www.nlassn.org

Beth Stoll, Editor
Jodie Fleck, Director of Conventions & Tours
Cody Nuernberg, Manager of Membership

Dedicated to providing information on issues important to the success of the lumber and building material industry in the upper Midwest.
Cost: $300.00
Frequency: Bi-Monthly
Circulation: 2200
Mailing list available for rent

16159 Classified Exchange
Miller Publishing Corporation
PO Box 34908
Memphis, TN 38184-0908

901-372-8280
800-844-1280; *Fax:* 901-373-6180
editor@millerwoodtradepub.com;
www.millerpublishing.com

Paul J Miller, President
Sue Putnam, Editor

Pages and pages of bargains, several pages on raw material and service sources for everything from lumber to curved plywood, from dry kilns to sawmill equipment and boilers. Special liquidations and auctions offering everything from soup to nuts.
Cost: $65.00
Frequency: Monthly

16160 Connected
Association of Millwork Distributors
10047 Robert Trent Jones Pkwy
Trinity, FL 34655-4649

727-372-3665
800-786-7274; *Fax:* 727-372-2879
marketing@amdweb.com; www.amdweb.com

Rosalie Leone, CEO

Keeps you abreast of the latest breaking news within the millwork industry regarding economics & finance; the current housing industry; legislative updates; codes, standards and the AMD Certification Program information, Education special offers as well as comprehensive Millwork News.
Frequency: Weekly

16161 Forestbytes
American Forests
734 15th Street NW
Suite 800
Washington, DC 20005

202-737-1944; www.americanforests.org
Social Media: Facebook, Twitter

Lynda Webster, Chair
Scott Steen, CEO

Features environmental stories and breakthroughs that impact our forests and trees and news and updates on American Forests projects and programs.
Frequency: Monthly
Founded in: 1990

16162 Forestry Source
Society of American Foresters
5400 Grosvenor Ln
Bethesda, MD 20814-2198

301-897-8720; *Fax:* 301-897-3690;
www.safnet.org
Social Media: Facebook, Twitter, LinkedIn

Michael T Goergen Jr, Executive VP/CEO
Joe Smith, Editor

Offers the latest information on national forestry trends, the latest developments in forestry at the federal, state, and local levels, the newest advances in forestry-related research and technology, and up-to-date information about SAF programs and activities.
Cost: $33.00
Frequency: Monthly
Founded in: 1900
Printed in 4 colors

16163 Import/Export Wood Purchasing News
Miller Publishing Corporation

PO Box 34908
Memphis, TN 38184-0908

901-372-8280
800-844-1280; *Fax:* 901-373-6180
editor@millerwoodtradepub.com;
www.millerpublishing.com

Paul J Miller, President
Sue Putnam, Editor

Read features about overseas buyers, U.S. factories buying imported forest products and North American exporters. Also carries forest products business trends on the domestic and international markets.
Cost: $75.00
Frequency: Bi-Monthly

16164 MSR Council Matters
MSR Lumber Producers Council
6300 Enterprise Lane
Madison, WI 53719

888-848-5339; *Fax:* 888-212-5110
info@msrlumber.org; www.msrlumber.org

Steve Hardy, President

Provides updates on issues affecting members and customers
Frequency: Monthly
Founded in: 1987

16165 National Frame Builders Association Newsletter
National Frame Builders Association
4700 W. Lake Avenue
Glenview, IL 60025

785-843-2444
800-557-6957; *Fax:* 847-375-6495
info@nfba.org; www.nfba.org

John Fullerton, VP
Tom Knight, President

Published by the National Frame Builders Association.

16166 National Wooden Pallet & Container Association: Newsletter
National Wooden Pallet & Container Association
1421 Prince Street
Suite 340
Alexandria, VA 22314-3501

703-519-6104; *Fax:* 703-519-4720
palletcomm@aol.com; www.nwpca.com

Bruce N Scholnick, President
Pamela Wilson, Publisher
Kathy Conroy, Marketing Director
Sam McAdow, Interim President
Susan Cheney, Membership Coordinator

Newsletter published by The National Wooden Pallet and Container Association.
Cost: $2995.00

16167 SFPA E-Newsletter
Southern Forest Products Association
2900 Indiana Ave
Kenner, LA 70065-4605

504-443-4464; *Fax:* 504-443-6612
mail@sfpa.org; www.sfpa.org

Digges Morgan, President
Richard Wallace, VP Communications
Tami Kessler, Corporate Secretary
Stephen P. Conwell, President
Tami Kessler, Corporate Secretary & Director

The Association and its members are committed to quality, and believe that Southern Pine forest products provide a smart, environmentally friendly way to meet our world's needs for a wide range of building and industrial products.
265 Members
Frequency: Weekly/Online

16168 Softwood Forest Products Buyer
Miller Publishing Corporation
PO Box 34908
Memphis, TN 38184-0908

901-372-8280
800-844-1280; *Fax:* 901-373-6180
editor@millerwoodtradepub.com;
www.millerpublishing.com

Paul J Miller, President
Sue Putnam, Editor

Provides you with interesting feature articles on purchasing, inventory control, marketing, production, utilization and distribution of Softwood forest products such as lumber, plywood, moulding, etc.
Cost: $65.00
Frequency: Bi-Monthly

16169 TPM Bulletin
Timber Products Manufacturers Association
951 E 3rd Avenue
Spokane, WA 99202-2287

509-535-4646; *Fax:* 509-534-6106
tpm@tpmrs.com; www.tpmrs.com

Dick Molenda, Interim President
Shelley Jeffers, Publications Coordinator

Provides insightful overviews of key employment issues that can impact every business.
Frequency: Monthly
Circulation: 250

16170 TPM Newsletter
Timber Products Manufacturers (TPM) Association
951 E 3rd Avenue
Spokane, WA 99202-2287

509-535-4646; *Fax:* 509-534-6106
tpm@tpmrs.com; www.tpmrs.com

Dick MoLenda, Interim President
Jeff Bosma, Chairman

Official newsletter of Timber Products Manufacturers (TPM) Association.
Cost: $195.00
250 Members
Frequency: Monthly
Circulation: 700
Founded in: 1916

16171 Timberline
Bear Creek Lumber
Po Box 669
Winthrop, WA 98862

800-597-7191; *Fax:* 509-997-2040
customerservice@bearcreeklumber.com;
www.bearcreeklumber.com
Social Media: Twitter, LinkedIn

Features articles about the timber industry, the construction industry, how-to information, and it also lets folks know what's new at Bear Creek Lumber.
Cost: $15.00
6000 Pages

16172 TreeWorker
Tree Care Industry Association
136 Harvey Road
Suite 101
Londonderry, NH 03053

603-314-5380
800-733-2622; *Fax:* 603-314-5386
tcia@tcia.org; www.tcia.org
Social Media: Facebook, Twitter, LinkedIn, Youtube

Mark Garvin, Interim CEO/President
Peter Gerstenberger, Sr Adv Safety/Standards/Compliance
Frequency: Monthly
Founded in: 1938

16173 Two-By-Four
Mountain States Lumber & Building Material Dealers
9034 E Easter Pl
#103
Centennial, CO 80112-2104

303-793-0859
800-365-0919; *Fax:* 303-290-9137
contact@mslbmda.org; www.mslbmda.org

Geri Adams, Executive Director

16174 Wood Design Focus
Forest Products Society
2801 Marshall Court
Madison, WI 53705-2295

608-231-1361; *Fax:* 608-231-2152
info@forestprod.org; www.forestprod.org
Social Media: Facebook, Twitter

Paul Merrick, President
Patrice Tardif, President-Elect
Timothy M. Young, Vice President
Stefan Bergmann, Executive Vice President

Online publication providing a communications link between design professionals, educators, reserachers, building code officials, and manufacturers of engineered wood products through the publication of technical articles related to contemporary engineered wood construction.
Cost: $125.00
Frequency: Quarterly
Founded in: 1947

16175 Wood Machining News
Wood Machining Institute
PO Box 476
Berkeley, CA 94701

510-448-8363; *Fax:* 925-945-0947
szymani@woodmachining.com;
www.woodmachining.com

Ryszard Szymani, Editor
Ryszard Szymani, Director

Information on the latest technological advances in the field of wood machining, including sawing, planning and sanding operations as well as the production of veneers and chips.
Cost: $72.00
Frequency: Fortnightly
Circulation: 600
Founded in: 1984

Magazines & Journals

16176 AMD Millwork Magazine
Association of Millwork Distributors
10047 Robert Trent Jones Pkwy
Trinity, FL 34655-4649

727-372-3665
800-786-7274; *Fax:* 727-372-2879
marketing@amdweb.com; www.amdweb.com

Rosalie Leone, CEO

Digital news journal distributed to AMD members and industry professionals with an interest in the millwork industry. An inside look at the heartbeat of AMD and offers industry insights found nowhere else.
Frequency: Monthly

16177 American Forests
American Forests
734 15th Street NW
Suite 800
Washington, DC 20005

202-737-1944; *Fax:* 202-955-4588;
www.americanforests.org
Social Media: Facebook, Twitter

Deborah Gangloff, Executive Director
Lydia Scalettar, Art Director

Updates on forest management and environmental policy, as well as news on the programs and policies of the American Forests organization.
Cost: $25.00
Frequency: Quarterly
Circulation: 25000
Founded in: 1875

16178 American Forests Magazine
American Forests
734 15th Street NW
Suite 800
Washington, DC 20005

202-737-1944; www.americanforests.org
Social Media: Facebook, Twitter

Lynda Webster, Chair
Scott Steen, CEO

Topics covered include urban forestry methods and visiting champion trees, fighting invasive species and learning about the many incredible creatures that make their homes in forests.
Frequency: Bi-Annually
Founded in: 1990

16179 Crossties
Railway Tie Association
115 Commerce Dr
Suite C
Fayetteville, GA 30214-7335

770-460-5553; *Fax:* 770-460-5573
ties@rta.org; www.rta.org

Talty O'Connor, President/CEO

Highlights new products, industry news, and personnel changes.
Cost: $35.00
Circulation: 3000
Founded in: 1983

16180 Crow's Weekly Market Report
CC Crow Publications
3635 N Farragut St
Portland, OR 97217-5954

503-241-7382; *Fax:* 503-646-9971
info@chadcrowe.com; www.chadcrowe.com
Social Media: Facebook, Twitter, LinkedIn

Chad Crowe, President
Sam Sherrill, Editor

Tracks the wood and lumber industry, providing customers with accurate and timely pricing and analysis.
Cost: $285.00
Frequency: Weekly
Circulation: 2000
Founded in: 1921
Mailing list available for rent

16181 Custom Woodworking Business
Vance Publishing
400 Knightsbridge Parkway
Lincolnshire, IL 60069

847-342-2600
800-343-2016; *Fax:* 847-634-4374
industrialinfo@vancepublishing.com;
www.iswonline.com
Social Media: Facebook, Twitter, Youtube

William C Vance, CEO
Helen Kuhl, Editor
Harry Urban, VP Publishing
Bill Esler, Associate Publisher/Editor-in-Chief
Rich Christianson, Associate Publisher/Editor-at-Large
Founded in: 1937

16182 Design Solutions Magazine
Architectural Woodwork Institute
46179 Westlake Drive
Suite 120
Potomac Falls, VA 20165

571-323-3636; *Fax:* 571-323-3630
info@awinet.org; www.awinet.org

Judy Durham, Executive VP
Philip Duvic, Marketing Director
Kirsten Ingham, President

Featuring beautiful woodwork projects manufactured by members of the Architectural Woodwork Institute (AWI). Many other related publications, including woodworking quality standards used by woodwork manufacturers and design professionals.
Cost: $25.00
Frequency: Quarterly
Circulation: 27000

16183 Evergreen Magazine
Evergreen Foundations
PO Box 1290
Bigfork, MT 59911

406-837-0966; *Fax:* 406-258-0815
editor@evergreenmagazine.com;
www.evergreenmagazine.com
Social Media: Facebook

James D Petersen, Publisher

Focuses on issues and events impacting forestry, forest communities, and the forest product industry. Includes profiles of industry leaders and advocates.
Frequency: Bi-Monthly
Circulation: 100000

16184 Fine Woodworking
Taunton Press
63 South Main Street
PO Box 5506
Newtown, CT 06470-2355

203-426-8171
800-477-8727; *Fax:* 203-426-3434
fwads@taunton.com; www.taunton.com

James Chiavelli, Publisher
Richard West, Advertising Manager

Published since 1975, written by woodworkers for woodworkers regularly shows the finest work in wood being done today.
Cost: $34.95
120 Pages
Frequency: 7 Issues (1yr)
Circulation: 250000
Founded in: 1980
Printed in 4 colors on glossy stock

16185 Forest Industries
Miller Freeman Publications
600 Harrison Street
6th Fl
San Francisco, CA 94107

415-947-6000; *Fax:* 415-947-6055;
www.mfi.com

Directed to foresters, loggers and manufacturers.
Cost: $55.00
90 Pages
Frequency: Monthly

16186 Forest Landowner Magazine
Forest Landowners Association
900 Circle 75 Pkwy Se
Suite 205
Atlanta, GA 30339-3075

404-325-2954
800-325-2954; *Fax:* 404-325-2955
info@forestlandowners.com;
www.forestlandowners.com

Scott P Jones, Executive VP
Joy Moore, Circulation Director

Provides members with applied, practical and current forestry information written by the most experienced and successful forestry professionals.
Cost: $50.00
Circulation: 9000
Founded in: 1941

16187 Forest Products Journal
Forest Products Society
2801 Marshall Ct
Madison, WI 53705-2295

608-231-1361; *Fax:* 608-231-2152
info@forestprod.org; www.forestprod.org
Social Media: Facebook, Twitter, LinkedIn

Carol Lewis, VP

Covers the latest research and technology from every branch of the forest products industry.
Cost: $155.00
Founded in: 1945

16188 Forests and People
Louisiana Forestry Association
PO Drawer 5067
Alexandria, LA 71307

318-443-2558; *Fax:* 318-443-1713
jtompkins@laforestry.com;
www.laforestry.com
Social Media: Facebook, Twitter

Janet Tompkins, Editor
Mike Merritt, President
Buck Vandersteen, Executive Director
Karla Johnson, Admin. Assistant/Annual Meeting
Debbie Dodd, Membership/Tree Farm Magazine
Cost: $250.00
36 Pages
Frequency: Quarterly
Circulation: 5800
ISSN: 0015-7589
Founded in: 1947
Printed in 4 colors on glossy stock

16189 Frame Building News
National Frame Builders Association
4700 W. Lake Avenue
Glenview, IL 60025

785-843-2444
800-557-6957; *Fax:* 847-375-6495
info@nfba.org; www.nfba.org
Social Media: Facebook

John Fullerton, VP
Tom Knight, President

The official publication of National Frame Builders Association.

16190 Great Lakes TPA Magazine
Great Lakes Timber Professionals Association
3243 Golf Course Road
PO Box 1278
Rhinelander, WI 54501-1278

715-282-5828; *Fax:* 715-282-4941
info@timberpa.com; www.timberpa.com

Henry Schienebeck, Executive Director & Editor

The magazine provides education and information on the practice and promotion of sustainable forestry and seeks to instill a sense of pride and professionalism among manufacturers, operators, transporters, landowners, and foresters.
Cost: $24.00
Frequency: Monthly
Circulation: 2500

16191 Hardwood Floors
National Wood Flooring Association
111 Chesterfield Industrial
Chesterfield, MO 63005-1219

636-519-9663
800-422-4556; *Fax:* 636-519-9664
info@nwfa.org; www.nwfa.org

Ed Korczak, Executive Director

An essential educational tool, with articles on everything from sanding and finishing techniques to industry trends and tips on running a profitable business.
Frequency: 6x/Year
Circulation: 25000

16192 International Journal of Forest Engineering
Forest Products Society
2801 Marshall Court
Madison, WI 53705-2295

608-231-1361; *Fax:* 608-231-2152
info@forestprod.org; www.forestprod.org
Social Media: Facebook, Twitter

Paul Merrick, President
Patrice Tardif, President-Elect
Timothy M. Young, Vice President
Stefan Bergmann, Executive Vice President

Committed to serving the international forest engineering community as the voice of new ideas and developments in forest engineering. Reporting on existing practices and innovations in forest engineering by scientists and professionals from around the world which promote environmentally sound forestry practices and contribute to sustainable forest management.
Frequency: Semiannually
Founded in: 1947

16193 International Wood: The Guide to Applications, Sources & Trends
International Wood Products Association
4214 King St
Alexandria, VA 22302-1555

703-820-6696; *Fax:* 703-820-8550
info@iwpawood.org; www.iwpawood.org

Brent McClendon, Executive VP/CAE
Annette Ferri, Member Services
Brigid Shea, Government Affairs
Annette Ferri, Director, Finance & Administration
Ashley A. Amidon, Manager, Government

Formerly Imported Wood, International Wood continues to lead with innovative new designs and new product applications.
Frequency: Annual
Circulation: 25000

16194 Journal of Forestry
Society of American Foresters
5400 Grosvenor Ln
Bethesda, MD 20814-2198

301-897-8720; *Fax:* 301-897-3690;
www.safnet.org

Michael T Goergen Jr, Executive VP/CEO
Matthew Walls, Publications Dir/Managing Editor

To advance the profession of forestry by keeping professionals informed about significant developments and ideas in the many facets of forestry: economics, education and communication, entomology and pathology, fire, forest ecology, geospatial technologies, history, international forestry, measurments, policy, recreation, silviculture, social sciences, soils anf hydrology, urban and community forestry, utilization and engineering, and wildlife management.
Cost: $85.00
Frequency: 8 Times
ISSN: 0022-1201
Founded in: 1902
Printed in 4 colors on glossy stock

16195 Loggers' World
Loggers World Publications
4206 Jackson Hwy
Chehalis, WA 98532-8425

360-262-3376
800-462-8283; *Fax:* 360-262-3337
logworld@aol.com; www.loggersworld.com

Mike Crouse, Publisher
Kevin Core, Advertising Manager
Finley Hays, Editor
Darin Burt, Writer

Accepts advertising.
Cost: $12.00
56 Pages
Frequency: Monthly
Circulation: 16,000
Founded in: 1966

16196 Logging & Sawmilling Journal
Logging & Sawmilling Journal
Po Box 86670
Vancouver, BC V7L-4L2

604-990-9970; *Fax:* 604-990-9971
stanhope@forestnet.com; www.forestnet.com
Social Media: Facebook

Rob Stanhope, Publisher
Lil Fawcus, Production Manager
Mailing list available for rent

16197 Lumber Cooperator
Northeastern Retail Lumber Association
585 N Greenbush Rd
Rensselaer, NY 12144-9615

518-286-1010
800-292-6752; *Fax:* 518-286-1755
rferris@nrla.org; www.nrla.org

Rita Ferris, President

Includes the latest industry, legislative and regulatory news, as well as issues and trends that most influence the lumber and building materials business. Readers gain insight into the newest methods, management techniques, new product ideas, family owned business concerns and key industry issues.
Cost: $40.00
100 Pages
Circulation: 5000
Founded in: 1894

16198 Lumberman's Equipment Digest
Lumbermen Online
PO Box 1146
Columbia, TN 38401

931-381-1638
800-477-7606; *Fax:* 931-388-3564
publisher@lumbermenonline.com;
www.lumbermenonline.com

Brady Carr, Publisher
Tammy Coffman, Advertising Manager
Shana Hibdon, Internet Technical Support
Gina High, Graphics Department
Cost: $38.00
Frequency: Monthly
Circulation: 35,000

16199 Millwork Magazine
Association of Millwork Distributors
10047 Robert Trent Jones Pkwy
New Port Richey, FL 34655-4649

727-372-3665
800-786-7274; *Fax:* 727-372-2879;
www.amdweb.com
Social Media: Twitter, LinkedIn

Rosalie Leone, CEO/ Secretary
Dan Barber, President
John Crowder, 1st VP
Mark Hefley, Associate VP
George Kessel, Treasurer

Articles of interest to AMD members.
1200 Members
Frequency: Monthly
Founded in: 1935

16200 Modern Woodworking
Modern Woodworking
90 West Afton Ave. #117
Yardley, PA 19067

267-519-1705
800-633-5953; *Fax:* 205-391-2081
Admin@tccmedia.com;
www.farmhausmodern.com

Brooke Wisdom, Executive Editor
W.W. Chip Wisdom, VP/Group Publisher
Mailing list available for rent

16201 National Hardwood Magazine
Miller Publishing Company
PO Box 34908
Memphis, TN 38184-0908

901-372-8280
800-844-1280; *Fax:* 901-373-6180
editor@millerwoodtradepub.com;
www.millerpublishing.com

Paul J Miller, President
Wayne Miller, VP
Sue Putnam, Editor

A monthly journal serving the hardwood industry including sawmillls, distillation, lumber yards, wholesalers and buyers and woodworkers.
Cost: $45.00
85 Pages
Frequency: Monthly
Circulation: 5000
Founded in: 1927
Printed in 4 colors on glossy stock

16202 Northern Journal of Applied Forestry
Society of American Foresters
5400 Grosvenor Ln
Bethesda, MD 20814-2198

301-897-8720
866-897-8720; *Fax:* 301-897-3690;
www.safnet.org
Social Media: Facebook, Twitter, LinkedIn

Matthew Walls, Publications Dir/Managing Editor
Kim C Steiner, Editor

Each regional journal of applies forestry focuses on research, practice, and techniques targeted to foresters and allied professionals in specific regions of the United States and Canada. This journal covers northeastern, midwestern, and boreal forests in the United States and Canada.
Cost: $75.00
Frequency: 4 Times
ISSN: 0742-6348

16203 Pallet Enterprise
Industrial Reporting
10244 Timber Ridge Dr
Ashland, VA 23005-8135

804-550-0323
800-805-0263; *Fax:* 804-550-2181
ed@ireporting.com; www.palletenterprise.com

Edward C Brindley Jr, Publisher
Chris Edwards, Production Manager
Chaille Brindley, Assistant Publisher
Scott Brindley, Marketing Director
Laura Seal, Circulation Manager

Written for those who manufacture, repair, sell or use wooden pallets and containers. Regular features include a market column, new products section and industry events.
Cost: $60.00
104 Pages
Frequency: Monthly
Circulation: 15000
Founded in: 1981
Printed in 4 colors on glossy stock

16204 PalletCentral
National Wooden Pallet & Container Association

1421 Prince Street
Suite 340
Alexandria, VA 22314-2805

703-519-6104; *Fax:* 703-519-4720;
www.nwpca.com

John T. Swenby, Chair
James Ruder, Chair-Elect
James Schwab, Secretary/ Treasurer
Bruce N. Scholnick, President

The technical journal for the solid wood packaging industry published by the NWPCA. First with essential news and innovations affecting wood packaging companies, going beyond reporting to provide useful analysis and strategies for coping with industry changes.
700+ Members
Frequency: Montly
Circulation: 6000
Founded in: 1947

16205 **Panel World**
Hatton-Brown Publishers
225 Hanrick Street(36104)
PO Box 2268
Montgomery, AL 36102-3317

334-834-1170
800-669-5613; *Fax:* 334-834-4525
mail@hattonbrown.com;
www.hattonbrown.com

Rich Donnell, Editor
Rhonda Thomas, Circulation Manager
Dan Shell, Managing Editor
Jennifer McCary, Associate Editor
Tonya Cooner, Associate Editor

For people who deal with production, sales, marketing, distribution, fabrication and utilization of veneer, plywood and other panel products.
Cost: $40.00
Circulation: 12850
Founded in: 1948
Printed in 4 colors on matte stock

16206 **Popular Woodworking**
F And W Publications
10151 Carver Road, Suite # 200
Blue Ash, OH 45242

513-531-2690; *Fax:* 513-531-1843
publicity@fwmedia.com;
www.fwpublications.com

David Nussbaum, CEO
Don Schroder, Ad Manager

Everything woodworkers need to develop their skills; in-depth tool reviews and tests, shop tips, finishing secrets, projects and more.
Cost: $28.00
104 Pages
Frequency: Monthly
Circulation: 240151
Founded in: 1981

16207 **Rural Builder**
F And W Publications
10151 Carver Road, Suite # 200
Blue Ash, OH 45242

513-531-2690; *Fax:* 715-445-4087
publicity@fwmedia.com;
www.fwpublications.com

Steve Shanesy, Publisher
Don Schroder, Advertising Manager

16208 **Southern Loggin' Times**
Hatton-Brown Publishers
PO Box 2268
Montgomery, AL 36102-2268

334-834-1170
800-669-5613; *Fax:* 334-834-4525
mail@hattonbrown.com;
www.hattonbrown.com

David H Ramsey, President
Rich Donnell, Editor

Monitors the south's forest products industry.
Cost: $65.00
Frequency: Monthly
Circulation: 13,408
ISSN: 0744-2106
Founded in: 1948
Printed in 4 colors on glossy stock

16209 **Southern Lumberman**
Hatton-Brown Publishers
PO Box 2268
Montgomery, AL 36102-2268

334-834-1170
800-669-5613; *Fax:* 334-834-4525
mail@hattonbrown.com;
www.hattonbrown.com

David H Ramsey, President
Rich Donnell, Editor

Industry news for sawmill operators and dimension manufacturers.
Cost: $21.00
60 Pages
Frequency: Monthly
Circulation: 13500

16210 **Southern Pine Inspection Bureau Magazine**
Southern Pine Inspection Bureau
PO Box 10915
Pensacola, FL 32524-0915

850-434-2611; *Fax:* 850-433-5594
spib@spib.org; www.spib.org

James Loy, President
Tom Jones, Executive Director
Founded in: 1940
Mailing list available for rent

16211 **Timber Harvesting**
Hatton-Brown Publishers
225 Hanrick Street (36104)
PO Box 2268
Montgomery, AL 36102-3317

334-834-1170
800-669-5613; *Fax:* 334-834-4525
mail@hattonbrown.com;
www.hattonbrown.com

Dave Ramsey, Co-Publisher
D K Knight, Co-Publisher
Rich Donnell, Editor

News and methods reported that are of particular interest to loggers.
Cost: $40.00
Frequency: Monthly
Circulation: 20130
ISSN: 0160-6433
Founded in: 1953
Printed in 4 colors on matte stock

16212 **Timber Processing**
Hatton-Brown Publishers
225 Hanrick Street
PO Box 2268
Montgomery, AL 36102

334-834-1170
800-669-5613; *Fax:* 334-834-4525
rich@hattonbrown.com;
www.hattonbrown.com

David H Ramsey, Co-Publisher
Rich Donnell, Editor-in-Chief
Dan Shell, Managing Editor

Timber Processing serves sawmill/chipmill operations; consultants in mill and processing operations; machinery manufacturers, dealers and distributors, others allied to the field.
Cost: $40.00
44 Pages
Circulation: 20780
ISSN: 0885-906X
Founded in: 1948
Printed in 4 colors on glossy stock

16213 **Timber West Journal**
Logging & Sawmilling Journal
Po Box 86670
Vancouver, BC V7L-4L2

604-990-9970
866-221-1017; *Fax:* 604-990-9971
timberwest@forestnet.com;
www.forestnet.com/timberwest
Social Media: Facebook

Sheila Ringdahl, Publisher
Diane Mettler, Managing Editor

Packed with valuable and useful stories on successful mechanized harvesting and wood processing techniques and equipment, special editorial features, plus timely information on legislation, industry news, annual events, and people and products pertinent to America's largest forestry market.
Cost: $20.00
48 Pages
Circulation: 10500
ISSN: 0192-0642
Founded in: 1975
Mailing list available for rent
Printed in 4 colors

16214 **Timberline**
Industrial Reporting
10244 Timber Ridge Dr
Ashland, VA 23005-8135

804-550-0323; *Fax:* 804-550-2181
editor@ireporting.com;
www.palletenterprise.com

Edward C Brindley Jr, Publisher
Tim Cox, Editor
Laura Seal, Circulation

Highlights sawmill, logging, and pallet interests including environmental issues, new machinery and technologies that impact the industry.
52 Pages
Frequency: Monthly
Circulation: 30000
Founded in: 1994
Mailing list available for rent: 28,000 names at $250 per M
Printed in 4 colors on newsprint stock

16215 **Tree Care Industry**
Tree Care Industry Association
136 Harvey Road
Suite 101
Londonderry, NH 03053

603-314-5380
800-733-2622; *Fax:* 603-314-5386
tcia@tcia.org; www.tcia.org
Social Media: Facebook, Twitter, LinkedIn, Youtube

Mark Garvin, Interim CEO/President
Peter Gerstenberger, Sr Adv Safety/Compliance/Standards

Informative articles on tree care issues, leading advertisers, and industry almanac, and cutting edge product news combine to make TCI Magazine a must-read for tree workers, tree care company owners, and anyone who wants a fresh, insightful look at the industry
Founded in: 1938

16216 **Tree Farmer Magazine, the Guide to Sustaining America's Family Forests**
American Forest Foundation
1111 19th St NW
Suite 780
Washington, DC 20036

202-463-2462; *Fax:* 202-463-2461
info@forestfoundation.org;
www.forestfoundation.org
Social Media: Facebook, Twitter, YouTube

Tom Martin, President & CEO
Brigitte Johnson APR, Director Communications, Editor

The official magazine of ATFS, this periodical provides practical, how-to and hands-on information and techniques, and services to help private fore landowners to become better stewards, save money and time, and add to the enjoyment of their land.

16217 **Wood Digest**
Cygnus Publishing
1233 Janesville Avenue
Fort Atkinson, WI 53538-0803

920-000-1111
800-547-7377; *Fax:* 920-563-1699
info@cygnus.com; www.cygnus.com

John French, CEO
John Anfderhaar, Associate Publisher
Paul Bowers, President
Jay Schneider, Publisher

Trade magazine, Accepts advertising.
64 Pages
Frequency: Monthly
Circulation: 51000
Founded in: 1965

16218 **Wood Finisher**
7616 Banning Way
Inver Grove Heights, MN 55077-5819
Mitchell Kohansek, Editor

Wood finishing information.
Cost: $10.00
20 Pages
Frequency: Monthly
Founded in: 1981

16219 **Wood and Fiber Science**
Society of Wood Science & Technology
PO Box 6155
Monona, WI 53716-6155

608-577-1342; *Fax:* 608-467-8979
vicki@swst.org; www.swst.org
Social Media: Facebook

Victoria Herian, Executive Director
James Funck, President Elect

Publishes papers with both professional and technical content. Original papers of professional concer, or based on research dealing with the science, processing, and manufacture of wood and composite products of wood or wood fiber origin are considered for publication. All papers are peer-reviewed and must be unpublished research not offered for publication elsewhere.
Cost: $250.00
Frequency: Quarterly
Circulation: 950
ISSN: 0735-6161
Founded in: 1958

16220 **Wood and Wood Products**
Vance Publishing
400 Knightsbridge Pkwy
Lincolnshire, IL 60069

847-634-2600; *Fax:* 847-634-4379
info@vancepublishing.com;
www.vancepublishing.com

William C Vance, Chairman
Peggy Walker, Wood & Wood Products

Leading woodworking industry publication for solid wood and panel technology.
140 Pages
Frequency: Monthly
Circulation: 48000
ISSN: 0043-7662
Founded in: 1937

16221 **World Wood Review**
Widman Publishing
601 West Broadway
Suite 400
Vancouver, BC V5Z 4C2

604-675-6923; *Fax:* 604-675-6924
tlhaugen@widman.com; www.widman.com

Janice Widman, Chair
Jason Roth, Director / Editor
Tamara Haugen, Director / Editor
Dick Brown, Associate Editor
Brian Haugen, Associate Editor

The premier newsletter serving the global wood products industry, with news of trends and developments in the solid wood and panel manufacturing sector.
Cost: $55.00
50 Pages
Frequency: Monthly

Trade Shows

16222 **AMD Annual Convention & Tradeshow**
Association of Millwork Distributors
10047 Robert Trent Jones Pkwy
Trinity, FL 34655-4649

727-372-3665
800-786-7274; *Fax:* 727-372-2879
marketing@amdweb.com; www.amdweb.com

Rosalie Leone, CEO

16223 **ATIC Annual Meeting**
7012 S Revere Parkway
Suite 140
Centennial, CO 80112

303-379-2955; www.aitc-glulam.org
Social Media: Facebook

R Michael Caldwell PE, Executive VP
Frequency: Annual
Founded in: 1952

16224 **American Forestry Association**
PO Box 2000
Washington, DC 20013-2000

202-955-4500

Billl Tikkala, Show Manager
Deborah Gangloff, Executive Director

30 booths of tree planting and care equipment.
1M Attendees
Frequency: November

16225 **Appalachian Hardwood Expo**
Mercer County Technical Education Center
105 Old Bluefield Road
Princeton, WV 24740-8901

304-425-4583

Linda Cox

100 tables.
2M Attendees
Frequency: June

16226 **Architectural Woodwork Institute Annual Convention**
46179 Westlake Drive
Suite 120
Potomac Falls, VA 20165

571-323-3636; *Fax:* 571-323-3630
info@awinet.org; www.awinet.org

Kimberly Haynes, Director Meetings & Conventions

Seminar, workshop and woodwork products such as casework, fixtures and panelings, equipment and supplies.

16227 **Forest Expo**
Prince George Regional Forest Exhibition Society
850 River Road
Prince George, BC V2L-5S8

250-563-8833; *Fax:* 250-563-3697;
www.cnre.ca

Trudy Swaan, General Manager

Provides a showcase to display the latest in new technology, equipment, supplies and services, as well as educate the forest sector and the general public about the importance of our forests.

16228 **Forest Products Machinery & Equipment Expo**
Southern Forest Products Association
2900 Indiana Avenue
Kenner, LA 70065

504-443-4464; *Fax:* 504-443-6612
mail@sfpa.org; www.sfpa.org

Digges Morgan, President
Richard Wallace, VP Communications
Tami Kessler, Corporate Secretary
Stephen P. Conwell, President
Tami Kessler, Corporate Secretary & Director

200+ exhibitors
3000 Attendees
Frequency: June, Biennial

16229 **Frame Building Expo**
National Frame Builders Association
4700 W. Lake Avenue
Glenview, IL 60025

785-843-2444
800-557-6957; *Fax:* 847-375-6495
info@nfba.org; www.nfba.org
Social Media: Facebook

John Fullerton, VP
Tom Knight, President

Containing 200 booths.
2000+ Attendees
Frequency: February

16230 **Greenbuild International Conference and Expo**
Engineered Wood Association
7011 S 19th Street
Tacoma, WA 98466-5333

253-565-6600; *Fax:* 253-565-7265
tanya.rosendahl@apawood.org;
www.apawood.org
Social Media: Facebook, Twitter

Tanya Rosendahl, Tradeshow Coordinator

16231 **HPVA Sping Conference**
Hardwood Plywood & Veneer
1825 Michael Faraday Dr
Reston, VA 20190-5350

703-435-2900; *Fax:* 703-435-2537
hpva@hpva.org; www.hpva.org

Clifford Howlett, President
Kip Howlett, HPVA President
Eva Mentel, Office Manager
Frequency: May

16232 **HPVA Winter Conference**
Hardwood Plywood & Veneer
1825 Michael Faraday Dr
Reston, VA 20190-5350

703-435-2900; *Fax:* 703-435-2537
hpva@hpva.org; www.hpva.org

Clifford Howlett, President
Kip Howlett, HPVA President
Eva Mentel, Office Manager
Frequency: November

16233 **Hardwood Manufacturers Association**
400 Penn Center Boulevard
Suite 530
Pittsburgh, PA 15235-5605
412-244-0440; *Fax:* 412-244-9090
Susan Regan, Executive VP
Offers 20 booths of sawmill and logging machinery and services.
300 Attendees
Frequency: March

16234 **IWPA Annual Convention**
International Wood Products Association
4214 King St
Alexandria, VA 22302-1555
703-820-6696; *Fax:* 703-820-8550
info@iwpawood.org; www.iwpawood.org
Brent McClendon, Executive VP/CAE
Annette Ferri, Member Services
Brigid Shea, Government Affairs
Annette Ferri, Director, Finance & Administration
Ashley A. Amidon, Manager, Government
The largest gethering solely dedicated to the North American imported wood products industry.
Frequency: April

16235 **International Woodworking Machinery and Furniture Supply Fair: USA**
Reed Exhibition Companies
1350 E Touhy Avenue
Des Plaines, IL 60018-3303
847-294-0300; *Fax:* 847-635-1571
Paul Pajor, National Marketing Manager
The largest woodworking machinery and furniture supply manufacturing exposition held in the Western Hemisphere. Exhibitors interface with North American furniture, cabinet, and woodworking manufacturers. One thousand booths.
37M Attendees
Frequency: August/Biennial

16236 **Lake States Logging Congress & Equipment Expo**
Great Lakes Timber Professionals Association
3243 Golf Course Road
PO Box 1278
Rhinelander, WI 54501-1278
715-282-5828; *Fax:* 715-282-4941
info@timberpa.com; www.timberpa.com
Henry Schienebeck, Executive Director & Editor
Held in either Michigan or Wisconsin, the Logging Congress is a 3-day expo that takes place during the Fall season throughout the Lake States region of the United States.
3500 Attendees
Founded in: 1945

16237 **Live Woods Show**
Pacific Logging Congress
PO Box 1281
Maple Valley, WA 98038
425-413-2808; *Fax:* 425-413-1359
rikki@pacificloggingcongress.com;
www.pacificloggingcongress.com
Rikki Wellman, Executive Director
Craig Olson, President
Ron Simon, Treasurer
3000+ Attendees
Frequency: September

16238 **Logging Congress Pacific**
2300 SW 6th Avenue
Suite 200
Portland, OR 97201-4915
Fax: 503-612-0344
Al Wilson, Executive Director
50 booths.
800 Attendees
Frequency: September

16239 **Lumbermen's Merchandising Conferences**
137 W Wayne Avenue
Wayne, PA 19087-4018
610-293-7000; *Fax:* 215-293-7098
Jack Reznor, Show Manager
Anthony Decarlo, President
325 booths.
1.6M Attendees
Frequency: March

16240 **MFMA Annual Conference**
Maple Flooring Manufacturers Association
111 Deer Lake Road
Suite 100
Deerfield, IL 60015
847-480-9138
888-480-9138; *Fax:* 847-480-9282
mcarson@maplefloor.org; www.maplefloor.org
Madhuri Carson, Conference Manager
Containing 50 booths.
300 Attendees
Frequency: Annual/March

16241 **NHLA Annual Convention & Exhibit Showcase North American Hardwood Lumber Indu**
National Hardwood Lumber Association
6830 Raleigh Lagrange Road
Memphis, TN 38184
901-377-1818; www.nhla.com
Lisa Browne, Convention Director
The premier networking opportunity for the Hardwood Industry. Provides attendees time for direct, personal contact with industry leaders and exhibitors, giving them from the opportunity to ask meaningful questions, view and compare products and services and strengthen business relationships.
Frequency: Annual

16242 **NWFA Wood Flooring Convention and Expo**
National Wood Flooring Association
111 Chesterfield Industrial Boulevard
Chesterfield, MO 63005
636-519-9663
800-422-4556; *Fax:* 636-519-9664;
www.nwfa.org
Michael Martin, CEO
The Wood Flooring Expo has become the international gathering place for wood flooring professionals: Manufacturers, Distributors, Dealer/Contractors, Inspectors, Installers, Import/Exporters, Architects & Designers of wood flooring.
2000 Attendees
Frequency: April

16243 **Northeastern Forest Products Equipment Expo**
Northeastern Loggers Association
3311 State Route 28 PO Box 69
Old Forge, NY 13420-0069
315-369-3078; *Fax:* 315-369-3736
nela@northernlogger.com
http://nefpexpo.net
Joseph Phaneuf, Show Manager
Annual expo on forest products equipment, suppliers, and services. Always listed as one of the top 100 shows in the U.S. with 200+ exhibitors and indoor/outdoor demonstrations.
6000 Attendees
Frequency: Annual/May

16244 **Northeastern Retail Lumber Association**
Northeastern Retail Lumber Association
585 N Greenbush Road
Rensselaer, NY 12144
518-286-1010
800-292-6752; *Fax:* 518-286-1755
rferris@nrla.org; www.nrla.org
Deborah Talar, Executive Assistant
Rita Ferris, President
500 booths or more of building materials and education relating to the lumber and building industry.
8M Attendees
Frequency: January

16245 **Northwestern Building Products Expo**
Northwestern Lumber Association
5905 Golden Valley Road
Suite 110
Minneapolis, MN 55422-4535
763-544-6822
888-544-6822; *Fax:* 763-595-4060
info@nlassn.org; www.nlassn.org
Sally Means, Director of Conventions
Jodie Fleck, Director of Conventions & Tours
Cody Nuernberg, Manager of Membership
Building material retailers and their contractors attend this trade show and conference for continuing education and cammeraderie
1200 Attendees
Frequency: Annual
Mailing list available for rent

16246 **Redwood Region Logging Conference California**
Redwood Region Logging Conference
5601 South Broadway Street
Eureka, CA 95503
707-443-4091; *Fax:* 707-443-0926;
www.rrlc.net/
Charles Benbow, Show Manager
100 booths of timber and forestry related products and services.
3M Attendees
Frequency: March

16247 **Retail Lumbermen's Association Northeast**
339 E Avenue
Rochester, NY 14604-2627
John Brill, Show Manager
681 booths of lumber and related services.
10M Attendees
Frequency: January

16248 **Sawmill Logging Equipment Expo East Coast**
220 E Williamsburg Road
PO Box 160
Sandston, VA 23150-0160
804-737-5625; *Fax:* 804-737-9437
info@exporichmond.com;
www.exporichmond.com
Mike Washko, Expo Manager
Logging and forestry production and distribution.
12M Attendees
Frequency: May

16249 **Southeastern Lumber Manufacturers Association**
Southeastern Lumber Manufacturers

200 Greencastle Road
Tyrone, GA 30290

770-631-6701; *Fax:* 770-631-6720;
www.slma.org/

Steve Roundtree, President
Bryan Smalley, President
Will Telligman, Government Affairs Manager
Beverly Knight, Accounting Manager

50 booths.
350 Attendees
Frequency: July

16250 Southern Forest Products Mid-Year Meeting
Southern Forest Products Association
2900 Indiana Avenue
Kenner, LA 70065

504-443-4464; *Fax:* 504-443-6612
mail@sfpa.org; www.sfpa.org

Digges Morgan, President
Richard Wallace, VP Communications
Tami Kessler, Corporate Secretary
Stephen P. Conwell, President
Tami Kessler, Corporate Secretary & Director

200+ exhibitors
3000 Attendees
Frequency: Annual

16251 Southern Forestry Conference
Forest Landowners Association
900 Circle 75 Pkwy Se
Suite 205
Atlanta, GA 30339-3075

404-325-2954
800-325-2954; *Fax:* 404-325-2955
info@forestlandowners.com;
www.forestlandowners.com

Lisa Newsome, Manager
Stacie Lewis, Managing Editor
Frequency: May
Founded in: 1941

16252 TCI Expo
Tree Care Industry Association
136 Harvey Road
Suite 101
Londonderry, NH 03053

603-314-5380
800-733-2622; *Fax:* 603-314-5386
tcia@tcia.org; www.tcia.org
Social Media: Facebook, Twitter, LinkedIn, Youtube

Mark Garvin, Interim CEO/President
Peter Gerstenberger, Sr Adv Safety/Compliance/Standards
3500 Attendees
Frequency: Annual
Founded in: 1938

16253 World of Wood Annual Convention
International Wood Products Association
4214 King Street W
Alexandria, VA 22302-1507

703-820-6696; *Fax:* 703-820-8550
info@iwpawood.org; www.iwpawood.org

Brent J McClendon, Executive VP/CAE
Annette Ferri, Member Services
Brigid Shea, Government Affairs
Annette Ferri, Director, Finance & Administration
Ashley A. Amidon, Manager, Government

A gethering for imported wood products industry importers, distributers, manufacturers, offshore suppliers and service providers.
220 Attendees
Frequency: Annual/Spring

Directories & Databases

16254 Cedar Shake and Shingle Bureau Membership Directory/Buyer's Guide
Cedar Shake & Shingle Bureau
PO Box 1178
Sumas, WA 98295-1178

604-820-7700; *Fax:* 604-820-0266
info@cedarbureau.com; www.cedarbureau.org

Lynne Christensen, Director of Operations
Barb Enns, Accountant
Dave Mooney, Cedar Quality Auditor
Sharron Beauregard, Accounting Assistant
Suzie Quigley, Customer Service Representative

About 102 member manufacturing mills in the Pacific Northwest and British Columbia, Canada; approximately 163 affiliated roofing applicators, builders, architects, remodelers and suppliers of related products and services.
Cost: $17.00
Frequency: SemiAnnual
Circulation: 450

16255 Dimension & Wood Components Buyer's Guide
Miller Publishing Corporation
Po Box 34908
Memphis, TN 38184-0908

901-372-8280
800-844-1280; *Fax:* 901-373-6180
editor@millerwoodtradepub.com;
www.millerpublishing.com

Paul J Miller, President
Sue Putnam, Editor

Instant access to manufacturers of furniture parts, mouldings, cabinet doors, stair parts, flooring, turnings, paneling, door parts, window parts, edge glued panels, etc. Gives the information on who to contact, firm name and address, phone number, fax number, number of employees, products manufactured, species of wood used, machining capabilities and marketing areas served.
Cost: $350.00

16256 Forest Products Export Directory
Miller Publishing Corporation
Po Box 34908
Memphis, TN 38184-0908

901-372-8280
800-844-1280; *Fax:* 901-373-6180
editor@millerwoodtradepub.com;
www.millerpublishing.com

Paul J Miller, President
Sue Putnam, Editor

The only directory published listing all the major exporters of North American forest products. Edited to help the oversease buyer find reliable suppliers for the wide variety of Softwood and Hardwood forest products available in North America.
Cost: $175.00

16257 Forest Products Research Society Membership Directory
2801 Marshall Ct
Madison, WI 53705-2295

608-231-1361; *Fax:* 608-231-2152
info@forestprod.org; www.forestprod.org

Carol Lewis, VP
Stefan A. Bergmann, Executive Vice President
Joe Gravunder, Publications Manager
Cost: $125.00
1900 Pages
Frequency: 10 Per Year
Circulation: 3500
Founded in: 1947

16258 Gebbie Press: All-In-One Media Directory
Gebbie Press
Po Box 1000
New Paltz, NY 12561

845-255-7560; *Fax:* 888-345-2790;
www.gebbieinc.com
Social Media: Facebook, Twitter, LinkedIn

Mark Gebbie, Associate Editor
Founded in: 1955

16259 Green Book's Hardwood Marketing Directory
Miller Publishing Corporation
Po Box 34908
Memphis, TN 38184-0908

901-372-8280
800-844-1280; *Fax:* 901-373-6180
editor@millerwoodtradepub.com;
www.millerpublishing.com

Paul J Miller, President
Sue Putnam, Editor

A sales booster that lists over 7,900 woodworking plants' Hardwood lumber and other Hardwood forest products purchasing needs. Gives up-to-date, documented facts on species, grades, thicknesses and quantities purchased by each plant annually in the U.S. and Canada.
Cost: $1200.00

16260 Green Book's Softwood Marketing Directory
Miller Publishing Corporation
Po Box 34908
Memphis, TN 38184-0908

901-372-8280
800-844-1280; *Fax:* 901-373-6180
editor@millerwoodtradepub.com;
www.millerpublishing.com

Paul J Miller, President
Sue Putnam, Editor

Instant access to over 5,000 woodworking and industrial plants' Softwood lumber purchasing needs with complete, up-to-date, documented facts on species, grades, thicknesses, and quantities of Softwood lumber and other Softwood forest products bought regularly.
Cost: $900.00

16261 Hardwood Manufacturers Association: Membership Directory
Hardwood Manufacturers Association
665 Rodi Road
Suite 305
Pittsburgh, PA 15235

412-244-0440
800-373-9663; *Fax:* 412-244-9090;
www.hardwoodinfo.com

Susan Regan, Executive VP

Over 100 companies with over 160 locations in the US.
Frequency: Annual December

16262 Hardwood Purchasing Handbook
Miller Publishing Corporation
Po Box 34908
Memphis, TN 38184-0908

901-372-8280
800-844-1280; *Fax:* 907-373-6180
editor@millerwoodtradepub.com;
www.millerpublishing.com

Paul J Miller, President
Sue Putnam, Editor

An easy-to-use digest size directory that has all the major Hardwood suppliers in the U.S.A. and Canada of Hardwood lumber, plywood, veneers, etc. Up-to-date sections describe Hardwood sawmills, wholesalers, distribution yards, etc. Com-

plete mailing addresses, phone numbers, fax numbers, email addresses, names of sales agents, main Hardwood species handled, specialty items listed and information on production facilities and shipping methods are given.
Cost: $175.00

16263 Imported Wood Purchasing Guide
Miller Publishing Corporation
Po Box 34908
Memphis, TN 38184-0908

901-372-8280
800-844-1280; *Fax:* 901-373-6180
editor@millerwoodtradepub.com;
www.millerpublishing.com

Paul J Miller, President
Sue Putnam, Editor

A wide variety of imported suppliers of lumber, mouldings, veneers, wall paneling, furniture components, flooring, plywood, hardboard, doorskins, millwork, etc.
Cost: $175.00

16264 Imported Wood: Guide To Applications, Sources and Trends
International Wood Products Association
4214 King St
Alexandria, VA 22302-1555

703-820-6696; *Fax:* 703-820-8550
info@iwpawood.org; www.iwpawood.org
Social Media: Facebook, Twitter, LinkedIn

Brent McClendon, Executive VP/CAE
Annette Ferri, Member Services
Brigid Shea, Government Affairs

An annual magazine featuring imported woods in applications, sustainable Forest Management issues and listing of IWPA members.
84 Pages
Frequency: Annual
Circulation: 15,000

16265 International Green Front Report
Friends of the Trees
PO Box 1064
Tonasket, WA 98855-1064
Fax: 509-485-2705
michael@friendsofthetrees.net

Michael Pilarski, Editor

Organizations and periodicals concerned with sustainable forestry and agriculture and related fields.
Cost: $7.00
Frequency: Irregular

16266 Lumbermen's Red Book
Lumbermens Credit Association
20 N Wacker Drive
Suite 1800
Chicago, IL 60606-2905

312-553-0943; *Fax:* 312-533-1842;
www.lumbermanscredit.com

PD McLaughlin, Editor

Approximately 39,000 manufacturers and distributors of lumber and wood products in the US and Canada.
Cost: $1780.00
Frequency: SemiAnnual

16267 North American Forest Products Export Directory
International Wood Trade Publications
1235 Sycamore View Road
Memphis, TN 38134-7646

901-752-1246; *Fax:* 901-373-6180

Producers, exporters, agents, etc. of lumber, plywood, etc. in the US and Canada.
Cost: $150.00
Frequency: Annual August
Circulation: 10,000

16268 Northeastern Retail Lumber Association Buyer's Guide
Northeastern Retail Lumber Association
585 N Greenbush Rd
Rensselaer, NY 12144-9615

518-286-1010
800-292-6752; *Fax:* 518-286-1755
rferris@nrla.org; www.nrla.org

Rita Ferris, President

Offers information on over 2,000 retail dealers in lumber and forest products located in the Northeastern states of the US.
Cost: $125.00
225 Pages
Frequency: Annual
ISSN: 0024-7294

16269 Random Lengths Big Book: Buyers' & Sellers' Directory of the Forest
Random Lengths Publications
PO Box 867
Eugene, OR 97440-0867

541-869-9925
888-686-9925; *Fax:* 800-874-7979
rlmail@rlpi.com; www.randomlengths.com

Dave Evans, Editor
Terri Richards, Editor

About 7,500 companies, consultants and associations involved in the softwood forest product industry in the US and Canada, including sawmills, treating plants, manufacturers of panels and specialty products, wholesalers and secondary manufacturers.
Cost: $188.00
Frequency: Annual February
Circulation: 2,200

16270 Rauch Guide to the US and Canadian Pulp & Paper Industry
Grey House Publishing
4919 Route 22
PO Box 56
Amenia, NY 12501

518-789-8700
800-562-2139; *Fax:* 845-373-6390
books@greyhouse.com; www.greyhouse.com
Social Media: Facebook, Twitter

Leslie Mackenzie, Publisher
Richard Gottlieb, Editor

Provides current market information and trends; industry economics and government regulations; company share data for each of the leading product categories; technology and raw material information; industry sources of further data; and unique profiles of 500+ pulp and paper manufacturers, a section which includes all known companies with pulp and paper sales at or over $15 million annually.
Cost: $595.00
400 Pages
ISBN: 1-592371-31-0
Founded in: 1981

16271 Timber Harvesting: Logger's Resource Guide
Hatton-Brown Publishers
Po Box 2268
Montgomery, AL 36102-2268

334-834-1170
800-669-5613; *Fax:* 334-834-4525
mail@hattonbrown.com;
www.hattonbrown.com

David H Ramsey, President
Rich Donnell, Editor
Cost: $20.00
88 Pages
Frequency: Annually, January
Circulation: 20,179
ISSN: 0160-6433
Printed in on glossy stock

16272 Where to Buy Hardwood Plywood, Veneer & Engineered Hardwood Flooring
Hardwood Plywood and Veneer Association
1825 Michael Faraday Drive
Reston, VA 20190-5350

703-435-2900; *Fax:* 703-435-2537
hpva@hpva.org; www.hpva.org

Kip Howlett, President
Eva Mentel, Office Manager
Ketti Tyree, Membership & Conventions Manager

The definitive annual guide to the species and products sold by HPVA members.
120 Pages
Frequency: Annual
Founded in: 1921

16273 Wood & Wood Products: Laminating Users Guide Issue
Louisiana Municipal Association
700 North 10th street
Baton Rouge, LA 70802

225-344-5001
800-234-8274; *Fax:* 225-344-3057;
www.lma.org

George Carter, Editor

List of approximately 100 manufacturers and importers of decorative overlays, wood substrates, adhesives, laminating equipment and laminated products.
Frequency: Annual June

16274 Wood Components Buyer's Guide
Wood Component Manufacturers Association
741 Butlers Gate NE
Suite 100
Marietta, GA 30068-4207

770-565-6660; *Fax:* 770-565-6663
wcma@woodcomponents.org;
www.woodcomponents.org

Steven V Lawser, Executive Director

Over 150 member manufacturers of wood components.
Cost: $5.00
Frequency: Annual Summer

16275 Wood Technology: Buyers' Guide Issue
Miller Freeman Publications
600 Harrison Street
Suite 400
San Francisco, CA 94107-1391

800-227-4675; *Fax:* 415-905-2630;
www.woodtechmag.com

David A Pease, Editorial Director

Companies supplying machinery, tools and other equipment to manufacturers of wood products worldwide.
Frequency: Annual

16276 Wood and Wood Products: Red Book Issue
Vance Publishing
400 Knightsbridge Parkway
Lincolnshire, IL 60069

847-634-2600; *Fax:* 847-634-4379;
www.vancepublishing.com

William C Vance, Chairman
Peggy Walker, President

Annual directory that is the editorial and advertising leader for the woodworking industry. Listings and specifications of more than 3,000 industry suppliers.
Cost: $40.00
Frequency: Annual
Circulation: 50,000

Industry Web Sites

16277 **http://gold.greyhouse.com**
G.O.L.D Grey House OnLine Databases
Grey House Publishing's online database platform, GOLD, offers Quick Search, Keyword Search and Expert Search for most business sectors including lumber and wood markets. The GOLD platform makes finding the information you need quick and easy - whether you're a novice searcher or an experienced database user. All of Grey House's directory products are available for subscription on the GOLD platform.

16278 **www.afandpa.org**
American Forest and Paper Association
Represents member companies and related trade associations which grow, harvest and process wood and wood fiber, manufacture pulp, paper and paperboard products from both virgin and recovered fiber and produce solid wood products.

16279 **www.afma4u.org**
American Furniture Manufacturers Association
Provides a uniform voice in the furniture industry.

16280 **www.aitc-glulam.org**
American Institute of Timber Construction
The national trade association of the structural glued laminiated (glulam) timber industry.

16281 **www.alsc.org**
American Lumber Standard Committee

16282 **www.amdweb.com**
Association of Millwork Distributors
Provides leadership, certification, education, promotion, networking and advocacy to, and for, the millwork distribution industry.

16283 **www.apawood.org**
Engineered Wood Association
A nonprofit trade association that represents US and Canadian manufacturers of structural engineered wood products, including plywood, oriented strand board (OSB), glued-laminated timber (glulam), wood i-joists and structural composite lumber.

16284 **www.bearcreeklumber.com**
Bear Creek Lumber
Publishes a newsletter called the Timberline.

16285 **www.big-creek.com**
Big Creek
Produces a newspaper

16286 **www.calredwood.org**
California Redwood Association
Authorized by Department of Commerce to develop and supervise redwood lumber grading.

16287 **www.capital-lumber.com**
Capital Lumber Company
Dedicated to being the leading distributor of materials in the Western United States.

16288 **www.construction.com**
McGraw-Hill Construction
McGraw-Hill Construction (MHC), part of The McGraw-Hill Companies, connects people and projects across the design and construction industry, serving owners, architects, engineers, general contractors, subcontractors, building product manufacturers, suppliers, dealers, distributors and adjacent markets.

16289 **www.fiberboard.org**
American Fiberboard Association
The national trade organization of manufacturers of cellulosic fiberboard products used for residential and commercial construction.

16290 **www.forestinfo.org**
Temperate Forest Foundation
Source for information which is understandable, unbiased, fast, accurate, and available in a wide variety of formats.

16291 **www.forestnet.com**
Logging & Sawmilling Journal
A journal that provides information on logginf and sawmilling.

16292 **www.forestprod.org**
Forest Products Society
Focus is on the development and research of information for the wood industry.

16293 **www.fpl.fs.fed.us/swst**
Society of Wood Science & Technology
Promotes policies and procedures which assure the wise use of wood and wood-based products; assures high standards for professional performance of wood scientists and technologists; foster educational programs at all levels of wood science and technolgoy and further the quality of such programs; represents the profession in public policy development.

16294 **www.gebbieinc.com**
Gebbie Press
A directory with all information that is needed for the lumber industry.

16295 **www.greyhouse.com**
Grey House Publishing
Authoritative reference directories for most business sectors including lumber and wood markets. Users can search the online databases with varied search criteria allowing for custom searches by product category, geographic area, sales volume, keyword, subject and more. Full Grey House catalog and online ordering also available.

16296 **www.hardboard.org**
American Hardboard Association
Represents major United States producers of hardwood.

16297 **www.hlma.org**
Pennsylvania Forest Products Association
Represents the state's entire forest products industry, including foresters, loggers, sawmills, and value-added processors.

16298 **www.iwpawood.org**
International Wood Products Association
International trade association representing companies handling imported wood products of all types.

16299 **www.lma.org**
Laminating Materials Association
Nonprofit trade group representing manufacturers and importers of decorative overlays, wood substrates, adhesives, laminating equipment and laminated products.

16300 **www.loggertraining.com**
A reference site for loggers in their pursuit of training programs where they work and live. Maintained by Northeastern Loggers' Association.

16301 **www.lumber.org**
North American Wholesale Lumber Association
NAWLA Bulletin is published monthly and includes industry and association news. The Association also produces the NAWLA Traders Market, an annual trade show bringing together over 2000 manufacturer and wholesale lumber traders at the premier event in the forest products industry. NAWLA also produces a variety of educational programs designed to enhance professionalism in the lumber industry.

16302 **www.maplefloor.org**
Maple Flooring Manufacturers Association
For manufacturers of northern hard maple solid strip flooring along with flooring contractors, distributors and providers of instalation-related products and services. Maintains technical standards for product quality, grading, shipping and packaging, and quality central.

16303 **www.millerpublishing.com**
Miller Publishing Corporation
Publishes many newspapers, magazines, and directories.

16304 **www.mslbmda.org**
Mountain States Lumber & Building Materials Dealer

16305 **www.nari.org**
National Association of the Remodeling Industry
Establishes and maintains a firm commitment to developing and sustaining programs that expand and unite the remodeling industry.

16306 **www.nlassn.org**
Northwestern Lumber Association
Retail lumber dealers in Iowa, Minnesota, North Dakota, and South Dakota.

16307 **www.nofma.org**
National Oak Flooring Manufacturers Association
Formulates and administers industry standards on hardwood floorings, inspection service, and semiannual Hardwood Flooring installation school.

16308 **www.nsdja.com**
National Sash and Door Jobbers Association
For wholesale millwork distribution companies.

16309 **www.nwfa.org**
National Wood Flooring Association
A not-for-profit trade association serving the wood flooring industry

16310 **www.nwpca.com**
National Wooden Pallet & Container Association
Represents wood and pallet container organizations.

16311 **www.osbguide.com**
Structural Board Association
Members are manufacturers of structural panels.

16312 **www.pacificloggingcongress.org**
Pacific Logging Congress
Fulfills the need to provide sound technical education about the forest industry.

16313 **www.pbmdf.org**
Composite Panel Association
For particle board manufacturers and suppliers.

16314 **www.postframe.org**
National Frame Builders Association
Building contractors, suppliers, design and code professionals and academic personnel specializing in the post frame construction industry.

16315 **www.sfpa.org**
Southern Forest Products Association
For lumber manufacturers across the mid-Atlantic and southern states as far west as Texas.

16316 **www.spib.org**
Southern Pine Inspection Bureau
Develops grading standards for Southern pine lumber and provides an inspection service and grade marking systems.

16317 **www.sweets.construction.com**
McGraw Hill Construction
In depth product information that lets you find, compare, select, specify and make purchase decisions in the industrial product marketplace.

16318 **www.swst.org**
Society of Wood Science & Technology
Promotes policies and procedures which assure the wise use of wood and wood-based products; assures high standards for professional performance of wood scientists and technologists; foster educational programs at all levels of wood science and technology and further the quality of such programs; represents the profession in public policy development.

16319 **www.toc.org**
TOC Management Services
Serves membership in the fields of labor, industrial, and employee relations. Provides counsel in wage and contract negotiations. Provides training and safety programs.

16320 **www.tpmrs.com**
Timber Products Manufacturers Association
Association of companies in the Timber and Wood products industry of the pacific northwest. TPM provides human resource and safety consulting, Training and employee benefits.

16321 **www.wdma.org**
Window & Door Manufacturers Association
Trade association representing approximately 145 U.S. and Canadian manufacturers and suppliers of windows and doors for the domestic and export market.

16322 **www.westernforestry.org**
Western Forestry and Conservation Association
Offers high-quality continuing education workshops and seminars for professional foresters throughout Oregon, Washington, Idaho, Montana, Northern California and British Columbia.

16323 **www.woodcomponents.org**
Wood Component Manufacturers Association
Represents manufacturers of wood component products for urniture, cabinetry, building products, and decorative wood products.

16324 **www.woodfloors.org**
National Wood Flooring Association
For distributors, manufacturers, retailers, and contractors.

16325 **www.woodtank.com**
National Wood Tank Institute
To promote the use and to guide the proper construction methods for wooden tanks as per NWTI S-82.

16326 **www.wrcla.org**
Western Red Cedar Lumber Association
Association of 26 quality producers of Western Red Cedar lumber products in Washington, Oregon, Canada.

16327 **www.wwpa.org**
Western Wood Products Association
Represents lumber manufacturers in 12 Western states and Alaska. Provides lumber quality control, technical support, and business information to supporting mills.

16328 **www2.dcn.org/orgs/wmmpa.wm**
Wood Moulding And Millwork Producers Association
Goal is to promote quality products produced by its members, to develop sources of supply, to promote optimum use of raw materials to standardize products, and to increase the domestic and foreign usage of moulding and millwork products.

Associations

16329 **ASM International**
ASM International
9639 Kinsman Rd
Materials Park, OH 44073-0002

440-338-5151
800-336-5152; *Fax:* 440-338-4634
info@jewishlibraries.org;
www.asminternational.org
Social Media: Facebook, Twitter, LinkedIn, RSS

Yossi Galron, Membership

The society for materials engineers and scientists, a worldwide network dedicated to advancing industry, technology and applications of metals and materials.
900 Members
Founded in: 1966

16330 **American Amusement Machine Association**
450 E. Higgins Road
Suite 201
Elk Grove Village, IL 60007

847-290-9088
jtally@alliant.edu; www.coin-op.org

Mary L Conlon
140 Members
Founded in: 1964

16331 **American Gear Manufacturers Association**
American Gear Manufacturers Association
1001 N. Fairfax Street
Suite 500
Alexandria, VA 22314-1587

703-684-0211; *Fax:* 703-684-0242
amia@amianet.org; www.agma.org
Social Media: Facebook, Twitter, Youtube

Caroline Frick, President and Director of the Board
Tyler Leshney, Secretary and Director of the Board
Colleen Simpson, Treasurer and Director of the Board
Laura Rooney, Managing Director
Beverly Graham, Membership Manager

Manufacturers of gears and geared speed changers. Involved in writing industry standards.
750 Members
Founded in: 1991

16332 **American Mold Builders Association**
American Mold Builders Association
7321 Shadeland Station Way
#285
Indianapolis, IL 46256

317-436-3102; *Fax:* 317-913-2445
webmgr@arl.org; www.amba.org
Social Media: Facebook, Twitter, LinkedIn, Flickr,YouTube, Google Plus

Larry Alford, President
Mary Case, Vice President/ President-Elect
Elliott Shore, Executive Director
Prudence S Adler, Associate Executive Director
Sue Baughman, Deputy Executive Director

Promotes the development, welfare and expansion of businesses engaged in the manufacture of molds and related tooling.
Cost: $50.00
124 Members
Frequency: Annual
Founded in: 1932

16333 **American Society of Mechanical Engineers**
Two Park Avenue
New York, NY 10016-5990

973-882-1170
800-843-2763; *Fax:* 202-429-9417
betaphimu@drexel.edu; www.asme.org
Social Media: Facebook, Twitter, LinkedIn, YouTube, Instagram

Amanda Ros, President
Eileen G Abels, PhD, Vice-President, President-Elect
Alison M. Lewis, PhD, Executive Director
Kathleen Inman, Treasurer
Erin Gabriele, Program Director

To promote and enhance the technical competency and professional well-being of the members, and through quality programs and activities in mechanical engineering, better enable its practitioners to contribute to the well being of human kind.
Founded in: 1948

16334 **American Textile Machinery Association**
American Textile Machinery Association
201 Park Washington Ct
Falls Church, VA 22046-4527

703-538-1789; *Fax:* 703-241-5603;
www.atmanet.org

Kelvin A Watson, President
Diane Covington, Secretary
Annie M Ford, Treasurer
Diane Covington, Secretary

ATMA's purpose is to advance the common interests of its members, improve business conditions within the US textile machinery industry from a global perspective and market the industry and members' machinery, parts and services.
Founded in: 1969

16335 **Associated Equipment Distributors**
600 22nd Street
Suite 220
Oak Brook, IL 60523

630-574-0650; *Fax:* 630-574-0132
cla@cathla.org; www.aednet.org
Social Media: Facebook

Mary Kelleher, President
N. Curtis LeMay, Vice President/Treasurer
Melanie Talley, Senior Association Coordinator
Bland O'Connor, Executive Director, CLA Office
1000 Members
Founded in: 1921

16336 **Association for Facilities Engineering**
8200 Greensboro Drive
Suite 400
McLean, VA 22102

571-395-8777; *Fax:* 571-766-2142
ccb@illinois.edu; www.afe.org
Social Media: Facebook

Dr. Deborah Stevenson, Director of the Center for Children
Michelle Biwer, Graduate Assistant
Lauren Gray, Graduate Assistant
Thaddeus Andracki, CCB Outreach & Communications

16337 **Association for Machine Translation in the Americas**

E-Mail: ccb@illinois.edu; www.amtaweb.org
Social Media: Facebook

Dr. Deborah Stevenson, Director of the Center for Children
Michelle Biwer, Graduate Assistant
Lauren Gray, Graduate Assistant
Thaddeus Andracki, CCB Outreach & Communications

16338 **Association for Manufacturing Technology**
American Machine Tool Distributors
7901 Westpark Drive
McLean, VA 22102-4206

703-893-2900
800-524-0475; *Fax:* 703-893-1151
sbrandenburg@amrms.com;
www.amtonline.org
Social Media: Twitter

Kendall Wiggin, President
Sandra Treadway, Vice President/President Elect
Kurt Kiefer, Secretary
Stacey Aldrich, Treasurer
Timothy Cherubini, Executive Director

Since 1925, the American Machine Tool Distributors' Association has been a major voice within the machine tool industry. The AMTDA represents independent distributors and worldwide builders of machine tools and related products used in the metalworking industry. The Association's mission is to provide marketers of manufacturing technology the essential services necessary to develop and perpetuate distribution businesses that make vital contributions to North American manufacturing.
53 Members
Founded in: 1973

16339 **Association of Computing Machinery**
2 Penn Plaza
Suite 701
New York, NY 10121-0701

212-626-0500
800-342-6626; *Fax:* 212-944-1318
sctseng@uci.edu; www.acm.org
Social Media: Facebook, Youtube

Sally C Tseng, Executive Director
Founded in: 1973

16340 **Association of Equipment Manufacturers**
6737 West Washington Street
Suite 2400
Milwaukee, WI 53214-5647

414-272-0943; *Fax:* 414-272-1170
aem@aem.org; www.aem.org
Social Media: Twitter

John Patterson, Chair
Leif J. Magnusson, Vice Chair
Renee Peters, Chief Financial Officer
Megan Tanel, VP, Exhibitions & Events
Luke, Anne Forristall, VP, Political & Public Affairs
850 Members

16341 **Association of Machinery and Equipment Appraisers**
Association of Machinery and Equipment
315 South Patrick Street
Alexandria, VA 22314-3532

703-836-7900
800-537-8629; *Fax:* 703-836-9303
csla@worldaccessnet.com; www.amea.org
Social Media: Facebook

Marcia Trauernicht, President
Maria Isabel Garcia, Second Vice President/Membership
Evelyn Pockrass, Treasurer
Dottie Lewis, Archives Coordinator
Judith Janzen, Administrator

Members are appraisers of the metalworking industry.
1500 Members
Founded in: 1967
Mailing list available for rent

16342 **Association of Vacuum Equipment Manufacturers International**
201 Park Washington Court
Falls Church, VA 22046-4527
703-538-3542; *Fax:* 703-241-5603
info@cni.org; www.avem.org
Social Media: Facebook, Twitter, LinkedIn, Youtube, Vimeo
Clifford A Lynch, Executive Director
Joan K. Lippincott, Asociate Executive Director
Sharon Adams, Administrative Assistant
Maurice-Angelo Cruz, Systems Coordinator
Jacqueline J Eudell, Office Manager
The only non-profit U.S. association dedicated fully to companies that manufacture vacuum equipment and supplies that serve and advance vacuum science and technology. AVEM promotes member interests and provides services to enhance the membership value and understanding of the global market.
202 Members
Founded in: 1990

16343 **Clinical Robotic Surgery Association**
Two Prudential Plaza
180 North Stetson, Suite 3500
Chicago, IL 60601
312-268-5754
gromero@clir.org; www.clinicalrobotics.com
Social Media: Facebook, Twitter, LinkedIn, Youtube
Charles Henry, President
Alice Anderson, Senior Program Officer
Nicole K. Ferraiolo, Program Officer
Sharon Ivy Weiss, Chief Operations Officer
Lizzi Albert, Administrative Coordinator
Founded in: 1997

16344 **Compressed Air and Gas Institutue**
Compressed Air and Gas Institutue
1300 Sumner Ave
Cleveland, OH 44115-2851
216-241-7333; *Fax:* 216-241-0105
jmhite0@dia.mil; www.cagi.org
Jackie Hite, President
Margaret Barron, Executive Direrctor
Chris Egan, Vice-President/President Elect
Robin Martindill, Secretary
Stan Cieplinski, Treasurer
An organization representing manufacturers of compressed air system equipment, including air compressors, blowers, pneumatic tools and air and gasdryingand filtration equipment.
Founded in: 1967

16345 **Concrete Sawing and Drilling Association**
Polycrystalline Products Association
100 2nd Ave S
Suite 402N
St. Petersburg, FL 33701
727-577-5004; *Fax:* 727-577-5012;
www.csda.org
Social Media: Facebook, Twitter, LinkedIn, Flickr, YouTube, Pinterest
Roberta Shaffer, Executive Director
Robin Hatziyannis, Editor-in-Chief/Education
Joseph S Banks, Business Manager
Ruby J Thomas, Head, Member Services
An industrial trade association of tool fabricators, machine tool builders, material suppliers, educators and users of polycrystalline products.
40 Members
Founded in: 1965

16346 **Contractors Pump Bureau**
Contractors Pump Bureau
6737 W Washington Street
Suite 2400
Milwaukee, WI 53214-5650
414-272-0943
866-AEM-0442; *Fax:* 414-272-1170
aem@aem.org;
www.aem.org/Groups/Groups/Group.asp?G=2
2
Social Media: Twitter
Jeff Davis, Chair
Juan Quiros, Senior Vice Chair
Andy Falco, Vice Chair
Nathan Burton, Technical & Safety Services Manager
A product group of the Association of Equipment Manufacturers, the CPB promotes matters of mutual interest to contractor pump users, manufacturers and parts and component suppliers. Membership is open to any AEM member in good standing actively engaged in the manufacture and distribution of portable contractor pumps within the USA, or supplying components to those manufacturers.
20 Members
Founded in: 1938

16347 **Converting Equipment Manufacturers Association**
201 Springs Street
Fort Mill, SC 29715
803-948-9470; *Fax:* 803-948-9471
info@hooverassociation.org;
www.cema-converting.org
Social Media: Facebook, Twitter, LinkedIn, YouTube
Charles Becker, President
Robert Downer, Vice President
Ryan Johnson, Financial Development
Brad Reiners, Communications Manager
Jerry Fleagle, IOM, CAE, Executive Director
Founded in: 1939

16348 **Conveyor Equipment Manufacturers Association (CEMA)**
5672 Strand CT
Suite 2
Naples, FL 34110
239-514-3441; *Fax:* 239-514-3470
shart@insurancelibrary.org; www.cemanet.org
Glenn Cryan, Executive Director
Meagan Stefanow, Reference Librarian
Sarah Hart, Reference Librarian
Involved in writing industry standards, the CEMA seeks to promote among its members and the industry standardization of design manufacture and application on a voluntary basis and in such manner as will not impede development of conveying machinery and component parts or lessen competition. CEMA sponsors an annual Engineering Conference that allows Member Company Engineers to meet and develop or improve CEMA Consensus Industry Standards and National Standards that affect the conveyor industry.
760+ Members
Founded in: 1887

16349 **Farm Equipment Manufacturers Association**
Farm Equipment Manufacturers Association
1000 Executive Parkway Dr
Suite 100
St Louis, MO 63141-6369
314-878-2304; *Fax:* 314-732-1480
richard.barry@ana.org; www.farmequip.org
Gertrude B. Hutchinson, President
June Levy, President
Warren Hawkes, VP
Wanda Hiestand, Treasurer
Jane Root, Secretary
An information gathering and distributing organization for farm equipment manufacturers and suppliers.
26 Members
Founded in: 1960

16350 **Fire Equipment Manufacturers' Association**
Fire Equipment Manufacturers' Association
1300 Sumner Avenue
Cleveland, OH 44115-2851
216-241-7333; *Fax:* 216-241-0105
janet.webster@oregonstate.edu;
www.femalifesafety.org
Kristen Anderson, President
Brian Voss, Secretary
Kristen LaBonte, Treasurer
Guillermina Cosulich, President-Elect
Kristen Anderson, President-Elect
The premier trade association representing leading brands, and spanning dozens of product categories, related to fire protection.
200 Members
Founded in: 1975

16351 **Fluid Power Safety Institute**
2170 South 3140 West
West Valley City, UT 84119
801-908-5456; *Fax:* 801-908-5734
iasl@mlahq.org; www.fluidpowersafety.com
Social Media: Twitter
Dr. Diljit Singh, President
Mihaela Banek Zorica, VP, Association Operations
Kay Hones, VP, Association Relations
Elizabeth Greef, VP, Advocacy & Promotion
Katy Manck, Treasurer

16352 **Fluid Power Society**
Fluid Power Society
1930 E Marlton Pike
Suite A2
Cherry Hill, NJ 08034-0054
856-489-8983
800-308-6005; *Fax:* 856-424-9248;
www.ifps.org
Duncan Campbell, President
Jack Tolbert, Vice President
Debra S. Nolan, CAE, Executive Director
Alan McIntire, Treasurer
Jack McLoraine, Director
International organization for fluid power and motion control professionals.

16353 **Food Processing Suppliers Association**
Food Processing Suppliers Association
1451 Dolley Madison Blvd
Suite 101
Mc Lean, VA 22101-3850
703-761-2600; *Fax:* 703-761-4334
admin@mola-inc.org; www.fpsa.org
Patrick McGinn, President
Mark Millidge, Vice President
Alison Mrowka, Secretary
Shannon Highland, Treasurer
Trade association for food and beverage processing suppliers.
630 Members
Founded in: 1983

16354 **Heat Exchange Institute**
Heat Exchange Institute
1300 Sumner Avenue
Cleveland, OH 44115-2851
216-241-7333; *Fax:* 216-241-0105
info@mlahq.org; www.heatexchange.org
Social Media: Facebook, LinkedIn, Youtube
Michelle Kraft, AHIP, President
Kevin Baliozian, Executive Director
Chris Shaffer, AHIP, Treasurer

Chris Shaffer, Director and Treasurer
Julia Esparza, Director

A non-profit trade association committed to the technical advancement, promotion and understanding of a broad range of utility and industrial-scale heat exchange and vacuum apparatus.
4500 Members
Founded in: 1898

16355 **Industrial Distribution Association**
Industrial Distribution Association
100 N 20th Street
4th Floor
Philadelphia, PA 19103

215-320-3862
866-460-2360; *Fax:* 215-564-2175;
www.ida-assoc.org
Social Media: Facebook, Twitter, YouTube

William J. Fehrman, President and CEO
Patrick J. Goodman, Executive Vice President
Maureen E. Sammon, Senior Vice President
Douglas L. Anderson, Executive Vice President

Promotes the industry and the use of converting equipment. Conducts research and compiles statistics for wholesalers of industrial equipment.
Founded in: 1971

16356 **International Association of Diecutting and Diemaking**
651 W Terra Cotta Ave
Suite 132
Crystal Lake, IL 60014

815-455-7519
800-828-4233; *Fax:* 815-455-7510
webmaster@mela.us; www.iadd.org
Social Media: Facebook, Twitter, LinkedIn

Roberta L. Dougherty, President
Jaleh Fazelian, Vice President/ Program Chair
William Kopycki, Secretary/ Treasurer
Marlis J. Saleh, Editor

A not-for-profit international trade association serving diecutters, diemakers, and industry suppliers worldwide. Provides conferences, educational and training programs, networking opportunities, a monthly magazine, technical articles, regional chapter meetings, publications and training manuals, recommended specifications, videos and surveys.
150 Members
Founded in: 1972

16357 **International Association of Machinists and Aerospace**
International Association of Machinists
9000 Machinists Pl
Upper Marlboro, MD 20772-2675

301-967-4500; *Fax:* 301-967-4588
execsecretary@mpla.us; www.goiam.org
Social Media: Facebook, Twitter, LinkedIn, Flickr, YouTube, Google+

Eric Stroshane, President
Mickey Coalwell, Vice-President/President Elect
Melanie Argo, Recording Secretary
Judy Zelenski, Executive Secretary
Roy Degler, Systems Administrator

Has an annual budget of approximately $101.3 million.
1600+ Members
Founded in: 1948

16358 **International Association of Professional Mechanical Engineers**
55 Public Square
Suite 612
Cleveland, OH 44113

216-453-0500
mla@areditions.com
iapme.org
Social Media: Facebook

Michael Colby, President
Pamela Bristah, Recording Secretary
Paul Cary, Administrative Officer
Linda W. Blair, Assistant Administrative Officer
Founded in: 1951

16359 **Machinery Dealers National Association**
Machinery Dealers National Association
315 S Patrick St
Alexandria, VA 22314-3532

703-836-9300
800-872-7807; *Fax:* 703-836-9303
bettyge@mchsi.com; www.mdna.org
Social Media: Facebook, Twitter

Sally Lindgren, President
Betty G. Ehlinge, Executive Director
Barbara Siemaszko, Secretary
Geoff Craven, Treasurer

Represents dealers of used industrial equipment.
Founded in: 1984

16360 **Manufacturers Alliance for Productivity and Innovation**
1600 Wilson Blvd
Suite 1100
Arlington, VA 22209-2594

703-841-9000; *Fax:* 703-841-9514
info@churchlibraries.org; www.mapi.net
Social Media: Facebook

A policy research organization whose members are companies drawn from the producers and users of capital goods and allied products. Includes leading companies in heavy industry, automotive, electronics, precision instruments, telecommunications, computers, office systems. aerospace, oil/gas, chemicals and similar high technology industries.
Founded in: 1958

16361 **Material Handling Institute**
Crane Manufacturers Association of America
8720 Red Oak Boulevard
Suite 201
Charlotte, NC 28217-3996

704-676-1190; *Fax:* 704-676-1199
nisohq@niso.org; www.mhia.org/psc

Mike Teets, Chair
Todd Carpenter, Executive Director / Secretary
Nettie Lagace, Associate Director for Programs
DeVonne Parks, Manager
Keith Webster, Treasurer

Supports crane equipment manufacturers.
70 Members
Founded in: 1939

16362 **Mechanical Power Transmission Association**
Mechanical Power Transmission Association
5672 Strand Ct.
Suite 2
Naples, FL 34110

239-514-3441; *Fax:* 239-514-3470
nls@loc.gov; www.mpta.org
Social Media: Facebook, Twitter, LinkedIn

Frank Cylke, Manager
Martinez Majors, IT Specialist
Alice G Freeman, Program Management Assistant
Michael M Moodie, Research/Development Officer

Formerly Multiple V-Belt and Mechanical Power Transmission Association.

16363 **National Fluid Power Association**
National Fluid Power Association
6737 W. Washington Street
Suite 2350
Milwaukee, WI 53214

414-778-3344; *Fax:* 414-778-3361;
www.nfpa.com
Social Media: Facebook, Twitter, LinkedIn, Flickr, Pinterest

Ursula Schwarz, Executive Director
Julie Drake, Chair

Members are companies which have designed, manufactured and nationally marketed a fluid power component for a least two years in the US.
55 Members
Founded in: 1978

16364 **National Tooling & Machining Association**
National Tooling & Machining Association
1357 Rockside Road
Cleveland, OH 44134

301-248-6200
800-248-6862; *Fax:* 216-264-2840
rscheier@gmail.com; www.ntma.org
Social Media: Facebook, Twitter, Flickr, RSS, Instagram

Deb Hoadley, President
Stephen Spohn, Vice President
David Bryan, Technology Contractor
Mary Ann Rupert, Conference Management Contractor
Robert Scheier, Library Association Administrator

Members are makers of jigs, molds, tools, gages, dies and fixtures for companies doing precision machining. Supports the NTMA - Committee for A Strong Economy.
Founded in: 1963

16365 **North American Equipment Dealers Association**
1195 Smizer Mill Rd
Fenton, MO 63026-3480

636-349-5000; *Fax:* 636-349-5443
info@archivists.org; www.naeda.com
Social Media: Facebook, Twitter, LinkedIn

Nancy Beaumont, Executive Director
Teresa Brinati, Director of Publishing
Solveig De Sutter, Director of Education
Tom Jurczak, Director of Finance
Matthew Black, Web and Information Systems

NAEDA and its affiliates provides a variety of educational, financial, legislative and legal services to equipment dealers in the United States and Canada.
3400 Members
Founded in: 1936

16366 **Outdoor Power Equipment and Engine Service Association**
Outdoor Power Equipment and Engine
37 Pratt Street
Essex, CT 06426-1159

860-767-1770; *Fax:* 860-767-7932
lfallon@solinet.net; www.opeesa.com

Gordon Baker, President
Beverly James, Treasurer
Lorene Flanders, Secretary
Diane N Baird, Treasurer

Members are distributors of outdoor power equipment to retailers with a minimum of $1 million gross sales. Associate membership is available for suppliers and finance companies associated with the industry.

16367 **Packaging Machinery Manufacturers Institute**
Packaging Machinery Manufacturers

11911 Freedom Drive
Suite 600
Reston, VA 20190

571-612-3200; *Fax:* 703-243-8556
sla@sla.org; www.pmmi.org
Social Media: Facebook, Twitter, LinkedIn, Youtube, Pinterest

Doug Newcomb, Deputy Chief Executive Officer
Quan O. Logan, Chief Technology Officer
Natasha Kenner, Director
Linda Broussard, Chief Financial Officer
Paula Diaz, Director, Membership

Trade association for manufacturers of packaging and packaging-related converting equipment. PMMI offers meetings, an inquiry service, statistics and surveys, and a business to business survey on its website. PMMI also offers several Pack Expos (packaging related tradeshows).
13M Members

16368 Powder Actuated Tool Manufacturers' Institute
Powder Actuated Tool Manufacturers
136 South Main Street
Suite 2e
Saint Charles, MO 63301

636-578-5510; *Fax:* 314-884-4414
drewwe@morrisville.edu
patmi.org
Social Media: Facebook, Twitter

Rebecca Hyams, President
Bill Jones, 1st Vice-President/President Elect
Laura Evans, 2nd Vice-President/Conference Chair
Carrie Fishner, Secretary
Greg Bobish, Treasurer

Represents manufacturers of construction tools used to fasten to and into steel and concrete.
348 Members
Founded in: 1968

16369 Power Conversion Products Council International
4 Hollis Street
PO Box 378
Sherborn, MA 01770

508-979-5935; *Fax:* 508-651-3920

Elizabeth Bevington-Chambers, Executive Director

Members are manufacturers and suppliers to the wall plug-in transformer/transformer charger/converter industry. Sponsor two meetings each year covering business and engineering topics.
50 Members
Founded in: 1974

16370 Power Tool Institute
1300 Sumner Ave
Cleveland, OH 44115-2851

216-241-7333; *Fax:* 216-241-0105
salis@salis.org; www.powertoolinstitute.com

Jane Shelling, Chair
Andrea Mitchell, Executive Director and Editor
Sheila Lacroix, Secretary
Karen Palmer, Treasurer

The preeminent organization for building global understanding of power tools and for maintaining high standards of safety and quality control in the industry.
160 Members
Founded in: 1988

16371 Power-Motion Technology Representative Association
Power-Motion Technology Representative
5353 Wayzata Blvd.
Suite 350
Minneapolis, MN 55416

949-859-2885
888-817-7872; *Fax:* 952-252-8096
info@tla-online.org; www.ptra.org
Social Media: Facebook, RSS

Nancy Friedland, President
Angela Weaver, VP
Laurie Murphy, Executive Secretary
Colleen Riley, Treasurer

To promote the science of power transmission/motion control engineering, to promote educational programs and activities and to promote representatives placed in the industry.
300 Members
Founded in: 1937

16372 Precision Machined Products Association
Precision Machined Products Association
6880 West Snowville Road
Suite 200
Brecksville, OH 44141

440-526-0300; *Fax:* 440-526-5803;
www.pmpa.org

Trudi Bellardo Hahn, Executive Director
C. Beth Fitzsimmons, Chairperson

Produces several educational opportunities for members, emphasizing quality assurance and emerging technologies. Sponsors the PMPA Political Action Committee.
Founded in: 1970

16373 Robotic Industries Association
Robotic Industries Association
900 Victors Way
Suite 140
Ann Arbor, MI 48108

734-994-6088; *Fax:* 734-994-3338
info@urbanlibraries.org;
www.roboticsonline.com
Social Media: Facebook, Twitter

Matt Poland, Chairman
Michael Sherrod, Vice Chair/Chair Elect
Gary Wasdin, Secretary/Treasurer
Lourdes Aceves, Project Manager, Edge
Mary Colleen Bragiel, Project Manager

Only trade group in North America specifically to serve the rototics industry.
150+ Members
Founded in: 1971

16374 Service Dealers Association
PO Box 73796
Houston, TX 77273-3063

281-443-3063; *Fax:* 817-921-3741

Melinda Delgado, Executive Director

Represents dealers and distributors of power equipment.
690 Members
Founded in: 1986

16375 Service Specialists Association
PO Box 936
Elgin, IL 60121

847-760-0067
800-763-5717; *Fax:* 330-722-5638
aaea@gandgcomm.com; www.truckservice.org
Social Media: Facebook, Twitter, LinkedIn

Den Gardner, Executive Director
Kenna Rathai, Associate Director
Kenna Rathai, Associate Executive Director

Members are persons, firms or corporations who have operated a full line heavy duty repair service shop for at least one year with sufficient inventory to service market area, having rebuilding department capable of making all necessary repairs.
Founded in: 1921

16376 Society of Manufacturing Engineers
Society of Manufacturing Engineers
1 SME Drive
PO Box 930
Dearborn, MI 48128

313-425-3000
800-733-4763; *Fax:* 313-425-3400;
www.sme.org

Donald Graul, Executive Director

Serves its members and others in the international manufacturing community by identifying, evaluating and explaining the adoption and integration of emerging information technologies to create business value.
1800 Members
Founded in: 1975

16377 Society of Robotic Surgery
Two Woodfield Lake
1100 E Woodfield Road, Suite 350
Schaumburg, IL 60173

847-517-7225
amwa@amwa.org; www.srobotics.org
Social Media: Facebook, Twitter, LinkedIn

Samantha Nelson, Program Assistant
Rachel Spassiani, Membership Associate & Publications
Melanie Canahuate, Education & Conference Assistant
Becky Phillips, Conference Program Manager
Lauren Ero, Education and Certificate Program
3.4M Members
Founded in: 1940

16378 The Association for Packaging and Processing Technologies
11911 Fredom Drive
Suite 600
Reston, VA 20190

571-612-3200; *Fax:* 703-243-8556
webeditor@asja.org; www.pmmi.org
Social Media: Facebook, Twitter, LinkedIn, Google+

Randy Dotinga, President
Sherry Beck Paprocki, Vice President
Alexandra Cantor Owens, Executive Director, ASJA
Neil O'Hara, Treasurer
Bruce Miller, Webmaster/IT Manager
1000+ Members
Founded in: 1948

16379 The FPDA Motion & Control Network
105 Eastern Avenue
Suite 104
Annapolis, MD 21403

410-940-6347
ata@atanet.org; www.fpda.org
Social Media: Facebook, Twitter

Caitilin Walsh, President
Walter W. Bacak, Executive Director
Boris M. Silversteyn, Secretary
Ted R. Wozniak, Treasurer
Teresa Kelly, Meetings Manager
11100 Members
Founded in: 1959

16380 Tooling Component Manufacturers Association
36505 Florida Avenue
Hemet, CA 92545-3534

Fax: 909-766-7443

Ray Fuhrer, Executive Secretary

Members are united primarily for the purpose of coordinating and standardizing sizes.
8 Members
Founded in: 1958

16381 Unified Abrasives Manufacturers' Association
30200 Detroit Road
Cleveland, OH 44145-1967

440-899-0010; *Fax:* 440-892-1404
pwa@prowriters.org; www.uama.org
Social Media: Twitter

Lee C Johns, President
400+ Members
Founded in: 1983

16382 Valve Manufacturers Association of America (VMA)
Valve Manufacturers Association of America
1050 17th St NW
Suite 280
Washington, DC 20036-5521

202-331-8105; *Fax:* 202-296-0378
beforecolumbusfoundation@gmail.com; www.vma.org

Gundars Strads, Executive Director

VMA represents the interests of nearly 100 U.S. and Canadian valve, actuator, and control Manufacturers who account for approximately 80% of the total industrial valve shipments out of U.S. and Canadian facilities. The American valve industry supplies approximately 35% of worldwide valve demand. VMA member companies employ 20,000 men and women directly in supporting jobs. VMA is the only organization exclusively serving U.S. and Canadian manufacturers of industrial valves, controls and actuator
Founded in: 1976

16383 Vibration Institute
Vibration Institute
2625 Butterfield Road
Suite 128N
Oak Brook, IL 60523-3415

630-654-2254; *Fax:* 630-654-2271
anneandhenrypaolucci@yahoo.com; www.vi-institute.org

Anne Paolucci, President

A not-for-profit organization dedicated to the exchange of practical vibration information on machines and structures.
Founded in: 1976

16384 Wood Machinery Manufacturers of America
9 Newport Dr.
Suite 200
Forest Hill, MD 21050

443-640-1052; *Fax:* 443-640-1031
info@wmma.org; www.wmma.org
Social Media: Facebook, Twitter, LinkedIn

Jamison Scott, President
Chris Hacker, Vice President
Fred Stringfellow, Executive Director

WMMA has worked to increase the productivity and profitability of U.S. machinery and tooling manufacturers and the businesses that support them.
Founded in: 1899

16385 Wood Machinery Maufacturers of America
Wood Machinery Maufacturers of America
9 Newport Drive
Suite 200
Forest Hill, MD 21050

443-640-1052; *Fax:* 443-640-1031
info@wmma.org; www.wmma.org
Social Media: Facebook, Twitter, LinkedIn

Jamison J. Scott, President
Chris Hacker, Vice President
Fred Stringfellow, Executive Director
Diane Schafer, Director of Meetings
Amy Chetelat, Director of Finance
Founded in: 1899

16386 Woodworking Machinery Industry Association
225 Reinekers Lane
Suite 410
Alexandria, VA 22314

860-350-WMIA; *Fax:* 860-354-0677
info@wmia.org; www.wmia.org
Social Media: Facebook, Twitter

Scott Mueller, President
Dave Rakauskas, Vice President
Jim Besonen, Secretary/Treasurer
Larry Hoffer, Executive Vice President
Liza Wentworth, Program Administrator
Founded in: 1977

Newsletters

16387 Association of Machinery and Equipment Appraisers - Newsletter
Association of Machinery and Equipment Appraisers
315 S Patrick St
Alexandria, VA 22314-3532

703-836-7900
800-537-8629; *Fax:* 703-836-9303
amea@amea.org; www.amea.org

Pamela Reid, Executive Director

Information about appraisers of the machinery equipment.
8 Pages
Circulation: 6800
Founded in: 1983
Mailing list available for rent: 282 names at $100 per M
Printed in 2 colors on matte stock

16388 CEMA Bulletin
Conveyor Equipment Manufacturers Association
5672 Strand Ct., Suite 2
Naples, FL 34110

239-514-3441; *Fax:* 239-514-3470; www.cemanet.org

Robert Reinfried, Executive Director

Association and conveyor industry news.
6 Pages
Circulation: 96
Founded in: 1933

16389 Caster and Wheel Handbook
Youngs
55 E Cherry Ln
Souderton, PA 18964-1550

215-723-4400
800-523-5454; *Fax:* 800-544-3239
custrep@youngscatalog.com; www.youngscatalog.com

Paul O Young Jr, President

Technical news and information.
Frequency: Monthly
Founded in: 1945

16390 Computer Aided Design Report
CAD/CAM Publishing
711 Van Nuys Street
San Diego, CA 92109-1053

858-488-0533; *Fax:* 858-488-0361
info@cadcampub.com; www.cadcampub.com/

Randall Newton, Editor

Uses of computers by engineers in the manufacturing trades.
Cost: $344.00
Frequency: Monthly
ISSN: 0276-749X
Founded in: 1977

16391 Computer Integrated Manufacture and Engineering
Lionheart Publishing
2555 Cumberland Pkwy Se
Suite 299
Atlanta, GA 30339-3921

770-432-2551; *Fax:* 770-432-6969

Explores cutting edge developments in manufacturing systems operation management.
Circulation: 24,000

16392 High-Tech Materials Alert
John Wiley & Sons
111 River St
Hoboken, NJ 07030-5790

201-748-6000
800-825-7550; *Fax:* 201-748-6088
info@wiley.com; www.wiley.com

William J Pesce, CEO

Details significant developments in high-performance materials ranging from alloys and metallic whiskers to ceramic and graphite fibers, their fabrication and industrial applications.
Cost: $1152.00
Frequency: Monthly
Founded in: 1807

16393 Industrial Health & Hazards Update
InfoTeam
PO Box 15640
Plantation, FL 33318-5640

954-473-9560; *Fax:* 954-473-0544

Merton Allen, Editor

Covers occupational safety, health, hazards, and disease, mitigatioin and control of hazardous situations; waste recycling and treaqtment; environmental pollution and control; product safety and liability; fires and explosions; plant and computer security,; air pollution; surface and ground water; wastewater; soil gases; combustion and incineration; earth warming; ozone layer depletion; electromagnetic radiation; toxic materials; and many other related topics.
Frequency: Monthlyth

16394 Innovators Digest
InfoTeam
PO Box 15640
Plantation, FL 33318-5640

954-473-9560; *Fax:* 954-473-0544

Merton Allen, Editor

A multidisciplinary publication covering developments in science, engineering, products, markets, business development, manufacturing and other technological developments having industrial or commercial significance.
Frequency: Bi-Weekly

16395 Intelligent Manufacturing
Lionheart Publishing
506 Roswell St Se
Suite 220
Marietta, GA 30060-4101

770-422-3139; *Fax:* 770-432-6969
lpi@lionhrtpub.com; www.lionhrtpub.com

John Llewellyn, Publisher
David Blanchard, Advertising Sales Manager
Marvin Diamond, Advertising Sales Manager

Provides expert solutions to manufacturing professionals covering production problems, devel-

opments in manufacturing systems.
Cost: $20.00
Frequency: Weekly
Circulation: 1598
Founded in: 1987

16396 Machinery Outlook
Manfredi & Associates
20934 W Lakeview Pkwy
Mundelein, IL 60060-9502
847-949-9080; *Fax:* 847-949-9910
info@manfredi.com;
www.machineryoutlook.com
Frank Manfredi, President
A newsletter about and for the construction and mining machinery industry.
Cost: $550.00
14 Pages
Frequency: Monthly
Founded in: 1984
Printed in one color on matte stock

16397 Machining Technology
Society of Manufacturing Engineers
1 SME Drive
PO Box 930
Dearborn, MI 48121
313-425-3000
800-733-4763; *Fax:* 313-425-3400
advertising@sme.org; www.sme.org
Mark Tomlinson, Executive Director/General Manager
Greg Sheremet, Publisher
Bob Harris, Director Finance
Covers all aspects of machining in manufacturing, milling, grinding, honing, etc.
Cost: $60.00
8 Pages
Frequency: Quarterly
Circulation: 3770
Founded in: 1932
Printed in 2 colors on matte stock

16398 Manufacturing Technology
National Technical Information Service
5285 Port Royal Rd
Springfield, VA 22161-0001
703-605-6000; *Fax:* 703-605-6900
info@ntis.gov; www.ntis.gov
Linda Davis, VP
Patrik Ekstrom, Business Development Manager
Reuel Avila, Managing Director
Covers CAD/CAM, robotics, robots, productivity, manufacturing, planning, processing and control, plant design and computer software.

16399 NTMA Record
Tooling
9300 Livingston Road
Fort Washington, MD 20744-4905
301-248-5071
800-248-6862; *Fax:* 301-248-7104;
www.ntma.org
Rob Akers, Operations Director/ Publisher
Richard Wills, CEO
Thomas Garcia, Manager, Marketing
Covers activities of 4,000 member companies of tool, die and precision machining industries.
Cost: $39.00
16 Pages
Frequency: Monthly
Circulation: 2000
Founded in: 1943

16400 Wood Machining News
Wood Machining Institute
PO Box 476
Berkeley, CA 94701
510-448-8363; *Fax:* 925-945-0947
szymani@woodmachining.com;
www.woodmachining.com
Ryszard Szymani, Director
Information on the latest technological advances in the field of wood machining, including sawing, planning and sanding operations as well as the production of veneers and chips and equipment associated with these operations. WMN also reports on new machinery, processes and software, cutting tools and machinery and worker safety.
Cost: $72.00
38448 Pages
Circulation: 600
ISSN: 0743-5232
Founded in: 1984

Magazines & Journals

16401 American Society of Mechanical Engineers
American Society of Mechanical Engineers
3 Park Ave
Suite 21
New York, NY 10016-5990
212-591-7000
800-843-2763; *Fax:* 202-429-9417
infocentral@asme.org; www.asme.org
Thomas Loughlin, Executive Director
John G Falcioni, Editor-in-Chief
Frequency: Monthly
Founded in: 1880

16402 American Tool, Die & Stamping News
Eagle Publications
42400 Grand River Ave
Suite 103
Novi, MI 48375-2572
248-347-3487
800-783-3491; *Fax:* 248-347-3492
info@ameritooldie.com;
www.ameritooldie.com
Arthur Brown, President
Joan Oakley, CEO
Applications, techniques, equipment and accessories of metal stamping, moldmaking, electric discharge machining; and new product information relating to the tool and die industry. Accepts advertising.
70 Pages
Circulation: 36000
ISSN: 0192-5709
Founded in: 1971
Printed in 4 colors on glossy stock

16403 Compressed Air Magazine
Ingersoll Rand Company
200 Chestnut Ridge Road
Woodcliff, NJ 07677
201-573-0123; *Fax:* 201-573-3172;
www.irco.com
Michele Zayle, Circulation Director
Thomas McAloon, Editor
A magazine of applied technology and industrial management for middle and upper level managers in diversified industries.
Cost: $15.00
44 Pages
Frequency: 8 per year
Circulation: 125,000
Printed in 4 colors on matte stock

16404 Contact
Furnas Electric Company
1000 McKee Street
Batavia, IL 60510-1682
630-879-6000; *Fax:* 630-879-0867
Steve Wilcox, Editor
Application of electric motor controls to electrically operated machinery and equipment.
Circulation: 4,000

16405 Cutting Edge
Int'l Assoc of Diecutting and Diemaking
651 W Terra Cotta Ave
Suite 132
Crystal Lake, IL 60014
815-455-7519
800-828-4233; *Fax:* 815-455-7510
ccrouse@iadd.org; www.iadd.org
Cindy Crouse, CEO
Jill May, Chapter Relations Coordinator
A technical journal and trade magazine written and edited specifically for diecutters, diemakers and industry suppliers who are faced with the need to stay ahead of technologies in an industry that is changing at breakneck speed.
Frequency: Monthly

16406 Diesel Progress: North American Edition
Diesel & Gas Turbine Publications
20855 Watertown Rd
Suite 220
Waukesha, WI 53186-1873
262-754-4100; *Fax:* 262-754-4175;
www.dieselspec.com
Michael Osenga, President
S Bollwahn, Circulation Manager
Geared towards readers interested in state-of-the-art systems technology. Features include new product listings, systems design, research and product testing as well as systems maintenance and rebuilding.
Frequency: Monthly
Circulation: 26011

16407 EE-Evaluation Engineering
Nelson Publishing Inc
2500 Tamiami Trl N
Nokomis, FL 34275-3476
941-966-9521; *Fax:* 941-966-2590;
www.healthmgttech.com
Social Media: Facebook
A Verner Nelson, President
Leading source of information for the electronics testing and evaluation market.
Founded in: 1962

16408 Elevator World
Elevator World
PO Box 6507
Mobile, AL 36660-0507
251-479-4514
800-730-5093; *Fax:* 251-479-7043
editorial@elevator-world.com;
www.elevator-world.com
T Bruce Mackinnon, CEO
Robert S Caporale, Senior VP/Editor
Patricia Cartee, VP/Commercial Operations
International journal for those involved in short-range vertical transportation, including manufacturers, contractors, maintainers, consultants and inspectors.
Cost: $75.00
170 Pages
Frequency: Monthly
Circulation: 7,000
Founded in: 1953
Printed in 4 colors on glossy stock

16409 Equip-Mart
Story Communications

116 N Camp Street
Seguin, TX 78155

830-303-3328
800-864-1155; *Fax:* 830-372-3011;
www.equip-mart.com

Tammy Reilly, Publisher

Largest industrial equipment magazine in North America. Received by manufacturig executives who purchase or sell industrial equipment, tools, supplies and accessories.
Frequency: Monthly
Circulation: 108,000

16410 **Gear Technology**
Randall Publishing Company
PO Box 1426
Elk Grove Village, IL 60009

847-437-6604; *Fax:* 847-437-6618;
www.geartechnology.com

Michael Goldstein, Publisher
William R Stott, Managing Editor
Dan Pels, Business Development Mana
Carol Tratar, Circulation Coordinator
Richard Goldstein, Vice President

Gear Technology offers technical articles from the top names in the industry; feature articles dealing with management and technology; top-notch tradeshow coverage; industry and products news.
Circulation: 13025
Founded in: 1934
Printed in 4 colors on glossy stock

16411 **High Performance Composites**
Ray Publishing
P.O.Box 992
Morrison, CO 80465-0992

303-467-1776; *Fax:* 303-467-1777
info@raypubs.com; www.compositeworld.com

Approach is technical, offering cutting-edge design, engineering, prototyping, and manufacturing solutions for aerospace and other traditional and emerging structural applications for advanced composites.

16412 **Home Medical Equipment News**
United Publications
106 Lafayette Street
PO Box 998
Yarmouth, ME 04096

207-846-0600; *Fax:* 207-846-0657;
www.hmenews.com

James G Taliaferro, CEO/President
Brenda Boothby, Circulation Director
Joline V Gilman, Production Director
Jim Sullivan, Editor
Rick Rector, Publisher

Serves home medical equipment providers.
Frequency: Monthly
Circulation: 17100
Founded in: 1995

16413 **Home Shop Machinist**
Village Press
2779 Aero Park Drive
PO Box 968
Traverse City, MI 49685-968

231-946-3712
800-327-7377; *Fax:* 231-946-3289
info@villagepress.com; www.villagepress.com

Robert Goff, Publisher
Neil Knopf, Editor
Joe D. Rice, Editor in Chief
Angela Sagi, Advertising Director

Articles on precision machining and metal working and how-to projects geared towards the amateur machinist and small commercial machine shops.
Cost: $25.00
Circulation: 28000

16414 **IEEE Transactions on Industry Applications**
IEEE Operations Center
PO Box 1331
Piscataway, NJ 08855-1331

732-981-0060; *Fax:* 732-981-1721
society-info@ieee.org; www.ieee.org

John Vig, CEO
Johnathan Dahl, Director of Sales and Marketing

The development and applications of electrical systems, apparatus, devices and controls to the processes and equipment of industry and commerce.
Cost: $515.00
Circulation: 5100
Founded in: 1980

16415 **InTech**
ISA Services
67 Alexander Drive
PO Box 12277
Research Triangle Park, NC 27709

919-549-8411; *Fax:* 919-990-9434
info@isa.org; www.isa.org

Greg Hale, Editor
Richard Simpson, Publisher

Covers the most recent developments in the instrumention, measurement and control market.
Frequency: Monthly
Circulation: 75000
Founded in: 1945

16416 **Industrial Machine Trader**
Heartland Industrial Group
1003 Central Avenue
PO Box 1415
Fort Dodge, IA 50501

515-955-1600
800-203-9960; *Fax:* 515-955-3753
ads@industrialgroup.com;
www.industrialmachinetrader.com

Tony Smith, Publisher
Gele Mckinney, President
Angi Hesterman, Circulation Manager

Industrial machinery equipment, suppliers and manufacturers.
Cost: $67.85
8 Pages
Frequency: Weekly
Circulation: 234000
Founded in: 1970

16417 **Industrial Market Place**
Wineberg Publications
7842 Lincoln Avenue
Skokie, IL 60077

847-676-1900
800-323-1818; *Fax:* 847-676-0063
info@industrialmktpl.com;
www.industrialmktpl.com

Joel Wineberg, President
Jackie Bitensky, Editor

Has advertisements on machinery, industrial and plant equipment, services and industrial acution in each issue.
Cost: $175.00
Frequency: Every 2 weeks
Circulation: 14,000
Founded in: 1951
Mailing list available for rent: 120 names at $70 per M
Printed in 4 colors on glossy stock

16418 **Journal of Engineering for Industry**
American Society of Mechanical Engineers
3 Park Ave
Suite 21
New York, NY 10016-5990

212-591-7000
800-843-2763; *Fax:* 212-591-7674
Infocentral@asme.org; www.asme.org

Richard E Feigel, President
David Soukup, Managing Director

Covers interfaces of mechanical engineering.
Cost: $40.00
Founded in: 1880

16419 **Journal of Materials Engineering and Performance**
ASM International
9639 Kinsman Road
Materials Park, OH 44073-0002

440-338-5151
800-336-5152; *Fax:* 440-338-4634
memberservice@asminternational.org;
www.asminternational.org
Social Media: Facebook, Twitter, LinkedIn

Jeane Deatherage, Administrator, Foundation Programs
Virginia Shirk, Foundation Executive Assistant

Peer-reviewed journal that publishes contributions on all aspects of materials selection, design, characterization, processing and performance testing. The journal for solving day-to-day engineering challenges - especially those involving components for larger systems.
Cost: $1965.00
Frequency: Bimonthly
Circulation: 305
Founded in: 1992

16420 **Journal of Thermal Spray Technology**
ASM International
9639 Kinsman Rd
Novelty, OH 44072-9603

440-338-5151; *Fax:* 440-338-4634
Cust-Srv@asminternational.org;
www.asminternational.org
Social Media: Facebook, Twitter, LinkedIn

Jeane Deatherage, Administrator, Foundation Programs
Virginia Shirk, Foundation Executive Assistant

Peer-reviewed journal which publishes contributions on all aspects, fundamental and practical, of thermal spray science, including processes, feedstock manufacture, testing and characterization. As the primary vehicle for thermal spray information transfer, its mission is to synergize the rapidly advancing thermal spray industry and related industries by presenting research and development efforts leading to advancements in implementable engineering applications of the technology.
Cost: $1577.00
Frequency: Bimonthly
Circulation: 680
Founded in: 1952

16421 **Locator Services**
Locator Online
315 S Patrick St
Suite 3
Alexandria, VA 22314-3532

703-836-9700
800-537-1446; *Fax:* 703-836-7665
sales@locatoronline.com;
www.locatoronline.com

Terry Pitman, Publisher

Used metalworking equipment.
Cost: $38.00
Frequency: Monthly
Circulation: 225000
Founded in: 1969

16422 **Machine Shop Guide**
Worldwide Communications

401 Worthington Avenue
Harrison, NJ 07029-2039

973-977-7555; *Fax:* 253-872-7603;
www.wctower.com

Robert L Hatschek, Executive Editor
Frederick Mason, Editor

Information on manufacturing technology, new applications for manufacturing technology and new products. Focus is metal cutting machines and tooling.
Frequency: 10 per year
Circulation: 102,893
Founded in: 1996
Printed in 4 colors on glossy stock

16423 **Machinery Trader**
Sandhills Publishing
PO Box 82545
Lincoln, NE 68501-2545

402-479-2181
800-247-4898; *Fax:* 402-479-2195
feedback@sandhills.com; www.sandhills.com

Tom Peed, CEO
Marva Wasser, Editor-in-Chief

Covering heavy equipment.
Cost: $59.00
160 Pages
Frequency: Weekly
Circulation: 20000
Founded in: 1978

16424 **Managing Automation**
Thomas Publishing Company
5 Penn Plz
Suite 10
New York, NY 10001-1860

212-695-0500; *Fax:* 212-290-7362
businesslists@thomaspublishing.com;
www.thomaspublishing.com

Carl Holst-Knudsen, CEO
Robert Malone, Editor
Heather L Mikisch, Publisher
Kim Vennard, Marketing Manager

Serves the needs of those managers and engineers responsible for the planning and implementation of factory automation at both the plant and enterprise levels.
Frequency: Monthly
Circulation: 100246
Founded in: 1898

16425 **Manufacturing Engineering**
Society of Manufacturing Engineers
1 SME Drive
#930
Dearborn, MI 48121
313-425-3000
800-733-4763; *Fax:* 313-425-3400
advertising@sme.org; www.sme.org

Mark Tomlinson, Executive Director
Greg Sheremet, Publisher
Gene Nelson, President

Serves metalworking industry machining, forming, inspection, assembly and processing operations.
Frequency: Monthly
Circulation: 111966
Founded in: 1932

16426 **Modern Machine Shop**
Gardner Publications
6915 Valley Ln
Cincinnati, OH 45244-3153

513-527-8800
800-950-8020; *Fax:* 513-527-8801
mmsmkt@gardnerweb.com;
www.gardnerweb.com

Rick Kline Sr, CEO
Mark D Albert, Manager
John Campos, Manager
Brian Wertheimer, Account Manager
Eddie Kania, Sales Manager

Reaches metalworking plants of all sizes - from small job shops to giant aerospace and automotive plants. It is edited for those involved in metalworking operations, particularly those performed on machine tools.
Cost: $4.00
Frequency: Monthly
Circulation: 107000
Founded in: 1928
Mailing list available for rent: 106M names
Printed in 4 colors on glossy stock

16427 **Motion Control**
ISA Services
PO Box 12277
Durham, NC 27709-2277

919-549-8411; *Fax:* 919-990-9434
info@isa.org; www.isa.org

Sam Batman, Editor
Richard Simpson, Publisher
Robert Renner, Executive Director

Information for those who design and maintain motion control systems.
Cost: $54.00
56 Pages
Circulation: 41000
ISSN: 1058-4644
Founded in: 1945
Printed in 4 colors on glossy stock

16428 **Motion System Distributor**
Penton Media
1166 Avenue of the Americas/10th Fl
New York, NY 10036

212-204-4200; *Fax:* 216-696-6662;
www.penton.com

Jane Cooper, Marketing
Chris Meyer, Director, Corporate Communications

Provides selling and technical information to individuals and distributors specializing in power transmission, motion control and fluid products.

16429 **NAEDA Buyer's Guide**
North American Equipment Dealers Association
1195 Smizer Mill Road
Fenton, MO 63026-3480

636-349-5000; *Fax:* 636-349-5443
naeda@naeda.com; www.naeda.com
Social Media: Twitter, LinkedIn

Annual directory of contact names, trade and product names of more than two thousand of the equipment industry's manufacturers and suppliers.
Cost: $35.00
5000 Members
Frequency: Annually
Founded in: 1900

16430 **OEM Worldwide**
Cygnus Publishing
PO Box 803
Fort Atkinson, WI 53538-0803

920-000-1111; *Fax:* 920-563-1699
tjheinlein@cableinet.co.uk;
www.cygnusb2b.com

John French, CEO
Leslie Shalabi, Publisher
James S Rank, VP
Sue Cullen, Advertising Manager
Brett Apold, Corporate Production Director

Designed to be a resource of operational and general productivity information for original equipment manufacturers in Europe, competing in the global marketplace.
Cost: $6.00
Frequency: Monthly
Circulation: 16800
Founded in: 1984

16431 **Outdoor Power Equipment**
1900 Arch Street
Philadelphia, PA 19103-1404
215-564-3484; *Fax:* 215-564-2175

Julie S Burns, Executive Director

Members are distributors of outdoor power equipment to retailers with a minimum of $1 million gross sales. Associate members are suppliers and finance companies.
150 Pages
Founded in: 1980

16432 **Plant Engineering**
Reed Business Information
30 Technology Parkway South
Suite 100
Norcross, GA 30092

646-746-6400
800-424-3996; *Fax:* 646-756-7583
webmaster@reedbusiness.com;
www.reedbusiness.com

John Poulin, CEO
Richard L Dunn, Editor
Gerard Van de Aast, Director
Carel de Bos, Chief Information Officer

The magazine for plant engineering professionals responsible for the maintenance, repair and operations of plant facilities, equipment and systems.
Cost: $3.00
Circulation: 116700

16433 **Processing Magazine**
Grand View Media Group
200 Croft Street
Suite 1
Birmingham, AL 35242

888-431-2877; *Fax:* 205-408-3797
webmaster@grandviewmedia.com;
www.gvmg.com/

Leading source for up-to-date product and equipment solutions.

16434 **Production Machining**
Gardner Publications
6915 Valley Ln
Cincinnati, OH 45244-3153

513-527-8800
800-950-8020; *Fax:* 513-527-8801
jjordan@gardnerweb.com;
www.gardnerweb.com

Rick Kline Sr, CEO
Leo Rakowski, Senior Editor
John Jordan, Assistant Editor
Lori Beckman, Managing Editor
John Campos, Manager
Frequency: Monthly
Circulation: 200000
Founded in: 1928

16435 **Pumps & Systems**
Randall Publishing Company
1900 28th Ave S
Suite 110
Homewood, AL 35209-2627

205-212-9402; *Fax:* 205-212-9452;
www.pump-zone.com

Walter Evans, President
George Lake, Associate Publisher
Scott Kidwell, Advertising Sales:
Tom Cory, Circulation
Robert Windle, CEO
Frequency: Monthly
Founded in: 2002

16436 Sensors Magazine
Advanstar Communications
7500 Old Oak Blvd
Cleveland, OH 44130-3343

440-243-8100; *Fax:* 440-891-2740
info@advanstar.com; www.act-europe.org

Barbara G Goode, Editor-in-Chief
Donna Pellerin George, Associate Editor
Joseph Loggia, CEO
Georgiann Decenzo, Director of Corporate marketing
Francis Heid, Vice President of Publishing

Primary source among design and production engineers of information on sensor technologies and products, and topic integral to sensor-based systems and applications. Provides practical and in-depth yet accessible information on sensor operation, design, application, and implementation within systems. Covers the effective use of state-of-the-art resources and tools that enable readers to get the maximum benefit from their use of sensors.
Frequency: Monthly
Circulation: 75000
Founded in: 1984

16437 Valve Magazine
Valve Manufacturers Association of America
1050 17th Street NW
Suite 280
Washington, DC 20036-5521

202-331-8105; *Fax:* 202-296-0378
wsandler@vma.org; www.vma.org

Bill Sandler, President
Marc Pasternak, VP

Promotion of significance and application of US and Canadian manufactured industrial valves and actuators.
Frequency: Quarterly
Circulation: 26000

16438 Vibrations Magazine
Vibration Institute
6262 Kingery Hwy
Suite 212
Willowbrook, IL 60527-2276

630-654-2254; *Fax:* 630-654-2271
information@vi-institute.org;
www.vi-institute.org

Ronald Eshleman, Executive Director

Provides current information about activities of the Vibration Institute and news about vibration technology. Each issue contains practical, technical articles and case histories.
Frequency: Quarterly
Founded in: 1975

16439 World Industrial Reporter
Keller International Publishing Corporation
150 Great Neck Rd
Suite 400
Great Neck, NY 11021-3309

516-829-9722; *Fax:* 516-829-9306;
www.supplychainbrain.com

Bryan DeLuca, Editor
Terry Beirne, Publisher
Jerry Keller, President
Mary Chavez, Director of Sales

New equipment, machinery and techniques for the industry.
34 Pages
Frequency: Monthly
Circulation: 37107
Founded in: 1882

Trade Shows

16440 ASME Annual Meeting
American Society of Mechanical Engineers
Three Park Avenue
New York, NY 10016

973-882-1170
800-843-2763; *Fax:* 212-591-7856
CustomerCare@asme.org; www.asme.org

Melissa Torres, Meetings Manager
Mary Jakubowski, Meetings Manager
Frequency: Annual/June

16441 ASME Gas Turbine Users Symposium (GTUS)
American Society of Mechanical Engineers/IGTI
Three Park Avenue
New York, NY 10016-5990

973-882-1170
800-843-2763; *Fax:* 404-847-0151
CustomerCare@asme.org; www.asme.org/igti

Stephanie Searsr, Coordinator, IGTI Conferences
Judy Osborn, Manager, IGTI Conferences & Expos

A show focused on the role gas turbines will play in meeting the nation's future energy demands, provides the information related to gas turbine operations, maintenance, advances, and design.
2000 Attendees
Frequency: Annual

16442 Association of Machinery and Equipment Appraisers Annual Conference
315 S Patrick Street
Alexandria, VA 22314-3501

703-836-7900
800-537-8629; *Fax:* 703-836-9303
amea@amea.org; www.amea.org

Lorna Lindsey, Manager
Mary Flynn, Executive Director

Exhibits of interest to machinery and equipment appraisers.
Founded in: 1982
Mailing list available for rent

16443 FloorTek Expo
American Floorcovering Alliance
210 West Cuyler St
Dalton, GA 30720-8209

706-278-4101
800-288-4101; *Fax:* 706-278-5323
afa@americanfloor.org; www.floor-tek.com

Wanda J Ellis, Executive Director

The only internationla flooring manufacturing tradeshow dedicated to the production and materials of the industry
3000+ Attendees
Frequency: Bi-Annual

16444 Gear Expo
American Gear Manufacturers Association
500 Montgomery Street
Suite 350
Alexandria, VA 22314-1581

703-684-0211; *Fax:* 703-684-0242;
www.gearexpo.com

Kurt Medert, VP

Biennial trade show held in October of the odd-numbered years. It is the only trade show devoted exclusively to the Gear Manufacturing process.
4.5M Attendees
Frequency: October
Founded in: 1987

16445 IADD/FSEA Odyssey
Int'l Assoc of Diecutting and Diemaking
651 W Terra Cotta Ave
Suite 132
Crystal Lake, IL 60014

815-455-7519
800-828-4233; *Fax:* 815-455-7510
cccrouse@iadd.org; www.iadd.org

Cindy Crouse, CEO
Jill May, Chapter Relations Coordinator

The premiere education and technology expo uniquely focused on diemaking, converting, foil stamping, embossing and bindery.
Frequency: Annual/May

16446 International Integrated Manufacturing
Reed Exhibition Companies
255 Washington Street
Newton, MA 02458-1637

617-584-4900; *Fax:* 617-630-2222

Elizabeth Hitchcock, International Sales

Expo and conference dedicated to the products and technology needed by engineering operations and management to automate and integrate manufacturing.
Frequency: March

16447 International Manufacturing Technology Show
7901 Westpark Drive
Mc Lean, VA 22102-4206

703-893-2900; *Fax:* 703-893-1151;
www.amtonline.org

John Byrd, President
Peter Eelman, VP Exhibitions

Manufacturing equipment trade show.
85M Attendees
Frequency: Biennial
Founded in: 1927

16448 International Woodworking Machinery and Furniture Supply Fair: USA
Reed Exhibition Companies
1350 E Touhy Avenue
Des Plaines, IL 60018-3303

847-294-0300; *Fax:* 847-635-1571

Paul Pajor, National Marketing Manager

The largest woodworking machinery and furniture supply manufacturing exposition held in the Western Hemisphere. Exhibitors interface with North American furniture, cabinet, and woodworking manufacturers. One thousand booths.
37M Attendees
Frequency: August/Biennial

16449 Job Shop Show: Midwest
Edward Publishing LLC
16 Waterbury Road
Prospect, CT 06712-1215

203-758-6658; *Fax:* 203-758-4476;
www.jobshoptechnology.com

Jennifer Bryda, Production Manager
Christoper Davis, Manager
Gerald Schmidt, President

A source for forming, fabricating, shaping, and assemblies. The show is designed to attract the highest caliber engineers and buyers from product manufacturers. There will be 170 exhibitors and booths.
1500 Attendees

16450 National Technical Training Symposium
Vibration Institute
6262 S Kingery Highway
Suite 212
Willowbrook, IL 60527

630-654-2254; *Fax:* 630-654-2271
information@vi-institute.org;
www.vi-institute.org

Ronald L Eshlemann, Director

Formerly the annual meeting, provides specific training in practical vibration technology.
Frequency: Annual

16451 Powder and Bulk Solids Conference and Exhibition
Reed Exhibition Companies
255 Washington Street
Newton, MA 02458-1637

617-584-4900; *Fax:* 617-630-2222

Elizabeth Hitchcock, International Sales

Equipment and technology for processing and handling of powder and bulk solids.
8.4M Attendees
Frequency: May

16452 South-Tec Machine Tool and Manufacturing Show
Society of Manufacturing Engineers
1 SME Drive
#930
Dearborn, MI 48128

313-425-3000
800-733-4763; *Fax:* 313-425-3400
advertising@sme.org; www.sme.org

Mark Tomlinson, Executive Director
Greg Sheremet, Publisher

A professional society dedicated to advancing scientific knowledge in the field of manufacturing and to applying its resources for researching, writing, publishing and disseminating information.
70M Attendees
Frequency: March
Founded in: 1932

Directories & Databases

16453 American Machine Tool Distributors Association Directory
1445 Research Bowl
Suite 450
Rockville, MD 20852-1421

301-738-1200; www.metalworld.com

Greg Safko, Editor
Ralph Nappi, President

Directory of services and supplies to the industry.
Cost: $60.00
150 Pages
Frequency: Annual
Founded in: 1925

16454 American Machinist Buyers' Guide
Penton Media
1166 Avenue of the Americas/10th Fl
New York, NY 10036

212-204-4200; *Fax:* 216-696-6662
information@penton.com; www.penton.com

Jane Cooper, Marketing
Pat Smith, Managing Editor
Chris Meyer, Director, Corporate Communications

Guide to over manufacturers of products and services used by metalworking industries.
Cost: $6.00
Frequency: Annual
Circulation: 80,000
Printed in 4 colors on glossy stock

16455 American Mold Builders Association
PO Box 404
Medinah, IL 60157-0404

630-980-7667; *Fax:* 630-980-9714
info@amba.org; www.amba.org

Jeanette Bradley, Editor
Kym Conis, Managing Director

Directory of services and supplies to the industry.
Cost: $25.00
50 Pages
Frequency: Annual

16456 American Textile Machinery Association Official Directory
201 Park Washington Ct
Falls Church, VA 22046-4527

703-538-1789; *Fax:* 703-241-5603
info@atmanet.org; www.atmanet.org

Harry W Buzzerd, Owner
Clay D Tyeryar, President/Assistant Treasurer
Susan Denston, Executive VP/Secretary
Judith O Buzzerd, Meetings Manager

The Directory of the American Textile Machinery Association/ATMA offers information on over 100 member textile machinery and accessory manufacturers. ATMA is a professional trade association devoted to the advancement of manufacturers of textile machinery, parts, and accessories in the textile industry.
100 Pages

16457 Directory of Machine Tools and Manufacturing
Association for Manufacturing Technology
7901 Westpark Drive
Mc Lean, VA 22102-4206

703-893-2900; *Fax:* 703-893-1151

Machine tools and related products built by members of the Association for Manufacturing Technology.
Frequency: Annual

16458 Equip-Mart
116 N Camp Street
Seguin, TX 78155
830-303-3328
800-864-1155; *Fax:* 830-372-3011;
www.equip-mart.com

Directory of available used metalworking equipment.
Frequency: Weekly

16459 ISA Directory
Instrumentation, Systems,and Automation Society
PO Box 12277
Durham, NC 27709-2277

919-549-8411; *Fax:* 919-990-9434
info@isa.org; www.isa.org

Premier guide to instrumentation, systems and automation
Printed in 4 colors

16460 Industrial Machine Trader
Heartland Industrial Group
1003 Central Avenue
PO Box 1415
Fort Dodge, IA 50501

515-955-1600
800-247-2000; *Fax:* 515-955-3753
igproduction@industrialgroup.com;
www.industrialgroup.com
Social Media: Facebook, Twitter, LinkedIn

Virginia Rodriguez, Publisher

Printed directory of available used metalworking equipment.
150+ Members
Frequency: Weekly
Founded in: 1966

16461 Locator Services
315 S Patrick St
Alexandria, VA 22314-3532

703-836-9700
800-537-1446; *Fax:* 703-836-7665
sales@locatoronline.com;
www.locatoronline.com

Terry Pitman, Publisher

Printed directory of available used metalworking equipment.
Frequency: Monthly
Circulation: 225,000

16462 Machine Design Product Locator
Penton Media
1166 Avenue of the Americas/10th Fl
New York, NY 10036

212-204-4200; *Fax:* 216-696-6662
information@penton.com; www.penton.com

Jane Cooper, Marketing
Chris Meyer, Director, Corporate Communications

Directory of services and supplies to the industry.
Cost: $35.00
325 Pages
Frequency: Annual
Circulation: 180,000
Printed in 4 colors on glossy stock

16463 Metalworking Machinery Mailer
Tade Publishing Group
29501 Greenfield Road
Suite 120
Southfield, MI 48076

248-552-8583
800-966-8233; *Fax:* 248-552-0466;
www.tadesite.com

Tom Lynch, Editor

Printed directory of available used metalworking equipment.
Frequency: Monthly

16464 Motion Control Technical Reference and Buyers Guide
ISA Services
PO Box 12277
Durham, NC 27709-2277

919-549-8411; *Fax:* 919-990-9434
info@isa.org; www.isa.org

The most comprehensive reference source for motion control market
Founded in: 2000
Printed in 4 colors

16465 Multimedia Monograph Series
SIGDA Multimedia

atrak.usc.edu/~sigda-mm/

Massoud Pedram, Program Director

Set of electronic media publications focusing on key talks/presentations given at various ACM sponsored conferences over the last few years.

16466 Orion Blue Book: Tools
Orion Research Corporation

14555 N Scottsdale Rd
Suite 330
Scottsdale, AZ 85254-3487

480-951-1114
800-844-0759; *Fax:* 480-951-1117;
www.bluebook.com

Roger Rohrs, Owner

List of manufacturers of tools.
Frequency: Annual

16467 Surplus Record Machinery & Equipment Directory
Thomas Scanlan
20 N Wacker Dr
Chicago, IL 60606-3004

312-372-9077; *Fax:* 312-372-6537
surplus@surplusrecord.com;
www.surplusrecord.com

Thomas Scanlan, Publisher

Listing over 55,000 items of used/surplus machine tools, machinery, electrical apparatus, and capital equipment by more than 1200 suppliers worldwide.
Cost: $33.00
736 Pages
Frequency: Monthly Magazine
Circulation: 150000
ISSN: 0039-615X
Founded in: 1924

16468 ThomasNet
Thomas Publishing Company, LLC
User Services Department
5 Penn Plaza
New York, NY 10001

212-695-0500
800-699-9822; *Fax:* 212-290-7362
contact@thomaspublishing.com;
www.thomasnet.com
Social Media: Facebook, Twitter, LinkedIn

Carl Holst-Knudsen, President
Robert Anderson, VP, Planning
Mitchell Peipert, VP, Finance
Ivy Molofsky, VP, Human Resources

A way to reach qualified businesses that list their company information on ThomasNet.com. Detailed profiles promote their products, services, capabilities and brands carried. The ThomasNet.com web site is the most up-to-date compilation of 650,000 North American manufacturers, distributors, and service companies in 67,000 industrial categories.
Founded in: 1898

16469 Used Machinery Buyer's Guide
Machinery Dealers National Association
315 S Patrick St
Alexandria, VA 22314-3532

703-836-9300
800-872-7807; *Fax:* 703-836-9303
office@mdna.org; www.mdna.org

Mark Robinson, Executive VP
Richard Levy CEA, President

Over 400 dealers in used capital equipment.
Frequency: Annual, September

Industry Web Sites

16470 http://gold.greyhouse.com
G.O.L.D Grey House OnLine Databases

Grey House Publishing's online database platform, GOLD, offers Quick Search, Keyword Search and Expert Search for most business sectors including machinery markets. The GOLD platform makes finding the information you need quick and easy - whether you're a novice searcher or an experienced database user. All of Grey House's directory products are available for subscription on the GOLD platform.

16471 www.amea.org
Association of Machinery and Equipment Appraisers

Members are appraisers of the metalworking industry.

16472 www.americanfloor.org
American Floorcovering Alliance

Promotes the industry's products and services to the world, and educates the members and others through seminars, press releases, and trade shows.

16473 www.avem.org
Association of Vacuum Equipment Manufacturers
International

The only non-profit U.S. association dedicated fully to companies that manufacture vacuum equipment and supplies.

16474 www.cemanet.org
Conveyor Equipment Manufacturers Association

Continues to be considered the resource for conveyor safety dimensional and application standards.

16475 www.fpmsa.org (or www.iefp.org)
Food Processing Machinery & Supplies Association

List of exhibitors from IEFP (links included).

16476 www.greyhouse.com
Grey House Publishing

Authoritative reference directories for most business sectors including machinery markets. Users can search the online databases with varied search criteria allowing for custom searches by product category, geographic area, sales volume, keyword, subject and more. Full Grey House catalog and online ordering also available.

16477 www.iadd.org
Int'l Association of Diecutting and Diemaking

A not-for-profit international trade association serving diecutters, diemakers, and industry suppliers worldwide. IADD provides conferences, educational and training programs, networking opportunities, a monthly magazine, technical articles, regional chapter meetings, publications and training manuals, recommended specifications, videos and surveys.

16478 www.mapi.net
Manufacturers Alliance/MAPI

A policy research organization whose members are companies drawn from the producers and users of capital goods and allied products. Includes leading companies in heavy industry, automotive, electronics, precision instruments, telecommunications, computers, office systems. aerospace, oil/gas, chemicals and similar high technology industries.

16479 www.mdna.org
Machinery Dealers National Association

Represents dealers of used industrial equipment.

16480 www.naeda.com
North American Equipment Dealers Association

Promotes the general welfare of retail agricultural, outdoor power, construction and large property equipment dealers in the United States and Canada.

16481 www.ntma.org
National Tooling and Machining Association

For makers of jigs, molds, tools, gages, dies and fixtures for companies doing precision machining.

16482 www.packexpo.com
Packaging Machinery Manufacturers Institute (PMMI)

For manufacturers of packaging and packaging-related converting equipment.

16483 www.pmpa.org
Precision Machined Products Association

Member companies are producers of high precision component products. Provides educational opportunities for members, emphasizing quality assurance and emerging technologies.

16484 www.polysort.com
Polysort.com

Includes materials, machinery and equipment, processors and industry services.

16485 www.taol\fema.com
Fire Equipment Manufacturers' Association

Members are companies making devices that control or extinguish fires in residential or commercial buildings.

16486 www.vma.org
Valve Manufacturers Association of America

Associations

16487 AAHC American Association of Healthcare
1205 Johnson Ferry Road
Suite 136-420
Marietta, GA 30068
404-661-1710
888-350-2242; *Fax:* 770-874-4401;
www.aahc.net

Linda Campbell, Executive Director

To serve as the preeminent credentialing, professional and practice development organization for the healthcare consulting profession; to advance the knowledge, quality and standards of practice for consulting to management in the healthcare industry; and to enhance the understanding and image of the healthcare consulting profession and member firms among its various publics.
Founded in: 1949

16488 AMR Management Services
201 East Main Street
Suite 1405
Lexington, KY 40507
859-514-9150; *Fax:* 859-514-9207
info@amrms.com; www.amrms.com
Social Media: Facebook, LinkedIn

Rebecca Klemm, President

Seeks to enhance members skills in organizational opportunities and in planning strategies to influence external events on international objectives.
400 Members
Founded in: 1982

16489 Academy of Human Resource Development
1000 Westgate Drive
Suite 252
St. Paul, MN 55114
651-290-7466; *Fax:* 651-290-2266
office@ahrd.org; www.ahrd.org
Social Media: Facebook, Twitter, LinkedIn, RSS

Ron Jacobs, President
Kathie Pugaczewski, CAE, CMP, Executive Director
Jeanne Demartino, Member Service Specialist
Jazzy McCroskey, Communications Specialist
Carissa Wolf, Meeting Planner
Founded in: 1993

16490 Adizes Network International
1212 Mark Ave
Carpinteria, CA 93013
805-565-2901; *Fax:* 805-565-0741
info@adizes.com; www.adizes.com
Social Media: Facebook, Twitter, LinkedIn, Google+

James C Morgan, Chairman and CEO
Dr Ichak Adizes, Professional Director
James Zukin, Senior Managing Director

Promotes Adizes management consulting as a profession. Facilitates discussion of ideas and conducts lectures and seminars.
115 Members
Founded in: 1973

16491 American Academy of Medical Administrators
American Academy of Medical Administrators
330 N Wabash Avenue
Suite 2000
Chicago, IL 60611
312-321-6815; *Fax:* 312-673-6705
info@aameda.org
aama.socious.com

John Garrity, Chairman
Kevin Baliozian, Executive Director
Eric Conde, MSA, CFAAMA, Chairman Elect
John Garrity, CFAAMA, Treasurer
Robert McKenney, PhD,FAAMA, Vice Chair

Department heads and administrators in areas of hospital and health administration.
Founded in: 1957

16492 American Association of Commerce Executives
American Chambers of Congress Executives
1330 Braddock Place
Suite 300
Alexandria, VA 22314
703-998-0072; *Fax:* 888-577-9883
webmaster@acce.org; www.acce.org
Social Media: Facebook, Twitter, LinkedIn, RSS

Joe Roman, Chairman of the Board
Mick Fleming, President
Tamara Philbin, COO and Membership Management
Chris Mead, SVP, Member & Sponsor Relations
Jacqui Cook, Chief Financial Officer

National association uniquely serving individuals involved in the management of chambers of all sizes. Chamber executives and professionals hold positions requiring leadership, vision and strong management skills. Devoted to helping chamber executives and their staffs' play a significant leadership role ing their communities.
1300 Members
Founded in: 1914

16493 American Business Women's Association
9820 Metcalf Ave
Suite 110
Overland Park, KS 66212
800-228-0007; *Fax:* 913-660-0101
webmail@abwa.org; www.abwa.org
Social Media: Facebook, Twitter, YouTube

Nancy Griffin, National President
Meg Bell, National VicePresident
Lisa Montross, National Secretary - Treasurer
Gina Berry, Vice President, District I
Frances Nicholson, Vice President, District II

16494 American Management Association
American Management Association
1601 Broadway
New York, NY 10019-7420
212-586-8100
800-262-9699; *Fax:* 212-903-8168;
www.amanet.org
Social Media: Facebook, Twitter, LinkedIn, YouTube

Edward T Reilly, CEO

Membership-based management development organization. AMA provides valuable and practical action-oriented learning programs to people at all levels, in all industries, from companies and agencies of all sizes. More than 500,000 AMA customers and members a year learn new skills and behaviors, gain more confidence, advance their careers through a wide range of seminars, conferences and executive forums, as well as publications, research, print and online self-study courses.
20000 Members
Founded in: 1923

16495 American Productivity and Quality Center
American Productivity and Quality Center
123 N Post Oak Ln
Third Floor
Houston, TX 77024-7797
713-681-4020
800-776-9676; *Fax:* 713-681-8578
cflett@apqc.org; www.apqc.org
Social Media: Facebook, Twitter, LinkedIn, Youtube, RSS

C. Jackson Grayson, Founder and Executive Chairman
Lisa Higgins, President
Carla O'Dell, Chief Executive Officer
Cindy Hubert, Executive Director
Mike Shea, Chief Financial Officer

Seeks to improve productivity and the quality of work life in the United States. Works with businesses, unions, academics and government agencies to improve productivity and quality.
300 Members
Founded in: 1977

16496 American Small Businesses Association
American Small Businesses Association
206 E College
Grapevine, TX 76034-2663
817-488-8770
800-801-2722; *Fax:* 817-251-8578

Bill Hill Sr, President
Wanda Johnson, Bookkeeper

Represents the interests of small businesses.
10M Members
Founded in: 1975

16497 American Society for Quality
American Society for Quality
600 N Plankinton Avenue
PO Box 3005
Milwaukee, WI 53201-3005
414-272-8575
800-248-1946; *Fax:* 414-272-1734
help@asq.org; www.asq.org
Social Media: Facebook, Twitter, LinkedIn, Youtube

Cecilia L. Kimberlin, Chairman
Bill Troy, Chief Executive Officer
Eric Hayler, Treasurer
Laurel Nelson-Rowe, Managing Director
Michelle Mason, Managing Director

ASQ's mission is to facilitate continuous improvement and increase customer satisfaction. Promotes quality principles, concepts and technologies. Provides information, contacts and opportunities to make things better in the workplace, in communities and in people's lives.
100M Members
Founded in: 1946

16498 American Society for the Advancement of Project Management
American Society for the Advancement of
6547 North Academy
#404
Colorado Springs, CO 80918
719-488-3850; *Fax:* 719-487-0637;
www.asapm.org

Joel Carboni, President
Tim Jaques, Vice President
Bill Duncan, Director of Certification
Thomas Baumann, Director of Education
John Colville, Director of Member Services

Standards and guidelines to define the work of project management personnel. Requirements to standardize the norms are collection, process and then institutionalization of the applied competence with acceptable protocols in managing the work for optimization of output. This includes the knowledge, experience and attitude of the manpower involved in the handling the assigned project.

16499 American Society of Association Executives
American Society of Association Executives
1575 I St NW
Washington, DC 20005-1103

202-371-0940
888-950-2723; *Fax:* 202-371-8315
ASAEservice@asaecenter.org;
www.asaecenter.org/

Abe Eshkenazi, Chair
Dana Anaman , CAE, Marketing Manager
Eyitemi Amorighoye, Director, Web Projects
Jenna Allen, Development Operations Manager
Francine Alestock, Executive Coordinator
24.5M Members
Founded in: 1920

16500 Association For Strategic Planning
Association for Strategic Planning
191 Clarksville Road
Princeton, NJ 08550

877-816-2080; *Fax:* 609-799-7032;
www.strategyplus.org
Social Media: Facebook, Twitter, LinkedIn, Youtube, Picasa

Neelima Firth, President
Lee Crumbaugh, Vice President
Tom Carter, Treasurer
Kimme Carlos, Executive Director
Dedicated to advancing thought and practice in strategy development and deployment for business, non-profit and government organizations. Provides opportunities to explore cutting-edge strategic planning principles and practices that enhance organizational success and advance members' and organizations' knowledge, capability, capacity for innovations and professionalism.
Founded in: 1999

16501 Association for Services Management International (AFSM)
Association for Services Management
17065 Camino San Bernardo
Suite 200
San Diego, CA 92127

858-674-5491
800-333-9786; *Fax:* 239-275-0794;
www.tsia.com
Social Media: Facebook, Twitter, YouTube, Google+, Blog

J.B. Wood, President and CEO
Ren, Grossrieder, SVP, Membership Development
Tom Rich, Vice President, IT
Trisha Bright, Vice President, Marketing
Thomas Lah, Executive Director
A global organization dedicated to furthering the knowledge, understanding, and career development of executives, managers and professionals in the high-technology service industry.
5000 Members
Founded in: 1975

16502 Association for Systems Management
Association for Systems Management
24587 Bagley Road
Cleveland, OH 44138
216-671-1919; *Fax:* 440-234-2930

Paula Winrod, Public Communication
Offers seminars and conferences in all phases of business systems and management.
5M Members
Founded in: 1947

16503 Association of Executive and Administrative Professionals
900 South Washington Street
Suite G-13
Falls Church, VA 22046-4009

703-237-8616; *Fax:* 703-533-1153
headquarters@theaeap.com; www.theaeap.com
Social Media: LinkedIn

Ruth Ludeman, Director
Has helped thousands of administrative and secretarial professionals grow in their chosen careers, and supported their efforts at becoming the best that they can be. Strives to provide its members with a pathway for setting and achieving accomplishments of all types and at all levels. Publishes a newsletter 11 times per year.
3000 Members
Founded in: 1975

16504 Association of Higher Education Facilities Officers (APPA)
1643 Prince St
Alexandria, VA 22314-2818

703-684-1446; *Fax:* 703-549-2772
webmaster@appa.org; www.appa.org
Social Media: Facebook, Twitter, LinkedIn, Youtube

Peter Strazdas, President
E. Lander Medlin, Executive Vice President
John F Bernhards, Associate Vice President
Norm Young, VP, Information and Research
Paul Wuebold, VP, Professional Affairs
APPA is an association dedicated to leadership in educational facilities management and the ongoing evolution of its professionals into influential leaders in education.
5500 Members
Founded in: 1914

16505 Association of Investment Management Sales Executives
Association of Investment Management
12100 Sunset Hills Road
Suite 130
Reston, VA 20190

703-234-4098; *Fax:* 703-435-4390
lyarborough@drohanmgmt.com;
www.aimse.org/

P. MacKenzie Hurd, CFA, President
Christopher D. Rae, Vice President
Kathy Hoskins, Executive Director
Katie Earley, Deputy Executive Director
Glenn Beales, Director of Finance
The AIMSE mission is to provide an educational forum for those employed in the investment management sales and marketing services profession worldwide. AIMSE fosters high ethical and professional standards among members regarding representation of investment products and services, with an educational emphasis on improving skills, enabling members to adapt to the changing needs of the marketplace.
1400 Members
Founded in: 1977

16506 Association of Management
Association of Management
920 Battlefield Boulevard
Suite 100
Chesapeake, VA 23322

757-482-2273; *Fax:* 757-482-0325
aomgt@aom-iaom.org; www.aom-iaom.org

Dr. Karin Klenke, Chairperson, Co-Founder and CEO
Dr. Willem Arthur Hamel, Co-Founder/President
T J Mills, VP Comptroller
Formerly the Association of Human Resources Management and Organizational Behavior (HRMOB).
3.5M Members
Founded in: 1979

16507 Association of Management Consulting Firms
Association of Management Consulting Firms
370 Lexington Avenue
Suite 2209
New York, NY 10017

212-262-3055; *Fax:* 212-262-3054
info@amcf.org; www.amcf.org
Social Media: Facebook, Twitter, LinkedIn, YouTube, RSS

Steve Goodrich, Chairman of the Board
Sally Caputo, President & Chief Operating Officer
Ayaka Sparks, Marketing & Events Coord.
Dina Bystryak, Marketing & Events Coordinator
MaryAnn Dogo, Admin Support & Project Coordinator
Seeks to unite management consulting firms in order to develop and improve professional standards and practice in the field. Offers information and referral services on management consultants.
65 Members
Founded in: 1929

16508 Automotive Trade Association Executives
Automotive Trade Association Executives
8400 Westpark Dr
Mc Lean, VA 22102-5116

703-821-7072; *Fax:* 703-556-8581
sjewett@nada.org; www.asna-atae.com

Stacey Castle, ATAE Chairman
Joe Rohatynski, Senior Editor
Promotes interests of executives of state and local auto dealers associations.
106 Members
Founded in: 2003

16509 Awards and Recognition Association
Awards and Recognition Association
8735 W. Higgins Road
Suite 300
Chicago, IL 60631

847-375-4800
800-344-2148; *Fax:* 847-375-6480
info@ara.org; www.ara.org
Social Media: Facebook, Twitter, Instagram

Mike May, President
Louise Ristau, CAE, Executive Director
Brian Fitzgerald, Senior Sales Manager
Tom Calvin, Sales Manager
Chris Schroll, Sales Manager
Membership organization of 4,000 companies dedicated to increasing the professionalism of recognition specialists and advancing the awards and engraving industry.
Founded in: 1993

16510 Best Employers Association
Best Employers Association
17701 Mitchell North
Irvine, CA 92614-6028

866-706-2225
800-237-8543; *Fax:* 949-553-0883
info@bestlife.com; www.beassoc.org/
Social Media: Facebook, Twitter, LinkedIn

Steve Course, President
Jennifer Bolton, Sales Account Manager
Ramon Duran, Sales Account Manager
Cristina Rios, Sales Account Manager
Dorothy Sehramm, Salews Account Manager

Providing group medical, dental, long-term disability, vision and life insurance to employers.
Founded in: 1970

16511 Business Management Daily
National Institute of Business Management
PO Box 9070
McLean, VA 22102-0070
703-058-8000
800-543-2055; *Fax:* 703-905-8040
Customer@BusinessManagementDaily.com; www.businessmanagementdaily.com
Social Media: Facebook, Twitter, LinkedIn, Google+
Steve Sturm, President
Career guidance for managers and executives.
Founded in: 1937

16512 Center for Breakthrough Thinking
Center for Breakthrough Thinking
PO Box 18012
Los Angeles, CA 90018
213-740-6415; *Fax:* 213-740-1120; www.cbttbd.atspace.cc
Social Media: Twitter
Dr Gerald Nadler, President
George Hathaway, Executive Vice President
Dr. William Chandon, Vice President
Mr. Steven S. Benson, Vice President - Development
Organized to promote and institutionalize the teaching and application of Breakthrough Thinking in universities, corporations and governments for solving problems, leveraging opportunities, and achieving change.
15 Members
Founded in: 1988

16513 Center for Creative Leadership
Center for Creative Leadership
One Leadership Place
PO Box 26300
Greensboro, NC 27410-6300
336-545-2810; *Fax:* 336-282-3284
info@ccl.org; www.ccl.org/Leadership/
Social Media: Facebook, Twitter, LinkedIn, Youtube, Google Plus, Pinteres
Odd Ingar Skaug, Chairman
John Alexander, President
An international, nonprofit educational institution devoted to behavioral science research, executive development and leadership education.
Founded in: 1970
Mailing list available for rent

16514 Center for Management Effectiveness
Center for Management Effectiveness
P. O. Box 1202
Pacific Palisades, CA 90272
310-459-6052; *Fax:* 310-459-9307
info@cmeinc.org; www.cmeinc.org
Social Media: Facebook, Twitter, LinkedIn, RSS
Jerry Feist, President
Ron Smith, General Manager
Rob Wood, Publications Director
Sam Erdman, Manager Information Systems
Christie Randolph, Management Consultants
Conducts management training programs and publishes self-scoring inventories, trainer guides and workbooks on stress management, resolution of conflict, risk taking, decision making and building managerial skills.
Founded in: 1981

16515 Center for Management Systems
Center for Management Systems
PO Box 159
Akron, IA 51001-0159
Fax: 712-568-3427
Provides specialized education to improve management skills.
70M Members
Founded in: 1978

16516 Center for Third World Organizing
Center For Third World Organizing
900 Alice Street
Suite 300
Oakland, CA 94607
510-433-0908; *Fax:* 510-433-0908; www.ctwo.org
Faron Mclurkin, Executive Director
Karey Leung, Research Director
Karissa Lewis, Senior Field Organizer
Avery Bizzell, Organiser
A national organization of books, periodicals and audiovisuals on transnational corporations and labor issues.
Founded in: 1980

16517 Christian Management Association
Christian Management Association
1825 Hamilton Drive
San Jose, CA 95125
408-703-6568; *Fax:* 408-703-6568
info@cmanational.org; www.christianmanagementassociation.org
Social Media: Facebook, Twitter, RSS
Frank Lofaro, CEO
Dick Bahruth, Senior Consultant
Sandy Huston, Member Services Manager
Joe Voorhies, Director Business Development
Charles S Blake, Director Finance
Designed to assist those involved in the management of Christian organizations.
3500+ Members
Founded in: 1976

16518 Club Managers Association of America
1733 King St
Alexandria, VA 22314-2720
703-739-9500; *Fax:* 703-739-0124
cmaa@cmaa.org; www.cmaa.org
Social Media: Facebook, Twitter, LinkedIn, Flickr
Tony D'Errico, CCM, CCE, President
Jill Philmon, CCM, CCE, Vice President
Jeff Morgan, FASAE, CAE, Chief Executive Officer
Seth Gregg, Chief Operating Officer
Margaret Meleney, Chief Financial Officer
Advances the professional of club management by fulfilling the educational and related needs of its members.
7000 Members
Founded in: 1927

16519 Construction Financial Management Association
100 Village Blvd.
Suite 200
Princeton, NJ 8540
609-452-8000
888-421-9996; *Fax:* 609-452-0474
info@cfma.org; www.cfma.org
Social Media: Facebook, Twitter, LinkedIn, YouTube
Stuart Binstock, President, CEO
Erica O'Grady, CAE, Vice President, Operations
Robert Rubin, CPA, VP, Finance & Admin.
Brian Summers, CAE, VP, Content Mgmt & Edu.
Ariel Sanchirico, Director, Online Learning
Founded in: 1981

16520 Data Processing Sciences Corporation
Data Processing Sciences Corporation
11370 Reed Hartman Hwy
Cincinnati, OH 45241
513-489-4200; *Fax:* 513-791-2371; www.dpsciences.com
Social Media: Facebook, Twitter, LinkedIn, Youtube, Google+
Kurt Loock, President
Scott Nesbitt, CEO
Stephen Vandegriff, EVP
Tim Shelton, CFO
DPS delivers solutions that simplify and manage technology for our clients so they can aggressively pursue their strategic business goals.

16521 Decision Sciences Institute
Decision Sciences Institute
C.T. Bauer College of Business
334 Melcher Hall, Suite 325
Houston, TX 77204-6021
713-743-4815; *Fax:* 713-743-8984
info@decisionsciences.org; www.decisionsciences.org
Social Media: Facebook, Twitter, LinkedIn
Morgan Swink, Publisher
Janelle Heineke, VP - Finance (Treasurer)
Gyula Vastag, VP - Global Activities
Kaushik Sengupta, VP - Marketing
Hope Baker, VP - Member Services
Scientific quantitative, behavioral and computational approaches to decision making.

16522 Distribution Business Management Association
2938 Columbia Ave
Suite 1102
Lancaster, PA 17603
717-295-0033; *Fax:* 717-299-2154
athorn@dbm-assoc.com; www.dcenter.com

16523 Diversified Business Communications
Diversified Business Communications
121 Free Street
Portland, ME 04101
207-842-5500; *Fax:* 207-842-5503
custserv@divcom.com; www.divbusiness.com
Theodore Wirth, President & Chief Executive Officer
Paul Clancy, Executive Vice President
Janice Rogers, Vice President, Human Resources
Vicki Hennin, Vice President, Strategic Marketing
Oakley R. Dyer, VP/Business Development
Has over 30 years of experience as trade magazine publishers and exhibition organizers. Provides exposition management services for associations and organizations seeking to expand domestically and overseas, as well as direct mail, internet, telemarketing campaigns and market research.
Founded in: 1949

16524 Employer Associations of America
262-696-3473
Vicki.Vought@mranet.org; www.eaahub.org
Mary Lynn Fayoumi, Chair
Vicki Vought, Executive Director
Clayton Kamida, Secretary - Treasurer
Cassie Schauer, Web Tech Specialist
Pam Estergard, Financial Services

16525 Employers Group
Employers Group
1150 S Olive St
Suite 2300
Los Angeles, CA 90015-2211
213-748-0421
800-748-8484; *Fax:* 213-742-0301
serviceone@employersgroup.com;

www.employersgroup.com
Social Media: Facebook, Twitter, LinkedIn

Mark Wilbur, CEO

Aims to provide human resources management, management counseling and educational programs. Offers unemployment insurance services, and workers compensation programs.
3.9M Members

16526 **Employers of America**
Employers of America
310 Meadow Lane
Mason City, IA 50401

641-424-3187
800-728-3187; *Fax:* 641-424-3187
employer@employerhelp.org;
www.employersgroup.com

Jim Collison, President

Provides information and guidance to employers, managers, and supervisors to empower employees and make great things happen.
1600 Members
Founded in: 1976

16527 **Financial Management Association International**
University of South Florida/College of Business
4202 E Fowler Ave
BSN 3416
Tampa, FL 33620-5500

813-974-2084; *Fax:* 813-974-3318
fma@coba.usf.edu; www.fma.org

Kose John, President
William G Christie, VP-Program
Ronald Masulis, VP-Global Services
Javier Estrada, VP-Practitioner Services
Jay R Ritter, President Elect

The mission of the FMA is to broaden the common interests between academicians and practitioners, provide opportunities for professional interaction between and among academicians, practitioners and students, promote the development and understanding of basic and applied research and of sound financial practices, and to enhance the quality of education in finance.
3000 Members
Founded in: 1970

16528 **Floodplain Management Association**
P.O. Box 712080
Santee, CA 92072

760-936-3676
admin@floodplain.org; www.floodplain.org
Social Media: Facebook, Twitter, LinkedIn, Google+

Thomas Plummer, Chair
Mark Seits, Vice Chair
Andrew Trelease, Treasurer
George Booth, Secretary
John Moynier, Director

16529 **Fulfillment Management Association**
Fulfillment Management Association
225 West 34th Street
Suite 946
New York, NY 10122

818-487-2090; *Fax:* 818-487-4501
info@the-mcma.org
the-mcma.org
Social Media: Facebook, Twitter, LinkedIn

Rochelle Boorstein, President
Suzanne Nicholas, Vice President
Raymond Dryden, Treasurer
Melissa Borduin, Executive Secretary
Jodi Sentementes, Recording Secretary

Educates, updates and maintains high standards of service in operations management and customer service. Sponsors four seminars per year. Members are direct mail fullfillment, marketing and circulation executives.
425 Members
Founded in: 1945

16530 **Independent Professional Representatives Organization (IPRO)**
Independent Professional Representatives
34157 West 9 Mile Road
Farmington Hills, MI 48335

248-474-0522
800-420-4268; *Fax:* 248-514-4418
ray@avreps.org; www.avreps.org
Social Media: Facebook, LinkedIn

Dave Humphries, President
Frank Culotta, Vice President
Mark Adams, Secretary
Mike Pecar, Treasurer

The mission of IPRO is to provide new avenues of networking; provide new and emerging resources for sound business management; enhance valuable dialogue and commmunication with business partners; and to continue to develop resources and benefits for individual members beyond the resources of individual firms.

16531 **Industrial Asset Management Council**
Industrial Asset Management Council
6625 The Corners Parkway
Suite 200
Peachtree Corners, GA 30092

770-325-3461; *Fax:* 770-263-8825
info@iamc.org; www.iamc.org
Social Media: Facebook, Twitter, LinkedIn, Pinterest, Tumblr, Blogger, St

Samantha L. Turner, Chair
Mr. Russell A. Burton, Vice Chair
J. Tate Godfrey, Executive Director
Rya Hazelwood, Director of Marketing & Conference
Joel Parker, Director of Research & Education

World's leading associates of industrial asset management and corporate real estate executives, their supplies and service providers and economic developers.
135 Members
Founded in: 1963

16532 **Information Resources Management Association**
Information Resources Management Association
701 E Chocolate Ave
Suite 200
Hershey, PA 17033-1240

717-533-8845; *Fax:* 717-533-8661
member@irma-international.org;
www.irma-international.org

Jan Travers, Executive Director
Sherif Kamel, Communications Director
Lech Janczewski PhD, IRMA World Representative Director
Gerald Grant, IRMA Doctoral Symposium Director
Paul Chalekian, IRMA United States Representative

An international professional organization dedicated to advancing the concepts and practices of information resources management in modern organizations. The primary objective of IRMA is to assist organizations and professionals in enhancing the overall knowledge and understanding of effective information resources management in the early 21st century and beyond.

16533 **Institute for Supply Management Association**
2055 E Centennial Circle
PO Box 22160
Tempe, AZ 85284-1802

480-752-6276
800-888-6276; *Fax:* 480-752-7890
custsvc@instituteforsupplymanagement.org;
www.ism.ws
Social Media: Facebook, Twitter, LinkedIn, Youtube, google Plus

Thomas K. Linton, Chair
Bill Michels, CPSM, C.P.M., Senior Vice President
Nora Neibergall, CPSM, C.P., Senior Vice President
Thomas W. Derry, Chief Executive Officer, ISM
Janis Kellerman, Senior Vice President/Corporate

The mission of ISM is lead supply management.
43000 Members
Founded in: 1915

16534 **Institute of Business Appraisers**
Institute of Business Appraisers
5217 South State Street
Suite 400
Salt Lake City, UT 84107
954-482-1812
800-299-4130; *Fax:* 866-353-5406
hqiba@go-iba.org; www.go-iba.org

Mark Walker, Board of Governor's Chair

The oldest professional society devoted solely to the appraisal of closely-held businesses.
3,000 Members
Founded in: 1978

16535 **Institute of Certified Business Counselors**
Institute of Certified Business Counselors
222 N. LaSalle Street
Suite300
Chicago, IL 60601

312-856-9590
877-844-2535; *Fax:* 503-292-8237
info@amaaonline.org; www.amaaonline.com
Social Media: Facebook, Twitter, LinkedIn, Google+

Michael Nail, Founder & Managing Director
Diane Niederman, Vice President of Alliances
MaryLou Nall, Operations Manager
Nancy Reyes, Member Services Administrator
Nilla Cooper, Director of Accounting

Premier association of skilled, experienced practitioners focused on the needs of businesses in ownership transition.
120 Members
Founded in: 1998

16536 **Institute of Management & Administration**
Institute of Management & Administration
3 Bethesda Metro Center
Suite 250
Bethesda, MD 20814-5377

703-341-3500
800-372-1033; *Fax:* 800-253-0332
customercare@bna.com; www.bna.com
Social Media: Facebook, Twitter, LinkedIn, YouTube

Gregory C. McCaffery, CEO & President
Sue Martin, Chief Operating Officer
Paul Albergo, Bureau Chief
Joe Breda, EVP, Product
Daniel M. Fine, EVP, Strategy

An independent source of exclusive business management information for experienced senior and middle management professionals.

16537 Institute of Management Accountant
Institute of Management Accountant
10 Paragon Dr
Suite 1
Montvale, NJ 07645-1760

201-573-9000
800-638-4427; *Fax:* 201-474-1600
ima@imanet.org; www.imanet.org
Social Media: Facebook, Twitter, LinkedIn, Youtube

Benjamin R. Mulling, Chair
Marc P. Palker, CMA, Chair - Elect
Jeffrey C. Thomson CMA, CAE, President

A subunit of the Institute of Management Accountants, with a network of 3,000 controllers incorporating newsletters and seminars.
70000 Members
Founded in: 1919

16538 Institute of Management Consultants - USA
Institute of Management Consultants - USA
2025 M St NW
Suite 800
Washington, DC 20036-2422

202-367-1261
800-221-2557; *Fax:* 202-367-2134
norm@ecksteinconsult.com; www.imcusa.org
Social Media: Facebook, Twitter, LinkedIn, RSS

Loraine Huchler CMC, P.E,

Chair and CEO
Cynthia E. Currence CMC, Director
Lee Czarapata CMC, Director
Don Matheson, Treasurer
Manola Robinson CMC, Director

IMC is the leading association representing management consultants in the United States, organized to establish consulting as a self-regulating profession, meriting public confidence and respect. Toward the achievement of this goal IMC awards the international appelation CMC for certified management consultants.

16539 Institute of Management and Administration
Institute of Management and Administration
3 Bethesda Metro Center
Suite 250
Bethesda, MD 20814-5377

703-341-3500
800-372-1033; *Fax:* 800-253-0332
customercare@bna.com; www.bna.com
Social Media: Facebook, Twitter, LinkedIn, YouTube

Gregory C. McCaffery, CEO & President
Sue Martin, Chief Operating Officer
Paul Albergo, Bureau Chief
Joe Breda, EVP, Product
Daniel M. Fine, EVP, Strategy

An independent source of exclusive business management information for experienced senior and middle management professionals.

16540 Int'l. Association of Healthcare Central Services Material Management
Int'l. Association of Healthcare
55 West Wacker Drive
Suite 501
Chicago, IL 60601

312-440-0078
800-962-8274; *Fax:* 312-440-9474
mailbox@iahcsmm.com; www.iahcsmm.org
Social Media: Facebook, Twitter, LinkedIn

David Jagrosse, CRCST, President
Susan Adams, Executive Director
Nick Baker, Certification Manager
Josephine Colacci, Advocacy
Elizabeth Berrios, Office Manager

Membership consists of persons serving in a technical, supervisory or management capacity in hospital central service departments responsible for the sterilization management and distribution of supplies.
9000 Members
Founded in: 1958

16541 International Association for Worksite Health Promotion
Association for Worksite Health Promotion
401 W. Michigan St.
Indianapolis, IN 46202

317-637-9200; *Fax:* 847-480-9282
iawhp@acsm.org
ww.acsm-iawhp.org
Social Media: Facebook, LinkedIn

George Pfeiffer, MSE, President
Charlie Estey, President-Elect
Stephen Cherniak, MS, MBA, Secretary/Treasurer
Wolf Kirsten, MS, Past President

Exists to advance the profession of worksite health promotion and the career development of its practitioners and to improve the performance of the programs they administer. Represents a variety of disciplines and worksites, for decision makers in the areas of health promotion/disease prevention and health care cost management.
3000 Members

16542 International Association of Administrative Professionals
10502 N. Ambassador Dr.
Suite 100
Kansas City, MO 64153

816-891-6600; *Fax:* 816-891-9118;
www.iaap-hq.org
Social Media: Facebook, Twitter, LinkedIn, Pinterest, RSS, YouTube

Wendy Melby, CAP-OM, Chair
Kristi Rotvold, CAP-OM, Chair-Elect
Jay Donohue,CAE, CMP, President & CEO
Melissa Mahoney, CAE, Senior Director, Operations
Melissa Sutphin, Executive Admin
Founded in: 1942

16543 International Council for Small Business
2201 G Street NW
Funger Hall Suite 315
Washington, DC 20052

202-944-0704; *Fax:* 202-994-4930
info@icsb.org; www.icsb.org
Social Media: Facebook, Twitter, Google+, RSS

Luca Iandoli, President
Dr. Robert S. Lai, President-Elect
Geralyn Franklin, VP/Finance/Control
Ayman El-Tarabishy, Executive Director
Michael Battaglia, Operations Manager

Founded in: 1955, the International Council for Small Business (ICSB) was the first international membership organization to promote the growth and development of small businesses worldwide. The organization brings together educators, researchers, policy-makers and practitioners from around the world to share knowledge and expertise in their respective fields.
4000+ Members
Founded in: 1955

16544 International Council of Management Consulting Institutes
International Council of Management
3860 BB NIJKERK Gld
P.O. Box 1058
Netherland

31 -0 3- 247; *Fax:* 31 -0 3- 246
info@icmci.org; www.icmci.org

Camera Gaylen, Executive Director
Michael Shays, Manager
John Roethle, Advisory Council

The global association of management consultants. The members of ICMCI are national institutes from around the world that certify professional management consultants. The ICMCI maintains an international code of professional conduct, an international uniform body of knowledge, and strict standards for certification and reciprocity between nations. It promotes professional development and networking between consultants and the highest standards of performance for clients.
39 Members
Founded in: 1987

16545 International Facility Management Association
International Facility Management
800 Gessner Rd.
Ste. 900
Houston, TX 77024-4257

713-623-4362; *Fax:* 713-623-6124
ifma@ifma.org; www.ifma.org
Social Media: Facebook, Twitter, LinkedIn, Youtube, Flickr, RSS

Michael D. Feldman, FMP, CM, Chair
Tony Keane, CAE, President and CEO
Maureen Ehrenberg, FRICS, First Vice President
William M. O'Neill, CFM, Second Vice President
Cheryl White, Director, Corporate Programs

Certifies facility, managers, conducts research, provides educational programs, recognizes facility management degree and certificate programs and produces World Workplace, the world's largest facility management conference and exposition.
Founded in: 1980

16546 International Leadership Association
1110 Bonifant Street
Suite 510
Silver Spring, MD 20910-3358

202-470-4818; *Fax:* 202-470-2724
ila@ila-net.org; www.ila-net.org
Social Media: Facebook, Twitter, LinkedIn, Google+, YouTube, Flickr

Cynthia Cherrey, President & CEO
Shelly Wilsey, Chief Operating Officer
Bridget Chisholm, Director of Conferences
Anita Marsh, Membership Manager
Jean Portianko, I.T. and Office Manager
Founded in: 1999

16547 International Personal Management and Association for Human Resources
Int'l Public Management Assoc for Human Resources
1617 Duke St
Alexandria, VA 22314-3406

703-549-7100; *Fax:* 703-684-0948
ipma@ipma-hr.org; www.ipma-hr.org
Social Media: Facebook, Twitter, LinkedIn

Neil Reichenberg, Executive Director
Sima Hassassian, Deputy Executive Director
Jenny Chang, Director of Communications

Jacob Jackovich, Assessment Services Coordinator
Andrey Pankov, Assessment Research Manager

Human resource professionals, representing the interests of over 6,000 individual and 1,300 agency members, at the federal, state and local levels of government. Promotes excellence in human resource management through the ongoing development of professional and ethical standards, and through its publishing and educational training programs.
6M Members
Founded in: 1906

16548 International Public Management Association
1617 Duke Street
Alexandria, VA 22314
703-549-7100; *Fax:* 703-684-0948
nreichenberg@ipma-hr.org; www.ipma-hr.org
Social Media: Facebook, Twitter, LinkedIn

Neil Reichenberg, Executive Director
Sima Hassassian, Deputy Executive Director
Gabrielle Voorhees, Controller
Jenny Chang, Director of Communications
Linda Sun, Director of China Programs
Founded in: 1906

16549 Life Office Management Association
Life Office Management Association
6190 Powers Ferry Road
Suite 600
Atlanta, GA 30339-5665
770-951-1770
800-968-1738; *Fax:* 770-984-0441
askloma@loma.org; www.loma.org
Social Media: Facebook, Twitter, LinkedIn, Youtube

Robert A Kerzner, CLU, ChFC, President and CEO
Jeffrey Hasty, FLMI, ACS, SVP/Corporate Secretary
Michele LaBouff, SVP, Human Resources
Kathy Milligan, FLMI, ACS, A, SVP, Education and Training
Ian J Watts, SVP/Managing Director, Intl. Ops

Insurance worldwide association of insurance companies specializing in research and education.
1250 Members
Founded in: 1924

16550 Marketing Management Association
www.mmaglobal.org
Social Media: Facebook, Twitter, LinkedIn, Google+, YouTube

Brain Vander Schee, President
Roscoe Hightower, Immediate Past President
Pam Kennett-Hensel, President Elect
Susan Geringer, VP, Marketing
Alex Miliovic
Founded in: 1977

16551 Medical Group Management Association
Medical Group Management Association
104 Inverness Terrace East
Englewood, CO 80112-5306
303-799-1111
877-275-6462; *Fax:* 303-643-9599
support@mgma.org; www.mgma.com
Social Media: Facebook, Twitter, LinkedIn, Youtube

Ronald S German, MBA, FACMPE, Chair of the Board
Kevin Spencer, Chief Operating Officer
Stephen A. Dickens, JD, FACMPE, F, Secretary/Treasurer

The oldest and largest professional membership association dedicated to medical practice management. Serves their members by offering timely and relevant networking and educational opportunities that keep the members up-to-date on the practice management field.
18M Members
Founded in: 1926

16552 National Association Executive Club
1300 L Street NW
Suite 1050
Washington, DC 20005-4107
202-043-3001; *Fax:* 202-783-4410

Steven Fier, Secretary
Angela West, Manager

Provides networking services and facilities.
500 Members
Founded in: 1953

16553 National Association for the Self-Employed
P.O. Box 241
Annapolis Junction, MD 20701-0241
800-649-6273
800-649-6273; www.nase.org
Social Media: Facebook, Twitter, LinkedIn, Youtube

Keith R. Hall, President/CEO
John K. Hearrell, VP, Membership & Affiliate Programs
Thom Childers, Software Developer/Database Admin
Rosie Farris, Accounts Payable
Cameron T. Brown, Systems Administrator

Goal is to promote small business growth through education and discounts earned through NASE negotiating power.
225M Members
Founded in: 1981
Mailing list available for rent

16554 National Association of Corporate Directors
2001 Pennsylvania Ave, NW
Suite 500
Washington, DC 20006
202-775-0509; *Fax:* 202-775-4857
Join@NACDonline.org; www.nacdonline.org
Social Media: Facebook, Twitter, LinkedIn, Youtube, RSS

Kenneth Daly, President/CEO
Katherine Davis, COO
Peter Gleason, Managing Director, CFO
Henry Stoever, Chief Marketing Officer
Judy Warner, Editor in Chief

A national non-profit membership organization dedicated exclusively to serving the corporate governance needs of corporate boards and individual board members.
15500 Members
Founded in: 1977

16555 National Association of Service Managers
PO Box 250796
Milwaukee, WI 53225
414-466-6060; *Fax:* 414-466-0840;
www.nasm.com
Social Media: Facebook

Ken Cook, Treasurer

Service manager association for professional development
100 Members
Founded in: 1955

16556 National Business Owners Association
480 Broadway
PO Box 3373
Saratoga Springs, NY 12866
202-839-9000
866-639-1669; *Fax:* 866-224-0609;
www.nawbo.org

Ed Bolen, President

A non-profit organization representing small business owners' interests and offers several money-saving services, valuable benefits and assistance.
4.5M Members
Founded in: 1986

16557 National Businesswomens Leadership Association
P.O. Box 419107
Kansas City, MI 64141-6107
913-432-7755
800-258-7246; *Fax:* 913-432-0824
cstserv@natsem.com;
www.nationalseminarstraining.com/AboutNBLA.cfm
Social Media: Facebook, Twitter, LinkedIn, Google+

Linda Truitt, President

Offers seminars and workshops on business related issues.
Founded in: 1986

16558 National Career Development Association
305 N. Beech Circle
Broken Arrow, OK 74012
918-663-7060
866-367-6232; *Fax:* 918-663-7058
webeditor@ncda.org; www.ncda.org
Social Media: Facebook, Twitter, LinkedIn, Pinterest

Cynthia Marco Scanlon, President
Mark Danaher, Past President
David M. Relie, President Elect
Deneen Pennington, Executive Director
Mary Ann Powell, CDF & Conference Director
Founded in: 1913

16559 National Committee for Quality Assurance
1100 13th Street NW
Suite 1000
Washington, DC 20005
202-955-3500; *Fax:* 202-955-3599
customersupport@ncqa.org; www.ncqa.org
Social Media: Facebook, Twitter, LinkedIn, Youtube, Google+, Pinterest

David Chin, MD, Chair
Margaret E. O'Kane, President
Tom Fluegel, Chief Operating Officer
Scott Hartranft, Chief Financial Officer
Rick Moore, Chief Information Officer

Independent, non profit organization dedicated to improving healthcare quality.
Founded in: 1990
Mailing list available for rent

16560 National Conference of Personal Managers
964 2nd Avenue
New York, NY 10022-6304
212-421-2670
866-91N-COPM; *Fax:* 212-838-5105
ncopmse@cox.net; www.ncopm.com/

Clinton Ford Billups Jr, National President
Jack Rollins, National First Vice President
Stanley Evans, National Second Vice President
Peggy Becker, National Secretary
Daniel Abrahamson, Eastern Executive Director

A personal manager is engaged in the occupation of advising and counseling talent and personalities in the entenainment industry. personal managers have the expertis to find and develop new talent and create opportunities for those artists which they represent.

16561 National Contract Management Association
21740 Beaumeade Circle
Suite 125
Ashburn, VA 20147
571-382-0082
800-344-8096; *Fax:* 703-448-0939
memberservices@ncmahq.org;
www.ncmahq.org
Social Media: Facebook, Twitter, LinkedIn, Youtube,Instagram
Russell J. Blaine, CPCM, Fellow, President
Michael Fischetti, J.D., CPCM,, Executive Director
John G. Horan, J.D., General Counsel
Penny L. White, J.D., Fellow, Director and Chair
Kim Rupert, CPCM, CFCM, Fe, Director and Chair, Finance
Formed in 1959 to foster the professional growth and educational advancement of its members.
19000 Members
Founded in: 1959

16562 National Employee Services and Recreation Association
Employee Services Management Association
568 Spring Road
Suite D
Elmhurst, IL 60126-3896
630-559-0020
esmahq@esmassn.org; www.esmassn.org
Pud Belek, President
Manufacturers and distributors offering products and services for employee discount programs and employee store merchandise to members.

16563 National Management Association
2210 Arbor Blvd
Moraine, OH 45439-1580
937-294-0421; *Fax:* 937-294-2374
nma@nma1.org; www.nma1.org
Social Media: Facebook, Twitter, LinkedIn, YouTube
William T Mahaffey, Chairman
Wendell M Pichon, Vice Chairman
Steve Bailey, CM, President
Sue Kappeler, CM, Vice President
Robin Furlong, Manager
Seeks to develop and recognize management as a profession and to promote the free enterprise system.
22000 Members
Founded in: 1925

16564 National Property Management Association
3525 Piedmont Road
Building 5, Suite 300
Atlanta, GA 30305
404-477-5811; *Fax:* 404-240-0998
hq@npma.org; www.npma.org
Social Media: Facebook, LinkedIn, YouTube
Marcia Whitson CPPM CF, National President
Cinda Brockman CPPM CF, Executive Vice President
Cheri Cross CPPM CF, Immediate Past President
Ivonne Bachar CPPM CF, VP, Administration
Rosanne Green CPPM CF, VP, Certification
Founded in: 1970

16565 National Small Business United
1156 15th St NW
Suite 1100
Washington, DC 20005-1755
202-293-8830
800-345-6728; *Fax:* 202-872-8543
info@nsba.biz; www.nsba.biz/
Social Media: Facebook, Twitter, LinkedIn, Google+, Stumbleupon
Tim Reynolds, Chair
C. Cookie Driscoll, First Vice Chair
Todd McCracken, President and CEO
Cynthia Kay, Vice Chair for Advocacy
Marc Amato, Vice Chair for Membership
Merged with Small Business United in 1986 and sponsors and supports the NSBU Political Action Committee.

16566 National Training Systems Association
2111 Wilson Boulevard
Suite 400
Arlington, VA 22201-3061
703-247-9471; *Fax:* 703-243-1659
jrobb@ndia.org; www.trainingsystems.org
Social Media: Facebook, Twitter, LinkedIn
De Voorhees, GD IT, Chairman
Pete Swan, VT MAK, Vice Chairman
James Robb, President
Debbie Dyson, Director/Exhibits
Patrick Rowe, Director of Membership Services
Represents companies in the simulation and training and training support industry. Provides forums, market surveys, and business development information and other services to members.
944 Members
Founded in: 1988

16567 Newspaper Association Managers
New England Press Association
PO Box 458
Essex, MA 01929
978-338-2555; *Fax:* 978-744-0333
mlpiper52@comcast.net;
www.nammanagers.com
Lisa Hills, President
Layne Bruce, Vice President
George White, Secretary
Tom Newton, Director
Robin Rhodes, Director
Executives of state, regional, national and international newspaper associations.
65 Members
Founded in: 1923

16568 North America Human ResourceManagement Association
E-Mail: casandra.merkel@shrm.org;
www.nahrma.org
Social Media: Facebook, Twitter, LinkedIn
Henry Jackson, President
Lic. Jorge Jauregui, HRMP, Immediate Past President
Cheryl Newcombe, Secretary/Treasurer
Founded in: 1997

16569 Operations Management Society
5400 Bosque Boulevard
Waco, TX 76710-4414
254-752-6315; *Fax:* 254-776-3767;
www.poms.org
Sushil Gupta, Ph.D, Executive Director
Dr. Metin Єakanyildirim, Associate Executive Director
Members are senior management and deans of business schools in the field of operations management.
Founded in: 1989

16570 Organization Development Institute
11234 Walnut Ridge Road
Chesterland, OH 44026-1240
440-729-7419; *Fax:* 440-729-9319
donwcole@aol.com; www.odinstitute.org
Social Media: Facebook, Twitter, LinkedIn
Dr. Donald W Cole RODC, President
Jim Gustafson, Editor Journal
Promotes the understanding of organization development and offers three categories of membership: professional consultant, regular and student. Offers the International Registry of O.D. Professionals and O.D. Handbook which lists names, addresses and E-mail addresses, publishes a monthly newsletter plus a quarterly journal of 100-150 pages. There are two conferences held every year, one in the USA and one International.
500 Members
Founded in: 1991

16571 Product Development and Management Association
330 N. Wabash Avenue
Suite 2000
Chicago, IL 60611
312-321-5145
800-232-5241; *Fax:* 312-673-6885
pdma@pdma.org; www.pdma.org
Social Media: Facebook, Twitter, LinkedIn
Charlie Noble, Chair
Charlie Noble, VP Academic Affairs
Peter Bradford, NPDP, VP of Certification
Peter Flentov, VP Chapters
Brad White, VP Conferences & Events
Provides essential information to help foster new product development, giving an overview of the total product innovation process and presenting the latest advancements in product innovation. Also assists managers in innovating and producing products more effectively and efficiently.
3200 Members
Founded in: 1976

16572 Production and Operations Management Society
www.poms.org
Sushil Gupta, Ph.D, Executive Director
Dr. Metin Єakanyildirim, Associate Executive Director
Founded in: 1989

16573 Professional Convention Management Association
35 East Wacker Drive
Suite 500
Chicago, IL 60601
312-423-7262
877-827-7262; *Fax:* 312-423-7222
communications@pcma.org; www.pcma.org
Social Media: Facebook, Twitter, LinkedIn, YouTube,Google+
Ray Kopcinski, CMP, Chairman of Board
Deborah Sexton, President and CEO
Jason Paganessi, Vice President, Business Innovation
Sherrif Karamat, CAE, BAS, MBA, Chief Operating Officer
Michelle Russell, Editor in Chief
PCMA delivers superior and innovative education, to promote the value of professional convention management.
6100 Members
Founded in: 1957

16574 **Professional Managers Association**
PO Box 77235
Washington, DC 20013
202-803-9597; *Fax:* 202-803-9044
info@promanager.org; www.promanager.org
Michael Leszcz, National President
Jeff Eppler, National Vice President
Jackie Jones, National Secretary
Tom Burger, Executive Director
Carlos Zepeda, National Treasurer
National membership association representing the interests of professional managers, management officials and non-bargaining unit employees in the federal government. Promote leadership and management excellence within the federal services.
10000 Members
Founded in: 1981

16575 **Project Management Institute (PMI)**
14 Campus Blvd
Newtown Square, PA 19073-3299
610-356-4600
855-746-4849; *Fax:* 610-482-9971
customercare@pmi.org; www.pmi.org
Social Media: Facebook, Twitter, LinkedIn, YouTube,Google+
Mark Langley, President & CEO
Michael Deprisco, Vice President
John J Doyle, MBA, Vice President, Finance
Craig Killough, Vice President, Organization Market
Dorothy McKelvy, MA, SPHR, Vice President, Human Resources
Fosters recognition of the need for project management professionalism. Offers professional certification and bestows awards.
105M Members
Founded in: 1969
Mailing list available for rent

16576 **Public Risk Management Association**
700 S. Washington St.
Suite 218
Alexandria, VA 22314
703-528-7701; *Fax:* 703-739-0200
info@primacentral.org; www.primacentral.org
Social Media: Facebook, Twitter, LinkedIn
Dean Coughenour, ARM, President
Regan Rychetsky, ABCP, Past President
Terri Evans, President-Elect
Marshall Davies, PhD, Executive Director
Jennifer Ackerman, CAE, Deputy Executive Director

16577 **Small Business Assistance Center**
90 Daniel Drive
Avondale, PA 19311
610-444-1720; *Fax:* 610-444-1724
inquire@sbacnetwork.org;
www.sbacnetwork.org
Provides information and assistance to small businesses. To train and consult entrepreneurs through information services, seminars and professional consultations.
Founded in: 1988

16578 **Society for Advancement of Management**
6300 Ocean Drive - OCNR 383
Unit - 5808
Corpus Christi, TX 78412-5807
361-825-3045
888-827-6077; *Fax:* 361-825-5609
moustafa@cob.tamucc.edu;
www.samnational.org
Social Media: Facebook, LinkedIn
Moustafa H Abdelsamad, President/CEO
R. Clifton Poole, Secretary
Kent Byus, Treasurer
SAM members come from a variety of disciplines - productions, finance, marketing, accounting and more who all share a common bond of interest in becoming stronger managers. SAM abounds with opportunities for professional development.
3000 Members
Founded in: 1912

16579 **Society for Human Resource Management**
SHRM/Society for Human Resource Management
1800 Duke St
Alexandria, VA 22314-3496
703-535-6000
800-283-7476
703-548-3440; *Fax:* 703-535-6490
shrmeducation@shrm.org.; www.shrm.org
Social Media: Facebook, Twitter, LinkedIn, YouTube, RSS, Google+
Bette J. Francis, SPHR, Chair
Henry G. Jackson, CPA, President and CEO
J. Robert Carr, J.D., SPHR, SVP, Membership, Marketing
Deb Cohen, Ph.D., SPHR, SVP, Knowledge Development
Brian K. Dickson, SVP, Professional Development
World's largest association devoted to human resource management. Serves the needs of the human resource management professional by providing the most essential and comprehensive set of resources available.
18500 Members
Founded in: 1948
Mailing list available for rent

16580 **Stage Managers' Association**
PO Box 275
Times Square Station
New York, NY 10108-0275
www.stagemanagers.org
Social Media: Facebook, Twitter, LinkedIn
Elynmarie Kazle, Chair
Mandy L. Berry, 1st Vice Chair
Hope Rose Kelly, 2nd Vice Chair
Eileen Arnold, Treasurer
Melissa A. Nathan, Secretary
Founded in: 1981

16581 **Strategic Management Association**
19102 South Blackhawk Parkway
Unit 25
Mokena, IL 60448-4066
815-806-4908;
www.strategicleadershipforum.org
Chris Glatz, Executive Director/Administration
The international society for strategic management and planning. Presents awards, conducts seminars and foundation research.
6.5M Members
Founded in: 1985

16582 **Strategic Management Society**
Rice Building, 815 W Van Buren Street
Suite 215
Chicago, IL 60607
312-492-6224; *Fax:* 312-492-6223
sms@strategicmanagement.net;
www.strategicmanagement.net
Social Media: Facebook, Twitter, LinkedIn, YouTube
Robert Hoskisson, President
Marjorie Lyles, President Elect
Jay Barney, Past President
Steven Floyd, Treasurer
Nikolaus Pelka, Executive Director
Founded in: 1981

16583 **Support Services Alliance**
Po Box 130
Schoharie, NY 12157-0130
518-295-7966
800-322-3920; *Fax:* 518-295-8556
membershipservices@ssamembers.com;
www.ssainfo.com
Steven Cole, President
Multi-state membership organization that provides cost-savings services and legislative representation for small businesses and the self-employed. Also offers services to the memberships of more than 100 affiliated state, regional and national associations.
50 Members
Founded in: 1977

16584 **The Association of State Floodplain Managers**
575 D'Onofrio Drive
Suite 200
Madison, WI 53719
608-828-3000; *Fax:* 608-828-6319;
www.floods.org
Social Media: Facebook, Twitter, LinkedIn
Bill Nechamen, Chair
Ceil Strauss, Vice Chair
Karen McHugh, Treasurer
Leslie Durham, Secretary
Chad Berginnis, Executive Director
Founded in: 1977

16585 **The Employers Association**
3020 W. Arrowood Road
Charlotte, NC 28273
704-522-8011; *Fax:* 704-522-8105
info@employersassoc.com;
www.employersassoc.com
Social Media: Facebook, Twitter, LinkedIn, RSS
Paul DeVine, Chairman
Paul DeVine, Vice Chairman
Kenny Colbert, President, CEO
Tom L. Barnhardt, Past Chairman
Cathy Graham, SPHR, Director, Benefit Services

16586 **The Sales Management Association**
E-Mail: support@salesmanagement.org;
www.salesmanagement.org
Social Media: Facebook, Twitter, LinkedIn, RSS
Robert J. Kelly, Chairman
Laura Hall, Managing Director

16587 **TheAmerican SocietyofAdministrative Professionals**
121 Free Street
Portland, ME 4101
888-960-ASAP; *Fax:* 207-842-5603
membership@asaporg.com; www.asaporg.com
Social Media: Facebook, Twitter, LinkedIn, Pinterest
Founded in: 2005

16588 **TheAssociationfor Financial Professionals**
4520 East West Highway
Suite 750
Bethesda, MD 20814
301-907-2862; *Fax:* 301-907-2864;
www.afponline.org
Social Media: Twitter, LinkedIn, YouTube, RSS
Anthony Scaglione, CTP, Chairman
Roberta Eiseman, CTP, Vice Chairman
Jeff Johnson, CTP, CPA, Vice Chairman
Ann Anthony, CTP, Board of Director
Terry Crawford, CTP, Board of Director

16589 **Turnaround Management Association Headquarters**
150 S Wacker Drive
Suite 900
Chicago, IL 60606
312-578-6900; *Fax:* 312-578-8336
info@turnaround.org; www.turnaround.org
Social Media: Facebook, Twitter, LinkedIn
Ronald R Sussman, Chairperson
Thomas M Kim, President
Gregory J. Fine, CAE, Chief Executive Officer
Jim Gavin, Chief Financial Officer
Jennifer Bethke, Chief Learning & Certification
The only international nonprofit association dedicated to corporate renewal and turnaround management. TMA's 9,000 members in 46 regional chapters comprise a professional community of turnaround practitioners, attorneys, accountants, investors, lenders, venture capitalists, appraiser, liquidators, executive recruiters and consultants. Three international conferences each year offer networking and educational sessions on the latest trends and best practices in the restructuring field.
9000 Members
Founded in: 1988

16590 **U.S. Workplace Wellness Alliance**
1615 H Street NW
Washington, DC 20062-2000
www.uswwa.org

16591 **WACRA: World Association for Case Method Research & Application**
23 Mackintosh Avenue
Needham, MA 02492-1218
781-444-8982; *Fax:* 781-444-1548
wacra@rcn.com; www.wacra.org
Dr Hans E Klein, President/Executive Director
Denise M. Smith, Executive Assistant
Dr. Amelia J. Klein, Director Education
Dr. Lars Bengtsson, Director Public Relations
Dr. Charles H. Patti, Director of Publications
Advancing the use of the case method and other interactive methodologies in teaching, training and planning.
2000 Members
Founded in: 1984

16592 **Wiley**
John Wiley & Sons
111 River Street
Hoboken, NJ 07030-5774
201-748-6000
800-825-7550; *Fax:* 201-748-6088
info@wiley.com; www.wiley.com
Matthew S. Kissiner, Chairman of the Board
Mark Allin, President and CEO
Vincent Marzano, Vice President & Treasurer
Ellis E. Cousens, Executive Vice President
John Kritzmacher, Executive Vice President
Provides information to help executives manage their companies effectively.

16593 **Women in Management**
Women in Management
PO Box 6690
Elgin, IL 60121-6690
877-946-6285; *Fax:* 847-683-3751
nationalwim@aol.com; www.wimonline.org
Dana Vierck, President
Ann Louis, Secretary
Tracey Carlstedt, Treasurer
Jane Gregory, Membership
Chris Awe, Administrator
Aims to promote self-growth in management. Sponsors speakers and discussion groups.
1.7M Members
Founded in: 1976

16594 **Young Presidents Organization**
600 East Las Colinas Boulevard
Suite 1000
Irving, TX 75039
972-587-1500
800-773-7976; *Fax:* 972-587-1611
askypo@ypo.org; www.ypo.org
Social Media: Facebook, Twitter, LinkedIn, YouTube, Google+, Instagram
Scott Mordell, Chief Executive Officer
Sean Magennis, Chief Operating Officer
Cynthia Abbott, Chief Marketing Officer
Terry Wilson, Chief Financial Officer
Dwight Moore, Chief Information Officer
Founded in: 1950

16595 **Young Presidents' Organization**
Young Presidents' Organization
600 East Las Colinas Boulevard
Suite 1000
Irving, TX 75039
972-587-1500
800-773-7976; *Fax:* 972-587-1611
askypo@ypo.org; www.ypo.org
Social Media: Facebook, Twitter, LinkedIn, Youtube, Google+, Instagram
Fulton Collins, Chairman
Scott Mordell, Chief Executive Officer
Members are corporate presidents under the age of fifty whose companies employ at least fifty employees.
8000 Members
Founded in: 1950

Newsletters

16596 **American Academy of Medical Administration Executive Newsletter**
701 Lee St
Suite 600
Des Plaines, IL 60016-4516
847-759-8601; *Fax:* 847-759-8602;
www.aameda.org
Renee Schleichar, CEO
Guy Snyder, Director of Education
Rhonda Guptill, Chief Financial Officer
Offers information and news to upper level administration of hospitals and medical institutions.
14 Pages
Frequency: BiWeekly

16597 **Best Practices Report**
Management Roundtable
92 Crescent St
Waltham, MA 02453-4315
781-891-8080
800-338-2223; *Fax:* 781-398-1889;
www.pharmcentric.com
A monthly newsletter on the best practices in product development. How to develop and deliver great products at the lowest cost in the shortest time.

16598 **Better Supervision**
Economics Press
12 Daniel Road
Fairfield, NJ 07004-2565
973-227-1224; *Fax:* 973-227-9742
Robert Guder, Publisher
Techniques for managing people successfully.
Cost: $1.00
Circulation: 43,000

16599 **Better Work Supervisor**
Clement Communications
Concord Industrial Park
Concordville, PA 19331
610-459-4200; *Fax:* 610-459-0936
Offers important information, articles and news to upper level management.
Cost: $48.50

16600 **Blue Ribbon Service**
Economics Press
12 Daniel Road
Fairfield, NJ 07004-2565
973-227-1224; *Fax:* 973-227-9742
Robert Guder, Publisher
Shows employees the importance of giving good customer service and methods of providing that service.
Circulation: 27,760

16601 **Bridging the Gap**
Section for Women in Public Administration
1301 Pennsylvania Avenue NW
Suite 700
Washington, DC 20004
202-393-7878; *Fax:* 202-638-4952
info@aspanet.org; www.aspanet.org
Social Media: Facebook, Twitter, LinkedIn
Circulation: 400
Founded in: 1939
Mailing list available for rent: 400 names

16602 **Bulletin to Management**
Bureau of National Affairs
1801 S Bell St
Arlington, VA 22202-4501
703-341-3000
800-372-1033; *Fax:* 800-253-0332
customercare@bna.com; www.bnabooks.com
Social Media: Facebook, Twitter, LinkedIn
Paul N Wojcik, CEO
Features summaries of current developments in human resource/personnel management and labor relations. Discusses real life job situations and provides policy guides on how companies have successfully handled employee related problems. Recurring features include statistics.
Cost: $317.00
Frequency: Weekly
Founded in: 1929

16603 **Business Journal**
Business Journals of North Carolina
120 W Morehead St
Suite 420
Charlotte, NC 28202-1874
704-973-1200
800-948-5323; *Fax:* 704-973-1201
charlotte@bizjournals.com;
www.citybiznetwork.com
George Conley, President
Robert Morris, Editor
David Harris, Managing Editor
72 Pages
Frequency: Weekly
ISSN: 0887-5588
Printed in 4 colors on newsprint stock

16604 **Business Courier**
101 W 7th St
Cincinnati, OH 45202-2306
513-621-6665
800-767-3263; *Fax:* 513-621-2462
borben@bizjournals.com;
www.bizjournals.com/cincinnati/
Douglas Bolton, Publisher
Rob Daumeyer, Editor
Cost: $83.00
Frequency: Weekly
Circulation: 11000
Founded in: 1947

16605 Case Strategies
Cutter Information Corporation
37 Broadway
Suite 1
Arlington, MA 02474-5500

781-648-1950
800-888-8939; *Fax:* 781-648-1950
service@cutter.com; www.cutter.com/

Paul Harman, Editor
Kim Leonard, Customer Service Director
Karen Coburn, CEO/President
Hillel Glazer, Senior Consultant
Ron Blitstein, Director

Objective, timely information to help you successfully integrate CASE into your organization.
Cost: $387.00
16 Pages
Frequency: Monthly
Founded in: 1986

16606 Cash Flow Enhancement Report
Institute of Management and Administration
3 Bethesda Metro Center
Suite 250
Bethesda, MD 20814-5377

703-341-3500
800-372-1033; *Fax:* 800-253-0332;
www.ioma.com

Focuses on business strategies for increasing liquidity.
Cost: $245.00
16 Pages
Frequency: Monthly

16607 Center for Creative Leadership Newsletter
Center for Creative Leadership
Attn: Client Services
PO Box 26300
Greensboro, NC 27438-6300

336-887-7210; *Fax:* 336-282-3284
info@ccl.org; www.ccl.org

Walter Ulmer Jr, Publisher
John Alexander, President, Chief Executive Officer

A newsletter featuring issues and observations on the behavioral science research and development field.
Frequency: Monthly
Circulation: 35000
Founded in: 1970

16608 Chief Executive Officers Newsletter
Center for Entreprenuel Management
47 West Street
Suite 5C
New York, NY 10014-4606

212-633-0060; *Fax:* 212-633-0063
mail@ceoclubs.org; www.ceoclubs.org

Joseph Mancuso, President
Christopher Jones, Office Manager

Unique management insights and sources for presidents of growing businesses.
Cost: $71.00
Frequency: Monthly
Circulation: 40000
Founded in: 1978

16609 Communications Insights
Comquest
112 Schubert Drive
Downingtown, PA 19335-3382

610-269-2100; *Fax:* 610-269-2275

Mark Schubert, Publisher

Tips and techniques for sucessful communication.

16610 Communique
213 W Institute Place
Suite 307
Chicago, IL 60610-3195

312-440-0078
800-962-8274; *Fax:* 312-440-9474
mailbox@iahcsmm.com; www.iahcsmm.com

Betty Hanna, Executive Director
Marilyn Corida, Secretary/Treasurer
Lisa Huber, President
Bruce T. Bird, President

Bi-monthly publication separates supervisors/directors from technicians.
Cost: $40.00
Frequency: 6/Annual
Circulation: 15M
ISBN: 1-605309-30-9

16611 Contractor's Business Management Report
Institute of Management and Administration
3 Bethesda Metro Center
Suite 250
Bethesda, MD 20814-5377

703-341-3500
800-372-1033; *Fax:* 800-253-0332;
www.ioma.com

Delivers practical, relevant, and insightful business management guidance to contractors, subcontractors and their consultants.
Cost: $424.00

16612 Corporate EFT Report
Phillips Publishing
95 Old Shoals Road
Arden, NC 28704

301-340-2100
866-599-9491
feedback@healthydirections.com;
www.healthydirections.com
Social Media: Facebook, Twitter

Newsletter on business, EFT operations for corporate cash managers.

16613 Corporate Examiner
Interfaith Center on Corporate Response
475 Riverside Dr
Suite 1842
New York, NY 10115-0034

212-870-2295; *Fax:* 212-870-2023
info@interfaithcommunity.org;
www.interfaithcommunity.org

Laura Morrison, Program Coordinator
Diane Bratcher, Editor

Analyzes corporate social responsibility issues and trends, reports corporate action news, reviews publications and media and presents the ideas and opinions of leaders of the corporate social responsibility movement.
Cost: $ 35.00
8 Pages
Circulation: 1500
Founded in: 1981
Printed in one color on matte stock

16614 Cost Controller
Siefer Consultants
PO Box 1384
Storm Lake, IA 50588-1384

712-732-7340; *Fax:* 712-732-7906

Dan Siefer, Publisher

Cost cutting techniques and ideas for business and industry.
Cost: $149.00
8 Pages
Frequency: Monthly

16615 Customer Communicator
Alexander Communications Group
1916 Park Ave
Suite 501
New York, NY 10037-3733

212-281-6099
800-232-4317; *Fax:* 212-283-7269
info@customerservicegroup.com;
www.customerservicegroup.com

Romauld Alexander, President
Adam Reif, Marketing Manager

Provides customer service representatives with the skills, techniques and motivation they need to be more productive.
Cost: $200.00
Frequency: Monthly
ISSN: 0145-8450
Founded in: 1990

16616 Customer Service Manager's Letter
Bureau of Business Practice
76 Ninth Avenue
7th Floor
New York, NY 10011

212-771-0600; *Fax:* 212-771-0885;
www.aspenlawschool.com
Social Media: Facebook, Twitter, LinkedIn

Mark Dorman, CEO
Gustavo Dobles, VP Operations

Specially designed to show managers how to reduce their costs, their customer base, and maximize their employee capability.
Cost: $179.00
8 Pages
Frequency: 2 per year
Circulation: 5200

16617 Daily Report for Executives
Bureau of National Affairs
1801 S Bell St
Arlington, VA 22202-4501

703-341-3000
800-372-1033; *Fax:* 800-253-0332
customercare@bna.com; www.bnabooks.com
Social Media: Facebook, Twitter, LinkedIn

Paul N Wojcik, CEO

A daily notification service covering legislative, regulatory, legal, tax and economic developments which affect both national and international businesses.
Cost: $9399.00
Frequency: Daily
ISSN: 0148-8155
Founded in: 1929

16618 Deal
The Deal, LLC.
14 Wall Street
New York, NY 10005

212-313-9200
888-667-3325
customerservice@thedeal.com;
www.thedeal.com
Social Media: Twitter

Mickey Hernandez, Advertising Sales
Elena Freed, Marketing

Dedicated solely to reporting and analyzing all the aspects of the booming, high stakes world of the deeal economy. Areas of coverage include mergers and acquisitions, IPO's, private equity, venture capital and bankruptcies. Published in newsletter and on website.
Cost: $249.00
26 Pages
Founded in: 1999

16619 Delphi Insight Series
Delphi Group

Ten Post Office Square
Suite 580
Boston, MA 02109-4603

617-247-1511
800-335-7440; *Fax:* 617-247-4957;
www.delphigroup.com

Thomas Koulopoulos, President
Hadley Reynolds, Director Research
Mary Ann Kozlowski, Director Public Relations

Timely and insightful analysis and review of the markets, developments, and business cases for knowledge management, corporate portals and e-business solutions. Incorporates original Delphi research findings. Written for all management titles. Includes weekly email news update on relevant issues and access to DelphiWeb, an extensive online resource of product and market information.
Cost: $20000.00
Frequency: Daily

16620 Directorship
Directorship Search Group
8 Sound Shore Drive
Suite 250
Greenwich, CT 06830-7276

203-618-7000; *Fax:* 203-618-7007;
www.directorship.com

Russell Reynolds Jr, CEO/President
Barrett Stephens, VP
J.P. Donlon, Editor-in-Chief

Articles and news of interest to CEOs and directors of public companies, on every aspect of corporate governance.
Cost: $395.00
12 Pages
ISSN: 0193-4279
Founded in: 1975
Printed in 4 colors on glossy stock

16621 EAP Link
International Education Services and Publishing
1537 Franklin Street
#201-203
San Francisco, CA 94109-4571

415-239-4171
800-551-3005

Kendall Van Blarcom, Publisher

International news for human resource professionals.
Cost: $197.00
8 Pages
Frequency: Monthly

16622 Employee Assistance Program Management Letter
Health Resources Publishing
1913 Atlantic Ave
Suite 200
Manasquan, NJ 08736-1067

732-292-1100
888-843-6242; *Fax:* 732-292-1111
info@healthresourcesonline.com;
www.healthresourcesonline.com

Robert K Jenkins, Publisher
Lisa Mansfield, Regional Director
Brett Powell, Regional Director
Alice Burron, Director

A monthly briefing on guidelines to help companies make decisions on managing their EAP programs. Contains information on what EAP's across the country are doing; help on policy issues dealing with and monitoring costs; framing coverages and limitations; and case histories.
Cost: $227.00
Frequency: Monthly
ISSN: 0896-0941
Founded in: 1978

16623 Enrollment Management Report
LRP Publications
747 Dresher Road Suite 500
PO Box 980
Horsham, PA 19044-980

215-840-0912
800-341-7874; *Fax:* 215-784-9639
webmaster@lrp.com; www.lrp.com

Jay Margolis, Editor

Provides solutions and strategies for recruitment, admissions, retention and financial aid for higher-education institutions. Shows readers how to face the challenge of working across departmental lines to improve retention rates and how to respond to the upcoming surge in non-traditional students who apply.
Cost: $198.00
Frequency: Monthly
Founded in: 1977

16624 Executive Administrator
Seifer Consultants
P.O.Box 1384
Storm Lake, IA 50588-1384
712-732-7340; *Fax:* 712-732-7906

John Siefer, Publisher

Management, job opportunities and news.
Cost: $70.00
Frequency: Monthly

16625 Executive Advantage
Briefings Publishing Group
1101 King St
Suite 110
Alexandria, VA 22314-2944

703-548-3800
800-888-2084; *Fax:* 703-684-2136;
www.briefings.com

Tina Ragland, Editorial Assistant
Lois Willingham, Marketing Manager
Deirdre Hackett, Executive Editor
William Dugan, Group Publisher
Michelle Cox, Publisher

A publication designed to help you learn the key interpersonal secrets to business success through proper etiquette and protocol.
Cost: $147.00
8 Pages
Frequency: Monthly
Founded in: 1981
Mailing list available for rent: 6000 names at $125 per M
Printed in 2 colors on matte stock

16626 Executive Edge
28 W 23rd Street
10th Floor
New York, NY 10010

212-367-4100; *Fax:* 212-367-4137

Rich Karlgaard, Publisher
David Hallerman, Editor

Covers quality customer service and marketing techniques.

16627 Executive Issues
Wharton School
255 S 38th St
Philadelphia, PA 19104-3706

215-386-8300; *Fax:* 215-573-6138
editor@wharton.upenn.edu;
www.wharton.upenn.edu

Jason Fisher, President

Discusses current business issues, business continuing information.
Circulation: 40000

16628 Executive Recruiter News
Kennedy Information
1 Phoenix Mill Lane
Floor 3
Peterborough, NH 03458

603-924-1006
800-531-0007
customerservice@kennedyinfo.com;
www.kennedyinfo.com

Joseph McCool, Editor
William Allen, Managing Director

The authoritative voice of the recruiting industry, covering news, analysis, practice, advice, proprietary data and opinion.
Cost: $229.00
8 Pages
Frequency: Monthly
ISSN: 0271-0781
Founded in: 1980
Printed in 2 colors on matte stock

16629 Executive Report on Managed Care
Health Resources Publishing
1913 Atlantic Ave
Suite 200
Manasquan, NJ 08736-1067

732-292-1100
888-843-6242; *Fax:* 732-292-1111
info@themcic.com;
www.healthresourcesonline.com

Robert K Jenkins, Publisher
Lisa Mansfield, Regional Director
Brett Powell, Regional Director
Alice Burron, Director

Bi-monthly report giving news of how major employers are implementing managed care programs. Helps companies prepare to evaluate and monitor various managed care proposals in terms of their cost effectiveness, quality and liability to the employer.
Cost: $497.00
Frequency: Weekly
ISSN: 0898-9753
Founded in: 1978

16630 Executive Report on Physician Organizations
Health Resources Publishing
1913 Atlantic Ave
Suite 200
Manasquan, NJ 08736-1067

732-292-1100
800-516-4343; *Fax:* 732-292-1111
info@themcic.com;
www.healthresourcesonline.com

Robert K Jenkins, Publisher
Lisa Mansfield, Marketing Assistant
Caroline Pense, Editor
Brett Powell, Regional Director
Alice Burron, Director

A bi-monthly newsletter published by Health Resources Publishing.
Cost: $197.00
Frequency: Monthly
Circulation: 5000
ISSN: 0898-9753
Founded in: 1978

16631 Executive Solutions
Dartnell Corporation
4660 N Ravenswood Avenue
Chicago, IL 60640-4510

773-907-9500
800-727-1227; *Fax:* 561-622-2423
customerservice@dartnellcorp.com;
www.dartnellcorp.com

Clark Fertridge, Publisher
John Aspley, Founder

Modern management techniques for executive training.

16632 Executive Wealth Advisory
National Institute of Business Management

Po Box 906
Williamsport, PA 17703-9933

703-058-8000
800-433-0622; *Fax:* 570-567-0166
customer@nibm.net; www.nibm.net

10 Pages
Frequency: Monthly
ISSN: 1049-4855

16633 Federal Personnel Guide
LRP Publications
360 Hiatt Drive
Palm Beach Gardens, FL 33418

561-622-6520
800-341-7874; *Fax:* 561-622-0757
webmaster@lrp.com; www.lrp.com

Kenneth Kahn, President

Annual almanac for US civilian federal personnel and training officers and individual federal and postal employees. An up-to-the-minute summary of rules and regulations affecting federal employees, including employment, pay and benefits.
Cost: $12.95
Circulation: 55000
ISBN: 1-881097-12-9
ISSN: 0163-7665
Founded in: 1978

16634 Financial Management Association International (FMA)
University of South Florida
4202 E Fowler Ave
Tampa, FL 33620-9951

813-974-2011; *Fax:* 813-974-5530;
www.usf.edu

Judy L Genshaft, President
William Christie, Financial Management Editor
Keith M Howe, Journal of Applied Finance Editor
James Schallheim, FMA Survey Synthesis Series Editor
John Finnerty, Editor FMA Online

Financial books, textbooks, databases, newspapers, research services, software and related products and services.
Frequency: Quarterly
Founded in: 1970
Mailing list available for rent

16635 Global Environmental Change Report
Cutter Information Corporation
111 Eighth Avenue 7th Floor
New York, NY 10011-5552

212-771-0600; *Fax:* 212-771-0885
jrohaly@aspenpublishers.com;
www.aspenlawschool.com

Wolters Kluwer, CEO
Richard Richard, Executive VP

An exclusive international service reporting on policy trends, industry actions and global environmental change.
Cost: $565.00
8 Pages
Frequency: Monthly

16636 HIPAA Bulletin for Management
Health Resources Publishing
1913 Atlantic Ave
Suite 200
Manasquan, NJ 08736-1067

732-292-1100
888-843-6242; *Fax:* 732-292-1111
info@healthresourcesonline.com;
www.healthresourcesonline.com

Robert K Jenkins, Publisher
Lisa Mansfield, Regional Director
Brett Powell, Regional Director
Alice Burron, Director

A monthly newsletter published by Health Resources Publishing.
Cost: $147.00
Frequency: Monthly
ISSN: 0898-9753
Founded in: 1978

16637 HMFA Healthcare Cost Containment Newsletter
Healthcare Finance Management Association
3 Westbrook Corporate Center
Suite 600
Westchester, IL 60154

708-531-9600; *Fax:* 708-531-0032;
www.hfma.org/publications/healthcarecost

Issues illustrate how to implement strategic cost management that will reduce labor and supply expenses, enhance operational efficiency, satisfy your patients, and improve your competitive position.
Cost: $125.00
Frequency: Quarterly

16638 HMFA Revenue Cycle Stragetist Newsletter
Healthcare Finance Management Association
3 Westbrook Corporate Center
Suite 600
Westchester, IL 60154

708-531-9600; *Fax:* 708-531-0032;
www.hfma.org/publications/

Improve your organization's bottom line while maintaining regulatory compliance.
Cost: $165.00
Frequency: Quarterly

16639 HR Briefings
Bureau of Business Practice
111 8th Avenue
New York, NY 10011

212-771-0733
800-243-1660; *Fax:* 800-901-9075;
www.aspenlawschool.com/

Alicia Pierce, President

Designed to help HR professionals become more effective on the job. It offers hands-on advice from other personnel managers who have experienced the kinds of problems facing readers.
Cost: $259.00
8 Pages
Frequency: Monthly
Founded in: 1925

16640 HR News
Int'l Public Management Assoc for Human Resources
1617 Duke St
Alexandria, VA 22314-3406

703-549-7100; *Fax:* 703-684-0948
ipma@pma-hr.org; www.ipma-hr.org

Neil Reichenberg, Executive Director
Sima Hassassian, COO
Tina Chiappetta, Sr Director Gov't Affairs/Comm
Frequency: Monthly
Circulation: 8000

16641 HR Weekly
SHRM/Society for Human Resource Management
1800 Duke St
Alexandria, VA 22314-3494

703-535-6000
866-898-4724; *Fax:* 703-535-6474
shrmeducation@shrm.org.; www.shrm.org
Social Media: Facebook, Twitter, LinkedIn, Youtube

Susan R Meisinger, CEO

Weekly e-newsletter highlighting critical HR/Human Resourace issues.

16642 HR on Campus
LRP Publications
747 Dresher Road
PO Box 980
Horsham, PA 19044-980

215-784-0912
800-341-7874; *Fax:* 215-784-9639
webmaster@lrp.com; www.lrp.com

Jay Margolis, Editor/publisher

Gives you the tools you need to solve your institution's human resource challenges. Provides pratical tips for handling real-life, day-to-day problems, along with the latest news and significant developments in higher education.
Cost: $165.00
Frequency: Monthly
Founded in: 1977

16643 HRmadeEasy
Employers of America
310 Meadow Lane
Mason City, IA 50401

641-424-3187
800-728-3187; *Fax:* 641-424-3187
employer@employerhelp.org;
www.employerhelp.org

Jim Collison, President

A weekly e-newsletter published by Employers of America.
Cost: $149.00
Frequency: Weekly
Circulation: 600
Founded in: 1976

16644 Hiring the Best
Briefings Publishing Group
1101 King St
Suite 110
Alexandria, VA 22314-2944

703-548-3800
800-888-2084; *Fax:* 703-684-2136;
www.briefings.com

Deirdre Hackett, Editor
William G Dugan, Publisher
Tina Ragland, Editorial Assistant
Lois Willingham, Marketing Manager

A publication designed to help executives recruit, screen, and retain the best employees.
Cost: $697.00
8 Pages
Frequency: Monthly
Circulation: 1300
Founded in: 1981
Mailing list available for rent: 6000 names at $125 per M
Printed in 2 colors on matte stock

16645 Human Resource Department Management Report
Institute of Management and Administration
3 Bethesda Metro Center
Suite 250
Bethesda, MD 20814-5377

703-341-3500
800-372-1033; *Fax:* 800-253-0332;
www.ioma.com

Shows HR department heads how to boost staff motivation and productivity, improve department automation, and cut costs while improving service.
Cost: $299.00
Frequency: Monthly

16646 Human Resources Management Reporter
Thomson Reuters

2395 Midway Rd
Carrollton, TX 75006

646-822-2000
800-431-9025; *Fax:* 888-216-1929
trta.lei-support@thomsonreuters.com;
www.ria.thomsonreuters.com

Elaine Yadlon, Plant Manager
Thomas H Glocer, CEO & Director
Robert D Daleo, Chief Financial Officer
Kelli Crane, Senior Vice President & CIO

For personnel practitioners.
Founded in: 1935

16647 ICSB Bulletin Updates
International Council for Small Business
2201 G Street NW
Suite 315
Washington, DC 20052

202-944-0704; *Fax:* 202-994-4930
icsb@gwu.edu; www.icsb.org
Social Media: Facebook, Twitter

Luca Iandoli, President
Dr. Robert S. Lai, President-Elect
Geralyn Franklin, VP/Finance/Control
Ayman El Tarabishy, Executive Director
Michael Bataglia, Operations Manager

Provides monthly updates on ICSB events, news, and relevant information.
4000+ Members
Frequency: Monthly
Founded in: 1955
Printed in 2 colors on glossy stock

16648 IOMA's Pay for Performance Report
Institute of Management and Administration
3 Bethesda Metro Center
Suite 250
Bethesda, MD 20814-5377

703-341-3500
800-372-1033; *Fax:* 800-253-0332;
www.ioma.com

Helps human resource and compensation executives improve their company's productivity through the use of variable pay and bonus programs for all types of employees.

16649 IOMA's Report on Managing Flexible Benefit Plans
Institute of Management and Administration
3 Bethesda Metro Center
Suite 250
Bethesda, MD 20814-5377

703-341-3500
800-372-1033; *Fax:* 800-253-0332;
www.ioma.com

Information to manage a firm's flex plan.
Cost: $245.00
16 Pages
Frequency: Monthly

16650 IT Services Business Report
Staffing Industry Analysts
881 Fremont Ave
Suite A3
Los Altos, CA 94024-5637

650-948-9303
800-950-9496; *Fax:* 650-232-2360;
www.sireport.com

Ron Mester, President/CEO
Peter Yessne, Chairman/Publisher

Business news and industry trends analysis for professionals.
Cost: $297.00
Frequency: Monthly
Founded in: 1989

16651 Information Advisor
Information Advisory Services
143 Old Marlton Pike
Medford, NJ 08055-8750

609-654-6266; *Fax:* 609-654-4309
dpanara@infotoday.com;
www.informationadvisor.com

Robert Berkman, Editor

Compares and evaluates business information services - print, online and CD-ROM. Covers international data, information quality, and new noteworthy products.
Frequency: Monthly
Circulation: 700

16652 International Management Council
608 S 114th Street
Omaha, NE 68154-3153

402-330-6310
800-688-9622; *Fax:* 402-330-7424;
www.cmc-global.org

Jodeen Sterba, National Administrator

Information on developing leadership and management skills through a network of shared experiences and education.
Printed in 2 colors on matte stock

16653 International Quality
Underwriters Laboratories
2600 N.W. Lake Rd.
Camas, WA 98607-8542

847-412-0136
877-854-3577; *Fax:* 360-817-6278
cec.us@us.ul.com; www.ul.com

Keith E Williams, CEO
John Drengenberg, Manager Consumer Affairs

Free standards and other quality management topics.
Frequency: Monthly
Circulation: 18000
Founded in: 1894

16654 Inventory Reduction Report
Institute of Management and Administration
3 Bethesda Metro Center
Suite 250
Bethesda, MD 20814-5377

703-341-3500
800-372-1033; *Fax:* 800-253-0332;
www.ioma.com

Focuses on reducing inventory costs, JIT methods and improving profitability.
Cost: $245.00
16 Pages
Frequency: Monthly

16655 Issues and Observations
Center for Creative Leadership & Jossay-Bass
350 Sansome Street
San Francisco, CA 94104-1304

415-334-4700
888-378-2537; *Fax:* 800-605-2665
info@ccl.org; www.ccl.org

John Alexander, President
Patricia Ohlott, President, Chief Executive Officer

Contains articles about leadership and management.
Cost: $99.00
Frequency: Quarterly
Circulation: 3000
ISSN: 1093-6092
Founded in: 1970

16656 Job Safety and Health
Bureau of National Affairs
1801 S Bell St
Arlington, VA 22202-4501

703-341-3000
800-372-1033; *Fax:* 800-253-0332;
www.bnabooks.com
Social Media: Facebook, Twitter, LinkedIn

Paul N Wojcik, CEO

A biweekly review of workplace health and safety regulations, policies, practices and trends.
Cost: $898.00
ISSN: 0149-7510
Founded in: 1929

16657 Jots and Jolts
Economics Press
12 Daniel Road
Fairfield, NJ 07004-2565

973-227-1224; *Fax:* 973-227-9742

John Beckley, Publisher

Monthly planner for supervisors; includes information management theory.
Cost: $1.00
Circulation: 32000

16658 Kennedy's Career Strategist
Career Strategies
1150 Wilmette Avenue
Wilmette, IL 60091-2603

847-251-1661
800-728-1709; *Fax:* 847-251-5191
mmkcareer@aol.com;
www.moatskennedy.com/newsletter.html

Marilyn Moat Kennedy, Editor
Linda Mitchell, Production Manager
Cost: $65.00
Frequency: Monthly
ISSN: 0891-2572
Founded in: 1986

16659 Laboratory Industry Report
Institute of Management and Administration
3 Bethesda Metro Center
Suite 250
Bethesda, MD 20814-5377

703-341-3500
800-372-1033; *Fax:* 800-253-0332;
www.ioma.com

An insider's view of the lab industry's most important business and financial trends.
Cost: $449.00

16660 Law Office Management & Administration Report
Institute of Management and Administration
3 Bethesda Metro Center
Suite 250
Bethesda, MD 20814-5377

703-341-3500
800-372-1033; *Fax:* 800-253-0332;
www.ioma.com

Covers the daily management concerns relevant for law firm administrators, office managers, and others.
Cost: $489.00
Frequency: Monthly
Founded in: 1983

16661 Leadership Strategies
Briefings Publishing Group
1101 King St
Suite 110
Alexandria, VA 22314-2944

703-548-3800
800-888-2084; *Fax:* 703-684-2136;
www.briefings.com

Deirdre Hackett, Editor
Jacqueline Stonis, Production Manager
William G. Duggan, Group Publisher
Lois Willingham, Marketing Manager

A publication designed to sharpen your management and leadership abilities, improve your productivity, and accelerate your professional

success.
Cost: $199.00
8 Pages
Frequency: Monthly
Circulation: 8500
Founded in: 1981
Mailing list available for rent: 7000 names at $125 per M
Printed in 2 colors on matte stock

16662 Management Policies and Personnel Law
Business Research Publications
1533 H Street NW
Suite 200W
Washington, DC 20005-1005
202-364-6473
800-822-6338; *Fax:* 202-466-3509
Susan Sonnesyn-Brooks, Editor
Leading newsletter designed to give managers an inside view into the best run companies.
Frequency: BiWeekly

16663 Manager's Legal Bulletin
Alexander Hamilton Institute
70 Hilltop Rd
Suite 220
Ramsey, NJ 07446-2816
201-825-3377
800-879-2441; *Fax:* 201-825-8696
custsvc@ahipubs.com; www.ahipubs.com
Schuyler T Jenks, President
Shows managers how to handle problems in the workplace without provoking lawsuits for illegal discrimination in hiring, firing, promotions, sexual harassment or discipline decisions.
Cost: $66.00
4 Pages
Frequency: Fortnightly
Circulation: 20000
Founded in: 1909
Mailing list available for rent: 8M names at $125 per M
Printed in 2 colors on matte stock

16664 Managing Benefits Plans
Institute of Management and Administration
3 Bethesda Metro Center
Suite 250
Bethesda, MD 20814-5377
703-341-3500
800-372-1033; *Fax:* 800-253-0332;
www.ioma.com
The result of combining two newsletters into one, stronger report. Managers who oversee the enrollment, communications, and administration of employee benefits are the best subscribers to MBP.
Cost: $399.00
Founded in: 1982

16665 Managing Customer Service
Institute of Management and Administration
3 Bethesda Metro Center
Suite 250
Bethesda, MD 20814-5377
703-341-3500
800-372-1033; *Fax:* 800-253-0332;
www.ioma.com
Boost the productivity, efficiency and visibility of your department, and keep it on the cutting edge.

16666 Managing Logistics
Institute of Management and Administration
3 Bethesda Metro Center
Suite 250
Bethesda, MD 20814-5377
703-341-3500
800-372-1033; *Fax:* 800-253-0332;
www.ioma.com
Covers new technologies and strategies, how to negotiate with outsourced service providers.

16667 Managing Training & Development
Institute of Management and Administration
3 Bethesda Metro Center
Suite 250
Bethesda, MD 20814-5377
703-341-3500
800-372-1033; *Fax:* 800-253-0332;
www.ioma.com
Covers all aspects of measuring, learning, development, getting employees trained for their jobs, and justifying the cost of training to upper management.

16668 Medical Group Management Update
Medical Group Management Association
104 Inverness Ter E
Englewood, CO 80112-5313
303-799-1111; *Fax:* 303-643-9599
infocenter@mgma.com; www.mgma.com
William Jessee, CEO
Eileen Barker, senior Vice President
Anders Gilberg, senior Vice President
Natalie Jamieson, Administrative Assistant
Monthly association newspaper offering up-to-the-minute articles on current legislation, practical management, health care trends, association activities and other timely subjects.
Frequency: Monthly

16669 Object-Oriented Strategies
Cutter Information Corporation
37 Broadway
Suite 1
Arlington, MA 02474-5500
781-648-1950
800-888-8939; *Fax:* 781-648-1950
service@cutter.com; www.cutter.com
Paul Harman, Editor
Kim Leonard, Customer Service Director
Karen Coburn, CEO
Hillel Glazer, Senior Consultant
Ron Blitstein, Director
Designed for managers and developers of object-oriented systems.
Cost: $495.00
16 Pages
Frequency: Monthly
Founded in: 1986

16670 Orlando Business Journal
Business Journals
Ste 700
255 S Orange Ave
Orlando, FL 32801-5007
407-649-8470
888-649-6254; *Fax:* 407-420-1625
orlando@bizjournals.com;
www.bizjournals.com/orlando
Ann Sonntag, Publisher
Ken Cogburn, Editor
Cindy Barth, Managing Editor
Sue Ross, Ad Director
Alan Byrd, Director of Marketing/Circulation
Cost: $79.00
64 Pages
Frequency: Weekly
ISSN: 8750-8686
Founded in: 1995
Printed in 4 colors on newsprint stock

16671 PMI Today
Project Management Institute
14 Campus Blvd
Newtown Square, PA 19073-3299
610-356-4600; *Fax:* 610-356-4647;
www.pmi.org
Gregory Balestrero, CEO
Mark Langley, Managing Director
Louis Mercken, Chairman
Van Goldfisher, Editor
Jane Farley, Secretary
A monthly newsletter published by the Project Management Institute.
6 Pages
Frequency: Monthly
Circulation: 150000
Founded in: 1969
Mailing list available for rent

16672 PSMJ Principal Strategies
PSMJ Resources
10 Midland Avenue
Newton, MA 02458-1000
617-965-0055
800-537-7765; *Fax:* 617-965-5152
info@psmj.com; www.psmj.com
Frank Stasiowski, Production Manager
Offers management tactics and techniques for the design industry.
Cost: $195.00
8 Pages
Frequency: Monthly
Founded in: 1974
*Mailing list available for rent*at $125 per M
Printed in 2 colors on matte stock

16673 PSMJ Project Delivery
PSMJ Resources
10 Midland Avenue
Newton, MA 02458-1000
617-965-0055
800-537-7765; *Fax:* 617-965-5152
info@psmj.com; www.psmj.com
Frank Stasiowski, Production Manager
Offers project management tactics and techniques to the design industry.
Cost: $196.00
8 Pages
Frequency: Monthly
*Mailing list available for rent*at $125 per M
Printed in 2 colors on matte stock

16674 Payroll Manager's Letter
Bureau of Business Practice
111 8th Avenue
7th Floor
New York, NY 10011
212-771-0600
800-638-8437
rfecustomer@aspenpubl.com;
www.aspenlawschool.com
Marc Jennings, VP
Gerry Centrowitz, VP, Marketing and Commu
Contains concise, plain-English explanations of the latest federal payroll developments which helps companies comply with rapidly changing employment tax and minimum wage/overtime laws.
Cost: $235.00
8 Pages
Circulation: 7000
Founded in: 1920
Printed in one color on glossy stock

16675 Personal Report for the Administrative Professional
National Institute of Business Management

1750 Old Meadow Rd
Suite 302
Mc Lean, VA 22102-4304

703-905-8000
800-543-2049; *Fax:* 703-905-8042
customer@nibm.net; www.nibm.net

Steve Sturm, President
Phil Ash, Marketing Director
Cost: $54.00
10 Pages
Frequency: Monthly
ISSN: 1049-4855
Founded in: 1937

16676 Preventing Business Fraud
Institute of Management and Administration
3 Bethesda Metro Center
Suite 250
Bethesda, MD 20814-5377

703-341-3500
800-372-1033; *Fax:* 800-253-0332;
www.ioma.com

Stop corporate fraud before it happens. Get guidance on how to avoid supplier collusion and kickbacks, false invoicing, health insurance and workers' compensation fraud, payroll, petty cash and T and E overstatements, theft of equipment and materials and more.

16677 Professional Advisor
Int'l Society of Speakers, Authors & Consultants
PO Box 6432
Kingwood, TX 77325-6432

281-441-3558; *Fax:* 281-441-3538

Bernard Zick, Publisher

Includes information of the consulting industry.
Cost: $120.00
10 Pages
Frequency: Monthly

16678 Profit Line
Ernst and Young
9920 Pacific Heights Blvd
Suite 200
San Diego, CA 92121

858-452-6800
800-200-7763; *Fax:* 858-452-6998;
www.profitline.com

Gary Martino, Chief Financial Officer

Business information newsletter for entrepreneurs.

16679 Quality Assurance Bulletin
Bureau of Business Practice
76 Ninth Avenue
7th Floor
New York, NY 10011

212-771-0600; *Fax:* 212-771-0885;
www.aspenlawschool.com
Social Media: Facebook, Twitter, LinkedIn

Mark Dorman, CEO
Gustavo Dobles, VP Operations

Helps quality professionals improve the company's question-answer function.
Cost: $118.80
8 Pages
Frequency: 2 per year

16680 Real Estate & Leasing Report
Business Journals
120 W Morehead St
Suite 420
Charlotte, NC 28202-1874

704-973-1200; *Fax:* 704-973-1201;
www.citybiznetwork.com

George Conley, President
Joanne Skoog, Editor
Cost: $70.00
70 Pages
Frequency: Weekly
ISSN: 0887-5588
Printed in 4 colors on newsprint stock

16681 Report on Salary Surveys
Institute of Management and Administration
3 Bethesda Metro Center
Suite 250
Bethesda, MD 20814-5377

703-341-3500
800-372-1033; *Fax:* 800-253-0332;
www.ioma.com

Analyzes data from major salary surveys released during the year by the biggest compensation survey companies, WorldatWork, SHRM, state HR societies, and the Big Four accounting firms, to give readers an overview of those expensive, hard-to-manage services.
Cost: $429.00
Founded in: 1993

16682 Rodenhauser Report
Consulting Information Services
191 Washington Street
Keene, NH 03431

603-355-1560; www.consultinginfo.com

Tom Rodenhauser, President

Rodenhauser Report is a monthly electronic briefing that forecasts consulting trends for senior management advisors and business executives.
Frequency: Monthly
Founded in: 1998

16683 Servicing Management
LDJ Corporation
100 Willenbrock Road
Oxford, CT 06478

203-755-0158
800-325-6745; *Fax:* 203-755-3480
info@servicingmgmt.com;
www.servicingmgmt.com

Paul Zackin, Publisher
Michael Bates, Editor
June Han, Circulation Manager
Jeanette Laliberte, Subscriptions

Delivers news and how-to advice to executives and personnel in the servicing of mortgage loans nationwide.
Cost: $48.00
Frequency: Monthly
Circulation: 18000
Founded in: 1969

16684 Small-Biz Growth
Support Services Alliance
PO Box 130
Schoharie, NY 12157-0130

518-295-7966
800-322-3920; *Fax:* 518-295-8556
info@ssamembers.com;
www.smallbizgrowth.com

Steven Cole, President

Keeps SSA members and their employees up-to-date on developments affecting small-business communties.
Cost: $25.00
Frequency: Monthly
Circulation: 17,000
Founded in: 1977

16685 Small-Business Strategies
Page Group
PO Box 116
Dundee, IL 60118-0116

847-695-7887

Phillip Grisolia, Publisher

Contains practical ideas for use in successfully starting and profitably managing small businesses. Accepts advertising.
Cost: $95.00
4 Pages
Frequency: BiWeekly

16686 Sound Thinking
Jay Mitchell Associates
PO Box 1285
Fairfield, IA 52556-0022

641-472-4087; *Fax:* 641-472-2071

Jay Mitchell, Publisher

Notes and comments on the radio industry and related fields, specializing in an outside-in view.
Cost: $65.00
2 Pages
Frequency: Monthly

16687 Source
Rachel PR Services
1650 S Pacific Coast Highway
Suite 200C
Redondo Beach, CA 90277-5625
Janis Brett-Elspas, Editor
Jamie Steiner, Advertising/Sales

Annual reference guide for job hunters in advertising, public relations, marketing and journalism offering more than 2,000 resources for finding jobs at all levels in all 50 states. Listings includes job banks, job hotlines, executive recruiters, books/directories, trade publications, industry associations and more.
Cost: $39.00
40 Pages
Frequency: Annual
Circulation: 30,000
Printed in on matte stock

16688 Southeastern Association Executive
Special Edition Publishing
999 Douglas Ave
Suite 3317
Altamonte Spgs, FL 32714-2063

407-862-7737; *Fax:* 407-862-8102
specedpub@earthlink.net;
www.specedpub.com

A Sciuto, Publisher
Nichole Wunduke, Editor
Betty Harper, Director of Sales & Marke

Monthly news magazine serving associations meetings and hospitality executives in the southeast .
25 Pages
Frequency: Monthly
Circulation: 5200
Founded in: 1973
Printed in 4 colors on glossy stock

16689 Staffing Industry Report
Staffing Industry Analysts
881 Fremont Ave
Suite A3
Los Altos, CA 94024-5637

650-948-9303
800-950-9496; *Fax:* 650-232-2360
memberservices@staffingindustry.com;
www.staffingindustry.com

Ron Mester, Managing Director
Tim Murphy, Editor
Joyce Routson, Managing Editor
Greg Palmer, CEO
Jason Ezratty, Managing Partner

A twice monthly newsletter for temporary help, staff leasing and employment service companies. Industry information, company news, training and automation resource reviews, financial coverage, labor demand and supply analysis, key interviews. Association news, public company stock tables. SI Report sponsors an annual Staffing Industry Executive Forum in April. Emphasis is on business news. Includes advertising supplement.
Cost: $385.00
Circulation: 3000
Founded in: 1989
Mailing list available for rent: 3500 names
Printed in 2 colors on matte stock

16690 Success in Recruiting and Retaining
National Institute of Business Management
1750 Old Meadow Rd
Suite 302
Mc Lean, VA 22102-4304

703-905-8000
800-543-2049; *Fax:* 703-905-8042
customer@nibm.net

Steve Sturm, President
10 Pages
Frequency: Monthly
ISSN: 1049-4855

16691 Successful Self-Management
Stahlka Associates
60 Westchester Road
Williamsville, NY 14221-5021

716-347-7070; *Fax:* 716-626-4188
wendystahlka@verizon.net;
www.stahlkamarketing.com

Clayton A Stahlka, Production Manager
Wendy Stahlka, President
Mastering changes in yourself and your environment to be the best you can be with what you have.
Cost: $24.00
5 Pages
Frequency: Quarterly
Circulation: 1800
Founded in: 1975
Printed in one color on matte stock

16692 Supplier Selection and Management Report
Institute of Management and Administration
3 Bethesda Metro Center
Suite 250
Bethesda, MD 20814-5377

703-341-3500
800-372-1033; *Fax:* 800-253-0332;
www.ioma.com

Focuses on supplier selection, partnering and management issues.
Cost: $289.00
16 Pages
Frequency: Monthly
Circulation: 180,000
Founded in: 1980

16693 Travel Manager's Executive Briefing
Health Resources Publishing
1913 Atlantic Ave
Suite 200
Manasquan, NJ 08736-1067

732-292-1100
888-843-6242; *Fax:* 732-292-1111
info@themcic.com;
www.healthresourcesonline.com

Robert K Jenkins, Publisher
Judith Granholm, Regional Director
Brett Powell, Regional Director
Alice Burron, Director
A digest published twice a month that covers developments in the field of travel and expense cost control. Topics include discounts in air fare, car rentals, hotel bills, travel alternatives, phone savings, planning for meetings trends in government legislation affecting business travel costs, and case histories of companies that have successfully cut costs. Ideal for travel managers of corporations, small businesses and nonprofit organizations.
Cost: $447.00
ISSN: 0272-569X
Founded in: 1978

16694 WACRA News
World Assoc for Case Method Research & Application
23 Mackintosh Avenue
Needham, MA 02492-1218

781-444-8982
800-523-6468; *Fax:* 781-444-1548
wacra@rcn.com; www.wacra.org

Dr Hans E Klein, President/Executive Director
Dr Charles H Patti, Publications Director

16695 WACRA Newsletter
World Assoc for Case Method Research & Application
23 Mackintosh Avenue
Needham, MA 02492-1218

781-444-8982
800-523-6468; *Fax:* 781-444-1548
hans.klein@wacra.org; www.wacra.org

Dr Hans E Klein, President/Executive Director
Dr Charles H Patti, Publications Director
Frequency: Biannual

16696 Wage-Hour Compliance Report
Institute of Management and Administration
3 Bethesda Metro Center
Suite 250
Bethesda, MD 20814-5377
703-341-3500
800-372-1033; *Fax:* 800-253-0332;
www.ioma.com

Covers white-collar exemptions, how to pay employees for rest and overtime periods, legal holidays, how to handle vacation, severance and negotiated termination pay rules, and give managers a concise rundown of new federal and state withholding and minimum wage changes, new rules, rates and requirements.

16697 What's Ahead in Personnel
Remy Publishing Company
1439 W Summerdale Ave
Suite 440
Chicago, IL 60640-2115

773-769-6760
800-542-6670; *Fax:* 773-464-0166;
www.passportnewsletter.com

Contains information on current HR trends, legal issues and company practices.
Frequency: SemiMonthly

16698 What's Working In Consulting
Kennedy Information
1 Pheonix Mill Lane
Floor 3
Fitzwilliam, NH 03447

603-924-1006
800-531-0007
customerservice@kennedyinfo.com;
www.kennedyinfo.com

Alan Weiss, Editor
Provides practical guidance on improving consulting skills and managing a consulting practice.
Cost: $197.00
Frequency: Monthly
ISSN: 1535-3036

16699 Women in Business
Business Journal of Portland
851 Sw 6th Ave
Suite 500
Portland, OR 97204-1342

503-274-8733
800-486-3289; *Fax:* 503-219-3450
borben@bizjournals.com;
www.bizjournals.com/portland

Craig Wessel, Publisher
Dan McMillan, Managing Editor
Rob Smith, Editor
George Vaughan, Advertising Director
Special supplement of The Business Journal that celebrates the achievements of women making a difference in the business world and community
Cost: $89.00
36 Pages
ISSN: 0742-6550
Printed in 4 colors on newsprint stock

16700 Work and Family Life
230 W 55th Street
Apartment 6B
New York, NY 10019-5212

212-557-3555; *Fax:* 212-557-6555
susan@workandfamilylife.com;
www.workandfamily.com

Ellen Galinsky, Executive Editor
Susan Ginsberg, Editor/Publisher
Anne Perryman, Editor
Susan Seitel, President
Provides information and practical solutions to a wide range of family, job and health issues. Purpose is to help readers find pleasure and satisfaction in their many roles at work, at home, and in their communities.
Cost: $ 295.00
Frequency: Monthly
Circulation: 50000
Founded in: 1984
Printed in 4 colors on matte stock

16701 Working Smart
National Institute of Business Management
1750 Old Meadow Rd
Suite 302
Mc Lean, VA 22102-4304

703-905-8000
800-543-2055; *Fax:* 703-905-8042
customer@nibm.net; www.nibm.net

Steve Sturm, President
Morey Stettner, Editor
Phil Ash, Marketing Director
Ready, relevant and reliable advice for managers on workplace issues.
Cost: $48.00
10 Pages
Frequency: Monthly
ISSN: 1049-4855
Founded in: 1937
Printed in 2 colors on matte stock

Magazines & Journals

16702 AFSM: Professional Journal
Assoication for Services Management International
11031 Via Frontera
Suite A
San Diego, CA 92127

239-275-7887
800-333-9786; *Fax:* 239-275-0794
info@afsmi.org; www.afsmi.org

Jb Wood, President/CEO
John Schoenewald, Executive Director
A journal aimed at management issues.
64 Pages
Frequency: Monthly
Founded in: 1975

16703 APICS: The Performance Advantage
APICS Association for Operations Management
8430 West Bryn Mawr Avenue
Suite 1000
Chicago, IL 60631

773-867-1777
800-444-2742; *Fax:* 773-639-3000
webmaster@apics.org.; www.apics.org
Social Media: Facebook, Twitter, LinkedIn, Youtube

Doug Kelly, Editor
Jennifer Procter, Managing Editor
Beth Rennie, Senior Editor

Provides comprehensive articles on enterprise resources planning, supply chain management, e-business, materials management and production and inventory management.
Cost: $65.00
64 Pages
Frequency: 10/Year
Circulation: 66,000
ISSN: 1056-0017
Mailing list available for rent: 40,000 names at $100 per M
Printed in 4 colors on glossy stock

16704 American Academy of Medical Administrators
American Academy of Medical Administrators
701 Lee St
Suite 600
Des Plaines, IL 60016-4516

847-759-8601; *Fax:* 847-759-8602;
www.aameda.org

Renee Schleichar, CEO
Holly Estal, Director of Education
Guy Snyder, Director of Education
Rhonda Guptill, Chief Financial Officer
24 Pages
Frequency: Quarterly
Founded in: 1957
Mailing list available for rent
Printed in 2 colors on glossy stock

16705 American Cemetery
Kates-Boylston Publications
11300 Rockville Pike
Suite 1100
Rockville, MD 20852

800-500-4585
800-500-4585; *Fax:* 301-287-2150
AmericanFD@aol.com;
www.kates-boylston.com

Adrian F Boylston, Publisher
Thomas Lorge, Executive Director
Thomas Parmalee, Executive Director
Amy Fidalgo, Production Manager

Features articles on cemetery administration, maintenance, sales and public relations. Also includes coverage of conventions, new cemeteries and new building ideas.
Cost: $39.95
Frequency: Monthly
Circulation: 5800

16706 American Small Businesses Association
206 E College St
Suite 201
Grapevine, TX 76051-5381

817-488-8770
800-801-2722; *Fax:* 817-251-8578

Bill Will Sr, President
Wanda Johnson, Bookkeeper

Represents the interests of small businesses.
Printed in on glossy stock

16707 Association Management Magazine
American Society of Association Executives
1575 I St Nw
Suite 11
Washington, DC 20005-1103

202-626-2700
888-950-2723; *Fax:* 202-371-8315
publicpolicy@asaenet.org; www.asaenet.org/

Karl Ely, Publisher
Keith C Skillman, Editor

Serves the field of trade business professional and philanthropic associations.
Cost: $30.00
Frequency: Monthly
Circulation: 22507
Founded in: 1920

16708 Benchmarking: A Practitioner's Guide for Becoming & Staying the Best
Quality & Productivity Management Association
300 N Martingale Road
Suite 230
Schaumburg, IL 60173-2407

Fax: 847-619-3383

William Ginnodo, Publisher
Lesley Williams, Publications Manager

Promotes benchmarking as a technique for comparing processes, products or services with the world's best encouraging ways to do things faster, better, and less cost.

16709 Bits and Pieces
Economics Press
12 Daniel Road
Fairfield, NJ 07004-2565

973-227-1224; *Fax:* 973-227-9742

Arthur Lenehan, Publisher

Management and common sense plus anecdotes and quotes.
Cost: $1.00
Circulation: 266,000

16710 Bloomberg Businessweek
Bloomberg
731 Lexington Avenue
New York, NY 10022

212-318-2000
800-955-4003; *Fax:* 212-617-5999;
www.bloomberg.com

Daniel L. Doctoroff, President/CEO
Peter T. Grauer, Chairman
Beth Mazzeo, Head of Global Data Products Div.
Thomas F. Secunda, Head of Global Financial Products
Matthew Winkler, Editor-in-Chief

Offers a global perspective to help senior executives profit from faster, smarter, and more informed decisions. Bloomberg Businessweek reaches more C-level executives than any other business magazine.
Cost: $4.95
Frequency: Weekly
Founded in: 1981

16711 Building Operating Management
Trade Press Publishing Corporation
2100 W Florist Avenue
Milwaukee, WI 53209-3799

414-228-7701; *Fax:* 414-228-1134
info@tradepress.com; www.tradepress.com

Edward Sullivan, Editor
Bobbie Reid, Production Director
Scott Cunningham, Associate Publisher
Eric Muench, Director of Circulation
Robert J Wisniewski, President/CEO

Serves the field of facilities management, encompassing commercial building: office buildings, real estate/property management firms, developers, financial institutions, insurance companies, apartment complexes, civic/convention centers, including members of the Building Owners and Managers Association
Frequency: Monthly
Circulation: 70000
Founded in: 1943

16712 Business Facilities
Group C Communications
PO Box 2060
Red Bank, NJ 07701-0901

732-842-7433
800-524-0337; *Fax:* 732-758-6634
webmaster@groupc.com; www.groupc.com

Edgar T Coene, President
Ted Coene, Publisher
Karim Khan, Editor
Beth Sicignano, Marketing Manager
Connie Donatantonio, Circulation Manager

Magazine covering the fields of corporation expansion, economic development and real estate.
Cost: $30.00
Frequency: Monthly
Circulation: 30309
Founded in: 1969

16713 Business First
Business News
455 S 4th St
Suite 278
Louisville, KY 40202-2551

502-583-1731; *Fax:* 502-587-1703
borben@bizjournals.com;
www.bizjournals.com

Tom Monahan, President
Carol Brando Timmons, Editor
Judith Berzof, Associate Editor
Rebecca Ray, Assistant Editor
Cost: $83.00
Frequency: Monthly

16714 C2M Consulting to Management
Journal of Management Consulting
858 Longview Road
Burlingame, CA 94010-6974

650-342-1954; *Fax:* 650-344-5005;
www.challenge2media.com

E Michael Shays, Publisher
Marsha Lewin, Chairman Editorial

The journal, which is read in over 60 countries, presents methods and processes for management consultants helping them to enlarge and perfect their skills and service to clients.
Cost: $80.00
Frequency: Quarterly
Circulation: 5000
ISSN: 0158-7778
Founded in: 1981

16715 CFO: the Magazine for Chief Financial Officers
CFO Publishing Corporation
253 Summer St
Suite 3
Boston, MA 02210-1114

617-345-9700; *Fax:* 617-951-4090;
www.cfo.com

Frank Quigley, President

Features insurance, cash management, taxes, benefits, accounting, buyers guide.
Circulation: 365,409

16716 COM-SAC, Computer Security, Audit & Control
Management Advisory Services & Publications

PO Box 81151
Wellesley Hills, MA 02481-0001

781-235-2895; *Fax:* 781-235-5446
Info@masp.com; www.masp.com

Presents tutorials and articles of current interest in computer security and audit, presents a comprehensive digest of all key articles and books published on the fields of computer security and control.
Cost: $98.00
Frequency: Quarterly
Founded in: 1973

16717 Central Penn Business Journal
Journal Publications
101 N 2nd Street
2nd Floor
Harrisburg, PA 17101-1600

717-236-4300; *Fax:* 717-909-6803
webmaster@journalpub.com;
www.centralpennbusiness.com

David A Schankweiler, Publisher
Gary Nalbandian, CEO/President
Jason Klinger, Editor

Provides comprehensive news for the business community.
Cost: $64.95
56 Pages
Frequency: Weekly
Circulation: 10,500
ISSN: 1058-3599
Founded in: 1985

16718 Chain Leader
Raymond Herrmann
2000 Clearwater Drive
Oak Brook, IL 60523

630-288-8242; *Fax:* 630-288-8215;
www.chainleader.com

Mary Boltz Chapman, Editor-in-Chief
Maya Norris, Managing Editor
Ray Herrmann, Publisher

Targets senior management of chain restaurant companies.
Frequency: Monthly
Circulation: 17323
Founded in: 1960

16719 Chief Executive
Chief Executive Group
110 Summit Avenue
Montvale, NJ 07645

201-930-5959; *Fax:* 201-930-5956
contact@chiefexecutive.net;
www.chiefexecutive.net

Carol Evans, Publisher
Robin Uhl, Circulation Manager
William J. Holstein, Editor-in-Chief
Edward M. Kopko, CEO/Chairman
Chris Chalk, Vice President of Sales

A journal of strategy and analysis by and for chief executives.
75 Pages
Frequency: Monthly
Circulation: 42000
Founded in: 1976

16720 Club Management Magazine
Finan Publishing Company
107 W Pacific
Saint Louis, MO 63119

314-961-6644; *Fax:* 314-961-4809;
www.cmaa.org

Thomas J Finan, Publisher/Editor
Dee Kaplan, Publisher
Dianne Dierkes, Circulation Manager

The resource for successful club operations.
Cost: $26.95
Frequency: 3 Issues a year
Founded in: 1927
Mailing list available for rent: 21,000 names
Printed in 4 colors on glossy stock

16721 Commitment Plus
Quality & Productivity Management Association
300 N Martingale Road
Suite 230
Schaumburg, IL 60173-2407

Fax: 847-619-3383

William Ginnodo, Editor/Author

This monthly newsletter is for managers who want to improve quality, productivity and service through people. It contains brief case studies, written primarily by QPMA staff, showing how operating managers, or their people, went about implementing improvements in their organizations' operating managers, and regularly reinforce the improvement message. This newsletter is free to members.
Cost: $95.00
4 Pages
Frequency: Monthly

16722 Competitive Intelligence Review
John Wiley & Sons
111 River St
Hoboken, NJ 07030-5790

201-748-6000
800-825-7550; *Fax:* 201-748-6088
info@wiley.com; www.wiley.com

William J Pesce, CEO

Collection and analysis of business information.
Cost: $68.95
Frequency: Quarterly
Circulation: 3250
Founded in: 1807

16723 Consulting Magazine
Kennedy Information
One Phoenix Mill Lane
Floor 3
Peterborough, NH 03458

603-924-1006
800-531-0007
bookstore@kennedyinfo.com;
www.kennedyinfo.com

Jack Sweeney, Editor-in-Chief
Mina Landrisina, Managing Director

The only magazine written exclusively for management consultants, consulting is dedicated to fostering performance excellence and career success. Consulting serves the information needs of those responsible for shaping the business strategies of their clients.
Cost: $99.00
Frequency: Monthly
ISSN: 1525-4321
Founded in: 1970

16724 Contingency Planning & Management
Witter Publishing Corporation
20 Commerce Street
Flemington, NJ 08822

908-788-0343; *Fax:* 908-788-3782;
www.witterpublishing.com

Bob Joudanin, Publisher
Paul Kirvan, Editor
Courtney Witter, Print Circulation/Subscriptions
Andrew Witter, President

Serves the fields of financial/banking, manufacturing industrial, transportation, utilities, telecommunications, health care, government, insurance and other allied fields.
Cost: $195.00
Frequency: Monthly
Founded in: 1987

16725 Contingency Planning & Recovery Journal
Management Advisory Services & Publications
PO Box 81151
Wellesley Hills, MA 02481-0001

781-235-2895; *Fax:* 781-235-5446
Info@masp.com; www.masp.com

The only independent quarterly that is membership and subscriber supported. It presents current state of affairs in emergency preparedness, contingency planning and business resumption planning and business continuity.
Cost: $ 75.00
16 Pages
Frequency: Quarterly
Founded in: 1972
Printed in 2 colors

16726 Corporate Meetings & Incentives
Penton Media Inc
10 Fawcett Street
Suite 500
Cambridge, MA 02138

847-763-9504
866-505-7173
shatch@meetingsnet.com;
www.meetingsnet.com
Social Media: Facebook, Twitter, LinkedIn

Susan Hatch, Editor

Serves those involved in organizing business meetings, conventions, corporate travel agencies, and related fields.
Cost: $87.00
Frequency: Monthly
Circulation: 32200
Founded in: 1980
Printed in 4 colors

16727 Corporate Security
Strafford Publications
PO Box 13729
Atlanta, GA 30324-0729

404-881-1141
800-926-7926; *Fax:* 404-881-0074
customerservice@straffordpub.com;
www.straffordpub.com

Richard Ossoff, Publisher
Joan McKenna, Editor
Marianne Mueller, Marketing

Intelligence briefing on the latest security developments, best practices, the most important trends and new technolgies.
Cost: $330.00
23 Pages
ISSN: 0889-0625
Founded in: 1984

16728 Cost Engineering Journal
AACE International
1265 Suncrest Towne Centre Drive
Morgantown, WV 26505-1876

304-296-8444
800-858-2678; *Fax:* 304-291-5728
info@aacei.org; www.aacei.org

Marvin Gelhausen, Managing Editor
Noah Kinderknecht, Editor

International hournal of cost estimation, cost/schedule control, and project management read by cost professionals around the world to get the most up-to-date information about the profession.
Frequency: Monthly
Founded in: 1956

16729 Crain's New York Business
Crain Communications

711 3rd Ave
New York, NY 10017-4014

212-210-0100; *Fax:* 212-210-0200;
www.crainsnewyork.com
Social Media: Facebook, Twitter, LinkedIn

Norm Feldman, President

Dedicated to exclusive coverage of business in New York City, Crain's keeps tabs on the people, the companies, the products, the politics and much more.
Frequency: Weekly
Circulation: 61000
Mailing list available for rent

16730 Customer Interaction Solutions
Technology Marketing Corporation
800 Connecticut Ave
1st Floor East
Norwalk, CT 06854-1936

203-852-6800
800-243-6002; *Fax:* 203-866-3326
tmc@tmcnet.com; www.tmcnet.com
Social Media: Twitter

Rich Tehrani, CEO

Dedicated to teleservices and e-services outsourcing, marketing and customer relationship management issues.
Frequency: Monthly
Founded in: 1972

16731 Decision Sciences Journal
Decision Sciences Institute
35 Broad Street
Atlanta, GA 30303

404-651-4000; *Fax:* 404-413-7714
dsi@gsu.edu; www.decisionsciences.org

Gary L Ragatz, President
Julie Kendall, Treasurer
Carol J. Latta, Executive Director
Terrell G. Williams, Marketing Director
Vicki Smith-Daniels, Editor

Scientific quantitative, behavioral and computational approaches to decision making.
Cost: $100.00
Frequency: Quarterly
Circulation: 5000
Founded in: 1968

16732 Destination KC
Show-Me Publishing
306 E 12th Street
Suite 1014
Kansas City, MO 64106

816-358-8700; *Fax:* 814-474-1111

Joe Sweeney, Editor-in-Chief

Kansas City's business relocation and information guide.
Cost: $36.00
984 Pages
Frequency: Monthly
ISSN: 1046-9958
Printed in 4 colors on glossy stock

16733 Direct
Primedia
1166 Avenue of the Americas/10th Fl
New York, NY 10036

212-204-4200; *Fax:* 913-514-6895
sales@rmsreprints.com; www.penton.com

Eric Jacobson, Senior VP
Charles Vietri, Managing Editor
Cheryll Richter, Marketing Manager
Andria Gennlauderslager, Circulation Manager
Chris Meyer, Director, Corporate Communications

Serves the marketing and media industries.
Circulation: 46500
ISSN: 1046-4174
Printed in 4 colors

16734 Director
NFDA Publications
13625 Bishops Dr
Brookfield, WI 53005-6607

262-789-1880
800-228-6332; *Fax:* 262-789-6977
nfda@nfda.org; www.nfda.org

Christine Pepper, CEO
Chris Raymond, Editor
Benjamin Lund, Assistant Editor
Fay Spano, Director of Public Relations

The Director is specifically designed to inform and educate the funeral service professional in today's world.
Cost: $45.00
114 Pages
Frequency: Monthly
Circulation: 14,761
ISSN: 0199-3186
Founded in: 1882
Printed in 4 colors on glossy stock

16735 Discovery
Cooper Group
381 Park Ave S
Suite 801
New York, NY 10016-8822

212-696-2512; *Fax:* 212-696-2517;
www.cooperdirect.com

Harold Cooper, CEO

Focusing on critical management issues that drive growth, profitability and shareholder value.
Cost: $10.00
Circulation: 1500
Founded in: 1984

16736 Economist
PO Box 58524
Boulder, CO 80322-8524

303-945-1917
800-456-6086; *Fax:* 303-604-7455
ukpressoffice@economist.com;
www.economist.com

Helen Alexander, CEO
Kate Cooke, Group Communications Manager
David Hanger, Publisher
James Wilson, Founder

The Economist is a news and business publication written for top business decision-makers and opinion leaders who need a wide range of information and views on world events. It explores the close links between domestic and international issues, business, finance, current affairs, science and technology.
160 Pages
Frequency: Weekly
Circulation: 1009759
ISSN: 0013-0613
Founded in: 1843
Printed in 4 colors on glossy stock

16737 Executive Update
Greater Washington Society of Assn Executives
1300 Pennsylvania Avenue NW
Washington, DC 20004

202-048-8014; *Fax:* 202-326-0995;
www.gwsae.org

Liz Whittenmore, Publisher
Scott Briscoe, Editor
Theresa Magner, Director Advertising
Jam Armstrong, Circulation Manager
Susane Sarsati, CEO/President

Association news aimed at the executive level.
120 Pages
Frequency: Monthly
Circulation: 13300
Founded in: 1980

16738 Expansion Management
Penton Media
1166 Avenue of the Americas/10th Fl
New York, NY 10036

212-204-4200; *Fax:* 216-696-6662
information@penton.com; www.penton.com

Jane Cooper, Marketing
Bill King, Chief Editor
Jodi Svenson, Production Manager
Chris Meyer, Director, Corporate Communications
Mary Abood, Vice President

Employs charts, graphs and art to lead readers through well organized sections, such as regional reviews, state reports, industry news, case studies and international reports. Addresses the key issues that attract executives in companies that need facts on resource management.
Frequency: Monthly
Circulation: 45015
Founded in: 1986

16739 Facilities Manager
APPA
1643 Prince St
Alexandria, VA 22314-2818

703-684-1446; *Fax:* 703-549-2772
lander@appa.org; www.appa.org

Steve Glazner, Editor
Anita Dosik, Managing Editor
Cost: $120.00
Frequency: Bimonthly
Circulation: 5,500
ISSN: 0882-7249

16740 Financial Management Journal
Financial Management Association International
4202 E Fowler Ave
Suite 3331
Tampa, FL 33620-9951

813-974-2084; *Fax:* 813-974-3318
fma@coba.usf.edu; www.fma.org

Jack S Rader, Executive Director
Jeffrey Coles, Advisory Editor

Financial Management serves both academicians and practitioners who are concerned with the financial management of non-financial businesses, financial institutions, and public and private not-for-profit organizations. The journal serves the profession by publishing significant new scholarly research in finance that is of the highest quality.
Frequency: Quarterly

16741 Financial Manager
Broadcast Cable Financial Management Association
550 W Frontage Rd
Suite 3600
Northfield, IL 60093-1243

847-716-7000; *Fax:* 847-716-7004
info@mediafinance.org; www.bcfm.com

Mary Collins, President
Jamie Smith, Director of Operations
Rachelle Brooks, BCCA Sales

A bi-monthly magazine published by the Broadcast Cable Financial Management Association.
Cost: $69.00
36 Pages
Circulation: 300
Founded in: 1961
Mailing list available for rent: 1100 names at $495 per M

16742 Forbes Magazine
Forbes Media LLC.

60 5th Ave
New York, NY 10011-8868

212-620-2200; *Fax:* 212-620-1857
readers@forbes.com; www.forbes.com

Malcolm S Forbes Jr, CEO
Bruce Rogers, VP Marketing
Paul Maidment, Executive Editor
Michael Smith Maidment, VP, GM Operations

A magazine giving detailed information about business and finance.
Frequency: Monthly

16743 Fortune Magazine
Time Inc./Time Warner
1271 Avenue of the Americas
16th Floor
New York, NY 10020-1393

212-522-1212
800-274-6800; *Fax:* 212-522-0602;
www.timeinc.com
Social Media: Facebook, Twitter

Laura Lang, CEO
Howard M. Averill, CFO
Leslie Picard, President
Stephanie George, Chief Marketing Officer
John Huey, Editor-in-Chief

FORTUNE is a global leader in business journalism. The magazine has a great history of providing analysis and news critical to business people.
Cost: $5.00
Frequency: Annual/18
Circulation: 1M
Founded in: 1930

16744 Global IT Consulting Report
Kennedy Information
1 Kennedy Place
Route 12 S
Fitzwilliam, NH 03447

212-973-3855

Martin Zook, Editor

The business of information technology consulting, featuring news, analysis, benchmasking data and our exclusive Intelligence Briefing.
Cost: $895.00
16 Pages
Frequency: Monthly

16745 Golf Course Management
Golf Course Superintendents Association of America
1421 Research Park Dr
Lawrence, KS 66049-3859

785-841-2240
800-472-7878; *Fax:* 785-832-4488
hrmail@gcsaa.org; www.gcsaa.org

Mark Woodward, CEO
Lacy Stattelman, Marketing Specialist
Carla Sturgeon, Sales Coordinator
Shelly Howard, Publications Coordinator

Golf Course Superintendent, economical, research and commercial interests concerned with golf course management and improvement. Provides information, education and representation for golf course managment profession.
Cost: $ 48.00
Frequency: Monthly
Circulation: 40000
ISSN: 0192-3048
Founded in: 1926

16746 HR Magazine
SHRM/Society for Human Resource Management
1800 Duke St
Alexandria, VA 22314-3494

703-535-6000
866-898-4724; *Fax:* 703-535-6474
shrmeducation@shrm.org.; www.shrm.org
Social Media: Facebook, Twitter, LinkedIn, Youtube

Susan R Meisinger, CEO
Leon Rubis, Editor

The world's leading HR resource, offering perspective and in-depth information to leading HR professionals for over 50 years.
Cost: $70.00
Frequency: Monthly
Circulation: 197000
ISSN: 1047-3149
Founded in: 1956

16747 IJCRA
World Assoc for Case Method Research & Application
23 Mackintosh Avenue
Needham, MA 02492-1218

781-444-8982
800-523-6468; *Fax:* 781-444-1548
wacra@rcn.com; www.wacra.org

Dr Hans E Klein, President/Executive Director
Dr Charles H Patti, Publications Director

Provides members and case writers and case teachers from around the world the opportunity to share their work with colleagues, to learn from colleagues and to create an international network for ccase writing, case teaching and interactive teaching applications.
Frequency: Quarterly
ISSN: 1554-7752

16748 Information Resources Management Journal
Information Resources Management Association
701 E Chocolate Ave
Suite 200
Hershey, PA 17033-1240

717-533-8845; *Fax:* 717-533-8861
members@irma-international.org;
www.irma-international.org

Jan Travers, Executive Director

An applied research, refereed, international journal providing coverage of challenges, opportunities, problems, trends, and solutions encountered by both scholars and practitioners in the field of information technology management.
Cost: $95.00
Frequency: Quarterly
ISSN: 1040-1628

16749 Institute of Management & Administration Newsletter
Institute of Management and Administration
3 Bethesda Metro Center
Suite 250
Bethesda, MD 20814-5377

703-341-3500
800-372-1033; *Fax:* 800-253-0332;
www.ioma.com

Monthly newsletter that offers information for all those involved in international sales, looking for new distribution channels and how to reduce exports costs and risks.
Circulation: 180,000

16750 International Cemetery & Funeral Management
International Cemetery & Funeral Association
1895 Preston White Drive
Suite 220
Reston, VA 20191-5434

703-391-8400
800-645-7700; *Fax:* 703-391-8416;
www.icfa.org

Susan Loving, Managing Editor
Larry Stuart Jr, General Manager

Serves as the primary communication vehicle for ICFA news, membership activities, legislation, marketing and management, including the financial aspects of cemetery and funeral home operation.
Cost: $25.00
64 Pages
Circulation: 6200
ISSN: 0270-5281
Founded in: 1887
Printed in 4 colors on glossy stock

16751 Journal of Corporate Renewal
Turnaround Management Association
150 S Wacker Drive
Suite 900
Chicago, IL 60606

312-578-6900; *Fax:* 312-578-8336
info@turnaround.org; www.turnaround.org
Social Media: Facebook, Twitter, LinkedIn

Lisa Poulin, President
Patrick Lagrange, Chairman
Linda Delgadillo, Executive Director

The only international nonprofit association dedicated to corporate renewal and turnaround management. TMA's 9,000 members in 46 regional chapters comprise a professional community of turnaround practitioners, attorneys, accountants, investors, lenders, venture capitalists, appraiser, liquidators, executive recruiters and consultants. Three international conferences each year offer networking and educational sessions on the latest trends and best practices in the restructuring field.
Frequency: 9/Year
Circulation: 9000+

16752 Journal of Information Technology Management
Association of Management
920 Battlefield Boulevard
Suite 100
Chesapeake, VA 23322

757-482-2273; *Fax:* 757-482-0325
aomgt@aom-iaom.org; www.aom-iaom.org

Dr Al Bento, Editor-in-Chief

A forum for the communication of solutions found by practitioners and academicians to the mulitfaceted problems associated with managing information and information technology as a corporate resource.
Frequency: Quarterly

16753 Journal of Management Systems
Association of Management
920 Battlefield Boulevard
Suite 100
Chesapeake, VA 23322

757-482-2273; *Fax:* 757-482-0325
aomgt@aom-iaom.org; www.aom-iaom.org

Dr John Saee, Editor-in-Chief

Promotes the integreation and cross-fertilization of the behavioral/organizational and information sciences and to encourage, sharpen and expand the dialogue between academicians and practitioners from an interdisiplinary perspective

16754 Journal of Quality Technology
American Society for Quality
600 N Plankinton Avenue
PO Box 3005
Milwaukee, WI 53201-3005

414-272-8575
800-248-1946; *Fax:* 414-272-1734
help@asq.org; www.asq.org
Social Media: Facebook, Twitter, LinkedIn

Roberto M Saco, President
Paul E Borawski, Executive Director
Erica Gumieny, Sales
Fay Spano, Communications/Media Relations

Published by the American Society for Quality, the JQT is a quarterly, peer-reviewed journal that focuses on the subject of quality control and the related areas of reliability and similar disciplines.
Cost: $30.00
100M Members
Frequency: Quarterly
Founded in: 1946

16755 MSI
Reed Business Information
30 Technology Parkway South
Suite 100
Norcross, GA 30092

630-574-0825
800-424-3996; *Fax:* 630-288-8781
webmaster@reedbusiness.com; www.reedbusiness.com

Jeff Greisch, President
Kevin Parker, Editorial Director
Jim Casella, CEO
Nancy Bartels, Senior Editor
Eric Roth, Circulation Manager
Frequency: Monthly
Founded in: 1977

16756 MWorld: Journal of the American Management Association
American Management Association
1601 Broadway
Suite 7
New York, NY 10019-7420

212-586-8100; *Fax:* 212-903-8168
customerservice@amanet.org; www.amanet.org

Edward T Reilly, CEO
Florence M Stone, Senior Vice President
Arthur Levy, Senior Vice President
Roger Kelleher, Manager
Jorge Rubio, Managing Director

Free quarterly management journal for American Management Association's executive and individual members.
48 Pages
Frequency: Quarterly
Circulation: 25,000
Founded in: 2002
Printed in 2 colors on glossy stock

16757 Maintenance Technology
Applied Technology Publications
1300 S Grove Ave
Suite 105
Barrington, IL 60010-5246

847-382-8100; *Fax:* 847-304-8603; www.mt-online.com

Arthur Rice, President/CEO
Bill Kiesel, Vice President/Publisher
Jane Alexander, Editor-In-Chief
Rick Carter, Executive Editor
Randy Buttstadt, Director of Creative Services

Maintenance Technology magazine serves the business and technical information needs of managers and engineers responsible for assuring availability of plant equipment and systems. It provides readers with articles on advanced technologies, strategies, tools, and services for the life-cycle management of capital assets.
Frequency: Monthly
Circulation: 50,827
Mailing list available for rent: 35,263 names at $$15 per M

16758 Manage
National Management Association
2210 Arbor Blvd
Suite A
Moraine, OH 45439-1580

937-294-0421; *Fax:* 937-294-2374
nma@nma1.org; www.nma1.org

Douglas Shaw, Publisher
Richard Hergert, Owner
Steve Bailey, CEO
Mike McCulley, Chief Operations Officer

Association news for executives.
32 Pages
Frequency: Quarterly
Founded in: 1925

16759 Management Consultants International
Kennedy Information
37 Beach Rd
Singapore 199597

65 -100-0688; *Fax:* 656-234-0688
corporate@cacmci.com; www.cacmci.com

News and business intelligence on management consulting worldwide. Monthly issues feature country by country surveys of local consulting firms.
Cost: $1122.00
16 Pages
Frequency: Monthly
ISSN: 0956-3253

16760 Medical Group Management Journal
Medical Group Management Association
104 Inverness Ter E
Englewood, CO 80112-5313

303-799-1111; *Fax:* 303-643-9599
infocenter@mgma.com; www.mgma.com

William Jessee, CEO
Eileen Barker, senior Vice President
Anders Gilberg, senior Vice President
Natalie Jamieson, Administrative Assistant

Encompasses pertinent problems, questions and issues relating to group practice management.
Frequency: Bi-Monthly

16761 New Mobility
PO Box 220
415 Horsham Road
Horsham, PA 19044

215-675-9133
888-850-0344; *Fax:* 215-675-9376
info@newmobility.com; www.newmobility.com
Social Media: Facebook, Twitter, MySpace

Tim Gilmer, Editor
Jean Dobbs, Editorial Director, VP
Kim Brennan, Circulation/List Manager
Amy Blackmore, VP of Sales
Jeff Leonard, SVP of Marketing + Communication

New Mobility encourages the integration of active-lifestyle wheelchair users into mainstream society, while simultaneously reflecting the vibrant world of disability-related arts, media, advocacy and philosophy. Our stories foster a sense of community.
Cost: $27.95
Frequency: Monthly

16762 Operations & Fulfillment
Primedia
11 River Bend Drive South
PO Box 4242
Stamford, CT 06907-242

203-589-9900
800-775-3777; *Fax:* 203-358-5823; www.multichannelmerchant.com

Sherry Chiger, Editorial Director
Melisa Dowling, Executive Editor
Len Roberto, Circulation Manager
Kate Dimarco, Creative Director of Production
Barry Litwin, VP Sales/Marketing

Provides executives information they can't get anywhere else and reach executives and managers with purchasing authority in all areas of operations management. Information on direct to customer fulfillment..
Cost: $85.00
Circulation: 40000
Founded in: 1984

16763 Organization Development Journal
Organization Development Institute
11234 Walnut Ridge Road
Chesterland, OH 44026-1240

440-729-7419; *Fax:* 440-729-9319; www.odinstitute.org/

Dr. Donald W Cole, Publisher
Dr. Donald W Cole, CEO/President
Jenny Maes, Editor

A journal published quarterly for human resource people, managers and organization development people. The most frequently cited OD/OB publication in the world.
Cost: $80.00
100 Pages
Frequency: Quarterly
Circulation: 700
ISSN: 0889-6402
Founded in: 1968
Mailing list available for rent: 9M names
Printed in one color on newsprint stock

16764 PM Network
Project Management Institute
14 Campus Blvd
Newtown Square, PA 19073-3299

610-356-4600; *Fax:* 610-356-4647; www.pmi.org

Gregory Balestrero, CEO
Louis J Mercken, Chair
Iain Fraser, Vice Chair
James McGeehan, Public Relations
Jane Farley, Secretary

A monthly magazine published by the Project Management Institute.
75 Pages
Frequency: Monthly
Mailing list available for rent

16765 Print Solutions Magazine
Document Management Industries Association
433 E Monroe Avenue
Alexandria, VA 22301-1693

703-836-6232
800-336-4641; *Fax:* 703-549-4966; www.printsolutionsmag.com/

Peter L Colaianni, Editor-in-Chief
Darin Painter, Managing Editor
Preeti Vasishtha, Assistant Editor
Andrew Brown, Assistant Editor

Source for marketing, management and product information.
Frequency: Monthly
Circulation: 42000
ISSN: 0532-1700
Founded in: 1962
Printed in 4 colors on glossy stock

16766 Professional Journal
AFSM International
11031 Via Frontera
Suite A
San Diego, CA 92127-1709

858-673-3055
800-333-9786; *Fax:* 239-275-0794; www.afsmi.org

John Schoenewald, Executive Director
Jb Wood, President/Ceo

A magazine for executives, managers and professionals in the high-technology services industry.
Cost: $90.00
114 Pages
Circulation: 7000
ISSN: 1049-2135
Founded in: 1975
Printed in 4 colors on glossy stock

16767 Project Management Journal
Project Management Institute
14 Campus Blvd
Newtown Square, PA 19073-3299

610-356-4600; *Fax:* 610-356-4647;
www.pmi.org

Gregory Balestrero, CEO
Mark Langley, Managing Director
Gary Boyler, Publisher
Dan Goldfischer, Editor in Chief
Beverly Cook, Production Manager

A quarterly journal published by the Project Management Institute.
65 Pages
Frequency: Quarterly
Mailing list available for rent

16768 Purchasing
Reed Business Information
6 Alfred Circle
Bedford, MA 00173

972-980-8810; *Fax:* 630-288-8686;
www.designnews.com
Social Media: Facebook, Twitter, LinkedIn

Kathy Doyle, Publisher
Lockie Montgomery, Production Manager
Anne Millen Porter, Business Manager
Paul Teague, Chief Editor.

About the purchasing professional in American industry.
Founded in: 1920

16769 Quality Engineering
American Society for Quality
600 N Plankinton Avenue
PO Box 3005
Milwaukee, WI 53201-3005

414-272-8575
800-248-1946; *Fax:* 414-272-1734
help@asq.org; www.asq.org
Social Media: Facebook, Twitter, LinkedIn

Roberto M Saco, President
Paul E Borawski, Executive Director
Erica Gumieny, Sales
Fay Spano, Communications/Media Relations

Co-published with Taylor and Francis, this journal is for professional practitioners and researchers whose goal is quality engineering improvements and solutions.
Cost: $34.75
100M Members
Frequency: Quarterly/Members Price
Founded in: 1946

16770 Quality Management Journal
American Society for Quality
600 N Plankinton Avenue
PO Box 3005
Milwaukee, WI 53201-3005

414-272-8575
800-248-1946; *Fax:* 414-272-1734
help@asq.org; www.asq.org
Social Media: Facebook, Twitter, LinkedIn

Roberto M Saco, President
Paul E Borawski, Executive Director
Erica Gumieny, Sales
Fay Spano, Communications/Media Relations

Published by the American Society for Quality, the QMT is a quarterly, peer-reviewed journal that focuses on the subject of quality management practice and provides a discussion forum for both practitioners and academics in the area of research.
Cost: $50.00
100M Members
Frequency: Quarterly
Founded in: 1946

16771 Quality Progress
American Society for Quality
600 N Plankinton Avenue
PO Box 3005
Milwaukee, WI 53201-3005

414-272-8575
800-248-1946; *Fax:* 414-272-1734
help@asq.org; www.asq.org
Social Media: Facebook, Twitter, LinkedIn

Roberto M Saco, President
Paul E Borawski, Executive Director
Erica Gumieny, Sales
Fay Spano, Communications/Media Relations

Published by the American Society for Quality, QP is a peer-reviewed journal that focuses on the subject of quality control, discussing the usage and implementation of quality principles including the subject areas of organizational behavior, knowledge management and process improvement.
Cost: $55.00
100M Members
Founded in: 1946

16772 Recruiting Trends
Kennedy Information
One Phoenix Mill Lane
Floor 3
Peterborough, NH 03458

603-924-1006
800-531-0007
customerservice@kennedyinfo.com;
www.kennedyinfo.com

Joseph McCool, Editor
Mina Landrisina, Managing Director

Provides strategies and tactics for creating and maintaining a competitive workforce.
Cost: $99.00
8 Pages
Frequency: Monthly
ISSN: 0034-1827
Founded in: 1970

16773 Retail Merchandiser
MacFadden Publishing
233 Park Ave S
6th Floor
New York, NY 10003-1606

212-979-4800; *Fax:* 212-979-7342;
www.retail-merchandiser.com

Jeff Friedman, Publisher
Greg Masters, Managing Editor
Toni Riggio, Sales Coordinator
Anita M Wise, Production Manager

Serves those in management positions of mass retail and discount companies.
Cost: $99.00
Frequency: Monthly
Circulation: 34,188
Founded in: 1961

16774 Risk Management
Risk & Insurance Management Society
655 3rd Avenue
2nd Floor
New York, NY 10017

212-286-9292; *Fax:* 212-286-9716
chapterservices@RIMS.org; www.rims.org

Ted Donovan, Publisher
Bill Coffin, Editor-in-Chief
Jared Wade, Associate Editor
Callie Nelson, Circulation Manager
Todd Lockwood, Advertising Sales Manager
Cost: $64.00
Frequency: Monthly
Circulation: 15000
Founded in: 1950

16775 SAM Advanced Management Journal
Society for Advancement of Management
Corpus Christi - College of Business
6300 Ocean Drive - Unit 5807
Corpus Christi, TX 78412-5807

361-825-6045; *Fax:* 361-825-2725
moustafa@cob.tamucc.edu;
www.samnational.org

Moustafa H. Abdelsamad, President/CEO
R. Clifton Poole, Secretary
S.G. Fletcher, Treasurer
Everette Anderson, VP, Sales & Marketing
Anthony Buono, Director

A quarterly, refereed publication especially designed for general managers.
Cost: $64.00
3000 Members
Frequency: Quarterly
Founded in: 1912

16776 SAM Management In Practice
Society for Advancement of Management
Corpus Christi - College of Business
6300 Ocean Drive, Unit 5807
Corpus Christi, TX 78412-5807

361-825-6045; *Fax:* 361-825-2725;
www.samnational.org

Moustafa H. Abdelsamad, President/CEO
R. Clifton Poole, Secretary
S.G. Fletcher, Treasurer
Everette Anderson, VP, Sales & Marketing
Anthony Buono, Director

A quarterly, refereed publication especially designed for general managers.
3000 Members
Frequency: Quarterly
Founded in: 1912

16777 Shelby Report
Shelby Publishing Company
517 Green St Nw
Gainesville, GA 30501-3300

770-534-8380; *Fax:* 770-535-0110;
www.shelbypublishing.com

Ron Johnston, President
Chuck Gilmer, Editor

Serving the grocery industry in Arizona, Arkansas, Colorado, Kansas, Louisana, Missouri, New Mexico, Oklahoma, and Texas,
Cost: $36.00
Frequency: Monthly
Circulation: 25201
Founded in: 1966

16778 Si Review
Staffing Industry Analysts
881 Fremont Ave
Suite A3
Los Altos, CA 94024-5637

650-948-9303
800-950-9496; *Fax:* 650-232-2360;
www.sireport.com

Ron Mester, President
Theresa Daly, Production Manager

Tools and techniques for staffing industry professionals. How-to's and survey articles for branch management, upper management, owners, and sales/service personnel in employment service companies. Display advertising included.
Cost: $99.00
Frequency: 22 issues per y
Founded in: 1989
Printed in 4 colors on glossy stock

16779 Software Quality Professional
American Society for Quality
600 N Plankinton Avenue
PO Box 3005
Milwaukee, WI 53201-3005

414-272-8575
800-248-1946; *Fax:* 414-272-1734
help@asq.org; www.asq.org
Social Media: Facebook, Twitter, LinkedIn

Roberto M Saco, President
Paul E Borawski, Executive Director
Erica Gumieny, Sales
Fay Spano, Communications/Media Relations

Published by the American Society for Quality, the SQP is a quarterly, peer-reviewed journal for software development professionals that focuses on the subject of quality practice principles in the implementation of software and the development of software systems.
Cost: $45.00
100M Members
Frequency: Quarterly
Founded in: 1946

16780 South Florida Business Journal
American City Business Journals
120 W Morehead St
Suite 400
Charlotte, NC 28202-1874

704-973-1000
800-486-3289; *Fax:* 704-973-1001
borben@bizjournals.com;
www.bizjournals.com

Whitney R Shaw, CEO
Megan Foley, Marketing Director
David Harris, Managing Editor

Covers all aspects of business in South Florida.
Cost: $99.00
Frequency: Weekly
ISSN: 1528-0527

16781 Staffing Management
SHRM/Society for Human Resource Management
1800 Duke St
Alexandria, VA 22314-3494

703-535-6000
866-898-4724; *Fax:* 703-535-6474
shrmeducation@shrm.org.; www.shrm.org
Social Media: Facebook, Twitter, LinkedIn, Youtube

Susan R Meisinger, CEO
Leon Rubis, Editor

Formerly known as Employment Management Today, this magazine provides information on the latest techniques and trends in recruiting and retaining your most important commodity: your employees.
Cost: $35.00
56 Pages
Frequency: Quarterly
Circulation: 10000
Founded in: 1995

16782 Supermarket News - Retail/Financial
Fairchild Publications
7 W 34th St
New York, NY 10001-8100

212-630-3880
800-204-4515; *Fax:* 212-630-3868
custserv@espcomp.com;
www.supermarketnews.com

Dan Bagan, Publishing Director
David Orgel, Editor-in-Chief
Christina Veiders, Managing Editor
Joy Kulick, Marketing
Cost: $45.00
Frequency: Weekly
ISSN: 0039-5803
Founded in: 1892

16783 Supervision Magazine
National Research Bureau
320 Valley St
Burlington, IA 52601-5513

319-752-5415; *Fax:* 319-752-3421
mail@national-research-bureau.com;
www.national-research-bureau.com

Diane M Darnall, President
Teresa Levinson, Editor

Dedicated to providing the most timely and relevant information to today's supervisors and managers.
Frequency: Monthly
Circulation: 1200
Founded in: 1930

16784 Supply Chain Management Review
Reed Business Information
225 Wyman St
Suite 3
Waltham, MA 02451-1216

781-734-8000; *Fax:* 781-734-8076;
www.reedbusiness.com

Mark Finklestein, President
Frank Quinn, Chief Editor
Susan Lacefield, Associate Editor
Mary Ann Gajewski, Production Manager
Stuart Whayman, CFO

Contains in-depth feature articles on various aspects of Supply Chain Management. SCM is the science of integrating the flow of goods and information from initial souring and purchasing, order processing and fulfillment, production planning and scheduling, inventory management, transportation, distribution and customer service. Each issue delivers in-depth feature articles from the thought leaders in the supply chain community.
Cost: $199.00
Circulation: 12000

16785 Supply Chain Technology News
Penton Media
1166 Avenue of the Americas/10th Fl
New York, NY 10036

212-204-4200; *Fax:* 216-696-6662
information@penton.com; www.penton.com

Jane Cooper, Marketing
Chris Meyer, Director, Corporate Communications

Focuses on the practical application of technology accross a broad range of supply chain functions.

16786 Tapping the Network Journal
Quality & Productivity Management Association
300 N Martingale Road
Suite 230
Schaumburg, IL 60173-2407

708-619-2909; *Fax:* 847-619-3383

William Ginnodo, Editor/Author

This quarterly publication is, By and For Organizational Change Agents. Most articles are written by QPMA members. Its purpose is to share - in a straightforward, factual and practical manner - what has been learned within the authors' organization during the course of a particular change effort. It is provided free to members, and made available to non-member subscribers.

16787 Training
50 S 9th Street
Minneapolis, MN 55402

612-333-0471; *Fax:* 612-333-6526;
www.vnu.com

Rob van den Bergh, CEO
Rob Ruijter, CFO
AC Nielsen, Marketing
Founded in: 1960

16788 WACRA: World Association for Case Method Research & Application
23 Mackintosh Avenue
Needham, MA 02492-1218

781-444-8982; *Fax:* 781-444-1548
wacra@rcn.com; www.wacra.org

Dr Hans E Klein, President/Executive Director
Denise Smith, Conference Office

Advancing the use of the case method and other interactive methodologies in teaching, training and planning.
Cost: $75.00
2000 Members
Circulation: digital
ISSN: 1931-7549
Founded in: 1984

16789 Warehousing Management
Reed Business Information
30 Technology Parkway South
Suite 100
Norcross, GA 30092

646-746-6400
800-424-3996; *Fax:* 646-756-7583
webmaster@reedbusiness.com;
www.reedbusiness.com

John Poulin, CEO
John R Johnson, Editor-in-Chief
James Reed, Owner
Jane Burgess, Marketing Director

Warehousing Management targets warehousing and distribution center operations managers with analysis, news, trends, equipment and events.
Circulation: 47185
Founded in: 1977

16790 Workgroup Computing Report
Patricia Seybold Group
Po Box 783
Needham Heights, MA 02492

617-742-5200
800-826-2424; *Fax:* 617-742-1028
feedback@customers.com; www.psgroup.com
Social Media: Twitter

Patricia Seybold, Founder/CEO

Provides information on implementing workflow, document management, groupware, and business process reengineering.
Cost: $440.00
Frequency: Monthly
Mailing list available for rent

16791 World
Economist
111 W 57th Street
The Economist Building
New York, NY 10019

212-541-5730; *Fax:* 212-541-9378
usrights@economist.com

Dudley Fishburn, Editor
David Hanger, Publisher
124 Pages
ISBN: 0-862181-66-6
Printed in 4 colors on glossy stock

16792 Young Presidents' Organization - Magazine
Young Presidents' Organization
451 Decker Drive
Suite 200
Irving, TX 75062-3954

972-504-4600; *Fax:* 972-650-4777;
www.ypo.org

Thomas Stauffer, Executive Director
Les Ward, Manager
Frequency: BiAnnual
Circulation: 8000
Printed in on glossy stock

Trade Shows

16793 AACE Annual Meeting
AACE International
1265 Suncrest Towne Centre Drive
Morgantown, WV 26505-1876

304-296-8444
800-858-2678; *Fax:* 304-291-5728
info@aacei.org; www.aacei.org
Social Media: Facebook, LinkedIn

Andrew S Dowd Jr, Executive Director
Jennie Amos, Marketing/Meetings Manager
Frequency: June

16794 AHRA Annual Meeting & Exposition
Association for Medical Imaging Management
490B Boston Post Road
Suite 200
Sudbury, MA 01776

978-443-7591
800-334-2472; *Fax:* 978-443-8046
info@ahraonline.org; www.ahraonline.org
Social Media: Facebook, Twitter, LinkedIn

Edward Cronin, Jr., CEO
Sarah Murray, Executive Assistant
Emily Ryan, Membership Coordinator
Debra Murphy, Publications Director

A resource and catalyst for the development of professional leadership in imaging sciences. A driving force toward improving the healthcare environment. Containing 171 booths and 171 exhibits.
5000 Members
Mailing list available for rent: 4000 names at $250 per M

16795 Administrative Assistants Executive Secretaries Seminar
PA Douglas & Associates
644 Strander Boulevard
#411
Seattle, WA 98188

206-244-6441; *Fax:* 780-444-8002;
www.padouglas.com

Dr. Paul A Douglas MBA, PhD, CMC, Leader

To provide seminars, workshops and educational materials to individuals from the United States, Canada, and Europe. Includes an intensive three-day workshop for exploring and developing intellectual, organizational and interpersonal abilities.
Founded in: 1975

16796 American Society of Association Executives Annual Meeting & Expo
American Society of Association Executives
The ASAE Building
1575 I Street NW
Washington, DC 20005

202-262-2723; *Fax:* 202-371-8315
publicpolicy@asaenet.org; www.asaenet.org

John Graham, Executive Director

Professional service companies that specialize in providing management services for association on a fee-for-service basis. Exhibits related to managing associations.
Frequency: Annual

16797 Annual Lean Six Sigma Conference
American Society for Quality
600 N Plankinton Avenue
PO Box 3005
Milwaukee, WI 53201-3005

414-272-8575
800-248-1946; *Fax:* 414-272-1734
help@asq.org; www.asq.org
Social Media: Facebook, Twitter, LinkedIn

Roberto M Saco, President
Paul E Borawski, Executive Director
Erica Gumieny, Sales
Fay Spano, Communications/Media Relations

An exclusive two-day briefing and networking event designed by and for the top practitioners in the Six Sigma community.
100M Members
Frequency: Annual/February
Founded in: 1946

16798 Annual Quality Audit Conference
American Society for Quality
600 N Plankinton Avenue
PO Box 3005
Milwaukee, WI 53201-3005

414-272-8575
800-248-1946; *Fax:* 414-272-1734
help@asq.org; www.asq.org
Social Media: Facebook, Twitter, LinkedIn

Roberto M Saco, President
Paul E Borawski, Executive Director
Erica Gumieny, Sales
Fay Spano, Communications/Media Relations

Topics of interest include: new innovating audit/process approaches, value added involvement, corporate expectations, corporate/social responsibility, auditing in the overall corporate scheme.
100M Members
Frequency: October
Founded in: 1946

16799 Annual Service Quality Conference
American Society for Quality
600 N Plankinton Avenue
PO Box 3005
Milwaukee, WI 53201-3005

414-272-8575
800-248-1946; *Fax:* 414-272-1734
help@asq.org; www.asq.org
Social Media: Facebook, Twitter, LinkedIn

Roberto M Saco, President
Paul E Borawski, Executive Director
Erica Gumieny, Sales
Fay Spano, Communications/Media Relations

The sessions we plan will help you to navigate through unpredictable consumer behavior and increasing competition to build a strong foundation for reaching superior levels of quality service.
100M Members
Frequency: September
Founded in: 1946

16800 Annual World Conference on Quality and Improvement
American Society for Quality
600 N Plankinton Avenue
PO Box 3005
Milwaukee, WI 53201-3005

414-272-8575
800-248-1946; *Fax:* 414-272-1734
help@asq.org; www.asq.org
Social Media: Facebook, Twitter, LinkedIn

Roberto M Saco, President
Paul E Borawski, Executive Director
Erica Gumieny, Sales
Fay Spano, Communications/Media Relations

Conference focuses on quality and improvement with more than 2,000 exhibits and attendees. Keynote speakers and sessions discuss quality tools, techniques and methodologies. Provides the opportunity for members to meet and network with colleagues in the industry.
100M Members
Frequency: May
Founded in: 1946

16801 Association for Services Management
11031 Via Frontera
Suite A
San Diego, CA 92127

239-275-7887
800-333-9786; *Fax:* 239-275-0794
info@afsmi.org; www.afsmi.org

John Schoenwald, Executive Director
Jb Wood, President/Ceo

Management convention and exposition.
Frequency: Fall

16802 Association for Strategic Planning Annual Conference
Association for Strategic Planning
12021 Wilshire Boulevard
Suite 286
Los Angeles, CA 90025-1200

877-816-2080; *Fax:* 323-954-0507;
www.strategyplus.org
Social Media: Facebook, Twitter, LinkedIn

Dr Stanley G Rosen, President
Janice Laureen, Executive Director

Nation's premier forum for professional discussion and exchange of information and experiences among strategic planning practitioners.
Frequency: February

16803 Association for Worksite Health Promotion Annual International Conference
60 Revere Drive
Suite 500
Northbrook, IL 60062-1577

847-480-9574; *Fax:* 847-480-9282;
www.awhp.org

Liz Freyn, Conference Manager

122 booths of information and supplies to promote and develop quality programs of health and fitness in business and industry. Seminar, workshop, conference, tours and luncheon.
950 Attendees
Founded in: 1974

16804 Association of Management Meeting
Association of Management
920 Battlefield Boulevard
Suite 100
Chesapeake, VA 23322

757-482-2273; *Fax:* 757-482-0325
aomgt@aom-iaom.org; www.aom-iaom.org

Dr Karin Klenke, Co-Founder/President
Dr WM A Hamel, CEO
T J Mills, VP Comptroller
800 Attendees
Frequency: Annual

16805 Chief's Edge
International Association of Fire Chiefs
4025 Fair Ridge Drive
Fairfax, VA 22033-2868

703-273-0911; *Fax:* 703-273-9363
education@iafc.org; www.iafc.org
Social Media: Facebook, Twitter

Mark Light, Executive Director & CEO
Lisa Yonkers, Director, Conferences & Education
Jason Nauman, Education & Learning Manager
Leanne Shroeder, Conference Manager

Fire service experts take participants through an intensive program that teaches lessons not taught in any school. Executive leadership program is designed for newly appointed fire chiefs and those preparing to become fire chiefs.
12000 Members
Founded in: 1873

16806 **Circulation Managers Association International**
11600 Sunrise Valley Drive
Reston, VA 20191-1412

703-506-1661

Joseph Forsee, Show Manager

100 booths exhibiting products such as news racks, rubber products and software.
225 Attendees
Frequency: June

16807 **Coaching and Teambuilding Skills for Managers and Supervisors**
SkillPath Seminars
6900 Squibb Road
PO Box 2768
Mission, KS 66201-2768

913-623-3900
800-873-7545; *Fax:* 913-362-4241
webmaster@skillpath.com; www.skillpath.com

One-day workshop to sharpen your leadership skills and boost your team's productivity. Various locations and dates.

16808 **Construction Specifications Institute Annual Show & Convention**
110 South Union Street
Suite 100
Alexandria, VA 22314

703-684-0300
800-689-2900; *Fax:* 703-684-8436
csi@csinet.org; www.csinet.org
Social Media: Facebook, Twitter, LinkedIn, Youtube,Slideshare,Flickr

Eugene A Valentine, President
W Richard Cooper, VP

Education sessions that focus on industry topics such as; Business and Professional Development, Design & Pre-Construction Activities, Facility Management, Formats & Documents, Legal, Public Facilities & Communities, Safety & Security, Specialty Construction, and Specifications.
6,000 Attendees
Frequency: Annual
Founded in: 1954

16809 **EMA Annual Conference & Exposition**
SHRM/Society for Human Resource Management
1800 Duke Street
Alexandria, VA 22314

703-535-6000
866-898-4724; *Fax:* 703-535-6474
shrmeducation@shrm.org.; www.shrm.org/
Social Media: Facebook, Twitter, LinkedIn, Youtube

Johnny C Taylor Jr, Chairman
Susan Meisinger, President/CEO
Robert O Gonzales, Secretary
Robb E Van Cleave, Treasurer

Conference devoted to employment management issues.
700 Attendees
Frequency: March/April

16810 **Financial Management Association International Annual Meeting**
University of South Florida
College of Business Administration/BSN 3331
4202 E Fowler Avenue
Tampa, FL 33620-5500

813-974-2084; *Fax:* 813-974-3318
fma@coba.usf.edu; www.fma.org/

Jonathan Karpoff, President Director
Jacqueline Garner, Vice President Financial Education
Rawley Thomas, VP Practitioner Services
Kenneth Eades, Vice President Global Services
Anthony Saunders, Vice President Annual Meeting

Annual meeting and exhibits of financial management related equipment, supplies and services.
Frequency: October

16811 **Fundamentals of Personnel Law for Managers and Supervisors**
Human Resources Council
6900 Squibb Road
PO Box 804441
Kansas City -4441

800-601-4636

Rose Miller, Trainer

One-day seminar covering the legal issues affecting everyday management of employees. Various locations and dates.

16812 **Hartford Conference on Leadership Development & Teambuilding**
SkillPath Seminars
6900 Squibb Road
PO Box 2768
Mission, KS 66201-2768

913-623-3900
800-873-7545; *Fax:* 913-362-4241
enroll@skillpath.net

Conference teaches practical leadership skills thorough real-life examples, pratical methods and techniques. Suitable for managers, supervisors, team leaders and team members.

16813 **ICSB Annual World Conference**
International Council for Small Business
2201 G Street NW
Suite 315
Washington, DC 20052

202-944-0704; *Fax:* 202-994-4930
icsb@gwu.edu; www.icsb.org
Social Media: Facebook, Twitter

Luca Iandoli, President
Dr. Robert S. Lai, President-Elect
Geralyn Franklin, VP/Finance/Control
Ayman El Tarabishy, Executive Director
Michael Battaglia, Operations Manager

Annual business conference attended by entrepreneurs, policy makers, business service providers and researchers.
4000+ Members
Founded in: 1955

16814 **IRMA Annual Conference**
Information Resources Management Association
701 E Chocolate Avenue
Suite 200
Hershey, PA 17033

717-533-8845; *Fax:* 717-533-8661
member@irma-international.org;
www.irma-international.org

Mehdi Khosrow-Pour PhD, President
Sherif Kamel PhD, Communications Director
Gerald Grant PhD, IRMA Doctoral Symposium Director
Lech Janczewski PhD, IRMA World Representative Director
Paul Chalekian, IRMA United States Representative

Provides forums for researchers and practitioners to share leading-edge knowledge in the global resource information management area. Various seminars, conventions and conferences, and other training programs are offered by IRMA throughout the year.
Frequency: May

16815 **Int'l. Association of Healthcare Central Svc. Material Management**
IAHCSMM Annual Conference
213 W Institute Place
Suite 307
Chicago, IL 60610-3195

312-440-0078
800-962-8274; *Fax:* 312-440-9474
mailbox@iahcsmm.com; www.iahcsmm.com

Betty Hanna, Executive Director
Marilyn Corida, Secretary/Treasurer
Lisa Huber, President
Bruce T. Bird, President

125 EXHIBITORSlication separates supervisors/directors from technicians.
600+ Attendees
Frequency: Annual

16816 **International Public Management Associatio n for Human Resources Trade Show**
Int'l Public Management Assoc for Human Resources
1617 Duke St
Alexandria, VA 22314-3406

703-549-7100; *Fax:* 703-684-0948;
www.ipma-hr.org

Neil Reichenberg, Executive Director
Sima Hassassian, COO
Tina Chiappetta, Sr Director Gov't Affairs/Comm
500 Attendees

16817 **Labor-Management Alliance (LMA)**
International Association of Fire Chiefs
4025 Fair Ridge Drive
Suite 300
Fairfax, VA 22033-2868

703-273-0911; *Fax:* 703-273-9363
jwoulfe@iafc.org; www.iafc.org

Mark Light, Executive Director & CEO
Karin Soyster Fitzgerald, Chief Operations Officer
Lisa Yonkers, Director, Conferences & Education
Jason Nauman, Education & Learning Manager
John Woulfe, Assistant Director, Hazmat

Provides exceptional networking opportunities and dynamic education to foster and enhance cooperative and collaborative labor-management relationships.
Frequency: Annual

16818 **National Quality Education Conference**
American Society for Quality
600 N Plankinton Avenue
PO Box 3005
Milwaukee, WI 53201-3005

414-272-8575
800-248-1946; *Fax:* 414-272-1734
help@asq.org; www.asq.org
Social Media: Facebook, Twitter, LinkedIn

Roberto M Saco, President
Paul E Borawski, Executive Director
Erica Gumieny, Sales
Fay Spano, Communications/Media Relations

Provides teachers, administrators, and support personnel opportunities to examine continuous improvement principles used in education. It provides resources and best practices to help you address requirements of No Child Left Behind, while helping you increase student achievement and improve overall performance.
100M Members
Frequency: November
Founded in: 1946

16819 New York Social Media Marketing Conference
SkillPath Seminars
6900 Sqibb Road
PO Box 2768
Mission, KS 66201-2768

913-623-3900
800-873-7545; *Fax:* 913-362-4241
webmaster@skillpath.com; www.skillpath.com

Steve Nichols, Customer Care Representative
Robb Garr, President

This state-of-the-art conference walks through everything needed to start using social media to drive real business results, even for someone who doesn't know the difference between a tweet and a like button. There's no reason to miss out any longer on the proven, bottom-line benefits of marketing with social media.
Frequency: Semi-Annual, April

16820 Project Management for IT Professionals
CompuMaster
6900 Squibb Road
PO Box 2973
Mission, KS 66201-1373

913-362-3900
800-867-4340; *Fax:* 913-432-4930
compumaster@mcimail.com;
www.compumaster.net

Casey Smith, Customer Service

A two-day workshop that will help you meet complex project deadlines and budgets. Held in various locations in November and December. Customization at your location available for groups of twenty or more.

16821 Society for Advancement of Management, Inc. (SAM)
Society for Advancement of Management
Corpus Christi - College of Business
6300 Ocean Drive, Unit 5808
Corpus Christi, TX 78412-5808

361-825-3045
888-827-6077; *Fax:* 361-825-5609
sam@samnational.org; www.samnational.org

Moustafa H. Abdelsamad, President/CEO
Ken E. Byus, Treasurer
Everette Anderson, VP, Sales & Marketing

Featuring speakers, sponsors, presentations, workshops and discussions.
2500 Members
Founded in: 1912

16822 Turnaround Management Association Annual Fall Conference
Turnaround Management Association
150 S Wacker Drive
Suite 900
Chicago, IL 60606

312-578-6900; *Fax:* 312-578-8336
info@turnaround.org; www.turnaround.org
Social Media: Facebook, Twitter, LinkedIn

Lisa Poulin, President
Patrick Lagrange, Chairman
Linda Delgadillo, Executive Director

The only international nonprofit association dedicated to corporate renewal and turnaround management. TMA's 9,000 members in 46 regional chapters comprise a professional community of turnaround practitioners, attorneys, accountants, investors, lenders, venture capitalists, appraiser, liquidators, executive recruiters and consultants. Three international conferences each year offer networking and educational sessions on the latest trends and best practices in the restructuring field.
600 Attendees
Frequency: Annual/Fall

16823 Turnaround Management Association Spring Conference
Turnaround Management Association
150 S Wacker Drive
Suite 900
Chicago, IL 60606

312-578-6900; *Fax:* 312-578-8336
info@turnaround.org; www.turnaround.org
Social Media: Facebook, Twitter, LinkedIn

Lisa Poulin, President
Patrick Lagrange, Chairman
Linda Delgadillo, Executive Director

The only international nonprofit association dedicated to corporate renewal and turnaround management. TMA's 9,000 members in 46 regional chapters comprise a professional community of turnaround practitioners, attorneys, accountants, investors, lenders, venture capitalists, appraiser, liquidators, executive recruiters and consultants. Three international conferences each year offer networking and educational sessions on the latest trends and best practices in the restructuring field.
600 Attendees
Frequency: Annual/Spring

16824 VCOS Symposium in the West
International Association of Fire Chiefs
4025 Fair Ridge Drive
Suite 300
Fairfax, VA 22033-2868

703-273-0911; *Fax:* 703-273-9363;
www.iafc.org

Mark Light, Executive Director & CEO
Lisa Yonkers, Director, Conferences & Education
Shannon Gilliland, Assistant Director, Conferences
Sara Stehle, Conference Specialist

Addresses the unique needs of volunteer and combination departmentsincluding transitioning from a volunteer to a combination department, recruitment and retention, leadership and management, staffing and more.
Frequency: Annual

16825 Volunteer & Combination Officers Section Symposium in the Sun
International Association of Fire Chiefs
4025 Fair Ridge Drive
Suite 300
Fairfax, VA 22033-2868

703-273-0911; *Fax:* 703-273-9363
sstehle@iafc.org; www.iafc.org

Mark Light, Executive Director & CEO
Lisa Yonkers, Director, Conferences & Education
Sara Stehle, Conference Specialist
Shannon Gilliland, Assistant Director, Conferences

Addresses the unique needs of volunteer and combination departments including transitioning from a volunteer to a combination department, recruitment and retention, leadership and management, staffing and more.
Frequency: Annual

16826 WACRA Annual Conference Research & Application
World Assoc for Case Method Research & Application
23 Mackintosh Avenue
Needham, MA 02492-1218

781-444-8982; *Fax:* 781-444-1548
hans.klein@wacra.org; www.wacra.org

Dr Hans E Klein, President/Executive Director
Dr Joelle Piffault, Director/Development/Membership
Dr Pavel Zufan, Director/Business/Economics

Directories & Databases

16827 ABI/INFORM
UMI/Data Courier
620 S 3rd Street
Suite 400
Louisville, KY 40202-2475

800-626-2823; *Fax:* 502-589-5572

This database contains more than 675,000 citations, appearing in over 900 international periodicals covering business and management related areas.

16828 ARMA International's Buyers Guide
ARMA International
11880 College Blvd
Suite 450
Overland Park, KS 66215

913-341-3808
800-422-2762; *Fax:* 913-341-3742
hq@arma.org; www.arma.org/conference
Social Media: Facebook, Twitter, LinkedIn

Formerly the Association of Record Managers and Administrators, this guide has 75-100 companies listed.

16829 Analysis of Workers' Compensation Laws
Chamber of Commerce of the United States
1615 H St Nw
Washington, DC 20062-0002

202-659-6000; *Fax:* 202-463-5836;
www.uschamber.org

Thomas J Donohue, CEO
Jean Hunt, Administrative Assistant

Offers a list of workers' compensation administrators.
Cost: $25.00
Frequency: Annual

16830 Association of Management Consulting Firms
AMCF
380 Lexington Avenue
Suite 1700
New York, NY 10168

212-551-7887; *Fax:* 212-551-7934
info@amcf.org; www.amcf.org

Elizabeth A Kovacs, President/CEO
Kathleen Fish, Director Programs
Samantha Colon, Executive Administrator

About 50 management consulting firms that are members of ACME.
Cost: $50.00
Frequency: Biennial
Founded in: 1929

16831 Business Information Desk Reference: Where to Find Answers to Questions
Palgrave Macmillan
175 5th Ave
New York, NY 10010-7728

212-982-3900; *Fax:* 212-307-5035;
www.ibtauris.com

Bruce McKenzie, President
Stuart Weir, Production Director
Paul Davighi, Marketing Director
Liz Stuckey, Secretary

Over 1,000 print material, online databases and federal agencies covering over 24 business areas are listed.

16832 Business Information Resources - Online Database
Grey House Publishing

4919 Route 22
PO Box 56
Amenia, NY 12501
518-789-8700
800-562-2139; *Fax:* 518-789-0556
gold@greyhouse.com
http://gold.greyhouse.com
Social Media: Facebook, Twitter

Leslie Mackenzie, Publisher
Richard Gottlieb, Editor

This one-stop, business building database provides immediate access to the resources you need for success in the industry of your choice. This is the kind of must have information that, before now, could take hours to find. With a subscription to the Directory of Business Information Resources - Online Database, you'll have immediate access to over 17,000 associations, magazines, journals, newsletters, trade shows, directories, databases, and web sites for 100 industry groups.
Founded in: 1981

16833 **Business Library**
Dow Jones & Company
4300 North Route 1
South Brunswick, NJ 08852
609-520-4000

Covers all types of topics and subjects that are of interest to US business markets.
Frequency: Full-text

16834 **Business Opportunities Handbook**
Enterprise Magazines
1020 N Broadway
Suite 111
Milwaukee, WI 53202-3157
414-272-9977; *Fax:* 414-272-9973;
www.franchisehandbook.com

Betsy Green, Owner

Over 2,500 listings of franchises, dealers and distributors that offer business opportunities to individuals.
Cost: $5.99
150 Pages
Frequency: Quarterly

16835 **Career Guide: Dun's Employment Opportunities Directory**
Dun & Bradstreet Information Service
3 Sylvan Way
Parsippany, NJ 07054-3822
973-605-6000; *Fax:* 973-605-9630

Offers information on more than 5,000 companies, leading employers of the United States, that provide career opportunities in sales, marketing and management.
Cost: $385.00
2700 Pages
Frequency: Annual

16836 **Company Intelligence**
Information Access Company
362 Lakeside Drive
Foster City, CA 94404-1171
650-378-5200
800-227-8431

Offers company news and financial information with an emphasis placed on hard-to-find privately held companies in the United States and worldwide.

16837 **Corporate Technology Database**
One Source Information Services
300 Baker Ave
Concord, MA 01742-2131
978-318-4300
800-554-5501; *Fax:* 978-318-4690
sales@onesource.com; www.onesource.com

Philip J Garlick, President
John Brewer, Vice Chairman
Brad Haigis, VP/Products
Beth Jacaruso, VP/Content

Offers profiles of over 45,000 public and private US corporations and operating units of large corporations that develop or manufacture some 100,000 high-technology products.
Frequency: Directory

16838 **Corporate Yellow Book**
Leadership Directories
104 5th Ave
New York, NY 10011-6901
212-627-4140; *Fax:* 212-645-0931
corporate@leadershipdirectories.com;
www.leadershipdirectories.com

David Hurvitz, CEO

Contact information for over 48,000 executives at over 1,000 companies and more than 9,000 board members and their outside affiliations.
Cost: $360.00
1,400 Pages
Frequency: Quarterly
ISSN: 1058-2098
Founded in: 1986

16839 **Directory of Business Information Resources**
Grey House Publishing
4919 Route 22
PO Box 56
Amenia, NY 12501
518-789-8700
800-562-2139; *Fax:* 845-373-6390
books@greyhouse.com; www.greyhouse.com
Social Media: Facebook, Twitter

Leslie Mackenzie, Publisher
Richard Gottlieb, Editor

The source for contacts in over 98 business areas, from advertising and agriculture to utilities and wholesalers. This carefully researched volume details, for each business industry, the associations representing each industry, the newsletters that keep members current, the magazines and journals that are important to the trade, the top conventions and industry web sites that provide important marketing information. Includes contact names with phone, fax, website and e-mail information.
Cost: $195.00
2300 Pages
Frequency: Annual
ISBN: 1-592371-93-0
Founded in: 1981

16840 **Directory of Executive Recruiters**
Kennedy Information
One Phoenix Mill Lane
Floor 3
Peterboro, NH 03458
603-924-1006
800-531-0007
customerservice@kennedyinfo.com;
www.kennedyinfo.com

Lists over 8,900 offices of 5,678 executive search firms in the US, Canada and Mexico. Includes key data and contact info on each firm. Directory is indexed by recruiter specialities, function, industry, key principals, and geography. Corporate edition is specially designed for corporate buyers of search services and search providers.
Cost: $179.95
1180 Pages
Frequency: Annual
ISBN: 1-885922-81-7
ISSN: 0090-6484

16841 **Directory of Management Consultants**
Kennedy Information
1 Phoenix Mill Lane
Floor 3
Peterborough, NH 03458
603-924-1006
800-531-0007
bookstore@kennedyinfo.com;
www.kennedyinfo.com

The premier directory of management consulting firms, published since 1979. The 10th edition profiles more than 2,400 firms in North America. Indexed by services, industries, geography, and key contacts.
Cost: $295.00
850 Pages
Frequency: Biennial
ISBN: 1-885922-69-8
ISSN: 0743-6890
Founded in: 1919
Mailing list available for rent: 7600 names at $200 per M

16842 **Directory of Management Information Systems Faculty**
Management Information Systems Research Center
355 Humphrey-271 9th Avenue S
Minneapolis, MN 55455
763-783-7496; *Fax:* 612-626-1316
jdegross@csom.umn.edu;
www.webfoot.csom.umn.edu

Gordon B Davis, Editor
Janice I DeGross, Manager
Kate Terry, Manager
Abby Pinto, Managing Director

College-level teachers of subjects related to management information systems and technology.
Cost: $25.00

16843 **Directory of Outplacement & Career Management Firms**
Kennedy Information
One Phoenix Mill Lane
Floor 3
Peterborough, NH 03458
603-924-1006
800-531-0007
customerservice@kennedyinfo.com;
www.kennedyinfo.com

Profiles 365 firms in 1,351 offices worldwide and identifies 1,875 key principals. Includes key data on revenues, staff sizes, fees & expense policies, and contact information. Indexed by industry specialty, geography and individual outplacement professional.
Cost: $129.00
606 Pages
ISBN: 1-885922-65-5

16844 **Directory of US Labor Organizations**
BNA Books
3 Bethesda Metro Center
Suite 250
Bethesda, MA 02814-5377
703-341-3500
800-372-1033; *Fax:* 800-253-0332
customercare@bna.com; www.bna.com

Gregory C McCaffery, President

Over 200 national unions and professional and state employees associations engaged in labor representation are profiled.
Cost: $55.00
110 Pages
Frequency: Annual

16845 **Diversity in Corporate America**
Hunt-Scanlon Corporation

700 Fairfield Avenue
Stamford, CT 06902

203-352-2920; *Fax:* 203-352-2930

James A Mueller, Founder
Scott Scanlon, CEO
Smooch S Reynolds, President
A David Brown, Managing Director
John D Delpino, Director - Executive Staffing

2,200 listings of executives responsible for managing corporate diversity in the US.
Cost: $179.00
Frequency: Biennial

16846 Employee Service Management: NESRA Buyers Directory

National Employee Services & Recreation Assn
568 Spring Road
Suite D
Elmhurst, IL 60126

630-559-0020; *Fax:* 630-559-0025
esmahq@esmassn.org; www.esmassn.org

Renee Mula, Editor

Includes a list of over 200 member manufacturers and distributors offering products and services for employee discount programs and employee store merchandise to members.
Frequency: Annual

16847 Employment, Hours and Earnings

US Department Of Commerce
200 Constitution Ave Nw
Washington, DC 20210-0001

202-693-5000; *Fax:* 202-219-8822
webmaster@dol.gov; www.dol.gov

Hilda L Solis, CEO
Sonya Carrion, Director

This database aimed at employees and management cover US employment, hours and earnings.

16848 Fortune Magazine

Time Inc./Time Warner
1271 Avenue of the Americas
16th Floor
New York, NY 10020-1393

212-522-1212
800-274-6800; *Fax:* 212-522-0602;
www.timeinc.com
Social Media: Facebook, Twitter

Laura Lang, CEO
Howard M. Averill, CFO
Leslie Picard, President
Stephanie George, Chief Marketing Officer
John Huey, Editor-in-Chief

FORTUNE is a global leader in business journalism. The magazine has a great history of providing analysis and news critical to business people.
Founded in: 1922

16849 Fortune: Deals of the Year Issue

Time Inc./Time Warner
1271 Avenue of the Americas
16th Floor
New York, NY 10020-1393

212-522-1212
800-274-6800; *Fax:* 212-522-0602;
www.timeinc.com

Laura Lang, CEO
Howard M. Averill, CFO
Leslie Picard, President
Stephanie George, Chief Marketing Officer
John Huey, Editor-in-Chief

Offers information on 50 of the largest United States corporate financial transactions, including mergers, acquisitions and leveraged buyouts.
Cost: $5.00
Frequency: Annual
Founded in: 1922

16850 Gale Group Management Contents

Gale/Cengage Learning
2250 Perimeter Park Drive
Suite 300
Morrisville, NC 27560

919-804-6400
800-334-2564; *Fax:* 919-804-6410
gale.content@A@cengage.com;
www.infotrac.galegroup.com
Social Media: Facebook, Twitter, LinkedIn, Youtube

Patrick C Sommers, President

A specialized database that provides current information on business practices and management techniques from key management journals. The database provides theoretical background and practical how to approaches to key management disciplines.
Frequency: Weekly

16851 International Directory of Executive Recruiters

Kennedy Information
One Phoenix Mill Lane
Floor 3
Peterborough, NH 03458

603-924-1006
800-531-0007
customerservice@kennedyinfo.com;
www.kennedyinfo.com

A comprehensive source of worldwide executive recruiting firms and consultancies. List full contact information for search firms in 60 countries. Indexed by management function, industry, firm, and search firm principals.
Cost: $149.00
800 Pages
ISBN: 1-885922-53-1

16852 International Registry of OD Professional

Organization Development Institute
11234 Walnut Ridge Road
Chesterland, OH 44026-1240

440-729-7419
donwcole@aol.com

Dr. Donald W Cole RODC, President

A who's who directory of services and supplies to the industry. Includes: The OD Code of Ethics; a Statement on the Knowledge and Skill Necessary for Competence in O.D.; a listing of not just names and addresses, but the credential of all those registered with us; a list of all the OD organizations in the world and all the OD/OB academic programs in the world.
Cost: $25.00
300 Pages
Frequency: Annual

16853 Labor Arbitration Information System

LRP Publications
747 Dresher Road, Suite 500
PO Box 980
Horsham, PA 19044-0980

215-840-0912; *Fax:* 215-784-9639
webmaster@lrp.com; www.lrp.com

Sandy Johnson, Director/Manager

Comprehensive indexing system for arbitration awards available. The easy-to-use, one-stop indexing system covers all the major arbitration reporting services including AAA, BNA, and CCH.
Cost: $515.00
Frequency: Monthly
Founded in: 1977

16854 Meeting the Needs of Employees with Disabilities

Resources for Rehabilitation
22 Bonad Road
Winchester, MA 01890

781-368-9094; *Fax:* 781-368-9096;
www.rfr.org

Offers various descriptions of organizations and products that assist those involved in the employment of people with disabilities.
Cost: $42.95
Frequency: Biennial

16855 SHRM Membership Directory Online

SHRM/Society for Human Resource Management
1800 Duke St
Alexandria, VA 22314-3494

703-535-6000
866-898-4724; *Fax:* 703-535-6474;
www.shrm.org
Social Media: Facebook, Twitter, LinkedIn, Youtube

Susan R Meisinger, CEO
Robert O Gonzales, Secretary
Robb E Van Cleave, Treasurer

An exclusive benefit for SHRM members, the SHRM Membership Directory Online is a searchable database catagorized by by name, title, company, company size, job function or location.

16856 Small Business Sourcebook

Gale/Cengage Learning
27500 Drake Road
Farmington Hills, MI 48331-3535

248-699-4253
800-877-4253; *Fax:* 877-363-4253
gale.galeord@cengage.com;
www.gale.cengage.com
Social Media: Facebook, Twitter, Youtube

Patrick C Sommers, President

In this two volume annotated guide you'll discover more than 340 specific small business profiles and 99 general small business topics, small business programs and assistance programs in the US, its territories and Canadian provinces and US federal government agencies and offices specializing is small business issues, programs and assistance.
Frequency: Annual/2 Volumes
ISBN: 1-414421-75-3

16857 Small Business or Entrepreneurial Related Newsletter

Prosperity & Profits Unlimited
PO Box 416
Denver, CO 80201-0416

303-573-5564

A Doyle, Editor

A mini directory of listings for small businesses.
Cost: $19.95
8 Pages
Frequency: Every 2 Years
Circulation: 2,500
Founded in: 1990
Printed in one color on matte stock

16858 Staffing Industry Sourcebook

Staffing Industry Analysts
881 Fremont Ave
Suite A3
Los Altos, CA 94024-5637

650-948-9303
800-950-9496; *Fax:* 650-232-2360;
www.sireport.com

Ron Mester, Manager
Jeff Reeder, Mgr Editor/SI Review
Sona Sharma, Mgr Editor/IT Serv Business Report
Linda Hubbard, Director of Marketing
Leslie Austin, Customer/Membership

Source Book, Facts and Figures for Market Research on the staffing industry.
Cost: $285.00
451 Pages
Frequency: BiAnnual
ISBN: 1-883814-10-3

16859 **Transnational Corporations and Labor: A Directory of Resources**
Third World Resources
1218 E 21st Street
Oakland, CA 94606
510-533-7583; *Fax:* 510-533-0923
Danielle Mahones, Executive Director
This directory is a source for books, periodicals and audiovisuals on transnational corporations and labor issues.
Cost: $14.95
160 Pages

Industry Web Sites

16860 **http://gold.greyhouse.com**
G.O.L.D Grey House OnLine Databases
Grey House Publishing's online database platform, GOLD, offers Quick Search, Keyword Search and Expert Search for most business sectors including management markets. The GOLD platform makes finding the information you need quick and easy - whether you're a novice searcher or an experienced database user. All of Grey House's directory products are available for subscription on the GOLD platform.

16861 **www.aahc.net**
AAHC American Association of Healthcare Consultant

16862 **www.aaimnhta.com**
American Association of Industrial Management
Dedicated to better management and the over-all objective which is the formulation of broad management principles and strategies that will insure sucessful management and promote the principles of free, private and competitive enterprise with individual opportunity and freedom under a constitutional government.

16863 **www.aameda.org**
American Academy of Medical Administrators
Department heads and administrators in areas of hospital and health administration.

16864 **www.afsmi.org**
AFSM International
A global organization dedicated to furthering the knowledge, understanding, and career development of executives, managers and professionals in the high-technology service industry.

16865 **www.amanet.org**
American Management Association
Offers a full range of business education and management development programs for indivudual and organizations in Europe, the Americas and Asia. Learn superior business skills and best management practices through a variety of seminars, conferences and special events.

16866 **www.amcf.org**
AMCF
Seeks to unite management consulting firms in order to develop and improve professional standards and practice in the field. Offers information and referral services on management consultants.

16867 **www.americanassocofindmgmt.com**
American Association of Industrial Management
Dedicated to better management and the formulation of broad management principles and strategies that will ensure sucessful management and promote the principles of free, private and competive enterprise with individual opportunity and freedom under a constitutional government.

16868 **www.aom-iaom.org**
Association of Management
Formerly the Association of Human Resources Management and Organizational Behavior.

16869 **www.apics.org**
APICS Association for Operations Management
The primary purpose of this specific industry group is to educate food and beverage manufacturers on effective marketing strategies, market trends and material management.

16870 **www.aspanet.org**
American Society for Public Administration
The nation's most respected society representing all forums in the public service arena. Advocate for greater effectiveness in government agents of goodwill and professionalism addressing key public service issues by promoting change at both the local and international levels, we can enhance the quality of lives worldwide.

16871 **www.awhp.org**
Association for Worksite Health Promotion
Exists to advance the profession of worksite health promotion and the career development of its practitioners and to improve the performance of the programs they administer. Represents a variety of disciplines and worksites, for decision-makers in the areas of health promotion/disease prevention and health-care cost management.

16872 **www.besthealthplans.com**
Best Employers Association
Market and administer medical and dental insurance for large and small groups. Specializes in group insurance and employee benefits.

16873 **www.bizintell.com**
Business Intelligence Association
Business to business research on a wide variety of industries. Specialize in primary and hard-to-find secondary information.

16874 **www.cmaa.org**
Club Managers Association of America
Professional association for managers of membership clubs. Members manage country, city, athletic, faculty, yacht, town and military clubs. Objectives to promote and advance friendly relations among persons connected with the management of clubs and other associations of similar character.

16875 **www.cmaonline.org**
The Christian Management Association
Designed to assist those involved in the management of Christian organizations.

16876 **www.cmeinc.org**
Center for Management Effectiveness
Conducts management training programs and publishes self-scoring inventories, trainer guides and workbooks on stress management, resolution of conflict, risk taking, decision making and building managerial skills.

16877 **www.corptech.com**
CORPTECH Information Services
Corporations and operating units of large corporations that develop or manufacture some 100,000 high-technology products.

16878 **www.emsnetwork.com/cbt**
Center for Breakthrough Thinking
Organized to promote and institutionalize the teaching and application of Breakthrough Thinking in universities, corporations and governments in solving problems, leveraging opportunities, and achieving change.

16879 **www.expedia.com**
Expedia.com
Internet travel service offers access to airlines, hotels, car rentals, vacation packages, cruises and corporate travel.

16880 **www.greyhouse.com**
Grey House Publishing
Authoritative reference directories for most business sectors including management markets. Users can search the online databases with varied search criteria allowing for custom searches by product category, geographic area, sales volume, keyword, subject and more. Full Grey House catalog and online ordering also available.

16881 **www.iamc.org**
Industrial Asset Management Council
Members are companies engaged in the management of two or more organizations on a professional client basis.

16882 **www.icmci.org**
ICMCI Intn'l Council of Mgnt Consulting Institutes
For national institutes from around the world that certify professional management consultants; promotes professional development and networking between consultants and the highest standards of performance for clients.

16883 **www.icsa.com**
International Customer Service Association
Dedicated to promoting the development and awareness of the customer service profession through networking, education and research.

16884 **www.icsb.org**
International Council for Small Business
Management development, resources, and metworking for small business professionals.

16885 **www.imc-ymca.org/join.html**
International Management Council
IMC provides individuals with opportunities for continually developing their leadership and management skills through a network of shared experiences and education.

16886 **www.imcusa.org/**
IMC-USA Institute of Management Consultants-USA
For management consultants in the United States, organized to establish consulting as a self-regulating profession, meriting public confidence and respect. Toward the achievement of this goal IMC awards the international appelation CMC for certified management consultants.

16887 **www.ioma.com**
Institute of Management & Administration
Organization helps to provides information and guidance to management teams for various businesses.

16888 **www.ipma-hr.org**
International/Public Management Assn For Human Res
Human resource professionals, representing the interests of over 6,000 individual and 1,300

agency members, at the federal, state and local levels of government. Promotes excellence in human resource management through the ongoing development of professional and ethical standards, and through its publishing and educational training programs.

16889 www.members.aol.com/odinst
Organization Development Institute

Promotes the understanding of organization development and offers three categories of membership: professional consultant, regular and student.

16890 www.mgma.com
Medical Group Management Association

The oldest and largest professional membership association dedicated to medical practice management. Serves their members by offering timely and relevant networking and educational opportunities that keep the members up-to-date on the practice management field.

16891 www.mt-online.com
Applied Technology Publications

MT-online.com is the premier source of capacity assurance and best practice solutions for manufacturing, process and service operations worldwide. Online home of Maintenance Technology magazie, the dynamic MT-online.com portal serves the critical technical, business and professional-development needs of engineers, managers and technicians from across all industrial, institutional and commercial sectors.

16892 www.nacdonline.org
National Association of Corporate Directors

Fosters research, surveys, seminars and director for corporate. Maintains placement service.

16893 www.naesaa.com
National Association of Executive Secretaries and Administrative Assistants

Publishes a newsletter 11 times per year.

16894 www.nsha.biz
National Small Business United

Volunteer-led association. Primary mission is to advocate state and federal policies that are beneficial to small business, the state and the nation and to promote the growth of free enterprise.

16895 www.pmi.org
Project Management Institute

Fosters recognition of the need for project management professionalism. Offers professional certification and bestows awards.

16896 www.promanager.org
Professional Managers Association

A national membership association representing the interests of professional managers, management officials and non-bargaining unit employees in the federal government.

16897 www.rbma.org
Radiology Business Management Association

Promotes management education and study of practice economics, legislative issues and consumer trends.

16898 www.samnational.org
Society for Advancement of Management

SAM members come from a variety of disciplines - productions, finance, marketing, accounting and more who share a common bond of interest in becoming stronger managers.

16899 www.shrm.org
Society for Human Resource Management

16900 www.shrm.org/ema
Society for Human Resources/Employment Mgt Assn

A national association comprised primarily of corporate human resource professionals responsible for hiring and staffing.

16901 www.ssainfo.com
Support Services Alliance

Multi-state membership organization that provides cost-savings services and legislative representation for small businesses and the self-employed. Also offers services to the memberships of more than 100 affiliated state, regional and national associations.

16902 www.wacra.org
World Assn for Case Method Research & Application

Members are professional and academicians with an interest in the use of the case method in teaching, training and planning. Interactive, innovative teaching and learning methods.

16903 www.ypo.org
Young Presidents' Organization

Members are corporate presidents under the age of fifty whose companies employ at least fifty employees.

Associations

16904 **APICS: Association for Operations Management**
8430 West Bryn Mawr Avenue
Suite 1000
Chicago, IL 60631

773-867-1777
800-444-2742; *Fax:* 773-639-3000;
www.apics.org
Social Media: Facebook, Twitter, LinkedIn, Youtube

Robert D Boyle, Chair of the Board
Abe Eshkenazi, CSCP, CPA,, Chief Executive Officer
Sharon Rice, Executive Director
Dean Martinez, Executive Vice President
Jennifer K Daniels, Vice President, Marketing

Provides lifelong learning for lifetime success. APICS certification programs, training tools and networking opportunities increase workplace performance. The society supports 20,000 manufacturing and service industry companies worldwide.
Cost: $110.00
60000 Members
Frequency: Membership/Professional
Founded in: 1957

16905 **ASM International**
9639 Kinsman Rd
Materials Park, OH 44073-0002

440-338-5151
800-336-5152; *Fax:* 440-338-4634
memberservices@asminternational.org;
www.asminternational.org
Social Media: Facebook, Twitter, LinkedIn

Prof. C. Ravi Ravindran, FASM, President
Dr. Sunniva R. Collins, FASM, Vice President
Thomas S Passek, Managing Director & Secretary
Jeane Deatherage, Administrator, Foundation Programs
Virginia Shirk, Foundation Executive Assistant

The society for materials engineers and scientists, a worldwide network dedicated to advancing industry, technology and applications of metals and materials.
35000 Members
Founded in: 1913

16906 **Adhesive & Sealant Council**
7101 Wisconsin Ave
Suite 990
Bethesda, MD 20814-4805

301-986-9700; *Fax:* 301-986-9795
data@ascouncil.org; www.ascouncil.org
Social Media: Twitter, LinkedIn

Traci Jensen, Chairman
William Allmond, President
Steve Duren, Senior Director, Member Services
Valeryia Mikharava, Director, Finance
Mark Collatz, Director, Government Relations

A North American trade association dedicated to representing the adhesive and sealant industry. ASC is bound by the collective efforts of its members, and strives to improve the industry operating government and strengthen its member companies.
Founded in: 1958

16907 **American Bearing Manufacturers Association**
330 North Wabash
Suite 2000
Chicago, IL 60611

202-367-1155; *Fax:* 202-367-2155
info@americanbearings.org;
www.americanbearings.org
Social Media: Facebook, Twitter

Chris Coughlin, Chair
Ben Succop, Vice Chair
Mark Thorsby, President & Secretary
Amanda Santoro, Director, Membership & Operations
Ashley Stenger, Director, Operations

Promotes bearing standardization. Sponsors Bearing Technical Committee.
Founded in: 1917

16908 **American Brush Manufacturers Association**
736 Main Ave, Suite 7
Durango, CO 81301

720-392-2262; *Fax:* 866-837-8450
info@abma.org; www.abma.org
Social Media: Facebook, Twitter, LinkedIn

David Park, Executive Director

Trade association representing North American manufacturers of brooms, brushes, mops and rollers.
175 Members
Founded in: 1917

16909 **American Machine Tool Distributors Association**
AMTDA
7901 Westpark Drive
McLean, VA 22102-4206

703-893-2900
800-524-0475; *Fax:* 703-893-1151
amt@amtonline.org; www.amtonline.org
Social Media: Facebook, Twitter, LinkedIn, YouTube

DouglasK. Woods, President
Amber L Thomas, Vice President - Advocacy
JefferyH Traver, Vice President - Business
PeterR. Eelman, Vice President - Exhibitions
LindaG Montfort, Vice President-Finance & HR

AMTDA will lead distributors of manufacturing technology by providing essential programs and services that help its members gain global recognition from customers and supplies as the preferred method of distribution.
Cost: $50.00
8-12 Pages
Frequency: Monthly
Circulation: 3400
Founded in: 1924

16910 **American Society for Quality**
American Society for Quality
600 N Plankinton Avenue
PO Box 3005
Milwaukee, WI 53201-3005

414-272-8575
800-248-1946; *Fax:* 414-272-1734
help@asq.org; www.asq.org
Social Media: Facebook, Twitter, LinkedIn, Youtube

John C. Timmerman, Chairman
Paul E Borawski, Executive Director
Jennifer Janzen, Director, Human Resources
Laurel Nelson-Rowe, Managing Director
Michelle Mason, Managing Director

ASQ's mission is to facilitate continuous improvement and increase customer satisfaction. Promotes quality principles, concepts and technologies. Provides information, contacts and opportunities to make things better in the workplace, in communities and in people's lives.
100M Members
Founded in: 1946

16911 **American Textile Machinery Association**
201 Park Washington Ct
Falls Church, VA 22046-4527

703-538-1789; *Fax:* 703-241-5603
info@atmanet.org; www.atmanet.org

Will Motchar, Chairman
Clay D Tyeryar, President/Assistant Treasurer
Harry W. Buzzerd, Jr., ATMA Management Counsel
Susan A. Denston, ATMA Executive Vice President
Carlos F. J. Moore, ATMA International Trade

The American Textile Machinery Association/ATMA's purpose is to advance the common interests of its members, improve business conditions within the US textile machinery industry from a global perspective and market the industry and members' machinery, parts and services.
Founded in: 1933

16912 **Association for Manufacturing Technology**
7901 Westpark Drive
McLean, VA 22102-4206
703-893-2900
800-524-0475; *Fax:* 703-893-1151
amt@amtonline.org; www.amtonline.org
Social Media: Facebook, Twitter, LinkedIn, YouTube

Douglas K Woods, President
Amber L Thomas, Vice President - Advocacy
JefferyH Traver, Vice President - Business
PeterR. Eelman, Vice President - Exhibitions
LindaG Montfort, Vice President-Finance & HR

Represents American providers of manufacturing machinery and equipment. Its goal is to promote technological advancements and improvements in the design, manufacture and sale of member's products in those markets and act as an industry advocate on trade organizations thoroughout the world.
Founded in: 1902

16913 **Association of Equipment Manufacturers**
6737 W Washington St
Suite 2400
Milwaukee, WI 53214-5650

414-272-0943
866-236-0442; *Fax:* 414-272-1170
aem@aem.org; www.aem.org
Social Media: Twitter

John Patterson, Chairman
Dennis Slater, President
Al Cervero, Vice President, Marketing
John Nowak, Chief Financial Officer
Anne Forristall Luke, Vice President, Political & Public

Composed of manufacturers of screens and feeders used in aggregates, mining and industrial processing. Promotes and furthers the interests of members in safety, production, engineering, government relations and other industry matters.
8 Members
Founded in: 1959

16914 **Battery Council International**
330 North Wabash Avenue
Suite 2000
Chicago, IL 60611

312-245-1074; *Fax:* 312-527-6640
info@batterycouncil.org;
www.batterycouncil.org
Social Media: Facebook, LinkedIn

Mark O. Thornsby, CAE, Executive Vice President

A not-for-profit trade association formed to promote the interests of an international lead-acid battery industry.
265 Members
Founded in: 1924

16915 Contract Packaging Association
One Parkview Plaza
Suite 800
Oakbrook Terrace, IL 60181

630-544-5053; *Fax:* 630-544-5055
info@contractpackaging.org;
www.contractpackaging.org
Social Media: Twitter, LinkedIn

Vicky Smitley, President
Chris Nutley, Past President
Tim Koers, Vice President
John Mazelin, Executive Director
Mark O' Malley, Treasurer

Formed for contract packaging firms and those businesses related to them. Promotes the growth and welfare of member firms.
155 Members
Founded in: 1992

16916 Conveyor Equipment Manufacturers Association (CEMA)
5672 Strand CT
Suite 2
Naples, FL 34110

239-514-3441; *Fax:* 239-514-3470
kim@cemanet.org; www.cemanet.org
Social Media: Facebook, Twitter, LinkedIn

Warren Chandler, President
Robert Reinfried, Executive Vice President
Jerry Heathman, Vice President
Jim McKnight, Secretary
Garry Abraham, Treasurer

Involved in writing industry standards, the CEMA seeks to promote among its members and the industry standardization of design manufacture and application on a voluntary basis and in such manner as will not impede development of conveying machinery and component parts or lessen competition. CEMA sponsors an annual Engineering Conference that allows Member Company Engineers to meet and develop or improve CEMA Consensus Industry Standards and National Standards that affect the conveyor industry.
96 Members
Founded in: 1933

16917 Flexible Packaging Association
185 Admiral Cochrane Drive
Suite 105
Annapolis, MD 21401

410-694-0800; *Fax:* 410-694-0900
fpa@flexpack.org; www.flexpack.org

Marla Donahue, President

One of the leading trade associations for converters of flexible packaging and suppliers to the industry. Also provides a wealth of information to its members through focused services and benefits of membership.

16918 Food & Beverage Marketplace Directory
Grey House Publishing
4919 Route 22
PO Box 56
Amenia, NY 12501-0056

518-789-8700
800-562-2139; *Fax:* 518-789-0556
books@greyhouse.com; www.greyhouse.com
Social Media: Facebook, Twitter

Richard Gottlieb, President
Leslie Mackenzie, Publisher

A three-volume set that is the most comprehensive resource in the food and beverage industry. Available in print, a subscription-based online database, as well as a mailing list and database formats.
Cost: $595.00
2000 Pages
Frequency: Annual
Founded in: 1981

16919 Grocery Manufacturers Association
1350 Eye St NW
Suite 300
Washington, DC 20005-3377

202-639-5900; *Fax:* 202-639-5932
info@gmaonline.org; www.gmabrands.com
Social Media: Facebook, Twitter, RSS

Pamela G Bailey, President
Jim Flannery, Senior Executive Vice President
Dr. Leon Bruner, DVM, Ph.D., Senior Vice President
Louis Finkel, Executive Vice President
Sean Darragh, Executive Vice President, Global

Manufacturers of food and nonfood products sold through the grocery trade. US sales are more than $500 billion, GMA members employ more than 2.5 million workers in the nation.
135 Members
Founded in: 1908

16920 International Packaged Ice Association
238 East Davis Blvd
Suite 213
Tampa, FL 33606

813-258-1690
jane@packagedice.com;
www.packagedice.com
Social Media: Facebook, YouTube

Bob Morse, Chairman
Bo Russell, Vice Chairman/Treasurer
John Smibert, Secretary/Assistant Treasurer
Mike Ringstaff, Associate Member

Manufacturers and distributors of ice and their suppliers.
150 Members
Founded in: 1917

16921 Manufacturers' Agents National Association
6321 W. Dempster Street
Suite 110
Morton Grove, IL 60053

949-859-4040
877-626-2776; *Fax:* 949-855-2973
MANA@MANAonline.org;
www.manaonline.org
Social Media: Facebook, Twitter, LinkedIn, YouTube,Google+

ken McGregor, Chairman
Charles Cohon, CPMR, President and CEO
Jerry Leth, Vice President and General Manager
Lisa Ball, Member Services Coordinator
Doug Bower, Director of Strategic Alliances

Association for independent agents and firms representing manufacturers and other businesses in specified territories on a commission basis, including consultants and associate member firms interested in the manufacturer/agency method of marketing.
Founded in: 1947

16922 Material Handling Institute
8720 Red Oak Blvd # 201
Suite 201
Charlotte, NC 28217-3996

704-676-1190; *Fax:* 704-676-1199
gbaer@mhia.org; www.mhi.org
Social Media: Facebook, Twitter, LinkedIn, Youtube, Blooger, RSS

Dave Young, Chairman
John Paxton, President
Gregg E. Goodner, Vice President

Industrial steel shelving is loaded by hand and generally stores materials that are small in size, with multiple parts stores on a given shelf separated by dividers, boxes and drawers.
400 Members
Founded in: 1945

16923 National Association of Display Industries
4651 Sheridan Street
Suite 470
Hollywood, FL 33021

954-893-7300; *Fax:* 954-893-7500
nadi@nadi-global.com; www.nadi-global.com

Klein Merriman, Executive Director
Tracy Dillon, Director Communications

A leading association for the visual merchandising profession. As visual merchandising has evolved over the years into playing an integral role in retail, NADI has always taken the lead in information and educating members. The association's already significant support for the visual design profession has grown with NADI's exclusive sponsorship of GlobalShop's Visual Merchandising Show and StoreXpo.
350 Members
Founded in: 1942

16924 National Association of Manufacturers
733 10th Street NW
Suite 700
Washington, DC 20001

202-637-3000
800-814-8468; *Fax:* 202-637-3182
manufacturing@nam.org; www.nam.org
Social Media: Facebook, Twitter, LinkedIn, Youtube, RSS, Flickr

Gregg M. Lundgren, Chairman
John F. Lundgren, Vice Chairman
Jay Timmons, President
Linda E. Kelly, Senior Vice President, Legal
Richard I. Klein, Senior Vice President

Enhances the competitiveness of manufacturers and improves American living standards by shaping a legislative and regulatory environment conductive to US economic growth and to increase understanding among policy makers, the media and the general public about the importance of manufacturing to America's economic strength.
14000 Members
Founded in: 1895

16925 National Automatic Merchandising Association
20 N Wacker Dr # 3500
Suite 3500
Chicago, IL 60606-3102

312-346-0370; *Fax:* 312-704-4140
dmathews@vending.org; www.vending.org
Social Media: Facebook, Twitter, YouTube

Howard Chapman, NCE, CCS, Chairman
Patrick Hagerty, Chair Elect
Heidi Chico, Vice Chair
Peter A. Tullio, Past Chair
Jeffery R. Smith, Secretary/Treasurer

Serves food and refreshment, vending, contract foodservice management and office coffee service industries.
2500 Members
Founded in: 1936

16926 North American Punch Manufacturers Association
21 Turquoise Avenue
Naples, FL 34114

239-775-7245; *Fax:* 239-775-7245;
www.exactapunch.com/associations.htm

Robert E May, Executive Secretary

Principal program of NAPMA is the standardization of all punches, dies and retainers manufactured by the various member companies.
23 Members
Founded in: 1963

16927 Pressure Vessel Manufacturers Association
800 Roosevelt Rd.
Building C,Suite 312
Glen Ellyn, IL 60137

630-942-6590; *Fax:* 630-790-3095
info@pvma.org; www.pvma.org/

Rick Fryda, President
Bill Kahl, Vice President
Brooke Cornard, Secretary/Treasurer
GregMc Rae, Director
Michael Pischke, Immediate Past President

Members are manufacturers of ASME code pressure vessels and suppliers, components and services to pressure vessel manfacturers.
31 Members
Founded in: 1975

16928 Production and Operations Management Society
Dept. of Management-Univ. of Baltimore
1420 N Charles Street
Baltimore, MD 21201-5720

410-837-4727; *Fax:* 410-837-5675;
www.poms.org/

Sushil Gupta, PhD, Executive Director
Chelliah Sriskandarajah, Ph.D., Associate Executive Director
Metin Єakanyildirim, Associate Professor of Operations

Members are professionals and academics with an interest in production and operations management.
1200 Members
Founded in: 1989

16929 Refractories Institute
1300 Sumner Avenue
Cleveland, OH 44115

216-241-7333; *Fax:* 216-241-0105
info@refractoriesinstitute.org;
www.refractoriesinstitute.org

Robert Crolius, President

National trade association for refractory manufacturers, suppliers of equipment and raw materials and installers of refractory products.
80 Members
Founded in: 1951

16930 Remanufacturing Industries Council
RICI
4401 Fair Lakes Ct
Suite 210
Fairfax, VA 22033-3848

Fax: 703-968-2878; www.rici.org
Social Media: Facebook, LinkedIn, Google+

Larry Rice, CEO

A coalition of associations and companies in the remanufacturing industry.
Founded in: 1997

16931 Remanufacturing Institute
Po Box 48
Lewisburg, PA 17837

570-523-0992; *Fax:* 705-555-5555
rgiuntini@reman.org; www.reman.org

Ron Giuntini, Executive Director

A coalition of associations and companies in the entire manufacturing industry. There are over 73,000 companies in this industry. Our goal is to unite them into a powerful organization.
11 Members
Founded in: 1997

16932 The Benchmarking Network
4606 Fm 1960 Rd W
Suite #250
Houston, TX 77069-4617

281-440-5044; *Fax:* 281-440-6677;
www.benchmarkingnetwork.com
Social Media: Facebook, Twitter

AMBC is a focused group of manufacturing process improvement professionals that looks to identify the best practices surrounding manufacturing issues for the overall operations of the members.

16933 Ultrasonic Industry Association
PO Box 2307
Dayton, OH 45401-2301

937-586-3725; *Fax:* 937-586-3699
uia@ultrasonics.org; www.ultrasonics.org

Mark Hodnett, President
Mark Schafer, VP
Ron Stault, Treasurer
Janet Devine, Secretary

Improving processes, techniques and materials through the application of ultasonic technology.
70 Members
Founded in: 1956

16934 United Association of Manufacturers Representatives
P.O. Box 4216
Dana Point, CA 92669

949-481-5214; *Fax:* 417-779-1576
info@uamr.com; www.uamr.com/

Karen Kittrell Mazzola, Executive Director

Benefits manufacturers and independent sales representatives and is a national marketing association.
3,000 Members
Founded in: 1965

16935 Waste Equipment Technology Association
4301 Connecticut Ave Nw
Suite 300
Washington, DC 20008-2304

202-244-4700
800-424-2869; *Fax:* 202-966-4824;
www.wasterecycling.org
Social Media: Facebook, Twitter, LinkedIn, Youtube

Mike Savage, Chairman
Sharon H. Kneiss, President and CEO
Philip Hagan, Director, Safety
Sheila R. Alkire, Director, Education
Catherine Maimon, Manager, Meetings

Manufacturers of waste handling, collection and processing equipment.
Founded in: 1972

Newsletters

16936 Infocus Newsletter
319 SW Washington Street
Suite 710
Portland, OR 97204-2618

503-227-3393; *Fax:* 503-274-7667

Lea Anne A Fuchs, President
Andy Palatka, Executive Director
Tonya Macalino, Adversiting and Sales

Infocus is a newsletter focused on industry topics and products.
Cost: $75.00
Circulation: 1,100
Founded in: 1960
Mailing list available for rent: 1M names at $200 per M

16937 Innovators Digest
InfoTeam
PO Box 15640
Plantation, FL 33318-5640

954-473-9560; *Fax:* 954-473-0544

Merton Allen, Editor

A multidisciplinary publication covering developments in science, engineering, products, markets, business development, manufacturing and other technological developments having industrial or commercial significance.
Frequency: Bi-Annual

16938 Intelligent Manufacturing
Lionheart Publishing
2555 Cumberland Pkwy Se
Suite 299
Atlanta, GA 30339-3921

770-432-2551; *Fax:* 770-432-6969
llewellyn@lionhrtpub.com

John Llewellyn, Publisher
David Blanchard, Editor

Provides expert solutions to manufacturing professionals covering production problems, developments in manufacturing systems.
Cost: $20.00
Circulation: 1,598

16939 Manufacturing Technology
National Technical Information Service
5285 Port Royal Rd
Springfield, VA 22161-0001

703-605-6000; *Fax:* 703-605-6900
info@ntis.gov; www.ntis.gov

Linda Davis, VP
Patrik Ekstr"m, Business Development Manager
Reuel Avila, Managing Director

Covers CAD/CAM, robotics, robots, productivity, manufacturing, planning, processing and control, plant design and computer software.

16940 News & Views
American Mold Builders Association
3601 Algonquin Rd
Suite 304
Rolling Meadows, IL 60008-3136

847-222-9402; *Fax:* 630-980-9714
info@amba.org; www.amba.org

Melissa Millhuff, Executive Director
Peter Manship, Managing Director
Kym Conis, Managing Director
Frequency: Quarterly
Circulation: 2000
Founded in: 1973

16941 Noise Regulation Report
Business Publishers
2222 Sedwick Drive
Durham, NC 27713

800-223-8720; *Fax:* 800-508-2592
custserv@bpinews.com; www.bpinews.com

Exclusive coverage of airport, highway, occupational and open space noise, noise control and mitigation issues.
Cost: $511.00
10 Pages
Frequency: 12 per year
Printed in on matte stock

16942 RPA Newsletter
Retail Packaging Association
2205 Warwick Way, Suite 110
Marriottsville, MD 21104

410-925-9809; *Fax:* 513-527-4999
info@retailpackaging.org;
www.retailpackaging.org

Joel Zaas, President
Frequency: Weekly
Founded in: 1989

16943 Service Management
National Association of Service Management
PO Box 250796
Milwaukee, WI 53225
414-466-6060; *Fax:* 414-466-0840;
www.nasm.com
Don Buelow, Publisher
Caryn Anderson, Editor
Ken Cook, Treasurer
Offers information on manufacturing and service companies.
40 Pages
Frequency: Quarterly
Circulation: 300

16944 Vision
Society of Manufacturing Engineers
1 SME Drive
PO Box 930
Dearborn, MI 48128
313-425-3000
800-733-4763; *Fax:* 313-425-3400
service@sme.org; www.sme.org
Mark Tomlinson, Executive Director
Greg Sheremet, Publisher
The newsletter highlights the latest developments in the machine vision industry including applications, techniques and methods.
Cost: $75.00
Frequency: Quarterly
Circulation: 1,100
ISSN: 1544-3531
Founded in: 1984

Magazines & Journals

16945 APICS: The Performance Advantage
APICS Association for Operations Management
5301 Shawnee Road
Alexandria, VA 22312-2317
703-548-8851; *Fax:* 703-354-8106
webmaster@apics.org; www.apics.org
Doug Kelly, Editor
Jennifer Procter, Managing Editor
Jeffery Raynes, CEO
Provides comprehensive articles on enterprise resources planning, supply chain management, e-business, materials management and production and inventory management.
Cost: $65.00
64 Pages
Circulation: 66000
ISSN: 1056-0017
Mailing list available for rent: 40,000 names at $100 per M
Printed in 4 colors on glossy stock

16946 Adhesives & Sealants
Business News Publishing Company
PO Box 400
Flossmoor, IL 60422
708-922-0761; *Fax:* 708-922-0762
mcphersont@bnpmedia.com;
www.adhesivesmag.com
Susan Love, Publisher
Teresa Mc Pherson, Editor
Kari Rowe, Circulation Manager
Violeta Ivezaj, Senior Marketing Manager
Cost: $33.00
Frequency: Monthly
Circulation: 15000
Founded in: 1926

16947 Adhesives Age
2 Grand Central Tower
140 East 45th Street,40th Floor
New York, NY 10017
212-884-9528; *Fax:* 212-884-9514
ltattum@chemweek.com; www.chemweek.com
Lyn Tattum, Group Vice President/Publisher
Joe Minnella, Global Sales Director
Adhesives Age provides readers with vital information: global industry coverage of the development, manufacture, and application of adhesives, sealants, and related products.
Cost: $75.00
62 Pages
Frequency: Weekly
Circulation: 22994
ISSN: 0001-821X
Founded in: 1958
Mailing list available for rent
Printed in 4 colors on glossy stock

16948 Advanced Materials & Processes
ASM International
9639 Kinsman Rd
Materials Park, OH 44073
440-338-5151
800-336-5152; *Fax:* 440-338-4634
memberservices@asminternational.org;
www.asminternational.org
Social Media: Facebook, Twitter, LinkedIn
Joseph M Zion, Publisher
Joanne Miller, Managing Editor
Margaret Hunt, Editor-in-Chief
Jeane Deatherage, Administrator, Foundation Programs
Virginia Shirk, Foundation Executive Assistant
AM&P, the monthly technical magazine from ASM International, is designed to keep readers aware of leading-edge developments and trends in engineering materials - metals and alloys, engineering polymers, advanced ceramics, and composites - and the methods used to select, process, fabricate, test, and characterize them.
Frequency: Monthly
Circulation: 32M
Founded in: 1977

16949 American Fastener Journal
Carol McGuire
11305 E. Monument Drive
Scottsdale, AZ 85262-4746
480-488-3500; *Fax:* 480-488-3247
mmcguire@fastenerjournal.com;
www.fastenerjournal.com
Mike McGuire, Publisher/Editor
Jackie McGuire, Executive Editor
Micki Leopard, Circulation Manager
This journal for the fastener industry covers technical articles, inspections, quality assurance, materials applications, specifications and standards, as well as manufacturer, distributors and supplier profiles. Publishes annual buyers guide - The American Fastener Source Guide
Cost: $45.00
Circulation: 13000
Founded in: 1981
Printed in 4 colors on glossy stock

16950 American Funeral Director
Kates-Boylston Publications
11300 Rockville Pike
Suite 1100
Rockville, MD 20852
800-500-4585
800-500-4585; *Fax:* 732-730-2515;
www.kates-boylston.com
Adrian F Boylston, Publisher
Thomas Parmalee, Executive Director
Amy Fidalgo, Production Manager
Articles on funeral home construction, finance, mortuary law, shipment of human remains by air transportation, sales and display methods, advertising and public relations, new equipment and other association activiies. Also includes personnel news about funeral directors and related supply firms.
Cost: $49.95
Frequency: Monthly
Circulation: 12168
Founded in: 1918

16951 CNC West
Arnold Publications
14340 Bolsa Chica Avenue E
PO Box 100
Westminster, CA 92684-100
714-899-0733; *Fax:* 714-899-0738
larnold@cnc-west.com; www.cnc-west.com
Shawn Arnold, Publisher
Chuck Bush, Editor
Shawn Arnold, CEO/President
Shawn Arnold, Circulation Manager
Shawn Arnold, Marketing Manager
News and trends on western jobshops and manufacturers
Cost: $32.50
Circulation: 22000
Founded in: 1981
Printed in 4 colors on glossy stock

16952 Card Manufacturing
International Card Manufacturing Association
PO Box 727
Princeton Junction, NJ 08550-727
609-799-4900; *Fax:* 609-799-7032
info@icma.com; www.icma.com
Lynn McCullough, Association Manager
Jeffrey E Barnhart, Communications Manager
Kaitlin Friedmann, Communications Manager
Al Vrancart, Founder
Advertiser supported trade magazine featuring industry news and features on all aspects of the plastic card production worldwide, and the news of the ICMA.
Cost: $75.00
Circulation: 3000

16953 Coatings World
Rodman Publishing
70 Hilltop Rd
Suite 3000
Ramsey, NJ 07446-1150
201-825-2552; *Fax:* 201-825-0553
info@rodpub.com;
www.nutraceuticalsworld.com
Social Media: Facebook, Twitter, LinkedIn
Rodman Zilenziger Jr, President
Matt Montgomery, VP
Coatings World is directed at industry personnel concerned with developing and manufacturing paints, coatings, adhesives and sealants. Feature articles and industry news are directed at chemists, formulators and all levels of management that must keep abreast of technical products and market developments.
Cost: $50.00
136 Pages
Frequency: Monthly
Circulation: 17315
ISSN: 1527-1129
Mailing list available for rent
Printed in 4 colors on glossy stock

16954 Composites Fabrication
Composites Fabricators Association

1010 N Glebe Rd
Suite 450
Arlington, VA 22201-4749

703-525-0714; *Fax:* 703-525-0743
info@acmanet.org; www.acmanet.org/

Elly Shariat, Marketing Manager
Andy Rusnak, Editor
Roxanne Fraver, Marketing & Circulation
Sabeena Hickman, Deputy Director
Jessica Howard, Production Manager

Presents information on new technology, trends and techniques for manufacturers in the fiberglass and composites industry.
Cost: $41.00
114 Pages
Circulation: 8000
ISSN: 1084-841X
Printed in 4 colors on glossy stock

16955 Consumer Goods Technology
Edgell Communications
4 Middlebury Boulevard
Randolph, NJ 07869

973-252-0100; *Fax:* 973-252-9020;
www.consumergoods.com

Andrew Gaffney, Group Publisher
Steve Rosenstock, Publisher
Tim Clark, Editor-in-Chief
Alliston Ackerman, Assistant Editor
Pat Wisser, Production Manager

Provides case histories, technology overviews, new products and industry news to assist corporations and management in the consumer goods industry.
Frequency: Monthly
Circulation: 25000
Founded in: 1984

16956 Contingency Planning & Management
Witter Publishing Corporation
20 Commerce Street
Flemington, NJ 08822

908-788-0343; *Fax:* 908-788-3782;
www.witterpublishing.com

Bob Joudanin, Publisher
Paul Kirvan, Editor In Chief
Courtney Writter, Circulation Manager
Andrew Witter, President

Serves the fields of financial/banking, manufacturing industrial, transportation, utilities, telecommunications, health care, government, insurance and other allied fields.
Frequency: Monthly
Founded in: 1987

16957 Contract Management
National Contract Management Association
1912 Woodford Road
Vienna, VA 22182-3728

703-489-9231
800-344-8096; *Fax:* 703-448-0939
memberservices@ncmahq.org;
www.ncmahq.org

Amy Miedema, Editor-in-Chief
Neal Couture, Executive Director

It covers the myriad aspects of government and commercial contract management. News and features provide information on such topics as procurement policy, on-the-job techniques, regulations, case law, ethics, contract administration, electronic commerce, international and small business matters, education and career development.
Cost: $75.00
80 Pages
Frequency: Monthly
Circulation: 22000
Founded in: 1959
Printed in 4 colors on glossy stock

16958 Control Design
Putman Media
555 W Pierce Rd
Suite 301
Itasca, IL 60143-2626

630-467-1300; *Fax:* 630-467-0197
lgoldberg@putman.net; www.putman.net

John Cappelletti, President
Mike Bacidore, Editor-in-Chief/Publisher
Anetta Gauthier, Production Manager
Lori Goldberg, Operations Manager

Markets to the manufacturing facilities under the government's standard industry classification (SIC) code 35, which manufacture a broad range of products from turbines, conveyors and machine tools to food processing, printing presses and computers.
Cost: $96.00
Circulation: 50,046
ISSN: 1094-3366
Founded in: 1938
Printed in 4 colors

16959 Design News
Reed Business Information
30 Technology Parkway South
Suite 100
Norcross, GA 30092

646-746-6400
800-424-3996; *Fax:* 646-756-7583
webmaster@reedbusiness.com;
www.reedbusiness.com

John Poulin, CEO
Karen Auguston Field, Editor-in-Chief
James Reed, Owner

Informs professionals in the technology industry of all the latest in new product introductions in fields such as bearings, fastening/joining and new technology.
Circulation: 170000

16960 Distributor's Link
4297 Corporate Sq
Naples, FL 34104-4754

239-643-2713
800-356-1639; *Fax:* 239-643-5220
leojcoar@linkmagazine.com;
www.linkmagazine.com/

Maryann Marzocchi, President
Tracey Lumia, Director of Sales and Marketing

Information aimed at the fastener distributors nationwide.
Cost: $45.00
Frequency: Quarterly
Circulation: 50000
Founded in: 1975

16961 Edplay
Fahy-Williams Publishing
PO Box 1080
Geneva, NY 14456-8080

315-789-0458
800-344-0559; *Fax:* 315-789-4263;
www.edplay.com

Kevin Fahy, Publisher
Tina Manzer, Editorial Director
Mark Stash, Art Director
Alyssa Lafaro, Associate Editor

Serves toy manufacturers and dealers. Offers product reviews, industry profiles, and reader surveys.
Circulation: 13000
Founded in: 1984

16962 Fastener Technology International
Initial Publications
PO Box 5451
Akron, OH 44334-0451

330-864-2122; *Fax:* 330-864-5298
mcnulty@fastenertech.com;
www.fastenertech.com

Job Lippincott, Publisher
Michael J. McNulty, Vice President and Editor

Contains articles on company profiles, new equipment, literature, products, fastener topics and patents.
Cost: $40.00
Circulation: 13,000
Founded in: 1981
Printed in 4 colors on glossy stock

16963 Fastening
Mike McGuire
293 Hopewell Drive
Powell, OH 43065-9350

614-848-3232
800-848-0304; *Fax:* 614-848-5045;
www.fastenerjournal.com

Mike McGuire, Publisher

In-depth and up-to-date information about fastening products, design/applications, people, companies, fastening industry events and specifications.
Cost: $30.00
Frequency: Quarterly
Circulation: 28,000
Founded in: 1995
Printed in 4 colors on glossy stock

16964 Forming & Fabricating
Society of Manufacturing Engineers
1 SME Drive
Box 930
Dearborn, MI 48128

313-425-3000
800-733-4763; *Fax:* 313-425-3400
advertising@sme.org; www.sme.org

Mark Tomlinson, Executive Director
Greg Sheremet, Publisher

News and features regarding the forming and fabricating industry with the intention of improving process productivity and project quality. Special focus on technology and its applications in manufacturing.
Frequency: Monthly
Circulation: 66616

16965 ITE Solutions
Institute of Industrial Engineers
25 Technology Pkwy S
Suite 150
Norcross, GA 30092-2946

770-449-0461; *Fax:* 770-263-8532
webmaster@iienet.org; www.iienet.org

16966 InTech
Instrumentation, Systems,and Automation Society
67 Alexander Drive
Research Triangle Park, NC 27709

919-549-8411; *Fax:* 919-990-9434
info@isa.org; www.isa.org

Richard Simpson, Publisher
Greg Hale, Editor
Rob Renner, Executive Officer
Chip Lee, Publication Director

Regular issue features include new product developments, new processes, research updates and general industry news.
Cost: $75.00
Frequency: Monthly
Circulation: 67000
Founded in: 1945

16967 Industrial Equipment News
Thomas Publishing Company

5 Penn Plz
Suite 10
New York, NY 10001-1860

212-695-0500
800-733-1127; *Fax:* 212-290-7362;
www.thomaspublishing.com

Carl Holst-Knudsen, CEO
Joseph Rosta, Editor-in-Chief
Marie Urbanowicz, Marketing Manager

Serves the industrial field including manufacturing, mining, utilities, construction, transportation,governmental establishments, and educational services.
Frequency: Monthly
ISSN: 0019-8258
Founded in: 1898

16968 Industrial Maintenance & Plant Operation
Reed Business Information
199 East Badger Road
Suite 201
Madison, WI 53713

973-920-7787; *Fax:* 973-920-7531
hpendrak@reedbusiness.com;
www.impomag.com

Scott Sward, Publisher
Rick Carter, Editor-in-Chief
R Reed, Owner
Kyle Orr, Circulation Manager
Hank Pendrak, Marketing Director
Circulation: 100000
Founded in: 1975

16969 Industrial Market Place
Wineberg Publications
7842 Lincoln Avenue
Skokie, IL 60077

847-676-1900
800-323-1818; *Fax:* 847-676-0063
info@industrialmktpl.com;
www.industrialmktpl.com

Joel Wineberg, President
Jackie Bitensky, Editor

Has advertisements on machinery, industrial and plant equipment and services and industrial auctions in each issue.
Cost: $175.00
Circulation: 14000
Founded in: 1951
Mailing list available for rent: 120 names at $70 per M
Printed in 4 colors on glossy stock

16970 Job Shop Technology
Edward Publishing
16 Waterbury Road
Prospect, CT 06712-1215

203-758-4474
800-317-0474; *Fax:* 203-758-3427;
www.jobshoptechnology.com

Mark W Shortt, Editor
Cindy Wilkinson, Circulation Director

Published to aid product manufacturers who outsource parts and manufacturing services. Specializes in manufacturing processes for the metals, plastics, rubber, and electronics industries, including virtually any outsourced manufacturing service.
Frequency: Quarterly
Circulation: 100,000
Founded in: 1986
Mailing list available for rent: 90875 names at $125 per M
Printed in 4 colors on glossy stock

16971 Journal of Coatings Technology
Federation of Societies for Coatings Technology
527 Plymouth Rd
Suite 415
Plymouth Meetin, PA 19462-1641

610-940-0777; *Fax:* 610-940-0292;
www.coatingstech.org

Robert F Ziegler, Publisher
Patricia D Ziegler, Administrative Assistant
Shelby Ferguson, Administrative Assistant
Chris Hobson, Communications Manager
Lance Edwards, Director

For the industrial and service organizations in paint and manufacturing plants, raw materials suppliers for coatings, printing inks and sealants.
Cost: $120.00
Frequency: Monthly

16972 Journal of Materials Engineering and Performance
ASM International
9639 Kinsman Road
Materials Park, OH 44073-0002

440-338-5151
800-336-5152; *Fax:* 440-338-4634
memberservice@asminternational.org;
www.asminternational.org
Social Media: Facebook, Twitter, LinkedIn

Jeane Deatherage, Administrator, Foundation Programs
Virginia Shirk, Foundation Executive Assistant

Peer-reviewed journal that publishes contributions on all aspects of materials selection, design, characterization, processing and performance testing. The journal for solving day-to-day engineering challenges - especially those involving components for larger systems.
Cost: $1965.00
Frequency: Bimonthly
Circulation: 305
Founded in: 1992

16973 Journal of Phase Equilibria
ASM International
9639 Kinsman Rd
Materials Park, OH 44072

440-338-5151
800-336-5152; *Fax:* 440-338-4634
memberservices@asminternational.org;
www.asminternational.org
Social Media: Facebook, Twitter, LinkedIn

Jeane Deatherage, Administrator, Foundation Programs
Virginia Shirk, Foundation Executive Assistant

Peer-reviewed journal that contains basic and applied research results, evaluated phase diagrams, a survey of current literature, and comments or other material pertinent to the previous three areas. The aim is to provide a broad spectrum of information concerning phase equilibria for the materials community.
Cost: $1965.00
Frequency: Bimonthly
Circulation: 305

16974 Journal of Process Control
Butterworth Heinemann
313 Washington Street
Newton, MA 02458-1626

617-928-5460; *Fax:* 781-933-6333

JD Perkins, Editor
T McAvoy, Regional Editor

Covers the application of control theory, operations research, computer science and engineering principles to the solution of process control problems.

16975 Journal of Quality Technology
American Society for Quality
600 N Plankinton Avenue
PO Box 3005
Milwaukee, WI 53201-3005

414-272-8575
800-248-1946; *Fax:* 414-272-1734
help@asq.org; www.asq.org
Social Media: Facebook, Twitter, LinkedIn

Roberto M Saco, President
Paul E Borawski, Executive Director
Erica Gumieny, Sales
Fay Spano, Communications/Media Relations

Published by the American Society for Quality, the JQT is a quarterly, peer-reviewed journal that focuses on the subject of quality control and the related areas of reliability and similar disciplines.
Cost: $30.00
100M Members
Frequency: Quarterly
Founded in: 1946

16976 Maintenance Technology
Applied Technology Publications
1300 S Grove Ave
Suite 105
Barrington, IL 60010-5246

847-382-8100; *Fax:* 847-304-8603;
www.mt-online.com

Arthur Rice, President/CEO
Bill Kiesel, Vice President/Publisher
Jane Alexander, Editor-In-Chief
Rick Carter, Executive Editor
Randy Buttstadt, Director of Creative Services

Maintenance Technology magazine serves the business and technical information needs of managers and engineers responsible for assuring availability of plant equipment and systems. It provides readers with articles on advanced technologies, strategies, tools, and services for the life-cycle management of capital assets.
Frequency: Monthly
Circulation: 50,827
Mailing list available for rent: 35,263 names at $$15 per M

16977 Managing Automation
Thomas Publishing Company
5 Penn Plz
Suite 10
New York, NY 10001-1860

212-695-0500
800-733-1127; *Fax:* 212-290-7362
contact@thomaspublishing.com;
www.thomaspublishing.com

Carl Holst-Knudsen, CEO
Greg MacSweeney, Managing Editor
Kim Vennard, Senior Marketing Manager
Shawn Jacobs, Director of Sales

Serves the needs of those managers and engineers responsible for the planning and implementation of factory automation at both the plant and enterprise levels.
Cost: $60.00
Frequency: Monthly
Circulation: 100246
Founded in: 1898

16978 Manufacturers Mart
Philip G Cannon Jr
PO Box 310
Georgetown, MA 01833-0410

978-352-3320
800-835-0017; *Fax:* 401-348-0797
info@manufacturersmart.com;
www.manufacturersmart.com

Phillip Cannon, Publisher
Linda Smith, Editor

Information and news on manufacturing companies with a regional focus in New England. New product articles, coverage of advances in technology, compliance issues, case studies, announcements and calendar events. Online

version includes searchable index of products and services.
32 Pages
Frequency: Monthly
Circulation: 30000
Founded in: 1978
Printed in 4 colors on newsprint stock

16979 Manufacturing Engineering
Society of Manufacturing Engineers
1 SME Drive
PO Box 930
Dearborn, MI 48128

313-425-3000
800-733-4763; *Fax:* 313-425-3400
advertising@sme.org; www.sme.org

Mark Tomlinson, Executive Director
Greg Sheremet, Publisher
Karen Manardo, Director of Communication
Tom Drozda, Publisher/Advertising

Serves metalworking industry machining, forming, inspection, assembly and processing operations.
Frequency: Monthly
Circulation: 1,11,966
Founded in: 1932

16980 Manufacturing News
Publishers & Producers
PO Box 36
Annandale, VA 22003

703-750-2664; *Fax:* 703-750-0064
editor@manufacturingnews.com;
www.manufacturingnews.com

Richard McCormack, Publisher/Editor

Gives in-depth analysis of critical manufacturing trends, insightful interviews with top players in industry and government and up-to-the-minute business news about issues that directly affect your ability to compete and prosper and takes a look at software and hardware, sucessful manufacturers, and profound technological changes.
Cost: $495.00
12 Pages
Frequency: Fortnightly
Circulation: 30,000
ISSN: 1078-2397
Founded in: 1994
Printed in on matte stock

16981 Manufacturing Systems
2000 Clearwater Drive
Oak Brook, IL 60523-8809

630-288-8000; *Fax:* 630-320-7373;
www.manufacturing.net

Michelle Palmer, Publisher
Mary Ann Brockway, Circulation Manager
David Greenfield, Editor

Information management for increased manufacturing productivity.
Cost: $6.00
Frequency: Monthly
Circulation: 114682

16982 Marketeer
1602 E Glen Avenue
Peoria, IL 61614-5451
VB Cook, Editor

New products for manufacturing.
Cost: $15.00
16 Pages
Frequency: Monthly
Founded in: 1952

16983 Marking Industry Magazine
Marking Devices Publishing Company
136 W Vallette St
Suite 6
Elmhurst, IL 60126-4377

630-832-5200; *Fax:* 630-832-5206;
www.markingdevices.com

David Hachmeister, President

New products, processes and services, MDAI and other association news, shows and seminars, sales and management methods.
Cost: $54.00
Frequency: Monthly
Circulation: 1300
Founded in: 1907

16984 Material Handling Equipment Distributors Association
Data Key Communications
201 US Highway 45
Vernon Hills, IL 60061-2398

847-680-3500; *Fax:* 847-362-6989
connect@mheda.org; www.mheda.org

Loren Swakow, President
Elizabeth Richard, Editor/Executive VP
Kathy Carter, Marketing Manager

Updates on technology, association news and announcements, industrial perspectives and outlook and new product information.
Cost: $24.00
Frequency: Quarterly
Circulation: 4000
Founded in: 1954

16985 Material Handling Network
Network Publishing
252 E Washington Street
East Peoria, IL 61611-338

309-699-4431
800-447-6901; *Fax:* 309-698-0801;
www.mhnetwork.com

Andra Stephens, Editor
Bob Behrens, General Manager
Andra Stephens, Advertising/Sales
Mindi Mitzelfelt, Graphic Designer

Monthly journal written for material handling distributors/dealers and people who sell racks, bins, conveyors, dock equipment, lift trucks, batteries, and pallet jacks - both power and non-power.
Cost: $65.00
156 Pages
Frequency: Monthly
Circulation: 12058
Founded in: 1981
Printed in 4 colors on n stock

16986 Material Handling Product News
Reed Business Information
225 Wyman St
Suite 3
Waltham, MA 02451-1216

781-734-8000; *Fax:* 781-734-8076;
www.reedbusiness.com

Mark Finklestein, President
Joseph Pagnotta, Editor-in-Chief
Joanna Schumann, Marketing Manager
Michael Holowchuck, Circulation Manager
Steve McCoy, Associate Publisher

Literature reviews, new product listings and new systems and services are featured regularly.
Frequency: Monthly
Founded in: 1977

16987 Materials at High Temperatures
Butterworth Heinemann
313 Washington Street
Newton, MA 02458-1626

617-928-5460; *Fax:* 781-933-6333

T Suzuki, Co-Editor
TB Gibbons, Co-Editor

Serves the needs of those developing and using materials for high temperature applications in the power, chemical, engine, processing and furnace industries.

16988 Mid-America Commerce & Industry
Mid-America Commerce & Industry
2432 Sw Pepperwood Rd
Topeka, KS 66614-5293

785-272-5280; *Fax:* 785-272-3729
maci@maci-mag.com; www.maci-mag.com/

David Lippe, President

Regional industrial magazine covering manufacturing in Missouri, Kansas, Nebraska, Oklahoma, Arizona and Iowa
Cost: $18.00
Frequency: Monthly

16989 Midrange ERP
MFG Publishing
9 W Street
Beverly, MA 01915-2225

978-927-1419; *Fax:* 978-921-1255;
www.mfgpublishing.com

Deborah A Turbide, Publisher

Planning and scheduling issues, polices and procedures, as well as system improvements.
Circulation: 40000
Founded in: 1996

16990 Modern Applications News
Nelson Publishing
2500 Tamiami Trl N
Nokomis, FL 34275-3476

941-966-9521; *Fax:* 941-966-2590
nelpub@ix.netcom.com;
www.healthmgttech.com
Social Media: Facebook

A Verner Nelson, President
John Mullaly, Editor
Bob Olree, Publisher
Joan Southerland, Marketing
Wyanne Harwell, Circulation Manager

Information includes coverage of abrasives and grinding, automated handling and robotics, CAD/CAM, coatings and finishings, coolants, lubricants and filters, cutting tools, heat treating, ID marking, lasers, machining centers, and shop control software.
Cost: $127.00
Frequency: Monthly
Circulation: 80340
Founded in: 1962

16991 NC Shop Owner
Penton Media
1166 Avenue of the Americas/10th Fl
New York, NY 10036

212-204-4200; *Fax:* 216-696-6662
information@penton.com; www.penton.com

Jane Cooper, Marketing
Chris Meyer, Director, Corporate Communications

News of industry events, new product information, updates on manufacturing technology and a special technology focus section.
Frequency: Semiannual
Circulation: 120,000

16992 National Association of Relay Manufacturers
2500 Wilson Boulevard
Arlington, VA 22201

703-907-8025; *Fax:* 703-875-8908
narm@ecaus.org; www.ecaus.org/narm

Electronical relay and associated switching devices. Engrs. Relay HB - 5th Edition - $60.00 plus $7.00 postage and handling; IRC Proceeding 2002 - $60.00 plus $7.00 postage and han-

dling
Cost: $60.00
Circulation: 1000
Founded in: 1947

16993 New Equipment Digest
Penton Media
1166 Avenue of the Americas/10th Fl
New York, NY 10036

212-204-4200; *Fax:* 216-696-6662
information@penton.com; www.penton.com

Chris Meyer, Director, Corporate Communications
Robert F King, Editor
Sarah Hughes, Production Manager
Bobbie Macy, Circulation Manager
David B. Nussbaum, CEO

Serves the general industrial field which include manufacturing, processing, engineering services, construction, transportation, mining, public utilities, wholesale distributors, educational services, libraries, and governmental establishments.
Frequency: Monthly
Circulation: 206154
Founded in: 1892

16994 Off-Highway Engineering
SAE
400 Commonwealth Dr
Warrendale, PA 15086-7511

724-776-4841
877-606-7323; *Fax:* 724-776-5760
sohe@sae.org; www.saesections.org

Richard O Schaum, President

Off-Highway Engineering serves the international off highway design and manufacturing field which consists of producers of construction, lawn and garden, agricultural equipment, and industrial vehicles. Also served are makers of engines and parts and components and others allied to the field.
Cost: $70.00
66 Pages
Circulation: 16308
ISSN: 1074-6919
Founded in: 1905
Printed in 4 colors on glossy stock

16995 Planning Guidebook
Reed Business Information
6 Alfred Circle
Bedford, MA 00173

972-980-8810; *Fax:* 617-558-4700
corporatecommunications@reedbusiness.com; www.designnews.com

William Shordon, Editor
Jim Casella, CEO

Offers information and news on manufacturing companies.
Frequency: Monthly
Founded in: 1946

16996 Plant
Rogers Media Publishing
777 Bay Street
Toronto, Ontario M5W1A

416-596-5729; *Fax:* 416-596-5552;
www.plant.ca

Joe Terrett, Editor
Kathy Smith, Production Manager
Jessica Jubb, Manager

PLANT serves manufacturing and processing industries in Canada.
Cost: $125.00
Frequency: 18 per year
ISSN: 0845-4213
Founded in: 1941

16997 Plant Services
Putman Media
555 W Pierce Rd
Suite 301
Itasca, IL 60143-2626

630-467-1300; *Fax:* 630-467-0197
mbrenner@putman.net; www.putman.net

John Cappelletti, CEO
Mike Bacidore, Editor-in-Chief
Mike Brenner, Group Publisher
Keith Larson, VP Content

For maintenance and engineering managers responsible for keeping manufacturing plants running efficiently.
Cost: $96.00
Circulation: 80100
Founded in: 1938
Mailing list available for rent: 10,000 names
Printed in 4 colors on glossy stock

16998 Plating and Surface Finishing
1155 Fifteenth Street, NW
Suite 500
Washington, DC 20005

202-457-8401; *Fax:* 407-281-6446
aesf@aesf.org; www.aesf.org

Jon Bednerik CAE, Publisher
Tom Urban, Advertising Manager
Donn Berry, Editor
Dan Denston, Executive Director
John Flatley, Senior Advisor and NASF Liaison

AESF is an international society that advances the science of surface finishing to benefit industry and society through education information and social involvement, as well as those who provide services, supplies and support to the industry.
Cost: $125.00
Frequency: Monthly
Circulation: 4000
Founded in: 1909

16999 Powder Coating
OSC Publishing
1300 E 66th Street
Minneapolis, MN 55423-2642

612-866-2242; *Fax:* 612-866-1939

Richard R Cress, Publisher
Richard Link, Manager

Our information focuses on the application, pre-treatment, materials, materials handling, and curing processes. Also features case histories.
Frequency: 9 per year
Circulation: 23587

17000 Precision Manufacturing
Minnesota Precision Manufacturing Association
3131 Fernbrook Ln N
Suite 111
Minneapolis, MN 55447-5336

763-473-4090; *Fax:* 763-473-2804;
www.mpma.com

Dennis A Olson, President
Garry Bultnick, Sales Manager
LuAnn Bartley, Executive Director

Publication for job shop owners, managers and engineers and industrial suppliers, distributors, OEM buyers and purchasing agents, manufacturing representatives and technical colleges.
Circulation: 7900
Founded in: 1958
Printed in on glossy stock

17001 Process Cooling & Equipment
Business News Publishing Company
1050 IL Route 83
Suite 200
Bensenville, IL 60106-1096

630-377-5909; *Fax:* 630-694-4002;
www.process-cooling.com

Katie Rotella, President
Linda Becker, Editor
Sean Meaney, Sales Manager

Focuses on temperatures down through cryogenic levels in industrial processes and in equipment cooling.

17002 Process Heating
Business News Publishing Company
155 Pfingsten Road
Suite 205
Deerfield, IL 60015
847-405-4000; *Fax:* 248-502-1001
PHeditors@bnpmedia.com;
www.process-heating.com
Social Media: Facebook, Twitter

Anne Armel, Publisher
Linda Becker, Associate Publisher/Editor
Beth McClelland, Production Manager
Sean Meaney, Sales Manager
Caroline Eychenne, European Sales Representative

Magazine covers heat processing at temperatures up to 1000 degrees F at end user and OEM plants in 9 industries. Follow us at twitter.com/ProcessHeating, www.facebook.com/ProcessHeating
Circulation: 25000
Founded in: 1994

17003 Products Finishing
Gardner Publications
6915 Valley Ln
Cincinnati, OH 45244-3153
513-527-8800
800-950-8020; *Fax:* 513-527-8801
narnold@gardnerweb.com;
www.gardnerweb.com

Rick Kline Sr, CEO
Matthew J Little, Editor
Nancy Eigel-Miller, Marketing Director
Nancy Arnold, Circulation Manager
John Campos, Manager

Covers production, management, engineering, design, etc. in plants where metal and plastic products are eletroplated, anodized, painted, buffed, cleaned or otherwise finished.
Cost: $89.00
Frequency: Monthly
Circulation: 42000
Founded in: 1928
Printed in 4 colors on glossy stock

17004 Progressive Distributor
Pfingsten Publishing
730 Madison Avenue
Fort Atkinson, WI 53538

920-563-5225
800-932-7732; *Fax:* 920-563-4269;
www.progressivedistributor.com

Rich Vurva, Editor
Pat OBrien, Executive Director
Mitch Bouchard, Secretary, Treasurer

Sales and marketing magazines for top manager, salespeople and marketing executives in industrial and construction distribution firms.
Circulation: 24337
Founded in: 1996
Printed in 4 colors on glossy stock

17005 Quality
Business News Publishing

1050 IL Route 83
Suite 200
Bensenville, IL 60106-1096

630-377-5909; *Fax:* 630-227-0204;
www.qualitymag.com

Katie Rotella, President
Thomas A Williams, Publisher
Christopher Sheehy, Manager

Quality is a monthly business publication serving the quality assurance and process improvement needs of more than 80,000 North American manufacturing professionals.
Cost: $75.00
74 Pages
Frequency: Monthly
Circulation: 64000
ISSN: 0360-9936
Founded in: 1962
Printed in 4 colors on glossy stock

17006 **Quality Engineering**
American Society for Quality
600 N Plankinton Avenue
PO Box 3005
Milwaukee, WI 53201-3005

414-272-8575
800-248-1946; *Fax:* 414-272-1734
help@asq.org; www.asq.org
Social Media: Facebook, Twitter, LinkedIn

Roberto M Saco, President
Paul E Borawski, Executive Director
Erica Gumieny, Sales
Fay Spano, Communications/Media Relations

Co-published with Taylor and Francis, this journal is for professional practitioners and researchers whose goal is quality engineering improvements and solutions.
Cost: $34.75
100M Members
Frequency: Quarterly/Members Price
Founded in: 1946

17007 **Quality Management Journal**
American Society for Quality
600 N Plankinton Avenue
PO Box 3005
Milwaukee, WI 53201-3005

414-272-8575
800-248-1946; *Fax:* 414-272-1734
help@asq.org; www.asq.org
Social Media: Facebook, Twitter, LinkedIn

Roberto M Saco, President
Paul E Borawski, Executive Director
Erica Gumieny, Sales
Fay Spano, Communications/Media Relations

Published by the American Society for Quality, the QMT is a quarterly, peer-reviewed journal that focuses on the subject of quality management practice and provides a discussion forum for both practitioners and academics in the area of research.
Cost: $50.00
100M Members
Frequency: Quarterly
Founded in: 1946

17008 **Quality Observer: ICSS Journal**
Quality University Press
3970 Chain Bridge Road
PO Box 1111
Fairfax, VA 22030-3316

703-691-9496; www.thequalityobserver.com

Johnson A Edosomwan, Editor

Case studies, interviews, international and national news and regular colums covering service in manufacturing, high-tech, government agencies and non-profit organizations.
Cost: $139.00
50 Pages
Frequency: 4 per year
Circulation: 15,000
ISSN: 1057-9583
Printed in 4 colors on glossy stock

17009 **Quality Progress**
American Society for Quality
600 N Plankinton Avenue
PO Box 3005
Milwaukee, WI 53201-3005

414-272-8575
800-248-1946; *Fax:* 414-272-1734
help@asq.org; www.asq.org
Social Media: Facebook, Twitter, LinkedIn

Roberto M Saco, President
Paul E Borawski, Executive Director
Erica Gumieny, Sales
Fay Spano, Communications/Media Relations

Published by the American Society for Quality, the QP is a peer-reviewed journal that focuses on the subject of quality control, discussing the usage and implementation of quality principles including the subject areas of organizational behavior, knowledge management and process improvement.
Cost: $55.00
100M Members
Founded in: 1946

17010 **Scan Tech News**
Reed Business Information
30 Technology Parkway South
Suite 100
Norcross, GA 30092

630-574-0825
800-424-3996; *Fax:* 630-288-8781
webmaster@reedbusiness.com;
www.reedbusiness.com

Jeff Greisch, President

Updates in trends in ADC technology and standards, the latest news from leading industry events, and product developments that streamline the flow of essential information in industrial settings.
Frequency: Monthly
Circulation: 82M

17011 **Software Quality Professional**
American Society for Quality
600 N Plankinton Avenue
PO Box 3005
Milwaukee, WI 53201-3005
414-272-8575
800-248-1946; *Fax:* 414-272-1734
help@asq.org; www.asq.org
Social Media: Facebook, Twitter, LinkedIn

Roberto M Saco, President
Paul E Borawski, Executive Director
Erica Gumieny, Sales
Fay Spano, Communications/Media Relations

Published by the American Society for Quality, the SQP is a quarterly, peer-reviewed journal for software development professionals that focuses on the subject of quality practice principles in the implementation of software and the development of software systems.
Cost: $45.00
100M Members
Frequency: Quarterly
Founded in: 1946

17012 **Solid State Technology**
PennWell Publishing Company
1421 S. Sheridan Road
Tulsa, OK 74112

918-835-3161
800-331-4463; *Fax:* 603-891-9294;
www.pennwell.com

Christine Shaw, VP
David Barach, Publisher

Serves firms involved in the manufacturing and testing of semi-conductor materials, equipment, device/circuits manufacturing and OEM manufacturing with in-house IC manufacturing facilities.
Cost: $213.00
Frequency: Monthly
ISSN: 0038-111X
Founded in: 1958
Mailing list available for rent

17013 **Solid Surface**
Cygnus Publishing
PO Box 803
Fort Atkinson, WI 53538-0803

920-000-1111
800-547-7377; *Fax:* 920-563-1699
paul.bowers@cygnuspub.com;
www.cygnusb2b.com

John French, CEO
Russ Lee, Editor
Paul Bowers, Group VP
Charlie Lillis, Content Licensing
Kathy Scott, Director of Public Relations

Solid surfaces link between fabricator, distributor, supplier, and manufacturer. It is dedicated to providing reliable and timely information, including updates on the latest fabrication trends and techniques, with a fresh perspective and a sense of humor.
Cost: $25.00
Circulation: 4,500
Founded in: 1966

17014 **Springs Manufacturer Institute**
Spring Manufacturers Institute
2001 Midwest Rd
Suite 106
Oak Brook, IL 60523-1378

630-495-8588; *Fax:* 630-495-8595
info@smihq.org; www.smihq.org

Lynne Carr, President
Rita Schauer, Editor
Kim Kostecki, Member Services Coordinator
Pashun McNulty, Financial Admin Coordinator
Russ Bryer, Secretary, Treasurer

Provides how-to and technical articles on inspection methods, design, finishes, manufacturing proccesses, materials and equipment, also contains financial and management articles on the interests of precision mechanical spring manufacturers.
130 Pages
Frequency: Quarterly
Circulation: 12,000
Printed in 4 colors on glossy stock

17015 **Supply Chain e-Business**
Keller International Publishing Corporation
150 Great Neck Rd
Suite 400
Great Neck, NY 11021-3309

516-829-9722; *Fax:* 516-829-9306;
www.supplychainbrain.com

Thomas A Foster, Editor-in-Chief
Russell W Goodman, Managing Editor
Jerry Keller, President
Mary Chavez, Director of Sales

Offers a thorough analysis of on-line solutions designed to help corporations achieve greater supply-chain visiblity and real-time connections with suppliers and customers
Frequency: Bi-Monthly
Circulation: 45M
ISSN: 1525-4887
Printed in 4 colors on glossy stock

17016 **Target**
Association for Manufacturing Excellence

380 W Palatine Road
Wheeling, IL 60090-5831

847-520-3282; *Fax:* 847-520-0163
info@ame.org; www.ame.org

Robert W Hall, Editor-in-Chief
Dick Barton, Director of Advertising

Contains coverage on educational events, opinion columns, a networking section and more, reflecting manufacturing competitiveness, and improvement concepts and activities for the members of the Association for Manufacturing Excellence and interested academia.
Cost: $125.00
Frequency: Quarterly
Circulation: 5000
Founded in: 1985

17017 US Industries Today
Postitive Publications
225 Madison Avenue
Morristown, NJ 07960

973-292-2600; *Fax:* 973-292-2696;
www.usitoday.com

Peter Mercer, Editor
Sabastian Fraser, CEO/President

Provides information on the latest developments across the whole range of the US manufacturing industry, covering stock market analysis, US business leaders, business profiles and industry sector reports, as well as new products and services.
Cost: $15.00
Circulation: 65000
Founded in: 1998

Trade Shows

17018 AES/EPA Conference/Exhibit: Environmental Control for Surface Finishing
American Electroplaters and Surface Finishers Soc.
1155 Fifteenth Street, NW
Suite 500
Washington, DC 20005

202-457-8401; *Fax:* 407-281-6446
exhibit@aesf.org; www.aesf.org

Kathy Shumacher, Show Manager
Dan Denston, Executive Director
John Flatley, Senior Advisor and NASF Liaison

One-hundred exhibitors of waste treatment, pollution control, surface finishing equipment and surfaces.
600 Attendees
Frequency: June

17019 AESF SUR/FIN Annual Technical Conference and Exhibit of Surface Finishers
American Electroplaters and Surface Finishers Soc.
1155 Fifteenth Street, NW
Suite 500
Washington, DC 20005

202-457-8401; *Fax:* 407-281-6446
exhibit@aesf.org; www.aesf.org

Dan Denston, Executive Director
John Flatley, Senior Advisor and NASF Liaison

More than 300 suppliers to the industry will attend.
Frequency: June

17020 AESF Week - Society's Annual Winter Meeting
American Electroplaters and Surface Finishers Soc.
1155 Fifteenth Street, NW
Suite 500
Washington, DC 20005

202-457-8401; *Fax:* 407-281-6446
exhibit@aesf.org; www.aesf.org

Dan Denston, Executive Director
John Flatley, Senior Advisor and NASF Liaison
Frequency: June

17021 AME Annual Conference
Association for Manufacturing Excellence
380 W Palatine Road
Suite 7
Wheeling, IL 60090-5863

847-520-3282; *Fax:* 847-520-0163
info@ame.org; www.ame.org

Vivian Bartt, Manager
Dick Barton, Director of Advertising
Frequency: November
Founded in: 1985

17022 AMSE International Manufacturing Science & Engineering Conference
American Society of Mechanical Engineers
Three Park Avenue
New York, NY 10016-5990

973-882-1170
800-843-2763
CustomerCare@asme.org; www.asme.org

The MSEC highlights cutting edge manufacturing research in technical paper, poster and panel sessions.
3200 Attendees
Frequency: Annual/Fall

17023 ASM Heat Treating Society Conference & Exposition
ASM International
9639 Kinsman Road
Materials Park, OH 44073

440-385-5151
800-336-5152; *Fax:* 440-338-4634
pamela.kleinman@asminternational.org;
www.asminternational.org
Social Media: Facebook, Twitter, LinkedIn

Pamela Kleinma, Senior Manager, Events
Kellye Thomas, Exposition Account Manager
Jeane Deatherage, Administrator, Foundation Programs
Virginia Shirk, Foundation Executive Assistant

Conference and exhibits of heat treating equipment and supplies plus information of interest to metallurgists, manufacturing, research and design technical professionals. 300 exhibitors.
3500 Attendees
Frequency: September, Bi-Annual
Founded in: 1974

17024 ASM Materials Science & Technology (MS&T)
ASM International
9639 Kinsman Road
Materials Park, OH 44073-0002

440-338-5151
800-336-5152; *Fax:* 440-338-4634
pamela.kleinman@asminternational.org;
www.asminternational.org
Social Media: Facebook, Twitter, LinkedIn

Pamela Kleinman, Senior Manager, Events
Kelly Thomas, Exposition Account Manager
Jeane Deatherage, Administrator, Foundation Programs
Virginia Shirk, Foundation Executive Assistant

Annual event focusing on testing, analysis, characterization and research of materials such as engineered materials, high performance metals, powdered metals, metal forming, surface modification, welding and joining. 350 exhibitors.
4,000 Attendees
Frequency: Annual/October
Founded in: 2005

17025 Adhesive and Sealant Council Fall Convention
Adhesive & Sealant Council
7101 Wisconsin Avenue
Suite 990
Bethesda, MD 20814

301-986-9700; *Fax:* 301-986-9795
data@ascouncil.org; www.ascouncil.org

Malinda Armstrong, Director, Meetings & Expositions
Frequency: October

17026 AeroMat Conference and Exposition
ASM International
9639 Kinsman Road
Materials Park, OH 44073-0002

440-385-5151
800-336-5152; *Fax:* 440-338-4634
kim.schaefer@asminternational.org;
www.asminternational.org
Social Media: Facebook, Twitter, LinkedIn

Kim Schaefer, Event Manager
Kelly Thomas, Exposition Account Manager
Jeane Deatherage, Administrator, Foundation Programs
Virginia Shirk, Foundation Executive Assistant

Conference for Aerospace Meterials Engineers, Structural Engineers and Designers. The annual event focuses on affordable structures and low-cost manufacturing, titanium alloy technology, advanced intermetallics and refractory metal alloys, materials and processes for space applications, aging systems, high strength steel, NDT evaluation, light alloy technology, welding and joining, and engineering technology. 150 exhibitors.
1500 Attendees
Frequency: Annual/June
Founded in: 1984

17027 Annual Elevator Convention and Exposition
356 Morgan Avenue
PO Box 6507
Mobile, AL 36660

251-479-4514
800-730-5093; *Fax:* 251-479-7043;
www.elevator-world.com

Ricia S Hendrick, President/Publisher
Robert Caporale, Senior VP and Editor
Frequency: Annual

17028 Annual Lean Six Sigma Conference
American Society for Quality
600 N Plankinton Avenue
PO Box 3005
Milwaukee, WI 53201-3005

414-272-8575
800-248-1946; *Fax:* 414-272-1734
help@asq.org; www.asq.org
Social Media: Facebook, Twitter, LinkedIn

Roberto M Saco, President
Paul E Borawski, Executive Director
Erica Gumieny, Sales
Fay Spano, Communications/Media Relations

An exclusive two-day briefing and networking event designed by and for the top practitioners in the Six Sigma community.
100M Members
Frequency: Annual/February
Founded in: 1946

17029 **Annual Meeting & Leadership Conference**
Private Label Manufacturers Association (PLMA)
630 Third Avenue
New York, NY 10017
212-972-3131; *Fax:* 212-983-1382
info@plma.com; www.plma.com
Brian Sharoff, President
Myra Rosen, VP
Tom Prendergast, Director, Research Services
Members look at key issues for the years ahead.
3200+ Members
Frequency: Annual
Founded in: 1979

17030 **Annual Quality Audit Conference**
American Society for Quality
600 N Plankinton Avenue
PO Box 3005
Milwaukee, WI 53201-3005
414-272-8575
800-248-1946; *Fax:* 414-272-1734
help@asq.org; www.asq.org
Social Media: Facebook, Twitter, LinkedIn
Roberto M Saco, President
Paul E Borawski, Executive Director
Erica Gumieny, Sales
Fay Spano, Communications/Media Relations
Topics of interest include: new innovating audit/process approaches, value added involvement, corporate expectations, corporate/social responsibility, auditing in the overall corporate scheme.
100M Members
Frequency: October
Founded in: 1946

17031 **Annual Service Quality Conference**
American Society for Quality
600 N Plankinton Avenue
PO Box 3005
Milwaukee, WI 53201-3005
414-272-8575
800-248-1946; *Fax:* 414-272-1734
help@asq.org; www.asq.org
Social Media: Facebook, Twitter, LinkedIn
Roberto M Saco, President
Paul E Borawski, Executive Director
Erica Gumieny, Sales
Fay Spano, Communications/Media Relations
The sessions we plan will help you to navigate through unpredictable consumer behavior and increasing competition to build a strong foundation for reaching superior levels of quality service.
100M Members
Frequency: September
Founded in: 1946

17032 **Annual World Conference on Quality and Improvement**
American Society for Quality
600 N Plankinton Avenue
PO Box 3005
Milwaukee, WI 53201-3005
414-272-8575
800-248-1946; *Fax:* 414-272-1734
help@asq.org; www.asq.org
Social Media: Facebook, Twitter, LinkedIn
Roberto M Saco, President
Paul E Borawski, Executive Director
Erica Gumieny, Sales
Fay Spano, Communications/Media Relations
Conference focuses on quality and improvement with more than 2,000 exhibits and attendees. Keynote speakers and sessions discuss quality tools, techniques and methodologies. Provides the opportunity for members to meet and network with colleagues in the industry.
100M Members
Frequency: May
Founded in: 1946

17033 **Association of Loudspeaker Mfg. & Acoustics (ALMA) Symposium**
ALMA International
55 Littleton Road
13B
Ayer, MA 01432
978-772-6977
management@almainternational.org;
www.almainternational.org
Spiro Iraclianos, President, VP
Unlike other audio-related events, ALMA Symposia focuses exclusively on products, services and technical and business topics relevant to the loudspeaker industry. Invited speakers present technical papers to keep attendees abreast of the latest developments and expert panelists discuss the latest topics. Training programs are also offered. Exhibit hall features more than 30 industry professionals.
100 Members
Frequency: Annual
Founded in: 1962

17034 **Atlantic Design Engineering**
Canon Communications
11444 W Olympic Boulevard
Suite 900
Los Angeles, CA 90064-1549
310-445-4200; *Fax:* 310-445-4299;
www.cancom.com/
Shannon Cleghorn, Customer & Media Coordinator
Erwin Laner, Promotional Manager
The Atlantic Design Engineering show serves the East Coast's design, process and manufacturing marketplace. Product classifications include Coatings & Finishes, composites, Computer Aided Design/Computer Aided Manufacturing, Electrical/Electronic, Electro Optical Components & Equipment, Engineered Safety Products, Engineering Management & Tools, Fasteners, Fluid Media, Fluid Power & Control and more. Held at the Jacob K. Javits Convention Center in New York, New York.
1319 Attendees
Frequency: June

17035 **BCI Annual Convention & Power Mart Expo**
Battery Council International
330 North Wabash Avenue
Suite 2000
Chicago, IL 60611
312-245-1074; *Fax:* 312-527-6640
info@batterycouncil.org;
www.batterycouncil.org
Social Media: Facebook, LinkedIn
Offers members the opportunity to exchange ideas and views with industry members from around the world in a working meeting atmosphere.
Frequency: Annual/Spring

17036 **CleanRooms East**
PennWell Conferences and Exhibitions
1421 S. Sheridan Road
Tulsa, OK 74112
918-835-3161
800-331-4463; *Fax:* 603-891-9200
andrear@pennwell.com; www.pennwell.com
Andrea Rollins, Show Manager
Lisa Gowern, Registration Manager
Meg Villeure, Conference Manager
CleanRooms shows, the international forums exclusively serving the contamination control industry, couples exhibits with 100% technology-driver conference programs.
3000 Attendees
Frequency: March
Mailing list available for rent

17037 **Close the Loop Technical Symposium**
2001 Midwest Road
Suite 106
Oak Brook, IL 60523-1335
630-495-8588; *Fax:* 630-495-8595;
www.smihq.org
Russ Bryer, Secretary, Treasurer
Jim Kobrinetz, Technical Director
Christy Johnson, Manager
Symposium will highlight the latest technolgy and best practice solutions to difficult technical problems that are regularly experienced by the spring designer, spring user and manufacturing personel.

17038 **Contract Packaging Association Annual Meeting**
Contract Manufacturing & Packaging
1601 Bond Street
Suite 101
Naperville, IL 60563
630-544-5053; *Fax:* 630-544-5055
info@contractpackaging.org;
www.contractpackaging.com
John Mazelin, President
John Riley, VP
Frequency: April

17039 **Dollar Store Expo**
Retail Dollar Store Association
11540 S Eastern Avenue
Suite 100
Henderson, NV 89052
702-893-9090
800-859-9247; *Fax:* 702-893-9227;
www.asdonline.com/info/dollar-store
Kristina Mullen, Show Manager
Wendy Witherspoon, Manager
Four-hundred and fifty booths for products that retail for a dollar or less. Wholesalers, distributors, manufacturers, importers and representatives for surplus, jewelry, hair and beauty, automotive, food items, household goods, gifts, toys, party supplies, seasonal and closeouts.
2,500 Attendees
Frequency: June
Founded in: 2002

17040 **Int'l Conference on Powder Injection Molding of Metals & Ceramics**
Innovative Material Solutions
605 Severn Drive
State College, PA 16803
814-867-1140; *Fax:* 814-867-2813
info@imspowder.com
Frequency: March

17041 **International Integrated Manufacturing Technology Trade Exhibition**
Reed Exhibition Companies
383 Main Avenue
Norwalk, CT 06851
203-840-4800; *Fax:* 203-840-4801
inquiry@reedexpo.com;
www.reedexpo.com/app/homepage
Elizabeth Hitchcock, International Sales
Expo and conference dedicated to the products and technology needed by engineering operations and management to automate and integrate manufacturing.
Frequency: June

17042 International Manufacturing Technology Show
7901 Westpark Drive
Mc Lean, VA 22102-4206
703-893-2900
800-828-7469; *Fax:* 703-827-5250
peelman@AMTonline.org; www.amtonline.org
Peter Eelman, VP Exhibitions
Michelle Edmonson, Exhibitions Operations Manager
Manufacturing equipment trade show.
85M Attendees
Frequency: Biennial
Founded in: 1927

17043 International Symposium for Testing & Failure Analysis
ASM International
9639 Kinsman Road
Materials Park, OH 44073
440-338-5151
800-336-5152; *Fax:* 440-338-4634
kim.schaefer@asminternational.org;
www.asminternational.org
Social Media: Facebook, Twitter, LinkedIn
Kim Schaefer, Event Manager
Kelly Thomas, Exposition Account Manager
Jeane Deatherage, Administrator, Foundation Programs
Virginia Shirk, Foundation Executive Assistant
Annual event focusing on microelectronic and elcetronic device failure analysis, techniques, EOS/ESD testing and descretes aimed at failure analysis engineers and managers, technisians and new failure analysis engineers. 200 exhibitors.
1100 Attendees
Frequency: Annual/November

17044 International Thermal Spray Conference & Exposition
ASM International
9639 Kinsman Road
Materials Park, OH 44073
440-338-5151
800-336-5152; *Fax:* 440-338-4634
natalie.nemec@asminternational.org;
www.asminternational.org
Social Media: Facebook, Twitter, LinkedIn
Natalie Neme, Event Manager
Kelly Thomas, Exposition Account Manager
Jeane Deatherage, Administrator, Foundation Programs
Virginia Shirk, Foundation Executive Assistant
Global annual event attracting professional interested in thermal spray technology focusing on advances in HVOF, plasma and detonation gun, flame spray and wire arc spray processes, performance of coatings, and future trends. 150 exhibitors.
1000 Attendees
Frequency: Annual/May

17045 Lean Management and Solutions Conference
Institute of Industrial Engineers
3577 Parkway Lane
Suite 200
Norcross, GA 30092
770-449-0460
800-494-0460; *Fax:* 770-441-3295
cs@iienet.org; www.iienet.org
Elaine Fuerst, Marketing Director
The place to find the leaders in lean management and all the tools that you need for success.
300 Attendees
Frequency: September

17046 METALfab
532 Forest Parkway
Suite A
Forest Park, GA 30297-6137
404-363-4009; *Fax:* 404-366-1852
nommainfo@nomma.org; www.nomma.org
Martha Pennington, Show Manager
Todd Daniel, Editor
Barbara Cook, Executive Director
Martha Pennington, Meetings Manager
Trade show sponsored by National Ornamental and Miscellaneous Metals Association.
1000 Attendees
Frequency: March

17047 Medical Design & Manufacturing Exhibition East/West
Canon Communications
11444 W Olympic Boulevard
Los Angeles, CA 15494
310-445-4200; *Fax:* 310-996-9499;
www.cancom.com
Shannon Cleghorn, Customer & Media Coordinator
Erwin Laner, Promotional Manager
Design, development, and manufacture of medical products, from high-volume, single-use disposables to next-generation diagnostic instruments and advanced imaging systems. Preview the latest advances in medical-grade materials, assembly components, electronics, machinery, software, systems, services, and more.
Frequency: May

17048 Medical Equipment Design & Technology Conference
Canon Communications
11444 W Olympic Boulevard
Los Angeles, CA 90064-1549
310-445-4200; *Fax:* 310-996-9499;
www.cancom.com
Shannon Cleghorn, Customer & Media Coordinator
Erwin Laner, Promotional Manager
Design, development, and manufacture of medical products, from high-volume, single-use disposables to next-generation diagnostic instruments and advanced imaging systems. Preview the latest advances in medical-grade materials, assembly components, electronics, machinery, software, systems, services and more.
Frequency: September

17049 Midwest Job Shop Show
Edward Publishing
16 Waterbury Road
Prospect, CT 06712-1215
203-758-4474; *Fax:* 203-758-4476;
www.jobshoptechnology.com
Jennifer Bryda, Production Manager
Christoper Davis, Manager
Gerald Schmidt, President
A source for forming, fabricating, shaping, and assemblies. The show is designed to attract the highest caliber engineers and buyers from product manufacturers. There will be 170 exhibitors and booths.
1500 Attendees

17050 National Manufacturing Week
Reed Exhibition Companies
383 Main Street
Norwalk, CT 06851
203-840-4800; *Fax:* 203-840-4801
inquiry@reedexpo.com;
www.reedexpo.com/app/homepage
Elizabeth Hitchcock, International Sales
The pre-eminent American forum for the display of industrial technology.
1.5M Attendees
Frequency: March

17051 National Plant Engineering and Facilities Management Show and Conference
Reed Exhibition Companies
383 Main Avenue
Norwalk, CT 06851
203-840-4800; *Fax:* 203-840-4801
inquiry@reedexpo.com;
www.reedexpo.com/app/homepage
Frequency: June

17052 National Quality Education Conference
American Society for Quality
600 N Plankinton Avenue
PO Box 3005
Milwaukee, WI 53201-3005
414-272-8575
800-248-1946; *Fax:* 414-272-1734
help@asq.org; www.asq.org
Social Media: Facebook, Twitter, LinkedIn
Roberto M Saco, President
Paul E Borawski, Executive Director
Erica Gumieny, Sales
Fay Spano, Communications/Media Relations
Provides teachers, administrators, and support personnel opportunities to examine continuous improvement principles used in education. It provides resources and best practices to help you address requirements of No Child Left Behind, while helping you increase student achievement and improve overall performance.
100M Members
Frequency: November
Founded in: 1946

17053 Pacific Design Engineering
Canon Communications
11444 W Olympic Boulevard
Los Angeles, CA 90064
310-445-4200; *Fax:* 310-996-9499;
www.cancom.com
Shannon Cleghorn, Customer & Media Coordinator
Erwin Laner, Promotional Manager
Serves the West Coast's dynamic design, process, and manufacturing marketplace. Product classifications include: Coatings and Finishes, Composites, Computer Aided Design/Computer Aided Manufacturing, Electrical/Electronic, Electrc Optical Compnents and Equipment, Engineered Safety Products, Engineering Management and Tools, Fasteners, Fluid Media, Fluid Power and Control.
Frequency: January

17054 Packaging & All That Jazz Trade Show
Retail Packaging Association
PO Box 43517
Cincinnati, OH 45243
513-527-4333; *Fax:* 513-527-4999
info@retailpackaging.org;
www.retailpackaging.org
Joel Zaas, President
Provides exhibitors and attendees opportunities to enjoy the great city of New Orleans and network and conduct business, all without losing valuable days in the office.
600 Attendees
Frequency: Annual

17055 Simulation Solutions Conference
Institute of Industrial Engineers

3577 Parkway Lane
Suite 200
Norcross, GA 30092

770-449-0460
800-494-0460; *Fax:* 770-441-3295
cs@iienet.org; www.iienet.org

Elaine Fuerst, Marketing Director

Simulation techniques. Tools and software used in a wide range of industries and applications.
250 Attendees

17056 South-Tec Machine Tool and Manufacturing Show
Society of Manufacturing Engineers
1 SME Drive
#930
Dearborn, MI 48121

313-425-3000
800-733-4763; *Fax:* 313-425-3400
service@sme.org; www.sme.org

Mark Tomlinson, Executive Director
Greg Sheremet, Publisher
70M Attendees
Founded in: 1932

17057 Southern Job Shop Show
Edward Publishing
16 Waterbury Road
Prospect, CT 06712-1215

203-758-4474; *Fax:* 860-768-4475;
www.jobshoptechnology.com

Mark W Shortt, Editor
Gerald Schmidt, President
Christopher Davis, Manager

The show is designed to attract the highest caliber engineers and buyers from your major DEM product manufacturers.
1500 Attendees
Frequency: March

17058 Spring World Expo
PO Box 1144
Highland Park, IL 60035

847-433-1335; *Fax:* 847-433-3769
info@casmi-springworld.org;
www.springworld.org

Gerald H Reese, Executive Director
Tracy Hodge, Director
4500 Attendees
Frequency: October

17059 World Adhesive & Sealant Conference
Adhesive & Sealant Council
7101 Wisconsin Avenue
Suite 990
Bethesda, MD 20814

301-986-9700; *Fax:* 301-986-9795
data@ascouncil.org; www.ascouncil.org
Social Media: Twitter, LinkedIn, RSS

Malinda Armstrong, Director, Meetings & Exhibitions
William Allmond, President
Traci Jensen, Chair

International event gathering together industry stakeholders from across the world for three days of keynote addresses, technical courses, and networking opportunities.
Frequency: Every Four Years/April

Directories & Databases

17060 Agricultural & Industrial Manufacturers Membership Directory
Agricultural & Industrial Manufacturers Rep Assn
7500 Flying Cloud Drive
Suite 900
Eden Prairie, MN 55344
952-253-6230
866-759-2467; *Fax:* 952-835-4774;
www.aimrareps.org

Michael J Kowalczyk, President
Ronald R Reed, VP
Cost: $25.00
Frequency: Annual October

17061 Directory of Manufacturing Research Centers
Manufacturing Technology Information
10 W 35th Street
Chicago, IL 60616-3717

312-431-1442
800-421-0586; *Fax:* 312-567-4736
info@iitri.org; www.iitri.org

Paula Marggraf, Editor
Cost: $75.00
Frequency: Irregular

17062 Directory of Waste Equipment Manufacturers and Distributors
WASTEC Equipment Technology Association
4301 Connecticut Ave NW
Suite 300
Washington, DC 20008-2304

202-966-4701; *Fax:* 202-966-4818;
www.wastec.org

Christine Hutcherson, Director Member Services
Bruce Parker, President
Gary T Satterfield, Executive VP
Sandra Price, Director Member Services

About 250 member manufacturers of waste handling, collection and processing equipment.
Cost: $5.00
Frequency: Annual

17063 Encyclopedia of American Industries
Grey House Publishing
4919 Route 22
PO Box 56
Amenia, NY 12501

518-789-8700
800-562-2139; *Fax:* 845-373-6390
books@greyhouse.com; www.greyhouse.com
Social Media: Facebook, Twitter

Leslie Mackenzie, Publisher
Richard Gottlieb, Editor

A two volume set, Volume I provides separate coverage of nearly 500 manufacturing industries, while Volume II presents nearly 600 essays covering the vast array of services and other non-manufacturing industries in the United States. Combined, these two volumes provide individual essays on every industry recognized by the U.S. Standard Industrial Classification (SIC) system.
Cost: $650.00
3000 Pages
ISBN: 1-592372-44-9
Founded in: 1981

17064 Manufacturers Representatives of America: Yearbook and Directory of Members
Manufacturers Representatives of America
PO Box 150229
Arlington, TX 76015-6229

817-465-5511; *Fax:* 817-561-7275

WR Bess, Executive Director

Several hundred independent manufacturers' representatives in paper, plastic, packaging and sanitary supplies.
Cost: $250.00
Frequency: Annual Fall
Circulation: 1,200

17065 Manufacturing & Distribution USA
Gale/Cengage Learning
27500 Drake Road
Farmington Hills, MI 48331-3535

248-699-4253
800-877-4253; *Fax:* 877-363-4253
gale.galeord@cengage.com;
www.gale.cengage.com
Social Media: Facebook, Twitter, Youtube

Patrick C Sommers, President

This new edition also features enhanced coverage of input-output data by industrial sector when available as well as classifications of leading public and private corporations in each industry.
ISBN: 1-414408-67-6

17066 Rauch Guide to the US Rubber Industry
Grey House Publishing
4919 Route 22
PO Box 56
Amenia, NY 12501

518-789-8700
800-562-2139; *Fax:* 845-373-6390
books@greyhouse.com; www.greyhouse.com
Social Media: Facebook, Twitter

Leslie Mackenzie, Publisher
Richard Gottlieb, Editor

Provides current market information and trends; industry economics and government regulations; company share data for each of the leading product categories; technology and raw material information; industry sources of further data; and unique profiles of 847 rubber manufacturers, a section which includes all known companies with rubber sales at or over $1 million annually.
Cost: $595.00
500 Pages
ISBN: 1-592371-30-2
Founded in: 1981

17067 Small Business Inovation Research
1000 Independence Avenue SW
Washington, DC 20585-1207

202-571-1300; www.sbir.gov

Lawrence Small, CEO
Frequency: Annual

17068 Sound and Vibration: Buyer's Guide Issue
Acoustical Publications
PO Box 40416
27101 E. Oviatt Road
Bay Village, OH 44140-0416

440-835-0101; *Fax:* 440-835-9303
sv@mindspring.com;
www.sandv.com.home/htm

Jack Mowry, Editor and Publisher
Scott J Lothes, Assistant Editor/Webmaster

This directory offers a list of manufacturers of products for noise and vibration control.
Frequency: Monthly
Circulation: 19,000
ISSN: 0-038181-09-9
Mailing list available for rent: 21M names
Printed in 4 colors on glossy stock

17069 ThomasNet
Thomas Publishing Company, LLC
User Services Department
5 Penn Plaza
New York, NY 10001

212-695-0500
800-699-9822; *Fax:* 212-290-7362

contact@thomaspublishing.com;
www.thomasnet.com
Social Media: Facebook, Twitter, LinkedIn

Carl Holst-Knudsen, President
Robert Anderson, VP, Planning
Mitchell Peipert, VP, Finance
Ivy Molofsky, VP, Human Resources

A way to reach qualified businesses that list their company information on ThomasNet.com. Detailed profiles promote their products, services, capabilities and brands carried. The ThomasNet.com web site is the most up-to-date compilation of 650,000 North American manufacturers, distributors, and service companies in 67,000 industrial categories.
Founded in: 1898

17070 **Who Audits America**
Data Financial Press
PO Box 668
Menlo Park, CA 94026-0668

650-321-4553; *Fax:* 650-321-4427

A who's who directory of services and supplies.
Cost: $133.00
600 Pages
Frequency: SemiAnnual

Industry Web Sites

17071 **http://gold.greyhouse.com**
G.O.L.D Grey House OnLine Databases

Grey House Publishing's online database platform, GOLD, offers Quick Search, Keyword Search and Expert Search for most business sectors including a wide variety of manufacturing markets. The GOLD platform makes finding the information you need quick and easy - whether you're a novice searcher or an experienced database user. All of Grey House's directory products are available for subscription on the GOLD platform.

17072 **www.abrasiveengineering.com**
Abrasive Grain Association

Members manufacture natural and artificial grains used in grinding wheels, coated abrasives etc.

17073 **www.aesf.org**
American Electroplaters and Surface Finishers Soc.

AESF is an international society that advances the science of surface finishing to benefit industry and society through education information and social involvement, as well as those who provide services, supplies and support to the industry.

17074 **www.agma.org**
American Gear Manufacturers Association

Manufacturers of gears and geared speed changers.

17075 **www.ahma.org**
American Hardware Manufacturers Association

Over 280 manufacturer representatives in the hardware industry.

17076 **www.amba.org**
American Mold Builders Association

Promotes the development, welfare, and expansion of businesses engaged in the manufacture of molds and related tooling.

17077 **www.amtda.org**
American Machine Tool Distributors Association

For distributors of manufacturing technology.

17078 **www.ararental.org**
American Rental Association

For rental business owners and equipment suppliers.

17079 **www.arcat.com**
National Association of Relay Manufacturers

NARM is a trade association for the electro-mechanical relay and associated switching devices industry. An affiliate of Electronic Industries Alliance.

17080 **www.asphaltinstitute.org**
Asphalt Institute

Conducts education, research, and engineering services related to asphalt products; conducts seminars and sells publications and videos on asphalt technology.

17081 **www.awci.com/**
American Watchmakers-Clockmakers Institute

Examines and certifies master watchmakers and clockmakers. Maintains a placement service. Conducts home study courses.

17082 **www.awci.org**
Association of the Wall and Ceiling Industries

Offers information on contractors, manufacturers, suppliers and organizations affiliated with the interior design, building and contracting community. Strives to provide services and undertake activities that enhance the members ability to operate a successful business.

17083 **www.bia.org**
Brick Industry Association

Supports the industry by rendering technical assistance to architects and designers, by providing marketing assistance to the industry, by monitoring and positively influencing governmental actions, by working to assure the long term availability of bricklayers and by providing other member services as appropriate.

17084 **www.cancentral.com**
Can Manufacturers Institute

Industry, environmental and consumer information.

17085 **www.carpet ushion.org**
Carpet Cushion Council

Encourages distribution and use of seperate carpet cushions. Works with regulatory agencies at the national, state and local levels.

17086 **www.cl2.com**
Chlorine Institute

Promotes safe handling of chlorine and caustic materials and sponsors awards.

17087 **www.cmit.edi.gatech.edu/**
Center for Manufacturing Information

Provides a non-instrusive environment in which manufacturers can objectively evaluate and compare the latest computer-based technologies.

17088 **www.cottonseed.com**
National Cottonseed Products Association

Services include the administration of trading rules and standards, a research program, information service center and product promotion of cotton seed food and feed products.

17089 **www.cti.org**
Cooling Technology

Seeks to improve technology, design and performance of water conservation apparatus. Provides inspection services and conducts research.

17090 **www.divbusiness.com**
Diversified Business Communications

Provides management services for associations and organizations seeking to expand domestically and overseas, as well as direct mail, internet, telemarketing campaigns and market research.

17091 **www.fluidcontrolsinstitute.org**
Fluid Controls Institute

Manufacturers of devices for fluid control, such as temperature and pressure regulators, strainers, gauges, control valves, solenoid valves, steam traps, etc.

17092 **www.fluidsealing.com**
Fluid Sealing Association

An international association of manufacturers of mechanical packings, sealing devices, gaskets, rubber expansion joints and allied products.

17093 **www.graphicsPor.org**
Graphics Products Association

Independent manufacturers and suppliers of paperboard packaging. Purposes are to futher development, use and sale of members product. Compiles statistics and bestows awards.

17094 **www.greyhouse.com**
Grey House Publishing

Authoritative reference directories for most business sectors including a wide variedy of manufacturing markets. Users can search the online databases with varied search criteria allowing for custom searches by product category, geographic area, sales volume, keyword, subject and more. Full Grey House catalog and online ordering also available.

17095 **www.housewares.org**
National Housewares Manufacturers Association

Links to other associations.

17096 **www.iccsafe.org/**
International Code Council

Nonprofit membership association with more than 16,000 members who span the building community, from code enforcement officials to materials manufacturers. Dedicated to preserving the public health, safety and welfare in the built environment through the effective use and enforcement of model codes.

17097 **www.icea.net**
Insulated Cable Engineers Association

Professional organization dedicated to developing cable standards for the electric power, control and telecommunications industries. Ensures safe, economical and efficient cable systems utilizing proven state-of-the-art materials and concepts. ICEA documents are of interest to cable manufacturers, architects and engineers, utility and manufacturing plant personnel, telecommunication engineers, consultants and OEMs.

17098 **www.ifai.com**
Industrial Fabrics Association International

Provides many products, services and programs to industry members.

17099 **www.ilma.org**
Independent Lubricant Manufacturers Association

Independent blenders and compounders of lubricants.

17100 **www.iopp.org**
Institute of Packaging Professionals

Association for packing professionals.

17101 www.ipc.org
IPC-Association Connecting Electronics Industries

Works to develop standards in circuit board assembly equipment. Brings together all players in the electronic interconnection industry, including designers, board manufacturers, assembly companies, suppliers and original equipment manufacturers. Offers workshops, conferences, meetings and online communications.

17102 www.isri.org
Institute of Scrap Recycling Industries

Members include processors, brokers and consumers of scrap metal, rubber, paper, textiles, plastics and glass.

17103 www.marinecanvas.com
Marine Fabricators Association

Firms and individuals engaged in the design, construction, and installation of marine fabric products. Provides certification and product standards.

17104 www.mechanical.com
Mechanical.Com

Manufacturing industry database.

17105 www.mep.nist.gov
Manufacturing Extension Partnership

A nationwide network of more thatn 70 not-for-profit centers whose sole purpose is to provide small and medium-sized manufacturers with the help they need to succeed.

17106 www.mfgworld.com/index.html
Manufacturing World Online

Manufacturing news, software, industry reports and links.

17107 www.mhia.org/psc/PSC_Products_Racks.cfm
Rack Manufacturers Institute

Makers of steel industrial storage racks.

17108 www.mt-online.com
Applied Technology Publications

MT-online.com is the premier source of capacity assurance and best practice solutions for manufacturing, process and service operations worldwide. Online home of Maintenance Technology magazie, the dynamic MT-online.com portal serves the critical technical, business and professional-development needs of engineers, managers and technicians from across all industrial, institutional and commercial sectors.

17109 www.naima.org
North American Insulation Manufacturers Assn

17110 www.nam.org
National Association of Manufacturers

Represents industry's views on national and international problems to government.

17111 www.naumd.com
North American Assoc. of Uniform Manufacturers

Promotes interests of manufacturers and distributors of uniforms and career wear.

17112 www.ncspa.org
National Corrugated Steel Pipe Association

NCSPA seeks to promote sound public policy relating to the use of corrugated steel drainage structures in private and public construction.

17113 www.nei.org
Nuclear Energy Institute

Members are of utilities, manufacturers of electrical generating equipment, researchers, architects, engineers, labor unions, and others interested in the generation of electricity by nuclear power.

17114 www.nomma.org
National Ornamental and Miscellaneous Metals Association

Publishes the Ornamental and Miscellaneous Metals Fabricator magazine. Holds annual convention and trade show (METALfab). Membership dues: $275 fabricators, $250 local supplier, $325 regional supplier, $425 nationwide supplier.

17115 www.nwpca.org
National Wooden Pallet & Container Association

Represents manufacturers, recyclers and distributors of pallets, containers and reels.

17116 www.p3-ny.org/
Women in Production

Promotes the interests of women in the production profession.

17117 www.patmi.org
Powder Actuated Tool Manufacturers Institute

Represents manufacturers of construction tools used to fasten to and into steel and concrete.

17118 www.powertoolinstitute.com
Power Tool Institute

Trade association representing manufacturers of power tools.

17119 www.reman.org
Remanufacturing Institute International

A coalition of associations and companies in the entire manufacturing industry. There are over 73,000 companies in this industry. Our goal is to unite them into a powerful organization.

17120 www.sawingassociation.com/
North American Sawing Association

17121 www.smma.org
SMMA: Small Motors & Motion Association

Manufacturing trade association. Members include electric motor and motion control companies, as well as suppliers, users, and associated businesses such as consultants, universities and distributors.

17122 www.steeltubeinstitute.org
Steel Tube Institute of North America

Members produce steel tubes and pipes from carbon, stainless or alloy steel for applications ranging from large structural tubing to small redrawn tubing.

17123 www.sunglassassociation.com
Sunglass Association of America

A nonprofit trade association of manufacturers and import-wholesale sunglasses, sunglass parts, components, materials, and reading glasses.

17124 www.thomasnet.com/index.html
Thomas Register of American Manufacturers

Industrial buying guide of US and Canadian manufacturers.

17125 www.tileusa.com
Tile Council of America

Manufacturers and suppliers of ceramic wall and floor tiles.

17126 www.tpatube.org
Tube & Pipe Association International

TPA is an educational technology association serving the metal tube and pipe producing and fabricating industries.

17127 www.ttmanet.org
Truck Trailer Manufacturers Association

News of interest to trailer manufacturers and suppliers.

17128 www.vending.org
National Automatic Merchandising Association

For makers and operators of automatic vending equipment.

17129 www.westernroofing.net/
Roof Tile Institute

Manufacturers of clay and concrete roof tiles. Emphasis is on technical issues and codes that involve tile. Has annual budget of approximately $300,000 a year. Publications available to members.

Associations

17130 Academy of Marketing Science
PO Box 248012
Coral Gables, FL 33124-8012

305-284-6673; *Fax:* 305-284-3762;
www.ams-web.org

Barry J. Babin, Co-Chair
Joseph F. Hair, Co-Chair
Adilson Borges, President
Harold W. Berkman, Executive Vice President/Director
D. Todd Donovan, Vice President, Membership
NA

Fosters education professional standards in marketing science. Sponsers the AMS Foundation which provides grants for the advancement of teaching and research.
1500 Members
Founded in: 1971

17131 American Association of Family & Consumer Sciences
400 N Columbus Street
Suite 202
Alexandria, VA 22314-2264

703-706-4600
800-424-8080; *Fax:* 703-706-4663
staff@aafcs.org; www.aafcs.org
Social Media: Facebook, Twitter, LinkedIn, Flickr, Pintrest

Duane Whitbeck, President
Carolyn Jackson, CEO
Gwynn Mason, Director of Communications

An association dedicated to Family & Consumer Sciences professionals. AAFCS strives to improve the quality and standards of individual and family life by providing educational programs, influencing public policy, and through communication.
10000 Members

17132 American Chamber of Commerce Executives
1330 Braddock Place
Suite 300
Alexandria, VA 22314

703-998-0072; *Fax:* 888-577-9883
webmaster@acce.org; www.acce.org
Social Media: Facebook, Twitter, LinkedIn, RSS

Betty Nokes, Chairman of the Board
Mick Fleming, President
Tamara Philbin, COO
Chris Mead, Senior VP, Members
Jacqui Cook, Chief Financial Officer
1300+ Members
Founded in: 1914

17133 American Marketing Association
American Marketing Association
311 S Wacker Dr # 5800
Suite 5800
Chicago, IL 60606-6629

312-542-9000
800-262-1150; *Fax:* 312-542-9001;
www.themarketingfoundation.org
Social Media: Facebook, Twitter, LinkedIn, Blog,Google+

Jerome D. Williams, Chairperson
Dennis L. Dunlap, Chief Executive Officer
Roger A. Kerin, Vice Chairperson
Donald R. Lehmann, Vice Chairperson
William Cron, Treasurer

A professional association for individuals and organizations involved in the practice, teaching and study of marketing worldwide.
40000 Members
Founded in: 1992
Mailing list available for rent

17134 Association for Innovative Marketing
34 Summit Avenue
Sharon, MA 02067-2149

781-784-8283; www.manta.com
Social Media: Facebook, Twitter, Google+

Facilitates sharing of innovative ideas; bestows awards, maintains library and speaker bureau.
Founded in: 1989

17135 Association for Postal Commerce
1800 Diagonal Road
Suite 320
Alexandria, VA 22314-2862

703-524-0096; *Fax:* 703-997-2414;
www.postcom.org

Gene Del Polito, President

National organization representing those who use, or who support, the use of mail as a medium for communication and commerce. Publishes a weekly newsletter covering postal policy and operational issues.
231 Members
Founded in: 1947

17136 Association of Marketing Service Providers
Mailing & Fulfillment Service Association
1800 Diagonal Road
Suite 320
Alexandria, VA 22314-2862

703-836-9200; *Fax:* 703-548-8204
mfsa-mail@mfsanet.org; www.epicomm.org
Social Media: Facebook, Twitter, LinkedIn, Youtube, RSS, Vimeo,Google+

Ken Garner, President/CEO
Tom Cobery, Vice President
Samantha Lake, Director of Marketing/Communication
Patty Dumas, Director of Accounting
Tyler T. Keeney, Director of Member Satisfaction

The national trade association for the mailing and fulfillment services industry.
Founded in: 1920
Mailing list available for rent

17137 Association of Marketing and Communication Professionals
127 Pittsburgh St.
Dallas, TX 75207

214-377-3524; *Fax:* 214-377-3548
info@amcpros.com
amcpros.com
Social Media: Facebook, LinkedIn, YouTube, Google+, RSS

Founded in: 1995

17138 Association of Sale Marketing Companies
1010 Wisconsin Avenue NW
Suite 900
Washington, DC 20007

202-337-9351; *Fax:* 202-337-4508;
www.ama.org

Mark Baum, President/CEO
Karen Connell, Contact

Provides referral service and other methods of assistance in locating sales and marketing companies.
250 Members
Founded in: 1995

17139 Biomedical Marketing Association
10293 N Meridian Street
Suite 175
Indianapolis, IN 46290

317-816-1640
800-278-7886; *Fax:* 317-816-1633
info@bmaonline.org; www.bmaonline.org

Michael L Boner, President

Builds diagnostic industry leadership by providing market education, professional development and a forum for fellowship and the exchange of ideas.

17140 Brand Activation Association
650 First Avenue
Suite 2-SW
New York, NY 10016-3207

212-420-1100; *Fax:* 212-533-7622
pma@pmalink.org; www.baalink.org/
Social Media: Facebook, Twitter, LinkedIn

Bonnie J Carlson, President
Noelle Boddewyn, Executive Assistant
Mike Kaufman, VP of Marketing
Marybeth Petescia, Marketing Manager
Christine Goonan, Director of Membership

Mission is to encourage the highest standards of excellence in promotion marketing. Represents member interests and promotes better understanding promotion in the marketing mix.
700 Members
Founded in: 1911

17141 Business Marketing Association
708 Third Avenue
Suite 123
New York, NY 10017

212-697-5950; *Fax:* 212-687-7310
info@marketing.org; www.marketing.org
Social Media: Facebook, Twitter, LinkedIn

Katherine Button Bell, Chairman
Stephen Liguori, Vice Chair
George Stenitzer, VP, Thought Leadership
Chris Schermer, VP, Marketing
Bob Felsenthal, VP, Membership

The Business Marketing Association/BMA, a preeminent service organization for professionals, provides expertise in business-to-business marketing and communications. The BMA offers an information-packed Website, online skills-building, marketing certification programs, and industry surveys and papers. In addition, members have the opportunity to interact with peers at seminars, chapter training programs and the BMA Annual Conference.
Founded in: 1922

17142 Business Marketing Association: Atlanta
2801 Buford Highway
Druid Chase Suite 375
Atlanta, GA 30329

404-641-9417
800-664-4262; *Fax:* 312-822-0054
info@bmaatlanta.com; www.bmaatlanta.com
Social Media: Facebook, Twitter, LinkedIn, Youtube

Martine Hunter, President
Rory Carlton, Treasurer
Eduardo Esparza, Co-Chair of Marketing
Mark Potter, Membership Chairperson
Nancy Bistritz, Public Relations

The Atlanta chapter of the BMA includes marketing executives from a variety of industries and backgrounds including research, advertising, promotions, events, Web development, printing and more. The BMA offers an information-packed Website, online skills-building, marketing certification programs, and industry surveys and papers. In addition, members have the opportunity to interact with peers at seminars,

participate in chapter training programs and the BMA Annual Conference.
Founded in: 1922

17143 Business Marketing Association: Boston
246 Hampshire Street
Cambridge, MA 02130

617-418-4000
800-664-4262; *Fax:* 312-822-0054
info@thebmaboston.com;
www.thebmaboston.com/

Michael Lewis, President
Will Robinson, VP Public Relations
Matthew Mamet, VP Internet Marketing
Larry Perreault, VP Finance
Chris Perkett, VP Programming

BMA Boston helps members improve their ability to manage business-to-business marketing and communications for greater productivity and profitability by providing unique access to information, ideas, and the experience of peers. The BMA offers an information-packed Website, online skills-building, marketing certification programs, and industry surveys and papers. In addition, members have the opportunity to interact with peers at seminars, chapter training programs and the BMA Annual Conference.

17144 Business Marketing Association: Houston
PO Box 710350
Houston, TX 77271-0350

713-723-1325; *Fax:* 713-723-1326
info@bmahouston.com; www.bmahouston.org
Social Media: Facebook, Twitter, LinkedIn, Youtube

Diana Salerno, President
Linda Ives, Executive Director
Megan Coffing, Vice President
Bob Wallace, Treasurer

Dedicated to serving the needs of business to business Associations worldwide.
Founded in: 1922

17145 Business Marketing Association: Hudson Valley
304 Wall Street
Kingston, NY 12401

845-340-4708
800-664-4262
alviankamaly@gmail.com; www.hvdma.org

Bud Clarke, President
Joan Giewat, First Vice President
June Bisel, Second Vice President
Rebecca D Jones, Treasurer
John Bassler, Secretary

Offers ways for its members to expand their business expertise and grow professionally.

17146 Business Marketing Association: Indy
8650 Commerce Park Place
Indianapolis, IN 46268

800-664-4262; *Fax:* 317-285-2068;
www.bmaindy.org

John Faust, President
Christine Johnston, Secretary
Judy Knafel, Treasurer

To promote the quality and effectiveness of Indiana-developed business-to-business marketing communications through the continuous learning of its members.

17147 Cable & Telecommunications Association for Marketing
120 Waterfront Street, Suite 200
National Harbor, MD 20745

301-485-8900; *Fax:* 301-560-4964
info@ctam.com; www.ctam.com
Social Media: Facebook, Twitter, LinkedIn, Youtube

Matrk Greatrex, Chair
Anne Cowan, President and CEO
Angie Britt, Vice President of Advanced Products
Jamia Bigalow, Vice Chair
Jonathan Hargis, Secretary / Treasurer

CTAM is dedicated to the discipline and development of consumer marketing excellence in cable television, new media and telecommunications services.
5500 Members
Founded in: 1976

17148 Communications Marketing Association
PO Box 5680
Lago Vista, TX 78645

512-656-7747
CMAExecDirector@aol.com;
www.cma-cmc.org
Social Media: Facebook, Twitter, LinkedIn, YouTube

Rex Reed, President
Larry Weber, Vice President
Karen Hollingsworth, Executive Director
Tony Fulton, Treasurer
Larry Seige, Secretary

17149 Communications Roundtable
1250 24th Street NW
Suite 250
Washington, DC 20037

202-755-5180; *Fax:* 202-466-0544;
www.roundtable.org

Michael Reichgut, Chairman
Shawn Dolley, CEO

Association of more than 20 public relations, marketing, graphics, advertising, training and other communications organizations with more than 12,000 professional members. The goals include furthering professionalism, cooperation between member organizations, career and employment support, and employer assistance.

17150 Construction Marketing Association
1220 Iroquois Ave.
Ste. #210
Naperville, IL 60563

630-868-5061;
www.constructionmarketingassociation.org
Social Media: Facebook, Twitter, LinkedIn, YouTube, Pinterest, Google+

Neil M. Brown, Chair/ Founder
Kevin Enke, Board Member, Rick
Kean O'Brien, Board Member
Deborah Hodges, Board Member
Founded in: 2009

17151 Construction Marketing Research Council C/O CMPA
4625 South Wendler Drive
Suite 111
Tempe, AZ 85282

602-431-1441; *Fax:* 602-431-0637;
www.nrc-cnrc.gc.ca/eng/rd/construction/index.html

Craig Schulz, President
Don Johnson, Director at Large
Jim McMahon, Treasurer

Members are professionals in the construction products industry with responsiblities for their firms' corporate strategic planning and the conduct of marketing research activities. Membership is restricted to the highest level marketing research or planning professional within a company.
25 Members
Founded in: 1992

17152 Council for Marketing and Opinion
470 Portage Lakes Dr
Suite 102
Akron, OH 44319

330-564-4211; *Fax:* 330-645-6750
info@cmoresearch.com
cmoresearch.com
Social Media: Facebook, Twitter, LinkedIn

S. Michelle Henry, President/Co-Founder
Amanda Barna, Vice President/Co-Owner
Anthony Matonis, Senior Dir., Research and Analytics
Ryan Thompson, Research Associate
Brandon Dalo, Research Operations Manager

A non-profit organization which works on behalf of the survery research industry to improve respondent cooperation in research, and to promote positive legislation and prevent restrictive legislation which could impact the survey research industry.
150+ Members
Founded in: 1992

17153 Data-Driven Marketing
Direct Marketing Association
1120 Avenue of the Americas
New York, NY 10036-6700

212-768-7277; *Fax:* 212-302-6714;
www.thedma.org
Social Media: Facebook, Twitter, LinkedIn

Gunther Schmachar, Chairman
Eva Reda, Vice Chairman
JoAnne Monfradi Dunn, CEO & President, Direct Marketing
Bruce Bieger, Senior Managing Director
Cathy Butler, SVP, Group Account Director

17154 Destination Marketing Association International
2025 M Street NW
Suite 500
Washington, DC 20036

202-296-7888; *Fax:* 202-296-7889
info@destinationmarketing.org;
www.destinationmarketing.org
Social Media: Facebook, Twitter, Google+

Joseph Marinelli, Chair
Alison Best, CDME, Chair Elect
David Adler, Founder/CEO
Stephanie Pace Brown, Secretary/ Treasurer
Cleo Battle, CDME, Immediate Past Chair

17155 Direct Marketing Association
1120 Avenue of the Americas
New York, NY 10036-6700

212-768-7277; *Fax:* 212-302-6714
customerservice@the-dma.org;
www.thedma.org
Social Media: Facebook, Twitter, LinkedIn

Gunther Schmachar, Chairman
Eva Reda, Vice Chairman
JoAnne Monfradi Dunn, CEO & President, Direct Marketing
Thomas J. Benton, Chief Operating Officer
Jerry Cerasale, J.D., Senior Vice President

The leading global trade association of businesses and nonprofit organizations using and supporting multichannel direct marketing tools and techniques. DMA advocates standards for responsible marketing, promotes relevance as the key to reaching consumers with desirable offers, and provides cutting edge research, education and networking opportunities to improve results throughout the end to end direct marketing process.
3100 Members
Founded in: 1917

17156 **Distributive Education Clubs of America**
1908 Association Dr # A
Reston, VA 20191-1594

703-860-5000; *Fax:* 703-860-4013
info@deca.org; www.deca.org
Social Media: Facebook, Twitter, LinkedIn, Youtube, RSS

Jim Brock, President
Edward Davis, Executive Director
Lynore Levenhagen, Secretary
Mary Peres, Treasurer

To enhance the co-curricular education of students with interest in marketing, management, and entrprenuership. Helps students to develop skills and competence for marketing careers, to build self-esteem, to experience leadership and to practice community service.
Founded in: 1946

17157 **Diving Equipment & Marketing Association**
858-616-6408
800-862-3483; *Fax:* 858-616-6495
info@dema.org; www.dema.org
Social Media: Facebook, Twitter, LinkedIn, Google+, YouTube, RSS, Instagr

Stephen Ashmore, President & Director
William Cline, Director
Jenny Collister, Director
Scott Daley, Director
Stuart Cove, Director
1300 Members

17158 **EMarketing Association**
40 Blue Ridge Dr.
Charlestown, RI 02813

800-496-2950
800-496-2950; *Fax:* 408-884-2461
admin@emarketingassociation.com; www.emarketingassociation.com
Social Media: Facebook, Twitter, LinkedIn

An international association of emarketing professionals. Members include governments, professionals and students involved with the emarketing arena. The eMA provides marketing resources, services, research, certifications, educational programs and events to its members and the marketing community.
2500 Members
Founded in: 1997

17159 **Electronic Retailing Association**
607 14th Street, NW
Suite 530
Washington, DC 20005

703-841-1751
800-987-6462; *Fax:* 425-977-1036
webadmin@retailing.org; www.retailing.org
Social Media: Facebook, Twitter, LinkedIn, Youtube.Flickr

Gregory Sater, Chairman of the Board
Julie Coons, President & CEO
Kevin Kelly, Chief Financial Officer
Bill McClellan, Vice President, Government Affairs
Dave Martin, Vice President, Marketing

The trade association that represents the leaders of direct response: members who maximize revenues through electronic retailing on television, online and on radio. ERA strives to protect the regulatory and legislative climate of direct response while ensuring a favorable landscape that enhances e-retailers' ability to bring quality products and services to the consumer.
Founded in: 1990

17160 **Entertainment Resource & Marketing Association**
2315 28th Street
Suite 204
Santa Monica, CA 90405

310-452-0426
Tami@erma.org; www.erma.org
Social Media: Facebook, Twitter, LinkedIn, Google+

Michael Schrager, President
Amy Ferguson, Vice President
Eric Dahlquist, Treasurer
Nikki David, Secretary
Tami Cooper, Ethics Committee

17161 **Foodservice Sales & Marketing Association**
1810-J York Road #384
Lutherville, MD 21093

800-617-1170
800-617-1170; *Fax:* 888-668-7496
info@fsmaonline.com; www.fsmaonline.com
Social Media: Facebook, Twitter, LinkedIn, Youtube

Stuart Wolff, Chairman of the Board
Rick Abraham, President & CEO
Sharon Boyle, Vice President
Jessica Muffoletto, Manager, Membership & Meetings
Barry Maloney, General Counsel

Specializes in selling food and related products to foodservice companies.
150 Members
Founded in: 2003
Mailing list available for rent

17162 **Global Retail Marketing Association**
www.thegrma.com
Social Media: Twitter, LinkedIn

Bill Brand, Advisory Board Member
Brian Beitler, Advisory Board Member
Ron Bonacci, Advisory Board Member
Lily Chang, Advisory Board Member
John Aylward, Advisory Board Member

17163 **Healthcare Public Relations & Marketing Association**
5406 Hazeltine Ave.
Sherman Oaks, CA 91401

714-647-2430
info@hprma.org; www.vnetitclients.com/hprma2
Social Media: Facebook, Twitter, LinkedIn

Pamela Westcott, President
Ava Alexander, Sponsorships
Jennifer Heinley, Secretary
Kathleen Curan, Communications
Lisa Killen, Membership

17164 **Hospitality Sales and Marketing Association**
7918 Jones Branch Drive
Suite 300
McLean, VA 22102

703-506-3280; *Fax:* 703-506-3266
info@hsmai.org; www.hsmai.org
Social Media: Facebook, Twitter, LinkedIn, Flicker

Rob Torres, Chair
Marina MacDonald, Vice Chair
Robert A. Gilbert, CHME, CHA, President & CEO
Juli Jones, Vice President
Fran Brasseux, CHSE, Executive Vice President
7000 Members
Founded in: 1927

17165 **Incentive Marketing Association**
4248 Park Glen Road
Minneapolis, MN 55416

952-928-4649
info@incentivemarketing.org; www.incentivemarketing.org
Social Media: Facebook, Twitter, LinkedIn

Sean Roark, CPIM, President
John Hornbogen, Executive Vice President
Susan Gray, Vice President
Karen Wesloh, Executive Director
Melissa Serres, Operations Director

Members are professional premium/incentive marketing executives.
500+ Members
Founded in: 1998

17166 **Incentive Performance Center**
5008 Castle Rock Way
Naples, FL 34112

914-591-7600; *Fax:* 239-775-7537
info@incentivecentral.org; www.incentivecentral.org

Howard C Henry, Executive Director/CAE

Your portal to new ways of achieving business goals by capturing the power of your best customers and employees.
150 Members
Founded in: 1984

17167 **Insurance Marketing & Communications Association**
4248 Park Glen Road
Minneapolis, MN 55416

952-928-4644; *Fax:* 952-929-1318
info@imcanet.com
imcanet.com
Social Media: Facebook, Twitter, LinkedIn, YouTube

Mark Friedlander, President
Gloria Grove, Executive Director
Anna Hargis, Executive Vice President
John Abbott, Member
Emily Hathcoat, Treasurer
Founded in: 1923

17168 **Internet Marketing Association**
10 Mar Del Rey
San Clemente, CA 92673

949-443-9300; *Fax:* 949-443-2215
imanetwork.org
Social Media: Facebook, Twitter, LinkedIn, RSS, Google+, YouTube

Sinan Kanatsiz, CIM, Chairman & Founder
Matthew Langie, CIM, Vice Chair of Education
Rachel Reenders, CIM, Executive Director
Vince Walden, Finance Director
David Steinberg, CIM, VP of Business Alliances
90000 Members
Founded in: 2001

17169 **Legal Marketing Association**
330 North Wabash Avenue
Suite 2000
Chicago, IL 60611-4267

312-321-6898; *Fax:* 312-673-6894
membersupport@legalmarketing.org; www.legalmarketing.org
Social Media: Facebook, Twitter, LinkedIn, Youtube

Betsi Roach, Executive Director
Susan Lane, Director of Operations
Adrianne Watson, Membership Services
Lizzie Duvall, Membership Services
Justine Gershak, Membership Services

LMA is a nonprofit organization dedicated to serving the needs and maintaining the profes-

sional standards of the men and women involved in marketing within the legal profession.
2700 Members
Founded in: 1985

17170 Life Insurance Direct Marketing Association
3227 S. Cherokee Lane
Suite 1320
Woodstock, GA 30188

770-516-0207
866-890-LEAD
info@lidma.org
lidma.org
Social Media: Facebook, Twitter, LinkedIn

Pat Wedeking, Chair
Byron Udell, President
Jeff McCauley, Vice President
Staci Birk, Director
Cynthia Farrow, Secretary/ Treasurer

17171 Manufacturers Agents National Association
16-A Journey
Suite 200
Aliso Viejo, CA 92656-3317

949-859-4040
877-626-2776; *Fax:* 949-855-2973
mana@manaonline.org; www.manaonline.org

Tom Hayward, CPMR, Chairman
Charles Cohon, CPMR, President and CEO
Jerry Leth, Vice President and General Manager
Lisa Ball, Member Services Coordinator
Doug Bower, Director of Strategic Alliances
6600 Members
Founded in: 1947

17172 Marketing Agencies Association Worldwide
60 Peachcroft Drive
Bernardsville, NJ 07924

908-428-4300; *Fax:* 908-766-1277
vincentsottosanti@maaw.org; www.maaw.org

Aldo Cundari, President
Aldo Cundari, 1st Vice President
Dan Mortimer, VP On-line Services
John Williams, Executive Director
Rick Shaver, Treasurer

The Marketing Agencies Association Worldwide (MAA) is the only global organization dedicated solely to the CEOs, Presidents,Managing Directors and Principals of top marketing services agencies.
75 Members
Founded in: 1963

17173 Marketing Education Association
PO Box 27473
Tempe, AZ 85285-7473

602-750-6735; www.nationalmea.org

Fosters the development and expansion of education for and about marketing as a descrete, clearly defined profession. Members are high school and postsecondary marketing educations as well as university-level teacher educations and collegiate marketing teacher education students.
Founded in: 1982

17174 Marketing Research Association
1156 15th Street NW
Suite 302
Washington, DC 20005

202-800-2545; *Fax:* 888-512-1050
membership@marketingresearch.org;
www.marketingresearch.org
Social Media: Facebook, Twitter, LinkedIn, Google+

David Almy, CEO

The Marketing Research Association's Blue Book Research Services Directory is the research industry number one reference source.
Founded in: 1957

17175 Marketing Science Institute
Marketing Science Institute
1000 Massachusetts Avenue
Cambridge, MA 02138-5396

617-491-2060; *Fax:* 617-491-2065
msi@msi.org; www.msi.org
Social Media: Facebook, Twitter, LinkedIn

Katherine N. Lemon, Executive Director
Marni Zea Clippinger, Chief Operating Officer
Earl Taylor, Chief Marketing Officer
Liza Hostetler-Ingalls, Administrative Assistant
Susan Keane, Editorial Director

MSI publishes research done on a variety of marketing topics, including: E - Commerce, Metrics, Branding, New Products and Innovations, Communications and more. Individual papers and subscriptions are available. We accept proposals and papers for grant consideration.
65 Members
Founded in: 1961

17176 Mass Marketing Insurance Institute
3007 Tilden Street, NW
Suite 7M-103
Washington, DC 20008

816-221-7575; *Fax:* 816-772-7765
Jeffrey.M.Collins@MedStar.net; www.mi2.org
Social Media: Twitter, Youtube, Pinterest, RSS, Googl

Greg Carlile, Executive Director
Laurie Weber, Associate Director

Provides a forum for professionals engaged in marketing, sales and administration of employee benefits such as worksite marketing, payroll deduction and other mass marketed services.

17177 Materials Marketing Associates
136 South Keowee Street
Dayton, OH 45402

937-222-1024; *Fax:* 937-222-5794
email@mma4u.com; www.mma4u.com

Kimberley Fantaci, President

Members are chemical distributors representing manufacturers marketing chemical raw material specialties to makers of coatings, inks, pharmaceuticals, adhesives, cosmetics, plastics, soaps, detergents, etc.
19 Members
Founded in: 1963

17178 Midwest Direct Marketing Association
P.O. Box 75
Andover, MN 55304

763-607-2943; *Fax:* 763-753-2240
office@mdma.org; www.mdma.org

Ben DuBois, Communications Director
Jolee Molitor, Programs Director
Vicki Erickson, Secretary/Treasurer
Jolee Moiltor, Past President

Dedicated to the advancement of professional and ethical practice of direct response marketing by members throughout the Upper Midwest.
600 Members
Founded in: 1960

17179 Mobile Marketing Association
41 E 11th St
11th Floor
New York, NY 10003

646-257-4515
northamerica@mmaglobal.com;
www.mmaglobal.com
Social Media: Facebook, Twitter, LinkedIn, Google+

Greg Stuart, Chief Executive Officer
Sheryl Daija, CSO & GM, Global Events
Chris Babayode, Managing Director, EMEA
Fabiano Destri Lobo, Managing Director, Latam
Michael Wis, SVP, Global Finance Administration
800 Members

17180 Multi-Level Marketing International Association
119 Stanford Court
Irvine, CA 92612-1671

949-854-0484; *Fax:* 949-854-7687
info@mlmia.com; www.mlmia.com
Social Media: Facebook, Twitter, LinkedIn

Doris Wood, Chairman/President Emeritus
Linda Bruno, Secretary

Seeks to strengthen and improve the Direct Sales/Network Marketing/Multi-Level Marketing industry in the United States and abroad.
Founded in: 1985

17181 Multicultural Marketing Resources
150 West 28th Street
Suite 1501
New York, NY 10001

212-242-3351; *Fax:* 212-691-5969
lisa@multicultural.com;
www.multicultural.com
Social Media: Facebook, Twitter, LinkedIn

Lisa Skriloff, President
Cassandra Richardson-Coughlin, Marketing/Sales Assistant
Kelleh Jian, Marketing/Sales Assistant
Mukti Ajmeri, Marketing/Sales Assistant
Nadia M, Marketing/Sales Assistant

A place where corporate executives can find diverse resources, experts and information on how to market to multicultural (ethnic and niche) consumer markets.
Founded in: 1994

17182 National Association of Display Industries
4651 Sheridan Street
Suite 470
Hollywood, FL 33021

954-893-7300; *Fax:* 954-893-7500;
www.nadi-global.com

Klein Merriman, Executive Director
Tracy Dillon, Director Communications

A leading association for the visual merchandising profession. As visual merchandising has evolved over the years into playing an integral role in retail, NADI has always taken the lead in informing and educating members. The association's already significant support of the visual design profession has grown with NADI's exclusive sponsorship of GlobalShop's Visual Merchandising Show and StoreXpo.
Founded in: 1942

17183 National Energy Marketers Association
3333 K Street, NW
Suite 110
Washington, DC 20007

202-333-3288; *Fax:* 202-333-3266;
www.energymarketers.com

Dan Verbanac, Chair, Executive Committee
Chris Hendrix, 1st Vice Chair, Executive Committee
Pierre Koshakji, 2nd Vice Chair, Executive Committee
Craig Goodman, President
Harry Warren, Chair Emeriti

17184 North American Farmers' Direct Marketing Association
62 White Loaf Road
Southampton, MA 1073
Fax: 413-233-4285; www.farmersinspired.com
Social Media: Facebook, Twitter, Pinterest, YouTube
Cynthia Chiles, President/ Chair
Charlie Touchette, Executive Director
Becky Walters, VP of Membership
Ben Beaver, VP of Education
Mike Dunn, Treasurer/ Finance Team Chair

17185 Performance Marketing Association
364 East Main St.
Suite 444
Middletown, DE 19709
805-233-7987
thepma.org
Social Media: Facebook, Twitter, LinkedIn, RSS, Google+
Brian Littleton, President
Tony Pantano, Treasurer
Tricia Meyer, Secretary
Todd Crawford, Board Member
Rachel Honoway, Board Member
20000 Members
Founded in: 2008

17186 Petroleum Marketers Association of America
1901 North Fort Myer Drive
Suite 500
Arlington, VA 22209
703-351-8000; *Fax:* 703-351-9160
info@pmaa.org; www.pmaa.org
Social Media: Facebook, Twitter
Grady Gaubert, Chairman
Mike Bailey, Vice Chair
Mark Whitehead, 2nd Vice Chair
Benny Hodges, Brands Division Director
Greg Benson, West Region Chair
Founded in: 1909

17187 Photo Marketing Association International
7918 Jones Branch Drive
Suite 300
McLean, VA 22102
703-665-4416
800-762-9287; *Fax:* 703-506-3266;
www.theimagingalliance.com
Social Media: Facebook, Twitter, LinkedIn
Allen Showalter, President
Robert L. Hanson, Vice President
Jim Esp, Executive Director/Secretary
Bill Eklund, Treasurer
18000 Members
Founded in: 1924

17188 Power Marketing Association
www.powermarketers.com
Ralph E. Beaty III, Membership/Communications Manager
Carol Ofiesh, Member Services Manager
Phil Ofiesh, Data Services Manager
Scott Spiewak, Publisher

17189 Private Label Manufacturers Association
630 Third Avenue
New York, NY 10017-6770
212-972-3131; *Fax:* 212-983-1382
info@plma.com; www.plma.com
Myra Rosen, Vice President
Brian Sharoff, President
Trade Association promoting the Private Label Industry.
3200+ Members
Founded in: 1979

17190 Produce Marketing Association
1500 Casho Mill Road
Newark, DE 19711
302-738-7100; *Fax:* 302-731-2409;
www.pma.com
Social Media: Facebook, Twitter, Pinterest, Flickr
Cathy Burns, President
Bryan Silbermann, Chief Executive Officer
Tony Parassio, Chief Operating Officer
Yvonne Bull, Chief Financial Officer
Margi Prueitt, Executive Director

17191 Producers Livestock Marketing Association
PO Box 540477
North Salt Lake, UT 84054-0477
801-936-2424
800-791-BEEF
homeoffice@producerslivestock.com;
www.producerslivestock.com
Rick O'Brien, General Manager
Brad Jones, Branch Manager
Bob Elliot, Assistant Branch Manager
Vivian Reed, Office Manager
Founded in: 1935

17192 Professional Insurance Marketing Association
35 E. Wacker Dr
Suite 850
Chicago, IL 60601-2106
817-569-PIMA; *Fax:* 312-644-8557
mona@pima-assn.org; www.pima-assn.org
Social Media: Twitter, LinkedIn
Daniel O'Brien, CLU, President
Mona F. Buckley, MPA, Chief Executive Officer
William Suneson, Secretary
Mark Kelsey, Treasurer
Dave Armstrong, Director
120 Members

17193 Promotion Industry Council
1805 N Mill Street
Naperville, IL 60563-1275
630-369-7781; *Fax:* 630-369-3773
Manufacturers, distributors and users of promotion premiums. Increases understanding of incentives and the premium promotion process.
100 Members
Founded in: 1940

17194 Re:Gender
11 Hanover Square
24th Floor
New York, NY 10005-2819
212-785-7335; *Fax:* 212-785-7350;
www.regender.org
Social Media: Facebook, Twitter, RSS
Lucie Lapovsky, Chair
Aine Duggan, President
Andrea Greenblatt, Vice President of Operations
Debbie Kellogg, Vice President for External Rel
Gail Cooper, Vice President for Programs
A network of 120 leading research, policy and advocacy centers committed to improving the lives of women and girls. Provides the latest news, information and strategies needed to ensure fully informed debates, effective policies and inclusive practices.
3,000 Members
Founded in: 1981

17195 Restaurant Marketing & Delivery Association
3636 Menaul Blvd.
Ste. 323
Albuquerque, NM 87110
E-Mail: membership@rmda.info;
www.rmda.info
Social Media: Facebook, Twitter, LinkedIn
Paul Birrell, President
David Farmer, Vice President
Wes Garrison, Treasurer
Anu Mehra, Convention
Luke Katuin, Technology
Founded in: 1990

17196 Sales and Marketing Executives International
PO Box 1390
Sumas, WA 98295-1390
312-893-0751; *Fax:* 312-893-0751
admin@smei.org; www.smei.org
Social Media: Facebook, Twitter, LinkedIn, Youtube, RSS,Blog
Clinton J. Schroeder MBA, CME, CS, Chairman
Willis Turner CAE CME CSE, President & Chief Executive Officer
Hans-Benno Mastboom, Senior Vice Chair
Antonio Rios-Ramirez, Senior Vice Chair
Nathalie Roemer CME, Secretary Treasurer
Members are most commonly professionals in the fields of sales and marketing management, market research management, sales training, distribution management and other senior executives in small and medium businesses.
10000 Members
Frequency: Annual Meeting (Fall)
Founded in: 1935

17197 Search Engine Marketing Professional Organization
401 Edgewater Pl.
Suite 600
Wakefield, MA 1880
718-876-8866
info@sempo.org; www.sempo.org
Social Media: Facebook, Twitter, LinkedIn, Blogpot, YouTube, Google+,Pint
Mike Grehan, Chair
Mike Gullaksen, President
Simon Heseltine, VP of Education
Marc Engelsman, VP of Research
Krista LaRiviere, VP of Local Group
Founded in: 2002

17198 Society for Marketing Professional Services
123 North Pitt Street
Suite 400
Alexandria, VA 22314
703-549-6117
800-292-7677; *Fax:* 703-549-2498
info@smps.org; www.smps.org
Social Media: Facebook, Twitter, LinkedIn, Youtube,Pinterest
Ronald D. Worth, CAE, FSMPS, CPS, CEO
Lisa Bowman, Senior Vice President
Mark DellaPietra, Vice President of Education
Tina Myers, CAE, Senior Vice President
Michele Santiago, Director of Marketing
Serving marketing and business development professionals employed by architectural, engineering and construction firms, SMPS provides education and networking opportunities tailored to build your bottom line.
5600 Members
Founded in: 1973
Mailing list available for rent: 6000 names at $200 per M

17199 **Society of Independent Gasoline Marketers**
3930 Pender Drive
Suite 340
Fairfax, VA 22030
703-709-7000; *Fax:* 703-709-7007
sigma@sigma.org; www.sigma.org
Tom Gresham, President
Kenneth A. Doyle, CAE, Executive Vice President
Mary Alice Kutyn, Director Meetings
Dennis Cuevas, Director of Education
Mary Alice Kutyn, Director of Meetings
Members are independent gasoline marketers.
270 Members
Founded in: 1958

17200 **Specialty Equipment Market Association**
1575 S. Valley Vista Drive
Diamond Bar, CA 91765-0910
909-610-2030; *Fax:* 909-860-0184
sema@sema.org; www.sema.org
Social Media: Facebook, Twitter, Google+
Dough Evans, Chairman
Christopher J. Kersting, President and CEO
George Afremow, Vice President
Steve McDonald, Vice President of Government Affair
John Kilroy, Vice President/General Manager, PRI
Represents the automotive aftermarket industry with government agencies and trade and consumer groups.
5200 Members
Founded in: 1963

17201 **Sport Marketing Association**
1972 Clark Ave.
Alliance, OH 44601
330-829-8207
smaoffice@mountunion.edu;
www.sportmarketingassociation.com
Social Media: Facebook, Twitter, LinkedIn
Jim Kadlecek, President
Khalid Ballouli, VP of Academic Affairs
Elizabeth Gregg, VP of Student Affairs
Steven McKelvey, VP of Industry Relations
Beth Grupsmith, Social Media Consultant
Founded in: 2002

17202 **Strategic Account Management Association**
10 N. Dearborn St.
2nd Floor
Chicago, IL 60602
312-251-3131; *Fax:* 312-251-3132
napolitano@strategicaccounts.org;
www.strategicaccounts.org
Social Media: Facebook, Twitter, LinkedIn, Pinterest, Google+
Bernard Quancard, President/CEO
Katherine Gotsick, Chief Operations Officer
Frankie Cusimano, Senior Manager, Membership
Matt Fegley, Chief Business Development Officer
Richard Rottsolk, Senior Manager, Corporate Resource
The Strategic Account Management Association is a non-profit organization devoted to developing and promoting the concept of customer-supplier partnering. SAMA is dedicated to the professional and personal development of the executives charged with managing national, global, and strategic account relationships, and to elevating the status of the profession as a whole. SAMA provides literature, training and research into best practices in large, complex, global customer account management.
2000 Members
Founded in: 1964

17203 **Thomson Reuters**
Thomson Reuters
2395 Midway Rd
Carrollton, TX 75006
646-223-4000
888-885-0206; *Fax:* 888-216-1929
trta.lei-support@thomsonreuters.com;
www.tax.thomsonreuters.com
David K R Thomson, Chairman
Thomas H Glocer, CEO & Director
Robert D Daleo, Chief Financial Officer
Kelli Crane, Senior Vice President & CIO
A national organization that focuses on marketing and sales intelligence for top level marketing executives.

17204 **Trade Show Exhibitors Association**
2214 NW 5th St.
Suite 1005
Bend, OR 97701
541-317-8768; *Fax:* 541-317-8749
tsea@tsea.org; www.tsea.org
Social Media: Facebook
Amanda Helgemoe, President
Michael Mulry, Vice President
Glenda Brundgardt, Treasurer
Chris Griffin, Secretary
Members are companies using exhibits for marketing, advertising or public relations.
1800 Members
Founded in: 1966

17205 **Transportation Marketing & Sales Association**
9382 Oak Avenue
Waconia, MN 55387
952-466-6270; www.tmsatoday.org/
Social Media: Facebook, Twitter, LinkedIn, YouTube
David Hoppens, Chairman
Dino Moler, President
Beth Carroll, VP-Administration & Finance
Candi Cybator, VP- Content & Strategy
Andy Williams, VP- Membership & Outreach
Founded in: 1924

17206 **Word of Mouth Marketing Association**
200 East Randolph Street
Suite 5100
Chicago, IL 60601
312-577-7610; *Fax:* 312-275-7687
membership@womma.org; www.womma.org
Social Media: Facebook, Twitter, LinkedIn, YouTube, Google+
Suzanne Fanning, President
Chris Spallino, Director of Marketing
Jennifer Connelly, Events Manager
Chelsea Hickey, Marketing Manager & Editor
The Word of Mouth Association is dedicated to word of mouth and social media marketing. It is the leader in ethical word of mouth marketing practices through eduation including the WOMMA summit, professional marketing opportunities and knowledge sharing.
Founded in: 2004

Newsletters

17207 **Advanced Selling Power**
Thompson Group
6850 Austin Center Blvd
Suite 100
Austin, TX 78731-3201
512-418-8869; *Fax:* 512-418-1209
carol@thompson-group.com;
www.thompson-group.com
Terry E Thompson, Publisher
Valerie A Canaday, Editor
Carol Thompson, President
Provides sales tactics, strategies and ideas to sales professinals and entrepreneurs. Each issue helps salespeople learn how to put together presentations, develop openings that keep customers interested, use testimonials correctly and more.
Cost: $10.00
Circulation: 1000
Founded in: 1993

17208 **Airline Financial News**
Phillips Business Information
1201 Seven Locks Road
Suite 300
Potomac, MD 20854-2931
301-541-1400; *Fax:* 301-309-3847
Grier Graham, Editor
Newsletter that provides the most timely financial reports and market analysis for the entire airline industry.
Cost: $695.00
Frequency: Weekly

17209 **Antin Marketing Letter**
Alan Antin/Antin Marketing Group
19888 Sw Monte Vista Dr
Suite 205
Beaverton, OR 97007-5412
503-356-0504; *Fax:* 913-663-5552;
www.commonsensemarketing.com
Brad Antin, President
Alan Antin, Director of Marketing
William Hammond, Director of Marketing
How-to info on marketing for professionals and entrepreneurs (service businessess, retailers, wholesalers, professional practice).
Cost: $197.00
Frequency: Monthly

17210 **Application Servers and Media Servers**
Probe Research
3 Wing Drive
Suite 240
Cedar Knolls, NJ 07927-1000
973-285-1500; *Fax:* 973-285-1519;
www.proberesearch.com
This bulletin describes the market for both applications and media servers; examines key issues and provides a profile of selected players in various product categories.

17211 **Art of Self Promotion**
Ilise Benun/Creative Marketing and Management
PO Box 23
Hoboken, NJ 07030
201-653-0783
800-737-0783; *Fax:* 201-222-2494
ilise@marketing-mentor.com;
www.artofselfpromotion.com
Lisa Cyr, Author
Ilise Benun, Marketing Manager
Nuts'n bolts for manageable marketing for small business owners and self employed professionals.
Cost: $100.80
8 Pages
Frequency: Quarterly
Founded in: 1995

17212 Association of Incentive Marketing News
Association of Incentive Marketing
1601 North Bond Street, Suite 303
Naperville, IL 60563

603-369-7780; *Fax:* 603-369-3773
karen@incentivemarketing.org;
www.incentivemarketing.org

George Meredith, Editor
Susan Peterson, Director of Membership
Nicole Sweigart, Administrative Director
Paul Cernohous, Director
Karen Renk, Executive Director

Articles cover promotion industry news and Association information and events.
Frequency: Quarterly
Circulation: 300

17213 Auctioneer
National Auctioneers Association
8880 Ballentine
Overland Park, KS 66214

913-541-8084; *Fax:* 913-894-5281
hcombest@auctioneers.org
auctioneers.org

Robert Shively, CEO
Wendy Dellinger, Advertising Manager
Steve Baska, Publications Editor
Ryan Putnam, Assistant Editor

Keeps members of the National Auctioneers Association informed of trends and legal issues related to auctioneering. Chronicles activities of the Association and its membership.
Frequency: Monthly
Circulation: 7000
Founded in: 1948

17214 Automated and Self-Provisioning Servers
Probe Research
3 Wing Drive
Suite 240
Cedar Knolls, NJ 07927-1000

973-285-1500; *Fax:* 973-285-1519;
www.proberesearch.com

A look at service provider implementation of automated and self - provisioning software systems. An explanation of the causes of delay and QoS degradation in IP networks.

17215 BDA
BDA News
900 W Sunset Boulevard
Suite 900
Los Angeles, CA 90069

310-712-0040; *Fax:* 310-712-0039;
www.bda.tv
Jill Masters, VP Member Services
Jim Chabin, President

Newsletter, awards annual, magazine and directory published by BDA for designers in the motion graphics industry.
Cost: $5.00
Frequency: Monthly
Circulation: 2000
Printed in 4 colors on glossy stock

17216 Bandwidth Management: Driving Profitablity to the Botton Line
Probe Research
3 Wing Drive
Suite 240
Cedar Knolls, NJ 07927-1000

973-285-1500; *Fax:* 973-285-1519;
www.proberesearch.com

Provides an analysis of the type of issues that require Bandwidth Management solutions. Makes a comparison of the types of technical solutions implemented in different parts of the network and the major benefits of each solution. Also analyzes the trends seen in IP traffic and inter - relationship with bandwidth management.

17217 Bulletproof Marketing for Small Businesses
Kay Borden/Franklin-Sarrett Publishers
3761 Vinyard Trce Ne
Marietta, GA 30062-5227

770-578-9410; *Fax:* 770-977-5495

Kay Borden, President

Publicity for small businesses, particularly producing news releases that get printed.
Cost: $15.00
Frequency: SemiAnnual
Founded in: 1994

17218 Business Owner
Mailing & Fulfillment Service Association
1421 Prince Street
Suite 410
Alexandria, VA 22314-2806

703-836-9200; *Fax:* 703-548-8204
mfsa-mail@mfsanet.org; www.mfsanet.org
Social Media: Facebook, Twitter, LinkedIn

David L Perkins Jr, Editor
Leo Raymond, Vice President

Developed specifically to communicate with owners and CEOs on issues unique to them. You'll receive a wealth of knowledge on growing your business, tax issues, insurance, estate planning, management, finance and much more.
Frequency: Bi-Monthly

17219 Business-2-Business Marketer
Business Marketing Association
Ste 123
1833 Centre Point Cir
Naperville, IL 60563-4848

630-544-5054; *Fax:* 630-544-5055
info@marketing.org; www.marketing.org
Social Media: Facebook, Twitter, LinkedIn

Jeffrey Hayzlett, Chairman
Gary Slack, Vice Chairman
Bob Goranson CBC, Treasurer

Editorial covers all apsects of integrated marketing disciplines, including: sales management, trade show marketing, datbase and direct mail marketing, presentations, telemarketing, public relations, advertising and electronic marketing.
Cost: $150.00
16 Pages
Circulation: 4300
ISSN: 1073-4538
Founded in: 1922
Printed in 4 colors on glossy stock

17220 Cable & Wireless
Probe Research
3 Wing Drive
Suite 240
Cedar Knolls, NJ 07927-1000

973-285-1500; *Fax:* 973-285-1519;
www.proberesearch.com

A look at cable & wireless IP infrastructure, how the company is operating it, and how it is managing services on its network.

17221 Cable Headed Equipment Markets Upstarts
Probe Research
3 Wing Drive
Suite 240
Cedar Knolls, NJ 07927-1000

973-285-1500; *Fax:* 973-285-1519;
www.proberesearch.com

This bulletin analyses the CMTS market and the role the equipment plays in the plans of the major cable operators to move towards the goal of full service operators. A market forecast is included and the major players profiled.

17222 Cambridge Reports Trends and Forecasts
Cambridge Reports
955 Massachusetts Ave
Suite 8
Cambridge, MA 02139-3178

617-661-0110; *Fax:* 617-661-3575

Gene Pokorny, Publisher

Key changes in consumer and public opinions.

17223 Career News Update
American Marketing Association
311 S Wacker Dr
Suite 5800
Chicago, IL 60606-6629

312-542-9000
800-262-1150; *Fax:* 312-542-9001;
www.marketingpower.com
Social Media: Facebook, Twitter, LinkedIn, Youtube

Dennis Dunlap, CEO

You'll receive the latest career and hiring advice as well as useful job resources and employment listings.
Frequency: Monthly
Mailing list available for rent

17224 Collegiate Trends
Strategic Marketing
550 N Maple Ave
Suite 102
Ridgewood, NJ 07450-1611

201-612-8100; *Fax:* 201-612-1444
weil@studentmonitor.com;
www.studentmonitor.com

Marketing and media trends for marketers targeting college students.
Cost: $95.00
Frequency: Quarterly
Founded in: 1987

17225 Colloquy
Frequency Marketing
PO Box 610
Milford, OH 45150-0610

513-248-2882; *Fax:* 513-248-2672
info_de@epsilon.com; www.epsilon.com

Bryan Kennedy, President/CEO
Jill Z. McBride, Chief Operating Officer
Catherine Lang, Chief Operating Officer
Paul Dundon, Chief Financial Officer
Jeanette Fitzgerald, General Counsel

Frequency Marketing, is the publisher of the COLLOQUY newsletter and COLLOQUY.com Web site, which are dedicated tot he discrimination of information about analysis of frequency marketing strategies and programs worldwide. COLLOQUY also provides educational and research services on a global basis to the loyalty marketing industry, and offers substantial news, research libraries and program archives to qualified subscribers at COLLOQUY.com.
Frequency: Quarterly
Circulation: 16,000+
Founded in: 1990

17226 Competitive Advantage
Competitive Advantage
PO Box 10828
Portland, OR 97296-0828

503-274-2953; *Fax:* 503-274-4349

Jim Moran, Publisher
Tonya Shrives, Promotional Director

Provides sales, marketing and management tools to make careers and companies more prosperous.
Circulation: 10,000

17227 Conference Board Management Briefing - Marketing
Conference Board
845 3rd Ave
Suite 2
New York, NY 10022-6600

212-759-0900; *Fax:* 212-980-7014
june.shelp@conference-board.org;
www.conference-board.org

Jonathan Spector, CEO

Trends and practices in marketing.
Frequency: Monthly

17228 Creative Marketing Newsletter
Association of Retail Marketing Services
10 Drs James Parker Boulevard
Suite 103
Red Bank, NJ 07701-1500

732-842-5070; *Fax:* 732-219-1938
info@goarms.com; www.goarms.com

Gerri Hopkins, Executive Director
Lisa McCauley, Administrative Director

Retail promotion marketing newsletter for supermarkets, convenience stores, drug chains and suppliers of retail promotions.
Frequency: Quarterly
Printed in 3 colors on matte stock

17229 Creative Selling
Bentley-Hall
120 E Washington St
Suite 913
Syracuse, NY 13202-4003

315-701-0308; *Fax:* 315-471-2138

Contains training material for sales managers and sales training managers.
Cost: $7.00
Circulation: 6,500

17230 Current Global Carrier Market Environment, Global Carrier
Probe Research
3 Wing Drive
Suite 240
Cedar Knolls, NJ 07927-1000

973-285-1500; *Fax:* 973-285-1519;
www.proberesearch.com

Addresses a sweeping review of current strategic, business, economic, financial, network technology, network operations and service portfolio topics now at work in global and international carriage. Also includes a discussion of the potential risk assessment value of existing and future bandwidth trading and arbitrage exchanges.

17231 Current Thinking on Network Evolution and Its Laws
Probe Research
3 Wing Drive
Suite 240
Cedar Knolls, NJ 07927-1000

973-285-1500; *Fax:* 973-285-1519;
www.proberesearch.com

This issue focuses on three laws of network evolution used by new entrants and by vendors. These three laws seem to be justified when the stock market rewarded new entrants with enormous valuations simply based on technology and expensive business plans. Now that the stock market no longer rewards such ventures, an analysis of these three laws is warranted and what impact thay have had on the carrier business.

17232 Customers First
Dartnell Corporation
4660 N Ravenswood Avenue
Chicago, IL 60640-4510

773-907-9500; *Fax:* 773-561-3801

Clark Fetridge, Publisher
Jim Nawrocki, Editor

A practical periodical that provides employees with an organized plan of action for building and improving customer relations.
Cost: $62.00

17233 Daily News E-Mail (3D)
Direct Marketing Association
1120 Avenue of the Americas
New York, NY 10036-6700

212-768-7277; *Fax:* 212-302-6714
customerservice@the-dma.org;
www.the-dma.org

Lawrence M Kimmel, CEO

Delivers the essential news, research, hot trends, and technological developments from the nations leading newspapers, trade publications, and the government all in an easy-to-read, time-saving format.

17234 Dartnell Sales and Marketing Executive Report
Dartnell Corporation
4660 N Ravenswood Avenue
Chicago, IL 60640-4510

773-907-9500
800-341-7874; *Fax:* 773-907-0645
infochicago@insightpd.com;
www.insightpd.com

Craig Scherer, Senior Partner
Anthony Annibale, General Manager
Cost: $168.00
Frequency: Monthly
Founded in: 1917

17235 Data Service: ISDN, Private Lines, Frame Relay and ATM
Probe Research
3 Wing Drive
Suite 240
Cedar Knolls, NJ 07927-1000

973-285-1500; *Fax:* 973-285-1519;
www.proberesearch.com

We survey and highlight four major data transport technologies detailing the technology's strengths, weakness, specific applications, and basic carrier strategies.

17236 Defining the M-Commerce Value Chain
Probe Research
3 Wing Drive
Suite 240
Cedar Knolls, NJ 07927-1000

973-285-1500; *Fax:* 973-285-1519;
www.proberesearch.com

Defines and unifies all participants in a mobile commerce transaction using the sentence Selecting, ordering and paying for items using a mobile device in a secure fashion. Examines the m-commerce business models selected carriers, ASPs and other vendors.

17237 Delaney Report
PRIMEDIA Intertec-Marketing & Professional Service
149 5th Avenue
#725
New York, NY 10010-6801
212-979-7881; *Fax:* 212-979-0691
tdrinfo@aol.com
http://www.delaneyreport.com

Thomas Delaney, Editor

Provides information on personnel changes, trade literature and indsutry events for advertising, media, media, and public relations executives. Reports on global news and developments.
Cost: $74.00

17238 Digital Subscriber Line Access Multiplexer Upstarts
Probe Research
3 Wing Drive
Suite 240
Cedar Knolls, NJ 07927-1000

973-285-1500; *Fax:* 973-285-1519;
www.proberesearch.com

This bulletin examines the major DSALM vendors and forecast the market for DSLAM ports and equipment revenue until 2006.

17239 Downtown Promotion Reporter
Alexander Communications Group
1916 Park Ave
Suite 501
New York, NY 10037-3733

212-281-6099
800-232-4317; *Fax:* 212-283-7269
info@downtowndevelopment.com;
www.downtowndevelopment.com

Romauld Alexander, President
Nadine Harris, Marketing Manager

Tested ideas for promotion, public relations, marketing, increasing business, participation, downtown image building, sales, and events.
Cost: $189.00
Frequency: Monthly
Founded in: 1954

17240 Drop Shippng News
Consolidated Marketing Services
PO Box 7838
New York, NY 10150

212-688-8797; *Fax:* 212-688-8797;
www.cmsassociates.com

Nicholas T Scheel, Editor/Publisher

Covers all facets of Drop Shipping; source directory for 300,000 consumer products. Book 'Drop Shipping' marketing methods.
Cost: $25.00
Frequency: Monthly
Founded in: 1977

17241 Dynamic Selling
Economics Press
12 Daniel Road
Fairfield, NJ 07004-2565

973-227-1224; *Fax:* 973-227-9742

Covers sales issues and ways to improve sales.

17242 Effective Telephone Techniques
Dartnell Corporation
4660 N Ravenswood Avenue
Chicago, IL 60640-4510

773-907-9500; *Fax:* 773-561-3801

Clark Fetridge, Publisher
Kim Anderson, Editor

Training bulletin helps your team build profitable customer relations with every call.
Cost: $62.00

17243 Empoyment Points
Mailing & Fulfillment Service Association
1421 Prince Street
Suite 410
Alexandria, VA 22314-2806

703-836-9200; *Fax:* 703-548-8204
mfsa-mail@mfsanet.org; www.mfsanet.org
Social Media: Facebook, Twitter, LinkedIn

Leo Raymond, Vice President

The content is written for business owners and operators who want to stay informed about current employment issues. The editorial is targeted

on human resource issues and employment practices in the mailing and fulfillment services industry.
Frequency: 4x/Year
Circulation: 2000

17244 Fiberoptics Market Intelligence
KMI Corporation
98 Spit Brook Rd
Suite 400
Nashua, NH 03062-5737

603-243-8100; *Fax:* 603-891-9172;
www.kmiresearch.com

Richard Mack, VP/General Manager
David Janoff, President
Kurt A Ruderman, Analyst/Editor

Markets, technologies, strategic planning, issues, standards and competition in the fiber optics industry.
Cost: $595.00
Frequency: Fortnightly
Founded in: 1974

17245 Frohlinger's Marketing Report
Marketing Strategist Communications
7 Coppel Drive
Tenafly, NJ 07670-2903

201-569-6088; *Fax:* 201-568-8538

Joseph Frohlinger, Editor/Publisher

Global marketing, advertising and media NL with emphasis on strategic and trend articles.
Cost: $200.00
Frequency: Bi-Monthly
Founded in: 1988

17246 Growth Strategies
Growth Strategies
2118 Wilshire Blvd
#826
Santa Monica, CA 90403-5704

310-721-6322; *Fax:* 310-828-0427

Roger Selbert, President

A newsletter published twice a monthly since 1981 has been presciently reporting on economic, social, political, technological, demographic, lifestyle, consumer, business, management, workforce and marketing trends.
Cost: $146.00
Frequency: Monthly
Founded in: 1981
Printed in 2 colors on glossy stock

17247 Guerrilla Marketing International
Cascade Seaview Corporation
PO Box 1336
Mill Valley, CA 94942-1336

415-383-5426; *Fax:* 415-381-8361

William Shear, Publisher

Marketing insights, trends and tips for small business.
Cost: $59.00
8 Pages
Frequency: Bi-Monthly
Founded in: 1989
Printed in one color on glossy stock

17248 Home Business Idea Possibility Newsletter
Prosperity & Profits Unlimited
PO Box 416
Denver, CO 80201-0416

303-573-5564

A Doyle, Editor

Possibilities for home businesses.
Cost: $7.50
4 Pages
Frequency: Annual
Circulation: 1,000
Founded in: 1996
Printed in one color on matte stock

17249 How Long Can Traffic Grow?
Probe Research
3 Wing Drive
Suite 240
Cedar Knolls, NJ 07927-1000

973-285-1500; *Fax:* 973-285-1519;
www.proberesearch.com

Carrier lack of agreement on standard metrics for traffic measurement allows for any interpretation of data, misleads investors and vendors. Optical networking's future depends on a more rational approach to traffic statistics. An assessment of the three drivers for optical networking are discussed.

17250 INFO Marketing Report
Towers Club Press
9170 NW 11th Avenue
Vancouver, WA 98665

360-574-3084

Jerry Buchanan, Editor

Focuses on marketing of HOW TO information in all its many forms: print, audio, video, public speaking, etc.
Cost: $69.95
Frequency: Monthly
Founded in: 1974

17251 Imaging Market Forum
Technology Marketing Corporation
800 Connecticut Ave
1st Floor East
Norwalk, CT 06854-1936

203-852-6800
800-243-6002; *Fax:* 203-866-3326
tmc@tmcnet.com; www.tmcnet.com
Social Media: Twitter

Rich Tehrani, CEO

Case studies and opinions.

17252 Incentive Marketing Association - Fast Take Newsletter
Incentive Marketing Association
4248 Park Glen Road
Minneapolis, MN 55416

952-928-4649
info@incentivemarketing.org;
www.incentivemarketing.org

Provides members with news and updates on association activities

17253 Infomercial Marketing Report
Steven Dworman and Associates
11533 Thurston Circle
Los Angeles, CA 90049-2426

310-472-6360

Steve Dworman, Editor/Publisher

Insider information on the infomercial industry.
Cost: $395.00
Frequency: Monthly

17254 Information Advisor
Information Today
143 Old Marlton Pike
Medford, NJ 08055-8750

609-654-6266
800-300-9868; *Fax:* 609-654-4309
custserv@infotoday.com; www.infotoday.com

Thomas H Hogan, President
Roger R Bilboul, Chairman Of The Board

Provides comprehensive evlauation of research tools, timely and specific information you will use, new sources valuable to researchers and head to head analysis of the most popular information services.
Cost: $165.00
Frequency: Monthly
Mailing list available for rent

17255 International Marketing Service Newsletter
IDG Communications
375 Cochituate Road
#9171
Framingham, MA 01701-4653
Frank Cutitta, Publisher

This newsletter concentrates on the overseas advertising and marketing industry.

17256 International Product Alert
Marketing Intelligence Service
482 N Main St
Canandaigua, NY 14424-1049

585-374-6326
800-836-5710; *Fax:* 585-374-5217;
www.productscan.com

Tom Vierhile, Editor

Reports product introductions from Europe, Asia and throughout the world.
Cost: $795.00
Frequency: Fortnightly
Founded in: 1983

17257 JonesReport
PO Box 50038
Indianapolis, IN 46250-7830

317-576-9889
800-878-9024; *Fax:* 317-576-0441
ctrmktg@jonesreport.com;
www.jonesreport.com

William Willburn, Publisher/President
William Willburn, Editor
Lue Dyar, Circulation Manager

Monthly newsletter for shopping center marketing professionals. Free Resource Guide in September. Salary Survey results in December. Christmas planner issues in April. STEALable marketing ideas in every issue. Sample copies are available.
Cost: $145.00
16 Pages
Frequency: Monthly
Circulation: 1000
Founded in: 1980
Mailing list available for rent: 6M names at $110 per M
Printed in 2 colors on matte stock

17258 Levin's Public Relations Report
Levin Public Relations & Marketing
2 East Ave
Suite 201
Larchmont, NY 10538-2419

914-834-2570; *Fax:* 914-834-5919;
www.saralevin.com

Sara B Levin, President
Sylvia Moss, Editor

Strategies, tactics for the CEO, VP Sales and Marketing seeking new marketing/public relations effectiveness.
Cost: $29.00
Frequency: Quarterly
Founded in: 1978

17259 Licensing Journal
PO Box 1169
Stamford, CT 06904-1169

203-358-0848

Charles Grimes, Publisher

A publication directed to leaders in the Intellectual Property, Technology and Entertainment

Communities. Accepts advertising.
Cost: $150.00
23 Pages
Frequency: Annual
Circulation: 1,000

17260 Licensing Letter
EPM Communications
19 W. 21st St., #303
New York, NY 10010
212-941-0099
888-852-9467; *Fax:* 212-941-1622
info@epmcom.com; www.epmcom.com
Ira Mayer, President
Michele Khan, Marketing
Contains features on licensed properties, market trends and survey analysis.
Cost: $467.00
Frequency: 22x Year
Founded in: 1977

17261 Long Haul Market
Probe Research
3 Wing Drive
Suite 240
Cedar Knolls, NJ 07927-1000
973-285-1500; *Fax:* 973-285-1519;
www.proberesearch.com
In this report, we take a look into the long haul market space and discuss some of the reasons - supply, demand and the resulting prices - that have reversed these service providers fortunes so dramatically over the past year or so. We also discuss long haul product lines, new networking technology and provide a table comparing market participants for convenient reference.

17262 M-Commerce Security
Probe Research
3 Wing Drive
Suite 240
Cedar Knolls, NJ 07927-1000
973-285-1500; *Fax:* 973-285-1519;
www.proberesearch.com
In this bulletin, we examine the issue of security in the m-commerce transaction and the technologies that are appering to address it. We also create international m-commerce forecasts by region.

17263 Mainly Marketing
Schoonmaker Associates
30150 Telegraph Road
Suite 155
Bringham Farms, MI 48025
248-594-7800; *Fax:* 866-211-5711;
www.mainlymkt.com
WK Schoonmaker, Publisher
Marketing high technology products.

17264 Make It Happen
Action Marketing
3747 NE Sandy Boulevard
Portland, OR 97232-1840
503-287-8321; *Fax:* 503-282-2980
CE Colwell, Publisher
Marketing news for starting a business and marketing products.

17265 Market: Africa/Mid-East
PRS Group
6320 Fly Rd
Suite 102
East Syracuse, NY 13057-9792
315-431-0511; *Fax:* 315-431-0200
custserv@prsgroup.com; www.prsgroup.com
Mary Lou Walsh, President
Patti Davis, Chairman
Ben McTernan, Managing Editor
Patty Redhead, Production Manager
Demographic and lifestyle information about consumers in Africa and the Middle East.
Cost: $397.00
Frequency: Monthly
Founded in: 1979

17266 Market: Asia Pacific
PRS Group
6320 Fly Rd
Suite 102
East Syracuse, NY 13057-9792
315-431-0511; *Fax:* 315-431-0200
custserv@prsgroup.com; www.prsgroup.com
Mary Lou Walsh, President
Patti Davis, Chairman
Ben McTernan, Managing Editor
Patty Redhead, Production Manager
Population and lifestyle trend information about consumers in the Asia-Pacific region.
Cost: $397.00
Frequency: Monthly
Circulation: 225
Founded in: 1979
Printed in 2 colors on matte stock

17267 Market: Latin America
PRS Group
6320 Fly Rd
Suite 102
East Syracuse, NY 13057-9792
315-431-0511; *Fax:* 315-431-0200
custserv@prsgroup.com; www.prsgroup.com
Mary Lou Walsh, President
Patti Davis, Chairman
Ben McTernan, Managing Editor
Patty Redhead, Production Manager
Population and lifestyle trend information about consumers in the Latin America region.
Frequency: Monthly
Founded in: 1979

17268 Marketing Academics Newsletter
American Marketing Association
311 S Wacker Dr
Suite 5800
Chicago, IL 60606-6629
312-542-9000
800-262-1150; *Fax:* 312-542-9001;
www.marketingpower.com
Social Media: Facebook, Twitter, LinkedIn, Youtube
Dennis Dunlap, CEO
This newsletter provides news and information that affect and inform this important constituency. It reviews Academic Council activities, profiles Academic SIGS and highlights upcoming events.
Mailing list available for rent

17269 Marketing Communications Report
14629 SW 104 Street
#272
Miami, FL 33186-4929
305-595-0063; *Fax:* 305-595-0380
Pete Silver, Editor
Highlights prevalent thoughts on successful marketing strategies and reviews new products.
Frequency: Monthly

17270 Marketing Dynamics
Recognition Technologies Users Association
10 High Street
Suite 630
Boston, MA 02110-1605
Fax: 617-426-8911
Franklin Cooper, Publisher
Focuses on strategic marketing and planning in technology and industrial areas including technology commercialization. Also features articles on government programs and how to participate in them. International market and business development also are featured.
Cost: $120.00
Frequency: Bi-Monthly
Circulation: 5,000
Printed in 2 colors on glossy stock

17271 Marketing Insights
WPI Communications
55 Morris Ave
Suite 300
Springfield, NJ 07081-1422
973-467-8700
800-323-4995; *Fax:* 973-467-0368
info@wpicomm.com; www.wpicomm.com
Steve Klinghoffer, President
Marilyn Lang, Chairman
Founded in: 1952

17272 Marketing Library Services
Information Today
143 Old Marlton Pike
Medford, NJ 08055-8750
609-654-6266
800-300-9868; *Fax:* 609-654-4309
custserv@infotoday.com; www.infotoday.com
Thomas H Hogan, President
Roger R Bilboul, Chairman Of The Board
Provides information professional in all types of libraries with specfic ideas for marketing their services.
Cost: $79.95
Frequency: Bi Monthly
ISSN: 0896-3908
Mailing list available for rent

17273 Marketing Matters Newsletter
American Marketing Association
311 S Wacker Dr
Suite 5800
Chicago, IL 60606-6629
312-542-9000
800-262-1150; *Fax:* 312-542-9001;
www.marketingpower.com
Social Media: Facebook, Twitter, LinkedIn, Youtube
Dennis Dunlap, CEO
This e-newsletter updates readers on the latest happenings in the marketing profession through news briefs, indepth features and interviews
Frequency: 2x/Monthly
Mailing list available for rent

17274 Marketing Power Newsletter
American Marketing Association
311 S Wacker Dr
Suite 5800
Chicago, IL 60606-6629
312-542-9000
800-262-1150; *Fax:* 312-542-9001;
www.marketingpower.com
Social Media: Facebook, Twitter, LinkedIn, Youtube
Dennis Dunlap, CEO
This update of the latest news, research and trends in the marketing industry and allied fields.
Frequency: Weekly
Mailing list available for rent

17275 Marketing Pulse
Unlimited Positive Communications
11 N Chestnut Street
New Paltz, NY 12561-1706
845-565-0615; *Fax:* 845-255-2231
Bill Harvey, Editor/Publisher

Focus on all aspects of new electronic media, advertising, entertainment, and marketing.
Cost: $300.00
Frequency: Monthly
Founded in: 1979

17276 **Marketing Report**
Progressive Business Publications
PO Box 3019
Malvern, PA 19355-0719

610-695-0201
800-220-5000; *Fax:* 610-647-8098
customer_service@pbp.com; www.pbp.com

Ed Satell, CEO
Christine Wheeler, Marketing Manager
Cost: $264.00
8 Pages
Founded in: 1989

17277 **Marketing Researchers Newsletter**
American Marketing Association
311 S Wacker Dr
Suite 5800
Chicago, IL 60606-6629

312-542-9000
800-262-1150; *Fax:* 312-542-9001;
www.marketingpower.com
Social Media: Facebook, Twitter, LinkedIn, Youtube

Dennis Dunlap, CEO

This e-newsletter provides members with content designed to educate and inform researchers or any member interested in marketing research topics.
Mailing list available for rent

17278 **Marketing Science Institute Newsletter**
Marketing Science Institute
1000 Massachusetts Ave
Suite 1
Cambridge, MA 02138-5379

617-491-2060; *Fax:* 617-491-2065
msi@msi.org; www.msi.org

Russ Winer, Executive Director
Leana McAlister, CEO

Focuses on people and events of MSI.
Circulation: 8000
Founded in: 1968

17279 **Marketing Technology**
Zhivago Marketing Partners
381 Seaside Dr
Jamestown, RI 02835-2376

401-423-2400; *Fax:* 401-423-2700
kristin@zhivago.com; www.zhivago.com

Kristin Zhivago, President
Philip Zhivago, CEO
Thomas Baker, Owner

Solutions to internal political problems encountered by high-tech marketers, critiques marketing campaigns, and discuss what's working.
Cost: $269.00
Frequency: Monthly
Founded in: 1970

17280 **Marketing Thought Leaders Newsletter**
American Marketing Association
311 S Wacker Dr
Suite 5800
Chicago, IL 60606-6629

312-542-9000
800-262-1150; *Fax:* 312-542-9001;
www.marketingpower.com
Social Media: Facebook, Twitter, LinkedIn, Youtube

Dennis Dunlap, CEO

These articles focus on the issues and concepts that shape marketing today and tomorrow.
Frequency: Monthly
Mailing list available for rent

17281 **Marketing to Emerging Minorities**
EPM Communications
19 W. 21st St., #303
New York, NY 10010

212-941-0099
888-852-9467; *Fax:* 212-941-1622
info@epmcom.com; www.epmcom.com

Ira Mayer, President
Michele Khan, Marketing
Melanie Shreffler, Editor

Research, trends and lifestyle coverage of minority markets.
Cost: $377.00
Frequency: Monthly

17282 **Marketscan International**
Miller Freeman Publications
2655 Seely Avenue
San Jose, CA 95134

408-943-1234; *Fax:* 408-943-0513

Paul W Kelash, Editor/Publisher

PC and Networking news in Europe, Asia, and Latin America.
Cost: $395.00
Frequency: Monthly
Founded in: 1987

17283 **Master Salesmanship**
Clement Communications
10 LaCrue Avenue
PO Box 36
Concordville, PA 19331

610-459-4200
888-358-5858; *Fax:* 610-459-4582
customerservice@clement.com;
www.clement.com

Andrew B Clancy, Managing Editor
George Clement, President

Newsletter for professional salespeople.
Cost: $156.00
Founded in: 1919

17284 **Meditation Software Market**
Probe Research
3 Wing Drive
Suite 240
Cedar Knolls, NJ 07927-1000

973-285-1500; *Fax:* 973-285-1519;
www.proberesearch.com

Examines the mediation market, the major and niche players, functionality of the solutions, and service provider deployments.

17285 **Multimedia Strategist**
Leader Publications
345 Park Avenue S
New York, NY 10010-1707

212-779-9200
800-888-8300; *Fax:* 212-696-1848
reprintscustomerservice@alm.com;
www.alm.com

Stuart M Wise, Editor
Kerry Kyle, Circulation Director
William L Pollak, CEO/President
Aric Press, Editorial Director
Kevin Vermeulen, Vice President, Group Publisher
Cost: $175.00
Frequency: Monthly
ISSN: 1080-3904
Founded in: 1997

17286 **New Account Selling**
Dartnell Corporation
4660 N Ravenswood Avenue
Chicago, IL 60640-4510

773-907-9500; *Fax:* 773-561-3801

Clark Fetridge, Publisher
Terry Breen, Editor

Timely and effective techniques for building sales and improving profits. Instructive series ideal for training new sales people and for increasing the productivity of your sales veterans.
Cost: $62.00

17287 **New Age Marketing Opportunities Newsletter**
New Editions International
PO Box 2578
Sedona, AZ 86339-2578

928-282-9574
800-777-4751; *Fax:* 928-282-9730;
www.newagemarket.com

Sophia Tarila PhD, Production Manager

Focuses on issues dealing with good marketing buys, resources and pertinent marketing programs dealing in the historic, visionary marketplace.
Cost: $24.00
4 Pages
Frequency: Bi-Monthly
Circulation: 450
Mailing list available for rent
Printed in one color on matte stock

17288 **Next Genaration IAD for SOHO Markets**
Probe Research
3 Wing Drive
Suite 240
Cedar Knolls, NJ 07927-1000

973-285-1500; *Fax:* 973-285-1519;
www.proberesearch.com

Examines the market for VoDSL - comapatible Integrated Access Devices (IAD) targeted toward SOHO customers. Identifies key issues associated with development, analyzes competitive dynamics and market requirements and reviews selected vendor products.

17289 **On The Move**
Transportation Marketing Communications Assoc
9382 Oak Avenue
Waconia, MN 55387

952-442-5638; *Fax:* 952-442-3941;
www.tmcatoday.org

John Ferguson, President
Tom Nightingale, VP
Tracy Robinson, Treasurer
Edward Moritz, Secretary
Brian Everett, Executive Director

Provides regular feature articles on ways to effectively create more impact in transportation marketing, sales and communications strategies.

17290 **Online Marketing Letter**
Cyberware Media
1005 Terminal Way
Suite 110
Reno, NV 89502

808-874-0089; www.cyberware.com

Jonathan Mizel, Editor/Publisher

Reviews the marketing of products and services over commercial online services of the internet.
Cost: $195.00
Frequency: Quarterly
Founded in: 1993

17291 **Online Marketplace**
Jupiter Communications Company

627 Broadway
2nd Floor
New York, NY 10012-2612

212-533-8885; *Fax:* 212-780-6075

Adam Schoenfeld, Editor
Gene DeRose, Publisher

Interactive transaction.
Cost: $545.00
Frequency: Monthly

17292 **Organized Executive**
Briefings Publishing Group
1101 King St
Suite 110
Alexandria, VA 22314-2944

703-548-3800
800-722-9221; *Fax:* 703-684-2136;
www.briefings.com

Stephanie Winston, Editor-in-Chief
Lois Willingham, Production Manager

A publication designed to help busy people more effectively master their activities and time by applying advanced organizational strategies developed by Stephanie Winston.
Cost: $97.00
8 Pages
Frequency: Monthly
Circulation: 30000
Founded in: 1981
Mailing list available for rent: 6000 names at $125 per M
Printed in 2 colors on matte stock

17293 **Overcoming Objections**
Dartnell Corporation
4660 N Ravenswood Avenue
Chicago, IL 60640-4510

773-907-9500; *Fax:* 773-561-3801

Clark Fetridge, Publisher
Christen Heide, Editor

Designed to give sales team practical responses to every objection they're likely to face and imparts proven techniques for turning every type of sales objection into a sales opportunity.
Cost: $62.00

17294 **Perspectives**
1375 King Avenue
PO 12279
Columbus, OH 43212-2220

614-486-6708
800-448-0398; *Fax:* 614-486-1819
service@mark-ed.com; www.mark-ed.org

J Gleason, President
Mary Carlisi, Production Manager

Information on education and marketing. Provides professional support and materials. Primary clients are schools, colleges and educational institutions.
Cost: $25.00
Circulation: 7500
Founded in: 1971
Printed in 4 colors on matte stock

17295 **Photo Marketing**
Photo Marketing Association International
3000 Picture Pl
Jackson, MI 49201-8853

517-788-8100; *Fax:* 517-788-8371;
www.theimagingalliance.com

Ted Fox, CEO
Terri Cameron, Publisher
Cost: $30.00
Frequency: Monthly
Founded in: 1980

17296 **PostScripts**
Mailing & Fulfillment Service Association
1421 Prince Street
Suite 410
Alexandria, VA 22314-2806

703-836-9200; *Fax:* 703-548-8204
mfsa-mail@mfsanet.org; www.mfsanet.org
Social Media: Facebook, Twitter, LinkedIn

Leo Raymond, Editor
Leo Raymond, Vice President

Each issue of PostScripts highlights a theme relevant to mailing or fulfillment operations, such as production management or information technology.
Frequency: 18x/Year
Circulation: 2800

17297 **Postal Points**
Mailing & Fulfillment Service Association
1421 Prince Street
Suite 410
Alexandria, VA 22314-2806

703-836-9200; *Fax:* 703-548-8204
mfsa-mail@mfsanet.org; www.mfsanet.org
Social Media: Facebook, Twitter, LinkedIn

Leo Raymond, Editor
Leo Raymond, Vice President

Deals exclusively with current and pending postal and delivery issues. Here you will find the facts and analysis of developing postal issues.
Frequency: 18x/Year

17298 **Premium Marketing Club of New York**
Association of Retail Marketing Services
10 Drs James Parker Boulevard
Suite 103
Red Bank, NJ 07701-1500

732-842-5070; *Fax:* 732-219-1938;
www.goarms.com

Gerri Hopkins, Executive Director
Lisa McCauley, Administrative Director

Provides education and networking information.
Frequency: 10 per year
Founded in: 1930
Printed in one color

17299 **Pricing Advisor**
Pricing Advisor
3535 Roswell Rd
Suite 59
Marietta, GA 30062-8828

770-509-9933; *Fax:* 770-509-1963
info@pricingsociety.com;
www.pricingsociety.com

Eric Mitchell, President
Michelle Darko, Editor
Sobem Nwoko, COO

Pricing strategy and tactics for marketing and corporate executives.
Cost: $400.00
8 Pages
Frequency: Monthly

17300 **Product Alert**
Marketing Intelligence Service
482 N Main St
Canandaigua, NY 14424-1049

585-374-6326
800-836-5710; *Fax:* 585-374-5217;
www.productscan.com

Christine Dengler, Marketing Manager
Tom Vierhile, CEO
Diane Beach, Editor

A twice-monthly briefing on new packaged goods introduced in North America. Featuring product pictures and descriptions with indexing provided in two convenient formats. Also available in a twice monthly, international version.
Cost: $795.00

17301 **Promos & Premiums**
New World Media
PO Box 95
Newton Centre, MA 02156

781-483-8967; *Fax:* 617-367-9151

Jennifer Sawyer English, Editor/Publisher
Barbara Kalunian, Publisher

Informs consumers, collectors, dealers, and marketing executives about the best special offers available nationwide.
Cost: $19.95
Frequency: Monthly
Founded in: 1994

17302 **Research Alert**
EPM Communications
19 W. 21st St., #303
New York, NY 10010

212-941-0099
888-852-9467; *Fax:* 212-941-1622
info@epmcom.com; www.epmcom.com

Ira Mayer, President
Michele Khan, Marketing
Melanie Shreffler, Editor

Analyzes research on consumer behavior and attitudes.
Cost: $389.00
Frequency: 24x Year

17303 **Revisiting R&D**
Probe Research
3 Wing Drive
Suite 240
Cedar Knolls, NJ 07927-1000

973-285-1500; *Fax:* 973-285-1519;
www.proberesearch.com

With the collapse of the bull market and the apparent collapse of viable wireline competition, the ILECs must focus on the role of wireless as a major competitor. The new Bush administration appears to be pro-ILEC and this will translate into a series of reglatory initiatives that may in total favor the ILECs R&D agendas have to shift to support innovative solutions in the access domain and in mobile.

17304 **Roper's Public Pulse**
Roper Starch Worldwide
29 W 35th Street
5th Floor
New York, NY 10001-2299

212-240-5300; *Fax:* 212-564-0465
dcrispell@roper.com; www.roper.com

Diane Crispell, Editor

Content includes the latest research on demographic trends, new insights from opinion research experts as to what Americans think, concise, brand-focused data, current consumer attitudes toward dozens of American themes, as well as news updates on special markets and brands.
Cost: $299.00
Frequency: Monthly
Circulation: 2000

17305 **SBC**
Probe Research
3 Wing Drive
Suite 240
Cedar Knolls, NJ 07927-1000

973-285-1500; *Fax:* 973-285-1519;
www.proberesearch.com

Discussion and analysis of ILEC/vendor market dynamics; case study of SBC's metro optical architecture; technology evolution; new services offered; incorporation of passive optical networking and metro DWDM rollouts; strategy going forward.

17306 Sales Bullet
Economics Press
12 Daniel Road
Fairfield, NJ 07004-2565

973-227-1224; *Fax:* 973-227-9742

Robert Guder, Editor
Diane Cody, Promotional Director

Covers the fundamental and subtleties of professional selling with methods, principles and ideas all salespoeple will find useful.
Circulation: 9,000

17307 Sales Manager's Bulletin
Bureau of Business Practice
76 Ninth Avenue
7th Floor
New York, NY 10011

212-771-0600; *Fax:* 212-771-0885;
www.aspenlawschool.com

Robert Becker, CEO
Gustavo Dobles, VP Operations

For front-line sales management. Focus on sales hiring, training, managing, motivation, results. Reports what people in sales management field are doing to produce measurable sales profits.
Cost: $9.00
Circulation: 4,290

17308 Sales Productivity Review
Penoyer Communications
PO Box 2509
Santa Clara, CA 95055-2509

408-248-5458
800-248-5458; *Fax:* 408-296-6917
info@penoyer.com; www.penoyer.com

Flyn Penoyer, President

Edited for sales management with an editorial focus that will assist in improving sales productivity and effectiveness.
Cost: $5.00
Frequency: 6 issues per ye

17309 Sales Promotion Monitor
Commerce Communications
418 N 3rd Street
Suite 303
Milwaukee, WI 55410-2444

414-225-9085; *Fax:* 414-225-9095
tom@com-broker.com; www.com-broker.com

K Sederberg, Publisher
Tom Millitzer, Contact

News and information concerning all aspects of sales promotion.

17310 Sales Rep's Advisor
Alexander Communications Group
1916 Park Ave
Suite 501
New York, NY 10037-3733

212-281-6099
800-232-4317; *Fax:* 212-283-7269
info@repsadvisor.com; www.repsadvisor.com

Romauld Alexander, President
Bill Keenan, Editor
Adam Reis, Marketing

For independent manufacturers sales representatives. Filled with concise advice and ideas for reducing costs and increasing profits.
Cost: $199.00
Frequency: Monthly
ISSN: 0278-5048
Founded in: 1954

17311 Sarah Stambler's E-Tactics Letter
E-Tactics
370 Central Park W
#210
New York, NY 10025-6517

212-222-1713; *Fax:* 212-678-6357
info@e-tactics.com; www.e-tactics.com

Sarah Stambler, President
Shlomo Bar-Ayal, Circulation Manager

Publication devoted to the creative use of electronic alternative media in the design and implementation of customer driven marketing, research and publication strategies.
Circulation: 5000
ISSN: 1070-809X
Founded in: 1984

17312 School Marketing Newsletter
School Market Research Institute
1721 Saybrook Road
PO Box 10
Haddam, CT 06438

860-345-8183
800-838-3444; *Fax:* 860-345-3985;
www.school-market.com

Bob Stimolo, Publisher
Lynn Stimolo, Account Executive
Sally Chittenden, Account Executive

How to articles, trends, original research, interviews with experts on school marketing Pre-K - 12th.
Cost: $119.00
12 Pages
Frequency: Monthly
Circulation: 500
ISSN: 0882-701X
Founded in: 1980
Printed in one color on matte stock

17313 Selling Advantage
Progressive Business Publications
PO Box 3019
Malvern, PA 19355-0719

610-695-0201
800-220-5000; *Fax:* 610-647-8098
webmaster@pbp.com; www.pbp.com

Ed Satell, CEO
Phillip Ahr, Editor

Business-to-business sales advice to assist sales staff and sales managers.
Cost: $94.56
Circulation: 60,000
Founded in: 1989

17314 Selling To Kids
Phillips Publishing
PO Box 611130
Potomac, MD 20859-2931

301-208-6787; *Fax:* 301-340-1451;
www.phillips.com/cgi/catalog/info?m2k

Angela Duff, Associate Publisher

Editorial offers news and practical advice on strategies in successful marketing. Includes information on market research, buying trends, and media opportunities and features news on conferences as well as a look at new products and services.
Cost: $495.00
Frequency: BiWeekly

17315 Selling to Seniors
CD Publications
8204 Fenton St
Silver Spring, MD 20910-4571

301-588-6380
800-666-6380; *Fax:* 301-588-6385
info@cdpublications.com;
www.cdpublications.com

Michael Gerecht, President
Jean Van Ryzin, Editor

Published as a subscriber driven newsletter targeting marketers and advertisers of products and services for the mature market.
Cost: $294.00
Frequency: Monthly
Founded in: 1961
Mailing list available for rent: 2,000 names at $160 per M

17316 Service Level Agreements
Probe Research
3 Wing Drive
Suite 240
Cedar Knolls, NJ 07927-1000

973-285-1500; *Fax:* 973-285-1519;
www.proberesearch.com

Details service level agreements that are being offered by several major service providers, and examines many of the popular software solutions taht are being used in their networks. Also a briefly discusses XML, and its potential uses.

17317 Siedlecki on Marketing
Richard Siedlecki Business & Marketing
4767 Lake Forrest Drive NE
Atlanta, GA 30342-2539

770-436-8271; *Fax:* 403-303-9939

Richard Siedlecki, Editor

Tips, techniques, and insights on marketing.
Cost: $49.00
6 Pages
Frequency: BiWeekly
Circulation: 500
Printed in one color on matte stock

17318 Strategic Health Care Marketing
Health Care Communications
11 Heritage Lane
PO Box 594
Rye, NY 10580-594

914-967-6741; *Fax:* 914-967-3054
healthcomm@aol.com;
www.strategichealthcare.com

Michele von Dambrowski, Editor/Publisher
Michele von Dambrowski, CEO

Business development and marketing startegies for health care executives.
Cost: $279.00
12 Pages
Frequency: Monthly
Circulation: 1200
Founded in: 1984
Printed in 2 colors on matte stock

17319 Subscribe
PO Box 194
Bryn Mawr, PA 19010-0194
Lynn Kerrigan, Editor
Gail Jennings, Administration

A newsletter offering marketing ideas to help gain new subscribers and retain old ones.
Cost: $49.00
Frequency: Quarterly

17320 Successful Closing Techniques
Dartnell Corporation
4660 N Ravenswood Avenue
Chicago, IL 60640-4510
773-907-9500; *Fax:* 773-561-3801

Clark Fetridge, Publisher
Terry Breen, Editor

Fail-safe techniques for acquiring bigger sales and more frequent closings.
Cost: $62.00

17321 Target Market News
Target Market News
228 S Wabash Ave
Suite 210
Chicago, IL 60604-2383

312-408-1881; *Fax:* 312-408-1867
TargetMarketNews@aol.com;

www.targetmarketnews.com
Social Media: Facebook, Twitter

Ken Smikle, President
Hallie Mummert, Editor

News and developments in the areas of black consumer marketing and black-oriented media.
Cost: $40.00
12 Pages
Frequency: Monthly
Founded in: 1988

17322 Trends Journal
Trends Research Institute
P.O.Box 3476
Kingston, NY 12402-3476

845-876-6700; *Fax:* 845-758-5252;
www.trendsresearch.com

Gerald Celente, Editor
Emily Arter, Manager

Offers the inside track on trends affecting your business, your profession, your life. Forecasts on over 300 trend categories - consumer, social, economic, political, media, health, family, education, and other domestic and international trends.
Cost: $185.00
Frequency: Quarterly
Founded in: 1980
Printed in 2 colors on glossy stock

17323 Upline
MLM Publishing
106 W South Street
Charlottesvle, VA 22902-5039

Fax: 434-979-1602

John Milton Fogg, Editor
Randolph Byrd, Publisher

Distribution training for network (multilevel) marketers.
Founded in: 1990

17324 Video Marketing Newsletter
Outback Group Productions
PO Box 872
Harrison, AR 72602-0872

Fax: 870-741-4727

Dan Reynolds, Editor/Publisher

Information, business opportunities, marketing tips, product reviews. For people interested in producing and marketing their own videos.
Cost: $185.00
Frequency: Monhtly
Founded in: 1989

17325 What's Working in Sales Management
Progressive Business Publications
PO Box 3019
Malvern, PA 19355-0719

610-695-0201
800-220-5000; *Fax:* 610-647-8098
webmaster@pbp.com; www.pbp.com

Ed Satell, CEO
Richard Kern, Editor

Sales management news and issues.
Cost: $264.00
Founded in: 1989

17326 Youth Markets Alert
EPM Communications
19 W. 21st St., #303
New York, NY 10010

212-941-0099
888-852-9467; *Fax:* 212-941-1622
info@epmcom.com; www.epmcom.com

Ira Mayer, President
Michele Khan, Marketing
Larissa Faw, Editor

Research reports on trends in youth response to marketing techniques and buying.
Cost: $447.00
Frequency: 24x Year

Magazines & Journals

17327 ADCLIP
National Research Bureau
320 Valley St
Burlington, IA 52601-5513

319-752-5415; *Fax:* 319-752-3421
mail@national-research-bureau.com;
www.national-research-bureau.com

Diane M Darnall, President
Nancy Heinzel, Circulation Manager

Individualized adclipping service providing market intelligence information on various retail operations. Includes full size, pages, market strategies, advertising promotion ideas, new store openings and more.

17328 Adage Global
Crain Communications
711 3rd Ave
New York, NY 10017-4014

212-210-0785; *Fax:* 212-210-0200
info@crain.com; www.crain.com

Norm Feldman, President
Scott Donaton, Editor
David Klein, Publisher
Philip Scarano, Circulation Director
Vanessa Reed, Marketing Director

Dedicated to being the world's essential advertising, marketing and media publication, with editors around the world, Adage covers topics of significance form Times Square to Taiwan.
Cost: $69.95
Frequency: Weekly
Circulation: 57,800
Founded in: 1943
Printed in 4 colors

17329 Advertising Age
Ad Age Group/Division of Crain Communications
711 3rd Ave
New York, NY 10017-4014

212-210-0785; *Fax:* 212-210-0465
jbloom@adage.com; www.adage.com

Norm Feldman, President

Editorial insights, exclusive analysis and proprietary data take readers beyond the day's news giving it context helping our audience understand ongoing and emerging trends.
Frequency: Weekly
Circulation: 56650

17330 Adweek
Prometheus Global Media
770 Broadway
New York, NY 10003-9595

212-493-4100; *Fax:* 646-654-5368;
www.prometheusgm.com
Social Media: Facebook, Twitter, RSS

Richard D. Beckman, CEO
James A. Finkelstein, Chairman
Madeline Krakowsky, Vice President Circulation
Tracy Brator, Executive Director Creative Service

Adweek is the source for advertising and agency news, information and opinion. Covering the industry from an agency perspective Adweek focuses on the image makersand those who create the strategy and the ads as well as those who buy the media and handle client relations.
Cost: $149.00
Frequency: Weekly
Circulation: 36032
Founded in: 1978

17331 Agency Sales Magazine
Manufacturers Agents National Association
16-A Journey
Suite 200
Aliso Viejo, CA 92656

949-859-4040
877-626-2776; *Fax:* 949-855-2973
mana@manaonline.org; www.manaonline.org

Jack Foster, Editor

Chronicling the changes which continue to take place nationwide that affect you and your business. Explores the latest tax developments, sales tips, market data, management aids, legal bulletins and more.
96 Pages
Frequency: Monthly
Circulation: 50000
Printed in on glossy stock

17332 Agri Marketing Magazine
Henderson Communications LLC
1422 Elbridge Payne Rd
Suite 250
Chesterfield, MO 63017-8544

636-728-1428; *Fax:* 636-777-4178
info@agrimarketing.com;
www.agrimarketing.com

Lynn Henderson, President

Covers the unique interests of corporate agribusiness executives, their marketing communications agencies, the agricultural media, ag trade associations and other ag related professionals.
Circulation: 8000
Founded in: 1962

17333 AgriSelling Principles and Practices
Henderson Communications LLC
1422 Elbridge Payne Rd
Suite 250
Chesterfield, MO 63017-8544

636-728-1428; *Fax:* 636-777-4178
info@agrimarketing.com;
www.agrimarketing.com

Lynn Henderson, President
Marilyn Holschuh, Editor

This 448-page book is utilized by many major agribusiness corporations and academic institutions for training its sales and marketing staff and or students.

17334 Brand Marketing
Fairchild Publications
7 W 34th St
New York, NY 10001-8100

212-988-2882; *Fax:* 212-630-3868
info@brandmarketingltd.com;
www.brandmarketingltd.com

Richard Faul, Publisher
Mary Berner, President

Covers how manufactureres launch and build brands, and how they leverage brand equity in new ways using new techniques. These ways include partnerships with retailers via trade marketing and information technology and a variety of cost-reduction strategies such as everyday low pricing and efficient consumer response.
Cost: $90.00
Frequency: Monthly
Circulation: 18,543

17335 Brandweek
Prometheus Global Media

770 Broadway
New York, NY 10003-9595

212-493-4100; *Fax:* 646-654-5368;
www.prometheusgm.com

Richard D. Beckman, CEO
James A. Finkelstein, Chairman
Madeline Krakowsky, Vice President Circulation
Tracy Brater, Executive Director Creative Service

Focuses on marketing strategy and services, brand identity, sponsorships, licensing, media usage and distribution and promotions.
Frequency: Weekly
Circulation: 25784
Founded in: 1991

17336 Broker News
Broker Publishing
PO Box 20287
Fountain Hills, AZ 85269-0287

480-816-1400
800-475-3565; *Fax:* 480-836-7767;
www.brokernews-online.com

Joanne Genualdi, Account Executive

Serving insurance producers and financial planners across the country.
Cost: $12.00
32+ Pages
Frequency: Bi-Monthly
Founded in: 1990

17337 BtoB Magazine
Ad Age Group/ Division of Crain Communications
711 3rd Ave
New York, NY 10017-4014

212-210-0785; *Fax:* 212-210-0200
info@crain.com; www.crain.com

Norm Feldman, President

Dedicated to integrated business to business marketing. Every page is packed with substance news, reports, technologies, benchmarks, best practices served up by the most knowledgeable journalists.
Frequency: Monthly
Circulation: 45000

17338 Business Journal
120 W Morehead Street
Suite 200
Charlotte, NC 28202

704-472-2340
800-948-5323; *Fax:* 704-973-1102
borben@bizjournals.com;
www.bizjournals.com/charlotte

Robert Morris, Editor
Megan Foley, Marketing Manager
Jeannie Falknor, Publisher

Provides marketing solutions and caring service.
Cost: $82.00
Frequency: Monthly

17339 CRM Magazine
Information Today
143 Old Marlton Pike
Medford, NJ 08055-8750

609-654-6266
800-300-9868; *Fax:* 609-654-4309
custserv@infotoday.com; www.infotoday.com

Thomas H Hogan, President
Roger R Bilboul, Chairman Of The Board

Offers vital information that will help you benefit from the experience of others in the industry.
Cost: $23.95
Mailing list available for rent: 4M names
Printed in 4 colors on glossy stock

17340 Catalog Success
North American Publishing Company
1500 Spring Garden St
Suite 1200
Philadelphia, PA 19130-4094

215-238-5300; *Fax:* 215-238-5342
phatch@napco.com; www.catalogsuccess.com

Ned S Borowsky, CEO
Matt Griffin, Associate Editor
Peggy Hatch, VP Group Publishing

Putting marketing management to the test.
Frequency: Monthly
Circulation: 20000
ISSN: 1524-2307
Founded in: 1999
Printed in 4 colors

17341 Chamber Executive Magazine
American Chamber of Commerce Executives
4875 Eisenhower Ave
Suite 250
Alexandria, VA 22304-4850

703-998-0072; *Fax:* 703-212-9512
webmaster@acce.org; www.acce.org
Social Media: Facebook, Twitter, LinkedIn

Mick Flemming, President
Frequency: 5X a year

17342 Circulation Management
Primedia
1166 Avenue of the Americas/10th Fl
New York, NY 10036

212-204-4200; *Fax:* 913-514-6895;
www.penton.com

Eric Jacobson, Senior VP
Ron Wall, Chief Officer
Chris Meyer, Director, Corporate Communications

Serves consumer/special interest and business/trade/association publications.
Frequency: Monthly
ISSN: 0888-8191
Founded in: 1986
Printed in 4 colors

17343 Connect
Media-Mark
114 Sansome St
Suite 1224
San Francisco, CA 94104-3803

415-743-6220; *Fax:* 415-421-6225
connect@media-mark.com;
www.media-mark.com

Art Garcia, Publisher

Features report on news-making agencies and corporate departments making news, as well as the people managing them, and rate/review PR services and products. Regular sections also report on international PR/marketing andmedia, women in marketing, investor relations, internet marketing, senior-level moves and promotions, account changes, trends, case studies and industry chatter.

17344 Consumer Goods Technology
Edgell Communications
4 Middlebury Boulevard
Randolph, NJ 07869

973-252-0100; *Fax:* 973-252-9020
cs@e-circ.net;
www.edgellcommunications.com

Gabriele A. Edgell, Chairman & CEO
Joe Skorupa, Editor-in-Chief
Andrew Gaffney, Group Publisher
Gerald Ryerson, President

Consumer Goods Technology serves manufacturers of accessories, shoes, apparel, appliances, consumer electronics, office products, automotive aftermarket products, seasonal merchandise, transporters of consumer products, consultants and others allied to the field.
Frequency: Monthly
Circulation: 25035
Founded in: 1984
Printed in 4 colors on glossy stock

17345 Currents
Council for Advancement & Support of Education
1307 New York Ave Nw
Suite 1000
Washington, DC 20005-4726

202-393-1301; *Fax:* 202-387-4973
memberservicecenter@case.org; www.case.org

John Lippincott, President
Deborah Bongiorno, Editor in chief
Tracy Baird, Marketing
Anne Eigeman, Editor

Offers articles on integrated marketing, technology and other industry related information.
Cost: $115.00
Frequency: Monthly
ISSN: 0748-478X
Founded in: 1975

17346 Customer Interaction Solutions
Technology Marketing Corporation
800 Connecticut Ave
1st Floor East
Norwalk, CT 06854-1936

203-852-6800
800-243-6002; *Fax:* 203-866-3326
tmc@tmcnet.com; www.tmcnet.com
Social Media: Twitter

Rich Tehrani, CEO
Tracey Schelmetic, Editorial Director

Dedicated to teleservices ans e-services outsoucing, marketing and customer relationship management issues.
Frequency: Monthly
Circulation: 13400

17347 CyberDealer
Meister Publishing Company
37733 Euclid Ave
Willoughby, OH 44094-5992

440-942-2000
800-572-7740; *Fax:* 440-975-3447;
www.meisternet.com

Gary Fitzgerald, President

Helps agricultural dealerships better manage their operations.
Frequency: 6 per year

17348 DECA Dimensions
Distributive Education Clubs of America
1908 Association Dr
Suite A
Reston, VA 20191-1594

703-860-5000; *Fax:* 703-860-4013
info@deca.org; www.deca.org

Edward Davis, Executive Director
Cindy Allen, Assistant Director
Christopher Young, Assistant Director

For student members interested in marketing, management, and entrepreneurial careers. Delivered to members in the classroom and integrated into the curriculum. Exhibitors welcome to our national and regional conferences.
Cost: $ 5.00
Circulation: 185,000
ISSN: 1060-6106
Founded in: 1948
Printed in 4 colors

17349 Daily Record
11 E Saratoga St
Baltimore, MD 21202-2199
410-752-3849; *Fax:* 410-752-2894
editor@mddailyrecord.com;
www.mddailyrecord.com
Chris Eddings, Publisher
Mark Chashir, Editor
Susan Hoettner, Marketing
Kris Chardo, Circulation Manager
Cost: $190.00
Frequency: Daily
Circulation: 9000
Founded in: 1888

17350 Dealerscope Merchandising
North American Publishing Company
1500 Spring Garden St
Suite 1200
Philadelphia, PA 19130-4094
215-238-5300
800-818-8174; *Fax:* 215-238-5342;
www.napco.com
Ned S Borowsky, CEO
Eric Schwartz, President
Grant Clauser, Editorial Director
David Dritsas, Editor-in-Chief
Sean Downey, Managing Editor
Offers news on the marketing of appliances and consumer electronics on a national and regional basis.
Frequency: Monthly
Circulation: 20000
Founded in: 1958

17351 Direct
Primedia
3585 Engineering Drive
Suite 100
Norcross, GA 30092
678-421-3000
800-216-1423; *Fax:* 212-206-3622;
www.primedia.com
Jack Condon, Chief Operating Officer
Ray Schultz, Editorial Director
Charles Vietri, Managing Editor
Elizabeth O'Connor, Publisher
Magazine of direct marketing management.
Cost: $85.00
Circulation: 46,527
Founded in: 1989

17352 Do-It-Yourself Retailing
5822 W 74th St
Indianapolis, IN 46278-1756
317-297-1190; *Fax:* 317-328-4354;
www.nrha.org
John Hammond, Executive Director

17353 Exhibitor Magazine
206 S Broadway
Suite 745
Rochester, MN 55903-0368
507-289-6556
888-235-6155; *Fax:* 507-289-5253;
www.exhibitoronline.com
Social Media: Facebook, Twitter, LinkedIn
Lee Knight, President
John Pavek, VP of Publishing
Mission is to provide trade show marketing professionals with the tools and education to produce high-performance programs with measurable results.
Cost: $78.00
Frequency: Monthly
ISSN: 0739-6821

17354 Greenville Magazine
303 Haywood Rd
Greenville, SC 29607-3426
864-271-1105; *Fax:* 864-271-1165;
www.greenvillemagazine.com
Paul Gesimondo, President
Features content summary, web-only extras, advertiser links, and access to reader service forms and various contests and programs.
Frequency: Monthly
Circulation: 10,002

17355 Journal of International Marketing
American Marketing Association
311 S Wacker Dr
Suite 5800
Chicago, IL 60606-6629
312-542-9000
800-262-1150; *Fax:* 312-542-9001;
www.marketingpower.com
Social Media: Facebook, Twitter, LinkedIn, Youtube
Dennis Dunlap, CEO
Presents scholarly and managerially relevant articles on international marketing.
Mailing list available for rent

17356 Journal of Marketing Research
American Marketing Association
311 S Wacker Dr
Suite 5800
Chicago, IL 60606-6629
312-542-9000
800-262-1150; *Fax:* 312-542-9001;
www.marketingpower.com
Social Media: Facebook, Twitter, LinkedIn, Youtube
Dennis Dunlap, CEO
Covers a wide range of marketing research concepts, methods and applications. You'll read about new techniques, contributions to knowledge based on experimental methods and developments in related fields that have a bearing on marketing research.
Mailing list available for rent

17357 Journal of Nonprofit & Public Sector Marketing
Taylor & Francis
325 Chestnut Street
Suite 800
Philadelphia, PA 19106
800-354-1420; *Fax:* 215-625-2940;
www.tandf.co.uk
Gillian Sullivan Mort, Editor
A peer reviewed journal devoted to the study of the adaption of traditional marketing principles for use by nonprofit organizations and government agencies.
Cost: $186.00
Frequency: Quarterly
Circulation: 500
ISSN: 1049-5142
Founded in: 1976

17358 Journal of Public Policy & Marketing
American Marketing Association
311 S Wacker Dr
Suite 5800
Chicago, IL 60606-6629
312-542-9000
800-262-1150; *Fax:* 312-542-9001;
www.marketingpower.com
Social Media: Facebook, Twitter, LinkedIn, Youtube
Dennis Dunlap, CEO
Each issue features a wide ranging forum for the research, findings and discussion of marketing subjects related to business and government.
Mailing list available for rent

17359 Journal of the Academy of Marketing Science
P.O. Box 248012
Coral Gables, FL 33124-8012
305-284-6673; *Fax:* 305-284-3762;
www.ams-web.org
Social Media: Facebook, Twitter, LinkedIn
Harold W. Berkman, Executive Vice President/Director
Adilson Borges, President
Promotes research and the dissemination of research results through the study and improvement of marketing as an economic, ethical and social force.
Cost: $112.00
112 Pages
Frequency: Bi-annually
Circulation: 1100
Founded in: 1965

17360 License Magazine
Advanstar Communications
641 Lexington Ave
Suite 8
New York, NY 10022-4503
212-951-6600; *Fax:* 212-951-6793
sekstract@advanstar.com;
www.licensemag.com
Joseph Loggia, CEO
Tony Lisanti, Editor
Detailed coverage and research on the $177+ billion licensed consumer product business including: retail and merchandising trends; promotional partnerships; available and recently granted property licenses; research reports; and case studies on licensed consumer product categories based on publishing and art, entertainment, brands, sports, fashion, home decor, and interactive media properties
Cost: $59.00
Frequency: Monthly
Circulation: 25000
Founded in: 1998
Printed in 4 colors

17361 Magnet Marketing & Sales
Graham Communications
40 Oval Rd
Suite 2
Quincy, MA 02170-3813
617-328-0069
800-659-0069; *Fax:* 617-471-1504;
www.grahamcomm.com
John R Graham, President
Cynthia Cantrell, Editor
John Graham, CEO
Jonathan Bloom, Marketing manager
A marketing and sales newsletter.
Cost: $18.95
9 Pages
Frequency: Quarterly
Printed in 2 colors on matte stock

17362 Marketing
Mane/Marketing
13901 NE 175th Street
#M
Woodinville, WA 98072-8548
425-487-9111; *Fax:* 425-487-3158
coff@marketings.com
Larry Coffman, Publisher
Features important area events, industry projects, awards and executives of note. Highlights

the latest information on marketing trends and pattern analysis. Free subscription.
Frequency: Monthly
Circulation: 11M

17363 Marketing Health Services
American Marketing Association
311 S Wacker Dr
Suite 5800
Chicago, IL 60606-6629

312-542-9000
800-262-1150; *Fax:* 312-542-9001;
www.marketingpower.com
Social Media: Facebook, Twitter, LinkedIn, Youtube

Dennis Dunlap, CEO

Specifically aimed at senior level healthcare marketers and managers, offers targeted information, practical strategies and thought provoking commentary to help achieve your goals and shape your vision
Frequency: Quarterly
Mailing list available for rent

17364 Marketing Management
American Marketing Association
311 S Wacker Dr
Suite 5800
Chicago, IL 60606-6629

312-542-9000
800-262-1150; *Fax:* 312-542-9001;
www.marketingpower.com
Social Media: Facebook, Twitter, LinkedIn, Youtube

Dennis Dunlap, CEO

Focuses on strategic marketing issues that marketing managers face every day.
Frequency: 6x/Year
Mailing list available for rent

17365 Marketing Recreation Classes
Learning Resources Network
1554 Hayes Drive
Manhattan, KS 66502-5068

785-539-5376; *Fax:* 888-234-8633
draves@lern.org; www.lern.org/

William Draves, Editor

This magazine offers information on marketing and advertising trends.
8 Pages
Frequency: Monthly
Founded in: 1980

17366 Marketing Research
American Marketing Association
311 S Wacker Dr
Suite 5800
Chicago, IL 60606-6629

312-542-9000
800-262-1150; *Fax:* 312-542-9001;
www.marketingpower.com
Social Media: Facebook, Twitter, LinkedIn, Youtube

Dennis Dunlap, CEO

Researchers and managers count on this resource to help stay on top of current methodologies and issues, management concerns and the latest books and software.
Frequency: Quarterly
Mailing list available for rent

17367 Marketing Science: INFORMS
INFORMS
7240 Parkway Dr
Suite 310
Hanover, MD 21076-1344

410-850-0300
800-446-3676; *Fax:* 410-757-3515
informs@informs.org; www.informs.org

Mark Doherty, Executive Director
Barry List, Director Marketing
Patricia Shaffer, Director Publications
Richard C Larson, President

Marketing journal offering marketing and advertising articles. Provides help for marketing decision makers and deeper understanding of marketing phenomena.
Cost: $172.00
Frequency: Quarterly
Circulation: 1800
ISSN: 0732-2399
Founded in: 1982

17368 Marketing to Women
EPM Communications
19 W. 21st St., #303
New York, NY 10010

212-941-0099
888-852-9467; *Fax:* 212-941-1622
info@epmcom.com; www.epmcom.com

Ira Mayer, President
Larissa Faw, Editor

Topics covers attitudes and buying behaviors of the female consumer, market segment demographics, gender gap and health issues, media preferences and the role of technology.
Cost: $35.00
Frequency: Monthly

17369 Marketrac
Marketrac San Diego
4 First American Way
Santa Ana, CA 92707

714-250-6400
800-345-7334; www.facorelogic.com

Gerald Schultz, Editor
Jim Lucich, Promotional Manager

Marketing communications: people, places, events, trends, new products, technology, public relations, advertising, broadcast, TV, radio, video production, promotions, market research, direct mail, trademark, copyright law, accounting, employee management printing, graphics, color separations, novelty promotions.
Cost: $15.00
32 Pages
Frequency: Monthly

17370 NAPRA ReView
109 N Beach Road
PO Box 9
Eastsound, WA 98245-9

360-376-2001
800-367-1907; *Fax:* 360-376-2704
marilyn@marilynmcguire.com;
www.napra.com

Erin Johnson, Advertising Sales
Marilyn McGuire, Editor
Marilyn McGuire, CEO/President
Frequency: 10 issues ayear
Circulation: 180000
Founded in: 1986

17371 POINT
Direct Marketing Association
1120 Avenue of the Americas
New York, NY 10036-6713

212-768-7277; *Fax:* 212-302-6714;
www.the-dma.org
Social Media: Facebook, Twitter, LinkedIn

John A. Greco Jr, President & CEO

DMA's digital magazine.

17372 POP Design
In-Store Marketing Institute
8550 W. Bryn Mawr
#200
Chicago, IL 60631

773-992-4450; *Fax:* 773-992-4455
info@instoremarketer.org; www.p2pi.org/

Peter Hoyt, President

Serves the news and product information needs of producers and designers of instore displays, signs and fixtures. Each issue features the latest trends and technologies vital to building and designing successful instore merchandising.
Frequency: Monthly
Circulation: 18000
Printed in 4 colors on glossy stock

17373 PSMJ Marketing Tactics
PSMJ Resources
10 Midland Avenue
Newton, MA 02458-1000

617-965-0055
800-537-7765; *Fax:* 617-965-5152
info@psmj.com; www.psmj.com

Frank Stasiowski, Production Manager

Provides marketing tactics and techniques for the design industry.
Cost: $267.00
8 Pages
Frequency: Monthly
Founded in: 1975
*Mailing list available for rent*at $125 per M
Printed in 2 colors on matte stock

17374 Personal Selling Power
1140 International Parkway
PO Box 5467
Fredericksburg, VA 22406-467

540-752-7000
800-752-7355; *Fax:* 540-752-7001
feedback@sellingpower.com;
www.sellingpower.com

John Nuzzi, VP / Associate Publisher
Laura Gschwandtner, CEO

Sales education/motivation magazine designed to train, educate, motivate salespeople.
Cost: $33.00
140 Pages
Frequency: 10 times a year
ISSN: 1093-2216
Printed in 4 colors on glossy stock

17375 Point of Purchase Magazine
1115 Northmeadow Parkway
Roswell, GA 30076

847-647-7987
800-241-9034; *Fax:* 847-647-9566
popmag@halldata.com; www.popmag.com

Murray Kasmenn, Publisher
Julie Andrews, Sales Manager
Larry Shore, Sales Manager
Ted Eshleman, Account Executive
Alison Medina, Executive Editor

Addresses the industry perspective of the brand marketer and the retailer and focuses on retail trends, case studies, statistics and profitability.
Cost: $60.00
Frequency: 9 per year
Circulation: 18,506

17376 Politically Direct
Direct Marketing Association
1120 Avenue of the Americas
New York, NY 10036-6700

212-768-7277; *Fax:* 212-302-6714
customerservice@the-dma.org;
www.the-dma.org

Lawrence M Kimmel, CEO

Published both in print and digital versions, this newsletter on DMA advocacy efforts keeps DMA members informed and involved in the politics and policies that impact them today and ahead of the curve on developments that will affect them tomorrow.

17377 PromaxBDA
PROMAX
1522 Cloverfield Blvd.
Suite E
Santa Monica, CA 90404
310-788-7600; *Fax:* 310-788-7616;
www.promaxbda.org
Jonathan Black-Verk, President & CEO
Jill Lindeman, General Manager
Magazine, newsletter and directory published by PROMAX for members only, promotion and marketing professionals in electronic media.
Frequency: Annual
Circulation: 2500
Founded in: 1952
Printed in 4 colors on glossy stock

17378 Quirk's Marketing Research Review
Quirk Enterprises
4662 Slater Rd
Eagan, MN 55122-2362
651-379-6200; *Fax:* 651-379-6205
info@quirks.com; www.quirks.com
Social Media: Facebook, Twitter, LinkedIn
Steve Quirk, President
Joe Rydholm, Editor
Evan Tweed, Vice President Sales
Alice Davies, Manager
Emphasizes marketing research case histories and techniques used by researchers in a variety of industries, from consumer products to advertising, includes directories of research services and new products and features personnel announcements.
Cost: $70.00
30000 Members
Circulation: 16013
Founded in: 1986
Mailing list available for rent: 17000 names
Printed in 4 colors on glossy stock

17379 Recharger Magazine
Recharger Magazine
1050 E Flamingo Rd
Suite N237
Las Vegas, NV 89119-7427
702-438-5557
877-902-9759; *Fax:* 702-873-9671
info@rechargermag.com;
www.rechargermag.com
Tom Enerson, Publisher
Amy Turner, Manager
Becky Fenton, Manager
Amy Weiss, Director
Nancy Calabrese, Sales Manager
Information including articles that cover business and marketing, technical updates, association and industry news, and company profiles. Related features focus on the importance of recycling, government legislation, and product comparisons.
Cost: $45.00
Frequency: Monthly
Circulation: 8000
Founded in: 1997

17380 Response TV
Advanstar Communications
Ste 300
17770 Cartwright Rd
Irvine, CA 92614-5815
714-513-8400
800-527-7008; *Fax:* 714-513-8412
george@directresponsetv.com;
www.directresponsetv.com
John Yarring, Publisher
Thomas Haire, Editor
Joe Logia, CEO/President
Jodi Dressig, Circulation manager
Gina Cohen, Manager
Addresses industry concerns regarding regulatory issues, production, fulfillment and aftermarketing. Designed for direct marketers, product owners and related agencies.
Cost: $39.00
Frequency: Monthly
Circulation: 21345
Founded in: 1993

17381 Sales Executive
Sales Marketing Executives of Greater New York
13 E 37th Street
#8
New York, NY 10016-2821
212-685-3613; *Fax:* 212-725-3752
Edward Glanegan, Publisher
Patricia Israel, Editor
For sales executives in New York.
Circulation: 2,500

17382 Sales Upbeat
Economics Press
12 Daniel Road
Fairfield, NJ 07004-2565
973-227-1224; *Fax:* 973-227-9742
John Beckley, Publisher
Robert Guder, Editor
Sales methods and techniques, quotes and anecdotes about selling.
Cost: $2.00
Circulation: 52,000

17383 Salesmanship
LRP Publications/Dartnell Corporation
PO Box 980
Horsham, PA 19044-0980
215-784-0912
800-341-7874; *Fax:* 215-784-9639
webmaster@lrp.com; www.lrp.com
Todd Lutz, CFO
Enhances training program with engaging and instructive reminders and shape-up tips that pay off in greater gains from sales force.
Cost: $62.00

17384 Say Yes Marketing Script Presentations
Frieda Carrol Communications
PO Box 416
Denver, CO 80201-0416
303-575-5676
This reference contains marketing presentations for various kinds of businesses.
Cost: $52.95

17385 Security Distributing & Marketing
Reed Business Information
1050 IL Route 83
Suite 200
Bensonville, IL 60106
630-616-0200; *Fax:* 630-227-0214;
www.sdmmag.com
Bill Zalud, Editorial Director
Susan Whitehurst, Production Manager
Lyn Sopala, Production Manager
Security Distributing and Marketing serves security installing dealers, security installing dealers with central station equipment, central station services, access control system specialists and systems integrators.
Cost: $82.00
104 Pages
Frequency: 19 per year
Circulation: 28,298
ISSN: 0049-0016
Founded in: 1971
Printed in 4 colors on glossy stock

17386 Selling Magazine
Selling Magazine
477 Madison Avenue
New York, NY 10022-5802
212-751-0485; *Fax:* 212-224-3592
Marjorie Weiss, Publisher
Selling is targeted to business-to-business salespeople.
Cost: $5.00
Circulation: 155162

17387 Senior Marketwatch
Campbell Associates
185 Martling Ave
Tarrytown, NY 10591-4703
914-332-1177; *Fax:* 914-332-1177
Arnold Thiesfeldt, Publisher
Features research based on tastes, trends, and resources of the senior market, as a means for advertisers and marketers to target and focus their products.
Cost: $242.00
12 Pages
Frequency: Monthly
Founded in: 1997

17388 Southern California Marketing Media
Southern California Marketing Media
5 Via Caseta
Rancho Santa Margarita, CA 92688-4947
949-713-3188; *Fax:* 714-713-3188
Gary Klayman, Publisher
Written to report on marketing strategies, techniques and new products for the Southern California area, includes various company, client and media updates, new trends, and guides to developing individualized marketing programs.

17389 Subscription Marketing
Blue Dolphin Communications
526 Boston Post Road
Wayland, MA 01778-1833
978-358-5795; *Fax:* 508-358-5795
subs@bluedolphin.com; www.bluedolphin.com
Donald L Nicholas, Publisher
Offers trade strategies for maximizing product profitability. Provides perspective on success and failure stories.
Cost: $195.00
Frequency: Monthly

17390 Supermarket News
Fairchild Publications
750 3rd Ave
New York, NY 10017-2703
212-630-4000
800-204-4515; *Fax:* 212-630-3563
customerservice@fairchildpub.com;
www.supermarketnews.com
Mary G Berner, CEO
David Merrefield, Editorial Director
Cost: $44.50
40 Pages
Frequency: Weekly
Circulation: 36346
ISSN: 0039-5803
Founded in: 1892

17391 **TODAY - The Journal of Work Process Improvement**
Recognition Technologies Users Association
185 Devonshire Street
Suite 770
Boston, MA 02110-1407
617-426-1167; *Fax:* 617-521-8675;
www.tawpi.org
Dan Bolita, Editor
Frank Moran, CEO/President
Jason Glass, VP Sales
Cost: $27.69
Circulation: 5000
ISSN: 1073-2233
Founded in: 1997
Printed in 2 colors on glossy stock

17392 **Target Marketing**
North American Publishing Company
1500 Spring Garden St
Suite 1200
Philadelphia, PA 19130-4094
215-238-5300; *Fax:* 215-238-5342;
www.targetmarketingmag.com
Social Media: Facebook, Twitter, LinkedIn
Ned S Borowsky, CEO
Lisa Yorgey, Managing Editor
Drew James, Sales Manager
Covers telemarketing, list rental, testing and management, circulation, catalogue and on-line/web marketing, and direct response advertising.
Cost: $65.00
Frequency: Monthly
Circulation: 42,000
Mailing list available for rent

17393 **Telemarketing & Call Center Solutions**
Technology Marketing Corporation
800 Connecticut Ave
1st Floor East
Norwalk, CT 06854-1924
203-852-6800
800-243-6002; *Fax:* 203-866-3326
tmc@tmcnet.com; www.tmcnet.com
Social Media: Twitter
Nadji Tehrani, President
Linda Driscoll, Editor
First and only authoritative guide to effective and profitable marketing through business telecommunications. Provides information on technology and services releases, new techniques and management strategies.
Cost: $7.00
Frequency: 24 times
Circulation: 31419
Founded in: 1972

17394 **Velocity**
Strategic Account Management Association
33 N La Salle Street
Suite 3700
Chicago, IL 60602
312-251-3131; *Fax:* 312-251-3132;
www.strategicaccounts.org
Greg Bartlett, Editor
Contains exclusive, in-depth articles on topics such as negotiation, customer management, internal alignment and effective team communications.
Cost: $65.00
52 Pages
Frequency: Quarterly
Circulation: 2000
Founded in: 1964
Printed in 4 colors

17395 **Wireless for the Corporate User**
Probe Research
3 Wing Drive
Suite 240
Cedar Knolls, NJ 07927-1000
973-285-1500; *Fax:* 973-285-1519
Jack Killion, Publisher
Edited for the corporate user/decision maker to keep abreast of the growth product and service offerings, the expanding uses and the technological, political and standardization issues of the wireless arena.
Circulation: 43000

17396 **World Trade**
BNP Media
2401 W. Big Beaver Rd, Suite 700
Troy, MI 48084
248-362-3700; www.bnpmedia.com
Social Media: Facebook, Twitter, LinkedIn
Katie Rotella, President
Cost: $37.00
58 Pages
Frequency: Monthly

Trade Shows

17397 **Annual Conference and Mailing Fulfillment Expo**
Mailing & Fulfillment Service Association
1421 Prince Street
Suite 410
Alexandria, VA 22314-2806
703-836-9200; *Fax:* 703-548-8204
mfsa-mail@mfsanet.org; www.mfsanet.org
Social Media: Facebook, Twitter, LinkedIn
Ken Garner, President
Jennifer Root, Director
Bill Stevenson, Director Marketing
Leo Raymond, Vice President
Quality educational sessions, industry specific exhibit hall, networking and more.
Frequency: Annual

17398 **Annual Conference for Catalog & Multichannel Merchants (ACCM)**
Direct Marketing Association
1120 Avenue of Americas
New York, NY 10036
212-768-7277; *Fax:* 212-302-6714;
www.the-dma.org
Social Media: Facebook, Twitter, LinkedIn
Julie Hogan, SVP Conference & Events
10M Attendees

17399 **Annual Conference on Healthcare Marketing**
Alliance for Healthcare Strategy & Marketing
11 S LaSalle Street
Suite 2300
Chicago, IL 60603
312-704-9700; *Fax:* 312-704-9709;
www.alliancehlth.org/hlthmktg
Workshop and social events plus 50 exhibits of marketing communications, health care information lines, stategic planning and more.
600 Attendees
Frequency: Annual
Founded in: 1984

17400 **Business Intelligence Conference**
The Conference Board
845 Third Avenue
New York, NY 10022
212-339-0345; *Fax:* 212-836-9740;
www.conference-board.org/intelligence.htm
Shows how you can utilize business intelligence in your own organization to enhance performace and drive results.
Frequency: June, Chicago

17401 **DMA Annual Conference & Exhibition**
Direct Marketing Association
1120 Avenue of Americas
New York, NY 10036-6700
212-768-7277; *Fax:* 212-302-6714
dmaconferences@the-dma.org;
www.the-dma.org
Lawrence M Kimmel, CEO
Julie A Hogan, SVP Conferences/Events
Brings together thousands of practitioners and experts from the entire marketing continuum to discuss solutions and best practices to achieve optimal channel mix and integration that lead to measurable results and increase real-time customer engagement.
12000 Attendees
Frequency: October

17402 **DMB: Direct Marketing to Business Conference**
Target Conference Corporation
11 Riverbend Drive S
Stamford, CT 06907-0949
203-358-9900; *Fax:* 203-358-5815
Ed Berkowitz
National conference for business to business direct marketers. 75 table tops
1000+ Attendees
Frequency: March
Mailing list available for rent

17403 **Direct Marketing Conference National Conference**
DMB Miami
Fontainebleau Hilton Resort and Towers
Miami, FL 33152
203-358-3751
800-927-5007; www.directmac.org
Information on improving R.O.I. and stay ahead of the competition, create customer centric business, synthesize traditional marketing strategies with the internet.

17404 **Electronic Retailing Association Annual Convention**
Electronic Retailing Association
607 14th Street, NW, Suite 530
Washington, DC 20005
703-841-1751
800-987-6462; *Fax:* 425-977-1036
contact@retailing.org; www.retailing.org
Social Media: Facebook, Twitter, LinkedIn, Youtube.Flickr
Karla Kelly, VP Meetings/Conventions
Christy Brzonkala Hopkins, Meetings Coordinator

17405 **Email Evolution Conference**
Direct Marketing Association
1120 Avenue of Americas
New York, NY 10036-6700
212-768-7277; *Fax:* 212-302-6714
dmaconferences@the-dma.org;
www.the-dma.org
Julie A Hogan, SVP Conference/Events
Lawrence M Kimmel, CEO
Focuses on the ever-changing and evolving world of email marketing, providing you with the best ways to capitalize on the high ROI this

low-cost communication tool can provide both on its own, and integrated with social, search, mobile, video and other email enhancers.
10M Attendees
Frequency: Annual/February

17406 Exhibitor Conference
Exhibitor Magazine Group
206 S Broadway
Suite 745
Rochester, MN 55904-6565

507-289-6556
888-235-6155; *Fax:* 507-289-5253
exhibitorshow@heiexpo.com;
www.exhibitoronline.com
Social Media: Facebook, Twitter, LinkedIn

Carol Fojtik, Managing Director/Sr Vice President

Conference program combined with exhibit hall featuring latest products and resources shaping the future of exhibiting and corporate event programs. Anyone responsible for planning, managing or implementing trade show or corporate event marketing functions should attend. Conference is held annually in Las Vegas, NV.
5M Attendees
Frequency: March, Las Vegas
Founded in: 1989

17407 FSMA Top 2 Top Conference
1810-J York Road #384
Lutherville, MD 21093
410-715-4084
800-617-1170; *Fax:* 888-668-7496
info@fsmaonline.com; www.fsmaonline.com

Bob Watson, Chair
Rick Abraham, President
Frequency: Annual/February
Mailing list available for rent

17408 High Performance Linux on Wall Street
Flagg Management
353 Lexington Avenue
New York, NY 10016

212-286-0333; *Fax:* 212-286-0086;
www.flaggmgmt.com

Russell Flagg, President

Featuring Linux and HPC futures discussions, virtualization, cloud computing and service-driven datacenters, open source meets low latency, VLDB architectures, cost reduction with Linux, and more.
1000 Attendees
Frequency: Annual
Founded in: 2001

17409 Incentive Marketing Association Annual Summit
Incentive Marketing Association
4248 Park Glen Road
Minneapolis, MN 55416

952-928-4649
info@incentivemarketing.org;
www.incentivemarketing.org

Karen Wesloh, Executive Director
Sean Roark, President

Gathering of experts and professionals in the incentive marketing industry to share ideas and discuss business growth.
Frequency: Annual

17410 MBA Research Conclave
MBAResearch and Curriculum Center
1375 King Avenue
PO Box 12279
Columbus, OH 43212

614-486-6708
800-448-0398; *Fax:* 614-486-1819;
www.mbaresearch.org

Marsha Dyer, Customer Service Manager
Kimberly Holstlaw, Executive Adminstrator
James Gleason, President/CEO

Containing 20 booths and 15 exhibits.
500 Attendees
Frequency: June
Founded in: 1971

17411 MDMA's Annual Direct Marketing Conference & Expo
Midwest Direct Marketing Association
P.O. Box 75
Andover, MN 55304

763-607-2943; *Fax:* 763-753-2240
office@mdma.org; www.mdma.org

Joan Forde, President
Cindy McCleary, Director

Containing 55 booths and 50 companies exhibiting.
Frequency: April
Mailing list available for rent: 1.1M+ names

17412 MFSA Midwinter Executive Conference
Mailing & Fulfillment Service Association
1421 Prince Street
Suite 410
Alexandria, VA 22314-2806

703-836-9200; *Fax:* 703-548-8204
mfsa-mail@mfsanet.org; www.mfsanet.org
Social Media: Facebook, Twitter, LinkedIn

Ken Garner, President
Jennifer Root, Director
Bill Stevenson, Director Marketing
Leo Raymond, Vice President

Will address financial operations and business valuation, marketing your own company, the changing world of postal regulations, technology in fulfillment, building a sales team, being strong in digital printing and the landscape of employment law.

17413 MLMIA Annual Corporate Convention and Expo
Multi-Level Marketing International Association
119 Stanford Court
Irvine, CA 92612-1671

949-854-0484; *Fax:* 949-281-2114
info@mlmia.com; www.mlmia.com
Social Media: Facebook, Twitter

Doris Wood, Chair/President Emeritus
Del Hickman, Executive Director
Eugene Argent, VP Support
Kate Jackson, Treasurer
Linda Bruno, Secretary

Seeks to strengthen and improve the Direct Sales/Network Marketing/Multi-Level Marketing industry in the United States and abroad. Members are companies which market their products and services directly to consumers through independent distributors, suppliers to the industry and distributors who interface with consumers.
Founded in: 1985

17414 Mailer Strategies Conference
Mailing & Fulfillment Service Association
1421 Prince Street
Suite 410
Alexandria, VA 22314-2806

703-836-9200; *Fax:* 703-548-8204
mfsa-mail@mfsanet.org; www.mfsanet.org
Social Media: Facebook, Twitter, LinkedIn

Ken Garner, President
Jennifer Root, Director
Bill Stevenson, Director Marketing
Leo Raymond, Vice President

This conference will focus solely on postal issues that are important to your operations.

17415 Marketing Federation's Annual Conference on Strategic Marketing
Marketing Federation
109 58th Avenue
Saint Petersburg, FL 33706-2203

727-363-7805; *Fax:* 727-367-6545

Greg Stemm

Offers attendees information on how to boost attendance at their seminars, conferences and expositions.

17416 NCDM Conference
Direct Marketing Association
1120 Avenue of Americas
New York, NY 10036-6700

212-768-7277; *Fax:* 212-302-6714
dmaconferences@the-dma.org;
www.the-dma.org

Julie A Hogan, SVP Conference/Events
Lawrence M Kimmel, CEO

Presents industry experts and hard-hitting case studies from a variety of verticals, such as financial services, retail, automotive, publishing, non-profit and many more, who will share the latest strategies and methodologies in gathering, analyzing, leveraging and protecting your most valuable business asset - customer data.
10M Attendees
Frequency: Annual/December

17417 NCDM Conferences National Center for Database Marketing
Primedia Business Exhibitions
11 River Bend S
PO Box 4254
Stamford, CT 06907

203-358-9900; *Fax:* 203-358-5815;
www.ncdmsummer.com or
www.ncdmwinter.com

Ed Berkowitz, Director Sales

A conference offering a highly qualified audience of database marketing decision-makers from all over the country, including a high concentration of marketers from the Midwest and West coast. Containing 210 booths and 100 exhibits.
2500 Attendees
Frequency: July/December

17418 National Conference on Operations & Fulfillment (NCOF)
Direct Marketing Association
1120 Avenue of Americas
New York, NY 1003-6700

212-768-7277; *Fax:* 312-302-6714
dmaconferences@the-dma.org;
www.the-dma.org

Julie A Hogan, SVP Conference/Events
Lawrence M Kimmel, CEO

Focus on innovative solutions for warehouse, distribution, operations, and ecommerce needs in the ever-changing world of operations and fulfillment.
10M Attendees
Frequency: Annual/April

17419 National Hispanic Market Trade Show and Media Expo (Se Habla Espanol)
Hispanic Business
5385 Hollister Avenue, Ste. 204
Santa Barbara, CA 93111

805-964-4554
800-806-4268; *Fax:* 805-964-5539
info@hispanstar.com;
www.expomediainc.com/en/home
Social Media: Facebook, Twitter, LinkedIn

John Pasini, Cfo/Coo

Annual show of 100 exhibitors of market/research, media, advertising, public relations, information services and recruitment.
1500 Attendees
Mailing list available for rent

17420 National Mail Order Merchandise Show
Expo Accessories
47 Main Avenue
Clifton, NJ 07014-1917

973-661-9681

Martin Deeks, Show Manager

300 booths.
5M Attendees
Frequency: January

17421 New York Nonprofit Conference
Direct Marketing Association
1120 Avenue of Americas
New York, NY 10036-6700

212-768-7277; *Fax:* 212-302-6714
dmaconferences@the-dma.org;
www.the-dma.org

Julie A Hogan, SVP Conference/Events
Lawrence M Kimmel, CEO

Discover which acknowledgement programs work best-and why, increase the revenue with membership options-as well as traditional fundraising appeals, learn how the Internet and e-mail campaigns can improve fundraising, lower costs and increase advocacy.
10M Attendees

17422 PROMO Live
Prism Business Media
PROMO Live
11 River Bend South
Stamford, CT 06907

508-743-0105
800-927-5007; *Fax:* 508-759-4552;
www.thepromoevent.com

Kim Stolfi, Conference/Show Coordinator
Florence Torres, Conference Program Manager
Frequency: Oct Chicago

17423 Photo Marketing Association International
3000 Picture Place
Jackson, MI 49201

517-788-8100; *Fax:* 517-788-8371;
www.theimagingalliance.com

Ted Fox, Executive Director
Mary Anne LaMarre, Operations Officer

Containing 3,230 booths and 645 exhibits. Promoting the growth of the photography industry through coorperation.
24M Attendees
Frequency: February

17424 Promo Expo
Promo Expo Sales
The Navy Pier
Chicago, IL 60606

800-927-5007; *Fax:* 203-358-3751;
www.promoexpo.com

The largest conference and exhibition dedicated to the promotion marketing industry, and the one event where you can meet with over four thousand promotion marketing decision makers.
Frequency: October

17425 Publishers Multinational Direct Conference
1501 3rd Avenue
New York, NY 10028-2101

212-734-7040; *Fax:* 212-986-3757

Alfred Goodloe, President

Offers publishers information and seminars on how to build sales and profits in foreign markets.
Frequency: March

17426 Securities Industry and Financial Markets Association (SIFMA) Annual Meeting
1101 New York Avenue NW
8th Floor
Washington, DC 20005

202-962-7300; *Fax:* 202-962-7305;
www.sifma.org
Social Media: Facebook, Twitter, LinkedIn

T Timothy Ryan Je, President/CEO
Randy Snook, Senior Managing Director/EVP
Donald D Kittell, CFO

The Securities Industry and Financial Markets Association/SIFMA Annual Meeting and Conference program addresses a variety of topics that may include competitiveness of the U.S. capital markets, global exchange consolidation, regulatory and legal initiatives, and trends in the fixed-income and capital markets.
Mailing list available for rent

17427 SourceMedia Conferences & Events
SourceMedia
One State Street Plaza
27th floor
New York, NY 10004

212-803-6093
800-803-3424; *Fax:* 212-803-8515
abconferences@sourcemedia.com;
www.sourcemedia.com/
Social Media: Facebook, Twitter, LinkedIn

James M Malkin, Chairman & CEO
William Johnson, CFO
Steve Andreazza, VP, Sales & Customer Service
Celie Baussan, SVP, Operations
Anne O'Brien, EVP Marketing & Strategic Planning

SourceMedia Conferences & Events attract over 20,000 attendees worldwide. The content embraces a variety of formats, including: conferences, executive roundtables, expositions, Web seminars, custom events and pod casts. With over 70 events annually, participants are provided with premier content as well as access to the industry's top solution providers. Markets served include: accounting; banking; capital markets; financial services; information technology; insurance; and real estate.
Mailing list available for rent

17428 TMCA Annual Conference & Marketing Expo
Transportation Marketing Communications Assoc
9382 Oak Avenue
Waconia, MN 55387

952-442-5638; *Fax:* 952-442-3941;
www.tmcatoday.org

John Ferguson, President
Tom Nightingale, VP
Tracy Robinson, Treasurer
Edward Moritz, Secretary
Brian Everett, Executive Director
200 Attendees
Frequency: Annual

Directories & Databases

17429 Adweek Directory
Prometheus Global Media
770 Broadway
New York, NY 10003-9595
212-493-4100; *Fax:* 646-654-5368;
www.prometheusgm.com

Richard D. Beckmand, CEO
James A. Finkelstein, Chairman
Madeline Krakowsky, Vice President Circulation
Tracy Brater, Executive Director Creative Service

Adweek Directories Online is where you will find searchable databases with comprehensive information on ad Agencies, brand marketers and multicultural media.
Frequency: Annual
Circulation: 800
Founded in: 1981

17430 Affluent Markets Alert
EPM Communications
488 E 18th Street
Brooklyn, NY 11226-6702

Fax: 718-469-7124

Offers complete coverage on affluent market trends containing complete contact and price information on books, monographs, journals and newspapers.
Frequency: Full-text

17431 AmericanProfile
Donnelley Marketing Information Services
25 Tremont Ave
#10250
Stamford, CT 06906-2330

203-325-9801
800-866-2255; *Fax:* 203-553-7276;
www.donnellyestates.com

Richard Donnelly, Owner

A database retrieval and reporting system that contains 1980 and 1990 census data, current year updates and 5-year projections of selected demographic characteristics and proprietary statistics.

17432 Annual Directory of Marketing Information Companies
American Demographics
PO Box 4949
Stamford, CT 06907-0949

203-358-9900

Offers a list of firms offering demographic and research services, data retrieval and analysis, market evaluation and forecasting.
Frequency: Annual
Circulation: 5,000

17433 Annual Mail Order Sales Directory & Mail Order 750 Report
Marketing Logistics

1460 Cloverdale Avenue
Highland Park, IL 60035-2817

847-831-1575

Arnold L Fishman, President

This comprehensive directory offers a list of mail order businesses reporting at least 5 million dollars in annual sales. The 750 report gives mail order companies, businesses and mail order catalogs, 250 listings of each.
Cost: $1095.00
Frequency: Annual

17434 **Boomer Report**
FIND/SVP
625 Avenue of the Americas
New York, NY 10011-2020

212-807-2656
800-346-3787; *Fax:* 212-645-7681

Andrew P Garvin, President

With over 77 million baby boomers, this report carefully tracks news stories, market surveys, and interviews the experts to help you spot opportunities and position your products.
Cost: $195.00
8 Pages
Frequency: Monthly

17435 **Bradford's Directory of Marketing Research Agencies & Consultants**
Bradford's Directory of Marketing Research Agency
9991 Caitlin Center
Manassas, VA 20110-4282

703-614-4000

Thomas Bradford, Owner

Over 2,500 companies that are involved in management or market research are listed.
Cost: $90.00
400 Pages
Frequency: Biennial
Circulation: 5,000

17436 **Business Marketing Association Membership Directory & Yellow Pages**
Business Marketing Association
Ste 123
1833 Centre Point Cir
Naperville, IL 60563-4848

630-544-5054; *Fax:* 630-544-5055
info@marketing.org; www.marketing.org
Social Media: Facebook, Twitter, LinkedIn

Jeffrey Hayzlett, Chairman
Gary Slack, Vice Chairman
Bob Goranson, Treasurer

Offers information on over 4,500 member business communications professionals in the field of advertising, marketing communications and marketing. Additional benefits of membership include opportunites for networking, professional development seminars, and access to marketing research and studies.
Frequency: Annual

17437 **Catalog Connection**
Holy B Pasiuk
210 E 5th Street
Greenville, NC 06437-0527

252-758-8612; www.catalogconnection.net

Over 400 companies that supply catalogs of their merchandise to consumers and businesses are profiled in this directory.
55 Pages
Frequency: Biennial

17438 **Catalog Handbook**
Enterprise Magazines
1020 N Broadway
Suite 111
Milwaukee, WI 53202-3157

414-272-9977; *Fax:* 414-272-9973;
www.franchisehandbook.com

Offers information on companies that offer product catalogs.
Cost: $6.99
106 Pages
Frequency: Quarterly
Circulation: 30,000
Founded in: 1989

17439 **Complete Directory of Mail Order Catalog Products**
Sutton Family Communications & Publishing Company
920 State Route 54 East
Elmitch, KY 42343

270-276-9500
jlsutton@apex.net

Theresa Sutton, Editor
Lee Sutton, General Manager

Print-out from database of wholesalers, manufacturers, distributors, importers and close-out houses. Database is updated daily to guarantee the most current and up-to-date sources available.
Cost: $157.50
100+ Pages

17440 **Direct Marketing Marketplace**
National Register Publishing
430 Mountain Ave.
Suite 400
New Providence, NJ 07974

800-473-7020; *Fax:* 908-673-1189
nrpeditorial@marquiswhoswho.com;
www.nationalregisterpub.com

Provides contact information for direct marketers, service firms and suppliers.

17441 **Directory Marketplace**
Todd Publications
PO Box 635
Nyack, NY 10960-0635

845-358-6213; *Fax:* 845-358-1059
toddpub@aol.com

Barry Klein, Editor

Directories and Reference Books for business, education, and libraries; news of new directories.
Cost: $25.00
Frequency: Bi-Monthly
Founded in: 1987

17442 **Directory of Franchising Organizations**
Pilot Books
127 Sterling Avenue
PO Box 2102
Greenport, NY 11944

631-477-0978
800-797-4568; *Fax:* 631-477-0978

Over 1,300 current franchise opportunities in 45 categories.
Cost: $12.95
Frequency: Annual
Circulation: 0
ISBN: 0-875762-15-8

17443 **Directory of Mail Order Catalogs**
Grey House Publishing
4919 Route 22
PO Box 56
Amenia, NY 12501

518-789-8700
800-562-2139; *Fax:* 845-373-6390
books@greyhouse.com; www.greyhouse.com
Social Media: Facebook, Twitter

Leslie Mackenzie, Publisher
Richard Gottlieb, Editor

The premier source of information on the mail order catalog industry. Covers over 13,000 consumer and business catalog companies with 44 different product chapters from Animals to Toys and Games.
Cost: $395.00
1600 Pages
Frequency: Annual
ISBN: 1-592373-96-8
Founded in: 1981

17444 **Directory of Mail Order Catalogs - Online Database**
Grey House Publishing
4919 Route 22
PO Box 56
Amenia, NY 12501

518-789-8700
800-562-2139; *Fax:* 845-373-6390
gold@greyhouse.com
http://gold.greyhouse.com
Social Media: Facebook, Twitter

Leslie Mackenzie, Publisher
Richard Gottlieb, Editor

Reach over 10,000 consumer catalog companies in one easy-to-use source with The Directory of Mail Order Catalogs - Online Database. Filled with business-building detail, each company profile gives you the information you need to access that organization quickly and easily. Listings provide key contacts, sales volume, employee size, printing information, circulation, list data, product descriptions and much more.
Frequency: Annual
Founded in: 1981

17445 **Entertainment Marketing Letter**
EPM Communications
19 W. 21st St., #303
New York, NY 10010

212-941-0099
888-852-9467; *Fax:* 212-941-1622
info@epmcom.com; www.epmcom.com

Ira Mayer, Owner
Terence Keegan, Editor

Database covering marketing techniques used in the entertainment industry.
Cost: $449.00
Frequency: 24 Issues/Year

17446 **Food & Beverage Market Place**
Grey House Publishing
4919 Route 22
PO Box 56
Amenia, NY 12501

518-789-8700
800-562-2139; *Fax:* 845-373-6390
books@greyhouse.com; www.greyhouse.com
Social Media: Facebook, Twitter

Leslie Mackenzie, Publisher
Richard Gottlieb, Editor

This information packed three-volume set is the most powerful buying and marketing guide for the US food and beverage industry. Includes thousands of industry freight and transportation listings.
Cost: $595.00
2000 Pages
Frequency: Annual
ISBN: 1-592373-61-5
Founded in: 1981

17447 **Food & Beverage Marketplace: Online Database**
Grey House Publishing

4919 Route 22
PO Box 56
Amenia, NY 12501

518-789-8700
800-562-2139; *Fax:* 518-789-0556
gold@greyhouse.com
http://gold.greyhouse.com
Social Media: Facebook, Twitter

Richard Gottlieb, President
Leslie Mackenzie, Publisher

This complete updated Food & Beverage Market Place: Online Database is the go-to source for the food and beverage industry. Anyone involved in the food and beverage industry needs this 'industry bible' and the important contacts to develop critical research data that can make for successful business growth.
Frequency: Annual
Founded in: 1981

17448 GreenBook: Worldwide of Market Research Companies and Services
NY American Marketing Association
116 East 27th Street
6th Floor
New York, NY 10016-1799

212-687-3280; *Fax:* 212-202-7920
info@greenbook.org; www.greenbook.org
Social Media: Twitter, LinkedIn

Lucas Pospichal, Managing Director

Comprehensive listings of over 1,500 market research firms in the US and Canada. Listings in over 300 service categories and market industries. The most reliable reference resource for buyers of marketing research services.
Cost: $350.00
880 Pages
Frequency: Yearly
Circulation: 4,500
Founded in: 1962

17449 Infomercial Marketing Sourcebook
Prometheus Global Media
770 Broadway
New York, NY 10003-9595

212-493-4100; *Fax:* 646-654-5368;
www.prometheusgm.com

Richard D. Beckman, CEO
James A. Finkelstein, Chairman
Madeline Krakowsky, Vice President Circulation
Tracy Brater, Executive Director Creative Service

A complete resource guide for everyone involved in the infomercial industry.

17450 International Directory of Marketing Research Companies & Services
New York Chapter/American Marketing Association
310 Madison Avenue
New York, NY 10017-6009

212-986-1418

Offers more than 1,500 marketing research consultants and suppliers of marketing research data.
Cost: $105.00
600 Pages
Frequency: Annual
Circulation: 6,000

17451 International Network Marketing Reference Book & Resource Directory
MLM Group Publications
12 Rose Center
Norwood, MA 02062-2603

Offers valuable information on over 800 companies in the multi-level marketing industry.
Cost: $15.75
85 Pages

17452 Leadership Library on Internet and CD-ROM
Leadership Directories
104 5th Ave
New York, NY 10011-6901

212-627-4140; *Fax:* 212-645-0931
info@leadershipdirectories.com;
www.leadershipdirectories.com

David Hurvitz, CEO

Makes all 14 leadership directories available over the Internet and on CD-ROM in one integrated directory. They provide subscribers with complete contact information in one database. Subscription includes Internet access and four CD-ROM editions quarterly.
Cost: $3065.00
Frequency: Updated Daily
ISSN: 1075-3869
Founded in: 1999
Mailing list available for rent
Printed in A colors on B stock

17453 MDMA Membership and Resource Directory
Midwest Direct Marketing Association
P.O. Box 75
Andover, MN 55304

763-607-2943; *Fax:* 763-753-2240
office@mdma.org; www.mdma.org

Ed Harrington, Manager
Cindy McCleary, Director
400 Pages
Frequency: April
Mailing list available for rent: 1.1M+ names

17454 Mail Order Business Directory
B Klein Publishers
PO Box 8503
Coral Springs, FL 33075-8503
Bernard Klein, Editor

A listing of over 12,000 corporations in the US and 500 international firms doing business by mail order and catalogs.
Cost: $95.00
400 Pages
Frequency: Annual

17455 Mail Order Product Guide
Todd Publications
PO Box 635
Nyack, NY 10960-0635
845-358-6213
800-747-1086

A listing of over 1,500 manufacturers and importers to the mail order industry worldwide.
Cost: $50.00
250 Pages
Frequency: Triennial
Circulation: 5,000

17456 Market Scope
Trade Dimensions
45 Danbury Rd
Wilton, CT 06897-4445

203-563-3000; *Fax:* 203-563-3131;
www.tradedimensions.com

Lynda Gutierrez, Managing Editor

The definitive source of market share and category sales data for supermarkets. The book configures the information in Trade Dimensions' database to determine market share by Nielsen, DMA, MSA and IRI definitions - over 300 markets in all. Market Scope also provides extensive category sales data as reported by Nielsen and IRI.
Cost: $325.00
Frequency: Annual

17457 Marketing Guidebook
Trade Dimensions
45 Danbury Rd
Wilton, CT 06897-4445

203-563-3000; *Fax:* 860-563-3131;
www.tradedimensions.com

Lynda Gutierrez, Managing Editor
Jane Sheulin, Editor

The 'blue book' sales and marketing professionals have depended on for 30 years. The directory details the supermarket industry from distribution standpoint, comprising over 800 profiles, organized into 52 market areas. Includes all grocery chains and wholesalers that do a minimum of $30 million in sales. Also includes food brokers, non-food distributors, and small wholesalers in each market.
Cost: $340.00
Frequency: Annual

17458 Marketing Made Easier: Directory of Mailing List Companies
Todd Publications
PO Box 635
Nyack, NY 10960-0635
845-358-6213
800-747-1056; *Fax:* 845-358-3203
toddpubQ@aol.com
toddpublications.com

Barry Klein, Editor

Over 1,100 companies that sell mailing lists and the type of lits they handle.
Cost: $55.00
100 Pages
Frequency: Biennial
Circulation: 5,000
ISBN: 0-915344-83-1
Founded in: 1972
Mailing list available for rent: 1,000 names at $100 per M
Printed in 2 colors

17459 Marketing Tools Directory
American Demographics
PO Box 4949
Stamford, CT 06907-0949
203-358-9900
800-832-1486; *Fax:* 607-273-3196

List of firms offering demographic and research services, data retrieval, and analysis, market evaluation and forecasting media services.
Frequency: Annual

17460 Marketing on a Shoestring: Low-Cost Tips for Marketing Products & Services
John Wiley & Sons
111 River St
Hoboken, NJ 07030-5790

201-748-6000
800-825-7550; *Fax:* 201-748-6088
info@wiley.com; www.wiley.com

William J Pesce, CEO

Business and professional associations that can assist individuals or companies in improving their marketing are profiled.
Cost: $14.95
236 Pages

17461 National Agri-Marketing Association
11020 King St
Suite 205
Overland Park, KS 66210-1201

913-491-6500; *Fax:* 913-491-6502
agrimktg@nama.org; www.nama.org
Social Media: Facebook, Twitter, LinkedIn, Youtube,Flickr

Jennifer Pickett, CEO
Vicki Henrickson, Vice President
2500 Pages
Frequency: Annual Spring
Founded in: 1956

17462 National Directory of Addresses and Telephone Numbers
Omnigraphics
2500 Penobscot Building
Detroit, MI 48226
313-961-1340
This new edition provides the most current names and addresses for businesses and services throughout the United States, arranged alphabetically and by business type.
Cost: $60.00
1,500 Pages
Frequency: Hardcover
ISBN: 0-780800-20-6

17463 National Trade and Professional Associations of the United States
Columbia Books
1212 New York Avenue NW
Suite 330
Washington, DC 20005-3987
202-641-1662
888-265-0600; *Fax:* 202-898-0775
info@columbiabooks.com;
www.columbiabooks.com
Buck Downs, Senior Editor
Lists 7,600 national trade associations, professional societies and labor unions. Five convenient indexes enable you to look up associations by subject, budget, geographic area, acronym and executive director. Other features include: contract information, serial publications, upcoming convention schedule, membership/staff size, budget figures, and background information.
Cost: $99.00
Frequency: Annual Feburary

17464 New Marketing Opportunities
New Editions International
PO Box 2578
Sedona, AZ 86339-2578
928-282-9574
800-777-4751; *Fax:* 928-282-9730;
www.newagemarket.com
Sophia Tarila, Author
Pat Bush, CEO
7,000 New Age and Metaphysical publishers, events, retailers, distributors, services, publications, reviewers, catalogers, media connections, internet connections, associations and other resources.
Cost: $139.95
Frequency: Annual
ISBN: 0-944773-18-4
Mailing list available for rent

17465 Procter & Gamble Marketing Alumni Directory
Ward Howell International
300 S Wacker Drive
Suite 2940
Chicago, IL 60606-6703
Membership directory listings.
120 Pages
Frequency: Annual

17466 Quirk's Marketing Research Review
Quirk Enterprises
PO Box 23536
Minneapolis, MN 55423-0536
952-854-5101; *Fax:* 612-854-8191
evan@quirks.com; www.quirks.com
Thomas Quirk, Publisher
Evan Tweed, Associate Publisher
Joseph Rydholm, Editor
Alice Davies, Manager
Publishing case histories and discussions of techniques which can be used by purchasers of research products and services. Also directories of research services. Accepts advertising.
Cost: $60.00
64 Pages
Frequency: 11 per year
Circulation: 15,500
Mailing list available for rent: 15.5M names
Printed in 4 colors on glossy stock

17467 Shop-at-Home Directory
Belcaro Group
7100 E Belvue
Suite 305
Greenwood Village, CO 80111
Marc Braunstein, President
This valuable informational source offers information on over 400 companies that offer direct mail order sales.
Cost: $3.00
60 Pages
Frequency: SemiAnnual

17468 Source Book Of Multicultural Experts
Multicultural Marketing Resources
101 5th Ave
Suite 10B
New York, NY 10003-1008
212-242-3351; *Fax:* 212-691-5969
lisa@multicultural.com;
www.multicultural.com
Social Media: Facebook, Twitter, LinkedIn
Lisa Skriloff, President
Agata Porter, Account Executive & Editor
Yartish Bullock-Okeke, Public Relations/Sales Manager
Melanie Eisenberg, Director, Client Services
Annette Chow, Director Sales/Business Development
An annual directory that includes companies with expertise in marketing to different cultural and lifestyle markets. Resources include how to reach ethnic consumers, and contacts and leads for possible business alliances.
Cost: $19.99
Frequency: Annually
Circulation: 4000
Founded in: 1994

17469 Sports Market Place Directory
Grey House Publishing
4919 Route 22
PO Box 56
Amenia, NY 12501
518-789-8700
800-562-2139; *Fax:* 518-789-0556
books@greyhouse.com; www.greyhouse.ocm
Social Media: Facebook, Twitter
Leslie Mackenzie, Publisher
Richard Gottlieb, Editor
For over 20 years, this comprehensive, up-to-date directory has offered direct access to the Who, What, When & Where of the Sports Industry. With this directory on your desk, you have a comprehensive tool providing current key information about the people, organizations and events involving the explosive sports industry at your fingertips.
Cost: $225.00
1800 Pages
Frequency: Annual
ISBN: 1-592373-48-8
Founded in: 1981

17470 State and Regional Associations of the United States
Columbia Books
1212 New York Avenue NW
Suite 330
Washington, DC 20005-3987
202-641-1662
888-265-0600; *Fax:* 202-898-0775
info@columbiabooks.com;
www.columbiabooks.com
Buck Downs, Senior Editor
Lists 7,200 of the largest and most significant state and regional trade and professional organizations in the US Look up associations by subject, budget, state, acronym, or chief executive. Also lists contract information, serial publications, upcoming convention schedule, membership/staff size, budget figures, and background information.
Cost: $79.00
Frequency: Annual March

17471 Who's Who: MASA Buyer's Guide to Blue Ribbon Mailing Services
Mailing & Fulfillment Service Association
1421 Prince Street
Suite 410
Alexandria, VA 22314-2806
703-836-9200; *Fax:* 703-548-8204;
www.mfsanet.org
Social Media: Facebook, Twitter, LinkedIn
Ken Garner, President
Bill Stevenson, Director Marketing
Leo Raymond, Vice President
Offers a detailed listing of suppliers of equipment, products and services to the direct mail industry, most containing a description of the specific products they provide.
Frequency: Annual

Industry Web Sites

17472 http://gold.greyhouse.com
G.O.L.D Grey House OnLine Databases
Grey House Publishing's online database platform, GOLD, offers Quick Search, Keyword Search and Expert Search for most business sectors including advertising and marketing markets. The GOLD platform makes finding the information you need quick and easy - whether you're a novice searcher or an experienced database user. All of Grey House's directory products are available for subscription on the GOLD platform.

17473 www.adweek.com
Adweek
Leading decision makers in the advertising and marketing field go to Adweek.Com everyday for breaking news, insight, buzz, opinion, analysis, research and classifieds. The resources of all six regional editions of Adweek, as well as the national edition of Brandweek are combined with the knowledge of our online editors and the multimedia/interactive capabilities of the web to deliver vital information quickly and effectively to our target audience.

17474 www.ama.org
American Marketing Association
Represents marketers and keeps members informed of trends in advertising. Fosters research, sponsors seminars and provides educational placement service.

17475 www.apmaw.org
Assn of Promotion Marketing Agencies Worldwide
A trade association of sales promotion agencies with at least two years experience.

17476 www.assist-intl.com
Assist International
International trade promotion and consulting firm: mailing lists, seminars, conferences, international business expo.

17477 **www.awmanet.org**
American Wholesale Marketers Association
Government affairs, trade shows, publications, and products.

17478 **www.bmahouston.org**
Business Marketing Association: Houston
Dedicated to serving the needs of business to business Associations worldwide.

17479 **www.choosecherries.org**
Cherry Marketing Institute
An organization providing cherry information and promoting material to food manufacturers, food service operators and others.

17480 **www.fmi.org**
Food Marketing Institute
Events, publications, industry and consumer information and media.

17481 **www.greyhouse.com**
Grey House Publishing
Authoritative reference directories for most business sectors including advertising and marketing markets. Users can search the online databases with varied search criteria allowing for custom searches by product category, geographic area, sales volume, keyword, subject and more. Full Grey House catalog and online ordering also available.

17482 **www.inma.org**
International Newspaper Marketing Association
Individuals in marketing, circulation, research and public relations of newspapers.

17483 **www.manaonline.org**
Manufacturers Agents National Association
A national organization for manufacturer's agents and manufacturers who contract for the services of these representatives.

17484 **www.mark-ed.org**
Marketing Education Center
Committed to education for and about marketing. Provides professional support and training materials. Primary clients are schools, colleges, and educational institutions.

17485 **www.marketing.org**
Business Marketing Association
Pre-eminent service organization for professional's in this vital industry.

17486 **www.marketingpower.com**
American Marketing Association
A professional association for individuals and organizations involved in the practice, teaching and study of marketing worldwide.

17487 **www.mfsanet.org**
Mailing & Fulfillment Service Association
The national trade association for the mailing and fulfillment services industry.

17488 **www.mlmia.com**
Multi-Level Marketing International Association
Seeks to strengthen and improve the multi-level marketing industry in the United States and abroad.

17489 **www.msi.org**
Marketing Science Institute
Seeks to improve marketing practice and education, conducts research.

17490 **www.nacda.com**
National Assn of Collegiate Marketing Admin.
Members are public relations and marketing professionals in college and university athletic departments. Promotes standards and provides professional support.

17491 **www.pdma.org**
Product Development and Management Association
International association serving those with a professional interest in improving the management of product innovation.

17492 **www.pma.com**
Produce Marketing Association
Products and services, issues and information, conventions and expos.

17493 **www.pmc-ny.com**
Premium Marketing Club of New York
Provides education and networking opportunities for members from all areas of the marketing field

17494 **www.printing.org**
Graphic Arts Marketing Information Service
A section of Printing Industries of American that provides market research and statistics to its members. Research is member selected and directed.

17495 **www.promax.tv**
PROMAX
International association of promotion and marketing, professionals in electronic media. Promotes the effectiveness of promotion and marketing within the industry and the academic community.

17496 **www.retailing.com**
Electronic Retailing Association
Members include infomercial producers, marketers, product developers, broadcasters and other industries serving the infomercial market.

17497 **www.riahome**
Research Institute of America
A national organization that focuses on marketing and sales intelligence for top level marketing executives.

17498 **www.sigma.org**
Society of Independent Gasoline Marketers
Members are independent gasoline marketers.

17499 **www.smps.org**
Society for Marketing Professional Services
Promotes new business development of architectural, engineering, planning, design and construction management firms.

17500 **www.strategicaccounts.org**
Strategic Account Management Association
Dedicated to the professional and personal development of the executives charged with managing national, global, and strategic account relationships, and to elevating the status of the profession as a whole.

17501 **www.teleport.com**
International Trade Resources
An overview of the steps required to market abroad. Updated guide to the web's best global business sites and more.

17502 **www.the-dma.org**
Direct Marketing Association
Leading global trade association of business and nonprofit organizations using and supporting direct marketing tools and techniques.

17503 **www.tpnregister.com**
TPN Register
Business to business marketplace.

International Trade Resources

17504 **Antigua and Barbuda Department of Tourism and Trade**
25 S.E. 2nd Avenue
Suite 300
Miami, FL 33131
305-381-6762; *Fax:* 305-381-7908;
www.antigua-barbuda.org
Byron Spencer, Manager

17505 **Austrian Trade Commission**
120 West 45th Street
9th Floor
New York, NY 10036
212-421-5250; *Fax:* 212-421-5251
newyork@advantageaustria.org;
www.advantageaustria.org/us
Peter Athanasiadis, Manager
Sabine Miller, Project Manager
Walter HAfle, Director

17506 **Belize Mission to the United Nations**
675 Third Avenue
Suite 1911
New York, NY 10017
212-986-1240; *Fax:* 212-593-0932
belize@un.int; www.un.int/belize/staff.htm
Janine Coye-Felson, Minister-Counsellor
Dina S. Shoman, Counsellor/Director of Trade
Alfonso Gahona, First Secretary

17507 **Botswana Embassy**
1531-1533 New Hampshire Avenue NW
Washington, DC 20036
202-244-4990; www.botswanaembassy.org
H.E. Ms. Tebelelo Seretse, Ambassador
Ms. Sophie Heide Mautle, Deputy Head of Mission

17508 **British Trade and Investment Office**
845 3rd Avenue
9th Floor
New York, NY 10022
212-745-0495
uktiusa@ukti.gsi.gov.uk; www.ukti.gov.uk
Social Media: Twitter, LinkedIn, YouTube, flickr
Nick Baird, Chief Executive Officer
Jon Harding, Chief Operating Officer
Crispin Simon, Managing Director, Trade
Michael Boyd, Managing Director
Sandra Rogers, Managing Director, Marketing

17509 **Bulgarian General Consulate**
121 E 62nd Street
New York, NY 10021
212-935-4646; *Fax:* 212-319-5955
consulate.newyork@mfa.bg;
www.consulbulgaria-ny.org

17510 **Business Council for the United Nations**
801 2nd Avenue
2nd Floor
New York, NY 10017
212-907-1300; *Fax:* 212-682-9185
unahq@unausa.org; www.unausa.org/bcun
Social Media: Facebook, Twitter, YouTube, flickr
Allison B MacEachron, Executive Director

17511 Chile Trade Commission
866 United Nations Plaza
Suite 603
New York, NY 10017
212-207-3266; *Fax:* 212-207-3649
Alejandro Cerda, Trade Commissioner

17512 Colombia Government Trade Bureau
1701 Pennsylvania Avenue, N W
Suite 560
Washington, DC 20006
202-887-9000; *Fax:* 202-223-0526
Fadul@coltrade.org

17513 Consulate General of Bahrain
866 2nd Avenue
14th Floor
New York, NY 10017
212-223-6200; *Fax:* 212-319-0687;
www.un.int/bahrain/consulate.html
Jassim Buallay, Manager

17514 Consulate General of Belgium
1065 Avenue of Americas
22nd Floor
New York, NY 10018
212-586-5110
212-586-7472; *Fax:* 212-582-9657
NewYork@diplobel.fed.be;
www.diplomatie.be/newyork/
Piet Morisse, Manager

17515 Consulate General of Bolivia
211 E 43rd Street
Suite 702
New York, NY 10017
212-599-6767; *Fax:* 212-687-0532
Jorge Heredia Cavero, Manager

17516 Consulate General of Brazil
1185 Avenue of the Americas
21st Floor
New York, NY 10036-2601
917-777-7777; *Fax:* 212-827-0225
cg.novayork@itamaraty.gov.br
http://novayork.itamaraty.gov.br/en-us/
Julio Cesar Gomes Dos Sant, Manager

17517 Consulate General of Costa Rica
14 Penn Plaza, #1202
225 West 34th Street
New York, NY 10122
212-509-3066
212-509-3066; *Fax:* 212-509-3068; *Fax:* 212-509-3068; www.costariica-embassy.org
Otto Barcas, Manager

17518 Consulate General of Germany
871 United Nations Plaza
New York, NY 10017
212-610-9700; *Fax:* 212-940-0402
Bernhard Von Der Planit, Manager

17519 Consulate General of Haiti
815 2nd Avenue
6th Floor
New York, NY 10017
212-697-9767; *Fax:* 212-681-6991;
www.haitianconsulate-nyc.org
Social Media: Facebook, Twitter
Marie Therese, Manager

17520 Consulate General of Honduras
255 West 36th Street
First Level
New York, NY 10018
212-714-9451; *Fax:* 212-714-9453;
www.hondurasemb.org
Social Media: Facebook, Twitter

17521 Consulate General of India
3 E 64th Street
New York, NY 10065
212-774-0600; *Fax:* 212-861-3788;
www.indiacgny.org
Social Media: Facebook, Twitter, Youtube
Dnyaneshwar M Mulay, Consul General
Mr. P.K. Bajaj, Consul (Head of Chancery)

17522 Consulate General of Indonesia
5 E 68th Street
New York, NY 10021
212-879-0600

17523 Consulate General of Israel
800 Second Avenue
New York, NY 10017
212-499-5000
info@newyork.mfa.gov.il; www.israelfm.org
Social Media: Facebook, Twitter, YouTube, flickr
Ido Aharoni, Consul General

17524 Consulate General of Kenya
866 UN Plaza
Suite 4016
New York, NY 10017
212-421-4741; *Fax:* 212-486-1985;
www.kenya.embassy-online.net/kenya-consulate-general-new-york.php
Rolando Visconti, Manager

17525 Consulate General of Lebanon
9 E 76th Street
New York, NY 10021
212-744-7905; *Fax:* 212-794-1510
lebconsny@aol.com; www.lebconsny.org/
Hassan Saad, Manager

17526 Consulate General of Lithuania
420 5th Avenue
3rd Floor
New York, NY 10018
212-354-7840
Rimantas Morkvenas, Manager

17527 Consulate General of Malta
249 E 35th Street
New York, NY 10016
212-425-2345

17528 Consulate General of Morocco
10 East 40th Street
New York, NY 10016
212-758-2625; *Fax:* 646-395-8077;
www.moroccanconsulate.com/
Ramon Xilotl, Manager

17529 Consulate General of Nicaragua
820, 2nd Avenue, 8th floor.,
Suite 802
New York, NY 10017
212-983-1981; *Fax:* 212-989-5528
info@ConsuladoDeNicaragua.com
consuladodenicaragua.com
Jose Flores, Manager
Nohelia Urcuyo, Consul

17530 Consulate General of Nigeria
828 2nd Avenue
New York, NY 10017
212-808-0301; *Fax:* 212-687-1476
cgnny@nigeriahouse.com;
www.nigeriahouse.com/
Social Media: Facebook

17531 Consulate General of Paraguay
801 2nd Avenue
Suite 600
New York, NY 10017
212-682-9441; *Fax:* 212-682-9443
info@consulparny.com;
www.consulparny.com/ingles/
Juan Baiardi, Manager

17532 Consulate General of Peru
215 Lexington Avenue
21st Floor
New York, NY 10016
212-481-7410; www.consuladoperu.com/

17533 Consulate General of Qatar
809 United Nations Plaza
4th Floor
New York, NY 10017
212-486-9335

17534 Consulate General of Russia
2790 Green St
San Francisco, CA 94123
415-928- 687; *Fax:* 415-929-0306;
www.consulrussia.org/eng

17535 Consulate General of Saudi Arabia
866 Second Avenue
5th Floor
New York, NY 10017
212-752-2740;
www.saudiembassy.net/embassy/us_offices.aspx
Abdulrahman Gdaia, Excellency

17536 Consulate General of Slovenia
600 3rd Avenue
24th Floor
New York, NY 10016
212-370-3007; *Fax:* 212-370-3581;
www.culturalprofiles.net/slovenia
Reimo Pettai, Manager
Sayed Jahangir, Director of Publications

17537 Consulate General of South Africa
333 E 38th Street
9th Floor
New York, NY 10016
212-213-4880; *Fax:* 212-213-0102
consulate.ny@foreign.gov.za;
www.southafrica-newyork.net/consulate/
Social Media: Facebook
George Monyemangene, Consul General

17538 Consulate General of St. Lucia
800 2nd Avenue
9th Floor
New York, NY 10017
212-499-5000
Julian Hunte, Manager

17539 Consulate General of Switzerland
633 3rd Avenue
30th Floor
New York, NY 10017
212-599-5700
Raymond Loretan, Excellency

17540 **Consulate General of Trinidad & Tobago**
125 Maiden Lane
Unit 4A, 4th Floor
New York, NY 10038

212-682-7272; *Fax:* 212-232-0368
consulate@ttcgny.com;
www.ttcgnewyork.com/
Social Media: Facebook, Twitter, You Tube

Hon Harold Robertson, Contact

17541 **Consulate General of Ukraine**
240 E 49th Street
New York, NY 10017

212-371-6965; *Fax:* 212-371-5547
gc_usn@mfa.gov.ua; www.ny.mfa.gov.ua/en

17542 **Consulate General of Uruguay**
420 Madison Avenue
6th Floor
New York, NY 10017

212-753-8191; *Fax:* 212-753-1603
consulado@consuladouruguaynewyork.com;
www.consuladouruguaynewyork.com/english-1/

Basil Bryan, Manager

17543 **Consulate General of Venezuela**
7 E 51st Street
New York, NY 10022

212-826-1660

17544 **Consulate General of the Commonwealth of the Bahamas**
231 E 46th Street
2nd Floor
New York, NY 10017

212-717-5643

Hon Eldred E Bethel, Contact

17545 **Consulate General of the Dominican Republic**
1715 22nd Street NW
Washington, DC 20008

202-332-6280; *Fax:* 202-265-8057

17546 **Consulate General of the Netherlands**
666 Third Avenue
19th Floor
New York, NY 10017

877-388-2443; *Fax:* 212-246-9769
nyc@minbuza.nl
http://ny.the-netherlands.org/
Social Media: Facebook, Twitter

Wanda Fleck, Manager

17547 **Consulate General of the Principality of Monaco**
565 5th Avenue
New York, NY 10017

212-286-0500

Magguy Maccario-Doyle, Manager

17548 **Consulate General of the Republic of Croatia**
369 Lexington Avenue
11th Floor
New York, NY 10017

212-972-2277

Abdul Seraj, Manager

17549 **Consulate General of the Republic of Belarus**
708 3rd Avenue
21st Floor
New York, NY 10017

212-682-5392

Sergei Kolos, Manager

17550 **Consulate of Guyana**
866 United Nations Plaza
New York, NY 10017

212-527-3215

Brentnold Evans, Manager

17551 **Consulate of the Republic of Uzbekistan**
866 United Nations Plaza
Suite 327-A
New York, NY 10017-7671

212-754-6178

17552 **Cyprus Embassy Trade Center**
13 E 40th Street
New York, NY 10016

212-213-9100; *Fax:* 212-213-2918
ctcny@cyprustradeny.org;
www.cyprustradeny.org/

Aristos Constantine, Trade Commissioner

The commission's primary role is to further and expand the economic interests of the Republic of Cyprus through promoting, facilitating and attracting foreign investment and fostering the expansion of exports of Cyprus' goods and services, in addition to monitoring related market and policy issues.

17553 **Department of Trade- Government of Antigua & Barbuda**
610 5th Avenue
Suite 311
New York, NY 10020

212-541-4117

17554 **Ecuadorian Consulate**
2535 15th Street NW
Washington, DC 20009

202-234-7200; *Fax:* 202-667-3482
consuladodc@ecuador.org; www.ecuador.us

Pablo Yanez, Consulate

17555 **Egyptian Consulate Economic & Commercial Office**
3521 International Ct. NW
Washingotn, DC 20008

202-895-5400; *Fax:* 202-244-4319
embassy@egyptembassy.net;
www.egyptembassy.net
Social Media: Facebook

Ayden Nour, Executive Director

17556 **Embassy of Australia**
1601 Massachusetts Avenue NW
Washington, DC 20036

202-797-3000; *Fax:* 202-797-3168;
www.usa.embassy.gov.au
Social Media: Facebook, Twitter

Kim Beazley, Ambassador

17557 **Embassy of Benin**
2124 Kalorama Road NW
Washington, DC 20008

202-232-6656; *Fax:* 202-265-1996
info@beninembassy.us; www.beninembassy.us

Cyrille Segbe Oguin, President

17558 **Embassy of Cambodia**
4530 16th Street NW
Washington, DC 20011

202-726-7742
202-726-7824; *Fax:* 202-726-8381;
www.embassyofcambodia.org
Social Media: Facebook

Hem Heng, Ambassador

17559 **Embassy of Ethiopia Trade Affairs**
3506 International Drive NW
Washington, DC 20008

202-364-1200; *Fax:* 202-587-0195
ethiopia@ethiopianembassy.org;
www.ethiopiaenmbassy.org

Girma Birru, Ambassador

17560 **Embassy of Finland**
3301 Massachusetts Avenue NW
Washington, DC 20008

202-298-5800; *Fax:* 202-298-6030
sanomat.was@formin.fi; www.finland.org
Social Media: Facebook, Twitter

Ritva Koukku-Ronde, Ambassador
Kristiina Vuorenp„„„, Assistant to the Ambassador
Tarja Thatcher, Social Secretary

17561 **Embassy of Georgia**
2209 Massachusettes Avenue, NW
Washington, DC 20008

202-387-2390; *Fax:* 202-387-0864
georgianconsulate1@verizon.net;
www.embassy.mfa.gov.ge

Temur Yakobashvili, Ambassador

17562 **Embassy of Grenada**
1701 New Hampshire Ave, NW
Washington, DC 20009-2501

202-265-2561; *Fax:* 292-265-2468
embassy@grenadaembassyusa.org;
www.grenadaembassyusa.org
Social Media: Facebook, Twitter, Google Plus

E. Angus Friday, Ambassador
Patricia D Clarke, Counsellor
Dianne C Perrotte, Administrative Assistant
Lucia Amedee, Receptionist/Office Assistant

17563 **Embassy of Jamaica (JAMPRO)**
1520 New Hampshire Ave, NW
Washington, DC 20036

202-452-0660; *Fax:* 202-452-0036
firstsec@jamaicaembassy.org;
www.embassyofjamaica.org

Dr Stephen Vasciannie, Ambassador

17564 **Embassy of Mali**
2130 R Street NW
Washington, DC 20008

202-332-2249; *Fax:* 202-332-6603
info@maliembassy.us; www.maliembassy.us

Al Maamoun Baba Lamine Keita, Ambassador
Muhamed Ouzouna Maiga, The First Counselor
Ahmadou Barazi Maiga, The Second Counselor
Salif Sanogo, The Third Counselor-Communication
Colonel Bourama Sangare, Defence Attache

17565 **Embassy of Mongolia**
2833 M Street NW
Washington, DC 20007

202-333-7117; *Fax:* 202-298-9227
dc@mongolianembassy.us;
www.mongolianembassy.us
Social Media: Facebook, Twitter, Youtube

H.E. Altangerel Bulgaa, Ambassador
Gansukh Damdin, Minister Counsellor, Deputy Chief

Munkhjargal Byamba, Counsellor
Colonel Boldbat Khasbazar, Defense Attache
Gantulga Chadraabal, Political Affairs/Counsellor

17566 Embassy of Panama
2862 McGill Terrace NW
Washington, DC 20008

202-483-1407
202-483-8416; *Fax:* 202-483-8413
info@embassyofpanama.org;
www.embassyofpanama.org
Social Media: Facebook

Mario E. Jaramillo, Ambassador

17567 Embassy of Tanzania
1232 22nd St, NW
Washington, DC 20037

202-884-1080
202-939-6125; *Fax:* 202-797-7408
ubalozi@tanzaniaembassy-us.org;
www.tanzaniaembassy-us.org

H.E. Liberata Mulamula, Ambassador
Lily Munanka, Minister
Paul Mwafongo, Minister Plenipotentiary, Economics
B. G.Emmanuel Maganga, Defense Attach
Edward Masanja, Financial Attache

17568 Embassy of Tunisia
1515 Massachusetts Avenue NW
Washington, DC 20005

202-862-1850; *Fax:* 202-862-1858;
www.tunconsusa.org/

Gordon Gray, Ambassador

17569 Embassy of Uganda
5911 16th Street NW
Washington, DC 20011

202-726-7100; *Fax:* 202-726-1727
owonekha@ugandaembassyus.org;
www.ugandaemb.org
Social Media: Facebook, Twitter

Oliver Wonekha, Ambassador
Alfred Nnam, Deputy Chief of Mission (DCM)
Dickson Ogwang, Minister Counselor
Patrick Muganda Guma, Counselor
Sam Bhoi Omara, First Secretary

17570 Embassy of Vietnam
1233 20th Street NW
Suite 400
Washington, DC 20036

202-861-0737; *Fax:* 202-861-0917
info@vietnamembassy.us;
www.vietnamembassy-usa.org

Nguyen Quoc Cuong, Ambassador

17571 Embassy of Zimbabwe
1608 New Hampshire Avenue
Washington, DC 20009

202-332-7100; *Fax:* 202-483-9326;
www.zimbabwe-embassy.us

Machivenyika Mapuranga, Ambassador
Richard T Chibuwe, Minister Counselor and Deputy Chief
R Matsika, Counselor
Whatmore Goora, Counselor (Political)
Col. George Chinoingira, Defence Attache

17572 Embassy of the Hashemite Kingdom of Jordan
3504 International Drive NW
Washington, DC 20008

202-966-2664; *Fax:* 202-966-3110;
www.jordanembassyus.org
Social Media: Facebook, Twitter, Youtube, Pintrest

Alia Hatoug Bouran, Ambassador

17573 Embassy of the Lao People's Democratic Republic
2222 S Street NW
Washington, DC 20008

202-332-6416
202-667-0076; *Fax:* 202-332-4923
embasslao@gmail.com; www.laoembassy.com

Seng Soukhathivong, Ambassador

17574 Embassy of the People's Republic of China
3505 International Place NW
Washington, DC 20008

202-495-2266; *Fax:* 202-495-2138
chinaembpress_us@mfa.gov.cn;
www.china-embassy.org

Zhang Yesui, Ambassador

17575 Embassy of the Republic of Angola
2100-2108 16th Street, NW
Washington, DC 20009

202-785-1156; *Fax:* 202-822-9049
angola@angola.org; www.angola.org

Alberto do Carmo Bento Ribeiro, Ambassador
Sofia Pegado da Silva, Minister Counselor
Manuel Francisco Louren‡o, First Secretary - Head of Consular
Ineclito Lima, First Secretary - Consular Section
Mercedes Quintino, First Secretary - Consular Section

17576 Embassy of the Republic of Fiji
2000 M Street,NW
Suite 710
Washington, DC 20036

202-466-8320; *Fax:* 202-466-8325
info@fijiembassydc.com;
www.fijiembassydc.com

Winston Thompson, Ambassador

17577 Embassy of the Republic of Latvia
2306 Massachusettes Ave, NW
Washington, DC 20008

202-328-2840; *Fax:* 202-328-2860
embassy.usa@mfa.gov.lv;
www.mfa.gov.lv/en/usa/
Social Media: Facebook, Twitter, Flickr

Andris Razans, Ambassador
Jurijs Pogrebnaks, Deputy Chief of Mission and Counsel
Vineta Mekone, Counsellor
Gita Leitlande, Defense Counsellor
Valts Vitums, First Secretary

17578 Embassy of the Republic of Liberia
5201 16th Street N. W.
Washington, DC 20011

202-723-0437; *Fax:* 202-723-0436;
www.liberianembassyus.org/

Charles Minor, President

17579 Embassy of the Republic of Yemen
2319 Wyoming Ave, NW
Washington, DC 20008

202-965-4760; *Fax:* 202-337-2017
ambassador@yemenembassy.org;
www.yemenembassy.org

Abdulwahab Abdulla Al-Hajjri, Ambassador
Nadia Hashem, Assistant to the Ambassador

17580 Embassy of the Republic of the Marshall Islands
2433 Massachusetts Avenue NW
Washington, DC 20008

202-234-5414; *Fax:* 202-232-3236;
www.rmiembassyus.org

Charles R. Paul, Ambassador

17581 Estonian Embassy in Washington
2131 Massachusetts Avenue NW
Washington, DC 20008

202-588-0101; *Fax:* 202-588-0108
Embassy.Washington@mfa.ee;
www.estemb.org

Marina Kaljurand, Ambassador
Tanel Sepp, Deputy Chief of Mission
Indrek Kannik, Counselor (Security Policy)
Oleg Dmitrijev, First Secretary (Political Affairs)
Marju Korts, Third Secretary (Economic Affairs)

17582 Fair Trading Commission
800 2nd Avenue
2nd Floor
New York, NY 10017

246-424-260; *Fax:* 246-424-0300
info@ftc.gov.bb; www.ftc.gov.bb

Peggy Griffith, CEO
Founded in: 1955

17583 French Trade Commission
1 E Wacker Drive
Suite 3730
Chicago, IL 60601

312-661-1880; *Fax:* 310-843-1700;
www.ubifrance.com
Social Media: Facebook, Twitter, LinkedIn

17584 Gambia Mission to the United Nations
800 2nd Avenue
Suite 400 F
New York, NY 10017

212-949-6640; *Fax:* 212-856-9820;
www.un.int/gambia

Tamsir Jallow, Ambassador

17585 General Consulate of Luxembourg
17 Beekman Place
New York, NY 10022

212-888-6664; *Fax:* 212-888-6116
newyork.cg@mae.etat.lu
http://newyork-cg.mae.lu/en/The-Consulate-General

Jean-Claude Knebeler, Consul General
Saba Amroun-Febres, Consular Officer

17586 Gibraltar Information Bureau
1156 15th Street NW
Suite 1100
Washington, DC 20005

202-452-1108; *Fax:* 202-452-1109

Perry Stieglitz, Executive Director

17587 Greek Trade Commission
150 E 58th Street
17th Floor
New York, NY 10155

212-751-2404; *Fax:* 212-593-2278

Yannis Papadimitriou, Manager

17588 Guatemala Trade Office
57 Park Avenue
New York, NY 10017

212-689-1014; *Fax:* 212-689-6414
guatrade@aol.com

Roberto Rosenberg, Manager

17589 Hong Kong Trade Development Council
219 East 46th Street
New York, NY 10017-2951

212-838-8688; *Fax:* 212-838-8941
new.york.office@hktdc.org; www.hktdc.com

Social Media: Facebook, Twitter, LinkedIn, Google+, YouTube, RSS, Weibo

Margaret Fong, Executive Director
Benjamin Chau, Deputy Executive Director
Raymond Yip, Deputy Executive Director
Ralph Chow, Regional Director, America

Promotes trade between the United States and Hong Kong.
Founded in: 1966

17590 Hungarian Trade Commission
425 Bloor Street, East
Suite 501
Toronto-Ontario M4W 3R4

416-923-3596; *Fax:* 416-923-2097

Gyula Cseko, Trade Commissioner

17591 Icelandic Consulate General
800 3rd Avenue
36th Floor
New York, NY 10022

212-593-2700
646-282-9360; *Fax:* 646-282-9369
icecon.ny@mfa.is; www.iceland.is/us/nyc
Social Media: Facebook

Hlynur Gudjonsson, Consul & Trade Commissioner
Berg_¢ra Laxdal, Cultural Representative
Founded in: 1939

17592 International Chamber of Commerce (ICC)
1212 Avenue of the Americas
New York, NY 10036-1689

212-703-5065; *Fax:* 212-575-0327;
www.iccwbo.org
Social Media: Facebook, Twitter, LinkedIn, Youtube

Gerard Worms, Chairman
Harold McGraw III, Vice-Chairman
Founded in: 1919

17593 Irish Trade Board
345 Park Avenue
17th Floor
New York, NY 10154

212-180-0800

Jean McCluskey, Marketing Executive

17594 Italian Trade Commission
33 East 67th Street
New York, NY 10065-5949

212-980-1500; *Fax:* 212-758-1050
newyork@ice.it;
www.italtrade.com/countries/americas/usa/newyork.htm

Michelle Jones, Editor
Robert Luongo, Executive Director

Developments in the Italian wine industry and market, as well as reviews of imported wines from Italy.

17595 Japanese External Trade Organization
1221 Avenue of the Americas
42nd Floor
New York, NY 10020

212-997-0400; *Fax:* 212-997-0464
jetrony@jetro.go.jp; www.jetro.org
Social Media: Facebook, Twitter

Masaki Fujihara, Director, Business Development
Daiki Nakajima, ICT/Environment

17596 Kazakhstan Mission to the United Nations
305 East 47th Street
3rd Floor
New York, NY 10017

212-230-1900; *Fax:* 212-230-1172
kazakhstan@un.int; www.kazakhstanun.org

Byrganym Aitimova, Ambassador
Akan Rakhmetulin, DeputyPermanent Representative
Israil Tilegen, Minister Counsellor
Ruslan Bultrikov, Counsellor
Tluezan Seksenbay, Counsellor

Historic contributions in the field of nucleardisarmamentand non-proliferation by voluntarily eliminating its nuclear arsenal, acceding to the NPT as a non-nuclear state and shutting down the former Semipalatinsk nuclear testing ground, thus ensuring global and regional stability
Founded in: 1992

17597 Korea Trade Promotion Center (KOTRA)
460 Park Avenue
14th Floor
New York, NY 10022

212-826-0900; *Fax:* 212-888-4930
kotrany@hotmail.com; www.kotrana.org

Sungpil Umo, President
Il Hoon Ko, Deputy Director

17598 Kyrgyzstan Mission to the United Nations
866 United Nations Plaza
Suite 477
New York, NY 10017

212-486-4214; *Fax:* 212-486-5259;
www.un.int/wcm/content/site/kyrgyzstan

Talaibek Kydyrov, Ambassador
Nuran Niyazaliev, Counsellor
Nurbek Kasymov, First Secretary
Diana Sarygulova, Third Secretary
Asel Davydova, Chief Administrative Specialist

Landlocked republic in the eastern part of Central Asia which is bordered in the north by Kazakhstan, in the east by China, in the south by China and Tajikistan, and in the west by Uzbekistan. Bishkek is the capital and largest city.
Founded in: 1993

17599 Malaysia Trade Commission
313 E 43rd Street
3rd Floor
New York, NY 10017

212-986-6310; *Fax:* 212-490-8576;
www.kln.gov.my

Hussein Haniff, Ambassador

17600 Mexico Trade Commission
757 3rd Avenue
Suite 2400
New York, NY 10017-2042

212-826-2978

17601 Moldova Mission to the United Nations
35 East 29th Street
New York, NY 10016

212-447-1867; *Fax:* 212-447-4067
unmoldova@aol.com;
www.un.int/wcm/content/site/moldova

Vlad Lupan, Ambassador
Larisa Miculet, Counsellor
Carolina Podoroghin, Third Secretary
Tatianana Dudnicenco, Chief Financial Officer
Litvac Sergiu, Administrator
Founded in: 1992

17602 New Zealand Trade Development Board
222 East 41st Street
New York, NY 10017-6739

212-497-0200

17603 Norwegian Trade Council
2720 34th Street NW
Washington, DC 20008

202-333-6000; *Fax:* 202-469-3990
emb.washington@mfa.no; www.norway.org
Social Media: Twitter, LinkedIn, Flickr, Instagram, Tumblr

Kare R.Aas, Ambassador
Lajla Jakhelin, Minister
Elin Kylvag, Personal Assistant
Berit Enge, Minister Counsellor

Innovation Norway promotes nationwide industrial development profitable to both the business economy and Norways national economy, and helps release the potential of different districts and regions by contributing towards innovation, internationalisation and promotion. Innovation Norway also promotes tourism to Norway

17604 Pakistan Trade Commission
12 E 65th Street
4th Floor
New York, NY 10021

212-879-5800

Abbas Zaidi, Manager

17605 Permanent Mission of Bangladesh to the United Nations
820 East Diplomat Center, 2nd Avenue
4th Floor
New York, NY 10017

212-867-3434; *Fax:* 212-972-4038
bangladesh@un.int;
www.un.int/wcm/content/site/bangladesh

A.K.Abdul Momen, Ambassador
Mustafizur Rahman, Permanent Representative
Andalib Elias, Counsellor
Samia Anjum, Counsellor

Peaceful settlement of disputes, promotion of human rights, protection of environment, sustainable development and so on.
Founded in: 1990

17606 Permanent Mission of Ghana to the United Nations
19 E 47th Street
New York, NY 10017

212-832-1300; *Fax:* 212-751-6743
ghanaperm@aol.com; www.un.int/ghana

Ken Kanda, Ambassador
William Kanyirige, Minister
Henry T.Menson, Minister-Counsellor
J.R Adogla, Minister-Counsellor
N.A Abayena, Counsellor
Founded in: 1957

17607 Permanent Mission of Myanmar (Formerly Burma)
10 E 77th Street
New York, NY 10075

212-744-1271; *Fax:* 212-744-1290
mynmarmnission@verizon.net;
www.myanmarmissionny.org

H.E.U. Kyaw Tin, Ambassador
A.Kyaw Zan, Minister counsellor
Ko Ko Shien, Minister Counsellor

17608 **Permanent Mission of Saint Vincent & the Grenadines to the United Nations**
800 2nd Avenue
Suite 400-G
New York, NY 10017
212-599-0950; *Fax:* 212-599-1020;
www.svg-un.org
Social Media: Facebook, Twitter, YouTube
Camillo M. Gonsalves, Ambassador
Nedra Miguel, Minister Counsellor
Mozart Carr, Attache
Maglyn Carrington, Secretary/Accountant
Primary channel for communications between the Vincentian Government and the United Nations in New York City.
Founded in: 1998

17609 **Permanent Mission of the Czech Republic to the United Nations**
1109-1111 Madison Avenue
New York, NY 10028
646-981-4001; *Fax:* 646-981-4099
un.newyork@embassy.mzv.cz;
www.mzv.cz/un.newyork
Social Media: Facebook, Twitter, LinkedIn
Edita Hrda, Amabassador
David Cervanka, Deputy Permanent Representative
Founded in: 1945

17610 **Permanent Mission of the Kingdom of Bhutan to the United Nations**
343 East 43rd Street
New York, NY 10017
212-682-2268; *Fax:* 212-661-0551
bhutan@un.int;
www.un.int/wcm/content/site/bhutan
Lhtu Wangchuk, Ambassador

17611 **Permanent Mission of the Republic of Sudan to the United Nations**
655 3rd Avenue
Suite 500-10
New York, NY 10017
212-593-0999
Jenine Selson, Manager

17612 **Permanent Mission of the Republic of Armenia to the United Nations**
119 E 36th Street
New York, NY 10016
212-752-3370
Andrezej Towpik, Manager

17613 **Permanent Mission of the Solomon Islands to the United Nations**
800 2nd Avenue
Suite 400
New York, NY 10017
212-599-6192; *Fax:* 212-661-8925;
www.un.int/wcm/content/site/solomonislands
Collin Beck, Ambassador
Hellen Beck, Counsellor
Vanessa M.Kenilorea, Third Secretary
B Jagne, Manager

17614 **Philippines Commercial Office**
556 5th Avenue
New York, NY 10036
212-764-1330

17615 **Poland Trade Commission**
675 3rd Avenue
19th Floor
New York, NY 10017
212-351-1713
Phyllis Poland, Owner

17616 **Portuguese Trade Commission**
590 5th Avenue
3rd Floor
New York, NY 10036
212-354-4403; *Fax:* 212-575-4737
chamber@portugal-us.com;
www.portugal-un.org

17617 **Romanian Consulate General**
11766 Wilshire Blvd
Suite 560
Los Angeles, CA 90025
310-444-0043; *Fax:* 310-445-0043
http://www.romanian.com
Corina Suteu, Manager
The Romanian projects are on hold, as inhouse resources were diverted to more lucrative projects hosted at NetSide. If you have an interst to develop something in Romanian, please let me know and perhaps we can work something out.

17618 **Singapore Trade Commission**
55 E 59th Street
Suite 21-B
New York, NY 10022
212-421-2869; *Fax:* 212-421-2206
newyork@contactsingapore.org
Kc Yeoh, Executive Director

17619 **Slovak Republic Mission to the United Nations**
866 United Nations Plaza
Suite 493
New York, NY 10017
212-980-1558

17620 **Swedish Trade Council**
150 N Michigan Avenue
Chicago, IL 60601
312-781-6222
Social Media: Facebook, Twitter
Stefam Bergstrom, Manager

17621 **Syrian Arab Republic Embassy**
2215 Wyoming Avenue NW
Washington, DC 20008
202-232-6313; *Fax:* 202-265-4585

17622 **Taiwan Trade Center**
5201 Great America Parkway
Suite 306
Santa Clara, CA 95054-112
408-988-5018; *Fax:* 408- 98-5029
office@taiwantradesf.org
http://sf.taiwantrade.com.tw/
Founded in: 1970

17623 **Tajikistan Mission to the United Nations**
136 E 67th Street
New York, NY 10021
212-744-2196; *Fax:* 212-472-7645
Khamrokhon Zaripov, President
Abduvokhid Karimov, Minister

17624 **Thailand Trade Center- Consulate General of Thailand**
401 N Michigan Avenue
Suite 544
Chicago, IL 60611
312-467-0044; *Fax:* 312-467-1690
ttcc@wwa.com

17625 **Trade Commission of Denmark**
285 Peachtree Road NE
Suite 920
Atlanta, GA 30303
404-588-1588; *Fax:* 678-904-9714
atlhkt@um.dk
Taksoe Jensen, Ambassador
Henrik Bronner, Manager

17626 **Trade Commission of Spain**
500 N Michigan Avenue
Suite 1500
Chicago, IL 60611
312-644-1154; www.spaintechnology.com

17627 **Turkish Trade Commission**
821 United Nations Plaza
4th Floor
New York, NY 10017
212-687-1530

17628 **Turkmenistan Mission to the United Nations**
866 United Nations Plaza
Suite 424
New York, NY 10017
212-486-8908; *Fax:* 212-486-2521
turkmenistan@un.int
Aksoltan Ataeva, Manager

17629 **United Nations Mission to El Salvador**
46 Park Avenue
New York, NY 10016
212-679-1616; *Fax:* 212-725-3467
elsalvador@un.int;
www.un.int/wcm/content/site/elsalvador
Antonio Montiero, Manager

Associations

17630 **AMT: Association for Manufacturing Technology**
7901 Westpark Dr
Mc Lean, VA 22102-4206

703-893-2900
800-524-0475; *Fax:* 703-893-1151
AMT@amtonline.org; www.amtonline.org
Social Media: Facebook, Twitter, LinkedIn, Youtube

Bob Simpson, President
Douglas K. Woods, First Vice Chairman
John Byrd, President

The Association For Manufacturing Technology represents and promotes U.S.-based manufacturing technology and its members-those who design, build, sell, and service the continuously evolving technology that lies at the heart of manufacturing
370 Members
Founded in: 1902

17631 **APMI International Advancement of Powder Metallurgy**
105 College Road E
Princeton, NJ 08540-6992
609-452-7700; *Fax:* 609-987-8523
info@mpif.org; www.mpif.org

Dean Howard, President
Michael E Lutheran, Director
C James Trombino CAE, Director

A non-profit professional society which promotes the advancement of powder metallurgy (PM) and particulate materials as a science. Its purpose is to disseminate and exchange information about PM and particulate materials through publications, conferences, and other activities of the society.
Founded in: 1959

17632 **ASM International**
9639 Kinsman Rd
Materials Park, OH 44072

440-338-5151
800-336-5152; *Fax:* 440-338-4634
memberservices@asminternational.org; www.asminternational.org
Social Media: Facebook, Twitter, LinkedIn

Stanley Theobald, Managing Director
Thomas S Passek, Association Managing Director
Joseph M Zion, Director, Sales & Marketing
Jeane Deatherage, Administrator, Foundation Programs
Virginia Shirk, Foundation Executive Assistant

The society for materials engineers and scientists, a worldwide network dedicated to advancing industry, technology and applications of metals and materials.
35000 Members
Founded in: 1913

17633 **ASM International Materials Information Society**
9639 Kinsman Road
Materials Park, OH 44073-0002

440-338-5151
800-336-5152
memberservicecenter@asminternational.org; www.asminternational.org
Social Media: Facebook, Twitter, LinkedIn

Founded in: 1913

17634 **Aluminum Anodizers Council (AAC)**
1000 North Rand Road
Suite 214
Wauconda, IL 60084

847-526-2010; *Fax:* 847-526-3993
mail@anodizing.org; www.anodizing.org
Social Media: LinkedIn

Represents the interests of aluminum anodizers worldwide and is the principal trade organization for the andozing industry in North America. It promotes the interests of its members through technical exchange, ongoing education, statistical data, market promotion and industry representation.
85 Members
Founded in: 1988

17635 **Aluminum Association**
Aluminum Association
1400 Crystal Drive
Suite 430
Arlington, VA 22209-2444

703-358-2960; *Fax:* 703-358-2961
info@aluminum.org; www.aluminum.org
Social Media: Facebook, Twitter, LinkedIn

J Stephen Larkin, President
Joe Quinn, VP, Public Affairs
Heidi Biggs Brock, President
Ryan Olsen, Vice President, Business Informatio

Members are manufacturers of aluminum mill products and producers of aluminum.
70 Members

17636 **Aluminum Extruders Council**
1000 North Rand Road
Suite 214
Wauconda, IL 60084

847-526-2010; *Fax:* 847-526-3993
mail@aec.org; www.aec.org
Social Media: Facebook, Twitter, LinkedIn, Blog

Matt McMahon, Chairman
Scott Kelley, Vice Chairman
Jeff Henderson, President
Nancy Molenda, Communications Manager

An international association dedicated to helping manufacturers, engineers, architects and others to discover why aluminum extrusoin is the preferred material process for better products
Founded in: 1950

17637 **American Association of Professional Farriers**
1313 Washington Street
Unit 5
Shelbyville, KY 40065

www.professionalfarriers.com

Dave Farley APF CF, President
Steve Prescott APF CJF, Vice President
Roy Bloom APF CJF, Treasurer
Jeff Ridley APF CJF TE, Immediate Past President
Bryan Quinsey, Executive Director
Founded in: 2011

17638 **American Ceramic Society**
600 N. Cleveland Ave.
Suite 210
Westerville, OH 43082

240-646-7054
866-721-3322; *Fax:* 240-396-5637
customerservice@ceramics.org; www.ceramics.org
Social Media: Facebook, Twitter, LinkedIn, RSS, Google+, YouTube

17639 **American Electroplaters and Surface Finishers Society (AESF)**
1155 15th Street NW
Suite 500
Washington, DC 20005

202-457-8401; *Fax:* 202-530-0659
info@aesf.org; www.aesf.org
Social Media: Facebook, Twitter, LinkedIn, RSS, Google+, YouTube

John Flatley, Executive Director
Courtney Mariette, Bookstore/Education
Holly Wills, Membership
Dan Denston, Executive Director
John Flatley, Senior Advisor and NASF Liaison

AESF is an international society that advances the science of surface finishing to benefit industry and society through education, information and social involvement, as well as those who provide services, supplies and support to the industry.
5000 Members
Founded in: 1911

17640 **American Farriers Association**
4059 Iron Works Pkwy
Suite 1
Lexington, KY 40511-8488

859-233-7411; *Fax:* 859-231-7862
info@americanfarriers.org; www.americanfarriers.org

Craig Trnka, President
Bob S.Earle, VP
Bryan Quinsey, Executive Director
Rachel Heighton, Office Manager
Founded in: 1971

17641 **American Foundry Society**
1695 N Penny Ln
Schaumburg, IL 60173-4555

847-824-0181
800-537-4237; *Fax:* 847-824-7848
library@afsinc.org; www.afsinc.org
Social Media: Facebook, Twitter, LinkedIn

Jerry Call, Executive VP
Ian Kay, VP
David Peterson, Membership Director
Trade association representing the interests of foundry workers across the nation. Offers publications, seminars and networking to promote business in the trade.
10000 Members
Founded in: 1896

17642 **American Galvanizers Association**
6881 S Holly Circle
Suite 108
Centennial, CO 80112

720-554-0900; *Fax:* 720-554-0909
aga@galvanizeit.org; www.galvanizeit.org
Social Media: Facebook, Twitter, LinkedIn, Google+, YouTube

John Gregor, President
Philip G. Rahrig, Executive Director

Non-profit dedicated to supporting galvanizers and promoting state-of-the-art technological developments in corrosion control.
Founded in: 1933

17643 **American Galvinizers Association**
6881 South Holly Circle,
Suite 108
Centennial, CO 80112

720-554-0900; *Fax:* 720-554-0909
aga@galvanizeit.org; www.galvanizeit.org

Social Media: Facebook, Twitter, LinkedIn, Google+, YouTube

Tommy Rose, President
John Gregor, First Vice President
Tim Pendley, Second Vice President
Philip G. Rahrig, Executive Director
Dr. Tom Langill, Technical Director
Founded in: 1933

17644 **American Institute of Mining, Metallurgical & Petroleum Engineers**
8307 Shaffer Parkway
Po Box 270728
Littleton, CO 80127-0013

303-948-4255; *Fax:* 303-948-4260
aime@aimehq.org; www.aimeny.org

Rick Rolater, Executive Director
James R Jorden, President

Organized and operated exclusively to advance, record and disseminate significant knowledge of engineering and the arts and sciences involved in the production and use of minerals, metals, energy sources and materials for the benefits of humankind, both directly as AIME and through memeber societies.

17645 **American Institute of Steel Construction**
One East Wacker Drive
Suite 700
Chicago, IL 60601-1802

312-670-2400; *Fax:* 312-670-5403
solutions@aisc.org; www.aisc.org
Social Media: RSS

Roger E. Ferch, President

17646 **American Iron & Steel Institute**
25 Massachusetts Ave., NW, Suite 800
Washington, DC 20001

202-452-7100; *Fax:* 202-496-9702
webmaster@steel.org; www.recycle-steel.org
Social Media: Facebook, Twitter, Youtube,Google+,Blog

Chip Foley, VP
David Bell, VP/CEO

Works with market development communications programs in automotive, construction and container markets.

17647 **American Society for Metals**
9639 Kinsman Road
Materials Park, OH 44073-0002

440-338-5151
800-336-5152
memberservicecenter@asminternational.org; www.asminternational.org
Social Media: Facebook, Twitter, LinkedIn

Founded in: 1913

17648 **American Welding Society**
8669 Doral Boulevard, Suite 130
Doral, FL 33166

305-443-9353
800-443-9353; *Fax:* 305-443-7559; www.aws.org
Social Media: Facebook, Twitter, Instagram

Ray Shook, Manager
Andy Cullison, Publisher
Amy Nathan, Public Relations Manager

Involved in writing industry standards.
48000 Members
Founded in: 1919

17649 **American Wire Cloth Institute**
25 North Broadway
Tarrytown, NY 10591

914-332-0040; *Fax:* 914-332-1541
info@hti.org; www.hti.org

Richard C Byrne, Executive Director

Formerly the Industrial Wire Cloth Institute (1978)
Founded in: 1933

17650 **American Wire Producers Association**
PO Box 151387
Alexandria, VA 22315

703-299-4434; *Fax:* 703-299-4434
info@awpa.org; www.awpa.org

Founded in: 1981

17651 **Artist-Blacksmiths Association of North America**
259 Muddy Fork Road
Jonesborough, TN 37659

423-913-1022; *Fax:* 423-913-1023
abana@abana.org; www.abana.org
Social Media: Facebook, Twitter

Eddie Rainey, President
Tina Chisena, First VP
John Fee, Second Vice President
Herb Upham, Secretary

For the professional and amateur blacksmith.
4500 Members
Founded in: 1973
Mailing list available for rent

17652 **Association for Iron & Steel Technology (AIST)**
186 Thorn Hill Rd
Warrendale, PA 15086-7528

724-814-3000; *Fax:* 724-814-3001
memberservices@aist.org; www.aist.org
Social Media: Facebook, Twitter, LinkedIn, YouTube

Ronald E Ashburn, Executive Director
Lori Wharrey, Board Administrator
Chris McKelvey, Assistant Board Administrator
Stacy Vermecky, Membership Services Manager
Penny English, Member Administrator

The Association for Iron & Steel Technology (AIST) is an international technical association representing iron and steel producers, their allied suppliers and related academia. The association is dedicated to advancing the technical development, production, processing and application of iron and steel.
12300 Members
Founded in: 2004

17653 **Association for Manufacturing Technology**
7901 Westpark Drive
McLean, VA 22102

703-893-2900
877-578-4000; *Fax:* 703-893-1151
amt@mfgtech.org; www.amtonline.org
Social Media: Facebook, Twitter, LinkedIn, YouTube

Douglas K. Woods, President
Amber Thomas, First Vice Chairman
John Byrd, President
Rebecca Stahl, Chief Financial Officer
Ian Stringer, Director

The Association For Manufacturing Technology represents and promotes U.S.-based manufacturing technology and its members-those who design, build, sell, and service the continuously evolving technology that lies at the heart of manufacturing

17654 **Association of Battery Recyclers**
PO Box 290286
Tampa, FL 33687

813-626-6151; *Fax:* 813-622-8387
joycemorales@aol.com
batteryrecyclers.com

Joyce Morales, Secretary/Treasurer

Investigates means and methods to achieve compliance with OSHA and EPA regulations impacting the secondary lead smelting industry.
Founded in: 1976

17655 **Association of Industrial Metallizers, Coaters and Laminators (AIMCAL)**
201 Springs Street
Fort Mill, SC 29715

803-948-9470; *Fax:* 803-948-9471
aimcal@aimcal.org; www.aimcal.org
Social Media: Facebook, Twitter

Dan Bemi, President
Danis Roy, VP
Craig Sheppard, Executive Director
Tracey Ingram, Senior Administrator
David Bryant, Treasurer

Nonprofit trade organization for makes of coated, laminated and metalized papers.
Founded in: 1970
Mailing list available for rent

17656 **Association of Steel Distributors**
401 N Michigan Avenue
Chicago, IL 60611

312-673-5793; *Fax:* 312-527-6705
headquarters@steeldistributors.org; www.steeldistributors.org
Social Media: Facebook, Twitter, LinkedIn, Instagram

Ron Pietrzak, Executive Director
Brain Robbins, President
Andy Gross, Executive Vice President
Mike Sawyer, Vice President
Bill Vitucci, Treasurer

ASD is a nonprofit organization, providing the steel distribution industry a forum for ideas exchange and market information.
Founded in: 1943

17657 **Association of Women in the Metal Industries**
19 Mantua Road
Mt Royal, NJ 08061

856-423-3201; *Fax:* 856-423-3420
awmi@talley.com; www.awmi.org
Social Media: Facebook, Twitter, LinkedIn

Haley Brust, Executive Director
Donna Peters, President
Carol Chizmar, Vice President
Lauren Lebakken, Secretary
Lauren Kerekes, Treasurer

An international, professional organization dedicated to promoting and supporting the advancement of women in the metal industries.
Founded in: 1981

17658 **Cast Iron Soil Pipe Institute**
2401 Fieldcrest Dr.
Mundelein, IL 60660

224-864-2910; www.cispi.org

Founded in: 1949

17659 **Cast Metals Institute**
1695 N Penny Ln
Schaumburg, IL 60173-4555

847-824-0181
800-537-4237; *Fax:* 847-824-7848

library@afsinc.org; www.afsinc.org
Social Media: Facebook, Twitter, LinkedIn

Mark Nagel, Executive VP
Sandy Salisbury-Linton, Vice Chairman

Supports all those involved in the cast metal industry. Hosts annual trade show.
Founded in: 1956

17660 Closure & Container Manufacturers Association

14070 Proton Rd.
Suite 100, LB 9
Dallas, TX 75244-3601

972-333-9107; *Fax:* 972-490-4219
office@bevtech.org; www.bevtech.org/
Social Media: Facebook, Twitter, LinkedIn

Brain Stegmann, President
Cloeann Durham, 1st Vice President
Sieg Muller, 2nd Vice President
Ron Puvak, Immediate Past President
Larry Hobbs, Executive Director

Conducts public relations for member companies and establishes industry standards.
38 Members
Founded in: 1984

17661 Copper Development Association

260 Madison Ave
New York, NY 10016-2403

212-251-7200
800-232-3282; *Fax:* 212-251-7234
questions@cda.copper.org; www.copper.org
Social Media: Facebook, Twitter, LinkedIn, Google+

Andrew G Kireta, President & CEO
Victoria Prather, Manager Communications
Michels Harold, VP Technaloy Services
Luis Lozano, Technical Consultant
Lorraine Herzing Mills, VP/Finance/Administration

Seeks to expand the uses and applications of copper and copper products. Responsible for industry-wide market statistics and research.
75 Members
Founded in: 1963

17662 Copper and Brass Servicenter Association

6734 w. 121st street
Suite 1019
overland park, KS 66209

913-396-0697; *Fax:* 913-345-1006;
www.copper-brass.org
Social Media: Facebook, Twitter, LinkedIn, YouTube, Flickr

Dick Farmer, President
Garret Herringdon, VP
Mark Wolman, Treasurer
Robbert James, Secretary
Cscott F. Immell, Immediate Past President

Distriburors (servicenters) of fabricated copper and copper alloy products (sheet, plate, coil, rod bar, tube, etc) and their brass mill suppliers.
75 Members
Founded in: 1951

17663 Ductile Iron Pipe Research Association

P.O. Box 19206
Suite O
Golden, CO 80402

205-402-8700; *Fax:* 205-402-8730
info@dipra.org; www.dipra.org
Social Media: Facebook, Twitter, YouTube

Jon R. Runge, CAE, President
Richard W Bonds, Technical Director
L. Gregg Horn, VP, Technical Services
Josh Blount, Staff Engineer/Project Manager

Established as the Cast Iron Pipe Publicity Bureau.
7 Members
Founded in: 1915

17664 Ductile Iron Society

15400 Pearl Rd
Suite 234
Strongsville, OH 44136-6017

440-665-3686; *Fax:* 440-878-0070
jwood@ductile.org; www.ductile.org

Robert O.Rourke, President
MIke Galvin, VP
Pete Guidi, Treasurer
James N.Wood, Executive and Technical Director
Patricio Gil, Past President

A technical society servicing the ductile iron industry. To advance the technology, art, science of ductile iron production and to disseminate all such information to the members.
102 Members
Founded in: 1958

17665 Edison Welding Institute

1250 Arthur E Adams Dr
Columbus, OH 43221-3585

614-688-5000; *Fax:* 614-688-5001
info@ewi.org; www.ewi.org
Social Media: Facebook, Twitter

Henry Cialone, President
Dr Karl Graff, Executive Director
Richard Rogovin, Chair

Companies and organizations with an interest in new developments in welding equipment and technology.

17666 Electrical Manufacturing & Coil Winding Association

PO Box 278
Imperial Beach, CA 91933-0278

619-435-3629; *Fax:* 619-435-3639
cthurman@earthlink.net; www.emcwa.org

Richard Duke, President
Charles Thurman, Executive Director
Don Stankiewicz, Vice President

A non-profit voluntary organization dedicated to the furtherance of the conception, research, design, manufacturing, marketing and use of electrical products. The Association provides an array of educational opportunities that enhance the development, knowledge, and use of electrical technology and products. Providing an annual forum to display products, ideas and innovations is a key element in this educational process.
400 Members
Founded in: 1973
Mailing list available for rent

17667 Fabricators & Manufacturers Association International

833 Featherstone Road
Rockford, IL 61107

815-399-8700
888-394-4362
info@fmanet.org; www.fmanet.org
Social Media: Facebook, Twitter, LinkedIn, YouTube, Google+

Ed Youdell, President & CEO

Organization seeking to improve the metal forming and fabricating industry.
2300 Members
Founded in: 1970

17668 Fabricators and Manufacturers Association

Fabricators and Manufacturers Association
833 Featherstone Road
Rockford, IL 61107-6302

815-399-8700; *Fax:* 815-484-7700
info@fmanet.org; www.fmanet.org
Social Media: Facebook, Twitter, LinkedIn

Gerald M Shankel, President/CEO
Jim Warren, Director/Membership + Education
Vicki Webb, Director/Information Technology
Mark Hoper, Director/Expositions
Michael Long, Director/Education
1500 Members
Founded in: 1971

17669 Forging Industry Association

1111 Superior Ave.
Suite 615
Cleveland, OH 44114

216-781-6260; *Fax:* 216-781-0102
info@forging.org; www.forging.org
Social Media: Facebook, Twitter, LinkedIn

Roy W. Hardy, President
Joe Boni, CFO
Don Farley, Director of Marketing
Theresa Ferry, Executive Assistant
Pat Kasik, Executive Assistant

17670 Global Platinum & Gold

5380 S 154th St
Gilbert, AZ 85298-6138

480-946-1242; *Fax:* 480-946-1242;
www.globalplatinumonline.com

A natural resources mining company engaged in the processing and commercial extraction of precious metals from complex ores.

17671 Gold Prospectors Association of America

43445 Business Park Drive
Suite #113
Temecula, CA 92590

951-699-4749
800-551-9707; *Fax:* 951-699-4062
info@goldprospectors.org;
www.goldprospectors.org
Social Media: Facebook, Twitter, LinkedIn, YouTube

Thomas Massie, CEO

GPAA is the largest recreational gold prospecting club. Owner of The Outdoor Channel, a cable TV channel featuring real outdoors for real people.
35M Members
Founded in: 1985

17672 Industrial Diamond Association of America

P.O. Box 29460
Columbus, OH 43229

614-797-2265
614-425-0712; *Fax:* 614-797-2264
tkane-ida@insight.rr.com;
www.superabrasives.org

Terry M. Kane, Executive Director

17673 Industrial Metal Containers Section of the Material Handling Institute

8720 Red Oak Boulevard
Suite 201
Charlotte, NC 28217-3996

704-676-1190; *Fax:* 704-676-1199
gbaer@mhia.org; www.mhi.org
Social Media: Facebook, Twitter, LinkedIn, YouTube

Dave Young, Chairman
John Patrox, President
Gregg E. Goodner, Vice President
Steve Buccella, VP, Corporate Sales/BD
Bryan Carey, President and CEO

Promotes the market and develops a code of ethics. Serves as liaison among members and other groups.
9 Members
Founded in: 1972

17674 Industrial Perforators Association
6737 W. Washington St
Milwaukee, WI 53214
414-389-8618; *Fax:* 414-276-7704
infof@iperf.org; www.iperf.org
Social Media: Facebook, Twitter
Delores Morris, Executive Secretary
Members are companies making perforated metal products.

17675 Innovative Material Solutions
225 Canterbury Drive
State College, PA 16803
814-867-1140; *Fax:* 814-867-2813
Supports all those involved in research in the materials industry. Hosts annual trade show.

17676 Institute of Scrap Recycling Industries
1615 L St NW
Suite 600
Washington, DC 20036-5664
202-662-8500; *Fax:* 202-626-0900
dennywhite@scrap.org; www.isri.org
Social Media: Facebook, Twitter, LinkedIn, YouTube
Robin K.Wiener, President
Sandy Bishop, VP Finance/Administration
Rachel Bookman, Admin Assistant
Thomas Crane, Director of Membership
ISRI provides education, advocacy, and compliance training while promoting public awareness of the role recycling plays in the U.S. economy, global trade, the environment and sustainable development.

17677 International Chromium Development Association
43 rue de la Chauss,e d'Antin
Paris 75009
014-076-0689; *Fax:* 014-076-0687
info@icdacr.com; www.icdacr.com
Samancor Chrome, Chairperson
Founded in: 1984

17678 International Copper Association
260 Madison Ave
16th Floor
New York, NY 10016-2403
212-251-7240; *Fax:* 212-251-7245
info@copperalliance.org;
www.copperalliance.org
Social Media: Facebook, Twitter, LinkedIn, Google+
Francis J Kane, President
Promoting the use of copper by communicating the unique attributes that make this sustainable element an essential contributor to the formation of life, to advances in science and technology, and to a higher standard of living worldwide.
Founded in: 1989

17679 International Council on Mining and Metals
35/38 Portman Square
London W1H 6LR
207-467-5070; *Fax:* 207-467-5071
info@icmm.com; www.icmm.com
Social Media: Twitter, LinkedIn, YouTube, RSS
Tom Butler, CEO
Aidan Davy, Deputy President
John Atherton, Director, Materials Stewardship
Ross Hamilton, Director, Environment and Climate C
Brigid Janssen, Director, Communications
Founded in: 2001

17680 International Hard Anondizing
P.O. Box 5
Moorestown, NJ 08054
856-234-0330; *Fax:* 856-727-9504
staff@ihanodizing.com; www.ihanodizing.com
Social Media: Facebook
Denise Downing, Executive Director
Formed by companies in the hard anodizing business to provide a forum for the exchange of technical information and to act as a clearing house for information about the industry.
Founded in: 1989

17681 International Lead Management Center
2525 Meridian Parkway
Suite 100
Durham, NC 27713
919-287-1872; *Fax:* 919-361-1957
info@ilmc.org; www.ilmc.org

17682 International Lead Zinc Research Organization
1822 NC Highway 54 East
Suite 120
Durham, NC 27713-5243
919-361-4647; *Fax:* 919-361-1957;
www.ilzro.org
Stephen Wilkinson, President
Judith Hendrickson, Corporate Secretary
Members are miners, smelters and refiners of lead and zinc. Supports research and development of new uses for the metals and refinement existing uses. Has an annual budget of approximately $5.3 million.
77 Members
Founded in: 1958

17683 International Magnesium Association
1000 N Rand Rd
Suite 214
Wauconda, IL 60084-1180
847-526-2010; *Fax:* 847-526-3993
info@intlmag.org; www.intlmag.org
Social Media: LinkedIn
Greg Patzer, Executive VP
Eileen Hoblit, Administrative Coordinator
Ken White, Chairman
Jan Guy, President
Dr. Karl Kainer, Immediate Past President
IMA is to promote the use of the metal magnesium in material selection and encourage innovative applications of the versatile metal.
125 Members
Founded in: 1943

17684 International Platinum GroupMetals Association
Schiess-Staett-Strasse 30
Germany, MU 80339
895-199-6770; *Fax:* 895-199-6719
info@ipa-news.com; www.ipa-news.com
Deon Carter, President
Steve Phiri, Director
Gabriele Randlshofer, Managing Director
Tania Bossi, Communications Manager
Julian K"hle, Government AffairsManager
Founded in: 1987

17685 International Precious Metals Institute
5101 N 12th Avenue
Suite C
Pensacola, FL 32504
850-476-1156; *Fax:* 850-476-1548
mail@ipmi.org; www.ipmi.org
Social Media: Facebook, LinkedIn, YouTube
Robert Ianniello, President
International association of producers, refiners, fabricators, scientists, users, financial institutions, merchants, private and public sector groups and the general precious metals community created to provide a forum for the exchange of information and technology.
Founded in: 1987

17686 International Thermal Spray Association
Post Office Box 1638
Painesville, OH 44077
440-357-5400; *Fax:* 440-357-5430
itsa@thermalspray.org; www.thermalspray.org
Social Media: Facebook, LinkedIn
Kathy M Dusa, Administrative Assistant
Bill Moiser, Chairman
Jim Rayan, Vice Chairman
David Wright, Executive Officer
Strengthens the level of awareness in general industry and government on the increasing capabilities and advantages of thermal spray technology for surface engineering through business opportunities, technical support and a social network. Contributes to growth and education in the thermal spray industry.
70 Members
Founded in: 1948

17687 International Titanium Association
11674 Huron Street
Suite 100
Northglenn, CO 80234
303-404-2221; *Fax:* 303-404-9111
ita@titanium.org; www.titanium.org
Social Media: titanium2011.pathable.com
Brett S.Paddock, President & CEO
Donn S.Hickton, VP
Hunter R.Dalton, Treasurer
Susan M.Abkowitz, Director
Jennifer Simpson, Executive Director
International Titanium Association is an international membership based trade association dedicated to the titanium metal industry. Established in 1984, ITA strives to connect the public interested in using titanium with specialists from across the globe who offer sales and technical assistance.
120 Members
Founded in: 1984

17688 Lead Industries Association
13 Main Street
Sparta, NJ 07871
973-726-5323; *Fax:* 973-726-4484;
www.leadinfo.com
Jeffrey T Miller, Executive Director
Nonprofit trade association representing the lead industries in the US and abroad. It collects and distributes information about the users of lead products in industry, vehicles, radioactive waste disposal and noise barriers. Its services are availble, generally free of charge, to anyone interested in the uses of lead and lead products.

17689 Machinery Dealers National Association
Machinery Dealers National Association

315 S Patrick St
Alexandria, VA 22314-3532

703-836-9300
800-872-7807; *Fax:* 703-836-9303
office@mdna.org; www.mdna.org
Social Media: Facebook, Twitter, LinkedIn, YouTube

Ron Shuster, President
Mark Robinson, Executive VP

Supports manufacturers involved in metal working machine tools. Publishes annual directory.

17690 Magnet Distributors and Fabricators Association
8 S Michigan Avenue
Suite 1000
Chicago, IL 60603

312-541-2667; *Fax:* 312-580-0165

August L Sisco, Executive Secretary

Distributors and magnetic materials and fabricators of magnetic components, plus suppliers to the distributor/fabricators.
31 Members
Founded in: 1991

17691 Metal Building Contractors and Erectors Association
PO Box 499
Shawnee Mission, KS 66201

913-432-3800
800-866-6722; *Fax:* 913-432-3803;
www.mbcea.org

Angela M Cruse, Executive Director
Tim Seyler, President

To support the professional advancement of metal building contractors, erectors, and the industry.
235 Members
Founded in: 1968

17692 Metal Building Manufacturers Association
1300 Sumner Avenue
Cleveland, OH 44115-2851

216-241-7333; *Fax:* 216-241-0105;
www.mbma.com
Social Media: Twitter, LinkedIn, Google+

Charles M Stockinger, General Manager
Charles E Praeger, Assistant General Manager
W Lee Shoemaker, Ph.D., P.E., Director of Research & Engineering
Dan J.Walker, Senior Technical Enginner
Jay D.Johnson, Director of Architectural Services

Promotes the design and construction of metal building systems in the low-rise, non-residential building marketplace.
Founded in: 1956

17693 Metal Construction Association
8735 W. Higgins Rd.
Suite 300
Chicago, IL 60631

847-375-4718; *Fax:* 847-375-6488
mca@metalconstruction.org;
www.metalconstruction.org
Social Media: Facebook, LinkedIn

Dedicated to promoting the use of metal in construction. Initiative include market development, educational programs, issue and product awareness compaigns and publication of technical guidelines and specifications manuals. Also monitors and confronts challenges affecting the industry such as code restructions.
100 Members
Founded in: 1983

17694 Metal Findings Manufacturers
30-R Houghton Street
Providence, RI 02904

401-861-4667; *Fax:* 401-861-0429
info@mfma.net; www.mfma.net

John Augustyn, Executive Officer

Makers of metal parts and fittings used in the assembly of jewelry.
Founded in: 1930

17695 Metal Injection Molding Association
105 College Road East
Princeton, NJ 8540

609-452-7700
609-987-8523; *Fax:* 609-987-8523
info@mpif.org; www.mimaweb.org

17696 Metal Powder Industries Federation
105 College Rd E
Princeton, NJ 08540-6692

609-452-7700; *Fax:* 609-987-8523
info@mpif.org; www.mpif.org

Michael Latheran, President, CEO
Jilliane Regan, VP
Jim Adams, Manager
James R.Dale, VP

As its name states, it is afederation of trade associations-six in all-that are concerned with some aspect of powder metallurgy, metal powders, or particulate materials.
210 Members
Founded in: 1944

17697 Metal Service Center Institute
4201 Euclid Ave
Suite 550
Rolling Meadows, IL 60008-2025

847-485-3000; *Fax:* 847-485-3001
info@msci.org; www.msci.org
Social Media: Facebook, Twitter, LinkedIn

Bob Weidner, President
Jonathan Kalkwarf, VP Finance/Administration
Rose Manfredini, VP Member Information Services
Chris Marti, VP Technology
375 Members
Founded in: 1907

17698 Metals Service Center Institute
4201 Euclid Ave
Rolling Meadows, IL 60008

847-485-3000; *Fax:* 847-485-3001
info@msci.org; www.msci.org
Social Media: Facebook, Twitter, LinkedIn

Bob Weidner, President/ Chief Executive Officer
Ann D'Orazio, Vice President, Marketing-Growth
Ashley DeVecht, Director of Communications
Rose Manfredini, Vice President, Membership
Chris Marti, Vice President, Research
400+ Members

17699 Mineral Information Institute
12999 E. Adam Aircraft Circle
Englewood, CO 80112-4167

303-948-4200; *Fax:* 800-763-3132
MEC@smenet.org;
www.MineralsEducationCoalition.org
Social Media: Facebook, Twitter, YouTube

Sharon Schonhaut, Director
Rebecca Smith, Curriculum Coordinator
Rachel Grimes, Outreach Coordinator
Carol Kiser, Purchases dept

Nonprofit organization dedicated to educating youth about the science of minerals and other natural resources and about their importance in our everyday lives.

17700 Minerals, Metals & Materials Society
184 Thorn Hill Road
Warrendale, PA 15086-7514

724-769-9000
800-759-4867; *Fax:* 724-776-3770
webmaster@tms.org; www.tms.org
Social Media: Facebook, LinkedIn, YouTube

James Robinson, Executive Director
Nellie Luther, Professional Affairs Coordinator
Gail Miller, Executive Assistant
Nancy Lesko, Executive & Board Administrator
Steve Reubi, Controller

Supports all those devoted to exploring the many aspects of materials science and engineering. Publishes monthly magazine.
Founded in: 1993

17701 Mining and Metallurgical Society of America
PO Box 810
Boulder, CO 80306-0810

303-444-6032; *Fax:* 415-897-1380
contactmmsa@mmsa.net; www.mmsa.net
Social Media: Facebook, Twitter, LinkedIn

Betty L. Gibbs, Executive Director
Matt Bender, President
Barney Guarnera, VP
Paul C. Jones, Treasurer
Michael Blois, Secretary

Concerned with the conservation of the nation's mineral resources and the best interest of the mining and metallurgical industries.
350 Members
Founded in: 1908

17702 National Association for Surface Finishing
1155 15th Street NW
Suite 500
Washington, DC 20005

202-457-8404; *Fax:* 202-530-0659;
www.nasf.org
Social Media: Facebook, Twitter

Erik Welys, President
Paul Brancato, VP
Brain Harrick, Secretary/Treasurer
Jery Wahlin, Executive

The National Association for Surface Finishing is a trade association whose mission is to promote the advancement of the surface finishing industry worldwide.

17703 National Association of Aluminum Developers
4201 Euclid Ave
Suite 550
Rolling Meadows, IL 60008-2025

847-485-3000; *Fax:* 847-485-3001
info@msci.org; www.msci.org
Social Media: Facebook, Twitter, LinkedIn

Bob Weidner, President
Jonathan Kalkwarf, VP Finance/Administration
Rose Manfredini, VP Member Information Services
Chris Marti, VP Technology
Ann Zastrow, VP

NAAD is the trade association of North American service centers and principal suppliers engaged in marketing aluminum products.
400 Members
Founded in: 1914

17704 National Blacksmiths and Welders
PO Box 123
Arnold, NE 69120

308-848-2913; www.arcat.com
Social Media: Facebook, Twitter, Google+

Dave Christen, President
Jim Lindquist, First Director

Gerry Westhoff, Second VP
James Holman, Executive Director

Blacksmiths, welders and manufacturing machine shops. Organize and offer assistance to state organizations for the advancement of their members with education and guiding measures for the present and future prospects of the trade.
175 Members
Founded in: 1895

17705 National Coil Coating Association
1300 Sumner Ave
Cleveland, OH 44115-2851

216-241-3333; *Fax:* 216-781-0621;
www.coilcoating.org
Social Media: Facebook, Twitter

NCCA is an established trade organization dedicated to the growth of coil coated products. A unified organization that provides resources and leadership in order to ensure that coil coated materials are the product of choice.
Founded in: 1962

17706 National Institute for Metal Working Skills
10565 Fairfax Boulevard
Suite 203
Fairfax, VA 22030

703-352-4971; *Fax:* 703-352-4991
kdoyle@nims-skills.com; www.nims-skills.org

James Wall, Executive Director
David Morgan, Director of Business Development
Catherine Ross, Accrediation Incharge

A nonprofit organization formed by metalworking trade associations, national labor organizations, a council of state governors, companies and educators to support the development of a skilled workforce for the metalworking industry.
Founded in: 1995
Mailing list available for rent

17707 National Ornamental & Miscellaneous Metals Association
P.O. Box 492167
Ste. 127 #311
Lawrenceville, GA 30049

888-516-8585; *Fax:* 888-279-7994
nommainfo@nomma.org; www.nomma.org
Social Media: Facebook, Twitter, LinkedIn, YouTube, Vimeo, Flickr

Allyn Moseley, President
Cathy Vequist, VP/Treasurer
Keith Majka, President-Elect
Mark Koenke, Immediate Past President
Todd Daniel, Executive Director

Supports all those involved in the ornamental and miscellaneous metal industry. Publishes bi-monthly magazine.
1000 Members
Founded in: 1958

17708 National Ornamental and Miscellaneous Metals
P.O. Box 492167
Ste. 127 #311
Lawrenceville, GA 30049

888-516-8585; *Fax:* 888-279-7994
nommainfo@nomma.org; www.nomma.org
Social Media: Facebook, Twitter, LinkedIn, YouTube

Todd Daniel, Executive Director
Liz Harris, Member Care & Operations Manager
Martha Pennington, Meetings & Exposition Manager
Allyn Moseley, President
Cathy Vequist, VP/Treasurer
Founded in: 1958

17709 National Tooling & Machining Association
National Tooling & Machining Association
1357 Rockside Road
Cleveland, OH 44134

800-248-6862
800-248-6862; *Fax:* 216-264-2840
info@ntma.org; www.ntma.org

Rob Akers, CEO
Rich Basalla, Membership Officer
Tiffany Bryson, Sales/Sponsorship Manager
John Capka, Chief Financial Officer

Trade organization representing the precision custom manufacturing industry throughout the US. Has an active safety & education program.
Founded in: 1972

17710 National Welding Supply Association
Fernley & Fernley
1900 Arch St
Philadelphia, PA 19103-1404

215-564-3484; *Fax:* 215-564-2175;
www.nwsa.com
Social Media: Facebook, Twitter

William R. Surman, President
William Mehlenbeck, Vice President
R.J Kuhn, Treasurer
Bryan Beck, Immediate Past President
Jay Armstrong, Director
1200 Members
Founded in: 1945

17711 Non-Ferrous Founders' Society
1480 Renaissance Drive
Suite 310
Park Ridge, IL 60068

847-299-0950; *Fax:* 847-299-3598
nffstaff@nffs.org; www.nffs.org
Social Media: Facebook, Twitter

James L Mallory, Executive Director
Jerrod A Weaver, Director Of Education and Training
Ryan J Moore, Member Services Manager

Manufacturers of bronze, brass and aluminum castings.
185 Members
Founded in: 1943

17712 North American Die Casting Association
3250 Arlington Heights Rd
Suite 101
Arlington Heights, IL 60004

847-279-0001; *Fax:* 847-279-0002
nadca@diecasting.org; www.diecasting.org
Social Media: Facebook, Twitter, LinkedIn, YouTube, Instagram

Neal Shapiro, Affairs Committee Chairman

Supports all those involved in the die casting industry. Publishes bi-monthly magazine.
Founded in: 1957

17713 Precision Metalforming Association
6363 Oak Tree Blvd
Cleveland, OH 44131-2500

216-901-9667; *Fax:* 216-901-9190
pma@pma.org; www.pma.org
Social Media: Facebook, Twitter, LinkedIn, YouTube

Nels Leutwiler, Chairman
Dennis J Keat, First Vice Chairman
Bernie Rosselli Jr, Second Vice Chairman/Treasurer
William Gaskin, President

Members include producers of metal stampings, spinnings, washers and precision sheet metal fabrications as well as suppliers of equipment, materials and services.
1300 Members
Founded in: 1913

17714 Resistance Welder Manufacturers
8669 NW 36 Street
Suite 130
Miami, FL 33166

305-443-9353; *Fax:* 305-442-7451;
www.aws.org/rwma/
Social Media: Facebook, LinkedIn

Mark Gramelspacher, Chairman
Ed Langhenry, Vice Chairman
Tom Snow, Vice Chairman

Strives to create widespread awareness and use of the various resistance welding processes and equipment, improve relations between individual manufacturers, foster higher ethical standards throughout the industry, develop industry standards to assist users of resistance welding equipment.
82 Members
Founded in: 1935

17715 Sheet Metal Workers International Association
1750 New York Avenue, NW
6th Floor
Washington, DC 20006

www.smwia.org

17716 Sheet Metal and Air Conditioning Contractors' National Association
4201 Lafayette Center Dr
Chantilly, VA 20151-1219

703-803-2980; *Fax:* 703-803-3732;
www.smacna.org
Social Media: Facebook, Twitter, LinkedIn, YouTube

Vincent Sandusky, CEO

An international trade association representing 4,500 contibuting contractor firms in the sheet metal and air conditioning industry. Develops technical standards and manuals addressing all facets of the sheet metal and air conditioning industry.
1944 Members
Founded in: 1943

17717 Silver Institute
1400 I Street, NW
Suite 550
Washington, DC 20005

202-835-0185; *Fax:* 202-835-0155
info@silverinstitute.org;
www.silverinstitute.org

Fernando Alanis, President
Mitchell Krebs, VP
Thomas Angelos, Treasurer
Michael Dirienzo, Executive Director and Secretary
Mark Spurbeck, Assistant Treasurer

International association of miners, refiners, fabricators and wholesalers of silver and silver products.
Founded in: 1971

17718 Silver Users Association
3930 walnut Street
Suite 210
Fairfax, VA 22030

703-934-0219
800-245-6999; *Fax:* 703-359-7562
sas@silversmithing.com;
www.silverusersassociation.org

Mike Merolla, President
John Gannon, VP

Represents the interests of corporations that make, sell and distribute products and services in

which silver is an essential part. SUA membership includes representatives from the photographic, electronic, silverware and jewelry industries; producers of semi-fabricated and industrial products; and, mirror manufacturers.
30 Members
Founded in: 1947

17719 Society of American Silversmiths
PO Box 786
West Warwick, RI 02893

401-461-6840; *Fax:* 401-461-0162
sas@silversmithing.com;
www.silversmithing.com

Jeffrey Herman, Founder/Executive Director
Founded to preserve the art and history of handcrafted holloware and flatware plus provide support, networking and greater access to the market for its artisan members. Artisans are silversmiths both practicing and retired who now or used to smith as a livelihood. Educates the public as to the aesthetic and investment value of this art form and demystifies silversmithing techniques through its literature and national exhibits.
240 Members
Founded in: 1989

17720 Society of Manufacturing Engineers
Society of Manufacturing Engineers
One SME Drive
PO Box 930
Dearborn, MI 48121

313-425-3000
800-733-4763; *Fax:* 313-425-3400
advertising@sme.org; www.sme.org
Social Media: Facebook, Twitter, LinkedIn, YouTube, Google+

Wayne F. Frost, President
Debbie Holton, Managing Director
Mark Tomlinson, Executive Director
Greg Sheremet, Publisher
Jeannine Kunz, Managing Director

Supports all those involved in the metalworking industry, specifically machining, forming, inspection, assembly and processing operations. Publishes magazine.
70M Members
Founded in: 1932

17721 Society of North American Goldsmiths
PO Box 1355
Eugene, OR 97440

541-345-5689; *Fax:* 541-345-1123;
www.snagmetalsmith.org
Social Media: Facebook, Twitter, LinkedIn

Nicole Jaquard, President
Peggy Eng, Conferences
Becky Mcdonah, Secretary
Anne Havel, Treasurer
Renee Zettle-Sterling, Past President

Promotes a favorable and enriching environment in which contemporary metalsmiths practice their art. One aspect of this process is educating the public about the quality and rich diversity within the field of metalsmithing. Exhibitions, public forums, lectures, and published documents are our primary methods of reaching out to the public. SNAG sponsors workshops, seminars, audio-visual services and an annual conference.
Founded in: 1969

17722 Specialty Steel Industry of North America
3050 K Street, N.W.
Washington, DC 20007

202-342-8630
800-982-0355; *Fax:* 202-342-8451;
www.ssina.com

17723 Steel Deck Institute
PO Box 25
Fox River Grove, IL 60021-0025

847-458-4647; *Fax:* 412-487-3326;
www.sdi.org

Steven A Roehrig, Managing Director
Trade association providing uniform industry standards for the engineering, design, manufacture and field usage of steel decks.
29 Members
Founded in: 1939

17724 Steel Door Institute
30200 Detroit Rd
Cleveland, OH 44145-1967

440-899-0010; *Fax:* 440-892-1404
info@steeldoor.org; www.steeldoor.org

Jeff Wherry, Executive Director
Producers of all metal frames and doors for commercial, industrial and residential construction.

17725 Steel Founders Society of America
780 McArdle Dr
Unit G
Crystal Lake, IL 60014-8155

815-455-8240; *Fax:* 815-455-8241
monroe@sfsa.org; www.sfsa.org
Social Media: Facebook

Raymond Monroe, Executive VP
Rick Boyd, Vice President of Technology
Kelly DiGiacomo, CPA, Director of Finance
Rob Blair, Manager of Information Services
David Poweleit, Director of Engineering
A technically oriented trade association serving the steel casting industry.
Founded in: 1902

17726 Steel Manufacturers Association
1150 Connecticut Ave NW
Suite 715
Washington, DC 20036-4131

202-296-1515; *Fax:* 202-296-2506;
www.steelnet.org

Philip K. Bell, President
Eric J. Stuart, VP, Energy & Environment
Adam B. Parr, VP, Policy & Communications
Annie Stefanec, Member Services Coordinator
The majority of SMA members are minimills companies engaged in electric air furnace/continuous caster steel productions as well as hot and cold rolling of steel mill products. A growing number of integrated steel producers are also members.

17727 Steel Plate Fabricators Association
944 Donata Ct
Lake Zurich, IL 60047-5025

847-438-8265; *Fax:* 847-438-8766
info@steeltank.com; www.steeltank.com
Social Media: Facebook, LinkedIn, Youtube

Anne Kiefer, Director Of Administration
Wayne B. Geyer, President
J Michael Braden, VP
Jerry Stetzler, Treasurer
Protection of the environment and preservation of air and water quality are key concerns for the owners and operators of tanks, pressure vessels, specialty fabrications and piping systems.
Founded in: 1916

17728 Steel Service Center Institute
701 West Mason Street
Springfield, OH 44128
217-528-4035
800-252-2516; *Fax:* 847-485-3001
info@ssci.org; www.ssoci.org
Social Media: Facebook

Thomas Conley, President
S Harbke, Director
570 Members
Founded in: 1909

17729 Steel Shipping Container Institute
120 Hatton Drive
Severna Park, MD 21146-4400

410-544-0385; *Fax:* 503-581-2221
snauman@industrialpackaging.org
whysteeldrums.org
Social Media: Facebook, Twitter, LinkedIn, YouTube, Google+

Kyle R. Stavig, Chairman
Leonard H. Berenfield, Vice Chairman
John McQuaid, Senior Advisor

17730 Steel Tank Institute
944 Donata Ct
Lake Zurich, IL 60047-5025

847-438-8265; *Fax:* 847-438-8766
info@steeltank.com; www.steeltank.com
Social Media: Facebook, LinkedIn, Youtube

Anne Kiefer, Director Of Administration
Wayne B. Geyer, President
J Michael Braden, VP
Jerry Stetzler, Treasurer
Protection of the environment and preservation of air and water quality are key concerns for the owners and operators of tanks, pressure vessels, specialty fabrications and piping systems.
Founded in: 1916

17731 Steel Tube Institute of North America
2516 Waukegan Road, Suite 172
Glenview, IL 60025

847-461-1701; *Fax:* 847-660-7981
sti@apk.net; www.steeltubeinstitute.org
Social Media: Facebook, LinkedIn

Timothy F Andrassy, Executive Director
Peggy Sams, Executive Assistant
Mary Gregel, Administrative Assistant
Dave Seeger, President
Members produce steel tubes and pipes from carbon, stainless or alloy steel, for applications ranging from large structural tubing to small redrawn tubing.
87 Members
Founded in: 1930

17732 The Aluminum Association
1400 Crystal Drive
Suite 430
Arlington, VA 22202

703-358-2960
info@aluminum.org; www.aluminum.org
Social Media: Facebook, Twitter, LinkedIn

Layle Smith, Chairman
Garney B. Scott, III, Vice Chairman
Michelle O'Neill, Second Vice Chair
Heidi Brock, President
Karen Bowden, Vice President, Administration

17733 The American Institute of Mining, Metallur gical and Petroleum Engineers
12999 East Adam Aircraft Circle
Englewood, CO 80112

303-325-5185; *Fax:* 888-702-0049
aime@aimehq.org; www.aimehq.org

Social Media: Facebook, LinkedIn, YouTube, RSS

Behrooz Fattahi, President
Garry W. Warren, President Elect
Nikhil C. Trivedi, President-Elect Designate
Dale E. Heinz, Past President
Drew Meyer, Trustee
Founded in: 1871

17734 The Fabricators & Manufacturers
833 Featherstone Road
Rockford, IL 61107

815-399-8700
888-394-4362; www.fmanet.org
Social Media: Facebook, Twitter, LinkedIn, YouTube, Google+

Edwin Stanley, Chair
Al Zelt, First Vice Chairman
Vivek Kumar Gupta, Second Vice Chairman
Lyle Menke, Secretary/ Treasurer
Carlos Borjas, Immediate Past Chair
Founded in: 1970

17735 The Minerals, Metals, and Materials Society
184 Thorn Hill Road
Warrendale, PA 15086-7514

800-759-4867; *Fax:* 724-776-3770
webmaster@tms.org; www.tms.org
Social Media: Facebook, LinkedIn, YouTube

Hani Henein, President
Elizabeth A. Holm, Past President
Patrice E. A. Turchi, Vice President
James Robinson, Secretary/ Executive Director
Robert W. Hyers, Financial Planning Officer

17736 The Silver Users Association
3930 walnut Street
Suite 210
Fairfax, VA 22030

703-934-0219
800-245-6999; *Fax:* 703-359-7562
sas@silversmithing.com;
www.silverusersassociation.org

Bill LeRoy, President
Mike Huber, Vice President
Jack Gannon, Immediate Past President
Bill Hamelin, Treasurer
John King, Secretary
Founded in: 1947

17737 Tube and Pipe Association International
833 Featherstone Road
Rockford, IL 61107

815-399-8700
888-394-4362; *Fax:* 815-484-7700;
www.fmanet.org
Social Media: Facebook, Twitter, LinkedIn, YouTube, Google+

Gerald Shankel, President
Mike Hedges, VP Finance/CFO

TPA is an educational technology association serving the metal tube and pipe producing and fabricating industries. It is an affiliate association of the Fabricators and Manufacturers Association International.
Founded in: 1970

17738 US Magnetic Materials Association
1120 East 23rd St.
Indianapolis, IN 46206

717-898-2294; www.usmagneticmaterials.com

Ed Richardson, Chairman/ President/ Treasurer
Peter Dent, Vice President
Daniel McGroarty, Vice President
Rob Strahs, Secretary/ Vice President
Kerry LaPierre, Board Member

17739 US Pipe and Foundry Company
Two Chase Corporate Drive
Suite 200
Birmingham, AL 35244

866-347-7473; *Fax:* 205-254-7494
info@uspipe.com; www.uspipe.com
Social Media: Facebook, Twitter, LinkedIn, YouTube, Google+

Paul Ciolino, Chief Executive Officer
Bob Waggoner, SVP, Marketing and Sales
Norb Gross, VP, Supply Chain & Logistics
Brad Overstreet, Chief Financial Officer
Vinod Upadhyay, VP, Information Technology

Supports all those involved with the foundry industry. Publishes semi-monthly newsletter.
Founded in: 1899

17740 Unified Abrasives Manufacturers Association
30200 Detroit Road
Cleveland, OH 44145-1967

440-899-0010; *Fax:* 440-892-1404
contact@uama.org; www.uama.org
Founded in: 1999

17741 United States Cutting Tool Institute
1300 Sumner Ave
Cleveland, OH 44115-2851

216-241-7333; *Fax:* 216-241-0105;
www.uscti.com

Charles M Stockinger, Secretary-Treasurer
Thomas Hagg, President
Steve Stokey, Senior Vice President
Philip Kurtz, Vice President

The premier trade association for all manufacturers of any type of cutting tools designed and sold to the metalworking, woodworking, and other industrial and consumer markets.
60 Members
Founded in: 1988

17742 Welding Research Council
PO Box 201547
Shaker Heights, OH 44122

216-658-3847; *Fax:* 216-658-3854
mprager@forengineers.org;
www.forengineers.org

Coordinates welding research.
Founded in: 1935

17743 Welding Research Council, Inc.
PO Box 201547
Shaker Heights, OH 44122

216-658-3847; *Fax:* 216-658-3854
mpc@forengineers.org; www.forengineers.org

Martin Prager, PhD, Executive Director

An outgrowth of the ASTM-ASME Joint Committee on the effect of temperature on the properties of metals which was founded in 1925 to meet the apparent need for information on the subject in the construction of central power stations.
600 Members
Founded in: 1966

17744 Wire Association International
71 Bradley Rd.
Suite 9
Madison, CT 06443

203-453-2777; *Fax:* 203-453-8384;
www.wirenet.org
Social Media: Facebook, Twitter, LinkedIn, YouTube

Steven J Fetteroll, Executive Director
Phyilis Conon, Technical Information Director

Technical association serving the global wire and cable industry by providing educational materials, sponsoring trade shows and international technical conferences.
Founded in: 1930

17745 Wiring Harness Manufacturers Association
15490 101st Ave. N.
Suite 100
Maple Grove, MN 55369

763-235-6467; *Fax:* 763-235-6461
whma@whma.org; www.whma.org

Andrew Larsen, Executive Director
Rick Bromn, Chairman
Donnie Hill, Vice Chairman/Secretary
Randy Olson, Treasurer
Lyle Fahning, Immediate Past Chair

To provide the cooperative forum through which members companies can solve both their specific problems and also help resolve industry problems.
4 Pages
Frequency: Quarterly
Circulation: 5,000

Newsletters

17746 Abrasive Users News Fax
Meadowlark Technical Services
144 Moore Rd
Butler, PA 16001-1312

724-282-6210; *Fax:* 724-234-2376
aes@abrasiveengineering.com;
www.abrasivesmall.com

Ted Giese, Executive Director

Newsletter from the Abrasive Engineering Society.
Cost: $50.00
Circulation: 500
Founded in: 1957

17747 American Iron and Steel Institute News
American Iron and Steel Institute
25 Massachusetts Ave., NW, Suite 800
Suite 705
Washington, DC 20001

202-452-7100; *Fax:* 202-496-9702
steelnews@steel.org; www.recycle-steel.org
Social Media: Facebook, Twitter, Youtube

Chip Foley, VP
Dave James, Marketing

Publication of the nonprofit trade organization representing approximately 65 percent of steel companies in the US, Canada and Mexico.
Circulation: 6000
Founded in: 1855

17748 American Metal Market
Michael G Botta
825 7th Avenue
New York, NY 10019-6014

212-887-8510; *Fax:* 212-887-8522
custserv@amm.com; www.amm.com

Gloria T LaRue, Editor
Catalino Abrei, Owner

A daily newspaper of the metals industry covering news and pricing information for corporate, purchasing and manufacturing management.
Frequency: Daily
Circulation: 10,500

17749 Building & Architecture News
Copper Development Association
260 Madison Ave
New York, NY 10016-2403

212-251-7200
800-232-3282; *Fax:* 212-251-7234
questions@cda.copper.org; www.copper.org

Andrew G Kireta, President & CEO
Victoria Prather, Manager Communications
Michels Harold, VP Technaloy Services

Arnold W Ray, VP Environmental Division
Lorraine Herzing Mills, VP/Finance/Administration
A special-edition newsletter that focuses onthe use of copper and copper alloys in commercial and residential design and construction.
Frequency: Monthly

17750 CBSA Capsules
Copper and Brass Servicenter Association
994 Old Eagle School Road
Suite 1019
Wayne, PA 19087
610-971-4850; *Fax:* 610-971-4859;
www.copper-brass.org
Daniel Erck, President
Robert A Lewis, VP
Content includes information about conventions and seminars, programs and activities sponsored by the CBSA, general business/industry news, legislation information and government regulations.
Cost: $35.00
6 Pages
Frequency: Monthly
Circulation: 200
Founded in: 1951

17751 Cables Industry Analyst
CRU International
6305 Ivy Ln
Suite 422
Greenbelt, MD 20770-6339
301-441-8997; *Fax:* 301-441-4726
sales@crugroup.com; www.crugroup.com
Florence Kauffman, VP
Written for managers and executives in the wire industry around the globe. Spotlights effective management techniques and superior administrative skills in the industry, profiles industry leaders, notes personnel movements and features general industry news.
Cost: $965.00
12 Pages
Frequency: Monthly
ISSN: 1368-4191

17752 Futuretech
John Wiley & Sons
111 River St
Hoboken, NJ 07030-5790
201-748-6000
800-825-7550; *Fax:* 201-748-6088
info@wiley.com; www.wiley.com
William J Pesce, CEO
Edited for product development and technology transfer engineers. Intelligence service that deals with new technologies with demonstrated commercial appeal still in the early stages of development in leading corporate, academic and university labs. Contains analysis and exploitation information.
Cost: $1500.00
24 Pages
Frequency: Monthly

17753 IMA Weekly Updates
1000 N Rand Rd
Suite 214
Wauconda, IL 60084-1180
847-526-2010; *Fax:* 847-526-3993
info@intlmag.org; www.intlmag.org
Greg Patzer, Executive Vice-President
Heidi Diederich, Administrative Coordinator
Develops international use and acceptance of magnesium metal and its alloys in all product forms. Members are organizations or individuals engaged in the production, manufacture or marketing of metallic magnesium or those supplying materials, equipment or consulting.
Cost: $90.00
Frequency: Weekly
Circulation: 5000
Founded in: 1943
Printed in 2 colors on glossy stock

17754 IMPI Conference
International Precious Metals Institute
5101 N 12th Avenue
Suite C
Pensacola, FL 32504
850-476-1156; *Fax:* 850-476-1548
mail@ipmi.org; www.ipmi.org
Robert Ianniello, President
annual conference holds technical sessions, evening social receptions and a golf tournament. Also some product demonstrations.
400 Attendees
Frequency: Annual

17755 MBCEA Newsletter
Metal Building Contractors & Erectors Association
PO Box 499
Shawnee Mission, KS 66201
913-432-3800; *Fax:* 913-432-3803
MBCEA@kc.rr.com; www.mbcea.org
Angela M Cruse, Executive Director
Tim Seyler, President
Official newsletter of the Metal Building Contractors and Erectors Association (MBCEA), a trade association, formed in 1968 to provide programs and services, as well as to support the interests of metal building contractors and erectors.

17756 Metal Construction Association
MCA Newsletter
4799 West Lake Street
Glenview, IL 60025
847-375-4718; *Fax:* 877-665-2234;
www.metalconstruction.org
Mark Engle, Executive VP
Julie Weldon, Chairman
Dedicated to promoting the use of metal in construction. Initative include market development, educational programs, issue and product awareness campaigns, and publication of technical guidelines and specifications manuals.
100 Pages
Frequency: Quartly
Founded in: 1983

17757 Precious Metals News
International Precious Metals Institute
5101 N 12th Avenue
Suite C
Pensacola, FL 32504
850-476-1156; *Fax:* 850-476-1548
mail@ipmi.org; www.ipmi.org
Robert Ianniello, President
Cost: $30.00
Frequency: Quarterly
Circulation: 1000
Founded in: 1976

17758 R&D Focus
International Lead Zinc Research Organization
2525 Meridian Parkway
PO Box 12036
Research Triangle Park, NC 27709-2036
919-361-4647; *Fax:* 919-361-1957
rputnam@ilzro.org; www.ilzro.org
Rob Putnam, Publisher
Doug Zabor, President
Reports on current research and development products in the metal industry.
Frequency: Quarterly
Circulation: 100
Founded in: 1958

17759 Steel Industry Weekly Review
2 Uxbridge Road
Scarsdale, NY 10583-2725
Karl Keffer, Publisher
Offers industry news for steel workers.
Cost: $75.00
Frequency: Monthly

17760 Titanium
International Titanium Association
2655 W Midway Blvd
Suite 300
Broomfield, CO 80020-7187
303-404-2221
299-942-5371; *Fax:* 303-404-9111
jsimpson@titanium.org; www.titanium.org
Frequency: Quarterly
Circulation: 5000
Founded in: 1960

17761 US Piper
US Pipe and Foundry Company
PO Box 10406
James Canada
Birmingham, AL 35202-406
205-547-7254; *Fax:* 205-254-7494;
www.uspipe.com
George Bogs, Publisher
Ray Torok, President
Walter Knollenberg, VP
Articles deal with advantages of using new products.
16 Pages
Circulation: 9000
Founded in: 1899

17762 WRC Bulletin
Welding Research Council
3 Park Avenue
27th Floor
New York, NY 10016-5902
212-591-7956; *Fax:* 212-591-7183
bulletinsales@forengineers.org;
www.forengineers.org/wrc
CR Felmley Jr, Publisher
Offers information and updates for the welding community.
Cost: $300.00
Frequency: Monthly
Circulation: 900

Magazines & Journals

17763 AISE Steel Technology
Association of Iron & Steel Engineers
186 Thorn Hill Road
Warrendale, PA 15086
724-776-6040; *Fax:* 724-776-1880
info@aist.org; www.aise.org
Ronald Ashburn, Managing Director
Marge Baker, Editor
Gerry Kane, Sales Manager
Karen Hadley, Managing Editor
Janet McConnell, Production Editor
Information relating to the design and construction of equipment, machinery and plants for the production and processing of iron and steel.
Cost: $115.00
Frequency: Monthly
Circulation: 8000
Founded in: 2004

17764 **APMI International**
105 College Road E
Princeton, NJ 08540-6622

609-452-7700; *Fax:* 609-987-8523
apmi@mpif.org; www.mpif.org

Christopher Adam, President
David L Schaefer, Director
Jim Adams, Manager

Monthly newsletter for all those involved the metal powder producing and consuming industries. Regular editorial features.
Founded in: 1965

17765 **Abrasives**
PO Box 11
Byron Center, MI 49315

616-530-3220; *Fax:* 616-530-6466;
www.abrasivesmagazine.com

Rose Trevino, Publisher/Editor

Covers research and development in the abrasives field including information about grinding and finishing applications.
Cost: $27.00
Frequency: Annual+
Circulation: 35000

17766 **Advanced Materials & Processes**
ASM International
9639 Kinsman Rd
Materials Park, OH 44073

440-338-5151
800-336-5152; *Fax:* 440-338-4634
memberservices@asminternational.org;
www.asminternational.org
Social Media: Facebook, Twitter, LinkedIn

Joseph M Zion, Publisher
Joanne Miller, Managing Editor
Margaret Hunt, Editor-in-Chief
Jeane Deatherage, Administrator, Foundation Programs
Virginia Shirk, Foundation Executive Assistant

AM&P, the monthly technical magazine from ASM International, is designed to keep readers aware of leading-edge developments and trends in engineering materials - metals and alloys, engineering polymers, advanced ceramics, and composites - and the methods used to select, process, fabricate, test, and characterize them.
Frequency: Monthly
Circulation: 32M
Founded in: 1977

17767 **Aluminum Recycling & Processing for Energy Conservation and Sustainability**
Aluminum Association
1525 Wilson Blvd
Suite 600
Arlington, VA 22209-2444

703-358-2960; *Fax:* 703-358-2961;
www.aluminum.org

John Green, Editor
Heidi Biggs Brock, President
Nicholas Adams, Vice President, Business
Frequency: Yearly

17768 **American Machinist**
Penton Media
1166 Avenue of the Americas/10th Fl
New York, NY 10036
212-204-4200; *Fax:* 216-696-6662
ameditor@penton.com; www.penton.com

Jane Cooper, Marketing
Patricia L Smith, Executive Editor
Charles Bates, Senior Editor
Jim Benes, Associate Editor
Chris Meyer, Director, Corporate Communications

Magazine of the manufacturing business. Plays an integral role in educating and informing our readers of the significant developments of manufacturing technology. The intent of every issue is to describe new metalworking technologies that help the readership speed production, cut costs, and stay competitive in the global market.
Frequency: Monthly
Circulation: 80000
Founded in: 1892
Printed in 4 colors

17769 **American Metal Market**
Reed Business Information
225 Park Avenue South
New York, NY 10003

646-274-6257; *Fax:* 630-288-8686;
www.amm.com
Social Media: Twitter, LinkedIn

Lawrence S Reed, President
Gloria LaRue, Editor-in-Chief
Catalino Abrei, Owner

Thoroughly covers the metals industry, from production to distribution to recycling. American Metal Market is comprehensive, timely, reliable and invaluable daily newspaper for today's metal industry professionals.
Cost: $725.00
16 Pages
Frequency: Daily
Circulation: 10000
Printed in on glossy stock

17770 **American Tool, Die & Stamping News**
Eagle Publications
42400 Grand River Ave
Suite 103
Novi, MI 48375-2572

248-347-3487
800-783-3491; *Fax:* 248-347-3492;
www.ameritooldie.com

Arthur Brown, President
Joan Oakley, CEO

Applications, techniques, equipment and accessories of metal stamping, moldmaking, electric discharge machining; and new product information relating to the tool and die industry. Accepts advertising.
70 Pages
Circulation: 36000
ISSN: 0192-5709
Founded in: 1971
Printed in 5 colors on glossy stock

17771 **Anvil Magazine**
PO Box 1810
Georgetown, CA 95634-1810

530-333-2142
800-942-6845; *Fax:* 530-333-2906;
www.anvilmag.com

Rob Edwards, Publisher
Timothy Sebastian, Editor-in-Chief
Jody Edwards, Advertising Manager

World-wide coverage of the blacksmithing and farrier trades.
Cost: $29.50
Frequency: Monthly
Circulation: 5000
Founded in: 1980

17772 **Anvil's Ring**
Artist-Blacksmith's Association of North America
259 Muddy Fork Road
Jonesborough, TN 37659

423-913-1022; *Fax:* 423-913-1023
areditor@abana.org; www.abana.org
Social Media: Facebook, Twitter

Dan Nauman, Editor

Covers such topics as architectural iron, decorative design, primitive artifacts, advice, and Association news. Also discusses supply sources, formal blacksmithing instruction and employment opportunities.
60 Pages
Frequency: Quarterly

17773 **Association of Iron and Steel Engineers Steel Technology**
Three Gateway Center
Suite 1900
Pittsburgh, PA 15222-1004

412-281-6323; *Fax:* 412-281-6216
rashburn@aist.org; www.aise.org

Ronald E Ashburn, Executive Director
Frank E Farmer, Graphic Designer
Chris Brown, Graphic Designer
Stacy Varmecky, General Manager

AISE Steel Technology is the monthly technical journal of AISE. Highly authorative, it contains exclusive technical information relating to all phases of iron and steelmaking and finishing.
50+ Pages
Frequency: Monthly
Printed in 4 colors

17774 **Automatic Machining Magazine**
Screw Machine Publishing Company
1066 Gravel Rd
Suite 201
Webster, NY 14580-1769

585-787-0820
800-610-6950; *Fax:* 585-787-0868;
www.automachmag.com

Wayne Wood, President

General industry news for professionals in the metal turning and cold forming fields.
Cost: $45.00
142 Pages
Frequency: Monthly
Circulation: 13000
Founded in: 1941
Printed in 4 colors on glossy stock

17775 **Casting World**
Continental Communications
104 Florence Ln
Fairfield, CT 06824-2215
203-255-7752; *Fax:* 203-377-7230

Wilburt W Troland, President

In-depth news on all aspects of ferrous and non-ferrous casting.
Cost: $99.00
Frequency: Quarterly
Circulation: 35000

17776 **Coil World**
CJL Publishing
8 High Point
Cedar Grove, NJ 07009

973-571-7155; *Fax:* 973-571-7102
philcola@optonline.net; www.coilworld.com

Philip E Colaiacovo, Editor-in-Chief/Publisher
Carl Hoffman, Circulation Manager
Shawn A Savage, Creative Director
A L Colaiacovo, Production/Advertising Svcs Manager

Offers articles on coil coating operations, fabricators, service centers, OEMs which use prepainted metals, new products, upcoming events, industry news, personnel announcements and committee updates.
Frequency: Quarterly
Circulation: 10000

17777 **Cutting Technology**
Penton Media

1166 Avenue of the Americas/10th Fl
New York, NY 10036

212-204-4200; *Fax:* 216-696-6662
information@penton.com; www.penton.com

Jane Cooper, Marketing
Patricia Smith, Executive Editor
Gil Apelis, Manager
Chris Meyer, Director, Corporate Communications

Covers the full gamut of information essential to the success and productivity of those involved in metalcutting manufacturing.
Cost: $35.00
Circulation: 40000
Founded in: 1892
Printed in 4 colors

17778 **Cutting Tool Engineering**
CTE Publications
40 Skokie Blvd
Suite 450
Northbrook, IL 60062-1698

847-498-9100
866-207-1450; *Fax:* 847-559-4444
alanr@jwr.com; www.ctemag.com

John Wm Roberts, CEO
Alan Richter, CEO
Alan Rooks, Director

Cutting Tool Engineering serves manufacturing plants in the metal working industries.
Cost: $65.00
72 Pages
Frequency: Monthly
Circulation: 34871
ISSN: 0011-4189
Founded in: 1955
Printed in 4 colors on glossy stock

17779 **Die Casting Engineer Magazine**
North American Die Casting Association
241 Holbrook Drive
Wheeling, IL 60090

847-279-0001; *Fax:* 847-279-0002
nadca@diecasting.org; www.diecasting.org
Social Media: Facebook, Twitter, LinkedIn, youtube, Flickr

Donna Peterson, Editor
Norwin A Merens, Managing Director

Provides members with the latest industry information, technology innovation and state-of-the-art developments. Each issue presents readers with up to date die casting news topics, opinion features of interest, and an editorial theme.
Cost: $150.00
1000 Pages
Frequency: Bi-Monthly
Founded in: 1989

17780 **Die Casting Management**
C-K Publishing
PO Box 247
Wonder Lake, IL 60097-0247

815-728-0912; *Fax:* 815-728-0912;
www.diecastmgmt.com

Rob Crofts, Publisher

The main content focuses on profitable management, and includes articles on finance, marketing, technology, engineering, industry developments, and government legislation.
Frequency: Bi-Monthly
Circulation: 4500

17781 **Ductile Iron News**
Ductile Iron Society
15400 Pearl Rd
Suite 234
Strongsville, OH 44136-6017

440-665-3686; *Fax:* 440-878-0070
jwood@ductile.org; www.ductile.org

Scott Gledhill, President
Patricio Gill, VP
Pete Guidi, Treasurer

The main material focuses on the technical data and applications, production statistics, and profiles of foundries.
Frequency: 3-4x/Year

17782 **Engineering and Mining Journal**
Mining Media
8751 E Hampden Ave
Suite C1
Denver, CO 80231-4930

303-751-5370; *Fax:* 303-283-0641
info@mining-media.com; www.e-mj.com

Peter Johnson, President
Steve Fiscor, Editor-in-Chief
Russ Carter, Managing Editor
Gina Tverdak, Assistant Editor

Serves the field of mining including exploration, development, milling, smelting, refining of metals and nonmetallics.
Cost: $79.00
Frequency: Monthly
Circulation: 10523
Founded in: 1866
Printed in 4 colors on glossy stock

17783 **Equip-Mart**
116 N Camp Street
Seguin, TX 78155

830-303-3328
800-864-1155; *Fax:* 830-372-3011;
www.equip-mart.com

James Story, President
Tammy Reilly, Publisher
Kim Wiemann, Circulation Manager

Used metalworking equipment.
Cost: $50.00
Frequency: Monthly
Circulation: 36000
Founded in: 1994

17784 **Fabricator**
Fabricators and Manufacturers Association
833 Featherstone Road
Rockford, IL 61107

815-227-8281
866-879-9144; *Fax:* 815-484-7700
dand@thefabricator.com;
www.thefabricator.com

Dan Davis, Executive Editor

North America's leading magazine for the metal forming and fabricating industry that delivers the news, technical articles, and case histories that enable fabricators to do their jobs more efficiently.
Cost: $75.00
Frequency: Monthly
Circulation: 55000
Founded in: 1970
Printed in 4 colors on glossy stock

17785 **Forging**
Penton Media
1166 Avenue of the Americas/10th Fl
New York, NY 10036

212-204-4200; *Fax:* 216-696-6662
forgeditor@penton.com; www.penton.com

Jane Cooper, Marketing
Robert Brooks, Editor
Melody Berendt, Circulation
Chris Meyer, Director, Corporate Communications

Dedicated to providing industrial part forgers with current market, product, process and equipment news and trend analysis.
Cost: $31.50
62 Pages
Circulation: 5000
ISSN: 1054-1756
Founded in: 1990
Printed in 4 colors on glossy stock

17786 **Foundry Management & Technology**
Penton Media
1166 Avenue of the Americas/10th Fl
New York, NY 10036

212-204-4200; *Fax:* 216-696-6662
jwright@penton.com; www.penton.com

Jane Cooper, Marketing
Dave Shanks, Publisher
Melody Berendt, Circulation Manager
Chris Meyer, Director, Corporate Communications

Received by management, production, engineering, research and technical professionals in the foundry industry.
Cost: $54.00
70 Pages
Frequency: Monthly
ISSN: 0360-8999
Printed in 4 colors on glossy stock

17787 **Gases & Welding Distributor**
Penton Media
1166 Avenue of the Americas/10th Fl
New York, NY 10036

212-204-4200; *Fax:* 216-696-6662
infomation@penton.com; www.penton.com

Jane Cooper, Marketing
Patricia L Smith, Executive Editor
Charles Bates, Senior Editor
Jim Benes, Associate Editor
Melody Berendt, Circulation Manager

Marketing, management and technology magazine that aids distributors of welding supplies, industrial/medical/specialty gases, and safety products to sell more effectively to diverse markets.
Cost: $55.00
74 Pages
Frequency: six issues ayea
ISSN: 1079-3909
Printed in 4 colors

17788 **Heat Treating Progress**
ASM International
9639 Kinsman Rd
Novelty, OH 44072-9603

440-338-5151
800-336-5152; *Fax:* 440-338-4634
MemberServiceCenter@asminternational.org;
www.asminternational.org

Stanley Theobald, Executive Director
Dean Peters, Editor-in-Chief
Lana Shapowal, Manager
Tina Long, Circulation Manager
Vin LeGendre, Publisher
Frequency: Monthly
Founded in: 1913

17789 **Industrial Paint & Powder Magazine**
Reed Business Information
30 Technology Parkway South
Suite 100
Norcross, GA 30092

630-574-0825
800-424-3996; *Fax:* 630-288-8781
webmaster@reedbusiness.com;
www.reedbusiness.com

Jeff Greisch, President

Coatings on manufacturing.
Cost: $55.00
Frequency: Monthly
Circulation: 38000
Founded in: 1924

17790 **Industrial Product Bulletin**
Gordon Publications
301 Gibraltar Drive
#650
Morris Plains, NJ 07950-3400
973-292-5100; *Fax:* 973-539-3476
Todd Baker, Publisher
Anita LaFond, Editor
Publication for executives and professionals in the process and metalworking industries.
Cost: $7.00
Circulation: 200,050

17791 **Inspection Trends**
American Welding Society
550 Nw 42nd Ave
Miami, FL 33126-5699
305-443-9353
800-443-9353; *Fax:* 305-443-7559
info@aws.org; www.aws.org
Ray Shook, President
Jeff Hufsey, Deputy Executive Director
Ray Shook, Executive Director
Kristin Campbell, Assistant Editor
Robert Pali, Treasurer
Our information assists inspection personnel through information and reports on new technology and equipment, tips on inspection techniques and interpretation, as well as by giving examples of practical methodology.
Cost: $50.00
Frequency: Quarterly
Circulation: 18000
Founded in: 1989

17792 **International Journal of Powder Metallurgy**
APMI International
105 College Road E
Princeton, NJ 08540-6992
609-452-7700; *Fax:* 609-987-8523
apmi@mpif.org; www.mpif.org/apmi
Dr Alan Lawley, Editor-in-Chief
Peter K Johnson, Contributing Editor
Embraces a wide range of materials and processes including classical press and sinter PM and advanced particulate materials.
Cost: $230.00
Frequency: Bi-Monthly
ISSN: 0888-7462

17793 **Iron & Steel Technology**
Association for Iron & Steel Technolgy (AIST)
186 Thorn Hill Rd
Warrendale, PA 15086-7528
724-814-3000; *Fax:* 724-814-3001
memberservices@aist.org; www.aist.org
Social Media: Facebook, Twitter, LinkedIn
Karen D Hickey, Managing Editor
Amanda Blyth, Technical Editor
Janet McConnell, Production Editor
The official monthly publication of AIST, this is the premier technical journal for metallurgical, engineering, operating and maintenance personnel in the global iron and steel industry.
Cost: $20.00
Frequency: Monthly
Circulation: 9600

17794 **Journal of Materials Engineering and Performance**
9639 Kinsman Road
Materials Park, OH 44073-2
440-338-5151; *Fax:* 440-338-4634
cust-srv@asminternational.org; www.asm-intl.org
Ash Khare, President
Stanley Theobald, Managing Director
Peer-reviewed journal which publishes contributions on all aspects of materials selection, design, characterization, processing and performance testing. The scope includes all materials used in engineering applications: those that typically result in components for larger systems.
Cost: $1184.00
Circulation: 645
Founded in: 1913

17795 **Journal of Minerals, Metals & Materials Society**
Minerals, Metals & Minerals Society
184 Thorn Hill Road
Warrendale, PA 15086-7511
724-776-9000; *Fax:* 724-776-3770
webmaster@tms.org; www.tms.org
Alexander R Scott, Executive Director
Robert Makowski, Communications Director
To promote the global science and engineering profession's concerned with minerals, metals and materials. Founded in 1871. Publishes a monthly magazine.
Cost: $20.00
Frequency: Monthly
Circulation: 10000
Founded in: 1880

17796 **Journal of Phase Equilibria**
ASM International
9639 Kinsman Rd
Materials Park, OH 44072
440-338-5151
800-336-5152; *Fax:* 440-338-4634
memberservices@asminternational.org; www.asminternational.org
Social Media: Facebook, Twitter, LinkedIn
Jeane Deatherage, Administrator, Foundation Programs
Virginia Shirk, Foundation Executive Assistant
Peer-reviewed journal that contains basic and applied research results, evaluated phase diagrams, a survey of current literature, and comments or other material pertinent to the previous three areas. The aim is to provide a broad spectrum of information concerning phase equilibria for the materials community.
Cost: $1965.00
Frequency: Bimonthly
Circulation: 305

17797 **Light Metal Age**
Fellom Publishing Company
170 S Spruce Ave
Suite 120
S San Francisco, CA 94080-4557
650-588-8832; *Fax:* 650-588-0901
lma@lightmetalage.com; www.buffalowildwings.com
Ann Marie Fellom, Publisher
Cost: $45.00
Frequency: Monthly
Circulation: 5000
ISSN: 0024-3345
Founded in: 1944
Printed in 4 colors on glossy stock

17798 **Locator Services**
Locator Online
315 S Patrick St
Suite 3
Alexandria, VA 22314-3532
703-836-9700
800-537-1446; *Fax:* 703-836-7665
webmaster@locatoronline.com; www.locatoronline.com
Terry Pitman, Publisher
Used metalworking equipment.
Frequency: Monthly
Circulation: 225000
Founded in: 1969

17799 **Machine Shop Guide**
Worldwide Communications
401 Worthington Avenue
Harrison, NJ 07029-2039
973-497-7555; *Fax:* 973-497-7556
Robert L Hatschek, Executive Editor
Information on manufacturing technology, new applications for manufacturing technology and new products.
Circulation: 102893

17800 **Manufacturers Showcase**
Heartland Communications Group
1003 Central Avenue
Po Box 1052
Fort Dodge, IA 50501
515-955-1600
800-203-9960; *Fax:* 515-955-3753;
www.industrialmachinetrader.com
Natalie Fevold, Operations Manager
Sandy Simonson, Sales Manager
A magazine for new metalworking machinery, tooling and supplies.
Frequency: Monthly

17801 **Manufacturing Engineering**
Society of Manufacturing Engineers
1 Sme Drive
PO Box 930
Dearborn, MI 48121
313-425-3000
800-733-4763; *Fax:* 313-425-3400
advertising@sme.org; www.sme.org
Mark Tomlinson, Executive Director
Greg Sheremet, Publisher
Gene Nelson, President
Serves metalworking industry machining, forming, inspection, assembly and processing operations.
Frequency: Monthly
Circulation: 111966
Founded in: 1932

17802 **Metal Architecture**
Modern Trade Communications
7450 Skokie Blvd
Suite 200
Skokie, IL 60077-3374
847-674-2200; *Fax:* 847-674-3676;
www.moderntrade.com
John Lawrence, President
Mark Wiebusch, Marketing & Operations
Shawn Zuver, Editorial & Production
Low-rise construction involving architects, engineers and specifiers.
Frequency: Monthly
Circulation: 29513

17803 **Metal Center News**
Reed Business Information
30 Technology Parkway South
Suite 100
Norcross, GA 30092
630-574-0825
800-424-3996; *Fax:* 630-288-8781

webmaster@reedbusiness.com;
www.reedbusiness.com

Jeff Greisch, President

Reports on verious phases of metal center operations.

17804 Metal Finishing
Elsevier Science
655 Avenue of the Americas
New York, NY 10010-5107

212-633-3800; *Fax:* 212-633-3850
PressOffice@elsevier.com; www.elsevier.com

Young Suk Chi, President
Patti Ann Frost, Managing Editor
Susan Canalizo, Director, Manager
Greg Valero, Manager

Finishes and finishing of metal products.
Cost: $87.00
Frequency: Monthly
Circulation: 19824
Founded in: 1903

17805 Metal Mecanica
Gardner Publications
901 poncedeleon blvd
sute 601
Coral Gables, FL 33134-3029

513-527-8977
800-950-8020; *Fax:* 305-448-9942;
www.metalmecanica.com

David Ash, President
Eduardo Tovar, Editor
Holgar Hilkinger, Circulation Manager
Alfredo Domador, Publisher
Circulation: 12157
Founded in: 1905

17806 MetalForming
Precision Metalforming Association
6363 Oak Tree Blvd
Cleveland, OH 44131-2500

216-901-9667; *Fax:* 216-901-9190
pma@pma.org;
www.metalformingmagazine.com

Brad Kuvin, Editor
Kathy DeLollis, Publisher
William Gaskin, President
Daniel Ellashek, VP
Lou Kren, Senior Editor

Edited for decision makers in the precision metal forming industry.
Cost: $59.95
100 Pages
Frequency: Monthly
Circulation: 60000
Founded in: 1967
Printed in 4 colors on matte stock

17807 Metallurgical and Materials Transactions
Minerals, Metals & Materials Society
184 Thorn Hill Road
Warrendale, PA 15086-7528

724-776-9000; *Fax:* 724-776-3770
webmaster@tms.org; www.tms.org

Robert Makowski, Publishing Director
Cost: $1467.00
Frequency: 13 issues
ISSN: 1073-5615

17808 Metalsmith
Society of North American Goldsmiths
5009 Londonderry Drive
Tampa, FL 33647-1336

813-977-5326; *Fax:* 813-977-8462
editor@snagmetalsmith.org;
www.snagmetalsmith.org

Suzanne Ramljak, Editor
Dana Singer, Executive Director
Ken Bova, President
Jean Savarese, Advertising Director
Ellen Laing, Program Manager

Information which explores new work in the jewelry, holloware, blacksmithing, and sculpture fields. Profiles of master metalsmiths are included.
Cost: $65.00
Circulation: 13,500
Founded in: 1969

17809 Metalworking Digest
Reed Business Information
30 Technology Parkway South
Suite 100
Norcross, GA 30092

973-920-7000
800-424-3996; *Fax:* 973-920-7531
webmaster@reedbusiness.com;
www.reedbusiness.com

Rich Stevancsecz, Editor
Joe May, Publisher
Cloin Ungaro, CEO/President
Steve Koppelman, Circulation Manager
R Reed, Owner
Frequency: Monthly
Circulation: 115000
Founded in: 1969

17810 Metalworking Distributor
Penton Media
1166 Avenue of the Americas/10th Fl
New York, NY 10036

212-204-4200; *Fax:* 216-696-6662
information@penton.com; www.penton.com

Jane Cooper, Marketing
Thomas Grasson, Editor
Susan Cubranich, Production Manager
Chris Meyer, Director, Corporate Communications

Publication exclusively devoted to distributors and wholesales in the metalworking industry to help improve marketing, management, and technology knowledge as well as provide information on new markets.
Frequency: Quarterly
Circulation: 5,000
Printed in 4 colors

17811 Modern Applications News
Nelson Publishing
2500 Tamiami Trl N
Nokomis, FL 34275-3476

941-966-9521; *Fax:* 941-966-2590;
www.healthmgttech.com
Social Media: Facebook

A Verner Nelson, President

Information includes coverage of abrasives and grinding, automated handling and robotics, CAD/CAM, coatings and finishings, coolants, lubricants and filters, cutting tools, heat treating, ID marking, lasers, machining centers, and shop control software.
Frequency: Monthly
Circulation: 84000
Founded in: 1967

17812 Modern Casting
American Foundrymen's Society
1695 N Penny Ln
Schaumburg, IL 60173-4555

847-824-0181
800-537-4237; *Fax:* 847-824-7848
circ@afsinc.org; www.afsinc.org

Jerry Call, Executive VP
Sandy Salisbury-Linton, Vice Chairman
Kyle Bauer, Editor
Barbara Jackowski, Circulation Manager
Alfred Spada, Editor-In-Chief

Designed to promote the technological advances in the industry.
Cost: $50.00
Frequency: Monthly
Circulation: 19000
Founded in: 1896

17813 Modern Machine Shop
Gardner Publications
6915 Valley Ln
Cincinnati, OH 45244-3153

513-527-8800
800-950-8020; *Fax:* 513-527-8801
mmsmkt@gardnerweb.com;
www.gardnerweb.com

Rick Kline Sr, CEO
Mark D Albert, Editor-in-Chief
Dianne Hight, Circulation Manager
John Campos, Manager
Brian Wertheimer, Account Manager

Reaches metalworking plants of all sizes - from small job shops to giant aerospace and automotive plants. It is edited for those involved in metalworking operations, particularly those performed on machine tools.
Cost: $89.00
Frequency: Monthly
Circulation: 107000
Founded in: 1928
Mailing list available for rent: 106M names
Printed in 4 colors on glossy stock

17814 Occupational Hazards
Penton Media
1166 Avenue of the Americas/10th Fl
New York, NY 10036

212-204-4200; *Fax:* 216-696-6662
information@penton.com; www.penton.com

Jane Cooper, Marketing
Bob Marinez, Publisher
David B Nussbaum, CEO
Jennifer Daugherty, Communications Manager
Chris Meyer, Director, Corporate Communications

Analysis of qualified recipients who have indicated that they recommend, select and/or buy the safety equipment, fire protection and other occupational health products.
65 Pages
Frequency: Monthly
Circulation: 65777
ISSN: 0029-7909
Founded in: 1892
Printed in 4 colors on glossy stock

17815 Ornamental and Miscellaneous Metals Fabricator
National Ornamental & Miscellaneous Metals Assn
532 Forest Parkway
Suite A
Forest Park, GA 30297-6137

404-363-4009; *Fax:* 404-366-1852
nommainfo@nomma.org; www.nomma.org

Curt Witter, CEO/President
Todd Daniel, Editor

Magazine published by National Ornamental and Miscellaneous Metals Association.
Cost: $30.00
Circulation: 10000
Founded in: 1958

17816 Platt's Metals Week
McGraw Hill
3333 Walnut Street
Boulder, CO 80301

720-548-5000
800-752-8878; *Fax:* 720-548-5701
metals@platts.com; www.mcgraw-hill.com

Jackie Roche, Editor-in-Chief
Terry McGraw, CEO

Harry Sachinsis, President
Jackie Roche, Publisher

Extensive price listings in four currencies.
Frequency: Weekly

17817 Powder Coating
OSC Publishing
1300 E 66th Street
Minneapolis, MN 55423-2642

612-866-2242; *Fax:* 612-866-1939

Richard R Cress, Publisher
Richard Link, Manager

Our information focuses on the application, pre-treatment, materials, materials handling, and curing processes. Also features case histories.
Cost: $95.00
Frequency: Monthly
Circulation: 23587

17818 Practical Welding Today
Fabricators and Manufacturers Association
833 Featherstone Road
Rockford, IL 61107-6302

815-399-8700; *Fax:* 815-484-7700
info@fmanet.org; www.fmanet.org

Gerald M Shankel, President/CEO
Michael Hedges, VP Finance/CFO
Scott Stevens, Publisher
Kim Clothier, Director of Circulation
Jim Gorzek, Marketing

Practical Welding Today is the only hands on, down-to-earth magazine with information that welders can use in the shop or out in the field. Published six times per year with more than 40,000 subcribers, it covers topics such as systems and equipment, safety, consumables, cutting and welding prep, welding inspection and more. In addition, Practical Welding Today has a regular lineup of application articles, welder profiles, product highlights and valuable buyers' guides.
Circulation: 40000
Printed in 4 colors on glossy stock

17819 Products Finishing
Gardner Publications
6915 Valley Ln
Cincinnati, OH 45244-3153

513-527-8800; *Fax:* 513-527-8801
narnold@gardnerweb.com;
www.gardnerweb.com

Rick Kline Sr, CEO
Beverly Graves, Manager
John Campos, Manager
Brian Wertheimer, Account Manager
Eddie Kania, Sales Manager

Covers production, management, engineering, design, etc. in plants where metal and plastic products are eletroplated, anodized, painted, buffed, cleaned or otherwise finished.
Cost: $89.00
Frequency: Monthly
Circulation: 45552
Founded in: 1928
Printed in 4 colors on glossy stock

17820 Projects in Metal
Village Press
2779 Aero Park Drive
PO Box 629
Traverse City, MI 49686-9101

231-463-3712; *Fax:* 231-946-3289
villagepre@aol.com;
www.members.aol.com/vpshop/pim/htm

Robert Goff, Publisher

In each issue you will find plans for valuable tools and accessories, and challenging hobby projects. Every project is complete in one issue.
Frequency: Bi-Monthly
Circulation: 15000

17821 Recycling Today
GIE Media
4012 Bridge Avenue
Cleveland, OH 44113-3320

216-961-4130
800-456-0707; *Fax:* 216-961-0364
btaylor@gie.net; www.recyclingtoday.com

Jim Keefe, Group Publisher
Brian Taylor, Editor
Richard Foster, CEO
Helen Duerr, Director of Production
Megan Ries, Advertising Coordinatior

Published for the secondary commodity processing/recycling market.
Cost: $30.00
Frequency: Monthly
Founded in: 1980

17822 SCRAP
Institute of Scrap Recycling Industries
1615 L Street NW
Suite 600
Washington, DC 20036-5664

202-662-8500; *Fax:* 202-626-0900
kentkiser@scrap.org; www.scrap.org

Kent Kiser, Publisher
Marian Weiss, Production Manager
Rachel H Pollack, Editor-In-Chief
Valerie Hillyer, Circulation/Advertising Associate

A bi-monthly magazine that covers all aspects of the international scrap recycling industry, including market trends, business management, personnel issues, equipment and technology, regulations and legislation, and more.
Cost: $36.00
16 Pages
Frequency: 6 per year
Circulation: 7400
ISSN: 1092-8618
Founded in: 1928

17823 Secondary Marketing Executive Magazine
Zackin Publications
100 Willenbrock Road
Oxford, CT 06478

203-262-4670
800-325-6745; *Fax:* 203-262-4680
info@secondarymarketingexec.com;
www.secondarymarketingexec.com
Social Media: Facebook, Twitter

Michael Bates, Publisher
Patrick Barnard, Editor
Vanessa Williams, Business Development

Delivers news, analysis and how-to advice to people involved in the buying and selling of mortgage loans and servicing rights nationwide.
Frequency: Monthly
Founded in: 1986

17824 Shop Owner
Penton Media
1166 Avenue of the Americas/10th Fl
New York, NY 10036

212-204-4200; *Fax:* 216-696-6662
information@penton.com; www.penton.com

Jane Cooper, Marketing
Thomas J Grasson, Editorial Director
Charles Bates, Senior Editor
Melody Berendt, Circulation Manager
Janet Marioneaux, Administrative Assistant

Digest-sized publication covering information essential to the success of the small to medium manufacturing shop.
Frequency: Quarterly
Circulation: 120000
Founded in: 1998
Printed in 4 colors

17825 Stamping Journal
Fabricators and Manufacturers Association
833 Featherstone Road
Rockford, IL 61107-6302

815-399-8700; *Fax:* 815-484-7700
info@fmanet.org; www.fmanet.org

Gerald Shankel, President/CEO
Michael Hedges, CFO
Scot Stevens, Publisher
Jim Gorzek, Sales Manager
Kim Clothier, Circulation Manager

Stamping Journal, the only North American magazine devoted exclusively to metal stamping, has been delivering the industry's latest techniques, news and ideas to subscribers worldwide for 13 years. Published six times per year, with more than 35,000 subscribers, Stamping Journal focuses on metal stamping technology including, tool and die, material handling, coil processing, stamping presses, press feeding, quick die change and more.
Cost: $65.00
Frequency: Monthly
Circulation: 35000
Founded in: 1970
Printed in 4 colors on glossy stock

17826 Tooling & Production
NP Communications, LLC
2500 Tamiami Trail N
Nokomis, FL 34275

941-966-9521; *Fax:* 941-966-2590
vnelson@nelsonpub.com;
www.toolingandproduction.com

Vern Nelson, Publisher/Editorial Director
Bob West, Managing Editor/Associate Publisher

Provides information to metalworking professionals working in large, high-throughput plants. Original editorial delivers technology, products, and processes applying to aerospace, automotive, medical equipment, mold, tool & die manufacturing, and much more.
100 Pages
Frequency: Monthly
Circulation: 70000
ISSN: 0040-9243
Founded in: 1934
Printed in 4 colors on glossy stock

17827 Tube & Pipe Journal
Fabricators and Manufacturers Association
833 Featherstone Road
Rockford, IL 61107-6302

815-998-8700; *Fax:* 815-484-7701
info@fmanet.org; www.fmanet.org

Gerald Shankel, President/CEO
Michael Hedges, CFO

The Tube and Pipe Journal is North America's only magazine devoted exclusively to metal tube and pipe manufacturing. Published 8 times per year and with more than 30,000 subscribers, TPJ covers topics such as tube producing, bending and forming, cutting and sawing, welding, tooling, coil and material handling, and more. TPJ also provides expanded coverage of hydroforming technology in the Hydroforming Journal, a separate supplement published four time per year alongside TPJ.
Cost: $200.00
Circulation: 30000
Founded in: 1970
Printed in 4 colors on glossy stock

17828 US Glass, Metal & Glazing
Key Communications

PO Box 569
Garrisonville, VA 22463

540-577-7174; *Fax:* 540-720-5687
info@glass.com; www.glass.com

Debra Levy, Publisher
Ellen Giard Chilcoat, Editor
Penny Stacey, Advertising Coordinator

Serves manufactures/fabricators, contract glaziers, distributors and wholesalers, retailors/dealers of glass/metal and or glass/metal products and other allied to the field.
Frequency: Monthly
Circulation: 15000
ISSN: 0041-7661
Founded in: 1995
Printed in 4 colors on glossy stock

17829 Welding Design & Fabrication
Penton Media
1166 Avenue of the Americas/10th Fl
New York, NY 10036

212-204-4200; *Fax:* 216-696-6662
information@penton.com; www.penton.com

Jane Cooper, Marketing
Dean Peters, Editor
David Nussbaum, CEO
Chris Meyer, Director, Corporate Communications

Reaches designers, engineers, managers, superviisors, and buyers in plants and field sites in the US and Canada who conduct welding and fabricating operations. Reports on processes and equipment, materials, safety, testing and inspection in the manufacturing of fabricated metal products, structural projects and equipment maintenance.
Frequency: Monthly
Circulation: 40000
Founded in: 1892
Printed in 4 colors

17830 Welding Innovation
James F Lincoln Arc Welding Foundation
22801 Saint Clair Ave
Cleveland, OH 44117-2524

216-481-4300; *Fax:* 216-383-8220;
www.jflf.org/

Roy Morrow, President
Richard D Seif, Chairman
Vicki Wilson, Administrative Assistant
Dave Manning, Executive Director

Informative articles related to welding steel structures such as bridges and buildings, as well as notices of related conferences.
Circulation: 40000
Founded in: 1936

17831 Welding Journal
American Welding Society
550 Nw 42nd Ave
Miami, FL 33126-5699
305-443-9353
800-443-9353; *Fax:* 305-443-7559
info@aws.org; www.aws.org

Ray Shook, President
Jefferey Weber, Publisher
Cecilia Barbier, Senior Coordinator Market
Robert Pali, Treasurer

Our feature articles include new product listings, book reviews and the application of new operating procedures.
Frequency: Monthly
Circulation: 46000
Founded in: 1919

17832 Wire Rope News & Sling Technology
Wire Rope News
PO Box 871
Clark, NJ 07066-871

908-486-3221; *Fax:* 732-396-4215
vsent@aol.com; www.wireropenews.com

Edward J Bluvias, Publisher
Conrad Miller, Editor

Wire Rope News & Sling Technology is edited for manufacturers and distributors of wire rope, chain, cordage, related hardware, and sling fabricators. Content includes technical articles, news, and reports describing the manufacture and use of wire rope in marine, construction, mining, aircraft and offshore drilling operations. Cordage, slings, chain and fittings are also covered. Editorial content contains articles about fabricating companies, new products and people in the news.
Cost: $20.00
Circulation: 4400
ISSN: 0740-1809
Founded in: 1979
Printed in 4 colors on glossy stock

Trade Shows

17833 AFS/CMI Advanced Foundry Operations Conference
American Foundrymen's Society
1695 N Penny Ln
Schaumburg, IL 60173-4555

847-824-0181
800-537-4237; *Fax:* 847-824-7848;
www.afsinc.org

Frequency: March

17834 AISTech Conference & Exposition
Association for Iron & Steel Technology
186 Thorn Hill Rd
Warrendale, PA 15086-7528

724-814-3000; *Fax:* 724-814-3001
memberservices@aist.org; www.aist.org
Social Media: Facebook, Twitter, LinkedIn

Ronald E Ashburn, Executive Director
William A Albaugh, Technology Programs Manager
Joann Cantrell, Publications Manager/Editor
Mark Didiano, Finance & Administration Manager
Stacy Varmecky, Membership Communications Manager

Featuring technologies from across the globe, allowing steel producers to compete in today's global market. Submit technical papers for presentation at the event. 300 exhibitors. Registration starts at $425.
4500 Attendees
Frequency: Annual/Spring

17835 ASM Heat Treating Society Conference & Exposition
ASM International
9639 Kinsman Road
Materials Park, OH 44073

440-385-5151
800-336-5152; *Fax:* 440-338-4634
pamela.kleinman@asminternational.org;
www.asminternational.org
Social Media: Facebook, Twitter, LinkedIn

Pamela Kleinma, Senior Manager, Events
Kellye Thomas, Exposition Account Manager
Jeane Deatherage, Administrator, Foundation Programs
Virginia Shirk, Foundation Executive Assistant

Conference and exhibits of heat treating equipment and supplies plus information of interest to metallurgists, manufacturing, research and design technical professionals. 300 exhibitors.
3500 Attendees
Frequency: September, Bi-Annual
Founded in: 1974

17836 ASM Materials Science & Technology (MS&T)
ASM International
9639 Kinsman Road
Materials Park, OH 44073-0002

440-338-5151
800-336-5152; *Fax:* 440-338-4634
pamela.kleinman@asminternational.org;
www.asminternational.org
Social Media: Facebook, Twitter, LinkedIn

Pamela Kleinman, Senior Manager, Events
Kelly Thomas, Exposition Account Manager
Jeane Deatherage, Administrator, Foundation Programs
Virginia Shirk, Foundation Executive Assistant

Annual event focusing on testing, analysis, characterization and research of materials such as engineered materials, high performance metals, powdered metals, metal forming, surface modification, welding and joining. 350 exhibitors.
4,000 Attendees
Frequency: Annual/October
Founded in: 2005

17837 Advanced Productivity Conference and Expo- Cleveland
Society of Manufacturing Engineers
1 SME Drive
PO Box 930
Dearborn, MI 48121

313-425-3000
800-733-4763; *Fax:* 313-425-3400
advertising@sme.org; www.sme.org

Mark Tomlinson, Executive Director
Greg Sheremet, Publisher

200 Exhibits of equipment, supplies and services for the tool and manufacturing engineering fields.
13800 Attendees
Frequency: Biennial
Founded in: 1984

17838 AeroMat Conference and Exposition
ASM International
9639 Kinsman Road
Materials Park, OH 44073-0002

440-385-5151
800-336-5152; *Fax:* 440-338-4634
kim.schaefer@asminternational.org;
www.asminternational.org
Social Media: Facebook, Twitter, LinkedIn

Kim Schaefer, Event Manager
Kelly Thomas, Exposition Account Manager
Jeane Deatherage, Administrator, Foundation Programs
Virginia Shirk, Foundation Executive Assistant

Conference for Aerospace Meterials Engineers, Structural Engineers and Designers. The annual event focuses on affordable structures and low-cost manufacturing, titanium alloy technology, advanced intermetallics and refractory metal alloys, materials and processes for space applications, aging systems, high strength steel, NDT evaluation, light alloy technology, welding and joining, and engineering technology. 150 exhibitors.
1500 Attendees
Frequency: Annual/June
Founded in: 1984

17839 American Foundrymen's Society Castings Congress and Cast Expo
505 State St
Des Plaines, IL 60016-2267

847-824-0181; *Fax:* 847-824-7845

Kristy Glass, Show Manager

300 booths including technical papers and panel sessions for the metal casting industry.
12000 Attendees
Frequency: Annual

17840 **American Society Engineers: Design International**
Systems and Design Group
3 Park Avenue
Floor 27
New York, NY 10016-5902

212-903-4160

Fred Goldfarb, Program Manager
Virgil Carter, CEO

150 booths.
2.5M Attendees
Frequency: August

17841 **American Welding Show**
American Welding Society
8669 Doral Boulevard, Suite 130
Doral, FL 33166

305-443-9353
800-443-9353; *Fax:* 305-443-7559;
www.aws.org

Ray Shook, Executive Director
Jefferey Weber, Publisher
Amy Nathan, Public Relations Manager

350 booths of welding and allied industries held in conjunction with metal form.
Frequency: Annual

17842 **American Zinc Association**
1112 16th Street NW
Suite 240
Washington, DC 20036-4818

202-478-8200; *Fax:* 202-835-0155
info@zinc.org; www.zinc.org

George Vary, Executive Director
David Adkins, Secretary
Frequency: February

17843 **Annual International Titanium Conference**
International Titanium Association
1871 Folsom Street
Suite 200
Boulder, CO 80302-5714

303-443-7515; *Fax:* 303-443-4406;
www.titanium.org

Amy Fitzgerald, Manager
800 Attendees
Frequency: October
Founded in: 1984

17844 **Artist-Blacksmiths Association of North America Conference**
Artist Blacksmith's Association of North America
259 Muddy Fork Road
Jonesborough, TN 37659

423-913-1022; *Fax:* 423-913-1023
abana@abana.org; www.abana.org
Social Media: Facebook, Twitter

Eddie Rainey, President

Meeting and exhibitions, workshops, demonstrations and artistic metalwork for the professional and amateur blacksmith.

17845 **Association of Industrial Metallizers, Coaters and Laminators Conference**
201 Springs Street
Fort Mill, SC 29708

803-802-7820; *Fax:* 803-802-7821
aimcal@aimcal.org; www.aimcal.org

Craig Sheppard, Executive Director
Erin Davis, Communications Manager

Displays relating to coaters and laminators, metallizers and producers of metallized film and or paper on continuous rolls, suppliers of plastic films, papers and adhesives.
Frequency: Annual
Founded in: 1970

17846 **Cast Expo**
Cast Metals Institute
1695 N Penny Ln
Schaumburg, IL 60173-4555

847-824-0181
800-537-4237; *Fax:* 847-824-7848;
www.castmetals.com
Social Media: Facebook, Twitter, LinkedIn

CastExpo attracts thousands of decision-making metalcasters from around the world, all of whom are looking for the latest advancements in equipment, technology and services to use in their own facilities.
Frequency: May

17847 **Electrical Manufacturing & Coil Winding Expo**
PO Box 278
Imperial Beach, CA 91933-0278

619-435-3629; *Fax:* 619-435-3639
cthurman@earthlink.net; www.emcwa.org

Richard Duke, President
Charles Thurman, Executive Director
Don Stankiewicz, Vice President

An annual technical conference and exhibition related to the manufacture of electrical products. Exhibitors include suppliers of materials and process equipment used in manufacturing electric motors, trnasformers, and other electrical devices. 150 exhibitors, free admission.
2000 Attendees

17848 **FABTECH International**
Fabricators and Manufacturers Association
833 Featherstone Road
Rockford, IL 61107-6302

815-399-8700; *Fax:* 815-399-7279;
www.fmametalfab.org

Mark Hoper, Director

Metal forming, fabricating, finishing and welding event that gives all the tools neded to improve productivity, increase profits and find new ways to survive in today's competitive business environment.
25000 Attendees
Frequency: Annual/November

17849 **Furnaces North America**
Metal Treating Institute
504 Osceola Ave
Jacksonville Beach, FL 32250

904-249-0448; *Fax:* 904-249-0459;
www.heattreat.net

Tom Morrison, Show Manager

North America's Premier Heat Treat Only Event, Furnaces North America 2012, will be held October 1-3, 2012 in Nashville, TN.
340 Members
1200 Attendees
Frequency: September
Founded in: 1933

17850 **International Anodizing Conference & Exposition**
Aluminum Anodizers Council (AAC)
1000 North Rand Road
Suite 214
Wauconda, IL 60084

847-526-2010; *Fax:* 847-526-3993
mail@anodizing.org; www.andoizing.org

Terry D Snell, Chairman
Todd Hamilton, Vice Chairman
Gregory T Rajsky CAE, President
120 Attendees
Frequency: Annual

17851 **International Symposium for Testing and Failure Analysis**
ASM International
9639 Kinsman Road
Materials Park, OH 44073-0002

440-385-5151; *Fax:* 440-338-4634

Jan DiRosa, Expositions Sales

Annual event focusing on microelectronic and electronic device failure analysis, techniques, EOS/ESD testing and discretes aimed at failure analysis engineers and managers, technicians and new failure analysis engineers. Santa Clara Convention Center, Santa Clara, California.
1,100 Attendees
Frequency: November

17852 **International Thermal Spray Conference & Exposition**
ASM International
9639 Kinsman Road
Materials Park, OH 44073

440-338-5151
800-336-5152; *Fax:* 440-338-4634
natalie.nemec@asminternational.org;
www.asminternational.org
Social Media: Facebook, Twitter, LinkedIn

Natalie Neme, Event Manager
Kelly Thomas, Exposition Account Manager
Jeane Deatherage, Administrator, Foundation Programs
Virginia Shirk, Foundation Executive Assistant

Global annual event attracting professional interested in thermal spray technology focusing on advances in HVOF, plasma and detonation gun, flame spray and wire arc spray processes, performance of coatings, and future trends. 150 exhibitors.
1000 Attendees
Frequency: Annual/May

17853 **Iron & Steel Exposition**
Association of Iron & Steel Engineers
3 Gateway Center
Suite 1900
Pittsburgh, PA 15222-1000

412-281-6323; *Fax:* 412-281-4657;
www.aise.org

Ronald E Ashiurn, Managing Director
Chris Brown, Graphic Designer
Stacy Varmecky, General Manager

Includes technical sessions and exhibits of equipment, supplies and services for the metals producing industry.
25M Attendees

17854 **MBCEA Annual Conference**
Metal Building Contractors & Erectors Association
PO Box 499
Shawnee Mission, KS 66201

913-432-3800; *Fax:* 913-432-3803;
www.mbcea.org

Angela M Cruse, Executive Director
Tim Seyler, President

Annual conference with the mission to support the professional advancement of metal building contractors, erectors and our industry.
Frequency: February

17855 **METALFORM**
Precision Metalforming Association
6363 Oak Tree Boulevard
Independence, OH 44131

216-901-8800; *Fax:* 216-901-9190
rjudson@pma.org; www.metalform.com

Amy Primiano, Director Expositions
William Gaskin, President

A regional networking and educational event that brings buyers and sellers from metal stamping

and fabricating markets together in a dynamic and interactive environment.
5,000 Attendees
Frequency: March

17856 **Metalworking Machine Tool Expo**
Marketing International Corporation
200 N Glebe Road
Suite 900
Arlington, VA 22203-3728
703-527-8000; *Fax:* 703-527-8006

Annual show of 100 machine tools suppliers.
8000 Attendees

17857 **NFFS Summit Conference**
Non-Ferrous Founders' Society
1480 Renaissance Drive
Suite 310
Park Ridge, IL 60068

847-299-0950; *Fax:* 847-299-3598
staff@nffs.org; www.nffs.org

Frequency: February

17858 **National Ornamental and Miscellaneous Metals Association**
532 Forest Parkway
Suite A
Forest Park, GA 30297-6137
404-363-4009; *Fax:* 888-279-7994
nommainfo@nomma.org; www.nomma.org

Barbara Cook, Executive Director
Todd Daniel, Editor
Cyndi Smith, Office Manager
Martha Pennington, Meetings/Exposition Manager

This annual convention and trade show — METALfab — is for all those involved in the ornamental and metallury industries.
900 Attendees
Founded in: 1958

17859 **PowderMet**
APMI International
105 College Road E
Princeton, NJ 08540-6992

609-452-7700; *Fax:* 609-987-8523
info@mpif.org; www.mpif.org

Nicholas T Mares, President
Michael E Lutheran, Director
C James Trombino CAE, Director

An annual international conference serving the powder metallurgy industry with a standalone exhibit featuring industry service providers and equipment suppliers.
1000 Attendees
Frequency: Annual

17860 **SMACNA Annual Convention**
Sheet Metal and Air Conditioning Contractor's Natl
4201 Lafayette Center Drive
Chantilly, VA 20151-1219

703-803-2980; *Fax:* 703-803-3732
info@smacna.org; www.smacna.org

Vincent R Sandusky, CEO

Sheet metal and air conditioning contractors explore the newest ideas, technologies, and trends in the construction industry.
Frequency: October

17861 **TMS Annual Meeting Exhibition**
Minerals, Metals & Materials Society
184 Thorn Hill Road
Warrendale, PA 15086
724-776-9000; *Fax:* 724-776-3770
webmaster@tms.org; www.tms.org

Cindy Wilson, Show Manager
Alexander Scott, Executive Director

International metals and materials exhibition. Production, processing, engineering and research. Held in Charlotte, North Carolina.
3,500 Attendees
Frequency: March

17862 **WESTEC-Advanced Productivity Expo**
Society of Manufacturing Engineers
1 SME Drive
PO Box 930
Dearborn, MI 48121
313-425-3000
800-733-4763; *Fax:* 313-425-3400
advertising@sme.org; www.sme.org

Mark Tomlinson, Executive Director
Greg Sheremet, Publisher

600 booths displaying machine tools and metalworking products and services.
40M Attendees
Frequency: Annual

Directories & Databases

17863 **Aluminum Association Aluminum Standards & Data**
Aluminum Association
900 19th Street NW
Washington, DC 20006-2105

202-862-5100

Contains the nominal composition and composition limits, typical mechanical and physical properties and tensile properties limits for US wrought aluminum alloys. Updated periodically.

17864 **Aluminum Extruders Council Buyer's Guide**
1000 North Rand Road
Suite 214
Wauconda, IL 60084

847-526-2010; *Fax:* 847-526-3993
mail@aec.org; www.aec.org
Social Media: LinkedIn

Matt McMahon, Chairman
Scott Kelley, Vice Chairman
Jeff Henderson, President
Nancy Molenda, Communications Manager

Offers listings of aluminum extruders.
Frequency: Annual
Founded in: 1950

17865 **DRI Steel Forecast**
DRI/McGraw-Hill
24 Hartwell Ave
Lexington, MA 02421-3103

781-860-6060; *Fax:* 781-860-6002
support@construction.com;
www.construction.com

Walt Arvin, President

This comprehensive database offers over 500 quarterly and annual forecasts on production, shipment, and consumption of raw steel and steel products in the United States.

17866 **Directory Iron and Steel Plants**
Association for Iron & Steel Technology
186 Thorn Hill Rd
Warrendale, PA 15086-7528

724-814-3000; *Fax:* 724-814-3001
memberservices@aist.org; www.aist.org
Social Media: Facebook, Twitter, LinkedIn

Ronald E Ashburn, Executive Director
William A Albaugh, Technology Programs Manager
Joann Cantrell, Publications Manager/Editor
Mark Didiano, Finance & Administration Manager
Stacy Varmecky, Membership Communications Manager

The Directory lists more than 2,000 companies and 17,500 individuals. Featuring data on essentially ever steel producer in the USA, Canada and Mexico, including names and titles of executive, enginnering, maintenance and operating personnel. Also includes an alpha listing of all major equipment, product and service providers to the international iron and steel industry, and a listing of associations affiliated with the industry, with complete geo-indexing. Softbound book with CD.
Cost: $95.00
Frequency: M-$95/NM-$135
ISBN: 1-935117-00-1

17867 **Dun's Industrial Guide: Metalworking Directory**
Dun & Bradstreet Information Service
3 Sylvan Way
Parsippany, NJ 07054-3822

973-605-6000
800-526-0651; *Fax:* 973-605-9630

Over 78,000 original equipment manufacturers, metal distributors, and machine tools/metalworking machinery distributors.
Cost: $775.00
Frequency: Annual

17868 **EDM Today Yearbook**
EDM Publications
230 W Parkway
Suite 3-1
Pompton Plains, NJ 07444-1065

973-831-1334; *Fax:* 973-831-1195

Jack Sebzda, Editor
Frequency: Annual

17869 **Economic Handbook of the Machine Tool Industry**
AMT - The Association for Manufacturing Technology
7901 Westpark Dr
Mc Lean, VA 22102-4206

703-893-2900; *Fax:* 703-893-1151
amt@amtonline.org; www.amtonline.org

Bob Simpson, President

Complete statistics for the US machine tool industry, including exports and imports.
Cost: $295.00
Frequency: Annual
Printed in one color on matte stock

17870 **Equip-Mart**
116 N Camp Street
Seguin, TX 78155

830-303-3328
800-864-1155; *Fax:* 830-372-3011;
www.equip-mart.com

Directory of available used metalworking equipment.
Frequency: Weekly

17871 **Foundry Management & Technology: Where to Buy Directory Issue**
Penton Publishing Company
1166 Avenue of the Americas/10th Fl
New York, NY 10036

212-204-4200; *Fax:* 216-696-1752
information@penton.com; www.penton.com

Dean Peters, Editor
Chris Meyer, Director, Corporate Communications

Listing of about 1,700 manufacturers of foundry products.
Cost: $15.00
Frequency: Annual, September
Circulation: 22,000

17872 Fundamentals of Steel Product Physical Metallurgy
Association for Iron & Steel Technology (AIST)
186 Thorn Hill Road
Warrendale, PA 15086-7528
724-814-3000; *Fax:* 724-814-3001
memberservices@aist.org;
www.steellibrary.com
Bruno C De Cooman, Author
John G Speer, Author
This directory is an introduction to steel products for industry professionals. With its readily accessible style, the book allows the reader to easily grasp important scientific topics that play an essential role in current steel research, product development and applications. ISBN: 978-1-935117-16-2
Cost: $110.00
Frequency: Annual

17873 Industrial Laser Review: Buyers' Guide of Companies & Products
PennWell Publishing Company
10 Tara Boulevard
5th Floor
Nashua, NH 03062-2800
603-891-0123; *Fax:* 603-891-0574;
www.industrial-lasers.com/index.html
David Belforte, Editor
Frequency: Annual July

17874 Industrial Machine Trader
Heartland Industrial Group
1003 Central Avenue
PO Box 1415
Fort Dodge, IA 50501
515-955-1600
800-247-2000; *Fax:* 515-955-3753
igproduction@industrialgroup.com;
www.industrialgroup.com
Social Media: Facebook, Twitter, LinkedIn
Virginia Rodriguez, Publisher
Printed directory of available used metalworking equipment.
150+ Members
Frequency: Weekly
Founded in: 1966

17875 International Lead and Zinc
WEFA Group
800 Baldwin Tower Boulevard
Eddystone, PA 19022-1368
610-490-4000; *Fax:* 610-490-2770
info@wefa.com; www.wefa.com
This database contains quarterly and annual time series on lead and zinc.

17876 International Powder Metallurgy Directory
Metal Powder Industries Federation
105 College Rd East
Princeton, NJ 08540-6692
609-452-7700; *Fax:* 609-987-8523
info@mpif.org; www.mpif.org
Michael Lutheran, President
Jim Adams, Director, Technical Services
C. James Trombino, Executive Director, CEO
Jillaine K. Regan, VP, Finance & Administration
Jessica Tamasi, Advertising & Exhibit Manager
Leading reference source for powder metallurgy parts producers and industry suppliers worldwide.
Cost: $30.00
210 Members
504 Pages
Frequency: Annual, Paperback
Founded in: 1944

17877 Iron and Manganese Ore Databook
Metal Bulletin
220 5th Avenue
New York, NY 10001-7708
212-136-6202
800-MET-L 25; *Fax:* 212-213-6273
John Bailey, Editor
Iron and manganese ore producers and traders worldwide.
Cost: $179.00
Frequency: Quadrennial

17878 Iron and Steel Works of the World
Metal Bulletin
220 5th Avenue
19th Floor
New York, NY 10001-7781
212-213-6202; *Fax:* 202-213-1870;
www.metalbulleton.com
Henry Cooke, Editor
Lists over 1,500 major iron and steel plants worldwide.
Cost: $439.00
730 Pages

17879 Locator Services
315 S Patrick St
Alexandria, VA 22314-3532
703-836-9700
800-537-1446; *Fax:* 703-836-7665
sales@locatoronline.com;
www.locatoronline.com
Terry Pitman, Publisher
Printed directory of available used metalworking equipment.
Frequency: Monthly
Circulation: 225,000

17880 Metal Bulletin's Prices and Data Book
Metal Bulletin
220 5th Avenue
19th Floor
New York, NY 10001-7781
212-213-6202; *Fax:* 212-213-1870
help@metalbulletin.com;
www.metalbulletin.com
Richard ODonoghue, Manager
Ania Tumm, Marketing Manager
Julius Pike, Account Manager
A list of national and international associations and trading organizations concerned with iron, steel and nonferrous ores and metals.
Cost: $165.00
Frequency: Annual

17881 Metal Casting Industry Directory
Penton Media
1166 Avenue of the Americas/10th Fl
New York, NY 10036
212-204-4200; *Fax:* 216-696-6662
information@penton.com; www.penton.com
Jane Cooper, Marketing
Chris Meyer, Director, Corporate Communications
Directory of services and supplies to the industry.
Cost: $425.00
300 Pages

17882 Metal Center News: Metal Distribution Issue
Hitchcock Publishing Company
191 S Gary Avenue
Carol Stream, IL 60188-2095
630-690-5600
Joseph Marino, Editor
Offers a list of producers and industrial metals and metal products, manufacturers of metal processing and handling equipment.
Cost: $25.00
Frequency: Annual
Circulation: 14,000

17883 Metal Finishing Guidebook Directory
Metal Finishing/Elsevier Science
360 Park Ave S
New York, NY 10010-1736
212-633-3980; *Fax:* 212-633-3913
metalfinishing@elsevier.com;
www.elsevier.com
Ys Chi, President
Patti Ann Frost, Managing Editor
Matthew Smaldon, Circulation Manager
Bill Godfrey, Chief Information Officer
Cost: $87.00
Founded in: 1962

17884 Metal Finishing: Guidebook Directory
Metal Finishing/Elsevier Science
650 Avenue of Americas
New York, NY 10011
212-633-5100; *Fax:* 212-633-5140;
www.metalfinishing.com
Eugene Nadel, Publisher
Don Walsh, Director of operations
Enthone Taps, Communications Manager
Jonathan Timms, Director of Marketing
Frequency: Annual January

17885 Metal Statistics
American Metal Market
350 Hudson Street
4th Floor
New York, NY 10014-4504
212-666-2420
800-662-4445; *Fax:* 212-519-7522
custserv@amm.com; www.amm.com
Gloria Larme, Editor-in-Chief
The statistical guide to North American metals. Hardcover $265.00, Softcover $185.00.
404 Pages
Frequency: Annual
ISBN: 0-910094-01-2
Founded in: 1908

17886 Metal Statistics: Ferrous Edition
American Metal Market
350 Hudson Street
4th Floor
New York, NY 10014-4504
212-662-2420
800-662-4445; *Fax:* 818-487-4550
custserv@amm.com; www.amm.com
Machael Botta, Publisher
Gloria LaRue, Editor-in-Chief
Statistics for North American metals, also Canadian and Mexican statistics, International tables and graphs, International trade labor contractsand recycling and scrap alternatives.
Cost: $265.00
Frequency: Annual
ISBN: 0-910094-00-4

17887 Metals Datafile
Materials Information
ASM International
Materials Park, OH 44073
440-930-4888; *Fax:* 440-338-4634
This database contains designation and specification numbers for ferrous and non-ferrous metals and alloys.
Frequency: Full-text

17888 Metalworking Machinery Mailer
Tade Publishing Group

29501 Greenfield Road; Suite 120
Southfield, MI 48076

248-552-8583
800-966-8233; *Fax:* 248-552-0466;
www.tadesite.com

Tom Lynch, Editor

Printed directory of available used metalworking equipment.
Frequency: Monthly

17889 **Mineral and Energy Information**
Mineral Information Institute
505 Violet St
Golden, CO 80401-6714

303-277-9190; *Fax:* 303-277-9198
mii@mii.org; www.mii.org

Profiles of associations, government agencies and special interest groups in North America that are sources of publications and products on mineral related subjects.
Cost: $15.00

17890 **Modern Machine Shop: CNC & Software Guide Software Issue**
Gardner Publications
6915 Valley Ln
Cincinnati, OH 45244-3153

513-527-8800; *Fax:* 513-527-8801;
www.gardnerweb.com

Rick Kline Sr, CEO
Richard Kline, Manager
John Campos, Manager
Brian Wertheimer, Account Manager
Eddie Kania, Sales Manager
Frequency: Annual April

17891 **Parts Cleaning: Master Source Buyer's Guide**
Witter Publishing Corporation
84 Park Avenue; Suite 32
Flemington, NJ 08822-1172

908-788-0343; *Fax:* 908-788-3782;
www.partscleaningweb.com

Andrew Witter, Owner
Frequency: Annual July

17892 **Pipe and Tube Mills of the World with Global Technical Data**
Preston Publishing Company
715 S Sheridan Rd
Tulsa, OK 74112-3139

918-834-2356; *Fax:* 918-299-4795;
www.prestonpipe.com

Richard Preston, Owner
LaSondra L O'Farrell, President

We also have a monthly trade journal The Preston Pipe and Tube Report.
Cost: $245.00; 842 Pages
Frequency: BiAnnual; *Founded in:* 1995
Printed in one color on matte stock

17893 **Powder Metallurgy Suppliers Directory**
Metal Powder Industries Federation
105 College Rd East
Princeton, NJ 08540-6692

609-452-7700; *Fax:* 609-987-8523
info@mpif.org; www.mpif.org

Michael Lutheran, President
Jim Adams, Director, Technical Services
C. James Trombino, Executive Director, CEO
Jillaine K. Regan, VP, Finance & Administration
Jessica Tamasi, Advertising & Exhibit Manager

Over 50 producers and suppliers of metal powder who belong to the Metal Powder Producers Association or Refractory Metals Association.
210 Members; *Frequency:* Paperback
Founded in: 1944

17894 **Precision Cleaning: Master Source Buyer's Guide**
Witter Publishing Corporation
84 Park Avenue; Suite 32
Flemington, NJ 08822-1172

908-788-0343; *Fax:* 908-788-3782;
www.precisioncleaningweb.com

Andrew Witter, Owner
Frequency: Annual

17895 **Purchasing Magazine**
Reed Business Information
275 Washington St
Newton, MA 02458-1611

617-964-3030; *Fax:* 617-558-4327;
www.designnews.com

About 1,800 metal producers, distributors, die casters, foundries, forgers, coil coaters and powder metals.
Cost: $15.00; *Frequency:* Annual

17896 **Reference Book for Metal Working Machinery**
Machinery Dealers National Association
1110 Spring St
Silver Spring, MD 20910-4019

301-585-9496
800-872-7807; *Fax:* 301-588-7830

Nearly 1,000 metal working machine tool manufacturers; international coverage.
Cost: $75.00

17897 **Serial Number Reference Book**
Machinery Dealers National Association
315 S Patrick St
Alexandria, VA 22314-3532

703-836-9300
800-872-7807; *Fax:* 703-836-9303
office@mdna.org; www.mdna.org

Mark Robinson, Executive VP
Richard Levy CEA, President

Sourcebook for metalworking machinery has been designed to lead the reader as quickly as possible to the specific serial number/age information he is seeking.
Cost: $29.95; 778 Pages

17898 **Silver Refiners of the World and their Identifying Ingot Marks**
Silver Institute
1112 16th St Nw; Suite 240
Washington, DC 20036-4818

202-347-8200; www.silverinstitute.org

Over 80 refiners in over 18 countries are profiled.
Cost: $33.00; 85 Pages

17899 **Welding Design & Fabrication**
Penton Media
1166 Avenue of the Americas/10th Fl
New York, NY 10036

212-204-4200; *Fax:* 216-696-6662
information@penton.com; www.penton.com

Jane Cooper, Marketing
Chris Meyer, Director, Corporate Communications

For owner operators and managers of professional welding shops.
Frequency: Annual, December

17900 **Who's Who in Powder Metallurgy Membership Directory**
Metal Powder Industries Federation
105 College Rd East
Princeton, NJ 08540-6692

609-452-7700; *Fax:* 609-987-8523
info@mpif.org; www.mpif.org

Michael Lutheran, President
Jim Adams, Director, Technical Services
C. James Trombino, Executive Director, CEO
Jillaine K. Regan, VP, Finance & Administration
Jessica Tamasi, Advertising & Exhibit Manager

An annual listing of the members of the APMI International and the Metal Powder Industries Federation.
Cost: $105.00; 210 Members
88 Pages; *Frequency:* Annual
ISSN: 0361-6304; *Founded in:* 1944

Industry Web Sites

17901 **http://gold.greyhouse.com**
G.O.L.D Grey House OnLine Databases

Grey House Publishing's online database platform, GOLD, offers Quick Search, Keyword Search and Expert Search for most business sectors including metals and metalworking markets. The GOLD platform makes finding the information you need quick and easy - whether you're a novice searcher or an experienced database user. All of Grey House's directory products are available for subscription on the GOLD platform.

17902 **www.ace.org**
Aluminum Extruders Council

An international trade association representing aluminum extruders.

17903 **www.aimcal.org**
Association of Industrial Metallizers, Coaters
and Laminators

Packaging equipment.

17904 **www.aisc.org**
American Institute of Steel Construction

Nonprofit trade association and technical institute established to serve the structural steel industry in the US. Our purpose is to promote the use of structural steel through research activities, market development, education, codes and specifacations, technical assistance, quality certifacation and standardization.

17905 **www.aise.org**
Association of Iron & Steel Engineers

Production and processing of iron and steel.

17906 **www.amea.org**
Association of Machinery and Equipment Appraisers

Members are appraisers of the metalworking industry.

17907 **www.asminternational.org**

ASM International provides information and networking for metals and materials professionals through its website.

17908 **www.aws.org**
American Welding Society

17909 **www.cbsa.copper-brass.org**
Copper and Brass Servicenter Association

Distributors of fabricated copper and copperalloy products, Sheets,plate, coil, rod, bar, pipe, tubing, etc.

17910 **www.cmadc.org**
Closure Manufacturers Association

Conducts public relations for member companies and establishes idustry standards.

17911 **www.coilcoaters.org**
National Coil Coaters Association

17912 **www.construction.com**
McGraw-Hill Construction

McGraw-Hill Construction (MHC), part of The McGraw-Hill Companies, connects people and projects across the design and construction industry, serving owners, architects, engineers, general contractors, subcontractors, building product manufacturers, suppliers, dealers, distributors and adjacent markets.

17913 www.copper.org
Copper Development Association
Seeks to expand the uses and applications of copper and copper products. Responsible for industry-wide market statistics and research.

17914 www.ductile.org
Ductile Iron Society
A technical society servicing the ductile iron industry. To advance the technology, art, science of ductile iron production and to disseminate all such information to the members.

17915 www.emcw.org
Electrical Manufacturing & Coil Winding Assn
Promotes welfare of the motor and coil industry. Offers courses and workshops.

17916 www.fmanet.org
Fabricators and Manufacturers Association
FMA is an educational association serving the metal forming and fabricating industry. Technology areas include sheet metal fabrucating, stamping, roll forming, coil processing, punching, and plate structural fabricating.

17917 www.forengineers.org/wrc
Welding Research Council
Coordinates welding research.

17918 www.greyhouse.com
Grey House Publishing
Authoritative reference directories for most business sectors, incluidng metal and metalworking markets. Users can search the online databases with varied search criteria allowing for custom searches by product category, geographic area, sales volume, keyword, subject and more. Full Grey House catalog and online ordering also available.

17919 www.ilzro.org
International Lead Zinc Research Organization
For miners, smelters and refiners of lead and zinc. Supports research and developement of new uses for the metals and refinement existing uses.

17920 www.intlmag.org
International Magnesium Association
Develops international use and acceptance of magnesium metal and its alloys in all product forms. Members are organizations or individuals engaged in the production, manufacture or marketing of metallic magnesium or those supplying materials, equipment or consulting.

17921 www.ipmi.org
International Precious Metals Institute
Miners, refiners, producers and users of precious metals, as well as research scientists and mercantilists.

17922 www.iss.org
Iron & Steel Society
Seeks to be the premier professional and technical society serving its members and advancing knowledge exchange in the global iron and steel industry. Publishes a monthly magazine.

17923 www.mbcea.org
Metal Building Contractors & Erectors Association
To support the professional advancement of metal building contractors, erectors, and the industry.

17924 www.mdna.org
Machinery Dealers National Association

17925 www.metalforming.com
Precision Metalforming Association
For producers of metal stampings, spinnings, washers and precision sheet metal fabrications as well as suppliers of equipment, materials and services.

17926 www.mfgtech.org
Association for Manufacturing Technology

17927 www.mhia.org
Material Handling Institute
Promotes the market and develops a code of ethics. Serves as liaison among members and other groups.

17928 www.mmsa.net
Mining and Metallurgical Society of America
A professional organization dedicated to increasing public awareness and understanding about mining and why mined materials are essential to modern society and human well being.

17929 www.mpif.org
Metal Powder Industries Federation
Promotes the science and industry of powder metallurgy through technical meetings, seminars, conferences, and publications.

17930 www.naad.org
National Association of Aluminum Distributors
NAAD is the trade association of North American service centers and principal suppliers engaged in marketing aluminum products.

17931 www.nffs.org
Non-Ferrous Founder's Society
Manufacturers of bronze, brass and aluminum castings.

17932 www.nwsa.com
Fernley & Fernley

17933 www.powdercoating.org
Powder Coating Institute

17934 www.scra.org/amc/tfa
Ferroalloys Association
Promotes the ferroalloy industry in the areas of technology, international trade, environment and health, safety and government relations.

17935 www.sdi.org
Steel Deck Institute
Trade association providing uniform industry standards for the engineering, design, manufacture and field usage of steel decks.

17936 www.silversmithing.com
Society of American Silversmiths
Founded to preserve the art and history of handcrafted holloware and flatware plus provide support, networking and greater access to the market forsilversmiths. Educates the public as to the aesthetic and investment value of this art form.

17937 www.smacna.org
Sheet Metal and Air Conditioning Contactor's Natl
An international trade association representing 4,500 contibuting contractor firms in the sheet metal and air conditioning industry. Develops technical standards and manuals addressing all facets of the sheet metal and air conditioning industry.

17938 www.spfa.org
Steel Plate Fabricators Association

17939 www.ssci.org
Steel Service Center Institute

17940 www.steel.org
American Iron and Steel Institute
Works to protect interests of manufacturers in the steel industry.

17941 www.steeldistributors.org/asd
Association of Steel Distributors
Bestows Steel Distributor of The Year Award and the Presidents Award of Merit.

17942 www.steelnews.com
Association for Iron and Steel Technology (AIST)
SteelNews.com is a publication created by the Association for Iron and Steel Technology (AIST) for the steel community. The site features daily updates of the latest global headlines.

17943 www.steeltubeinstitute.org
Steel Tube Institute of North America
Members produce steel tubes and pipes from carbon, stainless or alloy steel, for applications ranging from large structural tubing to small redrawn tubing.

17944 www.sweets.construction.com
McGraw Hill Construction
In depth product information that lets you find, compare, select, specify and make purchase decisions in the industrial product marketplace.

17945 www.taol.com/uscti
United States Cutting Tool Institute
For those in the domestic cutting tool market.

17946 www.thermalspray.org
International Thermal Spray Association
Strengthens the level of awareness in general industry and government on the increasing capabilities and advantages of thermal spray technology for surface engineering through business opportunities, technical support and a social network. Contributes to growth and education in the thermal spray industry.

17947 www.titanium.org
International Titanium Association
Contact ITA for mailing list price.

17948 www.uschamber.org/chamber/mall
Silver Users Association
Represents the interests of corporations that make, sell and distribute products and services in which silver is an essential part. SUA membership includes representatives from the photographic, electronic, silverware and jewelry industries; producers of semi-fabricated and industrial products; and, mirror manufacturers.

17949 www.wirenet.org
Wire Association International
Technical association serving the global wire and cable industry by providing educational materials, sponsoring trade shows and international technical conferences.

17950 www.zinc.org
American Zinc Association
Provides information on the zine industry and hosts international conference on zinc.

Associations

17951 Alabama Surface Mining Commission
PO Box 2390
Jasper, AL 35502

205-221-4130; *Fax:* 205-221-5077
asmc@asmc.alabama.gov;
www.surface-mining.state.al.us

Dr. Randall C. Johnson, Director
Ann Miles, Executive Secretary
Carla D.Lightsey, Chief Divison of SMCR
Milton McCarthy, Legal Division

Doing its part to balance civilization's demands for natural resources and environmental conservation in the state of Alabama.
Founded in: 1972

17952 Alaska Miners Association
121 W. Fireweed
Suite 120
Anchorage, AK 99503-4575

907-563-9229; *Fax:* 907-563-9225
ama@alaskaminers.org; www.alaskaminers.org
Social Media: Facebook, Twitter, LinkedIn, Google+

Jason Brune, President
Lorna Shaw, First Vice President
Mike Satre, SecondVice President
Kim Aasand, Treasurer
James Fueg, Past President

Works to promote the mining industry in Alaska. It advocates the development and use of Alaska's mineral resources to provide an economic base for the State. AMA monitors the activities of State and Federal Government, Congress and the Legislature that affect mineral development.

17953 American Association for Crystal Growth
6986 S. Wadsworth Court
Litteton, CO 80128

303-539-6907; *Fax:* 303-482-2775
AACG@comcast.net; www.crystalgrowth.org

Anthony L Gentile, Executive Administrator
David Bliss, Chairman
Russ Dupuis, Chair

AACG is a nonprofit technical membership organization where the primary function is a organic conference in the fall of crystal growth and characterization. A newsletter is published 3 times per year and distributed to members.
600 Members
Founded in: 1966

17954 American Coal Ash Association
38800 Country Club Drive
Suite 3050
Farmington Hills, MI 48331

720-870-7897; *Fax:* 720-870-7889
info@acaa-usa.org; www.acaa-usa.org

Thomas H Adams, Executive Director

To advance the management and use of coal combustion products in ways that are environmentally responsible, technically sound, commercially competitive, and supportive of a sustainable global community
126 Members
Founded in: 1968

17955 American Exploration and Mining Association
10 N Post St
Suite 305
Spokane, WA 99201-0722

509-624-1158; *Fax:* 509-623-1241
info@miningamerica.org;
www.miningamerica.org

Mari-Ann Green, President
Ron Parratt, 1st Vice President
Steve Alfers, 2nd Vice President
Shelia Bush, Secretary
Laura Skaer, Executive Director

Provides liaison between mining, industry and government. Offers short course on current technology.
2000 Members
Founded in: 1890

17956 American Geosciences Institute
4220 King St
Alexandria, VA 22302-1502

703-379-2480; *Fax:* 703-379-7563;
www.agiweb.org
Social Media: Facebook, Twitter

P.Patrick Leahy, Executive Director
Dr. Wayne D. Pennington, President
Dr. Sharon Mosher, President Elect
Ann Benow, Outreach and Development Director
Walter R.Sisson, Finance and administrator Director

A nonprofit federation of 45 geoscientific and professional associations that represents more than 120,000 geologists, geophysicists, and other earth scientists.
45 Members
Founded in: 1948

17957 American Institute of Mining, Metallurgical & Petroleum Engineers
12999 East Adam Aircraft Circle
Eglewood, CO 80112-5991

303-325-5185; *Fax:* 888-702-0049
aime@aimehq.org; www.aimehq.org
Social Media: Facebook, LinkedIn, YouTube, RSS

Brajendra Fattahi, President
Garry W. Warren, President-Elect
Nikhil C. Trivedi, President-Elect Designate
Dale E. Heinz, Past President
Drew Meyer, Trustee

Supporting member societies by exercising fiscal responsibility, distributing funds, facilitating interaction with the larger scientific and engineering community, enhancing collaboration among the member societies, and honoring the legacy and traditions of AIME.
130M Members
Founded in: 1871

17958 American Institute of Professional Geologists
1200 Washington St.
Thornton, CO 80241-3134

303-412-6205; *Fax:* 303-253-9220
aipg@aipg.org; www.aipg.org
Social Media: Facebook, LinkedIn

William J Siok, Executive Director
Wendy J.Davidson, Assistant Director
Cathy L.Duran, Professional Services
Cristie J.Valero, Office Assistant
Vickie Hill, Membership Services

Founded to certify the credentials of practicing geologists and to advocate on behalf of the profession.
5000 Members
Founded in: 1963

17959 Arizona Mining Association
916 W Adams St
Suite B-134
Phoenix, AZ 85007

602-266-4416; *Fax:* 602-230-8413;
www.azmining.org

Sydney Hay, President
June Castelhano, Administrative Assistant

Recognizes the importance of educating Arizona's citizens about the critical role the mining industry plays not only in our state and nation, but also in the world.
Founded in: 1965

17960 Arizona State Mine Inspectors
1700 West Washington
4th Floor
Phoenix, AZ 85007-4655

602-542-5971; *Fax:* 602-542-5335;
www.asmi.az.gov

John Stanford, Sr.Deputy Mine Inspector
Tim Evans, Assistant State Mine Inspector
Jack Speer, Deputy Mine Inspector Reclamation
Wiiliam Schifferns, Deputy Mine Inspector

Priority mission is to enforce state mining laws which protect mine employees, residents, and the Arizona environment. Focused on providing the best customer service to Arizona residents and mining enterprises.
330 Members
Founded in: 1912

17961 Association for Mineral Exploration British Columbia
889 W Pender Street
Suite 800
Vancouver, BC V6C-3B2

604-689-5271; *Fax:* 604-681-2363
info@amebc.ca; www.amebc.ca
Social Media: Facebook, Twitter

Gavin C Dirom, President/CEO
Rick Conte, Vice President
David McLelland, Chair
Diane Nicolson, Vice Chair
Sam Adkins, Director

AME BC is the predominant voice of mineral exploration and development in British Columbia.
5400 Members
Founded in: 1912

17962 Association of Bituminous Contractors
1250 Eye St NW
Suite 620
Washington, DC 20005-5976

202-296-5745; *Fax:* 202-331-8049

William H Howe, President

Members are general and independent contractors constructing coal mines and coal mine facilities and also bargains with the United Mine Workers.
150 Members
Frequency: Annual/March

17963 Association of Equipment Manufacturers
6737 West Washington Street
Suite 2400
Milwaukee, WI 53214-5647

414-272-0943; *Fax:* 414-212-1170
aem@aem.org; www.aem.org

James Ebbinghaus, VP

Representing manufacturers of architectural, construction, forestry, materials handling and liabilty equipment.

17964 Bureau of Land Management
1849 C Street NW
Room 5665
Washington, DC 20240

202-208-3801; *Fax:* 202-208-5242;
www.blm.gov
Social Media: Facebook, Twitter, LinkedIn, YouTube

Ted Bingham, President
Robert C Bruce, VP

17965 California Mining Association
1029 J Street
Suite 420
Sacramento, CA 95814

916-554-1000; *Fax:* 916-554-1042
spridmore@calcima.org; www.calcima.org

Adam Harper, Association Manager
Stephanie Pridmore, Association Administrator
Gary W. Hambly, President/CEO

Represents the breadth and depth of California's mining industry including producers of precious metals (such as gold and silver), industrial minerals (including borates, limestone, rare earth elements, clays, gypsum and tungsten) and rock, sand and gravel.

17966 Canadian Institute of Mining, Metallurgy and Petroleum
3500 de Maisonneuve Blvd. W.
Suite 1250
Westmount, QC H3Z-3C1

514-939-2710; *Fax:* 514-939-2714
cim@cim.org; www.cim.org
Social Media: Facebook, Twitter, LinkedIn, YouTube

Russell E Hallbauer, CIM President
Jean Vavrek, CIM Executive Director
Danielle Langlois, Director
Benoit Sawyer, Controller
Jasen Coady, Web Developer

The leading technical society of professionals in the Canadian minerals, metals, materials and energy industries.
12000 Members
Founded in: 1898

17967 China Clay Producers Association CCPA
113 Arkwright Landing
Macon, GA 31210

478-757-1211; *Fax:* 478-757-1949
info@georgiamining.org; www.kaolin.com/

Lee Lemke, Executive VP

The mission of the China Clay Producers Association is to promote the common business interest of producers of china clay and the development of coordinated policies, which assure the industry will continue to provide jobs and contribute to the Georgia economy. In addition, objectives also include informing members of proposed legislation, regulatory actions and other matters affecting the kaolin industry, and to maintain the industry's strong community commitment.
Founded in: 1978

17968 Colorado Mining Association
216 16th St
Suite 1250
Denver, CO 80202-5161

303-575-9199; *Fax:* 303-575-9194
colomine@coloradomining.org;
www.coloradomining.org
Social Media: Facebook, Twitter

Stuart Sanderson, President
Fred J. Menzer, Chairman
William Zisch, Chairman-Elect
Stephen A. Onorofskie, Treasurer

Composed of both small and large enterprises engaged in the exploration for, production and refining of, metals, coal, oil shale, and industrial minerals; firms that manufacture and distribute mining and mineral processing equipment and supplies; and other institutions providing services and supplies to the mineral industry.
Founded in: 1876

17969 Copper Development Association
260 Madison Ave
New York, NY 10016-2403

212-251-7200; *Fax:* 212-251-7234
questions@cda.copper.org; www.copper.org
Social Media: Facebook, Twitter, LinkedIn, Google+

Thomas S. Passek, President & CEO
Victoria Prather, Manager Communications
Michels Harold, VP Technaloy Services
Luis Lozano, Technical Consultant
Lorraine Herzing Mills, VP/Finance/Administration

Promoting the use of copper by communicating the unique attributes that make this sustainable element an essential contributor to the formation of life, to advances in science and technology, and to a higher standard of living worldwide.
75 Members
Founded in: 1963

17970 Desert Research Institute
2215 Raggio Pkwy
Reno, NV 89512-1095

775-673-7300; *Fax:* 775-673-7421;
www.dri.edu
Social Media: Facebook, Twitter

Stephen G Wells, President
Ellen Oppenheim, SVP, Finance & Admin/COO
Dr. Alan Gertler, VP, Research/Chief Science Officer
Chris Fritsen, VP, Academic and Faculty Affairs
Chris Ipsen, Assistant VP IT/CIO

A nonprofit statewide division of the university and community college system of Nevada, DRI pursues a full-time program of basic and applied environmental research on a local, national, and international scale. DRI employees nearly 400 full and part-time staff scientists, technicians, and support personnel.
Founded in: 1959

17971 Environmental Information Association
6935 Wisconsin Avenue
Suite 306
Chevy Chase, MD 20815-6112

301-961-4999
888-343-4342; *Fax:* 301-961-3094
info@eia-usa.org; www.eia-usa.org

Brent Kynoch, Managing Director
Kim Goodman, Membership and marketing Manager
Kelly Rut, Development Manager
Nehmesah Israel, Admin Assistant
Chris Gates, Treasurer

Providing the environmental industry with the information needed to remain knowledgeable, responsible, and competitive in the environmental health and safety industry.

17972 Excavation Engineering Associates
1352 SW 175th Street
Seattle, WA 98166

206-248-7388; *Fax:* 206-244-7994;
www.crimsonengineering.com
Social Media: Facebook, Twitter, LinkedIn, Google+

Estelle Friant, Secretary
James E.Friant, President

Underground excavation.

17973 Federal Mine Safety and Health Review Commission
1331 Pennsylvania Avenue, NW, Suite 520N
Suite 520N
Washington, DC 20004-1710

202-434-9900; *Fax:* 202-434-9906
fmshrc@fmshrc.gov; www.fmshrc.gov

Richard Baker, Executive Director

Independent adjudicative agency that provides administrative trial and apellate review of legal disputes arising under the Federal Mine Safety and Health Amendments Act of 1977 (mine act).

17974 Geological Society of America
PO Box 9140
Boulder, CO 80301-9140

303-357-1000
800-472-1988; *Fax:* 303-357-1070
gsa@geosociety.org; www.geosociety.org
Social Media: Facebook, Twitter, LinkedIn, YouTube

Jonathan G. Price, President
Claudia I. Mora, Vice President
Bruce R. Clark, Treasurer
Vicki McConnell, Executive Director/ Secretary
Nancy L. Wright, Technical Program Manager

Provides access to elements that are essential to the professional growth of earth scientists at all levels of expertise and from all sectors, academic, government, business, and industry. Membership unites thousands of earth scientists from every corner of the globe in a common purpose to study the mysteries of our planet and share scientific findings.
16000 Members
Founded in: 1888

17975 Gold Prospectors Association of America
43445 Business Park Drive
Suite #113
Temecula, CA 92590

951-699-4749
800-551-9707; *Fax:* 951-699-4062
info@goldprospectors.org;
www.goldprospectors.org
Social Media: Facebook, Twitter, LinkedIn, YouTube

Thomas Massie, CEO

GPAA is the largest recreational gold prospecting club. Owner of The Outdoor Channel, a cable TV channel featuring real outdoors for real people.
35M Members
Founded in: 1968

17976 Idaho Mining Association
802 W Bannock St
Suite 301
Boise, ID 83702-5840

208-342-0031; *Fax:* 208-345-4210
ima@mineidaho.com; www.mineidaho.com/
Social Media: Twitter

Randy Vranes, President
Corey Millard, 1st Vice President
Dennis Facer, 2nd Vice President
Jack Lyman, Executive Vice President

Founded to further the interests of Idaho's mining industry and minerals production. Mission is to act as the unified voice for its members to ensure the long-term health and well being of Idaho's mining industry.
Founded in: 1903

17977 International Lead Association
2 Bravingtons Walk
London N1 9AF

44 (0)20 7833 8090; *Fax:* 44 (0)20 7833 1611
enq@ila-lead.org; www.ila-lead.org
Social Media: Twitter, LinkedIn

Nonprofit trade association representing the lead industries in the US and abroad. It collects and distributes information about the users of lead products in industry, vehicles, radioactive waste disposal and noise barriers. Its services are availble, generally free of charge, to anyone interested in the uses of lead and lead products.

17978 Lignite Energy Council
1016 E. Owens Avenue
PO Box 2277
Bismarck, ND 58502-2277

701-258-7117
800-932-7117; *Fax:* 701-258-2755
lec@lignite.com; www.lignite.com
Social Media: Facebook, Twitter, LinkedIn, YouTube

Jason Bohrer, President/CEO
Alan Hodnik, Chairman
Robert McLennan, Chairman-Elect
Mike Jones, Ph. D., VP, Research and Development
Steve Van Dyke, VP, Communications

Regional Trade Association - promotes policies and activities that maintain a viable lignite industry and enhance development of our regions' lignite resources.
355 Members
Founded in: 1974

17979 Mine Safety Institue of America
319 Paintersville Road
Hunker, PA 15139

724-925-5150
sikora.lisa@dol.gov;
www.miningorganizations.org/msia.htm

Frank Linkous, President
Ronnie Biggerstaff, 1st VP
Joseph Sbaffoni, 2nd VP
William Gerringer, 3rd VP
Gerald E. Davis, Secretary/Treasurer

The objectives of the Mine Safety Institute of America is to provide successful educational programs, safer and healthier working conditions, more productivity in the mining industry, and support of good legislature pertaining to mining.
Founded in: 1908

17980 Mine Safety and Health Administration
1100 Wilson Blvd
21st Floor
Arlington, VA 22209-3939

202-693-9400
800-746-1553; *Fax:* 202-693-9401;
www.msha.gov

David G Dye, Executive Director

Administers the Federal Mine Safety and Health Act of 1977 (Mine Act) and enforces compliance with mandatory safety and health standards as a means to eliminate fatal accidents; to reduce the frequency and severity of nonfatal accidents, to minimize health hazards and to promote mineral processing operations in the US, regardless of size, employees, commodity mined or method of extraction.

17981 Mineral Economics and Management Society
Colorado School Of Mines
Golden, CO 49931

303-273-3150; *Fax:* 906-487-2944;
www.outreach.mines.edu

Patricia Dillon, President

A society for mineral, energy, and natural resource professionals who apply economics, finance and policy analysis to the issues facing the minerals and materials industries. These issues include supply and demand of mineral commodities, international trade in mineral and energy raw materials, environmental issues, natural resource, mineral and energy conservation, and related government policies.
200 Members
Founded in: 1991

17982 Mineral Information Institute
12999 E. Adam Aircraft Circle
Englewood, CO 80112

303-948-4236; *Fax:* 303-948-4265;
www.mineralseducationcoalition.org/
Social Media: Facebook, Twitter, LinkedIn, YouTube

Jaqueline S. Dorr, Manager

Nonprofit organization dedicated to educating youth about the science of minerals and other natural resources and about their importance in our everyday lives.

17983 Minerals, Metals & Materials Society
184 Thorn Hill Road
Warrendale, PA 15086-7514

800-759-4867
800-759-4867; *Fax:* 724-776-3770
webmaster@tms.org; www.tms.org
Social Media: Facebook, LinkedIn

James Robinson, Executive Director
Adrianne Carolla, Deputy Executive Director
Peter DeLuca, Accountant

Dedicated to the development and dissemination of the scientific and engineering knowledge bases for materials-centered technologies.

17984 Mining Foundation of the Southwest
PO Box 42317
Tucson, AZ 85733

520-577-7519; *Fax:* 520-577-7073
admin@miningfoundationsw.org;
www.miningfoundationsw.org

Thomas Aldrich, President
Amanda W. Brick, Executive Manager

Advances the science of mining and related industries by educating members and the public. Annual American Mining Hall of Fame First Saturday in December. A newsletter is published.
92 Members
Founded in: 1982

17985 Mining and Metallurgical Society of America
PO Box 810
PO Box 810
Boulder, CO 80306-0810

303-444-6032; *Fax:* 415-897-1380
contactmmsa@mmsa.net; www.mmsa.net
Social Media: Facebook, Twitter, LinkedIn

Alan K Burton, Business Manager
Mark leVier, President
Robert Schafer, VP
Kenneth Brunk, Treasurer

Concerned with the conservation of the nation's mineral resources and the best interest of the mining and metallurgical industries.
350 Members
Founded in: 1908

17986 National Association of State Land Reclamationists
Coal Research Center/Southern Illinois University
47 School Street
Suite 301
Philippi, WV 26416

304-940-0271; *Fax:* 618-453-7346
aharrington@crc.siu.edu
naslr.org

Sam Faith, President
Janet Yates, Vice President
Derek Giebell, Secretary/Treasurer
Jennifer Keese, Chairman

The National Association of State and Land Reclamationists advocates the use of research, innovative technology and professional discourse to foster the restoration of lands and waters affected by mining related activities.
140 Members
Founded in: 1972

17987 National Lime Association
200 N Glebe Rd
Suite 800
Arlington, VA 22203-3728

703-243-5463; *Fax:* 703-243-5489;
www.lime.org

William C.Herz, Executive Director
Arline Seeger, General Counsel
Hunter Prillaman, Director Of Government Affairs
Robert Hirsch, Director of Environment
Lori D.Oney, Admin Director

Trade association for US and Canadian manufacturers of high calcium quicklime, dolomitic quicklime and hydrated lime, collectively referred to as lime. NLA represents the interests of its members in Washington, provides input on standards and specifications for lime, and funds and manages research on current and new uses for lime.
63 Members
Founded in: 1902

17988 National Mining Association
101 Constitution Ave Nw
Suite 500 East
Washington, DC 20001-2133

202-463-2600; *Fax:* 202-463-2666
webmaster@nma.org; www.nma.org
Social Media: YouTube

Harry M. Conger, Chairman
Kevin Cruntchfield, Vice Chairman
Rich Nolan, Senior VP
Hal Quinn, President & CEO
Bruce Watzman, SVP, Regulatory Affairs

The voice of U.S. mining in Washington.
325 Members
Founded in: 1995

17989 National Ocean Industries Association
1120 G St NW
Suite 900
Washington, DC 20005-3801

202-347-6900; *Fax:* 202-347-8650
jwilliams@noia.org; www.noia.org
Social Media: Facebook, Twitter, LinkedIn, YouTube

Randall Luthi, President
Franki Stuntz, Sr.VP
Anna Chapman, VP, Conferences & Special Events
Nicoltte Nye, VP, Comm. &Industry Affairs
Jeff Vorberger, VP, Policy & Government Affairs

National organization engaged in offshore construction, drilling and petroleum production, geophysical exploration, ship building and re-

pair, deep-sea mining and related activities in the development and use of marine resources.
300 Members
Founded in: 1972

17990 **National Ready Mixed Concrete Association**
900 Spring St
Silver Spring, MD 20910-4015
240-485-1139; *Fax:* 301-585-4219
info@nrmca.org; www.nrmca.org
Social Media: Facebook, Twitter, LinkedIn, YouTube
Robert Garbini, President
Deana Angelastro, Executive Administrator
Allen Hamblen, Chairman
Ted Chandler, Vice Chairman
Scott Parson, Secretary/Treasurer
The mission of the National Ready Mixed Concrete Association is to provide exceptional value for our members by responsibly representing and serving the entire ready mixed concrete industry through leadership, promotion, education, and partnering to ensure ready mixed concrete is the building material of choice.
1200 Members
Founded in: 1930

17991 **National Stone, Sand & Gravel Association**
1605 King St
Alexandria, VA 22314-2726
703-525-8788
800-342-1415; *Fax:* 703-525-7782
jwilson@nssga.org; www.nssga.org
Social Media: Facebook, Twitter, LinkedIn, YouTube
Jennifer Joy Wilson, President & CEO
Gus Edwards, Executive Vice President
Janice B. Springs, Executive Assistant
Charles S. Luck IV, Chairman
Hal F. Williford Jr., First Vice Chairman
Represents the stone, sand and gravel — or aggregate — industries. Our members account for 90 percent of the crushed stone and 70 percent of the sand and gravel produced annually in the US.
25 Members
Founded in: 1916

17992 **Nevada Mining Association**
201 W. Liberty Street
Suite 300
Reno, NV 89501
775-829-2121; *Fax:* 775-852-2631;
www.nevadamining.org
Social Media: Facebook, Twitter, YouTube
Tim Crowley, President
Dylan Shaver, Public Affairs
Lauren Arends, Office Manager
Joseph Riney, Information System Administrator
Represents all aspects of the mining industry. Provides representation for the broad mining industry in public outreach activities such as public relations, media relations, and community relations.

17993 **North American Insulation Manufacturers Association**
11 Canal Center Plaza
Suite 103
Alexandria, VA 22314
703-684-0084; *Fax:* 703-684-0427;
www.naima.org
Mark Andrews, Chairman
Jeffrey Brisley, Vice Chairman
Cut Rich, President & CEO/ Treasurer
Angus Crane, Executive Vice President
An authoritative resource on energy-efficiency, sustainable performance, and the application and safety of fiber glass, rock wool, and slag wool insulation products. The voice of the insulation industry for architects and builders, design, process and maintenance engineers, contractors, code groups and standards organizations, government agencies, public interest, energy and environmental groups, and homeowners.

17994 **Perlite Institute**
2207 Forest Hills Drive
Suite A
Harrisburg, PA 17112
717-238-9723; *Fax:* 717-238-9985
info@perlite.org; www.perlite.org
Social Media: Facebook, Twitter
Matt Goecker, President
Matthew Malaghan, Vice President
Paul Dunlavey, Secretary/Treasurer
Denise Calabrese, Executive Director
An international association which establishes product standards and specifications, and which encourages the development of new product uses through research.
183 Members
Founded in: 1949

17995 **Rocky Mountain Association of Geologists**
910 16th St
Suite 1214
Denver, CO 80202-2997
303-573-8621; *Fax:* 303-476-2241
staff@rmag.org; www.rmag.org
Larry Rasmussen, President
Stephen Sturm, First VP
Catherine Campbell, Second VP
Barbara Kuzmic, Executive Director
2000 Members
Founded in: 1922

17996 **Silver Institute**
1400 I Street, NW
Suite 550
Washington, DC 20005
202-835-0185; *Fax:* 202-835-0155
info@silverinstitute.org;
www.silverinstitute.org
Robert Quartermain, President
Michael Dirienzo, Executive Director
International association of miners, refiners, fabricators and wholesalers of silver and silver products.

17997 **Silver Users Association**
3930 walnut Street
Suite 210
Fairfax, VA 22030
703-930-7790
800-245-6999; *Fax:* 703-359-7562
sas@silversmithing.com;
www.silverusersassociation.org
Bill Le Roy, President
Mike Huber, VP
John King, Secretary
Bill Hamelin, Treasurer
29 Members
Founded in: 1947

17998 **Silver Valley Mining Association**
604 Bank St.
Wallace, ID 83873
208-556-1621; www.silverminers.org
Dedicated to promoting the Silver Valley of northern Idaho and its mining industry. Informs the public of the history and merits of the region, serving various beneficiary needs of the mining industry, and serving those who work in the industry and the investing public.

17999 **Society for Mining, Metallurgy & Exploration**
12999 E. Adam Aircraft Circle
Englewood, CO 80112
303-948-4200
800-763-3132; *Fax:* 303-973-3845
sme@smenet.org; www.smenet.org
Social Media: Facebook, Twitter, LinkedIn, YouTube, Google+
John N. Murphy, President
Drew A. Meyer, President-Elect
Advances the worldwide mining and minerals community through information exchange and professional development.
13000 Members
Founded in: 1957

18000 **Society of Economic Geologists**
7811 Shaffer Pkwy
Littleton, CO 80127-3732
720-981-7874; *Fax:* 720-981-7874
seg@segweb.org; www.segweb.org
Social Media: Facebook, Twitter, LinkedIn, YouTube
Fran‡ois Robert, President
Robert P. Foster, President-Elect
A. James Macdonald, Vice President for Regional Affairs
Regina M. Baumgartner, VP, Student Affairs
Brian G Hoal, Executive Director
International organization of individual members with interests in the field of economic geology. Membership includes representatives from the industry, academia and government institutions. Annual meetings, publications, field conferences and short courses ensure active communication of economic geology related concepts with the membership and the economic geology profession at large.
3400 Members
Founded in: 1920

18001 **Society of Exploration Geophysicists**
8801 South Yale
Suite 500
Tulsa, OK 74137-3575
918-497-5500; *Fax:* 918-497-5557
web@seg.org; www.seg.org/index.shtml
Social Media: Facebook, Twitter, LinkedIn, YouTube, Google+
Dr. Bob A. Hardage, President
Dr. David James Monk, President-Elect
Dr. Wafik Bulind Beydoun, Vice-President
Nancy Jo House, Secretary/ Treasurer
Dr. Tamas Nemeth, Editor
The Society of Exploration Geophysicists/SEG is a not-for-profit organization that promotes the science of geophysics and the education of applied geophysicists. SEG fosters the expert and ethical practice of geophysics in the exploration and development of natural resources, in characterizing the near surface, and in mitigating earth hazards.
Founded in: 1930

18002 **Society of Mineral Analysts**
PO Box 50085
Sparks, NV 89435-0085
562-467-8980; www.sma-online.org
Social Media: Facebook, Twitter, LinkedIn
Patrick Brown, Director
The Society of Mineral Analysts is a non-profit organization, whose members are assayers, chemists, laboratory managers, geologists, suppliers and vendors both in and serving the mineral analysis industry.
250 Members
Founded in: 1986

18003 Solution Mining Research Institute
105 Apple Valley Circle
Clarks Summit, PA 18411

570-585-8092; *Fax:* 570-585-8091
info@solutionmining.org;
www.solutionmining.org

John O Voight, Executive Director
Carolyn L Diamond, Assistant Executive Director

Members are companies interested in the production of salt brine and solution mining of potash and soda ash, as well as production of slt covers, used for storage of oil, gas, chemicals, compressed air and waste.
100 Members
Founded in: 1958

18004 Sorptive Minerals Institute
1155 15th St NW
Suite 500
Washington, DC 20005-2725

202-289-2760; *Fax:* 202-530-0659
lcoogan@navista.net; www.sorptive.org

Lee Coogan, Executive Director

The Sorptive Minerals Institute represents the absorbent clay industry and is a not-for-profit industry trade association that would serve as the marketing, promotion and research arm of the absorbent clay indsutry with the goal of enhancing long-range growth and profitability.
Founded in: 1970

18005 Sulphur Institute
1020 19th Street NW, Suite 520
Washington, DC 20036

202-331-9660; *Fax:* 202-293-2940
sulphur@sulphurinstitute.org;
www.sulphurinstitute.org

Robert J Morris, President
Thomas W.Dunn, Director
Joshua C.Maak, Communications Manager
Donald S.Messik, VP,Communications

The Sulphur Institute (TSI) is an international, non-profit organization established in 1960. The Institute is the global advocate for sulphur, representing all stakeholders engaged in producing, consuming, trading, handling or adding value to sulphur. We seek to provide a common voice for all stakeholders to promote the uninterrupted, efficient and safe handling and transportation of all sulphur products while protecting the best interests of the environment
Founded in: 1960

18006 US Geological Survey
950 National Ctr
Reston, VA 20192-0001

703-648-4302; *Fax:* 703-648-6373
dc_va@usgs.gov; www.usgs.gov

Founded in: 1879

18007 United Mine Workers of America International Union
18354 Quantico Gateway Drive
Suite 200
Triangle, VA 22172

703-291-2400; *Fax:* 703-208-7227;
www.umwa.org

Cecil E Roberts, President
Daniel J Kane, Secretary/Treasurer

The United Mine Workers of America International Union is an organization with a diverse membership that includes coal miners, clean coal technicians, health care workers, truck drivers, manufacturing workers and public employees throughout the United States and Canada. The Union works to fight for safe workplaces, good wages and benefits, and fair representation.
120M Members
Founded in: 1890

18008 Utah Mining Association
136 S Main St
Suite 709
Salt Lake City, UT 84101-1683

801-364-1874; *Fax:* 801-364-2640
mining@utahmining.org; www.utahmining.org
Social Media: Facebook, Twitter

Mark Karll, Chairman
Greg Gergory, Vice Chairman
Mark Compton, President
Mike Brown, 1st Vice President
Chadd Baker, 2nd Vice President

Provides its members with full-time professional industry representation before the State Legislature; various government regulatory agencies on the federal, state and local levels; other associations, and business and industry groups. Helps to promote and protect the mining industry.
Founded in: 1915

18009 Vibrating Screen Manufacturers Association
6737 W Washington Street
Suite 2400
Milwaukee, WI 53214-5650

414-272-0943
866-236-0442; *Fax:* 414-272-1170
aem@aem.org; www.aem.org
Social Media: Twitter

Dennis Slater, President
Al Cervero, Senior VP

AEM is teh international trade and business development resource for companies that manufacture equipment, products andservices used worldwide in the construction, agricultural, minimg, forestry, and utility industries.
8 Members
Founded in: 1959

18010 Women in Mining National Organization
PO Box 260246
Lakewood, CO 80226-0246

303-298-1535
866-537-9697
wim@womeninmining.org;
www.womeninmining.org/aboutwim.htm

Betty Mahaffey, President
Christine Ballard, Vice President
Stephen Tibbals, Treasurer
Hannah McNally, Secretary

Women in Mining/WIM was founded in 1972 in Denver, Colorado, by several women whose intent was to facilitate education about the mining industry for themselves and for those not acquainted with the role the industry plays in their lives. In addition to providing valuable educations benefits, the WIM organization offers members an opportunity to become acquainted and work with others involved in the mining industry and thereby acquire new personal and professional contacts.
600 Members

18011 World Gold Council
510 Madison Ave
9th Floor
New York, NY 10022

212-317-3800; *Fax:* 212-688-0410;
www.gold.org
Social Media: Facebook, Twitter, Google+

Organization formed and funded by the world's leading gold mining companies with the aim of stimulating and maximizing the demand for, and holding of gold by consumers, investors, industry and the official sector.
Founded in: 1987

Newsletters

18012 AME BC News
Assoc for Mineral Exploration British Columbia
889 W Pender Street
Suite 800
Vancouver, BC V6C-3B2

604-689-5271; *Fax:* 604-681-2363
info@amebc.ca; www.amebc.ca

Gavin C Dirom, President/CEO

A member e-newsletter that captures essential mineral exploration and mining news, announces important upcoming events, gives an inside look at what is happening within AME BC, announces new and renewed members and more.
5400 Members
Frequency: Bi-Weekly
Founded in: 1912

18013 Alaska Geology Survey News
Alaska Division of Geological Survey
3354 College Rd
Fairbanks, AK 99709-3707

907-451-5000; *Fax:* 907-451-5050;
www.dggs.dnr.state.ak.us

Robert Swenson, Executive Director
Trudy Wassel, Business Manager
John Parrott, Manager

Alaska miners and earth scientists.
4 Pages
Frequency: Monthly
Printed in on glossy stock

18014 Ash at Work
American Coal Ash Association
15200 E Girard Ave
Suite 3050
Aurora, CO 80014-3955

720-870-7897; *Fax:* 720-870-7889
info@acaa-usa.org; www.acaa-usa.org

Thomas Adams, Executive Director

Association news. non-profit trade association.
160 Members
Frequency: 2x/Year
Founded in: 1968
Printed in 4 colors on glossy stock

18015 Bulletin
Northwest Mining Association
10 N Post St
Suite 220
Spokane, WA 99201-0722

509-624-1158; *Fax:* 509-623-1241;
www.nwma.org

Laura Skaer, Executive Director
Mike Heywood, Marketing Director

Published every six weeks. 12-16 page newsletter covering issues relevant to the hardrock mining industry.
Circulation: 1500
Founded in: 1895

18016 Coal Week International
McGraw Hill
PO Box 182604
Columbus, CO 43272

877-833-5524
800-752-8878; *Fax:* 614-759-3749
customer.service@mcgraw-hill.com;
www.mcgraw-hill.com

John Slater, Publisher

Offers information and news to and of the mining industry in North America.
Cost: $467.00
Frequency: Monthly
Founded in: 1884

18017 Coaldat Productivity Report
Pasha Publications
1600 Wilson Boulevard
Suite 600
Arlington, VA 22209-2510

703-528-1244
800-424-2908; *Fax:* 703-528-1253

Harry Baisden, Group Publisher
Michael Hopps, Editor
Kathy Thorne, Circulatin Manager

Shows quarterly and year-to-date total coal production in tons, productivity in tons per miner per day, average number of employees for each mine, mining methods used, controlling company, mine location, district number, union affiliation and whether the mine is surface or underground. Both a controlling company and a state/country format are available.
Cost: $545.00
60 Pages
Frequency: Quarterly

18018 Concentrates Newsletter
PO Box 42317
Tucson, AZ 85733

520-577-7519; *Fax:* 520-577-7073
admin@miningfoundationsw.org;
www.miningfoundationsw.org

Thomas Aldrich, President
Amanda W. Brick, Office Manager

Querterly newsletter providing members with news and updates regarding the Foundation
90 Pages
Frequency: Quarterly
Founded in: 1973

18019 Control
Putman Media Company
555 W Pierce Rd
Suite 301,Pierce Road
Itasca, IL 60143-2626

630-467-1300; *Fax:* 630-467-0197
jcappelletti@putman.net; www.putman.net

John Cappelletti, President
Walter Boies, Circulation Manager

Designed for instrumentation and control systems professionals.
Frequency: Fortnightly
Circulation: 35000
Founded in: 1945

18020 Legal Quarterly Digest of Mine Safety and Health Decisions
Legal Publication Services
888 Pittsford Mendon Center Road
Pittsford, NY 14534

585-582-3211; *Fax:* 585-582-2879
MineSafety@aol.com; www.minesafety.com

Ellen Smith, Owner/publisher
Melanie Aclander, Editor

Covers legal decisions on health and safety law in the mining industry.
Cost: $525.00
100 Pages
Frequency: Annual+
Founded in: 1991

18021 Machinery Outlook
Manfredi & Associates
20934 W Lakeview Pkwy
Mundelein, IL 60060-9502

847-949-9080; *Fax:* 847-949-9910
frank@manfredi.com;
www.machineryoutlook.com

Frank Manfredi, President

A newsletter about and for the construction and mining machinery industry.
Cost: $365.00
14 Pages
Frequency: Monthly
Founded in: 1984
Printed in one color on matte stock

18022 Mine Regulation Reporter
Pasha Publications
1600 Wilson Boulevard
Suite 600
Arlington, VA 22209-2509

703-528-1244
800-424-2908; *Fax:* 703-528-1253

Harry Baisden, Group Publisher
Michael Hopps, Editor
Kathy Thorne, Circulation Manager

The only biweekly newsletter and document service in the US for mine safety and environmental managers and attorneys. It covers mine safety, health and environmental regulations, legislation and court decisions that affect mine operations.
Cost: $785.00
Frequency: BiWeekly

18023 Mining and Metallurgical Society of America Newsletter
476 Wilson Avenue
Novato, CA 94947-4236

415-897-1380; *Fax:* 415-899-0262
contactmmsa@mmsa.net; www.mmsa.net

Alan K Burton, Executive Director

Society news and information for professionals in the mining industry.
6 Pages
Founded in: 1908

18024 The Outcrop
Rocky Mountain Association of Geologists
910 16th St
Suite 1214
Denver, CO 80202-2997

303-573-8621; *Fax:* 303-476-2241
staff@rmag.org; www.rmag.org
Social Media: Facebook, Twitter, LinkedIn

Larry Rasmussen, President
Barbara Kuzmic, Executive Director
Will Duggins, Managing Editor
Cheryl Fountain, Associate Editor

RMAG newsletter detailing member activities, organization events, and topics of interest.
2000 Members
Founded in: 1922

18025 Utah Mining Association Newsletter
Utah Mining Association
136 South Main Street
Suite 709
Salt Lake City, UT 84101-1683

801-364-1874; *Fax:* 801-364-2640
mining@utahmining.org; www.utahmining.org

Todd Bingham, President
Bryan Nielson, Chairman
Marilyn Tuttle, Office Manager

Provides updates on the mining industry.

18026 e-DIGEST & Washington Watch Newsletter
National Stone, Sand & Gravel Association
1605 King St
Alexandria, VA 22314-2726

703-525-8788
800-342-1415; *Fax:* 703-525-7782
jwilson@nssga.org; www.nssga.org

Jennifer Joy Wilson, President & CEO
Gus Edwards, Executive Vice President
Janice B. Springs, Executive Assistant

Member benefit of the NSSGA. Available online only.
25 Members
Frequency: Weekly
Founded in: 1916

Magazines & Journals

18027 ASH at Work
American Coal Ash Association
15200 E Girard Ave
Suite 3050
Aurora, CO 80014-3955

720-870-7897; *Fax:* 720-870-7889
info@acaa-usa.org; www.acaa-usa.org

Thomas H Adams, Executive Director

The only magazine covering all facets of the coal combustion products industry. Read by ACAA members and others interested in the use and management of coal combustion products.
126 Members
Frequency: Bi-Annually
Circulation: 10000
Founded in: 1968

18028 Alaska Miner
Alaska Miners Association
3305 Arctic Blvd
Suite 105
Anchorage, AK 99503-4575

907-563-9229; *Fax:* 907-563-9225
ama@alaskaminers.org; www.alaskaminers.org

Steven Borell, Executive Director

News and developments regarding Alaskan mining efforts.

18029 Alaska Miners Association Journal
Alaska Miners Association
3305 Arctic Boulevard
Suite 105
Anchorage, AK 99503-4575

907-563-9229; *Fax:* 907-563-9225
ama@alaskaminers.org; www.alaskaminers.org

Steven Borell, Executive Director

18030 CIM Magazine
Canadian Inst of Mining, Metallurgy & Petroleum
3400 de Maisonneuve Boulevard W
Suite 855
Montreal, QC H3Z-3B8

514-939-2710; *Fax:* 514-939-2714;
www.cim.org

Dawn Nelley, Publications

Provides important information on mine developments, new technologies, safety, HR, products and services, and business issues.
Frequency: 8x's a Year
Circulation: 11,289

18031 Coal
MacLean Hunter
29 N Wacker Drive
Floor 9
Chicago, IL 60606-3298

312-726-2802; *Fax:* 312-726-4103

Art Sanda, Editor
Elisabeth O'Grady, Executive Director

Articles cover maintenance and production of coal mines.
Cost: $62.50
Frequency: Monthly
Circulation: 22,000
Founded in: 1964

18032 Coal Age
Primedia
29 N Wacker Avenue
10th Floor
Chicago, IL 60606

312-726-2802; *Fax:* 312-726-2574;
www.coalage.com

Peter Johnson, Publisher
Stever P Fiscor, Editor-in-Chief
Ben Fromenthal, Production Manager

Geared primarily toward professionals in the coal mining and processing industries. Coal Age focuses on news, with in-depth features on coal mining operations and changing technologies.
Cost: $49.00
54 Pages
Frequency: Monthly
Circulation: 17900
ISSN: 1040-7820
Founded in: 1911
Printed in 4 colors on glossy stock

18033 Coal Journal
PO Box 3068
Pikeville, KY 41502-3068

606-432-0206; *Fax:* 606-432-2162

Terry L May, Publisher

Information concentrating on government regulations, emerging technologies and trade literature, and analyzes governmental actions and their impact on the coal industry.
Frequency: Quarterly
Circulation: 10000

18034 Coal People
Al Skinner Enterprises
PO Box 6247
Charleston, WV 25362-247

304-342-4129
800-235-5188; *Fax:* 304-343-3124
cpm@newwave.net; www.coalpeople.com

Al Skinner, Editor
Christina Karaum, Managing Editor
Beth Terranova, Sales Manager
Angela McNealy, Circulation Manager

Features special news and product sections for the coal industry. Home interest, historical pices, coal industry personalities.
Cost: $25.00
60 Pages
Frequency: 10 times ayear
Circulation: 11500
Founded in: 1976
Printed in 4 colors on glossy stock

18035 EARTH Magazine
American Geosciences Institute
4220 King St
Alexandria, VA 22302-1502

703-379-2480; *Fax:* 703-379-7563
agi@agiweb.org; www.earthmagazine.org
Social Media: Facebook, Twitter

Patrick Leahy, Executive Director
Dr. Wayne D. Pennington, President
Dr. Sharon Mosher, President Elect
Michael D. Lawless, Treasurer
Dr. Berry H. Tew, Jr., Secretary

The science behind the headlines.
Frequency: Monthly
Founded in: 1948

18036 Engineering & Mining Journal
Primedia Publishing
330 N Wabash Avenue
Suite 2300
Chicago, IL 60611

312-595-1080; *Fax:* 312-595-0295
info@mining-media.com; www.e-mj.com

Peter Johnson, Publisher
Steve Fiscor, Editor

Serves the field of mining including exploration, development, milling, smelting, refining of metals and nonmetallics
108 Pages
Frequency: Monthly
Circulation: 20589
ISSN: 0095-8948
Founded in: 1866
Printed in 4 colors on glossy stock

18037 Environmental & Engineering Geoscience
Geological Society of America
PO Box 9140
Boulder, CO 80301-9140

303-357-1019
800-472-1988; *Fax:* 303-357-1070
gsa@geosociety.org; www.geosociety.org
Social Media: Facebook, Twitter, LinkedIn, YouTube

John W. Geissman, President
George H. Davis, Vice President
Jonathan G. Price, Treasurer
John W. Hess, Executive Director/ Secretary

Contains new theory, applications, and case histories illustrating the dynamics of the fast-growing environmental and applied disciplines.
16000 Members
Frequency: Quarterly
Founded in: 1888

18038 GSA Today
Geological Society of America
PO Box 9140
Boulder, CO 80301-9140

303-357-1019
800-472-1988; *Fax:* 303-357-1070
gsa@geosociety.org; www.geosociety.org
Social Media: Facebook, Twitter, LinkedIn, YouTube

John W. Geissman, President
George H. Davis, Vice President
Jonathan G. Price, Treasurer
John W. Hess, Executive Director/ Secretary

Lead science articles are refereed and should present the results of exciting new research or summarize and synthesize important problems or issues.
16000 Members
Frequency: Monthly
Founded in: 1888

18039 Geology
Geological Society of America
PO Box 9140
Boulder, CO 80301-9140

303-357-1019
800-472-1988; *Fax:* 303-357-1070
gsa@geosociety.org; www.geosociety.org
Social Media: Facebook, Twitter, LinkedIn, YouTube

John W. Geissman, President
George H. Davis, Vice President
Jonathan G. Price, Treasurer
John W. Hess, Executive Director/ Secretary

Articles cover all earth-science disciplines and include new investigations and provocative topics. Professional geologists and university-level students in the earth sciences use this widely read journal to keep up with scientific research trends.
16000 Members
Frequency: Monthly
Founded in: 1888

18040 Geophysics
Society of Exploration Geophysicists
8801 South Yale
Suite 500
Tulsa, OK 74137-3575

918-497-5500; *Fax:* 918-497-5557
web@seg.org; www.seg.org/index.shtml
Social Media: Facebook, Twitter, LinkedIn

Dr. Bob A. Hardage, President
Dr. David James Monk, President-Elect
Dr. Wafik Bulind Beydoun, Vice-President
Nancy Jo House, Secretary/ Treasurer
Dr. Tamas Nemeth, Editor

Encompasses all aspects of research, exploration, and education in applied geophysics.
Founded in: 1930

18041 Geosphere
Geological Society of America
PO Box 9140
Boulder, CO 80301-9140

303-357-1019
800-472-1988; *Fax:* 303-357-1070
gsa@geosociety.org; www.geosociety.org
Social Media: Facebook, Twitter, LinkedIn, YouTube

John W. Geissman, President
George H. Davis, Vice President
Jonathan G. Price, Treasurer
John W. Hess, Executive Director/ Secretary

Electronic journal, peer-reviewed covering all geoscience disciplines in a medium that accommodates animations, sound, and movie files.
16000 Members
Frequency: Bimonthly
Founded in: 1888

18042 Geotimes
American Geological Institute
4220 King St
Alexandria, VA 22302-1502

703-379-2480; *Fax:* 703-379-7563;
www.agiweb.org/
Social Media: Facebook, Twitter

Dr. Wayne D. Pennington, President
Dr. Sharon Mosher, President Elect
Michael D. Lawless, Treasurer
Dr. Berry H. Tew, Jr., Secretary

Nonprofit federation of 40 geoscientific and professional associations that represents more than 100,000 geologists, geophysicsts, and other earth scientists. AGI provides information services to geoscientists, serves as a voice of shared interests in our profession, plays a major role in strengthening geoscience education, and strives to increase public awareness of the vital role the geosciences play in society's use of resources and interaction with the environment.
Cost: $42.95
250M Members
40 Pages
Frequency: Monthly
Circulation: 100000
Founded in: 1948

18043 Hydrogeology Journal
Geological Society of America
PO Box 9140
Boulder, CO 80301-9140

303-357-1019
800-472-1988; *Fax:* 303-357-1070
gsa@geosociety.org; www.geosociety.org
Social Media: Facebook, Twitter, LinkedIn, YouTube

John W. Geissman, President
George H. Davis, Vice President
Jonathan G. Price, Treasurer
John W. Hess, Executive Director/ Secretary

Features peer-reviewed papers on theoretical and applied hydrogeology. Describes worldwide progress in the science integrating subsurface

hydrology and geology with supporting disciplines.
16000 Members
Frequency: Bi-Monthly
Founded in: 1888

18044 JOM: The Member Journal of TMS
Minerals, Metals & Minerals Society
184 Thorn Hill Road
Warrendale, PA 15086-7514

724-776-9000
800-759-4867
724-776-9000; *Fax:* 724-776-3770
tmsgeneral@tms.org; www.tms.org
Social Media: Facebook, LinkedIn

Garry W. Warren, President
Wolfgang A. Schneider, Vice President
Warren Hunt, Jr., Secretary/ Executive Director
Adrian C. Deneys, Director/ Chair

A technical journal devoted to exploring the many aspects of materials science and engineering. Reports scholarly work that explores the state-of-the-art processing, fabrication, design, and application of metals, ceramics, plastics, composites, and other materials.
Cost: $131.00
Frequency: Monthly
Circulation: 10000
Founded in: 1948

18045 Journal of Electronic Materials
Minerals, Metals & Materials Society
184 Thorn Hill Road
Warrendale, PA 15086-7514

800-759-4867; *Fax:* 724-776-3770
webmaster@tms.org; www.tms.org
Social Media: Facebook, LinkedIn

Reports on the science and technology of electronic materials while examining new applications for semiconductors, magnetic alloys, insulators, and optical and display materials.
Frequency: Monthly

18046 Lithosphere
Geological Society of America
PO Box 9140
Boulder, CO 80301-9140

303-357-1019
800-472-1988; *Fax:* 303-357-1070
gsa@geosociety.org; www.geosociety.org
Social Media: Facebook, Twitter, LinkedIn, YouTube

John W. Geissman, President
George H. Davis, Vice President
Jonathan G. Price, Treasurer
John W. Hess, Executive Director/ Secretary

Peer-reviewed journal focusing on processes that affect the crust, upper mantle, landscapes, and/or sedimentary systems at all spatial and temporal scales.
16000 Members
Frequency: Bimonthly
Founded in: 1888

18047 Metallurgical and Materials Transactions
Minerals, Metals & Materials Society
184 Thorn Hill Road
Warrendale, PA 15086-7514

800-759-4867; *Fax:* 724-776-3770
webmaster@tms.org; www.tms.org
Social Media: Facebook, LinkedIn

Highly respected, peer-reviewed journals for metallurgy and materials science.
Frequency: Monthly

18048 Mine Safety and Health News
Legal Publication Services
888 Pittsford Mendon Center Road
Pittsford, NY 14534

585-582-3211; *Fax:* 585-582-2879
MineSafety@aol.com; www.minesafety.com

Ellen Smith, Owner
Melanie Aclander, Editor
Cost: $525.00
Founded in: 1991

18049 Mine and Quarry Trader
Primedia
7355 N Woodland Drive
PO Box 603
Indianapolis, IN 46206

317-991-1350
800-827-7468; *Fax:* 317-299-1356;
www.mineandquarry.com

John Owen, Production Manager
Colleen Leath, Circulation Director
Kyle Agert, Publisher
Laura Larahaag, Marketing
Ellen Rolett, Manager

Equipment and services geared to the mining, aggregate and heavy construction industries.
Cost: $21.00
76 Pages
Frequency: Monthly
Circulation: 34406
Founded in: 1976
Printed in 4 colors on matte stock

18050 Miners News
Miners News
9792 W Glen Ellyn Street
PO Box 4965
Boise, ID 83711

800-624-7212; *Fax:* 208-658-4901
minersnews@msn.com; www.minersnews.com

Gary White, Publisher
Shirley White, Public Relations

Information on mining history and provides insight into new technology and products used in mining.
Cost: $25.00
Circulation: 6512
ISSN: 0890-6157
Founded in: 1985

18051 Mines Magazine
Colorado School of Mines Alumni Association
1600 Arapahoe Street
PO Box 1410
Golden, CO 80402

303-733-3143; *Fax:* 303-273-3583;
www.minesmagazine.com
Social Media: Facebook, Twitter, LinkedIn

Nick Sutcliffe, Editor
Anita Pariseau, CEO/President
Amie Chitwood, Manager
Heidi Boersma, Administrative Assistant

Mines magazine is a critical communication serving the Colorado School of Mines community. Its mission is to keep readers informed about the school, to further the goals of the school and the alumni association, and to foster connectedness.
Cost: $35.00
Frequency: Quarterly
Circulation: 20000
Founded in: 1910
Printed in 4 colors on glossy stock

18052 Mining Record
Mining Record Company
PO Box 1630
Castle Rock, CO 80104-6130

303-888-8871
800-441-4708; *Fax:* 303-663-7823
customerservice@miningrecord.com;
www.miningrecord.com

Don E Howell, Editor
Dale Howell, Marketing

Has been in continuous publication for 115 years and is recognized as the industry's leading newspaper. Focuses on timely and credible news reporting on exploration, discovery, development, production, joint ventures, acquisitions, operating results, legislation, government reports and metals prices. Its readership is concentrated in the mining industry proper; mining companies and all individuals engaged in large or small mine production.
Cost: $45.00
16 Pages
Frequency: Monthly
Circulation: 5100
ISSN: 0026-5241
Founded in: 1889
Printed in on newsprint stock

18053 New Equipment Digest
Penton Media
1300 E 9th St
Suite 316
Cleveland, OH 44114-1503

216-696-7000; *Fax:* 216-696-6662
information@penton.com;
www.pentonmsc.com

Jane Cooper, Marketing
Jennifer Daugherty, Communications Manager
John DiPaola, Group Publisher
Robert F King, Editor
Bobbie Macy, Circulation Manager

Serves the general industrial field which includes manufacturing, processing, engineering services, construction, transportation, mining, public utilities, wholesale distributors, educational services, libraries, and governmental establishments.
Cost: $65.00
Frequency: Monthly
Circulation: 206000
Founded in: 1892

18054 North American Mining
Mining Media
1005 Terminal Way
#140
Reno, NV 89502-2179

775-323-1553; *Fax:* 775-323-1553

Dorothy Y Kosich, Editor

Information broken into departments which include environment, finance, government, management, new product news, profiles, safety issues and development technology updates.
Frequency: Bi-Monthly
Circulation: 7000

18055 Northern Miner
Southam Magazine Group
950 Wadsworth Boulevard
Suite 308
Lakewood, CO 80215

303-607-0853
800-459-8314; *Fax:* 303-607-0862
northernminer2@northernminer.com;
www.northernminer.com

John Cumming, Editor
Brian Warriner, Sales Representatives

News and information for the mining industry.
Cost: $89.00
Frequency: Weekly
Founded in: 1915
Printed in 4 colors on glossy stock

18056 Pay Dirt
Copper Queen Publishing Company

Copper Queen Plaza
PO Drawer 48
Bisbee, AZ 85603-48

520-432-2244; *Fax:* 520-432-2247

Gary Dillard, Editor
Caryl Larkins, CEO
Frank Barco, Publisher
Gruce Rubin, Marketing

Keeps readers informed on current mining developments, changes in policies and decisions by state and federal agencies affecting mining. Accepts advertising.
Cost: $30.00
34 Pages
Frequency: Monthly
Circulation: 2200
ISSN: 0886-0920
Founded in: 1938

18057 Pit & Quarry Magazine
The Aggregates Authority
1360 E. Ninth St.
Suite 1070
Cleveland, OH 44114

216-706-3700
800-669-1668; *Fax:* 216-706-3711
scarr@questex.com; www.pitandquarry.com

Sean Carr, Publisher

Exclusively for nonmetallic minerals producers.

18058 Professional Geologist
American Institute of Professional Geologists
1200 N Washington St
Suite 285
Thornton, CO 80241-3134

303-412-6205; *Fax:* 303-253-9220
aipg@aipg.org; www.aipg.org

William J Siok, Executive Director
Wendy Davidson, Assistant Director
Frequency: Bi-Monthly

18059 Reclamation Matters
American Society of Mining and Reclamation
1800 South Oak Street
Suite 100
Champaign, IL 61820-6974

859-335-6529
asmr@insightbb.com; www.asmr.us
Social Media: Facebook

Robert Darmody, Executive Secretary
Pete Stahl, President
Kimery Vories, President Elect
Richard Barnhisel, Editor-in-Chief

Dissemination of technical information relating to the reclamation of lands disturbed by mineral extraction. Members yearly issue is paid out of proceeding.
Cost: $10.00
Frequency: Twice A Year
Founded in: 1973

18060 Silver Valley Mining Journal
414 Sixth Street
Wallace, ID 83873

208-556-1621
silverminers@usamedia.tv;
www.silverminers.com

Provides information about silver mining.

18061 Skillings Mining Review
WestmorelandFlint
11 E Superior St
Suite 514
Duluth, MN 55802-3015

218-727-1552; *Fax:* 218-733-0463;
www.westmorelandflint.com

John Hyduke, President
Ivan Hohnstadt, General Manager
Holly Olson, Circulation Manager

Skillings Mining Review covers breaking news about mining companies and their suppliers, dynamics of the global marketplace, technical aspects of mining and processing, people in the industry and their contributions to it. Also production and shipping reports, and the latest news from coal and power industries.
Cost: $69.00
28 Pages
Frequency: Monthly
Circulation: 1500
ISSN: 0037-6329
Founded in: 1912
Printed in 4 colors on glossy stock

18062 The Leading Edge
Society of Exploration Geophysicists
8801 South Yale
Suite 500
Tulsa, OK 74137-3575

918-497-5500; *Fax:* 918-497-5557
web@seg.org; www.seg.org/index.shtml
Social Media: Facebook, Twitter, LinkedIn

Dr. Bob A. Hardage, President
Dr. David James Monk, President-Elect
Dr. Wafik Bulind Beydoun, Vice-President
Nancy Jo House, Secretary/ Treasurer
Dr. Tamas Nemeth, Editor

Gateway publication introducing new geophysical theory, instrumentation, and established practices to scientists in a wide range of geoscience disciplines. Most material is presented in a semitechnical manner that minimizes mathematical theory and emphasizes practical applications.
Frequency: Monthly
Founded in: 1930

18063 The Mountain Geologist
Rocky Mountain Association of Geologists
910 16th St
Suite 1214
Denver, CO 80202-2997

303-573-8621; *Fax:* 303-476-2241
staff@rmag.org; www.rmag.org

Larry Rasmussen, President
Barbara Kuzmic, Executive Director

RMAG's quarterly publication offering peer-reviewed articles from experts spanning a range of geologist sub-disciplines.
2000 Members
Frequency: Quarterly
Founded in: 1922

18064 United Mine Workers Journal
United Mine Workers of America
900 15th Street NW
Washington, DC 20005-2585

202-842-7200; *Fax:* 202-842-7227
sales@wmwa.net; www.wmwa.net

Doug Gibson, Editor

Information sent to members of the United Mine Workers of America, retirees, other labor unions, politicians and opinion makers in the United States and abroad. Reports on issues inside and outside the UMWA that are of interest to its members. Also contains features on politics, the arts, media and the culture of US workers.
Frequency: Monthly
Circulation: 200000

18065 Valley Gazette
Hometown Publications
1000 Bridgeport Ave
Suite 3-2
Shelton, CT 06484-4676

203-926-2080; *Fax:* 203-926-2091;
www.zwire.com

Gina Burkhart, CEO
Susane Hunter, Editor
Sharon Sakal, Circulation Manager
John Schneider, Marketing Manager
Frequency: Weekly
Circulation: 12322

18066 World Dredging, Mining & Construction
Placer Corporation
PO Box 17479
Irvine, CA 92623-7479

949-474-1120; *Fax:* 949-863-9261
info@worlddredging.com;
www.worlddredging.com

MJ Richardson, Publisher
Steve Richardson, Editor
Robert Lindaur, Circulation Manager

International and national news for the dredging.
Cost: $40.00
100 Pages
Frequency: Monthly
Circulation: 3400
ISSN: 1045-0343
Founded in: 1965
Printed in 4 colors on glossy stock

18067 World Mining Equipment
13544 Eads Road
Prairieville, LA 70769

225-673-9400; *Fax:* 225-677-8277
info@mining-media.com;
www.mining-media.com

Steve Fiscor, Editor in chief
Richard Johnson, Managing Editor
Russ Carter, Managing Editor
Victor Matteucci, National Sales Manager
Cost: $29.95
Frequency: Monthly
Circulation: 10,523
Founded in: 1866

Trade Shows

18068 ACAA Annual Meeting
American Coal Ash Association
38800 Country Club Drive
Farmington Hills, MI 48331-3439
720-870-7897; *Fax:* 720-870-7889
info@acaa-usa.org; www.acaa-usa.org

Thomas Adams, Executive Director
150 Attendees

18069 ASMA Annual Meeting
American Society of Mining and Reclamation
1800 South Oak Street
Suite 100
Champaign, IL 61820

217-333-9489; *Fax:* 859-335-6529
asmr@insightbb.com; www.asmr.us
Social Media: Facebook

Robert Darmody, Executive Secretary
Pete Stahl, President
Kimery Vories, President Elect

Approximately 30 exhibitors.
300 Attendees
Frequency: Annual

18070 Alaska Miners Association Convention
Alaska Miners Association

3305 Arctic Boulevard
Suite 105
Anchorage, AK 99503-4575

907-563-9229; *Fax:* 907-563-9225
ama@alaskaminers.org; www.alaskaminers.org

Steven Borell, Executive Director

Forty booths supporting businesses of the mining industry and state and federal agencies involved with regulating the industry.
500 Attendees
Frequency: Annual/March

18071 American Federation Mineralogical Society Rocky Mountain
816 Whipporwhill Sourt
Bartlesville, OK 74006

918-827-6405

T Alf, President

One hundred tables of gems, minerals and fossils for wholesale and retail dealers.
4M Attendees
Frequency: September

18072 American Gem & Mineral Suppliers Association
PO Box 741
Patton, CA 92369-0741

760-241-3191

Renata Williams, Executive Chairman

Ten booths.
100 Attendees
Frequency: February

18073 Arminera
Marketing International
200 N Glebe Road
Suite 900
Arlington, VA 22203

703-527-8000; *Fax:* 703-527-8006

Seminar, banquet and 400 exhibits of supplies, equipment and services for the mining industry.
8500 Attendees
Frequency: Biennial

18074 Ash at Work Transportation Research Board
American Coal Ash Association
15200 E Girard Ave
Suite 3050
Aurora, CO 80014-3955

720-870-7897; *Fax:* 720-870-7889
info@acaa-usa.org; www.acaa-usa.org

Thomas Adams, Executive Director

Non-profit trade association.
160 Members
Frequency: 2x/Year
Founded in: 1968
Printed in 4 colors on glossy stock

18075 EIA National Conference & Exposition
Environmental Information Association
6935 Wisconsin Avenue
Suite 306
Chevy Chase, MD 20815-6112

301-961-4999
888-343-4342; *Fax:* 301-961-3094
info@eia-usa.org; www.eia-usa.org

Dana Hudson, President
Mike Schrum, President Elect
Kevin Cannan, Vice President
Joy Finch, Secretary
Chris Gates, Treasurer

Providing the environmental industry with the information needed to remain knowledgeable, responsible, and competitive in the environmental health and safety industry.
Frequency: Annual/March

18076 MIACON Construction, Mining & Waste Management Show
Finocchiaro Enterprises
2921 Coral Way
Miami, FL 33145-3053

305-441-2865; *Fax:* 305-529-9217;
www.miacon.com

Michael Finocchiaro, President
Jose Garcia, VP
Justine Finocchiaro, Chief Operations

Annual show of 650 manufacturers, suppliers, distributors and exporters of equipment, machinery, supplies and services for the construction, mining and waste managment industries. There will be 600 booths.
10M Attendees
Frequency: December
Founded in: 1994

18077 MINExpo International
National Mining Association
101 Constitution Avenue NW
Suite 500 East
Washington, DC 20001-2133

202-463-2600; *Fax:* 202-463-2666;
www.minexpo.com

Harold P. Quinn, Jr., President & CEO

MINExpo is the mining industry's premier showcase for companies specializing in every facet of mining: open pit, underground, processing and preparation, mine site development, exploration and surveying, smelting and refining, and reclamation.
30000 Attendees
Frequency: Annual/September

18078 Mineral Exploration Roundup
Assoc for Mineral Exploration British Columbia
889 W Pender Street
Suite 800
Vancouver, BC V6C 3B2

604-689-5271; *Fax:* 604-681-2363
info@amebc.ca; www.amebc.ca
Social Media: Facebook, Twitter

Simone Hill, Acting Dir., Member Relations
Morgen Andoff, Acting Manager, Special Events
Roxanne Finnie, Manager, Member Relations

AME BC is the predominant voice of mineral exploration and development in British Columbia. AME BC represents members including geoscientists, prospectors, engineers, students, exploration and mining companies and suppliers who are engaged in mineral exploration and develoment in BC and throughout the world. AME BC annually hosts international guests from around the world during the annual Mineral Exploration Roundup conference that takes place every January.
5000 Members
Frequency: Annual/January
Founded in: 1912

18079 National Western Mining Conference & Exhibition
Colorado Mining Association
216 16th Street
Suite 1250
Denver, CO 80202-5161

303-575-9199; *Fax:* 303-575-9194
colomine@coloradomining.org;
www.coloradomining.org

Stuart Sanderson, President

Annual show of 90 exhibitors of equipment and support services for the mining industry.
1000 Attendees

18080 Northwest Mining Association Annual Meeting and Exposition
Northwest Mining Association
10 N Post Street
Suite 220
Spokane, WA 99201

509-624-1158; *Fax:* 509-623-1241;
www.nwma.com

Pat Nelsen, Operations Director

Annual mining convention in the US. Containing 335 booths, 280 exhibits and more than 20 technical sessions. The second largest annual mining convention in the USA. Founded in 1895.
2.5M Attendees
Frequency: December

18081 Randol Gold Forum
Randol International Limited
18301 W Colfax Avenue
#T1B
Golden, CO 80401-4834

303-526-7618; *Fax:* 303-271-0334
http://www.randol.com

Hans Von Michaelis, President
Patti Hamilton, Sales Coordinator

Mining companies exposition.
350 Attendees
Frequency: September

18082 Rapid Excavation Tunneling Conference Expo
PO Box 625002
Littleton, CO 80162-5002

303-973-9550

DD Daley, Meeting Manager

75 booths.
1M Attendees
Frequency: June

18083 SME Annual Meeting
Society of Mining, Metallurgy, and Exploration
12999 E. Adam Aircraft Circle
Englewood, CO 80112

303-948-4200
800-763-3132; *Fax:* 303-973-3845
sme@smenet.org; www.smenet.org
Social Media: Facebook, Twitter, LinkedIn

John N. Murphy, President
Drew A. Meyer, President-Elect
David L. Kanagy, Executive Director

Mine to Market: Now It's Global.
4M Attendees
Frequency: Annual/February

18084 UMA Annual Convention
Utah Mining Association
136 S Main St
Suite 709
Salt Lake City, UT 84101-1683

801-364-1874; *Fax:* 801-364-2640
mining@utahmining.org; www.utahmining.org

Todd Bingham, President
Terry Maio, Chairman
Marilyn Tuttle, Admininistrator
Frequency: August

Directories & Databases

18085 Coal Data
National Coal Association
100 Independence Ave, SW
Washington, DC 20585

202-586-8800

Offers important data on the 50 largest coal mines in the country.
Cost: $50.00

18086 Coal Mine Directory
Primedia

29 N Wacker Drive
10th Floor
Chicago, IL 60606-3203

312-726-2802
800-621-9907; *Fax:* 312-726-2574;
www.primediabusiness.com

Art Sanda, Editor
Patricia L Yos, Editor

Over 2,000 coal mines are profiled that are based in the United States and Canada.
Cost: $149.00
Frequency: Annual January
Circulation: 700

18087 DRI Coal Forecast
DRI/McGraw-Hill
24 Hartwell Ave
Lexington, MA 02421-3103

781-860-6060; *Fax:* 781-860-6002
support@construction.com;
www.construction.com

Walt Arvin, President

Offers valuable information on the mining of coal by supply region and producing state; total coal by demand region; cost and demand by the consumer sector.

18088 Engineering and Mining Journal: Buying Directory Issue
Primedia
29 N Wacker Drive
10th Floor
Chicago, IL 60606

312-726-2802
800-621-9907; *Fax:* 312-726-2574;
www.primediabusiness.com

Robert Wyllie, Editor

List of manufacturers and suppliers of mining equipment.
Cost: $35.00
Frequency: Annual November
Circulation: 23,000

18089 Expanded Shale, Clay and Slate Institute Roster of Members
Expanded Shale, Clay and Slate Institute
35 East Wacker Dr.
Suite 850
Chicago, IL 60601

801-272-7070; *Fax:* 312-644-8557
info@escsi.org; www.escsi.org

John Riese, President

About 15 producers by the rotary kiln method of lightweight aggregates of expanded shales, clays, and slates; international coverage.

18090 Geophysical Directory
Geophysical Directory
PO Box 130508
Houston, TX 77219-0508

713-291-1922
800-929-2462; *Fax:* 713-529-3646;
www.iagc.org

Claudia LaCalli, Editor
Stewart Schafer, Owner

About 4,500 companies that provide geophysical equipment, supplies or services and mining and petroleum companies that use geophysical techniques.
Cost: $135.00
400 Pages
Frequency: Annual March
Circulation: 2,000
Founded in: 1946
Mailing list available for rent: 2500 names
Printed in 4 colors on glossy stock

18091 Iron and Manganese Ore Databook
Metal Bulletin
220 5th Avenue
#Enus-19T
New York, NY 10001-7708

212-136-6202
800-MET-L 25; *Fax:* 212-213-6273

John Bailey, Editor

Iron and manganese ore producers and traders worldwide.
Cost: $179.00
Frequency: Quadrennial

18092 Keystone Coal Industry Manual
Primedia
29 N Wacker Drive
10th Floor
Chicago, IL 60611

312-726-2802
800-621-9907; *Fax:* 312-726-2574;
www.primediabusiness.com

Art Sanda, Editor
Patricia L Yos, Editor

Coal companies and mines, coke plants, coal preparation plants, domestic and export coal sales companies.
Cost: $260.00
Frequency: Annual January
Circulation: 1,400

18093 Landmen's Directory and Guidebook
American Association of Professional Landmen
4100 Fossil Creek Boulevard
Fort Worth, TX 76137-2723

817-847-7700; *Fax:* 817-847-7704
aapl@landman.org; www.landman.org

Le'ann Callihan, Editor/Publications Department

About 7,500 member specialists in assembling or disposing of land or rights required for oil, gas, coal andmineral exploration and exploitation in the US and Canada.
Cost: $100.00
Frequency: Annual November
Circulation: 7,500
ISSN: 0272-8370

18094 Minerals Yearbook
US Geological Survey
1730 E Parham Rd
Richmond, VA 23228-2202

804-261-2600; *Fax:* 804-261-2659
dc_va@usgs.gov; www.usgs.gov

Charles G Groats, Director

The Minerals Yearbook discusses the performance of the worldwide minerals and materials industry and provides background information to assist in interpreting that performance. Contents of the individual Minerals Yearbook volumes are, Volume I, Metals and Minerals, Volume II, Area Reports:Domestic, and Volume III, Area Reports: International.
200+ Pages
Frequency: Annual
Founded in: 1935

18095 Mining Directory
Metal Bulletin
220 5th Avenue
10th Floor
New York, NY 10001-7708

212-213-6202
800-MET-L 25; *Fax:* 212-213-6273
72610.3721@compuserve.com;
www.metbul.com/metbul/mbhome

Don Nelson, Editor

Offers valuable information on mines, mining equipment manufacturers, suppliers of equipment and services to the industry and industry consultants.
Cost: $158.00

18096 Mining Engineering: SME Membership Directory
Society of Mining, Metallurgy & Exploration
12999 E. Adam Aircraft Circle
Englewood, CO 80112

303-948-4200
800-763-3132; *Fax:* 303-973-3845
sme@smenet.org; www.smenet.org
Social Media: Facebook, Twitter, LinkedIn

John N. Murphy, President
Drew A. Meyer, President-Elect

A list of over 18,000 persons engaged in the location, exploration,treatment and marketing of all classes of minerals except petroleum.
Cost: $150.00
Frequency: Annual
Circulation: 20,000
ISSN: 0026-5187

18097 National Ocean Industries Association: Directory of Membership
National Ocean Industries Association
1120 G St NW
Suite 900
Washington, DC 20005-3801

202-347-6900; *Fax:* 202-347-8650;
www.noia.org

Tom Fry, President

Over 300 firms engaged in offshore construction, drilling and petroleum production, geophysical exploration, ship building and repair, deep-sea mining and related activities in the development and use of marine resources.
Frequency: Annual

18098 Pit & Quarry: Reference Manual & Buyers' Guide Issue
Advanstar Communications
2501 Colorado Avenue
Suite 280
Santa Monica, CA 90404-4503

310-857-7500; *Fax:* 310-857-7510
info@advanstar.com; www.advanstar.com

List of approximately 1,000 manufacturers and other suppliers of equipment, products and services to the nonmetallic mining and quarrying industry.
Cost: $25.00
Frequency: Annual
Circulation: 25,000

18099 Randol Buyer's Guide
Randol International Limited
18301 W Colfax Avenue
#T-2
Golden, CO 80401-4834

303-526-7618
800-726-3652; *Fax:* 303-278-9229
http://www.randol.com

Hans Von Michaelis, Editor

Approximately 10,000 companies that offer equipment and services used in the mining industry.
Cost: $35.00
Frequency: Annual
Circulation: 10,000

18100 Randol Mining Directory
Randol International Limited
18301 W Colfax Avenue
#T1B
Golden, CO 80401-4834

303-526-7618; *Fax:* 303-271-0334
http://www.randol.com

Hans Von Michaelis, President
Patti Hamilton, Sales Coordinator

The most comprehensive source of information on all mines in the USA. Used for systematic marketing to mines and exploration companies, statistical research and more, offering 10,000 industry contacts.

18101 **Rock Products: Buyer's Guide Issue**
Primedia
29 N Wacker Drive
10th Floor
Chicago, IL 60606
312-726-2802; *Fax:* 312-726-2574;
www.primediabusiness.com
Rick Marley, Editor
Scot Bieda, Publisher
David Pistello, Classified
List of about 1,500 providers worldwide of equipment and services for the nonmetallic mineral mining and processing industry.
Cost: $100.00
Frequency: Annual November
Circulation: 23,000

18102 **Silver Refiners of the World and their Identifying Ingot Marks**
Silver Institute
1112 16th St NW
Suite 240
Washington, DC 20036-4818
202-347-8200; www.silverinstitute.org
Over 80 refiners in over 18 countries are profiled.
Cost: $33.00
85 Pages

18103 **Western Mining Directory**
Howell Publishing Company
1758 Blake St
Denver, CO 80202-1226
303-296-8000
800-441-4748; *Fax:* 303-296-1123
Dave Howell, Owner
Directory of mining companies and mines nationwide.
Cost: $49.00
Circulation: 5,000
Founded in: 1968

18104 **World Aluminum: A Metal Bulletin Databook**
Metal Bulletin
220 5th Avenue
19th Floor
New York, NY 10001-7781
212-213-6202; *Fax:* 212-213-1870
help@metalbulletin.com;
www.metalbulletin.com
Richard ODonoghue, Manager
Ania Tumm, Marketing Manager
Julius Pike, Account Manager
Offers information on producers and traders of aluminum and aluminum alloys.
Cost: $247.00
540 Pages
ISSN: 0951-2233

18105 **World Mining Equipment**
Metal Bulletin
220 5th Avenue
New York, NY 10001
212-213-6202; *Fax:* 212-213-6619;
www.wme.com
Mike Woof, Editor
Manufacturers of mining equipment.
Cost: $246.00
66 Pages
Circulation: 13M
ISSN: 0746-729X
Printed in 4 colors on glossy stock

Industry Web Sites

18106 **http://gold.greyhouse.com**
G.O.L.D Grey House OnLine Databases
Grey House Publishing's online database platform, GOLD, offers Quick Search, Keyword Search and Expert Search for most business sectors including mining markets. The GOLD platform makes finding the information you need quick and easy - whether you're a novice searcher or an experienced database user. All of Grey House's directory products are available for subscription on the GOLD platform.

18107 **www.acaa-usa.org**
American Coal Ash Association
Promotes the beneficial use of coal cumbustion products.

18108 **www.aem.org**
Vibrating Screen Manufacturers Association

18109 **www.agiweb.org**
American Geological Institute
Provides information services to geoscientists, serves as a voice of shared interests in our profession.

18110 **www.aimeny.org**
American Institute of Mining & Petroleum Engineers
Organization was founded to further the arts and sciences employed to recover the earth's minerals and convert them to useful products.

18111 **www.aipg.org**
American Institute of Professional Geologists
Founded to certify the credentials of practicing geologists and to advocate on behalf of the profession.

18112 **www.alaskaminers.org**
Alaska Miners Association
Encourage and support responsible mineral production in Alaska.

18113 **www.amebc.ca**
Assn for Mineral Exploration British Columbia
Supports and promotes the mineral exploration community and related services by disseminating information to the public and governments, thereby assisting in the creation of wealth and jobs through sustainable mineral developement.

18114 **www.asmi.state.az.us**
State Mine Inspector

18115 **www.asmr.us**
American Society of Mining and Reclamation

18116 **www.azcu.org**
Arizona Mining Association
Provides information about mining, specifically copper mining and the impact it has on our lives.

18117 **www.blm.org**
Bureau of Land Management

18118 **www.calmining.org**
California Mining Association
Represents the breadth and depth of California's mining industry.

18119 **www.ces.ca.uky.edu/assmr**
American Society for Surface Mining & Reclamation
Dissemination of Technical information relating to the reclamation of lands disturbed by mineral extraction. Members yearly issue is paid out of proceedings. Membership dues - $50/regular; $10/students.

18120 **www.chamberofmines.bc.ca**
BC & Yukon Chamber of Mines
A list of mines in the Unites States.

18121 **www.cim.org**
Canadian Inst of Mining, Metallurgy & Petroleum
Strives to be the association of choice for professionals in the minerals industries.

18122 **www.coloradomining.org**
Colorado Mining Association
Serves as a spokesman for the mining industry in Colorado.

18123 **www.copper.org**
Copper Development Association

18124 **www.crc.siu.edu/nasir.htm**
National Association of State Land Reclamationists

18125 **www.crystalgrowth.org**
American Association for Crystal Growth
For those interested in organic crystal growth.

18126 **www.dri.edu**
Desert Research Institute
Information on basic and applied environmental research on a local, national, and international scale. For scientists, technicians, and support personnel.

18127 **www.fmshre.gov**
Federal Mine Safety and Health Review Commission

18128 **www.geosociety.org**
Geological Society of America

18129 **www.gold.org**
World Gold Council

18130 **www.goldprospecters.org**
Gold Prospectors Association

18131 **www.greyhouse.com**
Grey House Publishing
Authoritative reference directories for most business sectors, including mining markets. Users can search the online databases with varied search criteria allowing for custom searches by product category, geographic area, sales volume, keyword, subject and more. Full Grey House catalog and online ordering also available.

18132 **www.idahomining.org**
Idaho Mining Association
Founded to further the interests of Idaho's mining industry and minerals production.

18133 **www.kaolin.com**
China Clay Producers Association

18134 **www.leadinfo.com**
Lead Industries Association

18135 **www.lignite.com**
Lignite Energy Council
Promotes policies and directs activities that maintain a viable lignite industry and enhance the development of our regions lignite resources.

18136 **www.lime.org**
National Lime Association
Trade association for US and Canadian manufacturers of high calcium quicklime, dolomitic

quicklime and hydrated lime, collectively referred to as lime.

18137 **www.minecon.com/index.html**
Mineral Economics and Management Society

18138 **www.miningfoundationsw.org**
Mining Foundation of the Southwest

18139 **www.miningorganizations.org/msia.htm**
Mine Safety Institute of America

18140 **www.miningusa.com**
Mining Associations-National
A list of associations throughout the United States.

18141 **www.mmsa.net**
Mining and Metallurgical Society of America
A professional organization dedicated to increasing public awareness and understanding about mining and why mined materials are essential to modern society and human well being.

18142 **www.msha.gov**
Mine Safety and Health Administration

18143 **www.naima.org**
Mineral Insulation Manufacturers Association
Trade association of North American manufacturwers of fiberglass, rock wool, and slag wool insulation products.

18144 **www.nevadamining.org**
Nevada Mining Association
Represents all aspects of the mining industry in the state of Nevada.

18145 **www.nma.org**
National Mining Association
The only national trade organization represents the interests of mining before Congress, the Administration, federal agencies, the judiciary and the media.

18146 **www.noia.org**
National Ocean Industries Association
National organization engaged in offshore construction, drilling and petroleum production, geophysical exploration, ship building and repair.

18147 **www.nssga.org**
National Stone, Sand & Gravel Association

18148 **www.nwma.org**
Northwest Mining Association
Provides liaison between mining industry and government. Offers short course on current technology.

18149 **www.perlite.org**
Perlite Institute

18150 **www.pitandquarry.com**
The Aggregates Authority-Pit and Quarry
A magazine exclusively for nonmetallic minerals producers.

18151 **www.rheology.org**
Society of Rheology

18152 **www.rmag.org**
Rocky Mountain Association of Geologists

18153 **www.seg.org**
Society of Exploration Geophysicists

18154 **www.segweb.org**
Society of Economic Geologists
The society of economic geologists is an international organization of individual members with interest in the field of economic geology.

18155 **www.silverinstitute.org**
Silver Institute

18156 **www.silverminers.org**
Silver Valley Mining Association
dedicated to promoting the Silver Valley of northern Idaho and its mining industry.

18157 **www.smenet.org**
Society for Mining, Metallurgy & Exploration
Advances the worldwide mining and minerals community through information exchange and professional development.

18158 **www.solutionmining.org**
Solution Mining Research Institute

18159 **www.sorptive.org**
Sorptive Minerals Institute

18160 **www.sulphurinstitute.org**
Sulphur Institute

18161 **www.surface-mining.state.al.us**
Alabama Surface Mining Commission
Balance civilization's demands for natural resources and environmental conservation in the state of Alabama.

18162 **www.tmra.com**
Texas Mining & Reclamation Association

18163 **www.tms.org**
Minerals, Metals & Materials Society
Dedicated to the development and dissemination of the scientific and engineering knowledge bases for materials-centered technologies.

18164 **www.umwa.org**
United Mine Workers of America

18165 **www.usgs.gov**
US Geological Survey

18166 **www.utahmining.org**
Utah Mining Association
Helps to promote and protect the mining industry. Provides its members with full-time professional industry representation before the State Legislature; various government regularoty agencies on the federal, state and local levels, other associations, and business and industry groups.

18167 **www.womeninmining.org**
Women in Mining

Associations

18168 Academy of Motion Picture Arts and Sciences
8949 Wilshire Blvd
Beverly Hills, CA 90211-1972

310-247-3000; *Fax:* 310-271-3395;
www.oscars.org
Social Media: Facebook, Twitter, LinkedIn, Youtube

The Academy was founded to advance the arts and sciences of motion pictures; foster cooperation among creative leaders for cultural, educational and technological progress; recognize outstanding achievments; cooperate on technical research and improvement of methods and equipment; provide a common forum and meeting ground for various branches and crafts; represent the viewpoint of actual creators of the motion picture. Hosts annual Academy Awards.
6000 Members
Founded in: 1927

18169 Academy of Science Fiction Fantasy and Horror Films
334 W 54th St
Los Angeles, CA 90037-3806

323-752-5811; *Fax:* 323-752-5811
saturn.awards@ca.rr.com;
www.saturnawards.org
Social Media: Facebook, Twitter

Robert Holguin, President
Roger Fenton, VP
Michael Laster, Director

Culminated from the Count Dracula Society, the Academy hosts the annual Science Fiction Film Awards, called the Saturn Awards.
Founded in: 1972

18170 American Cinema Editors
100 Universal City Plaza
Verna Fields Building 2282 Room 190
Universal City, CA 91608

818-777-2900; *Fax:* 818-733-5023;
www.americancinemaeditors.org
Social Media: Facebook, Twitter

Alan Heim, President
Stephen Rivkin, VP
Lillian Bennson, Secretary
Ed Abroms, Treasurer
Jan Ambler, A.C.E

A non-profit corporation committed to the encouragement of mutually-beneficial dialogue with other members of the motion picture industry and to educating the general public. Holds the annual ACE Eddie Awards honoring the nominees for the Film Editing Award given by the Academy of Motion Pictures Arts and Sciences.
Founded in: 1950

18171 American Film Institute
2021 North Western Ave.
Los Angeles, CA 90027-1657
323-856-7600; *Fax:* 323-467-4578
information@afi.com; www.afi.com
Social Media: Facebook, Twitter, YouTube, Tumblr, Instagram

Bob Gazzale, President & CEO

The AFI is a nonprofit educational and cultural organization dedicated to preserving and honoring America's film heritage and educating its next generation of filmmakers.

18172 American Society of Cinematographers
1782 N Orange Drive
PO Box 2230
Hollywood, CA 90028

323-969-4333
800-448-0145; *Fax:* 323-882-6391
office@theasc.com; www.theasc.com
Social Media: Facebook, Twitter, YouTube ,Instagram, Vimeo

Daryn Okadaan, President
Michael Negrin, Secretary
Victor J Kemper, Treasurer
Rachael K. Bosley, Managing Director

The ASC is not a labor union or guild, but is an educational, cultural and professional organization. Membership is possible by invitation and is extended only to directors of photography with distinguished credits in the industry. Publishes 'American Cinematographer' magazine.
Founded in: 1919

18173 Art Directors Guild
11969 Ventura Blvd
Suite 200
Studio City, CA 91604-2619

818-762-9995; *Fax:* 818-762-9997
lydia@artdirectors.org; www.adg.org
Social Media: Facebook, Twitter, Instagram, Vimeo

Scott Roth, Executive Director
Lisa Frazza, Secretary
Michael Baugh, Treasurer
Sasha Aronson, Executive Assistant to Scott Roth
Alexandra Schaaf, Manager Membership Department

The creative talents that concieve and manage the background and settings for most films and television projects are members of the Art Directors Guild, Local 800. They and most other crafts of the entertainment industry are members of the International Alliance of Theatrical Stage Employees, Moving Picture Technicians, Artists and Allied Crafts of the United States, its Territories and Canada.
935 Members
Founded in: 1937

18174 Assistant Directors Training Program
15301 Ventura Blvd.
Bldg E #1075
Sherman Oaks, CA 91403

818-386-2545; *Fax:* 818-386-2876
mail@dgptp.org; www.trainingplan.org

Tom Joyner, Chair

Provides motion picture and television industry training as directed by the Alliance of Motion Picture and Television Producers and the Directors Guild of America.
Founded in: 1965

18175 Association of Cinema and Video Laboratories
Bev Wood C/O Deluxe Laboratories
1377 North Serrano Avenue
Hollywood, CA 90027

323-462-6171; *Fax:* 206-682-6649;
www.intersociety.org

Bev Wood, President
Chip Wilkenson, First VP
John Carlson, Second VP
Kevin Dillon, Treasurer
Bob Olson, Secretary

Provides opportunities for discussion and exchange of ideas in connection with administrative, technical and managerial problems in the motion picture and video industry. The Association is concerned with improvements in technical practices and procedures, public and industry relations, product specifications to vendors, the impact of current and impending governmental regulations, and any and all other areas of interest to the laboratory industry.
80 Members
Founded in: 1953

18176 Association of Talent Agents
9255 Sunset Blvd
Suite 930
Los Angeles, CA 90069-3317

310-274-0628; *Fax:* 310-274-5063;
www.agentassociation.com

Sandy Bresler, President
Sheldon Sroloff, VP
Jim Gosnell, Secretary/Treasurer
Karen Stuart, Executive Director
Shellie Jetton, Administrative Director

A non-profit trade association representing talent agencies in the industry. ATA is the voice of unified talent and literary agencies. ATA agencies represent the vast majority of working artists, including actors, directors, writers, and other artists in film, stage, television, radio, commercial, literary work, and other entertainment enterprises.
Founded in: 1937

18177 Casting Society of America
1149 N. Gower Street
Suite 110
Los Angeles, CA 90038

323-785-1011; *Fax:* 323-463-4753
info@castingsociety.com;
www.castingsociety.com

Richard Hicks, President
Matthew Lessall, Vice President
Sharon Bialy, Secretary
Mark Simon, Treasurer

CSA is the largest professional association of Casting Directors in the world. They work in all areas of entertainment in film, television and theatre. CSA continually seeks to expand their standing in the industry by providing information and opportunities that support is members.
500+ Members
Founded in: 1982

18178 Children in Film
11271 Ventura Blvd.
Studio City, CA 91604

818-432-7400
800-902-9001
contact@childreninfilm.com;
www.childreninfilm.com

Toni Casala, President
Trisha Noble, Director, Permit Services
Heather Broeker, Director, Marketing

To provide tools and information needed to successfully employ a child in the entertainment industry while also lending a healthy, positive view into the world of child actors.
Founded in: 2000

18179 Directors Guild of America
7920 W Sunset Blvd
Los Angeles, CA 90046-3347

310-289-2000
800-421-4173; *Fax:* 310-289-2029
LDavis@dga.org; www.dga.org

Jay Roth, President
Steven Soderbergh, National VP
Gilbert Cates, Secretary/Treasurer

The DGA represents Film and Television Directors, Unit Production Managers, First Assistant Directors, Second Assistant Directors, Technical Coordinators and Tape Associate Directors, Stage Managers and Production Assistants.

18180 Film Society of Lincoln Center
70 Lincoln Center Plz
New York, NY 10023-6595

212-875-5601; *Fax:* 212-875-5636
webmaster@filmlinc.com; www.filmlinc.com
Social Media: Facebook, Twitter, YouTube

Serge Joseph, Manager
Daniel H Stern, President
Wendy Keys, Secreatry
James Bouras, Treasurer
Lesli Klainberg, Executive Director

Celebrates American and international cinema, recognizes and supports new filmmakers, and enhances awareness, accessibility and understanding of the art among a broad and diverse film going audience. The Film Society is best known for two international festivals - the New York Film Festival and the New Directors/New Films festival.
Founded in: 1969

18181 Greek Americans in the Arts and Entertainment
3916 Sepulveda Blvd
Suite 107
Culver City, CA 90230

323-651-3507; *Fax:* 310-933-0250
info@americanhellenic.org;
www.americanhellenic.org
Social Media: Facebook, Twitter, LinkedIn

Dr. Menas Kafatos, Chairman
Eleftheria Polychronis, Vice President
Aris Anagnos, Vice President of Political Action
Dr. Tasos Chassiakos, VP, Culture & Education, Secretary
Alexander Mizan, Treasurer

Follows the legacy of Greek-Americans in the arts and entertainment field.

18182 Historians Film Committee
711 E. Boldt Way
Box 80
Appleton, WI 54911

920-832-6649; *Fax:* 202-544-8307
center@filmandhistory.org;
www.filmandhistory.org

Peter C Rollins, Editor-in-Chief

The Committee exists to further the use of film sources in teaching and research, to disseminate information about film and film use to historians and other social scientists, to work for an effective system of film preservation so that scholars may have ready access to film archives, and to organize periodic conferences dealing with film.
Founded in: 1970

18183 Hollywood Arts Council
PO Box 931056
Hollywood, CA 90093

323-462-2355; *Fax:* 323-465-9240;
www.hollywoodartscouncil.org
Social Media: Facebook, LinkedIn, YouTube

David Warren, Chairman
Matthew Leum, Vice Chair
Patti Negri, Secretary
Steven P. Tronson, Treasurer
Joni Labaqui, Director

Promotes, nurtures and supports the arts in Hollywood. Has served the community through advocacy, coalition building, free public arts events and after school programs.
400 Members
Founded in: 1978

18184 Independent Film & Television Alliance
10850 Wilshire Blvd
9th Floor
Los Angeles, CA 90024-4628

310-446-1000; *Fax:* 310-446-1600;
www.ifta-online.org
Social Media: Facebook, LinkedIn, YouTube

Michael Ryan, Chairman
Nicolas Chartier, Vice Chairperson
Kirk D' Amico, General Vice Chairperson
Charlotte Mickie, Vice Chairperson, Non-Californian
Lise Romanoff, Vice Chairperson/Secretary

A non-profit association whose mission is to provide the independent film and television industry with high-quality marketplace-oriented services and worldwide representation. The Alliance actively lobbies the United States and Eurpoean governments and the international organizations on measures that impact production and distribution.
Founded in: 1980

18185 International Animated Film Society
2114 W Burbank Blvd
Burbank, CA 91506-1232

818-842-8330; *Fax:* 613-232-6315
info@asifa-hollywood.org;
www.animationarchive.org

Amtran Manoogian, President

A California nonprofit organization established to promote and encourage the art and craft of animation. They support and encourage animation education, supports the preservation and critical evaluation of animation history, recognize achievement of excellence in the art and field of animation, strive to increase the public awareness of animation, act as a liaison to encourage the free exchange of ideas within the animation community, as well as a variety of other goals.
350 Members
Founded in: 1974

18186 International Cinematographers Guild
7755 W Sunset Boulevard
Hollywood, CA 90046

323-876-0160; *Fax:* 323-876-6383;
www.cameraguild.com
Social Media: Facebook, Twitter

Steven Poster, President
Lewis Rothenberg, National VP
Alan M. Gitlin, Secretary/Treasurer
Bruce C Doering, Executive Director

The International Cinematographers Guild welcomes camera professionals from across the United States and around the world.

18187 International Documentary Association
3470 Wilshire Boulevard
Suite 980
Los Angeles, CA 90010

213-232-1660; *Fax:* 213-232-1669
michael@documentary.org;
www.documentary.org
Social Media: Facebook, Twitter, LinkedIn, Youtube

Michael Lumpkin, Executive Director
Cindy Chyr, Development Director
Andrew Kaiser, Development Associate
Jina Chung, Associate
Amy Halpin, Manager

A nonprofit membership organization dedicated to supporting the efforts of nonfiction film and video makers throughout the United States and the world; promoting the documentary form; and expanding opportunities for the production, distribution, and exhibition of documentary.
2800+ Members
Founded in: 1982

18188 International Stunt Association
11331 Ventura Boulevard
Suite 100
Studio City, CA 91604

818-760-2072; *Fax:* 818-501-5656;
www.isastunts.com
Social Media: Facebook, Twitter

Leading the industry in exciting action while holding safety above all else, ISA is a fraternal organization whose membership is by invitation only. It is comprised of the top stuntment, stunt coordinators and second unit directors that Hollywood has to offer and a safety record that is second to none.
Founded in: 1980

18189 Motion Picture Association of America
15301 Ventura Boulevard
Building E
Sherman Oaks, CA 91403

818-995-6600; *Fax:* 818-285-4403;
www.mpaa.org

Christopher J Dodd, President/CEO

Serves as the voice and advocate of the American motion picture, home video and television industries. The association advocates for strong protection of the creative works produced and distributed by the industry, fights copyright theft around the world, and provides leadership in meeting new and emerging industry challenges.
7 Members
Founded in: 1922

18190 Motion Picture Editors Guild
7715 Sunset Boulevard
Suite 200
Hollywood, CA 90046

323-876-4770
800-705-8700; *Fax:* 323-876-0861
webmester@editorsguild.com;
www.editorsguild.com
Social Media: Facebook

Alan Heim, President
Gregg Rudloff, VP
Louis Bertini, Second Vice Presdient
Diane Adler, Secretary
Rachel B Igel, Treasurer

A national labor organization representing freelance and staff post-production professionals. MPED negotiates new collective bargaining agreements and enfoces existing agreements with employers involved in post-production. They provide assistance for securing better conditions, including but not limted to financial, medical, safety and artistic concerns.
6000 Members
Founded in: 1937

18191 Motion Picture Pilots Association
7435 Valjean Avenue
Van Nuys, CA 91406
818-947-5454; www.moviepilots.com

Cliff Fleming, Board Director
Dirk Vahle, Board Director
Rick Shuster, Board Director
Neil Looy, Board Director
Kevin LaRosa, Board Director

The MPPA promotes aviation safety and the interest of aviators working in the motion picture, television and entertainment industries; establishes, conducts and maintains such activities which promote higher aviation standards and better business methods as may assist in the advancement of aviation in the Entertainment Aviation Profession; cooperates with those

government agencies, industry organizations, entities or association whose objective is the betterment or advancement of the industry.
Founded in: 1997

18192 Motion Picture Sound Editors
10061 Riverside Dr.
PMB Box 751
Toluca Lake, CA 91602-2550

818-506-7731; *Fax:* 818-506-7732
info@mpse.org
mpse.org
Social Media: Facebook, Twitter, LinkedIn, YouTube

Frank Morrone, President
Mark Lanza, Vice President

Organization for the improvement of the professional status of sound editors.

18193 National Association of Theatre Owners
1705 N St. NW
Washington, DC 20036

202-962-0054
nato@natodc.com
natoonline.org

John Fithian, President & CEO

Exhibition trade organization that helps its members influence federal policy-making on issues of concern.

18194 Producers Guild of America
8530 Wilshire Blvd
Suite 450
Beverly Hills, CA 90211-3115

310-358-9020; *Fax:* 310-358-9520
info@producersguild.org;
www.producersguild.org

Marshall Herskovitz, President
Vance Van Paten, Executive Director
Grant Stoner, Director Membership
Courtney Cowan, Treasurer
Gale Ann Hurd, Secretary

The PGA represents, protects and promotes the interests of all members of the producing team by providing employment opportunities and health and welfare benefits for all members of the producing team; combating deceptive or uneraned credits within the producing team; and representing the interests of the entire producing team. The producing team consists of all those whose interdependency and support of each other are necessary for the creation of motion pictures and television programs.
500 Members
Founded in: 1950

18195 Society for Cinema & Media Studies
640 Parrington Oval
Wallace Old Science Hall Room 300
Norman, OK 73019

405-325-8075; *Fax:* 405-325-7135
office@cmstudies.org; www.cmstudies.org
Social Media: Facebook, Twitter

Steven Cohan, President
Victoria E. Johnson, Secretary
Amanda Klein, Treasurer
Jane Dye, Administrative Coordinator
Pamela Wojcik, President-Elect

A professional organization of college and university educators, filmmakers, historians, critics, scholars, and others devoted to the study of the moving image. The gaols of SCMS are to promote all areas of media studies within universities and two- and four-year colleges; to encourage and reward excellence in scholarship and writing; to facilitate and improve the teaching of media studies as disciplines and to advance multi-cultural awareness and interaction.
1M Members
Founded in: 1959

18196 Society of Camera Operators
PO Box 2006
Toluca Lake, CA 91610

818-382-7070; *Fax:* 323-856-9155;
www.soc.org
Social Media: Facebook, Twitter

Dan Dodd, Director
Mark August, President
Michael Scott, First VP
Mitch Dubin, Second VP
Lisa Stacilauskas, Third Vice President

Non-profit organization which advances the art and creative contribution of the operating cameraman in the Motion Picture and Television Industries.
Founded in: 1979
Mailing list available for rent

18197 Society of Motion Picture & Television Engineers
3 Barker Ave
5th Floor
White Plains, NY 10601-1509

914-761-1100; *Fax:* 914-761-3115;
www.smpte.org
Social Media: Facebook, Twitter, LinkedIn, Youtube

Barbara Lange, Executive Director
Sally-Ann D'Amato, Director Operations
Roberta Gorman, Manager
Peter Symes, Director Engineering
Amiee Ricca, Marketing and Communications

The SMPTE is the leading technical society for the motion imaging industry. It was founded to advance theory and development in the motion imaging field. Today, it publishes ANSI-approved Standards, Recommended Practices, and Engineering Guidelines. SMPTE holds conferences and local Section meetings to bring people and ides together, allowing for useful interaction and information exchange.
100 Members
Founded in: 1916

18198 Stuntmen's Association of Motion Pictures
5200 Lankershim Blvd.
Suite 190
North Hollywood, CA 91601

818-766-4334; *Fax:* 818-766-5943
hq@stuntmen.com; www.stuntmen.com

Chris Doyle, Manager
Alex Daniels, First VP
John Moio, Second VP
Oliver Keller, Secretary
Hugh Aodh O'Brien, Treasurer

Seeks to improve working conditions for stuntmen. Encourages members to uphold high professional standards.
135 Members
Founded in: 1961

18199 Stuntwomen's Association of Motion Pictures
3760 Cahuenga Blvd
Suite 104
Studio City, CA 91604-2411

818-588-8888
888-817-9267; *Fax:* 818-762-0907
INFO@STUNTWOMEN.COM;
www.stuntwomen.com
Social Media: Facebook

Jane Austin, President

A professional association for stuntwomen and stunt coordinators which seeks to uphold professional standards and improve working conditions.
Founded in: 1967

18200 Sundance Institute
1825 Three Kings Drive
PO Box 684429
Park City, UT 84060

435-658-3456; *Fax:* 435-658-3457
Institute@sundance.org; www.sundance.org
Social Media: Twitter, LinkedIn, Instagram

Robert Redford, President
Keri Putnam, Executive Director
Geoffrey Gilmore, Director Sundance Film Festival
Brooke McAffee, Director Finance
Ellen Oh, Associate Director Marketing

Non-profit organization dedicated to the discovery and development of independent artists and audiences. The Institute seeks to discover, support, and inspire independent film and theatre artists from the United States and around the world, and to introduce audiences to their new work. The Institutes programs include the annual Sundance Film Festival, held in Park City, Utah each January.
Founded in: 1981

18201 United Stuntwomen's Association
26893 Bouquet Canyon Rd.
Suite C, Box 218
Saugus, CA 91350

818-508-4651
usastunts@usastunts.com; www.usastunts.com

Bonnie Happy, President
Debbie Evans, Vice President

Trade association of professional stuntwomen, co-ordinators and second unit directors.
Founded in: 1984

18202 University Film and Video Association
UFVA Membership Office C/O Cheryl Jestis
University of Illinois Press
1325 South Oak Street
Champaign, IL 61820-6903

217-244-0626
866-244-0626; *Fax:* 217-244-9910
ufvahome@gmail.com; www.ufva.org
Social Media: Facebook, Twitter, LinkedIn, Instagram, YouTube

Francisco Menendez, President
Jennifer Machiorlatti, Executive VP
Brett Levner, Secretary
Tom Sanny, Treasurer
Cheryl Jestis, Membership Coordinator

Supports those interested in the fields of film and video production, history, criticism, and aesthetics. Provides training, education, and a quarterly magazine.
Cost: $75.00
Founded in: 1947

18203 Women in Film
6100 Wilshire Blvd
Suite 710
Los Angeles, CA 90048-5107

323-935-2211; *Fax:* 323-935-2212
info@wif.org; www.wif.org
Social Media: Facebook, Twitter, YouTube

Tichi Wilkerson-Kassel, Founder
Cathy Schulman, President
Glen Alpert, VP Membership
Nicole Katz, CFO
Gayle Nachlis, Executive Director

WIFs purpose is to empower, promote, nurture, and mentor women in the industry through a network of valuable contacts, events, and programs.
10000 Members
Founded in: 1974

Newsletters

18204 American Academy of Arts & Sciences Bulletin
American Academy of Arts & Sciences
136 Irving Street
Cambridge, MA 02138
617-576-5000; *Fax:* 617-576-5050
vsp@amacad.org; www.amacad.org
Leslie Berkowitz, President
Mark Robinson, Director, Operations
Paul Karoff, Director, Communications
Features the following departments: Academy News; Around the Country; Noteworthy; and Remembrance.
Frequency: 2x/year

18205 Festival Rag
541 Main Street
Union, WV 24983
Fax: 888-813-5457
markus@kemek.com;
www.kemek.com/independent-film/the-festival-rag
Markus Varjo, Publisher
Cil Ripley, Editor-In-Chief
Dave Roberts, Managing Editor
Carl Merrick, Content & Development
Dedicated to true independent filmmaking and filmmakers, and broadcast to thousands of media-industry subscribers. Provides information on film festivals worldwide, including interviews with filmmakers and programmers.

18206 Film Advisory Board Monthly
Film Advisory Board
263 W Olive Avenue
#377
Burbank, CA 91502
323-461-6541; *Fax:* 323-469-8541;
www.filmadvisoryboard.org
Social Media: Facebook, Twitter, LinkedIn
Janet Stokes, President
Information and news on the entertainment industry.
Frequency: Monthly
Founded in: 1975
Printed in one color on glossy stock

18207 Hollywood Arts Council
PO Box 931056
Hollywood, CA 90093
323-462-2355; *Fax:* 323-465-9240;
www.hollywoodartscouncil.org
Promotes, nurtures and supports the arts field in Hollywood. Newsletter is included with membership.
Founded in: 1978
Printed in 4 colors on glossy stock

18208 Preview Family Movie & TV Review
Movie Morality Ministries
6302 Riverside Dr
Irving, TX 75039
972-409-9960
800-807-8071; *Fax:* 785-255-4316
preview@fni.com; www.merchantcircle.com
Dave Haverty, President
Greg Shull, Editor
Susan Haverty, Desktop Publisher/Office Manager
Reviews current films and TV series from a Christian and family values perspective.
Cost: $34.00
Frequency: Monthly
ISSN: 0892-6468
Printed in 2 colors on matte stock

Magazines & Journals

18209 Advanstar
Advanstar Communications
641 Lexington Ave
Suite 8
New York, NY 10022-4503
212-951-6600; *Fax:* 212-951-6793
info@advanstar.com; www.advanstar.com
Joseph Loggia, CEO
News and features emphasize innovation in equipment technology and creative technique for editing, graphics, and special effects. Covers all budget levels from desktop post to feature films.
130 Pages
Frequency: Monthly
Circulation: 31464
Founded in: 1986

18210 American Cinematographer
American Society of Cinematographers
1782 North Orange Drive
PO Box 2230
Hollywood, CA 90078-2230
323-969-4333
800-448-0145; *Fax:* 323-876-4973
office@theasc.com; www.theasc.com
Covers feature films, television, commercials, music videos, digital video, new equipment, DVD and book releases and much more. An exploration and a reflection of today's cinematography. A publication of the American Society of Cinematographers.
Cost: $29.95
Frequency: Monthly
Circulation: 42000
Founded in: 1919
Mailing list available for rent

18211 Animation Magazine
Animation Magazine
26500 W.Agoura Rd
Suite 102
Calabasas, CA 91302
818-883-2884; *Fax:* 818-883-3773
info@animationmagazine.net;
www.animationmagazine.net
Jean Thoren, President
Promotes the art and business of animation and gives recognition to those animators and technicians who make the world of animation what it is today.
Cost: $50.00
Frequency: Monthly
Circulation: 30000
ISSN: 1041-617X
Founded in: 1986
Printed in 4 colors on glossy stock

18212 Celebrity Service
8833 W Sunset Boulevard
Suite 401
Los Angeles, CA 90069-2171
213-883-3671; *Fax:* 310-652-9244
Robert Dean, Manager/Director
A listing of celebrities names and addresses. Publisher of the Celebrity Bulletin informing the entertainment and news industry of which celebrities are traveling to Hollywood and New York
Frequency: Bi-Monthly

18213 Cineaste
Cineaste Magazine
243 5th Ave
Suite 706
New York, NY 10016
212-366-5720; *Fax:* 212-366-5724
cineaste@cineaste.com; www.cineaste.com
Gary Crowdus, Editor-in-Chief
Cynthia Lucia, Editor
Richard Porton, Editor
Dan Georgakas, Consulting Editor
Vicki Robinson, Production Assistant
An internationally recognized independent film magazine. Features contributions from many of America's most articulate and outspoken writers, critics and scholars. Focussing on both the art and politics of the cinema.
Cost: $ 20.00
Frequency: Quarterly
Circulation: 11000
ISSN: 0009-7004
Founded in: 1967
Mailing list available for rent

18214 Cinefantastique
CFQ Media
PO Box 34425
Los Angeles, CA 90034-0425
310-204-0825; *Fax:* 310-204-5882;
www.cfq.com
Frederick Clarke, Editor
Provides coverage of genre entertainment. Each issue features in-depth coverage of sci-fi, fantasy and horror films, TV, DVDs, games, toys, books, comics and more.
Cost: $34.95
Frequency: Monthly
Circulation: 40,000

18215 Cinefex
79 Daily Drive
#309
Camarillo, CA 93010
805-383-0800; *Fax:* 805-383-0803
advertising@cinefex.com; www.cinefex.com
A quarterly magazine devoted to motion picture special effects.
Cost: $32.00
180 Pages
Frequency: Quarterly
Circulation: 30000
ISSN: 0198-1056
Founded in: 1980
Printed in 4 colors

18216 Cinema Journal
University of Texas Press
2100 Comal
PO Box 7819
Austin, TX 78713-7819
512-471-7233
800-252-3206; *Fax:* 512-232-7178
utpress@uts.cc.utexas.edu;
www.utexas.edu/utpress
Sponsored by the Society for Cinema and Media Studies. The journal presents recent scholarship by SCMS members. It publishes essays on a wide variety of subjects from diverse methodological perspectives. A 'Professional Notes' section informs Society of Cinema and Media Studies readers about upcoming events, research opportunities, and the latest published research. Cinema Journal is a member of the CELJ, the Conference of Editors of Learned Journals.
Cost: $42.00
144 Pages
Frequency: Quarterly
Circulation: 2800
ISSN: 0009-7101
Founded in: 1950
Printed in on matte stock

18217 Daily Variety/Gotham
360 Park Avenue South
New York, NY 10010-3659

646-746-7001; *Fax:* 646-746-6977
vtccustserv@cdsfulfillment.com;
www.variety.com

Peter Bart, Editor-in-Chief
Timothy M Gray, Editor
Ted Johnson, Managing Editor
Kathy Lyford, Managing Editor
Phil Gallo, Associate Editor

Focus is on Broadway theater, network television headquarters, regional music business, and local film production. Explores the role of New York City in relation to the national and global entertainment industries.
Cost: $259.00
Frequency: Daily
Founded in: 1905

18218 Daily Variety/LA
5900 Wilshire Boulevard
Suite 3100
Los Angeles, CA 90036-3659

323-617-9100; *Fax:* 323-857-0494
vtccustserv@cdsfulfillment.com;
www.variety.com

Peter Bart, Editor-in-Chief
Timothy M Gray, Editor
Ted Johnson, Managing Editor
Kathy Lyford, Managing Editor
Phil Gallo, Associate Editor

Focus is on Hollywood, network television headquarters, regional music business, and local film production. Explores the role of Hollywood in relation to the national and global entertainment industries.
Cost: $259.00
Frequency: Daily
Founded in: 1905

18219 Documentary Magazine
International Documentary Association
3470 Wilshire Boulevard
Suite 980
Los Angeles, CA 90010

212-232-1660; *Fax:* 213-232-1669
tom@documentary.org; www.documentary.org
Social Media: Facebook, Twitter, LinkedIn, Instagram

Thomas White, Editor
Akiva Gottlieb, Associate Editor
Jina Chung, Manager Advertising Sales
Simon Kilmurry, Executive Director

Devoted exclusively to nonfiction media.
Cost: $55.00
2270 Members
Frequency: Quarterly
Founded in: 1982
Printed in 4 colors on glossy stock

18220 Film & History
Historians Film Committee
Lawrence University,Memorial Hall B5
711 E Boldt Way
Appleton, WI 54911

920-832-6649; www.h-net.org/~filmhis

Peter C Rollins, Director
Deborah Carmichael, Editor-in-Chief
Cynthia Miller, Associate Editor-in-Chief

An Interdisciplinary Journal of Film and Television Studies concerned with the impact of motion pictures on our society. Film and History focuses on how feature films and documentary films both represent and interpret history. Types of articles include: Analysis of individual films and/or television programs from a historical perspective, survey of documents related to the production of films, or analysis of history as explored through film.
Cost: $50.00
Frequency: Bi-annually
Circulation: 1000
ISSN: 0360-3695
Founded in: 1970

18221 Film & Video Magazine
110 William Street
11th Floor
New York, NY 10038

212-621-4900; *Fax:* 212-621-4635;
www.studiodaily.com/filmandvideo

Bryant Frazer, Editor-in-Chief
Pete Putman, Senior Editor
Alison Johns, Editor-in-Chief
Scott Gentry, Group Publisher
Jarrett Cory, Classified Sales

Covers new ideas in creating entertainment by focusing on technique in the production and finishing of features, TV programming, music videos and commercials. No longer publishes print copies, magazine is 100% digital
Frequency: Monthly
Founded in: 1983
Printed in 4 colors

18222 Film Journal International
VNU Business Media
770 Broadway,7th Floor
New York, NY 10003-9595

212-493-4097; *Fax:* 646-654-7694
subscriptions@filmjournal.com;
www.filmjournal.com

Penny Vane, President
Sid Holt, Editorial Director
Robert Sunshine, Publisher/Editor
Robin Klamfoth, Advertising Director
Kevin Lally, Executive Editor

A trade publication covering the motion picture industry, including theatrical exhibition, production, distribution, and allied activities. Articles report on US and international news, with features on current production, industry trends, theatre design, equipment, concessions, sound, digital cinema, screen advertising, and other industry-related news. Each issue also includes the Buying and Booking Guide, with comprehensive feature film reviews.
Cost: $65.00
Frequency: Monthly
Founded in: 1934
Mailing list available for rent

18223 Film Threat
Film Threat International Headquarters
5042 Wilshire Boulevard
PMB 1500
Los Angeles, CA 90036

Fax: 310-274-7985; www.filmthreat.com
Social Media: Facebook, Twitter

Mark Bell, Editor-in-Chief
Eric Campos, Senior Contributing Editor
Chris Gore, Founder/Publishjer

The print edition of Film Threat retired in 1997, but the legend has lived on as an internet journalism mainstay. FilmThreat.com delivers film reviews, film festival coverage, exclusive filmmaker interviews and original video content.
Cost: $10.50
Frequency: Bi-Monthly
Circulation: 100,000
Founded in: 1985

18224 Hollywood Life
Movieline Magazine
10537 Santa Monica Blvd
Suite 250
Los Angeles, CA 90025-4952

310-234-9501; *Fax:* 310-234-0332
hollywoodlife@pcspublink.com;
www.hollywoodlive.net

Anne Volokh, President

Formerly called Movieline, an entertainment lifestyle featuring interviews with stars, directors and producers; as well as information on celebrity shopping, up and coming talent, soundtracks, electronics and fashion associated with hollywood style and trends.
Cost: $13.75
Frequency: Monthly
Founded in: 1989
Printed in 4 colors on glossy stock

18225 Hollywood Reporter
Prometheus Global Media
770 Broadway
New York, NY 10003-9595

212-493-4100; *Fax:* 646-654-5368;
www.prometheusgm.com
Social Media: Facebook, Twitter, YouTube

Richard D. Beckman, CEO
James A. Finkelstein, Chairman
Madeline Krakowsky, Vice President Circulation
Tracy Brater, Executive Director Crative Service

Gives fresh ideas for film and TV. Covers the full spectrum of craft and commerce in the entertainment industry.
Cost: $199.00
Frequency: Weekly
Circulation: 34770

18226 International Cinematographers Guild Magazine
7755 W Sunset Blvd
Suite 300
Los Angeles, CA 90046-3911

323-876-0160; *Fax:* 323-876-6383
info@icgmagazine.com;
www.cameraguild.com

Steven Poster, President
John McCarthy, Marketing

Serves as the journal of 'how to' for film and digital techniques. It incorporates a wide range of editorial for specific job categories in relation to cinematography for Film/Hi-Def/Digital production and defines the tools and technology necessary for advancement in this field. The magazine is written for members of the International Cinematographers Guild, including cinematographers, camera operators, camera assistants, still photographers, publicists, film loaders, and others in the field.
Cost: $48.00
Frequency: Monthly
Founded in: 1929

18227 Journal of Film and Video
University Film and Video Association
University of Illinois Press
1325 S Oak Street
Champaign, IL 61820

217-244-0626
866-244-0626; *Fax:* 217-244-9910
journals@uiuc.edu; www.ufva.org

Stephen Tropiano, Editor
Cheryl Jestis, Membership

Focuses on scholarship in the fields of film and video production, history, criticism, and aesthetics. Topics include film and related media, education in these fields, and the function of film and video in society.
Cost: $40.00
Frequency: Quarterly
Circulation: 1200

18228 Journal of Popular Film and Television
Heldref Publications
1319 18th St Nw
Suite 2
Washington, DC 20036-1802
202-296-6267
800-365-9753; *Fax:* 202-296-5149
subscribe@heldref.org; www.heldref.org
James Denton, Executive Director
Gary Edgerton, Co-Executive Editor
Articles discuss networks, genres, series and audiences, as well as celebrity stars, directors and studios. Regular features include essays on the social and cultural background of films and television programs, filmographies, bibliographies, and commisioned book and video reviews.
Cost: $51.00
Frequency: Quarterly
ISSN: 0195-6051
Founded in: 1956

18229 Keyframe Magazine
DMG Publishing
2756 N Green Valley Pkwy
Suite 261
Henderson, NV 89014-2120
702-990-8656; *Fax:* 702-992-0471;
www.dmgpublishing.com
Dariush Derakhshani, Editor-in-Chief
Cheri Madison, Managing Editor
Charles Edgin, Editorial Director
Alice Edgin, Executive Editor
In response to reader requests, Keyframe is adding to its LightWave and Photoshop tutorials and content additional bonus pages covering other tools used by digital artists. As Keyframe evolves into this larger, better magazine, its new title with be HDRI 3D.
Cost: $54.00
Circulation: 9000
Founded in: 1997

18230 Millimeter Magazine
PO Box 2100
Skokie, IL 60076-7800
847-763-9504
866-505-7173; *Fax:* 847-763-9682;
www.millimeter.com
Cynthia Wisehart, Editor
In a fast-changing and challenging industry, Millimeter anticipates the future. Its early coverage of important technology-driven trends such as 24p production, desktop post, and digital cinema has helped readers remain competitive and plan their business investments. Millimeter is an authoritative resource for professionals in production, postproduction, animation, streaming, and visual effects for motion pictures, television and commercials.
Cost: $70.00
Frequency: Monthly

18231 Movie Collectors World
Arena Publishing
PO BOX 309
Fraser, MI 48026
586-774-4311; *Fax:* 703-940-4566;
www.mcwonline.com
Brian Bukantis, Editor
Leading collector's publication for collectors of movie memorabilia, with an emphasis on collectible movie posters. Each issue is filled with ads from dealers and collectors all over the world. In any monthly issue, you will find movie posters common and rare - everything from the 'Golden Age' to today's blockbusters.
Cost: $36.00
36-44 Pages
Frequency: Monthly
Circulation: 6000

18232 MovieMaker
MovieMaker Magazine
8328 De Soto Ave.
Canoga Park, CA 91304
310-742-7214
888-881-5861; *Fax:* 818-349-9922;
www.moviemaker.com
Timothy Rhys, Publisher/Editor-in-Chief
Jennifer M Wood, Editor
Phillip Williams, Editor at Large
Ian Bage, New Marketing Services
Liza Kelley, Production Manager
MovieMaker is the world's most widely - read independent movie magazine that focuses on the art and business of making movies. Its editorial mix is a progressive mix of in depth interviews and criticism combined by practical techniques and advice on financing, distribution and production strategies.
Cost: $18.00
Frequency: Quarterly
Circulation: 54000
Founded in: 1993
*Mailing list available for rent*at $175 per M

18233 Premiere Magazine
Hachette Filipacchi Media US Inc
1633 Broadway
Suite 41
New York, NY 10019-6708
212-767-6000; *Fax:* 212-481-6428;
www.premiere.com
Jessica Letkemann, Editor
Jennifer Cooper, Producer
A magazine for young adults, which focuses on the art and commerce of the film industry. Premiere's feature articles, profiles and monthly columns include original phtography, interviews with Hollywood's A-list and up-and-coming talent, studio heads and producers.

18234 Produced By
The Producers Guild of America
8530 Wilshire Blvd
Suite 450
Beverly Hills, CA 90211-3115
310-358-9020; *Fax:* 310-358-9520
info@producersguild.org;
www.producersguild.org
Vance Van Petter, Executive Director
Audra Whaley, Director Operations
Kyle Katz, Director Member Benefits
Chris Greenr, Director Communications
Dan Dodd, Advertising
Provided as a benefit with membership to the Producers Guild of America.
Frequency: Quarterly
Circulation: 325
Founded in: 1962

18235 Producer
Testa Communications
25 Willowdale Avenue
Port Washington, NY 11050-3779
516-767-2500; *Fax:* 516-767-9335
avvproducersguide.com
Randi Altman, Editor
Sande Seidman, Advertising Manager
Magazine aimed at producers, directors and creative people in the image and sound realms, with production stories on feature films, television, commercials, documentary, and corporate video projects. Accent is on the creative application of technology, following producers into the field and onto the studio set.
Cost: $15.00
Frequency: Bi-Monthly
Circulation: 18,300

18236 SMPTE Journal
Society of Motion Picture & Television Engineers
3 Barker Ave
Sute 5
White Plains, NY 10601-1509
914-761-1100; *Fax:* 914-761-3115;
www.smpte.org
Social Media: Facebook, Twitter
Kimberly Maki, Executive Director
Charlie Barone, Administrative Assistant
Featuring industry-leading papers and standards, each month the Journal keeps its members on the cutting edge of the industry. Each issue provides the latest research and papers, ranging in style from technical, scientific, and tutorial, to applications/practices. Readers are kept up-to-date on events and meetings, the latest publications and brochures, and new products and developments.
Cost: $140.00
Frequency: Monthly
Circulation: 10000
Founded in: 1916
Printed in on glossy stock

18237 San Francisco Cinematheque
San Francisco Cinematheque
145 Ninth Street
Suite 240
San Francisco, CA 94103
415-552-1990; *Fax:* 415-552-2067
sfc@sfcinematheque.org;
www.sfcinematheque.org
Stephen Anker, Executive Director
Alfonso Alvarez, Board Director
Gina Basso, Board Director
Aimee Friberg, Board Director
Jeff Lambert, Board Director
Supports risk-taking art, cutting edge artists and the boundless potential of creative expression.
Cost: $15.00
Frequency: Monthly
Founded in: 1961

18238 Script
Forum
5638 Sweet Air Road
Baldwin, MD 21013-9009
410-592-3466
888-245-2228; *Fax:* 410-592-8062
scriptmag@fwmedia.com; www.scriptmag.com
Social Media: Facebook, YouTube, RSS
Mark Madnick, Publisher
David Geatty, Founding Publisher
Shelly Mellot, Editor-in-Chief
Andrew Schneider, Managing Editor
Maureen Green, Editor
A leading source of information on the crage and business of writing for film and television. Each issues delivers informative articles on writing, developing and marketing screenplays and television scripts. Most articles are written by working writers. Additionally, development executives, agents, managers and entertainment attorneys contribute regularly.
Cost: $24.95
Frequency: Bi-Monthly
Circulation: 12000

18239 Starlog
1372 Broadway
2nd Floor
New York, NY 10018

212-689-2830
800-934-6788; www.starlog.com

David McDonnel, Editor
Norman Jacobs, Founder

Information on science fiction happenings in the movies and television industries.
Cost: $56.97
Frequency: Monthly
Circulation: 350000

18240 The Independent
independent-magazine.org
Social Media: Facebook, Twitter

Online source of information and inspiration for independent, grassroots and activist media makers.
Founded in: 2007

18241 Variety
Reed Business Information
5700 Wilshire Boulevard
Suite 120
Los Angeles, CA 90036-3659

323-857-6600
866-698-2743; *Fax:* 323-857-0494
VTCCustserv@cdsfulfillment.com;
www.variety.com

Charles C Koones, Publisher
Peter Bart, Editor-in-Chief
Timothy Gray, Editor
Kathy Lyford, Managing Editor
Christopher Wessel, Circulation Director

Variety covers all aspects of film, television and cable, homevideo, music, new media and technolgy, theater and finance. Topics run from people, companies, products and performances, to development, financing, distribution, regulation and marketing.
Cost: $259.00
Frequency: Weekly
Circulation: 35168
Founded in: 1905

Trade Shows

18242 American Film Institute Festival: AFI Fest
American Film Institute
2021 N Western Avenue
Los Angeles, CA 90027-1657

323-856-7896
866-234-3378; *Fax:* 323-856-9118
AFIFEST@AFI.com; www.afifest.com

Jennifer Morgerman, Publicity Director
Stacey Leinson, Publicity Manager
Lagan Sebert, Publicity Coordinator
John Wildman, Filmmaker Press Liaison
Alison Deknatel, Director Communications

A 10-day event held each November, the festival features a rich slate of films from emerging filmmakers, nightly red-carpet gala premieres and global showcases of the latest work from the great film masters. AFI runs concurrently with the American Film Market. Together, AFT Fest and AFM provide the film industry with the only concurrent festival/market event in North America.
60000 Attendees
Frequency: November
Founded in: 1986

18243 International Cinema Equipment (ICECO) Showest
Magna-Tech Electronic Company
5600 NW 32nd Avenue
Miami, FL 33142

305-573-7339; *Fax:* 305-573-8101;
www.showest.com

Steven H Krams, President
Dara Reusch, VP
Julio Urbay, VP International Sales/Marketing
Fancisco Blanco, VP Technical Services
Arturo Quintero, Architectural Design/Development

Annual convention for the Motion Picture industry. It is an international gathering devoted exclusively to the movie business. It is also the single largest international gathering of motion picture professionals and theatre owners in the world, with delegates from more than 50 countries in attendance each year.
Frequency: March
Founded in: 1975

18244 International Cinema Equipment Company ICECO Show East
Magna-Tech Electronic Company,Inc.
1998 NE 150th Street
North Miami, FL 33181
305-573-7339; *Fax:* 305-573-8101
iceco@aol.com; www.iceco.com

Steven H Krams, President
Dara Reusch, VP
Julio Urbay, VP International Sales/Marketing
Francisco Blanco, VP/Technical Services
Arturo Quintero, Architectural Design & Development

This annual convention brings together over 1300 colleagues from the motion picture industry in the United States, Latin America and the Caribbean. The convention provides information on industry trends, screen films and product reels, state-of-the-art theatre equipment along with services and technologies vital to the industry.
1300 Attendees
Founded in: 1975

18245 Moondance International Film Festival
Moondance International Film Festival
970 9th Street
Boulder, CO 80302

303-818-5771
director@moondancefilmfestival.com;
www.moondancefilmfestival.com
Social Media: Facebook, Twitter, LinkedIn

Elizabeth English, Festival Founder/Executive Director
Kyle/Erica Saylors, Festival Director/Event Coordinator
Karina Pyudik, Registration Coordinator
Douglis C Garvin, Special Events Coordinator
Roy Bodner, Publicist/Media Relations

The Festival's primary goal is to present films and scripts which have the power to raise awareness about vital social issues, educating writers and filmmakers, as well as festival audiences, and inspiring them to take positive action. The Festival's objective is to promote and encourage independent filmmakers, screenwriters, playwrights, and music composers and the best works in films, screenplays, stageplays, TV scripts, radioplays, film scores, lyrics, librettos, music videos, and short stor
Frequency: Annual
Founded in: 1999
Mailing list available for rent

18246 New York Film Festival
Film Society of Lincoln Center
70 Lincoln Center Plaza
New York, NY 10023

212-875-5610
888-313-6085
filminfo@filmlinc.com; www.filmlinc.com
Social Media: Facebook, Twitter

Rose Kuo, Executive Director
Richard Pena, Program Director
Lesli Klainberg, Managing Director

Celebrates American and international cinema and recognizes and supports new filmmakers.
Frequency: Annual

18247 Sundance Film Festival
Sundance Institute
1825 Three Kings Drive
PO Box 684426
Park City, UT 84060

435-658-3456; *Fax:* 435-658-3457
Institute@sundance.org; www.sundance.org

Robert Redford, Founder
Keri Putnam, Executive Director
Jill Miller, Managing Director

Annual festival held in Park City, Utah as a US showcase for American and International independent film. The Institute is dedicated to the development of artists of independent vision and the exhibition of their new work. Since its inception, the Institute has grown into an internationally recognized resource for thousands of independent artists.
Frequency: January
Founded in: 1981

18248 Telluride Film Festival
National Film Preserve
800 Jones Street
Berkeley, CA 94710

510-665-9494; *Fax:* 510-665-9589
mail@telluridefilmfestival.org;
www.telluridefilmfestival.org

Bill Pence, Founder
Stella Pence, Founder

Well situated on the international film festival calendar, Terruride takes place in Telluride, Colorado, and is defined by sense of purity and commitment.
Founded in: 1974

18249 Toronto International Film Festival
TIFF Bell Lightbox
350 King Street West
Toronto

888-599-8433; www.tiff.net

William Marshall, Founder
Piers Handling, Director & CEO
Noah Cowan, Artistic Director, Bell Lightbox
Cameron Bailey, Co-Director

Publicly attended film festival that takes place each September in Toronto, Ontario, Canada, showing upwards of 400 films from more than 60 countries. The festival is currently headquartered at TIFF Bell Lightbox, which opened in 2010.
Founded in: 1976
Mailing list available for rent

Directories & Databases

18250 Annual Index to Motion Picture Credits
Academy of Motion Picture Arts and Sciences
8949 Wilshire Blvd
Beverly Hills, CA 90211-1972

310-247-3000; *Fax:* 310-271-3395;
www.oscars.org

The Index is closely tied to the annual Academy Awards presentation. As part of the Academy Awards process, the Academy of Motion Picture Arts and Sciences gathers credits for each film hoping to qualify for awards. These credits, compiled and verified by the film's producer or dis-

tributor, are the core of the Annual Index and IMPC database. In addition to personal credits, IMPC also records index production and releasing dates, MPAA ratings, running times, color, language, and more.
Frequency: Annual
ISBN: 0-942102-37-1
ISSN: 0163-5123
Founded in: 1934

18251 **Blu-Book Production Directory**
Hollywood Creative Directory
5055 Wilshire Blvd
Los Angeles, CA 90036-6103

323-525-2369
800-815-0503; *Fax:* 323-525-2398
hcdcustomerservice@hcdonline.com;
www.hcdonline.com

Valencia McKinley, Manager

A comprehensive directory for professionals in the production and post-production industries. Provides current contact information needed to produce a film, TV program, commercial, or music video. The directory contains a special tabbed section on premier below-the-line craft professionals, along with selective credits, and has been expanded to include New York production facilities and services, making it one of the only bi-coastal resources of its kind.
Cost: $39.95
450 Pages
Frequency: Annual
ISBN: 1-928936-44-X

18252 **Boxoffice: Circuit Giants**
Boxoffice
PO Box 1634
Des Plains, IL 60019

212-627-7000; www.boxoffice.com

Peter Cane, Publisher
Joe Policy, CEO
Annlee Ellingson, Editor
Francesca Dinglasan, Senior Editor
Bob Vale, VP Advertising and Sales

Directory of the largest exhibition chains. Available to subscribers of Boxoffice magazine
Cost: $59.95
Frequency: Annual
Founded in: 1990

18253 **Boxoffice: Distributor Directory**
Boxoffice
PO Box 1634
Des Plains, IL 60019

212-627-7000; www.boxoffice.com

Peter Cane, Publisher
Joe Policy, CEO
Annlee Ellingson, Editor
Francesca Dinglasan, Senior Editor
Bob Vale, VP Advertising and Sales

Listings of studio and independent film suppliers. Available to subscribers of Boxoffice magazine
Cost: $59.95
Frequency: Annual
Founded in: 1990

18254 **Directors Guild of America Directory of Members**
Directors Guild of America
7920 W Sunset Blvd
Los Angeles, CA 90046-3347

310-289-2000
800-421-4173; *Fax:* 310-289-2029;
www.dga.org

Jay Roth, President
Morgan Rumpf, Director Communications
Paul Zepp, Membership Administrator
Darrell L Hop, Editor DGA Monthly/Website
Michael Apted, Secretary

The DGA represents Film and Television Directors, Unit Production Managers, First Assistant Directors, Second Assistant Directors, Technical Coordinators and Tape Associate Directors, Stage Managers and Production Associates. The Directory is available in print and on-line
Cost: $25.00
Frequency: Annual

18255 **Editors Guild Directory**
Motion Picture Editors Guild
7715 Sunset Boulevard
Suite 200
Hollywood, CA 90046

323-876-4770
800-705-8700; *Fax:* 323-876-0861
info@editorsguild.com; www.editorsguild.com

Ron Kutak, Executive Director
Tomm Carroll, Publications Director
Serena Kungr, Director Membership Services
Adriana Iglesias-Dietl, Membership Administrator
Tris Carpenter, Manager

An invaluable resource for producers, directors and post production professionals alike. It lists contact, credit, award and classification information for all of the Guild's active members at the time of publication, as well as a list of Oscar and Emmy winners for every year since the awards began. It also includes a retirees section.
Cost: $25.00
Frequency: Bi-Annual
Founded in: 1994

18256 **Film Journal: Distribution Guide Issue**
Film Journal International
770 Broadway
5th Floor
New York, NY 10003-9595

646-654-7680; *Fax:* 646-654-7694;
www.filmjournal.com

Robert Sunshine, Publisher/Editor
Kevin Lally, Executive Editor
Rex Roberts, Associate Editor
Andrew Sunshine, Advertising Director
Katey Rich, Editorial Assistant

The International Distribution and subdistribution Guide supplements the regular monthly Buying and Booking Guide. It is designed to furnish ready reference information on the who, what, where and how of theatrical sales. It lists the names, addresses, personnel, telephone numbers and product of domestic and international distributors, both major and independent, along with similar information on regional exchanges together with national companies they handle.
Frequency: Annual

18257 **Film Journal: Equipment Guide**
Film Journal International
770 Broadway
5th Floor
New York, NY 10003-9595

646-654-7680; *Fax:* 646-654-7694;
www.filmjournal.com

Robert Sunshine, Publisher/Editor
Kevin Lally, Executive Editor
Robin Klamfoth, Advertising Director
Rex Roberts, Associate Editor
Katey Rich, Editorial Assistant

The Equipment, Concessions and Services Guide is designed to provide ready reference information on the theatrical equipment and concessions industry. It lists in detail the company names, addresses, telephone numbers, personnel, affiliations and products of equipment and concession manufacturers and service companies, along with similar information on US and foreign service dealers and suppliers, arranged in alphabetical order according to state or country.
Frequency: Annual

18258 **Film Journal: Exhibition Guide**
Film Journal International
770 Broadway
5th Floor
New York, NY 10003-9595

212-493-4097; *Fax:* 646-654-7694
subscriptions@filmjournal.com;
www.filmjournal.com

Robert Sunshine, Publisher/Editor
Kevin Lally, Executive Editor
Robin Klamfoth, Advertising Director
Rex Roberts, Associate Editor
Sarah Sluis, Editorial Assistant

The exhibition Guide is an alphabetical listing designed to provide ready reference information on the leading theatrical motion picture circuits. It lists in comprehensive detail such data as company names, addresses and phone numbers, total screens and new screens projected, division office locations, top personnel, recent circuit acquisitions, and a state-by-state breakdown of screens.
Frequency: Annual
Founded in: 1934
Mailing list available for rent

18259 **Film Superlist: Motion Pictures in the Public Domain**
Hollywood Film Archive
8391 Beverly Blvd
Ste. 321
Los Angeles, CA 90048-2633

323-655-4968

Richard Baer, Executive Director

Created by Walter E. Hurst and updated by Richard Baer. 1992-1994. Three volumes to date, covering 50,000 films from the years 1894-1939, 1940-1949 and 1950-1959.

18260 **Grey House Performing Arts Directory**
Grey House Publishing
4919 Route 22
PO Box 56
Amenia, NY 12501

518-789-8700
800-562-2139; *Fax:* 845-373-6390
books@greyhouse.com; www.greyhouse.com
Social Media: Facebook, Twitter

Leslie Mackenzie, Publisher
Richard Gottlieb, Editor

The most comprehensive resource covering the Performing Arts. This directory provides current information on over 8,500 Dance Companies, Instrumental Music Programs, Opera Companies, Choral Groups, Theater Companies, Performing Arts Series, Performing Arts Facilities and Artist Management Groups.
Cost: $185.00
1200 Pages
Frequency: Annual
ISBN: 1-592373-76-3
Founded in: 1981

18261 **Grey House Performing Arts Directory - Online Database**
Grey House Publishing
4919 Route 22
PO Box 56
Amenia, NY 12501

518-789-8700
800-562-2139; *Fax:* 518-789-0556
gold@greyhouse.com;

www.gold.greyhouse.com
Social Media: Facebook, Twitter

Leslie Mackenzie, Publisher
Richard Gottlieb, Editor

The Grey House Performing Arts Directory - Online Database provides immediate access to dance companies, orchestras, opera companies, choral groups, theater companies, series, festivals and perfoming arts facilities across the country, or in their region, state, or in your own backyard. It offers unequaled coverage of the Performing Arts - over 8,500 listings - of the major performance organization, facilities, and information resources.
Frequency: Annual
Founded in: 1981

18262 **International Motion Picture Alamanc**
Quigley Publishing Company
64 Wintergreen Lane
Groton, MA 01450

860-228-0247
800-231-8239; *Fax:* 860-228-0157
quigleypub@aol.com;
www.quigleypublishing.com

William J Quigley, President/Publisher
Eileen Quigley, Editor

Contains over 400 pages of biographies and 500 pages of reference material. From 1928 to the present day, the complete set contains the biography of everyone who has ever been of importance to the Industry. Each edition includes thousands of company listings, credits for current films and films released in the prior ten years, statistics and awards and complete coverage of all aspects of the indiustry, including production, distribution and exhibition.
Cost: $175.00
Frequency: Annual

18263 **International Television and Video Almanac**
Quigley Publishing Company
64 Wintergreen Lane
Groton, MA 01450

860-228-0247
800-231-8239; *Fax:* 860-228-0157
quigleypub@aol.com;
www.quigleypublishing.com

William J Quigley, President/Publisher
Eileen Quigley, Editor

Each edition contains over 400 pages of biographies and an additional 500 pages of reference material on television programs, broadcast, cable and satellie, production services, the video industry, statistics and awards. Included are detailed listings for thousands of companies, as well as coverage outside the United States.
Cost: $175.00
Frequency: Annual
Founded in: 1955

18264 **Mini Reviews**
Cineman Syndicate
31 Purchase St
Suite 203
Rye, NY 10580-3013

914-967-5353; www.minireviews.com

John P McCarthy, Editor

An easy to read, easy to use guide for movie watchers updated weekly.
Frequency: Weekly
Founded in: 2000

18265 **Motion Picture TV and Theatre Directory**
Motion Picture Enterprises
PO Box 276
Tarrytown, NY 10591-0276

212-245-0969; *Fax:* 212-245-0974;
www.mpe.net

Neal R Pilzer, Publisher

The Guide is mailed to members of 59 trade associations, unions and professional societies; decision-makers at advertising agencies, production companies, TV stations, and government agencies; faculty and students of nearly 200 film schools; and other prime purchasers of film and TV equipment and services nationwide. Companies are listed both by category and company name. Listings include company name, address and telephone number as well as fax numbers, e-mail addresses, and web site URLs.
Cost: $18.80
335 Pages
Frequency: Annual
Circulation: 82500
Founded in: 1963

18266 **Movie World Almanac**
Hollywood Film Archive
8391 Beverly Blvd
PMB 321
Los Angeles, CA 90048-2633

323-655-4968

Richard Baer, Executive Director

Lists over 200 major American and foreign film distributors who handle old and contemporary films.

18267 **Reel Directory**
Lynetta Freeman
PO Box 1910
Boyes Hot Springs, CA 95416

415-531-9760; *Fax:* 707-581-1725
info@reeldirectory.com;
www.reeldirectory.com

Lynetta Freeman, Manager
Keith Marsalis, Director
Katie Carney, Director of Marketing

Source for Film, Video and Multimedia in Northern California.
Cost: $25.00
700 Pages
Frequency: Annual
Circulation: 5,000
Founded in: 1979

18268 **Studio Report: Film Development**
Hollywood Creative Directory
5055 Wilshire Blvd
Los Angeles, CA 90036-6103

323-525-2369
800-815-0503; *Fax:* 323-525-2398
hcdcustomerservice@hcdonline.com;
www.hcdonline.com

Valencia McKinley, Manager

The only directory of its kind, in print for the first time. A complete breakdown of film development project tracking. A-Z listings by title, spec screenplays sold, hot studio projects, cross-referenced by studio, production company and genre. The directory's main body consists of an alphabetical listing of all in-development projects that have achieved a forward-moving milestone some time in the last five months. Subsequent sections sort and cross-reference the information to highlight aspects
Cost: $19.95
190 Pages
ISBN: 1-928936-49-0

Industry Web Sites

18269 **http://gold.greyhouse.com**
G.O.L.D Grey House OnLine Databases

Grey House Publishing's online database platform, GOLD, offers Quick Search, Keyword Search and Expert Search for most business sectors including motion picture and entertainment markets. The GOLD platform makes finding the information you need quick and easy - whether you're a novice searcher or an experienced database user. All of Grey House's directory products are available for subscription on the GOLD platform.

18270 **www.actioncutprint.com**
Action-Cut-Print

Website for filmmakers, filmmaking resources, free ezine for directors, film and TV bookstore. The Director's Chair magazine by director Peter D. Marshall.

18271 **www.artdirectors.org**
Art Directors Guild

Conceive and manage the background and settings for most films and television projects.

18272 **www.asatalent.com**
ASA/Affordable Services

Entertainment services are brought to you as you need them and when you need them at the best price available. Security services, studio teachers, and medical services.

18273 **www.castingsociety.com**
Casting Society of America

An organization representing casting directors.

18274 **www.discoverhollywood.com**
Hollywood Arts Council

Promotes, nurtures and supports the arts field in Hollywood. Discover Hollywood on line.

18275 **www.documentary.org**
International Documentary Association

A nonprofit association founded to promote non-fiction film and video, to support the efforts of documentary film and video makers around the world, and to increase public appreciation and demand for the documentary.

18276 **www.greyhouse.com**
Grey House Publishing

Authoritative reference directories for most business sectors including motion picure and entertainment markets. Users can search the online databases with varied search criteria allowing for custom searches by product category, geographic area, sales volume, keyword, subject and more. Full Grey House catalog and online ordering also available.

18277 **www.iqfilm.org**
International Quorum of Film and Video Producers

Fosters the exchange of information and ideas. Seeks to raise professional standards. Disseminates information on new concepts and technology.

18278 **www.millimeter.com**
Millimeter Magazine

Authoritative resource for more than 33,000 qualified professionals in production, postproduction, animation, streaming and visual effects for motion pictures, television and commercials.

18279 **www.mpaa.org**
Motion Picture Association of America

Promotes high moral and artistic standards in motion picture production. Maintains Motion Picture Association Political Action Committee.

18280 **www.nyfa.com**
New York Film Academy

Educational institution devoted to providing focused filmmaking and acting instructions. Geared to offer an intensive, hands-on experience which gives students the opportunity to develop their creative skills to the fullest extent possible.

18281 www.oscars.org
Academy of Motion Picture Arts and Sciences

Current information on motion pictures, the arts and sciences, events and screenings.

18282 www.producersguild.com
Producers Guild of America

Members are producers of motion pictures and television shows mainly in the Los Angeles area.

18283 www.resumegenie.com

Motion Pictures job listings, salary information and job search tips.

18284 www.smpte.org
Society of Motion Picture & Television Engineers

Advances the practice and theory of engineering in television and film industry.

18285 www.stuntnet.com
International Stunt Association

Represents those involved in stunt work for the entertainment industry.

18286 www.stuntwomen.com
Stuntwomen's Association of Motion Pictures

A professional association for stuntwomen and stunt coordinators which seeks to uphold professional standards and improve working conditions.

18287 www.sundance.org
Sundance Institute

Nonprofit corporation dedicated to the support and development of emerging screenwriters and directors of vision. Hosts the Sundance Film Festival.

18288 www.wif.org
Women in Film

For global entertainment,communication and media industries. Focuses on contemporary issues facing women and provides an extensive network of valuable contacts, educational programs, scholars, film finishing funds, grants, community outreach, advocacy and practical services that promote, nurture and mentor women to achieve their highest potential.

Associations

18289 American Historic Racing Motorcycle Association
309 Buffalo Run
Goodlettsville, TN 37072
615-420-6435; *Fax:* 615-420-6438;
www.ahrma.org
Social Media: Facebook
Mark Hatten, Chairman
Matthew Benson, Communications Director
Mark Hatten, Treasurer
Rob Poole, Secretary
Carl Anderson, Treasurer
For individuals interested in vintage racing motorcycles.
5M Members
Founded in: 1989

18290 American Motorcyclist Association
13515 Yarmouth Dr
Pickerington, OH 43147-8273
614-856-1900
800-AMA-JOIN; *Fax:* 614-856-1920
tlindsay@ama-cycle.org;
www.americanmotorcyclist.com
Social Media: Facebook, YouTube
Rob Dingman, President
Maggie McNally, Chair
Perry King, Vice Chairman
Scott Papenfus, Marketing Director
Ken Ford, Assistant Treasurer
The association's purpose is to pursue, protect and promote the interests of motorcyclists, while serving the needs of its members.
270M Members
Founded in: 1924

18291 Antique Motorcycle Club of America
PO Box 663
Huntsville, AL 35804
256-509-9095
amcaExecutiveDirector@gmail.com
antiquemotorcycle.org
Social Media: Facebook, Instagram
Keith S. Kizer, Executive Director
The AMCA is the largest club of its kind in the United States.
11000 Members

18292 Breakdown & Legal Assistance for Motorcyclists
13047 Ventura Blvd
Suite 100
Studio City, CA 91604-2250
818-377-6280
800-424-5377; *Fax:* 818-377-6290
russbrown@russbrown.com;
www.russbrown.com
Social Media: Facebook, Twitter
J Russell Brown II, President
A support group for motorcyclists. Offers roadside assistance for emergencies and breakdowns. Attorney referral service specializing in motorcycle accident cases. Brochures and guest speakers available upon request, also offers a twenty-four hour toll-free hotline.
100M Members
Founded in: 1983

18293 Christian Motorcyclists Association
PO Box 9
Hatfield, AR 71945
www.cmausa.org
John Ogden Sr., Chairman & CEO
Interdenominational and evangelistic Christian ministry dedicated to reaching people for Christ through motorcycling.
Founded in: 1975

18294 Combat Veterans Motorcycle Association
www.combatvet.org
Non-profit organization of veteran motorcycle hobbyists whose charitable events raise money for veteran care facilities.
Founded in: 2001

18295 Harley Owners Group
National H.O.G. Office
PO Box 453
Milwaukee, WI 53201
800-258-2464; *Fax:* 414-343-4515;
www.harleydavidson.com
Social Media: Facebook, YouTube
James L Ziemer, President/CEO
Harley Davidson established the Harley Owners Group in response to a growing desire by Harley riders for an organized way to share their passion and show their pride.
60000 Members
Founded in: 1983

18296 Motorcycle & Moped Industry Council
716 Gordon Baker Road
Suite 100
North York, M2H 3B4, ON
416-491-4449
877-470-6642; *Fax:* 416-493-1985
info@mmic.ca; www.mmic.ca
Robert Ramsay, President
National nonprofit trade association which represents the responsible interest of the major motorcycle distributors, as well as the manufacturers, distributors and the retail outlets of motorcycle-related products and services, and individual owners and riders of motorcycles in Canada.
140 Members
Founded in: 1971

18297 Motorcycle Industry Council
2 Jenner Street
Suite 150
Irvine, CA 92618-3806
949-727-4211; *Fax:* 949-727-3313;
www.mic.org
Robert Moffit, Chairman
Tim Buche, President
David Kopf, Manager
A nonprofit national trade association created to represent the motorcycle industry.
Cost: $25.00
300 Members
Frequency: Annual
ISSN: 0149-3027
Founded in: 1914

18298 Motorcycle Riders Foundation
1325 G Street NW
Suite 500
Washington, DC 20005
202-546-0983; *Fax:* 202-546-0986
jeff@mrf.org; www.mrf.org
Kirk Willard, President
Mike Kerr, Vice President
Paulette Pinkham, Secretary
Chuc Coulter, Treasurer
Tiffany Latimer, Office Manager
To continue developing an aggressive, independent national advocate for the advancement of motorcycling and its associated lifestyle which is financially stable and exceeds the needs of motorcycling enthusiasts.
Founded in: 1987

18299 Motorcycle Safety Foundation
2 Jenner
Suite 150
Irvine, CA 92618-3812
949-727-3227
800-446-9227; *Fax:* 949-727-4217
MSF@msf-usa.org; www.msf-usa.org
Social Media: Facebook, Twitter, YouTube
Tim Buche, President
Founded by the five leading manufacturers and distributors of motorcycles for the purpose of public safety education.
7 Members
Founded in: 1972

18300 Women in the Wind
PO Box 8392
Toledo, OH 43605-0392
E-Mail: becky@womeninthewind.org;
www.womeninthewind.org
Becky Brown, Founder/Treasurer
Gale Collins, President
Lauranne Bailey, VP
Peggy Zeeb, Secretary
Seeks to promote a positive image for women motorcyclists. Educates members on maintenance and safety.
1000 Members
Founded in: 1979

Newsletters

18301 AHRMA Newsletter
American Historic Racing Motorcycle Association
PO Box 882
Wausau, WI 54402-0882
715-842-9699; *Fax:* 715-842-9545;
www.ahrma.org
Jeff Smith, Director
Matt Benson, Executive Director
David Lamberth, Executive Director
For individuals interested in vintage motorcycles.
Cost: $2.00
Circulation: 5,000

18302 MRF Reports
Motorcycle Riders Foundation
236 Massachusetts Ave Ne
Suite 204
Washington, DC 20002-4980
202-546-0983; *Fax:* 202-546-0986;
www.mrf.org
Eric Hampton, Editor/Publisher
Frequency: Bi-Monthly

Magazines & Journals

18303 American Motorcyclist
American Motorcyclist Association
13515 Yarmouth Dr
Pickerington, OH 43147-8273
614-856-1900
800-262-5646; *Fax:* 614-856-1920
membership@ama-cycle.org
http://www.americanmotorcyclist.com
Rob Dingman, President
Bill Wood, Editor-in-Chief
Grant Parsons, Managing Editor
John Holliday, Circulation

Magazine covers every facet of motorcycling. Each monthly issue details the people, places and events - from road rallies to road races - that make up the American motorcycling experience.
Cost: $39.00
Frequency: Monthly
Circulation: 260000
Founded in: 1924
Printed in 4 colors on glossy stock

18304 Biker
Paisano Publishers
PO Box 3075
Agoura Hills, CA 91376-3075

818-898-8740
800-962-985; *Fax:* 818-889-1252
easyridersevents.com

Joe Teresi, Publisher
Dean Shawier, Editor

Events and charity events for the motorcycle enthusiast.
Cost: $15.00
96 Pages
Founded in: 1971

18305 Cycle World
Hachette Filipacchi Media US
1499 Monrovia Ave
Newport Beach, CA 92663-2752

949-720-5300; *Fax:* 949-631-2374;
www.hfmus.com

Nancy Laporte, Executive Director
David Edwards, Editor-in-Chief

Publication for motorcycle enthusiasts.
Cost: $16.00
136 Pages
Frequency: Monthly
Circulation: 325000

18306 Cycling USA
United States Cycling Federation
1 Olympic Plz
Colorado Spring, CO 80909-5775

719-866-4581; *Fax:* 719-866-4628
web@usacycling.org; www.usacycling.org

Gerard Bisceglia, CEO
Sean Petty, Chief of Staff

Bike racing magazine.
Cost: $10.00
24 Pages
Circulation: 3000
Founded in: 1920

18307 Dealernews Magazine
Advanstar Communications
New York
New York, NY 10016-5778

212-951-6600
800-854-3112; *Fax:* 212-951-6793
info@advanstar.com; www.dealernews.com

Mike Vaughan, Publisher
Mary Slepicka, Associate Publisher
Arlo Redwine, Managing Editor

Written for and read by a qualified power sports dealer network and related industry associates. It features articles on merchandising, sales techniques and profiles of successful retailers. Industry trends and business conditions are monitored through exclusive industry research.
Frequency: Monthly
Circulation: 17535
Founded in: 1965
Printed in 4 colors on glossy stock

18308 Easyriders
Paisano Publishers
3547 Old Conejo Rd
Suite 106
Newbury Park, CA 91320

800-962-9857
800-825-7294; *Fax:* 805-375-4591
info@easyridersevents.com
easyridersevents.com

Joe Teresi, Publisher
Keith Ball, Editor
John Green, President

Motorcycle magazine.
Cost: $39.95
136 Pages
Frequency: Monthly
Founded in: 1971

18309 Motorcycle Dealer News
Edgell Communications
4500 Campus Drive
Suite 100
Santa Ana, CA 92705
Fax: 949-252-0499

Don Emde, Publisher

For dealers of power sports equipment and supplies.
Cost: $25.00

18310 Motorcycle Industry Magazine
Industry Shopper Publishing
PO Box 160
Gardnerville, NV 89410-160

775-782-0222
800-576-4624; *Fax:* 775-782-0266;
www.mimag.com

Rick Campbell, Publisher
Rick Campbell, Editor
Caroline Carr, Sales Manager

Provides information to the motorcycle and accessory dealer and or retailer on products, services, events and people aiming to maximize profitablity and growth, also includes personal watercraft vehicles, ATV's and snowmobiles.
Frequency: Monthly
Circulation: 14000
ISSN: 0884-626X
Founded in: 1976
Printed in 4 colors on glossy stock

18311 Shootin the Breeze
Women in the Wind
PO Box 8392
Toledo, OH 43605-0392

www.womeninthewind.org

Becky Brown, Founder
Gale Collins, President
Lauranne Bailey, VP
Peggy Zeeb, Secretary

Available to all Women in the Wind members.
Frequency: 6x/year

18312 The Antique Motorcycle
Antique Motorcycle Club of America
PO Box 3004
Westerville, OH 43086

740-803-2584
antiquemotorcycle.org

Greg Harrison, Editor
Paul Holdsworth, Director of Advertising

Official publication of The Antique Motorcycle Club of America, Inc.
Frequency: Bimonthly
Founded in: 2010

18313 Upshift Magazine
Motorcycle & Moped Industry Council
3000 Steeles Avenue East
Suite 201
Markham, Ontario L3R 4T9

416-491-4449
877-470-6642; *Fax:* 416-493-1985
info@mmic.ca; www.mmic.ca

Steve Thornton, Producer

Features articles and information on motorcycles.
Frequency: Quarterly

Trade Shows

18314 AMA Members Tour
American Motorcyclist Association
13515 Yarmouth Drive
Pickerington, OH 43147

614-856-1900; *Fax:* 614-856-1920
tlindsay@ama-cycle.org
http://www.americanmotorcyclist.com

Will Stoner, Director Special Events

The goal is to spread awareness of the benefits of membership and the importance of the work of the AMA does in protecting all motorcyclists' right to ride.
Frequency: Semi-Annual, June

18315 AMA Vintage Motorcycle Days
American Motorcyclist Association
13515 Yarmouth Drive
Pickerington, OH 43147

614-856-1900; *Fax:* 614-856-1920
tlindsay@ama-cycle.org;
www.amadirectlink.com

Will Stoner, Director Special Events

Will benefit the Motorcycle Hall of Fame Museum and will feature an exhibit of classic motorcycles and memorabilia.
Frequency: July

18316 Annual Meeting of the Minds
Motorcycle Riders Foundation
236 Massachusetts Avenue NE
Suite 510
Washington, DC 20002-4980

202-546-0983; *Fax:* 202-546-0986
downs@mrf.org; www.mrf.org

Carol Downs, Conference Director

Designed to educate and motivate those in the motorcyclists' rights community. The premier leadership conference that boasts an audience from across the nation and around the world.
Frequency: September

18317 Beast of the East
Motorcycle Riders Foundation
236 Massachusetts Avenue NE
Suite 510
Washington, DC 20002-4980

202-546-0983; *Fax:* 202-546-0986
downs@mrf.org; www.mrf.org

Carol Downs, Conference Director

Designed to educate and motivate those in the motorcyclists' rights community. These events are a great chance to meet other people who are as passionate about motorcyclists' rights as you are.
Frequency: April

18318 Best of the West
Motorcycle Riders Foundation
236 Massachusetts Avenue NE
Suite 510
Washington, DC 20002-4980

202-546-0983; *Fax:* 202-546-0986;
www.mrf.org

Carol Downs, Conference Director

Designed to educate and motivate those in the motorcyclists' rights community. These events are a great chance to meet other people who are as passionate about motorcyclists' rights as you are.
Frequency: June

18319 International Motorcycle Show
Advanstar Communications
201 E Sandpointe
Suite 600
Santa Ana, CA 92707
714-138-8400; *Fax:* 714-513-8481;
www.motorcycleshows.com
Jeff D'Entremont, Show Director
Leah Stevens, Account Manager
Chris Alonzo, Account Manager
Exposition for motorcyclists and enthusiasts.

18320 Los Angeles Calendar Motorcycle Show
Breakdown & Legal Assistance for Motorcyclists
13047 Ventura Boulevard
Suite 100
Studio City, CA 91604
323-321-1483
800-424-5377; *Fax:* 818-377-6290
russbrown@russbrown.com;
www.russbrown.com
Russ Brown, President
Biggest custom and performance streetbike event.
Frequency: July
Founded in: 1983

18321 Motocross American Reunion and Exhibit Grand Opening
American Motorcyclist Association
13515 Yarmouth Drive
Pickerington, OH 43147
614-856-1900
800-262-5646; *Fax:* 614-856-1920
americanmotorcyclist.com
Since 1924, the AMA has protected the future of motorcycling and promoted the cotorcycle lifestyle. As the world's largest motorcycling rights organization, the AMA advocates for motorcyclists' interests in the halls of local, state and federal government, the committees of international governing organizations, and the court of pulic opinion.
Frequency: July
Founded in: 1924

18322 Motorcycle and Parts
Glahe International
PO Box 2460
Germantown, MD 20875-2460
301-515-0012; *Fax:* 301-515-0016;
www.glahe.com
Exhibits of motorcycle equipment, supplies and services.

18323 Summer Nationals
Women in the Wind
PO Box 8392
Toledo, OH 43605-0392
www.womeninthewind.org
Becky Brown, Founder/Treasurer
Gale Collins, President
Lauranne Bailey, VP
Peggy Zeeb, Secretary
Frequency: July

Directories & Databases

18324 MSF Guide to Motorcycling Excellence
Motorcycle Safety Foundation
2 Jenner
Irvine, CA 92618-3812
949-727-3227; *Fax:* 949-727-4217;
www.msf-usa.org
Tim Buche, President
Covering the skills, knowledge and strategies for riding right. Subjects include: preparing yourself and your bike, developing street strategies, and advanced theory for experienced riders.
Cost: $24.95
176 Pages

18325 MilitaryBikers.org
www.militarybikers.org
Social Media: Facebook
Directory and discussion boards of military motorcycle clubs.

18326 Motorcycle Statistical Annual
Motorcycle Industry Council
2 Jenner Street
Suite 150
Irvine, CA 92618-3806
949-727-4211; *Fax:* 949-727-3313
This industry-related directory offers statistical information on US motorcycle manufacturers and distributors, as well as national and state motorcycle associations.
Cost: $25.00
Frequency: Annual
ISSN: 0149-3027

Industry Web Sites

18327 http://gold.greyhouse.com
G.O.L.D Grey House OnLine Databases
Grey House Publishing's online database platform, GOLD, offers Quick Search, Keyword Search and Expert Search for most business sectors including motorcycle and biking markets. The GOLD platform makes finding the information you need quick and easy - whether you're a novice searcher or an experienced database user. All of Grey House's directory products are available for subscription on the GOLD platform.

18328 www.ahrma.org
American Historic Racing Motorcycle Association
For individuals interested in vintage racing motorcycles.

18329 www.amadirectlink.com
American Motorcyclist Association
Covers every facet of motorcycling: the people, places and events that make up the American motorcycling experience. In addition, this award winning website offers profiles of issues affecting everyone who rides, and provides tools that help motorcyclists communicate directly with legislators, business leaders and the news media.

18330 www.greyhouse.com
Grey House Publishing
Authoritative reference directories for most business sectors including motocycle and biking markets. Users can search the online databases with varied search criteria allowing for custom searches by product category, geographic area, sales volume, keyword, subject and more. Full Grey House catalog and online ordering also available.

18331 www.mic.org
Motorcycle Industry Council
Nonprofit national trade association created to represent the motorcycle industry.

18332 www.mmic.ca
Motorcycle & Moped Industry Council
National nonprofit trade association which represents the responsible interest of the major motorcycle distributors, as well as the manufacturers, distributors and the retail outlets of motorcycle related products and services, and individual owners and riders of motorcycles in Canada.

18333 www.msf-usa.org
Motorcycle Safety Foundation
Founded by the five leading manufacturers and distributors of motorcycles for the purpose of public safety education.

18334 www.russbrown.com
Breakdown & Legal Assistance for Motorcyclists
A support group for motorcyclists. Offers roadside assistance for emergencies and breakdowns. Attorney referral service specializing in motorcycle accident cases. Brochures and guest speakers available upon request, also offers a twenty-four hour toll-free hotline.

Associations

18335 **AERA Engine Builders Association**
500 Coventry Lane
Suite 180
Crystal Lake, IL 60014

815-526-7600
888- 26-2372; *Fax:* 815-526-7601
info@aera.org; www.aera.org
Social Media: Facebook, Twitter

Rex B. Crumpton, Chairman
Steve Edmondson, First Vice Chairman
Bobby Kammerer, Second Vice Chairman
Steve Schoeben, Treasurer
Kevin Frische, Director

A specialized network of professional engine builders, rebuilders, production engine remanufacturers and installers.
Founded in: 1922

18336 **AUTOMOTIVE WHO'S WHO, Inc.**
AUTOMOTIVE WHO'S WHO, Inc
2899 East Big Beaver Road
#400
Troy, MI 48083

248-368-0200; *Fax:* 248-368-0202
info@automotivewhoswho.com;
www.automotivewhoswho.com

David M Bennett, Managing Director

Publishes an automotive original equipment suppliers directory and database for users by a wide range of industry professionals including top executives, site managers, engineers, buyers, consultants and researchers. The comprehensive directory covers the automotive manufacturing supply chain comprised of Tier I, II and III suppliers of parts, components, assemblies and related services.
Founded in: 1999

18337 **Advocates for Highway and Auto Safety**
750 1st St NE
Suite 901
Washington, DC 20002

202-408-1711; *Fax:* 202-408-1699
advocates@saferoads.org; www.saferoads.org
Social Media: Facebook, Twitter

Judith Lee Stone, President
Jacqueline Gillan, VP
Judie Pasquini, Director

An organization whose members advocate the support and advancement of highway and auto safety through the implementation of state and federal laws, programs and policies.
Founded in: 1989

18338 **Alliance of Automobile Manufacturers**
803 7th Street, N.W
Suite 300
Washington, DC 20001

202-326-5500; www.autoalliance.org
Social Media: Facebook, Twitter, YouTube, Google+, RSS

Mitch Bainwol, President/ CEO

An association of 12 of the largest car manufacturers, and is the leading advocacy group for the auto industry.

18339 **Alliance of State Automotive Aftermarket Associations**
5330 Wall Street
Suite 100
Madison, WI 53718

608-240-2066; *Fax:* 608-240-2069
info@asaaa.com; www.asaaa.com
Social Media: Facebook, Twitter, Google+, Pinterest

Skip Potter, President
Randy Lisk, VP
Gary Manke, Executive Director
Ben Welch-Bolen, CEO & Co-Owner
Tom Sepper, Chief Operating Officer

ASAAA consists of more than 10,000 members from both regional and state associations that support and represent the automotive aftermarket industry including that of parts and accessories, supplies and services.
10000 Members
Founded in: 1953

18340 **American Association of Motor Vehicle Administrators**
4301 Wilson Blvd
Suite 400
Arlington, VA 22203

703-522-4200; *Fax:* 703-522-1553
info@aamva.org; www.aamva.org
Social Media: Facebook, Twitter, LinkedIn, YouTube, Flickr

Neil D Schuster, President
Mark Saitta, VP
Claire O'Brian, Marketing

A nonprofit association that supports both state and provincial official members throughout North America who oversee the administration and enforcement of motor vehicle laws. Services include development and research in motor vehicle administration, law enforcement and highway safety as well as being an information clearinghouse.
Founded in: 1933

18341 **American Autoimmune Related Diseases Association**
22100 Gratiot Ave.
Eastpointe, MI 48021

586-776-3900
800-598-4668; *Fax:* 586-776-3900;
www.aarda.org
Social Media: Twitter, LinkedIn, YouTube

Betty Diamond, Chairperson
Noel R. Rose, Chairman Emeritus
Stanley M. Finger, Vice Chairperson
Virginia T. Ladd, President
John Kaiser, Treasurer

Includes patient information about autoimmunity and autoimmune related diseases.
Founded in: 1991

18342 **American Automobile Association**
1000 AAA Drive
Heathrow, FL 32746

407-444-4240
800-222-4357; *Fax:* 800-444-4247;
www.aaa.com

Robert Darbelnet, President
Jerry Cheske, Director Public Relations

Nation's largest motoring and leisure travel organization. AAA provides travel, insurance, financial and automotive related services. The not-for-profit, fully tax paying AAA has been a leader and advocate for the safety and security of all travelers.
45MM Members
Founded in: 1902

18343 **American Automotive Leasing Association**
675 North Washington Street
Suite 410
Alexandria, VI 22314

703-548-0777; *Fax:* 703-548-1925
sederholm@aalafleet.com; www.aalafleet.com

Pamela Sederholm, Executive Director
Traci Peters, Account Manager
Courtney Groff, Legislative Associate

A national industry association composed of commercial automotive fleet leasing and management companies.
Founded in: 1955

18344 **American Bus Association**
111 K Street NE
9th Floor
Washington, DC 20002

202-842-1645
800-283-2877; *Fax:* 202-842-0850
abainfo@buses.org; www.buses.org
Social Media: Facebook, Twitter, LinkedIn, YouTube

Thomas JeBran, Chair
John Meier, Vice Chair
Peter Pantuso, President & CEO
Frank Henry, Secretary/Treasurer

ABA supports 3,800 members consisting of motorcoach and tour companies in addition to organizations that represent the tourism and travel industry. ABA strives to educate consumers on the importance of highway and motorcoach safety.
Founded in: 1926

18345 **American Coatings Association**
1500 Rhode Island Ave., NW
Washington, DC 20005

202-462-6272; *Fax:* 202-462-8549
members@paint.org; www.paint.org
Social Media: Facebook, Twitter, LinkedIn, Hangout

J. Andrew Doyle, President/ CEO
Thomas J. Graves, Vice President
Allen Irish, Counsel/ Director
Jeff Wasikowski, Counsel
Nathan Perrine, CFO

18346 **American Highway Users Alliance**
1101 14th St NW
Suite 750
Washington, DC 20005-5608

202-857-1200; *Fax:* 202-857-1220
info@highways.org; www.highways.org
Social Media: Facebook, Twitter

Bill Graves, Chairman
Richard A. Coon, Vice Chairman
Thomas F. Jensen, Secretary
Roy E. Littlefield, Treasurer

A nonprofit trade association that actively advocates and promotes safe and uncongested highways and America's freedom of mobility.
Founded in: 1932

18347 **American International Automobile Dealers Association**
500 Montgomery Street
Suite 800
Alexandria, VA 22314

703-519-7800
800-462-4232; *Fax:* 703-519-7810
goaiada@aiada.org; www.aiada.org
Social Media: Facebook, Twitter, LinkedIn, YouTube

Jenell Rose, Chairwoman
Larry Kull, Chairman Elect
Bradley Hoffman, Vice Chair
Greg Kaminsky, Secretary/Treasurer

Lobbying and communications organization for American automobile dealerships that sell and service international nameplate brands.
11000 Members
Founded in: 1970

18348 **American Public Transportation Association**
1300IStreet NW
Suite 1200 East
Washington, DC 20005
202-496-4800; *Fax:* 202-496-4324
meetings2@apta.com; www.apta.com
Social Media: Facebook, Twitter, YouTube, Flickr, Blog
Michael Melaniphy, President & CEO
Petra Mollet, Chief of Staff
Rosemary Sheridan, VP, Marketing
Jeff Popovich, Chief Information Officer
Mary L. Childress, Chief Financial Officer
APTA is an international organization that supports and represents the transportation industry. Membership benefits include an annual association meeting, an international expo, membership directory, access to online publications, newsletters and electronic news service.
Founded in: 1882

18349 **American Society for Quality**
600 N Plankinton Avenue
PO Box 3005
Milwaukee, WI 53201-3005
414-272-8575
800-248-1946; *Fax:* 414-272-1734
help@asq.org; www.asq.org
Social Media: Facebook, Twitter, LinkedIn, YouTube, Google+
John C Timmerman, Chair
Paul E Borawski, CEO
Chava Scher, Treasurer
Fay Spano, Communications/Media Relations
An international organization with more than 90,000 members, the ASQ is an authoritative resource on quality that strives for improvement within the workplace and communities alike worldwide through the usage of advanced technology and training programs.
90M Members
Founded in: 1946

18350 **American Society of Body Engineers**
2122 15 Mile Rd
Suite F
Sterling Height, MI 48310-4853
586-268-8360; *Fax:* 586-268-2187
asbe@asbe.com; www.asbe.com
William Bonner, President
Jeff Grundy, Director
The American Society of Body Engineers is a non-profit corporation consisting of about 1,000 members within the industry including engineers, designers and suppliers. The organization strives to keep members current on the latest technological advancements within the field of automotive body engineering.
1000 Members
Founded in: 1945

18351 **American Trucking Association**
950 North Glebe Road
Suite 210
Arlington, VA 22203-4181
E-Mail: media@trucking.org; www.trucking.org
Social Media: Facebook, Twitter, YouTube, Flickr
Duane Long, Chairman
Pat Thomas, First Vice Chairman
Kevin W. Burch, Second Vice Chairman
Barry Pottle, Vice Chairman
Bill Graves, President
Founded in: 1933

18352 **Antique Automobile Club of America**
501 W. Governor Rd
P.O. Box 417
Hershey, PA 17033
717-534-1910; *Fax:* 717-534-9101
lgawel@aaca.org; www.aaca.org
Social Media: Facebook, YouTube
Don Barlup, President
Bob Parrish, Executive Vice President
Micky Bohne, Immediate Past President
John McCarthy, VP - Finance & Budget
Mel Carson, Secretary / Treasurer
America's premiere resource for the collectible vehicle community—includes publications, calendars, membership information, merchandise, photos, and forum.
Founded in: 1935

18353 **Antique Truck Club of America**
85 South Walnut Street
PO Box 31
Boyertown, PA 19512
610-367-2567; *Fax:* 610-367-9712
office@antiquetruckclub.org; www.antiquetruckclub.org
Social Media: Facebook
Fred Chase, President
Dave Lewis, Vice President
Tom Oehme, Treasurer
Mike Fowler, Secretary
An organization of persons who own or have an interest in antique commercial vehicles, and who wish to promote the preservation, restoration, operation and history of antique commercial vehicles.
Cost: $36.00
Frequency: Membership Fee
Founded in: 1971

18354 **Association for the Advancement of Automotive Medicine**
35 E Wacker Drive
Ste. 850
Chicago, IL 60601
847-844-3880; *Fax:* 312-644-8557
info@aaam.org; www.aaam.org
Social Media: LinkedIn
Frank A. Pintar, President
Brian N. Fildes, Immediate Past President
Gary A. Smith, President-Elect
Federico E. Vaca, Secretary
Kristy B. Arbogast, Treasurer
A professional multidisciplinary organization dedicated to limiting injuries from motor vehicle crashes.
Founded in: 1957

18355 **Association for the Advancement of**
PO Box 4176
Barrington, IL 60011-4176
847-844-3880; *Fax:* 847-844-3884
info@aaam.org; www.aaam.org
Frank A. Pintar, President
Gary A Smith, President Elect
Federico E Vaca, Secretary
Kristy B Arbogast, Treasurer
Founded in: 1957

18356 **Association of Diesel Specialists**
400 Admiral Boulevard
Kansas City, MO 64106
816-285-0810
888-401-1616; *Fax:* 847-770-4952
info@diesel.org; www.diesel.org
Chuck Oliveros, President
Carl Fergueson, VP
Al Roerts, Secretary
Laura Roundtree, Treasurer
The worldwide diesel industry's leading trade association, dedicated to the highest level of service on diesel fuel injection and related systems.
700+ Members
Founded in: 1956

18357 **Association of International Automobile Manufacturers**
1050 K Street, NW
Suite 650
Washington, DC 20001
202-650-5555; *Fax:* 703-525-8817
info@globalautomakers.org; www.globalautomakers.org
Social Media: Facebook, Twitter, RSS
Michael J Stanton, President
Ellen J Gleberman, Vice President/General Counsel
Jim Lentz, Chairman
John Mendel, Vice Chairman
Scott Becker, Treasurer
An international trade association that supports original equipment suppliers, automobile trade organizations and motor vehicle manufacturers. AIAM monitors government regulations and provides information and advocacy support relative to regulatory and legislative issues that directly affect the auto industry.

18358 **Auto Body Parts Association**
400 Putnam Pike
Suite J 503
Smithfield, RI 02917-2442
401-531-0809
800-323-5832; *Fax:* 401-262-0193
info@autobpa.com; www.autobpa.com
Dan Morrissey, Chairman
Jim Smith, President
Eric Taylor, Vice President
Michael Koren, Secretary
Dolores Richardson, Treasurer
An association of manufacturers, distributors, insurance and repair professionals which provide the collision repair industry with quality replacement parts.
140 Members
Founded in: 1980

18359 **Auto Care Association**
7101 Wisconsin Ave
Suite 1300
Bethesda, MD 20814-3415
301-654-6664; *Fax:* 301-654-3299
info@autocare.org; www.autocare.org
Social Media: Facebook, Twitter, Google+,YouTube
Richard Jago, Chairman
Michael Klein, Vice Chairman
Kathleen Schmatz, President & CEO
Mark Finestone, Vice President
Ira Davis, Secretary
Provides advocacy, educational, networking, technology, market intelligence and communications resources on auto care to its members.

18360 **Auto International Association**
7101 Wisconsin Avenue
Suite 1300
Bethesda, MD 20814
301-654-6664; *Fax:* 301-654-3299
aia@aftermarket.org; www.aiaglobal.org
Social Media: Facebook, Twitter, LinkedIn
Steve Bearden, Chair
Peter Klotz, Vice Chair
The Auto International Association (AIA) segment of the Automotive Aftermarket Industry Association promotes global trade in automotive products by providing a bridge between the inter-

national automotive community and the North American aftermarket.
Founded in: 1981

18361 Automatic Transmission Rebuilders Association
2400 Latigo Avenue
Oxnard, CA 93030

805-604-2000
866-464-2872; *Fax:* 805-604-2003
webmaster@atra.com; www.atra.com
Social Media: Facebook, Twitter, Google+

Dennis Madden, CEO
Jim Lyons, VP
Lance Wiggins, Director

Not-for-profit professional organization dedicated to the improvement and welfare of the automatic transmission repair industry for the benefit of the motoring public.
2000 Members
Founded in: 1954

18362 Automotive Aftermarket Industry Association
7101 Wisconsin Avenue
Suite 1300
Bethesda, MD 20814-3415

301-654-6664; *Fax:* 301-654-3299
info@autocare.org; www.autocare.org
Social Media: Facebook, Twitter, LinkedIn, Google+

Kathleen Schmatz, President
Susan Medick, COO & CFO
Rich White, Senior VP
Aaron Lowe, AAP, SVP, Regulatory & Gov. Affairs
Paul Fiore, Director, Government Affairs

A trade association consisting of more than 23,000 member companies and affiliates representing over 100,000 repair shops, distribution outlets, and parts stores.
23000 Members
Founded in: 1999

18363 Automotive Aftermarket Suppliers Association
PO Box 13966
Research Triangle Park, NC 27709-3966

919-549-4800; *Fax:* 919-549-4824
media@mema.org;
www.aftermarketsuppliers.org

Steve Handschuh, President
Bill Hanvey, Senior Vice President
Chris Gardner, Vice President
Ann Wilson, Senior Vice President
Margaret Beck, Senior Director

Automotive aftermarket supplier industry that provides a forum to address issues and resources that highlight the importance of purchasing quality parts backed by full-service suppliers.
Founded in: 1971

18364 Automotive Body Parts Association
400 Putnam Pike
Suite J 503
Smithfield, RI 02917-2442

401-531-0809
800-323-5832; *Fax:* 401-262-0193
info@autobpa.com; www.autobpa.com

Dan Morrissey, Chairman
Jim Smith, President
Eric Taylor, Vice President
Michael Koren, Secretary
Dolores Richardson, Treasurer

Members are companies that distribute, supply or manufacture automotive replacement body parts.
140 Members
Founded in: 1980

18365 Automotive Consulting Group
Automotive Consulting Group
4370 Varsity Dr.
Suite D
Ann Arbor, MI 48108

734-973-1110; *Fax:* 734-973-1118
acg@autoconsulting.com;
www.autoconsulting.com

Dennis Virag, President

Management consulting firm providing top line and bottom line business performance improvement services to the worldwide automotive industry.
Founded in: 1986

18366 Automotive Engine Rebuilders Association
500 Coventry Ln
Suite 180
Crystal Lake, IL 60014

815-526-7600
888-326-2372; *Fax:* 815-526-7601
info@aera.org; www.aera.org
Social Media: Facebook, Twitter

Rex B. Crumpton, Chairman
Steven Edmondson, First VC
Paul Hauglie, President
Steve Schoeben, Treasurer
Dwayne J. Dugas, Advisory Board Chairman

Network of specialists including production engine remanufacturers, installers, and professional engine rebuilders, provide services and support for the engine rebuilding industry.
Founded in: 1922

18367 Automotive Fleet and Leasing Association
N83 W13410 Leon Road
Menomonee Falls, WI 53051

414-386-0366; *Fax:* 414-359-1671
info@afla.org; www.afla.org
Social Media: Facebook, LinkedIn

Bill Elliott, Executive Director
Michael Bieger, President
Mary Sticha, Executive Vice President
Greg Haag, Communications & PR Manager

An organization consisting of more than 300 members that provides information, education and research on the fleet industry. Member benefits include annual conferences, educational seminars, the AFLA membership directory and more. The best source of information and contacts for automotive fleet and leasing professionals.
400 Members
Founded in: 1969

18368 Automotive Industry Action Group
26200 Lahser Road
Suite 200
Southfield, MI 48033-7100

248-358-3003; *Fax:* 248-799-7995
order_inquiry@aiag.org; www.aiag.org
Social Media: Facebook, Twitter

John Batchik, Chairman
David Kneisler, Vice Chairman
Scot Sharland, Executive Director

Composed of major North American vehicle manufacturers and their suppliers. Provides an open forum where members cooperate to develop and promote solutions that enhance prosperity in the automotive industry.
1000 Members
Founded in: 1982

18369 Automotive Lift Institute
80 Wheeler Ave
PO Box 85
Cortland, NY 13045

607-756-7775; *Fax:* 607-756-0888
info@autolift.org; www.autolift.org
Social Media: Facebook, Twitter, YouTube

Bob O'Gorman, President
Jeff Kritzer, Board of Directors

An association of manufacturers and distributors of automotive lifts used to raise motor vehicles for undercarriage work. Promotes awareness of safety measures used in operating lifts.
20 Members
Founded in: 1945

18370 Automotive Maintenance & Repair Association
725 E Dundee Road
Suite 206
Arlington Heights, IL 60004

847-947-2650; *Fax:* 202-318-0378
amra.org
Social Media: Facebook

Bill Ihnken, CEO
Chuck Abbott, Vice President, US Sales
Greg Dunkin, Vice President, Key Accounts
Amy Bonder, Vice President of Sales
Dennis Johndrow, Director of Compliance

A nonprofit trade association formally organized to represent the interests, common policies, and purposes of companies engaged in providing automotive maintenance and repair services, their suppliers, and related companies in the automotive industry when dealing with consumers.
Founded in: 1994

18371 Automotive Oil Change Association
330 North Wabash Avenue
Suite 2000
Chicago, IL 60611

312-321-5132
800-230-0702; *Fax:* 312-673-6832
info@aoca.org; www.aoca.org
Social Media: Facebook

Bryan White, President
David Haney, President
Dave Jensen, Vice President
Jim Grant, Secretary
Bob Falter, Treasurer

AOCA is a non-profit trade association that supports and represents more than 3,500 member facilities within the convenient automotive service industry. AOCA strives to educate consumers on the benefits of preventative auto maintenance, and the reliability of fast lube service centers.
3500 Members
Founded in: 1987

18372 Automotive Parts Remanufacturers Association
7250 Heritage Village Plaza
Suite 201
Gainesville, VA 20155

703-968-2772; *Fax:* 703-968-2878
info@apra.org; www.apra.org
Social Media: Facebook, Twitter, LinkedIn, YouTube

Omar Cueto, Chairman
Jay Robie, Vice President
Joe Kripli, President

Mission is to address the needs of the automotive and truck parts remanufacturing industry and to serve members by providing a wide range of quality products, services, workshops and education, through legislative advocacy, offering technical services, as well as arranging many

networking opportunities for members of the remanufacturing community.
1000 Members
Founded in: 1941

18373 Automotive Public Relations Council
Original Equipment Suppliers Association (OESA)
25925 Telegraph Rd.
Ste. 350
Southfield, MI 48033-2553

248-952-6401; *Fax:* 248-952-6404
info@oesa.org; www.oesa.org

Neil De Koker, President & CEO
Greg Janicki, Executive Director, Marketing

APRC is a professional organization for those within public relations that work in the automotive industry. Member benefits include access to industry news, discounted vendor services, and APRC conferences where members have the opportunity to meet and network with colleagues and practitioners in the automotive industry.
Founded in: 1998

18374 Automotive Recyclers Association
9113 Church St.
Manassas, VA 20110

571-208-0428
888-385-1005; *Fax:* 571-208-0430;
www.a-r-a.org
Social Media: Facebook, Twitter, Blog

Ricky Young, President
Mike Swift, First Vice President
RD Hooper, Second Vice President
Michael E. Wilson, Chief Executive
David Gold, Secretary

ARA is an international non-profit trade association with more than 3,000 members that supply equipment and services within the automotive recycling industry.
1000 Members
Founded in: 1943

18375 Automotive Service Association
8209 Mid Cities Blvd.
Suite 100
North Richland Hill, TX 76182-4712

817-514-2900
800-272-7467; *Fax:* 817-514-0770
asainfo@ASAshop.org; www.asashop.org
Social Media: Facebook, Twitter, LinkedIn

Donny Seyfer, AAM, Chairman
Roy Schnepper, Chairman Elect
Bill Moss, AAM, Secretary/Treasurer
Darrell Amberson, AAM, Immediate Past Chairman
John Cochrane, General Director

Leading organization for owners and managers of independent automotive service businesses that strive to deliver excellence in service and repairs to consumers.
8000 Members
Founded in: 1951

18376 Automotive Specialty Products Alliance
1667 K Street
NW Suite 300
Washington, DC 20006

202-862-3902; *Fax:* 202-223-2636
qbradley@consumered.org; www.inhalant.org
Social Media: Facebook, Twitter, YouTube

Colleen Creighton, Executive Director

Provides a unified industry voice for its members engaged in the automotive chemical and vehicle appearance product markets before state, regional and federal legislators and regulators.
Founded in: 1966

18377 Automotive Warehouse Distributors Association
7101 Wisconsin Avenue
Suite 1300
Bethesda, MD 20814-3415

301-654-6664; *Fax:* 301-654-3299
aaia@aftermarket.org; www.autocare.org
Social Media: Facebook, Twitter, LinkedIn, Google+

Kathleen Schmatz, President
Richard Jago, Chairman
Michael Klein, Vice Chairman
Mark Finestone, Treasurer
Ira Davis, Secretary

A trade association consisting of more than 600 members who are manufacturers and warehouse distributors, affiliates, marketing associations and others actively involved in the production, distribution and installation of motor vehicle parts, tools, services, accessories, equipment, materials and supplies. A segment of the Automotive Aftermarket Industry Association.
600 Members
Founded in: 1947

18378 Bearing Specialists Association
800 Roosevelt Rd
Bldg C, Suite 312
Glen Ellyn, IL 60137

630-858-3838; *Fax:* 630-790-3095
info@bsahome.org; www.bsahome.org
Social Media: Twitter, LinkedIn, RSS

Jack Simpson, President
Brian Negri, VP
Tim Breen, Treasurer
Jerilyn J. Church, Executive Secretary

BSA is a not-for-profit association that consists of companies that distribute factory-warranted ball, roller, and anti-friction bearings through authorized dealers. BSA provides members with the opportunity to network with others in the industry through meetings, seminars and educational programs at their annual convention.
100 Members
Founded in: 1966

18379 Brake Manufacturers Council
PO Box 13966
Research Triangle Park, NC 27709-3966

919-549-4800; *Fax:* 919-549-4824
media@mema.org;
www.aftermarketsuppliers.org

Frank Oliveto, Chairman
Walt Britland, Vice Chair
Terry Heffelfinger, Second Vice Chair
Jack Carney, Secretary
Bob Wilkes, Immediate Past Chairman

Obtaining and disseminating to members information on topics of interest to the brake parts industry.
Founded in: 1971

18380 California Autobody Association
P.O. Box 660607
Sacramento, CA 95866-0607

916-557-8100; *Fax:* 916-405-3529;
www.calautobody.com
Social Media: Facebook, LinkedIn

David Picton, 1st VP
Chuck Reyes, President

CAA is a non-profit trade association consisting of more than 1,000 members that support collision repair industry training and education with the goal of providing quality consumer repairs at reasonable prices.
1000+ Members
Founded in: 1967

18381 Car Care Council
7101 Wisconsin Ave
Suite 1300
Bethesda, MD 20814

240-333-1088; *Fax:* 301-654-3299
webmaster@aftermarket.org; www.carcare.org
Social Media: Facebook, Twitter, Pinterest, Instagram

Rich White, Executive Director
Ruth Elhinger, President

A nonprofit 501 (c) (3) educational foundation whose purpose is to educate motorists about the importance of maintenance repairs and entertainment for safer, cleaner, better-performing vehicles. Provides editorial and public service material for media use.
2000 Members
Founded in: 1968

18382 Center for Auto Safety
1825 Connecticut Ave NW
Suite 330
Washington, DC 20009-5708

202-328-7700; *Fax:* 202-387-0140;
www.autosafety.org

Clarence M Ditlow III, Executive Director

Provides consumers with advocacy support in Washington for auto quality and safety in addition to helping owners of unreliable vehicles by providing information relative to lemon laws, recalls, defect investigations, legislative issues in Congress and more.
15000 Members
Founded in: 1970

18383 Driving School Association of the Americas
3125 Wilmington Pike
Kettering, OH 45429

800-270-3722; *Fax:* 937-290-0696
info@thedsaa.org; www.thedsaa.org
Social Media: Facebook, Twitter

Charles Chauncy, President
Sheila Varnado, Executive VP
Robert Cole, Treasurer
Anthony Caracci, Secretary

A nonprofit organization for the purpose of raising the standards of educational methods in teaching drivers education, to promote traffic safety on the highways and streets, to publicize, inform and educate the general public to the need for more intensive driver training, safer roadways and all things relating there to.
58000 Members
Founded in: 1973

18384 Electric Auto Association
323 Los Altos Drive
Aptos, CA 95003
831-688-8669
contact@eaaev.org; www.electricauto.org
Social Media: Facebook

Ron Freund, Chairman
Marc Geller, Co-Chairman
Howard Clearfield, Treasurer
Guy Hall, Board Member
Terry Hershner, Board Member

A nonprofit educational organization that promotes the advancement and widespread adoption of battery electric vehicles.
Founded in: 1967

18385 Filter Manufacturers Council
10 Laboratory Drive
PO Box 13966
Research Triangle Park, NC 27709-3966

919-406-8846; *Fax:* 919-549-4824
jburkhart@mema.org;

www.aftermarketsuppliers.org
Social Media: Facebook

Steve Handschuh, President
Jack Cameron, VP

For manufacturers of vehicular and industrial filtration products in North America. Active in efforts to educate people on proper disposal of used oil filters.
Founded in: 1971

18386 Ford Dealers Alliance
401 Hackensack Avenue
Continental Plaza
Hackensack, NJ 07601

201-342-4542; *Fax:* 201-342-3997
fda@dealersalliance.org;
www.allianceford.com

A Michell Van Vorst, Executive Director
Edwin Mullane, President

Organization that strives to protect dealers against factory encroachment into retail.
15000 Members
Founded in: 1969

18387 Formula & Automobile Racing Association
786-571-6965
info@farausa.com; www.farausa.com
Social Media: Facebook, Twitter, YouTube, Instagram

Reinaldo "Tico Almeida, President
Carlos Mendez, Chief Operating Officer
Victor Leo, Driver Academy Director
Randy Almeida, Vice President
Bob Van Epps, Race Director

Provider of motorsports events for auto enthusiasts.

18388 Global Auto Makers
1050 K Street, NW
Suite 650
Washington, DC 20001

202-650-5555
info@globalautomakers.org;
www.globalautomakers.org
Social Media: Facebook, Twitter, RSS

Michael J Stanton, President & CEO
Ellen J Gleberman, Vice President/General Counsel
Scott Becker, Treasurer
David Zuchowski, Secretary
Michael J. Stanton, President & CEO

Working with industry leaders, legislators, regulators, and other stakeholders to create the kind of public policy that improves vehicle safety, encourages technological innovation, and protects the planet. Goal is to foster an open and competitive automotive marketplace that encourages investment, job growth, and development of more vehicles that enhance Americans' quality of life.
Founded in: 1961

18389 Global Automakers
1050 K Street, NW
Suite 650
Washington, DC 20001

202-650-5555
info@globalautomakers.org;
www.globalautomakers.org
Social Media: Facebook, Twitter, RSS

Jim Lentz, Chairman
John Mendel, Vice Chairman
John Bozella, Chief Executive Officer
David Zuchowski, Secretary
Scott Becker, Treasurer

A Washington, D.C.-based trade association and Lobby group whose members include international automobile and light duty truck manufacturers that design, build, and sell products in the United States.

18390 Golden Era Automobile Association
18021-150th Avenue East
Orting
Washington 98360

360-893-4227
AGW1886@aol.com; www.geaaonline.org

Henry Moebius, President

A car club that celebrates original cars, trucks, and motorcycles from 1915-1942 and World War II.

18391 Heavy Duty Manufacturers Association
10 Laboratory Drive
PO Box 13966
Research Triangle Park, NC 27709-3966

919-549-4800; *Fax:* 919-506-1465
info@hdma.org; www.hdma.org

Timothy R. Kraus, President
Jennifer Hjalmquist, Senior Director
Beth Barkovich, Director
Richard Anderson, Senior Market Research Analyst
Katelyn Litalien, Manager

Represents companies participating in the classes 4-8 medium and heavy truck original equipment and aftermarket parts manufacturing industry.
Founded in: 1983

18392 Independent Automotive Damage Appraisers Association
P.O. Box 12291
Columbus, GA 31917-2291

800-369-IADA; *Fax:* 888-IAD- NOW
admin@iada.org; www.iada.org

Mark Nathan, President
Bill Ambrosino, First Vice President
Michael E. Sellman, Secretary/ Treasurer
John Williams, Executive Vice President

Leader in the insurance/automotive industry in providing its members and the entire industry a forum for exchange of ideas and solutions to common problems in automotive appraisal and repair.
Founded in: 1947

18393 International Association of Auto Theft Investigators
PO Box 223
PO Box 223
Clinton, NY 13323-0223

315-853-1913; *Fax:* 315-883-1310
webmaster@iaati.org; www.iaati.org

John P O Byrne, President
John V Abounader, Executive Director
John V. Abounader, Executive Director

Formed to improve communication and coordination among the growing family of professional auto theft investigators.
4904 Members
Founded in: 1952

18394 International Automotive Technician's Network
640 W Lambert Road
Brea, CA 92821

714-257-1335
dmca-copyright@iatn.net; www.iatn.net
Social Media: Facebook, Twitter, LinkedIn

Monica Buchholz, Marketing

A group of professional automotive technicians from 153 countries who exchange technical knowledge and information with other members from around the world.
64601 Members

18395 International Carwash Association
230 East Ohio Street
uite 603
Chicago, IL 60611

888-422-8422
info@carwash.org; www.carwash.org
Social Media: Facebook, Twitter, LinkedIn

Gary Dennis, President
Pam Piro, Vice President
Eric Wulf, Chief Executive Officer
Claire Moore, Chief Operating Officer
Charnann Cox, Treasurer

A nonprofit trade group representing the retail and supply segmentsof the professional car wash industry in North America and around the globe.

18396 International Motor Press Association
4 Park Street
Harrington Park, NJ 07640

201-750-3533; *Fax:* 201-750-2010;
www.impa.org
Social Media: Facebook, Twitter

David Kiley, President
Mike Allen, First VP
Karl Greenberg, Second VP
Lisa Barrow, Secretary
Mike Geylin, Treasurer

Professional group of writers and editors producing auto articles for the press, radio or TV.

18397 International Show Car Association
1092 Centre Rd
Auburn Hills, MI 48326-2657

248-373-1700; www.theisca.com
Social Media: Facebook, Twitter

Bob Larivee, Owner
Bob Millard, General Manager

An organization of automotive enthusiasts who enjoy building, showing and viewing customs (cars, bikes and trucks), hot rods, competition cars, street machines and antique/restored vehicles.
Founded in: 1963

18398 Manufacturers of Emission Controls Association
2200 Wilson Blvd
Suite 310
Arlington, VA 22201

202-296-4797; *Fax:* 202-331-1388
asantos@meca.org; www.meca.org

Joseph Kubsh, Executive Director
Dr. Rasto Brezny, Deputy Director

Nonprofit association of the world is leading manufacturers of mobile source emission control manufacturers. Serves as a source of technical information on motor vehicle emission control technology.
Founded in: 1976

18399 Metropolitan Parking Association
299 Broadway
New York, NY 10007

212-406-3590

To promote and encourage ethical business practices among the operators of parking facilities, and to instill in public and non-public users of parking services confidence in the integrity and skills of parking operators.
400 Members
Founded in: 1981

18400 Micro-Reality Motorsports
PO 25 102 South Main Street
Cumberland, IA 50843

712-774-2577; *Fax:* 712-243-8552
nsei@metc.net; www.microreality.com

Kerry Namanny, President

Manufactures and promotes NASCAR micro-reality racing centers, plus several other sports and entertainment/promotions.
321 Members
Founded in: 1986

18401 Mobile Air Conditioning Society Worldwide
225 S Broad Street
PO Box 88
Lansdale, PA 19446

215-631-7020; *Fax:* 215-631-7017
macsworldwide@macsw.org; www.macsw.org
Social Media: Facebook, Twitter, LinkedIn, YouTube, Google+

Andrew Fiffick, Chairman
Gus Swensen, Vice Chair
Elvis Hoffpauir, President/COO
David Jack, Secretary
Peter Coll, Treasurer

Provides technical training, information and communication for the professionals in the automotive air conditioning industry.
1700 Members
Founded in: 1981

18402 Motor & Equipment Manufacturers Association
10 Laboratory Drive
PO Box 13966
Research Triangle Park, NC 27709-3966

919-549-4800; *Fax:* 919-406-1465
info@mema.org; www.mema.org
Social Media: Flickr

Steve Handschuh, President
Wendy Earp, Senior Vice President
Paul McCarthy, Vice President
Jo Anne Farr, Vice President
Leigh Merino, Senior Director

Represents more than 1,000 companies that manufacture motor vehiclecomponents and systems for the original equipment and aftermarket segments of the light vehicle and heavy-duty industries.

18403 Motor & Equipment Remanufacturers Association
25925 Telegraph Road
Suite 350
Southfield, MI 48033

248-750-1280; *Fax:* 248-750-1281
info@mera.org; www.mera.org
Social Media: Twitter, LinkedIn, YouTube, Instagram, Flickr

Shawn K. Zwicker, Chairman
Peter M. Butterfield, Vice Chairman
Michael Cardone Jr, Immediate Past Chairman
John R. Chalifoux, President & COO
Jack Vollbrecht, Senior Vice President

A trade group of many businesses, both large and small, in the remanufacturing industry.
Founded in: 1904

18404 Motor and Equipment Manufacturers Association
10 Laboratory Drive
PO Box 13966
Research Triangle Park, NC 27709-3966

919-549-4800; *Fax:* 919-406-1465
info@mema.org; www.mema.org
Social Media: Facebook, Twitter, LinkedIn, Flickr

Steve Handschuh, President
Robert E McKenna, CEO
Wendy Earp, CFO, Treasurer & Senior VP
Jo Ann Farr, VP, Human Resource

Serves manufacturers of all types of automotive and truck products through market research, legislative and regulatory representation and reporting, information services, industry networking and commercial services.
2000 Members
Founded in: 1904

18405 Motorcycle Industry Council
2 Jenner Street
Suite 150
Irvine, CA 92618-3806

949-727-4211; *Fax:* 949-727-3313
memberservices@mic.org; www.mic.org

A nonprofit, national trade association representing manufacturers and distributors of motorcycles, scooters, motorcycle/ATV parts and accessories.
Founded in: 1914

18406 NAFA Fleet Management Association
125 Village Boulevard Princeton Forrestal Villa
Suite 200
Princeton, NJ 08540

609-720-0882; *Fax:* 609-452-8004
info@nafa.org; www.nafa.org
Social Media: Facebook, Twitter, LinkedIn

Cluade T Masters, President
Ruth A Wolfson, Senior VP
Joanne Marsh, Director Marketing & Communications

Serving the needs of those managing fleets of automobiles, light duty trucks and/or vans for US and Canadian organizations. Offers statistical research, publications, including NAFA's Fleet Executive monthly magazine, regional meetings, government representation, conferences, trade shows and seminars.
3000+ Members
Founded in: 1957

18407 NARSA - The International Heat Transfer Association
3000 Village Run Road
Suite 103
Wexford, PA 15090-6315

724-799-8415; *Fax:* 724-799-8416
info@narsa.org; www.narsa.org

Maarten Taal, Chairman
Pat O' Connor, President
Mark Hicks, Vice President
Darlene Barlow, Secretary
Angelo Miozza, Treasurer

An association that has provided focus for the business of thermal management for transportation by providing commercial and technical forums that lead business development and product innovation for more than 58 years.
Founded in: 1954

18408 National Association of Automobile Museums
P.O. Box 271
Auburn, IN 46706

260-925-1444; *Fax:* 260-925-6266;
www.naam.museum

Terry Ernest, President
Mary Ann Porinchak, President Elect
Matthew G. Anderson, Secretary
Judy Endelman, Treasurer
Laura Brinkman, Executive Director

A professional center for automobile museums and affiliated organizations that supports, educates, and encourages members to operate according to professional standards of the museum industry.
Founded in: 1994

18409 National Auto Auction Association
5320 Spectrum Dr
Suite D
Frederick, MD 21703

301-696-0400; *Fax:* 301-631-1359
naaa@naaa.com; www.naaa.com
Social Media: Facebook, Twitter

Jack Neshe, President
Ellie Johnson, President-Elect
Mike Browning, Vice President
Frank Hackett, CEO
Steve McCannoughey, CFO

NAAA represents more then 317 auto auctions both domestic and international. With more than 8.9 million units sold each year. If there is one dominant theme that runs through the colorful history and phenomenal success of this entrepreneurial industry it is that auction business is all about people. NAAA is the net result of the people who pioneered and built it into one of the most respected trade associations in the world.
Founded in: 1948

18410 National Auto Body Council
7044 S. 13th St.
Oak Creek, WI 53154

414-908-4957; *Fax:* 414-768-8001;
www.nationalautobodycouncil.org
Social Media: Facebook, Twitter, YouTube

Nick Notte, President
Elizabeth Stein, Vice President
Brandon Devis, Past President
Rick E. Tuuri, Treasurer
Elizabeth Clark, Vice President

A nonprofit organization dedicated to promoting the professionalismand integrity of the collision industry through community service initiatives.
Founded in: 1990

18411 National Auto Sport Association
P.O. Box 2366
Napa Valley, CA 94558

510-232-6272; *Fax:* 510-277-0657
bizdev@drivenasa.com.prx2.unblocksit.es;
www.nasaproracing.com

An American motorsports organization promoting road racing and high-performance driver education.
Founded in: 1991

18412 National Automobile Dealers Association
8400 Westpark Drive
McLean, VA 22102

703-821-7000
800-252-6232
help@nada.org; www.nada.org
Social Media: Facebook, Twitter, LinkedIn, YouTube, Flickr

Forest McConnell, Chairman
William C Fox, Vice Chairman
Peter K Welch, President
Jeffrey B. Carlson, Secretary
George E. Nahas, Treasurer

Represents more than 19,700 new car and truck dealers, both domestic and international, with more than 43,000 separate franchises.
Founded in: 1917

18413 National Automotive Finance Association
7037 Ridge Road
Suite 300
Hanover, MD 21076-1343

410-712-4036
800-463-8955; *Fax:* 410-712-4038
inquire@nafassociation.com;

www.nafassociation.com
Social Media: LinkedIn

Asbel Perez-Viciedo, Chairman
Steve Hall, President
Scot Seagrave, Vice President
Ian Anderson, Vice President
Laurie Kight, Secretary
Founded in: 1996

18414 National Automotive Radiator Service Association
3000 Villiage Run Road
Suite 103, #221
Wexford, PA 15090-6315

724-799-8415
800-551-3232; *Fax:* 724-799-8416
info@narsa.org; www.narsa.org

Wayne Juchno, Executive Director
Douglas Shymoniak, Manager, Sales & New Business
Laressa Davis, Member Services Coordinator

Trade association serving the cooling system service industry and the public.
1500 Members
Founded in: 1953

18415 National Glass Association
1945 Old Gallows Rd
Suite 750
Vienna, VA 22182

703-442-4890
866-342-5642; *Fax:* 703-442-0630
administration@glass.org; www.glass.org
Social Media: Facebook, Twitter, LinkedIn

Nicole Harris, President & CEO
Nicole Harris, Vice President/Publisher
Tom Howhannesian, Chairman-Elect
Ken Mairotti, Treasurer
Michael Albert, Chairman

Provides information and education, as well as promote quality workmanship, ethics, and safety in the architectural, automotive and window and door glass industries. Acts as a clearinghouse for industry information, a catalyst in education and training matters, and a powerful voice on behalf of the members.
4000 Members
Founded in: 1948

18416 National Independent Automobile Dealers Association
2521 Brown Boulevard
Arlington, TX 76006-5203

817-492-2377
800-682-3837; *Fax:* 817-649-5866
mike@naida.com; www.niada.com

Karen Barbee, President
Michael R Linn, President
Steve Jordan, COO

Representing quality independent automobile dealers for almost 60 years. NIADA is here to assist members in becoming more successful within the used motor vehicle industry.
19000 Members
Founded in: 1946

18417 National Locksmith Automobile Association

630-837-2044
customerservice@thenationallocksmith.com;
www.thenationallocksmith.com
Social Media: Facebook

An organization of automotive specialists that service mechanical locks, produce duplicate keys of all types, and program transponders.

18418 National Motorists Association
402 W 2nd St
Waunakee, WI 53597

608-849-6000
800-882-2785; *Fax:* 888-787-0381
nma@motorists.org; www.motorists.org
Social Media: Facebook, Twitter

James Baxter, President
Gary Biller, Executive Director

Advocates, represents and protects the interests of North American motorists.
Cost: $35.00
Frequency: Annual Membership Dues
Founded in: 1982

18419 National Parking Association
1112 16th St NW
Suite 840
Washington, DC 20036

202-296-4336
800-647-7275; *Fax:* 202-296-3102
info@weareparking.org
weareparking.org
Social Media: Facebook, Twitter, LinkedIn, YouTube

Alan B. Lazowski, Chairman
Nicolle Judge, Chair Elect
Robert A. Zuritsky, Vice Chair
Frank Ching, Secretary
Christine Banning, President
Members are comprised of parking professionals in both the public and private sectors from across the country and around the world. NPA members are private operators, parking consultants, colleges and universities, municipalities, parking authorities, hospitals and medical centers and industry vendors.
2500 Members
Founded in: 1951

18420 National Truck Equipment Association
37400 Hills Tech Dr
Farmington Hill, MI 48331-3414

248-489-7090
800-441-6832; *Fax:* 248-489-8590
info@ntea.com; www.ntea.com
Social Media: Facebook, Twitter, LinkedIn, YouTube, Flickr, Instagram

James Carney, Executive Director
Frank Livas, First Vice President
Represents small to mid-sized companies that manufacture, distribute, install, buy, sell and repair commercial trucks, truck bodies, truck equipment, trailers and accessories.
1600 Members
Founded in: 1964

18421 National Wheel and Rim Association
3943-2 Baymeadows Road
Jacksonville, FL 32217

904-737-2900; *Fax:* 904-636-9881
info@cvsn.org; www.nationalwheelandrim.org

Dave Willis, President
Edward Neeley, Vice President
Andy Robblee, Treasurer
Angelo Volpe, Secretary/Executive VP

Represents warehouse distributors of wheels, rims and related parts.
230 Members
Founded in: 1924

18422 North American Automobile Trade Association
10 Four Seasons Place
10th Floor
Etobicoke, ON M9B 6H7

877-227-8878
naata@naata.org
naata.org
Social Media: Facebook, Twitter, LinkedIn, Flickr

Tahverlee Dunlop, President/ CEO
George Sahakian, Vice President
Andrew Pilsworth, Director
Jan Zurek, Director
Wouter VanEssen, Treasurer

Promotes the export of motor vehicles.
Founded in: 1996

18423 North American Council of Automotive Teachers (NACAT)
1820 Shiloh Road
Suite 1403
Tyler, TX 75703

903-747-8234; *Fax:* 843-556-7068
office@nacat.com; www.nacat.com
Social Media: Facebook, LinkedIn

Curt Ward, President
Patrick Brown-Harrison, Vice President/President Elect
Jim Voth, Secretary
Randy Nussler, Treasurer

Supports all educators in the automotive industry, with training and education, publications and seminars.
750 Members
Founded in: 1974

18424 Original Equipment Suppliers Association
25925 Telegraph Rd
Ste. 350
Southfield, MI 48033-2553

248-952-6401; *Fax:* 248-952-6404
info@oesa.org; www.oesa.org
Social Media: Facebook, LinkedIn, RSS

Julie A Fream, President &CEO
Neil De Koker, President Elect
Margaret Baxter, Senior VP, Operations
Dave Andrea, Senior VP, Industry Analysis
Glenn Stevens, Senior VP, Membership & Sales

Dedicated to advancing the business interests of companies supplying components, systems, modules, equipment, materials and services used in and by the original equipment automotive industry and to engage in activities in support of the welfare of the association membership. OESA is an affiliate of the Motor and Equipment Manufacturers Association.
340 Members
Founded in: 1998

18425 Overseas Automotive Council
10 Laboratory Drive
PO Box 13966
Research Triangle Park, NC 27709-3966

919-406-8854; *Fax:* 919-549-4824
bbrucato@aasa.mema.org;
www.aftermarketsuppliers.org
Social Media: Facebook, Twitter, LinkedIn

Mick Jordan, Chairman
Tim Vehlewald, 1st Vice Chair
Sharmila Kakac, Second Vice Chair
Ben Brucato, Executive Director
Bill Long, Managing Director

One of the oldest and most unique organizations in the global automotive aftermarket. Mission is to promote the sale of automotive products and services exported from North America, to enhance the prestige and goodwill of the global automotive aftermarket industry, to promote friendly trade relationships, cultural understanding and mutually beneficial cooperation among those engaged in the automotive aftermarket industry.
500+ Members
Founded in: 1923

18426 Performance Warehouse Association
41-701 Corporate Way
Suite 1
Palm Desert, CA 92260

760-346-5647; *Fax:* 760-346-5847;
www.pwa-par.org

Larry Pacey, Chairman
Ken Woomer, Chairman Elect
Trent Lowe, Treasurer

An organization of specialty automotive parts wholesalers joined together and dealing with management, financial and legislative matters.
10000 Members
Founded in: 1971

18427 Production Engine Remanufacturers Association
PO Box 250
Colleyville, TX 76034-0250

817-243-2646; *Fax:* 417-998-5056
jeopolich@pera.org; www.pera.org
Social Media: Facebook, LinkedIn

Nancie J. Boland, Executive VP
Robert P. McGraw, President

The Production Engine Remanufacturers Association is an association of individual and firm who remanufacture internal combustion enhgines or their major components or supply necessay components, supplies and eqipment required in the manufacturing process. The goal of PERA is to provide members with the opportinity to exchange ideas, methods and procedures necessary to efficiently produce remanufactured products which are equal or superior to origianl products in quality and performance.
Founded in: 1946

18428 Recreation Vehicle Dealers Association
3930 University Dr
Suite 300
Fairfax, VA 22030-2515

703-591-7130; *Fax:* 703-359-0152
info@rvda.org; www.rvda.org
Social Media: Facebook, Twitter, LinkedIn, YouTube

Mike Molino, President
Ronnie Hepp, VP of Administration
Hank Fortune, Director of Finance
Susan Charter, Associate Services Manager
John McCluskey, Chairman

National association advances the best interests of RV retailers through education, services, leadership and programs of market expansion that promote increased use and sale of RVs while enhancing their image.

18429 Recreational Vehicle Aftermarket Association
54 Westerly Road
Camp Hill, PA 17011

717-730-0300; *Fax:* 630-544-5055
ellenkietzmann@blueox.us;
www.rvaftermarket.org

Ellen Kietzmann, President
Ron Dempster, VP
Jess Fowler, Secretary
Bill Fudale, Treasurer

An organization for the suppliers, distributors and agents that represent the aftermarket segment of the RV industry.
110 Members
Founded in: 1969

18430 Retread and Repair Information Bureau
1013 Birch Street
Falls Church, VA 22046

703-533-7677
877-394-6811; *Fax:* 703-533-7678
info@retread.org; www.retread.org
Social Media: Facebook, Twitter, LinkedIn

David Stevens, Managing Director
Bob Majewski, President

Serving as the public relations arm of the retread industry. Gathering and disseminating information on retread passenger and truck tires to members and the general public.
500 Members
Founded in: 1973

18431 Rubber Manufacturers Association
1400 K St NW
Suite 900
Washington, DC 20005

202-682-4800; *Fax:* 202-682-4854
info@rma.org; www.rma.org
Social Media: Facebook, Twitter, YouTube

Charlie Cannon, President, CEO
Tracey Norberg, Senior VP
Dan Zielinski, Senior VP

National trade association for makers of tires and other rubber products.
100 Members

18432 Service Specialists Association
1221 Candlewick Dr NW
Suite 2B
Poplar Grove, IL 61065

847-760-0067
800-763-5717; *Fax:* 330-722-5638
trucksvc@aol.com; www.truckservice.org
Social Media: Facebook

Matt Thompson, President
Sean Ryan, Vice President
Toni Nastali, Treasurer
Billy Burkholder, Director
Nancy Hodges, Director

Members are persons, firms or corporations who have operated a full line heavy duty repair service shop for at least one year with sufficient inventory to service market area, having rebuilding department capable of making all necessary repairs.
140 Members
Founded in: 1981

18433 Society of Automotive Engineers
SAE Automotive Headquarters
755 W Big Beaver
Suite 1600
Troy, MI 48084-4906

724-776-4841
877-606-7323; *Fax:* 248-273-2494
CustomerService@sae.org; www.sae.org
Social Media: Facebook, Twitter, LinkedIn, Google+

Donald J Hillebrand, President
Mircea Gradu, VP, Automotive
Carol Story, Treasurer
David Schutt, CEO

Offers automotive engineers the technical information and expertise used in building, maintaining and operating self propelled vehicles for use on land, sea, air or space.
84000 Members
Founded in: 1905

18434 Society of Automotive Historians

E-Mail: webmaster@autohistory.org;
www.autohistory.org

Andrew Beckman, President
Edward Garten, Vice President
Bob Ebert, Secretary
Robert G. Barr, Director
Vince Wright, Director

Encourages research, preservation, recording, compilation, and publication of historical facts concerning the development of the automobile and related items throughout the world.
Founded in: 1969

18435 Society of Collision Repair Specialists
PO Box 909
Prosser, WA 99350

877-841-0660
877-841-0660; *Fax:* 877-851-0660
info@scrs.com; www.scrs.com
Social Media: Facebook, Twitter

Andy Dingman, Chairman
Kye Yeung, Vice Chair
Bruce Halcro, Treasurer
Brett Bailey, Secretary
Aaron Schulenburg, Executive Director

For owners and managers of auto collision repair shops, suppliers, insurance and educational associates and suppliers in the US, Canada, Australia and New Zealand. Distributes technical, management, marketing and sales information. Works to promote professionalism within the collision repair industry.
Founded in: 1983

18436 Society of Independent Gasoline Marketers of America
3930 Pender Drive
Suite 340
Fairfax, VA 22030

703-709-7000; *Fax:* 703-709-7007
sigma@sigma.org; www.sigma.org

Kenneth Doyle, Executive VP
Thomas Schmidt, First VP
Brian Beaver, Second VP

Supports independent fuel marketers and suppliers, providing training and education, publications and seminars.
250 Members
Founded in: 1958

18437 Specialty Equipment Market Association
1575 South Valley Vista Drive
Diamond Bar, CA 91765-0289

909-610-2030; *Fax:* 909-860-0184
sema@sema.org; www.sema.org
Social Media: Facebook, Twitter, Google+, Tumblr

Doug Evans, Chairman
Wade Kawasaki, Chair Elect
Christopher J Kirsting, President & CEO

This trade association consists of a diverse group of manufacturers, distributors, retailers, publishing companies, auto restorers, street rod builders, restylers, car clubs, race teams and more.
5700+ Members
Founded in: 1963

18438 The Aluminum Association
1400 Crystal Dr.
Suite 430
Arlington, CA 22202

703-358-2960
info@aluminum.org; www.aluminum.org
Social Media: Facebook, Twitter, LinkedIn

Heidi Brock, President
Karen Bowden, VP, Finance & Administration
Joe Quinn, VP, Public Affairs
Charles Johnson, VP, Policy
Ryan Olsen, VP, Business Info. & Statistics

The Aluminum Association's Aluminum Transportation Group promotes the use of aluminum in automobile and commercial vehicle manufacturing.

18439 The Recreation Vehicle Industry Association
1896 Preston White Drive
Reston, VA 20191

703-620-6003; *Fax:* 703-620-5071;
www.rvia.org

Derald Bontrager, Chairman
Robert L. Parish, First Vice Chairman
Garry Enyart, Second Vice Chairman
Kevin Phillips, Secretary
Matthew Miller, Treasurer
Founded in: 1963

18440 Tire Industry Association
1532 Pointer Ridge Pl
Suite G
Bowie, MD 207161883

301-430-7280
800-876-8372; *Fax:* 301-430-7283
info@tireindustry.org; www.tireindustry.org
Social Media: Facebook, Twitter, LinkedIn

Jason Littlefield, Executive VP
Bob Bignell, Executive Director

Representing all segments of the tire industry, including those that manufacture, repair, recycle, sell, service or use new or retreaded tires, and also those suppliers or individuals who furnish equipment, material or services to the industry.
5000 Members
Founded in: 2002

18441 Tire and Rim Association
175 Montrose West Ave
Suite 150
Copley, OH 44321-2793

330-666-8121; *Fax:* 330-666-8340
tra@us-tra.org; www.us-tra.org

Joseph Pacuit, Executive VP

Technical standardizing organization for tire, rim and valve manufacturers.
110 Members
Founded in: 1903

18442 Triangle Electric Auto Association
3702 Burwell Rollins CIR
Raleigh, NC 27612-5239

E-Mail: pppayments@rtpnet.org;
www.rtpnet.org

An association focused on the conversion of gas cars into electric cars.
Founded in: 1990

18443 United States Auto Club
USAC National Office
4910 West 16th Street
Speedway, IN 46224-0001

317-247-5151; *Fax:* 317-248-5584;
www.usacracing.com
Social Media: Facebook, Twitter

Kevin Miller, President

Supports all driving professionals and consumers with education, publications, driving and vacation tips. Publishes monthly magazine.

18444 United States Council for Automotive Research
1000 Town Center Drive
Suite 300
Southfield, MI 48075

248-223-9000; www.uscar.org

Steve Zimmer, Executive Director
Matt Liddane, Vice President
Paul Mascarenas, Chief Technical Officer
Jon Lauckner, Council Member

The collaborative automotive technology company for Chrysler Group LLC, Ford Motor Company, and General Motors.
Founded in: 1992

18445 Womens Automotive Association International
PO Box 2535
Birmingham, MI 48012

248-646-5250; *Fax:* 248-387-3550
lhswaai@aol.com; www.waai.com

Lorraine H Schultz, Founder/CEO
Lynn M. Wilhelm, Executive Director
Jennifer Michael, Treasurer
Ellen Mckoy, Vice President
Jody DeVere, Vice President

Dedicated to the development and advancement of women as automotive industry leaders. Today, the organization continues to thrive throughout the United States and Canada as the leading women's global organization dedicated to this purpose.
600 Members
Founded in: 1995

Newsletters

18446 AIAG e-News Brief
Automotive Industry Action Group
26200 Lahser Road
Suite 200
Southfield, MI 48033-7100

248-358-3570; *Fax:* 248-358-3253
inquiry@aiag.org; www.aiag.org

John Batchik, Chairman
David Kneisler, Vice Chairman
J. Scot Sharland, Executive Director

Global automotive industry news, member succes stories and need to know information on AIAG products and events.
1000 Members
Frequency: Monthly
Founded in: 1982

18447 Automotive Market Report
Automotive Auction Publishing
607 Laurel Drive
Monroeville, PA 15146-4405
412-373-6383; *Fax:* 412-373-6388

Clyde K Hillwig, Publisher

News items pertinent to auto auctions and the auto industry.
Frequency: BiWeekly
Circulation: 10000

18448 Automotive Week: Greensheet
Molinaro Communications
PO Box 355
Munroe Falls, OH 44262-0355

330-688-4960
877-694-6076; *Fax:* 866-926-0452
gary@thegreensheetonline.com;
www.thegreensheetonline.com

Gary Molinaro, Publisher/Editor
Marc Vincent, Managing Editor

Intelligence concerning the $270 billion independent automotive aftermarked. Breaking news & analysis not available anywhere else in the industry. Key moves in the retail and wholesale distribution channels, mergers & acquisitions; financial analysis of publicly-traded entities. Classified, non-product advertising accepted.
Cost: $225.00
4 Pages
Frequency: 48 issues
ISSN: 0889-3918
Founded in: 1975
Printed in on matte stock

18449 Car Dealer Insider
United Communications Group
9737 Washingtonian Blvd.
Suite 100
Gaithersburg, MD 20878-7364

301-287-2700; *Fax:* 301-287-2039;
www.ucg.com

Jill Gardner, Publisher
Donna Lawrence, Editor
Bruce Levenson, Co-Founder
Nancy Becker, Partner, President

Marketing intelligence for new car dealers includes dealer-tested tactics, best management practices and breaking news stories.
Frequency: Bi-Monthly
Founded in: 1977

18450 Chek-Chart Service Bulletin
Motor Information Systems/Chek-Chart
1301 W Long Lake Rd
Suite 200
Troy, MI 48098-6349

248-828-0000
800-426-6867; *Fax:* 248-828-0215

Paul M Eckstein, Manager
Anthony Mattar, Owner

Up-to-date information on all the new automotive developments from the car manufacturers. Information bulletin for service station dealers, mechanics, and instructors. Chek/Chart is part of MotorInformation Systems.

18451 EngiNEWS
Production Engine Remanufacturers Association
28203 Woodhaven Road
Edwards, MO 65326

417-998-5057; *Fax:* 417-998-5056
nancieboland@pera.org; www.pera.org
Social Media: Facebook, LinkedIn

Nancie J. Boland, Exutive VP
Robert P. McGraw, President

An semi-annual e-newsletter covering problems from airline fees to the amount of cars on the road and postives of new businesses involved in remanufacturing.
Frequency: Quarterly
Founded in: 1946
Mailing list available for rent: 200 names

18452 Executive Directors Report
Society of Collision Repair Specialists
PO Box 909
Prosser, WA 99350

509-735-0607
877-841-0660; *Fax:* 877-851-0660
info@scrs.com; www.scrs.com

Aaron Schulenburg, Executive Director
Luis Alonso, Treasurer
Linda Atkins, Administrative Assistant

Newsletter for owners and managers of auto collision repair shops, suppliers, insurance and educational associates and suppliers in the US, Canada, Australia and New Zealand. Technical, management, marketing and sales information. Free to members.
Frequency: Bi-Annually
Circulation: 6000
Founded in: 1982

18453 FirstUp: Daily News
American Int'l Automobile Dealers Association
211 N Union St
Suite 300
Alexandria, VA 22314-2643

703-519-7800
800-462-4232; *Fax:* 703-519-7810
goaiada@aiada.org; www.aiada.org
Social Media: Twitter

Jim Smail, Chairman
Ray Mungenast, Chairman-Elect

Jenell Ross, Vice Chair
Larry Kull, Secretary/ Treasurer
Cody Lusk, President

Conveys the day's auto-related news quickly, concisely, and accurately. Topics covered in FirstUp range from new vehicle releases, to the latest legislation concerning the auto industry.
11M+ Members
Frequency: Daily
Circulation: 30000
Founded in: 1970

18454 Fleet Administration News
PO Box 159
Litchfield Park, AZ 85340

623-772-9096; *Fax:* 623-772-9098
ncsfa.wildapricot.org

Joe O'Neill, Executive Director

NCSFA members are state government administrators responsible for vehicle fleet management.
Cost: $50.00
Frequency: Quarterly
Printed in on matte stock

18455 Fleet Perspectives
National Association of Fleet Administrators
125 Village Boulevard
Suite 200
Princeton, NJ 08540

609-720-0882; *Fax:* 609-452-8004
info@nafa.org; www.nafa.org
Social Media: Facebook, Twitter, LinkedIn

Phillip E. Russo, Executive Director
Patrick McCarron, Deputy Executive Director
Joanne Marsh, Director Marketing & Communications

Official e-newsletter for Public Service and Corporate fleet managers. Contains special profiles on NAFA Members, important fleet news, and informative articles that won't be found anywhere else.
3000+ Members
Frequency: Quarterly
Founded in: 1957

18456 FleetFOCUS
National Association of Fleet Administrators
125 Village Boulevard
Suite 200
Princeton, NJ 08540

609-720-0882; *Fax:* 609-452-8004
info@nafa.org; www.nafa.org
Social Media: Facebook, Twitter, LinkedIn

Phillip E. Russo, Executive Director

The focus for quick-reading highlights designed to give professional fleet managers the latest industry news.
2600+ Members
Frequency: Bi-Weekly

18457 Highway & Vehicle/Safety Report
Stamler Publishing Company
178 Thimble Island Road
PO Box 3367
Branford, CT 06405-1967

203-488-9808
800-422-4121; *Fax:* 203-488-3129;
www.trafficsafetynews.com

S Paul Stamler, Publisher
Suzanne Reutenauer, Circulation Manager

Business to business newsletter on the latest developments in transportation safety, regulations and new legislation, and new technology in the automotive industry.
Cost: $467.00
Frequency: Monthly
Founded in: 1973

18458 Highway Users In Action
American Highway Users Alliance
1101 14th St NW
Suite 750
Washington, DC 20005

202-857-1200; *Fax:* 202-857-1220
info@highways.org; www.highways.org
Social Media: Facebook, Twitter, YouTube

Bill Graves, Chairman
Richard A. Coon, Vice Chairman
Thomas F. Jensen, Secretary
Roy E. Littlefield, Treasurer

e-Newsletter with the latest, most recent Highway Users work on behalf of membership. Offers information affecting members.
Frequency: Bi-Annually
Founded in: 1932

18459 Hybrid & Electric Vehicle Progress
Alexander Communications Group
1916 Park Ave
8th Floor
New York, NY 10037-3733

212-281-6099
800-232-4317; *Fax:* 212-283-7269;
www.evprogress.com

Romauld Alexander, Owner
Laurence Alexander, CEO

News of hybrid and electric vehicle commercialization. Worldwide coverage focuses on news and data on both the technical and business aspects of the hybrid or electric vehicle industry.
Cost: $477.00
8 Pages
Frequency: Fortnightly
Circulation: 800
ISSN: 0190-4175
Founded in: 1954
Printed in 2 colors on matte stock

18460 IMPACT
International Motor Press Association
4 Park Street
Harrington Park, NJ 07640

201-750-3533; *Fax:* 201-750-2010
mike@jalopnik.com; www.impa.org

Mike Spinelli, President
John Matras, First VP
Mike Allen, Second VP
Frequency: Monthly

18461 Independent Gasoline Marketing (IGM)
Soc. of Independent Gasoline Marketers of America
3930 Pender Drive
Suite 340
Fairfax, VA 22030

703-709-7000; *Fax:* 703-709-7007
sigma@sigma.org; www.sigma.org

Kenneth Doyle, Executive VP
Marilyn Selvitelle, VP

Information for independent fuel marketers and suppliers on legislative issues, new market trends, equipment use and management techniques.
32 Pages
Circulation: 4000
Founded in: 1958
Printed in 4 colors on glossy stock

18462 Lemon Times
Center for Auto Safety
1825 Connecticut Ave NW
Suite 330
Washington, DC 20009-5725

202-328-7700; *Fax:* 202-387-0140;
www.autosafety.org

Clarence M Ditlow III, Executive Director
Sanja Pesek, Editor

Reports on the auto safety world of CAS, as well as covering safety litigation, secret warranties, crash tests, lemon laws, recalls, federal and state investigations.
Cost: $20.00
15000 Members
Frequency: Quarterly
Founded in: 1970

18463 Market Watch
AIADA
211 N Union St
Suite 300
Alexandria, VA 22314-2643

800-462-4232; *Fax:* 703-519-7810
goaiada@aiada.org; www.aiada.org
Social Media: Twitter

Jim Smail, Chairman
Ray Mungenast, Chairman-Elect
Jenell Ross, Vice Chair
Larry Kull, Secretary/ Treasurer
Cody Lusk, President

Emailed report providing a succinct rundown of the latest industry sales numbers and data. A summary of monthly trends, accompanied by easy-to-read charts and graphs, allows readers to track trends, note milestones, and react quickly to a shifting auto market.
11M+ Members
Frequency: Monthly
Founded in: 1970

18464 Motor
Hearst Business Communications
567 Robbins Dr
Suite 200
Troy, MI 48083-4515

248-585-1700; *Fax:* 248-828-7004
jlypen@motor.com; www.motor.com

Duane Harrison, Owner
Kevin Carr, President
Paul Moszak, Vice President/General Manager
Lori Aemiseqqer, Marketing
Richard Laimbeer, Publisher

Articles to keep readers up to date on the latest diagnostic techniques and service procedures. Management articles to help shop owners increase profitability, latest tools available, new products and industry news.
Cost: $48.00
Frequency: Monthly
Circulation: 138941
Founded in: 1903

18465 NACAT News
North American Council of Automotive Teachers
PO Box 80010
Charleston, SC 29416

843-556-7068; *Fax:* 843-556-7068
office@nacat.com; www.nacat.com

Patrick Brown Harrison, President
Rob Thompson, Vice President

Cutting edge automotive information for automotive educators. Also news of the organization and the automotive industry.
Circulation: 750
Founded in: 1974

18466 NAFA Fleetfocus
National Association of Fleet Administrators
125 Village Boulevard
Suite 200
Princeton, NJ 08540

609-720-0882; *Fax:* 732-494-6789
info@nafa.org; www.nafa.org

Philip Russo, Executive Director
Patrick McCarren, Deputy Executive Director
Joanne Marsh, Director Marketing

The focus for quick rading highlights designed to give professional fleet managers the latest industry news.
3000+ Members
Frequency: Weekly
Circulation: 3600
Founded in: 1946
Printed in one color on matte stock

18467 NPA NewsBrief
National Parking Association
1112 - 16th St NW
Suite 840
Washington, DC 20036-4880

202-296-4336
800-647-7275; *Fax:* 202-296-3102
info@weareparking.org
weareparking.org

Weekly newsletter offering updates and industry news for members.
Frequency: Weekly

18468 NPA eNews
National Parking Association
1112 - 16th St NW
Suite 840
Washington, DC 20036-4880

202-296-4336
800-647-7275; *Fax:* 202-296-3102
info@weareparking.org
weareparking.org

Montly electronic newsletter providing information on industry meetings, leadership opportunities, and industry updates and news.
Frequency: Monthly

18469 News & Views
Bearing Specialists Association
800 Roosevelt Road
Building C, Suite 312
Glen Ellyn, IL 60137

630-858-3838; *Fax:* 630-790-3095
info@bsahome.org; www.bsahome.org
Social Media: LinkedIn

Linda Miller, President
Richard W Church, Executive Director
Jerilyn J Church, Executive Secretary

Monthly newlsetter of BSA, the forum to enhance networking and knowledge sharing to promote the sale of bearings through authorized distributors. Available to members only.
100 Members
Frequency: E-Newlsetter for Members
Circulation: 400
Founded in: 1966

18470 Nozzle Chatter
Association of Diesel Specialists
400 Admiral Boulevard
Kansas City, MO 64106

816-285-0810; *Fax:* 847-770-4952
info@diesel.org; www.diesel.org
Social Media: Facebook, LinkedIn

Chuck Hess, President
Andy Girres, Vice President
Chuck Oliveros, Treasurer
Carl Fergueson, Secretary
David Fehling, Executive Director

Member benefit focusing on a variety of news, tips and information on the diesel industry. Contains information that will encourage the exchange of ideas among members; provides a forum for discussion and debate; allow for the fostering of new relationships and contacts; provide members with the knowledge and expertise of colleagues; and provide immediate access to information concerning training materials and publications through monthly reviews.
700+ Members
Frequency: Monthly
Founded in: 1956

18471 OAC Global Report
Overseas Automotive Council
PO Box 13966
Research Triangle Park, NC 27709-3966

919-549-4800; *Fax:* 919-549-4824
media@mema.org; www.tune-up.org

Margaret Beck, Senior Director
Steve Handschuh, President

Free to members.
Frequency: Monthly
Founded in: 1923

18472 Passenger Transport
American Public Transit Association
1666 K St NW
Suite 1100
Washington, DC 20006-1215

202-496-4800; *Fax:* 202-496-4324
ptsubscriptions@apta.com; www.apta.com

Michael Melaniphy, President/CEO
Petra Mollet, VP
Rosemary Sherid, Marketing

Information on federal legislative, administrative and regulatory developments, management and operations, new technology, and state and local developments in public transit.
Frequency: Bi-Weekly
Circulation: 5000
Founded in: 1882

18473 Power Report
JD Power and Associates Publications Division
2625 Townsgate Rd
Suite 100
Westlake Villag, CA 91361-5737

805-418-8000
888-537-6937; *Fax:* 805-418-8900
information@jdpa.com; www.jdpower.com

Finbarr O'Neill, CEO
Mary Ann Maskery, Editor
JD Power, Chairman

Focuses on what car buyers and owners feel about their current vehicles.
Cost: $299.00
Frequency: Monthly
Founded in: 1968

18474 Quality
BNP Media Company
155 N. Pfingsten Rd.
Suite 205
Deerfield, IL 60015

847-405-4044; *Fax:* 248-358-1024
dalpozzod@bnpmedia.com;
www.qulitymag.com
Social Media: Twitter

Taggart Henderson, Co-CEO
Darrell O. Dal Pozzo, Group Publisher
Chistopher Sheehy, Senior Audience Development Manager

A monthly business publication serving the quality assurance and process improvement needs of more than 64,000 manufacturing professionals. the magazine reports on the use of sound metrology methods, statistical analysis and process improvement techniques to significantly improve quality on the shop floor and in manufacturing planning.
1000 Members
Frequency: Monthly
Founded in: 1962

18475 Safety & Environment/ Working Conditions
Automotive Industry Action Group
26200 Lahser Road
Suite 200
Southfield, MI 48033-7100

248-358-3570; *Fax:* 248-358-3253
inquiry@aiag.org; www.aiag.org

John Batchik, Chairman
David Kneisler, Vice Chairman
J. Scot Sharland, Executive Director

Addresses emerging and global issues in safety, health and the environment affecting member companies and employees worldwide.
1000 Members
Frequency: Monthly
Founded in: 1982

18476 Service Executive
Automotive Week Publishing
PO Box 3495
Wayne, NJ 07474-3495

973-694-7792; www.auto-week.com

Marketing information for the independent automotive aftermarket. Fast-breaking news of new market entries and strategies; key retail and wholesale developments; merger, acquisition, bankruptcy reports; regular charts of the Top 25 market leaders in various segments (parts, chains, tune-up specialists, brake specialists, tire, fast lube, etc.). The market's sole weekly. Classified non-product advertising accepted.
Cost: $130.00
4 Pages
Frequency: Monthly
Founded in: 1975
Printed in on matte stock

18477 Shop Talk
IMACA Education Foundation
6410 Southwest Boulevard
Suite 212
Fort Worth, TX 76109-3920

817-732-4600; *Fax:* 817-732-9610;
www.imaca.org

Joan M Jones, Circulation Director

Technical and industry information for the mobile air conditioning industry.
Cost: $20.00
Founded in: 1958

18478 Show Stopper
International Show Car Association
1092 Centre Rd
Auburn Hills, MI 48326-2657

248-373-1700; www.theisca.com

Bob Larivee, Owner

Car association report about shows.

18479 Supply Chain Solutions
Automotive Industry Action Group
26200 Lahser Road
Suite 200
Southfield, MI 48033-7100

248-358-3570; *Fax:* 248-358-3253
inquiry@aiag.org; www.aiag.org

John Batchik, Chairman
David Kneisler, Vice Chairman
J. Scot Sharland, Executive Director

Important information on customs and supply chain security regulation; materials management and logistics best practices; and automatic identifications/ RFID standards.
1000 Members
Frequency: Monthly
Founded in: 1982

18480 The Insider
American Bus Association

111 K Street NE
9th Floor
Washington, DC 20002

202-842-1645; *Fax:* 202-842-0850
abainfo@buses.org; www.buses.org
Social Media: Facebook, Twitter, LinkedIn

James Jalbert, Chairman
Thomas JeBran, Vice Chairman
Frank Henry, Secretary/ Treasurer
Peter Pantuso, President & CEO
Brandon Buchanan, Director of Operations

First source of information for bus and tour operators, travel partners, manufacturers, suppliers, and policy-makers seeking original coverage on the motorcoach, tous, and travel industry, from legislation and regulation to news to grow readers' business.
Frequency: Bi-Monthly
Circulation: 10000
Founded in: 1926

18481 **Tire Business**
Crain Communications Inc
1725 Merriman Rd
Suite 300
Akron, OH 44313-5283

330-836-9180; *Fax:* 330-836-2831
info@crain.com; www.crain.com

William Morrow, Executive VP, Operations
Peter Brown, VP

Besides reporting on breaking news, Tire Business also compiles numerous rankings and industry statistics relating to the North American tire and automotive service markets, independent tire dealers, tire manufacturers, tire retreaders and the global tire market.
Frequency: Bi-Weekly
Circulation: 30000
Founded in: 1983

18482 **Today's Tire Industry**
Tire Industry Association
1532 Pointer Ridge Pl
Suite G
Bowie, MD 20716-1874

301-430-7280
800-876-8372; *Fax:* 301-430-7283
info@tireindustry.org; www.tireindustry.org

Kevin Rohlwing, Senior Vice President Of Training
Sandra Martinez, Director Operations
Dr.Roy Littlefield, Executive Vice President
Chris Marnett, Director Of Training

Features retail, management, personnel and industry related information.
Cost: $13.00

18483 **UPdate: Society of Automotive Engineers**
Society of Automotive Engineers
400 Commonwealth Dr
Warrendale, PA 15086-7511

724-776-4841
877-606-7323; *Fax:* 724-776-5760
update@sae.org; www.saesections.org

Richard O Schaum, President
Martha Schanno, Circulation Manager

Published to enhance communications with and among SAE members on such non-technical issues as society activities, meetings and members. Recruitment advertising is accepted.
Frequency: Monthly
Circulation: 65000
Founded in: 1905
Printed in 2 colors on newsprint stock

18484 **USAC News**
United States Auto Club
PO Box 24001
Indianapolis, IN 46224-0001

317-247-5151; *Fax:* 317-247-0123;
www.usacracing.com

Kevin Miller, President

Contains schedules and news from USAC divisions.
8 Pages
Frequency: Monthly
Founded in: 1982

18485 **Ward's Automotive Reports**
Ward's Communications
3000 Town Center
Suite 2750
Southfield, MI 48075-1245

248-799-2622
877-825-1815; *Fax:* 248-357-9747
wards@wardsauto.com; www.wardsauto.com

Tom Duncan, Publisher
Steve Finlay, Senior Editor
Jim Bush, Business Manager
Chris Lamphear, Marketing Manager

Automotive sales, production and inventory statistics, news and analysis.
Cost: $1195.00
8 Pages
Frequency: Weekly
Founded in: 1924
Printed in 2 colors on matte stock

18486 **Ward's Dealer Business**
PRIMEDIA Intertec-Technology & Transportation
3000 Town Center
Suite 2750
Southfield, MI 48075-1245

248-799-2622
877-778-2512; *Fax:* 248-357-9747
wards@wardsauto.com; www.wardsauto.com

Thomas Duncan, Group Publisher
Steve Finlay, Senior Editor
Steve Sindly, Editor
James Bush, Managing Director

Information for the management of US new car dealerships by covering profit building techniques and business expansions. Includes analysis of current automotive trends.
Cost: $36.00
Frequency: Monthly
Circulation: 32635

18487 **Ward's Engine and Vehicle Technology Update**
Ward's Communications
3000 Town Center
Suite 2750
Southfield, MI 48075-1245

248-799-2622; *Fax:* 248-357-9747
wards@wardsauto.com; www.wardsauto.com

Thomas Duncan, Group Publisher
Steve Finlay, Senior Editor
Barbara McClellan, Senior International Edit
James Bush, Managing Director
John Sousanis, Publication Manager

Review of the latest advances in engine and vehicle technology.
Cost: $935.00
8 Pages
Printed in 2 colors on ³ stock

Magazines & Journals

18488 **ACTION Magazine**
Mobile Air Conditioning Society Worldwide
225 S Broad Street
Lansdale, PA 19446

215-631-7020; *Fax:* 215-631-7017
info@macsw.org; www.macsw.org
Social Media: Facebook, Twitter, LinkedIn

The journal of record for the professional in the growing global mobile AC industry and changing heat transfer and engine cooling system marketplace. has access to the global design and service and repair experts in automotive, heavy-duty, off-road, and bus mobile A/C, heat transfer and engine cooling system industry.
1700 Members
Frequency: 8x Yearly
Circulation: 13000
Founded in: 1981

18489 **AGRR**
Key Communications
PO Box 569
Garrisonville, VA 22463

540-720-5584; *Fax:* 540-720-5687
news@glassbytes.com; www.agrrmag.com

Debra Levy, Publisher
Charles Cumpston, Editor

Source of unbiased, accurate information about the auto glass repair and replacement industry.
Frequency: Monthly
Circulation: 10,000
Founded in: 2001

18490 **Accident Analysis & Prevention**
AAAM
PO Box 4176
Barrington, IL 60011-4176

847-844-3880; *Fax:* 847-844-3884
info@aaam.org; www.aaam.org

Brian N. Fildes, Ph.D, President
Mary Pat McKay, MD, President-Elect
Kristy B. Arbogast, Ph.D, Secretary
Frances D. Bents, Treasurer

Provides wide coverage of the general areas relating to accidental injury and damage, including the pre-injury and immediate post-injury phases. Published papers deal with medical, legal, economic, educational, behavioral, theoretical or empirical aspects of transportation accidents, as well as with accidents at other sites.
Frequency: 6x Yearly
Founded in: 1957

18491 **Aftermarket Business Magazine**
Advanstar Communications
6200 Canoga Avenue
2nd Floor
Woodland Hills, CA 91367

81 -22 -403; *Fax:* 818-593-5020
jsavas@advanstar.com
aftermarketbusiness.com

Larry Silvey, Editor
Jim Savas, VP

Specializing in providing news, trends, research and analysis on aftermarket auto parts
Cost: $5.00
Frequency: Monthly
Circulation: 41,077
Founded in: 1936
Printed in on glossy stock

18492 **Alt Fuels Advisor**
Alexander Communications Group
1916 Park Ave
8th Floor, Suite 501
New York, NY 10037-3733

212-281-6099
800-232-4317; *Fax:* 212-283-7269;
www.altfuels.com

Romauld Alexander, Owner
Laurence Alexander, CEO

News and developments in alternative fuel vehicles, including natural gas, propane, CNG, ethanol, electric, hybrid and fuel cells. Alt Fuels brings together news of technical and business developments, usage, infrastructure and regulations for all types of alternative and clean fuel vehicles.
Cost: $367.00
Frequency: Monthly
ISSN: 1528-6746

18493 **American Rodder**
Buckaroo Communications
701 Arcturus Avenue
Oxnard, CA 93033

805-986-0400
866-515-5600; *Fax:* 810-735-6765;
www.superrod.com

Gerry Burgel, Editor
Debby Wheeler, Customer Service

Covers the street-rod and custom-car industries. Accepts advertising.
Cost: $39.99
100 Pages

18494 **Auto Laundry News**
EW Williams Publications
2125 Center Ave
Suite 305
Fort Lee, NJ 07024-5898

201-592-7007; *Fax:* 201-592-7171
philpl@ewwpi.com;
www.williamspublications.com

Andrew Williams, President
Stefan Budricks, Editor
Janys Kuznier, Circulation Director

Provides technical, operational, marketing, advertising, and managerial information for owners, operators, and investors in self services and automatic carwashes, as well as auto detailing information.
Cost: $56.00
Frequency: Monthly
Circulation: 17292
Founded in: 1953

18495 **Auto Remarketing**
Cherokee Publishing Company
301 Cascade Pointe Ln
Cary, NC 27513-5778

919-674-6020
800-608-7500; *Fax:* 919-674-6027;
www.autoremarketing.com

Ron Smith, CEO

Reports on changes in the automotive industry and their effects on the buying and selling of cars.
Cost: $24.95
Frequency: Monthly
Circulation: 22000
Founded in: 1990

18496 **Auto Rental News**
Bobit Business Media
3520 Challenger St
Torrance, CA 90503-1640

310-533-2400; *Fax:* 310-533-2500;
www.bobit.com

Edward J Bobit, CEO
Cathy Stephens, Executive Editor

For those involved in the renting of cars and trucks.
Cost: $30.00
Frequency: Monthly
Circulation: 16000

18497 **Auto Trim and Restyling News**
Bobit Publishing
3520 Challenger St
Torrance, CA 90503-1640

310-533-2400
800-241-9034; *Fax:* 310-533-2500;
www.bobit.com

Edward J Bobit, CEO
Travis Weeks, Group Publisher

Latest information on enhancing the appearance of cars with new upholstery, convertible tops and more.
Cost: $19.95
Frequency: Monthly
Founded in: 1955

18498 **AutoDealer**
AIADA
211 N Union St
Suite 300
Alexandria, VA 22314-2643

800-462-4232; *Fax:* 703-519-7810
goaiada@aiada.org; www.aiada.org
Social Media: Twitter

Jim Smail, Chairman
Ray Mungenast, Chairman-Elect
Jenell Ross, Vice Chair
Larry Kull, Secretary/ Treasurer
Cody Lusk, President

Offers members an in-depth look at America's international auto industry and provides thoughtful analysis of everything from cutting edge vehicle technology to legislation making its way through the halls of Congress. Features include exclusive interviews with auto executives, detailed political coverage, vehicle reviews, and member spotlights.
11M+ Members
Frequency: Quarterly
Founded in: 1970

18499 **AutoInc**
Automotive Service Association
8191 Precinct Line Road
Suite 100
Colleyville, TX 76034-7675

817-514-2900
800-272-7467; *Fax:* 817-514-0770
asainfo@ASAshop.org; www.asashop.org

Ron Nagy, Chairman
Darrell Amberson, Chairman-Elect
Frequency: Monthly
Founded in: 1951

18500 **AutoSmart**
Aegis Group-Publishers
30400 Van Dyke Avenue
Warren, MI 48093-2368

586-574-3400; *Fax:* 248-447-7566
campbell-ewald@c-e.com;
www.campbell-ewald.com

Jim Palmer, President
Bill Ludwig, Chairman, CEO
Jeremy Morris, Publisher

Published for Delco Electronics for car company decision makers who deal with such systems.
Frequency: Monthly

18501 **Autoglass**
National Glass Association
1945 Old Gallows Rd
Suite 750
Vienna, VA 22182

703-442-4890
866-342-5642; *Fax:* 703-442-0630
nicole@glass.org; www.glass.org

Phil James, CEO
Nancy Davis, Editor-in-Chief

Forum for owners, managers and distributors in glass replacement, repair, tinting, and also auto security fields. News and reports on insurance and legislative regulations. New product updates, news and technology information.
Cost: $24.95
Circulation: 7000
ISSN: 1047-2061
Founded in: 1948

18502 **Automotive Cooling Journal**
National Automotive Radiator Service Association
3000 Villiage Run Road
Suite 103, #221
Wexford, PA 15090-6315

724-799-8415
800-551-3232; *Fax:* 724-799-8416
info@narsa.org; www.narsa.org

Wayne Juchno, Executive Director
Douglas Shymoniak, Manager
Maarten Taal, President
Pat O'Connor, Vice President
Darlene Barlow, Secretary

Auto cooling system service data. Free to members.
Cost: $30.00
60 Pages
Frequency: Monthly
Circulation: 10000
Founded in: 1956

18503 **Automotive Design & Production**
Gardner Publications
705 S Main St
Suite 200
Plymouth, MI 48170-2089

734-416-9705; *Fax:* 734-416-9707
daver@autofieldguide.com; www.adp.com

Mike Vohland, Publisher
Lawrence S Gould, Contributing Editor
Rick Kline Jr, Publisher

Coverage of the automotive industry: suppliers, manufacturers from design through delivery.
Cost: $65.00
Frequency: Monthly
Circulation: 60,404
Founded in: 1928

18504 **Automotive Engineering International Magazine**
Society of Automotive Engineers
400 Commonwealth Dr
Warrendale, PA 15096-0001

724-772-8509
877-606-7323; *Fax:* 724-776-9765
customerservice@sae.org; www.sae.org

David Schutt, CEO
Kevin Jost, Editor
Brian Kaleida, Chief Information Officer

Cars, aircraft, trucks, off highway equipment, engines, materials, manufacturing and fuels have the Society of Engineers in common. The SAE is your one stop resource for technical information and expertise used in building, maintaining and operating self propelled vehicles for use on land, sea, air or space.
Cost: $120.00
125 Pages
Frequency: Monthly
Circulation: 124451
Founded in: 1905

18505 **Automotive Executive Magazine**
National Auto Dealers Association
8400 Westpark Dr
Mc Lean, VA 22102-3591

703-821-7150
800-252-6232; *Fax:* 703-821-7234
msaldana@nada.org; www.aemag.com

Tom Choy, Owner
Mark Stertz, President

Devoted exclusively to the automotive executive. Features that take on the new topics in the industry, and columns filled with practical, solid

business advice for each dealership department.
Cost: $24.00
40 Pages
Frequency: Monthly
Circulation: 23000
Founded in: 1917

18506 Automotive Fleet
Bobit Publishing Company
3520 Challenger St
Torrance, CA 90503-1640

310-533-2400
847-647-9780; *Fax:* 310-533-2500
Bobitpubs@halldata.com; www.bobit.com

Edward J Bobit, CEO
Ty Bobit, President

Improvements in operational, purchasing and management responsibilities.
Cost: $35.00
Frequency: Monthly
Circulation: 21037
Founded in: 1961

18507 Automotive Industries
Worldwide Purchasing Ltd
Versailles, KY 40383

313-262-5702
jal@autoindustry.us; www.ai-online.com

John Larkin, Publisher
Ed Richardson, Editor
Ben Adler, Finance
Nick Palmen, Associate Publisher

Offers information for vehicle producers and suppliers worldwide.
Cost: $70.00
Frequency: Monthly
Circulation: 85000
Founded in: 1895
Printed in on glossy stock

18508 Automotive Manufacturing & Production
Gardner Publications
6915 Valley Ln
Cincinnati, OH 45244-3153

513-527-8800
800-950-8020; *Fax:* 513-527-8801
rkline2@autofieldguide.com;
www.gardnerweb.com

Rick Kline Sr, CEO/Publisher
Richard Kline, VP

For engineers and managers who are concerned with improving manufacturing.
Cost: $89.00
110 Pages
Frequency: Monthly
Founded in: 1934

18509 Automotive News
Crain Communications
1155 Gratiot Ave
Detroit, MI 48207-2732

313-446-0450
877-812-1584; *Fax:* 313-446-1680
customerservice@autonews.com;
www.autonews.com

Richard Johnson, Managing Editor
Jason Stein, Editor
Tony Merpi, Director Of Marketing
Victor Galvan, Web Editor

Covers the manufacturing side of the automotive industry, including engineering, design, production and suppliers, with equal emphasis on the retail side of the industry, including the marketing, sales, service and resale of vehicles.
Frequency: Weekly
Circulation: 79000

18510 Automotive Recycling
Automotive Recyclers Association
9113 Church Street
Suite 1
Manassas, VA 20110-5457

571-208-0428
888-385-1005; *Fax:* 571-208-0430
michael@a-r-a.org; www.a-r-a.org

Michael E Wilson, CEO
Linda Pitman, President
Randy Reitman, Secretary

Offers information on the recycling of automobiles and automotive parts.
Cost: $40.00
Frequency: Bi-Monthly
Circulation: 1100
ISSN: 1058-9376
Founded in: 1943
Printed in on glossy stock

18511 Body Language
Automotive Body Parts Association
1510 Eldridge Parkway
Suite 110-168
Houston, TX 77077

281-531-0809
800-323-5832; *Fax:* 281-531-9411
info@autobpa.com; www.autobpa.com

Stanley Rodman, Executive Director
Nicholas Scheid, President

Published six times per year by the Automotive Body Parts Association, this newsletter keeps body shop operators and insurance industry executives up-to-date on the latest information concerning the manufacturing, distribution and importing of aftermarket body parts.
Cost: $80.00
146 Members
167 Pages
Circulation: 400
Founded in: 1980

18512 BodyShop Business
Babcox Publications
3550 Embassy Pkwy
Akron, OH 44333-8318

330-670-1234; *Fax:* 330-670-0874;
www.babcox.com

Bill Babcox, Owner
Georgina Carson, Editor
Bob Bissler, Senior Editor

Devoted to helping collision-repair shop owners and managers run more profitable businesses. Editorially, BodyShop business covers all aspects of collision repair, with a focus on how-to topics include management, dimensioning, straightening, welding, refinishing, law and technology.
Cost: $64.00
Frequency: Monthly
Circulation: 60145
Founded in: 1920

18513 Brake & Front End
Babcox Publications
3550 Embassy Pkwy
Akron, OH 44333-8318

330-670-1234; *Fax:* 330-670-0874
amarkel@babcox.com; www.babcox.com

Bill Babcox, Owner
Andrew Markel, Editor
Brad Mitchell, Circulation/IT Director

Has monthly service articles that feature the latest information on brake, chassis, exhaust, front end, front-wheel drive and wheel alignment. Each issue also profiles the newest product and service offerings from aftermarket suppliers.
Cost: $64.00
Frequency: Monthly
Circulation: 40,310
Founded in: 1920

18514 Cars & Parts
Amos Press
PO Box 4129
Sidney, OH 45365-4129

937-498-2111
800-448-3611; *Fax:* 937-498-0807
editorial@carsandparts.com;
www.amospress.com

Bruce D Boyd, CEO
Margie Bruns, Advertising Manager
Mark Kaufman, Associate Publisher

Focused to the serious collector car lobbyist. Each issue has an array of how-to articles, detailed coverage of feature cars and intriguing historical views of the auto companies and their most influential players. Additionally there are reports on major collector car shows and auctions including analysis of price trends on major categories of cars. Also included is a calendar of upcoming events: shows, auctions and swap meets. Finally, each issue has an extensive classified section.
Cost: $31.95
124 Pages
Frequency: Monthly
Founded in: 1957
Printed in 4 colors on glossy stock

18515 Counterman
Babcox Publications
3550 Embassy Pkwy
Akron, OH 44333-8318

330-670-1234; *Fax:* 330-670-0874;
www.babcox.com

Bill Babcox, Owner
Jon Owens, Publisher

Targeted at the needs of the jobber sales team — those who buy and sell parts, services, equipment, build brand awareness, preference and loyalty by recommending parts to the DIY customer and professional technician.
Cost: $ 110.00
Frequency: Monthly
Circulation: 50,000
Founded in: 1920

18516 Dealer
Horizon Communications
5201 Great America Pkwy
Floor 20, Suite 320
Santa Clara, CA 95054-1122

408-969-4888; *Fax:* 408-969-4895
jh@horizonpr.com; www.horizonpr.com

Mike Roscoe, Publisher

Information for automobile dealers on service, parts, used car merchandising, financing, body shop, planning and risk management.
Cost: $35.00
Frequency: Monthly
Circulation: 21178
Founded in: 1995

18517 Destinations
American Bus Association
111 K Street NE
9th Floor
Washington, DC 20002

202-842-1645; *Fax:* 202-842-0850
abainfo@buses.org; www.buses.org

Peter J Pantuso, CEO
Brandon Buchanan, Director of Operations
Clyde J. Hart Jr, Senior Vice President
Eric Braendel, CFO

Motorcoach travel across North America and Association news.
80 Pages
Frequency: Monthly
Circulation: 6000
Founded in: 1926
Printed in 4 colors on glossy stock

18518 Diesel Progress: North American Edition
Diesel & Gas Turbine Publications
20855 Watertown Rd
Suite 220
Waukesha, WI 53186-1873
262-754-4100; *Fax:* 262-754-4175
mosenga@dieselpub.com;
www.dieselspec.com
Michael Osenga, President
S Bollwahn, Circulation Manager
Geared towards readers interested in state-of-the-art systems technology. Features include new product listings, systems design, research and product testing as well as systems maintenance and rebuilding.
Frequency: Monthly
Circulation: 26,011
Founded in: 1837

18519 Double Clutch
Antique Truck Club of America
P.O. Box 31
85 South Walnut Street
Boyertown, PA 19512
610-367-2567; *Fax:* 610-367-9712
office@antiquetruckclub.org;
www.antiquetruckclub.org
Social Media: Facebook
Steve Skurnowicz, Magazine Committee Chair
Fred Chase, President
Magazine for antique truck enthusiasts.
Cost: $50.00
Founded in: 1971

18520 Dual News Magazine
Driving School Association of the Americas
3125 Wilmington Pike
Kettering, OH 45429
800-270-3722; *Fax:* 937-290-0696
info@thedsaa.org; www.thedsaa.org
Social Media: Facebook, Twitter
Sharon Postigo Fife, President
Robert Cole, Treasurer
Sheila Varnado, Executive VP
Debbie Prudhomme, Secretary
Keeping all driving school professionals informed of upcoming educational seminars, sharing ideas & opinions and introducing products and the like to driving educators. Represents a continuing commitment to the driving school industry.
58000 Members
Founded in: 1973

18521 Engine Builder
Babcox Publications
3550 Embassy Pkwy
Akron, OH 44333-8318
330-670-1234; *Fax:* 330-670-0874;
www.babcox.com
Bill Babcox, Owner
Doug Kaufman, Editor
Business magazine serving the machine shop, custom engine, production engine and small parts rebuilding markets. It delivers editorial excellence that reflects the growing sophistication of the rebuilding industry and aids its readers in the profitable operation of their businesses.
Cost: $64.00
72 Pages
Frequency: Monthly
Circulation: 19500
Founded in: 1920
Printed in 4 colors on glossy stock

18522 Engine Professional
Automotive Engine Rebuilders Association
500 Coventry Ln
Suite 180
Crystal Lake, IL 60014-7592
815-526-7600
866-326-2372; *Fax:* 815-526-7601
info@aera.org; www.aera.org
Social Media: Facebook, Twitter
David Bianchi, Chairman
John Goodman, President
Dean Yatchyshyn, Treasurer
Dwayne J. Dugas, 1st Vice Chairman
Ron McMorris, 2nd Vice Chairman
Packed with highly technical, application-driven articles that will help you and your business thrive.
Frequency: Quarterly
Founded in: 1922

18523 FLEETSolutions
National Association of Fleet Administrators
125 Village Boulevard
Suite 200
Princeton, NJ 08540
609-720-0882; *Fax:* 609-452-8004
info@nafa.org; www.nafa.org
Social Media: Facebook, Twitter, LinkedIn
Phillip E. Russo, Executive Director
Contains educational articles based on the eight disciplines of the fleet management profession.
2600+ Members
Frequency: Bi-Monthly

18524 Family Motor Coaching Magazine
8291 Clough Pike
Cincinnati, OH 45244-2796
513-474-3622
800-543-3622; *Fax:* 513-474-2332
membership@fmca.com; www.fmca.com
Don Eversman, Executive Director
Official publication of the Family Motor Coach Association, an organization for owners of self-contained motor homes. Publishes articles regarding motor home maintenance and repair, new products, travel destinations of interest to RV travelers and association news.
Cost: $24.00
Frequency: Monthly
Circulation: 98000

18525 Fleet Financials
Bobit Publishing Company
23210 Crenshaw Blvd
Suite 101
Torrance, CA 90505-3181
310-539-1969; *Fax:* 310-539-4329
mike.antich@bobit.com;
www.fleet-central.com
John Bebout, Owner
Features profiles of successfully managed fleets and analysis of lease verses company ownership.
Cost: $28.00
Frequency: Monthly
Circulation: 15500

18526 Global Insight
Motor and Equipment Manufacturers Association
10 Laboratory Drive
PO Box 13966
Research Triangle Park, NC 27709-3906
919-549-4800; *Fax:* 919-406-1465
info@mema.org; www.mema.org
Bob McKenna, President
Wendy Earp, VP
Frank Hampshire, Marketing
Member publication examines critical issues and challenges facing today's original equipment, aftermarket and heavy duty suppliers. Subscriptions and advertising available.
Frequency: Quarterly
Circulation: 2400
Founded in: 1904

18527 Hemmings Classic Car
Hemmings Motor News
PO Box 4317
Bennington, VT 05201
802-442-3101
800-227-4373; *Fax:* 802-447-9631
hmnmail@hemmings.com;
www.hemmings.com
Formerly the Special Interest Auto magazine, features contemporary road tests and in-depth automobile profiles, automotive design, engineering, styling and historical exposes, how-to restoration and technical articles, and profiles on specialists and shops specializing in the collector-car industry.
Frequency: Monthly
Founded in: 1954

18528 Hemmings Motor News
PO Box 100
Bennington, VT 05201
802-442-3101
800-227-4373; *Fax:* 802-447-9631
hmnmail@hemmings.com;
www.hemmings.com
Terry Ehrich, Publisher
Eileen Desmarais, Marketing
The bible of the car collector, this monthly magazine serves to enhance the experience of the car collector-enthusiast. Regular departments include vehicle and parts search, price checkers, dealers tips, hobby directory and more.
Cost: $31.95
Frequency: Monthly
Circulation: 210000
Founded in: 1954

18529 ImportCar
Babcox Publications
3550 Embassy Pkwy
Akron, OH 44333-8318
330-670-1234; *Fax:* 330-670-0874
mdellavalle@babcox.com; www.babcox.com
Bill Babcox, Owner
David Wooldridge, Publisher
Complete import service magazine. It is geared exclusively to the vehicle repair needs of import specialist technicians. The in-depth, technical nature of the magazine's editorial content helps technicians of all abilities do their jobs more efficiently and effectively.
Cost: $64.00
Frequency: Monthly
Circulation: 29190
Founded in: 1979

18530 Independent Battery Manufacturers
401 North Michigan Avenue
24th Floor
Chicago, IL 60611
312-644-6610; *Fax:* 312-527-6640
info@thebatteryman.com;
www.thebatteryman.com
Founded in: 1921

18531 International Collision Parts Industry Suppliers Guide
Automotive Body Parts Association

1510 Eldridge Parkway
Suite 110-168
Houston, TX 77077

281-531-0809
800-323-5832; *Fax:* 281-531-9411
info@autobpa.com; www.autobpa.com

Stanley Rodman, Executive Director
Nicholas Scheid, President

Covers the collision replacement parts industry.
146 Members
64 Pages
Frequency: Quarterly
Circulation: 2300
Founded in: 1980
Printed in 4 colors on glossy stock

18532 Journal of Quality Technology
American Society for Quality
600 N Plankinton Avenue
PO Box 3005
Milwaukee, WI 53201-3005

414-272-8575
800-248-1946; *Fax:* 414-272-1734
help@asq.org; www.asq.org

Roberto M Saco, President
Paul E Borawski, Executive Director
Erica Gumieny, Sales
Fay Spano, Communications/Media Relations

Published by the American Society for Quality, the JQT is a quarterly, peer-reviewed journal that focuses on the subject of quality control and the related areas of reliability and similar disciplines.
Cost: $30.00
100M Members
Frequency: Quarterly
Founded in: 1946

18533 LCT Magazine
Bobit Publishing Company
3520 Challenger St
Torrance, CA 90503-1640

310-533-2400
800-380-8335; *Fax:* 310-533-2500
webmaster@bobit.com; www.bobit.com

Edward J Bobit, CEO

Serves the limousine agency owner.
Cost: $28.00
Frequency: Monthly
Circulation: 10000
Founded in: 1961

18534 Limousine Digest
Digest Publications
29 Fostertown Road
Medford, NJ 08055

609-953-4900; *Fax:* 609-953-4905
info@limodigest.com; www.limodigest.com

Chris Weiss, Publisher
Susan Rose, Assistant Publisher
Iric Cohen, President

Information for owners and operators of limousine, livery and transportation fleets, including day to day operational information, industry trends, product reviews, technical advances, as well as success stories.
Cost: $24.95
100 Pages
Frequency: Monthly
Circulation: 12500
ISSN: 1095-8436
Founded in: 1990
Printed in 4 colors on glossy stock

18535 Locator
John Holmes Publishing Company
521 Main Street
PO Box 286
Whiting, IA 51063

712-458-2213
800-831-0820; *Fax:* 712-458-2687
sales@partslocator.com; www.partslocator.com

John Holmes, President
Charis Lloyd, VP
Wendy Lloyd, Marketing Director
Stacy Phillips, Editor

Nation's leading auto and truck parts magazine.
Cost: $29.00
250 Pages
Frequency: Monthly
Circulation: 18500
Founded in: 1957
Printed in 4 colors on newsprint stock

18536 Lubes-N-Greases
LNG Publishing Company
6105 Arlington Blvd
Suite G
Falls Church, VA 22044-2708

703-536-0800; *Fax:* 703-536-0803
info@Lngpublishing.com;
www.lngpublishing.com

Gloria Stienberg Briskin, Advertising Director
Nancy DeMarco, Publisher
Lisa Tocci, Managing Editor

The magazine of industry in motion.
Frequency: Monthly
Circulation: 17300
ISSN: 1080-9449
Founded in: 1995
Printed in 4 colors on glossy stock

18537 Lubricants World
4545 Post Oak Place
Suite 230
Houston, TX 77027

713-840-0378; *Fax:* 713-840-8585

Kathryn B Carnes, Editor

Professional journal for those in the oil and grease industry.

18538 MOVE
AAMVA
4301 Wilson Blvd
Suite 400
Arlington, VA 22203-1867

703-522-4200; *Fax:* 703-522-1553
info@aamva.org; www.aamva.org

Neil D. Schuster, President & CEO
Marc Saitta, Vice President & CFO

Provides members with practical and in-depth how-to information on a wide range of topics. Provides feature articles and departments that tackle issues facing today's administrators.
Frequency: Quarterly
Founded in: 1933
Printed in 4 colors

18539 MOVE Magazine
American Assn. of Motor Vehicle Administrators
Executive Plaza, 11350 McCormick Rd
Suite 900
Hunt Valley, MD 21031

410-584-1955; *Fax:* 410-584-1998;
www.aamva.org

Linda Lewis-Pickett, President/CEO
Bonnie L Rutledge, Editor

Journal of the voluntary, nonprofit, educational organization. AAMVA represents the state and provincial officials in the US, Canada and Mexico, who are responsible for the administration and enforcement of laws pertaining to the motor vehicle and its use.
Cost: $26.00
Frequency: Quarterly
Circulation: 32000
Founded in: 1996
Printed in 4 colors on glossy stock

18540 Market Analysis
Motor and Equipment Manufacturers Association
10 Laboratory Drive
PO Box 13966
Research Triangle Park, NC 27709-3966

919-549-4800; *Fax:* 919-406-1465
info@mema.org; www.mema.org

Bob McKenna, President
Wendy Earp, VP
Frank Hampshire, Marketing

Provides an analysis of how the vehicles parts industry is affected by the economy including informative news topics such as producer price indexes for parts and accessories, market data and more.
Frequency: Monthly
Founded in: 1904

18541 Modern Car Care
Virgo Publishing LLC
3300 N Central Ave
Suite 300
Phoenix, AZ 85012-2532

480-990-1101; *Fax:* 480-990-0819
jsiefert@vpico.com; www.vpico.com

John Seifert, CEO
Kelly Ridley, Executive VP, CFO
Heather Wood, VP,Human Resources

Magazine for automotive professionals.
Frequency: Monthly
Circulation: 20000
Founded in: 1986

18542 Motor Age
Chilton Company
300 Park Ave
Suite 19
New York, NY 10022-7409
212-751-3596
888-527-7008; *Fax:* 212-371-4058
info@advanstar.com; www.chiltonfunds.com

Richard L Chilton Jr, Chairman, CEO
Michael Clark, President, COO

Features developments in the auto industry.
Cost: $14.00
Frequency: Monthly
Circulation: 143,000
Founded in: 1992

18543 Motor Magazine
Hearst Business Communications
1301 Long Lake Road
Suite 300
Troy, MI 48098
248-585-1700
800-288-6828; *Fax:* 248-879-8603
motorbookscallcenter@motor.com;
www.motor.com

Duane Harrison, Owner
John Lypen, Editor
Richard Laimbeer, Publisher

Emphasis on repair and service end of automobile business for owners and managers.
Cost: $63.00
Frequency: Monthly
Circulation: 140000
Founded in: 1903

18544 Motor Trend
Primedia

6420 Wilshire Boulevard
Los Angeles, CA 90048-5502

323-822-2201; *Fax:* 323-782-2467;
www.motortrend.com

Tom Rogers, CEO
Eric Schwab, Advertising Manager
Peter Clancey, Marketing Executive

Comprehensive magazine offers the latest information and news on the automotive industry.
Cost: $47.88
Frequency: Monthly
Circulation: 999999
Founded in: 1988
Printed in 4 colors on glossy stock

18545 NADA'S Automotive Executive
National Automobile Dealers Association
8400 Westpark Dr
9th Floor, Suite 1
Mc Lean, VA 22102-3591

703-821-7000
800-252-6232; *Fax:* 703-821-7075
nadainfo@nada.org; www.nada.org

Phillip D Brady, President
Rick Wagoner, CEO

Provides up to the minute legislative, regulatory and state association news, also includes product development and implementation, labor relations and the economic climate.
Cost: $24.00
Frequency: Monthly
Circulation: 21850
Founded in: 1975

18546 NAPA Outlook
National Auto Parts Association
2999 Circle 75 Pkwy SE
Atlanta, GA 30339-3050

770-956-2200
877-794-9511; *Fax:* 770-956-2211
customersupport@napaonline.com;
www.napaautocare.com

Thomas C Gallagher, CEO

Ideas for business procedures for jobber store owners.
28 Pages
Frequency: Monthly
Founded in: 1925

18547 NASCAR Performance
Babcox Publications
3550 Embassy Pkwy
Akron, OH 44333-8318

330-670-1234; *Fax:* 330-670-0874
dkaufman@babcox.com; www.babcox.com

Bill Babcox, Owner
Doug Kaufman, Editor

Focuses on what goes on behind the scenes in NASCAR racing, and how that advanced technology transfers to automotive aftermarket applications. Professional NASCAR Garage is a quarterly supplement to all Babcox publications.
Founded in: 1920

18548 National Oil & Lube News
National Oil & Lube News
4418 74th St
Suite 66
Lubbock, TX 79424-2336

806-762-4464
800-796-2577; *Fax:* 806-762-4023
info@noln.net; www.noln.net

Garrett McKinnon, Editor
Steve Hurt, Co Publisher

Geared towards fast oil change and lubrication shop owners and managers. Information on the latest technology and environment concerns, also provides a link between shops and suppliers.
Cost: $29.00
76 Pages
Frequency: Monthly
Circulation: 17000
ISSN: 1071-1260
Founded in: 1986
Printed in 4 colors on glossy stock

18549 New England Automotive Report
Thomas Greco Publications
PO Box 734
Neptune, NJ 07753

732-922-8909; *Fax:* 732-922-9821
setlit4u@msn.com; www.aaspnj.org

Thomas Greco, Owner
Alicia D'Aquila, Editor
Charles Bryant, Executive Director

Provides reports on ideas, products and services to enhance collision repair productivity, also identifies insurance issues.
Cost: $48.00
85 Pages
Frequency: Monthly
Circulation: 4500
Founded in: 1996
Printed in 4 colors on glossy stock

18550 Old Cars Weekly
F+W Media
38 E. 29th Street
New York, NY 10016

212-447-1400; *Fax:* 212-447-5231
contact_us@fwmedia.com;
www.fwpublications.com

Jim Ogle, CFO
Sara Domville, President
Chad Phelps, Chief Digital Officer
David Nussbaum, CEO

Covers the entire field of collectible automobiles - from classic touring cars and roadsters of the early 1900s to the popular muscle cars of the 1960s and 1970s. Includes historical perspectives and facts on cars and their manufacturers, and reports on attractions at upcoming shows. Regular columns include 'New Products,' 'Questions & Answers,' 'Show Biz,' 'Bookmobile,' 'Restoration Basics,' and an extensive classified word ad section. Hundreds of car show listings are included.
Cost: $41.98
64 Pages
Frequency: Weekly
Circulation: 63104
Founded in: 1971

18551 PWA Conference
Performance Warehouse Association
41-701 Corporate Way
Suite 1
Palm Desert, CA 92260

760-346-5647; *Fax:* 760-346-5847
donnie@pedistributors.com; www.pwa-par.org

Donnie Eatherly, President
John Towle, Executive Director
Larry Pacey, Chairman
Trent Lowe, Treasurer
Frequency: September

18552 Parking Magazine
National Parking Association
1112 16th St NW
Suite 840
Washington, DC 20036-4880

202-296-4336
800-647-7275; *Fax:* 202-296-3102
info@weareparking.org
weareparking.org

Alan B. Lazowski, Chairman
Nicolle Judge, Chair Elect
Christine Banning, President
Alison Bibb-Carson, Managing Editor

Published by the National Parking Association.
Cost: $99.00
2500 Members
Frequency: Monthly
Circulation: 4000
ISSN: 0031-2193
Founded in: 1952
Mailing list available for rent: 2600 names at $250 per M
Printed in 4 colors

18553 Parts & People
Automotive Counseling & Publishing
899 Logan Street
Denver, CO 80203

303-765-4664; *Fax:* 303-765-4650;
www.partsandpeople.com

Lance Buchner, Owner
Rob Merwin, Editor

Collision and mechanical local and national news.
Cost: $36.00
Frequency: Monthly
Circulation: 59000
Founded in: 1986

18554 Parts Plus Magazine
3085 Fountainside Drive
#210
Germantown, TN 38138

901-727-8112
800-727-8112; *Fax:* 901-682-9098
info@networkhq.org; www.partsplus.com

Alan Bostwick, Executive VP

Published by the Association of Automotive Aftermarkets Distributors.
Cost: $29.95
Frequency: Monthly
Circulation: 5000
Founded in: 1965

18555 Professional Carwashing and Detailing
National Trade Publications
19 British American Blvd. West
Latham, NY 12110-2197

518-783-1281; *Fax:* 518-783-1386;
www.carwash.com

Tracy Aston-Martin, Vice President
Sandy Murphy, Publisher

Provides technical and marketing information to professional vehicle washing owners, managers and investors. Accepts advertising.
Cost: $42.00
76 Pages
Frequency: Monthly
Circulation: 19000
Founded in: 1976
Mailing list available for rent: 18M names at $125 per M
Printed in 4 colors on matte stock

18556 Professional Tool & Equipment News
1233 Janesville Avenue
Fort Atkinson, WI 53538

920-563-6388
888-966-3976; *Fax:* 920-563-1699
sales@pten.com; www.vehicleservicepros.com

Larry Greenberger, Publisher
Jacques Gordon, Editor
Sara Shelstrom, Publisher

Information for personnel and owners of general and specialty repair shops, including buying tools and equipment, technological innovations, new systems, time saving ideas and product re-

leases.
Cost: $32.00
Frequency: Monthly
Circulation: 105044
Founded in: 1996

18557 **Quality Engineering**
American Society for Quality
600 N Plankinton Avenue
PO Box 3005
Milwaukee, WI 53201-3005

414-272-8575
800-248-1946; *Fax:* 414-272-1734
help@asq.org; www.asq.org

James Rooney, Chair
Paul E Borawski, CEO
Erica Gumieny, Sales
Brian LeHouillier, Managing Director

Co-published with Taylor and Francis, this journal is for professional practitioners and researchers whose goal is quality engineering improvements and solutions.
Cost: $34.75
100M Members
Frequency: Quarterly/Members Price
Founded in: 1946

18558 **Quality Management Journal**
American Society for Quality
600 N Plankinton Avenue
PO Box 3005
Milwaukee, WI 53201-3005

414-272-8575
800-248-1946; *Fax:* 414-272-1734
help@asq.org; www.asq.org

James Rooney, Chair
Paul E Borawski, CEO
Erica Gumieny, Sales
Brian LeHouillier, Managing Director

Published by the American Society for Quality, the QMT is a quarterly, peer-reviewed journal that focuses on the subject of quality management practice and provides a discussion forum for both practitioners and academics in the area of research.
Cost: $50.00
100M Members
Frequency: Quarterly
Founded in: 1946

18559 **Quality Progress**
American Society for Quality
600 N Plankinton Avenue
PO Box 3005
Milwaukee, WI 53201-3005

414-272-8575
800-248-1946; *Fax:* 414-272-1734
help@asq.org; www.asq.org

James Rooney, Chair
Paul E Borawski, CEO
Erica Gumieny, Sales
Brian LeHouillier, Managing Director

Published by the American Society for Quality, the QP is a peer-reviewed journal that focuses on the subject of quality control, discussing the usage and implementation of quality principles including the subject areas of organizational behavior, knowledge management and process improvement.
Cost: $55.00
100M Members
Founded in: 1946

18560 **RV Trade Digest**
Cygnus Publishing
1233 Janesville Avenue
Fort Atkinson, WI 53538

920-000-1111
800-547-7377; *Fax:* 920-563-1699
editor@rvtradedigest.com;
www.cygnusb2b.com

John French, CEO
Tom Kohn, Executive Vice President
Paul Caplan, Senior Vice President
Paul Bonaiuto, CFO

Offers in-depth information to a trade audience of business professionals actively engaged in the manufacture, distribution and sales of RVs, supplies and accessories.
Cost: $40.00
Frequency: 9 issues (1year
Circulation: 16055
Founded in: 1966
Printed in 4 colors on glossy stock

18561 **Recyclers Power Source**
PO Box 556
Spirit Lake, IA 51360

712-336-5614
800-336-5614; *Fax:* 712-336-5617
jstahly@qwestoffice.net;
www.rpowersource.com

Laura Kabele
Julie Stahly

Purchasing guide for automotive recycling.
Frequency: Monthly

18562 **Reman Connection**
Automotive Parts Remanufacturers Association
7250 Heritage Village Plaza
Suite 201
Gainesville, VA 20155

703-968-2772; *Fax:* 703-968-2878
info@apra.org; www.apra.org

Omar Cueto, Chairman
Jay Robie, Vice President
Joe Kripli, President

Association magazine (replacing Global Connections) offers information on the remanufacturing industry including product updates, news features and more.
Cost: $35.00
1000 Members
Frequency: Monthly
Circulation: 10000+
Founded in: 1941

18563 **SAE Off-Highway Engineering**
Society of Automotive Engineers
400 Commonwealth Dr
Warrendale, PA 15096-0001

724-776-4841
877-606-7323; *Fax:* 724-776-0790
sohe@sae.org; www.sae.org

David Schutt, CEO
Brian Kaleida, Chief Information Officer

Member services and news, as well as activities including meetings, professional development seminars, publication introductions and education programs.
Cost: $70.00
Frequency: Monthly
Circulation: 58263
Founded in: 1905

18564 **SEMA News**
Performance Aftermarket Publishers
1575 South Valley Vista Drive
Diamond Bar, CA 91765

909-860-2030; *Fax:* 909-860-0184
editors@semanews.com; www.sema.org

Christopher Kersting, President
Peter MacGillivray, VP Communications

Covers specialty and performance segment of autos with the Auto Aftermarket, Specialty Equipment and Marketing Association.
Cost: $39.95
96 Pages
Frequency: Monthly
Circulation: 35000
Founded in: 1988
Printed in 4 colors on matte stock

18565 **School Bus Fleet**
Bobit Publishing Company
3520 Challenger St
Torrance, CA 90503-1640

310-533-2400; *Fax:* 310-533-2500
sbf@bobit.com; www.bobitbusinessmedia.com
Social Media: Facebook, Twitter, LinkedIn

Ty Bobit, CEO
Mark Hollenbeck, Associate Publisher
Frank DiGiacomo, Vice President Emeritus
James Blue, General Manager/Publisher

Published for persons involved with the transportation of school children grades K-12, includes articles on lowering costs, improving fleet operations, scheduling techniques, vehicle maintenance and federal regulatory issues.
Cost: $25.00
Frequency: Monthly
Circulation: 22000
Founded in: 1961

18566 **Software Quality Professional**
American Society for Quality
600 N Plankinton Avenue
PO Box 3005
Milwaukee, WI 53201-3005

414-272-8575
800-248-1946; *Fax:* 414-272-1734
help@asq.org; www.asq.org

James Rooney, Chair
Paul E Borawski, ASQ CEO
Erica Gumieny, Sales
William Mc Bee III, Treasurer
Brian Houillier, Managing

Published by the American Society for Quality, the SQP is a quarterly, peer-reviewed journal for software development professionals that focuses on the subject of quality practice principles in the implementation of software and the development of software systems.
Cost: $45.00
100M Members
Frequency: Quarterly
Founded in: 1946

18567 **Specialty Automotive Magazine**
Meyers Publishing
799 Camarillo Springs Rd
Camarillo, CA 93012-9468

805-445-8881; *Fax:* 805-445-8882
len@meyerspublishing.com;
www.meyerspublishing.com

Len Meyers, Owner
Len Meyers, Publisher
Andrew Meyers, Associate Publisher
Harriet Kaplan, Assistant Editor

For accessories and performance specialists, dedicated for car and truck product suppliers and installers. Various fatermaker segments are covered: street, track, van, truck, and off-road. Features cover: technology and trends, performance retailing, new product showcases, upgrade news, trade shows, legislation, advertising, OEM's industry news, and people on the move.
Cost: $10.00
Frequency: Monthly
Circulation: 25000
ISSN: 0894-7414
Founded in: 1983
Printed in 4 colors on glossy stock

18568 **Sport Truck & SUV Accessory Business**
Cygnus Publishing

1233 Janesville Avenue
Fort Atkinson, WI 53538

920-000-1111
800-547-7377; *Fax:* 920-563-1699;
www.cygnusb2b.com

John French, CEO
Pat Walker, Editor
Tom Kohn, Executive Vice President
Founded in: 1966

18569 Supercharger
Detroit Section Society of Automotive Engineers
28535 Orchard Lake Road
Suite 200
Farmington Hills, MI 48334

248-324-4445; *Fax:* 248-324-4449
jjablonski@sae-detroit.org;
www.sae-detroit.org

Charon Morgan, Chair
Terry Rhoades, Treasurer

The official publication of SAE Detroit Section that brings members together with news of upcoming tours, technical meetings, events and more.
Circulation: 16000
Printed in on glossy stock

18570 Tire Retread Information Packet & Buyers Guide
Tire Retread and Repair Information Bureau
1013 Birch Street
Falls Church, VA 22046

703-533-7677
877-394-6811; *Fax:* 703-533-7678
info@retread.org; www.retread.org

David Stevens, Managing Director
Bob Majewski, President
Eddie Burleson, Vice President
Phil Boarts, Secretary/Treasurer
Norm Ball, Director

Published by the Tire Retread Information Bureau.
380 Pages
Frequency: Weekly
Founded in: 1972

18571 Tire Review
Babcox Publications
3550 Embassy Pkwy
Akron, OH 44333-8318

330-670-1234; *Fax:* 330-670-0874
bbabcox@babcox.com; www.babcox.com

Bill Babcox, Owner
David Modiz, Group Publisher
Dave Wooldridge, Publisher

Designed to assist the independent retail tire dealer in his number one concern — profitability. It focuses on pricing strategies, marketing and effective advertising to meet the challenges of today's industry.
Cost: $64.00
84 Pages
Frequency: Monthly
Founded in: 1902

18572 Tow Times
TT Publications
203 West SR 434
Winter Springs, FL 32708

407-327-4817
800-308-3745; *Fax:* 407-327-2603
news@towtimes.com; www.towtimes.com

Clarissa Powell, Publisher
Tim Jackson, Editor
Dave Jones, President

Edited to review various aspects of the towing and road services. Accepts advertising.
Cost: $34.00
56 Pages
Frequency: Monthly
Founded in: 1983

18573 Toy Cars & Models
F+W Media
38 E. 29th Street
New York, NY 10016

212-447-1400; *Fax:* 212-447-5231
contact_us@fwmedia.com;
www.fwcommunity.com

Jim Ogle, CFO
Sara Domville, President
Chad Phelps, Chief Digital Officer
David Nussbaum, CEO

Provides comprehensive coverage of the model car hobby without bias toward scale, subject, manufacturer or material. Offers columns and news stories featuring models made of die-cast, white metal, plastic, resin and more while getting readers in touch with the manufacturers, distributors and retailers who sell these model cars. Monthly giveaways, reader polls and an active letters column give readers a chance to participate in their hobby.
Cost: $29.98
88 Pages
Frequency: Monthly
Circulation: 17916
Founded in: 1998

18574 Traffic Injury Prevention
AAAM
PO Box 4176
Barrington, IL 60011-4176

847-844-3880; *Fax:* 847-844-3884
info@aaam.org; www.aaam.org

Brian N. Fildes, Ph.D, President
Mary Pat McKay, MD, President-Elect
Kristy B. Arbogast, Ph.D, Secretary
Frances D. Bents, Treasurer

Bridging the disciplines of medicine, engineering, public health and traffic safety in order to foster the science of traffic injury prevention. The journal focuses on research, interventions and evaluations within the areas of traffic safety, crash causation, injury prevention and treatment.
Frequency: 6x Yearly
ISSN: 1538-9588
Founded in: 1957

18575 Truck & SUV Performance
Bobit Publishing Company
3520 Challenger St
Torrance, CA 90503-1640

310-533-2400; *Fax:* 310-533-2500
travis.weeks@bobit.com; www.bobit.com

Edward J Bobit, CEO
John Jeffries, Editor
Circulation: 32,000
Founded in: 1961

18576 Underhood Service
Babcox Publications
3550 Embassy Pkwy
Akron, OH 44333-8318

330-670-1234; *Fax:* 330-670-0874
bbabcox@babcox.com; www.babcox.com

Bill Babcox, CEO
Jeff Stankard, VP/ Group Publisher
Jennifer McMullen, Managing Editor

Meets the special needs of those technicians where most of their jobs involve the service and repair of under-the-hood systems. Answers the challenge of a continuing expansion of automotive technology.
Cost: $64.00
Frequency: Monthly
Circulation: 40500
Founded in: 1920

18577 Used Car Dealer Magazine
Nat'l Independent Automobile Dealers Association
2521 Brown Boulevard
Arlington, TX 76006-5203

817-492-2377
800-682-3837; *Fax:* 817-649-5866;
www.niada.com/

Michael R Linn, CEO/Publisher
Michael Harbour, Editor
Angela Ledbetter, Executive Assistant
Adrianne Argumaniz, Publication Manager

Information on auctions, profit center opportunities, trends in used car market, and updates on legislation. Coverage on association membership and the entire used vehicle industry.
Cost: $36.00
Circulation: 15000
Founded in: 1946
Printed in 4 colors on glossy stock

18578 Ward's Autoworld
Ward's Communications
3000 Town Center
Suite 2750
Southfield, MI 48075-1245

248-799-2622; *Fax:* 248-357-9747
wards@wardsauto.com; www.wardsauto.com

Thomas Duncan, Publisher
Drew Winter, Editor

News and analysis for automotive OEM professionals.
Cost: $55.00
130 Pages
Frequency: Monthly
Circulation: 102000
ISSN: 0043-0315
Founded in: 1924
Mailing list available for rent: 99,000 names
Printed in 4 colors on glossy stock

18579 Ward's Dealer Business
Ward's Communications
3000 Town Center
Suite 2750
Southfield, MI 48075-1245

248-799-2622; *Fax:* 248-357-9747
wards@wardsauto.com; www.wardsdealer.com

Thomas Duncan, Group Publisher
Drew Winter, Editor
Tony Noland, CEO
James Bush, Managing Director

News and analysis for auto dealership professionals.
80 Pages
Frequency: Monthly
Circulation: 27000
ISSN: 1086-1629
Founded in: 1924
Mailing list available for rent: 98,861 names
Printed in 4 colors

Trade Shows

18580 AAIW: Automotive Aftermarket Industry Week Expo
Overseas Automotive Council
10 Laboratory Drive
Po Box 13966
Reserach Triangle, NC 27709-3966

919-549-4800; *Fax:* 919-549-4824
media@mema.org; www.oac-intl.org

Jeremy Denton, Show Management

Containing 2,500 exhibits.
100M+ Attendees
Frequency: November

18581 AAMVA Annual International Conference
American Assoc. of Motor Vehicle Administrators
4301 Wilson Boulevard
Suite 400
Arlington, VA 22203
703-522-4200; *Fax:* 703-522-1553
info@aamva.org; www.aamva.org
Neil D Schuster, President
Marc Saitta, VP &CFO
Kathy King, Director Business Services
The annual conference of the American Association of Motor Vehicle Administrators during August that provides numerous exhibits, programs and presentations and the opportunity for members to meet and network with colleagues.
800 Attendees
Frequency: August
Founded in: 1933

18582 ABPA Trade Show Fair
Automotive Body Parts Association
1510 Eldridge Parkway
Suite 110-168
Houston, TX 77077
281-531-0809
800-323-5832; *Fax:* 281-531-9411
info@autobpa.com; www.autobpa.com
Stanley Rodman, Executive Director
Dolores Richardson, President
Trade show with 35 exhibitors and over 43 booths.
146 Members
Frequency: September
Founded in: 1980

18583 AFLA Annual Meeting and Conference
Automotive Fleet and Leasing Association
N83 W13410 Leon Road
Menomonee Falls, WI 53051
414-386-0366; *Fax:* 414-359-1671
info@afla.org; www.afla.org
Social Media: Facebook, LinkedIn
Bill Elliott, Executive Director
Michael Bieger, President
Mary Sticha, Executive Vice President
Greg Haag, Communications & PR Manager
Providing the opportunity and a forum for the exchange of information and ideas between related segments of the fleet industry.
400 Members
Frequency: Annual
Founded in: 1969

18584 AIAG AutoTech Conference
Automotive Industry Action Group
26200 Lahser Road
Suite 200
Southfield, MI 48033
248-358-3003; *Fax:* 248-799-7995
inquiry@aiag.org; www.aiag.org
Jhon Batchik, Chairman
David Kneisler, Vice Chairman
It's a venue where the collaboration between OEMs and suppliers is showcased through educational sessions, product and service exhibits and demonstrations, and networking opportunities.
3000 Attendees
Founded in: 1982

18585 ARA Annual Convention & Exposition
Automotive Recyclers Association
9113 Church Street
Manassas, VA 20110
571-208-0428
888-385-1005; *Fax:* 571-208-0430
michael@a-r-a.org; www.a-r-a.org
Michael Wilson, CEO
Kim Glasscock, Meetings & Expositions
Automotive recycling trade show. Containing over 150 booths and more than 100 exhibits. The 2006 trade show is scheduled for September 27th to September 30th in Indianapolis, Indiana and the 2007 trade show is scheduled for September 26th to September 29th in Orlando, Florida.
800 Attendees
Frequency: Annual/September

18586 ARTA Powertrain Expo
Automatic Transmission Rebuilders Association
2400 Latigo Avenue
Oxnard, CA 93030
805-604-2000
866-464-2872; *Fax:* 805-604-2003
dmadden@atra.com; www.atra.com
Dennis Madden, CEO
Jim Lyons, VP
Lance Wiggins, Director
Speakers on many subjects, providing information and tips for those within the transmission repair industry. Event provides the opportunity for members to meet and network.
2000 Members
Frequency: September
Founded in: 1954

18587 ASA Annual Convention
Automotive Service Association
8190 Precinct Line Road
Suite 100
Colleyville, TX 76034-7675
817-514-2900
800-272-7467; *Fax:* 817-514-0770
asainfo@ASAshop.org; www.asashop.org
Ron Pyle, President/Chief Staff Executive
Toni Slanton, Executive Director
Jhon Scully, Senior Vice President
Linda Ferguson, Program Administrator
Frequency: April/May

18588 American Engine Rebuilders Association Expo
American Engine Rebuilders Association
500 Coventry Lane
Suite 180
Crystal Lake, IL 60014
815-526-7600
888-326-2372; *Fax:* 815-526-7601
info@aera.org; www.aera.org
John Goodman, President
Dwayne J. Dugas, Chairman
Ron McMorris, First Vice Chairman
David Bianchi, Treasurer
550 exhibits with automotive services equipment, parts, tools, supplies and services. Seminar and dinner also offered.
6000 Attendees
Frequency: Annual
Founded in: 1974

18589 American Public Transportation Association Expo
American Public Transit Association
1666 K Street NW
Suite 1100
Washington, DC 20006
202-496-4800; *Fax:* 202-496-4324
meetings2@apta.com; www.apta.com
Michael Melaniphy, President
Gary Thomas, Chair
Rosemary Sherid, Marketing
Karen W. Harvey, Director Human Resources
Industry leaders from around the globe attend to meet suppliers of the latest public transportation products, services, and technologies designed to enhance the passenger experience and make your transit system more efficient and profitable.
15000 Attendees
Frequency: October 2008/2011
Founded in: 1882

18590 Annual Lean Six Sigma Conference
American Society for Quality
600 N Plankinton Avenue
PO Box 3005
Milwaukee, WI 53201-3005
414-272-8575
800-248-1946; *Fax:* 414-272-1734
help@asq.org; www.asq.org
James Rooney, Chair
Paul E Borawski, Executive Director
Erica Gumieny, Sales
Fay Spano, Communications/Media Relations
An exclusive two-day briefing and networking event designed by and for the top practitioners in the Six Sigma community.
100M Members
Frequency: Annual/February
Founded in: 1946

18591 Annual Quality Audit Conference
American Society for Quality
600 N Plankinton Avenue
PO Box 3005
Milwaukee, WI 53201-3005
414-272-8575
800-248-1946; *Fax:* 414-272-1734
help@asq.org; www.asq.org
James Rooney, Chair
Paul E Borawski, Executive Director
Erica Gumieny, Sales
Fay Spano, Communications/Media Relations
Topics of interest include: new innovating audit/process approaches, value added involvement, corporate expectations, corporate/social responsibility, auditing in the overall corporate scheme.
100M Members
Frequency: Annual/October
Founded in: 1946

18592 Annual Service Quality Conference
American Society for Quality
600 N Plankinton Avenue
PO Box 3005
Milwaukee, WI 53201-3005
414-272-8575
800-248-1946; *Fax:* 414-272-1734
help@asq.org; www.asq.org
James Rooney, Chair
Paul E Borawski, Executive Director
Erica Gumieny, Sales
Fay Spano, Communications/Media Relations
The sessions we plan will help you to navigate through unpredictable consumer behavior and increasing competition to build a strong foundation for reaching superior levels of quality service.
100M Members
Frequency: Annual/September
Founded in: 1946

18593 Annual World Conference on Quality and Improvement
American Society for Quality

600 N Plankinton Avenue
PO Box 3005
Milwaukee, WI 53201-3005

414-272-8575
800-248-1946; *Fax:* 414-272-1734
help@asq.org; www.asq.org

James Rooney, Chair
Paul E Borawski, Executive Director
Erica Gumieny, Sales
Fay Spano, Communications/Media Relations

Conference focuses on quality and improvement with more than 2,000 exhibits and attendees. Keynote speakers and sessions discuss quality tools, techniques and methodologies. Provides the opportunity for members to meet and network with colleagues in the industry.
100M Members
Frequency: Annual/May
Founded in: 1946

18594 Atlantic City Classic Car Show & Auction
Atlantic City Convention Center
One Convention Center Boulevard
Atlantic City, NJ 04801

609-449-2000; *Fax:* 609-449-2090;
www.acclassiccars.com
Social Media: Facebook, Twitter

Held annually, the AC Classic Car Show and Auction is the east coast's largest classic car show and auction.
60000 Attendees

18595 Auto Remarketing Convention
Auto Remarketing
Westview At Weston
301 Cascade Pointe Lane # 101
Cary, NC 27513

800-608-7500; *Fax:* 919-674-6027;
www.autoremarketing.com

Ron Smith, President

Executive conference focused on remarketing strategies for manufacturer, bank, finance, commercial and rental fleet/lease vehicles.
Frequency: February
Founded in: 1996

18596 Automotive Aftermarket Products Expo
Automotive Aftermarket Industry Association
7101 Wisconsin Avenue
Suite 1300
Bethesda, MD 20814-3415

301-654-6664; *Fax:* 301-654-3299
aaia@aftermarket.org; www.aftermarket.org

Kathleen Schmatz, President

Largest aftermarket trade show in North America, featuring over 1700 exhibitors of auto parts, accessories and services.
100M Attendees
Frequency: November

18597 Automotive Engine Rebuilders Association Expo
Automotive Engine Rebuilders Association
500 Coventry Lane
Suite 180
Crystal Lake, IL 60014-7592

815-526-7600
888-326-2372; *Fax:* 815-526-7601
info@aera.org; www.aera.org

John Goodman, President
Dwayne J. Dugas, Chairman
Ron McMorris, First Vice Chairman
David Bianchi, Treasurer

Demonstrations of the industry's latest technology in equipment, tools, supplies, parts, and services for automotive, heavy-duty, industrial, high-performance, marine, and specialty engines. Featuring the leading national and international companies showcasing the latest new products and services in the world of engine building, remanufacturing, and installation.

18598 BSA Convention
Bearing Specialists Association
800 Roosevelt Road
Building C, Suite 312
Glen Ellyn, IL 60137

630-858-3838; *Fax:* 630-790-3095
info@bsahome.org; www.bsahome.org
Social Media: LinkedIn

Linda Miller, President
Richard W Church, Executive Director
Jerilyn J Church, Executive Secretary
Kathy Fatz, Association Manager
Janet Arden, Publications Editor

The world's premier bearing industry event for authorized distributors of bearing products and services and the manufacturers of those products.
100 Members
Frequency: Annual
Founded in: 1966

18599 BSA Winter Meeting
Bearing Specialists Association
800 Roosevelt Road
Building C, Suite 312
Glen Ellyn, IL 60137

630-858-3838; *Fax:* 630-790-3095
info@bsahome.org; www.bsahome.org

Linda Miller, President
Jack Simpson, Vice President
Brian Negri, Treasurer
Kathy Fatz, Association Manager
Janet Arden, Publications Editor

BSA committees will be addressing many important issues and association projects at the Winter Meeting. Attending this meeting will help to influence the direction the industry takes over the coming years.
Frequency: Annual

18600 Chicago Auto Show
Chicago Automobile Trade Association
McCormick Place
2301 S Lake Shore Drive
Chicago, IL 60616

630-495-2282; *Fax:* 630-495-2260;
www.chicagoautoshow.com
Social Media: Facebook, Twitter, YouTube

Paul Brian, Director of Communications, CATA
Mark Bilek, Internet Director, CATA
Michelle Ferm, Communications Specialist, CATA
Dave Sloan, Auto Show General Manager
Sandi Potempa, Dir., Special Events & Exhibits

The Chicago Auto Show is the largest auto show in North America and has been held more times than any other auto exposition on the continent.
Frequency: Annual
Founded in: 1901

18601 Convergence Conference and Exhibition
Society of Automotive Engineers
755 W Big Beaver
Suite 1600
Troy, MI 48084

248-273-2455; *Fax:* 24- 27- 249
pkreh@sae.org; www.sae.org/convergence

Patti Kreh, Meetings, Exhibits Contact
Nori Fought, Meetings, Exhibits Contact
David Schutt, Chief Executive Officer

Serving the automotive and transportation electronics community by delivering relevant technology solutions and an electrifying line-up invited speakers and presenters.
8900+ Attendees
Frequency: October

18602 Dayton Auto Show
Hart Productions
60 N Second Street
Batavia, OH 45103

513-797-7900
877-704-8190; *Fax:* 513-797-1013
vicki@hartproductions.com;
www.hartproductions.com

Chip Hart, Show Management
Vicki Hart, Show Management
Vicki Diebold, Show Management
Trisha Marshall, Production Assistant
Victoria Hart, CFO

Annual auto show presented by the Dayton area Auto Dealers Association.
Frequency: March

18603 Heavy Duty Aftermarket Week
Association of Diesel Specialists
400 Admiral Boulevard
Kansas City, MO 64106

816-285-0810; *Fax:* 847-770-4952
info@diesel.org; www.diesel.org
Social Media: Facebook, LinkedIn

Chuck Hess, President
Andy Girres, Vice President
Chuck Oliveros, Treasurer
Carl Fergueson, Secretary
David Fehling, Executive Director

A distributor-focused business conference created by the industry's leading trade associations and marketing groups with a long-term goal of consolidating the many annual events on the industry calendar and to create the most valuable annual event for the heavy duty aftermarket. Heavy Duty Aftermarket Week is the largest North American gathering of the independent heavy-duty industry.
700+ Members
1800+ Attendees
Frequency: Annual/January
Founded in: 1956

18604 IAATI Annual Training Seminar
International Association of Auto Theft Investigators
PO Box 223
Clinton, NY

315-853-1913; *Fax:* 315-883-1310
jvabounader@iaati.org; www.iaati.org
Social Media: LinkedIn

Joe Broslus, President
John O'Byrne, VP
John V. Abounader, Executive Director
Marianne Finney, Marketing

Provides members who are auto theft investigators with resources to develop and maintain professional standards within the industry. Some of the topics covered range from arson and marine investigations to staged accident investigations. The 2012 seminar is in Kansas City, MO.
4904 Members
350 Attendees
Founded in: 1952

18605 International Autobody Congress and Exposition
Hanley-Wood
8600 Freeport Parkway
Suite 200
Irving, TX 75063

972-366-6324
888-529-1641; *Fax:* 972-536-6445

krobinson@hanleywood.com;
www.naceexpo.com

Linsay Roberts, Director
Ellen Pipkin, Show Manager

Specifically created for professionals involved in all aspects of the collision repair industry.
15M Attendees
Frequency: November

18606 International Big R Show
Automotive Parts Remanufacturers Association
7250 Heritage Village Plaza
Suite 201
Gainesville, VA 20155

703-968-2772; *Fax:* 703-968-2878
info@apra.org; www.apra.org

Omar Cueto, Chairman
Jay Robie, Vice President
Joe Kripli, President

Designed to attract rebuilders of a wide range of automotive and truck parts, exposing them to the key suppliers in this industry. Rebuilders specializing in electrical, c.v. joints, brake, clutch, transmissions, mechanical hydraulic, fuel systems, rack and pinion and air conditioning products will visit the show.
1000 Members
3000 Attendees
Frequency: Annual
Founded in: 1941

18607 LA Auto Show
Los Angeles Convention Center
1201 S Figueroa Street
Los Angeles, CA 90015

213-741-1151; www.laautoshow.com

The Los Angeles Auto Show is one of the top automotive events worldwide, bringing together the latest new vehicles from auto manufacturers around the world.

18608 MACS Convention and Trade Show
Mobile Air Conditioning Society Worldwide
225 S Broad Street
PO Box 88
Lansdale, PA 19446

215-631-7020; *Fax:* 215-631-7017
macsworldwide@macsw.org; www.macsw.org

David Jack, Secretary
Elvis Hoffpauir, President, CEO
Mary Koban, Director
Andrew Fiffick, Chairman
Peter Coll, Treasurer
2000 Attendees
Frequency: Annual

18609 NAAA Annual Conference
National Auto Auction Association
5320 Spectrum Drive
Suite D
Frederick, MD 21703

301-696-0400; *Fax:* 301-631-1359
naaa@naaa.com; www.naaa.com

Frank Hackett, Executive Director
Tom Dozier, Meetings Manager

Annual convention and exhibits of automobile and truck auction equipment, supplies and services.
Frequency: Fall

18610 NADA Convention & Expo
National Automobile Dealers Association
8400 Westpark Drive
Mc Lean, VA 22102-3522

703-217-7000
800-252-6232; *Fax:* 703-821-7075
nadainfo@nada.org; www.nada.org

Gary Heimes, Convention Director
Stephen R Pitt, Executive Director, Convention
Phillip Brady, President

Providing automobile dealers with the latest in cutting edge technology, products and services they need to impact the future success of their businesses.
25000 Attendees
Frequency: January/February

18611 NAFA Fleet Management Seminar
National Association of Fleet Administrators
125 Villiage Boulevard
Suite 200
Princeton, NJ 08540

609-720-0882; *Fax:* 609-452-8004
info@nafa.org; www.nafa.org

Phillip E Russo, Executive Director
Patrick McCarren, Deputy Executive Director
Joanne Marsdh, Director Marketing & Membership

Designed to provide comprehensive education to fleet managers like you who seek the fundamental principles and practices of successful fleet management.
3000+ Members
Founded in: 1957
Printed in on glossy stock

18612 NAFA Institute & Expo
National Association of Fleet Administrators
125 Villiage Boulevard
Suite 200
Princeton, NJ 08540

609-720-0882; *Fax:* 609-452-8004
info@nafa.org; www.nafa.org

Phillip E Russo, Executive Director
Patrick McCarren, Deputy Executive Director
Joanne Marsh, Director Marketing & Communications

To provide attendees and exhibitors alike with a more dynamic interaction on the exhibit hall floor and within concurrent sessions. An excellent opportunity to attend valuable education courses designed to benefit the veteran fleet professional as well as challenge first-time attendees!
3000+ Members
Frequency: April
Founded in: 1957
Printed in on glossy stock

18613 NARSA Annual Convention & Trade Show
National Automotive Radiator Service Association
3000 Villiage Run Road
Suite103, #221
Wexford, PA 15090-6315

724-799-8415
800-551-3232; *Fax:* 724-799-8416
info@narsa.org; www.narsa.org

Wayne Juchno, Executive Director
Douglas Shymoniak, Manager, Sales & New Business
Maarten Taal, President
Pat O'Connor, Vice President
Angelo Miozza, Treasurer

180 booths featuring seminars and workshops of parts, equipment and supplies.
1.8M Attendees
Frequency: Annual/November

18614 NPA Annual Convention & Expo
National Parking Association
1112 16th Street NW
Suite 300
Washington, DC 20036

202-296-4336
800-647-7275; *Fax:* 202-296-3102
info@weareparking.org
weareparking.org

Christine Banning, President
Christina Garneski, Vice President, Marketing & Comms
Stacy Hudson, Director, Business Development

Bringing together parking professionals from around the world with leading experts from business and industry to explore the latest trends and developments. The Convention also affords members an opportunity to share ideas and experiences and to explore the latest equipment and technologies at the Exposition.
Frequency: Annual
Founded in: 1955
Mailing list available for rent: 1700 names at $250 per M

18615 National Auto Glass Conference & Expo
National Glass Association
1945 Old Gallows Rd
Suite 750
Vienna, VA 22182

703-442-4890; *Fax:* 703-442-0630
attend@glass.org; www.glass.org

Phil James, President/CEO

Visit with over 50 companies and get informed about the latest technology and see products demonstrated live. Get answers to your technical questions and find out which solutions are right for your business.
800 Attendees
Frequency: Annual/May

18616 National Independent Automobile Dealers Association Convention & Expo
National Independent Automobile Dealers Assoc.
2521 Brown Boulevard
Arlington, TX 76006-5203

817-492-2377
800-682-3837; *Fax:* 817-649-5866
kimberly@niada.com; www.niada.com

Ginger Barrientez, Director of Events
Michael R Linn, President/CEO
Steven Jordan, COO

75 booths including automobile aftermarkets and finance companies.
Frequency: June

18617 National Quality Education Conference
American Society for Quality
600 N Plankinton Avenue
PO Box 3005
Milwaukee, WI 53201-3005

414-272-8575
800-248-1946; *Fax:* 414-272-1734
help@asq.org; www.asq.org

James Rooney, Chair
Paul E Borawski, CEO
Erica Gumieny, Sales
Fay Spano, Communications/Media Relations

Provides teachers, administrators, and support personnel opportunities to examine continuous improvement principles used in education. It provides resources and best practices to help you address requirements of No Child Left Behind, while helping you increase student achievement and improve overall performance.
100M Members
Frequency: Annual/November
Founded in: 1946

18618 New York International Auto Show
Jacob Javits Center
655 West 34th Street
New York, NY 10001

718-746-5300
800-282-3336; *Fax:* 718-746-9333;
www.autoshowny.com
Social Media: Facebook, Twitter, YouTube

The show offers virtually every make and model vehicle sold in the US under one roof giving consumers the unique opportunity to see everything the auto industry has to offer. From fuel-sipping economy cars to million dollar supercars, NYIAS has something for everyone.
Frequency: Annual

18619 North American Council of Automotive Teachers International Conference
North American Council of Automotive Teachers
PO Box 80010
Charleston, SC 29416

843-556-7068; *Fax:* 843-556-7068
office@nacat.com; www.nacat.com

Patrick Brown Harrison, President
Rob Thompson, Vice President
Curt Ward, Secretary
Chuck Ginther, Treasurer

Annual show of 70 exhibits and 50 seminars, suppliers, distributors, publishing companies and other trade organizations.
Frequency: July
Mailing list available for rent: 750 names at $165 per M

18620 North American International Auto Show
Detroit Auto Dealers Association
1900 W Big Beaver
Troy, MI 48084

248-643-0250; *Fax:* 248-637-0784
naiasmail@dada.org; www.naias.com

Rod Alberts, Executive Director
William Perkins, Chair

Annual show and exhibits of new automobiles and trucks, concept cars and van conversions.
808M Attendees
Frequency: January
Founded in: 1907

18621 PERA Annual Conference
Production Engine Remanufacturers Association
28203 Woodhave Road
Edwards, MO 65326

417-998-5057; *Fax:* 417-998-5056
nancieboland@pera.org; www.pera.org
Social Media: Facebook, LinkedIn

Nancie J. Boland, Executive VP
Robert P. McGraw, President

An opportunity to exchange ideas, methods and procedures necessary to efficiently produce remanufactured products which are equal or superior to original products in quality and performance. PERA adheres to and supports the premise that its members are dedicated to the highest business ethics, customer satisfaction, employee consideration and to the continual up-grading of the engine remanufacturing industry.
150 Attendees
Frequency: September / Seatle, WA
Founded in: 1946

18622 PWA Annual Conference
Performance Warehouse Association
41-701 Corporate Way
Suite 1
Palm Desert, CA 92260

760-346-5647; *Fax:* 760-346-5847
christina@pwa-par.org; www.pwa-par.org

John Towle, President
Larry Pacey, Chairman
Trent Lowe, Treasurer

This is an exclusive opportunity for manufacturers and distributors to meet in a private, business-like environment to discuss sales and marketing policies and programs.
165 Attendees
Frequency: Annual/September
Founded in: 1974

18623 Performance Racing Industry Trade Show
Performace Racing Industry
31706 South Coast Highway
Laguna Beach, CA 92651

949-499-5413; *Fax:* 949-499-0410
mail@performanceracing.com;
www.performanceracing.com

John Kilroy, Publisher/General Manager
Dan Schechner, Editor
Merredith Kaplan Burns, Managing Editor

Annual show. Features the latest in motorsports technology from 1400 companies with 4000 booths.
42000 Attendees
Frequency: Annual

18624 Philadelphia Auto Show
Philadelphia Convention Center
1101 Arch Street
Philadelphia, PA 19107

215-418-4700; www.phillyautoshow.com
Social Media: Facebook, Twitter

Recognized by the industry as one of the top shows in the country, the Philly Auto Show displays more than 700 vehicles from a variety of manufacturers.
Frequency: Annual

18625 RV Dealers International Convention & Expo
Recreation Vehicle Dealers Association
3930 University Drive
Fairfax, VA 22030-2515

703-591-7130; *Fax:* 703-359-0152
info@rvda.org; www.rvda.org

Mike Molino, CAE, President
Mary Anne Shreve, Editor

For RV retailers from across the U.S. and Canada.
Frequency: September
Mailing list available for rent: 1500 names

18626 RVAA Executive Conference
Recreational Vehicle Aftermarket Association
1833 Centre Point Circle
Suite 123
Naperville, IL 60563-9306

630-596-9004
info@rvaahq.org; www.rvaahq.org
Social Media: Facebook, Twitter

Patrick Farrey, Executive Director
Laura Hallen, Account Executive
Michael Greskiewicz, Expo Sales Manager
Meg Pawelski, Events & Awards Manager
Danielle Griffin, Communications Manager

An event which allows members to meet with each other to develop strategies for the coming year. It's the perfect opportunity for you to make the contacts and have the important face to face meeting time, with the potential partners that will enhance your success.
Frequency: October
Founded in: 1969

18627 SAE International Truck & Bus Meeting and Exhibition
Society of Automotive Engineers
755 W Big Beaver
Suite 1600
Troy, MI 48084

248-273-2455
877-606-7323; *Fax:* 248-273-2494
automotive_hq@sae.org; www.sae.org
Social Media: Facebook, Twitter, LinkedIn, YouTube, Google +

Dr. Rodica Baranescu, President
David Schutt, CEO
Nori Fought, Conference Service Representative
John Miller, Program Developer
Jack Pokrzywa, Operations Director

100 booths featuring suppliers of parts and components.
2.5M Attendees
Frequency: November

18628 SEMA International Auto Salon Trade Show
Specialty Equipment Market Association
1575 South Valley Vista Drive
Diamond Bar, CA 91765

909-610-2030
showinfo@sema.org; www.sema.org
Social Media: Facebook, Twitter, Google+

Christopher Kersting, President and CEO
Gary Vigil, Trade Show Director
Marel Del Rio, Trade Show Coordinator

When the sport-compact scene was just beginning, the show was launched to educate members about the growing market and to bring new buyers and opportunities to manufacturers.
Frequency: May
Founded in: 1998

18629 SEMA Offroad Convention
Specialty Equipment Market Association
1575 South Valley Vista Drive
Diamond Bar, CA 91765-0910

909-610-2030
sema@sema.org; www.phillyautoshow.com

Chris Kersting, President/CEO
Geoege Afremow, Vice President & CFO
Scooter Brothers, Chairman

Designed as a companion event to the well established SEMA Spring Expo, and as an extension of the SEMA Show, will target companies serving the recreational and performance off-road segments and aims to create new opportunities for this growing market.
Frequency: February

18630 SEMA Show
Specialty Equipment Market Association
1575 South Valley Vista Drive
Diamond Bar, CA 91765-0910

909-610-2030; *Fax:* 909-860-0184
sema@sema.org; www.sema.org

Chris Kersting, President/CEO
Geoege Afremow, Vice President & CFO
Scooter Scooter, Chairman

The premier automotive specialty performance products trade event in the world featuring performance, accessories, restoration and motorsports products.
100M Attendees
Frequency: November

18631 SEMA Spring Expo
Specialty Equipment Market Association

1575 South Valley Vista Drive
Diamond Bar, CA 91765-0910

909-610-2030
sema@sema.org; www.sema.org

Chris Kersting, President/CEO
Geoege Afremow, Vice President & CFO
Scooter Scooter, Chairman

The only trade show delivering the SEMA Show experience to the doorsteps of regional auto and truck parts and accessory businesses. We feature the leading companies that produce truck caps and accessories, automotive trim and restyling products, wheels and tires, gauges and instruments, performance parts and more.
Frequency: February

18632 SIGM Annual Meeting
Society of Independent Gasoline Marketers
3930 Pender Drive
Suite 340
Fairfax, VA 22030

703-709-7000; *Fax:* 703-709-7007
sigma@sigma.org; www.sigma.org

Kenneth Doyle, Executive Vice President
Susan Crosby, Director, Communication & Education
Mary Alice Kutyn, Director of Meetings
Nancy Muskett, Director, Advertising & Sponsorship
Marilyn Selvitelle, Director, Business Development

SIGMA meetings are valuable and varied, addressing topics of interest for branded or unbranded motor fuel marketers, those interested in alternative fuels, fuel suppliers, and of course administrative and financial discussions for all types of organizations.
Frequency: October

18633 SOUTHCON
Wescon
1230 Rosecrans Avenue
Suite 100
Manhattan Beach, CA 90266

310-524-4100
800-877-2668; *Fax:* 310-643-7328
j.cruz@ecishow.com; www.southcon.org

Joey Quesada Cruz, Show Management
Rod Mann, Conference Management

Issues that concern design, manufacturing and test departments. Instructors are leading experts in the topics they present.
10M Attendees
Frequency: February

18634 Supernationals Custom Auto Show
TNT Promotions Inc
PO Box 50386
Albuquerque, NM 87181-0386

505-480-0056
800-300-9381; www.thesupernationals.com

The premier annual automotive event in New Mexico. Attracts prominent street rods and customs from throughout the country, as well as local and regional vehicles for both show and competition display.
25000 Attendees
Frequency: Annual/February
Founded in: 1992

18635 TIA World Tire Expo
Tire Industry Association
1532 Pointer Ridge Place
Suite G
Bowie, MD 20716-1883

301-430-7280
800-876-8372; *Fax:* 301-430-7283
info@tireindustry.org; www.tireindustry.org

Gary Albright, President & CEO
Lary Brandt, CEO
Mike Berra Jr, Vice President
Eddie Burleson, General Manager

Providing an ideal forum for diverse individuals to meet, network and advance new business and marketing opportunities. This world-class exhibition is the number one showcase dedicated to those who have an interest in tire, rubber and transportation services.
Frequency: April

18636 WMDA Mega Show Annual Convention
WMDA Service Station & Automotive Repair Assoc.
1532 Pointer Ridge Place
Suite G
Bowie, MD 20716

301-390-0900
800-492-0329; *Fax:* 301-390-3161
mgates@wmda.net; www.wmda.net
Social Media: Facebook

Rick Agoris, President
Marta Gates, Director of Operations
Kirk McCauley, Director of Member Relations
Tirika Williams, Director of Finance

Featuring Over 225 Exhibits for the service station, automotive repair, car wash, convenience store & tire industries.
1500 Attendees

18637 iFlex Annual Conference
Automotive Oil Change Association
330 North Wabash Avenue
Suite 2000
Chicago, IL 60611

312-321-5132
800-230-0702; *Fax:* 312-673-6832
info@aoca.org; www.aoca.org

Bryan White, Executive Director
David Haney, President
Dave Jensen, Vice President
Bob Falter, Treasurer
Jim Grant, Secretary

Brings hundreds of vendors offering thousands of products and services to the fast lube industry and ancillary profit centers.
3000 Members
Frequency: Annual/April-May
Founded in: 1987

Directories & Databases

18638 American Bus Association's Motorcoach Marketer
American Bus Association
111 K Street NE
9th Floor
Washington, DC 20002

202-842-1645; *Fax:* 202-842-0850
abainfo@buses.org; www.buses.org

Thomas JeBran, President
John Meier, Vice Chairman
Frank Henry, Secretary/Treasurer

This directory is a comprehensive guide of the bus and travel industry offering information on hotels and sightseeing services, attractions, museums, restaurants and more.
500 Pages
Frequency: Annual
Founded in: 1926

18639 American Public Transit Association Membership Directory
American Public Transit Association
1666 K St NW
Suite 1100
Washington, DC 20006-1215

202-496-4800; *Fax:* 202-496-4324
hbrett@apta.com; www.apta.com

Michael Melaniphy, President/CEO
Petra Mollet, VP
Rosemary Sheridan, VP Communications and Marketing

A who's who directory of services and supplies within the public transportation industry.
Founded in: 1882

18640 Automotive Aftermarket Suppliers
Automotive Aftermarket Suppliers Association
10 Laboratory Drive
PO Box 13966
Research Triangle Park, NC 27709-3966

919-549-4800; *Fax:* 919-549-4824
media@mema.org;
www.aftermarketsuppliers.org

Steve Handschuh, President
Chris Gardner, VP
Margaret Beck, Marketing and Communications

Directory of automotive supply chains and jobbers/retailers in North America. Also, warehouse distributors and major programmed distribution groups.
Founded in: 1974

18641 Automotive Parts Remanufacturers Association Membership Directory
Automotive Parts Remanufacturers Association
7250 Heritage Village Plaza
Suite 201
Gainesville, VA 20155

703-968-2772; *Fax:* 703-968-2878
info@apra.org; www.apra.org

Omar Cueto, Chairman
Joe Kripli, President

Lists member companies and their products, addresses, phone and fax numbers, key personnel and sometimes even internet information. Keep this directory, your network resource for the automotive parts rebuilding industry, on your desk throughout the year.
Cost: $35.00
Frequency: Annual
Founded in: 1941

18642 ELM Guide to Automakers in North America
ELM International
PO Box 1740
East Lansing, MI 48826-1740

517-332-4900; *Fax:* 517-351-3032
contact_us@automotivesuppliers.com

The third edition of this guide contains more than 400 profiles that highlight the North American manufacturing operations of Chrysler, Ford, GM and all of the foreign owned automakers.
Cost: $350.00
Frequency: Semiannual

18643 ELM Guide to Japanese Affiliated Suppliers in North America
ELM International
PO Box 1740
East Lansing, MI 48826-1740

517-332-4900; *Fax:* 517-351-3032
contact_us@automotivesuppliers.com;
www.automotivesuppliers.com

Mark Santucci

Offers information on approximately 290 Japanese owned automotive original equipment components manufacturers that operate in North

America.
Cost: $350.00

18644 ELM Guide to US Automotive Sourcing
ELM International
PO Box 1740
East Lansing, MI 48826-1740
517-332-4900; *Fax:* 517-351-3032
contact_us@automotivesuppliers.com
Mark Santucci, Executive Director
Two volumes offering information on automotive original equipment manufacturer parts and components suppliers and profiles of plants belonging to 576 companies.
Cost: $775.00
1200 Pages

18645 NAFA's Professional Directory
National Association of Fleet Administrators
125 Village Boulevard
Suite 200
Princeton, NJ 08540
609-720-0882; *Fax:* 609-452-8004
info@nafa.org; www.nafa.org
Social Media: Facebook, Twitter, LinkedIn
Phillip E. Russo, Executive Director
Patrick McCarren, Executive Director
Mary Sticha, Vice President
Joanne Marsh, Director of Marketing
Gladys Reyes, Meeting & Event Planners
NAFA Member and Affiliate contact information.
2600+ Members
Frequency: Quarterly

18646 Old Cars Price Guide
F+W Media
38 E. 29th Street
New York, NY 10016
212-447-1400; *Fax:* 212-447-5231
contact_us@fwmedia.com;
www.fwpublications.com
Rick Groth, Publisher
Ron Kowalke, Editor
David Nussbaum, CEO
Sara Domville, President
The nation's most respected authority for pricing antique and collectible automobiles. The extensive price-guide section covers makes and models of domestic cars, from AMC to Willys, from model years 1901 to 1994. Also included are light-duty trucks and selected makes of imported cars. Cars are valued in six conditions - from 'Excellent' down to 'Parts Car.' Also includes columns and features on collectible cars.
Cost: $19.98
148 Pages
Frequency: Monthly
Circulation: 61000
Founded in: 1978

18647 PXN Parts Exchange New
15030 Avenue of Science
Suite 100
San Diego, CA 92128
858-946-1900
800-669-4237; *Fax:* 858-946-1073
ICSCUser@audatex.com; www.adpclaims.com
Social Media: Facebook, Twitter, LinkedIn, YouTube
Tony Aquila, Chairman, President & CEO
Jack Sanders, COO
Kamal Hamid, Director Investor Relations
Lisa Collins, Marketing Coordinator
Provides an electronic link from your ADP estimating system to comprehensive database of new replacement parts. Data on over three and a half million parts facilitates the writing of complete, cost-effective damage reports.

18648 RV Trade Digest
Cygnus Publishing
1233 Janesville Avenue
Fort Atkinson, WI 53538
920-000-1111
800-547-7377; *Fax:* 920-563-1699
info@cygnus.com; www.cygnus.com
John French, CEO
Paul Bonaiuto, CFO
Ed Wood, VP, HR and Communications
Kris Flitcroft, EVP-Residential, Construction, Mfg.
Blair Johnson, SVP, Business Development
Propriety BASE technology connecting businesses with multi-media content.
Cost: $40.00
40 Pages
Frequency: Bi-Monthly
Circulation: 15,000
Founded in: 1983
Printed in 4 colors on glossy stock

18649 Transmission Digest Buyer's Guide Issue
MD Publications
PO Box 2210
3057 E Cairo Street
Springfield, MO 65801-2210
417-866-3917
800-274-7890; *Fax:* 417-866-2781
bmace@mdpublications.com;
www.mdpublications.com
Carol Langsford, President
Michelle Dickeman, Vice President
Bob Mace, Publisher
Gary Sifford, Editor
Mike Anderson, Advertising Sales
List of over 500 manufacturers and distributors of products and services for the motor vehicle transmission repair industry.
Cost: $15.00
Printed in 4 colors on glossy stock

18650 Ward's Automotive Yearbook
Ward's Communications
3000 Town Center
Suite 2750
Southfield, MI 48075-1245
248-799-2622; *Fax:* 248-357-9747
tduncan@wardsauto.com; www.wardsauto.com
Social Media: Facebook, Twitter
Thomas Duncan, Group Publisher
James Bush, Managing Editor
David Zoia, Editorial Director
Drew Winter, Senior Editor
Chris Lamphear, Marketing Director
Directory of suppliers to the vehicle manufacturing industry. New vehicle sales, production and inventory data and new vehicle product information and statistics.
Cost: $475.00
500 Pages
Frequency: Annual
Circulation: 26,000
ISBN: 0-910589-15-1
Founded in: 1938

18651 Who Makes It and Where Directory
Tire Guides
1101 S Rogers Circle
Suite 6
Boca Raton, FL 33487-2748
561-997-9229; *Fax:* 561-997-9233
tireinfo@tireguides.com; www.tireguides.com
Nancy Garfield, Owner
James Garfield, Editor-in-Chief
Al Snyder, Contributing Editor
Jeff Chychrun, Associate Editor
Brand listings with manufacturer & distributor information; worldwide listing of web site addresses, fax numbers & U.S. toll free numbers.
Cost: $7.00
62 Pages
Frequency: Annual
Founded in: 1950

18652 Worldwide Automotive Supplier Directory
Society of Automotive Engineers
400 Commonwealth Drive
Warrendale, PA 15086-7511
724-776-4841
877-606-7323; *Fax:* 724-776-0790
customerservice@sae.org; www.sae.org
Social Media: Facebook, Twitter, LinkedIn, YouTube, Google+
David Schutt, President
Michael Thompson, Publisher
Melissa Bachman, Marketing
Peggy Bartlett, Corporate Sales
Directory features 10,000+ supplier listings from every major vehicle-producing region. And, it is the ONLY directory to provide information on a company's technical capabilities.
Cost: $329.00
Frequency: Annual
Circulation: 60,550
ISBN: 0-768015-36-7

Industry Web Sites

18653 http://gold.greyhouse.com
G.O.L.D Grey House OnLine Databases
Grey House Publishing's online database platform, GOLD, offers Quick Search, Keyword Search and Expert Search for most business sectors including automotive and transportation markets. The GOLD platform makes finding the information you need quick and easy - whether you're a novice searcher or an experienced database user. All of Grey House's directory products are available for subscription on the GOLD platform.

18654 www.aaam.org
Assn for the Advancement of Automotive Medicine
A professional multidisciplinary organization dedicated entirely to motor vehicle crash prevention and control.

18655 www.aamva.org
American Assn. of Motor Vehicle Administrators
Nonprofit organization represents state and provincial officials in the US and Canada who administer and enforce motor vehicle laws. Strives to develop model programs in motor vehicle administration, police traffic services and highway safety.

18656 www.aflaonline.com
Automotive Fleet & Leasing Association
Designed to improve communications among buyers, sellers, fleet administrators, lending institutions, lessors, used vehicle marketers and allied automotive service companies.

18657 www.aftermarket.org
Automotive Aftermarket Industry Association
For those involved in the motor vehicle replacement parts industry.

18658 www.aiada.org
American Int'l Automobile Dealers Assocation
Lobbying and communications organization for American automobile dealerships that sell and service international nameplate brands.

18659 www.aiag.org
Automotive Industry Action Group
Composed of major North American vehicle manufacturers and their suppliers. Provides an open forum where members cooperate to develop and promote solutions that enhance prosperity in the automotive industry.

18660 www.aoca.org
Automotive Oil Change Association
Representing the convenient automotive service industry. Dedicated to enhancing the competency of fast lube owners, educating the public about services our members offer and maintaining a favorable business environment for the industry as a whole.

18661 www.apra.org
Automotive Parts Rebuilders Association
Association of more than 1,500 member companies engaged in the rebuilding of automotive related hard parts, including starters, alternators, clutches, transmissions, brakes, drive shafts and other parts for passenger cars, trucks, off road, equipment and industrial uses.

18662 www.asq.org
American Society for Quality
The world's leading authority on quality that creates better workplaces and communitites worldwide by advancing learning, quality improvement, and knowledge exchange to improve business results.

18663 www.atra-gears.com
Automatic Transmission Rebuilders Association
Not for profit professional organization dedicated to the improvement and welfare of the automatic transmission repair industry for the benefit of the motoring public.

18664 www.autobpa.com
Automotive Body Parts Association
Members are companies that distribute, supply or manufacture automotive replacement body parts.

18665 www.autoconsulting.com
Automotive Consulting Group
Management consulting firm providing top line and bottom line business performance improvement services to the worldwide automotive industry.

18666 www.automotivefleetmgt.com
Automotive Fleet Management Corporation
Formed in order that financial institutions such as banks, credit unions and finance companies could repossess and dispose of their automotive collateral in a manner that is quick, efficient and cost effective.

18667 www.awda.org
Automotive Warehouse Distributors Association
Oldest organized group of warehouse distributors and their respective suppliers of parts, accessories tools and other supplies for the automotive aftermarket. In January 2004, AWDA joined forces with the Automotive Aftermarket Industry Association.

18668 www.buses.org
American Bus Association
Trade association for the North American bus industry.

18669 www.busesintl.com
Buses International Association
An organization of persons throughout the world who are professionally involved in the management of companies or organizations which operate or manufacture buses.

18670 www.carcare.org
Car Care Council
A nonprofit 501 (c) (3) educational foundation whose purpose is to educate motorists about the importance of maintenance repairs and entertainment for safer, cleaner better performing vehicles. Provides editorial and public service material for media use.

18671 www.classiccar.com
ClassicCar.Com
Offers classic car enthusiasts around the world an online community with chats, forums and discussion groups.

18672 www.diesel.org
Association of Diesel Specialists
The worldwide diesel industry's leading trade association, dedicated to the highest level of service on diesel fuel injection and related systems.

18673 www.edmunds.com
Edmunds.Com
Founded in: 1966 for the purpose of publishing new and used automotive pricing guides for automobile buyers.

18674 www.filtercouncil.org
Filter Manufacturers Council
For manufacturers of vehicular and industrial filtration products in North America. Active in efforts to educate people on proper disposal of used oil filters.

18675 www.forecast1.com
Forecast International
An electronic information/data service sourced from thousands of worldwide publications, in 15 languages. Provides concise passenger vehicles e-mail news and analysis summaries, news, trends and contract information with hyper-links to the source or a related website. Delivered 100 times a year.

18676 www.greyhouse.com
Grey House Publishing
Authoritative reference directories for most business sectors including automotive and transportation markets. Users can search the online databases with varied search criteria allowing for custom searches by product category, geographic area, sales volume, keyword, subject and more. Full Grey House catalog and online ordering also available.

18677 www.hemmings.com
Hemmings Motor News
Hemmings Motor News for the car collector and enthusiast.

18678 www.iaati.org
Int'l Association of Auto Theft Investigators
To improve communication and coordination among the growing family of professional auto theft investigators.

18679 www.impa.org
International Motor Press Association
Professional group of writers and editors producing auto articles for the press, radio or TV.

18680 www.macsw.org
Mobile Air Conditioning Society Worldwide
Provides technical training, information and communication for the professionals in the automotive air conditioning industry.

18681 www.mema.org
Motor and Equipment Manufacturers Association
Serves manufacturers of all types of automotive and truck products through market research, legislative and regulatory representation and reporting, information services, EDI network and credit reporting.

18682 www.naaa.com
National Auto Auction Association
Represents dealer wholesale auto auctions. Promotes exchange of ideas and public relations in the used car merchandising industry.

18683 www.nada.com
National Automobile Dealers Association
Provides representation for franchised new car and truck dealers in government, industry and public affairs. Provides counsel on legal and regulatory and political representation on Capital Hill.

18684 www.nafa.org
National Association of Fleet Administrators
Serving the needs of those managing fleets of automobiles, light duty trucks and/or vans for US and Canadian organizations. Offers statistical research, publications, regional meetings, government representation, conferences, trade shows and seminars.

18685 www.narsa.org
National Automotive Radiator Service Association
Trade association serving the cooling system service industry and the public.

18686 www.nascar.com
Turner Sports Interactive
Providing up-to-the-minute coverage on a 24-hour basis, NASCAR.COM delivers news, statistics and information on races, drivers, teams and industry events.

18687 www.nationalwheelandrim.org
National Wheel and Rim Association
Represents warehouse distributors of wheels, rims and related parts in the US and Canada.

18688 www.ncsfa.state.ut.us
National Conference of State Fleet Administrators
For state government administrators responsible for vehicle fleet management.

18689 www.ntea.com
National Truck Equipment Association
Represents small to mid-sized companies that manufacture, distribute, install, buy, sell and repair commercial trucks, truck bodies, truck equipment, trailers and accessories.

18690 www.partsplus.com
Association of Automotive Aftermarkets
Purchases and markets automotive replacement parts. Headquarters office for Parts Plus program distributors.

18691 www.pera.org
Production Engine Remanufacturers Association
The goal of the Production Engine Remanufacturers Association is to provide it's members with the opportunity to exchange the ideas, methods and procedures necessary to efficiently produce remanufactured products which are equal or superior to original products in quality and performance.

18692 www.pwa-par.com
Performance Warehouse Association
An organization of specialty automotive parts wholesalers joined together and dealing with management, financial and legislative matters.

18693 www.retread.org
Tire Retread Information Bureau

Serving as the public relations arm of the retread industry. Gathering and disseminating information on retread passenger and truck tires to members and the general public.

18694 www.rma.org
Rubber Manufacturers Association

National trade association for makers of tires and other rubber products.

18695 www.rvda.org
National RV Dealers Association

National association advances the best interests of RV retailers through education, services, leadership and programs of market expansion that promote increased use and sale of RVs as well as enhancement of the RV's image.

18696 www.scrs.com
Society of Collision Repair Specialists

For owners and managers of auto collision repair shops, suppliers, insurance and educational associates and suppliers in the US, Canada, Australia and New Zealand. Distributes technical, management, marketing and sales information. Works to promote professionalism within the collision repair industry.

18697 www.theautochannel.com
Auto Channel

Auto news, commentary and other useful information.

18698 www.tireindusty.org
Tire Industry Association

Representing all segments of the tire industry, including those that manufacture, repair, recycle, sell, service or use new or retreaded tires and also those suppliers or individuals who furnish equipment, material or services to the industry.

Associations

18699 Academy of Country Music
5500 Balboa Blvd
Suite 200
Encino, CA 91316-1505
818-788-8000; *Fax:* 818-788-0999
info@acmcountry.com; www.acmcountry.com
Drain Murphy, Chairman
David Young, Director Operations
Tiffany Moon, Secretary
Brandi Brammer, Project Manager
Tree Paine, Director Marketing
Involved in numerous events and activities promoting country music. Presents annual awards.
4M Members
Founded in: 1964

18700 Accordian Federation of North America
14126 E Rosencrans Boulevard
Santa Fe Springs, CA 90670
562-921-5058
afna@musician.org; www.afnafestival.org
Social Media: Facebook, Twitter, Google+
Madeleine D'Ablaing, President
Debbie Gray, VP
Oakley Yale, Secretary
Prisscilla Martinez, Treasurer
Larry Demian, Parliamentarian
Members are primarily teachers and music school owners with the primary purpose to encourage young people to pursue their music study. Holds festivals and competitions
75 Members
Founded in: 1972

18701 Accordionists & Teachers Guild International
813 West Lakeshore Drive
O'Fallon, IL 62269-1216
618-632-2859
amyjo@apci.net; www.accordions.com/atg
Amy Jo Sawyer, President
Joe Natole, First Vice President
Liz Finch, Second Vice President
Joan C. Sommers, Executive Secretary
ATG members are accordion teachers and professionals committed to furthering the progress of the accordion by improving teaching standards, music and all phases of music education.
Founded in: 1940

18702 Acoustical Society of America
1305 Walt Whitman Road
Suite 300
Melville, NY 11747-4300
516-576-2360; *Fax:* 631-923-2875
asa@acousticalsociety.org;
www.acousticalsociety.org
Christy K. Holland, President
Lily M. Wang, Vice President
David Feit, Treasurer
Christopher J. Struck, Standards Director
Susan E. Fox, Executive Director
Premier international scientific society in acoustics, dedicated to increasing and diffusing the knowledge of acoustics and its practical applications.

18703 American Choral Directors Association
545 Couch Drive
PO Box 2720
Oklahoma City, OK 73101-2720
405-232-8161; *Fax:* 405-232-8162;
www.acdaonline.org
Timothy Sharp, Executive Director
Jerry Mccoy, President
Haiary Aphelstadt, VP
Jo-Ann Miller, Treasurer
Nonprofit music-education organization whose central purpose is to promote excellence in choral music through performance, composition, publication, research and teaching. In addition, ACDA strives to elevate choral music's position in American society through arts advocacy. Holds annual convention.
Cost: $90.00
19500 Members
Founded in: 1959

18704 American College of Musicians
PO Box 1807
Austin, TX 78767
512-478-5775; *Fax:* 512-478-5843
ngpt@pianoguild.com; www.pianoguild.com
Richard Allison, President
Julia Kruger, VP
Provides student awards and teachers benefits.
Founded in: 1931

18705 American Composers Alliance
PO Box 1108
New York, NY 10040
212-568-0036
info@composers.com
composers.com
Social Media: Facebook, Twitter, YouTube
Gina Genova, Director
Music publisher and licensor representing Americans composing in the classical style.
Founded in: 1937

18706 American Federation of Musicians of the United States and Canada
1501 Broadway
Suite 600
New York, NY 10036-5501
212-869-1330; *Fax:* 212-764-6134
info@afm.org; www.afm.org
Social Media: Facebook, Twitter, YouTube
Thomas Lee, President
Linda Patterson, Executive Secreatry to President
AFM is an association of professional musicians united through their locals so that they can live and work in dignity; produce work that will be fulfilling and compensated fairly; have a meaningful voice in decisions that affect them; have the opportunity to develop their talents and skills; whose collective voice and power will be realized in a democratic and progressive union; and who oppose the forces of exploitation through their union solidarity.
10K Members
Founded in: 1896

18707 American Federation of Violin and Bow Makers
1121 East Avenue
Red Wing, MN 55066
929-216-0720
info@afvbm.org; www.afvbm.org
David Bonsey, President
Dan Weisshaar, Vice President
Yung Chin, Treasurer
Lisbeth Nelson Butler, Secretary
Members are those with recognized professional abilities and experience in either making or repairing violins and bows. They are elected to the Federation and are entitled to all privileges and duties of membership. The Federation has designed programs to held develop the technical skills and knowledge of the membership through seminars and regular meeting events. The Federation sponsors exhibitions as a forum for makers,musicians and the general public.
Founded in: 1980

18708 American Gamelan Institute
603-448-6060; *Fax:* 603-448-6060
agi@gamelan.org; www.gamelan.org
Founded in: 1983

18709 American Guild of Music
PO Box 599
Warren, MI 48090
248-686-1975
agm@americanguild.org;
www.americanguild.org
Barry Carr, President
Joanne Darby, Treasurer
Lorelei Eccleston Dart, First VP
Steve Petrunak, Second VP
The world's oldest international music organization. Its membership is open to independent music teachers, music store owners and their teaching staffs, music publishers and instrument manufacturers and music students.
6000 Members

18710 American Guild of Musical Artists
1430 Broadway
14th Floor
New York, NY 10018-3308
212-265-3687; *Fax:* 212-262-9088
agma@musicalartists.org;
www.musicalartists.org
Social Media: Facebook, Twitter
Alan S.Gordon, Executive Director
Gerry Angel, Director of Operations
Deborah A.Maher, Associate Executive Director
Gerry Angel, Director of Operations
AGMA is a labor union. It negotiates collective bargaining agreements for its members that provide them with these vital benefits: guaranteed salaries; rehearsal and overtime pay; regulated work hours; vacation and sick pay; access to low-cost health benefits; good-faith resolution of disputes; and protection of their legal and contractual rights.
5700 Members
Founded in: 1936

18711 American Guild of Organists
475 Riverside Drive
Suite 1260
New York, NY 10115-0055
212-870-2310; *Fax:* 212-870-2163
info@agohq.org; www.agohq.org
Social Media: Facebook, Twitter, LinkedIn, Google+
James Thomashower, Executive Director
Marcia Van Oyen, Director
Membership in the American Guild of Organists is primarily through local chapters, which hold regular meetings featuring performances, lectures, seminars, and discussions on a wide variety of topics. Many chapters also offer monthly newsletters, scholarship programs, musician placement services, and substitute referrals to employing institutions. Membership can also be without chapter affiliation.
20000 Members
Founded in: 1896

18712 American Harp Society
PO Box 278
Greenfield Center, NY 12833
518-893-7495; www.harpsociety.org

Ann Yeung, President
Barbara Lepke Sims, 1st VP
Carolyn Munford, 2nd VP
Erin Wood, Secretary
Ashanti Pretlow, Executive Secretary

Promotes and fosters the appreciation of the harp as a musical instrument, to encourage the composition of music for the harp and to improve the quality of performance of harpists.
Cost: $50.00
3000 Members
Founded in: 1962

18713 American Music Therapy Association
8455 Colesville Rd
Suite 1000
Silver Spring, MD 20910-3392

301-589-3300; *Fax:* 301-589-5175
info@musictherapy.org;
www.musictherapy.org
Social Media: Facebook, Twitter, YouTube

Andrea Farbman, Executive Director
Brian Abrams, Mid Atlantic Region President

The mission of the American Music Therapy Association is to advance public awareness of the benefits of music therapy and increase access to quality music therapy services in a rapidly changing world.
3800 Members
Founded in: 1998

18714 American Musical Instrument Society
1106 Garden Street
Hoboken, NJ 07030

201-656-0107
amis@guildassoc.com; www.amis.org
Social Media: Facebook

Albert R Rice, President
Carolyn Bryant, Vice-President
Deborah Check Reeves, Secretary
Joanne Kopp, Treasurer

Promotes better understanding of all aspects of history, design, construction, restoration, and usage of musical instruments in all cultures and from all periods. The membership of AMIS includes collectors, historians, curators, performers, instrument makers, restorers, dealers, conservators, teachers, students, and many institutional members.
Founded in: 1971

18715 American Musicological Society
194 Mercer St. Room 404
New York, NY 10012-1502

212-992-6340
877-679-7648; *Fax:* 212-885-4022
ams@ams-net.org; www.ams-net.org
Social Media: Facebook, Twitter, YouTube

Robert Judd, Executive Director
Al Hipkins, Office Manger
Melissa Kapocius, Secretary

A spcoety of professional musicologist and university educators. The annual meetings are held in the fall each year; 1007-Quebec; 2008-Nashville; 2009-Philedelphia.
3600 Members
Founded in: 1934

18716 American Orff-Schulwerk Association
PO Box 391089
Cleveland, OH 44139-8089

440-543-5366; *Fax:* 440-600-7332
info@aosa.org; www.aosa2.org

Katharine P. Johnson, Executive Director
Jo Ella Hug, President
Julie Scott, VP
Jennifer Hartman, Treasurer

Professional organization of music and movement educators dedicated to the creative teaching approach developed by Carl Orff and Gunild Keetman.
Cost: $70.00

18717 American School Band Directors Association
227 N 1st Street
PO Box 696
Guttenberg, IA 52052-0696

563-252-2500; *Fax:* 563-252-2500
asbda@alpinecom.net; www.asbda.com
Social Media: Facebook

Blair Callaway, President
Susan Barrett, Secretary
Blair Callaway, Treasurer
Dennis Hanna, Manager
Russ Hilton, Treasurer

Nationwide organization dedicated to the support of professional and college band conductors. Membership by invitation only.
1200 Members
Founded in: 1953

18718 American Society of Composers, Authors and Publishers (ASCAP)
1 Lincoln Plaza
New York, NY 10023-7097

212-621-6000; *Fax:* 212-621-8453
info@ascap.com; www.ascap.com
Social Media: Facebook, Twitter, LinkedIn, YouTube

Paul Williams, President/Chairman
James M Kendrick, Treasurer
Caroline Bienstock, Secretary
John Lofrumento, CEO

Performing rights organization created and controlled by composers, songwriters and music publishers. Protects the rights of its members by licensing and distributing royalties for the non-dramatic public performances of their copyrighted works. An online newsletter is also available filled with the most up-to-date information about professional opportunities, legislative issues, member benefits and more.
26000 Members
Founded in: 1914

18719 American Society of Music Arrangers and Composers
5903 Noble Ave
Van Nuys, CA 91411-3026

818-994-4661; *Fax:* 818-994-6181
asmac@theproperimageevents.com;
www.asmac.org
Social Media: Facebook, Twitter, LinkedIn, Youtube

Scherr Lillico, Executive Director
Duane L Tatro, Vice President
Ray Charles, Vice President

Professional society for arrangers, composers, orchestrators, and musicians. Monthly meetings with great speakers from the music industry.
500 Members
Founded in: 1938

18720 American Song Writers Association

205-815-8180
info@americansongwritersassociation.com;
www.americansongwritersassociation.com
Social Media: Facebook, Twitter, Pinterest

18721 American String Teachers Association
4155 Chain Bridge Rd
Fairfax, VA 22030-4102

703-279-2113; *Fax:* 703-279-2114
asta@astaweb.com; www.astaweb.com

Donna Hale, Executive Director
Beth Danner-Knight, Deputy Director
Mary Jane Dye, Deputy Director

A membership organization for string and orchestra teachers and players, helping them to develop and refine their careers. Members range from budding student teachers to artist-status performers, businesses who supply goods and services to the string and orchestra world plus colleges, universities, music programs and conservatories.
11300 Members
Founded in: 1946

18722 American Union of Swedish Singers

E-Mail: president@auss.org; www.auss.org
500+ Members

18723 American Viola Society
14070 Proton Rd
Suite 100
Dallas, TX 75244-3601

972-233-9107; *Fax:* 972-490-4219
info@avsnationaloffice.org;
www.americanviolasociety.org
Social Media: Facebook, Twitter

Nokunthula Ngwenyama, President
Madeline Crouch, General Manager
Karin Brown, Secretary
Michelle Sayles, Treasurer

An association for the promotion of viola performance and research. AVS membership is accompanied by two print issues of the Journal of the American Viola Society (JAVS) each year.
1000 Members

18724 Americana Music Association
The Factory at Franklin
PO Box 628
Franklin, TN 37065

615-386-6936; *Fax:* 615-386-6937
press@americanamusic.org;
www.americanamusic.org
Social Media: Facebook, Twitter, Pinterest, YouTube

Jed Hilly, Executive Director
Danna Strong, Director
Michelle Aquilato, Director of Marketing
Sarah Comardelle, Manager of Marketing
Whitney Holmes, Manager of Member Relations

18725 Association for Electronic Music
www.associationforelectronicmusic.org
Social Media: Twitter

Mark Lawrence, CEO

18726 Association of Concert Bands
6613 Cheryl Ann Drive
Independence, OH 44131-3718

800-726-8720; *Fax:* 216-524-1897;
www.acbands.org
Social Media: Facebook

Allen Beck, President
Nada Vencl, Secretary
Mike Montgomery, CIO
Howard Habenicht, Treasurer

The purpose of ACB is to encourage and foster adult concert community, municipal, and civic bands and to promote the performance of the

highest quality traditional and contemporary literature for band.
750 Members
Founded in: 1977

18727 Blues Foundation
421 S.Main St
Memphis, TN 38103-4464

901-527-2583; *Fax:* 901-529-4030
jay@blues.org; www.blues.org
Social Media: Facebook, Twitter, LinkedIn, YouTube, RSS

Jay Sieleman, President
Joey Whitmer, DeputuDirector
Cindy James, Membership
Chadd Webb, Treasurer

A nonprofit corporation which serves as the hub for the worldwide passion for Blues Music.
Founded in: 1980

18728 Carnatic Music Association of North America
P O Box 234
Fords, NJ 8863

908-521-0500
800-362-6137
webmaster@cmana.org; www.cmana.org

Aravind Narasimhan, President
Chithra Krishnan, Vice President
Rajesh Nathan, Secretary
Rhama Narayanan, Treasurer

18729 Chamber Music America
99 Madison Avenue
5th Floor
New York, NY 10016

212-242-2022; *Fax:* 646-430-5667;
www.chamber-music.org

Susan Dadian, Program Director
Margaret M Lioi, CEO
Louise Smith, Chair

Promotes artistic excellence and economic stability within the profession and to ensure that chamber music is a vital part of American life. Their vision is that chamber music serves as a model of cooperation and collaboration, that audiences become more committed to supporting chamber music and the professionals who devote their lives to this art form, and that opportunities for the performance of chamber music increase in traditional concert venues and beyond.
Founded in: 1977

18730 Chinese Arts and Music Association
P.O. Box 50531
Seattle, WA 98015-0531

206-817-6888
chinamusic@comcast.net;
www.uschinamusic.org

Warren Chang, President
Angel Yan, Board Member
Janelle Yeung, Board Member
Minghwa Chiem, Board Member
Buyun Zhao, Director

Dedicated to promoting Chinese classical music in the United States.

18731 Chorus America
1156 15th St NW
Suite 310
Washington, DC 20005-1747

202-331-7577; *Fax:* 202-331-7599
service@chorusamerica.org;
www.chorusamerica.org
Social Media: Facebook, Twitter, Youtube

Ann Meier Baker, President & Chief Executive Officer
Rollo Dilworth, Chairman
David C. Howse, Treasurer
Mary Lou Lyons, Secretary
Gayle M. Ober, Immediate Past Chair

Chorus America's mission is to build a dynamic and inclusive choral community so that more people are enriched by the beauty and power of choral singing.
2100 Members
Founded in: 1977

18732 Church Music Association of America
P.O. Box 4344
Roswell, NM 88202-4344

505-263-6298
contact@musicasacra.com;
www.musicasacra.com
Social Media: Facebook, Twitter, Google+

Founded in: 1964

18733 College Music Society
312 E Pine St
Missoula, MT 59802-4624

406-721-9616; *Fax:* 406-721-9419
cms@music.org; www.music.org
Social Media: Facebook, Twitter, LinkedIn, YouTube, Google+

Robby D Gunstream, Executive Director
David B. Williams, President

A consortium of college, conservatory, university and independent musicians and scholars interested in all disciplines of music. Its mission is to promote music teaching and learning, musical creativity and expression, research and dialogue, and diversity and interdisciplinary interaction.
9500 Attendees
Founded in: 1958

18734 Conductors Guild
719 Twinridge Ln
Richmond, VA 23235

804-553-1378; *Fax:* 804-553-1876
guild@conductorsguild.org;
www.conductorsguild.org
Social Media: Facebook, Twitter, LinkedIn

Amanda Burton Winger, Executive Director
Scott Winger, Assistant Director
David Leibowitz, Editor
Rufus Jones Jr, Editor

The Conductors Guild is the only music service organization devoted exclusively to the advancement of the art of conducting and to serving the artistic and professional needs of conductors.
1850+ Members
Founded in: 1975

18735 Contemporary Record Society
724 Winchester Road
Broomall, PA 19008

610-544-5920; *Fax:* 610-544-5920
crsnews@verizon.net;
www.mysite.verizon.net/vzeeewvp/contemporaryrecordsociety/

Caroline Hunt, Contact

Promotes both a fellowship in the musical arts between artists, composers and presenters and commercial recordingsa of participants in this endeavor. The intent of the Society is to advance the cause of music in the United States and throughout the world, promoting an association among its constituents. The scope of the Society's repertoire includes the musical masterworks of both well-known and relatively unknown composers of all periods.
Cost: $45.00
Founded in: 1981

18736 Country Music Association
One Music Circle S
Nashville, TN 37203

615-244-2840; *Fax:* 615-242-4783;
www.cmaworld.com
Social Media: Facebook, Twitter, YouTube, Instagram

Gary Overton, Chairman
Troy Tomlison, President
Jessie Schmidt, Secretary/Treasurer
Steve Moore, CEO

CMA is dedicated to bringing the poetry and emotion of Country Music to the World. They will continue a tradition of leadership and professionalism, promotoing the music and recognizing excellence in all its forms. They foster a spirit of community and sharing, and respect and encourage creativity and the unique contributions of everyone. It is a place to have fun and celebrate success.
5000+ Members
Founded in: 1958

18737 Country Radio Broadcasters
1009 16th Avenue South
Nashville, TN 37212

615-327-4487; *Fax:* 615-329-4492
news@crb.org;
www.countryradioseminar.com/
Social Media: Facebook, Twitter

Ed Salamon, Executive Director
Chasity Crouch, Business Manager
Bill Mayne, VP
Carole Bowen, Secretary
Jeff Walker, Treasurer

A nonprofit eductional organization. It is the principal entity that brings Country radio together with the Country music industry for learning opportunities that promote growth.
Founded in: 1969

18738 Creative Musicians Coalition
PO Box 6205
Peoria, IL 61601-6205

309-685-4843
800-882-4262; *Fax:* 309-685-4879
aimcmc@aol.com;
www.creativemusicianscoalition.com

Ronald Wallace, Founder/President

An international organization dedicated to the advancement of new music and the success of independent musicians.
1000 Members
Founded in: 1984

18739 East-2-West Marketing & Promotion
559 Wanamaker Road
Jenkintown, PA 19046-2219

215-884-3308; *Fax:* 215-884-1083;
www.musiciansnetwork.com

Jackie Paul, President/CEO

Marketing and promotion.
Mailing list available for rent

18740 Folk Alliance International
509 Delaware
#101
Kansas City, MO 64105

901-522-1170; *Fax:* 816-221-3658
fa@folk.org; www.folk.org/
Social Media: Facebook, Twitter, YouTube, Instagram

Lewis Meyers, Executive Director
Mary Sue Twohy, VP
Alan Korolenko, Secretary
Donald Davidoff, Treasurer
Lisa Schwartz, Secretary

The service association for the field, working on behalf of the folk music and dance industry year round. They offer a business directory of contacts for members, and a non-profit group exemption program for US-based organizations.
Cost: $70.00
Founded in: 1989

18741 Folklife Center Of International House
3701 Chestnut Street
Philadelphia, PA 19104

215-387-5125; *Fax:* 215-895-6550

Osagie Imasogie, President
Tanya Steinberg, Executive Director
William Parker, Director Of Communications Events

To present the highest caliber of traditional arts.

18742 Freelance Musicians' Association

E-Mail: info@freelancemusicians.org; www.freelancemusicians.org

18743 Gospel Music Association
741 cool Springs Blvd.
Franklin, TN 37067

615-242-0303; *Fax:* 615-254-9755
service@gospelmusic.org;
www.gospelmusic.org
Social Media: Facebook, Twitter, LinkedIn, Youtube

John Styll, President
Scott Brickell, Director
Charles Dorris, Founder/Chairman
Ed Harper, Director
Ed Leonard, Director

Our mission is to expose, promote and celebrate the gospel through music. GMA serves as a voice for the Christian music community. It provides an atmosphere in which artists, industry leaders, retail stores, radio stations, concert promoters and local churches can coordinate their efforts for the purpose of benefitting the industry as a whole, while remaining true to the purpose of communicating the gospel message.
Cost: $85.00
5000 Members
Founded in: 1964

18744 Guitar Accessory and Marketing Association (GAMA)
Po Box 757
New York, NY 10033

212-795-3630; *Fax:* 212-795-3630
assnhdqs@earthlink.net;
www.discoverguitar.com

Membership is comprised of guitar and guitar accessory manufacturers and various consumer magazines.
Founded in: 1933

18745 Guitar Foundation of America
PO Box 2900
Palos Verdes Peninsula, CA 78717

877-570-1651; *Fax:* 877-570-3409
info@guitarfoundation.org;
www.guitarfoundation.org
Social Media: Facebook, Twitter

Dr. Martha Masters, President
Jill Winchell, Operations Manager
Martha Masters, Executive VP
Jeff Cogan, VP
Robert Lane, Vice President/Secretary

Provides its members the combined advantages of a guitar society, a library, a publisher, a continuing education resource, and an artis council. The GFA is a non-profit educational and literacy organization devoted to furthering the knowledge of and interest in the guitar and its music.
Cost: $40.00
Founded in: 1973

18746 International Association for the Study of Popular Music

www.iaspm.net

Founded in: 1981

18747 International Association of Electronic Keyboard Manufacturers
305 Maple Avenue
Wyncote, PA 19095-3228
617-747-2816; www.iaekm.org

An association that comprises the global manufacturers of electronic keyboards and affiliated software and publications.

18748 International Association of Jazz Education
PO Box 724
Manhattan, KS 66505

785-776-8744; *Fax:* 785-776-6190;
www.iaje.org

Bill McFarlin, Executive Director
Chuck Owen, President
Ronald Carter, VP
Laura Johnson, Treasurer
Brian Coyle, Secretary

To ensure the continued development and growth of jazz through education and outreach.
Cost: $70.00
8000 Members
Founded in: 1989

18749 International Bluegrass Music Association
608 West, Irish Drive
Nashville, TN 37204

615-256-3222
888-438-4262; *Fax:* 615-256-0450
info@ibma.org; www.ibma.org
Social Media: Facebook, Twitter, LinkedIn, Youtube

Dan Hayes, Executive Director
Stan Zdonik, Vice Chair/Associations
Peter D'Addario, Treasurer
Lee Michael Demsey, Secretary

IBMA works together for high standards of professionalism, a greater appreciation for our music, and the success of the worldwide bluegrass community.

18750 International Clarinet Association
14070 Proton Rd
Suite 100 LB9
Dallas, TX 75244

972-233-9107; *Fax:* 972-490-4219
membership@clarinet.org; www.clarinet.org
Social Media: Twitter

John Cipolla, President
Tod Kerstetter, Treasurer
Caroline Hartig, Secretary
So Rhee, Executive Director

A community of clarinetists and clarinet enthusiasts that supports projects that will benefit clarinet performance; provides opportunities for the exchange of ideas, materials and information among its members; fosters the composition, publication, recording, and distribution of music for the clarinet; encourages the research and manufacture of a more definitive clarinet; and encourages and promotes the perfomance and teaching of a wide variety of repertoire for the clarinet.
4000 Members
Founded in: 1990

18751 International Computer Music Association
1819 Polk St.
Suite 330
San Francisco, CA 94109

Fax: 734-878-3031
icma@umich.edu; www.computermusic.org

Tom Erbe, President
Michael Gurevitch, VP, Membership
Margaret Schedel, VP, Conferences
Chryssie Nanou, Treasurer, Secretary
Christopher Haworth, Array Editor
Founded in: 1974

18752 International Horn Society

E-Mail: exec-secretary@hornsociety.org;
www.hornsociety.org

Jeffrey L. Snedeker, President
Kristina Mascher-Turner, Vice President
Annie Bosler, Secretary/Treasurer
Heidi Vogel, Executive Director
Cost: $35.00
3500+ Members
Founded in: 1970

18753 International Music Products Association NAMM
5790 Armada Drive
Carlsbad, CA 92008-4608

760-438-8001
800-767-6266; *Fax:* 760-438-7327
info@namm.org; www.namm.org
Social Media: Facebook, Twitter, YouTube, Pinterest

Larry Morton, President
Mark Goff, President/Owner
Joe lamond, President/CEO
Chris Martin, Chairman/CEO
Robin Walenta, President/CEO

An association whose mission is to unify, lead and strengthen the international music products industry and increase active participation in music making.
9000 Members
Founded in: 1901

18754 International Piano Guild
PO Box 1807
Austin, TX 78767

512-478-5775
ngpt@pianoguild.com; www.pianoguild.com

Richard Allison, President

A division of the American College of Musicians Professional society of piano teachers and music faculty members. Its primary function is to establish definite goals and awards for students of all levels, from the earliest beginner to the gifted prodigy. Its purpose is to encourage growth and enjoyment through the study of piano.
118m Members
Founded in: 1929

18755 International Polka Association
4608 S Archer Ave
Chicago, IL 60632-2932

773-254-7771
800-867-6552
ipa@internationalpolka.com;
www.internationalpolka.com
Social Media: Facebook, YouTube

Dave Ulczycki, President
Rick Rzeszutko, First VP
Fred Kenzierski, Second VP
Marlene Gill, Secretary
Linda Niewierowski, Treasurer

An educational and charitable organization for the preservation, promulgation and advancement of polka music and to promote, maintain and advance public interest in polka entertainment; to advance mutual interests and encourage greater cooperation among its members who are engaged in polka entertainment; and to encourage and pursue the study of polka music, dancing and traditional folklore. Responsible for the continued operation and growth of the Polka Music Hall of Fame and Museum.
Cost: $15.00
8M Members
Founded in: 1968

18756 **International Society of Folk Harpers and Craftsmen**
1614 Pittman Drive
Missoula, Mt 59803

406-542-1976
harps@thorharp.com;
www.folkharpsociety.org

Dave Kolacny, President
Timothy Habinski, First VP
Verlene Schermer, Second VP
Alice Williams, Secretary
Barbra Bailey Bradley, Treasurer

The mission of the ISFHC is: to promote the playing and enjoyment of the folk harp by all; to promote education, creation and development in the building of the folk harp; to increase awareness of professional folk harpers; and to increase public awareness of the music and joys of the folk harp.
Cost: $30.00
Founded in: 1985

18757 **Keyboard Teachers Association International**
361 Pin Oak Lane
Westbury, NY 11590-1941

516-333-3236; *Fax:* 516-997-9531;
www.musiciansnetwork.com

Dr. Albert DeVito, President

18758 **League of American Ochestras**
33 W 60th Street
New York, NY 10023-7905

212-262-5161; *Fax:* 212-262-5198
league@symphony.org;
www.americanorchestras.org

Henry Fogel, CEO
Jesse Rosen, President/CEO
Aja Stephens, Assistant to President
Steven C. Parrish, Vice Chair
Heather Noonan, Vice Chair

Provides leadership and service to American orchestras while communicating to the public the value and importance of orchestras and the music they perform. The League links a national network of thousands of musicians, conductors, managers, board members, volunteers, staff members and business partners, providing a wealth of services, information, and educational opportunities to its members.
1200 Members
Founded in: 1942
Mailing list available for rent

18759 **Metropolitan Opera Guild**
70 Lincoln Center Plz
New York, NY 10023-6593

212-769-7000; *Fax:* 212-769-7007
info@metguild.org;
www.metoperafamily.org/guild/
Social Media: Facebook, Twitter, LinkedIn, YouTube, Instagram

David Dik, Manager

Seeks to encourage the appreciation of opera and to support the Metorpolitan Opera. The guild provides programs and services in many areas designed to further these goals. Publishes monthly magazine and organizes special events throughout the year to raise funds.
100M Members
Founded in: 1935

18760 **Midland Center For The Arts Midland Music And Concert Series**
1801 W. St Andrews Road
Midland, MI 48640

989-631-8250; *Fax:* 989-631-7890
hohmeyer@mcfta.org; www.mcfta.org
Social Media: Facebook, Twitter, LinkedIn, Youtube

Michael Tiknis, President
James Hohmeyer, Artistic Director
Robb Wouose, Managing Director
Mark Bachman, Director
David Blakemore, Director

encourage concert audiences; Providing students with opportunities to experience professional performances.

18761 **Music Business Association**
1 Eves Drive
Suite 138
Marlton, NJ 8053

856-596-2221; *Fax:* 856-596-7299;
www.musicbiz.org
Social Media: Facebook, Twitter, RSS

Fred Beteille, Chairman
Steve Harkins, Vice Chairman
John Trickett, Treasurer
Ryan Redington, Secretary
James Donio, President

Membership organization promoting music commerce.

18762 **Music Critics Association of North America**
722 Dulaney Valley Rd.
#259
Baltimore, MD 21204

410-435-3881
info@mcana.org; www.mcana.org

Barbara Jepson, President
John Fleming, Vice President
James Bash, Treasurer
Roy C. Dicks, Secretary
Robert Leininger, Managing Director

An association for the promotion of high standards in classical music criticism.

18763 **Music Distributors Association**
14070 Proton Rd
Suite 100 LB9
Dallas, TX 75244-3601

972-233-9107; *Fax:* 972-490-4219
office@musicdistributors.org;
www.musicdistributors.org

International, nonprofit trade association representing and serving manufacturers, wholesalers, importers and exporters of musical instruments and accessories, sound reinforcement products and published music.
Cost: $675.00
Founded in: 1939

18764 **Music Library Association**
1600 Aspen Commons
Suite 100
Middleton, WI 53562

608-836-5825; *Fax:* 608-831-8200
mla@areditions.com;
www.musiclibraryassoc.org
Social Media: Facebook, Twitter

Michael Colby, President
Pamela Bristah, Secretary
Paul Cary, Admin Officer
Linda W.Blair, Admin Officer

Provides a forum for issues surrounding music, music in libraries, and music librarianship.
Cost: $90.00
Founded in: 1931

18765 **Music Performance Fund**
1501 Broadway
Suite 600
New York, NY 10036

212-391-3950; *Fax:* 212-221-2604
sramos@musicpf.org; www.musicpf.org
Social Media: Facebook

Den Beck, Trustee
Al Elvin, Director of Finance
Linda Williamson, Manager

A nonprofit public service organization headquartered in New York City. MPF is the world's largest sponsor of live, admission-free musical programs.
Founded in: 1948

18766 **Music Performance Trust Funds**
1501 Broadway
Suite 600
New York, NY 10036

212-391-3950; *Fax:* 212-221-2604
sramos@musicpf.org; www.musicpf.org
Social Media: Facebook

Dan Beck, Trustee
Vidrey Blackburn, Grant Review Process
Al Elvin, Director of Finance
Samantha Ramos, Team Member
Founded in: 1948

18767 **Music Publishers Association**
243 5th Ave
Suite 236
New York, NY 10016-8728

212-675-7354; *Fax:* 212-675-7381;
www.mpa.org

Kathleen Marsh, President
Bryndon Bay, Treasurer
Todd Vunderink, Secretary
Lauren Keiser, Second VP
75 Members
Founded in: 1895

18768 **Music Publishers Association of the United States**
243 5th Ave.
Suite 236
New York, NY 10016

212-675-7354; *Fax:* 212-675-7381
admin@mpa.org; www.mpa.org

Kathleen Marsh, President
Sean Patrick Flahaven, Vice President
Lauren Keiser, Second Vice President
Sonya Kim, Secretary
Erin Rogers, Treasurer

The MPA fosters communication among publishers, dealers, music educators, and all ultimate users of music. It is a nonprofit association which addresses itself to issues pertaining to every area of music publishing with an emphasis on the issues relevant to the publishers of print music for concert and educational purposes.
75 Members
Founded in: 1895

18769 **Music Teachers National Association**
1 W. 4th St.
Ste. 1550
Cincinnati, OH 45202-3004

513-421-1420
888-512-5278; *Fax:* 513-421-2503
mtnanet@mtna.org; www.mtna.org
Social Media: Facebook, Twitter

Gary L Ingle, Executive Director
Rebecca Grooms Johnson, NCTM, President
Karen Thickstun, NCTM, VP
Scott McBride Smith, NCTM, President-Elect
Sylvia Coats, NCTM, Secretary-Treasurer

The mission of the MTNA is to advance the value of music study and music making to society and to support the professionalism of music teachers.
24000 Members
Founded in: 1876
Mailing list available for rent: 23,000 names at $85 per M

18770 Music Video Production Association

E-Mail: infomvpa@gmail.com; www.mvpa.com

Coleen Haynes, President
Missy Galanadia, Vice President
Kim Dellara, Vice President
Grant Cihlar, Treasurer
Amanda Fox, Board of Director

18771 Music for All Foundation
39 W Jackson Place
Suite 150
Indianapolis, IN 46225

317-636-2263; *Fax:* 317-524-6200; www.musicforall.org

Eric Martin, President/CEO
Nancy H.Carlson, Executive VP/CFO
Carolyn Ealy, Education and Office Manager
Tonya Bullock, Accounting manager
Gayle W. Doster, Chairman

Committed to expanding the role of music and the arts in education, to heightening the public's appreciation of the value of music and arts education, and to creating a positive environment for the arts through societal changes.
Founded in: 1975
Mailing list available for rent

18772 Musical Box Society International
MBSI Member Registration
PO Box 10196
Springfield, MO 65808-0196

Fax: 417-886-8839; www.mbsi.org
Social Media: Facebook, Twitter, Digg, Yahoo, Reddit, StumbleUp

A nonprofit organization dedicated to the enjoyment, sstudy and preservation of all automatic musical instruments. Members receive the bimonthly scholarly journal, Mechanical Music, covering educational articles, relevant events, activities, news, information, and advertisements and the biennial, Directory of Members, Museums and Dealers. Hosts annual convention.
Cost: $55.00
2.8M Members
Founded in: 1949

18773 Musicians Foundation
875 Sixth Avenue
Suite 2303
New York, NY 10001-3507

212-239-9137; *Fax:* 212-239-9138
info@musiciansfoundation.org; www.musiciansfoundation.org
Social Media: Facebook, Twitter

BC Vermeersch, Executive Director
Hans E Tausig, President
Joseph Hertzberg, Treasurer

Representing interests on the condition and social welfare of professional musicians and their families. Provides emergency financial assistance to meet current living, medical and allied expenses.
Founded in: 1914

18774 National Academy of Recording Arts and Sciences
3030 Olympic Blvd.
Santa Monica, CA 90404

310-392-3777; *Fax:* 310-392-2188; www.grammy.org
Social Media: Facebook, Twitter, YouTube, Instagram

Ryan Seacrest, Honorary Chair
Tim Bucher, Chair
Geoff Cottrill, Vice Chair
Rachna Bhasin, Secretary/Treasurer
Rusty Rueff, Chair Emeritus
Founded in: 1988

18775 National Association for Music Education MENC
1806 Robert Fulton Drive
Reston, VA 20191

703-860-4000
800-336-3768; *Fax:* 703-860-1531; www.menc.org
Social Media: Facebook, Twitter, LinkedIn, Google+, Pinterest

John J Mahlmann, Executive Director
Lynn Brinckmeyer, President

Mission is to advance music education by encouraging the study and making of music by all.
Founded in: 1907

18776 National Association of Band Instrument Manufacturers
2026 Eagle Road
PO Box 51
Normal, IL 61761

309-452-4257; *Fax:* 309-452-4825
napbirt@napbirt.org; www.napbirt.org
Social Media: Facebook

Jerome Hershman, Contact
Bill Mathwes, Executive Director
Ross, Watkins

A trade association of band instrument manufacturers, importers and distributors including accessories selling to the trade only.
34 Members
Founded in: 1976

18777 National Association of College Wind and Percussion Instructor
Division of Fine Arts
Truman State University
Kirksville, MO 63501

660-785-4442; *Fax:* 660-785-7463
cmoore@fsu.edu; www.nacwpi.org
Social Media: Facebook

Chris Moore, President
Michael Dean, VP
Richard K Weerts, Executive Secretary/Treasurer

A forum for communication within the profession of applied music on the college campus. The Association is composed of university, college, and conservatory teachers.
Cost: $35.00
600 Members
Founded in: 1951

18778 National Association of Composers
P.O. Box 49256
Barrington Station
Los Angeles, CA 90049

www.music-usa.org/nacusa

Greg A. Steinke, Ph.D., President/ Chair
Wieslaw V Rentowski , Vice President
Sylvia Constantinidis, M.M., Secretary
Joe L. Alexander, Treasurer
Daniel Kessner, Past President
Founded in: 1933

18779 National Association of Negro Musicians Inc
931 Monroe Drive NE
Suite A102-159
Atlanta, GA 30308

404-647-7217; *Fax:* 404-745-0128; www.nanm.org
Social Media: Facebook, Twitter

Byron J. Smith, President
Geraldine Boone, First VP
Sylvia Turner Hollified, Second VP
Marydith Lawson, Executive Secretary
Daniel.J Long, Treasurer

Dedicated to the preservation, encouragement and advocacy of all genres of the music of African Americans. Holds a national convention in a different city eac year, offering a chance to participate in workshops, seminars, lectures and performances. NANM invites the professional artists, the educator, the student, the amateur, the lover of music to become a part of this organization's 'Pride in a Cultural Heritage.'
2.5M Members
Founded in: 1919

18780 National Association of Pastoral Musicians
962 Wayne Ave
Suite 210
Silver Spring, MD 20910-4461

240-247-3000
855-207-0293; *Fax:* 240-247-3001
npmsing@npm.org; www.npm.org

Richard B. Hilgartner, President
Kathleen Haley, Director Membership Services
Peter S. Maher, Chief Operating Officer
Paul Lagoy, Secretary & Mil Clerk

Fosters the art of musical liturgy. The members of NPM serve the Catholic Church in the United States as musicians, clergy, liturgists, and other leaders of prayer.
5000 Members
Founded in: 1976

18781 National Association of Professional Band Instrument Repair Technicians
2026 Eagle Road
PO Box 51
Normal, IL 61761

309-452-4257; *Fax:* 309-452-4825
napbirt@napbirt.org; www.napbirt.org
Social Media: Facebook

Bill Mathews, Executive Director
Ross Watkins, Admin. Manager

A nonprofit international educational association dedicated to the advancement of the craft of band instrument repair. Their mission is to promote the highest possible standards of band instrument repair, restoration and maintenance by providing members with multi-level professional development by offering technical training, continuing education and the publication of their bi-monthky trade journal.
Cost: $95.00
1300 Members
Founded in: 1976

18782 National Association of Recording Merchandisers
1 Eves Drive
Suite 138
Marlton, NJ 08053-3130

856-596-2221; *Fax:* 856-596-7299
donio@narm.com; www.musicbiz.org/
Social Media: Facebook, Twitter, RSS

Fred Beteille, Chair
Steve Harkins, Vice Chairman
John Trickett, Treasurer
Ryan Redington, Secretary
Jim Donio, President

A not-for-profit trade association that serves the music retailing community in the areas of networking, advocacy, information, education and promotion. Membership includes music and other entertainment retailers, wholesalers, distributorsm record labels, multimedia suppliers, and suppliers of related products and services, as well as individual professionals and educators in the music business field.
Founded in: 1958

18783 National Association of Schools of Music
11250 Roger Bacon Drive
Suite 21
Reston, VA 20190-5248

703-437-0700; *Fax:* 703-437-6312
info@arts-accredit.org; www.arts-accredit.org

Don Gibson, President
Mark Wait, VP
Mellasenah Y Morris, Treasurer

An organization of schools, conservatories, colleges and universities. NASM provides information to potential students and parents, consultations, stastistical information, professional development and policy analysis. It is the national accrediting agency for music and music-related disciplines.
635 Members
Founded in: 1924

18784 National Association of Teachers of Singing
9957 Moorings Drive
Suite 401
Jacksonville, FL 32257-2416

904-992-9101; *Fax:* 904-262-2587
info@nats.org; www.nats.org
Social Media: Facebook, Twitter, LinkedIn, YouTube, Pintrest, Flickr

Allen Henderson, Executive Director
Deborah Guess, Director of Operations
Amanda Wood, Membership & Program Coordinator
Linda J. Snyder, President
Karen Brunssen, President Elect

To encourage the highest standards of the vocal art and of ethical principles in the teaching of singing; and to promote vocal education and research at all levels, both for the enrichment of the general public and for the professional advancement of the talented.
7000 Members
Founded in: 1944

18785 National Ballroom and Entertainment Association
PO Box 274
Decorah, IA 52101-7600

563-382-3871
nbea@q.com; www.nbea.com
Social Media: Facebook

Larry Bowers, President
Pat Brannon, Vice President
John Matter, Executive Director
Ken Paulsen, Treasurer

National nonprofit association which advocates that social dancing is a life-long activity that contributes to the physical, mantal, and social well-being of an individual. They believe that social dancing should be preserved for current and future generations and introduced to today's youth as an alternate form of social interaction.
450 Members
Founded in: 1947

18786 National Band Association
Membership Office
745 Chastain Road-Ste 1140
PO Box 102
Kennesaw, GA 30144

601-297-8168; *Fax:* 601-266-6185
info@nationalbandassociation.org; www.nationalbandassociation.org
Social Media: Facebook, Twitter, RSS

Richard Good, President
Scott Casagrande, First VP
Scott Tobias, Second VP
Linda Moorehouse, Secretary/Treasurer
David Gregory, Advisor to the President

The purpose of the NBA to promote the musical and educational significance of bands and is dedicated to the attainment of a high level of excellence for bands and band music. It is open to anyone and everyone interested in bands, regardless of the length if his/her experience, type of position held, or the specific area at which he/she works. The membership roster includes men and women from every facet of the band world.
3M Members
Founded in: 1960

18787 National Endowment for the Arts
400 7th Street, SW
Washington, DC 20506-0001

202-682-5400
webmgr@arts.gov; www.arts.gov

Jane Chu, Chairman
Laura Callanan, Senior Deputy Chairman
Beth Bienvenu, Accessibility Director
Wendy Clark, Director of Museums
Ayanna N. Hudson, Arts Education Director

Independent federal agency that works with state arts agencies, local leaders, philanthropists and other federal agencies to give Americans opportunities to participate in the arts.

18788 National Federation of Music Clubs
1646 W Smith Valley Rd
Greenwood, IN 46142-1550

317-882-4003; *Fax:* 317-882-4019
info@nfmc-music.org; www.nfmc-music.org
Social Media: Facebook, Twitter, LinkedIn, Youtube

Carolyn Nelson, President
Michael Edwards, First VP
Kay Hawthorne, Secretary
Barbara Hildebrand, Treasurer
Jennifer Keller, Administrative Manager

NFMC provides opportunities for musical study, performance and appreciation to more than 200,000 senior, student and junior members in 6,500 music-related clubs and organizations nationwide. Members are professional and amateur musicians, vocalists, composers, dancers, performing artists, arts and music educators, music students, generous music patrons and benefactors, and music lovers of all ages.
170M Members
Founded in: 1898

18789 National Music Council of the United States
425 Park Street
Montclair, NJ 07043

973-655-7974
sandersd@mail.montclair.edu; www.musiccouncil.org

Michael Butera, President
Carolyn Nelson, First Vice President
Paul Williams, Second Vice President
Del R. Bryant, Third VP
Linda Lorence, Treasurer
Founded in: 1940

18790 National Opera Association
PO Box 60869
Canyon, TX 79016-0869

806-651-2857; *Fax:* 806-651-2958; www.noa.org
Social Media: Facebook

David Holley, President
Ruth Dobson, Vice President for Conventions
Paul Houghtaling, Vice President for Regions
Carol Ann Modesitt, Treasurer
Robert Hansen, Executive Director

The NOA seeks to promote a greater appreciation of opera and music theatre, to enhance pedagogy and performing activities, and to increase performance opportunities by supporting projects that improve the scope and quality of opera. Members in the United States, Canada, Europe, Asia and Australia participate in a wide array of activities in support of this mission.
775 Members
Founded in: 1955
Mailing list available for rent

18791 NationalAssociationofMusicMerchants
5790 Armada Drive
Carlsbad, CA 92008

760-438-8001
800-767-6266; *Fax:* 760-438-7327
info@namm.org; www.namm.org
Social Media: Facebook, Twitter, Pinterest, YouTube

Larry Morton, Chairman
Mark Goff, Vice Chairman
Robin Walenta, Treasurer
Chris Martin, Secretary
Joe Lamond, President/ CEO

18792 North American Basque Organizations
E-Mail: info@naBASQUE.org; www.nabasque.org

Valerie Arrechea, President
Mary Gaztambide, Vice President
Grace Mainvil, Treasurer
Marisa Espinal, Secretary
Kate Camino, Administrator
Founded in: 1973

18793 Opera America
330 7th Ave
16th Floor
New York, NY 10001-5248

212-796-8620; *Fax:* 212-796-8621
Info@operaamerica.org; www.operaamerica.org

Marc A Scorca, President
Frayda B. Lindemann, Chairman
Timothy O'Leary, Treasurer
James W Wright, Secretary
Rebecca Ackerman, Membership Manager

Opera America serves and strengthens the field of opera by providing a variety of informational, technical, and administrative resources to the greater opera community. Its fundamental mission is to promote opera as exciting and accessible to individuals from all walks of life.

18794 Organization of American Kodaly Educators
10801 National Blvd
Suite 405
Los Angeles, CA 90064

310-441-3555; *Fax:* 310-441-3577
info@oake.org; www.oake.org
Social Media: Facebook, Twitter, Google+

Joan Dahlin, Manager
Kevin Pearson, VP
Mary Neeley Stevens, Secretary

Kathy Hickey, Treasurer
Gary Shields, Administrative Director

The purpose of this organization is to promote Zoltan Kodaly's concept of Music for Everyone, through the improvment of music education in schools.
Founded in: 1973

18795 Pedal Steel Guitar Association
PO Box 20248
Floral Park, NY 11002-0248
516-616-9214; *Fax:* 516-616-9214
bobpsga@optonline.net; www.psga.org
Kelly Foster Griffin, President
Jane Smith, VP
Kathy Hickey, Treasurer
David Gadberry, Secretary
Doug Mack, Newsletter Editor

A nonprofit organization whose primary purpose is to share information on playing the steel guitar and in particular the pedal steel guitar. Publishes the Pedal Steel Newsletter ten times per year
1540 Members
Founded in: 1973

18796 Percussive Arts Society
110 W Washington Street
Suite A
Indianapolis, IN 46204
317-974-4488; *Fax:* 317-974-4499
percarts@pas.org; www.pas.org
Social Media: Facebook, Twitter, Instagram
Julie Hill, President
Georgr Barrett, VP
Dr. Chris Hanning, Secretary
Michael Balter, Treasurer
Jeffery Hartsough, Executive Director

A music service organization promoting percussion education, research, performance and appreciation throughout the world. Offers two print publications, the Percussive Arts Society International Headquarters/Museum and the annual Percussive Arts Society International Convention.
Cost: $85.00
7000 Members
Founded in: 1961

18797 Piano Technicians Guild
4444 Forest Ave
Kansas City, KS 66106
913-432-9975; *Fax:* 913-432-9986
ptg@ptg.org; www.ptg.org
Social Media: Facebook, Twitter, YouTube
Barbara Cassaday, Executive Director
Phil Bondi, RPT, President
Paul Brown, RPT, VP
Paul Adams, RPT, Secretary-Treasurer

A nonprofit organization serving piano tuners, technicians, and craftsmen throughout the world, organized to promote the highest possible service and technical standards among piano tuners and technicians.
4100 Members
Founded in: 1957

18798 Positive Music Association
www.positivemusicassociation.com
Sambodhi Prem, Composer/ Guitarist
400 Members
Founded in: 2003

18799 Production Music Association
9220 Sunset Blvd.
Suite 220
Los Angeles, CA 90069
www.pmamusic.com
Social Media: Facebook, Twitter, YouTube
Randy Thornton, Chairman
Adam Taylor, Vice Chairman
Ivy Tombak, Treasurer
Ron Mendelsohn, Secretary
Joel Goodman, Board Member
Founded in: 1997

18800 Recording Industry Association of America
1025 F ST N.W.
10th Floor
Washington, DC 20004
202-775-0101; www.riaa.com
Mitch Glazier, Sr. Executive Vice President
Steven M. Marks, Chief, Digital Business

18801 Retail Print Music Dealers Association
2650 Midway Rd
Suite 230
Carrolton, TX 75006
972-818-1333; *Fax:* 214-483-7004
cwilbur@penders.com; www.printmusic.org
Madeleine Crouch, Owner
Myrna Sislen, VP/Secretary
Christie Smith, VP/Treasurer

A professional trade organization founded to address the special needs and interests of the print music industry. RPMDA provides a common meeting ground for the congenial interchange of ideas among print music dealers; promotes ethical standards and policies in dealing with music publishers; promotes better dealer/publisher relations; serves the public and encourages music education; provides association-sponsored activities and publications that help its members prepare for future trends.
275 Members
Founded in: 1976

18802 Rhythm and Blues Foundation
P.O.Box 22438
Philadelphia, PA 19101
215-985-4822; *Fax:* 215-985-1195
info@rhythmblues.org;
www.rhythm-n-blues.org
Patricia Wilson Aden, Executive Director
Jim Fifield, Vice Chairman
Jeff Harleston, Treasurer
Kenneth Gamble, Secretary

Nonprofit service organization dedicated to the historical and cultural preservation of Rhythm and Blues music. The Foundation provides financial support, medical assistance and educational outreach through various grants and programs to support R&B amd Motown artists of the 40s, 50s, 60s and 70s.
Founded in: 1988

18803 Society of Professional Audio Recording Services
9 Music Square S
Suite 222
Nashville, TN 37203
800-771-7727; *Fax:* 214-722-1422
spars@spars.com; www.spars.com
Social Media: Facebook, Twitter, YouTube
Avatar Studios, President
Eric W Johnson, Secretary
Jessica Dally, Treasurer
Sherri Tantleff, Director

SPARS is dedicated to excellence through innovation, education and communication.
200 Members
Founded in: 1979
Mailing list available for rent

18804 Songwriters Guild of America
5120 Virginia Way
Suite C22
Brentwood, TN 37027
615-742-9945
800-524-6742; *Fax:* 615-630-7501
corporate@songwritersguild.com;
www.songwritersguild.com
Social Media: Facebook, Twitter, LinkedIn, RSS
Joe Whitt, Manager

Provides agreements between songwriters, composers and publishers. The SGA will take such lawful actions as will advance, promote and benefit the profession.
4000 Members
Founded in: 1931

18805 Sweet Adelines International
9110 S. Toledo
Tulsa, OK 74147-0168
918-622-1444
800-992-7464; *Fax:* 918-665-0894
admin@sweetadelineintl.org;
www.sweetadelineintl.org
Social Media: Facebook, Twitter, YouTube, Pinterest
Donna Kerley, Dicector Finance/Administration
Kelly Kirchoff, Director Communications
Jane Hanson, Marketing/Membership Coordinator
Kelly Bailey, Chief Executive Officer
Tammy Talbot, Chief Operating Officer

A worldwide organization of women singers committed to advancing the musical art form of barbershop harmony through education and performances. Their motto is to 'Harmonize the World.'
27000 Members
Founded in: 1945

18806 The Society for American Music
Stephen Foster Memorial
University of Pittsburgh
Pittsburgh, PA 15260
412-624-3031
sam@american-music.org;
www.american-music.org
Social Media: Facebook
Judy Tsou, Board of Trustee/ President
Kay Norton, Board of Trustee, VP
Sabine Feisst, Treasurer
Mariana Whitmer, Executive Director
Neil Lerner, Secretary
Founded in: 1975

18807 United States Germanic Music Association
E-Mail: mikesurrattmusic@gmail.com;
www.usgma.us

18808 World Piano Competition/AMSA
441 Vine St
Suite 1030
Cincinnati, OH 45202-2832
513-421-5342; *Fax:* 513-421-2672;
www.amsa-wpc.org
Gloria Ackerman, Founder, CEO
William Selnick, Treasurer
Stanley Aronoff, Event Chair
Leon Fleisher, President

Provides an continuum of services and role models to assist youth in need. Their task is to provide a venue of excitement and compassion to teach them to do their best to prepare for the enormous challenges they will face as they approach adulthood.
2.5M Members
Founded in: 1956

Newsletters

18809 American Guild Associate News Newsletter
American Guild of Music
PO Box 599
Warren, MI 48090-4905
248-686-1975; *Fax:* 630-968-0197
agm@americanguild.org;
www.americanguild.org
Richard Chizmadia, Editor-in-Chief
Offers information and news for professionals in the music profession.
Cost: $25.00
5000 Members
Frequency: Quarterly
Founded in: 1901

18810 American Music Center Opportunity Update
American Music Center
322 8th Ave
Suite 1001
New York, NY 10001-6774
212-366-5263; *Fax:* 212-366-5265
center@amc.net; www.amc.net
Joanne Cossa, Executive Director
A listing of composition competitions, calls for scores, workshops, and other opportunities delivered every month via e-mail to members of the American Music Center.
Frequency: Monthly
Founded in: 1939

18811 American Musical Instrument Society Newsletter
AMIS
1106 Garden Street
Hoboken, NJ 07030
201-656-0107
amis@guildassoc.com; www.amis.org
Albert R Rice, President
Carolyn Bryant, Vice-President
Deborah Check Reeves, Secretary
Joanne Kopp, Treasurer
Official notices and news of the Society's activites; short articles and communications; recent acquisition lists from member institutions; news of members; and classified ads.
Frequency: 2x/Year

18812 American Musicological Society Inc
University of Iowa
6010 College Station
Brunswick, ME 04011-8451
207-798-4243
877-679-7648; *Fax:* 207-798-4254
ams@ams-net.org; www.ams-net.org
Peter Alexander, Editor
Robert Judd, Executive Director
Al Hipkins, Office Manager
Melissa Kapocius, Secretary
The AMS Newsletter is published simiannually in February and August. The February Newsletter is mailed with the new Directory and Ballot each year. The August Newsletter is mailed with the Annual Meeting information and registration form each year.
Frequency: Semi-Annually
Founded in: 1934

18813 American School Band Directors Association Newsletter
American School Band Directors Association
227 N 1st Street
PO Box 696
Guttenberg, IA 52052-0696
563-252-2500; *Fax:* 563-252-2500
asbda@alpinecom.net; www.asbda.com
Monte Dunnum, President
Valerie Gaffney, Secretary
Blair Callaway, Treasurer
Reports and information for members of the ASBDA
Frequency: Quarterly
Founded in: 1953
Printed in 2 colors on matte stock

18814 American Viola Society Newsletter
American Viola Society
14070 Proton Rd
Suite 100
Dallas, TX 75244-3601
972-233-9107; *Fax:* 972-490-4219
stemple@comcast.net; www.madcrouch.com
Madeleine Crouch, President
A monthly e-newsletter. It contains announcements from the AVS, upcoming local chapter events, and other important items.
Frequency: Monthly

18815 Banjo Newsletter
PO Box 3418
Annapolis, MD 21403-0418
800-759-7425; *Fax:* 410-263-6503
bnl@infionline.net; www.banjonews.com
Newletter focusing on Bluegrass banjo music.
Mailing list available for rent

18816 Bluegrass Music Profiles
Bluegrass Publications
PO Box 850
Nicholasville, KY 40340-0850
859-333-6456
info@bluegrassmusicprofiles.com;
www.bluegrassmusicprofiles.com
Social Media: Facebook, Twitter
Information on Bluegrass music.

18817 Bluegrass Now
PO Box 2020
Rolla, MO 65402
573-341-7335; www.bluegrassnow.com
Information on Bluegrass music.

18818 Bluegrass Unlimited
PO Box 771
Warrenton, VA 20188-0771
540-349-8181
800-258-4727
info@bluegrassmusic.com;
www.bluegrassmusic.com
Information on Bluegrass music.
Mailing list available for rent

18819 Brooklyn Institute for Studies in American Music
Brooklyn College
2900 Bedford Ave
Brooklyn, NY 11210-2889
718-951-5000;
www.brooklyn.cuny.edu/bb/fac/american.htm
Karen L Gould, President
Music news and Academy activities.
Frequency: Semi-Annual
Founded in: 1861

18820 CMS Newsletter
College Music Society
312 E Pine Street
Missoula, MT 59802
406-721-9616; *Fax:* 406-721-9419
cms@music.org; www.music.org
Robby D Gunstream, Executive Director

18821 Dirty Linen
PO Box 6660
Baltimore, MD 21239-6600
410-583-7973; www.dirtylinen.com
Information on Bluegrass music.

18822 Early Music Newsletter
New York Recorder Guild
145 W 93 Street
New York, NY 10025-7559
212-662-2946
mzumoff@nyc.rr.com;
www.priceclan.com/nyrecorderguild/
Michael Zumoff, Executive Director
A publication of the New York Recorder Guild
10 Pages
Frequency: Monthly

18823 Flatpicking Guitar
High View Publications
PO Box 2160
Pulaski, VA 24301
540-980-0338
800-413-8296; *Fax:* 540-980-0557;
www.flatpick.com
Information on Bluegrass music and the Flatpick guitar.
Mailing list available for rent

18824 GMA Update
Gospel Music Association
PO Box 22697
Nashville, TN 37202
615-242-0303; *Fax:* 615-254-9755
info@gospelmusic.org; www.gospelmusic.org
John Styll, President
Jackie Patillo, Executive Director
GMA's industry e-newsletter available to any non-GMA member who wishes to receive it. Sent out once a month, GMA Update contains the latest news about the Christian music industry and valuable information about the GMA.
Frequency: Monthly
Mailing list available for rent

18825 GMAil
Gospel Music Association
PO Box 22697
Nashville, TN 37202
615-242-0303; *Fax:* 615-254-9755;
www.gospelmusic.org
John Styll, President
E-newsletter sent weekly to GMA members. Includes weekly music sales, charts, news, links to valuable resources, and information about upcoming GMA and industry events.
Frequency: Weekly
Founded in: 1964

18826 Girl Groups Gazette
PO Box 69A04
Department HSND
West Hollywood, CA 90069-0066
Louis Wendruck, Editor/Publisher
For fans of girl groups and female singers of the 1960's and 70's including photos, discographies, records, t-shirts, postcards, and videos.
Cost: $20.00
Frequency: Quarterly
Founded in: 1988

18827 In the Groove
Michigan Antique Phonograph Society

60 Central St
Battle Creek, MI 49017-3704

269-968-1299
antiquephono.org

Phil Stewart, Editor
Eileen Stewart, Editor

The Newsletter of the Michigan Antique Phonograph Society. Includes show, sales and auction announcements, MAPS chapter news, President's message, monthly feature articles, letters to the editor, and swap shop.
Cost: $25.00
24 Pages
Frequency: Monthly
Founded in: 1976

18828 **International Bluegrass Music Association**
IBMA
2 Music Cir S
Suite 100
Nashville, TN 37203-4381

615-256-3222
888-438-4262; *Fax:* 615-256-0450
info@ibma.org; www.ibma.org

Dan Hays, Executive Director

Information on Bluegrass music from the IBMA

18829 **Music for the Love of It**
67 Parkside Drive
Berkeley, CA 94705-2409

510-654-9134; *Fax:* 510-654-4656
tedrust@musicfortheloveofit.com;
www.musicfortheloveofit.com

Edgar Rust, Publisher/Editor
Janet Telford, Co-Editor

A newsletter for people everywhere who love making music. Every issues brings new enthusiasm, new ideas and new opportunities for making music.
Frequency: Bi-Monthly
ISSN: 0898-8757
Founded in: 1988
Printed in on matte stock

18830 **National Music Museum Newsletter**
National Music Museum
414 E Clark St
Vermillion, SD 57069-2307

605-677-5306; *Fax:* 605-677-6995
smm@usd.edu; www.usd.edu/smm/

Andre Larson, Director

Quarterly Newletter which includes feature articles written by the curatorial staff and lists recent acquisitions. Published in February, May, August and November. It is available with basic museum membership.
Cost: $35.00
Printed in 4 colors

18831 **No Depression**
908 Halcyon Avenue
Nashville, TN 37204

615-292-7084; www.nodepression.net

Information on Bluegrass music
Founded in: 1995

18832 **Notes a Tempo**
West Virginia University
Fairmount State University
1201 Locust Avenue
Fairmont, WV 26554

304-293-4841;
www.wvmea.tripod.com/Notes_a_Tempo_Winter_10.pdf

David Bess, Co-Editor
Becky Terry, Co-Editor

The official publication of the West Virginia Music Educators. Published Fall, Winter and Spring
20-32 Pages
Frequency: 3 per year
Circulation: 1115

18833 **Old Time Herald**
P.O.Box 61679
Durham, NC 27715-1679

919-286-2041
info@oldtimeherald.org;
www.oldtimeherald.org

Sarah Bryan, Editor-in-chief
Peter Honig, Business Director

Information on Bluegrass music
Mailing list available for rent

18834 **Pedal Steel Newsletter**
Pedal Steel Guitar Association
PO Box 20248
Floral Park, NY 11002-0248

516-616-9214; *Fax:* 516-616-9214
bobpsga@optonline.net; www.psga.org

Doug Mack, Editor
Bob Maickel, President

Dedicated to the art of playing pedal steel guitar. Every issue contains tablature arrangements of songs for the steel guitar as well as coming events, record reviews, product reports and news concerning the instrument.
Frequency: 10 x Per Year
ISSN: 1088-7954
Founded in: 1973
Mailing list available for rent

18835 **Percussion News**
Percussive Arts Society
110 W Washington Street
Suite A
Indianapolis, IN 46204

317-974-4488; *Fax:* 317-974-4499
percarts@pas.org; www.pas.org

Rick Mattingly, Editor
Hillary Henry, Art Director
Lisa Rogers, President

Newsletter devoted to membership activities. This colorful newsletter also features a Classified Advertising section. Percussion News is published in January, March, May, July, September and November.
Frequency: 6 Editions Per Year
Founded in: 1961
Mailing list available for rent

18836 **Rolling Stone**
Rolling Stone Magazine
1290 Ave of the Americas
2nd Floor
New York, NY 10104-0298

212-484-1616
800-283-1549; *Fax:* 212-484-1771;
www.rssoundingboard.com
Social Media: Facebook, Twitter, YouTube, RSS, Foursqare

Jann Wenner, President

A monthly newsletter geared for marketing, advertising and music exexecutives. It includes information on such matters as rock tours and musician endorsements, ad campaigns and rock contests.
Cost: $50.00
Frequency: Monthly
Founded in: 1967
Mailing list available for rent

18837 **Roots and Rhythm Newsletter**
Roots and Rhythm
PO Box 837
El Cerrito, CA 94530

510-526-8373
888-766-8766; *Fax:* 510-526-9001
roots@toast.net; www.rootsandrhythm.com

Frank Scott, Owner
Nancy Scott-Noennig, Co-Owner

Lists, reviews and makes available for sale, recordings of blues, rhythm and blues, rockabilly, country, folk, ethnic, nostalgia and jazz music. Each newsletter reviews about 400 items and lists another 500 without reviews.
Frequency: Bi-Monthly
Circulation: 10000
Founded in: 1974
Printed in 2 colors on newsprint stock

18838 **Sing Out!**
PO Box 5460
Bethlehem, PA 18015-0460

610-865-5366; *Fax:* 215-895-3052
info@singout.org; www.singout.org

Information on Bluegrass music
Mailing list available for rent

18839 **Tempo**
Academy of Country Music
5500 Balboa Blvd
Suite 200
Encino, CA 91316-1505

818-788-8000; *Fax:* 818-788-0999
info@acmcountry.com; www.acmcountry.com

Butch Waugh, Chairman

Devoted exclusively to the country music industry.
12 Pages
Frequency: Quarterly
Circulation: 4500
Founded in: 1964

18840 **The Voice**
1156 15th St NW
Suite 310
Washington, DC 20005-1747

202-331-7577; *Fax:* 202-331-7599
service@chorusamerica.org;
www.chorusamerica.org

Ann Meier Baker, President & Chief Executive Officer
1600 Members
Frequency: Quarterly
Circulation: 5000
ISSN: 1074-0805
Founded in: 1977

18841 **Westfield Center**
Westfield Center for Early Keyboard Studies
726 University Ave,Room 102
Cornell University
Ithaca, NY 14850-3914

607-255-3065
info@westfield.org; www.westfield.org

Annette Richards, Executive Director
Maja Anderson, Program Coordinator
Evan Cortens, Administrative Assistant

E-newsletter providing information to professional keyboard musicians.
12 Pages
Frequency: Monthly
Founded in: 1979

18842 **Women in Bluegrass Newsletter**
PO Box 2498
Winchester, VA 22604

800-227-2357;
www.murphymethod.com/womeninbluegrass.cfm

Information on women in bluegass music

Magazines & Journals

18843 AfterTouch: New Music Discoveries
Music Discovery Network
PO Box 6205
Peoria, IL 61601-6205

309-685-4843
800-882-4262; *Fax:* 309-685-4878
aimcmc@aol.com; www.musicdiscoveries.com

Ronald Wallace, Editor

A magazine for music lovers who would like to experience new sights and sounds and would like to keep their fingers on the pulse of the music industry.
Frequency: Annual
Circulation: 10,000
Founded in: 1984
Printed in on glossy stock

18844 American Music
University of Illinois Press
1325 South Oak Street
MC-566
Champaign, IL 61820-6903

217-244-0626
866-244-0626; *Fax:* 217-244-8082
journals@uillinois.edu;
www.press.uillinois.edu

Michael Pisani, Editor
Jeff McArdle, Journals Marketing/Advertising Mgr.

Publishes articles on American composers, performers, publishers, institutions, events, and the music industry as well as book and recording reviews, bibliographies, and discographies.
Cost: $45.00
Frequency: Quarterly
Circulation: 1650
ISSN: 0734-4392
Founded in: 1981
Mailing list available for rent: 1,650 names at $100 per M
Printed in 2 colors on glossy stock

18845 American Music Teacher
Music Teachers National Association
441 Vine St
Suite 505
Cincinnati, OH 45202-2813

513-421-1420
888-512-5278; *Fax:* 513-421-2503
mtnanet@mtna.org; www.mtna.org

Gary L Ingle, Executive Director
Gail Berenson, President
Janice Wenger, VP

Provides articles, reviews and regular columns that inform, educate and challenge music teachers and foster excellence in the music teaching profession.
Cost: $30.00
Circulation: 35000
Founded in: 1876
Mailing list available for rent: 24000 names at $85 per M
Printed in 4 colors on glossy stock

18846 American Organist
American Guild of Organists
475 Riverside Dr
Suite 1260
New York, NY 10115-0055

212-870-2310
800-246-5115; *Fax:* 212-870-2163
info@agohq.org; www.agohq.org
Social Media: Facebook

James Thomashower, Executive Director

Most widely read journal devoted to organ and choral music in the world. Officialjournal of the American Guild of Organists, the Royal Canadian College of Organists, and the Associated Pipe Organ Builders of America.
Cost: $ 52.00
Frequency: Monthly
Circulation: 24000
ISSN: 0164-3150
Founded in: 1967

18847 American String Teachers Journal
American String Teachers Association
4155 Chain Bridge Rd
Fairfax, VA 22030-4102

703-279-2113; *Fax:* 703-279-2114
asta@astaweb.com; www.astaweb.com

Donna Hale, Executive Director
Beth Danner-Knight, Deputy Director

Available to members. Provides an overview of current articles featured in the journal. Also answers questions about content, advertising, and contact information.
Cost: $90.00
Frequency: Quarterly
Circulation: 11,300
Mailing list available for rent: 10M+ names

18848 American Viola Society Journal
American Viola Society
14070 Proton Rd
Suite 100LB
Dallas, TX 75244-3601

972-233-9107; *Fax:* 972-490-4219
info@avsnationaloffice.org;
www.americanviolasociety.org

Nokuthula Ngwenyama, President
Karin Brown, Secretary
Michelle Sayles, Treasurer
Kathryn Steely, Webmaster

Peer reviewed journal which promotes interest in the viola.
Cost: $42.00
Frequency: Annually
Circulation: 1500
Founded in: 1984

18849 BMI Musicworld
Broadcast Music
7 World Trade Center
250 Greenwich Street
New York, NY 10007-0030

212-220-3000; *Fax:* 212-246-2163;
www.bmi.com

Del Bryant, CEO
John E Cody, COO/EVP

Performing rights organization. Articles of interest to the songwriting community.
Founded in: 1985

18850 Billboard Magazine
Prometheus Global Media
770 Broadwaye Blvd.
New York, NY 10003-9595

212-493-4100; *Fax:* 646-654-5368;
www.prometheusgm.com
Social Media: Facebook, Twitter

Richard D. Beckman, CEO
James A. Finkelstein, Chairman
Madeline Krakowsky, Vice President Circualtion
Tracy Brater, Executive Director Creative Service

Packed with in-depth music and entertainment features including the latest in new media and digital music, global coverage, music and money, touring, new artists, radio news and retail reports.
Cost: $149.00
Frequency: Weekly
Founded in: 1894

18851 CCM Magazine
Salem Publishing
402 BNA Drive
Suite 400
Nashville, TN 37217

615-386-3011; *Fax:* 615-386-3380;
www.ccmmagazine.com
Social Media: Facebook, Twitter, RSS

Jim Cumbee, President

The voice of Contemporary Christian Music. Each monthly issue features music news, exclusive interviews, and an in-depth look at the spiritual lives of today's leading Christian music artists.
Cost: $19.95
Frequency: Monthly
Founded in: 1978
Printed in 4 colors on glossy stock

18852 Callboard
Theatre Bay Area
1663 Mission St
Suite 525
San Francisco, CA 94103-2487

415-430-1140; *Fax:* 415-430-1145
tba@theatrebayarea.org;
www.theatrebayarea.org
Social Media: Facebook, Twitter, YouTube

Karen Mc Kevitt, Manager

Provides trade information for professionals in the Bay Area. The magazine contains the following departments: Letterbox, Inside the Industry, Community News, How Did They Do That, Keep An Eye On, Editors' Picks and Encore.
Cost: $65.00
Frequency: Monthly
ISSN: 1064-0703
Founded in: 1976
Printed in 2 colors on matte stock

18853 Chamber Music Magazine
Chamber Music America
UPS Box 458
243 Fifth Avenue
New York, NY 10016

212-242-2022; *Fax:* 212-242-7955;
www.chamber-music.org

Susan Dadian, Program Director
Margaret M Lioi, CEO
Louise Smith, Chair
Cost: $5.95
Frequency: Bi-Monthly
Circulation: 6000
Founded in: 1977

18854 Choral Journal
American Choral Directors Association
545 Couch Drive
Oklahoma City, OK 73102
405-232-8161; *Fax:* 405-232-8162;
www.acdaonline.org

Carroll Gonzo, Editor
Ron Granger, Managing Editor

Contains articles and columns of a scholarly and practical nature in addition to reviews of newly released CD recordings, books, and printed music.
Frequency: Monthly

18855 Clarinet Journal
International Clarinet Society
PO Box 5039
Wheaton, IL 60189-5039

630-665-3602; *Fax:* 630-665-3848
info@clarinet.org; www.clarinet.org

James Gillespie, Editor
So Rhee, Executive Director
Maxine Ramey, President
Caroline Hartig, Secretary
Tod Kerstetter, Treasurer

Contains articles in wide variety of areas written by performers and scholars.
Cost: $25.00
Frequency: Quarterly
Circulation: 3000

18856 Clavier
Instrumentalist Publishing Company
200 Northfield Road
Northfield, IL 60093-3390
847-446-5000
888-446-6888; *Fax:* 847-446-6263
editor@theinstrumentalist.com;
www.instrumentalistmagazine.com
Social Media: Facebook

James Rohner, Publisher
Judy Nelson, Editor

Provides new ideas and advice for piano teachers from leading educators. The focus of each issue is to offer practical advice for teachers. Articles include interviews with prominent performers, teachers and composers, the latest teaching methods, tributes to great artists of the past, and reviews of newly publshed music, educational software and videos.
Cost: $17.00
Frequency: 10X Per Year
Circulation: 16000
Founded in: 1965
Mailing list available for rent

18857 Close Up Magazine
Country Music Association
One Music Circle S
Nashville, TN 37203

615-244-2840; *Fax:* 615-242-4783
international@cmaworld.com;
www.cmaworld.com

Profiles of country music artists, various songwriters and industry news. Members of the Association receive the magazine as a benefit of their membership.
Circulation: 8000
Founded in: 1958

18858 Country Weekly Magazine
American Media Inc
1000 American Media Way
T-Rex Technology Center
Boca Raton, FL 33464-1000

561-997-7733; *Fax:* 561-989-1298;
www.nationalenquirer.com

David J Pecker, CEO

Devoted to country music and entertainment. Packed with feature articles and photos of country music personalities, music and video reviews, tour dates and late breaking news from the world of country music.
Cost: $34.95
Frequency: Bi-Weekly

18859 DJ Times
Testa Communications
25 Willowdale Avenue
Port Washington, NY 11050-3779

516-767-2500
800-937-7678; *Fax:* 516-767-9335
djtimes@testa.com; www.djtimes.com

Jim Tremayne, Editor-in-Chief
Steve Thorakos, Production Manager

Colorful tabloid magazine dedicated to professional mobile and club DJs. Specialized music sections, new product departments for sound and lighting, record reviews, business columns, informative entertainer profiles and more.
Cost: $19.40
Frequency: Monthly
Circulation: 30000
Founded in: 1988

18860 Diapason
Scranton Gillette Communications
3030 W Salt Creek Lane
Suite 201
Arlington Heights, IL 60005-5025

847-391-1000; *Fax:* 847-390-0408
jbutera@sgcmail.com; www.thediapason.com

Jerome Butera, Editor/Publisher
Joyce Robinson, Associate Editor

Devoted to the organ, the harpischord, the carillon, and church music. Includes feature articles, reviews, reports, news, organ specifications, and a calendar, as well as classified advertisements.
Cost: $35.00
Frequency: Monthly
ISSN: 0012-2378
Founded in: 1909

18861 Discoveries
700 East State Street
Ioal, WI 54990-0001

715-445-2214
800-258-0929; *Fax:* 715-445-4087;
www.discoveriesmag.com

Mark Williams, Publisher
Wayne Youngblood, Editorial Director
Cathy Bernardy, Associate Editor
Todd Whitesel, Associate Editor
Trevor Lauber, Advertising Sales Manager

Keeps close watch on market trends for collectible records, CDs and memorabilia. The Market Watch pages serve to interpret the mass of information available online and break it down to the most useful data collectors need. Each monthly issue is full of personality and opinion, with many reviews to help you determine where to spend your money. Coverage includes rock 'n' roll, rhythm &'blues, pop, doo-wop, classic jazz and country western recordings.
Cost: $28.00
Frequency: Monthly
Circulation: 10,859
Founded in: 1988

18862 Downbeat
102 N Haven Road
PO Box 906
Elmhurst, IL 60126

630-941-2030
800-554-7470; *Fax:* 630-941-3210
service@downbeat.com; www.downbeat.com

Kevin Maher, CEO

Monthly magazine includes such features as Readers Poll results, festival reviews, CD reviews, feature articles and more.
Cost: $29.95
Frequency: Monthly
Mailing list available for rent

18863 Electronic Musician
PRIMEDIA
6400 Hollis Street
Suite 12
Emeryville, CA 94608-1086

510-653-3307
emeditorial@prismb2b.com;
www.emusician.com
Social Media: Facebook, Twitter

Steve Oppenheimer, Editor-in-Chief
Joe Perry, Associate Publisher
Marie Briganti, List Manager

Magazine for musicians recording and producing music in a home or personal studio environment. They are a source of user-friendly technical information for musicans. Features include: Tech Page, ProFile, Working Musician, Sound Design Workshop, Making Tracks, Square One, Reviews, What's New, Master Class, Final Mix, and Editors Choice Awards.
Cost: $23.97
Frequency: Monthly
Circulation: 61102
Founded in: 1986
Mailing list available for rent

18864 Flute Talk
Instrumentalist Company
200 Northfield Road
Northfield, IL 60093-3390
847-446-5000
888-446-6888; *Fax:* 847-446-6263;
www.instrumentalistmagazine.com
Social Media: Facebook

Flute Talk is written for professional flute players, teachers, and advanced students. Frequent topics include performance analyses of flute repertoire, current teaching techniques, piccolo articles, interviews with prominent performers and teachers, and reviews of new music, recordings, and books for flutists.
Cost: $13.00
Frequency: 10 x Per Year
Circulation: 12000
Founded in: 1981

18865 Goldmine
700 E State Street
Iola, WI 54990-0001

715-445-2214
800-258-0929; *Fax:* 715-445-4087
susan.sliwicki@fwmedia.com;
www.goldminemag.com
Social Media: Facebook, YouTube, RSS, Pinterest

Jeff Pozorski, Publisher
Brian Earnest, Editorial Director
Peter Lindblad, Associate Editor
Tim Neely, Research Director
Trevor Lauber, Advertising Sales Manager

The world's largest marketplace for collectible records, CDs, and music memorabilia covering Rock N' Roll, Blues, Country, Folk, and Jazz. Large volumes of For Sale and Wanted ads are placed by collectors and dealers. Includes articles on recording stars of the past and present with discographies listing all known releases, a listing of upcoming record-and-CD-collector conventions, album reviews, hobby and music news, a collecting column, a letters section, and Collector Mania (Q&A).
Cost: $39.95
Frequency: Bi-Weekly
Circulation: 17026
Founded in: 1974
Mailing list available for rent

18866 Guitar One
Cherry Lane Magazines
6 E 32nd St
Suite 11
New York, NY 10016-5422

212-561-3000
800-825-4942; *Fax:* 212-447-6885;
www.guitarmag.com

Peter W Primont, CEO
Jonathan Simpson-Bint, President
Holly Klingel, VP Circulation
Steve Aaron, Publishing Director
Greg Di Benedetto, Publisher

Information on everything from the guitar equipment evaluations to news on the latest trends and technological developments to special insider pieces covering the sound secrets of today's top players.
Cost: $24.95
Frequency: Monthly
Circulation: 105,000
Founded in: 1985

18867 Guitar Review
Albert Augustine Limited
151 W 26th St
Suite 4
New York, NY 10001-6810

917-661-0220; *Fax:* 917-661-0223;
www.albertaugustine.com

Steven Griesgraber, President
Eliot Fisk, Associate Editor
David Starobin, Associate Editor
Ian Gallagher, Music Editor
Matthew Hough, Circulation

Scholarly articles related to the classical guitar.
Cost: $28.00
48 Pages
Frequency: Quarterly
Circulation: 4000
Founded in: 1946

18868 HipHop Weekly
Z & M Media
401 Broadway
New York, NY

212-696-0831; www.hiphopweekly.com
Social Media: Facebook, Twitter

Covers the entire hip hop culture.

18869 Instrumentalist
Instrumentalist Company
200 Northfield Road
Northfield, IL 60093-3390

847-446-5000
888-446-6888; *Fax:* 847-446-6263;
www.instrumentalistmagazine.com
Social Media: Facebook

A magazine school band and orchestra directors can depend on for practical information to use for then ensembles. The articles written by veteran directors and performers cover a wide range of topics, including rehearsal techniques, conducting tips, programming ideas, instrument clinics, repertoire analyses, and much more. Monthly new music reviews guide directors to selecting the best music for their students.
Cost: $21.00
Frequency: Monthly
Circulation: 16,000
Founded in: 1945
Printed in 4 colors

18870 International Musician
American Federation of Musicians
1501 Broadway
Suite 600
New York, NY 10036-5501

212-869-1330; *Fax:* 212-764-6134
info@afm.org; www.afm.org

Thomas Lee, President

Delivers the latest happenings in music. Focuses on the overall well-being of all musicians. Provides news pertaining to symphonic, rock, freelance, recording and touring musicians. IM features aricles on pressing issues sich as piracy, legislation, on-the-job struggles, and the effects of technology.
Cost: $25.00
Frequency: Monthly
Circulation: 110000
Founded in: 1896
Printed in on n stock

18871 JAMIA
American Musical Instrument Society
389 Main Street
Suite 202
Malden, MA 02148

781-397-8870; *Fax:* 781-397-8887
amis@guildassoc.com; www.amis.org

Stewart Carter, President
Joanne Kopp, Treasurer

Presents peer-reviewed articles that assist in both professionals and students to develop and apply biomedical and health informatics to patient care, teaching, research, and health care administration.
Frequency: Bi-Monthly
Founded in: 1971

18872 Jazz Education Journal
JazzTimes Magazine,Madavor Media
85 Quincy Ave
Suite 2
Quincy, MA 02169

617-706-9110; *Fax:* 617-536-0102;
www.jazztimes.com

Leslie M Sabina, Editor
Karen Mayse, Advertising

Provides news and information in the field of jazz education. Contains information of today's top jazz artists, reviews, transcriptions, industry news, and articles on improvisation, teaching techniques, history, performance, composition, arranging and music business.
Cost: $23.95
100 Pages
Circulation: 10,000
Founded in: 1968
Mailing list available for rent
Printed in on glossy stock

18873 Journal of American Organbuilding
American Institute of Organ Builders
PO Box 35306
Canton, OH 44735

330-806-9011; www.pipeorgan.org

Jeffrey L Weiler, Editor

Features technical articles, product and book reviews, and a forum for the exchange of building and service information and techniqes. Subscriptions are provided free to AIO members, and are available to non-members for $24.00 per year.
Cost: $24.00
Frequency: Quarterly
Founded in: 1974
Mailing list available for rent: 350 names at $250 per M
Printed in on glossy stock

18874 Journal of Music Theory
Yale University
Department of Music
PO Box 208310
New Haven, CT 06520-8310

203-432-2985; *Fax:* 203-432-2983
jmt.editor@yale.edu; www.yale.edu/jmt/

Ian Quinn, Editor
David Clampitt, Associate Editor
Richard Cohn, Associate Editor
Daniel Harrison, Associate Editor
Patrick McCreless, Associate Editor

Publishes peer-reviewed reseach in Music Theory.
Cost: $30.00
Frequency: Annual
Founded in: 1957

18875 Journal of Music Therapy
American Music Therapy Association
8455 Colesville Rd
Suite 1000
Silver Spring, MD 20910-3392

301-589-3300; *Fax:* 301-589-5175
info@musictherapy.org;
www.musictherapy.org

Andrea Farbman, Executive Director

Research in the area of music therapy and rehabilitation, a forum for authoratative articles of current music therapy research and theory, use of music in the behavioral sciences, book reviews, and guest editorials.
Cost: $120.00
Frequency: Quarterly
Circulation: 6000
ISSN: 0022-2917
Founded in: 1998

18876 Journal of Research in Music Education
MENC Subscription Office
PO Box 1584
Birmingham, AL 35201

800-633-4931; www.menc.org
Social Media: Facebook, Twitter

Keeps members informed of the latest music education research. Offers a collection of reports that includes thorough analyses of theories and projects by respected music researchers. Issued four times yearly.
Frequency: Quarterly
Founded in: 1907
Printed in on matte stock

18877 Journal of Singing
National Association of Teachers of Singing
9957 Moorings Drive
Suite 401
Jacksonville, FL 32257-2416

904-992-9101; *Fax:* 904-262-2587
info@nats.org; www.nats.org
Social Media: Facebook, Twitter, LinkedIn

Richard Dale Sjoerdsma, Editor-in-Chief
Kenneth Bozeman, Chair
Paul Witkowski, Marketing & Communications

The official journal of NATS, offering a wealth of research and insight from scholars and experts on teaching singing, with topics ranging from history and voice science to voice pedagogy.
Frequency: 5x times/year
Founded in: 1944

18878 Journal of the American Musicological Society
University of California Press, Journals Division
2000 Center Street Way
Suite 203
Berkeley, CA 94704-1223

510-643-7154; *Fax:* 510-642-9917
journals@ucpress.edu;
www.ucpressjournals.com

Bruce Alan Brown, Editor
Louise Goldberg, Assistant Editor
Julie Cumming, Book Review Editor

The JAMS publishes scholarship from all fields of musical inquiry: from historical musicology, critical theory, music analysis, iconography and organology, to performance practice, aesthetics and hermeneutics, ethnomusicology, gender and sexuality, popular music and cultural studies. Each issue includes articles, book reviews, and communications.
Cost: $42.00
Frequency: Tri-Annual
Circulation: 5000
ISSN: 0003-0139
Founded in: 1893

18879 Jukebox Collector Magazine
2545 SE 60th Court
Pleasant Hill, IA 50327-5099

515-265-8324; *Fax:* 515-265-1980
JukeboxCollector@att.net;
www.alwaysjukin.com

Rick Botts, Editor

Focuses on collectors of jukeboxes from the 40's, 50's, and 60's. There are approximately 150 jukeboxes for sale each month, along with show

events information. Accepts advertising.
Cost: $33.00
36 Pages
Frequency: Monthly
Circulation: 1800
Founded in: 1977

18880 Live Sound International
111 Speen Street
Framingham, MA 01701

415-387-4009
800-375-8015; *Fax:* 866-449-3761
amclean@livesoundint.com;
www.livesoundint.com

Mark Herman, Publisher
Jeff MacKay, Editor
Mitch Gallagher, Associate Editor
Sara Elliott, Advertising

The editorial focus is performance audio and event sound. Contains audio production techniques, new products, equipment applications and associated commercial concerns.
Cost: $60.00
Frequency: Monthly
Circulation: 20,000
Mailing list available for rent
Printed in on glossy stock

18881 Mix
Prism Business Media
6400 Hollis St
Suite 9
Emeryville, CA 94608-1052

510-658-3793
866-860-7087; *Fax:* 510-653-5142
mixeditorial@prismb2b.com;
www.mixonline.com

Melinda Paras, Owner
Erika Lopez, Associate Publisher
Tom Kenny, Editor
John Pledger, Publisher
Christen Pocock, Marketing Director

Mix covers a wide range of topics including: recording, live sound and production, broadcast production, audio for film and video, and music technology. In addition, Mix includes coverage of facility design and construction, location recording, tape/disc manufacturing, education, and other topics of importanct to audio professionals. Distributed in 94 countries.
Cost: $35.97
Frequency: Monthly
Circulation: 45244
Founded in: 1977

18882 Modern Drummer
Modern Drummer Publications
12 Old Bridge Rd
Cedar Grove, NJ 07009-1288

973-239-4140; *Fax:* 973-239-7139
mdinfo@moderndrummer.com;
www.moderndrummer.com

Isabel Spagnardi, Owner
Tracy A Kearns, Associate Publisher
Bill Miller, Editor-in-Chief
Rick Van Horn, Senior Editor
Adam Budofsky, Managing Editor

Every issue of Modern Drummer includes interviews with the world's leading drummers, a full roster of columns on all facets of drumming, complete drum charts, solos and patterns performed by your favorite players, insightful reviews on the hottest new geat, the best in CDs, books, and DVDs for drummers, and giveaways worth thousands of dollars.
Cost: $29.97
Frequency: Monthly
Circulation: 6000
ISSN: 1078-1757
Founded in: 1993
Mailing list available for rent
Printed in 4 colors on glossy stock

18883 Music
102 N Haven Road
PO Box 906
Elmhurst, IL 60126-2932

630-941-2030; *Fax:* 630-941-3210;
www.musicincmag.com

Zach Phillip, Editor
Kevin Maher, CEO
John Cahill, Eastern Advertising
Tom Burns, Western Advertising
Chris Maher, Classified Ads

Offered free to those involved in music products retailing. Delivers news you can use for the musical products industry. Geared toward store owners and managers in musical product retail and repair shops in the United States and Canada.
Frequency: 11 Per Year
Circulation: 8,949
Founded in: 1934

18884 Music & Sound Retailer
Testa Communications
25 Willowdale Avenue
Port Washington, NY 11050

516-767-2500
800-937-7678; *Fax:* 516-767-9335
testa@testa.com; www.testa.com

Brian Berk, Editor

News magazine serving owners, managers and sales personnel in retail musical-instument and sound-product dealershops. The magazine's emphasis is on full-line and combo dealerships offering guitars, drums, electronic keyboards and digital pianos, recording and sound-reinforcement products, lighting, DJ equipment, software, print and accessories. Recurring features include 'MI Spy,' 'Top Ten,' 'Veddatorial,' 'Selling Points,' and editor's letter
Cost: $18.00
Frequency: Monthly
Circulation: 11000
Founded in: 1985

18885 Music Row
1231 17th Avenue S
PO Box 158542
Nashville, TN 37215-8542

615-321-3617; *Fax:* 615-329-0852
sales@musicrow.com; www.musicrow.com

David M Ross, CEO/President

Written for people who work in the music business. Contents include record reviews, current news items, timely interviews or discovering hot talent first. Music Row subscriptions include six print issues per year, daily Afternoon News updates via e-mail and @Musicrow reports every Tuesday, Thursday and Friday via e-mail.
Cost: $159.00
Frequency: Six Per Year
Circulation: 14000
Founded in: 1981
Printed in 4 colors on glossy stock

18886 Music Trades Magazine
Music Trades
80 West Street
Englewood, NJ 07631-0432

201-871-1965
800-423-6530; *Fax:* 201-871-0455
music@musictrades.com;
www.musictrades.com

Brian Majeski, Publisher
Richard T Watson, Managing Editor
Juanita Hampton, Circulation Manager

A blend of industry news, hard sales and marketing data, trend analysis and management tips in every issue. Target audience is retailers, distributors, and manufacturers of musical instruments, professional audio equipment and related products, worldwide.
Cost: $16.00
Frequency: Monthly
Circulation: 7500
Founded in: 1890
Mailing list available for rent

18887 Music and Sound Journal
912 Carlton Road
Tarpon Spring, FL 34689

727-938-0571; www.masj.com

Don Kulak, Founder/Owner

Brings readers the future of sound today, with new music, experimental sound, cutting edge audio and acoustics and alternative media. MSJ is written for people who are discriminating about music, audio, and sound - people who want to improve their sonic environments on all levels, without having to study pages of data - people who want to more fully understand the profound impact sound has on every aspect of their daily lives.
ISSN: 1541-8545
Founded in: 1988

18888 Musical Merchandise Review
21 Highland Circle
Suite One
Needham, MA 02494

781-453-9310
800-964-5150; *Fax:* 781-453-9389
mprescott@symphonypublishing.com;
www.mmrmagazine.com

Lee Zapis, President
Sidney L Davis, Group Publisher
Richard E Kessel, Publisher/Advertising Sales
Maureen Johan, Classified Sales

Serves retailers of musical instruments, accessories, and related services as well as wholesalers, importers/exporters and manufacturers of related products. Its purpose is to communicate facts and ideas that will benefit musical merchandisers and their daily business operations as well as help them enhance their growth. Its editorial approach includes features on industry trends and innovations, new product promotion, in-store display techniques, financing, planning and dealer surveys.
Cost: $32.00
Frequency: Monthly
Founded in: 1879
*Mailing list available for rent*at $100 per M
Printed in 4 colors

18889 New on the Charts
Music Business Reference
70 Laurel Place
New Rochelle, NY 10801-7105

914-632-3349; *Fax:* 914-633-7690
lenny@notc.com; www.notc.com

Leonard Kalikow, Publisher/Editor

Circulation limited to professionals only, provides major signings, contracts and directories.
Cost: $365.00
Frequency: Monthly
Circulation: 5,000
ISSN: 0276-7031
Founded in: 1976

18890 Notes
Music Library Association
8551 Research Way
Suite 180
Middleton, WI 53562

608-836-5825; *Fax:* 608-831-8200
mla@areditions.com;
www.musiclibraryassoc.org

Michael Colby, President
Jane Gottlieb, Editor

18891 Opera America Newsline
Opera America
330 7th Ave
Suite 1600
New York, NY 10001-5248
212-796-8620; *Fax:* 212-796-8631
info@operaamerica.org;
www.operaamerica.org
Marc Scorca, President
Provides company news from around the world, articles on issues affecting the field, professional opportunities, and updates on OPERA America programs and activities. Complimentary subscription with all membership levels, excluding stand-alone professional subscriptions.
Frequency: 10X Per Year
Founded in: 1970

18892 Opera News
Metropolitan Opera Guild
70 Lincoln Center Plz
New York, NY 10023-6577
212-769-7000; *Fax:* 212-769-7007
info@metguild.org; www.metoperafamily.org
David Dik, Manager
Monthly magazine that reports on opera around the world. Issues include reviews of commercial recordings and live performances, profiles of artists and articles by eminent writers on the music scene.
Cost: $29.95
Frequency: Monthly
Circulation: 60000
Founded in: 1883

18893 Percussive Notes
Percussive Arts Society
110 W Washington Street
Suite A
Indianapolis, IN 46204
317-974-4488; *Fax:* 317-974-4499
percarts@pas.org; www.pas.org
Rick Mattingly, Editor
Hillary Henry, Managing Editor
The official journal of the Percussive Arts Society. Published in February, April, June, August, October and December, this magazine features a variety of articles and advertising aimed at professional and student percussionists. Regular sections are devoted to drumset, marching percussion, world percussion, symphonic percussion, technology, keyboard, health and wellness, research and reviews.
Cost: $85.00
Frequency: 6 Times Per Year
Circulation: 8000
Founded in: 1961
Mailing list available for rent

18894 Piano Guild Notes
Piano Guild Publications
PO Box 1807
Austin, TX 78767-1807
512-478-5775; *Fax:* 512-478-5843
ngpt@pianoguild.com; www.pianoguild.com
Richard Allison, President
Music industry publication focusing on Piano Guild members and activities.
Cost: $16.00
Frequency: Quarterly
Circulation: 11000
Founded in: 1929
Printed in 2 colors

18895 Piano Technicians Journal
Piano Technicians Guild
4444 Forest Avenue
Kansas City, KS 66106
913-432-9975; *Fax:* 913-432-9986
ptg@ptg.org; www.ptg.org
Barbara Cassaday, Executive Director
Jim Coleman Jr RPT, President
Norman R Cantrell RPT, VP
Monthly technical magazine covering all phases of working on pianos. Articles explore new tools, industry news and organizational issues. Feature articles range from setting up a repair shop to rebuilding techniques.
Cost: $ 150.00
Frequency: Monthly
Circulation: 4300
ISSN: 0031-9562

18896 Pitch Pipe
Sweet Adelines International
9110 S Toledo
PO Box 470168
Tulsa, OK 74137-0168
918-622-1444
800-992-7464; *Fax:* 918-665-0894
Joey@sweetadelineintl.org;
www.sweetadelineintl.org
Pat LeVezu, President
Joey Mechell Stenner, Editor
Kelly Kirchhoff, Director Communications
Official publication of Sweet Adelines International, the world's largest singing performance and music education organization for women. The Pitch Pipe informs, educates and recognizes the members who have made the organization a success. The subscription price for members is included in the annual per capita fee.
Cost: $12.00
Frequency: Quarterly
Circulation: 30,000
Founded in: 1947
Mailing list available for rent: 30M names
Printed in 4 colors on glossy stock

18897 Playback
American Society of Composers, Authors & Publisher
1 Lincoln Plz
New York, NY 10023-7097
212-621-6027
800-952-7227; *Fax:* 212-362-7328
Playback@ascap.com; www.ascap.com
Marilyn Bergman, President
Phil Crossland, Executive Editor
Jin Moon, Deputy Editor
Mike Barsky, Advertising
David Pollard, Design
The Society's magazine is loaded with full-color photos, features the latest news on ASCAP events, new member listings, legislative updates, feature articles on members, distribution info, upcoming workshops and showcases and much more.
Cost: $12.00
Frequency: Annual
Circulation: 100,000
ISSN: 1080-1391

18898 Pro Audio Review
IMAS Publishing
28 East 28th Street
12th Floor
New York, NY 22041
212-378-0400; *Fax:* 212-378-0470;
www.proaudioreview.com
John Gatski, Publisher/Executive Editor
Brett Moss, Managing Editor
Claudia Van Veen, Advertising
Reviews of the latest new equipment written by audio professionals in the field, from bench tests checking the specs, to new product announcements.
Cost: $24.95
Frequency: Monthly
Circulation: 26000
ISSN: 1083-6241
Founded in: 1995
Mailing list available for rent: 30,000 names at $145 per M
Printed in 4 colors on glossy stock

18899 Pro Sound News
United Business Media
28 East 28th Street
12th Floor
New York, NY 10019
212-378-0400; *Fax:* 212-378-2160
sedorusa@optonline.net;
www.governmentvideo.com
Gary Rhodes, International Sales Manager
Provides timely and accurate news, industy analysis, features and technology updates to the expanded professional audio community.
Cost: $30.00
Frequency: Monthly
Circulation: 250003
Printed in 4 colors

18900 RePlay Magazine
PO Box 572829
Tarzana, CA 91357-7004
818-776-2880; *Fax:* 818-776-2888
editor@replaymag.com; www.replaymag.com
Edward Adlum, President
Barry Zweben, Marketing
A trade publication for those within the coin-operated amusement machine industry, primarily distributors, manufacturers and operators of jukeboxes and games.
Cost: $65.00
Frequency: Monthly
Circulation: 36000
ISSN: 1534-2328
Founded in: 1975
Mailing list available for rent
Printed in 4 colors on glossy stock

18901 Rolling Stone Magazine
1290 Ave of the Americas
Floor 2
New York, NY 10104-0295
212-484-1616; *Fax:* 212-484-1771;
www.rssoundingboard.com
Social Media: Facebook, Twitter
Jann Wenner, President
Covers pop culture, politics etc in a massive amount of music articles, interviews, news, reviews, photos, and sound clips.

18902 Sheet Music Magazine
PO Box 58629
Boulder, CO 80323
914-244-8500
800-759-3036; *Fax:* 914-244-8560;
www.sheetmusicmagazine.com
Ed Shanaphy, Publisher
Features actual reproduction of popular songs, both words and music, articles on various aspects of musical performance and interest for many types of musicians, and self improvement features for keyboard and fretter instrument players. A single year's subscription brings you at least 66 great songs best-loved standards and today's most lyrical hits.
Cost: $22.97
Frequency: Bi-Monthly
Circulation: 50,000

18903 Society News
Contemporary Record Society

724 Winchester Road
Broomall, PA 19008

610-544-5920; *Fax:* 915-808-4232
crsnews@verizon.net;
www.mysite.verizon.net/vzeeewvp/contemporaryrecordsociety/id3.

Jack M Shusterman, Advertising

Offers opportunities to CRS consituents, progress notes on its associates, various awards and performance possibilities. The Society News offers feature articles of renowned composers/performers and reviews of music, recordings and music books.
Founded in: 1983

18904 **Southwestern Musician**
Texas Music Educators Association
7900 Centre Park
PO Box 140465
Austin, TX 78714-0465

512-452-0710
888-318-8632; *Fax:* 512-451-9213
rfloyd@tmea.org; www.tmea.org

Robert Floyd, Executive Director
Karen Kneten, Communications Manager
Tesa Harding, Advertising/Exhibit Manager
Laura Kocian, Financial Manager
Rita Ellinger, Membership Assistant

The official magazine of the TMEA. Publsihed monthly August through May. Included with membership. A President's newsletter is published each June when necessary to provide an update on TMEA activities. The purposed of this publication is to serve the music educators of Texas as a means of communication or professional philosophy and action and to promote the field of music education within the state.
Circulation: 14000
Founded in: 1938
Mailing list available for rent: 10,000 names
Printed in 4 colors on glossy stock

18905 **Symphony Magazine**
American Symphony Orchestra League
33 W 60th St
Suite 5
New York, NY 10023-7905

212-262-0638; *Fax:* 212-262-5198;
www.symphony.org

Henry Fogel, CEO
Stephen Alter, Advertising Manager
Michael Rush, Production Manager

Bimonthly magazine of the American Symphony Orchestra League. Discusses issues critical to the orchestra community and communicates the value and importance of orchestras and the music they perform. Publishes articles on compelling issues and trends relevant to the entire orchestra field. Its readers include professional staff, musicians, and board members in the orchestra industry and related fields; orchestra patrons and volunteers; and music critics and arts and media professionals.
Cost: $22.00
Frequency: Bi-Monthly
Circulation: 18000
Founded in: 1942
Mailing list available for rent
Printed in 4 colors

18906 **Symposium**
312 E Pine Street
Missoula, MT 59802

406-721-9616
800-729-0235; *Fax:* 406-721-9419
cms@music.org; www.music.org

Robby D Gunstream, Executive Director
Cynthia Taggart, President
Glenn Stanley, Editor

Serves as a vehicle for the dissemination of information and ideas on music in higher education. The content of the publication highlights concerns of general interest and reflects the work of the Society in the areas of music represented on its Board of Directors.
Frequency: One Per Year
Circulation: 8000
Founded in: 1968
Printed in one color on matte stock

18907 **Vibe**
E-Mail: vbecustserv@cdsfulfillment.com;
www.vibe.com

Mimi Valdez, Editor-In-Chief

Covers the trends, the events, and culture of the urban scene. Film, fashion and art to politics and music-pop, jazz, R&B, dance, hip hop, rap, house and more.
Cost: $11.95
Frequency: Monthly

Trade Shows

18908 **ASTA National Conference**
American String Teachers Association
4155 Chain Bridge Road
Fairfax, VA 22030

703-279-2113; *Fax:* 703-279-2114
asta@astaweb.com; www.astaweb.com

Donna Sizemore Hale, Executive Director
Beth Danner-Knight, Deputy Director
Jody McNamara, Deputy Director

Recognizing the wealth of our rich traditions as well as offer members new horizons in teaching and performing strings. Cost of attendance begins at $255. 150 exhibitors.
2000 Attendees
Frequency: Annual/March

18909 **ATG Annual Accordion Festival**
Accordionists & Teachers Guild International
813 West Lakeshore Drive
O'Fallon, IL 62269-1216

618-632-2859
amyjo@apci.net; www.accordions.com

Amy Jo Sawyer, President
Joe Natoli, First Vice President
Liz Finch, Second Vice President
Joan C. Sommers, Executive Secretary
Frequency: Annual
Founded in: 1940

18910 **American Choral Directors Association National Conference**
American Choral Directors Association
545 Couch Drive
Oklahoma City, OK 73102

405-232-8161; *Fax:* 405-232-8162;
www.acdaonline.org

Dr Tim Sharp, Executive Director

4 full days of concerts, interest sessions, exhibits, and networking.
Frequency: Annual/March

18911 **American Guild of Organists, National Conference**
475 Riverside Drive
Suite 1260
New York, NY 10115

212-870-2310; *Fax:* 212-870-2163
info@agohq.org; www.agohq.org

James Thomashower, Executive Director
Jennifer Madden, Manager Membership
Harold Calhoun, Mgr Competitions

Over 20 exhibits and a workshop for professional, amatuer and student organists.
Frequency: Biennial

18912 **American Harp Society National Conference**
3416 Primm Lane
Birmingham, AL 35216

205-795-7130; *Fax:* 205-823-2760
execsecretary@harpsociety.org;
www.harpsociety.org

Christa Grix, National Conference Chair
Lynne Aspnes, Conference Program Advisory Chair
Delaine Fedson, President

Conference will explore the mind-body-music connection, the creative process, and the connection between creativity and learning. The conference will include multiple disciplines including educators, composers, performers, therapists and practioners.
300 Attendees
Frequency: Annual
Founded in: 1962

18913 **American Institute of Organbuilders Annual Convention**
American Institute of Organ Builders
PO Box 130982
Houston, TX 77219

713-529-2212; *Fax:* 713-529-2212;
www.convention.pipeorgan.org

Rene Marceau, Convention Committee Chairman

Annual convention includes supplier exhibits, technical lectures, sight-seeing tours, professional examinations, lectures and organ demonstrations.
Frequency: October
Founded in: 1974
Mailing list available for rent: 350 names at $250 per M

18914 **American Music Therapy Conference**
National Music Therapy Association
8445 Colesville Road
Suite 1000
Silver Spring, MD 20910

301-589-3300; *Fax:* 301-589-5175;
www.musictherapy.org

Seminar and exhibits of publications, musical instruments, books, learning aids and recordings.
Frequency: November

18915 **American Musical Instrument Society**
1106 Garden Street
Hoboken, NJ 07030

202-656-0107
amis@guildassoc.com; www.amis.org

Susan Thompson, Program Co-Chair
Kathryn Libin, Program Co-Chair

A broad range of topics include the history, design, use, care and acoustics of musical instruments in all cultures and from all periods.
Frequency: Annual

18916 **American Musicological Society Annual Meeting**
American Musicological Society
194 Mercer St. Room 404
New York, NY 10012-1502

212-992-6340
877-679-7648; *Fax:* 212-995-4022
ams@ams-net.org; www.ams-net.org

Robert Judd, Executive Director

A society of professional musicologists and university educators. The annual meetings are held in the fall each year; 2007- Quebec; 2008- Nashville; 2009- Philadelphia.
2000 Attendees
Frequency: Annual
Founded in: 1948

Mailing list available for rent: 3515 names at $100 per M

18917 American Orff-Schulwerk Association National Conference
American Orff-Schulwerk Association
PO Box 391089
Cleveland, OH 44139-8089
440-543-5366; *Fax:* 440-600-7332
info@aosa.org; www.aosa2.org
Karen Medley, Conference Chair
One hundred exhibits of music, music books, software, insturments, and gifts in addition to National Conference of 2000+ music educators.
2400 Attendees
Frequency: November
Founded in: 1969

18918 American Symphony Orchestra League National Conference
33 W 60th Street
5th Floor
New York, NY 10023
212-262-5161; *Fax:* 212-262-5198;
www.symphony.org
Stephen Alter, Advertising and Meetings Manager
Meghan Whitbeck, Advertising/Meetings Coordinator
Henry Fogel, President/CEO
Ninety booths incorporating all facets of classical music industries including industry suppliers, music publishers and computer technology.
1200 Attendees
Frequency: June

18919 CMS National Conference
College Music Society
312 E Pine Street
Missoula, MT 59802
406-721-9616; *Fax:* 406-721-9419
cms@music.org; www.music.org
Robby D Gunstream, Executive Director
Presents higher education's broadest array of topics dealing with music. Attendees are faculty, administrators, graduate students, independent scholars, composers, publishers, and music business personnel who share a common interest and dedication to the improvement of music and its relationship to the other academic disciplines of higher education.
450 Attendees
Frequency: Annual/October

18920 Chamber Music America National Conference
Chamber Music America
305 7th Avenue
5th Floor
New York, NY 10001
212-242-2022; *Fax:* 212-242-7955;
www.chamber-music.org
Susan Dadian, Program Director
Margaret M Lioi, CEO
Louise Smith, Chair
700 Attendees
Frequency: Annual

18921 Chorus America Annual Conference
910 17th Street NW
Washington, DC 20006
202-776-0215; *Fax:* 202-776-0224
service@chorusamerica.org;
www.chorusamerica.org
Ann Meier Baker, President/CEO
Melanie Garrett, Membership Services Manager
This four day conference offers seminars, workshops, concerts, expert consultations and peer-group meetings in a friendly, dynamic environment.
500 Attendees
Frequency: June
Printed in 2 colors on matte stock

18922 Country Radio Seminar
Country Radio Broadcasters
819 18th Avenue S
Nashville, TN 37203
615-327-4487; *Fax:* 615-329-4492
info@crb.org; www.crb.org
Ed Salamon, Executive Director
Chasity Crouch, Business Manager
Carole Bowen, Secretary
Conference attendess include major radio groups and record labels as well as independents, Features include exhibits, seminars and shows.
2300 Attendees
Frequency: Annual
Founded in: 1969

18923 Folk Alliance Annual Meeting
Folk Alliance
510 South Main
1st Floor
Memphis, TN 38103
901-522-1170; *Fax:* 816-221-3658
fa@folk.org; www.folkalliance.org
200+ artists, 4 nights of show cases, four days of feature concerts, exhibit hall parties, panels, workshops, clinics and much more all under one roof.
3000 Attendees

18924 Gospel Music Week
Gospel Music Association
PO Box 22697
Nashville, TN 37202
615-242-0303; *Fax:* 615-254-9755
info@gospelmusic.org; www.gospelmusic.org
Jackie Patillo, Executive Director
Listen to new music as you experience over 100 eclectic performances throughout the week from today's top artists and tomorrow's hit-makers, invent new waysof enhancing your ministry through educational opportunities found in over 100 seminars and panels and through the sharing of your ideas with colleagues. Connect with your industry peers and friends at various networking opportunities including receptions, roundtables and more.
3,000 Attendees
Frequency: April
Founded in: 1964

18925 Gospel Music Workshop America
PO Box 34635
Detroit, MI 48208
313-898-6900; *Fax:* 313-898-4520;
www.gmwanational.org
Rev Albert L Jamison, Sr, Chair, Board of Directors
Sheila Smith, Director Operations
Mark Smith, Convention Manager
Conferences open with a highly spirited service including Sacraments, music from choirs within the GMWA, Psalmists and the preached Word. This is followed by lectures, speakers, preachers and over 100 courses offered during the week. Nightly musicals include chapter choirs and national recording artists. Midnight services are held which include music, preaching and various recordings by the Women's Division, Men's Division, Youth/Young Adult division and a service by Bishop Richard White.
16M Attendees
Frequency: August
Founded in: 1967

18926 International Association of Jazz Educators Conference
International Association of Jazz Education
PO Box 724
Manhattan, KS 66505
785-776-8744; *Fax:* 785-776-6190;
www.iaje.org
Bill McFarlin, Executive Director
This four-day conference fatures a 75,000 square-food music industry exposition, commission premieres, technology presentations, research papers, award ceremonies, and performances by over 500 of the world's most respected professional jazz groups and musicians.
8000 Attendees
Frequency: Annual

18927 International Computer Music Conference
International Computer Music Association
1819 Polk Street
Suite 330
San Francisco, CA 94109
Fax: 734-878-3031
icma@umich.edu; www.computermusic.org
Social Media: Facebook
Tae Hong Park, President
Margaret Schedel, VP of Conference
Chryssie Nanou, Treasurer/Secretary
Tom Erbe, VP, Membership
Sandra Neal, Administrative Assistant
The International Computer Music Association is an international affiliation of individuals and institutions involved in the technical, creative, and performance aspects of computer music. It serves composers, engineers, researchers and musicians who are interested in the integration of music and technology.
Founded in: 1974

18928 International Horn Competition of America
BGSU Continuing and Extended Education
14 College Park
Bowling Green, OH 43403-0200
509-963-1226; *Fax:* 509-963-1239;
www.ihcamerica.org
Jeffrey Snedeker, President
Andrew Pelletier, Host
International competition specifically for the horn as a solo instrument.
450 Attendees
Frequency: July

18929 International Horn Symposium
Central Washington University Music Department
400 E University Way
Ellensburg, WA 98926-7458
509-963-1226; *Fax:* 509-963-1239
gross@music.ucsb.edu; www.hornsociety.org
Jeffrey Snedeker, President
Kristina Mascher-Turner, Vice President
Annie Bosler, Secretary/Treasurer
Heidi Vogel, Executive Director
Features renowned hornists, guest ensembles, recitals and master classes
Frequency: Annual

18930 International Steel Guitar Convention
College Music Society
312 East Pine Street
Missoula, MT 59802
406-721-9616; *Fax:* 406-721-9419
cms@music.org; www.music.org
Social Media: Facebook, Twitter, YouTube, RSS
Dewitt Scott Sr, President
Mary Scott, Secretary

Sixty-five booths that provide entertainment from steel guitarists and various instruments including the bass guitar.
3M Attendees
Frequency: August

18931 Mid-South Horn Conference
Central Washington University Music Department
400 E University Way
Ellensburg, WA 98926-7458
509-963-1226; *Fax:* 509-963-1239;
www.hornsociety.org
Jeffrey Snedeker, President
Ellen Campbell, Event Host
Heidi Vogel, Membership Coordinator
Features renowned hornists, guest ensembles, recitals and master classes
450 Attendees
Frequency: March

18932 Midwest International Band & Orchestra Clinic
Midwest International Band & Orchestra Clinic
111 E Touhy Ave
Suite 250
Des Plaines, IL 60018
847-424-4163; *Fax:* 773-321-1509
info@midwestclinic.org;
www.midwestclinic.org
The purpose to the clinic is to raise the standards of music education, to develop new teaching techniqes, to examine, analyze, analyze and appraise literature dealing with music, demonstrations for the betterment of music education. 350 exhibitors, 565 booths, 30 concerts, and 50 instructional clinics.
12000 Attendees
Frequency: December

18933 Music Teachers National Association Convention
441 Vine Street
Suite 3100
Cincinnati, OH 45202
513-421-1420
888-512-5278; *Fax:* 513-421-2503
mtnanet@mtna.org; www.mtna.org
Gary L Ingle, Executive Director
Gail Berenson, President
Janice Wenger, VP
Atendees include independent music teachers, college faculty, students and parents from all over North America.
2500 Attendees
Frequency: Annual
Founded in: 1876
Mailing list available for rent: 23000 names at $85 per M

18934 NAMM: International Music Products Association
5790 Armada Drive
Carlsbad, CA 92008-4608
760-438-8001
800-767-6266; *Fax:* 760-438-7327
tradeshow@namm.com;
www.thenammshow.com
Joe Lamond, President
NAMM's trade shows are all about the experience. The experience of checking out the latest gear, of networking with other music product professionals, of attending free business-boosting classes. From the cook exhibits to the sizzling hot nightlife, music and music making always take center stage.
80000 Attendees
Frequency: January

18935 NATS National Conference
National Association of Teachers of Singing
9957 Moorings Drive
Suite 401
Jacksonville, FL 32257-2416
904-992-9101; *Fax:* 904-262-2587
info@nats.org; www.nats.org
Social Media: Facebook, Twitter, LinkedIn
Allen Henderson, Executive Director
Deborah Guess, Director of Operations
Paul Witkowski, Marketing & Communication
Amanda Wood, Membership & Program Coordinator
Gathers professionals, scholars, and experts worldwide to share ideas and participate in lectures, workshops, and demonstrations aimed at promotingvocal arts and the teaching of singing.
Frequency: June/July
Founded in: 1944

18936 National Association for Music Education Conference
1806 Robert Fulton Drive
Reston, VA 20191-4348
703-860-4000
800-336-3768; *Fax:* 703-860-1531;
www.menc.org
Social Media: Facebook, Twitter, LinkedIn
John J Mahlmann, Executive Director
Margaret Jamborsky, Director Meetings/Conventions
Elizabeth Lasko, Director Public Relations/Marketing
Amanda Kidwell, Membership Director
To advance music education by encouraging the study and making of music by all.
5M Attendees
Frequency: April

18937 National Association of Recording Merchandising Trade Show
9 Eves Drive
Suite 120
Marlton, NJ 08053-3130
856-596-2221; *Fax:* 859-596-3268;
www.namm.org
Social Media: Facebook, Twitter, RSS
Jim Donio, President
Pat Daly, Meeting Planner
Evelyn Dichter, Membership Coordinator
Susan L'Ecuyer, VP Communications/Marketing
One-on-One meeting opportunities, welcome reception, keynote speakers, marketplace exhibits, live performances, forums, receptions and awards dinner
3M Attendees
Frequency: April/May

18938 National Association of Schools of Music Annual Meeting
National Association of Schools of Music
11250 Roger Bacon Drive
Suite 21
Reston, VA 20190-5248
703-437-0700; *Fax:* 703-437-6312
info@arts-accredit.org; www.arts-accredit.org
Don Gibson, President
Mark Wait, VP
Mellasenah Y Morris, Treasurer
Frequency: November

18939 National Opera Association Conference
National Opera Association
PO Box 60869
Canyon, TX 79016
806-651-2857; *Fax:* 806-651-2958
rhansen@mail.wtamu.edu; www.noa.org
Social Media: Facebook, RSS
Robert Hansen, Executive Director
Robert Thieme, Editor
Annual conference and exhibits of opera related equipment, supplies and services.
775 Attendees
Frequency: Annual
Founded in: 1954

18940 Northeast Horn Workshop
Central Washington University Music Department
400 E University Way
Ellensburg, WA 98926-7458
509-963-1226; *Fax:* 509-963-1239
rdodsonw@mansfield.edu;
www.hornsociety.org
Jeffrey Snedeker, President
Rebecca Dodson, Workshop Host
Heidi Vogel, Membership Coordinator
Features renowned hornists, guest ensembles, recitals and master classes
450 Attendees
Frequency: February

18941 Opera America Conference
Opera America
330 7th Avenue
16th Floor
New York, NY 10001-5248
212-796-8620; *Fax:* 212-796-8631;
www.operaamerica.org
Social Media: RSS
Session topics include identifying ways to harness the power of the best new technologies, how to reach current and prospective audiences, how to gain support from donors, and how to enrich the lives of children and adults who are now downloading podcasts, reading blogs, and designing their own multimedia communications.
275 Attendees
Frequency: April

18942 Piano Technicians Guild Annual Convention
Piano Technicians Guild
4444 Forest Avenue
Kansas City, KS 66106
913-432-9975; *Fax:* 913-432-9986
ptg@ptg.org; www.ptg.org
Barbara J Cassaday, Executive Director
Jim Coleman Jr RPT, President
Norman R Cantrell RPT, VP
Come for the learning: find a hands-on class for your skill level; pick from sessions covering every type of piano service; squeeze in a mini-tech; prepare for the RPT exams; see the latest and greatest piano products.
650 Attendees
Frequency: June

18943 Sweet Adelines International Convention
Sweet Adelines International
PO Box 470168
Tulsa, OK 74147-0168
918-622-1444
800-992-7464; *Fax:* 918-665-0894;
www.sweetadelineintl.org
Kathy Hayes, Director Meetings/Corporate Service
Ruth Cameron, Meetings/Exhibits Coordinator
Jane Hanson, Marketing Coordinator
Connie Heyer, Membership Registrar
Kellye Kirchhoff, Director Communications

Heart-pounding chorus competitions, the rush and excitement of the quartet competition, education classes, shopping in the Harmony Bazaars and good times with old friends and new are all included in the International Convention.
8M Attendees
Frequency: October

18944 Winter Music Conference
3450 NE
12th Terrace
Fort Lauderdale, FL 33334
954-563-4444; *Fax:* 954-563-1599
info@wintermusicconference.com;
www.wintermusicconference.com
Regarded as the singular networking event in the dance music industry, attracting professionals from over 60 different countries.

18945 World of Bluegrass
International Bluegrass Music Association
2 Music Circle South
Suite 100
Nashville, TN 37203
615-256-3222
888-438-4262; *Fax:* 615-256-0450
info@ibma.org; www.ibma.org
Dan Hays, Executive Director
Nancy Cardwell, Special Projects Coordinator
Jill Snider, Member/Convention Services
Build relationships with event producers, record label reps, agents and managers, broadcasters, association leaders, educators, the media, instrument builders, artists and composers. Educational and networking events like seminars, facilitated discussions and workshops are the primary focus of the conference. Browse through 100+ booths in the Exhibit Hall. You will hear bluegrass music around the clock for seven days. The Highpoint of the Conference is the International Bluegrass Music Awards.
1,800 Attendees
Frequency: October

Directories & Databases

18946 American Music Center Directory
American Music Center
90 John Street
Suite 312
New York, NY 10038
212-645-6949; *Fax:* 212-366-5265
library@newmusicusa.org; www.amc.net
Joanne Cossa, Executive Director
Lyn Liston, Director New Music Information
Peter Shavitz, Director Development
Lisa Taliano, Director Information Technology
Carlos Camposeco, Director Finance and Administration
Mailing lists include all United States members; all International and United States members; Composer Members in the United States; Members in the New York City Metropolitan area; and Members in the United States and Canada.

18947 American Society of Composers, Authors and Publishers
American Soc. of Composers, Authors & Publishers
1 Lincoln Plz
New York, NY 10023-7097
212-621-6027; *Fax:* 212-621-8453;
www.ascap.com
Marilyn Bergman, President
Johnny Mandel, Writer Vice Chairman
Jay Morgenstern, Publisher Vice Chairman
Arnold Broido, Treasurer
Kathy Spanberger, Secretary
ASCAP created the dial-up ACE system as a useful tool for music professionals. An enhanced World Wide Web version of this database is now available. The database contains information on all compositions in the ASCAP repertory which have appeared in any of ASCAP's domestic surveys, including foreign compositions licensed by the ASCAP in the United States.
Frequency: Annual
Founded in: 1993

18948 AudArena International Guide
Billboard Directories
PO Box 15158
North Hollywood, CA 91615
818-487-4582
800-562-2706
info@billboard.com; www.orderbillboard.com
Arkady Fridman, Inside Sales Manager
Complete data on over 4,400 venues worldwide, including Amphitheaters, Arenas, Stadiums, Sports Facilities, Concert Halls and New Constructions. Also includes complete listings of companies offering services to the touring industry in the Facilty Buyer's Guide. The guide features contact names, phone and fax numbers, e-mail and web site addresses, market population, facility capacities and staging configurations, and rental fees and ticketing rights.
Cost: $99.00
325 Pages
Frequency: Annual

18949 Billboard Subscriber File
Edith Roman Associates
PO Box 1556
Pearl River, NY 10965
845-620-9000
800-223-2194; *Fax:* 845-620-9035;
www.edithroman.com
Steve Roberts, President
Wayne Nagrowski, E-Mail List Info Contact
Directory listees include booking agencies and agents, clubs, music publishers, promoters, radio stations, record labels, sound and lighting services, retailers, video, venues, wholesalers, equipment and manufacturing and general services.
Frequency: Annual

18950 Bluegrass Resource Directory
International Bluegrass Music Association
2 Music Cir S
Suite 100
Nashville, TN 37203-4381
615-256-3222
888-438-4262; *Fax:* 615-256-0450
info@ibma.org; www.ibma.org
Member Directory can only be accessed by IBMA members.
Cost: $25.00
88 Pages
Frequency: Annual

18951 Gospel Music Industry Directory
Gospel Music Association
P.O Box 22697
Nashville, TN 37202
615-242-0303; *Fax:* 615-254-9755
info@gospelmusic.org; www.gospelmusic.org
Social Media: Facebook, YouTube
John Styll, President
Scott Brickell, Director
Ed Harper, Director
Formerly called the Networking Guide, the GMA Music Industry Directory is a comprehensive listing of Christian and Gospel music artists, managers, booking agents, record companies, publishing companies and more. Active GMA Professional members get a copy of the directory free. Associate and Student GMA members can purchase one for a discounted rate.

18952 Grey House Performing Arts Directory
Grey House Publishing
4919 Route 22
PO Box 56
Amenia, NY 12501
518-789-8700
800-562-2139; *Fax:* 845-373-6390
books@greyhouse.com; www.greyhouse.com
Social Media: Facebook, Twitter
Leslie Mackenzie, Publisher
Richard Gottlieb, Editor
The most comprehensive resource covering the Performing Arts. This directory provides current information on over 8,500 Dance Companies, Instrumental Music Programs, Opera Companies, Choral Groups, Theater Companies, Performing Arts Series, Performing Arts Facilities and Artist Management Groups.
Cost: $185.00
1200 Pages
Frequency: Annual
ISBN: 1-592373-76-3
Founded in: 1981

18953 Grey House Performing Arts Directory - Online Database
Grey House Publishing
4919 Route 22
PO Box 56
Amenia, NY 12501-0556
518-789-8700
800-562-2139; *Fax:* 518-789-0556
gold@greyhouse.com;
www.gold.greyhouse.com
Social Media: Facebook, Twitter
Leslie Mackenzie, Publisher
Richard Gottlieb, Editor
The Grey House Performing Arts Directory - Online Database provides immediate access to dance companies, orchestras, opera companies, choral groups, theater companies, series, festivals and perfoming arts facilities across the country, or in their region, state, or in your own backyard. It offers unequaled coverage of the Performing Arts - over 8,500 listings - of the major performance organization, facilities, and information resources.
Frequency: Annual
Founded in: 1981

18954 International Buyers Guide
Billboard Directories
PO Box 15158
North Hollywood, CA 91615
818-487-4582
800-562-2706
info@billboard.com;
www.billboard.com/directories
Arkady Fridman, Inside Sales Manager
A must-have resource for doing business in the music industry, covers every aspect of the recording business worldwide. The latest edition includes contact information on: record labels, video and digital music companies, distributors and importers/exporters; music publishers and rights organizations - blank media manufacturers, pressing plants and services; manufacturers of jewel boxes and other packaging and equipment services; and suppliers of store fixtures, security and accessories.
Cost: $179.00
340 Pages
Frequency: Annual

18955 International Talent and Touring Guide
Billboard Directories

PO Box 15158
North Hollywood, CA 91615

818-487-4582
800-562-2706
info@billboard.com;
www.billboard.com/directories

Arkady Fridman, Inside Sales Manager

A reference guide for anyone who books, promotes or manages talent. Features over 30,000 listings, including 12,900 artists, managers and agents worldwide, including the USA and Canada. The guide includes contact names, phone and fax numbers, e-mail and website addresses, artists and their record labels, managers and agents, tour services and merchandise, sound and lighting vendors, equipment and instrument rentals, limo rentals, security services, plus national promoters and their key personnel
Cost: $139.00
242 Pages
Frequency: Annual

18956 **Keyboard Teachers Association International**
Dr. Albert DeVito
361 Pin Oak Lane
Westbury, NY 11590-1941

516-333-3236; *Fax:* 516-997-9531

Albert DeVito, President

Music teachers and those related to keeping members updated as to activity going on in music world.
Frequency: Quarterly
Founded in: 1963

18957 **MLA Membership Handbook**
Music Library Association
8551 Research Way
Suite 180
Middleton, WI 53562

608-836-5825; *Fax:* 608-831-8200;
www.musiclibraryassoc.org

Philip Vandermeer, President

A mailing list that is available for rental in a variety of formats.
Cost: $25.00
Founded in: 1931

18958 **Music Library Association Membership Directory**
Music Library Association
8551 Research Way
Suite 180
Middleton, WI 53562

608-836-5825; *Fax:* 608-831-8200
mla@areditions.com;
www.musiclibraryassoc.org

Jerry L. McBride, President

The MLA mailing list is available for rental in a variety of formats. Members include music librarians, librarians who work with music as part of their responsibilities, composers and music scholars, and others interested in the program of the association.

18959 **Musical America Directory**
Musical America
PO Box 1330
Highstown, NJ 08520

609-448- 334
800-221-5488; *Fax:* 609-371-7879
info@musicalamerica.com;
www.musicalamerica.com
Social Media: Facebook, Twitter, YouTube

Joyce Wasserman, Subscription Information
Bob Hudoba, Contact

Provides thousands of names, phone numbers, addresses, and Email and Web site addresses for manangers, orchestras, opera companies, festivals, presenters, venues and more around the world.
Cost: $125.00
Mailing list available for rent

18960 **Musician's Guide**
Billboard Directories
PO Box 15158
North Hollywood, CA 91615

818-487-4582
800-562-2706
info@billboard.com;
www.billboard.com/directories

Arkady Fridman, Inside Sales Manager

Everything the working musician needs to book gigs, contact record labels, find a manager, and locate tour services. The latest edition includes A & R Directory, Music Business Services, and City by City listings.
Cost: $15.95
170 Pages
Frequency: Annual

18961 **National Opera Association Membership Directory**
PO Box 60869
Canyon, TX 79016-0869

806-651-2857; *Fax:* 806-651-2958
rhansen@mail.wtamu.edu; www.noa.org
Social Media: Facebook, RSS

Robert Hansen, Executive Director
JoElyn Wakefield Wright, President
Edith Kirkpatrick Vrenios, VP Resources
Philip Hageman, Treasurer
Carol Notestine, Recording Secretary

Members of the National Opera Association are entitled to receive the NOA Freelance Artists and Production Resources databases, the NOA membership directory, and access to the NOA e-mail listserve.
Frequency: Annual
Mailing list available for rent

18962 **Orion Blue Book: Guitars and Musical Instruments**
Orion Research Corporation
14555 N Scottsdale Rd
Suite 330
Scottsdale, AZ 85254-3487

480-951-1114; *Fax:* 480-951-1117
sales@UsedPrice.com;
www.orionbluebook.com

Roger Rohrs, Owner

77,834 products listed; products listed from 1970s to present; over 450 manufacturers listed; 2 volumes - hardbound or on CD-ROM. Lists musical instruments from Accordians to Xylophones
Cost: $195.00
Frequency: Annual
Founded in: 1981

18963 **Orion Blue Book: Professional Sound**
Orion Research Corporation
14555 N Scottsdale Rd
Suite 330
Scottsdale, AZ 85254-3487

480-951-1114
800-844-0759; *Fax:* 480-951-1117
sales@UsedPrice.com;
www.orionbluebook.com

Roger Rohrs, Owner

Features over 48,964 products from the 1950's to present. Over 350 manufacturers listed. Comes in hardbound or on CD-ROM. Lists products from Cartridge Players to Wireless Microphone Systems.
Cost: $150.00
970 Pages
Frequency: Annual
Founded in: 1973

18964 **Orion Blue Book: Vintage Guitar**
Orion Research Corporation
14555 N Scottsdale Rd
Suite 330
Scottsdale, AZ 85254-3487

480-951-1114
800-844-0759; *Fax:* 480-951-1117
sales@UsedPrice.com;
www.orionbluebook.com

Roger Rohrs, Owner

Features more than 11,413 products from the 1800's to present. Over 30 manufacturers listed. Comes in hardbound or CD-ROM, Lists products from Banjos to Ukuleles.
Cost: $50.00
Frequency: Quarterly
Founded in: 1990

18965 **Record Retailing Directory**
Billboard Directories
PO Box 15158
North Hollywood, CA 91615

818-487-4582
800-562-2706
info@billboard.com;
www.billboard.com/directories

Arkady Fridman, Inside Sales Manager

Over 5,500 listings covering the entire retailing community. Provides access to major chain headquarters and local outlets; complete coverage of independent retailers; hard-to-find audiobook retailers; and the booming world of online record retailing, plus store genre or specialization; executives, owners, buyers and planners; address, phone, fax, email and web.
Cost: $215.00
Frequency: Annual

18966 **Source Directory of Books, Records and Tapes**
Sutton's Super Marketplace
153 Sutton Lane
Fordsville, KY 42343

270-276-9880
mtsutton32@earthlink.net; www.pubdisco.com

Jerry Sutton, Owner/Founder

Publishers, recording studios, wholesalers, distributors, manifacturers and importers. Approximatley 450 records. Changes daily as updated.
Cost: $55.20

18967 **Source Directory of Musical Instruments**
Sutton's Super Marketplace
153 Sutton Lane
Fordsville, KY 42343

270-276-9880
mtsutton32@earthlink.net; www.pubdisco.com

Jerry Sutton, Owner/Founder

Listings in directory include names, addresses, phone and fax numbers, and product descriptions from wholesale distributors, Importers, Manufacturers, Close-out houses and Liquidators. Updated daily.
Cost: $55.20

Industry Web Sites

18968 **http://gold.greyhouse.com**
G.O.L.D Grey House OnLine Databases

Grey House Publishing's online database platform, GOLD, offers Quick Search, Keyword Search and Expert Search for most business sectors including music and performance markets. The GOLD platform makes finding the information you need quick and easy - whether you're a novice searcher or an experienced database user. All of Grey House's directory products are available for subscription on the GOLD platform.

18969 **www.acdaonline.org**
American Choral Directors Association
Nonprofit music-education organization whose central purpose is to promote excellence in choral music through performance, composition, publication, research and teaching.

18970 **www.acmcountry.com**
Academy of Country Music
Involved in numerous events and activities promoting country music. Presents annual awards.

18971 **www.afm.org**
American Federation of Musicians of the United
States and Canada
Union representing over 100,000 professional musicians, performing in all genres of music.

18972 **www.afvbm.org**
American Federation of Violin and Bow Makers
Strives to elevate professional standards of craftmanship and ethical conduct among members. Helps members develop technical skills and knowledge.Research and study organization.

18973 **www.agohq.org**
American Guild of Organists
Promotes the organ in its historic and evolving roles and provides a forum for mutual support, inspiration, education and certification.

18974 **www.ascap.com**
American Society of Composers Authors & Publishers
Membership association of more than 260,000 US composers, song writers, lyricists and music publishers.

18975 **www.asmac.org**
American Society of Music Arrangers and Composers
Professional society for arrangers, composers, orchestrators, and musicians. Monthly meetings with great speakers from the music industry.

18976 **www.billboard.com**
The ultimate music industry research tool and information source. The Member Service database is state-of-the-art electronic information service, enabling users to efficiently access information from a variety of music industry databases via the World Wide Web.

18977 **www.chorusamerica.org**
Chorus America
National service for orchestral choruses, independent choruses and professional choruses.

18978 **www.clarinet.org**
International Clarinet Association
Seeks to focus attention on the importance of the clarinet and to foster communication of the fellowship between clarinetists.

18979 **www.cmaworld.com**
Country Music Association
Promotes and publicizes country music.

18980 **www.creativemusicalcoalition.com**
Creative Musician Coalition
A national organization that brings the world of new music to its readers. Includes in depth music reviews, informative artist interviews, interesting articles and feature columns, and valuable resource material.

18981 **www.flmusiced.org**
Florida Music Educators Association
Florida Music Educators Association and Florida School Music Association.

18982 **www.folkharpsociety.org**
International Society of Folk Harpers and Craftsmen
Conducts technical and artistic programs and promotes craft exchange.

18983 **www.gospelmusic.org**
Gospel Music Association
Dedicated to providing leadership, direction and unity for all facets of the gospel music industry. Through education, communication, information, promotion and recognition, the GMA is striving to help those involved in gospel music.

18984 **www.greyhouse.com**
Grey House Publishing
Authoritative reference directories for most business sectors including music and performance markets. Users can search the online databases with varied search criteria allowing for custom searches by product category, geographic area, sales volume, keyword, subject and more. Full Grey House catalog and online ordering also available.

18985 **www.guitarfoundation.org**
Guitar Foundation of America
Supports the serious studies of the guitar.

18986 **www.harpsociety.org**
American Harp Society
Improves the quality of the instrument and performance.

18987 **www.hornsociety.org**
International Horn Society
A national organization that focuses on music industry news and information.

18988 **www.iaekm.org**
International Association of Electronic Keyboard
Manufacturers
Global manufacturers of electronic kayboards and affiliated software and publications.

18989 **www.ibma.org**
World of Bluegrass
IBMA: working together for high standards of professionalism, a greater appreciation for our music, and the success of the world-wide bluegrass community.

18990 **www.imeamusic.org**
Indiana Music Educators Association
Supports and advances music education in Indiana.

18991 **www.internationalpolka.com**
International Polka Association
Educational organization concerned with the preservation and advancement of polka music. Operates the Polka Music Hall of Fame and Museum, and presents the International Polka Fesitval every year during the complete first weekend of August.

18992 **www.metguild.org**
Metropolitan Opera Guild
Seeks to promote greater understanding and interest in opera.

18993 **www.mpa.org**
Music Publishers Association of the United States
Encourages understanding of the copyright laws and works to protect musical works against infringements and piracy.

18994 **www.mtna.org**
Music Teachers National Association
This is a nonprofit organization of independent and collegiate music teachers committed to furthering the art of music through teaching, performance, composition and scholarly research.

18995 **www.music.org**
College Music Society
The Society is a national service organization for college conservatory and university music teachers.

18996 **www.musicalartists.org**
American Guild of Musical Artists
Exclusive bargaining agent for all concert musical artists.

18997 **www.musicdistributors.org**
Music Distributor Association
A trade association of 160 manufactures, importers, wholesalers of musical instruments and accessories, domestic and international selling to the trade only

18998 **www.musiclibraryassoc.org**
Music Library Association
Promotes growth and establishment in the use of music libraries, musical instruments and musical literature.

18999 **www.nacwpi.org**
National Association of College Wind and Percussion Instructors
Teachers of wind and percussion instruments in American colleges and universities.

19000 **www.napbirt.org**
National Association of Professional Band Instrument Repair Technicians
Promotes technical integrity in the craft. Surveys tools and procedures to improve work quality. Makes available emergency repair of band instruments. Provides placement services.

19001 **www.narm.com**
National Association of Recording Merchandisers
Not-for-profit trade association that represents the retailers, wholesalers, and distributors of prerecorded music in the United States.

19002 **www.nats.org**
National Association of Teachers of Singing
Promotes and encourages the highest standards of vocal education and research at all levels, both for the enrichment of the general public and for the professional advancement of the talented.

19003 **www.nbea.com**
National Ballroom and Entertainment Association
Provides exchange for owners and operators of ballrooms.

19004 **www.noa.org**
National Opera Association
To advance the appreciation, composition and production of opera.

19005 **www.npm.org**
National Association of Pastoral Musicians
Membership organization primarily composed of musicians, musician-liturgist, clergy, and other leaders of prayer devoted to serving the life

and mission of the Church through fosterering the art of musical liturgy in Roman Catholic worshiping communities in the United States.

19006 **www.nyssma.org**
New York State School Music Association
Advocates and improves the education in music of all people in New York State.

19007 **www.pas.org**
Percussive Arts Society
Promotes drums and percussion through a viable network of performers, teachers, students, enthusiasts and sustaining members. Offers publications, a worldwide network of the World Percussion Network, the Percussive Arts Society International Headquarters/Museum and the annual Percussive Arts Society International Convention.

19008 **www.pianoguild.com**
International Piano Guild
A division of the American College of Musicians Professional society of piano teachers and music faculty members. Sponsers national examinations.

19009 **www.printmusic.org**
Retail Print Music Dealers Association
The voice of the print music industry.

19010 **www.ptg.org**
Piano Technicians Guild
Conducts technical institutes at conventions and seminars. Promotes public education in piano care. Bestows awards. Publishes monthly technical journal by subscriptions.

19011 **www.spars.com**
Society of Professional Audio Recording Services
Members are individuals, companies and studios connected with the professional recording industry.

19012 **www.symphony.org**
American Symphony Orchestra League
The national nonprofit service and educational organization dedicated to strengthening symphony and chamber orchestras. It provides artistic, organizational and financial leadership and service to orchestral conductors, managers, volunteers and staff.

19013 **www.tmea.org**
Texas Music Educators Association
Promoting excellence in music education.

Associations

19014 **AAEI and FTA Western Regional Conference**
AAEI/FTA
Torrance, CA 90501

E-Mail: info@foreigntradeassociation.com; www.foreigntradeassociation.com
Social Media: Facebook, Twitter, LinkedIn

Tom Gould, President

Organization promotes growth of international trade in Southern California.

19015 **Alabama International Trade Center**
Alabama International Trade Center
University of Alabama
Tuscaloosa, AL

205-348-7621
aitc@ua.edu
aitc.ua.edu
Social Media: Facebook

Brian K. Davis, Director

Partnership between University of Alabama and U.S. Small Business Administration's export financing programs.
Founded in: 1979

19016 **American - Russian Business Council**

800-428-9308; www.russiancouncil.org
Social Media: Facebook, Twitter, LinkedIn

The Council is dedicated to promoting trade and investment between the two countries.
Founded in: 1994

19017 **American Association of Exporters and Impo rters (AAEI)**
1717 K Street NW
Suite 1120
Washington, DC 20006

202-857-8009; *Fax:* 202-857-7843; www.aaei.org
Social Media: Facebook, Twitter, LinkedIn

Marianne Rowden, President & CEO

Trade organization advocates on behalf of U.S. companies on trade policy issues.

19018 **American Australian Association**
50 Broadway
New York, NY 10004

212-338-6860; *Fax:* 212-338-6864
info@aaanyc.org; www.americanaustralian.org
Social Media: Facebook, Twitter, Pinterest

John Berry, President

The Association is dedicated to encouraging corporate, educational, economic and cultural ties between Australia and the United States.
Founded in: 1948

19019 **American Foreign Service Association**
2101 E St Nw
Washington, DC 20037-2990

202-338-4045; *Fax:* 202-338-6820
member@afsa.org; www.afsa.org
Social Media: Facebook, Twitter, Youtube, RSS

Hon. Barbara Stephenson, President
Hon. Charles A Ford, Treasurer
William Haugh, Secretary
Steve Morrison, FCS Vice President
Mark Petry, FAS Vice President

Missions are to enhance the effectiveness of the Foreign Service, to protect the professional interests of its members, to ensure the maintenance of high professional standards for both career diplomats and political appointeese, and to promote understanding of the critical role of the Foreign service in promoting America's national security and economic prosperity.
11M Members
Founded in: 1924

19020 **Association of Fish and Wildlife Agencies**
1100 First Street, NE
Suite 825
Washington, DC 20002

202-838-3474; *Fax:* 202-350-9869
info@fishwildlife.org; www.fishwildlife.org
Social Media: Facebook, Twitter, Blogger

Ron Regan, Executive Director
Carol Bambery, Association Counsel
Kathy Boydston, Wildlife & Energy Liasion
John Bloom, Accounting Manager
Arpita Choudhury, Science & Research Liasion

The organization that represents all of North America's fish and wildlife agencies that promotes sound management and conservation, and speaks with a unified voice on important fish and wildlife issues.
Founded in: 1902

19021 **Brazil - U.S. Business Council**
1615 H Street NW
Washington, DC 20062

202-463-5729
brazilcouncil@uschamber.com; www.brazilcouncil.org
Social Media: Facebook, Twitter, LinkedIn

Cassia Carvalho, Executive Director

The Council advocates for stronger economic and commercial ties between the two countries.

19022 **Bureau of Intelligence and Research (INR)**
Department of State
Washington, DC

www.state.gov/s/inr

Daniel B. Smith, Asst. Secy. of State

Intelligence bureau within U.S. Department of State supports U.S. diplomats.
Founded in: 1945

19023 **Business Council for International Underst anding (BCIU)**
1501 Broadway
Suite 2300
New York, NY 10036

212-490-0460; *Fax:* 212-697-8526; www.bciu.org
Social Media: Twitter, LinkedIn

Peter Tichansky, President & CEO

U.S. organization supports businesses pursuing global growth opportunities by facilitating relationships between business and government leaders worldwide.
200 Members

19024 **Center for Domestic Preparedness**
Federal Emergency Management Agency
61 Responder Dr.
Anniston, AL 36205

866-213-9553
cdp.dhs.gov
Social Media: Facebook, Twitter, YouTube

Mike King, Superintendent

Training center for emergency responders.
Founded in: 1998

19025 **Central Intelligence Agency (CIA)**
George Bush Center for Intelligence
Langley, VA

703-482-0623; *Fax:* 571-204-3800
cia.gov
Social Media: Facebook, Twitter, flickr, YouTube

John O. Brennan, Director

Civilian foreign intelligence service of the U.S. government.
Founded in: 1947

19026 **Citizens for Global Solutions**
420 7th St SE
Washington, DC 20003-2707

202-546-3950; *Fax:* 202-546-3749
info@globalsolutions.org; www.globalsolutions.org
Social Media: Facebook, Twitter, YouTube

Marvin Perry, CEO
Jordan Bankhead, MS, Chairman
Scott Paul,, Vice-Chair
Shirley Lee Davis, Secretary
Evan Freund, Treasurer

Nonprofit, tax deductible membership organization of 50 chapters and groups throughout the United States. We work to educate policy-makers and the American public on issues of global governance, international law and grassroots activism.
11000 Members
Founded in: 1978

19027 **Coast Guard Intelligence (CGI)**
U.S. Coast Guard
2703 Martin Luther King Jr. Ave. SE
Washington, DC 20593-7000

www.uscg.mil

RAdm Steven J. Andersen, Asst. Commandant

Military intelligence branch of U.S. Coast Guard and component of Central Security Service (CSS).
Founded in: 1915

19028 **Danish American Chamber of Commerce New Yo rk**
One Dag Hammarskjold Plaza
885 Second Ave., 18th Floor
New York, NY 10017-2201

646-790-7169
daccny@daccny.com; www.daccny.com
Social Media: Facebook, Twitter

Anne-Mette Andersen, Chairperson

Promotes business between Denmark and the U.S. by providing information and networking opportunities to members.

19029 **Defense Intelligence Agency (DIA)**
Department of Defense
Joint Base Anacostia-Bolling
Washington, DC 20340-5100

www.dia.mil

LG Vincent R. Stewart, Director

Intelligence service specializing in foreign governments and non-state actors.
Founded in: 1961

19030 **Florida Foreign Trade Association**
2335 NW 107 Ave.
Suite 2M30
Doral, FL 33172

305-471-0737
ffta.com
Social Media: Facebook, Twitter, LinkedIn, Instagram

Rafael Puga, President

FFTA is a not-for-profit promoting information exchange expanded participation in foreign trade.
Founded in: 1985

19031 Foreign Trade Association (FTA)
6216 E Pacific Coast Hwy.
Suite 407
Long Beach, CA 90803

888-223-6459; *Fax:* 310-220-4474
info@foreigntradeassociation.com;
www.foreigntradeassociation.com
Social Media: Facebook, Twitter, LinkedIn

Tom Gould, President

Organization promotes growth of international trade in Southern California.

19032 Intelligence Branch (IB)
Federal Bureau of Investigation
Washington, DC

www.fbi.gov

Eric Velez-Villar, Asst. Dir. for Intelligence Branch

FBI division responsible for intelligence functions including national security and homeland security.
Founded in: 2005

19033 Intelligence and National Security Allianc e (INSA)
4301 Wilson Blvd.
Suite 910
Arlington, VA 22203

703-224-4672; *Fax:* 571-777-8481;
www.insaonline.org
Social Media: Facebook, Twitter, LinkedIn, YouTube, flickr, Instagram

Letitia A. Long, Chair
Chuck Alsup, President

Public, private and academic leaders collaborate on intelligence and national security issues.
160 Members

19034 Intelligence and National Security Summit
Washington, DC

events.jspargo.com/inss16

Federal agency leaders and policymakers discuss U.S. intelligence priorities, challenges and opportunities.
3000 Members

19035 International Association of Official Human Rights Agencies
444 N Capitol Street NW
Suite 536
Washington, DC 20001

202-624-5410; *Fax:* 202-624-8185
iaohra@sso.org; www.iaohra.org

Jean Kelleher Niebauer, President
Alisa Warren, 2nd Vice President
Paula Haley, Secretary
Merrill Smith, Jr., Treasurer
Robin S. Toma, First Vice-President

Private non-profit corporation consisting of human rights agencies in the US and Canada. Provides opportunities and forums for the exchange of ideas and information among human rights advocates. Also provides training opportunities for members and other concerned groups and organizations.
200 Members
Founded in: 1968

19036 International City/County Management Association (ICMA)
777 North Capitol St. NE
Suite 500
Washington, DC 20002-4201

202-289-4262
800-745-8780; *Fax:* 202-962-3500
icma.org
Social Media: Facebook, Twitter, LinkedIn, YouTube, Pinterest, Flickr

Robert J. O'Neill, Executive Director

A worldwide organization for the advancement of professional local government.
Founded in: 1914

19037 International Economic Development Council
734 15th Street NW
Suite 900
Washington, DC 20005

202-223-7800; *Fax:* 202-223-4745;
www.iedconline.org/
Social Media: Facebook, Twitter, LinkedIn

Dyan Lingle Brasington, CEc, Chair
Jeff Finkle, CEcD, President/CEO
Katelyn Palomo, Executive Assistant
Swati Ghosh, Director, Research
Carrie Mulcaire, Director, Federal Grants

Nonprofit membership organization dedicated to helping economic developmers do their job more effectively and raising the profile of the profession. Members create more high-quality jobs, develop more vibrant communities, and generally improve the quality of life in their regions.
1.8M Members
Founded in: 1967

19038 International Trade Administration (ITA)
Department of Commerce
1401 Constitution Ave. NW
Washington, DC 20230

www.trade.gov
Social Media: Facebook, Twitter, LinkedIn

Letitia A. Long, Chair
Chuck Alsup, President

Promoting fair trade and an improved global business environment.
160 Members

19039 International Trade Club of Chicago (ITCC)
134 North LaSalle Street
Suite 1300
Chicago, IL 60602

312-423-5250
contact@itcc.org; www.itcc.org
Social Media: Twitter, LinkedIn

Fabrice Bonvoisin, President

Fosters expansion of international trade.
Founded in: 1919

19040 International Trade Commission (USITC)
500 E Street SW
Washington, DC 20436

202-205-2000; www.usitc.gov

Rhonda K. Schmidtlein, Chair

Quasi-judicial Federal agency investigates trade matters, such as dumping, in order to facilitate a rules-based international trading system.

19041 Interstate Council on Water Policy
505 North Ivy Street
Arlington, VA 22220-1707

703-243-7383; *Fax:* 301-984-5841
rpmueller1@mchsi.com; www.icwp.org
Social Media: Facebook, Twitter

Dru Buntin, 2nd Vice-Chairman
Ryan Mueller, Executive Director
Andrew Dehoff, Secretary & Treasurer
Jerry Schulte, 1st Vice Chairman

The ICWP is the national organization of state and regional water resources management agencies. It provides a means for members to exchange information, ideas and experience to work with federal agencies which share water management responsibilities.
70 Members
Founded in: 1959

19042 Interstate Oil and Gas Compact Commission
900 NE 23rd Street
Oklahoma City, OK 73105

405-525-3556
800-822-4015; *Fax:* 405-525-3592
communications@iogcc.ok.gov;
www.iogcc.state.ok.us

Mike Smith, Executive Director
Gerry Baker, Associate Executive Director
Hannah Barton, Member Services Coordinator
Amy Childers, Federal Projects Manager
Carol Booth, CommunicationsManager

A multi-state government agency that champions the conservation and efficient recovery of domestic oil and natural gas resources.
700 Members
Founded in: 1935

19043 Marine Corps Intelligence Activity (MCIA)
U.S. Marine Corps
Quantico, VA

www.hqmc.marines.mil/intelligence/Units/MCIA
Social Media: Facebook, Twitter, YouTube, flickr, Instagram

BGen Michael S. Groen, Director

Intelligence service to the Marine Corps and U.S. Intelligence Community.
Founded in: 1987

19044 National Association of Clean Air Agencies
444 N Capitol Street NW
Suite 307
Washington, DC 20001-1506

202-624-7864; *Fax:* 202-624-7863
4cleanair@4cleanair.org; www.4cleanair.org

Stu A Clark, Co-President
Merlyn Hough, Co-President
Bill Becker, Executive Director
Nancy Kruger, Deputy Director
Dave Klemp, Co-Vice President

Represents state and local air pollution control officers from over 150 major metropolitan areas and 53 states and territories.

19045 National Association of Export Companies (NEXCO)
PO Box 3949, Grand Central Station
New York, NY 10163

646-330-5168
director@nexco.org; www.nexco.org

Barney Lehrer, Board President

Trade association serving the international business community in New York City.
4000 Members
Founded in: 1963

19046 National Association of Foreign-Trade Zone s
National Press Building 529
14th Street NW, Suite 1071
Washington, DC 20045

202-331-1950; *Fax:* 202-331-1994;
www.naftz.org
Social Media: Facebook, Twitter, LinkedIn

Erik Autor, President

Promoter of U.S. Foreign-Trade Zones Program and its role in the changing environment of international trade.

19047 National Emergency Management Association
2760 Research Park Drive
Lexington, KY 40578

859-244-8000; *Fax:* 859-244-8239
nemaadmin@csg.org; www.nemaweb.org
Social Media: Facebook

Bryan Koon, President
Wendy Smith-Reeve, Vice President
Trina R. Sheets, NEMA Executive Director
Beverly Bell, Senior Policy Analyst
Karen Cobuluis, Meeting & Marketing Coordinator

A nonpartisan, nonprofit association dedicated to enhancing public safety by improving the nation's ability to prepare for, respond to, and recover from all emergencies, disasters, and threats to our nation's security. Provides national leadership and expertise in comprehensive emergency management, serves as a vital emergency management information and assistance resource, and advances continuous improvement in emergency management.
263 Members
Founded in: 1970

19048 National Foreign Trade Council
1625 K Street NW
Suite 200
Washington, DC 20006

202-887-0278; *Fax:* 202-452-8160
nftcinformation@nftc.org; www.nftc.org

Rufus H. Yerxa, President

The Council advocates for interests of American business in the world economy.

19049 National Geospatial-Intelligence Agency (N GA)
7500 GEOINT Dr.
Springfield, VA 22150

571-557-5400; www.nga.mil
Social Media: Facebook, Twitter, LinkedIn, YouTube

Robert Cardillo, Director
Susan Gordon, Deputy Director
Ed Mornston, Chief of Staff

Geospatial intelligence and combat support.
Founded in: 1996

19050 National Reconnaissance Office (NRO)
14675 Lee Rd.
Chantilly, VA 20151-1715

703-808-5050; *Fax:* 703-808-1171
publicaffairs@nro.mil; www.nro.gov
Social Media: Facebook, Twitter, YouTube

Betty Sapp, Director

One of the "big five" intelligence agencies, NRO provides satellite, signals, imagery and measurement intelligence to the U.S. government.
Founded in: 1961

19051 National Security Agency (NSA)
9800 Savage Rd.
Suite 6272
Ft. George G. Meade, MD 20755-6000

301-688-6524; www.nsa.gov

Adm Michael S. Rogers, Director

U.S. government organization responsible for global signals intelligence.

19052 North American Securities Administrators Association, Inc.
750 First Street NE
Suite 1140
Washington, DC 20002-8034

202-737-0900; *Fax:* 202-783-3571;
www.nasaa.org
Social Media: Facebook, RSS

Judith Shaw, President
Russ Iuculano, Executive Director
John H. Lynch, Deputy Executive Director
Joseph Brady, General Counsel
Michael Canning, Director of Policy

NASAA is the international organization representing securities administrators from all 50 states, the District of Columbia, Canada, Mexico and Puerto Rico, and is responsible for investor protection and education. NASAA recommends national policies in the securities industry and provides model legislation for state securities agencies to adopt affecting the regulation of broker/dealers and investment advisers. Consumers can contact NASAA to get phone numbers of state securities regulators.
66 Members
Founded in: 1919

19053 Office of Intelligence and Analysis (I&A)
Department of Homeland Security
DHS Nebraska Ave. Complex
Washington, DC

www.dhs.gov/office-intelligence-and-analysis

Gen Frank Taylor, Under Secretary of Homeland Secur.

The Office tracks terrorists and terrorist networks for Homeland Security.
Founded in: 2007

19054 Office of Intelligence and Counterintellig ence (OICI)
Department of Energy
1000 Independence Ave. SW
Washington, DC 20585

202-586-5000; www.energy.gov

Steven K. Black, Director

Intelligence gathering for the U.S. Department of Energy.
Founded in: 1977

19055 Office of National Security Intelligence (ONSI)
Drug Enforcement Administration
Washington, DC

www.dea.gov

Doug Poole, Chief of Intelligence
Founded in: 2006

19056 Office of Naval Intelligence (ONI)
U.S. Navy
4251 Suitland Rd.
Washington, DC 20395-5720

301-669-3001; www.oni.navy.mil
Social Media: Facebook

RAdm Robert D. Sharp, Commander

Military intelligence agency of the U.S. Navy.
Founded in: 1882

19057 Office of Terrorism and Financial Intellig ence (TFI)
Department of the Treasury
Washington, DC

www.treasury.gov

Leslie Ireland, Asst. Secy. for Intelligence

Treasury agency combats misuse of financial system by national security threats.
Founded in: 2004

19058 Office of the U.S. Trade Representative (U STR)
600 17th Street NW
Washington, DC 20508

ustr.gov

Michael Froman, United States Trade Representative

The USTR is a Cabinet-level position providing leadership on trade policy and negotiations.

19059 Organization of Women in International Tra de (OWIT)
OWIT International
c/o 1110 Vermont Ave. NW, Suite 715
Washington, DC 20005

E-Mail: info@owit.org; www.owit.org
Social Media: Facebook, Twitter, LinkedIn, YouTube

Andrea Ewart, President

Professional organization supporting the advancement of women in international trade.
2000 Members
Founded in: 1989

19060 The Agribusiness Council
PO Box 5565
Washington, DC 20016

202-296-4563
info@agribusinesscouncil.org;
www.agribusinesscouncil.org

Nick Hollis, President

Organization facilitating U.S. agribusiness participation in agricultural trade.

19061 The American Chamber of Commerce in New Ze aland
E-Mail: amcham@amcham.co.nz;
www.amcham.co.nz
Social Media: Twitter

Derek Syme, President

Promoting trade and investment between the United States and New Zealand for 50 years.

19062 The Association of Women in International Trade
c/o Affinity Strategies
100 M Street SE, Suite 600
Washington, DC 20003

202-684-3040
info@wiit.org
wiit.org
Social Media: Facebook, Twitter, LinkedIn

Evelyn Suarez, President

The Association promotes the professional development of women in international trade and business.

19063 The Center for Climate & Security
1025 Connecticut Ave. NW
Suite 1000
Washington, DC 20036

202-246-8612
climateandsecurity.org
Social Media: Facebook, Twitter, LinkedIn

Francesco Femia, Co-Founder & President
Caitlin Werrell, Co-Founder & President

Resource hub in the climate and security field.

19064 The International Trade Association of Gre ater Chicago (ITA/GC)
4610 N Kenton Ave.
Chicago, IL 60630

www.itagc.org
Social Media: Facebook, Twitter, LinkedIn

Arthur C. O'Meara, President

Association of manufacturers and service providers promotes international business.
500 Members
Founded in: 1985

19065 Twenty-Fifth Air Force (25 AF)
U.S. Air Force
Joint Base San Antonio
Lackland, TX

www.25af.af.mil
Social Media: Facebook, Twitter

MG Bradford Shwedo, Commander

Formerly Air Force Intelligence, Surveillance and Reconnaissance Agency.
Founded in: 1948

19066 US Army Intelligence and Security Command (INSCOM)
U.S. Army
Ft. Belvoir, VA

www.army.mil/inscom
Social Media: Facebook, Twitter

MG Christopher Ballard, Commander

Intelligence, security and information operations for U.S. Army and part of Central Security Service (CSS) within NSA.
Founded in: 1977

19067 United States Council for International Bu siness
1212 Avenue of the Americas
New York, NY 10036

212-354-4480; *Fax:* 212-575-0327;
www.uscib.org
Social Media: Facebook, Twitter, LinkedIn, YouTube

Peter M. Robinson, President & CEO

The Council promotes American business views on international policy issues, works to harmonize international trade and commercial practices and helps shape the international regulatory environment.
300 Members
Founded in: 1945

19068 Washington International Trade Association
1300 Pennsylvania Ave. NW
Suite G-329
Washington, DC 20004

202-312-1600; *Fax:* 202-312-1601
wita@wita.org
wita.org
Social Media: Facebook, Twitter, LinkedIn, YouTube

Ken Levinson, Executive Director

Non-partisan forum for discussion of international trade and economic issues.
Founded in: 1982

19069 World Trade Organization (WTO)
Geneva, Switzerland

www.wto.org

Roberto Azevedo, Director-General

Forum for governments to negotiate trade agreements and settle trade disputes.
164 Members
Founded in: 1995

Newsletters

19070 BNA's Eastern Europe Reporter
Bureau of National Affairs
1801 S Bell St
Arlington, VA 22202-4501

703-341-3000
800-372-1033; *Fax:* 800-253-0332
customercare@bna.com; www.bnabooks.com

Paul N Wojcik, CEO
William A. Beltz

This is just one of many biweekly notification services covering legislative, regulatory and legal developments affecting business, trade and investment in Eastern Europe and the former Soviet Union.
Cost: $1750.00
Frequency: Bi-annually

19071 EuroWatch
WorldTrade Executive
PO Box 761
Concord, MA 01742

978-287-0301; *Fax:* 978-287-0302
info@wtexec.com; www.wtexec.com

Alison French, Production Manager

Analyzes the most recent EU judicial and legislative developments. Covers EU trade issues, labor issues, single market and currency issues, EU and individual country business law, trademark issues.
Cost: $797.00

19072 International Association of Emergency Managers
201 Park Washington Court
Falls Church, VA 22046-4513

703-538-1795; *Fax:* 703-241-5603
info@iaem.com; www.iaem.com

Elizabeth B Armstrong, Executive Director
Sharon L Kelly, Member Director
Elizabeth B Armstrong, CEO
Karen Thompson, Editor
Dawn Shiley, Communication Manager

Representatives of city and county government departments responsible for emergency management and disaster preparedness.
Cost: $160.00
20 Pages
Frequency: Monthly
Circulation: 2700
Founded in: 1952
Printed in 2 colors on matte stock

19073 NASAA Insight
NA Securities Administrators Association
750 First Street NE
Suite 1140
Washington, DC 20002-8034

202-737-0900; *Fax:* 202-783-3571;
www.nasaa.org
Social Media: Facebook

Jack Herstein, President
Preston DuFauchard, President-Elect
Rick Hancox, Secretary
Fred J. Joseph, Treasurer

Designed to keep readers informed of recent NASAA activities.
Frequency: Quarterly
Founded in: 1919

19074 Worldwide Government Report
Worldwide Government Directories
7979 Old Georgetown Road
Suite 900
Bethesda, MD 20814-2429

301-258-2677
800-332-3535; *Fax:* 301-718-8494

Jonathan Hixon, Publisher

Each issue provides detailed reports of elections, government and military turnover. Events covered include ousted heads of state, reshuffled governments, changes in ruling majorities, analyses of recent elections, outlooks for upcoming elections, and senior military appointments.
Cost: $247.00
Frequency: Monthly

Magazines & Journals

19075 Armed Forces Journal
6883 Commercial Dr
Springfield, VA 22159

800-368-5718
armylet@atpco.com; www.defensenews.com

Mark Winans, VP
Elaine Howard, President/CEO
Alex Neill, Managing Editor
Jim Tice, Senior Writer
David Smith, Marketing

The leading joint service monthly magazine for officers and leaders in the US military community. AFJ has been providing essential review and analysis on key defense issues for more than 140 years. Offers in-depth coverage of military technology, procurement, logistics, strategy, doctrine and tactics. Also covers special operations, US Coast Guard and US National Guard developments.
Cost: $55.00
Frequency: Monthly
Circulation: 1MM

19076 C41SR Journal
Defense News
6883 Commercial Dr
Springfield, VA 22159
800-368-5718
armylet@atpco.com; www.defensenews.com

Mark Winans, VP
Elaine Howard, President/CEO
Alex Neill, Managing Editor
Jim Tice, Senior Writer
David Smith, Marketing

Dedicated to the rapidly advancing, high-tech realm of military intelligence, surveillance and reconnaissance. It was the first major periodical to specifically serve this key area of military growth and development, and has a strong following in the world's network-centric warfare community.
Cost: $55.00
Frequency: Monthly
Circulation: 1MM

19077 Defense News
6883 Commercial Dr
Springfield, VA 22151-4202

703-750-9000
800-424-9335; *Fax:* 703-658-8412
armylet@atpco.com; www.defensenews.com

Mark Winans, VP
Elaine Howard, President/CEO
Alex Neill, Managing Editor
Jim Tice, Senior Writer
David Smith, Marketing

Provides the global defense community with the latest news and analysis on defense programs, policy, business and technology. With bureaus and reporters around the world, Defense News sets the standard for accuracy, credibility and timeliness in defense reporting. Circulates to top leaders and decisionmakers in North America and in Europe, Asia and the Middle East.
Cost: $55.00
Frequency: Weekly
Circulation: 1MM

19078 Economic Development Journal
International Economic Development Council

734 15th Street NW
Suite 900
Washington, DC 20005

202-223-7800; *Fax:* 202-223-4745;
www.iedc.org

Jeff Finkle, President & CEO
Dennis G. Coleman, Chair
Jay C. Moon, Vice Chair
Paul Krutko, Secretary/ Treasurer

Premier publication of IEDC's diverse and dynamic discipline, featuring in-depth accounts of important programs, projects, and trends from the US and around the world.
1.8M Members
Frequency: Quarterly
Founded in: 1967

19079 Foreign Service Journal
American Foreign Service Association
2101 E St NW
Washington, DC 20037-2990

202-338-4045
800-704-2572; *Fax:* 202-338-6820
member@afsa.org; www.afsa.org

Susan R. Johnson, President
Andrew Winter, Treasurer

Each issue covers foreign affairs from an insider's perspective, providing thoughtful articles on international issues, the practice of diplomacy and the US Foreign Service.
Cost: $40.00
68 Pages
Frequency: Monthly
Circulation: 12500
ISSN: 0146-3543
Founded in: 1924
Printed in on glossy stock

19080 International Debates
Congressional Digest Corporation
4416 E West Hwy
Suite 400
Bethesda, MD 20814-4568

301-634-3113
800-637-9915; *Fax:* 301-634-3189
info@congressionaldigest.com;
www.pro-and-con.org/

Griff Thomas, President
Page Robinson, Publisher

Independent journal featuring controversies before the United Nations and other international forums. Each issue covers an important and timely international issue and includes in-depth background information, key documents, and diverse global perspectives.
Frequency: 9x Yearly
Founded in: 1921

19081 Journal of Food Protection
International Association for Food Protection
6200 Aurora Ave
Suite 200W
Urbandale, IA 50322-2864

515-276-3344
800-369-6337; *Fax:* 515-276-8655
info@foodprotection.org;
www.foodprotection.org
Social Media: Facebook, Twitter, LinkedIn

Lisa Hovey, Managing Editor
Didi Loynachan, Administrative Editor

Internationally recognized as the leading publication in the field of food microbiology, each issue contains scientific research and authoritative review articles reporting on a variety of topics in food science pertaining to food safety and quality.
Cost: $335.00
Frequency: Monthly
Circulation: 11000+
ISBN: 0-362028-X -
Founded in: 1911
Mailing list available for rent: 3000+ names at $150 per M
Printed in 4 colors on glossy stock

19082 Navy News and Undersea Technology
Pasha Publications
1616 N Fort Myer Drive
Suite 1000
Arlington, VA 22209-3107

703-528-1244
800-424-2908; *Fax:* 703-528-1253

Harry Baisden, Group Publisher
Thomas Jandl, Editor
Tod Sedgwick, Publisher

This report on the Navy, as well as the Marine Corps and naval developments overseas. Frequently cited by experts in the field as the source for breaking developments in submarine and anti-submarine warfare technology, this newsletter sets the standard for Navy reporting.
Cost: $545.00
Frequency: Weekly

19083 Parameters
US Army War College
122 Forbes Ave
Suite C34
Carlisle, PA 17013-5220

717-245-3131; *Fax:* 717-245-3323;
www.strategicinstitute.army.mil/pubs/parameters

Robert J Ivany, Manager

Refereed journal of ideas and issues. Provides a forum for mature thought on the art and science of land warfare, joint and combined matters, national and international security affairs, military strategy, military leadership and management, military history, ethics, and other topics of significant and current interest to the US Army and the Department of Defense.
Cost: $26.00
Frequency: Quarterly
Circulation: 1300

19084 Training & Simulation Journal
6883 Commercial Dr
Springfield, VA 22159

800-368-5718
armylet@atpco.com; www.defensenews.com

Mark Winans, VP
Elaine Howard, President/CEO
Alex Neill, Managing Editor
Jim Tice, Senior Writer
David Smith, Marketing

About trends in the global military training and simulation market, and a forum for market leaders to obtain and exchange information on emerging issues, new technologies, and new products.
Cost: $55.00
Frequency: Bi-Monthly
Circulation: 1MM

Trade Shows

19085 AAEI Annual Conference
American Association of Exporters and Importers
1717 K Street NW
Suite 1120
Washington, DC 20006

202-857-8009; *Fax:* 202-857-7843;
www.aaei.org/news/events
Social Media: Facebook, Twitter, LinkedIn

Marianne Rowden, President & CEO

Association's annual education event provides the latest industry information and networking opportunities.

19086 Climate and National Security Forum
The Center for Climate and Security
Washington, DC

climateandsecurity.org/category/events
Social Media: Facebook, Twitter, LinkedIn

Francesco Femia, Co-Founder & President
Caitlin Werrell, Co-Founder & President

Discussions regarding risks and opportunities related to climate change and security.

19087 Department of Commerce Trade Missions
Department of Commerce
1401 Constitution Ave. NW
Washington, DC 20230

www.export.gov/Trade-Missions
Social Media: Facebook, Twitter, LinkedIn, YouTube

Trade missions organized by the Department of Commerce put U.S. firms in direct contact with potential clients, foreign industry executives and government officials.

19088 Discover Global Markets
Department of Commerce
1401 Constitution Ave. NW
Washington, DC 20230

2016.export.gov/discoverglobalmarkets
Social Media: Facebook, Twitter, LinkedIn, YouTube

Conference series put on by the U.S. Commercial Service of the Department of Commerce, designed to help U.S. businesses grow exports.

19089 IAEM Annual Conference
International Association of Emergency Managers
201 Park Washington Court
Falls Church, VA 22046

703-538-1795; *Fax:* 703-241-5603
info@iaem.com; www.iaem.com

Provides a forum for current trends and topics, information about the latest tools and technology in emergency management and homeland security, and advances IAEM-USA committee work. Sessions encourage stakeholders at all levels of government, the private sector, public health and related professions to exchange ideas on collaborating to protect lives and property from disaster.
1000 Attendees
Frequency: Annual/November

19090 Marine West Military Expo
Nielsen Business Media, USA
1145 Sanctuary Parkway
Suite 355
Alpharetta

703-488-2762

Ron Bates, Event Organizer

This event is fully dedicated to the defense industry. The event will showcase the latest products and equipments used for marine and related industry at one place. The visitors will be the military professionals, equipment buyers, decision makers and the other people related to the field of defense.
Frequency: Annual/February

19091 NEMA Mid-Year Conference
National Emergency Management Association
PO Box 11910
Lexington, KY 40578

859-244-8000; *Fax:* 859-244-8239
nemaadmin@csg.org; www.nemaweb.org

Jim Mullen, President
John Madden, Vice President
Charley English, Treasurer

Tom Sands, Secretary
Brenda Bergeron, Legal Counsel

Gives the opportunity to discuss important issues in the field of emergency management and homeland security. Also hear from respected leaders working on many of these issues. Opportunities to meet and network with peers are invaluable in these times of rapid change and economic challenges.
Frequency: Annual/March

19092 **UDT: Undersea Defense Technology Conference and Exhibition**
Reed Exhibition Companies
255 Washington Street
Newton, MA 02458-1637

617-584-4900; *Fax:* 617-630-2222
Social Media: Facebook, Twitter, LinkedIn

Elizabeth Hitchcock, International Sales

The world's leading exhibition and conference for undersea defence and security. Gain access to the latest technologies, connect with existing suppliers and create new business relationships. Gives the invaluable opportunity to network across the global maritime community. Suppliers exhibiting; UUVs and components, acoustic technologies, maritime surveillance solutions, harbour and port security products, mine detection systems, and submarine hardware and electronics.
Frequency: Annual/May

19093 **UNA-USA Annual Meeting**
United Nations Association of the USA
1800 Massachusetts Avenue NW
Suite 400
Washington, DC 20036

202-887-9040; *Fax:* 202-887-9021
inquiries@un.org; www.unausa.org

Patrick Madden, Executive Director

Brings together UNA-USA's constituencies for a variety of skills trainings, issue briefings, networking opportunities and capacity-building.
400 Attendees
Frequency: Annual/November

Directories & Databases

19094 **Daily Defense News Capsules**
United Communications Group
11300 Rockville Pike
Suite 1100
Rockville, MD 20852-3030

301-816-8950; *Fax:* 301-816-8945

Greg Beaudoin, Editor

This database offers the complete text of Periscope - Daily Defense News Capsules, that provide abstracts of international press coverage of military and defense news.

19095 **Defense Industry Charts**
Carroll Publishing
4701 Sangamore Rd
Suite 155S
Bethesda, MD 20816-2532

301-263-9800
800-336-4240; *Fax:* 301-263-9805
info@carrollpub.com; www.carrollpub.com

Tom Carroll, President

19000 key personnel in top US defense contractors, including major aerospace, electronic, military hardware, information technology and systems integration companies. Serves as a road map to the critical players in this important industry.
Cost: $2050.00
Frequency: Quarterly

19096 **Defense Programs**
Carroll Publishing
4701 Sangamore Rd
Suite 155S
Bethesda, MD 20816-2532

301-263-9800
800-336-4240; *Fax:* 301-263-9805
info@carrollpub.com; www.carrollpub.com

Tom Carroll, President

Detailed description of more than 2,000 military research, development, test and evaluation programs and projects.
Cost: $1060.00
Frequency: Quarterly

19097 **Defense and Foreign Affairs Handbook**
International Strategic Studies Association
PO Box 19289
Alexandria, VA 22320-0289

703-548-1070; *Fax:* 703-684-7476
dfa@strategicstudies.org;
www.strategicstudies.org

Gregory Copley, Editor

Important global reference encyclopedia for most world leaders .Comprehensive chapters on 238 countries and territories worldwide, with each chapter giving full cabinet and leadership listings, history, recent developments, demographics, economic statistics, political and constitutional data, news media,defense overview, defense structure.
Cost: $297.00
2500 Pages
Frequency: Monthly
Circulation: 4,000
ISBN: 1-892998-06-8
Founded in: 1976

19098 **Foreign Consular Offices in the United States**
Bureau of Public Affairs/US Department of State
2201 C Street NW
Washington, DC 20520-0001

202-647-6141

A complete and official listing of the foreign consular offices in the US, and recognized consular officers. Compiled by the US Department of State, with the full cooperation of the foreign missions in Washington, it is offered as a convenience to organizations and persons who must deal with consular government agencies, state tax officials, international trade organizations, chamber of commerce, and judicial authorities.
Cost: $4.00
290 Pages
Frequency: Annual

19099 **IAEM Directory**
International Association of Emergency Managers
111 Park Pl
Falls Church, VA 22046-4513

703-538-1795; *Fax:* 703-241-5603
info@iaem.com; www.iaem.com

Shan Coffin, Editor
Sharon L Kelly, Circulation Director
Cost: $100.00
Circulation: 8,000

19100 **Kaleidoscope: Current World Data**
ABC-CLIO
PO Box 1911
Santa Barbara, CA 93102-1911

805-968-1911; *Fax:* 805-685-9685
CustomerService@abc-clio.com;
www.abc-clio.com

Ron Boehm, CEO

This comprehensive database takes a look at all aspects of the American culture. Listings of information include statistics and factual information on the population, culture, economy, military forces, government, and political systems of countries around the world, the US States and Canadian provinces.
Frequency: Full-text

19101 **Military Biographical Profiles**
CTB/McGraw Hill
20 Ryan Ranch Rd
Monterey, CA 93940-5770

831-393-0700
800-538-9547; *Fax:* 831-393-6528
CTBTechnicalSupport@CTB.com;
www.ctb.com

Ellen Haley, President
Sandor Nagy, Chief Operating Officer

Offers valuable information on US military officers and Department of Defense officials.
Frequency: Full-text

19102 **Profiles of Worldwide Government Leaders**
Worldwide Government Directories
7979 Old Georgetown Road
Suite 900
Bethesda, MD 20814-2429

301-258-2677
800-332-3535; *Fax:* 301-718-8494

Jonathan Hixon, Publisher

Spanning 195 countries, includes comprehensive biographical snapshots of as many as 30 or more ministers from each country. The material is obtained from primary and secondary sources including embassies, government ministries, offices of the United States government and proprietary global network of correspondents.
Cost: $297.00
850+ Pages
Frequency: Annual

19103 **The World Factbook**
Central Intelligence Agency
Office of Public Affairs
Washington, DC 20505

703-482-0623; *Fax:* 571-204-3800
cia.gov
Social Media: Facebook, Twitter, flickr, YouTube

Annual publication of the CIA contains information on the history, people, government, etc., of 267 world entities.
Cost: $89.00
Frequency: Annual
Founded in: 1981

19104 **Worldwide Directory of Defense Attorneys**
Worldwide Government Directories
7979 Old Georgetown Road
Suite 900
Bethesda, MD 20814-2429

301-258-2677
800-332-3535; *Fax:* 301-718-8494

Jonathan Hixon, Publisher

One-of-a-kind resource covering military and civilian defense and national security agencies from the ministry of defense down to service branches in 195 countries worldwide.
Cost: $647.00
1,100 Pages
Frequency: Annual

19105 **Worldwide Government Directory**
Worldwide Government Directories

7979 Old Georgetown Road
Suite 900
Bethesda, MD 20814-2429

301-258-2677
800-332-3535; *Fax:* 301-718-8494

Jonathan Hixon, Publisher

Offers valuable information on every senior government official in the executive, legislative, and judicial branches as well as the diplomatic and defense communities of 195 countries worldwide. Plus senior officials in over 100 international organizations. Each entry includes name, address, title, telephone, telex, facsimile number, and more. Also included are current state agencies and corporations, official forms of address, international dialing codes and central bank information.
Cost: $347.00
1,400 Pages
Frequency: Annual

19106 **Worldwide Government Directory with International Organizations**
1414 22nd Street NW
Washington, DC 20037-1003

202-887-8500
800-432-2250; *Fax:* 800-380-3810;
www.cqpress.com

Linda Dziobek, Editor

Coverage includes over 1800 pages of executive, legislative and political branches; heads of state, ministers, deputies, secretaries and spokespersons as well as state agencies, diplomats and senior level defense officials. Also covers the leadership of more than 100 international organizations.
Cost: $450.00
1700 Pages
Frequency: Annually

Industry Web Sites

19107 **Office of the Director of National Intelli gence**
Office of the Director of National Intelligence
Washington, DC 20511

703-733-8600; www.dni.gov

James R. Clapper, Director of National Intelligence
Stephanie O'Sullivan, Principal Deputy DNI

ODNI is responsible for integrating the intelligence collection and analysis of the 16 member agencies of the Intelligence Community.

19108 **export.gov**
International Trade Administration
1401 Constitution Ave. NW
Washington, DC 20230

www.export.gov
Social Media: Facebook, Twitter, LinkedIn, YouTube

Market intelligence, advice and tools for U.S. companies looking to succeed in global markets.

19109 **www.cued.org**
National Council for Urban Economic Development

National membership organization serving public and private participants in economic development across the United States and in international settings. CUED provides information to its members who build local economies through the tools used for job creation, attraction and retention. Members include public economic development directors, chamber of commerce staff, utility executives and academicians, plus the many other professionals who help design and implement development programs.

19110 **www.foodprotection.org**
International Association for Food Protection

The International Association for Food Protection founded in 1911, is a nonprofit educational association with a mission to provide food safety professionals worldwide with a forum to exchange information on protecting the food supply. The Association is comprised of a cross-section of over 3,000 members from 50 nations. Affiliate chapters are located in the United States, Canada and South Korea.

19111 **www.intelligencecareers.gov**
www.intelligencecareers.gov

Tool for exploring careers in the 17 federal intelligence agencies.

19112 **www.iogcc.state.ok.us**
Interstate Oil and Gas Compact Commission

Represents the governors of 37 states that produce virtually all the domestic oil and natural gas in the United States.

19113 **www.napawash.org**
National Academy of Public Administration

An independent, non-profit organization chartered by Congress to improve governance at all levels- local, regional, state, national and international.

19114 **www.nasaa.org**
North American Securities Administrators Assoc

NASAA is the international organization representing 66 securities administrators from all 50 states, the District of Columbia, Canada, Mexico and Puerto Rico, and is responsible for investor protection and education. NASAA recommends national policies in the securities industry and provides model legislation for state securities agencies to adopt affecting the regulation of broker/dealers and investment advisers. Consumers can contact NASAA to get phone numbers of state securities regulators.

19115 **www.nbpc.net**
National Border Patrol Council

A labor union representing employees of the US border patrol.

19116 **www.nemaweb.org**
National Emergency Management Association

Members include federal agencies, local emergency management representatives and interested individuals, associations and corporations.

19117 **www.sso.org**
Intl Assoc of Official Human Rights Agencies

Members are state and local government human rights and human relations agencies.

19118 **www.sso.org/iafwa**
Intl Assoc of Fish and Wildlife Agencies

Established as the National Association of Game Commissioners.

19119 **www.water.dnr.state.sc.us/water/icwp**
Interstate Council on Water Policy

Members are state and regional agencies concerned with conservation and environmental issues.

International Trade Resources

19120 **Albania to the United Nations**
320 E 79th Street
New York, NY 10075

212-249-2059; *Fax:* 212-535-2917
albania.un@albania-un.org;
www.albania-un.org
Social Media: Facebook, Twitter, LinkedIn

Ferit Hoxha, Ambassador
Petrik Jorgi, Minister Counselor
Olisa Cifligu, Second Secretary
Ermal Frasheri, Advisor, Legal Issues

19121 **United States Census Bureau**
Department of Commerce
4600 Silver Hill Rd.
Washington, DC 20233

800-923-8282; www.census.gov/foreign-trade
Social Media: Facebook, Twitter, YouTube

Peter M. Robinson, President & CEO

Foreign Trade is the official source for U.S. import and export statistics and information on export regulations.
300 Members
Founded in: 1945

19122 **stopfakes.gov**
International Trade Administration
Office of Intellectual Property Rights
14th St. and Constitution Ave. NW
Washington, DC 20230

866-999-4258; www.stopfakes.gov

U.S. government tools and resources on intellectual property rights help businesses secure IP rights at home and abroad.

Associations

19123 **ARMA International**
11880 College Blvd
Suite 450
Overland Park, KS 66210

913-341-3808
800-422-2762; *Fax:* 913-341-3742
hq@arma.org; www.arma.org
Social Media: Facebook, Twitter, LinkedIn

Marilyn Bier, Executive Director
Peter Kurilecz, IGP, CRM, CA, President
Tera Ladner, J.D., IGP, CRM, President-Elect
Brenda Prowse, CRM, Treasurer
Fred Pulzello, IGP, CRM, Immediate Past President

A not-for-profit professional association and the authority on managing records and information.
11000 Members
Founded in: 1955

19124 **Business and Institutional Furniture Manufacturers Association**
678 Front Avenue NW
Suite 150
Grand Rapids, MI 49504-5368

616-285-3963; *Fax:* 616-285-3765
email@bifma.org; www.bifma.org
Social Media: Facebook, Twitter, LinkedIn

Sylvain Garneau, President
Thomas Reardon, Executive Director
Don Van Winkle, Vice President
Franco Bianchi, Treasurer

BIFMA is a not-for-profit trade association of furniture manufacturers and suppliers, addressing issues of common concern.
245+ Members
Founded in: 1973

19125 **Graphic Arts Information Network**
200 Deer Run Road
Sewickley, PA 15143

412-741-6860
800-910-4283; *Fax:* 412-741-2311
printing@printing.org; www.printing.org/
Social Media: Facebook, Twitter, LinkedIn, RSS

Michael F Makin, President

Members are companies printing labels for food or consumer products.
40 Members

19126 **Independent Office Products & Furniture Dealers Association**
3601 E. Joppa Road
Baltimore, MD 21234

410-931-8100; *Fax:* 410-931-8111
info@iopfda.org; www.nopanet.org/
Social Media: Twitter, LinkedIn

Mike Tucker, President
Paul Miller, Director Government Affairs
Paula Kreuzburg, M.D
Alicia Ellis, Director, Marketing

Association for independent office product and office furniture dealers. IOPFDA is comprised of the National Office Products Alliance (NOPA) and the Office Furniture Dealers Alliance (OFDA).
1500 Members
Founded in: 1904

19127 **National Office Products Alliance**
3601 E Joppa Rd.
Baltimore, MD 21234

410-931-8100; *Fax:* 410-931-8111;
www.nopanet.org

Paula Kreuzburg, Executive Director

Information and resources to promote the success of member dealers.

19128 **Office Furniture Dealers Alliance**
3601 E Joppa Rd.
Baltimore, MD 21234

410-931-8100; *Fax:* 410-931-8111
info@ofda.org; www.ofdanet.org
Social Media: LinkedIn

Rod Manson, Chair
Paula Kreuzburg, Executive Director

The Alliance's mission is to provide independent dealers with information and tools to help them succeed in a changing industry.
1200 Members

19129 **Office Furniture Distribution Association**
P.O. Box 2548
Secaucus, NJ 07096

517-467-9355; *Fax:* 517-467-9056
theofda@yahoo.com; www.theofda.org

75 Members
Founded in: 1923

19130 **Office Products Representatives**
3131 Elbee Road
Dayton, OH 45439

937-297-2250
800-447-1684; *Fax:* 937-297-2254
info@oprareps.org; www.oprareps.org

Carol Hinton, Owner
100 Members
Founded in: 1974

19131 **Office Products Wholesalers Association**
5024 Campbell Boulevard
Baltimore, MD 21236

410-931-8100; *Fax:* 410-931-8111
info@BusinessSolutionsAssociation.com;
www.opwa.org

Cal Clemons, Executive Vice President
Paula Kreuzberg, Associate Director

Members are chief executives of office product wholesalers and manufacturers.
165 Members
Founded in: 1995

19132 **Society for Service Professionals in Printing**
433 E Monroe Ave
Alexandria, VA 22301-1645

703-684-0044
866-600-8820; *Fax:* 703-548-9137;
www.sspp.org

Peter Colaianni, Executive Director
Marj Green, Director

Individual membership society dedicated to the needs of customer service professionals in the printing industry.
8 Members
Founded in: 1993

Newsletters

19133 **BTA Hotline Online**
Business Technology Association
12411 Wornall Rd
Suite 200
Kansas City, MO 64145-1212

816-941-3100
800-325-7219; *Fax:* 816-941-2829
info@bta.org; www.bta.org

Brent Hoskins, Executive Director
Rob Richardson, President

Current copier/printer and network systems industry news.
Founded in: 1926

19134 **Digital Image Review**
Buyers Laboratory
20 Railroad Avenue
Hackensack, NJ 07601-3309

201-896-6439; *Fax:* 201-488-0461
info@buyerslab.com; www.buyerslab.com

Daria Hoffman, Managing Editor
Michael Danziger, CEO

Devoted to digital topics, all types of digital office products, industry news and trends, trade show, pricing changes and much more.
Cost: $305.00
16 Pages
Frequency: Monthly
Founded in: 1961

19135 **Executary**
National Association of Executive Secretaries
900 S Washington Street
Suite G13
Falls Church, VA 22046-4009

703-237-8616; *Fax:* 703-533-1153
headquarters@theaeap.com; www.theaeap.com
Social Media: LinkedIn

Ruth Ludeman, Director

Packed with practical advice on various issues of interest to administrative professionals. Seeks to support AEAP's mission to assist members in achieving their career goals by keeping you informed of advances and changes in the administrative profession.
Frequency: 10x/Year
Mailing list available for rent: 5000 names

19136 **Form & Document Industry Newsletter**
1147 Fleetwood Avenue
Madison, WI 53716-1417

888-367-3078
bfma@bfma.org; www.bfma.org

Robin Miller, President
Olufunke Somefun, VP Programs
Ray Killam, VP Operations/ Acting CFO

Industry newsletter containing educational articles and rules on the latest processes, techniques and products in the form and document industry. Library rate is $35.00 per year.
Cost: $50.00
38574 Pages
Circulation: 700
Founded in: 1958
Mailing list available for rent: 1000 names at $400 per M

19137 **Jot and Jolts**
Economics Press
12 Daniel Road
Fairfield, NJ 07004-2565

973-227-1224
800-526-2554; *Fax:* 973-227-8360;
www.epinc.com

Monthly planner for supervisors to the office products industry.
Cost: $16.20
26 Pages
Frequency: Monthly
Printed in on glossy stock

19138 **MFP Report**
Bissett Communications

Apt 44
20919 Bloomfield Ave
Lakewood, CA 90715-1840

562-809-8917; *Fax:* 562-809-1627
http://www.mfpreport.com

Brian R Bissett, Publisher

A newsletter providing information on manufacturers, suppliers, sellers, and managers of multifunction peripherals and connected office equipment of the latest MFP business, market and technology issues and their impact.
Frequency: Monthly

19139 Scanner
Private Label Manufacturers Association (PLMA)
630 Third Avenue
New York, NY 10017-6506

212-972-3131; *Fax:* 212-983-1382
info@plma.com; www.plma.com

Brian Sharoff, President
Myra Rosen, VP
Tom Prendergast, Director, Research Services

News and information for the private label industry.
3200+ Members
6 Pages
Frequency: Quarterly
Circulation: 12000
Founded in: 1979

Magazines & Journals

19140 Better Buys for Business
Progressive Business Publications
PO Box 3019
Malvern, PA 19355-0719

610-695-0201
800-247-2185; *Fax:* 610-647-8098
webmaster@pbp.com; www.pbp.com

Ed Satell, CEO
Steve Hannaford, Editor

Publishes 10 non-advertising buyer's guides for office equipment (copiers, printers, fax machines and scanners), with objective, unbiased information and evaluations. Each issue includes in-depth write-ups on all manufacturers and their models, easy to read specifications and price charts to compare models and Editor's Choice selections - awarded to the best machines in each product category
Cost: $149.00
Circulation: 4,000
ISSN: 1084-2055
Founded in: 1980
Printed in 4 colors on matte stock

19141 Business Documents
North American Publishing Company
1500 Spring Garden St
Suite 1200
Philadelphia, PA 19130-4094

215-238-5300
800-627-2689; *Fax:* 215-238-5342;
www.napco.com

Ned S Borowsky, CEO
Brian C Ludwick, Publisher

For professional buyers of forms, labels and electronic systems. Emphasizes internal and external design, production and management of business documents either as traditionally printed forms or electronically generated documents.
Cost: $24.00
42 Pages
Frequency: Monthly
Founded in: 1958
Mailing list available for rent
Printed in 2 colors on matte stock

19142 Business Forms, Labels & Systems
North American Publishing Company
1500 Spring Garden St
Suite 1200
Philadelphia, PA 19130-4094

215-238-5300
800-627-2689; *Fax:* 215-238-5342
webmaster@napco.com; www.napco.com/

Ned S Borowsky, CEO
Judith Cavaliere, Publisher
Maggie DeWitt, Senior Editor
Cynthia Graham, Associate Editor
Jennifer Hans, Associate Editor

For independent manufacturers and distributors in the forms and systems industry. Emphasizes product applications, marketing and sales ideas and new technology.
Cost: $49.00
Frequency: Monthly
Circulation: 12000
Founded in: 1958
Mailing list available for rent
Printed in 4 colors on glossy stock

19143 Business Solutions
Corry Publishing
5539 Peach Street
Erie, PA 16506

814-380-0025
800-290-5460; *Fax:* 814-864-2037
editor@corrypub.com; www.corrypub.com

John Clifton, Group Publisher
Melinda Reed-Fadden, Circulation Manager
Dan Schell, Editor
Carrie Brocious, Marketing Director
Jim Roddy, President

Informative magazine including analysis of technological and marketing developments.
Frequency: Monthly
Circulation: 43000
Founded in: 1980

19144 Digital Information Network
Buyers Laboratory
20 Railroad Avenue
Hackensack, NJ 07601-3309

201-587-0828; *Fax:* 201-488-0461
info@buyerslab.com; www.buyerslab.com

Daria Hoffman, Managing Editor

A comprehensive test report service which provides test reports on all the office products BLI evaluates. Subscribers will also get a sixteen page monthly newsletter called Digital Imaging Review, and will recieve a copy of BLI's Multifunctional Specification Guide, Facsimile-Based Products, Copier-Based Products and the Printer Specification Guide, as well as updated specifications throughout the term of their subscription.
Cost: $755.00

19145 Hard Copy Supplies Journal
Lyra Research
PO Box 9143
Newtonville, MA 02640-9143

617-454-2600; *Fax:* 617-454-2601;
www.lyra.com

Charles LeCompte, Publisher
Frank Stefansson, CEO/President
Jim Forrest, Managing Editor
Jennifer Sprague, Vice President of Sales
Andre Rebelo, Marketing Manager

In-depth coverage of current innovations in marketing materials and media, including ink jet cartridges, toner, paper and film, and monitors the fast-moving corporate developments, such as lawsuits, mergers, distribution, tactics, and marketing campaigns.
Cost: $550.00
Frequency: Monthly
Circulation: 2,000
Founded in: 1991

19146 Information Management Magazine
ARMA International
11880 College Blvd
Suite 450
Overland Park, KS 66210

913-341-3808
800-422-2762; *Fax:* 913-341-3742
hq@arma.org; www.arma.org

Marilyn Bier, Executive Director
Jody Becker, Associate Editor
Brenda Prowse, Treasurer

The leading source of information on topics and issues central to the management of records and information worldwide. Each issue features insightful articles written by experts in the management of records and information.
Cost: $115.00
Frequency: Bi-monthly
Circulation: 11000
ISSN: 1535-2897
Mailing list available for rent: 9000 names
Printed in 4 colors on glossy stock

19147 Mail: Journal of Communication Distribution
Excelsior Publications
One Millstone Road
Gold Key Box 2425
Milford, PA 18337

570-861-1969; *Fax:* 570-686-3495

Francis P Ruggiero, Publsher
Circulation: 43000

19148 Office Dealer
Quality Publishing
252 N Main Street
Suite 200
Mount Airy, NC 27030-3810

336-783-0000; *Fax:* 336-783-0045
bcomer@os-od.com; www.os-od.com/

Richard Kunkel, Publisher
Simon DeGroot, Editorial Director
Bessie Comer, Sales/Advertising Coor
Scott Cullen, Managing Editor
Debbie Hooker, Director of Publishing Services

Information including the latest industry news pertaining to resellers, plus office dealer conventions and other newsworthy events.
Circulation: 17020

19149 Office Solutions
Quality Publishing
252 N Main Street #200
PO Box 1028
Mount Airy, NC 27030-3810

336-783-0000; *Fax:* 336-783-0045
osod@os-od.com; www.os-od.com

Richard Kunkel, Publisher
Simon Degroot, Editorial Director
Debbey Hooker, Circulation Manager
Bill Middleton, Marketing Manager
Scott Cullen, Managing Editor

Information on state of the art, survey and overview of articles and product offerings. Emphasis on personal computing, software, telecommunications, personnel and financial management.
Cost: $36.00
Circulation: 81250
Founded in: 2003

19150 Office Systems Research Journal
SW Missouri Council of Governments

901 S National Avenue
Springfield, MO 65804

417-836-5000; *Fax:* 417-836-4146;
www.smsu.edu

Diane May, Executive Director

A journal offering research and news of the office supplies and products industry.
Cost: $35.00
Circulation: 400

19151 Office Technology
Business Tchnology Association
12411 Wornall Rd
Suite 200
Kansas City, MO 64145-1212

816-941-3100
800-325-7219; *Fax:* 816-941-2829
info@bta.org; www.bta.org
Social Media: Facebook, Twitter, LinkedIn

Brent Hoskins, Executive Director
Rob Richardson, President
Cost: $100.00
Frequency: Monthly
Circulation: 3500
ISBN: 1-092916-9 -
Founded in: 1927
Mailing list available for rent: 1200 names

19152 Print Solutions Magazine
Document Management Industries Association
433 E Monroe Avenue
Alexandria, VA 22301-1693

703-836-6232; *Fax:* 703-549-4966;
www.printsolutionsmag.com

Peter L Colaianni CAE, Editor-in-Chief

Source for marketing, management and product information.
Cost: $49.00
276 Pages
Frequency: Monthly
ISSN: 0532-1700
Printed in 4 colors on glossy stock

19153 Recharger Magazine
Recharger Magazine
1050 E Flamingo Rd
Suite N237
Las Vegas, NV 89119-7427

702-438-5557
877-902-9759; *Fax:* 702-873-9671
info@rechargermag.com;
www.rechargermag.com

Phyllis Gurgevich, Publisher
Amy Turner, Managing Editor
Michael MacDonald, Graphics Director
Sara Feest, Sales Assistant
Monica Miceli, Associate Editor

Information including articles that cover business and marketing, technical updates, association and industry news, and company profiles. Related features focus on the importance of recycling, government legislation, and product comparisons.
Cost: $45.00
Frequency: Monthly
Circulation: 8000

Trade Shows

19154 ARMA International Conference & Expo
ARMA International
11880 College Blvd
Suite 450
Overland Park, KS 66215

913-341-3808
800-422-2762; *Fax:* 913-341-3742
hq@arma.org; www.arma.org/conference
Social Media: Facebook, Twitter, iConference

Carol Jorgenson, Meetings/Education Coordinator
Wanda Wilson, Senior Manager, Conferences
Elizabeth Zlitni, Exposition Manager

Conference, seminar, workshop, banquet, award ceremony and 175 exhibits of micrographics, optical disk, automated document storage and retrieval systems and more technology of interest to information professionals.
3500 Attendees
Frequency: Annual
Founded in: 1956

19155 American Business Women's Association Convention
9100 Ward Parkway
PO Box 8728
Kansas City, MO 64114

816-361-6621
800-228-0007; *Fax:* 816-361-4991
abwa@abwa.org; www.abwa.org

Wendy Mabrey, Corporate Sponsorship Coordinator
Carolyn Elman, Executive Director

One-hundred exhibits of equipment, supplies and services for women in business, seminar and banquet.
2000 Attendees
Frequency: November

19156 American Society for Training & Development Conference & Exposition
American Society for Training & Development
1640 King Street
PO Box 1443
Alexandria, VA 22313-2043

703-683-8100; *Fax:* 703-683-8103
customercare@astd.org; www.astd.org

Michael Neff, Executive Director
2000 Attendees

19157 Business Show
INPEX
217 9th Street
Pittsburgh, PA 15222-3506

412-881-1300
800-544-6739; *Fax:* 412-288-4546;
www.inventionshow.com/

Nevin Arora, Product Manager

Annual show of 150 exhibits of office furniture, supplies and machines; computers; media; specialty items; financial services; printing services; security systems; entertainment; cellular phones and pagers; sinage; travel agencies; audio-visual equipment and car rental agencies.
5000 Attendees

19158 Business Technology Association National Conference
Business Technology Association
12411 Wornall Road
Suite 200
Kansas City, MO 64145-1212

816-941-3100
800-325-7219; *Fax:* 816-941-4838
info@bta.org; www.bta.org
Social Media: Facebook, Twitter, LinkedIn

Brent Hoskins, Executive Director
Ron Richardson, President
Frequency: Annual
Founded in: 1926
Mailing list available for rent: 1200 names

19159 Document World/American Business Equipment and Computer Show
Key Productions
116 Murphy Road
Hartford, CT 06114-2121

860-247-8363

Eldred Codling, Show Manager

Features exhibits of computer software, hardware, supplies and services.
6M Attendees
Frequency: April

19160 National Stationery Show
George Little Management
10 Bank Street
White Plains, NY 10606-1954

914-486-6070
800-272-7469; *Fax:* 914-948-6180; www.

Lori Robinson, VP
Kelly Bristol, Assistant Show Manager
George Little II, President

A show for greeting cards and social stationery, writing instruments and home office products, party ware and giftwrap, scrapbooking and craft supplies, albums, frames and much more.
14000 Attendees
Frequency: May

Directories & Databases

19161 ARMA International's Buyers Guide
ARMA International
11880 College Blvd
Suite 450
Overland Park, KS 66215

913-341-3808
800-422-2762; *Fax:* 913-341-3742
hq@arma.org; www.arma.org/conference

75-100 companies listed. Free.

19162 Directory of Mail Order Catalogs
Grey House Publishing
4919 Route 22
PO Box 56
Amenia, NY 12501

518-789-8700
800-562-2139; *Fax:* 845-373-6390
books@greyhouse.com; www.greyhouse.com
Social Media: Facebook, Twitter

Leslie Mackenzie, Publisher
Richard Gottlieb, Editor

The premier source of information on the mail order catalog industry. Covers over 13,000 consumer and business catalog companies with 44 different product chapters including office supplies, stationery and more.
Cost: $395.00
1900 Pages
Frequency: Annual
ISBN: 1-592373-96-8
Founded in: 1981

19163 Directory of Mail Order Catalogs - Online Database
Grey House Publishing
4919 Route 22
PO Box 56
Amenia, NY 12501

518-789-8700
800-562-2139; *Fax:* 845-373-6390
gold@greyhouse.com
http://gold.greyhouse.com
Social Media: Facebook, Twitter

Leslie Mackenzie, Publisher
Richard Gottlieb, Editor

Reach over 10,000 consumer catalog companies in one easy-to-use source with The Directory of Mail Order Catalogs - Online Database. Filled with business-building detail, each company profile gives you the information you need to ac-

cess that organization quickly and easily. Listings provide key contacts, sales volume, employee size, printing information, circulation, list data, product descriptions and much more.
Frequency: Annual
Founded in: 1981

19164 Orion Blue Book: Copier
Orion Research Corporation
14555 N Scottsdale Rd
Suite 330
Scottsdale, AZ 85254-3487

480-951-1114
800-844-0759; *Fax:* 480-951-1117
support@orionbluebook.com;
www.orionbluebook.com/

Roger Rohrs, Owner

List of manufacturers of copiers and other office equipment.
Cost: $39.00
Frequency: Annual

Industry Web Sites

19165 http://gold.greyhouse.com
G.O.L.D Grey House OnLine Databases

Grey House Publishing's online database platform, GOLD, offers Quick Search, Keyword Search and Expert Search for most business sectors, including office supplies and services makrets. The GOLD platform makes finding the information you need quick and easy - whether you're a novice searcher or an experienced database user. All of Grey House's directory products are available for subscription on the GOLD platform.

19166 www.americanpayroll.org
American Payroll Association

Association of payroll and human resource professionals. Website furthers information exchange and meeting announcements.

19167 www.bfma.org
Business Forms Management Association

For form systems professionals interested in the effective capture distribution and management of information in electronic and paper forms.

19168 www.bifma.org
Business and Institutional Furniture Manufacturers
Association

The voice of the office furniture industry, BIFMA members are manufacturers and suppliers of goods and services to the industry.

19169 www.dmia.org
Document Management Industries Association

19170 www.greyhouse.com
Grey House Publishing

Authoritative reference directories for most business sectors including office products and services markets. Users can search the online databases with varied search criteria allowing for custom searches by product category, geographic area, sales volume, keyword, subject and more. Full Grey House catalog and online ordering also available.

19171 www.iopfda.org
Independent Office Products & Furniture Dealers
Association

Association for independent office product and office furniture dealers. IOPFDA is comprised of the National Office Products Alliance (NOPA) and the Office Furniture Dealers Alliance (OFDA).

19172 www.oprareps.org
Office Products Representatives Association

Provides programs and services that promote the role of the independant manufactures' representative in the various distribution channels within the entire office products industry.

19173 www.sspp.org
Society for Service Professionals in Printing

Individual membership society dedicated to the needs of customer service professionals in the printing industry.

19174 www.theofda.org
Office Furniture Distribution Association

Associations

19175 American Forest & Paper Association
1111 19th St NW
Suite 800
Washington, DC 20036-3652

202-463-2700
800-878-8878; *Fax:* 202-463-2785
info@afandpa.org; www.afandpa.org
Social Media: Facebook, Twitter, LinkedIn, YouTube

James B. Hannan, Chairman
Doyle R. Simons, 1st Vice Chairman
Alexander Toeldte, 2nd Vice Chairman
Donna A. Harman, President & CEO
Jan A. Poling, Vice President & Secretary

To provide significant value to member companies through outstanding performance in those areas that are key to members' success and where an association can be more effective than individual companies.
Founded in: 1993

19176 American Paper Machinery Association
201 Park Washington Ct
Falls Church, VA 22046-4527

703-538-1787; *Fax:* 703-241-5603
apmahq@aol.com; www.papermachinery.org

Clay D Tyeryar, Chief Administrative Executive
Judith O Buzzerd, Manager Meetings
Sharon Kelly, Coordinator Member Services

To promote the global common interests, image and business relations of the membership.
35 Members
Founded in: 1971

19177 Association of Independent Corrugated Converters
113 S. West Street
3rd floor
Alexandria, VA 22314

703-836-2422
877-836-2422; *Fax:* 703-836-2795
info@aiccbox.org; www.aiccbox.org
Social Media: Facebook, Twitter, LinkedIn, YouTube

A Steven Young, President
Maria Frustaci, Administrative Director
David Core, CAE, Director Education
Taryn Pyle, Director Meetings
Chris Richards, Webmaster/Systems Manager

Represents and protects, the business interests of the independent sector of the corrugated packaging industry. Dedicated to strengthening the independent's position in the marketplace through programs and publications that empower our members to compete successfully in a rapidly changing industry and an increasingly competitive and global business environment.
750 Members
Founded in: 1974

19178 Fibre Box Association
500 Park Boulevard
Suite 985
Itasca, IL 60143

847-364-9600; *Fax:* 847-364-9639
fba@fibrebox.org; www.fibrebox.org
Social Media: LinkedIn

Bill Hoel, Chairman
Peter Watson, First Vice Chairman
Douglas Bonsik, Second Vice-Chairman
Dennis J. Colley, President
Mike Waite, Immediate Past Chairman

A non-profit association that represents and serves the corrugated industry. It also brings together the North American manufacturers to improve the overall well being of the industry and to provide an array of services that enable member companies to conduct their business more effectively , responsibly and efficiently.
170 Members
Founded in: 1940

19179 Foodservice/Packaging Institute
7700 Leesburg Pike
Suite 421
Falls Church, VA 22043

703-592-9889; *Fax:* 703-592-9864
fpi@fpi.org; www.fpi.org
Social Media: Facebook, Twitter, LinkedIn, Blog

Lynn Dyer, President
Natha Dempsey, VP
Caron Mason, Communications Manager
Jennifer Goldman, Manager

A national association comprised of manufacturers and suppliers of single-use foodservice packaging products.
25 Members
Founded in: 1933

19180 Forest Resources Association, Inc.
1901 Pennsylvania Ave. NW
Suite 303
Washington, DC 20006

202-296-3937; *Fax:* 202-296-0562;
www.forestresources.org
Social Media: Facebook, Twitter, YouTube

Deb Hawkinson, President
Neil Ward, Vice President

Promotes sustainable use of forest resources in the interests of its members.

19181 International Corrugated Packaging Foundation
113 S West Street
Alexandria, VA 22314-2858

703-549-8580; *Fax:* 703-549-8670
info@icpfbox.org; www.icpfbox.org
Social Media: Twitter

Steven Landal, Chairman
Richard M Flaherty, President
Thomas W.H. Walton, Vice Chairman
A Steven Young, Treasurer
Paul Vishny, Secretary

An industry led philantrophic organization dedicated to building a knowledgeable workforce for the corrugated packaging industry.
Founded in: 1985

19182 International Council of Forest and Paper Associations
E-Mail: info@icfpa.org; www.icfpa.org

Elizabeth de Carvalhaes, President

Worldwide network of forest and paper associations advocates for industry at international level.

19183 International Molded Fiber Association
355 Lexington Avenue
Floor 15
New York, NY 10017

262-241-0522; *Fax:* 262-241-3766
Alan@IMFA.org; www.imfa.org
Social Media: Facebook, Twitter, LinkedIn

Cassandra Niesing, Asst. Director
Joseph Grygny, Chairman

Acts as an information center for the molded fiber industry with worldwide membership of users and manufacturers of molded fiber producs. Promotes use of natural and recycled fibers.
Founded in: 1996

19184 National Council for Air and Stream Improvement
PO Box 133138
Research Triangle Park, NC 27709-3318

919-941-6400; *Fax:* 919-941-6401
ryeske@ncasi.org; www.ncasi.org

NCASI's mission is to serve the forest products industry as a center of excellence for providing technical information and scientific research needed to achieve the industry's environmental goals and principles.
Founded in: 1943

19185 National Paper Trade Association
330 North Wabash Avenue
Suite 2000
Chicago, IL 60611

312-321-4092
800-355-6782; *Fax:* 312-673-6736
NPTA@goNPTA.com; www.gonpta.com
Social Media: Facebook, Twitter, YouTube

Greg Savage, Chairman
Donald C Clampitt, First Vice Chairman
Travis M. Mlakar, Second Vice Chairman
William Frohlich, President
Hilton Maze, Treasurer

Supports all those professionals in the paper, packaging and allied products distribution industries. Publishes monthly magazine.
2000 Members
Founded in: 1903

19186 National Paperbox Association
1901 Pennsylvania Avenue NW
Suite 1508
Washington, DC 20006

202-466-7252; *Fax:* 413-747-7777;
www.paperbox.org
Social Media: Facebook, Twitter, LinkedIn, YouTube

Ben Markens, President
Lou Kornet, Vice President
Kim Guarnaccia, Director of Marketing
Brian Chaisson, Director of Industry Benchmarking
Jennie Markens, Director of General Leaders

Serves as the voice of the paperbox and packaging industry. Also represents the concerns of boxmaker nationally, internationally and at the local level through its Regional Divisions. Publishes bi-monthly magazine and holds an annual convention.
100 Members
Founded in: 1839

19187 Paper Distribution Council
National Paper Trade Association
330 North Wabash Avenue
Suite 2000
Chicago, IL 60611

312-321-4092; *Fax:* 312-673-4092
NPTA@goNPTA.com; www.gonpta.com
Social Media: Facebook, Twitter, YouTube

Greg Savage, Chairman
Donald C Clampitt, First Vice Chairman
Travis M. Mlakar, Second Vice Chairman
William Frohlich, President
Hilton Maze, Treasurer

Association for paper, packaging and applied products distribution channels.
35 Members
ISBN: 1-092807-3 -
Founded in: 1958

19188 **Paper Industry Management Association**
15 Technology Parkway South
Norcross, GA 30092

770-209-7230; *Fax:* 770-209-7359;
www.imaweb.com
Social Media: Facebook, Twitter, Youtube

Ralph W Feck, President
Terry M Gallagher, Regional VP
Jim Weir, Executive VP/COO
Julie Weldon, Senior Manager
Patrick Andrus, Marketing Coordinator

Contributes to the strength of the international pulp and paper community by providing the means for our members to address relevant industry issues and to develop their management and leadership skills.
4500 Members
Founded in: 1919

19189 **Paper Shipping Sack Manufacturers Association**
5050 Blue Church Road
Coopersburg, PA 18036

610-282-6845; *Fax:* 610-282-1577
admin@pssma.org; www.pssma.org

Richard E. Storat, President
Ross Barett, Chairman
Donald P Belmont, Vice Chairman

Provides its member companies with programs and services which further the industry's objectives and in doing so promote and enhance the welfare of the industry.
45 Members
Founded in: 1933

19190 **Paperboard Packaging Council**
1350 Main Street
Suite 1508
Springfield, MA 01103-1670

413-686-9191; *Fax:* 413-747-7777;
www.ppcnet.org
Social Media: Facebook, Twitter, LinkedIn, YouTube

Ben Markens, President
Lou Kornet, Vice President

Members are companies making folding cartons. Provides publications and instructional materials on the paper industry and recycling.
92 Members
Founded in: 1929

19191 **Technical Association of the Pulp & Paper Industry**
15 Technology Parkway South
Norcross, GA 30092

770-446-1400
800-322-8686; *Fax:* 770-446-6947
webmaster@tappi.org; www.tappi.org

Larry N Montague, CEO
Chris Luettgen, Chair
Paul R. Durocher, Vice Chair

To engage the people and resources of our association in providing technically sound solutions to the workplace problems and opportunities that challenge our current and future members.
12000 Members
ISSN: 0734-1415
Founded in: 1915

19192 **United Paperworkers International Union**
33 Gilmer Street SE
PO Box 3967
Atlanta, GA 30303-3202

404-413-2000; *Fax:* 404-651-4314
libdgg@langate.gsu.edu; www.library.gsu.edu
Social Media: Facebook, Twitter, LinkedIn, YouTube, Instagram, Flickr, Vi

Mike Dees, President

Bestows awards and conducts training seminars.
Founded in: 1972

Newsletters

19193 **American Forest & Paper Association Report**
American Forest & Paper Association
1111 19th St NW
Suite 800
Washington, DC 20036-3652

202-463-2700; *Fax:* 202-463-2785
info@afandpa.org; www.afandpa.org

Covers events of the paper, wood and forest industry. Distribution is limited to association members only.
Cost: $1200.00
4 Pages
Frequency: Weekly
Founded in: 1993

19194 **Conservatree Greenline**
Greenline Publications
PO Box 590780
San Francisco, CA 94159-780

415-386-8646; *Fax:* 415-391-7890;
www.conservatree.com

Alan Davis, Founder/Publisher
Susan Kinsella, Editor

Reports on efforts and achievements by businesses on the environmental front.
Cost: $59.00
Circulation: 25000
Founded in: 1976

19195 **Essential Resources, LLC**
45 S Park Pl
Suite 330
Morristown, NJ 07960-3924

908-832-6979; *Fax:* 908-832-6970

Newsletters for plastic, chemical, pharmaceutical, and packaging industries.
5-15 Pages

19196 **Official Board Markets**
Advanstar Communications
2835 N Sheffield Avenue
Suite 226
Chicago, IL 60657-9213

312-553-8922; *Fax:* 312-553-8929;
www.packaging-online.com

Mark Arzoumanian, Editor-in-Chief
Esther Durkalski, Managing Editor

Covers the corrugated container and folding carton converting industries.
Cost: $180.00
24 Pages
Frequency: Weekly
Circulation: 5900
Founded in: 1915
Printed in on glossy stock

19197 **Seaboard Bulletin**
International Paper
PO Box 1200
Bucksport, ME 04416-1200

207-469-1700; *Fax:* 207-469-1705

David Bailey, President

Paper industry news.

Magazines & Journals

19198 **Asia Pacific PaperMaker**
Paper Industry Management Association
4700 West Lake Avenue
Glenview, IL 60025-1485

847-375-6860; *Fax:* 877-527-5973
info@pimaweb.org; www.pima-online.org

Jim Weir, Executive VP/CEO
Patrick Andrus, Marketing Coordinator
Patrick Filippelli, Sales Manager
Sarah Walsh, Administrative Assistant
Mary Cornell, Account Manager
Founded in: 1919

19199 **Board Converting News**
NV Business Publishers Corporation
43 Main St
Avon By the Sea, NJ 07717-1051

732-502-0500; *Fax:* 732-502-9606
tvilardi@NVPublications.com;
www.nvpublications.com

Ted Vilardi, Owner
Jim Curley, Editor-in-Chief
Robyn Smith, Executive Publisher
Gail Kalina, Production Manager
Dan Brunton, Managing Director

News for the corrugated box and folding carton industry along with box and carton transacted prices.
Cost: $180.00
140 Pages
Frequency: Weekly

19200 **Converting Magazine**
Reed Business Information
2000 Clearwater Dr
Oak Brook, IL 60523-8809

630-574-0825; *Fax:* 630-288-8781
psaran@reedbusiness.com;
www.reedbusiness.com

Jeff Greisch, President
Mark Spaulding, Editor-in-Chief
Steve Reiss, VP
Frequency: Monthly
Circulation: 4000

19201 **Distribution Sales & Management**
National Paper Trade Association
500 B1 - County Boulevard
Suite 200E
Farmingdale, NY 11735-5402

631-777-2223; *Fax:* 631-777-2224;
www.goNPTA.com

Debra Ray, Editor
Bill Fronlinch, Publisher

The business magazine for the paper, packaging and allied products distribution channel.
Cost: $49.00
48 Pages
Frequency: Monthly
Circulation: 17000
ISSN: 1092-8073
Founded in: 1959
Printed in on matte stock

19202 **European PaperMaker**
Paper Industry Management Association
1699 Wall Street
Suite 212
Mount Prospect, IL 60056

847-699-1706; *Fax:* 847-956-0520;
www.pima-online.org

Mary Cornell, Account Manager

19203 **International Paper Board Industry**
Brunton Publications & NV Public

43 Main Street
Avon By The Sea, NJ 07717-1051

732-502-0500; *Fax:* 732-502-9606
jcurley@NVPublications.com;
www.nvpublications.com

Mike Brunton, Publisher
Jim Curley, Editor-in-Chief
Gail Kalina, Production Manager
Tom Vilardi, President
Dan Brunton, Managing Director

Information on corrugated paper and converting industry, encompassing news and production worldwide.
Cost: $60.00
Frequency: Monthly
Circulation: 10021

19204 Latin American PaperMaker
Paper Industry Management Association
1699 Wall Street
Suite 212
Mount Prospect, IL 60056

847-956-0250; *Fax:* 847-956-0520
info@pima-online.org; www.pima-online.org

Ralph W. Feck, President
Jim Weir, COO/Executive VP
Patrick Andrus, Marketing Coordinator
Patrick Filippelli, Sales Manager
Sarah Walsh, Administrative Assistant
Founded in: 1919

19205 Mill Trade Journal's Recycling Markets
NV Business Publishers Corporation
43 Main St
Avon By the Sea, NJ 07717-1051

732-502-0500
800-962-3001; *Fax:* 732-502-9606
advertising@NVPublications.com;
www.nvpublications.com

Ted Vilardi, Owner
Roy Bradbrook, Editor
Jim Curley, Editor-in-Chief
Gail Kalina, Production Manager
Robyn Smith, Executive Publisher

Information on recycling mills paper stock, scrap metal and plastics brokers and dealers used by the municipal governments and private organizations as a basis for letting contracts.
Cost: $130.00
Frequency: Fortnightly
Circulation: 3625
Founded in: 1984
Printed in 2 colors on matte stock

19206 NPTA Distribution Sales & Management
111 Great Neck Road
Suite 418
Great Neck, NY 11021-5402

516-829-3070; *Fax:* 516-829-3074

19207 North American PaperMaker
Paper Industry Management Association
4700 West Lake Avenue
Glenview, IL 60025-1485

847-375-6860; *Fax:* 877-527-5973
info@pimaweb.org; www.pima-online.org

Jim Weir, Executive VP/COO
Pam Oddi, Administrative Assistant
Patrick Filippelli, Sales Manager
Patrick Andrus, Marketing Coordinator
Julie Weldon, Senior Manager
Founded in: 1919

19208 Paper Age Magazine
O'Brien Publications
20 Schofield Rd
Suite 200B
Cohasset, MA 02025-1922

781-749-5255; *Fax:* 781-749-5896;
www.paperage.com

John O'Brien, Owner
John O'Brien, Managing Editor
Michael O'Brien, Publisher

For management and supervisory personnel of pulp, paper and paperboard mills. Tabloid-sized magazine covering the pulp, paper and converting industry, with a unique mix of timely and insightful coverage of corporate strategies, mill operations, technological innovations, industry issues, as well as analysis of the latest production and marketing trends.
Cost: $90.00
Circulation: 36156
Founded in: 1884

19209 Paper Industry Equipment Magazine
PO Box 5675
Montgomery, AL 36103

604-264-1158
888-224-6611; *Fax:* 604-264-1367
info@paperindustrymag.com;
www.paperindustrymag.com

Tim Shaddick, Publisher
Peter N Williamson, Editor

Services and equipment for the pulp/paper industry.
Cost: $12.00
32 Pages
Circulation: 1900
Founded in: 1984
Printed in 4 colors on glossy stock

19210 Paper Stock Report: News and Trends of the Paper Recycling Markets
McEntee Media Corporation
13727 Holland Road
Brook Park, OH 44142

216-362-7979; *Fax:* 216-362-6553;
www.recyle.cc

Ken McEntee, President

Covers news and trends of the scrap paper markets.
Cost: $115.00
Frequency: BiWeekly
Founded in: 1990

19211 Paper, Paperboard and Wood Pulp Monthly Statistical Summary
American Forest & Paper Association
1111 19th St NW
Suite 800
Washington, DC 20036-3652

202-463-2700
800-878-8878; *Fax:* 202-463-2700
info@afandpa.org; www.afandpa.org

Donna Harman, CEO
Henson Moore, President

For the pulp and paper industry.
Cost: $435.00
Frequency: Monthly
Founded in: 1878

19212 Recycled Paper News
McEntee Media Corporation
9815 Hazelwood Ave
Strongsville, OH 44149-2305

440-238-6603; *Fax:* 440-238-6712
info@recycle.cc; www.recycle.cc

Ken Mc Entee, Owner

Coverage of markets and environmental issues related to recycled paper and environmentally friendly paper making process.
Cost: $235.00
Frequency: Monthly
Founded in: 1990

19213 Solutions! for People, Processes and Paper
TAPPI and PIMA
15 Technology Parkway S
Norcross, GA 30092

770-446-1400
800-322-8686; *Fax:* 770-446-6947
webmaster@tappi.org; www.tappi.org

Larry N Montague, CEO
Thomas J Garland, Vice Chairman

19214 TAPPI Journal
Technical Association of the Pulp & Paper Industry
15 Technology Parkway S
Norcross, GA 30092

770-446-1400
800-322-8686; *Fax:* 770-446-6947
webmaster@tappi.org; www.tappi.org

Larry N Montague, CEO
Thomas J Garland, Vice Chairman

Serves domestic and international pulp, paper, paperboard, packaging and converting industries; manufacturers and suppliers of machinery, equipment, chemicals and other material.
Cost: $350.00
130 Pages
Frequency: Monthly
Circulation: 40637
ISSN: 0734-1415
Founded in: 1915
Printed in 4 colors on glossy stock

19215 Walden's Paper Report
Walden-Mott Corporation
225 N Franklin Tpke
Ramsey, NJ 07446-1600

201-818-8630
888-292-5336; *Fax:* 201-818-8720
editorial@walden-mott.com;
www.waldenmott.com

Alfred F Walden, President
Linda Colhen, Director of Operations
Kirk Hardy, Director of Operations

Reports on company expansions and general financial notes on the manufacturers, as well as personnel changes and appointments. Concise review of news on the North American paper industry.
Cost: $240.00
8 Pages
Circulation: 500
Founded in: 1884

Trade Shows

19216 Annual Information Technology Conference
PIMA-Paper Industry Management Association
4700 West Lake Avenue
Glenview, IL 60025-1485

847-375-6860; *Fax:* 877-527-5973
info@pimaweb.org; www.pimaweb.org

Carol Waugh, Meetings Manager

Three-day conference to bring together IT and process control professionals from around the world to share their knowledge of information technology in the pulp and paper industry and to promote systems applications. The only IT conference planned for and by IT professionals.
500 Attendees
Frequency: Annual, April

19217 **International Bioenergy and Bioproducts Conference (IBBC)**
Technical Association of the Pulp & Paper Industry
15 Technology Parkway S
Norcross, GA 30092

770-446-1400
800-322-8686; *Fax:* 770-446-6947
webmaster@tappi.org; www.tappi.org

Norman F. Marsolan, Chair
Thomas J. Garland, Vice Chair
Larry N. Montague, President & CEO

Focusing on technical advancements and commercialization of bioconversion technologies that leverage the forest products manufacturing infrastructure and will include technical presentations, expert panels, case studies, and reports from projects that address feedstock and harvesting improvements to increase yield and quality of biomass, and much more.
500 Attendees
Frequency: Annual/October

19218 **National Paper Trade Association Convention Expo**
National Paper Trade Association
111 Great Neck Road
Suite 418
Great Neck, NY 11021-5497

516-829-3070; *Fax:* 312-673-6736
bill@goNPTA.com; www.gonpta.com

William Frohlich, President

Annual convention of 135 manufacturers, suppliers and distributors of paper products, including packaging materials, health care disposables, industrial and retail packaging supplies, sanitary supplies and computer equipment.
3000 Attendees
Frequency: Annual September
Founded in: 1903

19219 **National Stationery Show**
George Little Management
10 Bank Street
White Plains, NY 10606-1954

914-486-6070
800-272-7469; *Fax:* 914-948-6180; www.

Lori Robinson, VP
Kelly Bristol, Assistant Show Manager
George Little II, President

A show for greeting cards and social stationery, writing instruments and home office products, party ware and giftwrap, scrapbooking and craft supplies, albums, frames and much more.
14000 Attendees
Frequency: May

19220 **National Trade Association Paper Plastics Allied Products Exposition**
National Paper Trade Association
111 Great Neck Road
Suite 418
Great Neck, NY 11021-5402

516-829-3070
bill@goNPTA.com; www.gonpta.com

William Frohlich, President

Industrial and retail packaging, computer products and supplies and equipment. 30 booths.
7M Attendees
Frequency: October

19221 **Paper, Plastics and Allied Products Exposition**
National Paper Trade Association
111 Great Neck Road
Suite 418
Great Neck, NY 11021-5497

516-829-3070; *Fax:* 516-829-3074;
www.gonpta.com

William Frohlich, President

Annual show and exhibits of industrial papers, plastics and plastic products allied to the paper industry.
7000 Attendees

19222 **Pulp and Paper**
Glahe International
PO Box 2460
Germantown, MD 20875-2460

301-515-0012; *Fax:* 301-515-0016

Exhibits of equipment, supplies and services for the pulp and paper industries.

Directories & Databases

19223 **Directory of Corrugated Plants**
Fibre Box Association
2850 Golf Road
Suite 412
Rolling Meadows, IL 60008

847-364-9600; *Fax:* 847-364-9639
shuske@fibrebox.org; www.fibrebox.org

Sharlene Huske

Lists companies and their related plant facilities that manufacture corrugated and solid fiber paperboard products in North America.
Cost: $200.00

19224 **Grade Finder's Competitive Grade Finder**
Grade Finders
622 Exton Commons
Exton, PA 19341

610-524-7070; *Fax:* 610-524-8912
info@gradefinders.com;
www.gradefinders.com

Mark A Subers, President
Phyllis Subers, Office Manager

List of about 5500 manufacturers and distributors of paper. Also lists 6,000 grades of paper competitive classification.
Cost: $60.00
700 Pages
Frequency: Annual April
Circulation: 13,000
ISBN: 0-929502-14-0
Founded in: 1967
Printed in one color on matte stock

19225 **Grade Finder's Paper Buyers Encyclopedia**
Grade Finders
622 Exton Commons
Exton, PA 19341

610-524-7070; *Fax:* 610-524-8912
info@gradefinders.com;
www.gradefinders.com

Mark Subers, President

A list of about 6,700 manufacturers, converters and suppliers to the paper industry. In addition, it lists over 4,000 grades of paper categorized into competitive classifications showing each grades rating, opacity, color availability, etc. Also contains an extensive how-to buy paper section.
Cost: $150.00
530 Pages
Frequency: Annual
Circulation: 7000

19226 **National Institute of Packaging and Handling Logistics Engineers**
5903 Ridgeway Drive
Grand Prairie, TX 75052

817-466-7490
866-464-7453; *Fax:* 570-523-0606
admin@niphle.com; www.niphle.com
Social Media: Facebook, Twitter, LinkedIn

Richard D Owen, Executive Director

An assemblage of professionals whose interest in the complex and diverse practice of distribution and logistics is a common bond.

19227 **PIMA Buyers Guide**
Paper Industry Management Association
4700 W Lake Avenue
Glenview, IL 60025-1485

847-375-6860; *Fax:* 877-527-5973;
www.pimaweb.org

Jospeh Agnew, Editor
Pam Oddi, Editorial Support

Directory aimed at the paper and pulp industry offering various information on manufacturers of chemicals and supplies used in the manufacturing of paper.
Cost: $120.00
60 Pages
Frequency: Annual
Circulation: 2,000
Printed in on matte stock

19228 **Rauch Guide to the US and Canadian Pulp & Paper Industry**
Grey House Publishing
4919 Route 22
PO Box 56
Amenia, NY 12501

518-789-8700
800-562-2139; *Fax:* 845-373-6390
books@greyhouse.com; www.greyhouse.com
Social Media: Facebook, Twitter

Leslie Mackenzie, Publisher
Richard Gottlieb, Editor

Provides current market information and trends; industry economics and government regulations; company share data for each of the leading product categories; technology and raw material information; industry sources of further data; and unique profiles of 500+ pulp and paper manufacturers, a section which includes all known companies with pulp and paper sales at or over $15 million annually.
Cost: $595.00
400 Pages
ISBN: 1-592371-31-0
Founded in: 1981

19229 **TAPPI Membership Directory and Company Guide**
Technical Association of the Pulp & Paper Industry
15 Technology Parkway S
Norcross, GA 30092

770-446-1400
800-322-8686; *Fax:* 770-446-6947
webmaster@tappi.org; www.tappi.org

Larry N Montague, CEO
Thomas J Garland, Vice Chairman

About 35,000 member executives, managers, engineers, technologists and superintendents in the pulp, paper, packaging, converting, non-wovens and allied industries.
Cost: $140.00
Frequency: October

19230 **Walden's ABC Guide and Paper Production Yearbook**
Walden-Mott Corporation

225 N Franklin Tpke
Ramsey, NJ 07446-1600

201-818-8630; *Fax:* 201-818-8720;
www.waldenmott.com

Alfred F Walden, President
Kirk Hardy, Director of Operations

Offers a large list of manufacturers and suppliers of printing papers.
Cost: $117.50
300 Pages
Frequency: Annual January

Industry Web Sites

19231 http://gold.greyhouse.com
G.O.L.D Grey House OnLine Databases

Grey House Publishing's online database platform, GOLD, offers Quick Search, Keyword Search and Expert Search for most business sectors including paper and allied products markets. The GOLD platform makes finding the information you need quick and easy - whether you're a novice searcher or an experienced database user. All of Grey House's directory products are available for subscription on the GOLD platform.

19232 www.afandpa.org
American Forest and Paper Association

Serves forest, paper, paperboard and wood products packaging industry

19233 www.fibrebox.org
Fibre Box Association

For national corrigated manufacturers.

19234 www.fpi.org
Foodservice & Packaging Institute

Manufacturers, suppliers and distributors of one-time use products used for food service, as well as packaging products made from paper, plastic, aluminum and other materials. Membership dues based on sales.

19235 www.gonpta.com
National Paper Trade Association

Association for paper, packaging and applied products distribution channel.

19236 www.greyhouse.com
Grey House Publishing

Authoritative reference directories for most business sectors including paper and allied products markets. Users can search the online databases with varied search criteria allowing for custom searches by product category, geographic area, sales volume, keyword, subject and more. Full Grey House catalog and online ordering also available.

19237 www.tappi.org
Technical Association of the Pulp & Paper Industry

Associations

19238 **Actors Equity Association**
165 W 46th St
New York, NY 10036-2500

212-869-8530; *Fax:* 212-719-9815;
www.actorsequity.org

Alan Eisenberg, CEO
Mark Zimmerman, President
David Lotz, National Director of Communications
Mary Lou Westerfield, Natioanl Director Policy
Flora Stamatiades, National Director Organizing

A labor union that represents Actors and Stage Managers in the United States. Seeks to advance, promote and foster the art of live theatre as an essential component of our society. Negotiates wages and working conditions and provides a wide range of benefits, including health and pension plans.
45000 Members
Founded in: 1913

19239 **African Performing Arts Association**
PO Box 660573
Atlanta, GA 30366

www.africanperformingarts.org

Founded in: 2001

19240 **Alternate ROOTS**
115 Martin Luther King Jr Dr.
Suite 200
Atlanta, GA 30303

404-577-1079; *Fax:* 404-577-7991
ennis@alternateroots.org;
www.alternateroots.org
Social Media: Facebook, Twitter, Flickr

19241 **American Alliance for Theatre and Education**
4908 Auburn Avenue
Bethesda, MD 20814-3474

301-200-1944; *Fax:* 301-280-1682
info@aate.com; www.aate.com
Social Media: Facebook, Twitter, LinkedIn, RSS

Gary Minyard, President
Kelly Prestel, Treasurer
Amy P.Jenson, Advocacy Director
Jeremy Kisling, Communications Director
Mitch Mattson, Planning Director

The national voice for theatre and education, representing artists and educators serving young people in theatre and education. Its members play a vital role in advocating for the interests of children who benefit from theatre in their communities and classrooms. AATE embraces diversity and encourages inclusion of all races, social classes, ages, genders, religions, sexual orientations, national organizations and abilities.
700 Members
Founded in: 1986

19242 **American Association of Community Theatre**
1300 Gendy Street
Fort Worth, TX 76107-4036

817-732-3177
866-687-2228; *Fax:* 817-732-3178
info@aact.org; www.aact.org
Social Media: Facebook, Twitter, LinkedIn

Julie Crawford, Executive Director
Murray Chase, President
Carole Ries, Executive Vice President
Frank Peot, Secretary
Michael Fox, Treasurer

The national voice of community theatre, representing the interests of its members and over 7,000 theatres across the US and with the armed services overseas. Its mission is to foster the encouragement and development of, and commitment to, the highest standards by community theatres, including standards of excellence for production, management, governance, community relations and service.
Founded in: 1986
Mailing list available for rent: 10000 names at $180 per M

19243 **American Composers Forum**
75 West 5th Street
Suite 522
Saint Paul, MN 55102-1439

651-228-1407; *Fax:* 651-291-7978
lhoeschler@gmail.com;
www.composersforum.org
Social Media: Facebook, Twitter

Mary Ellen Childs, Chair
Patrick Castillo, Vice Chair
Dan Thomas, Vice Chair
David Ranheim, Secretary
Sam Hsu, Treasurer
2000 Members
Founded in: 1973

19244 **American Dance Therapy Association**
10632 Little Patuxent Pkwy
Suite 108
Columbia, MD 21044-3263

410-997-4040; *Fax:* 410-997-4048
info@adta.org; www.adta.org
Social Media: Facebook, Twitter, Pinterest, YouTube

Gloria Farrow, Manager
Jody Wager, President
Gloria J Farrow, Operations Director
Meghan Dempsey, Treasurer
Gail Wood, Secretary

Professional organization of dance movement therapists, with members both nationally and internationally; offers training, research findings, and a newsletter. Holds annual conference.
1.1M Members
Founded in: 1966

19245 **American Disc Jockey Association**
20118 N 67th Avenue
Suite 300-605
Glendale, AZ 85308

888-723-5776
888-723-5776; *Fax:* 866-310-4676
office@adja.org; www.adja.org
Social Media: Facebook, Twitter, YouTube

Rob Snyder, Director

An association of professional mobile entertainers. Encourages success for its members through continuous education, camaraderie, and networking. The primary goal is to educate Disc Jockeys so that each member acts ethically and responsibly.

19246 **American Federation of Musicians of the United States and Canada**
1501 Broadway
Suite 600
New York, NY 10036-5501

212-869-1330; *Fax:* 212-764-6134
info@afm.org; www.afm.org
Social Media: Facebook, Twitter, YouTube

Thomas Lee, President
Linda Patterson, Executive Secreatry to President

AFM is an association of professional musicians united through their locals so that they can live and work in dignity; produce work that will be fulfilling and compensated fairly; have a meaningful voice in decisions that affect them; have the opportunity to develop their talents and skills; whose collective voice and power will be realized in a democratic and progressive union; and who oppose the forces of exploitation through their union solidarity.
10K Members
Founded in: 1896

19247 **American Indian Registry for the Performing Arts**
1717 N Highland
Suite 614
Los Angeles, CA 90028

213-962-6574;
www.afn.org/~native/orgnztns.htm

Organization of American Indian performers and technical personnel in the entertainment field.

19248 **American Institute of Organ Builders**
PO Box 35306
Canton, OH 44735

330-806-9011
robert_sullivan@pipeorgan.org;
www.pipeorgan.org
Social Media: Twitter

Philip Parkey, President
Michael Lauffer, Vice President
Louis E Patterson, Secretary
Charles R Eames, Treasurer
Joseph O'Donnell, Secretary

Sponsors training seminars, quarterly journal and annual convention for pipe organ builders and service technicians.
385 Members
Founded in: 1974
Mailing list available for rent: 350 names at $250 per M

19249 **American Institute of Organbuilders**
PO Box 35306
Canton, OH 44735

330-806-9011
robert_sullivan@pipeorgan.org;
www.pipeorgan.org
Social Media: Facebook

Philip Parkey, President
Michael Lauffer, Vice President
Robert Sullivan, Executive Secretary
Joseph O'Donnell, Secretary
Charles R. Eames, Treasurer
Founded in: 1974

19250 **Americans for the Arts**
1000 Vermont Avenue, NW
6th Floor
Washington, DC 20005

202-371-2830; *Fax:* 202-371-0424;
www.americansforthearts.org
Social Media: Facebook, Twitter, LinkedIn, YouTube, Pinterest

Abel Lopez, Chair
Ramona Baker, Vice Chair
C. Kendric Fergeson, Immediate Past Chair
Michael Spring, Secretary
Julie Muraco, Treasurer
Founded in: 1960

19251 **Associated Pipe Organ Builders of America**
P.O. Box 8268
Erie, PA 8268

800-473-5270
800-473-5270; www.apoba.com

Bob Rusczyk, Executive Director
Richard Parsons, President
Paul Lytle, Vice President
Randall Dyer, Secretary
Seth Marshall, Treasurer

A professional association of North American firms engaged in building traditional pipe organs. Members are a select group of organbuilders who have passed stringent membership requirements which include commitment

to principles regarding the use of electronic technology in organ building.
27 Members

19252 **Association for Theatre in Higher Education**
1000 Westgate Dr.
Suite 252
St. Paul, MN 55114

651-288-3430
800-918-9216; *Fax:* 651-290-2266
info@athe.org; www.athe.org
Social Media: Facebook

Eric Ewald, Executive Director
Patricia Ybarra, President
Karen Jean Martinson, Secretary
Scott Shattuck, Treasurer

ATHE serves the interests of its diverse individual and organization members. Its vision is to advocate for the field of theatre and performance in higher education. It serves as an intellectual and artistic center for producing new knowledge about theatre and performance-related disciplines. cultivating vital alliances with other scholarly and creative disciplines, linking with professional and community-based theatres, and promoting access and equity.
1700 Members
Founded in: 1986

19253 **Association of Arts Administration Educators**
Bolz Center for Arts Administration
188 Hanford Street
Columbus, OH 43206

312-469-0795; *Fax:* 608-265-2735
info@artsadministration.org;
www.artsadministration.org
Social Media: Facebook, Twitter, RSS

Andrew Taylor, President/Director
John McCann, VP
Phyllis Johnson, Treasurer
Stephen Boyle, Secretary

The Association of Administration Educators (AAAE) is an international organization incorporated as a nonprofit institution within the United States. Its mission is to represent college and university graduate and undergraduate programs in the arts administration, encompassing training in the management of visual, performing, literary, media, cultural and arts service organizations.
Founded in: 1975

19254 **Association of Hispanic Arts**
P.O.Box 1169
El Barrio, NY 10029

212-876-1242
888-876-1240; *Fax:* 212-876-1285
informacion@latinoarts.org; www.nalac.org

Nicholas L Arture, Executive Director
Julia L Gutierrez-Rivera, Program Officer/Arts Service Coord.
Crystal Chaparro, Office Assistant
Gregory Castro, Comptroller
Brenda L Jiminez, Board Chair

A nonprofit arts service organization serving the Latino arts and cultural community. AHA was established out of the need to create funding and presenting opportunities for individual Latino artists and cultural organizations whose contributions were unrecognized and whose efforts were underserved by mainstream public and private institutions.
Founded in: 1975

19255 **Association of Performing Arts Presenters**
1211 Connecticut Ave NW
Suite 200
Washington, DC 20036-2716

202-833-2787
888-820-2787; *Fax:* 202-833-1543
info@artspresenters.org; www.apap365.org/
Social Media: Facebook, Twitter, YouTube

Sandra Gibson, President
Dr. Michael Blachly, Chair
Brain Jose, Vice Chairman
Nicole Borrelli Hearn, Vice Chair
Todd Wetzel, Treasurer

A national membership and advocacy organization dedicated to bringing performing artists and audiences together.
1900 Members
Founded in: 1957

19256 **Broadcast Music Incorporated BMI**
7 World Trade Center
250 Greenwich Street
New York, NY 10007-0030
212-220-3000; *Fax:* 212-246-2163
newyork@bmi.com; www.bmi.com
Social Media: Facebook, Twitter, LinkedIn, YouTube, Pinterest, RSS, Insta

Del Bryant, CEO
John E Cody, COO/Executive VP

American performing rights organization that represents approximately 300,000 songwriters, composers and music publishers in all genres of music. The nonprofit company collects license fees on behalf of those American creators it represents, as well as thousands of creators from around the world who chose BMI for representation in the US. These fees are then distributed as royalties to the writers, composers and copyright holders it represents.
300m Members
Founded in: 1939

19257 **Chinese Music Society of North America**
PO Box 5275
Woodridge, IL 60517-0275

630-910-1551; *Fax:* 630-910-1561;
www.chinesemusic.net

Sin-Yan Shen, President
Kok-Koon Ng, VP
Yuan-Yuan Lee, Executive Director
Billie Jefferson, Artistic Administrator
Der-Tung Yuan, Membership

A national nonprofit organization founded to increase and diffuse the knowledge of Chinese music and performing arts. Today it has grown to become the national association of Chinese musicians and scholars and National and International organization specializing in Research and Educational Material in English concerning Music/Theater/Dance and Musical Instruments from China and Non-Western Cultures.
Founded in: 1969

19258 **Chorus America**
P.O. Box 2646
Suite 310
Arlington, VA 22202-0646

202-331-7577; *Fax:* 202-331-7599
webmaster@chorusamerica.org;
www.chorusamerica.org
Social Media: Facebook, Twitter, YouTube, Google+

Rollo Dilworth, Chairman
Gayle. M Ober, Immediate Past Chairman
Mitch Menchaca, Interim CEO
Michael McCarthy, Treasurer
Mary Lyons, Secretary
2000 Members
Founded in: 1977

19259 **Classical Action**
165 W 46th St
Suite 1300
New York, NY 10036-2514

212-997-7717; *Fax:* 212-840-0551
classicalaction@broadwaycares.org;
www.classicalaction.org
Social Media: Facebook, Twitter

Charles Hamlen, Founding Director
Chris Kenney, Associate Director

Since 1993, Classical Action has provided a unified voice for all those within the performing arts community to help combat HIV/AIDS and the devastating effects of this epidemic.
Founded in: 1993

19260 **Conductors Guild**
719 Twinridge Ln
Richmond, VA 23235
804-553-1378; *Fax:* 804-553-1876
guild@conductorsguild.org;
www.conductorsguild.org
Social Media: Facebook, Twitter, LinkedIn

Gordon Johnson, President
Amanda Burton Winger, Executive Director
Erin Freeman, VP
Christopher Blair, Treasurer
David Leibowitz, Secretary

The Conductors Guild is the only music service organization devoted exclusively to the advancement of the art of conducting and to serving the artistic and professional needs of conductors.
1850+ Members
Founded in: 1975

19261 **Congress on Research in Dance**
7044 South 13th Street
Oak Creek, WI 53154

414-908-4951; *Fax:* 414-768-8001
info@cordance.org; www.cordance.org

Anne Flynn, President
Helen Thomas, Chair, Editorial Board
Petri Hoppu, Vice President
Bridget Cauthery, Treasurer

A not-for-profit, interdisciplinary organization with an open, international membership. Its purposes are: to encourage research in all aspects of dance, including related fields; to foster the exchange of ideas, resources, and methodology, through publication, international and regional conferences and workshops; to promote the accessibility of research materials.
Cost: $35.00
750 Members
Founded in: 1965
Mailing list available for rent

19262 **Costume Society of America**

www.costumesocietyamerica.com
Social Media: Facebook, Twitter, LinkedIn, YouTube

19263 **Country Dance & Song Society**
116 Pleasant St
Suite 345
Easthampton, MA 01027-2759
413-203-5467; *Fax:* 413-203-5471
office@cdss.org; www.cdss.org
Social Media: Facebook, Twitter, Instagram, YouTube, Flickr

Rima Dael, Executive/Artistic Director
Carol Compton, Financial Manager
Christine Dadmun, Membership Admin
Bob Blondin, Business Manager
Robin Hayden, Development Director

A national organization dedicated to the preservation and promotion of English and Anglo-American traditional and historical folk dance, music and song. Composed of individual members and affiliate groups, it functions both as an international service bureau and as a facilitator in building and maintaining local and regional dance, music and song communities. It exists to meed needs for community-based activity, for active participation, and for sharing and keeping historical and folk
3400 Members
Founded in: 1915

19264 **Dance Critics Association**
Old Chelsea Station
PO Box 1882
New York, NY 10011

732-643-4008
dancecritics@hotmail.com;
www.dancecritics.org

Kena Herod, Co-Chair
Linda Traiger, Co-Chair

Encourages excellence in dance criticism through education, research and the exchange of ideas. Produces quarterly newsletter.
Cost: $50.00
300 Members
Founded in: 1973

19265 **Dance Educators of America**
PO Box 740387
Suite262
Boynton Beach, FL 33474

914-636-3200
800-329-3868; *Fax:* 914-636-5895
info@dancedea.com;
www.usadance.dancedea.com/
Social Media: Facebook, Twitter, Youtube

Vickie Sheer, Executive Director
Fran Peters, President
Charles Kelley, Treasurer
Robyn Bourdeau, Chief Financial Officer
Stephen Ball, Events and DEA Coordinator

Dedicated to improving the quality and teaching abilities of its member teachers and enhancing their education of students, as well as furthering the professional and ethical standards in the performing arts and of dance in all its form. Membership is limited to qualified teachers.
Cost: $150.00
1800 Members
Founded in: 1932

19266 **Dance Films Association**
252 Java Street
Suit 333
Brooklyn, NY 11222

347-505-8649; *Fax:* 212-727-0765
info@dancefilms.org; www.dancefilms.org
Social Media: Facebook, Twitter, Vimeo

Deidra Towers, Executive Director
Latika Young, Education Director
Anna Brady Nuse, Festival Coordinator
Julian Barnett, Research/Development

Supports all those professionals in both the dance and the film community. Publishes bi-monthly magazine.
Cost: $50.00
Founded in: 1956

19267 **Dance Masters of America**
PO Box 610533
Bayside, NY 11361

718-255-4013; *Fax:* 718-225-4293
dmamann@aol.com; www.dma-national.org

Shely Pack Manning, National President
Robert Mann, National Executive Secretary
Charleen Locascio, National Treasurer

An international organization of dance educators who have been certified by test to teach whose main focus is advancing the art of dance and improving the practice of its teaching.
2.5M Members
Founded in: 1884

19268 **Dance USA**
1111 16th St NW
Suite 300
Washington, DC 20036-4830

202-833-1717; *Fax:* 202-833-2686
danceusa@danceusa.org; www.danceusa.org
Social Media: Facebook, Twitter, YouTube, Vimeo

Amy Fitterer, Executive Director
Tom Thielen, Director Finance/Operations
Katherine Fabian, Membership Manager
Dough Singleton, Chair
Andrea Clark-Smith, Vice Chair

Provides a forum for the discussion of issues of concern to members and a support network for exchange of information.
400 Members
Founded in: 1982

19269 **Dance/USA**
1111 16th Street NW Ste. 300
Washington, DC 20036
202-833-1717; www.danceusa.org
Social Media: Facebook, Twitter, YouTube, Vimeo

Dough Singleton, Chair
Charlotte Ballet, Chair Elect
Andrea Clark-Smith, Vice Chair
Sarah Thompson, Secretary
Robert Dorf, Treasurer

19270 **Dramatists Guild of America**
1501 Broadway
Suite 701
New York, NY 10036-5505

212-398-9366; *Fax:* 212-944-0420;
www.dramatistsguild.com

Ralph Sevush, Executive Director Business Affairs
Gary Garrison, Executive Director Creative Affairs
Abby Marcus, Managing Director
Roland Tec, Director of Membership

The Dramatists Guild of America was established over eighty years ago, and is the only professional association that advances the interests of playwrights, composers, lyricists and librettists writing for the living stage.
6000+ Members
Founded in: 1964

19271 **Educational Theatre Association**
2343 Auburn Ave
Cincinnati, OH 45219-2819

513-421-3900; *Fax:* 513-421-7077;
www.schooltheatre.org
Social Media: Facebook, Twitter, Instagram, YouTube

Jay Seller, President
Frank Pruet, VP
Julie Woffington, Executive Director
Jim Flanagan, Director of Operations
Ginny Butsch, Community Manager

EdTA is a professional organization for theatre educators. In addition to providing professional development, advocacy, and networking support to its members, Edta oprtates the International Society, an honorary organization for high school and middle school theatre students.
4600+ Members
Founded in: 1929

19272 **Esperanza Performing Arts Association**
Po Box 502591
San Diego, CA 92150

858-391-1311
info@esperanzaarts.org;
www.esperanzaarts.org

Alan Cox, Executive Director
Adam Stout, Assistant Director

19273 **Fractured Atlas**
248 W. 35th Street, 10th Fl.
New York, NY 10001

888-692-7878; *Fax:* 212-277-8025
support@fracturedatlas.org;
www.fracturedatlas.org
Social Media: Facebook, Twitter, LinkedIn

Holly Sidford, Chair
Russell Wills Taylor, Vice Chair
Adam Forest Huttler, Executive Director
Adam Huttler, Secretary
Alanna Weifenbach, Treasurer
Founded in: 1998

19274 **Fritz and Lavinia Jensen Foundation**
Foundation for the Carolinas
220 N Tryon Street
Charlotte, NC 28202

704-641-4691; *Fax:* 704-973-4599
info@jensenfoundation.org;
www.jensenfoundation.org

Ann Todd, Competition Coordinator
Jane W. Pardue, President
R. Benjamin Leaptrott, Jr., Vice President
Oliver Worthington, Vice President
Gene Hoots, Trustee

Sponsors voice competitions supporting opera and other classical singers.

19275 **Gina Bachauer International Piano Foundation**
138 W Broadway
Suite 220
Salt Lake City, UT 84101-1913

801-297-4250; *Fax:* 801-521-9202
info@bachauer.com; www.bachauer.com
Social Media: Facebook, Twitter, Flickr, Google+, YouTube

Thomas Holst, Manager
Kimi Kawashima, Manager
Arlo McGinn, Secretary
Nathan Morgan, Treasurer
Kary Billings, Chairman

The mission of the Foundation is to further the pianistic art, foster excellence in performance and teaching, develop opportunities for pianists beyond the scope of the organization and offer leadership in developing a musically-educated community.
Founded in: 1976

19276 **Guild of American Luthiers**
8222 S Park Ave
Tacoma, WA 98408-5226

253-472-7853; *Fax:* 253-472-7853
orders@luth.org; www.luth.org
Social Media: Facebook

Debra G Olsen, Executive Director
Tim Olsen, Editor
Kurt Kendall, Membership

Manufacturers and repairs stringed instruments; offers quarterly journal and triennial meeting.
Cost: $45.00
3000 Members
Founded in: 1972

19277 **Institute of Outdoor Drama**
201 Erwin Building
Mail Stop 528
Greenville, NC 27858-4353

252-328-5363; *Fax:* 252-328-0968;
www.outdoor-theatre.org
Social Media: Facebook, Twitter, RSS

Michael C. Hardy, Director
Susan D. Phillips, Business Manager
Founded in: 1963

19278 **International Computer Music Association**
1819 Polk Street
Suite 330
San Francisco, CA 94109

Fax: 734-878-3031
icma@umich.edu; www.computermusic.org
Social Media: Facebook

Tae Hong Park, President
Margaret Schedel, VP Of Conference
Michael Gurevich, Vice President for Membership
Tae Hong Park, Vice President for Preservation
Chryssie Nanou, Treasurer/Secretary

The International Computer Music Association is an international affiliaton of individuals and institutions involved in the technical, creative, and performance aspects of computer music. It serves composers, engineers, researchers and musicians who are interested in the integration of music and technology.
Cost: $63.52
450 Members

19279 **International Festivals and Events Association**
2603 W Eastover Ter
Boise, ID 83706-2800

208-433-0950; *Fax:* 208-433-9812
nia@ifea.com; www.ifea.com
Social Media: Facebook, Twitter, LinkedIn, YouTube

Steven Schmader, President
Nia Hovde, VP/Marketing

A voluntary association of events, event producers, event suppliers, and related professionals and organizations whose common purpose is the production and presentation of festivals, events, and civic and private celebrations.
2000 Members
Founded in: 1956

19280 **International Performing Arts for Youth**
1315 Walnut Street
Suite 320
Philadelphia, PA 19107

267-690-1325; *Fax:* 267-519-3343;
www.ipayweb.org

Ms. Peg Schuler-Armstrong, President
Ms. Pamela K. Lieberman, Vice President
Ms. Mary Kate Barley-Jenkins, Immediate Past President
Jeremy Boomer Stacey, Executive Director
Ms. Nadine Carew, Treasurer
Founded in: 2001

19281 **International Planned Music Association**
5900 S Salina Street
Syracuse, NY 13205

315-469-7711; *Fax:* 315-469-8842;
www.ipmanet.com

Bob Bobuk, President
Gary Alshouse, VP
Barb Cowsert, Secretary
Jon Baker, Treasurer
Jack Carroll, General Counsel

IPMA is a trade organization made up of providers of planned and programmed music services and key vendors. The Associatin exists to provide members with a common ground on which to share informatio about running exciting, profitable franchises and to provide associate members with opportunities to expand their sales in markets all over the world.
200 Members

19282 **International Society for the Performing Arts**
630 9th Avenue
Suite 213
New York, NY 10036-4752

212-206-8490; *Fax:* 212-206-8603;
www.ispa.org
Social Media: Facebook, Twitter, Pinterest

Anthony Sargent, Chair
Jeff Daniel, Treasurer
Margia Claudia, Secretary
Johann Zietsman, CEO
Lynne Caruso, Membership Manager

A nonprofit organization of executives and directors of concert and performance halls, festivals, performing companies, and artists competitions; government cultural officials; artists' managers; and other interested parties with a professional involvement in the performing arts around the world, and in every arts disciplie. The purpose of ISPA is to develop, nurture, energize and educate an international network of arts leaders and professionals who are dedicated to advancing its field.
600 Members
Founded in: 1949

19283 **International Theatre Equipment Association**
770 Broadway
5th Floor
New York, NY 10003-9595

646-654-7680; *Fax:* 212-257-6428;
www.itea.com

Robert Sunshine, Executive Director
Barry Ferrell, President
Jack Panzeca, VP
Joe DeMeo, Treasurer
Sarah Fuller, Secretary

Fosters and maintains professional, business and social relationships among its members within all segments of the motion picture industry. Bestows annual Teddy Award to manufacturer of the year and the annual Rodney Award to dealer of the year.
Cost: $375.00
180 Members
Founded in: 1971

19284 **International Ticketing Association**
10401 N Meridian St
Suite 300
Indianapolis, IN 46290

212-629-4036; *Fax:* 212-629-8532
info@intix.org; www.intix.org
Social Media: Facebook, Twitter, LinkedIn

Jennifer Aprea, Board Chair
Gary Lustig, Chair-Elect
Mardi S Dilger, Past Chair
Jena L Hoffman, President
Amber E Kinney, Treasurer

Non-profit association committed to the improvement, progress and advancement of ticket management. Provides educational programs, trade shows, conducts surveys, conference proceedings, and its valuable membership directory.
Founded in: 1982

19285 **Jazz Education**
3303 South Rice, Suite 107
PO Box 8031
Houston, TX 77056

713-839-7000; *Fax:* 715-839-8266;
www.jazzeducation.org
Social Media: Facebook, LinkedIn

Tracy Scott, Executive Director

Nonprofit music organization providing worthwhile educational activities for school-aged youth in the field of music. Includes many subjects not covered by school systems. Promotes appreciation and understanding of Jazz.
Founded in: 1970

19286 **League of American Orchestras**
33 West 60th Street
New York, NY 10023

212-262-5161; *Fax:* 212-262-5198
member@americanorchestras.org;
www.americanorchestras.org
Social Media: Facebook, Twitter, YouTube

Patricia A Richards, Chair
Steven C. Parrish, Vice Chair
Jesse Rosen, President/ CEO
Barry A Sanders, Secretary
Robert A Peiser, Treasurer
800 Members
Founded in: 1942

19287 **League of American Theatres and Producers**
729 Seventh Avenue
5th Floor
New York, NY 10019

212-764-1122; *Fax:* 212-944-2136
league@broadway.org;
www.broadwayleague.com
Social Media: Facebook, Twitter, LinkedIn, Pinterest, Instagram, YouTube

Charolette St Martin, Executive Director
Colin Gibson, Director Finance
Jane Svendsen, Director Marketing
Ed Sandler, Director Membership Services

National trade association for the commercial theatre industry whose principal activity is negotiation of labor contracts and government relations.
400 Members
Founded in: 1930

19288 **League of Historic American Theatres**
9 Newport Drive
Suite 200
Forest Hill, MD 21050

443-640-1058
877-627-0833; *Fax:* 443-640-1031
info@lhat.org; www.network.lhat.org

Frances Holden, Executive Director
Thomas Johnson, VP
Alice North, Treasurer
John Bell, Chair
Don Telford, Immediate Past Chair

The League of Historic American Theatres, a nonprofit membership association, promotes the rescue, rehabilitation and sustainable operation of historic theatres throughout North America. Founded in 1976, the League serves its members through educational programs, publications, specialized services and an annual conference and theatre tour.
500+ Members
Founded in: 1976

19289 **Literary Managers and Dramaturgs of the Americas**
PO Box 36
New York, NY 10129

212-561-0315
800-680-2148

lmdanyc@hotmail.com; www.lmda.org
Social Media: Facebook, Twitter

Brain Quirt, Chair
Beth Blickers, President
Danielle Carroll, Administrative Director
Nichole Gantshar, Treasurer
Richard Wolfe, VP

The mission of the LMDA is to affirm the role of dramaturg, to expande the possibilities of the field to other media and institutions and to cultivate, develop and promote the function of dramaturgy and literary management.
500 Members

19290 Mid-Atlantic Arts Foundation
201 N Charles Street
Suite 401
Baltimore, MD 21201-4102

410-539-6656; *Fax:* 410-837-5517
info@midatlanticarts.org;
www.midatlanticarts.org
Social Media: Facebook, Twitter, YouTube, Pinterest

Alan Cooper, Executive Director
E Scott Johnson, Secretary

MAAF celebrates, promotes and supports the richness and diversity of the region's art resources and works to increase access to the arts and other cultures of the region and the world.
40000 Members
Founded in: 1979
Mailing list available for rent: 30,000 names

19291 Music Distributors Association
14070 Proton Road
Suite 100 LB 9
Dallas, TX 75244-3601

972-233-9107; *Fax:* 972-490-4219
office@musicdistributors.org;
www.musicdistributors.org

An international nonprofit trade association representing and serving manufacturers, wholesalers, importers and exporters of musical instruments and accessories, sound reinforcement products and published music.
Cost: $675.00
Founded in: 1939

19292 National Alliance for Musical Theatre
520 Eighth Avenue
Suite 301
New York, NY 10018

212-714-6668; *Fax:* 212-714-0469
info@namt.org; www.namt.org
Social Media: Facebook, Twitter, RSS, YouTube

Michael G. Murphy, Treasurer
Paige Price, Vice President
Betsy King Militello, Executive Director
Wayne Bryan, Secretary
Jeff Loeb, President

Not-for-profit working for the advance of musical theatre.
30000 Members
Founded in: 1985

19293 National Association for Drama Therapy
Suite 101
Suite 220
Albany, NY 12203

888-416-7167; *Fax:* 518-463-8656
office@nadta.org; www.nadta.org
Social Media: Facebook, Twitter, YouTube, Instagram

Nadya Trytan, President
Jeremy Segall, MA, RDT, LCAT, VP
Whitney Sullivan, RDT, LCSW, Secretary
Dani York, RDT, LCAT, Treasurer
Nancy Sondag, Membership

A nonprofit association which establishes and upholds high standards of professional competence and ethics among drama therapists; to develop criteria for training and registration; to sponsor publications and conferences; and to promote the profession of drama therapy through information and advocacy.
Founded in: 1979

19294 National Association for Music Education
1806 Robert Fulton Drive
Reston, VA 20191

703-860-4000
800-336-3768; *Fax:* 703-860-1531;
www.nafme.org
Social Media: Facebook, Twitter, LinkedIn, Google+, Pinterest

Lynn M Brinckmeyer, President

The mission of MENC is to advance music education by encouraging the study and making of music by all. MENC offers more than 100 books, videos and compact discs, as well as two general-interest magazines on music education and four more closely targeted journals.
Founded in: 1907
Mailing list available for rent: 60,000 names

19295 National Association of Latino Arts and Cultures
1208 Buena Vista
San Antonio, TX 78207

210-432-3982; *Fax:* 210-432-3934
info@nalac.org; www.nalac.org
Social Media: Facebook, Twitter

Maria L¢pez De L,on, Executive Director

A nonprofit dedicated exclusively to serving Latino arts communities.
Founded in: 1989

19296 National Association of Performing Arts Managers and Agents
459 Columbus Avenue
#133
New York, NY 10024

E-Mail: tuluck@fairpoint.net;
www.napama.org

Jerry Ross, President
David Wannen, Vice President
Jeff Laramie, Vice President
Laurelle Favreau, Secretary
Robin Pomerance, Treasurer
Founded in: 1979

19297 National Corporate Theatre Fund
505 Eighth Avenue
Suite 2303
New York, NY 10018

212-750-6895; *Fax:* 212-750-6977;
www.theatreforward.org
Social Media: Facebook, Twitter, YouTube

Richard Thomas, Honorary Chair
James S Turley, Chairman
Gretchen Shugart, President
Bruce R Ewing, Secretary
Frank Orlowski, Treasurer

19298 National Costumers Association
6000 E. Evans Ave.
#3-205
Denver, CO 80222

317-351-1940
800-622-1321; *Fax:* 317-351-1941
office@costumers.org; www.costumers.org

Janie Westendorf, President
Deborah Meredith, First Vive President
Linda Adams Foat, Second VP
Jennifer Skarstedt, Secretary/Treasurer

The objectives on the NCA are to establish and maintain professional and ethical standards of business in the costume industry. They encourage and promote a greater and more diversified use of costumes in all fields of human activity. They provide trade information, cooperation and friendship among its members together with a sound public relations policy.
400 Members
Founded in: 1923

19299 National Dance Association
1900 Association Dr
Reston, VA 20191-1502

703-476-3400
800-213-7193; *Fax:* 703-476-9527
nda@aahperd.org; www.aahperd.org/nda
Social Media: Facebook, Twitter

Colleen Dean, Manager
Marcey E Siegel, VP Dance Education
Mary Ann Laverty, VP Dance Performance

A nonprofit service organization dedicated to increasing knowledge, improving skills and encouraging sound professional practices in dance education while promoting and supporting creative and healthy lifestyles through high quality dance programs.
2000 Members
Founded in: 1932

19300 National Dance Education Organization
8609 2nd Avenue
Suite 203 B
Silver Spring, MD 20910

301-585-2880; *Fax:* 301-585-2888
info@ndeo.org; www.ndeo.org

Susan McGreevy-Nichols, Executive Director
Patricia Cohen, Treasurer

A nonprofit organization dedicated to promoting standards of excellence in dance education.
2000 Members
Founded in: 1998

19301 National Endowment for the Arts
1100 Pennsylvania Ave NW
Washington, DC 20506

202-682-5400; *Fax:* 202-682-5611
webmgr@arts.gov; www.arts.gov
Social Media: Facebook, Twitter

Dana Gioia, CEO
Guilomar Barbi, Scheduler
Sarah Cook, Executive Assistant
Jon P Peede, Counselor to the Chairman
Sydney Smith, Administrative Specialist

The National Endowment for the Arts, an investment in America's living heritage, serves the public good by nurturing the expression of human creativity, supporting the cultivation of community spirit, and fostering the recognition and appreciation of the excellence and diversity of our nation's artistic accomplishments.

19302 National Music Publishers Association
101 Constitution Avenue NW
Suite 705 East
Washington, DC 20001

202-742-4375; *Fax:* 202-393-6673
pr@nmpa.org; www.nmpa.org
Social Media: Facebook, Twitter, YouTube, Instagram

Martin Bandier, President/CEO
John Eastman, Director

The NMPA is committed to promoting and advancing the interests of music publishers and their songwriting partners. Their goal is to foster a business climate that allows its members to thrive creatively and financially.
800 Members
Founded in: 1917

19303 National Performance Network
1024 Elysian Fields Avenue
New Orleans, LA 70117
504-595-8008; *Fax:* 504-595-8006
info@npnweb.org; www.npnweb.org
Social Media: Facebook, Twitter
Abe Rybeck, Chair
Yolanda Cesta Cursach, Vice Chair
MK Wegmann, President/ CEO
Meena Natarajan, Secretary
Shannon Daut, Treasurer
Founded in: 1985

19304 National Piano Travelers Association
401 Sawkill Road
PO Box 2264
Kingston, NY 12401-2264
845-338-1464; *Fax:* 845-338-5751;
www.pianotravelers.com
Roy Chandler, President
Bob dove, VP
Dawn Demars, Secretary/Treasurer
Buys and sells pianos.
110 Members

19305 Network of Ensemble Theaters
PO Box 83526
Portland, OR 97283
E-Mail: info@ensembletheaters.net;
www.ensembletheaters.net
Laurie McCants, President
August Schulenburg, Vice President
Mark Valdez, Executive Director
Cynthia Ling Lee, Secretary
Bruce Allardice, Treasurer
Founded in: 1995

19306 New England Theatre Conference
215 Knob Hill Drive
Hamden, CT 06518
617-851-8535; *Fax:* 203-288-5938
mail@netconline.org; www.netconline.org
James Fergudon, President
Jeffrey Watts, Executive VP
Jamie Taylor, VP Administration/Finance
Chris Crossen-sills, Executive Secretary
Jim Quinn, Clerk of the Corporation
Non-profit corporation, composed of individuals and organizations in the six-State region of New England, who are active and interested in the performing arts. The NETC promotes excellence in theatre for their region, and supports quality theatre and performance in all of its diversity.
500 Members
Founded in: 1952

19307 New Music USA
90 Broad St.
Suite 1902
New York, NY 10004
212-645-6949
info@newmusicusa.org;
www.newmusicusa.org
Social Media: Facebook, Twitter, Vimeo
Ed Harsh, President & CEO
Frederick Peters, Chair
Part of the Performing Arts Alliance, New Music USA advocates for the creation and performance of new music.

19308 North American Drama Therapy Association
Suite 101
Suite 220
Albany, NY 12203
888-416-7167
888-416-7167; *Fax:* 518-463-8656;
www.nadta.org
Social Media: Facebook, Twitter, YouTube, Instagram
Nadya Trytan, President
Jason Butler, President-Elect
Jeremy Segall, Vice President
Whitney Sullivan, Secretary
Dani York, Treasurer
Founded in: 1979

19309 North American Performing Arts Managers and Agents
459 Columbus Ave
Suite 133
New York, NY 10024-5129
212-362-8304
800-867-3281
info@napama.org; www.napama.org
Richard Baird, Owner
David Wannen, VP
Jerry Ross, VP
Susan Endrizzi Moris, Secretary
Robin Pomerance, Treasurer
National nonprofit trade association dedicated to promoting the professionalism of its members and the vitality of the performing arts. NAPAMA promotes the mutual advancement and the best interests of performing arts managers and agents; promotes open discourse among members and within the larger field; gives active consideration and expression of opinion on questions affecting the industry and develops and encourages ethical and sound business practices.
Cost: $150.00
Founded in: 1979

19310 OPERA America
330 Seventh Avenue
New York, NY 10001
212-796-8620; *Fax:* 212-796-8621
Info@operaamerica.org;
www.operaamerica.org
Social Media: Facebook, Twitter, Google+, YouTube
Dr. Frayda B. Lindemann, Chairman
Susan F. Morris, Vice Chairman
Marc A. Scorca, President/ CEO
William Florescu, Secretary
Timothy O'Leary, Treasurer
Founded in: 1973

19311 Oratorio Society of New York
1440 Broadway
23rd Floor
New York, NY 10018-9759
212-400-7255
president@oratoriosocietyofny.org;
www.oratoriosocietyofny.org
Social Media: Facebook, Twitter, Youtube
Richard A Pace, Chairman & President
Mary J.Knight, Vice President
Marie Gangemi, Treasurer
Jay Jacobson, Secretary
Kent Tritle, Music Director
New York City's second oldest cultural organization. On December 25, 1874 the society began what has become an unbroken tradition of annual performances of Handel's Messiah (at Carnegie Hall since its opening in 1891).
Founded in: 1873

19312 Performing Arts Alliance
1211 Connecticut Ave. NW
Suite 200
Washington, DC 20036
202-207-3850; *Fax:* 202-833-1543
info@theperformingartsalliance.org;
www.theperformingartsalliance.org
Social Media: Facebook, Twitter
Mario Garcia Durham, Chair
The Alliance advocates for federal policy that fosters the contributions to society of America's professional nonprofit arts organizations and artists.
30K Members
Founded in: 1977

19313 Performing Arts Association
719 Edmond St
St Joseph, MO 64501-2268
816-279-1225
info@paastjo.org;
www.saintjosephperformingarts.org
Social Media: Facebook, Twitter
David Cripe, President
Elaine Smith, VP
Debbie Demuth, Secretary
Kim Lueger, Treasurer
Beth Sharp, Director
Mission is to provide a diverse selection of performing arts in the St. Joseph area by presenting programs that foster, increase and promote public knowledge and appreciation of music, theatre and dance and lectures on subjects of cultural interests.
Founded in: 1979

19314 Performing Arts Medicine Association
PO Box 117
Englewood, CO 80151
303-808-5643; *Fax:* 866-408-7069
webmaster@artsmed.org; www.artsmed.org
Social Media: Facebook, Twitter, LinkedIn
Julie Massaro, Executive Director
Mary Fletcher, Consultant
John Chong, President
Dorry Allen, Manager of Member Services
Organization for physicians and other professionsl persons who are involved in treatment and/or research in the field of Performing Arts Medicine.
Founded in: 1989

19315 Piano Manufacturers Association
14070 Proton Road
Suite 100
Dallas, TX 75244
972-233-9107; *Fax:* 972-490-4219;
www.pianonet.com
Donald W Dillon, Executive Director
Piano industry trade association.
Founded in: 1991

19316 Piano Technicians Guild
4444 Forest Avenue
Kansas City, KS 66106
913-432-9975; *Fax:* 913-432-9986
ptg@ptg.org; www.ptg.org
Social Media: Facebook, Twitter, YouTube
Barbara Cassaday, Executive Director
Jim Coleman, President
Norman R. Cantrell, VP
Phil A Bondi, Secretary/Treasurer
A nonprofit organization serving piano tuners, technicians, and craftsman throughout the world, organized to promote the highest possible service and technical standards among piano tuners and technicians.
4100 Members
Founded in: 1957

19317 Production Music Library Association
1600 Aspen Commons
Suite 100
Middleton, WI 53562
608-836-5825; *Fax:* 608-831-8200
mla@areditions.com;

www.musiclibraryassoc.org
Social Media: Facebook, Twitter

Jerry L McBride, President
Michael Colby, VP
Pamela Bristah, Secretary

Provides a forum for issues surrounding music, music in libraries, and music librarianship. Members include music librarians, librarians who work with music as part of their responsibilities, composers and music scholars, and others interested in the program of the association.
20 Members
Founded in: 1931

19318 Professional Women Singers Association
P.O. Box 29
Deer Park, NY 11729

212-969-0590; *Fax:* 928-395-2560
professionalwomensingers@gmail.com;
www.womensingers.org
Social Media: Facebook

Elissa Weiss, President
Allison Atteberry, First VP
Sarah Downs, Second VP
Ruth Ann Cunningham, Secretary
Mary Lou Zobel, Treasurer

Non-profit networking organization for professional women singers. The group sponsors concerts, master classes and seminars for both singers and the community at large.
40 Members
Founded in: 1982

19319 Roundalab - International Association of Round Dance Teachers
2803 Louisiana Street
Longview, WA 98632-3536

360-423-7423
877-943-2623
roundalab@roundalab.org; www.roundalab.org
Social Media: Facebook

Frank & Sandy Hartzel, General Chairman
Terri & Tim Wilaby, Vice Chairman
Mary & Bob Townsend-Manning, Marketing Membership

Supports all those involved in the field of round dancing. Publishes quarterly magazine.
Founded in: 1974
Mailing list available for rent

19320 Screen Actors Guild - American Federation of Television and Radio Artists
5757 Wilshire Blvd
7th Floor
Los Angeles, CA 90036-3600

323-954-1600
855-724-2387; *Fax:* 323-549-6792
sagaftrainfo@sagaftra.org; www.sagaftra.org
Social Media: Facebook, Twitter, Instagram, YouTube, RSS

Gabrielle Carteris, President
David White, National Executive Director
Duncan Crabtree-Ireland, Chief Operating Officer
Mary Cavallaro, Chief Broadcast Officer
Pam Greenwalt, Chief Communications & Marketing

Formerly the Screen Actors Guild. Labor union affiliated with AFL-CIO which represents actors in film, television and commercials. The Guild exists to enhance actors' working conditions, compensation and benefits and to be a powerful, unifed voice on behalf of artists' rights.

19321 Society of American Magicians
PO Box 510260
Saint Louis, MO 63151-0260

314-846-5659; *Fax:* 314-846-5659
rmblowers@aol.com; www.magicsam.com
Social Media: Facebook, Twitter

J.Christopher Bontjes, President
Bruce Kalver, First VP
Mike Miller, Second VP
Chuck Lehr, Secretary
Mary Ann Blowers, Treasurer

Founded to promote and maintain harmonious fellowship among those interested in magic as an art, to improve ethics of the magical profession, and to foster, promote and improve the advancement of magical arts in the field of amusement and entertainment. Membership includes professional and amateur magicians, manufacturers of magical apparatus and collectors.
5.5M Members
Founded in: 1902

19322 Society of Stage Directors & Choreograhers
321 W. 44th Street
Suite 804
New York, NY 10036

212-391-1070; *Fax:* 212-302-6195
Info@SDCweb.org; www.sdcweb.org
Social Media: Facebook, Twitter, LinkedIn, Google+, Instagram

Susan H Schulman, President
John Rando, Executive Vice President
Leigh Silverman, Vice President
Oz Scott, Secretary
Ethan McSweeny, Treasurer
Founded in: 1965

19323 Society of Stage Directors and Choreographers
321 W. 44th Street
Suite 804
New York, NY 10036-5653

212-391-1070
800-541-5204; *Fax:* 212-302-6195
Info@SDCweb.org; www.sdcweb.org
Social Media: Facebook, Twitter, LinkedIn, Google+, Instagram

Susan H Schulman, President
John Rando, Executive Vice President
Leigh Silverman, Vice President
Oz Scott, Secretary
Ethan McSweeny, Treasurer

An independent labor union representing directors and choreographers in American theatre.
1700 Members
Founded in: 1965
Mailing list available for rent

19324 Southern Arts Federation
1800 Peachtree St NW
Suite 808
Atlanta, GA 30309-2512

404-874-7244; *Fax:* 404-873-2148;
www.southarts.org
Social Media: Facebook, Twitter, LinkedIn

Susie Surkamer, Executive Director
Stephanie Conner, Secretary
Ken May, Treasurer
David Batley, Marketing/Communications Director

In partnership with nine state arts agencies: promotes and supports arts regionally, nationally and internationally; enhances the artistic excellence and professionalism of Southern Arts Organizations and artists; serves the diverse population of the south.
Founded in: 1975

19325 Stage Directors and Choreographers Foundation
321 W. 44th Street
Suite 804
New York, NY 10036

212-391-1070; *Fax:* 212-302-6195
Info@SDCweb.org; www.sdcfoundation.org
Social Media: Facebook, Twitter, LinkedIn, Google+, Instagram

Susan H Schulman, President
John Rando, Executive Vice President
Leigh Silverman, Vice President
Oz Scott, Secretary
Ethan McSweeny, Treasurer
Founded in: 1965

19326 The Actors' Fund
729 Seventh Avenue, 10th floor
New York, NY 10019

212-221-7300
info@actorsfund.org; www.actorsfund.org
Social Media: Facebook, Twitter, LinkedIn, YouTube

Brian Stokes Mitchell, Chairmen
Philip S. Birsh, Vice Chair
Marc Grodman, Secretary
Abby Schroeder, Assistant Secretary
Steve Kalafer, Treasurer
Founded in: 1882

19327 The United States Disc Jockey Association
Post Office Box 43252
Nottingham, ML 21236

443-903-2013
support@usdja.com; www.usdja.com
Social Media: Facebook, Twitter, Vimeo

Jason Walsh, President

19328 Theatre Authority
165 West 46th Street
New York, NY 10036

212-869-8530; *Fax:* 212-719-9815;
www.actorsequity.org/benefits/theatreauthority.asp

Presides over theatrical agencies and performing arts organizations.

19329 Theatre Bay Area
1119 Market Street
2nd Floor
San Francisco, CA 94103

415-430-1140; *Fax:* 415-430-1145
tba@theatrebayarea.org;
www.theatrebayarea.org
Social Media: Facebook, Twitter, Pinterest, YouTube

Karen Mc Kevitt, Executive Director
Dale Albright, Director, Member Services
Clayton Lord, Director, Audience Development

Theatre Bay Area's mission is to unite, strengthen and promote the theatre community in the San Francisco Bay Area, working on behalf of their conviction that the performing arts are an essential public good, critical to a healthy and truly democratic society, and invaluable as a source of personal enrichment and growth.
3,000 Members
Founded in: 1976

19330 Theatre Communications Group
520 8th Ave
24th Floor
New York, NY 10018-8666

212-609-5900; *Fax:* 212-609-5901
tcg@tcg.org; www.tcg.org
Social Media: Facebook, Twitter, Instagram

Theresa Eyring, Executive Director
Jennifer Cleary, Director of Membership

The mission of the TCG is to strengthen, nurture and promote the professional not-for-profit American theatre. TCG believes that their diversity as a field is their greatest strength. They celebrate differences in aesthetic, culture, organizational structure, and geography. They believe that every theatre makes a contribution to the greater field as a whole, that every performance expands the artistic vocabulary for us all, and that we all benefit from one another's presence.
Cost: $39.95
14000 Members
Frequency: Monthly
Founded in: 1961

19331 Theatre Development Fund
520 Eight Avenue
Suite 801
New York, NY 10018-6507

212-912-9770
info@tdf.org; www.tdf.org
Social Media: Facebook, Twitter, YouTube, Google+

Earl D. Weiner, Chairman
Sandra Kresch, Vice Chairman
Robert T. Goldm Treasurer, Deborah Hartnett Secretary

Not-for-profit service organization for the performing arts. TDF administers a wide range of audience development and financial assistance programs that encourage production of new plays and musicals and enable more New Yorkers and visitors to enjoy the riches and variety of the city's theatre, dance and music.
Cost: $25.00
Founded in: 1968

19332 US Institute for Theatre Technology
315 S Crouse Ave
Suite 200
Syracuse, NY 13210-1835

315-463-6463
800-938-7488; *Fax:* 315-463-6525
info@.usitt.org; www.usitt.org
Social Media: Facebook, Twitter, LinkedIn, Instagram, Pinterest

Carol Carrigan, Manager
Patricia Dennis, Secretary
Travis DeCastro, Treasurer

Association of design, production and technology professionals in the performing arts and entertainment industry whose mission is to promote the knowledge and skills of its members. International in scope, USITT draws its board of directors from across the US and Canada. Sponsors projects, programs, research, symposia, exhibits and annual conference. Disseminates information on aesthetic and technical developments.
3700 Members
Founded in: 1960

19333 USA Dance Inc
PO Box 152988
Cape Coral, FL 33915-2988

800-447-9047; *Fax:* 239-573-0946
central-office@usadance.org
usadance.org
Social Media: Facebook, Twitter, LinkedIn, YouTube

Lydia Scardina, National President
Bill Rose, Sr.Vice President
Greg Warner, National Secretary
Esther Freeman, National Treasurer
Ken Richards, VP, Dance Sports

Nonprofit organization working to promote ballroom dancing, both as a recreational activity and as a competitive sport, and to educate the public about the mental, physical and social benefits of dance.
23000 Members
Founded in: 1965

19334 United Square Dancers of America

E-Mail: usda@usda.org; www.usda.org
Social Media: Facebook

Mike Matsko, President
L Paul Schmidt, Vice President
Jim Maczko, Past President
Milene McCall, Secretary
Jim Taylor, Treasurer
Founded in: 1981

19335 United States Association of Fringe Festivals
www.fringefestivals.us

Association of alternative performing arts festivals.

19336 United States Institute for Theatre Technology
315 South Crouse Avenue
Suite 200
Syracuse, NY 13210

315-463-6463
800-938-7488; *Fax:* 800-938-7488
info@usitt.org; www.usitt.org
Social Media: Facebook, Twitter, LinkedIn, Instagram, Pinterest

Lea Asbell Swanger, President
Carolyn Satter, Vice President
David Grindle, Executive Director
Jimmie Byrd, Secretary
Dan Culhane, Treasurer
Founded in: 1960

19337 Voice and Speech Trainers Association

773-888-2782
president@vasta.org; www.vasta.org

Lynn Watson, President
Betty Moulton, President Elect
Mandy Rees, Past President
Melanie Julian, Secretary
Artemis Preeshl, Treasurer
Founded in: 2005

19338 Women in the Arts Foundation
C/O E Butler
245 Broome Street
New York, NY 10002

212-941-0130
info@nyartistsequity.org;
www.nyartistsequity.org/
Social Media: Twitter, Instagram

Regina Stewart, Executive Director
Eric Butler, Executive Coordinator
Linda Butti, Executive Coordinator
Sari Menna, Financial Coordinator

WIA works to overcome discrimination against women artists. They provide information to help women function effectively as professional artists. WIA is open to all women interested in the arts.
150 Members
Founded in: 1971

19339 Writers Guild of America
7000 West Third Street
Los Angeles, CA 90048

323-951-4000; *Fax:* 323-782-4800;
www.wga.org
Social Media: Facebook, Twitter, YouTube,RSS

Chris Keyser, President
Howard A. Rodman, Vice President
Carl Gottlieb, Secretary/ Treasurer
Billy Ray, Board of Directors
Shawn Ryan, Board of Directors
Founded in: 1921

Newsletters

19340 American Dance
240 West 14th Street
New York, NY 10011

212-932-2789
info@americandanceguild.org;
www.americandanceguild.org
Social Media: Facebook

Gloria McLean, President
Tina Croll, VP

Contains articles on member news, dance, and education.
Frequency: 4 per year
Founded in: 1956

19341 Artsearch
Theatre Communications Group
520 8th Ave
Suite 305
New York, NY 10018-4156

212-609-5900; *Fax:* 212-609-5901
tcg@tcg.org; www.tcg.org

Theresa Eyring, Executive Director

Artsearch is divided into five main categories: Administration, Artistic, Production/Design, Career Development, and Education.
Cost: $75.00
Frequency: Bi-Monthly
ISSN: 0730-9023
Founded in: 1961
Printed in on newsprint stock

19342 Broadside
Theatre Library Association
New York Public Library for Performing Arts
40 Lincoln Center Plaza
New York, NY 10023

E-Mail: info@tla-online.org;
www.tla-online.org/publications/broadside.htm
l

Nancy Friedland, President
Angela Weaver, VP
Rebecca Lord, Executive Secretary
Collen Reilly, Treasurer

Features articles and news items related to exhibitions and collections, information about TLA-sponsored events, book reviews, and other items of interest in the fields of theatre, film, and dance.
ISSN: 0068-2748
Founded in: 1937

19343 Country Dance and Song Society News
Country Dance and Song Society
116 Pleasant St
Suite 345
Easthampton, MA 01027-2759

413-203-5467; *Fax:* 413-203-5471
news@cdss.org; www.cdss.org

Caroline Batson, Editor
Rima Dael, Executive Director
Bob Blondin, Business Manager

A selection of articles, letters and poems. CDSS News is available as a benefit of membership in the Country Dance and Song Society.
ISSN: 1070-8251
Founded in: 1915

19344 **DNBulletin**
151 W 30th Street
Suite 202
New York, NY 10001

212-564-0985; *Fax:* 212-216-9027
dnbinfo@dancenotation.org;
www.dancenotation.org

Senta Driver, Editor

Dance news for consumers and professionals.
Founded in: 1940
Printed in 2 colors on matte stock

19345 **Dancedrill**
3101 Poplarwood Court
Suite 310
Raleigh, NC 27604-1010

919-872-7888; *Fax:* 919-872-6888

Susan Wershing, Publisher
Kay Crawford, Editor

Publication informs members of dance drill teams and their directors.
Frequency: 4 per year

19346 **Dramatists Guild Newsletter**
Dramatists Guild of America
1501 Broadway
Suite 701
New York, NY 10036-5505

212-398-9366; *Fax:* 212-944-0420;
www.dramaguild.com

Ralph Sevush, Executive Director

Supplement to 'The Dramatist,' available only to Guild members, includes bi-monthly reports from New York and Los Angeles, advice from the Business Affairs Department, the latest information on submission and career development opportunities, and reminders of approaching deadlines.

19347 **INTIX Bulletin**
International Ticketing Association
One College Park, 8910 Purdue Road
Suite 480
Indianapolis, IN 46268

212-629-4036; *Fax:* 212-628-8532
info@intix.org; www.intix.org

Jena L Hoffman, President
Kathleen O'Donnell, Director

E-bulletin provides news from the International Ticketing Association including information about upcoming events, conferences and exhibitions, industry news.
1200 Members
Frequency: Monthly
ISSN: 1071-6254
Founded in: 1979
Printed in 4 colors on glossy stock

19348 **In Focus**
National Association of Theatre Owners
13190 SW 68th Parkway
Suite 200
Portland, OR 97223-8368

503-207-4700
877-388-8385; *Fax:* 503-207-1937
http://www.infocus.com

19349 **In Theater**
Parker Publishing & Communications
214 Sullivan St
Suite 2C
New York, NY 10012-1354

212-228-1225; *Fax:* 212-719-4477;
www.parker-publishing.com

Emily Parker, President

Offers the reader a behind-the-scenes perspective of how a show is technically conceived, rehearsed and staged. Regular departments center on drama and musical reviews, listings of shows in major cities and columnist options.
Cost: $78.00
Frequency: Weekly
Circulation: 71,068

19350 **InLEAGUE**
League of Historic American Theatres
2105 Laurel Bush Rd
Suite 201
Bel Air, MD 21015

443-640-1058
877-627-0833; *Fax:* 443-640-1031
info@lhat.org; www.lhat.org

Frances Holden, Executive Director
John Bell, VP
Darlene Smolik, Treasurer
Edward Kelsey, Secretary

Quarterly newsletter which reports news from historic theatre progects around the country and features articles on all facets of historic theatre restoration and operation. The newsletter solicits articles and information from the membership.
Frequency: Quarterly
Founded in: 1976

19351 **Job Contact Bulletin**
Southeastern Theatre Conference
1175 Revolution Mill Dr.
Studio 14
Greensboro, NC 27405

336-272-3645; *Fax:* 336-272-8810
arpil@setc.org; www.setc.org

April J'C Marshall, Contact
Jack Benjamin, President
H. Duke Guthrie, Treasurer

On-line employment listing of Classified Ads for theatrical positions, auditions, and more.
Founded in: 1949

19352 **Performing Arts Insider**
PAI C/O Total Theater
PO Box 31
Greeley, CO 80632

970-405-3077
totalpost@totaltheater.com
performingartsinsider.com
Social Media: Facebook, Twitter

A leading source of information about the perfoming arts in New York City and around the country. Each issue includes day-by-day calendar listings of shows on broadway, off and off-off broadway, plus dance, opera, cabaret and special events. Also includes comprehensive theatre guides, listing the author, director, cast, designers, synopsis, theater and box office details, as well as contact information for producers, press agents, general managers and casting directors.
Cost: $275.00
Frequency: Monthly+9 Mid-Month Updat
Founded in: 1944
Printed in on matte stock

19353 **SETC News**
Southeastern Theatre Conference
1175 Revolution Mill Dr.
Studio 14
Greensboro, NC 27405

336-272-3645; *Fax:* 336-272-8810;
www.setc.org

Deanna Thompson, Editor
Jack Benjamin, President
H. Duke Guthrie, Treasurer

Provides news and important information to members of the Southeaster Theatre Conference on upcoming SETC events, advocacy efforts, awards and competitions as well as items of special interest to the various divisions and interest areas. In addition, SETC News publishes news about people and organizations based in the Southeast.
Circulation: 4000
Founded in: 1949

19354 **Spotlight**
American Association of Community Theatre
1300 Gendy Street
Forth Worth, TX 76107

817-732-3177
866-687-2228; *Fax:* 817-732-3178
info@aact.org; www.aact.org
Social Media: Facebook, Twitter, LinkedIn

Julie Crawford, Executive Director
Murray Chase, President
David Cockerell, Marketing/Communications Director

News and updates on issues pertinent to community theatre.
Cost: $2.00
24 Pages
Circulation: 2000
Founded in: 1958
Mailing list available for rent: 9,500 names at $180 per M
Printed in on matte stock

19355 **Technical Brief**
Yale School of Drama
222 York Street
PO Box 208244
New Haven, CT 06520

203-432-8188; *Fax:* 203-432-8129
bronislaw.sammler@yale.edu;
www.technicalbrief.org

Ben Sammler, Editor
Dan Harvey, Editor

Produced for technical managers in theater. Written by professionals for professionals, its purpose is simple: communication. Technical Brief provides a dailogue between technical practitioners from the several performing arts who all share similar problems.
Cost: $15.00
Frequency: 3 X Year
Founded in: 1924

19356 **Women in the Arts Bulletin**
Women in the Arts Foundation
32-35 30th Street
D24
Long Island City, NY 11106

212-941-0130
reginas@anny.org;
www.womenintheartsfoundation.org

Erin Butler, Editor
Regina Stewart, Executir Director
Sandra Cockerham, President

Gallery information and reviews. Women in the Arts Foundation works to overcome discrimination against women artists.
Frequency: Monthly
Founded in: 1971

Magazines & Journals

19357 **American Dancer**
USA Dance
PO Box 152988
Cape Coral, FL 33915-2988

800-447-9047; *Fax:* 239-573-0946;
www.usadance.org

Shawn Fisher, Editor

News of interests to dance enthusiasts.
Cost: $25.00
Frequency: Bi-Monthly
Circulation: 23000

19358 American Theatre Magazine
Theatre Communications Group
520 8th Ave
Suite 305
New York, NY 10018-8666

212-609-5900; *Fax:* 212-609-5901
custserve@tcg.org; www.tcg.org

Jim O'Quinn, Editor in Chief
Nicole Estvanik Taylor, Managing Editor
Cost: $35.00

19359 Applause Magazine
Denver Center for Performing Arts
1101 13th St
Denver, CO 80204-5319

303-893-3272
800-641-1222; *Fax:* 303-893-3206;
www.denvercenter.org

Randy Weeks, President
Daniel L. Ritchie, Chairman &CEO

A publication of the Denver Center Theatre Company and Dever Center Attractions
Frequency: 8-10 per year
Founded in: 1988
Printed in 4 colors on glossy stock

19360 Asian Pacific American Journal
Asian American Writers Workshop
16 W 32nd St
Suite 10A
New York, NY 10001-1093

212-494-0061; *Fax:* 212-494-0062
desk@aaww.org; www.aaww.org

Ken Chen, Executive Director
Jeannie L Wong, Adminstrative Director
Anjali Goyal, Programs Assistant
Jeffrey Lin, Designer
Hanya Yanagihara, Journal Editor

Features include short fiction, poems, essays, stage scripts, translations and artwork.
Frequency: Semi-Annual
ISSN: 1067-778X
Founded in: 1992

19361 Back Stage
770 Broadway 7th Floor
New York, NY 10003

212-493-4420
800-658-8372
advertising@backstage.com;
www.backstage.com

Charles Weiss, Manager
Jamie Painter Young, Editor-in-Chief
Jenelle Riley, Film/TV Editor
Leonard Jacobs, Theatre Editor
Sherry Eaker, Editor-at-Large

Four print, four interactive and two face-to-face publications. Provides casting, news, articles and other resources for working actors, cingers, dancers and behind-the-scenes staff and crew.
Cost: $84.00
Circulation: 30,000
Founded in: 1960
Mailing list available for rent

19362 Bomb Magazine
New Art Publications
80 Hanson Pl
Suite 703
Brooklyn, NY 11217-1506

718-636-9100
866-354-0334; *Fax:* 718-636-9200
info@bombsite.com; www.bombsite.com
Social Media: Facebook, Twitter, YouTube

Betsy Sussler, Publisher/Editor
Mary-Ann Monforton, Associate Publisher
Nell McClister, Senior Editor
Lucy Raven, Managing Editor
Paul W Morris, Director Marketing/Special Projects

Focuses on contemporary art, literature, theater, film, music.
Cost: $495.00
Frequency: Quarterly
Circulation: 60,000
Founded in: 1981
Mailing list available for rent
Printed in 4 colors on matte stock

19363 BoxOffice Magazine
BoxOffice Media
9107 Wilshire Blvd.
Suite 450
Beverly Hills, CA 90210-4241

310-876-9090; www.boxoffice.com

Peter Crane, Publisher
Kenneth James Bacon, Creative Director
Phil Contrino, Editor
Amy Nicholson, Editor

The premier trade magazine covering the latest developments in the movie industry, from films in production to digital cinema and everything in between.
Founded in: 1948

19364 Callaloo
Johns Hopkins University Press
2715 N Charles St
Baltimore, MD 21218-4363

410-516-6900
800-537-5487; *Fax:* 410-516-6998;
www.press.jhu.edu/journals/callaloo

William Brody, President
Kyle G Dargan, Managing Editor

Journal of African and African-American issues. Content includes original works by, and critical studies of, black writers worldwide. Offers a rich mixture of fiction, poetry, plays, critical essays, cultural studies, interviews, and visual art, as well as special thematic issues.
Frequency: Quarterly
Circulation: 2,500
ISSN: 0161-2492
Founded in: 1976

19365 Canadian Theatre Review
University of Toronto Press
5201 Dufferin Street
Toronto, ON M3H-5T8

416-667-7810
800-221-9985; *Fax:* 416-667-7881
journals@utpress.utoronto.ca;
www.utpjournals.com
Social Media: Facebook, Twitter, Blog

Anne Marie Corrigan, VP
Audrey Greenwood, Advertising/Marketing Coordinator

Provides critical analysis and innovative coverage of current developments in Canadian theatre. Advocates new issues and artists. Publishes at least one significant new playscript per issue. Each issue includes at least one complete playscript related to the issue theme, insightful articles, and informative reviews.
Cost: $40.00
Frequency: Quarterly
ISSN: 0315-0836
Founded in: 1974
*Mailing list available for rent*at $250 per M

19366 Confrontation
CW Post Campus English Department
720 Northern Blvd
Greenvale, NY 11548-1300

516-626-0099; *Fax:* 516-299-3566;
www.liunet.bkstore.com

Jayne Mo, Manager

Brings new talent to light in the shadows cast by well-known authors. Each issue contains orignal work by famous and by lesser known writers.
Cost: $10.00
Frequency: Twice Yearly
Founded in: 1968

19367 Contact Quarterly Journal of Dance and Improvisation
Contact Collaborations
PO Box 603
Northampton, MA 01061

413-586-1181; *Fax:* 413-586-9055
info@contactquarterly.com;
www.contactquarterly.com

Lisa Nelson, Co-Editor
Nancy Stark Smith, Co-Editor
Melinda Buckwalter, Associate Editor
Kristin Horrigan, Operations Manager/Advertising
Bill McCully, Development/Marketing

A journal of dance, improvisation, performance and contemporary movement arts. Presents materials that spring from the experience of doing. Encourages articulation and dialogue and stimulates activity and exploration within the field of movement and its performance.
Cost: $22.00
Frequency: BiAnnual
Founded in: 1978

19368 Cue Magazine
PO Box 2027
Burlingame, CA 94011-2027

415-348-8004; *Fax:* 650-348-7781;
www.cuemagazines.com

Devoted to the Northern California, Seattle and Portland commercial film, video and multimedia industries and locations that support production.
Frequency: Monthly

19369 Dance Chronicle
Taylor & Francis Group
270 Madison Ave
Floor 4
New York, NY 10016-0601

212-679-3853; *Fax:* 212-564-7854;
www.summitcom.com

George Dorris, Co-Editor
Jack Anderson, Co-Editor
Edwin Bayrn, Associate Editor

Covers a wide variety of topics, including dance and music, theater, film, literature, painting and aesthetics.
Cost: $465.00
Frequency: TriAnnual
ISSN: 0147-2526

19370 Dance Magazine
Macfadden Performing Arts Media
333 7th Avenue
11th Floor
New York, NY 10001

212-979-4800; www.dancemagazine.com

Amy Cogan, VP/Group Publisher
Karen Hildebrand, VP Editorial
Jessi Petrov, Publishing/Marketing Director
Wendy Perron, Editor-in-Chief

The must read magazine for professional and aspiring dancers. From Broadway to ballet and tap to hip hop, not other magazine keeps you in touch with what is going on in all disciplines of dance.
Cost: $34.95
Frequency: Monthly
Circulation: 300,000
ISSN: 0011-6009
Founded in: 1927
Printed in 4 colors on glossy stock

19371 Dance Research Journal
Congress on Research in dance

7044 South 13th Street
Oak Creek, WI 53154

414-908-4951; *Fax:* 414-768-8001
info@cordance.org; www.cordance.org

Ann Dils, Co-Editor
Jill Green, Co-Editor

Published three times a year by the Congress on Research in Dance, this journal carries scholarly articles, book reviews, lists of books and journals received, and reports of scholarly conferences, archives and other projects of interest to the field.
Frequency: 3x/Year
Founded in: 1965
Mailing list available for rent

19372 Dance Spirit
Macfadden Performing Arts Media, LLC
333 7th Avenue
11th Floor
New York, NY 10001

212-979-4800; www.dancespirit.com

Amy Cogan, VP/Group Publisher
Karen Hildebrand, VP Editorial
Jessi Petrov, Publishing/Marekting Director
Kayte Lydon, Editor-in-Chief

Dedicated to inspiring the next generation of dancers. Packed with expert advice on dance techniques and performing, health and nutrition tips and the latest styles to keep you looking your best from studio to stage to school.
Cost: $16.95
Frequency: 10 Per Year
Founded in: 1980

19373 Dance Teacher Magazine
Macfadden Performing Arts Media
333 7th Avenue
11th Floor
New York, NY 10001

212-979-4800; *Fax:* 646-459-4900;
www.dance-teacher.com

Amy Cogan, VP/Group Publisher
Karen Hildebrand, VP Editorial/Editor-in-Chief
Jessie Petrov, Publishing/Marketing Director

The only magazine written just for dance professionals. Packed with useful ideas that will help you and your students become better dancers.
Cost: $24.95
Frequency: Monthly
Circulation: 60000
Founded in: 1979
Printed in 4 colors

19374 Dance on Camera Journal
Dance Films Association
48 W 21st St
Suite 907
New York, NY 10010-6989

212-727-0764; *Fax:* 212-727-0764
info@dancefilms.org; www.dancefilms.org
Social Media: Facebook, Twitter

Deidra Towers, Executive Director
Marta Renzi, President
Harry Streep, VP
Amy Meharg, Treasurer
Nolini Barretto, Secretary

Subjects range from reviews and essays, news items regarding dance films, festivals, opportunites, and issues facing artists
Frequency: Bi-Monthly
Founded in: 1956

19375 Dance/USA Journal
Dance/USA
1111 16th St Nw
Suite 300
Washington, DC 20036-4830

202-833-1717; *Fax:* 202-833-2686
danceusa@danceusa.org; www.danceusa.org

Andrea Snyder, Executive Director
Tom Thielen, Director Finance/Operations
Katherine Fabian, Membership Manager

The journal features articles on issues of importance to the dance community; news stories relating to arts and dance; essays from leaders in the dance field; notes on changes, transitions and opportunties in the field; calendar of up coming events; and highlights of Dance/USA sponsored events. Subscription is free to members of Dance/USA.
Cost: $40.00
28-36 Pages
Frequency: Quarterly
Founded in: 1982
Printed in 2 colors on glossy stock

19376 Descant
50 Baldwin Street
PO Box 314 Station P
Toronto, ON M5S-2S8

416-593-2557; *Fax:* 416-593-9362;
www.descant.ca
Social Media: Facebook

Karen Mulhallen, Editor-in-Chief
Vera DeWaard, Managing Editor
Mary Newberry, Project Manager
Stacey May Fowles, Circulation Manager
Pasha Malla, Director of Outreach

A quarterly journal publishing new and established contemporary writers and visual artists from Canada and around the world. Devoted to the discovery and development of new writers, and places their work in the company of celebrated writers.
Cost: $28.00
Frequency: Quarterly
Circulation: 1200
ISSN: 0382-909X
Founded in: 1970
Mailing list available for rent

19377 Drama Review
MIT Press
55 Hayward Street
Cambridge, MA 02142-1493

617-253-5646
800-207-8354; *Fax:* 617-258-6779
journals-info@mit.edu; www.mitpress.mit.edu
Social Media: Facebook, Twitter, RSS

Rebbecca Mc Leod, Owner

TDR focuses on performances in their social, economic, and political conctexts. It emphasizes experimental, avant-garde, intercultural and interdisciplinary performance. TDR covers dance, theatre, performance art, visual art, popular entertainment, media, sports, rituals, and performance in politics and everyday life.
Frequency: Quarterly
Founded in: 1955

19378 Dramatics Magazine
Educational Theatre Association
2343 Auburn Ave
Cincinnati, OH 45219-2819

513-421-3900; *Fax:* 513-421-7077
jpalmarini@schooltheatre.org
schooltheatre.org
Social Media: Facebook, Twitter

Donald A Corathers, Publications Director
James Palmarini, Editor

Dramatics is the only magazine that is edited exclusively for students and teachers of theatre. Contents include practical articles about acting, directing, playwriting, design, and technical theatre; interviews with working professionals that illuminate the process of becoming a theatre artist; options for higher education and training in theatre; playscripts; reports on new shows and other important events in the theatre world; book, video, and CD-ROM reviews, and more.
Cost: $27.00
4000 Members
Frequency: 9x/ A Year
Circulation: 34100
ISSN: 0012-5989
Founded in: 1929

19379 Encore Performance Publishing
PO Box 95567
South Jordan, UT 84095-0567

801-282-8159
encoreplay@aol.com; www.encoreplay.com

Michael C Perry, President

Publishes a variety of publications for those professionals in the performing arts industry.

19380 Gospel Today
Gospel Today
PO Box 800
Fairburn, GA 30213

770-719-4825; *Fax:* 770-716-2660
admin@gospeltoday.com;
www.gospeltoday.com

Dr Teresa Hairston, Publisher

To provide a quality publication to inspire, educate, inform, and empower readers towards standards of Godly excellence.
Cost: $17.97
Frequency: 8 Per Year
Circulation: 250000
Founded in: 1989
Printed in 4 colors on glossy stock

19381 Hispanic Arts News
Association of Hispanic Arts
1025 Connecticut Ave
Suite 1000
Washington, DC 20036

202-657-5158
888-876-1240; *Fax:* 202-478-2767;
www.hispanics.einnews.com
Social Media: Facebook, Twitter

Features in depth articles on the local and national arts community, including artist profiles and a calendar of events.
Frequency: 9 Per Year
Mailing list available for rent: 5000 names at $80 per M

19382 JazzTimes
JazzTimes Magazine
Madavor Media,85 Quincy Ave
Suite 2
Quincy, MA 02169

617-706-9110
800-437-5828; *Fax:* 617-536-0102;
www.jazztimes.com

Glen Sabin, CEO
Eric Wynne, Consumer Advertising Director

JazzTimes contains extensive news coverage, award winning jazz journalism, hundreds of CD, Book and Video reviews, World class photography and award winning graphics, informative features and columns, special theme issues, special directories, readers poll and critic pics, and sound$weeps giveaways and prizes.
Cost: $23.95
Frequency: 10 Issues per y
Circulation: 86000
Founded in: 1980

19383 Journal of Arts Management, Law, Society
Heldref Publishers

325 Chestnut Street
Suite 800
Philadelphia, PA 19106
215-625-8900
800-354-1420; *Fax:* 202-296-5149
customer.service@taylorandfrancis.com;
www.heldref.org

James Denton, Executive Director

A resource for arts policymakters and analysts, sociologists, arts and cultural administrators, educators, trusteed, artists, lawyers, and citizens concerned with the performing, visual, and media arts as well as cultural affairs. Articles, commentaries, and reviews of publications address marketing, intellectual property, arts policy, arts law, governance, and cultural production and dissemination, from a variety of philosophical, disciplinary, and national and international perspectives.
Cost: $79.00
Frequency: Monthly
ISSN: 1063-2921
Founded in: 1956

19384 Journal of Dance Education
National Dance Education Organization
8609 2nd Avenue
Suite 203 B
Silver Spring, MD 20910

301-585-2880; *Fax:* 301-585-2888
info@ndeo.org; www.ndeo.org
Social Media: Facebook, Twitter

Susan McGreevy-Nichols, Executive Director
Jane Bonbright EdD, Executive Director
Patricia Cohen, Treasurer
Cost: $90.00
Frequency: Quarterly
Circulation: 2000
ISSN: 1529-0824

19385 Lighting Dimensions
Primedia Business
249 W 17th St
New York, NY 10011-5382

212-206-1894
800-827-3322; *Fax:* 212-514-3719
lightingdimensions.com

Doug MacDonald, Group Publisher
David Johnson, Associate Publisher/Editorial
Marian Sandberg-Dierson, Editor
Mark Newman, Managing Editor
Jennifer Hirst, Director

Trade publication for lighting professionals in film, theatre, television, concerts, clubs, themed environments, architecctural, commercial, and industrial lighting. Sponsors of the LDI Trade Show and the Broadway Lighting Master Classes.
Cost: $34.97
Frequency: 12/year
Circulation: 14,177
Founded in: 1989

19386 Mid-Atlantic Events Magazine
1800 Byberry Road
Suite 901
Huntingdon Valley, PA 19006

215-947-8600
800-521-8588; *Fax:* 215-947-8650
editor@eventsmagazine.com;
www.eventsmagazine.com
Social Media: Facebook, Twitter, YouTube

Jim Cohn, Publisher
Rich Kupka, Editor
Fred Cohn, VP Sales
Katie O'Connell, Director Sales/Marketing
Dana Kurtbek, Production

Focused on Hospitality in the Mid-Atlantic area. It assists the Associations, Corporations, Government, Group and Independent Meeting, Event and Travel Planners who are responsible for arranging Conventions, Trade Shows, Hotel Accommodations, Corporate/Group Travel, Meetings, Seminars, Conferences, Symposiums, Site Selections, Special Events, Banquets, Entertainment, Corporate Golf Outings and Golf Tournaments, Company Picnics, Team Building, Retreats, Board Meetings, Training & Development.
Circulation: 26000
ISSN: 0896-3967
Founded in: 1987
Mailing list available for rent
Printed in 8 colors on glossy stock

19387 National Squares
National Square Dance Convention
C/O Gene and Connie Triplett
2760 Polo Club Boulevard
Matthews, NC 28105

704-847-1265
Richp27890@aol.com;
www.nationalsquaredanceconvention.com

Dick/Linda Peterson, Editors
Gene/Connie Triplett, Circulation Managers
Dick/Linda Peterson, Public Relations

A national square dance magazine published by the National Executive Committee of the National Square Dance Convention.
Cost: $7.00
Frequency: Quarterly

19388 New England Theatre Journal
New England Theatre Conference
215 Knob Hill Drive
Hamden, CT 06518

617-851-8535; *Fax:* 203-288-5938
mail@netconline.org; www.netconline.org

Sabine Klein, President
Jeffrey Watts, Executive VP
Charles Emmons, VP Administration/Finance

Scholarly publication produced once per year. Includes book and theatre reviews, historical analyses, and other well-written articles by noted authors. Free to NETC members. Specifically designed to provide members, and others interested in live theatre arts, with the information and resources they need to enhance their careers, promote their groups, and sharpen their theatre skills.
Cost: $10.00
Frequency: Annual
Founded in: 1952

19389 Nouveau Magazine
Barbara Tompkins
5933 Stoney Hill Rd
New Hope, PA 18938-9602

215-794-5996; *Fax:* 215-794-8305;
www.nouveaumagazine.com

Barbara Tompkins, Publisher

Features theater reviews.
Frequency: Monthly
Founded in: 1981
Printed in 4 colors on glossy stock

19390 OffBeat
OffBeat
421 Frenchmen St
Suite 200
New Orleans, LA 70116-2039

504-944-4300
877-944-4300; *Fax:* 504-944-4306
offbeat@offbeat.com; www.offbeat.com
Social Media: Facebook, Twitter, Flickr

Jan Ramsy, Publisher
Joseph L Irrera, Managing Editor
Bunny Matthews, Senior Editor
Michael Jastroch, Magazine Design/Production
Doug Jackson, Distribution Manager

Consumer-oriented music magazine focusing on New Orleans and Louisiana music. Regular columns on Cajun music, zydeco, traditional and contemporary jazz, brass band (Mardi Gras second-line music), New Orleans R & B, Louisiana and delta blues, Gospel, modern and roots rock and our internationally-appreciated culture and cusine. Information on music fairs and festivals in the region is given.
Cost: $29.00
Frequency: Monthly
Circulation: 50000
ISBN: 1-090081-0 -
Founded in: 1985
Mailing list available for rent: 15000 names
Printed in 4 colors on newsprint stock

19391 Performing Arts Insider Magazine
PAI C/O Total Theater
PO Box 31
Greeley, CO 80632

970-405-3077
paipress@aol.com;
www.performingartsinsider.com

David Lefkowitz, Publisher/Editor
Richmond Shepard, Publisher
J. Weil, Advertising Sales

Includes day-by-day calendar listings of shows on Broadway, Off and Off-Off Broadway, plus dance, opera, cabaret and special events. Also included are comprehensive theater guides, listing the author, director, cast, designers, synopsis, theater and box office details, as well as contact information for producers, press agents, general managers and casting directors.
Cost: $275.00
Frequency: Monthly+9 Updates
Circulation: 2000
Founded in: 1944

19392 Performing Arts Resources
Theatre Library Association
New York Public Library for Performing Arts
40 Lincoln Center Plaza
New York, NY 10023

E-Mail: info@tla-online.org;
www.tla-online.org/publications/par.html

Nancy Friedland, President
Angela Weaver, VP
Rebecca Lord, Executive Secretary
Colleen Reilly, Treasurer

Features articles on resource materials in the fields of theatre, popular entertainment, film, television and radio, information on public and private collections, and essays on conservation and collection management of theatre arts materials.
Cost: $30.00
Frequency: Irregular
Circulation: 500
ISSN: 0360-3814
Founded in: 1974

19393 Playbill
34-15 61st Street
Woodside, NY 11377

212-557-5757; *Fax:* 212-682-2932
agans@playbill.com; www.playbill.com

Andrew Gans, Editor

The exclusive magazine for Broadway and Off-Broadway theatregoers, providing the information necessary for the understanding and enjoyment of each show, including features articles and columns by and about theatre personalities, entertainment, travel, fashion, dining and other editorial pieces geared to the lifestyle of the upscale, active theatre attendee. Playbill also serves New York's three most prominent performing arts venues - the Metropolitan Opera House, Lincoln Center and Carnegie Hall
Cost: $24.00
Frequency: Monthly
Founded in: 1884

19394 Plays: Drama Magazine for Young People
Plays Magazine
PO Box 600160
Newton, MA 02460
617-630-9100
800-630-5755; *Fax:* 617-630-9101;
www.playsmag.com
Elizabeth Preston, Editor
Includes eight to ten royalty-free one-act plays, arranged by age level. Modern and traditional plays for the celebration of all important holidays and occasions. Adaptable to all cast sizes with easy to follow instructions for settings and costumes. A complete source of original plays and programs for school-age actors and audiences.
Cost: $39.00
Frequency: 7 X Per Year
Circulation: 6000
Founded in: 1940
Printed in on matte stock

19395 Pointe Magazine
Macfadden Performing Arts Media LLC
333 7th Avenue
11th Floor
New York, NY 10001
212-979-4800; www.pointemagazine.com
Amy Cogan, VP/Group Publisher
Karen Hildebrand, VP Editorial
Jessie Petrov, Publishing/Marketing Director
Dedicated exclusively to the world of ballet.
Frequency: Bi-Monthly
Circulation: 120000

19396 Pollstar: Concert Hotwire
Pollstar
4697 W Jacquelyn Ave
Fresno, CA 93722-6443
559-271-7900; *Fax:* 559-271-7979
info@pollstar.com; www.pollstar.com
Gary Smith, COO
Shari Rice, VP
Gary Bongiovanni, CEO
Trade publication for the concert industry offering global coverage and information including concert tour schedules, ticket sales information and more.
Cost: $449.00
Frequency: Weekly
Circulation: 20000
Printed in 4 colors

19397 Shakespeare Bulletin
University of North Carolina
Department of English
9201 University City Boulevard
Charlotte, NC 28223
www.shakespeare-bulletin.org
Seymour Isenberg, Founding Editor
Andrew James Hartley, Editor
Jeremy Lopez, Theatre Review Editor
Genevieve Love, Book Review Editor
Kirk Melnikoff, Shakespeare on Film Editor
A peer-reviewed journal of performance and criticism and scholarship which provides commentary on Shakespeare and Renaissance drama through feature articles, thatre and film reviews, and book reviews. The journal is a member of the Conference of Editors of Learned Journals.
Cost: $35.00
Frequency: Quarterly
ISSN: 0748-2558
Founded in: 1982
Mailing list available for rent
Printed in on matte stock

19398 Show Music
Po Box A
East Haddam, CT 06423-0466
860-873-8664; *Fax:* 860-873-2329
rklink@goodspeed.org; www.showmusic.org
Ryan Klink, Managing Editor
Maz O Preeo, Editor-In-Chief
Internationally acclaimed by professionals and fans as the premier magazine covering musical theatre around the world. Show music combines insightful interviews and reviews of productions, recordings, videos and books.

19399 Sondheim Review
PO Box 11213
Chicago, IL 60611-0213
773-275-4254
800-584-1020; *Fax:* 773-275-4254
info@sondheimreview.com;
www.sondheimreview.com
Dedicated to the work of the musical theater and Broadway's foremost composer and lyricist, Stephen Sondheim. Each issue containes news, interviews, upcoming productions in the area, puzzles and more.
Cost: $19.95
Frequency: Quarterly
Circulation: 40000
ISSN: 1076-450X
Founded in: 1994
Mailing list available for rent: 6,000 names at $105 per M
Printed in on glossy stock

19400 Southern Theatre
Southeastern Theatre Conference
1175 Revolution Mill Dr.
Studio 14
Greensboro, NC 27405
336-272-3645; *Fax:* 336-272-8810
setc@setc.org; www.setc.org
Elizabeth Baun, Executive Director
April J'Callahan Marshall, Professional Theatre Services Mgr
Hardy Koenig, Educational Services Manager
Spotlights people, places and organizations within the region that are paving new paths in theatre. Includes low-cost strategies for design success, tips on hot markets for playwrights, new books of special interest, innovative ideas for marketing theatre, inside track on new trends and some of the region's up-and-coming theatre stars. Subscription is free with SETC membership.
Cost: $18.75
Frequency: Quarterly
Circulation: 4000+
Founded in: 1949

19401 Spectrum
110 S Jefferson Street
Dayton, OH 45402-3412
937-220-1600
800-247-1614; *Fax:* 937-220-1642;
www.thinktv.org
Social Media: Facebook, Twitter, YouTube
Jerry Kathman, President&CEO
Brad Mays, Treasurer
Alisa Poe, Secretary
ThinkTV's monthly member magazine. Contains program listings for both ThinkTV 16 and ThinkTV14 as well as interesting feature stories, station news and more.
Frequency: Weekly
Circulation: 18000
Founded in: 1959

19402 Stage of the Art
American Alliance for Theatre and Education
4908 Auburn Avenue
Bethesda, MD 20814-3474
301-200-1944; *Fax:* 301-280-1682;
www.aate.com
Social Media: Facebook, Twitter, RSS
David Young, Editor
JoBeth Gonzalez, Director Publications/Research
Published by the American Alliance for Theatre and Education.
Mailing list available for rent: 700 names at $150 per M

19403 Stagebill
Stagebill
144 E 44th Street
New York, NY 10017
212-476-0640; *Fax:* 212-983-5976
bmattison@stagebill.com;
www.avant-rus.com/stagebill
Fred B Tarter, Chairman/President/CEO
Gerry Byrne, Chairman/President/CEO
Ben Mattison, Editorial Contact
Publisher of the program magazines for the leading, theaters, symphonies, dance companies and performing arts centers in the United States. A national performing arts magazine.
Frequency: Monthly
Founded in: 1924

19404 Stages
Curtains
301 W 45th Street
Apartment 5A
New York, NY 10036-3825
Fax: 201-836-4107
Frank Scheck, Editor
Cost: $20.00
Frequency: Monthly
Circulation: 35,000

19405 TD & T: Theatre Design & Technology
US Institute for Theatre Technology
315 South Crouse Avenue
Suite 200
Syracuse, NY 13210
315-463-6525; *Fax:* 315-463-6525;
www.usitt.org
Social Media: Facebook, Twitter
David Roger, Editor
Arnold Wengrow, Book Review Editor
Michelle Smith, Membership/Advertising Manager
N Deborah Hazlett, Art Director
Published by United States Institute for Theatre Technology. Focuses on USITT's ten interest areas: architecture, costume design and technology, education, engineering, health and safety, lighting, management, scene design, sound design, and technical production.
3700 Members
Frequency: Quarterly

19406 Teaching Theatre Journal
Educational Theatre Association
2343 Auburn Ave
Cincinnati, OH 45219-2819
513-421-3900; *Fax:* 513-421-7077
jpalmarini@schooltheatre.org
schooltheatre.org
Social Media: Facebook, Twitter
Donald A Corathers, Publications Director
James Palmarini, Editor
For professional theatre educators. A typical issue includes an article on acting, directing, playwriting, or technical theatre; a profile of an outstanding educationl theatre program; a piece on curriculum design, assessment, or teaching methodology; and reports on current trends or is-

sues in the field, such as funding, standards, or certification.
4000 Members
Frequency: Quarterly
Circulation: 4000
ISSN: 1077-2561
Founded in: 1929

19407 **Technical Brief**
Yale School of Drama
222 York Street
PO Box 208244
New Haven, CT 06520

203-432-8188; *Fax:* 203-432-8129
bronislaw.sammler@yale.edu;
www.technicalbrief.org

Ben Sammler, Co-Editor
Don Harvey, Co-Editor

Written by professionals for professionals, providing a dialogue between technical practitioners from the several performing arts. The succinct articles, complete with mechanical drawings, represent the best solutions to recurring technical problems. Published October, January and April.
Cost: $15.00
Frequency: 3X Per Year
Founded in: 1924

19408 **Theater Magazine**
Yale School of Drama
1120 Chapel Street
P.O Box 1257
New Haven, CT 06505

203-432-1234; *Fax:* 203-432-6423
yalerep@yale.edu; www.yale.edu/drama

Tom Sellar, Editor
Laraine Sammler, Business Manager
Alex Grennan, Director of Business/Comm

Periodicals, essays and articles of the Yale School of Drama.
Cost: $22.00
Frequency: Annual+
Circulation: 2500
Founded in: 1924
Mailing list available for rent: 1.5M names
Printed in one color on matte stock

19409 **Theatre Bay Area Magazine**
1663 Mission Street
Suite 525
San Francisco, CA 94103

415-430-1140; *Fax:* 415-430-1145
tba@theatrebayarea.org;
www.theatrebayarea.org
Social Media: Facebook, Twitter, YouTube

Karen Mc Kevitt, Executive Director
Dale Albright, Director, Member Services
Clayton Lord, Director, Audience Development
Cost: $5.95
Frequency: Monthly
Circulation: 4500

19410 **Theatre Bill**
Jerome Press
332 Congress St
Suite 2
Boston, MA 02210-1217

617-423-3400; *Fax:* 617-423-7108;
www.showofthemonthtravel.com

Jerome Rosenfeld, Owner

19411 **Theatre Journal**
Johns Hopkins University Press
2715 N Charles St
Baltimore, MD 21218-4363

410-516-6900
800-537-5487; *Fax:* 410-516-6968
webmaster@jhupress.jhu.edu;
www.press.jhu.edu

William Brody, President
David Z Saltz, Co-Editor
Sonja Arsham Kuftinec, Performance Review Editor
James Peck, Book Review Editor
Bob Kowkabany, Managing Editor

One of the most authoritative and useful publications of theatre studies available today. Theatre Journal features social and historical studies, production reviews, and theoretical inquiries that analize dramatic texts and production. Official journal of the Association for Theatre in Higher Education.
Cost: $40.00
Frequency: Quarterly
Circulation: 2492
ISSN: 0192-2882
Founded in: 1878
Mailing list available for rent

19412 **Theatre Symposium**
Auburn University
1175 Revolution Mill Dr.
Studio 14
Greensboro, NC 27405

336-272-3645; *Fax:* 336-272-8810
setc@setc.org; www.setc.org

M Scott Phillips, Editor

An annual publication of works of scholarship resulting from a single topic meeting held on a southeastern university campus each year. Available to adult members only. A copublication of the Southeaster Theatre Conference and the University of Alabama Press.

19413 **Theatre Topics**
Johns Hopkins University Press
2715 N Charles St
Baltimore, MD 21218-4363

410-516-6900
800-537-5487; *Fax:* 410-516-6998
webmaster@jhupress.jhu.edu;
www.press.jhu.edu

William Brody, President
Sandra G Shannon, Co-Editor
DeAnna Toten Beard, Book Review Editor
Elanore Lampners, Managing Editor
Beverley Pevitts, Founding Editor

Focuses on performance studies, dramaturgy, and theatre pedagogy. Concise and timely articles on a broad array of practical, performance-oriented subjects, with special attention to topics of current interest to the profession. Keeps readers informed of the latest developments on the stage and in the classroom. The official journal of the Association for Theatre in Higher Education. Published in March and September.
Cost: $32.00
Frequency: Semi-Annually
Circulation: 1528
ISSN: 1054-8378
Founded in: 1878
Mailing list available for rent

19414 **Youth Theatre Journal**
American Alliance for Theatre and Education
4908 Auburn Ave
Bethesda, MD 20814

301-200-1944; *Fax:* 301-235-7108
info@aate.com; www.aate.com

A scholarly journal dedicated to advancing the study and practice of theatre and drama with, for, and by the people of all ages. It is concerned with all forms of scholarship of the highest quality that inform the fields of theatre for young audiences and drama/theatre education.
Cost: $25.00
Frequency: 2x/Year
Circulation: 1000
ISSN: 0892-9092
Mailing list available for rent: 700 names at $150 per M

Trade Shows

19415 **AACT WorldFest**
American Association of Community Theatre
1300 Gendy Street
Fort Worth, TX 76107-4036

817-732-3177
866-687-2228; *Fax:* 817-732-3178
info@aact.org; www.aact.org
Social Media: Facebook, Twitter, LinkedIn

Julie Crawford, Executive Director
Murray Chase, President
Carole Ries, Executive Vice President

The international gathering of community theatre professionals for a week-long showcase of performances from theatre troupes around the world.
Frequency: Every 4 Years

19416 **CinemaCon**
National Association of Theatre Owners
750 1st St NE
Suite 1130
Washington, DC 20002-4241

202-962-0054; *Fax:* 202-962-0370
nato@natodc.com; www.natoonline.org

John Fithian, President
Gary Klein, VP
Kathy Conroy, Executive Director

A gathering of cinema owners and operators.
4000 Members
Frequency: Annual/March

19417 **Community Theatre Management Conference**
American Association of Community Theatre
1300 Gendy Street
Fort Worth, TX 76107-4036

817-732-3177
866-687-2228; *Fax:* 817-732-3178
info@aact.org; www.aact.org
Social Media: Facebook, Twitter, LinkedIn

Julie Crawford, Executive Director
Murray Chase, President

Educational conference for professionals working in theatre management.
Frequency: Annual

19418 **Congress on Research in Dance Annual Conference**
Congress on Research in Dance
7044 South 13th Street
Oak Creek, WI 53154

414-908-4951; *Fax:* 414-768-8001
info@cordance.org; www.cordance.org

Anne Flynn, President
Petri Hoppu, Vice President
Cindy Lemek, CORD Association Manager
Frequency: November

19419 **EXPO**
Theatre Bay Area

870 Market Street
Suite 375
San Francisco, CA 94102-3002

415-430-1140; *Fax:* 415-430-1145
dale@theatrebayarea.org;
www.theatrebayarea.org

Dale Albright, Director of Individual Services

Theatre Bay Area's EXPO is where attendees can meet those kinds of businesses that might offer services to the theatre community: theatre companies, actors, etc. There are also break-out sessions discussing issues of interest to the theatre community.
500+ Attendees
Frequency: May

19420 **EdTA Thespian Festival**
Educational Theatre Association
2343 Auburn Ave
Cincinnati, OH 45219-2819

513-421-3900; *Fax:* 513-421-7077;
www.schooltheatre.org
Social Media: Facebook, Twitter

Michael Peitz, Executive Director
Gloria McIntyre, President
Jay Seller VP

The premiere showcase for high school theatre, drawing students and teachers from throughout the United States and abroad.
3000 Attendees

19421 **Educational Theatre Association Conference**
Educational Theatre Association
2343 Auburn Ave
Cincinnati, OH 45219-2819

513-421-3900; *Fax:* 513-421-7077;
www.schooltheatre.org
Social Media: Facebook, Twitter

Michael Peitz, Executive Director
Gloria McIntyre, President
Jay Seller VP
400 Attendees
Frequency: Annual

19422 **International Association of Venue Managers**
International Association of Assembly Managers
635 Fritz Drive
Suite 100
Coppell, TX 75019-4442

972-906-7441
800-935-4226; *Fax:* 972-906-7418;
www.iaam.org

Steven Peters, President
Robyn Williams, First Vice President
Frequency: Annual

19423 **NDEO National Conference**
National Dance Education Organization
8609 2nd Avenue
Suite 203 B
Silver Spring, MD 20910

301-585-2880; *Fax:* 301-585-2888
info@ndeo.org; www.ndeo.org

Susan McGreevy-Nichols, Executive Director
Jane Bonbright EdD, Executive Director
Patricia Cohen, Treasurer

Provides 200+ professional development sessions for artists, educators and administrators teaching or supporting dance education programs in PreK-12, colleges/universities, private studio/schools of dance, community centers and performing arts organizations.
800 Attendees
Frequency: Annual

19424 **National AACTFest**
American Association of Community Theatre
1300 Gendy Street
Fort Worth, TX 76107-4036

817-732-3177; *Fax:* 817-732-3178
info@aact.org; www.aact.org

Julie Crawford, Executive Director
Murray Chase, President

National theatre festival showcasing the top acts of AACT's state and regional festivals, as well as offering theatre management conference, workshops, and social networking opportunities.
Frequency: Annual

19425 **National Black Theatre Festival**
610 Coliseum Drive
Suite 1
Winston-Salem, NC 27106

336-723-2266
nbtf@bellsouth.net; www.nbtf.org

Patrice Toney, President
Frequency: Annual, Winston-Salem

19426 **National Square Dance Convention**
PO Box 5790
Topeka, KS 66605-5790

317-635-4455; www.57nsdc.com

Ernie Stone, Executive Committee
Barbara Stone, Executive Committee

250 booths and 250 exhibitors.
20M+ Attendees
Frequency: June

19427 **New England Theatre Conference**
215 Knob Hill Drive
Hamden, CT 06518

617-851-8535; *Fax:* 203-288-5938
mail@netconline.org; www.netconline.org

Sabine Klein, President
Jeffrey Watts, Executive VP
Charles Emmons, VP Administration/Finance

Promoting excellence in theatre, a conference of New England's oldest, largest regional theatre association.
800+ Attendees
Frequency: November
Founded in: 1952

19428 **North Carolina Southeastern Theatre Conference**
1175 Revolution Mill Drive
Suite 14
Greensboro, NC 27405-0868

336-272-3645; *Fax:* 336-272-8810
info@setc.org; www.setc.org

Betsey Baun, Executive Director
April Marshall, Contact/Pro. Theatre Services

Join over 4,000 Theatre Artists for education, exchanges, ideas, products, networking and great theatre. Convention activities include keynote speakers, auditions, guest speakers, festivals, design competition, commercial and educational expo exhibits, scholarship awards, social events and workshops.
4000+ Attendees

19429 **Prescott Park Arts Festival**
105 Marcy Street
PO Box 4370
Portsmouth, NH 03802-4370

603-436-2848; *Fax:* 603-436-1034
info@prescottpark.org; www.prescottpark.org
Social Media: Facebook

Ben Anderson, Executive Director
John Moynihan, General Manager
Catherine Wejchert, Development Coordinator

Provide a financially accessible, quality multi-arts festival to a diverse audience.

19430 **TCG National Conference**
Theatre Communications Group
520 8th Ave
24th Floor
New York, NY 10018-4156

212-609-5900; *Fax:* 212-609-5901
tcg@tcg.org; www.tcg.org

Theresa Eyring, Executive Director
Jennifer Cleary, Membership Director

19431 **US Institute for Theatre Technology Annual Conference & Stage Expo**
USITT
315 S Crouse Avenue
Suite 200
Syracuse, NY 13210
315-463-6463
800-938-7488; *Fax:* 315-463-6525
info@usitt.org; www.usitt.org
Social Media: Facebook, Twitter, LinkedIn

Carl Lefko, President
Patricia Dennis, Secretary
Travis DeCastro, Treasurer

The Conference offers over 175 sessions featuring design, technology, costume, sound, architecture, management, engineering, and production. The Stage Expo showcases businesses, products, services, and eductional opportunities in the performing arts and entertainment industry. With over 150 exhibitors, Stage Expo provides conference attendees with the opportunity to see the newest and best products and services on the market today.
3700 Members
3800 Attendees
Frequency: March
Founded in: 1960

Directories & Databases

19432 **Academy Players Directory**
2210 W Olive Avenue
Suite 320
Burbank, CA 91506

310-247-3058; *Fax:* 310-550-5034
info@playersdirectory.com;
www.playersdirectory.com

The Players Directory appeared in 1937 as the first reliable casting directory that listed both featured stars and extras. Today, more than 16,000 actors are included.
Cost: $75.00
Founded in: 1937

19433 **American Association of Community Theatre Membership Directory**
American Association of Community Theatre
1300 Gendy Street
Forth Worth, TX 76107-4036

817-732-3177
866-687-2228; *Fax:* 817-732-3178
info@aact.org; www.aact.org

Julie Crawford, Executive Director
Murray Chase, President
Carole Ries, Executive Vice President
David Cockerell, Marketing/Communications Director

The database includes addresses for over 7,000 community theatre organizations in the USA. Only available to members.
Founded in: 1980
Mailing list available for rent: 10000 names at $180 per M

19434 **Americans for the Arts Field Directory**
Americans for the Arts
1 E 53rd St
2nd Floor
New York, NY 10022-4242
212-223-2787; *Fax:* 212-980-4857;
www.artsactionfund.org
Social Media: Facebook, Twitter, RSS, You Tube
Suzanne Niemeyer, Editor
Robert L Lynch, President/CEO
Liz Bartolomeo, Public Relations/Marketing Coord
Chad Bauman, Director Print/Multimedia
Graham Dunstan, Assoc Director Publication Sales
A must-have resource for anyone working in the arts and community development. The directory provides contact information for local, state, regional, and national arts service organizations-more than 4,000 entries broken down by state and region. Also includes contact information for professional consultants working in the nonprofit arts field. A great networking tool.
Cost: $35.00
262 Pages

19435 **Association of Performing Arts Presenters Membership Directory**
APAP
1211 Connecticut Ave NW
Suite 200
Washington, DC 20036-2716
202-833-2787
888-820-2787; *Fax:* 202-833-1543
info@artspresenters.org;
www.artspresenters.org
Sandra Gibson, President
Sean Handerhan, Marketing
An invaluable resource for keeping in touch with colleagues. Puts more than 1,450 presenters, service organizations, artists, management companies, consultants, and vendors at your fingertips. An excellent networking tool for everyone on your staff.
1900 Members
Frequency: Annual
Founded in: 1957

19436 **Complete Catalogue of Plays**
Dramatists Play Service
440 Park Ave S
New York, NY 10016-8012
212-683-8960; *Fax:* 212-213-1539;
www.dramatists.com
Social Media: Facebook
Stephen Fultan, President
Rafael J Rivera, VP Finance/Administration
Michael Q Fellmeth, VP Publications/IT
Tamra Feifer, Director Operations
The Complete Catalogue is published in odd years and the Supplement of New Plays in even years. Both books are distributed, without charge, to current customers in the Fall of each year.
412 Pages
Founded in: 1936

19437 **Costume Designers Guild Directory**
Costumer Designers Guild
4730 Woodman Avenue
Suite 430
Sherman Oaks, CA 91423-2400
818-905-1557; *Fax:* 818-905-1560;
www.costumedesignersguild.com
Cheryl Downey, Executive Director
Deborah N Landis, President
Directory includes members' names, classification, and other statistical information.
Frequency: Annual

19438 **Dance Annual Directory**
Dance Magazine
333 7th Ave
11th Floor
New York, NY 10001-5109
212-979-4800; *Fax:* 212-979-4817;
www.dancemagazine.com
Karla Johnson, Publisher
Emily Macel, Editor
Karen Hildebrand, Editorial Director
Wendy Perron, Editor-in-Chief
Hanna Rubin, Managing Editor
Reach 300,000+ dancers, dance teachers, and dance professionals in the dance world.
Cost: $100.00
Frequency: Annual

19439 **Dance Magazine College Guide**
Dance Magazine
333 7th Ave
11th Floor
New York, NY 10038-3900
212-979-4800; *Fax:* 212-979-4817
subscriptions@dancemagazine.com;
www.dancemagazine.com
Karla Johnson, President
Karen Hildebrand, Editorial Director
Wendy Perron, Editor-in-Chief
Hanna Rubin, Managing Editor
Kate Lydon, Education Editor
With over 500+ listings, Dance Magazine College Guide is a comprehensive source for dance degree programs in higher education. Find application deadlines and audition dates. Get student perspectives and career advice. Online database offers the ability to identify programs that match an individual's personal criteria for degree, type of dance, location, department size, tuition and more.
Cost: $29.95
Frequency: Annual

19440 **Dance Magazine: Summer Dance Calendar Issue**
Dance Magazine
33 W 60th Street
Floor 10
New York, NY 10023-7905
212-245-9050
800-331-1750; www.dancemagazine.com
A list of dance workshops and special programs for students are listed.
Cost: $3.95
Frequency: Annual
Circulation: 100,000

19441 **Dance/USA Annual Directory and List-Serv**
Dance/USA
1111 16th St NW
Suite 300
Washington, DC 20036-4830
202-833-1717; *Fax:* 202-833-2686
danceusa@danceusa.org; www.danceusa.org
Andrea Snyder, Executive Director
Tom Thielen, Director Finance/Operations
Katherine Fabian, Membership Manager
On-going list-servs keep many peer councils in touch throughout the year, by providing a quick and easy connection to peer counseling when members have an immediate question or problem. Information about dance companies, schools, presenters, service organizations and commercial suppliers is included in the annual copy of Dance Annual Directory.
Frequency: Annual
Circulation: 400+

19442 **Directory of Theatre Training Programs**
Theatre Directories
P.O.Box 2409
Manchester Center, VT 05255-2409
802-867-9333; *Fax:* 802-867-2297
info@theatredirectories.com;
www.theatredirectories.com
Peg Lyons, Editor
PJ Tumielewicz, Editor
Profiles admissions, tuition, faculty, curriculum, facilities, productions and philosophy of training at 475 programs in the US, Canada and abroad: Colleges, Universities, Conservatories, Undergraduate and Graduate degrees. Includes Combined Auditions information. Indexed by degrees offered in each program.
Cost: $39.50
ISBN: 0-933919-61-1

19443 **Dramatics College Theatre Directory**
Educational Theatre Association
2343 Auburn Ave
Cincinnati, OH 45219-2815
513-421-3900; *Fax:* 513-421-7077;
www.edta.org
Social Media: Facebook, Twitter
Michael Peitz, Executive Director
Gloria McIntyre, President
Jay Seller, VP
Lists more than 250 college, university, and conservatory theatre programs, offering a sketch of each based on information provided by the schools. The listings can be used to measure each school against one's own criteria for location, setting, courses of study, admission requirements, and cost. Find out which programs offer merit scholarships and grants and how those funds are awarded. Use the contact information to get in touch with the programs that seem to offer the best fit for your needs
Cost: $9.00
Frequency: Annual

19444 **Dramatics Magazine: Summer Theatre Directory**
Educational Theatre Association
2343 Auburn Ave
Cincinnati, OH 45219-2815
513-421-3900; *Fax:* 513-421-7077;
www.edta.org
Social Media: Facebook, Twitter
Michael Peitz, Executive Director
Gloria McIntyre, President
Jay Seller, VP
Lists nearly 200 summer theatre programs and stock companies, offering a sketch of each based on factual information provided by the schools, camps, and theatre companies. The listings can be used to measure each program against one's own criteria for location, setting, housing, courses of study, admission requirements and fees.
Cost: $9.00
Frequency: Annual

19445 **Dramatist's Sourcebook**
Theatre Communications Group
520 8th Ave
24th Floor
New York, NY 10018-4156
212-609-5900; *Fax:* 212-609-5901
tcg@tcg.org; www.tcg.org
Theresa Eyring, Executive Director
Kelly Haydon, Database Manager
Jennifer Cleary, Director Membership
Terence Nemeth, Publisher
Kathy Sova, Editorial Director
Completely revised, with more than 900 opportunities for playwrights, translators, composers,

lyricists, and librettists, as well as opportunities for screen, radio, and television writers. Thoroughly indexed, with a calendar of deadlines. The Sourcebook contains scrip-submission procedures for more than 350 theatres seeking new plays; guidelines for more than 150 prizes; and sections on agents, fellowships and residencies.
Cost: $22.95
Frequency: Annual
ISBN: 1-559362-94-4
Founded in: 1980

19446 Dramatists Guild Annual Resource Directory
Dramatists Guild of America
1501 Broadway
Suite 701
New York, NY 10036-5505
212-398-9366; *Fax:* 212-944-0420;
www.dramaguild.com
Ralph Sevush, Executive Director
The Resource Directory is an annual sourcebook available only to Guild members, sent automatically as one of the privileges of Guild members. It includes lists of conferences and festivals, contests, producers, publishers, agents and attorneys, fellowships and grants, and workshops throughout the US and the world.
Frequency: Annual

19447 Encyclopedia of Exhibition
National Association of Theatre Owners
750 1st St Ne
Suite 1130
Washington, DC 20002-4241
202-962-0054; *Fax:* 202-962-0370
nato@natodc.com; www.natoonline.org
John Fithian, President
Gary Klein, VP
Kathy Conroy, Executive Director
Packed with information on film grosses, upcoming releases, and filmgoer demographics. Also features a directory of international and domestic exhibitors and distributors, cinema companies ranked by screen count, trade publications and more
Cost: $500.00
Frequency: Annual

19448 Feedback Theatrebooks and Prospero Press
Feedback Theatrebooks & Prospero Press
PO Box 174
Brooklin, ME 04616
207-359-2781; *Fax:* 207-359-5532
Publishes theatre histories, cookbooks, directories, anthologies of plays, plays published before WWII, and format guidelines for playwrights.

19449 Grey House Performing Arts Directory
Grey House Publishing
4919 Route 22
PO Box 56
Amenia, NY 12501
518-789-8700
800-562-2139; *Fax:* 845-373-6390
books@greyhouse.com; www.greyhouse.com
Social Media: Facebook, Twitter
Leslie Mackenzie, Publisher
Richard Gottlieb, Editor
The most comprehensive resource covering the Performing Arts. This directory provides current information on over 8,500 Dance Companies, Instrumental Music Programs, Opera Companies, Choral Groups, Theater Companies, Performing Arts Series, Performing Arts Facilities and Artist Management Groups.
Cost: $185.00
1200 Pages
Frequency: Annual
ISBN: 1-592373-76-3
Founded in: 1981

19450 Grey House Performing Arts Directory - Online Database
Grey House Publishing
4919 Route 22
PO Box 56
Amenia, NY 12501-0056
518-789-8700
800-562-2139; *Fax:* 518-789-0556
gold@greyhouse.com;
www.gold.greyhouse.com
Social Media: Facebook, Twitter
Leslie Mackenzie, Publisher
Richard Gottlieb, Editor
The Grey House Performing Arts Directory - Online Database provides immediate access to dance companies, orchestras, opera companies, choral groups, theater companies, series, festivals and perfoming arts facilities across the country, or in their region, state, or in your own backyard. It offers unequaled coverage of the Performing Arts - over 8,500 listings - of the major performance organization, facilities, and information resources.
Frequency: Annual
Founded in: 1981

19451 Money for Film and Video Artists
Americans for the Arts
1 E 53rd St
2nd Floor
New York, NY 10022-4242
212-223-2787; *Fax:* 212-980-4857;
www.artsactionfund.org
Social Media: Facebook, Twitter, RSS, You Tube
Suzanne Niemeyer, Editor
Robert L Lynch, President/CEO
Liz Bartolomeo, Public Relations/Marketing Coord
Chad Bauman, Director Print/Multimedia
Graham Dunstan, Assoc Director Publication Sales
A comprehensive resource guide to fellowships, grants, awards, low-cost facilities, emergency assistance programs, technical assistance, and support services. Entries include contact information; type of award and/or scope of service; eligibilty requirements; application procedures; deadlines and more.
Cost: $14.95
317 Pages
ISBN: 1-879903-09-1

19452 Money for International Exchange in the Arts
Americans for the Arts
1 E 53rd St
2nd Floor
New York, NY 10022-4242
212-223-2787; *Fax:* 212-980-4857;
www.artsactionfund.org
Social Media: Facebook, Twitter, RSS, You Tube
Suzanne Niemeyer, Editor
Robert L Lynch, President/CEO
Liz Bartolomeo, Public Relations/Marketing Coord
Chad Bauman, Director Print/Multimedia
Graham Dunstan, Assoc Director Publication Sales
This resource includes grants, fellowships and awards for travel and work abroad; support and technical assistance for international touring and exchange; international artists' residencies; programs that support artists' professional development, and more. Indexed by region, discipline and type of support.
Cost: $14.95
122 Pages
ISBN: 1-879903-01-6

19453 Money for Performing Artists
Americans for the Arts
1 E 53rd St
2nd Floor
New York, NY 10022-4242
212-223-2787; *Fax:* 212-980-4857;
www.artsactionfund.org
Social Media: Facebook, Twitter, RSS, You Tube
Suzanne Niemeyer, Editor
Robert L Lynch, President/CEO
Liz Bartolomeo, Public Relations/Marketing Coord
Chad Bauman, Director Print/Multimedia
Graham Dunstan, Assoc Director Publication Sales
Lists awards, grants, fellowships, competitions, auditions, workshops, and artists' colonies, as well as emergency and technical assistance programs.
Cost: $12.00
240 Pages
ISBN: 0-915400-96-0
Founded in: 1991

19454 Money for Visual Arts
Americans for the Arts
1 E 53rd St
2nd Floor
New York, NY 10022-4242
212-223-2787; *Fax:* 212-980-4857;
www.artsactionfund.org
Social Media: Facebook, Twitter, RSS, You Tube
Suzanne Niemeyer, Editor
Robert L Lynch, President/CEO
Liz Bartolomeo, Public Relations/Marketing Coord
Chad Bauman, Director Print/Multimedia
Graham Dunstan, Assoc Director Publication Sales
A guide to grants, fellowships, awards, artist colonies, emergency and technical assistance, and support services. Entries include contact information; type of award and/or scope of service; eligibility requirements; application procedures; deadlines, and more.
Cost: $14.95
340 Pages

19455 Musical America International Directory of the Performing Arts
Commonwealth Business Media
50 Millstone Rd
Suite 200
East Windsor, NJ 08520-1418
609-371-7700
800-221-5488; *Fax:* 609-371-7879
info@musicalamerica.com;
www.musicalamerica.com
Stephanie Challener, Publisher
Sedgwick Clark, Editor
Susan Elliot, News Editor
Bob Hudoba, Data Editor
Features over 14,000 detailed listings of worldwide arts organizations, including key contact information such as name, address, phone, fax, Web site and E-mail addresses, budget category, type of event and seating capacity. In addition, through advertising, over 10,000 artists are indexed in the alphabetical and categorical indexes. Categories include artist managers, orchestras, opera companies, concert series, festivals, competitions, music schools and departments, record companies, and more.
Founded in: 1898

19456 **NYC/On Stage**
Theatre Development Fund
520 Eight Avenue
Suite 801
New York, NY 10018-6507
212-912-9770
info@tdf.org; www.tdf.org
Social Media: Facebook
Earl D. Weiner, Chair
Sandra Kresch, Vice Chairman
Robert T. Goldman, Treasurer
Deborah Hartnett, Secretary
Theater, dance, and music companies and performing arts centers in New York City.
Founded in: 1995

19457 **National Network For Artist Placement**
National Network for Artist Placement
935 W Avenue 37
Los Angeles, CA 90065
323-222-4035
800-354-5348
NNAPnow@aol.com;
www.americansforthearts.org
Warren Christensen, Consultant
Internship opportunities in dance, music, theatre, art and film.
Cost: $85.00
375 Pages
Frequency: Bi-Annual
ISBN: 0-945941-13-7

19458 **Opera America Membership Directory**
Opera America
330 7th Ave
16th Floor
New York, NY 10001-5248
212-796-8620; *Fax:* 212-796-8631
info@operaamerica.org;
www.operaamerica.org
Social Media: YouTube
Marc Scorca, President
Directory of Opera America's Company, Business, Library, and Affilliate Members, indexed alphabetically and geographically. Includes the Annual Report to Members, a description of Opera America's programs and services, and a list of individual members.
Cost: $25.00
Frequency: Annual

19459 **Plays and Playwrights**
International Society of Dramatists
1638 Euclid Avenue
Miami Beach, FL 33139-7744
305-882-1864
http://blog.nytesmallpress.com/
Offers valuable information on over 1,000 dramatists producing works in English.
Cost: $29.95
200 Pages
Frequency: Annual
Circulation: 10,000

19460 **Regional Theatre Directory**
Theatre Directories
P.O.Box 2409
Manchester Center, VT 05255-2409
802-867-9333; *Fax:* 802-867-2297;
www.theatredirectories.com
Peg Lyons, Editor
PJ Tumielewicz, Editor
Profiles over 400 theatres including dinner theatres, equity and non-equity. Find out when/where auditions are held, when resumes shoul be sent, housing and transportation policy, and general description of company. If you want to find a job or an internship as an actor, designer, technician or staff in a professional regional or dinner theatre anywhere in the country, this directory can help you.
Cost: $29.50
Frequency: Annual
ISBN: 0-933919-63-8
Founded in: 1984

19461 **ShowBiz Bookkeeper**
Theatre Directories
P.O.Box 2409
Manchester Center, VT 05255-2409
802-867-9333; *Fax:* 802-867-2297
info@theatredirectories.com;
www.theatredirectories.com
The tax record-keeping system for professionals working in the arts.
Cost: $22.95

19462 **Stars in Your Eyes...Feet on the Ground**
Theatre Directories
P.O.Box 2409
Manchester Center, VT 05255-2409
802-867-9333; *Fax:* 802-867-2297
info@theatredirectories.com;
www.theatredirectories.com
PJ Tumielewicz, Editor
Peg Lyons, Editor
For teens who want to act...Practical advice for young actors: learning how show business works; agents and managers; local cable shows and television commercials; auditioning for stage, student films and TV; choosing a school; dealing with rejection; parental support and more. Written by a 19-year old professional actress.
Cost: $16.95
ISBN: 0-933919-42-5

19463 **Student's Guide to Playwriting Opportunities**
Theatre Directories
P.O.Box 2409
Manchester Center, VT 05255-2409
802-867-9333; *Fax:* 802-867-2297
info@theatredirectories.com;
www.theatredirectories.com
Michael Write, Directory Editor
Christi Pyland, Directory Editor
PJ Tumielewicz, Theatre Directories, Inc Editor
Peg Lyons, Theatre Directories, Inc Editor
An essential tool for every high shool or college student with an interest in playwriting. Comprehensive listings of 79 academic programs and another 80 professional development programs geared for the young writer. New essays on the art, process and business of playwriting.
Cost: $23.95
128 Pages
ISBN: 0-933919-53-0

19464 **Summer Theatre Directory**
Theatre Directories
P.O.Box 2409
Manchester Center, VT 05255-2409
802-867-9333; *Fax:* 802-867-2297
info@theatredirectories.com;
www.theatredirectories.com
Opportunities at over 350 summer theatres, theme parks, and summer training programs.
Cost: $29.50

19465 **Theatre Profiles Database**
Theatre Communications Group
520 8th Ave
24th Floor
New York, NY 10018-4156
212-609-5900; *Fax:* 212-609-5901
tcg@tcg.org; www.tcg.org
Theresa Eyring, Executive Director
Kelly Haydon, Database Manager
Jennifer Cleary, Director Membership
Terence Nemeth, Publisher
Kathy Sova, Editorial Director
Online database of more than 400 theatre members in 47 states, 17,000 individual members, 100 Trustee Leadership Network members and a growing number of University, Funder and Business Affiliates.
Frequency: Annual

19466 **Whole Arts Directory**
Midmarch Arts Press
300 Riverside Dr
Apartment 8A
New York, NY 10025-5279
212-666-6990; *Fax:* 212-865-5510;
www.midmarchartspress.org
Cynthia Navaregga, Manager
Directory to arts resources, organiztions, museums, galleries, colonies, retreats, art therapy, information services, and much more. Highly useful material for all artists, students, organizations and institutions.
Cost: $12.95
175 Pages
ISBN: 0-960247-67-x
Founded in: 1987
Printed in on matte stock

Industry Web Sites

19467 **http://gold.greyhouse.com**
G.O.L.D Grey House OnLine Databases
Grey House Publishing's online database platform, GOLD, offers Quick Search, Keyword Search and Expert Search for most business sectors including performing arts markets. The GOLD platform makes finding the information you need quick and easy - whether you're a novice searcher or an experienced database user. All of Grey House's directory products are available for subscription on the GOLD platform.

19468 **www.aact.org**
American Association of Community Theatre
Non-profit corporation fostering excellence in community theatre productions and governance through community theatre festivals, educational opportunity publications, network, resources, and website.
Founded in: 1980

19469 **www.aahperd.org/nda**
National Dance Association
A nonprofit service organization dedicated to increasing knowledge, improving skills and encouraging sound professional practices in dance education while promoting and supporting creative and healthy lifestyles through high quality dance programs.

19470 **www.aate.com**
American Alliance for Theatre and Education
Members are artists, teachers and professionals who serve youth theatres and theatre educational programs.

19471 **www.absolutewrite.com**
Absolute Write
Advice for writers, including playwrights.

19472 **www.actorsequity.org**
Actors Equity Association
Labor union affiliated with AFL-CIO which represents actors in film, television and commercials.

19473 **www.actorsite.com**
Actor Site
Audition and other information.

19474 **www.actorsource.com**
Actorsource
Extensive information and resources for actors.

19475 **www.actorstheatre.org**
Actors Theatre of Louisville
Supports new playwrights. For information on entering a play, click Humana Festival.

19476 **www.adta.org**
American Dance Therapy Association
Founded in: 1966; professional organization of dance movement therapists, with members both nationally and internationally; offers training, research findings, and a newsletter.

19477 **www.aislesay.com**
Aislesay
Internet magazine of stage reviews and opinions.

19478 **www.americandanceguild.org**
American Dance Guild
Non-profit membership organization; sponsors professional seminars, workshops, a student scholarship and other projects and institutes programs of national significance in the field of dance.

19479 **www.americantheaterweb.com**
American Theater Web
Find theaters, Broadway shows and musicals.

19480 **www.answers4dancers.com**
Answers for Dancers
Dance Magazine sponsors this site.

19481 **www.artsmed.org**
Performing Arts Medicine Association
Organization for physicians and professionals interested in the research of Performing Arts Medicine.

19482 **www.artspresenters.org**
Association of Performing Arts Presenters
Celebrates rich and diverse performing arts to the public.

19483 **www.artstabilization.org**
National Arts Strategies
Offers training and technical assistance to arts organizations.

19484 **www.athe.org**
Association for Theatre in Higher Education
Promotes quality in theatre education.

19485 **www.bachauer.com**
Gina Bachauer International Piano Foundation
Produce a yearly piano international competition

19486 **www.backstage.com**
Backstage.com
Information for actors, casting calls, film reviews, auditions and acting jobs.

19487 **www.backstagejobs.com**
Theatre Design and Technical Jobs Page
Employment opportunities.

19488 **www.backstageworld.com**
Backstage World
Post your resume and search for design and technical job opportunities worldwide.

19489 **www.bmi.com**
BMI
Secures the rights of songwriters/composers. Collects license fees for the public performance of music and pays royalties to its copyright owners.

19490 **www.catf.org**
Contemporary American Theater Festival
Dedicated to providing and developing new American Theater.

19491 **www.cincinnatiarts.org**
Cincinnati Arts Association
Dedicated to supporting performing and visual arts.

19492 **www.classicalaction.org**
Classical Action
Provides a unified voice for all those within the performing arts community to help combat HIV/AIDS.

19493 **www.computermusic.org**
International Computer Music Association
Supports the performance aspects of computer music; publishes newsletter and holds annual conferance.

19494 **www.conductorsguild.org**
Conductors Guild
Dedicated to encouraging the highest standards in the art and profession of conducting. Founded in 1975.

19495 **www.contactimprov.net**
Contact Improv
Improvisation for dancers.

19496 **www.costume-con.org**
Costume Connections
Costume conferences.

19497 **www.costume.org**
International Costumers' Guild
An affiliation of amateur hobbyist and professional costumers.

19498 **www.costumegallery.com**
Costume Gallery
A central location on the web for fashion and costume since 1996.

19499 **www.costumers.org**
National Costumers Association
Seeks to establish and maintain professional and ethical standards of business in the costume industry.

19500 **www.costumes.org**
Costumer's Manifesto
Online book, information and links.

19501 **www.costumesocietyamerica.com**
Costume Society of America
Education, research, presentation and design.

19502 **www.creativedir.com**
Creative Directory Services
Diectory of suppliers for costumes, sets, special effects and stunts.

19503 **www.criticaldance.com**
Dance Critics Association
Critical dance forum and ballet dance magazine

19504 **www.csulb.edu/~jvancamp/copyrigh.html**
Csulb.edu
Copyrighting choreographic works.

19505 **www.csusa.org/face/index.htm**
Friends of Active Copyright Education
Playwrights should click on Words, then Copyright Basics.

19506 **www.cyberdance.org**
Cyber Dance
Collection of links to modern dance and classical ballet resources.

19507 **www.danceart.com/edancing**
Danceart.com
Ballet and dance art, features, chat and more.

19508 **www.dancenotation.org**
Dance Notation Bureau
Notation basics, Notated Theatrical Dances Catalogue and links.

19509 **www.dancepages.com**
Dance Pages.com
Offers resources to dance teachers.

19510 **www.dancer.com/dance-links**
Dance Links
Links to many dance sites.

19511 **www.danceusa.org**
Dance/USA
Provides a forum for the discussion of issues of concern to membersand a support network for exchange of information; also bestows awards.

19512 **www.deadance.com**
Dance Educators of America
Promotes the education of teachers in the performing arts.

19513 **www.dma-national.org**
Dance Masters of America
An organization of dance teachers.

19514 **www.dramaguild.com**
Dramatists Guild
Comprehensive organization that deals solely with Broadway and off-Broadway producers, off-off-Broadway groups, agents, theatres and sources of grants.

19515 **www.dramaleague.org**
Drama League
Seeks to strengthen American theatre through the nurturing of stage directors.

19516 **www.dtw.org**
Dance Theater Workshop
Identifies, presents and supports independent contemporary artists and dance companies to advance dance and live performances in New York and worldwide.

19517 **www.edta.org**
Educational Theater Association
Theater educators working to increase support for theater programs in the educational system.

19518 **www.esperanzaarts.org**
Esperanza Performing Arts Association

19519 **www.etecnyc.net**
Entertainment Technology Online
For employment in design and technical theatre, click on Classifieds. Also offers resources and buyers guides for theatrical lighting.

19520 **www.gmn.com**
Global Music Network
Go backstage, watch rehearsals, listen to performances of classical and jazz artists.

19521 **www.goldmime.com**
Goldston Mime Foundation: School for Mime
Holds summer seminars and workshops.

19522 **www.greyhouse.com**
Grey House Publishing
Authoritative reference directories for most business sectors including performing arts markets. Users can search the online databases with varied search criteria allowing for custom searches by product category, geographic area, sales volume, keyword, subject and more. Full Grey House catalog and online ordering also available.

19523 **www.harada-sound.com/sound/handbook**
Kai's Sound Handbook
Information for sound designers.

19524 **www.heniford.net/1234**
Small Cast One-Act Guide Online
List of short plays.

19525 **www.ifea.com**
International Festivals and Events Association
Network for planning events and exchange programs; publishes quarterly magazine.

19526 **www.intix.org**
International Ticketing Association
Not-for-profit association representing 22 countries worldwide and more than 1,200 members. Committed to the improvement, progress and advancement of ticket management, and to reach this goal provides educational programs, trade shows, conducts surveys and conference proceedings and produces a membership directory.

19527 **www.ispa.org**
International Society for the Performing Arts
Foundation
Supports international cooperation, facilitates networking and enhances professional dialogue.

19528 **www.jensenfoundation.org**
Fritz and Lavinia Jensen Foundation
Sponsors competitions.

19529 **www.latinoarts.org**
Association of Hispanic Arts
A multidisciplinary organization which supports Hispanic arts organizations and individual artists with technical assistance. The organization facilitates projects and programs designed to foster the appreciation, growth, and well being of the Latino cultural community. It's quarter publication, AHA; Hispanic Arts News, features in depth articles on the local and national arts community, including artist profiles and a calendar of events.

19530 **www.lib.colum.edu/costwais.html**
Costume Image Database
Access costume images.

19531 **www.light-link.com**
Lightsearch.com
Lists of lighting equipment suppliers.

19532 **www.livebroadway.com**
League of American Theatres and Producers
National trade association for the commercial theatre industry whose principal activity is negotiation of labor contracts and government relations.

19533 **www.lmda.org**
Literary Managers and Dramaturgs of the Americas
Voluntary membership organization.

19534 **www.luth.org**
Guild of American Luthiers
Manufacturers and repairs stringed instruments; offers quarterly journal and triennial meeting.

19535 **www.lycos.com**
Lycos
Click Arts and Entertainment, then Dance, Theatre or Performing Arts.

19536 **www.magicsam.com**
Society of American Magicians
Founded to promote and maintain harmonious fellowship among those interested in magic as an art, to improve ethics of the magical profession, and to foster, promote and improve the advancement of magical arts in the field of amusement and entertainment. Membership includes professional and amateur magicians, manufacturers of magical apparatus and collectors.

19537 **www.makeupmag.com**
Make-Up Artist Magazine
Make-up artist magazine online.

19538 **www.members.aol.com/thegoop/gaff.html**
Gaff Tape Webring
Tech theatre.

19539 **www.midatlanticarts.org**
Mid Atlantic Arts Foundation
Provides leadership and support for artists and arts organizations in the Mid-Atlantic region and beyond.

19540 **www.milieux.com/costume**
Costume Source
Provides online sources for materials, costumes, accessories and books.

19541 **www.mtishows.com**
Music Theatre International
Scripts, cast recordings, study guides, production slides and other resources.

19542 **www.musicalamerica.com**
Musicalamerica.com
Late-breaking industry news, full search capabilities, immediate interaction between Presenter and Artist Manager/Artist.

19543 **www.musicianshealth.com**
Chiropractic Performing Arts Association
To educate amateur and professional entertainers, musicians and dancers about reaching optimum health potential through natural, drug-free, conservative chiropractic care.

19544 **www.nadt.org**
National Association for Drama Therapy
Promotes the profession of Drama Therapy.

19545 **www.namm.org**
NAMM-International Music Products Association
Offers professional development seminars; sells musical instruments and allied products.

19546 **www.napama.org**
North American Performing Arts Managers and Agents
A cooperative voice in a competitive business.

19547 **www.natoonline.org**
National Association of Theatre Owners
Exhibition trade organization, representing more than 30,000 movie screens in all 50 states, and additional cinemas in 50 countries worldwide.

19548 **www.nbtf.org**
National Black Theatre Festival

19549 **www.netconline.org**
New England Theatre Conference
Non-profit educational corporation founded to develop, expand and assist theatre activity in community, educational and professional levels in New England. Holds annual auditions.

19550 **www.netsword.com/stagecombat.html**
Netsword
Lessons on stage combat.

19551 **www.newplaysforchildren.com**
New Plays Online
Plays for children and young adults.

19552 **www.nmpa.org**
National Music Publishers' Association
Publishes a quarterly newsletter and holds an annual meeting.

19553 **www.ntcp.org**
Non-Traditional Casting Project
Promotes inclusive practices in television, theatre and film.

19554 **www.nyfa.org**
New York Foundation for the Arts
Employment openings in the arts.

19555 **www.nypl.org/reseach/lpa/lpa.html**
New York Public Library for the Performing Arts
Primary research collection.

19556 **www.nytimes.com**
New York Times on the Web
Arts and Theatre contains play reviews.

19557 **www.oobr.com**
Off-Off-Broadway Review
Lists information on off-off broadway shows such as: title of show, author, director, producing company, theatre, address, box-office phone number, dates and times, admission price and contact info.

19558 **www.opencasting.com**
Open Casting
Bulletin board containing auditions, crew calls, casting notices and links.

19559 **www.paastjo.org**
Performing Arts Association
Provides a diverse selection of performing arts.

19560 **www.pen.org**
PEN: American Center
Site of the international literary community organization.

19561 **www.performingarts.net**
Performing Arts Online
Dedicated to the perpetuation of quality performing arts.

19562 **www.pianonet.com**
Piano Manufacturers Association International
Manufacturers and suppliers of pianos and parts; holds annual trade show.

19563 **www.pipeorgan.org**
American Institute of Organ Builders
Sponsers training seminars, quarterly journal and annual convention for pipe organ builders and service technicians.

19564 **www.plasa.org**
Professional Lighting and Sound Association
Web site for PLASA, a leading trade body for Lighting and Sound Professionals.

19565 **www.playbill.com**
Playbill Online
Listings for Broadway and off Broadway theatre productions. Also guides for sites, including summer stock, national touring shows and regional theatres worldwide.

19566 **www.playwrights.org**
Playwrights Center of San Francisco
Playwrites directory.

19567 **www.playwrightshorizons.org**
Playwrights Horizon
At home page click arrow. On next page click working with PH. You will see Writing Submissions.

19568 **www.playwrightsproject.com**
Playwrights Project
Promotes literacy, creativity and communication skills in young people through drama-based activities.

19569 **www.press.jhu.edu/press/journals/paj**
Johns Hopkins University Press
A journal of performance and art.

19570 **www.press.jhu.edu/press/journals/tj**
Johns Hopkins University Press
Theatre Journal

19571 **www.press.jhu.edu/press/journals/tt**
Johns Hopkins University Press
Theatre Topics

19572 **www.proppeople.com**
Proppeople.com
Online home for props professionals.

19573 **www.renfaire.com/Language/index.html**
Renfaire.com
Lessons on proper Elizabethan accents.

19574 **www.rigging.net**
Rigger's Page
Technical information on stage rigging equipment.

19575 **www.roundalab.org**
Roundalab
A professional international society of individuals who teach round dancing at any phase.

19576 **www.safd.org**
Society of American Fight Directors
Promotes safety in directing staged combat and theatrical violence.

19577 **www.sagaftra.org**

19578 **www.sapphireswan.com/dance**
Dance Directory
Dance resources.

19579 **www.setc.org**
Southeastern Theatre Conference
Annual conventions include auditions.

19580 **www.sfballet.org**
San Francisco Ballet Association
Provides a repertoire of classical and contemporary ballet; to provide educational opportunities for professional dancers and choreographers; to excel in ballet, artistic direction and administration.

19581 **www.southarts.org**
Southern Arts Federation
Serves as the leadership voice to increase the regional, national and international awareness and prominence of Southern arts. Creates mechanisms and partnerships to expand local, regional, national and international markets for Southern arts.

19582 **www.spolin.com**
Spolin Center
Information on improvisational theatre.

19583 **www.ssdc.org**
Society of Stage Directors and Choreographers
An independent labor union representing directors and choreographers in American theatre.

19584 **www.stage-directions.com**
Stage Directions Magazine
The practical and technical side of theatrical operations.

19585 **www.stageplays.com/markets.htm**
Playwrights Noticeboard
Information on contests, publishing and production opportunities.

19586 **www.stetson.edu/csata/thr_guid.html**
McCoy's Guide to Theatre and Performance Studies
A brief guide to internet resources in theatre and performance studies put out by Stetson University.

19587 **www.summertheater.com**
Directory of Summer Theater in the United States
Search for summer theater opportunities by alphabetized listings or geographic region.

19588 **www.talkinbroadway.com**
Talkin' Broadway
Theatrical events and information on and off Broadway and other selected geographical locations.

19589 **www.tcg.org**
Theatre Communications Group
Supports alliances among playwrights, theatres and communities. Promotes not-for-profit theatre and offers resources to jobseekers. Offers financial support to designers and directors through its Career Development Program.

19590 **www.tdf.org**
Theatre Development Fund
Not-for-profit service organization. Provides support for every area of the dance, music and professional theatre field. Founded 1968.

19591 **www.teleport.com/~bjscript/index.htm**
Essays on the Craft of Dramatic Writing
Essays on writing a screenplay, play or novel.

19592 **www.theatre-resource.com**
Theatre Resource
Career and employment information.

19593 **www.theatrebayarea.org**
Theatre Bay Area
Serving more than 400 member theatre companies and 3,000 individual members in the San Francisco Bay Area and Northern California, Theatre Bay Area provides monthly classes, workshops, events, information and publications.

19594 **www.theatrecrafts.com**
Theatrecrafts.com
Practical information about technical theatre techniques for theatre folk at any level.

19595 **www.theatrejobs.com**
Theatrejobs.com
Online job placement. Festival listings, summer stock, assistantships, apprenticeships, fellowships and internships.

19596 **www.theatrelibrary.org/links**
Performing Arts Links
General resources including applied and interactive theatre, performing arts data service and art sites. Digital librarian includes glossary of technical theatre terms.

19597 **www.theatrelibrary.org/links/index.html**
Theatrelibrary.org
Master categories are Theatre, Dance, Cinema and Reviews.

19598 **www.thecastingnetwork.com/webring.html**
Casting Network.com
By and for actors.

19599 **www.theplays.org**
Electronic Literature Foundation
William Shakespeare's plays online.

19600 **www.top20performingarts.com**
Top 20 Performing Arts
Online directory for Perfoming Arts education.

19601 **www.towson.edu/worldmusiccongresses**
World Music Congresses
1997-2010 World Cello Congress' II-V, 2004 The First World Guitar Congress and 2008 World Guitar Congress II. Celebrations of music with international gatherings of the world's greatest musicians, composers, conductors, instrument manufacturers students, and music lovers from around the globe.

19602 **www.unc.edu/depts/outdoor**
Institute of Outdoor Drama
Summer jobs for all theatrical personnel.

19603 **www.ups.edu/professionalorgs/dramaturgy**
Dramaturgy Northwest
Relevant information for all dramaturgs.

19604 **www.urta.com**
University/Resident Theatre Association
Coalition of theatre training programs. Sponsors unified auditions.

19605 **www.usabda.org**
USA Dance
Non-profit organization working to promote ballroom dancing, both as a recreational activity and as a competetive sport.

19606 **www.usitt.org**
United States Institute for Theatre Technology
The association of design, production and technology professionals in the performing arts and entertainment industry whose mission is to promote the knowledge and skills of its members. International in scope, USITT draws its board of directors from across the US and Canada. Sponsors projects, programs, research, symposia, exhibits, and annual conference. Disseminates information on aesthetic and technical developments.

19607 **www.variety.org**
Variety

e-version of the show business newspaper.

19608 www.vcu.edu/artweb/playwriting
Playwriting Seminars

An opinionated web companion on the art and craft of playwriting for theatre and dance.

19609 www.vl-theatre.com
WWW Virtual Library

Links to theatre and drama resources. Updated daily.

19610 www.writersguild.com
Writers Guild of America

List of Agents and information on Mentor program.

19611 www.wwar.com
World Wide Arts Resources

Links to Theatre and Dance.

19612 www2.sundance.org
Sundance Institute

Information on the Sundance Theatre Laboratory summer workshop for directors, playwrights, choreographers, solo performers and composers. For information on submitting a play, click Theatre Program on home page.

Associations

19613 AAPG Foundation
PO Box 979
Tulsa, OK 74101-0979
918-560-2644
855-302-2743; *Fax:* 918-560-2642
foundation.aapg.org
Social Media: Facebook, Twitter
David Curtiss, Executive Director
The Foundation supports the geosciences by providing funding for educational and research programs.
Founded in: 1967

19614 ADSC International Association of Foundation Drilling
8445 Freeport Parkway Suite 325
Irving, TX
469-359-6000; *Fax:* 469-359-6007
adsc@adsc-iafd.com; www.adsc-iafd.com
Social Media: Facebook, Twitter, LinkedIn
Al Rasband, President
Martin McDermott, Vice President
Lance Kitchens, Treasurer
Rick Marshall, Director
Greg Sullivan, Director

19615 American Association of Drilling Engineers
P.O. Box 107
Houston, TX 77001
281-293-9800
info@aade.org; www.aade.org
Social Media: Facebook
Geree Wald Morton, President
Randy Thomas, Vice President
Duane Halverson, Treasurer
Jannie Snelson, Secretary
Bob Vaughn, Executive Director
Founded in: 1978

19616 American Association of Petroleum Geologists
1444 S. Boulder
PO Box 979
Tulsa, OK 74119
918-584-2555
800-364-2274; *Fax:* 918-560-2665
bulletin@aapg.org; www.aapg.org
Social Media: Facebook, Twitter, LinkedIn, YouTube
Paul Weimer, President
Denise M. Cox, Secretary
Edward Beaumont, President-Elect
James S. McGhay, Treasurer
Stephen E. Laubach, Editor
Supports those professionals involved in the field of geology as it relates to petroleum, natural gas, and other energy products. Publishes monthly journal of peer-reviewed articles.
30000 Members
Founded in: 1917

19617 American Association of Petroleum Geologis
P.O. Box 979
Tulsa, OK 74101-0979
918-560-2644
855-302-2743; *Fax:* 918-560-2642
foundation.aapg.org
Social Media: Facebook, Twitter, Stumbleupon
David Curtiss, Executive Director
David E. Lange, Deputy Executive Director
April Stuart, Program Coordinator
Tamra Campbell, Administrative Assistant
Karen Piqune, Librarian
Founded in: 1967

19618 American Association of Professional Landmen
800 Fournier Street
Fort Worth, TX 76102
817-847-7700; *Fax:* 817-847-7704
aapl@landman.org; www.landman.org
Social Media: Facebook, Twitter, LinkedIn, YouTube
Jack C. Richards, President
Jim R. Dewbre, 1st Vice President
Melanie Bell,CPL, Executive VP
Bernard J. Ulicy, 2nd Vice President
C.Craig Young, Sr.Director
AAPL's mission is to promote the highest standards of performance for all land professionals, to advance their stature and to encourage sound stewardship of energy and mineral resources.
7000 Members
Founded in: 1955

19619 American Fuel & Petrochemical Manufacturer s
1667 K Street NW
Ste. 700
Washington, DC 20006
202-457-0480; *Fax:* 202-457-0486;
www.afpm.org
Social Media: Facebook, Twitter, RSS
David Lamp, Chairman
Gregory J. Goff, Vice Chair
Charles T. Drevna, Executive Assistant
Rich Moskowitz, General Counsel
Diana Cronan, Communications Director
450 Members
Founded in: 1902

19620 American Gas Association
400 N Capitol Street NW
Washington, DC 20001
202-824-7000; *Fax:* 202-824-7092
ykorolevich@aga.org; www.aga.org
Social Media: Facebook, Twitter, LinkedIn, Myspace, Flickr
Terry D. McCallister, Chairman
Dave McCurdy, President & CEO
Ralph A. LaRossa, 1st Vice Chair
Pierce H. Norton II, 2nd Vice Chair
Gregg S. Kantor, Immediate Past Chairman
The American Gas Association advocates the interests of its members and their customers, and provides information and services promoting efficient demand and supply growth and operational excellence in the safe, reliable and efficient delivery of natural gas.
Founded in: 1918

19621 American Institute of Mining Metallurgical & Petroleum Engineers
12999 East Adam Aircraft Circle
Englewood, CO 80112
303-325-5185; *Fax:* 888-702-0049
aime@aimehq.org; www.aimehq.org
Social Media: Facebook, LinkedIn, YouTube, RSS
Brajendra Fattahi, President
Garry W. Warren, President-Elect
Nikhil C. Trivedi, President-Elect Designate
Dale E. Heinz, Past President
Drew Meyer, Trustee
AIME is and shall be a New York State Nonprofit Corporation organized and operated to advance and disseminate, through the programs of the Member Societies, knowledge of engineering and the arts and sciences involved in the production and use of minerals, metals, energy sources and materials for the benefit of humankind, and to represent AIME and the Member Societies within the larger engineering community.
90000 Members
Founded in: 1871

19622 American Oil & Gas Historical Society
1201 15th Street
Ste 300
Washington, DC 20005
aoghs.org
Social Media: Facebook, Twitter, LinkedIn, Google+
Bruce A. Wells, Executive Director
Founded in: 2003

19623 American Petroleum Institute
1220 L St NW
Washington, DC 20005-4070
202-682-8000; *Fax:* 202-682-8232;
www.api.org
Social Media: Facebook, Twitter, YouTube, Flickr
Jack N.Gerard, President & CEO
The only national trade association that represents all aspects of America's oil and natural gas industry. Members are producers, refiners, suppliers, pipeline operators and marine transporters, as well as service and supply companies that support all segments of the industry.
400+ Members
Founded in: 1919

19624 Association of Desk and Derrick Clubs
5321 South Sheridan Road
Suite 24
Tulsa, OK 74145
918-622-1749; *Fax:* 918-622-1675
ado@addc.org; www.addc.org
Social Media: Facebook, Twitter, YouTube
Linda Rodgers, President
Connie Harrison, Vice President
Maggi Franks, Treasurer
Babara Ann Pappas, Secretary
Sheryl Minear, RP, Parliamentarian
Founded in: 1949

19625 Association of Drilled Shaft Contractors
8445 Freeport Parkway
Suite 325
Irving, TX 75063
469-359-6000; *Fax:* 469-359-6007
adsc@adsc-iafd.com; www.adsc-iafd.com
Social Media: Facebook, LinkedIn
Tom Witherspoon, President
Tom Tuozzolo, Vice President
Luke Schuler, Treasurer
Tom Bird, Chairman
A professional, internationa, nonprofit trade association representing the anchored earth retention, drilled shaft, micropile, and other heavy civil construction/design industries. Members include specialty subcontractors, manufacturers and suppliers, academicians and design engineers in the private and public sectors.
Founded in: 1972

19626 Association of Energy Service Companies
14531 FM 529
Suite 250
Houston, TX 77095-3528
713-781-0758
800-672-0771; *Fax:* 713-781-7542;
www.aesc.net
Social Media: Facebook, Twitter, LinkedIn
Kenny Jordan, Executive Director
Patty Jordan, Publisher/Sales Manager
Angla Fails, Administrative Manager
Roni Ashley, Director Accounting Services
Professional trade association for well-site service contractors and businesses providing goods

and services to well-site contractors. Develops and sells training and safety materials.
600 Members
Founded in: 1956

19627 Association of International Petroleum Negotiators
11767 Katy Freeway
Suite 412
Houston, TX 77079

281-558-7715; *Fax:* 281-558-7073
president@aipn.org; www.aipn.org

John Bowman, President
Judith Kim, VP - Communication
Steven Otillar, VP - Education
Kimberly Reeder, VP - Membership
Joseph Wesley, VP - Planning
Founded in: 1982

19628 Association of Oil Pipe Lines
1808 Eye St NW
Suite 300
Washington, DC 20006-5423

202-408-7970; *Fax:* 202-280-1949
aopl@aopl.org; www.aopl.org
Social Media: Facebook, Twitter

Andrew J.Black, President
Steven M.Kramer, General Counsel
John Stoody, Director
Heather Keith, Director
Rekha Chandrasekher, Industry Analyst

Acts as an information clearinghouse for the public, the media and the pipeline industry; provides coordination and leaderships for the industry's ongoing joint Environmental Safety Initiative; and represents common carrier crude and product petroleum pipleines in Congress, before regulatory agencies, and in the federal courts.
47 Members
Founded in: 1947

19629 Association of Petroleum Industry Cooperative Managers
www.apicom.org

Founded in: 1972

19630 Association of Petroleum Surveying & Geomatics
www.apsg.info
Social Media: Facebook, Twitter, LinkedIn

Jackie Portsmouth, Chairman
Ashok Wadwani, Vice Chair
Kevin Crozier, Nominations Chair
Alma Alling, Communications Chair
Robert Edwards, Secretary/ Treasurer
Founded in: 1998

19631 Concrete Sawing & Drilling Association
100 2nd Ave South
Ste 240N
St. Petersburg, FL 33701

727-577-5004
info@CSDA.org; www.csda.org
Social Media: Facebook, Twitter, YouTube, Instagram

Judith O'Day, President
Kevin Baron, Vice President
Patrick O'Brien, Executive Director
Jim Dvoratchek, Past President
Mike Orzechowski, Secretary/ Treasurer

19632 Coordinating Research Council
5755 North Point Parkway
Suite 265
Alpharetta, GA 30022-3067

678-795-0506; *Fax:* 678-795-0509
jantucker@crcao.com; www.crcao.org

Brent Bailey, Executive Director
Christopher Tennant, Deputy Director
Debra Carter, Controller
Betty Taylor, Administrative Assistant
Jan Beck, Committee Coordinator and Webmaster

A nonprofit organization that directs, through committee action, engineering and environmental studies on the interaction between automotive/other mobility equipment and petroleum products.
1M Members
Founded in: 1942

19633 Council of Petroleum Accountants Societies
445 Union Blvd.
Suite 207
Lakewood, CO 80228

303-300-1311
877-992-6727; *Fax:* 303-300-3733;
www.copas.org
Social Media: Facebook, Twitter, LinkedIn

Tom Wierman, Executive Director
Cheri McCallister, Administrator
Anita Hartz, Creative Specialist
Rich Moring III, President
Jeff Wright, Vice President

Members are accountants involved in, or closely related to, the oil and gas industry. Also provides ethical standards for energy accountants and is the certification organization for the Accredited Petroleum Accountant program.
3200 Members
Founded in: 1961

19634 Domestic Petroleum Council
101 Constitution Avenue NW
Suite 800
Washington, DC 20001-2133

202-742-4300; www.dpcusa.org/

William F Whitsitt, President

To work constructively for sound energy, environmental and related public policies that encourage responsible exploration, development, and production of natural gas and crude oil to meet consumer needs and fuel our economy.
24 Members
Founded in: 1975

19635 Drilling Engineering Association
10370 Richmond Ave, Suite 760
Houston, TX 77042

713-292-1945; *Fax:* 713-292-1946
dea-global.org

Ben Bloys, Chairman
David Dowell, Advisory Board Member
Glenda Wylie, Advisory Board Member
Robert Estes, Advisory Board Member
Scott Maddox, Secretary/ Treasurer

19636 Energy Security Council
9720 Cypresswood Dr.
Suite 206
Houston, TX 77070

281-587-2700; *Fax:* 281-807-6000
mindy@energysecuritycouncil.org;
www.energysecuritycouncil.org

Rob Ream, Chairman
Rick Powers, Vice-Chairman
Butch Brazell, Director of Global Security
Clete Buckaloo, Director of Law Enforcement
Kent Chrisman, Director of Corp. Security & Admin.

Founded as Petroleum Industry Security Council and assumed its current name in 1999. Provides support to security professionals and business developers in the energy industry.
450 Members
Founded in: 1976

19637 Energy Telecommunications and Electrical Association
5005 Royal Lane
Suite 116
Irving, TX 75063

888-503-8700; *Fax:* 972-915-6040;
www.entelec.org
Social Media: LinkedIn

Dan Mueller, President
Michael Burt, 1st Vice President
James Coulter, 2nd Vice President
Becky Holland, 3rd Vice President
Richard Nation, Secretary/ Treasurer

A user association that focuses on communications and control technologies used by petroleum, natural gas, pipeline and electric utility companies. Primary goal is to provide education for its members.
Founded in: 1928

19638 Energy Traffic Association
3303 Main Street Corridor
Houston, TX 77002

713-528-2868; *Fax:* 713-464-0702
russell@energytraffic.org;
www.energytraffic.org

Ralph Lopez, President
Renee Ahmed, Vice President/ Secretary
Russell Powell, Executive Director
Roger Rood, Immediate Past President
Tonya Svoboda, Board member

A nonprofit educational association of logistics professionals in the energy industry. Membership consists of managers of energy industry logistics departments and those logistics providers serving the energy industry.
100 Members
Founded in: 1941

19639 Fiberglass Tank and Pipe Institute
14323 Heatherfield
Suite 101
Houston, TX 77079-7407

713-690-7777; *Fax:* 713-690-2842
info@fiberglasstankandpipe.com;
www.fiberglasstankandpipe.com

Bobby Jin, President

The fiberglass-reinforced, thermosetting, plastic tank and pipe manufacturing industry. Members are domestic manufacturers.
5 Members
Founded in: 1987

19640 Foundation Drilling Magazine
Association of Drilled Shaft Contractors
8445 Freeport Parkway
Suite 325
Irving, TX 75063

469-359-6000; *Fax:* 469-359-6007
adsc@adsc-iafd.com; www.adsc-iafd.com
Social Media: Facebook, Twitter, LinkedIn

Tom Witherspoon, President
Tom Tuozzolo, Vice President
Luke Schuler, Treasurer
Tom Bird, Chairman

The best news source within our industry. Filled with information about design, projects and updates on what's going on where, Foundation Drilling Magazine is devoted to reporting on the drilled shaft, anchored retention, and other related industries.
Frequency: 8x Yearly
Founded in: 1972

19641 **Gas Research Machinery Council**
3030 LBJ Freeway
Suite 1300
Dallas, TX 75234

972-620-4026; *Fax:* 972-620-1613
memberservices@southerngas.org; www.gmrc.org

Craig Linn, Chairman
Roland Trevino, Vice Chairman
Mike Grubb, President & CEO
Jane Butler, Vice President
Scott Schubring, Project Supervisory Committee

Members are companies in the natural gas, oil and petrochemical industries in mechanical and fluid systems design.
75 Members
Founded in: 1952

19642 **Independent Liquid Terminals Association**
1005 North Glebe Road
Suite 600
Arlington, VA 22201

703-875-2011; *Fax:* 703-875-2018
info@ilta.org; www.ilta.org

E David Doane, President
Melinda Whitney, Director/Government Affairs
Eric W. Thomas, Chairman
John G. McGrossin, Treasurer
Seph E. Shotwell, Secretary

Supports all those bulk, liquid terminal owners/operators and establishments supplying equipment, goods and services to the bulk liquid terminaling industry. Publishes monthly newsletter.
Founded in: 1974

19643 **Independent Lubricant Manufacturers**
400 N Columbus St
Suite 201
Alexandria, VA 22314-2264

703-684-5574; *Fax:* 703-836-8503
ilma@ilma.org; www.ilma.org
Social Media: Facebook, Twitter

Celeste Powers, Executive Director
Martha Jolkovski, Director Publications/Advertising
Glenn Boyle, Second Vice President
Dixon W Benz II, Executive Sales Manager

Independent blenders and compounders of lubricants.
Founded in: 1976

19644 **Independent Terminal Operators Association**
1150 Connecticut Avenue NW
9th Floor
Washington, DC 20036-4129

202-828-4100; *Fax:* 202-828-4130
wbode@bode.com

William H Bode, Secretary & General Counsel

Represents indepedent petroleum distributors.
15 Members
Founded in: 1970

19645 **Institute of Gas Technology**
1700 S Mount Prospect Rd
Des Plaines, IL 60018-1804

847-768-0500; *Fax:* 847-768-0501
publicrelations@gastechnology.org; www.gastechnology.org
Social Media: Facebook, Twitter, LinkedIn, YouTube

David Carroll, President & CEO
Chris Herman, Treasurer & CFO
Paul Chromek, General Counsel & Secretary

An independent, not-for-profit center for energy and environmental research, development, education and information. Main function is to perform sponsored and in-house research, development and demonstration, provide educational programs and services, and disseminate scientific and technical information.
Founded in: 1941

19646 **International Association for Energy Economics**
28790 Chagrin Blvd.,
Ste 350
Clevelend, OH 44122

216-464-5365
iaee@iaee.org; www.iaee.org

Peter R. Hartley, President
Anne Neumann, VP - Publication
Jurgis Vilemas, VP -Finance
Lori Smith Dschell, VP -Communications
Ponald D. Ripple, VP -Conferences

19647 **International Association of Directional Drilling**
281-288-6484; www.iadd-intl.org

Jim Oberkircher, Founder/ CEO
Arstrong Lee Agbaji, Assistant Director
Bill Bailey, Board Member
Ed Dew, Board Member
Chris McCartney, Board Member

19648 **International Association of Drilling Contractors**
10370 Richmond Ave
Suite 760
Houston, TX 77042-9687

713-292-1945; *Fax:* 713-292-1946
info@iadc.org; www.iadc.org
Social Media: Facebook, Twitter, LinkedIn, RSS

Stephen Colville, President and CEO
Tap Powell, Executive VP
Mike Killalea, Group VP
Jason McFarland, Corporate Development
Mike Dubose, VP-Interantional Dept

Dedicated to enhancing the interests of the oil-and-gas and geothermal drilling and completion industry worldwide
1239 Members
Founded in: 1940

19649 **International Coiled Tubing Association**
PO Box 1082
Montgomery, TX 77356

936-520-1549; *Fax:* 832-201-9977
ababin@icota.com; www.icota.com

Alan Turner, Sr.Co-Chair
Jason Skufca, Executive Director
David Larimore, Treasurer
Allison Babin, Secretary
Federico Botero, Board Member
7 Members
Founded in: 1994

19650 **International Energy Credit Association**
1120 Route 73
Suite C
Mt. Laurel, NJ 08054

856-380-6854; *Fax:* 856-439-0525
ieca@ahint.com; www.ieca.net
Social Media: Facebook, Twitter, LinkedIn

Zachary Starbird, President
James Hawkins, 1st VP
John Early, Treasurer
Jamie Swartz, VP Education
Steve Harwitz, Director-Environment Regulations

Members are credit and financial executives with companies whose product is a petroleum derivative.
800 Members
Founded in: 1923

19651 **International Geophysical Association**
1225 North Loop West
Suite 220
Houston, TX 77008

713-957-8080; *Fax:* 713-957-0008
info@iagc.org; www.iagc.org
Social Media: Facebook, Twitter, Youtube

Nikki Martin, President
Walt Rosenbusch, VP
Gail Adams, VP of Communications
Dr.Robert Gisiner, Director of Marine Environment
Criss Rennie, Director-Membership

Represents the industry that provides geophysical services to the oil and gas industry.
203 Members
Founded in: 1971

19652 **International Oil Scouts Association**
PO Box 940310
Houston, TX 77094-7310

512-472-8138; www.oilscouts.com
Social Media: Facebook

Pam Florek, President
Christi Sarat, Executive VP
Don Grimm, Second VP
Lisa Bonin, Secretary
Ty Cline, VP Finance

Compiles statistics on exploration and development wells in the United States. Offers professional development and scholarship programs.
175 Members
Founded in: 1924

19653 **International Slurry Surfacing Association**
3 Church Cir
PMB 250
Annapolis, MD 21401

410-267-0023; *Fax:* 410-267-7546
krissoff@slurry.org; www.slurry.org
Social Media: Facebook, Twitter

Rusty Price, President
Carter Dabney, Vice President
Rex Eberly, Secretary
Eric Reimschiissel, Treasurer
Bob Jerman, Technical Director

A non profit association dedicated to the interests, education, and success of slurry surfacing professionals and corporations around the world.
200 Members
Founded in: 1963

19654 **International Union of Petroleum and Industrial Workers**
8131 E Rosecrans Avenue
Paramount, CA 90723

562-630-6232
800-624-5842; *Fax:* 562-408-1073
petroleumworkers@aol.com
Social Media: Facebook

George R Beltz, International President
Pamela Parlow, Internat'l Secretary/Tresurer
5000 Members
Founded in: 1951

19655 **Interstate Natural Gas Association of America**
20 F Street, NW
Suite 450
Washington, DC 20001

202-216-5900; *Fax:* 202-216-0870;
www.ingaa.org

Donald F. Santa, Jr., President & CEO
Richard R Hoffmann, Executive Director
Catherine J Landry, Director of Communications
James O'Bryant, Researcher & Comm Assistant
Martin E. Edwards, VP, Legislative Affairs

Trade association of natural gas pipelines in the United States, Canada, Mexico and Europe.
25 Members
Founded in: 1944

19656 **Interstate Oil and Gas Compact Commission**
900 NE 23rd Street
Oklahoma City, OK 73105

405-525-3556; *Fax:* 405-525-3592
communications@iogcc.ok.gov;
www.iogcc.state.ok.us

Mary Fallin, Chairman
David Porter, Vice Chairman
Michael Teague, 2nd Vice Chairman
Mike Smith, Executive Director
Gerry Baker, AssociateExecutive Director

The members are states that produce oil or gas; associate states support the conservation of America's energy resources. Also establishes rules andguidelines for the proper maintenance of wells.
700 Members
Founded in: 1935

19657 **Liaison Committee of Cooperating Oil and Gas Association**
1718 Columbus Road SW
PO Box 535
Granville, OH 13023-0535

740-587-0444; *Fax:* 202-857-4799
stewart@ooga.org;
www.energyconnect.com/liason

Thomas E Stewart, Secretary/Treasurer

Established to facilitate communication among state and regional oil and gas associations.
25 Members
Founded in: 1957

19658 **Mid-Continent Oil and Gas Association**
730 North Blvd.
Baton Rouge, LA 70802

225-387-3205; *Fax:* 225-344-5502;
www.lmoga.com
Social Media: Facebook, Twitter, Flickr

Chris John, President
Tyler Gray, General Counsel
Brent Golleher, Director of Government
Richard Metcalf, Director of Environmental Affairs
Ashley Cain, Manager of Communications

At the forefront of the continually changing legal, legislative and regulatory issues facing a growing and diverse membership.
7.5M Members
Founded in: 1917

19659 **NLGI**
249 SW Noel
Suite 249
Lee's Summit, MO 64063

816-524-2500; *Fax:* 816-524-2504
nlgi@nlgi.org; www.nlgi.org
Social Media: LinkedIn

David J Como, Vice President
Kim Smallwood, Secretary
Joe Kaperick, Treasurer
Kimberly Hartley, Executive Director
Marilyn Brohm, Manager, Membership & Market

Members are companies that manufacture and market all types of lubricating greases, additive or equipment suppliers, and research and educational groups whose interests are primarily technical.
280 Members
Founded in: 1933

19660 **NORA Association of Responsible Recyclers**
7250 Heritage Village Plaza
Suite 201
Gainesville, VA 20155

703-753-4277; *Fax:* 703-753-2445
sparker@noranews.org; www.noranews.org

Bill Hinton, President
Chirs Bergstrom, Executive Vice President
Roy Schumacher, Vice President
Scott D Parker, Executive Director
Casey Parker, Associate Director

Members are companies that reprocess used antifreeze, wastewater, oil filters, chemicals and companies that provide products or services to the industry.
211 Members
Founded in: 1985

19661 **National Association of Convenience Stores**
1600 Duke Street
Alexandria, VA 22314

703-684-3600; *Fax:* 703-836-4564
panderson@nacsonline.com;
www.nacsonline.com
Social Media: Facebook, Twitter, LinkedIn, YouTube, Instagram

Henry Armour, President and CEO
Paige Anderson, Director, Government Relations
Amy Ashley-Burke, Director
Laura Beck, Marketing Specialist
Reed Armstrong, Products & Services Manager
Founded in: 1961

19662 **National Association of Division Order Analysts**
PO Box 2300
Lee's Summit, MO 64063

972-715-4489
administrator@nadoa.org; www.nadoa.org
Social Media: Facebook, Twitter, LinkedIn, RSS

Nancy Cemino, President
Brenda Pirrozzolo, 1st VP/Finance
Sandi Rupprecht, 2nd VP/Site Selection
Jean Hinton, Treasurer
Michele Lawton, Recording Secretary
900 Members
Founded in: 1974

19663 **National Association of Oil and Energy Services Professionals**
PO Box 67
East Petersburg, PA 17520

717-625-3076
888-552-0900; *Fax:* 717-625-3077
jgarber@thinkoesp.org; www.naohsm.org
Social Media: Facebook, Twitter, LinkedIn, YouTube

Al Breda, President
Ralph Adams, Vice-President
Mike Hodge, Treasurer
Paul Cuprewich, Secretary
George Fantacone, Vice President

Members are oil heat service managers and small business owners. Also provides members with technical tapes, books and speakers to train thei employee technicians.
1500 Members
Founded in: 1952

19664 **National Association of Petroleum Investment Analysts**
415 Hayward Mill Road
Concord, MA 01742-4604

978-369-0084; *Fax:* 978-369-0086
dbm@napia.org; www.napia.org

Gregory B. Barnett, Membership Chairman
Michael D. Smolinski, President
D. Barry McKennitt, Executive Director
Tyler Dann II, Board Member
Nancy J. F. Prue, Board Member
Founded in: 1974

19665 **National Association of Royalty Owners**
15 W 6th St
Suite 2626
Tulsa, OK 74119

918-794-1660
800-558-0557; *Fax:* 918-794-1662
NARO@NARO-us.org; www.naro-us.org
Social Media: Facebook, Twitter

Candice Brewer, President
James Elder, Vice President
Emily Wagner, Corporate Secretary
JIm Leonard, Treasurer

Assists mineral and royalty owners in the effective management of their mineral properties. Provides information on tax, regulatory, and legislative matters. Conducts seminars and bestows awards.
5M Members
Founded in: 1980

19666 **National Drilling Association**
4036 Center Rd
Suite B
Brunswick, OH 44212

877-632-4748
877-632-4748; *Fax:* 216-803-9900
info@nda4u.com; www.nda4u.com
Social Media: Facebook, LinkedIn

Dan Dunn, President
Michael Willey, Vice President
Larry Gibel, Secretary/ Treasurer
Timothy Augustine, Director

A non-profit trade association of contractors, manufacturers and affiliated members from the drilling industry representing the geotechnical, environmental and mineral exploration sectors of this industry.
250+ Members
Founded in: 1972

19667 **National Ocean Industries Association**
1120 G St NW
Suite 900
Washington, DC 20005

202-347-6900; *Fax:* 202-347-8650
jwilliams@noia.org; www.noia.org
Social Media: Facebook, Twitter, LinkedIn, YouTube, Google+

Randall Luthi, President
Franki Stunz, Sr.Vice President
Ann Chapman, VP Conferences and Events
Megan Bel Miller, VP Government Relations
Nicoltte Nye, VP Communications

Represents all facets of the domestic offshore and related industries. Member companies are dedicated to the development of offshore oil and natural gas for the continued growth and security of the US.
320+ Members
Founded in: 1972

19668 National Petrochemical & Refiners Association
1667 K Street, NW
Suite 700
Washington, DC 20006
202-457-0480; *Fax:* 202-457-0486
info@afpm.org; www.afpm.org
Social Media: Facebook, Twitter
Gregory J Goff, Chairman
Lawrence M Ziemba, Vice Chair
Chet Thompson, President
Brandon E Williams, Executive Vice President
Rebecca H Adler, Senior director, Communications
Association that represents the petrochemical and refining industries, sponsors periodic conferences, and seeks to inform policymakers and the public. Issues include the recycling of used oils and other liquid wastes.
450 Members
Founded in: 1902

19669 National Petroleum Council
1625 K St NW
Suite 600
Washington, DC 20006
202-393-6100; *Fax:* 202-331-8539
info@npc.org; www.npc.org
Charles D. Davidson, Chair
Rex W. Tillerson, Vice Chair
Marshall W. Nichols, Executive Director
Ernest J. Moniz, Secretary
Self-supporting, federal advisory body to the Secretary of Energy established in 1946 at the request of President Truman.
191 Members
Founded in: 1946

19670 National Petroleum Energy Credit Association
1302 Clayton Nolen Drive
Horseshoe Bay, TX 78657
830-220-3797; *Fax:* 817-796-1080
ContactUs@npeca.org; www.npeca.org
Mike Swillo, President
Mark L. Macha, 1st Vice President
Della White, 2nd Vice President
Laura Roussel, 3rd Vice President
Terry Faber, Secretary
Founded in: 1935

19671 National Propane Gas Association
1899 L St NW
Suite 350
Washington, DC 20036
202-466-7200; *Fax:* 202-466-7205
info@npga.org; www.npga.org
Charlie Ory, Chairman
Stuart Weidie, Chairman-Elect
Jerry Brick, Vice-Chairman
Richard Roldan, President & CEO
Chris Earhart, Treasurer
Members are producers and distributors of liquified petroleum gas and equipment manufacturers.
3500 Members
Founded in: 1931

19672 National Stripper Well Association
1201 15th St NW
Suite 300
Washington, DC 20005
202-857-4722; *Fax:* 202-857-4799
webmaster@ipaa.org; www.ipaa.org
Social Media: Facebook, Twitter, LinkedIn, Youtube
Michael Watford, Chairman
Mark K.Miller, Vice Chair
Diemer True, Treasurer
Barry Russell, President & CEO
This operates under the Independent Petroleum Association, which is an informed voice for the exloration and production segment of the industry. It provides economic and statistical information, and develops investment symposia and other opportunities for its members.
1600+ Members
Founded in: 1929

19673 Natural Gas Supply Association
1620 Eye St., NW
Suite 700
Washington, DC 20006
202-326-9300; *Fax:* 202-326-9330;
www.ngsa.org
Social Media: Twitter
Bill Green, Chairman
Frans Everts, Vice Chair
Dean E. Wiggins, President
A.Scott Moore, Secretary-Treasurer
Represents U.S.-based producers and marketers of natural gas on issues that affect the natural gas industry, including the residential and industrial consumers who rely on the fuel for a myriad of purposes.
14 Members
Founded in: 1965

19674 Newport Associates
7400 E Orchard Road
Suite 320
Englewood, CO 80111-2528
Fax: 303-779-0908
Association for over 450 oil companies in over 20 world regions.

19675 Nuclear Energy Institute
1201 F St., NW
Suite 1100
Washington, DC 20004-1218
202-739-8000; *Fax:* 202-785-4019
webmaster@nei.org; www.nei.org
Social Media: Facebook, Twitter, LinkedIn, Google+, YouTube, Pinterest, F
Donald E. Brandt, Chairman
Christopher M. Crane, President & CEO
Marvin S. Fertel, President & CEO
Alexande W. Flint, Senior Vice President
Maria G. Korsnick, Chief Operating Officer
Members are of utilities, manufacturers of electrical generating equipment, researchers, architects, engineers, labor unions, and others interested in the generation of electricity by nuclear power.
350 Members
Founded in: 1984

19676 Paper, Allied-Industrial, Chemical and Energy Workers International Union
3340 Perimeter Hill Drive
Nashville, TN 37211
615-834-8590; *Fax:* 615-731-6362
jhill@isdn.net; www.paceunion.org
Jim Pannell, VP
Lynne Baker, Associate Director Communications
Joan Hill, Director Research & Education
Elaine Piper, Owner
Work to make life better for the workers and their families.
320M Members
Founded in: 1884

19677 Petroleum Equipment & Services Association
2500 Citywest Blvd
Suite 1110
Houston, TX 77042-3049
713-932-0168
info@pesa.org
pesa.org
Social Media: Facebook, Twitter, LinkedIn, Google+, YouTube
Gary Halverson, Chairman
Saeid Rahimian, Vice Chairman
Burk L. Ellison, First VP
Leslie Shockley Beyer, President
Molly Smart, Vice President of Communications
200 Members
Founded in: 1933

19678 Petroleum Equipment Institute
PO Box 2380
Tulsa, OK 74101-2380
918-494-9696; *Fax:* 918-491-9895;
www.pei.org
Social Media: Facebook, Twitter, LinkedIn, Google+
Kevin McKinney, President
Steve Trabilsy, Vice President
Robert Renkes, Executive Vice President
Robert Peavey, Treasurer
Members are makers and distributors of equipment used in service stations, bulk plants and other petroleum marketing facilities.
1600+ Members
Founded in: 1951
Mailing list available for rent: 1600 names at $275 per M

19679 Petroleum Investor Relations Association
2800 Post Oak Boulevard
Suite 5450
Houston, TX 77056
713-621-7800; *Fax:* 978-369-0086
chris.pitre@rowancompanies.com;
www.rowancompanies.com
Thomas P. Burke, President
W.Matt Ralls, Executive Chairman
Stephen Butz, Executive VP & Treasurer
Mark A. Keller, Executive Vice President
Melanie M. Trent, Company Secretary
Represents investor communications professional in the peroleum and natural gas industry
100 Members
Founded in: 1923

19680 Petroleum Marketers Association
1901 Fort Myer Dr
Suite 1200
Arlington, VA 22209-1609
703-351-8000; *Fax:* 703-351-9160;
www.pmaa.org
Daniel F Gilligan, President
Nancy Kniher, Director Member Service
Cost: $50.00
700 Members

19681 Petroleum Marketers Association of America
1901 North Fort Myer Drive
Suite 500
Arlington, VA 22209
703-351-8000; *Fax:* 703-351-9160
info@pmaa.org; www.pmaa.org
Social Media: Facebook, Twitter
Grady Gaubert, Chairman
Mike Bailey, Vice Chair
Mark Whitehead, 2nd Vice Chair
Rob Underwead, President
Sherri Stone, Vice President
Founded in: 1909

19682 **Petroleum Retailers & Auto Repair Association**
1051 Brinton Road
Suite 304
Pittsburgh, PA 15221

412-241-2380; *Fax:* 412-241-2815
web-email-2010@prara.com; www.prara.com

Jeff Decker, President
Dennis Budzynski, 1st Vice President
Gauttam Patel, 2nd Vice President
Nancy Maricondi, Executive Director
Ray Moore, Treasurer
Founded in: 1937

19683 **Petroleum Technology Transfer Council**
PO Box 710942
Oak Hill, VA 20171

703-620-4797; *Fax:* 571-485-8255
hq@pttc.org; www.pttc.org
Social Media: Facebook

J.C. Hall, Chairman
Barry Tew, Vice Chairman
Mary Carr, Executive Director
Jeremy Viscomi, Executive Director
Kathy Chapman, Director of Operations

Fosters the effective transfer of exploration and production technology to US petroleum producers through regional resource centers, workshops, websites, publications, etc.
Founded in: 1993

19684 **Pipeline Research Council International**
3141 Fairview Park Drive
Suite 525
Falls Church, VA 22042

703-205-1600; *Fax:* 703-205-1607
gtenely@prci.com; www.prci.org

Phillip DePriest, Chairman
Jeff Whiworth, Vice Chairman
Cliff Johnson, President
Michael P. Whelan, Director
Gary Choquette, Senior Program Manager

Sponsors research on technical issues facing the natural gas transmission industry. Members are companies operating pipeline systems.
78 Members
Founded in: 1952
Mailing list available for rent

19685 **Rocky Mountain Oil and Gas Association**
1900 Grant Street
Denver, CO 80203

303-860-0099; *Fax:* 303-861-0373

Jess D Cooper, General Manager
Linda Swain, Manager

A trade association, representing oil and gas industries.
600 Members
Founded in: 1920

19686 **Service Station Dealers of America**
1532 Pointer Ridge Place
Suite G
Bowie, MD 20716

301-390-4405; *Fax:* 301-390-3161
mgates@wmda.net; www.ssda-at.com
Social Media: Facebook, Twitter

Peter S Kischak, President
Fred Bordoff, 1st Vice President
Billy Hillmuth, 2nd Vice President
Hugh Campbell, Treasurer

Service Station Dealers of America/National Coalition of Petroleum Retailers and Allied Trades is a national association composed of individual and state affiliate associations representing service station dealers, repair facilities, car washes and convenience stores.
Founded in: 1947

19687 **Society of Independent Gasoline Marketers**
3930 Pender Drive
Suite 340
Fairfax, VA 22030

703-709-7000
sigma@sigma.org; www.sigma.org

Tom Gresham, President
David Baker, 1st Vice President
William Bradford, 2nd Vice President
Liz Menz, Education Director
Nancy Muskett, Marketing Director
260 Members
Founded in: 1958

19688 **Society of Petroleum Engineers**
222 Palisades Creek Drive
Richardson, TX 75080

972-952-9393
800-456-6863; *Fax:* 972-952-9435
spedal@spe.org; www.spe.org
Social Media: Facebook, Twitter, LinkedIn, YouTube, Instagram

Nathan Meehan, President
Janeen Judah, VP Finance
Mark A. Rubin, CEO & Executive VP
Stephen Graham, Chief Operations Officer
Cordella Wong, Managing Director

Supports those professionals involved in the field of exploration, drilling, production, and reservoir management, as well as related manufacturing and service organizations. Publishes monthly magazine.
12400 Members
Founded in: 1957

19689 **Society of Petroleum Evaluation Engineers**
5535 Memorial Drive
Houston, TX 77007

713-651-1639; *Fax:* 713-951-9659
info@spee.org; www.spee.org

Gary Gonzenbach, President
Dee Patterson, Vice President
Floyd Siegle, Secretary/Treasurer
Brad DeWitt, Director

Members are engineers specializing in the fields of petroleum and natural gas properties.
495 Members
Founded in: 1962

19690 **Society of Petrophysicists and Well Log Analysts**
8866 Gulf Freeway
Suite 320
Houston, TX 77017

713-947-8727; *Fax:* 713-947-7181;
www.spwla.org
Social Media: Facebook, Twitter, LinkedIn

Thaimar Ramirez, President
Luiz Quintero, President-Elect
Brett L.Wendt, VP Technology
Oliver Mullin, VP Publications

Provides information services to scientists in the petroleum and mineral industries, serves as a voice of shared interests in our profession, plays a major role in strengthening petrophysical education, and strives to increase the awareness of the role petrophysics has in the Oil and Gas Industry and the scientific community.
3300 Members
Founded in: 1959

19691 **Solution Mining Research Institute**
105 Apple Valley Circle
Clarks Summit, PA 18411

570-585-8092; *Fax:* 570-585-8091
info@solutionmining.org;
www.solutionmining.org
Social Media: LinkedIn

Dr. Benoit Brouard, President
Kerry L. DeVries, Vice President
Dr. Fritz Wilke, Secretary-Treasurer
Klaus Buschbom, Program Chairman
John O. Voigt, Executive Director

Members are companies interested in the production of salt brine and solution mining of potash and soda ash, as well as production of salt covers, used for storage of oil, gas, chemicals, compressed air and waste.
100 Members
Founded in: 1965

19692 **Southern Gas Association**
3030 LBJ Freeway
Suite 1500
Dallas, TX 75234

972-620-8505; *Fax:* 972-620-1613
memberservices@southerngas.org;
www.southerngas.org
Social Media: Facebook, Twitter, YouTube, RSS

Henry P. Linginfelter, Chairman
Frank Yoho, 1st Vice Chair
Jerry L. Morris, 2nd Vice Chair
Mike Grubb, President & CEO
Kimberly Watson, Secretary - Treasurer

116 Members
Founded in: 1908

19693 **Spill Control Association of America**
103 Oronoco Street
Suite 200
Alexandria, VA 22314

571-451-0433; *Fax:* 443-640-1086
info@scaa-spill.org; www.scaa-spill.org

Rick Lewis, President
Devon Grennan, VP
Nelson Fetgatter, Treasurer
Robert Chambers, Secretary
John Allen, Executive Director

Members are companies concerned with cleaning up spills of oil and hazardous products and manufacturers of specialized products for spill control.
Founded in: 1973

19694 **The Independent Petroleum Association of America**
1201 15th St NW
Suite 300
Washington, DC 20005

202-857-4722; *Fax:* 202-857-4799;
www.ipaa.org
Social Media: Facebook, Twitter, LinkedIn, YouTube

Michael Watford, Chairman
Mark Miller, Vice Chairman
Barry Russell, President & CEO
Diemer TRUE, Treasurer
Lee O. Fuller, Executive Vice President

Members are small producers of oil and natural gas and their suppliers.
5500 Members
Founded in: 1929

19695 The National Petroleum Management Association
10908 Courthouse Rd
Ste 102-301
Fredericksburg, VA 22408

540-507-4371; *Fax:* 540-507-4372;
www.npma-fuelnet.org

Jack Lavin, President
Alan Reynolds, VP - Communication
Ruth Lavin, Marketing Officer
Erin Creese, San Antonio Office Manager
Al Pond, Board Member

19696 The Society of Exploration Geophysicists
8801 South Yale
Suite 500
Tulsa, OK 74137-3575

918-497-5500; *Fax:* 918-497-5557;
www.seg.org/seg
Social Media: Facebook, Twitter, LinkedIn, YouTube, Google+, Instagram

Michael C. Forrest, Chair
Dr. John Holloway, President
Alison W. Small, Treasurer
William L. Abriel, President-Elect
Dr. Eve S. Sprunt, First Vice President

19697 Tubular Exchanger Manufacturers Association, Inc.
25 North Broadway
Tarrytown, NY 10591

914-332-0040; *Fax:* 914-332-1541
tema@tema.org; www.tema.org

Richard C Byrne, Secretary

Sets standards for the industry, known as TEMA Standards, which are sold to the chemical processing and petroleum refining industries
18 Members
Founded in: 1939

19698 US Oil & Gas Association
1101 K Street NW
Suite 425
Washington, DC 20005

202-638-4400; www.usoga.org
Social Media: Facebook, Twitter

Walter G. Mayfield, Chairman
Albert L. Modiano, President
Tim Stewart, Vice President
Founded in: 1917

19699 Western Petroleum Marketers Association
PO Box 571500
Salt Lake City, UT 84157-1500

801-263-9762
888-252-5550; *Fax:* 801-262-9413
info@wpma.com; www.wpma.com
Social Media: Facebook, Twitter, LinkedIn, YouTube

Brad Bell, President
Rick Reese, 1st Vice President
Ron Berry, 2nd Vice President
Mark Lytle, 3rd Vice President
Gregg Benson, Senior PMAA Director

Trade magazine for petroleum marketers, c-store owners, and businesses associated with petroleum marketing.
700 Members
Founded in: 1953

19700 Western States Petroleum Association
1415 L St
Suite 600
Sacramento, CA 95814

916-498-9203; *Fax:* 916-444-5745;
www.wspa.org
Social Media: Facebook, Twitter

Catherine Reheis-Boyd, President
Tupper Hull, Vice President
Steven Arita, Senior Environmental Coordinator
Barbara Chichester, Bookkeeper

Trade association that represents the full spectrum of those companies that refine, produce, transport, and market petroleum and petroleum products in six western states: Arizona, California, Oregon, Nevada, Hawaii and Washington.
35 Members
Founded in: 1907

Newsletters

19701 Butane-Propane News
PO Box 660698
Arcadia, CA 91066-698

626-357-2168
800-214-4386; *Fax:* 626-303-2854;
www.bpnews.com

Natalie Peal, Publisher
Ann Rey, Editorial Director

Petroleum and propane industry news.
Cost: $32.00
Frequency: Monthly
Founded in: 1939

19702 Clean-Coal/Synfuels Letter
McGraw Hill
PO Box 182604
Columbus, OH 43272

614-304-4000
877-833-5524; *Fax:* 614-759-3749
customer.service@mcgraw-hill.com;
www.mcgraw-hill.com
Social Media: Facebook, Twitter, You Tube

John Higgins, Publisher

Provides worldwide coverage of the development of clean-coal technologies.
Cost: $840.00
6 Pages
Frequency: Monthly
Founded in: 1899

19703 Cold Water Oil Spills
Cutter Information Corporation
37 Broadway
Suite 1
Arlington, MA 02474-5500

781-648-1950
800-888-8939; *Fax:* 781-648-1950
service@cutter.com; www.cutter.com

Kim Leonard, Editor
Karen Coburn, Senior Consultant
Hillel Glazer, Senior Consultant
Ron Blitstein, Director

Clean up and control of oil spills in cold and icy waters.
Cost: $175.00
Founded in: 1986

19704 Fuel Line
National Petrochemical & Refiners Association
1667 K Street, NW
Suite 700
Washington, DC 20006-1654

202-457-0480; *Fax:* 202-457-0486
info@npra.org; www.npra.org

Charles Drevna, President
Gerald R. Van De Velde, CFO
Rebbie J. Riley, Executive Assistant

Addresses motor fuels regulations, policy and related issues. Available online only for NPRA members.
450 Members
Frequency: Weekly

19705 Gas Daily
1200 G Street NW
#1000
Washington, DC 20005

202-383-2100
800-752-8878; *Fax:* 202-383-2125
support@platts.com; www.gasdaily.com

Mark Davidson, Publisher
Bill Loveless, Director
Larry Foster, Director
Dixie Barrett, Vice President

Information on spot prices cash markets and regulatory developments for the natural gas industry.
Cost: $2255.00
Frequency: Daily

19706 Gas Storage Report
Pasha Publications
1600 Wilson Boulevard
#600
Arlington, VA 22209-2510

703-528-1244; *Fax:* 703-528-7821;
www.pasha.com

Jeff Pruzan, Editor

Detailed charts that list monthly storage activity of all interstate pipelines and covers all phases of the underground storage of natural gas.
Cost: $495.00
Frequency: Monthly

19707 Golob's Oil Pollution Bulletin
World Information Systems
PO Box 535
Cambridge, MA 02238-0535
Fax: 617-492-3312

Richard S Golob, Publisher
Roger B Wilson Jr, Editor

Provides news analysis on oil pollution prevention, control and cleanup. Covers oil spills worldwide, regulations, legislation and court decisions, technical reports, new equipment and products, contract opportunities and awards, and conference notices.
Cost: $335.00
Frequency: BiWeekly
Circulation: 20,000

19708 Green Room Report
National Petrochemical & Refiners Association
1667 K Street, NW
Suite 700
Washington, DC 20006-1654

202-457-0480; *Fax:* 202-457-0486
info@npra.org; www.npra.org

Charles Drevna, President
Gerald R. Van De Velde, CFO
Rebbie J. Riley, Executive Assistant

Addresses current environmental and safety events, including regulation and policy issues of EPA and OSHA. Available only online to NPRA members.
450 Members
Frequency: Weekly

19709 **Gulf of Mexico Newsletter**
Offshore Data Services
3200 Wilcrest Dr
Suite 170
Houston, TX 77042-3366

832-463-3000; *Fax:* 832-463-3100;
www.ods-petrodata.com

Thomas E Marsh, President
Hannah Hartland, Chairman

Aimed at the supply and service people of the off-shore oil and gas industry in the Gulf of Mexico, covers all significant industry news and events, and summarizes construction and field development activities.
Cost: $259.00
Frequency: Weekly
Circulation: 2150
Founded in: 2002

19710 **Hart's Renewable Fuel News**
Hart Evepy Publishing LP
1201 Seven Locks Road
#300
Potomac, MD 20854

301-354-2100; *Fax:* 301-424-7260;
www.worldfuels.com

Rachel Gantz, Editor
Robert Gaph, Executive Editor
Jack Peckham, Executive Editor
Theresa Ward, Managing Editor

Refinery updates, oxygenation schemes, capital spending, strategic alliances and essential business intelligence on corporate moves.
Cost: $1495.00
Frequency: Weekly
Founded in: 1973

19711 **ILMA Compoundings**
Independent Lubricant Manufacturers Association
400 N Columbus St
Suite 201
Alexandria, VA 22314-2264

703-684-5574; *Fax:* 703-836-8503
ilma@ilma.org; www.ilma.org

Celeste Powers, Executive Director
Martha Jolkovski, Director Publications/Advertising

Focuses on legislative, regulatory, marketing and industry news of concern to independent blenders and compounders of high-quality lubricants. Accepts advertising.
Cost: $150.00
20 Pages
Frequency: Monthly
Circulation: 1800
Founded in: 1948

19712 **Independent Liquid Terminals Association Newsletter**
Independent Liquid Terminals Association
1444 I St Nw
Suite 400
Washington, DC 20005-6538

202-842-9200; *Fax:* 703-875-2018
info@ilta.org; www.ilta.org

E David Doane, President
Gwen Butler, Office Manager

Monthly publication detailing federal, state and local legislative and regulatory action, ILTA response and ILTA events. Geared specifically to bulk liquid terminal owners/operators and establishments supplying equipment, goods and services to the bulk liquid terminaling industry.
8 Pages
Frequency: Monthly
Printed in 2 colors

19713 **Institute of Gas Technology**
Institute of Gas Technology
1700 S Mount Prospect Rd
Des Plaines, IL 60018-1804

847-768-0500; *Fax:* 847-768-0501
publicrelations@gastechnology.org;
www.gastechnology.org

David Carroll, President/CEO
Edward Johnston, Managing Director
Carol Worster, Manager

Newsletter
Cost: $495.00
Founded in: 1945

19714 **International Directory of Oil Spills and Control Products and Services**
Cutter Information Corporation
37 Broadway
Suite 1
Arlington, MA 02474-5500

781-648-8700; *Fax:* 781-648-8707
consortium@cutter.com; www.cutter.com
Social Media: Facebook, Twitter, LinkedIn, RSS

Verna Allee, Senior Consultant

Products and services listed by category.
Cost: $75.00

19715 **International Gas Technology Highlights**
Institute of Gas Technology
1700 S Mount Prospect Rd
Des Plaines, IL 60018-1804

847-768-0664; *Fax:* 847-768-0669
gtiadmin@gastechnology.org;
www.gastechnology.org

David Carroll, President/CEO
Edward Johnston, Managing Director

A biweekly newsletter covering international developments in energy with a focus on natural gas.
Cost: $100.00
4 Pages
Circulation: 1600
Founded in: 1946
Printed in 2 colors on matte stock

19716 **International Oil News**
William F Bland
709 Turmeric Ln
Durham, NC 27713-3103

919-544-1717; *Fax:* 919-544-1999
mbs@PetroChemical-News.com;
www.petrochemical-news.com/pcn.htm

Susan Kensil, President
Mollie B Sandor, Circulation Director

A weekly report of current news about all areas of the international petroleum industry, exploration, production, processing, transportation and marketing.
Cost: $857.00
Frequency: Weekly
Founded in: 1963

19717 **International Summary and Review of Oil Spills**
Cutter Information Corporation
37 Broadway
Suite 1
Arlington, MA 02474-5500

781-648-8700; *Fax:* 781-648-8707;
www.cutter.com

Verna Allee, Senior Consultant

International coverage of the gas and oil industry.
Cost: $100.00
Frequency: Monthly
Founded in: 1986

19718 **LNG Observer**
Institute of Gas Technology
1700 S Mount Prospect Rd
Des Plaines, IL 60018-1804

847-768-0664; *Fax:* 847-768-0669;
www.gastechnology.org

David Carroll, President/CEO

A bimonthly publication covering the worldwide liquefied natural gas industry, including political developments, technology, economics, statistics and interviews with industry leaders.
Cost: $395.00
24 Pages
Frequency: Bi-Monthly
Circulation: 2,000
ISBN: 1-053694-9 -

19719 **Leading Edge**
Society of Exploration Geophysicists
PO Box 702740
Tulsa, OK 74170-2740

918-497-5500; *Fax:* 918-497-5557
web@seg.org; www.seg.org
Social Media: Facebook, Twitter, LinkedIn

Mary Fleming, Executive Director
Vladimir Grechka, Editor
David J Monk, President
Richard D Miller, First V.P
Dennis A Cooke, Second V.P.

19720 **Lundberg Letter**
Lundberg Survey
911 Via Alondra
Camarillo, CA 93012-8048

805-383-2400
800-660-4574; *Fax:* 805-383-2424
lsi@lundbergsurvey.com;
www.lundbergsurvey.com

Trilby Lundberg, President

News on the US gasoline and diesel market. Retail and wholesale prices, market shares, consumption, taxes, station populations and consumer trends.
Cost: $399.00
Founded in: 1950

19721 **NGI's Daily Gas Price Index**
Intelligence Press
PO Box 70587
Washington, DC 20024

202-583-2596
800-427-5747; *Fax:* 202-318-0597
subscriptions@intelligencepress.com
intelligencepress.com

Ellen Beswick, Publisher
Mike Nazzaro, Managing Editor
Alexander Steis, Managing Editor

Gas industry news, reports and statistics.
Cost: $1045.00
Frequency: Daily

19722 **National Association of Royalty Owners**
12316 Andrews Drive
Suite B
Oklahoma City, OK 73120-5779

405-573-2972
800-558-0557; *Fax:* 405-286-9402
naro@naro-us.org; www.naro-us.org

Paul Covert, VP
Wana Box, President
David Guest, Manager

Newsletter for members. Also a book is available Look Before You Lease.
Cost: $6.50
Frequency: Monthly
Founded in: 1980

19723 Natural Gas Intelligence Price Index
22648 Glenn Drive
Suite 305
Sterling, VA 20164

703-318-8848
800-427-5747; *Fax:* 703-318-0597
info@naturalgasintel.com;
www.naturalgasintel.com
Social Media: Facebook, Twitter, LinkedIn

Ellen Beswick, Founder & Editor-in-Chief
Dexter Steis, Executive Publisher
Alexander Steis, Managing Editor

Price indexes available daily and weekly. Natural Gas Intelligence (NGI) is a leading provider of natural gas and market data to the energy industry. Since the first issue of Natural Gas Intelligence was published in 1981, NGI has provided key natural gas pricing, news and analysis relied upon daily by thousands of industry participants in the Americas, Europe, and Asia.
Cost: $1195.00
Frequency: Weekly
Founded in: 1981

19724 Natural Gas Week
Energy Intelligence Group
1401 New York Ave Nw
Suite 500
Washington, DC 20005-2102

202-393-5113; *Fax:* 202-393-5115
info@accion.org; www.accion.org

Maria Otero, President
Mike Sultan, Managing Director
John Lwande, Managing Director
Melissa Baez, Project Manager

Economics news covering the gas industry.
Cost: $1860.00
20 Pages
Frequency: Weekly
Founded in: 1985
Printed in 2 colors on matte stock

19725 News Fuel & Vehicles Report
Inside Washington Publishers
1919 S Eads St
Suite 201
Arlington, VA 22202-3028

703-418-3981
800-424-9068; *Fax:* 703-416-8543
support@iwpnews.com; www.iwpnews.com

Latest news, research and reports on alternative fuels and vehicles development aimed toward the program managers, lobbyists, policy makers, and auto, oil and corn chemical industries.
Cost: $985.00
Founded in: 1980

19726 Ocean News & Technology
Technology Systems Corporation
PO Box 1096
Palm City, FL 34991-7174

772-221-7720; *Fax:* 772-221-7715
techsystems@sprintmail.com;
www.ocean-news.com

Dan White, Editor
Sharon White, Circulation Manager

Magazine focusing on the major business areas of the ocean industry. News articles and technology developments are covered in areas including defense, offshore oil, diving, science, environment and marine.
Cost: $45.00
Founded in: 1981

19727 Offshore Rig Newsletter
Offshore Data Services
3200 Wilcrest Dr
Suite 170
Houston, TX 77042-3366

832-463-3000; *Fax:* 832-463-3100;
www.ods-petrodata.com

Thomas E Marsh, President
Barry Young, Chairman

Emerging markets, accidents, new technology, financing schemes, insurance trends, rig construction, moves, sales, and rates, labor problems, attrition, marketing strategies, and the corporate activities of drilling contractors.
Cost: $220.00
Frequency: Monthly
Circulation: 900
Founded in: 1973

19728 Oil Daily
Energy Intelligence Group
1401 New York Ave Nw
Suite 500
Washington, DC 20005-2102

202-393-5113; *Fax:* 202-393-5115
info@accion.org; www.accion.org

Maria Otero, President
John Lwande, Managing Director
Melissa Baez, Project Manager

Magazine on the petroleum and oil industry, available on line.
Cost: $1880.00
Frequency: Daily
Circulation: 60000
Founded in: 1951

19729 Oil Express
United Communications Group
11300 Rockville Pike
Street 1100
Rockville, MD 20852-3030

301-287-2700; *Fax:* 301-816-8945
webmaster@ucg.com; www.ucg.com

Benny Dicecca, President

Information for gasoline marketers.
Cost: $447.00
8 Pages
Frequency: Monthly
Founded in: 1977

19730 Oil Spill Intelligence Report
Aspen Publishers
111 8th Ave
Suite 700
New York, NY 10011-5207

212-771-0600
800-234-1660; *Fax:* 212-771-0885;
www.aspenlawschool.com

Richard Kravits, Executive VP
Gerry Centrowitz, Marketing/Communications Manager

Provides timely coverage of oil spills worldwide.
Cost: $695.00
6 Pages
Frequency: Weekly
Founded in: 1978

19731 Oil Spill United States Law Report
Aspen Publishers
76 Ninth Avenue
7th Floor
New York, NY 10011

212-771-0600
800-638-8437; www.aspenlawschool.com

Mark Dorman, CEO
Gustavo Dobles, VP Operations

Professionals who need to stay abreast of US federal and state regulations.
Cost: $7.67
12 Pages
Frequency: Monthly

19732 Oil, Gas and Petrochem Equipment
PennWell Publishing Company
1421 S Sheridan Rd
Tulsa, OK 74112-6619

918-835-3161
800-331-4463; *Fax:* 918-831-9476;
www.pennwell.com

Robert Biolchini, President
Tim L Tobeck, Group Publisher
J B Avants, Publisher & Editor

The petroleum industry's only all new products and services magazine. Each month it announces the newest developments in equipment, products, systems and services for drilling, production, refining, petrochemical manufacturing, pipeline/storage and gas processing.
Cost: $35.00
Frequency: Monthly
Circulation: 32000
Founded in: 1955
Mailing list available for rent: 32,000 names
Printed in 4 colors on glossy stock

19733 PIW's Oil Market Intelligence
286 Madison Ave
Suite 14
New York, NY 10017-6368

212-557-3000; *Fax:* 212-557-5051;
www.piw.pubs.com

Offers information on oil and gas stocks and bonds.
Frequency: Monthly

19734 PTTC Network News
Petroleum Technology Transfer Council
16010 Barkers Point Lane
Suite 220
Houston, TX 77079

281-921-1720; *Fax:* 281-921-1723
hq@pttc.org; www.pttc.org

Kristi Lovendahl, Webmaster/Newsletter Editor
Norma Gutierrez, Circulation Director
Donald Duttlinger, Executive Director
Russell Lindsay, Advertising Sales Director

16 page newsletter with east to read summaries of new oil and natural gas technologies.
Frequency: Quarterly
Circulation: 17000
Founded in: 1994

19735 PetroChemical News
William F Bland
PO Box 16666
Chapel Hill, NC 27516-6666

919-490-0700; *Fax:* 919-490-3002

Susan D Kensil, Editor

A fast, accurate report of significant world petrochemical developments.
Cost: $739.00
4 Pages
Frequency: Weekly

19736 Petroleum Intelligence Weekly
5 E 37th St
Suite 5
New York, NY 10016-2807

212-532-1112; *Fax:* 212-532-4479
info@energyintel.com; www.energyintel.com

Tom Wallin, President
Peter Kemp, Editor
Raja W. Sidawi, Chairman
Sarah Miller, Editor-at-Large

News of the oil and gas industries worldwide.
Cost: $3340.00
Frequency: Weekly
Founded in: 1961

19737 Platt's Oilgram News
McGraw Hill

3333 Walnut Street
Boulder, CO 80301-2525

720-485-5000
800-752-8878; *Fax:* 720-548-5701
support@platts.com; www.platts.com
Social Media: Facebook, Twitter, LinkedIn, YouTube,LinkedIn,RSS,Blog

O Marashian, Publisher
James Keener, Marketing
Harry Sachinsis, President

News of the oil and gas industries worldwide.
Frequency: Daily
Founded in: 1888
Mailing list available for rent

19738 **Public Gas News**
American Public Gas Association
201 Massachusetts Ave Ne
Suite C-4
Washington, DC 20002-4957

202-464-0240; *Fax:* 202-464-0246
website@apga.org; www.apga.org

Bert Kalisch, President
Bob Beauregard, Marketing
Chuck Warrington, Managing Director

Written for public gas managers to keep them apprised of industry news.
Cost: $50.00
Circulation: 1000
Founded in: 1961
Printed in on matte stock

19739 **Security Watch**
National Petrochemical & Refiners Association
1667 K Street, NW
Suite 700
Washington, DC 20006-1654

202-457-0480; *Fax:* 202-457-0486
info@npra.org; www.npra.org

Charles Drevna, President
Gerald R. Van De Velde, CFO
Rebbie J. Riley, Executive Assistant

Important security-related events, announcements, and background stories from government and industry. Written for members of the refining and petrochemical industries who have facility security responsibilities.
450 Members
Frequency: Weekly

19740 **Tech Update**
National Petrochemical & Refiners Association
1667 K Street, NW
Suite 700
Washington, DC 20006-1654

202-457-0480; *Fax:* 202-457-0486
info@npra.org; www.npra.org

Charles Drevna, President
Gerald R. Van De Velde, CFO
Rebbie J. Riley, Executive Assistant

Highlights developments in safety, plant security, technology, government regulations, and NPRA technical meetings for the petroleum refining and petrochemical industries.
450 Members
Frequency: Bi-Weekly

19741 **WPMA Weekly Update**
Western Petroleum Marketers Association
PO Box 571500
Murray, UT 84157

801-263-9762
888-252-5550; *Fax:* 801-262-9413
info@wpma.com; www.wpma.com

Gene Inglesby, Executive Director
Rob Franklin, President
Bob Ogan, VP

E-newsletter.
Frequency: Weekly
Founded in: 1953

19742 **Washington Report**
Interstate Natural Gas Association of America
555 13th St Nw
Suite 300W
Washington, DC 20004-1109

202-637-8600; *Fax:* 202-637-8615;
www.stonebridge-international.com

Anthony S Harrington, CEO
Samuel Berger, Manager

Natural gas newsletter places a special emphasis on developments that affect the interstate pipeline industry. It covers Congress, the Federal Energy Regulatory Commission and other federal agencies, state and Canadian regulatory boards and company news.

19743 **Weekly Propane Newsletter**
Butane-Propane News
PO Box 660698
Arcadia, CA 91066-0698

626-357-2168; *Fax:* 626-303-2854;
www.bpnews.com

Natalie Peal, Publisher
Kurt Ruhl, National Sales Manager

Weekly updates and rates on the propane and gas industry.
Cost: $205.00
8 Pages
Frequency: Weekly
Circulation: 2000
Founded in: 1939
Printed in one color on matte stock

19744 **Western Petroleum Marketers Association**
PO Box 571500
Salt Lake, UT 84157-1500

801-263-9762; *Fax:* 801-262-9413
info@wpma.com; www.wpma.com
Social Media: Facebook, Twitter

Gene Inglesby, Executive Director
Sandra Peterson, Editor
Brett Adams, President
Robert Fung, First V.P
Lary Poulton, Second V.P.

Accepts advertising.
Founded in: 1953

19745 **World Gas Intelligence**
575 Broadway
New York, NY 10012-3230

212-941-5500; *Fax:* 212-941-5509;
www.piw.pubs.com

Edward L Morse, Publisher
Jocelyn Strauber, Circulation Director

International coverage of the oil and gas industry.
Cost: $985.00
Frequency: SemiMonthly
Mailing list available for rent

Magazines & Journals

19746 **AAPG Bulletin**
American Association of Petroleum Geologists
PO Box 979
Tulsa, OK 74101-979

918-584-2555; *Fax:* 918-560-2632
bulletin@aapg.org; www.aapg.org

Beverly Molyneux, Managing Editor
David Curtiss, CEO/President
Larry Nations, Marketing

Peer reviewed articles that cover major extent and detailed geologic data. Information on petroleum, natural gas, and other energy products.
Cost: $305.00
Frequency: Monthly
Circulation: 30000
ISSN: 0149-1423
Founded in: 1917

19747 **AAPG Explorer**
American Association of Petroleum Geologists
1444 S Boulder Avenue
PO Box 979
Tulsa, OK 74101-979

918-584-2555
800-288-7636; *Fax:* 918-560-2665
postmaster@aapg.org; www.aapg.org

Patrick J F Gratton, President
Ernest A Mancini, Editor
Brenda Merideth, Advertising Sales Manager

News for explorationists of oil, gas and minerals as well as for geologists with environmental and water well concerns.
Cost: $50.00
Frequency: Monthly
Circulation: 30000
ISBN: 0-195298-6 -
Founded in: 1917
Printed in 4 colors on matte stock

19748 **American Gas Magazine**
American Gas Association
400 N Capitol Street NW
Suite 450
Washington, DC 20001

202-824-7000; *Fax:* 202-824-7092;
www.aga.org
Social Media: Facebook, Twitter, YouTube,RSS,Flickr

Dave McCurdy, CEO
Kevin Hardardt, CFO/CAO
Ysabel Korolevich, Membership Services
Frequency: 10x/Year
Founded in: 1918

19749 **American Oil and Gas Reporter**
National Publishers Group
PO Box 343
Derby, KS 67037

316-788-6271
800-847-8301; *Fax:* 316-788-7568;
www.fiest.com

Charlie Cookson, Publisher
Bill Campbell, Managing Editor

The American Oil & Gas Reporter serves the exploration, drilling and production segments of the oil and gas industry.
Cost: $65.07
Frequency: Monthly
Circulation: 7384
Founded in: 1958

19750 **BIC - Business & Industry Connection**
BIC Alliance
Po Box 3502
Covington, LA 70434

985-893-8692; *Fax:* 985-893-8693
bic@bicalliance.com; www.bicalliance.com

Jamie Craig, Editor
Earl Heard, CEO/President
Kathy Dugas, Administrator
Joe Storer, Manager

Information on oil and gas, refining, petrochemical, environmental, construction, engineering, pulp and paper, state agencies and municipalities business.
Cost: $45.00
Circulation: 75000

19751 **Bloomberg Natural Gas Report**
Bloomberg Financial Markets
100 Business Park Drive
Princeton, NJ 08542-840

609-279-3000
800-395-9403; *Fax:* 917-369-7000
munis@bloomberg.com;
www.bloomberg.com/energy

Michael Bloomberg, Publisher
Ronald Henkoff, Editor

News, interviews, and analysis of topics of importance to all levels of the natural gas market.
12 Pages
Frequency: Weekly
Circulation: 1700
Founded in: 1980

19752 **Butane-Propane News**
Butane-Propane News
PO Box 660698
Arcadia, CA 91006

626-357-2168
800-214-4386; *Fax:* 626-303-2854;
www.bpnews.com

Natalie Peal, Publisher
Ann Rey, Editorial Director
Kurt Ruhl, Sales Manager

Petroleum and propane industry news.
Cost: $32.00
56 Pages
Frequency: Monthly
Circulation: 16500
Founded in: 1939
Printed in 4 colors on glossy stock

19753 **Coal People**
Al Skinner Enterprises
PO Box 6247
Charleston, WV 25362-0247

304-342-4129
800-235-5188; *Fax:* 304-343-3124
cpm@newwave.net; www.coalpeople.com

A Skinner, Owner
Christina Karawan, Managing Editor
Beth Terranova, Sales Manager
Angela McNealy, Circulation Manager
C K Lane, Senior Vice President

Features special news and product sections for the coal industry.
Cost: $25.00
60 Pages
Circulation: 11500
Founded in: 1976
Printed in 4 colors on glossy stock

19754 **Compressor Tech Two**
Diesel & Gas Turbine Publications
20855 Watertown Rd
Suite 220
Waukesha, WI 53186-1873

262-754-4100; *Fax:* 262-754-4175
slizdas@dieselpub.com; www.dieselspec.com

Michael Osenga, President
Brent Haight, Managing Editor
Kara Kane, Advertising Manager
Christa Johnson, Production Manager
Sheila Lizdas, Circulation Manager

Covers oil and gas exploration, drilling, oilfield contracting, gas and petrochemical pipeline and storage, as well as petrochemical, hydrocarbon and gas processing industries.
Circulation: 12000

19755 **Diesel Progress: North American Edition**
Diesel & Gas Turbine Publications
20855 Watertown
Suite 220
Waukesha, WI 53186-1873

262-754-4100
800-558-4322; *Fax:* 262-832-5075
mosenga@dieselpub.com;
www.dieselspec.com

Michael Osenga, President
Sheila Lizdas, Circulation Manager
Lynne Diefenbach, Advertising Manager
Christa Johnson, Production Manager

Geared towards readers interested in state-of-the-art systems technology. Features include new product listings, systems design, research amd product testing as well as systems maintenance and rebuilding.
Frequency: Monthly
Circulation: 26011
Founded in: 1969

19756 **Drill Bits**
National Drilling Association
1545 W 130th St
Suite A2
Hinckley, OH 44233-9121

330-273-5756
877-632-4748; *Fax:* 216-803-9900
info@nda4u.com; www.nda4u.com

Peggy McGee, President
Dan Dunn, VP
Jim Howe, Secretary/Treasurer
Tim Cleary, Board of Directors
R. Alan Garrard, Board of Directors

A non-profit trade association of contractors, manufacturers and affiliated members from the drilling industry representing the geotechnical, environmental and mineral exploration sectors of this industry.
250+ Members
Frequency: 2 X/Year
Founded in: 1972

19757 **Drilling Contractor**
International Association of Drilling Contractors
10370 Richmond Ave
Suite 760
Houston, TX 77042-9687

713-292-1945; *Fax:* 713-292-1946
info@iadc.org; www.iadc.org

Lee Hunt, President
Tom Terrell, Senior VP Business Development

All drilling, all completing, all the time.
Cost: $50.00
40 Pages
Frequency: 6x/Year
Circulation: 34500
Printed in 4 colors

19758 **Energy Markets**
Hart Publications
4545 Post Oak Place
#210
Houston, TX 77027

713-993-9320; *Fax:* 713-840-8585

Linda K Rader, Editor
Robert C Jarvis, Publisher

Energy Markets serves the following energy industry business classifications: utilities, municipalities, consultants and financial services, regulators, and other companies allied to or supportive of the energy industry.
Frequency: Monthly
Circulation: 25,751
Founded in: 1993

19759 **Energy Network**
Gulf Publishing Company
PO Box 2608
Houston, TX 77252

713-529-4301
800-231-6275; *Fax:* 713-520-4433
store@gulfpub.com; www.gulfpub.com
Social Media: Twitter, LinkedIn, RSS,YouTube

John D Royall, President/CEO
Ron Higgins, VP Sales/Publisher

Edited for companies that sell products to the oil and gas industry.
Founded in: 1916
Mailing list available for rent

19760 **Fuel Oil News**
Hunter Publishing Limited
3100 S King Dr
Suite 1004
Chicago, IL 60616-3483

312-567-9981; *Fax:* 312-846-4632;
www.fueloilnews.com

Luke Hunter, Partner
Joanne Juda, Circulation Director
Kate Kenny, Publisher
Keith Reid, Senior Editor
Patricia McCartney, Associate Editor

For home heating oil retailers.
Cost: $28.00
70 Pages
Frequency: Monthly
Circulation: 18000
Founded in: 1935
Printed in 4 colors on glossy stock

19761 **Gas Turbine World**
Pequot Publishing
PO Box 447
Southport, CT 36490

203-259-1812; *Fax:* 203-254-3431
http://www.gtwbooks.com

Robert Farmer, Editor
Victor Debiasi, Publisher
Janes Janson, Marketing
Peg Walker, Circulation Manager

Serves the electric, utility and non-untility power generation, oil/gas production and processing industries.
Cost: $135.00
Frequency: Weekly
Circulation: 11000
Founded in: 1979

19762 **Gas Utility Manager**
James Informational Media
6301 Gaston Avenue
#541
Dallas, TX 75214-6204

214-827-4630; *Fax:* 847-391-9058;
www.betterroads.com

Mike Porcaro, Publisher
Mike Porcaro, CEO/President
Carole Spohr, Marketing Manager
Stacy Stiglic, Circulation Manager
Ruth Stidger, Editor

Federal and international regulations, new supply projects, research and development projects and gas industry news.
Cost: $95.00
40 Pages
Frequency: Annual+
Circulation: 40000
Founded in: 1931

19763 **Georgia Petroleum Marketer**
Georgia Oilmen Association

1775 Spectrum Drive
Suite 100
Lawrenceville, GA 30043

770-995-7570; *Fax:* 770-995-9757
rlane@gaoilassoc.com;
www.georgiaoilmensassoc.com

Roger T Lane, President/Editor
Mary R Franklin, Associate Editor
100 Pages
Frequency: Annual
Circulation: 800

19764 Hart's E & P
Hart Publications
1616 S Voss Rd
Suite 1000
Houston, TX 77057-2641

713-993-9320; *Fax:* 713-840-8585
directoryeditor@hartenergy.com;
www.hartenergy.com

Rich Eichler, CEO
Joe Fisher, Senior Vice President
Kristine Klavers, Senior Vice President
Frederick Potter, Executive Vice President

Technical approaches and improvements related to both offshore and land drilling and extraction of petroleum products, also new product information and personality profiles.
Cost: $59.00
Frequency: Monthly
Circulation: 25000

19765 Hart's Gas/LPG Markets
Hart Publications
6011 Executive Drive
#200
Rockville, MD 20852-3804

301-468-1039; *Fax:* 301-468-1039;
www.hartpub.com

Robert Gough, Editor

Financial reports on individual natural gas and liquid gasoline companies, their stock analysis, value and future mergers or acquisitions that may affect the pricing of gasoline or companies involved in the industry.
Cost: $ 1497.00
Frequency: Monthly

19766 Hart's Oil & Gas Interests
Hart Publications
6011 Executive Boulevard
#200
Rockville, MD 20852-3804

301-468-1039; *Fax:* 301-468-1039;
www.hartpub.com

Brian Crotty, Group Publisher

Designed to keep readers abreast of developments and investment ideas in the petroleum and natural gas industry.
Frequency: Monthly

19767 Hart's Oil & Gas Investor
Hart Publications
1616 S Voss Rd
Suite 1000
Houston, TX 77057-2641

713-993-9320
800-874-2544; *Fax:* 713-840-8585
directoryeditor@hartenergy.com;
www.hartenergy.com

Rich Eichler, CEO
Leslie Haines, Editor-in-Chief
Nissa Darbonne, Executive Editor
Kristine Klavers, Senior Vice President
Frederick Potter, Executive Vice President

Company performance, investment forecasts, economic outlooks, management strategy reports, focusing on the financial aspects of the petroleum and natural gas industry.
Cost: $297.00
Frequency: Monthly
Circulation: 5100
Printed in 4 colors

19768 Hart's World Refining
Hart Publications
4545 Post Oak Place
Suite 210
Houston, TX 77027-3105

713-993-9320
800-874-2544; *Fax:* 713-840-8585;
www.hartpub.com

David Coates, Publisher
Jeremy Grunt, Executive Editor
Terry Higgins, Executive Publisher
Robert Gough, Editorial Director
Rich Eichler, President

Covers projects, financing and market developments, along with feedstock and product supply, demand, pricing information, technical and regulatory events associated with the manufacture, supply, and use of transportation fuels refining technologies, business strategies and fuel policy legislation.
Cost: $149.00
Circulation: 15,693
Founded in: 1980

19769 Hydrocarbon Processing
Gulf Publishing Company
PO Box 2608
Houston, TX 77252-2608

713-529-4301
800-231-6275; *Fax:* 713-520-4433
store@gulfpub.com; www.gulfpub.com
Social Media: Twitter, LinkedIn, RSS,YouTube

John D Royall, President/CEO
Ron Higgins, VP Sales/Publisher

Concentrates on the problems facing management and technical personnel in the worldwide hydrocarbon processing industry. Accepts advertising.
Cost: $120.00
Frequency: Monthly
Circulation: 30000
Founded in: 1916
Mailing list available for rent
Printed in on glossy stock

19770 Journal of Geophysical Research
American Geophysical Union
2000 Florida Ave Nw
Washington, DC 20009-1277

202-462-6900
800-966-2481; *Fax:* 202-328-0566
usaha@usaha.org; www.agu.org
Social Media: Facebook, Twitter, LinkedIn, YouTube,RSS,Flickr,Blog

Christine McEntee, Executive Director
John Orcutt, Publisher

There are five sections covering soid earth, oceans, atmosphere, planets, and space physics.
Cost: $20.00
Frequency: Monthly
Circulation: 10,000
Founded in: 1919

19771 Journal of Petroleum Technology
Society of Petroleum Engineers
PO Box 833836
Richardson, TX 75083-3836

972-952-9300
800-456-6863; *Fax:* 972-952-9435
service@spe.org; www.spe.org

Mark Rubin, Executive Director
Giovanni Paccaloni, President
Paul Thone, Senior Manager of Sales
Niki Bradbury, Managing Director

Journal of Petroleum Technology serves the field of exploration, drilling, production, and reservoir management as well as related manufacturing and service organizations.
98 Pages
Frequency: Monthly
Circulation: 51205
Founded in: 1949
Printed in 4 colors on glossy stock

19772 LP/Gas
Advanstar Communications
131 W 1st St
Duluth, MN 55802-2065

218-740-7200
800-346-0085; *Fax:* 218-740-7079
info@advanstar.com; www.advanstar.com

Kent Akervik, Manager
Sean Carr, Publisher
Joseph Loggia, CEO
Kris Meyer, Circulation Manager
Brian Kanaba, National Sales Manager

The propane industry's premier information source.
Cost: $30.00
36 Pages
Frequency: Monthly
Circulation: 15320
ISSN: 0024-7103
Printed in 4 colors on glossy stock

19773 Landman
American Association of Professional Landmen
4100 Fossil Creek Boulevard
Fort Worth, TX 76137-2723

817-847-7700; *Fax:* 817-847-7704
aapl@landman.org; www.landman.org

Le'ann Callihan, Editor
Robin Forte, President

Accepts advertising.
Cost: $50.00
76 Pages
Founded in: 1955

19774 Lubricants World
4545 Post Oak Place
Suite 230
Houston, TX 77027

713-840-0378; *Fax:* 713-840-0379

Kathryn B Carnes, Editor

19775 NLGI Spokesman
National Lubricating Grease Institute
4635 Wyandotte St
Suite 202
Kansas City, MO 64112-1537

816-931-9480; *Fax:* 816-753-5026
nlgi@nlgi.org; www.nlgi.org

Kim Bott, Executive Director
Kim Bott, Administrative Assistant

About 50% of technical or scientific information amied at the manufacturers, users and suppliers of lubricating grease.
Cost: $53.00
Frequency: Monthly
Circulation: 2500
Founded in: 1933

19776 National Petroleum News
Bel-Av Communications
359 Galahad Rd
Bolingbrook, IL 60440-2108

www.npnweb.com

Keith Reid, Editor-in-Chief
Debra Reschke, Managing/Research Editor

The independent voice of the petroleum industry, content is aimed at the owner, operator or senior manager-the people who make the big decisions

that require capital, time and resources.
Cost: $64.00
90 Pages
Frequency: Monthly
Circulation: 38000
Founded in: 1909

19777 Natural Gas Fuels
RP Publishing
2696 S Colorado Blvd
Suite 595
Denver, CO 80222-5944

303-863-0521; *Fax:* 303-863-1722
info@rppublishing.com;
www.rppublishing.com

Frank Rowe, President

Technological advances, marketing strategies, legislative activities, successful applications, and corporate and government initiatives to promote natural gas-powered vehicles
Circulation: 7000
Founded in: 1992

19778 O&A Marketing News
KAL Publications
559 S Harbor Blvd
Suite A
Anaheim, CA 92805-4547

714-563-9300; *Fax:* 714-563-9310;
www.kalpub.com

Kathy Laderman, President
Doreen Philbin, Advertising Sales Manager
Jim Penn, Circulation Manager
Linda Squeo, Marketing Manager

Coverage of industry events and related shows for wholesale and retail marketers of gasoline, oil and automotive service replacement products in the thirteen Pacific-Western states.
Cost: $20.00
Circulation: 7000
Founded in: 1966

19779 Offshore
PennWell Publishing Company
1421 S Sheridan Rd
Tulsa, OK 74112-6619

918-835-3161
800-331-4463; *Fax:* 918-831-9476
Headquarters@PennWell.com;
www.pennwell.com

Robert Biolchini, President
Biol Chini, CEO
Tommie Grigg, Circulation Manager
Elbon Ball, Editor
Jayne Gilfinger, Marketing Manager

Offshore serves the international oil and gas industry in its marine/offshore operations.
Cost: $75.00
186 Pages
Frequency: Monthly
Circulation: 40000
ISSN: 0030-0608
Founded in: 1910
Mailing list available for rent
Printed in 4 colors on glossy stock

19780 Oil & Gas Journal
PennWell Publishing Company
1700 West Loop S
#1000
Houston, TX 77027-3005

713-621-9720; *Fax:* 713-963-6285
sales@pennwell.com; www.ogjonline.com

Tom T Terrell, Publisher
Tim Sullivant, Regional Sales Manager
Mike Moss, Regional Sales Manager

Detailed interpreation and information of the world developments in the oil and gas industry
Cost: $79.00
Frequency: Weekly
Circulation: 36090
Founded in: 1990
Printed in 4 colors on glossy stock

19781 Oil Spill Contingency Planning: A Global Perspective
Aspen Publishers
76 Ninth Avenue
7th Floor
New York, NY 10011

212-771-0600
800-638-8437; wwww.aspenlawschool.com

Mark Dorman, CEO
Gustavo Dobles, VP Operations

Hands-on guidebook to contingency planning for oil spills.
Cost: $195.00

19782 Oilheating
Industry Publications
3621 Hill Rd
Parsippany, NJ 07054-1001

973-331-9545; *Fax:* 973-331-9547;
www.spraytechnology.com
Social Media: Facebook

Cynthia Hundley, Publisher

Addresses issues on dispatching and delivery efficiency, residential and commercial fuel oil use, as well as sales and services of oilfired equipment.
Cost: $42.00
Frequency: Monthly
Circulation: 13280
ISSN: 1092-6003
Founded in: 1922
Mailing list available for rent

19783 Petroleo International
Keller International Publishing Corporation
150 Great Neck Rd
Suite 400
Great Neck, NY 11021-3309

516-829-9722; *Fax:* 516-829-9306;
www.supplychainbrain.com

Victor Prieto, Editor
Sean Noble, Publisher
Steve Kann, Circulation Manager
Jerry Keller, President
Mary Chavez, Director of Sales

Spanish language petroleum/petrochemical magazine.
100 Pages
Circulation: 10,314
Founded in: 1943

19784 SPE Drilling & Completion
Society of Petroleum Engineers
PO Box 833836
Richardson, TX 75083-3836
972-529-9300
800-456-6863; *Fax:* 972-952-9435
service@spe.org; www.spe.org

Giovanni Paccaloni, President
Shashana Pearson, Editor
Mary Jane, Advertising Manager
Georgeann Bilich, Publisher
Niki Bradbury, Managing Director

Technical papers selected for the drilling profession reviewed by peers on topics such as casing, instrumentation, bit technology, fluids, measurment, deviation control, telemetry, completion and well control.
Cost: $60.00
Frequency: Quarterly
Circulation: 3588
Founded in: 1984

19785 Sea Technology Magazine
Compass Publications, Inc.
1501 Wilson Blvd
Suite 1001
Arlington, VA 22209-2403

703-524-3136; *Fax:* 703-841-0852
oceanbiz@sea-technology.com;
www.sea-technology.com
Social Media: Twitter

Amos Bussmann, President/Publisher
Joy Carter, Circulation Manager
Meghan Ventura, Managing Editor

Worldwide information leader for marine/offshore business, science and engineering. Read in more than 110 countries by management, engineers, scientists and technical personnel working in industry, government and education.
Cost: $40.00
Frequency: Monthly
Circulation: 16304
ISSN: 0093-3651
Founded in: 1960
*Mailing list available for rent*at $80 per M
Printed in 4 colors

19786 Today's Refinery
Chemical Week Associates
2 Grand Central Tower,140 East 45th Street
40th floor
New York, NY 10017

212-884-9528; *Fax:* 212-884-9514
ltattum@chemweek.com; www.chemweek.com
Social Media: Twitter, RSS,Blog

John Rockwell, VP
Joe Minnella, Global Sales Director
LYN TATTUM, Publisher
Robert Westervelt, Editor-in-Chief

Editorials from industry leaders focusing on current problems facing the industry. Highlights on legistation, activity, government regulations,and reports on major industry meetings.
Frequency: Monthly
Circulation: 10,000
Mailing list available for rent

19787 Utility & Pipeline Industries
WMO DannHausen Corporation
330 North Wabash
Suite 3201
Chicago, IL 60611

312-628-5870; *Fax:* 312-628-5878
wod@dannhausen.com;
www.gasindustries.com

Bob Higgins, Publisher
Heidi Liddle, Production Manager
Karen Ebbesmeyer, Circulation Manager
Ruth W. Stidger, Editor-in-Chief
Cory Sekine Pettite, Managing Editor

Market to federal agencies, bureaus, government departments and toll authorities. Accepts advertising.
Cost: $20.00
62 Pages
Frequency: Monthly
Circulation: 10680

19788 Washington Report
National Ocean Industries Association
1120 G St Nw
Suite 900
Washington, DC 20005-3801

202-347-6900; *Fax:* 202-347-8650;
www.noia.org
Social Media: Facebook, Twitter, YouTube

Tom Fry, President
Franki K Stuntz, Director Administration
Nolty J Thuriot, Director Congressional Affairs
Frequency: Bi-Weekly

19789 Well Servicing
Workover Well Servicing Publications

10200 Richmond Avenue
Suite 275
Houston, TX 77042

713-781-0758
800-692-0771; *Fax:* 713-781-7542
kjordan@aesc.net; www.aesc.net

Kenny Jordan, Executive DIrector
Polly Fisk, Editor
Patty Jordan, Circulation

New products listing and reviews, field reports, and information on companies in the industry. Written and edited for energy service company professionals, and oil & gas operations.
40 Pages
Circulation: 11000
ISSN: 0043-2393
Founded in: 1956

19790 Western Petroleum Marketers News Magazine
Western Petroleum Marketers Association
PO Box 571500
Murray, UT 84157

801-263-9762
888-252-5550; *Fax:* 801-262-9413
info@wpma.com; www.wpma.com

Gene Inglesby, Executive Director
Rob Franklin, President
Bob Ogan, VP
Frequency: Quarterly

19791 World Oil
Gulf Publishing Company
PO Box 2608
Houston, TX 77252

713-529-4301
800-231-6275; *Fax:* 713-520-4433
store@gulfpub.com; www.gulfpub.com
Social Media: Twitter, LinkedIn, RSS,YouTube

John D Royall, President/CEO
Ron Higgins, VP Sales/Publisher

Reaches the exploration, drilling, producing, and well servicing segments of the oil and gas industry.
Cost: $34.00
100 Pages
Frequency: Monthly
Circulation: 36000
ISSN: 0043-8790
Founded in: 1916
Mailing list available for rent
Printed in 4 colors on glossy stock

Trade Shows

19792 American Association of Petroleum Geologists Annual Convention/Expo
American Association of Petroleum Geologists
PO Box 979
Tulsa, OK 74119

918-584-2555
800-364-2274; *Fax:* 918-560-2665
convene@aapg.org; www.aapg.org
Social Media: Facebook, Twitter, LinkedIn, YouTube

Randa Reeder-Briggs, Annual Meeting Manager
Melissa Howerton, Annual Meeting Assistant
Steph Benton, Exhibit Manager
Rick Fritz, Executive Director
Edward 'Ted' Beaumont, President

Exhibits of instrumentation, equipment, supplies, services and publications for petroleum geologists, geophysicists and engineers.
7000 Attendees
Frequency: Annual/April

19793 American School of Gas Measurement Technology Meeting
PO Box 3991
Houston, TX 77253-3991

903-486-7875; *Fax:* 512-267-9243;
www.asgmt.com

Seminar, workshop, and tours, plus 95 exhibits of gas measurement, equipment, supplies and services.
600 Attendees
Frequency: Annual
Founded in: 1927

19794 Asia Pacific Improved Oil Recovery Conference
Society of Petroleum Engineers-Texas
222 Palisades Creek Drive
PO Box 833836
Richardson, TX 75083-3868

972-952-9300; *Fax:* 972-952-9435;
www.spe.org

Oil recovery exhibition.
Mailing list available for rent

19795 Beaumont Industrial Petrochemical Trade Show
Lobos Services
16016 Perkins Road
Baton Rouge, LA 70810-3631

225-751-5626

Debbie Balough, Show Manager

Informs local industry of the full array of industrial equipment for the chemical industries.
5M Attendees
Frequency: January

19796 Circum-Pacific Council Energy Mineral Resources
5100 Westheimer Road
Houston, TX 77056-5596

713-709-9071; *Fax:* 713-622-5360

Mary Stewart, Show Manager
Napoleon Carcamo, Owner

50 booths.
1.2M Attendees
Frequency: November

19797 Eastern Oil and Gas Equipment Show
Pennsylvania Oil and Gas Association
412 N 2nd Street
Harrisburg, PA 17101-1342

717-939-9551

Stephen Rhoads, Show Manager

175 booths displaying new technologies, products and services relating to the oil and gas industries.
1M Attendees
Frequency: June

19798 Entelec Conference & Expo
Energy Telecommunications and Electrical Assoc
5005 W Royal Lane
Suite 116
Irving, TX 75063

972-929-3169
888-503-8700; *Fax:* 972-915-6040
blaine@entelec.org; www.entelec.org

Blaine Siske, Executive Manager
Susan Joiner, Exhibits Manager
Michael Blurt, President
James C Coulter, First V.P
Kenneth Clouse, Second V.P.

To bring together communications and control technology professionals from the petroleum, natural gas, pipeline, and electric utility companies for three days of quality training, seminars, exhibits and networking.
Frequency: Annual/May
Founded in: 1928

19799 Europe International Offshore Exchange
222 Palisades Creek Drive
Richardson, TX 75080-2040
Donna Anderson, Show Manager

1,100 booths.
21M Attendees
Frequency: September

19800 International Thermal Spray Conference & Exposition
ASM International
9639 Kinsman Road
Materials Park, OH 44073

440-338-5151
800-336-5152; *Fax:* 440-338-4634
natalie.nemec@asminternational.org;
www.asminternational.org
Social Media: Facebook, Twitter, LinkedIn

Natalie Neme, Event Manager
Kelly Thomas, Exposition Account Manager

Global annual event attracting professional interested in thermal spray technology focusing on advances in HVOF, plasma and detonation gun, flame spray and wire arc spray processes, performance of coatings, and future trends. 150 exhibitors.
1000 Attendees
Frequency: Annual/May

19801 Landman
American Association of Petroleum Landmen
4100 Fossil Creek Boulevard
Fort Worth, TX 76137-2723

817-847-7700; *Fax:* 817-847-7704
http://www.landman.org

Carolyn Stephens, Editor
Le Ann Pembroke, Advertising Manager

50 booths.
1.5M Attendees
Frequency: June

19802 Liquified Gas Association Southwest
PO Box 9925
Austin, TX 78766-0925

Fax: 512-834-0758

Cheryl Tomanetz, Show Manager

125 booths.
1.8M Attendees
Frequency: September

19803 Liquified Natural Gas
Reed Exhibition Companies
255 Washington Street
Newton, MA 02458-1637

617-584-4900; *Fax:* 617-630-2222

Elizabeth Hitchcock, International Sales

Presentation for the liquefied natural gas industry.
2.5M Attendees
Frequency: May

19804 Liquified Petroleum Gas Exposition Midwest
4100 Country Club Drive
Jefferson City, MO 65109-0302
573-634-5345; *Fax:* 573-893-2623

Emma Krommel, Show Manager

100 booths of large transport and bobtail delivery trucks.
1M Attendees
Frequency: June

19805 **Midwest Petroleum & Convenience Tradeshow**
Illinois Petroleum Marketers Association
PO Box 12020
Springfield, IL 62791-2020
217-544-4609; *Fax:* 217-789-0222
Bill Fleischli, Executive VP, Managing Editor
Suppliers and manufacturers to petroleum marketing and convenience store trades, including pumps, computers, trucks, safety devices, canopies, car washes and tank testing. 300 booths.
4M Attendees
Frequency: June

19806 **National Petro Refiners Association Refinery Petrochemical Plant**
1899 L Street NW
Suite 1000
Washington, DC 20036-3810
202-457-0480
http://www.npra.org
Robert Dzuiban, Show Manager
Robert Slaughter, President
A forum for the exchange of technical information and services to the petroleum industry.
1.3M Attendees
Frequency: May

19807 **Offshore Technology Conference**
222 Palisades Creek Drive, Richardson
Richardson, TX 75080-2040
972-952-9494
866-229-2386; *Fax:* 972-952-9435
service@spe.org; www.spe.org
Alan Wegener, Show Manager
Niki Bradbury, Managing Director
Consisting of a forum to disseminate technical information for the advancement of engineering.
30M Attendees
Frequency: May

19808 **Petroleum Computer Conference**
Society of Petroleum Engineers
222 Palisades Creek Drive
Richardson, TX 75080-2040
972-952-9300; *Fax:* 972-952-9435
service@spe.org; www.spe.org
Niki Bradbury, Managing Director
Annual show of 50 microcomputer manufacturers and suppliers who provide hardware and software to the petroleum industry.
650 Attendees

19809 **Petroleum Equipment Institute (CONVEX) and Exhibits**
Petroleum Equipment Institute
PO Box 2380
Tulsa, OK 74101-2380
918-494-9696; *Fax:* 918-491-9895;
www.pei.org
Connie Dooley, Administrative Director
Robert Renkes, Marketing Director
Sarah West, Marketing Director
Rick Long, General Manager
Annual show of manufacturers of petroleum marketing equipment. There are 215 exhibiting companies with 675 booths.
4500 Attendees
Frequency: October
Founded in: 1951

19810 **Society Petro Engineers Annual Meeting**
PO Box 833836
Richardson, TX 75083-3836
972-952-9300; *Fax:* 972-952-9435
Lois Woods, Show Manager
Mark Rubin, Executive Director
Conference with exhibits of drilling and production equipment and materials.
10M Attendees
Frequency: September

19811 **Society Petro Engineers Permian Basin Oil Gas Recovery Conference and Expo**
PO Box 833836
Richardson, TX 75083-3836
972-952-9300
Susan Bell, Event Manager
70 booths.
400 Attendees
Frequency: March

19812 **Society Petro Engineers Petroleum Computer Conference and Expo**
PO Box 833836
Richardson, TX 75083-3836
972-952-9300
Georgie Cumiskey, Event Manager
30 booths of microcomputer hardware and software for the petroleum industry.
300 Attendees
Frequency: July

19813 **Society Petro Engineers Production Operations Symposium**
PO Box 833836
Richardson, TX 75083-3836
972-952-9300
Karen Rodgers, Event Manager
Mark Rubin, Executive Director
70 booths of oil and gas industry related products and services.
1M Attendees
Frequency: March

19814 **Society Petro Engineers Rocky Mountain**
PO Box 833836
Richardson, TX 75083-3836
972-952-9300
Georgie Cumiskey, Event Manager
60 booths.
300 Attendees
Frequency: April

19815 **Society Petro Engineers Western Regional Meeting**
PO Box 833836
Richardson, TX 75083-3836
972-952-9300
Lois Woods, Exchange Manager
Mark Rubin, Executive Director
65 booths.
700 Attendees
Frequency: May

19816 **Society of Petro Engineers Eastern Regional Meeting**
PO Box 833836
Richardson, TX 75083-3836
972-952-9300
Susan Bell, Event Manager
Mark Rubin, Executive Director
Offers a forum for the exchange of ideas between petroleum and gas engineers.
500 Attendees
Frequency: October

19817 **Society of Petro Engineers Enhanced Oil Recovery Symposium and Exchange**
PO Box 833836
Richardson, TX 75083-3836
972-952-9300
Georgie Cumiskey, Event Manager
Mark Rubin, Executive Director
100 booths.
1.6M Attendees
Frequency: April

19818 **Southeast Petro Food Marketing Expo**
7300 Glenwood Avenue
Raleigh, NC 27612
919-782-4411; *Fax:* 919-782-4414;
www.sepetro.org
Sharon Vinson, Show Manager
550 booths and 400+ exhibitors serving the petroleum and convenience store industries in the southeast.
2,000 Attendees
Frequency: March

19819 **WPMA Convention & Convenience Store Expo**
Western Petroleum Marketers Association
Po Box 571500
Salt Lake, UT 84157-1500
801-263-9762; *Fax:* 801-262-9413
info@wpma.com; www.wpma.com
Social Media: Facebook, Twitter
Gene Inglesby, Executive Director
Jan Roothoff, Administration Director
In addition to Las Vegas entertainment and special events, the convention offers keynote speakers around current issues and topics, as well as workshops. Over 400 exhibits. Registration costs vary.
3750 Attendees
Frequency: Annual/Winter

19820 **Western Petroleum Marketers Convention & Convenience Store Expo**
Western Petroleum Marketers Association
PO Box 571500
Salt Lake, UT 84157-1500
801-263-9762
888-252-5550; *Fax:* 801-262-9413
info@wpma.com; www.wpma.com
Social Media: Facebook, Twitter
Gene Inglesby, Executive Director
Jan Roothoff, Administration Director
Bob Ogan, VP
430 booths.
3500 Attendees
Frequency: February

19821 **World Gas Conference**
American Gas Association
400 N Capitol Street NW
Washington, DC 20001
202-824-7000; *Fax:* 202-824-7092
ykorolevich@aga.org; www.aga.org
Social Media: Facebook, Twitter, LinkedIn, Myspace, Flickr
John W. Somerhalder, II, Chairman
Dave McCurdy, President & CEO
Lawrence T. Borgard, 1st Vice Chair
Ronald W. Jibson, 2nd Vice Chair
Information towards building a sustainable future for the gas industry.
Frequency: Quadrennial
Founded in: 1918

Directories & Databases

19822 APILIT
American Petroleum Institute
275 7th Avenue
9th Floor
New York, NY 10001-6708
212-989-9001; *Fax:* 212-366-4298
Over 500,000 citations are offered from 1978, to the literature related to the oil refining and petrochemical industries.

19823 Africa-Middle East Petroleum Directory
PennWell Directories
1700 West Loop S
Suite 1000
Houston, TX 77027-3005
713-621-9720
800-752-9764; *Fax:* 281-499-6310
susana@penwell.com;
www.petroleumdirectories.com
Jonelle Moore, Editor
Tim Sullivant, Manager
A directory for: associations, government agencies, drilling, exploration and production of natural gas, petrochemicals, pipeline operators etc.
Cost: $125.00
156 Pages

19824 American Oil and Gas Reporter Directory
Domestic Petroleum Publishers
PO Box 343
Derby, KS 67037-0343
316-788-6271; *Fax:* 316-788-7568
Bill Campbell, Editor
Charlie Cookson, Publisher
State oil and gas regulatory agencies.
Cost: $25.00
Frequency: Annual March
Circulation: 13,540

19825 American Oil and Gas Reporter: American Drilling Rig Directory Issues
National Publishers Group
PO Box 343
Derby, KS 67037-0343
316-788-6271; *Fax:* 316-788-7568
Bill Campbell, Editor
Charlie Cookson, Publisher
List of contractors engaged in onshore drilling for petroleum and gas.
Cost: $25.00
Frequency: SemiAnnual
Circulation: 13,540

19826 American Oil and Gas Reporter: Directory of Crude Oil Purchasers Issue
Domestic Petroleum Publishers
PO Box 343
Derby, KS 67037-0343
316-788-6271; *Fax:* 316-788-7568
Bill Campbell, Editor
Charlie Cookson, Publisher
List of companies buying crude oil in the US.
Cost: $25.00
Frequency: Annual July
Circulation: 13,540

19827 Armstrong Oil Directories
Armstrong Oil
Po Box 52106
Amarillo, TX 79159-2106
806-457-9300; *Fax:* 806-457-9301
support@armstrongoil.com;
www.armstrongoil.com
Alan Armstrong, Owner
Directory of services and supplies to the industry.
Cost: $53.50
300 Pages
Frequency: Annual

19828 Brown's Directory of North American and International Gas Companies
Advanstar Communications
131 W 1st St
Duluth, MN 55802-2065
218-740-7200
800-346-0085; *Fax:* 218-740-7079
info@advanstar.com; www.advanstar.com
Kent Akervik, Manager
Joseph Loggia, CEO
Operating gas companies, brokers and refineries are listed in this comprehensive directory with worldwide coverage.
Cost: $265.00
350 Pages
Frequency: Annual
Circulation: 1,000

19829 Canadian Oil Industry Directory
PennWell Directories
1700 West Loop S
Suite 1000
Houston, TX 77027-3005
713-621-9720
800-752-9764; *Fax:* 281-499-6310
susana@penwell.com;
www.petroleumdirectories.com
Susan Anderson, Editor
Tim Sullivant, Manager
A directory for: associations, government agencies, drilling contractors, engineering, construction, exploration, production, petrochemicals, pipeline operators, etc.
Cost: $135.00

19830 Congress Legislative Directory
American Gas Association
1515 Wilson Boulevard
Suite 100
Arlington, VA 22209-2469
703-841-8400
Offers information on members of both houses of the United States Congress, federal government agencies relevant to the natural gas industry.
Cost: $10.00
220 Pages
Frequency: Annual

19831 Contracts for Field Projects & Supporting Research on Enhanced Oil Recovery
US Department of Energy
PO Box 1398
Bartlesville, OK 74005
918-336-0307; *Fax:* 918-337-4418
Herbert A Tiedemann, Editor
Energy Department technical project officers and contractors.
97 Pages
Frequency: Quarterly
Founded in: 1997

19832 Crude Oil Analysis Data Bank
PO Box 2565
Bartlesville, OK 74005-2565
918-336-2400
Contains over 9,000 analyses, obtained from the Bureau of Mines, of worldwide crude oil deposits.
Frequency: Full-text

19833 DRI/Platt's Oil Prices
DRI/McGraw-Hill
24 Hartwell Ave
Lexington, MA 02421-3103
781-860-6060; *Fax:* 781-860-6002
support@construction.com;
www.construction.com
Walt Arvin, President
Database provides weekly, monthly and daily time series of worldwide petroleum product prices.

19834 Drilling & Well Servicing Contractors
Midwest Publishing Company
2230 E 49th Ste E
Tulsa, OK 74105-8771
918-582-2000
800-829-2002; *Fax:* 918-587-9349
info@midwestpub.com; www.midwestpub.com
Will L Hammack, Owner
Approximately 4,000 drilling and well servicing contractors, equipment suppliers, manufacturers and service companies.
Cost: $150.00
Frequency: Annual, September
Founded in: 1943

19835 Dwight's Offshore and Bid Data
Dwight's Energydata
1633 Firman Drive
Suite 100
Richardson, TX 75081-6790
972-783-8002
800-468-3381; *Fax:* 972-783-0058
This large database offers the most current information on bids, lease ownership data, and competitive intelligence data on the petroleum industry.

19836 Fuel Oil News-Source Book Issue
Fuel Oil News
3496 E Lake Lansing Road
Suite 150
East Lansing, MI 48823-6223
517-337-4040; www.fueloilnews.com
Offers a list of over 600 manufacturers and suppliers of oil handling, heating and delivering companies.
Cost: $10.00
Frequency: Annual
Circulation: 17,000

19837 GOA Membership Directory
Georgia Oilmen Association
1775 Spectrum Drive
Suite 100
Lawrenceville, GA 30043-5745
770-995-7570; *Fax:* 770-995-9757
kcarter@gaoilassoc.com;
www.georgiaoilmensassoc.com
Roger T Lane, President/Editor
Mary R Franklin, Associate Editor
Karen Carter, Executive Assitant
Directory of active and associate members and other valuable information.
Cost: $250.00
42 Pages
Frequency: Monthly
Circulation: 1,300
Printed in on glossy stock

19838 Gas and Oil Equipment Directory
Underwriters Laboratories
2600 N.W.Lake Rd
Camas, WA 98607-8542

847-412-0136
877-854-3577; *Fax:* 847-272-8129;
www.ul.com
Social Media: Facebook, Twitter, YouTube

Keith E Williams, CEO
John Drengenberg, Manager Consumer Affairs

Companies that have qualified to use the UL listing mark or classification marking on or in connection with products that have been found to be in compliance with UL's requirements.
Cost: $9.00
Frequency: Annual October

19839 Hart Energy Publishing
4545 Post Oak Place Drive
Suite 210
Houston, TX 77027-3105

713-993-9320
800-874-2544; *Fax:* 713-840-8585
jeff@grainnet.com; www.hartenergy.com

Jeff Miller, Director Marketing
Matt Beltz, Marketing Associate
Rich Eichler, President
Kristine Klavers, Senior Vice President
Frederick Potter, Executive Vice President

Hart Energy Publishing is the worldwide leader in energy industry publishing. With fiver energy magazines, E & P, Oil and Gas investors, Pipeline gas technology, energy markets and world refining. Hart Energy Publishing also has a range of newsletters and centers devoted to the downstream Energy industry.
15 Pages
Frequency: Monthly

19840 Hart Publications
4545 Post Oak Place Drive
Houston, TX 77027-3105

713-993-9320
800-874-2544; *Fax:* 713-840-8585;
www.hartpub.com

Gina Acosta, Fulfillment
Rich Eichler, President

Directories, magazines and newsletters of the oil and gas industry
15 Pages
Frequency: Annually

19841 International Oil Spill Control Directory
Cutter Information Corporation
37 Broadway
Suite 1
Arlington, MA 02474-5500

781-648-8700; *Fax:* 781-648-8707
consortium@cutter.com; www.cutter.com
Social Media: Facebook, Twitter, LinkedIn, RSS

Verna Allee, Senior Consultant
Karen Coburn, President & CEO
Paul Bergeron, CFO & COO
Anne Mullaney, Vice-President

Offers valuable information on more than 1,000 suppliers of more than 3,500 oil spill cleanup, prevention and control products and services.
Cost: $95.00
225 Pages
Frequency: Annual

19842 Marketers, Purchasers & Trading Companies
Midwest Publishing Company
2230 E 49th Ste E
Tulsa, OK 74105-8771

918-582-2000
800-829-2002; *Fax:* 918-587-9349
info@midwestdirectories.com;
www.midwestdirectories.com

Will Hammack, Editor

Over 5,300 purchasers, marketers and traders of refined products, crude oil and natural gas.
Cost: $145.00
Frequency: Annual October

19843 McGraw-Hill GasWire
DRI/McGraw-Hill
24 Hartwell Ave
Lexington, MA 02421-3103

781-860-6060; *Fax:* 781-860-6002
support@construction.com;
www.construction.com

Walt Arvin, President

Contains news and analyses of the US natural gas market.
Frequency: Full-text

19844 Member Directory and Oil & Gas Agencies
Interstate Oil and Gas Compact Commission
PO Box 53127
Oklahoma City, OK 73152-3127

405-525-3556
800-822-4015; *Fax:* 405-525-3592
iogcc@iogcc.state.ok.us;
www.iogcc.state.ok.us

Christine Hansen, Executive Director
Alesha Leemaster, Communications Manager

About 600 state representatives to the commission from 29 oil and gas producing states and seven associate states and committee members from related industries and government agencies.
Cost: $11.00
Frequency: Annual

19845 NOIA Leaders
National Ocean Industries Association
1120 G St NW
Suite 900
Washington, DC 20005-3801

202-347-6900; *Fax:* 202-347-8650;
www.noia.org
Social Media: Facebook, Twitter, YouTube

Tom Fry, President
Franki K Stuntz, Director Administration
Nolty J Thuriot, Director Congressional Affairs
Frequency: Annual
Founded in: 1972

19846 National Petroleum News: Buyer's Guide Issue
2101 S Arlington Heights Road
Arlington Heights, IL 60005-4185

847-427-9512; *Fax:* 847-427-2041

Jim Bursch, Publisher
Don Smith, Editor

A comprehensive listing of products and services for the petroleum industry.
Cost: $30.00
Frequency: Annual
Circulation: 18,000

19847 National Petroleum News: Market Facts Issue
2101 S Arlington Heights Road
Arlington Heights, IL 60005-4185

847-427-9512; *Fax:* 847-427-2041

Jim Bursch, Publisher
Don Smith, Editor

Offers the industry's most up-to-date compilation of petroleum/convenience store facts, figures and trends.
Cost: $75.00
Frequency: Annual
Circulation: 18,000

19848 Natural Gas Industry Directory
PennWell Directories
1700 West Loop S
Suite 1000
Houston, TX 77027-3005

713-621-9720
800-752-9764; *Fax:* 281-499-6310;
www.petroleumdirectories.com

Susan Anderson, Editor
Tim Sullivant, Manager

Major divisions of the natural gas industry worldwide.
Cost: $165.00

19849 Offshore Services and Equipment Directory
Greene Dot
11686 Jocatal Center
San Diego, CA 92127-1147

858-485-0189; *Fax:* 858-485-5139

Renee Garza, Editor

About 5,000 suppliers of equipment and services to the offshore petroleum exploration and production industry worldwide.
Cost: $235.00
Frequency: Annual May
Circulation: 4,000

19850 Oil and Gas Directory
Geophysical Directory
Po Box 130508
Houston, TX 77219-0508

713-529-1922
800-929-2462; *Fax:* 713-529-3646;
www.iagc.org

Stewart Schafer, Owner

Valuable information is listed on over 5,000 companies worldwide that are involved in petroleum exploration and drilling.
Cost: $130.00
700 Pages
Frequency: Annual, October
Circulation: 2,000
Founded in: 1970

19851 Oil and Gas Field Code Master List
US Energy Information Administration
1000 Independence Av SW
#E1-231
Washington, DC 20585-0001

202-586-8800; *Fax:* 202-586-0727;
www.eia.doe.gov

John H Weiner, Executive Director

All identified oil and gas fields in the US.
Cost: $27.00
Frequency: Annual December

19852 Permit Data On-Line
Petroleum Information Corporation
PO Box 2612
Denver, CO 80201-2612

303-595-7500
800-645-3282

Oil well drilling permits granted by regional governmental agencies.
Frequency: Weekly

19853 PetroProcess HSE Directory
Atlantic Communications LLC
1635 W Alabama St
Houston, TX 77006-4101

713-831-1768; *Fax:* 713-523-7804
info@oilonline.com; www.oilonline.com

Shaun Wymes, President
Rob Garza, General Manager
Graham Thomson, General Manager
Ray Vanegas, Manager

Doug Duguid, Managing Director
Cost: $79.00
650 Pages
Frequency: Annual
Founded in: 1990

19854 Petroleum Equipment Directory
Petroleum Equipment Institute
6514 E 69th St
Tulsa, OK 74133-1729

918-494-9696; *Fax:* 918-491-9895
rrenkes@pei.org; www.pei.org

Robert N Renkes, Executive VP
Sarah West, Marketing Director
Rick Long, General Manager

Member manufacturers, distributors and installers of petroleum marketing equipment worldwide are offered.
Cost: $50.00
395 Pages
Frequency: Annual
Circulation: 3,000

19855 Petroleum Marketers Association of America Directory
Petroleum Marketers Association of America
1901 Fort Myer Dr
Suite 500
Arlington, VA 22209-1609

703-351-8000
800-300-7622; *Fax:* 703-351-9160
http://www.pmaa.org

Daniel F Gilligan, President
Sarah Dodge, Director/Legislative Affairs
Patricia Murrey, Director/Administration
Holly Tuminello, VP
Izua Yang, Manager/Communications/Conferences

About 45 state and regional member associations. A national organization representing the nation's independent petroleum marketers.
Cost: $50.00
Frequency: Annual February
Circulation: 2,000

19856 Petroleum Marketing Management Buyers Guide
Graphic Concepts
1801 Rockville Pike
Suite 330
Rockville, MD 20852-1633

A list of suppliers of products, equipment and services to combination gas station owners and convenience stores.
Frequency: Annual
Circulation: 20,000

19857 Petroleum Software Directory
PennWell Publishing Company
3050 Post Oak Boulevard
Suite 200
Houston, TX 77056-6570

713-219-9720
800-752-9764; *Fax:* 713-963-6228
susana@pennwell.com

More than 800 companies that produce over 1,800 micro-, mini- and mainframe computer software packages designed for petroleum industry applications.
Cost: $195.00
Frequency: Annual June
Circulation: 1,000

19858 Petroleum Supply Annual
Superintendent of Documents
1000 Independence Ave SW
Washington, DC 20585

202-586-8800
http://www.eia.doe.gov/oil_gas/petroleum/data_publications/petrol

Contains information on the supply and disposition of crude oil and petroleum products. Reflects data collected by the petroleum industry during 1998 through annual and monthly surveys, it is divided in to two volumes. The first volume contains three sections, Summary Statistics, Detailed Statistics, and Refinery Capacity, each with final annual data. Volume 1 cost is $17.00, volume 2 $51.00
175 Pages
Frequency: Annual
Founded in: 1999

19859 Pipeline & Gas Journal: Buyer's Guide Issue
Oildom Publishing Company of Texas
PO Box 941669
Houston, TX 77094-8669

281-558-6930; *Fax:* 281-558-7029;
www.oildompublishing.com

Jeff Share, Editor

List of over 700 companies supplying products and services used in construction and operation of cross country pipeline and gas distribution systems.
Cost: $75.00
Frequency: May

19860 Pipeline & Gas Journal: Directory of Pipeline Operating Companies
Oildom Publishing Company of Texas
PO Box 941669
Houston, TX 77218-9368

281-558-6930; *Fax:* 281-558-7029;
www.oildompublishing.com

Jeff Share, Editor
Oliver Klinger, Editor

List of companies operating oil and gas transmission pipelines worldwide.
Cost: $80.00
Frequency: September
Circulation: 27,000

19861 Platts Insight
The McGraw-Hill Companies
1221 Avenue of the Americas
New York, NY 10020

212-904-2000
power@platts.com; www.platts.com

Glenn Goldberg, President, Information & Media

A comprehensive look at the energy industry, with year end outlook editions on global energy, sustainability, electric power, nuclear and more.

19862 SPE: Annual Membership Directory
Society of Petroleum Engineers
PO Box 833836
Richardson, TX 75083-3836

972-952-9300
800-456-6863; *Fax:* 972-952-9435

Georgeann Bilich, Editor

List of 52,000 member petroleum engineers.
Cost: $150.00
Frequency: Annual May
Circulation: 5,000

19863 Supply, Distribution, Manufacturing and Service
Midwest Publishing Company
2230 E 49th Ste E
Tulsa, OK 74105-8771

918-582-2000
800-829-2002; *Fax:* 918-587-9349
info@midwestdirectories.com;
www.midwestdirectories.com

Will Hammack, Editor

8,000 oil well supply stores, service companies and equipment manufacturers.
Cost: $165.00
Frequency: Annual, September
Founded in: 1943

19864 TULSA Database
Petroleum Abstracts
101 Harwell
Tulsa, OK 74104-3189

918-631-2297
800-247-8678; *Fax:* 918-599-9361;
www.tulsaworld.com

Pam Weaver, Assistant Director
David Brown, Assistant Director of Marketing
Pam Jenni, Managing Editor

Contains more than 700,000 citations, with abstracts, to the worldwide literature and patents on the exploration, development and production of petroleum resources.
Frequency: Weekly Updates

19865 US Non-Utility Power Directory on CD-ROM
PennWell Publishing Company
PO Box 1260
Tulsa, OK 74101-1260

918-835-3161
800-752-9764; *Fax:* 918-831-9555

Gockel Delma, Sales

Offers a unique source of information to industry professionals including a listing of over 1,423 plant locations including project names, site addresses, plant types, fuels, installed capacity, power contract information, operating control systems, ownership and more.
Cost: $695.00
Frequency: Annual

19866 US Offshore Oil Company Contact List
Offshore Data Services
PO Box 19909
Houston, TX 77224-1909

713-781-7094; *Fax:* 713-781-9594

Marie Sheffer, Editor
Linda Parino, Circulation Director

Approximately 265 oil companies with US offshore leases.
Cost: $135.00
Frequency: Annual
Circulation: 800
ISBN: 1-058587-7 -
Mailing list available for rent

19867 USA Oil Industry Directory
PennWell Publishing Company
3050 Post Oak Boulevard
Suite 200
Houston, TX 77056-6570

713-219-9720
800-752-9764; *Fax:* 713-963-6228
susana@pennwell.com

Laura Bell, Editor
Susan Anderson, Publisher

Over 3,600 independent oil producers, fund companies, petroleum marketing companies, crude oil brokers and integrated oil firms.
Cost: $165.00
Frequency: Annual October
Circulation: 5,000

19868 USA Oilfield Service, Supply and Manufacturers Directory
PennWell Publishing Company

3050 Post Oak Boulevard
Suite 200
Houston, TX 77056-6570

713-219-9720
800-752-9764; *Fax:* 713-963-6228
susana@pennwell.com

Guntis Moritis, Editor

About 3,600 companies that provide oilfield equipment, supplies and services to the oil industry.
Cost: $145.00
Frequency: Annual October
Circulation: 2,500

19869 West Coast Petroleum Industry Directory
Economic Insight
3004 Sw 1st Ave
Portland, OR 97201-4708

503-222-2425; *Fax:* 503-242-2968
info@econ.com; www.econ.com

Sam Van Vactor, President

Individuals and companies that refine, buy and sell oil and petroleum products are listed.
Cost: $85.00
204 Pages
Frequency: Quarterly

19870 World Oil-Marine Drilling Rigs
Gulf Publishing Company
3301 Allen Parkway
Houston, TX 77019-1896

713-294-4301

Offers information on over 600 mobile and self-contained drilling rigs including submersibles, drillships and barges.
Cost: $11.00
Frequency: Annual
Circulation: 30,000

Industry Web Sites

19871 http://gold.greyhouse.com
G.O.L.D Grey House OnLine Databases

Grey House Publishing's online database platform, GOLD, offers Quick Search, Keyword Search and Expert Search for most business sectors including petroleum and allied services markets. The GOLD platform makes finding the information you need quick and easy - whether you're a novice searcher or an experienced database user. All of Grey House's directory products are available for subscription on the GOLD platform.

19872 www.aesc.net
Association of Energy Service Companies

Professional trade association for well-site service contractors and businesses providing goods and services to well-site contractors. Develops and sells training and safety materials.

19873 www.aopl.org
Association of Oil Pipe Lines

Assembles statistics and other data relating to the pipeline industry for presentation to Congress, government departments, trade associations, and the public.

19874 www.api.org
American Petroleum Institute

Seeks to maintain cooperation between government and industry, fosters foreign and domestic trade in American petroleum products, conducts research.

19875 www.bpnews.com
Butane-Propane News

Petroleum and propane industry news.

19876 www.entelec.org
Energy Telecommunications and Electrical Assoc

A user association focusing on communications and control technologies used by petroleum, natural gas, pipeline and electric utility companies.

19877 www.greyhouse.com
Grey House Publishing

Authoritative reference directories for most business sectors including petroleum and allied products marktes. Users can search the online databases with varied search criteria allowing for custom searches by product category, geographic area, sales volume, keyword, subject and more. Full Grey House catalog and online ordering also available.

19878 www.iadc.org
International Association of Drilling Contractors

Conducts educational and training programs. Sponsors safety contest and bestows awards.

19879 www.igt.org
Institute of Gas Technology

An independent not-for-profit center for energy and environmental research, development, education and information. Main function is to perform sponsored and in-house research, development and demonstration, provide educational programs and services, and disseminate scientific and technical information.

19880 www.iosc.org
Oil Spill Conference

Strives to create a global colloquim for public, government and business ideas addressing all aspects of oil spills impacting the environment. International exchange of information and ideas dealing with spill prevention, planning, response and restoration processes, protocols and technology.

19881 www.liquidrecyclers.org
NORA, An Association of Responsible Recyclers

Members are companies that reprocess used antifreeze, wastewater, oil filters, chemicals and companies that provide products or services to the industry.

19882 www.naro-us.org
National Association of Royalty Owners

Assists mineral and royalty owners in the effective management of their mineral properties. Provides information on tax, regulatory, and legislative matters. Conducts seminars and bestows awards.

19883 www.noraoil.com
National Oil Recyclers Association

Members are companies that reprocess used oil into fuel oil or recycle antifreeze, wastewater, oil filters and companies that provide products or services to the industry.

19884 www.npc.org
National Petroleum Council

Self-supporting federal advisory body to the Secretary of Energy established in 1946 at the request of President Truman.

19885 www.npga.org
National Propane Gas Association

Members are producers and distributors of liquefied petroleum gas and equipment manufacturers.

19886 www.npradc.org
National PetroChemical & Refiners Association

Members are petroleum, petrochemical and refining companies.

19887 www.oilscouts.org
International Oil Scouts Association

Compiles statistics on exploration and development wells in the US. Offers professional development and scholarship programs.

19888 www.pei.org
Petroleum Equipment Institute

Members are makers and distributors of equipment used in service stations, bulk plants and other petroleum marketing facilities.

19889 www.pttc.org
Petroleum Technology Transfer Council

Fosters the effective transfer of exploration and production technology to US petroleum producers through regional resource centers, workshops, websites, publications, etc.

19890 www.spwla.org
Society of Professional Well Log Analysts

Promotes the evaluation of formations, through well logging techniques, in order to locate gas, oil and other minerals.

19891 www.wspa.org
Western States Petroleum Association

For companies that refine, produce, transport, and market petroleum and petroleum products in six western states: Arizona, California, Oregon, Nevada, Hawaii and Washington.

Associations

19892 ASPCA
424 E 92nd St
New York, NY 10128-6804
212-876-7566; *Fax:* 212-876-0014
publicinformation@aspca.org; www.aspca.org
Social Media: Facebook, Twitter, Pinterest, YouTube, Google+
Tim F. Wray, Chair
Frederick Tanne, Vice- Chair
Frederik Gradin, Treasurer
Sally Spooner, Secretary
Matthew Bershadker, President & CEO
Society for the humane treatment of animals, established in 1866.
300+ Members
Founded in: 1866

19893 American Animal Hospital Association
12575 W Bayaud Ave
Lakewood, CO 80228-2021
303-986-2800; *Fax:* 303-986-1700;
www.aaha.org
Social Media: Facebook, Twitter, LinkedIn, Youtube
John Albers, Executive Director
Ellin Davis, Secretary
A group of hospitals and animal practitioners serving the industry.
33000 Members
Founded in: 1933

19894 American Cat Fanciers Association
PO Box 1949
Nixa, MO 65714-1949
417-725-1530; *Fax:* 417-725-1533
ACFA@aol.com; www.acfacat.com
Doug Blackmore, President
Alan Lanners, First VP
Donald Finger, Second VP
Cindy Skeen, Executive Director
Central registry for cats. Sanctions shows, publishes a bimonthly newsletter, offers a yearbook and maintains pedigree records.
800 Members
Founded in: 1955

19895 American Farriers Association
4059 Iron Works Pkwy
Suite 1
Lexington, KY 40511
859-233-7411
877-268-4505; *Fax:* 859-231-7862
info@americanfarriers.org;
www.americanfarriers.org
Social Media: Facebook
Thomas Dubois, President
Jon Johnson, President-Elect
Dave Johnson, Vice President
Bruce Worman, Treasurer
Donnie Perkinson, Secretary
To further the professional development of farriers, to provide leadership and resource for the benefit of the farrier industry, and to improve the welfare of the horse through continuing farrier education.
2.4M Members
Founded in: 1971

19896 American Federation of Aviculture
STAT Marketing
11240 Waples Mill Road
Suite 200
Fairfax, VA 22030
703-281-4043; *Fax:* 703-359-7562
info@aaham.org; www.aaham.org
Social Media: Facebook, Twitter, LinkedIn, YouTube, Google+, Pinterest
Christine Stottlemyer, Chair
Victoria Di Tomaso, President
John Currier, First VP
Lori Sickelbaugh, Second VP
Amy Mitchell, Treasurer
Information for manufacturers, suppliers, distributors and retailers of exotic birds and related products, including feed, seeds, cages, toys, vitamins and minerals.
Founded in: 1968

19897 American Humane Association
1400 16th Street NW
Suite 360
Washington, DC 20036
818-501-0123
800-227-4645; *Fax:* 818-762-0908
info@americanhumane.org;
www.americanhumane.org
Social Media: Facebook, Twitter, LinkedIn, YouTube, RSS, Pinterest
Robin R. Ganzert, President & CEO
Audrey Lang, Sr. Vice President
Clifford Rose, Chief Financial Officer
Stephanie Carmody, General Counsel
Kwane Stewart, National Director
Protects children and animals from cruelty, neglect, abuse, and exploitation.
Founded in: 1877

19898 American Kennel Club
260 Madison Ave
New York, NY 10016
212-696-8200; *Fax:* 212-696-8239
info@akc.org; www.akc.org
Social Media: Facebook, Twitter, YouTube, Pinterest, Google+, I
Ronald Menaker, Chairman
Carl C. Ashby, Vice Chairman
Dennis B. Sprung, President
James P. Crowley, Executive Secretary
Joseph V. Baffuto Jr., Chief Financial Officer
The principical registry of pure-bred dogs in the United States. More ways to enjoy your dog.
15000 Members
Founded in: 1884

19899 American Morgan Horse Association
4066 Shelburne Rd
Suite 5
Shelburne, VT 05482
802-985-4944; *Fax:* 802-985-8897
info@morganhorse.com
morganhorse.com
Social Media: Facebook, Twitter, Youtube, Pinterest
Jeff Gove, President
Kris Breyer, Vice President
Carol Fletcher, Vice President of Finance
Julie Broadway, Executive Director
Information for Morgan horse breeders and owners.
7000 Members
Founded in: 1909

19900 American Paint Horse Association
2800 Meacham Boulevard
Fort Worth, TX 76137
817-834-2742; *Fax:* 817-834-3152
askapha@apha.com; www.apha.com
Social Media: Facebook, Twitter, YouTube
Ron Shelly, President
Susie Shaw, President-Elect
George Ready, Vice President
Dr. Craig Wood, Senior Committee Member
Billy L. Smith, Executive Director
Information for owners and riders of American Paint Horses.
55000 Members
Founded in: 1960

19901 American Pet Products Association
255 Glenville Rd.
Greenwich, CT 06831
203-532-0000
800-452-1225; *Fax:* 203-532-0551;
www.americanpetproducts.org
Bob Vetere, President & CEO
Andrew Darmohraj, EVP & COO
Trade association of manufacturers, manufacturers' representatives, importers and livestock suppliers.
1200 Members
Founded in: 1958

19902 American Pet Products Manufacturers Association
255 Glenville Road
Greenwich, CT 06831
203-532-0000
800-452-1225; *Fax:* 203-532-0551
andy@appma.org;
www.americanpetproducts.org
Robert Merar, Chairman
Bob Vetere, President & CEO
Andrew Darmohraj, Executive Vice President & COO
Steve Ware, Treasurer
Edith Martingnetti, General Mgr/Exhibitor Registration
Information for manufacturers of pet products and service providers in the pet industry.
Frequency: Annual
Founded in: 1958

19903 American Rabbit Breeders Association
PO Box 5667
Bloomington, IL 61702
309-664-7500; *Fax:* 309-664-0941
info@arba.net
arba.net
Josh Humphries, President
Randy Shumaker, VP
Eric Stewart, Executive Director
David Freeman, Treasurer
Roger Hassenpflug, Director
Information for rabbit breeders and owners.
23000 Members
Founded in: 1910

19904 American Veterinary Medical Association
1931 N Meacham Rd
Suite 100
Schaumburg, IL 60173-4360
847-303-6142
800-248-2862; *Fax:* 847-925-1329
sgranskog@avma.org; www.avma.org
Social Media: Facebook, Twitter, LinkedIn, YouTube, Flickr
Tim Frey, Manager
Michael Walters, Director Communications Division
Dr. Gail Golab, Assistant Director
Publishes various journals and information for members. Acts as a clearinghouse for veterinarians.
86500 Members
Founded in: 1863

19905 **Animal Health Institute**
1325 G St NW
Suite 700
Washington, DC 20005-3127
202-637-2440; *Fax:* 202-393-1667
rphillips@ahi.org; www.ahi.org
Social Media: Facebook, Twitter, Flickr, YouTube
Alexander S.Mathews, President & CEO
Ron Phillips, VP Legislative/Public Affairs
Dr Richard A A.Carnevale, VP, Regulator
Dr Kent McClure, General Counsel
Carolyn S Ayers, VP, Admin. & Finance
Represents manufacturers of animal health care products.
24 Members
Founded in: 1941

19906 **Animal Legal Defense Fund**
170 East Cotati Avenue
Cotati, CA 94931
707-795-2533; *Fax:* 707-795-7280
info@aldf.org; www.aldf.org
Social Media: Facebook, Twitter, YouTube, Pinterest
Sarah Luick, Chair
Marilyn Forbes, Vice- Chair
Lisa Brewer, Secretary
Jim Rockenbach, Treasurer
Stephen Wells, Executive Director
Information on animal protection, wildlife conservation and animal rights.
10000 Members
Founded in: 1979

19907 **Association of Pet Dog Trainers**
The Association of Pet Dog Trainers
2365 Harrodsburg Road A325
Lexington, KY 40504
800-738-3647; *Fax:* 864-331-0767
education@apdt.com; www.apdt.com
Social Media: Facebook, Twitter, LinkedIn
Amber Burckhalter, Board Chair
Jill-Marie O'Brien, Board Vice-Chair
Robin Bennet, Board Treasurer
Casey Lomanaco, Board Secretary
Megan Armstrong, Board Member
Enhancing the human/dog relationship by educating trainers, other animal professionals and the public and advocating dog friendly training.
6000 Members
Founded in: 1993

19908 **Delta Society**
875 124th Ave NW
Suite 101
Bellevue, WA 98005
425-679-5500
800-869-6898; *Fax:* 425-679-5539
info@deltasociety.org
petpartners.org
Social Media: Facebook, Twitter, LinkedIn, YouTube, Pinterest, Instagram
C. Annie Magnant, President & CEO
David E. Williams, Chief Medical Officer
Linda Dicus, Executive Assistant
Chris Calabro, Director of Technology
Mary M. Callahan, Senior National Director
Information on human-animal interactions. Service Dog Center provides information and advocacy for dogs trained to assist people with disabilities. Pet Partners Program trains volunteers, health professionals, animals for animal-assisted therapy and activities.
4.6M Members
Founded in: 1977

19909 **International Association of Pet Cemeteries & Crematories**
4991 Peachtree Road
Atlanta, GA 30341
518-594-3000
800-952-5541; *Fax:* 770-457-8160
info@iaopc.com; www.iaopc.com
Angie Hansen, President
Robert Blosser, Vice President
Debra Bjorling, Treasurer
Scott Hunter, Advisory Council
Donna Bethune, Executive Administrator
Educates the public on pet burials and the disposal of sick and diseased animals to eliminate contamination of ground and water. Conducts workshops and research projects.
175 Members
Founded in: 1971

19910 **International Boarding & Pet Services Asso**
1702 E Pikes Peak Avenue
Colorado Springs, CO 80909
719-667-1600; *Fax:* 719-667-0116
info@abka.com; www.ibpsa.com
James Krack, Executive Manager
Information about the pet industry products, including pet foods, supplements, retail supplies, construction materials, cages, computers and software.
Founded in: 1977

19911 **International Professional Groomers**
6475 Wallace Rd NW
Salem, OR 97304
503-551-2397; *Fax:* 503-581-1220
info@ipgicmg.com; www.ipgicmg.com
Social Media: Facebook, Twitter
Linda Easton, President
Represents the professional pet grooming industry, providing continuing education to members and public information on the proper care treatment. also publishes a quarterly newsletter.
500 Members
Founded in: 1988

19912 **National Association of Professional Pet Care**
1120 Route 73
Suite 200
Mt. Laurel, NJ 08054
856-439-0324; *Fax:* 856-439-0525
napps@petsitters.org; www.petsitters.org
Social Media: Facebook, Twitter, LinkedIn, Google+, Pinterest
Yvette Gonzales, President
Jessica Abernathy, President Elect
Cyndy Lippert, Secretary-Treasurer
Cathleen Delaney, Administrative Director
Kara Jenkins, Director
Nonprofit organization dedicated to serving the needs of professional pet care providers. Promotes ethical standards and fosters cooperation among members in the pet care industry.
2200+ Members
Founded in: 1989

19913 **National Congress of Animal Trainers**
23675 W Chardon Rd
Grayslake, IL 60030-9584
847-546-0717; *Fax:* 847-546-3454
John F Cuneo, President
For trainers and breeders of rare animals.
300 Members

19914 **National Dog Groomers Association of American**
PO Box 101
Clark, PA 16113
724-962-2711; *Fax:* 724-962-1919
ndga@nationaldoggroomers.com; www.nationaldoggroomers.com
Social Media: Facebook
Jeffrey Reynolds, Executive Director
Wendy Booth, Certification Coordinator
Sue Zecco, Contest Coordinator
To unite groomers through membership and offer optional certification testing throughout the United States.
2.4M Members
Founded in: 1969

19915 **National Humane Education Society**
PO Box 340
Charles Town, WV 25414-0340
304-725-0506; *Fax:* 304-725-1523
information@nhes.org; www.nhes.org
Social Media: Facebook, Twitter, YouTube
Anna C Briggs, Founder
James D Taylor, President
Cynthia L Taylor, Vice President
Virginia Dungan, Treasurer
Christina B Fernandez, Secretary
Mission to foster a sentiment of kindness to animals.
400M+ Members
Founded in: 1948

19916 **National Pigeon Association**
17128 Colima Drive Unit 603
Hacienda Heights, CA 91745
626-820-8080
npasecretary@yahoo.com; www.npausa.com
Social Media: Facebook, Twitter
Jerry Gagne, President
Lennie Mefferd, Secretary/Treasurer
Tim Stajkowski, Eastern Vise President
Roger Hansen, Western Vice President
Special information for members.
Founded in: 1920

19917 **National Taxidermists Association**
PO Box 384
Pocahontas, IL 62275
618-669-2929; *Fax:* 618-669-2909
nationaltaxidermistassoc@frontier.com; www.nationaltaxidermists.com
Social Media: Facebook, Twitter, YouTube, Google+, Pinterest
Michelle Burkholder, President
Russell Knight, Vice President
Harry Whitehead, Treasurer
Tim Thacker, Secretary
Garvice Thomas, Board of Directors
Preserving animals to their natural form.
2500 Members
Founded in: 1972

19918 **PETCO Foundation**
654 Richland Hills Dr.
San Antonio, TX 78245
858-453-7845
888-824-7257; *Fax:* 858-909-2618; www.petco.com
Social Media: Facebook, Twitter, Instagram
Brian Devine, Chairman
Charlie Piscitello, President
Judith Munoz, Vice President
Susanne Kogut, Executive Director
Rana Smith, Director
We put animals first. The Petco Foundation supports community organization and efforts that enhance the lives of companion animals.
Founded in: 1999

19919 People for the Ethical Treatment of Animals (PETA)
501 Front Street
Norfolk, VA 23510
757-622-7382; *Fax:* 757-622-0457
info@peta.org; www.peta.org
Social Media: Facebook, Twitter, Pinterest, Google+
Ingrid Newkirk, President
Opposes all forms of animal exploitation. Seeks to educate the public on what the group sees as the three major institutionalized cruelty issues: the exploitation and abuse of animals in experimentation, the manufacturing of fur apparel, and slaughtering for human consumption.
80000 Members
Founded in: 1980

19920 Pet Care Services Association
2760 N Academy Boulevard
Suite 120
Colorado Springs, CO 80917
719-667-1600
877-570-7788; *Fax:* 719-667-0116
info@petcareservices.org;
www.petcareservices.org
Joan Saunders, CEO
Seeks to upgrade the industry through educational programs and conventions. Promotes code of ethics and accreditation programs for kennel operators.
2400 Members
Founded in: 1977

19921 Pet Food Institute
2025 M St NW
Suite 800
Washington, DC 20036
202-367-1120; *Fax:* 202-367-2120
info@petfoodinstitute.org;
www.petfoodinstitute.org
Duane H Ekedahl, Executive Director
Represents dog and cat food manufacturers. Supporting initiative to advance the quality of dog and cat food. Supporting research in pet nutrition and the important role of pets in our society. Promoting the overall care and well-being of pets.
100 Members
Founded in: 1958

19922 Pet Industry Distributors Association
3465 Box Hill Corporate Center Dr.
Suite H
Abingdon, MD 21009
443-640-1060; *Fax:* 443-640-1086
pida@kingmgmt.org; www.pida.org
Social Media: LinkedIn
Scott Rath, Chairman
Mark Smith, Vice Chairman
Jeff Boyd, Secretary/Treasurer
Steven T. King, President
Marci Hickey, Director of Meetings
Represents wholesaler-distributors of pet products, providing training and education to members.
190 Members
Founded in: 1968

19923 Pet Industry Joint Advisory Council
1615 Duke Street
Suite 100
Alexandria, VA 22314
202-452-1525
800-553-7387; *Fax:* 202-452-1516
info@pijac.org; www.pijac.org
Social Media: Facebook, Twitter
Ken Oh, Chair
Andy Ponte, First Vice-Chair
Marcie Whichard, Second Vice-chair
Laura Reid, Secretary/Treasurer
Edwin Sayres, President & CEO
Monitors federal and state regulations and legislation affecting industry. Sponsors research and educational projects including certification programs in veterinary care and husbandry for companion animals, in-store training videos, etc.
1500 Members
Founded in: 1971

19924 Pet Lovers Association
PO Box 145
Joppa, MD 21085
410-679-0978
Elden Harrison, President
Advises pet owners of their responsibilities.
Founded in: 1983

19925 Pet Pride
P.O. Box 1055
Pacific Palisades, CA 90272
310-836-5427; www.petpride.org
Ruth Argust, President
Public education programs for proper cat care.
50000 Members
Founded in: 1965

19926 Pet Sitters International
201 East King Street
King, NC 27021-9163
336-983-9222; *Fax:* 336-983-5266
info@petsit.com; www.petsit.com
Social Media: Facebook, Twitter, LinkedIn, YouTube, Google+
Terry Chance, Marketing Director
Beth Stultz, Marketing Manager
Chris Sutphin, Member Services Manager
Patti Moran, President
Mike Moran, Vice President
Society of professional pet sitters. Membership provides valuable benefits - educational resources for those engaged in the pet-sitting industry. Also provides a forum to network with peers who share a common vision of excellence in at-home pet care.
7000 Members
Founded in: 1994

19927 PetCenter.Com: Internet Animal Hospital PetFoodDirect.com
189 Main Street
Harleysville, PA 19438
215-513-1999; *Fax:* 215-513-7286; www.thepetcenter.com
T J Dunn, Jr DVM, Director
Award winning virtual animal hospital for dog and cat love. Mission of providing dog and cat caretakers with a better understanding of the medical and surgical treatment of pets. Created by veterinarians under the direction of Dr T.J. Dunn, all articles are presented in non-medical terms, just as if the veterinarian was speaking to you personally in a real exam room. Associated with PetFoodDirect.com

19928 PetFoodDirect.com
189 Main St
Harleysville, PA 19438
215-513-1999
877-738-3663; *Fax:* 215-513-7286;
www.petfooddirect.com
Social Media: Facebook, Twitter
Brock Weatherup, CEO
Jon Roska, Jr, Founder & VP of Merchandising
Rose Hamilton, Chief Marketing Officer
Matthew Murray, VP, Finance
Joe Falkenstein, CFO & VP of Operations
Largest pure play entailer for premium pet food, supplies and accessories on the internet. Our customers can order from a huge selection of pet products, have access to value-added services, including information on pet healthcare and nutrition.
Founded in: 1997

19929 US Animal Health Association
4221 Mitchell Ave
Saint Joseph, MO 64507
816-671-1144; *Fax:* 816-671-1201
usaha@usaha.org; www.usaha.org
Dr. Bruce King, President
Dr. David Schmitt, President-Elect
Dr. Boyd Parr, First Vice President
Barbara Determan, Second Vice President
Dr. Kristin Haas, Third Vice President
Science-based, non-profit, voluntary organization. Concerning disease eradication, animal health, emerging diseases, food safety, public health, animal welfare, and international trade.
1400 Members
Founded in: 1897

19930 United Kennel Club
100 E Kilgore Rd
Kalamazoo, MI 49002-5584
269-343-9020; *Fax:* 269-343-7037
conformation@ukcdogs.com;
www.ukcdogs.com
Tanya Raab, President
Todd Kellam, Senior Vice President
Angela Smith, Senior Director of Research & Dev
Taylor Armstrong, Customer Service Manager
Allen Gingerich, Senior Director of Hunting Events
Responsible for dog pedigrees and transfer of ownership of pedigree dogs. Best registry of pure-bred dogs.
50 Members
Founded in: 1898

19931 Western and English Sales Association
451 E 58th Avenue
Suite 4128
Denver, CO 80216
303-295-1040
800-295-1041; *Fax:* 303-295-0941
info@denver-wesa.com;
www.denver-wesa.com
Social Media: Facebook
Mark Broughton, Chairperson
Scott Piper, President
Gerald Adame, Vice President
Tracy Patterson, Secretary
Jay Phillips, Treasurer
Trade association
1200 Members
Founded in: 1921

19932 World Pet Association
135 West Lemon Ave.
Monrovia, CA 91016
626-447-2222; *Fax:* 626-447-8350
info@wpamail.org
worldpetassociation.org
Jim Boschee, Chairman
Michael Twain, CFO
Vic Mason, 1st Vice Chair
Barry Berman, 2nd Vice Chair
Pete Risano, Secretary
A non-profit, membership-controlled trade association organized to represent its members and the interests of the companion animal and product industry. America's oldest pet industry trade association. Our mission is to promote responsible pet care worldwide.

19933 World Society for the Protection of Animals
89 South Street
2nd Floor
Boston, MA 02111

508-879-8350
800-833-9772; *Fax:* 212-564-4250
wspa@wspausa.com; www.wspa.usa.org
Social Media: Facebook, Twitter, YouTube

Laura Simpson, USA Director
Peter Davies, Director General
Robert S Cummings, President
John Bowen, Secretary
Carter Luke, Treasurer

International animal protection news reports. Lobbies for effective animal welfare laws and provides educational material.
12 Members

Newsletters

19934 ASPCA Report
424 E 92nd St
New York, NY 10128-6804

212-876-7566; www.aspca.com

Janice Borzendowski, Publisher
Ed Sayres, Director
Kathryn Investigations, Director
Bonnie Shelter, Operations Manager

Pet care news, issues, features and reviews.
Frequency: Weekly
Founded in: 1866

19935 Animals International
World Society for the Protection of Animals
34 Deloss Street
Framingham, MA 01702

508-879-8350; *Fax:* 508-620-0786
wspa@wspausa.com;
www.wspa-international.org/

Laura Salter, USA Director
Susan Sherwin, Press Contact

International animal protection news reports.
Cost: $10.00
12 Pages
Frequency: Quarterly
Founded in: 1981

19936 Animals' Advocate
Animal Legal Defense Fund
170 E Cotati Avenue
Cotati, CA 94931-4474

707-795-2533; *Fax:* 707-795-7280
info@aldf.org; www.aldf.org/action.htm

Stephen Wells, Executive Director

A newsletter offering information on animal protection, wildlife conservation and animal rights.
4 Pages
Frequency: Monthly

19937 Anthrozoos
Delta Society
875 124th Ave Ne
Suite 101
Bellevue, WA 98005-2531

425-226-7357; *Fax:* 425-235-1076
info@deltasociety.org; www.deltasociety.org

Lawrence Norvell, CEO
Robert T Franklin, Secretary
Stephanie LaFarge, Secretary
David BellRetired, Treasurer

Scientific journal on the interactions of people, animals and nature.
Cost: $40.00
72 Pages
Frequency: Quarterly
Circulation: 800
Founded in: 1977

19938 Association of Pet Dog Trainers Newsletter
750 Executive Center Dr
Box 35
Greenville, SC 29615

864-331-0764
800-738-3647; *Fax:* 856-439-0525
information@apdt.com; www.apdt.com

Richard Spencer, Executive Director
Pat Miller, Treasurer
Sue Pearson, Treasurer
Kellyann Conway-Payne, Vice President
Pia Silvani, Secretary

Building better trainers through education.
Founded in: 1993

19939 Cat Industry Newsletter
Good Communications
PO Box 10069
Austin, TX 78766-1069

512-454-9062
800-968-1738; *Fax:* 512-454-3420;
www.petfoodindustry.com

Ross Becker, Editor

Business newsletter for catfood, cat products and cat litter industries. Covers business news, marketing, new products in the pipeline, industry data.
Cost: $295.00
6 Pages
Frequency: Monthly
ISSN: 1074-7788
Founded in: 1992
Printed in on matte stock

19940 Dog Industry Newsletter
Good Communications
PO Box 10069
Austin, TX 78766-1069

512-454-9062
800-968-1738; *Fax:* 512-454-3420;
www.petfoodindustry.com

Ross Becker, Editor

Business newsletter for petfood,and pet products industries.Covers business news, marketing, new products in the pipeline, industry data.
Cost: $295.00
10 Pages
Frequency: Monthly
ISSN: 1074-777X
Founded in: 1990
Printed in on matte stock

19941 Humane News
Associated Humane Societies
124 Evergreen Ave
Newark, NJ 07114-2133

973-824-7080; *Fax:* 973-824-5937
associatedhumane@aol.com;
www.associatedhumanesocieties.org

Roseann Trezza, Executive Director

News concerning animal welfare.
24 Pages
Frequency: Monthly
Circulation: 75000
Founded in: 1906

19942 IPG Newsletter
International Professional Groomers
6475 Wallace Rd NW
Salem, OR 97304-9743

847-758-1938
800-258-4765; *Fax:* 847-758-8031;
www.ipgcmb.com

Judy Kurpiel, President

A quarterly newsletter published by the International Professional Groomers.
6 Pages
Frequency: Quarterly
Circulation: 500
Founded in: 1988

19943 International Pet Industry News
Good Communications
PO Box 10069
Austin, TX 78766-1069

512-454-9062
800-968-1738; *Fax:* 512-454-3420;
www.petfoods.com

Ross Becker, Editor

Business newsletter for internatioal petfood, pet products industries. Covers business news, marketing, new products in the pipeline, industry data.
Cost: $295.00
8 Pages
Frequency: Monthly
ISSN: 1074-780X
Founded in: 1993
Printed in on matte stock

19944 K-9 Courier
PO Box 49
Jerico Springs, MO 64756

Monthly newsletter for breeders.
Frequency: Monthly

19945 Pet Gazette
Gazette Publishing
1309 N Halifax Avenue
Daytona Beach, FL 32118-3658

E-Mail: editor@petgazette.net;
www.petgazette.net

Robin Nudd, Advertising Coordinator
Amy McWilliams, Circulation

Pictures, anecdotes, cartoons and more for the pet industry.
Cost: $12.50
24 Pages
Frequency: Quarterly
Circulation: 300

19946 Pet Partners Newsletter
Delta Society
875 124th Ave Ne
Suite 101
Bellevue, WA 98005-2531

425-226-7357; *Fax:* 425-235-1076
info@deltasociety.org; www.deltasociety.org

Lawrence Norvell, CEO
Stephanie LaFarge, Secretary
David BellRetired, Treasurer

How-to newsletter for pet owners who volunteer in animal-assisted therapy and activity programs.
Cost: $6.00
2 Pages
Frequency: Monthly
Circulation: 2500
Founded in: 1977

19947 Pet Planet Newsletter
PO Box 150899
Denver, CO 80215-0899

303-986-2800; *Fax:* 303-986-1700;
www.healthypet.com

John W Albers, Executive Director
Gregg Takashima, Vice President

A group of hospitals and animal practitioners serving the industry.
Cost: $60.00
64 Pages
Frequency: Bi-Monthly
Circulation: 14,000
Founded in: 1985
Printed in on glossy stock

19948 Pet Stuff
Pet Stuff
608 Tumbleweed Lane
Fall Brook, CA 92028-9446

760-728-9306; *Fax:* 760-728-9735

Robert Tanner, Publisher

A direct co-op mailing service to the pet industry. Accepts advertising.
Frequency: BiWeekly

19949 PetLetter
Pet Industry Joint Advisory Council
1146 19th St NW
Suite 350
Washington, DC 20036-2438

202-452-1525
800-553-7387; *Fax:* 202-452-1516
info@pijac.org; www.pijac.org

Michael Addox, VP & General Counsel
Michael Canning, President

Contains a breadth of information on the current status of pending state and federal legislation, science and educational program news, the release of PIJAC publications, other PIJAC news, and a list of the newest Certified Anical Specialists

19950 Veterinary Industry Newsletter
Good Communications
PO Box 10069
Austin, TX 78766-1069

512-454-9062
800-968-1738; *Fax:* 512-454-3420;
www.petfoodsnews.com

Ross Becker, Editor

Business newsletter for petfood, animal health and veterinary industries.Covers business news, marketing, new products in the pipeline, industry data.
Cost: $295.00
10 Pages
Frequency: Monthly
ISSN: 1074-7796
Founded in: 1993
Printed in one color on matte stock

19951 Watchbird
PO Box 56218
Phoenix, AZ 85079

602-484-0931; *Fax:* 602-484-0109
webmaster@afabirds.org; www.afabirds.org/

Jerry Crowley, Executive VP
S Rosenbeltt, Circulation Director
Benny Gallaway, President

Journal on conservation, education, bird keeping and breeding.
Circulation: 6000
Founded in: 1974

Magazines & Journals

19952 Animal Fair
7 Penn Plaza
11th Floor
New York, NY 10001

212-629-0392; *Fax:* 212-988-7486
editor@animalfair.com; www.animalfair.com

Wendy Diamond, Editorial Director
Wendy Diamond, CEO/President
Cost: $19.95
Frequency: Bi-annually
Founded in: 1999

19953 Aquarium Fish Magazine
Fancy Publications
PO Box 6050
Mission Viejo, CA 92690

949-855-8822; *Fax:* 949-855-3045
aquariumfish@fancypubs.com;
www.animalnetwork.com

Devoted to pet stores and readers who keep freshwater and saltwater species of tropical fish.
Cost: $15.97
Frequency: Monthly
Circulation: 49,700
Founded in: 1905

19954 Bird Talk
Fancy Publications
3 Burroughs
Irvine, CA 92618

949-855-8822; *Fax:* 949-855-3045;
www.birdtalkmagazine.com

Edward Bauman, Editor

Pet news.
Cost: $13.99
64 Pages
Frequency: Monthly
Founded in: 1983

19955 BirdTimes
Pet Publishing
7-L Dundas Circle
Greensboro, NC 27407

336-292-4047; *Fax:* 336-292-4272;
www.petpublishing.com

Mike Hammond, Publisher
Cost: $17.97
Circulation: 50000
ISSN: 1096-7923
Founded in: 1992
Printed in 4 colors on glossy stock

19956 Bloodlines
United Kennel Club
100 E Kilgore Rd
Portage, MI 49002-5584

269-343-9020; *Fax:* 269-343-7037
webmaster@ukcdogs.com; www.ukcdogs.com

Wayne Cavanaugh, President
Rosie Reeds, Advertising

A comprehensive publication covering breeding, showing and registering of animals.
Cost: $24.00
Frequency: Monthly
Founded in: 1898

19957 Cat Fancy Magazine
Fancy Publications
3 Burroughs
Irvine, CA 92618

949-855-8822; *Fax:* 949-855-3045;
www.animalnetwork.com

Susan Logan, Editor
Sandy Meyer, Managing Editor

Offers information to cat owners and pet shop owners regarding cats.
Cost: $14.99
Frequency: Monthly
Founded in: 1965

19958 Cats & Kittens
Pet Publishing
7-L Dundas Circle
Greensboro, NC 27407

336-292-4047; *Fax:* 336-292-4272;
www.petpublishing.com

Mike Hammond, Publisher
Rita Davis, Editor

Cat enthusiast magazine.
Cost: $19.97
52 Pages
Circulation: 50000
ISSN: 1079-8285
Founded in: 1998
Printed in 4 colors on glossy stock

19959 Cats Magazine
PRIMEDIA Enthusiast Group
3585 Engineering Drive
Suite 100
Norcross, GA 30092

678-421-3000
800-216-1423; *Fax:* 212-745-0121;
www.primedia.com

Mike Carney, Publisher
Doug Stange, Editor
Kelly P Conlin, CEO

For cat owners.
Founded in: 1989

19960 Dog & Kennel
Pet Publishing
7-L Dundas Circle
Greensboro, NC 27407

336-292-4047; *Fax:* 336-292-4272;
www.petpublishing.com

Mike Hammond, Publisher
Rita Davis, Editor

Dog enthusiast magazine.
Cost: $4.99
64 Pages
Circulation: 50000
ISSN: 1079-8277
Founded in: 1996
Printed in 4 colors on glossy stock

19961 Dog Fancy Magazine
Fancy Publications
3 Burroughs
Irvine, CA 92618

949-855-8822
800-546-7730; *Fax:* 949-855-3045;
www.animalnetwork.com

Susane Chney, Editor
Scott Montey, Publisher
Dock Style, CEO/President
Christy Chism, Circulation Manager
Steven Sapoher, Marketing Manager

A magazine covering the world of dogs.
Cost: $96.00
Frequency: Monthly

19962 Dog World Magazine
Charels A Tupta
3 Burroughs
Irvine, CA 92618

949-855-8822
800-361-8056; *Fax:* 949-855-3045;
www.dogworld.co.uk

Charels A Tupta, Publisher
Donna Marcel, Chairman

Written for the serious dog enthusiast, Dog World is the authority on dog care. Special editorial on behavior, nutrition, health care and training, plus thousands of classified and display listings in every issue.
Cost: $14.99
132 Pages
Frequency: Monthly
Circulation: 64876
Founded in: 1916

19963 Dogs USA
Fancy Publications
3 Burroughs
Irvine, CA 92618

949-855-8822; *Fax:* 949-855-3045;
www.animalnetwork.com

Edward Bauman, Editor

Registration, breeding, pedigree news, bloodlines, etc. for dogs.
Cost: $5.95
Frequency: Annual

19964 Equestrian Retailer
Morris Communications
PO Box 7980
Colorado Springs, CO 80907-5339
719-633-5524; *Fax:* 719-633-1392;
www.equestrianretailer.com
Rick Swan, Associate Publisher
Kathy Swan, Executive Editor
William S Morris, President
Karen Ficklin, Circulation Manager
Rob Fulkerson, General Manager
Serves to promote profitablity in the equine industry.
60 Pages
Circulation: 11000
Founded in: 1998
Printed in 4 colors on matte stock

19965 Freshwater and Marine Aquarium Magazine
RC Modeler Corporation
PO Box 487
Sierra Madre, CA 91025-0487
626-355-1476
800-523-1736; *Fax:* 626-355-6415;
www.fishchannel.com/fama
Patricia Crews, President
A magazine aimed at aquarium pertaining to fish and marine life, hobboyists.
Cost: $22.00
200 Pages
Frequency: Monthly
Circulation: 65000
Founded in: 1978
Printed in 4 colors on glossy stock

19966 Good Dog!
PO Box 10069
Austin, TX 78766-1069
512-454-9062
800-968-1738; *Fax:* 512-454-3420
help@gooddogmagazine.com;
www.gooddogmagazine.com
Judith Becker, Editor
Ross Becker, Publisher
Consumer magazine for dog owners. Nationally known for its test reports on dog food and products for dogs. Also publishes books on dog food, puppy selection and genetics.
Cost: $12.00
36 Pages
Circulation: 40000
ISSN: 0899-6024
Founded in: 1988
Printed in 4 colors

19967 NAPPS Network
Association of Professional Pet Sitters
15000 Commerce Parkway
Suite C
Mt Laurel, NJ 08054
856-439-0324; *Fax:* 856-439-0525
napps@ahint.com; www.petsitters.org
Sally Liddick, Co-Director
Charlotte Reed, Editor/Publisher
Jerry Wentz, President
Caitlin Dougherty, Manager
Kimberly Libucki, Administrative Assistant
Official publication of the Association of Professional Pet Sitters.
Frequency: Quarterly
Circulation: 1500
Founded in: 1989

19968 Pet Age Magazine
HH Backer Associates
18 S Michigan Ave
Suite 1100
Chicago, IL 60603-3233
312-578-1818; *Fax:* 312-578-1819
hhbacker@hhbacker.com; www.hhbacker.com
Patty Backer, President
Karen MacLeod, Editor in Chief
Mark Mitera, VP
Beth Morrissey, Production Coordinator
Cathy Foster, Senior Editor
Pet AGE helps pet/pet suppliers ratailers suceed in today competive marketplace. Editorial features emphasize progressive management and trends and issues. Accepts advertising.
Cost: $70.00
80 Pages
Frequency: Monthly
Circulation: 23076
ISSN: 0098-5406
Founded in: 1965
Printed in on glossy stock

19969 Pet Business Magazine
Pet Business
333 7th Ave
11th Floor
New York, NY 10001-5004
212-979-4861; *Fax:* 646-674-0102;
www.petbusiness.com
Craig Rexford, VP
Mike Burnette, Founder
Jerry Thom, Founder
David Litwak, Editor In Chief
Nisa Cirulnick, Sales & Marketing Coordinator
Trade magazine for the pet industry. News, new products, animal care and legislative topics. Accepts advertising.
Cost: $49.97
Circulation: 24,000
Founded in: 1973
Mailing list available for rent: 19.5M names
Printed in 4 colors on glossy stock

19970 Pet Product News Magazine
Fancy Publications
3 Burroughs
PO Box 6040
Irvine, CA 92618
949-855-8822; *Fax:* 949-855-3045;
www.animalnetwork.com
Edward Bauman, Editor
Journal focusing on new products and other industry news.

19971 Pet Sitter's World
Pet Sitters International
201 E King St
King, NC 27021-9161
336-983-9222; *Fax:* 336-983-5266
info@petsit.com; www.petsit.com
Patti Moran, President
Designed to educate pet sitters and affiliated firms on pet-sitting industry business practices, ideas, products, field-tested consumer tips and trends
Cost: $36.00
56 Pages
Frequency: Bimonthly
Circulation: 8500
Founded in: 1985
Printed in on glossy stock

19972 Petfood Industry
WATT Publishing Company
303 N Main Street
Suite 500
Rockford, IL 61101
815-966-5400; *Fax:* 815-966-6416;
www.wattnet.com
James Watt, Chairman/CEO
Greg Watt, President/COO
Jeff Swanson, Publishing Director
The leading global information source for the petfood manufacturing industry, connecting manufacturing organizations with their supplier counterparts.
Cost: $48.00
46 Pages
Frequency: Monthly
Circulation: 9795
ISSN: 0031-6245
Founded in: 1959
Printed in 4 colors on glossy stock

Trade Shows

19973 AVMA Annual Convention
American Veterinary Medical Association
1931 N Meacham Road
Suite 100
Schaumburg, IL 60173-4360
847-036-6142
800-248-2862; *Fax:* 847-925-1329;
www.avma.org
Social Media: Facebook, Twitter, LinkedIn, YouTube
Larry Corry DVM, 2009-10 President
Larry Kornegay DVM, 2009-10 President-Elect
Seminar and more than 300 exhibits of products, materials, equipment, data, and services for veterinary medicine. Education and hands-on labs, exhibit hall, charitable events and networking
10000 Attendees
Frequency: Annual/July

19974 America's Family Pet Expo
World Wide Pet Supply Association
406 S 1st Avenue
Arcadia, CA 91006-3829
626-447-2222
800-999-7295; *Fax:* 626-447-8350;
www.wwpsa.com
Rick Newman, President
Lewis M Sutton, CFO
Steve Segner, First VP
Russ Feller, Second Vice President
Dr. Robert Bray, Equine Outreach
Brings together all elements of the companion animal world and promotes responsible pet ownsership. Demonstrations, speakers, product exhibits, hobbyist shows, rides for the children, contests and more. 500 booths. April, Orange County, CA
80M Attendees
Frequency: April/September
Founded in: 1990

19975 American Animal Hospital Association Annual Meeting
American Animal Hospital Association
12575 W Bayaud Avenue
Lakewood, CO 80228
303-986-2800; *Fax:* 303-986-1700;
www.aahanet.org
Donna Johnson, Exhibit Coordinator
Chuck Potter, Annual Meeting Manager
John Albers, Executive Director

250 scientific displays related to small animal veterinary care, computer software, marketing consulting services and pet care products.
3000 Attendees
Frequency: Annual
Founded in: 1933

19976 American College of Veterinary Opthalmologists Conferΐnce
2316 West Northern Avenue
Phoenix, AZ 85021
602-995-2871; *Fax:* 602-995-1770
Lisa Schultz, Practice Manager
Meeting and 30 exhibits of opthamology equipment and information.
400 Attendees
Frequency: Annual

19977 American College of Veterinary Surgeons - Veterinary Symposium
American College of Veterinary Surgeons
19785 Crystal Rock Dr,
Suite 305
Germantown, MD 20874
301-916-0200; *Fax:* 301-916-2287
acvs@acvs.org; www.acvs.org
Ann T Loew, Executive Director
William B Henry, VP
Mark Markel, Chair
Marvin L Olmstead, ACVS President
Ann Loew, Executive Director
Over 150 exhibits featuring veterinary equipment, supplies and services.
1500 Attendees
Frequency: October 5-7
Founded in: 1965

19978 American Federation of Aviculture Inc
STAT Marketing
PO Box 91717
Austin, TX 78709
512-585-9800; *Fax:* 512-858-7029
afaoffice@afabirds.org; www.afabirds.org
Social Media: Facebook, Twitter
Nancy Speed, National President
Linda Sheaffer, Chair
Jamie Whittaker, First VP
Brent Gattis, Second VP
Brent Andrus, CFO
Annual convention for manufacturers, suppliers, distributors and retailers of exotic birds and related products, including feed, seeds, cages, toys, vitamins and minerals. 65 booths.
750 Attendees
Founded in: 1974

19979 American Humane Association Annual Meeting and Training Conference
American Humane Association
1400 16th Street NW
Suite 360
Washington, DC 20036
303-792-9900
800-227-4645; *Fax:* 818-762-0908
info@americanhumane.org;
www.americanhumane.org
Social Media: Facebook, Twitter, RSS,YouTube,Pinterest
Robert R Ganzert, President/CEO
Clifford Rose, CFO
Over 50 exhibits of animal welfare equipment, including pet food, cages, trucks, id programs and veterinary services. Breakfast, luncheon, reception.
700 Attendees
Frequency: Annual
Founded in: 1982

19980 American Morgan Horse Association Grand National Show
3 Bostwick Road
PO Box 960
Shelburne, VT 05482-0960
802-985-4944; *Fax:* 802-985-8897
info@morganhorse.com
morganhorse.com
Raymond Gifford, Show Manager
Fred Braden, Executive Director
Offers you a way to enjoy your Morgan in a competitive setting, while enjoying the company of other Morgan exhibitors. 30 booths.
8M Attendees
Frequency: October

19981 American Paint Horse Association World Championship Horse Shows
PO Box 961023
Fort Worth, TX 76161-0023
817-834-2742; *Fax:* 817-834-3152
http://www.apha.com
Carl Parker, President
Richard Cox, VP
Alice Singleton, Senior Committee Member
Ed Robert, Executive Secretary
A 14 day annual event that has become the proving ground for competitors striving to show that they ride or own the best American Paint Horses in the world. 100 booths.
5M Attendees
Frequency: July

19982 American Pet Products Manufacturers Association National Tradeshow
255 Glenville Road
Greenwich, CT 06831
203-532-0000
800-452-1225; *Fax:* 203-532-0551
andy@appma.org;
www.americanpetproducts.org
Bob Vetere, COO/Managing Director
Jennifer Bilbao, Marketing/PR Administrator
Andrew Darmohraj, VP/Deputy Managing Director
Jamie Cavanaugh, Trade Show Coordinator
Edith Martingnetti, General Mgr/Exhibitor Registration
Breakfast, reception, and 1400 pet products manufacturers exhibits.
Frequency: Annual
Founded in: 1959

19983 American Rabbit Breeders Association National Convention
8 Westport Court
Bloomington, IL 61704
309-664-7500; *Fax:* 309-664-0941
arba.net
Glen Carr, Executive Director
Seminar, banquet, luncheon and 1500 rabbit breeders exhibits.
3000 Attendees
Frequency: Annual
Founded in: 1910

19984 American Veterinary Medical Association Annual Convention
American Veterinary Medical Association
1931 N Meacham Road
Suite 100
Schaumburg, IL 60173
847-036-6142; *Fax:* 847-925-1329
convention@avma.org; www.avma.org
Dr Bonnie Beaver, President
David Little, Director
Seminar and 310 exhibits of products, materials, equipment, data, and services for veterinary medicine.
10000 Attendees
Frequency: Annual

19985 Annual Pet Industry Trade Show
World Wide Pet Supply Association
406 S 1st Avenue
Arcadia, CA 91006-3829
626-447-2222; *Fax:* 626-447-8350;
www.wwpsa.com
Doug Poindexter, Executive VP
A comprehensive collection of exhibits and educational events unparalleled in the industry.

19986 Global Pet Expo
American Pet Products Association
255 Glenville Rd.
Greenwich, CT 06831
203-532-0000
800-452-1225; *Fax:* 203-532-0551
globalpetexpo@americanpetproducts.org
globalpetexpo.org
Social Media: Facebook, Twitter, Flickr, YouTube
Andrew Darmohraj, Executive Vice President & COO
Tracey Wilson, Show Manager
Sarah Bopp, Associate Manager
Pet industry's largest annual trade show featuring buyers from more than 80 countries.
Frequency: Annual

19987 HH Backer Pet Industry Christmas Trade Show
HH Backer Associates
200 S Michigan Avenue
Suite 840
Chicago, IL 60604
312-663-4040; *Fax:* 312-663-5676
hhbacker@hhbacker.com; www.hhbacker.com
Patty Backer, President/Publisher
Karen Long MacLeod, Assoc Publisher/Editor in Chief
M Christopher Mitera, VP
Colette Fairchild, CMP, Trade Show Director
Julie Wichert, Sales Manager
Containing 1000 plus booths and 550 plus exhibits consisting of pet supplies, products and services.
9M Attendees
Frequency: October
Founded in: 1967

19988 HH Backer Pet Industry Spring Trade Show
HH Backer Associates
200 S Michigan Avenue
Suite 840
Chicago, IL 60604
312-663-4040; *Fax:* 312-663-5676
hhbacker@hhbacker.com; www.hhbacker.com
Patty Backer, President/Publisher
Karen Long MacLeod, Assoc Publisher/Editor in Chief
M Christopher Mitera, VP
Collette Fairchild, CMP, Trade Show Director
Julie Wichert, Sales Manager
Containing 1000 plus booths and 550 plus exhibits consisting of pet supplies, products and services.
10M Attendees
Frequency: April
Founded in: 1967

19989 International Boarding & Pet Services Asso Annual Convention & Trade Show
1702 E Pikes Peak Avenue
Colorado Springs, CO 80909
719-667-1600; *Fax:* 719-667-0116
info@abka.com; www.ibpsa.com
James Krack, Executive Manager
Kathryn Eddy, Show Manager
Annual show and exhibit of pet industry products, including pet foods, supplements, retail supplies, construction materials, cages, computers and software.
300 Attendees
Frequency: October
Founded in: 1977

19990 NAPPS Annual Convention: National Assoc. of Professional Pet Sitters
17000 Commerce Parkway
Suite C
Mt. Laurel, NJ 08054
856-439-0324; *Fax:* 856-439-0525
napps@ahint.com; www.petsitters.org
Felicia Lembesis, Administrative Director
Rebecca Haines, Registration Coordinator
Kelly Calzaretta, Meeting/Exhibit Manager
Cathe Delaney, Membership Coordinator
Caitlin Dougherty, Manager
Exhibits, business sessions and networking opportunities. Provide tools and support to foster the success of members' businesses. To promote the value of pet sitting to the public and the advocate the welfare of animals.
Frequency: September

19991 National Lawn & Garden Show
Controlled Marketing Conferences
PO Box 1771
Monument, CO 80132
719-488-0226
888-316-0226; *Fax:* 719-488-8168
nlginfo@nlgshow.com; www.nlgshow.com
Robert Mikulas, President
Chris Wolf, VP
This event is run in conjunction with the National Lawn and Garden Show.
3000 Attendees
Frequency: June

19992 National Pigeon Association
1717 SE 43rd Terrace
Topeka, KS 66609-1728
785-267-5732; *Fax:* 785-783-2846
secretary@npausa.com; www.npausa.com
Frank Barrachina, President
Pat Avery, Secretary, Treasurer
James Avery, Secretary/Treasurer
Jerry McCalmon, Show Manager
Special information and exhibits about our members and the hobby of pigeon raising.
500 Attendees
Frequency: January
Founded in: 1920

19993 Pet Exposition Trade Show
Pet Industry Distributors Association
2105 Laurel Bush Road
Suite 200
Bel Air, MD 21015
443-640-1060; *Fax:* 443-640-1086
pida@kingmgmt.org; www.pida.org
Steven T King CAE, President
Fred Schober, Chairman
Perry Parks, 2nd Vice Chairman
Randy Reber, Secretary/Treasurer
Steven T King, President
Containing 500 booths and 300 exhibits.
3000 Attendees
Frequency: March
Founded in: 1968

19994 Pet Food Institute Meeting and Trade Show
Pet Food Institute
2025 M Street NW
Washington, DC 20036
202-367-1120; *Fax:* 202-367-2120
info@petfoodinstitute.org;
www.petfoodinstitute.org
Stephen Payne, Public Relations Manager
Duane Ekedahl, Executive Director
Annual exhibits of equipment, supplies and services for manufacturers of commercially prepared dry, semi-moist and canned pet foods.
250 Attendees
Frequency: October

19995 Petfood Forum
WATT Publishing Company
303 N Main Street
Suite 500
Rockford, IL 61101
815-966-5400; *Fax:* 815-966-6416;
www.wattnet.com
Tim Phillips, Editor
Clay Schreiber, Publisher
James Watt, Owner
A technical trade show and symposium for the pet food industry including manufacturers, suppliers to the industry as well as other pet food professsionals. Containing 143 booths.
850 Attendees
Frequency: April
Founded in: 1993
Mailing list available for rent

19996 Quest for Excellence
Pet Sitters International
201 East King Street
King, NC 27021-9163
336-983-9222; *Fax:* 336-983-3755
info@petsit.com; www.petsit.com
Kay Calzemari, Operating Manager
Beth Stoltz, Member Service Coordinator
Amy Woodleaf, Manager/Membership
John Long, Public Relations Coordinator
Dotty Shantz, Member Service
Containing 20+ exhibits.
250 Attendees
Frequency: September
Founded in: 1994

19997 Super Zoo Annual WWPSA Pet Industry Trade Show
World Wide Pet Supply Association
406 S 1st Avenue
Arcadia, CA 91006-3829
626-447-2222; *Fax:* 626-447-8350;
www.wwpsa.com
Caryn Cohan-Bates, Manager
America's oldest pet industry trade show offering over 450 exhibitors with 850 booths. Seminars, workshops, grooming events and more are held for retailers and wholesalers.
9000 Attendees
Frequency: July
Founded in: 1951

19998 Tufts Animal Expo
Hynes Convention Center
900 Boylston Street
Boston, MA 02115
617-954-2000
800-845-8800; *Fax:* 617-954-2125;
www.mccahome.com
Animal care professionals addressed the social and medical impact pets have on human lives.
7000 Attendees
Frequency: October

19999 World of Private Label International Trade Show
Private Label Manufacturers Association (PLMA)
630 Third Avenue
New York, NY 10017
212-972-3131; *Fax:* 212-983-1382
info@plma.com; www.plma.com
Brian Sharoff, President
Myra Rosen, VP
Tom Prendergast, Director, Research Services
This show has brought retailers together with manufacturers to help them find new products, make new contacts, and discover new ideas that will help their private label programmers succeed and grow.

Directories & Databases

20000 American Humane Association Directory
American Humane Association
1400 16th Street NW
Suite 360
Washington, DC 20036
303-792-9900
800-227-4645; *Fax:* 818-762-0908
info@americanhumane.org;
www.americanhumane.org
Social Media: Facebook, Twitter, RSS,YouTube,Pinterest
Robert R Ganzert, President
Clifford Rose, CFO
Animal protection agencies; Canadian and some other foreign agencies are available; national and individual state editions are available.

20001 Directory of Animal Care and Control Agencies
American Humane Association
63 Inverness Dr E
Englewood, CO 80112-5117
303-792-9900
800-227-4645; *Fax:* 303-792-5333
info@americanhumane.org;
www.americanhumane.org
Marie Wheatley, President
Over 6,000 animal protection agencies; Canadian and some other foreign agencies are available; national and individual state editions are available.
Cost: $75.00

20002 Market Research Report
Animal Health Institute
1325 G St NW
Suite 700
Washington, DC 20005-3127
202-637-2440; *Fax:* 202-393-1667
amathews@ahi.org; www.ahi.org
Alexander Mathews, President
Dr Richard A Carnevale, VP Regulatory, Scientific, Int'l
Ron Phillips, VP/Legislative/Public Affairs

Sandra L Phelan, Director Regulatory Affairs
Carolyn S Ayers, VP Administration/Finance

An annual directory published by the Animal Health Institute.
Cost: $150.00
50 Pages
Frequency: Annual
Founded in: 1941

20003 **Pets/Animals Forum**
CompuServe Information Service
5000 Arlington Centre Blvd
Columbus, OH 43220-5439
614-326-1002
800-848-8199

This database provides a forum for the discussion of typical house and exotic pets.
Frequency: Bulletin Board

20004 **Veterinary Economics**
Veterinary Healthcare Communications
8033 Flint
Lenexa, KS 66214
913-492-4300
800-255-6864; *Fax:* 913-492-4157;
www.vetmedpub.com

Daniel R. Verdon Chapman, Executive Director
Ray Click, VP/General Manager

Publishes two monthly magazines, a full drug list resource, and business books; conducts the Central Veterinary Conference trade show; rents its mail lists and does custom communication projects.
Frequency: Monthly
Circulation: 52,000
Mailing list available for rent: 48M+ names
Printed in 4 colors on matte stock

Industry Web Sites

20005 **http://gold.greyhouse.com**
G.O.L.D Grey House OnLine Databases

Grey House Publishing's online database platform, GOLD, offers Quick Search, Keyword Search and Expert Search for most business sectors including pet and pet supply markets. The GOLD platform makes finding the information you need quick and easy - whether you're a novice searcher or an experienced database user. All of Grey House's directory products are available for subscription on the GOLD platform.

20006 **www.aahanet.org**
American Animal Hospital Association

A group of hospitals and animal practitioners serving the industry.

20007 **www.abka.com**
American Boarding Kennels Association

Seeks to upgrade the industry through educational programs and conventions. Promotes code of ethics and accreditation programs for kennel operators.

20008 **www.ahi.org**
Animal Health Institute

Resource for you to learn more about how animals health products work, how they are used and their many benefits.

20009 **www.akc.org**
American Kennel Club

The principal registry of pure-bred dogs in the US.

20010 **www.allpets.com**
Dog.com

Best selection of dog supplies and prices, news and forum about dogs, health issues, grooming and the well-being for our four-legged friends.

20011 **www.apdt.com**
Association of Pet Dog Trainers

Official web site of the association. Includes members in the news, training events, industry news, trainer search engine, conference news and merchandise.

20012 **www.aspca.org**
ASPCA

Society for the humane treatment of animals, established in 1866.

20013 **www.avma.org**
American Veterinary Medical Association

Publishes various journals and information for members. Acts as a clearinghouse for veterinarians.

20014 **www.deltasociety.org**
Delta Society

Information on human-animal interactions. Service Dog Center provides information and advocacy for dogs trained to assist people with disabilities. Pet Partners Program trains volunteers, health professionals, animals for animal-assisted therapy and activities.

20015 **www.greyhouse.com**
Grey House Publishing

Authoritative reference directories for most business sectors including pet and pet supply markets. Users can search the online databases with varied search criteria allowing for custom searches by product category, geographic area, sales volume, keyword, subject and more. Full Grey House catalog and online ordering also available.

20016 **www.nhes.org**
National Humane Education Society

Fights for the prevention of cruelty to animals in any form. Fostering a sentiment of kindness since 1948.

20017 **www.npausa.com**
National Pigeon Association

Special information for members and for the hobby of pigeon raising.

20018 **www.peta.org**
People for the Ethical Treatment of Animals (PETA)

Opposes all forms of animal exploitation. Seeks to educate the public on what the group sees as the three major institutionalized cruelty issues: the exploitation and abuse of animals in experimentation, the manufacturing of fur apparel, and slaughtering for human consumption.

20019 **www.petfoodinstitute.org**
Pet Food Institute

Represents the manufacturer of 97% of all dog and cat food produced in the US. Dedicated to promoting the overall care and well-being of pets. Research in pet nutrition, proper feedings and pet care.

20020 **www.petpride.org**
Pet Pride

Operates a no kill free shelter for the lifetime of homeless cats.

20021 **www.petsit.com**
Pet Sitters International

Society of professional pet sitters. Membership provides valuable benefits - educational resources for those engaged in the pet-sitting industry. Also provides a forum to network with peers who share a common vision of excellence in at-home pet care.

20022 **www.petsitters.org**
National Association of Professional Pet Sitters

The only non-profit organization dedicated to serving the needs of professional pet care providers. Promotes ethical standards and fosters cooperation among members in the pet care industry.

20023 **www.pida.org**
Pet Industry Distributors Association

Represents wholesaler-distributors of pet products, providing training and education to members.

20024 **www.pijac.org**
Pet Industry Joint Advisory Council

Monitors federal and state regulations and legislation affecting the industry. Sponsors research and educational projects including certification programs in veterinary care and husbandry for companion animals, in-store training videos, etc.

20025 **www.usaha.org**
United States Animal Health Association

Science-based, non-profit, voluntary organization. Members are state and federal animal health officials, universities, veterinarians, livestock producers, research scientists, and extension services all to control livestock diseases in the US.

20026 **www.wspa.americas.org**
The Resource Center of the Americas

International animal protection news reports. Informs, educates and organizes economic justice and cross-cultural understanding in the Americas.

20027 **www.wwpsa.com**
World Wide Pet Supply Association

Seeks to advance the economic interests of members. Promotes responsible pet ownership. Sponsors consumer and trade shows for the pet industry.

Associations

20028 Academy of Managed Care Pharmacy
100 N Pitt St
Suite 400
Alexandria, VA 22314-3141

703-683-8416
800-827-2627; *Fax:* 703-683-8417
sandres@amcp.org; www.amcp.org
Social Media: Facebook, Twitter, LinkedIn

Judy Cahill, Executive Director
Elaine Manieri, Director
Cathryn A Carroll, PhD, Treasurer

Promotes the development and application of appropriate and accessible medication therapy. Represents professional pharmacists and associates practicing in managed care settings.
4800 Members
Founded in: 1989
Mailing list available for rent

20029 Academy of Managed Care Pharmacy (AMCP)
100 North Pitt Street
Suite 400
Alexandria, VA 22314

703-683-8416
800-827-2627; *Fax:* 703-683-8417
memberservices@amcp.org; www.amcp.org
Social Media: Facebook, Twitter, LinkedIn

Dana Davis McCormick, President
Raulo S Frear, President Elect
Kim A. Caldwell, Past President
Stanley E. Ferrell, Director
H Eric Cannon, Treasurer
6000 Members

20030 Accreditation Council for Pharmacy Education
135 S. LaSalle Street
Suite 4100
Chicago, IL 60603-4810

312-664-3575; *Fax:* 312-664-4652
info@acpe-accredit.org;
www.acpe-accredit.org
Social Media: Facebook

Janet Cline, Chair
Tian Merren Owens, Vice Chair
Stephanie F. Gardner, President
Bruce Canaday, Vice President
Michael A. Mone, Secretary/Treasurer

A nonprofit accreditation national agency.
Founded in: 1932

20031 American Association of Colleges of Pharmacy
1727 King St
Alexandria, VA 22314-2700

703-739-2330; *Fax:* 703-836-8982
mail@aacp.org; www.aacp.org
Social Media: Facebook, Twitter, LinkedIn, YouTube

Lucinda Maine, Executive VP
Kenneth W Miller, Senior VP
Daniel J Cassidy, COO

National organization representing the interests of pharmaceutical education and educators. Comprising all 111 US pharmacy colleges and schools including more than 5,000 faculty, 50,000 students enrolled in professional programs and 4,000 individuals pursuing graduate study. AACP is committed to excellence in pharmaceutical education.
3670 Members
Founded in: 1900
Mailing list available for rent

20032 American Association of Pharmaceutical Scientists
2107 Wilson Blvd
Suite 700
Arlington, VA 22201-3042

703-243-2800; *Fax:* 703-243-9650
aaps@aaps.org; www.aaps.org
Social Media: Facebook, Twitter, LinkedIn, YouTube

Gene Fiese, President
Patrick Deluca, President Elect
Peter Inchauteguiz, Director Marketing
James Greif, Communcations Specialist
Maureen Downs, Director of Finance

Aims to advance science through the open exchange of scientific knowledge, serve as an information resource and contribute to human health through pharmaceutical research and development.
11000 Members
Founded in: 1986
Mailing list available for rent

20033 American Association of Pharmacy Technicians (AAPT)
PO Box 1447
Greensboro, NC 27402

336-333-9356
877-368-4771; *Fax:* 336-333-9068
aapt@pharmacytechnician.com;
www.pharmacytechnician.com
Social Media: Facebook, Twitter

Judy Neville, BS, CPhT, President
Susan Jeffery, VP
Danalynne Young, BS, CPhT, Secretary
Bobbie Craddock, CPhT, Treasurer

Provides leadership and represents the interests of its members to the public as well as health care organizations. Promotes safe efficacious and cost effective dispensing, distribution and use of medications. Provides continuing education programs and services to help technicians update their skills and keep pace with changes in pharmacy services. Promotes pharmacy technicians as an integral part of the patient care team.
850 Members
Founded in: 1979

20034 American Association of Pharmacy Technicia
P.O. Box 1447
Greensboro, NC 27402

336-333-9356
877-368-4771; *Fax:* 336-333-9068
aapt@pharmacytechnician.com;
www.pharmacytechnician.com
Social Media: Facebook, Twitter

Judy Neville, BS, CPhT, President
Judy Neville, Vice President
Ann Barlow Oberg, Immediate Past President
Danalynne Young, BS, CPhT, Secretary
Bobbie Craddock, Treasurer
Founded in: 1979

20035 American Chemical Society
1155 16th St Nw
Washington, DC 20036-4892

202-872-4600
800-333-9511; *Fax:* 202-872-4615
service@acs.org; www.acs.org
Social Media: Facebook, Twitter, LinkedIn, Google+

Madeleine Jacobs, CEO
Diane Grob Schmidt, President
John Crum, Executive Director
Thomas R Gilbert, Director

Supports scientists and other professionals working in the field of drug discovery. Publishes monthly magazine.
159K Members
Founded in: 1876

20036 American Clinical Laboratory Association
1100 New York Ave Nw
Suite 880
Washington, DC 20005-6172

202-637-9466; *Fax:* 202-637-2050
info@clinical-labs.org; www.acla.com
Social Media: Facebook, Twitter, RSS

Alan Mertz, President
Julie Khani, SVP
Francesca Fierro O'Reilly, Vice President Government Affairs
Thomas Sparkman, Vice President Government Affairs
Peter M Kazon, Legal Counsel

Members are clinical laboratories licensed and regulated under medicare and the interstate laboratory program.
Founded in: 1971

20037 American College of Apothecaries
2830 Summer Oaks Dr
Bartlett, TN 38134-3811

901-383-8119; *Fax:* 901-383-8882
aca@acainfo.org; www.acainfo.org

D C Huffman, Executive VP
Jeffrey Denton, President
Randall S Myers, VP

Disseminates and translates knowledge, research data and recent developments in professional pharmacy practice for the benefit of pharmacists, pharmacy students and the public. This is achieved through regular distribution of periodicals, development of major publications and continuing education courses on clinical and administrative topics and conducting educational conferences.
1M Members
Founded in: 1940

20038 American College of Clinical Pharmacology
21750 Red Rum Drive
Suite 137
Ashburn, VA 20147

571-291-3493; *Fax:* 571-918-4167
Info@ACCP1.org; www.accp1.org
Social Media: Facebook, LinkedIn

Lisa Von Moltke, President
Krista K Levy, Executive Director
Keri J Sperry, Director of Education
Erica Serow, Manager of meetings

A national organization of clinical pharmacology healthcare professionals who seek to advance clinical pharmacology.
Founded in: 1969

20039 American College of Clinical Pharmacy
13000 W. 87th Street Parkway
Suite 650
Lenexa, KS 66215-4530

913-492-3311; *Fax:* 913-492-0088
accp@accp.com; www.accp.com

Michael S Maddux, Pharm.D., FCCP, Executive Director

Professional and scientific society that provides leadership, education, advocacy and resources enabling clinical pharmacists to achieve excellence in practice and research. Membership is composed of practitioners, scientists, educators, administrators, students, residents, fellows and

others committed to excellence in clinical pharmacy and patient pharmacotherapy.
Founded in: 1979

20040 **American College of Medical Quality**
5272 River Road
Suite 630
Bethesda, MD 20816

301-718-6516
800-924-2149; *Fax:* 301-656-0989
acmq@acmq.org; www.acmq.org
Social Media: Facebook, LinkedIn

Prathibha Varkey, President
Mark Lyles, MD, MBA, FACMQ, President-Elect
Donald E Casey, Jr MD, MPH, VP

The mission of the American College of Medical Quality is to provide leadership and education in healthcare quality management.
900 Members
Founded in: 1972

20041 **American Council on Pharmaceutical Education**
20 N Clark Street
Suite 2500
Chicago, IL 60602

312-664-3575; *Fax:* 312-664-4652

Robert Buchman, Executive Director

Promotes the education of pharmaceutical medicine.

20042 **American Institute of the History of Pharmacy**
777 Highland Ave
Madison, WI 53705-2222

608-262-5378; *Fax:* 608-262-3397
Institute@aihp.org;
www.pharmacy.wisc.edu/aihp
Social Media: Facebook, LinkedIn

Dr. Gregory Higby, Executive Director
Dr. Elaine C Stroud, Assistant Director
Beth D Fisher, Assoc. Dir. Curatorial Affairs
Joseph Gabriel, Ph.D., Historian
William Zellmer, President

Non-profit national organization devoted to advancing knowledge and understanding of the place of pharmacy in history. Contributes to the understanding of the development of civilization by fostering the creation, preservation, and dissemination of knowledge concerning the history and related humanistic aspects of the pharmaceutical field.
900 Members
Founded in: 1941

20043 **American Pharmacists Association**
2215 Constitution Ave NW
Washington, DC 20037-2985

202-628-4410
800-237-2742; *Fax:* 202-783-2351
infocenter@aphanet.org; www.pharmacist.com
Social Media: Facebook, Twitter, LinkedIn, YouTube, RSS

Thomas E Menighan, CEO
Elizabeth Keyes, Chief Operating Officer
Joseph J Janela, CFO

It is the largest association of pharmacists in the United States, whose mission is to provide information, education, and advocacy to empower its members to improve medication use and advance patient care.
60000 Members
Founded in: 1852

20044 **American Public Health Association**
800 I Street NW
Washington, DC 20001-3710

202-777-2742; *Fax:* 202-777-2534
coments@apha.org; www.apha.org
Social Media: Facebook, Twitter

Jay M Bernhardt, Vice Chair
Gene Lutz, President
Georges Benjamin, Executive Director
Jose F Cordero, Member Services
Louise A Anderson, Director Operations

Brings together researchers, health service providers, administrators, teachers and other health workers in a unique, multidisciplinary environment of professional exchange, study and action in the effort to prevent disease and promote health.
50000 Members
Founded in: 1872

20045 **American Society for Automation in Pharmacy**
492 Norristown Road
Suite 160
Blue Bell, PA 19422

610-825-7783; *Fax:* 610-825-7641;
www.asapnet.org

Tammy Devine, President
Tim Tannert, R.Ph, Vice President
Chuck Welch, Secretary/Treasurer

Assists its members in advancing the application of computer technology in the pharmacist's role as care giver, in the efficient operation of a pharmacy and promoting standards, legislation and guidelines.
350 Members
Founded in: 1988

20046 **American Society for Clinical Pharmacology and Therapeutics**
528 N Washington St
Alexandria, VA 22314

703-836-6981
info@ascpt.org; www.ascpt.org
Social Media: Facebook, Twitter, LinkedIn, Google+

Mario L Rocci, Jr., PhD, President
Julie A Johnson, PharmD, President Elect
Russ B. Altman, Immediate Past President
Gregory L. Kearns, Secretary/Treasurer
Sharon J. Swan, Chief Executive Officer

Focuses on improving the understanding and use of existing drug therapies and developing safe and more effective treatments for the future.
2200 Members
Founded in: 1900

20047 **American Society for Parenteral & Enteral Nutrition**
8630 Fenton Street
Suite 412
Silver Spring, MD 20910

301-587-6315
800-727-4567; *Fax:* 301-587-2365
aspen@nutr.org; www.nutritioncare.org
Social Media: Facebook, Twitter, LinkedIn, YouTube

Marion F Winkler, President
Vincent W Vanek, VP
Robin Kriegel, CAE, Executive Director
Joanne Kieffer, Director Finance

Promotes professional communication among and within professional disciplines in the broad field of clinical nutrition including parenteral and enteral nutrition (tube feeding) through national and regional meetings, local seminars, scientific, clinical and educational exhibits and publications.
6000 Members
Founded in: 1979

20048 **American Society for Pharmacy Law**
3085 Stevenson Drive
Suite 200
Springfield, IL 62703

217-529-6948; *Fax:* 217-529-9120
info@aspl.org; www.aspl.org
Social Media: LinkedIn

Laura Carpenter, President
Brian Guthrie, Director
Janet Bascom, Member Services Director
Nathela Chatara, CAE, Executive Director
Jim Boyd, Treasurer

An organization of pharmacists and lawyers who are interested in the law as it applies to the pharmacy industry.
Founded in: 1974

20049 **American Society of Consultant Pharmacists**
1321 Duke St
Alexandria, VA 22314-3563

703-739-1300
800-355-2727; *Fax:* 703-739-1321
info@ascp.com; www.ascp.com
Social Media: Facebook, Twitter, LinkedIn, YouTube

Frank Grosso, RPh, Executive Director and CEO
Kelly Jennings, Chief Financial Officer
Cindy S. Porter, RPh, VP Education & Foundation Dev.
Debbie Furman, VP Membership & Strategic Alliances
Arnold E. Clayman, VP Pharmacy Practice & Government

The international professional association that provides leadership, education, advocacy and resources to advance the practice of senior care pharmacy.
6500+ Members
Founded in: 1969

20050 **American Society of Consultant Pharmacists Foundation**
1321 Duke Street
Alexandria, VA 22314-3563

703-739-1300
800-355-2727; *Fax:* 703-739-1500
info@ascpfoundation.org;
www.ascpfoundation.org

Nancy L Losben, Chairman
Frank Grosso, Executive Director
Jan Allen, Treasurer
Carla McSpadden, Board of Trustees
Ross W. Brickley, Board of Trustees

A charitable organization affiliated with the American Society of Consultant Pharmacists. It sponsors research, administers programs, holds traineeships in pharmacy practice, and performs other educational and outreach functions.
Founded in: 1982

20051 **American Society of Health-System Pharmacists**
7272 Wisconsin Ave
Bethesda, MD 20814-4861

301-657-3000
866-279-0681; *Fax:* 301-664-8877;
www.ashp.org
Social Media: Facebook, Twitter, LinkedIn, YouTube

John A Armitstead, President
Paul W Abramowitz, EVP/CEO

An association that brings together health-system pharmacists who practice in hospitals, health maintenance organizations, long-term care facilities, home care, and other components of health care systems. ASHSP has a long history of medication error prevention efforts and believe the

mission of pharmacists is to help people make the best use of medicines.
31M Members
Founded in: 1942
Mailing list available for rent

20052 American Society of Pharmacognosy
E-Mail: j.porter@usciences.edu; www.pharmacognosy.us/
Social Media: Facebook, Twitter, LinkedIn, RSS
Brad Moore, Chair
Phil Crews, President
Ed Kennelly, Vice President
William J. Keller, Secretary
Jim McAlpine, Treasurer
A scientific society that promotes the growth and development of pharmacognosy through presentation of research achievements and publication of meritous research.
1100 Members
Founded in: 1959

20053 Aspirin Foundation of America
529 14th St NW
Suite 807
Washington, DC 20045-1801
202-393-0000
800-432-3247; *Fax:* 202-737-8406
info@aspirin.org; www.aspirin.org
A non-profit educational foundation with a membership of companies engaged in the manufacture, preparation, compounding or processing of aspirin and aspirin products. AFA serves as a central source of information on the health benefits of aspirin and aspirin products, when used as directed.
Founded in: 1981

20054 Association of Clinical Research Professionals
99 Canal Center Plaza
Suite 200
Alexandria, VA 22314
703-254-8100; *Fax:* 703-254-8101
office@acrpnet.org; www.acrpnet.org
Social Media: Facebook, Twitter, LinkedIn, YouTube
Norbert Clemens, MD, PhD, CPI, Chair, Board of Trustees
Thomas L Adams, CAE, President/CEO
James Thomasell, Director Finance
The Academy of Clinical Research Professionals and the Academy of Pharmaceutical Physician and Investigators are affiliates of ACRP. The Academy asministers non-physician certification programs and govermmental affairs activities. APPI represents all physician members of ACRP.
21000 Members
Founded in: 1976

20055 Board of Pharmacy Specialties
2215 Constitution Avenue NW
Washington, DC 20037-2985
202-429-7591; *Fax:* 202-429-6304; www.bpsweb.org
Social Media: Facebook, Twitter, YouTube
Sharon M Durfee, Chair
William Evans, Chair Elect
A post-licensure certification agency that improves patient care bypromoting the recognition and value of specialized training, knowledge, and skills in pharmacy and specialty board certification of pharmacists.
Founded in: 1973

20056 College of Psychiatric and Neurologic Pharmacists
8055 O Street
Suite S113
Lincoln, NE 68510
402-476-1677; *Fax:* 888-551-7617
info@cpnp.org; www.cpnp.org
Social Media: Facebook, Twitter, LinkedIn, YouTube, Google+
Ray Love, President
Christopher Thomas, President-Elect
Steven Burghart, Past President
Jennifer Zacher, PharmD, BCPP, Secretary
Robert Haight, PharmD, BCPP

, Treasurer

Organization that advances the reach and practice of neuropsychiatric pharmacists.
Founded in: 1998

20057 Drug Information Association
800 Enterprise Road
Suite 200
Horsham, PA 19044-3595
215-442-6100; *Fax:* 215-442-6199
dia@diahome.org; www.diaglobal.org
Social Media: Facebook, Twitter, LinkedIn
Paul Pomerantz BA MBA, Worldwide Executive Director
Lisa Zoks BA, Worldwide Dir Met/Communications
Provides a neutral global forum for the exchange and dissemination of information on the discovery, development, evaluation and utilization of medicines and related health care technologies. Through these activities the DIA provides development opportunities for its members.
20000 Members
Founded in: 1964

20058 Drug, Chemical & Associated Technologies Association
One Union St
Suite 208
Robbinsville, NJ 8691
609-208-1888
800-640-3228; *Fax:* 609-208-0599; www.dcat.org
Social Media: Facebook, LinkedIn
George Svokos, President
Folker Ruchatz, First Vice President
Milton Boyer, Second Vice President
Margaret M. Timony, Executive Director
David Beattie, Director
A nonprofit, member-supported business development association for the global pharmaceutical manufacturing industry.
Founded in: 1890

20059 Drug, Chemical & Associated Technologies
One Union St
Suite 208
Robbinsville, NJ 08691-3162
609-208-1888; *Fax:* 609-448-1944; www.dcat.org
Margaret Timony, Executive Director
James K Martin, Senior Vice President
Bob Kanuga, Vice President
The premier business development association whose membership is comprised of companies that manufacture, distribute or provide services to the pharamceutical, chemical, nutritional and related industries.
Founded in: 1890

20060 Federation of Pharmacy Networks
30131 Town Center Drive
Suite 100
Laguna Niguel, CA 92677
949-495-5257; *Fax:* 949-495-1258
info@fpn.org; www.fpn.org
Don Anderson, President
Tom Scono, Vice President
Carol Carlson, CEO
Cathi Clark, Secretary
Curtis Woods, Treasurer
An organization of independent pharmacy group purchasing organizations established for the purpose of providing a forum for its members to exchangeideas that promote, advance and ensure the future of independent pharmacy.

20061 Food & Drug Law Institute
1155 15th Street NW
Siute 910
Washington, DC 20005-2706
202-371-1420
800-956-6293; *Fax:* 202-371-0649
comments@fdli.org; www.fdli.org
Social Media: Facebook, LinkedIn
Amy Comstock Rick, JD, President & CEO
Iris V. Stratton CPA, VP Finance & Administration
Michael Sprott, Membership Manager
A nonprofit, educational organization dedicated to improving the understanding of the laws, regulations, and policies affecting health care technologies, food and cosmetics. FDLI is neutral, nonpartisan and does not lobby or advocate positions on any issue.
550+ Members
Founded in: 1949

20062 Food and Drug Administration
10903 New Hampshire Avenue
Silver Spring, MD 20993
888-463-6332; www.fda.gov
Social Media: Facebook, Twitter, YouTube, Flickr
Margaret A Hamburg, Commissioner of Food and Drugs
Walter S Harris, Deputy Commissioner for Operations
James Tyler, Chief Financial Officer
Denise Esposito, Chief of Staff
Mitch Zeller, Director
A federal agency of the United States Department of Health and Human Services that is responsible for protecting and promoting public health through the regulation and supervision of food safety, tobacco products, dietary supplements, prescription and over-the counter medications, vaccines, animal foods, veterinary products, etc.

20063 Generic Pharmaceutical Association
777 Sixth Street, NW
Suite 510
Washington, DC 20001
202-249-7100; *Fax:* 202-249-7105
info@gphaonline.org; www.gphaonline.org
Social Media: Facebook, Twitter, LinkedIn, Google+, YouTube
Chester Davis, Jr, President
David Gaugh, R.Ph, Senior Vice President
Doug Boothe, Secretary/Treasurer
Represents the manufacturers and distributors of finished generic pharmaceutical products, manufacturers and distributors of bulk active pharmaceutical chemicals, and suppliers of other goods and services to the generic pharmaceutical industry.

20064 Healthcare Distribution Management Association
901 N Glebe Rd
Suite 1000
Arlington, VA 22203-1853

703-787-0000; *Fax:* 703-812-5282;
www.healthcaredistribution.org
Social Media: Twitter, LinkedIn

Ted Scherr, President/CEO
Nancy E Hanagan, Executive VP/COO
Susan Mirvis, Senior VP Marketing/Communications

An organization representing all major constituents of healthcare product distribution management.

20065 Hematology/Oncology Pharmacy Association
8735 W. Higgins Road
Suite 300
Chicago, IL 60631

877-467-2791
board@hoparx.org; www.hoparx.org

John Kuhn, Chair
Barry Goldspiel, Vice Chair
Scott Soefge, President
Helen Marshall, Secretary
Jolynn Sessions, Treasurer

A nonprofit professional organization created to help oncology and hematology.
Founded in: 1995

20066 IAGIM
4901 Midtown Lane PBG
Florida 33418

561-376-2224
info@iagim.org; www.iagim.org

Publishes generic pharmaceutical journals and technical handbooks.

20067 Independent Pharmacy Cooperative
1550 Columbus St
Sun Prairie, WI 53590-3901

608-825-9556
800-755-1531; *Fax:* 608-825-1535
member.services@ipcrx.com; www.ipcrx.com

Don Anderson, CEO
Gary Helgerson, COO
Chuck Benjamin, CFO

Provides member pharmacies with the lowest possible contract pricing on quality products and services.
4500 Members
Founded in: 1984

20068 Institute for Safe Medication Practices
200 Lakeside Drive
Suite 200
Horsham, PA 19044

215-947-7797; *Fax:* 215-914-1492;
www.ismp.org
Social Media: Facebook, Twitter

Michael R Cohen, RPh, MS, ScD, President
Mark J Cziraky, PharmD, Executive Vice President
Judy Smetzer, Vice President
Susan F. Paparella, Vice President
Russell H. Jenkins, Medical Director

A nonprofit organization devoted entirely to medication error prevention and safe medication use.
Founded in: 1975

20069 International Pharmaceutical Excipients Council of the Americas
3138 N. 10th Street
Suite 500
Arlington, VA 22201

571-814-3449; *Fax:* 703-525-5157
ipecamer@ipecamericas.org;
www.ipecamericas.org

Kimberly Beals, Executive Director
Tammy Kramer, Office Manager
Valeria Stewart, Training Coordinator
Linda A. Herzog, Technical & Membership Operations

Members are companies with an interest in the otherwise inert chemicals used as vehicles for medicines. IPEC is a federation of three independent regional associations headquartered in the US. and Japan. Each association focuses its attention on the applicable laws, regulations, science and business practices of its region to accomplish its members goals.
300 Members
Founded in: 1991

20070 International Pharmaceutical Federation
2517 JP The Hague
The Netherlands

170-302-1970; *Fax:* 170-302-1999;
www.fip.org
Social Media: Facebook, Twitter, LinkedIn

Luc Besancon, Chief Executive Officer
Rachel Van Kesteren, Executive Secretary
Paula Cohen, Secretary
Carola Van der Hoeff, Chief Operating Officer
Lin-Nam Wang, Communication Manager

An international federation of national organizations that represent pharmacists and pharmaceutical scientists.
Founded in: 1912

20071 International Society for Pharmacoepidemiology
5272 River Road
Suite 630
Bethesda, MD 20816

301-718-6500; *Fax:* 301-656-0989
ISPE@paimgmt.com; www.pharmacoepi.org
Social Media: Facebook, LinkedIn, YouTube

Sonia Hernandez-Diaz, FISPE, President
Kiyoshi Kubota, FISPE, President Elect
Alison Bourke, Vice-President Finance
Mark H. Epstein, Executive Secretary
Andrew Jerdonek, Account Manager

A nonprofit international professional membership organization dedicated to advancing the health of the public by providing a forum for the open exchange of scientific information and for the development of policy, education, and advocacy for pharmacoepidemiology, pharmacovigilance, drug use research, outcomes research, comparative effectiveness research, and therapeutic risk management.

20072 International Society for Pharmaceutical Engineering (ISPE)
600 N. Westshore Blvd
Suite 900
Tampa, FL 33609

813-960-2105; *Fax:* 813-264-2816
ask@ispe.org; www.ispe.org
Social Media: Facebook, Twitter, LinkedIn, Myspace, YouTube

John Bournas, President & CEO
Victoria Smoke, CFO
Kindra Bess, Director, Event Operations
Gloria Hall, Editor & Director of Publications
Karleen Kos, VP of Member Relations

Global society for technical professionals in pharmaceutical manufacturing and drug development sectors.
2000 Members
Founded in: 1980

20073 Joint Commission on the Accreditation of Healthcare Organizations
601 13th Street, NW
Suite 560
Washington, DC 20005

630-792-5800; *Fax:* 630-792-5005;
www.jointcommission.org
Social Media: Facebook, Twitter, LinkedIn, YouTube, Google+

Mark R Chassin, President
Anne Marie Benedicto, Executive Vice President
Ann Jacobson, Executive Director
Amy Panagopoulos, Senior Director
Anita Giuntoli, Director

A nonprofit organization that accredits and certifies more than 20,500 health care organizations and programs in the United States.
Founded in: 1951

20074 Lambda Kappa Sigma (International Professional Pharmacy Fraternity)
P.O. Box 570
Muskego, WI 53150-0570

800-LKS-1913; *Fax:* 262-679-4558
ExecutiveDirector@lks.org; www.lks.org
Social Media: Facebook, Twitter

Jenny Brandt, President
Patti Lozano, Vice President
Joan Rogala, Executive Director
Kim Hancock, Secretary
Sandy Mullen, Treasurer

An international professional pharmacy fraternity open to undergraduate and graduate pharmacy students and participating pharmacists. It also provides lifelong opportunities for women in pharmacy.
25000 Members
Founded in: 1913

20075 National Alliance of State Pharmacy Associations
2530 Professional Road
Suite 202
Richmond, VA 23235

804-285-4431
804-612-6555
rsnead@naspa.us; www.naspa.us
Social Media: Facebook, Twitter, LinkedIn

Mike Larkin Kansas, President
Pat Epple Pennsylvania, President-Elect
Joni Cover Nebraska, 1st Vice President
Jon Roth, 2nd Vice President
Louise Jones Alabama, Secretary/Treasurer

Promotes leadership, sharing, learning, and policy exchange among state pharmacy associations and pharmacy leaders nationwide, and provides education and advocacy to support pharmacists, patients, and communities working together to improve public health.
Founded in: 1927

20076 National Alliance of State Pharmacy
2530 Professional Rd
Suite 202
Richmond, VA 23235-3217

804-285-4431; *Fax:* 804-285-4227
becky@naspa.us; www.naspa.us
Social Media: Twitter

Rebecca Snead, Executive Director
Joni Cover Nebraska, First VP
400 Members
Founded in: 1927

20077 National Association of Boards of Pharmacy
1600 Feehanville Dr
Mount Prospect, IL 60056
847-698-6227
800-774-6227; *Fax:* 847-391-4502
custserv@nabp.net; www.nabp.net
Social Media: RSS
Joseph L Adams, RPh, Chairperson
Edward G McGinley, MBA, RPh, President
Jeanne D Waggener, RPh, Treasurer
Serves all American boards of pharmacy in matters of interstate reciprocity of licensure and licensing as well as other matters of mutual concern.
Founded in: 1904

20078 National Association of Chain Drug Stores
413 N Lee Street
PO Box 1417-D49
Alexandria, VA 22313-1480
703-549-3001; *Fax:* 703-836-4869;
www.nacds.org
Social Media: Facebook, Twitter, LinkedIn, YouTube
Randy Edeker, Chairman
Martin Otto, Vice Chairman
Craig L Fuller, President/CEO
Mark Griffin, Director
David Bernauer, Treasurer
Association for manufacturers or suppliers of chain drug store equipment, supplies and services.
210 Members
Founded in: 1933

20079 National Community Pharmacists Association
100 Daingerfield Road
Alexandria, VA 22314
703-683-8200
800-544-7447; *Fax:* 703-683-3619
info@ncpanet.com; www.ncpanet.org
Social Media: Facebook, Twitter, Google+, YouTube
Bradley Arthur, President
Bruce Roberts RPh, Executive VP/CEO
Represents pharmacy owners, managers and employees of nearly 25,000 independent community pharmacies across the US.
60000 Members
Founded in: 1898

20080 National Council for Prescription Drug Programs
9240 E Raintree Dr
Scottsdale, AZ 85260-7518
480-477-1000; *Fax:* 480-767-1042
info@ncpdp.org; www.ncpdp.org
Lee Ann Stember, President
Dennis Kitterman, Director Marketing Communications
Phillip D Scott, SVP Sales/Marketing
Joanne Longie, VP Operations
Members are computer companies, drug manufacturers, drug store chains, drug wholesalers, insurers, mail order prescription drug companies, pharmaceutical claim processors, prescription drug providers, software vendors, service organizations, government agencies and others with a interest in drug program administration standardization.
1350 Members
Founded in: 1977

20081 National Institute for Pharmacist Care Outcomes
100 Daingerfield Road
Alexandria, VA 22314
703-683-8200; *Fax:* 703-683-3619
kathryn.kuhn@ncpanet.org; www.ncpanet.org
Social Media: Facebook, Twitter, Google+
Kathryn Kuhn, Executive Director, NIPCO Programs
Eleanor Nespica, Coordinator, NIPCO Programs
Mike Clark, Manager
Bradley Arthur, President
The national accrediting organization for pharmacist care education and training programs leading to the pharmacist care diplomate credential. A leading authority in helping community pharmacists develop new market niches in disease management and wellness.

20082 National Pharmaceutical Alliance
427 King Street
Suite 222
Alexandria, VA 22314
703-836-8816; *Fax:* 919-469-5858;
www.npa.org
Cristina Sizemore, Executive Director
Deborah Kline, Manager Communications
Represents the interests of small pharmaceutical companies and allied industries.
Founded in: 1993

20083 National Pharmaceutical Association
107 Kilmayne Drive
Suite C
Cary, NC 27511
877-215-2091; *Fax:* 919-469-5858
npha@npha.net; www.npha.net
Social Media: Facebook, Twitter
Dr. Carleton Maxwell, President
Erica Hanesworth, President Elect
Cornetta Levi, Immediate Past-President
Gayle Tuckett, Secretary
Joseph T. Lee, Treasurer
A nationwide, professional organization of pharmacists.
Founded in: 1950

20084 National Pharmaceutical Council
1717 Pennsylvania Ave., NW
Suite 800
Washington, DC 20006
703-620-6390; *Fax:* 202-827-0314
info@npcnow.com; www.npcnow.org
Social Media: Facebook, Twitter, LinkedIn, YouTube
Daniel Leonard, President
Pat Adams, VP Business Operations
Gary Persinger, VP Health Care Systems
Richard Levy, VP Scientific
Jeffery Warren, Senior Advisor
Represents major, research-intensive, pharmaceutical companies. Conducts national and state studies, holds educational forums and generates publications for consumer and for health care cost containment programs.
31 Members
Founded in: 1953

20085 National Pharmacy Purchasing Association
4747 Morena Blvd
Suite 340
San Diego, CA 92117-3468
858-581-6373
888-544-6772; *Fax:* 858-581-6372
info@pharmacypurchasing.com;
www.pharmacypurchasing.com
Social Media: Facebook, Twitter
Dale J Kroll, President & CEO
Francine Morgano, Vice President
Michael Thomas, Event & Editorial Assistant
Debby Flannery, Advisory Board
Deb Harden, Advisory Board
An association that promotes the profession of pharmacy purchasing and offers educational opportunities for pharmacy buyers. Members include pharmacy buyers and managers from private, nonprofit, or government-run institutional facilities that work to promote the profession of pharmacy purchasing and offerseducational opportunities for pharmacy buyers.
Founded in: 1991

20086 National Pharmacy Technician Association
PO BOX 683148
Houston, TX 77268
888-247-8700; *Fax:* 888-247-8706
mikej@pharmacytechnician.org;
www.pharmacytechnician.org
Social Media: Facebook, Twitter, LinkedIn, YouTube, RSS
Mike Johnston, Chairman
Robin Luke, President
Wendy Meigs, Board Member
Carol Reyes, Board Member
Rhonda Wilson, Board Member
The world's largest professional organization established specifically for pharmacy technicians.
Founded in: 1999

20087 New York State Council of Health-Systems Pharmacists
210 Washington Ave
Albany, NY 12203
518-456-8819
518-456-8819; *Fax:* 518-456-9319
nyschpweb@nyschp.org; www.nyschp.org
Social Media: Facebook, Twitter, LinkedIn
Stephanie Seyse, President
Joseph Pinto, President Elect
Monica Mehta, Vice President
Shaun C. Flynn, Executive Director
Philip Manning, Treasurer
Provides leadership and resources to promote quality pharmaceuticalservices directed at appropriate medication therapy and positive patient outcomes.
2200 Members

20088 Pan American Health Organization
525 Twenty-third Street, N.W.
Washington, DC 20037
202-974-3000; *Fax:* 202-974-3663;
www.paho.org
Social Media: Facebook, Twitter, LinkedIn, YouTube, Flickr, RSS
The world's oldest international public health agency that providestechnical cooperation and mobilizes partnerships to improve health and quality of life in the countries of the Americas.
Founded in: 1902

20089 Parenteral Drug Association
3 Bethesda Metro Center
Suite 1500
Bethesda, MD 20814
301-860-0293; *Fax:* 301-986-0296
info@pda.org; www.pda.org
Social Media: Twitter, LinkedIn, YouTube
Vince R Anicetti, Chairman
Richard Jahnson, President and CEO
Wanda Neal-Ballard, Director Programs/Meetings

Lance K Hoboy, MBA, VP Finance
Matthew Clark, Director Marketing

A non-profit international association of scientists involved in the development, manufacture, quality control and regulation of pharmaceuticals/biopharmaceuticals and related products. The association also provides educational opportunities for government and university sectors that have a vocational interest in pharmaceutical/biopharmaceutical sciences and technology.
10500 Members
Founded in: 1946

20090 Pediatric Pharmacy Advocacy Group
5865 Ridgeway Center Parkway
Suite 300
Memphis, TN 38120-4014

901-820-4434; *Fax:* 901-767-0704
membership@ppag.org; www.ppag.org
Social Media: Facebook, Twitter, LinkedIn

Jared Cash, PharmD, President
Lisa Lubsch, PharmD, President-Elect
Kimberly Novak, PharmD, Secretary
Jeffrey Low, Treasurer
Matthew R. Helms, Executive Director

A nonprofit organization that strives to improve the health of children.
800 Members
Founded in: 1990

20091 Pennsylvania Pharmacists Association
508 North Third Street
Harrisburg, PA 17101

717-234-6151
ppa@papharmacists.com;
www.papharmacists.com
Social Media: Facebook, Twitter, LinkedIn, YouTube, Flickr

Donna Hazel, President
Eric Pusey, President-Elect
Nicholas Leon, First Vice President
Nicholas Leon, Second Vice President
Eric Esterbrook, Immediate Past President

A professional membership society of registered pharmacists, student pharmacists, pharmacy technicans, and others who reside, work, attend college,or are interested in pharmacy in Pennsylvania.
Founded in: 1878

20092 Pharmaceutical Care Management Association
325 7th St. NW
9th Fl.
Washington, DC 20004

202-756-5700; *Fax:* 202-756-5708;
www.pcmanet.org
Social Media: Facebook, Twitter

Mark Merritt, President & CEO
Brenda Palmer, Chief Financial Officer
Brian McCarthy, Chief Operating Officer

National association of pharmacy benefit managers.
Founded in: 2009

20093 Pharmaceutical Outsourcing Management Association
8865 W Okeechobee Boulevard
Suite 202
West Palm Beach, FL 33411
561-795-5503; *Fax:* 561-795-5503;
www.pharmoutsourcing.com

Shannon Brome-Ward, President
Linda Wauk, VP
Charles Calvert, Treasurer
Fran Grote, Secretary

Established as a forum to exchange ideas and experiences about outsourcing in the pharmaceutical industry.
Founded in: 1995

20094 Pharmaceutical Research and Manufacturers of America
950 F Street, NW
Suite 300
Washington, DC 20004

202-835-3400
newsroom@phrma.org; www.phrma.org
Social Media: Facebook, Twitter, YouTube, Flickr, Google+

Kenneth C Frazier, Chairman
George A Scangos, Chairman Elect
Jack Bailey, President
Joaquin Duato, Treasurer

Mission is to conduct effective advocacy for public policies that encourage discovery of important new medicines for patients by pharmaceutical/biotechnology research companies.
Founded in: 1958

20095 Pharmacy Benefit Management Institute, Inc .
2901 N Dallas Pkwy
Ste 420
Plano, TX 75093

480-730-0814; *Fax:* 480-222-4229
jlutz@pbmi.com; www.pbmi.com
Social Media: LinkedIn

Jane Lutz, Executive Director
Kathleen Fairman, Vice President
Linda DeChant, Director of Sales
Julie Blackman, Marketing Manager
Shelly Carey, Research Director

Pharmacy benefit management education, research, and consulting.

20096 Pharmacy Technician Certification Board
2215 Constitution Avenue NW
Suite 101
Washington, DC 20037

800-363-8012; *Fax:* 202-888-1699
contact@ptcb.org; www.ptcb.org
Social Media: Facebook, Twitter

Paul Abramowitz, Chair
Paul Abramowitz, Vice Chair
Thomas Menighan, Executive Vice President
Everett B. McAllister, Executive Director & CEO
Larry Wagenknecht, Treasurer

Develops, maintains, promotes, and administers a nationally accredited certification and recertification program for pharmacy technicians to enablethe most effective support of pharmacists to advance patient safety.
Founded in: 1995

20097 Pinoy Pharmacy
www.pinoypharmacy.com
Social Media: Facebook, Twitter

An online community for Filipino pharmacy professionals around the world.

20098 Professional Compounding Centers of America
9901 South Wilcrest Drive
Houston, TX 77099

281-933-6948
800-331-2498; *Fax:* 281-933-6627
customerservice@pccarx.com;
www.pccarx.com
Social Media: Facebook, Twitter, LinkedIn, YouTube, Flickr

Provides independent pharmacists with a complete support system forcompounding unique dosage forms.
3900 Members
Founded in: 1981

20099 Regulatory Affairs Professionals Society
5635 Fishers Lane
Suite 550
Rockville, MA 20852

301-770-2920; *Fax:* 301-770-2924
raps@raps.org; www.raps.org
Social Media: Facebook, Twitter, LinkedIn, YouTube, Google+, Flickr

Donald A Middlebrook, Chairman
Rainer Voelksen, President
Martha A. Brumfield, President Elect
Salma Michor, Secretary/Treasurer
Gautam Maitra, Director

The largest global organization of and for those involved with the regulation of healthcare and related products, including medical devices, pharmaceuticals, biologics and nutritional products.
Founded in: 1976

20100 Roundtable of Toxicology Consultants
P.O. Box 98224
Raleigh, NC 27624

E-Mail: toxconsultants@earthlink.net;
www.toxconsultants.com

Jane Allen, President
Joann Schuh, President Elect
Dave Hobson, Past President
Lori Dostal, Secretary
Merrill Osheroff, Treasurer

An organization of independently practicing toxicologists dedicatedto solving the problems for clients.
Founded in: 1986

20101 Society for Laboratory Automation and Screening
100 Illinois Street
Ste. 242
St. Charles, IL 60174
630-256-7527
877-990-7527
slas@slas.org; www.slas.org
Social Media: Facebook, Twitter, LinkedIn, YouTube

Dean Ho, Ph.D., President
Richard Eglen, Ph.D., Vice President
Alastair Binnie, Director
Michele A Cleary, Ph.D., Secretary
Mike Snowden, Ph.D., Treasurer

A global community of more than 18,000 scientists from academia, government and industry collectively focused on leveraging the power of technologyto achieve scientific objectives.
18000 Members
Founded in: 2009

20102 Society of Critical Care Medicine
500 Midway Drive
Mount Prospect, IL 60056
847-827-6869; *Fax:* 847-827-6886
info@sccm.org; www.sccm.org
Social Media: Twitter, Google+

J. Christopher Farmer, President
David J Martin, Chief Executive Officer
Dorothy Suwanski, Executive Assistant
Ellen Turney, Human Resources Manager
Karen Boman, Business Analyst

The largest multiprofessional organization dedicated to ensuring excellence and consistency in the practice of critical care.

20103 **Southeastern Society of Health-System Pharmacists**

www.smshp.org
Social Media: Facebook, Twitter

A regional association representing pharmacists and related personnel associated with organized health-care settings.

20104 **Student National Pharmaceutical Association**

PO Box 761388
San Antonio, TX 78245

210-383-7381; *Fax:* 210-579-1059
contactsnpha@snpha.org; www.snpha.org
Social Media: Facebook, Twitter, YouTube, Instagram

Joshua Blackwell, PharmD, Executive Chairman
Jessie Nai Hwang, President
Gevorg Martirosyan, President Elect
Dr. Carmita Coleman, Executive Director
Kyle Brown, Vice President

An educational service association of pharmacy students who are concerned about pharmacy and healthcare related issues, and the poor minority representation in pharmacy and other health-related professions.
Founded in: 1972

Newsletters

20105 **AACP News**

American Association of Colleges of Pharmacy
1727 King St
Suite 210
Alexandria, VA 22314-2700

703-739-2330; *Fax:* 703-836-8982;
www.aacp.org

Lucinda Maine, Executive VP
Kenneth W Miller, Senior VP
Daniel J Cassidy, COO

Activities and issues in pharmacy education. 12 pages, free to members. Published since 1874.
Cost: $35.00
Frequency: Monthly
Circulation: 300
Founded in: 1900
Mailing list available for rent: 300 names
Printed in on newsprint stock

20106 **ACCP Report**

American College of Clinical Pharmacy
13000 W. 87th St Parkway
Lenexa, KS 66215-4530

913-492-3311; *Fax:* 913-492-0088
accp@accp.com; www.accp.com

George Puiges, Publisher
Bruce Mueller, Editor
Micheal Maddux, Executive Director
Jon Poynter, Project Manager, Membership
Kimma Sheldon, Medical Editor

The American College of Clinical Pharmacy (ACCP) is a professional and scientific society that provides leadership, education, advocacy, and resources enabling clinical pharmacists to achieve excellence in practice and research.
Cost: $45.00
Frequency: Monthly
Circulation: 12000

20107 **Alternative Medicine Alert**

American Health Consultants
3525 Piedmont Rd Ne
Building Six, Suite 400
Atlanta, GA 30305-1578

404-467-4243
800-688-2421; *Fax:* 404-262-7837;
www.ahcpub.com

Jeff Mac Donald, CEO

Reports on studies of herbs in medicine, reactions in relation to different herbs. Studies that are out and those being done.
Cost: $299.00
Frequency: Monthly
Mailing list available for rent
Printed in 4 colors on matte stock

20108 **Annals of Pharmacotherapy**

Harvey Whitney Books Company
8044 Montgomery Road
PO Box 42696
Cincinnati, OH 45242-0696

513-793-3555
877-742-7631; *Fax:* 513-793-3600
customer-services@theannals.com;
www.theannals.com

Tina Whitney, Finance Executive
Eugene Sorkin, Associate Editor
Harvey Whitney, CEO
Greg Johnson, Marketing
Ann Brandwieve, Circulation Manager

For 38 years this independent peer reviewed journal has been dedicated to the advancement of pharmacotherapy. Article categories include; original research, comprehensive reviews, case reports, editorials, and letters. special article features include new drug evaluations, therapeutic controversies, recent theraputic advances, international reports, continuing education articles, and more.
Cost: $158.00
Frequency: Monthly
Circulation: 50000
ISSN: 1060-0280
Founded in: 1967
Printed in 4 colors on glossy stock

20109 **Chapter News**

American College of Cardiology
76 S State Street
Concord, NH 03301-3520

603-228-1231; *Fax:* 603-228-2118
assnrhc@aol.com

Walter Perry, Executive Director

Newsletter for cardiovascular specialists in Maine, New Hampshire and Vermont.
Frequency: Quarterly
Mailing list available for rent

20110 **Clin-Alert-Newsletter**

Technomic Publishing Company
300 S Riverside Plz
Suite 1200
Chicago, IL 60606-6637

312-876-0004; *Fax:* 312-876-1158
foodinfo@technomic.com;
www.technomic.com

Ronald Paul, President
Darren Tristano, Executive Vice President
Neil Stern, Senior Partner

This unique adverse drug reaction/interaction reporting service presents-in newsletter format-a summary of adverse clinical events, collected from 103 key medical and research journals from around the world. Approximately 360 abstracts per year.
Cost: $155.00
8 Pages
Frequency: Semimonthly
ISSN: 0069-4770
Printed in 2 colors

20111 **Clinical Investigator News**

CTB International Publishing
PO Box 218
Maplewood, NJ 07040-218

973-966-0997; *Fax:* 973-966-0242
info@ctbintl.com; www.ctbintl.com

FG Racioppi, Marketing Director
William Robison, Circulation Manager

Alerts independent investigators to existing or emerging opportunities to participate in clinical trials of drugs and maintain a steady flow of studies. Covers preclinical development through Phase II/III, approvals and post-marketing surveillance (PMS) studies.
Cost: $647.00
48 Pages
Frequency: Monthly
Founded in: 1980
Mailing list available for rent
Printed in one color on newsprint stock

20112 **Clinical Trials Monitor**

CTB International Publishing
PO Box 218
Maplewood, NJ 07040-218

973-966-0997; *Fax:* 973-379-0242
info@ctbintl.com; www.ctbintl.com

Oykue Brogna, Publisher
Christopher Brogna, Editor

Tracks clinical trials planned, underway, completed or abandoned. Lists the drug, the company, the indication, phase or stage, principal investigator, where and when trials will be held, enrollment plans and proposed end points. Reports results at meetings, and in journals.
Cost: $1197.00
64 Pages
Frequency: Monthly
Founded in: 1985
Printed in one color on newsprint stock

20113 **Consumer Pharmacist**

Elba Medical Foundation
PO Box 494
Metairie, LA 70004

504-889-7070; *Fax:* 504-889-7060

John DiMaggio, Publisher

Drug information newsletter.
Cost: $30.00
Frequency: Monthly

20114 **DIA Newsletter**

Drug Information Association
800 Enterprise Rd
Suite 200
Horsham, PA 19044-3595

215-442-6100; *Fax:* 215-442-6199
dia@diahome.org; www.diahome.org
Social Media: Facebook, Twitter, LinkedIn, YouTube

Ling Su, President
John Roberts, Treasurer
Paul Pomerantz,MBA, Worldwide Executive Director

Association activities, technical developments, supplying, and production of drugs.
Cost: $40.00
20 Pages
Frequency: Monthly
Founded in: 1964

20115 **Diagnostics Intelligence**

CTB International Publishing
PO Box 218
Maplewood, NJ 07040-218

973-966-0997; *Fax:* 973-966-0242
info@ctbintl.com; www.ctbintl.com

Oyque Brogna, CEO/President
F Racioppi, Marketing Director

Covers the latest in research, development, new product language, regulatory affairs, patents, litigations, opportunities and finance in the invitro diagnostics business.
Cost: $578.00
20 Pages
Frequency: Monthly
Mailing list available for rent
Printed in one color on newsprint stock

20116 Drug Development Pipeline
CTB International Publishing
PO Box 218
Maplewood, NJ 07040

973-966-0997; *Fax:* 973-966-0242
info@ctbintl.com; www.ctbintl.com/

FG Racioppi, Marketing Director
Chris Brogna, President
Laszlo Novak, Editor

Newsletter that summarizes the changes in the drug development plans of US and Canadian pharmaceutical companies. Each issue will alert the reader to more than 120 products that are moving through the pipeline.
Cost: $198.00
Frequency: Monthly
Founded in: 1982
Mailing list available for rent
Printed in one color on newsprint stock

20117 Emerging Pharmaceuticals
CTB International Publishing
PO Box 218
Maplewood, NJ 07040-218

973-966-0997; *Fax:* 973-966-0242
info@ctbintl.com; www.ctbintl.com

FG Racioppi, Marketing Director

Covers the earliest stage of drug development, from discovery through preclinical trials. Alerts readers to news and insights about novel compounds, innovative screening methods and candidates for the R&D pipeline.
Cost: $542.00
14 Pages
Frequency: Monthly
Mailing list available for rent
Printed in one color on newsprint stock

20118 FDC Reports: Gold Sheet
FDC Reports
5550 Friendship Boulevard
Suite 1
Chevy Chase, MD 20815-7278

301-657-9830
800-332-2181; *Fax:* 301-656-3094
fdc.customer.service@elsevier.com;
www.fdcreports.com

Bill Paulson, Editor
Michael Magoulias, VP Sales/Marketing
Mike Squires, CEO/President
William Paulson, Executive Editor

A specialized publication which focuses each month on important changes in FDA's policies for regulating good manufacturing practices for pharmaceutical companies and their suppliers. Since 1967, this publication has provided quality control officials with the latest useful information on state-of-the-art production and quality control techniques.
Cost: $595.00
Frequency: Monthly
ISSN: 1530-6194
Founded in: 1939
Mailing list available for rent
Printed in 2 colors on matte stock

20119 FDC Reports: Green Sheet
FDC Reports
5550 Friendship Boulevard
Suite 1
Chevy Chase, MD 20815-7256

301-657-9830; *Fax:* 301-656-3094;
www.fdcreports.com

Mike Squires, President
Michael Koppenhoffer, Editor

For nearly 40 years The Green Sheet has been an independent source of news and information on the pharmacy profession and the pharmaceutical distribution system. This four-page publication provides pharmacists, wholesalers, drugstore managers and trade relations executives with concise coverage of: professional policy; national and state pharmacy association activities; reimbursement issues; new drug introductions and pharmaceutical pricing and deals.
Cost: $65.00
4 Pages
Frequency: Weekly
Founded in: 1939

20120 FDC Reports: Pink Sheet
FDC Reports
5550 Friendship Boulevard
Suite 1
Chevy Chase, MD 20815-7256

301-657-9830
800-332-2181; *Fax:* 301-656-3094
PinkEditor@elsevier.com;
www.fdcreports.com

Wallace Werble Jr, Publisher
Janet Coleman, Editor
Mike Squires, CEO/President
Shawn Smith, Marketing
Emily Brainard, Circulation Manager

Provides in-depth weekly news and analysis about developments affecting the prescription medicines. The publication closely tracks regulatory policies and actions by FDA, FTC, HCFA, Congress, the courts and other key federal and state agencies with jurisdiction over the drug industry. Regular coverage areas include: NDA and Generic Drug approvals, FDA recalls and seizures, mergers, the R&D pipeline, biotechnology start-ups and new product activity.
Cost: $1580.00
35 Pages
Frequency: Weekly
ISSN: 1068-5324
Founded in: 1939

20121 FDC Reports: Tan Sheet
FDC Reports
5550 Friendship Boulevard
Suite 1
Chevy Chase, MD 20815-7256

301-657-9830; *Fax:* 301-656-3094
FDC.Customer.Service@Elsevier.com;
www.fdcreports.com

Mike Squires, CEO/President
Ramsey Baghdadi, Editor
Michael Magoulias, Marketing Manager
Emily Brainard, Circulation Manager

Provides in-depth coverage of nonprescription pharmaceuticals and dietary supplement/nutritionals. Spectrum of coverage includes: regulatory activities of FTC, CPSC and FDA, including monograph and non-monograph decisions, enforcement actions, advisory committee reviews and approvals; Congressional hearings and legislation; business and marketing news such as Rx-to-OTC switches, product development and new product introductions; FDA recalls and seizures and regular listing of product trademarks
Cost: $1285.00
Frequency: Weekly
ISSN: 1068-5316
Founded in: 1939

20122 FDLI Prospectus
Food & Drug Law Institute
1155 15th Street NW
Suite 800
Washington, DC 20005
202-371-1420
800-956-6293; *Fax:* 202-371-0649
comments@fdli.org; www.fdli.org

Michael D. Levin-Epstein, Vice President, Publications
Abby C. Foster, Managing Editor
weekly e-newsletter
Frequency: Weekly

20123 Food and Drug Letter
FDAnews
300 N Washington St
Suite 200
Falls Church, VA 22046-3441

703-538-7600
888-838-5578; *Fax:* 703-538-7676
customerservice@fdanews.com;
www.fdanews.com

Cynthia Carter, President
Michael Miven, Editor
Maritva Lizama, Marketing
J T Hrontith, Sales Director

Provides reliable, in-depth analysis of how FDA's regulations and procedures will affect your current decisions and long-term plans and gives you in-depth interpretation to tell you why FDA is making or proposing revisions.
Cost: $1095.00
8 Pages
Frequency: Annual+

20124 Health News Daily
FDC Reports
5550 Friendship Boulevard
Suite 1
Chevy Chase, MD 20815-7256

301-657-9830
800-332-2181; *Fax:* 301-656-3094;
www.healthnewsdaily.com

Jim Chicca, Editor
Mike Squires, Executive Director

Provides up-to-the-minute coverage on a broad spectrum of health care issues including pharmaceuticals, medical devices and diagnostics, biomedical research, federal health policy and legislation, Medicare-Medicaid, technology reimbursement and cost-containment. Special emphasis is placed on federal regulatory and legislative developments. Published each business day, the publication draws on the expertise of more than 40 F-D-C reports editors and reporters.
Cost: $ 1480.00
Frequency: Daily
Founded in: 1939

20125 International Pharmaceutical Regulatory Monitor
Omniprint
9700 Philadelphia Ct
Lanham, MD 20706-4405

301-731-7000
800-345-2611; *Fax:* 301-731-7001;
www.omniprint.net

Ken Kaufman, President
Stephen Brown, VP

Comprehensive reports on the world's drug and biotechnology regulations for testing and marketing; provides actual regulatory documents (English texts).
Cost: $595.00
60 Pages
Frequency: Monthly
ISSN: 0888-6393
Founded in: 1973

Mailing list available for rent
Printed in 2 colors on matte stock

20126 Mealey's Emerging Drugs & Devices
LexisNexis Mealey's
555 W 5th Avenue
Los Angeles, CA 90013
213-627-1130
mealeyinfo@lexisnexis.com;
www.lexisnexis.com/mealeys
Tom Hagy, VP/General Manager
Maureen McGuire, Editorial Director
Tom Moylan, Editor
The report covers cases involving a variety of prescription drug vaccines, implants and devices. Duract, Parlodel, Accutane, fen-phen, Rezulin, Propulsid, dietary supplements and blood products are among the topics tracked. Medical devices covered include heart catheters, breast implants, heart valves, intraocular lenses, jaw implants, joint replacements, latex gloves, pacemakers, pedicle screws, penile implants, and surgical lasers.
Cost: $1249.00
100 Pages
Frequency: Semi-Monthly
Founded in: 1996

20127 Mealey's Litigation Report: Baycol
LexisNexis Mealey's
555 W 5th Avenue
Los Angeles, CA 90013
213-627-1130
mealeyinfo@lexisnexis.com;
www.lexisnexis.com/mealeys
Tom Hagy, VP/General Manager
Maureen McGuire, Editorial Director
Dylan McGuire, Editor
This report tracks the litigation surrounding Baycol and other statin-based anti-cholesterol drug cases. Since the voluntary withdrawl of Bayer's Baycol and Lipobay brand cerivastatin anti-cholesterol drugs, numerous complaints have been filed. The report will cover hard-to-find filings, new complaints, class actions, MDL developments, trial updates and more.
Cost: $950.00
100 Pages
Frequency: Monthly
Founded in: 2002

20128 Mealey's Litigation Report: Fen-Phen/Redux
LexisNexis Mealey's
555 W 5th Avenue
Los Angeles, CA 90013
213-627-1130
mealeyinfo@lexisnexis.com;
www.lexisnexis.com/mealeys
Tom Hagy, VP/General Manager
Maureen McGuire, Editorial Director
Michael Lefkowitz, Editor
The report provides detailed coverage of the litigation surrounding fen-phen, Redux and other diet drugs. The report covers new filings, class actions, MDL proceedings, trials, settlements, rulings, medical studies, FDA activity and more.
Cost: $995.00
100 Pages
Frequency: Monthly
Founded in: 1997

20129 NABP Newsletter
National Association of Boards of Pharmacy
700 Busse Highway
Park Ridge, IL 60068
847-698-6227
800-774-6227; *Fax:* 847-698-0124
custserv@nabp.net; www.nabp.net
Malcom Broussard, Chairperson
Michael Burlson, President
Joseph Adams, Treasurer
Provides coverage of issues important to those who practice pharmacy and those who regulate that practice. Information about NABP's competency assessment and licensure transfer programs, news about the boards of pharmacy, and articles that impact the practice and regulation of pharmacy appear in each issue.
Cost: $35.00
Frequency: 10 Per Year

20130 NCPA Newsletter
National Community Pharmacists Association
100 Daingerfield Road
Alexandria, VA 22314
703-683-8200
800-544-7447; *Fax:* 703-683-3619
info@ncpanet.com; www.ncpanet.org
Mike Conlan, VP Publications
Chris Linville, Managing Editor
Stay up-to-date on the latest developments in legislation, federal regulation, pharmacy news, and other important events with the NCPA Newsletter. Independent pharmacists get the information they need to understand the policies, politics, and government actions that affect independent pharmacy practice. Annual subscription is included in NCPA memership dues.
Cost: $50.00

20131 Nation's Health
American Public Health Association
800 I Street NW
Washington, DC 20001-3710
202-777-2742; *Fax:* 202-777-2534
membership.mail@apha.org; www.apha.org
Social Media: Facebook, Twitter, LinkedIn, YouTube, Blogs
Georges C Benjamin, Executive Director
Mazin Abdelgader, Publication Services
Michele Late, Executive Editor
For the latest news on public health, public health professionals, legislators and decision-makers. This newsletter is part of APHA membership.
Cost: $50.00
Frequency: 10 Per Year

20132 PDA Letter
Parenteral Drug Association
1894 Preston White Drive
Reston, VA 20191-5433
703-620-6390; *Fax:* 703-476-0904
info@npcnow.org; www.npcnow.org
Walter L Morris, III, Senior Editor
Designed to keep members informed of the latest information in the regulatory arena along with scientific happenings within the Association and the industry. It also contains details on upcoming PDA events, as well as worldwide Chapter activities.
Frequency: Monthly
Founded in: 1949

20133 Pharmaceutical & Med Packaging News
Canon Communications
11444 W Olympic Blvd
Suite 900
Los Angeles, CA 90064-1555
310-445-4200; *Fax:* 310-445-4299
feedback@cancom.com; www.cancom.com
Klaus Weinmann, CEO
Rudolf Hotter, COO
Frequency: Monthly
Founded in: 1992

20134 Pharmaceutical News Daily
CTB International Publishing
PO Box 218
Maplewood, NJ 07040
973-966-0997; *Fax:* 973-966-0242
info@ctbintl.com; www.ctbintl.com
Kris Brogina, CEO/President
Kistine Yanicek, Editor
Oykue Brogina, Publisher
T Tseng, Circulation Manager
This daily electronic newsletter updates the highly competitive pharmaceutical and biotechnology industries. Delivered by e-mail.
Cost: $279.00
Frequency: Daily
Founded in: 1984
Mailing list available for rent
Printed in one color on newsprint stock

20135 Pharmacist's Letter
Therapeutic Research
3120 W March Lane
PO Box 8190
Stockton, CA 95208-190
209-472-2240; *Fax:* 209-472-2249;
www.pletter.com
Jeff Jellin, Publisher
A newsletter to pharmacists offering coverage of drug development, production, distribution, legislation, safety and other issues concerning the industry.
Cost: $85.00
ISSN: 0883-0371

20136 Pharmacy Practice News
McMahon Group
545 W 45th St
8th Floor
New York, NY 10036-3409
646-557-0966; *Fax:* 646-957-7230
davidb@mcmahonmed.com;
www.strategiesinmedicine.com
Raymond Mc Mahon, CEO
Van Velle, President
David Bronstein, Editor-in-Chief
Marsha Radebaugh, Circulation Manager
Michelle McMohan, Creative Director
Created to inform hospital pharmacists of the latest news on drugs, nutrition, research and trends in the pharmaceutical industry.
Cost: $60.00
Frequency: Monthly
Circulation: 45460
Founded in: 1972

20137 Pharmacy Student
APLA
2215 Constitution Avenue NW
Washington, DC 20037-2977
202-429-7576
Rick Harding, Publisher
Practical information to help pharmacy students grow.
Cost: $35.00
Frequency: Monthly
Circulation: 100000

20138 Pharmacy Today
American Pharmacists Association

2215 Constitution Avenue NW
Washington, DC 20037-2977

202-429-7557
800-237-2742; *Fax:* 202-783-2351
pt@aphanet.org; www.pharmacists.org

Frank Bennicasa, Publisher
L Michael Posey, Editor
Carli Richard, Managing Editor

Offering readers profiles of practices that employ unique MTM techniques to effectively serve their patients. Readers can use these profiles as models to develop and improve their own MTM practice, increase patient adherence, and build patient loyalty.
Cost: $200.00
Frequency: Monthly
ISSN: 1042-0991
Founded in: 1962

20139 Prescriber's Letter
Therapeutic Research
PO Box 8190
Stockton, CA 95208

209-472-2240; *Fax:* 209-472-2249;
www.pletter.com

Jeff Jellin PharmD, Publisher

A newsletter to pharmacists offering coverage of drug development, production, distribution, legislation, safety and other issues concerning the industry.
Cost: $85.00
ISSN: 1073-7219

20140 Preventive Medicine Update
HealthComm International
5800 Soundview Drive
PO Box 1729
Gig Harbor, WA 98335-2000

253-858-3315
800-843-9660; *Fax:* 253-851-9749

Jeffrey Bland, CEO/Contact

20141 Psoriasis Resource
National Psoriasis Foundation
6600 Sw 92nd Ave
Suite 300
Portland, OR 97223-7195

503-244-7404
800-723-9166; *Fax:* 503-245-0626
getinfo@npfusa.org; www.psoriasis.org

Pam Field, CEO
Bill Taggart, Managing Editor
Gail Zimmerman, CEO

A newsletter published for members of the National Psoriasis Foundation. Highlights interesting articles on psoriasis products and medications andother health related topics. Contains advertisements for psoriasis-related products and services.
16 Pages
Circulation: 40000
Mailing list available for rent: 28000 names
Printed in 2 colors on matte stock

20142 Results Newsletter
American Clinical Laboratory Association
1100 New York Ave Nw
Suite 725
Washington, DC 20005-6172

202-637-9466; *Fax:* 202-637-2050
info@clinical-labs.org; www.acla.com

Alan Mertz, President
Frequency: Monthly
Mailing list available for rent

20143 Rx Ipsa Loquitur
American Society for Pharmacy Law
1224 Centre West Dr
Suite 400
Springfield, IL 62704-2184

217-698-6163; *Fax:* 217-698-6164;
www.aspl.org

Michael Monson, Owner
Francis B Palumbo, Director
Pamela Tolson CAE, Executive Director
William Fassett, Treasurer

Featuring recent court decisions, legislative and regulatory news, and other current pharmacy law news and articles.
Frequency: Bi-Monthly

20144 Washington Drug Letter
FDAnews
300 N Washington St
Suite 200
Falls Church, VA 22046-3441

703-538-7600
888-838-5578; *Fax:* 703-538-7676
customerservice@fdanews.com;
www.fdanews.com

Cynthia Carter, President
Maritza Lizama, Marketing Director

Summaries of FDA regulatory changes and key legislation that affects prescription and over the counter drugs. Each weekly issue brings you up-to-date on pre approval and post approval issues that directly impact your operation.
Cost: $897.00
Frequency: Weekly

Magazines & Journals

20145 AAPS Newsmagazine
American Association of Pharmaceutical Scientists
2107 Wilson Blvd
Suite 700
Arlington, VA 22201-3042

703-243-2800; *Fax:* 703-243-9054
aaps@aaps.org; www.aaps.org

John Lisack, Executive Director
Karol Shadle, Associate Director
Maria Nadeau, Member Groups Manager
Me'Gesha Portlock, Administrative Assistant

Exclusive to AAPS members. Features expanded coverage of the industry, complete with expert information on marketplace trends, regulatory matters, and career opportunities.
Mailing list available for rent

20146 AAPS Online Buyers Guide
American Association of Pharmaceutical Scientists
2107 Wilson Blvd
Suite 700
Arlington, VA 22201-3042

703-243-2800; *Fax:* 703-243-9054
aaps@aaps.org; www.aaps.org

John Lisack, Executive Director
Karol Shadle, Associate Director
Maria Nadeau, Member Groups Manager
Me'Gesha Portlock, Administrative Assistant

comprehensive sourcebook you need as a pharmaceutical scientist. Research the more than 500 companies providing the products and service you need. You can browse the entire Online Buyers Guide or you can refine your search by Company Name, Region, Business Category, or Keyword.
Mailing list available for rent

20147 AAPS PharmSciTech Journal
American Association of Pharmaceutical Scientists
2107 Wilson Blvd
Suite 700
Arlington, VA 22201-3042

703-243-2800; *Fax:* 703-243-9054
aaps@aaps.org; www.aaps.org

John Lisack, Executive Director
Karol Shadle, Associate Director
Maria Nadeau, Member Groups Manager
Me'Gesha Portlock, Administrative Assistant

An online-only journal published and owned by the American Association of Pharmaceutical Scientists. The journal's mission is to disseminate scientific and technical information on drug product design, development, evaluation and processing to the global pharmaceutical research community, taking full advantage of web-based publishing by presenting innovative text with 3-D graphics, interactive figures and databases, video and audio files.
ISSN: 1530-9932
Mailing list available for rent

20148 America's Pharmacist
National Community Pharmacists Association
100 Daingerfield Road
Alexandria, VA 22314

703-683-8200
800-544-7447; *Fax:* 703-683-3619
info@ncpanet.com; www.ncpanet.org

Mike Conlan, VP Publications/Editor
Chris Linville, Managing Editor

This informative magazine gives 25,000 independent pharmacists insight into current issues that affect independent pharmacy and NCPA's activities to address those issues. Also; it serves the readers by including monthly articles on clinical topics, a continuing education series for pharmacists who want to earn CE credit, information on how to manage finances, and proven tips on better marketing, as well as profiles of NCPA members from across the country. Annual subscription included in dues.
Cost: $50.00
Frequency: Monthly

20149 American Institute of the History of Pharmacy
777 Highland Ave
Madison, WI 53705-2222

608-262-5378; *Fax:* 608-262-3397
aihp@aihp.org; www.aihp.org/

Dr. Gregory Higby, Executive Director
Dr. Elaine Stroud, Assistant Director
Beth Fisher, Assoc. Dir. Curatorial Affairs

Articles on pharmaceutical history and usage.
Cost: $50.00
200 Pages
Frequency: Quarterly
Circulation: 1200
Founded in: 1960
Printed in on glossy stock

20150 American Journal of Health-System Pharmacy
American Society of Health-System Pharmacists
7272 Wisconsin Ave
Bethesda, MD 20814-4861

301-657-3000
866-279-0681; *Fax:* 301-664-8877
ajhp@ashp.org; www.ashp.org
Social Media: Facebook, Twitter, LinkedIn, YouTube

Kathryn Shultz, President
Paul Abramowitz, CEO
Philip Schneider, Treasurer

The journal for pharmacists practicing in all area's of acute care, ambulatory care, home care,

long term care, HMO's, PPO's, and PBM's.
Cost: $165.00
54 Pages
Frequency: Bi-Weekly
Circulation: 42,000
ISSN: 1079-2082
Printed in 2 colors on glossy stock

20151 American Journal of Medical Quality
American College of Medical Quality
4334 Montgomery Ave
Suite B
Bethesda, MD 20814-4415
301-913-9149
800-924-2149; *Fax:* 301-913-9142
acmq@acmq.org; www.acmq.org
Bridget Brodie, Manager
Frequency: Bi-Monthly

20152 American Journal of Pharmaceutical Education
American Association of Colleges of Pharmacy
1727 King St
Alexandria, VA 22314-2700
703-739-2330; *Fax:* 703-836-8982;
www.aacp.org
Lucinda Maine, Executive VP
Kenneth W Miller, Senior VP
Daniel J Cassidy, COO
Official publication of the American Association of Colleges of Pharmacy. Dedicated to all those with interest in professional, graduate, and post-graduate pharmaceutical education. Its purpose is to documnet and advance pharmaceutical education in the United States and Internationally. Features original research articles, editorials, reports on the state of pharmaceutical education, descriptions of teaching innovations, and book reviews.
Cost: $65.00
120 Pages
Frequency: Quarterly
Circulation: 3200
ISSN: 0002-9459
Founded in: 1937
Printed in one color on matte stock

20153 American Journal of Public Health
American Public Health Association
800 I Street NW
Washington, DC 20001-3710
202-777-2742; *Fax:* 202-777-2534;
www.apha.org
Social Media: Facebook, Twitter, LinkedIn, YouTube, Blogs
Mary E Northridge PhD, Editor-in-Chief
Provides in-depth information in the field of public health. Research and program evaluations are accompanied by authoritative editorials, throught-provoking commentary, and timely health policy analysis.
Cost: $419.00
120 Pages
Frequency: Monthly
Founded in: 1990

20154 BioPharm
Advanstar Communications
6200 Canoga Avenue
2nd Floor
Woodland Hills, CA 91367
818-593-5000; *Fax:* 818-593-5020
biopharminternational.com
Joseph Loggia, President
Chris DeMoulin, VP
Susannah George, Marketing Director
Publication taking a practical approach to the technology and business of developing and manufacturing biotechnology-derived pharmaceutical products. Regular topics include process development, downstream processing, facilities design, emerging technologies and regulatory compliance.
Cost: $64.00
Frequency: Monthly
Circulation: 29,200
ISSN: 1040-8304
Founded in: 1987

20155 Chain Drug Review
Racher Press
220 5th Avenue
New York, NY 10001
212-213-6000; *Fax:* 212-725-3961
info@racherpress.com; www.racherpress.com
Kevin Burke, VP/Group Advertising
Jeff Woldt, VP/Editorial Director
David Pinto, Editor
Chain Drug Review serves the chain drug industry.
Cost: $185.00
Frequency: Bi-weekly
Circulation: 54000
Founded in: 1978
Printed in 4 colors on glossy stock

20156 Chemistry
American Chemical Society
1155 16th St Nw
Washington, DC 20036-4892
202-872-4600
800-227-5558; *Fax:* 202-872-4615
help@acs.org; www.acs.org
Madeleine Jacobs, CEO
Judith L Benham, Board Chair
Published for members, student affiliates, and those interested in learning more about the chemical sciences and the American Chemical Society.

20157 CleanRooms Magazine
PennWell Publishing Company
98 Spit Brook Rd
Suite 100
Nashua, NH 03062-5737
603-891-0123; *Fax:* 603-891-9294
georgem@pennwell.com; www.pennwell.com
Christine Shaw, VP
James Enos, Publisher
Bob Johnson, Sales & Marketing Manager
Serves the contamination control and ultrapure materials and process industries. Written for readers in the microelectronics, pharmaceutical, biotech, health care, food processing and other user industries. Provides technology and business news and new product listings.
Cost: $97.00
Frequency: Monthly
Circulation: 35031
Founded in: 1987

20158 Community Pharmacist
ELF Publications
5285 W Louisiana Ave
Lakewood, CO 80232-5976
303-975-0075
800-922-8513; *Fax:* 303-975-0132
mcasey@elfpublications.com;
www.elfpublications.com
Judy Lane, Owner
Ronald R Quam, Editor/Publisher
Pharmacy trade journal that meets the professional educational needs of today's practitioner
Cost: $12.00
40 Pages
ISSN: 1096-9179
Founded in: 1972
Printed in 4 colors on glossy stock

20159 Contract Pharma
Rodman Publishing
70 Hilltop Rd
3rd Floor
Ramsey, NJ 07446-1150
201-825-2552; *Fax:* 201-825-0553
info@rodpub.com;
www.nutraceuticalsworld.com
Rodman Zilenziger Jr, President
Matt Montgomery, VP
A global publication providing most up-to-date news, outsourcing information, business trends, commentary, and viewpoints to the Pharmaceutical and Biopharmaceutical outsourcing industry.
Frequency: Monthly
Circulation: 20026
Founded in: 1999

20160 DIA Global Forum
Drug Information Association
800 Enterprise Road
Suite 200
Horsham, PA 19044-3595
215-442-6100; *Fax:* 215-442-6199
dia@diahome.org; www.diahome.org
Paul Pomerantz BA MBA, Worldwide Executive Director
Lisa Zoks BA, Worldwide Dir Mktg/Communications
Presents important news from DIA conferences and workshops, reports of the Board of Directors and the regional advisory councils that directly impact DIA members, as well as practical tips, regulatory and global updates, upcoming DIA events, program notes, and more.
Frequency: Bi-Monthly
Circulation: 20000
ISSN: 1944-1991
Printed in 4 colors

20161 DVM News
Advanstar Communications
8033 Flint St
Lenexa, KS 66214-3335
913-492-4300
800-255-6864; *Fax:* 913-492-4157
dverdon@advanstar.com; www.dvm360.com
Rebecca Turner Chapman, VP
Information from veterinary medicine covering news, features, practice management and new products and services.
Cost: $4.00
Frequency: Monthly
ISSN: 0012-7337
Founded in: 1987

20162 Drug Information Journal
Drug Information Association
800 Enterprise Road
Suite 200
Horsham, PA 19044-3595
215-442-6100; *Fax:* 215-442-6199
dia@diahome.org; www.diahome.org
Paul Pomerantz BA MBA, Worldwide Executive Director
Lisa Zoks BA, Worldwide Dir Mktg/Communications
Purpose is to disseminate information on manual and automated drug research, development, and information systems; to foster communication between educational, research, industrial and governmental personnel engaged in drug information activities; and to provide a forum for the development of improved methods of presenting research data generated from chemical, toxicologic, pharmacologic, and clinical studies.
Frequency: Bi-Monthly
Circulation: 20000
ISSN: 0092-8615
Founded in: 1964

20163 Drug Store News
Lebhar-Friedman

425 Park Ave
New York, NY 10022-3526

212-756-5088; *Fax:* 212-838-9487
editor@drugstorenews.com;
www.drugstorenews.com

Heather Martin, Manager
J Rodger Friedman, CEO

Publication consists of merchandising trends and pharmacy developments. Provides extensive coverage of every major segment of chain drug retailing and combination stores.
Cost: $119.00
Circulation: 45000
Founded in: 1925

20164 Drug Topics
Medical Economics Publishing
5 Paragon Dr
Montvale, NJ 07645-1791

973-944-7777; *Fax:* 973-944-7778
drug.topics@Medec.com; www.drugtopics.com

Jim Granto, Publisher
Heather Schlosser, National Account Manager

Information on the distributing and dispensing drug trade.
Cost: $61.00
Printed in 4 colors on glossy stock

20165 Food & Drug Packaging
Stagnito Publishing Group
155 Pfingston Road
Suite 205
Deerfield, IL 60015

847-205-5660; *Fax:* 847-205-5680
gvansomeren@stagnito.com; www.fdp.com
Social Media: Facebook, Twitter, LinkedIn, you tube

Lisa McTigue Pierce, Editor-in-Chief
Blayne Long, Senior Marketing Manager
Geneine Van Someren, Circulation Manager
Vince Miconi, Advertising Production Manager
George Misko, Regional Sales Manager

Food and Drug Packaging serves industries engaged in packaging food, beverages, pharmaceuticals, cosmetics and consulting/engineering firms.
Frequency: Monthly
Circulation: 75140
Founded in: 1959

20166 Food and Drug Law Journal
Food & Drug Law Institute
1155 15th Street NW
Suite 800
Washington, DC 20005

202-371-1420
800-956-6293; *Fax:* 202-371-0649
comments@fdli.org; www.fdli.org

Michael D. Levin-Epstein, Vice President, Publications
Abby C. Foster, Managing Editor

Award-winning journal offering scholarly, in-depth, analytical articles, providing insight into action of the FDA, FTC, and USDA, how the courts interpret these actions, and the reaction of the industry.
Cost: $379.00
Frequency: Quarterly
ISSN: 1064-590x

20167 Formulary
Advanstar Communications
6200 Canoga Avenue
2nd Floor
Woodland Hills, CA 91367

818-593-5000; *Fax:* 818-593-5020
info@advanstar.com; www.advanstar.com

Joseph Loggia, President
Chris DeMoulintein, VP
Susannah George, Marketing Director

Peer-reviewed publication providing drug information for physicians, pharmacists, and other health care professionals who influence the selection and use of drugs in hospitals, HMO's, and other managed care settings.
Cost: $61.00
Frequency: Monthly
Circulation: 51402
ISSN: 1082-801X
Founded in: 1992
Mailing list available for rent

20168 HealthCare Distributor
ELF Publications
5285 W Louisiana Ave
Lakewood, CO 80232-5976

303-975-0075
800-922-8513; *Fax:* 303-975-0132
elfpub@qwest.net; www.elfpublications.com

Judy Lane, Owner
Ronald R Quam, Editor/Publisher
Chuck Austin, Senior Editor
Jerry Lester, Director of Sales

Multi-market publication devoted to the issues and opportunities facing the wholesale drug, chain drug, medical/surgical and home care products distribution industries
Cost: $12.00
80 Pages
Frequency: Bi-annually
Circulation: 12000
ISSN: 1096-9160
Founded in: 1972
Printed in 4 colors on glossy stock

20169 Hospital Pharmacy
Facts and Comparisons
111 Westport Plz
Suite 300
St Louis, MO 63146-3011

314-216-2100
800-223-0554; *Fax:* 314-878-5563
service@drugfacts.com;
www.factsandcomparisons.com

John Pins, VP

Provides pharmacists with peer-reviewed articles and monthly features covering clinical and administrative areas such as drug use, drug distribution systems in hospitals and health-systems, automation, medication errors and adverse events, Joint Commission drug-related material and current FDA drug information.
Cost: $124.95
Frequency: Monthly
ISSN: 0018-5787
Founded in: 1965

20170 Inform
American Oil Chemists' Society
2710 S Boulder
Urbana, IL 61802-6996

217-359-2344; *Fax:* 217-351-8091
kheine@aocs.org; www.aocs.org
Social Media: Facebook, Twitter, LinkedIn, Blog

Jody Schonfeld, Publications Director
Kimmy Farris, Production Editor
Kathy Heine, Managing Editor

Member benefit pmagazine providing international news on fats, oils, surfactants, detergents, and related materials.
Cost: $175.00
462 Pages
Frequency: Monthly
Circulation: 3700
ISSN: 0897-8026
Founded in: 1909
Printed in on glossy stock

20171 International Pharmaceutical Abstracts
American Society of Health-System Pharmacists
7272 Wisconsin Ave
Bethesda, MD 20814-4861

301-657-3000
866-279-0681; *Fax:* 301-664-8877
ipa@ashp.org; www.ashp.org

Mark Woods, President

These reports offering the latest in the development of drugs overseas, clinical use, cosmetics and, alternative and herbal medicine. Reports on pharmacy practice are also included.
Cost: $240.00
Frequency: Monthly
Circulation: 31,000
ISSN: 0020-8264
Founded in: 1936

20172 Journal of Managed Care Pharmacy
Academy of Managed Care Pharmacy
100 N Pitt St
Suite 400
Alexandria, VA 22314-3141

703-683-8416
800-827-2627; *Fax:* 703-683-8417
sandres@amcp.org; www.amcp.org
Social Media: Facebook, Twitter, LinkedIn

Douglas Burgoyne, President
Robert Gregory, Treasurer

Features articles on trends and recent developments in managed care pharmacy, updates from pharmacy educators about the inclusion of managed care topics in cirricula and news and information about the academy and it's activities.
Cost: $60.00
Frequency: Bi-Monthly

20173 Journal of Parenteral and Enteral Nutrition
Amer. Society for Parenteral & Enteral Nutrition
8630 Fenton Street
Suite 412
Silver Spring, MD 20910-3803

301-587-6315
800-727-4567; *Fax:* 301-587-2365
jpen@nutr.org; www.nutritioncare.org
Social Media: Facebook, Twitter

Is the premier scientific journal of nutrition and metabolic support. It publishes original, peer-reviewd studies that define the cutting edge of basic and clinical research in the field. It explores the science of optimizing the care of patients receiving enteral or IV therapies. This is included as benefits of membership in ASPEN.
Cost: $90.00
Frequency: Fortnightly
Circulation: 7800
ISSN: 0148-6071
Founded in: 1977

20174 Journal of Pharmaceutical Innovation
Int'l Society for Pharmaceutical Engineering
3109 W Dr Martin Luther King Jr Boulevard
Suite 250
Tampa, FL 33607

813-960-2105; *Fax:* 813-264-2816
ask@ispe.org; www.ispe.org

Gloria N Hall, Editor & Director of Publications
Lynda Goldbach, Publications Manager
Amy Lecceardone, Publications Coordinator
Valerie Adams, Advertising Sales Coordinator
Frequency: 4/Year
Circulation: 2000

20175 Journal of Pharmaceutical Marketing and Management
Taylor & Francis Group LLC

325 Chestnut St
Suite 800
Philadelphia, PA 19106-2614

215-625-8900
800-354-1420; *Fax:* 215-625-2940
haworthorders@taylorandfrancis.com;
www.taylorandfrancis.com

Kevin Bradley, President

The journal maintains a vigorous policy of publishing quality research reports of interest to individuals involved in the manufacturing, wholesale, institutional, retail, regulatory, organizational and academic components of the pharmaceutical industry.
Frequency: Quarterly

20176 Journal of Pharmaceutical Sciences
Wiley InterScience
350 Main St
Malden, MA 02148-5089

781-388-8250
800-835-6770; *Fax:* 781-388-8210
cs-journals@wiley.com; www.wiley.com

Amy Yodaniss, VP
Julie Fisher, Assistant Editor
Roger Hall, VP
Laurie Beagell, Circulation Manager

A comprehensive look at the world of drugs and pharmaceuticals.
Frequency: Monthly
Circulation: 225

20177 Journal of Pharmacy Practice
Technomic Publishing Company
PO Box 3535
Lancaster, PA 17601

717-291-5609
800-233-9936; *Fax:* 717-295-4538
aflannery@techpub.com; www.techpub.com

Amy Flannery, Marketing

The journal provides useful, timely reports on the most challenging issues of pharmacy today and anticipates the unique demands of this rapidly changing field. Each issue's single-topic format and thoughtful, readable analysis gives a better grasp of difficult problems and provides immediately useful information.
Cost: $210.00
80 Pages
ISSN: 0897-1900
Printed in 2 colors on matte stock

20178 Journal of Pharmacy Technology
Harvey Whitney Books Company
PO Box 42696
Cincinnati, OH 45242-696

513-793-3555
877-742-7631; *Fax:* 513-793-3600
customerserv@jpharmtechnol.com;
www.jpharmtechnol.com

Harvey Whitney, Publisher/Editor
Eugene Sorkin, Associate Editorial
Ann Brandewiede, Circulation Manager

Latest information on drugs, for health professionals. Topics covered include new drug profiles, education and training, legal dilemmas, drug distribution, products and equipment and continuing education.
Cost: $122.00
Circulation: 1000
ISSN: 8755-1225

20179 Journal of Surfactants and Detergents
American Oil Chemists' Society
2710 S Boulder
Urbana, IL 61802-6996

217-359-2344; *Fax:* 217-351-8091
general@aocs.org; www.aocs.org
Social Media: Facebook, Twitter, LinkedIn, Blog

Jody Schonfeld, Publications Director
Pam Landman, Journals Coordinator
Kimmy Farris, Production Editor

Dedicated to the practical and theoretical aspects of oleochemical and petrochemical surfactants, soaps and detergents. This growing scientific journal publishes peer-reviewed research papers, and reviews related to surfactants and detergents technologies.
Cost: $457.00
Frequency: Quarterly
Founded in: 1998

20180 Journal of the American Oil Chemists' Society
American Oil Chemists' Society
2710 S Boulder
Urbana, IL 61802-6966

217-359-2344; *Fax:* 217-351-8091
general@aocs.org; www.aocs.org
Social Media: Facebook, Twitter, LinkedIn, Blog

Jodey Schonfeld, Publications Director
Pam Landman, Journals Coordinator
Kimmy Farris, Production Editor

The leading source for technical papers related to the fats and oils industries. A peer-reviewed journal devoted to fundamental and practical research, production, processing, packaging and distribution in the growing field of fats, oils, proteins and other related substances.
Cost: $619.00
Frequency: Monthly
Founded in: 1947

20181 Journal of the American Pharmacists Association
American Pharmacists Association
2215 Constitution Ave NW
Washington, DC 20037-2985

202-628-4410
800-237-2742; *Fax:* 202-783-2351;
www.pharmacist.com
Social Media: Facebook, Twitter, YouTube

L Michael Posey, Editor
L Douglas Reid, Editor-In-Chief

The official peer-reviewed journal of APhA, provides information on pharmaceutical care, drug therapy, diseases and other health issues, trends in pharmacy practice and therapeutics, informed opinion, and original research.
ISSN: 1544-3191

20182 Lipids
American Oil Chemists' Society
2710 S Boulder
Urbana, IL 61802-6996

217-359-2344; *Fax:* 217-351-8091
general@aocs.org; www.aocs.org
Social Media: Facebook, Twitter, LinkedIn, Blog

Jody Schonfeld, Publications Director
Pam Landman, Journals Coordinator
Kimmy Farris, Production Editor

Scientific journal features full-length original research articles, short communications, methods papers and review articles on timely topics. All papers are meticulously peer-reviewed and edited by some of the foremost experts in their respective fields.
Cost: $461.00
Frequency: Monthly
Founded in: 1966

20183 MPMN: Medical Product Manufacturing News
UBM Canon
2901 28th St
Ste. 100
Santa Monica, CA 90045

310-445-4200; *Fax:* 310-445-4299
john.bethune@cancom.com;
www.devicelink.com
Social Media: Twitter

Shana Leonard, Editor in Chief
Bob Michaels, Managing Editor

A product tabloid magazine that provides information on the new products and services available to medical device manufacturers.
Frequency: 10x/yr

20184 Med Ad News
Canon Communicaitons Pharmaceutical Media Group
828A Newtown Yardley Road
Newtown, PA 18940

215-944-9800; *Fax:* 215-867-0053
sandra.baker@cancom.com;
www.pharmalive.com

Christiane Truelove, Editor

Provides extensive coverage and incisive analyses of issues, events, trends and strategies shaping pharmaceutical business, marketing and sales.
Frequency: Monthly

20185 Modern Drug Discovery
American Chemical Society
1155 16th St Nw
16th Street NW
Washington, DC 20036-4892

202-872-4600
800-227-5558; *Fax:* 202-872-4615
service@acs.org; www.acs.org

Madeleine Jacobs, CEO/Executive Director

Reports matters of interest to scientists and other professionals working in the field of drug discovery.
Frequency: Monthly

20186 Monitor
Association of Clinical Research Professionals
1012 14th Street NW
Suite 108
Washington, DC 20006

202-737-8100; *Fax:* 202-737-8101
acrp@associationhq.com; www.acrpnet.org

Sharada Gilkey, Editor-in-Chief

Features peer-reviewed articles, columns, and home study.
Frequency: Quarterly

20187 Nutrition in Clinical Practice
Amer. Society for Parenteral & Enteral Nutrition
8630 Fenton Street
Suite 412
Silver Spring, MD 20910

301-587-6315
800-727-4567; *Fax:* 301-587-2365
aspen@nutr.org; www.nutritioncare.org
Social Media: Facebook, Twitter

Bridget Hollick, Managing Editor

This compliments the Journal of Parenteral and Enteral Nutrition with practical information and advice. It provides peer-reviewed clinical studies, reviews, techniques and procedures, teaching cases, clinical observations, and nutrition news. Included as benefits of membership is ASPEN.
Cost: $45.00
Frequency: Bi-Monthly
ISSN: 0884-5336

20188 PDA Journal of Pharmaceutical Science and Technology
Parenteral Drug Association
1894 Preston White Drive
Reston, VA 20191-5433

703-620-6390; *Fax:* 703-476-0904
infoQnpcnow.com; www.npcnow.org

Lee Kirsch, Editor

One of the most relevant and outstanding peer-reviewed scientific and technical papers in the pharmaceutical/biopharmaceutical industry. The Journal is distributed to members as a membership benefit.
Frequency: Bi-Monthly

20189 Pharmaceutical & Medical Packaging News
Canon Communications
11444 W Olympic Blvd
Suite 900
Los Angeles, CA 90064-1555

310-445-4200; *Fax:* 310-445-4299
feedback@cancom.com; www.pmpnews.com

Charlie McCurdy, President
Daphne Allen, Editor
Justine Hamilton, Marketing Director
Peter Manfre, Account Executive

Information and news on events, new technology, industry trends, regulatory matters, and health care trade associations for professionals involved in the pharmaceutical and medical product packaging industry.
Cost: $150.00
Frequency: Monthly
Circulation: 20,000
ISSN: 1081-5481
Founded in: 1978

20190 Pharmaceutical Engineering
Int'l Society for Pharmaceutical Engineering
3109 W Dr Martin Luther King Jr Boulevard
Suite 250
Tampa, FL 33607

813-960-2105; *Fax:* 813-264-2816
ask@ispe.org; www.ispe.org

Gloria N Hall, Editor & Director of Publications
Lynda Goldbach, Publications Manager
Amy Lecceardone, Publications Coordinator
Valerie Adams, Advertising Sales Coordinator

Journal is published bi-monthly for members only and is considered by ISPE members to be the number one member benefit. Feature articles provide practical application and specification information on the design, construction, supervision and maintenance of process equipment, plant systems, instrumentation and facilities.
Frequency: Bi-monthly
Circulation: 2000

20191 Pharmaceutical Executive
Advanstar Communications
131 W 1st St
Duluth, MN 55802-2065

218-740-7200
800-598-6008; *Fax:* 218-723-9537
info@advanstar.com; www.advanstar.com

Kent Akervik, Manager
Kim Brown, Producation Manager

Publication designed to meet the diverse management and marketing needs of professionals in the pharmaceutical industry worldwide. Editorial provides useful information on marketing, sales and promotion, as well as legal and regulatory issues.
Cost: $70.00
Frequency: Monthly
Circulation: 16237
ISSN: 0279-6570
Founded in: 1987
Mailing list available for rent

20192 Pharmaceutical Processing
Reed Business Information
100 Enterprise drive
Suite 600
Rockaway, NJ 07866-912

973-920-7000
800-222-0289; *Fax:* 973-920-7531;
www.reedbusiness.com

Tim Canny, Publisher
Mike Auerbach, Editor
R Reed, Owner

Contents include news on new products/equipment/services, case history and application articles focusing on equipment, instrumentation, process systems, packaging, validation and outsourcing services offered to the pharmaceutical marketplace.
Frequency: Monthly
Circulation: 31075
Founded in: 1984

20193 Pharmaceutical Research
Plenum Publishing Corporation
233 Spring St
New York, NY 10013-1522

212-242-1490; *Fax:* 212-807-1047
info@plenum.com; www.plenum.com

Wolfgang Sadee, Editor

Research reports and summaries of the latest in development of certain drugs and pharmaceuticals.
Cost: $49.95
Frequency: Monthly
Founded in: 1998

20194 Pharmaceutical Technology Magazine
Advanstar Communications
485 Route One South
Building F, First Floor
Iselin, NJ 08830

732-596-0276; *Fax:* 732-596-0005
mtracey@advanstar.com; www.pharmtech.com

Mike Tracey, Publisher
Douglas McCormick, Editor in Chief
Paul Milazzo, Director of Sales
Tria Deibert, Marketing Director

Provides authoritative and timely information covering all aspects of conventional and biotech pharmaceutical manufacturing including: applied research and development, drug delivery, solid dosage, manufacturing machinery and equipment, information technologies, contract services, biotechnology trends, and regulatory issues.
Frequency: Monthly
Circulation: 33691
Founded in: 1987

20195 Pharmacy Times
Romaine Pierson Publishers
666 Plainsboro Rd
Plainsboro, NJ 08536

609-716-7777; *Fax:* 609-716-4747
cms@skainfo.com; www.pharmacytimes.com
Social Media: Facebook, Twitter, LinkedIn, YouTube

Emilie McCardell, Editor-In-Chief
Cam Bishop, CEO
James Granato, Publisher
James Marshal, Production Director
Margaret P. Roeske, Associate Editor

News, analysis and trends in the pharmaceutical business.
Cost: $65.00
Frequency: Monthly
Circulation: 174,104
Founded in: 1897

20196 Pharmacy West
Western Communications
Po Box 6020
Bend, OR 97708-6020

541-382-1811; *Fax:* 541-385-5802

Gordon Black, President

Distributed to pharmacies in the thirteen western states.
Cost: $18.00
Frequency: Monthly

20197 Profile of Pharmacy Faculty
American Association of Colleges of Pharmacy
1727 King St
Alexandria, VA 22314-2700

703-739-2330; *Fax:* 703-836-8982;
www.aacp.org

Lucinda Maine, Executive VP
Kenneth W Miller, Senior VP
Daniel J Cassidy, COO

Provides statistics describing faculty at U.S. colleges and schools of pharmacy including a summary of the demographics, teaching discipline, rank, highest degree earned, tenure status, type of appointment, and salary of over 3,000 full time faculty members. Updated annually.
Cost: $25.00

20198 Scrip Magazine
1775 Broadway
Suite 511
New York, NY 10019

212-262-8230; *Fax:* 212-262-8234
chonour@ThetaReports.com

An in-depth view of the issues and challenges facing all sectors of the pharmaceutical industry worldwide. Analytical features are written by pharmaceutical experts and opinion leaders as well as specialist journalists.
Frequency: Monthly

20199 The Consultant Pharmacist
American Society of Consultant Pharmacists
1321 Duke St
Suite 120
Alexandria, VA 22314-3563

703-739-1300
800-355-2727; *Fax:* 703-739-1321
info@ascp.com; www.ascp.com
Social Media: Facebook, Twitter, LinkedIn, YouTube, Blogs

Frank Grosso, RPh, Executive Director & CEO
Marlene Bloom, Editor
Debbie Furman, Circulation

Official peer reviewed journal of the American Society of Consultant Pharmacists. Editorial deals with geriatric pharmacotherapy.
76 Pages
Circulation: 11000
Founded in: 1969
Printed in 4 colors on glossy stock

20200 Update Magazine
Food & Drug Law Institute
1155 15th Street NW
Suite 800
Washington, DC 20005

202-371-1420
800-956-6293; *Fax:* 202-371-0649
comments@fdli.org; www.fdli.org
Social Media: Facebook, Twitter, LinkedIn

Michael D. Levin-Epstein, Vice President, Publications
Erin M Jones, Membership and Marketing
Susan C Winckler, President & CEO

Update brings you the latest news from FDLI and the industry, featuring viewpoints on trends, artilces on topics of regulatory concern, changes at the FDA, news about FDLI activities, and recurring columns about current events in the industry. Free to individuals within FDLI member

organizations.
Cost: $100.00
Frequency: Bimonthly

Trade Shows

20201 AACP Annual Meeting and Seminars
American Association of Colleges of Pharmacy
1727 King Street
Alexandria, VA 22314

703-739-2330; *Fax:* 703-836-8982;
www.aacp.org

Lucinda L Maine, Executive VP
Kenneth W Miller, Senior VP
Daniel J Cassidy, COO

A chance to learn and exchange ideas on pharmacy education and recent innovations in health care.
Frequency: July

20202 AACP Institute
American Association of Colleges of Pharmacy
1727 King Street
Alexandria, VA 22314

703-739-2330; *Fax:* 703-836-8982;
www.aacp.org

Lucinda L Maine, Executive VP
Kenneth W Miller, Senior VP
Daniel J Cassidy, COO
Frequency: May

20203 AAPS Annual Meeting & Expo
American AssociationOf Pharmaceutical Scientists
2107 Wilson Boulevard
Suite 700
Arlington, VA 22201-3042

703-243-2800; *Fax:* 703-243-9650
aaps@aaps.org; www.aaps.org

John Lisack, Executive Director
Maureen Downs, Director Finance

925 booths of raw materials, supplies and equipment, research and contract service labs, computer software, packaging and more.
Frequency: Annual November
Mailing list available for rent

20204 AAPT Annual Convention
American Association of Pharmacy Technicians
PO Box 1447
Greensboro, NC 27402

877-368-4771; *Fax:* 336-333-9068
aapt@pharmacytechnician.com;
www.pharmacytechnician.com

Sandra Covington, President
Susan Jeffery, VP

Education programs and services to help technicians update their skills to keep pace with changes in the pharmacy services.
Frequency: August

20205 ACLA Annual Meeting
American Clinical Laboratory Association
1250 H Street NW
Suite 880
Washington, DC 20005

202-637-9466; *Fax:* 202-637-2050
info@clinical-labs.org; www.acla.com

Aan Mertz, President
JoAnne Glisson, VP
Jason DuBois, VP of Govt. Relations
Francesca O'Reilly, VP of Govt. Affairs

Dedicated to providing the latest information for clinical laboratories.
Frequency: January
Founded in: 1971

20206 ACMP Conference
Academy of Managed Care Pharmacy
100 N Pitt Street
Suite 400
Alexandria, VA 22314-3134

703-683-8416
800-827-2627; *Fax:* 703-683-8417
sadres@amcp.org; www.amcp.org
Social Media: Facebook, Twitter, LinkedIn

Aimee O'Conner, Assistant Director

Offers an exciting lineup of speakers, workshops, and topical sessions designed to meet the challenges of today's pharmacist practicing in a dynamic and constantly evolving managed care environment.
Frequency: October

20207 APHA Annual Meeting & Exposition
American Public Health Association
800 I Street NW
Washington, DC 20001-3710

202-777-2742; *Fax:* 202-777-2534
diane.lentini@apha.org; www.apha.org

Diane Lentini, Meetings Manager
Gene Lutz, President
Georges C Benjamin, Executive Director
Jose F Cordero, Member
Louise A Anderson, Director Operations

The premier platform to share successes and failures, discover exceptional best practices and learn from expert colleagues and the latest reasearch in the field.
13000 Attendees
Frequency: November

20208 ASCP Annual Meeting
American Society of Consultant Pharmacists
1321 Duke Street
Suite 120
Alexandria, VA 22314-3563

703-739-1300
800-355-2727; *Fax:* 703-739-1321
info@ascp.com; www.ascp.com
Social Media: Facebook, Twitter, LinkedIn, Vimeo

Jackie Hajji, Director Meetings/Conventions
Frank Grosso, RPh, Executive Director & CEO
Nicole J. Brandt, Chairman
Joseph Marek, President

Annual meeting of 300 exhibitors of pharmaceuticals, drug distribution systems, packaging equipment, computers, durable medical equipment and medical supplies.
2000 Attendees
Frequency: November
Founded in: 1969
Mailing list available for rent: 6500 names

20209 ASHP Summer Meeting
American Society of Health-System Pharmacists
7272 Wisconsin Avenue
Bethesda, MD 20814-4836

301-657-3000
866-279-0681; *Fax:* 301-664-8857;
www.ashp.org

Janet A Silvester R.Ph.,MBA, President

Offers a variety of programming, and delivers expertise on subject areas that are crucial to advancing a professional practice. Series programming, learning communities, and updates on hot topics, combined with exhibits and a variety of networking opportunities.
Frequency: June

20210 ASPL Developments in Pharmacy Law Seminar
American Society for Pharmacy Law
1224 Centre W
Suite 400B
Springfield, IL 62704

217-391-0219; *Fax:* 217-793-0041;
www.aspl.org

Melissa Madigan, President
Francis B Paulumbo, Director
Pamela Tolson, CAE, Executive Director
William Fassett, Treasurer

An annual highlight with nationally renowned speakers and panelists discussing issues pertaining to pharmacy law. This seminar has evolved into an excellent educational opportunity for practicing pharmacists, attorneys, and academicians with the opportunity to gain both pharmacy and legal continuing education credits.
Frequency: Annual

20211 Academy of Pharmaceutical Research and Science Convention
American Pharmaceutical Association
2215 Constitution Avenue NW
Washington, DC 20037

202-429-7524
800-237-2742; *Fax:* 202-628-0443;
www.aphanet.org

Windy K Christner, Meetings/Expositions

Main exhibits, pharmaceutical equipment supplies and services.
Frequency: Annual

20212 American Association of College Pharmacies
1727 King Street
Alexandria, VA 22314

703-739-2330; *Fax:* 703-836-8982;
www.aacp.org

Lucinda L Maine, Executive VP
Kenneth W Miller, Senior VP
Daniel J Cassidy, COO

Educational association representing pharmacy scientists, educators and administrators.
2.3M Attendees
Frequency: July

20213 American College of Medical Quality Annual Meeting
American College of Medical Quality
4334 Montgomery Avenue
Suite B
Bethesda, MD 20814

301-913-9149
800-924-2149; *Fax:* 301-656-0989
acmq@aol.com; www.acmq.org
Social Media: Facebook, Twitter, LinkedIn

Alan Krumholz, MD, President
James D. Cross, President-elect
Andrew Jerdonek, Executive Director
Donald Casey, Jr MD, Treasurer

Annual show and 10-20 exhibits of computer hardware and software, pharmaceuticals, medical publications and related equipment, supplies and services.
150 Attendees
Founded in: 1973

20214 American Pharmacists Annual Meeting & Expo
American Pharmacists Association
2215 Constitution Avenue, NW
Washington, DC 20037

202-429-7593
800-237-2742; *Fax:* 203-737-3211
lmace@aphanet.org; www.aphameeting.org

Laura Larson, Exposition & Exchange Information

Todd McDonald, Meeting Schedule Information
Lindsey Mace, General Conference Assistant
Kristen Binaso, Sponsorship Coordinator
Stacy Berkowitz, Educational Coordinator

The APhA Annual Meeting and Exposition provides information on the latest trends and best practices in pharmacy, while providing attendees the opportunity to share experiences and ideas with 7,000 pharmacy professionals from every practice setting; chain, independent, hospital, federal, long-term care, nuclear, and more.
Frequency: Annual/Spring

20215 Annual NCPA Convention & Trade Exposition
National Community Pharmacists Associations
100 Daingerfield Road
Alexandria, VA 22314

703-683-8200
800-544-7447; *Fax:* 703-683-3619
info@ncpanet.com; www.ncpanet.org

Litsa Deck, Director Convention/Trade Expos

Workshops and education programs pretaining to Pharmacy industry.
Frequency: October
Mailing list available for rent

20216 Annual North American Conference and European Annual Conference
Association of Clinical Research Professionals
1012 14th Street NW
Suite 108
Washington, DC 20006

202-737-8100; *Fax:* 202-737-8101
acrp@associationhq.com; www.acrpnet.org

Robin Newman, Vice Chair
Thomas L Adams, CAE, President/CEO
Larry J Medley, CAE, Director Finance
Alan Armstrong, Director Marketing/COO

The world's leading conferences for clinical research professionals, presenting diverse educational opportunities and face-to-face interactions with industry experts.
Frequency: April, September

20217 DCAT Western Education Conference
Drug, Chemical & Associated Technologies
1 Washington Boulevard
Suite 7
Robbinsville, NJ 08691

609-448-1000
800-640-3228; *Fax:* 609-448-1944
info@dcat.org; www.dcat.org
Social Media: Facebook, LinkedIn

Brooke DiGiuseppe, Meeting Services
Margaret Timony, Senior Manager
Jacklyn Vitelli, Deputy Executive Director
Jeanne Motola, Administrative Assistant

Gain important insights into issues and trends that will affect the future of the nutrition and health industry. Participate in discussion on key business issues with industry experts.
Frequency: April

20218 DIA Annual Meeting
Drug Information Association
800 Enterprise Road
Suite 200
Horsham, PA 19044-3595

215-442-6100; *Fax:* 215-442-6199
dia@diahome.org; www.diahome.org

Paul Pomerantz BA MBA, Worldwide Executive Director
Lisa Zoks BA, Worldwide Dir Mktg/Communications

20219 Distribution & Logistics Conference
National Association of Chain Drug Stores
413 N Lee Street
PO Box 1417 D-49
Alexandria, VA 22313-1480

703-549-3001; *Fax:* 703-836-4869;
www.nacds.org
Social Media: Facebook, Twitter, LinkedIn, YouTube

Greg Wasson, Chairman
Bob Narveson, Vice Chairman
John Standley, Treasurer

This unique conference explores and evaluates current systems and emerging technologies, and helps retailers and suppliers forge stronger links through supply chain management. The exhibit hall allows leading industry consultants and vendors to demonstrate their products and services.
Frequency: March

20220 Distribution Management Conference & Expo
Healthcare Distribution Management Association
900 N Glebe Road
Suite 1000
Arlington, VA 22203

703-787-0000; *Fax:* 703-935-3200
lburke@hdmanet.org;
www.healthcaredistribution.org

John Grey, President and CEO
Ann Bittman, EVP and COO
Patrick Kelly, SVP

Provides the latest information on the most important topics affecting healthcare distribution.
Frequency: June

20221 FDLI & FDA Annual Conference
Food and Drug Law Institute
1155 15th Street NW
Suite 800
Washington, DC 20005

202-371-1420
800-956-6293; *Fax:* 202-371-0649
comments@fdli.org; www.fdli.org

Susan C. Winckler, President & CEO
Iris V. Stratton CPA, VP Finance & Administration
Michael Sprott, Membership Manager

Bringing together high-ranking officials from the food and drug industry together with top executives.
550+ Members
Founded in: 1949

20222 HDMA Annual Meeting
Healthcare Distribution Management Association
900 N Glebe Road
Suite 1000
Arlington, VA 22203

703-787-0000; *Fax:* 703-935-3200
lburke@hdmanet.org;
www.healthcaredistribution.org

John Grey, President and CEO
Ann Bittman, EVP and COO
Patrick Kelly, SVP

Provides a unique opportunity for senior-level retailer and supplier member executives to interact and discuss strategic issues.
Frequency: October

20223 IPC Annual Meeting
Independent Pharmacy Cooperative
1550 Columbus Street
Sun Prairie, WI 53590

608-259-9556
800-755-1531; *Fax:* 800-274-5525
staff@ipcrx.com; www.ipcrx.com

Mike Flint, President/CEO
Gary Helgerson, COO
Chuck Benjamin, CFO

A venue to provide independent pharmacies vital information to maximize their store's profitability
Frequency: July

20224 ISPE Annual Meeting
Int'l Society for Pharmaceutical Engineering
3109 W Dr. Martin Luther King Jr Boulevard
Suite 250
Tampa, FL 33607

813-960-2105; *Fax:* 813-264-2816
ask@ispe.org; www.ispe.org

Education and training on topics pretaining to the pharmaceutical manufacturing industry.
Frequency: Annual

20225 Midyear Industry & Technology Issues Conference
American Society for Automation in Pharmacy
492 Norristown Road
Suite 160
Blue Bell, PA 19422

610-825-7783; *Fax:* 310-825-7641;
www.asapnet.org

WA Lockwood, Executive Director

Learn about the industry and technology issues facing the pharmacy market today.
Frequency: June

20226 NABP's Annual Meeting
National Association of Boards of Pharmacy
700 Busse Highway
Park Ridge, IL 60068

847-698-6227
800-774-6227; *Fax:* 847-698-0124
custserv@nabp.net; www.nabp.net

Carmen A Catizone, Executive Director/Secretary

Building regulatory foundation for patients safety.
Frequency: May

20227 NABP's Fall Educational Conference
National Association of Boards of Pharmacy
700 Busse Highway
Park Ridge, IL 60068

847-698-6227
800-774-6227; *Fax:* 847-698-0124
custserv@nabp.net; www.nabp.net

Malcom Broussard, Chairperson
Michael Burlson, President
Joseph Adams, Treasurer
Frequency: December

20228 NACDS Annual Meeting
National Association of Chain Drug Stores
413 N Lee Street
Alexandria, VA 22314

703-549-3001; *Fax:* 703-836-4869;
www.nacds.org

Jodi Witmer, Executive Director
Terry Arth, VP Meetings/International Programs
Larry Lotridge, VP Conference Exhibits

This meeting provides a stage to meet and discuss strategic issues with key trading partners: Strategic Exchange Appointments in which to do business, participants and sponsors from dozens of relevant companies.
1M Attendees
Frequency: April

20229 NCPA Annual Conference on National Legislation and Government Affairs
National Community Pharmacists Associations

100 Daingerfield Road
Alexandria, VA 22314

703-683-8200
800-544-7447; *Fax:* 703-683-3619
info@ncpanet.com; www.ncpanet.org

Litsa Deck, Director Convention/Trade Expos

An opportunity to be an insider to discuss community pharmacy issues on Capitol Hill with the people that can make things happen. It will enhance your understanding of the political process and the many legislative issues that will have a dramatic impact on the way you deliver health care in the coming years.
Frequency: April

20230 NCPA Annual Meeting
National Council of State Pharmacy Association
5501 Patterson Avenue
Suite 200
Richmond, VA 23226

804-285-4145; *Fax:* 804-285-4227
becky@ncspae.org; www.ncspae.org

Rebecca P Snead, Executive Vice President
Brad Hall, Executive Director

Offers cutting-edge training for professionals from every facet of the pharmacy industry. Learn the latest about prescription drugs, natural products, and over-the-counter remedies. Discover new products and services from the industry's leading manufacturers, and gain knowledge and insights to better aid patients and advance your career.
Frequency: October

20231 NCPDP's Annual Conference
National Council for Prescription Drug Programs
9240 E Raintree Drive
Scottsdale, AZ 85260-7518

480-477-1000; *Fax:* 480-767-1042
ncpdp@ncpdp.org; www.ncpdp.org

Beth Fagan, Meeting Planning
Lee Ann Stember, President

Topic will be Building New Technologies. Offers educational sessions, a trade show, kenote speakers and more.
Frequency: March

20232 National Clinical Issues Forum: Metabolic Syndrome
American Pharmaceutical Association Foundation
2215 Constitution Avenue NW
Washington, DC 20037

202-297-7524
800-237-APHA; *Fax:* 202-429-6300
info@aphafoundation.org;
www.aphafoundation.org

Carol Bugdalski-Stutrud, Director
Carl Emswiller, Director
Hazel Pipkin, VP
Marie Michnich, Director Health Policy Program
Michael Stewart, Director Public Relations

To provide an opportunity for the exchange of information between leading clinical pharmacists from across the U.S. who are providing innovative patient care services for people afflicted with the co-morbidities of diabetes, hypertension and hyperlipidemia.
Frequency: May

20233 National Community Pharmacists Association Convention and Exhibition
National Community Pharmacists Association
100 Daingerfield Road
Alexandria, VA 22314-2833

703-683-8200
800-544-7447; *Fax:* 703-683-3619
info@ncpanet.com; www.ncpanet.org

Litsa Deck, Director Convention/Meetings
Faith James, Coordinator Convention/Meetings
Deleisa Johnson, VP Public Relations

Annual show of 450 exhibitors of pharmaceutical and related equipment, supplies and services.
Frequency: October, Florida

20234 National Conference on Advances in Perinatal and Pediatric Nutrition
Amer. Society for Parenteral & Enteral Nutrition
8630 Fenton Street
Suite 412
Silver Spring, MD 20910

301-587-6315
800-727-4567; *Fax:* 301-587-2365
aspen@nutr.org; www.nutritioncare.org
Social Media: Facebook, Twitter

Marion F Winkler, President
Vincent W Vanek, VP
Robin Kriegel, CAE, Executive Director
Joanne Kieffer, Director Finance

The purpose of the conference is to increase knowledge and awareness of the nutritional requirements of these special need patients. Has been planned for dieticians, nurses, obstetricians, neonatologiests, pediatricians, pediatric gastroenterologists, pharmacists, and other health care professionals involved in the care of high risk pregnant mothers, premature infants, and pediatric patients.
Frequency: July

20235 PCMA Annual Meeting
Pharmaceutical Care Management Association
325 7th St. NW
9th Fl.
Washington, DC 20004

202-756-5700; *Fax:* 202-756-5708;
www.pcmanet.org
Social Media: Facebook, Twitter

Mark Merritt, President & CEO

The industry's annual event for decision makers.
Frequency: Annual
Founded in: 2009

20236 RX Expo: An Educational Forum and Buying Show
National Community Pharmacists Association
100 Daingerfield Road
Alexandria, VA 22314-2833
703-683-8200
800-544-7447; *Fax:* 703-683-3619
info@ncpanet.com; www.ncpanet.org

Stephen Giroux PD, President
Bruce Roberts RPh, Executive VP/CEO

Annual show and exhibits of general gifts, sundries and seasonal items, over the counter products, health and beauty aids, electronic products, prescription drug products, personal care products, home health care products, IV products and related products.
1700 Attendees

20237 USP Annual Scientific Meeting
United States Pharmacopeial Convention
12601 Twinbrook Parkway
Rockville, MD 20852-1790

301-810-0667
800-227-8772; *Fax:* 301-816-8148
support@usp.org; www.usp.org

Anju K Malhotra, Manager Conferences/Meetings
Roger Williams, Executive Director

Open to the public and serves as an interactive forum where USP and its stakeholders can discuss new direction and standards that affect the pharmaceutical industry. The meeting provides attendees an opportunity to better understand the scope of USP's scientific work and provide input on key standards-setting issues.
Frequency: September

20238 Western Section Meeting of the Triological Society
Triological Society
555 N 30th Street
Omaha, NE 68131-2136

402-346-5500; *Fax:* 402-346-5300
info@triological.org; www.triological.org

I Kaufman Arenberg, MD, Executive Director

Annual show of 30 exhibitors of medical services and supplies related to Otolaryngology.
152 Attendees
Frequency: May

Directories & Databases

20239 American Drug Index
Lippincott Williams & Wilkins
16522 Hunters Green Pkwy
PO Box 1600
Hagerstown, MD 21740

301-223-2300
800-638-3030; *Fax:* 301-223-2400;
www.lww.com
Social Media: Facebook, Twitter

Norman Billups, Editor
Shirley Billups, Editor

Contains more than 22,000 entries. Practical features include: alphabetically listed drug names, extensive cross-indexing, complete information on the distributor's brand name, manufacturer, generic and/or chemical names, chemical strength and much more useful information. Electronic version available.
Cost: $69.95
1088 Pages
Frequency: Annual, Hardcover
ISBN: 1-574391-33-X

20240 Annual Meeting & Showcase
Academy of Managed Care Pharmacy
100 N Pitt St
Suite 400
Alexandria, VA 22314-3141

703-683-8416
800-827-2627; *Fax:* 703-683-8417
sandres@amcp.org; www.amcp.org
Social Media: Facebook, Twitter, LinkedIn

Douglas Burgoyne, President
Robert Gregory, Treasurer

Nationally reowned keynote speakers, new research presentations, achievement awards, competitions and Board inaugurations fill the agenda for managed care pharmacy's premier event.
Frequency: April

20241 CSO Directory
Drug Information Association

800 Enterprise Road
Suite 200
Horsham, PA 19044-3595

215-442-6100; *Fax:* 215-442-6199
dia@diahome.org; www.diahome.org

Paul Pomerantz BA MBA, Worldwide Executive Director
Lisa Zoks BA, Worlwide Dir Mktg/Communications

One of the industry's most respected and comprehensive reference guides, compiles company descriptions and contact information from hundreds of companies that provide services for every phase of the clinical trial and drug development process.

20242 DCAT Digest and Directory of Membership
Drug, Chemical & Associated Technologies
1 Washington Blvd
Suite 7
Robbinsville, NJ 08691-3162

609-448-1000
800-640-3228; *Fax:* 609-448-1944
info@dcat.org; www.dcat.org
Social Media: Facebook, LinkedIn

Margaret Timony, Executive Director
Lynda M Doyle, Senior Manager
Jacklyn Vitelli, Deputy Executive Director
Jeanne Motola, Administrative Assistant

Keeping members in touch with their colleagues throughout the industry.

20243 DIOGENES
FOI Services
704 Quince Orchard Rd
Gaithersburg, MD 20878-1700

301-975-9400; *Fax:* 301-975-0702
infofoi@foiservices.com;
www.foiservices.com

John Carey, President
Marlene Bobka, Vice President of Services

This comprehensive database contains citations to more than 1 million unpublished US Food and Drug Administration regulatory documents covering prescription and over-the-counter drugs.
Founded in: 1975

20244 DRUGDEX System
Thompson Micromedex
6200 South Syracuse Way
Suite 300
Greenwood Village, CO 80111-4740

303-679-9500
800-525-9083; *Fax:* 303-486-6464;
www.micromedex.com
Social Media: Facebook

This comprehensive database covers all aspects of drugs and their use, including investigational, FDA-approved, and OTC preparations.
Frequency: Full-text

20245 DataStat
NDCHealth
3975 Research Park Drive
Ann Arbor, MI 48108

734-994-0540
800-225-5632; *Fax:* 734-663-9084
mweindorf@datastat.com; www.datastat.com

Marielle Weindorf, Senior Research Director
Ellen Johnson
Randolph Hutto, EVP Business Development
Charles W Miller, EVP Corporate Initiatives

This comprehensive database offers descriptions of drug interactions at the ingredient level for individual drugs and therapeutic classes of drugs.
Frequency: Full-text
Founded in: 1967

20246 Directory of Hospital Personnel
Grey House Publishing
4919 Route 22
PO Box 56
Amenia, NY 12501

518-789-8700
800-562-2139; *Fax:* 845-373-6390
books@greyhouse.com; www.greyhouse.com
Social Media: Facebook, Twitter

Richard Gottlieb, President
Leslie Mackenzie, Publisher

A Who's Who of the hospital universe that makes it easy to get in touch with over 10,000 key decision makers. Comprehensive data includes listing of US hospitals, detailed contact information, number of physicians and employees, teaching affiliations, accreditation and much more.
Cost: $325.00
2300 Pages
ISBN: 1-592372-86-4
Founded in: 1981

20247 Directory of Hospital Personnel - Online Database
Grey House Publishing
4919 Route 22
PO Box 56
Amenia, NY 12501

518-789-8700
800-562-2139; *Fax:* 845-373-6390
gold@greyhouse.com
http://gold.greyhouse.com
Social Media: Facebook, Twitter

Richard Gottlieb, President
Leslie Mackenzie, Publisher

The DHP Online Database is the best resource you can have at your fingertips when researching or marketing a product or service to the hospital market. A 'Who's Who' of the hospital universe, this database puts you in touch with over 140,000 key decision-makers at 5,800 hospitals nationwide.
Founded in: 1981

20248 Drug Store and HBC Chains
Chain Store Guide
3922 Coconut Palm Dr
Tampa, FL 33619-1389

813-627-6700
800-778-9794; *Fax:* 813-627-7094
info@csgis.com; www.csgis.com

Mike Jarvis, Publisher
Chris Leedy, Advertising Sales

Tap into the lucrative drug industry with profiles on more than 1,700 US and Canadian companies operating two or more retail drug stores, deep discount stores, health and beauty care (HBC) stores, cosmetic stores or vitamin stores that have industry sales of at least $250,000. This powerful database empowers you to sell and market your products successfully by reaching more than 8,300 key decision makers.
Cost: $335.00

20249 Drug and Cosmetic Industry Catalog
Advanstar Communications
One Park Avenue
New York, NY 10016

212-797-7631; *Fax:* 212-951-6793
info@advanstar.com; www.advanstar.com

Eric Lisman, Executive VP

Over 1,000 manufacturers and suppliers of packaging equipment, private formulas and raw materials used in the drug and cosmetics industries are profiled.
Cost: $25.00
270 Pages
Frequency: Annual
Circulation: 4,000
Mailing list available for rent

20250 FDC Reports: The NDA Pipeline
FDC Reports
5550 Friendship Boulevard
Suite 1
Chevy Chase, MD 20815-7278

301-657-9830; *Fax:* 301-664-7238
fdc.customer.service@elsevier.com;
www.fdcreports.com

Karl Uhlendo, Executive Editor
Mike Squires, President

The NDA Pipeline is a searchable database available through the Web that contains up-to-date coverage of over 900 companies and more than 7,00 approval records. The NDA Pipeline tracks drug and biological product research, clinical trials and approvals. It also includes a comprehensive listing of products in research, descriptions of phases of development and licensing information and linked articles from The Pink Sheet and other FDC Reports publications.
900 Pages
Frequency: Annual
ISSN: 7012-8630
Founded in: 1939

20251 GAMP Good Practice Guide
Int'l Society for Pharmaceutical Engineering
3109 W Dr. Martin Luther King Jr Boulevard
Suite 250
Tampa, FL 33607

813-960-2105; *Fax:* 813-264-2816
ask@ispe.org; www.ispe.org

Provides new comprehensive guidance on meeting current regulatory expectations for compliant electronic records and signatures, which includes the need for record integrity, security, and availability throughout the required retention period. This is achieved by well documented, validated systems, and the application of appropriate operational controls.

20252 ISPE Good Practice Guide
Int'l Society for Pharmaceutical Engineering
3109 W Dr. Martin Luther King Jr Boulevard
Suite 250
Tampa, FL 33607

813-960-2105; *Fax:* 813-264-2816
ask@ispe.org; www.ispe.org

Provides a standard methodology for use in testing the containment efficiency of solids handling systems used in the pharmaceutical industry under closely defined conditions. It covers the main factors that affect the test results for specific contained solids handling systems, including material handled, room environment, air quality, ventilation and operator technique.

20253 Ident-A-Drug Reference
Therapeutic Research
3120 W March Lane
PO Box 8190
Stockton, CA 95219-0190

209-472-2240; *Fax:* 209-472-2249;
www.pletter.com

Jeff Jellin, PharmD, Editor

It gives you all the drug identification information found on this web site for more than 30,000 entries.
Cost: $85.00
704 Pages
ISBN: 0-967613-65-5

20254 InVitro Diagnostics Industry Directory
CTB International Publishing

PO Box 218
Maplewood, NJ 07040-0218

973-966-0997; *Fax:* 973-966-0242
info@ctbintl.com; www.ctbintl.com

Lists address, phone and fax number of invitro diagnostics companies, suppliers, distributors, regulatory agencies, professional societies and trade associations worldwide and contains over 2,300 entries worldwide-more than 1,200 contact names.
Cost: $277.00
ISBN: 1-887566-17-1
Printed in one color on matte stock

20255 International Pharmaceutical Abstracts Database
Thomson Scientific
1500 Spring Garden St
Philadelphia, PA 19130-4067

215-386-0100
800-336-4474; *Fax:* 215-386-2911
ts.info.na@thomson.com; www.thomson.com

Robert C Cullen, President/CEO
Craig Soderstrom, VP Office of CEO
Kristen McCarthy, VP Marketing/Communications
James Smith, Chief Operating Officer

These reports offering the latest in the development of drugs overseas, clinical and inventigotional use, cosmetics and, alternative and herbal medicine. Reports on pharmacy practice are also included.
ISSN: 0020-8264

20256 NABP Manual
National Association of Boards of Pharmacy
700 Busse Highway
Park Ridge, IL 60068

847-698-6227
800-774-6227; *Fax:* 847-698-0124
custserv@nabp.net; www.nabp.net

Malcom Broussard, Chairperson
Michael Burlson, President
Joseph Adams, Treasurer

Developed to be read in conjunction with state laws. It presents general information essential to all board of pharmacy members, and serves as a valuable reference for new board members. The manual is ideal for compiling and cross-referencing amendments and other records.
Cost: $25.00

20257 Natural Medicines Comprehensive Database
Therapeutic Research
PO Box 8190
Stockton, CA 95208-0190

209-472-2240; *Fax:* 209-472-2249;
www.pletter.com

Jeff Jellin, PharmD, Editor

Provides you with monographs on each natural ingredient plus updated helpful charts and tables.
Cost: $85.00
2000 Pages
ISBN: 0-967613-68-X

20258 Pharma Industry Directory
CTB International Publishing
PO Box 218
Maplewood, NJ 07040

973-966-0997; *Fax:* 973-966-0242
info@ctbintl.com; www.ctbintl.com

This is divided into 4 sections. The first section contains a complete alphabetical listing of the names, addresses, and phone and fax numbers of over 1,300 companies. The other sections are alphabetical listings of the companies with tables identifying them as to the fields they are involved in. The last section is a business index.
Cost: $250.00
ISBN: 1-887566-21-X
Printed in one color on matte stock

20259 Pharmaceutical News Index
UMI/Data Courier
620 S 3rd Street
Suite 400
Louisville, KY 40202-2475

502-583-4111
800-626-2823; *Fax:* 502-589-5572

Contains the latest US and international information about pharmaceutial, cosmetics, medical devices, and related health industries.

20260 Physicians' Desk Reference
Thomson Medical Economics
5 Paragon Drive
Montvale, NJ 07645-1742

201-358-7500
800-442-6657; *Fax:* 201-573-8999
PDRbookstore@medec.com; www.pdr.net

Thomas Eck, Marketing Manager

Physicians have turned to PDR for the latest word in prescription drugs for 57 years. Today, it is considered the standard prescription drug reference and can be found in virtually every phyician's office, hospital and pharmacy in the US.
Cost: $92.95
3,000 Pages
Frequency: Hardcover

20261 Roster of Faculty and Professional Staff
American Association of Colleges of Pharmacy
1727 King St
Suite 210
Alexandria, VA 22314-2700

703-739-2330; *Fax:* 703-836-8982;
www.aacp.org

Lucinda Maine, Executive VP
Kenneth W Miller, Senior VP
Daniel J Cassidy, COO

A directory of more than 5,000 full and part-time pharmacy faculty members including mailing and e-mail addresses, phone and fax numbers, degrees, and disciplines. Also included is valuable information about AACP such as officers, committee members, staff, and addresses and phone numbers for affiliated associations and corporations. $10 AACP Member.
Cost: $100.00
Frequency: November
Mailing list available for rent

Industry Web Sites

20262 http://gold.greyhouse.com
G.O.L.D Grey House OnLine Databases

Grey House Publishing's online database platform, GOLD, offers Quick Search, Keyword Search and Expert Search for most business sectors including drug, pharmaceutical and healthcare markets. The GOLD platform makes finding the information you need quick and easy - whether you're a novice searcher or an experienced database user. All of Grey House's directory products are available for subscription on the GOLD platform.

20263 www.aacp.org
American Association of Colleges of Pharmacy

National organization representing the interests of pharmaceutical education and educators. Comprising all 83 US pharmacy colleges and schools including more than 4,000 faculty, 36,000 student enrolled in professional programs and 3,600 individuals pursuing graduate study, AACP is committed to excellence in pharmaceutical education.

20264 www.aaps.org
American Association of Pharmaceutical Scientists

Aims to advance science through the open exchange of scientific knowledge, serve as an information resource and contribute to human health through pharmaceutical reseach and development.

20265 www.accp.com
American College of Clinical Pharmacy

Professional and scientific society that provides leadership, education, advocacy and resources enabling clinical pharmacists to achieve excellence in practice and research.

20266 www.acrpnet.org
Association of Clinical Research Professionals

Provides global leadership for the clinical research profession by promoting and advancing the highest ethical standards and practices.

20267 www.aihp.org
American Instiute of the History of Pharmacy

Supplies information regarding pharmaceutical history and usage.

20268 www.apha.org
American Public Health Association

Brings together researchers, health service providers, administrators, teachers and other health workers in a unique, multidisciplinary environment of professional exchange, study and action on the effort to prevent disease and promote health.

20269 www.asapnet.org
American Society for Automation in Pharmacy

Is to assist its members in advancing the application of computer technology in the pharmacists role as caregiver and in the efficient operation and management of a pharmacy.

20270 www.ashp.org
American Society of Health-System Pharmacy

An association that brings together health-system pharmacists and addresses their concerns.

20271 www.aspl.org
American Society for Pharmacy Law

An organization of pharmacists and lawyers who are interested in the law as it applies to the pharmacy industry.

20272 www.diahome.org
Drug Information Association

Association for those interested in technical developments, supply, and production of drugs. Exchanges and disseminates information by continuing to provide a neutral forum, respecting and welcoming all participants and offering quality driven programming.

20273 www.fdli.org
Food and Drug Law Institute

Nonprofit educational organization dedicated to improving the understanding of the laws, regulations and policies affecting the food, drug, medical device and biologics industries. A neutral, non-partisan organization that does not lobby.

20274 www.greyhouse.com
Grey House Publishing

Authoritative reference directories for most business sectors including drug, pharmaceutical and healthcare markets. Users can search the online databases with varied search criteria allowing for custom searches by product category, geographic area, sales volume, keyword, subject and more. Full Grey House catalog and online ordering also available.

20275 www.ipecamericas.org
International Pharmaceutical Excipients Council

Members are companies with an interest in the otherwise inert chemicals used as vehicles for medicines. Federation of three independent regional industry associations headquartered in the US. Each association focuses its attention on the applicable law, regulations, science and business practices of its region. The three associations work together on excipient safety and public health issues, in connection with international trade matters, and to achieve harmonization of regulatory standards.

20276 www.ncpanet.org
National Community Pharmacists Association

Represents independent pharmacists, provides support for undergraduate pharmacy education.

20277 www.npa.org
National Pharmaceutical Alliance

Represents the interests of small pharmaceutical companies and allied industries.

20278 www.nutritioncare.org
American Soc. for Parenteral & Enteral Nutrition

Strives to be a conduit amoung those interested in Nutrition Support.

20279 www.pda.org
Parenteral Drug Association

Members are makers of parenteral (injectable) drugs and other pharmaceuticals, as well as suppliers, academia and regulatory bodies. Our mission is to advance the pharmaceutical and biopharmaceutical technology internationally by promoting scientifically sound and practical technical information and education for industry and regulatory issues.

20280 www.pdr.net
Thomson Medical Economics

Physicians have turned to PDR for the latest word on prescription drugs for 57 years. Today it is considered the standard prescription drug reference and can be found in virtually every phyician's office, hospital and pharmacy in the US.

20281 www.pharmacist.com
American Pharmacists Association

APhA was the first established national professional society of pharmacists, founded in 1852 as the American Pharamceutical Assocation. It is the largest assocation of pharamcists in the US, whose mission is to provide information, education, and advocacy to empower its members to improve medication use and advance patient care.

20282 www.pharmacytechnician.com
American Association of Pharmacy Technicians

Provides leadership and represents the interests of its members to the public as well as healthcare organizations. Promotes the safe, effectacious, and cost effective dispensing distribution and use of medications. Provides continuing education programs and services to help technicians update their skills to keep pace with changes in pharmacy services.

20283 www.thompson.com
Thompson Scientific and Healthcare

Professionals in business, government, law and academia have reliedon us for the most authorative, timely and practical guidance available.

20284 www.usp.org
United States Pharmacopeia

Helps to ensure that consumers recieve quality medicines by establishing state-of-the-art standards that pharmaceutical manufacturers must meet. We provide standards for more than 3,800 medicines, dietary supplements and other health care products.

Associations

20285 Advertising Photographers of America
419 Lafayette St,2nd Floor
New York, NY 10003
212-807-0399; *Fax:* 212-727-8120
jocelyn@apany.com; www.apanational.com
Martin Trailer, President
Matthew Klein, VP
Julia Graham, Director
Our goal is to establish, endorse and promote professional practices, standards and ethics in the photographic and advertising community.
650 Members
Founded in: 1981

20286 American Photographic Artists Guild
568 Main Street
Wilbraham, MA 01095
785-883-4166
katfalls@tdi.net; www.useassociations.com
D John McCarthy, President
Joanie Ford, Historian/Merits/Degrees
Miles Andonov, Education
Lori Smith, Membership/Public Relations
Joanie Ford, Chairman
Encourages a better understanding between the photographer, the color artist and the retoucher. Conducts educational programs, sponsors competitions and bestows awards.
Founded in: 1966

20287 American Photography Association
407-536-4611
877-627-2360;
www.americanphotographyassociation.org
Social Media: Facebook, Twitter
To promote the interest, appreciation and participation in photography by all levels of photographers.

20288 American Photograpic Artists
5042 Wilshire Blvd
#321
Los Angeles, CA 90036
apanational.org
Social Media: Facebook, Twitter, LinkedIn, Vimeo
Tony Gale, National Board President
Michael Grecco, National Board EVP
John Durant, National Board SVP
Lee White, National Board Vice President
Andrew Strauss, National Board Treasurer
A not-for-profit organization for professional photographers.
Founded in: 1981

20289 American Society for Photobiology
1313 Dolley Madison Blvd
Suite 402
McLean, VA 22101
785-865-9405
800-627-0326; *Fax:* 785-843-6153
headquarters@photobiology.org;
www.photobiology.org
Social Media: Facebook, LinkedIn
Keith Cengel, President
Georg Wondrak, President-Elect
David Drupa, Executive Secretariat
Don Forbes, Secretary
Teresa Busch, Treasurer
Founded to further the scientific study of the effects of light on all living organisms.
1600 Members
Founded in: 1972

20290 American Society for Photogrammetry and Remote Sensing
5410 Grosvenor Lane
Suite 210
Bethesda, MD 20814-2160
301-493-0290; *Fax:* 301-493-0208;
www.asprs.org
Social Media: Facebook, Twitter
Dr. E. Lynn Usery, President
Dr. Charles K. Toth, President Elect
Rebecca A. Morton, Vice President
Roberta E. Lenczowski, National Director
Dr. Donald T. Lauer, Treasurer
A professional scientific association to advance the knowledge of and improve mapping sciences.
7000 Members
Founded in: 1934

20291 American Society of Media Photographers
150 North 2nd Street
Philadelphia, PA 19106
215-451-2767
info@asmp.org
asmp.org
Social Media: Facebook, Twitter, LinkedIn
Jenna Close, Chair
Luke Copping, Vice-Chair
Mark Green, Treasurer
Irene Owsley, Secretary
Tom Kennedy, Executive Director
A trade association which protects and promotes the interests of photographers whose work is for publication.
Founded in: 1942

20292 American Society of Photographers
3120 N. Argonne Dr.
Milwaukee, WI 53222
414-871-6600; *Fax:* 978-272-5201
jonallyn@aol.com; www.asofp.com
Social Media: Facebook, Twitter, Instagram
Randy McNeilly, Chairman of the Board
Kalen Henderson, President
Jessica Vogel, President Elect
Dennis Hammon, Vice President
Gabriel I. Alonso, Secretary Treasurer
Membership requirements include membership in Professional Photographers of America and either a Master of Photography, a Photographic Craftsmen, or a photographic specialist. Publishes a quarterly newsletter.
850 Members
Founded in: 1937

20293 American Society of Picture Professionals
201 E 25th St.,
Suite 11c
New York, NY 10010
516-500-3686; *Fax:* 424-247-9844
aspp-ny@aspp.com; www.aspp.com
Social Media: Facebook, Twitter, LinkedIn, YouTube, RSS
Sam Merrell, Executive Director
Cecilia de Querol, National President
Steve Spelman, Secretary
Mary F Loftus, Treasurer
Anita Dunca, Membership Co-Chair
Members are image producers, stock photo agencies, and image users.Provides networking and educational opportunities in the image transaction industry.
800 Members
Founded in: 1969

20294 Antique and Amusement Photographers International
P.O.Box 3094
McDonough, GA 30253
860-578-2274; *Fax:* 877-865-1052
info@oldtimephotos.org;
www.oldtimephotos.org
Social Media: Facebook, Twitter, LinkedIn, Pinterest
Derrick Gillikin, President
Susan K. Crutchfield, Executive Director
Michele Powers, Secretary
Sarana Rogers, Treasurer
Trent Edwards, Vice President
Members are photography studies and photographers, primarliy in the US and Canada, specializing in costume photography and suppliers to the industry.
200 Members
Founded in: 1990

20295 Association of International Photography Art Dealers
2025 M Street NW
Suite 800
Washington, DC 20036
202-367-1158; *Fax:* 202-367-2158
info@aipad.com; www.aipad.com
Social Media: Facebook, Twitter, Instagram, Flickr, Vimeo
Catherine Edelman, President
Kraige Block, Vice President
Richard Moore, Treasurer
Larry Miller, Secretary
Meredith Y. Robertson, Executive Director
Galleries and private dealers in fine photography who have been in business for at least three years.
Founded in: 1979

20296 BioCommunications Association
220 Southwind Lane
Hillsborough, NC 27278
919-245-0906
office@bca.org; www.bca.org
Social Media: Facebook, Twitter, LinkedIn, YouTube
Nancy Hurtgen, Executive Director
Connie Johansen, President
James Koepfler, Secretary/ Treasurer
Susanne Loomis, Vice President
Karen M. Hensley, Dir. Of Communications
Made up of professionals who create and use the highest quality images and presentations in visual communications media for teaching and documentation in the life sciences and medicine.
140 Members
Founded in: 1931

20297 Center for Photography at Woodstock
59 Tinker St
Woodstock, NY 12498
845-679-9957; *Fax:* 845-679-6337
info@cpw.org; www.cpw.org
Social Media: Facebook, Twitter, Flickr, Vimeo, Instagram
Howard Greenberg, Founder, Chair
Clinton Cargill, Vice President
Jed Root, Treasurer
Andy Young, Secretary
Ariel Shanberg, Executive Director
The Center for Photography at Woodstock is a not-for-profit, artist-centered organization dedicated to supporting artists working in photography and related media and engaging audiences through opportunities in which creation, discovery, and education are made possible.
Founded in: 1977

20298 Council on Fine Art Photography
5613 Johnson Ave
Bethesda, MD 20817-3503

301-897-0083

Lowell Anson Kenyon, Executive Director

Members are fine art photographers employing silver processes.
50 Members
Founded in: 1982

20299 Digital Media Licensing Association
3165 S. Alma School Road
#29-261
Chandler, AZ 85248-3760

714-815-8427
cathy@digitalmedialicensing.org;
www.pacaoffice.org
Social Media: Facebook, Twitter, LinkedIn, RSS, Skype

Sarah Fix, President
Elena Flanagan-Eister, Vice President
Chris Carey, Treasurer
Julie Zentmaier, Secretary
Cathy Aron, Executive Director

A community of visual media licensing professionals.
100+ Members
Founded in: 1951

20300 Evidence Photographers International Council
229 Peachtree St. NE
#2200
Atlanta, GA 30303

570-253-5450
800-356-3742; *Fax:* 404-614-6406
csc@evidencephotographers.com;
www.evidencephotographers.com
Social Media: Facebook

Claire White, Association Director

A non profit educational and scientific organization with the primary purpose is the advancement of forensic photography/videography in civil evidence and law enforcement.
2000 Members
Founded in: 1968

20301 IEEE Standards Association
445 Hoes Lane
Piscataway, NJ 08854-4141

732-981-0060; *Fax:* 732-562-1571
i3amembership@i3a.org
standards.ieee.org
Social Media: Facebook, Twitter, LinkedIn

Bruce Kraemer, President
John Kulick, Chairman
Yatin Trivedi, Treasurer
Konstantinos Karachalios, Secretary
Phil Wennblom, Corporate Advisory Group

Formerly (1997) National Association of Photographic Manufacturers and (2001) Photographic and Imaging Maufacturers Association. The Silver Council is a program sponsored by I3A that monitors environmental regulation of commercial silver use. Membership fee varies,based on annual sales.
81 Members
Founded in: 1946

20302 Independent Photo Imagers
2518 Anthem Village Drive
Suite 104
Henderson, NV 89052

702-617-1141; *Fax:* 702-617-1181
info@ipiphoto.com; www.ipiphoto.com
Social Media: Facebook, Twitter, LinkedIn, YouTube, Pinterest, Instagram

Joel Miller, Chairman
Ron Mohney, Executive Director
T.K. Broecker, Treasurer
Koby Marowelli, Secretary
Larry Steiner, Vice Chairman

An association of independent photographers, who use various means of developing their pictures.
45 Members
Founded in: 1982

20303 International Color Consortium
1899 Preston White Drive
Reston, VA 20191

703-264-7200; www.color.org

Max Derhak, Co-Chair
William Li, Co-Chair
Ray Cheydleur, Vice Chair
Deborah Orf, Secretary
Phil Green, Technical Secretary

An association to promote the use and adoption of open, vendor-neutral, cross-platform color management.
Founded in: 1993

20304 International Fire Photographers Association
143 40th Street
New Orleans, LA 70124

504-482-9616; *Fax:* 504-486-4946
president@ifpaonline.com
ifpafirephotos.org/
Social Media: Facebook, Twitter, Google+, Yahoo

Chris E Mickal, President
Michael Heller, VP

Promote professionalism in all aspects of fire photography, specifically in the fields of fire, educational, and investigative photography and the recognition of all fire photography organizations as an important tool in the fire service and law enforcement
200 Members
Founded in: 1964

20305 International Graphic Arts Education Association
1899 Preston White Drive
Reston, VA 20191

703-758-0595; www.igaea.org

Monika Zarzycka, President
Kelly Glentz Brush, Secretary
Dr. Jerry Waite, Treasurer
Tony Cimaglia, First Vice-President (Publications)
Michael Williams, President-Elect

An association of educators in partnership with industry, dedicated to sharing theories, principles, techniques, and processes relating to graphic communications and imaging theory.
800 Members
Founded in: 1923

20306 Naples Art Association
The von Liebig Art Center
585 Park St.
Naples, FL 34102

239-262-6517; www.naplesart.org
Social Media: Facebook, Twitter, LinkedIn, Pinterest, YouTube

Andrew Sroka, Board President
Aimee Schlehr, Executive Director
Shea Lindner, Programs Manager
Maureen Christensen, Development Director
Callie Spilane, Education Director

A nonprofit organization to promote and advance education, interest and participation in the visual arts.
Founded in: 1956

20307 National Association of Photo Equipment Technicians
300 Picture Place
Jackson, MI 49201

517-788-8100; *Fax:* 517-788-8371;
www.arcat.com

William Covey, Executive Liaison

Provides information on the photogrpahic industry to those engaged in the photographic repair.
250 Members
Founded in: 1973

20308 National Association of Quick Printers (NAQP)
One Meadowlands Plaza
Suite 1511
East Rutherford, NJ 07073

201-634-9600
800-642-6275; *Fax:* 201-634-0324
webmaster@napl.org; www.naqp.com
Social Media: Facebook, Twitter, LinkedIn, YouTube,RSS, Pinterest, Google

Joseph Truncale, President & CEO
Nigel Worme, Chairman
Willam Gavigan, Treasurer/ Secretary
Niels Winther, Vice Chairman
Mike Philie, Senior Vice President

Furthers the business of quick printers, copy shops, and small format commercial printers. Also welcomes manufacturers and suppliers of equipment and consumables, trade publications, and consultants to the quick print industry.
900 Members
Founded in: 1975

20309 National Photograpic Society
15 Woodbine Farm Business Park
Threemilestone, UK

843-289-0615; www.thenps.com
Social Media: Facebook, Twitter, Google+, RSS

Rod Pascoe, Chairman
Stu Cooper, Mentor and Trainer
Sarah Fitzgerald, Liaison Manager
Paul Spiers, Head of marketing
Susan Hurren, Social Media and Press

A society for both professional as well as enthusiast photographers.

20310 National Press Photographers Association
120 Hooper Street
Athens, GA 30602-3018

706-542-2506; *Fax:* 919-383-7261
info@nppa.org
nppa.org
Social Media: Facebook, Twitter, LinkedIn, Vimeo

Akili Ramsess, Executive Director
Melissa Lyttle, President
Michael King, Vice President
Seth Gitner, Secretary
Carolyn Hall, Treasurer

Sponsors numerous, annual television and print media workshops. Conducts annual competition for news photos and television news film. Monthly magazine job information bank given to all members.
6500+ Members
Founded in: 1946

20311 National Stereoscopic Association
Portland, OR

503-771-4440
strwld@teleport.com
stereoworld.org
Social Media: Facebook

Lawrence Kaufman, Chairman
Lee Pratt, President

John Bueche, Vice President
Carl Bowers, Treasurer
Ronald Gold, Vice President, Marketing

A nonprofit organization to promote research, practice, collection and use of vintage and contempory stereoviews, stereo cameras and equipment.
Founded in: 1974

20312 North American Nature Photography Association
6382 Charleston Road
Alma, IL 62807

618-547-7616; *Fax:* 618-547-7438
info@nanpa.org; www.nanpa.org
Social Media: RSS

Gabby Salazar, President
Sean Fitzgerald, President-Elect
Susan Day, Executive Director
Bruce Haley, Treasurer
Clay Bolt, Board Member

Committed solely to serving the field of nature photography. Provides education, information develops standards and promotes nature photography as an art form and teaching medium.
Founded in: 1993

20313 North American Nature Photography Associat ion
6382 Charleston Road
Alma, IL 62807

618-547-7616; *Fax:* 618-547-7438
info@nanpa.org; www.nanpa.org
Social Media: Facebook, Twitter, LinkedIn, RSS, Google+

Gabby Salazar, President
Sean Fitzgerald, President Elect
Bruce Haley, Past-President, Treasurer
Clay Bolt, Board Member
Gary Farber, Board Member

An organization dedicated to photography of nature.

20314 PERA
Pera Innovation Park, Nottingham Rd.
Melton Mowbray
Leicestershire, UK LE13 0PB

166-450-1501
800-776-8616; *Fax:* 408-512-5254
enquiries@peraconsulting.com; www.pera.com
Social Media: Facebook, Twitter

Glyn Goddard, Non-Executive Director
Dean Hallam, Chief Financial Officer
Alan Baxter, Non Executive Director
John Hill, Executive Chairman
Paul Trantor, Chief Executive Officer

An association for production equipment rental personnel and organizations.
75 Members
Founded in: 1973

20315 Photo Chemical Machining Institute
11 Robert Toner Blvd
234
North Attleboro, MA 02763

508-385-0085; *Fax:* 508-232-6005
cflaherty@pcmi.org; www.pcmi.org

Catherine Flaherty, Executive Director
William Fox, President
Mike Lynch, Vice-President
Eric Kemperman, Treasurer
Philip Greiner, Secretary

Members are companies producing metal products through photo chemical machining. In addition the Institute includes companies that service the PCM industry and supply its needs.
210 Members
Founded in: 1967

20316 Photo Marketing Association International
718 Jones Branch Drive
Suite 300
McLean, VA 22102

703-665-4416
800-762-9287; *Fax:* 703-506-3266;
www.theimagingalliance.com
Social Media: Facebook, Twitter, LinkedIn

Gabrielle Mullinax, President
Georgia McCabe, CEO/ Executive Director
Jerry Sullivan, Vice-President
Lisa Otto, Treasurer
Mark Klostermeyer, Sr. Vice President

A national organization of associations and manufacturers and suppliers of photographic equipment; also members of the National Association of Photo Equipment Technicians and of the Professional School Photographers of America.
18000 Members
Founded in: 1924

20317 Photographic Society of America
8241 S Walker Avenue
Suite 104
Oklahoma City, OK 73139

405-843-1437
855-772-4636; www.psa-photo.org

Charlie Burke, President
Elena McTighe, Executive Vice President
Dana Cohoon, Treasurer
Stan Bormann, Secretary
Ralph Durham, Conference Vice President

Worldwide interactive organization for anyone interested in photography, professional or serious amateur. Offers a wide variety of activities, monthly magazine, photo and digital competitions, study groups via mail and Internet, how-to programs, an annal conference, and many other activites and services.
Founded in: 1934

20318 Photoimaging Manufacturers and Distributor s Association
7600 Jericho Turnpike
Suite 301
Woodbury, NY 11797

516-802-0895; *Fax:* 516-364-0140
jackie@pmda.com; www.pmda.com
Social Media: Facebook, Twitter, LinkedIn

Dan Unger, President
Michelle Fernandez, VP
Jay Kelbley, VP
Jim Malcolm, VP
Jerry Grossman, Executive Director

Contributes to the progress and welfare of the photoimaging industry.
Founded in: 1939

20319 Picture Agency Council of America
23046 Avenida De La Carlota
Suite 600
Laguna Hills, CA 92653

714-815-8427; *Fax:* 949-679-8224
execdirector@pacaoffice.org;
www.stockindustry.org

Cathy Aron, Executive Director
Maria Kessler, President

Trade association for stock picture companies in North America. Serves member agencies, their clients and their contributing photographers by promoting communication among photo agencies and other professional groups.
150 Members
Founded in: 1951

20320 Professional Aerial Photographers' Association
12069 Cessna Place
Brookshire, TX 77423

703-887-8703; *Fax:* 703-281-6700
cboyle@boyleconsulting.com
professionalaerialphotographers.com

Chuck Boyle, President
Laura Boyko, VP, Programs
Kent Larson, VP, Membership
John Mooney, Treasurer, Secretary
Julie Belanger, ExecutiveDirector

A professional trade organization for aerial photographers.
Founded in: 1974

20321 Professional Photographer Magazine
229 Peachtree St NE
Suite 2200
Atlanta, GA 30303

404-522-8600
800-742-7468; *Fax:* 404-614-6406
ppmag@omeda.com; www.ppmag.com
Social Media: Facebook, Twitter, Pinterest

David Trust, CEO
Bob Lloyd, President
Dana Groves, Marketing Executive

Portrait, commercial, wedding, industrial and specialized photographers and photographic artists.
28000 Members
Founded in: 1869

20322 Professional Photographers Association
Professional Photographers Assoc. of New England
PO Box 568
Durham, NH 3824

603-868-2970; *Fax:* 860-423-9402;
www.ppane.com
Social Media: Facebook, YouTube

Lorraine Bedell, President
Steve Lourenco, President Elect
Madonna Lovett, Vice President of Programs
Fred Stiteler, Executive Secretary
Alison Miniter, Vice President of Comm
1000 Attendees
Frequency: September
Founded in: 1860

20323 Professional Photographers of America
229 Peachtree St. NE
Suite 2200
Atlanta, GA 30303

404-522-8600; *Fax:* 404-614-6400;
www.ppa.com
Social Media: Facebook, Twitter, LinkedIn, Google+, Instagram, YouTube

Susan Michal, Chairman
Michael Timmons, President
Lori Craft, Vice President
Rob Behm, Treasurer
Stephen Thetford, Director

A nonprofit trade association for photographers.
Founded in: 1869

20324 Professional Picture Framers Association
83 South Street Unit
#303
Freehold, NJ 7728

732-536-5160
800-762-9287; *Fax:* 517-788-8371
info@ppfadirectory.com; www.ppfa.com
Social Media: Facebook, Twitter, LinkedIn

John Pruitt CPF, President
Fran Gray MCPF, VP

A trade association of manufacturers, wholesalers, print publishers, importers and retailers selling art, framing and related supplies.
3000 Members
Founded in: 1971

20325 Professional Travelogue Sponsors
El Camino College Foundation
16007 Crenshaw Boulevard
Torrance, CA 90506
310-329-5345
800-832-5345; *Fax:* 310-715-7875
artstickets@elcamino.edu;
www.elcamino.edu/centerforthearts
Social Media: Facebook, Twitter, YouTube, Instagram, Flickr
Thomas Fallow, President
Bruce Spain, Executive Director
Rick Christophersen, Director
Sara Hamilton, Administrative Assistant
Nancy Adler, Production Manager
Currently the largest documentary Travel Film Program Sponsor and Presenter.
55 Members
Founded in: 1967

20326 Professional Women Photographers
Metropolitan Opera Guild
119 W. 72nd St.
#223
New York, NY 10023
212-867-7745
pwp@pwponline.org; www.pwponline.org
Social Media: Facebook, Twitter, LinkedIn, Amazon, RSS
Beth Shaw, President
Fredda Gordon, Vice President
Francoise Jeanpierre, Treasurer
Joann Frechette, Secretary
Elizabeth Currier, Membership
To support and promote the work of women photographers through the sharing of ideas, resources and experience, to provide educational forums to engourage artistic growth and photographic development, and to stimulate public interst in and support for the art of photography
170 Members
Founded in: 1975
Mailing list available for rent

20327 SPIE, the international society for optics and photonics
1000 20th Street
Bellingham, WA 98225-6705
360-676-3290
888-504-8171; *Fax:* 360-647-1445
customerservice@spie.org; www.SPIE.org
Social Media: Facebook, Twitter, LinkedIn, RSS, YouTube, Blogspot
Prof. Toyohiko Yatagai, President
Dr. Eugene G. Arthurs, CEO
Dr. Glenn D. Boreman, Vice President
Gary Spiegel, Secretary/ Treasurer
Dr. Robert A. Lieberman, President-Elect
Members are scientists, engineers, researchers and companies interested in technology and applications of optical, electro-optical, fiber-optic, laser, and photonic systems.
14000 Members
Founded in: 1955

20328 Silver Users Association
3930 Walnut St.
Suite 210
Fairfax, VA 22030
703-930-7790; *Fax:* 703-359-7562
pmiller@mwcapitol.com;
www.silverusersassociation.org
Social Media: Facebook
Paul A Miller, Executive Director
Bill LeRoy, President
Mike Huber, VP
John King, Secretary
Bill Hammerle, Treasury
Represents manufacturers and distributors of products in which silver is an essential element. Works for the recognition of silver as a commodity and the removal of governmental regulations which retard its free exchange in commerce both foreign and domestic. Also helps provide a stable trading climate in the metal, it monitors the silver market to insure that silver information available to the industry and public is accurate.
45 Members
Founded in: 1947

20329 Society for Photographic Education
2530 Superior Avenue
Suite 403
Cleveland, OH 44114
216-622-2733; *Fax:* 216-622-2712
membership@spenational.org;
www.spenational.org
Social Media: Facebook, Twitter, Instagram
Jeff Curto, National Board Chair
Anne Massoni, Vice-Chair
James Wyman, Executive Director
Lupita Murillo Tinnen, Treasurer
Robin Germany, Secretary
The Society for Photographic Education is a non-profit membership organization that provides a forum for the discussion of photogrphy and related media as a means of creative expression and cultural insight. Through its interdisciplinary porgrams, services and publications, the society seeks to promote a broader understanding of the medium in all its forms, and to foster the development of its practice, teaching, scholarship and criticism.
1800 Members
Founded in: 1963

20330 Society of American Travel Writers
One Parkview Plaza
Suite 800
Oakbrook Terrace, IL 60181
312-420-6846; *Fax:* 414-359-1671
info@satw.org; www.satw.org
Social Media: Facebook, Twitter, LinkedIn
Paul Lasley, President
Barbara Orr, Vice President
Peggy Bendel, Secretary
Tom Adkinson, Treasurer
Catherine Hamm, President-Elect
Photographers and 35 associate member representatives of airlines, hotels, resorts, tourist agencies and public relations firms.
Founded in: 1955

20331 Student Photographic Society
229 Peachtree St. NE
Suite 2200
Atlanta, GA 30303
888-722-1334
info@studentphoto.com
studentphoto.com
Social Media: Facebook, Twitter, Google+
Susan Michal, Chairman
Michael Timmons, President
Lori Craft, Vice President
Rob Behm, Treasurer
Stephen Thetford, Director
Provides career building resources, networking opportunities and information for photography students.
Founded in: 1999

20332 Take Great Pictures
109 White Oak Lane
Suite 72F
Old Bridge, NJ 08857
732-679-3460; *Fax:* 516-364-0140
webmaster@TakeGreatPictures.com;
www.takegreatpictures.com
Social Media: RSS
Willard Clark, Executive Director
Founded as Photographic Merchandising and Distributing Association and became Photographic Manufacturers and Distributors Association before assuming its present name in 1999. Membership is $500/year for associate members and $1,000/year for voting members.
20000 Members
Founded in: 1939

20333 The Association of Independent Architectural Photographers
32 West 200 South
Suite 219
Salt Lake City, UT 84101
801-738-8786
aiap@photographer.org; www.aiap.net
A professional organization for architectural photographers.

20334 The Society for Photographic Education
2530 Superior Avenue
Suite 403
Cleveland, OH 44114
216-622-2733; *Fax:* 216-622-2712
membership@spenational.org;
www.spenational.org
Social Media: Facebook, Twitter, Instagram
Jeff Curto, National Board Chair
Anne Massoni, Vice-Chair
James Wyman, Executive Director
Lupita Murillo Tinnen, Treasurer
Robin Germany, Secretary
A nonprofit ogranization for the advancement of education in photography.
1800 Members
Founded in: 1963

20335 University Photographers Association of America
SUNY Brockport
350 New Campus Drive
Brockport, NY 14420-2931
716-395-2133; *Fax:* 662-915-1298
jdusen@brockport.edu; www.upaa.org
Glenn Carpenter, President
Robert Jordan, VP
Nick Romanenko, Treasurer
Mark Carriveau, Secretary
Bill Bitzinger, Board Member
Members are college and university photographers who are concerned with the application and practice of photography.
250 Members
Founded in: 1961

20336 Wedding & Portrait Photographers International (WPPI)
85 Broad St.
11th Floor
New York, NY 10004
646-654-4500; *Fax:* 310-846-4770;
www.wppionline.com
Social Media: Facebook, Twitter, YouTube, Instagram
Stephen Sheanin, CEO/President
John McGeary, Senior Vice President
Lauren Wendle, VP, Publisher
Neeta Lakhani, Operations Manager
Jason Groupp, Director

Promotes high artistic and technical standards. Serves as a forum for an exchange of technical knowledge. Members are offered the opportunity to purchase special products and services.
2.8M Members
Founded in: 1978

20337 Wedding Photojournalist Association
www.wpja.com
A resource of photojournalists and candid wedding photographers.
Founded in: 2002

20338 White House News Photographers Association
7119 Ben Franklin Station
Washington, DC 20044-7119
202-785-5230
info@whnpa.org; www.whnpa.org
Social Media: Facebook, Twitter
Whitney Shefte, President
Jim Bourg, Vice President
Jon Elswick, Treasurer
Joshua Roberts, Secretary
Dennis Brack, Ex Officio
Volunteer association of professional photographers covering the Washington political venue. Activities include educational seminars, work with high school students and an annual awards contest. Our work is seen in newspapers, magazines, television and on the Internet.
500 Members
Founded in: 1941

20339 Worldwide Community of Imaging Association
2282 Springport Road
Suite F
Jackson, MI 49202
517-788-8100
800-762-9287; *Fax:* 517-788-8371;
www.theimagingalliance.com
Social Media: Facebook, Twitter, LinkedIn
Bill Eklund, President
Gabrielle Mullinax, Senior Vice President
Jerry Sullivan, Vice President
Mark Klostermeyer, MCPF, Treasurer
Jim Esp, Secretary, Executive Director
United diverse professionals in the imaging industry worldwide.
Founded in: 1924

Newsletters

20340 American Society of Media Photgraphers Bulletin
Photo District News
150 North Second Street
Philadelphia, PA 19106
215-451-2767; *Fax:* 215-451-0880
info@asmp.org; www.asmp.org
Social Media: Facebook, Twitter, LinkedIn
Holly Hughes, Editor
Jeffery Roberts, President
Member publication that addresses the news and preoccupations of the photography industry.
Frequency: Quarterly
Circulation: 5500
Founded in: 1944

20341 BCA News
BioCommunications Association
220 Southwind Lane
Hillsborough, NC 27278-7907
919-245-0906; *Fax:* 919-245-0906
khensley@mdanderson.org; www.bca.org
Social Media: Facebook, Twitter, LinkedIn, Blog,Tumblr
Karen Hensley, Editor
Susanne Loomis, President
Joseph Kane, Vice-President
James Koepfler, Secretary-Treasurer
Keeps members informed about such things as annual meetings, chapter activities, awards and member updates.
Frequency: 2-3x/Year

20342 Dance on Camera Journal
Dance Films Association
48 W 21st St
Suite 907
New York, NY 10010-6989
212-727-0764; *Fax:* 212-727-0764;
www.dancefilms.org
Deidra Towers, Executive Director
Louise Spain, CEO
The only service organization in the world dedicated to both the dance and the film community.
Cost: $45.00
Circulation: 350
Founded in: 1956

20343 Future Image Report
Future Image
520 South El Camino Real
Suite 206A
San Mateo, CA 94402
650-579-0493
800-749-3572; *Fax:* 650-579-0566;
www.futureimage.com
Alexis J Gerard, Editor/Publisher
Paul Worthington, Managing Editor
Heidy Bravo, Circulaion Manager
News and analysis of technology and market developments in photo-digital imaging, for management-level industry professionals.
Cost: $500.00
Founded in: 1991

20344 Light Impressions Review
PO Box 940
Rochester, NY 14603-0940
716-271-8960
William Edwards, Publisher
Lance Speer, Director
Photography notes and news.
Cost: $15.00
16 Pages
Frequency: Monthly

20345 NTIS Alert- Photography & Recording Devices
National Technical Information Service
5285 Port Royal Rd
US Department of Commerce
Alexandria, VA 22312
703-605-6000
800-553-6847; *Fax:* 703-605-6900
info@ntis.gov; www.ntis.gov
Linda Davis, VP
Cost: $140.00
Founded in: 1955

20346 Photo Marketing
Photo Marketing Association International
2282 Springport Road
Suite F
Jackson, MI 49202
517-788-8100
800-762-9287; *Fax:* 517-788-8371;
www.theimagingalliance.com
Social Media: Facebook, Twitter, LinkedIn
Ted Fox, CEO
Allen Showalter, President
Mark Klostermeyer, Vice-President
Robert L Hanson, Treasurer
News of interest to the photo business on both a national and international basis.
Cost: $5.00
4 Pages
Frequency: Monthly
Circulation: 12,141
Founded in: 1925

20347 PhotoDaily
PhotoSource International
1910 35th Ave
Pine Lake Farm
Osceola, WI 54020-5602
715-248-3800
800-624-0266; *Fax:* 715-248-7394
info@photosource.com; www.photosource.com
Rohn Engh, President
Bruce Swenson, Production Manager
Jonna Zehma, Editor
Pairs photographers with the picture needs of magazine and book editors.
Cost: $330.00
Frequency: Daily
Founded in: 1976

20348 Photobulletin
PhotoSource International
1910 35th Ave
Osceola, WI 54020-5602
715-248-3800
800-624-0266; *Fax:* 715-248-7394
info@photosource.com; www.photosource.com
Rohn Engh, President
Lists photographic needs of photobuyers buying in the top-notch markets.
Frequency: Daily
Founded in: 1980
Printed in one color

20349 Photofinishing News
Photofinishing News
219 Lafeyette Avenue
Westwood, NJ 07675-904
201-819-2533
hans@photo-news.com; www.photo-news.com
Hans Kuhlman, Editor
Technical / marketing coverage of worldwide photography / photo-imaging industry, reviews of new products, tradeshows and market statistics.
Cost: $150.00
12 Pages
ISBN: 0-889239-3 -
ISSN: 1536-6553
Founded in: 1970
Printed in one color on matte stock

20350 Photograph Collector
340 East Richardson Avenue
Suite 200
Langhorne, PA 19047-2824
215-891-0214
info@photoreview.org; www.photoreview.org
Stephen Perloff, Editor
News and analysis for collectors, curators and dealers. Current coverage of the auction market, trends, discoveries, museums and trade shows. Accepts advertising.
Cost: $149.95
8 Pages
Frequency: Monthly
ISBN: 0-271083-8 -
Founded in: 1980
Printed in one color on matte stock

20351 Professional Photographers Association of New England
98 Windham Street
PO Box 316
Willimantic, CT 06226-316

203-488-2334
860-423-1402; *Fax:* 860-423-9402;
www.ppane.com

Harvey Goldstein, Editor
Ruth Clegg, CEO/President
Circulation: 1000
Founded in: 1961
Printed in on glossy stock

Magazines & Journals

20352 Advanced Imaging
Cygnus Publishing
102 Wilmont Road
Suite 470
Deerfield, IL 60015-3601

847-405-0257
larry.adams@cygnusb2b.com;
www.cygnusb2b.com

Dave Brambert, Group Publisher
Larry Adams, Editor-in-Chief
Richard Reiff, President
Hank Russell, Managing Editor

Contains information on professional photographic techniques and new approaches in all forms of media.
Cost: $60.00
Frequency: Monthly
Circulation: 44009
Founded in: 1966

20353 Afterimage
Visual Studies Workshop
31 Prince Street
Rochester, NY 14607-1405

585-442-8676; *Fax:* 585-442-1992
info@vsw.org;
www.vsw.org/afterimage/index.html

Karen VanMeenen, Editor
Joanna Heatwole, Managing Editor

Geared toward media arts and photography artists, curators, academics, administrators and students. Features photography, independent film and video coverage, artist's books, alternative publishing and cultural studies issues. Also highlights conference and festival reports and scholarly feature articles.
Cost: $33.00
Circulation: 10000
Founded in: 1980

20354 American Photo
1633 Broadway
43rd Floor
New York, NY 10019

212-676-6000
800-274-4514; *Fax:* 212-489-4217;
www.hfmus.com/

David Schonauer, Editor-in-Chief
Krissa Cavouras, Associate Editor
Richard Rabinowitz, Publisher

Profiles of professional photographers and other photographic topics.
Cost: $4.99
Frequency: 6 Issues per year
Circulation: 27,733
Founded in: 1888

20355 Aperture
Aperture Foundation
547 W 27th St
Suite 4
New York, NY 10001-5511

212-505-5555
800-825-0061; *Fax:* 212-979-7759
info@aperture.org; www.aperture.org

Michael Culloso, President
Cathy Kaplan, Vice-Chairman
Frederick Smith, Treasurer

Dedicates itself to celebrating the finest in creative photography. Through the periodicals exquisitely reproduced images, rivaling the quality of the photographers' original prints, subscribers experience a wealth of challenging, beautiful pictures on a series of significant topics. Accepts advertising.
Cost: $40.00
80 Pages
Frequency: Quarterly
Founded in: 1952
Mailing list available for rent

20356 Exposure
Society for Photographic Education
2530 Superior Avenue
Suite 403
Cleveland, OH 44114

216-622-2733; *Fax:* 216-622-2712
membership@spenational.org;
www.spenational.org

Virginia Morrison, Executive Director
Nina Barcellona, Advertising & Publications
Meghan Borato, Registrar
Carla Pasquale, Office/Accounts Manager
Cost: $15.00
Frequency: Biannual
Mailing list available for rent: 700 names

20357 History of Photography
Routledge Publishing
7625 Empire Drive
Florence, KS 41042-2919

800-354-1420
orders@taylorandfrancis.com;
www.taylorandfrancis.com

Graham Smith, Editor
Ann Haddrell, Advertising Manager

An international publication devoted to the history and criticism of the basic sematic unit of all modern media.
Cost: $396.00
92 Pages
Frequency: Annual+
ISSN: 0308-7298
Founded in: 1977

20358 Imaging Business
Cygnus Business Media
3 Huntington Quadrangle
Suite 301N
Melville, NY 11747-4618

631-845-2700
800-308-6397; *Fax:* 631-845-7109
bill.schiffner@cygnuspub.com;
www.labsonline.com

Bill Schiffner, Associate Publisher

Formerly called Photographic Processing. Covers photographic equipment, processing, suppliers and dealers. No longer in publication, but last six years of issues available in online archive.
Cost: $66.00
Frequency: Monthly
Circulation: 21000
ISSN: 0031-8744
Founded in: 1936
Printed in 4 colors

20359 News Photographer
National Press Photographers Association
120 Hooper Street
Athens, GA 30602-3018

706-542-2506; *Fax:* 919-383-7261
info@nppa.org; www.nppa.org
Social Media: Facebook, Twitter, LinkedIn, Vimeo

Akili Ramsess, Executive Director
Melissa Lyttle, President
Tom Burton, Interim Editor

Features articles, news and profiles about still and television news photography.
Cost: $38.00
Frequency: Monthly
Circulation: 10500
ISSN: 0199-2422
Founded in: 1946
Mailing list available for rent: 9,500 names at $50 per M
Printed in 4 colors

20360 Outdoor Photographer
Werner Publshing Corporation
12121 Wilshire Blvd
Suite 1200
Los Angeles, CA 90025-1168

310-820-1500; *Fax:* 310-826-5008
editors@outdoorphotographer.com;
www.outdoorphotographer.com
Social Media: Facebook, Twitter

Steve Warner, Owner
Ibarionex Perello, Associate Editor
Cost: $14.97
Founded in: 1965
Mailing list available for rent

20361 PC Photo
Werner Publishing
12121 Wilshire Blvd # 1200
12th Floor
Los Angeles, CA 90025-1168

310-820-1500; *Fax:* 310-826-5008;
www.wernerpublishing.com

Steve Werner, Owner
Rob Shepherd, Editor

Covers the new desktop darkroom or home photo lab technologies, trends and methods. Designed to stimulate desktop photographers through the listing of new products and technologies.
Cost: $11.97
Founded in: 1965

20362 PCPhoto Magazine
Werner Publishing Corporation
12121 Wilshire Blvd
Suite 1200
Los Angeles, CA 90025-1176

310-820-1500; *Fax:* 310-826-5008;
www.wernerpublishing.com

Steve Werner, Owner

Shows you how to enjy the exciting and affordable new world of computers and photography. Features step-by-step instructions, evaluations of the latest equipment, tips from the pros, and more!
Cost: $11.97
Frequency: 9 Issues
Mailing list available for rent

20363 PHOTO Techniques
Preston Publications
6600 W Touhy Ave
Niles, IL 60714-4516

847-647-2900; *Fax:* 847-647-1155
jwhite@phototechmag.com;
www.prestonpub.com

Tinsley Preston, Owner
Joe White, Editor
Connie Turgon, Marketplace Advertising

PHOTO Techniques offers practical articles that help solve shooting, processing, lighting and

printing problems. This is the one magazine that walks you step by step through new techniques. Every other issue contains a digital section. Departments you can rely on include; Master Printing Class, David Vestal's commentary, Photochemistry and more. There are valuable guides to cameras, papers, films, useful accessories and darkroom suppliers.
Cost: $27.99
Founded in: 1979
Mailing list available for rent: 30,000 names at $145 per M

20364 Photo District News
Prometheus Global Media
770 Broadway
New York, NY 10003-9595

212-493-4100; *Fax:* 646-654-5368;
www.prometheusgm.com

Richard D. Beckman, CEO
James A. Finkelstein, Chairman
Madeline Krakowsky, Vice President Circulation
Tracy Brator, Executive Director Creative Service

Delivers the information photographers need to survive in a competitive business from marketing and business advice to legal issues, photographic techniques, new technologies and more.
Frequency: Monthly
Founded in: 1980

20365 Photo Insider
123 US Hwy 46 (West)
Fairfield, NJ 07004

973-377-2007
800-631-0300; www.photoinsider.com
Social Media: Facebook, Twitter, LinkedIn, YouTube,Foursquare,Flickr,Pint

Founded in: 1947

20366 Photo Lab Management
PLM Publishing
1312 Lincoln Boulevard
Santa Monica, CA 90401-1706

310-451-1344; *Fax:* 310-395-9058;
www.plmpublishing.co.uk/home.htm

Claire F Irwin, Editor
Paula L McCulloch, Publishing Director
John DH Colley, Marketing Manager

Specifically for those who work in the photo lab business. Contains articles on personnel and technical information.
Cost: $15.00
52 Pages
Frequency: Monthly
Founded in: 1979

20367 Photo Marketing
Photo Marketing Association International
2282 Springport Road
Suite F
Jackson, MI 49202

517-788-8100
800-762-9287; *Fax:* 517-788-8371;
www.theimagingalliance.com
Social Media: Facebook, Twitter, LinkedIn

Ted Fox, CEO
Allen Showalter, President
Mark Klostermeyer, Vice-President
Robert L Hanson, Treasurer

Directed to the marketing and advertising professionals, offers information on marketing photography nationally and internationally.
Cost: $50.00
80 Pages
Frequency: Monthly
Circulation: 12141
Founded in: 1924

20368 Photo Metro
1590 Golden Gate Avenue
San Francisco, CA 94115

415-243-9917; *Fax:* 415-243-9919;
www.photometro.com

Henry Brimmer, Publisher

Image-oriented magazine dedicated to photography, features portfolios, interviews and book reviews. Accepts advertising.
Cost: $20.00
32 Pages
Frequency: Monthly
Founded in: 1982

20369 Photo Stock News
1910 35th Road
Pine Lake Farm
Osceola, WI 54020

715-248-3800; *Fax:* 715-248-7394
info@photosource.com; www.photosource.com
Social Media: Facebook, Twitter

Ron Engh, Editor
Angela Dober, Managing Editor

Contains information of interest to freelance stock photographers, includes the latest industry trends and strategies. Regular issue features include Electronic Highway.
Frequency: 12 per year

20370 PhotoStockNotes
PhotoSource International
1910 35th Ave
Osceola, WI 54020-5602

715-248-3800
800-624-0266; *Fax:* 715-248-7394
info@photosource.com; www.photosource.com

Rohn Engh, Owner
Angela Dober, Managing Editor

Trends in the editorial stock photo industry.
Cost: $36.00
3 Pages
Frequency: Monthly
Founded in: 1976

20371 Photography Quarterly
Center for Photography at Woodstock
59 Tinker St
Woodstock, NY 12498-1236

845-679-9957; *Fax:* 845-679-6337
info@cpw.org; www.cpw.org
Social Media: Facebook, Twitter

Ariel Shanberg, Executive Director
Akemi Hiatt, Program Associate
Lawrence Lewis, Operations Manager
Lindsay Stern, Education Coordinator

Founded in: 1977, tthe Center for Photography at Woodstock is a not-for-profit 501 (c)3 artist-centered organization dedicated to supporting artists working in photography and related media and engaging audiences through opportunities in which creation, discovery and education are made possible.
Cost: $25.00
Frequency: Quarterly
Circulation: 2500
ISSN: 0890-4639
Founded in: 1977
Printed in one color on glossy stock

20372 Photoletter
PhotoSource International
1910 35th Ave
Osceola, WI 54020-5602

715-248-3800
800-624-0266; *Fax:* 715-248-7394
info@photosource.com; www.photosource.com

Rohn Engh, Owner

A publication covering the world of photography.
Cost: $264.00
4 Pages
Frequency: Weekly

20373 Photopro Magazine
Patch Communications
5211 S Washington Avenue
Titusville, FL 32780-7315

321-268-5010; *Fax:* 321-267-1894

Christi Ashby, Publisher
Suzanne Odistro, Advertising Manager

A professional trade publication covering photography nationally and internationally.
Cost: $16.95
80 Pages
Frequency: Monthly
Founded in: 1990

20374 Picture Magazine
319 Lafayette Street
No 135
New York, NY 10012
212-352-2700; *Fax:* 212-352-2155
picmag@aol.com; www.picturemagazine.com

Brock Wylan, Pulisher
Katherine Nguyen, Associate Editor

Phot industry trade publication.

20375 Popular Photography
Hachette Filipacchi Magazines
1633 Broadway
43rd Floor
New York, NY 10019-6708

212-767-6000
800-876-6636; *Fax:* 212-767-5600
popphoto@neodata.com;
www.popularphotography.com

Alain Lemarchand, CEO
Tami Kelly, Founder
Nate Silver, Founder

A publication offering information and updates to the photography world.
Cost: $12.00
80 Pages
Frequency: Monthly
ISSN: 0032-4582

20376 Popular Photography & Imaging American PHOTO Magazine
Bonnier Corp
1633 Broadway
Suite 4200
New York, NY 10019-6708
212-767-6000; *Fax:* 212-767-5600;
www.popphoto.com
Social Media: Facebook, Twitter, RSS
Jeffrey Roberts, Publisher
Russell Brock, Associate Editor

Comprehensive coverage of the latest equipment, inspiring images by leading photographers, in-depth how-to articles and wuthoritative reports. Draws upon top professionals in the field to inform committed readers who are passionate about pictures.
Mailing list available for rent

20377 Professional Photographer
PPA Publications
229 Peachtree Street NE
International Tower, Suite 2200
Atlanta, GA 30303-1608

404-522-8600
800-786-6277; *Fax:* 404-614-6405
ppa@bframe.com; www.ppmag.com

Cameron Bishopp, Senior Manager Publications
Jeff Kent, Senior Editor
Dana Groves, Marketing Executive

Business magazine for professional photographers. Delivers valuable articles packed with money making ideas to improve photography techniques and business skills. Accepts advertising.
Cost: $27.00
80 Pages
Frequency: Monthly
Circulation: 30000
Founded in: 1910

20378 Rangefinder Magazine
Rangefinder Publishing
6255 W Sunset Blvd
Los Angeles, CA 90028
323-817-3500; *Fax:* 323-817-1994;
www.rangefindermag.com
Steve Sheanin, CEO
Bill Hurter, Editor
Includes product and new equipment reviews, lighting and technical pieces, how-to's, promotion and marketing stories, portraiture tips, accessories and system round-ups, computer technology, black-and-white shooting, lens reviews, processing techniques
Frequency: Monthly

20379 Select Magazine
Select Worldwide
18-20 Farringdon Lane
1st Floor Clerks Court
London UK EC1R 3AU
4.40207E+12; *Fax:* 4.40207E+12;
www.select-magazine.com
Social Media: Twitter, Blog
Joe Carbonara, Managing Editor
Select is used worldwide by creative decision makers in the advertising, graphic design, fashion and retail world.
Frequency: 2x/Year
Circulation: 7500

20380 Shutterbug
Shutterbug
261 Madison Avenue
6th Floor
New York, NY 10016
212-915-4157
800-829-3340
editorial@shutterbug.com;
www.shutterbug.com
Social Media: Facebook, Twitter, Instagram
Keith Pray, Publisher
Joanne George, Advertising Representative
Genny Breslin, National Account Manager
Offers articles, insights, news, and how-tos from professional photographers to amateur and novice photographers.
Cost: $17.95
Frequency: Monthly
Founded in: 1989

20381 Studio Photography
Cygnus Business Media
1233 Janesville Avenue
Fort Atkinson, WI 53538
631-963-6200
800-547-7377; www.imaginginfo.com/spd/
Social Media: RSS
Liz Vickers, Group Publisher
Alice B Miller, Editor
Jackie Dandoy, Circulation Manager
Ashley Birkholz, Classified Sales
Barry Ancona, List Rental Manager
Formerly Studio Photography & Design. Showcases the hottest portrait, wedding, commercial, digital, and travel photographers every month. It is also supported by a selection of supplementary guides, tech tips, tutorials, and product round-ups.
Frequency: Monthly
Circulation: 50000
Founded in: 1936

Trade Shows

20382 ASPRS Annual Conference
American Society for
Photogammetry/Remote Sensing
5410 Grosvenor Lane
Suite 210
Bethesda, MD 20814-2160
301-493-0290; *Fax:* 301-493-0208
asprs@asprs.org; www.asprs.org
Social Media: Facebook, Twitter
James Plasker, Executive Director
Kimberly A Tiley, Assistant Executive Director
Jesse Winch, Program Manager
Educational sessions and exhibits committed to advancing knowledge in the mapping sciences and promoting the responsible application of photogrammetry, remote sensing and related technologies.

20383 BIOCOMM
BioCommunications Association
220 Southwind Lane
Hillsborough, NC 27278-7907
919-245-0906; *Fax:* 919-245-0906
office@bca.org; www.bca.org
Social Media: Facebook, Twitter, LinkedIn
Nancy Hurtgen, Manager Central Office
Susanne Loomis, President
Joseph Kane, Vice-President
James Koepfler, Secretary-Treasurer
Includes a packed program of seminars, workshops, a juried media salon, and commercial exhibits to provide attendees with inspiration and the latest information on visual media in the life sciences.
Frequency: Annual

20384 PMA Annual Convention and Trade Show
3000 Picture Place
Jackson, MI 49201
517-885-5980; *Fax:* 517-788-8371;
www.theimagingalliance.com
Rod Folland, Trade Exhibit Sevices Executive
Mary Anne LaMarre, Operations Officer
Ted Fox, Executive Director
Formerly the Photo Marketing Association, PMA is a global forum for photo imaging industry education, networking and introductions of new products and technologies. Includes conferences and meetings of the Association of Professional Color Imagers, the Digital Imaging Marketing Association, the Photo Imaging Education Association, the Professional Picture Framers Association, the Professional Scrapbook Retailers Organization and the Professional School Photographers Association.
24M Attendees
Frequency: February/March

20385 Photohistory
Photographic Historical Society
PO Box 39563
Rochester, NY 14604-9563
585-461-4545
Triennial show and exhibits of cameras and photographic images.
Frequency: October, Rochester

20386 Photovision
Glahe International
PO Box 2460
Germantown, MD 20875-2460
301-515-0012; *Fax:* 301-515-0016
Exhibits of photography equipment, supplies and services.

20387 Professional Photographer American Expo
Professional Photographers of America
229 Peachtree Street NE
International Tower, Suite 2200
Atlanta, GA 30303-1608
404-522-8600; *Fax:* 404-614-6401
http://www.ppa.com
Dana Groves, Advertising Director
Devoted to new technologies in the photography field. 300 booths.
5M Attendees
Frequency: July

20388 SPE Regional & National Conference
Society for Photographic Education
2530 Superior Avenue
Suite 403
Cleveland, OH 44114
216-622-2733; *Fax:* 216-622-2712
membership@spenational.org;
www.spenational.org
Virginia Morrison, Executive Director
Nina Barcellona, Advertising & Publications
Meghan Borato, Registrar
Carla Pasquale, Office/Accounts Manager
1000 Attendees
Frequency: Annual

20389 SPIE Photonics West
1000 20th Street
PO Box 10
Bellingham, WA 38227-0010
360-676-3290
888-504-8171; *Fax:* 360-647-1445
help@spie.org; www.SPIE.org
Social Media: Facebook, Twitter, LinkedIn
Eugene G Arthurs, Executive Director
Conference proceedings, and SPIE digital library.
14000 Members
Founded in: 1955

20390 WPPI Conference & Expo
Wedding & Portrait Photographers International
85 Broad St.
11th Fl.
New York, NY 10004
646-846-4500; *Fax:* 310-846-4770;
www.wppionline.com/wppi-show.shtml
Industry event for wedding and portrait photographers and filmmakers.
13000 Attendees

Directories & Databases

20391 Complete Directory of Film & Photo Products
Sutton Family Communications & Publishing Company
920 State Route 54 East
Elmitch, KY 42343
270-276-9500
jlsutton@apex.net
Theresa Sutton, Publisher
Lee Sutton, Editor
Print-out from database of wholesalers, manufacturers, distributors, importers and close-out houses. Database is updated daily to guarantee the most current and up-to-date sources avail-

able.
Cost: $34.50
100 Pages

20392 Directory of Free Stock Photography
Infosource Publishing
10 E 39th Street
6th Floor
New York, NY 10016-0111
212-683-8905
Offers valuable information on federal, state and local governments which will provide photographs free of charge for commercial use.
Cost: $14.50
150 Pages
Frequency: Biennial

20393 Green Book: Directory of Natural History and General Stock Photography
AG Editions
41 Union Sq W
Suite 525
New York, NY 10003-3230
212-929-0959; *Fax:* 212-924-4796
info@agpix.com; www.ag-editions.com
Ann Guifoyle, Editor
Sharon Powers, Manager
Over 400 photographers and photo agencies that provide stock photography.
Cost: $28.00
368 Pages
Frequency: Biennial
Circulation: 6500
Founded in: 1986

20394 Guide to Photography Workshops
Shaw Guides
P.O. Box 231295
New York, NY 10023
212-799-6464; *Fax:* 212-724-9287
http://photoworkshops.shawguides.com
Workshops are profiled that are aimed at amateurs and professionals, including photo tours, studio intensives and specialized instruction.
Cost: $19.95
300 Pages
Frequency: Biennial

20395 Hemingway's Glamour Photographer's Resource Directory
Looking Glass Photography
5975 Keller Road
Saint Louis, MO 63128-3359
314-849-8952
Buyers of glamour photography, including film and video producers are profiled.
Cost: $40.00
200 Pages
Frequency: Biennial
Circulation: 1,000

20396 Industrial Photography: Gold Book Issue
PTN Publishing Company
445 Broadhollow Road
Melville, NY 11747-3669
516-465-7684
Steve Shaw, Editor
A list of manufacturers of photographic equipment and supplies, motion picture laboratories, videotape production facilities, equipment rental services, custom developing services and photographic repair services.
Cost: $5.75
Frequency: Annual December
Circulation: 40,000

20397 Orion Blue Book: Camera
Orion Research Corporation
14555 N Scottsdale Rd
Suite 330
Scottsdale, AZ 85254-3487
480-951-1114
800-844-0759; *Fax:* 480-951-1117;
www.bluebook.com
Roger Rohrs, Owner
List of manufacturers of cameras.
Frequency: Annual

20398 Photographer's Complete Guide to Exhibition & Sales Spaces
Consultant Press
13 Laight St
#201
New York, NY 10013-2119
212-431-3130
Bob Speirs, Owner
Directory of services and supplies to the industry.
Cost: $24.95
280 Pages

20399 Photographic Trade News: Master Buying Guide
Cygnus Business Media
445 Broad Hollow Road
Melville, NY 11747-3669
631-845-2700; *Fax:* 631-845-2723;
www.photolife.com
Offers a list of manufacturers and distributors of photographic equipment and photography associations.
Frequency: Annual

20400 Photography Forum
CompuServe Information Service
5000 Arlington Centre Blvd
Columbus, OH 43220-5439
614-326-1002
800-848-8199
Offers a forum for the discussion of photography on both the amateur and professional levels.
Frequency: Bulletin Board

20401 Photography RoundTable
GE Information Services
401 N Washington Street
Rockville, MD 20850-1707
301-388-8284
Cathy Ge, Owner
Provides a forum for the exchange of photography tips and information.
Frequency: Bulletin Board

20402 Who's Who in Photographic Management
Photo Marketing Association International
2282 Springport Road
Suite F
Jackson, MI 49202
517-788-8100
800-762-9287; *Fax:* 517-788-8371;
www.theimagingalliance.com
Social Media: Facebook, Twitter, LinkedIn
Ted Fox, CEO
Allen Showalter, President
Mark Klostermeyer, Vice-President
Robert L Hanson, Treasurer
Over 15,500 members of the association and manufacturers and suppliers of photographic equipment; also members of the National Association of Photo Equipment Technicians and of the Professional School Photographers of America.
Cost: $75.00
Frequency: Annual

Industry Web Sites

20403 http://gold.greyhouse.com
G.O.L.D Grey House OnLine Databases
Grey House Publishing's online database platform, GOLD, offers Quick Search, Keyword Search and Expert Search for most business sectors including photography markets. The GOLD platform makes finding the information you need quick and easy - whether you're a novice searcher or an experienced database user. All of Grey House's directory products are available for subscription on the GOLD platform.

20404 www.aspp.com
American Society of Picture Professionals
Members are image producers, stock photo agencies, and image users.Provides networking and educational opportunities in the image transaction industry.

20405 www.bca.org
BioCommunications Association
Made up of professionals who create and use the highest quality images and presentations in visual communications media for teaching and documentation in the life sciences and medicine.

20406 www.cpw.org
Center for Photography at Woodstock
Founded in: 1977, the Center for Photography at Woodstock is a not-for-profit 501(c)3 artist-centered organization dedicated to supporting artists working in photography and related media and engaging audiences through opportunities in which creation, discovery and education are made possible.

20407 www.editorialphoto.com
Editorial Photographers
Internet discussion forum on business issues with more than 3000 subscribers participating from over 30 countries around the globe. Via the forum photographers exchange information on business practices, copyright and contract concerns. Useful resources such as sample business forms, publisher contract reviews and more can be found here.

20408 www.greyhouse.com
Grey House Publishing
Authoritative reference directories for most business sectors including photography markets. Users can search the online databases with varied search criteria allowing for custom searches by product category, geographic area, sales volume, keyword, subject and more. Full Grey House catalog and online ordering also available.

20409 www.nppa.org
National Press Photographers Association
Sponsors numerous annual television and print media workshops. Conducts annual competition for newsphotos and television newsfilm. Monthly magazine job information bank given to all members.

20410 www.ppa.com
Professional Photographers of America
Portrait, commercial, wedding, industrial and specialized photo- graphers and photographic artists.

20411 www.stockindustry.org
Picture Agency Council of America
The trade association for stock picture agencies in North America.

Associations

20412 ASM International
9639 Kinsman Rd
Materials Park, OH 44073-0002

440-338-5151
800-336-5152; *Fax:* 440-338-4634
memberservices@asminternational.org;
www.asminternational.org
Social Media: Facebook, Twitter, LinkedIn

Nichol Campana, Director of Devlpt & Operations
Jeane Deatherage, Administrator
Mary A. Jerson, Administrative Assistant
Virginia Shirk, Foundation Ex Assistant
Terry F. Mosier, Managing Director

The society for materials engineers and scientists, a worldwide network dedicated to advancing industry, technology and applications of metals and materials.
35000 Members
Founded in: 1913

20413 American Chemistry Council
American Chemistry Council
700 Second St.,NE
Washington, DC 20002

202-249-7000; *Fax:* 202-249-6100
api@plastics.org; www.polyurethane.org
Social Media: Facebook, Twitter, LinkedIn, RSS

Anne Womack Koltan, VP of Communications
Nacole B. Hinton, Managing Dir. Of Human Resources
Calvin M. Dooley, President and CEO
Dell Perelman, Chief of staff and General Counsel
Raymond O'Bryan, CFO & Chief Administration Officer

API is composed of companies that supply polyurethane resins or chemicals used in polyurethane resins, manufacture polyurethanes, produce machinery used in the manufacture or processing polyurethane, or engage in the business of applying polyurethane products in end use applications. API consists of several groups that focus on critical industry issues such as product stewardship, recycling, communications.
80 Members
Founded in: 1977

20414 American Composites Manufacturers Association
3033 Wilson Blvd
Suite 420
Arlington, VA 22201

703-525-0511; *Fax:* 703-525-0743
info@acmanet.org; www.acmanet.org
Social Media: Facebook, Twitter, LinkedIn, RSS

Tom Dobbins, President
Jeff Craney, Chairman
Kevin Barnett, Chairman-Elect/ Treasurer
Kimberly Howard, Secretary
Leon Garoufalis, Vice Chairman

Presents information on new technology, trends and techniques for manufacturers in the fiberglass and composites industry.
600 Members
Founded in: 1979

20415 American Electroplaters and Surface Finishers Society (AESF)
1155 15th Street NW
Suite 500
Washington, DC 20005

202-457-8404; *Fax:* 202-530-0659
info@aesf.org; www.aesf.org
Social Media: Facebook, Twitter, LinkedIn, RSS, Google+

John Flatley, Executive Director
Courtney Mariette, Bookstore/Education
Melissa Walker, Membership
Carrie Hoffman, Deputy Executive Director

AESF is an international society that advances the science of surface finishing to benefit industry and society through education, information and social involvement, as well as those who provide services, supplies and support to the industry.
5000 Members
Founded in: 1909

20416 American Plastics Council
American Chemistry Council
700 Second St.,NE
Washington, DC 20002

202-249-7000
800-243-5790; *Fax:* 202-249-6100;
www.plastics.org
Social Media: Facebook, Twitter, LinkedIn, RSS

Calvin M Dooley, President
Anne Womack Koltan, VP of Communications
Nacole B. Hinton, Managing Dir. Of Human Resources
Dell Perelman, Chief of staff and General Counsel
Raymond O'Bryan, CFO & Chief Administration Officer

Major trade association for the US plastics industry. We demonstrate that plastics are a responsible choice and promote the countless ways that plastics make lives better, healthier and safer.
24 Members

20417 American Society for Plasticulture
526 Brittany Drive
State College, PA 16803

814-238-7045; *Fax:* 814-238-7051;
www.plasticulture.org

Henry Taber, President
William Tietjen, Chairman
Patricia Heuser, Executive Director
Jodi Fleck-Arnold, VP

Promotes research, education and technology application for plastics used in agricultural and horticultural production systems. Hosts a congress every year or so; published proceedings of research presentations.
100 Members
Founded in: 1962

20418 Association of Industrial Metallizers, Coaters and Laminators
201 Springs Street
Fort Mill, SC 29715

803-948-9470; *Fax:* 803-948-9471
aimcal@aimcal.org; www.aimcal.org

Dan Bemi, President
Danis Roy, Vice President
David Bryant, Treasurer
Craig Sheppard, Executive Director
Dante Ferrari, Directors at Large

Nonprofit trade organization for makers of coated, laminated and metalized papers. AIMCAL serves as the global forum for the flexible metallizing, coating and laminating industry by providing resources, services and information. AIMCAL collects and distributes information to increase industry knowledge, while fostering an environment that builds relationships and a spirit of cooperation between member companies worldwide.
260 Members
Founded in: 1970

20419 Association of Postconsumer Plastic Recyclers
1001 G Street, NW
Suite 500 West
Washington, DC 20001

202-316-3046; www.plasticsrecycling.org
Social Media: Facebook, Twitter, LinkedIn

Steve Alexander, Executive Director
Josh Standish, Technical Director
Dave Cornell, Technical Consultant
Kara Pochiro, Communications Director
Liz Bedard, Rigids Program Director

Represents companies that acquire, reprocess and sell the output of more than 90 percent of the post-consumer plastic processing capacity in North America.
Founded in: 1992

20420 Association of Rotational Molders International
800 Roosevelt Rd
Suite C-312
Glen Ellyn, IL 60137

630-942-6589; *Fax:* 630-790-3095
info@rotomolding.org; www.rotomolding.org
Social Media: Facebook, LinkedIn

Adam Webb, Managing Director
Corey Claussen, President
Dru Laws, Treasurer/Secretary
Conchita Miranda, Vice President
Rick Church, Executive Dircetor

Seeks to increase awareness of roto-molding, exchange technical information, provide education, and standardize production guidelines.
425 Members
Founded in: 1976

20421 Berkshire Plastics Network
Downtown Pittsfield Office
66 Allen Street
Pittsfield, MA 01201

413-499-4000
800-438-9572; *Fax:* 413-447-9641
info@berkshirechamber.com;
www.berkshirechamber.com
Social Media: Facebook, Twitter, LinkedIn, YouTube

Linda Gaspardi Febles, Chair
Jonathan Butler, President & CEO
June Roy-Martin, VP Member Services
Lori Gazzillo, Chair-Elect
Chip Moore, Treasurer

A consortium of more than 40 independent companies, representing virtually every discipline in the design and production of molds, components and plastic products.

20422 International Association of Plastics Distribution
6734 W 121st St
Overland Park, KS 66209

913-345-1005; *Fax:* 913-345-1006
iapd@iapd.org; www.iapd.org
Social Media: Facebook, Twitter, LinkedIn, YouTube, Flickr

Susan E. Avery, Chief Executive Officer
Kevin Short, President
Mitch Opalich, Vice-President
Wayne Gono, Executive Committee Member
Tyler Booth, Member

The International Association of Plastics Distribution, founded in 1956, is an international trade association comprised of companies engaged in the distribution and manufacture of plastics materials. Represented are materials in semi-finished stock shapes, such as sheet, rod, tube, pipe, valves, fittings, film and related products. Members' materials are produced and distributed for a

wide variety of engineering and high performance applications.
Founded in: 1956

20423 **International Molded Fiber Association**
355 Lexington Avenue, Floor 15
New York, NY 10017

262-241-0522; *Fax:* 262-241-3766
Alan@IMFA.org; www.imfa.org
Social Media: Facebook, Twitter, LinkedIn

Cassandra Niesing, Asst. Director
Joseph Grygny, Chairman/ Founder
Hubert Ranger, Founder

Acts as an information center for the molded fiber industry with worldwide membership of users and manufacturers of molded fiber producs. Promotes use of natural and recycled fibers.
Founded in: 1997

20424 **National Association for PET Container Resources**
7310 Turfway Road
Suite 550
Florence, KY 41042

859-372-6635; *Fax:* 707-935-1998
n4mayshun@napcor.com; www.napcor.com
Social Media: Facebook

Rick Moore, Executive Director
Resa Dimino, Director of Public Policy
Kate Eagles, Project Director

National association for the PET plastic industry. Promotes the use of PET plastic packaging and facilitates the recycling of PET containers.
13 Members
Frequency: Bi-Monthly
Founded in: 1987

20425 **National Certification In Plastics (NCP)**
Society of the Plastics Industry
1667 K St NW
Suite 1000
Washington, DC 20006-1620

202-496-4400
888-627-3660; *Fax:* 202-496-4444
ncp@socplas.org; www.eric.gov

Barbara Darby, Manager Plastics Learning Network
Barry Eisenberg, Director Communications/Marketing

The National Certification in Plastics (NCP) program is a national, voluntary certification examination that tests plastics operations employees' skills and knowledge. The National Certification in Plastics exam tests the knowledge and skill level of plastics operations employees in one of the four major plastics processes - injection molding, extrusion, thermoforming or blow molding.The NCP program is sponsored by the Society of the Plastics Industry.

20426 **Plastic Pipe and Fittings Association**
800 Roosevelt Rd
Building C, Suite 312
Glen Ellyn, IL 60137

630-858-6540; *Fax:* 630-790-3095;
www.ppfahome.org
Social Media: Facebook, RSS

Richard W Church, Executive Director

The Plastic Pipe and Fittings Association (PPFA) is a national trade association comprised of member companies that manufacture plastic piping, fittings and solvent cements for plumbing and related applications, or supply raw materials, ingredients or machinery for the manufacturing process.
Founded in: 1978

20427 **Plastic Shipping Container Institute**
5614 Connecticut Avenue, N.W
#284
Washington, DC 20015

202-253-4347; *Fax:* 202-330-5092;
www.pscionline.org

David H Baker, General Counsel

The Plastic Shipping Container Institute (PSCI) is an international organization of producers of plastic pails (rigid, plastic shipping containers). The Institute's mission is to promote the common interests of, and the general well being of, the plastic shipping container industry, including consideration of local, state and federal regulatory and legislative issues and international trade issues impacting customers, suppliers and consumers.
Founded in: 1967

20428 **Plastics Institute of America**
University of Massachusetts Lowell, Plastics Engin
Ball Hall Room 204
One University Avenue
Lowell, MA 01854

978-934-2575; *Fax:* 978-934-3089
contactus@plasticsinstitute.org;
www.plasticsinstitute.org

Aldo Crugnola, Executive Director
Angelo Sabatalo, Chair Elect
Dan Mielcarek, Chair
Nick R. Schott, Secretary/ Director of Training
Marlene Gosling, Treasurer

The Plastics Institute of America is a not-for-profit educational and research organization dedicated to providing service to the plastics industries. We support, foster and guide plastics education and research at all levels to ensure the continued growth of the industry. Since our founding the Institute has held to this mission with ongoing educational programs and resources for skilled workers, professionals and industry executives.
Founded in: 1961

20429 **Plastics Learning Network**
Society of the Plastics Industry
7 North Laurens Street
Greenville, SC 29601

864-239-2939; *Fax:* 864-239-0549;
www.plasticsnews.com

Barbara Darby, Manager Plastics Learning Network
Barry Eisenberg, Director Communications/Marketing

Training opportunities are available for plastics employers and employees through the Plastics Learning Network (PLN) which is sponsored by the Society of the Plastics Industry's (SPI). Courses from qualified instructors are presented as on-site courses tailored to individual work schedules. Courses currently available are Operator Training in Injection Molding and Extrusion. Financial aid is available.
Founded in: 2001

20430 **Plastics Pipe Institute**
105 Decker Court
Suite 825
Irving, TX 75062

469-499-1044; *Fax:* 469-499-1063
info@plasticpipe.org; www.plasticpipe.org
Social Media: Facebook, LinkedIn, YouTube

Tony Radoszewski, President
Lance MacNevin, Director of Engineering
Sarah Patterson, Technical Director
Dana gecker, Marketing Communications Manager
Vicki Hackett, Office Manager/Executive Assistant

The major trade association representing all segments of the plastics piping industry. As an association, PPI focuses collaborative efforts to accumulate data, concentrate facts and target resources toward advancements in applications and increases in widespread usage.
300 Members
Founded in: 1950

20431 **Plastics USA**
1667 K St.NW.
Suite 1000
Washington, DC 20006

202-974-5200; *Fax:* 202-296-7005
tradeshows@socplas.org; www.socplas.org
Social Media: Facebook, Twitter, LinkedIn

Adam Krumhans, Trade Show Coordinator
Donald Duncan, President

Plastics USA, sponsored by The Society of the Plastics Industry/SPI, is held once every three years. The three-day trade show and educational program, which is sponsored by the Society of Plastics Engineers, has proven to be an ideal business forum for the North American plastics industry. Last held in Chicago in 2001, Plastics USA attracted over 15,000 attendees and the show featured 435 exhibiting companies occupying 95,000 square feet of exhibit space.
12M Members

20432 **Polymer Processing Institute**
New Jersey Institute Of Technology University Heig
Guttenberg Information Technologies Center
Suite 3901
Newark, NJ 07102-1982

973-596-5256; *Fax:* 973-642-4594;
www.polymers-ppi.com

Ming-Wan Young, Ph.D, President
Costas G. Gogos, Ph.D, Senior Advisor/President Emeritus
Mariann Pappagallo, Administrative Consultant
Niloufar Faridi, Ph.D, Senior Technical Consultant
Linjie Zhu, Ph.D., Technical Director

The Polymer Processing Institute is an independent research corporation headquartered at New Jersey Institute of Technology, Newark, New Jersey. Its mission is to assist industry by implementing the advanced knowledge in the field of polymer technology and related areas through sponsored research, development and education, and to disseminate information via technology transfer.
Founded in: 1999

20433 **Polystyrene Packaging Council (PSPC)**
American Chemistry Council
700 Second St.,NE
Washington, DC 20002

202-249-7000; *Fax:* 202-249-6100;
www.polystyrenerecyclingnetwork.com
Social Media: Facebook, Twitter, RSS

Michael H. Levy, Senior Director
Annie F. Walton, Administrative Assistant
Calvin M. Dooley, President and CEO
Dell Perelman, Chief of staff and General Counsel

PSPC, a business unit of the American Plastics Council, is a nonprofit trade association dedicated to providing accurate information on the environmental impact of polystyrene packaging, including polystyrene recycling programs. PSPC's membership includes manufacturers of polystyrene resin, polystyrene foam and rigid food service packaging.

20434 SPI
1667 K St NW
Suite 1000
Washington, DC 20006
202-974-5200
888-627-3660; *Fax:* 202-296-7005;
www.plasticbag.com
Social Media: Facebook, Twitter, LinkedIn

Donna Dempsey, Executive Director
Betsy Coleman, Assistant Director
Yvonne Wade, Assistant Manager
Jack Riopelle, Chairman
John Wilhite, Vice Chairman

Members are US and Canadian manufacturers of plastic retail bags. A business unite of the Society of the Plastics Industry, Inc. that actively promotes the growth of the plastic film and bag industry. FBF membership includes companies that are in the plastic bag segment of the industry as well as those in the film sector.
50 Members
Founded in: 1937

20435 Society of Plastics Engineers
6 Berskshire Blvd
Suite 306
Bethel, CT 6801

203-775-0471; *Fax:* 203-775-8490
info@4spe.org; www.4spe.org
Social Media: Facebook, Twitter, LinkedIn, RSS

Susan Oderwald, Executive Director
Dick Cameron, President
Dr. Jaime A. Gomez, Vice President/Treasurer
Monica Verheij, Vice President/Secretary
William De Vos, Chief Executive Officer

The premier source of peer-reviewed technical information for plastics professionals. SPE takes action every day to help individuals and companies in the plastics industry succeed by spreading knowledge, strengthening skills, and promoting plastics.
15000 Members
Founded in: 1942

20436 Society of the Plastics Industry
1425 K Street NW
Suite 500
Washington, DC 20005

202-974-5200; *Fax:* 202-296-7005
feedback@plasticindustry.org;
www.plasticsindustry.org
Social Media: Facebook, Twitter, LinkedIn, YouTube

William Cartuaex, President
Fred Daniell, Chair
James Murphy, Vice Chair
Wylie Royce, Treasurer
Tad McGwire, Secretary

Trade association representing one of the largest manufacturing industries in the US. Members represent the entire plastics industry supply chain, including processors, machinery and equipment manufacturers and raw material suppliers. The US plastics industry employs 1.5 million workers and provides $304 billon in annual shipment.
1100 Members
Founded in: 1937

20437 Thermoforming Institute
1667 K St NW
Suite 240
Washington, DC 20006-1620

202-974-5200; *Fax:* 202-296-7005;
www.thermoforminginstitute.org
Social Media: Facebook, Twitter, LinkedIn

William Cartuaex, President
Gene Janders, VP Trade Shows

A business unit of the Society of the Plastics Industry, Incorporated,the Thermoforming Institute is comprised of principal officers of companies or divisions significantly engaged in the manufacture of custom thermoformed products.
1200 Members
Founded in: 1937

Newsletters

20438 ACM Monthly
Composite Market Reports
PO Box 137
Gilbert, AZ 85299-0137

480-507-6882; *Fax:* 480-507-6986
info@compositemarketreports.com;
www.compositemarketreports.com/

John R. White, Executive Director/CEO
Patricia Ryan, Operations/COO
Russell Harris, Director Financial Services
Wayne Graves, Director Information Systems
Brian Hebert, Marketing/Communications Manager

Reports on market and technology intelligence for materials suppliers.

20439 Additives for Polymers
Reed Elsevier Science Direct
9555 Springboro Pike
Miamisburg, OH 45342

937-865-6800; *Fax:* 937-865-1349
s.barrett@elsevier.com; www.elsevier.com

Guy Kitteringhem, Publisher
A Weawer, Editor
S. Barrett, Program Editor
Marike Westra, Director Corporate Relations
Ylann Schemm, Communications Executive

Each issue identifies and details relevant materials and products, new applications, new research and technical developments, newly issued US and British patents.
Frequency: Monthly
Founded in: 1887
Printed in on matte stock

20440 Advanced Materials & Composites News
Composites Worldwide
991 C Lomas Santa Fe Drive
PMB469
Solana Beach, CA 92075-2141

858-755-1372; *Fax:* 858-755-5271
compositesnews@adelphia.net;
www.compositesnews.com

Steve Loud, Editor
Susan Loud, Managing Editor

Focuses on the processes, applications markets, design, international activities and more related to composites and other advanced materials, particularly for civil engineering and construction, but for all markets and structural applications, including aerospace, transportation, and industrial.
Cost: $598.00
Circulation: 1000

20441 Composite Industry Monthly
Composite Market Reports
PO Box 137
Gilbert, AZ 85299

480-507-6882; *Fax:* 480-507-6986
info@compositemarketreports.com;
www.compositemarketreports.com

William Benjamin, Publisher
John R. White, Executive Director/CEO
Patricia Ryan, Operations/COO
Wayne Graves, Director Information Systems
Russell Harris, Director Financial Services

Market and technology intelligence for users, prime and sub-contractors, universities, government and others.
Cost: $1495.00
Frequency: Monthly
Circulation: 8177
Founded in: 1971

20442 Modern Plastics Worldwide
Canon Communications
11444 W Olympic Blvd
Suite 900
Los Angeles, CA 90064-1555

310-445-4200; *Fax:* 310-445-4299
info@modplas.com; www.modplas.com/

Charlie Mc Curdy, President
Kevin O'Grady, Publisher

Industry trends and developments. Accepts advertising.
Cost: $150.00
125 Pages
Frequency: Monthly

20443 POF Newsletter
Information Gatekeepers
PO Box 35880
Brighton, MA 02135-1000
617-782-5033
800-323-1088; *Fax:* 617-782-5735
info@igigroup.com; www.igigroup.com

Paul Polishuk, CEO
Bev Wilson, Managing Editor
Will Ashley, IT Director/Media Manager

Covers recent developments in the plastic optical fiber industry. Also provides updates on components, systems, applications, standards and a calendar of related events.
Cost: $395.00
Founded in: 1977

20444 Plastic Focus
Plastics Connection
PO Box 814
Amherst, MA 01004-0814

413-549-5020; *Fax:* 413-549-9955;
www.trplastics.com

Michael L Berins, Publisher
Armando Honegger, CEO

Newsletter for buyers, sellers, and users of plastic.
Cost: $275.00
Frequency: Bi-Weekly

20445 Plastics Brief Newsletter
Plastic Marketing News Brief Market Search
2727 North Holland Sylvania Road
Suite A
Toledo, OH 43615-1800

419-535-7899; *Fax:* 419-535-1243;
www.sagepub.com

James Best, Publisher

For plastic sales and marketing executives. Covers new materials, new applications, market trends, price changes.
Cost: $249.00
Frequency: Monthly

20446 Plastics Machinery & Auxiliaries
Canon Communications
Ste 370
3300 E 1st Ave
Denver, CO 80206-5806

303-321-2322; *Fax:* 303-321-3552;
www.pma-magazine.com/

Merle R. Snyder, Editor
Jamie Quanbeck, Online Editor
Heidi Hill, Managing Editor
Kate Hunley, Associate Editor

Plastics Machinery & Auxiliaries provides readers with a forum for learning about new products and services used in a wide range of plastics processes. Plastics Machinery & Auxiliaries is distributed free of charge to qualified professionals in the plastics processing industry, in the USA and Canada.

20447 Plastics News
Crain Communications
1725 Merriman Rd
Suite 300
Akron, OH 44313-5283

330-836-9180; *Fax:* 330-836-2831
info@crain.com; www.crain.com

Robert S Simmons, VP
Linda Whelan, Marketing Manager

Delivers breaking news, features, detailed rankings, economic data and materials pricing to readers around the world.
Frequency: Weekly
Circulation: 60054
Founded in: 1989

20448 Plastics Recycling Update
PO Box 42270
Portland, OR 97242-0270

503-233-1305; *Fax:* 503-233-1356
info@resource-recycling.com;
www.resource-recycling.com/rr.html
Social Media: Facebook, Twitter, RSS

Jerry Powell, Editor/Publisher
Rick Downing, Advertising Director
Dylan de Thomas, Managing Editor
Mary Lynch, Assistant Publisher
Chad Powell, Director of Research

Resource Recycling is the journal of recycling and composting professionals. Each month, the latest information is provided about post-consumer waste recovery efforts including: collection system assessments; processing developments; markets analyses, and legislative and regulatory reviews. Additional features includes special commodity and regular departments on equipment, recycling and composting programs, association and state activities.
Cost: $58.00
Frequency: Monthly
ISSN: 0147-2429
Founded in: 1981
Printed in 2 colors

20449 Plastics Week
Market Search
Laguna Beach, CA

949-212-7400; www.plasticsweek.com

James R Best, Publisher
Linda Best, Production Manager
Jim Best, Editor
Jim Best, CEO

Weekly newletters on plastics. Focusing on strategies, markets, technology, recycling and environmental issues.
Cost: $480.00
6 Pages
Founded in: 1961

20450 Polymer Blends, Alloys, and Interpenetrating Polymer Networks
Sage Publications
2455 Teller Rd
Newbury Park, CA 91320-2234

805-499-9774
800-818-7243; *Fax:* 805-499-0871
info@sagepub.com; www.sagepub.com

Blaise R Simqu, CEO
David P McCune, Director

Survey and summary of the growing literature and patents in the promising area of plastics technology. Each issue provides new information on chemistry, properties and performance, testing, processing, and application.
Cost: $ 455.00
40 Pages
Frequency: Monthly
ISSN: 0893-6684
Printed in 2 colors on matte stock

20451 Rubber and Plastics News
Crain Communications
1725 Merriman Rd
Suite 300
Akron, OH 44313-5283
330-836-9180; *Fax:* 330-836-2831
info@crain.com; www.crain.com

Robert S Simmons, VP

It provides news, features, technical and marketing information in print and daily on the Internet to rubber manufacturers, suppliers, consultants and laboratories worldwide.
Frequency: Bi-Weekly
Circulation: 16387

Magazines & Journals

20452 Advanced Composites Monthly
Composite Market Reports
PO Box 137
Gilbert, AZ 85299-0137

480-507-6882; *Fax:* 480-507-6986
info@compositemarketreports.com;
www.compositemarketreports.com

William Benjamin, President/Editor
Chris Red, Market Research
Cher Benjamin, VP
Joe Benjamin, Office Manager

Provides information to personnel at all levels in the advanced composite manufacturing industry.
10 Pages
Frequency: Monthly
Founded in: 1975

20453 Advanced Materials & Processes
ASM International
9639 Kinsman Rd
Materials Park, OH 44073

440-338-5151
800-336-5152; *Fax:* 440-338-4634
memberservices@asminternational.org;
www.asminternational.org

Joseph M Zion, Publisher
Thomas S. Passek, Managing Editor
Margaret Hunt, Editor-in-Chief

AM&P, the monthly technical magazine from ASM International, is designed to keep readers aware of leading-edge developments and trends in engineering materials - metals and alloys, engineering polymers, advanced ceramics, and composites - and the methods used to select, process, fabricate, test, and characterize them.
Frequency: Monthly
Circulation: 32M
Founded in: 1977

20454 Digest of Polymer Developments
STR-Specialized Technology Resources
10 Springborn Ctr
Enfield, CT 06082-4814

860-749-8371; *Fax:* 860-749-8234;
www.strlab.com

Dennis Jilot, CEO

Covers domestic and international information on new plastics applications, potential growth and market performance, as well as current events in the plastics and allied chemicals industries. Contains a cumulative index by market and another by plastics materials for quick reference.
Cost: $625.00

20455 GraFiber News
Composite Market Reports
PO Box 137
Gilbert, AZ 85299-0137

480-507-6882; *Fax:* 602-507-6986;
www.compositemarketreports.com

William Benjamin, President/Publisher/Editor/CEO
Cher Benjamin, VP
Chris Red, Market Research
Joe Benjamin, Office Manager

Provides global coverage of the aerospace industry for advanced material suppliers.
Cost: $2556.25
10 Pages
Frequency: Monthly
ISSN: 1058-9023
Founded in: 1973
Printed in 4 colors on matte stock

20456 IAPD Magazine
International Association of Plastics Distribution
6734 W 121st St
Leawood, KS 66209-2002

913-345-1007; *Fax:* 913-345-1006
iapd@iapd.org; www.iapd.org

Deborah Hamlin, Manager
Patrick M Foose, Board President
Howard J Natal, VP Board of Directors

Published by the International Association of Plastics Distributors/IAPD, the magazine provides information on the plastics industry with special emphasis on profitability and advances in technology. IAPD fosters the development of the plastics industry through the collection, production and dissemination of quality information and education, and by being a catalyst in assuring proactive representation in the governmental and public arenas.
Cost: $90.00
68 Pages
Frequency: Monthly
Circulation: 10000
Founded in: 1956
Printed in 4 colors on glossy stock

20457 Injection Molding Magazine
Canon Communications
11444 W Olympic Blvd
Ste.900
Los Angeles, CA 90064

310-445-4200; www.immnet.com
Social Media: Facebook, Twitter, LinkedIn

Paul Miller, President/CEO
Stephen Corrick, Publisher/VP/Sales & Marketing
Jeff Tade, Publications Production Manager
Willy Bruijns-Miller, VP Circulation

Custom and captive molding operations, product design, moldmaking, processing information, new materials and equipment, and management issues are the editorial focus.
Cost: $168.57
Frequency: Monthly
Circulation: 37500
Founded in: 1999

20458 Journal of Cellular Plastics
Sage Publications
2455 Teller Rd
Newbury Park, CA 91320-2234

805-499-9774
800-818-7243; *Fax:* 805-499-0871
journals@sagepub.com; www.sagepub.com

Blaise R Simqu, CEO

A permanent record for international achievements in the science, technology, and economics of cellular plastics. It has been a major source of information on this topic for 35 years. Each issue presents outstanding technical advances in

chemistry, formulation, processing, testing, properties, performance, and applications.
Cost: $901.00
96 Pages
Frequency: Bi-Monthly
ISSN: 0021-955X
Printed in 2 colors on matte stock

20459 Journal of Composite Materials
Sage Publications
2455 Teller Rd
Newbury Park, CA 91320-2234

805-499-9774
800-818-7243; *Fax:* 805-499-0871
journals@sagepub.com; www.sagepub.com

Blaise R Simqu, CEO
Thomas Hahn, Editor

The leading medium for composite materials technology transfer. Featuring original studies from international material scientists, the journal seeks to emphasize practical applications with no compromise in technical integrity.
Cost: $4576.00
96 Pages
Frequency: Bi-Monthly
ISSN: 0021-9983
Founded in: 1965
Printed in 2 colors on matte stock

20460 Journal of Elastomers and Plastics
Sage Publications
2455 Teller Rd
Newbury Park, CA 91320-2234
805-499-9774
800-818-7243; *Fax:* 805-499-0871
journals@sagepub.com; www.sagepub.com

Blaise R Simqu, CEO
S. Qutubuddin, Editorial Board

The latest contributions to the technology and properties of elastomers and related polymeric products. Major emphasis is placed on specialty and high performance elastomers. The journal regularly presents current information on the chemistry, processing, properties, and applications of recently developed and improved elastomeric materials.
Cost: $867.00
96 Pages
Frequency: Quarterly
ISSN: 0095-2443
Printed in 2 colors on matte stock

20461 Journal of Materials Engineering and Performance
American Society for Metals
9639 Kinsman Road
Materials Park, OH 44073-0002

440-338-5151
800-336-5152; *Fax:* 440-338-4634
memberservices@asminternational.org;
www.asminternational.org

Gernant E. Maurer, President
Thomas S. Passek, Managing Director

Peer-reviewed journal that publishes contributions on all aspects of materials selection, design, characterization, processing and performance testing. The scope includes all materials used in engineering applications, those that typically result in components for larger systems.
Cost: $1397.00
Frequency: Bimonthly
Circulation: 645

20462 Journal of Materials Processing
Elsevier ScienceDirect
360 Park Ave S
New York, NY 10010-1736

212-989-5800
888-437-4636; *Fax:* 212-633-3990
journals@sagepub.com; www.elsevier.com

Erik Engstrom, CEO
J. Gunasekera, Regional Editor North America

Original papers developments in traditional and innovative processing technologies for metals, polymers, composites, ceramics, and specialty materials. The scope is international and interdisciplinary.
Cost: $5208.00
96 Pages
Frequency: 42 Issues Per Year
ISSN: 0924-0136
Printed in 2 colors on matte stock

20463 Journal of Phase Equilibria
ASM International
9639 Kinsman Rd
Materials Park, OH 44073-0002

440-338-5151
800-336-5152; *Fax:* 440-338-4634
memberservices@asminternational.org;
www.asminternational.org

Gernant E. Maurer, President
Thomas S. Passek, Managing Director

Peer-reviewed journal that contains basic and applied research results, evaluated phase diagrams, a survey of current literature, and comments or other material pertinent to the previous three areas. The aim is to provide a broad spectrum of information concerning phase equilibria for the materials community.
Cost: $1965.00
Frequency: Bimonthly
Circulation: 305
Mailing list available for rent

20464 Journal of Plastic Film & Sheeting
Sage Publications
2455 Teller Rd
Newbury Park, CA 91320-2234

805-499-9774
800-818-7243; *Fax:* 805-499-0871
journals@sagepub.com; www.sagepub.com

Blaise R Simqu, CEO

The Journal of Plastic Film and Sheeting improves communication concerning plastic film and sheeting with major emphasis on the propagation of knowledge which will serve to advance the science and technology of these products and thus better serve industry and the ultimate consumer. The journal reports on the wide variety of advances that are rapidly taking place in the technology of plastic film and sheeting.
Cost: $795.00
88 Pages
Frequency: Quarterly
ISSN: 8756-0879
Printed in 2 colors on matte stock

20465 Journal of Polymer Science
John Wiley & Sons
111 River St
Hoboken, NJ 07030-5790

201-748-6000; *Fax:* 201-748-6088
info@wiley.com; www.wiley.com

William J Pesce, CEO

The Journal of Polymer Science provides a continuous forum for the dissemination of thoroughly peer-reviewed, fundamental, international research into the preparation and properties of macromolecules. Part A: Polymer Chemistry is devoted to studies in fundamental organic polymer chemistry and physical organic chemistry. Polymer Physics (Part B) details contemporary research on all aspects of polymer physics.
200 Pages
Frequency: 48 Issues Per Year
ISSN: 0887-624X

20466 Journal of Reinforced Plastics and Composites
Sage Publications
2455 Teller Rd
Newbury Park, CA 91320-2234

805-499-9774
800-818-7243; *Fax:* 805-499-0871
journals@sagepub.com; www.sagepub.com

Blaise R Simqu, CEO
Christos C. Chamis, Editorial Board

The Journal of Reinforced Plastics and Composites presents research studies on a broad range of today's reinforced plastics and composites. The journal provides a permanent record of achievements in the science, technology, and economics of reinforced plastics and composites. Reports on special topics are regularly included such as recycling, environmental effects, novel materials, computer-aided design, predictive modelling, and composite materials.
Cost: $4509.00
Frequency: 18 Times Per Year
ISSN: 0731-6844
Founded in: 1962

20467 Journal of Thermoplastic Composite Materials
Sage Publications
2455 Teller Rd
Newbury Park, CA 91320-2234

805-499-9774
800-818-7243; *Fax:* 805-499-0871
journals@sagepub.com; www.sagepub.com

Blaise R Simqu, CEO
M.N. Ghasemi Jejhad, Associate Editor

An international forum for the presentation of new advances in the technology of this class of materials. Emphasis is given to the fundamental areas of new material development and characterization, design, rheological behavior in short, discontinuous, and continuous fiber systems; process development, manufacturing science, matrix-fiber interphase charaterization; short and long-term performance prediction; and engineering data base assistance for thermoplastic composites.
Cost: $1186.00
96 Pages
Frequency: Bi-Monthly
ISSN: 0892-7057
Printed in 2 colors on matte stock

20468 Journal of Vinyl and Additive Technology
John Wiley & Sons
111 River St
Hoboken, NJ 07030-5790

201-748-6000; *Fax:* 201-748-6088
subinfo@wiley.com; www.wiley.com

William J Pesce, CEO
Elliot L. Weinberg, Associate Editor

Journal of Vinyl and Additive Technology is a peer-reviewed technical publication for new work in the fields of polymer modifiers and additives, vinyl polymers and selected review papers. Over half of all papers in JVAT are based on technology of additives and modifiers for all classes of polymers: thermoset polymers and both condensation and addition thermoplastics. Papers on vinyl technology include PVC additives.
Cost: $336.00
Frequency: Quarterly
Circulation: 625
ISSN: 1083-5601
Founded in: 1942

20469 Journal of Wide Bandgap Materials
Sage Publications
2455 Teller Rd
Newbury Park, CA 91320-2234
805-499-9774
800-818-7243; *Fax:* 805-499-0871
journals@sagepub.com; www.sagepub.com
Blaise R Simqu, CEO
Shojiro Komatsu, Editorial Advisory Board
The Journal of Wide Bandgap Materials is an international journal publishing original peer-reviewed papers on fundamental, experimental and theoretical developments in the science and engineering of wide bandgap materials. The Journal provides a broad-based forum for the publication and sharing of ongoing research and development efforts in the field of wide bandgap materials.
Cost: $245.00
96 Pages
Frequency: Quarterly
ISSN: 1524-511X
Printed in 2 colors on matte stock

20470 Medical Plastics & Biomaterials
Canon Communications
11444 W Olympic Blvd
Suite 900
Los Angeles, CA 90064-1555
310-445-4200
800-243-9696; *Fax:* 310-445-4299;
www.cancom.com
Charlie Mc Curdy, President
Tonna Anuligo, Technical Editor
Kevin O'Grady, Group Publisher
Technical information on the full range of plastics and biomaterials used in manufacturing and packaging medical products.
Cost: $59.00
Frequency: Monthly
Circulation: 61200
Founded in: 1978

20471 Modern Plastics
Canon Communications
11444 W Olympic Blvd
Suite 900
Los Angeles, CA 90064-1555
310-445-4200; *Fax:* 310-445-4299;
www.modplas.com/
Social Media: Facebook, Twitter, LinkedIn
Charlie Mc Curdy, President
Kevin O'Grady, Publisher
Serves companies utilizing plastics. Developments in resin technology, machinery/processing techniques and additive innovation.
Cost: $59.00
Frequency: Monthly
Circulation: 50300
Founded in: 1978

20472 PM/USA Green Sheet
Marketing Handbook
PO Box 243687
Boynton Beach, FL 33424-3687
561-732-5858; *Fax:* 561-732-2607
results@greensheetads.com;
www.greensheetads.com
Lee Noe, Publisher/Editor
Bob Miller, Technical Director
For those responsible for manufacturing operations.
Cost: $45.00
Frequency: Monthly
Founded in: 1972

20473 Plastics Business News
Plastics Universe
2727 Holland Sylvania Road
Suite A
Toledo, OH 43615
419-535-7899; *Fax:* 419-535-1243
mberins@javanet.com;
www.plasticx.com/pub/plast_11.html
Michael L. Berins, Publisher
A weekly newsletter published for the professionals in the plastic industry. Covers advances in materials and processes, pricing, new applications and markets, international competition, etc.
Cost: $327.00
Frequency: Weekly
Founded in: 1972

20474 Plastics Distributor and Fabricator Magazine
KLW Enterprises
PO Box 669
LaGrange, IL 60525-0669
708-588-1845; *Fax:* 708-588-1846
pdfm@plasticsmag.com;
www.plasticsmag.com
David Whelan, Editor/Publisher
Riia O'Donnell, Associate Editor
Lynette Zeitler, Art Director
Contains industry and products news relevant to the manufacture, distribution and fabrication of plastic rod, sheet and tube.
Founded in: 1983
Printed in 4 colors on glossy stock

20475 Plastics Engineering
Society of Plastics Engineers
13 Church Hill Rd
Newtown, CT 06470
203-775-0471; *Fax:* 203-775-8490
info@4spe.org; www.4spe.org
Susan Oderwald, Executive Director
Communication to SPE's global audience of plastics professionals about current developments in the industry, technology, and activities of the Society.
Frequency: Monthly
Circulation: 35000

20476 Plastics Focus
Plastics Universe
2727 Holland Sylvania Road
Suite A
Toledo, OH 43615
419-535-7899; *Fax:* 419-535-1243
James Best, CEO
Bi-Monthly updates on new applicationsand markets for plastics, new polymers, alloys and blends as well as machinery, processing developments, and international competitions and opportunities.
Cost: $295.00

20477 Plastics Hotline
Industry Marketing Solutions
809 Central Avenue
PO Box 893, 2nd Floor
Fort Dodge, IA 50501-1052
888-247-2006; *Fax:* 515-574-2237
steve@plasticshotline.com;
www.plasticshotline.com
Social Media: Facebook, Twitter, LinkedIn, YouTube
Steve Scanlan, Publisher
Jim Rykhus, List Marketing Specialist
Cara Jondle, Tradeshow & Marketing Manager
Jody Kirchoff, Operations
Plastics Hotline has been published since 1983. This weekly periodical continues to be the National Marketplace for Plastic Processors to buy and sell equipment, parts and services.
Cost: $69.00
Frequency: Weekly
Founded in: 1990

20478 Plastics Machining & Fabricating
Onsrud Cutter
800 Liberty Dr
Libertyville, IL 60048-2374
847-362-1560; *Fax:* 847-362-5028
info@plasticsmachining.com;
www.plasticsmachining.com
Harry Urban, Publisher
Plastics Molding & Fabricating is an online technical and management magazine dedicated to the secondary plastics processing industry. It is edited for qualified professionals whose operations include: machining, milling, fabricating, forming, bending, bonding, molding, printing and finishing of plastics. Editorial subjects include case studies, technology updates, trends & news and opinion pieces.
Frequency: Bi-Monthly
Circulation: 15,015

20479 Plastics Technology
Gardner Publications
6915 Valley Ln
Cincinnati, OH 45244-3153
513-527-8800
800-950-8020; *Fax:* 513-527-8801
cnorman@gardnerweb.com;
www.gardnerweb.com
Rick Kline Sr, CEO
Sherry Fuchs, Managing Editor
Theresa Basso, Production Editor
Joe Grande, Senior Editor
A premier source of technical and business information for plastics processors, each issue reports on technological innovations and developments in the plastics processing market and reaches more than 47,000 processors who depend on authoritative coverage on applying new technology, evaluating products and practical manufacturing.
Frequency: Monthly
Circulation: 47559
Founded in: 1928

20480 Polymer Engineering & Science
John Wiley & Sons
111 River St
Hoboken, NJ 07030-5790
201-748-6000; *Fax:* 201-748-6088
subinfo@wiley.com; www.wiley.com
William J Pesce, CEO
Alan J Lesser, Associate Editor
Laura Espinet, Journal Production
Kim Thompkins, Advertising/Media
Presents papers of fundamental significance to engineers and scientists interested in polmeric materials.
Cost: $545.00
Frequency: Monthly
Circulation: 86000
Founded in: 1945

Trade Shows

20481 ANTEC
Society of Plastics Engineering
13 Church Hill Road
Newtown, CT 06470
203-775-0471; *Fax:* 203-775-8490
info@4spe.org; www.4spe.org
Susan Oderwald, Executive Director
The largest technical conference for the plastics industry

20482 ASM Heat Treating Society Conference & Exposition
ASM International
9639 Kinsman Road
Materials Park, OH 44073

440-385-5151
800-336-5152; *Fax:* 440-338-4634
pamela.kleinman@asminternational.org; www.asminternational.org

Pamela Kleinma, Senior Manager, Events
Kellye Thomas, Exposition Account Manager

Conference and exhibits of heat treating equipment and supplies plus information of interest to metallurgists, manufacturing, research and design technical professionals. 300 exhibitors.
3500 Attendees
Frequency: September, Bi-Annual
Founded in: 1974

20483 ASM Materials Science & Technology (MS&T)
ASM International
9639 Kinsman Road
Materials Park, OH 44073-0002

440-338-5151
800-336-5152; *Fax:* 440-338-4634
pamela.kleinman@asminternational.org; www.asminternational.org

Pamela Kleinman, Senior Manager, Events
Kelly Thomas, Exposition Account Manager

Annual event focusing on testing, analysis, characterization and research of materials such as engineered materials, high performance metals, powdered metals, metal forming, surface modification, welding and joining. 350 exhibitors.
4,000 Attendees
Frequency: Annual/October
Founded in: 2005

20484 AeroMat Conference and Exposition
ASM International
9639 Kinsman Road
Materials Park, OH 44073-0002

440-385-5151
800-336-5152; *Fax:* 440-338-4634
kim.schaefer@asminternational.org; www.asminternational.org

Kim Schaefer, Event Manager
Kelly Thomas, Exposition Account Manager

Conference for Aerospace Meterials Engineers, Structural Engineers and Designers. The annual event focuses on affordable structures and low-cost manufacturing, titanium alloy technology, advanced intermetallics and refractory metal alloys, materials and processes for space applications, aging systems, high strength steel, NDT evaluation, light alloy technology, welding and joining, and engineering technology. 150 exhibitors.
1500 Attendees
Frequency: Annual/June
Founded in: 1984

20485 Association of Industrial Metallizers, Coaters and Laminators
201 Springs Street
Fort Mill, SC 29715

803-948-9470; *Fax:* 803-948-9471
aimcal@aimcal.org; www.aimcal.org

Craig Sheppard, Executive Director
Caleb Howe, Communications Manager
Ed Cohen, Technical Consultant
Norma Bryant, Office Manager

Displays relating to coaters and laminators, metallizers and producers of metallized film and or paper on continuous rolls, suppliers of plastic films, papers and adhesives.
Frequency: Annual
Founded in: 1970

20486 Health Pack Innovative Technology Conference
1833 Centre Point Circle
Suite 123
Naperville, IL 60563

630-544-5051; *Fax:* 630-544-5055
info@healthpack.net; www.healthpack.net

Heather Jayson, Show Coordinator
Steve Bunell, Operations Manager
Curtis Larson, Program Coordinator
John Spitzley, Program Co-Chairman
Angela Holty, Owner

Unique annual conference focuses exclusively on medical device packaging, bringing together medical device manufacturers, packaging materials suppliers and converters, contract packagers, test labs, and other service providers. Food and beverage functions served in the exhibition area provide repeated opportunities for networking between exhibitors, attendees, and conference speakers. Conference location in St. Petersburg, Florida, 20 booths.
100 Attendees
Frequency: March

20487 International Association of Plastics Distributors Convention
6734 W 121st Street
Overland Park, KS 66209

913-345-1005; *Fax:* 913-345-1006
iapd@iapd.org; www.iapd.org

Susan E Avery, Executive Director
Patrick M Foose, Board President
Howard J Natal, VP Board of Directors

IAPD is an international trade association comprised of companies engaged in the distribution and manufacture of plastics materials. The annual convention features numerous exhibits that represent a variety of materials in the plastics industry including semi-finished stock shapes, such as sheet, rod, tube, pipe, valves, fittings, film and related products. 76 booths.
450 Attendees
Frequency: September
Founded in: 1956

20488 International Plastics Show
1801 K Street NW
Suite 1000
Washington, DC 20006

202-974-5200; *Fax:* 202-296-7005
tradeshows@socplas.org; www.socplas.org or www.npe.org

Ken Rietz, President
Brigid Hughes, Director Trade Show Promotions
Adam Krumhansl, Trade Show Coordinator

Containing 2,000 exhibits.
85M+ Attendees
Frequency: June

20489 National Agricultural Plastics Congress
American Society for Plasticulture
526 Brittany Drive
State College, PA 16803

814-238-7045; *Fax:* 814-238-7051; www.plasticulture.org

William Tietjen, Chairman Plastics Congress
Henry Taber, President
Jodi Fleck-Arnold, VP
Edward Carey, Secretary/Treasurer
Patricia Heuser, Executive Director

Plastic products used in agriculture. 15-25 booths.
150 Attendees
Frequency: March/November

20490 National Plastics Exposition
Society of the Plastics Industry
1667 K Street NW
Suite 1000
Washington, DC 20006

202-974-5200; *Fax:* 202-296-7005
feedback@plasticsindustry.org; www.plasticsindustry.org
Social Media: Facebook, Twitter, LinkedIn

William R Carteaux, President/CEO
Jon Kurrie, VP Government Affairs/Public Policy
Al Damico, Executive VP

This expo features exhibits of molded, extruded, fabricated, laminated and calendered plastics, raw materials, machinery and laboratory equipment for the industry.
75M Attendees
Frequency: June

20491 PLASTEC East Trade Show
Canon Communications
11444 West Olympic Boulevard
Los Angeles, CA 90064-1549

310-445-4200; *Fax:* 310-996-9499; www.plasteceast.com

Diane O'Connor, Trade Show Director
Shannon Cleghorn, Customer & Media Coordinator

Five co-located shows, 1,750 plastic exhibitors. The Trade Show takes place every 2 years, in odd years.
32000 Attendees

20492 PLASTEC West Trade Show
Canon Communications
2901 28th Street
Suite 100
Santa Monica, CA 90405

310-445-4200; *Fax:* 310-996-9499
Tssalesadmin@ubm.com; www.plastecwest.com
Social Media: Twitter

Diane O'Connor, Trade Show Director
Jane Sullivan, Exhibit Contact

Five co-located shows, 3,000 exhibitors, trade show features plastics, packaging and manufacturing industries.
45000 Attendees
Frequency: January/February

20493 POLYCON
International Cast Polymer Association
3033 Wilson Blvd
Suite 4200
Arlington, VA 22201

703-525-0511; *Fax:* 703-525-0743; www.icpa-hq.org

Jeanne McCormack, Director Conferences & Meetings
Elizabeth Cookson, Mgr Conferences & Program Dvlpmt
Debbie Cannon, President

The program includes three days of in-depth educational programming, exhibits, a product showcase, and more. Sponsored annually by the International Cast Polymer Association/ICPA, POLYCON is the largest convention and trade show for the cast polymer industry. Over 800 industry professionals attend the convention to network, attend educational sessions, and visit with over 70 exhibitors.
Frequency: Annual

20494 PPI Annual Meeting
Plastics Pipe Institute

105 Decker Court
Suite 2
Irving, TX 75062
469-499-1044; *Fax:* 469-499-1063
info@plasticpipe.org; www.plasticpipe.org
Tony Radoszewski, Executive Director
Camille Rubeiz, Director Engineering
Stephen Boros, Technical Director
Frequency: May

20495 Polyurethanes Technical Conference
Alliance for the Polyurethanes Industry
700 Second St.,NE
Arlington, VA 22209
703-741-5103; *Fax:* 703-741-5655;
www.polyurethane.org
Richard E Mericle, Executive Director
Kaye Robinson, Conference Planning Committee
Semi-annual trade show for the polyurethanes industry in North America. International technical conference and exposition will feature technical and industry issues sessions, poster session and exhibits.
Frequency: September/October
Founded in: 1977

Directories & Databases

20496 American Mold Builders Association/AMBA Membership Directory
American Mold Builders Association
3601 Algonquin Rd
Suite 207
Rolling Meadows, IL 60008-3136
847-222-9402; *Fax:* 630-980-9714
info@amba.org; www.amba.org or amba.org/adOppGrid.php
Melissa Millhuff, Executive Director
AMBA represents nearly 325 member companies comprised of approximately 9,000 employees and representing just over $2 billion in annual tooling sales. Members span 35 states with 12 chapter affiliations. AMBA member companies serve original equipment manufacturers in every industry including automotive, medical, electronics/electrical, toys, recreation and sporting goods, building and construction, lawn and garden, consumer, and industrial. Free to members and available to others for $50.00.
Cost: $50.00
Frequency: Annual
Circulation: 2,200
Founded in: 1973

20497 Handbook of Plastic Compounds, Elastomers and Resins
John Wiley & Sons
10475 Crosspoint Blvd
Indianapolis, IN 46256-3386
317-572-3000; *Fax:* 317-572-4000;
www.wiley.com
Lou Peragallo, Manager
Michael Ash, Editor
Directory of services and supplies to the industry. A complete, accurate, and current data source on primary material tradename products for the rubber and plastic industries. This handbook gives short, easy-to-find information on over 15,000 chemical trademark products currently sold throughout the world.
Cost: $385.00
ISBN: 0-471188-30-1

20498 IAPD Membership Directory
International Association of Plastics Distribution
6734 W 121st St
Overland Park, KS 66209-2002
913-345-1005; *Fax:* 913-345-1006
iapd@iapd.org; www.iapd.org
Susan Avery, Executive Director
The IAPD Membership Directory lists almost 400 companies by membership category with their locations, phone and fax numbers, key personnel and plastics products. There is also a listing of companies by geographical location, as well as an alphabetical listing of individuals from the various companies.
Cost: $150.00
Frequency: Annual May

20499 Plastics Business News
Plastics Universe
2727 Holland Sylvania Road
Suite A
Toledo, OH 43615
419-535-7899; *Fax:* 419-535-1243
mberins@javanet.com;
www.plasticx.com/pub/plast_11.html
Michael L. Berins, Publisher
Offers information on the plastics industry, forecasts, mergers, and new product developments.
Cost: $327.00
Frequency: Weekly
Founded in: 1972

20500 Plastics Compounding Redbook
Advanstar Communications
2501 Colorado Avenue
Suite 280
Santa Monica, CA 90404
310-857-7500; *Fax:* 310-857-7510
info@advanstar.com; www.advanstar.com
Joseph Loggia, CEO
Chris DeMoulin, VP
Susannah George, Marketing Director
List of suppliers — over 1,000 — of resin, additives, fillers and other materials compounding equipment and services to the plastic industry.
Cost: $150.00
280 Pages
Frequency: Annual
Circulation: 12,000

20501 Plastics Digest/PA Index
IHS/Information Handling Services
15 Inverness Way E
Englewood, CO 80112-5710
303-736-3000
800-525-7052; *Fax:* 303-736-3150;
www.ihsenergy.com
Social Media: Facebook, Twitter, LinkedIn
Jerre Stead, CEO
Michael Armstrong, Director
A list of over 200 manufacturers and suppliers of plastics materials are listed in this comprehensive directory. CD format only.
Cost: $768.00

20502 Plastics Engineering Handbook of the Society of the Plastics Industry
Society of the Plastics Industry
1667 K St NW
Suite 1000
Washington, DC 20006-1620
202-974-5200
800-541-0736; *Fax:* 202-296-7005
feedback@plasticsindustry.org;
www.plasticsindustry.org
Social Media: Facebook, Twitter, LinkedIn
William Cartuaex, President
Jon Kurrie, VP Government Affairs/Public Policy
Al Damico, Executive VP
Educational groups, associations, consultants and providers of technical data, literature and materials to the reinforced plastics industry.
Cost: $175.00

20503 Plastics News Datebook Online
Crain Communications
1725 Merriman Rd
Suite 300
Akron, OH 44313-5283
330-836-9180; *Fax:* 330-836-2831
info@crain.com; www.crain.com
Robert S Simmons, VP
Linda Whelan, Marketing Manager
This business to business buyers guide highlights products and services such as extruders, sheet manufacturers, film, rod and sheet suppliers, processors, roto-molding equipment, injection molding, polyurethane machinery, resin producers and compounders. The Plastics News Online Directory helps you, as a BtoB buyer, research products and make smart buying decisions.

20504 Plastics News Web Watch Directory
Crain Communications
1725 Merriman Rd
Suite 300
Akron, OH 44313-9006
330-836-9180
800-678-9595; *Fax:* 330-836-2831
editorial@plasticsnews.com; www.crain.com
Robert S Simmons, VP
Anthony Eagan, Publisher
Contains processors, primary equipment, auxiliary equipment, resin suppliers, compounders, recyclers, tooling and molds, design and prototyping, trade associations, industry services and more.
154 Pages
ISSN: 1042-802X
Printed in 4 colors on glossy stock

20505 Rauch Guide to the US Adhesives & Sealants Industry
Grey House Publishing
4919 Route 22
PO Box 56
Amenia, NY 12501
518-789-8700
800-562-2139; *Fax:* 845-373-6390
books@greyhouse.com; www.greyhouse.com
Social Media: Facebook, Twitter
Leslie Mackenzie, Publisher
Richard Gottlieb, Editor
Contains information providing data on industry economics, government regulations, technology, raw materials, products and markets in addition to industry activities, organizations and sources of information on trade shows, exhibits, professional associations and societies. Provides unique profiles of more than 700 suppliers.
Cost: $595.00
361 Pages
ISBN: 1-592371-29-9
Founded in: 1981

20506 Rauch Guide to the US Plastics Industry
Grey House Publishing
4919 Route 22
PO Box 56
Amenia, NY 12501-0056
518-789-8700
800-562-2139; *Fax:* 518-789-0556
books@greyhouse.com; www.greyhouse.com
Social Media: Facebook, Twitter
Leslie Mackenzie, Publisher
Richard Gottlieb, Editor
Offers comprehensive data on the $182 billion industry, the Guide is a highly valued industry re-

source covering the economics, processes, materials, sales and activities of leading U.S. plastics producers. Additional features include a personnel index with key industry executives and an enhanced company listing containing detailed information indicating subsidiary, division or parent information, Internet site addresses, E-mail addresses, and key contacts.
Cost: $595.00
646 Pages
ISBN: 1-592371-28-0
Founded in: 1981

20507 Who's Who in World Petrochemicals and Plastics
Reed Business Information
3355 West Alabama
Suite 700
Houston, TX 77098
713-523-2613
888-525-3255; *Fax:* 713-525-2659
csc@icis.com; www.icis.com/
Jamie Reed, Owner
Andy Soloman, Global Editorial Director
Chrissy Salisbury, Manager
More than 9,600 individuals from 3,700 petrochemical and plastic companies worldwide.
Cost: $276.00
Frequency: Annual November
Circulation: 1,500

20508 Worldwide Petrochemical Directory
PennWell Directories
1455 West Loop South
Suite 400
Houston, TX 77027-3005
713-621-9720
800-736-6935; *Fax:* 713-963-6285
billw@pennwell.com; www.pennwell.com
Bob Tippee, Editor
David Nakamura, Refining/Petrochemical Editor
Guntis Moritis, Production Editor
Tim Sullivant, Manager
2,980 operative petrochemical plants with 8,675 personnel in 4,320 locations are listed with their parent companies, plant locations, products produced, capacities, and current production volumes if available. Approximately 9,340 locations having 13,145 Email and 4,330 Website addresses are listed for engineering, construction, manufacturing, supply and service companies with a description of products and services provided. Included are 350 cross-references reflecting mergers and acquisitions.
Cost: $150.00
Frequency: Annual November
Circulation: 3,500
Mailing list available for rent

Industry Web Sites

20509 http://gold.greyhouse.com
G.O.L.D Grey House OnLine Databases
Grey House Publishing's online database platform, GOLD, offers Quick Search, Keyword Search and Expert Search for most business sectors including plastics markets. The GOLD platform makes finding the information you need quick and easy - whether you're a novice searcher or an experienced database user. All of Grey House's directory products are available for subscription on the GOLD platform.

20510 www.aimcal.org
Association of Industrial Metallizers, Coaters
and Laminators
Packaging equipment.

20511 www.americanmanufacturers.com
AmericanManufacturers.com
Product exchanges and electronic requests for quotes.

20512 www.apexq.com
American Plastics Exchange
Molders and extruders can review data sheets and bid for prime virgin resin.

20513 www.ariba.com
Ariba
Allows buyers and sellers to find trading partners and negotiate prices.

20514 www.assettrade.com
AssetTrade.com
Used equipment and machinery.

20515 www.berkshireplastics.org
Berkshire Plastics Network
Consortium of more than 40 independent companies, representing virtually every discipline in the design and production of molds, components and plastics products.

20516 www.chematch.com
CheMatch.com
Buyers and sellers exchange for plastic materials.

20517 www.chemconnect.com
ChemConnect
Buyers and sellers can find partners and negotiate price.

20518 www.chemcross.com
ChemCross
Online trading offered by Asian producers of plastics and chemicals.

20519 www.commerxplasticsnet.com
Commerx
Online training.

20520 www.dovebid.com
DoveBid
Bidding on used equipment, as well as capital assets.

20521 www.e-resin.com
e-Resin.com
Direct negotiation with suppliers for additives, materials and finished products.

20522 www.efodia.com
eFodia
Online purchasing of chemical processing, compounding and additives, other materials.

20523 www.elastomersolutions.com
ElastomerSolutions
Online trading for the elastomers industry.

20524 www.ewinwin.com
eWinWin
Associations, cooperatives, buyers and suppliers can employ an aggregation system for lower priced purchases.

20525 www.freemarkets.com
FreeMarkets
Reverse auction in which suppliers submit online bids for commodities, services, parts and materials.

20526 www.getplastic.com
GetPlastic.com
Materials designed for those who purchase resins.

20527 www.greyhouse.com
Grey House Publishing
Authoritative reference directories for most business sectors including plastics markets. Users can search the online databases with varied search criteria allowing for custom searches by product category, geographic area, sales volume, keyword, subject and more. Full Grey House catalog and online ordering also available.

20528 www.i2i.com
Industry to Industry
Buying and selling of plastics.

20529 www.justforplastics.com
Justforplastics.com
Marketplace for plastic services, tooling, equipment and products.

20530 www.mfgconnect.com
Mfgconnect.com
Exchange product development information and CAD files prior to bidding on contracts.

20531 www.napcor.com
National Association for Pet Container Resources
National trade association which promotes the recycling of pet con-tainers and the usage of pet plastic.

20532 www.omnexus.com
Omnexus Corporation
Trading in equipment, services, materials and tooling for central injection and blow molders.

20533 www.onechem.com
OneChem
Software applications and transactional storefront for global commercial transactions in plastics and chemicals.

20534 www.packagingexchange.com
PackagingExchange.Com
Storefront transactions and online auction for packaging products, equipment and materials.

20535 www.packexpo.com
Packexpo.com
Source for packaging materials, machinery, parts and services.

20536 www.packtion.com
Packtion Corporation
Informational tools and exchange opportunites for packaging services.

20537 www.plasticlink.com
PlasticLink.Com
Materials, equipment and products for thermoformers, extruders and semifinished shape processors.

20538 www.plasticpipe.org
Plastics Pipe Institute
The major trade association representing all segments of the plastics piping industry. As an association, PPI focuses collaborative efforts to accumulate data, concentrate facts and target resources toward advancements in applications and increases in widespread usage.

20539 www.plastics.org
American Plastics Council
Gateway to plastics on the internet.

20540 www.plasticsandchemicals.com
Plasticsandchemicals.com
Bid-based marketplace.

20541 www.plasticsbin.com
NetVendor
Trading in scrap resin and surplus plastic inventory.

20542 **www.plasticsindustry.org**
Society of the Plastics Industry
The Society of the Plastics Industry is the trade association representing one of the largest manufacturing industries in the US. SPI's 1,500 members represent the entire plastics industry supply chain, including processors, machinery and equipment manufacturers and raw material suppliers. The US plastics industry employs 1.5 million workers and provides $304 billon in annual shipment.

20543 **www.plasticsrecycling.org**
AssociationOd Postconsumer Plastic Recyclers
Represents companies that acquire, reprocess and sell the output of more than 90 percent of the post-consumer plastic processing capacity in North America.

20544 **www.plasticulture.com**
American Society for Plasticulture
Promotes research, education, and technology application for plastics used in agricultural and horticultural production systems. Hosts a congress every year or so; published proceedings of research presentations.

20545 **www.polymeradditives.com**
PolymerAdditives.com
Purchase brand-name polymer additives online.

20546 **www.polymersite.com**
PolymerSite.com/PolySort
Exchange site for resins and compounds. Flexible negotiations in a sealed bid environment.

20547 **www.polyurethane.org**
Alliance for the Polyurethanes Industry
For companies that supply polyurethane resins or chemicals used in polyurethane resins, manufacture polyurethanes, produce machinery used in the manufacture or processing polyurethane, or engage in the business of applying polyurethane products in end use applications.

20548 **www.primeadvantage.com**
Prime Advantage Corporation
Buying consortium offers volume discounts on resins and components.

20549 **www.sorcity.com**
Sorcity.com
Reverse auction in which buyer files request for quote and supplier bids.

20550 **www.supplierone.com**
SupplierOne.com
Supply chain management and e-marketplace for manufactured components.

20551 **www.thedock.com**
The Dock Exchange
Buying and selling of equipment online.

20552 **www.theplasticsexchange.com**
ThePlasticsExchange.com
Trading in commodity prime resins.

20553 **www.worldwideplastics.com**
TheBuyersNet.com
Catalog of semifinished materials.

Associations

20554 American Society of Plumbing Engineers
6400 Shafer Ct.
Suite 350
Rosemont, IL 60018-4914

847-296-0002; *Fax:* 847-296-2963
info@aspe.org; www.aspe.org

Billy Smith, Executive Director/CEO, Secretary
Mitch Clemente, President
David E. DeBord, Vice President, Education
Chris Graham, Treasurer
Scott Steindler, Vice President, Technical

The American Society of Plumbing Engineers (ASPE) is a professional organization dedicated to the advancement of the science of plumbing engineering, to the professional growth and advancement of its members and the health, welfare and safety of the public. The Society disseminates technical data and information, sponsors activities that facilitate interaction with fellow professionals, and, through research and education, expands the base of knowledge of the plumbing engineering industry.
6000+ Members
Founded in: 1964

20555 American Society of Sanitary Engineering
18927 Hickory Creek Dr.
Suite 220
Mokena, IL 60448

708-995-3019; *Fax:* 708-479-6139;
www.asse-plumbing.org

John F. Flader, Treasurer
Douglas A. Marian, International President
Scott Hamilton, Executive Director
Michele Kilpatrick, Administrative asst.
Dana Colombo, Vice President

Members are from all segments of the plumbing industry, including contractors, engineers, inspectors, journeymen, apprentices and others who are involved in various segments of the industry. Provides information, an opportunity to exchange ideas, solve problems and offers a forum where all sides can express their views.
300 Members
Founded in: 1906

20556 American Supply Association
1200 N. Arlington Heights Rd.
Suite 150
Itasca, IL 60143

630-467-0000; *Fax:* 630-467-0001
info@asa.net; www.asa.net
Social Media: Facebook, Twitter, LinkedIn

Michael Adelizzi, Executive VP, Secretary
John Strong, Chairman
Rick Fantham, President
Steve Cook, Treasurer
Tim Milford, President-Elect

ASA is a not-for-profit national organization serving wholesale distributors and their suppliers in the plumbing, heating, cooling and industrial pipe, valves, and fittings industries. ASA provides a forum for trading partners from around the country to discuss critical issues facing them, and offers a menu of products and services uniquely geared to their needs.
800 Members
Founded in: 1969

20557 International Association of Plumbing and Mechanical Officials (IAPMO)
4755 E Philadelphia Street
Ontario, CA 91761

909-472-4100
800-854-2676; *Fax:* 909-472-4150
info@iapmo.org; www.iapmo.org
Social Media: Facebook, Twitter, LinkedIn

Bruce Pfeiffer, President
DJ Nunez, Vice Pesident
Russ Chaney, CEO
David Straub, Treasurer/ Secretary
Neil Bogatz, General counsel

IAPMO has been protecting the public's health and safety for more than eighty years by working in concert with government and industry to implement comprehensive plumbing and mechanical systems around the world.
5000 Members
Founded in: 1926

20558 Manufacturers Standardization Society
127 Park St NE
Vienna, VA 22180-4602

703-281-6613; *Fax:* 703-281-6671
info@msshq.org; www.mss-hq.org

Robert O'Neill, Executive Director

The Manufacturers Standardization Society (MSS) of the Valve and Fittings Industry is a non-profit technical association organized for development and improvement of industry, national and international codes and standards for valves, valve actuators, valve modifications, pipe fittings, pipe hangers, flanges, and associated seals.
Cost: $1800.00
Founded in: 1924

20559 Midwest Distributors Association (MWDA)
1200 N. Arlington Heights Rd.
Suite 150
Itasca, IL 60143

630-467-0000; *Fax:* 312-464-0091;
www.mwda.net

Dave Poteete, President
Ryan Curry, Secretary/ Treasurer
Todd Restel, President-Elect
Chris Murin, Executive Director
John Bennerotte, Director

The mission of the MWDA is to professionally promote the improvement of the industry by providing quality programs, educational and training opportunities to improve operational efficiency and marketing effectiveness, and by facilitating the exchange of ideas and information throughout the distribution channel. The MWDA serves the states of Illinois, Iowa, Kansas, Minnesota, Missouri, Nebraska, North Dakota, South Dakota, Upper Michigan and Wisconsin.
110 Members
Founded in: 1942

20560 National Kitchen and Bath Association
687 Willow Grove St
Hackettstown, NJ 07840

908-850-1206
800-843-6522; *Fax:* 908-852-1695
feedback@nkba.org; www.nkba.org
Social Media: Facebook, Twitter, LinkedIn, Pinterest

Maria Stapperfenne, President
Mark Kovich, President-Elect
Denise M. Dick, Vice President
Blue Arnold, Secretary
Lorenzo Marquez, Treasurer

The NKBA enhances the success of its members in the kitchen and bath industry through networking, education, certification, marketing and business tools, leadership opportunities, and the annual Kitchen/Bath Industry Show.
40000 Members
Founded in: 1963

20561 North Central Wholesalers Association/NCWA
7107 Crossroads Blvd
Suite 106
Brentwood, TN 37027

615-371-5004; *Fax:* 615-371-5444
terry@northcentralwholesalers.org;
www.northcentralwholesalers.org

Howard Wolff, President
Jock Castoldi, Treasurer
Russ Visner, Director

The NCWA serves wholesale distributors of plumbing, heating, cooling and piping products in Indiana, Michigan, Ohio, Western Pennsylvania and West Virginia, sponsoring educational conferences and offering networking opportunities. During the year NCWA offers its members seminars, workshops, newsletters, industry statistics, an annual regional convention and other traditional trade association programs.
75 Members
Founded in: 2003

20562 Pacific Southwest Distributors Association
7345 E Evans Rd
No. 7
Scottsdale, AZ 85260

480-991-5703; *Fax:* 480-991-5704
rbluth@qwestoffice.net; www.thepsda.info

Bob Bluth, Owner
Michael Adelizzi, Executive Vice President

Made up of distributors of heating, cooling and plumbing supplies.
Founded in: 1946

20563 Plastic Pipe and Fittings Association
800 Roosevelt Rd
Building C, Suite 312
Glen Ellyn, IL 60137

630-858-6540; *Fax:* 630-790-3095;
www.ppfahome.org
Social Media: Facebook, RSS

Richard W Church, Executive Director

The Plastic Pipe and Fittings Association (PPFA) is a national trade association of member companies that manufacture plastic piping, fittings and solvent cements for plumbing and related applications, and supply raw materials, ingredients or machinery for the manufacturing process. The PPFA provides relevant information needed to properly design, specify and install plastic piping systems, promoting an understanding of the environmental impact and benefits of thermoplastic piping products.
78 Members
Founded in: 1978

20564 Plumbing Heating Cooling Contractors Association
180 South Washington Street
Suite 100
Falls Church, VA 22046

703-237-8100
800-533-7694; *Fax:* 703-237-7442
naphcc@naphcc.org; www.phccweb.org
Social Media: Facebook, Twitter, LinkedIn, RSS

Kevin Tindall, President-Elect
Elicia Magruder, Vice President of Communications
Michael Copp, Executive Vice President
Steven A. Rivers, President
Laurie Crigler, Secretary

National organization designed for suppliers of equipment, supplies and services for the plumbing, heating and cooling industries.
3700 Members
Founded in: 1883

20565 Plumbing Manufacturers International
1921 Rohlwing Rd
Unit G
Rolling Meadows, IL 60008
847-481-5500; *Fax:* 847-481-5501;
www.pmihome.org
Social Media: Facebook, Twitter, LinkedIn, YouTube, Google+
Fernando Fernandez, President
Paul Patton, Vice- President
Barbara C. Higgens, CEO/Executive Director
Peter Jahrling, Treasurer
Tim Kilbane, Immediate Past President
The Plumbing Manufacturers Institute (PMI) is the trade association of plumbing products manufacturers. The Institute functions as a sounding board for its members, a source for industry and market information, and as a coordinating and decision-making body for dealing with industry issues. It is active in many arenas as it helps develop and maintain standards and codes, and works closely with government agencies at all levels - federal, state and local.
44 Members
Founded in: 1975

20566 Plumbing and Drainage Institute
800 Turnpike Street
Suite 300
North Andover, MA 01845
978-557-0720
800-589-8956; *Fax:* 978-557-0721
pdi@PDIonline.org; www.pdionline.org
William Whitehead, Executive Director
An association of manufacturers of engineered plumbing products. Our members and licensees make products such as; flood drains, roof drains, sanitary floor drains, cleanouts, water hammer arresters, swimming pool drains, backwater valves, grease interceptors, fixture supports and other drainage specialties.
14 Members

20567 Plumbing and Mechanical Contractors Association of Oregon
14695 SW Millikan Way
Beaverton, OR 97006
503-626-6666; *Fax:* 503-626-6630
fwall@pmcaoregon.com;
www.pmcaoregon.com
Frank Wall, Executive Director
250 Members
Founded in: 1980

20568 Southern Wholesalers Association
201 Seaboard Lane
7107 Crossroads Blvd
Suite 106
Brentwood, TN 37027
615-371-5004; *Fax:* 615-371-5444
terry@southernwholesalers.org;
www.southernwholesalers.org
Social Media: Facebook
Travis Elrod, President
Brendan Donahue, First VP/ Treasurer
John Simmons, Second VP
Harry Hays, Chairman Ex-Officio
Coley Herin, Chairman of the Board
The Southern Wholesalers Association is a regional association composed of leading Wholesalers of plumbing, heating, and cooling equipment and supplies; pipe, valves and fittings; and water systems throughout the southeast, as well as, Associate Member suppliers and reps to the phcp, pvf and water systems industry.
850 Members
Founded in: 1928

20569 United Association
Three Park Place
Annapolis, MD 21401
410-269-2000; *Fax:* 410-267-0382;
www.ua.org
Social Media: Facebook, Twitter, YouTube
William P. Hite, General President
Mark McManus, General Secretary-Treasurer
Union of plumbers, fitters, welders and service techs.
370K Members
Founded in: 1889

20570 Valve Manufacturers Association of America
1050 17th Street NW
Suite 280
Washington, DC 20036-5521
202-331-8105; *Fax:* 202-296-0378
wsandler@vma.org; www.vma.org
Greg Rogowski, Chairman
Bob Kemple, Vice Chairman
William S. Sandler, President
Marc Pasternak, Vice President
Judy Tibbs, Director of Education
VMA represents the interests of nearly 100 U.S. and Canadian valve actuator, and control manufacturers who account for approximately 80% of the total industrial valve shipments out of U.S. and Canadian facilities. The American valve industry supplies approximately 35% of worldwide valve demand. VMA member companies employ 20,000 men and women directly in supporting jobs. VMA is the only organization exclusively serving U.S. and Canadian manufacturers of industrial valves, controls and actuator
100 Members
Founded in: 1938

20571 Western Suppliers Association
3423 Investment Blvd
Suite 204
Hayward, CA 94545
510-670-0962
800-752-8833; *Fax:* 510-670-9081
info@wsagroup.org;
www.westernsuppliersassociation.com
Richard Amaro, President
Frank Nisonger, Vice President
Ted Green, Treasurer
Glenn Kunishige, Director
Frank Mullin, Advisory Director
A regional office that represents various wholesalers in the heating, plumbing and piping fields.
Founded in: 1952

Newsletters

20572 Plumbing Systems & Design
2980 River Rd
Des Plaines, IL 60018
847-296-0002; *Fax:* 773-695-9007
info@aspe.org; www.psdmagazine.com
Gretchen Pienta, Managing Editor
David Jern, Executive Publisher
Rachel Boger, Graphic Designer
Richard Albrecht, Website
Industry leading technical publication with ASPE news and features. Free to ASPE members and subscribers.
Frequency: Monthly
Circulation: 27000
Founded in: 1965
Printed in on glossy stock

Magazines & Journals

20573 Directory of Listed Plumbing Products Official Magazine
Int'l Assn of Plumbing & Mechanical Officials
4755 E Philadelphia St
Ontario, CA 91761-2816
909-472-4100; *Fax:* 909-472-4150;
www.iapmo.org
Social Media: Facebook, Twitter, LinkedIn, YouTube
Gary Hice, VP
Dan Daniels, President
Russ Chancy, CEO
Dwight Perkins, Senior Director
Cost: $75.00
7000 Members
1300 Pages
Frequency: 6x Yearly
Circulation: 26,000
Founded in: 1926

20574 OFFICIAL Magazine
Int'l Assn of Plumbing & Mechanical Officials
4755 E Philadelphia St
Ontario, CA 91761-2816
909-472-4100
800-854-2676; *Fax:* 909-472-4150
info@iapmo.org; www.iapmo.org
Gary Hile, President
Bruce Pfeiffer, VP
Russ Chancy, CEO
The nation's leading source for information about plumbing and mechanical safety codes. This publication is geared toward plumbers, mechanical contractors, manufacturers and government safety officials who need to know safety code information
Cost: $75.00
9000 Members
Frequency: Bi-Monthly
Circulation: 26000
Founded in: 1958

20575 PM Engineer
Business News Publishing Company
155 N Pfingsten Rd
#205
Deerfield, IL 60015
630-377-5909; *Fax:* 248-502-1023
privacy@BNPMedia.com;
www.pmengineer.com
Bob Miondonski, Group Publisher & Editor
Mike Miazga, Ednior Editor
Julius Ballanco, Editorial Director
Suzette Rubio, Online Editor
John Siegenthaler, Hydronics Editor
Provides technical sheets, manufacturer product brochures, news features and analysis of useful industry information on the engineering and design of plumbing, piping, hydronics, cooling/heating, and fire protection/sprinkler systems. Free to trade engineers.
80 Pages
Circulation: 25000
Printed in 4 colors on glossy stock

20576 PM Plumbing & Mechanical
Business News Publishing Company
155 N Pfingsten Rd
#205
Deerfield, IL 60015
630-377-5909; *Fax:* 248-502-1023
privacy@BNPMedia.com; www.pmmag.com/
Bob Miondonski, Group Publisher & Editor
Mike Miazga, Ednior Editor

Julius Ballanco, Editorial Director
Suzette Rubio, Online Editor
John Siegenthaler, Hydronics Editor

Serves plumbing, hydronic heating and mechanical contractors.
Frequency: Monthly
Circulation: 45091

20577 Plumbing Engineer
TMB Publishing
2165 Shermer Rd
Suite A
Northbrook, IL 60062-5474

847-564-1127; *Fax:* 847-564-1264
editor@plumbingengineer.com;
www.plumbingengineer.com

John Mesenbrink, Chief Editor
Marilyn Cunningham, Assistant Editor
Cate Brown, Production Manager
Sadie Bechtold, Production Assistant
Mark Bruno, Art Director

Offers news and updates to plumbing engineers and manufacturers.
Cost: $35.00
Frequency: Monthly
Founded in: 1973

20578 Plumbing Standards
American Society of Sanitary Engineering
901 Canterbury Rd
Suite A
Cleveland, OH 44145-1480

440-835-3040; *Fax:* 440-835-3488;
www.asse-plumbing.org

James Bickford, President
Donald R Jr. Summers, First VP
Steve Silber, Second VP
Scott Hamilton, Third VP
Ron Murray, Immiate Past President

Topics include standards information, updates, water, wastewater, plumbing design guidelines, and technical information pertaining to the water industry.
Cost: $12.00
Frequency: Quarterly
Circulation: 15000
Founded in: 1906

20579 Reeves Journal
23421 South Pointe Drive
Suite 280
Laguna Hills, CA 92653

949-830-0881; *Fax:* 949-859-7845
hendersont@bnpmedia.com;
www.reevesjournal.com

Ellyn Fishman, Publisher
Kati Larson, Advertising Sales
Jack Sweet, Editor
Souzan Azar, Production

Reeves Journal, one of the oldest publications in the plumbing industry, addresses the regional opportunities and challenges facing plumbing/heating/cooling-phc contractors, wholesalers and engineers in the 14 western United States, focusing on the products, issues, codes and regulations relevant to the phc industry.
Frequency: Monthly
Founded in: 1926

20580 Supply House Times
American Supply Association
155 N Pfingsten Rd
#205
Deerfield, IL 60015

312-464-0090; *Fax:* 312-464-0091
info@asa.net; www.supplyht.com

Bob Miondonski, Group Publisher & Editor
Mike Miazga, Ednior Editor
Julius Ballanco, Editorial Director
Suzette Rubio, Online Editor
John Siegenthaler, Hydronics Editor

Articles on plumbing, heating, cooling, and piping products.
50 Pages
Frequency: 6x Yearly
Circulation: 2,500
Mailing list available for rent: 4,000 names
Printed in 4 colors on matte stock

20581 United Association Journal
United Association
Three Park Place
Annapolis, MD 21401

410-269-2000; *Fax:* 410-267-0382;
www.ua.org

William P. Hite, President
Mark McManus, General Secretary/Treasurer

Official publication of the United Association of Journeymen and Apprentices of the Plumbing and Pipe Fitting Industry.
Frequency: Monthly
Circulation: 315000
ISSN: 0095-7763
Founded in: 1889

20582 Valve Magazine
Valve Manufacturers Association of America
1050 17th Street NW
Suite 280
Washington, DC 20036-5521

202-331-8105; *Fax:* 202-296-0378
wsandler@vma.org; www.valvemagazine.com

William S Sandler, President
Judy Tibbs, Associate Publisher/Editor-in-Chief
Sue Partyke, Advertising Director
Chris Guy, New Products, Media & Industry News
Michelle Wandres, Art Director/Production Manager

Promotion of significance and application of US and Canadian manufactured industrial valves and actuators.
Frequency: Quarterly
Circulation: 2600

Trade Shows

20583 ASPE Engineered Plumbing Exposition
National Trade Show Productions
313 South Patrick Street
Alexandria, VA 22314-1117

703-683-8500
800-687-7469; *Fax:* 703-836-4486;
www.ntpshow.com/ or www.aspe.org

Robert E Harar, Chairman and CEO
Karin Frendrich, Chief Operating Officer
Jennifer Hoff, Executive Director

A biennial exhibits trade show for the plumbing and engineering industry, the Engineered Plumbing Exposition, sponsored by the American Society of Plumbing Engineers/ASPE, is a gathering of plumbing, engineering and design products, equipment and services. Everything from pipes to pumps to fixtures, from compressors to computers and consulting services, is on display to allow engineers and specifiers to view the newest and most innovative design materials available to them.
7000 Attendees
Founded in: 1964

20584 Business and Education Conference
Int'l Assoc of Plumbing and Mechanical Officials
4755 E Philadelphia Street
Ontario, CA 91761

909-472-4100
800-854-2676; *Fax:* 909-472-4150
info@iapmo.org; www.iapmo.org

GP Russ Chaney, Chief Executive Officer
Gaby Davis, Director of Worldwide Operations
Neil Bogatz, General Counsel
Monte Bogatz, Associate General Counsel
Tricia Schwenke, Executive Assistant

IAPMO's annual conference brings together the public health and safety officials dedicated to plumbing and mechanical systems. for more than eighty years this venue allows for the free flow of information about changes in these necessary systems and provides technical education allowing these professionals hig competency in the associated cides and standards.
9000 Members
600 Attendees
Frequency: Annual/September
Founded in: 1923

20585 Directory of Listed Plumbing Products Annual Conference
Int'l Assn of Plumbing & Mechanical Officials
4755 E Philadelphia St
Ontario, CA 91761-2816

909-472-4100; *Fax:* 909-472-4150;
www.iapmo.org
Social Media: Facebook, Twitter, LinkedIn, YouTube

Gary Hice, VP
Dan Daniels, President
Russ Chancy, CEO
Dwight Perkins, Senior Director
7000 Members
450 Attendees
Founded in: 1926

20586 MSS Annual Meeting
Manufacturers Standardization Society
127 Park St NE
Vienna, VA 22180-4602

703-281-6613; *Fax:* 703-281-6671
orders@mss-hq.org; www.mss-hq.org

Robert O'Neill, Executive Director
Frequency: Annual/May
Founded in: 1924

20587 Mid-Atlantic Plumbing Heating Cooling Expo
Reber-Friel Company
221 King Manor Drive
Suite A
King Of Prussia, PA 19406-2500

610-272-4020; *Fax:* 610-272-5190

Richard Retzback, Show Manager

350 booths featuring products and services used by the plumbing, heating and cooling industries.
4.3M Attendees
Frequency: Annual/November

20588 National Plumbing, Heating, Cooling and Piping Products Exposition
American Supply Association
222 Merchandise Mart Plaza
Suite 1400
Chicago, IL 60654

312-464-0090; *Fax:* 312-464-0091
info@asa.net; www.asa.net/

Karen Weeks, Show Manager
Bob Higgason, Owner
George Conyngham Jr., President
Colin Perry, Treasurer
Inge Calderon, Secretary

Offers information and a forum for the exchange of ideas among plumbing, heating and cooling engineers.
11M Attendees

20589 NetworkASA
American Supply Association
222 Merchandise Mart
Suite 1400
Chicago, IL 60654
312-464-0090; *Fax:* 312-464-0091
info@asa.net; www.asa.net
Ruth Mitchell, Meetings/Conventions Director
For distributors and manufacturers in the PHCP/PVF industry. Provides information and opportunities that cannot be found with other organizations or events.
Frequency: Annual

20590 Spring Septic System Conference
Granite State Designers & Installers Association
53 Regional Drive
Concord, NH 03301-3520
603-228-1231; *Fax:* 603-228-2118
info@gsdia.org; www.gsdia.org
Carl Hagstrom, Director
Randy Orvis, Director
Conference and trade show with 30 exhibitors and booths for septic system professionals and other allied industries.
400 Attendees
Frequency: Annual/March

Directories & Databases

20591 Complete Directory of Plumbing Products
Sutton Family Communications & Publishing Company
National Fleamarketeer
155 Sutton Lane
Fordsville, KY 42343
270-740-0870
jlsutton@apex.net;
www.suttoncompliance.com
Theresa Sutton, Editor
Lee Sutton, General Manager
Print-out from database of wholesalers, manufacturers, distributors, importers and close-out houses. Database is updated daily to guarantee the most current and up-to-date sources available.
Cost: $55.20
100+ Pages

20592 Directory of Custom Compounders
Delphi Marketing Services
400 E 89th Street
Apartment 2J
New York, NY 10128-6728
Dr. Newman Giragosian, Editor
Offers information on manufacturers of custom mixtures of plastics and resins.
Cost: $295.00
115 Pages
Frequency: Annual

20593 Directory of Listed Plumbing Products
Int'l Assn of Plumbing & Mechanical Officials
4755 E Philadelphia St
Ontario, CA 91761-2816
909-472-4100; *Fax:* 909-472-4150;
www.iapmo.org
Leticia Wilson, Manager
Dan Daniels, VP
Russ Chancy, Executive Director
Directory of products and supplies to the plumbing industry.
Cost: $93.00
1300 Pages
Frequency: Monthly

20594 Plumbing Engineer: Product Directory Issue
TMB Publishing
2165 Shermer Rd
Suite A
Northbrook, IL 60062-5474
847-564-1127; *Fax:* 847-564-1264
editor@plumbingengineer.com;
www.tmbpublishing.com
John Mesenbrink, Chief Editor
Marilyn Cunningham, Assistant Editor
Cate Brown, Production Manager
Sadie Bechtold, Production Assistant
Mark Bruno, Art Director
Over 400 plumbing products from approximately 250 manufacturers.
Frequency: Annual/January
Circulation: 2,6104

20595 Who's Who in the Plumbing-Heating-Cooling Contracting Business
Nat'l Assn of Plumbing-Heating-Cooling Contractors
180 South Washington Street
PO Box 6808
Falls Church, VA 22046-2900
703-237-8100
800-533-7694; *Fax:* 703-237-7442
naphcc@naphcc.org; www.phccweb.org
Frank Maddalon, President
Keith Bienvenu, President-Elect
David Dugger, VP
Kevin Tindall, Secretary
Gerry Kennedy, Executive VP
About 6,000 professional plumbing/heating/cooling contractors and member firms.
Cost: $75.00
Frequency: Annual
Circulation: 15,000
Founded in: 1883

Industry Web Sites

20596 http://gold.greyhouse.com
G.O.L.D Grey House OnLine Databases
Grey House Publishing's online database platform, GOLD, offers Quick Search, Keyword Search and Expert Search for most business sectors including plumbing and heating markets. The GOLD platform makes finding the information you need quick and easy - whether you're a novice searcher or an experienced database user. All of Grey House's directory products are available for subscription on the GOLD platform.

20597 www.asa.net
American Supply Association
For industry wholesale distributors and manufacturers.

20598 www.aspe.org
American Society of Plumbing Engineers
Seeks to resolve professional problems in plumbing engineering. Operates a certification program.

20599 www.asse-plumbing.org
American Society of Sanitary Engineering
Members are from all segments of the plumbing industry, including contractors, engineers, inspectors, journeymen, apprentices and others involved in the industry. Provides information, the opportunity to exchange ideas, solve problems and offers forum where all sides can express their views.

20600 www.construction.com
McGraw-Hill Construction
McGraw-Hill Construction (MHC), part of The McGraw-Hill Companies, connects people and projects across the design and construction industry, serving owners, architects, engineers, general contractors, subcontractors, building product manufacturers, suppliers, dealers, distributors and adjacent markets.

20601 www.greyhouse.com
Grey House Publishing
Authoritative reference directories for most business sectors including plumbing and heating markets. Users can search the online databases with varied search criteria allowing for custom searches by product category, geographic area, sales volume, keyword, subject and more. Full Grey House catalog and online ordering also available.

20602 www.iapmo.org
Int'l Assoc of Plumbing and Mechanical Officers
IAPMO has been protecting the public's health and safety for more than eighty years by working in concert with government and industry to implement comprehensive plumbing and mechanical systems around the world.

20603 www.pdionline.org
Plumbing and Drainage Institute
For manufacturers of engineered plumbing products, flood drains, roof drains, sanitary floor drains, cleanouts, water hammer arresters, swimming pool drains, backwater valves, grease interceptors, fixture supports, and other drainage specialties.

20604 www.sweets.construction.com
McGraw Hill Construction
In depth product information that lets you find, compare, select, specify and make purchase decisions in the industrial product marketplace.

20605 www.uboiler.com
Uniform Boiler and Pressure Vessel Laws Society
Established to promote uniformity in rules, laws and regulations for boiler and pressure vessel safety based on the requirements of the American Society of Mechanical Engineers Boiler and Pressure Vessel Code and other related national standards.

20606 www.vma.org
Valve Manufacturers Association of America

Associations

20607 Amalgamated Printers Association
3019 Elm Lane
Middleton, WI 53562

406-928-4757
TWOEMPRESS@aol.com
apa-letterpress.com
Social Media: Facebook, Twitter, LinkedIn, Google+, Pinterest

Sky Shipley, President
Joe Warren, VP
Cindy Iverson, Secretary/Treasurer
Howard Gelbert, Director
David Kent, Archivist

The Amalgamated Printers' Association was organized in 1958 as a hobby printers group so that members could improve their skills, expand their knowledge, and exchange samples of their letterpress work in addition to encouraging excellence of printing content, design, and techniques.
150 Members
Founded in: 1958

20608 American Printing History Association
PO Box 4519
Grand Central Station
New York, NY 10163

E-Mail: secretary@printinghistory.org
printinghistory.org

Robert McCamant, President

Membership organization promoting the study of the history of printing and related arts such as calligraphy and typography.

20609 Assoc. Suppliers of Printing, Publishing & Converting Technologies
1899 Preston White Drive
Reston, VA 20191

703-264-7200; *Fax:* 703-620-0994
npes@npes.org; www.npes.org

Ralph J. Nappi, President
Michael Ring, Chairman
Mal Baboyian, Treasurer
Mark J. Nuzzaco, Secretary
Marc Olin, Vice President & General Manager

The Association for Suppliers of Printing , Publishing and Converting Technologies is a trade association that represents manufacturers, importers and distributors of equipment, supplies, systems and software used in every printing, publishing and converting process from design to distribution. Virtually all industry products and processes are represented by the member companies, which range in size from under $1 million in annual sales revenue to more than $1 billion.
600 Members
Founded in: 1933

20610 Binding Industries of America
Printing Industry of Illinois
200 Deer Run Road
Sewickley, PA 15143

412-741-6860
800-910-4283; *Fax:* 412-741-2311
printing@printing.org;
www.bindingindustries.org
Social Media: Facebook, Twitter, LinkedIn, Google+, Pinterest

Frederick A. Hartwig, Manager, Environment ane Health
Gary A. Jones, Assistant Vice President
Chris Eckhart, Chairman
Chris Webbert, Vice-Chairman

A trade association representing bindery and looseleaf manufacturers, graphic finishers, and supplies to those industries
350 Members
Founded in: 1955

20611 Book Manufacturers' Institute (BMI)
2 Armand Beach Drive
Suite 1B
Palm Coast, FL 32137-2612

386-986-4552; *Fax:* 386-986-4553
info@bmibook.com; www.bmibook.org

Daniel N Bach, Executive VP & Secretary
Jac B. Garner, President
Kent H. Larson, President-Elect/ Vice President
Paul Genovesse, Treasurer
Robert J. Boyd, General counsel

Since 1933, the Book Manufacturers' Institute, Inc. (BMI) has been the leading nationally recognized trade association of the book manufacturing industry. BMI member companies annually produce the great majority of books ordered by the U. S. book publishing industry. Today, BMI is a vital part of the industry, playing a leading role by providing an intra-industry communications link among book manufacturers, publishers, suppliers and governmental bodies.
90 Members
Founded in: 1933

20612 Center for Book Arts
28 W 27th St
3rd Floor
New York, NY 10001

212-481-0295; *Fax:* 212-481-9853
info@centerforbookarts.org;
www.centerforbookarts.org
Social Media: Facebook, Twitter, YouTube, Flickr, Instagram

Andrew W Mellon, Chair
Brian Hannon, Vice Chair
Robert J. Ruben, MD & Co Chair
Nancy Macomber, Treasurer
David W. Lowden, Secretary

The Center for Book Arts is dedicated to preserving the traditional crafts of book-making, as well as exploring and encouraging contemporary interpretations of the book as an art object. Each year the Center offers three terms of courses, workshops and seminars taught by experienced book artists, and providing hands-on training in all aspects of traditional and contemporary bookmaking, including bookbinding, letterpress printing, papermaking, and other associated arts.
Founded in: 1974

20613 Flexographic Technical Association Inc.
3920 Veterans Memorial Highway
Suite 9
Bohemia, NY 11716-1074

631-737-6020; *Fax:* 631-737-6813
memberinfo@flexography.org;
www.flexography.org
Social Media: Twitter, LinkedIn

Allen J. Marquardt, Chair
Jack Fulton, Vice Chair
Howard B. Vreeland, Chair-elect
Mark Cisternino, President
Dan Doherty, Treasurer

Technical society devoted exclusively to the flexographic printing industry.
1500 Members
Founded in: 1958

20614 Gravure Association of the Americas
8281 Pink Lake Rd.
Denver, NC 28037

201-523-6042; *Fax:* 201-523-6048
gaa@gaa.org; www.gaa.org
Social Media: Facebook, LinkedIn

Philip Pimlott, Executive Director

The Association promotes gravure printing, a high-tech process that runs on the fastest and widest presses in the world.
Founded in: 2013

20615 In-Plant Printing and Mailing Association
455 S. Sam Barr Drive
Suite 203
Keaney, MO 64060

816-919-1691; *Fax:* 816-902-4766
ipmainfo@ipma.org; www.ipma.org
Social Media: Facebook, Twitter, LinkedIn, YouTube, Google+

Carma Goin, Executive Director
Rob Lingard, President
Tammy Golden, Secretary/Treasurer
Mike Lincoln, President-Elect
Dwayne Magee, Membership Representative

The professional association for all segments of the in-house corporate printing and mailing professionals who work for educational institutions, the government, and private industry.
600 Members
Founded in: 1964

20616 International Waterless Printing Association
International Waterless Printing Association
5 Southside Dr Unit 11-328
Clifton Park, NY 12065

518-387-9321
800-850-0660; *Fax:* 518-310-2383
info@waterless.org; www.waterless.org

John O'Rourke, Vice president
Brian Amos, Secretary
Julie Leonhard, Treasurer
Joel Friedman, Executive Director
Ruud Kempers, Director European Operations

Dedicated to the informational and educational needs of its printer and sponsor members. Seeks to inform designers and print buyers about the many benefits the process offers.
Founded in: 1993

20617 Printing Brokerage Buyers Association
1530 Locust Street
Mezanine 124
Philadelphia, PA 19102

215-821-6581
866-586-9391; *Fax:* 561-845-7130;
www.pbba.org
Social Media: RSS

Vincent Mallardi, Chairman

Promotes business relationships among brokers, buying groups, manufacturers and related companies. Sets standards, codes and supplies information and referrals.

20618 Printing Impressions
North American Publishing Company (NAPCO)
1500 Spring Garden St
12th Floor
Philadelphia, PA 19130

215-238-5338
888-889-9491; *Fax:* 212-238-5280
webmaster@napco.com; www.piworld.com

Social Media: Facebook, Twitter, LinkedIn, Yahoo,Windows Live

Rosemary Sirico, President
Diane Pesce, VP
Mark T. Michelson, Editor-in-Chief
Erik Cagle, Senior Editor, PI Weekly Editor
Alex Schwartz, Senior Editor, PI Weekly Editor

Promotes the interests of women in the production profession.
Founded in: 1966

20619 Printing Industries of America
301 Brush Creek Road
Warrendale, PA 15086-7529

412-741-6860
800-910-4283; *Fax:* 412-741-2311
info@printing.org; www.printing.org
Social Media: Facebook, Twitter, LinkedIn, Pinterest

Michael F. Makin, Ex-Officio
Mr Michael S Wurst, Treasurer
Paul L Cousineau, Chairman, Research Committee
David A. Olberding, Chairman of the Board of Directors
Bradley L. Thompson, 1st Vice Chairman

A graphic arts trade association representing our members in this industry. Printing Industries of America, along with its affiliates, delivers products and services that enhance the growth, efficiency and profitability of its members and the industry through advocacy, education, research and technical information
10000 Members
Founded in: 1887

20620 Printing Industries of New England
5 Crystal Pond Road
Southborough, MA 01772

508-804-4100
800-365-7463; *Fax:* 508-804-4119;
www.pine.org
Social Media: Facebook, Twitter, LinkedIn

Tad Parker, President
Kurt Peterson, Chairman
Bob Clement, Secretary/Treasurer
Justin Pallis, Vice Chairman
Mike Peluso, Member at Large

Serves more than 450 commercial printing and graphic communications companies throughout five New England states. Provides products and services on an ongoing basis to help member companies operate more profitably.
450 Members
Founded in: 1887

20621 Printing Industries of Northern California
665 3rd St
Suite 500
San Francisco, CA 94107

415-495-8242
800-659-3363; *Fax:* 800-824-1911
info@vma.bz
main.vma.bz
Social Media: Facebook, Twitter, LinkedIn, Google+, Pinterest, YouTube, V

Frank Parks, Chairman
John Crammer, 1st Vice Chairman
Arnold Greenfield, Ex Officio
Dan Nelson, President
David Katz, Vice President

The Printing Industries of Northern California (PINC) is a non-profit trade association serving several industry segments in Northern California, primarily the print production and print buying segments.

20622 Printing Industry Association of the South
305 Plus Park Blvd
Nashville, TN 37217

615-366-1094; *Fax:* 615-366-4192
info@pias.org; www.pias.org

Ed Chalifoux, President

The Printing Industry Association of the South (PIAS), a non-profit trade association, is dedicated to assisting the entire industry to continue to expand in the region and help the industry prosper across the seven-state region of Alabama, Arkansas, Kentucky, Louisiana, Mississippi, Tennessee and West Virginia.
520 Members

20623 Printing and Graphic Communications Association
6411 Ivy Lane
Suite 700
Greenbelt, MD 20770

www.pgca.org

Serves the graphic communications community in the Washington, D.C. metropolitan area.
Founded in: 1914

20624 Society for Service Professionals in Printing (SSPP)
Document Management Industries Association
433 E Monroe Ave
Alexandria, VA 22301-1645

703-684-0044
877-777-7398; *Fax:* 703-548-9137
ssppinfo@sspp.org; www.sspp.org

Peter Colainni, Executive Director
Marj Green, Director
Kevin Cooper, Billing Coordinator
Pam Decker, Webmaster

A national organization that focuses on rates, service and trends in the printing industry for consumers. SSPP provides information about both printing and customer service to its members through three monthly newsletters and special interest bulletins. SSPP sponsors the national Certification Examination for Printing Service Specialists (CPSS), which recognizes those printing service specialists who have attained a proscribed body of knowledge about both printing and customer service.
Cost: $150.00

20625 Specialty Graphic Imaging Association
10015 Main St
Fairfax, VA 22031

703-385-1335
888-385-3588; *Fax:* 703-273-0456;
www.sgia.org
Social Media: Facebook, Twitter, LinkedIn, Wordpress

Michael Robertson, President
James Gill, Associate Vice Chairman
Hoddy Peck, Chairman
Lynn Krinsky, Treasurer
Scott Crosby, Secretary

Participants include corporations, institutions and individuals interested in screen printing and digital imaging. Conducts technical research and training workshops.
Founded in: 1986

20626 The 3D Printing Association
Silicon Valley Center
2570 N First St.
San Jose, CA 95131

408-600-2647;
www.the3dprintingassociation.org

The Association supports and represents all interests in the 3D printing industry.
Founded in: 2013

Newsletters

20627 Binding Edge
Printing Industry of Illinois
200 Deer Run Road
Sewickley, PA 15143

412-741-6860
800-910-4283; *Fax:* 412-741-2311
gain@piagatf.org; www.bindingindustries.org
Social Media: Facebook, Twitter, LinkedIn

Michael Makin, President/CEO
Justin Goldstein, Manager

Includes articles designed to help bindery and loose leaf facilities improve their processes and keep up on the latest technologies.
Frequency: Quarterly
Circulation: 12000

20628 Business Printing Technologies Report
DMIA
433 East Monroe Avenue
Alexandria, VA 22301-1645

703-836-6232; *Fax:* 703-836-2241;
www.dmia.org

Timothy J Mehl, President
Peter L Colaianni, Executive VP
Brad Holt, VP Media/Publications
Robert O'Connell, Treasurer
Marj Green, VP Operations

Offers a complete overview of the printing industry.
Frequency: Annual
Circulation: 5600
Founded in: 1955

20629 Economic Edge
National Association for Printing Leadership
One Meadowlands Plaza
Suite 1511
East Rutherford, NJ 07073

201-634-9600
800-642-6275; *Fax:* 201-634-0324
webmaster@napl.org; www.napl.org
Social Media: Facebook, Twitter, LinkedIn, YouTube,RSS

Joseph Truncale, President
Timothy Fischer, Executive VP/COO

Economic analysis of the graphic arts industry.
Cost: $150.00
12 Pages
Frequency: Quarterly
Founded in: 1933

20630 Footprints
Footprint Communications
1339 Massachusetts Street
Lawrence, KS 66044

800-488-8316; *Fax:* 785-832-0087
mike@footcom.com; www.footprints.com

Dick Vinocur, Publisher

A newsletter for the printing industry reporting news, management, marketing and financial data (including industry stock indexes), product introductions, personnel changes, association affairs and recent acquisitions and mergers.

Footprints also reports on exhibits, shows, meetings and conferences in the graphic arts industry.
Cost: $327.00
Frequency: Fortnightly

20631 Graphic Arts Monthly Online
Reed Business Information
4709 Golf Road
Skokie, IL 60076

800-217-7874; *Fax:* 630-288-8781
psaran@reedbusiness.com;
www.reedbusiness.com

Jeff Greisch, President
Bill Esler, Editor-in-Chief
Lisa Cross, Web Site Editor
Stephanie Kauffman, Reprint Management Services
Mark Kelsey, CEO

Graphic Arts Monthly Online is a subscriber-based Web portal for printing professionals and print buyers featuring current and archived news, research and business tools, online classifieds, used equipment marketplace and online training and education.
Cost: $159.00
Frequency: Monthly

20632 Graphic Communicator
Graphic Communications International Union
25 Louisiana Avenue N.W
Washington, DC 20001

202-624-6800; *Fax:* 202-721-0600
webmessenger@gciu.org; www.gciu.org
Social Media: Facebook, Twitter

James P Hoffa, President
Ken Hall, Secretary-Treasurer

Tabloid size newspaper for and about members of the GCIU. The international union represents workers in the printing/publishing industry. Members range from desktop operators to paper handler.
Cost: $12.00
Circulation: 100000
Founded in: 1983

20633 NAQP Network
National Association for Printing Leadership
One Meadowlands Plaza
Suite 1511
East Rutherford, NJ 07073

201-634-9600
800-642-6275; *Fax:* 201-634-0324
webmaster@napl.org; www.naqp.com
Social Media: Facebook, Twitter, LinkedIn, YouTube,RSS

Joseph P Truncale, President & CEO
Dean D' Ambrosi, Vice President
Carol Rocke, Marketing Coordinator

Editorial content covers technological advances, product news, profiles on industry leaders, and club events.
Frequency: Monthly
Circulation: 900

20634 Printing News
Cygnus Publishing
3 Huntington Quadrangle
Suite 301N
Melville, NY 11747-3601

631-845-2700
800-308-6397; *Fax:* 631-249-5774
editor@printingnews.com;
www.printingnews.com
Social Media: Facebook, Twitter, LinkedIn

David Kastriner, Publisher
Michael Zerner, Associate Publisher
David Lindsay, Editor-in-Chief
Rachel Frank, Editor

Includes timely news and information on a variety of subjects including technological breakthroughs, industry trends, marketing, finance, as well as industry leader and corporate profiles.
Cost: $39.95
Frequency: Weekly
Circulation: 9000
Founded in: 1928
Mailing list available for rent

20635 SGIA Journal
Specialty Graphic Imaging Association
10015 Main St
Fairfax, VA 22031-3489

703-385-1335
888-385-3588; *Fax:* 703-273-0456
sgia@sgia.org; www.sgia.org
Social Media: Facebook, Twitter, LinkedIn

Michael Robertson, President
Sondra Fry Benoudiz, VP Membership
Lynn Krinsky, Chairman
Pete Gallo, First Vice Chairman
Tim Markley, Second Vice Chairman

Provides members with access to information relative to industry trends and the latest news such as emerging markets, government regulations, and technological developments.
Cost: $149.00
Frequency: Bi-Monthly
Circulation: 3800
Founded in: 1948
Printed in 2 colors on glossy stock

20636 Signature Service
Signature Service Real Estate Rainier
302 Binghampton Street W
PO Box 8
Rainier, WA 98576

360-446-4646
877-446-4647; *Fax:* 360-446-2400;
www.signatureservice.com

Peter Colaianni, Executive Director
Marj Green, Director
Kevin Cooper, Billing Coordinator
Pam Decker, Webmaster

Newsletter covering rates, service and trends in the printing industry for consumers.
Cost: $115.00
8 Pages
Frequency: Monthly
Circulation: 2000

Magazines & Journals

20637 American InkMaker
Cygnus Publishing
PO Box 803
Fort Atkinson, WI 53538-0803

920-000-1111
800-547-7377; *Fax:* 920-563-1699
Rich.Reiff@CygnusPub.com;
www.cygnusb2b.com

John French, CEO
Robert Stange, Senior VP Marketing

Offers information to the professional ink manufacturer. The editorial content consists of contributed technical papers and nontechnical features about trends, technology and global happenings to help our readers to improve their profitability in addition to featuring a monthly interview with printers.
Cost: $46.00
Circulation: 3800
Founded in: 1923

20638 American Printer
American Printer
2100 West Loop South
Suite 900
Houston, TX 77027-3515

713-300-0674
info@AmericanPrinter.com;
www.americanprinter.com
Social Media: Facebook, Twitter, RSS

Katherine O'Brien, Editor
Michael P Koch, Senior Art Director
Denise Kapel, Managing Editor
Carrie Cleaveland, Assistant Editor
Jill Roth, Director Brand Development

Regular issue features include new products listings, new equipment technology and reports on system developments.
Frequency: Monthly
Circulation: 86037
Founded in: 1883
Mailing list available for rent

20639 Awards & Engraving Magazine
National Business Media
PO Box 1416
Broomfield, CO 80038-1416

303-469-0424
800-669-0424; *Fax:* 303-469-5730
steve@nbm.com; www.nbm.com
Social Media: Facebook, Twitter, LinkedIn

Bob Wieber, President
Dave Pomeroy, Publisher

Content includes a special focus, and regular articles on signage, the glass market, business management, people profiles, and advances in technology.
Cost: $38.00
Frequency: Monthly
Founded in: 1985

20640 Big Picture
325 Public Street
Providence, RI 02905

401-752-3442
800-421-1321; *Fax:* 401-752-3528
webmaster@bigpicturelearning.org;
www.bigpicture.org

Tedd Swormstedt, CEO
Ronald A. Wolk, Chairman

This publication reports on digital printing of visual communications with coverage of digital printing from image capture and processing to finishing and display.
Frequency: Monthly
Circulation: 48000
Founded in: 1996

20641 Dealer Communicator
Fichera Communications
441 South State Road 7
Suite 14
Margate, FL 33068-2823

954-971-4360
800-327-8999; *Fax:* 954-971-4362
omike@dealercommunicator.com;
www.dealercommunicator.com

Orazio Fichera, Publisher/President
Particia Leavitt, VP

Provides national and international coverage for the graphic arts and printing industries.
Cost: $30.00
32 Pages
Frequency: Monthly
Circulation: 13619
Founded in: 1982
Printed in 4 colors on glossy stock

20642 Digital Graphics
National Business Media

PO Box 1416
Broomfield, CO 80038-1416

303-469-0424
800-669-0424; *Fax:* 303-465-3424
kmergent@nbm.com; www.nbm.com
Social Media: Facebook, Twitter, LinkedIn

Bob Wieber, President
Ken Mergentime, Editor

Regular departments track public stock comapnies of interest to the industry, report on international graphics news and highlight recent technological advances.
64 Pages
Frequency: Monthly
Circulation: 18583
Founded in: 1985
Printed in 4 colors

20643 Digital Output
Rockport Custom Publishing
100 Cummings Ctr
Suite 321E
Beverly, MA 01915-6101

978-921-7850; *Fax:* 978-921-7870
edit@rockportpubs.com;
www.rockportpubs.com

Thomas Tetreault, CEO
Lynn Weese, Account Executive

Provides case studies and trend updates, as well as discussing how and why companies integrate and coordinate their marketing strategies.
Frequency: 12 + 2 Buyers Guides

20644 Document Processing Technology
RB Publishing Company
2424 American Lane
PO Box 259906
Madison, WI 53725-9906

608-277-8785
800-536-1992; *Fax:* 608-241-8666
rbpub@rbpub.com; www.rbpub.com

Ron Brent, Publisher/President
Allison Lloyd, Managing Editor
Marll Thiede, Executive Editor/VP
Rachel Spahr, Circulation Manager
Tonjia Weber, Production Manager

Covers digital printing, publishing and distribution. Feature and special topic articles focus on industry trends, technology and strategies for high-volume document processors.
Frequency: Monthly
Circulation: 10000
Founded in: 1988

20645 Electronic Publishing
PennWell Publishing Company
1421 S Sheridan Rd
Tulsa, OK 74112-6619

918-835-3161
800-331-4463; *Fax:* 918-831-9476
Headquarters@PennWell.com;
www.pennwell.com

Robert Biolchini, President
Courtney E Howard, Managing Editor
Frank J Romano, Sr Contributing & Founding Editor
Nancy A Hitchcock, Senior Associate Editor

For those who communicate in print, including service bureaus, printers, prepress houses and desktop publishers, it provides latest products, news and related developments.
Cost: $59.00
Frequency: Monthly
Circulation: 68441
Founded in: 1910
Mailing list available for rent

20646 Flash Magazine
BlackLighting
252 Riddle Pond Road
West Topsham, VT 05086

800-252-2599
800-252-2599; *Fax:* 802-439-6462
salesBL@BlackLightning.com;
www.flashweb.com

Walter Vose Jeffries, Publisher

Flash Magazine was started in 1989 and is all about desktop publishing, book-on-demand binding, inkjet & laser printinting, heat transfers and other topics of interest to the small time publisher and graphic artist. The Flash is filled with great how-to articles that will help you take care of your printer, do maintenance & repairs yourself, teach you about graphics, digital photography, scanning and laser etching glass and book-on-demand publishing, binding and so much more.
Cost: $20.00
Frequency: Monthly
Circulation: 112000

20647 Flexo Magazine
Flexographic Technical Association
3920 Veterans Memorial Highway
Suite 9
Bohemia, NY 11716

631-737-6020; *Fax:* 631-737-6813
membership@flexography.org;
www.flexography.org
Social Media: Facebook, LinkedIn

Robert Moran, Publisher
Christian Bonawandt, Editor

Trade publication for the flexographic printing industry.
1300 Members
Frequency: Monthly

20648 Forms & Direct Mail Manufacturer's Marketplace
Bulls-Eye Communications
211 Champion Avenue
Webster, NY 14580

585-265-3045

Marsha A Thompson, Editor

The resource magazine of business forms and direct mail printers. Spotlights news and products in the industry.
Cost: $49.00
Frequency: Bi-Monthly
Circulation: 4,870

20649 Graphic Communications World
Hayzlett & Associates
3313 South Western Avenue
Sioux Falls, SD 57106

605-355-5531; *Fax:* 605-275-2087;
www.hayzlett.com/index.htm

Jeanette Clinkunbroomer, Editor
Jeff Hayzlett, Owner

Offers a comprehensive overview of the graphic arts and communications industry.
Cost: $347.00
Frequency: Monthly
Founded in: 1968

20650 Gravure
Gravure Association of America
1200A Scottsville Road
Rochester, NY 14624-5703

585-436-2150; *Fax:* 585-436-7689
lwshatch@gaa.org; www.gaa.org

Laura Wayland-Smith Hatch, Editor
William Martin, President/CEO

Editorial coverage focuses on the technical developments in gravure printing, the financial performance of the industry and association member activities.
Cost: $67.00
Circulation: 3500
ISSN: 0894-4946
Founded in: 1987
Printed in 4 colors on matte stock

20651 High Volume Printing (HVP)
Innes Publishing Company
28100 North Ashley Circle
PO Box 7280
Libertyville, IL 60048

847-816-7900
800-247-3306; *Fax:* 847-247-8855
meinnes@innespub.com; www.innespub.com

Mary Ellen Innes, Publisher
Ray Roth, Editor
Barb Pettersen, Circulation Manager
Mary Ellin Innes, President
Judy Abbott, Administrative Assistant

HVP offers a strategic mix of management and production-oriented editorial content, and has consistently led in coverage of new technologies and regulatory issues. It focuses on the bottom-line realities involved in merging tomorrow's technologies with today's operating environment. Subjects include prepress, press, and postpress equipment and technology, sales and marketing management, training, regulatory issues and more.
Circulation: 39057
Founded in: 1982

20652 IPA Bulletin
IPA: Association of Graphic Solutions Providers
7200 France Ave S
Suite 223
Edina, MN 55435-4309

952-896-1908
800-255-8141; *Fax:* 708-596-5112
bessie@ipa.org; www.ipa.org

Steven Bonnoff, Executive Director
Becky Walroth, Editorial Assistant
Steven Bonoff, President

Association news offering information on prepress and graphic arts.
Cost: $20.00
6 Pages
Circulation: 2,100
ISSN: 1539-137X
Founded in: 1911
Printed in 4 colors on glossy stock

20653 In Plant Graphics
North American Publishing Company
1500 Spring Garden St
Suite 1200
Philadelphia, PA 19130-4094

215-238-5300; *Fax:* 215-238-5342;
www.ipgonline.com

Ned S Borowsky, CEO
Glen Reynolds, Publisher
Dorlissa Goodrich, Production Manager
Maggie Tajack, Advertising Promotion Manager
Brian Ludwig, Group Publisher

Articles include management advice, technical information, industry news and reader profiles.
Cost: $65.00
60 Pages
Frequency: Monthly
Circulation: 20,000
ISSN: 1087-2817
Founded in: 1996
Printed in 4 colors on glossy stock

20654 In Plant Printer
Innes Publishing Company

28100 North Ashley Circle
Suite 101
Libertyville, IL 60048

847-816-7900
800-247-3306; *Fax:* 847-247-8855;
www.innespub.com

Mary Ellin Innes, President
Jack Klasnic, Editor
Barbara Pettersen, Circulation Manager
Teri Saeed, Production Manager
Judy Abbott, Administrative Assistant

Serves printing, graphics and typesetting facilities located in business, industry, education, government, hospitals, associations, and nonprofit organizations.
Cost: $110.00
70 Pages
Frequency: Monthly
Circulation: 247637
ISSN: 0891-8996
Founded in: 1977
Printed in 4 colors on glossy stock

20655 Ink World
Ink World Direct Limited
108 Queens Road
Nuneaton, WI 07446-1150

800-011-2011
info@rodpub.com; www.ink-world.com

Rodman Zilenziger Jr, President
Matt Montgomery, VP

Covers the printing inks, coatings and allied industries.
64 Pages
Frequency: Monthly
Circulation: 6187
Founded in: 1994
Printed in 4 colors on glossy stock

20656 Inside Finishing Magazine
Foil & Speciality Effects Association
2150 Southwest Wesport Drive
Suite 101
Topeka, KS 66614

785-271-5816; *Fax:* 785-271-6404
fseamail@fsea.com; www.fsea.com

Jeff Peterson, Executive Director
Gayla Peterson, Sales Director
Kym Conis, Assistant Director
Eric.J Carter, Art Director & Webmaster

A quarterly magazine published by the Foil Stamping and Embossing Association, Inside Finishing has a targeted circulation of 6,000 graphic finishing decision makers. These include trade finishers, folding carton companies, greeting card manufacturers, and commercial printers with finishing/bindery operations. It also includes a small percentage of graphic designers involved in the foil stamping and embossing industry, and, of course, industry suppliers to the graphic finishing industry.
56 Pages
Frequency: 4 issues
Founded in: 1994

20657 Instant and Small Commercial Printer ISCP
Innes Publishing Company
28100 North Ashley Circle
PO Box 7280
Libertyville, IL 60048-7280

847-816-7900
800-247-3306; *Fax:* 847-247-8855;
www.innespub.com

Dan Innes, Publisher
Linda Casey, Editor
Barb Pettersen, Circualtion MAnager
Mary Ellin Innes, President

ISCP magazine publishes how-to articles and case histories on printing and photocopy reproduction. Emphasis on desktop publishing and short-run digital technologies reflects the growth of this service in instant printing operations. Management stories are aimed at helping the publication's largely entrepreneurial audience grapple successfully with everyday problems and spot new opportunities for growth.
Frequency: Monthly
Circulation: 413671
Founded in: 1982

20658 Label & Narrow Web Industry
Rodman Publishing
70 Hilltop Rd
Suite 3000
Ramsey, NJ 07446-1150

201-825-2552; *Fax:* 201-825-0553
label@rodpub.com;
www.labelandnarrowweb.com
Social Media: Facebook, Twitter, LinkedIn, RSS

Rodman J. Zilenziger Jr, President
Matthew Montgomery, VP
Kathleen Scully, Publisher
Steve Katz, Editor
Catherine Diamond, Associate Editor

Label and Narrow Web serves manufacturers of label and narrow web including labels, tags, tape, materials, substrates, machinery, and equipment and others allied to the field.
80 Pages
Circulation: 11000
ISSN: 1095-3248
Founded in: 1996
Mailing list available for rent
Printed in 4 colors on glossy stock

20659 New England Printer and Publisher
Printing Industries of New England
5 Crystal Pond Rd
Southborough, MA 01772-1758

508-804-4100
800-365-7463; *Fax:* 508-804-4119
jtepper04@pine.org; www.pine.org

John Scibelli, Manager
Joe La Valla, Chairman
Brie Drummond, Production Manager
Kurt Peterson, Vice-Chairman
Bob Clement, Secretary-Treasurer

Trade magazine for printers and publishers.
Cost: $2.40
48 Pages
Frequency: Monthly
Circulation: 4000
Founded in: 1938
Printed in 4 colors on matte stock

20660 New Pages: Alternatives in Print and Media
New Pages Press
PO Box 1580
Bay City, MI 48706

989-671-0081; *Fax:* 313-743-2730
newpagesonline@hotmail.com;
www.newpages.com

Casey Hill, Publisher
Denise Hill, Editor

News and information for bookstores and libraries.
Cost: $12.00
64 Pages
Frequency: Quarterly

20661 Newspapers & Technology
Conley Magazines
1623 Blake Street
Suite 250
Denver, CO 80202
303-575-9595; *Fax:* 303-575-9555;
www.newsandtech.com/

Mary Van Meter, Publisher
Chuck Moozakis, Editor-in-Chief
Tara McKeekin, Editor
Hays Goodman, Associate Editor/Webmaster

Newspapers & Technology is a monthly trade publication for newspaper publishers and department managers involved in applying and integrating technology. Written by industry experts, News & Tech provides regular coverage of the following departments: prepress, press, postpress and new media.
Circulation: 16,874

20662 PC Presentations Productions
Pisces Publishing Group
1400 South Nova Road
Suite 303
Daytona Beach, FL 32114-5851

203-877-1927; *Fax:* 203-877-1927;
www.piscespub.com

Don Johnson, Editor/Publisher
Douglas Finlay, Managing Editor

PC Presentations Productions is a free online magazine intended for both the high-end professional and the student. Graphic and video tutorials for intermediate and advanced content producers are regular features as are HTML and Javascript tutorials and Website design tutorials intended for students and others wishing to add these skills.
Frequency: Weekly
ISSN: 1065-9699

20663 Package Printing
North American Publishing Company
1500 Spring Garden St
Suite 1200
Philadelphia, PA 19130-4094

215-238-5300
800-627-2689; *Fax:* 215-238-5342
customerservice@napco.com;
www.packageprinting.com
Social Media: Facebook, Twitter, LinkedIn, Yahoo,Windows Live

Ned S Borowsky, CEO
Brian Ludwick, Publisher
Robert Margulies, Sales Manager
Megan Wolf, Assistant Editor
Sean Sams, Advertising Account Manager

Trade publication serving the business and technology needs of presidents and CEOs of flexible packaging, tag and label, folding rigid boxes and directing operations.
Cost: $99.50
75 Pages
Frequency: Monthly
Circulation: 24000
Founded in: 1958
Mailing list available for rent

20664 Paper Magazine
365 Broadway
6th Floor
New York, NY 10013

212-226-4405
800-829-9160; *Fax:* 212-226-0062
edit@papermag.com; www.papermag.com

Sharon Phair, Advertising & Marketing
Kim Hastreiter, Publisher
Alexis Swerdloff, Executive Editor
Nobu Massiah, Editor
Carol Lee, Creative Director

PAPER Magazine focuses on the latest trends in pop culture, style, music and film, including information on New York art exhibits, club listings, literary events, movie reviews and shows. Includes night-life guide.
Cost: $9.97
Frequency: 10 Issues Per Year
Circulation: 90,000
Founded in: 1984

20665 Print Business Register
Cygnus Business Media

3 Huntington Quadrangle
Suite 301 North
Melville, NY 11747

631-845-2700
800-308-6397; *Fax:* 631-845-2741;
www.cygnusb2b.com
Social Media: Facebook

Michael Zerner, Publisher
Rachel Frank, Editor

Editorial material reports on mergers, acquisitions, reorganizations and major issues affecting the marketplace of the commercial printing industry.
Frequency: Weekly
Circulation: 650
Mailing list available for rent

20666 Print Magazine
RC Publications
38 east 29th street, 4th floor
New York, NY 10016

212-447-1400; *Fax:* 212-447-5231
info@printmag.com; www.printmag.com
Social Media: Facebook, Twitter, Flickr

Joel Toner, Publisher

Regular highlights include advertising and promotion design, corporate identity, design education and film/TV production. Also covered are creative trends and technological advances in photography, printing, web design, illustration, motion graphics and packaging. Includes profiles of visual artists, ad agencies and graphic design firms.
Cost: $37.00
Frequency: Monthly
Circulation: 54149
Mailing list available for rent

20667 Print Solutions Magazine
Document Management Industries Association
330 N Wabash Ave
Suite 2000
Chicago, IL 60611

800-230-0175; *Fax:* 312-673-6880;
www.psda.org

Peter L Colaianni CAE, Editor-in-Chief
Preeti Vasishtha, Assistant Editor
Lashell Stratton, Assistant Editor
Rebecca Trela, Assistant Editor

The independent's source for marketing, management and product information.
Cost: $49.00
276 Pages
Frequency: Monthly
Circulation: 42000
ISSN: 0532-1700
Founded in: 1962
Printed in 4 colors on glossy stock

20668 Print on Demand Business
Cygnus Business Media
1233 Janesville Avenue
Fort Atkinson, WI 53538

631-845-2700
800-547-7377; *Fax:* 631-845-2741
info@cygnus.com; www.cygnusb2b.com/

Bob Hall, Executive Editor
Denise Gustavson, Managing Editor
Paul Bonaiuto, CFO
John French, CEO

Editorial includes a look at new products, industry news, updated technology, tips on the best equipment and a look ahead with an upcoming calendar of events.
Frequency: Bi-Monthly

20669 Printing Impressions
North American Publishing Company
1500 Spring Garden St
Suite 1200
Philadelphia, PA 19130-4094

215-238-5300
800-627-2689; *Fax:* 215-238-5342
mmichelson@napco.com; www.napco.com

Ned S Borowsky, CEO
Chris Bauer, Managing Editor
Tunisia Bey, Circulation Manager

Offers news, articles, updates, statistics, research reports and more for the printing industry including printers involved in commercial and newspaper printing and trades.
Frequency: Weekly
Circulation: 83035
Founded in: 1958
Mailing list available for rent

20670 Printing Industry Association of the South - Magazine
Printing Industry Association of the South
PO Box 290249
Nashville, TN 37229-0249

615-366-1094; *Fax:* 615-366-4192
info@pias.org; www.pias.org

Ed Chalifoux, President
James Tepper, Board Member

Print industry information. Free with membership.
Frequency: Monthly
Circulation: 5000
Printed in 4 colors on glossy stock

20671 Printing Manager
National Association of Printing Leadership
One Meadowlands Plaza
Suite 1511
East Rutherford, NJ 07073

201-634-9600
800-642-6275; *Fax:* 201-634-0324
webmaster@napl.org; www.napl.org

Joseph P Truncale, President/CEO
Timothy Fischer, Executive Vp/COO

Provides current news for printing executives including the latest industry, marketing and management news.
40 Pages
Frequency: Quarterly
Circulation: 6000
Founded in: 1933
Mailing list available for rent
Printed in 4 colors

20672 Printing News Magazine
Cygnus Business Media
3 Huntington Quadrangle
Suite 301N
Melville, NY 11747

631-845-2700; *Fax:* 631-845-2741
editor@printingnews.com;
www.printingnews.com
Social Media: Facebook, Twitter, LinkedIn, RSS

David Nathenson, Publisher
Michael Zerner, Associate Publisher
David Lindsay, Editor-in-Chief
Rachel Frank, Editor

News and information on the graphic arts industry in New York, Connecticut, New Jersey and Pennsylvania.
Cost: $39.95
44 Pages
Circulation: 7000
Founded in: 1937

20673 Printing News Online
Cygnus Business Media
3 Huntingon Quadrangle
Suite 301N
Melville, NY 11747

631-845-2700
800-308-6397; *Fax:* 631-845-2741;
www.printingnews.com
Social Media: Facebook, Twitter, LinkedIn, RSS

David Nathenson, Publisher
Michael Zerner, Associate Publisher
David Lindsay, Editor-in-Chief
Rachel Frank, Editor

Includes timely news and information on a variety of subjects including technological breakthroughs, industry trends, marketing, finance, as well as industry leader and corporate profiles.

20674 Publishing Executive
North American Publishing Company
1500 Spring Garden St
Suite 1200
Philadelphia, PA 19130-4094

215-238-5300; *Fax:* 215-238-5342;
www.printmediamag.com/

Ned S Borowsky, CEO
Noelle Skodzinski, Editor-in-Chief
Matt Steinmetz, Associate Editor
Rhoda Dixon, Circulation Manager
Candas Carmen, Associate Publisher

Publishing Executive (formerly PrintMedia) delivers information to magazine publishers, associations, corporate publishers, advertising and marketing agencies.
Circulation: 17500

20675 Quick Printing
Cygnus Business Media
3 Huntington Quadrangle
Suite 301 North
Melville, NY 11747-803

631-845-2700
800-308-6397; *Fax:* 631-845-2741
Bob@quickprinting.com;
www.quickprinting.com
Social Media: Facebook

Jann Levesque, Group Publisher
Kelley Holmes, Publisher
Bob Hall, Editor
Denise Gustavson, Managing Editor

Business journal for those in the printing business.
Cost: $66.00
Frequency: Monthly
Circulation: 48000
Founded in: 1937
Mailing list available for rent

20676 SGIA Journal
Specialty Graphic Imaging Association
10015 Main St
Fairfax, VA 22031-3489

703-385-1335
888-385-3588; *Fax:* 703-273-0456
sgia@sgia.org; www.sgia.org
Social Media: Facebook, Twitter, LinkedIn

Michael Robertson, President
Sondra Fry Benoudiz, VP Membership

Published quarterly in January, April, July and October.
Circulation: 14000
Founded in: 1948

20677 Screen Printing
ST Media Group International
11262 Cornell Park Dr
Cincinnati, OH 45242-1812

513-421-2050
800-421-1321; *Fax:* 513-421-5144

customer@stmediagroup.com;
www.stmediagroup.com

Tedd Swormstedt, CEO
Brian Foos, CFO
Mark Kissling, Director

Screen printing professionals have relied on Screen Printing for landmark coverage of the latest techniques and technologies that save time, energy and money.
Frequency: Monthly
Circulation: 17000
Founded in: 1953
Mailing list available for rent: 17,000 names at $200 per M

20678 Signs of the Times & Screen Printing en Espanol
ST Media Group International
11262 Cornell Park Dr
Cincinnati, OH 45242-1812

513-421-2050
800-421-1321; *Fax:* 513-421-5144
customer@stmediagroup.com;
www.stmediagroup.com

Tedd Swormstedt, CEO
Brian Foos, CFO
Mark Kissling, Director

Covering the industries of signmaking, screen printing and digital imaging for Spanish speaking visual communications markets.
Frequency: Monthly
Circulation: 17000
Founded in: 1906
Mailing list available for rent

20679 Wide Format Imaging Magazine
Cygnus Publishing
3 Huntington Quadrangle
Suite 301 North
Melville, NY 11747

631-845-2700
800-308-6397; *Fax:* 631-845-2741;
www.wide-formatimaging.com
Social Media: Facebook, Twitter, LinkedIn, RSS

David Nathenson, Publisher
Karen Lowry-Hall, Editor
Denise M Gustavson, Managing Editor/Web Editor
Charlie Lillis, Director Content Licensing
Katie Brennan, Vice President

Wide Format Imaginging Magazine provides information on new technologies, analysis of new products, business management tips, and profiles of significant people in the industry. The magazine is a monthly business publication serving 18,000 wide-format professionals. These mostly small business owners are responsible for wide- and large-format drawings, blueprints, soft signage, outdoor signage, posters, POP displays, digital fine art printmaking, and large trade show graphics.
Cost: $25.00
Frequency: Monthly
Mailing list available for rent

Trade Shows

20680 BIA Mid Management Conference
Printing Industry of Illinois
200 Deer Run Road
Sewickley, PA 15143

412-741-6860
800-910-4283; *Fax:* 412-741-2311
printing@printing.org;
www.bindingindustries.org
Social Media: Facebook, Twitter, LinkedIn

Michael Makin, President/CEO
Justin Goldstein, Manager

Brings together mid-managers from trade binderies, graphic finishing, information packaging, custom loose leaf manufacturing, and the suppliers to those industries.
600 Attendees
Frequency: Annual/May

20681 CMM International
Romeland house
Romeland Hill
St Albans
Herdfordshire

212-268-4160; *Fax:* 212-268-4178
info@mackbrooks.co.uk; www.cmmshow.com

The premier converting and package printing event for thousands of professionals.
Frequency: June4-7 Chicago
Founded in: 1978

20682 Graphic Arts
Graphic Arts Show Company
1899 Preston White Drive
Reston, VA 20191-5468

703-264-7200; *Fax:* 703-620-9187
info@gasc.org; www.gasc.org

Chris Price, VP
Kelly Kilga, Director Operations
Ralph Nappi, President

One of America's foremost regional prepress, printing, publishing, and converting trade shows. 300 booths, 70,000 square feet.
18000 Attendees
Frequency: March
Founded in: 1982

20683 Graphics of the Americas
Printing Association of Florida
6275 Hazeltine National Drive
Orlando, FL 32822

407-240-8009
800-331-0461; *Fax:* 407-240-8333
gain@piagatf.org; www.goa.2013.com

Bill Maguire, Chairman
Larry Kudeviz, Treasurer
Rob Hasson, First Vice Chairman
Art Abbott, Second Vice Chairman
George Ryan, CEO

We are the second largest Graphic Arts and Converting show in America. We give you two vital markets, Southeast US and Latin America: Mexico, South America, Central America and the Caribbean. Our 28 year track record reflects our success with both exhibitors and show visitors.
20000 Attendees

20684 Gutenberg Festival
American Printer
2100 West Loop South
Suite 900
Houston, TX 77027-3515

713-300-0674
info@AmericanPrinter.com;
www.americanprinter.com
Social Media: Facebook, Twitter, RSS

Kelly Kilga, Conference/Show Operations Director
Lilly Kinney, Conference Manager
Tina Scott, Exhibit Sales Director
Chrissie Hahn, Exhibit Sales Manager

The top printing event on the west coast and the only place to see live running equipment both traditional and digital.
15000 Attendees
Frequency: April
Mailing list available for rent

20685 Interquest
Interquest Ltd.
513-D Stewart Street
Charlottesville, VA 22902

434-979-9945; *Fax:* 434-979-9959
iquest@inter-quest.com; www.inter-quest.com

David Davis, Director

Interquest analysts will present key results from the company's latest research in the field.
Frequency: March

20686 Labelexpo America
Tarsus Group Plc
E-Mail: sales@labelexpo.com;
www.labelexpo-americas.com

Label, printing, decoration, web printing and converting industry's largest expo.
Frequency: Sept, Chicago

20687 National Association of Professional Print Buyers
15050 Northeast 20th Avenue
Suite A
North Miami, FL 33181-1123

305-956-9563

Vincent Mallardi, Executive Director
400 booths.
2.5M Attendees
Frequency: April
Founded in: 1969

20688 Non-Impact Printing Conference and Exhibit
IS&T-The Society for Imaging Science & Technology
7003 Kilworth Lane
Springfield, VA 22151-4008

703-642-9090; *Fax:* 703-642-9094
info@imaging.org; www.imaging.org

Robert R Buckley, President
Ingeborg Tastl, Secretary
Scott Silence, Treasurer

Annual conference and exhibits of non-impact printing equipment, supplies and services, including printer components, printer consumables, paper and document handling devices and display units.
620 Attendees

20689 Print
Graphic Arts Show Company
1899 Preston White Drive
Reston, VA 20191-5435

703-264-7200; *Fax:* 703-620-9187
info@gasc.org; www.gasc.org

Ralph Nappi, President
Chris Price, Vice President
Kelly Kilga, Director Communications
Lilly Kinney, Conference Manager

This is the largest, most comprehensive event for the commercial, package printing and converting industry in the world in 2013. This huge international event held every four years offers you more running machinery under one roof than any other event anywhere.
40000 Attendees
Frequency: September/Annual
Founded in: 1968
Mailing list available for rent

20690 Print Media Conference & Expo
c/o North American Publishing Company
1500 Spring Garden St, Suite 1200
Philadelphia, PA 19130-4094

888-627-2630; *Fax:* 215-409-0100;
www.pubxpo.com

20691 SGIA Technology Show
Specialty Graphic Imaging Association

10015 Main Street
Fairfax, VA 22031-3489

703-385-1335
888-385-3588; *Fax:* 703-273-0456
sgia@sgia.org; www.sgia.org
Social Media: Facebook, Twitter, LinkedIn

Michael Robertson, President/CEO
Sondra Fry Benoudiz, VP Membership

Technologies showcased include: embossing, printing, graphics, digital imaging, screen printing and embroidering.
14000 Attendees
Frequency: September
Founded in: 1948

20692 Tools of Change for Publishing Conference
O'Reilly Media, Inc.
1005 Gravenstein Highway North
Sebastopol, CA 95472

707-827-7019
800-889-8969; *Fax:* 707-824-8268
orders@oreilly.com; www.oreilly.com
Social Media: Facebook, Twitter, YouTube,RSS

Gina Blaber, Vice President, Conferences
Suzanne Axtell, Communications Manager
Shirley Bailes, Speaker Manager

Expect coverage with a range of practical, in-depth sessions that cover the innovations rocking every aspect of the art, craft, and business of publishing in the 21st century.
Frequency: February

20693 Vue/Point Conference
Graphic Arts Show Company
1189 Preston White Drive
Reston, VA 22091-4367

703-264-7200; *Fax:* 703-620-9187
info@gasc.org; www.gasc.org

David Poulos, Conference Coordinator

Presents topics via panel discussions composed of printing professionals who are willing to share their experiences.

Directories & Databases

20694 Coldset Web Offset Directory
Printing Industries of America/Graphic Arts
200 Deer Run Rd
Sewickley, PA 15143-2600

412-741-6860
800-910-4283; *Fax:* 412-741-2311; www.printing.org
Social Media: Facebook, Twitter, LinkedIn

Michael F Makin, President
Eric Delzer, Chairman

Over 600 printing firms with more than 1,000 presses in the US, Puerto Rico and Canada are profiled.
Cost: $120.00
Frequency: BiAnnual

20695 Corporate and Incentive Travel
Coastal Communications Corporation
2700 N Military Trail
Suite 120
Boca Raton, FL 33431-6394

561-989-0600; *Fax:* 561-989-9509;
www.themeetingmagazines.com

Harvey Grotsky, Publisher/Editor-In-Chief
Susan Wycoff Fell, Managing Editor
Susan S Gregg, Managing Editor
Mitch D Miller, Creative Director

Read by over 40,000 ABC audited meeting and incentive travel planners and key executives responsible for meeting decisions. Articles range monthly from in-depth how-to's, to issue oriented features, examinations of professional concerns, thoroughly researched destination reports, and columns by industry experts
Cost: $50.00
Frequency: Annual
Circulation: 60,000
Founded in: 1983
Mailing list available for rent

20696 Directory International Suppliers/Printing Publishing/Converting Technologies
Association for Suppliers of Printing, Publishing
& Converting Technologies
1899 Preston White Drive
Reston, VA 20191-4367

703-264-7200; *Fax:* 703-620-0994
npes@npes.org; www.npes.org

Ralph J Nappi, President
Douglas Sprei, Director Marketing/Communications
Jesus A Romero, Database Manager
Steve Prejsner, Manager of Technology

An online, freely accessible, association database of NPES member companies and more than 500 products, searchable by product category, keyword or company name.
220 Pages
Frequency: Biennial

20697 Heatset Web Offset Directory
Printing Industries of America/Graphic Arts
200 Deer Run Rd
Sewickley, PA 15143-2600

412-741-6860
800-910-4283; *Fax:* 412-741-2311
gain@piagatf.org; www.printing.org
Social Media: Facebook, Twitter, LinkedIn

Michael Makin, President
Eric Delzer, Chairman

Offers information on nearly 500 heatset web printing firms in the United States, Puerto Rico and Canada including products produced.
Cost: $50.00
110 Pages
Frequency: BiAnnually

20698 In Plant Reproductions: Buyer's Guide Issue
North American Publishing Company
1500 Spring Garden St
Suite 1200
Philadelphia, PA 19130-4094

215-238-5300
800-627-2689; *Fax:* 215-238-5342

Ned S Borowsky, CEO

Firms that manufacture or supply equipment, materials and services to printing facilities of firms or organizations, including art, paste-up and copy preparation, mailing systems, darkroom equipment, presses, paper, word processing, computerized composition and electronic publishing.
Cost: $35.00
Frequency: Annual December
Circulation: 41,000

20699 International Directory of Private Presses
Educators Research Service
2443 Fair Oaks Boulevard
Suite 316
Sacramento, CA 95825-7684

www.briarpress.org

Offers valuable information on over 1,200 private presses and hobbyist printers worldwide.
Cost: $50.00
300 Pages
Frequency: Annual

20700 Print Image International
401 N Michigan Avenue
Suite 2100
Chicago, IL 60611-4245

312-268-8015
800-234-0640; *Fax:* 312-321-6869;
www.printimage.org

John Giles, Editor
Steve Johnson, President
300 Pages

20701 Rauch Guide to the US Ink Industry
Grey House Publishing
4919 Route 22
PO Box 56
Amenia, NY 12501-0056

518-789-8700
800-562-2139; *Fax:* 518-789-0556
books@greyhouse.com; www.greyhouse.com
Social Media: Facebook, Twitter

Leslie Mackenzie, Publisher
Richard Gottlieb, Editor

The Guide to this complex and diffuse $4.2 billion ink industry provides market facts and figures in a highly organized format, ideal for today's busy personnel. The report serves as a ready-reference for top executives as well as the industry newcomer.
Cost: $595.00
700 Pages
ISBN: 1-592371-26-4
Founded in: 1981

20702 Rauch Guide to the US and Canadian Pulp & Paper Industry
Grey House Publishing
4919 Route 22
PO Box 56
Amenia, NY 12501-0056

518-789-8700
800-562-2139; *Fax:* 518-789-0556
books@greyhouse.com; www.greyhouse.com
Social Media: Facebook, Twitter

Leslie Mackenzie, Publisher
Richard Gottlieb, Editor

Provides current market information and trends to; industry economics and government regulations; company share data for each of the leading product categories; technology and raw material information; industry sources of further data; and unique profiles of 500+ pulp and paper manufacturers, a section which includes all known companies with pulp and paper sales at or over $15 million annually.
Cost: $595.00
400 Pages
ISBN: 1-592371-31-0
Founded in: 1981

20703 Who's Who SGIA
Specialty Graphic Imaging Association
10015 Main St
Fairfax, VA 22031-3489

703-385-1335
888-385-3588; *Fax:* 703-273-0456

sgia@sgia.org; www.sgia.org
Social Media: Facebook, Twitter, LinkedIn

Michael Robertson, President
Sondra Fry Benoudiz, VP Membership
Circulation: 3,800
Founded in: 1948

Industry Web Sites

20704 http://gold.greyhouse.com
G.O.L.D Grey House OnLine Databases

Grey House Publishing's online database platform, GOLD, offers Quick Search, Keyword Search and Expert Search for most business sectors including printing and allied markets. The GOLD platform makes finding the information you need quick and easy - whether you're a novice searcher or an experienced database user. All of Grey House's directory products are available for subscription on the GOLD platform.

20705 www.fsea.com
Foil Stamping and Embossing Association

For companies engaged in the process of hot stamping or embossing in the graphics industry and companies that manufacture, distribute or provide services to the hot stamping/embossing industry.

20706 www.gaa.org
Gravure Association of America

Members are gravure printers, converters, suppliers and users.

20707 www.greyhouse.com
Grey House Publishing

Authoritative reference directories for most business sectors including printing and allied markets. Users can search the online databases with varied search criteria allowing for custom searches by product category, geographic area, sales volume, keyword, subject and more. Full Grey House catalog and online ordering also available.

20708 www.iaphc.org
International Assn of Printing House Craftsmen

A voluntary graphic arts organization in which many people share their knowledge and their skill with one another. Open to anyone in any part of the graphic arts community who wish technical information.

20709 www.ipa.org
International Prepress Association

Members produce pre-press material for the graphics industry.

20710 www.magazine.org
Magazine Publishers of America

Promotes magazines as an advertising medium. Provides information services and assistance to members in areas of circulation marketing.

20711 www.napim.org
National Association of Printing Ink Manufacturers

Purpose is to represent the printing ink industry in the U.S.A.

20712 www.napl.org
National Association for Printing Leadership

Promotes the interests in leadership for priniting professionals.

20713 www.npes.org
NPES-Association for Suppliers of Printing
&
Publishing Technology

Members are manufacturers and distributors of graphic arts equipment, systems, software and supplies. Promotes marketing, safety and industry standards, international trade and government relations.

20714 www.pbbai.net
Printing Brokerage Buyers Assoc International

Promotes business relationships among brokers, buying groups, manufacturers and related companies. Sets standards and codes and supplies information and referrals.

20715 www.pgca.org
Printing and Graphic Communications Association

Serving the graphic communications community in the Washington, D.C. metropolitan area.

20716 www.pias.org
Printing Industry Association of the South

Represents the print industry.

20717 www.pinc.org
Print Buyers Association

For professionals in print buying.

20718 www.pine.org
Printing Institute of New England

20719 www.polymers.com
Polymers DotCom

20720 www.printing.org
Printing Industries of America (PIA)

The largest graphic arts organization founded over 100 years ago.

20721 www.teched.Vt.edu/gcc
Graphic Comm Central

Web portal for education in the graphic communications industry.

20722 www.waterless.org
Waterless Printing Association

Dedicated to the informational and educational needs of its printer and sponsor members.

Associations

20723 American Society of Health Care Marketing
1 N Franklin Street
Chicago, IL 60606-3421

773-327-1064; *Fax:* 312-422-4579

20724 Arthur W Page Society
230 Park Avenue
Suite 455
New York, NY 10169

212-400-7959; *Fax:* 347-474-7399
rbolton@awpagesociety.com;
www.awpagesociety.com
Social Media: Twitter, LinkedIn, YouTube, RSS

Roger Bolton, President
Gary Sheffer, Chairman
Valerie Di Maria, Secretary
Robert De Fillippo, Treasurer
Sally Benjamin Young, Vice Chair

Professional public relations organization with a single mission, to strengthen the management policy role of the chief public relations officer. Conducts seminars and conferences.
397 Members
Founded in: 1983

20725 Association of Women in Communications
3337 Duke Street
Alexandria, VA 22314

703-370-7436; *Fax:* 703-342-4311
info@womcom.org; www.womcom.org
Social Media: Facebook, Twitter, LinkedIn, YouTube, Google+

Mitzie Zerr, Chair
Linda Timm Hankmeier, Director
Lisa Angle, Secretary
Missy Kruse, Vice Chair
Pat Meads, Treasurer

Professional organization that champions the advancement of women across all communications disciplines by recognizing excellence, promoting leadership and positioning its members at the forefront of the evolving communications era. Hosts a bi-annual conference.
3500 Members
Founded in: 1909

20726 Baptist Communicators Association
1519 Menlo Drive
Kennesaw, GA 30152

770-425-3728; www.baptistcommunicators.org
Social Media: Facebook, Twitter, Vimeo, Wordpress

Ian Richardson, President
Joe Westbury, Treasurer
Shawn Hendricks, President-Elect
Barbara L. Denman, Program Chair-Elect
Brian Hobbs, Program Chairs

PR and Journalism professionals.
300 Members
Founded in: 1953

20727 Business Marketing Association: Atlanta
2801 Buford Highway, Druid Chase
Suite 375
Atlanta, GA 30329

404-641-9417
800-664-4262; *Fax:* 312-822-0054
info@bmaatlanta.org
bmaatlanta.org
Social Media: Facebook, Twitter, LinkedIn, Google+

Moira Vetter, President
Mark Towery, President Elect
Subodh Singh, VP Member Services
Khoi Ta, VP Young Professionals
Mark Miranda, VP Sponsorship

The Atlanta chapter of the BMA includes marketing executives from a variety of industries and backgrounds including research, advertising, promotions, events, Web development, printing and more. The BMA offers an information-packed Website, online skills-building, marketing certification programs, and industry surveys and papers. In addition, members have the opportunity to interact with peers at seminars, participate in chapter training programs and the BMA Annual Conference.
Founded in: 1922

20728 Business Marketing Association: Boston
246 Hampshire Street
Cambridge, MA 02130

617-418-4000
800-664-4262; *Fax:* 312-822-0054;
www.thebmaboston.com

Michael Lewis, President
Will Robinson, VP Public Relations
Matthew Mamet, VP Internet Marketing
Larry Perreault, VP Finance
Chris Perkett, VP Programming

BMA Boston helps members improve their ability to manage business-to-business marketing and communications for greater productivity and profitability by providing unique access to information, ideas, and the experience of peers. The BMA offers an information-packed Website, online skills-building, marketing certification programs, and industry surveys and papers. In addition, members have the opportunity to interact with peers at seminars, chapter training programs and the BMA Annual Conference.

20729 Communications Roundtable
1250 24th Street NW
Suite 250
Washington, DC 20037

202-755-5180; *Fax:* 202-466-0544;
www.roundtable.org

Michael Reichgut, Chairman
Shawn Dolley, CEO

Association of more than 20 public relations, marketing, graphics, advertising, training and other communications organizations with more than 12,000 professional members. The goals include furthering professionalism, cooperation between member organizations, career and employment support, and employer assistance.

20730 Consultants in Public Relations SA
4200 Massachusetts Avenue NW
Washington, DC 20016

202-244-2580; *Fax:* 202-224-2581

John M Reed, Chairman
Founded in: 1970

20731 Council of Communications Management
65 Enterprise
Aliso Viejo, CA 92656

866-463-6226; *Fax:* 303-850-6819
info@thecommunicationexchange.org;
www.ccmconnection.com
Social Media: Facebook, LinkedIn

Becky Healy, President
Barry Mike, Past President
Kerrin Nally, Secretary
Jeff Kosiorek, Vice President
Michael Rudnick, Treasurer

Established more than 40 years ago as a forum for seasoned professionals to share best practices in organizational communications.
Founded in: 1955

20732 Council of Public Relations Firms
32 East 31st Street
9th Floor
New York, NY 10016

646-588-0139; *Fax:* 646-651-4770;
www.prfirms.org
Social Media: Twitter, LinkedIn, YouTube,RSS, Pinterest, Flickr

Kathy Cripps, President
Matt Shaw, Senior Vice President
Bryan Harris, Treasury
Aaron Schoenherr, Secretary
Chris Graves, Chairman
100+ Members

20733 Entertainment Publicists Professional Society
PO Box 5841
Beverly Hills, CA 90209

E-Mail: info@eppsonline.org;
www.eppsonline.org

Rick Markovitz, President

The Society has chapters in Los Angeles and New York. Members work in publicity, promotions and marketing.
Founded in: 1991

20734 Hispanic Public Relations Association
PO Box 86760
Los Angeles, CA 90086-0760

E-Mail: info@hpra-usa.org; www.hpra-usa.org
Social Media: Facebook, Twitter

Andy Checo, President

The HPRA's mission is the professional development and advancement of its members and the practice of Hispanic public relations.
Founded in: 1984

20735 Institute for Public Relations
University of Florida
PO Box 118400
2096 Weimer Hall
Gainesville, FL 32611-8400

352-392-0280; *Fax:* 352-846-1122
ace@ifas.ufl.edu; www.instituteforpr.org
Social Media: Facebook, Twitter, LinkedIn, YouTube,RSS

Dr. Tina McCorkindale, President & CEO
Kenneth Makovsky, Co-Chairs
Jenn Moyer, Foundations Operations Manager
Gary Sheffer, Treasurer
Dr. Sarab Kochhar, Director of Research

Improving the effectiveness of organizations by advancing the professional knowledge and practice of public relations through research and education.
Founded in: 1956
Mailing list available for rent

20736 International Association of Business Communicators
601 Montgomery Street
Suite 1900
San Francisco, CA 94111
415-544-4700
800-776-4222; *Fax:* 415-544-4747
member_relations@iabc.com; www.iabc.com
Social Media: Facebook, Twitter, LinkedIn, YouTube, Pinterest, Google+, I

Michael Ambjorn, Chair
Dianne Chase, Vice Chair
Sharon L. Hunter, Director
Ginger D. Homan, Secretary/ Treasurer
Carlos Fulcher, Executive Director

International knowledge network for professionals engaged in strategic business communication management.
12000 Members
Founded in: 1970

20737 **Original Equipment Suppliers Association**
Original Equipment Suppliers Association
25925 Telegraph Rd
Suite 350
Southfield, MI 48033-2553
248-952-6401; *Fax:* 248-952-6404
info@oesa.org; www.autopr.org
Social Media: Facebook, Twitter, LinkedIn, RSS, Tumblr
Daniel E. Sceli, Chair
Samir Salman, Vice Chairman
Julie A Fream, President & CEO
Joseph B. Anderson Jr., Director
Jacqui Dedo, Senior Advisor
Provides a forum for information exchange among communication professionals with the automotive industry. Two conferences are held every year, topics are integrated marketing, communications and the automotive industry.
450 Members
Founded in: 1998

Newsletters

20738 **Bulldog Reporter**
InfoCom Group
5900 Hollis Street
Suite L
Emeryville, CA 94608-2008
510-653-3035
800-959-1059; *Fax:* 510-596-9331;
www.infocomgroup.com
James Sinkinson, Publisher
Tim Gray, President
Emphasis on placement opportunities and media profiles, as well as personnel changes at media outlets throughout the US.
Cost: $599.00
Frequency: Fortnightly
Circulation: 5000
Founded in: 1980

20739 **Contacts: Media Pipeline for PR People**
Larimi Communications Association
500 Executive Boulevard
Ossining on Hudson, NY 10562-1114
914-923-9400; *Fax:* 914-923-9484
info@mercommawards.com;
www.mercommawards.com/
Michael M Smith, Publisher
Madeleine Gillis, Editor
Provides pipeline of communications between what an editor needs and a public relations person can supply.
Cost: $287.00
1 Pages
Frequency: Weekly
Founded in: 1975
Printed in one color

20740 **Downtown Promotion Reporter**
Alexander Communications Group
1916 Park Ave
Suite 501
New York, NY 10037-3733
212-281-6099
800-232-4317; *Fax:* 212-283-7269
info@downtowndevelopment.com;
www.downtowndevelopment.com/
Romauld Alexander, President
Tested ideas for promotion, public relations, marketing, increasing business, participation, downtown image building, sales, and events.
Cost: $189.00
Frequency: Monthly
ISSN: 0363-2830

20741 **Healthcare PR & Marketing News**
Phillips Business Information
1201 Seven Locks Road
Suite 300
Potomac, MD 20854-2931
301-354-1400; *Fax:* 301-340-1451
Sharmi Banik, Editor
Kismet Toksu Gould, Publisher
Issues faced by health care executives in PR firms and hospitals. Regular features include industry surveys, case studies and executive profiles.
Cost: $397.00
Frequency: Bi-Monthly
Founded in: 1992

20742 **High-Tech Hot Sheet**
Hot Sheet Publishing
114 Sansome Street
Suite 1224
San Francisco, CA 94104
415-421-6225; *Fax:* 415-421-6225
Art Gracia, Editor/Publisher
Reporting updates and changes in staff, beat assignments, new publications, suspension of publishing in high-tech media.
Cost: $395.00
Frequency: Monthly
Founded in: 1987

20743 **Holmes Report**
Holmes Group
271 W 47th St
Suite 23A
New York, NY 10036-1447
212-333-2300; *Fax:* 212-333-2624
gdrury@holmesreport.com;
www.holmesreport.com
Paul Holmes, President
Greg Drury, Managing Editor
Arun Sudhaman, Managing Editor
Source of information for public relations and corporate communications professionals.
Cost: $290.00
Frequency: Weekly
Circulation: 15,000
ISBN: 0-972364-50-1
Founded in: 2001
Printed in 4 colors on glossy stock

20744 **Interactive PR & Marketing News**
Phillips Publishing
1201 Seven Locks Road
#300
Potomac, MD 20854-2931
301-354-1400; *Fax:* 301-424-8602;
www.phillips.com
Angela Duff, Publisher
Covers the latest trends and news on the World Wide Web and Internet markets and looks at their users.
Cost: $347.00
Frequency: 23 per year
Circulation: 5M

20745 **Interactive Public Relations**
Ragan Communications
316 N Michigan Ave
Suite 400
Chicago, IL 60601-3773
312-960-4100
800-493-4867; *Fax:* 312-960-4106
cservice@ragan.com; www.ragan.com
Jim Ylisela, Publisher
Mark ragan, CEO
Kasia Chalko, Marketing Director
Includes targeted newsletters in the areas of employment communication, Web PR, organizational writing and editing, sales and marketing, media relations, motivational management, and investor relations.
Cost: $279.00
Founded in: 1970

20746 **Jack O'Dwyer's Newsletter**
JR O'Dwyer Company
271 Madison Ave
Suite 600
New York, NY 10016-1013
212-683-2750; *Fax:* 212-683-2750
jack@odwyerpr.com; www.odwyerpr.com
Jack O'Dwyer, President
Fay Shapiro, Publisher
Eileen Kelly, Sales Manager
John ODwyer, Advertising Sales Manager
Covers current happenings in both electronic and print media, including new PR products and accounts, PR campaigns, and books about public relations.
Cost: $295.00
Frequency: Weekly
Founded in: 1970

20747 **Levin's Public Relations Report**
Levin Public Relations & Marketing
2 East Ave
Suite 201
Larchmont, NY 10538-2419
914-834-2570; *Fax:* 914-834-5919;
www.saralevin.com
Sara B Levin, President
Sylvia Moss, Editor
Strategies, tactics for the CEO, VP Sales and Marketing seeking new marketing/public relations effectiveness.
Cost: $29.00
Frequency: Monthly
Founded in: 1984

20748 **Media Relations Insider**
InfoCom Group
124 Linden Street
Oakland, CA 94607
510-596-9300
800-959-1059; www.infocomgroup.com
Social Media: Facebook, Twitter, LinkedIn, RSS
Eastern and Western editions give you media news and exclusive interviews with top business journalists in your region.
Cost: $399.00
Frequency: Monthly
Mailing list available for rent

20749 **Media Relations Report**
Ragan Communications
316 N Michigan Ave
Suite 400
Chicago, IL 60601-3773
312-960-4100
800-493-4867; *Fax:* 312-960-4106
cservice@ragan.com; www.ragan.com
Jim Ylisela, Publisher
Mark Ragan, CEO
Cost: $28.92
Frequency: Monthly
Circulation: 1000
Founded in: 1975
Mailing list available for rent
Printed in 2 colors on matte stock

20750 **MediaQuest**
MediaQuest Publishing
PO Box 9222
Boston, MA 02114-0996
617-536-5353; *Fax:* 617-367-9151
Barbara Kalunian, Editor/Publisher
Media placement becomes easier for PR professionals through behind the scenes interviews

with leading journalists at top broadcast and print outlets.
Cost: $295.00
Frequency: Bi-Monthly
Founded in: 1990

20751 Memo to the President
American Association State Colleges & Universities
1307 New York Ave Nw
Suite 5
Washington, DC 20005-4723
202-293-7070
800-542-2062; *Fax:* 202-296-5819
chilcotts@aascu.org; www.aascu.org
Edward Elnendorf, President
Susan M Chilcott, Editor
Cost: $100.00
6 Pages
Frequency: Monthly
Circulation: 1200
ISSN: 0047-6692
Founded in: 1961
Printed in 2 colors on matte stock

20752 O'Dwyers Washington Report
JR O'Dwyer Company
271 Madison Ave
#600
New York, NY 10016-1013
212-683-2750; *Fax:* 212-683-2750
jack@odwyerpr.com; www.odwyerpr.com
Jack O'Dwyer, President
Kevin McCowley, Advertising Sales Manager
John ODwyer, Advertising Sales Manager
Covers Washington public relations and public affairs lobbying news.
Cost: $95.00
8 Pages

20753 Opportunity
Career Skills Press/Brody Communications
815 Greenwood Ave
Suite 8
Jenkintown, PA 19046-2800
215-886-1688
800-726-7936; *Fax:* 215-886-1699
info@brodypro.com; www.brodypro.com
Marjorie Brody, President
Miryam S Raddy, Marketing Manager
Feature products published by Career Skills Press unit.
4 Pages
Frequency: Quarterly
Circulation: 10000
Founded in: 1983
Printed in 4 colors on glossy stock

20754 PR Intelligence Report
Lawrence Ragan Communications
316 N Michigan Ave
Suite 400
Chicago, IL 60601-3773
312-960-4100; *Fax:* 312-960-4106
cservice@ragan.com; www.ragan.com
Jim Ylisela, Publisher
Mark Regan, CEO
Digs below the surface to provide the details, insights and information you need to improve your career, make your next campaign a success, or avoid costly mistakes.
Cost: $279.00
8 Pages
Circulation: 1000
Founded in: 1970
Printed in 2 colors on matte stock

20755 PR News
Phillips Business Information
4 Choke Cherry Rd
Fl 2
Rockville, MD 20850-4024
301-450-0035; *Fax:* 301-340-3169;
www.prandmarketing.com
Matthew Schwartz, Editor
Diane Schwartz, Publisher
Briefing on the latest PR trends, what's working and what's not. We feature case studies of successful PR campaigns.
Cost: $697.00
10 Pages
Frequency: Weekly
Founded in: 1944

20756 PR Reporter
Lawrence Ragan Communications
316 N Michigan Ave
Suite 400
Chicago, IL 60601-3773
312-960-4100
800-493-4867; *Fax:* 312-960-4106
cservice@ragan.com; www.ragan.com
Jim Ylisela, Publisher
Mark Ragan, President
Rebecca Anderson, Managing Editor
Weekly publication dedicated to the behavioral aspects of public relations, public affairs and communication strategies. Its quick read format keeps you up to date on the latest theories, research, public opinions, case studies and successful public relations techniques.
Frequency: Weekly
Founded in: 1970

20757 PR Tactics
Public Relations Society of America
33 Maiden Ln
Suite 11
New York, NY 10038-5150
212-460-1400; *Fax:* 212-995-0757
helpdesk@prsa.org; www.prsa.org
Catherine Bolton, President
Philip Bonaventura, Chief Financial Officer
Cost: $75.00
32 Pages
Frequency: Monthly
Circulation: 25000
Founded in: 1947
Printed in 4 colors on newsprint stock

20758 PR Watch
Center for Media and Democracy
520 University Ave
Suite 227
Madison, WI 53703-4929
608-260-9713; *Fax:* 608-260-9714
editor@prwatch.org; www.prwatch.org
Lisa Graves, Executive Director
Dave Ross, Secretary
Sheldon Rampton, Research Director
Kristian Knutsen, Administrative Assistant
Investigates and exposes how the public relations industry and other professional propagandists manipulate public information, perceptions and opinion on behalf of governments and special interests.
Frequency: Quarterly
Founded in: 1993

20759 PR Week
114 W 26th Street
3rd Floor
New York, NY 10001
646-638-6000; *Fax:* 646-638-6115
letters@prweek.com; www.prweek.com
Lisa Kirk, Publishing Director
Julia Hood, Editor-in-Chief
Cutting-edge newsletter of public relations.
Frequency: Weekly

20760 Partyline Publishing
PartyLine Publishing Company
35 Sutton Place
New York, NY 10022-2464
212-755-3487; *Fax:* 212-755-4859;
www.partylinepublishing.com
Morton Yarmon, Editor
Betty Yarmon, Publisher/Editor-in-chief
Weekly media newsletter, delivered by E-mail, that informs their readers of the latest happenings in the media world...new editors, new publications, new networks, new shows on existing networks, new producers, any and all media news.
Cost: $139.50
Frequency: Weekly
Circulation: 1,400
Founded in: 1960

20761 Pro Motion
Beyond the Byte
PO Box 388
Fallston, MD 21047
410-877-3524
800-861-1235; *Fax:* 410-877-7064;
www.pro-motionsnetwork.com
Emily Laisy, President
News of interest to Media Escort and publicists.
Cost: $12.00
4 Pages
Frequency: Quarterly
Circulation: 325
ISSN: 0886-6104
Founded in: 1985
Printed in one color on matte stock

20762 Public Relations Career Opportunities
CEO Update
1575 I Street NW
#1190
Washington, DC 20005-1105
202-408-7900; *Fax:* 202-408-7907
James Zaniello, Editor
Public relations and publis affairs job opportunities compensating $35,000 plus nationwide.
Cost: $217.00
Frequency: Bi-Monthly
Founded in: 1986

20763 Ragan's Interactive Public Relations
Lawrence Ragan Communications
316 N Michigan Ave
Suite 400
Chicago, IL 60601-3773
312-960-4100
800-878-5331; *Fax:* 312-960-4106
cservice@ragan.com; www.ragan.com
Jim Ylisela, Publisher
Dedicated to helping PR people navigate cyberspace.
Cost: $269.00
8 Pages
Frequency: Monthly
Circulation: 800
Founded in: 1970
Printed in 2 colors on matte stock

20764 Ragan's Media Relations Report
Lawrence Ragan Communications
316 N Michigan Ave
Chicago, IL 60601-3773
312-960-4100
800-493-4867; *Fax:* 312-960-4106
cservice@ragan.com; www.ragan.com
Jim Ylisela, Publisher
David Murray, Editor
Diane Tillman, Marketing Manager
Content focuses on personal changes, moves and additions in various media, including television,

radio and print. Offers tips on angles to take, interviews top journalists on what type of information they prefer, and continuously updates contact numbers and addresses.
Cost: $317.00
Frequency: Monthly
Founded in: 1970
Printed in 2 colors on matte stock

20765 West Coast PR Newsletter
West Coast MediaNet
5928 Lindley Avenue
Encino, CA 91316-1047

818-893-3449; *Fax:* 818-776-1930;
www.westcoastprjobs.com

Darren Shuster, Publisher
Ken West, Manager

Delivers in-depth inteviews and features, new media contacts and personnel updates, tips from experts in various fields, and listings of new PR markets. Regular coverage includes media web site and book reviews, as well as how-to articles, all with a West Coast angle.
Cost: $75.00
16 Pages
Frequency: 12 issues
Circulation: 1M

Magazines & Journals

20766 ACH Product & Marketing Handbook for Financial Institutions & Companies
NACHA: The Electronic Payments Association
13450 Sunrise Valley Drive
Suite 100
Herndon, VA 20171

703-561-1100; *Fax:* 703-787-0996
info@nacha.org; www.nacha.org

Janet O Estep, CEO
Marcie Haitema, Chairperson

Designed for full financial institutions and companies to assist them in understanding ACH products and services-their benefits, risk management considerations, marketing techniques and FAQs from both corporate and consumer perspectives.
Cost: $70.00
Frequency: Annual+

20767 Communication World
Int'l Association of Business Communicators
601 Montgomery Street
Suite 1900
San Francisco, CA 94111

415-544-4700; *Fax:* 415-544-4747
cwmagazine@iabc.com; www.iabc.com

Natasha Nicholson, Executive Editor
Sue Khodarahmi, Managing Editor
Sue Cavallaro, Production Editor

Covers the latest in communication research, technology and trends through in-depth reports and insightful interviews.
Cost: $150.00
Frequency: Bi-Monthly
Founded in: 1970

20768 Currents
Council for Advancement & Support of Education
1307 New York Ave Nw
Suite 1000
Washington, DC 20005-4726

202-393-1301; *Fax:* 202-387-4973
memberservicecenter@case.org; www.case.org

Deborah Bangiorno, Editor
Donald Falkenstein, Vice President of Finance
Will Hayden, Production Coordinator
John Lippincott, President
Marla Misek, Senior Editor

Offers information on campus fund raising, public relations,and alumni administration.
Cost: $115.00
Circulation: 15000
Founded in: 1974

20769 International Public Relations Review
18 W Church Street
Saint Frederick, MD 31701

229-567-8074; *Fax:* 912-845-2991

John Reed, Publisher

Public relations international communications issues for senior level PR professionals.

20770 Jack O'Dwyer's Services Report
JR O'Dwyer Company
271 Madison Ave
Suite 600
New York, NY 10016-1013

212-683-2750; *Fax:* 212-683-2750
jack@odwyerpr.com; www.odwyerpr.com

Jack O'Dwyer, Owner
John ODwyer, Advertising Sales Manager
Eileen Kelly, Sales Manager

Information on film, videotape, database and release distribution industries which serve public relations professionals.
Cost: $45.00
Frequency: Monthly
Circulation: 4500
Founded in: 1980

20771 Jack O'Dwyers Washington Report
JR O'Dwyer Company
271 Madison Ave
Suite 600
New York, NY 10016-1013

212-683-2750; *Fax:* 212-683-2750
jack@odwyerpr.com; www.odwyerpr.com

Jack O'Dwyer, Owner
John ODwyer, Advertising Sales Manager
Cost: $60.00
Frequency: Weekly
Founded in: 1970

20772 Managing Media Relations in a Crisis
NACHA: The Electronic Payments Association
13450 Sunrise Valley Drive
Suite 100
Herndon, VA 20171

703-561-1100; *Fax:* 703-787-0996
info@nacha.org; www.nacha.org

Janet O Estep, CEO
Marcie B Haitema, Chairperson

This guide is designed to assist your organization to develop, test and execute a crisis communication plan. Understand how to address the issues, know whom to call and in what order to alert them, which vendors you can count on to help, and how to develop a means to track the crisis as it grows or abates.
Cost: $30.00

20773 Public Relations Quarterly
Howard Penn Hudson
44 W Market Street
PO Box 311
Rhinebeck, NY 12572-311

845-876-2081
800-572-3451; *Fax:* 845-876-2561;
www.hudsonsdirectory.com

Howard Penn Hudson, Editor/Publisher
Elaine F Newman, Executive Editor
Berecah Sullivan, Circulation Manager
Nichole Latierre, Marketing Manager

Independent public relations magazine, now 48 years old, presenting articles and columns on the theory and process of public relations and communications.
Cost: $65.00
Frequency: Quarterly
ISSN: 0033-3700
Founded in: 1955
Printed in on matte stock

20774 Public Relations Review
Elsevier
6277 Seaharbor Drive
Orlando, FL 32887

877-839-7126; www.elsevier.com

Jan D Achenbach, Editor-In-Chief
Bill Godfrey, Chief Information Officer
David Clark, Senior Vice President

Covers public relations, education, government, survey research, public policy, history and bibliographies.
Cost: $110.00
Frequency: 12 issues
Circulation: 1M
ISSN: 0363-0111

20775 Public Relations Strategist
Public Relations Society of America
33 Maiden Ln
Suite 11
New York, NY 10038-5150

212-460-1400; *Fax:* 212-995-0757
william.murray@prsa.org; www.prsa.org

Gary McCormick, Chairman/CEO
William Murray, President & COO
Philip Bonaventura, CFO
Jeneen Garcia, Vice President

With emphasis on the issues and trends affecting public relations management, it examines the changing concepts and challenges current practices with relevant, original and thought-provoking articles.
Cost: $100.00
Frequency: 4 issues per ye
Circulation: 20538
Founded in: 1947

20776 Public Relations Tactics
Public Relations Society of America
33 Maiden Ln
Suite 11
New York, NY 10038-5150

212-460-1400; *Fax:* 212-995-0757
helpdesk@prsa.org; www.prsa.org

Gary McCormick, Chairman/CEO
Gale Spreter, Marketing Manager
Alison Stateman, Managing Editor
Catherine A Bolton, Executive Director
Philip Bonaventura, Chief Financial Officer

News, trends and how-to information for public relations people.
Cost: $75.00
Frequency: Monthly
Circulation: 20538
Founded in: 1947

20777 Reputation Management
Editorial Media & Marketing International

708 3rd Avenue
Frnt 2
New York, NY 10017-4201

212-687-5260; www.prcentral.com

Kara T Ingraham, Publisher/COO

Editorial focuses on finance, marketing, human resources, government and society. Highlights domestic and international corporate news presenting observations and perspectives vital to the industry.
Cost: $52.00
Frequency: Bi-Monthly
Circulation: 12M
Founded in: 1995

Trade Shows

20778 American Society of Health Care Marketing and Public Relations Trade Show
1 N Franklin Street
31st Floor
Chicago, IL 60606-3421

773-327-1064; *Fax:* 312-422-4579

Lauren Barnett, Executive Director

Sixty booths of communications, printing, computer equipment, public relations and fund raising consultants in the health care profession.
600 Attendees
Frequency: September

20779 Arthur W Page Society
Arthur W Page Society
317 Madison Ave
Suite 1607
New York, NY 10017-5201

212-400-7959; *Fax:* 347-474-7399;
www.awpagesociety.com
Social Media: Facebook, Twitter, YouTube,RSS

Roger Bolton, President
Gary Shepper, Chairman
Valerie Di Maria, Secretary
Frequency: Annual/September
Founded in: 1986

20780 National Hispanic Market Trade Show and Media Expo (Se Habla Espanol)
Hispanic Business Inc
5385 Hollister Avenue
Suite 204
Santa Barbara, CA 93111

800-806-4268; *Fax:* 805-964-5539
info@hispanstar.com; www.expomediainc.com
Social Media: Facebook, Twitter, LinkedIn

John Pasini, Cfo/Coo

Annual show of 100 exhibitors of market/research, media, advertising, public relations, information services and recruitment.
1500 Attendees

20781 National School for Public Relations
15948 Derwood Rd
Rockville, MD 20855

301-519-0496; *Fax:* 301-519-0494
info@nspra.org; www.nspra.org

Mildred Wainger, Administration Services

Offers information and news for professionals in the field of public relations.
600 Attendees
Frequency: July

20782 Strategic Media Relations Conference
Ragan Communications
316 N Michigan Avenue
Chicago, IL 60601

312-960-4100
800-878-5331; *Fax:* 312-960-4106
cservice@ragan.com; www.raganinstitute.com

Showcase of best practices for winning top media coverage in a new era. Learn how peers have garnered more ink, managed crises, built their brands and gone global. Attend pre- and post-conference sessions that provide career-boosting skills in crisis survival, media training, online media relations, PR writing, persuasive communications, PR management, digital PR and pitching stories.
Frequency: March

Directories & Databases

20783 Adweek Directory
Prometheus Global Media
770 Broadway
New York, NY 10003-9595

212-493-4100; *Fax:* 646-654-5368;
www.prometheusgm.com

Richard D. Beckman, CEO
James A. Finkelstein, Chairman
Madeline Krakowsky, Vice President Circulation
Tracy Brater, Executive Director Creative Service

Adweek Directories Online is where you will find searchable databases with comprehensive information on ad agencies, brand marketers and multicultural media.
Frequency: Annual
Circulation: 800
Founded in: 1981

20784 Bacon's Newspaper & Magazine Directories
Cision U.S., Inc.
322 South Michigan Avenue
Suite 900
Chicago, IL 60604

312-263-0070
866-639-5087
info.us@cision.com
us.cision.com

Joe Bernardo, President & CEO
Heidi Sullivan, VP & Publisher
Valerie Lopez, Research Director
Jessica White, Research Director
Rachel Farrell, Research Manager

Two volume set listing all daily and community newspapers, magazines and newsletters, news service and syndicates, syndicated columnists, complete editorial staff listings of each publication provided, covers U.S., Canada, Mexico, and Carribean.
Cost: $350.00
4,700 Pages
Frequency: Annual
ISSN: 1088-9639
Founded in: 1951
Printed in one color on matte stock

20785 Bacon's Radio/TV/Cable Directory
Cision U.S., Inc.
332 South Michigan Avenue
Suite 900
Chicago, IL 60604

312-263-0070
866-639-5087
info.us@cision.com; www.us.cision.com

Joe Bernardo, President & CEO
Heidi Sullivan, VP & Publisher
Valerie Lopez, Research Director
Jessica White, Research Director
Rachel Farrell, Research Manager

Includes comprehensive coverage for contact and programming information for more than 3,500 televsion networks, cable networks, television syndicators, television stations, and cable systems in the United States and Canada.
Cost: $350.00
Frequency: Annual
ISSN: 1088-9639
Printed in one color on matte stock

20786 Burrelle's Media Directory
BurrellesLuce
75 E Northfield Rd
Livingston, NJ 07039-4532

973-992-6600
800-631-1160; *Fax:* 973-992-7675
inquiry@burrellesluce.com;
www.burrellesluce.com
Social Media: Facebook, Twitter, LinkedIn, RSS

Robert C Waggoner, CEO

Approximately 60,000 media listings in North America. Listings cover newspapers, magazines (trades and consumer), broadcast, and internet outlets.
Cost: $795.00
Frequency: Annual

20787 Corporate Yellow Book
Leadership Directories
104 5th Ave
New York, NY 10011-6901

212-627-4140; *Fax:* 212-645-0931
corporate@leadershipdirectories.com;
www.leadershipdirectories.com

David Hurvitz, CEO

Contact information for over 48,000 executives at over 1,000 companies and more than 9,000 board members and their outside affiliations.
Cost: $360.00
1,400 Pages
Frequency: Quarterly
ISSN: 1058-2098
Founded in: 1986

20788 Leadership Library in Print
Leadership Directories
104 5th Ave
New York, NY 10011-6901

212-627-4140; *Fax:* 212-645-0931
info@leadershipdirectories.com;
www.leadershipdirectories.com

David Hurvitz, CEO

Complete set of all 14 leadership directories. Provides subscribers with complete contact information for the 400,000 individuals who constitute the institutional leadership of the US.
Cost: $2300.00
Frequency: Semiannually
Founded in: 1996

20789 O'Dwyer's Directory of Corporate Communications
JR O'Dwyer Company
271 Madison Ave
Suite 600
New York, NY 10016-1013

212-683-2750; *Fax:* 212-683-2750
jack@odwyerpr.com; www.odwyerpr.com

Jack O'Dwyer, Owner
John ODwyer, Advertising Sales Manager

Public relations departments are profiled that represent the United States companies that are listed on the New York Stock Exchange.
Cost: $110.00
400 Pages
Frequency: Annual

20790 PR News
Phillips Business Information

7811 Montrose Road
Potomac, MD 20854
301-340-2100
feedback@healthydirections.com;
www.healthydirections.com

This database offers information on public relations issues.
Cost: $597.00
Frequency: 48 issues

20791 PR Newswire
150 E 58th Street
31st Floor
New York, NY 10155-0002

212-355-0090; *Fax:* 212-832-9406

This comprehensive database offers current news, financial news, earnings statements, mergers, acquisitions, proxy contests and general features pertaining to the public relations industry.
Frequency: Directory

20792 Public Relations Tactics
Public Relations Society of America
33 Maiden Ln
New York, NY 10038-5150

212-460-1400; *Fax:* 212-995-0757
william.murray@prsa.org; www.prsa.org

Catherine Bolton, Manager

List of products and services used by public relations professionals worldwide.
Frequency: Annual June

20793 Public Relations Tactics: Register Issue/The Blue Book
Public Relations Society of America
33 Maiden Ln
New York, NY 10038-5150

212-460-1400; *Fax:* 212-995-0757
william.murray@prsa.org; www.prsa.org

Catherine Bolton, Manager

About 17,000 public relations practitioners in business government education etc., who are members.
Cost: $100.00
Frequency: Annual July

20794 Publicity at Your Finger Tips
Federal Systems
PO Box 298-L
Oliver Springs, TN 37840-0298

865-483-3579

Offers a comprehensive list of magazines, newspapers and other publications in the United States that provide publicity for businesses, churches and charitable organizations.
Cost: $24.95

20795 Staffing Industry Supplier Directory and Buyers Guide
Staffing Industry Analysts
881 Fremont Ave
Suite A3
Los Altos, CA 94024-5637

650-948-9303
800-950-9496; *Fax:* 650-232-2360;
www.sireport.com

Ron Mester, Manager

Complete listing of suppliers and products for temporary help, placement and recruiting firms in the staffing industry.
Cost: $89.50
295 Pages
Frequency: Annual
ISBN: 1-883814-11-1

Industry Web Sites

20796 http://gold.greyhouse.com
G.O.L.D Grey House OnLine Databases

Grey House Pubishing's online database platform, GOLD, offers Quick Search, Keyword Search and Expert Search for most business sectors including public relations and media markets. The GOLD platform makes finding the information you need quick and easy - whether you're a novice searcher or an experienced database user. All of Grey House's directory products are available for subscription on the GOLD platform.

20797 www.absolutelypr.com
Absolutely Public Relations

Results-driven media relations - local, trade, national.

20798 www.achieva.info
ACHIEVA

20799 www.aem.org
Construction Equipment Advertisers and Public
Relations Council

A council of AEM that works to promote marketing, sales and advertising of construction equipment.

20800 www.afgcan.org
AFHCAN Project

20801 www.aprc-online.org
Automotive Public Relations Council

Provides a forum for information exchange among communication professionals with the automotive industry.

20802 www.bloomgross.com
Bloom Gross & Associates

Executive recruitment firm with corporate communications, public relations, marketing/branding/market research, and direct marketing/sales promotion practice areas.

20803 www.case.org
Council for the Advancement and Support of Ed.

Offers information on campus fund raising, public relations and alumni administration.

20804 www.cof.org
Council on Foundations

Non profit trade association for foundations

20805 www.greyhouse.com
Grey House Publishing

Authoritative reference directories for most business sectors including public relations and media markets. Users can search the online databases with varied search criteria allowing for custom searches by product category, geographic area, sales volume, keyword, subject and more. Full Grey House catalog and online ordering also available.

20806 www.iabc.com
International Association of Business Communicators

An international association for members who are professionals in organizational communications and public relations. Accepts advertising.

20807 www.instituteforpr.com
Institute for Public Relations

To improve the effectiveness of organizations by advancing the professional knowledge and practice of public relations through research and education.

20808 www.kscpublivrelations.com
KSC Public Relations

Full-service advertising, public relations and marketing firm serving real estate developers, health care automotive, and manufacturers.

20809 www.magnetcom.com
Magnet - Communications

Public relations firm.

20810 www.mediaaccessgroup.com
Media Access Group

20811 www.multicultural.com
Multicultural Marketing Resources Asian American
Advertising Federation

A public relations/marketing firm where corporate executives will find diverse resources, experts and information on how to market to multicultural (ethnic and niche) consumer markets.

20812 www.niri.org
National Investor Relations Institute

Professional association of corporate officers and investors relations consultants.

20813 www.petersgrouppr.com
PetersGroup Public Relations

Provides a full range of marketing and public relations programs to national and international businesses. The agency works closely with technology clients ranging from Funded start-ups to Fortune 500 companies, to integrate the right mix of research, strategy, positioning and media to help customers meet their ongoing business and communication goals.

20814 www.pinnacleww.com
Pinnacle Worldwide

For independent public relations firms in major markets around the globe.

20815 www.progressivepr.com
PPR Communications

20816 www.prpublishing.com
Public Relations Publishing Company

Case studies, research and trends in public relations and information on issues of importance to PR professionals.

20817 www.prsa.org
Public Relations Society of America

A major professional association of public relations practitioners.

20818 www.prweek.com
PR Week

20819 www.silveranvil.org
Silver Anvil Resource Center

Online database of public relations campaigns.

20820 www.washingtonpost.com
Washington Post

20821 www.wepr.org
Women Executives in Public Relations

Provides a support network for women in public relations. Offers grants and scholarships for courses in public relations and for college students studying communications.

Associations

20822 Alliance for Audited Media
48 W Seegers Road
Arlington Heights, IL 60005-3913

224-366-6939; *Fax:* 224-366-6949
service@accessabc.com
auditedmedia.com
Social Media: Facebook, Twitter, LinkedIn, YouTube, Instagram

Christina Meringolo, Chairwoman
Scott Kruse, Vice Chair
Tom Drouillard, President/Managing Director
Edward Boyd, Secretary
Liberta Abbondante, Treasurer

The world's largest circulation-auditing organization, ABC provides circulation data on 1,400+ newspapers and more than 1,100 periodicals to ABC-member publications, advertisers and advertising agencies.
4.1M+ Members
Founded in: 1914

20823 Alliance of Area Business Publications
2512 Artesia Blvd
Suite 200
Redondo Beach, CA 90278

310-379-8261; *Fax:* 310-379-8283
aabpstaff@gmail.com; www.bizpubs.org
Social Media: RSS

C James Dowden, Executive Director
Jeff Nutall, President
Lisa Jones, Vice President
Joel Zwiebel, Secretary-Treasurer
Shelly Elmore, Director

Represents metropolitan area and state wide business to business publications with conventions, newsletters, and other services.
1.2M Members
Founded in: 1979

20824 American Black Book Writers' Association
269 S Beverly Drive Street 2600
Beverly Hills, CA 90212
310-306-4042

Will Gibson, President

Members include all African Americans who are involved with any aspects of the publishing industry.
4M Members

20825 American Book Producers Association
31 W 8th Street
2nd Floor
New York, NY 10011

917-741-1919
800-209-4575; *Fax:* 212-675-1364
office@ABPAonline.org; www.abpaonline.org
Social Media: Facebook

Richard Rothschild, President
David Katz, Manager
Nancy Hall, Vice President
Valerie Tomaselli, Treasurer
Michael Centore, ABPA Administrator

Increases the book industry's awareness of members capabilities and exchanges information on improving business. Develops concepts for books and other publications.
Founded in: 1980

20826 American Booksellers Association
333 Westchester Avenue
Suite S202
White Plains, NY 10604

914-406-7500
800-637-0037; *Fax:* 914-417-4013
info@bookweb.org; www.bookweb.org
Social Media: Facebook, Twitter, YouTube

Oren Teicher, CEO
Betsy Burton, President
Robyn DesHotel, Chief Financial Officer
Robert Sindelar, Vice President/ Secretary
Joy Dallangra-Sanger, Senior Program Officer

Trade organization pledge to protecting the well-being of book retailers and promoting the availability of books.
2000 Members
Founded in: 1900

20827 American Library Association
50 E Huron St
Chicago, IL 60611-2795

312-944-6780
800-545-2433; *Fax:* 312-440-9374
ala@ala.org; www.ala.org
Social Media: Facebook, Twitter, LinkedIn, Stumbleupon, Friendfeed, Reddi

Robert E. Banks, Executive Board Member
Keith Michael Fiels, Executive Director
Sari Feldman, President
Mario Gonzalez, Treasurer
Dr. Julie B. Todaro, President-Elect

To provide leadership for the development, promotion, and improvement of library and information services and the profession of librarianship in order to enhance learning and ensure access to information for all.
65000 Members
Founded in: 1876

20828 American Society of Journalists & Authors
355 Lexington Avenue
15th Floor
New York, NY 10017-6603

212-997-0947; *Fax:* 212-937-2315
staff@asja.org; www.asja.org
Social Media: Facebook, Twitter, LinkedIn, Google+, Instagram

Alexandra Canto Owens, Executive Director
Neil O'Hara, Treasurer
Randy Dotinga, President
Sherry Beck Paprocki, Vice-President
Sandra Lamb, Secretary
1200 Members
Founded in: 1948

20829 Antiquarian Booksellers Association of America
20 W 44th St
Suite 507
New York, NY 10036

212-944-8291; *Fax:* 212-944-8293
sbenne@abaa.org; www.abaa.org
Social Media: Facebook, Twitter, RSS

Susan Benne, Executive Director
Thomas Goldwasser, President
Mary Gilliam, Vice-President/ Secretary
Charles Kutcher, Treasurer

A trade association of rare book dealers.
480 Members
Founded in: 1949

20830 Arizona Book Publishing Association
6340 South Rural Road
#118-152
Tempe, AZ 85283

602-274-6264
info@azbookpub.com; www.azbookpub.com

Sam Henrie, President
Mike Wentz, Managing Editor

20831 Associated Church Press
924 Woodcrest Way
Oviedo, FL 32762

407-341-6615; *Fax:* 407-386-3236
AssociatedChurchPress@gmail.com;
www.theacp.org
Social Media: Facebook, Twitter, RSS

Joe Thoma, Executive Director
Cynthia Martens, President
Carlos Medley, Treasurer
Terri Lackey, Associate Director
Charlotte Indico, Associate Director

Aims to share ideas and concerns in religious publishing and to stimulate higher standards of religious journalism to exert a more positive influence.
240 Members
Founded in: 1916

20832 Association for Information and Image Management
1100 Wayne Avenue
Suite 1100
Silver Spring, MD 20910

301-587-8202
800-477-2446; *Fax:* 301-587-2711
aiim@aiim.org; www.aiim.org
Social Media: Facebook, Twitter, LinkedIn, RSS, YouTube, Google+

Paul Engel, Chairman
Anthony Peleska, Vice Chair
Timothy Elmore, Immediate Past Chair
Mark Patrick, Executive Committee Member at Large
Daniel Antion, Treasurer

Members are users and manufacturers of equipment and supplies of the information and image industry.
10M Members
Founded in: 1943

20833 Association of American Publishers (AAP)
455 Massachusetts Avenue NW
Suite 700
Washington, DC 20001

202-347-3375; *Fax:* 202-347-3690
info@publishers.org; www.publishers.org
Social Media: Facebook, Twitter, LinkedIn, RSS

Tom Allen, President & CEO
Brian Murray, Chair
Y.S. Chi, Vice Chair
W.Drake McFeely, Treasurer
Bert Ramlow, Executive Assistant & CEO

AAP is the trade association for the US book publishers, providing advocacy and communications on behalf of the industry. AAP represents the industry's priorities on policy, legislative and regulatory issues regionally, nationally and worldwide. These include protection of intellectual property rights and worldwide copyright enforcement, digital and new technology issues, funding for education and libraries, tax and trade, censorship and literacy.
400+ Members
Founded in: 1970

20834 Association of American University Presses
28 West 36th Street
Suite 602
New York, NY 10018

212-989-1010; *Fax:* 212-989-0275
info@aaupnet.org; www.aaupnet.org
Social Media: Facebook, Twitter, RSS

Peter Berkery, Executive Director
Tim Muench, Assistant Director
Meredith Babb, President

Susan Doerr, Treasurer
David Hamrick, President Elect

Members are university presses and a limited number of presses of non-degree-granting scholarly institutions.
125 Members
Founded in: 1937
Mailing list available for rent: 2.2M names

20835 Association of Catholic Publishers
4725 Dorsey Hall Dr.
Suite 1, PMB 709
Ellicott City, MD 21042

410-988-2926; *Fax:* 410-571-4946;
www.catholicpublishers.org

Therese Brown, Executive Director

Catholic publishers and content producers.

20836 Association of Directory Publishers
116 Cass Street
PO Box 1929
Traverse City, MI 49684

800-267-9002; *Fax:* 231-486-2182
hq@adp.org; www.adp.org
Social Media: Facebook, Twitter, LinkedIn, YouTube

Laura Hill, Chairman
Todd McKnight, First Vice Chairman
Jim Hail, Treasurer
Danny Bills, Secretary
Cindi A. Aldrich, President/CEO

240 Members
Founded in: 1898

20837 Association of Directory Publishers (ADP)
116 Cass St.
Traverse City, MI 49684

800-267-9002; *Fax:* 231-486-2182
hq@adp.org; www.adp.org
Social Media: Facebook, Twitter, LinkedIn, YouTube

Cindi A. Aldrich, President & CEO
Laura Hill, Chairman

The association is the communication link to the Telephone Directory industry. It provides a forum for the exchange of ideas and information among publishers of telephone, city and special interest directories and provides continuous training to assist in the enhancement of the publisher's operation.
240 Members
Founded in: 1898

20838 Association of Free Community Papers
135 Old Cove Rd
Suite 210
Liverpool, NY 13090

877-203-2327; *Fax:* 781-459-7770
loren@afcp.org; www.afcp.org
Social Media: Facebook, Twitter, LinkedIn, YouTube, Instagram

Loren Colburn, Executive Director
Carol Toomey, President
Karen Sawicz, Secretary / Treasurer
Greg Birkett, 1st Vice President
Shane Goodman, 2nd Vice President

Offers national classified advertising placement services; conducts charitable programs, sponsors competition, compiles statistics.
250 Members
Founded in: 1951

20839 Association of Medical Media
1120 Route 73
Suite 200
Mount Laurel, NJ 08054

856-380-6814; *Fax:* 856-439-0525
info@ammonline.org; www.ammonline.org
Social Media: Facebook, Twitter, LinkedIn

Lisa Trofe, Executive Director

Members of this nonprofit are medical publishing firms, content providers and others in the medical communications field.

20840 Author's Coalition of America
P.O. Box 929
Pentwater, MI 49449

231-869-2011; *Fax:* 313-882-3047
dkelly@authorscoalition.org;
www.authorscoalition.org

Dorien Kelly, Assistant Administrator

An organization of U.S. based authors and creators united to receive and distribute non-title specific reprographic royalties to member organizations, assist in further development of collective licensing programs and act for the general benefit of authors. The ACA is an association of twenty independent authors' organizations representing text writers, songwriters, visual artists, illustrators and photographers.
80000 Members
Founded in: 1994

20841 Book Industry Study Group (BISG)
1412 Broadway
21st Floor, Office 19
New York, NY 10018

646-336-7141; *Fax:* 646-336-6214
info@bisg.org; www.bisg.org
Social Media: Facebook, Twitter, LinkedIn, RSS

Maureen McMahon, Chair
Peter Balis, Vice President
Brian O'Leary, Executive Director
Kim Graff, Operations Manager

BISG is the leading US book trade association for standardized best practices, research and education.
170 Members
Founded in: 1975

20842 Book Manufacturers' Institute
2 Armand Beach Drive
Suite 1B
Palm Coast, FL 32137-2612

386-986-4552; *Fax:* 386-986-4553
info@bmibook.com; www.bmibook.org

Daniel N Bach, Executive VP
Kent H Larson, Vice President/ President- Elect
Jac B Garner, President
Paul Genovese, Treasurer
Jackie Murray, Conference Coordinator

Since 1933, the Book Manufacturers' Institute, Inc (BMI) has been the leading nationally recognized trade association of the book manufacturing industry. BMI member companies annually produce the great majority of books ordered by the U.S. book publishing industry. Today, BMI is a vital part of the industry, playing a leading role by providing an intra-industry communications link among book manufacturers, publishers, suppliers and governmental bodies.
94 Members
Founded in: 1933

20843 Community of Literary Magazines and Presses
154 Christopher St.
Suite 3C
New York, NY 10014-9110

212-741-9110; *Fax:* 212-741-9112
info@clmp.org; www.clmp.org
Social Media: Facebook, Twitter

Jeffrey Lependorf, Executive Director

Organization serving independent literary publishers.
Founded in: 1967

20844 Guild of Book Workers
521 5th Avenue
New York, NY 10175

212-292-4444
secretary@guildofbookworkers.org;
www.guildofbookworkers.org

Jennifer Evers, Membership Chair
Mark Andersson, President
Bexx Caswell, Vice President
Catherine Burkhard, Secretary
Alicia Bailey, Treasurer

To broaden public awareness of the hand book arts, to stimulate commissions of fine bindings, and to stress the need for sound book conservation and restoration.
900+ Members
Founded in: 1906

20845 Impact Publishers, Inc.
Impact Publishers
5674 Shattuck Avenue
Oakland, CA 94609

805-466-5917
800-748-6273; *Fax:* 800-652-1613
customerservice@newharbinger.com;
www.newharbinger.com
Social Media: Facebook, Twitter, Pinterest

Offers the finest in practical, reader-friendly help on a wide variety of personal interpersonal matters: relationships, divorce recovery, parenting, stress, personal growth, and mental health.
Founded in: 1973

20846 Independent Book Publishers Association
1020 Manhattan Beach Blvd
Suite 204
Manhattan Beach, CA 90266

310-546-1818; *Fax:* 310-546-3939
info@ibpa-online.org; www.ibpa-online.org
Social Media: Facebook, Twitter, LinkedIn, Flickr, RSS

Angela Bole, Executive Director
Rana DiOrio, Secretary
Florrie Binford-Kichler, President
Rob Price, Treasurer
Peter Goodman, Chair

Provides cooperative marketing programs, education and advocacy within the publishing industry.
4000+ Members
Founded in: 1983

20847 Independent Free Papers of America
104 Westland Drive
Columbia, TN 38401

931-922-4171
800-441-4372; www.ifpa.com
Social Media: Facebook, Twitter, LinkedIn

Doug Fabian, President
Jane Means, Vice President
Danielle Burnett, CADNET Director
Douglas Fry, Executive Director
Mark Helmer, Treasurer

Bestows awards and compiles statistics.
300 Members
Founded in: 1980

20848 International Digital Enterprise Alliance
1600 Duke Street
Suite 420
Alexandria, VA 22314

703-837-1070; *Fax:* 703-837-1072
info@idealliance.org; www.idealliance.org

David Steinhardt, CEO
Steve Bonoff, Executive Vice President
Joe Duncan, Chairman
Marriott Winchester, Vice-Chairman
Neil Johnson, Treasurer

Founded as The Graphic Communications Association , was formed to help member companies apply the latest computer-related technologies to all forms of print and electronic publishing
Founded in: 1966

20849 Jenkins Independent Publishers
Jenkins Group
1129 Woodmere Ave.
Suite B
Traverse City, MI 49686

231-330-0445
800-706-4636; *Fax:* 231-933-0448;
www.bookpublishing.com

Jerrold R. Jenkins, Chairman And CEO

Provides comprehensive marketing and custom book publishing services for independent and small press book publishers.
160 Members
Founded in: 1996

20850 Magazine Publishers of America
757 Third Avenue
11th Floor
New York, NY 10017

212-872-3700; *Fax:* 212-888-4217
mpa@magazine.org; www.magazine.org
Social Media: Facebook, Twitter, LinkedIn, YouTube,Pinterest

Nancr Telliho, Interim President & CEO
Andrew Clurman, Executive Assistant
Stephen M. Lacy, Chairman
Thomas Harty, Treasurer
Eric Zinczenko, Secretary

Promotes magazines as an advertising medium. Provides information services and assistance to members in areas of circulation marketing.
240 Members
Founded in: 1919

20851 National Association of Hispanic Publications, Inc.
529 14th St. NW
Suite 923
Washington, DC 20045

202-662-7250; www.nahp.org
Social Media: Facebook, Twitter

Martha Montoya, President

Trade advocacy organization promoting Spanish-language newspapers, magazines and related media.

20852 National Association of Desktop Publishers
462 Old Boston Road
Topsfield, MA 01983-1232

978-876-6855
800-874-4113
nadtp@aol.com

Barry Harrigan, Owner

Trade organization which serves the desk top publishing industry and offers information resources.
5M Members
Founded in: 1987

20853 National Association of Hispanic Publications
National Press Building
529 14th Street NW
Suite 923
Washington, DC 20045

202-662-7250; *Fax:* 703-610-9005
directory@nahp.org; www.nahp.org
Social Media: Facebook, Twitter

Clara Escobedo, President
Martha Montoya, Vice President, Membership
Christina Monte Scott, Treasurer
Norma Condreay, Secretary
Jesus Cobian, Membership Chair

Promotes the Hispanic print media as a valuable means of communication. Works to ensure that member publications are listed in National Media Directories.
200 Members
Founded in: 1982

20854 National Association of Independent
PO Box 430
Highland City, FL 33846-0430

863-648-4420
naip@aol.com; www.publishersreport.com

Betty A Lampe, Executive Director

Assists and educates small publishing companies. Conducts seminars on marketing strategies, target audience, and techniques of book distribution. Especially helpful for the beginning or self-publisher.
500 Members
Founded in: 1979

20855 National Association of Publishers' Representatives
2800 W. Higgins Road
Suite 440
Hoffman Estates, IL 60169

877-263-9640; *Fax:* 847-885-8393
info@napronline.org; www.naproline.org
Social Media: Facebook, LinkedIn

Darren Dunay, President
Everett Knapp III, Chairman
Craig Pitcher, Vice President
Jan Zeman, Secretary/Treasurer
David Bayard, Board of Directors

Provides information for publishers' representatives selling advertising space.
250 Members
Founded in: 1950

20856 National Music Publishers Association
975 F Street, NW
Suite 375
Washington, DC 20004

202-393-6672; *Fax:* 202-393-6673
admin@mpa.org; www.nmpa.org
Social Media: Facebook, Twitter, YouTube, Instagram

David Israelite, President/CEO
Chris Clyde, Senior Vice President
Todd Vunderink, Secretary
Caroline Bienstock, Treasurer
Irwin Robinson, Chairman

An advocate for the protection of music copyrights.
800 Members
Founded in: 1917

20857 National Newspaper Association
900 Community Drive
Springfield, IL 62703

217-241-1400; *Fax:* 217-241-1301
membership@nna.org; www.nnaweb.org
Social Media: Facebook, Twitter, RSS

Matthew Paxton, President
Susan Rowell, Vice President
Dennis DeRossett, Chief Operating Officer
Tonda Rush, Director, Public Policy
Lynne Lance, Director, Membership Services

Industry trade newspaper. Accepts advertising.
2100 Members
Founded in: 1885

20858 National Paper Trade Association
330 North Wabash Avenue
Suite 2000
Chicago, IL 60611

312-321-4092
800-355-6782; *Fax:* 312-673-6736;
www.gonpta.com
Social Media: Twitter, LinkedIn, YouTube

William Frohlich, President
Sean Samet, Executive Vice President
Hilton Maze, Chairman
Don Clampitt, Treasurer
Kevin Gammonley, CEO

An Association for the paper, packaging, and supplies distribution industry.
2000 Members
Founded in: 1903

20859 Newspaper Association of America
4401 Wilson Blvd
Suite 900
Arlington, VA 22203

571-366-1000; *Fax:* 571-366-1195
joan.mills@naa.org; www.naa.org
Social Media: Facebook, Twitter, LinkedIn, YouTube, RSS, Google+

Robert J. Dickey, Past Chairman
Stephen P. Hills, Vice Chairman
Tony W. Hunter, Secretary
Donna Bareett, Chairman
Michael J. Klingensmith, Treasurer

Founded by the merger of seven associations serving the newspaper industry. Focuses on the major issues that affect today's newspaper industry public policy and legal matters, advertising revenue growth and audience development across the medium's broad portfolio of products and digital platforms.
2000 Members
Founded in: 1992

20860 Online Publishers Association (OPA)
1350 Broadway
Suite 606
New York, NY 10018

646-473-1000; *Fax:* 646-473-0200
info@digitalcontentnext.org
digitalcontentnext.org
Social Media: Facebook, Twitter, LinkedIn, Google+

Michael Zimbalist, Chairman
Krishan Bhatia, Vice Chairman
Drew Schutte, Treasurer
David Payne, Secretary
Marty Moe, President

The Online Publishers Association (OPA) is a not-for-profit trade organization dedicated to representing high-quality online content providers before the advertising community, the press, the government and the public.
Founded in: 2001

20861 PSP American Medical Publishers Committee
Association of America Publishers, Inc

71 Fifth Avenue
2nd Floor
New York, NY 10003-3004

212-255-0200; *Fax:* 212-255-7007
jtagler@publishers.org; www.PSPcentral.org

Patrick J. Kelly, Chair
Susan King, Vice Chair
Jennifer Crewe, Editorial Director
H. Frederick Dylla, Executive Director & CEO
Thomas Easley, Senior Vice President

The primary goals of the PSP/AMPC are to educate, advocate, engage in outreach and philanthropy and frame issues of relevance to medical publishers, including promoting a positive image of scientific and medical publishing.
300 Members
Founded in: 1960

20862 Science Fiction & Fantasy Writers of America
PO Box 3238
Enfield, CT 06083-3238

www.swfa.org
Social Media: Facebook, Twitter

Cat Rambo, President
Kate Baker, Operations Manager

Professional organization for writers of fantasy, science fiction and related genres. Host of the Nebula Awards.

20863 Society for Collegiate Journalists
1584 Wesleyan Drive
Virginia Inesleyan College
Norfolk, VA 23502-5599

757-455-3419; *Fax:* 757-461-5025
wjruehlmann@vwc.edu; www.scj.us
Social Media: Facebook

Mary Beth Earnheardt, Executive Director
Frank Barnas, President
Vivian Wagner, Second VP
Martha Collins, Third V.P
Rick Stewart, First Vice President

A collegiate journalism organization.
800 Members
Founded in: 1909

20864 Society for Scholarly Publishing
10200 W 44th Ave
Suite 304
Wheat Ridge, CO 80033

303-422-3914; *Fax:* 720-881-6101
info@sspnet.org; www.sspnet.org
Social Media: Facebook, Twitter, LinkedIn, RSS

Howard Ratner, Past President
Melanie Dolechek, Executive Director
Ann Michael, President
Byron Laws, Secretary/Treasurer
Rick Anderson, President-Elect

A group that represents scholarly publications, such as journals, university publications and magazines.
800 Members
Founded in: 1978

20865 Society of National Association Publications
12100 Sunset Hills Road
Suite 130
Reston, VA 20190

703-234-4063; *Fax:* 703-435-4390
info@associationmediaandpublishing.org
associationmediaandpublishing.org
Social Media: Facebook, Twitter, LinkedIn, Flickr

John T. Adams, Executive Director
Angel Alvarez-Mapp, President
John Falcioni, Vice President
Joe Vallina, Treasurer
Carla Kalogeridis, Editorial Director

Develops standards for editorial and advertising content of association and professional society magazines.
1045 Members
Founded in: 1963

20866 Software & Information Industry Association
1090 Vermont Ave NW
6th Floor
Washington, DC 20005-4905

202-289-7442
800-388-7478; *Fax:* 202-289-7097
piracy@siia.net; www.siia.net
Social Media: Facebook, Twitter, LinkedIn

Ken Wasch, President
Tom Davin, Senior Vice President & MD
Tom Meldrum, Vice President
Heather Farley, COO
David Foster, CEO

Members are microcomputer software firms. Services include data collection program, software protection, contracts reference disk, conferences and lobbying.
1200 Members
Founded in: 1984

20867 Special Libraries Association
331 S Patrick St
Alexandria, VA 22314-3501

703-647-4900; *Fax:* 703-647-4901
sla@sla.org; www.sla.org
Social Media: Facebook, Twitter, LinkedIn, Youtube, RSS

Tom Rink, President-Elect
Jill Strand, President
John DiGilio, Treasurer
Linda Broussard, Chief Financial Officer
Doug Newcomb, Chief Executive Officer

International association of information professionals who work in special libraries serving business, research, government and institutions that produce specialized information.
7000 Members
Founded in: 1856

20868 Specialized Information Publishers Association
1090 Vermont Ave NW
Sixth Floor
Washington, DC 20005-4095

202-289-7442
800-356-9302; *Fax:* 202-289-7097;
www.sipaonline.com
Social Media: Facebook, Twitter, LinkedIn, Digg, Google+

Henry Greene, Executive Director
Ken Wasch, President
Keith Kupferschmid, General Counsel and SVP
Tom Davin, Senior Vice President
Tom Meldrum, Vice President, Finance

International trade association serving the interests of publishers of newsletters and specialized information services.
450 Members
Founded in: 1977
*Mailing list available for rent*at $65 per M

20869 The Association of Publishers for Special Sales
PO Box 9725
Colorado Springs, CO 80932-0725

719-924-5534; *Fax:* 719-213-2602
community.bookapss.org
Social Media: Facebook, Twitter, Google+, Yahoo

Scott Flora, Consultant
Brian Jud, Executive Director
June Hyjek, Manager
Sarah Tufano, Administrative Assistant
Kim Tuttle, Executive Assistant

A nonprofit trade association for independent presses and self-publishers who want to produce better books and market them successfully. SPAN offers a monthly newsletter with information-rich articles and great benefits.
1300 Members
Founded in: 1996

20870 University of Denver
Sturm Hall
2000 East Astbury Ave
Denver, CO 80208

303-871-2570; *Fax:* 303-871-2501
pi-info@du.edu;
www.du.edu/publishinginstitute
Social Media: Facebook, Twitter, YouTube, Flickr

Jill Smith, Director
Jennifer Conder, Associate Director
Margaret Shaheen, Program Administrator

A certificate program that combines workshops in editing and marketing with lecture/teaching sessions conducted by leading experts from all areas of publishing.
Founded in: 1864

20871 Western Publications Association
823 Rim Crest Dr
Westlake Village, CA 91361

805-495-1863
888-735-1545; *Fax:* 866-735-1545
wpa@wpa-online.org; www.wpa-online.org
Social Media: Facebook, Twitter, LinkedIn, RSS

Jane Silbering, Executive Director
Jennifer Hamilton Bingo, Vice President
Norb Garrett, President
John Brooks, Treasurer/ Secretary
Darren Buford, Director

Represents magazine publishing companies and companies related to publishing industry, in the western United States.
200 Members
Founded in: 1951

20872 Women in Production
276 Bowery
New York, NY 10012

212-334-2106; *Fax:* 212-431-5786
admin@p3-ny.org; www.p3-ny.org

Rosemary Sirico, President
Diane Pesce, VP

Nonprofit profesional and educational association whose mission is to facilitate career growth and education through peer support and the exchange of information.
500 Members
Founded in: 2003

20873 Women's National Book Association
PO Box 237
FDR Station
New York, NY 10150

212-208-4629; *Fax:* 212-208-4629
info@wnba-books.org; www.wnba-books.org
Social Media: Facebook, Twitter, LinkedIn, RSS

Carin Siegfried, President
Jane Kinney-Denning, Vice President
Shannon Janeczek, Secretary
Gloria Toler, Treasurer
Valeri Tomaselli, Past President

An organization of women and men in all occupations allied to the book industry.
800 Members
Founded in: 1917

20874 Yellow Pages Publishers Association
Connell Corporate Park
400 Connell Drive
Suite 1100
Berkeley Heights, NJ 07922-2747

908-286-2380; *Fax:* 908-286-0620
KimberlyEnik@ypassociation.org;
www.yellowpageblues.com
Social Media: Facebook, Twitter, LinkedIn, YouTube,Blog

George Burnett, Chairman
Dennis Payne, Vice Chairman
Neg Norton, President

Trade association which represents the Yellow Pages industry. YPPA's publisher members collectively produce over 96 percent of all directories published in the United States and account for 99 percent of the revenues generated by Yellow Pages advertising.
340 Members
Founded in: 1988

Newsletters

20875 AAP Monthly Report
Association of American Publishers
71 5th Ave
Suite 2
New York, NY 10003-3004

212-255-1407; *Fax:* 212-255-7007
jtagler@publishers.org; www.pspcentral.org

John Tagler, VP/Executive Director
Sara Pinto, Director
Kate Kolendo, Project Manager

A report offering information and news to the publishing community.
Cost: $800.00

20876 American Book Producers Association Newsletter
American Book Producers Association
151 W 19th Street
3rd Floor
New York, NY 10011

917-741-1919
800-209-4575; *Fax:* 212-675-1364
office@abpaonline.org; www.abpaonline.org

David Rubel, Publisher
Dan Tucker, Co-President
David Katz, Manager
Richard Rothschild, President
Kirsten Hall, Administrator

Trade association of independent book producers in the United States and Canada.
6 Pages
Frequency: Monthly
Circulation: 2500
Founded in: 1980
Printed in 2 colors on matte stock

20877 Augsburg Fortress Newsletter for Church Leaders
Augsburg Fortress
PO Box 1209
Minneapolis, MN 55440-1209

612-330-3300
800-328-4648; *Fax:* 800-722-7766;
www.augsburgfortress.org

Roderick Olson, Publisher

Monthly newsletter designed to equip pastors, church leaders, Christian leaders, Christian Educators and volunteers with valuable and timely resources, promotions, and ministry ideas.
Frequency: Monthly eNewsletter

20878 BISG Bulletin
Book Industry Study Group
1412 Broadway
21st Floor, Office 19
New York, NY 10018

646-336-7141; *Fax:* 646-336-6214
info@bisg.org; www.bisg.org
Social Media: Facebook, Twitter, LinkedIn, RSS

Brian O'Leary, Executive Director
Kim Graff, Operations Manager
Maureen McMahon, Chair
Peter Balis, Vice President

News and information from the Book Industry Study Group regarding book industry technologies, conferences, opinions, policy development, supply chain and more.
Founded in: 1976

20879 Book Arts
Center for Book Arts
28 W 27th St
Suite 3
New York, NY 10001-6906

212-481-0295; *Fax:* 212-481-9853
info@centerforbookarts.org;
www.centerforbookarts.org
Social Media: Facebook, Twitter, YouTube,Flickr

Alexander Campos, Executive Director

Center news and activities.
Founded in: 1974

20880 Book News
American Book Producers Association
151 W 19th Street
3rd Floor
New York, NY 10011

917-741-1919
800-209-4575; *Fax:* 212-675-1364
office@abpaonline.org; www.abpaonline.org

Richard Rothschild, President
Bok Hee, Manager
Bill Raggio, Contact

Monthly newsletter is part of the membership benefits; provides a transcript of the monthly member luncheon's speaker, as well as association and member news.
Frequency: Benefit of Membership
Founded in: 1980

20881 Bookselling This Week
American Booksellers Association
200 White Plains Rd
Suite 600
Tarrytown, NY 10591

800-637-0037; *Fax:* 914-591-2720
info@bookweb.org; www.bookweb.org

Oren Teicher, CEO
Len Viahos, COO
Ellie Chang, CFO
Frequency: Weekly
Circulation: 10000

20882 Educational Marketer
Simba Information
60 Long Ridge Rd
Suite 300
Stamford, CT 06902-1841

203-325-8193
888-297-4622; *Fax:* 203-325-8975
customerservice@simbainformation.com;
www.simbanet.com/

Linda Kopp, Publisher

Reports on the entire educational publishing spectrum from el-hi to College. It covers the complete range of print and electronic tools including software, and multimedia materials. It details mergers, acquisitions, financial reports, distribution, adoption and enrollment trends, legislative issues
Cost: $650.00
8 Pages
Founded in: 1989
Printed in 4 colors

20883 Exchange
Association of American University Presses
Rm 602
30 W 36th St
New York, NY 10018-8063

212-989-1010; *Fax:* 212-989-0275
aaupnet.org/

Hollis Holmes, Publisher
Peter J Givler, Executive Director
Rachel Weiss, Marketing Manager
Latasha Watters, Marketing Coordinator

Reports on issues relevant to scholarly publishing.
Cost: $10.00
16 Pages
Frequency: Quarterly

20884 Footprints Newsletter
Evangelical Christian Publishers Association
4816 S Ash Ave
Suite 101
Tempe, AZ 85282-7735

480-966-3998; *Fax:* 480-966-1944
info@ecpa.org; www.ecpa.org

Mark Kuyper, President
Kelly Gallagher, VP
Dave Bird, Marketing

An international, not-for-profit, trade organization serving its industry by promoting excellence and professionalism, sharing relevant data, stimulating Christian fellowship, raising the effectiveness of member houses, and equipping them to meet the needs of the changing marketplace.
Frequency: Monthly
Circulation: 280

20885 Fusion Magazine
Newspaper Association of America
4401 Wilson Blvd
Suite 900
Arlington, VA 22203-4195

571-366-1000; *Fax:* 571-366-1195
joan.mills@naa.org; www.naa.org
Social Media: Facebook, Twitter, LinkedIn, YouTube,RSS

Reggie Hall, Senior VP
James M Moroney, Chairman
Robert Dickey, Secretary
Donna Barrett, Treasurer
Robert M Nutting, Vice Chairman

This newsletter focuses on the business of diversity within the newspaper industry. In it you will find new strategies for making diversity work in advertising, news and editorial, circulation, marketing, production, human resources and the business office.
Frequency: Quarterly
Mailing list available for rent

20886 Guild of Book Workers-Newsletter
Guild of Book Workers
521 5th Avenue
17th Floor
New York, NY 10175-1799

212-285-5581
palimpsest.stanford.edu/byorg/gbw

Margaret Johnson, Publisher
Bernadette Callery, Membership Secretary

Information for the book arts field.
Circulation: 800

20887 Hotline
1825 Ponce de Leon
Suite 429
Coral Gables, FL 33133
703-992-9339
800-356-9302; *Fax:* 703-992-7512
sipa@online.com; www.hotline.com
Henry Greene, Executive Director
Furthers the professional and economic interests of members. Future plans include seminars, research and representing members before federal agencies. Available only to members.
Founded in: 1977
Printed in one color on matte stock

20888 Independent Book Publishers Association Newsletter
Independent Book Publishers Association
1020 Manhattan Beach Blvd
Suite 204
Manhattan Beach, CA 90266
310-546-1818; *Fax:* 310-546-3939
info@ibpa-online.org; www.ibpa-online.org
Social Media: Facebook, Twitter, LinkedIn, Flickr,RSS
Terry Nathan, Executive Director
Lisa Krebs, Assistant Director
Steve Mettee, Board Chair
Roy M Carlisle, Treasurer
Florrie Kichler, President
Publicity, sales, legal, and marketing opportunities and news articles for independent book publishers.
Frequency: Monthly
Circulation: 6000

20889 Independent Publishers Trade Report
PO Box 176
Southport, CT 06490-176
860-669-5848; *Fax:* 203-332-7629
Henry Berry, Publisher
News and information for independent publishers, monthly column in the COSMEP Newsletter.

20890 Independent Small Press Review
WHW Publishing
930 Via Fruteria
Santa Barbara, CA 93110-2322
609-408-8000; www.ifpa.com
Gary Rudy, Executive Director
Offers a comprehensive look at the concerns and issues of the small business publisher.

20891 John Kremer's Book Marketing Tip of the Week
Open Horizons Publishing
PO Box 2887
Taos, NM 87571
575-751-3398
800-796-6130; *Fax:* 575-751-3100
info@bookmarket.com; www.bookmarket.com
John Kremer, Editor
Robert Sanny, Advertising/Sales Manager
Email newletter offering new PR and sales leads and tips every week.
Frequency: Weekly
Founded in: 1982
Mailing list available for rent

20892 Lifelong Learning Market Report
Simba Information
60 Long Ridge Rd
Suite 300
Stamford, CT 06902-1841
203-325-8193
888-297-4622; *Fax:* 203-325-8975
customerservice@simbainformation.com; www.simbanet.com
Linda Kopp, Publisher
News and analysis for content and service providers of corporate training and professional development materials. Includes news on merger and aczuisitions, industry financial performance and trends, product development and distribution.
Cost: $625.00
Founded in: 1989

20893 MBR Bookwatch
Midwest Book Review
278 Orchard Drive
Oregon, WI 53575-1129
608-835-7937
mbr@execpc.com; www.midwestbookreview.com
James A Cox, Editor-in-Chief
A monthly online book review publication that will showcase the reviews and commentaries of those MBR editors and specialized reviewers who've demonstrated expertise in their field. Bookwatch will also feature author interviews and editorial observations of various aspects of the publishing world, offered by knowledgeable and articulate participants.
140 Pages
Frequency: Monthly
Circulation: 30,000
Founded in: 1976

20894 National Association of Professional Print Buyers
15050 NE 20th Avenue
Suite A
North Miami, FL 33181-1123
305-956-9563
Vincent Millardi, Publisher
Accepts advertising.
Cost: $315.00
296 Pages
Frequency: Monthly

20895 NewsInc.
Cole Group
PO Box 719
Pacifica, CA 94044-719
650-557-9595; *Fax:* 650-475-8479
admin@colegroup.com; www.colegroup.com
David M Cole, Publisher/Editor
Marge Wetmore, Circulation Manager
The weekly newsletter about the business of the newspaper business, written for media executives and the investments community. subscriptions available in digital or print formats, as well as for archive access.
Cost: $99.00
Frequency: 48/Yr, for Digital Access
Founded in: 1989

20896 Newsletter on Newsletters
Newsletter on Newsletters
PO Box 348
Rhinebeck, NY 12572-0348
845-876-5222; *Fax:* 845-876-4943; www.newsletteronnewsletters.com
Paul Swift, Editor
Graphics, editorial, promotions, management and reports on the entire newsletter industry.
Cost: $275.00
Founded in: 1970

20897 Online Publishing Update E-Newsletter
Newspaper Association of America
4401 Wilson Blvd
Suite 900
Arlington, VA 22203-4195
571-366-1000; *Fax:* 571-366-1195; www.naa.org
Social Media: Facebook, Twitter, LinkedIn, YouTube,RSS
Reggie Hall, Senior VP
James M Moroney, Chairman
Robert Dickey, Secretary
Donna Barrett, Treasurer
A round-up of news, research, industry trends, best practices and more, focusing on items of interest to newspaper and digital media executives. Online Publishing Update e-newsletter is published every Monday, Wednesday and Friday.
Frequency: 3x/Weekly

20898 PMA Newsletter
Publishers Marketing Association
627 Aviation Way
Manhattan Beach, CA 90266-7107
310-372-2732; *Fax:* 310-374-3342
info@ibpa-online.org; www.atlanticpublishers.com
Terry Nathan, Executive Director
Publishing law, copyrighting, marketing, business management all directed toward the independent book publishing community.
Frequency: Monthly
Circulation: 10000
Founded in: 1983

20899 Personal Composition Report
Graphic Dimensions
134 Caversham Woods
Pittsford, NY 14534-2834
585-381-3428
Michael Kleper, Publisher
Covers all aspects of electronic publishing and imaging including news, reviews and in-depth analysis. Begun in 1979 by Professor Michael Kleper of RIT, the newsletter has provided consistent, valuable information for its readers.
Cost: $100.00
16 Pages
Frequency: Annual
Printed in one color on matte stock

20900 Pleasures of Publishing
Columbia University
2960 Broadway
New York, NY 10027-6900
212-854-1754; *Fax:* 212-749-0397; www.columbia.edu
Robert Kasdin, Executive VP
Mathew Martg, Marketing
Industry news.

20901 Professional Publishing Report
Simba Information
60 Long Ridge Rd
Suite 300
Stamford, CT 06902-1841
203-325-8193; *Fax:* 203-325-8915
customerservice@simbainformation.com; www.simbanet.com
Linda Kopp, Publisher
Charlie Friscia, Marketing
John Fuller, Executive Editor
Newletter focuses on the $10 billion professional publishing industry. Features in-depth analysis of each of the four major professional publishing categories: scientific/technical, medical, legal and business. Provides revenue breakdowns by media and market, merger and acquisition news, and analysis of market trends.
Cost: $715.00
Founded in: 1989

20902 Publishers Monthly Domestic Sales
Association of American Publishers
50 F St Nw
Suite 400
Washington, DC 20001-1565

202-347-3375; *Fax:* 202-347-3690
info@publishers.org; www.publishers.org

Tom Allen, CEO
Katie Blough, Editor
Patricia Schroeder, President
Tina Jordan, Vice President
Kate Kolendo, Project Manager

Sales charts, index and rates for the publishing community.
Frequency: Monthly
Founded in: 1970

20903 Publishers Multinational Direct
Direct International
1501 Third Avenue
New York, NY 10028-2101

212-861-4188; *Fax:* 212-628-5070;
www.publishersmultinational.com

Alfred Goodloe, Editor

National and international coverage of the publishing community including printing, prepress and direct marketing.
Cost: $195.00
Frequency: Monthly

20904 Publishers Report
National Association of Independent Publishers
PO Box 430
Highland City, FL 33846-430

863-648-4420; *Fax:* 836-648-4420
naip@aol.com; www.publishersreport.com

Betsy A Lampe, Publisher

Provides a clearinghouse of information on small/independent publishing for its members. Accepts advertising. Departments include: 'New Books, Audios & Videos,' It's a Date,' 'NAIP Book Review,' 'New Media Sources,' 'Wanted,' 'In the Know,' 'F41,' and various others helpful for new publishers and self-publishers.

20905 Publishers' Auxiliary
National Newspaper Association
900 Community Drive
Springfield, IL 62703

217-241-1400; *Fax:* 217-241-1301
membership@nna.org; www.nnaweb.org
Social Media: Facebook, Twitter

Matthew Paxton, President
Tonda Rush, Director, Public Policy
Stan Schwartz, Managing Editor

Providing personnel announcements, new technology, economic trends, and new publicaiton and distribution methods for executives in the newpaper industry.
Founded in: 1865

20906 Publishing Markets
Reed Business Information
275 Washington St
Newton, MA 02458-1611

617-964-3030; *Fax:* 617-558-4327;
www.designnews.com

Deborah Selsky, Publisher
San Buchan, Editor

Economic and demographic trends that affect the book publishing market.
Cost: $129.00

20907 Publishing Poynters
Para Publishing
PO Box 8206-240
Santa Barbara, CA 93118-8206

805-968-7277
800-727-2782; *Fax:* 805-968-1379;
www.parapublishing.com
Social Media: Facebook, Twitter

Dan Poynter, Editor
Becky Carbone, Production Manager

Book publishing news and ideas: marketing, promotion and distribution.
Cost: $9.95
20 Pages
Frequency: Monthly
Circulation: 16000
ISSN: 1530-5694
Founded in: 1969
Printed in one color

20908 Report on Preschool Programs
Business Publishers,Inc
2222 Sedwick Drive
Durham, NC 27713

800-223-8720; *Fax:* 800-508-2592
custserv@bpinews.com; www.bpinews.com

The one source to turn to for timely, accurate coverage of important developments in Head Start, child care, health care, special education and much more.
Cost: $357.00
8 Pages
Founded in: 1963

20909 SPAN
Small Publishers Association of North America
1618 W Colorado Avenue
Colorado Springs, CO 80904-4029

719-475-1726; *Fax:* 719-471-2182
span@spannet.org; www.spannet.org

Marilyn Ross, Editor
Cathy Bowman, Production Manager

Includes money-making articles and book industry information.
24 Pages
Frequency: Monthly
Circulation: 4000
Founded in: 1996

20910 SPAN Internet Newsletter
Small Publishers Association of North America
PO Box 9725
Colorado Springs, CO 80932-0725

719-924-5534; *Fax:* 719-213-2602
brad@spannet.org; www.spannet.org
Social Media: Facebook, Twitter

Marilyn Ross, Executive Director/Editor
Tom Ross, VP

The SPAN Internet Newsletter features timely and useful information on many aspects of writing and the publishing industry, including articles on book marketing and publicity in addition to providing links to industry related Websites.
Frequency: Monthly
Circulation: 4000
Founded in: 1996

20911 Small Publisher Co-Op
Nigel Maxey
1521 SE Palm Court
PO Box 1620
Stuart, FL 34994-1620

772-287-8117
spcoop@hotmail.com; www.spco-op.com

Niyel Maxey, President/Editor
Kevin Hawken, Member Service Manager

This monthly newsletter offers a guide to publishing and marketing books, reports, periodicals, etc.
Cost: $15.00
Circulation: 5900

20912 Span Connection
Small Publishers Association of North America
PO Box 1306
Buena Vista, CO 81211-1306

719-395-4790; *Fax:* 719-395-8374;
www.spannet.org

Scoot Flora, Editor
Scoot Flora, CEO

Wide variety of news and information about small-scale and individual publishing.
Cost: $105.00
Frequency: Monthly
Circulation: 4000
Founded in: 1996

20913 Specialty Directory Publishing Market Forecast
Simba Information
60 Long Ridge Rd
Suite 300
Stamford, CT 06902-1841

203-325-8193
888-297-4622; *Fax:* 203-325-8975
info@simbanet.com; www.simbanet.com

Kathy Mickey, Managing Editor/Analyst
David Goddard, Senior Editor/Analyst
Michael Norris, Senior Editor/Analyst

Complete market size, revenue and growth figures and forecasts including revenues driven by electronic products and exclusive reanking of leading publishers by revenue.
Cost: $495.00
Frequency: Anually
Founded in: 1989

20914 The Bookwoman
Women's National Book Association
PO Box 237
FDR Station
New York, NY 10150

212-208-4629; *Fax:* 212-208-4629;
www.wnba-books.org
Social Media: Facebook, Twitter, LinkedIn, RSS

Joan Gelfand, President
Mary Grey James, Vice President/President-Elect
Ruth Light, Secretary
Margaret E Auer, Treasurer
Shannon Janeczek, The Bookwoman, Managing Editor

Bi-annual journal for members of the Women's National Book Association. Stories of interest for people in the world of books. Book review are includes, how-to information and chapter news from across the United States. Ad space available.
2 Pages
Frequency: Biennial
Circulation: 1000
Founded in: 1917

Magazines & Journals

20915 American Libraries Magazine
50 East Huron Street
Chicago, IL 60611

800-545-2433; *Fax:* 312-944-7841
membership@ala.org; www.ala.org

Keith Fields, Publisher, ALA Executive Director
Mary Mackay, Marketing & Sales Director
Camila Alire, ALA President

News and information on legislation concerning libraries, new publications and technology issues
Cost: $70.00
Frequency: 10x/Yr $ incl in ALA dues
Circulation: 60,000
ISSN: 0002-9769
Founded in: 1876

20916 Book Dealers World
North American Bookdealers Exchange
PO Box 606
Cottage Grove, OR 97424

541-942-7455; *Fax:* 541-942-7455;
www.bookmarketingprofits.com

Al Galasso, Editorial Director
Steve Sherman, Publisher

The book marketing magazine for independent publishers and mail order entrepreneurs. A publication of the North American Book Dealers Exchange, an international book marketing organization, specializing in cooperative opportunities at trade shows, in mail order, press releases and more.
Cost: $45.00
32 Pages
Frequency: Quarterly
Circulation: 10000
ISSN: 1098-8521
Founded in: 1980
Printed in on newsprint stock

20917 Book Promotion Hotline
Ad-Lib Publications
51 1/2 W Adam
PO Box 1102
Fairfield, IA 52556-3226

515-472-6617
800-669-0773; *Fax:* 641-472-3186

Marie Kiefer, Editor/Publisher

Provides media contacts and other marketing sources of interest to the publisher/marketing trade.
Cost: $150.00
4 Pages
Frequency: Weekly
Circulation: 1,000

20918 Booklist
American Library Association
50 E Huron St
Chicago, IL 60611-2788

312-280-2518
800-545-2433
kfiels@ala.org; www.ala.org

Keith Michael Fiels, Executive Director
Mary Ellen Quinn, Editor

The purpose of this guide is to provide information on materials worthy of consideration for purchase by small and medium sized public libraries.
Cost: $79.95
Founded in: 1876

20919 CBA Marketplace
Association for Christian Retail
9240 Explorer Drive
Suite 200
Colorado Spring, CO 80920

719-265-9895
800-252-1950; *Fax:* 719-272-3510
info@cbaonline.org; www.cbaonline.org

Bill Anderson, President/CEO
Cliff Goins, Treasurer
Greg Thornton, Director of Publications
George Thomsen, Chairman
Robin Hogan, Secretary

Resource for Christian retailers & suppliers.
Cost: $59.95
Frequency: Monthly
Circulation: 8000
Mailing list available for rent

20920 Christian Retailing
Strang Communications Company
600 Rinehart Rd
Lake Mary, FL 32746-4868

407-333-0600; *Fax:* 407-333-7100;
www.strang.com

Stephen Strang, CEO
Tircia Stafford, Circulation Director

A trade journal designed to inform Christian bookstore owners about books, music and gifts, videos, etc. Also it features topics to help retailers run a successful business.
Cost: $75.00
72 Pages
Frequency: Monthly
Circulation: 10000
Founded in: 1975

20921 Circulation Management
PRIMEDIA Intertec-Marketing & Professional Service
PO Box 4235
Stamford, CT 06907-0235

212-475-2212; *Fax:* 203-358-5823;
www.circman.com

Roberta Thomas, Publisher

Subscriptions, renewals, direct mail, list selection, circulation planning, data management, fulfillment and list management.
Cost: $39.00
Frequency: Monthly
Circulation: 10,000

20922 Collegiate Journalist
Society for Collegiate Journalists
1584 Wesleyan Drive
Virginia Wesleyan College
Virginia Beach, VA 23502-5599

757-455-3419; *Fax:* 757-461-5025
wjruehlmann@vwc.edu; www.scj.us

J D Tarpley, Publisher
William Ruehlmann, CEO/President
Adam Earnheardt, Editor

For editors of yearbooks, magazines and newspapers.
Cost: $5.00
28 Pages
Frequency: Monthly

20923 Complete Guide to Self-Publishing
Communication Creativity
425 Cedar
Buena Vista, CO 81211-0909

719-395-8659
800-331-8355; *Fax:* 719-395-8374

Marilyn Ross, Publisher
Matthew Sullivan, Editor

The most comprehensive resource available about the business of publishing. Offers everything you need to know to write, publish, promote and sell books.
Cost: $19.99
521 Pages
ISBN: 1-582970-91-2

20924 Desktop Publishers Journal
462 Boston Street
Topsfield, MA 01983

Fax: 800-492-1014; www.dtpjournal.com

Barry Harrigan, Contact

Offers a comprehensive array of news, analysis, features and reviews on the latest products and services on the market today.
Cost: $15.00
Frequency: 12 issues

20925 Editor & Publisher
Editor & Publisher International Yearbook
11 W 19th Street
10th Floor
New York, NY 10011-4234

212-291-1259; *Fax:* 212-691-7287;
www.mediainfo.com

Michael Parker, President

Covers all facets of the newspaper business today and is regarded as the bible of the newspaper industry.
Cost: $184.00
Frequency: 46 issues
Founded in: 1884

20926 Editorial Eye
EEI Communications
66 Canal Center Plz
Suite 200
Alexandria, VA 22314-5507

703-683-0683; *Fax:* 703-683-4915
info@eeicommunications.com;
www.eeicom.com

James T Degrafferei, CEO
Robin Cormier, VP
Candee Wilson, Director
Linda B. Jorgensen, Editor

Offering information on written excellence, editorial information and communication skills for readers.
Cost: $125.00
Frequency: Monthly
Founded in: 1972

20927 Electronic Publishing
PennWell Publishing Company
10 Tara Boulevard
5th Floor
Nashua, NH 03062-2880

603-891-0123; *Fax:* 603-891-0539
genepri@pennwell.com;
www.electronic-publishing.com

Gene Pritchard, Publisher

For those who communicate in print, including service bureaus, printers, prepress houses and desktop publishers, it provides latest products, news and related developments.
Cost: $45.00
Frequency: Monthly
Circulation: 68,441

20928 F&W Publications
1507 Dana Avenue
Cincinnati, OH 45207

513-396-6160; *Fax:* 513-531-1025;
www.writersdigest.com

Jeff Lapin, President

Articles that reflect the current state of American freelance writing.
72 Pages
Frequency: 8 per year
Circulation: 85,000
ISBN: 7-148602-50-8
Founded in: 1930

20929 FLEXO Magazine
Flexographic Technical Association Inc
900 Marconi Avenue
Ronkonkoma, NY 11779-7212

631-737-6020; *Fax:* 631-737-6813;
www.flexography.org

Robert Moran, President
Christian Bonawandt, Editor

Up-to-date on the changes and advances in the rapidly-expanding flexographic industry.
Cost: $55.00
Frequency: Monthly

20930 Folio: Magazine for Magazine Management
Red 7 Media, LLC

10 Norden Place
Norwalk, CT 06855
203-854-6730; *Fax:* 203-854-6735
tsilber@red7media.com; www.foliomag.com
Stefanie Botelho, Associate Editor
Kerry Smith, President /CEO
Dan Trombetto, Group Creative Director
Tony Silber, General Manager
John Ellertson, Director Advertising Sales Manager
Written for the people who run the nation's magazines. Offers authoritative intelligence on the magazine market to enable industry professionals to navigate the widening range of strategic options. Every issue delivers features on the people and technologies that are transforming the magazine business, along with useful columns and departments, thought-provoking analysis and tactical advice for building successful magazines.
Cost: $96.00
Frequency: Monthly
Circulation: 11550
Founded in: 1971

20931 ForeWord Reviews
ForeWord Magazine
425 Boardman Avenue
Traverse City, MI 49684
231-933-3699; *Fax:* 231-933-3899;
www.forewordreviews.com
Victoria Sutherland, Owner
Stacy Price, Director Advertising Sales
Review books and other servies for authors and small publishers.
Cost: $40.00
Frequency: Monthly
Circulation: 20000
Founded in: 1998
Printed in 4 colors on 6 stock

20932 INFO FLEX
Flexographic Technical Association Inc
3920 Veterans Memorial Highway
Suite 9
Bohemia, NY 11716
631-737-6020; *Fax:* 631-737-6813
memberinfo@flexography.org;
www.flexography.org
Mark Cisternino, President
Greg Platt, Chairman
Dan Doherty, Treasurer
Jason Barrier, Director
The show floor boasts 200+ booths manned by flexography's leading suppliers, as well as a presentation theater, and educational pavilion, a social event and more
Frequency: Annual/May

20933 Independent Publisher Magazine
Jenkins Group
1129 Woodmere Avenue
Suite B
Traverse City, MI 49686-4275
231-933-0445
800-706-4636; *Fax:* 231-933-0448;
www.bookpublishing.com
Jerrold R Jenkins, President
Jim Barmes, Editor
Andrew Pargel, Marketing Manager
Trade journal for the independent publishing, community, university presses, librarians, bookstores and professionals.
Cost: $40.00
Frequency: Monthly
Circulation: 8000
Founded in: 1988
Mailing list available for rent: 42M names
Printed in 4 colors on glossy stock

20934 Information Publishing: Business/ Professional Markets & Media
Simba Information
60 Long Ridge Rd
Suite 300
Stamford, CT 06902-1841
203-325-8193; *Fax:* 203-325-8915
simbainfo@simbanet.com; www.simbanet.com
Linda Kopp, Publisher
Donna Devall, Marketing Director
Charlie Friscia, Director of Advertising
Demonstrates how publishers are profiting from media. Discover the opportunities in newsletters, directories, books, magazines, journals and electronic information services. More than 300 pages of information and analysis, 100 tables and charts, financial and operating information on more than 50 key publishing companies, 16 principal information markets reviewed in-depth, with five year forecasts by market and by media.
Cost: $1995.00
Founded in: 1989

20935 Inside Edge
International Publishing Management Association
1205 W College Street
Liberty, MO 64068
816-781-1111; *Fax:* 660-781-2790
ipmainfo@ipma.org; www.ipma.org
Larry Aaron, Executive Director
Susan Murphy, Editor
Jack Welch, CEO
Lea Holt, Director
Offers information on the association's activities, industry trends, and corporate publishing facility profiles.
Cost: $50.00
24 Pages
Frequency: Monthly
Circulation: 1500
Mailing list available for rent: 2M names

20936 MultiMedia & Internet @Schools
Information Today
143 Old Marlton Pike
Medford, NJ 08055-8750
609-654-6266
800-300-9868; *Fax:* 609-654-4309
custserv@infotoday.com; www.infotoday.com
Thomas H Hogan, President
Roger R Bilboul, Chairman Of The Board
John C Yersak, Vice President
Sue Hogan, Director
John Brokenshire, CFO
A practical guide for K-12 library media specialists, technology coordinators and other educators with information on how to get high-performance learning from technology-based school products, services and resources.
Cost: $ 39.95
Frequency: 6 issues/yr
Mailing list available for rent: 4M names
Printed in 4 colors on glossy stock

20937 New Age Publishing and Retailing Alliance Trade Journal
PO Box 9
Eastsound, WA 98245-0009
360-376-2702; *Fax:* 360-376-2704
Marilyn McGuire, Executive Director
Carole Scarfuto, Administrative Director
Covers the publishing and retailing trades.
Frequency: Bi-Monthly
Circulation: 10,000

20938 NewsInc
PO Box 719
Pacifica, CA 94044-719
650-557-9595; *Fax:* 650-557-9696
news@newsinc.net; www.newsinc.net
David Cole, Publisher/Editor
Cost: $147.00
Frequency: Weekly
Founded in: 1989

20939 Newspapers & Technology
Conley Magazines
1623 Blake Street
Suite 250
Denver, CO 80202
303-575-9595; *Fax:* 303-575-9555;
www.newsandtech.com/
Mary Van Meter, Publisher
Chuck Moozakis, Editor-in-Chief
Tara McMeekin, Editor
Hays Goodman, Associate Editor/Webmaster
Newspapers & Technology is a monthly trade publication for newspaper publishers and department managers involved in applying and integrating technology. Written by industry experts, News & Tech provides regular coverage of the following departments: prepress, press, postpress and new media.
Circulation: 16,874
Mailing list available for rent

20940 Poets & Writer's Magazine
Poets & Writers
150 Broadway
New York, NY 10038-4381
212-566-2424; *Fax:* 212-587-9673
editor@pw.org; www.pettuswilliams.com
Marvin K Pettus, President
Christine Cassidy, Marketing Director
William Hayes, Finance Executive
Interviews, essays, grants and awards, practical information for poets and writers.
Cost: $19.95
Circulation: 60000

20941 Progressive Review
1312 18th Street NW
5th Floor
Washington, DC 20036
202-835-0770; *Fax:* 202-835-0779
news@prorev.com; www.prorev.com
Sam Smith, Editor
Frequency: Monthly
Founded in: 1964

20942 Publish
462 Boston Street
Suite 310
Topsfield, MA 01983
978-887-6855; *Fax:* 978-887-9245
Barry Harrigan, Owner

20943 Publishers Weekly
PO Box 51593
Harlan, IA 51593
800-278-2991; *Fax:* 712-733-8019
pwycustserv@cdsfulfillment.com;
www.publishersweekly.com
Social Media: Facebook, Twitter, LinkedIn, RSS
Jim Milliot, Co-Editorial Director
Michael Coffey, Co-Editorial Director
Diane Roback, Children's Book Editor
Louisa Ermelino, Reviews Director
Calvin Reid, News Editor
PW is the international journal of book publishing and bookselling including business news, re-

views and bestseller lists targeted at publishers, booksellers, librarians and literary agents.
Frequency: Weekly
Founded in: 1872

20944 Publishing & Production Executive
Mark Hertzog
1500 Spring Garden Street
Suite 1200
Philadelphia, PA 19130

215-238-5300; *Fax:* 215-238-5457;
www.ppe-online.com

Allison Schill Eckel, Managing Editor
Gretchen Kirby, Editor

Addresses technological trends and issues relevant to print production managers specializing in books, magazines, catalogs, agency or corporate communications.
Frequency: 12 per year
Circulation: 30,000

20945 Quill
PO Box 94080
Palatine, IL 60094-v
765-653-3333
800-789-1331; *Fax:* 800-789-8955;
www.quill.com

20946 Searcher: Magazine for the Database Professional
Information Today
143 Old Marlton Pike
Medford, NJ 08055-8750

609-654-6266
800-300-9868; *Fax:* 609-654-4309
custserv@infotoday.com; www.infotoday.com
Social Media: Facebook, Twitter

Thomas H Hogan, President
Roger R Bilboul, Chairman Of The Board

Explores and deliberates on a comprehensive range of issues important to the professional database researcher. Combines evaluations of data content with discussions of delivery media.
Cost: $86.95
Frequency: 10 issues/yr
Mailing list available for rent: 4M names
Printed in 4 colors on glossy stock

20947 Student Press Review
Columbia University
2960 Broadway
New York, NY 10027-6900

212-854-1754; *Fax:* 212-749-0397
cspa@columbia.edu; www.columbia.edu

Robert Kasdin, Executive VP
Helen F Smith, Editor
Edmund J Sullivan, Publisher

Reports and advises on high school and college student media. Offers how-to articles and features to improve student newspapers, magazines and yearbooks in schools, colleges, and universities.
Frequency: Quarterly
Circulation: 2200
Founded in: 1925

20948 Volt Report on Directory Publishing
Volt Directory Marketing
1800 Byberry Road
Suite 800
Huntingdon Valley, PA 19006-3520

800-677-3839; *Fax:* 215-938-5549

Kathy Wolden, Editor

As the monitor of the directory publishing industry, the Morgan report provides news on the people, companies, products and opportunities shaping the industry today. Includes practical how-to guidance on key facets of the directory publishing process as well as strategic overviews.
Cost: $95.00
12 Pages
Frequency: Monthly

20949 Writer Magazine
21027 Crossroads Circle
PO Box 1612
Waukesha, WI 53187-1612

262-796-8776
800-533-6644; *Fax:* 262-796-1615
corporate.kalmbach.com

Sylvia Burack, Publisher
Elfrieda Abbe, Executive Vice President
Chuck Croft, Executive Vice President

Practical guide to instruct, inform, and inspire writers as they work toward the goal of publication. Writers of short stories, novels, poetry, plays or science fiction, readers will find straightforward advice, up-to-date market lists and tips on manuscript submission.
Cost: $29.00
Frequency: Monthly
Circulation: 43000
Founded in: 1987

20950 Writer's Digest
F&W Publications
4700 E Galbraith Rd
Cincinnati, OH 45236-2726

513-531-2690
800-258-0929; *Fax:* 513-531-1843
WritersDig@fwpubs.com;
www.fwpublications.com

David Nussbaum, CEO
Jim Ogle, Chief Financial Officer
Kate Rados, Marketing Director
Stacie Berger, Communications Director

Information and how to tips for freelance writers.
Cost: $19.96
Frequency: Monthly
Founded in: 1920

Trade Shows

20951 AAP General Annual Meeting
Association of American Publishers (AAP)
455 Massachusetts Avenue NW
Suite 700
Washington, DC 20001-2777

202-347-3375; *Fax:* 202-347-3690
info@publishers.org; www.publishers.org
Social Media: Twitter

Karen Abramson, President & CEO
Tina Jordan, Vice President
Allan R Adler, VP for Legal & Government Affairs
Jay Diskey, Executive Director, School Division
Gail Kump, Director, Membership Marketing

Discussion topics include the state of digital content, distribution channels and copyright protection as seen through the prism of publishers and their historic partners.
200 Members
Frequency: Annual

20952 ADP Annual Convention and Partners Trade Show
Association of Directory Publishers
116 Cass St.
Traverse City, MI 49684

800-267-9002; *Fax:* 231-486-2182
adp.org/node/669
Social Media: Facebook, Twitter, LinkedIn, YouTube

Cindi A. Aldrich, President & CEO
Valerie Donn, Director of Meetings & Events
Frequency: Annual

20953 American Library Association Annual Conference
American Library Association
50 E Huron Street
Chicago, IL 60611

800-545-2433
customerservice@ala.org; www.ala.org

Loriene Roy, President
Keith Michael Fiels, Executive Director

Annual meeting and exhibits of books, periodicals, reference works, audio visual equipment, films, data processing services, computer hardware and software, library equipment and supplies.

20954 American Medical Publishers' Association Annual Meeting
71 Fifth Avenue
2nd Floor
New York, NY 10003

212-255-0200; *Fax:* 212-255-7007
jtagler@publishers.org; www.pspcentral.org
Social Media: LinkedIn

John Tagler, VP/Executive Director
Sara Pinto, Director
Kate Kolendo, Project Manager

Information provided to medical publishing field.
Frequency: Annual
Founded in: 1960

20955 Association of American University Presses Conference
Association of American University Presses
71 W 23rd Street
Suite 901
New York, NY 10010-3264

212-989-1010; *Fax:* 212-989-0275
annualmeeting@aaupnet.org; www.aaupnet.org

Peter Givler, Executive Director
Timothy Muench, Assistant Director

Annual conference and exhibits of equipment, supplies and services for scholarly publishing divisions of colleges and universities.
125 Attendees
Frequency: Annual

20956 Association of College and Research Libraries
American Library Association
50 E Huron Street
Chicago, IL 60611-5295

312-280-2511
800-545-2433; *Fax:* 312-280-2520
customerservice@ala.org; www.ala.org/acrl

Mary Ellen Davis, Executive Director

Two hundred exhibitors with computers and web products, audiovisual products, furniture and library equipment.
3000 Attendees
Frequency: Biennial
ISSN: 0099-0086
Founded in: 1978
Mailing list available for rent

20957 Association of Free Community Papers
1630 Miner Street
Suite 204, Box 1989
Idaho Springs, CO 80452

877-203-2327; *Fax:* 781-459-7770;
www.afcp.org

Craig Mullin, Executive Director
Brianne Janes, Graphic Designer

Exhibits for publishers of free circulation papers and shopping/advertising guides.
Frequency: Annual
Founded in: 1951

20958 Book Expo America
Reed Exhibitions
383 Main Avenue
Norwalk, CT 06851

203-404-4800
800-840-5614
cmuller@reedexpo.com;
www.bookexpoamerica.com
Social Media: Facebook, Twitter, LinkedIn, YouTube,Pinterest

Courtney Muller, Event Manager
Cathy Glickstein, Registration
Lisa Montanaro, Sales Executive

Sponsored by American Booksellers Association and Association of American Publishers. More than 2,000 exhibits, 500 authors, over 60 conference sessions as well as a special area for rights business, all the latest titles across genres, uncover hidden gems, network, and meet the industry contacts to put you instantly on top of what you need to know for your business and job.
Frequency: May/June
Founded in: 2000

20959 Christian Booksellers Association
9240 Explorer Drive
Colorado Springs, CO 80920

800-252-1950; *Fax:* 719-272-3510
info@cbaonline.org; www.cbaonline.org

Bill Anderson, President
Mike Regennitter, Executive Director
Scott Graham, Director

Exhibition and sales of Christian oriented products to include categories of books and Bibles, music, framed art, jewelry, videos, clothing gifts, cards, stationary, children products, computer software, church supplies, curriculum and store supplies.
12M Attendees
Frequency: July

20960 Digital Book Printing Forum
Interquest Ltd.
513-D Stewart Street
Charlottesville, VA 22902

434-979-9945; *Fax:* 434-979-9959
iquest@inter-quest.com; www.inter-quest.com

David Davis, Director

Interquest analysts will present key results from the company's latest research in the field.
Frequency: March

20961 Digital Book World
Fax: new

Jeremy Greenfield, Editorial Director
Raymond Kyle, Business Development Manager
Gary Lynch, Group Publisher
Amanda Malek, Online Product Development

A year-round platform offering educational and networking resoruces for consumer publishing professionals and their partners - including agents ,booksellers and technology vendors - online and in person

20962 FFTA Annual Forum & INFO FLEX Exhibition
Flexographic Technical Association Inc
3920 Veterans Memorial Highway
Suite 9
Bohemia, NY 11716

631-737-6020; *Fax:* 631-737-6813
memberinfo@flexography.org;
www.flexography.org

Mark Cisternino, President
Joe Tuccitto, Director of Education
Doreen Monteleone, Director Environmental Affairs
Sharon Cox, Director of Marketing
Katie Dubois, Creative Services Manager

Presents the most promising technological advances and emerging market opportunities to keep you and your company up to date.
1600+ Attendees

20963 FOLIO Show
Red 7 Media, LLC
10 Norden Place
Norwalk, CT 06855

203-854-6730; *Fax:* 203-854-6735;
www.folioshow.com/
Social Media: Facebook, Twitter, LinkedIn

Tony Silberg, Publisher/General Manager
John Ellertson, Group Sales Director
Magan Sprenger, Account Executive
Tania Babiuk, Account Executive
Kerry Smith, President

Biennial show and exhibits of publishing supplies, paper, printing equipment, color separators, fulfillment houses, lists and related equipment, supplies and services to the magazine and book publishing trades.
7,000 Attendees

20964 InfoCommerce
InfoCommerce Group Inc
2 Bala Plaza
Suite 300
Bala Cynwyd, PA 19004

610-649-1200; *Fax:* 610-471-0515
rchristensen@infocommercegroup.com;
www.infocommercegroup.com

Roxanne Christensen, Dir Awards Conferences & Consulting

Convenes all kinds of publishers who are bound only by their ability and willingness to take risks.
Frequency: Oct, Philadelphia

20965 NCRW Annual Conference
National Council for Research on Women
11 Hanover Square
24th Floor
New York, NY 10005-2819

212-785-7335; *Fax:* 212-785-7350
ncrw@ncrw.org; www.ncrw.org

Mariam K Chamberlain, Founding President
Linda G Basch, President
Frequency: June

20966 New England Booksellers Association Annual Trade Show
1770 Massachusetts Avenue
#332
Cambridge, MA 02140

617-576-3070
800-466-8711; *Fax:* 617-576-3091;
www.newenglandbooks.org/

Allan Schmid, President
Dale Szczeblowski, VP

Offers the opportunity for publishers to get their products in the hands of the booksellers in an area with one of the highest concentrations of readers in the country. This traditional multi-media exhibition is the largest of the regional conference in bookseller attendance.
2M+ Attendees
Frequency: September/October

20967 Publishing Institute
Publishing Institute
University of Denver
2000 E. Asbury Ave
Denver, CO 80208

303-832-5280; *Fax:* 303-871-2501
pi-info@du.edu;
www.du.edu/publishinginstitute

Elizabeth Geiser, Director
Joyce Meskis, Director

A certificate program that combines workshops in editing and marketing with lecture/teaching sessions conducted by leading experts from all areas of publishing.
90 Attendees
Frequency: July-August

20968 Publishing University
Independent Book Publishers Association
1020 Manhattan Beach Blvd
Suite 204
Manhattan Beach, CA 90266

310-546-1818; *Fax:* 310-546-3939
info@ibpa-online.org; www.ibpa-online.org

Terry Nathan, Executive Director
Lisa Krebs, Assistant Director
Steve Mettee, Board Chair
Roy M Carlisle, Treasurer
Florrie B Kichler, President

A 2-day publishing conference focusing on education and networking, 40 exhibitors.
300 Attendees
Frequency: Annual

20969 Small Press Book Fair
Small Press Center
20 W 44th Street
New York, NY 10036-6604

212-764-7021; *Fax:* 212-354-5365
smallpress@aol.com; www.smallpress.org

Mary Bertschmann, Chair
Lloyd Jassin, Vice Chair
Mashala Solammi, Owner

One of the major book fairs for small press. Containing 100 booths and 100 exhibits.
2,500 Attendees
Frequency: March

20970 Tools of Change for Publishing Conference
O'Reilly Media, Inc.
1005 Gravenstein Highway North
Sebastopol, CA 95472

707-827-7000
800-998-9938; *Fax:* 707-829-0104
conf-webmaster@oreilly.com;
www.oreilly.com
Social Media: Facebook, Twitter, LinkedIn, RSS

Gina Blaber, Vice President, Conferences
Suzanne Axtell, Communications Manager
Shirley Bailes, Speaker Manager

Expect coverage with a range of practical, in-depth sessions that cover the innovations rocking every aspect of the art, craft, and business of publishing in the 21st century.
Frequency: February
Mailing list available for rent

20971 Writing Academy Seminar
Writing Academy
4010 Singleton Road
Rockford, IL 61114

815-877-9675; www.wams.org/indexhtm

Annual seminar and exhibits by Christian writers.

20972 Yellow Pages Publishers Association Convention
Yellow Pages Publishers Association
116 Cass Street
Traverse City, MI 49684

800-267-9002; *Fax:* 231-486-2182
hq@adp.org; www.adp.org/

R. Lawrence Angove, President
Bonnie Pintozzi, COO
Vernon Smith, Treasurer

Annual convention and exhibits of equipment, supplies and services for the publication of Yellow Pages telephone directories.

Directories & Databases

20973 2,224 Public Libraries Data Files
Open Horizons Publishing
PO Box 2887
Taos, NM 87571

575-751-3398
800-796-6130; *Fax:* 575-751-3100
info@bookmarket.com; www.bookmarket.com

John Kremer, Editor
Robert Sanny, Advertising/Sales Manager

Database features 2,224 general public libraries, with name and address; no phone, fax, or email. Download in your choice of formats along with an information sheet.
Cost: $40.00
Frequency: Database
Founded in: 1982

20974 Advertising and Publicity Resources for Scholarly Books
Association of American University Presses
Rm 602
30 W 36th St
New York, NY 10018-8063

212-989-1010; *Fax:* 212-989-0275
info@aaupnet.org; www.aaupnet.org

Peter Givler, Executive Director
Timothy Muench, Marketing Coordinator
Latasha Watters, Marketing Coordinator

This comprehensive directory lists periodicals which accept advertising or review copies of scholarly publications.
Cost: $189.00
425 Pages

20975 Alternative Publications: A Guide to Directories and Other Sources
Mcfarland & Company
Po Box 611
Jefferson, NC 28640-0611

336-246-4460; *Fax:* 336-246-5018
info@mcfarlandpub.com;
www.mcfarlandpub.com
Social Media: Facebook, Twitter, LinkedIn

Robert Franklin, President

Offers indexes and abstracts, review sources and bibliographies dealing with alternative publications.
Cost: $18.95
96 Pages

20976 American Book Producers Directory
American Book Producers Association
160 5th Avenue
New York, NY 10010-7003

212-645-2368
800-209-4575; *Fax:* 212-242-6799
office@ABPAonline.org; www.abpaonline.org

David Rubel, President
David Katz, Treasurer
Valerie Tomaselli, Treasurer
Nancy Hall, Vice President
40 Pages
Circulation: 2,000
Founded in: 1980
Printed in 2 colors on matte stock

20977 American Book Trade Directory
Information Today
143 Old Marlton Pike
Medford, NJ 08055-8750

609-654-6266
800-300-9868; *Fax:* 609-654-4309
custserv@infotoday.com; www.infotoday.com
Social Media: Facebook, Twitter

Thomas H Hogan, President
Roger R Bilboul, Chairman Of The Board

A US book trade community. Profiles 25,500 retail and antiquarian book dealers, plus 1,200 book and magazine wholesalers, distributors, and jobbers in all 50 states and US territories.
Cost: $299.00
1800 Pages
ISBN: 1-573872-12-1

20978 American Directory of Writer's Guidelines
Dustbooks
PO Box 100
Paradise, CA 95967-0100

530-877-6110
800-477-6110; *Fax:* 530-877-0222
directories@dustbooks.com;
www.dustbooks.com

Brigitte M Phillips, Editor
Susan D Klassen, Editor
Doris Hall, Editor

These guidelines help writers target their submissions to the exact needs of the individual publisher. A compilation of information for freelancers from more than 1,500 magazine editors and book publishers.
Cost: $29.95
752 Pages
ISBN: 1-884956-40-8

20979 Association of American University Presses Directory
Association of American University Presses
Rm 602
30 W 36th St
New York, NY 10018-8063

212-989-1010; *Fax:* 212-989-0275
info@aaupnet.org;
www.aaup.uchicago.edu/aaup_home.html

Peter Givler, Executive Director
Timothy Muench, Assistant Director

114 presses and affiliates worldwide.
Cost: $14.95
Frequency: Annual November

20980 Bacon's Newspaper & Magazine Directories
Cision U.S., Inc.
322 South Michigan Avenue
Suite 900
Chicago, IL 60604

312-263-0070
866-639-5087
info.us@cision.com
us.cision.com

Joe Bernardo, President & CEO
Heidi Sullivan, VP & Publisher
Valerie Lopez, Research Director
Jessica White, Research Director
Rachel Farrell, Research Manager

Two volume set listing all daily and community newspapers, magazines and newsletters, news service and syndicates, syndicated columnists, complete editorial staff listings of each publication provided, covers U.S., Canada, Mexico, and Carribean.
Cost: $350.00
4,700 Pages
Frequency: Annual
ISSN: 1088-9639
Founded in: 1951
Printed in one color on matte stock

20981 Bacon's Radio/TV/Cable Directory
Cision U.S., Inc.
332 South Michigan Avenue
Suite 900
Chicago, IL 60604

312-263-0070
866-639-5087
info.us@cision.com; www.us.cision.com

Joe Bernardo, President & CEO
Heidi Sullivan, VP & Publisher
Valerie Lopez, Research Director
Jessica White, Research Director
Rachel Farrell, Research Manager

Includes comprehensive coverage for contact and programming information for more than 3,500 televsion networks, cable networks, television syndicators, television stations, and cable systems in the United States and Canada.
Cost: $350.00
Frequency: Annual
ISSN: 1088-9639
Printed in one color on matte stock

20982 Book Marketing 105: Choosing a Book Distribution System
Open Horizons Publishing
PO Box 2887
Taos, NM 87571

575-751-3398
800-796-6130; *Fax:* 575-751-3100
info@bookmarket.com; www.bookmarket.com

John Kremer, Editor
Robert Sanny, Advertising/Sales Manager

A mini-guide including criteria for deciding how to distribute books. Also includes complete information on 30 distributors, 4 library distributors, 89 book publishers who also distribute for other publishers, 3 sales reps to the chains, 27 bookstore wholesalers, 34 library wholesalers, and 23 Spanish-launguage wholesalers. Plus a sample distribution contract.
Cost: $30.00
Frequency: Ebook Download
Founded in: 1982

20983 BookStats
Association of American Publishers (AAP)
455 Massachusetts Avenue NW
Suite 700
Washington, DC 20001-2777

202-347-3375; *Fax:* 202-347-3690
info@publishers.org; www.publishers.org
Social Media: Twitter

Karen Abramson, President & CEO
Tina Jordan, Vice President
Allan R Adler, VP for Legal & Government Affairs
Jay Diskey, Executive Director, School Division
Gail Kump, Director, Membership Marketing

Provides a comprehensive view of the size and shape of the US book publishing industry measured by publisher net unit and dollar sales.
Frequency: Annual

20984 Business Info USA
InfoUSA
5711 S 86th Cir
Omaha, NE 68127-4146

402-593-4500
888-260-7943; *Fax:* 402-331-6287;
www.infousa.com

Vinod Gupta, CEO
Karen Peters, Account Executive
Cost: $2750.00
Frequency: Monthly
Circulation: 4000000
Founded in: 1972

20985 Business Periodicals Index
HW Wilson Company

950 Dr Martin L King Jr Blvd
Bronx, NY 10452-4297

718-588-8405
800-367-6770; *Fax:* 718-590-1617;
www.hwwilson.com

Harold Regan, CEO
Kathleen McEvoy, Director of Public Relations

Designed for businesses, business schools and libraries, business periodicals index covers English-language business periodicals and trade journals. Users enjoy quick access to feature articles, product reviews, interviews, biographical sketches, corporate profiles, obituaries, surveys, book reviews, reports from associations, societies, trade shows and conferences, and more. The database also provides SIC codes for industries and names of corporations used as subject headings.

20986 **Catalog Sales Data Files**
Open Horizons Publishing
PO Box 2887
Taos, NM 87571

575-751-3398
800-796-6130; *Fax:* 575-751-3100
info@bookmarket.com; www.bookmarket.com

John Kremer, Editor
Robert Sanny, Advertising/Sales Manager

Database features the top 1,350 catalogs, internet bookstore sites, chain store outlets, wholesalers, distributors, and other special sales outlets. Includes catalog names, buyers, addresses, phone and fax numbers, emails, website, types of books carried, and other important details.
Cost: $30.00
Frequency: Database
Founded in: 1982

20987 **Celebrate Today**
Open Horizons Publishing
PO Box 2887
Taos, NM 87571

575-751-3398
800-796-6130; *Fax:* 575-751-3100
info@bookmarket.com; www.bookmarket.com

John Kremer, Editor
Robert Sanny, Advertising/Sales Manager

Database with 18,290 holidays, special days, weeks, months and historical anniversaries. Searchable by subject interest. Includes contact info and websites in most cases. Useful for setting pub dates and doing PR tie-ins.
Cost: $30.00
Frequency: Database
Founded in: 1982

20988 **Complete Directory of Large Print Books and Serials**
4919 Route 22
PO Box 56
Amenia, NY 12546

518-789-8700
800-562-2139; *Fax:* 518-789-0556
customerservice@greyhouse.com;
www.greyhouse.com

R R Bowker

Provides nine easy to use indexes including Title, Author, General Reading Subject, Textbook Subject, Children's Subject, Serials Subject, and Serials Title. For easy acquisition, full contact information on publishers, wholesalers and distributors is provided in a separate index.
Frequency: Annual
ISBN: 0-835249-41-6

20989 **Corporate Yellow Book**
Leadership Directories
398 RXR Plaza
Uniondale, NY 11556

516-730-1900
corporate@leadershipdirectories.com;
www.corporate.yellowbook.com

David Hurvitz, CEO
Bryan Turner, CFO
Jim McCusker, President

Contact information for over 48,000 executives at over 1,000 companies and more than 9,000 board members and their outside affiliations.
Cost: $400.00
1,400 Pages
Frequency: Quarterly
ISSN: 1058-2098
Founded in: 1986

20990 **Directories in Print**
Gale/Cengage Learning
10650 Toebben Drive
Independence, KY 41051

800-824-5179
800-354-9706; *Fax:* 800-487-8488
higheredcs@cengage.com; www.gale.com

Patrick C Sommers, President

Describes more than 16,000 active rosters, guides and other print and nonprint address lists published in the United States and worldwide.
Frequency: Annual
ISBN: 1-414421-75-3

20991 **Directory of Poetry Publishers**
Dustbooks
PO Box 100
Paradise, CA 95967-0100

530-877-6110
800-477-6110; *Fax:* 530-877-0222
directories@dustbooks.com;
www.dustbooks.com

Len Fulton, Editor

Over 2,100 magazines, small and commercial presses and university presses that accept poetry for publication.
Cost: $25.95
300 Pages
Frequency: Annual
Circulation: 2,000
ISBN: 0-916685-47-0

20992 **Directory of Small Magazines Press Magazine Editors & Publishers**
Dustbooks
PO Box 100
Paradise, CA 95967-0100

530-877-6110
800-477-6110; *Fax:* 530-877-0222
directories@dustbooks.com;
www.dustbooks.com

Len Fulton, Editor

This directory contains more than 7,500 listings of editors and publishers in alphabetical order, along with their associated publishing companies, their addresses, phones, e-mail addresses and Web pages. Includes self publishers.
Cost: $25.95
460 Pages
Frequency: Annual
Circulation: 1,000
ISBN: 0-913218-28-6
Founded in: 1967
Mailing list available for rent

20993 **Editor & Publisher International Yearbook**
Editor & Publisher Company
770 Broadway
New York, NY 10003-9595

212-291-1259
800-336-4380; *Fax:* 646-654-5370;
www.editorandpublisher.com

Sid Holt, Editor-in-Chief
Greg Mitchell, Editor
Michael Parker, President

Daily and Sunday newspapers in the US and Canada; weekly newspapers; foreign daily newspapers; special service newspapers; newspaper syndicates; news servides; journalism schools; foreign language and Black newspapers in the US; news, picture and press services; feature and news syndicates; comic and magazine services; advertising clubs; trade associations; clipping bureaus; house organs; journalism awards; manufacturers of equipment and supplies.
Cost: $230.00
Frequency: Annual March

20994 **Editor & Publisher Market Guide**
Editor & Publisher Company
770 Broadway
New York, NY 10003-9595

212-291-1259
800-336-4380; *Fax:* 646-654-5370;
www.editorandpublisher.com

Sid Holt, Editor-in-Chief
Greg Mitchell, Editor
Michael Parker, President

More than 1,700 newspaper markets in the US and Canada.
Cost: $100.00
Frequency: Annual November
Circulation: 4,500

20995 **Editor & Publisher: Journalism Awards and Fellowships Directory Issue**
Editor & Publisher Company
770 Broadway
New York, NY 10003-9595

212-291-1259
800-336-4380; *Fax:* 646-654-5370;
www.editorandpublisher.com

Sid Holt, Editor-in-Chief
Greg Mitchell, Editor
Michael Parker, President

Over 500 cash prizes, scholarships, fellowships and grants available to journalists and students for work on special subjects or in specific fields.
Cost: $4.00
Frequency: Annual December
Circulation: 28,500

20996 **Grey House Publishing**
4919 Route 22
PO Box 56
Amenia, NY 12546

518-789-8700
800-562-2139; *Fax:* 518-789-0556
customerservice@greyhouse.com;
www.greyhouse.com

Leslie Mackenzie, Publisher
Richard Gottlieb, Editor

Publishes over 100 titles including reference directories in the areas of business, education, health, statistics and demographics, as well as educational encyclopedias and business handbooks. All titles offer detailed information in well-organized formats. Many titles available online.
Founded in: 1981

20997 **IBPA Directory**
Independent Book Publishers Association

627 Aviation Way
Manhattan Beach, CA 90266

310-318-2270; *Fax:* 310-374-3342
info@ibpa-online.org; www.ibpa-online.org

Terry Nathan, Executive Director
Lisa Krebs, Assistant Director

A directory of members and one of regional affiliates is available online with multi-level search options.

20998 **International Directory of Little Magazines & Small Presses**
Dustbooks
PO Box 100
Paradise, CA 95967-0100

530-877-6110; *Fax:* 530-877-0222
directories@dustbooks.com;
www.dustbooks.com

Len Fulton, Editor

Lists more than 4,000 book and magazine publishers of literary, avant garde, cutting-edge contemporary, left wing, right wing and radical chic fiction to non-fiction essays, reviews, artwork, music, satire, criticism, commentary, letters, parts of novels, longpoems, concrete art, collages, plays, news items and more.
Cost: $55.00
Frequency: Annual/Cloth
Circulation: 1,000
ISBN: 0-916685-49-7

20999 **International Literary Market Place**
Information Today
143 Old Marlton Pike
Medford, NJ 08055-8750

609-654-6266
800-300-9868; *Fax:* 609-654-4309
custserv@infotoday.com; www.infotoday.com
Social Media: Facebook, Twitter

Thomas H Hogan, President
Roger R Bilboul, Chairman of the Board
John C Yersak, Vice President
John Brokenshire, CFO

The directory of the international book publishing industry with 16,500 up to date profiles with book related concerns, including trade organizations, distributors, dealers, literary associations, trade publications, book trade events, and other resources conveniently organzied in a country by counrty format
Cost: $240.00
1800 Pages
ISBN: 1-573871-75-3

21000 **Livestock Publications Council Membership Directory**
Livestock Publications
910 Currie Street
Fort Worth, TX 76107

817-336-1130; *Fax:* 817-232-4820
dianej@flash.net;
www.livestockpublications.com

Offers information on over 100 US and Canadian LPC-member livestock magazines, newspapers and newsletters.

21001 **Magazines for Libraries**
R R Bowker LLC
630 Central Ave
New Providence, NJ 07974-1506
908-286-0288
888-269-5372; *Fax:* 908-219-0098
info@bowker.com; www.bowker.com

Magazines for Libraries provides the serials information you need to build and maintain a quality collection that best meets the needs of your library's users.
Frequency: Triennial
ISBN: 1-600301-16-2

21002 **National Journal**
National Journal
600 New Hampshire Ave NW
Washington, DC 20037-2403

202-739-8400
800-207-8001; *Fax:* 202-833-8069
service@nationaljournal.com;
www.nationaljournal.com

John Fox Sullivan, President
Steve Hull, Senior VP
Timothy B Clark, VP

Publishes directories in the area of government.

21003 **Progressive Periodicals Directory**
Progressive Education; PO Box 120574
Nashville, TN 37212-0574

615-367-1874

Craig T Canan, Editor

About 600 social-concerns periodicals.
Cost: $16.00

21004 **Publishers, Distributors and Wholesalers of the United States**
R R Bowker LLC
630 Central Ave
New Providence, NJ 07974-1506

908-286-0288
888-269-5372; *Fax:* 908-219-0098
info@bowker.com; www.bowker.com

R R Bowker

In this 2 volume set locate publishers, museum and association imprint and trade organizations that publish, software firms, audio-cassette producers and even publishers that have gone out of business.
Frequency: 2 Volumes; *ISBN:* 0-835249-66-9

21005 **Publishing & Production Executive: Who's Who of Suppliers and Services**
North American Publishing Company
1500 Spring Garden St
Suite 1200
Philadelphia, PA 19130-4094

215-238-5300
800-777-8074; *Fax:* 215-238-5342
customerservice@napco.com; www.napco.com

Ned S Borowsky, CEO

Directory of services and supplies to the industry.
Circulation: 30,000
Mailing list available for rent

21006 **Single Unit Supermarkets Operators**
Chain Store Guide
3922 Coconut Palm Dr
Tampa, FL 33619-1389

813-627-6700
800-778-9794; *Fax:* 813-627-7094
info@csgis.com; www.csgis.com

Mike Jarvis, Publisher
Shami Choon, Manager

Discover more than 7,100 single-unit supermarkets with annual sales topping $500,000 dollars. This comprehensive desktop reference makes it easy to reach our compiled list of 21,000 key executives and buyers, plus their primary wholesalers.
Cost: $335.00; 725 Pages
Frequency: Annual;

21007 **Small Publishers Association of North America (SPAN)**
PO Box 1306
Buena Vista, CO 81211-1306

719-395-4790; *Fax:* 719-395-8374;
www.spannet.org

Marilyn Ross, Executive Director/Editor
Tom Ross, VP
Cathy Bowman, Production Manager

Online resource for book publishing know-how. Works to advance the image and profits of self publishers and independent publishers through education and marketing opportunities.

21008 **Something About the Author**
Gale/Cengage Learning
Po Box 09187
Detroit, MI 48209-0187

248-699-4253
800-877-4253; *Fax:* 248-699-8049
gale.galeord@cengage.com; www.gale.com

Patrick C Sommers, President

An easy to use source for librarians, students and other researchers each volume in this series provides illustrated biographical profiles of approximately 75 children's authors and artists. This critically acclaimed series covers more than 12,000 individuals, ranging from established award winners to authors and illustrators who are just beginning their careers.
ISBN: 1-414442-17-3

21009 **Standard Periodical Directory**
Oxbridge Communications
39 W. 29 St.; # 301
New York, NY 10001

212-741-0231
800-955-0231; *Fax:* 212-633-2938
custserv@mediafinder.com;
www.mediafinder.com

Patricia Hagood, President

Circulation, advertising and list rental info for more than 75,000 North American periodicals.
Cost: $1495.00; 2,326 Pages
Frequency: Annual; *Circulation:* 3,500
ISBN: 1-891783-23-8; *ISSN:* 0085-6630
Founded in: 1964; Printed in 4 colors

21010 **Top 700 Independent Bookstores**
Open Horizons Publishing
PO Box 2887
Taos, NM 87571

641-472-6130
800-796-6130; *Fax:* 641-472-1560
info@bookmarket.com; www.bookmarket.com

John Kremer, Editor
Robert Sanny, Advertising/Sales Manager

Database of 790 stores with address, book buyer, owner, event coordinator, phone, fax, email, website and more. Lists the largest bookstores that work with authors and that buy from indy book publishers. Compiled from industry news, author and publisher recommendations, and research.The report comes as a data file download in your choice of Access, Excel, comma- or tab-delimited ASCII, d-Base or rich text format.
Cost: $40.00; *Frequency:* Database
Founded in: 1982

21011 **Ulrich's Periodicals Directory**
R R Bowker LLC
630 Central Ave
New Providence, NJ 07974-1506

908-286-1090
888-269-5372; *Fax:* 908-219-0098
info@bowker.com; www.bowker.com

Michael Cairns, CEO
Annie Callanan, COO

An essential reference tool for any serials librarian the Ulrich's Periodicals Directory™ is overflowing with the latest international bibliographic information on journals, magazines and newspapers.

Industry Web Sites

21012 **http://gold.greyhouse.com**
G.O.L.D Grey House OnLine Databases
Grey House Publishing's online database platform, GOLD, offers Quick Search, Keyword Search and Expert Search for most business sectors including publishing and allied markets. The GOLD platform makes finding the information you need quick and easy - whether you're a novice searcher or an experienced database user. All of Grey House's directory products are available for subscription on the GOLD platform.

21013 **www.aaup.princetou.edu**
Exchange
Reports on issues relevant to scholarly publishing.

21014 **www.aaupnet.org/membership/directory**
Association of American University Presses
Members are university presses and a limited number of presses of non-degree-granting scholarly institutions.

21015 **www.abaa.org**
Antiquarian Booksellers Association of America
A trade association of rare book dealers.

21016 **www.abpaonline.org**
American Book Producers Association
Increases the book industry's awareness of members capabilities and exchanges information on improving business. Develops concepts for books and other publications.

21017 **www.accessabc.com**
Audit Bureau of Circulations
The world's largest circulation-auditing organization, ABC provides circulation data on 1,400+ newspapers and more than 1,100 periodicals to ABC-member publications, advertisers and advertising agencies.

21018 **www.ampaonline.org**
American Medical Publishers' Association
Information provided to the medical publishing field.

21019 **www.bisg.org**
Book Industry Study Group
Promotes and supports research, enabling various sectors of the industry to develop and expand their professional and business plans. Book Industry Study Group has various paperback publications.

21020 **www.bizpubs.org**
Alliance of Area Business Publications
Represents metropolitan area and state-wide business to business publications with conventions, newsletters, and other services.

21021 **www.bookbuilders.org**
Bookbuilders West
A nonprofit organization that provides a forum for publishers and suppliers to share experiences via dinners, social events and educational seminars.

21022 **www.bookmarketingprofits.com**
North American Bookdealers Exchange
Independent publishers and mail order entrepreneurs. An international book marketing organization specializing in cooperative opportunities at trade shows, in mail order, press releases, and more.

21023 **www.bookpublishing.com**
Jenkins Independent Publishers

21024 **www.catholicpress.org**
Catholic Press Association of the US and Canada

21025 **www.clmp.org**
Council of Literary Magazines and Presses
Membership is open to any noncommercial literary magazine or press that publishes at least one or more books per year.

21026 **www.columbia.edu/eu/cspa**
Columbia Scholastic Press Association
International student press association composed of writing students, journalists and faculty advisers in schools and colleges through educational conferences, idea exchanges and recognition programs.

21027 **www.du.edu/pi**
Publishing Institute
A national organization that combines workshops in editing and marketing with lecture/teaching sessions conducted by leading experts from all areas of publishing.

21028 **www.ecpa.org**
Evangelical Christian Publishers Association
Promotes excellence and professionalism, shares relevant data, and equips Christian publishers to meet the needs of the changing marketplace.

21029 **www.flexography.org**
Flexographic Technical Association

21030 **www.flexography.org/flexsys/index.cfm**
Flexographic Technical Assn Education & Training
Magazine publishing.

21031 **www.greyhouse.com**
Grey House Publishing
Authoritative reference directories for most business sectors including publishing and allied markets. Users can search the online databases with varied search criteria allowing for custom searches by product category, geographic area, sales volume, keyword, subject and more. Full Grey House catalog and online ordering also available.

21032 **www.interquest.Com**
Fax: new
A market and technology research and consulting firm in the field of digital printing and publishing that produces studies on topics such as digital printing, transactional printing, variable imaging, etc.

21033 **www.ipma.org**
International Publishing Management Association
The professional association for in-house corporate publishing professionals who work for educational institutions, governments and private industry.

21034 **www.naa.org**
Newspaper Association of America
Founded by the merger of seven associations serving the newspaper industry. Focuses on the major issues that affect today's newspaper industry public policy and legal matters, advertising revenue growth and audience development across the medium's broad portfolio of products and digital platforms.

21035 **www.ncrw.org**
National Council for Research on Women
A network of 120 leading research, policy and advocacy centers dedicated to improving the lives of women and girls. Provides the latest news, analysis and strategies needed to ensure fully informed debates, effective policies and inclusive practices.

21036 **www.newsletters.org**
Newsletter & Electronic Publishers Association
International trade association serving the interests of publishers of newsletters and specialized information services.

21037 **www.nmpa.org**
National Music Publishers' Association

21038 **www.p3-ny.org/**
Partnership in Print Production
Promotes the interests of women.

21039 **www.pacificpress.com**
Pacific Press Publishing Association
Promotes the interests of publishing, press, and media professionals.

21040 **www.papertrade.com**
National Paper Trade Association

21041 **www.publishers.org**
Association of American Publishers
Principal trade association for the US book publishing industry members comprise most of the major commerical book publishers in the US, as well as smaller and medium-sized houses, not-for-profit publishers, university presses, and scholarly societies.

21042 **www.publishersreport.com**
National Association of Independent Publishers
Assists and educates small publishing companies. Conducts seminars on marketing strategies, target audience, and techniques of book distribution. Especially helpful for the beginning or self-publisher.

21043 **www.snaponline.org**
Society of National Association Publications
Develops standards for editorial and advertising content of association and professional society magazines.

21044 **www.spannet.org**
Small Publishers Association of North America
For independent presses and self-publishers who want to produce better books and market them more successfully.

21045 **www.sspnet.org**
Society for Scholarly Publishing
A group that represents scholarly publications, such as journals, university publications and magazines.

21046 **www.theacp.org**
Associated Church Press
Aims to share ideas and concerns in religious publishing and to stimulate higher standards of religious journalism to exert a more positive influence.

21047 **www.thomson.com**
Thomson.Com
A shared Web service that provides critical tools for more than 35 publishers.

21048 **www.wpa-online.org**
Western Publications Association
Represents magazine publishing companies and companies related to publishing industry, in the western United States.

Associations

21049 Accredited Review Appraisers Council
ARAC
303 W Cypress Street
San Antonio, TX 78212

800-486-3676; www.arac.lincoln-grad.org

Provides education and designation in appraisal and real estate review.

21050 American Association of Certified Wedding Planners
210 W College St
Suite 400
Grapevine, TX 76051

214-342-2378
president@aacwp.org; www.aacwp.org
Social Media: Facebook, Twitter, Instagram

Trudy Baade, President
Wendy Kidd, Vice-President
Micki Novak, Treasurer
Jenny Cline, Secretary
Jennifer Ashford, Education

A national organization that offers designations to qualified appraisers, teaches courses on latest appraisal information and offers courses on home inspection.

21051 American College of Real Estate Lawyers
11300 Rockville Pike
Suite 903
Rockville, MD 20852
301-816-9811; *Fax:* 301-816-9786
webmaster@acrel.org; www.acrel.site-ym.com

Roger D. Winston, President
Jay A. Epstein, President-Elect
Steven A. Waters, Vice President
Peter Aitelli, Secretary
Marilyn C. Maloney, Treasurer

Members are CPAs working in the real estate field.

21052 American Homeowners Foundation
6776 Little Falls Rd
Arlington, VA 22213-1213

703-536-7776
800-489-7776; *Fax:* 703-536-7079;
www.americanhomeowners.org

Bruce Itahn, President

A national consumer organization representing the nation's 75 million homeowners.
Founded in: 1984

21053 American Industrial Real Estate
Pacific Financial Center
500 North Brand
Suite 900
Glendale, CA 91203
213-687-8777; *Fax:* 213-687-8616
jcruz@airea.com; www.airea.com
Social Media: Facebook, Twitter

Joy D'La Cruz, Chief Operations Officer
Tim Hayes, Executive Director
Joseph T. Faulkner, President
Louis J. Tomaselli, Vice-President
Joseph Lin, President Elect

Encourages high professional standards. Has developed industrial multiple listing system and standard lease form. Publishes a quarterly newsletter.
1600 Members
Founded in: 1960

21054 American Land Title Association
1800 M Street, NW
Suite 300S
Washington, DC 20036-5828

202-296-3671
800-787-ALTA; *Fax:* 202-223-5843
service@alta.org; www.alta.org
Social Media: Facebook, Twitter, LinkedIn, YouTube, Google+

Michelle L. Korsmo, CEO
Jack Rattikin, Chair, Finance Committee
John M. Hollenbeck, President
Steven G. Day, Treasurer
Daniel D. Mennenoh, President-Elect

Trade organization for title insurers, abstractors and agents.
4600+ Members
Founded in: 1907
Mailing list available for rent: 3000 names at $500 per M

21055 American Planning Association
205 N. Michigan Ave
Suite 1200
Chicago, IL 60601

312-431-9100; *Fax:* 312-786-6700
CustomerService@planning.org;
www.planning.org
Social Media: Facebook, Twitter, LinkedIn, YouTube, Flickr, RSS

James Drinan, Executive Director/CEO
Caroline Rhea, President
Ann Simms, Chief Operating Officer
Harriet Bogdanowicz, Chief Communications Officer
Mark Ferguson, Chief Information Officer

A public interest and research organization representing practicing planners, officials, and citizens involved with urban and rural planning issues. APA's objective is to encourage planning that will meet the needs of people and society more effectively.
Founded in: 1978

21056 American Rental Association
1900 19th St
Moline, IL 61265

309-764-2475
800-334-2177; *Fax:* 309-764-1533
ara@ararental.org; www.ararental.org

Christine Wehrman, CEO/ Executive Vice-President
Terry Turner, President
Paul Phelon, Chairman
Roger Vajgrt, President-Elect
Mark Gilbertson, SIG Chair

Benefits members (rental business owners and equipment suppliers) by promoting, representing and enhancing the rental industry, resulting in improved rental services to the public.
8600 Members
Founded in: 1955

21057 American Resort Development Association
1201 15th St Nw
Suite 400
Washington, DC 20005-2842

202-371-6700; *Fax:* 202-289-8544;
www.ardafoundation.org

Howard C. Nusbaum, President & CEO
Darla Zanini, Executive Vice President
Robert A. Miller, Chairman
Lan Wang, Research Director
Randall Upchurch, Vice Chairman

International trade association composed of resort developers and resort industry suppliers.
1000 Members
Founded in: 1982

21058 American Society of Appraisers
11107 Sunset Hills Rd
Suite 310
Reston, VA 20190

703-478-2228
800-272-8258; *Fax:* 703-742-8471
asainfo@appraisers.org; www.appraisers.org
Social Media: Facebook, Twitter, LinkedIn, YouTube

Jim Hirt, Chief Executive Officer
Susan Fischer, Governance Manager
Linda B. Trugman, International President
Sharon A. Desfor, International Secretary/ Treasurer
Susan Golashovsky, International Vice President

Professional association of appraisers of all disciplines.
5000 Members
Founded in: 1936

21059 American Society of Farm Managers and Rural Appraisers
950 S Cherry St
Suite 508
Denver, CO 80246-2664

303-758-3513; *Fax:* 303-758-0190;
www.asfmra.org
Social Media: Facebook, Twitter, LinkedIn

Douglas W Slothower, Executive VP
LeeAnn E. Moss, Academic Vice President
Michael J. Krause, First Vice President
Fred L. Hepler, President
Merrill E. Swanson, President-Elect

Premier professional organization for professionals who provide management, consultation and valuation services on rural and agricultural assets. Provides members with the resources, information and leadership that enables them to provide valuable services to the agricultural community.
Founded in: 1929

21060 Asian Real Estate Association of America
3990 Old Town Ave.
C304
San Diego, CA 92110

619-795-7873; *Fax:* 619-795-7822
contact@areaa.org; www.areaa.org
Social Media: Facebook, Twitter, LinkedIn, Instagram

Carmen Chong, Chairwoman

Represents the interests of the Asian real estate market.

21061 Building Owners and Managers Association International
1101 15th Street., NW
Suite 800
Washington, DC 20005

202-408-2662; *Fax:* 202-326-6377
info@boma.org; www.boma.org
Social Media: Facebook, Twitter, LinkedIn, YouTube, Pinterest

Brian M. Hartnetiaux, Chair-Elect
Kent C. Gibson, Chair & Chief Elected Officer
Henry Chamberlain, Presdent & COO
Robert M. Brierley, Vice Chair
Daniel W. Chasney, Secretary/Treasurer

Owners and managers of commercial office buildings.
7.5M Members
Founded in: 1907

21062 Commercial Real Estate Women
655 15th Street NW
Washington, DC 20005
202-737-3262
jennyw@crewnetwork.org; www.crewdc.org
Social Media: LinkedIn

Pam Zandy, Director of Special Events
Bari Nichols, President
Nancy Petrash, Treasurer
Susan Denner, Director of Communications
Michelle Kilby, President-Elect

Provides a forum for women who are involved in commercial real estate and wish to network as well as reap the benefits of their courses.
9000 Members
Founded in: 1989

21063 Commercial-Investment Real Estate Institute
430 N Michigan Avenue
Suite 800
Chicago, IL 60611
312-321-4460; www.ccim.com
Social Media: Facebook, Twitter, Google+, RSS

Walter S. Clements, Executive VP
Mark Macek, President
Steven W. Moreira, President-Elect
Robin L. Webb, First Vice-President
Charles C. Connely, Treasurer

Functions as a professional association of real estate practitioners who have successfully completed its certification program or are striving toward it.
4M Members

21064 Community Associations Institute
6402 Arlington Blvd
Suite 500
Falls Church, VA 22042
703-970-9220
888-224-4321; *Fax:* 703-970-9558
CAI-INFO@CAIonline.org;
www.caionline.org
Social Media: Facebook, Twitter, LinkedIn, Vimeo

Composed of community and condominium associations managers, management companies and other business partners.
33500 Members
Founded in: 1973

21065 CoreNet Global
CoreNet Global Inc
133 Peachtree ST NE
Suite 3000
Atlanta, GA 30303
404-589-3200
800-726-8111; *Fax:* 404-589-3201;
www.corenetglobal.org
Social Media: Facebook, Twitter, LinkedIn, YouTube, Google+, RSS

Angela Cain, CEO
Jim Scannell, Chairman
John Davis, Controller
Larry Bazrod, COO
Damion Daubon, Office Manager

Formerly NACORE International.
9000 Members

21066 Council of Real Estate Brokerage Managers
Country Radio Broadcaster's Inc
430 N. Michigan Ave.
Chicago, IL 60611
615-327-4487
800-621-8738; *Fax:* 312-329-8882
info@crb.com; www.crb.com
Social Media: Facebook, Twitter, LinkedIn

Bette McTamney, President
Ginny Shipe, CEO
Tara Maric, Director of Member services
Michael Bindman, Finance Vice President
Adorna Carroll, President-Elect

Members are real estate firm owners and managers.
7000 Members
Founded in: 1968

21067 Council of Residential Specialists
430 N Michigan Ave
3rd Floor
Chicago, IL 60611
312-321-4400
800-462-8841; *Fax:* 312-329-8551
crshelp@crs.com; www.crs.com
Social Media: Facebook, Twitter, LinkedIn, YouTube, Google+, RSS

Lana Vukovljak, CEO
Dale Carlton, Chair
Janelle Pfleiger, Vice Chair
Mary McCall, Chair of Nominating
Leigh Brown, 1st VP

Seeks to establish cooperation among brokers engaged in buying, selling, trading and leasing of real estate.
40000 Members
Founded in: 1976

21068 Council of Residential Specialties
430 N Michigan Ave
3rd Floor
Chicago, IL 60611
312-321-4400
800-462-8841; *Fax:* 312-329-8551
crshelp@crs.com; www.crs.com
Social Media: Facebook, Twitter, LinkedIn, YouTube, Google+, RSS

Lana Vukovljak, CEO
Dale Carlton, Chair
Janelle Pfleiger, Vice Chair
Mary McCall, Chair of Nominating
Leigh Brown, 1st VP

A council of the Realtors National Marketing Institute.
40000 Members
Founded in: 1976

21069 Counselors of Real Estate
430 N Michigan Ave
Chicago, IL 60611
312-329-8427; *Fax:* 312-329-8881
info@cre.org; www.cre.org

Mary Walker Fleischmann, President & CEO
Noah D. Shlaes, Chair of the Board
James S. Lee, First Vice Chair
Brent A. Palmer, Second Vice Chair
John J. Hentschel, Liaison Viice Chair

Association members provide the public with expert, objective advice on property and land related matters. Individuals invited to join are awarded the CRE designation.
1100 Members
Founded in: 1953

21070 Institute for Responsible Housing Preservation
799 9th Street NW
Suite 500
Washington, DC 20001-4501
202-585-8000; *Fax:* 202-585-8080
jlesk@nixonpeabody.com;
www.nixonpeabody.com
Social Media: Facebook, Twitter, LinkedIn, YouTube, RSS

Margaret Wagner, Vice president
Greg Gossard, Treasurer
Alex Viorst, President
Brian Poulin, Chairman
Steve Whyte, Secretary

IRHP members are owners and managers of Low Income Housing Preservation and Resident Housing Act housing and ELIHPA housing and concerned professionals.
Founded in: 1989

21071 Institute of Real Estate Management
430 N Michigan Ave
Chicago, IL 60611
800-837-0706; *Fax:* 800-338-4736
getinfo@irem.org; www.irem.org
Social Media: Facebook, Twitter, LinkedIn, YouTube

Alfred Ojejinmi, Senior Vice President
J. Benjamin McGrew, Secretary/ Treasurer
Cheryl Ann Gray, Senior Vice President
Christopher Mellen, President
Michael T. Lanning, President-Elect

Awards property manager certificate to qualifying individuals and accreditates management organizations and management firms. Offers management courses.
40000 Members
Founded in: 1976

21072 International Council of Shopping Centers
1221 Ave of the Americas
41st Floor
New York, NY 10020-1099
646-728-3800; *Fax:* 732-694-1690
membership@icsc.org; www.icsc.org
Social Media: Facebook, Twitter, LinkedIn, YouTube, Google+, Pinterest, I

Michael P Kercheval, CEO
Jennifer Collin, Manager, Membership Development
Glen Hale, CFO
Sheri Pupello, Member Communications
Michelle Anderson, Education Coordinator

Fosters professional standards of performance in the development, construction, financing, leasing, management and operation of shopping centers throughout the world.
70000 Members
Founded in: 1957

21073 International Exchangers Association
PO Box L
Rancho Santa Fe, CA 92067-0560
973-496-5784; *Fax:* 973-496-5784

Works to standardize procedures and establish professional ethics.
3.2M Members
Founded in: 1978

21074 International Real Estate Federation
1050 Connecticut Ave NW
Suite 500
Washington, DC 20036
202-772-3308
bill@fiabci-usa.com; www.fiabci-usa.com

Ruth Kruger, President
Bill Endsley, Secretary General
Susan Greenfield, Treasurer
Lance Fulford, Vice President
Maire Rosol, President-Elect

Encourages private ownership of real property and understanding of property rights and obligations.

21075 **International Real Estate Institute**
810 N Farrell Drive
Palm Springs, CA 92262

760-327-5284
877-743-6799; *Fax:* 760-327-5631
support@assoc-hdqts.org; www.irei-assoc.org

Ross Ford III, President & CEO
Bill Merrell, Executive Director

An organization comprised of thousands of real estate professionals from over 98 countries around the world. Acts as a voting member of, and property advisor to, the United Nations. Members specialize in real estate and property management. Arranges and promotes international educational real estate seminars.
2000 Members
Founded in: 1975

21076 **Maine Apartment Owners and Managers Association, Inc.**
P.O. Box 282
Bath, ME 04530

207-623-3480
800-204-4311
maoma@maoma.org;
www.maineapartmentowners.com

A national organization that presents the facts and information builder/developer/owners/manager members need to keep abreast of in the world of multi-family housing. Monthly issue will bring the reader timely insight on real estate, tax news, financing techniques, and effective management procedures, and keeps readers aware of the new developments in the condominium market.

21077 **Mortgage Bankers Association of America**
Mortgage Bankers Association
1919 M Street NW
5th Floor
Washington, DC 20036

202-557-2700
800-793-6222
membership@mortgagebankers.org;
www.mortgagebankers.org
Social Media: Facebook, Twitter, LinkedIn, YouTube

Bill Emerson, Chairman
David H. Stevens, President/CEO
Rodrigo Lopez, Chairman-Elect
J. David Motley, Vice-Chairman
Marcia Davies, Chief Operating Officer

Seeks to improve methods of originating, servicing and marketing loans.
2.8M Members
Founded in: 1914

21078 **National Affordable Housing Management**
400 N Columbus Street
Suite 203
Alexandria, VA 22314

703-683-8630; *Fax:* 703-683-8634;
www.nahma.org
Social Media: Facebook, Twitter, LinkedIn, YouTube

Kris Cook, Executive Director
Brenda Moser, Director, Meetings & Membership
Larry Keys, Director, Govt. Affairs
Rajni Agarwal, Director, Finance & Administration
Scott McMillen, Coordinator, Govt. Affairs

Trade association representing individuals involved in the management of affordable multifamily housing.
Founded in: 1990

21079 **National Apartment Association**
4300 Wilson Blvd
Suite 400
Arlington, VA 22203

703-518-6141; *Fax:* 703-248-9440
webmaster@naahq.org; www.naahq.org
Social Media: Facebook, Twitter, LinkedIn, YouTube, Google+, Pinterest, F

Doug Culkin, President &CEO
Chanal Thomas, Office Manager
Judy Reynolds, Senior Manger, Governance
Bob Pinnegar, EVP & COO
Lynn Miller, Administrator

The largest organization dedicated solely to rental housing-serves 26,000 rental housing professionals representing 3.4 million apartments nationwide. NAA lobbies for the industry, provides education programs, publishes Units Magazine, and conducts an annual Education Conference and Trade Show.
68000 Members
Founded in: 1939

21080 **National Association of Home Builders**
1201 15th St NW
Washington, DC 20005

202-266-8200
800-368-5242; *Fax:* 202-266-8400
info@nahb.org; www.nahb.org
Social Media: Facebook, Twitter, LinkedIn, Pinterest, Google+

Gerald M Howard, CEO
Tom Woods, Chairman
Ed Brady, 1st Vice Chairman of the Board
Granger MacDonald, 2nd Vice Chairman of the Board
Randy Noel, 3rdVice Chairman

Represents the building industry by serving its members and affiliated state and local builders associations.
1.4M Members
Founded in: 1942

21081 **National Association of Housing Cooperatives**
1444 I Street NW
Suite 700
Washington, DC 20005-6542

202-737-0797; *Fax:* 202-216-9646
info@nahc.coop; www.coophousing.org
Social Media: Facebook, Twitter

Linda Brockway, Treasurer
Ralph J. Marcus, Chairman
Gregory J. Carlson, President
Fred Gibbs, Vice President
Anne Hills, Secretary

A nonprofit national federation of housing cooperatives, professionals, organizations and individuals promoting the interests of cooperative housing communities. Housing cooperatives are a form of multi family home ownership.
1000 Members
Founded in: 1952

21082 **National Association of Master Appraisers**
303 W Cypress St
San Antonio, TX 78212-5512

210-271-0781
800-229-6262; *Fax:* 210-225-8450
djd@masterappraisers.org;
www.masterappraisers.org

Del Martinez, Manager
Christopher Deane, Marketing And Production Manager

Provides basic and advanced courses in techniques, management practices and marketing strategies. Offers designations in real estate appraisal MRA (Master Residential Appraisers), MFLA (Master Farm & Land Appraiser) and MSA (Master Senior Appraiser).

21083 **National Association of Real Estate Investment Trusts**
1875 I St NW
Suite 600
Washington, DC 20006

202-739-9400
800-3 N-REIT; *Fax:* 202-739-9401
info@nareit.org; www.reit.com
Social Media: Facebook, Twitter, LinkedIn, Google+, YouTube, RSS

Steven A. Wechsler, President &CEO
David B. Henry, 1st Vice Chair
Edward J. Fritsch, 2nd Vice Chair
Timothy J. Naughton, Treasurer
David J. Neithercut, Chairman

NAREIT is the representative voice for U.S. REITs and publicly traded real estate companies worldwide. Members are real estate investment trusts and other businesses that own, operate and finance income-producing real estate, as well as those firms and individuals who advise, study and service these businesses.

21084 **National Association of Realtors**
430 N Michigan Ave
Chicago, IL 60611-4087

312-645-7730
800-874-6500; *Fax:* 312-329-8576;
www.realtor.org
Social Media: Facebook, Twitter, LinkedIn, Skype, Google+

Dale Stinton, CEO
Tom Salomone, President-Elect
Chris Polychron, President
Mike McGrew, Treasurer
Bill Brown, First Vice President

Promotes education, high professional standards and modern techniques of real estate work.
1.1M Members
Founded in: 1908

21085 **National Association of Residential Property Managers**
638 Independence Parkway
Suite 100
Chesapeake, VA 23320

757-466-3336
800-782-3452; *Fax:* 866-466-2776
info@narpm.org; www.narpm.org
Social Media: Facebook, Twitter, LinkedIn, RSS

Andrew Propst, President
Gail S. Phillips, Executive Director
Bart Sturzl, President-Elect
Leeann Ghiglione, Treasurer
Stephen D. Foster, Past President

Provides education and publications for the single-family residential property manager.
Founded in: 1987

21086 **National Association of Review Appraisers and Mortgage Underwriters**
810 N. Farrell Drive
Palm Springs, CA 92262

760-327-5284
877-743-6805; *Fax:* 760-327-5631
support@assoc-hdqts.org; www.naramu.org

Robert G Johnson, Executive Director
Fred Simon, Production Manager

Conducts educational seminars. Maintains library, speakers bureau and operates a placement service.
6.5M Members
Founded in: 1976

21087 National Council of Exchangors
11 West Main Street
Suite 223
Belgrade, MT 59714

858-222-1608; *Fax:* 928-771-2323
admin@ncexchangors.com;
www.ncexchangors.com

Michael Libster, President & Chair
Kenneth L Kisner, Ex. President
Alex Ruggieri, Secretary
William Jones, Treasurer

A non-profit association and is a nationwide network of real estate professionals who specilize in marketing real estate equities primarily through the medium of the real estate exchange. This network is comprised of local groups organized into regional chapters.
400+ Members

21088 National Low Income Housing Coalition
1000 Vermont Ave
Suite 500
Washington, DC 20005

202-662-1530; *Fax:* 202-393-1973
info@nlihc.org; www.nlihc.org
Social Media: Facebook, Twitter, LinkedIn, Blog

Sheila Crowley, President &CEO
Malik Siraj Akbar, Communications Specialist
Khara Norris, Director of Administration
Andrew Aurand, Vice President for Research
Josephine Clarke, Executive Assistant

A national nonprofit organization representing housing advocates, organizers, tenants and professionals in the housing field. The Coalition advocates, represents and educates for decent housing and neighborhoods for all low-income people. It works with Congress and the executive branch to obtain adequate Federal support for low-income housing and related programs.
Founded in: 1974

21089 National Property Management Association
3525 Piedmont Road, Building 5
Suite 300
Atlanta, GA 30305

404-477-5811; *Fax:* 404-240-0998
hq@nmpa.org; www.npma.org
Social Media: Facebook, LinkedIn

Cinda Brockman, Executive Vice President
Marcia Whitson, National President
Ivonne Bachar, Vice President of Administration
Rosanne Green, Vice President of Certification
Jessica Dzara, Vice President of Comm & Marketing

Nonprofit professional association dedicated to the cost effective management of personal property and fixed assets.
3700 Members
Founded in: 1970

21090 National Real Estate Investors Association
7265 Kenwood Rd.
Suite 368
Cincinnati, OH 45236

859-261-3335
888-762-7342; *Fax:* 859-422-4916
info@nationalreia.com; www.nationalreia.com
Social Media: Facebook, Twitter

Rebecca Mc Lean, Executive Director
Scott Whaley, VP
Anna Mills, Treasurer
Lisa Kay Hansen, Secretary
Charles Tassell, Director of Governmental Affairs

Coalition of trade associations serving real estate investors, landlords and owners. Provides education and product services for officers and members.
115 Members
Founded in: 1985

21091 National Residential Appraisers Institute
Registered Financial Planners Institute
2001 Cooper Foster Park Rd
Amherst, OH 44001

440-935-1698; *Fax:* 888-254-5314
info@repi.com; www.nraiappraisers.com

Brian Schreiber, President
Jack Braman, Vice President/Education Director
Adrian Fredrick, Secretary
Rich Farina, Director

Promotes professionalism in the evaluation of residential real estate and requires demonstration appraisals and testing for professional certification.
451 Members
Founded in: 1977

21092 National Society of Environmental Consultants
Po Box 12528
San Antonio, TX 78212-0528

210-225-2897
800-486-3676; *Fax:* 210-225-8450;
www.nsec.lincoln-grad.org

Deborah Deane, President

Provides standards, education and a forum for real estate environmental site consultants. Provides a designation program for individuals doing environmental assessments and promotes education and further information about real estate environmental problems.

21093 National Society of Professional Surveyors
National Society of Professional Surveyors
5119 Pegasus Court
Suite Q
Frederick, MD 21704

240-439-4615; *Fax:* 240-439-4952
curtis.sumner@nsps.us.com; www.acsm.net
Social Media: Facebook, Twitter, YouTube

Curt Sumner, Executive Director
Jon Warren, President
Rick Howard, Chairman
Jan Fokens, Vice President
Robert Miller, Treasurer

Organization of professionals for networking and education in the topographical field.
5500 Members
Frequency: Annual
Founded in: 1942

21094 National Trust for Historic Preservation
2600 Virginia Avenue
Suite 1100
Washington, DC 20037

202-588-6000
800-944-6847; *Fax:* 202-588-6038
info@savingplaces.org
savingplaces.org
Social Media: Facebook, Twitter, Pinterest, Instagram, YouTube

Stephanie K. Meeks, President &CEO
Tabitha Almquist, Chief of Staff
Carla Washinko, Chief Financial & Admin Officer
Paul Edmondson, Chief Legal Officer
Amy Maniatis, Chief Marketing officer

A private, nonprofit membership organization dedicated to saving historic places and revitlizing America's communities. Also provides leadership, education, advocacy, and resources to save America's diverse historic places and revitalize the communities.
270k Members
Founded in: 1949
Mailing list available for rent

21095 Neighborhood Reinvestment Corporation
92 Argonaut
Suite 255
Aliso Viejo, CA 92656-3100

949-770-2000
800-808-3372; *Fax:* 949-770-2157
sales@federalregister.com;
www.federalregister.com

Supplies training, grants, developmental assistance, and a range of other technical services designed to help the local partnerships achieve substantially self-reliant neighborhoods. The goal is to improve a neighborhood's housing and physical conditions, build a positive community image, and establish a healthy real estate market and a core of neighbors capable of managing the continued health of their neighborhood.
Founded in: 1978

21096 Professional Certification Board
Po Box 12528
San Antonio, TX 78212-0528

210-225-2897
800-486-3676; *Fax:* 210-225-8450;
www.nsec.lincoln-grad.org

Deborah Deane, President

Provides education and board certificates for the real estate appraisal specialties of manufactured housing valuation, business valuation and litigation management.

21097 Professional Housing Management Association
154 Fort Evans Road NE
Leesburg, VA 201176

703-771-1888; *Fax:* 703-771-1888
mkcooper@earthlink.net; www.phma.com
Social Media: Facebook, Twitter, LinkedIn, Flickr

Barry Scribner, Treasurer
Del Eulberg, President
Elijah A. Wilki Wilkerson, Executive Vice President
Jon R. Moore, Exective Director
Chris Cole, Secretary

Members are federal government employees, civilian or military, who are directly involved in housing management or provides direct support to the field.
3,120 Members
Founded in: 1973

21098 Property Owners Association
1072 Madison Ave
Lakewood, NJ 08701

732-780-1966; *Fax:* 732-780-1611
info@poanj.org; www.poanj.org
Social Media: Facebook, Twitter

Jeffery Feld, Sergeant-At-Arms
Marc Tunis, Treasurer
Larry Rosen, President
Derek Reed, Vice President
Jerry Cheslow, Secretary

The Property Owners Association of New Jersey, Inc. brings together owners and operators of residential real estate, interested persons, and related industry personnel for educational and information sharing purposes.
550 Members
Founded in: 1949

21099 Real Estate Buyers Agent Council
430 N Michigan Avenue
Chicago, IL 60611
800-648-6224
800-648-6224; *Fax:* 312-329-8632
REBAC@realtors.org; www.rebac.net
Social Media: Facebook, Twitter, LinkedIn, YouTube
Walter T McDonald, President
Larry Von Feldt, VP/Liaison to Gov Affairs
Pat Kaplan, VP Liaison to Committees
Amy Gunaka, Marketing Manager
Represents professional real estate agents who act as buyers' agents.
50000 Members
Founded in: 1988
Mailing list available for rent

21100 Real Estate Capital Resources Association
1350 I Street NW
Washington, DC 20005-3305
202-663-3740; *Fax:* 202-371-0069
G David Fensterheim, Executive Director
Represents firms that provide third party work-out and capital recovery services in connection with distressed real estate and real estate related assets.
100 Members
Founded in: 1989

21101 Real Estate Educators Association
7739 E Broadway
Suite 337
Tuscon, AZ 85710
520-609-2380; *Fax:* 856-423-3420
MemberCare@reea.org; www.reea.org
Social Media: Facebook, Twitter
Michael McAllister, President
Melissa Kleeman-Moy, Secretary
Bill Aaron, Treasurer
Tina Lapp, President-Elect
Kris Inman, Executive Director
Individuals involved in training and education.
1,400 Members
Founded in: 1979

21102 Real Estate Information Providers Association
1420 16th Street NW
Washington, DC 20036-2218
202-298-8169; *Fax:* 202-332-2301; www.reipa.com
Randy Dyer, Executive Director
Supports professional information providers in the real estate industry.
Founded in: 1995

21103 Real Estate Roundtable
801 Pennsylvania Ave NW
Suite 720
Washington, DC 20004
202-639-8400; *Fax:* 202-639-8442
info@rer.org; www.rer.org
William C. Rudin, Chairman
Jeffrey D DeBoer, President/CEO
Jeanne Kane, Chairman-Elect
Debra A. Cafaro, Secretary
Thomas M. Flexner, Treasurer
Actively involves public and private real estate owners, advisors, builders, investors, lenders and managers on key tax, capital and credit, energy, environmental and homeland security policy issues in Washington. Its members are senior principals from every spectrum of the commercial real estate industry and leaders of major national real estate trade associations.
230 Members
Founded in: 1999

21104 Realtors Land Institute
430 N Michigan Ave
Floor 11
Chicago, IL 60611
312-329-8440
800-441-5263; *Fax:* 312-329-8633
rli@realtors.org; www.rliland.com
Social Media: Facebook, Twitter, LinkedIn, Google+
Michele Cohen, Executive VP
Teri Jensen, President
Bob Turner, President-Elect
Brandon Rogillio, Vice President
George Clift, Immediate Past President
Promotes competence and accredits members. Maintains educational programs for real estate brokers.
1.9M Members
Founded in: 1944

21105 Society of Industrial and Office Realtors
1201 New York Ave NW
Suite 350
Washington, DC 20005-6126
202-449-8200; *Fax:* 202-216-9325
membership@sior.com; www.sior.com
Social Media: Facebook, Twitter, LinkedIn, Pinterest, Google+, Youtube
Richard Hollander, Executive VP
Allen Gump, President
Geoffrey Kasselman, President-Elect
Del Markward, Vice-President
Jack Whalen, Treasurer
Active members are brokers, consultants and appraisers.
3100 Members
Founded in: 1939

21106 SourceMedia
One State Street Plaza
27th floor
New York, NY 10004
212-803-8200
800-803-3424; *Fax:* 212-843-9608
custserv@sourcemedia.com; www.sourcemedia.com
Douglas J. Manoni, CEO
Michael P. Caruso, CFO
David Longobardi, EVP & Chief Content Officer
Minna Rhee, Chief Digital Officer
Marianne Collins, Chief Revenue Officer
SourceMedia provides market information, including news, analysis, and insight to the financial services and related industries such as accounting and technology, through its publications, industry-standard data applications, seminars and conferences. The informational services that SourceMedia delivers are available in print or online, including newspapers and magazines, reference directories, database products, software, web seminars and live events.

21107 The American Real Estate & Urban Economics Association
821 Academic Way,223 RBB
Tallahassee, FL 32306-1110
850-644-7898; *Fax:* 850-644-4077
elaffitte@fsu.edu; www.areuea.org
Stuart Rosenthal, President
Edward Coulson, First VP
Marsha J. Courchane, Executive Vice President
Liz Laffitte, Executive Director
David H. Downs, Treasurer
Addresses academic and commercial concerns in real estate and commercial economics.
1200 Members
ISSN: 1080-8620
Founded in: 1964

21108 Women's Council of Realtors
430 N Michigan Ave
Chicago, IL 60611
312-329-8483
800-245-8512; *Fax:* 312-329-3290
wcr@wcr.org; www.wcr.org
Social Media: Facebook, Twitter, LinkedIn, Pinterest, Instagram
Jeff Hornberger, Executive Vice President
Carol Raabe, VP Operations
Sindy Ready, President
Jo Ann Stevens, Financial Secretary
Melissa Zimbelman, President-elect
Provides opportunities for women in real estate at the local, state and national level. Offers courses in leadership training and referral and relocation buisness.
40000 Members
Founded in: 1938

21109 Worldwide ERC
4401 Wilson Blvd
Suite 510
Arlington, VA 22203
703-842-3400; *Fax:* 703-527-1552
CustomerCare@WorldwideERC.org; www.erc.org
Social Media: Facebook, Twitter, LinkedIn, Pinterest
Peggy Smith, President & CEO
Robert J. Horsley, Vice Chair- Finance
Dale L. Collins, Chair-Elect
Cindy Salter, Chairman
Sharon Byrnes, Vice Chair-Talent Community
A national organization that examines key issues affecting the relocation industry for the benefit of corporations, government agencies, and firms or individuals providing specific services to relocated employees and their families. Accepts advertising.
1600 Members
Founded in: 1964

Newsletters

21110 ACREL News
American College of Real Estate Lawyers
11300 Rockville Pike
Suite 903
Rockville, MD 20852-3034
301-816-9811; *Fax:* 301-816-9786
webmaster@acrel.org; www.acrel.site-ym.com
Roger D. Winston, President
Frequency: Monthly

21111 AOMA Newsletter
Apartment Owners & Managers Assn of America
65 Cherry Avenue
Cherry Plaza
Watertown, CT 06795
Fax: 860-274-2580
Robert J McGough, Editor
Pietro
Each month the AOMA newsletter presents the facts and information builder/developer/owners/manager members need to keep abreast of in the world of Multi-Family housing. Every monthly issue will bring the reader timely insight on Real Estate, tax news, financing techniques, and effective management procedures, and keeps readers aware of the new developments in the condominium market.
Cost: $125.00
Frequency: 12 issues
Circulation: 6,200
Mailing list available for rent
Printed in one color

21112 **ASFMRA News**
Amer. Society of Farm Managers & Rural Appraisers
950 S Cherry St
Suite 508
Denver, CO 80246-2664
303-758-3513; *Fax:* 303-758-0190
asfmra@agri-associations.org;
www.asfmra.org
Cheryl L Cooley, Manager Communications
Thomas V. Boyer, President
Informs ASFMRA members of education, member, event, meeting and government issues.
Cost: $24.00
Founded in: 1929
Mailing list available for rent: 2500 names at $1M per M

21113 **Accredited Review Appraiser**
Accredited Review Appraisers Council
303 W Cypress Street
San Antonio, TX 78212-5512
800-486-3676; *Fax:* 210-225-8450
arac.lincoln-grad.org
Deborah J Deane, Publisher
Rachel L Phelps, Marketing Manager
Offers information on appraisals and real estate reviews.
8 Pages
Frequency: Quarterly
Founded in: 1987
Printed in one color on matte stock

21114 **Advise and Counsel**
National Association of Counselors
303 W Cypress St
San Antonio, TX 78212-5512
210-271-0781
800-229-6262; *Fax:* 210-225-8450
djd@masterappraisers.org;
www.masterappraisers.org
Offers information on real estate and appriasal counseling services.
Cost: $45.00
8 Pages
Frequency: Quarterly
Circulation: 4000

21115 **American Chapter News**
American Chapter International Real Estate Assn
30700 Russell Ranch Road
Westlake Village, CA 91362
805-557-2300; *Fax:* 805-557-2680;
www.realtors.com
Teresa Salmon, Publisher
International real estate news and information.
Cost: $110.00
8 Pages
Frequency: Monthly

21116 **American Industrial Real Estate Association Newsletter**
American Industrial Real Estate Association
700 S Flowers Street
Suite 600
Los Angeles, CA 90017
213-687-8777; *Fax:* 213-687-8616
support@airea.com; www.airea.com
Ron Surace, COO
6 Pages
Frequency: Quarterly
Founded in: 1964
Printed in 3 colors on glossy stock

21117 **American Society of Farm Managers and Rural Appraisers Newsletter**
Amer. Society of Farm Managers & Rural Appraisers
950 S Cherry St
Suite 508
Denver, CO 80246-2664
303-758-3513; *Fax:* 303-758-0190
asfmra@agri-associations.org;
www.asfmra.org
Cheryl L Cooley, Manager Communications/IT/PR
Hope S. Evans, Membership Coordinator
Provides professionals involved in rural property issues such as management and appraisal, with information on the industry as well as educational opportunities. Includes membership and information from the American Society of Farm Manager and Rural Appraisers.
Cost: $30.00
Frequency: Annual+
ISSN: 1076-3856
Founded in: 1929
Mailing list available for rent: 2500 names at $1M per M
Printed in 2 colors on glossy stock

21118 **Andrews Report**
Report Publications
9595 Whitney Drive
#100
Indianapolis, IN 46280
William Woburn, Publisher
For owners and operators of small shopping centers.
Cost: $147.00
12 Pages
Frequency: Monthly

21119 **Apartment Management Newsletter**
AMN Publishing
PO BOX 352
Massapequa, NY 11758
516-551-5343
amnpub@aol.com
propertymanagementnewsletters.com
Helene Mandelbaum, Editor
Vera West, Circulation Manager
News and information for apartment owners and managers, including tips and techniques for marketing, maintenance, personnel and compliance with national laws and requirements.
Cost: $6.00
Founded in: 2001

21120 **Apartment Management Report**
Apartment Owners & Managers Assn of America
65 Cherry Avenue
Cherry Plaza
Watertown, CT 06795-238
Fax: 860-274-2580
Robert J McGough, Editor
Janet Pietro, Circulation Manager
Researched and written for the owner/manager, overall property manager, and for the on site managers. Typical in depth subjects cover the nuts and bolts of every day management. Research reports on tenant renting strategies, model apartments, security, outside maintenance, how to avoid and handle tenant complaints, and more.
Cost: $72.85
6 Pages
Frequency: Monthly
Circulation: 6200
Mailing list available for rent: 6000 names
Printed in one color

21121 **Asset Watch**
LDI Publishing
1401 16th Street NW
Washington, DC 20036-2201
202-232-2144; *Fax:* 202-232-4757
Steve Sullivan, Publisher
News and analysis of federal asset sales RDIC, LRTC, HUD, etc., contracting and resolutions.
Cost: $475.00
6 Pages
Frequency: 5 per year

21122 **Asset-Backed Alert**
Harrison Scott Publications
5 Marine View Plz
Suite 301
Hoboken, NJ 07030-5722
201-386-1491
800-283-9363; *Fax:* 201-659-4141
info@hspnews.com; www.hspnews.com
Andy Albert, Chairman/Publisher
Thomas J Ferris, Director
Michelle Lebowitz, Director
A weekly update on global securitization
Cost: $2297.00
20 Pages
Frequency: Weekly
Circulation: 500
Founded in: 1990
Mailing list available for rent: 900 names at $400 per M
Printed in one color on matte stock

21123 **Bulletin**
Property Management Association
7508 Wisconsin Ave
Suite 4
Bethesda, MD 20814-3561
301-657-9200; *Fax:* 301-907-9326
info@pma-dc.org; www.pma-dc.org
Tom Cohn, Executive Director
News and events surrounding the real estate industry.
Cost: $100.00
24 Pages
Frequency: Monthly

21124 **Commercial Lease Law Insider**
Brownstone Publishers
149 5th Ave
Suite 10
New York, NY 10010-6832
212-473-8200; *Fax:* 212-473-8786
vendomecs@qualitycustomercare.com;
www.brownstone.com
John M Striker Esq, Publisher
Nicole Lefton Esq, Editor
Commercial leasing strategies, techniques and insights with practical aids such as model lease clauses, checklists, do's and dont's, as well as coverage of new court decisions affecting commercial leases. Readership consists of commercial property owners, managers and real estate attorneys.
Cost: $337.00
Frequency: Monthly
*Mailing list available for rent*at $110 per M
Printed in 2 colors on matte stock

21125 **Commercial Property News**
Miller Freeman Publications
600 Harrison Street
Suite 400
San Francisco, CA 94107-1391
Fax: 415-905-2239
David Nussbaum, Publisher
Maxine Jaffe, Editor
Tabloid newspaper edited for commercial property professionals.
Cost: $4.00
Circulation: 34,000

21126 **Commercial Real Estate Digest**
Vestal Communications
334 Humphrey Drive
Evergreen, CO 80439-9655
Robert Vestal, Publisher

Master copy newsletter allowing unlimited copy additions before subscriber prints and distributes to clients.
Cost: $495.00
2 Pages
Frequency: Quarterly

21127 **Community Association Law Reporter**
Community Associations Institute
6402 Arlington Blvd
Suite 500
Falls Church, VA Falls Chur

Fal-s C-urch
888-224-4321; *Fax:* 703-970-9558
caidirect@caionline.org; www.caionline.org

Daniel Brannigan, Editor
Information on legal cases and court decisions concerning condominium, cooperative and homeowner associations.
Cost: $208.00
8 Pages
Frequency: Monthly
Founded in: 1973

21128 **Community Associations Institute News**
Community Associations Institute
6402 Arlington Blvd
Suite 500
Falls Church, VA Falls Chur

Fal-s C-urch
888-224-4321; *Fax:* 703-970-9558
caidirect@caionline.org; www.caionline.org

Daniel Brannigan, Editor
Real estate news and reports.
Frequency: Monthly
Founded in: 1973

21129 **Community Management**
Community Associations Institute
6402 Arlington Blvd
Suite 500
Falls Church, VA Falls Chur

Fal-s C-urch
888-224-4321; *Fax:* 703-970-9558
caidirect@caionline.org; www.caionline.org

Daniel Brannigan, Editor
Bimonthly newsletter of news, strategies and trends written especially for managers of condominium and homeowner associations. This easy to read, award-winning newsletter comes packed with how-to information on such subjects as cutting expenses, complying with federal laws, working effectively with boards of directors, ensuring community safety and resolving disputes. It often features case studies of succcessful new approaches in community association management and operations.
Cost: $59.00
8 Pages
Founded in: 1973

21130 **Daily Commerce**
Daily Journal Corporation
PO Box 54026
Los Angeles, CA 90054-0026

213-229-5300; *Fax:* 213-229-5481;
www.dailyjournal.com

Gerald L Salzman, CEO
Ray Chagolla, Circulation Manager
Lisa Churchill, Editor
personnel announcements, datebook information, consumer news, and the internet, information on government foreclosers, default notices, lending reports and probate estate sales.
Cost: $237.00
Frequency: Monthly
Circulation: 10000

21131 **Environmental Consultant**
National Society of Environmental Consultants
PO Box 12528
San Antonio, TX 78212-0528

210-225-2897
800-486-3676; *Fax:* 210-225-8450
nsec.lincoln-grad.org/

Deborah Deane, President
Offers information, articles and news of interest to real estate environmental site consultants.
Cost: $50.00
16 Pages
Frequency: Quarterly
Circulation: 4000
Founded in: 1992

21132 **Housing Affairs Letter**
CD Publications
8204 Fenton St
Silver Spring, MD 20910-4571

301-588-6380
800-666-6380; *Fax:* 301-588-6385
info@cdpublications.com;
www.cdpublications.com

Michael Gerecht, President
Tom Edwards, Editor
The latest news on housing activity nationwide, including private, public and subsidized housing, legislation and regulations.
Cost: $559.00
Frequency: Weekly
Founded in: 1961
Mailing list available for rent: 2,000 names at $160 per M

21133 **Housing the Elderly Report**
CD Publications
8204 Fenton St
Silver Spring, MD 20910-4571

301-588-6380
800-666-6380; *Fax:* 301-588-6385
info@cdpublications.com;
www.cdpublications.com

Michael Gerecht, President
Jeff Pines, Editor
News and advice for owners and managers of long-term care facilities on marketing and managing all types of elderly housing, with profiles of new senior housing projects, business reports and an exclusive annual salary survey.
Cost: $294.00
Frequency: Monthly
Founded in: 1961
Mailing list available for rent: 2,000 names at $160 per M

21134 **Inside IREM**
Institute of Real Estate Management
430 N Michigan Ave
Suite 7
Chicago, IL 60611-4011

312-329-6000; *Fax:* 312-661-0217
info@crs.com; www.irem.org

Russell Salzman, CEO
Membership newsletter for members of the Institute of Real Estate Management. It includes news on IREM policies, programs and new products. Federal, state and local legislative developments affecting real estate and asset management are also reported.
40000 Pages
Founded in: 1976

21135 **Inspector**
American Society of Home Inspectors
932 Lee Street
Suite 101
Des Plaines, IL 60016-3520

847-759-2820
800-248-2744; *Fax:* 847-759-1620
webmaster@ashi.org; www.ashi.org

Richard Clough, Executive Director
Paul Christensen, President
Newsletter for members of New England chapter of American Society of Home Inspectors.
Cost: $250.00
Frequency: Monthly
Circulation: 6000
Founded in: 1976

21136 **International Real Estate Newsletter**
1224 N Nokomis NE
Alexandria, MN 56308-5072

320-763-4648; *Fax:* 320-763-9290
iami@iami.org; www.iami.org/

David Held, Production Manager
Robert Johnson, CEO
A compilation of international real estate information which is disseminated to the International Real Estate Institute's membership and to other subscribers. This publication also reviews the latest accomplishments of the Institute and those of its high quality professional members.
Cost: $29.50
4 Pages
Frequency: Monthly
Founded in: 1975
Printed in one color on newsprint stock

21137 **Ledger Quarterly**
Community Associations Institute
6402 Arlington Blvd
Suite 500
Falls Church, VA Falls Chur

Fal-s C-urch
888-224-4321; *Fax:* 703-970-9558
caidirect@caionline.org; www.caionline.org

Quarterly newsletter of financial news for condominium, cooperative and homeowner associations. If you participate in any way in the financial management of an association, this eight-page newsletter is a resource you should have. It's absolutely vital for keeping up-to-date on trends in asssociation accounting practices, calculating the best strategies to minimize association taxes, and advising the board on investments.
Cost: $67.00
Frequency: Quarterly
Circulation: 12000+
Founded in: 1973

21138 **Mac News**
Mid-Atlantic Council of Shopping Centers
8811 Colesville Road
Silver Spring, MD 20910-4343

301-890-1467

Tom Cohn, Publisher
News of the council.
Cost: $100.00
20 Pages
Frequency: Monthly

21139 **Managing Housing Letter**
CD Publications
8204 Fenton St
Silver Spring, MD 20910-4571

301-588-6380
800-666-6380; *Fax:* 301-588-6385
info@cdpublications.com;
www.cdpublications.com

Michael Gerecht, President
Charles Wisniowski, Editor
News and advice for owners, managers and professionals dealing with apartments and the real

estate industry.
Cost: $269.00
Frequency: Monthly
Founded in: 1978
Mailing list available for rent: 2,000 names at $160 per M

21140 Mobilehome Parks Report
Thomas P Kerr
3807 Pasadena Ave
Suite 100
Sacramento, CA 95821-2880

916-971-0489
800-392-5180; *Fax:* 916-971-1849
tkerr@aol.com; www.aol.com

Reports on trends, issues, court decisions, legislation, financing and other matters of concern to owners and developers of manufactured housing communities. Valuable to attorneys and others who specialize in this segment of the Housing Industry.
Cost: $125.00
8 Pages
Frequency: Monthly
Circulation: 350
Founded in: 1998
Printed in one color on matte stock

21141 National Association of Neighborhoods Newsletter
1300 Pennsylvania Avenue
NW Suite 700
Washington, DC 20004

202-332-7766; *Fax:* 202-332-2314
staff@nanworld.org; www.nanworld.org

C Y Doyd, Editor
Ricardo C Byrd, President

Offers news and information to the community real estate industry.
Frequency: Quarterly
Circulation: 10,000
Founded in: 1975

21142 New England Real Estate Journal
East Coast Publications
PO Box 55
Accord, MA 02018

781-878-4540
800-654-4993; *Fax:* 781-871-1853
nerej@rejournal.com; www.rejournal.com

Tom Murray, Publisher
David Denelle, Editor

Business publication for the commercial-industrial-investment real estate industries.
Cost: $2.00
Frequency: Weekly
Circulation: 13000
Founded in: 1961
Printed in on newsprint stock

21143 Professional Apartment Management
Brownstone Publishers
149 5th Ave
Suite 10
New York, NY 10010-6832

212-473-8200
800-643-8095; *Fax:* 212-473-8786
custserv@brownstone.com;
www.brownstone.com

Mary Lopez, Production Manager
Michael Koplin, Circulation Director

Strategies, techniques and suggestions for attracting and retaining paying tenants, and avoiding legal disputes. Includes model language for leases, sample ads, plus coverage of legal issues, recent court decisions and the like.
Cost: $217.00
Frequency: Monthly
Founded in: 1972
Printed in 2 colors on matte stock

21144 Real Estate Alert
Harrison Scott Publications
5 Marine View Plz
Suite 301
Hoboken, NJ 07030-5722

201-386-1491; *Fax:* 201-659-4141
info@hspnews.com; www.hspnews.com

Andy Albert, Chairman/President
Michelle Lebowitz, Director

Contains information for real estate and financial professionals looking for opportunities to buy or manage assets.
Cost: $1397.00
8 Pages
Frequency: Weekly
Circulation: 300+
Founded in: 1989
Printed in 4 colors

21145 Real Estate Asset Manager
Lincoln Graduate Center - Executive Offices
PO Box 12528
San Antonio, TX 78212-0528

210-225-2897
800-531-5333; *Fax:* 210-225-8450;
www.lincoln-grad.org

Debroah Deane, President
Rachel Phelps, Marketing Manager

Offers news and information on environmental concerns, real estate and appraisals.
8 Pages

21146 Real Estate Brokers Insider
Alexander Communications Group
1916 Park Ave
Suite 501
New York, NY 10037-3733

212-281-6099
800-232-4317; *Fax:* 212-283-7269
info@brokersinsider.com;
www.brokersinsider.com/

Romauld Alexander, President
Nadine Harris, Marketing Manager

Provides agency broker/owners with in depth information on how to run their businesses better.
Cost: $247.00
8 Pages
Frequency: Fortnightly
ISSN: 1086-2935
Founded in: 1978

21147 Real Estate Economics
AREUEA
PO Box 9958
Richmond, VA 23228-1148

866-273-8321; *Fax:* 877-273-8323;
www.areuea.org

Susan Watcher, Publisher
David C. Ling, Editor

Discussions on topics such as housing prices, office markets, real estate valuation and appraisal.
Cost: $100.00
Frequency: Quarterly
Founded in: 1964

21148 Real Estate Investor's Monthly
John T Reed Publishing
342 Bryan Dr
Alamo, CA 94507-2858

925-820-6292; *Fax:* 925-820-1259
johnreed@johntreed.com; www.johntreed.com

John T Reed, President

Information for owners who manage and own their own property, suggestions for increasing their investment returns.
Cost: $125.00
8 Pages
Frequency: Monthly
Circulation: 500
Founded in: 1980

21149 Tax Credit Advisor
1400 16th St Nw
Suite 420A
Washington, DC 20036-2216

202-939-1790; *Fax:* 202-265-4435
info@housingonline.com;
www.housingonline.com

Peter Bell, President
Glenn Petherick, Executive Director
Thom Amdur, Executive Director
David Abromowitz, Secretary

Monthly newsletter providing comprehensive coverage of all aspects of the federal low-income housing tax credit program, the primary incentive for low-income apartment development. Covers legislation, IRS rules, equity and debt programs, and market trends.
Cost: $269.00
12 Pages
Frequency: Monthly
Circulation: 750

21150 Upward Directions
Community Associations Institute
6402 Arlington Blvd.
Suite 500
Falls Church, VA 22042

703-970-9220
888-224-4321; *Fax:* 703-970-6558;
www.caionline.org

Tom Skiba, CEO

NBBC-CAM's quarterly newsletter for the further education and professional development of CMCA Certificants. Program news, updates on state credentialing activities, legislation and regulation and continuing education opportunities make this newsletter required reading for Certified Managers of Community Associations (CMCA's. Everything you need to know to earn, maintain and optimize the benefits from manager certification from the National Board of Certification.
Frequency: Quarterly

Magazines & Journals

21151 ALQ Real Estate Intelligence Report
Common Communications
PO Box 5702
Portsmouth, NH 03802-5702

800-299-9961
800-299-9961; *Fax:* 603-436-5202;
www.reintel.com

Pat Remick, Editor
Frank Cook, Publisher

A close examination of buyer agency movement, services rendered by brokerages, the impact of technology on real estate and success stories.
Cost: $200.00
Frequency: Quarterly
Founded in: 1989

21152 Affordable Housing Finance
Alexander & Edwards Publishing
33 New Montgomery St
Suite 290
San Francisco, CA 94105-4520

415-315-1241
800-989-7255; *Fax:* 415-315-1248;
www.hanleywood.com

Rob Britt, Manager
Andre Shashaty, President
Susan Piel, Conference Director
Michael Premsrirat, Circulation Manager
Carol Yee, Office Manager

Offers practical information on obtaining debt and equality financing from federal, state, and local governments as well as private resources. In-depth coverage on the federal low-income housing tax credit program, tax-exempt bond financing, corporate tax credit investigation.
Cost: $119.00
Frequency: Monthly
Circulation: 9000

21153 Alliance
John W Yopp Publications
6540 Julian Road
Gainesville, GA 30506-5550

800-849-9677; *Fax:* 800-849-8418
info@jwyopp.com; www.jwyopp.com

Mary Y Cronley, Associate Pubisher/Editor
Natalie Gilmer, Accounts Manager

Articles provide news and information on topics of interest, including marketing and sales, pre-need campaigns and other operational topics.
Frequency: Monthly
Circulation: 8000
Founded in: 1919

21154 American Cemetery
Kates-Boylston Publications
11300 Rockville Pike
Suite 1100
Rockville, MD 20852

800-500-4585
800-500-4585; *Fax:* 301-287-2150
AmericanFD@aol.com;
www.kates-boylston.com

Adrian F Boylston, Publisher
Thomas Lorge, Executive Director
Thomas Parmalee, Executive Director
Amy Fidalgo, Production Manager

Features articles on cemetery administration, maintenance, sales and public relations. Also includes coverage of conventions, new cemeteries and new building ideas.
Cost: $39.95
Frequency: Monthly
Circulation: 5800

21155 Apartment Age Magazine
Apartment Association of Greater Los Angeles
621 S Westmoreland Ave
Los Angeles, CA 90005-3962

310-536-0281; *Fax:* 213-382-3970
webmaster@aagla.org; www.aagla.org

Charles Isham, VP
Kevin Postema, Editor/Advertising Director
Larry Cannizzaro, President

Serving the interests of residential rental property owners.
Cost: $48.00
80 Pages
Frequency: Monthly
Circulation: 40000
ISSN: 0192-0030

21156 Apartment Finance Today Magazine
Hanley Wood LLC
One Thomas Circle, NW
Suite 600
Washington, DC 20005

202-452-0800; *Fax:* 202-785-1974;
www.hanleywood.com

John McManus, Editorial Director
Shabnam Mogharabi, Editor-In-Chief

Provides in-depth and inbiased reporting and insightful alaysis for owners, developers and asset managers.
Cost: $29.00
80 Pages
Circulation: 11784
ISSN: 1097-4059
Founded in: 1995
Printed in 4 colors on glossy stock

21157 Apartment News
Arizona Multi-Housing Consulting Corporation
5110 N 44th Street
Suite L160
Phoenix, AZ 85018-2107

602-224-0135
800-316-6403; *Fax:* 602-224-0657
info@azama.org; www.azama.org

Terry Feinberg, President
Mitchell McBay, Marketing Manager
Erick Richard, Editor
Wayne Kaplan, Director of Community Relations
Marilyn Everroad, Events Manager

Articles on state and national government affairs, education, marketing, crime prevention, maintenance and legal issues relating to the Arizona multihousing industry.
Cost: $50.00
Frequency: Monthly
Circulation: 2500
Founded in: 1964
Printed in on glossy stock

21158 Area Development
Halcyon Business Publications
400 Post Avenue
Westbury, NY 11590-2267

516-338-0900; *Fax:* 516-338-0100;
www.areadevelopment.com

Dennis Shea, Publisher/CEO
Geraldie Gambale, Editor
Gertrude Staudt, Circulation Manager

Focuses on the factors necessary for a successful corporate expansion or relocation, labor, taxes, incentives, quality of life, market access, and transportation.
Cost: $75.00
Circulation: 45000
Founded in: 1970

21159 Brownfield Renewal
Brownfield Renewal
2200 E Devon Ave
Suite 354
Des Plains, IL 60018

312-488-4830; *Fax:* 312-488-4220
editorial@brownfieldrenewal.com;
www.brownfieldrenewal.com

Steve Dwyer, Editorial Director
Monica Acuna, Circulation Director

Dedicated to the remediation, redevelopment and reuse of brownfields.
Cost: $79.95
Frequency: Bimonthly
ISSN: 1554-8791
Founded in: 1999

21160 Building Operating Management
Trade Press Publishing Corporation
2100 West Florist Avenue
Milwaukee, WI 53209-3799

414-228-7701; *Fax:* 414-228-1134
info@tradepress.com; www.tradepress.com

Scott G Holverson, Regional Sales Manager
Edward Sullivan, Editor
Eric Muench, Director of Circulation
Bobbie Reid, Production Director
Robert Wisniewski, President/CEO

Serves the field of facilities management, encompassing commercial building: office buildings, real estate/property management firms, developers, financial institutions, insurance companies, apartment complexes, civic/convention centers, including members of the Building Owners and Managers Association
Frequency: Monthly
Circulation: 70000
Founded in: 1915

21161 Business Facilities
Group C Communications
PO Box 2060
Red Bank, NJ 07701-0901

732-842-7433
800-524-0337; *Fax:* 732-758-6634
jsemple@groupc.com; www.groupc.com

Edgar T Coene, President
Jim Semple, Production Manager
Mary McCandless, Production Manager
Bill MacRae, Marketing Director

Magazine covering the fields of corporation expansion, economic development and real estate.
Cost: $30.00
Frequency: Monthly
Circulation: 43500
Founded in: 1968

21162 Business Journal
120 W Morehead Street
Suite 200
Charlotte, NC 28202

704-347-2340
800-948-5323; *Fax:* 704-973-1102
borben@bizjournals.com;
www.bizjournals.com/charlotte

Robert Morris, Editor
David Harris, Managing Editor
Kim Moser, Advertising Assistant
Megan Foley, Marketing Director
Jeannie Falknor, Publisher

Provides marketing solutions and caring service.
Cost: $82.00
Frequency: Daily

21163 CF Industrial Reporter
Clayton-Fillmore
PO Box 480894
Denver, CO 80248-894

303-663-0606; *Fax:* 303-663-1616;
www.clayfil.com

Howard Treibitz, Editor

Briefs of the markets broken down into specific cities, includes briefs of the economy and average manufacturing.
Cost: $189.00
Frequency: Monthly

21164 Commercial
Oakland Press
28 W Huron St
Pontiac, MI 48342-2100

248-745-4794
248-332-1988; *Fax:* 248-332-3003

Edward Moss, Owner

A showcase of available commercial properties in the region.
Cost: $18.00
Frequency: Monthly
Circulation: 30,000

21165 Common Ground
Community Associations Institute
6402 Arlington Blvd
Suite 500
Falls Church, VA Falls Chur
Fal-s C-urch
888-224-4321; *Fax:* 703-970-9558
caidirect@caionline.org; www.caionline.org

Dori Meinert, Editor

CAI's award-winning bimonthly magazine for condominium and homeowner associations, managers and other industry professionals. Would you like to learn how a Web site can help

your community association? Or peruse tips on cutting your budget? Or find out about the New Urbanism and other community development trends? Stay informed and involved via features and departments on the legal, political mechanical, personal, and day-to-day realities of community association life.
Cost: $69.00
Frequency: Monthly
Founded in: 1978

21166 **Comparative Statistics of Industrial and Office Real Estate Markets**
Society of Industrial & Office Realtors
1201 New York Ave NW
Suite 350
Washington, DC 20005-6126
202-449-8200; *Fax:* 202-216-9325
admin@sior.com; www.sior.com
Richard Hollander, Executive VP
Craig S Meyer, President
A comprehensive publication that summarizes the results of a nationwide survey of industrial and office real estate market activity.
Cost: $135.00
300 Pages
Frequency: Annual+
Circulation: 3000

21167 **Connections**
Women's Council of Realtors
430 N Michigan Ave
Chicago, IL 60611-4011
312-329-8483
800-462-8841; *Fax:* 312-329-3290
info@crs.com; www.wcr.org
Gary Krysler, Executive Director
Carol Raabe, VP Operations
Top producers in the real estate industry share their strategies for success.
32 Pages
Circulation: 14000
Founded in: 1966
Printed in 4 colors on matte stock

21168 **Cooperative Housing Journal**
National Association of Housing Cooperatives
630 Eye St NW
Washington, DC 20001-3736
202-289-3500; *Fax:* 202-289-8181
nahro@nahro.org; www.nahro.org
Saul Ramirez, Executive Director
Deniz Tunder, Editor
Articles of lasting value to leaders in cooperative housing.
Cost: $25.00
Circulation: 3000
Founded in: 1933

21169 **Cooperator**
Yale Robbins Publications
102 Madison Ave
5th Floor
New York, NY 10016-7417
212-683-5700; *Fax:* 212-545-0764
mrosales@mrofficespace.com; www.mrofficespace.com
Yale Robbins, Owner
Pam Liebman, CEO/President
Judith C Grover, Managing Editor
George Rubin, Circulation Manager
Ellen Levy, Advertising Manager
Articles covering management, maintenance business, finance, law, interior design and related topics.
Cost: $30.00
Frequency: Monthly
Circulation: 75000
Founded in: 1985
Printed in 4 colors

21170 **Daily Record**
11 E Saratoga St
Baltimore, MD 21202-2199
410-752-3849; *Fax:* 410-752-2894
editor@mddailyrecord.com; www.mddailyrecord.com
Chris Eddings, Publisher
Suzanne Fischer-Huettner, VP Sales
Christopher J Chardo, Circulation Director
Mark R Cheshire, Editor-in-Chief
Jeffrey Raymond, Editor
Cost: $190.00
Frequency: Daily
Founded in: 1888

21171 **Development**
National Assn of Industrial & Office Properties
2201 Cooperative Way
3rd floor
Herndon, VA 20171-4583
703-904-7100
800-666-6780; *Fax:* 703-904-7942
feedback@naiop.org; www.naiop.org
Thomas Bisacquino, President
Shirley A Maloney, Publisher
Articles pertaining to industrial and office real estate - development, ownership, management, investment, financing, leasing, etc.
Cost: $65.00
72 Pages
Frequency: Quarterly
Circulation: 14000
ISSN: 0888-6067
Founded in: 2000
Printed in 4 colors on glossy stock

21172 **Developments**
American Resort Development Association
1201 15th St NW
Suite 400
Washington, DC 20005-2842
202-371-6700; *Fax:* 202-289-8544
hnusbaum@arda.org; www.ardafoundation.org
Howard Nusbaum, President
Serves the timeshare industry.
Frequency: Monthly
Circulation: 1,000
Founded in: 1978

21173 **Financial Freedom Report**
2450 Fort Union Boulevard
Salt Lake City, UT 84121-3337
Fax: 801-944-4334
Carolyn Tice, Editor
An investor's information services company which specializes in home business start-up, analysis, acquisition and maintenance of real property.
Cost: $119.00
72 Pages
Frequency: 4 issues
Founded in: 1976

21174 **First Tuesday**
Realty Publications
PO Box 20069
Riverside, CA 92516-69
909-781-7300; *Fax:* 909-781-4721
Fred Crane, Publisher
Provides practical assistance to real estate professional. Includes legal and economic updates affecting the commercial and residential developments.
Frequency: Monthly
Circulation: 5000

21175 **Global Property Investor**
Alexander & Edwards Publishing
220 Sansome Street
11th Floor
San Francisco, CA 94104-2326
415-151-1241
800-989-7255; *Fax:* 415-249-1595; www.housingfinance.com
Shabnam Mogharabi, Director
Christine Serlin, Executive Editor
Objective, independent journal covering commercial property investment and development trends with readership in Europe, Asia and North America.

21176 **Hotel Journal**
Stacey Horowitz
45 Research Way
Suite 106
East Setauket, NY 11733
631-246-9300; *Fax:* 631-246-9496; www.hoteljournal.com
Stacey Silver, Group Publisher
Stefani C O'Connor, Executive News Editor
Cathy Urell, Senior Desk Editor
Barbara Jordan, Production Manager
Hope Rosenzweig, Advertising Manager
Cost: $85.00
Frequency: Monthly

21177 **In Business**
Business Information
2718 Dryden Drive
Madison, WI 53704
608-246-3599; *Fax:* 608-246-3597
Jody Glynn Patrick, Publisher
Joseph Vanden Plas, Editor
The business magazine for the Greater Madison Market.
48 Pages
Frequency: Monthly
Circulation: 15,000
ISSN: 0192-7450

21178 **Ingram's**
Show-Me Publishing, Inc
PO Box 411356
Kansas City, MO 64141-1356
816-842-9994; *Fax:* 816-474-1111
editorial@ingramsonline.com; www.ingramsonline.com
Joe Sweeney, Editor-in-Chief/Publisher
Jack Cashill, Executive Editor
Kansas City's business magazine.
Cost: $36.00
114 Pages
Frequency: Monthly
ISSN: 1046-9958
Printed in 4 colors on glossy stock

21179 **Institutional Real Estate Letter**
Institutional Real Estate
2274 Camino Ramon
San Ramon, CA 94583
925-244-0500; *Fax:* 925-244-0520; www.irei.com
H Lawrence Hull Jr, Chairman
Geoffrey Dohrmann, CRE, Founder/President/CEO
Larry Gray, Editorial Director
Offers analysis of market trends related to pension fund investment in real estate.
Cost: $2495.00
Frequency: Monthly
Founded in: 1987

21180 **International Real Estate Journal**
International Real Estate Institute

810 N Farrell Drive
Palm Springs, CA 92262

760-327-5284
877-743-6799; *Fax:* 760-327-5631
info@irei-assoc.org; www.irei-assoc.org

Roger Wood, Production Manager
James Held, Production Manager
Robert Johnson, CEO

A full color magazine dedicated to discussing and promoting real estate opportunities all over the world. The articles cover a wide array of international Real Estate topics and are written by top international professionals.
Frequency: Monthly
Circulation: 10,000
Founded in: 1977

21181 Journal of Property Management
Institute of Real Estate Management
430 N Michigan Ave
Suite 7
Chicago, IL 60611-4011

312-329-6000; *Fax:* 312-661-0217
custserv@irem.org; www.irem.org

Russell Salzman, CEO
Anthony Smith, President

Features articles on management, leasing and development of all property types.
Cost: $69.95
Circulation: 18000
Founded in: 1976

21182 Journal of Real Estate Taxation
Thomson Reuters
195 Broadway
New York, NY 10007

817-332-3709
800-431-9025; *Fax:* 888-216-1929
ria.thomsonreuters.com

Paul D Carman, Editor-in-Chief
Robert J Murdich JD, Managing Editor

Complete, ongoing coverage of all aspects of real estate tax planning. In-depth articles by leading attorneys, accountants, and real estate authorities keep you abreast of the latest developments and how they affect real estate tax planning.
Cost: $315.00
Frequency: Quarterly

21183 MB News
Monument Builders of North America
401 N Michigan Avenue
Suite 2200
Chicago, IL 60611-4267

800-233-4472; *Fax:* 312-673-6732;
www.monumentbuilders.org

Greg Patzer, Executive VP
Marty Kraslen, Manager

The Monument Builders of North America represent the leading retail, wholesale and manufacturing and supply firms of the monument industry. Articles promote public interest, knowledge and appreciation of memorialization.
Cost: $70.00
Frequency: 12 issues
Circulation: 1400

21184 Midwest Real Estate News
The Law Bulletin Publishing Company
415 N State St
Suite 1
Chicago, IL 60654-8116

312-644-7800; *Fax:* 312-644-4255
dwalsh@lbpc.com; www.lawbulletin.com

Lanning Macfarland Jr, President
Tricia Haddon, Associate Publisher
Bob Craig, Editor
Robert Carr, Associate editor

The Midwest's only commercial real estate source.
Cost: $60.00
Frequency: Monthly
Circulation: 16914
Founded in: 1854
Printed in 4 colors on glossy stock

21185 Mobility Magazine
Worldwide ERC
4401 Wilson Boulevard
Suite 510
Arlington, VA 22203

703-842-3400; *Fax:* 703-527-1552
webmaster@worldwideerc.org;
www.worldwideerc.org

Anita Brienza GMS, SVP Communications/Marketing
Frank Mauck, Managing Editor

Relocation leaders share experiences, offer new solutions to age-old challenges, set industry trends, describe best practices and policies, as well as comment on key issues affecting the relocation profession.
Cost: $48.00
68 Pages
Frequency: Monthly
Circulation: 12500
Founded in: 1960

21186 Mortgage and Real Estate Executives Report
PO Box 64833
Saint Paul, MN 55164-0833

212-929-7500
800-950-1205; *Fax:* 212-367-6718

21187 Multifamily Executive
MGI Publications
1 Thomas Cir NW
Suite 600
Washington, DC 20005-5803

202-452-0800; *Fax:* 202-785-1974
arice@hanleywood.com;
www.hanleywood.com

Ed McNeill, President
Stephanie Davis, Production Manager
Alison Rice, Editor
Nicola Pellegrini, Marketing
J Michael Boyle, Publisher

Software and technology innovations, legislation, property development, management and renovation topics. Subscription free to qualified individuals.
Frequency: Monthly
Circulation: 25000
ISSN: 1089-4721
Founded in: 1976
Printed in 4 colors on glossy stock

21188 National Real Estate Investor
Penton Media
249 W 17th Street
New York, NY 10011

212-204-4200
david.bodamer@penton.com;
www.nreionline.com

Marianne Rivera, Publisher
David Bodamer, Editorial Director
Susan Piperato, Managing Editor

The leading authority on commercial real estate trends. Readers represent a cross-section of dissciplines-brokerage, construction, owner/development, finance/investment, property managment, corporate real estate, and real estate services.
Circulation: 33000
Founded in: 1939

21189 National Relocation & Real Estate Magazine
RISMedia, Inc
69 E Avenue
Norwalk, CT 06851

203-855-1234
800-724-6000
realestatemagazinefeedback@rismedia.com
rismedia.com

John Featherston, Publisher
Steve Empey, CEO

Information on emerging trends and important issues affecting the various industries that are involved in relocating people and the home buying process.
Cost: $42.84
Frequency: Monthly
Circulation: 34,500
Founded in: 1985

21190 New Homes Guide
4902 Eisenhower Boulevard
Suite 216
Tampa, FL 33634

813-823-3535; *Fax:* 813-290-7380

Emily Boyd, Manager
Sharon Kirkbride, Contact

21191 Office & Industrial Properties
MGI Publications
301 Oxford Valley Road
#1301
Yardley, PA 19067-7706

215-321-5112; *Fax:* 215-321-5122

Edward McNeill Jr, President/Editor-in-Chief

Contains business, technology, design and financial aspects concerning large private properties.
Cost: $36.00
Frequency: Bi-Monthly
Circulation: 15,000

21192 Office Buildings Magazine
Yale Robbins Publications
102 Madison Ave
5 Floor
New York, NY 10016-7417

212-683-5700
800-411-2229; *Fax:* 212-545-0764
mrosales@mrofficespace.com;
www.mrofficespace.com

Yale Robbins, Owner
Henry Robbins, Marketing
Debbie Estock, Editor
Dane Pedupo, Circulation

Offers information on appraising and betterment of the real estate community in major markets in the Northeast.
Cost: $675.00
Frequency: Annual+
Founded in: 1982
Printed in 4 colors

21193 Pest Control
Questex Media
600 Superior Ave E
Suite 1100
Cleveland, OH 44114-2614

216-706-3620
800-669-1668; *Fax:* 216-706-3711
pestcon@questex.com; www.questex.com

Tony Davino, Executive VP
Matt Waddell, Publisher
Matt Simoni, Sales Manager
Frank Andorka, Editorial Director

Serves the structural pest control industry.
Frequency: Monthly
Circulation: 21600
ISSN: 0031-6121

Founded in: 1933
Printed in 4 colors on glossy stock

21194 Plants, Sites & Parks
12350 NW 39th Street
Suite 101
Coral Springs, FL 33065
954-753-2660
800-753-2660; *Fax:* 954-755-7048
Kevin Castellani, Group Publisher
Steve Chaffin, Publisher/Editor-in-Chief
Lisa M Bouchey, Managing Editor
Industrial office and economic development, facility planning and site selection for manufacturing and service industries.
Circulation: 44,500

21195 Professional Report
Society of Industrial & Office Realtors
1201 New York Ave NW
Suite 350
Washington, DC 20005-6126
202-449-8200; *Fax:* 202-216-9325
admin@sior.com; www.sior.com
Richard Hollander, Executive VP
Craig S Meyer, President
Articles by industry experts focusing on new paradigm in the practice of commercial real estate.
Cost: $295.00
Frequency: Quarterly
Circulation: 2,200
Founded in: 1991

21196 RCI Timeshare Business
RCI
PO Box 80229
Indianapolis, IN 46280-0229
317-805-9000; *Fax:* 317-805-9618
alyssa.chase@rci.com; www.rci.com
Alyssa Chase, Editor
Katherine Jones, Publisher
David Tontius, CEO/President
Serves timeshare resorts/developers, hoteliers, operations and others allied to the field.
42 Pages
Frequency: Monthly
Circulation: 9000
Founded in: 1974
Printed in 4 colors on glossy stock

21197 RCI Ventures Magazine
RCI
9998 N Michigan Road
Carmel, IN 46032
317-059-9584; *Fax:* 317-805-9507
alyssa.chase@rci.com; www.rciventures.com
Alyssa Chase, Editor
Nicole Keller, Senior Editor
Gathering of more than 4,000 of timesharing's best and brightest executives.
Frequency: April
Circulation: 35000
ISSN: 1099-6753
Printed in 4 colors on 6 stock

21198 Real Estate Business
Realtors National Marketing Institute
430 N Michigan Avenue
#300
Chicago, IL 60611-4002
312-321-4400; *Fax:* 312-329-8882;
www.crs.com
Sara Patterson, Editor-in-Chief
Eric Berkland, Marketing
Nina Cottrell, CEO
Ron Canning, Vice President
Information for real estate agents and brokers engaged in US residential sales activities.
Cost: $24.00
64 Pages
Circulation: 48000
Founded in: 1976

21199 Real Estate Executive
Sunshine Media
735 Broad Street
Suite 708
Chattanooga, TN 37402
423-266-3234
800-624-7496; *Fax:* 423-266-7960
info@sunshinemedia.com;
www.sunshinemedia.com
Tony Young, President
Jim Martin, President/CEO
David McDonald, Publisher
About real estate professionals from real estate professionals. Reaches 100 percent of the professional real estate audience in each market it serves. Each issue profiles a leading realty executive or agency within your local real estate market, as well as an assortment of new products, services and innovations.
Cost: $36.00
Frequency: Monthly
Circulation: 3000
Founded in: 1996

21200 Real Estate Finance Journal
Thomson Reuters
610 Opperman Drive
Eagan, MN 55123
652-168-7700; www.west.thomson.com
Examines the opportunities and pitfalls facing real estate owners, developers, investors and lenders. Focuses on financing, liability, investments, taxes and asset management.
Cost: $558.00
Frequency: Quarterly

21201 Real Estate Finance Today
Mortgage Bankers Association of America
1919 Pennsylvania Avenue NW
Washington, DC 20006-3404
202-557-2700
membership@mortgagebankers.org;
www.mortgagebankers.org
Features inside news reports on events and trends affecting the residential and commercial mortgage markets.

21202 Real Estate Forum
Real Estate Media
120 Broadway
Suite 5
New York, NY 10271
212-929-6976; www.reforum.com
Michael G Desiato, VP/Group Publisher
Sule Aygoren Carranza, Editor
Paul Bubny, Managing Editor
Alexa Faulkner, Circulation
The one source for market intelligence and business generation.
Frequency: Monthly
Circulation: 53821
Founded in: 1940

21203 Real Estate Review
Thomson Reuters
195 Broadway
Suite 4
New York, NY 10007-3124
646-822-2000
800-231-1860; *Fax:* 646-822-2800
trta.lei-support@thomsonreuters.com;
www.ria.thomsonreuters.com
Elaine Yadlon, Plant Manager
Thomas H Glocer, CEO & Director
Robert D Daleo, Chief Financial Officer
Kelli Crane, Senior Vice President & CIO
Information on financing, mortgage banking, investments, and related legal and tax issues, also covers US commercial, industrial and residential development.
Frequency: Quarterly
Circulation: 5,500

21204 Real Property, Property and Trust Journal
American Bar Association
321 N Clark St
Chicago, IL 60654-7598
312-988-5000
800-285-2221; *Fax:* 312-988-6281
askaba@abanet.org; www.abanet.org
Tommy H Wells Jr, President
Jennifer Collins, Advertising Sales Coordinator
Scholarly articles in the fields of estate planning, trust law and real property law.
Cost: $60.00
Frequency: Quarterly
Founded in: 1878

21205 Realtor Magazine
New York State Association of Realtors
430 N Michigan Avenue
Suite 430
Chicago, IL 60611-4087
800-874-6500; *Fax:* 312-329-5978
narpubs@realtors.org
realtormag.realtor.org
Stacey Mancrieff, Editor
Frank Sibley, Senior VP/Publisher
Christina H Spira, Managing Editor
Wanda Clark, Publications Assistant
Pamela G Kabati, Vice President / Editorial Director
The business tool for real estate professionals. The New York Report is given after page 8.
Cost: $56.00
70 Pages
Frequency: Monthly
ISSN: 1522-0842
Founded in: 1908
Printed in 4 colors on glossy stock

21206 Rental Management
1900 19th Street
Moline, IL 61265-4179
309-764-2475
800-334-2177; *Fax:* 309-764-1533;
www.ararental.org
Chris Wehrman, Executive VP
Joe Lynch, Deputy Executive VP
A monthly magazine published by the American Rental Association
Frequency: Monthly
Circulation: 18000

21207 Residential Specialist
430 N Michigan Ave
Suite 3
Chicago, IL 60611-4011
312-828-9129; *Fax:* 312-329-8882
info@crs.com; www.crs.com
Nina Cottrell, CEO
Eric Berkland, Director Marketing
Carol Raabe, Vice President of Operations
Carlee Londo, Marketing Manager
Richard Lawson, Director of Products

Published by the Council of Residential Specialists.
Cost: $29.95
64 Pages
Circulation: 40000
Founded in: 1976

21208 Site Selection Magazine
Conway Data
6625 the Corners Pkwy
Suite 200
Peachtree Corners, GA 30092-3334
770-446-6996; *Fax:* 770-263-8825;
www.conway.com
Adam Jones-Kelley, Managing Director
Loura Lyne, President
Julie Clark, Circulation Manager
Focus is on political, international and quality of life issues, also provides development groups, business parks, labor factors, relevant technology, real estate and finance information.
Cost: $90.00
Frequency: Monthly
Circulation: 45000
Founded in: 1954

21209 Timeshare Business
RCI
PO Box 80229
Indianapolis, IN 46280-0229
317-805-9000; *Fax:* 317-805-9618
alyssa.chase@rci.com; www.rci.com
Alyssa Chase, Editor
Nicole keller, Senior Associate Editor
Rita Corea, Circulation Manager
Magazine for resort developers, property managers, sales and marketing professionals, homeowners association boards, and other key personnel in the timeshare industry.
42 Pages
Frequency: Monthly
Circulation: 35000
ISSN: 1099-6753
Founded in: 1974
Printed in 4 colors on 6 stock

21210 US Sites & Development
Vulcan Publications
PO Box 12846
Birmingham, AL 35202-2846
205-328-6198; www.vulcanpub.com
Val Carrier, Publisher
Includes tax laws, real estate trends, as well as labor and work force issues.

21211 Unique Homes
327 Wall St
Princeton, NJ 08540-1518
609-688-1110
877-688-1110; *Fax:* 609-688-0201
krussell@uniquehomes.com;
www.uniquehomes.com
Kathleen Carlin-Russell, Manager
Lauren Baier Kim, Managing Editor
Cheryl Jock, Production Manager
Robert Burke, Custom Publishing Manager
Cost: $24.97
Circulation: 54,856
Founded in: 1978

21212 Units Magazine
National Apartment Association
4300 Wilson Boulevard
Siote 400
Arlington, VA 22203
703-518-6141; *Fax:* 703-248-9440
webmaster@naahq.org; www.naahq.org
Doug Culkin, President
Paul Bergeron, Communications Director
Contains news and information essential to all facets of the apartment industry-with a focus eacho month on managemetn, marketing, maintenance and politics.
Cost: $99.00
80 Pages
Frequency: Monthly
Circulation: 80,000
Printed in on glossy stock

21213 Vacation Industry Review
Interval International
PO Box 431920
Miami, FL 33243-1920
305-666-1861; *Fax:* 305-663-2227;
www.resortdeveloper.com
Craig M Nash, CEO
Alina Betancourt, Account Executive
Ximena Villegas, Account Executive
Vacation Industry Review is a quarterly trade publication covering the global timeshare, fractional, vacation ownership resort industry. It discusses industry issues and trends and showcases new resort developments and key markets. It also covers products and services of interest to the industry, and the activities of prominent individuals and companies.
48/64 Pages
Frequency: Quarterly
Circulation: 28,000
Founded in: 1984
Printed in 4 colors on glossy stock

21214 Vacation Ownership World
CHB Company
8701 Collins Ave Ph
Miami, Fl 33154
305-864-6083; *Fax:* 305-864-6085;
www.vomagazine.com
Jon Paulisin, Publisher/President
Lou Skidmore, Editor
Howard White, Circulation Manager
News and feature stories, in depth analysis of the issues and trends affecting the industry of global timesharing.
Founded in: 1984

21215 Valuation Insights & Perspectives
Appraisal Institute
550 W Van Buren St
Suite 1000
Chicago, IL 60607-3850
312-335-4100; *Fax:* 312-335-4400
puborders@appraisalinstitute.org;
www.appraisalinstitute.org
Fred Grubbe, CEO
Larisa Phillips, President
Offers a collection of high interest articles, and features industry and institute news section and columns on legal matters, technology, marketing and timely appraisal issues.
Cost: $48.00
18 Pages
Frequency: Quarterly
Circulation: 82000
Founded in: 1996
Printed in 4 colors on glossy stock

Trade Shows

21216 American Congress on Surveying & Mapping Annual Conference
6 Montgomery Village Avenue
Suite 403
Gaithersburg, MD 20879
240-680-0765; *Fax:* 240-632-1321
curtis.sumner@acsm.net; www.acsm.net
Curt Sumner, Executive Director
Ilse Genovese, Communications Director
Bob Jupin, Accounting Manager
One hundred and thirty exhibits of industry related equipment, supplies and services plus workshop and conference.
2000 Attendees
Frequency: Annual
Founded in: 1954

21217 American Land Tree Association Annual Convention
1828 L Street NW
Suite 705
Washington, DC 20036-5104
202-296-3671
http://www.alta.org
James Maher, VP
1M Attendees
Frequency: October

21218 American Real Estate Society Annual Meeting
American Real Estate Society
Cleveland State University-BU327
Dept. Finance, Business College
Cleveland, OH 44114
216-687-4732; *Fax:* 216-687-9331;
www.aresnet.org
Annual meeting and 10 exhibitors that are publishers, data providers, technical foundtions. Exhibits relate to decision-making within real estate finance, real estate market analysis, investment, valuation, development and other areas related to real estate.
300 Attendees
Frequency: April

21219 American Society of Appraisers International Appraisal Conference
11107 Sunset Hills Rd
Suite 310
Reston, VA 20190
703-478-2228
800-272-8258; *Fax:* 703-742-8471
asainfo@appraisers.org; www.appraisers.org
Social Media: Facebook, Twitter, LinkedIn, YouTube
Jane Grimm, Executive VP
Susan Fischer, Governance Manager
Jack Washbourn, President
Exhibits for professional appraisers.
5000 Members
Frequency: Annual
Founded in: 1936

21220 Apartment Association of Greater Dallas Annual Trade Show
4230 LBJ Freeway
Suite 140
Dallas, TX 75244
972-385-9091; *Fax:* 972-385-9412
pkelley@aagdallas.com; www.aagdallas.com
Paula Kelley CMP, Director of Events
Gerry Henigsman, Executive Assistant
Marsha Stephenson, Executive Assistant

Bradley Elliott, Director of Communications
Donna Derden, Vice President

Tours and 240 displays of industry related supplies and services.
3000 Attendees
Frequency: April
Founded in: 1963

21221 Apartment Association of Metro Denver Educational Expo and Trade Show
650 S Cherry Street
Suite 635
Denver, CO 80246
303-290-0403; *Fax:* 303-329-0403
Mark Williams, Executive Director
Seminar, reception and 142 exhibits of property management equipment, supplies, services and information.
1500 Attendees
Frequency: Annual

21222 BOMA Winter Business Meeting & Leadership Conference
Building Owners & Managers Association Int'l
1201 New York Avenue NW
Suite 300
Washington, DC 20005
202-408-2662; *Fax:* 202-371-0181
info@boma.org; www.boma.org
Henry Chamberlain, President/CEO
Laura Best, Conference Director
Opportunity for business professionals to discuss problems, security, exchange ideas and share experience and knowledge.
Frequency: January

21223 BUILDINGS-New York
Reed Exhibition Companies
383 Main Avenue
Norwalk, CT 06851-1543
203-840-4800; *Fax:* 203-840-9570
Annual show of 425 exhibitors of products and services for the building owner, developer, manager, co-ops and superintendents in the commercial and residential real estate market, including asbestos abatement, waterproofing, restoration, financial services, utilities, laundry equipment, cleaning services, computer software, elevators, heating and air conditioning, light safety/security, renovation and restoration.
9,000 Attendees

21224 Coldwell Bankers Annual National Show
27271 Las Ramblas
Mission Viejo, CA 92691-6386
949-673-3650; *Fax:* 973-496-5784
Sandra Deering, Manager
Seventy-five booths.
4.5M Attendees

21225 MIPIM
Reed Exhibition Companies
255 Washington Street
Newton, MA 02458-1637
617-584-4900; *Fax:* 617-630-2222
Elizabeth Hitchcock, International Sales
International property market conference.
4M Attendees
Frequency: March

21226 National Association of Realtors Meetings and Trade Show
430 N Michigan Avenue
Chicago, IL 60611-4087
312-645-7730
800-874-6500
infocentral@realtors.org; www.realtor.org
Karen Crafton, Convention Executive Secretary
Sue Gourley, Conventions VP
Terrence McDermott, CEO
Bill Armstrong, Treasurer
Seminars and networking, plus updates in the industry. More than 200 exhibiting companies.
6500 Attendees
Frequency: May

21227 National Association of Realtors Trade Exposition
National Association of Realtors
430 N Michigan Avenue
Chicago, IL 60611-4002
312-645-7730; *Fax:* 312-329-8882
info@crs.com; www.crs.com
Sara Patterson, Director Communications
Terrence McDermott, Vice President
Ron Canning, Vice President
Spring show of 250 exhibitors of real estate industry equipment, supplies and services, including hardware and software, marketing programs, office products, mortgage and financial services and insurance.
40000 Attendees
Founded in: 1976

21228 Old House New House Home Show
4051 E Main Street
St Charles, IL
630-515-1160
kp@corecomm.net; www.kennedyproductions.com
Social Media: Facebook
Beth Wall, Contact
Discover the latest innovations, seeing creative solutions and gathering the motivation to tackle home improvement projects.
Frequency: Sept/Oct Illinois

21229 Real Show
Journal of Property Management
430 N Michigan Avenue
Chicago, IL 60611-4002
312-329-6064; *Fax:* 312-329-8882
info@crs.com; www.crs.com
Sara Patterson, Director Communications
Ron Canning, Vice President
A trade show with 275 exhibitors and 450 booths, for professional owners and managers of investment residential and commercial property.
40000 Attendees
Founded in: 1976

21230 Realmart
National Association of Industrial & Office Prop.
Woodlyn Park-2201 Coop. Way
Herndon, VA 22071
703-267-6665; *Fax:* 703-904-7974
garvin@naiop.org
Annual show of 100 suppliers of companies catering to the commercial real estate industry.
1,000 Attendees

21231 Realtors Conference & Expo
National Association of Realtors
430 North Michigan Ave.
Chicago, IL 60611
800-874-6500
convinfo@realtors.org; www.realtor.org/convention.nsf
Social Media: Facebook, Twitter, LinkedIn, YouTube
Dale Stinton, Chief Executive Officer
Chris Polychron, President
Networking, educational sessions on timely topics and a vendor expo.
Frequency: Annual

21232 SourceMedia Conferences & Events
SourceMedia
One State Street Plaza
27th floor
New York, NY 10004
212-803-6093
800-803-3424; *Fax:* 212-803-8515; www.sourcemedia.com/
James M Malkin, Chairman & CEO
William Johnson, CFO
Steve Andreazza, VP, Sales & Customer Service
Celie Baussan, SVP, Operations
Anne O'Brien, EVP Marketing & Strategic Planning
SourceMedia Conferences & Events attract over 20,000 attendees worldwide. The content embraces a variety of formats, including: conferences, executive roundtables, expositions, Web seminars, custom events and pod casts. With over 70 events annually, participants are provided with premier content as well as access to the industry's top solution providers. Markets served include: accounting; banking; capital markets; financial services; information technology; insurance; and real estate.
Mailing list available for rent

21233 Trade Expo
Professional Housing Management
PO Box 4251
Leesburg, VA 20177
703-327-6873
800-543-7188; *Fax:* 703-327-4005
phmainfo@earthlink.net; www.phma.com
Jon Moore, Director
Mona Pearson, Trade Expo Coordinator
At the expo there will be 230 booths with 150 exhibitors.
1,200 Attendees
Frequency: January

Directories & Databases

21234 America's Top-Rated Cities
Grey House Publishing
4919 Route 22
PO Box 56
Amenia, NY 12501
518-789-8700
800-562-2139; *Fax:* 518-789-0556
books@greyhouse.com; www.greyhouse.com
Social Media: Facebook, Twitter
Leslie Mackenzie, Publisher
Richard Gottlieb, Editor
Provides current, comprehensive statistical information in one easy-to-use source on the 100 top cities that have been cited as the best for business and living in the US. Available as a four volume set or individual volumes (Southern, Western, Central and Eastern)
Cost: $225.00
2000 Pages
ISBN: 1-592373-49-6
Founded in: 1981

21235 America's Top-Rated Smaller Cities
Grey House Publishing

4919 Route 22
PO Box 56
Amenia, NY 12501

518-789-8700
800-562-2139; *Fax:* 845-373-6390
books@greyhouse.com; www.greyhouse.com
Social Media: Facebook, Twitter

Leslie Mackenzie, Publisher
Richard Gottlieb, Editor

America's Top-Rated Smaller Cities provides current, comprehensive data on 110 US cities, all top-ranked by population growth, median income, unemployment rate and crime rate. This informative handbook allows readers to see, at a glance, a concise social, business, economic, demographic and environmental profile of each city, including brief evaluative comments.
Cost: $195.00
1800 Pages
ISBN: 1-592372-84-8
Founded in: 1981

21236 American Resort Development Association: Membership Directory
American Resort Development Association
1201 15th St Nw
Suite 400
Washington, DC 20005-2842

202-371-6700; *Fax:* 202-289-8544
hnusbaum@arda.org; www.ardafoundation.org

Howard Nusbaum, President
Lou Ann Burney, VP
Rob Dumm, Finance
Alexa Antonuk, Communications Manager

Over 800 member firms in the resort development industry, including developers, finance companies, architectural firms, audiovisual companies, direct mail companies, rental and vacation exchange companies and law firms.
Frequency: Annual Winter

21237 American Society of Appraisers Directory
American Society of Appraisers
11107 Sunset Hills Rd
Suite 310
Reston, VA 20190

703-478-2228
800-272-8258; *Fax:* 703-742-8471
asainfo@appraisers.org; www.appraisers.org
Social Media: Facebook, Twitter, LinkedIn, YouTube

Jane Grimm, Executive VP
Susan Fischer, Governance Manager
Jack Washbourn, President

Directory of association members who are accredited appraisers.
Cost: $12.50
5000 Members
Circulation: 8,000
Founded in: 1936

21238 Buyers Broker Registry
Who's Who in Creative Real Estate
PO Box 23275
Ventura, CA 93002-3275

Offers valuable information on over 650 real estate agents in the United States who have met performance requirements set by the publisher.
Cost: $25.00
136 Pages
Frequency: Annual

21239 CRB/CRS Referral Directory
Realtors National Marketing Institute
430 N Michigan Avenue
Suite 300
Chicago, IL 60611-4002

Fax: 312-329-8882
http://www.crs.com

Gwen Voelker, Editor

Aimed at the real estate industry, this directory lists over 32,000 real estate brokerage managers and residential sales specialists.
Cost: $45.00
776 Pages
Frequency: Annual
Circulation: 32,000

21240 CRE Member Directory
Counselors of Real Estate
430 N Michigan Ave
Chicago, IL 60611-4019

312-329-8427; *Fax:* 312-329-8881;
www.cre.org

Mary Fleischmann, President
Frequency: Annual March

21241 Commercial Investment Real Estate
CCIM Institute
430 N Michigan Ave
Chicago, IL 60611-4011

312-321-4460; *Fax:* 312-321-4530
magazine@ccim.com; www.ccim.com

Jonathan Falk, Manager
Ken Setlak, Chief Financial Officer
Sara Drummond, Executive Editor

Directory of services and supplies to the industry.
40000 Pages
Founded in: 1976

21242 Comparative Guide to American Suburbs
Grey House Publishing
4919 Route 22
PO Box 56
Amenia, NY 12501

518-789-8700
800-562-2139; *Fax:* 845-373-6390
books@greyhouse.com; www.greyhouse.com
Social Media: Facebook, Twitter

Leslie Mackenzie, Publisher
Richard Gottlieb, Editor

Covers statistics on the 2,000+ suburban communities surrounding the 60 largest metropolitan areas - their population characteristics, income levels, economy, school systems and important data on how they compare to one another.
Cost: $150.00
1000 Pages
ISBN: 1-592371-80-9
Founded in: 1981

21243 Crime in America's Top-Rated Cities
Grey House Publishing
4919 Route 22
PO Box 56
Amenia, NY 12501

518-789-8700
800-562-2139; *Fax:* 845-373-6390
books@greyhouse.com; www.greyhouse.com
Social Media: Facebook, Twitter

Leslie Mackenzie, Publisher
Richard Gottlieb, Editor

Details over twenty years of crime statistics in all major crime categories: violent crimes, property crimes and total crime. Conveniently arranged by city, it offers details that compare the number of crimes and crime rates for the city, suburbs and metro area with national crime trends for violent, property and total crimes. Statistics on anti-crime programs, crime risk, hate crimes, illegal drugs, law enforcement, correctional facilities, death penalty, laws and much more.
Cost: $155.00
839 Pages
ISBN: 1-891482-84-X
Founded in: 1981

21244 Crittenden's Real Estate Buyers Directory
Crittendon Research
250 Bel Marin Keys Boulevard
Novato, CA 94949-5727

415-382-2400
800-421-3483; *Fax:* 415-382-2476;
www.crittendenonline.com

John Goodwin, Editor/Publisher
Vitlario Laeson, Marketing Director
Pati Bess, Customer Service Director

A list of over 500 real estate buyers, including private institutional investors, banks, pension funds and real estate investment trusts.

21245 Crittendon Directory of Real Estate Financing
Crittendon Research
250 Bel Marin Keys Boulevard
Novato, CA 94949-5727

415-382-7790; *Fax:* 415-382-2476

Listing of over 400 major lenders, investors and joint ventures enagged in commercial and residential real estate financing and investing.
Cost: $387.00
500 Pages
Frequency: Semiannual

21246 DAMAR Real Estate Information Service Online Database
3550 W Temple Street
Los Angeles, CA 90004-3620

800-873-2627

This comprehensive database offers real estate information, with an emphasis on California.
Frequency: Full-text

21247 Directory of 2,500 Active Real Estate Lenders
International Wealth Success
PO Box 186
Merrick, NY 11566-0186
516-766-5850
800-323-0548; *Fax:* 516-766-5919
admin@iwsmoney.com; www.iwsmoney.com

Tyler G Hicks, President
Lists 2,500 names and addresses of direct lenders or sources of information on possible lenders for real estate.
Cost: $25.00
197 Pages
Frequency: Annually
ISBN: 1-561503-37-1
Founded in: 1985

21248 Directory of Accredited Real Property Appraisers
American Society of Appraisers
PO Box 17265
Washington, DC 20041-7265

202-337-0037
800-272-8258; *Fax:* 202-742-8471

Rebecca Ewing, Publication Manager

Approximately 1,700 urban, residential, rural, ad valorem and timberland appraisers; limited international coverage.
Frequency: Annual January

21249 Directory of Professional Appraisal Services
American Society of Appraisers

PO Box 17265
Washington, DC 20041-7265

202-337-0037
800-272-8258; *Fax:* 202-742-8471
asainfo@appraisers.org; www.appraisers.org

Rebecca Ewing, Publisher/Editor

Over 3,000 tested and accredited members appraisers of real and personal property, businesses, machinery and equipment are listed.
Cost: $10.00
275 Pages
Frequency: Annual
Circulation: 8,000

21250 Directory of Real Estate Development and Related Education Programs
Urban Land Institute
625 Indiana Avenue NW
Suite 400
Washington, DC 20004-2923

202-247-7116

Over 60 programs are profiled that are currently being offered at colleges and universities in the area of real estate.
Cost: $19.00
132 Pages
Frequency: Biennial

21251 ERC Directory of Real Estate Appraisers and Brokers
Employee Relocation Council
1720 N Street NW
Washington, DC 20036-2900

202-857-0857

Tina Lung, Editor
Cost: $35.00
1,100 Pages
Frequency: Annual

21252 European Investment in United States Real Estate
Mead Ventures
PO Box 44952
Phoenix, AZ 85064-4952

Investors, developers and brokers located in Europe are the focus of this valuable directory.
Cost: $195.00
406 Pages
Frequency: Annual

21253 Executive Guide to Specialists in Industrial and Office Real Estate
Society of Industrial & Office Realtors
1201 New York Ave NW
Suite 350
Washington, DC 20005-6126

202-449-8200; *Fax:* 202-216-9325
admin@sior.com; www.sior.com

Richard Hollander, Executive VP
Craig S Meyer, President

Thousands of specialists are listed that are integrated with industrial real estate and related industries.
Cost: $60.00
210 Pages
Frequency: Annual

21254 FDIC: Investment Properties Publication
Federal Deposit Insurance Corporation
550 17th St Nw
Washington, DC 20429-0002

202-000-1111; *Fax:* 202-898-8595

Mitchell L Glassman, Plant Manager

Offers information on properties owned by the Federal Deposit Insurance Corporation, including land, commercial real estate, multifamily dwellings and hotels and motels.
200 Pages
Frequency: Quarterly

21255 Guide to Real Estate and Mortgage Banking Software
Real Estate Solutions
2609 Klingle Road NW
Washington, DC 20008-1202

202-362-9854

Lists approximately 500 real estate and mortgage banking computer software, hardware and products.
Cost: $49.95
640 Pages
Frequency: Biennial

21256 Income & Cost for Organization & Servicing of 1-4 Unit Residential Loans
Mortgage Bankers Association of America
1919 Pennsylvania Avenue NW
Washington, DC 20006-3404

202-557-2700
membership@mortgagebankers.org;
www.mortgagebankers.org

Annual report provides data and analysis on the income and expenses associated with the organization, warehousing, marketing and servicing or one-to-four-unit residential marketing loans.
80 Pages
Frequency: $150 Member/$300 Non

21257 Japanese Investment in US Real Estate Review
Mead Ventures
PO Box 44952
Phoenix, AZ 85064-4952

Fax: 602-234-0076

This is a complete database listing documenting Japanese purchases of US golf courses, houses, office buildings and industrial properties.
Frequency: Full-text

21258 Journal of the American Society of Farm Managers and Rural Appraisers
ASFMRA
950 S Cherry St
Suite 508
Denver, CO 80246-2664

303-758-3513; *Fax:* 303-758-0190
asfmra@agri-associations.org;
www.asfmra.org

Cheryl L Cooley, Manager Communications/PR
Mailing list available for rent: 2500 names at $1M per M

21259 Major Cities Canada
Grey House Publishing
4919 Route 22
PO Box 56
Amenia, NY 12501

800-562-2139; *Fax:* 845-373-6390; *Fax:* new;
www.greyhouse.ca

Richard Gottlieb, President

Provides an in-depth comparison and analysis of the 50 most populated cities in Canada. Split into 4 major categories; background, study rankings, development offices, and statistical tables
Cost: $180.00
793 Pages

21260 Million Dollar Guide to Business and Real Estate Loan Sources
International Wealth Success
PO Box 186
Merrick, NY 11566-0186

516-766-5850
800-323-0548; *Fax:* 516-766-5919
admin@iwsmoney.com; www.iwsmoney.com

Tyler G Hicks, President

Lists hundreds of business and real estate lenders, giving their lending data in very brief form.
Cost: $25.00
201 Pages
Frequency: Annually
Founded in: 1990

21261 Monthly Resort Real Estate Property Index
MDR Telecom
4742 La Villa Marina
Unit A
Marina Del Rey, CA 90292-7086

Mario Collura, Editor

Offers information on resort timeshares and resort condominiums for rent or sale.
Cost: $10.00
80 Pages
Frequency: Monthly

21262 Mortgage Banking Performance Report
Mortgage Bankers Association of America
1919 Pennsylvania Avenue NW
Washington, DC 20006-3404

202-557-2700
membership@mortgagebankers.org;
www.mortgagebankers.org

The report includes an annual summary, is a financial statement analysis of mortgage banking company performance.
80 Pages
Frequency: $125 Member/$175 Non
Founded in: 1992

21263 Mortgage Banking Sourcebook
Mortgage Bankers Association of America
1919 Pennsylvania Avenue NW
Washington, DC 20006-3404

202-557-2700
membership@mortgagebankers.org;
www.mortgagebankers.org

Comprehensive directory to federal and state government agencies, industry trade associations colleges and universities, and other organizations and sources of information on mortgage lending, Includes an entire network of industry contact complete with addresses, telephone and fax numbers and internet website addresses.
Cost: $40.00
144 Pages
Founded in: 1997

21264 Mortgage Finance Database
Mortgage Bankers Association of America
1919 Pennsylvania Avenue NW
Washington, DC 20006-3404

202-557-2700; www.mortgagebankers.com

This database contains the most comprehensive and up-to-date collection of mortgage-related variables currently available.

21265 National Association of Independent Fee Appraisers: Membership Directory
National Association of Independent Fee Appraisers
7501 Murdoch Avenue
Saint Louis, MO 63119-2810

314-645-7583; *Fax:* 314-781-2872

Donna Walters, Publications

Five thousand and five hundred independent real estate appraisers.
Frequency: Annual January

21266 **National Association of Master Appraisers Membership Directory**
National Association of Master Appraisers
303 W Cypress St
San Antonio, TX 78212-5512

210-271-0781
800-229-6262; *Fax:* 210-225-8450;
www.masterappraisers.org

Del Martinez, Manager
Christopher Deane, Marketing And Production Manager

Approximately 3,500 real estate appraisers.
Frequency: Annual January
Circulation: 3,500

21267 **National Association of Real Estate Appraisers**
P.O. Box 879
Palm Springs, CA 92263

76- 32- 528
877-815-4172; *Fax:* 760-327-5631
info@narea-assoc.org; www.narea-assoc.org

Dallas Martin, President

A complete guide to the REIT industry with approximately 240 real estate investment trusts, and over 1,000 associate members listed.
Cost: $695.00
600 Pages
Frequency: Annual

21268 **National Association of Real Estate Companies: Membership Directory**
National Association of Real Estate Companies
216 W Jackson Blvd
Suite 625
Chicago, IL 60606-6945

312-263-1755; *Fax:* 312-750-1203
info@narec.org; www.narec.org

Kim Klein, Administrator

About 200 real estate development companies.
Frequency: Quarterly

21269 **National Directory of Exchange Groups**
Creative Real Estate Magazine
PO Box L
Rancho Santa Fe, CA 92067-0560

858-756-1441; *Fax:* 818-156-1111

Lists over 125 professional real estate marketing groups practicing tax-deferred real estate exchanges.
Cost: $72.00
48 Pages
Frequency: Monthly
Circulation: 51,000
ISBN: 0-194722-2 -

21270 **National Real Estate Directory**
Real Estate Publishing Company
P.O. Box 180635
Coronado, CA 92118

866-431-5223; *Fax:* 619-615-2350;
www.national-real-estate-directory.com

Over 22,000 federal and state agencies, offices and departments related to the regulation of real estate, real estate associations and publications are listed.
Cost: $29.95
110 Pages
Frequency: Biennial

21271 **National Real Estate Investor Sourcebook**
Primedia
5680 Greenwood Plaza Boulevard
Suite 300
Greenwood Village, CO 80111

303-741-2901; *Fax:* 720-489-3101;
www.primediabusiness.com

Barbara Katinsky, Editor

List of about 7,000 companies and individuals in 18 real estate fields.
Cost: $78.95
Frequency: Annual, September
Circulation: 33,000

21272 **National Referral Roster**
Candy Holub
615 5th Street SE
Cedar Rapids, IA 52401-2158

319-364-6167
800-553-8878; *Fax:* 319-369-0029;
www.roster.com

Candy Holub, Publisher
Mary Richeson, Business Developer
Joey Grim, Business Developer

Approximately 90,000 Real Estate offices nationwide. Provides an effective, comprehensive and easy-to-use tool for realtors to make successful referrals to other relators nationwide.
Cost: $95.00
936 Pages
Frequency: Annual
Circulation: 18,000
ISSN: 1075-1084
Founded in: 1923
Printed in 2 colors on newsprint stock

21273 **National Toll-Free 800 Guide to Real Estate Publications and Publishers**
Real Estate Publishing Company
4580 Brookside Rd
Cameron Park, CA 95682-9619

530-677-3864

Joe Wgle, President

Directory of publications to the industry.
Cost: $15.95
82 Pages
Frequency: Biennial

21274 **Nelson's Directory of Institutional Real Estate**
Nelson Publications
2500 Tamiami Trl N
Nokomis, FL 34275-3476

941-966-9521; *Fax:* 941-966-2590;
www.healthmgttech.com

A Verner Nelson, Owner
Marcia Boysen, Editor

Institutional investors who invest in real estate: investment managers, real estate service firms, insurance companies, plan sponsors, corporations and REIT's.
Cost: $335.00
Frequency: Annual August

21275 **One List Directory**
MRH Associates
365 Willard Avenue
Suite 2K
Newington, CT 06111-2373

800-727-5478

Over 700 companies and 6,000 company divisions are involved as listees in this comprehensive directory. Included is a section of over 12,000 contact personnel in the real estate and construction industry.
Cost: $545.00
750 Pages
Frequency: Annual

21276 **Professional Relocation and Real Estate Services Directory**
Relocation Information Service
113 Post Road E
2nd Floor
Westport, CT 06880-3410

203-256-1079; *Fax:* 203-227-3800

Offers over 6,000 real estate brokerage companies, appraisal firms, home inspectors and services companies.
Cost: $95.00
800 Pages
Frequency: Annual
Circulation: 35,000

21277 **Profiles of America**
Grey House Publishing
4919 Route 22
PO Box 56
Amenia, NY 12501

518-789-8700
800-562-2139; *Fax:* 845-373-6390
books@greyhouse.com; www.greyhouse.com
Social Media: Facebook, Twitter

Leslie Mackenzie, Publisher
Richard Gottlieb, Editor

This four volume set details over 40,000 places, from the biggest metropolis to the smallest unincorporated hamlet and provides statistical details and information on over 50 different topics including: geography, climate, population, economy, income, taxes, education, housing, health and environment, public safety, transportation, presidential election results and more.
Cost: $795.00
10000 Pages
ISBN: 1-891482-80-7

21278 **Profiles of...Series - State Handbooks**
Grey House Publishing
4919 Route 22
PO Box 56
Amenia, NY 12501

518-789-8700
800-562-2139; *Fax:* 845-373-6390
books@greyhouse.com; www.greyhouse.com
Social Media: Facebook, Twitter

Leslie Mackenzie, Publisher
Richard Gottlieb, Editor

Each state-by-state volume in this new series provides at-a-glance detailed demographic and statistical data on every populated place in the state, along with easy-to-use comparative rankings. Series includes 20 states. Additional states added each year.
Founded in: 1981

21279 **Real Estate & Land Use Regulation in Eastern and Central Europe**
WorldTrade Executive
PO Box 761
Concord, MA 01742-0761

978-287-0301; *Fax:* 978-287-0302;
www.wtexec.com

Alison French, Production Manager

Topics covered include: leasing in Russia: helpful hints for tenants; a guide to government agencies regulating development in Moscow and St. Petersburg; current law and practice for the Russian real estate market; the real estate lease in the Czech Republic; environmental considerations for acquisition of property in Hungary.
Cost: $135.00

21280 **Real Estate Books and Periodicals in Print**
Real Estate Publishing Company

PO Box 41177
Sacramento, CA 95841-0177

530-677-3864

John Johnsich, Publisher

Over 400 publishers of real estate books and periodicals and their product lines are profiled in this directory.
Cost: $29.95
256 Pages
Frequency: Annual
ISBN: 0-914256-33-5
Founded in: 1975

21281 Real Estate Data
DataQuick Information Systems
9620 Towne Centre Dr
San Diego, CA 92121-1963

858-455-6900
800-863-INFO; *Fax:* 858-455-7848
customercare@dataquick.com;
www.dataquick.com

Sara Stephenson, Marketing

More than 12 million developed and undeveloped real properties in California, Arizona, Nevada, Oregon and Washington.
Frequency: Daily

21282 Real Estate RoundTable
GE Information Services
801 Pennsylvania Ave
NW Suite 720
Washing, DC 20004

202-639-8400; *Fax:* 202-639-8442
info@rer.org; www.rer.org

Cathy Ge, Owner
Clifton Rodgers, Senior Vice President

This database provides a forum for discussions between professional realtors and individuals interested in the buying and selling of residential and commercial property.
Frequency: Bulletin Board

21283 Real Estate Software Directory and Catalog
Z-Law Software
PO Box 40602
Providence, RI 02940-0602

401-273-5588
800-526-5588; *Fax:* 401-421-5334;
www.z-law.com
Social Media: Facebook

Gary L Sherman, President

A comprehensive guide to real estate and mortgage banking software. Includes IBM and MAC applications for realtors, landlords, property managers, investors, developers, attorneys, contractors, appraisers, loan agents, and anyone in real estate.
Frequency: SemiAnnual

21284 Timeshare Multiple Listing Service
MDR Telecom
11965 Venice Boulevard
Suite 204
Los Angeles, CA 90066-3954

323-539-9701
800-423-6377; *Fax:* 310-915-7212
triwest@att.net; www.triwest-timeshare.com

Mario A Collura, Production Manager
Mario A Collura, Author

Approximately 6,000 pieces of timeshare real estate in the US, Mexico, and Carribean.
Cost: $10.00
60 Pages
Frequency: Monthly
ISBN: 1-888176-11-3
Founded in: 1984

21285 Timeshare Vacation Owners HIP Resort Directory
TRI Publishing
11965 Venice Boulevard
Suite 204
Los Angeles, CA 90066-3954
800-423-6377; *Fax:* 310-915-7212;
www.triwest-timeshare.com

Mario A Collura, President
Viccie Mac, Managing Editor

This is the only combined resort directory for buyers, owners and industry professionals. Over 3,000 resorts.
Cost: $18.95
111 Pages
Frequency: Every 2 Years
ISBN: 1-888176-12-1
Founded in: 1995

21286 US Real Estate Register
Barry
312 Main St
Wilmington, MA 01887-2791

978-658-7174

Joe Barry, Owner

Offers information on real estate departments of large national companies, industrial organizations and chambers of commerce involved in real estate development.
Cost: $58.00
575 Pages
Frequency: Annual

21287 United National Real Estate Catalog
United National Real Estate
4700 Belleview Avenue
Kansas City, MO 64112-1315

816-561-1115
800-999-1020; *Fax:* 816-231-5599

James Marinovich

Offers information on several thousand farms, ranches and country estates.
Cost: $4.95
200 Pages
Frequency: Semiannual

21288 Who's Who in Luxury Real Estate
JBL
2110 Western Avenue
Seattle, WA 98121-2110

206-441-7900
800-488-4066; *Fax:* 206-441-5297

Approximately 500 international luxury real estate brokers.
Cost: $19.95
Frequency: Annual

Industry Web Sites

21289 http://gold.greyhouse.com
G.O.L.D Grey House OnLine Databases

Grey House Publishing's online database platform, GOLD, offers Quick Search, Keyword Search and Expert Search for most business sectors including real estate and allied markets. The GOLD platform makes finding the information you need quick and easy - whether you're a novice searcher or an experienced database user. All of Grey House's directory products are available for subscription on the GOLD platform.

21290 www.aagdallas.com
Apartment Association of Greater Dallas

21291 www.airea.com
American Industrial Real Estate Association

Encourages high professional standards. Has developed industrial multiple listing system and standard lease form. Publishes a quarterly newsletter

21292 www.americanhomeowners.org
American Homeowners Foundation

Serves as an educational and research consumer group offering books, model contracts, special studies, home buying, selling,investing, building, financing and remodeling.

21293 www.appraisalinstitute.org
Appraisal Institute

Promotes a code of ethics and uniform standards of the real estate appraisal practice. Publishes periodicals, books and appraisal-related materials, and sponsors courses and seminars.

21294 www.appraisers.org
American Society of Appraisers

Professional association of appraisers of all kinds.

21295 www.areuea.org
American Real Estate and Urban Economics Assoc

Addresses academic and commercial concerns in real estate and commercial economics.

21296 www.asfmra.org
American Soc of Farm Managers and Rural Appraisers

Provides professionals involved in rural property issues such as management and appraisal, with information on the industry as well as educational opportunities. Includes membership and information from the American Society of Farm Manager and Rural Appraisers.

21297 www.commercialsources.com

The official commercial real state site of the National Association Of Realtors.

21298 www.crb.com
Council of Real Estate Brokerage Managers

Members are real estate firm owners and managers.

21299 www.cre.org
Couselors of Real Estate

Association members provide the public with expert, objective advice on property and land related matters. Individuals invited to join are awarded the CRE designation.

21300 www.creonline.com
6440 Sky Pointe Dr.
Suite 140-187
Las Vegas, NV 89131

810-793-0261; www.creonline.com
Social Media: Facebook, Twitter, LinkedIn

Jeanne Ekhaml, Operations

State-by-state and county-by-county listing of real estate investment clubs.

21301 www.erc.org
Employee Relocation Council

A national organization that examines key issues affecting the relocation industry for the benefit of corporations, government agencies, and firms or individuals providing specific services to relocated employees and their families. Accepts advertising.

21302 www.fiabci-usa.com
FIABCI-USA

Encourages private ownership of real property and understanding of property rights and obligations.

21303 www.greyhouse.com
Grey House Publishing

Authoritative reference directories for most business sectors including real estate and allied markets. Users can search the online databases with varied search criteria allowing for custom searches by product category, geographic area, sales volume, keyword, subject and more. Full Grey House catalog and online ordering also available.

21304 www.homestore.com

Homestore.com's family of sites is the leading destination for the home and the real estate- related information on the Internet. Provides informatin on Finance and Insurance, Home Improvement, Decorating, Lawn and garden, Home Electronics amd more.

21305 www.iaia.org
International Association for Impact Assessment

IAIA provides a forum for the exchange of the ideas and experiences to stimulate innovation in assessing, managing and mitigating the consequences of development.

21306 www.icsc.org
International Council of Shopping Centers

Fosters professional standards of performance in the development, construction, financing, leasing, management and operation of shopping centers throughout the world.

21307 www.nahma.org
National Affordable Housing Management Association

Trade association representing companies and individuals involved in the management of affordable multifamily housing.

21308 www.npma.org
National Property Management Association

Represents asset management professionals and keeps members a breast of trends in asset accountability technologies. Sponsors seminars, training courses: certification program.

21309 www.realtor.com
National Association of Realtors

Seeks to establish cooperation among brokers engaged in buying, selling, trading and leasing for realestate.

21310 www.realtylocator.com
Realty Locator

Over 100,000 real estate links nationwide in 10,000 cities and towns in all 50 states.

21311 www.reea.org
Real Estate Educators Association

Individuals involved in training and education.

21312 www.reipa.com
Real Estate Information Providers Association

Supports professional information providers in the real estate industry.

21313 www.relibrary.com/index.html
Real Estate Library

Contains essential resources for buyers, sellers, home owners and real estate professionals.

21314 www.rfpi.com/wrai.htm
National Residential Appraisers Institute

Promotes professionalism in the evaluation of residential real estate and requires demonstration appraisals and testing for professional certification.

Associations

21315 American Bakers Association
601 Pennsylvania Ave., NW
Suite 230
Washington, DC 20004

202-789-0300; *Fax:* 202-898-1164
info@americanbakers.org
americanbakers.org
Social Media: Twitter, LinkedIn, YouTube, RSS

Rich Scalise, Chairman
Fred Penny, First Vice Chairman
Bradley K. Alexander, Second Vice Chairman
Robb MacKie, President/ CEO
Erin Sharp, Treasurer

Represents the interests of bakers.
Founded in: 1897

21316 American Bakers Institute
1300 I St Nw
Suite 700W
Washington, DC 20005

202-789-0300; *Fax:* 202-898-1164
info@americanbakers.org;
www.americanbakers.org
Social Media: Twitter, LinkedIn, YouTube, RSS

Robb Mac Kie, President & CEO
James Hamilton, Counsel
Howard R. Alton, Chairman
Lee Sanders, Secretary
Albert Lepage, Treasurer

Association comprised of wholesale bakers.
300 Members
Founded in: 1897

21317 American Culinary Federation
180 Center Place Way
St. Augustine, FL 32095

800-624-9458; *Fax:* 904-940-0741
acf@acfchefs.net; www.acfchefs.org
Social Media: Facebook, Twitter, LinkedIn, RSS, Flickr

Thomas J. Macrina, President
Michael Ty, Immediate Past President
William Tillinghast, Treasurer
Kyle Richardson, Secretary
Brian A. Hardy, Vice President, Central Region

Professional chefs' organization.
Founded in: 1929

21318 American Culinary Federation: Chef & Child Foundation
180 Center Place Way
St Augustine, FL 32095

904-824-4468
800-624-9458; *Fax:* 904-825-4758
acf@acfchefs.net; www.acfchefs.org
Social Media: Facebook, Twitter, Flickr, RSS

Heidi Cramb, Executive Director
Thomas J. Macrina, Presiednt
James Taylor, Secretary
William Tillinghast, Treasurer
Michael Ty, Immediate Past President

Seeks to teach children proper nutrition and feed hungry children in the US.
20000 Members
Founded in: 1929

21319 American Hotel and Lodging Association
1250 I Street, NW
Suite 1100
Washington, DC 20005

202-289-3100; *Fax:* 202-289-3199
eiinfo@ahla.com; www.ahla.com
Social Media: Facebook, Twitter, LinkedIn

Jim Abrahamson, Chair
Mark Carrier, Vice Chair
Geoff Ballotti, Secretary/ Treasurer
Katherine Lugar, President/ CEO
Joori Jeon, Executive Vice President & CFO

Organization focused on the needs of every aspect of the lodging industry.

21320 American Institute of Baking
1213 Bakers Way
Manhattan, KS 66505-3999

785-537-4750
800-633-5137; *Fax:* 785-537-1493
sales@aibonline.org; www.aibonline.org
Social Media: Facebook, Twitter, LinkedIn

Andrew Biane, President, CEO
Susan Hancock, Vice President, Innovation
Maureen Olewnik, Senior Vice President
Doug Markham, Director, People Processes
Tom Ogle, Chief Financial Officer

Committed to protecting the safety of the food supply chain worldwide and providing high value technical programs.
Founded in: 1919

21321 American Institute of Wine and Food
P.O. Box 973
Belmont, CA 94002-0973

415-508-6790
info@aiwf.org; www.aiwf.org
Social Media: Facebook

Frank Giaimo, National Chair
Mary Chamberlin, National Vice Chair
Drew Jaglom, National Secretary
George Linn, National Treasurer
Joyce Kucharvy, Director

A nonprofit organization dedicated to advancing the understanding, appreciation and quality of wine and food.
6000+ Members
Founded in: 1981

21322 American Knife Manufacturers Association Association
30200 DetroitRd.
Westlake, OH 44145

440-899-0010; *Fax:* 440-892-1404;
www.americanknife.org
Social Media: Facebook, Twitter, LinkedIn, You Tube

J. Jeffery Wherry, Executive Director
Rick Joswick, VP
Alan Peppel, Treasurer
Bob Clemence, President
Gregory Borrosch, Associate Member Representative

The Corporation is organized and shall operate to promote the best interests of the machine knives and cutlery industry and its members.
23 Members
Founded in: 1951

21323 American Personal & Private Chef Associati on
4572 Delaware Street
San Diego, CA 92116

619-294-2436
800-644-8389
webmaster@personalchef.com;
www.personalchef.com
Social Media: Facebook, Twitter, LinkedIn, Pinterest

Candy Wallace, Founder, Executive Director

Organization for professional chefs.

21324 American Restaurant Association
PO Box 51482
Sarasota, FL 34232

941-379-2228
info@americanrestaurantassociation.com;
www.americanrestaurantassociation.com

Jerry Dalton, Vice President of Commodities

An organization for the entire restaurant business.
Founded in: 1996

21325 American Society of Baking
7809 N Chestnut Avenue
Kansas City, MO 64119

800-713-0462; *Fax:* 888-315-2612
info@asbe.org; www.asbe.org
Social Media: Facebook, Twitter, Google+

Ramon Rivera, Chairman
Mario Somoza, 1st Vice Chairman
Wendi Ebbing, 2nd Vice Chairman
Bill Zimmerman, 3rd Vice Chairman
Teresa Ruder, Secretary/ Treasurer

Promoting the advancement of baking science and technology through the exchange of information and interaction among baking industry professionals.
Founded in: 1924

21326 Association of Correctional Food Service Affiliates
PO Box 10065
Burbank, CA 91510

818-843-6608; *Fax:* 818-843-7423;
www.acfsa.org
Social Media: Facebook, Twitter, LinkedIn, Shutterfly

Laurie Maurino, President
Robin Sherman, Past President
Timothy Thielman, Vice President
Carlos Salazar Jr., VP Elect / Treasurer
Linda Mills, Secretary

An organization dedicated to advancing all aspects of food service in correctional facilities.
Founded in: 1969

21327 Commercial Food Equipment Service Association
3605 Centre Circle
Fort Mill, SC 29715

336-346-4700
336-346-4745; *Fax:* 336-346-4745
pault@cfesa.com; www.cfesa.com
Social Media: Facebook, LinkedIn, YouTube

Paul Toukatly, President
John Schwindt, Vice President
Gary Potvin, Vice President
Wayne Stoutner, Treasurer
David Hahn, Secretary

An organization for certified technicians servicing food equipment.
Founded in: 1963

21328 Cookie and Snack Bakers Association
7517 Winton Drive
Indianapolis, IN 46268

888-789-3090
casba.us

William H. Bennett, President
Kevin Boyle, Immediate Past President
Tom Lugar, Treasurer
Mike Kriegermeier, Secretary
Craig S. Parrish, Executive Director

An organization for cookie and snack bakers.
Founded in: 1970

21329 **Cookware Manufacturers Association**
PO Box 531335
Birmingham, AL 35253-1335

205-592-0389; *Fax:* 205-599-5598
hrushing@usit.net; www.cookware.org
Social Media: Facebook, Twitter, LinkedIn, Pinterest

Jay Zalinskas, President
Gene Karlson, VP
Hugh J Rushing, Executive VP

Represents manufactures of cookware and bakeware in the US and Canada. Publishes consumer guides to cookware and engineering standards for industry.
21 Members
Founded in: 1920

21330 **Council of State Restaurant Associations**
2055 L St. NW
Washington, DC 20036

202-973-5377
admin@staterestaurantassociations.org
staterestaurantassociations.org

Stan Harris, President
Adam Mills, Vice President
Lynn Minges, Secretary/Treasurer
Anuja Miner, Executive Vice President

The Council works to promote the success of State Restaurant Associations.
Founded in: 1914

21331 **Foodservice Consultants Society International**
P.O. Box 4961
Louisville, KY 40204

502-379-4122
Info@fcsi.org; www.fcsi.org
Social Media: Facebook, Twitter

Jonathan Doughty, President
James Petersen, FCSI, Treasurer/ Secretary
Toni Clarke, FCSI, Board of Director
William Taunton, FCSI, Board of Director
Martin Rahmann, FCSI, Board of Director

A foodservice association with members in over 30 countries.
1000+ Members
Founded in: 1955

21332 **Green Restaurant Association**
89 South Street
Suite 802
Boston, MA 2111

617-737-3344
info@dinegreen.com; www.dinegreen.com
Social Media: Facebook, Twitter

Nonprofit organization that provides information and resources for making aspects of restaurants more eco-friendly.
Founded in: 1990

21333 **Home Baking Association**
2931 SW Gainsboro Road
Topeka, KS

785-478-3283; *Fax:* 785-478-3024
hbapatton@aol.com; www.homebaking.org
Social Media: Facebook, Twitter, Flickr

Sam Garlow, President
Tom Payne, 1st Vice President
Eric Wall, 2nd Vice President

National organization promoting scratch baking education and practice.
Founded in: 1951

21334 **International Association of Culinary Professionals**
1221 Avenue of the Americas
42nd floor
New York, NY 10020

646-358-4957
866-358-4951; *Fax:* 866-358-2524
membership@iacp.com; www.iacp.com
Social Media: Facebook, Twitter, Vimeo, YouTube

Martha Holmberg, Chief Executive Officer
Shani Phelan, Member Programs & Operations
Margaret Crable, Communications & Marketing Manager
Glenn Mack, Chair

A not for profit organization whose members represent virtually every profession in the culinary universe: teachers, cooking school owners, caterers, writers, chefs, media cooking personalities, editors, publishers, food stylists, food photographers, restauranteurs, leaders of major food corporations and vintners. Literally a who's who of the food world. Founded in 1978.
3000 Members
Founded in: 1978

21335 **International Caterers Association**
3601 East Joppa Road
Baltimore, MD 21234

410-931-8100; *Fax:* 410-931-8111
paulak@clemonsmgmt.com
internationalcaterers.org
Social Media: Facebook, Twitter, Instagram

Robin Selden, President
Jennifer Perna, Immediate Past President
Frank Christian, Treasurer
Karen O'Connor, Treasurer
Paula Kreuzberg, Executive Director

Organization for catering professionals.

21336 **International Food Service Executives Association Headquarters**
4955 Miller Street
Suite 107
Wheat Ridge, CO 80033

702-838-8821
800-893-5499; *Fax:* 303-420-9579
ifseahqoffice@gmail.com; www.ifsea.com
Social Media: Facebook, Twitter, LinkedIn

Grant Thompson, Chairman of the Board
Edward Manley, President/COO
David Orosz, International Chairman of the Board
Gina Vance, International Chairman of the Board

Provides education and community service to the foodservice industry.
3,000 Members
Founded in: 1901

21337 **James Beard Foundation**
167 W 12th St
New York, NY 10011

212-675-4984
800-362-3273; *Fax:* 212-645-1438
info@jamesbeard.org; www.jamesbeard.org
Social Media: Facebook, Twitter

Susan Ungaro, President
Mitchell Davis, Executive Vice President
Marilyn Platzer, Chief Financial & Operating Officer
Nancy Kull, Executive Asst. to the President
Anna Mowry, Special Projects Manager

Nonprofit organization dedicated to preserving the country's culinary heritage and fostering the appreciation and development of gastronomy by recognizing and promoting excellence in all aspects of the culinary arts.
Founded in: 1986

21338 **Mobile Industrial Caterers' Association**
7300 Artesia Boulevard
Buena Park, CA 90621-1804

714-632-6800; *Fax:* 714-632-5405;
www.mobilecaterers.com

Kelly Ramirez, Executive Director

Aids with problems common within the industry through exchange of ideas, advice on legal problems, safety standards and licensing regulations.
185 Members
Founded in: 1964

21339 **National Association for Catering and Events**
10440 Little Patuxent Parkway
Suite 300
Columbia, MD 21044

410-290-5410; *Fax:* 410-630-5768
INFO@NACE.NET; www.nace.net
Social Media: Facebook, Twitter, LinkedIn, Pinterest, YouTube

Joe Mahoney, President
Bonnie Fedchock, Executive Director
Donnell Bayot, Second Vice President
Kate Patay, CPCE, Secretary/ Treasurer
Lisa Hopkins Barry, Immediate Past President

Serves catering professionals and the vendors and suppliers that support them.
4000+ Members
Founded in: 1950

21340 **National Bar & Restaurant Management Association**
307 Jackson Avenue W
Oxford, MS 38655

662-236-5510
800-247-3881; *Fax:* 662-236-5541
jrobinson@oxpub.com; www.nightclub.com
Social Media: Facebook, Twitter, LinkedIn, Instagram, Vimeo

Jon Taffer, President
Leo J. Squatrito, VP, Sale & Marketing
Erica Walsh, Marketing Manager
Greg Goulski, Director of Sales, Digital Media
Kristen Santoro, Content & Conference Dircetor

21341 **National Council of Chain Restaurants**
1101 New York Ave NW
Washington, DC 20005

202-783-7971
800-673-4692; *Fax:* 202-737-2849
purviss@nrf.com
nrf.com
Social Media: Facebook, Twitter, LinkedIn, YouTube, Instagram, Flickr

Matthew R. Shay, President
Kip Tindell, Chairman
Cicely Simpson, Treasurer
Mindy F. Grossman, Secretary
Mary Schell, Vice Chairman

A division of the National Retail Federation, NCCR was formed by a group of foodservice and restaurant executives who felt that they were not receiving adequate government relations representation from existing organizations. The NCCR helps shape federal legislative and regulatory issues that are of uniform significance to our member companies. Comprised of nearly 40 of the largest chain restaurant companies in the country.
Frequency: Inquire For Membership
Founded in: 1965

21342 National Restaurant Association
2055 L Street NW
Suite 700
Washington, DC 20036

202-331-5900
800-424-5156; *Fax:* 202-331-2429;
www.restaurant.org
Social Media: Facebook, Twitter, YouTube

Jack Crawford, Chair
Joe Kadow, Vice Chair
Jeff Davis, Treasurer
Dawn Sweeney, President/ Chief Executive Officer
Ed Beck, SVP, Technology

Striving to help members build customer loyalty, find financial success and provide rewarding careers in foodservice.
Founded in: 1919

21343 North American Association of Food Equipment Manufacturers
161 North Clark Street
Suite 2020
Chicago, IL 60601

312-821-0201; *Fax:* 312-821-0202
info@nafem.org; www.nafem.org
Social Media: Facebook, Twitter, LinkedIn

Deirdre Flynn, Executive Vice President
Michael L. Whiteley, President
Joseph Carlson, Secretary/ Treasurer
Kevin Fink, President-Elect
Marianne Byrne, Marketing Manager

Dealers and distributors of foodservice equipment and supplies.
700 Members
Founded in: 1979

21344 North American Association of Foodservice Equipment Manufacturers
161 North Clark Street
Suite 2020
Chicago, IL 60601

312-821-0201; *Fax:* 312-821-0202
info@nafem.org; www.nafem.org
Social Media: Facebook

Michael L. Whiteley, CFSP, President
Kevin Fink, CFSP, President-Elect
Joseph Carlson, CFSP, Secretary/Treasurer
Deirdre Flynn, CFSP, Executive Vice President
Charlie Souhrada, CFSP, Director, Member Services

Trade association for foodservice and food equipment manufacturers.

21345 Professional Chef's Association
P.O. Box 453
Frederick, CO 80530

720-379-8759
info@ProfessionalChef.com
professionalchef.com
Social Media: Facebook, Twitter, LinkedIn

Organization for professional chefs.
Founded in: 1997

21346 Restaurant Facility Management Association
5600 Tennyson Parkway
Suite 265
Plano, TX 75024

972-805-0905; *Fax:* 972-805-0906;
www.rfmaonline.com

Kevin Carringer, Chair
Annaji Sailer, Board Vendor Representative
Roger Goldstein, Immediate Past Chair
John F. Getha, Treasurer
Nic Mclaughlin, Secretary

Association for restaurant facility management professionals.

21347 United States Personal Chef Association
7680 Universal Blvd.
Suite 550
Orlando, FL 32819

800-995-2138
info@uspca.com; www.uspca.com
Social Media: Facebook, Twitter, LinkedIn, RSS, Google+, YouTube

Larry Lynch, President
Robert Lynch, Vice President
Vince Likar, Director of Member Service
Annise Jackson, Manager of Membership
Dan Chancellor, Marketing Manager

Organization offering all the necessary resources for those interested in starting their own personal chef business.
Founded in: 1991

Newsletters

21348 AEPMA News & Views
American Edged Products Manufacturers Association
21165 Whitfield Pl
Suite 105
Sterling, VA 20165

703-433-9281; *Fax:* 703-433-0369
info@aepma.org; www.aepma.org

David Barrack, Executive Director
Robert Clemence, VP
Tom Arrowsmith, Treasurer

Serves the marketing and manufacturing of the cutlery industry.
Frequency: Twice/Year

21349 American Culinary Federation Newsletter
American Culinary Federation
180 Center Place Way
St Augustine, FL 32095-8859

904-824-4468
800-624-9458; *Fax:* 904-825-4758;
www.acfchefs.org

Heidi Cramb, Executive Director
Edward G Leonard, President
Brent T. Frei, Director of Marketing
Kay Orde, Editor
Michael Feierstein, Administrative Assistant

The official membership newsletter of the American Culinary Federation.
Frequency: Monthly
Circulation: 21000
Founded in: 1929
Printed in 2 colors on matte stock

21350 Baker's Math
American Bakers Institute
1300 I St Nw
Suite 700W
Washington, DC 20005-7203

202-789-0300; *Fax:* 202-898-1164;
www.americanbakers.org

Robb Mac Kie, President

21351 CHRIE Communique
Int'l Council on Hotel, Restaurant Institute Edu.
2810 North Parham Road
suite 230
Richmond, VA 23294-3006

804-747-4971; *Fax:* 804-346-5009
publications@chrie.org; www.chrie.org

Dale Gaddy, Publisher
Mike Zema, President
Kathy McCarty, CEO
Joseph Bradley, Treasurer

Monthly newsletter offering information on industry, significant hospitality and tourism education job listings.
Cost: $65.00
Frequency: Monthly
Circulation: 1800
Founded in: 1946

21352 Cameron's Foodservice Marketing Reporter
Cameron's Publications
5423 Sheridan Drive
PO Box 676
Williamsville, NY 14231

519-586-8785; *Fax:* 519-586-8816;
www.cameronpub.com

Nina T Cameron, Editor
Bob McClelland, Publisher
Peggy Kelly, Circulation Manager

Successful promotion and advertising case histories for the restaurant and hotel industry.
Cost: $197.00
Frequency: Fortnightly
Founded in: 1970

21353 Center of the Plate
American Culinary Federation
180 Center Place Way
St Augustine, FL 32095-8859

904-824-4468
800-624-9458; *Fax:* 904-825-4758
acf@acfchefs.net; www.acfchefs.org

Heidi Cramb, Executive Director
Edward Leonard, Administrative Assistant
Michael Feierstein, Administrative Assistant
Bryan Hunt, Graphic Designer
Patricia Carroll, Director of Communications

Official membership newsletter of the American Culinary Federation.
Cost: $50.00
Frequency: Monthly
Circulation: 25000+
Founded in: 1929

21354 Wine on Line Food and Wine Review
Enterprise Publishing
PO Box 328
Blair, NE 68008-0328

402-426-2121; *Fax:* 402-426-2227;
www.enterprisepub.com

Mark Rhoades, President
Dough Barber, Editor
Lynette Hansen, Sales Manager
Bill Smutko, Circulation Manager
Dave Smith, Production Manager

Reviews, feature articles and information on all areas of food and wine, including restaurants, hotels, trains and airlines. Accepts advertising.
Cost: $36.00
10 Pages
Circulation: 13150
Founded in: 1800

Magazines & Journals

21355 Chain Store Information Guide
3922 Coconut Palm Dr
Tampa, FL 33619
800-778-9794; *Fax:* 813-627-6888;
www.chainstoreguide.com

A national organization that serves the commercial and institutional food and lodging industry.
Founded in: 1967

21356 Cheers
257 Park Avenue S
3rd Floor, Suite 303
New York, NY 10010

212-967-1551; *Fax:* 646-654-2099

John Eastman, Owner

Every issue is designed to help on-premise operators enhance the profitability of their beverage operations.

21357 Chef
Talcott Communications Corporation
20 N Wacker Dr
Suite 3900
Chicago, IL 60606-3188

312-726-2410; *Fax:* 312-726-2554;
www.ucco.com/tc.htm

Laura Herold, President
Rob Benes, Senior Editor
Morgan Holzman, Contributing Editor
David Pizzimenti, Circulation Manager

Information on food production and presentation, includes chef profiles, trend studies, marketing information and restaurant profiles.
Cost: $32.00
Frequency: Monthly
Circulation: 38769
ISSN: 1087-061X
Founded in: 1956
Printed in 4 colors on glossy stock

21358 Coffee & Cuisine
Coffee Talk
1218 3rd Avenue
#1315
Seattle, WA 98101-3021

206-521-7247; *Fax:* 206-623-0446;
www.coffeecuisine.com

Kerri Goodman, Publisher

Covers new products, personnel moves, industry news, how to articles, education, and techniques to increase sales growth for the coffee, cold beverage and foodservice industry.
Cost: $36.00
Frequency: Monthly
Circulation: 30000

21359 Cooking for Profit
CP Publishing
PO Box 267
Fond du Lac, WI 54936-267

920-923-3700; *Fax:* 920-923-6805
comments@cookingforprofit.com;
www.cookingforprofit.com

Colleen Phalen, Editor-in-Chief

Paid subscription trade magazine targeted to foodservice owners, managers and chefs. Each month features current trends in food preparation with step-by-step recipes and photographs; effective management techniques; and the latest in foodservice equipment — all written by industry experts. Also features in-depth profiles of a successful foodservice operation.
Cost: $26.00
28 Pages
Frequency: Monthly
Founded in: 1932
Printed in 4 colors on glossy stock

21360 Cornell Hotel & Restaurant Administration Quarterly
Elsevier Science Publishing Company
537 Statler Hall
Ithaca, NY 14853-6902

607-255-9780; *Fax:* 607-254-2922
hosp_research@cornell.edu;
www.hotelschool.cornell.edu

Dr. Michael Sturman, Editor
Glenn Withiam, Executive Editor
Nicole Roach, Marketing

A journal devoted to the development and exchange of management ideas for the hospitality industry.
Cost: $113.00
Frequency: Quarterly
Circulation: 4500
Founded in: 1963

21361 Culinary Trends
Culinary Trends Publications
6285 E Spring Street
#107
Long Beach, CA 90808-4000

310-496-2558; *Fax:* 310-421-8993;
www.culinarytrends.com

Fred Mensigna, Publisher
Linda Mensinga, Editor

Information for food and beverage managers along with managers of hotels and restaurants.
Cost: $21.60
Frequency: Quarterly
Circulation: 10000

21362 El Restaurante Mexicano
Maiden Name Press
1010 Lake St
Suite 604
Oak Park, IL 60301-1136

708-848-3200
800-407-5845; *Fax:* 708-445-9477
kfurore@restmex.com; www.restmex.com

Joe Madden, President
Kathleen Furore, Managing Director
Jessica Pantanini, Managing Director

A bilingual magazine featuring industry specific food news, features restaurant profiles and new product information for personnel of restaurants serving mexican/southwestern menu items nationwide.
Cost: $18.00
Circulation: 27000
Founded in: 1997

21363 FEDA News & Views
Foodservice Equipment Distributors Association
223 W Jackson Boulevard
#620
Chicago, IL 60606-6911

312-427-9605; *Fax:* 312-427-9607
feda@feda.com; www.feda.com

Stacy Ward, Managing Editor
Ray Herrick, Executive VP
Adela Ramos, Administration Director, Manager
Bruce Gulbas, President

Focus is on sales, technology, new products and other areas of benefit to dealers, as well as industry trends and news.
Cost: $150.00
Circulation: 1200
Founded in: 1933

21364 Food & Beverage News
Food & Beverage News
1886 W Bay Drive
#E6
Largo, FL 33770-3017

727-585-7745; *Fax:* 727-585-7245;
www.fbnews.com

Dennis J Regan, Publisher

News on the latest liquor law, new products, and government legislation.
Cost: $28.00
Frequency: Monthly
Circulation: 16,880

21365 Food Arts Magazine
M Shanken Communications
387 Park Ave S
Suite 8
New York, NY 10016-8872

212-684-4224; *Fax:* 212-684-5424;
www.cigaraficionado.com

Marvin Shanken, Publisher

A magazine devoted to the restaurant industry.
Cost: $40.00
Frequency: Monthly
Founded in: 1988

21366 Foodservice Equipment & Supplies Specialist
Reed Business Information
1350 E Touhy Avenue
Des Plaines, IL 60018-3358

630-320-7000; *Fax:* 630-288-8686;
www.reedbusiness.com

Mitchell Schechter, Editor-in-Chief
Niles Crum, Publisher

Magazine for professionals who specify, sell and distribute foodservice equipment, supplies and furnishings.
Cost: $69.95
64+ Pages
Frequency: Monthly
Circulation: 27M
Founded in: 1947
Printed in 4 colors on glossy stock

21367 Foodservice Equipment Reports
Robin Ashton
2000 Clearwater Drive
Oak Brook, IL 60523-3358

630-288-8000
800-446-6551; *Fax:* 630-288-8265
webmaster@reedbusiness.com;
www.reedbusiness.com

Josph Carbonara, Editor-in-Chief
Maureen Slocum, Publisher
Keithy Mcnamara, Marketing
katy Tucker, Circulation Manager
Jeff Greisph, CEO

Geared toward manufacturers of foodservice equipment and their agencies.
Cost: $106.90
Frequency: Monthly
Circulation: 22719
Founded in: 1947

21368 Franchise Times
2808 Anthony Lane S
Minneapolis, MN 55418

612-767-3200
800-528-3296; *Fax:* 612-767-3230
info@franchisetimes.com;
www.franchisetimes.com

Mary Jo Larson, Publisher
Nancy Weingartner, Executive Editor
Beth Ewen, Managing Editor

Investigative pieces, analysis and profiles to help franchisors, franchisees and vendors improve their businesses.
Frequency: 10x/year

21369 Fresh Cup Magazine
Fresh Cup Publishing Company

537 SE Ash Street Suite 300
PO Box 14827
Portland, OR 97293-827

503-236-2587
800-868-5866; *Fax:* 503-236-3165
jan@freshcup.com; www.freshcup.com

Julie Beals, Editor
Nicole Maas, Sales/Marketing Associate
Bill Berninger, Circulation Director
Ward Barbee, Publisher
Jan Gibson, Owner
Cost: $57.00
68 Pages
Frequency: Monthly
Circulation: 14000
Founded in: 1992
Printed in 4 colors on glossy stock

21370 Full-Service Restaurant

www.fsrmagazine.com
Social Media: Facebook, Twitter

Greg Sanders, Group Publisher
Connie Gentry, Editor

Ideas and insights for decision-makers in full-service restaurant industry.
Founded in: 2012

21371 Gourmet News
Oser Communications Group
1877 N Kolb Road
Tucson, AZ 85715

520-721-1300; www.gourmetnews.com

Rocelle Aragon, Editor
Kate Seymour, Senior Associate Publisher

The business newspaper for the gourmet industry.
40 Pages
Frequency: Monthly
Circulation: 23381
ISSN: 1052-4630
Founded in: 1991
Printed in 4 colors on glossy stock

21372 Journal of Foodservice Business Research
Taylor & Francis
325 Chestnut Street
Suite 800
Philadelphia, PA 19106

800-354-1420; *Fax:* 215-625-2940;
www.tandf.co.uk

David A Cranage, Editor

Features articles from international experts in various disciplines, including management, marketing, finance, law, food technology, nutrition, psychology, information systems, anthropology, human resources, and more.
Cost: $ 92.00
Frequency: Quarterly
ISSN: 1537-8020
Founded in: 1978

21373 Midsouthwest Restaurant
3800 North Portland Avenue
Oklahoma City, OK 73112-2982

405-942-8181
800-375-8181; *Fax:* 405-942-0541;
www.okrestaurants.com

Jim Hopper, President/CEO
Shannon Moad, Editor
Debra Bailey, Deputy Director
Frequency: Quarterly
Circulation: 2500
Founded in: 1933

21374 Nation's Restaurant News
Lebhar-Friedman Publications
425 Park Ave
Suite 6
New York, NY 10022-3526

212-756-5220; *Fax:* 212-756-5250
info@lf.com

Lebhar Friedman, Publisher
Michael Cardillo, VP Sales
Leslie Wolowitz, Advertising

Serves commercial and onsite food service and lodging establishments including restaurants, schools, universities, hospitals, nursing homes and other health and welfare facilities, hotels and motels with food service, government installations, clubs and other related firms.
Cost: $44.95
Frequency: Weekly
Circulation: 85999
Founded in: 1925
Mailing list available for rent: 100,000 names at $100 per M
Printed in 4 colors on matte stock

21375 National Culinary Review
American Culinary Federation
180 Center Place Way
St Augustine, FL 32095-8859

904-824-4468
800-624-9458; *Fax:* 904-825-4758;
www.acfchefs.org

Heidi Cramb, Executive Director
Edward G Leonard, Administrative Assistant
Michael Feierstein, Administrative Assistant
Bryan Hunt, Graphic Designer
Patricia Carroll, Director of Communications
Accepts advertising.
Cost: $50.00
Frequency: Monthly
Founded in: 1929

21376 National Dipper
US Exposition Corporation
1028 W. Devon Avenue
Elk Grove Village, IL 60007

847-301-8400; *Fax:* 847-301-8402
lynda@nationaldipper.com;
www.nationaldipper.com

Lynda Utterback, Publisher

Information for retail ice cream and frozen yogurt owners and operators, includes changes and developments in the business.
Cost: $55.00
Circulation: 17000
Founded in: 1985
Printed in 4 colors on glossy stock

21377 Quick Service Restaurant

www.qsrmagazine.com
Social Media: Facebook, Twitter

Greg Sanders, Group Publisher
Sam Oches, Editor

Leading source of news about "limited-service" restaurant industry.

21378 Restaurant Digest
Panagos Publishing
3930 Knowles Avenue
#305
Kensington, MD 20895-2428

301-929-6200; *Fax:* 301-929-6550;
www.foodservicedepot.com

Bruce Panagos, Publisher

Developments and news of interest to owners, managers, and operators of dining and entertainment establishments in the region.

21379 Restaurant Hospitality
Donohue/Meehan Publishing
1801 E 9th St
Suite 920
Cleveland, OH 44114-3103

216-931-7258; *Fax:* 216-696-1752
rheditor@penton.com;
www.restaurant-hospitality.com

Jeff Donohoe, President
Jess Grossberg, Publisher
Gail Bellamy, Managing Editor
Sue Apple, Production Manager
Frequency: Monthly
Circulation: 117,721
Founded in: 1892

21380 Restaurant Marketing
Oxford Publishing
Ste 1
1903b University Ave
Oxford, MS 38655-4150

662-236-5510
800-247-3881; *Fax:* 662-281-0104;
www.restaurant-marketing.net

Frequency: Bi-Monthly

21381 Restaurant Wine
Wine Profits
PO Box 222
Napa, CA 94559-222

707-224-4777; *Fax:* 707-224-6740;
www.restaurantwine.com

Ronn Wiegand, Publisher
Paul Grieco, Co-Owner

Information on the marketing of wine in restaurants, hotels and clubs, wine and food pairing ideas and review of wines.
Cost: $99.00
Frequency: Monthly
Circulation: 3000
ISSN: 1040-7030
Printed in 2 colors on matte stock

21382 Restaurants & Institutions
Reed Business Information
2000 Clearwater Dr
Oak Brook, IL 60523-8809

630-574-0825; *Fax:* 630-288-8781
jamie.popp@reedbusiness.com;
www.reedbusiness.com

Jeff Greisch, President
Scott Hume, Managing Editor

Commercial and noncommercial foodservice establishments including restaurant, hotels, motels, fast-food chains,coffee shops, food stores with foodservice
Frequency: Monthly
Circulation: 155512
Founded in: 1937
Printed in 4 colors on glossy stock

21383 Restaurants USA
National Restaurant Association
1200 17th St NW
Washington, DC 20036-3006

202-331-5900
800-424-5156; *Fax:* 202-331-2429;
www.restaurant.org

Dawn M Sweeney, CEO
Sarah Hamaker, Treasurer
Phil Hickey, Treasurer

A trade magazine offering information for restaurant owners and managers, including industry trends, operational pointers, management principles and association activities.
Cost: $125.00
48 Pages
Frequency: Monthly
Circulation: 44000
Founded in: 1980
Printed in 4 colors

21384 Restaurants, Resorts & Hotels
Publishing Group
PO Box 318
Trumbull, CT 06611-0318

860-279-0149; *Fax:* 203-254-7104

James Martone, Publisher

Information on new products, supplies, food and equipment for those executives and managers who have responsibility for the food.
Cost: $24.00
Frequency: Monthly
Circulation: 97,000

21385 Southeast Food Service News
8805 Tamiami Trail N #301
Naples, FL 34108

239-514-1258
efischer@sfsn.com; www.sfsn.com
Social Media: Y

Elliott R Fischer, Marketing Director
John P Hayward, Account Executive
Elsie Olson, Production Manager
Frequency: Monthly
Founded in: 1977

21386 Southwest Food Service News
4011 W Plano Pkwy
Suite 121
Plano, TX 75093-5620

972-943-1254; *Fax:* 972-943-1258;
www.southwestfoodservice.com

Sam Ballard, Publisher

21387 Total Food Service
PO Box 2507
Greenwich, CT 06836-2507

203-661-9090; *Fax:* 203-661-9325;
www.totalfood.com

Fred Klashman, President

21388 Yankee Food Service
Griffin Publishing Company
201 Oak St
Suite A
Pembroke, MA 02359

781-294-4700
866-677-4700; *Fax:* 781-829-0134
info@griffinpublishing.net;
www.griffinpublishing.net

Kevin Griffin, President
Lynda Bassett, Editor
Henry Zacchini, Associate Publisher
Karen Harty, Vice President
Julie Mignosa, Office Manager

Reports news and happenings of the food service industry in New England.
Cost: $47.00
48 Pages
Frequency: Monthly
Circulation: 26110
Founded in: 1979

Trade Shows

21389 AEPMA Annual Meeting
American Edged Products Manufacturers Association
21165 Whitfield Pl
Suite 105
Sterling, VA 20165

703-433-9281; *Fax:* 703-433-0369;
www.aepma.org

David Barrack, Executive Director
Robert Clemence, VP
Tom Arrowsmith, Treasurer

Offering training and certificate programs, and management courses.
Frequency: Annual

21390 American Culinary Federation Central Regional Conference
American Culinary Federation
10 San Bartola Drive
Saint Augustine, FL 32085

904-824-4468
800-624-9458; *Fax:* 904-825-4758
acf@acfchefs.net; www.acfchefs.org

Brent Frei, Director Marketing
Michael Baskette, Administrative Assistant
Michael Feierstein, Administrative Assistant
Bryan Hunt, Graphic Designer
Patricia Carroll, Director of Communications

Culinary equipment, supplies and services. Seminars, workshops, cooking demos, more.

21391 American Culinary Federation National Convention
10 San Bartola Drive
Saint Augustine, FL 32086

904-824-4468
800-624-9458; *Fax:* 904-825-4758
acf@acfchefs.net; www.acfchefs.org

Brent Frei, Director Marketing
Michael Baskette, Administrative Assistant
Michael Feierstein, Administrative Assistant
Bryan Hunt, Graphic Designer
Patricia Carroll, Director of Communications

200 booths of products and foodstuffs for the food service industry. Seminars, workshops, cooking demos, more.

21392 American Culinary Federation Northeast Regional Conference
American Culinary Federation
10 San Bartola Drive
Saint Augustine, FL 32086

904-824-4468
800-624-9458; *Fax:* 904-825-4758
acf@acfchefs.net; www.acfchefs.org

Brent Frei, Director Marketing
Michael Baskette, Administrative Assistant
Michael Feierstein, Administrative Assistant
Bryan Hunt, Graphic Designer
Patricia Carroll, Director of Communications

Culinary equipment, supplies and services. Seminars, workshops, cooking demos, more.

21393 American Culinary Federation Southeast Regional Conference
American Culinary Federation
10 San Bartola Drive
Saint Augustine, FL 32086

904-824-4468
800-624-9458; *Fax:* 904-825-4758
acf@acfchefs.net; www.acfchefs.org

Brent Frei, Director Marketing
Michael Baskette, Administrative Assistant
Michael Feierstein, Administrative Assistant
Bryan Hunt, Graphic Designer
Patricia Carroll, Director of Communications

Culinary equipment, supplies and services. Seminars, workshops, cooking demos, more.

21394 American Culinary Federation Western Regional Conference
American Culinary Federation
10 San Bartola Drive
Saint Augustine, FL 32086

904-824-4468
800-624-9458; *Fax:* 904-825-4758
acf@acfchefs.net; www.acfchefs.org

Brent Frei, Director Marketing
Michael Baskette, Administrative Assistant
Michael Feierstein, Administrative Assistant
Bryan Hunt, Graphic Designer
Patricia Carroll, Director of Communications

Culinary equipment, supplies and services. Seminars, workshops, cooking demos, more.

21395 Annual Hotel, Motel and Restaurant Supply Show of the Southeast
Leisure Time Unlimited
708 Main Street
PO Box 332
Myrtle Beach, SC 29577

843-448-9483
800-261-5991; *Fax:* 843-626-1513
hmrss@sc.rr.com; www.hmrsss.com

Brooke P Baker, Show Director

Trade show for the hospitality industry.
23000 Attendees
Frequency: January
Founded in: 1975

21396 Fancy Food Show
Specialty Food Association, Inc.
136 Madison Avenue
12th Floor
New York, NY 10016

212-482-6440; *Fax:* new;
www.specialtyfood.com

Mike Silver, Chair
Becky Renfro Borbolla, Treasurer
Dennis Deschaine, Past Chairperson
Shawn McBride, Vice Chair
Matt Nielsen, Secretary

Over 80,000 on-trend and best-in-class products, including confections, cheese, coffee, snacks, spices, ethnic, natural, organic and more. 1,300 exhibitors representing specialty foods and beverages from across the United States and 35 countries and regions.

21397 Hospitality Food Service Expo Southeast and Atlanta International Wine
Reed Business Information
275 Washington Street
Boston, MA 02458

617-261-1166; *Fax:* 617-558-4327;
www.cahners.com

Patrick Paleno, Show Manager
Barry Reed Jr, CFO
Stuart Whayman, CFO

400 booths featuring educational seminars, culinary salon, and exhibits of products and services.
12M Attendees
Frequency: October

21398 National Restaurant Association: Restaurant, Hotel-Motel Show
1200 17th Street NW
Washington, DC 20036-3006

202-331-5900
http://www.nraef.org

Reed Hayes, President, Chief Operating Officer
Steven Anderson, President

1,800 booths for the food service industry exhibiting food and beverages.
105M Attendees
Frequency: May

21399 Restaurant Innovation Summit
National Restaurant Association
2055 L St. NW
Suite 700
Washington, DC 20036

202-331-5900
800-424-5156; *Fax:* 202-331-2429;
www.restaurant.org/Events-Networking/Events
Social Media: Facebook, Twitter

Jack Crawford, Chairman

Innovations in technology and how they may be applied to the restaurant industry.
Frequency: Annual

21400 Year of Enchantment
Int'l Council on Hotel, Restaurant Institute Edu.
1200 17th Street NW
Washington, DC 20036-3006
202-467-6300
publications@chrie.org; www.chrie.org
Susan Gould, Manager
Joseph Bradley, Treasurer
Containing 70+ booths and 50+ exhibits.
750 Attendees
Frequency: August
Founded in: 1946

Directories & Databases

21401 Chain Restaurant Operators Directory
Chain Store Guide
3922 Coconut Palm Dr
Tampa, FL 33619-1389
813-627-6700
800-972-9202; *Fax:* 813-627-7094
info@csgis.com; www.csgis.com
Mike Jarvis, Publisher
Arthur Sciarrotta, Senior VP
Discover more than 5,600 listings and more than 26,000 unique personnel within the Restaurant Chain, Foodservice Management, and Hotel/Motel Operator markets in the U.S. and Canada. Each company must have at least $1 million in annual sales either system wide or industry and have two or more units/accounts.
Cost: $335.00
Frequency: Annual

21402 Culinary Collection Directory
International Association/Culinary Professionals
304 W Liberty Street
Suite 201
Louisville, KY 40202
502-587-7953
800-928-4227; *Fax:* 502-589-3602
info@iacp.com; www.iacp.com
Kerry Edwards, Sr Member Services Representative
Trina Gribbins, Manager
Teachers, cooking school owners, caterers, writers, chefs, media cooking personalities, editors, publishers, food stylists, food photographers, restauranteurs, leaders of major food corporations and vintners. Literally a who's who of the food world.

21403 Food & Beverage Market Place
Grey House Publishing
4919 Route 22
PO Box 56
Amenia, NY 12501
518-789-8700
800-562-2139; *Fax:* 845-373-6390
books@greyhouse.com; www.greyhouse.com
Social Media: Facebook, Twitter
Leslie Mackenzie, Publisher
Richard Gottlieb, Editor
This information packed three-volume set is the most powerful buying and marketing guide for the US food and beverage industry. Includes thousands of industry freight and transportation listings.
Cost: $595.00
2000 Pages
Frequency: Annual
ISBN: 1-592373-61-5
Founded in: 1981

21404 Food & Beverage Marketplace: Online Database
Grey House Publishing
4919 Route 22
PO Box 56
Amenia, NY 12501
518-789-8700
800-562-2139; *Fax:* 845-373-6390
gold@greyhouse.com;
www.gold.greyhouse.com
Social Media: Facebook, Twitter
Richard Gottlieb, President
Leslie Mackenzie, Publisher
This complete updated Food & Beverage Market Place: Online Database is the go-to source for the food and beverage industry. Anyone involved in the food and beverage industry needs this 'industry bible' and the important contacts to develop critical research data that can make for successful business growth.
Frequency: Annual
Founded in: 1981

21405 Getaways for Gourmets in the Northeast
Wood Pond Press
365 Ridgewood Rd
West Hartford, CT 06107-3517
860-521-0389; *Fax:* 860-313-0185;
www.green-cuisine.com
Richard M Woodworth, Owner
Directory of services and supplies to the industry.
Cost: $14.95
514 Pages

21406 High Volume Independent Restaurants Database
Chain Store Guide
3922 Coconut Palm Dr
Tampa, FL 33619-1389
813-627-6700
800-778-9794; *Fax:* 813-627-7094
info@csgis.com; www.csgis.com
Mike Jarvis, Publisher
Shami Choon, Manager
Covers this growing niche through its nearly 5,900 listings featuring casual dining, family restaurants and fine dining establishments. Plus, access to over 15,000 key personnel names puts you in contact with key decision makers.
Cost: $335.00
1,000 Pages
Frequency: Annual

21407 International Association of Culinary Professionals
1221 Avenue of the Americas
42ns Floor
New York, NY 10020
646-358-4957
866-358-4951; *Fax:* 866-358-2524
info@iacp.com; www.iacp.com
Social Media: Facebook, Twitter, YouTube, Vimeo
Martha Homberg, Chief Executive Officer
Shani Phelan, Member Programs & Operations Mgr
Margaret Crable, Communications & Marketing
A not for profit organization whose members represent virtually every profession in the culinary universe: teachers, cooking school owners, caterers, writers, chefs, media cooking personalities, editors, publishers, food stylists, food photographers, restauranteurs, leaders of major food corporations and vintners. Literally a who's who of the food world. Founded in 1978.
3000+ Members
Founded in: 1978

21408 Restaurant Hospitality: Hospitality 500 Issue
Penton Media
1166 Avenue of the Americas
New York, NY 10036
212-204-4200; *Fax:* 216-696-6662
information@penton.com; www.penton.com
Social Media: Facebook, Twitter, LinkedIn
Jane Cooper, Marketing
Chris Meyer, Director
Bev Walter, Service Manager
500 independent restaurants selected on basis of sales.
Cost: $25.00
Frequency: Annual, June
Circulation: 123,000

21409 Restaurants and Institutions: Annual 400 Issues
Reed Business Information
1350 E Touhy Avenue
Suite 200E
Des Plaines, IL 60018-3358
847-962-2200; *Fax:* 630-288-8686;
www.reedbusiness.com
Roland Dietz, CEO
Stuart Whayman, CFO
Cost: $25.00
Frequency: Annual
Circulation: 16,000

21410 Zagat.com Restaurant Guides
Zagat Survey
4 Columbus Cir
New York, NY 10019-1180
212-977-6000; *Fax:* 212-977-9760
customerservice@zagat.com; www.zagat.com
Tim Zagat, CEO
Zagat.com was launched in May of 1999 and contains the most trusted and authoritive dining information online for over 20,000 restaurants in twenty eight cities worldwide, with 17 more cities to be added shortly. Based in New York City, the Zagat survey was founded in 1979 by Tim and Nina Zagat.

Industry Web Sites

21411 http://gold.greyhouse.com
G.O.L.D Grey House OnLine Databases
Grey House Publishing's online database platform, GOLD, offers Quick Search, Keyword Search and Expert Search for most business sectors including restaurant markets. The GOLD platform makes finding the information you need quick and easy - whether you're a novice searcher or an experienced database user. All of Grey House's directory products are available for subscription on the GOLD platform.

21412 www.acfchefs.org
American Culinary Federation
Member organization of professional chefs and cooks. Certifies chefs, accredits culinary programs and promotes culinary arts.

21413 www.chefcertification.com
American Culinary Federation
Offers the required courses for ACF certification online.

21414 www.chowbaby.com
This web site is search engine for restaurants.It makes finding the perfect eatery close to your

home or travel destination. Online reservations, maps, menus and more. You can search by Internatinal Location, US Location, US Map, or Cuisine type.

21415 www.chrie.org
Int'l Council on Hotel, Restaurant Institute Edu.

To enhance professionalism at all levels of the hospitality and tourism industry through education and training.

21416 www.greyhouse.com
Grey House Publishing

Authoritative reference directories for most business sectors including restaurant markets. Users can search the online databases with varied search criteria allowing for custom searches by product category, geographic area, sales volume, keyword, subject and more. Full Grey House catalog and online ordering also available.

21417 www.iacp.com
International Association of Culinary Professionals

A not for profit organization whose members represent virtually every profession in the culinary universe: teachers, cooking school owners, caterers, writers, chefs, media cooking personalities, editors, publishers, food stylists, food photographers, restauranteurs, leaders of major food corporations and vintners. Literally a who's who of the food world. Founded in 1978.

21418 www.ifsea.org
International Food Service Executives

Provides education and community service to the foodservice industry.

21419 www.restaurant.org
National Restaurant Association

Trends, government affairs, training, research, dining guides and links.

21420 www.therestaurantfinder.com

This search engine help to find restaurants by type or location.

Associations

21421 American Beverage Licensees
5101 River Rd
Suite 108
Bethesda, MD 20816-1560
301-656-1494; *Fax:* 301-656-7539
info@ablusa.org; www.ablusa.org
Social Media: Facebook, Twitter, RSS
John D. Bodnovich, Executive Director
Warren Scheidt, President
Raymond Cox, Treasurer
Terry Harvath, Vice President
John Moran, Vice President
Supports all those involved with the retailing of beverages.
20000 Members

21422 American Booksellers Association
333 Westchester Avenue
Suite S202
White Plains, NY 10604
914-406-7500
800-637-0037; *Fax:* 914-417-4013
info@bookweb.org; www.bookweb.org
Social Media: Facebook, Twitter, YouTube
Oren Teicher, CEO
Dan Cullen, Content Officer
Eleanor Chang, CFO
Betsy Burton, President
Robert Sindelar, Vice President/Secretary
Trade organization pledge to protecting the well-being of book retailers and promoting the availability of books.
2000 Members
Founded in: 1900

21423 American Collegiate Retailing Association
Loyola University/Department of Marketing
6363 Saint Charles Avenue
New Orleans, LA 70118-6195
504-865-2011; *Fax:* 504-865-3496;
www.acraretail.org
Rodney Runyan, President
Jane Swinney, Vice President
Robert Paul Jones, Secretary
Susan S. Fiorito, Treasurer
Leigh Sparks, Member-at-Large
Organization of faculty from colleges with a background in retailing.
400 Members
Founded in: 1950

21424 American Mobile Retail Association
213-785-4783
info@americanmra.com
americanmobileretailassociation.blogspot.ca
Social Media: Facebook, Twitter
Stacey Jischke-Steffe, Co-Founder/President
Jeanine Romo, Co-Founder/Vice President
Support and assistance for mobile retailers.

21425 Associated Surplus Dealers/Associated Merchandise Dealers
ASD/AMD Merchandise Group
2950 31st Street
Suite 100
Santa Monica, CA 90405-3037
310-396-6006
800-421-4511; *Fax:* 310-399-2662;
www.merchandisegroup.com
Leading producer of trade shows and publications in the variety and general merchandise industry.
15000 Members
Founded in: 1961

21426 Association for Retail Technology
1101 New York Ave NW
Washington, DC 20005
202-783-7971
800-673-4692; *Fax:* 202-737-2849
arts@nrf.com; www.nrf.com
Social Media: Facebook, Twitter, LinkedIn, YouTube, Instagram, Flickr
Matthew Shay, President and CEO
Carleen Kohut, COO
Mallory Duncan, SVP& General Counsel
David French, SVP, Govt. Relations
Mike Gatti, SVP, Member Relations
Subsidiary of the National Retail Federation, this is a retailer-driven membership organization dedicated to creating an international, barrier-free technology environment for retailers. ARTS was established to ensure that technology works to enhance a retailer's ability to develop store level business solutions and avoid situations that limit a retailer's ability to implement change while providing industry standards designed to provide greater value at lower costs.
175 Members
Founded in: 1993

21427 Association of Retail Marketing Services
10 Drs James Parker Boulevard
Suite 103
Red Bank, NJ 07701-1500
732-842-5070
866-231-6310; *Fax:* 732-219-1938
info@goarms.com; www.goarms.com
Gerri Hopkins, Executive Director
Lisa McCauley, Administrative Director
Supports all those involved with the marketing of all aspects of the retail industry, manufacturing, distribution, representation.
100 Members
Founded in: 1957

21428 Black Retail Action Group
68 East 131st Street
Suite 704
New York, NY 10037
212-234-3050; *Fax:* 212-234-3053
info@bragusa.org
bragusa.org
Social Media: Instagram
Nicole Cokley-Dunlap, Co-President
Shawn R.Outler, Co-President
Regina Gwynn, Vice President-Operations
Leslie Smith, Vice President-Finance
Juanita Fields, Secretary
500 Members
Founded in: 1970

21429 Christian Booksellers Association (CBA)
1365 Garden of the Gods Rd
Suite 105
Colorado Spring, CO 80907
719-265-9895
800-252-1950; *Fax:* 719-272-3508
info@cbaonline.org; www.cbaonline.org
Social Media: Facebook, Twitter
Curtis Riskey, President
Sue Smith, Chairman
Bob Hawkins. Jr, Secretary
Bill Couey, Treasurer
Robin Hogan, Vice Chairman
Provides products and services to assist and support Christian retail stores.
3.4M Members
Founded in: 1950

21430 Comics Professional Retail Organization
PO Box 16804
Irvine, CA 92623-6804
714-446-8871; www.comicspro.org
Social Media: Facebook, Twitter
Peter Dolan, President
The voice of direct-market comic book retailers.

21431 Electronic Retailing Association
607 14th Street, NW
Suite 530
Washington, DC 20005
703-841-1751
800-987-6462; *Fax:* 425-977-1036
webadmin@retailing.org; www.retailing.org
Social Media: Facebook, Twitter, LinkedIn, YouTube, Flickr
Julie Coons, President and CEO
Gregory Sater, Chairman
Chris Reinmuth, Secretary
Christopher Hearing, Treasurer
Poonam Khubani, Chairman-Elect
To foster growth, development and acceptance of the rapidly growing direct response industry worldwide for the companies who use the power of electronic media to sell goods and services to the public.
Founded in: 1990
Mailing list available for rent

21432 Franchise Consultants International Association
5147 S Angela Road
Memphis, TN 38117-3454
901-368-3881; *Fax:* 202-628-0812
Social Media: Facebook, Twitter, LinkedIn
William Richey, Executive Director
Seeks to coordinate effective and professional franchise consulting, serves as a clearinghouse and operates a library.
800 Members
Founded in: 1980

21433 Institute of Store Planners
25 N Broadway
Tarrytown, NY 10591-3221
914-332-1806; *Fax:* 914-332-1541;
www.retaildesigninstitute.org
Richard C Byrne, Manager
Kenneth Nisch, VP
Ronald Kline, Chairman
Richard Byrne, Manager
Provides a forum for debate and discussion by store design experts and retailers. Sponsors student design programs.
1300 Members
Founded in: 1961

21434 International Center for Companies of Food
Shuwaikh Industrial Area. Block 143
Street 111
Shuwaikh, KU 70655
965-483-8750; *Fax:* 965-484-0125;
www.international-center.com
Social Media: Facebook, Twitter, LinkedIn
Shaker Al-Samman, MD
Provides management research on problems related to food distribution and serves as an international forum where food chain store executives can meet to exchange ideas and information.
500 Members
Founded in: 1960

21435 International Council of Shopping Centers
1221 Ave of the Americas
41 St. Fl.
New York, NY 10020-1099
646-728-3800; *Fax:* 732-694-1690
membership@icsc.org; www.icsc.org
Social Media: Facebook, Twitter, LinkedIn, YouTube, Pinterest, Google+, I
Sheri Pupello, Member Communcations Representative
Cecilia Perrino, Customer Service/ InfoCenter
Glen Hale, CFO
Jesse Tron, Director, Communications
Jennifer Collin, Manager, Membership Development
Supports all those involved with any aspect of shopping centers.
70000 Members
Founded in: 1957

21436 International Franchise Association
1900 K Street, NW
Suite 700
Washington, DC 20006
202-628-8000; *Fax:* 202-628-0812;
www.franchise.org
Social Media: Facebook, Twitter, LinkedIn, YouTube, Instagram
Robert Cresanti, President
Melanie Bergeron, Chair of the Board
Aziz Hashim, Vice Chairman
Shelly Sun, Treasurer
Liam Brown, Secretary
Membership consists of companies franchising the distribution of goods or services.
Founded in: 1997

21437 International Map Trade Association
2629 Manhattan Avenue
PMB 281
Hermosa Beach, CA 90254
310-376-7731; *Fax:* 949-458-0300;
www.imiamaps.org
Chris Knoebel, President
Sanford J Hill, Executive Director
Membership comprised of retail stores featuring maps, travel books, globes, and travel products, plus publishers and manufacturers producing these products. Publishes a monthly newsletter.
800 Members
Founded in: 1981

21438 International Premium Cigar & Pipe Retailers Association
4 Bradley Park Ct
Suite 2H
Columbus, GA 31904-3637
706-494-1143; *Fax:* 706-494-1893
info@rtda.org; www.ipcpr.org
Social Media: Facebook, Twitter, LinkedIn, YouTube
Finnie Helmuth, President
Craig Cass, 1st Vice President
Ken P. Neumann, 2nd Vice President
John Anderson, Treasurer
Greg Zimmerman, Secretary
Trade association of high quality tobacconists.
2,350 Members
Founded in: 1933

21439 Marine Retailers Association of America
8401 73rd Ave. N.
Suite 71
Minneapolis, MN 55428
763-315-8043; *Fax:* 708-763-9236
matt@mraa.com; www.mraa.com
Social Media: Facebook, Twitter, LinkedIn, RSS
Matt Gruhn, President
Liz Walz, Vice President
Randy Wattenbarger, Chairman
Joe Lewis, Vice Chairman
Joe Hoffmaster, Secretary/ Treasurer
Raising the standards of retailing within the industry. Promotes activities for the recreational boating industry and holds seminars to improve management.
2.5M Members
Founded in: 1972

21440 Museum Store Association
3773 E Cherry Creek North Dr
Suite 755
Denver, CO 80209
303-504-9223; *Fax:* 303-504-9585
info@museumstoreassociation.org;
www.museumdistrict.com
Social Media: Facebook, Twitter, LinkedIn, Pinterest
Stuart Hata, First Vice President
David Duddy, President
Alice McAuliffe, Treasurer
Jama Rice, Executive Director/ CEO
Julie Steiner, Second Vice President
2500 Members
Frequency: April, Annually
Founded in: 1955

21441 National Advisory Group
2063 Oak Street
Jacksonville, FL 32204
904-845-5989
nagconvenience.com
Social Media: Facebook
Joseph Howton, Executive VP
Mary Banmiller, President
Bill Donahe, Publisher
Ben Jatlow, Chairman
This association represents senior level management of retail companies organized to enhance buying power, merchandising programs and an exchange of ideas. Membership dues: Retail Average $300, Associations $350.
500 Members
Founded in: 1983

21442 National Association General Merchandise Representatives
1037 Us Highway 46
Suite C102
Clifton, NJ 07013-2461
973-614-9211; *Fax:* 973-916-1986
frankp@performancesales.com;
www.nagmr.com
Social Media: Facebook, Twitter, Pinterest, RSS
David Perrone, President
Jordan Stone, Vice President
Ronald Ross, Treasurer
Rich Siporin, Secretary
Bruce Funk, Director
A professional association of consumer product brokers representing leading manufacturers to the drug, mass merchandise and food trade.

21443 National Association of Catalog Showrooms
PO Box 736
Northport, NY 11768-0736
631-754-4364; *Fax:* 631-754-4364;
www.businessfinance.com
Social Media: Facebook, Twitter, LinkedIn
Members are catalog showroom operators and catalog publishers & associate members are suppliers.
350 Members
Founded in: 1972

21444 National Association of Chain Drug Stores
1776 Wilson Blvd
Suite 200
Arlington, VA 22209
703-549-3001; *Fax:* 703-836-4869
contactus@nacds.org; www.nacds.org
Social Media: Facebook, Twitter, LinkedIn, YouTube, Flickr
Steven C Anderson, President/CEO
Randy Edeker, Chairman
Juna Ortiz, Treasurer
Martin Otto, Vice Chairman
Jose Barra, Director
The chief purpose of NACDS is to represent the views and policy positions of member chain drug companies.
105 Members
Founded in: 1933

21445 National Association of College Stores
528 E Lorain St
Oberlin, OH 44074-1298
440-775-7777
800-622-7498; *Fax:* 440-774-5315
service@nacscorp.com; www.nacscorp.com
Kurt K. Schoen, President & COO
Marc Fleischaker, Secretary/ Legal Counsel
Brian E Cartier, CEO
Frank Sulen, CFO & Treasurer
Steve Alb, Chairperson
Provides educational and support services and products to college stores. Promotes business methods and ethics. Conducts manager certification, educational services and research.
3.9M Members
Founded in: 1963

21446 National Association of Convenience Stores
1600 Duke Street
Alexandria, VA 22314
703-684-3600
877-684-3600; *Fax:* 703-836-4564;
www.nacsonline.com
Social Media: Facebook, Twitter, LinkedIn, YouTube, Instagram
Henry Armour, Staff Liason
R. Timothy Columbus, Legal Counsel
Kathy LeBeouf, Executive Director
Brian E Cartier, CEO
Jack Kofdarali, Chairman
Association supporting key industry trends and innovative practices of convenience store companies.
2.3M Members
Founded in: 1961
Mailing list available for rent

21447 National Association of Music Merchants
5790 Armada Dr
Carlsbad, CA 92008
760-438-8001
800-767-6266; *Fax:* 760-438-7327
info@namm.org; www.namm.org

Social Media: Facebook, Twitter, YouTube, Pinterest

Joe Lamond, President
Chris Martin, Treasurer
Joel Menchey, Secretary
Mark Goff, Chairman
Robin Valenta, Vice Chairman

Retailers of musical instruments.
3.6M Members

21448 National Association of Resale Professionals

PO BOX 190
St Clair Shores, MI 48080

586-294-6700
800-544-0751; *Fax:* 586-588-7018
info@narts.org; www.narts.org

Adele R. Meyer, Executive Director
Gail A. Seigel, Director of Membership Services

A national trade association for owners and managers of resale thrift shops. Purpose is to provide educational networking to promote the industry.
1100+ Members
Founded in: 1984

21449 National Automatic Merchandising Association

20 N Wacker Dr
Suite 3500
Chicago, IL 60606

312-346-0370
800-331-8816; *Fax:* 312-704-4140
jbradshaw@vending.org; www.vending.org
Social Media: Facebook, Twitter, x, YouTube

Howard Chapman, Chairman
Peter A. Tullio, Past Chair
Heidi Chico, Vice Chairman
Patrick Hagerty, Chair-Elect
Carla Balakgie, President & CEO

Collectively advancing and promoting the automatic merchandising and coffee service industries, members include service companies, equipment manufacturers and suppliers of products and services to operating service companies.
1250+ Members
Founded in: 1936

21450 National Council of Chain Restaurants

325 7th St NW
Suite 1100
Washington, DC 20004

202-783-7971
800-673-4692; *Fax:* 202-737-2849
info@nrf.com; www.nccr.net

Chip Kunde, Chairman
Rob Green, Executive Director
Scott Vinson, Vice President
Cicely Simpson, Treasurer
Lynn Liddle, Secretary

The leading trade association exclusively representing chain restaurant companies. Working to advance sound public policy that best serves the interests of restaurant businesses and the millions of people they employ.
Founded in: 1965

21451 National Grocers Association

1005 N Glebe Rd
Suite 250
Arlington, VA 22201-5758

703-516-0700; *Fax:* 703-516-0115;
www.nationalgrocers.org
Social Media: Facebook, Twitter, LinkedIn

Peter J. Larkin, President & CEO
Charlie Bray, Executive Vice President
Rich Niemann, Chairman
Cheryl Sommer, Treasurer
Rich McMenamin, Secretary

Works to advance understanding, trade, and cooperation in the food industry. Represents members interests before the government. Offers store planning, and engineering, training and advertising.
1.5M Members
Founded in: 1982

21452 National Ice Cream Retailers Association

1028 West Devon Ave.
Elk Grove Village, IL 60007

847-301-7500
866-303-6960; *Fax:* 847-301-8402
info@nicra.org; www.nicra.org
Social Media: Facebook

Lynda Utterback, Executive Director
Carl Chaney, President
Neil McWilliams, Vice President
Jim Oden, President-Elect
Nanette Frey, Past President

Members are in retail frozen dessert businesses. Some offer food services either full of limited and some operate convenience stores. The common denominator is that all members offer frozen desserts for take home or on site consumption.
350 Members
Founded in: 1933

21453 National Restaurant Association

2055 L St. NW
Suite 700
Washington, DC 20036

202-331-5900
800-424-5156; *Fax:* 202-331-2429;
www.restaurant.org
Social Media: Facebook, Twitter, YouTube

Jack Crawford, Chair
Joe Kadow, Vice Chair
Jeff Davis, Treasurer
Dawn Sweeney, President & CEO
Ed Beck, Chief Information Officer & SVP
60000 Members
Founded in: 1917

21454 National Restaurant Association Education Foundation

2055 L St. NW
Washington, DC 200036

312-715-1010
800-424-5156; *Fax:* 312-583-9767
rgifford@restaurant.org; www.nraef.org
Social Media: Facebook, Twitter, YouTube, Tumblr, Pinterest

Michael A. Hickey, Chair
Gregory J. Hamer, Treasurer
Lorna C. Donatone, Vice-Chairman
Dawn Sweeney, President & CEO
Rob Gifford, Executive Vice President

NRAEF is the philanthropic foundation of the National Restaurant Association. Committed to enhancing the restaurant industry's service to the public through education, community engagement and promotion of career opportunities.
Founded in: 1987

21455 National Retail Federation

1101 New York Ave NW
Washington, DC 20005

202-783-7971
800-673-4692; *Fax:* 202-737-2849;
www.nrf.com
Social Media: Facebook, Twitter, LinkedIn, YouTube, Instagram, Flickr

Matthew R. Shay, President/CEO
Mindy F. Grossman, Vice Chair
Autor Erik, Vice President
Kip Tindell, Chairman
Kip Tindell, Treasurer & Chairman of Finance

Retail trade association with membership that comprises all retail formats and channels of distribution including department, specialty, discount, catalog, Internet and independent stores. NRF members represent an industry that encompasses more than 1.4 million US retail establishments which employ more than 23 million people — about one in five American workers — and registered 2002 sales of $3.6 trillion. NRF's international members operate stores in more than 50 nations.
55M Members
Founded in: 1990

21456 National Shoe Retailers Association

7386 N. La Cholla Blvd
Tucson, AZ 85741

520-209-1710
800-673-8446; *Fax:* 410-381-1167
info@nsra.org; www.nsra.org
Social Media: Facebook, Twitter, LinkedIn, Google+, Pinterest

Jeff Greenberg, Board Chairman
Chuck Schuyler, President
Lenny Comeras, Vice Chairman
Rick Ravel, Past Chairman
Jeanette Riechers, Vice Chairman

Membership association for independent shoe ratailers. Provides busisness services such as credit-card processing and shipping at special low members only prices. Also provides educational and training programs, consulting and other services.
1400 Members
Founded in: 1912

21457 National Ski & Snowboard Retailers Association

1601 Feehanville Drive
Suite 300
Mount Prospect, IL 60056

847-391-9825
888-527-1168; *Fax:* 847-391-9827
info@nssra.com; www.nssra.com

Larry Weindruch, President
Paul Prutzman, Chairman

The retail voice for the ski and snowboard industries and provides information and services you need to operate more successfully.
250 Members
Founded in: 1987

21458 National Sporting Goods Association

1601 Feehanville Drive
Suite 300
Mount Prospect, IL 60056

847-296-6742
800-815-5422; *Fax:* 847-391-9827
info@nsga.org; www.nsga.org

Ken Meehan, Chairman of the Board
Matt Carlson, President/CEO
Dan Wiersma, CFO
Randy Nill, Treasurer/ Chairman-Elect
Jeff Rosenthal, Past chairman

Association of retailers, manufacturers and suppliers of sports equipment, footwear and apparel.
2000+ Members
Founded in: 1929

21459 North American Equipment Dealers Association

1195 Smizer Mill Rd
Fenton, MO 63026

636-349-5000; *Fax:* 636-349-5443
naeda@naeda.com; www.naeda.com
Social Media: Facebook, Twitter

Richard Lawhun, President
Joe Nash, Immediate Past President
Mark Foster, 2nd Vice Chair & Secretary
Brian Carpenter, First Vice Chair & Treasurer
Blaine Bingham, Chairman

NAEDA and its affiliates provides a variety of educational, financial, legislative and legal services to equipment dealers in the United States and Canada.
5000 Members
Founded in: 1900

21460 North American Retail Dealers Association
222 South Riverside Plaza
Suite 2100
Chicago, IL 60606

312-648-0649
800-621-0298; *Fax:* 312-648-1212
nardasvc@narda.com; www.narda.com
Social Media: Facebook, LinkedIn

Leon Barbachano, Chairman
Timothy W. Seavey, First Vice Chairman
Leon Barbachano, Second Vice Chairman
Michael Fischer, Past Chairman & Treasurer
Otto Papasadero, Executive Director

A national organization of association members, independent retailers selling and servicing major appliances, consumer electronics products, furniture and computers. Emphasis is placed on ideas that help readers become better, more profitable businesses. Articles are featured regularly on displays, salesmanship, financial analysis and service management.
1000 Members
Founded in: 1943

21461 Oriental Rug Importers Association
400 Tenafly Road
Suite 699
Tenafly, NJ 7670

201-866-5054; *Fax:* 201-866-6169
llaufer@oria.org; www.oria.org

Lucille Laufer, Executive Director
Reza Momeni, President
Kami Navid, Vice-President
Behrooz Hakimian, Treasurer
Ramin Kalaty, Secretary

Membership is concentrated in the New York area.
Founded in: 1958

21462 Point-of-Purchase Advertising Internationa l
440 N. Wells Street
Suite 740
Chicago, IL 60654

312-863-2900; *Fax:* 312-229-1152;
www.popai.com
Social Media: Facebook, Twitter, LinkedIn, Pinterest

Michelle Adams, Chairman
Keith Arndt, Co-Vice Chair
Scott Eisen, Treasurer
Bob Zanotti, Co-Vice Chair
Madeline Baumgartner, Market Research Manager

Supports all those involved with in-store promotional programs — and research on marketing and retail trends.
1400 Members
Founded in: 1936

21463 Professional Audio-Video Retailers Association
10 E 22nd Street
Suite 310
Lombard, IL 60148-6191

630-268-1500
800-621-0298; *Fax:* 630-953-8957

Debra Smith, Executive Director

Supports owners and operators of independently owned, audio/video stores. Members includes manufacturers of high-end audio/video equipment.
204 Members
Founded in: 1979

21464 Professional Sales Association
5045 Park Ave West
Suite 1B
Seville, OH 44273

330-299-7343; *Fax:* 300-408-0075;
www.profsales.com

Jim Mcgonical, President
Charlie Martin, Central Regional Manager
Alex Marsden, Eastern Regional Manager

An organization of manufacturers' representative firms which sell hardware, housewares, lawn and garden products and traffic appliances to the retail trade.
25 Members
Founded in: 1969

21465 Retail Advertising & Marketing Association
328 7th St Nw
Suite 1100
Washington, DC 20004

202-626-8181
800-673-4692; *Fax:* 202-737-2849
gattim@nrf.com; www.rama-nrf.org
Social Media: Facebook, Twitter, LinkedIn, Google+

Libby Landen, VP, Strategic Marketing
Mike Gatti, Executive Director
Kelly Gilmore, Senior Vice president
Kathy Grannis, Manager, Media Relations
Marcia Tabler, RAMA Consultant

Provides visionary leadership that promotes creativity, innovation and excellence within all marketing disciplines that strategically elevates our members and our industry.
1600 Members
Founded in: 1952

21466 Retail Industry Leaders Association
1700 N Moore St
Suite 2250
Arlington, VA 22209

703-841-2300; *Fax:* 703-841-1184
suzie.squier@rila.org; www.rila.org
Social Media: Facebook, Twitter, LinkedIn

Hubert Joly, Director At- Large
Richard Dreiling, Chairman
Eric Wiseman, Treasurer
William Rhodes III, Vice Chairman
Robert Niblock, Secretary

Retail Industry Leaders Association is a trade association of the lasgest and fastest growing companies in the retail industry, its members include over 400 retailers, product manufacturers, and service suppliers.
400+ Members
Founded in: 1969

21467 Retail Merchants Association
5101 Monument Ave.
Richmond, VA 23230

804-662-5500
866-750-2532; *Fax:* 804-662-5507
info@retailmerchants.com;
www.retailmerchants.com
Social Media: Facebook, Twitter, LinkedIn

Nancy C. Thomas, President & CEO

The Association is dedicated to helping local retailers and small businesses grow.
Founded in: 1906

21468 Retail Packaging Association
105 Eastern Avenue
Suite 104
Annapolis, MD 21403

410-940-6459; *Fax:* 410-263-1659
info@retailpackaging.org;
www.retailpackaging.org

Tony Van Belkom, President
Bob Gant, VP
Jatin Patel, Treasurer~
Denise Cabera, Secretary

Serves its members and the entire retail packaging industry. Also organizes the largest trade show and conference of its kind in the US. A self-governed not-for-profit organization comprised of professionals involved in all facets of production and distribution of retail packaging products.
Founded in: 1989

21469 Retail Systems Alert Group
377 Elliot Street Po Box 332
Newton Upper Falls, MA 02464

617-527-4626; *Fax:* 617-527-8102
info@retailsystems.com;
www.retailsystems.com

Brian Kilcourse, President
Tom Friedman, Chairman
Karen Moss, Editor
Lisa Gayle, Advertising Manager

Retail Systems Alert Group has helped companies reach a highly qualified audience of Extened Retail Industry professionals through advertising, sponsorship, research, and exhibiting opportunities.
Founded in: 1870

21470 Scuba Retailers Association
4 Florence Street
Somerville, MA 02145

617-623-7722
Social Media: Facebook, Twitter, LinkedIn

James Estabrook, Executive Director

Members are stores selling scuba and association underwater equipment.
500 Members
Founded in: 1989

21471 Small Business Technology Council
National Small Business Association
1156 15th St Nw
Suite 1100
Washington, DC 20005

202-662-9700
800-835-6728
alec@sbtc.org; www.sbtc.org
Social Media: Facebook, Twitter, RSS

James Morrison, President
Robert Schmidt, Co-Chair
Heidi Jacobus, Co-Chair
Jere Glover, Executive Director
Larry Nannis, Treasurer

Working with and providing web sites for the very small business.
120 Members
Founded in: 2000

21472 Vacuum and Sewing Dealers Trade Association
2724 2nd Ave
Des Moines, IA 50313-4933

515-282-9101
800-367-5651; *Fax:* 515-282-4483;
www.vdta.com

Craig Dorman, Sales
Charley Dunham, Chairman
Judy Patterson, President
Marlin Graham, Vice-President
Beth Vitiritto, Managing Editor

Seeks to increase the independent vacuum cleaner and sewing machine dealer market share.
20,00 Members
Founded in: 1981

21473 Wine and Spirits Guild of America
3530 Vinings Ridge Court
Atlanta, GA 30339

770-956-8808; *Fax:* 770-988-8634
info@wineandspiritsguild.com;
www.wineandspiritsguild.com

Barbara Owen, Conference Manager
Brad Feuerbacher, President
Cedric Matin, Ex-Officio President & Director
David Jabour, 2nd Vice President and Treasurer
Gary Fisch, 1st Vice President

Promotes the exchange of information on merchandising, marketing and buying of wines and spirits.
40 Members
Founded in: 1948

Newsletters

21474 American Collegiate Retailing Association Newsletter
Loyola University/Department of Marketing
PO Box 121
New Orleans, LA 70118

504-865-2011; *Fax:* 504-865-3851
admit@loyno.edu; www.loyno.edu

Kevin Wildes, President
Alice Glenn, Secretary
Cynthia Tucker, Editor
Mary Degnan, Marketing Manager
Janice Long, Circulation Manager

Educational retailing news and information.
Frequency: Quarterly
Founded in: 1923

21475 Bookselling This Week
American Booksellers Association
200 White Plains Rd
Suite 600
Tarrytown, NY 10591

800-637-0037; *Fax:* 914-591-2720
info@bookweb.org; www.bookweb.org

Oren Teicher, CEO
Len Viahos, COO
Ellie Chang, CFO
Frequency: Weekly
Circulation: 10000

21476 Campus Marketplace
National Association of College Stores
500 E Lorain St
Oberlin, OH 44074-1238

440-775-0120
800-622-7498; *Fax:* 440-775-4769
webteam@nacs.org; www.nacs.org

Brian Cartier, CEO
Carrie Tompkins, Editor

Weekly newsletter covering college store industry: sales, trends, news, personnel and address changes for stores as well as vendors.
Frequency: Monthly
Circulation: 4000
Founded in: 1982

21477 For the President's Eyes Only
Bureau of Business Practice
76 Ninth Avenue
7th Floor
New York, NY 10011

212-771-0600; *Fax:* 212-771-0885;
www.aspenlawschool.com

Robert Becker, CEO
Gustavo Dobles, VP Operations

Provides the latest information on areas of vital interest to the head of the company.
12 Pages
Frequency: 2 per year

21478 Insider
Trade Dimensions
45 Danbury Rd
Wilton, CT 06897-4445

203-563-3000; *Fax:* 203-563-3131;
www.tradedimensions.com

Brain Thomas, Editor
Kristina Castle, Circulation Coordina

Shopping center weekly newsletter that profiles the latest retailer expansion plans, giving - in addition to the numbers of stores operated and planned, the areas targeted, and the type of locations sought - a thumbnail sketch of what makes the concept unique, and what the company specifically looks for in a site.
Cost: $299.00
Frequency: Weekly
Founded in: 1970

21479 International Map Trade Association
2629 Manhattan Avenue
PMB 281
Hermosa Beach, CA 90254-2447

310-376-7731; *Fax:* 949-458-0300;
www.imiamaps.org

Sandy Hill, Executive Director
Linda Hill, Editor

Membership comprised of retail stores featuring maps, travel books, globes, and travel products, plus publishers and manufacturers producing these products. Publishes a monthly newsletter
Cost: $60.00
20 Pages
Frequency: Monthly
ISSN: 1065-6324
Founded in: 1981
Printed in on matte stock

21480 Mouser Report
CAMCO
124 E Carolina Avenue
Crewe, VA 23930-1802

434-645-1993
800-448-8595; *Fax:* 434-645-8232

Charles Mouser, Publisher
Brend DeLuca, Circulation Director

Newsletter covers the latest trends in retail and advertising.
Cost: $96.00
16 Pages
Frequency: Monthly

21481 NRF-BTM Retail Executive Opinion Survey
National Retail Federation
325 7th St
Suite 1101
Washington, DC 20004-2808

202-783-7971
800-673-4692; *Fax:* 202-737-2849;
www.nrf.com
Social Media: Facebook, Twitter, LinkedIn

Matthew Shay, President
Scott Krugman, Publisher
Mader Richard, Executive Director
Michael Gatti, VP/Marketing
David French, VP

Gathers the opinions of the industry's top executives on trends in merchandising, hiring, sales expectations, customer traffic and special seasonal related developments.
Frequency: Monthly

21482 NRF/BIGresearch Consumer Intentions and Actions Survey
National Retail Federation
325 7th St Nw
Suite 1101
Washington, DC 20004-2808

202-783-7971
800-673-4693; *Fax:* 202-737-2849;
www.nrf.com

Matthew Shay, President
Scott Krugman, Publisher
Mader Richard, Executive Director
Michael Gatti, VP/Marketing
David French, VP

Index on consumer shopping behavior. The survey also gauges consumer spending during holidays.
Frequency: Weekly

21483 NSSRA Newsletter
National Ski and Snowboard Retailers Association
1604 Feehanville Drive
Suite 300
Mount Prospect, IL 60056-6213

847-228-8277; *Fax:* 847-439-0111
info@nssra.com; www.nssra.com

Larry Weindruch, President
Paul Prutzman, Chairman

Keeps members informed on critical industry issues, such as guidelines, litigation exposure and marketing
Frequency: Quarterly
Circulation: 1000

21484 National Research Bureau Newsletter
National Research Bureau
320 Valley St
Burlington, IA 52601-5513

319-752-5415; *Fax:* 319-752-3421
contactus@supervisionmagazine.com;
www.national-research-bureau.com

Diane M Darnall, President
William H. Wood, Founder

A newsletter is created for a company by combining a customized masthead with a four page, monthly issue of helpful information on a business field selected by the company.
4 Pages
Frequency: Daily
Founded in: 1933
Printed in 3 colors

21485 Retail CEO Insider
National Retail Federation
325 7th St Nw
Suite 1100
Washington, DC 20004-2808

202-783-7971
800-673-4693; *Fax:* 202-737-2849;
www.nrf.com
Social Media: Facebook, Twitter, LinkedIn, You Tube

Matthew Shay, President
Scott Krugman, Publisher
Mader Richard, Executive Director
Michael Gatti, VP/Marketing
David French, VP

Two-page private news briefing for CEOs, chairpersons and presidents of National Retail Federation member companies. Provides concise, bullet-point coverage of issues facing the industry in the style of the Kiplinger Washington Letter, with a heavy emphasis on government affairs and public policy. Distributed to approximately 650 C-level executives.
Frequency: Monthly

21486 Retail Sales Outlook
National Retail Federation

325 7th St Nw
Suite 1101
Washington, DC 20004-2808

202-783-7971
800-673-4693; *Fax:* 202-737-2849;
www.nrf.com
Social Media: Facebook, Twitter, LinkedIn

Matthew Shay, President
Scott Krugman, Publisher
Mader Richard, Executive Director
Michael Gatti, VP/Marketing
David French, VP

Economic analysis of the retail industry.
Frequency: Quarterly

21487 Shopping Center Management Insider
6 East 32nd St
8th Floor
New York, NY 10016

212-812-8420
800-519-3692
info@vendomegrp.com;
www.vendomegrp.com

Steven Gordon Esq, Editor

Tested management techniques, legal insights and how-to guidelines for running a shopping center or mall. Includes model notices to tenants, letters, agreements, rules, etc.
Cost: $297.00
Frequency: Monthly
Founded in: 1985
Printed in 2 colors on matte stock

21488 T-Shirt Business Info Mapping Newsletter
Prosperity & Profits Unlimited
PO Box 416
Denver, CO 80201-0416

303-575-5676

A Doyle, Editor

How-to T-shirt business and information.
Cost: $8.00
8 Pages
Frequency: Annual
Circulation: 1,450
Founded in: 1989
Printed in one color on matte stock

Magazines & Journals

21489 Accessory Merchandising
Vance Publishing
400 Knightsbridge Pkwy
Lincolnshire, IL 60069-3628

847-634-2600; *Fax:* 847-634-4379
mreckling@vancepublishing.com;
www.vancepublishing.com

Peggy Walker, President
Chandra Palermo, Editor
Michael R. Reckling, Group Publisher
Steven J. Kulikowski, Marketing Manager
Douglas Riemer, Circulation Director

21490 Army/Navy Store & Outdoor Merchandiser
445 Broad Hollow Road
Suite 21
Melville, NY 11747

631-845-2700; *Fax:* 631-845-2797

Military surplus, workwear, casual apparel, camping, hunting and sporting goods, and outdoor clothing industries.
Cost: $25.00
Frequency: Monthly
Circulation: 12M

21491 Barnard's Retail Trend Report
Barnard Enterprises
17 Kenneth Road
Upper Montclair, NJ 07043-2541

973-655-8888; www.retailtrends.com

Kurt Barnard, Publisher/Editor
Jim Adamson, CEO

Forecasts market trends in the retailing industry and on consumer spending.
Cost: $179.00
10 Pages
Circulation: 1200
Founded in: 1984
Printed in 2 colors on newsprint stock

21492 Casual Living
Reed Business Information
2000 Clearwater Dr
Oak Brook, IL 60523-8809

630-574-0825; *Fax:* 630-288-8781;
www.reedbusiness.com

Jeff Greisch, President
Mark Kelsey, MD
Jeremy Knibbs, Chief Executive

21493 Chain Merchandiser
Merchandising Publications Company
PO Box 95C
Baker City, OR 97814-0095

Fax: 541-523-2063

Ruth Sanders, Business Manager
Henry Von Morpurgo, Editor/Publisher

A national service and promotion program incorporating Specialty Foods and Beverages and Deli-Dairy World. Devoted to improved merchandising methods at every level of the marketing and distributing processes - from the field and factory and warehouse to retail sales persons - to provide better customer values, lower costs and greater profits.

21494 Chain Store Age
Lebhar-Friedman
425 Park Ave
Suite 6
New York, NY 10022-3526

212-756-5088
800-216-7117; *Fax:* 212-838-9487
info@lf.com; www.nrn.com

Heather Martin, Manager
John Rapuzzi, Group Publisher
Antonia Peterson, Desk Editor
J Roger Friedman, President

Offers a full overview of chain stores, including management, operation, construction and modernization, store equipment, real estate and advertising.
Frequency: Monthly
Circulation: 35551
Founded in: 1925

21495 College Store
Executive Business Media
PO Box 1500
Westbury, NY 11590-0812

516-334-3030; *Fax:* 516-334-3059
webteam@nacs.org; www.nacs.org

Cynthia D'Angelo, President
Ron Stevens, Editor

Covers the college bookstore market retail industry.
Cost: $40.00
40 Pages
Frequency: Bi-Monthly
Circulation: 6,800

21496 College Store Executive
Executive Business Media
825 Old Country Road
PO Box 1500
Westbury, NY 11590-812

516-334-3030; *Fax:* 516-334-3059
ebm-mail@ebmpubs.com; www.ebmpubs.com

Ken Baglino, Editor
Nancy Wilderwith, Advertising Manager

A merchandising and news magazine edited for those responsible for buying and merchandising products for college retail stores.
Cost: $35.00
36 Pages
Circulation: 8547
ISSN: 0010-1141
Founded in: 1970
Printed in 4 colors on glossy stock

21497 College Store Magazine
National Association of College Stores
500 E Lorain St
Oberlin, OH 44074-1238

440-775-0120
800-622-7498; *Fax:* 440-775-4769
webteam@nacs.org; www.nacs.org

Brian Cartier, CEO
Keith Galestock, Editor
Tara Ellis, Associate Editor

Covers the college store industry's long term issues and trends, focusing on retailing, technology and serving campus communities.
Cost: $66.00
Mailing list available for rent

21498 DSN Retailing Today
Lebhar-Friedman
425 Park Ave
Suite 6
New York, NY 10022-3526

212-756-5088
800-216-7117; *Fax:* 212-838-9487;
www.dsnretailingtoday.com

Heather Martin, Manager
Tim Craig, Editor-in-Chief
Tony Lisanti, Editorial Director
Roger Friedman, CEO

Leading international newspaper serving the growing mass market.
Frequency: Monthly
Circulation: 34000
Founded in: 1925

21499 Dealerscope
North American Publishing Company
1500 Spring Garden St
Suite 1200
Philadelphia, PA 19130-4094

215-238-5300
800-818-8174; *Fax:* 215-238-5342;
www.dealerscope.com
Social Media: Facebook, Twitter, LinkedIn

Ned S Borowsky, CEO
David Dritsas, Editor-in-Chief
Eric Schwartz, President/Publishing
Rhoda Dixon, Circulation Manager
Suzanne DeFruscio, Advertising Promotion Manager

Dedicated to delivering peer-based knowledge and experience, Dealerscope is the ultimate vehicle for presenting product and service solutions to the consumer.
Founded in: 1958

21500 Display & Design Ideas
Shore Varrone

6255 Barfield Road
#200
Atlanta, GA 30328-4332

404-848-0077; *Fax:* 404-252-4436;
www.svi-atl.com

Doug Hope, Publisher
Steve Kaufman, Editor
Lee Pritcher, Owner

Product news and design solutions for those in the retail chain indusrty.
Cost: $60.00
Frequency: Monthly
Circulation: 18,039

21501 Do-It-Yourself Retailing
5822 W 74th St
Indianapolis, IN 46278-1756

317-297-1190; *Fax:* 317-328-4354
vecchie@sbcglobal.net; www.nrha.org

John Hammond, Executive Director
Kevin Hohman, Publisher
Frequency: Monthly
Circulation: 44333

21502 Drug Store News
Lebhar-Friedman
425 Park Ave
Suite 6
New York, NY 10022-3526

212-756-5088; *Fax:* 212-838-9487;
www.drugstorenews.com

Heather Martin, Manager
Tony Lisanti, Editor

Publication consists of merchandising trends and pharmacy developments. Provides extensive coverage of every major segment of chain drug retailing and combination stores.
Cost: $189.00
Frequency: Weekly
Circulation: 40000
Founded in: 1925

21503 Edplay
Fahy-Williams Publishing
PO Box 1080
Geneva, NY 14456-2137

315-789-0458
800-344-0559; *Fax:* 315-789-4263;
www.fwpi.com

J Kevin Fahy, Publisher
Tina Manzer, Editorial Director
Jason Hagerman, Advertising Account Rep
Bradley G Gordner, Senior Editor
Tricia King, Office Manager

Serves toy manufacturers and dealers. Offers product reviews, industry profiles, and reader surveys.
Cost: $22.00
Frequency: Quarterly
Circulation: 7684

21504 Flea Markets Magazine
FleaMarkets.com
1156 15th St NW
Suite 1100
Washington, DC 20005-1755

202-293-8830
800-835-6728; www.fleamarkets.com

Todd McCracken, President

A quarterly magazine published by FleaMarkets.com.
Cost: $15.00
Frequency: Quarterly
Circulation: 3000
Founded in: 1989

21505 Gacs Today
Naylor Publications
PO Box 855
Snellville, GA 30078-855

770-736-9723; *Fax:* 770-736-9725;
www.gacs.com

Jim Tudor, CEO
Frequency: Quarterly
Circulation: 2500
Founded in: 1973

21506 Garden Center Merchandising & Management
Branch-Smith Publishing
PO Box 1868
Fort Worth, TX 76101-1868

817-882-4110
800-433-5612; *Fax:* 817-882-4121;
www.gardencentermac.com

David Branch, President
Terri Smith, Director Circulation
Carol Miller, Editor
Frequency: Monthly
Circulation: 15143
Founded in: 1915

21507 Garden Center Products & Supplies
Branch-Smith Publishing
PO Box 1868
Fort Worth, TX 76101-1868

817-882-4110
800-433-5612; *Fax:* 817-882-4121;
www.branchsmith.com

David Branch, President
Patrice Kuhl, Publisher/Sales Director
Frequency: Monthly
Founded in: 1910

21508 Hearth & Home
Village West Publishing
PO Box 1288
Laconia, NH 03247-2008

603-528-4285
800-258-3772; *Fax:* 603-524-0643;
www.homehearth.com

Richard Wright, Editor
Jackie Avignone, Sales Manager

Information for retailers and others selling hearth products, patio furnishing, barbecues, spas, garden accessories, and other outdoor products.
Cost: $11.95
Circulation: 18000
ISSN: 0273-5695
Founded in: 1980

21509 International Gaming and Wagering Business
BNP Media
PO Box 1080
Skokie, IL 60076-9785

847-763-9534; *Fax:* 847-763-9538
igwb@halldata.com; www.igwb.com
Social Media: Facebook, Twitter, LinkedIn

James Rutherford, Editor
Lynn Davidson, Marketing
Tammie Gizicki, Director

Focuses on business strategy, legislative information, food service and promotional concerns.
Frequency: Monthly
Circulation: 25000

21510 Kitchenware News
United Publications
PO Box 1056
Yarmouth, ME 04096-2056

207-846-0600; *Fax:* 207-846-0657;
www.kitchenwares.com

Brooke Taliaferro, President
Jim McNeil, Publisher

News and information on the latest products and equipment for the retail kitchenware industry.
Cost: $45.00
Frequency: Monthly
Circulation: 12,117

21511 MMR/Mass Market Retailers
Racher Press
220 5th Avenue
New York, NY 10001-7798

212-213-6000; *Fax:* 212-725-4594
info@racherpress.com;
www.massmarketretailers.com

Susan Schinitsky, Publisher
David Pinto, Editor
John Dioguardi, Director Sales/Marketing
Kevin Burke, Group Advertising Director
Pam Vandernoth, Circulation Director

News, analysis, trends, and events for drug, discount, and supermarket chain executives.
Cost: $185.00
Circulation: 21645
Founded in: 1984

21512 Magazine Retailer
MetaMedia
124 W 24th Street
#3-D
New York, NY 1011-1920

212-989-6978; *Fax:* 212-255-7143

David Orlow, Publisher
Djalal Mohammadi, President

Merchandising tips, new tiles, publication changes, consumer purchasing trends, industry news and media impact on sales.
Cost: $19.00
Frequency: Quarterly
Circulation: 10,326

21513 Mass Market Retailer
Racher Press
220 5th Avenue
New York, NY 10001-7708

212-213-6000; *Fax:* 212-725-3961;
www.massmarketretailers.com

Susan Schinitsky, Publisher
David Pinto, Editor
Susan Schinitsky, CEO/President
John Dioguardi, Marketing
Pam Vandernoth, Circulation Manager

News and information on the drug store chain industry.
Cost: $35.00
30 Pages
Founded in: 1984

21514 Military Market
Gannet Company
6883 Commercial Dr
Springfield, VA 22151-4202

703-750-8643; *Fax:* 703-750-8717
rhynema@atpco.com; www.gannett.com

Dennis V Washburn, CEO
David Craig, Managing Editor

Provides trade information, trends, and news for military commisionary and post/base exchange managers.
Cost: $84.00
Frequency: Monthly
Circulation: 12000
Founded in: 1940

21515 Museum Store Magazine
Museum Store Association

4100 E Mississippi Ave
Suite 800
Denver, CO 80246-3055

303-504-9223; *Fax:* 303-504-9585
membership@museumdistrict.com;
www.museumdistrict.com

Beverly J Barsook, Executive Director
Amy Nicholas, Editor
Cost: $34.00
Frequency: Quarterly
Circulation: 3000
Founded in: 1955
Printed in 4 colors on glossy stock

21516 Museums & More Specialty Shops Product News
Museums & More Specialty Product News
PO Box 128
Sparta, Mi 49345-2122

616-887-9008; *Fax:* 616-887-2666;
www.museumsandmore.com

Julie McCallum, Editor
Jon Kaufman, Publisher

Product highlights and marketing strategies for the owners and oporators of gift shops in museums and other public attractions.
Cost: $35.00
Frequency: Quarterly
Circulation: 28014

21517 NACS SCAN
National Association of Convenience Stores
1600 Duke St
Suite 700
Alexandria, VA 22314-3436

703-684-3600; *Fax:* 703-836-4564
webmaster@nacsonline.com;
www.nacsonline.com

Hank Armour, President

A bi-monthly magazine offering information on key industry trends and innovative practices of convenience store companies.
Cost: $840.00
Frequency: Monthly
Circulation: 3000
Founded in: 1961

21518 NAEDA Equipment Dealer
North American Equipment Dealers Association
1195 Smizer Mill Rd
Fenton, MO 63026-3480

636-349-5000; *Fax:* 636-349-5443
naeda@naeda.com; www.naeda.com
Social Media: Twitter, LinkedIn

Paul Kindinger, President/CEO
Michael Williams, VP, Government Relations/Treasurer
Terry Leath, Executive Assistant
Roger Gjellstad, First Vice Chair
Lester Killebrew, Chairman

Monthly management and merchandising magazine featuring articles about successful dealers, new products, new technology, industry news and much more.
Cost: $40.00
5000 Members
Frequency: Monthly
Circulation: 9,500
ISSN: 1074-5017
Founded in: 1900
Printed in 4 colors on glossy stock

21519 NARDA Independent Retailer
North American Retail Dealers Association
10 E 22nd Street
Suite 310
Lombard, IL 60148-6191

630-953-8950
800-621-0298; *Fax:* 630-953-8957;
www.narda.com

Tom Drake, CEO/President
Gennifer Michalek, Chairman

Emphasis is placed on ideas that help readers become better, more profitable businesses. Articles are featured regularly on displays, salesmanship, financial analysis and service management.
Cost: $78.00
36 Pages
Frequency: Monthly
Circulation: 2000
ISSN: 1098-9714
Founded in: 1943
Mailing list available for rent: 2,000 names
Printed in 4 colors on glossy stock

21520 New Age Retailer
Continuity Publishing
2183 Alpine Way
Bellingham, WA 98226-8045

360-676-0789
800-463-9243; *Fax:* 360-676-0932;
www.newageretailer.com

Molly Trimble, CEO
Ray Hemachandra, Editor-in-Chief
Laurel Leigh, Editor
Stephanie R Hager, Circulation Manager
Ellen Koolen, Production Manager

Provides information on new products and business to business trade magazine that supports store owners by providing independent product reviews, retail advice and coverage of the new age and spirtual lviing industry.
Cost: $ 85.00
192 Pages
Circulation: 10000
Founded in: 1987
Mailing list available for rent: 6,000 names at $150 per M

21521 POP Design
In-Store Marketing Institute
7400 Skokie Blvd
Skokie, IL 60077-3339

847-675-7400; *Fax:* 847-675-7494
info@instoremarketer.org;
www.instoremarketer.org
Social Media: Facebook, Twitter, LinkedIn

Peter Hoyt, President

Serves the news and product information needs of producers and designers of instore displays, signs and fixtures. Each issue features the latest trends and technologies vital to building and designing successful instore merchandising.
Frequency: Monthly
Circulation: 18000
Printed in 4 colors on glossy stock

21522 POPAI News
Point-of-Purchase Advertising Institute
1600 Duke Street
Suite 400
Alexandria, VA 22314

703-373-8815; *Fax:* 703-373-8801
bcotter@popai.com; www.popai.com
Social Media: Facebook, Twitter, LinkedIn

Berk Cotter, Director Member Services
Richard Blatt, CEO/President
Stephen Morant, Manager Production Services
Sean Simmons, General Manager

Provides the point-of-purchase industry with coverage of marketing and retail trends, with an emphasis on in-store promotional programs. Editorial offers coverage of marketing programs, display case histories, preview of new promotional campaigns, sales volume and trends. Accepts advertising.
Cost: $40.00
Frequency: Monthly
Founded in: 1940

21523 Pollution Engineering
Reed Business Information
2000 Clearwater Dr
Oak Brook, IL 60523-8809

630-574-0825; *Fax:* 630-288-8781
greenr@bnpmedia.com;
www.reedbusiness.com
Social Media: Facebook, Twitter, LinkedIn

Jeff Greisch, President
Erin Puranananda, Marketing Manager
Seth Fisher, Products Editor
Mark Kelsey, Chief Executive Officer

Serves the field of pollution control in manufacturing industries, utilities, consulting engineers and constructors. Also serves government agencies including administration of federal, state and local environmental programs.
Frequency: Monthly
ISSN: 0032-3640
Founded in: 1977

21524 Publishers Weekly
PO Box 51593
Harlan, IA 51593

800-278-2991; *Fax:* 712-733-8019
pwycustserv@cdsfulfillment.com;
www.publishersweekly.com
Social Media: Facebook, Twitter, LinkedIn

George Slovik, President
Michael Coffey, Co-Editorial Director
Diane Roback, Children's Book Editor
Louisa Ermelino, Reviews Director
Calvin Reid, News Editor

PW is the international journal of book publishing and bookselling including business news, reviews and bestseller lists targeted at publishers, booksellers, librarians and literary agents.
Frequency: Weekly
Founded in: 1872

21525 Retail Cost of Doing Business
American Floorcovering Association
2211 E Howell Avenue
Anaheim, CA 92806-6009

714-572-8370

Offers an overview of the retail trade.
Frequency: Annual

21526 Retail Focus
National Sporting Goods Association
1601 Feehanville Drive
Suite 300
Mount Prospect, IL 60056

847-296-6742
800-815-5422; *Fax:* 847-391-9827
info@nsga.org; www.nsga.org

Bob Dickman, Chairman of the Board
Matt Carlson, President/CEO
Dan Kasen, Director of Information Services

Magazine for members only
Frequency: Bi-Monthly
Mailing list available for rent

21527 Retail Observer
Retail Observer
1442 Sierra Creek Way
San Jose, CA 95132-3618

408-272-8974
800-393-0509; *Fax:* 408-272-3344
info@retailobserver.com;
www.retailobserver.com/

Chuck Edmonds, Publisher
Lee Boucher, Editor

Edited for owners, managers and retail sales personnel of appliance stores, home entertainment stores and kitchen and bath dealers.
Frequency: Monthly
Circulation: 11750

21528 Retail Systems Alert
Retail Systems Alert Group
PO Box 332
Newton Upper Falls, MA 02464-02

617-527-4626; *Fax:* 617-527-8102;
www.retailsystems.com

Thomas H Friedman, Publisher

Provides updated information on automation news and trends, including decision systems, information systems implementation, in-store merchandise management, and case studies of retailers.
Cost: $295.00
8 Pages
Frequency: Monthly
Founded in: 1988

21529 Retail Systems Reseller
Edgell Communications
4 Middlebury Boulevard
Suite 107
Randolph, NJ 07869-1111

973-252-0100; *Fax:* 973-252-9020;
www.edgellcommunications.com

Michael Kachmar, Publisher
Joseph S King, Editor-in-Chief
Gabriele A Edgell, CEO
Dan Ligorner, Director of Marketing

Offers information to retailers, dealers, systems integraters, VARs, VADs, etc., on retail technology for small to mid-size retailers.

21530 RetailTech
770 Broadway
New York, NY 10003-9522

646-654-7480; *Fax:* 646-654-7568;
www.retail-merchandiser.com

21531 STORES Magazine
National Retail Federation
325 7th St NW
Suite 1101
Washington, DC 20004-2808

202-783-7971
800-673-4693; *Fax:* 202-737-2849
pennw@nrf.com; www.nrf.com
Social Media: Facebook, Twitter, LinkedIn

Matthew Shay, President
Scott Krugman, Publisher
Mader Richard, Executive Director
Michael Gatti, VP/Marketing
David French, VP

Magazine of the National Retail Federation. Provides timely information of importance to senior retail headquarters executives. Every issue reports on trends in retail technology, credit and payment systems, logistics and supply chain and other vital store operations.
Cost: $120.00
Frequency: Monthly
Circulation: 35000

21532 Succe$$ful $ource$
Sutton Family Communications & Publishing Company
155 Sutton Lane
Fordsville, KY 42343

270-740-0870
jlsutton@apex.net;
www.suttoncompliance.com

Theresa Sutton, Publisher

The #1 trade magazine for multi-billion dollar flea market industry.
Cost: $5.00
Circulation: 100000
Founded in: 1977

21533 Supermarket News
Fairchild Publications
750 3rd Ave
New York, NY 10017-2703

212-630-4000
800-204-4515; *Fax:* 212-630-3563;
www.supermarketnews.com

Mary G Berner, CEO
David Merrefield, Editorial Director
Dan Bagan, Publishing Director
David Orgel, Editor-in-Chief
Cost: $44.50
40 Pages
Frequency: Weekly
Circulation: 36346
ISSN: 0039-5803
Founded in: 1892

21534 Today's Grocers
Florida Grocer Publications
PO Box 430760
S Miami, FL 33246

305-661-0792
800-440-3067; *Fax:* 305-661-6720

Jack Nobles, Publisher
Dennis Kane, Editor

Provides the latest food industry news and trends to Florida, Georgia, Alabama, Louisiana, Mississippi and the Carolinas.
Cost: $29.00
24 Pages
Frequency: Monthly
Circulation: 19,000
ISSN: 1529-4420
Founded in: 1956
Printed in on newsprint stock

Trade Shows

21535 ASD/AMD Houston Variety Merchandise Show
ASD/AMD Merchandise Group
2950 31st Street
Suite 100
Santa Monica, CA 90405

310-396-6006
800-421-4511; *Fax:* 310-399-2662;
www.merchandisegroup.com

Julie Ichiba, Show Director

Our newest variety and general merchandise trade show offers buyers in the southwestern US and Mexico terrific product sourcing opportunities for all types of popular consumer goods.
12000 Attendees

21536 ASD/AMD Las Vegas Trade Show
ASD/AMD Merchandise Group
2950 31st Street
Suite 100
Santa Monica, CA 90405

310-396-6006
800-421-4511; *Fax:* 310-399-2662;
www.merchandisegroup.com

Julie Ichiba, Show Director

The summer edition of the largest variety merchandise event in the US attracts over 50,000 buyers to Las Vegas. Tens of thousands of unique products in hundreds of popular consumer product categories are on display at this even
50000 Attendees
Frequency: August

21537 ASD/AMD's Atlantic City Variety Merchandise Show
ASD/AMD Merchandise Group
2950 31st Street
Suite 100
Santa Monica, CA 90405

310-396-6006
800-421-4511; *Fax:* 310-399-2662;
www.merchandisegroup.com

Julie Ichiba, Show Director

Held in Atlantic City, New Jersey, this event is a popular destination for east coast retailers to make deals and place orders for variety and general merchandise in hundreds of popular consumer categories before the summer selling season begins.
10000 Attendees
Frequency: May

21538 ASD/AMD's Fall Variety Merchandise Show
ASD/AMD Merchandise Group
2950 31st Street
Suite 100
Santa Monica, CA 90405

310-396-6006
800-421-4511; *Fax:* 310-399-2662;
www.merchandisegroup.com

Julie Ichiba, Show Director

The fall edition of the general merchandise event on the east coast takes place in New York City. It's the last opportunity of the year for retailers to place orders for goods before the busy holiday buying season.
12000 Attendees
Frequency: September

21539 ASD/AMD's Las Vegas Merchandise Expo
ASD/AMD Merchandise Group
2950 31st Street
Suite 100
Santa Monica, CA 90405
310-396-6006
800-421-4511; *Fax:* 310-399-2662;
www.merchandisegroup.com

Julie Ichiba, Show Director

Held in Las Vegas, Nevada, this event is strategically timed for western US retailers to stock their shelves with quality, value-priced variety and general merchandise in between our larger Las Vegas Trade Shows in March and Agust.
5,000 Attendees
Frequency: June

21540 ASD/AMD's New York Variety Merchandise Show
ASD/AMD Merchandise Group
2950 31st Street
Suite 100
Santa Monica, CA 90405

310-396-6006
800-421-4511; *Fax:* 310-399-2662;
www.merchandisegroup.com

Julie Ichiba, Show Director

Held in New York City, this event is the first opportunity of the New Year for variety and general merchandise retailers to stock their shelves after the holidays with popular, value-priced consumer goods in hundreds of product categories.
12500 Attendees
Frequency: January

21541 ASD/AMD's Orlando Variety Merchandise Show
ASD/AMD Merchandise Group

2950 31st Street
Suite 100
Santa Monica, CA 90405

310-396-6006
800-421-4511; *Fax:* 310-399-2662;
www.merchandisegroup.com

Julie Ichiba, Show Director

Held in Orlando, Florida, this event is a popular destination for southeastern US retailers to make deals and place orders for variety and general merchandise in hundreds of popular consumer categories.
5,500 Attendees
Frequency: April

21542 Accent on Design
George Little Management
10 Bank Street
Suite 1200
White Plains, NY 10606-1954

914-486-6070
800-272-7469; *Fax:* 914-948-2867;
www.nyigf.com

Elizabeth Murphy, Manager
George Little II, President

370 booths of the latest and most innovative gift lines such as decorative accessories and home furnishings.
50M Attendees
Frequency: August
Founded in: 1984

21543 American Beverage Licensees Annual Convention & Trade Show
National Association of Beverage Retailers
5101 River Road
Suite 108
Bethesda, MD 20816-1560

301-656-1494; *Fax:* 301-656-7539;
www.ablusa.org

Harry Wiles, Executive Director
Shawn Ross, Office Manager

Annual show of 75 manufacturers, suppliers and distributors of alcoholic beverages.
1,000 Attendees

21544 Associated Surplus Dealers/Associated Merchandise Dealers Trade Show
ASD/AMD Merchandise Group
2950 31st Street
Suite 100
Santa Monica, CA 90405

310-255-4633
800-421-4511; *Fax:* 310-399-3662;
www.merchandisegroup.com

Sam Bundy, Group President

Gifts, souvenirs and assorted merchandise for professional buyers.
15000 Attendees
Frequency: Annual/March

21545 Book Expo America
Reed Exhibitions
383 Main Avenue
Norwalk, CT 06851

203-404-4800
800-840-5614
cmuller@reedexpo.com;
www.bookexpoamerica.com
Social Media: Facebook, Twitter, LinkedIn

Courtney Muller, Event Manager
Cathy Glickstein, Registration

Sponsored by American Booksellers Association and Association of American Publishers. More than 2,000 exhibits, 500 authors, over 60 conference sessions as well as a special area for rights business, all the latest titles across genres, uncover hidden gems, network, and meet the industry contacts to put you instantly on top of what you need to know for your business and job.
Frequency: May/June
Founded in: 2000

21546 CMM International: FLEX Expo
Bruno Blenheim
Fort Lee Executive Park
Fort Lee, FL 07024

800-829-3976; *Fax:* 201-346-1602

Nick Helyer, President

Exhibits by franchisers and sellers to the franchise industry. 125 booths.
5M Attendees
Frequency: June

21547 Customer Relationship Management Course: C RMretail
National Retail Federation
325 7th Street NW
Suite 1101
Washington, DC 20004

202-783-7971; *Fax:* 202-737-2849
exhibit@nrf.com; www.nrf.com
Social Media: Facebook, Twitter, LinkedIn

Michaal Tuttle, Director Exhibits
Cindy Shin, Director Sales

CRMretail is a cross-industry conference, bringing together retail business leaders and the leading technology companies, solutions providers, consultants and academicians in the field of customer relationship management. Annual CRMretail research conducted by Gartner Dataquest is also released at this conference.
200 Attendees
Frequency: Late Spring
Founded in: 1993

21548 Green Profit's Retail Experience
Green Profit Magazine
335 N River Street
Batavia, IL 60510

630-208-9080
888-888-0013; *Fax:* 630-208-9350
info@ballpublishing.com;
www.ballpublishing.com/conferences

Michelle Mazza, Show Manager

Educational event and tradeshow dedicated exclusively to garden center retailing. Covers topics from store layout and design to merchandising strategies and business management. 20 booths
300 Attendees
Frequency: September
Founded in: 2006

21549 International Council of Shopping Centers Fall Convention Trade & Exposition
International Council of Shopping Centers
1221 Ave Of The Americas
41st Fl
New York, NY 10020-1099

646-728-3800; *Fax:* 732-694-1755
icsc@icsc.org; www.icsc.org

Michael Kercheval, President/CEO
Denise Adrian, Director Of Marketing

21550 International Franchise Association Expo
1501 K St NW
Suite 350
Washington, DC 20005-1412

202-628-8000; *Fax:* 202-628-0812

Matthew Shay, President
Patricia Langfeld, VP

75 booths.
1M Attendees
Frequency: February

21551 Internet Retailer Conference & Exhibition
Internet Retailer
300 S Wacker Drive
Suite 602
Chicago, IL 60606

Fax: 312-362-9532; www.internetretailer.com
Social Media: Facebook, Twitter, LinkedIn

Learn the strategies, practices and tools to lift your site into e-retailing's second decade of growth. Network with your peers in the only show serving e-retailers from all merchant channels.
Frequency: Annual

21552 Logistics
Retail Industry Leaders Association
1700 N Moore Street
Suite 2250
Arlington, VA 22209

703-841-2300; *Fax:* 703-841-1184;
www.imra.org

Britt Wood, VP
Sean Nodland, Manager

This event brings together retailers, consumer product companies, and suppliers of goods and service logistics side of business
400 Attendees
Frequency: February

21553 Loss Prevention Conference & Exhibition
National Retail Federation
325 7th Street NW
Suite 1100
Washington, DC 20004

202-783-7971; *Fax:* 202-737-2849
exhibit@nrf.com; www.nrf.com
Social Media: Facebook, Twitter, LinkedIn

Michaal Tuttle, Director Exhibits
Scott Krugman, Publisher
Mader Richard, Executive Director
Michael Gatti, VP/Marketing
David French, VP

Major conference for Loss Prevention, Internal Audit and Risk Management professionals in the retail industry.
1500 Attendees
Frequency: June
Founded in: 1993

21554 Loss Prevention, Auditing & Safety Conference
Retail Industry Leaders Association
1700 N Moore Street
Suite 2250
Arlington, VA 22209

703-841-2300; *Fax:* 703-841-1184
rhett.asher@retail-leaders.org;
www.retail-leaders.org
Social Media: Facebook, Twitter, LinkedIn

Rhett Asher

Annual information exchange.
325 Attendees
Frequency: April

21555 Marketing Conference
International Mass Retail Association
1700 N Moore Street
Suite 2250
Arlington, VA 22209

703-841-2300; *Fax:* 703-841-1184;
www.imra.org

Peter Kim, Owner

21556 NACS Show Annual Meeting and Exposition
National Association of Convenience Stores

1600 Duke Street
Alexandria, VA 22314

703-684-3600; *Fax:* 703-836-4564
nacs@nacs.com; www.nacsshow.com

Jane Berzan, VP Events/Mktg/Supplier Relations
Sherry Romello, Director Meetings and Conventions
24000 Attendees
Frequency: October

21557 National Lawn & Garden Controlled Marketing Conference
Controlled Marketing Conferences
PO Box 1771
Monument, CO 80132

719-488-0226
888-316-0226; *Fax:* 719-488-8168;
www.nlgshow.com

Robert Mikulas, President
Chris Wolf, VP

This year CMC events will be linked to the National Lawn ans Garden Show - The Expo Division. Don't miss out on the industries most important lawn and garden headlines event.
3000 Attendees
Frequency: June

21558 National Retail Federation Annual Conference and Expo
National Retail Federation
325 7th Street NW
Suite 1100
Washington, DC 20004-2808

202-783-7971; *Fax:* 202-783-0581
webmaster@nrf.com; www.nrf.com

Michaal Tuttle, Director Exhibits
Cindy Shin, Director Sales
Tracy Mullin, President

600 booths exhibiting the latest in retail technology, new developments in credit validation, security and materials handling.
12M Attendees
Frequency: January

21559 Retail Advertising Conference: RAC
Retail Advertising & Marketing International
325 7th Street NW
Suite 1100
Washington, DC 20004

202-626-8183; *Fax:* 202-737-2849;
www.rama-nrf.org

Mike Gatti, VP Marketing

Definitive event for retail advertising and marketing professionals each year featuring the RAC Awards gala dinner and Retail Hall of Fame induction annually.
1000 Attendees
Frequency: February

21560 Retail Promotion Show
Association of Retail Marketing Services
10 Drs James Parker Boulevard
Suite 103
Red Bank, NJ 07701-1500

732-842-5070
866-331-6310; *Fax:* 732-219-1938;
www.goarms.com

Gerri Hopkins, Executive Director

Annual show of 65 manufacturers, suppliers, distributors and representatives of dinnerware, glassware, housewares, books, videos, games, sweepstakes, dolls and plush toys suppliers used as retail promotions.
1200 Attendees
Frequency: March, Annual

21561 Shop.org Annual Summit
Shop.org
325 7th Street NW
Suite 1100
Washington, DC 20004

202-626-8183; *Fax:* 202-626-8191;
www.shop.org

Diane Furstenberg, COO
Lane Bryant, VP Marketing

Provides a unique opportunity for Internet and multi-channel retail industry leaders to exchange ideas, perspectives, opportunities and challenges in an intimate and comfortable setting. The Summit features dialogues with distinguished keynote speakers, provocative panels and debates on timely issues, and important original research.
600 Attendees
Frequency: September

21562 Shop.org Members' Forum
Shop.org
325 7th Street NW
Suite 1100
Washington, DC 20004

202-626-8183; *Fax:* 202-626-8191;
www.shop.org

Diane Furstenberg, COO
Lane Bryant, VP Marketing

Attendees see presentations for an online holiday recap and new multichannel retail research sessions as well as roundtable discussions and other networking events.
350 Attendees
Frequency: January

21563 Southern Convenience Store & Petroleum Show
PO Box 855
Snellville, GA 30078

770-736-9723; *Fax:* 770-736-9725
jtudor@aol.com; www.gacs.com

Jim Tudor, President

Contains 250 exhibits.
3,000 Attendees
Founded in: 2003

21564 Store Fixturing Show
Shore Varrone
6255 Barfield Road NE
Suite 200
Atlanta, GA 30328-4332

404-848-0077
800-241-9034; *Fax:* 770-252-4436

Russ Eisenhardt, VP Trade Shows
Lee Pritcher, Owner

The largest annual store design event in the world. The event also includes The Visual Merchandising Show, the Retail Operations & Construction Expo, the POPAI Expo and the Exhibit Ideas Show. 800 exhibitors in total.
15M Attendees
Frequency: April

21565 Store Operations & Human Resources Conference
International Mass Retail Association
1700 N Moore Street
Suite 2250
Arlington, VA 22209

703-841-2300; *Fax:* 703-841-1184;
www.imra.org

This educational event provides attendees with an opportunity to learn from experts in their fields on the most pressing topics of the day

Directories & Databases

21566 Annual Trade Show Directory
Forum Publishing Company
383 E Main St
Centerport, NY 11721-1538

631-754-5000; *Fax:* 631-754-0630;
www.forum123.com

Martin Stevens, Owner

Over 1,800 merchandise trade shows throughout the United States and Canada.
Cost: $39.95
312 Pages
Frequency: Annual

21567 Association of Retail Marketing Services Membership Directory
Association of Retail Marketing Services
10 Drs James Parker Boulevard
Suite 103
Red Bank, NJ 07701-1500

732-842-5070; *Fax:* 732-219-1938;
www.goarms.com

Gerri Hopkins, Executive Director
Lisa McCauley, Administrative Director

Membership directory.
Cost: $25.00
Frequency: Annual

21568 Directory of Convenience Stores
Trade Dimensions
45 Danbury Rd
Wilton, CT 06897-4445

203-563-3000; *Fax:* 860-563-3131;
www.tradedimensions.com

Jennifer Gillbert, Editor
Lynda Guticulez, Managing Editor

The directory comprises nearly 1,500 detailed profiles on the companies you need to do business with - extensive dependable information on the grocery industry's most volatile segment.
Cost: $245.00
Frequency: Annual

21569 Directory of High Discount Merchandise Sources
B Klein Publishers
Po Box 6578
Delray Beach, FL 33482-6578

561-496-3316; *Fax:* 561-496-5546

Bernard Klein, Owner

Approximately 1,200 sources of products offered at high discounts.
Cost: $35.00
Frequency: Annual

21570 Directory of Mail Order Catalogs
Grey House Publishing
4919 Route 22
PO Box 56
Amenia, NY 12501

518-789-8700
800-562-2139; *Fax:* 845-373-6390
books@greyhouse.com; www.greyhouse.com
Social Media: Facebook, Twitter

Leslie Mackenzie, Publisher
Richard Gottlieb, Editor

The premier source of information on the mail order catalog industry. Covers over 13,000 consumer and business catalog companies with 44 different product chapters from Animals to Toys and Games.
Cost: $395.00
1900 Pages
Frequency: Annual

ISBN: 1-592373-96-8
Founded in: 1981

21571 **Directory of Mail Order Catalogs - Online Database**
Grey House Publishing
4919 Route 22
PO Box 56
Amenia, NY 12501
518-789-8700
800-562-2139; *Fax:* 845-373-6390
gold@greyhouse.com
http://gold.greyhouse.com
Social Media: Facebook, Twitter
Leslie Mackenzie, Publisher
Richard Gottlieb, Editor
Reach over 10,000 consumer catalog companies in one easy-to-use source with The Directory of Mail Order Catalogs - Online Database. Filled with business-building detail, each company profile gives you the information you need to access that organization quickly and easily. Listings provide key contacts, sales volume, employee size, printing information, circulation, list data, product descriptions and much more.
Frequency: Annual
Founded in: 1981

21572 **Directory of Major Malls**
PO Box 837
Nyack, NY 10960-0837
845-348-7000; *Fax:* 845-426-0802
Tama J Shor, Editor/Publisher
Murray Shor, Consulting Publisher
Contains 2865 listings with over 1800 leasing/site plans of major malls, with many showing the anchors, design layout, intersecting streets, peripheral land, and major highways.
ISBN: 0-932599-13-3

21573 **Directory of Mass Merchandisers**
Trade Dimensions
45 Danbury Rd
Wilton, CT 06897-4445
203-563-3000; *Fax:* 860-563-3131;
www.tradedimensions.com
Lynda Gutierrez, Managing Editor
Jennifer Gilbert, Editor
This directory defines this complex class of retail trade. Includes profiles of the chains and leading mass merchandisers by market area. Also includes HBC suppliers and store type breakdowns by state/region.
Cost: $245.00
Frequency: Annual

21574 **Discount & General Merchandising Stores**
Chain Store Guide
3922 Coconut Palm Dr
Tampa, FL 33619-1389
813-627-6700
800-972-9292; *Fax:* 813-627-7094
info@csgis.com; www.csgis.com
Mike Jarvis, Publisher
Shami Choon, Manager
This database is an in-depth look at the mass-merchandising segment, bringing you access to more than 7,000 listings along with over 23,000 key personnel. This report includes targeted research from sectors such as Discount Department Stores, General Merchandise Stores, Dollar Stores, Automotive Aftermarket Retailers and Computer & Consumer Electronics Chains.
Cost: $335.00
720 Pages
Frequency: Annual

21575 **Discount Merchandiser**
McFadden Publishing Company
233 Park Ave S
6th Floor
New York, NY 10003-1606
212-979-4800; *Fax:* 212-979-7342
Steven Jacober, Editor
Profiles of the top 55 chains and list of top 85 discount merchandising companies.
Cost: $40.00
Frequency: Annual June

21576 **International Franchise Association - Franchise Opportunities Guide**
1501 K St NW
Suite 350
Washington, DC 20005-1412
202-628-8000; *Fax:* 202-628-0812;
www.franchise.org
Matthew Shay, President
This directory lists over 3,000 companies offering franchises.
Cost: $21.00
300 Pages
Frequency: SemiAnnual

21577 **Leading Chain Tenants Database**
Chain Store Guide
3922 Coconut Palm Dr
Tampa, FL 33619-1389
813-627-6700
800-778-9794; *Fax:* 813-627-7094
info@csgis.com; www.csgis.com
Mike Jarvis, Publisher
Arthur Sciarrotta, Senior VP
Information on more than 8,600 retailers in the U.S. and Canada with over 32,000 personnel contacts. This database will lead you to new real estate prospects across a vast range of industries. Whether you are in real estate development, leasing or sales, the opportunities are endless.
Cost: $365.00

21578 **NRB Shopping Center Directory**
Trade Dimensions
45 Danbury Rd
Wilton, CT 06897-4445
203-563-3000; *Fax:* 860-563-3131;
www.nrbonline.com
Patricia Kelly, Managing Editor
Stephanie Strano, Circulation Director
The most comprehensive book on shopping centers available. Encompassing over 37,000 centers from neighborhood to super regional, the Directory is organized into four volumes: East, Midwest, South, West. A fifth volume is dedicated exclusively to the industry's top contacts, comprising the names and contact information for anyone who owns, leases, or manages three or more centers.
Cost: $325.00
Frequency: Annual

21579 **Outlet Project Directory**
Value Retail News
29399 Us Highway 19 N
Suite 370
Clearwater, FL 33761-2138
727-781-7557
800-669-1020; *Fax:* 727-536-4389;
www.valueretailnews.com
Cher Russell-Street, Editor
Factory outlet projects.
Cost: $179.00
Frequency: SemiAnnual

21580 **Outlet Retail Directory**
Off-Price Specialists, Value Retail News
14250 49th St N
Clearwater, FL 33762-2800
727-464-6460; *Fax:* 727-453-7419
James Pierce, Manager
Over 500 outlet retail chains are profiled.
280 Pages
Frequency: Semiannual

21581 **Products & Services Directory**
Value Retail News
29399 Us Highway 19 N
Suite 370
Clearwater, FL 33761-2138
727-781-7557
800-669-1020; *Fax:* 727-536-4389;
www.valueretailnews.com
Cher Russell-Street, Editor
More than 2,000 service companies specializing in outlet or off-price retailing and development industries.
Cost: $49.00
Frequency: Annual

21582 **Productscan Online**
Marketing Intelligence Service
6473 State Route 64
Naples, NY 14512-9726
585-374-6326; *Fax:* 585-374-5217;
www.productscan.com
Tom Vierhile, Manager
Julie Fox, Finance Executive
This database is dedicated solely to new launches of consumer packaged goods. Includes label copy, in-depth reports on innovations, and product pictures capable of statistical analysis and manufacturer history reports.
Cost: $ 3995.00

21583 **Retail Industry Buying Guide: STORES Magazine**
National Retail Federation
325 7th St NW
Suite 1100
Washington, DC 20004-2808
202-783-7971
800-673-4693; *Fax:* 202-737-2849
pennw@nrf.com; www.nrf.com
Social Media: Facebook, Twitter, LinkedIn
Matthew Shay, President
Scott Krugman, Publisher
Mader Richard, Executive Director
Michael Gatti, VP/Marketing
David French, VP
Capital spending in the products and services that are imperitive to running a smooth and efficient retail operation were particularly hard hit in the past year. In the face of continued uncertainty, it's essential that retailers make informed decisions on how to best invest their limited capital to ensure a positive return on their investment. This directory is that source of information.
Frequency: Monthly
Circulation: 35000

21584 **Retail Tenant Directory**
Trade Dimensions
45 Danbury Rd
Wilton, CT 06897-4445
203-563-3000; *Fax:* 860-563-3131;
www.tradedimensions.com
Garrett Van Siclen, Publisher
Thomas Donato, Editor
Complete and accurate details for 5,000+ growing retailers that are looking for space. Holding company section lists corporate profiles for major parent companies which own two or more major retail chains in the US. Individual company profiles include retail classifications, total number of stores, operating names, sales volume,

who to contact, extensive site selection criteria including demographic preferences, expansion plans, acquisitions, format changes and more.
Cost: $ 345.00
1500 Pages
Frequency: Annual
ISBN: 0-911790-29-2

21585 **Shippers Guide to Department & Chain Stores Nationwide**
Shippers Guides
PO Box 112
Duarte, CA 91009-0112
626-357-6430; *Fax:* 626-357-6366
Profiles over 1,000 department stores and chain stores and information about routing and freight movement.
Cost: $349.00
350 Pages
Frequency: Annual
Mailing list available for rent: 1,000 names at $299 per M

21586 **Shopping Center Directory**
National Research Bureau
333 W Wacker Drive
Suite 900
Chicago, IL 60606-1284
312-346-3900
This large directory offers information on over 30,000 shopping centers in four regional volumes.
Cost: $225.00
3,200 Pages
Frequency: Annual

21587 **Single Unit Supermarkets Operators**
Chain Store Guide
3922 Coconut Palm Dr
Tampa, FL 33619-1389
813-627-6700
800-778-9794; *Fax:* 813-627-7094
info@csgis.com; www.csgis.com
Mike Jarvis, Publisher
Shami Choon, Manager
Discover more than 7,100 single-unit supermarkets with annual sales topping $500,000 dollars. This comprehensive desktop reference makes it easy to reach our compiled list of 21,000 key executives and buyers, plus their primary wholesalers.
Cost: $335.00
725 Pages
Frequency: Annual

21588 **Stores: Top 100 Retailers Issue**
National Retail Federation
325 7th St NW
Suite 1100
Washington, DC 20004-2808
202-783-7971
800-673-4694; *Fax:* 202-737-2849
pennw@nrf.com; www.nrf.com
Social Media: Facebook, Twitter, LinkedIn
Matthew Shay, President
Scott Krugman, Publisher
Mader Richard, Executive Director
Michael Gatti, VP/Marketing
David French, VP
100 US retail companies having largest estimated sales during preceding year.
Cost: $75.00
Frequency: Annual July
Circulation: 35,000

21589 **Supermarket, Grocery & Convenience Stores**
Chain Store Guide
3922 Coconut Palm Dr
Tampa, FL 33619-1389
813-627-6700
800-778-9794; *Fax:* 813-627-7094
info@csgis.com; www.csgis.com
Mike Jarvis, Publisher
Shami Choon, Manager
Contains information on close to 3,400 U.S. and Canadian supermarket chains, each with at least $2 million in annual sales - one of the most profitable segments in this sector of the economy. The companies in this database operate over 41,000 individual supermarket, superstore, club store, gourmet supermarkets and combo-store units. A special convenience store section profiles 1,700 convenience store chains operating over 85,000 stores.
Cost: $335.00
Frequency: Annual

21590 **Top Shopping Centers: Major Markets 1-50**
National Research Bureau
333 W Wacker Drive
Suite 900
Chicago, IL 60606-1284
312-346-3900
Cost: $895.00

21591 **US Trade Pages**
Global Source
1511 K Street NW
Washington, DC 20005-1403
Kara Kent, Editor
These directories including a volume on Brazil, Chile, Canada, Mexico, Venezuela, and Argentina list trade associations and professional services that provide information on imports and exports between the US and the above listed companies.
Cost: $59.95
Frequency: 6 Volumes

21592 **World Federation of Direct Selling Associations Directory**
WFDSA
1776 K St Nw
Washington, DC 20006-2304
202-546-5330; *Fax:* 202-453-9010;
www.wfdsa.org
Social Media: Facebook, Twitter, LinkedIn
A Harold, President
Founded in: 1789

Industry Web Sites

21593 **http://gold.greyhouse.com**
G.O.L.D Grey House OnLine Databases
Grey House Publising's online database platform, GOLD, offers Quick Search, Keyword Search and Expert Search for most business sectors including retailing markets. The GOLD platform makes finding the information you need quick and easy - whether you're a novice searcher or an experienced database user. All of Grey House's directory products are available for subscription on the GOLD platform.

21594 **www.aamp.com**
American Association of Meat Processors
The membership consists of small to medium sized meat, poultry and food businesses including: packers, processors, wholesalers, home food service businesses, retailers, deli and catering operators. AAMP is also affiliated with 34 state, regional and provincial organizations which represent meat and poultry businesses.

21595 **www.bookweb.org**
American Booksellers Association
Trade association for retail booksellers. Not for profit.

21596 **www.fdi.org**
International Center for Companies of Food Trade
and Industry/North America
Provides management research on problems related to food distribution and serves as an international forum where food chain store executives can meet to exchange ideas and information.

21597 **www.fleamarkets.org**
National Flea Market Association
Represents Flea Market and Swap Meet owners and managers and disseminates information to the general public and media regarding the flea market industry worldwide.

21598 **www.goarms.com**
Association of Retail Marketing Services
Approximately 60 retailers involved in the ARMS retail promotion show, held annually.

21599 **www.greyhouse.com**
Grey House Publishing
Authoritative reference directories for most business sectors including retail markets. Users can search the online databases with varied search criteria allowing for custom searches by product category, geographic area, sales volume, keyword, subject and more. Full Grey House catalog and online ordering also available.

21600 **www.ispo.org**
Institute of Store Planners
Provides a forum for debate and discussion by store design experts and retailers. Sponsors student design programs.

21601 **www.maptrade.org**
International Map Trade Association
Membership comprised of retail stores featuring maps, travel books, globes, and travel products, plus publishers and manufacturers producing these products. Publishes a monthly newsletter

21602 **www.mraa.com**
Marine Retailers Association of America
Promotes activities for the recreational boating industry and holds seminars to improve management.

21603 **www.nacs.org**
National Association of College Stores
Provides educational and support services and products to college stores. Promotes business methods and ethics. Conducts manager certification, educational services and research.

21604 **www.nag-net.com**
Convenience Stores/Petroleum Marketers Association
This association represents senior level management of retail companies organized to enhance buying power, merchandising programs and an exchange of ideas. C-Stores/Petroleum Marketers membership dues: Retail Av. $300, Assoc. $500

21605 **www.nagmr.org**
National Association General Merchandise Repr
A professional association of consumer product brokers representing leading manufacturers to the retail trade.

21606 **www.narda.com**
North American Retail Dealers Association
A national organization of association members, independent retailers selling and servicing major appliances, consumer electronics products, furniture and computers. Emphasis is placed on

ideas that help readers become better, more profitable businesses. Articles are featured regularly on displays, salesmanship, financial analysis and service management.

21607 www.nationalPawnbrokers.org
National Pawnbrokers Association
Nonprofits organization that supports all those involved with the retail pawnbrokers.

21608 www.nationalgrocers.org
National Grocers Association
Works to advance understanding, trade, and cooperation in the food industry. Represents members interests before the government. Offers store planning, and engineering, training and advertising.

21609 www.nicyra.org
National Ice Cream & Yogurt Retailers Association
Members are in retail frozen dessert businesses. Some offer food services either full of limited and some operate convenience stores. The common denominator is that all members offer frozen desserts for take-home or on-site consumption.

21610 www.nrf.com
National Retail Federation
Retail trade association with membership that comprises all retail formats and channels of distribution including department, specialty, discount, catalog, Internet and independent stores. NRF members represent an industry that encompasses more than 1.4 million US retail establishments which employ more than 23 million people — about one in five American workers — and registered 2002 sales of $3.6 trillion. NRF's international members operate stores in more than 50 nations.

21611 www.nsgachicagoshow.com
National Sporting Goods Association
Members consist of retailers, wholesalers, suppliers, sales agents and media. Sponsor of NSGA World Sports EXPO, held annually in Chicago, and the NSGA Management Conference. Has an annual budget of approximately $8 million.

21612 www.nssra.com
National Ski & Snowboard Retailers Association
The retail voice for the ski and snowboard industries and provides information and services you need to operate more successfully.

21613 www.retailsystems.com
Retail Systems Alert Group
For retail and supply chain professionals. Access to community centers, newsletter information, and online ordering information is also available.

21614 www.rtda.org
Retail Tobacco Dealers of America
Trade association of high quality tobacconists.

21615 www.shop.org
Shop.org
Association for retailers online. It's where professional retailerscome together to garner the insight, knowledge and intellegence to make better decisions in the evolving world of the Internet and multi-channel retailing.

21616 www.smallbusinesslocator.com
Small Business Association
Providing information to mom and pop businesses.

Associations

21617 Acrylonitrile Group
1250 Connecticut Ave Nw
Suite 700
Washington, DC 20036

202-419-1500; *Fax:* 202-659-8037
angroup@regnet.com; www.angroup.org

Robert J Fensterheim, Executive Director

Represents producers and users of the industrial chemical used to make plastics, fibers and synthetic rubber products.
Founded in: 1981

21618 American Chemical Society: Rubber Division
411 Wolf Ledges
Suite 201
Akron, OH 44311

330-972-7814; *Fax:* 330-972-5269;
www.rubber.org

John Long, Councilor
Leo Goss, Chair-Elect
Terry DeLapa, Chair
William Stahl, Treasurer
Jerry McCall, Secretary

The Rubber Division of the American Chemical Society is a professional organization dedicated to providing educational programs, technical resources and other vital services for the people associated with rubber and affiliated industries.
Founded in: 1909

21619 Association for Rubber Products Manufacturers
7321 Shadeland Station Way
Suite 285
Indianapolis, IN 46256

317-863-4072; *Fax:* 317-913-2445;
www.arpminc.com

Association dedicated to helping industry executives improve their businesses.
Founded in: 2010

21620 Engineering with Rubber: How to Design Rubber Components
American Chemical Society: Rubber Division
411 Wolf Ledges
Suite 201
Akron, OH 44311
330-972-7814; *Fax:* 330-972-5269;
www.rubber.org

John Long, Councilor
Leo Goss, Chair-Elect
Terry DeLapa, Chair
William Stahl, Treasurer
Jerry McCall, Secretary

Teaches the beginning engineer the principles of rubber science and technology-what rubber is, how it behaves, and how to design simple engineering components.
Founded in: 1909

21621 International Institute of Synthetic Rubber Producers, Inc.
3535 Briapark Drive
Suite 250
Houston, TX 77042

713-783-7511; *Fax:* 713-783-7253
info@iisrp.com; www.iisrp.com

Juan Ramon Salinas, Managing Director/CEO
Roxanna Bauza-Petrovic, General Director of Programs
Sue Flynn, Executive Assistant/ Event Coor
Robin Boyd, Manager of Accounts
Mary O'Connor, European Section Secretariat

International trade association for synthetic rubber producers to receive and benefit from statistical, environmental, and technical information in order to keep abreast of the world's market growth and events.
50 Members
Founded in: 1960

21622 North American Recycled Rubber Association
1621 Mcewen Drive
Unit 24
Whitby Ontario, CA L1N-9A5

905-433-7669; *Fax:* 905-433-0905;
www.recycle.net

Diane Sarracini, Contact

Created to bring together the various stakeholders affiliated with the recycled rubber industry.
Founded in: 1994

21623 Polyurethane Foam Association
9724 Kingston Pike
334 Lakeside Plaza
Loudon, TN 37774

865-657-9840; *Fax:* 865-381-1292
rluedeka@pfa.org; www.pfa.org

Robert Luedeka, Executive Director

The mission of the Polyurethane Foam Association (PFA) is to educate customers and other groups about flexible polyurethane foam (FPF) and to promote its use in manufactured and industrial products.
Founded in: 1980

21624 Rubber & Plastics News
1725 Merriman Rd.
Akron, OH 44313-5251

330-836-9180; *Fax:* 330-836-2831;
www.rubbernews.com
Social Media: Facebook, Twitter, LinkedIn

Domestic and international rubber industry news as well as new technology and products.
Frequency: 25x/year
Founded in: 1971

21625 Rubber Division, American Chemical Society
411 Wolf Ledges
Suite 201
Akron, OH 44311

330-972-7814; *Fax:* 330-972-5269;
www.rubber.org

John Long, Councilor
Leo Goss, Chair-Elect
Terry DeLapa, Chair
William Stahl, Treasurer
Jerry McCall, Secretary

Rubber division of the American Chemical Society is a professional association dedicated to providing educational programs, technical resources and other vital services for the people associated with rubber and affiliated industries. Serves as a global resource for networking and partnerships with academics and industry.
Founded in: 1909

21626 Rubber Manufacturers Association
1400 K St Nw
Suite 900
Washington, DC 20005

202-682-4800; *Fax:* 202-682-4854
info@rma.org; www.rma.org
Social Media: Facebook, Twitter, YouTube

Charlie Cannon, President & CEO
Tracey Norberg, Senior Vice President, General Coun
Daniel Zielinski, Senior Vice President, Public Affai

National trade association for makers of tires and other rubber products.
100 Members
Founded in: 1915

21627 Rubber Pavements Association
10000 N. 31st Ave
Suite D-408
Phoenix, AZ 85051
480-517-9944
877-517-9944; *Fax:* 480-517-9959
dougc@rubberpavements.org;
www.rubberpavements.org

Mark Belshe, Executive Director
Guadalupe Dickerson, Office Manager
Cliff Ashcroft, President

Dedicated to encouraging greater usage of high quality, cost effective asphalt pavements containing recycled tire rubber.
Founded in: 1985

21628 Single Ply Roofing Institute
465 Waverley Oaks Road
Suite 421
Waltham, MA 02452

781-647-7026; *Fax:* 781-647-7222
info@spri.org; www.spri.org

SPRI represents sheet membrane and related component suppliers in the commercial roofing industry.
Founded in: 1981

21629 Society of the Plastics Industry
1425 K Street NW
Suite 500
Washington, DC 20005

202-974-5200
202-296-7005; *Fax:* 202-296-7005;
www.plasticsindustry.org
Social Media: Facebook, Twitter, LinkedIn, YouTube

William Cartuaex, President

Represents the entire plastics industry in a manner that promotes development of the industry and enhances public understanding of its contributions while meeting the needs of society and providing value to members.
Founded in: 1937

21630 Tire Industry Association
1532 Pointer Ridge Place
Suite G
Bowie, MD 20716-1883

301-430-7280
800-876-8372; *Fax:* 301-430-7283
info@tireindustry.org; www.tireindustry.org
Social Media: Facebook, Twitter, LinkedIn

Roy Littlefield, Executive VP
Mike Wolfe, Treasurer
Tom Formanek, Secretary
Freda0 Pratt-Boyer, President
Ken Brown, Past President

TIA is an international association representing all segments of the tire industry, including those that manufacture, repair, recycle, sell, service or use new or retreaded tires, and also those suppliers or individuals who furnish equipment, material or services to the industry. TIA was formed by the July 2002 merger of the International Tire & Rubber Association (ITRA) and the Tire Association of North America (TANA).
7000+ Members
Founded in: 2002

21631 Tire Retread and Repair Information Bureau
1013 Birch St.
Falls Church, VA 22046

703-533-7677
877-394-6811; *Fax:* 703-533-7678

info@retread.org; www.retread.org
Social Media: Facebook, Twitter, YouTube

David Stevens, Managing Director
Brian Hayes, President
Phil Boarts, Secretary/ Treasurer
Eddie Burleson, Vice President
Mike Berra, Director

Our goal is to provide the motoring public (both in the private and public sectors) with the most up-to-date information about the economic and environmental benefits of tire retreading and tire repairing.
Founded in: 1974

21632 Tread Rubber Manufacturers Group
Piper and Marbury
1200 19th Street NW
Washington, DC 20036-2430

202-614-4171

Works to improve tire retreading techniques and to safeguard the public interest in retreading.

Newsletters

21633 Rubber Chemistry and Technology
Rubber Division, American Chemical Society
PO Box 499
Akron, OH 44325-3801

330-972-7883; *Fax:* 330-972-5269

Lu Ann Blazeff, Publisher

Information on materials and equipment pertaining to the rubber industry. Accepts advertising.
Cost: $487.50
Frequency: 5 Times per Year

21634 Rubber and Plastics News
Crain Communications
1725 Merriman Rd
Suite 300
Akron, OH 44313-5283

330-836-9180
800-678-9595; *Fax:* 330-836-2831
editorials@rubbernews.com; www.crain.com

Robert S Simmons, VP
Edward Noga, Editor

Discusses production, research and development, management, sales and marketing.
Cost: $79.00
24 Pages
Frequency: Monthly
Circulation: 16258
Founded in: 1971
Printed in 4 colors on glossy stock

21635 Worldwide Rubber Statistics
Int'l Institute of Synthetic Rubber Producers
2077 S Gessner Rd
Suite 133
Houston, TX 77063-1150

713-783-7511; *Fax:* 713-783-7253
orderfs@iisrp.com; www.iisrp.com
Social Media: Facebook, Twitter, LinkedIn

Jim Mc Graw, CEO
Dr K Leon Loh Sr, Senior Director of Programs
Sue Flynn, Executive Assistant
Robin Boyd, Manager of Accounts

Guide to the synthetic and natural rubber industry, including Centrally Planned Economy Countries.
Cost: $1050.00
40 Members
Founded in: 1960

Magazines & Journals

21636 Global Tire News.com
Rubber & Plastic News
1725 Merriman Rd
Suite 300
Akron, OH 44313-5283

330-836-9180
330-836-9180; *Fax:* 330-836-1005
dsector@crain.com; www.rubbernews.com
Social Media: Facebook, Twitter, LinkedIn

Dave Cielasko, Publisher
Don Sector, Advertising Coordinator
Mike McNulty, Rubber & Plastics News Staff Writer
Brent Weaver, Classified Coordinator

Provides rubber industry information relative to tire manufacturers; top tire company managers; plant listings and other data. Subscription to annual publication includes access to Global Tire News.com.
Cost: $79.00
Frequency: Annual

21637 Rubber World
Lippincott & Peto
PO Box 5451
Akron, OH 44334-0451

330-864-2122; *Fax:* 330-864-5298
jhl@rubberworld.com; www.rubberworld.com

Job Lippincott, President
Dennis Kennelly, VP Sales
Don R Smith, Editor
Darlene Ballard, Director of Marketing Services
Jill Rohrer, Managing Editor

Provides complete technical coverage to the rubber industry.
Cost: $34.00

Trade Shows

21638 International Latex Conference
Crain Communications
1725 Merriman Road
Suite 300
Akron, OH 44313-5283

330-836-9180; *Fax:* 330-836-1005
cstevens@crain.com; www.rubbernews.com

Twelve exhibitors with 12 booths.
Frequency: July

21639 International Tire Exhibition and Conference
Crain Communications
1725 Merriman Road
Suite 300
Akron, OH 44313-5283

330-836-9180; *Fax:* 330-836-1005
cstevens@crain.com; www.rubbernews.com

One-hundred and thirty exhibitors with 110 booths.
Frequency: September

21640 Rubber Expo
American Chemical Society-Rubber Division
PO Box 499
Akron, OH 44309-0499

330-972-7814
800-227-5558; *Fax:* 330-972-5269
help@acs.org; www.chemistry.org

Sherri L Poorman, Exhibition Manager

Biennial show of 300 manufacturers and suppliers of equipment, supplies and services for the rubber industry, including machinery, chemicals, raw rubber, finished rubber products, quality control equipment and related equipment.
8,000 Attendees
Frequency: October, Cleveland

21641 Rubber Mini Expo
American Chemical Society-Rubber Division
PO Box 499
Akron, OH 44309-0499

330-972-7814; *Fax:* 330-972-5269
shbarr@rubber.org; www.rubber.org

Sue Barr, Exposition & Future Sites Manager

Biennial show of 150 manufacturers, suppliers and custom services for the rubber industry, including machinery, chemicals, raw rubber, finished rubber products, quality control equipment and related equipment.
3000 Attendees
Frequency: October

21642 Rubber and Plastics Industry Conference of the United Steelworkers of America
5 Gateway Center
Pittsburgh, PA 15220

412-562-6971; *Fax:* 412-562-6963

John Sellers, Executive VP
90M Attendees
Founded in: 1935

Directories & Databases

21643 Rauch Guide to the US Rubber Industry
Grey House Publishing
4919 Route 22
PO Box 56
Amenia, NY 12501

518-789-8700
800-562-2139; *Fax:* 845-373-6390
books@greyhouse.com; www.greyhouse.com
Social Media: Facebook, Twitter

Leslie Mackenzie, Publisher
Richard Gottlieb, Editor

Provides industry structure and current market information about the $39 billion US rubber industry which faces intense inter-material competition and severe government regulation. The report contains a wealth of marketing and related technical information about the busines.
Cost: $595.00
500 Pages
ISBN: 1-592371-30-2
Founded in: 1981

21644 Rubber World Blue Book: Materials, Compounding and Machinery
Lippincott & Peto
Po Box 5451
Akron, OH 44334-0451

330-864-2122; *Fax:* 330-864-5298;
www.rubberworld.com

Job Lippincott, Owner

Over 850 suppliers of over 8,000 chemicals, materials and compounding ingredients for rubber manufacturers.
Cost: $103.00
Frequency: Annual
Circulation: 4,000

21645 Rubber World: Custom Mixers Directory
Lippincott & Peto

Po Box 5451
Akron, OH 44334-0451

330-864-2122; *Fax:* 330-864-5298;
www.rubberworld.com

Job Lippincott, Owner

A list of rubber manufacturers providing custom mixes.
Cost: $3.00
Frequency: Annual

21646 Rubber World: Machinery Suppliers Issue
Lippincott & Peto
Po Box 5451
Akron, OH 44334-0451

330-864-2122; *Fax:* 330-864-5298;
www.rubberworld.com

Job Lippincott, Owner

Lists suppliers of used and rebuilt machinery and instrumentation and test equipment to the rubber industry.
Cost: $3.00
Frequency: Annual
ISBN: 0-035957-2 -

21647 Rubber and Plastics News: Rubicana Issue
Crain Communications
1725 Merriman Rd
Suite 300
Akron, OH 44313-5283

330-836-9180
800-678-9595; *Fax:* 330-836-2831;
www.crain.com

Robert S Simmons, VP

A list of over 1,000 rubber product manufacturers and suppliers of equipment, services and materials.
Cost: $85.00
Frequency: Annual
Circulation: 15,000

Industry Web Sites

21648 http://gold.greyhouse.com
G.O.L.D Grey House OnLine Databases

Grey House Publishing's online database platform, GOLD, offers Quick Search, Keyword Search and Expert Search for most business sectors including rubber markets. The GOLD platform makes finding the information you need quick and easy - whether you're a novice searcher or an experienced database user. All of Grey House's directory products are available for subscription on the GOLD platform.

21649 www.greyhouse.com
Grey House Publishing

Authoritative reference directories for most business sectors including rubber markets. Users can search the online databases with varied search criteria allowing for custom searches by product category, geographic area, sales volume, keyword, subject and more. Full Grey House catalog and online ordering also available.

21650 www.iisrp.com
Int'l Institute of Synthetic Rubber Producers
For manufacturers of synthetic rubber.

21651 www.itra.com
International Tire and Rubber Association
Information on tire retreading and repairing, new tires, scrap tire reduction and removal equipment, rubber recycling technologies, recycled rubber products and allied services including brake equipment, wheel alignment, tire balancers, tire changers, service trucks, marketing/sales and management programs and computer systems.

21652 www.rma.org
Scrap Tire Management Council
For tire manufacturers marketers of scrap tires.

21653 www.rubbernews.com
Rubber & Plastics News
1725 Merriman Rd.
Akron, OH 44313-5251

330-836-9180; *Fax:* 330-836-2831;
www.rubbernews.com

Website of Rubber & Plastics News magazine. Updated daily with an online archive, statistics and rankings.

Associations

21654 **AAA Foundation for Traffic Safety**
607 14th Street NW
Suite 201
Washington, DC 20005

202-638-5944; *Fax:* 202-638-5943
info@aaafoundation.org;
www.aaafoundation.org
Social Media: Facebook, Twitter, RSS

Peter Kissinger, President/CEO
Kenneth Johnson, Treasurer
Laura Dunn, Manager of Research & Communication
Paul C. Petrillo, Chairman
John Tomlin, Secretary

AAA Foundation for Traffic Safety is dedicated to saving lives and reducing injuries on the roads. It is a not-for-profit, publicly-supported charitable educational and research organization.
Founded in: 1947

21655 **ASIS International**
1625 Prince St
Alexandria, VA 22314-2818

703-519-6200
888-968-1968; *Fax:* 703-519-6299
asis@asisonline.org; www.asisonline.org
Social Media: Facebook, Twitter, LinkedIn, You Tube

David C. Davis, President-Elect
Dave N. Tyson, President
Thomas J. Langer, Treasurer
Richard E. Chase, Secretary
Richard E. Widup, Chairman

The largest organization for security professionals. ASIS is dedicated to increasing the effectiveness and productivity of security professionals by developing educational programs and materials that cover broad security interests, such as the ASIS Annual Seminar and Exhibits, as well as specific topics. ASIS also advocates the role and value of the security management profession to the media, governmental entities, and the public.
Founded in: 1955

21656 **Academy of Security Educators & Trainers**
16 Penn Plaza
Suite 1570
New York, NY 10001

212-268-4555
800-947-5827; *Fax:* 212-563-4783;
www.academyofsecurity.org

Dr Richard W Kobetz, Executive Director
Jerry Heying, President
Mary E Kobetz, Secretary-Treasurer

Non-profit organization of security professionals dedicated to exploring the large spectrum of issues confronting the security field. Meetings are held to discuss, design, develop, and exchange thoughts and ideas in an open forum. Awards the CST (certified security trainer) designation.
300 Members
Founded in: 1980

21657 **Advanced Medical Technology Association: AdvaMed**
701 Pennsylvania Ave Nw
Suite 800
Washington, DC 20004-2654

202-783-8700; *Fax:* 202-783-8750
info@advamed.org; www.advamed.org
Social Media: Facebook, Twitter, LinkedIn, You Tube

Stephen J Ubl, President/CEO
David Nexon, Senior Executive VP
Kenneth Mendez, Sr. Executive Vice President
Vincent Forlenza, Chairman
Jason Rupp, Vice President

Dedicated to providing members with the advocacy, information, education and tangible solutions necessary for success in a world of increasingly complex medical regulations.
1300 Members
Founded in: 1975

21658 **Advocates for Highway and Auto Safety**
750 1st St NE
Suite 1130
Washington, DC 20002

202-408-1711; *Fax:* 202-408-1699
advocates@saferoads.org; www.saferoads.org
Social Media: Facebook, Twitter

Judith Lee Stone, President
Jacqueline Gillan, VP
Judie Pasquini, Director
Peter Kurdock, Advocates' State Coordinator

An organization whose members advocate the support and advancement of highway and auto safety through the implementation of state and federal laws, programs and policies.
Founded in: 1989

21659 **American Association for Aerosol Research (AAAR)**
12100 Sunset Hills Road
Suite 130
Reston, VA 20190
703-437-4377; *Fax:* 800-485-3106
info@aaar.org; www.aaar.org

Jay Turner, President
Allen Robinson, Vice President Elect
Sheryl Ehrman, Vice President
Linsey Marr, Treasurer
Suresh Dhaniyala, Secretary

AAAR is a nonprofit professional organization for scientists and engineers who wish to promote and communicate technical advances in the field of aerosol research. The Association fosters the exchange of information among members and with other disciplines through conferences, symposia and publication of a professional journal. Committed to the development of aerosol and its application to important social issues, AAAR offers an international forum for education, communication and networking.
1000 Members
Founded in: 1982

21660 **American Association of Occupational Health Nurses**
2920 Brandywine Rd # 100
Suite 100
Chamblee, GA 30341-5539

770-455-7271; *Fax:* 850-484-8762;
www.aaohn.org
Social Media: Facebook, Twitter, LinkedIn

Ann Cox, Executive Director

AAOHN is a principal force in developing and promoting the profession of occupational and environmental health nursing by providing education, resources, and advocacy.
Founded in: 1942

21661 **American Association of Poison Control Centers**
3201 New Mexico Ave
Suite 310
Washington, DC 200016

202-362-3867
800-222-1222; *Fax:* 202-362-8377;
www.poison.org
Social Media: Facebook

Toby Litovitz, Executive Director

Nonprofit nationwide organization of poison centers and others interested in the prevention and treatment of poisoning. Promotes the reduction of injury, illness and death from poisonings through public and professional education and scientific research. Promotes universal access to certified regional poison centers.
Founded in: 1980

21662 **American Bio-Recovery Association**
39 St.Mary Street
Norwalk, OH 44857

419-663-2819
888-979-2272; *Fax:* 440-499-9959;
www.americanbiorecovery.org

Andrew Yurchuck, President
Eric Morse, Vice President
Robert O'Connor, Secretary
Barbara Jones, Treasurer

A nationwide non-profit association of crime and trauma scene recovery professionals who are dedicated to upholding the highest technical, ethical and educational guidelines of the biohazard remediation industry.

21663 **American Biological Safety Association**
1200 Allanson Rd
Mundelein, IL 60060-3808

847-949-1517
866-425-1385; *Fax:* 847-566-4580
info@absa.org; www.absa.org

Edward Stygar III, Executive Director
Marian Downing, President
Melissa Moreland, President-Elect
Carol McGhan, Treasurer
Scott Alderman, Councilor

ABSA's goals are to provide a professional association that represents the interest and needs of practitioners of biological safety, and to providea forum for the continued and timely exchange of biosafety information.
Founded in: 1984

21664 **American Chemical Society**
1155 16th St NW
Washington, DC 200036

202-872-4600
800-333-9511; *Fax:* 202-872-4615
help@acs.org; www.acs.org
Social Media: Facebook, Twitter, LinkedIn, Google+

Thomas M. Connelly, CEO
Madeleine Jacobs, Executive Director
Diane Grob Schmidt, President
Pat N. Confalone, Chair
George M. Bodner, Director Publications

Supports chemists and companies who work with chemicals and their by-products.
158 M Members
Founded in: 1876

21665 **American College of Occupational and Environmental Medicine**
25 Northwest Point Blvd
Suite 700
Elk Grove Village, IL 60007-1030

847-818-1800; *Fax:* 847-818-9266
acoeminfo@acoem.org; www.acoem.org
Social Media: Twitter, YouTube

Kathryn L. Mueller, Past President
Charles M. Yarborough III, Vice President
Mark A. Roberts, President
James A. Tacci, President-Elect
Jeffery S. Harris, Secretary-Treasurer

Occupational and environmental medicine is devoted to the prevention and management of occupational and injury, illness and disability, and promotion of health and productivity of workers, thier families and communities.
5000 Members
Founded in: 1916

21666 American Conference of Governmental Industrial Hygienists
1330 Kemper Meadow Drive
Cincinnati, OH 45240

513-742-2020; *Fax:* 513-742-3355
mail@acgih.org; www.acgih.org
Social Media: Facebook, Twitter, LinkedIn, Google+

J. Torey Nalbone, Chair
Shannon Henshaw Gaffney, Vice Chair
John S. Morawetz, Secretary/ Treasurer
A. Anthony Rizzuto, Executive Director
Susan Arnold, Director

A member-based organization and community of professionals that advances worker health and safety through education and the development and dissemination of scientific and technical knowledge.
Founded in: 1938

21667 American Correctional Association
206 N. Washington Street
Alexandria, VA 22314

703-224-0000; *Fax:* 703-224-0179
IndiaV@aca.org; www.aca.org
Social Media: Facebook, Twitter, LinkedIn, YouTube

Mary L. Livers, President
Lanette C. Linthicum, President-Elect
Daron Hall, Past President
James A Gondles, Secretary
Gary C. Mohr, Treasurer

Formerly known as the National Prison Association.
Founded in: 1870

21668 American Fire Safety Council
1909 K St Nw
Suite 400
Washington, DC 20006-1168

202-338-0022; *Fax:* 202-955-6215;
www.fire-safety.net
Social Media: Facebook, Twitter, LinkedIn

Mike Heimowitz, President

Improving fire safety through enhancement of fire codes and standards and promoting responsible use of flame retardants and flame retardant products. AFSC was created to provide a stronger and broader voice on advocacy and safety issues.
Founded in: 2003

21669 American Fire Sprinkler Association
12750 Merit Drive
Suite 350
Dallas, TX 75251

214-349-5965; *Fax:* 214-343-8898
afsainfo@firesprinkler.org;
www.firesprinkler.org
Social Media: Facebook, Twitter, LinkedIn, YouTube, Flickr

Steve Muncy, President
Frank Mortl III, Executive Vice President
Joseph A. Heinrich, Chairman
Michael F. Meehan, First Vice-Chairman
Thomas J. McKinnon, Treasurer

Nonprofit international association representing open shop fire sprinkler contractors, dedicated to the educational advancement of its members and promotion of the use of automatic sprinkler systems. Offers a convention and exhibition, correspondence course, monthly magazine and a monthly newsletter.
900 Members
Founded in: 1981

21670 American Gas Association
400 N Capitol Street NW
Suite 450
Washington, DC 20001

202-824-7000; *Fax:* 202-824-7092
ykorolevich@aga.org; www.aga.org
Social Media: Facebook, Twitter, LinkedIn, YouTube, Wordpress, Instagram

Dave McCurdy, President/CEO
Gregg S. Kantor, Immediate Past Chairman
Pierce H. Norton II, 2nd Vice Chairman
Terry D. McCallister, Chairman
Ralph A. LaRossa, 1st Vice Chairman

The American Gas Association advocates the interests of its members and their customers, and provides information and services promoting efficient demand and supply growth and operational excellence in the safe, reliable and efficient delivery of natural gas.
200 Members
Founded in: 1918

21671 American Industrial Hygiene Association
3141 Fairview Park Drive
Suite 777
Falls Church, VA 22042

703-849-8888; *Fax:* 703-207-3561
infonet@aiha.org; www.aiha.org
Social Media: Facebook, Twitter, LinkedIn, YouTube, RSS

Steven E. Lacey, PhD, CIH, CSP, President
Cynthia A. Ostrowski, CIH, Vice President
J. Lindsay Cook, CIH, CSP, Treasurer
Kathleen S. Murphy, CIH, Secretary
Deborah Imel Nelson, PhD, CIH, President-Elect

AIHA promotes healthy and safe environments by advancing the science, principles, practice, and value of industrial hygiene and occupational and environmental health and safety.
10000 Members
Founded in: 1939

21672 American Insurance Association
2101 L Street, NW
Suite 400
Washington, DC 200037

202-828-7100; *Fax:* 202-293-1219
info@aiadc.org; www.aiadc.org
Social Media: Facebook, Twitter, LinkedIn, YouTube, RSS

Leigh Ann Pusey, President/CEO
J. Stephen Zielezienski, SVP & General Counsel
Joseph Digiovanni, SVP, State Affairs
David S. Lauer, VP/ Treasurer
Peter R. Foley, VP, Claims Administration

A property, casualty insurance trade organization representing more than 40,000 insurers that write more than $120 billion in premiums each year. AIA member companies offer all types of property-casualty insurance, including personal and commercial auto insurance, commercial property and liability coverage for small businesses, worker's compensation, medical malpractice coverage, and product liability insurance.
40000 Members
Founded in: 1866

21673 American National Standards Institute ANSI
1899 L Street, NW
11th Floor
Washington, DC 20036

202-293-8020; *Fax:* 202-293-9287
info@ansi.org; www.ansi.org
Social Media: Facebook, Twitter, LinkedIn, YouTube, Google+

Joe Bhatia, President/CEO
Susan Bose, Manager Membership Services
Tricia Power, Manager, Corporate Governance
James T. Pauley, Chairman
Patricia A. Griffin, Vice President and General Counsel

To enhance the global competition of business and quality of life by promoting and facilitating voluntary consensus standards and conformity assessment systems, and safeguarding their integrity.
1000 Members
Founded in: 1916

21674 American Polygraph Association
PO Box 8037
Chattanooga, TN 37414-0037

423-892-3992
800-272-8037; *Fax:* 423-894-5435
manager@polygraph.org; www.polygraph.org
Social Media: Facebook, Twitter

Lisa Jacocks, National Office Manager
Walt Goodson, President
Raymond Nelson, Chairman
Gordon L. Vaughan, General Counsel
Darryl Starks, Vice-President Government

Representing experienced polygraph examiners in private business; law enforcement and government. Professional APA polygraph examiners administer hundreds of thousands of polygraph exams each year worldwide. The APA establishes standards of ethical practices, techniques, instrumentation and research, as well as provides advanced training and continuing education programs.
2700+ Members
Founded in: 1966

21675 American Public Health Association
800 I Street NW
Washington, DC 20001

202-777-2742; *Fax:* 202-777-2534
comments@apha.org; www.apha.org
Social Media: Facebook, Twitter

Dr Georges C Benjamin, Executive Director
Shiriki Kumanyika, President
Richard J. Cohen, Treasurer
Jose Fernandez-Pena, Vice Chair
Camara P. Jones, President Elect

Influencing policies and setting priorities for over 125 years. Thoughout its history it has been in the forefront of numerous efforts to prevent disease and promote health.
Founded in: 1872

21676 American Red Cross
2025 E. St.,NW
Washington, DC 20006

202-303-5214
800-733-2767; *Fax:* 202-639-3021;
www.redcross.org
Social Media: Facebook, Twitter, Flickr, YouTube

Gail J McGovern, President/CEO
Bonnie McElveen-Hunter, Chairman
Brian J. Rhoa, CFO
David Meltzer, General Counsel
Jennifer L. Hawkins, Corporate Secretary

The American Red Cross is where people moblilze to help their neighbors across the street, across the country and across the world, in emergencies. Each year, in communities large and small, victims of some 70,000 disasters turn to the nearly one million volunteers and 35,000 employees of the Red Cross.
31000 Members
Founded in: 1881

21677 American Safety & Health Institute
4148 Louis Avenue
Holiday, FL 34691

727-437-7560
800-682-5067

info@ashinstitute.org; www.ashinstitute.org
Social Media: Facebook, Twitter, LinkedIn

Frank Swiger, Manager

Nonprofit association of professional safety & health educators providing nationally recognized training programs through more than 5000 approved training centers across the US and in several foreign countries.
30000 Members
Founded in: 1996

21678 American Society for Industrial Security

1625 Prince Street
Alexandria, VA 22314-2882

703-519-6200; *Fax:* 703-519-6299
asis@asisonline.org; www.asisonline.org
Social Media: Facebook, Twitter, LinkedIn, YouTube

Dave N. Tyson, President
Michael J Stack, CEO
Thomas J. Langer, Treasurer
Richard E. Chase, Secretary
Richard E. Widup, Chairman

ASIS International (ASIS) is the largest organization for security professionals, with more than 33,000 members worldwide. ASIS is dedicated to increasing the effectiveness and productivity of security professionals by developing educational programs and materials that address broad security interests, such as the ASIS Annual Seminar and Exhibits, as well as specific security topics.
33000 Members
Founded in: 1955

21679 American Society for Nondestructive Testing

1711 Arlingate Lane
PO Box 28518
Columbus, OH 43228-0518

614-274-6003
800-222-2768; *Fax:* 614-274-6899;
www.asnt.org
Social Media: Facebook, Twitter, LinkedIn, YouTube

Arnold Bereson, Executive Director
Roger Engelbart, Vice- President
David Mandina, Secreatry/ Treasurer
Robert J. Potter, Chair
Raymond G. Morasse, President

ASNT is the world's largest technical society for nondestructive tests (NDT) professionals.
15000 Members
Founded in: 1941

21680 American Society of Crime Laboratory Directors (ASCLD)

139A Technology Drive
Garner, NC 27529

919-773-2044; *Fax:* 919-861-9930
president@ascld.org; www.ascld.org
Social Media: Facebook, Twitter, LinkedIn, RSS

Jody Wolf, President
Cicilia Doyle, Secretary
Jeremy Triplett, President-Elect
Jean Stover, Executive Director
Ramona Robertson, Administrative Assistant

The American Society of Crime Laboratory Directors (ASCLD) is a nonprofit professional society of crime laboratory directors and forensic science managers dedicated to providing excellence in forensic science through leadership and innovation.
Founded in: 1973

21681 American Society of Criminology

1314 Kinnear Rd
Suite 212
Columbus, OH 43212-1156

614-292-9207; *Fax:* 614-292-6767
asc@asc41.com; www.asc41.com
Social Media: Facebook, Twitter

Ruth Peterson, President-Elect
Chris Eskridge, Executive Director
Candace Kruttscnitt, President
Eric Baumer, Vice President
Bonnie Fisher, Treasurer

The American Society of Criminology is an international organization concerned with criminology, embracing scholary, scientific and profesional knowledge concerning the etiology, prevention, control, and treatment of crime and delinquency.

21682 American Society of Industrial Security

1625 Prince St
Alexandria, VA 22314-2882

703-519-6200; *Fax:* 703-519-6299
asis@asisonline.org; www.asisonline.org
Social Media: Facebook, Twitter, LinkedIn, YouTube

Richard E. Widup, Chairman
Dave N. Tyson, President
Michael J. Stack, CEO
Thomas J. Langer, Treasurer
Richard E. Chase, Secretary

The largest international organization for professionals who are responsible for security, including managers and directors of security.
33000 Members
Founded in: 1955

21683 American Society of Mechanical Engineers

Two Park Ave
New York, NY 10016-5990

800-843-2763
800-843-2763
973-882-1170; *Fax:* 202-429-9417
CustomerCare@asme.org; www.asme.org
Social Media: Facebook, Twitter, LinkedIn

K.Keith Roe, President- Nominee
Julio Guerrero, President
J.Robert Sims, Immediate Past President
James W. Coaker, Secretary/ Treasurer
Thomas G. Loughlin, Executive Director

Through its initiatives in education, advocacy and public policy, the ASME. Foundation impacts all aspects of the mechanical engineering community.
1.4M Members
Founded in: 1880

21684 American Society of Safety Engineers

520 N. Northwest Hwy
Park Ridge, IL 60068

847-699-2929; *Fax:* 847-768-3434
customerservice@asse.org; www.asse.org
Social Media: Facebook, Twitter, LinkedIn, Instagram

Michael Belcher, President
Fred J. Fortman, Secretary & Executive Treasurer
Thomas F. Cecich, President-Elect
James D. Smith, Senior Vice President
Stephanie A. Helgerman, VP, Finance

The oldest and largest professional safety organization. Its members manage, supervise and consult on safety, health, and environmental issues in industry, insurance, government and education.
36000 Members
Founded in: 1911

21685 American Traffic Safety Services Association

15 Riverside Parkway
Suite 100
Fredericksburg, VA 22406-1022

540-368-1701
800-272-8772; *Fax:* 540-368-1717
memberservices@atssa.com; www.atssa.com
Social Media: Facebook, Twitter, YouTube

Scott Seeley, Chairman
Debra Ricker, Chairman Elect
Juan Arvizu, At-large-Director
Sue Reiss, Foundation President (Non-Voting)
Craig Sliter, Guardrail Services Div Director

The American Traffic Safety Services Association, is an international trade association founded in 1969. It has has represented companies and individuals in the traffic control and roadway safety industry.
11630 Members
Founded in: 1969

21686 American Welding Society

8669 NW 36 St.
Suite 130
Miami, FL 33126-6672

305-443-9353
800-443-9353; *Fax:* 305-443-7559
info@aws.org
awsnow.org
Social Media: Facebook, Twitter, Instagram

David J. Landon, President
David L. McQuaid, Vice President
John R. Bray, Vice President
Dale Flood, Vice President
Robert G. Pali, Treasurer

The mission of the American Welding Society is to advance the science, technology and application of welding and allied joining and cutting processes, including brazing, soldering and thermal spraying.
70000 Members
Founded in: 1919

21687 Associated Locksmiths of America

3500 Easy St
Dallas, TX 75247

214-819-9733
800-532-2562; *Fax:* 214-819-9736
jim@aloa.org; www.aloa.org
Social Media: Facebook, Twitter, LinkedIn

David Lowell, Executive Director
Charles Gibson, Secretary

ALOA is an international professional organization of highly qualified security professionals engaged in consulting, sales, installation and maintenance of locks, keys safes, premises security, access controls, alarms, and other security related endeavors.
10M Members
Founded in: 1956

21688 Association of Air Medical Services

909 N. Washington St.
Suite 410
Alexandria, VA 22314

703-836-8732; *Fax:* 703-836-8920
information@aams.org; www.aams.org

Dawn Mancuso, Executive Director
Dave Evans, Chair
Graeme Field, Vice Chair
Rick Sherlock, CEO & President
Douglas A. Garretson, Treasurer

AAMS is built on the idea that representation from a variety of medical transport services and businesses can be brought together to share information, collectively resolve problems and pro-

vide leadership in the medical transport community.
581 Members
Founded in: 1980

21689 Association of Certified Fraud Examiners
716 West Ave
Austin, TX 78701-2727

512-478-9000
800-245-3321; *Fax:* 512-478-9297
MemberServices@acfe.com; www.acfe.com
Social Media: Facebook, Twitter, LinkedIn

John D. Gill, VP- Education
James D. Ratley, President/CEO
Joseph T. Wells, Chairman
Bruce Dorris, Program Director & Vice President
Jeanette LeVie, Vice President- Administration

The mission of the Association of Certified Fraud Examiners is to reduce the incidence of fraud and white-collar crime and to assist its members in its dectection and prevention.
75000 Members
Founded in: 1988

21690 Association of Christian Investigators
2553 Jackson Keller
Suite 200
San Antonio, TX 78230

210-342-0509; *Fax:* 210-342-0731
kelmar@kelmarpi.com; www.a-c-i.org

Kelly E Riddle, President
Hugo Briseno, Director, Georgia
Timothy Friend, Director, California (Northern)
Andrew Smart, Director, Alabama
Paul Jacob, Director, Alaska

Provides a spirit-filled organization that promoste the investigative profession in a non-competitive atmosphere. Provides an environment in which investigators can create meaningful and long-term relationships with other investigators outside the professional bonds.
1000+ Members
Founded in: 1996

21691 Association of Contingency Planners
136 Everett Road
Albany, NY 12205

414-908-4945
800-445-4227; *Fax:* 414-768-8001
staff@acp-international.com;
www.acp-international.com
Social Media: Facebook, Twitter, LinkedIn

Leo A Wrobel, President
Bonnie Canal, Chairman
Michael Carver, Treasurer
Steve Elliot, Board Member
Michael J. Morganti, Secretary

Nonprofit trade association dedicated to fostering continued professional growth and development in effective contingency and business resumption planning.
2300 Members
Founded in: 1983

21692 Association of Professional Industrial Hygienists
2288 Gunbarrel Rd
Ste 154/364
Chattanooga, TN 37421

888-481-3006; www.apih.us

Offers credentialing to industrial hygienists.
Founded in: 1994

21693 Association of Public Safety Communication Officials-International
351 N Williamson Boulevard
Daytona Beach, FL 32114-1112

386-322-2500
888-272-6911; *Fax:* 386-322-2501
apco@apcointl.org; www.apcointl.org
Social Media: Facebook, Twitter, LinkedIn, psconnect

John W. Wright, Immediate Past President
Brent Lee, President
Cheryl J. Greathouse, 1st VP
Martha K. Carter, 2nd VP
Derek Poarch, Ex-Officio

The Association of Public-Safety Communications Officials International (APCO) is a member driven association of communications professionals that provides leadership; influences public safety communications decisions of government and industry; promotes professional development; and, fosters the development and use of technology for the benefit of the public.
16000 Members
Founded in: 1932

21694 Association of State Dam Safety Officials
239 S. Limestone
Lexington, KY 40508

859-550-2788
info@damsafety.org; www.damsafety.org
Social Media: Facebook, Twitter, LinkedIn, YouTube

Jim Pawloski, President
Dusty Myers, President Elect
Tom Woosley, Past President
Roger Adams, Secretary
Jon Garton, Treasurer

Organization for safety officials overseeing state dams.
3000 Members
Founded in: 1983

21695 Association of State Floodplain Managers
575 D'Onoforio Drive
Suite 200
Madison, WI 53719

608-828-3000; *Fax:* 608-828-6319
asfpm@floods.org; www.floods.org
Social Media: Facebook, Twitter, LinkedIn, Tumblr

Larry A Larson, DirectorEmeritus, Sr. Policy Adviso
Maria Cox Lamm, Vice Chair
Karen McHugh, Treasurer
Leslie Durham, Secretary
Ceil C. Strauss, Chair

It is the mission of the Association to mitigate the losses, costs and human suffering caused by flooding and to promote wise use of the natural and beneficial functions of floodplains.
6500 Members
Founded in: 1976

21696 Automatic Fire Alarm Association
81 Mill Street
Suite 300
Gahanna, OH 43230

614-416-8076
844-438-2322; *Fax:* 614-453-8744
fire-alarm@afaa.org; www.afaa.org
Social Media: Facebook, Twitter, LinkedIn, Yahoo

Jack McNamara, President/Executive Director
Rick Heffernan, Secretary
Randall L. Hormann, Administrative Director
William Koffel, Vice President
Rodger Reiswig, Treasurer

Striving to be the foremost industry advocate organization dedicated to improving the quality, reliability and value of fire and life safety systems.
Founded in: 1953

21697 Aviation Safety Institute
PO Box 2480
Carlingford, NS 2118

128-819-2455; *Fax:* 128-572-5248
enquiry@asi.net.au; www.asi.net.au
Social Media: Twitter, LinkedIn

Edward H Wachs, President/Chair
Thomas Clevinger, VP/Treasurer
Richard Davies, Managing Director
Melinda Brennan, Manager-WHS
Kevin Mulholland, Manager-Audit

An aviation safety research center established in 1973. Studying the most overlooked, most important area of aviation safety.
Founded in: 2008

21698 Board of Certified Safety Professionals
2301 W. Bradley Avenue
Champaign, IL 61821

217-359-9263; *Fax:* 217-359-0055
bcsp@bcsp.org; www.bcsp.org
Social Media: Facebook, Twitter, LinkedIn, Google+

Cece M Weldon, President
John E. Hodges, Vice President
Jack H. Dobson, Treasurer
Teresa M. Turnbeaugh, CEO, Secretary
Guy Snyder, CFO

Operating solely as a peer certification board with the purpose of certifying practitioners in the safety profession.
Founded in: 1969
Mailing list available for rent: 20,000 names

21699 Business Disaster Preparedness Council
Lee County Emergency Management
PO Box 398
Ft. Meyers, FL 33902-398

239-399-9779; *Fax:* 941-477-3636
board@leegov.com

Bob Lee, Owner

Public and private partnership whose goal it is to assist business in planning for and recovering from natural disasters and emergencies.
Founded in: 1998

21700 CPWR: Center for Construction Research and Training
8484 Georgia Ave
Suite 1000
Silver Spring, MD 20910

301-578-8500; *Fax:* 301-578-8572
cpwrwebsite@cpwr.com; www.cpwr.com
Social Media: Facebook, Twitter, RSS, YouTube

Sean McGarvey, President
Richard Resnick, Vice President/ General Counsel
Chris Trahan, Deputy Director
Erich J. Stafford, Executive Director
Brent Booker, Secretary/ Treasurer

CPWR is committed to preventing illness, injury, and death in the construction industry through its safety and health research, broad network of trainers, and on-going outreach to workers and employers.
Founded in: 1990

21701 **Canada Safety Council**
1020 Thomas Spratt Place
Ottawa, ON K1G 5L5

613-739-1535; *Fax:* 613-739-1566
canadasafetycouncil.org
Social Media: Facebook, Twitter

Jack Smith, President
Raynald Marchand, General Manager, Programs
Judy Lavergne, Secretary
Peter Slivar, Manager, Finance & Administration
Lewis Smith, Communications

The Canada Safety Counil is a national, non-government, charitable organization dedicated to safety. Mission is to lead in the national effort to reduce preventable deaths, injuries and economic loss in public and private places throughout Canada.
Founded in: 1968

21702 **Canadian Alarm & Security Association**
50 Acadia Avenue
Suite 201
Markham, ON L3R 0B3

905-513-0622
800-538-9919; *Fax:* 905-513-0624;
www.canasa.org
Social Media: Facebook, Twitter, LinkedIn

JF Champagne, Ex-Officio
Carl Jorgensen, Vice president
Carol Cairns, Treasurer
Kevin Hincks, Secretary
Philippe Bouchard, President

A national non-profit organization dedicated to promoting the interests of its members and the safety and security of all Canadians.
Founded in: 1977

21703 **Central Station Alarm Association**
8150 Leesburg Pike
Suite 700
Vienna, VA 22182

703-242-4670; *Fax:* 703-242-4675
techadmin@csaaintl.org
csaaintl.org
Social Media: Facebook, Twitter, LinkedIn, RSS

Jay Hauhn, Executive Director
Joe Nuccio, First Vice President
Pamela Petrow, President
Graham Westphal, Secretary
Ivan Spector, Treasurer

Represents companies offering security (alarm) monitoring systems through a central station. It also represents companies that provide services and products to the industry.
300+ Members
Founded in: 1950

21704 **Clery Center**
110 Gallagher Road
Wayne, PA 19087

484-580-8754
888-251-7959; *Fax:* 484-580-8759
clerycenter.org
Social Media: Facebook, Twitter, LinkedIn, YouTube

Constance B. Clery, Co-Founder & Chairwoman
Howard K. Clery, Co-Founder
Benjamin F. Clery, Treasurer
Roger Carolin, Chairman
Christopher F. McConnell, Vice Chairman

A non-profit organization whose mission is to prevent violence, substance abuse and other crimes in college and university campus communities across the United States, and to compassionately assist the vicitims of these crimes.
Founded in: 1987

21705 **Commercial Vehicle Safety Alliance**
6303 Ivy Lane
Suite 310
Greenbelt, MD 20770-6319

301-830-6143; *Fax:* 301-830-6144
cvsahq@cvsa.org; www.cvsa.org
Social Media: Facebook, Twitter, LinkedIn, YouTube

Collin B. Mooney, Executive Director
Maj. Jay Thompson, President
Julius Debuschewitz, Vice President
Capt. Christoph Turner, Secretary

The Commercial Vehicle Safety Alliance (CVSA) is a nonprofit organization, established to promote an environment free of commercial vehicle accidents and incidents. Our mission is to promote commercial motor vehicle safty and security by providing leadership to enforcement, industry and policy makers.
540 Members
Founded in: 1980

21706 **Computer Security Institute**
350 Hudson St.
Suite 300
New York, NY 10014

415-947-6320; *Fax:* 415-947-6023;
www.gocsi.com
Social Media: Facebook, Twitter, LinkedIn

Jody Nurre, Sales Director
Mary Griffin, Membership Director
Robert Richardson, Director
Terri Curran, Director
Cheryl Jackson, Information Systems

Computer Security Institute serves the needs of information security professionals through membership, educational events, security surveys and awareness tools.
Founded in: 1974

21707 **Consumer Data Industry Association**
1090 Vermont Ave NW
Suite 200
Washington, DC 20005-4964

202-371-0910; *Fax:* 202-371-0134
cdia@cdiaonline.org; www.cdiaonline.org

Norm Magnuson, VP
Betty Byrnes, Member Services

The Consumer Data Industry Association is an international trade association, founded in 1906, that represents consumer information companies that provide fraud prevention and risk management products, credit and mortgage reports, tenant and employment screening services, check fraud and verification services, and collection services.
140 Members
Founded in: 1906

21708 **Conveyor Equipment Manufacturers Association (CEMA)**
5672 Strand CT
Suite 2
Naples, FL 34110

239-514-3441; *Fax:* 239-514-3470
phil@cemanet.org; www.cemanet.org
Social Media: Facebook, Twitter, LinkedIn

Jerry Heathman, President
Garry Abraham, Vice President
Robert Reinfried, Executive VP
Paul Ross, Secretary
E.A. Thompson, Tresaurer

Involved in writing industry standards, the CEMA seeks to promote among its members and the industry standardization of design manufacture and application on a voluntary basis and in such manner as will not impede development of conveying machinery and component parts or lessen competition. CEMA sponsors an annual Engineering Conference that allows Member Company Engineers to meet and develop or improve CEMA Consensus Industry Standards and National Standards that affect the conveyor industry.
96 Members
Founded in: 1933

21709 **Council of International Investigators**
PO Box 565
Elmhurst, IL 60126-0565

630-501-1880
888-759-8884; *Fax:* 206-367-8777
office@cii2.org; www.cii2.org
Social Media: Facebook, LinkedIn

Galen Clements, Executive Regional Director
Sheila Ponnosamy, President
Eduard Sigrist, Past president/ Treasurer
Anne Styren, Secretary
Bert Falbaum, VP/ Executive Regional Director

The Council of International Investigators was formed to encourage a greater association among owners and operators of investigation agencies while developing mutual trust and respect.
Founded in: 1955

21710 **Council on Certification of Health, Environmental & Technologists**
2301 W. Bradley Avenue
Champaign, IL 61821

217-359-9263; *Fax:* 217-359-0055
cchest@cchest.org; www.cchest.org
Social Media: Facebook, Twitter, LinkedIn, Google+

Angie Kluth, Chief accounting Officer
Andrea Kamradt, Examination Manager
Treasa Turnbeaugh, CEO
Robert Schneller, COO
Teresa Hasken, CFO

CCHEST is recognized as the leader in high-quality, third-party accredited health, safety, and environmental credentialing for technologists, technicians, supervisors, and workers.
3000 Members
Founded in: 1969

21711 **Dangerous Goods Advisory Council**
7501 Greenway Center Drive
Suite 760
Greenbelt, MD 20770

202-289-4550; *Fax:* 202-289-4074
info@dgac.org; www.dgac.org
Social Media: Facebook, Twitter

Del Billings, Technical director
Vaughn Arthur, Secretary & President
Barbara Lantry-Miller, Treasurer
Ben Barrett, Chair
Greg Allen, Vice Chair

DGAC fulfills its mission by providing education, technical assistance and information to the private and public sectors. Members incude shippers in the chemical, petroleum, and pharmaceutical industries, manufacturers, carriers, container manufacturers and reconditioners, emergency/waste clean-up companies, trade associations, and others involved in the transport of dangerous goods.
Founded in: 1978

21712 **Electrical Safety Foundation International**
1300 N 17th Street
Suite 900
Rosslyn, VA 22209

703-841-5935; *Fax:* 703-841-3329
info@esfi.org; www.esfi.org
Social Media: Facebook, Twitter, LinkedIn, YouTube

Stephen Sokolow, Chairman
John Engel, Vice Chairman
Brett Brenner, President

Kevin Cosgriff, Treasurer
Patrick Davin, Secretary

The mission of the Electrical Safety Foundation International (ESFI) is to advocate electrical safety in the home and in the workplace in order to reduce electrically-related fatalities, injuries and property loss. ESFI is committed to: Being the unbiased authority in electrical safety issues for consumers, the workforce, and the media; Identifying and addressing evolving electrical safety needs; Advocating safety technology, compliance with codes and standards, and risk-reducing behaviors.
Founded in: 1994

21713 Electronic Security Association
6333 North State Highway 161
Suite 350
Irving, TX 75038

972-807-6800
888-447-1689; *Fax:* 972-807-6883;
www.esaweb.org
Social Media: Facebook, Twitter, LinkedIn

Marshall Marinace, President
Dee Ann Harn, Vice President
Merlin Guilbeau, Executive Director
Jon Sargent, Secretary
Steve Paley, Treasurer

Trade association representing the electronic security industry.
Founded in: 1948

21714 Environmental Information Association
6935 Wisconsin Ave
Suite 306
Chevy Chase, MD 20815-6112

301-961-4999
888-343-4342; *Fax:* 301-961-3094
info@eia-usa.org; www.eia-usa.org
Social Media: Twitter, Google+

Kevin Cannan, President
Chris Gates, President-Elect
Mike Schrum, Past President
Robert De Malo, Secretary
Kyle Burroughs, Treasurer

Nonprofit organization dedicated to providing environmental information to individuals, members and industry. Disseminates information on the abatement of asbestos and lead-based paint, indoor air quality, safety and health issues, analytical issues and environmental site assessments.

21715 Executive Protein Institute
Executive Protection Institute
16 Penn Plaza
Suite 1130
New York, NY 10001

212-268-4555; *Fax:* 212-563-4783
info@personalprotection.com;
www.personalprotection.com
Social Media: Facebook, LinkedIn

John Negus, Asst. Executive Director
Jerry Heying, Executive Director
Eugene R. Ferrara, Chief Instructor
John F. Musser, Chief to Staff
Ana Paula Alfonso, Operations Director

A non-profit professional society whose members include academics, trainers, students, law enforcement and government officials, self-employed professionals, security officers, directors from major intenational corporations, security service organizations, and communications, energy, retail, chemicals, insurance, petroleum and utility companies.
2800 Members
Founded in: 1978

21716 False Alarm Reduction Association
10024 Vanderbilt Circle
Unit 4
Rockville, MD 20850

301-519-9237; *Fax:* 301-519-9508
info@faraonline.org; www.faraonline.org

Brad Shipp, Executive Director
Kerri McDonald, President
Nadya Morgan, Vice President-Electronics Security
Tammy Foxworth, Vice President-Fire
Steven Heggemann, Treasurer

Primarily made up of persons employed by government and public safety agencies in charge of, or working in, False Alarm Reduction Units. The goal is to assist these individuals in reducing false alarms for their jurisdiction.
Founded in: 1997

21717 Federal Law Enforcement Officers Association
7945 MacArthur Blvd.
Suite 201
Cabin John, MD 20818

202-870-5503
866-553-5362; *Fax:* 717-932-2262
fleoa@fleoa.org; www.fleoa.org
Social Media: Facebook, Twitter

Jon Adler, National President
Nate Catura, National Executive VP
Chris Schoppmeyer, Vice President-Agency Affairs
Lazaro Cosme, Vice President-Operations
Frank Terreri, Vice President-Legislative Affairs

Founded by a group of concerned federal agents from Customs, the IRS, FBI and INS, its goal is to assure that legal assistance and representation are a phone call away.
24000 Members
Founded in: 1977

21718 Financial & Security Products Association (FSPA)
1024 Mebane Oaks Rd.
Suite 273
Mebane, NC 27302

919-648-0664
800-843-6082; *Fax:* 919-648-0670
info@fspa1.com; www.fspa1.com
Social Media: LinkedIn

Linda Abell, Chairman
L.A Smith, President
Fred Wheeler, Director
Gene Polito, Vice President
Kevin Callahan, Secretary/ Treasurer

Independent dealers, manufacturers and associates whose outstanding products and services give financial institutions a crucial edge in performance, efficiency and economy.
Founded in: 1973

21719 Fire Apparatus Manufacturers' Association (FAMA)
PO Box 3065
Ocala, FL 34478

352-843-3404; *Fax:* 781-334-2911
office@fama.org; www.fama.org

Harold Boer, President
Bruce Whitehouse, VP

Membership association for manufacturers of emergency vehicles and components affixed to or carried upon the vehicle.
125 Members
Founded in: 1946

21720 Fire Equipment Manufacturers' Association
1300 Sumner Avenue
Cleveland, OH 44115

216-241-7333; *Fax:* 216-241-0105;
www.femalifesafety.org
Social Media: LinkedIn, YouTube, Wordpress, Slideshare

The premier trade association representing leading brands, and spanning dozens of product categories, related to fire protection.
27 Members
Founded in: 1925

21721 Fire Suppression Systems Association
3601 East Joppa Road
Baltimore, MD 21234

410-931-8100; *Fax:* 410-931-8111
fssa@clemonsmgmt.com; www.fssa.net
Social Media: Facebook, Twitter, LinkedIn

Scott Bailey, Director
Eric Burkland, Immediate Past President
Ray Aldridge, Vice President
Helen Lowery, Secretary/ Treasurer
Tim Carman, President

An organization of manufacturers, suppliers, and design-installers, dedicated to providing a higher level of fire protection. Members are specialists in protecting high value special hazardareas from fire.
Founded in: 1982

21722 Flight Safety Foundation
801 N. Fairfax Street
Suite 400
Alexandria, VA 22314-1774

703-739-6700; *Fax:* 703-739-6708
wahdan@flightsafety.org;
www.flightsafety.org
Social Media: Facebook, Twitter, LinkedIn

Jon Beatty, President/CEO
Stephanie Mackin, Support Services Manager
David Barger, Treasurer
Ken Hylander, Chair
Kenneth P. Quinn, General Counsel & Secretary

Flight Safety Foundation is an independent, nonprofit, international organization engaged in research, auditing, education, advocacy and publishing to improve aviation safety. The Foundation's mission is to pursue the continuous improvement of global aviation safety and the prevention of accidents.
1000+ Members
Founded in: 1947

21723 Homeland Security Industries Association
666 11th Street NW
Suite 315
Washington, DC 20001

202-386-6471; *Fax:* 202-331-8191
info@hsianet.org; www.hsianet.org

Brenda Boone, Owner

Nonprofit group providing a mechanism for government and the private sector to coordinate on a wide range of homeland security issues. Monitors legislation, regulations and hearings, provides training, and develops position papers reflecting industry concerns.
200+ Members
Founded in: 2002

21724 Institute for Health & Productivity Management
17470 N. Pacesetter Way
Scottsdale, AZ 85255
480-305-2100; *Fax:* 480-305-2189
sean@ihpm.org; www.ihpm.org
Sean Sullivan, President/CEO
Bill Williams, Senior VP & Co-Founder
Pamella Thomas, Chief Medical Officer
Steve Priddy, Executive Director
Deborah Love, EVP & COO
Nonprofit organization making employee health an investment in corporate success through enhanced workplace performance.
Founded in: 1997

21725 Institute for Intergovernmental Research
PO Box 12729
Tallahassee, FL 32317-2729
850-385-0600; *Fax:* 850-422-3529
nygc@iir.com; www.iir.com
Keith G Burt, Advisory Board
Emory B. Williams, Chairman
John Czernis, President
Meena Harris, Executive Vice President
R. Clay Jester, Senior Vice President

21726 Insurance Institute for Highway Safety
1005 N Glebe Rd
Suite 800
Arlington, VA 22201
703-247-1500; *Fax:* 703-247-1588
rrader@iihs.org; www.iihs.org
Social Media: Twitter, YouTube, RSS
Adrian Lund, President
Russ Rader, SVP, Communications
Eric Williams, Counsel
Shelly Shelton, Senior Legal Administrator
Brenda O'Donnell, VP, Insurer Relations
The Insurance Institute for Highway Safety is a nonprofit research and communications organization funded by auto insurers.
Founded in: 1959

21727 Int'l Association for Counterterrorism & Security Professionals
PO Box 10265
Arlington, VA 22210
201-461-5422; www.iacsp.com
Steven Fustero, Executive Director
Our goals include creating a center of information and educational services for those concerned about the challenges now facing all free societies, and promoting professional ethics in the counter terrorism field.
Founded in: 1992

21728 International Association For Healthcare Security and Safety
PO Box 5038
Glendale Heights, IL 60139
630-529-3913
888-353-0990; *Fax:* 630-529-4139
info@iahss.org; www.iahss.org
Social Media: Facebook, Twitter, LinkedIn
David LaRose, President
Jeff A. Young, President Elect
Ben Scaglione, Vice President/Secretary
Colleen Kucera, Executive Director
Nancy Felesena, Executive Assistant
An association dedicated to professionals involved in managing and directing security and safety in healthcare establishments.
Founded in: 1968

21729 International Association for Identification
2131 Hollywood Blvd.
Suite 403
Hollywood, FL 33020
954-589-0628; *Fax:* 954-589-0657;
www.theiai.org
Social Media: Facebook
Bridget Lewis, President
Harold Ruslander, 1st Vice President
Steve Johnson, Board Chair/Past President
Phyllis Karasov, legal Counsel
Glen Calhoun, COO
This is a forum where forensic specialists worldwide can interact as a whole. The main focus of any forensic organization is training and research to ensure all specialists maintain the highest levels of integrity and professionalism in order to meet the constant challenges to our individual disciplines.
Founded in: 1915

21730 International Association for Computer Systems
6 Swarthmore Lane
Dix Hills, NY 11746
631-499-1616; *Fax:* 631-462-9178
iacssjalex@aol.com; www.iacss.com
Robert J Wilk, President
Promotes the security of computer information systems. Certifies individuals as Computer Systems Security Professionals.
Founded in: 1981

21731 International Association for Healthcare Security and Safety
PO Box 5038
Glendale Heights, IL 60139
630-529-3913
888-353-0990; *Fax:* 630-529-4139
info@iahss.org; www.iahss.org
Social Media: Facebook, Twitter, LinkedIn
David LaRose, President
Richard Dufresne, Sr., Member-at-Large
Jeff A. Young, President-Elect
Dana Frentz, VP/Treasurer
Ben Scaglione, VP/Secretary
Nonprofit professional organization of healthcare security and safety executives around the world. Works to improve and professionalize security and safety in healthcare facilities through the exchange of information and experiences among members. A magazine, newsletter and an annual meeting are benefits of membership.
1700 Members
Founded in: 1968

21732 International Association of Arson Investigators
2111 Baldwin Ave
Suite 203
Crofton, MD 21114
410-451-3473
800-468-4224; *Fax:* 410-451-9049;
www.firearson.com
Social Media: Facebook, Twitter, LinkedIn, YouTube
Daniel Heenan, President
George Codding, 1st VP
Soctt Bennett, 2nd VP
Peter Mansi, Immediate Past President
Kevin Crawford, Director
Dedicated to improving the professional development of fire and explosion investigators by being the global resource for fire investigation, technology and research
7500 Members
Founded in: 1949

21733 International Association of Black Professional Firefighters
1200 G St. nW
Suite 800
Washington, DC 20005
202-434-4526
877-213-2170; *Fax:* 202-434-8707
evpiabpff@yahoo.com; www.iabpff.org
Social Media: Facebook, Twitter, LinkedIn
James Hill, President
Sam Aubrey Jr., Treasurer
Kenyatta Smith, EVP
Melanie Anderson, Financial Secreatry
Freddie Jackson, Sergeant at Arms
Promotes interracial progress throughout the fire service and encourages African American firefighters to seek elevated ranks. Offers an annual convention, education courses an an online resource page.
Founded in: 1970

21734 International Association of Bomb Technicians and Investigators
1120 International Parkway
Suite 129
Fredericksburg, VA 22406
540-752-4533; *Fax:* 540-752-2796
admin@iabti.org; www.iabti.org
Social Media: Facebook, Twitter, LinkedIn
James T. Wooten, International Director
The IABTI is an independent, non-profit, professional association formed for countering the criminal use of explosives. This is accomplished through the exchange of training, expertise and information among personnel employed in the fields of law enforcement, emergency services, the military, forensic science and other related fields.
Founded in: 1973

21735 International Association of Campus Law Enforcement Administrators
342 N Main Street
West Hartford, CT 06117-2507
860-586-7517; *Fax:* 860-586-7550
info@iaclea.org; www.iaclea.org
Social Media: Facebook
Patricia Patton, Director
David L Perry, Immediate Past President
Willaim F Taylor, President
Randy A Burba, President- Elect
Jasper Cooke, VP for Finance
Advances public safety for educational institutions by providing educational resources, advocacy and professional development.
Founded in: 1958

21736 International Association of Chiefs of Police
44 Canal Center Plaza
Suite 200
Alexandria, VA 22314
703-836-6767
800-THE-IACP; *Fax:* 703-836-4543;
www.theiacp.org
Social Media: Facebook, Twitter, LinkedIn, RSS, YouTube
Rechard Beary, President
Vincent Talucci, Executive Director/CEO
Gwen Boniface, Deputy Executive Director
John Firman, Director of Strategic Partnerships
Paul Santiago, Director of Intl. Policing Division
The association's goals are to advance the science and art of police services; to develop and disseminate improved administrative. technical and opreration practices and promote their use in police work; to foster police cooperation and the exchange of information and experience among police administrators throughout the world; to

bring about recruitment and training in the police profession of qualified person.
15000 Members
Founded in: 1893

21737 International Association of Crime Analysts
9218 Metcalf Ave.
Suite 364
Overland Park, KS 66212
919-940-3883
800-609-3419
iaca@iaca.net; www.iaca.net
Social Media: Facebook, Twitter, LinkedIn, RSS
Ericka Jackson, VP, Membership
Carolyn Cassidy, President
Tony Berger, VP, Administration
Eric Drifmeyer, Treasurer
Dawn Clausius, Secretary
The International Association of Crime Analysts was formed in 1990 to help crime analysts around the world improve their skills and make valuable contacts, to help law enforcement agencies make the best use of crime analysis, and to advocate for standards of performance and technique within the profession itself. This is accomplished through training, networking, and publications.
Founded in: 1990

21738 International Association of Dive Rescue Specialists
8103 East US Highway
36, Box 171 Avon
INDIANA, US 46123
317-464-9787
800-423-7911; *Fax:* 317-641-0730
dowens@iadrs.org; www.iadrs.org
Social Media: Twitter
Blades Robinson, Executive Director
Steven Orusa, Operations Director
David Owens, Dir. Of communications
Fred Jackson, Advisory Board
Steve Fleming, Board of Directors
IADRS is dedicated to helping water rescue professionals stay informed about advances in training, equipment, and life saving techniques.
Founded in: 1977

21739 International Association of Fire Chiefs
4025 Fair Ridge Drive
Suite 300
Fairfax, VA 22033-2868
703-273-0911; *Fax:* 703-273-9363
thicks@iafc.org; www.iafc.org
Social Media: Facebook, Twitter, RSS
Mark W. Light, Executive Director
Karen Soyster Fitzgerald, Chief Operations Officer
Chief John Sinclair, President & Chairman
Chief Thomas Jenkins, First Vice President
Chief Gary Curmode, Second Vice President
Provides leadership to career and volunteer chief, chief fire officers and managers of emergency service organization throughout the inernational community through vision, information, education, services and representation to enhance their professionalsim and capabilities.
12000 Members
Founded in: 1873

21740 International Association of Firefighters
1750 New York Ave
Nw Suite 300
Washington, DC 20006-5395
202-737-8484; *Fax:* 202-737-8418
pr@iaff.org; www.iaff.org
Social Media: Facebook, Twitter, Youtube, Flickr, Pinterest
Harold Schaitberger, President
Jim Lee, Chief of Operations
Peter L. Gorman, Chief of Staff
Thomas H. Miller, Secretary/ Treasurer
William Romaka, 1st VP
Represents city and county firefighters and state and federal workers such as forestry firefighters and emergency medical workers at certain industrial facilities. Addressed are health and safety, labor relations, training, hazardous materials and burn injuries and education.
240k Members
Founded in: 1903

21741 International Association of Personal Protection Agents
PO Box 266
Arlington Heights, IL 60006-0266
847-870-8007; *Fax:* 847-870-8990
proproserv@aol.com; www.iappa.net
Social Media: Facebook
Stephen R. Barnhart, Executive Director
Charles Mallice, Operations & Training Director
Nikolai Ehlers, CCPA, Senior Security Consultant
James A. King, Chief Advisor
Arnaldo B. Merli, CCPA, International Security Consultant
Professional, nonprofit membership body open to military and civilian law enforcement personnel and people from the public and private sector who are engaged in the protection of royalty, presidential, state and diplomatic officials, government, military and corporate executives, personalities from the entertainment world and those involved in witness and prisoner protection.
Founded in: 1989

21742 International Association of Professional Security Consultants
575 Market St.
Suite 2125
San Francisco, CA 94105
415-536-0288; *Fax:* 415-764-4915
iapsc@iapsc.org; www.iapsc.org
Social Media: LinkedIn
Harold Gillens, President
Alan Brockbank, Vice President
Kerry Parker, Executive Director
Ken Wheatley, Secretary
Lynda Buel, Treasurer
The International Association of Professional Security Consultants (IAPSC) is a widely recognized consulting association in the security industry. Its rigid membership requirements ensure that potential clients may select from the most elite group of professional, ethical and competent security consultants available to them.
Founded in: 1984

21743 International Biometrics & Identification Association
1090 Vermant Avenue
NW, 6th Floor
Washington, DC 20005
202-789-4452; *Fax:* 202-289-7097
ibia@ibia.org; www.ibia.org
Social Media: Facebook, Twitter, RSS
Raffie Beroukhim, Director
Christer Bergman, Secretary
Robert Harbour, President and Chairman of the Board
Walter Hamilton, Vice Chairman
Mike DePasquale, Treasurer
IBIA provides strong and growing value to its members, expanding business opportunities for the industry, advocating government support for the useof biometrics in leading commercial and public-sector applications, and reporting on key issues of strategic importance to the membership.
Founded in: 1998

21744 International Biometrics Industry Association
1090 Vermont Avenue,
NW, 6th Floor
Washington, DC 20005
202-789-4452; *Fax:* 202-289-7097
ibia@ibia.org; www.ibia.org
Social Media: Facebook, Twitter, RSS
Robert Harbour, Chairman/ President
Walter Hamilton, Vice Chairman
Raffie Beroukhim, Director
Christer Bergman, Secretary
Mike DePasquale, Treasurer
Trade association representing developers, manufacturers and integrators of biometric hardware and software.
Founded in: 1998

21745 International Centre for the Prevention of Crime
465 rue St-Jean Street
Bureau 803
Montreal, QU H2Y-2R6
514-288-6731; *Fax:* 514-288-8763
cipc@cipc-icpc.org;
www.crime-prevention-intl.org/english
Social Media: Facebook, Twitter, LinkedIn
Vincenzo Castelli, Administrator
Erich Marks, VP
Chantal Bernier, President
Elizabeth Johnston, Secretary
Paul Girard, Treasurer
The ICPC is an international forum for national government local authorities, public agencies, specialized institutions, and non-government organisations of exchange experience, consider emerging knowledge, and improve policies and programs in crime prevention and community safety. ICPC staff monitors developments, provides direct assistance to members, and contributes to public knowledge and understanding in the field.
Founded in: 1994

21746 International Consumer Product Health & Safety Organization
7044 S. 13th Street
Oak Creek, WI 53154
414-908-4930; *Fax:* 301-601-3543
customercare@icphso.org; www.icphso.org
Social Media: Twitter, LinkedIn
Rick Brenner, Vice President
Alan Kaufman, President
Nancy Cowles, President-Elect
D Fenton, Executive Director
Ann Weeks, Past President
ICPHSO holds a unique position in its ability to attract the interest of a broad range of health and safety professionals and interested consumers, world-wide.
Founded in: 1993

21747 International Fire Service Training Association
930 N Willis
Stillwater, OK 74078
405-744-5723; *Fax:* 405-744-8204
customer.service@osufpp.org; www.ifsta.org
Social Media: Facebook, Twitter, LinkedIn
Robert Moore, State Fire Organization
Steve Ashbrock, Fire Dept.
Steve Austin, Fire Service Affiliate
Mike Wieder, Fire Organisation
Scott D. Kerwood, Fire Department
Nonprofit organization associated with Fire Protection Publications, a department of the College

of Engineering, Architecture and Technology at Oklahoma State University.
Founded in: 1934

21748 **International Foundation for Protection Officers**
1250 Tamiami
Tr. N Ste.206
Naples, FL 34102

239-430-0534; *Fax:* 239-430-0533
adminifpo@earthlink.net; www.ifpo.org
Social Media: Facebook, Twitter, LinkedIn

Sandi J Davies, Executive Director
Michael Stroberger, Secretary/Treasurer
Rck Daniels, Chairman
Karl Poulin, Director
Tom M. Conley, Past Chairman

Nonprofit organization for the purpose of facilitating the training and certification needs of protection officers and security supervisors from both the commercial and proprietary sectors.
Founded in: 1988

21749 **International High Technology Crime Investigation Association**
3288 Goldstone Drive
Roseville, CA 95747

916-408-1751; *Fax:* 916-384-2232
info@htcia.org; www.htcia.org
Social Media: Facebook, Twitter, LinkedIn

Shadi Hayden, President
Tom Quilty, Past President
Peter Morin, 1st Vice President
Steve Branigan, Secretary
Matt Samuelson, Treasurer

Designed to encourage, promote, aid and effect the voluntary interchange of data, information, experience, ideas and knowledge about methods, processes, and techniques relating to investigations and security in advanced technologies among its membership.
3500 Members
Founded in: 1984

21750 **International Hologram Association**
2149 Cascade Ave
Suite 106
Hood River, OR 97031-1087

541-386-9449; *Fax:* 541-386-1564;
www.hairmasterssalon.com

More than 60 of the worlds leading hologram manufacturers are members. Dedicated to promoting the interests of those quality hologram manufacturers worldwide and to helping our customers to achieve their security, packaging graphic and other objectives through the effective use of holography.
Founded in: 1993

21751 **International Hologram Manufacturers Association**
4 Windmill Business Village
Brooklands Close, SU TW167DY

193-278-5680; *Fax:* 193-278-0790
info@ihma.org; www.ihma.org

Mike Messmer, Chairman
Nuray Yilmaz, Board Member
Umendra Gupta, ASPA Representative
Diana Newcomb, Board Member
Rajan Thomas, Asian Representative

A not for profit organization serving the hologram manufacturing industry.
Founded in: 1993

21752 **International Locksmiths Association**
PO Box 9560
Naperville, IL 60567-0560

866-745-5625; www.ilanational.org

Tom Ripp, Director/Co-Chair
Larry Bowman, Vice President
Kurt Kloeckner, Treasurer
Kevin T. Piiper, National President
John Rendle, Secretary

Members are locksmiths, carpenters and building engineers who are employed by colleges, universities, hospitals, companies and government facilities. Dedicated to the education of members and the benefit of our institutions.

21753 **International Municipal Signal Association**
597 Haverty Court
Suite 100
Rockledge, FL 32955

321-392-0500
800-723-4672; *Fax:* 321-806-1400
info@imsasafety.org; www.imsasafety.org
Social Media: Facebook, Twitter, LinkedIn

Douglas M. Aiken, Deputy Executive Director
Mike Flanigan, Past President
Hans Kristensen, President
Kan Balltrip, President-Elect
Leonard Addair, Director-at-Large

Basic purpose of the organization is to keep its members and others in the profession, up-to-date on proper procedures of construction and maintenance of signal systems and informed on new products and equipment developments.
10000 Members
Founded in: 1896

21754 **International Photoluminescent Safety**
2001 Jefferson Davis Highway
Suite 1004
Arlington, VA 22202-3617

703-416-0060; *Fax:* 703-416-0014
info@plsafety.org; www.plsafety.org

Tom Thompson, Executive Director

A leader in the marine safety and implementation of the highest possible performance, manufacturing maintenance, service and training standards, for all lifesaving, survival and emergency rescue equipment.
131 Members
Founded in: 1986

21755 **International Process Servers Association**
2854 Larimer St
Denver, CO 80205

585-232-8590
800-611-2774; *Fax:* 877-824-2482
richard@processservers.com;
www.iprocessservers.com

Unifies process servers in the United States and throughout the world, as the single greatest resource for all process servers and private investigators.

21756 **International Safety Equipment Association**
1901 N Moore Street
Suite 808
Arlington, VA 22209-1762

703-525-1695; *Fax:* 703-528-2148
isea@safetyequipment.org;
www.safetyequipment.org
Social Media: Facebook, Twitter, LinkedIn

Daniel K Shipp, President
Nate Kogler, Public Affairs Director
Craig Wallentine, Office Services Manager
Eric Beck, Chairman
Brian Lyons, Past Chairman

Trade association in the US for companies that manufacture safety equipment. Member companies are world leaders in the design and manufacture of clothing and equipment used in factories, construction sites, hospitals and clinics, farms, schools, laboratories, and in the home — anywhere people are doing work. Our common goal is to protect the health and safety of people exposed to hazardous and potentially harmful environments.
Founded in: 1933

21757 **International Security Management Association**
PO Box 623
Buffalo, IA 52728-0623

563-381-4008
800-368-1894; *Fax:* 563-381-4283
susan.pohlmann@isma.com
isma.com/

Tim Janes, President
Mike Howard, Executive Director
Damin Memeekin, Second VP
Mary Welsh, Deputy Executive Director

ISMA's mission is to provide and support an international forum of selected security executives whose combined expertise wil be utilized in a synergistic manner in developing, assimilating, sharing knowledge within security disciplines for the ultimate purpose of enhancing professional and business standards.
400 Members
Founded in: 1983

21758 **International System Safety Society**
PO Box 70
Unionville, VA 22567-0070

540-854-8630; *Fax:* 540-854-4561;
www.system-safety.org
Social Media: Facebook, LinkedIn

Dr. Rod Simmons, President
Bob Schmedake, Immediate Past President
Pam Kniess, Executive Secretary
Chuick Muniak, Executive Vice President
Clif Ericson, Treasurer

The System Safety Society is a non-profit organization dedicated to supporting the safety professional in the application of system engineering and systems management to risk analysis. The Society is international in scope and draws members throughout the world.
4500 Members
Founded in: 1962

21759 **International of Personal Protection Agents**
PO Box 266
Arlington Heights, IL 60006-0266

847-870-8007; *Fax:* 847-870-8990
proproserv@aol.com; www.iappa.net
Social Media: Facebook

Dr. Stephen Barnhart, Executive Director
Charles Mallice, Operations &Training Director
Mr Nikolai Ehlers, Senior Security Consultant
Mr James A King, Chief Advisor
Mr Chris Menary, National Director

Professional, nonprofit membership body open to military and civilian law enforcement personnel and people from the public and private sector who are engaged in the protection of royalty, presidential, state and diplomatic officials, government, military and corporate executives, personalities from the entertainment world and those involved in witness and prisoner protection.
Founded in: 1989

21760 **Investigators of America**
PO Box 4243
Downey, CA 90241

562-869-2535
877-393-7792; *Fax:* 562-869-5268
dkalepi@earthlink.net;
www.investigatorsofamerica.com

John R. Spencer, Director
Dave Blair, Director
Roberto A. Rivera, Director

Edwin C. Hodges, Director
Steven Rambam, Director

Investigators of America is a rapidly growing association comprised of elite private investigators, insurance adjusters, and expert witnesses across the United States with affiliates in other countries.

21761 Laser Institute of America
13501 Ingenuity Dr
Suite 128
Orlando, FL 32826

407-380-1553
800-345-2737; *Fax:* 407-380-5588
lia@lia.org; www.lia.org
Social Media: Facebook, Twitter, LinkedIn, Google+

Yongfeng Lu, Past President
Lin Li, President Elect
Rodert Thomas, President
Stephen Capp, Treasurer
Paul Denney, Secretary

The Laser Institute of America is the professional membership society dedicated to fostering lasers, laser applications and safety worldwide. Its mission is to foster lasers, laser applications, and laser safety worldwide. Serving the industrial, medical, research and government communities, LIA offers technical information and networking opportunities to laser users from around the globe.
1200 Members
Founded in: 1968

21762 Mine Safety and Health Administration
1100 Wilson Blvd
21st Floor
Arlington, VA 22209-3939

202-693-9400
800-746-1553; *Fax:* 202-693-9401;
www.msha.gov
Social Media: Facebook, Twitter

David G Dye, Executive Director

Mission is to enforce compliance with mandatory safety and health standards as a means to eliminate fatal accidents, reduce the frequency and severity of nonfatal accidents, minimnize health hazards, and to promote improved safety and health conditions in national mines.
Founded in: 1978

21763 Motorcycle Safety Foundation
2 Jenner
Suite 150
Irvine, CA 92618

800-446-9227
msf@msf-usa.org; www.msf-usa.org
Social Media: Facebook, Twitter, YouTube

Russ Brenan, Chair
Joseph Dagley, Vice Chair
Tim Buche, President & CEO
Robert Gladden, Vice President
Steve Piehl, Secretary/ Treasurer

Provides information on rider training, licensing, and goverment relations.

21764 National Alarm Association of America
PO Box 3409
Dayton, OH 45401

937-461-2208
800-283-6285; *Fax:* 937-461-4759;
www.arcat.com

Gene Riddlebaugh, President
Grant Angell, Senior VP Associate Affairs
Ricardo Gonzales, Vice President

Mission is to advance the welfare of members through the free exchange, among members of ideas and the dissemination of information concerning trade practices, business conditions, technical developments, within the industry, and any related subject of concern to the security industry.
Founded in: 1984

21765 National Association of Elevator Safety Authorities
PO Box 640
Rochester, WA 98579

360-292-4968
800-746-2372; *Fax:* 360-292-4973
dotty@naesai.org; www.naesai.org

George W. Gibson, Advisor
Douglas S Warne, President
Dean G Mclellan, VP
Fredick C Slater, Treasurer
Michael Stewart, Secretary

Elevator inspector certification and continuing education.
2500 Members
Founded in: 1969

21766 National Association of Fire Equipment Distributors
180 N. Wabash Avenue
Suite 401
Chicago, IL 60601

312-461-9600; *Fax:* 312-461-0777
dharris@nafed.org; www.nafed.org
Social Media: Facebook, LinkedIn, YouTube

Ed Hugill, President
Danny Harris, Ex Officio
Tim Krulan, Treasurer
George Seymour, President Elect
Bill Johnson, Director

Mission is to improve the economic environment, business performance, and technical competence in the fire protection industry.
Founded in: 1963

21767 National Association of Fraud Investigators
2519 NW 23rd St.
Suite 204
Oklahoma City, Ok 73107

405-833-2327
RBrown2150@aol.com; www.nafraud.com

Established to improve communications and expand the network of professional fraud investigators.

21768 National Association of Legal Investigators
235N Pine Street
Lansing, MI 48933

517-702-9835
866-520-NALI; *Fax:* 517-372-1501;
www.nalionline.org
Social Media: Facebook, Twitter

Don C. Johnson, National Director
Jayne McElfnesh, Assistant National Director
Andi Murphy, National Secretary
Julian Vail, Association Management
Nicole Bocra Gray, Regional Director- Northeast Region

Membership in NAL is open to all professional legal investigators who are actively engaged in negligence investigations for plaintiff and/or criminal defense, and who are employed by investigative firms, law firms or public defender agencies.
Founded in: 1967

21769 National Association of Safety Professionals
1531 South
Post Road
Shelby, NC 28152

800-922-2219; *Fax:* 704-487-1579
info@naspweb.com; www.naspweb.com
Social Media: Facebook, Twitter

Eric Gislason, Executive Director
Jon Beard, IT Analyst

A nonprofit membership organization providing training, consultative services as well as certifications.
10000 Members

21770 National Association of Security Companies
444 North Capitol Street, NW
Suite 345
Washington, DC 20001

202-347-3257; *Fax:* 202-393-7006
information@nasco.org; www.nasco.org

Jim McNulty, Chair
Stephen Kasloff, 1st Vice Chair
Julie Payne, 2nd Vice Chair
Lynn Oliver, Secretary
David Buckman, Treasurer

To promote standards and professionalism for private security officers and within contract security.

21771 National Burglar & Fire Alarm Association
2300 Valley View Lane
Suite 230
Irving, TX 75062

214-260-5970
888-447-1689; *Fax:* 214-260-5979;
www.alarm.org
Social Media: Facebook, Twitter, YouTubee

Merlin Guilbeau, Executive Director
Georgia Calaway, Communications/PR Director
Founded in: 1948

21772 National Classification Management Society
994 Old Eagle School Rd
Suite 1019
Wayne, PA 19087-1866

610-971-4856; *Fax:* 610-971-4859
info@classmgmt.com; www.classmgmt.com
Social Media: Facebook, Twitter, LinkedIn

Sharon K. Tannahill, Executive Director
Mr. Dennis Arriage, President
Mrs. Aprilli Abbott, Vice President
Dean Young, Treasurer
Ms. Debbie Young, Secretary

Advancing the practice of classification management in the disiplines of industrial security, information security, government designated unclassified information, and intellectual property, and to foster the highest qualities of security professionalism among its members.
1,300 Members
Founded in: 1964

21773 National Council of Investigation & Security Services
7501 Sparrows Point Boulevard
Baltimore, MD 21219-1927

800-445-8408; *Fax:* 410-388-9746
nciss@comcast.net; www.nciss.org

Carolyn Ward, Executive Director
Francie Koehler, Past President
Debbie Anderson, Secretary
Don C. Johnson, CLI
Bill Fletcher, Treasurer

A cooperative of those companies and associations responsible for providing private security

and investigation services to the legal profession, business community, government and the public.
1300 Members
Founded in: 1975

21774 National Counterterrorism Center
National Counterterrorism Center
Washington, DC 20511

703-733-8600
nctcpao@nctc.gov; www.nctc.gov
Social Media: Facebook, Twitter, YouTube, RSS, Tumblr, Flickr

Nicholas J. Rasmussen, Director
John J. Mulligan, Deputy Director

The primary organization in the United States Government for integrating and analyzing all intelligence pertaining to counterterrorism.

21775 National Crime Justice Association
720 7th Street NW
Third Floor
Washington, DC 20001

202-628-8550; *Fax:* 202-448-1723
info@ncja.org; www.ncja.org
Social Media: Facebook, Twitter, LinkedIn, Pinterest, RSS

Cabell C. Cropper, Executive Director
Lisa Nine Accordini, Senior Staff Associate
Bethany Broida, Director of Communications
Robert Greeves, Senior Policy Adviser
Janene Scelza, Web Manager

Exists to promote the developemtn of justice systems in states, tribal nations, and units of local government that enhance public saftety ; prevent and reduce the harmful effects of criminal and delinquent behavior on victims, individuals and communities; adjudicate defendants and sanction offenders fairly and justly; and that are effective and efficient.
Founded in: 1971

21776 National Crime Prevention Council
1201 Connecticut Avenue, NW
Suite 200
Washington, DC 20036

202-466-6272; *Fax:* 202-296-1356
webmaster@ncpc.org; www.ncpc.org

David A. Dean, Chairman
Ann M. Harnkins, President & CEO
Jean Adnopoz, Secretary
John p. Box, Treasurer
Robert F. Diegelman, Vice Chair

Aids people in keeping themselves, their families, and their communities safe from crime. NCPC produces tools that communities can use to learn crime prevention strategies, engage community members, and coordinate with local agencies.
136 Members
Founded in: 1979

21777 National Defense Industrial Association
2111 Wilson Blvd
Suite 400
Arlington, VA 22201-3061

703-522-1820; *Fax:* 703-522-1885
info@ndia.org; www.ndia.org
Social Media: Facebook, Twitter, LinkedIn, YouTube, Pinterest, Google+

Mckinley Craig, President & CEO
O'Connell Cyndi, Web Operations
Barry D. Bates, VP, Operations
Goodman Will, VP, Government Policy
Dino Pignotti, VP, Advertising

A leading defense idustry association whose mission is to promote national security through a variety of means, including education, training and advocacy.
28100 Members
Founded in: 1919

21778 National Electrical Manufacturers
1300 17th St N
Suite 900
Arlington, VA 22209

703-841-3200; *Fax:* 703-841-5900
webmaster@nema.org; www.nema.org
Social Media: Facebook, Twitter, LinkedIn, RSS, YouTube, Google+

Kevin J. Cosgriff, President
Donald J. Hendler, Chairman
Maryrose Sylvester, Vice Chair
David G. Nord, Treasurer
John W. Estey, Board Committee Chairman

NEMA's mission is to promote the competitiveness of its member companies by providing quality services that will impact positively on standrds, government regulation and market economics.
400 Members
Founded in: 1926

21779 National Emergency Equipment Dealers Association
8421 Frost Way
Annandale, VA 22003

703-280-4622; *Fax:* 703-280-0942
KentonP1@aol.com; www.femsa.org
Social Media: Facebook, Twitter, LinkedIn, Pinterest, Google+, Tumblr

Kenton Pattie, Executive Director

Serves dealers who sell and service fire, rescue, and emergency rescue systems equipment and apparatus. Preserves and strengthens the free market system for dealers through advocacy, information and training. Assists dealers profitably deliver high quality products and support to the nation's emergency services.
Founded in: 1915

21780 National Fire Protection Association
1 Batterymarch Park
Quincy, MA 02169-7471

617-770-3000
800-344-3555; *Fax:* 617-770-0700
publicaffairs@nfpa.org; www.nfpa.org
Social Media: Facebook, Twitter, LinkedIn, YouTube, Google+, RSS, Pintere

Jim Pauley, President/CEO
Randolph W. Tucker, 1st VP
Ernest J. Grant, Chairman
Amy R. Action, Secretary
Thomas A. Lawson, Treasurer

The mission of the NFPA is to reduce the worldwide burden of fire and other hazards on the quality of life by providing and advocating consensus codes and standards, research, training and education.
75000 Members
Founded in: 1896

21781 National Fire Sprinkler Association
40 Jon Barrett Rd.
Patterson, NY 12563

845-878-4200; *Fax:* 845-878-4215
info@nfsa.org; www.nfsa.org
Social Media: Facebook, Twitter, LinkedIn, YouTube, Google+

Russell P. Fleming, Executive Vice President
Alan Wiginton, Director
Dennis Coleman, Chairman
James Boulanger, Treasurer
Larry Thau, Vice Chair

The goal is to create a market for the widespread acceptance of competently installed automatic fire sprinkler systems in new and existing construction. Members are makers and installers of automatic fire sprinklers and related equipment.
Founded in: 1905

21782 National Floor Safety Institute (NFSI)
PO Box 92607
Southlake, TX 76092

817-749-1700; *Fax:* 817-749-1702
info@nfsi.org; www.nfsi.org
Social Media: Facebook, Twitter, LinkedIn

Richard Bing, Senior Marketing Manager
Russell Kendzior, President & Chairman
Howard W. Harris, Treasurer
Steven C. Spencer, Vice President
Beth B Risinger, CEO/Executive Director

Mission is to aid in the prevention of slip-and-fall accidents through education, training and recearch. The NFSI is led by a fifteen-member Board of Directors representing product manufacturers, insurance underwriters, trade associations, and independent consultants.
Founded in: 1997

21783 National Institute for Occupational Safety & Health
1600 Clifton Rd
Atlanta, GA 30329-4027

404-639-3385
800-232-4636; *Fax:* 513-533-8573
eidtechinfo@cdc.gov;
www.cdc.gov/niosh/homepage.html
Social Media: Facebook, Twitter, RSS, MySpace, YouTube, Flickr

John Howard MD, Director
Hubert H Humphrey, Chief of Staff
Max Lum EdD, Assoc Director Health

To promote health and quality of life by preventing and controlling disease, injury, and disability.

21784 National Institute of Standards and Technology (NIST)
100 Bureau Dr
Stop 1070
Gaithersburg, MD 20899-1070

301-975-6478
800-877-8339; *Fax:* 301-948-6107
inquiries@nist.gov; www.nist.gov
Social Media: Facebook, Twitter, LinkedIn, RSS, YouTube, Flickr

W. Watt Starnes, CEO
Dr. William E. May, Director
Kevin Kimball, Chief of Staff
George Jenkins, Chief Financial Officer
Heather Mayton, Executive Officer

Promotes US innovation and industrial competitiveness by advancing measurement science, standards, and technology in ways that enhance economic security and improve quality of life. It's four cooperative programs are NIST Laboratories, Baldrige National Quality Program, Manufacturing Extension Partnership, and Advanced Technology Program.
Founded in: 1901

21785 National Nuclear Security Administration
1000 Independence Ave.,
S.W.
Washington, DC 20585

202-586-5000
800-342-5363; *Fax:* 202-586-7371;
www.nnsa.energy.gov
Social Media: Facebook, Twitter, YouTube, Flickr, RSS

Frank G. Klotz, Administrator
Madelyn Creedon, Principal Deputy Administrator
Annie Harrington, Deputy Administrator
Bruce Diamond, General Counsel
Deborah Wilbar, Associate Administrator

Organization for advancing nuclear sciences, technologies and engineering.
Founded in: 2000

21786 National Safety Council
1121 SpringLake Dr.
Itasca, IL 60143-3201
630-285-1121
800-621-7619; *Fax:* 630-285-1434
customerservice@nsc.org; www.nsc.org
Social Media: Facebook, Twitter, LinkedIn, YouTube, Google+
Deborah Hersman, CEO
John P. Surma, Chairman
Patrick Phelan, Chief Financial Officer
Shay Gallagher, Vice President
Jeane Wrenn, Senior Director/General Counsel
Nonprofit, nongovernmental, international public service organization dedicated to protecting life and promoting health.
48000 Members
Founded in: 1913

21787 National Safety Management Society
PO Box 4460
Walnut Creek, CA 94596-0460
800-321-2910
nsmsinc@yahoo.com; www.nsms.us
Social Media: Facebook, Twitter, LinkedIn, RSS
Roosevelt Smith, President
John H Bridges III, Director
Jeffery Chung, Board Member
Marilyn Clark Alston, Board Member
Charles W. McGlothlin, Board Member
Mission is to support managers and their employees in their responsibility to assure the safety of all employees.
Founded in: 1966

21788 National Sheriffs' Association
1450 Duke Street
Alexandria, VA 22314
800-424-7827; *Fax:* 703-838-5349
mkendall@sheriffs.org; www.sheriffs.org
Social Media: Facebook, Twitter, LinkedIn, Google+
John E. Aubrey, Immediate Past President
John Thompson, Interim Executive Director
Linda Foldvik, Director of Finance
Miriam Kendall, Executive Secretary
Fred G. Wilson, Director of Outreach & Law
An organization to promote criminal justice, homeland security and public safety.
Founded in: 1940

21789 National Society of Professional Insurance Investigators
PO Box 88
Delaware, OH 43015
888-677-4498; *Fax:* 740-369-7155
nspii@nspii.com; www.nspii.com
Social Media: LinkedIn, RSS
Micheal E. Jacobs, President
Jeffrey W. Ferrand, First VP
Michall Beagle, Secretary/Membership Chairman
A professional society for research and education.
590 Members
Founded in: 1983

21790 National Tooling & Machining Association
1357 Rockside Road
Cleveland, OH 44134
301-248-6200
800-248-6862; *Fax:* 216-264-2840
info@ntma.org; www.ntma.org
Social Media: Twitter, LinkedIn
Jeff Kelly, CEO
John Belza, President
Supports its members through education, training and resources.
2700 Members
Founded in: 1943

21791 NationalAssociationof SchoolSafetyand Law Enforcement Officials
19411 S. W. 308thStreet
Homestead, FL 33030
305-905-1323; *Fax:* 305-247-9915;
www.nassleo.org
Social Media: Facebook, Twitter
Augustine Pescatore, Chairman
Larry D. Johnson, President
Chief Ian Moffett, President Elect
Hector Garcia, Secretary
Rudy Perez, Treasurer
Provides levels of resources for school law enforcement and safety officials.

21792 Professional Investigators & Security Association
PO Box 3307
Fairfax, VA 22038-3307
703-818-0552; *Fax:* 703-818-0551
kbreenpi@yahoo.com; www.vapisa.com
Social Media: Facebook, Twitter
Kristopher W. Wilgus, 1st, Vice President
Susan Spofford, 2nd Vice President
Nicole Bocra Grray, President
Vacant T.B.A., Secretary
Narma J. Duncan, Treasurer
PISA is recognized as the preeminent professional organization representing members of the Private Security Services.
Founded in: 1984

21793 Professional Records & Information Service s Management
8735 W Higgins Rd
Suite 300
Chicago, IL 60631
847-375-6344
800-336-9793; *Fax:* 847-375-6343
info@prismintl.org; www.prismintl.org
Social Media: Facebook, Twitter, LinkedIn
Dave Bergeson, Executive Director
Chad Sorrell, President
Chris Kelly, Vice President
Michael Fruchter, Secretary/ Treasurer
Chris Pearson, Asst. Secretary
A nonprofit trade association for the commercial information management industry whose vision is to be the primary global resource for commercial information management outsourcing providers.
Founded in: 1930

21794 SAFE Association
PO Box 130
Creswell, OR 97426-0130
541-895-3012; *Fax:* 541-895-3014
safe@peak.org; www.safeassociation.com
Social Media: Facebook
Barr Shope, President
Joe Spinosa, President-Elect
Mathew Wawrowski, Vice President
Jerry Ride, Treasurer
Alex Mc Gill, Secretary
Dedicated to the preservation of human life. Provides a common meeting ground for the sharing of problems, ideas and information.
Founded in: 1956

21795 Safe & Vault Technicians Association
3500 Easy St
Dallas, TX 75247
214-819-9733
800-532-2562; *Fax:* 214-819-9736;
www.savta.org
Charles Gibson, President
Provides a host of benefits to help its members stay informed, solving day to day problems, and out-performing the competition. Has helped thousands of safe and vault techicians achiveve personal and professional success.
Founded in: 1986

21796 Safety Equipment Distributors Association
1901 North Moore Street
Suite 808
Arlington, VA 22209-1762
703-525-1695; *Fax:* 703-528-2148;
www.safetycentral.org
Social Media: Facebook, Twitter, LinkedIn
Eric Beck, Chairman
Brian Lyons, Past Chairman
Daniel K. Shipp, President
Sheila Eads, Vice Chairman
Jim Johnson, General Manager
The Saftey Equipment Distributor's Association is the trade association comprised of companies that distribute safety equipmant and related products and services. Its member companies are leaders in the distribution of personal protective equipment to a broad spectrum of users, including general industry, construction, municipalities, utilities, schools and laboratories.
175 Members
Founded in: 1933

21797 Safety Glazing Certification Council
P.O. Box 730
100 W. Main St.
Sackets Harbor, NY 13685
315-646-2234; *Fax:* 315-646-2297
staff@amscert.com; www.sgcc.org
John Kent, Administrative Staff
Peter Weismantle, President
Richard Paschel, Vice President
June Willcott, Secretary
Elaine S. Rodman, Treasurer
Nonprofit corporation that provides for the certifacation of safety glazing materials, comprised of safety glazing manufacturers and other parties concerned with public safety. SGCC is managed by a board of directors comprised of representatives from the safety glazing industry and the public interest sector.
105 Members
Founded in: 1971

21798 Scaffold & Access Industry Association
400 Admiral Blvd
Kansas City, MO 64106
816-595-4860
866-687-7115; *Fax:* 602-257-1166
rjm@scaffold.org; www.scaffold.org
Social Media: Facebook, Twitter, LinkedIn, RSS
Paula Manning, President Elect
Mike Russell, President
Frank Frietsch, Treasurer
Ted Beville, Vice President
Colby Hubler, Secretary
Nonprofit organization which promotes scaffold safety and education through its publications, conventions, tradeshows and training programs.
Founded in: 1972

21799 Scaffold and Access Industry Association
400 Admiral Blvd
Kansas City, MO 64106

816-595-4860; *Fax:* 816-472-7765
info@saiaonline.org; www.saiaonline.org
Social Media: Facebook, Twitter, LinkedIn, RSS

Mike Russell, President
Paula Manning, President Elect
Ted Beville, Vice President
Colby Hubler, Secretary
Frank Frietsch, Treasurer

To promote, represent and enhance the access, scaffolding and forming industry for the benefit of its members.
Founded in: 1972

21800 Security Hardware Distributors Association
105 Eastern Avenue
Suite 104
Annapolis, MD 21403

410-940-6346; *Fax:* 410-263-1659
info@shda.org; www.shda.org

Sean Steinmann, President
Rob Justen, Director
Karen Hoffman-Kahl, Immediate Past President
John Burke, Vice President
David Swartz, Treasurer

Offers education and services to its members.
150 Members
Founded in: 1940

21801 Security Industry Association
8405 Colesville Road
Suite 500
Silver Spring, MD 20910

301-804-4700
866-817-8888; *Fax:* 301-804-4701
info@siaonline.org; www.siaonline.org
Social Media: Facebook, Twitter, LinkedIn, YouTube

Denis Hebert, Chairman Elect
Herve Fages, Vice Chairman
Scott Schafer, Treasurer
V. John Storia, Chairman
John Romanowich, Secretary

SIA is dedicated to promoting growth, advancement, and professionalism within the security industry. Its activities fall into four core concentrations: government relations, research & technology, education & training, and standards.
510 Members
Founded in: 1969

21802 Semiconductor Environmental Safety & Health Association
1313 Dolley Madison Boulevard
Suite 402
McLean, VA 22101

703-790-1745; *Fax:* 703-790-2672
BBurk@Burkinc.com; www.seshaonline.org
Social Media: Facebook, Twitter, LinkedIn

Hilary Matthews, President
Brett J Burk, Executive Director
Steven Roberge, Treasurer
Raymond Mvdaid, Secretary
Paul M Connor, President-Elect

SESHA is the premier association serving the global semiconductor and associated technology industries by providing education and professional development.
1500 Members
Founded in: 1978

21803 Society for Occupational & Environmental Health
1010 Vermont Ave., NW
Suite 513
Washington, DC 20005

202-347-4976; *Fax:* 202-347-4950
kkirkland@aoec.org; www.soeh.org

Ronald Denny Dobbin CIH, President
Katherine H. Kirkland, Executive Director
Sarah Shiffert, Association Director
Mark Catlin, Governing Board

The Society plays a unique, integrating role by bringing together professionals in government, and academia. It reduces occupational and environmental hazards through the presentation of scientific data and the dynamic exchange of information across institutions and disciplines.
Founded in: 1972

21804 Society of Fire Protection Engineers
9711 Washingtonian Blvd
Suite 380
Gaithersburg, MD 20878

301-718-2910; *Fax:* 240-328-6225
sfpehqtrs@sfpe.org; www.sfpe.org
Social Media: Facebook, Twitter, LinkedIn, YouTube, RSS

Milosh Puchovsky, President-Elect
Michael Madden, President
Carl F. Baldassarra, President-Elect
Jack Poole, Secretary
Peter Willse, Vice President

The purpose of the Society is to advance the science and practice of fire protection engineering and its allied fields, to maintain a high ethical standard among its members and to foster fire protection engineering education. The Society provides a program of educational offerings and provides technical publications.
4500 Members
Founded in: 1950

21805 The American Association of Safety Council s
www.safetycouncils.org

Jim Meade, President
Darby Vorce, Vice President
Dianna Braud, Past President
Lynndee Riley, Secretary
Toni Burrows, Treasurer

An international association of safety professionals

21806 The Association of State Floodplain Managers
575 D'Onofrio Drive
Suite 200
Madison, WI 53719

608-828-3000; *Fax:* 608-828-6319
memberhelp@floods.org; www.floods.org
Social Media: Facebook, Twitter, LinkedIn, Google+, Tumblr

Maria Cox Lamm, Vice Chair
Ceil Strauss, Chair
Chad Berginnis, Executive Director
Leslie Durham, Secretary
Karen McHugh, Treasurer

To promote education, policies and activities that mitigate current and future losses, costs and human suffering caused by flooding.

21807 The International Biometric Society
1444 I Street, NW
Suite 700
Washington, DC 20005

202-712-9049; *Fax:* 202-216-9646
ibs@biometricsociety.org;
www.biometricsociety.org
Social Media: Facebook, Twitter, LinkedIn

John Hinde, President
Elizabeth Thompson, President Elect
Dee Ann Walker, Executive Director
Jose Pinheiro, Director
James Carpenter, Secretary/ Treasurer

21808 The National Burglar & Fire Alarm
440 North Broad Street
Suite 130
Philadelphia, PA 19130

215-400-6428; *Fax:* 215-400-4717
secretary@nassleo.org; www.alarm.org
Social Media: Facebook, Twitter, YouTube

21809 The World Institute for Security Enhancement

702-722-7779
training@worldinstitute.org;
www.worldinstitute.org

G.F. Bryant, Executive Director
Henry D Infante, Director of Operations
Rubern Bala, Director of International Marketing
M Gregory Scott, Director of Intnl. Investigations
Lisa A Kane, Director of Health

21810 Transportation Security Administration

866-289-9673
TSA-ContactCenter@tsa.dhs.gov;
www.tsa.gov
Social Media: Facebook, Twitter, LinkedIn, YouTube

Peter Neffenger, Administrator
Kenneth Fletcher, Chief Risk Officer
Thomas McDaniels, Chief of Staffs
Francine Kerner, Chief Counsel
Pat Rose, Finance
Founded in: 2001

21811 U.S. Fire Administration
16825 S. Seton Ave.
Emmitsburg, MD 21727

301-447-1000
888-382-3827; *Fax:* 301-447-1441
netcadmissions@fema.dhs.gov;
www.usfa.fema.gov
Social Media: Facebook, Twitter, YouTube

Ernest Mitchell, US Fire Administrator
Kyle Blackman, Executive Officer
Vanetta Huff, Secretary
Angela Cunningham, Administrative Specialist
Elizabeth Miller, Budget Analysis

21812 U.S. Security Associates
200 Mansell Court Fifth Floor
Roswell, GA 30076

770-625-1500
800-730-9599; www.ussecurityassociates.com
Social Media: Facebook, Twitter, LinkedIn, YouTube, Google+

Founded in: 1993

21813 Underwriters Laboratories
333 Pfingsten Rd
Northbrook, IL 60062-2096

847-412-0136; *Fax:* 847-272-8129
northbrook@us.ul.com; www.ul.com
Social Media: Facebook, Twitter, LinkedIn, YouTube, Google+, Pinterest

Christian Anschuetz, SVP & Chief Information Officer
Terry Brady, SVP & Chief Legal Officer
Adrian Groom, SVP & Chief Human Resources Officer
Michael Saltzman, SVP & CFO
Barbara Guthrie, SVP & Public Safety Officer

Underwriters Labdoratories Inc. is an independent, not-for-profit product-safty testing and certification organization, that has been testing products for safety for more than a century.
Founded in: 1894

21814 United States Association of Professional Investigators
175 Hutton Ranch Rd
Ste 103-165
Kalispell, MO 59901

877-894-0615; *Fax:* 877-851-0794
infor@usapi.org; www.usapi.org
Social Media: Twitter

Randy Torgerson, President
fred Ritz, Vice President
Leah Ritz, Executive Director
Stephane Juneau, CFO

21815 United States Marine Safety Association
5050 Industrial Road
Suite 2
Wall Township, NJ 07727

732-751-0102; *Fax:* 732-751-0508
fhornig@vanebrothers.com; www.usmsa.org

Frank Hornig, President
Karen Hansen, Vice President
Tom Thompson, Executive Director
Maureen Fackenthal, Administrative Director
Dan Connor, Treasurer

21816 United States Society on Dams
1616 Seventeenth Street
Suite 483
Denver, CO 80202

303-628-5430; *Fax:* 303-628-5431
stephens@ussdams.org; www.ussdams.org

John S. Wolfhope, President
Dean B. Durkee, Secretary-Treasurer
Daniel L. Wade, Vice President
Larry D. Stephens, Executive Director
John D. Rice, Board of Director

21817 Veterans of Safety
22 Logan Street
New Bedford, MA 02740
660-543-4281
info@vetsofsafety.org; www.vetsofsafety.org

Warren K Brown, Past President
Dr Nigel Ellis, VP
Dianna Bryant, Executive Director
Wendell W. Wahlstedt, President
Christopher M Gates, Counsil of Ambassadors

Our mission is the promotion of safety, health, and environmental awareness by using and making available the lifetime experience of professionals throughout the world.
Founded in: 1941

21818 Western States Auto Theft Investigators Association Southern Chapter
6 Hutton Centre Drive
Suite 1040
Santa Ana, CA 92707

714-434-9600
webmaster@wsati.org; www.wsati.org
Social Media: Facebook, Twitter

Heather Roberts, Secretary
Brian Yori, VP
Aristeed Powell, President
Jeff Enfield, Treasurer
Richard O. Knapp, Legal Counsel

A non-profit organization that is comprised of professionals representing law enforcement, rental car and insurance companies, and other individuals whose goal is to reduce vehicle theft.
Founded in: 1965

21819 Women Investigators Association
PO Box 18305
Encino, CA 91416

800-603-3524
womeninvas@aol.com; www.w-i-a.org

Debra J Burdette, Executive Director
Robinette Desrochers, VP/Membership Director

Offering education and training, certification, networking, group discounts and represents women in our industry to the media.

Newsletters

21820 ACP Sentinel
Association of Contingency Planners
7044 S 13th St
Oak Creek, WI 53154-1429

414-768-8000
800-445-4227; *Fax:* 414-768-8001;
www.naspa.com

Scott Sherer, Executive Director
Shirley Runnels, Membership

News and event information for national and local chapters dedicated to fostering continued professional growth and development in effective contingency and business planning.
Cost: $75.00
Frequency: Quarterly
Founded in: 1983

21821 American Society of Crime Laboratory Directors
139K Technology Drive
Garner, NC 27529

919-773-2044; *Fax:* 919-773-2602
info@nfstc.org; www.ascld.org

William E Marbaker, President
Susan C Scholl, Membership

Contains useful information and news to maintain and improve communications among crime laboratory directors and their staff.
Cost: $100.00
Frequency: Quarterly
Founded in: 1973

21822 CGAA Signals
Central Station Alarm Association
8150 Leesburg Pike
Suite 700
Vienna, VA 22182-2721

703-242-4670; *Fax:* 703-242-4675
communications@csaaul.org; www.csaaul.org

Stephen P Doyle, Executive VP/CEO
Celia Besore, VP Marketing & Programs
300+ Members
Frequency: Quarterly
Circulation: 1200
Founded in: 1950

21823 Councilor
Safety & Health Council of Northern New England
57 Regional Dr
Suite 6
Concord, NH 03301-8518

603-228-1401
800-834-6472; *Fax:* 603-224-0998
safety@shcnne.org; www.shcnne.org

Lyman Cousens, Executive Director

Covers current regulatory issues as well as health and safety information. Free to members.
16 Pages
Frequency: Monthly
Founded in: 2004
Printed in 2 colors on matte stock

21824 Emergency Preparedness News
Business Publishers
2601 University Boulevard W
#200
Silver Spring, MD 20902

301-929-5700
800-274-6737; *Fax:* 301-949-8844
custserv@bpinews.com; www.bpinews.com

Adam P Goldstein, Publisher
Deborah Eby, Editor
David Henderson, Director
Melissa Worcester, Service

Dedicated solely to disaster management: from securing pre-disaster mitigation and counter terrorism funds, to staying prepared for hurricanes, terrorist threats, fires, floods and other natural disasters. Only available online now.
Cost: $357.00
Frequency: Monthly
ISSN: 0275-3782

21825 FAMA Flyer
Fire Apparatus Manufacturers' Association
PO Box 397
Lynnfield, MA 01940-0397

781-334-2911; *Fax:* 781-334-2911
info@fama.org; www.fama.org

Grady North, President
Greg Kozey, VP

A newsletter that is written specifically for Fire Apparatus Manufactures and Fire Associations across the United States.
Frequency: 3x/Yr
Circulation: 500

21826 HTCIA Newsletter
3288 Goldstone Drive
Roseville, CA 95747

916-408-1751; *Fax:* 916-408-7543;
www.htcia.org

Carol Hutchings, Executive Director

For members only
Frequency: Quarterly

21827 Homeland Security & Defense
McGraw Hill
1200 G St Nw
Suite 900
Washington, DC 20005-3821

202-383-2377; *Fax:* 202-383-2438;
www.aviationweek.com

Jennifer Michels, President
Paul Hoversten, Managing Editor
Mark Lipowicz, Publisher
Iain Blackhall, Managing Director

News items for defense and homeland security professionals. Available in print or electronically.
Cost: $595.00
Frequency: Weekly
Founded in: 1920

21828 Nine Lives Associates: Newsletter
Executive Protection Institute
PO Box 802
Berryville, VA 22611

540-554-2540; *Fax:* 540-554-2558
info@personalprotection.com;
www.personalprotection.com

Ronald J. Wilczynski, President
Tom Quilty, VP
Peter Morin, Tresurer
Jose Soltero, Secretary

Personal protection news and announcements for member graduates of Executive Protection Institute.
Founded in: 1980

21829 Progress
National Association of Elevator Safety
6957 Littlerock Road SW
Suite A
Tumwater, WA 98512

360-292-4968
800-746-2372; *Fax:* 360-292-4973
dotty@naesai.org; www.naesai.org
Social Media: Facebook, Twitter, LinkedIn

Dotty Stanlaske, Executive Director
Dean McLellan, President
Bill Snyder, VP

Informs members of the newest developments in the elevator industry; listings of all currently-scheduled seminars, updated classes and workshops; a message from the Executive Director with news from the main office; articles addressing code questions and issues; news from around the globe and advertising opportunities.
Frequency: Monthly

21830 Progress Report: The Foundation Newsletter
AAA Foundation for Traffic Safety
14th Street NW
Suite 201
Washington, DC 20005

202-638-5944; *Fax:* 202-638-5943;
www.aaafoundation.org

Fairley Mahlum, Communications Director
Frequency: Monthly

21831 Protection News
International Foundation for Protection Officers
PO Box 771329
Naples, FL 34107-1329

239-430-0534; *Fax:* 239-430-0533
sandi@ifpo.com; www.ifpo.org

Sandi J Davies, Executive Director
Michael Stroberger, Secretary/Treasurer

Circulation to all IFPO members and candidates in associated programs. Publication is designed to keep professionals current on trends within the security industry and is full of valuable information and commentary pertinent to the enhancement of life, safety and property protection.
Cost: $18.00
Frequency: Quarterly
Founded in: 1988

21832 SAFE Symposium News
SAFE Association
PO Box 130
Creswell, OR 97426

541-895-3012; *Fax:* 541-895-3014
safe@peak.org; www.safeassociation.com
Social Media: Facebook

Al Loving, President
John Fair, President-Elect

The SAFE Association is dedicated to the preservation of human life. It provides a common meeting ground for the sharing of problems, ideas and information. SAFE is a non-profit international association headquartered in Oregon, with chapters located throughout the world. SAFE publishes a quarterly Newsletter and Proceedings of the Annual SAFE Symposium. These publications are valuable reference sources for the professional involved in all forms of safety and survival.
1100+ Attendees
Frequency: Quarterly
Founded in: 1954

21833 SIA News
Security Industry Association
8405 Colesville Road
Suite 500
Alexandria, MD 20109

301-804-4700
866-817-8888; *Fax:* 301-804-4701
info@siaonline.org; www.siaonline.org

Richard Chace, CEO
Rand Price CAE, COO
Donald Erickson, Government Relations Director

Informs and educates members and prospective members of SIA activities, news, and information. Available online only.
Frequency: 2 X'S Monthly
ISSN: 1071-6713
Founded in: 1969

21834 Safety Compliance Letter
Bureau of Business Practice
111 Eight Avenue
New York, NY 10011

800-638-8437; www.aspenlawschool.com

Alicia Pierce, Publisher
Michele Rubin, Editor

Monitors and reports on the regulatory environment and provides subscribers with up-to-date information in a concise and easy-to-read format, with references and resources (including internet addresses) to get additional help on particular topics.
Cost: $289.00
Frequency: Monthly
ISBN: 9-900003-20-0
Founded in: 1920

21835 Salt & Highway Deicing
Salt Institute
700 N Fairfax St
Suite 600
Alexandria, VA 22314-2085

703-549-4648; *Fax:* 703-548-2194
info@saltinstitute.org; www.saltinstitute.org

Richard L Hanneman, President
Tammy Goodwin, Administrative Director

A quarterly e-newsletter published by the Salt Institute.
Frequency: Quarterly
Circulation: 8000
Founded in: 1914
Printed in on glossy stock

21836 Security Director's Report
Institute of Management and Administration
1 Washington Park
Suite 1300
Newark, NJ 07102

212-244-0360; *Fax:* 973-622-0595;
www.ioma.com

Designed to help security directors keep pace with the rapidly evolving world of corporate security. Alerts to critical news, import new security products, and up-to-date advice that you need to know to effectively manager your security department.
Cost: $419.00
Frequency: Monthly

21837 Signal
American Traffic Safety Services Association
15 Riverside Parkway
Suite 100
Fredericksburg, VA 22406-1022

540-368-1701
800-272-8772; *Fax:* 540-368-1717;
www.atssa.com
Social Media: Facebook, Twitter

James Baron, Communications Director

Covers legislative updates, industry news and meeting information, as well as other items of interest to the roadway safety industry as is a full-color publication.
Frequency: Quarterly

21838 Society Update
American Society of Safety Engineers
1800 E Oakton Street
Des Plaines, IL 60018

847-699-2929; *Fax:* 847-768-3434
customerservice@asse.org; www.asse.org
Social Media: Facebook

Fred J Fortman, Executive Director
Jim Drzewiecki, Finance/Controller Director
Diane Hurns, Manager Public Relations Department

Membership benefit via e-mail with news, information on training, plus happenings in the 150 chapters throughout the US.
Cost: $60.00
Founded in: 1911

21839 Workplace Substance Abuse Advisor
LRP Publications
PO Box 24668
West Palm Beach, FL 33416-4668

561-622-6520
800-341-7874; *Fax:* 561-622-0757
custserve@lrp.com; www.lrp.com

Kenneth Kahn, President

Current developments affecting how your workplace deals with alcohol and drug abusing employees. Comprehensive overview of all the areas you need to know to create and maintain an effective substance abuse program in your company.
Cost: $377.00
Frequency: 2 X'S Month
Founded in: 1977

Magazines & Journals

21840 Access Control & Security Systems
PRIMEDIA Business Magazines & Media
1166 Avenue of the Americas
Shawnee Mission, NY 10036

212-204-4200; *Fax:* 913-514-6895;
www.penton.com

Eric Jacobson, Senior VP
Gregg Herring, Publisher
Paul Rothman, Associate Editor
Brenda Wiley, Advertising Production Manager
Marty McCallen, National Sales Manager

Product overview articles and columns cover topics on door entry, CCTV, operators and gates, sensors and perimeter security.
Frequency: Monthly
Circulation: 38000+
Founded in: 1905

21841 Business & Legal Reports
Business & Legal Reports
PO Box 6001
Old Saybrook, CT 06475-6001

860-510-0100
800-727-5257; *Fax:* 860-510-7225
service@blr.com; www.blr.com

Robert L Brady, CEO
Peggy Carter-Ward, Editor-in-Chief

Provides essential tools for safety and environmental compliance and training needs.
32 Pages

21842 Campus Safety Journal
Bricepac

12228 Venice Boulevard Suite 541
PO Box 66515
Los Angeles, CA 90066

310-390-5277; *Fax:* 310-390-4777;
www.campusjournal.com

Pat Restivo, Circualtion
John Horn, President

Provides a vehicle for communicating campus safety and security issues to all interested parties at the middle, secondary, college and university levels.
40 Pages
Frequency: Monthly
Circulation: 20000
Founded in: 1992
Printed in 4 colors on glossy stock

21843 **Compliance Magazine**
Briefings Media Group
PO Box 787
Williamsport, PA 17703

800-791-8699; *Fax:* 570-320-2079;
www.compliancemag.com

Betty Hintch, Editor
Laura Daugherity, Production Coordinator

Compliance Magazine offers the latest in government regulations, including the materials and information needed to stay in compliance, safety trends, and a complete Safety Buyers' Guide.
Frequency: Annual
Founded in: 1985

21844 **Computer Fraud & Security**
Elsevier Science
360 Park Ave S
New York, NY 10010-1736

212-633-3980; *Fax:* 212-633-3913;
www.elsevier.com

Provides practical, usable information to effectively manage and control computer and information security within commercial organizations.
Frequency: Monthly
ISSN: 1361-3723
Founded in: 1979

21845 **Computer Security Journal**
Computer Security Institute
600 Harrison Street
San Francisco, CA 94107

415-947-6320; *Fax:* 415-947-6023
csi@cmp.com; www.gocsi.com
Social Media: Facebook, Twitter, LinkedIn

Russell Kay, Publisher

Keeps you informed with comprehensive, practical articles, case studies, reviews and commentaries written by knowledgeable computer security professionals.
Cost: $224.00
Frequency: Quarterly
Circulation: 3000
Founded in: 1974

21846 **Computers & Security**
Elsevier Science
360 Park Ave S
New York, NY 10010-1736

212-633-3980; *Fax:* 212-633-3913;
www.elsevier.com
Social Media: Facebook, Twitter, LinkedIn

Provides a blend of leading edge research and sound practical management advice.
Frequency: Monthly
ISSN: 0167-4048
Founded in: 1997

21847 **Corporate Security**
Strafford Publications
PO Box 13729
Atlanta, GA 30324-0729

404-881-1141
800-926-7926; *Fax:* 404-881-0074
custserv@straffordpub.com;
www.straffordpub.com

Richard Ossoff, President
George Coleman, Manager

Intelligence briefing on the latest security developments, best practices, the most important trends and new technolgies.
Cost: $330.00
Frequency: Bi-Monthly
ISSN: 0889-0625
Founded in: 1984

21848 **EMS Product News**
Cygnus Publishing
PO Box 803
Fort Atkinson, WI 53538-0803

920-000-1111
800-547-7377; *Fax:* 920-563-1699
Ronnie.Garret@cygnuspub.com;
www.cygnusb2b.com
Social Media: Facebook, Twitter, LinkedIn

John French, CEO
Nancy Perry, Editor

Product information written with the emergency medical service professional in mind.
Cost: $53.00
Frequency: 6 Issues
Circulation: 20000

21849 **Emergency Medical Product News**
Cygnus Business Media
PO Box 803
Fort Atkinson, WI 53538-0803

920-000-1111
800-547-7377; *Fax:* 920-563-1699;
www.cygnusb2b.com

John French, CEO
Ronnie Garrett, Director of Public Relations
Kathy Scott, Director of Public Relations
Paul Bonaiuto, CFO

A bi-monthly tabloid-sized magazine showcasing new products in the Emergengy Medical Technician's scope of use.

21850 **Emergency Medical Services**
Cygnus Business Media
PO Box 803
Fort Atkinson, WI 53538-0803

920-000-1111; *Fax:* 920-563-1699
scott.cravens@cygnusb2b.com;
www.cygnusb2b.com
Social Media: Facebook, Twitter, LinkedIn

John French, CEO
Nancy Perry, Associate Publisher

A magazine designed for both career and volunteer EMS professionals. This magazine has been rated number one for editorial quality, reader interest and advertising pages.
Frequency: Monthly

21851 **Fire & Arson Investigator Magazine**
International Association of Arson Investigators
2111 Baldwin Ave
Suite 203
Crofton, MD 21114

410-451-3473; *Fax:* 410-451-9049;
www.firearson.com

David Nichols, President
Cost: $75.00
Frequency: Quarterly

21852 **Fire EMS**
PennWell
PO Box 1260
Tulsa, OK 74101-1260

918-835-3161
800-331-4463; *Fax:* 918-831-9497
headquarters@pennwell.com;
www.pennwell.com
Social Media: Facebook, Twitter

Robert F Biolchini, CEO
Junior Isles, Publisher/Editor

News, product information and feature articles of interest to paramedics.
Cost: $30.00
Frequency: Monthly
Printed in 4 colors on glossy stock

21853 **Fire Engineering**
PennWell
PO Box 1260
Tulsa, OK 74101-1260

918-835-3161
800-962-6484; *Fax:* 918-831-9497
dianef@pennwell.com; www.pennwell.com
Social Media: Facebook, Twitter

Robert F Biolchini, CEO
Diane Feldman, Executive Editor
Bobby Halton, Editor-in-Chief

Provides education and training to the fire service through a hands-on, technically oriented editorial package.
Cost: $29.95
106 Pages
Frequency: Monthly
Circulation: 44824
ISSN: 0015-2587
Printed in 4 colors on glossy stock

21854 **Fire Protection Engineering**
Society of Fire Protection Engineers
7315 Wisconsin Ave
Suite 620E
Bethesda, MD 20814-3234

301-718-2910; *Fax:* 301-718-2242;
www.sfpe.org

David D Evans, Executive Director
Rebecca Salzman, Membership Coordinator
Samuel Dannaway, Publisher
James D Mike, President

Technical magazine advancing the science and practice of fire protection and its allied fields.
Cost: $145.00
Frequency: Quarterly
Circulation: 4500
Founded in: 1950

21855 **IMSA Journal**
International Municipal Signal Association
165 E Union Street
PO Box 539
Newark, NY 14513-0539

315-331-2182
800-723-4672; *Fax:* 315-331-8205
info@imsasafety.org; www.imsasafety.org

Marilyn Lawrence, Publisher & Executive Director
Sharon Earl, Editor

Each issue focuses on different topics, including Dispatch/Public Safety Telecommunications, Fire Alarm Interior, Fire Alarm Municipal, FCC Licensing, Flagging, Roadway Lighting, Signs & Markings, Traffic Signal Systems, Two-Way Radios, Wireless Data, Wireless Traffic Control, and Work Zone Safety.
Cost: $700.00
Frequency: Bimonthly
Circulation: 12,000
ISSN: 1064-2560

21856 **Industrial Hygiene News**
Rimbach Publishing

8650 Babcock Blvd
Suite 1
Pittsburgh, PA 15237-5010

412-364-5366
800-245-3182; *Fax:* 412-369-9720
info@rimbach.com; www.rimbach.com

Norberta Rimbach, President
Karen Galante, Circulation Manager

Articles, news and product information for professionals in Occupational Health and Industrial Hygiene.
Circulation: 60,111
Founded in: 1978

21857 Industrial Safety & Hygiene News
Business News Publishing
2401 W Big Beaver RD
Suite 700
Troy, MI 48084

248-244-6498
800-837-7370; *Fax:* 248-244-6439;
www.ishn.com
Social Media: Facebook, Twitter, LinkedIn

Katie Rotella, President
Dave Johnson, Editor
Randy Green, Advertising Manager

Feature articles and product information for safety, health and environmental professionals. Free subscription to qualified professionals.
Cost: $58.00
Frequency: Monthly
Founded in: 1926

21858 Infection Control Today
Virgo Publishing LLC
3300 N Central Ave
Suite 300
Phoenix, AZ 85012-2532

480-675-9925; *Fax:* 480-990-0819
peggyj@vpico.com; www.vpico.com

Jenny Bolton, President
Kelly Ridley, VP
Jennifer Janos, Controller

Infection Control Today provides science based articles for the general ward, operating room, sterile processing and environmental services departments of healthcare facilities as well as for the public health community.
Mailing list available for rent: 30000+ names

21859 Journal of Fire Sciences
Sage Publications
2455 Teller Rd
Newbury Park, CA 91320-2234

805-499-9774
800-818-7243; *Fax:* 805-499-0871
info@sagepub.com; www.sagepub.com
Social Media: LinkedIn

Blaise R Simqu, CEO

Reporting new developments in related technology. Peer-reviewed articles by recognized specialists from around the world. In-depth articles provide new science based information useful in materials research and product development.
Cost: $1281.00
88 Pages
Frequency: Bi-Monthly
ISSN: 0734-9041
Founded in: 1965
Printed in 2 colors on matte stock

21860 Journal of Occupational and Environmental Medicine (JOEM)
American College of Occupational/Environmental Med
25 Northwest Point Blvd
Suite 700
Elk Grove Village, IL 60007

847-818-1800; *Fax:* 847-818-9266
acoeminfo@acoem.org; www.acoem.org

Barry Eisenberg, Executive Director
Marianne Dreger, Communications Director

The official publication of the ACOEM, the Journal provides the latest data on reseach, as well as practical information for use in everyday practice. Readers find articles, case reviews, news and calendar of events, book reviews, and information about new product offerings.
Cost: $338.00
Frequency: Monthly/Free for Members
ISSN: 1076-2752
Founded in: 1916

21861 Journal of Security Education
Academy of Security Educators & Trainers
PO Box 802
Berryville, VA 22611

540-554-2540; *Fax:* 540-554-2558;
www.tandfonline.com

Dr Richard W Kobetz, Executive Director
Dr HHA Cooper, President
Mary E Kobetz, Secretary-Treasurer

21862 Law and Order Magazine
Hendon Publications
130 Waukegan Rd
Suite 202, 2nd Floor
Deerfield, IL 60015-4912

847-444-3300
800-843-9764; *Fax:* 847-444-3333
info@hendonpub.com; www.hendonpub.com

Henry Kingwill, President
Henry Kingwill, Publisher
Kathryn Murnik, Director

Latest news of interest to police and law enforcement professionals. New product and service information, available in print and online.
Cost: $24.95
Frequency: Monthly
Circulation: 32304
Founded in: 1953

21863 Materials Evaluation
American Society for Nondestructive Testing
1711 Arlingate Lane
PO Box 28518
Columbus, OH 43228-518

614-274-6003
800-222-2768; *Fax:* 614-274-6899
kwie@asnt.org; www.asnt.org

Paul McIntire, Publication Manager
Betsy Blazar, Marketing Manager
Shelby Reeves, Owner
Wayne Hollile, Executive Director

Research, reviews and information of nondestructive testing materials. Provides members and subscribers the latest news and technical information concerning this industry.
Cost: $10.00
Frequency: Monthly

21864 National Defense Magazine
National Defense Industrial Association
2111 Wilson Blvd
Suite 400
Arlington, VA 22201-3061

703-522-1820
703-247-9469; *Fax:* 703-522-1885
info@ndia.org; www.ndia.org

Lawrence Farrell, President
Sandra I Erwin, Editor
Sharon Foster, Circulation Manager

Places main focus on issues concerning the U.S. defense industry. Provides the trends in national security, including technology advancement, acquisition policy, critical industry sectors, and marketing are editorial staples.
Cost: $40.00
Frequency: Monthly
Circulation: 30000
ISSN: 0092-1491
Founded in: 1946

21865 National Fire Protection Association Newsletter
National Fire Protection Association
1 Batterymarch Park
Quincy, MA 02169-7471

617-770-3000
800-344-3555; *Fax:* 617-770-0700
publicaffairs@nfpa.org; www.nfpa.org

James M. Shannon, President/CEO
Peg O'Brien, Administrator - Public Affairs
Sharon Gamache, Executive Director
Bruce Mullen, CFO
Paul Crossman, VP, Marketing

Written for various fire safety professionals and covers major topics in fire protection and suppression. The Journal carries investigation reports written by NFPA specialists, special NFPA statistical studies on large-loss fires, multiple deaths, fire fighter deaths and injuries and others annually and articles on fire protection advances, public education and information of interest to NFPA members.
75000 Members
Frequency: Monthly
Founded in: 1896

21866 National Locksmith
National Publishing Company
1533 Burgundy Pkwy
Streamwood, IL 60107-1811

630-837-1250; *Fax:* 630-837-1210
natllock@aol.com; www.locksmithledger.net

Marc Goldberg, Publisher
Greg Mango, Editor

New products, marketing, sales, merchandising, and the array of factors involved in successful locksmith enterprises and services. Informs professionals about the latest news and techniques in security.
Cost: $46.00
Frequency: Monthly
Circulation: 17000
Founded in: 1983

21867 Occupational Hazards
Penton Media
1166 Avenue of the Americas
Suite 316
Cleveland, NY 10036

212-204-4200; *Fax:* 216-696-6662
information@penton.com; www.penton.com

Jane Cooper, Marketing
Bob Marinez, Publisher
Rob Howlette, Advertising Manager
Chris Meyer, Director
Bev Walter, Customer Service

Analysis of qualified recipients who have indicated that they recommend, select and/or buy the safety equipment, fire protection and other occupational health products.
Cost: $50.00
65 Pages
Frequency: Monthly
Circulation: 71,000
ISSN: 0029-7909
Founded in: 1892
Printed in 4 colors on glossy stock

21868 Oregon Investigator
PO Box 2705
Portland, OR 97208

866-584-8645
webmaster@oali.org; www.oali.org

Ted J Tolliver, Executive Director
Patricia Vollbrect, President

Official journal of the organization setting a standard of excellence among investigators. Legislative issues and news of upcoming seminars.
Founded in: 1983

21869 Pest Control Technology
GIE Media
4012 Bridge Avenue
Cleveland, OH 44113

216-961-4130
800-456-0707; *Fax:* 216-961-0364;
www.pctonline.com

Dan Moreland, Publisher
Jodi Dorsch, CEO

Directed towards technological and educational advancement in the pest control industry.
Cost: $35.00
76 Pages
Frequency: Monthly
ISSN: 0730-7608
Founded in: 1972
Printed in 4 colors on glossy stock

21870 Pollution Equipment News
Rimbach Publishing
8650 Babcock Blvd
Suite 1
Pittsburgh, PA 15237-5010

412-364-5366
800-245-3182; *Fax:* 412-369-9720
info@rimbach.com; www.rimbach.com

Norberta Rimbach, President
Karen Galante, Circulation Manager
Paul Henderson, VP of Sales and Marketing
Richard Rimbach, Owner

Provides information to those responsible for selecting products and services for air, water, wastewater and hazardous waste pollution abatement.
Frequency: Bi-Annually
Circulation: 91000
Founded in: 1968

21871 Process Safety Progress
John Wiley & Sons
1475 Crosspoint Boulevard
Indianapolis, IN 46256

877-762-2974; *Fax:* 800-597-3299;
www.wiley.com
Social Media: LinkedIn

D A Crowl, Editor
Joseph F Louvar, Editor

Practical information for engineering professionals. Focuses on chemical and hydrocarbon safety, loss prevention and health.
Cost: $345.00
Frequency: Quarterly
ISSN: 1066-8527
Founded in: 1908

21872 Professional Safety
American Society of Safety Engineers
1800 E Oakton Street
Des Plaines, IL 60018

847-699-2929; *Fax:* 847-768-3434
customerservice@asse.org; www.asse.org
Social Media: Facebook, Twitter

Fred Fortman, Executive Director
Jim Drzewiecki, Finance/Controller Director
Diane Hurns, Manager Public Relations Department

Journal of the well known professional safety, health and environmental organization. Articles provide in-depth examination of health and safety concerns.
Cost: $60.00
Frequency: Monthly
Founded in: 1990

21873 Public Safety Communications/APCO Bulletin
Association of Public-Safety Comm Officials Int'l
351 N Williamson Boulevard
Daytona Beach, FL 32114-1112

386-322-2500
888-272-6911; *Fax:* 386-322-2501
apco@apcointl.org; www.apcointl.org/
Social Media: Facebook, Twitter, LinkedIn, You Tube

Toni Edwards, Managing Editor
George S Rice Jr, Executive Director
Susan Stowell, Member Services Director
Garry Mendez, Marketing/Communications Director
Robert Gurss Esq., Legal/Government Affairs Director

Newsletter dedicated to the enhancement of public safety communications and to serving its more than 15,000 members, the people who use public safety communications systems and services. Subscription is a member benefit.
Frequency: Monthly
Circulation: 13000
ISSN: 1526-1646
Founded in: 1935

21874 Quality Digest
Quality Control International
555 East Avenue
P.O. Box 1769
Chico, CA 95926

530-893-4095; *Fax:* 530-893-0395
qualitydigest@qualitydigest.com;
www.qualitydigest.com
Social Media: Facebook

Michael Richman, Managing Editor
Dirk Dusharme, Technical Editor
Scott Papon, Publisher
April Johnson, Circulation Manager

Serves the field of quality-related activites in manufacturing, financial services, communications, utilities, transportation, government, military, retail, educational institutions, health care, consulting, aerospace, software, agricultural, forestry, fishing, mining, construction and other industries. Available in print and free online.
Cost: $59.00
Frequency: Monthly
ISSN: 1049-8699
Founded in: 1981

21875 SAFE Newsletter
SAFE Association
PO Box 130
Creswell, OR 97426

541-895-3012; *Fax:* 541-895-3014
safe@peak.org; www.safeassociation.com

Marcia Baldwin, President
Bryan Billings, President-Elect
Frequency: 4-6x/Year
Circulation: 1000
Founded in: 1957

21876 SC Magazine
Haymarket Media
161 Worcester Road
Suite 201
Framingham, MA 01701

508-879-9792; *Fax:* 508-879-2755;
www.scmagazine.com
Social Media: Facebook, Twitter, LinkedIn
Illena Armstrong, Editor-in-Chief
Gil Torren, Sales Director
Sherry Oommen, Circulation Director

Covers all industries that use information security systems. Provides data on information security products, services, market trends and industry developments.
Cost: $60.00
133 Pages
Frequency: Monthly
Circulation: 40,000
ISSN: 1096-7974
Founded in: 1999
Printed in 4 colors

21877 Safe & Vault Technology
Safe & Vault Technicians Association
3500 Easy St
Dallas, TX 75247-6416

214-819-9771; *Fax:* 214-819-9736;
www.savta.org

Charles Gibson, President
Mike Oelert, Editor

Industry news, reviews, announcements and new products of paticular interest to readers.
Cost: $45.00
Frequency: Monthly
Circulation: 3000
Founded in: 1986

21878 Safety & Health
National Safety Council
PO Box 558
Itasca, IL 60143-0558

630-775-2213
800-621-7615; *Fax:* 630-285-1315
info@nsc.org; www.nsc.org

Alan C McMillan, CEO
Melissa J Ruminski, Managing Editor
Suzanne Powills, Publisher

Coverage of safety news and changes, trade shows and training courses.
Cost: $58.50
Frequency: Monthly
Founded in: 1954
Mailing list available for rent

21879 Security Dealer
Cygnus Publishing
PO Box 803
Fort Atkinson, WI 53538-0803

920-000-1111
800-547-7377; *Fax:* 920-563-1699;
www.cygnusb2b.com

John French, CEO
Susan Brady, Editor-in-Chief
Susan Whitehurst, Group Publisher

Trade publication for those in the electronic burglary and fire alarm system business.
Cost: $112.00
Frequency: Monthly
Circulation: 25500
Founded in: 1966

21880 Security Distributing and Marketing
Business News Publishing
1050 IL Route 83
Suite 200
Bensenville, IL 60106-1096

630-377-5909; *Fax:* 630-227-0214;
www.sdmmag.com

Katie Rotella, President
Laura Stepanek, Editor
Russ Gager, Senior Editor

Information source for the electronic security, life safety and home systems industries. Subscription free to professionals.
Frequency: Monthly
Circulation: 28000

21881 Security Industry Buyers Guide
ASIS International

21882 Security Magazine
Business News Publishing
2401 W Big Beaver Rd
Suite 700
Troy, MI 48084-3333

248-362-3700; *Fax:* 248-362-0317;
www.bnpmedia.com

Mitchell Henderson, CEO
Mark McCourt, Publisher
Russ Gager, Senior Editor
Laura Stepanek, Editor
Mark McCourt, Pulisher

Covers all types of businesses, including industrial manufacturing, service companies, institutions and government, as well as consulting, design, and integrator firms that specify security. News, columns and security product information. No charge to professionals.
Frequency: Monthly
Circulation: 40590
Founded in: 1964
Printed in 4 colors on glossy stock

21883 Security Management
American Society for Industrial Security
1625 Prince Street
Alexandria, VA 22314-2818

703-519-6200
800-368-5685; *Fax:* 703-519-6299
sharowitz@asisonline.org;
www.securitymanagement.com

Denny White, Publisher
Sherry Harowitz, Editor-in-Chief
Carlton Purvis, Associate Editor

Features, news and trends in the security world. In print and online.
Cost: $48.00
Frequency: Monthly
Founded in: 1955

21884 Security Products
Stevens Publishing Corporation
5151 Belt Line Rd
10th Floor
Dallas, TX 75254-7507

972-687-6700; *Fax:* 972-687-6767;
www.stevenspublishing.com

Craig S Stevens, President
Margaret Perry, Circulation Director
Russell Lindsay, Publisher
Ralph Jensen, Editor
Karina Sanchez, Managing Editor

Offers examples of security solutions set by such facilities as casinos and hospitals, and explores such issues as false alarm reduction and personnel training, it also highlights new technologies.
Cost: $75.00
Frequency: Monthly
Circulation: 65000
Founded in: 1925

21885 Security Sales & Integration
Bobit Publishing Company
3520 Challenger St
Torrance, CA 90503-1640

310-533-2400; *Fax:* 310-533-2500;
www.bobit.com

Edward J Bobit, CEO
Scott Goldfine, Editor-in-chief
Michael Zawinski, Publisher

News, feature articles, columnists and new products in the field ofelectronic security.
Cost: $15.00
Frequency: Monthly
Founded in: 1981

21886 Security and Privacy
IEEE Computer Society
10662 Los Vaqueros Drive
PO Box 3014
Los Alamitos, CA 90720-1314

714-821-8380
800-272-6657; *Fax:* 714-821-4010
help@computer.org;
www.computer.org/security

Angela Burgess, Publisher
Kathy Clark-Fisher, Lead Editor
Georgann Carter, Circulation Manager
George Cybenko, Editor-in-Chief

Trans-border data flow issues, protocols, database management and security. Available online to members and in print to others.
Cost: $29.00
Frequency: 6 Issues/Year
Circulation: 1600
Founded in: 1979

21887 Sound & Video Contractor
Primedia
PO Box 12914
Overland Park, KS 66282

913-341-1300; *Fax:* 913-967-1903;
www.svconline.com

Michael Goldman, Editor
Cynthia Wisehart, Editorial Director
Charissa Young, Associate Editor

Contains information on sound systems, video display, security, CCTV, home theater, and automation. Delivers in depth instruction and examples of successful installations, fundamental acoustical and video theory and news on new technologies affecting the systems contracting business.
Cost: $35.00
Frequency: Monthly
Circulation: 21000
Founded in: 1983
Mailing list available for rent: 20,500 names at $110 per M

21888 The Poison Line
American Association of Poison Control Centers
3201 New Mexico Ave NW
Suite 310
Washington, DC 20016-2739

202-895-4259
800-222-1222; *Fax:* 202-362-8377
info@aapcc.org; www.poison.org

M Litovitz, Executive Director
Frequency: Biannual
Founded in: 1958

21889 Underground Focus
Planet Underground
411 South Evergreen
Manteno, IL 60950

815-468-7814; *Fax:* 815-468-7644;
www.underspace.com
Social Media: Facebook, Twitter, LinkedIn

Ron Rosencrans, Founder
Amy Chmura, Editor

Documents the importance of careful excavation and helps them get the budgets to do the job. Powerfully dramatizes the need for underground damage prevention, excavation safety, and the hazards of not protecting the subsurface infrastructure.
Cost: $25.00
46 Pages
Circulation: 21800
ISSN: 1090-400X
Founded in: 1986
Printed in 4 colors on glossy stock

Trade Shows

21890 AAAR Annual Meeting
American Association for Aerosol Research
15000 Commerce Parkway
Suite C
Mount Laurel, NJ 08054

856-439-9080; *Fax:* 856-439-0525
dbright@ahint.com; www.aaar.org

Lynn Russell, Program Chair
Melissa Baldwin, Executive Director

Exibits related to aerosol research in areas including industrial process, air pollution, and industrial hygiene. Over 600 professionals attend.
600 Attendees
Frequency: Annual, October

21891 ASFPM Annual Conference
Association of State Floodplain Managers
2809 Fish Hatchery Road
Suite 204
Madison, WI 53713

608-274-0123; *Fax:* 608-274-0696
asfpm@floods.org; www.floods.org

Larry Larson, Executive Director
Becky Head, Member Services Coordinator

Focus on floodproofing techniques, materials, floodproofing and elevation contractors, current issues and programs, new federal tax impications and the various means of funding floodproofing projects. implications. Held June in Norfolk, VA.
Frequency: Annual
Founded in: 1951

21892 ASIS International
1625 Prince Street
Alexandria, VA 22314-2818

703-519-6200; *Fax:* 703-519-6299
asis@asisonline.org; www.asisonline.org

Shannon Burch, Exhibits Manager
Michael Stack, Executive Director

Exhibits related to loss prevention and security for public and private organizations. Held September 24-26, 2007 at the Las Vegas Convention Center in Las Vegas, Nevada.
Frequency: September
Founded in: 1955

21893 America's Fire & Security Expo
ROC Exhibitions
1963 University Lane
Lisle, IL 60532

630-271-8210; *Fax:* 630-271-8234
info@rocexhibitions.com;
www.americassecurity.com

Jerry Carter, Marketing Director

Annual 3 day marketplace featuring state-of-the-art security products, systems and services. Over 50 free educational sessions. Emphasis on the markets of Latin America, the Caribbean and the Southeastern US.
Frequency: July

21894 American Biological Safety Association Conference
1200 Allanson Road
Mundelein, IL 60060-3808

847-949-1517
847-566-4580; *Fax:* 847-566-4580;
www.absa.org

LouAnn Burnett, Chair

Exhibits of biological safety equipment, supplies and services. Held October at the Opryland Hotel in Nashville, Tennessee.
300 Attendees
Frequency: October
Founded in: 1984

21895 American Fire Sprinkler Association Annual Convention & Exhibition
American Fire Sprinkler Association
12750 Merit Drive
Suite 350
Dallas, TX 75251
214-349-5965
847-949-1517; *Fax:* 214-343-8898
afsainfo@firesprinkler.org; www.firesprinkler.org
Steve Muncy, President
Janet Knowles, VP/Makreting & Communications
120 exhibits of sprinkler heads, pipe, hangers, tools and other equipment. Seminar, workshop and tours. Held September in Phoenix, Arizona.
1000 Attendees
Frequency: September
Founded in: 1981

21896 American Industrial Hygiene Association Conference & Exposition
American Industrial Hygiene Association
3141 Fairview Park Drive
Suite 777
Falls Church, VA 22042
703-849-8888; *Fax:* 703-207-3561
infonet@aiha.org; www.aiha.org
Social Media: Facebook, Twitter, LinkedIn
Bethany Chirico, Director, Global Meetings & Expos
Alison Daniels, Manager, Expositions
Laura Cilano Garcia, Program Director
Steven E. Lacey, President
Conference for occupational and environmental health and safety professionals around the globe. Held June in Philadelphia, Pennsylvania.
10000 Members
4,000 Attendees
Frequency: Annual
Founded in: 1939

21897 American Society for Nondestructive Testing Conference
1711 Arlingate Lane
PO Box 28518
Columbus, OH 43228-0518
614-274-6003
800-222-2768; *Fax:* 614-274-6899
kwie@asnt.org; www.asnt.org
Michael O'Toole, Senior Manager Conferences
Jacquie Giunta, Meeting Coordinator
Ruth Staat, Exhibit/Event Supervisor
Seminar, conference and 150 exhibits of nondestructive testing equipment, services, supplies and laboratory representatives. Holds a smaller conference in the spring. Held November in Las Vegas, Nevada.
3000 Attendees
Frequency: Fall

21898 American Society of Crime Laboratory Directors Annual Symposium
139 Technology Drive
Suite K
Garner, NC 27529-7970
919-773-2044; *Fax:* 919-773-2602;
www.ascld.org
Bill Marbaker, President
Devoted to providing training in leadership and management techniques in the field of forensic science. Also offers membership the opportunity to network with other laboratory directors.
Frequency: October

21899 American Society of Safety Engineers Professional Development Conference
American Society of Safety Engineers
1800 E Oakton Street
Des Plaines, IL 60018
847-699-2929; *Fax:* 847-768-3434
customerservice@asse.org; www.asse.org
Fred Fortman, Executive Director
Jim Drzewiecki, Finance/Controller Director
Diane Hurns, Manager Public Relations Department
Annual conference and expo of 250 manufacturers and suppliers of safety equipment and health products. Held June
3500 Attendees
Frequency: June

21900 Annual American Occupational Health Conference
American College of Occupational/Environmental Med
25 Northwest Point Blvd
Suite 700
Elk Grove Village, IL 60007
847-818-1800; *Fax:* 847-818-9266
acoeminfo@acoem.org; www.acoem.org
Social Media: Facebook, Twitter, LinkedIn, You Tube
Barry Eisenberg, Executive Director
Marianne Dreger, Communications Director
AOHC
Frequency: Annual/Spring

21901 Applied Ergonomics Conference
Institute of Industrial Engineers
3577 Parkway Lane
Suite 200
Norcross, GA 30092
770-449-0461
800-494-0460; *Fax:* 770-263-8532
cs@iienet.org; www.iienet.org/annual
Carol LeBlanc, Conference Manager
An exclusive event for ergonomists, engineers, and safety professionals. The conference focuses on how companies have successfully implemented programs that provide excellent return on their ergonomics investment. Held May Nashville, Tennessee.
800 Attendees
Frequency: March
Founded in: 1998

21902 Associated Locksmiths of America & Safe and Vault Tech Security Expo
Associated Locksmiths of America
3500 Easy Street
Dallas, TX 75247-6416
214-819-9733
800-532-2562
convention@aloa.org; www.aloa.org
Social Media: Facebook
Karen Lyons, Conventions/Meetings
Kim Hammond, Exhibits/Sales
Features industry innovation, training, networking and education in the security world. Over 350 exhibitors with cash and carry merchandise. Held July, in Charlotte, North Carolina.
4000 Attendees
Frequency: July
Founded in: 1956

21903 BOMA Annual Convention
Building Owners & Managers Association Int'l
1201 New York Avenue NW
Suite 300
Washington, DC 20005
202-408-2662; *Fax:* 202-326-6377
info@boma.org; www.boma.org
Social Media: Facebook, Twitter, LinkedIn
Henry Chamberlain, President/COO
Kurt R Padavano, Chairman & CEO
Richard Gringer, Chair
Ray Mackry, Circulation Manager
Opportunity for business professionals to discuss problems, security, exchange ideas and share experience and knowledge. Held July 21-24, 2007 at the Jacob K Javits Convention Center in New York City.
Frequency: July

21904 Bomb Technicians & Investigators Annual Conference
PO Box 160
Goldvein, VA 22720-0160
540-752-4533; *Fax:* 540-752-2796
admin@iabti.org; www.iabti.org
Ralph Way PhD, Executive Director
Speakers on the latest information on bomb and bio threats.Attendes are in the fields of law enforcement, fire and emergency services, the military, forensic science and other related fields.
Founded in: 1973

21905 CSAA Electronic Security Forum & Exposition
Central Station Alarm Association
440 Maple Avenue E
Suite 201
Vienna, VA 22180
703-242-4670; *Fax:* 703-242-4675
meetings@csaaul.org; www.csaaul.org
John McDonald, Meetings/Conferences
Exhibitors, speakers and workshops for the alarm and security professional. Held May
Frequency: May

21906 California Alarm Association Winter Convention
3401 Pacific Avenue
Suite 1C
Marina del Rey, CA 90292
310-305-1277
800-437-7658; *Fax:* 310-305-2077
info@caaonline.org; www.caaonline.org
Jon Sargent, President
Jerry Lenander, Executive Director
George DeMarco, Southern VP
Ron Galippo, Secretary
Annual meeting of state trade association comprised of licensed alarm company operators and suppliers of products and services. Nearly 200 alarm companies and 50 suppliers are members. Alarm companies represent 70% of the electronic security industry in California. Held December in San Francisco, California.
Frequency: December

21907 Campus Law Enforcement Administrators Annual Conference
342 N Main Street
Hartford, CT 06117-2507
860-586-7517; *Fax:* 860-586-7550
info@iaclea.org; www.iaclea.org
Delores Stafford, President
Carol Ewing, Professional Development
Presentations on sucessful or new programs and current trends.
Frequency: June

21908 Campus Safety Conference
Bricepac

12228 Venice Boulevard
PO Box 66515
Los Angeles, CA 90066

310-390-5277; *Fax:* 800-758-0935;
www.campusjournal.com

Sandra Watson, Conferences/Training

Training conference designed especially for campus safety professionals at both the secondary school and higher education levels. Features more than 13 seminars of critical importance to campus safety decision makers and staff.
Frequency: 2 Days/November

21909 Card Tech/Secur Tech: CTST Conference & Exhibition
SourceMedia
One State Street Plaza
27th Floor
New York, NY 10004

212-258-6093
800-803-3424; *Fax:* 212-803-8515;
www.ieee.org
Social Media: Facebook, Twitter, LinkedIn

Nicoal Crawford, Director of Operations
Nikole Tenbrink, Custom Events

250 booth exhibit hall, seminars, luncheons and keynote speakers in the advanced card and biometric technology field. Explores real world applications in several industries including financial services, goverment and security. Held May in San Francisco, California.
50000 Attendees
Frequency: April

21910 Computer Security Conference & Expo
Computer Security Institute
600 Harrison Street
San Francisco, CA 94107

415-947-6320; *Fax:* 415-947-6023;
www.gocsi.com
Social Media: Facebook, Twitter

Jennifer Stevens, Conference Director

Annual event with over 150 educational sessions and exhibitor hall. Held October in Orlando, Florida.
Frequency: November

21911 Convention & Traffic Expo
American Traffic Safety Services Association
15 Riverside Parkway
Suite 100
Fredericksburg, VA 22406-1022

540-368-1701
800-272-8772; *Fax:* 540-368-1717;
www.atssa.com

Joe Jeffrey, Chairman

The premier meeting place for roadway professionals around the world. The program and exhibits are dedicated to issues and products related to all aspects of temporary traffic control and roadway safety.
Frequency: Annual/February

21912 Counterterrorism & Security Professionals Annual Conference
PO Box 10265
Arlington, VA 22210

201-461-5422; www.iacsp.com

Steven Fustero, Executive Director

We believe that all elements of the world's societies must become better educated about the threats of terrorism as a first step toward developing innovative and effective countermeasures to combat these ongoing threats. A better informed society will result in a freer one.
Frequency: May
Founded in: 1992

21913 Crime Analysts Annual Conference
9218 Metcalf
PMB 364
Overland Park, KS 66212
919-940-3883
nfritz@du.edu; www.iaca.net

Noah Fritz, Director
Christopher Bruce, VP Administration

Annual themed conference helping crime analysts around the world improve their skills and make valuable contacts. Aids law enforcement agencies in making the best use of crime analysis and advocates for standards of performance and technique within the profession itself.
Frequency: October
Founded in: 1990

21914 Disaster Response & Recovery Exposition NDMS Conference
J Spargo & Associates
11208 Waples Mill Road
Suite 112
Fairfax, VA 22030

703-631-6200
800-564-4220; *Fax:* 703-654-6931;
www.drrexpo.com
Social Media: Facebook, Twitter, LinkedIn

Nathan Wills, Account Manager

Held in conjunction with the NDMS Conference; it is an opportunity for local, State and Federal public health practitioners and policy makers to discover the latest equipment, technologies and services available.
2700 Attendees
Frequency: August

21915 Eastern Ergonomics Conference & Exposition
Continental Exhibitions
370 Lexington Avenue
New York, NY 10017

212-370-5005
800-222-2596; *Fax:* 212-370-5699
information@ergoexpo.com;
www.ergoexpo.com

Lenore Kolb, Vice President of Sales
Walter Chamizon, President

Learn how to use ergonomics to increase productivity and safety at over 80 educational sessions. Try new products from over 100 companies, in over 2,000 square feet of floor space.
Frequency: June

21916 Emergency Preparedness & Response Conference & Exposition: READY
National Trade Productions
313 S Patrick Street
Alexandria, VA 22314

703-683-8500
800-687-7469; *Fax:* 703-706-8234
ready@ntpshow.com; www.readyinfousa.com

Janie Bridgeman, Sales Director
Maria Chaloux, Industry Relations

Annual symposium and trade show for personnel from federal, state and local agencies to learn about the latest emergency response equipment, technology, strategies and applications.
Frequency: July

21917 Emergency Response Conference & Expo
PBI Media
1201 Seven Locks Road
Suite 300
Potomac, MD 20854

301-541-1400; *Fax:* 301-309-3847;
www.pbimedia.com

Robert Lewis, Conference Coordinator

Annual event for first responders and the companies who support them, working together on land, air and sea to save lives and property. Conference and exhibitors.
Frequency: November

21918 Energy Security Expo
EJ Krause & Associates
6550 Rock Spring Drive
Suite 500
Bethesda, MD 20817-1126

301-493-5500; *Fax:* 301-493-5705;
www.pipelinesecurity.com

Michael Rosenburg, Show Manager
Edward Krause, President

Intensive conference with workshops led by leading international experts from government and industry. Exhibit area featuring technologies, products and services for pipeline and energy infrastructure including oil, gas, electric grids, power plants and dams.
Frequency: May

21919 Fire-Rescue International
International Association of Fire Chiefs
4025 Fair Ridge Dr
Fairfax, VA 22033-2868

703-273-0911; *Fax:* 703-273-9363;
www.iafc.org
Social Media: Facebook, LinkedIn

Al H. Gillespie, President & Chairman of the Board
Hank Clemmensen, First Vice President
William R. Metcalf, Second Vice President
Richard Carrizzo, Treasurer
Luther L. Fincher, Jr., Director-At-Large

FRI education covers all areas of the emergency service: navigating the political environment, managing change, ethical leadership, EMS issues, career development and moor. Exhibitors showcase the newest fire service innovations in apparatus, technology, equipment, gear and more.
12000 Members
Founded in: 1873

21920 Fire-Rescue Med (FRM)
International Association of Fire Chiefs
4025 Fair Ridge Drive
Suite 300
Fairfax, VA 22033-2868

703-273-0911; *Fax:* 703-273-9363;
www.iafc.org

Mark Light, Executive Director & CEO
Lisa Yonkers, Director, Conferences & Education
Leanne Shroeder, Conference Manager
Shannon Gilliland, Assistant Director, Conferences

Each spring, Fire-Rescue Med is the conference for fire-based EMS leaders, providing education and training on hiring and retaining EMTs, public and private integration challenges, embracing technology, billing for services, illness prevention programs and more.
Frequency: Annual

21921 Gov't Convention on Emerging Technologies Partnerships for Homeland Security
National Conference Services
6440-C Dobbin Road
Columbia, MD 21045

301-596-8899
888-603-8899; *Fax:* 301-596-6274;
www.federalevents.com

Fredrick Martin, Director
Anne Slobodien, Chief Executive Officer

Forum for representatives from federal, state and local governments, along with the private sector

to collaborate on and experiment with information technology that addresses mission needs critical to homeland security. Exhibits, workshops and simulation exercises.
Frequency: January

21922 GovSec
National Trade Productions
313 S Patrick Street
Alexandria, VA 22314

703-838-8500; *Fax:* 703-836-4486;
www.govsecinfo.com

Denise Medved, General Manager

Provides a full spectrum of security solutions for federal, state, and local governments tasked with developing comprehensive strategies that address physical security, information security and cyber security needs. Educational programs held in conjunction with displays of a wide variety of security products and services designed specifically for government users.
Frequency: Annual/May

21923 HTCIA International Training Conference & Expo
Int'l High Technnology Crime Investigation Assoc
3288 Goldstone Drive
Roseville, CA 95747

916-408-1751; *Fax:* 916-408-7543;
www.htcia.org

Carol Hutchings, Executive Director
Ronald J Wilczysnki, First VP/Conference Chair

Intended to attract participants from all over the world to take advantage of the training and networking opportunities that is offered.
Frequency: Annual

21924 Homeland Security Expo & Conference
E-Gov Conferences
3141 Fairview Park Drive
Suite 777
Falls Church, VA 22042-4507

703-876-5060
800-746-0099; *Fax:* 703-876-5059
info@e-gov.com; www.homeecexpo.com

Mike Smoyer, General Manager

Keynote presentations, conference sessions, plenary session and exhibition of solutions and technologies to enhance homeland security efforts.
Frequency: November/December

21925 IMSA Conference
International Municipal Signal Association
165 E Union Street
PO Box 539
Newark, NY 14513-0539

315-331-2182
800-723-4672; *Fax:* 315-331-8205
info@imsasafety.org; www.imsasafety.org
Social Media: Facebook, Twitter, LinkedIn

Marilyn Lawrence, Executive Director/Publisher
Sharon Earl, Executive Assistant/Assitant Editor

Schools, technical sessions, exhibit floor and product demos.
1300 Attendees

21926 ISC Expo International Security Conference and Expo-Las Vegas
Reed Exhibition Companies
383 Main Avenue
Norwalk, CT 06851

203-840-4800; *Fax:* 203-840-9322
inquiry@isc.reedexpo.com; www.iscwest.com
Social Media: Facebook, Twitter, LinkedIn

Amie Cangelosi, Marketing Coordinator
Kara Buonanno, Marketing/Conference Manager

From around the globe, every relevant manufacturer, product, service and industry expert will be on hand for three days under one roof.
Frequency: March/April

21927 ISC: International Security Conference & Expo
Reed Exhibitions
383 Main Avenue
Norwalk, CT 06851

203-840-4800; *Fax:* 203-840-9322
inquiry@isc.reedexpo.com; www.isceast.com
Social Media: Facebook, Twitter, LinkedIn

Amie Cangelosi, Marketing Coordinator
Kara Buonanno, Marketing/Conference Manager

From around the globe, relevant manufacturers, products, services and industry experts will be on hand under one roof.
Frequency: November

21928 Inside ID: Identification Solutions Mega Show
Inside ID
8900 Saunders Lane
Bethesda, MD 20817

301-365-0186; *Fax:* 301-365-2519;
www.insideid.com

Ben Miller, President
Liz Wenchel, CEO

Helps define and center the evolution of the emerging disipline of Identity Management. Education and displays of new products and technologies in identification. Facilitates the marketplace of buyers and sellers, provides a broad-based forum, and gathering place for standards groups and associations around the world.

21929 International Cargo Security Council
1400 I Street NW
Suite 1050
Washington, DC 20005-2209

202-821-1787; *Fax:* 410-956-0679
icsc@cargosecurity.com; www.securecargo.org

Joe Baker Jr, Executive Director
Ellen Parkereman, Meeting Director

Workshops and 60 booth exposition for cargo transportation and security professionals from the entire spectrum of cargo security: air, truck, rail maritime and intermodal.
450 Attendees
Frequency: Annual
Founded in: 1973

21930 International Consumer Product Health & Safety Organization Annual Meeting
PO Box 1785
Germantown, MD 20875-1785

301-601-3240; *Fax:* 301-601-3543
icphso@aol.com; www.icphso.org

Dedicated to the health and safety issues related to consumer products manufactured and marketed in the global marketplace. Serving both health and safety professionals and consumers by sponsoring national and regional workshops. Annual meeting and training syposium.
Frequency: March
Founded in: 1993

21931 NAESA Annual Workshop
National Association of Elevator Safety
6957 Littlerock Road SW
Suite A
Tumwater, WA 98512

360-292-4968
800-746-2372; *Fax:* 360-292-4973
dotty@naesai.org; www.naesai.org
Social Media: Facebook, Twitter, LinkedIn

Dotty Stanlaske, Executive Director
Dean McLellan, President
Bill Snyder, VP
Frequency: August

21932 National Council of Investigation & Security Annual Conference
7501 Sparrows Point Boulevard
Baltimore, MD 21219-1927

800-445-8408; *Fax:* 410-388-9746
nciss@comcast.net; www.nciss.org

Carolyn Ward, Executive Director
Francie Koehler, President
Bruce Hulme, Legislative Director

State associations and firms providing contract security services and investigative services. Our cooperative effort includes a legislative watch and providing accurate information reguarding our profession.
Frequency: March

21933 National Ergonomics Conference & Exposition
Continental Exhibitions
370 Lexington Avenue
New York, NY 10017

212-370-5005
800-222-2596; *Fax:* 212-370-5699
lkolb@ergoexpo.com; www.ergoexpo.com

Lenore Kolb, Vice President of Sales
Walter Chamizon, President

Learn how to use ergonomics to increase productivity and safety at over 80 educational sessions. Try new products from over 100 companies, in over 2,000 square feet of floor space.
Frequency: December

21934 National Fire Protection World Safety Conference & Exposition
National Fire Protection Association
1 Batterymarch Park
Quincy, MA 02169-7471

617-770-3000
800-344-3555; *Fax:* 617-770-0700
publicaffairs@nfpa.org; www.nfpa.org

James M. Shannon, President/CEO
Peg O'Brien, Administrator - Public Affairs
Sharon Gamache, Executive Director
Bruce Mullen, CFO
Paul Crossman, VP, Marketing

Professional development, networking and hundreds of booths from key industry suppliers.
75000 Members
Frequency: May
Founded in: 1896

21935 National Safety Council Congress Expo
National Safety Council
1121 Spring Lake Drive
Itasca, IL 60143

630-775-2213
800-621-7619; *Fax:* 630-285-0798
customerservice@nsc.org
http://congress.nsc.org

Nancy Gavin, Expo Manager
Christine Paplaczyk, Exhibit Sales
Alan McMillan, CEO

Annual event for safety, health and the environment.
16000 Attendees
Frequency: September

21936 **Police and Security Expo**
PO Box 20068
Sarasota, FL 34276-0368
609-466-2111
800-323-1927; *Fax:* 609-466-2675
webmaster@police-security.com;
www.police-security.com
Displaying goods, products and services for law enforcement and security professionals.
Frequency: June

21937 **Professional Security Consultants Annual Conference**
525 SW 5th Street
Suite A
Des Moines, IA 50309-4501
515-282-8192; *Fax:* 515-282-9117
iapsc@iapsc.org; www.iapsc.org
David G Aggleton, President
Robert A Schultheiss, VP
Dick Goodson, Executive Director
Harold Gillens, Secretary
Frank Pisciotta, Treasurer
Seeks to enhance members knowledge through seminars, training programs, and educational materials. Works to foster public awareness of the security consulting industry.
Frequency: April
Founded in: 1984

21938 **Professional Security Alliance Conference & Exhibits**
PSA Security Network
12011 N Tejon Street
Denver, CO 80234
303-520-0137; *Fax:* 303-252-1741
lisa@psasecurity.com; www.psasecurity.com
Lisa Speyer, Conference/Marketing
Shelley Binder, Customer/Vendor Service
Michelle Medina, Membership
For corporate management, salespeople, project managers and other technicians for PSA member companies. Educational sessions and pavillion featuring video surveillance, access control and biometrics.

21939 **Prove It! Measuring Safety Performance Symposium**
American Society of Safety Engineers
1800 E Oakton Street
Des Plaines, IL 60018
847-699-2929; *Fax:* 847-768-3434
customerservice@asse.org; www.asse.org
Social Media: Facebook
Terrie S. Norris, President
Richard A. Pollock, President Elect
Kathy Seabrook, Senior Vice President
Fred J. Fortman, Jr., Secretary & Executive Director
James D. Smith, Vice President, Finance
Demonstrate the performance of your safety program and the value of safety. This symposium will show you how and the rewards are great. Develop leading indicators specific to safety, learn what and how to measure, and learn to use metrics to improve safety performance.
30000 Members
Founded in: 1911

21940 **Rocky Mountain Health & Safety Conference**
Colorado Safety Association
4730 Oakland Street
Suite 500
Denver, CO 80239
303-373-1937; *Fax:* 303-373-1955
info@coloradosafety.org;
www.coloradosafety.org
Melodye Turek, President
Jan Harris, Finance Manager
Judy Sapp, Manager
Over 100 exhibitors of safety products, regulatory compliance updates and networking. Educational sessions are offered on various safety topics.
Frequency: April
Founded in: 1968

21941 **SAFE Association Annual Symposium**
SAFE Association
PO Box 130
Creswell, OR 97426
541-895-3012; *Fax:* 541-895-3014
safe@peak.org; www.safeassociation.com
Social Media: Facebook
Marcia Baldwin, President
Bryan Bailey, President-Elect
Presentation topics range from desert survival to the latest aircraft passenger egress aids, cockpit design, restraint systems, and school bus design to international symbols related to transportation and safety, and crew training. Attended by an international group of professionals who are there to share problems and solutions in the field of safety and survival.
1200+ Attendees

21942 **SAFE Symposium**
SAFE Association
PO Box 130
Creswell, OR 97426
541-895-3012; *Fax:* 541-895-3014
safe@peak.org; www.safeassociation.com
Social Media: Facebook
Al Loving, President
John Fair, President-Elect
The SAFE Association is dedicated to the preservation of human life. It provides a common meeting ground for the sharing of problems, ideas and information. SAFE is a non-profit international association headquartered in Oregon, with chapters located throughout the world. SAFE publishes a quarterly Newsletter and Proceedings of the Annual SAFE Symposium. These publications are valuable reference sources for the professional involved in all forms of safety and survival.
1100+ Attendees
Frequency: Quarterly
Founded in: 1954

21943 **Safetech**
Safe & Vault Technicians Association
3003 Live Oak Street
Dallas, TX 75204-6128
214-199-9771; *Fax:* 214-827-1810;
www.savta.org
Joanne Mims, Conventions/Meetings Manager
Annual symposium and trade show for professionals in the valuables protection industry.
Frequency; March

21944 **Securing New Ground**
Securing New Ground
10100 Sherman Road
Chardon, OH 44024
440-286-4900; *Fax:* 440-286-9169
info@securingnewground.com;
www.securingnewground.com
Dini Jones, Conference Coordinator
Rebecca Reed, Manager
Annual 2 day conference with influential people impacting the security industry. Learn about financing, new trends and opportunities for the security industry. Breakfast, lunch and reception included.
Frequency: October

21945 **Security Canada Trade Shows**
Canadian Alarm & Security Association
610 Alden Road
Suite 100
Markam, ON L3R-9Z1
905-513-0622; *Fax:* 905-513-0624;
www.canasa.org
Tracy Cannata, Executive Director
Joyce Everton, Administrative Manager
Lynne Hewiston, Trade Show Manager
Offering four shows annually. Security Canada East is in April, Security Canada Atlantic is in September, Security Canada West is in June and Security Canada Central is in October. These gaterings offer professional development, information, networking and new products to dealers, distributors, manufacturers and monitoring companies across Canada.
Founded in: 1977

21946 **Sensors Expo & Conference**
Advanstar Communications
1 Phoenix Mill Lane
Peterborough, NH 03458
603-924-5400; *Fax:* 603-924-5401;
www.sensorsexpo.com
Cathy Walters, Show Director
Jeanne DuVal, Sales Manager
Informative, sensor related sessions, exhibits and special events for thousands of professionals who will help shape the future of sensing technology.
Frequency: June

21947 **Texas Association of Fire Educators Annual Instructors Conference**
13492 Research Boulevard
Suite 120, PMB 262
Austin, TX 78750-2254
www.tx-tafe.org
Alan Storck, President
Tim Sendelbach, VP
Jim Lee, Secretary
Patricia Clinton, Treasurer
Annual gathering for state fire safety instructors to network and learn the latest in the industry.
Frequency: January

21948 **Texas Burglar & Fire Alarm Assn. Annual Meeting, Trade Show & Golf Classic**
PO Box 59982
Dallas, TX 75229-1982
877-908-2322; *Fax:* 877-908-2522
president@tbfaa.org; www.tbfaa.org
Rex Adams, President
JD Benfer, VP
Jan Wilson, Secretary
Malcolm Reed, Treasurer
Annual gathering of a large number of professional security and fire alarm companies that operate in the state of Texas.
Frequency: October

21949 **US Maritime Security Expo**
EJ Krause & Associates

6550 Rock Spring Drive
Suite 500
Bethesda, MD 20817-1126

301-493-5500; *Fax:* 301-493-5705;
www.maritimesecurityexpo.com

Lindsey Field, Show Manager
Edward Krause, President

Annual conference and exhibitor hall attended by those who protect ports, harbors, bridges, cargo containers, power plants, off shore oil rigs, railroads, cargo and passenger ships.
Frequency: September

21950 Wildland Urban Interface Conference
International Association of Fire Chiefs
4025 Fair Ridge Drive
Suite 300
Fairfax, VA 22033-2868

703-273-0911; *Fax:* 703-273-9363;
www.iafc.org

Mark Light, Executive Director & CEO
Lisa Yonkers, Director, Conferences & Education
Shannon Gilliland, Assistant Director, Conferences
Leanne Shroeder, Conference Manager

Brings together leaders from the local, state and federal levels to collaborate against the fastest growing fire threat in the world. From education and mitigation, suppression strategies, high-hazard operations to policy, WUI addresses the toughest challenges facing the wildland firefighting community.

Directories & Databases

21951 American Society for Industrial Security: Annual Membership Directory
American Society for Industrial Security
1625 Prince Street
Alexandria, VA 22314-2818

703-519-6200
800-368-5685; *Fax:* 703-519-6299
asis@asisonline.org; www.asisonline.org

Keith Goins, Membership Manager
Michael Stack, Executive Director

25,000 member management specialists in the private and public sectors who formulate security policy and direct security programs to prevent terrorism, dcoument piracy. Available as a membership benefit only.

21952 BCSP Directory and International Registry of Certified Safety Professionals
Board of Certified Safety Professionals
2301 W. Bradley Avenue
Champaign, IL 61874-9571

217-359-9263; *Fax:* 217-359-0055
bcsp@bcsp.org; www.bcsp.org

Thomas L Adams, Executive Director

Directory includes over 10,000 safety professionals holding the Certified Safety Professional (CSP) or Associate Safety Professional (ASP) designation.
Circulation: 20000
Founded in: 1969
Mailing list available for rent: 20,000 names
Printed in on matte stock

21953 Business Insurance Directory of Safety Consultants & Rehabilitation Mgt.
Crain Communications
360 N Michigan Ave
Chicago, IL 60601-3800

312-649-5200; *Fax:* 312-649-7937
KCrain@crain.com; www.crain.com

Keith Crain, CEO
Ronnie Drachman, Director Communications

List of more than 150 employee safety consultants and over 70 employee rehabilitation management providers.
Cost: $4.00
Frequency: Annual
Circulation: 53,000

21954 Central Station Alarm Association Directory
8150 Leesburg Pike
Suite 201
Vienna, VA 22182-2721

703-242-4670; *Fax:* 703-242-4675;
www.csaaul.org

Steve Doyle, Executive Director
Celia Besore, Director Marketing/Communications
Cost: $195.00
94 Pages
Frequency: Annual
Circulation: 1,000

21955 Computer Security Buyers Guide
Computer Security Institute
600 Harrison Street
San Francisco, CA 94107-1387

415-947-6320
800-227-4675; *Fax:* 415-905-2218
wwilson@infi.com; www.gocsi.com/csi

Patrice Rapalus, Editor

About 650 suppliers and consultants of computer security products, including communications and network security, disaster recovery, media security, personnel security and security training.
Cost: $197.00
Frequency: Annual
Circulation: 4,500

21956 Directory of Mail Drop Addresses and Zip Codes
Fraud & Theft Information Bureau
8400 96th Ct S
Boynton Beach, FL 33472-4400

561-732-3653; *Fax:* 561-732-4928;
www.fraudandtheftinfo.com

Pat Ford, Owner
Pearl Say, Editor/VP

Identifies every one of the 35,000 mail drops used by credit card thieves to steel your merchandise. Thousands of credt card thieves use thse address, which sound like residential addresses, to hide their identity and true address while stealing from you with stolen credit card numbers.
Cost: $605.50
Frequency: Annual
ISBN: 0-914801-07-4
Founded in: 1982

21957 Disaster Resource Guide
Disaster Resource Guide
PO Box 15243
Santa Ana, CA 92735

Fax: 714-558-8901;
www.disaster-resource.com

Articles, business resources and product information for public and private emergency preparedness. Free of charge if subscriber is registered annually.
Frequency: Annual

21958 Fire Protection Equipment Directory
Underwriters Laboratories
333 Pfingsten Rd
Northbrook, IL 60062-2096

847-412-0136
877-854-3577; *Fax:* 847-272-8129
cec@us.ul.com; www.ul.com
Social Media: Facebook, Twitter, LinkedIn, You Tube

Keith E Williams, CEO
John Drengenberg, Manager Consumer Affairs

Companies that have qualified to use the UL listing mark or classification marking on or in connection with products that have been found to be in compliance with UL's requirements.
Cost: $35.00
Frequency: February

21959 Fire Resistance Directory
Underwriters Laboratories
333 Pfingsten Rd
Northbrook, IL 60062-2096

847-412-0136
877-854-3577; *Fax:* 847-272-8129
cec@us.ul.com; www.ul.com
Social Media: Facebook, Twitter, LinkedIn, You Tube

Keith E Williams, CEO
John Drengenberg, Manager Consumer Affairs

Companies that have qualified to use the UL listing mark or classification marking on or in connection with products that have been found to be in compliance with UL's requirements. 4 book set.
Cost: $110.00
Frequency: February

21960 Fire Retardant Chemicals Association: Membership Directory
Fire Retardant Chemicals Association
851 New Holland Avenue
Lancaster, PA 17601-5644

202-530-4590; *Fax:* 717-295-4538;
www.fireretardants.org

Approximately 35 member manufacturers and distributors of chemical fire retardants and related supplies.

21961 Fire Suppression Systems Association: Membership Directory
Fire Suppression Systems Association
5024 Campbell Boulevard
Suite R
Baltimore, MD 21236

410-931-2374; *Fax:* 410-931-8111

Approximately 120 member companies that design, manufacture, distribute, install or repair and maintain fire suppression systems.
Frequency: Annual

21962 Grey House Homeland Security Directory
Grey House Publishing
4919 Route 22
PO Box 56
Amenia, NY 12501

518-789-8700
800-562-2139; *Fax:* 845-373-6390
books@greyhouse.com; www.greyhouse.com
Social Media: Facebook, Twitter

Leslie Mackenzie, Publisher
Richard Gottlieb, Editor

Features the latest contact information for government and private organizations involved with Homeland Security along with the latest product information. The directory provides detailed profiles of nearly 1,500 Federal & State Organizations & Agencies and over 3,000 Officials and Key Executives involved with Homeland Secu-

rity.
Cost: $195.00
800 Pages
ISBN: 1-592371-96-5
Founded in: 1981

21963 Grey House Homeland Security Directory - Online Database
Grey House Publishing
4919 Route 22
PO Box 56
Amenia, NY 12501
518-789-8700
800-562-2139; *Fax:* 845-373-6390
gold@greyhouse.com;
www.gold.greyhouse.com
Social Media: Facebook, Twitter
Leslie Mackenzie, Publisher
Richard Gottlieb, Editor
This comprehensive database presents a wide range of information that is scattered and hard to find elsewhere, providing subscribers with access to the most comprehensive, up-to-date and detailed information on the nation's homeland security contacts and services. This online database contains over 1,100 profiles of Federal and State agencies and companies along with the names of 11,000 key contacts.
Founded in: 1981

21964 Grey House Safety & Security Directory
Grey House Publishing
4919 Route 22
PO Box 56
Amenia, NY 12501
518-789-8700
800-562-2139; *Fax:* 845-373-6390
books@greyhouse.com; www.greyhouse.com
Social Media: Facebook, Twitter
Leslie Mackenzie, Publisher
Richard Gottlieb, Editor
Comprehensive guide to the safety and security industry, including articles, checklists, OSHA regulations and product listings. Focuses on creating and maintaining a safe and secure enviroment, and dealing specifically with hazardous materials, noise and vibration, workplace preparation and maintenance, electrical and lighting safety, fire and rescue and more.
Cost: $165.00
1600 Pages
ISBN: 1-592373-75-5
Founded in: 1981

21965 Grey House Transportation Security Directory
Grey House Publishing
4919 Route 22
PO Box 56
Amenia, NY 12501
518-789-8700
800-562-2139; *Fax:* 845-373-6390
books@greyhouse.com; www.greyhouse.com
Social Media: Facebook, Twitter
Leslie Mackenzie, Publisher
Richard Gottlieb, Editor
Information on everything from Regulatory Authorities to Security Equipment, this top-flight database brings together the relevant information necessary for creating and maintaining a security plan for a wide range of transportation facilities.
Cost: $195.00
800 Pages
ISBN: 1-592370-75-6
Founded in: 1981

21966 Kodex Security Equipment/Systems Database
Security Defense Systems
139 Chestnut Street
#626
Nutley, NJ 07110-2311
973-235-0606
800-325-6339; *Fax:* 973-235-0132;
www.securitydefense.com
More than 32,000 manufacturers and distributors worldwide of home and office security equipment and systems.
Cost: $295.00
Frequency: Biennial

21967 Material Safety Data Sheet Reference
C&P Press
565 5th Ave
5th Floor
New York, NY 10017-2413
212-587-8620; *Fax:* 646-733-6010;
www.pharmpress.com
Regulatory and product safety requirements. Contains full text MSDS's for products listed in the Crop Protection Reference plus additional safety information such as DOT shipping information, SARA Title III regulations, Hazardous Chemical inventory reporting information plus much more. Available in print, database, continually updated electronic version or CD-ROM.

21968 NFPA Journal: Buyers' Guide
National Fire Protection Association
1 Batterymarch Park
Quincy, MA 02169-7471
617-770-3000
800-344-3555; *Fax:* 617-770-0700
publicaffairs@nfpa.org; www.nfpa.org
James M. Shannon, President/CEO
Peg O'Brien, Administrator - Public Affairs
Sharon Gamache, Executive Director
Bruce Mullen, CFO
Paul Crossman, VP, Marketing
List of manufacturers and consultants of fire protection, fire safety and fire service products.
Cost: $30.00
75000 Members
Frequency: February
Circulation: 95,000
Founded in: 1896

21969 National Directory of Fire Chiefs & EMS Administrators
National Public Safety Information Bureau
2173 Church Street, Suite 201
PO Box 365
Stevens Point, WI 54481-0365
715-345-2772
800-647-7579; *Fax:* 715-345-7288
info@safetysource.com;
www.safetysource.com
Laura Gross, Vice President of Procurement
Steve Cywinski, Account Manager
John Diser, Account Manager
Christina Scott, Business Development Manager
Vital contact resource for busy professionals. Contact nearly every fire and emergency department in the US, nearly 35,000 departments.
Cost: $129.00
Frequency: June
Circulation: 10000
Founded in: 1964

21970 National Directory of Law Enforcement Administrators
National Public Safety Information Bureau
2173 Church Street, Suite 201
PO Box 365
Stevens Point, WI 54481-0365
715-345-2772
800-647-7579; *Fax:* 715-345-7288
info@safetysource.com;
www.safetysource.com
Laura Gross, Vice President of Procurement
Steve Cywinski, Account Manager
John Diser, Account Manager
Christina Scott, Business Development Manager
Listing of police departments, sheriffs, criminal prosecutors, state law enforcement, criminal investigation and homeland security agencies.
Cost: $129.00
Frequency: June
Circulation: 10000
ISBN: 1-880245-22-1
Founded in: 1964

21971 National Work Zone Safety Information Clearinghouse
Texas Transportation Institute
3135 Tamu
College Station, TX 77843-0001
979-845-1715
888-447-5556
workzone@tamu.edu; www.wzsafety.tamu.edu
Cooperative partnership between the American Road and Transportation Builders Association and the Texas Transportation Institute. Offers information traffic accidents and crashes, equipment and technology, legislation, research projects and training.

21972 Security Industry Sourcebook
PRIMEDIA Business Magazines & Media
1166 Avenue of the Americas
Shawnee Mission, NY 66282-2901
212-204-4200; *Fax:* 913-514-6895;
www.penton.com
Eric Jacobson, Senior VP
Listings of over 600 manufacturers and distributors of security and safety products.
Frequency: Annual
Circulation: 28,400

21973 Society of Fire Protection Engineers: Membership Roster
Society of Fire Protection Engineers
7315 Wisconsin Ave
Suite 1225W
Bethesda, MD 20814-3234
301-718-2910; *Fax:* 301-718-2242
info@aiia-sfpe.org; www.sfpe.org
Pamela A Powell, Editor
Kathleen Almond, Executive Director
Allan Freedman, Executive Director
Frequency: Annual February

Industry Web Sites

21974 http://gold.greyhouse.com
G.O.L.D Grey House OnLine Databases
Grey House Publishing's online database platform, GOLD, offers Quick Search, Keyword Search and Expert Search for most business sectors including safety and security markets. The GOLD platform makes finding the information you need quick and easy - whether you're a novice searcher or an experienced database user. All of Grey House's directory products are be available for subscription on the GOLD platform.

21975 www.abih.org
American Board of Industrial Hygiene
Information on credentials for Certified Industrial Hygienist status.

21976 www.afaa.org
Automatic Fire Alarm Association
Members are made up of manufacturers, installers and others interested in fire alarm and detec-

tion equipment. Seminars are conducted on a national basis.

21977 www.allbounty.com
North American Recovery Network
Worldwide portal for agents of collateral repossesion and bail bonds. Chats, forums and industry news.

21978 www.aloa.org
Associated Locksmiths of America
News and event information for the locksmith industry. Maintains referral service and offers insurance and bonding programs.

21979 www.alw.nih.gov/Security/security
Center for Information Technology
Computer security information and links.

21980 www.apco911.org
Association of Public-Safety Communications Officials International
Dedicated to the enhancement of public safety communications and to serving its more than 15,000 members, the people who use public safety communications systems and services.

21981 www.asisonline.org
American Society for Industrial Security
Organization which features ideas and practices for business and industrial security managers.

21982 www.asse.org
American Society of Safety Engineers
Information for members on upcoming meetings, training and local chapters.

21983 www.atssa.org
American Traffic Safety Services Association
Promotes uniform use of lights, signs, pavement markings and barricades. Distributes technical information and sponsors training courses for worksite traffic supervisors.

21984 www.bioxs.com
Bio XS
Biometrics newsletter updated weekly. Features company profiles and new products.

21985 www.buildershardware.com
Builders Hardware Manufacturers Association
Code & life safety regulation information concerning locks and builders hardware.

21986 www.businesssecuritytips.com
Security Industry Association
Provides businesses with technology specific information and helps business owners and managers understand how available technology can be be better utilized.

21987 www.ccohs.ca
Canadian Centre for Occupational Safety & Health
Information on safety and industrial health topics in Canada.

21988 www.cdc.gov/niosh/homepage.html
National Institute for Occupational Safety/Health
Information on chemical safety, emergency response, injuries, construction, mining, agriculture concerns, respirators and much more.

21989 www.cert.org
Carnegie Mellon Software Engineering Institute
News, statistics and helpful articles relating to computer security.

21990 www.chemsafety.gov
US Chemical Safety & Hazard Investigation Board
Investigative reports of chemical safety incidents and an archive of completed investigations and recommondations made to regulators.

21991 www.cisecurity.org
Center for Internet Security
Helps organizations around the world effectively manage the risks related to internet security.

21992 www.csrc.nist.gov
National Institute of Standards & Technology
Information, links and white papers from the Information Technology Laboratory, the Computer Security Division and the Computer Security Resource Center.

21993 www.disaster-resource.com
Disaster Resource Guide
News, articles, business resources and product highlights for security and business managers as well as contingency planners who are in charge of emergency business recovery.

21994 www.eia-usa.org
Environmental Information Association
Nonprofit organization dedicated to providing environmental information to individuals, members and the industry. Disseminates information on the abatement of asbestos and lead-based paint, indoor air quality, safety and health issues, analytical issues and environmental site assessments.

21995 www.fama.org
Fire Apparatus Manufacturers' Association
Membership association for manufacturers of emergency vehicles and components affixed to or carried upon the vehicle.

21996 www.findbiometrics.com
Topickz
Showcases new technologies in biometric security and provides links to companies providing them.

21997 www.first.org
Forum of Incident Response and Security Teams
Brings together a variety of computer security incident response teams from government, commercial and academic organizations. This site encourages cooperation in incident prevention, rapid reaction to incidents and to promote information sharing.

21998 www.fraud.org
National Consumers League
Your source for Internet and telemarketing fraud information.

21999 www.fraudandtheftinfo.com
Fraud and Theft Information Bureau
Provides problem solving, crime prevention, money saving manuals and fraud blocker databases.

22000 www.fssa.net
Fire Suppression Systems Association
Association news and events for designers, suppliers and installers of special hazard fire suppression equipment, gases and detectors.

22001 www.ginetwork.com
Global Investigators Network
Worldwide internet based organization for private investigators.

22002 www.gocsi.org
Computer Security Institute
Information on computer and network security.

22003 www.greyhouse.com
Grey House Publishing
Authoritative reference directories for most business sectors including safety and security markets. Users can search the online databases with varied search criteria allowing for custom searches by product category, geographic area, sales volume, keyword, subject and more. Full Grey House catalog and online ordering also available.

22004 www.highwaysafety.org
Insurance Institute for Highway Safety
Vehicle safety news and statistics from traffic and motor vehicle safety organization supported by auto insurers.

22005 www.htcia.org
Int'l High Technology Crime Investigation Assoc
Designed to encourage, promote, aid and effect the voluntary interchange of data, information, experience, ideas and knowledge about methods, processes, and techniques relating to investigations and security in advanced technologies among its membership.

22006 www.imsasafety.org
International Municipal Signal Association
Basic purpose of the organization is to keep its members and others in the profession, up-to-date on proper procedures of construction and maintenance of signal systems and informed on new products and equipment developments.

22007 www.infoguys.com
Spyville
Process servers associations, articles and certification information, forensic experts and a searchable database for private investigators or those seeking to hire one.

22008 www.infosecuritymag.techtarget.com
Tech Target
Online information technology magazine.

22009 www.intsi.org
International Security Industry Organization
Dedicated to improving effcient communication to all stakeholders in the security industries and provides them with the necessary information to be more effective in their daily tasks.

22010 www.investigativeprofessionals.com
Investigative Professionals
Consult with a professional investigator, accomplish a people locator search, do a background check, conduct your own investigation or get information on becoming a private investigator.

22011 www.issa.org
Information Systems Security Association
International computer system information from an organization of security professionals and practitioners.

22012 www.museum-security.org
Museum Security Network
Free internet service and mailing list for museum security professionals, curators, librarians, registrar and specialized police.

22013 www.naaa.org
National Alarm Association of America
Alarm dealers association offers training, tips, an online newsletter and other member benefits.

22014 www.ndia.org
National Defense Industrial Association
To provide legal and ethical forum for the interchange of ideas between the government and in-

dustry to resolve industrial problems of joint concern.

22015 **www.net-security.org**
Help Net Security
Daily updated security related site.

22016 **www.nfpa.org**
National Fire Protection Association
The mission of the NFPA is to reduce the worldwide burden of fire and other hazards on the quality of life by providing and advocating consensus codes and standards, research, training and education.

22017 **www.nnsa.doe.gov**
National Nuclear Security Administration
Increasing public awareness of nuclear security and current energy issues. Links to website of supporting offices.

22018 **www.nsi.org**
National Security Institute
Features industry and product news, computer alerts, travel advisories, a calender of events, a directory of products and services and access to a virtual security library.

22019 **www.ope.ed.gov/security**
Campus Security Statistics
Direct link to reported criminal offenses for over 6000 colleges and universities in the US. If you are considering a college in a large urban city, a small liberal arts college, a specialized college or a community college you can find their security statistics here.

22020 **www.osh.net**
Workcare
Links to health and safety news. Offers online newslettter free to subscribers.

22021 **www.osha.gov**
Occupational Safety & Health Administration
Regulations and standards for worker safety in the US. Also included are a searchable database of recent safety violation citations, electronic safety lessons for many industries, a spot where workers can report safety concerns, safety tipsheets and a section for Spanish speaking workers.

22022 **www.osha.gov/dop/nacosh.html**
Nat'l Advisory Comm. on Occupational Safety/Health
News releases, federal register notices, reports, meeting agendas and contact information for the 12 members representing management, labor, occupational health and safety and the public. This group advises the secretaries of labor and health and human services on occupational safety and health programs and policies.

22023 **www.pavnet.org**
Partnership Against Violence Network
Virtual library of information about violence and youth-at-risk, representing data from seven different Federal agencies.

22024 **www.personalprotection.com**
Nine Lives Associates
Information on programs which emphasize personal survival skills and techniques for the protection of others. Information on training and list of protective agents and consultants.

22025 **www.picoffeshop.com**
PI Coffee Shop
Articles and a national forum of interest to private investigators.

22026 **www.pimall.com**
PI Mall
Information for private investigator contacts, products, training and services.

22027 **www.processervers.com**
International Process Servers Association
Resource for process servers and private investigators. Message board and searchable database by zipcode to locate a local process server.

22028 **www.ready.gov**
US Government
Updates and information on how the Department of Homeland Security is working to keep America safe.

22029 **www.rims.org**
Risk & Insurance Management Society
Information on worker's compensation, enterprise risk, risk management and financing, corporate governance and risk management.

22030 **www.rmsecgroup.com**
Risk Management Security Group
Addresses general aviation and cargo security concerns, training for professional transportation personnel, provides threat vulnerability assessments and literature.

22031 **www.safeassociation.com**
SAFE Association
Website of the nonprofit organization dedicated to the preservation of human life. It provides a common meeting ground for the sharing of problems, ideas and information.

22032 **www.saferoads.org**
Advocates for Highway and Auto Safety
Information on road safety issues, federal programs, polls, reports and helpful links for consumers, safety and law enforcement agencies, insurance agents and organizations.

22033 **www.safetycentral.org**
Safety Equipment Distributors Association
Represents wholesale-distributors of safety equipment and works to enhance and improve distribution through excellence in communications, training, education and services.

22034 **www.safetyhealthmanager.org**
National Safety Management Society
A professional society dedicated to the advancement of new concepts of accident prevention and loss control, promoting safety management.

22035 **www.safetysmart.com**
Bongarde Holdings
Safety education products and information.

22036 **www.safetysource.com**
National Public Safety Information Bureau
News, events, web guide and public safety shopping for professionals in corrections, EMS, fire and police departments.

22037 **www.securityfocus.com**
Symantec
Offers a forum for objective reporting by security experts on the latest computer security threats and prevention.

22038 **www.securitysales.com**
Security Sales & Integration
Breaking news of electronic security concerns and articles from the current issue of Security Sales & Integration.

22039 **www.siaonline.org**
Security Industry Association
Promotes growth, expansion and professionalism within the security industry. Online newsletter has the daily top ten headlines in security.

22040 **www.stats.bls.gov**
Bureau of Labor Statistics
Data on workplace injuries, illnesses and fatalities.

22041 **www.terrorismcentral.com**
Terrorism Central
Responding to the need for a single, trusted source of information about terrorism and related security issues, this central information repository comprises original and secondary sources spanning decades of research.

22042 **www.ul.com/auth/tca**
Underwriters Laboratories
Code Authority — online newsletter for the code community.

22043 **www.vpppa.org**
Voluntary Protection Program Participant's Assoc.
Information on the Occupational Safety and Health Administration's Voluntary Protection Participant program for companies.

22044 **www.whitehouse.gov/homeland**
Whitehouse
Updates of Homeland Security department and staff activities, list of state homeland security officers and contact information.

22045 **www1.blr.com**
Business & Legal Reports
Provides essential tools for safety and environmental compliance and training needs.

Associations

22046 **International Network for Social Network Analysis**
1404 1/2 Adams Avenue
Huntington, WV 25704
304-208-8001; *Fax:* 304-523-9701
support@insna.org; www.insna.org
Social Media: Facebook, Twitter
Laura Skvoretz, Chair/ Treasurer
John Skvoretz, President
Katherine Fraust, Vice President
Yanjie Bian, Board Member
Ulrik Brandes, Board Member
The International Network for Social Network Analysis was developed for researchers interested in social network theory and understanding the online world. Members discuss the virtual community, the virtual workplace and social support.
Founded in: 1977

22047 **Social Media Association**
socialmediaassoc.com
Social Media: Facebook, Twitter, LinkedIn, RSS, Google+, Pinterest
Paul Rubell, President
Hilary Topper, Founder
Paul Biedermann, Creative Director/Owner
Beth Granger, Board Member
Donna Rivera-Downey, Chief Marketing & Communications
Social Media Association brings together the media community both online and offline. Members are interested in business and innovation through social, digital and future media.

22048 **Social Media Club**
Post Office Box 14881
San Francisco, CA 94114-0881
socialmediaclub.org
Social Media: Facebook, Twitter, LinkedIn, YouTube, Google+, Pinterest
Golden Ashby, President
Ali Sabkar, Founder
Cynthia Johnson, Editorial Director
Naomi Assaraf, Sponsorship Director
Anders Abrahamsson, International Web Editorial
Social Media Club was founded to host conversations around the world that explore key issues facing society as technologies transform the way we connect, communicate, collaborate and relate to each other.
300 Members
Founded in: 2006

22049 **Social Media Professional Association**
530 Lytton Avenue
Palo Alto, CA 94301
650-600-3844
800-123-4567;
www.socialmediaprofessionalassociation.com
Social Media: Facebook, Twitter, LinkedIn, YouTube, Google+, Pinterest
The Social Media Professional Association provides training, education, and advocacy for its members. It also offers a Social Media Marketing Certification program that aids existing business owners and entrepreneurs as they grow or start new businesses in the social media and mobile web marketing fields.

22050 **The Internet Association**
Washington, DC
E-Mail: news@internetassociation.org
internetassociation.org
Social Media: Facebook, Twitter, LinkedIn, RSS, Google+, Flickr, YouTube,
Michael Beckerman, President
Oisin Hanrahan, CEO and Co-founder
The Internet Association represents America's leading internet companies and their global community of users. They are dedicated to policy solutions that protect internet innovations and empowers users.

22051 **The Social Network Association**
E-Mail: info@thesocialnetworkassociation.com
thesocialnetworkassociation.com
Social Media: Facebook, Twitter, Google+, RSS
Jim Nico, Founder and CEO
Dr. Jane Bellan Karwoski, PhD, MSW, Chief Science Officer
Terry Monoson-Nico, Program Director
Daniel Goodsell, General Counsel
Gian Brown, Member, Advisory Board
The Social Network Association is a collaborative industry forum enabling social networking businesses and users to collectively identify and resolce common issues in a productive environment. It provides a comprehensive suite of applications and services to all its members.
Founded in: 2011

22052 **Word of Mouth Marketing Association**
200 East Randolph Street
Suite 5100
Chicago, IL 60601
312-577-7610; *Fax:* 312-275-7687
membership@womma.org; www.womma.org
Social Media: Facebook, Twitter, LinkedIn, YouTube, Google+, RSS
Suzanne Fanning, President
Harvey Morris, Vice President
Jennifer Connelly, Events Manager
Leah Marshall, Director of Development
Pam Smith, Editorial Director
Founded in: 2004

22053 **eMarketing Association**
40 Blue Ridge Dr.
Charlestown, RI 02813
800-496-2950; *Fax:* 408-884-2461
ema@emarketingassociation.com
emarketingassociation.com
Social Media: Facebook, Twitter, LinkedIn, RSS
eMarketing Association is the world's largest association of online marketers. Members meet and network with the top leaders in the eMarketing arena, through its Power Networking Party which helps businesses with new and significant marketing efforts.

Newsletters

22054 **A Formula for Fueling Ad Agency New Business Through Social Media**
American Association of Advertising Agencies
1065 Avenue of the Americas
16th Floor
New York, NY 10018
212-682-2500; *Fax:* 212-682-8391;
www.aaaa.org
Social Media: Facebook, Twitter, LinkedIn
Nancy Hill, President
Michael D. Donahue, Executive Vice President
Laura J. Bartlett, CFO & COO
Michele Adams, Board Secretary
Designed to focus and kick-start your agency's understanding, participation, credibility and leadership in social media with less expense, time and frustration. Created for C level and senior executives charged with the responsibility of new business development.

22055 **NRB Today**
National Religious Broadcasters
9510 Technology Dr
Manassas, VA 20110-4149
703-330-7100; *Fax:* 703-330-7100
info@nrb.org; www.nrb.org
Social Media: Facebook
Frank Wright, President/CEO
Linda Smith, EVP/COO
Kenneth Chan, Director of Communications
This weekly newsletter by National Religious Broadcasters covers the latest news from the association and NRB's member organizations. The newsletter also serves as a source for tips, trends, and insights relevant to Christian communicators across the spectrum. Topics include audience building, branding, business strategy, innovation, job hunting, leadership, management, marketing, social media, and web strategy. NRB Today also features occasional columns, movie reviews, and product reviews.
Founded in: 1944

Magazines & Journals

22056 **The Social Media Monthly**
www.thesocialmediamonthly.com
A monthly magazine for all things involving social media.

Trade Shows

22057 **ANA Digital & Social Media Conference**
Association of National Advertisers
708 Third Avenue
33 Floor
New York, NY 10017
212-697-5950; *Fax:* 212-661-8057
info@ana.net; www.ana.net
Social Media: Facebook, Twitter, LinkedIn, YouTube
Bob Liodice, President & CEO
Christine Manna, COO
William Zengel, EVP
Discussing how to use social media to impact the consumer decision journey and how to effectively partner with other companies to maximize social media reach and more.

22058 **International Network for Social Network Analysis**
1404 1/2 Adams Avenue
Huntington, WV 25704
304-208-8001; *Fax:* 304-523-9701;
www.insna.org
Social Media: Facebook, Twitter
Laura Skvoretz, Chair/ Treasurer
John Skvoretz, President
Katherine Fraust, Vice President
Yanjie Bian, Board Member
Ulrik Brandes, Board Member
The International Network for Social Network Analysis was developed for researchers interested in social network theory and understanding the online world. Members discuss the virtual community, the virtual workplace and social support.
Founded in: 1977

22059 New York Social Media Marketing Conference
SkillPath Seminars
6900 Sqibb Road
PO Box 2768
Mission, KS 66201-2768

913-623-3900
800-873-7545; *Fax:* 913-362-4241
webmaster@skillpath.com; www.skillpath.com

Steve Nichols, Customer Care Representative
Robb Garr, President

This state-of-the-art conference walks through everything needed to start using social media to drive real business results, even for someone who doesn't know the difference between a tweet and a like button. There's no reason to miss out any longer on the proven, bottom-line benefits of marketing with social media.
Frequency: Semi-Annual, April

22060 Response Expo
201 Sandpointe Ave
Suite 500
Santa Ana, CA 92707-8700

714-338-6700
800-854-3112; *Fax:* 714-513-8482
thaire@questex.com;
www.responsemagazine.com
Social Media: Facebook, Twitter, LinkedIn, YouTube

Thomas Haire, Editor
Don Rosenberg, VP
Kristina Kronenberg, Marketing Director

Focuses on the evolution of consumers from passive watchers to active and empowered brand evangelists. Technology and social media have enabled and encouraged consumers to engage and interact with content. Learn how to take DR marketing from traditional campaign management to the future of customer engagement.
Frequency: Monthly
Circulation: 12000
Founded in: 1987

22061 Social Media Association
socialmediaassoc.com/events
Social Media: Facebook, Twitter, LinkedIn, RSS, Google+, Pinterest

Paul Rubell, President
Hilary Topper, Founder
Paul Biedermann, Board Member
Beth Granger, Board Member
Donna Rivera-Downey, Board Member

Social Media Association brings together the media community both online and offline. Members are interested in business and innovation through social, digital and future media.

22062 Social Media Club
Post Office Box 14881
San Francisco, CA 94114-0881
socialmediaclub.org/events
Social Media: Facebook, Twitter, LinkedIn, YouTube, Google+, Pinterest

Golden Ashby, President
Ali Sabkar, New Chapter MD
Cynthia Johnson, Editorial Director
Naomi Assaraf, Sponsorship Director
Anders Abrahamsson, International Web Editorial

Social Media Club was founded to host conversations around the world that explore key issues facing society as technologies transform the way we connect, communicate, collaborate and relate to each other.
300 Members
Founded in: 2006

22063 Transformation LA
American Association of Advertising Agencies
1065 Avenue of the Americas
16th Floor
New York, NY 10018

212-682-2500; *Fax:* 212-682-8391
kipp@aaaa.org; www.aaaa.org
Social Media: Facebook, Twitter, LinkedIn

Nancy Hill, President
Chris Weil, Chair
Andrew Bennett, Director at Large
Sharon Napier, Secretary/Treasurer

Talent recruitment and retention; regulatory updates; mobility; social media; and growing your business are a few of the sessions scheduled. Tour some of the entertainment capital's most creative facilities, including innovative 4A's member agencies.

22064 Word of Mouth Marketing Association
65 E. Wacker Place
Suite #500
Chicago, IL 60601

312-853-4400; *Fax:* 312-275-7687
membership@womma.org;
www.womma.org/events-education/events
Social Media: Facebook, Twitter, LinkedIn, YouTube, Google+

Suzanne Fanning, President
Chris Spallino, Director of Marketing
Jennifer Connelly, Events Manager
Chelsea Hickey, Marketing Manager & Editor
Founded in: 2004

Associations

22065 **ADMA Annual Meeting**
Alaskan Dog Mushers Association
PO Box 70662
Fairbanks, AK 99707-0662

907-457-6874; *Fax:* 907-479-3516
adma@sleddog.org; www.sleddog.org
Social Media: Facebook

Dawn Brown, Secretary
Shannon Erhart, Trustee
Paula Ciniero, President
Casey Thompson, Vice President

Alaskan Dog Mushers Association annual meeting

22066 **ATP Tour**
Association of Tennis Professionals
201 ATP Tour Boulevard
Ponte Vedra Beach, FL

904-856-6400
800-527-4811; *Fax:* 904-285-5966;
www.atptennis.com
Social Media: Facebook, Twitter, Instagram, Google+,Youtube

Giorgio di Palermo, Player Representative
Mark Young, Vice Chairman
Flip Galloway, Chief Operating Officer
Chris Kermode, Executive Chairman & President
Mark Webster, Tournament Representative

Operates the official tennis computer ranking system. Administers entry system for international tennis circuit and tennis system. Membership restricted to male, touring, professional tennis players.
Founded in: 1972

22067 **Academy for Sports Dentistry**
P.O. Box 364
Farmersville, IL 62533

800-273-1788
217-227-3431; *Fax:* 217-227-3438
sportsdentistry@consolidated.net;
www.academyforsportsdentistry.org
Social Media: Facebook, Twitter

Shelly Lott, Executive Secretary
James Lovelace, President
Wayne Nakamura, President-Ellet
E. Jan Chithalen, Treasurer
W Robert Howarth, Immediate Past President
Founded in: 1983

22068 **Adventure Cycling Association**
150 East Pine Street
PO Box 8308
Missoula, MT 59807

406-721-1776
800-755-2453; *Fax:* 406-721-8754
info@adventurecycling.org;
www.adventurecycling.org
Social Media: Facebook, Twitter, Flickr, YouTube, Instagram, Pi

Leigh Carter, General Manager
Andy baur, Secretary
Andrew Huppert, Treasurer
Donna O'Neal, Vice- President
Wally Werner, President

Their mission is to inspire people of all ages to travel by bicycle for fitness, fun and self-discovery. A non-profit organization, it is a resource offering many programs for cyclists, including a national network of bicycle touring routes and organized trips.
42000 Members
Founded in: 1972

22069 **Aerobics and Fitness Association of America**
15250 Ventura Blvd
Suite 200
Sherman Oaks, CA 91403-3297

818-905-0040
877-968-7263; *Fax:* 818-788-6301
contactafaa@afaa.com; www.afaa.com
Social Media: Facebook, Twitter, LinkedIn, Google+, Pinterest, Youtube, I

Linda Pfeffer, President

Association for the education, certification and training of exercise instructors; information resource center for consumers.
Founded in: 1983

22070 **Amateur Athletic Union of the United States**
PO Box 22409
Lake Buena Vista, FL 32830

407-934-7200
800-AAU-4USA; *Fax:* 407-934-7242;
www.aausports.org
Social Media: Facebook, Twitter, YouTube, Pinterest, Instagram

Dr. Roger Goudy, President/CEO
James Parker, Director Sports
Rachel D'Orazio, Director Marketing/Websites
Pam Marshall, Director Sponsorship
Cynthia Diaz, Director Finance

The AAU hosts the Junior Olympic Games, 30 youth sports programs, 25 adult sports programs, awards over 200,000 championship medals annually, partnered with Walt Disney World to host events at Disney's Wide World of Sports Complex, and presents an annual James E. Sullivan memorial award.
500M Members
Founded in: 1888

22071 **Amateur Softball Association**
2801 NE 50th St.
Oklahoma City, OK 73111

405-424-5266; www.asasoftball.com
Social Media: Facebook, Twitter, YouTube, Instagram

Craig Cress, Executive Director
Shirley Adkins, Executive Secretary
Mark Loehrs, Chief Financial Officer
Steve Walker, Director of Operations
Savannah Edwards, Director of I.T
Founded in: 1933

22072 **American Academy of Podiatric Sports Medicine**
109 Greenwich Dr
Walkersville, MD 21793-9121

352-620-8562
888-854-3338
301-845-9887; *Fax:* 352-620-8765
info@aapsm.org; www.aapsm.org
Social Media: Facebook

Rita J. Yates, Executive Director
David Jenkins, President
Maggie Fournier, Secretary-Treasurer
Alex Kor, Vice-President
Amol Saxena, Director

Serves to advance the understanding, prevention and management of lower extremity sports and fitness injuries. They believe that providing such knowledge to the profession and the public will optimize enjoyment and safe participation in sports and fitness activities. They accomplish this mission through professional education, scientific research, public awareness and membership support.
800 Members
Founded in: 1970

22073 **American Alliance for Health, Physical Education, Recreation and Dance**
1900 Association Dr
Reston, VA 20191-1598

703-476-3400
800-213-7193; *Fax:* 703-476-9527;
www.aahperd.org
Social Media: Facebook, Twitter, LinkedIn, Pinterest, Instagram

Steve Jefferies, President
Charlene Burgeson, Executive Director
Hans Van Der Mars, Program Director
E. Paul Roetert, CEO
Dolly D. Lambdin, President-Elect

Organization that provides educational programs, resources and support for professionals within the fields of health, physical education, recreation and dance.
25000 Members
Founded in: 1885

22074 **American Amateur Baseball Congress**
100 W Broadway
Farmington, NM 87401

505-327-3120
800-557-3120; *Fax:* 505-327-3132
info@aabc.us; www.aabc.us

Richard Neely, President
Mike Diamond, Executive VP
Tedra Liessmann, Secretary/Treasurer
Rusty Hill, Legal Advisor

Provides profressive and continuous organized competition for sub teens through adults.bers.
250M Members
Founded in: 1935

22075 **American Association of Collegiate Registrars and Admissions Officers**
One Dupont Circle NW
Suite 520
Washington, DC 20036

202-293-9161
202-296-3359; *Fax:* 202-872-8857;
www.aacrao.org
Social Media: Facebook, Twitter, LinkedIn, Google+

Michael Reilly, Executive Director
Melanie Gottlieb, Deputy Director
Gene Parker, Administrative Assistant
Charles Han, Asst Director, IT
Martha Henebry, Director of Operations

22076 **American Baseball Coaches Association**
4101 Piedmont Parkway
Suite C
Greensboro, NC 27410

336-821-3140; *Fax:* 336-886-0000
abca@abca.org; www.abca.org
Social Media: Facebook, Twitter, LinkedIn, Google+

Bill Arce, Director
Dave Keilitz, Executive Director
Scott Berry, Immediate Past President
Mark Johnson,, Chair
Ed BlankMeyer, President

Association of Baseball Coaches in the United States.
6500 Members
Founded in: 1945

22077 **American Camp Association**
5000 State Road 67 N
Martinsville, IN 46151-7902

765-342-8456
800-428-2267; *Fax:* 765-342-2065
pr@acacamps.org; www.acacamps.org

Social Media: Facebook, Twitter, LinkedIn, Google+, RSS, YouTube, Pintere

Tom Holland, CEO
Tisha Bolger, Chair
Craig whiting, Treasurer
Rue Mapp, Vice-Chair
Steve Baskin, Board Members

Formerly known as the American Camping Association, is a community of camp professionals who have joined together to share their knowledge and experience and to ensure the quality of camp programs.
6700 Members
Founded in: 1910

22078 American Canoe Association
503 Sophia Street
Suite 100
Fredericksburg, VA 22401

540-907-4460; *Fax:* 888-229-3792
aca@americancanoe.org;
www.americancanoe.org
Social Media: Facebook, Twitter, LinkedIn, Google+, YouTube, Pinterest, I

Jerry Dunne, At-Large
Wade Blackwood, Executive Director
Katie Hansen, Membership
Christopher Stec, Chief Operating Officer

A nationwide non-profit organization that is in service to the broader paddling public by providing education on matters related to paddling, supporting stewardship of the paddling environment, and enabling programs and events to support paddlesport recreation.
50000 Members
Founded in: 1880

22079 American College of Sports Medicine
401 W Michigan St
Indianapolis, IN 46202-3233

317-637-9200; *Fax:* 317-634-7817
publicinfo@acsm.org; www.acsm.org
Social Media: Facebook, Twitter, YouTube, Pinterest, Instagram

Asker Jeukendrup, Corporate Representative
Henry S. Miller, Director
Carol Ewing Garber, President-Elect
Dave Hillery, Treasurer
James Pivarnik, Foundation President

The ACSM promotes and integrates scientific research, education, and practical applications of sports medicine and exercise science to maintain and enhance physical performance, fitness, health, and quality of life.
20000 Members
ISBN: 0-195913-1 -
Founded in: 1954

22080 American Council on Exercise
4851 Paramount Dr
San Diego, CA 92123

858-576-6500
888-825-3636; *Fax:* 858-576-6564
support@acefitness.org; www.acefitness.org
Social Media: Facebook, Twitter, LinkedIn, Google+, Pinterest, Youtube, R

Scott Goudeseune, President & CEO
Nancy Travanian, Chair
John Ellis, Vice Chair
Ariane Amiri, Treasurer
Michele Stanten, Secretary

A nonprofit organization committed to enriching quality of life through safe and effective physical activity. ACE protects all segments of society against ineffective fitness products, programs and trends through its ongoing public education, outreach and research. ACE further protects the public by setting certification and continuing education standards for fitness professionals.
Founded in: 1985

22081 American Cutting Horse Association
P.O. Box 2443
Brenham, TX 77834

979-836-3370; *Fax:* 979-251-9971
achacutting@yahoo.com; www.achacutting.org
Social Media: Facebook

Ryan Combs, Board Member
Jason Borchardt, President
David Wilson, Vice-President
Cary Sims, Treasurer
Trent Bell, Board Member

22082 American Fastpitch Association
2926 Calle Frontera
San Clemente, CA 92673

949-291-8783; *Fax:* 888-630-1320
info@afasoftball.com; www.afasoftball.com
Social Media: Instagram

Ron Gossmer, National Director
Clarence Davis, Fastpitch Director/UIC
Joey Markakis, Slow Pitch Director

Represents those individuals engaged in amateur softball.
250M Members
Founded in: 1980

22083 American Football Coaches Association
100 Legends Lane
Waco, TX 76706

254-754-9900; *Fax:* 254-754-7373
info@afca.com; www.afca.com

Grant Teaff, Executive Director
Gary Darnell, Associate Executive Director
Vince Thompson, Director of Media Relations
Adam Guess, Managing Director of Finance
Janet Robertson, Director of Conferences & Events
11,00 Members
Founded in: 1921

22084 American Greyhound Track Operators Association
Palm Beach Kennel Club
1111 North Congress Avenue
West Palm Beach, FL 33409

561-688-5799; *Fax:* 801-751-2404;
www.agtoa.com

Juan Fra, President
Dennis Bicsak, Office Coordinator
Sally Briggs, 1st VP
Michael Corbin, Treasurer
Harold Purnell, Counsel
Founded in: 1946

22085 American Hockey Coaches Association
7 Concord Street
Gloucester, MA 01930

781-245-4177; *Fax:* 781-245-2492
ahcahockey@comcast.net;
www.ahcahockey.com
Social Media: Facebook, Twitter, LinkedIn, YouTube, RSS

Joe Bertagna, Executive Director
Brian Riley, President
Kathy Bertagna, Membership Administrator
Bruce Delventhal, Treasurer
Brett Peterson, Past President

Maintains the highest possible standards in hockey and the hockey profession
Founded in: 1947

22086 American Orthopaedic Society for Sports Medicine
9400 W. Higgind Rd
Suite 300
Rosemont, IL 60018

847-292-4900
877-321-3500; *Fax:* 847-292-4905
aossm@aossm.org; www.sportsmed.org
Social Media: Facebook, Twitter

Susan Serpico, Executice Asst.
Charles A. Bush-Joseph MD, VP
Bruce Reider MD, Journal Editor
Irvin E Bomberger, Executive Director
Camille Petrick, Managing Director

A national organization of orthopaedic surgeons specializing in sports medicine, including national and international sports medicine leaders.
2000 Members
Founded in: 1972

22087 American Recreation Coalition
1225 G St. NW
Suite 650
Washington, DC 20005-3832

202-682-9530; *Fax:* 202-682-9529
bnasta@funoutdoors.com;
www.funoutdoors.com
Social Media: Facebook, Twitter

Derrick Crandall, President & CEO
Catherine Ahern, VP, Member Services
Melinda Meade, Director of Communications
Tom Georgevits, Dir. Of Partner Projects

A non-profit Washington based federation that provides a unified voice for recreation interests to conserve their full and active participation in government policy making on issues such as public land management. ARC works to build public-private partnerships to enhance and protect outdoor recreation opportunities and resources.
100+ Members
Founded in: 1979

22088 American Running Association
4405 East West Hwy
Suite 405
Bethesda, MD 20814

301-913-9517
800-776-2732; *Fax:* 301-913-9520;
www.americanrunning.org
Social Media: LinkedIn

David Watt, Executive Director
Maria Kolanowsk, Project Coordinator
Barb Baldwin, Project Consultant

A leading voice and center for information on sports' running medicine. The 'ARA Clinic' provides personal feedback from a select cadre of physicians and sports medicine personnel.
10000 Members
Founded in: 1968

22089 American Society of Golf Course Architects
125 N Executive Dr
Suite 302
Brookfield, WI 53005

262-786-5960; *Fax:* 262-786-5919
info@asgca.org; www.asgca.org
Social Media: Facebook, Twitter, LinkedIn

Rick Robbins, Immediate Past President
Lee Schmidt, President
Steve Smyers, Vice President
Greg Martin, Treasurer
John Sanford, Secretary

A non-profit organization comprised of leading golf course designers in North America. ASGCA is actively involved in many issues realted to the game of golf, including responsible environmental designs.
185 Members
Founded in: 1946

22090 American Spa and Health Resort
PO Box 585
Lake Forest, IL 60045
847-234-8851; *Fax:* 847-295-7790
Social Media: Facebook
Melanie Ruehle, Contact
Seeks to establish and maintain high standards of quality in US health spas.
Founded in: 1982

22091 American Volleyball Coaches Association
2365 Harrodsburg Road
Suite A325
Lexington, KY 40504
859-226-4315
866-544-2822; *Fax:* 859-226-4338
members@avca.org; www.avca.org
Social Media: Facebook, Twitter, YouTube, Pinterest
Kathy Deboer, Executive Director
Ross Brown, Assistant Executive Director
Anne Kordes, President
Kevin Hambly, President Elect
Kim Norman, NAIA Rep
To advance the development of the sport of volleyball by providing all coaches with educational programs, a forum for opinion exchange and recognition opportunities.
4900 Members
Founded in: 1981

22092 Aquatic Exercise Association
PO Box 1609
Nokomis, FL 34274-1609
941-486-8600
888-232-9283; *Fax:* 941-486-8820;
www.aeawave.com
Social Media: Facebook
Julie See, President/ Education Director
Angie Proctor, Executive Director
Dan Yeats, Event Operations Coordinator
Troy Nelson, Administrative Services Coordinator
Donna Blackmon, Operations Administrator
A not-for-profit educational organization dedicated to the growth and development of the aquatic fitness industry and the safety of the public served.
6,000 Members
Founded in: 1984
Mailing list available for rent: 85,000 names

22093 Archery Range and Retailers Organization
156 N Main St
Suite D
Oregon, WI 53575
608-835-9060
800-234-7499; *Fax:* 608-835-9360;
www.archeryretailers.com
Kent Colgrove, Secretary
Martin Stubstad, President
Ervin Wagner, Treasurer
Ron Pelkey, Director
Will Moulton, Vice President
A national organization of porfessional full time archery ranges and pro shops.
140 Members
Founded in: 1968

22094 Archery Trade Association
PO Box 70
New Ulm, MN 56073-0070
507-233-8130
866-266-2776; *Fax:* 507-233-8140
info@archerytrade.org; www.archerytrade.org
Social Media: Facebook, Twitter
Scoff Henrikson, President/CEO
Mark Copeland, Director of Marketing
Jeff Adee, Executive Asst. to the President
Peter Gussie, Communiactions coordinator
Benjamin Summers, Dir. Of finance & Operations
Formerly the Archery Manufacturers and Merchants Organization, provides the core funding and direction for two foundations critical to the future of archery and bowhunting.
Founded in: 1947

22095 Association for the Advancement of Applied Sports Psychology
8365 Keystone Crossing
Suite 107
Indianapolis, IN 46240
317-205-9225; *Fax:* 317-205-9481
info@appliedsportpsych.org;
www.appliedsportpsych.org
Social Media: Facebook, Twitter, YouTube
Robert Schinke, Ed.D., President
Brent Walker, Ph.D., President-Elect
Jonathan Metzler, Ph.D., CC-AAS, Past-President Elect
Rebecca Concepcion, Ph.D., Secretary-Treasurer
Kent Lindeman, CMP, Executive Director
Founded in: 1986

22096 Association of Diving Contractors International
5206 Fm 1960 Rd W
Suite 202
Houston, TX 77069
281-893-8388; *Fax:* 281-893-5118
rroberts@adc-int.org; www.adc-int.org
Social Media: Facebook, Twitter, LinkedIn
Phil Newsum, Executive Director
Claudio Castro, At Large Executive Committee Member
Robbie Mistretta, Treasurer
Jay Crofton, 1st VP
Craig Fortenbery, President
The Association of Diving Contractors International, Inc. was founded in 1968 by a small group of diving companies. Their goal was to create a non-profit organization to cultivate and promote the art and science of commercial diving, establish uniform safe standards for commercial divers, and encourage industry-wide observance of these standards.
500 Members
Founded in: 1968

22097 Association of Volleyball Professionals
2183 Fairview Road
Suite 222
Costa Mesa, CA 92627
949-646-4600
contact@avp.com; www.avp.com
Social Media: Facebook, Twitter, LinkedIn, Instagram, YouTube
Founded in: 1983

22098 Athletic Equipment Managers Association
207 E, Bodman
Bement, IL 61813
217-678-1004; *Fax:* 217-678-1005;
www.equipmentmanagers.org
Social Media: Facebook, Twitter, LinkedIn
Kelly Jones, Certification Steering Committee
Mike Royster, Executive Director
Matthew Althoff, Associate Executive Director
Dan Siermine, President
Meli Resendiz, VicePresident
The purpose of the AEMA is to promote, advance, and improve the Equipment Managers Profession in all of its many phases.
700 Members
Founded in: 1973
Mailing list available for rent

22099 Billiard and Bowling Institute of America
PO Box 6363
West Palm Beach, FL 33405
561-835-0077; *Fax:* 561-659-1824
bbia@billiardandbowling.org;
www.billiardandbowling.org
Jeff Mraz, President
Corey Dykstra, VP
Hank Boomershine, Secretary/ Treasurer/ Con. Chairman
Skip Nemecek, Director
Mike Judy, Director
A not-for-profit association formed to service the billiard and bowling industries. The BBIA network is uniquely structured to open channels of communication between manufacturers and distributors in order to assist and improve members' business operations. BBIA provides an innovative forum for billiard and bowling businesses to share ideas, gain information, gather feedback and explore the dynamics of the product pipeline between manufacturer and end user.
150 Members
Founded in: 1940

22100 Bowling Proprietors' Association of America
621 Six Flags Drive
Arlington, TX 76011
817-649-5105
800-343-1329; *Fax:* 817-633-2940
answer@bpaa.com; www.bpaamax.com
Vladmir Wapensky, Executive Director
Supports the Bowling Proprietors' Association of American Political Action Committee.
3.6M Members
Founded in: 1932

22101 College Swimming Coaches Association of America
1640 Maple
#803
Evanston, IL 60201
847-833-3478
r-groseth@northwestern.edu; www.cscaa.org/
Social Media: Twitter, LinkedIn, YouTube
Joel Shinofield, Executive Director
Bill Wadley, President
Maureen Travers, Secretary
Chuck Knoles, Treasurer
Bob Pearson, Sergeant-At-Arms
The oldest organization of college coaches in America; a professional organization of college swimming and diving coaches dedicated to serving and providing leadership for the advancement of the sport of swimming at the collegiate level.
Founded in: 1922

22102 Cross Country Ski Areas Association
P.O. Box 818
Woodstock, VT 05091
802-236-3021
reese@xcski.org; www.xcski.org
Social Media: Facebook, Twitter, Instagram
Reese Brown, President/Executive Director
A non-profit organization representing member ski service providers. The association's purpose is to promote the growth and improve the quality of cross country ski operations in North America.
350 Members
Founded in: 1977

22103 Disabled Sports USA
451 Hungerford Dr.
Suite 100
Rockville, MD 20850

301-217-0960; www.disabledsportsusa.org
Social Media: Facebook, Twitter, YouTube

Kirk Bauer, Executive Director

Providing opportunities to participate in sports, regardless of ability.
Founded in: 1967

22104 Football Writers Association of America (FWAA)
18652 Vista Del Sol Dr
Dallas, TX 75287-4021

972-713-6198
tigerfwaa@aol.com;
www.sportswriters.net/fwaa
Social Media: Twitter

Lee Barfknecht, President
Steve Richardson, Executive director
George Schroeder, Board of Director
Mark Anderson, 1st VP
David Jones, 2nd VP

Established to improve working conditions in college press boxes.
900 Members
Founded in: 1941
Mailing list available for rent: 800 names at $50 per M

22105 Golf Coaches Association of America
1225 West Main Street
Suite 110
Norman, OK 73069

405-329-4222
866-422-2669; *Fax:* 405-573-7888
info@collegiategolf.com;
www.collegiategolf.com
Social Media: Facebook, Twitter

Conrad Ray, President
Andrew Sapp, 1st Vice President
Ryan Klatt, Director of Operations
Gregg Grost, CEO
Todd Sattefield, Past President

Founded in: 1958

22106 Golf Superintendents Association of America
1421 Research Park Dr
Lawrence, KS 66049

785-841-2240
800-472-7878; *Fax:* 785-832-3643
mbrhelp@gcsaa.org; www.gcsaa.org
Social Media: Facebook, Twitter

J. Rhett Evans, CEO
Keith A. Ihms, Immediate Past President
William H. Maynard, Secretary /Treasurer
Peter J Grass, Vice President
John J. O'Keefe, President

Provides education programs in formal settings and at home through videotapes and correspondence courses. Administers professional certification programs, publishes magazines and multiple newsletters, conducts and supports research, provides scholarship opportunities, offers employment assistance and career development support, promotes the image of the golf course superintendent through cable TV program 'Par For The Course' and other vehicles. Provides leadership in governmental issues.
22000 Members
Founded in: 1926

22107 Harness Tracks of America
4640 E Sunrise Dr
Suite 200
Tucson, AZ 85718-4576

520-529-2525; *Fax:* 520-529-3235;
www.harnesstracks.com
Social Media: Facebook, Twitter

Paul J. Estok, Executive VP &General Counsel
Paul Fontaine, President
Hugh Mitchell, Chairman
Christopher Mcerlean, Treasurer
Jason Settlemoir, VP

Mission is to help members obtain their economic objectives by promoting live racing, enhancing and preserving the integrity and image of the sport, and providing information to members and the general public about the sport and the significant economic impact of the industry.
35 Members

22108 Ice Skating Institute
6000 Custer Rd
Bldg 9
Plano, TX 75023

972-735-8800; *Fax:* 972-735-8815
isi@skateisi.org; www.skateisi.org
Social Media: Facebook, Twitter, LinkedIn, Pinterest, Google+

Peter Martell, Executive Director
Elizabeth Kibat, Controller
Jeff Anderson, Administrative Service Manager
Sandey Carlsen, Membership Coordinator
Angela Tooley, Administrative Assistant

Industry trade association dedicated to providing leadership, education and services to the ice skating industry.
64500 Members
Founded in: 1959

22109 International Federation of American Football
79 Rateau Street
La Courneuve 93120

E-Mail: info@ifaf.org; www.ifaf.org
Social Media: Twitter, YouTube

Makato Keneuji, Senior Vice President
Scott Hallenbeck, Treasurer
Elesa Zehndorfer, Secretary
Founded in: 1896

22110 International Professional Rodeo Association
1412 S Agnew Ave
Oklahoma City, OK 73108

405-235-6540; *Fax:* 405-235-6577;
www.iprarodeo.com

Ronnie Williams, Chief Field Representative
Tom Schick, Chairman
Lindsay Whelchel, Membership/Receptionist
Dale Yerigan, General manager
Tammie Hiatt, IFR Tradshow Coordinator

Governing body for professional rodeo. 500 rodeos across USA and Canada, $5 million prize money per year, 5 million fans.
3500 Members
Founded in: 1960

22111 International Sports Heritage Association
PO Box 2384
Florence, OR 97439

541-991-7315; *Fax:* 541-997-3871
info@sportsheritage.org;
www.sportsheritage.org
Social Media: Facebook, Twitter

Karen Bednarski, Executive Director
Marjorie Snyder, President
Susan Wasser, First Vice President
Paula Homan, Second Vice President
Megan Gardner, Treasurer

The mission of ISHA is to educate, promote and support organizations and individuals engaged in the celebration of sports heritage.
140+ Members
Founded in: 1971

22112 Ladies Professional Golf Association
100 International Golf Dr
Daytona Beach, FL 32124-1092

386-274-6200; *Fax:* 386-274-1099;
www.lpga.com
Social Media: Facebook, Twitter, RSS, YouTube, Instagram, Pinte

Carolyn Bivens, CEO
Karen Durkin, EVP/Chief Marketing Officer
Christopher Higgs, Senior VP/COO
Ken Wooten, VP Finance
Micahael Whan, Commissioner

The LPGA is a non-profit organization involved in every facet of golf. In addition to staging the LPGA Tour, the LPGA is also committed to advancing women, youth and the sport of golf through expanding the programs of the LPGA Teaching and Club Professional Division, as well as increasing contributions of the organization and its tournaments to charity.
Founded in: 1959

22113 League of American Bicyclists
1612 K Street NW
Suite 1102
Washington, DC 20006-2850

202-822-1333; *Fax:* 202-822-1334
bikeleague@bikeleague.org;
www.bikeleague.org
Social Media: Facebook, Twitter, LinkedIn, Google+

Alex Doty, Executive Director
Bill Nesper, Deputy Director, Programs & Ops
Kevin Dekkinga, Member Services Coordinator
Lorna Green, Operations, Manager
Founded in: 1880, the League is the only national membership organization of bicyclists in the United States. The League works to promote and encourage bicycling for recreation and transportation, and to protect and defend the rights of bicyclists through advocacy and education.
Founded in: 1880

22114 Melbourne Greyhound Park
1100 N Wickham Rd
Melbourne, FL 32935

321-259-9800; *Fax:* 321-259-3437;
www.mgpark.com
Social Media: Facebook, Twitter, YouTube, RSS

James J O'Brien, General Manager

Trade association representing the interest of and providing services to greyhound racetrack owners and operators via government advocacy, information sharing, annual conference and trade shows.
35 Members
Founded in: 1971
Mailing list available for rent

22115 National Aeronautic Association
1 Reagan National Airport
Suite 202
Washington, DC 20001-6015

703-416-4888
800-644-9777; *Fax:* 703-416-4877
naa@naa.aero; www.naa-usa.org

Jonathan Gaffney, President
George Carneal, General Counsel
Walter J. Boyne, Chairman
Roy Kiefer, Treasurer
Elizabeth Matarese, Secretary

A non-profit association dedicated to the advancement of the art, sport and science of aviation in the United States. The official record-keeper for United States aviation.
3000 Members
Founded in: 1922

22116 National Amateur Baseball Association
PO Box 705
Bowie, MD 20718
410-721-4727; *Fax:* 410-721-4940
nabf1914@aol.com; www.nabf.com
Social Media: Facebook
Thomas Stout, Director
Derel J Topik, First VP
Glenn McNish, Second VP
Connie Brown, Third VP
Charles Blackburn Jr, Executive Director
The oldest continually operated national basesball organization in the country.
10M Members
Founded in: 1914

22117 National Archery Association (USA Archery)
4065 Sinton Road
Suite 110
Colorado Springs, CO 80907
719-866-4576; *Fax:* 719-632-4733;
www.usarchery.org
Social Media: Facebook, Twitter, YouTube, Instagram, Google+, P
Denise Parker, CEO
Sheri Rhodes, Chairman
Denise Parker, Chief Executive Officer
Amber Hildebrand, Accounting Assistant
Cindy Clark, Office/Finance Manager
Formed to develop and promote the sport of archery. Recognized by the US Olympic committee as the national governing body for the olympic sport of archery. The NAA selects and trains mens and womens archery teams to represent the US in international, pan american and olympic competitions.
8500 Members
Founded in: 1894

22118 National Association of Basketball Coaches
1111 Main St
Suite 1000
Kansas City, MO 64105-2136
816-878-6222; *Fax:* 816-878-6223;
www.nabc.com
Social Media: Facebook, Twitter
Paul Hewitt, 4th VP
Jeff Jones, 3rd VP
Ron Hunter, 2nd VP
Page Moir, 1st VP
Phil Martelli, President
Promotes the advancement and opportunities for coaches and teachers in the sport of basketball.
5000 Members
Founded in: 1927

22119 National Association of Collegiate Directors of Athletics
24651 Detroit Rd
Cleveland, OH 44145
440-892-4000; *Fax:* 440-892-4007;
www.nacda.com
Social Media: Facebook, Twitter
Erin Dengler, Manager-Communications
Ryan Virtue, Manager- Affiliate Associations
Jason Galaska, Asst. Executive Director
Bob Vecchione, Executive Director
Noreen Byrne, Business Manger
Professional association for college atheltics directors, assistants and conference administrators.
Provides educational opportunities and serves as a vehicle for networking and the exchange of information to others in the college sports profession.
1.5M Members
Founded in: 1965

22120 National Association of Collegiate Women Athletic Administrators
2024 Main Street
#1W
Kansas City, MO 64108
816-389-8200; *Fax:* 816-389-8220;
www.nacwaa.org
Social Media: Facebook, Twitter, LinkedIn, YouTube, Pinterest
Joan McDermott, President
Lynn Hickey, President Elect
Chris Plonsky, Past President
Erin McDermott, Treasurer
Lori Mazza, Secretary

22121 National Association of Professional Baseball Leagues
1325 Franklin Ave.
Suite 160
Garden City, NY 11530
727-822-6937; *Fax:* 727-821-5819
inquire@napw.com; www.napw.com
Social Media: Facebook, Twitter, LinkedIn, Pinteresr
Mike Moore, President
RJ Sparks, Promotional Director
Two hundred and seventy booths.
2.5M Members

22122 National Association of Sporting Goods Wholesalers
1 Parkview Plaza
Suite 123
Oakbrook Terrace, IL 60181
630-596-9006; *Fax:* 630-544-5055
info@nasgw.org; www.nasgw.org
Social Media: Facebook, Twitter, Flickr
Kenyon Gleason, President
Peter Brownell, Chairman
Brad Burney, Vice Chair & Director
Mike Halleron, Treasurer
Maurice Desmarais, President & Secretary
Serves as a liaison with other sporting goods associations. The NASGW is the organizer and sponsor of the industry's annual meeting/expo event.
400 Members
Founded in: 1953

22123 National Association of Sports Commissions
9916 Carver Rd.
Suite 100
Cincinnati, OH 45242
513-281-3888; *Fax:* 513-281-1765
info@SportsCommissions.org;
www.sportscommissions.org
Social Media: Facebook, Twitter, LinkedIn, Pinterest, YouTube, WordPress
Kevin Smith, CSEE, Chairman
Greg Ayers, CSEE, Vice Chairman/Chair-Elect
Ralph Morton, CSEE, Treasurer
Mike Anderson, CSEE, Secretary
Terry Hasseltine, CSEE, Immediate Past Chair
Founded in: 1992

22124 National Association of Sports Officials
2017 Lathrop Ave
Racine, WI 53405
262-632-5448
800-733-6100; *Fax:* 262-632-5460
naso@naso.org; www.referee.com
Social Media: Facebook, Twitter
Barry Mano, President
Marc Ratner, Chair
Anita Ortega, Vice Chair
Henry Zaborniak, Treasurer
Nonprofit 501(c)(3), educational association providing individual benefits such as training materials, liability and assault protection insurance and more to sports officials of all sports and every level.
16000 Members
Founded in: 1976

22125 National Association of Student Financial Aid Administrators
1101 Connecticut AvenueNW
Suite 1100
Washington, DC 20036-4303
202-785-0453; *Fax:* 202-785-1487;
www.nasfaa.org
Social Media: Facebook, Twitter, LinkedIn, YouTube, Google+
Eileen O'Leary, National Chair
Dan Mann, National Chair-Elect
Craig Munier, Past National Chair
Justin Draeger, President
Lori Vedder, Treasurer

22126 National Athletic Trainers Association
1620 Valwood Parkway
Suite 115
Carrollton, TX 75006
214-637-6282
860-437-5700; *Fax:* 214-637-2206
webmaster@nata.org; www.nata.org
Social Media: Facebook, Twitter, LinkedIn
Eve Becker-Doyle, Executive Director
Teresa Foster Welch, Assistant Executive Director
Karen Peterson, Manager Executive Operations
Ellen Satlof, Public Relations Manager
Cynthia Nadel, Marketing Coordinator
Association for professionals in athletic training.
28000 Members
Founded in: 1950

22127 National Athletics Trainers' Association
1620 Valwood Parkway
Suite 115
Carrollton, TX 75006
214-637-6282
860-437-5700; *Fax:* 214-637-2206;
www.nata.org
Social Media: Facebook, Twitter, LinkedIn
Jim Thornton, MS, ATC, CES, President
MaryBeth Horodyski, EdD, Vice President
Marjorie Albohm, Past President
Tim Weston, MEd, ATC, Board of Director, District 1
Michael Goldenberg, MS, ATC, Board of Director, District 2
35,00 Members
Founded in: 1950

22128 National Basketball Athletic Trainers Association
400 Colony Square
Suite 1750
Atlanta, GA 30361
404-892-8919; *Fax:* 404-892-8560
rmallernee@mallernee-branch.com;
www.nbata.com
Tom Badenour, Chairman
A satelite of the National Athletic Trainers Association. Members are athletic trainers in the NBA.
60 Members
Founded in: 1974

22129 National Bicycle Dealers Association
3176 Pullman St.
Suite 117
Costa Mesa, CA 92626

949-722-6909; *Fax:* 949-722-1747
info@nbda.com; www.nbda.com

Dan Thornton, Chairman
James Moore, President
Jim Carveth, First VP
Jeff Koenig, Second VP
Chris Kegel, Secretary

The mission of the NBDA is to inspire and serve the specialty bicycle retailer through communicating the value and needs of the specialty bicycle retailer, enhancing the specialty bicycle retailer's profitability, and promoting the passion for cycling. The NBDA is a non-profit association promoting the interests of every specialty bicycle retailer in the United States.
2M Members
Founded in: 1946

22130 National Collegiate Athletic Association
700 W. Washington Street
P.O. Box 6222
Indianapolis, IN 46206-6222

317-917-6222; *Fax:* 317-917-6888;
www.ncaa.org
Social Media: Facebook, Twitter, YouTube, Instagram

Mark Emmert, President

22131 National Cutting Horse Association
260 Bailey Avenue
Fort Worth, TX 76107

817-244-6188; *Fax:* 817-244-2015
info@nchacutting.com; www.nchacutting.com
Social Media: Facebook, Twitter, RSS

Keith Deaville, President
Ernie Beutenmiller, VP
Jeff Hooper, Executive Director

Members are individuals and organizations interested in the development of superior horses and the refinement of the cutting horse competition.
20500 Members
Founded in: 1946

22132 National Fastpitch Coaches Association
2641 Grinstead Drive
Louisville, KY 40206

502-409-4600; *Fax:* 502-409-4622
nfca@nfca.org; www.nfca.org
Social Media: Facebook, Twitter, LinkedIn

Rhonda Revelle, President
Kathryn Gleason, First VP
Kate Drohan, Second VP

The professional growth organization for fastpitch softball coaches from all competitives levels of play.
4100 Members
Founded in: 1983

22133 National Golf Cart Manufacturers Association
NGCMA Attn: Fred Somers, Jr.
2 Ravinia Drive
Suite 1200
Atlanta, GA 30346

770-394-7200; *Fax:* 770-454-0138
membership@ngcma.org; www.ngcma.org

Fred L Somers, Jr, Secretary & General Counsel

Non-profit national trade association comprised of the leading golf car and personal transport vehicle manufacturers. NGCMA sponsors the development and maintenance of ANSI sanctioned standards to establish safety specifications for the design and operation of golf cars and PTVs driven by electric motors and internal combustion engines for golf cars.
Founded in: 1984

22134 National Golf Foundation
501 N Highway A1A
Suite 401
Jupiter, FL 33477-4577

561-744-6006
888-275-4643; *Fax:* 561-744-6107
general@ngf.org; www.ngf.org
Social Media: Facebook, Twitter, LinkedIn

Joseph Beditz, President/CEO
Greg Nathan, Sr. Vice President/ Membership

The National Golf Foundation, founded in 1936 and based in Jupiter, Fla., is the industry's knowledge leader on the U.S. golf economy and leading provider of golf industry databases. NGF delivers independent and objective narket intelligence, insights and trends to fulfill its mission: To Keep Golf Businesses Ahead of the Game.
4000 Members
Founded in: 1936

22135 National High School Baseball Coaches Association
PO Box 12843
Tempe, AZ 85284

602-615-0571; *Fax:* 480-838-7133
rdavini@cox.net; www.baseballcoaches.org

Ron Davini, Executive Director

Provides services and recognition for baseball coaches and to help promote and represent high school baseball across this country.
1600 Members
Founded in: 1991

22136 National Hockey League
1185 Avenue of the Americas
Floor 15
New York, NY 10036

212-789-2000; *Fax:* 212-789-2020;
www.nhl.com
Social Media: Facebook, Twitter, LinkedIn

Gary Bettman, Commissioner
William Daly, Deputy Commissioner
John Collins, COO

The NHL is one of the four major professional sports associations in North America, with 30 professional ice hockey franchises in the US and Canada.

22137 National Junior College Athletic Association
1631 Mesa Ave
Suite B
Colorado Springs, CO 80906

719-590-9788; *Fax:* 719-590-7324
meleicht@njcaa.org; www.njcaa.org
Social Media: Facebook, Twitter, Pinterest

Mary Ellen Leicht, Executive Director
Mark Krug, Ass. Executive Director
Bryce Roderick, President

The purpose of the NJCAA is to promote and foster junior college athletics on intersectional and national levels so that results will be consistent with the total educational program of its members.
525 Members
Founded in: 1938

22138 National Pro Fastpitch
3350 Hobson Pike
Hermitage, TN 37076

615-232-2900; *Fax:* 615-232-8880
info@profastpitch.com; www.profastpitch.com
Social Media: Facebook, Twitter, YouTube, Instagram

Cheri Kempf, Commissioner
Gaye Lynn Wilson, Vice President
Ed Whipple, Supervisor of Officials
Cynthia Gerken, NPF Travel Agent
Nikki Worthman, NPF Intern

22139 National Recreation and Park Association
22377 Belmont Ridge Road
Ashburn, VA 20148-4501

703-858-0784
800-626-6772; *Fax:* 703-858-0794
info@nrpa.org; www.nrpa.org
Social Media: Facebook, Twitter, LinkedIn, YouTube, Pinterest

Jodie H Adams, President
John Crosby, Marketing
Jessica Lytle, Director

Advancing parks, recreation and environmental conservation efforts that enhance the quality of life for all people.
Founded in: 1965

22140 National Rifle Association of America
11250 Waples Mill Rd
Fairfax, VA 22030-7400

703-267-1400; *Fax:* 703-267-3970
membership@nrahq.org; www.home.nra.org
Social Media: Facebook, Twitter

Oldest sportsmen's organization in the US. Maintains the NRA Political Victory Fund and supports the Institute for Legislative Action. Has an annual budget over $140 million.
4 Members
Founded in: 1871

22141 National Soccer Coaches Association of America
30 W. Pershing Rd.
Suite 350
Kansas City, MO 64108

816-471-1941; *Fax:* 816-474-7408
info@nscaa.com; www.nscaa.com

George Perry, President
Mike Jacobs, VP, Events
Amanda Vandervort, VP, Marketing
Charlie Slagle, VP, Education
Lesle Gallimore, VP, Membership
Founded in: 1941

22142 National Sporting Goods Association
1601 Feehanville Dr
Suite 300
Mt Prospect, IL 60056

847-296-6742
800-815-5422; *Fax:* 847-391-9827
info@nsga.org; www.nsga.org
Social Media: Facebook, Twitter, LinkedIn, Flickr, YouTube

Ken Meehan, Chairman
Randy Nill, Treasurer/Chairman Elect
Matt Carlson, President

Association of retailers, manufacturers and suppliers of sports equipment, footwear, and apparel.
2000+ Members
Founded in: 1929

22143 National Strength and Conditioning Association
1885 Bob Johnson Dr.
Colorado Springs, CO 80906

719-632-6722
800-815-6826; *Fax:* 719-632-6367;
www.nsca.com

Steven J. Fleck, PhD, President
Todd Miller, PhD, Vice President

Colin Wilborn, PhD, Treasurer-Secretary
Michael Embree, Executive Director
Levi Boren, PhD, Sr. Director of Certification
Founded in: 1978

22144 National Youth Sports Coaches Association
2050 Vista Parkway
West Palm Beach, FL 33411
636-797-5334
800-688-5437; *Fax:* 561-684-2546
nysca@nays.org; www.nays.org
Social Media: Facebook, Twitter, LinkedIn, YouTube, RSS, Pinterest, Googl
Represents coaches involved in youth athletics.
Founded in: 1981

22145 Pop Warner Little Scholars
586 Middletown Boulevard
Suite C-100
Langhorne, PA 19047-1867
215-752-2691; *Fax:* 215-752-2879
webmaster@popwarner.com; www.popwarner.com
Social Media: Facebook, Twitter, LinkedIn, YouTube, Rss
Jon Butler, Executive Director
Mary Fitzgerald, COO
Lisa Moroski, National Cheer/Dance Commissioner
A national youth football and cheerleading organization that provides assistance to its various chapters.
400M Members
Founded in: 1929

22146 Professional Association of Diving
30151 Tomas
Rcho Sta Marg, CA 92688-2125
949-858-7234
800-729-7234; *Fax:* 949-267-1267
webmaster@padi.com; www.padi.com
Social Media: Facebook, Twitter, YouTube
Brian Cronin, CEO
Certifies scuba diving instructors. Provides education/training materials and retail support to its members.
67M Members
Founded in: 1966

22147 Professional Association of Volleyball Officials
PO Box 780
Oxford, KS 67119
888-791-2074; *Fax:* 620-455-3800
pavo@pavo.org; www.pavo.org
Julie Voeck, President
Joan Powell, President
Crystal Lewis, Board Delegate
Ben Jordan, Director Examinations
Karen Gee, Director Finance
The Professional Association of Volleyball Officials is dedicated to improving the quality of volleyball officiating for all rules codes and skill levels. PAVO strives to increase the number of competent officials through education and mentoring and promotes involvement in the governing bodies of other volleyball officiating groups.
2M Members

22148 Professional Baseball Athletic Trainers Society
1201 Peachtree St Ne
Suite 1750
Atlanta, GA 30361-6320
404-875-7990; *Fax:* 410-730-2219; www.pbats.com
Social Media: Facebook, Twitter, RSS
Jamie Reed, President
Jim Carroll, Director Public Relations
Serve as an educational resource for the Major League and Minor League baseball athletic trainers. Serves its members by providing for the continued education of the athletic trainer as it relates to the profession, helping improve his understanding of sports medicine so as to better promote the health of his constituency - professional baseball players.
60 Members
Founded in: 1983

22149 Professional Bowlers Association
615 Second Ave
Seattle, WA 98104
206-332-9688; *Fax:* 206-332-9722
info@pba.com; www.pba.com
Social Media: Facebook, Twitter, Youtube, RSS
Fred Schreyer, CEO
Steve Miller, Board Member
Lisa Gil, VP Brand Communications
Acts on behalf of professional bowlers.
3800 Members
Founded in: 1958

22150 Professional Football Athletic Trainer Society
1201 Peachtree St Ne
Suite 1750
Atlanta, GA 30361-6320
404-875-7990; *Fax:* 404-892-8560; www.pfats.com
Social Media: Facebook, Twitter, Youtube, RSS
Rollin E Mallernee II, President
Professional association whose members are the athletic trainers of the NFL. They provide, lead and manage helathcare for the NFL athletes, club employees and members of the NFL community. Dedicated to insuring the highest quality health care is practiced. Guided by the profesional integrity and ethical standards of its members and by the unity they share.
650 Members
Founded in: 1982

22151 Professional Golfers Association (PGA)
100 Ave of the Champions
Palm Beach Gdns, FL 33418
561-624-8400; *Fax:* 561-624-8448; www.pga.com
Social Media: Facebook, Twitter, Google+
Ted Bishop, President
Derek Sprague, Vice President
Paul Levy, Secretary
Peter Bevacqua, CEO
The world's largest working sports organization comprised of more than 25,000 men and women PGA professionals to promote the game of golf to everyone, and to promote its members as leaders in the golf industry.
28000 Members
Founded in: 1916

22152 Professional Inline Hockey Association
1733 East Harrisburg Pike
Middletown, PA 17057
719-200-4208
info@thepiha.com; www.thepiha.com
Charles Yoder, Founder
CJ Yoder, President
Jami Yoder, VP
Jim Vanhorn, Chief Financial Officer
Denis Jelcic, Commissioner

22153 Professional Skaters Association
3006 Allegro Park Ln Sw
Rochester, MN 55902
507-281-5122; *Fax:* 507-281-5491
office@skatepsa.com; www.skatepsa.com
Social Media: Facebook, Twitter, LinkedIn, Pinterest, YouTube
Jimmie Santee, Executive Director
Kelley Morris, First VP
Jackie Brenner, Third VP
Donna Wells, Administrative Assistant
Barb Yackel, Marketing & Events
An international organization responsible for the education of skating coaches. Membership is offered to coaches in every discipline and at all levels, as well as to performing professionals, judges, eligible skaters and friends or patrons of the sport of figure skating.
6000 Members
Founded in: 1938

22154 Roller Skating Association
6905 Corporate Dr
Indianapolis, IN 46278
317-347-2626; *Fax:* 317-347-2636
rsa@rollerskating.com; www.rollerskating.org
Social Media: Facebook, Twitter, LinkedIn, YouTube, Pinterest, Google+
Robert Bentley, President
Michael Jacques, VP
Brian Molony, Treasurer
Jim McMahon, Executive Director
A trade association representing skating center owners and operators; teachers, coaches and judges of roller skating; and manufacturers and suppliers of roller skating equipment.
1000 Members
Founded in: 1937

22155 SHAPE America
1900 Association Dr.
Reston, VA 20191
800-213-7193; *Fax:* 703-476-9527; www.shapeamerica.org
Social Media: Facebook, Twitter, Instagram, Pinterest
Steve Jefferies, President
E. Paul Roetert, Chief Executive Officer
The Society of Health and Physical Educators is a national membership organization for committed to youth fitness and excellence in physical education.
Founded in: 1885

22156 Society for American Baseball Research
555 N. Central Ave.
#416
Phoenix, AZ 85004
602-496-1460
800-969-7227; *Fax:* 602-595-5690
info@sabr.org; www.sabr.org
Social Media: Facebook, Twitter, Youtube
Vince Gennaro, President
Bill Nowlin, VP
Todd Lebowitz, Secretary
F X Flinn, Treasurer
Emily Hawks, Director

Foisters the study of baseball past and present and provides an outlet for educational, historical and research information about the game.
6700 Members
Founded in: 1971
Mailing list available for rent: 25000 names at $85 per M

22157 Sporting Arms and Ammunition Manufacturers Institute
11 Mile Hill Rd
Newtown, CT 06470-2359
203-426-4358; *Fax:* 203-426-3592;
www.saami.org
Steve Sanetti, President
Rick Patterson, Managing Director
SAAMI is an association of the nation's leading manufacturers of sporting firearms, ammunition, and components.
Founded in: 1926

22158 Sporting Goods Agents Association (SGAA)
PO Box 998
Morton Grove, IL 60053
847-296-3670; *Fax:* 847-827-0196
sgaa998@aol.com; www.sgaaonline.org
Social Media: LinkedIn
Skip Nipper, President
Lois Halinton, Chief Operating Officer
International trade association of independent and established sporting goods agents.
500 Members
Founded in: 1934

22159 Sporting Goods Manufacturers Association
8505 Fenton Street
Suite 211
Silver Spring, MD 20910
301-495-6321; *Fax:* 301-495-6322
info@sfia.org; www.sfia.org
Tom Cove, President & CEO
Chip Baldwin, CFO
Bill Sells, VP, Government Relations
Ron Rosenbaum, SVP, Marketing & Business Dev
Jan Ciambor, Office Manager
SGMA is the trade association of North American manufacturers, producers, and distributers of sports apparel, athletic footwear, fitness, and sporting goods equipment. SGMA represents and supports its members through programs and strategies for sports participation, market intelligence, and public policy.
1000 Members
Founded in: 1906

22160 Sports Turf Managers Association
805 New Hampshire St
Suite E
Lawrence, KS 66044
785-843-2549
800-323-3875; *Fax:* 785-843-2977;
www.stma.org
Social Media: Facebook, LinkedIn
Tom Cove, President
David Pinsonneault, President Elect
Rene Aspiron, VP
Allen Johnson, Secretary/Treasurer
Chip Baldwin, CFO
Grounds care for golf and athletic fields.
2500 Members
Founded in: 1981

22161 Sportsplex Operators and Developers
Westgate Station
PO Box 24263
Rochester, NY 14624-0263
585-426-2215; *Fax:* 585-247-3112
info@sportsplexoperators.com;
www.sportsplexoperators.com
John Fitzgerald, President
Diane Aselin, Executive VP
Don Aselin, Executive Director
Norm Rice, Canadian Vice President
Kelly Tharp, Secretary
SODA was formed to meet the needs of the private concerns, public agencies, and other organizations that own or maintain sports complex facilities.
300 Members
Founded in: 1981

22162 Tennis Industry Association
117 Executive Center
1 Corpus Christie Place
Hilton Head Island, SC 29928
843-686-3036; *Fax:* 843-686-3078
info@tennisindustry.org;
www.tennisindustry.org
Social Media: Facebook, Twitter, LinkedIn, YouTube, Google+, RSS, Pintere
Jon Muir, President
Jolyn DeBoer, Executive Director
Brian O'Donnell, National Coordinator
To educate the marketplace, fund research and market intelligence and supply this reliable industry data to our member companies. The TIA is the Information source and clearing house for positive tennis news that we supply to TIA members, tennis publications and to the mainstream media in cooperation with the USTA.
800 Members
Founded in: 1974

22163 The College Golf Foundation
1225 West Main Street
Suite 110
Norman, OK 73069
405-329-4222; *Fax:* 405-573-7888
info@collegiategolf.com;
www.collegiategolf.com
Social Media: Facebook, Twitter
Conrad Ray, President
Andrew Sapp, 1st Vice President
Greg Sands, 2nd Vice President
Mark Crabtree, 3rd Vice President
Todd Sattefield, Past President
Founded in: 1958

22164 The United States Association of Blind Athletes
1 Olympic Plaza
Colorado Springs, CO 80909
719-866-3224; *Fax:* 719-866-3400;
www.usaba.org
Social Media: Facebook, Twitter
Dave Bushland, President
Tracie Foster, Vice President
Gary Remensnyyder, Treasurer
Trishca Zorn-Hudson, Secretary
Mark A. Lucas, MS, Executive Director

22165 U.S. Track & Field and Cross Country Coaches Association
1100 Poydras Street
Suite 1750
New Orleans, LA 70163
504-599-8900; *Fax:* 504-599-8909
sam@ustfccca.org; www.ustfccca.org
Social Media: Twitter, RSS
Sam Seemes, CEO
Damon Martin, President
Sandra Ford-Centonze, Secretary
Larry Cole, Treasurer
Dave Svoboda, Director of Operations
A non-profit professional organization that represents men's and women's cross country and track & field coaches in the United States.
8000 Members

22166 U.S. Track & Field and Cross Country Coach es Association
1100 Poydras Street
Suite 1750
New Orleans, LA 70163
504-599-8900; *Fax:* 504-599-8909;
www.ustfccca.org
Social Media: Facebook, RSS
Damon Martin, President
Larry Cole, Treasurer
Sandra Ford-Centonze, Secretary
Sam Seemes, Chief Executive Officer
Dave Svoboda, Director of Operations
8,000 Members

22167 US Field Hockey Association
1 Olympic Plaza
Colorado Springs, CO 80909
719-866-4567; *Fax:* 719-632-0979
usfha@usfieldhockey.com;
www.usfieldhockey.com
Social Media: Facebook, Twitter, LinkedIn, YouTube, Pinterest, Google+
Steve Looke, Executive Director
Simon Hoskins, Marketing Director
Represents field hockey, professional and amateur sports.
14000 Members
Founded in: 1928

22168 US Handball Association
2333 N Tucson Blvd
Tucson, AZ 85716
520-795-0434
800-289-8742; *Fax:* 520-795-0465
handball@ushandball.org; www.ushandball.org
Social Media: Facebook, Twitter, Vimeo
Mike Steele, President
LeaAnn Martin, VP
Tom Sove, VP
Mike Driscoll, Treasurer - Southwest Region
Vern Roberts, Executive Director
Organization that runs all the tournaments for the professional and amateur players. Home of the Handball Hall of Fame.

22169 US Lacrosse
113 W University Pkwy
Baltimore, MD 21210
410-235-6882; *Fax:* 410-366-6735
info@uslacrosse.org; www.uslacrosse.org
Social Media: Facebook, Twitter, Youtube, Google+, Instagram
Steve Stenersen, President & CEO
Bill Schoonmaker, VP, Strategy & Business Development
Cara Morris, VP, Finance & Administration
Ann Kitt Carpenetti, VP, Lacrosse Operations
Mark Hogan, VP, Brand Marketing & Membership
The national governing body of men's and women's lacrosse. Through responsive and effective leadership, the organization provides programs and services to inspire participation while protecting the integrity of the sport. Known as the resource center for the sport, US Lacrosse is devoted to growing the game responsibly, providing programs and services to develop the game nationally, publishing Lacrosse Magazine & LaxMagazine.com, hosting events, and preserving the history of the game.
300M Members
Founded in: 1998

22170 US Olympic Committee
One Olympic Plaza
Colorado Springs, CO 80909
719-632-5551
888-222-2313; *Fax:* 719-632-0250;
www.teamusa.org
Social Media: Facebook, Twitter, Youtube, Instagram
Scott Blackmun, Chief Executive Officer
Lawrence Probst, Chairman
Morane Kerek, Chief Financial Officer
Lisa Baird, Chief Marketing Officer
Larry Buendorf, Chief Security Officer
The national committee for the US handles the preparation of the US Olympic, Paralympic and Pan American Games teams.
Founded in: 1978

22171 US Professional Tennis Association
3535 Briarpark Drive
Suite One
Houston, TX 77042
713-978-7782
800-877-8248; *Fax:* 713-978-7780
uspta@uspta.com; www.uspta.com
Social Media: Facebook, Twitter, LinkedIn, YouTube, Pinterest, Google+, I
John Embree, CEO
Fred Viancos, Director of Professional Dev.
Kathy Buchanan, Director of Computer Services
Julie Myers, Director of Creative Services
Ellen Weatherford, Controller
A nonprofit association for professional tennis teachers.
14000 Members
Founded in: 1927

22172 US Raquetball Association
AARA National Office
1685 W Uintah Street
Ste. 103
Colorado Springs, CO 80904-2906
719-635-5396; *Fax:* 719-635-0685
sczarnecki@usra.org; www.usra.org
Social Media: Facebook, Twitter, YouTube, Instagram
Larry Haemmerle, President
Jason Thoerner, VP
Steve Czarnecki, Executive Director
Peggine Tellez, Manager, Sport Development
Myles Hayes, Coordinator, Membership Services
A nonprofit corporation designed to promote the development of competitive and recreational racquetball in the United States. The association offers a 'competitive license' membership for a one year term at $30.00 annually. A lifetime membership is also offered.
40M Members
Frequency: 6 Per Year
Circulation: 25,000
Founded in: 1968
Mailing list available for rent

22173 US Ski & Snowboard Association
1 Victory Lane
PO Box 100
Park City, UT 84060
435-649-9090; *Fax:* 435-649-3613
info@ussa.org
usskiteam.com
Social Media: Facebook, Twitter, YouTube, Instagram
Tiger Shaw, President/CEO
Calum Clark, Vice President, Events
Luke Bodensteiner, EVP, Athletics
Brooke McAffee, VP/CFO
Michael Jaquet, VP, Chief Marketing Officer
The national governing body for Olympic skiing and snowboarding.
30000 Members
Founded in: 1904

22174 US Soccer Federation
1801 S Prairie Ave
Chicago, IL 60616
312-808-1300; *Fax:* 312-808-1301
centercircle@ussoccer.org; www.ussoccer.com
Social Media: Facebook, Twitter, YouTube, Google+, Instgram, Vi
Sunil K Gulati, President
Mike Edwards, EVP
Dan Flynn, CEO/Secretary General
The governing body of soccer in all its form in the United States. US Soccer has helped chart the course for the sport in the USA for 90 years.
Founded in: 1913

22175 US Speedskating
5662 Cougar Lane
Kearns, UT 84118
801-417-5360; *Fax:* 801-417-5361
tmorris@usspeedskating.org;
www.usspeedskating.org
Social Media: Facebook, Twitter, Youtube
Ted Morris, Executive Director
Dale Schoon, Director of Finance
Matt Whewell, Communications Director
Angela Bond, Membership Coordinator
Shane Domer, Sports Science Director
Devoted to speedskating and its participants on the national and international levels.
2000 Members
Founded in: 1966

22176 US Squash Racquet Association
555 Eighth Ave
Suite 1102
New York, NY 10018-4311
212-268-4090; *Fax:* 212-268-4091
membership@ussquash.com;
www.ussquash.org
Social Media: Facebook, Twitter, LinkedIn, Youtube, Flickr
John A Fry, Chair
David Keating, District Associations
F. Gilpin Lane, Athlete Representative
Michelle Quibell, Athlete Representative
Tim Wyant, Ex Officio
The USSRA is the national governing body for the sport of squash racquets in the United States. A nonprofit, service organization whose primary function is that of management and maintenance of all squash related activities for a growing membership- driven organization.
8000 Members
Founded in: 1907

22177 US Synchronized Swimming
132 E Washington Street
Suite 820
Indianapolis, IN 46204
317-237-5700; *Fax:* 317-237-5705
marketing@usasynchro.org;
www.usasynchro.org
Social Media: Facebook, Twitter, YouTube, Pinterest, Instagarm
Judy McGowan, President
Sheila McNabb, VP Competitive Operations
Krista Bessinger, VP, Education & Certification
Nancy Rosengard, VP, Marketing & Member Services
Britt Rooney, Treasurer
Dedicated to the promotion of synchronized swimming. Sanctions and governs all synchronized swimming in the US and selects and trains National and Olympic Teams to represent the US in international competitions.
6000 Members

22178 US Track and Field
132 East Washington Street,
Suite 800
Indianapolis, IN 46204
317-261-0500; *Fax:* 317-261-0481;
www.usatf.org
Social Media: Facebook, Twitter, You Tube
Max Siegel, CEO
Renee Washington, COO
Jill Geer, CPAO
Norman Wain, General Counsel
Carmen Triplet, Special Event Manager
The national governing body for track and field, long-distance running and race waling in the United States.
Founded in: 1878

22179 US Volleyball Association
Suite 700
Los Gatos, CA 95031
E-Mail: volleyballorg@hotmail.com;
www.volleyball.org
Promotes volleyball in the US trains the USA men's and women's teams promotes beach and grassroots volleyball in the United States.
140M Members
Founded in: 1928

22180 USA Basketball
5465 Mark Dabling Boulevard
Colorado Springs, CO 80918-3842
719-590-4800; *Fax:* 719-590-4811;
www.usab.com
Social Media: Facebook, Twitter, Google+, YouTube
Jerry Colangelo, Chairman
Chauncey Billups, Athlete Representative
Kim Bohuny, NBA Representative
Jim Carr, National Organizations Rep.
Bob Gardner, NFHS Representative
Founded in: 1934

22181 USA Deaf Sports Federation
PO Box 22011
Santa Fe, NM 87502
605-367-5760; *Fax:* 605-782-8441
support@usdeafsports.org;
www.usdeafsports.org
Social Media: Facebook, Twitter, RSS, YouTube
Jack C. Lamberton, President
Jeffrey L. Salit, Vice President
Mark Apodaca, Chief Financial Officer
Danny Lacey, Chief Development Officer
Brianne Burger, Secretary
Founded in: 1945

22182 USA Gymnastics
132 E Washington Street
Suite 700
Indianapolis, IN 46204
317-237-5050
800-345-4719; *Fax:* 317-237-5069
membership@usagym.org;
www.usa-gymnastics.org
Social Media: Facebook, Twitter, LinkedIn, YouTube, Instagram
Peter Vidmar, Chairman
Steve Penny, President
Paul Parilla, Vice Chair
Jim Morris, Treasurer
Gary Anderson, Secretary
The sole national governing body for the sport of gymnastics in the United States. USA Gymnastics creates, organizes and conducts clinics, training camps, team competitions and other aspects of athlete, coach and official selection and development.
13000 Members
Founded in: 1963

22183 USA Hockey
1775 Bob Johnson Dr
Colorado Spring, CO 80906-4090
719-576-8724; *Fax:* 719-538-1160
usah@usahockey.org; www.usahockey.com
Social Media: Facebook, Twitter, LinkedIn
Dave Ogrean, Executive Director
Mike Bertsch, Marketing & Communications
Kim Folsom, Executive Assistant
Rae Briggle, Member Services
Casey Jorgensen, General Counsel
Promotes the sport of hockey. USA Hockey is the national governing body for the sport of ice hockey in the US.
600K Members
Founded in: 1937

22184 USA Roller Sports
PO Box 6579
Lincoln, NE 68506
402-483-7551; *Fax:* 402-483-1465;
www.usarollersports.org
Social Media: Facebook, Twitter, You Tube
George Kolibaba, Chairman/President
David Adamy, VP
The national governing body for all amateur skating sports including artistic, roller, and speed skating.
15K Members
Founded in: 1937

22185 USA Swimming
One Olympic Plaza
Colorado Springs, CO 80909
719-866-4578; www.usaswimming.org
Chuck Wielgus, Executive Director
Pat Hogan, Club Development Managing Director
Mike Unger, Assistant Executive Director
Jim Harvey, Chief Financial Officer
Frank Busch, National Team Director
Devoted to the sport of swimming and its enjoyment nationwide. Governing body for the sport of swimming.
400,0 Members
Founded in: 1844

22186 USA Table Tennis
4065 Sinton Road
Suite 120
Colorado Springs, CO 80907
719-866-4583; *Fax:* 719-632-6071
admin@usatt.org; www.usatt.org
Social Media: Facebook, Twitter, LinkedIn, YouTube, Pinterest, Instagarm,
Gordon Kaye, CEO
Doru Gheorghe, COO/High Performance Director
Teresa Benavides, Financial Director
Andy Horn, Membership Director
Tiffany Oldland, Sanctioning & Ratings Manager
Dedicated to the promotion of the sport of table tennis and sponsors the US team. Membership dues are $40 per year for adults and $20 for those 17 years old and under.
9000+ Members
Founded in: 1933

22187 USA Track & Field
USA Track & Field
132 East Washington Street, Suite 8
Indianapolis, IN 46204
317-261-0500; *Fax:* 317-261-0481;
www.usatf.org
Max Siegel, CEO
Renee Washington, COO
Jill Geer, CPAO
Norman Wain, General Counsel
Carmen Triplet, Special Event Manager
Founded in: 1878

22188 USA Water Ski Association
1251 Holy Cow Rd
Polk City, FL 33868
863-324-4341; *Fax:* 863-325-8259
usawaterski@usawaterski.org;
www.usawaterski.org
The national governing body for organized water skiing in the United States. A member of the International Water Ski Federation (World Governing Body), the Pan American Sports Association and the United States Olympic Committee.
37500 Members
Founded in: 1939

22189 USA Weightlifting
1 Olympic Plz
Colorado Spring, CO 80909-5764
719-866-4508; *Fax:* 719-866-4741
usaw@usaweightlifting.org;
www.usaweightlifting.org
Michael Masik, CEO, General Secretary
Laurie Lopez, Director, Operations
Carissa Gump, Director, Corp. Services
Phil Andrews, Director, Events & Programs
USA Weightlifting is the National Governing Body (NGB) for the Olympic sport of weightlifting in the United States. USA weightlifting is a member of the United States Olympic Committee and a member of the International Weightlifting Federation. As the NGB, USA Weightlifting is responsible for conducting Olympic weightlifting programs throughout the country. The organization conducts a variety of programs that will ultimately develop Olympic, World Championship and Pan American Games' winners.
Cost: $20.00
4000 Members
Frequency: Quarterly
Circulation: 4500
Founded in: 1981

22190 United States Amateur Boxing
1 Olympic Plz
Colorado Spring, CO 80909
719-866-2300; *Fax:* 719-866-2132
media@usoc.org; www.usaboxing.org
Anthony Bartkowski, Executive Director
Betsy McCallister, Executive Assistant
Brian Lawrence, CFO
Lynette Smith, Director, Membership Services
The national governing body for Olympic-style boxing. It is responsible for the administration, development and promotion of Olympic-style boxing in the United State.
7000 Members
Founded in: 1981

22191 United States Bowling Congress
621 Six Flags Dr
Arlington, TX 76011
817-385-8200
800-514-2695; *Fax:* 817-385-8260;
www.bowl.com
Social Media: Facebook, Twitter, LinkedIn, You Tube
Andrew Cain, President
Frank Wilkinson, VP
Tamoria Adams, Director
Tim Payne, Chief Information Officer
Kevin Dornberger, Director, Team USA
Established in 2005 as the organization to serve amateur adult and youth bowlers of the United States. It resulted from the merger of the American Bowling Congress, Young American Bowling Alliance and USA Bowling. USBC is the national governing body for bowling as recognized by the United States Olympic Committee.
3 M Members
Founded in: 2005

22192 United States Canoe Association
509 S Bishop Ave
Secane, PA 19018
610-405-5008; www.uscanoe.com
Susan Williams, President
Joan Theiss, Insurance Coordinator

22193 United States Extreme Sports Association
6350 Lake Oconee Parkway
Suite 102-128
Greensboro, GA 30642
877-900-8737
info@usesa.org; www.usesa.org

22194 United States Fencing Association
1 Olympic Plz
Colorado Spring, CO 80909-5760
719-866-4444; *Fax:* 719-866-4645
info@usfencing.org; www.usfencing.org
Social Media: Facebook, Twitter, LinkedIn, You Tube
Donald Anthony Jr., Chairman
Sam Cheris, Treasurer
Nathan Anderson, Secretary
National Governing Body for the sport of fencing in the United States. Their mission is to develop fencers to achieve international success and to administer and promote the sport in the USA.
9M Members
Founded in: 1891

22195 United States Golf Association
PO Box 708
Far Hills, NJ 07931
908-234-2300; *Fax:* 908-234-9687
mediarelations@usga.org; www.usga.org
Social Media: Facebook, Twitter, LinkedIn, You Tube
Walter W Driver Jr, President
James E Reinhart, VP
David Fay, Executive Director
An association of member clubs and courses. Conducts the US Open and Women's Open Championships, the Walker and Curtis Cup matches and ten national amateur championships.
7.5M Members
Founded in: 1894

22196 United States Harness Writers Association
PO Box 1314
Mechanicsburg, PA 17055
717-766-3219; www.ushwa.org
Steve Wolf, President
Chris Tully, First VP
Tim Bojarski, Second VP
Judy Davis-Wilson, Treasurer
Jerry Connors, Secretary
Members are media members who cover the sport of harness racing.
300 Members
Founded in: 1947

22197 United States Parachute Association
5401 Southpoint Centre Boulevard
Fredricksburg, VA 22407
540-604-9740; *Fax:* 540-604-9741
uspa@uspa.org; www.uspa.org
Social Media: Facebook, Twitter, LinkedIn, YouTube, RSS
Jay Stokes, President
Randy Allison, Vice President

Sherry Butcher, Secretary
Lee Schlichtemeier, Treasurer
BJ Worth, Chairman

The USPA is a voluntary membership organization of individuals who enjoy and support the sport of skydiving. The purpose of USPA is three-fold: to promote safe skydiving through training, licensing, and instructor qualification programs; to ensure skydiving's rightful place on airports and in the airspace system; and to promote competition and record-setting programs.
33000 Members
Founded in: 1946

22198 United States Racquet Stringers
PO Box 3392
Duluth, GA 92084

760-536-1177; *Fax:* 760-536-1171
usra@racquettech.com; www.racquettech.com

David Bone, Executive Director
Dianne Pray, Membership Coordinator
Crawford Lindsey, Editor/Webmaster
Kristine Thom, Production Manager

Educates constituencies to better understand, service, perform with, and enjoy the technological wonders known as racquests, strings, balls, courts, shoes, and stringing machines.
7000 Members
Founded in: 1975

22199 United States Tennis Association
70 West Red Oak Lane
White Plains, NY 10604

914-696-7000; www.usta.com
Social Media: Facebook, Twitter, YouTube

Katrina Adams, Chairman, CEO & President
Andy Andrews, First Vice President
Tommy Ho, Vice President
Don Tisdel, Vice President
Patrick Galbraith, Secretary-Treasurer
Founded in: 1881

22200 United States Trotting Association
750 Michigan Ave
Columbus, OH 43215

614-224-2291
877-800-8782; *Fax:* 614-224-4575
stats@ustrotting.com; www.ustrotting.com
Social Media: Facebook, Twitter, LinkedIn, You Tube

Ivan L Axelrod, Chairman
E Phillip Langley, President
Russell C Williams, Vice Chair
Mike Tanner, VP
Richard Brandt Jr., Treasurer

The USTA licenses owners, trainers, drivers and officials; formulates the rules of racing; maintains and disseminates racing information and records; serves as the registry for the Standardbred breed; endeavors to ensure the integrity of harness racing; insists on the humane treatment of Standardbreds; and promotes the sport of harness racing and the Standardbred breed.
Founded in: 1939

22201 United States Water Fitness Association
P.O. Box 243279
Boynton Beach, FL 33424-3279

561-732-9908; *Fax:* 561-732-0950
info@uswfa.org; www.uswfa.com

John R Spannuth, President/CEO
Marion Frega, Assistant to President

Nonprofit educational organization that promotes aquatics throughout the US and other countries. Publishes the National Aquatics Newsletter, names the 100 top programs and aquatics in the country, by state and in 25+ categories. Conducts a wide variety of national aquatics certifications including Water Fitness Instructors (primary and masters), aquatic directors, coordinators of water fitness programs. Conducts annual international aquatics conference.
Founded in: 1988

22202 United States of America Cricket Association
8461 Lake Worth Road
Suite B-1-185
Lake Worth, FL 33467

561-839-1888
lbrulport@usaca.org; www.usaca.org
Social Media: Facebook, Twitter

Gladstone Dainty, President
Michael Gale, 1st Vice President
Rafey Syed, 2nd Vice President
John Thickett, Treasurer
Mascelles Bailey, Secretary

22203 Western Fairs Association
1776 Tribute Rd
Suite 210
Sacramento, CA 95815-4495

916-927-3100; *Fax:* 916-927-6397
stephenc@fairsnet.org; www.fairsnet.org

Stephen J Chambers, Executive Director
Jon Baker, VP
Carrie Wright, Marketing
Nichole Farley, Marketing
Lori Hanley, Communications Manager

A non-profit association with members throughout the Western United States and Canada that strives to promote industry standards. Membership includes access to conventions and trade shows, educational training programs as well as legislative advocacy support.
2000 Members
Founded in: 1922

22204 Women's Basketball Coaches Association
4646 Lawrenceville Hwy.
Lilburn, GA 30047

770-279-8027; *Fax:* 770-279-8473
membership@wbca.org; www.wbca.org
Social Media: Facebook, Twitter, RSS

Sue Semrau, President
Coquese Washington, VP
Charli Turner Thorne, Past President
Matthew Mitchell, Secretary
Danielle Donehew, Executive Director
Founded in: 1981

22205 Women's National Basketball Association
645 Fifth Avenue
New York, NY 10022

www.wnba.com
Social Media: Facebook, Twitter, YouTube, Instagram

22206 Women's Sports Foundation
Eisenhower Park
East Meadow, NY 11554

516-542-4700
800-227-3988; *Fax:* 516-542-4716
info@womenssportsfoundation.org; www.womenssportsfoundation.org
Social Media: Facebook, Twitter

Billie Jean King, Founder
Donna Lopiano, CEO
Allison Sawyer, Senior Communications Coordinator

Disseminates information as well as encourages girls and women in sports and physical activity. Organization offers free access to quarterly electronic newsletter, Women's Sports Experience, that provides general updates on the world of girls'and women's sports as well as the Foundation's work.
4000 Members
Circulation: 15000
Founded in: 1974

22207 YMCA of the USA
101 N Wacker Dr
Suite 1400
Chicago, IL 60606-1784

312-977-0031
800-872-9622; www.ymca.net
Social Media: Facebook

Neil Nicoll, CEO

Provides national and state branch divisions.
20.1M Members

22208 ational Federation of State High School Associations
PO BOX 690
Indianapolis, IN 46206

317-972-6900; *Fax:* 317-822-5700; www.nfhs.org
Social Media: Twitter

Tom Welter, President
Gary Musselman, President-Elect
Gary Ray, B.O.D., Section 2
Jerome Singleton, B.O.D., Section 3
Marty Hickman, B.O.D., Section 4
Founded in: 1920

Newsletters

22209 AAPSM Newsletter
American Academy of Podiatric Sports Medicine
109 Greenwich Dr
Walkersville, MD 21793-9121

352-620-8562
888-854-3338; *Fax:* 352-620-8765
info@aapsm.org; www.aapsm.org
Social Media: Facebook

Rita Yates, Executive Director
David M Davidson, Director

A quarterly newsletter published by the American Academy of Podiatric Sports Medicine.
12 Pages
Frequency: Quarterly
Circulation: 700
Founded in: 1970
Mailing list available for rent: 600 names at $125 per M

22210 ARC e-Newsletter
American Recreation Coalition
1225 New York Ave NW
Suite 450
Washington, DC 20005

202-682-9530; *Fax:* 202-682-9529
jmitchelle@funoutdoors.com; www.funoutdoors.com

Derrick Crandall, President
Catherine Ahern, VP
Julia Mitchell, Director of Partnership Programs

A monthly e-newsletter distributed via e-mail.
Frequency: Monthly, e-Newsletter
Circulation: Variable

22211 BCA Newsletter
National High School Baseball Coaches Association
PO Box 12843
Tempe, AZ 85284

602-615-0571; *Fax:* 480-838-7133
rdavini@cox.net; www.baseballcoaches.org

Ron Davini, Executive Director

22212 Behind the Seams
National Amateur Baseball Federation
PO Box 705
Bowie, MD 20715

301-625-5005; *Fax:* 301-352-0214
NABF1914@aol.com; www.nabf.com
Social Media: Facebook

J Patrick Eaken, Editor
Charles M Blackburn, Executive Director

The official newsletter of the National Amateur Baseball Federation. Sent to NABF league members.
Frequency: Quarterly
Founded in: 1914

22213 CSCAA Newsletter
College Swimming Coaches Association of America
1640 Maple
#803
Evanston, IL 60201

847-833-3478
r-groseth@northwestern.edu; wwww.csaa.org

Bob Groseth, Executive Director
George Kennedy, President

22214 Field Hockey News
US Field Hockey Association
1 Olympic Plaza
Colorado Springs, CO 80909

719-866-4567; *Fax:* 719-632-0979
usfha@usfieldhockey.com;
www.usfieldhockey.com
Social Media: Facebook, Twitter, LinkedIn, You Tube
Steve Looke, Executive Director
Simon Hoskins, Marketing Director
Frequency: Seasonally

22215 Hunting Report for Big Game Hunters
Oxpecker Enterprises
Ste 523
9200 S Dadeland Blvd
Miami, FL 33156-2713

305-670-1361
800-272-5656; *Fax:* 305-716-1376
Subscriptions@HuntingReport.com;
www.huntingreport.com
Social Media: Facebook, Twitter, LinkedIn

Don Causey, President/Publisher
Nick Titus, Production Manager

Provides information on hunting opportunities and conditions in the US, Africa and other parts of the world.
Cost: $60.00
Frequency: Monthly
ISSN: 1052-4746
Founded in: 1980

22216 Hunting Report: Birdshooters and Water
Oxpecker Enterprises
Ste 523
9200 S Dadeland Blvd
Miami, FL 33156-2713

305-670-1361; *Fax:* 954-370-1376
subscriptions@huntingreport.com;
www.huntingreport.com
Social Media: Facebook, Twitter, LinkedIn

Don Causey, Publisher

Serving the Sportsman who travels.
Cost: $45.00
14 Pages
Frequency: Monthly
Circulation: 1850
Founded in: 1983
Printed in 2 colors on matte stock

22217 InBrief
Sporting Goods Manufacturers Association
8505 Fenton Street
Silver Spring, MD 20910

301-495-6321; *Fax:* 301-495-6322
info@sgma.com; www.sgma.com

Tom Cove, President & CEO
Bill Sells, VP Government Relations
Chip Baldwin, CFO
Mike May, Director Communications

Newsletter with information about and for manufacturers in the sporting goods industry.
Frequency: Bi-weekly

22218 International Sports Heritage Association
PO Box 2384
Florence, OR 97439

541-991-7315; *Fax:* 541-997-3871
info@sportsheritage.org;
www.sportsheritage.org
Social Media: Facebook, Twitter

Karen Bednarski, Executive Director
Mike Gibbons, President
Rick Wells, First Vice President
Meg Snyder, Second Vice President
Ben Sopp, Treasurer

E-Newsletter
140+ Members
Frequency: Quarterly
Founded in: 1971

22219 Leader Board
Golf Course Superintendents Association of America
1421 Research Park Dr
Lawrence, KS 66049-3859

785-841-2240
800-472-7878; *Fax:* 785-832-4488
infobox@gcsaa.org; www.gcsaa.org
Social Media: Facebook, Twitter

Mark Woodward, CEO
Melissa Householder, Communications Coordinator
Ed Hiscock, Editor-In-Chief

Bi-monthly newsletter for golf facility decision makers, including superintendents and their employers, presenting timely and useful informaiton about golf course management in a quick easy-to-read format.
Frequency: Monthly
Circulation: 40000
Founded in: 1926

22220 Media Sports Business
Kagan Research
1 Lower Ragsdale Dr
Building One Suite 130
Monterey, CA 93940-5749

831-624-1536
800-307-2529; *Fax:* 831-625-3225
info@kagan.com; www.kagan.com

Tim Baskerville, President
Tom Johnson, Marketing Manager

Statistics of a different kind. How much media pay to carry sports events, the impact of media on pro sports franchises, and more. Scores big with major league and media players. Three month trial available.
Cost: $945.00
Frequency: Monthly
Founded in: 1969

22221 NASGW Newsletter
National Association of Sporting Goods Wholesalers
1833 Centre Point Circle
Suite 123
Naperville, IL 60563

630-596-9006; *Fax:* 630-544-5055
nasgw@nasgw.org; www.nasgw.org
Social Media: Facebook, LinkedIn
Maurice Desmarais, President
Jack Baumler, Chairman
Kent Williams, Vice Chair
Peter Brownell, Treasurer

Non-profit trade association of wholesalers, distributors and manufacturers. Serves as a liason with other sporting goods associations. The NASGW is the organizer and sponser of the industry's annual meeting/expo event.
400 Members
Founded in: 1953

22222 NSGA Sporting Goods Alert
National Sporting Goods Association
1601 Feehanville Dr
Suite 300
Mt Prospect, IL 60056-6035

847-296-6742; *Fax:* 847-391-9827
info@nsga.org; www.nsga.org

Jeff Rosenthal, Chairman of the Board
Matt Carlson, President/CEO
Dan Kasen, Director of Information Services

News and rule changes affecting team dealers. Newsletter is free to members.

22223 NSGA Team Line-Up
National Sporting Goods Association
1601 Feehanville Dr
Suite 300
Mt Prospect, IL 60056-6035

847-296-6742; *Fax:* 847-391-9827
info@nsga.org; www.nsga.org

Ken Meehan, Chairman of the Board
Matt Carlson, President/CEO
Dustin Dobrin, Director of Information Services

News and rule changes affecting team dealers. Newsletter is free to members.
Frequency: Weekly

22224 National High School Baseball Coaches Association
PO Box 12843
Tempe, AZ 85284

602-615-0571; *Fax:* 480-838-7133
rdavini@cox.net; www.baseballcoaches.org

Ron Davini, Executive Director

Association news, information, coaching articles.
Frequency: 2x/Year
Circulation: 1500+
Founded in: 1991

22225 Newsline
Golf Course Superintendents Association of America
1421 Research Park Dr
Lawrence, KS 66049-3859

785-841-2240
800-472-7878; *Fax:* 785-832-4488
infobox@gcsaa.org; www.gcsaa.org
Social Media: Facebook

Mark Woodward, CEO

Membership newsletter highlighting programs and services, and featuring news about the association, its members, the golf course management profession and industry.
Founded in: 1926

22226 Parachutist
United States Parachute Association

5401 Southpoint Centre Boulevard
Fredricksburg, VA 22407

540-604-9740; *Fax:* 540-604-9740
uspa@uspa.org; www.uspa.org
Social Media: Facebook, Twitter, LinkedIn, YouTube, RSS

Elijah Florio, Editor in Chief
Laura Sharp, Managing Editor
Guilherme Cunha, Advertising Manager, Web Developer
David Cherry, Graphic Designer

The official newsletter of the USPA.
33000 Members
Founded in: 1946

22227 **Running & FitNews**
American Running Association
4405 East-West Highway
Suite 405
Bethesda, MD 20814

800-776-2732
800-776-2732; *Fax:* 301-913-9520
milerun@americanrunning.org; www.americanrunning.org
Social Media: Facebook, LinkedIn

David Watt, Executive Director
Barbara Baldwin, Projects Consultant
Jeff Venables, Editor
Jeff Harbison, President
Bill Young, Secretary/Treasurer

running, health and sports medicine e-newsletter.
Founded in: 1968

22228 **Sport Scene**
North American Youth Sport Institute
4985 Oak Garden Drive
PO Box 957
Kernersville, NC 27285

336-784-4926
800-767-4916; *Fax:* 336-784-5546
jack@naysi.com; www.naysi.com
Social Media: Facebook

Jack Hutslar, Publisher/Editor

News, features, tips, reviews, statistics, and summaries for people who work with tots, children and teens in fitness, recreation, education, sport and health with the focus on management, resources latest coaching and teaching methods, do's and dont's, safety, program ideas, legal issues, and training programs for leaders. Goal is to provide current information to improve learning while making activities more safe and positive so children can have more fun.
Cost: $ 16.00
Frequency: 6X/yr
ISBN: 0-270181-2 -
Founded in: 1979

22229 **Team Marketing Report**
Team Marketing Report
1653 North Wells St
Suite 2F
Chicago, IL 60614-3962

312-280-2311
847-256-2564; *Fax:* 312-280-2322;
www.teammarketing.com
Social Media: Facebook, Twitter, LinkedIn

Becky Vallett, Executive Editor
Dan Bulla, Editor-at-Large / Director of Sales

Information on rates, ticket prices, and consumer attitudes, new ideas to help increase sales and exposure through the sports market.
Cost: $195.00
Frequency: Monthly
Founded in: 1988

22230 **Winning Edge Newsletter**
1001 Diamond Ridge
Suite 800
Jefferson City, MO 65109

573-635-1660; *Fax:* 573-635-8233
hq@somo.org; www.somo.org
Social Media: Facebook, Twitter, LinkedIn, YouTube, RSS

Mark Musso, President
Mandi Steward Mueller, Public Relations Coordinator
Diannah White, Chief Communications Officer
Randy Bohem, Chair
Don Spear, Member

Publication produced for the athletes, volunteers and supports of the Special Olympics.
Frequency: Quarterly
Founded in: 1983

Magazines & Journals

22231 **ADDvantage**
US Professional Tennis Association
3535 Briarpark Drive
Suite 1
Houston, TX 77042-5245

713-978-7782
800-877-8248; *Fax:* 713-978-7780
uspta@uspta.org; www.uspta.com

Shawna Riley, Editor
Kim Forrester, Managing Editor

A monthly magazine published by the US Professional Tennis Association. Available through membership only.
36 Pages
Frequency: Monthly
Circulation: 13,000
Founded in: 1927
Printed in 4 colors on glossy stock

22232 **AKWA Magazine**
Aquatic Exercise Association
201 Tamiami Trail
PO Box 1609
Nokomis, FL 34274-1609

941-486-8600
888-232-9283; *Fax:* 941-486-8820;
www.aeawave.com

Angie Nelson, Executive Director
Julie See, President
Kim Huff, Director of Marketing

The aqautics fitness industry's leading magazine. Brings professionals the most up to date and innovative ideas in programming, management, safety and nutrition for group exercise and personal training in the pool. Available to AEA members with their $65.00 membership.
Circulation: 6000
Founded in: 1987
Mailing list available for rent: 90M names
Printed in 4 colors on glossy stock

22233 **American Firearms Industry**
AFI Communications
2400 E Las Olas Boulevard
#397
Fort Lauderdale, FL 33301

954-467-9994; *Fax:* 954-463-2501
webmaster@amfire.com; www.amfire.com
Social Media: Facebook, Twitter, LinkedIn

Andrew Molchan, Editor
Alexandra Molchan, Circulation Manager
Kathleen Molchan, Sales Manager

A business-to-business trade magazine containing articles and information centered on the retailing of firearms and shooting products. Areas covered are: handguns, revolvers, pistols, rifles, shotguns, ammunition, rifle scopes, reloading, holsters, hunting accessories, gun parts, cutlery, knives, archery, bows, crossbows, camping, camouflage, black powder, smokeless powder, binoculars, safes, gunlocks, air guns, used gun news and political news and views relatingto firearms and the industry.
Cost: $18.00
Frequency: Monthly
Circulation: 34
Founded in: 1973

22234 **American Fitness**
Aerobics and Fitness Association of America
15250 Ventura Blvd
Suite 200
Sherman Oaks, CA 91403-3297

818-905-0040
877-968-7263; *Fax:* 818-990-5468
contactafaa@afaa.com; www.afaa.com

Linda Pfeffer, President
Roscoe K Fawcett Jr, Publisher

The official publication of the Aerobics and Fitness Association of America. Known for reporting health-related fitness research, current trends, advances in equipment and training applications.
Cost: $27.00
Frequency: Bi-annually
Circulation: 100,000
Founded in: 1983

22235 **American Hunter**
National Rifle Association
11250 Waples Mill Rd
Fairfax, VA 22030-7400

703-267-1400
877-672-2000
americanhunter.org
Social Media: Facebook, Twitter, LinkedIn, YouTube, RSS

Mark A Keefe IV, Editor

American Hunter offers expertise on how and where to hunt all types of North American game and encourages readers to take advantage of the rich opportunities and to pass along the tradition to the next generation.

22236 **American Paddler**
American Canoe Association
7432 Alban Station Boulevard
Suite B-232
Springfield, VA 22150

703-451-0141; *Fax:* 703-451-2245
aca@americancanoe.org; www.acanet.org

Marty Bartels, Publisher

22237 **American Quarter Horse Journal**
American Quarter Horse Association
1600 Quarter Horse Drive
PO Box 200
Amarillo, TX 79104

806-764-4888; *Fax:* 806-349-6400;
www.aqha.com

Bill Brewer, Executive VP
Jim Jennings, Publisher

Industry magazine for Quarter Horse breeders, farm managers and owners.
Cost: $25.00
550 Pages
Frequency: Monthly
Circulation: 66575
Founded in: 1948
Printed in 4 colors on glossy stock

22238 **American Rifleman**
National Rifle Association

11250 Waples Mill Rd
Fairfax, VA 22030-7400

703-267-1400
800-672-3888; *Fax:* 703-267-3971
publications@nrahq.org;
www.nrapublications.org
Social Media: Facebook, Twitter, LinkedIn, YouTube, RSS

Mark Keefe IV, Editor-In-Chief

Premier magazine for shooting and firearms enthusiasts. Coverage is devoted to rifles, shotguns, handguns, ammunition, reloading, optics and shooting accessories.
Cost: $35.00
Frequency: Monthly
Circulation: 100000
Founded in: 1975

22239 Americas 1st Freedom
National Rifle Association
11250 Waples Mill Rd
Fairfax, VA 22030-7400

703-267-1400
877-672-2000; *Fax:* 703-267-3971
publications@nrahq.org;
www.nrapublications.org
Social Media: Facebook, Twitter, LinkedIn, YouTube, RSS

Mark Keefe IV, Editor-In-Chief

NRA's pure news magazine. Its mission is to deliver professional, compelling, accurate, timely and hard-hitting journalism that tells the truth about the threats to our Second Amendment rights. Subscription complementary with membership in NRA. Otherwise $9.95
Founded in: 1975

22240 Aquatic Therapy and Fitness Research
Aquatic Exercise Association
PO Box 1609
Nokomis, FL 34274-1609

941-486-8600
888-232-9283; *Fax:* 941-486-8820
info@aeawave.com; www.aeawave.com
Social Media: Facebook, Twitter, LinkedIn, YouTube, RSS

Angie Proctor, CEO
Julie See, President
Kim Huff, Director of Marketing

Journal. Peer-reviewed publication providing documentated opinions of industry leaders. A multidisciplinary publication, each issue includes two focus areas. Subscription included with AEA membership.
Cost: $65.00
Frequency: Monthly
Circulation: 6000
Founded in: 1984

22241 Aquatics International
Leisure Publications
6222 Wilshire Blvd.
Los Angeles, CA 90020-4244

323-644-4801
888-269-8410; *Fax:* 323-964-4842;
www.aquaticsintl.com
Social Media: Facebook, Twitter, LinkedIn, YouTube, RSS

Garry Carter, Sales Manager
Steve Honum, Account Executive
Theresa Wrong, Sales Manager

Articles of interest to colleges and schools; municipal, county and state pool facilities; hotels, resorts and country clubs; fitness clubs; rehab centers; YMCAs; military facilities; and waterparks.
Cost: $30.00
Frequency: 11X/Yr
Circulation: 30000
Mailing list available for rent

22242 Arabian Horse World
Arabian Horse World
624 South Main Street
Suite 201
Templeton, CA 93456

805-771-2300
800-955-9423; *Fax:* 805-927-6522
info@arabianhorseworld.com;
www.arabianhorseworld.com
Social Media: Facebook

Denise Hearst, Publisher
Mary Jane Parkinson, Editor
Kristin Youngberg, Managing Editor

Our philosophy at Arabian Horse World is to promote the Arabian - through education and entertainment - to new levels of appreciation and usefullness. Show results and breeding farms are featured.
Cost: $40.00
Frequency: Monthly
Circulation: 15000
Founded in: 1990
Printed in 4 colors on glossy stock

22243 Archery Business Magazine
Grand View Media Group
14505 21st Ave N
Suite 202
Plymouth, MN 55447

763-473-5800
800-766-0039; *Fax:* 763-473-5801
pbrady@affinitygroup.com;
www.bowhuntingworld.com
Social Media: Facebook

Steve Schiffman, Publisher
Mark Melotik, Editor
Patty Brady, Advertising
Steven Hedlund, President

Controlled circulation trade magazine covering the business side of bowhunting and archery: trade news, industry statistics, marketing and product trends, new product research and development, tips for better business management and effective training.
Frequency: Monthly
Circulation: 11000+
Founded in: 1975

22244 Arrow Trade Magazine
3479 409th Ave NW
Braham, MN 55006-3340

320-396-3473
888-796-2083; *Fax:* 320-396-3206
timdehn@arrowtrademag.com;
www.arrowtrademagazine.com
Social Media: Facebook, Twitter

Tim Dehn, Publisher
Matt Granger, Advertising
Rachel Givens, Subscriptions

A business magazine published for retailers, distributors, sales representatives and manufacturers of bowhunting equipment and camouflage clothing.
Founded in: 1997

22245 Athletic Management
MAG
2488 N Triphammer Road
Ithaca, NY 14850

607-257-6970; *Fax:* 607-257-7328
info@athleticbid.com;
www.momentummedia.com

Mark Goldberg, President
Eleanor Frankel, Editor

Free to college athletic administrators and high school athletic directors in the US and Canada. The editorial mission of Athletic Management is to help Athletic Directors enhance their operations, to share new ideas, and cover pertinent news topics. Feature stories and regular sections address the various facets of managing an athletic department.
Cost: $25.00
Frequency: Weekly
Circulation: 30200
Founded in: 1988
Printed in 4 colors on glossy stock

22246 Bass Times
ESPN

334-272-9530
customerservice@bassmaster.com
sports.espn.go.com/outdoors/bassmaster

Bass Times is packed with news and information for serious bass fishermen. The perfect compliment to Bassmaster Magazine.
Cost: $12.00
Frequency: Monthly

22247 Bassmaster
ESPN

334-272-9530
sports.espn.go.com/bassmaster
Social Media: Facebook, Twitter, LinkedIn, YouTube, RSS

Bassmaster Magazine monthly.
Frequency: Monthly

22248 Bicycle Friendly America Magazine
League of American Bicyclists
1612 K St NW
Suite 1102
Washington, DC 20006-2850

202-822-1333; *Fax:* 202-822-1334
bikeleague@bikeleague.org;
www.bikeleague.org
Social Media: Facebook, Twitter, LinkedIn, YouTube, RSS

Alex Doty, Executive Director
Karen Jenkins, Chair
Lorna Green, Operations Manager

Contains cycling stories; how-to articles; health; legal and safety columns; legislative updates, fitness, cycling technique and travel.
Frequency: Bi-Monthly
Circulation: 325000

22249 Black's Buyers Directory
PO Box 2029
Red Bank, NJ 07701
732-224-8700
800-224-9464; *Fax:* 732-741-2827;
www.fieldandstream.com
Social Media: Facebook, Twitter, LinkedIn, YouTube, RSS

James F Black Jr, Publisher
Lois Re, Editor
Christopher Pluck, Owner

The complete buyer's guide to equipment. A one-stop source of information on anything and everything that's archery/bowhunting.
Founded in: 2001

22250 Bowlers Journal International
Luby Publishing Company
122 S Michigan Ave
Suite 1506
Chicago, IL 60603-6148

312-341-1110; *Fax:* 312-341-1469
email@bowlersjournal.com;
www.lubypublishing.com

Keith Hamilton, President
Mason King, Editor
Emily Kupper, Circulation Director
Bob Nieman, Editor

Information geared toward all levels of industry personnel. Regular issue features include new products listings, tournament reviews, personal-

ity profiles and proprietor workshops.
Cost: $24.00
Frequency: Monthly
Circulation: 22319
Founded in: 1913

22251 **Bowling Center Management**
Bowling Proprietors Association of America
122 S Michigan Avenue
Suite 1506
Chicago, IL 60603-6107

312-341-1110; *Fax:* 312-341-1180
bowlctrman@aol.com; www.bcmmag.com
Social Media: Facebook, Twitter, LinkedIn

Mike Panozzo, Publisher
Bob Nieman, Editor
Emily Kupper, Circulation Director
Mason King, Editor

Information designed for bowling center owners to help them in the operation and management of their centers.
Cost: $60.00
Frequency: Monthly
Circulation: 5000
Founded in: 1995

22252 **By Design**
American Society of Golf Course Architects
125 N Executive Dr
Suite 302
Brookfield, WI 53005-6035

262-786-5960; *Fax:* 262-786-5919
info@asgca.org; www.asgca.org
Social Media: Facebook, Twitter

Chad Ritterbusch, Executive Director

E-Magazine highlighting the work of ASGCA golf course architects worldwide. Subscribe at no charge at www.asgca.org
185 Members
Frequency: Quarterly
Circulation: 6000
Founded in: 1946

22253 **Camping Magazine**
American Camp Association
5000 State Road 67 N
Martinsville, IN 46151-7902

765-342-8456
800-428-2267; *Fax:* 765-342-2065
pr@acacamps.org; www.acacamps.org
Social Media: Facebook, Twitter, LinkedIn

Peg Smith, CEO
Kim Bruno, Communication/Development Head
Terrie Nicodemus, Manager

The official publication of the American Camp Association. Experts in the camp field contribute informative articles and essays on current advances in camp management, staffing and human resources, programming, risk management, special populations and diversity, health and wellness, and more.
Cost: $24.95
Founded in: 1920
Mailing list available for rent

22254 **Coaching Management**
MAG
2488 N Triphammer Road
Ithaca, NY 14850-5220

607-257-6970; *Fax:* 607-257-7328
info@athleticbid.com;
www.momentummedia.com
Social Media: Facebook, Twitter, LinkedIn

Mark Goldberg, Publisher/CEO
Eleanor Frankel, Editor
Dave Dubin, Circulation Director

Information including team equipment, apparel, injury prevention, conditioning, as well as field, stadium and court maintenance and improvement. Primary feature articles cover a wide range of coaching tools and techniques.
Frequency: Bi-annually
Circulation: 20556
Founded in: 1988
Mailing list available for rent

22255 **Coaching Volleyball**
American Volleyball Coaches Association
2365 Harrodsburg Road
Suite A325
Lexington, KY 40504

859-226-4315
866-544-2822; *Fax:* 859-226-4338
members@avca.org; www.avca.org
Social Media: Facebook, Twitter, LinkedIn, YouTube, RSS

Leah DeBoer, Executive Director
Leah Brock, Communications Manager
Frequency: Bi-Monthly

22256 **Cross Country Skier**
PO Box 550
Cable, WI 54821

715-798-5500
800-827-0607; *Fax:* 715-798-3599
info@crosscountryskier.com;
www.crosscountryskier.com
Social Media: Facebook, Twitter, LinkedIn

Ron Bergin, Owner

The journal of nordic skiing - destinations, news, training and technique, waxing, competition, equipment and new products, and great features on all facets of the sport of cross country skiing.

22257 **Cutting Horse Chatter**
National Cutting Horse Association
260 Bailey Avenue
Fort Worth, TX 76107

817-244-6188; *Fax:* 817-244-2015;
www.nchacutting.com

Chubby Turner, President
Chris Benedict, VP
Jeff Hooper, Executive Director
Rick Ivey, Tresurer
Alan Gold, Director Marketing
Frequency: Monthly
Circulation: 20500

22258 **Deer & Deer Hunting**
F+W Media
38 E. 29th Street
New York, NY 10016

212-447-1400; *Fax:* 212-447-5231
contact_us@fwmedia.com;
www.fwpublications.com

Hugh McAloon, Publisher

Edited for serious, year-round whitetail hunting enthusiasts and focuses on hunting techniques, deer biology and behavior, deer management, habitat requirements, the natural history of deer, and hunting ethics. Contains how-to articles designed to help hunters be successful. Regular columns and departments include book reviews, Deer Browse (unusual observations by hunters), new products, an editor's column, letters from readers, Deer Behavior, Can You Outsmart This Deer? and Q&A.
Cost: $19.99
Circulation: 212500
Founded in: 1977
Mailing list available for rent

22259 **Fantasy Sports**
F+W Media
38 E. 29th Street
New York, NY 10016

212-447-1400; *Fax:* 212-447-5231
contact_us@fwmedia.com;
www.fwpublications.com

Tom Kessenich, Editor
David Nussbaum, Chair
Jim Ogle, Finance/Administration
Sara Domville, President
Phil Graham, VP

The essential manual for those who participate in Rotisserie and other fantasy sports leagues. Reports extensive statistics to help managers in making personnel moves. Also includes recommendations on who to draft or trade. The April and May issues focus on baseball. The August and September issues focus on football. An up-to-the-minute, online version is also available fo a small fee at www.fantasysportsmag.com
Cost: $9.97
132 Pages
Frequency: 4 Per Year
Circulation: 78,767
Founded in: 1989
Mailing list available for rent

22260 **Fastpitch Delivery**
National Fastpitch Coaches Association
2641 Grinstead Drive,
Suite D
Louisville, KY 42046

502-409-4600; *Fax:* 502-409-4622
nfca@nfca.org; www.nfca.org
Social Media: Facebook, Twitter, LinkedIn, YouTube, RSS

Lacy Lee Baker, Executive Director
Hildred Deese, Senior Director of Events
Frequency: Monthly
Founded in: 1982

22261 **Fishermen's News**
Philip's Publishing Group
2201 W Commodore Way
Seattle, WA 98199-1298

206-284-8285
800-258-8609; *Fax:* 206-284-0391
circulation@rhppublishing.com;
www.pacmar.com

Peter Philips, Publisher
Lisa Albers, Managing Editor
Bill Forslund, Advertising Manager
Maggie Cheung, Circulation Manager
Sharon Adjiri, Production Manager

In addition to important fisheries news, every month they bring readers important information and lessons on Safety, entertaining pieces about commercial fishing history, a commercial listing of fishing vessels and equipment in their classified section, updated information on seafood market trends and important notices about all the meetings and conferences occurring on the West Coast.
Cost: $21.00
Frequency: Monthly
Circulation: 14,933
Founded in: 1945
Printed in 4 colors on newsprint stock

22262 **Fishing Tackle Retailer**
ESPN Productions
3500 Blue Lake Drive
Birmingham, AL 35243

407-566-2277; *Fax:* 334-279-7148;
www.bassmaster.com
Social Media: Facebook, Twitter, LinkedIn, YouTube, RSS

Clem Dippel, Publisher
Scott Wall, Advertising Sales

Information to inform and instruct America's fishing tackle retailers, merchandisers, and distributors on merchandise and sales techniques

used to sell fishing tackle.
Cost: $4.00
Frequency: 11X/yr
Circulation: 17720
Founded in: 1980
Printed in 4 colors

22263 Funworld
Int'l Association of Amusement Parks & Attractions
1448 Duke St
Alexandria, VA 22314-3403

703-836-3677; *Fax:* 703-836-2824
alee@IAAPA.org; www.iaapa.org
Social Media: Facebook, Twitter, LinkedIn, YouTube

Charlie Bray, President/CEO
Susan Mosedale, Executive VP
Jan McCool, Executive
Roxanne Pope, Assistant to the President

Funworld Magazine is a service for IAAPA members and provides discussion and illustrative examinations of the amusement and attractions industry form members to stay current and connected. The magazine contains features that analyze various aspects of the amusement business including safety, thrill rides, financial issues, event coverage and profiles of member and non-member facilities from around the world.
Cost: $45.00
Circulation: 8,500
Founded in: 1917

22264 Golf Business
National Golf Course Owners Association
291 Seven Farms Dr
Suite 2
Daniel Island, SC 29492-8000

843-881-9956
800-933-4262; *Fax:* 843-856-3288
golfbusiness@ngcoa.org; www.ngcoa.org
Social Media: Facebook, Twitter, YouTube

Michael Hughes, CEO
Joe Rice, Publisher
Frank Santangelo, Manager

The official publication of the National Golf Course Owners Association. The editorial content is designed to promote the exchange of information and ideas among course owners and senior industry executives to improve the profitability of their operations. Golf Business is dedicated to serving the entire interest of the golf course operation.
Cost: $35.00
Frequency: Monthly
Circulation: 20000
Founded in: 1971
Printed in 4 colors on glossy stock

22265 Golf Course Management
Golf Course Superintendents Association of America
1421 Research Park Dr
Lawrence, KS 66049-3859

785-841-2240
800-472-7878; *Fax:* 785-832-4488;
www.gcsaa.org
Social Media: Facebook, Twitter

Mark Woodward, CEO
Scott Hollistor, Editor
Bunny Smith, Managing Editor
Mark Gabrick, Sr Manager Corp Sales/Marketing

Official monthly magazine of Golf Course Superintendents Association of America and golf course management industry's leading professional journal. Includes scientific, technical and practical management articles.
Cost: $60.00
Frequency: Monthly
Circulation: 40,000
Founded in: 1932

22266 Golf Course News
4012 Bridge Avenue
Cleveland, OH 44113

216-961-4130; *Fax:* 216-961-0364;
www.golfnewsmag.com

Kevin Gilbride, Publisher
John Walsh, Editor
Richard Foster, CEO
Chris Foster, President/COO
Doug Adams, Director Marketing

Focuses on course maintenance and management, new course openings, and awards and promotions. New products related to the industry and environment and government issues.
Cost: $45.00
Circulation: 30000

22267 Golf Inc Magazine
Cypress Manazines
250 Bei Marin Key Boulevard, #A
PO Box 1150
Novato, CA 94949-5727

415-382-2400
800-436-6149; *Fax:* 415-382-2416
mikeb@cypressmagazines.com;
www.golfincmagazine.com

Jack Crittenden, President
Kim Boalick, Advertising
Mindy Heral, Marketing
Jim Dunlap, Editor-in-Chief

Provides news, success stories and benchmark data for all aspects of the golf course industry - including development, operations, marketing, retail, turf, sales and driving range.
Cost: $65.00
Frequency: Monthly
Circulation: 15000

22268 Golf Range Times
Forecast Golf Group
P.O.Box 3106
Glen Allen, VA 23058-3106

804-379-5760; *Fax:* 804-378-5780
info@forecastgolf.com; www.forecastgolf.com

James E Turner, Publisher/Editor
Betty Jo Bass, Advertising Manager

Information on Golf Range industry changes and closings, new ranges, and development information and services.
Cost: $49.95
Frequency: Monthly
Circulation: 6000
Founded in: 1990

22269 Golfdom
Questex Medica Group
PO Bo 5057
Brentwood, TN 37024
615-377-3322
866-344-1315; *Fax:* 615-377-3322
questex@sunbeltfs.com; www.golfdom.com

Patrick Jones, Publisher
Larry Aylward, Editor

Publication is written for golf course architects, superintendents, management companies, owners, developers, consultants and others in the industry with an interest in golf course design, construction, remodeling and related business and management topics. Subscription is free to Golf course superintendents, owners and managers. Individuals who are not qualified as superintendents, owners and managers can subscribe at the current subscription rate.
Cost: $30.00
Circulation: 3000
Founded in: 1927

22270 Government Recreation & Fitness
Executive Business Media
825 Old Country Road
PO Box 1500
Westbury, NY 11590

516-334-3030; *Fax:* 516-334-3059
ebm-mail@ebmpubs.com; www.ebmpubs.com

Murry Greenwald, Publisher
Paul Ragnoz, Managing Editor

Government Recreation and Fitness reaches recreation and fitness professionals in every department and agency of the federal government, goes directly to the people who purchase your products, and covers both appropriated and nonappropriated fund budgets. Subscription is free to managers and operators of fitness centers and recreation facilities at US military bases, federal agencies and offices as well as procurement agents for these facilities and others allied to the field
Cost: $35.00
Frequency: 15 issues per year
Circulation: 9974
ISSN: 1086-7899
Founded in: 1994
Printed in 4 colors on glossy stock

22271 Gun & Knife Show Calendar
F+W Media
38 E. 29th Street
New York, NY 10016

212-447-1400; *Fax:* 212-447-5231
contact_us@fwmedia.com;
www.fwpublications.com
Social Media: Twitter

Hugh McAloon, Publisher
Bruce Wolberg, Ad Manager
John Koenig, Editor'

A compilation of gun shows and knife shows held throughout the country, and is intended to be used as a complete guide for anyone who attends or displays at these shows. Regular listings include the dates of the show, the address, the city, state, number of tables, and the cost of tables. For attendees, the show hours and the cost of admission are listed. Shows are listed for a full year ahead and there is no charge to list a show.
Cost: $15.95
88 Pages
Frequency: Quarterly
Circulation: 5758
Founded in: 1952

22272 Hockey Business News
Straight Line Communications
12327 Santa Monica Boulevard
#202
Los Angeles, CA 90025-2552

310-207-9916; *Fax:* 310-442-6663
hbn@artnet.net

Mark Brown, Publisher

Features articles on ice hockey news and events, Canadian and international news, industry trends and forecasts and new products.
Cost: $60.00
Frequency: 9 per year
Circulation: 5,000

22273 Horseman's Journal
National Horsemen's Administration Corporation
870 Corporate Drive
Suite 300
Lexington, KY 40503

859-259-0451
866-245-1711; *Fax:* 859-259-0452
racing@hpba.org; www.hbpa.org

Richard E Glover, Editor
Sandy Erreguin, Advertising Director

Official magazine of the National Horsemen's Benevolent and Protective Association. Designed to give owners and trainers of racehorses

information helpful for the running of their horse related businesses.
56 Pages
Circulation: 32,000
Founded in: 1942
Printed in 4 colors on glossy stock

22274 ISI EDGE
Ice Skating Institute
600 Custer Rd
Bldg 9
Plano, TX 75023

972-735-8800; *Fax:* 972-735-8815
isi@skateisi.org; www.skateisi.org

Peter Martell, Executive Director

Professional journal for the ice skating industry. Focuses on the needs and interests of the industry's managers, skating and hockey directors, instructors, and builders/suppliers.
Frequency: Bi-Monthly

22275 Inside Archery
2960 N Academy Boulevard
Suite 101
Colorado Springs, CO 80917

719-495-9999; *Fax:* 719-495-8899
info@insidearchery.com;
www.fieldandstream.com
Social Media: Twitter, LinkedIn

Bill Krenz, President/Editor
Sherry Krenz, VP/Publisher

The Archery Industry Authority
Founded in: 1997

22276 International Bowling Industry
13245 Riverside Drive
Suite 501
Sherman Oaks, CA 91423

818-789-2695; *Fax:* 818-789-2812
info@bowlingindustry.com;
www.bowlingindustry.com
Social Media: Twitter, LinkedIn

Scott Frager, Publisher & Editor
Nick West, Associate Publisher
Fred Groh, Managing Editor
Patty Heath, Office Manager

Information on customer services, new products, industry trends, new concepts in management and marketing techniques, and employee motivation.
Cost: $32.00
Frequency: Monthly
Circulation: 10,205

22277 International Gaming and Wagering Business
BNP Media
PO Box 1080
Skokie, IL 60076-9785

847-763-9534; *Fax:* 847-763-9538
igwb@halldata.com; www.igwb.com

James Rutherford, Editor
Lynn Davidson, Marketing
Tammie Gizicki, Director

Focuses on business strategy, legislative information, food service and promotional concerns.
Frequency: Monthly
Circulation: 25000

22278 Journal of Sport and Social Issues
Sage Publications
2455 Teller Road
Newbury Park, CA 91320

800-818-7243; *Fax:* 800-583-2665
journals@sagepub.com;
www.sagepublications.com
Social Media: Facebook

CL Cole, Editor

Brings together the latest research, discussion and analysis on contemporary sport issues.
Cost: $552.00
Frequency: Quarterly
ISSN: 0193-7235

22279 Lacrosse Magazine
113 W University Pkwy
Baltimore, MD 21210-3301

410-235-6882; *Fax:* 410-366-6735
info@uslacrosse.org; www.laxmagazine.com
Social Media: Facebook, Twitter, LinkedIn, Live Blogs

Steve Stenersen, President
Bill Schoonmaker, COO
Bill Rubacky, Managing Director of Marketing
Kira Muller, Director of Advertising Sales

The most widely circulated publication for the sport of lacrosse, Lacrosse Magazine connects the sport's community, educates players, coaches and officials, entertains fans and keeps the membership of US Lacrosse informed.
Frequency: Monthly
Circulation: 300M
ISSN: 1069-5893
Founded in: 1982

22280 Master Skier
PO Box 187
Escabana, MI 49829

906-789-1139; www.masterskier.com

Journal dedicated to the skiing industry. Delivered to 51,000 readers in 19 countries.
Founded in: 1986
Mailing list available for rent

22281 Medicine and Science in Sports and Exercise
American College of Sports Medicine
401 W Michigan Street
PO Box 1440
Indianapolis, IN 46206

317-347-7817; *Fax:* 317-634-7817
msse@acsm.org; www.acsm.org

Kent B Pandolf, Editor-in-Chief
Gay Smith, Editor

Scientific research, education, and practical applications of sports medicine and exercise science to maintain and enhance physical performance, fitness, health and quality of life.
Cost: $300.00
Frequency: Monthly
Circulation: 14842
ISSN: 0195-9131
Founded in: 1968
Printed in 4 colors on matte stock

22282 Military Trader
F+W Media
38 E. 29th Street
New York, NY 10016

212-447-1400; *Fax:* 212-447-5231
contact_us@fwmedia.com;
www.fwpublications.com
Social Media: Facebook, Twitter, LinkedIn, Live Blogs

Rick Groth, Publisher
John Adams-Graf, Editor
David Nussbaum, Chair
Jim Ogle, Finance
David Blansfield, President

For military collectors, the best monthly source of news, features, collecting advice, shows, and events. Each issue offers thousands of 'For Sale' and 'Wanted' mlitary collectibles from hundreds of dealers and collectors. This is where to go when you are trying to buy or sell vintage military uniforms, pins, medals, helmets, ammunition, firearms, flags, and other militaria.
Cost: $19.00
56 Pages
Frequency: Monthly
Circulation: 9414
Founded in: 1975

22283 Military Vehicles
F+W Media
38 E. 29th Street
New York, NY 10016

212-447-1400; *Fax:* 212-447-5231
contact_us@fwmedia.com;
www.fwpublications.com
Social Media: Facebook, Twitter, LinkedIn, Live Blogs

Bill Reed, President
John Adams-Graf, Editor
David Nussbaum, Chair
Jim Ogle, Finance
David Blansfield, President

Each issue includes news, vintage military photos, collecting advice, market information, show listings, and extensive display and classified advertising sections offering to buy and sell hundreds of jeeps, tanks, trucks, vehicle parts, and accessories from dealers and enthusiasts all over the world. Other regular features include book and media reviews, letters to the editor, tech topics, weapons & replicas, models & toys, and internet sightings.
Cost: $23.98
176 Pages
Circulation: 19,000
Founded in: 1952

22284 NJCAA Review
National Junior College Athletic Association
1631 Mesa Ave Suite B
Suite 103
Colorado Springs, CO 80920

719-590-9788; *Fax:* 719-590-7324
meleicht@njcaa.org; www.njcaa.org
Social Media: Facebook, Twitter

Mary Ellen Leicht, Executive Director
Mark Krug, Director Sports Information/Media
Marry Elen, Director
Dee Dorus, Administrative Assistant
Cost: $30.00
Frequency: 10x/Year
Circulation: 2500
Founded in: 1989

22285 NRA InSights
National Rifle Association
11250 Waples Mill Rd
Fairfax, VA 22030-7400

703-267-1400
800-672-3888; www.nrapubliIcations.org
Social Media: Twitter, LinkedIn

NRAs official publication for its Junior members. Designed to motivate its readers to participate in all aspects of the shooting sports. Features personality profiles on top junior shooters, hunting stories, how-to pieces, program announcements, product surveys, safety features and educational information about firearms. Subscription included in membership dues.

22286 Online Magazine
Information Today
143 Old Marlton Pike
Medford, NJ 08055-8750

609-654-6266
800-300-9868; *Fax:* 609-654-4309
custserv@infotoday.com; www.infotoday.com

Thomas H Hogan, President
Roger R Bilboul, Chairman Of The Board

Online is written for information professionals and provides articles, product reviews, case stud-

ies, evaluation and informed opinion about selecting, using and managing electronic information products, plus industry and professional information about onlline database systems.
Cost: $115.00
Frequency: Monthly
Founded in: 1976

22287 Outdoors Magazine
Elk Publishing
531 Main St
Colchester, VT 05446-7222

802-879-2013
800-499-0447; *Fax:* 802-860-0005
info@outdoorsmagazine.net;
www.elkpublishing.com

James Austin, Publisher

A monthly publication covering hunting, fishing and wildlife issues in Vermont, New York, Maine, Massachusetts and Connecticut.
Cost: $18.95
Frequency: Monthly
Circulation: 10000
ISSN: 1096-1976
Founded in: 1996
Printed in 4 colors on matte stock

22288 PGA TOUR Partners Magazine
North American Media Group
12301 Whitewater Dr
Suite 260
Minnetonka, MN 55343-4103

952-936-9333
800-688-7611; *Fax:* 952-936-9169
NAMGhq@namginc.com; www.namginc.com

Seth Hoyt, Publisher

An exclusive, members-only publication filled with tips and techniques that can be used to improve your game, from the first tee to the 18th green.
Frequency: Bi-Monthly
Circulation: 1.3 m
Founded in: 1978

22289 Paddler
Paddle Sport Publishing
122 South Orange Av.
Steamboat Springs, CO 80477-5450

970-879-1450
888-774-7554; *Fax:* 970-870-1404
circulation@paddlermagazine.com;
www.paddlermagazine.com

Eugene Buchanan, Publisher/Editor
Tom Bie, Managing Editor

Each issues is filled with stories on places to paddle, skill enhancement, gear reviews, environmental issues, industry updats and profiles of leading paddlers.
Cost: $18.00
Frequency: Monthly
Circulation: 5527
Printed in 4 colors on glossy stock

22290 Parachutist Magazine
United States Parachute Association
5401 Southpoint Centre Blvd
Fredericksburg, VA 22407-2612

540-604-9740; *Fax:* 540-604-9741
uspa@uspa.org; www.uspa.org
Social Media: Facebook, Twitter

Jay Stokes, President
Randy Allison, VP
Sherry Butcher, Secretary & National Director
Lee Schlichtemeier, Treasurer
Jan Meyer, National Director

Supporting safe skydiving and those individuals who practice the sport. The magazine discusses issues dealing with training, safety, equipment, and networking the worldwide community of skydivers.
Cost: $4.50
112 Pages
Frequency: Monthly
Circulation: 35000
Founded in: 1946

22291 Pool and Spa News
Leisure Publications
6222 Wilshire Blvd
Los Angeles, CA 90020-4244

323-644-4801
888-269-8410; *Fax:* 323-801-4986
poolspanews@hanleywood.com;
www.poolspanews.com
Social Media: Facebook, Twitter, LinkedIn

Dick Coleman, Publisher
Erika Taylor, Editor
Steve Schlange, Marketing Manager
Scot Christ, Accountant

Pool and Spa News goals are: to furnish information to help pool and spa professionals function better in their businesses; to showcase products that can be sold or used in the industry; to help make their business life easier and more rewarding.
Cost: $16.50
Frequency: Semi-Monthly
Founded in: 1960
Mailing list available for rent

22292 Powersports Business
Ehlert Publishing Group
3300 Fernbrook Lane N
Suite 200
Plymouth, MN 55447

763-383-4400
800-848-6247; *Fax:* 763-383-4499
customerservice@powersportsbusiness.com;
www.powersportsbusiness.com
Social Media: Facebook, Twitter, LinkedIn

Mark Adams, CEO
Dave McMahon, Editor

Gives dealers, distributors, and manufacturers timely business news and analysis every three weeks.
Frequency: Weekly
Circulation: 18000
Founded in: 1969

22293 Pro Football Weekly
302 Saunders Rd
Suite 100
Riverwoods, IL 60015-3897

847-940-1100
800-331-7529; *Fax:* 847-940-1108;
www.profootballweekly.com
Social Media: Facebook, Twitter, LinkedIn

Hub Arkush, President

Seeks to bring the best coverage in the NFL to its readers.
Cost: $49.95
Frequency: Weekly
Founded in: 1967

22294 Professional Skater
Professional Skaters Association
3006 Allegro Park Ln SW
Rochester, MN 55902-4159

507-280-6812; *Fax:* 507-281-5491
office@skatepsa.com; www.skatepsa.com

Jimmie Santee, Executive Director

A bi-monthly magazine published by the Professional Skater Association.
Cost: $19.95
40 Pages
Frequency: Bi-Monthly
Founded in: 1984

22295 QUAD Off-Road Magazine
Transworld Publishing
Ste 150
2052 Corte Del Nogal
Carlsbad, CA 92011-1491

760-722-7777; *Fax:* 760-722-0653
jasonyoung@twsnet.com; www.neodata.com

Jason Young, Publication Contact

Quad off-road magazine delivers all things ATV: Breathtaking photography, tons of practical tips, the hottest nwe products, Quad comparison tests, ARV adventure stories, and much more.
Cost: $9.97
Frequency: Monthly

22296 Quarter Horse Racing Journal
American Quarter Horse Association
PO Box 200
Amarillo, TX 79168-0001

806-376-4811; *Fax:* 806-349-6411;
www.aqha.com
Social Media: Facebook, Twitter, LinkedIn, You Tube

Jim Helzer, President

News and races, health and management, business and industry, winner's circle, the handicapper, horse health, quarter paths, sports medicine, finish line and others are featured articles.
Frequency: Monthly

22297 Racquetball Magazine
USA Racquetball
4244 Russet Court
Lilburn, GA 80904-2906

770-972-2303; *Fax:* 719-635-0685
rjohn@usra.org; www.racqmag.com

Jim Hiser, Executive Director
Kevin Joyce, Director Membership
Melody Weiss, Director Finance
Heather Fender, Executive Assistant/Event Coord
Ed Mazur, President

Geared toward a readership of informed, active enthusiasts who seek entertainment, instruction and accurate reporting of events. Available by subscription through the US Racquetball Association National Office.
Cost: $20.00
64 Pages
Frequency: Bi-Monthly
Circulation: 16,000
ISSN: 1060-877X
Founded in: 1990
Printed in 4 colors on glossy stock

22298 Recreational Ice Skating
Ice Skating Institute
6000 Custer Rd
Bldg 9
Plano, TX 75023

972-735-8800; *Fax:* 972-735-8815
editor@skateisi.org; www.skateisi.org

Peter Martell, Executive Director

Distributed to ISI individual skater members, skating coaches, and rinks and pro shops worldwide. Written for and about ice skating enthusiasts and focuses on promoting ice skating as recreation and sport.
Frequency: Quarterly

22299 Referee
National Association of Sports Officials
2017 Lathrop Ave
Racine, WI 53405-3758

262-632-5448
800-733-6100; *Fax:* 262-632-5460
questions@referee.com; www.referee.com
Social Media: Facebook, Twitter, LinkedIn

Barry Mano, President

Monthly magazine published by the National Association of Sports Officials. Containes interviews, feature articles, late-breaking news,

personality profiles, investigative reports, health, legal and tax tips, and a wide range of technical information for many sports.
Cost: $44.95
80 Pages
Frequency: Monthly
Circulation: 77000
Founded in: 1976
Printed in 4 colors on glossy stock

22300 Ride BMX
Transworld Magazines
353 Airport Road
Oceanside, CA 92054

760-722-7777; *Fax:* 760-722-0653
jasonyoung@twsnet.com; www.neodata.com
Social Media: Facebook, Twitter, LinkedIn

Jason Young, Publication Contact

Publication with information for BMX riders.
Cost: $15.97
Frequency: Monthly

22301 Rodale's Scuba Diving
F+W Media
38 E. 29th Street
New York, NY 10016

212-447-1400; *Fax:* 212-447-5231
contact_us@fwmedia.com;
www.fwpublications.com
Social Media: Facebook, Twitter, LinkedIn

Edited to provide information about the practice of diving, dive travel opportunities, the marine environment, the reader's health and safety and the dive equipment on which they depend. Travel editorial focuses on both domestic and international dive travel and equipment editorial offers readers comparative product reviews.
Cost: $16.97
Frequency: 11 Per Year
Circulation: 187,059
Founded in: 1992

22302 Shooting Illustrated
National Rifle Association
11250 Waples Mill Rd
Fairfax, VA 22030-7400
703-267-1400
877-672-2000; www.nrapublications.org
Social Media: Facebook, Twitter, LinkedIn

Aaron Carter, Associate Editor

Comprehensive, timely and all-inclusive. In its pages you will find the best gun writers in the world, assembled to bring you the latest information on rifles, pistols or shotguns. From handloading to gunsmithing to highpower competition; from varmint rifles to rifles for the world's biggest game; from competition pistols to heavy field revolvers.
Cost: $9.95

22303 Shooting Industry
12345 World Trade Drive
San Diego, CA 92128-3102

858-674-4898
858-605-0254; *Fax:* 619-297-5353
subs@shootingindustry.com;
www.shootingindustry.com
Social Media: Facebook, Twitter, LinkedIn

Russ Thurman, Editor
Brian Friesen, Sales Manager

A trade publication covering the hunting and shooting industries. This publication is available to select dealers and select police personnel only. Dealers must have a current Federal Firearms License and no less than two additional credentials. Police personnel must have a letter from their Police Chief or Range Officer requesting a subscription (on department letterhead).
Cost: $25.00
Frequency: Monthly
Founded in: 1955

22304 Shooting Sports Retailer
SSR Communications
200 Croft Street
Suite 1
Birmingham, AL 35242

205-408-3766; *Fax:* 212-944-1884
stuart@grandviewmedia.com;
www.shootingsportsretailer.com

Glenn Karaban, President

Features articles on shooting sports equipment, sales techniques, new products, sales aids, and potential problems for the wholesale seller of shooting equipment.
Frequency: Monthly
Circulation: 17463
Founded in: 1980

22305 Shooting Sports USA
National Rifle Association
11250 Waples Mill Rd
Fairfax, VA 22030-7400

703-267-1400
877-672-2000; www.nrapublications.org
Social Media: Facebook, Twitter

Information for the competitive shooter, from smallbore to high power, air action pistol and everything in between.
Cost: $9.95

22306 Single Shot Rifle Journal
American Single Shot Rifle Association
PO Box 1162
Niles, MI 49120

269-687-9550
journaleditor@assra.com; www.assra.com

Gary Staup, President
John Merz, VP
D. Wayne Stiles, Editor

The official magazine of The American Single Shot Rifle Association. Susbscription is included with membership in the ASSRA.
Cost: $35.00
60 Pages
Frequency: Bi-Monthly
Circulation: 2400
Founded in: 1948
Printed in on matte stock

22307 Ski Area Management
Beardsley Publishing Corporation
45 Main Street North
PO Box 644
Woodbury, CT 06798

203-263-0888; *Fax:* 203-266-0452
news@saminfo.com; www.saminfo.com

Jennifer Rowan, Publisher
Olivia Rowan, Marketing/Associate Publisher
Donna Jacobs, V.P./Administration
Rick Kahl, Editor
Ann Hasper, Senior Editor

SAM magazine is the professional trade publication for the mountain resort market. It is a bi-monthly, all-paid publication.
Cost: $48.00
Frequency: Monthly
Circulation: 3992
Founded in: 1962
Printed in 4 colors on glossy stock

22308 Ski Magazine
929 Pearl Street
5720 Flatiron Parkway
Boulder, CO 80301

303-448-7600
800-678-0817; *Fax:* 303-442-6321;
www.skimag.com
Social Media: Facebook, Twitter, LinkedIn, You Tube

Kendall Hamilton, Editor-In-Chief
Greg Ditrinco, Executive Editor
Kim Beekman, Managing Editor
Samantha Berman, Senior Editor

Includes information on travel, gear, instruction, snow reports, mountain cams, and gift shops.
Cost: $11.00
Frequency: 8X/year

22309 SkiTrax Magazine
260 Spadina Avenue
Suite 200
Toronto, Canada M5V1P9, ON

416-977-2100
866-754-8729; *Fax:* 416-977-9200;
www.skitrax.com
Social Media: Facebook, Twitter, LinkedIn, You Tube

North America's premier nordic publication is the official magazine of the USSA and CCC and offers the broadest coverage of nordic skiing available. Coverage includes comprehensive Annual North American Buyer's Guide; local touring centers and exotic backcountry hide-a-ways; complete North American and international competition coverage; regular tips on products; training, technique, telemark, masters, and waxing; extensive calendar of events; plus much more.

22310 Soccer Journal
National Soccer Coaches Association of America
6700 Squibb Road
Suite 215
Mission, KS 66202

913-362-1747
800-458-0678; *Fax:* 913-362-3439;
www.nscaa.com

The official publication of the National Soccer Coaches of America. Produced exclusively for soccer coaches. Each issue contains technical and tactical articles, news and updates on important events, thoughts from opinion leaders in the sport and features on the interesting people and issues of the game. Subscription included in NSCAA membership.
Cost: $50.00
Frequency: 8X/Year
Circulation: 18000
Founded in: 1941

22311 Speedway Illustrated
Speedway Illustrated
107 Elm St
Salisbury, MA 01952-1803

978-465-9099
888-837-3684; *Fax:* 978-465-9033
editorial@speedwayillustrated.com;
www.speedwayillustrated.com

Dick Berggren, VP
Steve Chryssos, Advertising Manager
Lynne Henry, Advertising Sales

They'll show you how to build and race your own car, and take you inside at NASCAR's hottest teams and stars.
Cost: $19.94
Frequency: Monthly
Circulation: 150000
Founded in: 2000

22312 Sporting Goods Business
VNU Business Publications
2900 Veterans Hwy
Bristol, PA 19007-1606

847-763-9050
800-464- 759; *Fax:* 847-763-9037
info@sgdealer.com;
www.sportinggoodsbusiness.com
Social Media: Facebook, Twitter

Michael Marchesano, President
Derek Irwin, CFO
Sid Holt, Editorial Director

Covers information on all facets of sporting goods, including industry news, sales volume analysis, market events coverage, and other statistics, also covers store operation, merchandising, pricing, promotion, cost control, and sales training.
Cost: $75.00
Frequency: Monthly
Circulation: 27,374
Founded in: 1905

22313 Sporting Goods Dealer
VNU Publications
PO Box 1184
Skokie, IL 60076-8194

847-763-9050
800-464- 759; *Fax:* 847-763-9037
info@sgdealer.com; www.sgdealer.com
Social Media: Facebook, Twitter

Michael Marchesano, President/CEO
Sid Holt, Editorial Director
Derek Irwin, CFO

Sporting Goods Dealer offers reporting on industry insiders, new products, and merchandising trends affecting team dealers and retailers that service schools, colleges, and pro and local teams.
Cost: $75.00
Circulation: 10000
Founded in: 1905

22314 Sporting News
Sporting News Publishing Company
PO Vox 51570
Boulder, CO 80322-1510

314-997-7111
800-777-6785; *Fax:* 314-993-7798;
www.sportingnews.com

Pete Spina, Publisher
Kathy Kinkeade, VP

A comprehensive publication covering sporting goods manufacturers, retailers, wholesalers and distributors.
Cost: $15.97
Frequency: Bi-Monthly

22315 Sports Illustrated
Time Life Building
New York, NY 10020-1393

212-229-9797; *Fax:* 212-467-4049;
www.sportsillustrated.cnn.com

John Huey, Editor-in-Chief
Terry McDonell, Editor, Time Inc. Sports Group
Paul Fichtenbaum, Managing Editor, SI.com

Sports Illustrated is the most respected voice in sports journalism, which reaches a weekly audience of nearly 21 million adults, and SI.com, the 24/7 sports news website that delivers up to the minute news, scores, statistics and in-depth analysis.
Cost: $39.95
Frequency: 56 Issues/Year

22316 Sports Illustrated for Kids
Sports Illustrated
1271 Ave of the Americas
Suite 32
New York, NY 10020-1401

212-522-1212
212-467-4049; *Fax:* 212-522-0318;
www.sikids.com
Social Media: Facebook

Bob Der, Managing Editor & Publisher
Beth Power Bugler, Creative Director
Justin Tejada, Assistant Managing Editor
Paul Ulane, Senior Producer, sikids.com

Great action photos, easy-to-read stories about star athletes, helpful instructional tips from the pros, humor, comics and activities.
Cost: $24.95
Frequency: Monthly

22317 SportsTravel Magazine
Schneider Publishing Company
11835 W Olympic Blvd
Suite 1265
Los Angeles, CA 90064-5814

310-577-3700
877-577-3700; *Fax:* 310-577-3715
info@schneiderpublishing.com;
www.schneiderpublishing.com
Social Media: Facebook, Twitter, LinkedIn

Tim Schneider, President
Lisa Furfine, Associate Publisher
Jason Gewirtz, Managing Editor/SportsTravel

SportsTravel magazine is the event organizer's guide to successfully creating and staging sports events. SportsTravel provides information on sports destinations and venues, transportation and accommodations, bidding for events, sponsorships, and marketing. SportsTravel facilitates relationships among sports governing bodies, host destinations, sponsors, and suppliers.
Cost: $48.00
Circulation: 14,000
ISSN: 1091-5354
Founded in: 1997
Printed in 4 colors on glossy stock

22318 Sportsbusiness Journal
Business Journals Inc
120 W Morehead St
Suite 420
Charlotte, NC 28202-1874

704-973-1200
800-829-9389; *Fax:* 704-973-1201
citybiz@bizjournals.com;
www.citybiznetwork.com

George Conley, President

Provides important news information sports industry executives need to be successful in the fast paced world of sports business
Cost: $249.00
Frequency: 49X/Year
Circulation: 17,000
Founded in: 1998

22319 Squash Magazine
23 Cynwyd Road
PO Box 1216
Bala Cynwyd, PA 19004-5216

610-667-4006; *Fax:* 610-667-6539;
www.us-squash.org
Social Media: Facebook, Twitter

Craig W Brand, Executive Director
Keith Klipstein, Executive Director

Articles on the sport of squash racquets in the United States.
Cost: $35.00
Frequency: 10 per year

22320 Synchro Swimming USA
US Synchronized Swimming
132 E Washington Street
Suite 800
Indianapolis, IN 46204-3674

317-237-5700; *Fax:* 317-237-5705
marketing@usasynchro.org;
www.usasynchro.org

Terry Harper, Executive Director
Taylor Payne, Media Relations Director
Jordan Dillon, Business Development Director
Judy McGowan, President
Frequency: Quarterly
Circulation: 6000

22321 TEE Time Magazine
PO Box 225
Whitman, MA 02382

781-447-2299; *Fax:* 781-447-7773;
www.teetime-mag.com
Social Media: Facebook, Twitter

Mary Porter, Editor
Karen Christoforo, Sales

The Mid-Atlantics region's most comprehensive golf magazine. Each issue includes golf instruction, profiles of Mid-Atlantic personalities, course reviews and more.
Cost: $12.95
64 Pages

22322 Training & Conditioning
MAG
20 East Lake Rd.
Ithaca, NY 14850-5220

607-257-6970; *Fax:* 607-257-7328
info@athleticbid.com;
www.momentummedia.com

Mark Goldberg, Publisher
Diedra Harkenrider, East and Southeast US Sales Rep
Pennie Small, Manager

Articles on injury protection and treatment, rehabilitation, strength and speed training, as well as cardiovascular equipment for competitive athletes.
Frequency: BiMonthly
Circulation: 27,400

22323 Transworld Motocross
Transworld Publications
353 Airport Road
Oceanside, CA 92054

760-722-7777; *Fax:* 760-722-0653;
www.neodata.com

Jason Young, Publications Contact
Al Crolius, Manager

Magazine designed for the motocross enthusiast.
Cost: $16.97
Frequency: Monthly

22324 Transworld Skateboarding Business
Transworld Business Subscriptions
2052 Corte del Nogal
Suite 100
Carlsbad, CA 92011

760-722-7777
850-682-7644; *Fax:* 760-722-0653;
www.twsbiz.com
Social Media: Facebook, Twitter, LinkedIn

Larry Balma, Publisher
Brad McDonald, Manager

Geared toward skateboard retailers, apparel chain buyers, and manufacturers of skateboard products, includes new product information, industry news, and technical innovations.
Cost: $16.97
Frequency: Monthly
Circulation: 14500

22325 Transworld Snowboarding
Transworld Business
Ste 150
2052 Corte Del Nogal
Carlsbad, CA 92011-1491

760-722-7777
850-682-7644; *Fax:* 760-722-0653;
www.twsnow.com
Social Media: Facebook, Twitter, LinkedIn

Larry Balma, Publisher
Brad McDonald, Manager

Articles on industry news, retailer surveys, new products, and technical studies.
Cost: $14.97
Frequency: 9/Year
Circulation: 20000

22326 Transworld Surf
Transworld Publishing
Ste 150
2052 Corte Del Nogal
Carlsbad, CA 92011-1491

760-722-7777
850-682-7644; *Fax:* 760-722-0653
jasonyoung@twsnet.com; www.neodata.com
Social Media: Facebook, Twitter, LinkedIn

Jason Young, Publications Contact
Brad McDonald, Manager
Magazine for surfing enthusiasts.
Cost: $12.00
Frequency: Monthly

22327 Trapper & Predator
F+W Media
38 E. 29th Street
New York, NY 10016

212-447-1400; *Fax:* 212-447-5231
contact_us@fwmedia.com;
www.fwpublications.com

Hugh McAloon, Publisher
Paul Wait, Editor
Contains news, in-depth features, and how-to tips on trapping, the art of predator calling, and animal damage control. Contributors include the top names in the business. Regular columns and departments include The Fur Shed, Let's Swap Ideas, Q&A, and news from state trapping associations nationwide.
Cost: $18.95
Frequency: 10 Per Year
Circulation: 38,260
Founded in: 1975

22328 Turkey & Turkey Hunting
F+W Media
38 E. 29th Street
New York, NY 10016

212-447-1400; *Fax:* 212-447-5231
contact_us@fwmedia.com;
www.fwpublications.com

Hugh McAloon, Publisher
Paul Wait, Editor
Edited for serious, technical, year-round, gun and bow turkey hunters. Features emphasize success and enjoyment of the sport. Articles focus on hunting, scouting, turkey behavior and biology, hunting ethics, new equipment, methodologies, turkey management, and current research. Columns include Tree Call,Mail Pouch, Turkey Biology, a Q&A column, Hunter's Library, Turkey Gear, and Last Call.
Cost: $15.95
Frequency: 6 Per Year
Circulation: 68,962
Founded in: 1991

22329 USA Table Tennis
USA Table Tennis
1 Olympic Plaza
Colorado Springs, CO 80909-5746

719-866-4583; *Fax:* 719-632-6071;
www.usatt.org
Social Media: Facebook, Twitter

Michael Cavanaugh, CEO
Dedicated to providing readers with all of the tools and information necessary to follow or participate in this life-long sport.
9000 Members
Frequency: 6x/Year
Circulation: 8000
Founded in: 1935

22330 Velobusiness
Inside Communications
1830 55th St
Boulder, CO 80301-2700

303-440-0601; *Fax:* 303-444-6788

Felix Magowan, President
Trends in the market, new product develoment updates and spot news reports, also includes testing and performance evaluations, as well as marketing, merchandising and sales techniques.
Cost: $35.00
Frequency: Monthly
Circulation: 10,560

22331 Woman's Outlook
National Rifle Association
9582 Hamilton Ave
Huntington Beach, CA 92646

800-565-6651
877-672-2000; www.womenoutlook.com

Created especially for women. Covers topics from personal protection and home security to general firearms safety and recreation. Subscription complimentary with membership in NRA. Otherwise $9.95

22332 Woodall's Campground Management
Woodall Publishing Company
PO Box 8600
Ventura, CA 93002-8600

805-667-2001
877-680-6155; *Fax:* 805-667-4122
info@woodallpub.com;
www.affinitygroup.com

Michael A Schneider, CEO
Kristopher Bunker, Editor
Terry Thompson, Advertising
Information for campground owners and managers, provides methods of management and industry trends along with reports from independent and franchise campgrounds, public parks and state associations.
Cost: $24.95
Frequency: Monthly
Circulation: 10,000
Founded in: 1935

Trade Shows

22333 AACCA Spirit Coaches Conference
American Association of Cheerleading Coaches
6745 Lenox Center Court
Suite 318
Memphis, TN 38115

800-533-6583; *Fax:* 901-251-5851;
www.aacca.org

Jim Lord, Executive Director
Michle Ziegler, Instructor
The official NFHS Sprit Coaches Education Program.
Frequency: Annual
Founded in: 1988

22334 AAU Annual Convention
Amateur Athletic Union
1910 Hotel Plaza Boulevard
PO Box 22409
Lake Buena Vista, FL 32830

407-934-7200; *Fax:* 407-934-7242
pam@aausports.org; www.aausports.org
Social Media: Facebook, Twitter

Pam Marshall, Convention Contact
John Hodges, Exhibitor Information
Bobby Dodd, President/CEO
National Convention of the Amateur Athletic Union.

22335 ASA Sportfishing Summit
American Sportfishing Association
225 Reinekers Lane
Suite 420
Alexandria, VA 22314

703-519-9691; *Fax:* 703-519-1872
mjwilliamson@asafishing.org;
www.asafishing.org
Social Media: Facebook, Twitter
Mary Jane Williamson, Communications Director
Amy Yohanes, Administrative Services Manager
Gordon Robertson, VP
Patrick Egan, Manager
ASA's membership meeting and premier networking event. From special sessions, to business workshops tp association committee meeting, the Summit provides a wide-range of opportunities to gain information on the most relevant issues facing the sportfishing industry.
Frequency: October

22336 ASGCA Meeting
American Society of Golf Course Architects
125 N Executive Dr
Suite 302
Brookfield, WI 53005-6035

262-786-5960; *Fax:* 262-786-5919
info@asgca.org; www.asgca.org
Social Media: Facebook, Twitter

Chad Ritterbusch, Executive Director
Bob ~ Cupp, President
Rick Robbin, VP
Lee Schmidt, Treasurer
Steve Smyers, Secretary
Combines golfing experiences with informational seminars and social engagements to form a trulyuniqie atmosphere that makes for both an enjoyable and educational meeting experience.
185 Members
Founded in: 1946

22337 AVCA Annual Convention
American Volleyball Coaches Association
2365 Harrodsburg Road
Suite A325
Lexington, KY 40504
859-226-4315
866-544-2822; *Fax:* 859-226-4338
members@avca.org; www.avca.org
Social Media: Facebook, Twitter, LinkedIn

Kathy DeBoer, Executive Director
Will Engle, Assistant Director, Events
A gathering of volleyball coaches and vendors
1700 Members
Frequency: Annual

22338 Action Sports Retailer Trade Exhibit West Fall and Spring
ASR Trade Expo
31910 Del Obispo
Suite 200
San Juan Capistrano, CA 92675

949-226-5744; *Fax:* 949-226-5659;
www.asrbiz.com

Tina Middleton, Marketing Director
Lisha Steinkoenig, Registration Coordinator
Megan Lara, Expo Coordinator
Provides the ultimate showcase of the action sports and youth lifestyle market by attracting the world's largest and most powerful brands and buyers representing such diverse markets as surf, skate, swim, snow, footwear and fashion.
10M Attendees
Frequency: September/February

22339 Allegheny Sport, Travel and Outdoor Show
Expositions

PO Box 550
Edgewater Branch
Cleveland, OH 44107-0550

216-529-1300
800-600-0307; *Fax:* 216-529-0311;
www.sportandtravel.com

Chris Fassnacht, Show Producer

Dedicated to hunting, shiftin and camping. Features hundreds of state-of-the-art exhibitors, dozens of live demonstrations, and a top notch line-up of seminar experts.
Frequency: Annual
Founded in: 1985

22340 Amateur Softball Association of America
2801 NE 50th Street
Oklahoma City, OK 73111

405-424-5266; *Fax:* 405-424-3855;
www.asasoftball.com

Bill Plummer III, Hall of Fame/Trade Show Manager
Ron Radigonda, Executive Director

Annual meeting of the Amateur Softball Association.
1000+ Attendees
Frequency: Annual/November
Founded in: 1933

22341 American Alliance for Health, Physical Education, Recreation & Dance Expo
1900 Association Drive
Reston, VA 20191

703-476-3400
800-213-7193; *Fax:* 703-476-9527
conv@aahperd.org; www.aahperd.org
Social Media: Twitter

Danny Ballard, President
Judith C Young, VP
Paula Kun, Marketing
Shannon Mueller, Director

National convention and exposition that features many exhibits focusing on products, services and equipment within the fields of health, physical education, recreation and dance.
5000 Attendees
Frequency: Annual/April
Founded in: 1879

22342 American Baseball Coaches Association Convention
108 S University Avenue
Suite 3
Mount Pleasant, MI 48858-2327

989-775-3300; *Fax:* 989-775-3600
abca@abca.org; www.abca.org
Social Media: Facebook, Twitter

Nick Phillips, Membership/Convention Coordinator
4000 Attendees
Frequency: Annual

22343 American Bowling Congress Annual Convention
United States Bowling Congress
5301 South 76th Street
Greendale, WI 53129

414-216-6400
800-514-2695; *Fax:* 414-421-8560
bowlinfo@bowl.com; www.bowl.com

Annual conference of the United States Bowling Congress whose mission is to ensure the integrity and protect the future of the sport by providing programs and services and enhancing the bowling experience.

22344 American Camp Association Conference & Exhibits
American Camp Association
5000 State Road 67 N
Martinsville, IN 46151-7902

765-342-8456
800-428-2267; *Fax:* 765-342-2065;
www.aca-camps.org
Social Media: Facebook, Twitter, LinkedIn

Tisher Bolger, President
Scott Brody, VP
Steve Baskin, Treasurer Board of Directors
Peg Smith, CEO

One hundred and forty to one hundred and fifty booths of arts and crafts, computer software, sporting goods, waterfront equipment and more plus a seminar and workshop.
1,200 Attendees
Frequency: Annual
Founded in: 1943

22345 American College of Sports Medicine Annual Meeting
401 W Michigan Street
Indianapolis, IN 46202

317-637-9200; *Fax:* 317-634-7817
acsm@acsm.org; www.acsm.org
Social Media: Facebook, Twitter, LinkedIn, You Tube

James R Whitehead, Executive VP
Janet Walberg Rankin, President

One hundred and eighty-five exhibits of sports equipment, publications, supplies and services, conference and banquet. CME credits available for a nominal fee at time of registration.
5000 Attendees
Frequency: Annual
Founded in: 1954

22346 American Football Coaches Association Convention
American Football Coaches Association
100 Legends Lane
Waco, TX 76706

254-754-9900; *Fax:* 254-754-7373;
www.afca.com
Social Media: Facebook, Twitter

Grant Teaff, Executive Director

120 booths of equipment, supplies and services relevant to the game of football. Three-day event includees coaching clinic, awards luncheon and Coach of the Year dinner.
6000 Attendees
Frequency: Annual/January
Founded in: 1921

22347 American Greyhound Track Operators Association
Palm Beach Kennel Club
1111 North Congress Avenue
West Palm Beach, FL 33409

561-688-5799; *Fax:* 801-754-2404;
www.agtoa.com
Social Media: Facebook, Twitter

Richard Winning, President
Dennis Bicsak, Managing Coordinator
Dennis Bicsak, Managing Coordinator
Michael Corbin~, Treasurer

A forum for all those affiliated with the sport to exchange ideas and to develop new techniques for the improvement and growth of the greyhound industry.
400 Attendees
Frequency: Annual/March

22348 American Hockey Coaches Association Convention
American Hockey Coaches Association
7 Concord Street
Gloucester, MA 01930

781-245-4177; *Fax:* 781-245-2492
ahcahockey@comcast.net;
www.ahcahockey.com
Social Media: Facebook, Twitter, LinkedIn

Joe Bertagna, Executive Director
George Gwozdecky, President
Kevin Sneddon, VP/Convention Planning

70 exhibits of ice hockey equipment and supplies plus worksop and banquet.
500 Attendees
Frequency: Annual/April
Founded in: 1960

22349 American Orthopaedic Society for Sports Medicine Annual Meeting
American Orthopaedic Society for Sports Medicine
6300 N River Road
Suite 500
Rosemont, IL 60018-4229

847-292-4900
877-321-3500; *Fax:* 847-292-4905
aossm@aossm.org; www.sportsmed.org

Michelle Schaffer, Exhibits Coordinator
Camille Petrick, Manager

130 exhibits of equipment supplies and services for sports medicine and related fields. Banquet and tours available.
1,500 Attendees
Frequency: June/July
Founded in: 1972

22350 American Swimming Coaches Association
5101 NW 21st Avenue
Suite 200
Fort Lauderdale, FL 33309

954-563-4930
800-356-2722; *Fax:* 954-563-9813;
www.swimmmingcoach.org
Social Media: Facebook

John Leonard, Executive Director
Lori Klatt, Marketing

Annual convention
1.5M Attendees
Frequency: September

22351 American Youth Soccer Organization
12501 S Isis Avenue
Hawthorne, CA 90250

310-643-6455
800-872-2976; *Fax:* 310-643-5310;
www.soccer.org

Rick Smith, Executive Director

The AYSO annual general meeting is your opportunity to represent your region, area or section on a national level.
800 Attendees
Frequency: Annual

22352 Archery Trade Show
Archery Trade Association
PO Box 70
Suite 310
Minnesota, UT 84107

507-233-8130
866-266-2776; *Fax:* 507-233-8140
info@archerytrade.org; www.archerytrade.org
Social Media: Facebook, Twitter

Jay McAnich, President/CEO
Denise Parker, VP/Director Marketing
Cindy Brophy, Manager Tradeshow/Membership Svces
Kelly A. Kelly, Executive Assistant
Kurt Weber, Director of Marketing

Formerly the Archery Manufacturers and Merchants Organization (AMO), the ATA provides

the core funding and direction critical to the future of archery and bowhunting. The trade show features 499 exhibitors cover 155,500 square feet.
8000 Attendees
Frequency: Annual

22353 **Arnold Sports Festival**
Arnold Sports Festival
1215 Worthington Woods Blvd.
Worthington, OH 43805
614-431-2600; *Fax:* 516-625-1023
lpinney@arnoldexpo.com; www.arnoldsportsfestival.com
Social Media: Facebook, Twitter
Lucy Pinneyr, Event Chair
Brent LaLonda, Media Contact
Five days of fitness equipment, sports entertainment, supplements, apparel and athletic stars, with more than 17,000 competitive athletes in 40 sporting events. Over 500 exhibitors and 150,000 visitors; takes place during the Arnold Sports Festival
150M+ Attendees
Frequency: March
Founded in: 1976

22354 **Athletic Equipment Managers Association Convention**
723 Keil Ct
Bowling Green, OH 43402-2235
www.equipmentmanagers.org
Sporting goods equipment manufacturers.
300 Attendees
Frequency: June

22355 **BCA Convention**
National High School Baseball Coaches Association
PO Box 12843
Tempe, AZ 85284
602-615-0571; *Fax:* 480-838-7133
rdavini@cox.net; www.baseballcoaches.org
Ron Davini, Executive Director

22356 **Billiard & Home Leisure Expo**
Billiards Congress of America
4345 Beverly Street
Suite D
Colorado Springs, CO 80918
719-264-8300; *Fax:* 719-264-0900; www.bcaexpo.com
Social Media: Facebook, Twitter, LinkedIn
Rob Johnson, Chief Executive Officer
Lynda Bradt, Business Accountant
Shane Tyree, Membership & Communications Manager
This show hosts nearly 300 companies in 1400 booths, featuring every product line in the home recreation industry, from billiard and game tables, cues and cue accessories, cloth, balls and apparel, to spas, bowling, darts, foosball, art, home furnishings, novelty items, outdoor living, books, publications, video games, coin-op, pinball, jukeboxes, gaming and much more.
Founded in: 1948

22357 **Bowling Proprieters Association of America International Bowl Expo**
615 Six Flags Drive
PO Box 5802
Arlington, TX 76011-6347
800-343-1329
888-649-5585; *Fax:* 817-633-2940; www.bpaa.com
Social Media: Facebook, Twitter, LinkedIn
Lee Ann Norton, Director Meetings/Events
Laurie Clower, Executive Assistant~
Judy King, Director of Finance
The bowling industry's premier event. Brings together thousands of bowling industry professionals in one place. You can find the latest trends, bowling-related products and services, marketing ideas, profit center opportunities, and tools to help you spread the excitement of bowling throughout your communities. Trade show showcases the latest products and services from more than 300 companies in over 900 exhibit booths.
5000 Attendees
Frequency: June
Founded in: 1932

22358 **CMAA Annual Conference**
Club Managers Association of America
1733 King Street
Alexandria, VA 22314
703-739-9500; *Fax:* 703-739-0124
cmaa@cmaa.org; www.smaa.org
Social Media: Facebook, Twitter, LinkedIn, You Tube
Jim Singerling, Executive VP
Club Managers Association of America Annual World Conference. This International Conference brings together club industry professionals from around the world for five days of challenging education, entertaining social events and an industry trade show.
Founded in: 1990

22359 **CSCAA National Convention & Clinic**
College Swimming Coaches Association of America
1640 Maple
#803
Evanston, IL 60201
847-833-3478
r-groseth@northwestern.edu; www.collegecoaches.org
Social Media: Facebook, Twitter, LinkedIn
Bob Groseth, Executive Director
George Kennedy, President
Founded in: 1990

22360 **Colorado RV Adventure Travel Show**
Industrial Expositions
1675 Larimer, Suite 700
PO Box 480084
Denver, CO 80248-0084
303-892-6800
800-457-2434; *Fax:* 303-892-6322
info@iei-expos.com; www.bigasalloutdoors.com
Social Media: Facebook, Twitter, LinkedIn
Jeff Haughton, President
Dianne Seymour, Expo Manager
Recreational vehicles, accessories and travel.
18000 Attendees
Frequency: Annual/January
Founded in: 1990

22361 **Colorado RV, Sports, Boat and Travel Show**
Industrial Expositions
1675 Larimer Street
Suite 700
Denver, CO 80202
303-892-6800
800-457-2434; *Fax:* 303-892-6322
dseymour@iei-expos.com; www.bigasalloutdoors.com
Social Media: Facebook, Twitter, LinkedIn
Jeff Haughton, President
Dianne Seymour, Expo Manager
Annual trade show of recreational vehicles, sports, boats and travel.
Founded in: 1990

22362 **Crescent Ski Council**
PO Box 17944
Greenville, SC 29606-8944
864-229-7488; *Fax:* 864-235-2504; www.crescentskicouncil.org
Social Media: Facebook, Twitter, LinkedIn, You Tube
Michelle Shuford, Contact
Exhibits of snow ski resorts and related lodging services. 50 booths.
500 Attendees
Frequency: April
Founded in: 1969

22363 **Cross Country Ski Areas Association Annual Conference**
Cross Country Ski Areas Association
P.O. Box 818
Woodstock, VT 05091
802-236-3021
reese@xcski.org; www.xcski.org
Social Media: Facebook, Twitter, Instagram
Reese Brown, President/ Executive Director
Jo Jo Toeppner, Chairman
Bringing together cross country ski enthusiasts to participate in workshops and forums on topics including interactive grooming, maintenance, and snowmaking elements.
Cost: $475.00
350 Members
Frequency: Annual
Founded in: 1977

22364 **DEMA/Diving Equipment & Marketing Association Trade Show**
3750 Convoy Street
Suite 310
San Diego, CA 92111-3741
858-616-6408
800-862-3483; *Fax:* 858-616-6495
info@dema.org; www.dema.org
Social Media: Facebook, Twitter, LinkedIn, You Tube
Christine Von Steiger, Exhibit Space Sales
Tom Markusson, Sponsorship Sales
Tom Ingram, Executive Director
Stephen Ashmore, President
Annual trade show produced by the Diving Equipment & Marketing Association.
10M Attendees
Frequency: Annual

22365 **Eastern Fishing and Outdoor Exposition**
International Sport Show Producers Association
PO Box 4720
Portsmouth, NH 03802-4720
603-431-4315; *Fax:* 603-431-1971
info@sportshows.com; www.sportshows.com
Social Media: Facebook, Twitter, LinkedIn, You Tube
Paul Fuller, President
Over 450 exhibitors representing the entire world of fishing and hunting.
45k Attendees
Frequency: Annual/February
Founded in: 1996
Mailing list available for rent

22366 **Eastern Iowa Sportshow**
Iowa Show Productions
PO Box 2460
Waterloo, IA 50704
319-232-0218; *Fax:* 319-235-8932
info@iowashows.com; www.iowashows.com
Social Media: Facebook, Twitter, LinkedIn
See a huge display of fishing boats, family sport boats, personal watercraft, pontoons, tent camp-

ers, travel trailers, fifth wheels, vans, and motorhomes. Plus boat accessories, truck toppers, motorcycles, ATVs, fishing camps, fly-ins, outposts, Lake Erie Walleye charters, family resorts, Lake Michigan sportfishing, houseboat rentals, Golf vacations, canoe outfitters, big game outfitters, tourism associations, campgrounds, camping gear, fishing tackle, archery equipment, targets, decoys, calls.

22367 Fall RV & Van Show
O'Loughlin Trade Shows
PO Box 80750
Portland, OR 97280-1750

503-246-8291; *Fax:* 503-246-1066;
www.oloughlintradeshows.com
Social Media: Facebook, Twitter, LinkedIn

Peter O'Loughlin, Show Manager

Portland, OR. Recreational vehicles and vans
Frequency: September

22368 Fly Fishing Show - Denver
854 Opossum Lake Road
Carlisle, PA 17013

717-243-6733
800-420-7582; *Fax:* 717-243-8603
flyfishingshow@aol.com;
www.flyfishingshow.com
Social Media: Facebook, Twitter

Barry Serviente, Executive Director

Annual fly fishing show.

22369 Football Officials Association Southwest Convention
Dallas Football Officials Association
2005 Fairmeadow
Richardson, TX 75080

972-235-9110; *Fax:* 972-235-7675
dfoasecretary@aol.com; www.dfoa.com

David Tucker, Registration
Mike Woodard, President

Texas Association of Sports Officials annual convention.
1.8M Attendees
Frequency: Annual

22370 Fred Hall's Western Fishing Tackle & Boat Show: Delmar
Fred Hall & Associates
PO Box 2925
Camarillo, CA 93011

805-389-3339; *Fax:* 805-389-1219

Bart Hall, Show Manager

Featuring all forms of outdoor recreation including boats, fishing tackle, adventure travel and recreational vehicles.

22371 Golf Course Superintendents Association of America
GCSAA
1421 Research Park Drive
Lawrence, KS 66049-3858

785-841-2240
800-472-7878; *Fax:* 785-832-4455;
www.golfindustryshow.com
Social Media: Facebook, Twitter, LinkedIn, You Tube

Julia Ozark, Sr Trade Show Manager
Caroline Gollier, Trade Show Project Manager
Scotti Corley, Meeting/Trade Show Coordinator
Kelly Jo Springirth, Director Exhibit Services
Steve Mona, CEO

Trade show designed for the owners/operators of golf facilities and the professional members of the golf course and club management industries. The event combines education, networking and solutions for golf course superintendents, owners/operators, general managers, chief operating officers, architects and builders.
25M Attendees
Frequency: February

22372 Grand Center Boat Show
Show Span
2121 Celebration Drive NE
Grand Rapids, MI 49525

616-447-2860
800-328-6550; *Fax:* 616-447-2861
events@showspan.com; www.showspan.com
Social Media: Facebook, Twitter, LinkedIn

Carolyn Alt, Manager

Held at the Grand Center in Grand Rapids, Michigan. Every kind of boat under the sun. Over 400 boats.
82000 Attendees
Frequency: February

22373 Great Lakes Athletic Trainers
8015 Kersey Drive
Indianapolis, IL 46236

815-455-3860; *Fax:* 815-477-6907;
www.glata.org
Social Media: Facebook, Twitter, LinkedIn

Mark Schauer, Co Coordinator
Kevin Gerlach, Co Coordinator

Annual meeting and symposium.
1M Attendees
Frequency: March

22374 Greater Cincinnati Golf Show
North Coast Golf Productions
PO Box 372
Twinsburg, OH 44087-0372

330-963-6963
800-939-0040; *Fax:* 330-487-0352
consumer@northcoastgolfshows.com;
www.cincinnatigolfshow.com
Social Media: Facebook, Twitter, LinkedIn

America's favorite consumer golf show.

22375 ICAST
American Sportfishing Association
1001 North Fairfax Street
Suite 501
Alexandria, VA 22314

703-519-9691; *Fax:* 703-519-1872
mdelvalle@asafishing.org; www.asafishing.org
Social Media: Facebook, Twitter, LinkedIn

Maria del Valle, ICAST Director
Kenneth Andres, ICAST Associate
Gordon Robertson, VP
Mary Jane Williamson, Communications Director

The sportfishing industry's largest trade event is a major catalyst for sales and a terrific networking opportunity for the sportfishing community
Frequency: July

22376 ISHA Annual Conference
International Sports Heritage Association
PO Box 2384
Florence, OR 97439

541-991-7315; *Fax:* 541-997-3871
info@sportsheritage.org;
www.sportsheritage.org
Social Media: Facebook, Twitter, LinkedIn

Karen Bednarski, Executive Director
Sheila Kelly, President
Mike Gibbons, First Vice President
Pete Fierle, Second Vice President
Ed Harris, Treasurer

Session discussions, educational sessions and speakers
140+ Members
Founded in: 1971

22377 Ice Skating Institute
6000 Custe Rd.
Bldg. 9
Plano, TX 75023

972-735-8800; *Fax:* 972-735-8815
isi@skateisi.org; www.skateisi.org
Social Media: Facebook

Peter Martell, Executive Director

The industry's leading trade show where you're sure to find the technical information, products and suppliers you need to run your business every day. Who should attend: Arena owners and managers; Hockey and figure skating coaches and instructors; Ice arena programming directors; Operations personnel; builders and suppliers to the industry.
Frequency: Annual/May

22378 International Pool & Spa Expo
PO Box 612128
Dallas, TX 75261-2128

972-536-6350
888-869-8522; *Fax:* 972-536-6364;
www.poolandspaexpo.com

Tina Brinkley, Operations Coordinator
Kathy Ruff, Operations Manager
Tracy Beaulieu, Conference Manager
Vila Snider, Registration Manager
Donna Bellantone, Assoc Show Director

Latest trends, newest products, and innovative ways to increase sales and add profits to your business.
16M Attendees
Frequency: November

22379 Kansas Sports, Boat and Travel Show
Industrial Expositions
PO Box 480084
Denver, CO 80248

303-892-6800
800-457-2434; *Fax:* 303-892-6322
dseymour@iei-expos.com;
www.bigasalloutdoors.com

Jeff Haughton, President
Dianne Seymour, Expo Manager

Annual show produced by Industrial Expositions.
Frequency: Annual

22380 Let's Play Hockey International Expo
Let's Play Hockey
2721 East 42nd Street
Minneapolis, MN 55406

612-729-0023; *Fax:* 612-729-0259
letsplay@letsplayhockey.com;
www.letsplayhockey.com

Doug Johnson, Contact
Doug Johnson, Publisher
Kevin Kurtt, Editor

Hockey Industry Trade Show. Five days of events. Seminars, races, tournaments, awards banquet, expo demo day, Hall of Fame display, buying group meetings and more.
Founded in: 1999

22381 Lincoln Boat, Sport and Travel Show
Egan Enterprises
4100 North 84th Street
Lincoln, NE 68505-5465

402-466-8102; *Fax:* 402-467-5630;
www.nebraskasportshow.com

Pat Egan, Contact Person

Equipment and supplies for the outdoor life.
Frequency: Annual

22382 Management Conference & Team Dealer Summit
National Sporting Goods Association

1601 Feehanville Drive
Suite 300
Mount Prospect, IL 60056

847-966-6742
800-815-5422; *Fax:* 847-391-9827
conference@nsga.org; www.nsga.org

Jeff Rosenthal, Chairman of the Board
Matt Carlson, President/CEO
Dan Kasen, Director of Information Services

The Sporting Goods industry's premier educational and networking event, featuring programming aimed at ensuring business' success, brings together leaders and industry insiders for engaging conversations and stimulating presentations.

22383 NABC Convention & MarketPlace
National Association of Basketball Coaches
1111 Main St
Suite 1000
Kansas City, MO 64105-2116

816-878-6222; *Fax:* 816-878-6223;
www.nabc.com

Jim Haney, Executive Director
Reggie Minton, Deputy Executive Director
Kevin Henderson, Associate Executive Director
Dottie Yearout, Director of Membership Services
Janelle Guidry, Convention Manager

The Convention offers Professional Development Clinics
Frequency: Annual/Spring

22384 NACDA Convention
Nat'l Assoc of Collegiate Directors of Athletics
24651 Detroit Road
Westlake, OH 44145

440-892-4000; *Fax:* 440-892-4007;
www.nacda.com
Social Media: Facebook, Twitter, LinkedIn

Michael Cleary, Executive Director

Devoted to examining contemporary problems facing today's athletics administrator. Caters to administrators in all levels of intercollegiate athletics with general sessions for the entire membership and breakout sessions which are geared to the specific needs of administrators at all levels of the NCAA, NAIA, and NJCAA

22385 NASC Sports Event Symposium
9916 Carver Road
Suite 100
Cincinnati, OH 45242

513-281-3888; *Fax:* 513-281-1765
info@nascsymposium.com;
www.nascsymposium.com
Social Media: Facebook, Twitter, LinkedIn

Don Schumacher, Executive Director
Beth Hecquet, Director of Meetings and Events

National Association of Sports Commissions. Representing more than 550 organizations. Attendees are provided with new ideas, practical tips and the hottest trends.
550 Members
Founded in: 1992

22386 NASGW Annual Meeting and Expo
National Association of Sporting Goods Wholesalers
1833 Centre Point Circle
Suite 123
Naperville, IL 60563

630-596-9006; *Fax:* 630-544-5055;
www.nasgw.org
Social Media: Facebook, Twitter, LinkedIn

Maurice Desmarais, President
Jack Baumler, Chairman
Kent Williams, Vice Chair
Peter Brownell, Treasurer

Educational, marketing and communications opportunity for the hunting and shooting sports wholesaler, manufacturer and sales professional.
400 Members
Founded in: 1954

22387 NCAA Annual Convention

317-917-6222; *Fax:* 317-917-6888;
www.ncaasports.com
Social Media: Facebook, Twitter, LinkedIn

Trade show and convention
Frequency: January
Founded in: 1915

22388 NFCA National Convention
National Fastpitch Coaches Association
100 G T Thames Drive
Suite D
Starkville, MS 39759

662-320-2155; *Fax:* 662-320-2283
nfca@nfca.org; www.nfca.org
Social Media: Facebook, Twitter, LinkedIn

Lacy Lee Baker, Executive Director
Hildred Deese, Senior Director of Events
Frequency: Annual, December

22389 NSAA National Convention and Trade Show
National Ski Areas Association
133 S Van Gordon Street
Suite 300
Lakewood, CO 80228

303-987-1111; *Fax:* 303-986-2345
nsaa@nsaa.org; www.nsaa.org
Social Media: Facebook, Twitter, LinkedIn

Michael Berry, President
Keri Hone, Director Events/Projects
Tom Moore, Director Conventions/Meetings
Kate Powers, Director Member Services
Amy Steele, Director Sponsorships

Annual convention of the National Ski Areas Association

22390 National Association of Basketball Coaches Annual Convention
1111 Main Street
Suite 1000
Kansas City, MO 64105-2136

816-878-6222; *Fax:* 816-878-6223;
www.nabc.org
Social Media: Facebook, Twitter, LinkedIn

James Haney, Executive Director
Reggie Minton, Deputy Executive Director
Kevin Henderson, Associate Executive Director

Approximately 150 booths offering services and resources for Basketball Coaches.
3M Attendees
Frequency: March/April

22391 National Institute for Golf Management
National Golf Foundation
1150 South US Highway One
Suite 401
Jupiter, FL 33477

561-744-6006
888-275-4643; *Fax:* 561-744-6107
general@ngf.org; www.ngf.org
Social Media: Facebook, Twitter, LinkedIn

Annual golf institute sponsored by the National Golf Foundation.
Frequency: Annual

22392 National Intramural Recreational Sports Association
4185 SW Research Way
Corvallis, OR 97333-1067

541-766-8211; *Fax:* 541-766-8284
nirsa@nirsa.org; www.nirsa.org
Social Media: Facebook, Twitter, LinkedIn

Kent Blumenthal, Executive Director
Dr. William N. Wasson, Owner

This show provides an annual marketplace for athletic and recreational equipment, supplies and services.
1.6M Attendees
Frequency: Annual/April
Founded in: 1950

22393 National Recreation and Park Association's Conference and Exposition
National Recreation and Park Association
22377 Belmont Ridge Road
Ashburn, VA 20148

703-858-0784; *Fax:* 703-858-0794
info@nrpa.org; www.nrpa.org

Britt Esen, Director
Jodie H Adams, President
John Crosby, Marketing

Provides targeted learning opportunities specifically for parks and recreation directors, supervisors and managers, community center directors, recreation programmers, natural resources personnel, therapeutic recreation specialists, citizen advocates and students.
4000 Attendees
Founded in: 1965

22394 National Soccer Coaches Association of America
800 Ann Avenue
Kansas City, KS 66101

913-362-1747
800-458-0676; *Fax:* 913-362-3439
nscaa.com
Social Media: Facebook, Twitter, LinkedIn

Joe Cummings, CEO and Executive Director
Tommy Reder, CFO

Every coach who attends will find something new to add to their soccer reperoire. The trade show consists of more than 300 companies. Attendees can examine the latest soccer-related technology and equipment.
30m Members
9000 Attendees
Frequency: Annual/January
Founded in: 1941

22395 National Trappers Association Sports Show
2815 Washington Avenue
Bedford, IN 47421

812-277-9670
866-680-8727; *Fax:* 812-277-9672
ntaheadquarters@nationaltrappers.com;
www.nationaltrappers.com

Kraig Kaatz, President
Chris Flynn, VP
Kraig Kaatz, General Organizer

300 booths including outdoor sports supplies and dealers.
6M Attendees
Frequency: Annual/August

22396 New York National Boat Show
National Marine Manufacturers Association

148 West 37th Street
11th Floor
New York, NY 10018

212-984-7007; *Fax:* 212-564-2728;
www.nyboatshow.com
Social Media: Facebook, Twitter

Jonathon Pritko, Show Manager
Bob MkAlpine, Exhibitor Relationship Manager
Dan Castellano, Exhibitor Relationships Manager
Elba-Rosales Rise, Show Administrator
Josh Rosales, Operation Coordinator

Annual boat show held at Jacob Javitz Convention Center in New York
Frequency: January

22397 North American Society for Sport Management Conference
North American Society for Sport Management
Slippery Rock University
West Gym 014
Slippery Rock, PA 16057

724-738-4812; *Fax:* 724-738-4858
nassm@sru.edu; www.nassm.com
Social Media: Facebook, Twitter

North American Society for Sport Management annual convention and trade show.

22398 Northwest Sportshow
General Sports Shows
3539 Hennepin Avenue
Minneapolis, MN 55408-3830

612-827-5833
800-777-4766; *Fax:* 612-827-1424

David Perkins, President

Public show offering the finest presentation of outdoor recreation and marine products and services.
205M Attendees
Frequency: March

22399 Outdoorama Family Sport and Travel Show
Michigan United Conservation Clubs
2101 Wood Street
PO Box 30235
Lansing, MI 48909

517-371-1041
800-777-6720; *Fax:* 517-371-1505
membership@mucc.org; www.mucc.org
Social Media: Facebook, Twitter, LinkedIn

Sam Washington, Executive Director
Kelly Snyder, Event/Fundraising Assistant
Evan Steiner, Events/Fundraising Specialist

Michigan's favorite outdoor show featuring over 200,000 square feet of exhibit space dedicated to the latest in fishing and hunting equipment, fishing and power boats, recreational vehicles, outdoor gear and vacationing destinations throughout North America. Four-hundred plus booths.
42000 Attendees
Frequency: February
Founded in: 1974

22400 PTR International Tennis Symposium
Professional Tennis Registry
P.O. Box 4739
Hilton Head Island, SC 29938

843-785-7244
800-421-6289; *Fax:* 843-686-2033
ptr@ptrtennis.org; www.ptrtennis.org
Social Media: Facebook, Twitter, LinkedIn

Dan Santorum, Chief Executive Officer
Julie Jilly, VP Marketing & Special Events
Helma Cap, Membership Director
Peggy Edwards, Director, Communications

Symposium of professional tennis teachers and coaches. PTR has excellent relationships and partnerships with industry leaders such as the USTA, Tennis Industry Association, the ITF and many National Tennis Federations.
15000 Members
Frequency: 2x Per Year
Founded in: 1976

22401 Pop Warner Little Scholars Convention
586 Middletown Boulevard
Suite C-100
Langhorne, PA 19047-1867

215-752-2691; *Fax:* 215-752-2879
webmaster@popwarner.com;
www.popwarner.com
Social Media: Facebook, Twitter

Jon Butler, Executive Director
Mary Fitzgerald, COO
Lisa Moroski, National Cheer/Dance Commissioner
1000 Attendees
Frequency: Bi-Annual

22402 Professional Golfers Association Merchandise Show
Reed Exhibitions
383 Main Avenue
Norwalk, CT 06851

203-404-4800
800-840-5628; *Fax:* 203-840-9628
inquiry@pga.reedexpo.com;
www.pgamerchandiseshow.com
Social Media: Facebook, Twitter

Kara Codio, Marketing/Conference Manager
Sherry Major, Media Relations Manager
Jay Andronaco, Event Marketing Manager

The PGA Merchandise Show provides a snap-shot of the industry as a whole and access to products and services that pertain to every aspect of the game. It is the focal point for new product introductions, professional development programs, business meetings and more.
30M Attendees
Frequency: January

22403 Professional Golfers Association Golf Show
Sydney Convention and Exhibition Centre
Darling Harbour
Sydney
Australia NSW 2000
www.pgaexpo.com
Social Media: Facebook, Twitter, LinkedIn

International PGA Golf Show. 2006 Show held in Australia
50000 Attendees
Frequency: Annual

22404 RSA Convention and Trade Show
Roller Skating Association International
6905 Corporate Drive
Indianapolis, IN 46278

317-347-2626; *Fax:* 317-347-2636
rsa@rollerskating.com; www.rollerskating.org
Social Media: Facebook, Twitter, LinkedIn, You Tube

Bobby Braun, President
Ron Liette, VP
John Purcell, Executive Director

Helping roller skating industry professionals discover ways to build strong foundations for their businesses.
1000 Members
Frequency: annual
Founded in: 1937

22405 Rocky Mountain Snowmobile Expo
Industrial Expositions
1675 Larimer Street
Suite 700
Denver, CO 80202

303-892-6800
800-457-2434; *Fax:* 303-892-6322
dseymour@iei-expos.com;
www.bigasalloutdoors.com
Social Media: Facebook, Twitter

Jeff Haughton, President
Diane Seymour, Expo Manager

Large display of snowmobiles and accessories, meet performance experts, resorts and lodges, winter clothing, ice fishing, winter travel destinations, snowmobile adventure theatre, avalanche awareness, swap meet and more.

22406 SHOT Show: Shooting Hunting Outdoor Trade Show
Reed Exhibition Companies
28 The Quadrant
Richmond 6851

203-404-4800
800-840-5628; *Fax:* 203-840-9628;
www.reedexpo.com

Worldwide annual gathering that unites manufacturer and retailer and all other industry stakeholders to trade, source and learn about the latest products, innovations and trends in the shooting sports industry.
15M Attendees
Frequency: January

22407 SIA Snow Show
SnowSports Industries America
8377-b Greensboro Drive
McLean, VA 22102-3587

703-556-9020; *Fax:* 703-821-8276
siamail@snowsports.org;
www.siasnowshow.com
Social Media: Facebook, Twitter, LinkedIn, YouTube, Wikipedia, Vimeo

From fashion to skis and snowboards to Nordic, snowshoes, outdoor and basic essentials, the SIA Snow Show previews the entire winter sports market and then deads to the on-snow demo to try it all out on snow.
700+ Members
19M Attendees
Frequency: Annual/January
Founded in: 1954

22408 Saltwater Fishing Expo
Eastern Fishing and Outdoor Exposition
PO Box 4720
Portsmouth, NH 03802

603-431-4315; *Fax:* 603-431-1971;
www.sportshows.com

The Saltwater Fishing Expo is expecting over 300 exhibitors representing the entire spectrum of saltwater sportfishing. There will be dozens of seminars throughout the three days of the show, which will be presented by experts who are at the top of their game.

22409 San Mateo Inernational Sportsmen's Expo
International Sportsmen's Exposition
PO Box 2569
Vancouver, WA 98668-2569

360-693-3700
800-545-6100; *Fax:* 360-693-3352;
www.sportsexpos.com

Brian Layng, President/CEO
Rick Flattum, Director Operations
Heidi Crannell, Marketing Coordinator
Bruce Tarbet, Sponsorship/Advertising
Brent Layng, Sales Manager

Fishing, hunting, outdoor sports and destination travel show. Connect with new dealers and network with other exhibitors.

22410 Ski Dazzle Ski Show and Snowboard Expo: Chicago
Ski Dazzle
P.O. Box 1839
Laguna Beach, CA 92651

949-497-4977; *Fax:* 949-497-4123
snowdog@skidazzle.com; www.skidazzle.com
Social Media: Facebook, Twitter, LinkedIn, You Tube

Judy Gray, Owner
Jim Foster, Owner

Hundreds of local, national and international exhibitors including over 85 resorts, ski and snowboard retailers, manufacturers, a huge ski and snowboard sale, and lots of surprises. Over 250 exhibit booths showcasing core companies of skiing and snowboarding.

22411 Ski Dazzle: The Los Angeles Ski Show & Snowboard Expo
P.O. Box 1840
Laguna Beach, CA 92651-1839

949-497-4977; *Fax:* 949-497-4123
snowdog@skidazzle.com; www.skidazzle.com
Social Media: Facebook, Twitter, LinkedIn, You Tube

Judy Gray, Co-Owner
Jim Foster, Owner

Consumer ski show and snowboard expo at the Los Angeles Convention Center offering 350 ski and snowboard related exhibits. Excellent sponsor and promotional opportunities for 18-49 demographic audience.
90000 Attendees
Frequency: November

22412 Soaring Society of America Annual Convention
5425 West Jack Gomez Boulevard
P.O. Box 2100
Hobbs, NM 88241

575-392-1177; *Fax:* 575-392-8154
feedback@ssa.org; www.ssa.org

C Wright, Executive Director

Annual convetion of the Soaring Society of America.

22413 Sporting Goods Manufacturers Markets
1150 17th Street NW
8th Floor
Washington, DC 20036-1604

202-775-1762; *Fax:* 202-296-7462
info@sgma.com; www.sgma.com

Tom Cove, President/CEO
Gregg Harrlety, VP
Kalinda Mathis, Director Marketing

Retailers, distributors, wholesalers, importers/exporters and other buyers of sports related products come for 10,000 exhibits of sports apparel, footwear, accessories and e-commerce products and services.
80000 Attendees
Frequency: Spring/Fall

22414 Sports Licensing & Entertainment Marketplace Tailgate Picnic Show
Showproco, LLC
1450 NE 123rd Street
North Miami, FL 33161

305-893-8771
800-327-3736; *Fax:* 305-893-8783;
www.showproco.com
Social Media: Facebook, Twitter, LinkedIn

Tom Cove, President
Stanley Schwartz, Director

A show dedicated to sports licensed apparel & products with participation from major sports licensors and their licensees. In conjunction will be the Tailgate & Picnic Show, which will bring together all of the products sports fans want to buy. Attendees will represent everything from sporting goods stores to fan shops, grocery to gift shops, drug stores to convenience stores and more.
Frequency: November

22415 Strictly Sail Pacific
Jack London Square
Oakland, CA

800-817-7245; *Fax:* 401-847-2044
info@sailamerica.com; www.strictlysail.com
Social Media: Facebook, Twitter, LinkedIn

Cynthia Goss, Contact

Annual Boat Show. A mix of boats and gear, seminars and special events. It will feature over 300 exhibitors from 25 states and over 90 seminars.

22416 Surf Expo
Surf Expo Offices
990 Hammond Drive
Suite 325
Atlanta, GA 30328

678-817-7970
800-947-7873; *Fax:* 404-220-3030
rturner@surfexpo.com; www.surfexpo.com

Where manufacturers and retailers in the boardsports, and swim and resort industries have come together in a business-first buying and selling environment.
8M Attendees
Frequency: Twice Annually

22417 US Gymnastics Federation
US Gymnastics Congress
Pam American Plaza
201 South Capitol, Suite 300
Indianapolis, IN 46225

317-237-5050; *Fax:* 317-692-5212;
www.usagym.org

Steve Penny, President

Three days of eduction with over 135 sessions offered. Lectures given by recognized top people in the field. Sessions on coaching, judging, business, preschool, recreational, sports science, fitness, Group Gymnastics and cheerleading. The Trade Show exhibit hall will feature 200 booths of products and information from over 85 different Industry Member vendors.
2M Attendees
Frequency: Annual

22418 US Lacrosse National Convention
113 W University Pkwy
Baltimore, MD 21210-3301

410-235-6882; *Fax:* 410-366-6735
info@uslacrosse.org; www.uslacrosse.org
Social Media: Facebook, Twitter

Steve Stenersen, President
Bill Schoonmaker, COO
Bill Rubacky, Managing Director of Marketing
Kira Muller, Director of Advertising Sales

Billed as the unofficial start to lacrosse season, the event gathers the best the sport has to offer; providing the largest educational opportunity with over 5,000 coaches, officials, vendors and administrators in attendance. Over 100 exhibitors
5000 Attendees
Frequency: Annual

22419 USA Track and Field Annual Meeting
One RCA Dome
Suite 140
Indianapolis, IN 46225

317-261-0500; *Fax:* 317-261-0481
membership@usatf.org; www.usatf.org
Social Media: Facebook, Twitter, LinkedIn

Jill Geer, Public Relations

Annual meeting of the USA Track and Field organization.
Frequency: Annual

22420 USTFCCCA Annual Coaches Convention
U.S. Track & Field and Cross Country Coaches Assoc
1100 Poydras Street
Suite 1750
New Orleans, LA 70163

504-599-8900; *Fax:* 504-599-8909
sam@ustfccca.org; www.ustfccca.org
Social Media: Facebook, Twitter, LinkedIn

Sam Seemes, CEO
Mike Corn, Assistant Director
Sylvia Kamp, Administrator
Tom Lewis, Director of Communications

22421 Underwater Intervention
5206 FM 1960 West
Suite 202
Houston, TX 77069

281-893-8539
800-316-2188; *Fax:* 281-893-5118
rroberts@adc-int.org;
www.underwaterintervention.com/
Social Media: Facebook, Twitter, LinkedIn

Rebecca Roberts, Show Manager
Roff Saxon, Executive Director

Conference covering all aspects of underwater operations. Next trade show is scheduled for 2007 with 200+ booths, sponsored by both the Marine Technology Society and the Association of Diving Contractors International.
2500 Attendees
Founded in: 1991

22422 WBCA National Convention
Women's Basketball Coaches Association
4646 Lawrenceville Highway
Lilburn, GA 30047

770-279-8027; *Fax:* 770-279-8473;
www.wbca.org
Social Media: Facebook, Twitter

Beth Bass, CEO
Shannon Reynolds, COO
Seana Peck, Manager Marketing
Stephanie S Baron, Director Events
Dorinda Schremmer, Director Membership/Conventions

Women's Basketball Coaches Association national convention. Held annually.
Founded in: 1981

22423 Water Ski and Wakeboard Expo
1251 Holy Cow Road
Polk City, FL 33868

863-324-4341; *Fax:* 863-325-8529
usawaterski@usawaterski.org;
www.usawaterski.org
Social Media: Facebook, Twitter, LinkedIn

Annual event of the USA Water Ski Organization.
Frequency: Annual

22424 Western Fairs Association Annual Trade Show
Western Fairs Association

1776 Tribute Road
Suite 210
Sacramento, CA 95815-4495

916-927-3100; *Fax:* 916-927-6397
stephenc@fairsnet.org; www.fairsnet.org
Social Media: Facebook, Twitter, YouTube

Rick Pickering, President
Jon Baker, VP
Stephen J Chambers, Executive Director
Nichole Farley, Marketing

Meet face to face with buyers from the Fair and Festival Industry across the Western United States. Acts, attractions, services, supplies, commericial exhibitors and more.
2000 Members
Frequency: Annual/Jan
Founded in: 1922

22425 **Western States Toy and Hobby Show**
Western Toy and Hobby Representative Association
PO Box 2250
Pomona, CA 91786

909-899-3753; *Fax:* 951-277-1599
toyshow@wthra.com; www.wthra.com
Social Media: Facebook, Twitter

Phylis St John, Show Director

If it's for kids, it's here. Show is for trade members only, not open to the public.
3000 Attendees
Frequency: March

22426 **World Fishing and Outdoor Exposition**
Eastern Fishing and Outdoor Exposition
PO Box 4720
Portsmouth, NH 03802-4720

603-431-4315; *Fax:* 603-431-1971
info@sportshows.com; www.sportshows.com
Social Media: Facebook

You'll find the entire world of fishing and hunting and much more.
Frequency: Annual
Founded in: 1978

22427 **World Fly Fishing Expo**
Eastern Fishing and Outdoor Exposition
PO Box 4720
Portsmouth, NH 03802-4720

603-431-4315; *Fax:* 603-431-1971
info@sportshows.com; www.sportshows.com
Social Media: Facebook

This expo has all the major manufacturers of fly rods and reels, fly fishing accessories, fly tying materials, guides and lodges.
Frequency: Annual

Directories & Databases

22428 **Amusement Park Guide**
Globe Pequot Press
246 Goose Ln
Suite 200
Guilford, CT 06437-2186

203-458-4500; *Fax:* 203-458-4601;
www.globepequot.com

James Joseph, President

The complete guide to the amusement parks in the United States and Canada gives the latest details about new rides at each park, with a special focus on roller coasters.
Cost: $14.95
ISBN: 0-762725-37-0

22429 **Athlete and Celebrity Address Directory/Autograph Hunter's Guide**
Global Sports Productions
16810 Crystal Drive East
Suite 101
Santa Monica, CA 90404-2702

310-454-9480; *Fax:* 310-454-6590
globalnw@earthlink.net;
www.sportsbooksempire.com
Social Media: Facebook

Ed Kobak, Owner
Greg Andrews, VP Operations

Complete source of athlete and sports personality addresses from baseball, basketball, football, hockey, golf, tennis, soccer, boxing and autosports. Also included are television, movie and other celebrities' addresses.
Cost: $ 29.95
198 Pages
Frequency: Annual
ISBN: 0-966796-17-9
Founded in: 2005

22430 **Baseball Bluebook**
8373 N Cedar Hills Lane
Fair Grove, MD 65648

417-833-6550; *Fax:* 417-833-9911
dj@baseballbluebook.com;
www.baseballbluebook.com

Dennis Wubbena, Owner
Eric Wubbena, President

Directory of baseball club personnel at all levels of play. Spiral bound directory contains Major Leagues, Minor Leagues and Independent League Personnel, contact information and schedules
Cost: $55.00
500 Pages
Frequency: Annual
Founded in: 1909

22431 **Complete Directory of Fishing Tackle**
Sutton Family Communications & Publishing Company
155 Sutton Lane
Fordsville, KY 42343

270-740-0870
jlsutton@apex.net;
www.suttoncompliance.com

Jerry Sutton, Contact

Listings in directory include names, addresses, phone and fax numbers, and product descriptions from wholesale distributors, Importers, Manufacturers, Close-out houses and liquidators.
Cost: $72.20
100+ Pages

22432 **Complete Directory of Outdoor Products**
Sutton Family Communications & Publishing Company
155 Sutton Lane
Fordsville, KY 42343

270-740-0870
jlsutton@apex.net;
www.suttoncompliance.com

Jerry Sutton, Manager

Print-out from database of wholesalers, manufacturers, distributors, importers and close-out houses. Database is updated daily to guarantee the most current and up-to-date sources available.
Cost: $95.20
100+ Pages

22433 **Complete Directory of Sporting Goods**
Sutton Family Communications & Publishing Company
155 Sutton Lane
Fordsville, KY 42343

270-740-0870
jlsutton@apex.net;
www.suttoncompliance.com

Jerry Sutton, Manager

Print-out from database of wholesalers, manufacturers, distributors, importers and close-out houses. Database is updated daily to guarantee the most current and up-to-date sources available.
Cost: $139.00
100+ Pages

22434 **Computer Sports World**
675 Grier Drive
Las Vegas, NV 89119-3738

702-735-0101
800-321-5562; *Fax:* 702-294-1322
dandros@vegasinsider.com;
www.cswstats.com

Statistical information on all aspects of the sports industry.
Frequency: Full-text
Founded in: 1983

22435 **Encyclopedia of Sports Business Contacts**
Global Sports Productions
1223 Broadway
Suite 101
Santa Monica, CA 90404-2702

310-395-6533; *Fax:* 310-454-6590
globalnw@earthlink.net;
www.sportsbooksempire.com
Social Media: Facebook, Twitter

Ed Kobak, President

This huge book covers the business side of sports with addresses, telephone and fax numbers, emails, websites and entire contact personnel from sports organizations, teams, leagues, publications, lawyers and agents, corporate sponsors, sports marketing and management firms and others.
Cost: $79.95
600 Pages
Frequency: Annual
Founded in: 2005

22436 **Golf Traveler**
Affinity Group
64 Inverness Dr E
Englewood, CO 80112-5114

303-728-7428
800-234-3450; *Fax:* 303-728-7257;
www.affinitygroup.com

Bruce Hoster, Manager

Golf courses and affiliated resorts are listed.
Cost: $2.50
88 Pages
Frequency: BiMonthly
Circulation: 75,000

22437 **International Sports Directory**
Global Sports Productions
1223 Broadway
Suite 101
Santa Monica, CA 90404-2702

310-395-6533; *Fax:* 310-454-6590
globalnw@earthlink.net;
www.sportsbooksempire.com

Ed Kobak, Owner

This all-in-one directory covers the entire world of sports from A to Z. Included are addresses, e-mails, websites, telephone and fax numbers and contact personnel from sports organizations, clubs, teams and publications. The most comprehensive sports directory available, covering both

national and international listings.
Cost: $29.95
500 Pages
Frequency: Annual
ISBN: 1-891655-02-7
Founded in: 1980

22438 Motor Sports Forum
Racing Information Systems
2314 Harriman Ln
Unit A
Redondo Beach, CA 90278-4426

310-374-3750
racing@motorsportsforum.com;
www.motorsportsforum.com

Michael F Hollander, Editor-in-Chief
Bab Karambelas, Senior Editor

This database contains information on auto racing in the United States and Canada.
Frequency: Bulletin Board

22439 News/Retrieval Sports Report
Dow Jones & Company
1155 Avenue of the Americas
New York, NY 10036-2717

212-597-5756; *Fax:* 212-416-4348;
www.dowjones.com

Offers information on sports news stories and statistics from United Press International.
Frequency: Full-text

22440 Orion Blue Book: Guns and Scopes
Orion Research Corporation
14555 N Scottsdale Rd
Suite 330
Scottsdale, AZ 85254-3487

480-951-1114
800-844-0759; *Fax:* 480-951-1117;
www.orionbluebook.com

Roger Rohrs, Owner

List of manufacturers of guns. Current issue contains 18,543 products. Lists products from 1800's to present. Over 300 manufacturers listed.
Cost: $45.00
480 Pages
Frequency: Annual
Founded in: 1992

22441 Parks Directory of the United States
Omnigraphics
615 Griswold Street
Detroit, MI 48226

313-961-1340
800-234-1340; *Fax:* 313-961-1383
editorial@omnigraphics.com;
www.omnigraphics.com

Darren L Smith, Editor

Covers nearly 5,000 national and state parks, and other designated recreational, scenic, and historic areas in the United States and Canada. It provides up-to-date contact and descriptive information for every national and state park in the U.S.
Cost: $185.00
1,100 Pages
Frequency: Biennial
ISBN: 0-780806-63-8

22442 Q&A Booklets
Sporting Goods Agents Association
14555~N~Scottsdale~Rd
Scottsdale~, AZ 60053

847-296-3670; *Fax:* 847-827-0196
sgaa998@aol.com; www.sgaaonline.org

Skip Nipper, President
Lois Halinton, Chief Operating Officer

Sporting Goods Agents Association booklets for manufacturers and agents. Answers questions such as: Why should I use an independent agent rather than hire my own salespeople? What are the most important aspects to examine when I interview an agency? What are independent sporting goods agents and what do they do? What factors should be considered when forming a territory to cover. And more.
Cost: $15.00

22443 Recreation Facilities Products & Services
Sutton Family Communications & Publishing Company
155 Sutton Lane
Fordsville, KY 42343

270-740-0870
jlsutton@apex.net;
www.suttoncompliance.com

Jerry Sutton, Manager

Print-out from database of wholesalers, manufacturers, distributors, importers and close-out houses. Database is updated daily to guarantee the most current and up-to-date sources available. Accepts advertising.
Cost: $97.20
100+ Pages

22444 Recreational Sports Directory
National Intramural Recreational Sports Assn
4185 Sw Research Way
Corvallis, OR 97333-1067

541-766-8211; *Fax:* 541-766-8284
nirsa@nirsa.org; www.nirsa.org

Kent Blumenthal, Executive Director

Directory of services and supplies to the industry.
Cost: $20.00
400 Pages
Frequency: Annual
Circulation: 1,500

22445 Sporting News Baseball Guide
Sporting News Publishing Company
10176 Corporate Square Drive
Suite 200
Saint Louis, MO 63132-2924

314-997-7111; *Fax:* 314-993-7798;
www.sportingnews.com

Jim Nuckols, CEO

A list of National and American League and their affiliate minor leagues.
Cost: $12.95
Frequency: Annual

22446 Sporting News Football Register
Sporting News Publishing Company
10176 Corporate Square Drive
Suite 200
Saint Louis, MO 63132-2924

314-997-7111; *Fax:* 314-993-7798;
www.sportingnews.com

Jim Nuckols, CEO

Directory of services and supplies to the industry.
Cost: $12.95
430 Pages
Frequency: Annual

22447 Sports Address Bible and Almanac
Global Sports Productions
1223 Broadway
Suite 101
Santa Monica, CA 90404-2702

310-395-6533; *Fax:* 310-454-6590
globalnw@earthlink.net;
www.sportsbooksempire.com

Ed Kobak, Owner
Greg Andrews, VP Operations

Over 7,500 sports listings from professional, semi-pro, Olympic and amateur, collegiate and interscholastic sports organizations, leagues, teams, halls of fame, media outlets and more.
Cost: $34.95
505 Pages
Frequency: Biennial
ISBN: 1-891655-11-6
ISSN: 0743-4561
Founded in: 1998

22448 Sports Market Place Directory
Grey House Publishing
4919 Route 22
PO Box 56
Amenia, NY 12501

518-789-8700
800-562-2139; *Fax:* 845-373-6390
books@greyhouse.com; www.greyhouse.com
Social Media: Facebook, Twitter

Leslie Mackenzie, Publisher
Richard Gottlieb, Editor

For over 20 years, this comprehensive, up-to-date directory has offered direct access to the Who, What, When & Where of the Sports Industry. With this directory on your desk, you have a comprehensive tool providing current key information about the people, organizations and events involving the explosive sports industry at your fingertips.
Cost: $225.00
1800 Pages
Frequency: Annual
ISBN: 1-592373-48-8
Founded in: 1981

22449 Sports Market Place Directory - Online Database
Grey House Publishing
4919 Route 22
PO Box 56
Amenia, NY 12501

518-789-8700
800-562-2139; *Fax:* 845-373-6390
gold@greyhouse.com;
www.gold.greyhouse.com
Social Media: Facebook, Twitter

Leslie Mackenzie, Publisher
Richard Gottlieb, Editor

For over 20 years, this comprehensive, up-to-date directory provides current key information about the people, organizations and events involving the sports industry including, contact information and key executives for single sports organizations, multi-sport organizations, media, sponsors, college sports, manufacturers, trade shows and more.
Founded in: 1981

22450 Sports RoundTable
GE Information Services
401 N Washington Street
Rockville, MD 20850-1707

301-388-8284

Cathy Ge, Owner

This database provides coverage of major professional, amateur and collegiate sports including football, basketball, baseball, and hockey.
Frequency: Full-text

22451 SportsAlert
Comtex Scientific Corporation
911 Hope Street
#4838
Stamford, CT 06907-2318

Fax: 203-358-0236; www.sportsalert.net

This database contains sports news and statistics providing real-time coverage of US and international professional, collegiate and amateur athletic events.
Frequency: Full-text

22452 **Tennis-Places to Play: Camps and Clinics Issue**
Golf Digest Tennis NY Times Magazine Group
5520 Park Avenue
Trumbull, CT 06611-3400
203-373-7000; *Fax:* 203-371-2162
Directory of services and supplies to the industry.
Cost: $2.50
Frequency: Annual
Circulation: 800,000

Industry Web Sites

22453 **http://gold.greyhouse.com**
G.O.L.D Grey House OnLine Databases
Grey House Publishing's online database platform, GOLD, offers Quick Search, Keyword Search and Expert Search for most business sectors including sports and recreation markets. The GOLD platform makes finding the information you need quick and easy - whether you're a novice searcher or an experienced database user. All of Grey House's directory products are available for subscription on the GOLD platform.

22454 **www.aahperd.org**
American Alliance for Hlth, Phys. Edu. Rec. Dance

22455 **www.aahperd.org/uawgs**
National Association for Girls and Women in Sports
A non-profit organization serving the needs of teachers, coaches and participants of sports programs for girls and women.

22456 **www.aapsm.org**
American Academy of Podiatric Sports Medicine
The American Academy of Podiatric Sports Medicine was founded in San Francisco by a group of podiatric sports physicians who had the insight to realize the need for a podiatric sports medicine association devoted to the treatment of athletic injuries. Today the AAPSM has over 500 members.

22457 **www.aausports.org**
Amateur Athletic Union of the United States

22458 **www.abca.org**
American Baseball Coaches Association
Formerly called the American Association of College Baseball Coaches.

22459 **www.aca-camps.org**
American Camping Association
Educational programs. Legislative monitoring, child and youth development.

22460 **www.acanet.org**
American Canoe Association
Promotes the sport of canoeing and its safety, recreational and conservation

22461 **www.acsm.org**
American College of Sports Medicine
The ACSM promotes and integrates scientific research, education, and practical applications of sports medicine and exercise science to maintain and enhance physical performance, fitness, health, and quality of life.

22462 **www.adventurecycling.org**
Adventure Cycling Association
Developes road and mountain bike routes, runs bike tours and eventsand also acts as information resource for bicyclists planning trips.

22463 **www.aeawave.com**
Aquatic Exercise Association
Covers topics relating to aquatic fitness and therapy including industry trends, research, programs, exercises and products.

22464 **www.afaa.com**
Aerobics and Fitness Association of America
Association for the education, certification and training of exercise instructors; information resource center for consumers.

22465 **www.ahcahockey.com**
American Hockey Coaches Association
Helps maintain the highest possible standards in hockey and the hockey profession.

22466 **www.americanrunning.org**
American Running Association
To encourage all people, from youth to adults, to improve their health and fitness by walking and running, and maintaining an active and healthy lifestyle.

22467 **www.asgca.org**
American Society of Golf Course Architects
A non-profit organization comprised of leading golf course designers in North America. ASGCA is actively involved in many issues realted to the game of golf, including responsible environmental designs.

22468 **www.athleticclubs.com**
Athletic Net
Click on links to find fitness, sports medicine, general health and wellness, government sites, directories, nutrition and newsgroups.

22469 **www.avca.org**
American Volleyball Coaches Association
To develop and grow the sport of volleyball

22470 **www.baseballcoaches.org**
National High School Baseball Coaches Association
Provides services and recognition for baseball coaches and to help promote and represent high school baseball across the country.

22471 **www.bikeleague.org**
League of American Bicyclists

22472 **www.collegecoaches.org**
College Swimming Coaches Association of America
The oldest organization of college coaches in America; a professional organization of college swimming and diving coaches dedicated to serving and providing leadership for the advancement of the sport of swimming at the collegiate level.

22473 **www.greyhouse.com**
Grey House Publishing
Authoritative reference directories for most business sectors including sports and recreation markets. Users can search the online databases with varied search criteria allowing for custom searches by product category, geographic area, sales volume, keyword, subject and more. Full Grey House catalog and online ordering also available.

22474 **www.iasv.net**
International Academy of Sports Vision
Promotes education, research and development of sports visions. Publishes Sportsvision Magazine and annual scientific journal. Mission is to prevent eye injuries and imprrove visual performance in sports.

22475 **www.instituteofdiving.com**
Institute of Diving
Membership includes sports, commercial and military divers with the purpose being to operate the Museum of Man in the Sea, publish a newsletter, provide a technical library, offer an information exchange, and promote programs and projects for the improvement of knowledge about the underwater world.

22476 **www.iprarodeo.com**
International Professional Rodeo Association
Governing body for professional rodeo. 500 rodeos across USA and Canada, $5 million prize money per year, 5 million fans.

22477 **www.lpga.com**
Ladies Professional Golf Association
For women and youth golfers.

22478 **www.naa-usa.org**
National Aeronautic Association
Members include aerospace corporations, aero clubs, affiliates and major national sporting aviation organizations.

22479 **www.nabc.com**
National Association of Basketball Coaches
Promotes the advancement and opportunities for coaches and teachers in the sport of basketball.

22480 **www.nabf.com**
National Amateur Baseball Association
Promotes amateur baseball and the industry in general.

22481 **www.nacola.com**
Nat'l Assoc of Collegiate Directors of Athletics
Professional association for college atheltics directors, assistants and conference administrators. Provides educational opportunities and serves as a vehicle for networking and the exchange of information to others in the college sports profession.

22482 **www.nasgw.org**
National Association of Sporting Goods
Non-profit trade association of wholesalers, distributors and manufacturers. Serves as a liason with other sporting goods associations.

22483 **www.naso.org**
National Association of Sports Officials
Not-for-profit 501(c)(3) educational association providing individual benefits such as training materials, liability and assault protection insurance and more to sports officials of all sports and every level.

22484 **www.nauticalworld.com**
Nautical World
Dedicated to bringing all related web sites within easy access to watersports enthusiasts. This search engine has been designed to locate advertiser's information within Nautical World but will also offer access to other watersport related web sites as well. Offers sections on marine electronics and hardware, sailing, boats, dock supplies, fishing accessories, diving accessories, industry news, watersports, weather forecasting and more.

22485 **www.nays.org**
National Youth Sports Coaches Association
Represents coaches involved in youth athletics.

22486 **www.nfca.org**
National Fastpitch Coaches Association
The professional growth organization for fastpitch softball coaches from all competitives levels of play.

22487 **www.nflalumni.org**
National Football League Alumni
Provides a forum for those individuals retired from the NFL but still playing an active role.

22488 **www.ngf.org**
National Golf Foundation
Provides market research and serves as an information clearinghouse for the industry. Conducts seminars for golf teachers, coaches and professionals. Conducts golf course development feasibility studies for developers.

22489 **www.njcaa.org**
National Junior College Athletic Association
NJCAA members are two year institutions recognized by the American Association of Community and Junior Colleges.

22490 **www.nra.org**
National Rifle Association
Oldest sportsmen's organization in the US. Maintains the NRA Political Victory Fund and supports the Institute for Legislative Action.

22491 **www.nsga.org**
National Sporting Goods Association
Association of retailers, manufacturers and suppliers of sports equipment, footwear, and apparel.

22492 **www.nsgachicagoshow.com**
Athletic Goods Team Distributors
Strives to keep athletic team dealers informed of rule changes that affect equipment sales.

22493 **www.pga.com**
Professional Golfers Association of America
The world's largest working sports organization comprised of more than 25,000 men and women PGA professionals to promote the game of golf to everyone, and to promote its members as leaders in the golf industry.

22494 **www.popwarner.com**
Pop Warner Little Scholars
A national youth football and cheerleading organization that provides assistance to its various chapters.

22495 **www.r-sports.com**
Sporting Goods Agents Association
International trade association of independent and established sporting goods agents.

22496 **www.restaurantreport.com/top100**
Resturant Report On-Line
Includes top 100 food sites, feature stories, newsletters, buyer's guide, marketplace, hospitality jobs.

22497 **www.rollerskating.com**
Roller Skating Association
Exists for private businessmen and women engaged in the enterprise of roller skating.

22498 **www.rollerskating.org**
Roller Skating Association International
A trade association representing skating center owners, operators; teachers, coaches and judges of roller skating; and manufacturers and suppliers of roller skating equipment.

22499 **www.sabr.org**
Society for American Baseball Research
Membership association whose purpose is to facilitate and disseminate baseball research.

22500 **www.sgma.com**
Sporting Goods Manufacturers Association
For manufacturers, producers, and distributers of sports apparel, athletic footwear, fitness, and sporting goods equipment.

22501 **www.skateisi.org**
Ice Skating Institute
Industry trade association dedicated to providing leadership, education and services to the ice skating industry.

22502 **www.sportsheritage.org**
International Sports Heritage Association
The mission of ISHA is to educate, promote and support organizations and individuals engaged in the celebration of sports heritage.

22503 **www.sportsmarketplce.com**
Grey House Publishing
Provides organizations' contact information with detailed descriptions including: key contacts, physical, mailing, email and web addresses plus phone and fax numbers.

22504 **www.sportsmed.org**
American Orthopaedic Society for Sports Medicine
Promotes the prevention, recognition and orthopedic treatment of sports injuries.

22505 **www.sportsplexoperators.com**
Sportsplex Operators and Developers of Association
SODA was formed to meet the needs of the private concerns, public agencies, and other organizations that own or maintain sports complex facilities.

22506 **www.teamusa.org**
US Olympic Committee
The national committee for the US. Handles the preparation of the US Olympic, Paralympic and Pan American Games teams.

22507 **www.tennisindustry.org**
Tennis Industry Association
To educate the marketplace, fund research and market intelligence and supply this reliable industry data to our member companies. The TIA is the Information source and clearing house for positive tennis news that we supply to TIA members, tennis publications and to the mainstream media in cooperation with the USTA.

22508 **www.usa-swimming.org**
USA Swimming
Devoted to the sport of swimming and its enjoyment nationwide.

22509 **www.usahockey.com**
USA Hockey
Promotes the sport of hockey.

22510 **www.usarchery.org**
National Archery Association
Supports archers while aiming to advance the sport of archery in the US. Monthly newsletter, Nock-Nock, provides communication among the NAA office, NAA clubs, state associations and the individual members of the NAA. Provides members with news and tournament results ranging from the local and state level to international competition.

22511 **www.usatt.org**
USA Table Tennis
Dedicated to the promotion of the sport of table tennis and sponsors the US team. Membership dues are $30 per year for adults and $20 for those 18 years old and under.

22512 **www.usawaterski.org**
USA Water Ski Association
Encourages interest in the sport as well as training and safety.

22513 **www.usaweightlifting.org**
USA Weightlifting
USA Weightlifting is the National Governing Body (NGB) for the Olympic sport of weightlifting in the United States. USA weightlifting is a member of the United States Olympic Committee and a member of the International Weightlifting Federation. As the NGB, USA Weightlifting is responsible for conducting Olympic weightlifting programs throughout the country. The organization conducts a variety of programs that will ultimately develop Olympic, World Championship and Pan American Games' winners.

22514 **www.usfencing.org**
United States Fencing Association
Promotes the sport of fencing in the US.

22515 **www.usfieldhockey.com**
US Field Hockey Association
Represents field hockey, professional and amateur sports.

22516 **www.ushandball.org**
US Handball Association
Organization that runs all the tournaments for the professional and amateur players. Home of the Handball Hall of Fame.

22517 **www.usolimplc.com**
United States Amateur Boxing
Promotes the sport of boxing nationwide.

22518 **www.uspa.org**
United States Parachute Association
A not-for-profit membership association dedicated to the promotion of safe skydiving and the support of those who enjoy it. Sponsors Instructor Rating Program to train and certify instructors, jump masters and examiners.

22519 **www.usra.org**
US Raquetball Association
A nonprofit corporation designed to promote the development of competitive and recreational racquetball in the United States. The association offers a 'competitive license' membership for a one year term at $15.00 annually, or at discounted longer term rates. A lifetime membership is also offered. A 'Club Recreational Membership' program is offered for an annual fee of $150.00 with a reduced AARA recreational membership available to club members for $3.00 per player.

22520 **www.usskiteam.com, www.ussnowboardteam.com**
US Ski & Snowboard Association
Association for skiing and snowboarding nationwide.

22521 **www.usspeedskating.org**
US Speedskating
Devoted to speedskating and its participants on the national and international levels.

22522 **www.ustfccca.org**
U.S. Track & Field and Cross Country Coaches Assoc
A non-profit professional organization that represents men's and women's cross country and track & field coaches in the United States.

22523 **www.uswfa.com**
United States Water Fitness Association
Nonprofit educational organization that promotes aquatics throughout the United States and other countries. Publishes the National Aquatics Newsletter, names the 100 top US water fitness programs and program 5 aquatics in the country,

by state and in 25+ categories. Conducts a wide variety of national aquatics certifications including Water Fitness Instructors (primary and masters), aquatic directors, coordinators of water fitness programs. Conducts annual international aquatics conference.

22524 www.volleyball.org
US Volleyball Association
Promotes volleyball in the US trains the USA men's and women's teams promotes beach and grassroots volleyball in the United States.

22525 www.voyager.net/aabc
American Amateur Baseball Congress
Provides administrative services for amateur baseball youth through adults. 250,000 members.

22526 www.ymca.net
YMCA of the USA
Provides national and state branch divisions.

Associations

22527 Allied Stone Industries
PO Box 288145
Chicago, IL 60628-8145

773-928-4800; *Fax:* 773-928-4129;
www.alliedstone.com
Social Media: Facebook, Twitter

Gary Ballerini, President
Pam Pine, VP
Brundene Van Ness, President-Elect
Butch Coleman, Treasurer
Bill Halquist, Secretary

Quarries, fabricators and dealers in stone and concrete.
55 Members
Founded in: 1950

22528 American Concrete Institute
38800 Country Club Drive
PO Box 9094
Farmington Hills, MI 48331

248-848-3700; *Fax:* 248-848-3701
ron.burg@concrete.org; www.concrete.org
Social Media: Facebook, Twitter, LinkedIn, Youtube

Anne M Ellis, President
William B Rushing, VP
Sharon L Wood, VP
Ronald G Burg, Executive VP

ACI is a scientific and educational society representing the interests of concrete users concerned with the design, construction, or maintenance of concrete structures. Conventions and meetings, monthly periodicals and special publications; chapter activities; and technical committees all provide a forum for concrete interests to discuss problems relating to concrete.
20000 Members
Founded in: 1904

22529 American Concrete Pavement Association
9450 W Bryn Mawr Ave.
Suite 150
Rosemont, IL 60018

847-966-2272; *Fax:* 847-966-9970
acpa@acpa.org; www.pavement.com
Social Media: Facebook, Twitter, LinkedIn, Youtube

Jerry Voigt, CEO & President
Mike Lipps, Chairman
Steve Jackson, Vice Chairman
Lori Tiefenthaler, 2nd Vice Chair
Glenn Eder, Treasurer

ACPA is committed to promoting the quality and superiority of concrete pavements. It leads and assists its members in market development, technical expertise, design innovation, research, and public relations. ACPA's membership includes contractors, cement companies, material suppliers, equipment manufacturers and suppliers, ready mix producers, allied associations, bonding and insurance companies, and consulting firms.
Founded in: 1963

22530 American Concrete Pipe Association
8445 Freeport Parkway
Suite 350
Irving, TX 75063-2595

972-506-7216; *Fax:* 972-506-7682
info@concrete-pipe.org;
www.concrete-pipe.org
Social Media: Facebook, Twitter, LinkedIn, Youtube, Pinterest

Michael D. Kusch, Chairman
A. C. Gossett, III, Vice Chairman
Darren Wise, Secretary
Brian Rhees, Treasurer
Matt Childs, P.E., President

The American Concrete Pipe Association (ACPA) is a nonprofit organization, composed primarily of manufacturers of concrete pipe and related conveyance products located throughout the United States, Canada and in over 40 foreign countries.
145 Members
Founded in: 1907

22531 American Natural Soda Ash Corporation
15 Riverside Avenue
2nd Floor
Westport, CT 06880

203-226-9056; *Fax:* 203-227-1484
contact@ansac.org; www.ansac.com
Social Media: Facebook, Twitter

Donna McSwain-Santos, Marketing

ANSAC markets, sells and distributes high quality soda ash to over 40 countries around the world.
Founded in: 1984

22532 American Society of Concrete Contractors
2025 S Brentwood Blvd
Suite 105
St Louis, MO 63144-1850

314-962-0210
866-788-2722; *Fax:* 314-968-4367
questions@ascconline.org;
www.ascconline.org
Social Media: Facebook, Twitter, LinkedIn, Pinterest

Scott M. Anderson, President
Anthony R. DeCarlo, Jr., VP
Chris Forster, VP
Mario Garza, VP
Keith Wayne, Treasurer/Secretary

The American Society of Concrete Contractors/ASCC seeks to continually advance the qualifications of concrete constructors and encourage greater interaction between designer and constructor. Publishes the Contactor's Guide to Quality Concrete Construction jointly with ACI. Issues Safety Alerts, Safety Bulletins, and a Safety Manual as well as a troubleshooting newsletter, management reports, and a members bulletin.

22533 Concrete Employers Association
900 Spring Street
Silver Spring, MD 20910

240-485-1139
888-846-7622; *Fax:* 301-585-4219
rgarbini@nrmca.org; www.nrmca.org
Social Media: Facebook, Twitter, LinkedIn, Youtube

Robert Garbini, President
Deana Angelastro, Executive Administrator
Allen Hamblen, Chairman
Ted Chandler, Vice Chairman
Scott Parson, Secretary/Treasurer

Concrete plant manufacturers.
Founded in: 1930

22534 Concrete Foundations Association
113 W First Street
PO Box 204
Mount Vernon, IA 52314

319-895-6940; *Fax:* 320-213-5556
info@cfawalls.org; www.cfawalls.org

David Martinson, President
Dennis Purinton, Vice-President
Phillip Marone, Secretary
Doug Herbert, Treasurer
Jim Bartley, Past-President

Members are residential foundation contractors and their suppliers. The association produces promotional, marketing and technical materials for members' potential customers; provides its members with newsletters, industry publications, and seminar and trade show opportunities; develops specifications, technical information, and safety programs; and represents its members on national code bodies.
300 Members
Founded in: 1975

22535 Concrete Polishing Association of America
38800 Country Club Dr.
Farmington Hills, MI 48331
443-249-7919
info@cpaa-us.org; www.cpaa-us.org
Social Media: Facebook, Twitter

Chad Gill, President

Supporting and shaping the concrete polishing industry.
Founded in: 2009

22536 Concrete Promotion Council of Northern California
6966 Sunrise Boulevard
Suite 329
Citrus Heights, CA 95610

916-952-0437
888-633-0393; *Fax:* 831-302-7330
Paulette.Salisbury@cncement.org;
www.cpcnc.org

Paulette Salisbury, Interim Director
Bill Albanese, President Board of Directors
Jeff Nehmens, Treasurer Board of Directors
Dave Bearden, Member Board of Directors
Curt Higgins, Member Board of Directors

A member of the Pacific Southwest Concrete Alliance, composed of companies from all parts of the Northern Californian concrete industry including ready mix suppliers, cement producers, admixture manufacturers, concrete contractors as well as members of the public and private design committees. Their mission is to increase the quantity and diversity of quality concrete projects in Northern California through providing educational opportunities to the Professional Design Community.

22537 Concrete Reinforcing Steel Institute
933 N Plum Grove Road
Schaumburg, IL 60173-4758

847-517-1200; *Fax:* 847-517-1206
brisser@crsi.org; www.crsi.org
Social Media: Facebook, Twitter, LinkedIn

David McDonald, President
Joe Culligan, Chief Financial Officer
Steven Hawkins, Sr., VP, Marketing
David McDonald, Managing Director
Barbara Burchett, Government Affairs

Conducts research and provides technical information on reinforced concrete design and construction practices.
1600 Members
Founded in: 1924

22538 Concrete Sawing and Drilling Association
100 2nd Ave S
Suite 402N
St Petersburg, FL 33701

727-577-5004; *Fax:* 727-577-5012
info@csda.org; www.csda.org
Social Media: Facebook, LinkedIn, Youtube

Kevin Baron, President
Jack Sondergard, VP
Mike Orzechowski, Secretary/Treasurer
Patrick O'Brien, Executive Director

To promote the use of professional specialty sawing and drilling contractors and their methods.
525 Members
Founded in: 1972

22539 Expanded Shale Clay and Slate Institute
35 E Wacker Drive
Suite 850
Chicago, IL 60601

801-272-7070; *Fax:* 312-644-8557
info@escsi.org; www.escsi.org
Social Media: LinkedIn, Youtube

John Riese, President

Sponsors research at engineering schools, educational seminars and develops industry standards.
Founded in: 1908

22540 Indiana Limestone Institute of America
1502 I Street
Suite 400
Bedford, IN 47421

812-275-4426; *Fax:* 812-279-8682;
www.iliai.com

Jim Owens, Technical Director
Todd Schnatzmeyer, Executive Director
Dave Morthland, Office Manager

The trade association which represents quarries and fabricators of Indiana Limestone, as well as associate members who supply goods or services to the industry, ILIA's charte is to eductate and promote
90 Members
Founded in: 1928

22541 International Cast Polymer Alliance
3033 Wilson Blvd
Suite 420
Arlington, VA 22201

703-525-0511; *Fax:* 703-525-0743;
www.icpa-hq.org

Debbie Cannon, President
John Webster, President Elect
Jack Simmons, Secretary
Jamie Myers, Immediate Past President

Formerly known as the Cultured Marble Institute, is a nonprofit organization representing over 300 members including manufacturers, suppliers, fabricators, and installers of cultured marble, cultured granite, cultured onyx, and solid surface kitchen and bath products.

22542 Marble Institute of America
380 E. Lorain Street
Suite 100
Oberlin, OH 44074

440-250-9222; *Fax:* 440-774-9222
miainfo@marble-institute.com;
www.marble-institute.com
Social Media: Facebook, Twitter, LinkedIn, Youtube

Jonathan Zanger, President
Tony Malisani, VP
Dan Rea, Secretary
David Castelucci, Treasurer

The Marble Institute of America (MIA) is the authoritative source of information on standards of natural stone workmanship and practice and the suitable application of natural stone products.
2000 Members
Founded in: 1907

22543 Masonry Society
105 South Sunset Street
Suite Q
Longmont, CO 80501-6172

303-939-9700; *Fax:* 303-541-9215
info@masonrysociety.org;
www.masonrysociety.org
Social Media: LinkedIn

Dr. Russell Brown, President
Scott Walkowicz, President-Elect
Jerry Painter, Vice President
Philip Samblanet, Executive Director
Susan Scheurer, TMS Meeting Planner

Dedicated to the advancement of scientific, engineering, architectual and construction knowledge of masonry. Promotes research and education and disseminates information on masonry materials, design, construction. Publishes newsletters, codes & specifications and material on masonry design.
700 Members
Founded in: 1977

22544 National Concrete Burial Vault Association
136 South Keowee Street
Dayton, OH 45402
407-788-1996
888-88 -NCBV; *Fax:* 937-222-5794
info@ncbva.org; www.ncbva.org

Jerry Russell, President
Mark Bates, President Elect
Steve Handley, Secretary/Treasurer
Michael Crummitt, Immediate Past President
Ed Bruns, Director

A voluntary nonprofit organization of concrete burial vault manufacturers throughtout the United States and Canada. The purpose of the organization is to provide a unified voice for the concrete burial vault industry regardless of product affiliation, brand recognition or location.
350 Members
Founded in: 1930

22545 National Concrete Masonry Association
13750 Sunrise Valley Dr
Herndon, VA 20171-4662

703-713-1900; *Fax:* 703-713-1910
info@ncma.org; www.ncma.org
Social Media: Facebook, Twitter, LinkedIn, Pinterest

Robert Thomas, President
Ron Churchill, Director of Sales
Joseph Bowen, Chairman
Patrick Sauter, Chairman-Elect
Dale Puskas, Past Chairman

The national trade association representing the concrete masonry industry. The association is involved in a broad range of technical, research, marketing, government relations and community activities.
Founded in: 1918

22546 National Lime Association
200 N Glebe Rd
Suite 800
Arlington, VA 22203-3728

703-243-5463; *Fax:* 703-243-5489
wcherz@lime.org; www.lime.org
Social Media: Facebook

William C Herz, Executive Director
Jonathan De'Ath, Director
Hunter L. Prillaman, Director, Govt. Affairs
Lori D Oney, Director, Finance, Administration
Robert A. Hirsch, Director, Environment

Trade association for US and Canadian manufacturers of high calcium quicklime, dolomitic quicklime and hydrated lime, collectively referred to as lime. NLA represents the interests of its members in Washington, provides input on standards and specifacations for lime, and funds and manages research on current and new uses for lime.
Founded in: 1902

22547 National Precast Concrete Association
200 North Glebe
Suite 200
Arlington, IN 46032

317-571-9500
800-366-7731; *Fax:* 317-571-0041
npca@precast.org; www.precast.org
Social Media: Facebook, Twitter, LinkedIn, Youtube, RSS, Flickr

William C. Herz, MPH, Executive Director
Phillip Cutler, VP, Technical Services
Lori D. Oney, VP, Finance & Administration
Brenda Ibitz, VP, Development & Member Services
Bob Whitmore, VP, Communications & Public Affairs

An international trade organization, NPCA represents manufacturers of plant produced precast concrete products and companies that provide the equipment, supplies and services to make these products. NPCA also provides technical information throught nine product committees, which consist of members who concentrate on specific product lines within the precast industry.
1100 Members
Founded in: 1965

22548 National Ready Mixed Concrete Association
900 Spring St
Silver Spring, MD 20910-4015

301-587-1400
888-846-7622; *Fax:* 301-585-4219
info@nrmca.org; www.nrmca.org
Social Media: Facebook, Twitter, LinkedIn, Youtube

Robert Garbini, President
Deana Angelastro, Executive Administrator
Allen Hamblen, Chairman
Ted Chandler, Vice Chairman
Scott Parson, Secretary/Treasurer

NRMCA represents its membership of ready mixed concrete producrs in market development, technical research, engineering advances, government relations, and regulatory issues. In addition to conducting educational seminars, workshops, conferences and trade shows, NRMCA disseminates a wide variety of publications for its members, ranging from Congressional digests and promotion pointers to driver education.
Founded in: 1930

22549 Ornamental Concrete Producers Association
759 Phelps Johnson Rd
Leitchfield, KY 42754
270-879-6319; *Fax:* 218-751-2186
delpreus@paulbunyan.net;
www.ornamentalconcrete.org

Del Preuss, Executive Director
Robert Garbini, President
Shawnita Dickens, Manager

An international nonprofit educational association comprised of producers and suppliers.
Cost: $50.00
500 Members
Founded in: 1991

22550 Portland Cement Association
5420 Old Orchard Road
Skokie, IL 60077-1083

847-966-6200; *Fax:* 847-966-9781
info@cement.org; www.cement.org
Social Media: Facebook, Twitter, LinkedIn, YouTube

James Toscas, President/CEO
John Stull, Chair
Karl Watson Jr., Vice-Chair

Tom Beck, President
Steve Ambrose, Vice President

The Portland Cement Association represents cement companies in the United States and Canada. It conducts market development, engineering, research, education, and public affairs programs.
Founded in: 1916

22551 Post-Tensioning Institute
Bldg Main
38800 Country Club Dr
Farmington Hills, MI 48331-3439

248-848-3180; *Fax:* 248-848-3181
info@post-tensioning.org;
www.post-tensioning.org
Social Media: Facebook, Twitter, LinkedIn

Theodore L Neff, Executive Director
Robert Sward, President
David Martin, VP
Guy Cloutier, Secretary
Marc Khoury, Past President

Provides research, technical development, marketing and promotional activities for companies engaged in post-tensioned prestressed construction. Members include fabricators and manufacturers.
900 Members
Founded in: 1976

22552 Refractories Institute
1300 Sumner Avenue
PO Box 8439
Cleveland, OH 44115

216-241-7333; *Fax:* 216-241-0105;
www.refractoriesinstitute.org

Robert Crolius, President

A trade association which promotes the interests of the refractories industry. TRI has a long tradition of providing support and services to manufacturers of refractory materials and products and suppliers of raw materials, equipment, and services to the refractories industry.
80 Members
Founded in: 1951

22553 Specialty Minerals
Minerals Technology
405 Lexington Ave
New York, NY 10174-0002

212-986-2486
800-801-1031; *Fax:* 610-882-8726;
www.mineralstech.com

Joseph C Muscari, Executive Chairman
Robert S Wetherbee, President & CEO
Douglas T Dietrich, Senior VP/CFO
D J Monagle III, Senior VP/Managing Director
Thomas J Meek, Senior VP/General Counsel/Secretary

A subsidiary of Minerals Technology, Inc., a resource and technology based organization that develops and produces performance-enhancing minerals, mineral-based and synthetic mineral products for the paper, steel, polymer, healthcare and other manufacturing industries on a worldwide basis.
Founded in: 1992

22554 Tilt-Up Concrete Association
113 First Street W
PO Box 204
Mount Vernon, IA 52314-0204

319-895-6911; *Fax:* 320-213-5555
info@tilt-up.org; www.tilt-up.org
Social Media: Facebook, Twitter, LinkedIn, You Tube

Kimberley Corwin, President
Shane Miller, President Elect
Andrew S McPherson, Treasurer
James M Williams, Secretary

TCA members include contractors, suppliers, architects, and engineers dedicated to the advancement of quality tilt-up concrete construction. Activities include a national promotional program, information clearinghouse, educational seminars, referral service, achievement awards program, development of codes and standards, and a quarterly magazine.
Founded in: 1986

Newsletters

22555 Concrete Openings
Concrete Sawing and Drilling Association
13577 Feather Sound Drive
Suite 560
Clearwater, FL 33762

727-577-5004; *Fax:* 727-577-5012
info@csda.org; www.csda.org
Social Media: Facebook, LinkedIn

Patrick O'Brien, Executive Director
500 Members
300 Attendees
Frequency: Quarterly
Circulation: 17000
Founded in: 1972

22556 Cutting Edge
Marble Institute of America
28901 Clemens Road
Suite 100
Cleveland, OH 44145

440-250-9222; *Fax:* 440-250-9223
miainfo@marble-institute.com;
www.marble-institute.com

Gary Distelhorst, Executive VP/CEO
Helen Distelhorst, Director Meetings/Special Events
Jim Hieb, VP
Frequency: Monthly
Circulation: 1500

22557 Refractory News
Refractories Institute
630 Smithfield Street
Suite 1160
Pittsburgh, PA 15222-3907

412-281-6787; *Fax:* 412-281-6881
triassn@aol.com; www.refractoriesinstitute.org
Social Media: Facebook, Twitter

Flo Story, Editor

A monthly newsletter featuring timely industry news, information on federal regulations, member updates, announcements on seminars, and the latest refractory information and statistics.
Cost: $24.00
4 Pages
Frequency: Monthly
Circulation: 700
Founded in: 1951
Mailing list available for rent
Printed in 2 colors on matte stock

Magazines & Journals

22558 ACI Materials Journal
American Concrete Institute
38800 Country Club Drive
PO Box 9094
Farmington Hills, MI 48333-9094

248-848-3700; *Fax:* 248-848-3701
shannon.hale@concrete.org;
www.concrete.org/pubs/journals/mjhome.asp

Shannon M Hale, Technical Editor
Carl R Bischof, Senior Editor Publishing Services
Renee J Lewis, Publishing & Event Services
Douglas J Sordyl, Marketing/Sales/Industry Relations
Donna G Halstead, Finance & Administration

ACI Materials Journal contains individually authored papers as well as papers developed for convention sessions. These papers address structural research, materials research, design theory, structural analysis, and state-of-the-art reviews.
Founded in: 1904
Mailing list available for rent

22559 ACI Structural Journal
American Concrete Institute
38800 Country Club Drive
PO Box 9094
Farmington Hills, MI 48333-9094

248-848-3700; *Fax:* 248-848-3701
shannon.hale@concrete.org;
www.concrete.org/pubs/journals/sjhome.asp

Shannon M Hale, Technical Editor
Carl R Bischof, Senior Editor Publishing Services
Renee J Lewis, Publishing & Event Services
Douglas J Sordyl, Marketing/Sales/Industry Relations
Donna G Halstead, Finance & Administration

ACI Structural Journal contains individually authored papers as well as papers developed for convention sessions. These papers address structural research, materials research, design theory, structural analysis, and state-of-the-art reviews.
Founded in: 1904
Mailing list available for rent

22560 Cement Americas
Primedia
11555 Central Parkway
10th Floor
Chicago, IL 60606

312-726-2802; *Fax:* 312-726-2574;
www.cementamericas.com

Steven Prokopy, Editor
Norm Rose, Sales

Cement Americas provides comprehensive coverage of the North and South American cement markets from raw materials extraction to delivery and transportation to the end user. Production-oriented articles focus on areas where the market activity is at its greatest. Coverage of new ideas, technological improvements, industry trends, and views from leading figures in the cement industry ensure that Cement Americas remains the cement industry journal of the Americas.
ISSN: 0035-7464
Printed in 4 colors on glossy stock

22561 Concrete InFocus
Naylor Publications
5950 NW 1st Pl
Gainesville, FL 32607-6018

352-332-1252
800-369-6220; *Fax:* 352-331-3525
chodges@naylor.com; www.naylor.com
Social Media: Facebook, Twitter, LinkedIn, You Tube

Michael Moss, President

Magazine that's mailed to 5,000+ industry personnel.

22562 Concrete International
American Concrete Institute
38800 Country Club Drive
PO Box 9094
Farmington Hills, MI 48333-9094

248-848-3700; *Fax:* 248-848-3701
ron.burg@concrete.org; www.concrete.org

Carl R Bischof, Senior Editor
Ronald G Burg, Executive Vice President

The circulation is concentrated among the most important professionals in the concrete field; the engineers, architects, contractors, manufacturers, and technicians largely responsible for the advancement of concrete technology and practice.
Frequency: Monthly
Circulation: 20000

22563 Concrete Masonry Designs
NCMA
13750 Sunrise Valley Dr
Herndon, VA 20171-4662

703-713-1900; *Fax:* 703-713-1910
ncma@ncma.org; www.ncma.org

Robert Thomas, President
Ron Churchill, Director Of Sales

Highlights concrete masonry applications, best practice tips, specifications and details. Also showcases concrete masonry landscape products.
Cost: $1.00
Frequency: Monthly
Circulation: 25000
Founded in: 1918
Printed in 4 colors on glossy stock

22564 Concrete Openings
Concrete Sawing and Drilling Association
13577 Feather Sound Drive
Suite 560
St Petersburg, FL 33762

727-577-5004; *Fax:* 727-577-5012
info@csda.org; www.concreteopenings.com
Social Media: Facebook

Cherryl O'Brien, Editor
Russell Hitchen, Associate Editor
Patrick O'Brien, Publisher

The official magazine of the Concrete Sawing & Drilling Association. Editorial contributions are welcomed and advertisements are encouraged.
Frequency: Quarterly
Circulation: 16000
ISSN: 1093-6483

22565 Concrete Producer
Hanley Wood
426 S Westgate
Addison, IL 60101

630-543-0870; *Fax:* 847-564-9287
ryelton@hanleywood.com;
www.theconcreteproducer.com

Richard Yelton, Editor-in-Chief
Tom Bagsarian, Managing Editor
Chari O'Rourke, Circulation Manager

Written for decision-making professionals who buy and specify materials, plant equipment, accessories, trucks, and related products used in the major concrete-producing market segments. Each issue offers money saving operational tips, management advice, new products and technology, and solutions to complex concrete-production questions.

22566 Contemporary Stone & Tile Design
Business News Publishing Company
299 Market Street
Suite 320
Saddle Brook, NJ 07663

201-845-5035; *Fax:* 201-291-9002;
www.stoneworld.com

Alex Backrach, Publisher
Michael Reis, Editor

Promotes the benefits of natural stone and ceramic tile to a readership of architects, interior designers, specifiers and consumers. Practical tips and commentary on stone and tile design are included, featuring interviews with architects and designers from the world's leading firms.
Cost: $125.00
Frequency: Quarterly
Circulation: 21000
Founded in: 1987

22567 MC
National Precast Concrete Association
10333 N Meridian St
Suite 272
Indianapolis, IN 46290-1081

317-571-9500
800-366-7731; *Fax:* 317-571-0041
rhyink@precast.org; www.precast.org

Ty Gable, President
Brenda Ibitz, Manager Advertising

MC magazine features detailed articles about the latest industry technologies and developments, perspectives on current industry events, profiles on leading precast concrete companies and case studies of various manufactured concrete applications.
Frequency: Bi-Monthly

22568 Masonry Construction
Hanley Wood
426 S Westgate
Addison, IL 60101

630-543-0870; *Fax:* 847-564-9287
ryelton@hanleywood.com;
www.masonryconstruction.com
Social Media: Facebook, Twitter

Richard Yelton, Editor-in-Chief
Ron Holzhauer, Deputy Editor
Kari Moosman, Associate Editor
Ted Worthington, Managing Editor
Chari O'Rourke, Circulation Manager

Masonry Construction brings together the complex and fragmented components of the masonry industry—contractors, general contractors, architects, engineers, and producers—providing technical advice, innovative methods and materials, state-of-the-art projects, and essential product information.

22569 Precast
National Precast Concrete Association
1320 City Center Drive
Suite 200
Carmel, IN 46032

317-571-9500
800-366-7731; *Fax:* 317-571-0041
npca@precast.org; www.precast.org

Ty Gable, President
Brenda Ibitz, VP Development and Member Services
Frequency: Bi-Monthly
Circulation: 5000

22570 Professional Builder
Reed Business Information
8878 Barrons Blvd
Littleton, CO 80129-2345

303-470-4000
800-446-6551; *Fax:* 303-470-4691
subsmail@reedbusiness.com;
www.reedbusiness.com

Tim Myers, Executive
Stuart Whayman, Finance
Nathan Cahill, HR

The magazine for professionals within the residential building industry. Articles cover industry news, company profiles, market reports, construction technology and merchandising information needed to successfully complete each job.
Frequency: Monthly
Founded in: 1977

22571 Rock Products
Primedia
29 N Wacker Drive
10th Floor
Chicago, IL 60606

312-726-2802; *Fax:* 312-726-2574;
www.rockproducts.com

Rick Markley, Editor
Scott Bieda, Publisher
Sean ~ Carr, Sales Manager

The aggregate industry's journal of applied technology.
Frequency: Monthly
ISSN: 0035-7464
Founded in: 1905

22572 Stone World
BNP Media
210 E State Rt 4
Suite 203
Paramus, NJ 07652-5103

201-291-9001; *Fax:* 201-291-9002
info@stoneworld.com; www.stoneworld.com

Alex Bachrach, Publisher

A source of information on stone use in architecture and interior design as well as stone production, distribution, installationm and maintenance.

Trade Shows

22573 CSDA Convention and Tech Fair
Concrete Sawing and Drilling Association
13577 Feather Sound Drive
Suite 560
Clearwater, FL 33762

727-577-5004; *Fax:* 727-577-5012
info@csda.org; www.csda.org
Social Media: Facebook, LinkedIn

Patrick O'Brien, Executive Director
500 Members
300 Attendees
Frequency: Annual
Founded in: 1972

22574 Composites and Polycon Convention
American Composites Manufacturers Association
1010 North Glebe Road
Suite 450
Arlington, VA 22201

703-525-0511; *Fax:* 703-525-0743
info@acmanet.org; www.acmanet.org

Three-day convention. Attendees will have the opportunity to choose from 100 presentations, live demonstrations and technical papers. Covering every level of expertise from beginer to advanced, industry experts will address dozens of subject areas in the most striking detail, from technical to production to regulatory to management and more.
Frequency: Annual

22575 Manufactured Concrete Products Exposition
National Concrete Masonry Association
13750 Sunrise Valley Drive
Herndon, VA 20171-4662

703-713-1900; *Fax:* 703-713-1910
ncma@ncma.org; www.ncma.org

Mark Hogan, President
Ron Churchill, Director Of Sales

The Manufactured Concrete Products Exposition is brought to you by a partnership between the National Concrete Masonry Association, the Interlocking Concrete Paving Institute and the American Concrete Pipe Association.
Frequency: Annual

22576 **National Concrete Burial Vault Association Convention**
NCBVA
195 Wekiva Springs Road
Suite 200
Longwood, FL 32779
407-788-1996; *Fax:* 407-774-6751;
www.ncbva.org
Thomas A Monahan, Executive Director
Heather Jones, Conventions/Event Planning
Convention held annually. Includes awards banquet, installation of officers and more.
Frequency: Annual

22577 **PTI Technical Conference and Exhibition**
Post-Tensioning Institute
38800 Country Club Drive~
Farmington Hills, MI 48331
248-848-3180; *Fax:* 248-848-3181
info@post-tensioning.org;
www.post-tensioning.org
Ted Neff, Executive Director
Larry Krauser, President
Marc Khoury, VP
Robert Sward, Secretary
Earn CEUs, attend technical sessions, awards events, exhibits, and ask-the-expert forum.
Frequency: May

22578 **Precast Show**
National Precast Concrete Association
1320 City Center Drive
Suite 200
Carmel, IN 46032-1074
317-571-9500
800-366-7731; *Fax:* 317-571-0041
npca@precast.org; www.precast.org
Social Media: Facebook, Twitter, LinkedIn, You Tube
Ty Gable, President
Erica Wells, Director Meetings
Trade show for the precast concrete industry, containing 300 booths and 300 exhibits.
3000 Attendees
Frequency: Annual

22579 **StonExpo**
Marble Institute of America
28901 Clemens Road
Suite 100
Cleveland, OH 44145
440-250-9222; *Fax:* 440-250-9223;
www.marble-institute.com
Gary Distelhorst, EVP/CEO
Helen Distelhorst, Meetings/Special Events Director
Where fabricators, installers and distributors can experience everything from natural stone extracted from quarries around the world, to the most technologically advanced fabricating machinery, to the beautiful finished product: exquisite countertops that are installed in both residential and commercial properties today.
Frequency: Annual/January

22580 **World of Concrete Exposition**
Post Tensioning Institute
8601 North Black Canyon Highway
Suite 103
Phoenix, AZ 85021
602-870-7540; *Fax:* 602-870-7541
info@post-tensioning.org;
www.post-tensioning.org
Seminars, exhibits and trade shows. Sponsored by the Post-Tensioning Institute.
36M Attendees
Frequency: January/Febuary

Directories & Databases

22581 **CSDA Resource Guide & Membership Directory**
Concrete Sawing and Drilling Association
100 2nd Avenue S
Suite 402N
St. Petersburg, FL 33701
727-577-5004; *Fax:* 727-577-5012
info@csda.org; www.csda.org
Patrick O'Brien, Executive Director
Cost: $12.00
500 Members
97 Pages
Founded in: 1972

22582 **Dimension Stone Design Manual**
Marble Institute of America
28901 Clemens Rd
Suite 100
Cleveland, OH 44145-1166
440-250-9222; *Fax:* 440-250-9223
mia@marble-institute.com;
www.marble-institute.com
Gary Distelhorst, Executive VP
Helen Distelhorst, Director Meetings/Special Events
Jim Hieb, VP
Michael A. Twiss, President
An authoritative source for guidelines on using natural stone in architectural designs. Contents include sections on granite, marble, limestone, serpentine, travertine, quartz-based stone and slate with product descriptions and technical data; general installation guidelines; guidelines and typical detailing for horizontal surfaces, vertical surfaces, wet areas, furniture and countertops; maintenance of exterior/ interior stone installations; and a glossary of terms relating to dimension stone.
Cost: $90.00
350 Pages
Founded in: 1960

22583 **Dimension Stones of the World: Book of Color Plates**
Marble Institute of America
28901 Clemens Rd
Suite 100
Cleveland, OH 44145-1166
440-250-9222; *Fax:* 440-250-9223
mia@marble-institute.com;
www.marble-institute.com
Gary Distelhorst, Executive VP
Helen Distelhorst, Director Meetings/Special Events
Jim Hieb, VP
Michael A. Twiss, President
This set contains over 600 full color reproductions of granites, limestones, marbles, onyx, quartz based stone, slate and travertine. On the reverse side of each page are the ASTM test values for absorbption, density, compressive strength, hardness and flexural strength. Also listed for each stone are primary name, country of origin, quarry location, geological age, color range, recommended usage and available sizes.
Cost: $330.00
Founded in: 1960

22584 **Online MCP**
American Concrete Institute
38800 Country Club Drive
PO Box 9094
Farmington Hills, MI 48333-9094
248-483-3700; *Fax:* 248-848-3801
shannon.hale@concrete.org; www.concrete.org
William R Tolley, Executive VP
Douglas J Sordyl, Marketing/Sales/Industry Relations
Donna G Halstead, Finance/Administration
Shannon M Hale, Technical Editor
Carl R Bischof, Senior Editor Publishing Services
Contains all of the ACI documents you need to answer your questions about code requirements, specifications, tolerance, concrete proportions, construction methods, evaluations of test results, and many more topics.
Founded in: 1994
Mailing list available for rent

22585 **Stone World Annual Buyer's Guide**
Stone World Magazine
210 Route 4 East
Suite 311
Paramus, NJ 90001
201-291-9001; *Fax:* 201-291-2002
info@stoneworld.com; www.stoneworld.com
Social Media: Facebook, Twitter
Alex Bachrach, Publisher
Michael Reis, Senior Editor/Associate Publisher
Comprised of six sections covering: stone suppliers, fabricating equipment and suppliers, installation and stone care materials and supplies, associations, services, trade shows and organizers.
Cost: $6.00
Frequency: Annual
Circulation: 22,000
Founded in: 1984

Industry Web Sites

22586 **http://gold.greyhouse.com**
G.O.L.D Grey House OnLine Databases
Grey House Publishing's online database platform, GOLD, offers Quick Search, Keyword Search and Expert Search for most business sectors including stone and concrete markets. The GOLD platform makes finding the information you need quick and easy - whether you're a novice searcher or an experienced database user. All of Grey House's directory products are available for subscription on the GOLD platform.

22587 **www.construction.com**
McGraw-Hill Construction
McGraw-Hill Construction (MHC), part of The McGraw-Hill Companies, connects people and projects across the design and construction industry, serving owners, architects, engineers, general contractors, subcontractors, building product manufacturers, suppliers, dealers, distributors and adjacent markets.

22588 **www.crsi.org**
Concrete Reinforcing Steel Institute
Conducts research and provides technical information on reinforced concrete design and construction practices.

22589 **www.csda.org**
Concrete Sawing and Drilling Association
To promote the use of professional specialty sawing and drilling contractors and their methods.

22590 **www.greyhouse.com**
Grey House Publishing
Authoritative reference directories for most business sectors including stone and concrete markets. Users can search the online databases with

varied search criteria allowing for custom searches by product category, geographic area, sales volume, keyword, subject and more. Full Grey House catalog and online ordering also available.

22591 www.icri.org
International Concrete Repair Institute

To improve the quality of repair, restoration, and protection of concrete and other structures.

22592 www.marble-institute.com
Marble Institute of America

Importers, finishers, wholesalers, fabricators, quarriers and exporters of stone for both interior and exterior application as well as suppliers of machines, tools and services.

22593 www.masonryinstitute.org
1315 Storm Pkwy.
Torrance, CA 90501-5041
310-257-9000; *Fax:* 310-257-1942;
www.masonryinstitute.org

Source for contacts and publications in the masonry industry.
Founded in: 1957

22594 www.post-tensioning.org
Post-Tensioning Institute

Provides research, technical development, marketing and promotional activities for companies engaged in post-tensioned prestressed construction. Members include fabricators and manufacturers.

22595 www.precast.org
National Precast Concrete Association

22596 www.sweets.construction.com
McGraw Hill Construction

In depth product information that lets you find, compare, select, specify and make purchase decisions in the industrial product marketplace.

Associations

22597 **4G Americas**
1750 - 112th Avenue NE, Suite B220
Bellevue, WA 98004
425-372-8922; *Fax:* 425-372-8923
vicki.livingston@4gamericas.org;
www.4gamericas.org
Social Media: Facebook, Twitter, LinkedIn
Chris Pearson, President
Vicki Livingston, Head of Comm./Analyst Relations
Jose Otero, Director
Paul Mankiewich, Director
Bob Suffern, Director

22598 **Advanced Television Systems Committee**
1776 K St. NW
8th Floor
Washington, Dc 20006-2340
202-872-9160; *Fax:* 202-872-9161;
www.atsc.org
Social Media: Facebook, Twitter
Founded in: 1982

22599 **American Radio Relay League**
225 Main St
Newington, CT 06111-1494
860-594-0200
888-277-5289; *Fax:* 860-594-0259;
www.arrl.org
Social Media: Facebook, Twitter, Youtube, RSS
David Sumner, CEO
Joel Harrison, President
Barry Shelley, CFO
Harold Kramer, COO
National membership association for amateur radio operators.
170m Members
Founded in: 1914

22600 **Antenna Measurement Techniques Association**
6065 Roswell Road
Atlanta, GA 30328
770-864-3488; *Fax:* 770-864-3491
president@amta.org; www.amta.org
Social Media: LinkedIn, RSS
Peter Collins, President
John Demas, VP
Dennis Lewis, Secretary
Dave Pinnell, Treasurer
Nonprofit professional organization open to individuals with an interest in antenna measurements. Areas of interest include: measurement facilities, unique or innovative measurement techniques, test instrumentation and systems, RCS measurements, compact range design and evaluation, near-field techniques and their applications, and the practical aspects of measurement problems and their solutions.
400 Members
Founded in: 1979

22601 **Armed Forces Communications and Electronics Association**
AFCEA International Headquarters
4400 Fair Lakes Ct
Suite 100
Fairfax, VA 22033-3899
703-631-6100
800-336-4583; *Fax:* 703-631-6169
service@afcea.org; www.afcea.org
Social Media: Facebook, Twitter, LinkedIn, Google+, YouTube, Slideshare,
LtGen Robert M. Shea, USMC (Ret.), President/CEO
Linda Gooden, Chair
Brig Gen John Meincke, Vice Chairman
Patrick Miorin, Treasurer/EVP/CFO
James L. Griggs Jr., VP/CIO/CTO
A non-profit international association dedicated to supporting global security by providing an ethical environment that encourages a close cooperative relationship among civil government agencies, the military and industry.
Cost: $35.00
31000 Members
Founded in: 1946

22602 **Assn. of Public-Safety Communications Officials International**
351 N Williamson Boulevard
Daytona Beach, FL 32114-1112
386-322-2500
888-272-6911; *Fax:* 386-322-2501
apco@apcointl.org; www.apcointl.org
Social Media: Facebook, Twitter, LinkedIn, Youtube
Brent Lee, President
Cheryl J. Greathouse, 1St VP
Martha K. Carter, 2nd VP
Doreen Geary, Accounting
Meghan Architect, Publications
A not-for-profit professional organization dedicated to the enhancement of public safety communications. Exists to serve the people who manage, operate, maintain, and supply the communications systems used to safeguard the lives and property of citizens everywhere.
16000 Members
Founded in: 1935

22603 **Association for Local Telecommunications Services**
900 17th St NW
Suite 400
Washington, DC 20006-2507
202-296-6650; *Fax:* 202-296-7585
membership@alts.org; www.comptelascent.org
Earl Comstock, CEO
COMPTEL is the leading industry accociation representing communications service providers and their supplier partners.

22604 **Association of Teleservices International**
222 S Westmonte Drive
Suite 101
Altamonte Springs, FL 32714
603-362-9489
866-896-2874; *Fax:* 407-774-6440
admin@atsi.org; www.atsi.org
Social Media: Facebook, Twitter, LinkedIn
Jeff Zindel, President
Doug Robbins, VP
Josue Leon, VP, Secretary
JoAnn Fussell, VP, Treasurer
Gary Edwards, Chairman
Promotes fair competition through appropriate regulation and legislation; provides research and development provides support services and educational opportunities to address challenges in operating environments; in encourages and maintains the high standards of ethics and service.
800+ Members
Founded in: 1942

22605 **Broadcast Designers' Association International**
5700 Wilshire Blvd
Suite 275
Los Angeles, CA 90036
310-788-7600; *Fax:* 310-788-7616;
www.promaxbda.org
Social Media: Facebook, Twitter, LinkedIn, RSS
Steve Kazanjian, President
Stacy LA Cotera, General Manager
Randy Smith, CFO
Lucian Cojescu, Chief Information Officer
Association for manufacturers or suppliers of broadcast design equipment, supplies and services.

22606 **CDMA Development Group**
575 Anton Blvd.
Suite 440
Costa Mesa, CA 92626
714-545-5211
888-800-CDMA; *Fax:* 714-545-4601
cdg@cdg.org; www.cdg.org
Social Media: Facebook, Twitter, RSS
Mark S. Richer, President
Jerry Whitaker, Vice President
Lindsy Shelton Gross, Director of Communications
Daro Bruno, Office Manager
Founded in: 1993

22607 **Carnegie Mellon University: Information Networking Institute**
Electrical & Computer Engineering Department
4616 Henry Street
Pittsburgh, PA 15213
412-268-7195; *Fax:* 412-268-7196
ini@cmu.edu; www.ini.cmu.edu
Social Media: Facebook, Twitter, LinkedIn, Youtube, Flickr,Google+
Dena Haritos Tsamitis, Director
Lynn Carroll, Assistant Director
Andrew Pueschel, Project Manager/Events/Marketing
Chriss Swaney, Director Public Relations
Sean O'Leary, Manager
The Information Networking Institute was established by Carnegie Mellon as the nation's first research and education center devoted to Information Networking.
Founded in: 1989

22608 **Cellular Telecommunications Industry**
CTIA
1400 16th St NW
Suite 600
Washington, DC 20036-2225
202-785-0081; *Fax:* 202-785-0721;
www.ctia.org
Social Media: Facebook, Twitter, LinkedIn, Youtube, Flickr,Google+
Meredith Attwell Baker, President & CEO
Tom Power, Senior VP, General Counsel
Scott Bergmann, VP, Regulatory Affairs
Jot Carpenter, VP, Govt. Affairs
Rocco Carlitti, SVP/CFO
An international organization representing all sectors of wireless communications. As a non-profit membership organization, they represent service providers, manufacturers, wireless data and Internet companies and other contributors to the wireless universe.
Founded in: 1984

22609 **Center for Strategic and International Studies**
1616 Rhode Island Avenue, NW
Washington, DC 20036

202-887-0200; *Fax:* 202-775-3199;
www.csis.org
Social Media: RSS

John J. Hamre, President and CEO
Carig Cohen, Executive Vice President
Jon B. Alterman, SVP
David J. Berteau, SVP & Director
Alice Blevins, SVP for Operations
Founded in: 1962

22610 **Competitive Telecommunications Association**
1200 G St. NW, Suite 350
Washington, DC 20005

202-296-6650; *Fax:* 202-296-7585;
www.comptel.org
Social Media: Facebook, Twitter, LinkedIn

Deborah Ward, Chairwoman
Chris Murray, Vice Chairman
Jim Butman, Treasurer
Ron Beaumont, Director
Bill Barloon, Director
Founded in: 1981

22611 **Enterprise Wireless Alliance**
2121 Cooperative Way
Suite 225
Herndon, VA 20171

703-528-5115
800-482-8282; *Fax:* 703-524-1074
Info@EnterpriseWireless.org;
www.enterprisewireless.org

Catherine Leonard, Chairman
David Reeves, Vice Chairman
Mark E Crosby, President/CEO
Gordon Day, Treasurer
Sarah Beerbower, Director, Sales and Services

Formerly ITA and AMTA, works to preserve spectrum rights and access for enterprise wireless customers.
400 Members
Founded in: 1985

22612 **Geospatial Information & Technology Association**
1360 University Ave. West
Suite 455
St. Paul, MN 55104-4086

E-Mail: president@gita.org; www.gita.org
Social Media: Facebook, Twitter, LinkedIn, YouTube

Mark Limbruner, President
Elizabeth Bialek, Treasurer
Eric Hoogenraad, Secretary
Matthew Thomas, President Elect
Rebecca Shumate, At-Large Board Member

22613 **Kagan Research**
1 Lower Ragsdale Dr
Building One Suite 130
Monterey, CA 93940-5749

831-624-1536
800-307-2529; *Fax:* 831-625-3225
info@kagan.com; www.kagan.com
Social Media: Facebook, Twitter, LinkedIn, Youtube, Google+

Mike Chinn, President
Tom Corbitt, Chief Administration Officer
Dan Oakey, Chief Contracts Officer

Provides knowledge, insight and industry perspectives, anticipates trends, projects revenues, tracks financing and values the debt and equity of hundreds of privately held and publicly traded media and communications companies.
Founded in: 1969

22614 **National Association of Broadcasters**
1771 N St. NW
Washington, DC 20036

202-429-5300
800-NAB-EXPO
nan@nab.org; www.nab.org
Social Media: Facebook, Twitter, LinkedIn, YouTube

David Lougee, President
Elizabeth Neuhoff, CEO
Gordon H. Smith, CEO & President
Brian Lawlor, Member, Executive Committee
Don Benson, Member, Executive Committee

22615 **National Cable & Telecommunications Association**
25 Massachusetts Ave. NW
Suite 100
Washington, DC 20001

202-222-2300
info@ncta.com; www.ncta.com
Social Media: Facebook, Twitter, LinkedIn

Michael Powell, President & CEO
Neil Smit, Chairman

Trade association for U.S. cable industry.
200 Members

22616 **National Cable andTelecommunications**
25 Massachusetts Avenue, NW
Suite 100
Washington, DC 20001

202-222-2300; *Fax:* 202-222-2514
webmaster@ncta.com; www.ncta.com
Social Media: Facebook, Twitter, LinkedIn

Michael Powell, President & CEO
James M. Assey, Executive Vice President
K. Dane Snowden, Chief of Staff
Bruce Carnes, SVP, Finance & Administration
William Check, SVP, Science & Technology
200 Members

22617 **National Exchange Carrier Association**
80 S Jefferson Rd
Suite 1
Whippany, NJ 07981-1009

973-599-0580
800-228-8597; *Fax:* 973-884-8469
webmastr@neca.org; www.neca.org
Social Media: Facebook, Twitter

William Hegman, CEO
Peter A Dunbar, VP/CFO
James W Frame, VP Operations
Regina McNeil, VP/General Counsel/Corp Secretary
Ed Buchanan, Chair

NECA administer's the FCCs access charge plan. They file access charge tariffs with the FCC, collect and validate cost and revenue data, ensure compliance with FCC rules, distribute revenues from access charges among pool members, process FCC regulatory fees, and offer training and education on a wide variety of telecom topics.
1500 Members
Founded in: 1983

22618 **National Telephone Cooperative Association**
4121 Wilson Blvd
Suite 1000
Arlington, VA 22203-4145

703-351-2000; *Fax:* 703-351-2001
contact@ntca.org; www.ntca.org
Social Media: Facebook, Twitter, LinkedIn, YouTube

Shirley Bloomfield, CEO
James M. Dauby, President
Doug Boone, VP
William P. Hegmann, Secretary/Treasurer
Don Richards, General Counsel

Non-profit association offering a wide array of member services including a government affairs program; expert legal and industry representation; a broad range of educational services; a comprehensive assortment of regular and special publications and public relations programs; and a well-rounded complement of national and regional meetings.
900 Members
Founded in: 1954

22619 **Organization for the Promotion and Adv. of Small Telecommunications**
4121 Wilson Boulevard
Suite 1000
Arlington, VA 22203

703-351-2000; *Fax:* 703-351-2001;
www.ntca.org
Social Media: Facebook, Twitter, LinkedIn, YouTube

James M. Dauby, President
Shirley Bloomfield, CEO
Doug Boone, VP
William P. Hegmann, Secretary/Treasurer
Don Richards, General Counsel

Protects the interests of small, rural, independent commercial telephone companies and cooperatives that have less than 50,000 access lines.
900 Members
Founded in: 1963

22620 **Personal Communications Industry**
500 Montgomery Street
Suite 700
Alexandria, VA 22314

703-390-0300
800-759-0300; *Fax:* 703-836-1608;
www.pcia.com
Social Media: Facebook, Twitter, LinkedIn

Thomas A Murray, Chairman
Steven Marshall, Vice Chairman
David E. Weisman, Treasurer
Jonathan S Adelstein, President & CEO
Tim House, VP, External Relations

Represents companies that develop, own, manage and operate towers, commercial rooftops and other facilities for the provision of all types of wireless, broadcasting and telecommunication services. PCIA is dedicated to advancing an understanding of the benefits of wireless services and required infrastructure to local and federal government officials and communities at large.
3000 Members
Founded in: 1949

22621 **Power and Communication Contractors Association**
1908 Mt. Vernon Ave.
2nd Floor
Alexandria, VA 22301

703-212-7734
800-542-7222; *Fax:* 703-548-3733
info@pccaweb.org; www.pccaweb.org

Timothy Killoren, President
Todd Myers, President-Elect
James Dillahunty, 1st Vice President
Larry Pribyl, 2nd Vice President
John Fluharty, II, Secretary

A national trade association for companies constructing electric power facilities, including transmission and distribution lines and substations and telephone, fiber optic, and cable television systems.
300 Members
Founded in: 1945

22622 Satellite Broadcasting and Communications Association
1100 17th St. NW
Ste. 1150
Washington, DC 20036
202-349-3620
800-541-5981; *Fax:* 202-318-2618
info@sbca.org; www.sbca.org
Social Media: Facebook, Twitter, LinkedIn, YouTube
Andrew Reinsdorf, Chairman
Jeffery Blum, Vice Chairman
Joseph Widoff, Executive Director
Benjamin Rowan, Education Manager
Abdul Salam, Sr. Director of Finance & HR
Founded in: 1994

22623 Satellite Industry Association
www.sia.org
Social Media: LinkedIn
Bill Weller, Chairman
Stacy Fuller, Vice Chairman
Sam Black, Acting President
Dean Hirasawa, Communications Manager
Jennifer Williams, Office Manager
Founded in: 1995

22624 Society for Technical Communication
9401 Lee Highway
Suite 300
Fairfax, VA 22031
703-522-4114; *Fax:* 703-522-2075;
www.stc.org
Social Media: Facebook, Twitter, LinkedIn, YouTube
Katherine Brown-Hoekstra, President
Bernard Aschwanden, Vice President
Chris Lyons, Chief Executive Officer
Kimberly Kelly, Education Manager
Molly Jin, Director of Meetings and Education
Founded in: 1957

22625 Society of Broadcast Engineers
9102 N Meridian St
Suite 150
Indianapolis, IN 46260-1896
317-846-9000; *Fax:* 317-846-9120
mclappe@sbe.org; www.sbe.org
Social Media: Facebook, Twitter, LinkedIn, YouTube
Jerry Massey, President
James E. Leifer, VP
Andrea Cummins, Treasurer
Ted Hand, Secretary
John Poray, CAE, Executive Director
SBE provides members with the opportunity to network and share ideas and information in keeping current with the ongoing changes within the industry. Members can attend annual conferences and expositions, have access to educational opportunities and obtain professional certification.
5100+ Members
Founded in: 1964
Mailing list available for rent: 5700 names at $170 per M

22626 Society of Cable Telecommunications Engineers
140 Philips Rd
Exton, PA 19341-1318
610-363-6888
800-542-5040; *Fax:* 610-363-5898
information@scte.org; www.scte.org
Social Media: Facebook, Twitter
Tony Werner, Chairman
Bill Warga, Vice Chairman
Steve Williams, Secretary
Christine Whittaker, Treasurer
Mark Dzuban, President/CEO
A nonprofit, professional organization committed to advancing the careers of cable telecommunications professionals and serving their industry through excellence in professional development, information and standards.
15000 Members
Founded in: 1969

22627 Society of Satellite Professionals
New York Information Technology Center
250 Park Ave
7th Floor
New York, NY 10177
212-809-5199; *Fax:* 212-825-0075;
www.sspi.org
Social Media: Facebook, Twitter, LinkedIn, YouTube
Chris Stott, Chairman & CEO
Bryan McGuirk, President
Doug Boone, VP
William P. Hegmann, Secretary/Treasurer
Don Richards, General Counsel
A nonprofit association that serves people working in the satellite industry in countries arount the world. Professional development society of the global satellite industry.
1000 Members
Founded in: 1983

22628 Society of Telecommunications Consultants
13275 State Highway 89
PO Box 70
Old Station, CA 96071
530-335-7313
800-782-7670; *Fax:* 530-335-7360;
www.stcconsultants.org
Social Media: Facebook, Twitter, Pinterest
Cathy Cimaglia, Administration Manager
The STC is an international organization of independent telecommunications and information technology consultants who serve clients in business and government.
180 Members
Founded in: 1976

22629 Telecom Association
31500 Grape Street #3-307
Lake Elsinore, CA 92532
www.telecomassociation.com
Social Media: Facebook, Twitter, LinkedIn, YouTube
Nancy Hagen Baldwin, President
Dan Baldwin, Executive Director
Kathleen Brown, Administrator
3800 Members
Founded in: 1995

22630 Telecom Pioneers
1801 California Street
Suite 225
Denver, CO 80202-2932
303-571-1200
800-872-5995; *Fax:* 303-572-0520
info@telecompioneers.org;
www.telecompioneers.org
Gloria Pazel, Chairman
Ann Smalley, Vice Chairman
Charlene Hill, Executive Director
Michael Sears, Past Chairman
Formerly known as the Telephone Pioneers of America, TelecomPioneers is comprised of nearly 620,000 current and retired telecommunications employees who have joined together to make their communities better places in which to live and work
Founded in: 1911

22631 Telecommunications Industry Association (TIA)
1320 N Courthouse Rd
Suite 200
Arlington, VA 22201-3834
703-907-7700; *Fax:* 703-907-7727
tia@tiaonline.org; www.tiaonline.org
Social Media: Facebook, Twitter
Grant Seiffert, President
Jennifer Pentecost Sims, Treasurer
Scott Belcher, CEO
Ed Mikoski, Standards/Business Development
Mark Walker, Chair
The Telecommunications Industry Association/TIA represents providers of information, communications and entertainment technology products and services for the global marketplace through its core competencies in standards development, domestic and international policy advocacy, and facilitating member business opportunities. The association facilitates the convergence of new communications networks while working for a competitive and innovative market environment.

22632 Telework Coalition
204 E St Ne
Washington, DC 20002-4923
202-266-0046
info@telcoa.org; www.telcoa.org
Social Media: Facebook, Twitter, LinkedIn
Chuck Wilsker, President
Jack Heacock, Senior VP & Co-Founder
Enabling virtual, mobile and distributed work through education, technology and legislation.

22633 The National Communication Association
1765 N Street NW
Washington, DC 20036
202-464-4622; *Fax:* 202-464-4600
inbox@natcom.org; www.natcom.org
Social Media: Facebook, Twitter, YouTube, Blog
Carole Blair, President
Christina S. Beck, First Vice President
Stephen J. Hartnett, Second Vice President
Nancy Kidd, Executive Director
Mark Fernando, Chief Of Staff
Founded in: 1914

22634 United Communications Group
9737 Washingtonian Blvd
Suite 200
Gaithersburg, MD 20878-7364
301-287-2700; *Fax:* 301-287-2039
info@ucq.com; www.ucg.com
Todd Foreman, Partner-CEO
Nancy Becker, Partner-President
Steve McVearry, General Counsel
Jon Slabaugh, Managing Director, Business Dev
Chris Dingee, CFO
A portfolio of highly focused business and professional publishing companies providing guidance, information, analysis, data and solutions to over two million clients worldwide.
Founded in: 1977

22635 United States International Telecommunication Union Association
E-Mail: cherie.mills@pillsburylaw.com;
www.usitua.org
Audrey Allison, Chair
The USITUA is a U.S. industry forum on International Telecommunication Union policy matters.

22636 United States Telecom Association
607 14th St Nw
Suite 400
Washington, DC 20005-2000

202-326-7300; *Fax:* 202-315-3603
membership@ustelecom.org;
www.ustelecom.org
Social Media: Facebook, Twitter, LinkedIn, YouTube

Walter B McCormick Jr, President/CEO
Robert A. Hunt, Chairman
Alan J. Roth, SEVP
Jonathan Banks, SVP, Law & Policy
Mark Kulish, SVP, Administration & CFO

Trade association representing service providers and suppliers for the telecom industry.
1200 Members

22637 Wireless Communications Alliance
1510 Page Mill Rd.
Palo Alto, CA 94304

E-Mail: promote@wca.org; www.wca.org
Social Media: Facebook, Twitter, LinkedIn

Founded in: 1994

22638 Wireless Internet Service Providers Association
1095 Hilltop Drive #317
Redding, CA 96003

260-622-5776
866-317-2851
tcoffey@wispa.org; www.wispa.org
Social Media: Facebook, Twitter, LinkedIn, Google+, Tumblr

Alex Phillips, President
Chuck Hogg, Vice President
Mark Radabaugh, Treasurer
Dennis Burgess, Secretary
Trina Coffey, Dir., Operations/Event Management
800 Members

Newsletters

22639 Broadband
IGI Group
1340 Soldiers Field Road
Suite 2
Brighton, MA 02135

617-782-5033
800-323-1088; *Fax:* 617-782-5735
info@igigroup.com; www.igigroup.com

Paul Polishuk, President/CEO
Hui Pan, Conference Director
Bev Wilson, Managing Editor
Will Ashley, IT Director/Media Manager

The Broadband Newsletter covers such subjects as: growth in broadband access such as ADSL, cable modems, satellite and fixed wireless; spending plans of the telcos and MSOs for broadband access; important applications that will drive the market; and growth of the internet based on fast internet access.
Cost: $695.00
Frequency: Monthly
Circulation: 1500
Founded in: 1977
Mailing list available for rent

22640 Broadband Advertising
Kagan World Media
1 Lower Ragsdale Dr
Building One, Suite 130
Monterey, CA 93940-5749

831-624-1536
800-307-2529; *Fax:* 831-625-3225
info@kagan.com; www.kagan.com

Tim Baskerville, President
Tom Johnson, Marketing Manager

Provides critical information about how and where advertising sales will intersect across all broadband platforms. Includes data and analysis previously published in Internet Advertising and Cable TV advertising
Cost: $1095.00
Frequency: Monthly
Founded in: 1969

22641 Broadband Technology
Kagan World Media
1 Lower Ragsdale Dr
Building One Suite 130
Monterey, CA 93940-5749

831-624-1536
800-307-2529; *Fax:* 831-625-3225
info@kagan.com; www.kagan.com

Tim Baskerville, President
Tom Johnson, Marketing Manager
Michael Schroeder, Manager

Incisive, thorough reports on deployments of bundled services, high-spped data, digital video and telephony. Analyzes and projects growth of set-top boxes, modems, switches, routers and other infrastructure. Provides data and stats on services offered and plant construction by cable, DSL, satellite, wireless and wired phone providers.
Cost: $1045.00
Frequency: Monthly
Founded in: 1969

22642 Broadcast Investor
Kagan World Media
1 Lower Ragsdale Dr
Building One Suite 130
Monterey, CA 93940-5749

831-624-1536
800-307-2529; *Fax:* 831-625-3225
info@kagan.com; www.kagan.com

Tim Baskerville, President
Tom Johnson, Marketing Manager

The market's most comprehensive sourve of current and historical data on valuations, deals and finance. Trends, forecasts, data.
Cost: $1295.00
Frequency: Monthly
Founded in: 1969

22643 CBQ-Communication Booknotes Quarterly
Lawrence Erlbaum Associates
10 Industrial Avenue
Mahwah, NJ 07430

201-258-2200; *Fax:* 201-760-3735;
www.leaonline.com/loi/cbq

Christopher Sterling, Editor
James K Bracken, Assistant Editor

Descriptive reviews of new publications and websites.
Cost: $350.00
Frequency: Quarterly
ISSN: 1094-8007
Founded in: 1969

22644 Cable Program Investor
Kagan World Media
1 Lower Ragsdale Dr
Building One, Suite 130
Monterey, CA 93940-5749

831-624-1536
800-307-2529; *Fax:* 831-625-3225
info@kagan.com; www.kagan.com

Tim Baskerville, President
Tom Johnson, Marketing Manager

Provides exclusive data and analysis, deal benchmarks and balance sheet assessments. It covers home shopping networks, programming trends, multichannel penetration by platform and ratings data.
Cost: $1045.00
Frequency: Monthly
Founded in: 1969

22645 Cable TV Investor
Kagan World Media
1 Lower Ragsdale Dr
Building One,Suite 130
Monterey, CA 93940-5749

831-624-1536
800-307-2529; *Fax:* 831-625-3225
info@kagan.com; www.kagan.com

Tim Baskerville, President
Tom Johnson, Marketing Manager

Provides information on the data, the deals, the valuation metrics, the distillation of information into intelligence. The information you want and need to remain competitive
Cost: $1295.00
Frequency: Monthly
Founded in: 1969

22646 Cable TV Law Reporter
Kagan World Media
1 Lower Ragsdale Dr
Building One Suite 130
Monterey, CA 93940-5749

831-624-1536
800-307-2529; *Fax:* 831-625-3225
info@kagan.com; www.kagan.com

Tim Baskerville, President
Tom Johnson, Marketing Manager

The quintessential library of cable court cases, arbitrations, legal precedents. Labeled and catalogued for easy reference. Required reading for attorneys, government regulators and top executives. Three month trial available.
Cost: $995.00
Frequency: Monthly
Founded in: 1969

22647 Communication
National Technical Information Service
5285 Port Royal Rd
Springfield, VA 22161-0001

703-605-6000; *Fax:* 703-605-6900
customerservice@ntis.gov; www.ntis.gov

Linda Davis, VP
Bruce Borzino, Director

Covers common carrier and satellite communications, information theory, graphics, policies, regulations, studies, radio and television.
Founded in: 1991

22648 Communications Daily
Warren Publishing
2115 Ward Ct Nw
Washington, DC 20037-1209

202-872-9200
800-771-9202; *Fax:* 202-318-8350
info@warren-news.com;
www.warren-news.com

Brig Easley, Executive VP/Controller
Paul Warren, Chair/Publisher
Daniel Warren, President/Editor

Daily publication for the entire telecommunications indusrty.
Frequency: Daily
Circulation: 70000+
Founded in: 1945

22649 Fiber Optic Sensors and Systems
IGI Group
1340 Soldiers Field Road
Suite 2
Brighton, MA 02135
617-782-5033
800-323-1088; *Fax:* 617-782-5735
info@igigroup.com; www.igigroup.com
Paul Polishuk, CEO
Hui Pan, Conference Director
Bev Wilson, Managing Editor
Covers procurements, contract awards, requests for qualifications and proposals, reports on market studies, patents filed and awarded, new product announcements, new technology, market forecasts, reviews of important contracts, important conferences and trade shows, and Japanese and European developments.
Cost: $695.00
Frequency: Monthly
Founded in: 1977

22650 Fiber Optics News
Phillips Business Information
1201 Seven Locks Road
Potomac, MD 20854-2931
301-354-1400; *Fax:* 301-340-0542
stephenh@pennwell.com;
www.lightwaveonline.com
Ellen Hamm, Publisher
Mark Mikolas, Editor
Stephen Hardy, Editorial Director
Fiber optics in the telecommunications fields.
Cost: $37.00

22651 Fiber Optics Weekly Update
IGI Group
1340 Soldiers Field Road
Suite 2
Brighton, MA 02135
617-782-5033
800-323-1088; *Fax:* 617-782-5735
info@igigroup.com; www.igigroup.com
Paul Polishuk, CEO
Hui Pan, Conference Director
Bev Wilson, Managing Editor
Yesim Taskor, Controller
Covers procurements, new contracts, company buyouts, new products, important publications, latest news, planned projects, financial reports, market forecasts, conference and trade show reviews, joint ventures, contract awards, impact of technology, and international developments.
Cost: $695.00
Frequency: Weekly
Founded in: 1977

22652 Fiber Optics and Communications
IGI Group
1340 Soldiers Field Road
Suite 2
Brighton, MA 02135
617-782-5033
800-323-1088; *Fax:* 617-783-5735
editor@igigroup.com; www.igigroup.com
Paul Polishuk, Publisher
Hui Pan, Conference Director
Bev Wilson, Managing Editor
Yesim Taskor, Controller
Fiber optics is spreading rapidly into all major high and low tech fields. This newsletter helps relieve the pressure on busy executives by reviewing over 300 sources on a regular basis and providing only the most relevant information.
Cost: $695.00
Frequency: Monthly
Founded in: 1977

22653 Fixed Wireless
IGI Group
1340 Soldiers Field Road
Suite 2
Brighton, MA 02135
617-782-5033
800-323-1088; *Fax:* 617-782-5735
editor@igigroup.com; www.igigroup.com
Paul Polishuk, CEO
Hui Pan, Conference Director
Bev Wilson, Managing Editor
Yesim Taskor, Controller
Tracks technological breakthroughs, network developments, market trends, contacts and examines who the players are in this re-emerging market.
Cost: $695.00
Frequency: Monthly
Founded in: 1977

22654 Home Networks
IGI Group
1340 Soldiers Field Road
Suite 2
Brighton, MA 02135
617-782-5033
800-323-1088; *Fax:* 617-782-5735
info@igigroup.com; www.igigroup.com
Paul Polishuk, Publisher/CEO
Hui Pan, Conference Director
Bev Wilson, Managing Editor
Yesim Taskor, Controller
The market for home networks is driven by the 15 million homes with two or more PCs requiring interconnection and new housing units being built for tomorrow's home network environment. This newsletter keeps you connected to this rapidly developing arena of opportunities.
Cost: $695.00
Frequency: Monthly
Founded in: 1977

22655 Interval
Society of Cable Telecommunications Engineers
140 Philips Road
Exton, PA 19341-1318
610-363-6888
800-542-5040; *Fax:* 610-363-5898
scte@scte.org; www.scte.org
Mark Durbaz, President/CEO
Catty Oaks, VP
Serving the members of SCTE, Interval highlights the events of the Society and it's Chapters.
Cost: $40.00
Circulation: 15000
Founded in: 1969

22656 Kagan Media Money
Kagan World Media
1 Lower Ragsdale Dr
Building One, Suite 130
Monterey, CA 93940-5749
831-624-1536
800-307-2529; *Fax:* 831-625-3225
info@kagan.com; www.kagan.com
Tim Baskerville, President
Tom Johnson, Marketing Manager
Sandie Borthwick, Executive Director
Designed to continually focus on the essential trends and hottest topics. Each issue is jammed with leading media indicators, media merger and acquisition data, handy benchmarks and reference charts and the most thought-provoking and insightful analysis.
Cost: $1245.00
Frequency: 48 issues per y
Founded in: 1969

22657 LAN Newsletter
IGI Group
1340 Soldiers Field Road
Suite 2
Brighton, MA 02135
617-782-5033
800-323-1088; *Fax:* 617-782-5735
editor@igigroup.com; www.igigroup.com
Paul Polishuk, President/CEO
Hui Pan, Conference Director
Bev Wilson, Managing Editor
Yesim Taskor, Controller
Provides information on new developments and products in the LAN-local area network-industry. Discusses both foreign and domestic markets, including new LAN purchases and installation and management changes.
Cost: $695.00
Frequency: Monthly
Circulation: 12000
Founded in: 1977

22658 LAN Product News
Worldwide Videotex
Po Box 3273
Boynton Beach, FL 33424
561-738-2276
markedit@juno.com; www.wvpubs.com
Provides news and information on the computer Local Area Network (LAN) industry. Covers new hardware and software products, as well as research and development.
Cost: $25.00
Frequency: Monthly

22659 MIC/TECH Data Communications
1111 Marlkress Road
Cherry Hill, NJ 08003-2334
856-489-4310
800-678-4642; *Fax:* 856-424-1999
Lawrence Feidelman, Publisher
Michael Smith, Editor
Carol Bell, Advertising/Sales
Complete performance and pricing of modems, multiplexus, networks and processing.
Cost: $920.00
Frequency: Daily

22660 Microcell Report
150 E 2nd Street
New York, NY 10009-8400
800-883-8989; *Fax:* 212-366-9798
Roger Newell, Publisher
A monthly report on personal communication services including advanced digital mobile telephone applications. Covers regulatory, technical and communication aspects of PCS which includes wireless LANS and PBX.
Cost: $397.00
10 Pages
Frequency: Monthly

22661 Microwave News
Microwave News
155 East 77th Street
New York, NY 10075
212-517-2800; *Fax:* 212-734-0316
info@microwavenews.com;
www.microwavenews.com
Social Media: Twitter
Louis Slesin, Editor & Publisher
Health issues relating to non-ionizing radiation.
Frequency: 6 issues per year
Founded in: 1981

22662 **Modem Users News**
Worldwide Videotex
Po Box 3273
Boynton Beach, FL 33424
561-738-2276
markedit@juno.com; www.wvpubs.com
Provides the latest news and information on software, hardware, supplies and services for individuals and companies who communicate via modems in computer and/or facsimile applications. Contains detailed information, prices, and evaluations of products ranging from protable laptop PC and fax boards, to a wide range of accessible services.
Cost: $25.00
Frequency: Monthly

22663 **Newsletter**
United Communications Group
11300 Rockville Pike
#1100
Rockville, MD 20852-3012
301-816-8950; *Fax:* 301-816-8945
ccmi@ucg.com; www.ucg.com
Sean Oberle, Publisher
Todd Foreman, CEO
Jon Slabaugh, MD
Stephanie Tamburello, HR
Editorial content provides hands-on advice on how to improve their services and reduce their overall operating expenses.
Cost: $379.00
Frequency: BiMonthly

22664 **North American Telecom Newswatch**
United Communications Group
11300 Rockville Pike
Street 1100
Rockville, MD 20852-3012
301-287-2700; *Fax:* 301-816-8945;
www.ucg.com
Benny Dicecca, President
Todd Foreman, CEO
Jon Slabaugh, MD
Stephanie Tamburello, HR
The news that impacts daily business operations, including equipment updates, regulation issues, long distance and internet useage, and wireless financials.
Founded in: 1977

22665 **Online Newsletter**
Information Intelligence
PO Box 31098
Phoenix, AZ 85046-1098
602-996-2283; www.infointelligience.com
Richard Huleatt, Publisher/Editor
Covers all on-line services, suppliers, vendors, CD-ROM data bases, microcomputers and associated equipment.
Cost: $6.25
9 Pages
Frequency: 10 per year
Founded in: 1980
Printed in on newsprint stock

22666 **Optical Networks and WDM**
IGI Group
1340 Soldiers Field Road
Suite 2
Brighton, MA 02135
617-782-5033
800-323-1088; *Fax:* 617-782-5735
info@igigroup.com; www.igigroup.com
Paul Polishuk, CEO
Hui Pan, Conference Director
Bev Wilson, Managing Editor
Yesim Taskor, Controller
The WDM newsletter provides worldwide coverage of technology, markets and applications. Covers such subjects as: WDM systems, MAN applications, Gigabit networks, ATM, financials reports, premise wiring, optical amplifiers, optical networks, new products, network management, standards, optical cross connects, frame relay, competitive analysis, manufacturers strategies, optical access, regulations, tariffs, technology, broadband servies, WANs, market forecasts, BOC strategies and more.
Cost: $695.00
Frequency: Monthly
Founded in: 1977

22667 **Photonics Components/Subsystems**
IGI group
1340 Soldiers Field Road
Suite 2
Brighton, MA 02135
617-782-5033
800-323-1088; *Fax:* 617-782-5735
info@igigroup.com; www.igigroup.com
Paul Polishuk, Publisher
Hui Pan, Conference Director
Bev Wilson, Managing Editor
Yesim Taskor, Controller
Provides worldwide coverage of technology, markets, and applications. Some subjects covered include: market forecasts, product comparisons, new products, contract awards, new technologies, start-up funding, customer requirements, standards, industry trends, photonics automation, systems developments, licensing, competitive assessments, mergers and acquisitions, and pricing trends.
Cost: $695.00
Frequency: Monthly
Founded in: 1977

22668 **Plastic Optical Fiber (POF)**
IGI Group
1340 Soldiers Field Road
Suite 2
Brighton, MA 02135
617-782-5033
800-323-1088; *Fax:* 617-782-5735
editor@igigroup.com; www.igigroup.com
Paul Polishuk, CEO
Hui Pan, Conference Director
Bev Wilson, Managing Editor
Yesim Taskor, Controller
Some of the subjects covered are: applications, products, imaging, patents, technology, market research, suppliers, publications, standards, sensors, cost analyses, mergers, audio systems, lighting/illuminations, medical acquisitions, medical, market opportunities, contracts awarded, automotive, licensing opportunities, RFPs, component costs, investments and signs.
Cost: $395.00
Frequency: 6 issues per yr
Founded in: 1977

22669 **SCTE Interval**
Society of Cable Telecommunications Engineers
140 Philips Road
Exton, PA 19341-1318
610-363-6888
800-542-5040; *Fax:* 610-363-5898
scte@scte.org; www.scte.org
Mark Durbaz, President/CEO
Catty Oaks, VP
SCTE's monthly newsletter keeps members abreast of association events, activities and member accomplishments.
Cost: $40.00
Circulation: 15,000
Founded in: 1969

22670 **Satellite News**
Phillips Publishing
7811 Montrose Road
Potomac, MD 20854
301-340-2100
866-599-9491
feedback@healthydirections.com;
www.healthydirections.com
Satellite telecommunications.
Frequency: Monthly
Founded in: 1985

22671 **Society of Telecommunications Consultants Newsletter**
Society of Telecommunications Consultants
13275 State Highway 89
PO Box 70
Old Station, CA 96071
530-335-7313
800-782-7670; *Fax:* 530-335-7360
stchdq@stcconsultants.org;
www.stcconsultants.org
Cathy Cimaglia, Administrative Manager
Mark Durbaz, President/CEO
Catty Oaks, VP
A newsletter for update and informational purposes.
Frequency: Quarterly
Founded in: 1969

22672 **State & Local Communications Report**
BRP Publications
1333 H Street NW
Suite 100 E
Washington, DC 20005-4746
202-312-6060
800-822-6338; *Fax:* 202-842-3047
Lynn Stanton, Editor
Victoria Mason, Publisher
Premier biweekly news service covering state and local communications issues. The in-depth reporting includes regular coverage of such timely topics as legislation and regulation, new state regulatory activities and important business and industry developments in the areas of telephone, data and enhanced services.
Cost: $599.00
8 Pages
Frequency: BiWeekly

22673 **State Telephone Regulation Report**
Telecom Publishing Group
1101 King Street
Suite 444
Alexandria, VA 22314-2944
703-683-4100
800-327-7205; *Fax:* 703-739-6490
Chris Vestal, Publisher
Herbert Kirchoff, Editor
Analysis of state telecommunications legislation.
Cost: $535.00
12 Pages
Frequency: BiWeekly
Printed in 2 colors on matte stock

22674 **Submarine Fiber Optic Communications Systems**
IGI Group
1340 Soldiers Field Road
Suite 2
Brighton, MA 02135
617-782-5033
800-323-1088; *Fax:* 617-782-5735
editor@igigroup.com; www.igigroup.com
Paul Polishuk, Publisher
Hui Pan, Conference Director
Bev Wilson
Yesim Taskor, Controller

Provides a monthly market intelligence report on new developments in markets, technology and applications. Of special interest will be developments in optical amplifier technology, solutions, Wavelength Division Multiplexing and how these are having an impact on the Submarine Fiber Optic business
Cost: $695.00
Frequency: Monthly
Founded in: 1977

22675 TR Wireless News
BRP Publications
1333 H Street NW
Suite 100 E
Washington, DC 20005-4707

202-312-6060
800-822-6338; *Fax:* 202-842-3047

Victoria Mason, Publisher
Andrew Kreig, President

Montiors regulatory, technological and market developments in the rapidly expanding wireless communications industry. It covers new services, corporate activity, and licensing and specturm allocation in the areas of personal communication services.
Cost: $597.00
Frequency: BiWeekly

22676 TV Program Investor
Kagan World Media
1 Lower Ragsdale Dr
Building One, Suite 130
Monterey, CA 93940-5749

831-624-1536
800-307-2529; *Fax:* 831-625-3225
info@kagan.com; www.kagan.com

Tim Baskerville, President
Tom Johnson, Marketing Manager

More than just a newsletter, practically a seminar on how much programs cost and what they are worth. Exclusive spreadsheets with estimates of what goes between the commercials. Three month trial available.
Cost: $895.00
Frequency: Monthly
Founded in: 1969

22677 Telco Competition Report
BRP Publications
1333 H Street NW
Suite 100 E
Washington, DC 20005-4746

202-312-6060
800-822-6338; *Fax:* 202-842-3047

Victoria Mason, Publisher
Brian Hammond, Editor

Provides important information on events and issues surrounding the $90 billion local exchange markets. Each issues covers the continuing regulatory, financial, strategic and technological ramifications of local exchange competition, including the second and third-tier cities being targeted by competitions and strategies for success.
Cost: $596.00
20 Pages
Frequency: BiWeekly

22678 Tele-Service News
Worldwide Videotex
Po Box 3273
Boynton Beach, FL 33424

561-738-2276
markedit@juno.com; www.wvpubs.com

Provides news and information on the telephone industry. Covers services, products, research and development and business plans of RBOCs (Regional Bell Operating Companies), long distance carriers, and independent vendors.
Cost: $25.00
Frequency: Monthly

22679 Telecom Daily Lead from US Telecom Association
SmartBrief
1401 H Street
N.W, Suite 600
Washington, DC 20005

202-326-7300; *Fax:* 202-326-7333
webmaster@smartbrief.com;
www.dailylead.com/usta

Portia Krebs, VP Communications
Jason Ross, Lead Editor
Eric Hoffman, Sales Account Director

Free daily newsbriefing, delivered by e-mail, that covers the telecom industry's top news stories.
Frequency: Daily
Circulation: 11000

22680 Telecom Outlook
Market Intelligence Research Company
2525 Charleston Road
Mountain View, CA 94043-1626
Wyman Bravard, Publisher

Reports on the telecommunications industry.
Frequency: Monthly

22681 Telecom Standards
IGI Group
1340 Soldiers Field Road
Suite 2
Brighton, MA 02135

617-782-5033
800-323-1088; *Fax:* 617-782-5735
editor@igigroup.com; www.igigroup.com

Paul Polishuk, President/CEO
Hui Pan, Conference Director
Bev Wilson, Managing Editor
Yesim Taskor, Controller

Provides coverage of standards activities around the world, schedules of standards meetings, the availablity of standards, and how to obtain standards, minutes of standards meetings and drafts of standards.
Cost: $695.00
Frequency: Monthly
Founded in: 1977

22682 Telecommunications Mergers and Acquisitions
IGI group
1340 Soldiers Field Road
Suite 2
Brighton, MA 02135

617-782-5033
800-323-1088; *Fax:* 617-782-5735
editor@igigroup.com; www.igigroup.com

Paul Polishuk, President/CEO
Hui Pan, Conference Director
Bev Wilson, Managing Editor
Yesim Taskor, Controller

Covers worldwide developments in the telecommunications mergers and acquisitions. In addition to reporting to these activities, the newsletter analyzes potential merger and acquisition candidates, summarizes in an easy-to-read form trends by different companies and industry requirements.
Cost: $695.00
Frequency: Monthly
Founded in: 1977

22683 Telecommunications Reports International
BRP Publications
111 Eighth Avenue
7th Floor
New York, NY 10011-4707

212-771-0600
800-234-1660; *Fax:* 212-771-0885
jrohaly@aspenpublishers.com;
www.aspenlawschool.com

Andrew Jacobson, Publisher
George Brandon, Editor
Jim Monahan, President
Richard H Kravitz, Execitive VP

International telecom policy and trade issues, global services, satellites, tariffs and financial developments.
Cost: $1789.00
Frequency: 24 issues per y

22684 Telemarketing Update
Prosperity & Profits Unlimited
PO Box 416
Denver, CO 80201-0416

303-573-5564

AC Doyle, Publisher

Telemarketing script presentation suggestions and ideas.
Cost: $200.00
8 Pages
Frequency: Annual
Circulation: 2,000
Printed in on matte stock

22685 Telemarketing Update-Catering Service Business Script Presentations
Prosperity & Profits Unlimited
PO Box 416
Denver, CO 80201-0416

303-573-5564

A Doyle, Editor

Catering service telemarketing script presentations.
Cost: $19.95
10 Pages
Frequency: Irregular
Circulation: 2,100
Founded in: 1990
Printed in one color on matte stock

22686 VoiceNews
Stoneridge Technical Services
PO Box 1891
Rockville, MD 20849-1891

301-424-0114; *Fax:* 301-424-8971

William Creitz, Publisher/Editor

Covers voice technology for telecommunications and office automation: voice messaging, voice response, speech recognition, speech synthesis.
Cost: $25.00

22687 Why Not An Answering Service?
Prosperity & Profits Unlimited
PO Box 416
Denver, CO 80201-0416

303-573-5564

A Doyle, Editor

Offers information and ideas on telephone answering service possibilities.
Cost: $29.95
73 Pages
Frequency: Every Five Years
Circulation: 5,000
Founded in: 1989
Printed in on matte stock

22688 Wireless Market Stats
Kagan World Media

1 Lower Ragsdale Dr
Building One Suite 130
Monterey, CA 93940-5749

831-624-1536
800-307-2529; *Fax:* 831-625-3225
info@kagan.com; www.kagan.com

Tim Baskerville, President
Tom Johnson, Marketing Manager

In-depth analysis of metropolitan and rural cellular market efficiency, plus operating statistics, private deal market data, economic and demographic data for narrowband and broadband PCS, ESMR, paging and more.
Cost: $1095.00
Frequency: Monthly
Founded in: 1969

22689 Wireless Satellite and Broadcasting
IGI Group
1340 Soldiers Field Road
Suite 2
Brighton, MA 02135

617-782-5033
800-323-1088; *Fax:* 617-782-5735
editor@igigroup.com; www.igigroup.com

Paul Polishuk, Publisher
Hui Pan, Conference Director
Bev Wilson, Managing Editor

Subjects covered include: market opportunities, technology, international developments, regulation/policy, standards, applications, procurements, PCN, market forecasts, new products, mergers/acquisitions, joint ventures and more.
Cost: $695.00
Frequency: Monthly
Founded in: 1977

22690 Wireless Telecom Investor
Kagan World Media
1 Lower Ragsdale Dr
Building One, Suite 130
Monterey, CA 93940-5749

831-624-1536
800-307-2529; *Fax:* 831-625-3225
info@kagan.com; www.kagan.com

Tim Baskerville, President
Tom Johnson, Marketing Manager

Exclusive analysis of private and public values of wireless telecommunications companies, including cellular telephone, ESMR and PCS. Exclusive databases of subscribers, market penetrations, market potential, industry growth. Catching super-fast growth in a capsule.
Cost: $1095.00
Frequency: Monthly
Founded in: 1969

22691 Wireless Week
Chilton Company
600 S Cherry Street
Suite 400
Denver, CO 80246-1706

303-393-7449; *Fax:* 303-399-2034

Tom Brooksher, Publisher
Judith Lockwood, Editor

Covers the wireless telecommunications industry.
Circulation: 32,000

22692 Worldwide Videotex Update
Worldwide Videotex
Po Box 3273
Boynton Beach, FL 33424

561-738-2276
markedit@juno.com; www.wvpubs.com

Reports news and information on videotex, The Internet, online services, electronic mail, satellite communications and television related technologies, such as teleconferencing and teletext.
Cost: $25.00
Frequency: Monthly

22693 XDSL
IGI Group
1340 Soldiers Field Road
Suite 2
Boston, MA 02135

617-782-5033
800-323-1088; *Fax:* 617-782-5735
bmark@igigroup.com; www.igigroup.com

Paul Polishuk, President/CEO
Hui Panb, Conference Director
Bev Wilson, Managing Editor

Subjects covered include: field trials, applicatins, competition ffrom cable and satellite, new products, Telco plans, fiber optics, market forecasts, techology developments, wireless, major player strategies, cable modems, ISDN and more.
Cost: $695.00
Frequency: Monthly
Founded in: 1977

Magazines & Journals

22694 ACUTA Journal of Communications Technology in Higher Education
ACUTA
152 W Zandale Drive
Suite 200
Lexington, KY 40503-2486

859-278-3338; *Fax:* 859-278-3268
pscott@acuta.org; www.acuta.org
Social Media: Facebook

Pat Scott, Editor
Tamara Closs, President
Jerry A Simmer, Director
Corinne Harrison, Executive Officer
Tom Chappel, Finance & Administration

Journal is distributed to telecom, information management professionals at colleges and universities, along with industry professionals with products and services for the higher education vertical market.
Cost: $80.00
48 Pages
Frequency: Quarterly
Circulation: 2320
ISSN: 1097-8658
Founded in: 1997
Mailing list available for rent: 2,300 names
Printed in 4 colors on matte stock

22695 ARRL The National Association for Amateur Radio
American Radio Relay League
225 Main St
Newington, CT 06111

860-594-0200
888-277-5289; *Fax:* 860-594-0259;
www.arrl.org

David Sumner, CEO
Kay Craigie, President
Bob Inderbitzen, Marketing Manager

Geared at the IRF and amatuer radio operators industry, provides information on communications theory and technical advances in design and construction. The official journal of the American Radio Relay League.
Cost: $24.00
156M Members
Frequency: Monthly
Circulation: 146000
Founded in: 1914

22696 America's Network
Questex Media Group
201 Sandpointe Ave
Suite 500
Santa Ana, CA 92707-8716

714-338-6700
800-854-3112; *Fax:* 714-513-8481;
www.americasnetwork.com

Paul Semple, Publisher
Bill Pettit, National Sales Director

Independent reporting and business analysis of telecommunications technologies for today's public network.
Cost: $100.00
Frequency: Monthly
Circulation: 60,006

22697 Audiotex Update
Worldwide Videotex
PO Box 3273
Boynton Beach, FL 33424-3273

561-738-2276
markedit@juno.com; www.wvpubs.com

Mark E Wright, Editor

Provides the latest news and infromation about the audiotex industry, including voice processing information, products, services, as well as research and development.
Cost: $165.00
Frequency: Monthly
Founded in: 1981

22698 B/OSS
Virgo Publishing LLC
3300 N Central Ave
Suite 300
Phoenix, AZ 85012-2532

480-675-9925; *Fax:* 480-990-0819
mikes@vpico.com; www.vpico.com
Social Media: Facebook, Twitter, LinkedIn

Jenny Bolton, President
John Siefert, CEO
Kelly Ridley, VP
Troy Bix, Publisher

Source for news and analysis for telecommunications support systems as they take a leading role in creating and supporting service differentiation in the communications marketplace.
Circulation: 20000
Founded in: 1986
Printed in on glossy stock

22699 Business Communications Review
BCR Enterprises
Ste 200
3025 Highland Pkwy
Downers Grove, IL 60515-5668

630-986-1432
800-227-1234; *Fax:* 630-323-5324;
www.bcr.com

Fred Knight, Publisher

Offers a complete package of the latest information for persons associated with the communications industry.
Cost: $45.00
80 Pages
Frequency: Monthly
Founded in: 1971

22700 CTI the Authority on Computer, Internet, & Network Telephony
Technology Marketing Corporation
1 Technology Plz
Norwalk, CT 06854-1936

203-852-6800
800-243-6002; *Fax:* 203-853-2845;
www.tmcnet.com
Social Media: Facebook, Twitter

Rich Tehrani, CEO
Anthony Graffeo, National Advertising Sales Manager
Greg Galitzine, Editorial Director

Provides tutorials, application stories, and new product listings and reviews, as well as service information. Emphasizes furthering the development, implementation and use of CTI technology.
Frequency: Monthly
Circulation: 50256
Founded in: 1998

22701 Cabling Business
Cabling Publications
12035 Shiloh Rd
Suite 350
Dallas, TX 75228-1549

214-322-8171; *Fax:* 214-319-6077
russell@cablingbusiness.com;
www.cablingbusiness.com
Social Media: Facebook, Twitter

Stephen Paulov, President
Christy Sheeran, Business Manager
Rita Paulov, Senior Sales Associate
David Deal, Webmaster
Margaret Patterson, Managing Editor

New product information, troubleshooting hints, and information on installation and repair.
Frequency: Monthly
Circulation: 24070
Mailing list available for rent

22702 Cabling Installation & Maintenance
PennWell Publishing Company
1421 S Sheridan Rd
Tulsa, OK 74112-6619

918-831-9421
800-331-4483; *Fax:* 918-831-9476
patrick@pennwell.com; www.pennwell.com

Robert Biolchini, President
Steve Smith, Executive Editor

Emphasizes the problem solving aspects of cable installation in telecommunications, data, and video systems.
Frequency: Monthly
Circulation: 23604
Founded in: 1993

22703 Call Center Magazine
Miller Freeman Publications
11 Est 19th Street
3rd Floor
New York, NY 10011

212-600-3000
800-672-6111; *Fax:* 212-691-1191;
www.callcentermagazine.com

Keith Dawson, Editor
Max Steiger, Sales Manager

Dedicated to providing in-depth and unbiased product and strategic information for call center executives.
Frequency: Monthly
Circulation: 32904

22704 Communication Theory
International Communication Association
U de Montreal, Department de Communication
1500 21st Street
Washington, DC 20026

202-955-1444; *Fax:* 202-955-1448
communicationtheory@umontreal.ca.;
www.icahdq.org
Social Media: Facebook, Twitter, LinkedIn

Francois Cooren, Editor

Publishes research articles, theoretical essays, and reviews on topics of broad theoretical interest from across the range of communication studies. Recognizes that approaches to theory develpment and explication are diverse.
Mailing list available for rent

22705 Communication Yearbook
International Communication Association
Ohio University, School of Communication Study
1501 21st Street
Washington, DC 20026

202-955-1445; *Fax:* 202-955-1449
communicationtheory@umontreal.ca.;
www.icahdq.org
Social Media: Facebook, Twitter, LinkedIn

Dr Christina S. Beck, Editor

Features state-of-the discipline literature reviews of communication research. Highlights reviews of research exploring communication concepts that span traditional 'division' divides, issues of central importance to the accomplishment of communication in a variety of contexts and for diverse communicators throughout the world.
Founded in: 1913
Mailing list available for rent

22706 Communications Billing Report
Telecommunications Reports International
76 9th Ave. 7th fl
#100-E
Washington, NY 10011

21- 77- 071; *Fax:* 212-771-0732
joseph.rohaly@wolterskluwer.com;
www.tr.com
Social Media: Facebook, Twitter, LinkedIn

Victoria Mason, Editor-in-Chief

Content provides hard-to-find facts on such issues as developing internet electronic payment systems, keeping on top of new outsourcing opportunities, enhancing customer care and back office functions and making the most of new software developments.
Cost: $765.00
Frequency: BiWeekly

22707 Communications Crossroads
United States Telecom Association
1401 H St NW
Suite 600
Washington, DC 20005-2110

202-326-7300; *Fax:* 202-326-7333;
www.usta.org
Social Media: Facebook, Twitter, LinkedIn, You Tube

Walter Mc Kormick, President
James Cooconi, VP
Robert Curry, Tresurer
Robert Hunt, Secretary

Dedicated to the success stories, investment opportunities and industry events that herald the future of small and rural carriers.
Cost: $60.00
Circulation: 3500
Founded in: 2006

22708 Enterprise Wireless Magazine
Enterprise Wireless Association
8484 Westpark Drive
Suite 630
McLean, VA 22102-5117

703-528-5115
800-482-8282; *Fax:* 703-524-1074
customerservice@enterprisewireless.org;
www.enterprisewireless.org
Social Media: Facebook, Twitter

Mark Crosby, President/CEO
Andre Cote, Senior VP
Ila Dudley, VP Spectrum Management
Ron Franklin, VP Membership/Business Development

Covers how wireless meets the operational needs of business and industrial enterprise users. Used extensivley throughout the year by your prospects to stay informed of technical, industry and association information, and as a comprehensive buyers' guide for the products and services they use most often.
Frequency: Quarterly

22709 Global Telephony
Primedia
3585 Engineering Drive
Suite 100
Norcross,, GA 30092
678-421-3000
800-216-1423; *Fax:* 312-595-0295;
www.primediabusiness.com
Social Media: Facebook, Twitter, LinkedIn, You Tube

Larry Lannon, Publisher
Carol Wilson, Editor

Telephony delivers timely and intelligent coverage of the news, technologies and business strategies driving the industry.
Frequency: 24/Yr
Circulation: 63,500

22710 Handbooks of Communication Series
International Communication Association
Dept of Comm, University of Colorado at Boulder
1500 21st Street
Washington, DC 20026

202-955-1444; *Fax:* 202-955-1448
communicationtheory@umontreal.ca.;
www.icahdq.org
Social Media: Facebook, Twitter, LinkedIn

Robert T Craig, Editor
Linda Bathgate, Senior Editor

Publishes research articles, theoretical essays, and reviews on topics of broad theoretical interest from across the range of communication studies. Recognizes that approaches to theory develpment and explication are diverse.
Mailing list available for rent

22711 Human Communication Research
International Communication Association
Dept of Communication Arts & Science,234 Sparks
1500 21st Street
Washington, DC 20026

202-955-1444; *Fax:* 202-955-1448
communicationtheory@umontreal.ca.;
www.icahdq.org
Social Media: Facebook, Twitter, LinkedIn

James P Dillard, Editor

Publishes research articles, theoretical essays, and reviews on topics of broad theoretical interest from across the range of communication studies. Recognizes that approaches to theory develpment and explication are diverse.
Frequency: Quarterly
Mailing list available for rent

22712 ICA Communique
International Communications Association
1500 21st St NW
1500 21st Street
Washington, DC 20026

202-955-1444; *Fax:* 202-955-1448
communicationtheory@umontreal.ca.;
www.icahdq.org
Social Media: Facebook, Twitter, LinkedIn

M Haley, Executive Director

Publishes research articles, theoretical essays, and reviews on topics of broad theoretical interest from across the range of communication studies. Recognizes that approaches to theory develpment and explication are diverse.
Cost: $135.00
Frequency: 10/Year
Mailing list available for rent

22713 IEEE Communications Magazine
Institute of Electrical & Electronics Engineers
3 Park Ave
Suite 17
New York, NY 10016-5997

212-419-7900; *Fax:* 212-752-4929
publications@comsoc.org; www.ieee.org
Social Media: Facebook, Twitter, LinkedIn, You Tube

Daniel J Senese, CEO
Jack Howell, Executive Director

Written in tutorial applications-driven style by the industry's leading experts. IEEE Communications Magazine delivers usable information on the latest international coverage of current issues and advances in key areas.
Cost: $ 20.00
Frequency: Monthly
Circulation: 43832

22714 IEEE Network
IEEE Operations Center
PO Box 1331
Piscataway, NJ 08855-1331

732-981-0060; *Fax:* 732-981-1721
publications@comsoc.org; www.cosmoc.org

John Vig, CEO

The magazine of Global Internetworking provides the most current information for communications professionals involved with the interconnection of computing systems.
Frequency: Bi-Monthly

22715 Intele-Card News
Quality Publishing
523 N Sam Houston Parkway E
Suite 300
Houston, TX 77060

281-272-2744
800-792-6397; *Fax:* 281-847-5752;
www.intelecard.com

Theresa Ward, Editor-in-Chief
Jo Ann Davy, Managing Editor
Laurette Veres, Owner

Reports on news and events impacting the business of telephone cards, identifies significant trends and profiles industry newsmakers.
Frequency: Monthly
Circulation: 12000
Founded in: 1995

22716 Journal of Communication
International Communication Association
Department of Communication-101 Burton Hall
University of Oklahoma
Norman, OK 73019

405-325-9503
joc@ou.edu; www.icahdq.org

Michael Pfau, Editor

A general forum for communication scholarship and publishes articles and book reviews examining a broad range of issues in communication theory and research. Publishes the best available scholarship on all aspects of communication.

22717 Journal of Computer-Mediated Communication
International Communication Association
1500 21st Street
Washington, DC 20026

202-955-1444; *Fax:* 202-955-1448
jcmc.indiana.edu
Social Media: Facebook, Twitter, LinkedIn

Susan C Herring, Editor

Publishes research articles, theoretical essays, and reviews on topics of broad theoretical interest from across the range of communication studies. Recognizes that approaches to theory develpment and explication are diverse.
Mailing list available for rent

22718 Lightwave
PennWell Publishing Company
1421 S Sheridan Rd
Tulsa, OK 74112-6619

918-831-9421
800-331-4483; *Fax:* 918-831-9476
stephenh@pennwell.com; www.pennwell.com

Robert Biolchini, President
Carrie Meadows, Managing Editor
Meghan Fuller, Senior News Editor
Matt Vincent, Associate Editor/Web Editor

An international journal of fiber optics that covers all applications of the technology in telecommunications, data communications, broadcast and cable TV and specialized military applications.
Cost: $137.00
224 Pages
Frequency: Monthly
ISSN: 0741-5834
Founded in: 1910
Printed in 4 colors on matte stock

22719 Locating, Testing and Repairing
Stober Research and Communications
PO Box 517
McHenry, IL 60051

815-385-6123; *Fax:* 815-385-7151;
www.ltrmag.com
Social Media: Facebook, Twitter

L Jack Stober, Publisher

Information on copper and fiber optic sets available for telecommunication applications, as well as listings of companies and categories of this equipment. Regular departments contain fault locating and test equipment tips, a new product showcase and a look at new industry literature.
Cost: $100.00
Frequency: Quarterly
Circulation: 27355
Founded in: 1998

22720 Mobile Communication Business
Phillips Business Information
7811 Montrose Road
Potomac, MD 20854

301-340-2100
feedback@healthydirections.com;
www.healthydirections.com
Social Media: Facebook, Twitter

Don Steele, Editor

Offers information and the latest technological advances in telecommunications.
Frequency: Monthly
Founded in: 1985

22721 Multimedia Telecommunication News
Stoneridge Technical Services
PO Box 1891
Rockville, MD 20849-1891

301-424-0114; *Fax:* 301-424-8971
techwriter@stoneridgetech.com;
www.stoneridgetech.com

William W Creitz, Editor

Focuses on new products, applications, technological developments, markets and company activites.
Frequency: Monthly

22722 NTCA Exchange
National Telephone Cooperative Association
4121 Wilson Blvd
Suite 1000
Arlington, VA 22203-4145

703-351-2000; *Fax:* 703-351-2001;
www.ntca.org

Michael E Brunner, CEO

Bi-monthly newsletter examining association and member news, including profiles, business tips and member updates.
Cost: $15.00
Frequency: Bi-Monthly
Circulation: 5100
Founded in: 1980

22723 Network Magazine
CMP Media
245 Blackfriars Road
Manhasset, NY 11030

516-562-5000
866-880-8219; *Fax:* 516-562-7013;
www.cmp.com

Art Wittmann, Editor
Paula McGinlinchey, Publisher

Network Magazine serves communications carriers, communications service providers including interexchange/PTT's/long distance carriers, business services (non-computer) and other industry organizations.
Cost: $175.00
162 Pages
Frequency: Monthly
Circulation: 125000
ISSN: 1093-8001
Founded in: 1986
Printed in 4 colors on matte stock

22724 Networks Update
Worldwide Videotex
Po Box 3273
Boynton Beach, FL 33424

561-738-2276
markedit@juno.com; www.wvpubs.com
Social Media: Facebook, Twitter

Provides the latest news and information about the computer network industry. This includes national, international, public, private, and military network products, services, companies, marketing strategies, and research and development.
Cost: $25.00
Frequency: Monthly

22725 Opastco Roundtable
OPASTCO
2020 K Street
Suite 700
Washington, DC 20006

202-659-5990; *Fax:* 202-659-4619
roundtable@opastco.org; www.opastco.org

John Rose, President
Caurey Watson, Administrative Services Manager

Provides practical, how-to information that small local exchange carriers can use in their day-to-day operations, as well as plain English explanations of industry issues and technologies.
Frequency: BiMonthly

22726 Outside Plant
Practical Communications
220 N Smith St
Suite 228
Palatine, IL 60067-2488

847-202-4683; *Fax:* 847-639-9542
sharon@ospmag.com; www.ospmag.com

Sharon Stober, VP/Editorial Director
Karen Adolphson, Managing Editor
Mary Beth Koelling, Executive Director Sales/Marketing

Magazine for telecom outside plant professionals. Reaches ASP engineers, planners, managers

and technicians in Bell and independent phone companies.
Cost: $30.00
100 Pages
Frequency: Monthly
Circulation: 25000
Founded in: 1983

22727 **POINT**
Direct Marketing Association
1120 Avenue of the Americas
New York, NY 10036-6713

212-768-7277; *Fax:* 212-768-4547;
www.the-dma.org
Social Media: Facebook, Twitter

John A. Greco Jr, President & CEO

DMA's digital magazine.

22728 **Pen Computing Magazine**
Pen Computing Publishing Office
120 Bethpage Road
Suite 300
Hicksville, NY 11801

516-433-8725; *Fax:* 516-433-8724
cb@pencomputing.com;
www.pencomputing.com

Howard Borgen, Publisher
Lisa Krebs, VP Advertising
Wayne Laslo, Advertising Manager
Conrad H Blickenstorfer, Editor-in-Chief
David MacNeill, Executive Editor

Bi-Monthly print journal of pen-based and mobile computing. Hardware and software reviews, expert opinions, feature articles, case studies, how-to, industry news, technical primers and more.
Cost: $18.00
Frequency: Bi-Monthly
Circulation: 79515
Founded in: 1993

22729 **Politically Direct**
Direct Marketing Association
1120 Avenue of the Americas
New York, NY 10036-6700

212-768-7277; *Fax:* 212-302-6714
customerservice@the-dma.org;
www.the-dma.org

Lawrence M Kimmel, CEO

Published both in print and digital, this newsletter on DMA advocacy efforts keeps DMA members informed and involved in the politics and policies that impact them today and ahead of the curve on developments that will affect them tomorrow.
Frequency: Quarterly

22730 **RCR Wireless News**
Crain Communications
1746 Cole Blvd
Suite 150
Lakewood, CO 80401-3208

303-733-2500
888-909-9111; *Fax:* 303-733-9941
subs@crain.com; www.crain.com

Mary Pemberton, Marketing
Tracy Ford, Associate Publisher/Editor
Dan Meyer, Managing Editor
Pete Racelis, President

News and analysis of the wireless communications industry.
Cost: $69.00
Frequency: Weekly
Circulation: 65000
Founded in: 1981
Printed in on matte stock

22731 **Satellite Business News**
Satellite Business News
1990 M Street NW
Suite 510
Washington, DC 20036-3102

202-785-0505; *Fax:* 202-785-9291
general.mail@satbiznews.com;
www.satbiznews.com

Bob Scherman, Publisher
Jeffrey Williams, Managing Editor
Charlie Ergen, CEO/President

Up-to-date news on satellite television industry, upcoming events, and new technology for the industry.
Cost: $44.75
Frequency: Bi-annually
Circulation: 565700
Founded in: 1983

22732 **Satellite News**
Phillips Business Information
6181 Executive Blvd
Rockville, MD 20852-3901

301-881-7516
866-279-1930; *Fax:* 301-424-2709
information@phillips.com; www.phillips.com

Donald Phelps, President
Robert Phillips, CEO

Information on satellite launches, companies rebounding from losses, blows to competitors and regulatory issues.
Frequency: Weekly
Circulation: 18000
Founded in: 1974

22733 **Satellite Week**
Warren Publishing
2115 Ward Ct NW
Washington, DC 20037-1209

202-872-9200
800-771-9202; *Fax:* 202-318-8350
info@warren-news.com;
www.warren-news.com

Brig Easley, Executive VP
Paul Warren, Chair/Publisher
Daniel Warren, President/Editor

The definitive weekly source for fast-breaking, international news on space communications policy, regularion, technology and business. Offers up-to-date, comprehensive reports on new technologies, notices of international advances, details about regulation and deregularion, satellite marketplace intelligence, news of DBS developments, and continuous coverage of what industry leaders are doing and saying.
Frequency: Weekly
Founded in: 1945

22734 **Sound & Communications**
Testa Communications
25 Willowdale Avenue
Port Washington, NY 11050-3779

516-767-2500
800-937-7678; *Fax:* 516-767-9335
testa@testa.com;
www.testacommunications.com
Social Media: Facebook, Twitter

Vincent P Testa, President
David A. Silverman, Editor

Covers sound, display, security and multimedia systems, also theory and applications.
Frequency: Monthly
Circulation: 22500
Founded in: 1955

22735 **Sound & Video Contractor**
Primedia
PO Box 12914
Overland Park, KS 66282

913-341-1300; *Fax:* 913-967-1903;
www.svconline.com

Mark Johnson, Editor
Trevor Boyer, Associate Editor
Trevor Boyer, Associate Editor

Contains information on sound systems, video display, security, CCTV, home theater, and automation. Delivers in depth instruction and examples of successful installations, fundamental acoustical and video theory and news on new technologies eaffecting the systems contracting business.
Cost: $35.00
Frequency: Monthly
Circulation: 21,000
Founded in: 1983
Mailing list available for rent: 20,500 names at $110 per M

22736 **Sys Admin**
CMP Media
303 Second Street
Suite 200
Lawrence, KS 94107

415-947-6000; *Fax:* 785-841-2047;
www.sysadminmag.com

Amber Ankerhola
Deirdre Blake, MD

SYS ADMIN serves the Unix and Linux system administration market.
Cost: $39.00
100 Pages
Frequency: Monthly
Founded in: 1992
Printed in on glossy stock

22737 **TELEconference Magazine**
Applied Business Telecommunications
201 Sandpoint Ave
Suite 600
Santa Ana, CA 92707-8700

714-513-8400
800-854-3112; *Fax:* 714-513-8680;
www.advanstar.com

Keith Gallagher, Publisher
Paul DeVeaux, Editor

Devoted to the field of teleconferencing and contains in-depth articles to provide updates on audio/graphic and video teleconferencing applications, trends and developments.
Cost: $10.00
Circulation: 15000
Founded in: 1992

22738 **Telecommunications**
Horizon House Publications
685 Canton St
Norwood, MA 02062-2608

781-762-1319; *Fax:* 781-769-5037;
www.horizonhouse.com

Charles A Ayotte, CEO
Robert Bass, Production Manager
Bob Wallace, Editor
William Harrison, Manager
William Bassy, President

Communication technology and market developments for users, service providers and manufacturers worldwide.
Frequency: Monthly
Circulation: 80854
Founded in: 1960

22739 **Telephone IP News**
Worldwide Videotex

Po Box 3273
Boynton Beach, FL 33424

561-738-2276
markedit@juno.com; www.wvpubs.com

Provides news and information concerning the information provider (IP) industry for telephone services and two-way paging and wireless information services. Reports on new products available to providers and monitors public service commission rulings as they aplly to information services.
Cost: $25.00
Frequency: Monthly

22740 Telephony
Telephony Division
One IBM Plaza
Suite 2300
Chicago, IL 10151

312-595-1080; *Fax:* 312-595-0296
telephony@prismb2b.com; www.primedia.com

Mark Hickey, Publisher
Dan O'Shea, Editor-in-Chief
Kim Brower, Marketing Manager

Written for professionals involved in management, construction, maintenance and marketing of modern telecommunication systems. Focus is on new, technical advances, filed applications and management techniques.
Cost: $3.00
Frequency: Weekly
Circulation: 59000
Founded in: 1989

22741 VON
Virgo Publishing LLC
3300 N Central Ave
Suite 300
Phoenix, AZ 85012-2532

480-675-9925; *Fax:* 480-990-0819
mikes@vpico.com; www.vpico.com
Social Media: Facebook, Twitter

Jenny Bolton, President

Global information on IP Communications strategy.
Mailing list available for rent: 22000+ names at $var per M

22742 Wire Journal International
Wire Association International
1570 Boston Post Road
PO Box 578
Guilford, CT 06437

203-453-2777; *Fax:* 203-453-8384
mmarselli@wirenet.org; www.wirenet.org
Social Media: Facebook, Twitter

Brian A Bouvier, President
Steven J Fetteroll, Executive Director
Mark A Marselli, Editor-in-Chief
Janice E Swindells, Director of Marketing Services
Robert J Xeller, Director Sales

The leading technical publication for the wire and cable industry. Written for executives, engineers, technical and sales professionals, and purchasing agents engaged in the manufacture of ferrous and nonferrous wire and cable; electrical wire and cable; fiber optic cable; and formed and fabricated wire products.
Frequency: Monthly
Circulation: 13434
Founded in: 1930
Printed in 4 colors on glossy stock

22743 Worldwide Telecom
Worldwide Videotex
Po Box 3273
Boynton Beach, FL 33424

561-738-2276
markedit@juno.com; www.wvpubs.com
Social Media: Facebook, Twitter

Provides the latest news and information on international telecommunication products, services, and contracts. The emphasis is on U.S. telecommunications companies doing business in foreign markets and on products with a potential market overseas.
Cost: $25.00
Frequency: Monthly

22744 Yellow Pages Industry Sourcebook
SIMBA Information
60 Long Ridge Rd
Suite 300
Stamford, CT 06902-1841

203-325-8193; *Fax:* 203-325-8915
info@simbanet.com; www.simbanet.com

Linda Kopp, Publisher
Kathy Mickey, Managing Editor

Lists key officers, revenues, leading books, major accounts, sales offices and suppliers for more than 1500 firms involved in yellow pages publishing.
Cost: $99.00

22745 xchange
Virgo Publishing LLC
3300 N Central Ave
Suite 300
Phoenix, AZ 85012-2532

480-675-9925; *Fax:* 480-990-0819
mikes@vpico.com; www.vpico.com

Jenny Bolton, President
John Siefert, CEO
Kelly Ridley, VP
Katherine Clements, Publisher

Provides in-depth, executive-level news and analysis regarding strategy, technology and regulation to help communications service providers create new revenue, lower costs and achieve sustainable business models.
Frequency: Annual+
Circulation: 35,003
Founded in: 1996

Trade Shows

22746 AFCEA TechNet Asia-Pacific
Armed Forces Communications and Electronics Assn
4400 Fair Lakes Court
Fairfax, VA 22033

703-631-6200
800-564-4220; *Fax:* 703-654-6931;
www.afcea.org

Paul doCarmo, Assistant Director/Exhibit Sales
Connie Shaw, Exhibit Sales Account Manager
Herbert Browne, President

Military, government and industry communications and electronics professionals gather to see exhibits of communications and electronics equipment, supplies and services.
2000 Attendees
Frequency: November/Annual
Founded in: 1985

22747 AFCEA Technical Committee Tech Forum TechNet International
AFCEA Headquarters
4400 Fair Lakes Court
Fairfax, VA 22033-3899

703-631-6100
800-336-4583; *Fax:* 703-631-6169
service@afcea.org; www.afcea.org

Herbert Browne, President
Paul doCarmo, Assistant Director/Exhibit Sales
Connie Shaw, Exhibit Sales Account Manager

One of the nation's largest C4I conventions and expositions and features numerous professional development opportunities and tremendous networking opportunies.
Founded in: 1985

22748 AFCEA/USNI West Conference & Exposition
Armed Forces Communications and Electronics Assn
4400 Fair Lakes Court
Fairfax, VA 22033

703-631-6200
800-564-4220; *Fax:* 703-654-6931;
www.afcea.org

Paul doCarmo, Assistant Director/Exhibit Sales
Connie Shaw, Exhibit Sales Account Manager
Herbert Browne, President

Over 350 of the industry's most recognized defense and technology organizations showcase their technology products and services to top decision-makers from the US Pacific Fleet, Naval Station San Diego, Space & Warfare Command, Naval Base Coronado, Camp Pendleton Marine Corps Base and many other west coast military and government facilities.
6000 Attendees
Frequency: January/Annual
Founded in: 1985

22749 AIIM Annual Conference and Expo
Association for Information and Image Management
1100 Wayne Avenue
Suite 1100
Silver Spring, MD 20910-5603

301-587-8202
800-477-2446; *Fax:* 301-587-2711
aiim@aiim.org; www.aiim.org
Social Media: Facebook, Twitter

Jan Andersson, Chair
Robert Zagami, Vice Chair

The leading industry event for Enterprise Content and Document Management, which encompasses the technologies and strategies used to capture, manage, share, and store documents and digital content.
Frequency: April

22750 APCO Annual Conference & Expo
Assoc of Public-Safety Commun Officials Intl
351 N Williamson Boulevard
Daytona Beach, FL 32114-1112

386-322-2500
888-272-6911; *Fax:* 386-322-2501
apco@apcointl.org; www.apcointl.org/
Social Media: Facebook

George S Rice Jr, Executive Director
Barbara Myers, Conference Services Director
Brigid Blaschak, Tradeshow Manager
Patricia Giannini, Senior Meeting Coordinator
Garry Mendez, Marketing/Communications Director

The Association of Public-Safety Communications Officials International/APCO 's Annual Conference brings together more than 300 vendors to give you hands-on demonstrations of new technologies you might use in your agency or call centers. The Conference also offers sessions on personal and professional development and a variety of technical skills. Banquet, breakfast and

exhibitors of radio, computer, and supporting equipment companies.
6000 Attendees
Frequency: Annual
Founded in: 1935

22751 Annual Conference for Catalog & Multichannel Merchants (ACCM)
Direct Marketing Association
1120 Avenue of Americas
New York, NY 10036

212-768-7277; *Fax:* 212-768-4547;
www.the-dma.org

Julie Hogan, SVP Conference & Events
10M Attendees

22752 Antenna Measurement Techniques Association Show
6065 Roswell Road
Suite 2252
Atlanta, GA 30328

770-864-3488; *Fax:* 770-864-3491;
www.amta.org
Social Media: Facebook, Twitter

Janet O'Neil, Contact

Antenna test equipment, supplies and services for government, private and institutional laboratories involved in design and development.

22753 Association for Communications Technology Professionals in Higher Education
ACUTA
152 W Zandale Drive
Suite 200
Lexington, KY 40503-2486

859-278-3338; *Fax:* 859-278-3268
kbowman@acuta.org; www.acuta.org
Social Media: Facebook, Twitter, LinkedIn, You Tube

Kellie Bowman, Registration
Jeri Semer, Executive Director

Annual conference and exhibits of educational telecommunications equipment, supplies and services. Containing 95 booths.
600 Attendees
Frequency: Annual
Founded in: 1971

22754 Association of Teleservices International Conference
ATSI
12 Academy Avenue
Atkinson, NH 03811

866-896-2874; *Fax:* 703-435-4390
admin@atsi.org; www.atsi.org
Social Media: Facebook, Twitter, LinkedIn, You Tube

Lori Jenkins, President
Marcy Hewlett, Convention Chair

Exhibits of interest to telephone answering and voice message providers.
800+ Attendees
Founded in: 1942

22755 Cable-Tec Expo
Society of Cable Telecommunications Engineers
140 Philips Road
Exton, PA 19341-1318

610-524-1725
800-542-5040; *Fax:* 610-363-5898
info@scte.org
expo.scte.org
Social Media: Facebook, Twitter, LinkedIn, You Tube

Heather Gosciniak, Director

The Society's Cable-Tec Expo is the premier industry hardware exhibition that also offers an engineering conference, workshops and meetings. Expo contains more than 500 booths and 400 exhibits.
12M Attendees
Frequency: Annual

22756 Call Center Conference and Exposition
CMP Media
11 West 19th Street
New York, NY 10011

888-428-3976; *Fax:* 212-600-3080;
www.callcenterweek.com
Social Media: Facebook, Twitter, LinkedIn, You Tube

Joni Mitchell, Marketing Manager
Joy Cerequas, Director Events

125 booths, plus conference covering all applications of new technologies and services in call processing, transaction processing and telemarketing.
2.5M Attendees
Frequency: February

22757 Email Evolution Conference
Direct Marketing Association
1120 Avenue of Americas
New York, NY 10036-6700

212-768-7277; *Fax:* 212-302-6714
dmaconferences@the-dma.org;
www.the-dma.org

Julie A Hogan, SVP Conference/Events
Lawrence M Kimmel, CEO

Focuses on the ever-changing and evolving world of email marketing, providing you with the best ways to capitalize on the high ROI this low-cost communication tool can provide both on its own, and integrated with social, search, mobile, video and other email enhancers.
10M Attendees
Frequency: Annual/February

22758 Entelec Conference & Expo
Energy Telecommunications and Electrical Assoc
5005 Royal Lane
Suite 116
Irving, TX 75063

888-503-8700; *Fax:* 972-915-6040
info@entelec.org; www.entelec.org
Social Media: Facebook, Twitter, LinkedIn

Blaine Siske, Executive Manager
Amanda Prudden, Association Manager

22759 Enterprise Wireless
Enterprise Wireless Alliance
8484 Westpark Drive
Suite 630
McLean, VA 22102-5117

703-528-5115; *Fax:* 703-524-1074
customerservice@enterprisewireless.org;
www.enterprisewireless.org
Social Media: Facebook, Twitter, LinkedIn

Mark Crosby, President/CEO
Andre Cote, Senior VP
Ila Dudley, VP Spectrum Management
Ron Franklin, VP Membership/Business Development

Co-hosted by AAPC and USMSS, this trade show and conference is for wireless service providers, manufacturers, systems integrators an denterprise users to showcase innovative new wireless products.

22760 IEEE Communications Expo IEEE Globecom
J Spargo & Associates
11208 Waples Mill Road
Suite 112
Fairfax, VA 22030

703-631-6200
800-564-4220; *Fax:* 703-654-6931;
www.ieee.org

Connie Shaw, Exhibit Sales Account Manager

In addition to targeting IEEE Communications Society members, also draws companies from Silicon Valley, Northern California, and the Pacific Rim, who manufacture or distribute products or services to support wireless technologies, optical networking, the Internet, or the telecom marketplace.
2000 Attendees
Frequency: November

22761 INTX
National Cable & Telecommunications Association
25 Massachusetts Ave. NW
Suite 100
Washington, DC 20001

202-222-2300
webmaster@ncta.com; www.ncta.com
Social Media: Facebook, Twitter, LinkedIn

Michael Powell, President & CEO

The Internet & Television Expo
Frequency: Annual/Spring
Founded in: 2015

22762 International Wireless Communication Expo
6300 S Syracuse Way
Suite 650
Englewood, CO 80111-6726

303-904-0407
rugianskis@prismb2b.com;
www.iwceexpo.com
Social Media: Facebook, Twitter, LinkedIn

Rita Ugianskis, Group Show Director
Laura Magliola, Marketing Manager
Stacey Orlick, Director
Catherine E. Campfield, Co-ordinator
Angela Wood, Conference Program Manager

The one place where all industries and communications professionals come together to share thoughts and ideas on wireless communications technologies.
6.5M Attendees
Frequency: March

22763 NATOA Annual Conference
Nat'l Assn of Telecommunication Officer & Advisors
3213 Duke Street
Suite 695
Alexandria, VA 22314

703-519-8035; *Fax:* 703-519-7080
info@natoa.org; www.natoa.org
Social Media: Facebook, Twitter

Elizabeth Beaty, Executive Director
Jennifer Harman, Manager
Tonya Rideout, Deputy

Containing 30 booths featuring telecommunications equipment and supplies. Cable operators and local governments. Educational sessions topics include technology, competitive markets, programming, and cable franchise administration.
700 Attendees
Frequency: September

22764 NCDM Conference
Direct Marketing Association

1120 Avenue of Americas
New York, NY 10036-6700

212-768-7277; *Fax:* 212-302-6714
dmaconferences@the-dma.org;
www.the-dma.org

Julie A Hogan, SVP Conferences/Events
Lawrence M Kimmel, CEO

Presents industry experts and hard-hitting case studies from a variety of verticals, such as financial services, retail, automotive, publishing, non-profit and many more, who will share the latest strategies and methodologies in gathering, analyzing, leveraging and protecting your most valuable business asset - customer data.
10M Attendees
Frequency: Annual/December

22765 NEAX 2400 IMS Users Group
40 Marsh Wall
Columbia, CT 29221-0886

803-798-4800; www.necusergroup.com
Social Media: Facebook, Twitter

Carlisle Reames, Contact

15 booths of educational sessions for NEC 2400 DBX systems users.
350 Attendees
Frequency: April

22766 NXTcomm
Telecommunications Industry Association/TIA
2500 Wilson Boulevard
Suite 300
Arlington, VA 22201-3834

703-907-7700; *Fax:* 703-907-7727
gseiffert@tiaonline.org;
www.tiaonline.org/business/events/TIATradeshows.cfm
Social Media: Facebook, Twitter, LinkedIn

Grant Seiffert, President
Mike Nunes, Government Relations Director
Lora Magruder, Member Relations Director
Daniel J. Pigott, Chairman of the Board
Thomas Stanton, Vice Chair

NXTcomm is an industry event uniting the premier information and communications technology suppliers with the world's leading communications and entertainment companies. Connect with 450+ exhibitors and 20,000+ attendees. Soak up essential knowledge during insider-led conferences. The global forces that are driving communications-based innovation are here.

22767 National Conference on Operations & Fulfillment (NCOF)
Direct Marketing Association
1120 Avenue of Americas
New York, NY 10036-6700

212-768-7277; *Fax:* 212-302-6714
dmaconferences@the-dma.org;
www.the-dma.org

Julie A Hogan, SVP Conference/Educational Services
Lawrence M Kimmel, CEO

Focuses on innovative solutions for warehouse, distribution, operations, and ecommerce needs in the ever-changing world of operations and fulfillment.
10M Attendees
Frequency: Annual/April

22768 New York Nonprofit Conference
Direct Marketing Association
1120 Avenue of Americas
New York, NY 10036-6700

212-768-7277; *Fax:* 212-302-6714
dmaconferences@the-dma.org;
www.the-dma.org

Julie A Hogan, SVP Conference/Events
Lawrence M Kimmel, CEO

Discover which acknowledgement programs work best-and why, increase revenue with membership options-as well as traditional fundraising appeals, learn how the internet and e-mail campaigng can improve fundraising, lower costs and increase advocac
10M Attendees

22769 PCCA Annual Convention
Power and Communication Contractors
1908 Mt. Vernon Ave
Suite 200
Alexandria, VA 22314

703-212-7734
800-542-7222; *Fax:* 703-548-3733
info@pccaweb.org; www.pccaweb.org
Social Media: Facebook, Twitter

Kevin Mason, President
Larry Libla, President-Elect
Frequency: March

22770 TechNet North 2006
AFCEA Canada & AFCEA International
102 Centrepointe Drive
Ottawa, ON K2G-6B1

613-786-2619; *Fax:* 613-230-1554;
www.technetnorth.com
Social Media: Facebook, Twitter

Kevin d'Entremont, Exhibit Director
Rick Tachuk, Marketing & Communications Director

Delivers an inovative professional development conference and a major trade exhibition focused on the latest C4ISR solutions, products and technologies for the North American defense and security sectors.

22771 Telecom
607 14th Street
Suite 600
Washington, DC 20005-2164

202-547-2680; *Fax:* 202-326-7333;
www.usta.org
Social Media: Facebook, Twitter, LinkedIn, You Tube

Walter B McCormick Jr, President/CEO
Jaonne Hovis, Chair
Tony Prez, Director

Conference and exhibition offers a variety of educational sessions, special interest seminars and keynote speakers. The show features an estimated 160 exhibitors.
1300 Attendees
Frequency: Annual

22772 Utilities Telecommunications Council Annual Conference and Exhibition
Utilities Telecommunications Council
1129 20th St.NW
Suite 350
Washington, DC 20036

202-872-0030; *Fax:* 202-872-1331
marketing@utc.org; www.utc.org
Social Media: Facebook, Twitter, LinkedIn

Connie Durcsase, President
Mike Oldak, VP & General Counsel
Karnel Thomas, VM- Member Services
Kathleen Fitzpatric, VP- Operations

Annual conference and exhibits of telecommunications equipment and services.
1,000 Attendees
Founded in: 1948

22773 Wire Expo
Wire Association International
1570 Boston Post Road
PO Box 578
Guilford, CT 06437-0578

203-453-2777; *Fax:* 203-453-8384;
www.wirenet.org
Social Media: Facebook, Twitter

Livia Jacobs, Manager Convention/Events
Nicholas Nickoletopoulos, President
Steven J. Fetteroll~, Executive Director
Robert J. Xeller, Sales

Wire Expo provides you with ready-made opportunities—including meeting with more than 450 suppliers on the show floor. You'll gain manufacturing and technical information by attending short courses and listening to some of the 75+ paper that will be presented at WCTS. Social events also provide oppertunities to make conections with other professionals in the wire industry.
4000 Attendees
Frequency: May/June
Founded in: 1930

Directories & Databases

22774 Audiotex Directory
ADBG Publishing
PO Box 25929
Los Angeles, CA 90025-0929

310-914-9000; *Fax:* 310-479-0654;
www.krango.com
Social Media: Facebook, Twitter

Larry Podell, Editor

Over 1,200 product and service suppliers in the voice processing fax, and audiotex fields, including hardware, software, vendors, telephone companies, service bureaus, audio programmers, and consultants
Cost: $50.00
Frequency: Annual

22775 Bacon's Radio/TV/Cable Directory
Cision U.S., Inc.
332 South Michigan Avenue
Suite 900
Chicago, IL 60604

312-263-0070
866-639-5087
info.us@cision.com; www.us.cision.com

Joe Bernardo, President & CEO
Heidi Sullivan, VP & Publisher
Valerie Lopez, Research Director
Jessica White, Research Director
Rachel Farrell, Research Manager

Includes comprehensive coverage for contact and programming information for more than 3,500 televsion networks, cable networks, television syndicators, television stations, and cable systems in the United States and Canada.
Cost: $350.00
Frequency: Annual
ISSN: 1088-9639
Printed in one color on matte stock

22776 Communication News: Network Access Directory
Nelson Publishing
2500 Tamiami Trl N
Nokomis, FL 34275-3476

941-966-9521; *Fax:* 941-966-2590;
www.healthmgttech.com
Social Media: Facebook, Twitter, LinkedIn

A Verner Nelson, Owner
Cost: $7.00
Frequency: Annual, June
Circulation: 71,000
Mailing list available for rent

22777 **Communications News: Broadband Directory**
Nelson Publishing
2500 Tamiami Trl N
Nokomis, FL 34275-3476
941-966-9521; *Fax:* 941-966-2590;
www.healthmgttech.com
Social Media: Facebook, Twitter, LinkedIn
A Verner Nelson, Owner
Cost: $7.00
Frequency: Annual, December
Circulation: 71,000
Mailing list available for rent

22778 **Communications News: PBX/CTI Directory**
Nelson Publishing
2500 Tamiami Trl N
Nokomis, FL 34275-3476
941-966-9521; *Fax:* 941-966-2590;
www.healthmgttech.com
Social Media: Facebook, Twitter, LinkedIn
A Verner Nelson, Owner
Cost: $7.00
Frequency: Annual, April
Circulation: 71,000
Mailing list available for rent

22779 **Communications News: Test Directory**
Nelson Publishing
2500 Tamiami Trl N
Nokomis, FL 34275-3476
941-966-9521; *Fax:* 941-966-2590;
www.healthmgttech.com
Social Media: Facebook, Twitter, LinkedIn
A Verner Nelson, Owner
Cost: $7.00
Frequency: Annual, February
Circulation: 71,000
Mailing list available for rent

22780 **Communications News: Video/ Audioconferencing Directory**
Nelson Publishing
2500 Tamiami Trl N
Nokomis, FL 34275-3476
941-966-9521; *Fax:* 941-966-2590;
www.healthmgttech.com
Social Media: Facebook, Twitter, LinkedIn
A Verner Nelson, Owner
Cost: $7.00
Frequency: Annual, October
Circulation: 71,000
Mailing list available for rent

22781 **Communications News: Wireless Directory**
Nelson Publishing
2500 Tamiami Trl N
Nokomis, FL 34275-3476
941-966-9521; *Fax:* 941-966-2590;
www.healthmgttech.com
Social Media: Facebook, Twitter, LinkedIn
A Verner Nelson, Owner
Cost: $7.00
Frequency: Annual, August
Circulation: 71,000
Mailing list available for rent

22782 **Complete Directory of Telephones & Accessories**
Sutton Family Communications & Publishing Company
155 Sutton Lane
Fordsville, KY 42343
270-740-0870
jlsutton@apex.net;
www.suttoncompliance.com
Social Media: Facebook, Twitter
Theresa Sutton, Editor
Lee Sutton, General Manager
Print-out from database of wholesalers, manufacturers, distributors, importers and close-out houses. Database is updated daily to guarantee the most current and up-to-date sources available.
Cost: $55.20
100+ Pages

22783 **Corporate Yellow Book**
Leadership Directories
104 5th Ave
New York, NY 10011-6901
212-627-4140; *Fax:* 212-645-0931
info@leadershipdirectories.com;
www.leadershipdirectories.com
Social Media: Facebook, Twitter
David Hurvitz, CEO
Contact information for over 48,000 executives at over 1,000 companies and more than 9,000 board members and their outside affiliations.
Cost: $420.00
1,400 Pages
Frequency: Quarterly
ISSN: 1058-2098
Founded in: 1986

22784 **Directory of Communications Professionals**
National Assn of Regulatory Utility Commissioners
1101 Vermont Ave NW
Suite 200
Washington, DC 20005-3553
202-898-2200; *Fax:* 202-898-2213;
www.naruc.org
Social Media: Facebook, Twitter
Charles Gray, Executive Director
Philip Jones, President
Offers information on consultants and other professionals active in regulated telecommunications.
Cost: $33.00
240 Pages
Frequency: Annual

22785 **International Fiber Optics Yellow Pages**
Information Gatekeepers
214 Harvard Avenue
Suite 200
Allston, MA 02134-4641
617-232-3111
800-323-1088; *Fax:* 617-734-8562
webmaster@igigroup.com;
www.fiberopticsyp.com
Social Media: Facebook, Twitter
Will Ashley, Contact
The most extensive Fiber Optics reference volume available anywhere. This directory is still the world's only source book devoted exclusively to Fiber Optics.
Cost: $89.95
Frequency: Annual
Founded in: 1977

22786 **LATA Directory**
Center for Communications Management
11300 Rockville Pike
Suite 1100
Rockville, MD 20852-3003
301-770-7490; *Fax:* 301-287-2445;
www.lataweb.com
Social Media: Facebook, Twitter
Ronald Canter, Owner
Offers information on local access transport areas by states.
Cost: $195.00
220 Pages
Frequency: Annual

22787 **Local Calling Area Directory**
Center for Communications Management
11300 Rockville Pike
Suite 1100
Rockville, MD 20852-3003
301-770-7490; *Fax:* 301-287-2445;
www.lataweb.com
Social Media: Facebook, Twitter
Ronald Canter, Owner
Offers area codes and their zones or exchanges in cities of 100,000 or more in population.
Cost: $795.00
1,050 Pages
Frequency: Annual

22788 **Lynx Global Telecom Database**
Lynx Technologies
710 Route 46 East
PO Box 368
Little Falls, NJ 07424-0368
973-256-7200; *Fax:* 973-882-3583;
www.lynxtech.com
Social Media: Facebook, Twitter
Kathleen Elsayed, Production Manager
Mike Salerno, Circulation Director
350 telecommunications carriers services in approximately 200 countries, territories and other political divisions.

22789 **Network Management Guidelines and Contact Directory**
Network Operations Forum
1200 G Street NW
Washington, DC 20005-3814
202-347-1228; *Fax:* 202-393-5453
Over 25 telecommunications companies.

22790 **North American Telecommunications Association - Sourcebook**
2000 P St NW
Suite 550
Washington, DC 20036-6921
202-419-0412; www.naaee.org
Brian Day, Executive Director
Sue Bumpous, Communications Manager
Offers a wide array of information on manufacturers and suppliers of non-utility telephone terminal equipment.
Cost: $53.00
208 Pages

22791 **Outside Plant: Directory of Outside Plant Contractors Issue**
Practical Communications
PO Box 183
Cary, IL 60013-0183
847-639-2200; *Fax:* 847-639-7598
John Saxtan, Editor
Offers a list of over 800 contractors in the telecommunications industry that specialize in outside plant projects.
Cost: $30.00
Frequency: Annual
Circulation: 20,000

22792 **Phillips Satellite Industry Directory**
Phillips Business Information

1201 Seven Locks Road
Potomac, MD 20854-2931

301-354-1400
800-777-5006; *Fax:* 301-309-9473

Minica Kenny, Editor
Don Pazour, CEO

Over 6,000 contacts and more than 3,800 hardware and technical service companies, transponder brokers and resellers, consultants, communications attorneys, publishers, uplinks and downlinks, video conference suppliers, related trade associations, government agencies and satellite telecommunications carriers.
Cost: $257.00
Frequency: Annual January

22793 Phillips Who's Who in Electronic Commerce
Phillips Business Information
1201 Seven Locks Road
Potomac, MD 20854-2931

301-354-1400
800-777-5006; *Fax:* 301-309-9473

Jennifer O Newman, Editor
Don Pazour, CEO

Service providers, value-added banks and networks, software vendors, associations, user groups, consultants, business and technical services for electronic commerce industry.
Cost: $199.00
Frequency: Annual

22794 Pocket Guides to the Internet: Terminal Connections
Information Today
143 Old Marlton Pike
Medford, NJ 08055-8750

609-654-6266
800-300-9868; *Fax:* 609-654-4309
custserv@infotoday.com; www.infotoday.com
Social Media: Facebook, Twitter

Thomas H Hogan, President
Roger R Bilboul, Chairman Of The Board

Unix/VMS systems and other basic terminal applications and telecommunications programs.
Cost: $9.95

22795 Q-TEL 1000
United Communications Group
11300 Rockville Pike
P.O Box: 217
Rockville, MD 20852-3030

301-816-8950
800-526-5307; *Fax:* 858-674-5491;
www.qtel.qa
Social Media: Facebook, Twitter

This database offers information on telecommunications charges.
Frequency: Full-text
Mailing list available for rent

22796 RCR Publications
RCR Publications
1746 Cole Boulevard
Suite 150
Golden, CO 80401

303-733-2500
800-678-9696; *Fax:* 303-733-9941
mbush@crain.com; www.rcrnews.com

Melodye Bush, Database Coordinator

Offers a wide variety of information on cellular and personal communications industries. Includes detailed information on carriers and vendors around the world.
Cost: $950.00
Frequency: Annual
Founded in: 1991

22797 RCR's Cellular Database
RCR Publications
1746 Cole Boulevard
Suite 150
Golden, CO 80401

303-733-2500
800-678-9696; *Fax:* 303-733-9941
mbush@crain.com; www.rcrnews.com

Melodye Bush, Database Coordinator

Offers a wide variety of information on cellular communications industry. Includes detailed information on cellular carriers and vendors.
Cost: $300.00
Frequency: Annual
Founded in: 1991

22798 RCR's PCS Database
RCR Publications
1746 Cole Boulevard
Suite 150
Golden, CO 80401

303-733-2500
800-678-9696; *Fax:* 303-733-9941
mbush@crain.com; www.rcrnews.com

Melodye Bush, Database Coordinator

Offers a wide variety of information on the personal communications industry. Includes detailed information on PCS carriers and vendors.
Cost: $300.00
Frequency: Annual
Founded in: 1991

22799 Satellite Industry Directory
Phillips Business Information
1201 Seven Locks Road
Suite 300
Potomac, MD 20854-2931

301-354-1400; *Fax:* 301-309-9473

Monica Kenny, Editor

Profiles operational and planned satellite systems, equipment and service providers, satellite brokers, uplinkers/downlinkers and more.
Cost: $247.00
750 Pages
Frequency: Annual

22800 Sbusiness
AFSM International
17065 Camino San Bernardo
Suite 200
San Diego, CA 92127-1709

858-673-3055
800-333-9786; *Fax:* 239-275-0794;
www.afsmi.org
Social Media: Facebook, Twitter

John Shoenewald, Executive Director
Jb Wood, President/CEO

The professional journal for customer service and support managers.
Cost: $60.00
100 Pages
Frequency: Bi-Monthly
Circulation: 10000
Founded in: 1975
Mailing list available for rent

22801 TCP/IP for the Internet
Mecklermedia Corporation
20 Ketchum Street
Westport, CT 06880-5908

203-341-2806; *Fax:* 203-454-5840

Marshall Breeding, Editor

Standard network protocol for data transmission over the global internet - products and packages for Unix, DOS, Windows and Macintosh platforms.
Cost: $24.95

22802 Telecommunications Directory
Gale/Cengage Learning
10650 Toebben Drive
Detroit, KY 41051

248-699-4253
800-877-4253; *Fax:* 248-699-8049
gale.galeord@cengage.com; www.gale.com
Social Media: Facebook, Twitter

Patrick C Sommers, President

Provides detailed information on telecommunications companies providing a range of products and services from cellular communications and local exchange carriers to satellite services and Internet service providers.
ISBN: 1-414419-80-5

22803 Telecommunications Export Guide
North American Telecommunications Association
2000 P St NW
Suite 550
Washington, DC 20036-6921

202-419-0412; www.naaee.org

Brian Day, Executive Director
Sue Bumpous, Communications Manager

Offers a list of over 135 foreign telecommunications agencies, and federal and state government agencies concerned with exports in the United States.
Cost: $103.00

22804 Telemarketing and Call Center Solutions Buyer's Guide and Directory Issue
Technology Marketing Corporation
800 Connecticut Ave
1st Floor East
Norwalk, CT 06854-1936

203-852-6800
800-243-6002; *Fax:* 203-853-2845
tmc@tmcnet.com; www.tmcnet.com
Social Media: Facebook, Twitter, LinkedIn, You Tube

Rich Tehrani, CEO
Nanji Tehrani, Chair
David Rodriguez, President/Assistant Treasurer
Michael Genaro, VP

Over 1100 domestic and foreign suppliers of equipment products and services to the telecommunications/telemarketing industry.
Cost: $25.00
Frequency: Annual December
Founded in: 1972

22805 Telephone Industry Directory
Phillips Business Information
1201 Seven Locks Road
Suite 300
Potomac, MD 20854-2931

301-354-1400; *Fax:* 301-349-9473

Jennifer Newman, Assistant Managing Editor

Offers valuable information on over 4,800 manufacturers, distributors and suppliers to the telecommunications industry.
Cost: $249.00
750 Pages
Frequency: Annual

22806 Voice Mail Reference Manual and Buyer's Guide
Robins Press
2675 Henry Hudson Parkway W
Apartment 6J
Bronx, NY 10463-7741

718-548-7245
800-238-7130; *Fax:* 718-548-7237
robinspr@ix.netcom.com;
www.mmdimensions.com/telstore

Marc Robins, Publisher

Offers information on over 60 suppliers of about 90 voice mail systems and service bureaus.
Cost: $65.00
384 Pages
Frequency: Annual
Mailing list available for rent: 10M names
Printed in 2 colors on matte stock

22807 **Voice Processing Printed Circuit Cards: A Sourcebook of Suppliers & Products**
Robins Press
2675 Henry Hudson Parkway W
Apartment 6J
Bronx, NY 10463-7741
718-548-7245

Offers a list of over 50 vendors of voice processing circuit cards and related technology worldwide.
Cost: $150.00
Frequency: Annual

22808 **World Satellite Almanac**
Phillips Business Information
1201 Seven Locks Road
Suite 300
Potomac, MD 20854-2931
301-354-1400; *Fax:* 301-340-1520
Monica Kenny, Editor

All commercial satellite systems and operators are profiled.
Cost: $247.00; 700 Pages
Frequency: Annual

22809 **World Telecommunications Tariff Directory**
Lynx Technologies
PO Box 368
Little Falls, NJ 07424-0368
973-256-7200

A comprehensive directory of over 1,200 Local Exchange Carriers and other telecom companies make up this directory. Includes a detailed index for easy cross-referencing by company name, contacts, titles, geographical region, services provided, email and more.
Cost: $699.00; 9,000 Pages

Industry Web Sites

22810 **http://gold.greyhouse.com**
G.O.L.D Grey House OnLine Databases

Grey House Publishing's online database platform, GOLD, offers Quick Search, Keyword Search and Expert Search for most business sectors including telecommunications and media markets. The GOLD platform makes finding the information you need quick and easy - whether you're a novice searcher or an experienced database user. All of Grey House's directory products are available for subscription on the GOLD platform.

22811 **www.adweek.com**
ADWEEK

Leading decision makers in the advertising and marketing field go to Adweek.Com every day for breaking news, insight, buzz, opinion, analysis, research and classifieds. The resources of all six regional editions of Adweek, as well as the national edition of Brandweek are combined with the knowledge of our online editors and the multimedia-interactive capabilities of the web to deliver vital information quickly and effectively to our target audience.

22812 **www.alts.org**
Association of Local Telecommunications Services

Represents state and local telecommunications offices.

22813 **www.amtausa.org**
American Mobile Telecommunications Association

Membership is made up of operators in the 220 MHz, 450 MHz, 800 MHz and 900 MHz bands, as well as product and service providers for the industry. Many members are exploring other areas of the mobile telecommunications industry — digital SMR, Personal Communications Services, data communications, mobile satellite, cable telephony and international wireless interests. AMTA is working with its members and with government to insure that those areas can be pursued successfully.

22814 **www.arrl.org**
American Radio Relay League

National membership association for amateur radio operators.

22815 **www.atis.org**
Alliance for Telecommunications Industry Solutions

Membership organization that provides the tools necessary for the industry to identify standards, guidelines and operating procedures that make the interoperability of existing and emerging telecommunications proiducts and services possible.

22816 **www.atsi.org**
Association of Telemessaging Services International

Promotes fair competition through appropriate regulation and legislation; provides research and development provides support services and educational opportunities to address challenges in operating environments; in encourages and maintains the high standards of ethics and service.

22817 **www.floridapsc.com**
Telecommunications Cooperative Network

Offers group purchasing discounts on long-distance telephone services, equipment counseling, and analysis of communications needs.

22818 **www.greyhouse.com**
Grey House Publishing

Authoritative reference directories for most business sectors including telecommunications and media markets. Users can search the online databases with varied search criteria allowing for custom searches by product category, geographic area, sales volume, keyword, subject and more. Full Grey House catalog and online ordering also available.

22819 **www.icea.net**
Insulated Cable Engineers Association

Professional organization dedicated to developing cable standards for the electric power, control and telecommunications industries. Ensures safe, economical and efficient cable systems utilizing proven state-of-the-art materials and concepts. ICEA documents are of interest to cable manufacturers, architects and engineers, utility and manufacturing plant personnel, telecommunication engineers, consultants and OEMs.

22820 **www.igigroup.com**
Information Gatekeepers

Provides worldwide coverage of wireless LAN's, LAN interconnection, wireless in-building and major applications such as point-of-sales, portable computer interconnections and remote data collection.

22821 **www.imc.org**
Internet Email Consortium

Information about IMC and its members, all the internet email standards and more.

22822 **www.isoc.org**
Internet Society

International, professional membership organization focusing on standards, education and policy issues.

22823 **www.kagan.com**
Wireless/Private Cable Investor

The original bible of the wireless cable, multipoint distribution pay TV industry. Published continuously since 1972, this newsletter is the window on cable competition. Three month trial available.

22824 **www.ntca.org**
National Telephone Cooperative Association

Represents both cooperative and commercial, independent rural phone companies.

22825 **www.pcca.org**
Power and Communication Contractors

A national trade association for companies constructing electric power facilities, including transmission and distribution lines and substations and telephone, fiber optic, and cable television systems.

22826 **www.scte.org**
Society of Cable Telecommunications Engineers

For people engaged in engineering, construction, installation, manufacture, technical direction, management, regulation, or administration of broad band communications technologies.

22827 **www.steconsulting.org**
Society of Telecommunications Consultants

The Society of Telecommunications Consultants is aprofessional association of Independent telecommunications consultants who provide expert, non based councel to business industry service organizations and government, worldwide. It serves its constituency by providing educational business and networking opportunities and by negotiating tangible and intangible benefits. The STC also serves as a resource, connecting end users to consultants to business, educational and promotrional opportunities.

22828 **www.telecommagazine.com**
Telecommunications Industry Association

This magazine reports on carrier class and wide area communications technologies for service providers and their corporate network customers worldwide. Coverage includes technology, product, market and application information for serious communications professionals, interexchange, cellular/wireless/satellite carriers, cable companies as well as commercial users and government agencies in the communications industry.

22829 **www.telecommute.org**
Telecommuting Advisory Council

A comprehensive monthly digest of news about employer-sponsored telecommuting programs for employers working at home or elsewhere off-site. Contains case studies, international news, technology updates, legal and regulatory news, and managerial topics.

22830 **www.usta.org**
United States Telecom Association

Broad based association for the local exchange carrier industry worldwide.

Associations

22831 **Acrylic Council**
1285 Avenue of the Americas
35th Floor
New York, NY 10019
212-397-4600; *Fax:* 212-554-4042;
www.fabriclink.com
Social Media: Facebook, Twitter
Lynn Misiak, Executive Director
A business league created to provide products in facilities maintained in the US. Educates the retailer and consumer of the benefits of acrylic fiber.

22832 **Amalgamated Clothing and Textile Workers Union**
1710 Broadway
New York, NY 10019-5254
212-255-9655; www.acronymfinder.com
Social Media: Facebook, Twitter
Jack Sheinkman, President
William Towne, Manager
Sponsors and supports the Political Action Committee in this field.
249M Members
Founded in: 1976

22833 **American Flock Association**
PO Box 1090
Suite C
Cherryville, NC 28021
617-303-6288; *Fax:* 704-671-2366
info@flocking.org; www.flocking.org
Social Media: LinkedIn, YouTube, Pinterest
Karl Spilhaus, President
Steve Rosenthal, Managing Director
Provides positive leadership to foster a strong flock industry in North America.
60 Members
Founded in: 1984

22834 **American Home Sewing & Craft Association**
PO Box 369
Monroeville, PA 15146
412-372-5950; *Fax:* 412-372-5953
info@sewing.org; www.sewing.org
Handicraft and collectibles forum

22835 **American Sheep Industry Association**
9785 Maroon Circle
Suite 360
Englewood, CO 80112
303-771-3500; *Fax:* 303-771-8200;
www.sheepusa.org
Social Media: Facebook
Burton Pfliger, President
Mike Corn, VP
Benny Cox, Secretary/Treasurer
A federation of state associations dedicated to the welfare and profitability of the sheep industry.
8000+ Members
Founded in: 1865

22836 **American Textile Machinery Association**
201 Park Washington Ct
Falls Church, VA 22046-4527
703-538-1789; *Fax:* 703-241-5603
info@atmanet.org; www.atmanet.org
Social Media: Facebook, Twitter
Will Motchar, Chairman
Mike Viniconis, Vice Chairman
Clay D Tyeryar, President & Assistant Treasurer
Allen Moore, Vice Chairman/Treasurer
Susan A Denston, Executive VP & Secretary
The American Textile Machinery Association/ATMA's purpose is to improve business conditions within the textile machinery industry of the United States within a global context; to encourage the use of the products of the industry; and to protect, promote, foster and advance the common interests of the members as manufacturers and distributors of textile machinery and parts and machinery accessory to textile machinery on a worldwide basis.
1.5M Members
Founded in: 1933

22837 **American Yarn Spinners Association**
PO Box 99
Gastonia, NC 28053
704-824-3522; *Fax:* 704-824-0630;
www.aysa.org
Social Media: Facebook, Twitter
Michael Hubbard, Executive Director
Provides full service to the sales yarn industry.
100 Members
Founded in: 1967

22838 **Association of Georgia's Textile, Carpet, & Consumer Products Manufacturers**
50 Hurt Plz Se
Suite 985
Atlanta, GA 30303-2941
404-688-0555; *Fax:* 404-584-0720
info@gamfg.org; www.gamfg.org
Social Media: Facebook, Twitter
Lee Bryan, Chairman
Del Land, Vice Chairman
G L Bowen III, President
Kevin Thieneman, Treasurer
Charles B Jones III, VP & General Counsel
Founded in: 1900

22839 **Association of Knitted Fabrics**
1001 Connecticut Ave NW
Suite 315
Washington, DC 20036
202-822-8028; *Fax:* 202-822-8029;
www.nationaltextile.org
Social Media: Facebook, Twitter
William L Jasper, Chairman
James C Self III, Vice Chairman
Augustine Tantillo, President
Sarah Pierce, Senior VP
Mike Hubbard, VP
Manufacturers of knitted cotton and wool products.
6 Members
Founded in: 1935

22840 **Carpet & Rug Institute: West**
100 South Hamilton Street
Suite 3
Dalton, CA 30720
706-278-3176; *Fax:* 706-278-8835;
www.carpet-rug.com
Social Media: Facebook, Twitter, LinkedIn, Youtube, Google+
Terri Caputo, President
Founded in: 1791
Mailing list available for rent

22841 **Cotton Council International**
1521 New Hampshire Avenue NW
Washington, DC 20036
202-745-7805; *Fax:* 202-483-4040
cottonuse@cotton.org; www.cottonusa.org
Social Media: Facebook, Twitter, YouTube, Pinterest
James L Webb, Chairman
John A Burch, President
T Jordan Lea, First VP
Dahlen K Hancock, Second VP
Keith T Lucas, Treasurer

22842 **Craft Yarn Council**
3740 N. Josey Lane
Suite 102
Carrollton, TX 75007
972-325-7232; *Fax:* 972-215-7333;
www.craftyarncouncil.com
Social Media: Facebook, Youtube, Google+
Michael Hubbard, Secretary/Treasurer
Mary Colucci, Executive Director
The Craft Yarn Council represents the leading yarn companies, accessory manufacturers, magazine, book publishers, and consultants in the yarn industry.
Founded in: 1981

22843 **Durene Association of America**
194 S South St
Gastonia, NC 28052-4125
704-865-1651; *Fax:* 704-824-0638
Russell Duren, President
Develops and uses tests to determine quality. Licenses manufacturers to use Durene identification on products.
4 Members
Founded in: 1929

22844 **Elastic Fabric Manufacturers Council**
230 Congress Street
Boston, MA 02110
617-542-8220; *Fax:* 617-542-2199;
www.textilenta.org
Provides exchange and management services, trade promotions, statistical programs and information bulletins.
32 Members
Founded in: 1915

22845 **Electrostatic Discharge Association**
7900 Turin Road
Building 3
Rome, NY 13440-2069
315-339-6937; *Fax:* 315-339-6793
info@esda.org; www.esda.org
Social Media: Facebook, Twitter, LinkedIn
Donn Bellmore, President
Leo G Henry, Senior VP
Professional voluntary association dedicated to advancing the theory and practice of electrostatic discharge avoidance. Initial emphasis on the effects of ESD on electronic components has broadened to include textiles, plastics, web processing, explosives, clean rooms and graphic arts. Expands ESD awareness through educational programs, development of standards, tutorials, publications, local chapters, symposia and certification.
Founded in: 1982

22846 **Hard Fibers Association**
120 Genesee Street
Suite 601
Auburn, NY 13021-3603
315-520-0871; *Fax:* 315-255-3292
John Hurd, President
Importers and distributors of sisal, abaca and other hard fibers.

22847 **Home Sewing Association**
PO Box 369
Monroeville, PA 15146
412-725-5950; *Fax:* 412-372-5953
info@sewing.org; www.sewing.org
Joyce Perhac, Manager

Represents most facets of the home sewing industry. National trade association for independent sewing machine dealers and distributors.
1.5M Members
Founded in: 1912

22848 INDA Association of Nonwoven Fabrics
1100 Crescent Green
Suite 115
Cary, NC 27518

919-459-3700; *Fax:* 919-459-3701
info@inda.org; www.inda.org
Social Media: Facebook, Twitter, LinkedIn, RSS

Robert Lovegrove, Chairman
Karen Castle, Vice Chairperson Planning
Renita Jones Anderson, Vice Chairperson Finance
Todd Bassett, Past INDA Chairman
Joan Izzo, Director of Marketing

Mission is to promote the value and profitability of the global nonwovens/engineered fabrics industry to benefit the members.
300 Members
Founded in: 1968

22849 Industrial Fabrics Association International
1801 County Road BW
Roseville, MN 55413-4061

651-222-2508
800-225-4324; *Fax:* 651-631-9334
generalinfo@ifai.com; www.ifai.com
Social Media: Facebook, Twitter, LinkedIn, YouTube

Stephen M Warner, President

A not-for-profit trade association that represent the international specialty fabrics marketplace that facilitates the development, application and promotion of products manufactured by the diverse membership.
2000 Members

22850 Institute of Textile Technology
North Carolina State University
3426 College of Textiles
NSCU Centennial Campus
Raleigh, NC 27695-8301

919-513-7704
888-348-3512; *Fax:* 919-882-9410;
www.ittorissa.org
Social Media: Facebook, Twitter

W Gilbert O'Neal, President & CEO
George Edmunds, VP

A graduate school supported in part by member companies. Publishes the Textile Technology Digest.

22851 International Society of Industrial Fabric
1801 County Road B W
Roseville, MN 55113-4061
651-222-2508
800-225-4324; *Fax:* 651-631-9334
generalinfo@ifai.com; www.ifai.com
Social Media: Facebook, Twitter, LinkedIn, Youtube

Mark J Hennessy, President & CEO
Todd V Lindemann, VP, Conference Management
Pam Egan-Blahna, Director, Human Resource
Dan McCarthy, VP, Finance/CFO
Andrew M Aho, Director, Membership & Divisions

A not-for profit trade association whose more than 2,000 member companies represent the international specialty fabrics marketplace. Members range in size from one-person shops to multinational corporations; member products span the entire spectrum of the specialty fabrics industry from fiber and fabric suppliers to manufacturers of end products, equipment and hardware.
350 Members
Founded in: 1912

22852 International Textile & Apparel Association
PO Box 70687
Knoxville, TN 37938-0687

865-992-1535
executivedirector@itaaonline.org;
www.itaaonline.org
Social Media: Facebook, Twitter, RSS

Nancy Rutherford, Executive Director

Professional association for 1,000 college professors of clothing and textile studies.
Founded in: 1935

22853 Knitted Textile Association
1701 K St. NW
Suite 625
Washington, DC 20006

202-822-8028; *Fax:* 202-822-8029
spierce@ncto.org; www.ncto.org
Social Media: Facebook, Twitter, LinkedIn, YouTube

Jeffrey Price, Chairman
Rob Chapman, Vice Chairman
Augustine Tantillo, President
Sara Beatty, Secretary
Robin Haynes, Treasurer

The KTA is an active participant in the International Mechinery and Equipment exhibition that takes place in Textile Hall in Greenville, South Carolina and highlights the latest in knitting and related dying and finishing equipment.

22854 Narrow Fabrics Institute
1801 County Road BW
Roseville, MN 55113-4061

651-225-6920; *Fax:* 651-631-9334
generalinfo@ifai.com; www.narrowfabrics.org
Social Media: Facebook, Twitter, LinkedIn, Youtube

Mary J Hennessy, President & CEO
Todd V Lindemann, VP, Conference Management
Pam Egan-Blahna, Director, Human Resource
Dan McCarthy, VP, Finance/CFO
Andrew M Aho, Director, Membership & Divisions

Conducts research, sells abrasior rods, and compiles statistics on narrow fabrics
40 Members
Founded in: 1956

22855 National Cotton Batting Institute
4322 Bloombury St
Southaven, MS 38672

901-218-2393; *Fax:* 662-449-0046;
www.natbat.com
Social Media: Facebook, Twitter

Weston Arnall, President
Greg Windsperger, VP
Fred Middleton, Executive Secretary-Treasurer

NCBI respresents U.S. companies that manufacture and sell batting for use in mattresses, futons, home furnishing, and upholstered products. It provides a range of services to assist its members in expanding markets, monitoring and contributing to legislative and regulatory decisions that affect the industry, and conducting consumer education and information programs.
27 Members
Founded in: 1954

22856 National Cotton Council of America
1918 N Parkway
Memphis, TN 38112-5000

901-274-9030; *Fax:* 901-725-0510;
www.cotton.org
Social Media: Facebook, Twitter

Sledge Taylor, Chairman
Shane Stephens, Vice Chairman
Meredith B Allen, VP
Sid Brough, VP
John C Fricke, VP

The council serves as the central forum for consensus-building among producers, ginners, warehousers, merchants, cottonseed processors/dealers, cooperatives and textile manufacturers.

22857 National Council for Textile Education
Georgia Institute of Technology
1701 K St. NW
Suite 625
Washington, DC 20006

202-822-8028; *Fax:* 202-822-8029
spierce@ncto.org; www.ncto.org
Social Media: Facebook, Twitter, LinkedIn, YouTube

Jeffrey Price, Chairman
Augustine Tantillo, President
Sara Beatty, Secretary
Robin Haynes, Treasurer
Rob Chapman, Vice Chairman

Members are administrators of college textile departments whose curriculum comprise science-based programs with substantial laboratory and plant experience.

22858 National Council of Textile Organizations
1701 K St. NW
Suite 625
Washington, DC 20006

202-822-8028; *Fax:* 202-822-8029;
www.ncto.org
Social Media: Facebook, Twitter, LinkedIn, YouTube

Augustine Tantillo, President & CEO
Jeffrey Price, Chairman

The voice of the U.S. textile industry.

22859 National Knitwear & Sportswear Association
1701 K St. NW
Suite 625
Washington, DC 20006

202-822-8028; *Fax:* 202-822-8029
spierce@ncto.org; www.ncto.org
Social Media: Facebook, Twitter, LinkedIn, YouTube

Jeffrey Price, Chairman
Rob Chapman, Vice Chairman
Augustine Tantillo, President
Sara Beatty, Secretary
Robin Haynes, Treasurer

Represents U.S. manufacturers and contractors, designing studios and related business engaged in the production of knitted sportswear and knitted products of all types.

22860 Northern Textile Association
1701 K St. NW
Suite 625
Washington, DC 20006

202-822-8028; *Fax:* 202-822-8029
spierce@ncto.org; www.ncto.org
Social Media: Facebook, Twitter, LinkedIn, YouTube

Jeffrey Price, Chairman
Rob Chapman, Vice Chairman

Augustine Tantillo, President
Sara Beatty, Secretary
Robin Haynes, Treasurer

The KTA is an active participant in the International Mechinery and Equipment exhibition that takes place in Textile Hall in Greenville, South Carolina and highlights the latest in knitting and related dying and finishing equipment.

22861 Restoration Industry Association
2025 M Street, NW
Suite 800
Rockville, MD 20852

202-367-1180
800-272-7012; *Fax:* 202-367-2180
info@restorationindustry.org;
www.restorationindustry.org
Social Media: Facebook, Twitter, LinkedIn

Scott Stamper, President
Chuck Violand, First Vice President
Mark Springer, Vice President
Jack A. White, Secretary
Larry Holder, Treasurer

A trade association for cleaning and restoration professionals worldwide, and the foremost authority, trainer and educator in the industry.
1100 Members
Founded in: 1946

22862 Schiffi Lace & Embroidery Manufacturers Association
26 Industrial Ave
Suite 2
Fairview, NJ 07022-1600

201-840-7611; *Fax:* 201-943-7793
info@schiffli.org; www.schiffli.org
Social Media: Facebook, Twitter

August Bischoff, President
Vincent Mesiano, VP

Crafted lace, and embroidery that adorns lingerie and dresses t towels, sheets, curtains, tablecloths, patches, logos and much more.
Founded in: 1848

22863 Secondary Materials and Recycled Textiles Association
3465 Box Hill Corp. Center Drive
Suite H
Abingdon, MD 21009

443-640-1050; *Fax:* 443-640-1086
Heather@KINGmgmt.org; www.smartasn.org
Social Media: Facebook, Twitter, LinkedIn, Youtube

Jeff Pearl, President
Eric Stubin, Vice President
David Bloovman, 2nd Vice President
E. Carle Shotwell, Treasurer
Lou Buty, Immediate Past President

A dynamic international association which seeks to strengthen the economic opportunities of its members. Promotes the interdependence of all its industry segments by providing a common forum for networking, education, and trade.
Founded in: 1932

22864 Shippers of Recycled Textiles
7910 Woodmont Ave # 1405
Bethesda, MD 20814-3082

301-907-0001; *Fax:* 301-656-1079
smartinfo@kingmgmt.org; www.sorti.org
Social Media: Facebook, Twitter

Eric Stubin, President
Robert Goode, Treasurer
Lou Buty, VP
75 Members
Founded in: 1988

22865 Southern Textile Association
PO Box 66
Gastonia, NC 28053-0066

704-215-4543; *Fax:* 704-215-4160;
www.southerntextile.org
Social Media: Facebook, Twitter

Judson L. Boehmer, Chairman
Todd Wemyss, President
Mike Kingsmore, First VP
Carson Copeland, Second VP
Lillian G. Link, Secretary/Treasurer

Represents the textile and clothing industry in the South.
Founded in: 1908

22866 Surface Design Association
PO Box 20430
Albuquerque, NM 87154

707-829-3110; *Fax:* 707-829-3285
info@surfacedesign.org;
www.surfacedesign.org
Social Media: Facebook, Twitter, LinkedIn

Astrid Bennett, President
Jennifer Reis, VP
Joyce Martelli, Treasurer
Tedd Milder, Secretary
Danielle Kelly, Executive Director

Aims to stimulate, promote and improve education in the area of surface design, to encourage the surface designer as an individual artist and to provide a forum for exchange of ideas through conferences and publications.
Founded in: 1977
*Mailing list available for rent*at $75 per M

22867 TRI/Princeton
601 Prospect Ave
PO Box 625
Princeton, NJ 08540

609-430-4820; *Fax:* 609-683-7836
info@triprinceton.org; www.triprinceton.org
Social Media: Facebook, Twitter, LinkedIn

Kurl L Adams, Chair
David Graham, Vice Chairman
Yash K Kamath, Research Director
Robert J. Bianchin, Chairman of the Board
Kurt L. Adams, Vice Chair

Provides advanced research and education in polymers, fibers, films, personal care and porous materials.
40 Members
Founded in: 1930

22868 Textile Care Allied Trades Association
271 Us Highway 46
Suite C205
Fairfield, NJ 07004-2432

973-244-1790; *Fax:* 973-244-4455
info@tcata.org; www.tcata.org
Social Media: Facebook, Twitter, LinkedIn

David Cotter, CEO
Cheryl Paglia, Office Manager

Represents the interests of distributors and manufacturers of equipment and supplies for the cleaning industry.

22869 Textile Rental Services Association
1800 Diagonal Rd
Suite 200
Alexandria, VA 22314-2842

703-519-0029
877-770-9274; *Fax:* 703-519-0026
trsa@trsa.org; www.trsa.org
Social Media: Facebook, Twitter, LinkedIn, Youtube, RSS

Greg Jelpema, Chairman
Robert Doud, Executive Director
Joseph Ricci, President & CEO
Tom Newell, Vice President of Operations
Kevin Schwalb, Vp of Government Relations

Covers the uniform, linen supply, health care and dust control service markets.
Founded in: 1912

22870 The Knitting Guild Association (TKGA)
1100-H Brandywine Boulevard
Zanesville, OH 43701-7303

740-452-4541; *Fax:* 740-452-2552
tkga@tkga.com; www.tkga.com
Social Media: Facebook, Twitter, Pinterest

Penny Sitler, Executive Director

Membership organization for knitters with focus on knitting education and enhancing knitters skills.
11000 Members
Founded in: 1984

Newsletters

22871 Embroidery News
Schiffi Lace & Embroidery Manufacturers Assn
596 Anderson Avenue
Suite 203
Cliffside Park, NJ 07010-1831

201-943-7757; *Fax:* 201-943-7793

Leonard Seiler, Editor
Eugene Schrouzol, Publisher

Newsletter for the embroidery industry.
Frequency: BiMonthly
Circulation: 500

22872 Marine Textiles
RCM Enterprises
12 Oaks Center #922
Wayzata, MN 55391

800-451-9278

Mara Sidney, Publisher
Jim Penningroth, Editor

Serves firms in the boating market who use fabrics and furnishings. Accepts advertising.
Cost: $28.00

Magazines & Journals

22873 AATCC Review
American Assoc Textile Chemists and Colorists
1 Davis Dr
Research Triangle Park, NC 27709-2215

919-549-8141
800-360-5380; *Fax:* 919-549-8933
danielsj@aatcc.org; www.aatcc.org
Social Media: Facebook, Twitter, LinkedIn

John Daniels, Executive VP
Debra Hibbard, Executive Assistant
Charles E Gavin, Treasurer
Brenda Jones, Production Manager

Covers all aspects of design, dyeing, printing, finishing, and testing as they relate to textile manufacturing, including fibers, fabrics of all types, garments, carpets, home textiles, and industrial products.
Frequency: Monthly
ISSN: 1532-8813
Founded in: 1997
Mailing list available for rent
Printed in 4 colors on glossy stock

22874 Cleaning & Restoration Magazine
Restoration Industry Association

12339 Carroll Avenue~
Suite K
Rockville, MD 20852

301-231-6505
800-272-7012; *Fax:* 301-231-6569
info@restorationindustry.org;
www.restorationindustry.org

Donald E Manger, Executive Director
Patricia L Harman, Communications Director
Valorie D. Seely, Accountant

Trade journal covering fire and water damage restoration, rug and textile cleaning, indoor air quality and business issues.
Frequency: Monthly
Circulation: 6000

22875 Fabric Architecture
Industrial Fabrics Association International
1801 County Road B W
Roseville, MN 55113-4061

651-222-2508
800-225-4324; *Fax:* 651-631-9334
bnwhite@ifai.org; www.ifai.com

Stephen Warner, CEO

Strives to inform architects, designers, landscape architects, engineers and other specifiers about architectural fabric structutres, the fibers and fabrics used to make them, their design possibilities, their construction, and issues regarding their applicability and acceptance.
Cost: $39.00
Frequency: Bi-Monthly

22876 Geotechnical Fabrics Report
Industrial Fabrics Association International
1801 County Road B W
Roseville, MN 55113-4061

651-222-2508
800-225-4324; *Fax:* 651-631-9334
generalinfo@ifai.com; www.ifai.com

Stephen Warner, CEO
James Dankert, Managing Editor
Stephen B Duerk, Chairman
Beth L Hungiville, Managing Director
Miller Weldmaster, Director

Peer reviewed technical journal for civil engineers using geosynthetics in road construction, errosion control, hazardous waste, drainage, containment and reinforcement.
Cost: $49.00
Circulation: 16,000
ISSN: 0882-4983
Founded in: 1988
Printed in 4 colors on glossy stock

22877 Home Textiles Today
Reed Business Information
360 Park Ave S
New York, NY 10010-1737

646-746-6400
800-446-6551; *Fax:* 646-756-7583
corporatecommunications@reedbusiness.com;
www.reedbusiness.com

John Poulin, CEO
Mark Fraser, Publisher

Textile industry news, reports, research and summaries for the professional.
Circulation: 8000
Founded in: 1979

22878 IFAI'S Marine Fabricator
Industrial Fabrics Association International
1801 County Road B W
Roseville, MN 55113-4061

651-222-2508
800-225-4324; *Fax:* 651-631-9334
generalinfo@ifai.com; www.ifai.com

Stephen Warner, CEO
George K Ochs, Chairman
Jeffrey W Kirk, Vice Chairman

Publication contains articles designed for beginning to intermediate level fabricators, advanced techniques and technology, profiles, business tips, industry news, new products and publications, and showcases of fabricators' craftmanship.
Frequency: Quarterly
Circulation: 5000
Founded in: 1964

22879 Impressions Magazine
Miller Freeman Publications
13760 Noel Rd
Suite 500
Dallas, TX 75240-7336

972-239-3060
800-527-0207; *Fax:* 972-419-7825

Carl Piazza, Publisher
Laura Gonz, Editor

Covers the textile screen printing imprinted sportswear retailing, and commercial embroidery industry. Accepts advertising.
Cost: $36.00
250 Pages
Frequency: Annual

22880 Industrial Fabric Products Review
Industrial Fabrics Association International
1801 County Road B W
Roseville, MN 55113-4061

651-222-2508
800-225-4324; *Fax:* 651-631-9334
generalinfo@ifai.com; www.ifai.com

Stephen Warner, CEO

Keeps individuals up to date on the information needed to keep their business growing, including reports on traditional or emerging markets and end products worldwide; forecasts and analyses of industry trends, announcements of new technologies in fibers, fabrics, equipment and treatments, and profiles of growth-oriented businesses and prodcuts.
Cost: $69.00
Frequency: Monthly
Founded in: 1915

22881 Journal of Engineered Fibers & Fabrics
INDA Association of Nonwoven Fabrics
1100 Crescent Green
Suite 115
Cary, NC 27511

919-233-1210; *Fax:* 919-233-1282;
www.inda.org
Social Media: Facebook, Twitter, LinkedIn

Rory Holmes, President
Peggy Blake, Director of Marketing
Ian Butler, Director Market Research
Todd~ Bassett, Managing Director
Monica Moretti, Tresurer

International peer reviewed scientific eJournal that publishes original R&D on all aspects o ffabric technologies and their value chain from raw materials to end-use products.
Frequency: Quarterly
Circulation: 3000
Founded in: 1968

22882 Journal of Industrial Textiles
851 New Holland Avenue
Suite 3535
Lancaster, PA 17604

717-291-5609
800-233-9936; *Fax:* 717-295-4538;
www.journals.sagepub.com/home/jit

22883 Marine Fabricator
Industrial Fabrics Association International
1801 County Road BW
Roseville, MN 55413

651-222-2508
800-225-4324; *Fax:* 651-631-9334
cptschida@ifai.com; www.ifai.com
Social Media: Facebook, Twitter, LinkedIn

Galynn Nordstrom, Senior Editor

Educates and informs 5,000 marine shop professionals and also provides reportage that reflects the innovations and trends of the industry.
Cost: $34.00
Frequency: Bi-Monthly

22884 Nonwovens Industry
Rodman Publishing
70 Hilltop Rd
Suite 3000
Ramsey, NJ 07446-1150

201-825-2552; *Fax:* 201-825-0553
info@rodpub.com;
www.nutraceuticalsworld.com
Social Media: Facebook, Twitter, LinkedIn

Rodman Zilenziger Jr, President
Matt Montgomery, VP

Written for nonwoven roll goods producers, converters and end-use manufacturers.
70 Pages
Frequency: Monthly
Circulation: 11000
Founded in: 1970

22885 Nonwovens World
MTS Publications
4100 S 7th Street
Kalamazoo, MI 49009-8461

269-375-1236; *Fax:* 269-375-6710
admin@marketingtechnologyservice.com;
www.marketingtechnologyservice.com

James P Hanson, Editor
Cindy Costello, Circulation Manager
Wayne C Carter, Advertising Sales Director

Covers new products, as well as production and marketing strategies.
Circulation: 10384
Founded in: 1986

22886 Sheep Industry News
9785 Maroon Circle
Suite 360
Englewood, CO 80112

303-771-3500; *Fax:* 303-771-8200;
www.sheepusa.org
Social Media: Facebook

Clint Krebs, President
Peter Orwick, Executive Director
Rita Kourlis Samuelson, Wool Marketing Director

A federation of state associations dedicated to the welfare and profitability of the sheep industry.
Cost: $25.00
8000+ Members
Frequency: Monthly
Circulation: 8000
Founded in: 1865

22887 Surface Design Journal
PO Box 360
Sebastopol, CA 95473-360

707-829-3110; *Fax:* 707-829-3285;
www.surfacedesign.org
Social Media: Facebook, Twitter, LinkedIn

Jason Pollen, President

Professional organization of more than 2,000 textile artists, designers for industry, and academicians.
Cost: $8.00
52 Pages
Frequency: Quarterly
Circulation: 6000
Founded in: 1977

22888 Textile Rental Magazine
Textile Rental Services Association
1800 Diagonal Rd
Suite 200
Alexandria, VA 22314-2842

703-519-0029
877-770-9274; *Fax:* 703-519-0026
trsa@trsa.org; www.trsa.org
Social Media: Facebook, Twitter, LinkedIn, You Tube

Roger Cocivera, President/CEO
Jack Morgan, Editor

Packed with valuable tips and ideas.
Frequency: Monthly

22889 Textile Research Journal
TRI Princeton
PO Box 625
Princeton, NJ 08542

609-924-3150; *Fax:* 609-683-7836;
www.triprinceton.com

Dr. Gail R Eaton, President

Provides advanced research and education in polymers, fibers, films, personel care and porous materials.
Frequency: Monthly
Founded in: 1930

Trade Shows

22890 American Home Sewing & Craft Association Sewing & Craft Show: AHSCA
American Home Sewing and Craft Association
1350 Broadway
Suite 1601
New York, NY 10018

212-714-1633; *Fax:* 212-714-1655
info@sewing.org; www.sewing.org

200 exhibits of fabric, notions, patterns, sewing and knitting machines, crafts and trimmings. Attended by professionals from major chain stores, independent retailers, wholesalers and manufacturers.
3000 Attendees
Frequency: Semiannual

22891 American Textile Machinery Exhibition International
Textile Hall Corporation
PO Box 5823
Greenville, SC 29606

864-331-2277; *Fax:* 864-331-2282

Butler Mullins, Director

Exhibition of machinery, supplies and services required for manufacture of yarn and fiber, for the weaving, knitting and dying/printing/finishing processes, for manufacture of non-wovens and for plant maintenance.
10000 Attendees
Frequency: September

22892 Apparel Printing and Embroidery Expo
Primedia
3585 Engineering Drive
Suite 100
Norcross, GA 30092

678-421-3000; *Fax:* 913-967-1898;
www.primediabusiness.com

Joanie Forsythe, Sales Manager
Arlene Mayfield, President
Scott Asher, VP

Semi-annual show of 200 manufacturers, suppliers and distributors of commercial screen printing and embroidery equipment and supplies, computer graphic systems and softgoods such as T-shirts, sweats, jackets and caps.
3000 Attendees

22893 Apparel Show of the Americas
Bobbin Publishing/Miller Freeman
PO Box 279
Euless, TX 76039

817-215-1600
800-693-1363; *Fax:* 817-215-1666;
wwwmfi.com

Betty Webb, Trade Show Director

Conference, seminar and 329 exhibits of equipment, fabrics, accessories and services for sewn products and apparel.
5790 Attendees
Frequency: Annual
Founded in: 1992

22894 Association of Specialists in Cleaning & Restoration Convention
Restoration Industry Association
9810 Patuxent Woods Drive
Suite K
Columbia, MD 21046-1595

443-878-1000
800-272-7012; *Fax:* 443-878-1010
info@restorationindustry.org;
www.restorationindustry.org
Social Media: Facebook, Twitter, LinkedIn, You Tube

Donald E Manger, Executive Director
Patricia L Harman, Communications Director

Annual convention and exhibits of carpet, upholstery and draperies cleaning and restoration equipment, duct cleaning supplies and services, 100+ booths.
600 Attendees
Frequency: Annual
Founded in: 1945

22895 Filtration: International Conference & Exposition
INDA Association of Nonwoven Fabrics
1100 Crescent Green
Suite 115
Cary, NC 27511

919-233-1210; *Fax:* 919-233-1282;
www.inda.org
Social Media: Facebook, Twitter, LinkedIn

Rory Holmes, President
Peggy Blake, Director of Marketing
Ian Butler, Director Market Research/Stats

The North American Show for all aspects of filter media. One-stop shopping where you can compare products and prices. See state-of-the-art products. Great networking experience.
1400 Attendees
Frequency: Annual

22896 Geosynthetics
Industrial Fabrics Association International
1801 County Road BW
Roseville, MN 55113

651-222-2508
800-225-4324; *Fax:* 651-631-9334
confmgmt@ifai.com; www.ifaiexpo.info
Social Media: Facebook, Twitter, LinkedIn

Beth Wistrcill, Conference Manager

Features design, engineering strategies and cost-saving geosynthetics solutions.
Frequency: February

22897 IDEA, International Engineered Fabrics Con ference + Expositions
INDA Association of Nonwoven Fabrics
1100 Crescent Green
Suite 115
Cary, NC 27518

919-233-1210; *Fax:* 919-233-1282;
www.inda.org
Social Media: Facebook, Twitter, LinkedIn

Dave Rousse, President
Joan Izzo, Director of Marketing
Brad Kalil, Director Market Research/Stats

See, touch and buy state-of-the-art engineered fabrics. Compare all the components used to make first class fabrics-raw materials, chemicals, machinery and converting and finishind services.
5200 Attendees
Frequency: Triennial

22898 IFAI Annual Expo
Industrial Fabrics Association International
1801 County Road BW
Roseville, MN 55113

651-222-2508
800-225-4324; *Fax:* 651-631-9334
http://www.ifaiexpo.com

Beth Wistrcill, Conference Manager
Miller Weldmaster, Director
JoAnne Ferris, Director of Marketing

A trade event on the America's for the technical textiles and specialty fabrics industry.
Frequency: Annual/September

22899 International Engineered Fabrics
INDA Association of Nonwoven Fabrics
1100 Crescent Green
Suite 115
Cary, NC 27511

919-233-1210; *Fax:* 919-233-1282;
www.inda.org
Social Media: Facebook, Twitter, LinkedIn

Rory Holmes, President
Peggy Blake, Director of Marketing
Ian Butler, Director Market Research/Stats

See, touch and buy state-of-the-art engineered fabrics. Compare all the components used to make first class fabrics-raw materials, chemicals, machinery and converting and finishind services.

22900 International Fashion and Boutique Shows
100 Wells Avenue
#9103
Newton, MA 02459-3210

617-731-8316

Samuel Starr, Show Manager

1,800 booths.
30M Attendees
Frequency: January

22901 International Fastener Exposition
PEMCO
383 Main Avenue
Norwalk, CT 06851-1543

203-840-7700; *Fax:* 630-260-0395

Barbara Silverman, VP, Show Manager
Laura Rezek, Advertising

450 booths developed specifically for the fastener manufacturing and precision formed parts industry.
4.8M Attendees
Frequency: March

Directories & Databases

22902 ATI's Textile Red Book: America's Textile Industries
Billian Publishing Company

2100 Powers Ferry Rd SE
Suite 300
Atlanta, GA 30339-5055

770-955-5656
800-533-8484; *Fax:* 770-952-0669;
www.billian.com

Jim Borneman, President
Dave Ramsays, Database Sales
Douglas Billian, Owner

Comprehensive reference guide for the textile industry. Includes over 6,000 mills in the US, Canada and Mexico. In addition to providing the complete contact information for the plant, each listing gives key personnel, products produced, fibers processed and mill equipment used.
Cost: $160.00
Frequency: Annual
ISSN: 1047-6903

22903 **America's Textiles International**
Billian Publishing Company
2100 Powers Ferry Rd SE
Suite 300
Atlanta, GA 30339-5055

770-955-5656; *Fax:* 770-952-0669;
www.billian.com

Annual directory provides the complete contact information - including Web sites and e-mail addresses for over 2,400 equipment, technology and service providers to the textile industry.
Frequency: Annual
Circulation: 32,000
ISSN: 0890-9970
Founded in: 1887

22904 **Davison's Textile Blue Book**
Davison Publishing Company
PO Box 1289
Concord, NC 28026-1289

704-785-8700
800-328-4766; *Fax:* 704-785-8701;
www.davisonpublishing.com

Carol Nealy, Advertising Manager

5,400 mills, dryers, finishers, in the United States, Canada, and Mexico.
Cost: $165.00
800 Pages
Frequency: Annual
ISBN: 0-875150-69-1
Founded in: 1866

22905 **Interior Textiles Fabric Resource Directory**
Wool Bureau/Atlanta Merchandise Mart
240 Peachtree Street NW
Suite 6F11
Atlanta, GA 30303-1361

404-577-4320

Approximately 108 manufacturers and suppliers of wool and wool blend upholsteries, wallcoverings and draperies.
45 Pages

22906 **International Textile & Apparel Association Membership Directory**
PO Box 1360
Monument, CO 80132-1360

719-488-3716
info@itaaonline.org; www.itaaonline.org

Sandra S Hutton, Executive Director

Professional association for 1,000 college professors of clothing and textile studies.
8-12 Pages
Frequency: 6 per year
Circulation: Members
Founded in: 1944

22907 **Knitted Textile Association: Official Resource Guide and Fact Book**
Knitted Textile Association
386 Park Avenue
New York, NY 10016-8804

212-545-9014; *Fax:* 212-889-6160

Peter Adelman, Editor

A list of over 150 member manufacturers, suppliers and distributors of knitted fabric products and services.
Cost: $10.00
Frequency: Annual

22908 **Knitting Times: Buyers' Guide Issue**
National Knitwear & Sportswear Association
386 Park Avenue S
New York, NY 10016-8804

212-545-9014; *Fax:* 212-532-0766

Dawne G Shink, Editor

List of about 4,500 suppliers and manufacturers of chemicals, contract, management and computer services, cutting room equipment, dyeing, finishing and printing equipment, knitted and woven fabrics, fibers and yarn, interfacing, pressing and steaming, knitting, sewing and trimming equipment, materials handling and plant control services.
Cost: $25.00
Frequency: Annual, September
Circulation: 10,000

22909 **LDB Interior Textiles Buyers' Guide**
EW Williams Publications
342 Madison Avenue
Room 1901
New York, NY 10173-1999

212-697-1122; *Fax:* 212-661-1713
ldb342@aol.com

Renee Bennett, Editor-in-Chief
Aleksandra Kazimierska, Directory Manager
Janys Kuznier, Circulation Director

Over 2,000 manufacturers, importers and suppliers of home fashions products and services, decorative fabric converters and alternative window coverings, fabricators, manufacturer's representatives and others allied to the home fashions trade.
Cost: $40.00
Frequency: Annual June
Circulation: 12,000

22910 **Narrow Fabrics Institute: Buyer's Guide**
Narrow Fabrics Institute
345 Cedar Street
Suite 800
Saint Paul, MN 55101-1004

800-225-4324; *Fax:* 651-222-8215

Approximately 34 producers of narrow fabrics for use in automotive medical, lifting, environmental safety, recreational, military, air cargo, trucks, and other fields, requiring industrial fabrics.
Frequency: Annual fall

22911 **Textile Chemist and Colorist Buyers Guide**
American Assoc Textile Chemists and Colorists
PO Box 12215
Research Triangle Park, NC 27709-2215

919-549-8141
800-360-5380; *Fax:* 919-549-8933
danielsj@aatcc.org; www.aatcc.org

John Daniels, Executive VP
Debra Hibbard, Executive Assistant
Charles E Gavin, Treasurer
Brenda Jones, Product Orders

Over 500 dye, pigments, machinery and equipment manufacturers are profiled.
ISBN: 0-040490-0 -
Founded in: 1921
Mailing list available for rent

22912 **Textile Technology Digest**
2551 Ivy Road
Charlottesville, VA 22903

434-296-5511; *Fax:* 434-296-2957;
www.ittorissa.org

Offers abstracts to worldwide literature from more than 1,300 sources annually such as proceedings, trade literature and other sources collected by the institutes library. The CD-ROM quarterly is available for $1,710 plus shipping. Network licenses begin at $500 for up to 10 simultaneous users.
Cost: $545.00
Frequency: Monthly
Founded in: 1944

22913 **Wool Source List**
Kairalla Agency
27 Raymond Street
Manchester, MA 01944-1614
Eleanor Kairalla, Executive Director

Conducts trade and consumer polls on woolen apparel.
360 Pages
Founded in: 1939

Industry Web Sites

22914 **http://gold.greyhouse.com**
G.O.L.D Grey House OnLine Databases

Grey House Publishing's online database platform, GOLD, offers Quick Search, Keyword Search and Expert Search for most business sectors including textile markets. The GOLD platform makes finding the information you need quick and easy - whether you're a novice searcher or an experienced database user. All of Grey House's directory products are available for subscription on the GOLD platform.

22915 **www.aatcc.org**
American Association of Textile Chemists & Colorists

22916 **www.atmanet.org**
American Textile Machinery Association

Advances the common interests of its members, works to improve business conditions within the US textile machinery industry from a global perspective and markets the industry and members' machinery, parts and services.

22917 **www.carpet-rug.com**
Carpet & Rug Institute

22918 **www.cottoninc.com**
Cotton

22919 **www.fibersource.com**
American Fiber Manufacturers Association

Trade association for US companies that manufacture synthetic and cellulostic fibers. The industry employs 30,000 people and produces over 9 billion pounds of fiber in the US. The association maintains close ties to other manufactured fiber trade associations worldwide.

22920 **www.flocking.org**
American Flock Association

Fosters the use of flocked products. Strives to improve and advance flocking technology.

22921 **www.greyhouse.com**
Grey House Publishing

Authoritative reference directories for most business sectors including textile markets. Users can search the online databases with varied search criteria allowing for custom searches by product category, geographic area, sales volume, keyword, subject and more. Full Grey House catalog and online ordering also available.

22922 **www.ifai.com**
Industrial Fabrics Association International

Association of geosynthetics, fabricators, installers, equipment manufacturers, suppliers, testing firms, consultants, and educators, who produce textiles, nets, mats, grids, and other products. Industrial Fabrics Association International is the industry's first source for technical fabric resources and information.

22923 **www.inda.org**
INDA Association of Nonwoven Fabrics Industries

22924 **www.itt.edu**
Institute of Textile Technology

A graduate school supported in part by member companies. Publishes the Textile Technology Digest.

22925 **www.sewing.org**
Home Sewing Association

Represents most facets of the home sewing industry. National trade association for independent sewing machine dealers and distributors.

22926 **www.sleepproducts.org**
International Sleep Products Association

Maintains a strong organization to influence government actions, inform and educate the membership and act on industry issues to enhance the growth,profitability and stature of the sleep products industry. Provides members with information and services to manage their business more effectively and efficiently. Publishes a magazine devoted exclusively to the mattress industry, BEDtimes covers a broad range of issue and news important to the industry.

22927 **www.smartasn.org**
Shippers of Recycled Textiles

22928 **www.textilenta.org**
Northern Textile Association

Textile manufacturing trade association.

22929 **www.triprinceton.org**
TRI Princeton

TRI/Princeton provides advanced research and education in polymers, fibers, films, personel care, and porous materials.

Associations

22930 American Wholesale Marketers Association
11311 Sunset Hills Road
Suite 530
Reston, VA 20190
703-208-3358
800-482-2962; *Fax:* 703-573-5738
info@cdaweb.net; www.cdaweb.net
Social Media: Facebook, Twitter, LinkedIn
Scott Ramminger, President & CEO
Chad Owen, First Vice Chairman
Susie Douglas Munson, Second Vice Chairman
Meredith Kimbrell, Director, Education
Robert Sincavich, Chairman
A trade association supporting the confectionary, tobacco and allied products industries through programs and services. members include wholesale distributors, manufacturers, and other allieds to the industry.
1000 Members
Founded in: 1942

22931 Association of Dark Leaf Tobacco Dealers
2500 S Main St
Springfield, TN 37172-0638
615-384-9576; *Fax:* 615-384-6461
info@hailcotton.com; www.hailcotton.com
Mike De la Fargue, President & CEO
Tom Wilks, Executive VP
Roderick Roe, CFO
Andy Spies, Executive VP Sales
Eric Van Der Linden, Executive VP
An affiliate of Burley and Dark Leaf Tobacco Export Association.
Founded in: 1902

22932 Bright Belt Warehouse Association
PO Box 120004
Raleigh, NC 27606
919-828-8988; *Fax:* 919-821-2092
Association of flue-cured tobacco warehousemen.

22933 Burley Stabilization Corporation
835 Bill Jones Industrial Dr.
Springfield, TN 37172
615-212-0508; *Fax:* 866-828-6501
burleytobacco@aol.com;
www.burleystabilization.com
George Marks, President
Joe K Thomas III, VP
Charlie C Finch, Managing Director
Association of Burley tobacco warehouses in Kentucky, Tennessee, Ohio, Missouri, Indiana, Virginia, West Virginia and North Carolina.

22934 Burley Tobacco Growers Cooperative Association
620 S Broadway
Lexington, KY 40508-3149
859-252-3561; *Fax:* 859-231-9804
stephanie@burleytobacco.com;
www.burleytobacco.com
Pat Raines, President
Eddie Warren, VP
Robert Reed Bush Sr., Secretary
Al Pedigo, Treasurer
Steve Pratt, General Manager
Burley tobacco grower cooperative

22935 Cigar Association of America
1100 G Street NW
Suite 1050
Washington, DC 20005-7405
202-223-8204
866-482-3570; *Fax:* 202-833-0379;
www.cigarassociation.org
Social Media: Facebook, Twitter, LinkedIn, Pinterest
Dan Carr, Chairman
Craig Williamson, President
Consists of cigar manufacturers, importers and major industry suppliers. Provides government relations and statistical services to the industry and promotes the image of the cigar.
60 Members
Founded in: 1937

22936 Eastern Dark-Fired Tobacco
1109 S Main St
Springfield, TN 37172-3509
615-384-4543; *Fax:* 615-384-4545
Dan Borthick, President
Association of North Central Tennessee and South Central Kentucky growers that produce Type 22 Dark fire-cured and Type 35 Dark air-cured (one sucker) tobacco.

22937 Flue-Cured Tobacco Cooperative
1304 Annapolis Dr
Raleigh, NC 27608-2130
919-821-4560; *Fax:* 919-821-4564
arnoldh3151@ipass.net;
www.ustobaccofarmer.com
Tommy Bunn, President/CEO
Stuart Thompson, CEO
Edward Kacsuta, Chief Financial Officer
Mike Lynch, Senior VP, Global Sales & Marekting
Sam Tie, Manager, Human Resource
Marketing cooperative which administers price support and provides %100 US flue-cured tobacco direct to purchasers.
Founded in: 1946

22938 Friends of Tobacco
403 B East New Bern Road
Kinston, NC 20501
919-522-4769; *Fax:* 919-522-4769
fot@fujipub.com
fujipub.com/fot
Gary Corbett, President
Nonprofit organization promoting the economic importance of tobacco and freedom of choice in using tobacco products.
16000 Members
Founded in: 1991

22939 Retail Tobacco Dealers of America
14611 Goodrich Dr NW
Suite 2H
Gig Harbor, WA 98329
253-857-8934; *Fax:* 253-857-0143
info@fujipub.com; www.rtda.org
Social Media: Facebook, Twitter, LinkedIn, Youtube
Joe Row, Executive Director
Represents and assists retail tobacconists.
Founded in: 1993

22940 Specialty Tobacco Council
102 W Third Street
Suite 200-B
Winston-Salem, NC 27101
336-723-4311; *Fax:* 336-759-0965
hroemer@specialtytobacco.org
specialtytobacco.org
Henry C Roemer III, Executive Director
Represents manufacturers and importers of specialty tobacco products.
Founded in: 1984

22941 Tobacco Associates
1306 Annapolis Drive
Suite 102
Raleigh, NC 27608-2136
919-821-7670; *Fax:* 919-821-7674
tar@tobaccoassociatesinc.org;
www.tobaccoassociatesinc.org
Kirk Wayne, President
Hank Mozingo, VP
Veronica Martins, Office Manager
Mission is to enhance understanding of US flue-cured tobacco and assist manufacturers interested in adding quality US leaf to their products.
Founded in: 1947
Mailing list available for rent

22942 Tobacco Association of the United States
PO Box 8019
Princeton, NC 08543-8019
609-275-4900; *Fax:* 609-275-8379
tma@tma.org; www.tma.org
Tommy Bunn, Executive VP
Promotes market for US leaf tobacco.
100 Members
Founded in: 1915

22943 Tobacco Growers Association of North Carolina
3901 Barrett Dr
Suite 202
Raleigh, NC 27609-6611
919-781-0066; *Fax:* 919-781-0066
grahamboyd@nc.rr.com; www.tganc.com
Graham Boyd, Executive VP
Commodity association for North Carolina tobacco growers.
10000 Members
Founded in: 1981

22944 Tobacco Merchants Association
PO Box 8019
Princeton, NJ 08543-8019
609-275-4900; *Fax:* 609-275-8379
tma@tma.org; www.tma.org
Social Media: Facebook, Twitter
Farrell Delman, President
Mark Schoenseld, Editor
Roberta Crosdy, Marketing Manager
Mark Schoenseld, Publisher
Tobacco trade association and source of current information on the tobacco industry.
170 Members
Founded in: 1915

Newsletters

22945 Tobacco Barometer
Tobacco Merchants Association of the United States
PO Box 8019
Princeton, NJ 08543-8019
609-275-4900; *Fax:* 609-275-8379
tma@tma.org; www.tma.org
Social Media: Facebook, Twitter
Mark Schoenseld, Editor
Roberta Crosdy, Marketing Manager
Mark Schoenseld, Farrell
Delman President
Tobacco industry news.
Frequency: Monthly
Founded in: 1915

22946 **Tobacco Products Litigation Reporter**
TPLR
PO Box 1162
Back Bay Annex
Boston, MA 02117-1162
617-373-2026; *Fax:* 617-437-3672;
www.tplr.com
Richard Daynard, Publisher
Lissy Friedman, Publication Director
Mark Gottlieb, Legal Editor
Tobacco industry news.
Cost: $995.00; *Frequency:* 8 issues per year
Founded in: 1950

22947 **Tobacco on Trial**
Tobacco Products Liability Project
102 The Fenway
Cushing Hall, Suite 117
Boston, MA 02115-5098
617-373-2026; *Fax:* 617-373-3672;
www.tobacco-on-trial.com
Richard A Daynard, Publisher
Susan L Frank, Editor
Mark Gottlieb, Executive Director
Richard A Daynard, President
Tobacco industry news.
Cost: $95.00; *Founded in:* 1979

Magazines & Journals

22948 **Smokeshop**
Lockwood Trade Journal
26 Broadway; Suite 9M2
New York, NY 10004-1777
212-391-2060
800-766-2633; *Fax:* 212-827-0945
sales@smokeshopmag.com;
www.lockwoodpublications.com
Robert Lockwood, CEO
Edward Hoyt III, Editor
Bob Olesen, Advertising Sales Manager
Retail tobacco dealer's prevailing source for industry news designed to help readers operate their business more successfully.
Cost: $24.00; *Founded in:* 1970

22949 **Tobacco International**
Lockwood Trade Journal
26 Broadway; Suite 9M2
New York, NY 10004-1777
212-391-2060; *Fax:* 212-827-0945
sales@smokeshopmag.com;
www.lockwoodpublications.com
Robert Lockwood, CEO
Edward Hoyt III, Editor
Bob Olesen, Advertising Sales Manager
This trade publication offers information and news on the importing and exporting of tobacco.
Cost: $25.00; *Frequency:* Monthly
Founded in: 1970

22950 **Tobacco Reporter**
SpecComm International
3000 Highwoods Boulevard; Suite 300
Raleigh, NC 27604-1029
919-878-0540; *Fax:* 919-876-8531
customerservice@tobaccoreporter.com;
www.tobaccoreporter.com
Cost: $36.00; ISSN: 0361-5593

22951 **Tobacco Retailer**
Bel-Av Communications
359 Galahad Rd
Bolingbrook, IL 60440-2108
www.tobaccoretailer.com
Charlie Forman, Group Publisher
Richard Brandes, Editor-in-Chief
Features sales, marketing and operations articles, news and new products, personnel advice, cigar reviews, updates on the National Association of Tobacco Outlets and profiles of leading retailers.
Cost: $29.00; *Frequency:* Bi-Monthly
Circulation: 15000; *Founded in:* 1998

22952 **Tobacco Science**
2016 Fanning Bridge Road
Fletcher, NC 28732
828-684-3562; *Fax:* 828-684-8715
pam_puryear@ncsu.edu;
www.tobaccoscience.com
Dr David Shew, Editor
Pam Puryear, Managing Editor
Scientific journal containing technical reports on tobacco and tobacco smoke.

22953 **Tobacconist**
SpecComm International
3101 Poplarwood Court; Suite 115
Raleigh, NC 27604-1029
919-872-5040; *Fax:* 919-876-6531
mjackson@speccomm.com;
www.tobacconistmagazine.com
Dayton Matlick, Publisher
Ed O'Connor, Advertising/Sales Manager
Dayton Matlick, Editor
Dayton Matlick, CEO
A business publication for retail tobacconists in the United States that includes information ranging from critical issues to new products and business advice.
Cost: $28.00; *Frequency:* Quarterly

Trade Shows

22954 **AWMA Expo**
American Wholesale Marketers Association
1128 16th Street NW
Washington, DC 20036-4808
202-463-2124
800-642-2962; *Fax:* 202-467-0559
robertp@awmanet.org; www.cdaweb.net
Robert Pignato, VP Marketing/Industry Affairs
Annual show of 4500 manufacturers and suppliers of confectionery, tobacco, snack foods, juice, novelties and related products.

22955 **Retail Tobacco Dealers of America Trade Show**
4 Bradley Park Court
Suite 2H
Columbus, GA 31904-3637
706-494-1143; *Fax:* 706-494-1893
rtda@msn.com; www.rtda.org
Ira Fader Jr, Show Manager
Trade show for premium tobacco products. Not open to the public. For the benefit of association members only. Containing 950 booths and 6,400 exhibits.
5,500 Attendees; *Frequency:* July

Directories & Databases

22956 **Tobacco Barometer: Cigarettes and Cigars/ Smoking, Chewing and Snuff**
Tobacco Merchants Association of the United States
PO Box 8019
Princeton, NJ 08543-8019
609-275-4900; *Fax:* 609-275-8379;
www.tma.org
Farrell Delman, President
These two databases offers information on every aspect of the tobacco industry.
Frequency: Full-text

22957 **Tobacco Reporter's Global Tobacco Industry Guide**
SpecComm International
3000 Highwoods Boulevard
Suite 300
Raleigh, NC 27604-1029
919-878-0540; *Fax:* 919-876-8531
sales@tobaccoreporter.com;
www.tobaccoreporter.com
Noel Morris, Publisher
Taco Tuinstra, Managing Editor
Directory of tobacco suppliers, leaf dealers, processors, manufacturers, brokers, marketing boards and associations.
Cost: $78.00; *Frequency:* Annual

Industry Web Sites

22958 **http://gold.greyhouse.com**
G.O.L.D Grey House OnLine Databases
Grey House Publishing's online database platform, GOLD, offers Quick Search, Keyword Search and Expert Search for most business sectors including tobacco markets. The GOLD platform makes finding the information you need quick and easy - whether you're a novice searcher or an experienced database user. All of Grey House's directory products are available for subscription on the GOLD platform.

22959 **www.awmanet.org**
American Wholesale Marketers Association
A trade association representing corporations in the wholesale tobacco industries.

22960 **www.buycheapcigarettes.com**
We offer discount cigarettes and tobacco products. Cigarettes and tobacco products are for consumer use only. Minimum order is 3 Cartons.

22961 **www.freedomnet.org/tobacco.html**
Pipe Tobacco Council
Consists of manufacturers and importers of smoking tobacco in the United States. Provides government relations and statistical services to the industry.

22962 **www.greyhouse.com**
Grey House Publishing
Authoritative reference directories for most business sectors including tobacco markets. Users can search the online databases with varied search criteria allowing for custom searches by product category, geographic area, sales volume, keyword, subject and more. Full Grey House catalog and online ordering also available.

22963 **www.paylesscigarettes.com**
Sells dicount cigarettes and tobacco products.

22964 **www.taxfreetobacco.com**
Sells dicount cigarettess.

22965 **www.thetobaccoshop.com**
Offers discount cigarettes and tobacco products.

22966 **www.tobaccoassociatesinc.org**
Website of the association representing US flue-cured tobacco producers.

22967 **www.ustobaccofarmer.com**
Information of interest to tobacco farmers.

Associations

22968 ABF Freight Systems
3801 Old Greenwood Road
PO Box 10048
Fort Smith, AR 72917-0048

479-785-8700
800-610-5544; *Fax:* 479-785-8701
customercare@abf.com; www.abfs.com
Social Media: Facebook, Twitter, LinkedIn, Google+

Robert A Davidson, CEO
Shannon Lively, Vive President of Transportation

Concentrates on national and regional transportation of general commodities freight, involving primarily LTL shipments. Mission is to provide reliable transportation services in a responsible manner to meet customers' unique needs.

22969 AIT Worldwide Logistics
701 N Rohlwing Rd
Itasca, IL 60143-1348

815-229-7700
800-669-4248; *Fax:* 630-766-0205
info@aitworldwide.com;
www.aitworldwide.com
Social Media: Facebook, Twitter, LinkedIn, You Tube

Vaughn Moore, President & CEO
Keith Tholan, Executive VP, Sales
Joe Kayser, Executive VP, Finance
Ray Fennelly, Executive VP, Global Development
Chris Jostes, Ocean Transport Coordinator

AIT Worldwide Logistics provides customers with inovative high-tech support and customization that enhances every shipment by tailoring the technology to the systems of each individual customer. AIT distinguishes itself by offering customers a variety of value-added services to enhance supply chain efficiencies: custom-built IT solutions, flexible worldwide service offerings by ground, air, ocean and rail, an extensive global network, competitive price structure, and superior customer service.

22970 APL Logistics
16220 N Scottsdale Rd
Suite 400
Scottsdale, AZ 85254-1720

602-586-4800
800-666-2723; *Fax:* 602-586-4585;
www.apllogistics.com/wps/portal/apll

Beat Simon, President
Kurt Breinlinger, Chief Commercial Officer
Danny Goh, Chief Operations Officer
David Frentzel, VP, Contract Logistics
David Howland, VP, Land Transport Services

APL provides customers around the world with container transportation services through a network combining high-quality intermodal operations with state-of-the-art information technology.

22971 Advanced Transit Association
9019 Hamilton Drive
Fairfax, VA 22031-3075

703-591-8328; www.advancedtransit.org

Tom Richert, Chairman
Catherine G Burke, President
Bob Dunning, VP
Jerry Kieffer, Manager

Supports the transportation association.
100 Members

22972 Air Courier Conference of America
Express Delivery & Logistics Association
400 Admiral Blvd
Kansas City, MO 64106

703-998-7121
816-221-0254; *Fax:* 703-998-7123
jmorris@aircour.org;
www.expressassociation.org
Social Media: LinkedIn

George Trapp, President
Jim Conway, Executive Director
Ken Bowman, Dir of Strategic Initiatives
Jennifer Crane, Associate Director

Air courier and air package delivery companies.

22973 Air Line Pilots Association, International
1625 Massachusetts Ave NW
Washington, DC 20036

703-689-2270; www.alpa.org
Social Media: Facebook, Twitter, YouTube

Tim Canoll, President
Joe DePete, First Vice-President
Bill Couette, Vice President-Administration
W. Randolph Helling, Vice-President-Finance
Rick Dominguez, Executive Administrator

International association for airline pilots
Founded in: 1931

22974 Air Transport Research Society
3433 Van Munching Hall
University of Maryland
College Park, MD 20742

301-405-2204; *Fax:* 301-314-1023
atrs@rhsmith.umd.edu; www.atrsworld.org

Tae H. Oum, Founder, Chair
Martin Dresner, President, CEO
Anming Zhang, VP, Research
Sveinn Gudmundsson, VP, External
Christian Hofer, VP, Programs

A Society for researchers in the field of air transportation
Founded in: 1995

22975 Aircraft Owners and Pilots Association (AOPA)
421 Aviation Way
Frederick, MD 21701

301-695-2000
800-872-2672; *Fax:* 301-695-2375;
www.aopa.org
Social Media: Facebook, Twitter, LinkedIn, Pinterest, Google+

Mark Baker, President & CEO
James W. Minow, Executive Director
Bruce Landsberg, Senior Safety Advisor

For pilots and aircraft owners
Founded in: 1939

22976 Airlines for America (A4A)
1301 Pennsylvania Ave. NW
Suite 1100
Washington, DC 20004

202-626-4000
ata@airlines.org; www.airlines.org
Social Media: Facebook, Twitter, LinkedIn, YouTube

Nicholas E. Calio, President & CEO
Paul R. Archambeault, SVP, CFO & COO
David A. Berg, SVP, General Counsel & Secretary
Christine M. Burgeson, SVP, Global Govt. Affairs
Jean Medina, SVP, Communications

Airlines for America advocates for a safe, secure and healthy U.S. airline industry.
Founded in: 1936

22977 America's Independent Truckers' Association
P.O. Box 1250
Clinton, MS 39060

601-924-9606
844-464-2482; www.aitaonline.com
Social Media: Facebook, Twitter

Larry Daniel, Founder

Created to serve independent owner operators and small to medium sized fleet owners.
Founded in: 1997

22978 American Association of Airport Executives
601 Madison Street
Suite 400
Alexandria, VA 22314

703-824-0504; *Fax:* 703-820-1395
member.services@aaae.org; www.aaae.org
Social Media: Facebook, Twitter, LinkedIn, RSS, Pinterest, YouTube

Jeffrey A. Mulder, Chair
Carl D. Newman, 1st Vice Chair
Scott A. Brockman, 2nd Vice Chair
Janne M. Olivier, Secretary/Treasurer
Brad Van Dam, Senior VP, Federal Affairs

The professional association that represents airport management personnel at public-use commercialand general aviation airports in the US
Founded in: 1928

22979 American Association of Motor Vehicle Administrators
4401 Wilson Boulevard
Suite 700
Alexandria, VA 22203

703-522-4200; www.aamva.org
Social Media: Facebook, Twitter, LinkedIn, Flickr, YouTube

Anne Ferro, President & CEO
Whitney Brewster, Executive Director
Terri L. Coombes, Deputy Chief of Staff
Stephen Campbell, Commissioner
Heidi Francis, Assistant Deputy Minister

Non-governmental, voluntary organization who strives to develop model programs in motor vehicle administration
Founded in: 1933

22980 American Association of Port Authorities
1010 Duke Street
Alexandria, VA 22314-3589

703-684-5700; *Fax:* 703-684-6321
info@aapa-ports.org; www.aapa-ports.org
Social Media: Facebook, Twitter, LinkedIn

Kristin Decas, Chairman
Kurt J. Nagle, President & CEO
Jean C. Godwin, Executive Vice President
Colleen O'sullivan, Finance & Human Resources
Maria Estevez, Administrative Assistant

Trade association founded in 1912 that represents over 130 port authorities in the western hemisphere
Founded in: 1912

22981 American Association of Railroad Superintendents
425 Third Street SW
Washington, DC 20024

202-639-2100; *Fax:* 630-762-0755
media@aar.org; www.aar.org
Social Media: Facebook, Twitter, LinkedIn, Youtube

Edward R. Hamberger, President
John Gray, SVP, Policy and Economics
Ian Jefferies, SVP, Government Affairs

Jeffrey Marsh, SVP, Finance and Administration
Patricia M. Reilly, SVP, Communications

Operating department officers of railroads.
500 Members
Founded in: 1881

22982 American Association of State Highway & Transportation
444 N Capitol St NW
Suite 249
Washington, DC 20001-1539

202-624-5800; *Fax:* 202-624-5806
info@aashto.org; www.transportation.org
Social Media: Facebook, Twitter, LinkedIn, You Tube

Bud Wright, Executive Director
Jenet Adem, Director, Finance & Administration
Clarisse Bernardes Coble, Human Resources Manager
Tony Bianchi, Associate Project Director
Belinda Bates, Senior Graphic Designer

Representing highway and transportation departments in the 50 states, the District of Columbia, and Puerto Rico. It represents all five transportation modes: air, highways, public transportation, rail ,and water. Its primary goal is to foster the development, operation, and maintenance of an integrated national transportation system.
Founded in: 1981

22983 American Association of State Highway and Transportation Officials
444 North Capitol Street N.W.
Suite 249
Washington, DC 20001

202-624-5800; *Fax:* 202-624-5806
info@aashto.org; www.transportation.org
Social Media: Facebook, Twitter, LinkedIn, YouTube

Bud Wright, Executive Director
Jenet Adem, Director of Finance
Tony Bianchi, Associate Project Director
John Boyd, Senior Communications Editor
Lloyd Brown, Director of Communications

A standards-setting body which publishes specifications, test protocols anf guidelines used in highway design and construction across the United States

22984 American Automobile Association
1000 AAA Drive
Heathrow, FL 32746-5062

407-444-7966; *Fax:* 800-222-4357;
www.aaa.com

22985 American Bus Association
111 K Street NE
9th Floor
Washington, DC 20002

202-842-1645
800-283-2877; *Fax:* 202-842-0850
abainfo@buses.org; www.buses.org
Social Media: Facebook, Twitter, LinkedIn

Peter J Pantuso, President & CEO
Brandon Buchanan, Director, Operations
Clyde J Hart Jr., Senior VP, Govt. Affairs & Policy
Norm Litter, VP, Regulatory & Industry Affairs
Eric Braendel, CFO

ABA supports 3,800 members consisting of motorcoach and tour companies in addition to organizations that represent the tourism and travel industry. ABA strives to educate consumers on the importance of highway and motorcoach safety.
Founded in: 1926

22986 American Commodity and Shipping
2102-D Gallows Rd.
Vienna, VA 22182

703-848-9422; *Fax:* 703-848-9424
info@americancommodity.com;
www.americancommodity.com
Social Media: Facebook, Twitter, LinkedIn

22987 American Concrete Pavement Association
9450 W Bryn Mawr Ave.
Suite 150
Rosemont, IL 60018

847-966-2272
acpa@acpa.org; www.pavement.com
Social Media: Facebook, Twitter, LinkedIn, YouTube

Mike Lipps, Chairman
Steve Jackson, Vice Chairman
Lori Tiefenthaler, 2nd Vice Chair
Jerry Voigt, President, CEO
Glenn Eder, Treasurer

Trade association that exclusively represents the interests of those involved with the design, construction and preservation of concrete pavements.
Founded in: 1963

22988 American Council of Highway Advertisers
PO Box 809
North Beach, MD 20714

301-386-3330

22989 American Moving and Storage Association
1611 Duke St
Alexandria, VA 22314-3406

703-683-7410; *Fax:* 703-683-7527;
www.moving.org
Social Media: Facebook, Twitter, LinkedIn, Pinterest

Linda Bauer Darr, CEO
Sandy Lynch, SVP

Represents members including interstate moving and storage companies, local movers, international movers plus industry suppliers and state association members. AMSA's chief goals include strong support for effective government regulations and policies that protect consumers while allowing members to provide quality service at compensatory prices, and ensuring that consumers understand the value of professional moving and storage services.
3200 Members
Founded in: 1936

22990 American Public Transportation Association
1300 I Street NW
Suite 1200 East
Washington, DC 20005

202-496-4800; *Fax:* 202-496-4324
meetings2@apta.com; www.apta.com
Social Media: Facebook, Twitter, LinkedIn, Youtube, Flickr, Blog

Michael P Melaniphy, President & CEO
Petra Mollet, Chief Of Staff
Pamela L Boswell, VP, Workforce Development
Mary Childress, CFO
Art Guzzetti, VP, Policy

APTA is an international organization that supports and represents the transportation industry. Membership benefits include an annual association meeting, an international expo, membership directory, access to online publications, newsletters and electronic news service.
Founded in: 1882

22991 American Railway Development Association
500 New Jersey Avenue, NW
Suite 400
Washington, DC 20001

202-715-1259; *Fax:* 952-828-9751
info@amraildev.com; www.amraildev.com/
Social Media: Facebook, Twitter, LinkedIn

Stephanie Johnson, President
Alan Sisk, First VP
Gary Rozmus, Second VP
Mark Holder, Secretary/Treasurer

Members are marketing, real estate and industrial development officers of railroads. Objectives are to foster the industrial, real estate, natural resources and market development activities of North American railroads and through the advancement of ideas and education of its members, further promote the effectiveness of railway development and related work.
200 Members
Founded in: 1906

22992 American Railway Engineering and Maintenance-of-Way Association
4501 Forbes Blvd
Suite 130
Lanham, MD 20706-4362

301-459-3200; *Fax:* 301-459-8077
bcaruso@arema.org; www.arema.org
Social Media: Facebook, LinkedIn

Beth Caruso, Executive Director & CEO
Vickie Fisher, Director, Finance
Stacy Spaulding, Executive & Board Operations
Janice Clements, Director, Membership
Christy Thomas, Events Manager

Fosters concern for design, construction and maintenance of bridges, buildings, water service facilities and other railway structures.
5400 Members
Founded in: 1891

22993 American Road and Transportation Builders
1219 28th St NW
Washington, DC 20007-3389

202-289-4434; *Fax:* 202-289-4435
general@artba.org; www.artba.org

David S. Zachry, Chairman
Bob Alger, Senior Vice Chair
Matt Cummings, First Vice Chair
Tom Hill, Treasurer
Pete Ruane, Secretary

Offers information and resources for members associated with the transporation building industry.
Founded in: 1902

22994 American Short Line & Regional Railroad Association
50 F Street, N.W.
Suite 7020
Washington, DC 20001

202-628-4500; *Fax:* 202-628-6430
lbdarr@aslrra.org; www.aslrra.org

Linda Bauer Darr, President & Treasurer
Keith T. Borman, VP, General Counsel
Kathleen M. Cassidy, VP, Member Services
Jo E. Strang, VP, Regulatory Affairs
Jenny M. Bourque, Director

An association of North American short line and regional railroads

22995 **American Short Line Railroad Association**
50 F Street NW
Suite 7020
Washington, DC 20001-1536
202-628-4500; *Fax:* 202-628-6430
aslrra@aslrra.org; www.aslrra.org
Linda Bauer Darr, President & Treasurer
Keith T Borman, VP, General Counsel
Jenny M Bourque, Director, Marketing
Kathleen M Cassidy, VP, Meetings & Member Services
Jenny M. Bourque, Director
Monitors and reports legislative and regulatory activities.
750 Members
Founded in: 1913

22996 **American Society of Transportation & Logistics**
8430 W Bryn Mawr Ave
Suite 1000
Chicago, IL 60631
773-867-1777; *Fax:* 773-639-3000;
www.astl.org
Social Media: Facebook, Twitter, LinkedIn
George Yarusavage, CTL C.P.M., Chairman
William J. Ferreira, Vice Chairman
Laurie Denham, PLS, President
Mike A. Regan, DLP, Treasurer
Evelyn Thomchick, CTL, Secretary
Professional organization for transportation and logistics professionals.
Founded in: 1946

22997 **American Space Transportation Association**
General Dynamics
1801 Alexander Bell Drive
Reston, VA 20191-4400
703-548-2723
800-548-2723; *Fax:* 703-295-6222;
www.asce.org
Social Media: Facebook, Twitter, LinkedIn, YouTube, Google+
Patrick J Natale, Executive Director
Pete Shavalay, CFO
Thomas Smith, Deputy Executive Director
The successor organization to the Ad Hoc Industry Group promoting the development of commercial space transportation in the United States.
25 Members
Founded in: 1852

22998 **American Towman Network**
7 West Street
Warwick, NY 10990
201-722-3000
800-732-3869; *Fax:* 201-722-3010
towcrazy@wrecker.com; www.towman.com
Social Media: Facebook, RSS
Jim Sorrenti, Editor
Steven Calitri, Editor in Chief
Henry Calitri, Exhibit Sales

22999 **American Traffic Safety Services Association**
15 Riverside Parkway
Suite 100
Fredericksburg, VA 22406-1022
540-368-1701
800-272-8772; *Fax:* 540-368-1717;
www.atssa.com
Social Media: Facebook, Twitter, YouTube
Scott Seeley, Chairman
Debra Ricker, Chairman Elect
Kathleen Holst, Past President
Henry Ross, Past President
Peter Speer, Past President
An international trade association with the core purpose to advance roadway safety.
Founded in: 1969

23000 **American Truck Historical Society**
10380 N Ambassador Dr.
Suite 101, P.O. Box 901611
Kansas City, MO 64153
816-891-9900; *Fax:* 816-891-9903
don@aths.org; www.aths.org
Social Media: Facebook, Twitter, YouTube
Don Bretthauer, Executive Director
Shelley Ruhlman, Managing Director
Melinda Hunsberger, Director of Finance
Courtney Dery, Library Director
Jan Martin, Support Systems Specialist
Collects and preserves the history of antique trucks and the industry.
Founded in: 1971

23001 **American Trucking Association**
950 North Glebe Road
Suite 210
Arlington, VA 22203-4181
703-838-1700
866-821-3468; *Fax:* 703-838-8884
atamembership@trucking.org;
www.trucking.org
Social Media: Twitter
Pat Thomas, Chairman
Bill Graves, President & CEO
Kevin W. Burch, ATA First Vice Chairman
David Manning, ATA Second Vice Chairman
John M Smith, Secretary
Largest national trade association for the trucking industry.
Founded in: 1933

23002 **American Underground Space Association**
12999 E. Adam Aircraft Circle
Englewood, CO 80112
303-948-4200
800-763-3132; *Fax:* 303-973-3845
cs@smenet.org; www.auca.org
Social Media: Facebook, Twitter, LinkedIn
William W Edgerton, Chair
Arthur D Silber, Vice Chairman
700 Members
Founded in: 1976

23003 **American Waterways Operators**
801 N Quincy St
Suite 200
Arlington, VA 22203-1708
703-841-9300; *Fax:* 703-841-0389;
www.americanwaterways.com
Social Media: Facebook, Twitter, LinkedIn
Buckley McAllister, Chairman
Frank Morton, Vice Chairman
George Foster, Treasurer
Thomas A. Allegretti, President & CEO
Mary J. Anastacio, Manager - Finance
Members include domestic carriers transporting commodities by water, shipyards, terminals and affiliated, business.
375 Members

23004 **Association for Commuter Transportation**
1330 Braddock Place
Suite 350
Alexandria, VA 22314-6405
571-699-3064
888-719-5772
info@actweb.org; www.actweb.org
Social Media: Facebook, Twitter
Caryn Souza, Director
Marlon Powell, Adminstrative Assistant
Kevin Oliff, Marketing & Outreach Specialist
Jason Pavluchuk, Govt. Relations Specialist
ACT provides you with the resources of an international organization and the support of a regional affiliate of experienced Transportation Demand Management professionals.
810 Members
Founded in: 1991

23005 **Association for Women in Aviation Maintenance**
2330 Kenlee Drive
Cincinnati, OH 45230
386-416-0248; *Fax:* 386-236-0517;
www.awam.org
Social Media: Facebook, LinkedIn
Lynette Ashland, President
Jane Shelton, Vice President
Teressa Stark, Treasurer
Laura Gordon, Secretary
Anna Romer, Director | Scholarship Co-Chair
An organization formed for the purpose of championing women's professional growth and enrichment in the aviation maintenance fields.

23006 **Association of Air Medical Services**
909 N. Washington Street
Suite 410
Alexandria, VA 22314-3143
703-836-8732; *Fax:* 703-836-8920
information@aams.org; www.aams.org
Dawn Mancuso, Executive Director
Shirley Scholz, VP
Rick Sherlock, President
Yogendra Sheth, Finance & Accounting Manager
Voluntary nonprofit organization, encourages and supports its members in maintaining a standard of performance reflecting safe operations and efficient, high quality patient care. Built on the idea that representation from a variety of medical transport services and businesses can be brought together to share information, collectively resolve problems and provide leadership in the medical transport community.

23007 **Association of American Railroads**
425 Third Street SW
Suite 114
Washington, DC 20024-3217
202-639-2100
media@aar.org; www.aar.org
Social Media: Facebook, Twitter, LinkedIn, YouTube
Edward R. Hamberger, President & CEO
Patricia M. Reilly, SVP, Communications
Jeffrey Marsh, SVP, Finance & Administration
Ian Jefferies, SVP, Government Affairs
John Gray, svp, Policy and Economics
Presently serves a joint agency of its individual railroad members to ensure an efficient nationwide rail system.
Founded in: 1934

23008 **Association of Metropolitan Planning Organizations**
444 North Capitol Street, NW
Suite 345
Washington, DC 20000
202-624-3680; *Fax:* 202-624-3685;
www.ampo.org
Richard Perrin, President
Elaine Clegg, Vice President
R. Todd Ashby, Executive Director
Rich Denbow, Director of Technical Programs
Levon Boyagian, Policy Consultant
A nonprofit organization serving metropolitan planning organizations.
Founded in: 1994

23009 Association of Railway Museums
PO Box 370
Tujunga, CA 91043-0370
818-951-9151; *Fax:* 818-951-9151;
www.railway.museums.org
Ellen Fishburn, Secretary
Paul Hamond, President
The association of railway museums is for the preservation of railway equipment, artifacts and history.
125 Members
Founded in: 1961

23010 Automotive Parts Remanufacturers Association
7250 Heritage Villa Plaza
Suite 201
Gainesville, VA 20155
703-968-2772; *Fax:* 703-753-2445
info@apra.org; www.apra.org
Social Media: Facebook, Twitter, LinkedIn, YouTube
Omar Cueto, Chairman
Jay Robie, Vice President
Joe Kripli, President
Association for remanufacturers of automotive parts.
Founded in: 1941

23011 BAX Global
440 Exchange
Irvine, CA 92602
602-458-6200
800-225-5229; www.baxglobal.com
Social Media: Twitter
Joseph L Carnes, President
Jay Arnold, VP Human Resources
Specializes in managing the movement of heavy-weight packages and cargo of all shapes and sizes.

23012 Boat Owners Association of the United States
880 South Pickett Street
Alexandria, VA 22304-4606
703-461-2878
membership@boatus.com; www.boatus.com
Social Media: Facebook, Twitter, YouTube, Google+
Richard Schwartz, Chairman, Founder
Margaret Podlich, President
Adam Wheeler, VP and Director of Towing
Heather Lougheed, VP, Membership
John Condon, AVP, Towing Operations
Association of boat owners offering various services, supporting recreational boat and trailer towing activities.
Founded in: 1966

23013 Brotherhood of Locomotive Engineers and Trainmen
Standard Building
1370 Ontario St.
Mezzanine, OH 44113-1702
216-241-2630; *Fax:* 216-241-6516
PresStaff@ble-t.org; www.ble-t.org
Dennis R. Pierce, National President
E. Lee Pruitt, First Vice President
Marcus J. Ruef, VP, Director of Arbitration
Gil L. Gore, Michael D., Vice President
A trade organization for railroad workers.

23014 Brotherhood of Maintenance of Way Employee s
41475 Gardenbrook Road
Novi, MI 48375-1328
248-662-2660; *Fax:* 248-662-2659;
www.bmwe.org
Freddie N. Simpson, National Division President
Perry Geller, National Div. Secretary-Treasurer
David R. Scoville, Vice President- Western Region
Roger Sanchez, Vice President- South Region
David D. Joynt, Vice President at Large
A national union representing the workers who build and maintain the tracks, bridges, building and other structures of the railroads.

23015 Brotherhood of Railroad Signalmen
917 Shenandoah Shores Rd
Front Royal, VA 22630-6418
540-622-6522; *Fax:* 540-622-6532
kelly@brs.org; www.brs.org
Social Media: Facebook, Twitter, RSS
W Dan Pickett, President
Walter A Barrows, Treasurer
Floyd Mason, VP
Mike S. Baldwin, Research
National organization representing the men and women who install and maintain signal systems for most of the nation's railroads.
ISSN: 0037-5020
Founded in: 1901

23016 Carrier Information Exchange
4601 N Fairfax Drive
Suite 1160
Arlington, VA 22203
703-841-6374; *Fax:* 703-841-6370
mcinfosupport@egov.com; www.mcinfo.org

23017 Center for Transportation and the Environment (CTE)
730 Peachtree Street
Suite 760
Atlanta, GA 30308
678-244-4150; *Fax:* 678-244-4151; www.cte.tv
Eric Sonnichsen, Chairman
Joe Beno, Treasurer
John Sleconich, Secretary
James B. Martin, M.C.E., P.E., Associate Director
Eugene Murray, B.A., Distance Learning Specialist
A nonprofit organization to improve the efficiency and sustainability of the energy ad transportation systems.
Founded in: 1991

23018 Commercial Vehicle Safety Alliance
6303 Ivy Lane
Suite 310
Greenbelt, MD 20770-631
301-830-6144
cvsahq@cvsa.org; www.cvsa.org
Social Media: Facebook, Twitter, LinkedIn, YouTube
A nonprofit organization dedicated to improving the safety of commercial vehicles.

23019 Committee for Better Transit
38 W Cliff Street
Somerville, NJ 08876
E-Mail: brooklynbus@hotmail.com;
www.brooklynbus.tripod.com
The Committee for Better Transit is a forty-one year old New York Metropolitan independent transit advocacy organization comprised of transit experts and users, which seeks cost effective user-friendly solutions to transit challenges.

23020 Council of Fleet Specialists
315 Delaware Street
Kansas City, MO 64105-1256
816-421-2600; *Fax:* 816-421-0515
UJ Reese, Executive VP
Members are distributors of parts and services for heavy-duty trucks.
210 Members
Founded in: 1967

23021 Driver Employee Council of America
1001 G St Nw
Suite 500-W
Washington, DC 20001-4564
202-434-4100; *Fax:* 202-842-0011
info@khlaw.com; www.khlaw.com
Social Media: LinkedIn, RSS
Jerome H Heckman, Partner
Members are companies leasing truck drivers to private carriers.
43 Members
Founded in: 1992

23022 Energy Traffic Association
935 Eldridge Road
Suite 604
Sugar Land, TX 77478
832-474-3564; www.energytraffic.org
Ralph Lopez, President
Renee Ahmed, VP & Secretary
Russell Powell, Executive Director
Formed by the merger of the Oilfield Supply Traffic Association and the Shippers Oil Field Traffic Association, ETA serves the oil and gas industry in transportation, distribution and logistics. Members are energy industry transportation, distribution, purchasing and logistics managers, and transportation and logistics providers.
Founded in: 1997

23023 Expediting Management Association
Livingston, TN
931-823-1122; *Fax:* 403-201-6402;
www.expedite.org
Katherine Rench, C.E.M, President
Glenda Warman, VP
Linda Strauss, Secretary
David Kern, Treasurer
Patricia Murphy, Executive Administrator
The Expediting Management Association, Inc. will maintain a certification program for it's memebers giving them the opportunity to achieve recognition from their peers in the association and industry.
200 Members
Founded in: 1972

23024 Express Carriers Association
9532 Liberia Ave.
Suite 752
Manassas, VA 20110
703-361-1058; *Fax:* 703-361-5274
eca@expresscarriers.com;
www.expresscarriers.com
Paul Steffes, President
Jim Luciani, 1st VP
Mike Coyle, Second VP
Jim King, Treasurer
Jim Bernecker, Secretary
The mission of the ECA is to develop business between carriers, shippers and vendors of products and services to the transportation industry.

23025 Fleet Management Institute (NAFA)
125 Village Boulevard
Suite 200
Princeton, NJ 08540
609-720-0882; *Fax:* 609-452-8004
info@nafa.org; www.nafa.org

Social Media: Facebook, Twitter, LinkedIn, YouTube

Patricia Murtaugh, Assistant Executive Director
Joanne Marsh, Manager

23026 Flight Safety Foundation
801 N. Fairfax Street
Suite 400
Alexandria, VA 22314-1774

703-739-6700; *Fax:* 703-739-6708
wahdan@flightsafety.org
flightsafety.org
Social Media: Facebook, Twitter, LinkedIn

Ken Hylander, Chair
David McMillan, Past Chair
Jon Beatty, President and CEO
David Barger, Treasurer
Kenneth P. Quinn, General Counsel and Secretary

Independent, nonprofit international oganization engaged in research, auditing, education, advocacy and publishing to imporove flight safety.
Founded in: 1947

23027 Gemini Shippers Group
137 West 25th Street
3rd Floor
New York, NY 10001

212-947-3424; *Fax:* 212-629-0361
info@geminishippers.com;
www.geminishippers.com
Social Media: Facebook, Twitter, LinkedIn, Google+

Sara L. Mayes, CEO and President
Kenneth O'Brien, Chief Operating Officer
Nicole Uchrin, Managing Director
Rich Moore, Sales Director
Arlene L. Blocker, Membership Director

Shippers association with global contracts for all commodities.
200 Members
Founded in: 1916

23028 Heavy Duty Representatives Association
160 Symphony Way
Elgin, IL 847-760-00

330-725-7160
800-763-5717; *Fax:* 330-725-7160
trucksvc@aol.com; www.hdra.org

Larry Rossenthal, President
Walt Sirman, Vice President
John Stojak, Secretary

Independent sales agencies which sell heavy-duty components to the trucking and aftermarket industries.

23029 High Speed Grand Transportation
1010 Massachusetts Avenue NW
Washington, DC 20001

202-789-8107; www.hsgt.org

23030 Highway Users Federation for Safety and
PO Box 6285
Olympia, WA 98507-1904

253-376-8492; www.acronymfinder.com
Social Media: Facebook

Diane Steed, President

The Highway Users Federation (WHUF) is an association concerned ith increasing capacity and safer on Highways.

23031 Independent Truck Owner-Operators
1 NW OOIDA Drive
Grain Valley, MI 64029

816-229-5791
800-444-5791
Jim_Johnston@ooida.com; www.ooida.com
Social Media: Facebook, Twitter, YouTube

Jim Johnston, President
Todd Spencer, EVP
Woody Chambers, General VP
Robert Esler, Secretary
Bill Rode, Treasurer

Trade association for business and human resources equipment financing.
15000 Members
Founded in: 1973

23032 Institute of Transportation Engineers
1627 Eye St NW
Suite 600
Washington, DC 20006

202-785-0060; *Fax:* 202-785-0609
ite_staff@ite.org; www.ite.org
Social Media: Facebook, Twitter, LinkedIn, YouTube, Google+, Pinterest

Zaki Mustafa, President
W Hibbett Neel Jr., VP
16000 Members
Founded in: 1930

23033 Insurance Institute for Highway Safety
988 Dairy Road
Ruckersville, VA 22968

434-985-4600; *Fax:* 434-985-2202
rrader@iihs.org; www.iihs.org
Social Media: Twitter, RSS, YouTube

Adrian Lund, President
Russ Rader, SVP, Communications
Shelley Shelton, Sr. Legal Associate
Brenda O'Donnell, VP, Insurer Relations
Chamelle Matthew, Sr. Communications Specialist

Independent, nonprofit research and communications organization dedicated to reducing highway crash death, injuries and property damage losses.
Founded in: 1959

23034 Intermodal Association of North America
11785 Beltsville Dr.
Suite 1100
Calverton, MD 20705-4049

301-982-3400; *Fax:* 301-982-4815
iana@intermodal.org; www.intermodal.org
Social Media: Facebook, Twitter, LinkedIn

Adriene B. Bailey, Chairman
Michael B. Wilson, Vice Chairman
David W. Manning, Treasurer
Joanne F. Casey, President & CEO

Promotes the benefits and growth of intermodal freight transportation.
1000+ Members
Founded in: 1991

23035 International Association of Structural Movers
PO Box 2104
Neenah, WI 54956-2104

803-951-9304; *Fax:* 920-486-1519
info@iasm.org; www.iasm.org
Social Media: Facebook, LinkedIn, YouTube, Google+

Jim Herman, President
Don Toothman, Jr., VP
Natalie Hammer, Secretaty/Treasurer

Members are movers of heavy structural products, trusses, houses, machinery and masonry structures.
385 Members
Founded in: 1983

23036 International Brotherhood of Teamsters
25 Louisiana Ave Nw
Washington, DC 20001-2130

202-624-6800; *Fax:* 202-624-6918;
www.teamster.org
Social Media: Facebook, Twitter, Google+

James P Hoffa, President
Ken Hall, Secretary/Treasurer

Affiliated with the AFL-CIO.
1.3MM Members
Founded in: 1954

23037 International Council of Cruise Lines
910 SE 17th Street
Suite 400
Fort Lauderdale, FL 33316

754-224-2200; *Fax:* 754-224-2250
info@cruising.org; www.cruising.org
Social Media: Facebook, Twitter, LinkedIn, Pinterest

Cindy D'Aoust, CEO
Tom Fischetti, CFO
Bud Darr, SVP Tech & Regulatory Affairs
Lorri Christou, SVP Marketing & Communications
Mike McGarry, SVP, Public Affairs

Dedicated to the promotion and growth of the cruise industry.
Founded in: 1975

23038 International Furniture Transportation and Logistics Council
PO Box 889
Gardner, MA 01440-0889

978-632-1913; *Fax:* 978-630-2917
jsears@iftlc.org; www.iftlc.org
Social Media: Twitter

Raynard F Bohman Jr, Managing Director

Members are furniture manufacturers, retrilers, carriers, wholesalers and warehouses of allied products.
300 Members

23039 International Light Transportation Vehicle Association
5579-B Chamblee Dunwoody Road
Atlanta, GA 30338
E-Mail: fsomers@ILTVA.org; www.iltva.org

Caleb Chesser, President
Fred Somers, General Counsel & Secretary

Organization dedicated to ensuring best practices and safety standards for light vehicle transportation.
Founded in: 1984

23040 International Marine Transit Association
34 Otis Hill Road
Hingham, MA 02043

781-749-0078; *Fax:* 781-749-0078;
www.interferry.com
Social Media: Twitter, RSS

Mike Grainger, Chairman
John Steen-Mikkelsen, President
Mike Corrigan, Treasurer
Len Roueche, Secretary

Membership includes ferry operators, naval architects, manufacturers, suppliers, and others in the ferry industry around the world.
400 Members
Founded in: 1976

23041 International Parking Institute
1330 Braddock Place
Suite 350
Alexandria, VA 22314

571-699-3011; *Fax:* 703-566-2267
ipi@parking.org; www.parking.org
Social Media: Facebook, Twitter, LinkedIn, YouTube, Pinterest, Instagram

Liliana Rambo, CAPP, Chair of the BOD
Kim Jackson, CAPP, Chair-elect
Cindy Campbell, Past Chair
Rick Decker, CAPP, Treasurer
Shawn D. Conrad, CAE, Executive Director

Organization that provides educational and technical services to parking professionals and to the public.
Founded in: 1962

23042 International Road Federation
500 Montgomery Street
Fifth Floor
Alexandria, VA

703-535-1001; *Fax:* 703-535-1007
info@IRFnews.org; www.irfnet.org
Social Media: Facebook, Twitter, LinkedIn, Flickr

A service organization for better road transportation systems.
Founded in: 1948

23043 International Safe Transit Association
1400 Abbot Rd
Suite 160
East Lansing, MI 48823-1900

517-333-3437
888-367-4782; *Fax:* 517-333-3813
ista@ista.org; www.ista.org
Social Media: Facebook, Twitter, LinkedIn

Edward A Church, President
A J Gruber, VP, Technical Services
Lisa Bonsignore, VP, Special Events
Larry Dull, VP, Sustainable Solutions
Kathy A Joneson, VP, Communications

Members are shippers, carriers, manufacturers, packagers, package designers and testing laboratories, included in transport packaging.
750 Members
Founded in: 1948
Mailing list available for rent: 4000 names at $500 per M

23044 Interstate Trucking Association
Express Carriers Association
9532 Liberia Avenue
#752
Manassas, VA 20110

703-361-1058
866-322-7447; *Fax:* 703-361-5274
eca@expresscarriers.com; www.expresscarriers.com

Paul Steffes, President
Jim Luciani, First VP
Mike Coyle, Second VP
Jim King, Treasurer
Jim Bernecker, Secretary

Organization of newly enacted state legislation regulations having direct impact on vehicle operations, fuel taxes, registration size and weight.

23045 Lake Carriers Association
20325 Center Ridge Road
Suite 720
Rocky River, OH 44116-3508

440-333-4444; *Fax:* 440-333-9993
info@lcaships.com; www.lcaships.com
Social Media: Twitter

James H I Weakley, President
Glen G Nekvasil, VP
Harold W Henderson, General Counsel
Thomas G. Rayburn, Director of Env.& Reg. Affairs
Katherine A. Gumeny, Secretary/Treasurer

Members are US- Flag Great Lakes vessel operators engaged in transporting iron ore, coal, grain, limestone, cement and petroleum products.
Founded in: 1880

23046 Landstar Global Logistics
13410 Sutton Park Drive S
Jacksonville, FL 32224

904-398-9400
800-872-9400
corpcomm@landstar.com; www.landstar.com
Social Media: Facebook, LinkedIn

Henry H Gerkens, Chairman, President & CEO
Jim B Gattoni, Executive VP, CFO
Joe Beacorn, VP & Chief Safety Operations Office
Larry S Thomas, VP/Chief Information Officer
Michael Kneller, VP, General Counsel & Secretary

Mission is to be the leading non-asset based provider of transportation capacity delivering safe, sepcialized transportation services to customers worldwide utilizing a network of agents, third-party capacity owners and employees.

23047 Light Truck Assessory Alliance
SEMA
1575 S.Valley Vista Drive
Diamond Bar, CA 91765-0910

909-396-0289
info@sema.org; www.sema.org
Social Media: Facebook, Twitter, Google+

Nate Shelton, Chairman
Doug Evans, Chair-Elect
Christopher J Kersting, President & CEO
George Afremow, VP, CFO
Tom Myroniak, VP, Marketing & Market Research

A national organization with 150 manufacturers of truck caps and light truck accessories.

23048 Mid-West Truckers Association
2727 N Dirksen Pkwy
Springfield, IL 62702-1490

217-525-0310; *Fax:* 217-525-0342
info@mid-westtruckers.com; www.mid-westtruckers.com
Social Media: Facebook, YouTube

Don Schaefer, Executive Vice President
Matt Wells, Associate Director
Jeanne Campo, Secretary/Treasurer
Candy Wendt, Drug & Alcohol Supervisor
Diana McMahan, Membership Coordinator

Serves the trucking industry by lobbying on their behalf, assisting with registration, license plate procurement and group insurance programs. Conducts educational programs, has own self-funded workers compensation insurance program. Trade association represents truck owners in 14 states.
3000 Members
Founded in: 1962

23049 Motor Transport Management Group
PO Box 605
Rillito, AZ 85654

520-616-0175; *Fax:* 208-561-2980; www.transportationmg.com
Social Media: Facebook

23050 National Air Carrier Association
1000 Wilson Boulevard
Suite 1700
Arlington, VA 22209-3928

703-358-8060; *Fax:* 703-358-8070; www.naca.cc

Oakley Brooks, President
Paul H Doell, Director, Govt. Affairs
George R Paul, Director Technical Services
Paul H Doell, Director Government Affairs
7 Members
Founded in: 1962

23051 National Air Traffic Controllers Association
1325 Massachusetts Avenue N.W.
Washington, DC 20005

202-628-5451
800-266-0895; *Fax:* 202-628-5767; www.natca.org
Social Media: Facebook, Twitter, LinkedIn, YouTube, Instagram

Paul Rinaldi, President
Trish Gilbert, Executive Vice President
Mike MacDonald, Regional VP
Kevin Peterson, Regional VP
Jim Ullmann, Regional VP

Members are controllers in public and private sectors and Federal Aviation Administration engineers.

23052 National Air Transportation Association
818 Connecticut Avenue, NW
Suite 900
Washington, DC 22302-1507

202-774-1535
800-808-6282; *Fax:* 703-845-8176; www.nata.aero
Social Media: Facebook, Twitter, LinkedIn, RSS

Andy Priester Scheeringa, Chairman
Marty Hiller, Vice Chairman
Thomas L Hendricks, President
Greg Schmidt, Treasurer
Guy Hill, Jr., Secretary

Aggressively promotes safety and the success of aviation service businesses through its advocacy efforts before government, the media and the public as well as by providing valuable programs and forums to further its members' prosperity.
1800 Members
Founded in: 1940

23053 National Asphalt Pavement Association
5100 Forbes Blvd
Lanham, MD 20708

301-731-4748
888-468-6499; *Fax:* 301-731-4621; www.asphaltpavement.org

A trade association that exclusively represents the interests of the asphalt pavment matieral producer and paving contractor on the national level with Congress, government agenices and other national trade and business organizations.

23054 National Association of Freight & Logistics
P.O.Box 60944
Dubai

714-343-1112; *Fax:* 714-343-1105; www.nafl.ae

David Phillips, President
Kevin Ennis, VP
Nadia Abdul Aziz, Secretary General
Suman Chakrabarti, Treasurer

Previously the National Committee of Freight Forwarders, the NAFL brings together in one body all the major players in the freight fowarding, logistics, and shipping industries.
Founded in: 1992

23055 National Association of Rail Shippers
77 K Street NE
8th Floor
Washington, DC 20002-4681
202-650-6500
800-432-2250; *Fax:* 972-644-8208;
www.rollcall.com
Social Media: Facebook, Twitter, LinkedIn, You Tube
Charlie Mitchell, VP
Laurie Battaglia, Publisher
Strives to provide a sound transporation system. Bestows annual Award of Excellence.
2M Members
Founded in: 1937

23056 National Association of Railroad Passengers
505 Capitol Court NE
Suite 300
Washington, DC 20002-7706
202-408-8362; *Fax:* 202-408-8287
narp@narprail.org; www.narprail.org
Social Media: Facebook, Twitter, Google+
Jim Mathews, President & CEO
Sean Jeans-Gail, VP
Robert J. Stewart, Chairman
Carol Haslett, Vice Chair
Stephen J. Salatti, Secretary
Seeks to increase public awareness of rail passenger service and its benefits. Works for a national transportation policy.
12M Members
Founded in: 1967

23057 National Association of Small Trucking Companies
2054 Nashville Pike
Gallatin, TN 37066
615-451-4555
800-264-8580; *Fax:* 615-451-0041
david.owen@nastc.com; www.nastc.com
Social Media: Twitter
David Owen, President
Buster Anderson, Executive Vice President
Dana Campbell, Vice President Of Operations
Hunter Owen, VP, Sales and Marketing
Angel Clark, Director of Safety & Compliance
Association for small trucking fleets and companies.
Founded in: 1989

23058 National Association of State Aviation Officials
8400 Westpark Dr.
2nd Floor
McLean, VA 22102
703-454-0649
info@nasao.org; www.nasao.org
Social Media: Facebook, Twitter, LinkedIn
Gary Cathey, Chairman
Brad Brandt, Vice Chairman
Ronnie Mitchell, Treasurer
Carol L. Comer, Immediate Past Chairman
Greg Principato, President/ CEO
Established to ensure uniformity of safety measures and to standardize airport regulations.
Founded in: 1931

23059 National Association of Truck Stop Operators
1330 Braddock Place
#501
Alexandria, VA 22314-1483
703-549-2100
800-956-9160; *Fax:* 703-684-4525
editor@natso.com; www.natso.com
Social Media: Facebook, Twitter, Youtube, RSS
Tom Heinz, Chairman
Thomas M O'Brien, Secretary/Treasurer
Lisa J Mullings, President & CEO
Taryn Brice-Rowland, Director of Member Engagement
Roger Cole, Editor, Biz Brief
NATSO is the professional association of America's $42 billion travel plaza and truckstop industry. NATSO represents the industry on legislative and regulatory matters; serves as the official source of information on the diverse travel plaza and truckstop industry; provides education to its members; conducts an annual convention and trade show; and supports efforts to generally improve the business climate in which its members operate.
1230+ Members
Founded in: 1990

23060 National Automobile Dealers Association
8400 Westpark Dr
Mc Lean, VA 22102-3591
703-821-7000
800-252-6232; *Fax:* 703-821-7234
help@nada.org; www.nada.org
Social Media: Facebook, Twitter, LinkedIn, Flickr, Youtube
Bill Fox, Chairman
Jeff Carlson, Vice Chairman
Peter Welch, President
Joe Cowden, EVP/COO/CFO
David Regan, EVP, Legislative Affairs
Manufacturers, suppliers and distributors of products and services designed to control dealership expenses, help merchandising or improve profitability.
19700 Members
Founded in: 1917

23061 National Business Aviation Association
1200 G Street NW
Suite 1100
Washington, DC 20005
202-783-9000; *Fax:* 202-331-8364
info@nbaa.org; www.nbaa.org
Social Media: Facebook, Twitter, LinkedIn
Paul Anderson, Chairman
Lloyd "Fig" Newton, Vice Chairman/ Treasurer
Edward M. Bolen, President & CEO
Steve Brown, Chief Operating Officer
Marc Freeman, Chief Financial Officer
Promotes the aviation interests of organizations utilizing general aviation aircraft for business purposes.
Founded in: 1947

23062 National Business Travel Association
123 North Pitt Street
Alexandria, VA 22314-3234
703-684-0836; *Fax:* 703-342-4324
info@nbta.org; www.gbta.org
Social Media: Facebook, Twitter, LinkedIn, You Tube
Christle Johnson, President & CEO
Mark Ziegler, Vice President
Hema Shah, Chief Financial Officer
Hayford Mensah, CPA, Director, Finance
Getnesh Made, Manager, Finance
Offers over 1,300 corporate travel managers and allied members in the United States and Canada.
7000+ Members
Founded in: 1968

23063 National Center for Bicycling and Walking
1612 K Street, NW
Suite 802
Washington, DC 20006
202-223-3621
info@bikewalk.org; www.bikewalk.org
Mark Plotz, Senior Associate / Program Manager
John Williams, CenterlinesEditor
Jim Johnston, Web/Systems Administrator
A resident program at the Project for Public Spaces, Inc.
Founded in: 1977

23064 National Child Transport Association
Hall of States
444 N Capitol St Nw
Suite 438
Washington, DC 20001-1505
202-624-7710; *Fax:* 202-624-5899
bthompson@ncsha.org; www.ncsha.org
Social Media: Facebook, Twitter
Barbara J Thompson, Executive Director
Cary D Knox, Executive Office Admin
Thomas R. Gleason, President
Grant S. Whitaker, Vice President
Ralph M. Perrey, Secretary/Treasurer
Thirty booths.
1.2M Members

23065 National Customs Brokers and Forwarders
1200 18th St Nw
Suite 901
Washington, DC 20036-2572
202-466-0222; *Fax:* 202-466-0226
staff@ncbfaa.org; www.ncbfaa.org
Social Media: Facebook, Twitter, LinkedIn
Darrell Sekin, Jr., Chairman
Geoffrey Powell, President
Amy Magnus, VP
Scott E. Larson, Treasurer
William S. App, Jr., Secretary
Learn about new business leads, stay on top of Customs Service and other agency regulations that will impact your operations and provide invaluable professional development resources for your employees.
600+ Members
Founded in: 1897

23066 National Defense Transportation Association (NDTA)
50 S Pickett Street
Suite 220
Alexandria, VA 22304
703-751-5011; *Fax:* 703-823-8761
info@ndtahq.com; www.ndtahq.com
Social Media: Facebook, Twitter, LinkedIn
Mark H. Buzby RADM, USN (Ret.), President & COO
Jim Veditz COL, USA (Ret.), Senior VP Operations
Lee Matthews, VP, Marketing & Corp. Development
Patty Casidy, VP, Finance
Rebecca Jones, Executive Asst. To President
Intended as a liasion between government, military and private transportation officials.
7800 Members
Founded in: 1944

23067 National Food Distributors Association
401 N. MIchigan Avenue
Suite 2200
Chicago, IL 60611-4267
312-644-6610; *Fax:* 212-482-6459
info@allfoodbusiness.com;
www.allfoodbusiness.com
An organization comprised of independent store-to-door service distributors and suppliers of specialty food items.
2100 Members
Founded in: 1952

23068 National Industrial Transportation League
1700 N Moore St
Suite 1900
Arlington, VA 22209-1931
703-524-5011; *Fax:* 703-524-5017
info@nitl.org; www.nitl.org
Social Media: Twitter
Bruce J Carlton, President & CEO
Ellie Gilanshah, VP, Finance, Admin & Membership
Doug J. Kratzberg, Chairman
Mary Pileggi, 1st Vice Chairman
Gary A. Palmer, 2nd Vice Chairman
Provides information to the industrial transportation industry, including computer services software and innovations for transportation operations.
600 Members
Founded in: 1907

23069 National Institute of Certified Moving Consultants
1420 King Street
Alexandria, VA 22314-2794
703-683-7410
800-538-6672; *Fax:* 703-683-7527
cert@nicet.org; www.nicet.org
Social Media: Facebook, LinkedIn
Michael A Clark, Chief Operating Executive
Ahmed Farouki, Senior Director, Technical Services
Regina L. Stevenson, Director, Administrative Services
Brian Gifford, Director, Quality Management
Paul L. Stockman, Manager, Certification Services
Awards the certified moving consultant designation to those who have passed an exam testing their liability.
Founded in: 1961

23070 National Institute of Packaging and Handling Logistics Engineers
5903 Ridgeway Drive
Grand Prairie, TX 75052
817-466-7490
866-464-7453; *Fax:* 570-523-0606
admin@niphle.com; www.niphle.com
Social Media: Facebook, Twitter, LinkedIn
Sean Kerins, President
An assemblage of professionals whose interest in the complex and diverse practice of distribution and logistics is a common bond.
600 Members
Founded in: 1956

23071 National Marine Representatives Associatio n
PO Box 360
Gurnee, IL 60031
847-662-3167; *Fax:* 847-336-7126
info@nmraonline.org; www.nmraonline.org
Rob Gueterman, President
Brandon Flack, Past President
Keith LaMarr, Vice President
Neal Tombley, Treasurer
Clayton Smith, Secretary
A national organization serving marine industry sales representatives and the manufacturers who sell marine products.
Founded in: 1960

23072 National Motor Freight Traffic Association
1001 North Fairfax Street
Suite 600
Alexandria, VA 22314-1798
703-838-1810
866-411-6632; *Fax:* 703-683-6296
customerservice@nmfta.org; www.nmfta.org
Social Media: LinkedIn
Paul Levine, Executive Director
Joel Ringer, Chairman, CCSB
Urban Jonson, Chief Technology Officer
Leslie Tate, Finance & HR Manager
Urban Jonson, Chief Technology Officer
Provides expertise in freight classification, packaging, and transportation codes.

23073 National Motorcoach Network/Byways Magazin
PO Box 1088
Mount Jackson, VA 22842
540-477-3202
800-469-0062; *Fax:* 540-477-3858
stephen.kirchner@gmail.com;
www.motorcoach.com/byways
Founded in: 1983

23074 National Parking Association
1112 16th St Nw
Suite 840
Washington, DC 20036-4880
202-296-4336
800-647-7275; *Fax:* 202-296-3102
info@npapark.org; www.npapark.org
Social Media: Facebook, Twitter, LinkedIn, YouTube
Mark Muglich, Chairman
Alan B. Lazowski, Chair Elect
Nicolle Judge, Vice Chair
David Damus, Secretary
Robert A Zuritsky, Treasurer
Proudly serving the nation's parking industry since 1951. Our members are comprised of parking professionals in both the public and private sectors from across the country and around the world. NPA members are private operators, parking consultants, colleges and universities, municipalities, parking authorities, hospitals and medical centers and industry vendors.
2500+ Members
Founded in: 1951
Mailing list available for rent

23075 National Private Truck Council
950 N Glebe Rd
Suite 530
Arlington, VA 22203-4183
703-683-1300; *Fax:* 703-683-1217
tmoore@nptc.org; www.nptc.org
Social Media: Facebook, Twitter, LinkedIn, Youtube, Flickr, RSS
Gary S Petty, President & CEO
Tom Moore, CTP, SVP
Serena Porter, Membership Manager
George Mundell, EVP & COO
Rick Schweiter, General Counsel & Govt. Affairs
Distributors, shippers, processors, jobbers and manufacturers who transport their own goods and are owners of their own truck fleets. Sponsors national safety contests, safety seminars, management workshops, fleet management certification.
650 Members
Founded in: 1939

23076 National Private Truck Council
950 N. Glebe Road
Suite 2300
Arlington, VA 22203-4183
703-683-1300; *Fax:* 703-683-1217;
www.nptc.org
Social Media: Facebook, Twitter, LinkedIn, Flickr, YouTube, RSS
Tom Moore, CTP, Senior Vice President
George Mundell, Executive Vice President & COO
Gary F. Petty, President & CEO
Serena Porter, Membership Manager
Rick Schweitzer, General Counsel & Gov. Affairs
National trade association dedicated exclusively to representing private motor carrier fleets.
Founded in: 1939

23077 National School Transportation Association
122 South Royal Street
Alexandria, VA 22314
703-684-3200
800-222-6782; *Fax:* 703-684-3212
info@yellowbuses.com; www.yellowbuses.org
Social Media: Facebook, Twitter, LinkedIn, YouTube
Todd Monteferrario, President
Steve Hey, President Elect
Blake Krapf, Secretary/Treasurer
Ronna Weber, Executive Director
Meaghan Allain, Membership & Ops Coor.
Strives to provide safe transportation, foster safety, and an atmosphere conducive to private enterprise.
3M Members
Founded in: 1964

23078 National Small Shipments Traffic
330 N Wabash Avenue
Suite 2000
Chicago, IL 60611
202-367-1174; *Fax:* 202-686-2877
info@nasstrac.org; www.nasstrac.org
Social Media: Facebook, Twitter, LinkedIn
Doug Easley, Chairperson
Chris Norek, Ph.D., President
Terri Reid, 1st VP
Marc Feeser, 2nd VP
Tom Wenzinger, Treasurer
Members are truck, air, rail and sea shippers of freight weighing less than 10,000 pounds.
250 Members
Founded in: 1952

23079 National Truck Equipment Association
37400 Hills Tech Dr
Farmington Hill, MI 48331-3414
248-489-7090
800-441-6832; *Fax:* 248-489-8590
info@ntea.com; www.ntea.com
Social Media: Facebook, Twitter, LinkedIn, Flickr, YouTube, Instagram
Steve Carey, Executive Director
Carole Vartanian, Accounting Manager
Derek Eng, Director of Information Technology
Sheree Campbell, Executive Assistant
Michelle Kubitz, Director of Events
NTEA currently represents nearly 1,600 small to mid sized companies that manufacture, distribute, install, buy, sell and repair commercial trucks, truck bodies, truck equipment, trailers and accessories. The major commercial truck

chassis manufacturers also belong to the NTEA as associate members.
1800 Members
Founded in: 1964

23080 National Truck Leasing System
2651 Warrenville Road
Suite 560
Oakbrook Terrace, IL 60515
630-538-8878
800-729-6857; *Fax:* 630-953-0040
eventsadmin@nationalease.com;
www.nationalease.com
Social Media: Facebook, Twitter, LinkedIn, Google+
John Grainger, President
Members are independent truck leasing companies.
Founded in: 1944

23081 National Truck and Heavy Equipment Claims Council (NTHECC)
PO Box 5928
Fresno, CA 93755-5928
559-431-3774; *Fax:* 559-436-4755;
www.nthecc.org
Betty Clayton, President
Ed Williams, President Elect
Kelly R. Reich, Past President
Shane Carder, Secretary
Darrell W. Bickley, Treasurer
Repair and manufacturing facilities, insurance companies and adjusters concerned with insuring of heavy equipment and trucks. Promotes safety.
125 Members
Founded in: 1961

23082 National Truckers Association, Inc.
E-Mail: info@nationaltruckers.com;
www.nationaltruckers.com
Information and services for independent owner operators and small fleets.

23083 National Trucking Industrial Relations
908 King Street
Alexandria, VA 22314-3067
703-836-5506; www.all-acronyms.com
Social Media: Facebook
Trucking executives and lawyers concerned with personnel and labor relations issues.
128 Members
Founded in: 1987

23084 National Waterways Conference
110 N Glebe Rd.
Suite 1010
Arlington, VA 22201
703-224-8007; *Fax:* 866-371-1390
amy@waterways.org; www.waterways.org
Jim Oliver, Chairman
Jamie McCurry, Vice Chairman
Amy W. Larson, Esq.,, President
Randy Richardson, VP
Carole Wright, Director of Internal Operations
Dedicated to a greater understanding of the widespread public benefits of the American waterways system.
350 Members
Founded in: 1960

23085 Natural Gas Vehicles for America
400 N Capitol St Nw
Washington, DC 20001-1511
202-824-7360; *Fax:* 202-824-7087
rkolodziej@ngvamerica.org;
www.ngvamerica.org
Social Media: Facebook, Twitter, LinkedIn, YouTube
Matthew Godlewski, President
Jeffrey Clarke, Gen. Counsel & Dir., Reg. Affairs
Paul Kerkhoven, Director, Government Affairs
Lucas Blanchard, Dir., Ops, Membership & Planning
Dan Bowerson, Director, Technology & Dev.
Members are organizations with an interest in encouraging the development of natural gas powered vehicles.
250 Members
Founded in: 1988

23086 Network of Employers for Traffic Safety
344 Maple Avenue, West
#357
Vienna, VA 22180-5162
703-755-5350
888-221-0045
sgillies@trafficsafety.org
trafficsafety.org
Jack Hanley, Executive Director
Susan Gillies, Administrative Lead
Joseph L. McKillips, CSP, Chair
Focused on improving traffic safety.

23087 North American Shippers Association
1600 St. Georges Ave
PO Box 249
Rahway, NJ 07065
732-680-4540; *Fax:* 732-388-6580
nasaships@hillebrandgroup.com;
www.nasaships.com
Case Pieterman, Executive Director
Stephen Ballas, President
Members are shippers of wine and alcoholic beverages.
430 Members
Founded in: 1987

23088 North American Transportation Council
427 Garrison Rd.
Unit 3 & 4
Fort Erie, ON L2A 6E6
800-559-7421; *Fax:* 905-994-0117
info@fca-natc.org; www.natc.com
Dave Sirgey, President
Mary Anne Vehrs, Sales & Marketing
Julie Gauthier, Administrative Assistant
Diane Sheppard, Accounting Supervisor
Jon Ainsworth, Manager, IT & Dev
Represents Canadian and US based motor carriers engaged in for-hire trucking in the North American transborder market.

23089 NorthAmerican Transportation Association
9120 Double Diamond Parkway
Ste 346
Reno, NV 89521-4842
800-805-0040; www.ntassoc.com
Social Media: Facebook, Twitter, LinkedIn, YouTube
Association of transportation safety and compliance professionals serving the motor carrier industry.
Founded in: 1989

23090 Owner Operator Independent Drivers
1 NW OOIDA Drive
Grain Valley, MI 64029-1000
816-229-5791
800-444-5791; *Fax:* 816-229-0518
webmaster@ooida.com; www.ooida.com
Social Media: Facebook, Twitter, Youtube
Jim Johnston, President
Todd Spencer, EVP
Woody Chambers, General VP
Robert Esler, Secretary
Bill Rode, Treasurer
National association for owner-operators, professional drivers and small fleet owners. Lobbies federal and state government and advises on all legislation affecting the trucking industry. Provides insurance, financial products and business services.
15000 Members
Frequency: Monthly
Circulation: 200000
Founded in: 1973

23091 Owner Operators of America
PO Box 582
Orchard Park, NY 14127-0582
Merchants providing goods and services to truck drivers, operators and owners. Seeks to protect the status, interests and image of truck drivers. Offers discounts on fuel, tires, food, repairs, parts and insurance. Provides tax filing assistance. Sponsors trade shows, conferences and public relations programs.
250 Members
Founded in: 1982

23092 Passenger Vessel Association
103 Oronoco Street
Suite 200
Alexandria, VA 22314-1549
703-518-5005
800-807-8360; *Fax:* 703-518-5151
pvainfo@passengervessel.com;
www.passengervessel.com
Social Media: Facebook
Dave Anderson, President
Margo Marks, Vice President
Jeff Whitaker, Secretary/Treasurer
John Groundwater, Executive Director
Edmund Welch, Legislative Director
Represents operators of tours, excursions, ferries, charter vessels, dinner boats and other small passenger vessels.
600 Members
Founded in: 1971

23093 Professional Truck Driver Institute
Express Carriers Association
555 E Barddock Road
Alexandria, VA 22314
703-647-7015
866-322-7447; *Fax:* 703-836-6610
dheller@truckload.org; www.ptdi.org
David Money, Chairman
Kevin Bursch, Vice Chair
Mary Beth McCollum, Secretary
David Heller, Director
Marlene Dakita, Certification Coordinator
The nation's foremost advocate of optimum standards and professionalism for entry level truck driver training.
60 Members
Founded in: 1986

23094 Professional Truck Driving Institute
555 E. Braddock Road
Alexandria, VA 22314
703-647-7015; *Fax:* 703-846-6610
dheller@truckload.org; www.ptdi.org
David Money, Chairman
Kevin Bursch, Vice Chair
Mary Beth McCollum, Secretary
David Heller, Director
Marlene Dakita, Certification Coordinator

Advocates of truck-driver training standards, driver professionalism and safety.
Founded in: 1986

23095 Professional Trucking Services Association
United Truckers Service
1001 Bayhill Drive
Suite 300
San Bruno, CA 94066
650-260-3170; *Fax:* 770-929-3201;
www.allbusiness.com
Social Media: Facebook, Twitter, Youtube, RSS, Google+

Members are service bureaus which assist trucking companies in obtaining licensing and permits.
52 Members
Founded in: 1984

23096 Railway Industrial Clearance Association
8900 Eastloch Dr.
Suite 215
Spring, TX 77379
281-826-0009; www.rica.org

Rick Ford, Chairman
Kelli Collins, President
Justin Gilmet, VP
Mike Scott, Treasurer
Mark Lockwood, Secretary

Representation includes all aspects of logistics associated with the movement of dimensional cargo via rail.
400+ Members
Founded in: 1969

23097 Railway Supply Institute
425 Third Street, S.W.
Suite 920
Washington, DC 20024
202-347-4664; *Fax:* 202-347-0047
simpson@rsiweb.org; www.rsiweb.org
Social Media: Twitter, LinkedIn

Thomas D Simpson, President
Nicole B Brewin, VP, Govt. Affairs
Robyn M. Leach, VP, Administration
Amanda T. Patrick, CEM, Trade Shows & Marketing
Brian M. Kellman, Membership & Grassroots Coordinator

The railway equipment and supply industry.
300 Members
Founded in: 1908

23098 Railway Systems Suppliers
13133 Professional Drive
Suite 100
Jacksonville, FL 32225
904-379-3366; *Fax:* 904-379-3941
rssi@rssi.org; www.rssi.org

N. Michael Choat, President
Walter Winzen, Executive VP
Franklin Brown, 1st VP
Phil Hess, 2nd VP
Michael A. Drudy, Exe. Director/Secretary/Treasurer

A trade association serving the communication and signal segment of the rail transportation industry. Manages an annual trade show.
260+ Members
Founded in: 1966

23099 Regional Airline Association
2025 M Street NW
Washington, DC 20036-3309
202-367-1170; *Fax:* 202-367-2170
registration@raa.org; www.raa.org
Social Media: Facebook, Twitter, YouTube

Faye Malarkey Black, President
Stacey Bechdolt, Senior VP, Operations & Safety
Allie Cortes, Associate
Liam Connolly, Senior Director- Regulatory Affairs
Staci Morgan, Operations Manager

Membership consists of more than 70 airlines and 350 associate members that provide goods and services.
300 Members
Founded in: 1975

23100 Shippers Oil Field Traffic Association
907 Kiowa Drive E
Gainesville, TX 76240-9575
940-668-7735; *Fax:* 940-668-7212;
www.all-acronyms.com
Social Media: Facebook, Twitter

50 Members
Founded in: 1941

23101 Society of Automotive Engineers
400 Commonwealth Dr
Warrendale, PA 15096
724-776-4841
877-606-7323; *Fax:* 724-776-0790
customerservice@sae.org; www.sae.org
Social Media: Facebook, Twitter, LinkedIn, Google+

David L. Schutt, PhD, Chief Executive Officer
Gregory L. Bradley, Esq., General Counsel
Sandra L. Dillner, Director of Human Resources
Brian Kaleida, Chief Information Officer
Frank Menchaca, Chief Product Officer

Offers automotive engineers the technical information and expertise used in building, maintaining and operating self propelled vehicles for use on land, sea, air or space.

23102 Space Transportation Association
4305 Underwood Street
University Park, MD 20782
703-855-3917
rich@spacetransportation.us;
www.spacetransportation.us

Richard Coleman, President
Ty McCoy, Chairman

Represents the interests of organizations which intend to develop, build, operate and use space transportation vehicles and systems in order to provide reliable, economical, safe and routine access to space for public and private entities.
20 Members
Founded in: 1989

23103 Specialized Carriers and Rigging
5870 Trinity Parkway
Suite 200
Centreville, VA 20120
703-698-0291; *Fax:* 571-722-1698
info@scranet.org; www.scranet.org
Social Media: Facebook, Twitter, LinkedIn

Alan Barnhart, Chairman
Bruce Forster, President
John McTyre, VP
Delynn Burkhalter, Treasurer
Terry Young, Assistant Treasurer

Members are carriers, crane and rigging operators and millwrights engaged in the transport of heavy goods.
1300 Members
Founded in: 1959

23104 Taxicab, Limousine & Paratransit Association
3200 Tower Oaks Boulevard
Suite 220
Rockville, MD 20852
301-984-5700; *Fax:* 301-984-5703
info@tlpa.com; www.tlpa.org

Alfred La Gasse III, CEO
Harold Morgan, Executive VP
Leah New, Manager, Communications
Michelle A Jasper, Manager, Meetings
Ayesha Plaskett, Office Assistant

Members include owners of taxicab, limousine, airport shuttle, paratransit and nonemergency medical transportation fleets.
1107 Members
Founded in: 1917
Mailing list available for rent: 6,000 names at $100 per M

23105 The American Road & Transportation Builders Association
1219 28th Street, N.W.
Washington, DC 20007
202-289-4434
info@artba.org; www.artba.org
Social Media: Facebook, Twitter, LinkedIn, YouTube, Google+

David S. Zachry, Chairman
Bob Alger, Senior Vice Chairman
Matt Cummings, First Vice Chairman
Rob Charter, Vice Chairman At-Large
Tom Hill, Treasurer

National transportation construction trade group.
Founded in: 1902

23106 The Associated General Contractors of America
2300 Wilson Blvd.
Suite 300
Arlington, VA 22201
703-548-3118
800-242-1767; *Fax:* 703-548-3119
info@agc.org; www.agc.org
Social Media: Facebook, Twitter, LinkedIn, YouTube

Charles L. Greco, President
Mark Knight, Senior Vice President
Art Daniel, Vice President
Joseph Stella, Treasurer
Stephen E. Sandherr, CEO

Trade association for the construction industry.
26000 Members
Founded in: 1918

23107 The Association Of American Truckers
P.O. Box 230369
Montgomery, AL 36123-0369
800-426-6221; *Fax:* 334-269-1352
will@americantruckersonline.com;
www.americantruckersonline.com

Provides insurance and other trucking related products for the American Trucking Associations.

23108 The Institute of Navigation
8551 Rixlew Ln.
STE 360
Manassas, VA 20109
703-366-2723; *Fax:* 703-366-2724
membership@ion.org; www.ion.org
Social Media: Facebook, Twitter, LinkedIn, YouTube

Lisa Beaty, Executive Director
Rick Buongiovanni, IT Director
Ken Esthus, Marketing Director

Miriam Lewis, Program/Author Liaison
Megan Andrews, Senior Meeting Manager

Nonprofit professional society dedicated to the advancement of the art and sciece of positioning, radar and navigation.
Founded in: 1945

23109 The Intelligent Transportation Society of America (ITS America)
1100 New Jersey Ave. SE
Suite 850
Washington, DC 20003

202-484-4847
800-374-8472
info@itsa.org; www.itsa.org
Social Media: Facebook, Twitter, LinkedIn, YouTube, Flickr

Jill M. Ingrassia, Chair
Chris Murray, Vice Chair
Dana Christensen, Treasurer
Regina Hopper, President and CEO
Michael Eason, Chief Financial Officer

Organization dedicated to advancing the research, development and design of surface transportation systems.
1200+ Members
Founded in: 1991

23110 The National Customs Brokers & Forwarders Association of America
1200 18th Street, NW
#901
Washington, DC 20036

202-466-0222; *Fax:* 202-466-0226;
www.ncbfaa.org
Social Media: Facebook, Twitter, LinkedIn

Darrell Sekin, Jr., Chairman, Board
Geoffrey Powell, President
Scott E. Larson, Treasurer
William S. App, Jr., Secretary
Amy Magnus, VP

Represents and supports members of the US freight forwarding industry providing education and publications.
970+ Members
Founded in: 1987

23111 The Trucking Industry Defense Association
3601 E. Joppa Road
Baltimore, MD 21234

410-931-8100; *Fax:* 410-931-8111
info@tida.org; www.tida.org
Social Media: LinkedIn

Joel B. Schechter, President
Dana Hoffman, Secretary
William Schrank, General Counsel
Tim Sullivan, Treasurer
Ren,e Theragood, Executive Director

A nonprofit assocation devoted to sharing knowledge and resources for defense of the trucking industry.

23112 Transport Workers Union of America
501 3rd Street NW
9th Floor
Washington, DC 20001

202-719-3900; *Fax:* 202-347-0454;
www.twu.org
Social Media: Facebook, Twitter, Youtube, Flickr

Harry Lombardo, President
John Samuelson, Executive VP
Alex Garcia, Secretary/Treasurer

Chartered by the Congress of Industrial Organizations.
110M Members
ISBN: 0-039865-9 -
Founded in: 1934

23113 Transportation Clubs International
P.O. Box 426
Union, WA 98592

877-858-8627;
www.transportationclubsinternational.com

Members are individuals in all phases of transportation, traffic management and physical distribution.
10M Members

23114 Transportation Institute
5201 Auth Way
Camp Springs, MD 20746-4211

301-423-3335; *Fax:* 301-423-0634
info@trans-inst.org; www.trans-inst.org

James L Henry, Chairman & President
Jerome K Welsch Jr, COO
Robert E Johnston, Executive VP

Members are US flag shipping, towing and dredging companies.
100 Members
Founded in: 1967

23115 Transportation Intermediaries Association
1625 Prince St
Suite 200
Alexandria, VA 22314-2883

703-299-5700
888-910-4747; *Fax:* 703-836-0123
info@tianet.org; www.tianet.org
Social Media: Facebook, Twitter, LinkedIn

Robert Voltmann, President/CEO
Cindy Amos, Dir. Education & Meeting
Nancy O'Liddy, Dir. Policy & TIA Services
Valerie Sumner, Meetings Manager
Roberta Sumner, Meetings Manager

Education and policy organization for North American transportation intermediaries. The only national association representing the interests of all third party transportation service providers. Members include logistics management firms, property brokers, perishable commodities brokers, freight forwarders, intermodal marketers and ocean and air forwarders.
700 Members
Founded in: 1977

23116 Transportation Loss Claim and Security
120 Main Street
Huntington, NY 11743-6906

631-549-8988; *Fax:* 631-549-8962;
www.tlcouncil.org

Reed Tepper, Chairman
Nadia Martin, CCP, President
Phillip Lamb, Secretary/Treasurer
Curtis Hart, Vice President
Kristen Walberg, CCP, Regional Director

A nonprofit trade association dedicated to the prevention of freight loss, damage and delay, the promulgation of reasonable liability rules, laws and claim policies.
660 Members
Founded in: 1974

23117 Transportation Loss Prevention & Security Association
155 Polifly Road
Hackensack, NJ 07601

732-350-3776
eloughman@nakblaw.com; www.tlpsa.org

William D Bierman, Executive Director
Edward M Loughman, Assistant to Executive Director

Originally a combination of the National Freight Claim Council and the Transportation Loss Prevention and Security Council, this independent association supports all persons who have an interest in loss and damage claims and security issues. Members include carriers, shippers, vendors, law enforcement, attorneys, insurance carriers, third-party logistics, etc.
Founded in: 2000

23118 Transportation Research Board
500 Fifth Street NW
Washington, DC 20001

202-334-2934; *Fax:* 202-334-2527
rallen@nas.edu; www.trb.org
Social Media: Facebook, Twitter, LinkedIn

Janet M. McNaughton, Senior Editor
Rosa P Allen, Administrative Coordinator
Cynthia M Baker, Executive Assistant
Anthony T Bailey, Financial Associate
Thomas R. Menzies, Senior Program Officer

23119 Transportation Research Forum
Department 2880
PO Box 6050
Fargo, ND 58108-6050

701-231-7766; *Fax:* 701-231-1945
info@trforum.org; www.trforum.org
Social Media: Facebook, LinkedIn

Pat McCarthy, Executive VP
David Ripplinger, President
P.S. Sriraj, VP, Membership
Marla Westervelt, VP, Public Relations
Joe Schwieterman, VP, Chapter Relations

An independent organization of transportation professionals.
300 Members
Founded in: 1958

23120 Truck Frame and Axle Repair Association
3741 Enterprise Drive SW
Rochester, MN 55902-0122

800-232-8272; *Fax:* 813-626-5385
w.g.reich@att.net; www.taraassociation.com
Social Media: Facebook

Paul Jones, President
Ken Dias, Consultant
Bill Hinchcliffe, Secretary/Treasurer

For operators and owners of heavy duty truck repair facilities, fleet managers, truckers and insurance damage appraisers.
110 Members
Founded in: 1966

23121 Truck Renting and Leasing Corporation
675 N Washington Street
Suite 410
Alexandria, VA 22314

703-299-9120
800-426-1420; *Fax:* 703-299-9115;
www.trala.org

Jack Jacoby, President & CEO
Peter Einisman, Manager of Government Relations
Shannon Davison, Director of Communications & Events
Tonya Gibbs, VP, Finance & Business Operations
Andrew Stasiowski, Director, Govt. Relations

A multi-national technology company, NRLC monitors legislation and other issues affecting the truck/trailer leasing and rental industry. It also manufacturers heavy-duty, on-and-off-road trucks worldwide.
275 Members
Founded in: 1978

23122 Truck Trailer Manufacturers Association
7001 Heritage Village Plaza
Suite 220
Gainesville, VA 20155

703-549-3010; *Fax:* 703-549-3014
ttma@erols.com; www.ttmanet.org

Jeff Sims, President
John Freiler, Engineering Manager
Nancy Livingston, Administration

A national organization of truck and tank trailer manufacturers and 120 suppliers to the industry.
Founded in: 1941

23123 Truck and Heavy Equipment Claims Council
PO Box 5928
Fresno, CA 93755-5928

559-431-3774; *Fax:* 559-436-4755;
www.nthecc.org

Betty Clayton, President
Ed Williams, President Elect
Kelly R. Reich, Past President
Shane Carder, Secretary
Darrell W. Bickley, Treasurer

Repair and manufacturing facilities, insurance companies and adjusters concerned with insuring of heavy equipment and trucks. Promotes safety.
45 Members
Founded in: 1961

23124 Truck-Frame Axle Repair Association
www.taraassociation.com
Social Media: Facebook

Paul Jones, President
Ken Dias, Consultant
Bill Hinchcliffe, Secretary/Treasurer

Association for truck frame and axle repairers.

23125 Trucker Buddy International
3200 Rice Mine Rd
Tuscaloosa, A 35406

05 -48 -261
800-692-8339
info@truckerbuddy.org;
www.truckerbuddy.org
Social Media: Facebook, Twitter

K.C. Brau, President
Elizabeth Barna, Vice President
Brad Williamson, Secretary
Steve Sichterman, Treasurer
Randy Schwartzenburg, Executive Director

A nonprofit organization for educating and mentoring schoolchildren via trucker penpals.
Founded in: 1992

23126 Truckload Carriers Association
555 East Braddock Road
Alexandria, VA 22314-2182

703-838-1950; *Fax:* 703-836-6610
tca@truckload.org; www.truckload.org
Social Media: Facebook, Twitter, LinkedIn, Youtube, Flickr

Russell Stubbs, Chairman
John Lyboldt, President
William Giroux, Executive Vice President
Tomora Brown, Membership Liaison

The Truckload Carriers Association (TCA) represents nearly 700 companies working in and serving the truckload freight industry. Collectively, TCA member companies employ several hundred thousand people across the U.S. and Canada. TCA is the only national trade association whose collective sole focus is thetruckload segment of the motor carrier industry. The association represents dry van, refrigerated, flatbed, and intermodal container carriers across North America and Mexico.
800 Members
Founded in: 1938

23127 United Bus Owners of America
113 S West Street
4th Floor
Alexandria, VA 22314-2824

703-838-8262
800-424-8262; *Fax:* 703-838-2950
info@uma.org; www.uma.org
Social Media: Facebook, Twitter, LinkedIn, Youtube

Victor S Parra, President & CEO
Ken Presley, VP, Industry Relations & COO
Maggie Masterson, Meetings & Operations Director
Terri Tackett, Marketing & Membership Director
Brian Annett, Chairman

Serves the bus industry, with particular emphasis on group travel and tourism.
800 Members
Founded in: 1971

23128 United States Telecom Association
607 14th St Nw
Suite 400
Washington, DC 20005-2000

202-326-7300; *Fax:* 202-315-3603
membership@ustelecom.org;
www.ustelecom.org
Social Media: Facebook, Twitter, LinkedIn, Youtube

Walter B. McCormick, Jr., President/CEO
Robert A. Hunt, Chairman of the Board
Alan J. Roth, Senior Executive Vice President
Mark Kulish, SVP, Admin & CFO
Anne Veigle, SVP, Communications

Trade association representing service provides and suppliers for the telecom industry.
Cost: $699.00

23129 United Truckers Association
9090 FM 1026
Gouldbusk, TX 76845

484-681-9283; *Fax:* 956-425-9350
info@utatruckers.com;
www.unitedtruckersassociation.com

Assocation for truck drivers.
Founded in: 1995

23130 Used Truck Association
325 County Club Drive
Suite A
Stockbridge, GA 30281

817-439-3900
877-438-7882; *Fax:* 817-439-3609
contact@uta.org; www.uta.org
Social Media: Facebook, LinkedIn

Rick Clark, President
Craig Kendall, VP
Angelique Pierce, Secretary
Brock Frederick, Treasurer
Marty Crawford, President Emeritus

Used truck manufacturers and dealerships.
800 Members
Founded in: 1988

23131 Wine and Spirits Shippers Association
11800 Sunrise Valley Dr
Suite 332
Reston, VA 20191-5302

207-805-1664
800-368-3167; *Fax:* 703-860-2422
info@wssa.com; www.wssa.com
Social Media: Facebook, Twitter, LinkedIn, RSS

Alison Leavitt, Managing Director
Gretchen Veevaert, Program Coordinator
Cecilia Borruso, Contract Supervisor/Pricing Analyst
Heather Randolph, Director of Operations
Louis Healey, President

Provides members with services that allow for the efficient and economical transportation of alcoholic beverages.
320 Members
Founded in: 1976

23132 Women's Transportation Seminar: National
1701 K St Nw
Suite 800
Washington, DC 20006-1504

202-955-5085; *Fax:* 202-955-5088
membership@wtsinternational.org;
www.wtsinternational.org
Social Media: Facebook, Twitter, LinkedIn, Pinterest, Instagram

Beverley Swaim-Staley, Chair
Diane Woodend Jones, Vice Chairman
Felicia Boyd, Secretary
Rina Cutler, Treasurer
Marcia Ferranto, President/CEO
5000+ Members
Founded in: 1977

23133 Womens Transportation Seminar
1701 K St Nw
Suite 800
Washington, DC 20006-1504

202-955-5085; *Fax:* 202-955-5088
membership@wtsinternational.org;
www.wtsinternational.org
Social Media: Facebook, Twitter, LinkedIn, Pinterest, Instagram

Beverley Swaim-Staley, Chair
Diane Woodend Jones, Vice Chairman
Felicia Boyd, Secretary
Rina Cutler, Treasurer
Marcia Ferranto, President/CEO
5000+ Members
Founded in: 1977

23134 World Organization of Dredging
Post Office Box 2035
Spotsylvania, VA 22553

619-839-9474; *Fax:* 360-750-1445
tmverna@westerndredging.org; www.woda.org

Anders Jensen, President
Dr A Csiti, General Manager
Rashyan Allays, Secretary
Thomas M. Verna, Executive Director

Develops professionalism in individuals involved in the dredging industry.
2700 Members
Founded in: 1981

Newsletters

23135 ABA Insider
American Bus Association
111 K Street NE
Suite 575
Washington, DC 20005-5923

202-842-1645; *Fax:* 202-842-0850
abainfo@buses.org; www.buses.org

Peter J Pantuso, CEO
Eron Shosteck, Marketing

ABA's biweekly newsletter that keeps members informed on the travel, tourism and motorcoach industry.
Frequency: Biweekly
Founded in: 1926

23136 Advanced Transit News
Advanced Transit Association

PO Box 162
Palo Alto, CA 94302

800-779-0544
800-779-0544; *Fax:* 800-779-0544
jpaskry@davinciglobal.com;
www.advancedtransit.org

Catherine G. Burke, President
Bob Dunning, VP
Lawrence Fabian, Publisher

Offers information on the American transit system.
100 Pages
Frequency: Quarterly
Founded in: 1953
Printed in one color on matte stock

23137 American Trucker
PRIMEDIA Intertec-Technology & Transportation
PO Box 12901
Shawnee Mission, KS 66282-2901

913-341-1300
800-827-7468; *Fax:* 913-514-6895;
www.trucker.com

Eric Jacobson, Senior VP
Coleen Liatch, Supervisor

Information for those interested in the truck industry. Contains articles on new and used trucks, supplies, equipment, financing, pricing, and other truck related services.
Cost: $21.00
Frequency: Monthly
Circulation: 600000
Founded in: 1926

23138 Center for Microcomputers in Transportation
512 Weil Hall
PO Box 116585
Gainesville, FL 32611

352-392-7575
800-226-1013; *Fax:* 352-389-2324
mctrans@ce.ufl.edu; www.mctrans.ce.ufl.edu

Mark Newman, Associate Director
Max Crumit, Executive Vice President
Kirk Hatfield, Director
Founded in: 1986

23139 Dispatch & Division Newsletters
Taxicab, Limousine & Paratransit Association
3200 Tower Oaks Blvd
Suite 220
Rockville, MD 20852

301-984-5700; *Fax:* 301-984-5703
info@tlpa.org; www.tlpa.org

Alfred LaGasse, CEO
Victor Dizengoff, President

Dispatch features articles on industry business issues, provides advice on running a transportation company, and comes with division specific bi-monthly newsletters.
Frequency: Bimonthly
Circulation: 6000

23140 Dual News
Driving School Association of America
11 W Pomona Boulevard
Monterey Park, CA 91754

Fax: 626-722-0485

George Hensel, Publisher

Association news for student driving instructors and educational personnel.
Frequency: BiWeekly
Circulation: 5,000

23141 Fleet Street
Greenwich Consulting
15821 Fetlock Lane
Chino Hills, CA 91709

909-606-2271; *Fax:* 909-597-7759

Karen Edward, Publisher

Consulting newsletter geared toward Distribution and Fleet Management Executives - Provides transportation managers with cost-cutting methodogies.
Circulation: 15500

23142 HazMat Transport News
Business Publishers
8737 Colesville Road
Suite 1100
Silver Spring, MD 20910-3925

301-876-6300
800-274-6737; *Fax:* 301-587-4530
custserv@bpinews.com; www.bpinews.com

Leonard A Eiserer, Publisher
Beth Early, Operations Director

Regulatory and legislative development affecting hazardous materials transportation. In-depth coverage on research and special programs administration, hazmat regulation programs and enforcement actions.
Cost: $447.00
Founded in: 1963

23143 Inside DOT and Transportation Week
King of Communications Group
1325 Massachusetts Ave Nw
Suite 310
Washington, DC 20005-4194

240-455-6801
800-926-5464; *Fax:* 240-628-5774;
www.king-com.com

F King, President
Dave Ahearn, Editor
Wenita Lhill-waddell, Marketing
Linda Gasparello, General Manager

Offers information to persons working in the transportation profession.
Cost: $1300.00
12 Pages
Frequency: Daily
Founded in: 1973
Printed in one color on newsprint stock

23144 Interstate Information Report
Express Carriers Association
9532 Liberia Avenue,
Suite 130
Manassas, VA 20190-3233

703-361-1058
866-322-7447; *Fax:* 704-435-4390
eca@expresscarriers.com;
www.expresscarriers.com

Carrie Ehlers, President
Stuart Hyden, First Vice President

Compilation of newly enacted state legislation regulations having direct impact on vehicle operations, fuel taxes, registration size and weight.

23145 Legislative Alert
Taxicab, Limousine & Paratransit Association
3200 Tower Oaks Blvd
Suite 220
Rockville, MD 20852

301-984-5700; *Fax:* 301-984-5703
info@tlpa.org; www.tlpa.org

Alfred LaGasse, CEO
Victor Dizengoff, President

TLPA's members-only bulletin of early alerts to critical changes in the industry, announcing threats and opportunities on issues that are before Congress and federal agencies. Organizes operators to take action, and provides knowledge and awareness.
Circulation: 6000

23146 McTrans
Center for Microcomputers in Transportation
512 Weil Hall
PO Box 116585
Gainesville, FL 32611

352-392-7575
800-226-1013; *Fax:* 352-389-2324
mctrans@ce.ufl.edu; www.mctrans.ce.ufl.edu

CE Wallace, Publisher
Mark Newman, Associate Director
Max Crumit, Executive Vice President
Kirk Hatfield, Director

Information about microcomputer software and resources in transportation.
Circulation: 8,000
Founded in: 1986

23147 Owner Operator News
PO Box 582
Orchard Park, NY 14127-0582

Fax: 716-941-5582

Charles DeVaul, Publisher

Trucking news and information.
Frequency: Monthly

23148 Passenger Transport
American Public Transit Association
1666 K St Nw
Suite 1100
Washington, DC 20006-1215

202-496-4800; *Fax:* 202-496-4324
hbrett@apta.com; www.apta.com

Karol J Popkin, CEO
Petra Mollet, VP
Rosemary Sherid, Marketing

Information on federal legislative, administrative and regulatory developments, management and operations, new technology, and state and local developments in public transit.
Cost: $75.00
Frequency: B-Weekly
Circulation: 5000
Founded in: 1882

23149 Proclaim
Slesia Companies
619 Broad Creek Dr
Fort Washington, MD 20744-5800

301-292-1970; *Fax:* 301-292-1787
silesia-aroma.com

Dale L Anderson, President

Covers transportation freight claims.
Frequency: Monthly

23150 Rider's Digest
Metropolitan Atlanta Road Transit
2424 Piedmont Rd Ne
Atlanta, GA 30324-3311

404-848-5000; *Fax:* 404-848-5098
schedinfo@itsmarta.com; www.itsmarta.com

Nathaniel P Ford Sr, CEO

Public transportation news.
Frequency: Monthly

23151 TransitPulse
Trans 21
55 Virginia St
Dorchester, MA 02125-2352

617-825-9687; *Fax:* 617-482-7417

Lawrence J Fabin, Publisher

Newsletters and faxed advisory service on worldwide developments in Automated People

Movers.
Cost: $75.00
4 Pages
Frequency: BiMonthly
Circulation: 500
Printed in one color on matte stock

23152 Transport Workers Union of America
Transport Workers Union of America
1700 Broadway
Suite 2
New York, NY 10019-5905

212-259-4900; *Fax:* 202-347-0454
mailbox@twu.org; www.twu.org

James Little, President
David Rosen, General Counsel
Alex Garcia, Director

Chartered by the Congress of Industrial Organizations.
Frequency: Monthly
ISBN: 0-039865-9 -
Founded in: 1934

23153 Transportation Intermediaries Update
Transportation Intermediaries Association
1625 Prince St
Suite 200
Alexandria, VA 22314-2883

703-299-5700; *Fax:* 703-836-0123
voltmann@tianet.org; www.tianet.org

Robert Voltmann, President

Education and policy organization for North American transportation intermediaries. TIA is the only national association representing the interests of all third party transportation service providers. The members of TIA include logistics management firms, property brokers, perishable commodities brokers, freight forwarders, intermodal marketers, ocean and air forwarders, and NVOCC's.
700 Pages
Frequency: Monthly

23154 Truck Equipment News
National Truck Equipment Association
37400 Hills Tech Dr
Farmington Hill, MI 48331-3414

248-489-7090
800-441-6832; *Fax:* 248-489-8590
info@ntea.com; www.ntea.com

James Carney, Executive Director
Dennis Jones, First Vice President

Covers NTEA and member/industry activities, business management issues, technical topics, excise tax applications, sales/marketing management topics, legislative and regulatory news, monthly new truck retail sales figures, NTEA/industry events calendar, and other current topics of interest to industry members.
Cost: $72.00
150 Pages
Frequency: Monthly
Circulation: 1600
Founded in: 1964

23155 Trucker Publications
Trucker Publications
PO Box 3413
Little Rock, AR 72203-3413

501-666-0500; *Fax:* 501-666-0700;
www.thetrucker.com

Ray Wittenberg, Publisher

Up to date, comprehensive coverage of news affecting both drivers and management, including regulatory issues, road conditions, fuel, and current trends in technology.
Cost: $21.50
Frequency: BiWeekly
Circulation: 27,500

23156 Truckload Authority
Truckload Carriers Association
555 East Braddock Road
Suite CS-4
Alexandria, VA 22314-2182
703-838-1950; *Fax:* 703-836-6610
tca@truckload.org; www.truckload.org
Social Media: Facebook, Twitter, LinkedIn

Chris Burruss, President
Deborah Sparks, VP
Gary Salisbury, Chairman

Offers industry insights for truckload carrier executives.
850 Members
Frequency: Monthly
Founded in: 1938

23157 Truckload Carriers Report
Truckload Carriers Association
555 E Braddock Road
Suite CS-4
Alexandria, VA 22314-2182

703-838-1950; *Fax:* 703-836-6610
tca@truckload.org; www.truckload.org

John Lyboldt, President
William Giroux, Executive Vice President
Russell Stubbs, Chairman
Bianca Gibson, Executive Editor

A newsletter for truckload carriers executives. Free to association members.
Frequency: Weekly
Founded in: 1938
Mailing list available for rent

23158 US Rail News
Business Publishers
222 Sedwick Dr
Suite 101
Durham, NC 27713

800-223-8720; *Fax:* 800-508-2592
custserv@bpinews.com; www.bpinews.com

Reports on the trends, legislation, regulations, acquisitions, business opportunities and technological developments that directly affect the rail industry.
Cost: $437.00
Frequency: 25 per year
Founded in: 1963

23159 Urban Transport News
Business Publishers
8737 Colesville Road
Suite 1100
Silver Spring, MD 20910-3928

301-876-6300
800-274-6737; *Fax:* 301-587-4530
custserv@bpinews.com; www.bpinews.com

Leonard A Eiserer, Publisher
Beth Early, Operations Director

Comprehensive briefings on trends, regulations, legislation, business and technological developments in the mass transit area.
Cost: $437.00
Founded in: 1963

Magazines & Journals

23160 Air Medical Journal
526 King Street
Suite 415
Alexandria, VA 22314-3143

703-836-8732
800-525-3712; *Fax:* 703-836-8920
information@aams.org; www.aams.org

Renee Holleran, Editor
Dawn M Mancuso, Director
John Fiegel, Director

An association of health care entities operating helicopter transport services. Magazine is published, price included in membership.
375 Pages
Founded in: 1980
Printed in on glossy stock

23161 American Journal of Transportation
Fleur de Lis Publishing
1354 Hancock Street
Suite 300
Quincy, MA 02169

617-328-5005
800-599-6358; *Fax:* 617-328-5999
editorial@ajot.com; www.ajot.com/

George Lauriat, Editor
Ann Radwan, Associate Editor
William Bourbon, Publisher
Bob Kirk, Production Manager
Kristen Davis, Graphic Designer

Newspaper serving the shipping, trucking, air freight and railroad industries in the US and Canada.
Cost: $98.00
Frequency: Weekly
Circulation: 8115
ISSN: 1529-1820
Founded in: 1994
Printed in on newsprint stock

23162 American Mover
American Movers Conference
1611 Duke St
Alexandria, VA 22314-3406

703-683-7410; *Fax:* 703-683-7527
info@moving.org; www.moving.org

Linda Bauer Darr, CEO
Joseph M Harrison, President
Carol Laird, Production Manager
Norma Gyovai, Advertising Manager

This publication covers the moving and storage industry.
Cost: $60.00
24 Pages
Frequency: Monthly
Circulation: 3700
Founded in: 1958

23163 American Shipper
Howard Publications
300 W Adams Street Suite 600
PO Box 4728
Jacksonville, FL 32201-4728

904-355-2601
800-874-6422; *Fax:* 904-791-8836;
www.americanshipper.com

Nancy Barry, Production Manager
Hayes Howard, Publisher
Kerry Cowart, Circulation Manager
James Blaeser, Sales Associate

Provides those involved in domestic and global supply chain management with news and information of a strategic nature, useful in the formation of logistics polices and partnerships.
Cost: $36.00
104 Pages
Frequency: Monthly
Circulation: 13705
ISSN: 1074-8350
Founded in: 1951
Printed in 4 colors on glossy stock

23164 American Trucker
Primedia
7355 Woodland Drive
Indianapolis, IN 46278-1769

317-991-1350
800-827-7468; *Fax:* 317-299-1356;
www.trucker.com

Dallas Nauert, Production Manager
Diana Starks, Circulation Director

A trade publication featuring new and used trucks, trailors,parts and services for the heavy duty trucking industry.
Cost: $21.00
Frequency: Monthly
Circulation: 930338
Founded in: 1975
Printed in 4 colors on matte stock

23165 Analysis of Class I Railroads
Association of American Railroads
425 Third Street SW
Suite 1144
Washington, DC 20024-3217
202-639-2100
media@aar.org; www.aar.org
Social Media: Facebook, Twitter, LinkedIn
Edward R. Hamberger, President & CEO
Tom White, Editor
Patricia M. Reilly, SVP, Communications
Offers information on the railroad travel industry.
Cost: $400.00
Frequency: Annual
Founded in: 1934

23166 Atlantic Northeast Rails & Ports
162 main street
Yarmouth, ME 04096
207-846-3549; *Fax:* 603-215-4482;
www.atlanticnortheast.com
Chop Hardenbergh, CEO/President
Cost: $375.00
Frequency: Monthly
Circulation: 300
Founded in: 1994

23167 Better Roads
WMO DannHausen Corporation
PO Box 558
Park Ridge, IL 60068
847-696-2391; *Fax:* 847-696-3445
Wm O Dannhausen, Publisher
Market to federal agencies, bureaus, government departments, states, counties township road and city public works.
Cost: $26.96
Frequency: Monthly
Circulation: 38406
Founded in: 1769

23168 Brotherhood of Locomotive Engineers
Brotherhood of Locomotive Engineers
1370 Ontario St
Cleveland, OH 44113-1701
216-241-2630; *Fax:* 216-241-6516
policy@ble.org; www.ble.org
Ed Rodzwicz, CEO
John Bentley, Editor

23169 Bus Conversions Magazine
MAK Publishing
7246 Garden Grove Boulevard
Westminster, CA 92683
714-799-0062; *Fax:* 714-799-0042
editor@busconversions.com;
www.busconversions.com
Michael A Kadletz, Publisher
Rikki Gee, Publication Manager
how-to, full color, monthly magazine that includes photos, floor plans, helpful hints and guides for buying, selling, selecting, and converting a bus to an RV or executive entertainer's coach. Features pages of classified ads and valuable info on maintaining, operating and updating your coach.
Cost: $38.00
72 Pages
Circulation: 8000
ISSN: 1070-6526
Founded in: 1992
Printed in 4 colors on glossy stock

23170 Bus Ride
Friendship Publications
4742 N 24th St
Suite 340
Phoenix, AZ 85016-4884
602-265-7600
800-541-2670; *Fax:* 602-277-7588
steve@busride.com; www.busride.com
Steve Kane, Publisher/Editor-in-Chief
Wayne Bryan, Editor
Donna Arnseth, Circulation Administrator
Maria Jolly, Assistant Editor
Valerie Valtierra, Production Director
Bus industry trade journal with articles about bus companies, training agencies and manufacturers and suppliers to the bus industry.
Cost: $39.00
120 Pages
Frequency: Monthly
Circulation: 16000
Founded in: 1965
Printed in 4 colors on glossy stock

23171 Chief Logistics Officer
Penton Media
1166 Avenue of the Americas/10th
Suite 316
Cleveland, NY 10036
212-204-4200; *Fax:* 216-696-6662
information@penton.com; www.penton.com
Jane Cooper, Marketing
Perry A Trunick, Editor
Maryann Jovorek, Production Manager
Chris Meyer, Director
Magazine for supply chain leaders, supplement to Transportation and Distribution.
Cost: $50.00
48 Pages
Frequency: Quarterly
Circulation: 12M
Founded in: 1960
Printed in 4 colors on glossy stock

23172 Classic Trains
James Folcum
21027 Crossroads Circle
Waukesha, WI 53187
262-796-8776; *Fax:* 262-796-1615;
www.classictrain.com
Rob McGornigal, Editor
Mike Yuhaf, Advertising Manager
Publication features stories on antique and old trains.

23173 Commercial Carrier Journal
Randall-Reilly
3200 Rice Mine Road NE
Tuscaloosa, AL 35406
800-633-5953; *Fax:* 610-964-4647;
www.ccjdigital.com
Jeff Crissey, Editor
Covering fleet management topics from technology to equipment.
Frequency: Monthly
Circulation: 96500
Founded in: 1934

23174 Contracting for Transportation & Logistics Services
120 Main Street
Huntington, NY 11743-6906
631-270-0100; *Fax:* 516-549-8962
tcpc@transportlaw.com;
www.transportlaw.com
William J Augello, Executive Director
Published by the Transportation Consumer Protection Council.
Cost: $48.00
Founded in: 2001

23175 Corporate Procedures for Shipping & Receiving
120 Main Street
Huntington, NY 11743-6906
631-270-0100; *Fax:* 516-549-8962
tcpc@transportlaw.com;
www.transportlaw.com
William J Augello, Executive Director
Published by the Transportation Consumer Protection Council.
Cost: $95.00
Founded in: 1998

23176 Defense Transportation Journal
National Defense Transportation Association
50 S Pickett Street
Suite 220
Alexandria, VA 22304-7206
703-751-5011; *Fax:* 703-823-8761
info@ndtahq.com; www.ndtahq.com
LTG Kenneth Wykle, President
Karen Schmitt, Managing Editor
The official publication of the National Defense Transportation Association and the only publication for the government and military transportation industry.
Cost: $35.00
Frequency: Bi-Monthly
Circulation: 8500

23177 Destinations
American Bus Association
700 13th St NW
Suite 575
Washington, DC 20005-5923
202-842-1645
800-283-2877; *Fax:* 202-842-0850
abainfo@buses.org; www.buses.org
Peter J Pantuso, CEO
Eron Shosteck, Marketing
Motorcoach travel across North America and Association news.
80 Pages
Frequency: Monthly
Circulation: 6000
Founded in: 1926
Printed in 4 colors on glossy stock

23178 Diesel Equipment Superintendent
Business Journals
50 Day Street
Norwalk, CT 06854-3100
203-853-6015; *Fax:* 203-852-8175
James Jones, Editor
Maintenance management in areas of selection, of heavy duty trucks and trailers.
Cost: $25.00
100 Pages
Frequency: Monthly
Founded in: 1923

23179 Digest
American Bus Association
700 13th St NW
Suite 575
Washington, DC 20005-5923
202-842-1645
800-283-2877; *Fax:* 202-842-0850
abainfo@buses.org; www.buses.org
Peter J Pantuso, CEO
Judi Bredemeier, Editor
Chrystal Farmer, Marketing Manager
Michael Hayes, Publisher

Legislation news.
Cost: $150.00
Circulation: 3200
Founded in: 1996
Printed in 2 colors on matte stock

23180 Direction
American Moving and Storage Association
1611 Duke St
Alexandria, VA 22314-3406

703-683-7410; *Fax:* 703-683-7527;
www.moving.org

Matthew Hicks, Advertising
John Parkinson, Editorial
Allison Bresky, Production

Provides news and in-depth feature articles to provide members with vital information to help operate their companies more profitably.
Cost: $35.00
Frequency: Bi-Monthly
Circulation: 4000

23181 Fastline Catalog
Fastline Media Group
4900 Fox Run Road
P.O. Box 248
Buckner, KY 40010-0248

502-222-0146
800-626-6409; *Fax:* 502-222-0615;
www.fastline.com
Social Media: Facebook, Twitter

William Howard, Editor
Susan Arterburn, Marketing Director
Pat Higgins, Vice President, Sales

Nationwide and regional picture buying guides for the trucking industry.
Frequency: Monthly
Founded in: 1978

23182 Fleet Equipment Magazine
Maple Publishing Company
3550 Embassy Parkway
Akron, OH 44333-8318

330-670-1234; *Fax:* 330-670-0874;
www.truklink.com

Tom Gelinas, Editor
Bill Babcox, President
Robert Dorn, Publisher
Kelly McAleese, Ad Services Manager
Lindsey Fritz, Circulation Manager

Edited for fleet equipment managers of truck fleets.
Cost: $82.00
Frequency: Monthly
Circulation: 61,571
Founded in: 1974

23183 Fleet Owner Magazine
Primedia
11 River Bend Drive South
PO Box 4949
Stamford, CT 06907-949

203-358-9900; *Fax:* 203-358-5811
frcs@pbsub.com; www.fleetowner.com

Thomas Duncan, Vice President
Jim Mele, Editor-in-Chief
David Cullen, Executive Editor

Monthly business magazine serving executives and managers in commercial trucking fleets.
Cost: $40.00
Frequency: Monthly
Founded in: 1928

23184 Freight Claims in Plain English
120 Main Street
Huntington, NY 11743-6906

631-270-0100; *Fax:* 516-549-8962
tcpc@transportlaw.com;
www.transportlaw.com

William J Augello, Executive Director

Published by the Transportation Consumer Protection Council.
Cost: $100.00
Founded in: 1995

23185 Freight Claims: Filing & Recovery
120 Main Street
Huntington, NY 11743-6906

631-270-0100; *Fax:* 516-549-8962
tcpc@transportlaw.com;
www.transportlaw.com

William J Augello, Executive Director

Published by the Transportation Consumer Protection Council.
Cost: $48.00
Founded in: 2001

23186 Go-West Magazine
Motor Transport Management Group
3251 Beacon Road
West Sacramento, CA 95691-3475

916-373-3630; *Fax:* 916-852-5707

Jim Beach, Editor

Complete overview of the transportation industry.
Frequency: Monthly

23187 Guide to Transportation After the Sunsetting of the ICC
120 Main Street
Huntington, NY 11743-6906
631-270-0100; *Fax:* 516-549-8962
tcpc@transportlaw.com;
www.transportlaw.com

William J Augello, Executive Director

Published by the Transportation Consumer Protection Council.
Cost: $75.00
Founded in: 1997

23188 Heavy Duty Trucking
Newport Communications
38 Executive Park
Suite 300
Irvine, CA 92614-6755

949-261-1636; *Fax:* 949-261-2904
webmaster@truckinginfo.com;
www.truckinginfo.com

Doug Condra, President
Susan Condra, Circulation Manager
Susan Patterson, Marketing
Marty Mc Collan, Publisher

National business magazine for managers of medium and heavy duty truck fleets, and manufacturers and dealers of those trucks and the components used to build them.
Cost: $65.00
Frequency: Monthly
Circulation: 90000
Founded in: 1922
Printed in 4 colors on glossy stock

23189 Hemispheres
Pace Communications
PO Box 13607
Greensboro, NC 27415-3607

336-378-6065
800-346-1336; *Fax:* 336-275-2864;
www.pacecommunications.com

Bonnie McElveen, CEO
Leigh Klee, Chief Financial Officer
Ed Calfo, Executive Vice President

Children's magazine for US airline fliers.
Frequency: Monthly
Circulation: 60000
Founded in: 1973

23190 High Performance Composites
Ray Publishing
P.O.Box 992
Morrison, CO 80465-0992

303-467-1776; *Fax:* 303-467-1777;
www.compositeworld.com

Approach is technical, offering cutting-edge design, engineering, prototyping, and manufacturing solutions for aerospace and other traditional and emerging structural applications for advanced composites.

23191 ITE Journal
Institute of Transportation Engineers
1099 14th St NW
Suite 300E
Washington, DC 20005-5924

202-289-0222; *Fax:* 202-289-7722
ite_staff@ite.org; www.it.org

Thomas Brahms, CEO
Shannon Gore Peters, Editor
Christina Denekas, Circulation Manager
Richard T Romer, International President

Provides timely news and information on subjects of interest to professionals responsible for traffic engineering, transportation planning, ITS, transit, safety, demand management, education etc.
Cost: $100.00
300 Pages
Frequency: Monthly
Circulation: 7500
Founded in: 1930

23192 Inbound Logistics Magazine
Thomas Publishing Company
5 Penn Plaza
New York, NY 10001-1810

212-950-0500; *Fax:* 212-629-1565
editor@inboundlogistics.com;
www.inboundlogistics.com

Keith Biondo, Publisher
Felecia Stratton, Editor
Carolyn Smolin, Circulation Manager
Robert Malone, Executive Editor

Accepts advertising.
Frequency: Monthly
Circulation: 55050
Founded in: 1981

23193 Institute of Transportation Engineering Journal
Institute of Transportation Engineering
1627 Eye St. NW
Suite 600
Washington, DC 20006

202-785-0060; *Fax:* 202-785-0609
ite_staff@ite.org; www.ite.org

Thomas Brahms, CEO
Christina Denekas, Marketing Manager
Marianne Saglam, Communications & Media Sr. Director

Dedicated to the transportation engineering field. A journal is published for members only.
Cost: $65.00
Frequency: Monthly
Circulation: 17000
Founded in: 1930

23194 International Rail Journal
Simmons-Boardman Publishing Corporation
345 Hudson St
Suite 1201
New York, NY 10014-7123

212-620-7200; *Fax:* 212-633-1165
db@railjournal.co.uk;
www.simmonsboardman.com

Arthur J McGinnis Jr, President

Covers the rapidly developing railway marketplace for railway and rail transit managers and engineers, suppliers and consultants worldwide.
Frequency: Monthly
Circulation: 100960
Founded in: 1960

23195 Journal of HazMat Transportation
Packaging Research International
404 Price St
West Chester, PA 19382-3531

610-436-8292
877-429-7447; *Fax:* 610-436-9422;
www.hazmatship.com

Vincent A Vitollo, Owner

A professionally prepared technical reporting system, focused exlusively on explaining changes to the hazardous materials transportation regulations. Thoroughly covers and provides technical reviews of the US 49CFR, International Civil Aviation Organization Technical Instructions, the International Maritime Dangerous Goods Code, and the European Road and Rail Regulations.
Cost: $209.00
Circulation: 1000
Founded in: 1990
Printed in 4 colors on matte stock

23196 Journal of the Transportation Research Forum
Transportation Research Forum
Department 2880
PO Box 6050
Fargo, ND 58108-6050

701-231-7766; *Fax:* 701-231-1945
info@trforum.org; www.trforum.org

Richard Gritta, President
Starr McMullen, VP

Contains original manuscripts which are timely in scope and germane to transportation
300 Members
Frequency: 3x/Year
Founded in: 1958

23197 Keep on Truckin' News
Mid-West Truckers Association
2727 N Dirksen Pkwy
Springfield, IL 62702-1490

217-525-0310; *Fax:* 217-525-0342
info@mid-westtruckers.com;
www.trucknews.com

Don Schaefer, President

For members of Mid-West Association.
64 Pages
Frequency: Monthly
Circulation: 4000
Founded in: 1964
Printed in 4 colors on glossy stock

23198 Land Line Magazine
1 NW OOIDA Drive
Grain Valley, MO 64029-712

816-229-5791
800-444-5791; *Fax:* 816-443-2227
info@landlinemag.com;
www.landlinemag.com

Todd Spencer, Editor-in-Chief
Sandi Soendker, Publisher
Jim Johnson, CEO/President
Mike Schermoly, Marketing
Pam Perry, Circulation Manager

Edited for the owner/operator and independent trucker and small fleet operator who drive heavy duty trucks.
13 Pages
Frequency: Monthly
Circulation: 200000+
Founded in: 1973
Printed in 4 colors on glossy stock

23199 Light & Medium Truck
TT Publishing
2200 Mill Road
Alexandria, VA 22314-4654

703-838-1770; *Fax:* 703-548-3662
bharmon@trucking.org; www.ttnews.com

Bruce Harmon, Managing Editor
Debra Devine, Production Coordinator
Stanford Erickson, Associate Publisher
Scott Smith, Circulation Manager
Paul Rosenthal, Marketing Manager

Provides information for day to day management of a company using light to medium duty trucks, such as equipment safety, alternative fuels, maintenance and government regulations.
Frequency: Monthly
Circulation: 50509
Founded in: 1945

23200 Locomotive Engineers Journal
Brotherhood of Locomotive Engineers
1370 Ontario St
Standard Building
Cleveland, OH 44113-1701

216-241-2630; *Fax:* 216-241-6516
execstaff@ble.org; www.ble.org

Ed Rodzwicz, CEO
Kathleen Policy, Associate Editor
Don M Hahs, President

Designed to meet the information needs of professional engineers throughout North America, also for railroad enthusiasts.
Cost: $10.00
Frequency: Quarterly
Circulation: 54000
Founded in: 1863

23201 Logistics Management & Distribution Report
Reed Business Information
225 Wyman St
Suite 3
Waltham, MA 02451-1216

781-734-8000
800-662-7776; *Fax:* 781-734-8076
lm@reedbusiness.com; www.reedbusiness.com

Mark Finklestein, President
Peter Bradley, CFO
Stuart Whayman, CFO

Logistics Management and Distribution Report is written for managers and professionals in charge of traffic, transportation, purchasing, inventory control, containerization and warehousing the functions of physical distribution and business logistics. Covers marketing and operating strategies, cost reduction opportunities and governmental regulation and law.
Frequency: Monthly
Circulation: 30,000
Founded in: 1977

23202 Marine Digest & Transportation News
Marine Publishing
1710 South Norman Street
Seattle, WA 98144-1234

206-709-1840; *Fax:* 206-324-8939;
www.marinedigest.com

Peter Hurme, Publisher/Senior Editor
Gary Greenewald, Circulation Manager
Tom Henning, Sales/Marketing Manager
M Daigle, Owner

Serves the maritime shipping community primarily in the western United States. Updates on new products, suppliers, legislation and insurance are featured.
Cost: $28.00
Frequency: Monthly
Circulation: 7200
Founded in: 1922

23203 Mass Transit Magazine
Cygnus Publishing
PO Box 803
Fort Atkinson, WI 53538-0803

920-000-1111; *Fax:* 920-563-1699;
www.cygnusb2b.com

John French, CEO
Carie Grall, Associate Publisher
Paul Bowers, Group VP
Debbie Dumke, Manager
Deb Krause, National Accounts Manager
Cost: $120.00
Frequency: Monthly
Founded in: 1966

23204 Mid-West Truck Trader
Heartland Communications
15400 Knoll #500
Dallas, TX 75248

800-247-2000; *Fax:* 515-574-2213

Bruce Foval, Editor

Trucking industry news and views.
Cost: $59.00
56 Pages
Frequency: Monthly
Founded in: 1976

23205 Milk & Liquid Food Transporter
Brady Company
N80w12878 Fond Du Lac Ave
Menomonee Falls, WI 53051-4410

262-255-0100; *Fax:* 262-255-3388;
www.bradycorp.com

Kathy Wall, President

Information for owners, operators and managers of companies that haul milk or other liquid foods in sanitary or food grade tankers. Publication covers maintenance, association news, state of the industry, business management, and activities of independent haulers.
Cost: $12.00
Frequency: Monthly
Circulation: 4,100

23206 Modern Bulk Transporter
Tunnell Publications
PO Box 66010
Houston, TX 77266

713-523-8124; *Fax:* 713-523-8384

Charles Wilson, Editor
Robin Anderson, Advertising Director

Serves the truck industry that transports petroleum and petroleum products. Accepts advertising.
Cost: $25.00
Frequency: Monthly

23207 Movers News
New York State Movers & Warehousemen's Association
125 Maiden Lane
11th Floor
New York, NY 10038

212-635-0510; *Fax:* 212-635-0511
nymovers@msn.com;
www.movernet.com/nysmwa

David Blake, Editor
John Palisand, President

Association news.
Cost: $24.00
Frequency: BiMonthly
ISSN: 8750-1155
Founded in: 1937

23208 NATSO Truckers News
Newport Communications

PO Box W
Newport Beach, CA 92658-8910

949-261-1636; *Fax:* 949-261-2904;
www.heavytruck.com

W Dewey Clower, Publisher

Provides industry news, legislation affecting drivers, product developments, and on road service.
Cost: $20.00
Frequency: Monthly
Circulation: 182,716

23209 National Bus Trader
National Bus Trader
9698 W Judson Rd
Polo, IL 61064-9015

815-946-2341; *Fax:* 815-946-2347;
www.busmag.com

Larry Plachno, CEO

Equipment magazine for over-the-road and integral buses in the United States and Canada.
Cost: $25.00
Frequency: Monthly
Circulation: 7000
ISSN: 0194-939X
Founded in: 1977
Printed in on glossy stock

23210 New Equipment Digest
Penton Media
1166 Avenue of the Americas/10th
Suite 316
New York, NY 10036

212-204-4200; *Fax:* 216-696-6662
information@penton.com; www.penton.com

Jane Cooper, Marketing
Tom Sockel, Associate Editor
Robert King, Editor
Sarah Hughes, Production Manager
Bobbie Macy, Circulation Manager

Serves the general industrial field which includes manufacturing, processing, engineering services, construction, transportation, mining, public utilities, wholesale distributors, educational services, libraries and governmental establishments.
Frequency: Monthly
Circulation: 206154
Founded in: 1936

23211 Newport's Road Star
Newport Communications
38 Executive Park
Suite 300
Irvine, CA 92614-6755

949-261-1636
800-233-1911; *Fax:* 949-261-2904
ssturgess@truckinginfo.com;
www.truckinginfo.com

Doug Condra, President
Faye Solem, Circulation Manager
Steve Sturgess, Editor

Monthly magazine for professional long-distance tractor-trailer drivers, who either own their own trucks or drive for trucking companies.
Frequency: Monthly
Circulation: 153000
Founded in: 1898

23212 Oklahoma Motor Carrier
Okalhoma Trucking Association
7201 N Classen Boulevard
Suite 106
Oklahoma City, OK 73116-620

405-843-9488
800-368-9576; *Fax:* 405-843-7310;
www.oktrucking.org

Dan Case, Executive Director
Craig Schneithorst, Chairman

Official publication of Associated Motor Carriers of Oklahoma, the state trade association for the trucking industry.
30 Pages
Frequency: Quarterly
Circulation: 3000
Founded in: 1932
Printed in 4 colors

23213 Over the Road
Ramp Publishing Group
PO Box 549
Roswell, GA 30077

770-587-0311; *Fax:* 770-642-8874;
www.ramppub.com

Marvin Shefsky, Publisher

Information for professional truck drivers, owners, operators, and fleet drivers on current events, industry news, driver profiles, and employment opportunities.
Cost: $30.00
Frequency: Monthly
Circulation: 116624

23214 Overdrive Magazine
Randall Publishing Company
PO Box 2155
Tuscaloosa, AL 35403-2155

205-758-2585
800-633-5953; *Fax:* 205-758-2593
editors@overdriveonline.com;
www.randallpub.com

Wayne Randall, President
Brad Holthaus, Publisher
Linda Longton, Editor

For the owner/operator and small fleet operator.
Cost: $30.00
Frequency: Monthly
Circulation: 104753
Founded in: 1934
Printed in 4 colors on glossy stock

23215 Owner Operator
Reed Business Information
2000 Clearwater Dr
Oak Brook, IL 60523-8809

630-574-0825; *Fax:* 630-288-8781;
www.reedbusiness.com

Jeff Greisch, President

For independent truckers and small fleet owners.
Frequency: Monthly

23216 P&D Magazine
Motor Transport Management Group
3251 Beacon Road
West Sacramento, CA 95691-3475

916-373-3630; *Fax:* 916-852-5707

Robert L Titus, Publisher

Edited for the needs of pick up and delivery.
Cost: $5.00
Circulation: 33,571

23217 PC-Trans
University of Kansas
2011 Learned Hall
Lawrence, KS 66044-7526

785-864-2700; *Fax:* 785-864-5655
mgivechi@ku.edu; www.ku.edu

Lisa Harris, Editor
Mehrdad Givechi, Manager
Alice Kuo, Advertising
Pat Weaver, Director

Software reviews and miscellaneous computer information for transportation professionals.
Circulation: 13000
Founded in: 1872

23218 Pro Trucker
Ramp Publishing Group
PO Box 549
Roswell, GA 30077-549
770-587-0311
800-878-0311; *Fax:* 770-642-8874;
www.protruckeronline.com

Greg McClendon, Sales Manager
Marvin Shefsky, Publisher

Professional truck drivers, owners, operators, and fleet drivers, information on interviews, industry news, employment information, distribution locations and leasing options for the professional drivers.
Frequency: Monthly
Circulation: 116000
Founded in: 1981

23219 Progressive Railroading
Trade Press Publishing Corporation
PO Box 694
Milwaukee, WI 53201-694

414-271-5011; *Fax:* 414-228-1134;
www.facilities.com

Steve Bolte, Publisher
Pat Foran, Editor
Tim Rowe, Marketing
Wendy Melnick, Production Manager
Robert J Wisniewski, CEO

Feature includes management techniques, purchasing developments, engineering innovations and general industry news.
Cost: $55.00
Frequency: Monthly
Circulation: 25,207
Founded in: 1994

23220 Protecting Shippers' Interests
120 Main Street
Huntington, NY 11743-6906

631-270-0100; *Fax:* 516-549-8962
tcpc@transportlaw.com;
www.transportlaw.com

William J Augello, Executive Director

Published by the Transportation Consumer Protection Council.
Cost: $75.00
Founded in: 1997

23221 RV Business
TL Enterprises
3601 Calle Tecate
Camarillo, CA 93012-5056

805-987-1800; *Fax:* 805-389-0484
tlecs@magserv.com; www.rvbusiness.com

Katherine Sharma, Editor
Denielle Sternburg, Business Manager
Sherman Goldenberg, Publisher

Reports on various aspects of the recreational vehicle industry, including forecasting trends, new technologies, marketing and business concepts.
Cost: $12.00
Frequency: Monthly

23222 Rail News Update
Association of American Railroads
425 Third Street SW
Suite 114
Washington, DC 20024-3217

202-639-2100; www.aar.org
Social Media: Facebook, Twitter, LinkedIn

Edward R. Hamberger, President & CEO
Patricia M. Reilly, SVP, Communications

Publishes pertinent new in the railroad industry especially covering Washington news. Covers Department of Transportation and Interstate Commerce activities.
Frequency: BiWeekly

23223 Railroad Facts
Association of American Railroads

425 Third Street SW
Suite 114
Washington, DC 20024-3217

202-639-2100
media@aar.org; www.aar.org
Social Media: Facebook, Twitter, LinkedIn

Offers statistical information and research reports on railroad travel.
Cost: $60.00
Frequency: Annual
Founded in: 1934

23224 Railroad Ten-Year Trends
Association of American Railroads
425 Third Street SW
Suite 114
Washington, DC 20024-3217

202-639-2100
media@aar.org; www.aar.org
Social Media: Facebook, Twitter, LinkedIn

Edward Hamberger, President & CEO
Tom White, Editor

Offers historical facts and perspectives on America's railroad industry.
Cost: $95.00
Founded in: 1934

23225 Railway Age
Simmons-Boardman Publishing Corporation
345 Hudson St
Suite 1201
New York, NY 10014-7123

212-620-7200; *Fax:* 212-633-1165;
www.simmonsboardman.com

Arthur J McGinnis Jr, President

Emphasis is placed on technology, operations, strategic planning, marketing and other issues such as legislative, labor and management developments.
Frequency: Monthly
Circulation: 260030
Founded in: 1876

23226 Railway Track and Structures
Simmons-Boardman Publishing Corporation
345 Hudson St
Suite 1201
New York, NY 10014-7123

212-620-7200; *Fax:* 212-633-1165;
www.simmonsboardman.com

Arthur J McGinnis Jr, President

A technical magazine designed to meet the information needs of the roadway and other civil engineering related departments of North American rail freight and passenger operators.
Frequency: Monthly
Circulation: 8541

23227 Refrigerated Transporter
Penton
PO Box 66010
Houston, TX 77266

713-523-8124
800-880-0368; *Fax:* 713-523-8384
refrigeratedtransporter.com

Ray Anderson, Publisher

23228 Road King
Hammock Publishing
28 White Bridge Road
Suite 209
Nashville, TN 37205

615-385-9745; *Fax:* 615-386-9349;
www.roadking.com

Rex Hammock, President

Focuses on trucking lifestyles, achievements and interests. Offers articles on equipment and driver success.
Cost: $15.00
Frequency: BiMonthly
Circulation: 222,590

23229 School Bus Fleet
Bobit Publishing Company
3520 Challenger St
Torrance, CA 90503-1640

310-533-2400; *Fax:* 310-533-2500;
www.bobit.com

Edward J Bobit, CEO
Cliff Henke, Editor

A magazine that serves the field of pupil transportation, to public and private schools and to independent contract operators transporting students.
Cost: $42.00
Frequency: Monthly
Circulation: 24000
Founded in: 1961

23230 Shippers' Domestic Truck Bill of Lading & Common Carrier Rate Agreement Kit
Transportation & Logistics Council
120 Main Street
Huntington, NY 11743

631-549-8988; *Fax:* 631-549-8962
tlc@transportlaw.org; www.tlccouncil.org

Diane Smid, Membership Secretary
Judy Selvaggio, Administrative Secretary
George Pezold, Executive Director

Published by the Transportation Consumer Protection Council.
Cost: $50.00
Frequency: Monthly
Founded in: 1974

23231 Signalman's Journal
Brotherhood of Railroad Signalmen
601 W Golf Road
Box U
Mount Prospect, IL 60056-4276

847-439-3732; *Fax:* 847-439-3743
signalman@brs.org; www.brs.org

W Dan Pickett, President
Walter A Barrows, Treasurer

Information concerning railroad signaling devices, equipment and apparatus, also includes current events and items pertaining to railroad signalmen.
40 Pages
Frequency: Quarterly
Circulation: 10700
ISSN: 0037-5020
Founded in: 1901
Printed in 4 colors on glossy stock

23232 Southern Motor Cargo
477 S Shady Grove Road
Memphis, TN 38120-2512

901-346-5943; *Fax:* 901-276-5400

Wallace Witmer Jr, Editor

Offers information on shipping.
Cost: $30.00
66 Pages
Frequency: Monthly
Founded in: 1945

23233 Speedlines
High Speed Grand Transportation Association
1010 Massachusetts Avenue NW, #110
Washington, DC 20001-5402

202-789-8107; *Fax:* 212-789-8109;
www.hsgt.org

Mark Dysart, Editor

Exclusively devoted to the High Speed Ground Transportation Association covering broad policy debates, state activity reports, federal developments and technological papers.
Frequency: Quarterly
Circulation: 3,200

23234 Structural Mover
International Association of Structural Movers
PO Box 2637
Lexington, SC 29071-2637

803-951-9304; *Fax:* 803-951-9314;
www.iasm.org

N Eugene Brymer, Staff Executive

A magazine written specifically for members of the International Association of Structural Movers. Subcription to quarterly magazine included in price of membership to IASM.
Frequency: Quarterly
Circulation: 500

23235 Successful Dealer
Kona Communications
707 Lake Cook Road
Deerfield, IL 60015

847-498-3180
800-767-5662; *Fax:* 847-498-3197
truckbooks@konacommunications.com;
www.successfuldealer.com

Denise Rondini, Editorial Director
James D Moss, Publisher
James D Moss, President
Tom Cory, Circulation Manager
John S Dickson, National Sales Manager

Edited for the dealer organization covering dealerships, selling and servicing medium to heavy-duty trucks, trailers and construction equipment. Accepts advertising.
Cost: $50.00
52 Pages
Frequency: bi-monthly
Circulation: 23000
ISSN: 0161-6080
Founded in: 1918
Printed in g colors on 4 stock

23236 Teamster Magazine
International Brotherhood of Teamsters
25 Louisiana Ave NW
Washington, DC 20001-2130

202-624-6800; *Fax:* 202-624-6918
communications@teamster.org;
www.teamster.org

James P Hoffa Jr, President
Per Bernstein, Editor-in-Chief

Affiliated with the AFL-CIO. Magazine is published for members only of 30 pages.
Cost: $12.00
Circulation: 1.4 mill
Founded in: 1903

23237 Traffic Management
Reed Business Information
275 Washington St
Newton, MA 02458-1611

617-964-3030; *Fax:* 617-630-3730
webmaster@reedbusiness.com;
www.designnews.com

Mitch MacDonald, Editor
Ron Bondlow, Publisher

Accepts advertising.
100 Pages
Frequency: Monthly
Circulation: 73000
Founded in: 1982

23238 Traffic World
Journal of Commerce

33 Washington Street
13th Floor
Newark, NJ 07102

973-848-7000
800-255-1341; *Fax:* 973-848-7068;
www.trafficworld.com

William B Cassidy, Managuing Editor

Discusses all facets of the transportation industry. Also online at www.joc.com.
Cost: $174.00
Frequency: Weekly
Founded in: 1907

23239 Trailer/Body Builders
Penton
PO Box 66010
Houston, TX 77266

713-523-8124
800-880-0368; *Fax:* 713-523-8384;
www.trailer-bodybuilders.com

Ray Anderson, Publisher

Serves the truck trailer and truck body manufacturing industry. Accepts advertising.
Cost: $25.00
Frequency: Monthly
Circulation: 15500
Founded in: 1960

23240 Transport Fleet News
Transport Publishing
1962 N Bissell Street
#3
Chicago, IL 60614-5015

773-058-8540

Lillana Rogala, Publisher

Industry news and product for fleet supervisors.
Circulation: 10,500

23241 Transport Topics
Express Carriers Association
950 N. Glebe Road
Suite 210
Arlington, VA 22203

703-838-1770
866-322-7447; *Fax:* 703-838-7916
habramso@ttnews.com; www.ttnews.com

Bruce harmon, Managing Editor
Neil Abt, News Editor
Nancy Baily, Copy Editor

Trucking industry news, features and analysis.

23242 Transportation & Distribution
Penton Media
1166 Avenue of the Americas/10th
Suite 316
New York, NY 10036

212-204-4200; *Fax:* 216-696-6662
editor@logisticstoday.com; www.penton.com

Jane Cooper, Marketing
Antoinette Sanchez-Perkins, Circulation Manager
Newt Barret, Publisher
Dave Blanchard, Editor
David Nussbaum, CEO

Serves the information needs of logistics professionals, identifying trends and providing expert views on strategic, management and operational subjects affecting logistics. Accepts advertising.
Cost: $60.00
78 Pages
Frequency: Monthly
Circulation: 85000
Founded in: 1960
Printed in 4 colors on glossy stock

23243 Transportation Equipment News
Vulcan Publications
PO Box 55886
Birmingham, AL 35255

205-328-6198; *Fax:* 205-987-2882;
www.vulcanpub.com

Ian Greenspan, Publisher

Extensive coverage of government regulations, recruiting and training issues as well as buying and leasing, maintenance and industry trade shows.

23244 Transportation Leader
Taxicab, Limousine & Paratransit Association
3200 Tower Oaks Blvd
Suite 220
Rockville, MD 20852

301-984-5700; *Fax:* 301-984-5703
info@tlpa.org; www.tlpa.org

Alfred LaGasse, CEO
Victor Dizengoff, President

Leading resource for news and information on issues, trends, and people in the private, for-hire passenger transportation industry. Provides readers with an array of features, articles, and columns that include information on managing a transportation company, industry trends, driver's tips, an industry calendar of events, coverage of TLPA events, and advertisements from the industry's leading suppliers.
Cost: $4.00
48 Pages
Frequency: Quarterly
Circulation: 6000
Founded in: 1920
Mailing list available for rent: 6,000 names at $100 per M
Printed in 4 colors on glossy stock

23245 Truck Accessory News
Bobit Publishing
3520 Challenger St
Torrance, CA 90503-1640

310-533-2400; *Fax:* 310-533-2500;
www.bobit.com

Edward J Bobit, CEO
Travis Weeks, Publisher
Jerry Martin, Circulation Manager

Provides information on product and merchandise trends, covers industry news on retail activities, and interviews top executives and buyers.
Cost: $37.00
Frequency: Monthly
Circulation: 10000
Founded in: 1961

23246 Trucker's Connection
Megan Cullingford
5960 Crooked Creek Road
Suite 15
Norcross, GA 30092

770-416-0927; *Fax:* 770-416-1734;
www.truckersconnection.com

Dan Barnhill, Editor
Reid Ramsay, Production Manager
Megan Cullingford, General Manager
David Guthrie, Advertising Sales

Published for the use of long haul, over-the-road truck drivers, owner operators, small trucking company fleet owners, safety and recruiting of personnel for trucking companies in the US and Canada.
Frequency: Monthly
Circulation: 16,5,000
Founded in: 1986
Printed in 4 colors on glossy stock

23247 Truckin'
McMullen Argus Publishing
2400 E Katella Avenue
11th Floor
Anaheim, CA 92806-6832

714-939-2559; *Fax:* 714-978-6390
info@primedia.com;
www.primediaautomotive.com

Steve Parr, CEO
Susan Brocett, Marketing Manager
Brad Christopher, Publisher
Steve Warner, Editor
Jerome Dziechiasz, Sales Manager

Provides information on testing new trucks, reviewing accessories and trucking' activities.
Cost: $24.95
Frequency: Monthly
Circulation: 180000

23248 Trucking Technology
167 Cherry Street
Suite 430
Milford, CT 06460-3466

203-882-9485

23249 World Wide Shipping (WWS)
World Wide Shipping Guide
16302 Byrnwyck Ln
Odessa, FL 33556-2807

813-920-4788; *Fax:* 813-920-8268
info@wwship.com; www.wwship.com

Lee Di Paci, Publisher
Barbara Edwards, Marketing Manager
Bob Susor, Marketing Manager

Dedicated to the interests of North American exporters, importers, distributors, freight forwarders, NVOCC's and customs brokers requiring freight tranportation services and equipment.
Cost: $32.00
32 Pages
Frequency: Fortnightly
Circulation: 9000
ISSN: 1060-7900
Founded in: 1919
Printed in 4 colors on glossy stock

Trade Shows

23250 AAR Annual Convention and Exhibit
Railway Systems Suppliers
9306 New Lagrange Road
Suite 100
Louisville, KY 40242
502-327-7774; *Fax:* 502-327-0541
rssi@rssi.org; www.rssi.org

Donald Remaley, Executive Director
Franklin Brown, President

Railroad signal and communication equipment displays, annual meeting & banquet.
Frequency: Annual
Founded in: 1960

23251 AREMA Annual Conference & Exposition
American Railway Engineering & Maintenance-of-Way
4501 Forbes Boulevard
Suite 130
Lanham, MD 20706

301-459-3200; *Fax:* 301-459-8077
dknight@arema.org; www.arema.org

Beth Caruso, Executive Director & CEO
Stacy Spaulding, Senior Director, Board Operations
Desiree Knight, Director, Conferences & Seminars

Approximately 198 exhibitors from all segments of the railway engineering and maintenance industry, in addition to the conference talks, semi-

nars, and events. Advanced registration for non-members starts at $760.
1600 Attendees
Frequency: Bi-Ennial

23252 ARTBA National Convention
American Road and Transportation Builders Assn
1219 28th St NW
Washington, DC 20007-3389
202-289-4434; *Fax:* 202-289-4435
general@artba.org; www.artba.org
Pete Ruane, President
Matt Jeanneret, Sr. VP, Communications/Marketing
Jaime Mahoney, Publications Manager
Liz Cavallaro, Sales Manager
Tom Hill, Treasurer
Frequency: Annual/Fall

23253 American Bus Marketplace
1015 15th Street NW
Washington, DC 20005-2605
202-842-9100
800-283-2877; *Fax:* 202-842-0850
Katie Robbins
Sales and marketing event for the North American group travel industry. 350 booths.
2M Attendees
Frequency: December

23254 American Car Rental Association Convention
11250 Roger Bacon Drive
#8
Reston, VA 20190
703-787-7718; *Fax:* 703-435-4390;
www.acraorg.com
Gwendolyn Hogan
One hundred exhibits of cars, vans, buses, computers, equipment and services for car rental company owners and officers. Conference, reception and dinner.
600 Attendees
Frequency: Annual
Founded in: 1978

23255 American Public Transportation Association Expo
1666 K Street NW
Suite 1100
Washington, DC 20006
202-496-4800; *Fax:* 202-496-4324
meetings2@apta.com; www.apta.com
William W Millar, President
Petra Mollet, VP
Rosemary Sherid, Marketing
Seminar, workshop, conference, luncheon, banquet, tours and 800 exhibits for the planning designing and finance and operation of public transportation.
15000 Attendees
Frequency: October 2008/2011
Founded in: 1882

23256 American Truck Dealers Convention and Equipment Exposition
National Automobile Dealers Association
8400 Westpark Drive
Mc Lean, VA 22102-3522
703-217-7000; *Fax:* 703-821-7075;
www.nada.org
Gary Heimes
Annual show of 100 manufacturers, suppliers and distributors of products and services designed to control dealership expenses, help merchandising or improve profitability.
2,500 Attendees
Founded in: 1963

23257 American Trucking Association Management Conference and Exhibition
American Trucking Association
2200 Mill Road
Alexandria, VA 22314-4677
703-838-1700
800-282-5463; *Fax:* 703-838-5720
trucking@cais.com; www.trucking.org
Bill Graves, President
Annual show of 168 exhibitors of equipment, supplies and services related to the trucking industry.
1,500 Attendees
Frequency: Annual
Founded in: 1984

23258 Association for Commuter Transportation Convention
808 17th Street NW
Suite 200
Washington, DC 20006-3910
202-393-3497
tmi.cob.fsu.edu/act
Elizabeth Stutts, President
Kenneth M Sufka, Executive Director
Shamus Misek, VP
Kim Tabah, Director of Development
Barbara Ash, Communications Manager
Thirty booths.
300 Attendees
Frequency: September

23259 Association of Railway Museums Convention
Association of Railway Museums
PO Box 370
Tujunga, CA 91043-0370
818-951-9151; *Fax:* 818-951-9151
Paul Hammond, President ARM
Annual show and exhibits for the preservation of railway equipment, artifacts and history. Seminar, tours, banquet and dinner.
125 Attendees
Frequency: October
Founded in: 1961

23260 Biodiesel Investor Conference
Platts
24 Hartwell Avenue
Lexington, MA 02421
781-860-6100
866-355-2930
registration@platts.com; www.platts.com
Frequency: June Houston

23261 ECA Shipper: Carrier Marketplace
Express Carriers Association
9532 Liberia Avenue
Manassas, VA 20110
703-361-1058
866-322-7447; *Fax:* 703-361-5274
eca@expresscarriers.com;
www.expresscarriers.com
Carrie Ehlers, President
Stuart Hyden, First Vice President
Premier business to business event featuring one on one interviews between shippers, carriers and vendors of products/services to the transportation industry.
300+ Attendees
Frequency: April
Founded in: 1997

23262 Education Conference & Expo
American Moving and Storage Association
1611 Duke St
Alexandria, VA 22314-3406
703-683-7410; *Fax:* 703-683-7527;
www.moving.org
Linda Bauer Darr, CEO
Sandy Lynch, SVP
The largest gathering of moving and storage industry professionals in the country. With more than 30 education sessions and over 10 hours of dedicated network time, the conference & expo offers countless opportunities to further your career while making new business contacts.
Frequency: Annual/March

23263 Fleet Management Institute (NAFA) Convention
100 Wood Avenue S
Suite 310
Iselin, NJ 08830
732-494-8100; *Fax:* 732-494-6789
info@nafa.org; www.nafa.org
Patricia Murtaugh, Assistant Executive Director
Joanne Marsh, Manager
Fleet management education and automobile parts and services, as well as maintenance for business and public service vehicles. 250 booths
2M Attendees
Frequency: April/May

23264 Institute of Transportation Engineers Annual Meeting
Institute of Transportation Engineers
525 School Street SW
Suite 410
Washington, DC 20024-2729
202-548-8050; *Fax:* 202-863-5486;
www.ite.org
Marianne Wool, Manager
Shannon Gore Peters, Editor
Annual meeting of 100 exhibitors of transportation equipment, supplies and services.
2,000 Attendees
Frequency: Las Vegas

23265 Intermodal EXPO
Intermodal Association of North America
11785 Beltsville Dr.
Suite 1100
Calverton, MD 20705-4049
301-982-3400; *Fax:* 301-982-4815
shanelle.casey@intermodal.org
intermodalexpo.org
Social Media: Facebook, Twitter, LinkedIn
Edgar Martinez, Exhibits & Sponsorship
Shanelle Casey, Registration
Forum for information exchange on issues facing intermodal supply chain.
1800 Attendees
Founded in: 1991

23266 International Association of Structural Movers Annual Convention
PO Box 600
Oakton, VA 22124
703-648-3225; *Fax:* 503-543-6697;
www.iasm.org
Containing 20 booths and 15 exhibits.

23267 International Public Transit Expo
Pemco/Professional Expo Management Company
191 S Gary Avenue
Carol Stream, IL 60188-2092
630-690-5600; *Fax:* 203-840-9662
Barbara Silverman, VP

The world's largest transit industry event offering a chance for top transit officials to meet with manufacturers from around the world.
16M Attendees
Frequency: October

23268 International Truck and Bus Expo
Society of Automotive Engineers
400 Commonwealth Drive
Warrendale, PA 15096-0001
724-772-8548; *Fax:* 724-776-0790;
www.sae.org
Andrew Brown, Treasurer

23269 Light Truck Accessory Expo
Truck Cap and Accessory Association
6564 Loisdale Court
Suite 430
Springfield, VA 22150-1812
703-822-0707
800-283-8242; *Fax:* 703-922-7806
Kendra Moore, Director Meetings/Marketing
Annual show of 150 manufacturers of truck caps and light truck accessories.
2,500 Attendees

23270 Link
R&D Associates
16607 Blanco Road
Suite 305
San Antonio, TX 78232-1940
210-682-4302; *Fax:* 830-493-8036
David Dee, Editor
Articles of interest to the food, food packaging, food processing and foodservice industry. 50 booths.
300 Attendees
Frequency: Spring/Fall

23271 Mid-West Truck & Trailer Show
2727 N Dirksen Pkwy
Springfield, IL 62702-1490
217-525-0310; *Fax:* 217-525-0342
info@midwesttruckshow.com;
www.midwesttruckshow.com
Social Media: Facebook
Don Schaefer, President
Serves trucking industry by lobbying on their behalf, assisting with registration, license plate procurement and group insurance programs. Conducts educational programs, has own self-funded workers compensation insurance program. Trade association represents truck owners in 14 states.
2700 Members
Founded in: 1962

23272 Midwest Truck Show
Mid-West Truckers Association
2727 N Dirksen Parkway
Springfield, IL 62702
217-525-0310; *Fax:* 217-525-0342
info@mid-westtruckers.com;
www.mid-westtruckers.com
Don Schaefer, Executive VP
Annual show and exhibits of trucks, trailers, financing information, computers, insurance information and related equipment, supplies and services. Containing 200 booths and 150 exhibitors.
6,000 Attendees
Frequency: February

23273 NDTA Forum & Expo
National Defense Transportation Association
50 S Pickett Street
Suite 220
Alexandria, VA 22304-7206
703-751-5011; *Fax:* 703-823-8761
info@ndtahq.com; www.ndtahq.com
LTG Kenneth Wykle, President
COL Dennis Edwards, VP Marketing
A key element in the Association's fulfillment of its educational and professional development missions and it also offers outstanding opportunities for networking and mentoring.
1200 Attendees
Frequency: Annual/September

23274 National Industrial Transportation League Trade Show
1700 N Moore St
Suite 1900
Arlington, VA 22209-1931
703-524-5011; *Fax:* 703-524-5017
info@nitl.org; www.nitl.org
Arthur E. Cole, President
Michael J Barr, First Vice Chairman
Peter Gatti, Executive VP
Annual show of 250 exhibitors of computer services software and innovations for transportation operations.
600 Members
Founded in: 1907

23275 National Private Truck Council Management/ Education Conference
National Private Truck Council
66 Canal Center Plaza
Alexandria, VA 22314-1591
703-683-1300; *Fax:* 703-683-1217
Gary Petty, CEO
Annual conference and exhibits of equipment, supplies and services for processors, shippers, distributors and retailers who operate their own truck fleets to advance their primary nontransportation business enterprises.

23276 North American Truck Show
North American Expositions Company
33 Rutherford Avenue
Boston, MA 02129-3795
617-242-6092
800-225-1577; *Fax:* 617-242-1817;
www.truckingexpo.com
Gregory Soughlin, Show Manager
Six hundred booths.
25M Attendees
Frequency: May

23277 Railway Interchange Annual Conference
American Railway Engineering & Maintenance-of-Way
4501 Forbes Boulevard
Suite 150
Lanham, MD 20706-4362
301-459-3200; *Fax:* 301-459-8077
bcaruso@arema.org; www.arema.org
Beth Caruso, Executive Director & CEO
Vickie Fisher, Director, Finance
Stace Spaulding, Executive & Board Operations
Desiree Knights, Director, Conferences & Seminars
Lindsay Hamilton, Director, Marketing & Communication

23278 TLPA Annual Convention & Trade Show
Taxicab, Limousine & Paratransit Association
3200 Tower Oaks Boulevard
Suite 220
Rockville, MD 20852
301-984-5700; *Fax:* 301-984-5703;
www.tlpa.org
Alfred La Gasse III, Executive VP
Victor Dizengoff, President
Shares information vital to owners or taxicab, limousine, airport shuttle, paratransit and nonemergency medical transportation fleets. 100 suppliers and exhibitors of the newest products available to the industry.
1000 Attendees
Frequency: Annual

23279 TransComp Exhibition
National Industrial Transportation League
1700 N Moore Street
Suite 1900
Arlington, VA 22209-1931
703-524-5011; *Fax:* 703-524-5017
info@nitl.org; www.nitl.org
Ellie Gilanshah, VP Finance and Membership
3000 Attendees
Frequency: November
Founded in: 1907

23280 Transportation Intermediaries Annual Convention & Trade Show
Transportation Intermediaries Association
1625 Prince St.
Suite 200
Alexandria, VA 22314
703-299-5700; *Fax:* 703-836-0123
info@tianet.org; www.tianet.org
Robert Voltmann, President/CEO
Larry Fisher, Contact
Education and policy organization for North American transportation intermediaries. TIA is the only national association representing the interests of all third party transportation service providers. The members of TIA include logistics management firms, property brokers, perishable commodities brokers, freight forwarders, intermodal marketers, ocean and air forwarders, and NVOCC's.
700 Attendees
Founded in: 1978

23281 Transportation Research Forum Annual Meeting
Transportation Research Forum
Department 2880
PO Box 6050
Fargo, ND 58108-6050
701-231-7766; *Fax:* 701-231-1945
info@trforum.org; www.trforum.org
Richard Gritta, President
Starr McMullen, VP
300 Members
Founded in: 1958

23282 Truck Show Las Vegas
Independent Trade Show Management
1155 Chess Drive
Suite 102
Foster City, CA 94404-1117
650-349-4876
800-227-5992; *Fax:* 650-349-5169
rsherrard@truckshow.com;
www.truckshow.com
Sue K Fena, Sr. Show Coordinator
Roger Sherrard, President
The premier commercial truck and equipment show in the USA. Containing 2,500 booths and 350 exhibits, also offers seminars and workshops on current topics in the trucking industry.
20M Attendees
Frequency: June

Founded in: 1961
Mailing list available for rent

23283 Truckerfest
Newport Communications
38 Executive Park
Suite 300
Irvine, CA 92614-6755

949-261-1636
800-233-1911; *Fax:* 949-261-2904;
www.truckerfest.com

Bud Farquhar, Show Manager
BJ Iverson, Events Coordinator

Trucker appreciation event at Alamo Travel Plaza, Reno, NV. Truck Parade, trucker games, music, free dinners, truck beauty contest, and fireworks. Containing 75 booths and 60 exhibits.
10M Attendees
Frequency: August

23284 Trucking Show Mid-America
1404 Browns Lane
Suite E
Louisville, KY 40207

www.truckingshow.com

Timothy Young, Show Manager

Four hundred and fifty booths displaying the latest in trucking.
35M Attendees
Frequency: March

23285 Truckload Carriers Association Annual Convention
Truckload Carriers Association
555 East Braddock Road
Suite CS-4
Alexandria, VA 22314-2182

703-838-1960; *Fax:* 703-836-6610
tca@truckload.org; www.truckload.org
Social Media: Facebook, Twitter, LinkedIn, YouTube, Flickr

Russell Stubbs, Chairman
John Lyboldt, President
William Giroux, Executive Vice President
Tomora Brown, Membership Liaison

Annual convention bringing together professionals from across the truckload carrier industry for 3.5 days of networking, speakers, and exhibitors.
900 Members
Frequency: Annual/March
Founded in: 1938

23286 Women's Transportation Seminar
Women's Transportation Seminar
1 Walnut Street
Boston, MA 02108-3616

617-367-3273; *Fax:* 617-227-6783

Annual seminar and exhibits of transportation equipment, supplies and services.

23287 Work Truck Show
National Truck Equipment Association
37400 Hills Tech Drive
Farmington Hills, MI 48331-3414

248-489-7090
800-441-6832; *Fax:* 248-489-8590
info@ntea.com; www.ntea.com

Tom Rawson, President
Dennis Jones, First Vice President

Annual business to business event designed to bring together distributors, upfitters, manufacturers, buyers and users of work trucks in all industries including delivery, government, construction and landscaping.
7,000 Attendees
Frequency: March

Directories & Databases

23288 AAA Bridge and Ferry Directory
American Automobile Association
1000 AAA Drive
Heathrow, FL 32746-5062

407-444-7966

Melanie Fuller, Highway Infoformation Coordinator

Offers information on over 500 toll facilities in the US, Canada and Mexico that enable automobiles and passengers to complete toll non-highway portions of their journey.
Cost: $12.50
103 Pages
Frequency: Annual

23289 ARTBA Transportation Officials & Engineers Directory
American Road and Transportation Builders Assn
1219 28th St NW
Washington, DC 20007-3389

202-289-4434; *Fax:* 202-289-4435
general@artba.org; www.artba.org

Pete Ruane, President
Matt Jeanneret, Sr. VP, Communications/Marketing
Jaime Mahoney, Publications Manager
Liz Cavallaro, Sales Manager
Tom Hill, Treasurer

An annual survey of local, state and federal transportation agencies offered as a pocket-sized publication and as a mergeable Excel spreadsheet. The TO&E Directory includes key information about more than 6,000 state and local transportation departments and authorities, including URLs and e-mail addresses. From $195 for members to get the pocket edition to $475 for non-members to get the Excel version.
6300 Members
Frequency: Annual
Founded in: 1902

23290 Affiliated Warehouse Companies Directory
Affiliated Warehouse Companies, Inc
PO Box 295
Hazlet, NJ 07730-0295

732-739-2323; *Fax:* 732-739-4154
sales@awco.com; www.awco.com

Jim McBride, President
Patrick McBride, Vice President

Third party logistics and public warehousing, marketing and sales company. Directory is free.
Founded in: 1953
Mailing list available for rent: 8,500 names at $100 per M
Printed in 4 colors

23291 Air CargoWorld & Traffic World
Knight-Ridder Financial
75 Wall Street
Floor 23
New York, NY 10005-2833

212-429-2307; *Fax:* 212-372-7148

Offers valuable information on cash, futures and options markets.

23292 Airline, Ship & Catering: Onboard Service Buyer's Guide & Directory
International Publishing Company of America
664 La Villa Dr
Miami Springs, FL 33166-6030

305-887-1700; *Fax:* 305-885-1923

Alexander Morton, Owner

Offers information on over 6,000 airlines, railroads, ship lines and termianl restaurants.
Cost: $125.00
Frequency: Annual
Circulation: 6,000

23293 American Bus Association's Motorcoach Marketer
American Bus Association
700 13th St NW
Suite 575
Washington, DC 20005-5923

202-842-1645; *Fax:* 202-842-0850
abainfo@buses.org; www.buses.org

Peter J Pantuso, CEO
Eron Shosteck, Marketing

This directory is a comprehensive guide of the bus and travel industry offering information on hotels and sightseeing services, attractions, museums, restaurants and more.
500 Pages
Frequency: Annual
Founded in: 1926

23294 American Public Transit Association Membership Directory
American Public Transit Association
1666 K St NW
Suite 1100
Washington, DC 20006-1215

202-496-4800; *Fax:* 202-496-4324
hbrett@apta.com; www.apta.com

Karol J Popkin, CEO
Petra Mollet, VP
Rosemary Sherid, Marketing

A who's who directory of services and supplies within the public transportation industry.
Founded in: 1882

23295 American Shortline Railway Guide
Kalmbach Publishing Company
Po Box 1612
Waukesha, WI 53187-1612

262-796-8776; *Fax:* 262-796-1615;
www.trains.com

Gerald Boettcher, President

Directory of services and supplies to the industry.
Cost: $18.95
320 Pages

23296 Bus Garage Index
Friendship Publications
PO Box 1472
Spokane, WA 99210-1472

800-541-2670; *Fax:* 509-325-0405

Bruce Sankey, President
Leslie Maris, VP Marketing
Linda Metler, Production Manager

Offers information on over 900 garages and service centers in the United States and Canada offering services to buses on charter service and tours.
Cost: $28.00
140 Pages
Circulation: 3,000
Mailing list available for rent: 14M names
Printed in 4 colors on glossy stock

23297 Bus Industry Directory
Friendship Publications

PO Box 1472
Spokane, WA 99210-1472

800-541-2670; *Fax:* 509-325-0405

Bruce Sankey, President/Publisher
Leslie Maris, VP Marketing

A comprehensive list of over 4,500 intercity and charter bus companies and local transit authorities in the United States and Canada.
Cost: $78.00
500 Pages
Frequency: Annual
Mailing list available for rent: 14M names
Printed in 4 colors on glossy stock

23298 **Carrier Routing Director**
Transportation Technical Services
500 Lafayette Boulevard
Fredericksburg, VA 22401-6070

540-899-9872
800-666-4887; *Fax:* 888-665-9887;
www.ttstrucks.com

Thomas R Fugee, Executive VP

Two thousand six hundred top common and contract carriers, toll-free faxes, states served + Canadian provinces and Mexico, equipment types, commodities.
Cost: $145.00
Frequency: Annual
Founded in: 1992

23299 **DRI Transportation Detail**
DRI/McGraw-Hill
24 Hartwell Ave
Lexington, MA 02421-3103

781-860-6060; *Fax:* 781-860-6002
support@construction.com;
www.construction.com

Walt Arvin, President

This time series contains annual and quarterly data describing aspects of the transportation industry.

23300 **Defense Transportation Journal NDTA Almanac**
National Defense Transportation Association
50 S Pickett Street
Suite 220
Alexandria, VA 22304-7206

703-751-5011; *Fax:* 703-823-8761
info@ndtahq.com; www.ndtahq.com
Social Media: Facebook, Twitter, LinkedIn, You Tube

LTG Kenneth Wykle, President
COL Dennis Edwards, VP Marketing

Reference book of Military/Government/Transportation industry companies and executives
128 Pages

23301 **Directory of Shippers**
Transportation Technical Services
500 Lafayette Boulevard
Fredericksburg, VA 22401-6070
540-899-9872
800-666-4887; *Fax:* 888-665-9887;
www.ttstrucks.com

Thomas R Fugee, Executive VP

Compilateion of 14,000 logistics executives. Key information on 13,500 companies, phone, fax-e-mail, addresses, SIC's, revenue. Great marketing sales and research tool.
Cost: $170.00
Frequency: Annual
Founded in: 1992

23302 **Directory of Transportation Professionals**
National Assn of Regulatory Utility Commissioners
PO Box 684
Washington, DC 20044-0684

202-898-2200

Offers valuable information on over 100 regulated transportation firms and professionals.
Cost: $20.00
150 Pages
Frequency: Annual

23303 **Directory of Truck Dealers**
Transportation Technical Services
500 Lafayette Boulevard
Fredericksburg, VA 22401-6070

540-899-9872
800-666-4887; *Fax:* 888-665-9887;
www.ttstrucks.com

Thomas R Fugee, Executive VP

Unique, extensive list of 2,700 of the nation's kmid-size/heavy truck dealers. Address, brands sold, serviced, keky contacts, phone and fax.
Cost: $95.00
Frequency: Annual
Founded in: 1992

23304 **Fleet Owner-Specs and Buyers' Directory Issue**
Primedia
1166 Avenue of the Americas/10th Fl
Shawnee Mission, NY 10036

212-204-4200; *Fax:* 913-514-6895;
www.penton.com

Eric Jacobson, Senior VP
Tom Moore, Editor
Chris Meyer, Director

Lists of manufacturers of equipment and materials used in the operation, management and maintenance of truck and bus fleets.
Cost: $5.00
Frequency: Annual October
Circulation: 100,250

23305 **Foreign Flag Merchant Ships Owned by US Parent Companies**
US Department of Transportation
400 7th Street SW
Room 8117
Washington, DC 20590-0001

202-366-4000

Directory of services and supplies to the industry.
20 Pages
Frequency: SemiAnnual

23306 **Greenwood's Guide to Great Lakes Shipping**
Freshwater Press
1700 E 13th Street
Suite 3-R
Cleveland, OH 44114-3213

216-241-0373; *Fax:* 216-781-6344;
www.greenwoodsguide.com

Michael Dills, VP/General Manager

Offers companies that ship water-carried commodities and service firms on the Great Lakes Seaway systems. Details of vessels, dock facilities, shipyards, etc.
Cost: $71.00
650 Pages
Frequency: Annual
Circulation: 2,500
Founded in: 1960
Printed in on glossy stock

23307 **Grey House Transportation Security Directory**
Grey House Publishing
4919 Route 22
PO Box 56
Amenia, NY 12501

518-789-8700
800-562-2139; *Fax:* 845-373-6390
books@greyhouse.com; www.greyhouse.com
Social Media: Facebook, Twitter

Leslie Mackenzie, Publisher
Richard Gottlieb, Editor

Provides information on everything from Regulatory Authorities to Security Equipment, this top-flight directory brings together the relevant information necessary for creating and maintaining a security plan for a wide range of transportation facilities.
Cost: $195.00
800 Pages
ISBN: 1-592370-75-6
Founded in: 1981

23308 **Heavy Duty Representatives Profile Directory**
Heavy Duty Representatives Association
160 Symphony Way
Elgin, IL 60120

847-760-0067
800-763-5717; *Fax:* 330-722-5638
trucksvc@aol.com
hdra.org

Larry Rosenthal, President
Walt Sirman, Vice President
John Stojack, Secretary

About 60 independent sales agencies which sell heavy-duty components to the trucking and aftermarket industries.
Frequency: Annual January

23309 **Heavy Duty Trucking: CFS Buyers Guide**
Newport Communications Div.-HIC Corporation
38 Executive Park
Suite 300
Irvine, CA 92614-6755

949-261-1636; *Fax:* 949-261-2904

Doug Condra, Publisher

Five hundred Council of Fleet Specialists member manufacturers and wholesalers specializing in heavy-duty truck parts and repairs.
Cost: $45.00
Frequency: Annual January
Circulation: 98,502

23310 **Inland River Guide**
Waterways Journal
319 N 4th St
Suite 650
St Louis, MO 63102-1994

314-241-7354; *Fax:* 314-241-4207
info@waterwaysjournal.net;
www.waterwaysjournal.net

H Nelson Spencer Iii, Publisher
John S Shoulberg, Editor/Associate Publisher
Ed Rahe, Advertising Sales
Alan Bates, Manager
Marie Rausch, Advertising Sales Director

The only directory published specifically for the benefit of the companies doing business along the inland and intracoastal waterways. It contains vital information about companies servicing all industry segments.
Cost: $65.00
600+ Pages
Frequency: Annual
Circulation: 3,000
Founded in: 1972

23311 **Inland River Record**
Waterways Journal

319 N 4th St
Suite 650
St Louis, MO 63102-1994
314-241-7354; *Fax:* 314-241-4207
hnspencer@waterwaysjournal.net;
www.waterwaysjournal.net
H Nelson Spencer III, Publisher
John S Shoulberg, Manager
Alan Bates, Manager
Marie Rausch, Advertising Sales Director
Lists in detail more than 3,500 commercial towboats and tugs, U.S. engineer vessels and Coast Guard vessels navigating the Mississippi and Ohio, their tributaries and the Gulf Intracoastal Waterway.
Cost: $37.50
475 Pages
Frequency: Annual
Circulation: 3,000

23312 **Leonard's Guide National Third Party Logistics Directory**
GR Leonard & Company
49 E Huntington Dr
Arcadia, CA 91006-3210
626-574-1800
800-574-5250; www.leonardsguide.com
David Ercolani, President
Approximately 2,000 transportation brokers and third party logistics firms and brokerages in the US and Canada.
Cost: $75.00
Frequency: Annual Spring

23313 **Light List**
United States Coast Guard
2100 2nd Street SW
Washington, DC 20593-0002
202-488-8157; *Fax:* 202-366-5063
Offers information to the shipping industry in the form of lights. This comprehensive directory offers a list of lights, fog signals, daybeacons, radiobeacons and LORAN stations operated or authorized by the US Coast Guard. Various volumes are offered.
Cost: $25.00
200+ Pages
Frequency: Volumes

23314 **Mass Transit: Consultants Issue**
Cygnus Publishing
Po Box 803
Fort Atkinson, WI 53538-0803
920-000-1111; *Fax:* 920-563-1699;
www.cygnusb2b.com
John French, CEO
Kathy Scott, Director of Public Relations
Paul Bonaiuto, CFO
Offers listings of over 300 urban transportation architects, designers, engineers and other specialists serving the urban transportation industry.
Frequency: BiMonthly

23315 **Mexican Motor Carrier Directory**
Transportation Technical Services
500 Lafayette Boulevard
Fredericksburg, VA 22401-6070
540-899-9872
800-666-4887; *Fax:* 888-665-9887;
www.ttstrucks.com
Thomas R Fugee, Executive VP
Unique, extensive and key information on 500 Mexican carriers.
Cost: $145.00
Frequency: Annual

23316 **NARUC Compilation of Transportation Regulatory Policy**
National Assn of Regulatory Utility Commissioners
PO Box 684
Washington, DC 20044-0684
202-898-2200
http://www.naruc.org
Offers a list of over 100 regulatory agencies in the United States and Canada for the transportation industry.
Cost: $33.00

23317 **NTEA Membership Roster & Product Directory**
National Truck Equipment Association
37400 Hills Tech Dr
Farmington Hill, MI 48331-3414
248-489-7090
800-441-6832; *Fax:* 248-489-8590
info@ntea.com; www.ntea.com
James Carney, Executive Director
Dennis Jones, First Vice President
Over 1,600 manufacturers and distributors of commercial trucks, bodies, trailers and related equipment. Information includes: product info, membership category, affiliate membership, join date, address, phone and fax numbers, e-mail address, Web site address.
Cost: $50.00
Frequency: Annual
Founded in: 1964

23318 **National Customs Brokers and Forwarders Association of America**
National Customs Brokers & Forwarders Association
1200 18th St NW
Suite 901
Washington, DC 20036-2572
202-466-0222; *Fax:* 202-466-0226;
www.ncbfaa.org
Barbara Reilly, Executive VP
About 600 customs brokers, international air cargo agents, and freight forwarders in the United States.
Cost: $24.00
Frequency: Annual

23319 **National Industrial Transportation League Reference Manual**
National Industrial Transportation League
1700 N Moore St
Suite 1900
Arlington, VA 22209-1931
703-524-5011; *Fax:* 703-524-5017
info@nitl.org; www.nitl.org
Bruce J Carlton, President
Frequency: SemiAnnual

23320 **National Institute of Packaging, Handling and Logistic Engineers**
NIPHLE
5903 Ridgeway Drive
Grand Prairie, TX 75052
817-466-7490
866-464-7453; *Fax:* 570-523-0606;
www.niphle.org
Richard D Owen, Executive Director
Founded in: 1956

23321 **National Motor Carrier Directory**
Transportation Technical Services
500 Lafayette Boulevard
Fredericksburg, VA 22401-6070
540-899-9872
800-666-4887; *Fax:* 888-665-9887;
www.ttstrucks.com
Thomas R Fugee, Executive VP
CEO, fleet size, toll-free/fax number, revenue, SCAC, trailer type, TK or LTL, trucks plus tractors owned and leased and more.
Cost: $395.00
1982 Pages
Frequency: Annual
Founded in: 1992

23322 **National Private Truck Council: Official Membership Directory**
2200 Mill Road
Suite 350
Alexandria, VA 22314
703-683-1300; *Fax:* 703-683-1217;
www.nptc.org
Gary Petty, President/CEO
Richard LaRoche, Director Membership
The only organization that represents the interests and concerns of private fleets — companies that use in-house or dedicated truck fleets to support distribution of their products. The directory includes members listed by: company, individual and industry. Both private fleet and supplier members are listed.
Cost: $145.00
100 Pages
Frequency: Annual
Printed in 4 colors on glossy stock

23323 **Pacific Shipper's Transportation Services Directory**
PRIMEDIA Information
10 Lake Drive
Hightstown, NJ 08520-5321
609-371-7700
800-224-5488; www.primediainfo.com
Amy Middlebrook, Editor
John Capers III, Publisher
John Murphy, Circulation Director
Offers valuable information on coastal transportation operations and support services on the Pacific Coast.
Cost: $202.00
730 Pages
Frequency: Annual
Printed in 4 colors on newsprint stock

23324 **Private Fleet Directory**
Transportation Technical Services
500 Lafayette Boulevard
Fredericksburg, VA 22401-6070
540-899-9872
800-666-4887; *Fax:* 888-665-9887;
www.ttstrucks.com
Thomas R Fugee, Executive VP
Over 26,000 private fleets in the US that transport their own freight (Wal-Mart, Ace Hardware, Toys R Us).
Cost: $295.00
1,900 Pages
Frequency: Annual July
Founded in: 1992

23325 **Railway Line Clearances**
Commonwealth Business Media
10 Lake Drive
Hightstown, NJ 08520-5321
609-371-7703
800-224-5488; *Fax:* 609-371-7830;
www.cbizmedia.com
Alan Glass, Chairman/CEO
Susan Murray, Publisher
Kathy Keeney, Associate Publisher
This directory offers weight limitations, heights and widths of clearances for railroads in North America and Canada, parts of the United States, clearance contacts and AAR rules and regulation.
Cost: $200.00
Frequency: Annual
Printed in 2 colors on matte stock

23326 Refrigerated Transporter: Warehouse Directory Issue
Penton
PO Box 66010
Houston, TX 77266
713-523-8124
800-880-0368; *Fax:* 713-523-8384
refrigeratedtransporter.com
Ray Anderson, Publisher
Listing of approximately 265 refrigerated warehouses in the US and Canada.

23327 Survey of State Travel Offices
United States Travel Data Center
1100 New York Avenue NW
Washington, DC 20005-3934
202-326-7300; *Fax:* 202-408-1255
Patrick Thompson, Editor
State and territorial government agencies responsible for travel and travel promotion in their states.
Cost: $475.00
Frequency: Annual March

23328 Transportation Management Association Directory
Association for Commuter Transportation
1518 K St NW
Suite 503
Washington, DC 20005-1203
202-737-2926; *Fax:* 202-347-8847
info@nadca.com; www.nadca.com
Kenneth Sufka, Executive Vice President
Over 50 established transportation management associations in the United States are the focus of this comprehensive directory.
123 Pages
Circulation: 400

23329 Transportation Research Board Directory
Transportation Research Board
2101 Constitution Ave Nw
Washington, DC 20418-0007
202-334-2933; *Fax:* 202-334-2527
TABSales@nas.edu;
www.nationalacademies.org/trb
Robert Skinner, CEO
Directory lists organizations and committee members with an interest in transportation. Individual affiliate information is no longer available in print or in electronic format.
Frequency: Annual

23330 Truck Trailer Manufacturers Association: Membership Directory
Truck Trailer Manufacturers Association
8506 Wellington Road
Suite 101
Alexandria, VA 20109
703-549-3010; *Fax:* 703-549-3014
ttma@erols.com; www.ttmanet.org
Richard Bowling, President
About 100 truck and tank trailer manufacturers and 120 suppliers to the industry.
Cost: $135.00
Frequency: Annual

23331 Trucksource: Sources of Trucking Industry Information
Express Carriers Association
9532 Liberia Avenue
Suite 130
Manassas, VA 20110
703-361-1058
866-322-7447; *Fax:* 703-361-5274
eca@expresscarriers.org;
www.expresscarriers.com
Carrie Ehlers, President
Stuart Hyden, First Vice President
Features over 1,000 sources of information on the trucking industry, including industry reports, videos, periodicals and databases about the motor carrier industry.

23332 USTA Industry Directory
United States Telecom Association
1401 H St NW
Suite 600
Washington, DC 20005-2110
202-326-7300; *Fax:* 202-326-7333;
www.usta.org
Walter McKormick, President
Joan Johnson, Secretary
Comprehensive directory of over 1200 local exchange carriers and other telecom companies make up this directory. Includes a detailed index for easy cross-referencing by company name, contacts, titles, geographical region, services provided, e-mail and more. USTA's directory is your gateway to the telecom industry.
Cost: $699.00
Frequency: Annual

23333 Vocational Equipment Directory for GMC Truck Dealers
Verbiest Publishing Company
1155 Henrietta Street
Birmingham, MI 48009-1906
Directory of services and supplies to the industry.
Cost: $25.00
200 Pages
Frequency: Annual
Circulation: 6,000

23334 WESTLAW Transportation Library
West Publishing Company
610 Opperman Drive
Eagan, MN 55123-1340
651-687-7327; www.westgroup.com
This database offers information on US transportation laws.
Frequency: Full-text

Industry Web Sites

23335 http://gold.greyhouse.com
G.O.L.D Grey House OnLine Databases
Grey House Publishing's online database platform, GOLD, offers Quick Search, Keyword Search and Expert Search for most business sectors including transportation markets. The GOLD platform makes finding the information you need quick and easy - whether you're a novice searcher or an experienced database user. All of Grey House's directory products are available for subscription on the GOLD platform.

23336 www.aar.org
Association of American Railroads
Seeks to advance knowledge of scientific and economic location, construction, maintenance and operation of railroad.

23337 www.apta.com
American Public Transit Association
Maintains biographical archives and operates a placement service.

23338 www.buses.org
American Bus Association
Trade association for the North American bus industry.

23339 www.expedia.com
Expedia.com
Internet travel service offers access to airlines, hotels, car rentals, vacation packages, cruises and corporate travel.

23340 www.expresscarriers.com
Conducts research, promotes federal standards of construction, design, use and operation of tank trucks.

23341 www.gams.org
Association of Air Medical Services
An association of health care entities operating helicopter transport services.

23342 www.greyhouse.com
Grey House Publishing
Authoritative reference directories for most business markets including transportation markets. Users can search the online databases with varied search criteria allowing for custom searches by product category, geographic area, sales volume, keyword, subject and more. Full Grey House catalog and online ordering also available.

23343 www.hotwire.com
Hotwire.com
Internet travel service offering discounts on flights, hotels, car rentals, packages and cruises.

23344 www.iasm.org
International Association of Structural Movers
Members are movers of heavy structural products, trusses, houses and machinery and masonry structures.

23345 www.iccl.org
Internhational Council of Cruise Lines
For North American oceangoing, overnight major cruise line companies.

23346 www.intermodal.org
Intermodal Association of North America
Members are motor, rail and water transportation companies. Promotes the benefits and growth of intermodal freight transportation.

23347 www.ista.org
International Safe Transit Association
Members are shippers, carriers, manufacturers, packagers, package designers and testing laboratories, included in transport packaging.

23348 www.ite.org
Institute for Transportation Engineering
Dedicated to the transportation engineering field.

23349 www.moving.org
American Moving and Storage Association
Represents members including interstate moving and storage companies, local movers, international movers plus industry suppliers and state association members. AMSA's chief goals include strong support for effective government regulations and policies that protect consumers while allowing members to provide quality service at compensatory prices, and ensuring that consumers understand the value of professional moving and storage services.

23350 www.narprail.org
National Association of Railroad Passengers
Seeks to increase public awareness of rail passenger service and its benefits. Works for a national transportation policy.

23351 www.natso.com
NATSO

NATSO is the professional association of America's $42 billion travel plaza and truckstop industry. NATSO represents the industry on legislative and regulatory matters; serves as the official source of information on the diverse travel plaza and truckstop industry; provides education to its members; conducts an annual convention and trade show; and supports efforts to generally improve the business climate in which its members operate.

23352 **www.nbta.org**
National Business Travel Association

Offers over 1,300 corporate travel managers and allied members in the United States and Canada.

23353 **www.ndtahq.com**
National Defense Transportation Association

Intended as a liasion between government, military and private transportation officials.

23354 **www.nitl.org**
National Industrial Transportation League

Annual show of 250 exhibitors of computer services software and innovations for transportation operations.

23355 **www.nptc.org**
National Private Truck Council

Distributors, shippers, processors, jobbers and manufacturers who transport their own goods and are owners of their own truck fleets.

23356 **www.ntea.com**
National Truck Equipment Association

For small to mid-sized companies that manufacture, distribute, install, sell and repair commercial trucks, truck bodies, truck equipment, trailers and accessories.

23357 **www.ooida.com**
Owner Operator Independent Drivers Association

For owner-operators, professional drivers and small fleet owners.

23358 **www.ptdi.org**
Professional Truck Driver Institute

Advocate of optimum standards and professionalism for entry-level truck driver training.

23359 **www.raa.org**
Regional Airline Association

Membership consists of more than 70 airlines, plus 350 Associate members provide goods and services.

23360 **www.railway.museums.org**
Association of Railway Museums

The association of railway museums is for the preservation of railway equipment, artifacts and history.

23361 **www.rampages.onramp.net/~nars/**
National Association of Rail Shippers

Strives to provide a sound transporation system. Bestows annual Award of Excellence.

23362 **www.rpi.org**
Railway Progress Institute

The railway equipment and supply industry.

23363 **www.rssi.org**
Railway Systems Suppliers

A trade association serving the communication and signal segment of the rail transportation industry. Manages an annual trade show.

23364 **www.scooltrans.com**
National School Transportation Association

Strives to provide safe transportation, foster safety, and an atmosphere conducive to private enterprise.

23365 **www.scranet.org**
Specialized Carriers and Rigging Association

Members are carriers, crane and rigging operators and millwrights engaged in the transport of heavy goods.

23366 **www.specialtyfoods.org**
National Food Distributors Association

An organization comprised of independent store-to-door service distributors and suppliers of specialty food items.

23367 **www.teamster.org**
International Brotherhood of Teamsters

Affiliated with the AFL-CIO.

23368 **www.terry.org**
International Marine Transit Association

Membership includes ferry operators, naval architects, manufacturers, suppliers, and others in the terry industry around the world.

23369 **www.tianet.org**
Transportation Intermediaries Association

For North American transportation intermediaries including logistics management firms, property brokers, perishable commodities brokers, freight forwarders, intermodal marketers, ocean and air forwarders.

23370 **www.travel.yahoo.com**
Yahoo.com

Internet travel service providing access to flights, hotels, car rentals, vacation packages and cruises.

23371 **www.travelocity.com**
Sabre Holdings

Travel service offering consumers access to hundreds of airlines and thousands of hotels, as well as cruise, last-minute and vacation packages and best-in-class car rental companies.

23372 **www.truckline.com**
American Trucking Association

23373 **www.ttmanet.org**
Truck Trailer Manufacturers Association

A national organization of truck and tank trailer manufacturers and 120 suppliers to the industry.

23374 **www.tww.org**
Transport Workers Union of America

Chartered by the Congress of Industrial Organizations.

23375 **www.waterways.org**
National Waterways Conference

For shippers, barge lines and local port authorities working to promote a better understanding of the public value of the American waterways system.

23376 **www.weareparking.org**
National Parking Association

Social Media: Facebook, Twitter, LinkedIn

For operators of public and private parking facilities, including government, hospitals, colleges, universities and others.

23377 **www.woda.org**
World Organization of Dredging Associations

Develops professionalism in individuals involved in the dredging industry.

Associations

23378 **American Bus Association**
111 K Street NE
9th Floor
Washington, DC 20002

202-877-2208
800-283-2877; *Fax:* 202-842-0850
abainfo@buses.org; www.buses.org
Social Media: Facebook, Twitter, LinkedIn, YouTube

Peter J Pantuso, President & CEO
Roderick Lewis, Director, Membership & BD
Suzanne Te Beau Rohde, VP, Govt. Affairs & Policy
Brandon Buchanan, Director of Regulatory Affairs
Daniel Hoff, Director, Gov Affairs & Policy

ABA supports 3,800 members consisting of motorcoach and tour companies in addition to organizations that represent the tourism and travel industry. ABA strives to educate consumers on the importance of highway and motorcoach safety.
Founded in: 1926

23379 **American Council of Highway Advertisers**
1101 14th St., NW
Suite 1030
Washington, DC 20005-5635

202-857-0044; *Fax:* 202-857-7809
info@crp.org; www.opensecrets.org
Social Media: Facebook, Twitter, LinkedIn, RSS, YouTube

Sheila Krumholz, Executive Director
Jacob Hileman, IT Director
Sarah Bryner, Research Director
Viveca Novak, Editorial & Communications Director
Dan Auble, Senior Researcher
Founded in: 1983

23380 **American Society of Travel Agents (ASTA)**
675 N. Washington Street
Suite 490
Alexandria, VA 22314

703-739-2782
800-275-2782; *Fax:* 703-684-8319
askasta@asta.org; www.asta.org
Social Media: Facebook, Twitter, LinkedIn

Zane Kerby, President & CEO
Paul Ruden, EVP, Legal & Industry Affairs
Eben Peck, SVP, Government & Industry Affairs
Mark Meader, VP, Industry Affairs
Sue Sheats, VP, Business Development

Promotes and encourages travel among people of all nations. Serves as an information resource for the travel industry.
21M Members
Founded in: 1931

23381 **Association of Corporate Travel Executives**
510 King Street
Suite 220
Alexandria, VA 22314-2964

262-763-1902
800-375-2283; *Fax:* 613-836-0619
info@acte.org; www.acte.org
Social Media: Facebook, Twitter, LinkedIn, YouTube, RSS

Kurt Knackstedt, President
Greeley Koch, Executive Director
Jeff Kurn, Treasurer
Greeley Koch, Chief Staff Officer
Amber Kelleher, Global Engagement

Provides a forum for the discussion of ideas and information related to the corporate travel industry. Conducts educational programs and conferences.
700 Members
Founded in: 1988
Mailing list available for rent

23382 **Association of Group Travel Executives**
AH Light Company
510 King Street
Suite 220
Alexandria, VA 22314

262-763-1902
800-375-2283; *Fax:* 908-273-2344
info@acte.org; www.acte.org
Social Media: Facebook, Twitter, LinkedIn, YouTube, RSS

Kurt Knackstedt, President
Greeley Koch, Executive Director
Jeff Kurn, Treasurer
Greeley Koch, Chief Staff Officer
Amber Kelleher, Global Engagement

Affiliated with the Travel Industry Association of America.
675 Members
Founded in: 1988

23383 **Association of Retail Travel Agents**
4320 North Miller Road
Scottsdale, AZ 85251

800-969-6069; *Fax:* 866-743-2087;
www.arta.travel
Social Media: Facebook, Twitter, LinkedIn, You Tube

Nancy Linares, Board of Director

Promotes the interests of retail travel agents through representation on industry councils and testimony before Congress. Conducts joint marketing and educational programs.
2800 Members
Founded in: 1963

23384 **Association of Travel Marketing Executives**
PO Box 3176
West Tisbury, MA 02575

508-693-0550; *Fax:* 508-693-0115
kzern@atme.org; www.atme.org
Social Media: Facebook, Twitter, LinkedIn, Flickr

Kristin Zern, Executive Director
Henry Harteveldt, Chairman
Susan Black, Vice Chairman
Jeffrey DeKorte, Secretary
Jacqueline Johnson, Treasurer
Founded in: 1980

23385 **Association of Travel Marketing Executives**
PO Box 3176
West Tisbury, MA 02575

508-693-0550; *Fax:* 508-693-0115
kzern@atme.org; www.atme.org
Social Media: Facebook, Twitter, LinkedIn, Flickr

Kristin Zern, Executive Director
Henry Harteveldt, Chairman
Susan Black, Vice Chairman
Jeffrey DeKorte, Secretary
Jacqueline Johnson, Treasurer

Travel and tourism reports.
Founded in: 1980

23386 **Caribbean Hotel Association**
2655 Le Jeune Rd
Suite 910
Coral Gables, FL 33134

305-443-3040; *Fax:* 305-675-7977
membership@caribbeanhotelandtourism.com; www.caribbeanhotelandtourism.com
Social Media: Facebook, Twitter, LinkedIn

Richard Doumeng, Chairman
Emil Lee, President
Karolin Troubetzkoy, 1st VP
Stuart Bowe, 2nd VP
Karen Whitt, 3rd VP

Mission is to optimize the full potential of the Caribbean hotel and tourism industry by serving member needs and building partnerships. It's a LLC registered in the Cayman Islands, with offices in San Juan, Puerto Rico and Miami, FL.
Founded in: 1959

23387 **Greater Independent Association of National Travel Services**
915 Broadway
20th Floor
New York, NY 10010-7130

212-627-0001; *Fax:* 212-627-1110;
www.giantstravel.com
Social Media: Twitter, Youtube

Desiree Gruber, President
Susan Shapiro, Executive Director

Aims to establish a travel industry marketing cooperative. Holds regional workshops and seminars.
1.8M Members
Founded in: 1968

23388 **Hospitality Sales & Marketing Association International**
1760 Old Meadow Road
Suite 500
McLean, VA 22102

703-506-3280; *Fax:* 703-506-3266
info@hsmai.org; www.hsmai.org
Social Media: Facebook, Twitter, LinkedIn, Flickr

Rob Torres, Chairman
Jeff Senior, Chair Elect
Mark Thompson, Secretary/Treasurer
Marina MacDonald, Vice Chair
Robert A. Gilbert, CHME, CHA, President & CEO

The hospitality industry's source for knowledge, community, and recognition for leaders committed to professional development, sales growth, revenue optimization, marketing and branding.
7000 Members
Founded in: 1927

23389 **International Association of Convention and Visitor Bureaus**
2025 M St Nw
Suite 500
Washington, DC 20036-3349

202-296-7888; *Fax:* 202-296-7889
info@destinationmarketing.org;
www.destinationmarketing.org
Social Media: Facebook, Twitter, LinkedIn, Google+, YouTube, Flickr, Slid

Charles Jeffers II, Interim CEO & COO
Valencia Bembry, SVP
Stephanie Ann Russell, Executive Assistant
Christine Shimasaki, CDME, CMP, Managing Director
Elaine Rosquist, CMP, Director of Services

Promotes sound professional practices in the solicitation and servicing of meetings and conventions. Members represent travel/tourism related

businesses. Publications include an electronic newsletter and online directory.
Founded in: 1914
Mailing list available for rent: 1200 names at $400 per M

23390 International Association of Travel
PO Box D
Hurleyville, NY 12747

845-434-7777

Promotes accurate reporting on fields of aviation, travel, tourism and airports.
50+ Members
Founded in: 1988

23391 National Association of Business Travel Agents
National Association of Business Travel Agents
1920 L St. NW
Suite 300
Washington, DC 20036-2365

202-463-6223; *Fax:* 202-463-6239
nabe@nabe.com; www.nabe.com
Social Media: Twitter

Tom Beers, Executive Director
Colette Brissett, Administrative Director
Chris Jonas, Director, Comm. and Programs
Suzanne Clegg, Events Coordinator
Robert Crow, Editor, Business Economics

NBTA is a forum bringing together business travel buyer and supplier professionals from around the world. Membership includes access to the industry's premier network of corporate and government travel decision-makers and purchasers, a monthly e-newsletter as well as a quarterly publication, world-wide and local events, CTE opportunities and professional certificate programs.
Founded in: 1959

23392 National Association of RV Parks and Campgrounds
9085 E. Mineral Circle
Suite 200
Centennial, CO 80112

303-681-0401
800-395-2267; *Fax:* 303-681-0426
info@arvc.org; www.arvc.org
Social Media: Facebook, Twitter, LinkedIn, Youtube

Paul Bambei, President/CEO
Candra Talley, Membership Program Manager
Barb Youmans, Senior Director of Education
Jennifer Schwartz, Vice President, Marketing
Molly Martin, Marketing Coordinator

The association actively protects the best interests of its members on a federal level and provides awareness and assistance against government legislation & regulations at all levels(national, state and local).
3100 Members
Founded in: 1966
Mailing list available for rent: 3,200 names

23393 National Motorcoach Network
PO Box 1088
Mount Jackson, VA 22842

540-477-3202
800-469-0062; *Fax:* 540-477-3858
stephen.kirchner@gmail.com;
www.motorcoach.com/byways

Founded in: 1983

23394 National Tour Association
101 Prosperous Place
Suite 350
Lexington, KY 40509
859-264-6540
800-682-8886; *Fax:* 859-264-6570
pam.inman@ntastaff.com; www.ntaonline.com
Social Media: Facebook, Twitter, LinkedIn, Youtube, Google+, Instagram

Pam Inman, President
Catherine Prather, Executive Vice President
Doug Rentz, Director, Communication & Marketing
Dawn Pettus, Manager, Events

The National Tour Association is an organization of nearly 4,000 international tourism professionals focused on the development, promotion and increased use of tour operators packaged travel.
4000 Members
Founded in: 1951
Mailing list available for rent

23395 Office of General Supply and Services
1800 F Street, NW
Washington, DC 20405

202-564-2480
866-606-8220
NCSCcustomer.service@gsa.gov;
www.gsa.gov
Social Media: Facebook, Twitter, Youtube, RSS

Adam Neufeld, Deputy Administrator
Denise Turner Roth, Administrator
Katy Kale, Chief Of Staff
Reginald Cardozo, Deputy Chief of Staff
Norman Dong, Public Buildings Service

The Office of General Supplies and Services (GSS) is responsible for acquisition services and comprehensive supply chain management, including excess/surplus federal property.
Founded in: 1949

23396 Passenger Vessel Association
103 Oronoco Street
Suite 200
Alexandria, VA 22314-1549

703-518-5005
800-807-8360; *Fax:* 703-518-5151
pvainfo@passengervessel.com;
www.passengervessel.com
Social Media: Facebook

John Groundwater, Executive Director
Margo Marks, Vice President
Leslie Kagarise, Director of Finance
Lee Hill, Chief Financial Officer
Edmund Welch, Legislative Director

Represents operators of tours, excursions, ferries, charter vessels, dinner boats and other small passenger vessels.
600 Members
Founded in: 1971

23397 Receptive Services Association
2365 Harrodsburg Road
Suite A325
Lexington, KY 40504

859-219-3545
866-939-0934; *Fax:* 859-226-4404
headquarters@rsaa.com; www.rsana.com
Social Media: Facebook, Youtube

Matt Grayson, Executive Director
Rachel Gates, Member Services Administrator
Toby Bishop, Sales Manager
Jonathan Zuk, Chairman
Veronique Hubert, Vice Chairman

Helping receptive operators serve international tour companies through partnerships with North American suppliers.
570 Members

23398 Recreational Vehicle Industry Association
1896 Preston White Drive
Reston, VA 20191

703-620-6003; *Fax:* 703-620-5071;
www.rvia.org

David Humphreys, President

The national trade association representing recreation vehicle manufacturers and their component parts suppliers who build more than 98% of all RVsproduced in the U.S.
Founded in: 1963

23399 Society of American Travel Writers
One Parkview Plaza
Suite 800
Oakbrook Terrace, IL 60181

414-359-1671; *Fax:* 414-359-1671
info@satw.org; www.satw.org
Social Media: Facebook, Twitter, LinkedIn

Paul Lasley, President
Annette Thompson, Immediate Past President
Barbara Orr, Vice President, Membership
Tom Adkinson, Treasurer
Peggy Bendel, Secretary

Photographers and 35 associate member representatives of airlines, hotels, resorts, tourist agencies and public relations firms.
Founded in: 1955

23400 Society of Incentive and Travel Executives
330 N Wabash Ave
Chicago, IL 60611

312-321-5148; *Fax:* 312-527-6783
site@siteglobal.com; www.siteglobal.com
Social Media: Facebook, Twitter, LinkedIn, Youtube

Kevin M. Hinton, CEO
Ashley Mayrisch, Marketing Coordinator
Maggie Vaulman, Membership Associate
Adrianne Stokes, Operations Associate
Murphy Goodworth, Global Conference Director

An individual membership society covering 70 countries. Members are corporate users, airlines, Tourist Boards, cruise lines, destination management companies, consultants, hotels/resorts, travel agents, incentive travel houses and publications.
2000 Members
Founded in: 1973

23401 Travel Industry Association of America
1100 New York Ave Nw
Suite 450
Washington, DC 20005-3934

202-408-8422; *Fax:* 202-408-1255;
www.tia.org

Roger J Dow, President & CEO
Todd Davidson, Treasurer & Director
Bonnie L Carlson, Secretary & Director

Members are hotels, airlines and travel agencies interested in promoting increased travel to and within the US.
2100 Members
Founded in: 1941

23402 Travel and Tourism Research Association
5300 Lakewood Road
Whitehall, MI 49461

248-708-8872; *Fax:* 248-814-7150
info@ttra.com; www.ttra.com

Dan Mishell, Chairman
Jeffrey Eslinger, President
Susan Bruinzeel, 1st VP/Conference Chair

Dr. Marion Joppe, 2nd VP/Membership Chair
John Markham, Treasurer
Founded in: 1970

23403 U.S. Travel Association
1100 New York Ave. NW
Suite 450
Washington, DC 20005
202-408-8422; *Fax:* 202-408-1255
feedback@ustravel.org; www.ustravel.org
Todd Davidson, Chair
Roger J. Dow, President
The Association advocates for the importance of travel, and the freedom to travel, to a healthy U.S. economy.

23404 Volunteers for Peace
7 Kilburn Street
Suite 316
Belmont, VT 05401
802-598-0052
vfp@vfp.org; www.vfp.org
Social Media: Facebook, Twitter
Matt Messier, Executive Director
Alexandra Smith, International Placement Coordinator
Ton Sherman, President
Lila Hobbes, Secretary, Treasurer
A Vermont nonprofit membership organization promoting over 3000 international voluntary service projects in 100 countries. Workcamps are an affordable way to travel, live and work abroad.
2000 Members
Founded in: 1982

Newsletters

23405 AAA World
2040 Market Street
Philadelphia, PA 19103
215-851-0291
800-763-9900; *Fax:* 215-851-0297
letters@aaaworld.com; www.aaaworld.com
Allen EeWalle, CEO
Sandy Kaden, Circulation Manager
Promotes travel destinations, gives advice on traveling and helpful automobile information.
Cost: $71.00
Circulation: 2.1 mill
Founded in: 1900

23406 ABA Insider
American Bus Association
111 K Street NE
9th Floor
Washington, DC 20002
202-842-1645; *Fax:* 202-842-0850
abainfo@buses.org; www.buses.org
Peter J Pantuso, CEO
Buchcannon Brandon, Director of Operations
Hart Clyde, Senior VP of Government Affairs
Hoff Daniel, Director of ABA Foundation & Policy
Jones Patrick, Legislative & Communications Coordi
ABA's biweekly newsletter that keeps members informed on the travel, tourism and motorcoach industry.
Frequency: Biweekly
Founded in: 1926

23407 Caribbean Reporter
Caribbean Hotel Association
18 Calle Marseilles
San Juan, PR 907-1682
787-725-2901; *Fax:* 787-725-9180;
www.chahotels.com
Beverly Telemague, Publisher
Membership news.
Cost: $4.99
Frequency: Monthly
Founded in: 1959

23408 Entree Travel Newsletter
Entree Publishing
PO Box 5148
Santa Barbara, CA 93150-5148
805-969-5848; *Fax:* 805-969-5849
wtomicki@aol.com; www.entreenews.com
William Tomicki, Editor/Publisher
Travel, fashion and beauty ideas, sports and photography, wines and restaurants reviews new literature, music and film of interest to the travel and food enthusiast.
Cost: $75.00
Frequency: Monthly
Circulation: 8000
Printed in one color on matte stock

23409 IACVB e-News
Int'l Association of Convention & Visitor Bureaus
2025 M St Nw
Suite 500
Washington, DC 20036-3349
202-296-7888; *Fax:* 202-296-7889;
www.destinationmarketing.org
Michael D Gehrisch, CEO
Kristen Clemens, Editor
An electronic newsletter published by the International Association of Convention and Visitor Bureaus. Available with membership.
Frequency: Weekly
Circulation: 1300
Founded in: 1914
Mailing list available for rent: 1200 names at $400 per M

23410 Ocean and Cruise News
PO Box 329
Northport, NY 11768
203-329-2787; *Fax:* 203-329-2767
news@wocls.org; www.wocls.org/
Tom Cassidy, VP
Geroge Devol, President
Complete news on cruises.
Cost: $30.00
Frequency: Monthly
Circulation: 7000
Founded in: 1980

23411 Travel Industry Association of America Newsletter
Travel Industry Association of America
1100 New York Ave Nw
Suite 450 W
Washington, DC 20005-6130
202-408-8422; *Fax:* 202-408-1255;
www.tia.org
Roger J Dow, CEO
C Betsi, Marketing Manager
Kathy Keefe, Editor
Travel information.
Cost: $1350.00
Frequency: Monthly
Circulation: 3500
Founded in: 1941
Printed in 3 colors on glossy stock

23412 Travel Management Newsletter
Reed Travel Group
500 Plaza Dr
Secaucus, NJ 07094-3619
201-902-1800; *Fax:* 202-902-2053;
www.tmdaily.com
Steve Bailey, Publisher
Discusses the news and views of the travel professional.
Cost: $735.00
Frequency: Weekly

23413 Travel Manager's Executive Briefing
Health Resources Publishing
1913 Atlantic Ave
Suite 200
Manasquan, NJ 08736-1067
732-292-1100
800-516-4343; *Fax:* 732-292-1111
info@themcic.com;
www.healthresourcesonline.com
Robert K Jenkins, Publisher
Lisa Mansfield, Marketing Assistant
Read by travel managers of major corporations, Fortune 500 companies and corporate travel agencies twice a month to get up to the minute developments in the important field of travel and expense cost control.
Cost: $447.00
ISSN: 0272-569x

23414 Travel Weekly
500 Plaza Drive
Secaucus, NJ 07094-3685
201-902-1696; *Fax:* 201-902-2053;
www.travelweekly.com
William D Scott, Publisher
Industry news, articles and stories on the travel industry.
Cost: $26.00
Frequency: BiWeekly

23415 Travel and Tourism Executive Report
10200 W 44th Avenue
Suite 304
Wheat Ridge, CO 80033-2840
303-463-2887
Francine Butler, Executive Director
Established as the Travel Research Association as the result of a merger.
750 Pages

23416 Travelwriter Marketletter
21553 Center Point Circle
Ashburn, VA 20147
571-214-9086; *Fax:* 208-988-7672;
www.travelwriterml.com
Mimi Backhausen, Editor & Publisher
A monthly newsletter for travel writers and travel photographers. It's mainly about marketing travel articles, photography and travel books; also describes free trips for professional travel writers.
Cost: $75.00
10 Pages
Frequency: Monthly
Circulation: 1000
ISSN: 0738-9093

23417 Tuesday Newsletter
National Tour Association
101 Prosperours Place
Suite 350
Lexington, KY 40509
859-264-6540
800-682-8886; *Fax:* 859-264-6570
chorton@multibriefs.com
ntaonline.com
Social Media: Facebook, Twitter, LinkedIn
Pam Inman, President
Doug Rentz, Director, Communication & Marketing
The National Tour Association is an organization of nearly 4,000 North American tourism professionals focused on the development, promotion and increased use of tour operators packaged

travel.
Cost: $36.00
Frequency: Monthly
Circulation: 5000
Founded in: 1998
Mailing list available for rent: 3,800 names

Magazines & Journals

23418 ABC Preferred Flight Planner: Europe- Middle East-Africa
ABC Corporate Services/Reed Travel Group
500 Plaza Drive
Secaucus, NJ 07094-3619
201-678-8775; *Fax:* 201-902-2053;
www.infotec-travel.com
Luis Murcia, Owner
Offers information on properties and locations of interest to corporate business travelers.
250 Pages
Frequency: SemiAnnual
Circulation: 65,000

23419 ASTA Agency Management
Miller Freeman Publications
2655 Seely Avenue
San Jose, CA 95134
408-943-1234; *Fax:* 408-943-0513
Mary Pat Sullivan, Publisher
Provides concise and useful information on trends in the industry and practical ideas regarding the profitable administration of travel agencies.
Cost: $36.00
Frequency: Monthly
Circulation: 35,182

23420 ASU Travel Guide
448 Ignacio Boulevard
Suite 333
San Rafael, CA 94949-5539
415-898-9500
866-459-0300; *Fax:* 415-898-9501;
www.asutravelguide.com
Christopher Gil, Managing Editor
Hank Sousa, VP
Provides information concerning worldwide travel destinations and other locales of interest to travelers and the bargains and discounts available to airline employees.
352 Pages
Frequency: Quarterly
Circulation: 700000
Founded in: 1971
Printed in 4 colors on glossy stock

23421 Bank Travel Management
Group Travel Leader
301 East High Street
Lexington, KY 40507
859-253-0455; *Fax:* 859-253-0499;
www.banktravelmanagement.com
Mac Lacy, President & Publisher
Herb Sparrow, Executive Editor
Brian Jewell, Associate Editor
Kelly Tyner, Director of Sales & Marketing
Stacey Bowman, National Account Manager
Regular sections include: The Banker's Box, managing your senior program, and marketing your trips, with special features on personal travel accounts, trends in travel and banking clubs. Subscriptions are complimentary for qualified travel planners.
Cost: $49.00
Frequency: 6/Year
Circulation: 4100
Founded in: 1994

23422 Bus Tours Magazine
National Bus Trader
9698 W Judson Rd
Polo, IL 61064-9015
815-946-2341; *Fax:* 815-946-2347
nbt@busmag.com; www.busmag.com
Larry Plachno, President
Shaye Hall, Assistant Editor
Nancy Ann Plachno, Business Manager
Focuses on the operations, arrangements and marketing techniques used to plan these excursions as well as what's new in the industry.
Cost: $10.00
Frequency: Monthly
Circulation: 7,200
Founded in: 1979

23423 Byways
National Motorcoach Network
42 Cabin Hill Lane
Mt Jackson, VA 22842
540-773-3323
800-469-0062; *Fax:* 540-477-3858
stephen.kirchner@gmail.com;
www.motorcoach.com/byways
Social Media: Facebook, Twitter, LinkedIn
Stephen M Kirchner, Publisher/Editor
Featuring North America's leading travel destinations. Includes riverboat gambling updates and special reports on the top 50 motorcoach destinations.
48 Pages
Frequency: Bi-Monthly
Circulation: 20000
Founded in: 1983

23424 City Visitor
Travelhost
5755 Granger Road
Independence, OH 44131
972-556-0541; *Fax:* 972-432-8729;
www.travelhost.com
James E Buerger, President
Travelhost is an in room publisher edited for the business and vacation traveler, with news features and general information relating to travel, recreation, business, new products and services and leisure activities.
Cost: $33.00
Frequency: Monthly
Founded in: 1967

23425 Conde Nast Traveler Business Extra
Conde Nast
4 Times Sq
14th Floor
New York, NY 10036-6561
212-286-2860; *Fax:* 212-286-5960;
www.condenast.com
Charles H Townsend, CEO
Relates to gathering information for tourism.

23426 Corporate & Incentive Travel
Coastal Communications Corporation
2700 N Military Trail
Suite 120
Boca Raton, FL 33431
561-989-0600; *Fax:* 561-989-9509
ccceditor1@att.net;
www.themeetingmagazines.com
Harvey Grotsky, Publisher/Editor-In-Chief
Susan Wyckoff Fell, Managing Editor
Susan Gregg, Managing Editor
The magazine for corporate meetings and incentive travel planners. In-depth editorial focus on site selection, accommodations and transportation, current legislation, conference, seminar and training facilities, budget and cost controls, and destination reports. Regular features highlight industry news and developments, trends and personalities, meeting values, facilities, and destinations.
Frequency: Monthly
Circulation: 40,000
Founded in: 1983

23427 Corporate and Incentive Travel
Coastal Communications Corporation
2700 N Military Trail
Suite 120
Boca Raton, FL 33431-6394
561-989-0600; *Fax:* 561-989-9509;
www.themeetingmagazines.com
Harvey Grotsky, President & CEO
Susan Wyckoff Fell, Managing Editor
Susan S Gregg, Managing Editor
This magazine is edited for corporate meeting planners with the responsibility for staging and planning meetings, incentive travel programs, conferences and conventions.
Frequency: Monthly
Founded in: 1983

23428 Country Discoveries
5400 S 60th Street
Greendale, WI 53129-1404
414-423-0100
800-344-6913; *Fax:* 414-423-8463;
www.reimanpub.com
Focuses on backwoods travel in both the United States and Canada.
Cost: $14.98
Founded in: 1965

23429 Courier
National Tour Association
101 Prosperous Place
Suite 350
Lexington, KY 40509
859-264-6540
800-682-8886; *Fax:* 859-264-6570
questions@ntastaff.com
ntaonline.com
Pam Inman, President
Bob Rouse, Editor-in-Chief
Courier Magazine helps readers to meet their responsibilities involved with their jobs.
Cost: $36.00
Frequency: Monthly
Circulation: 6000
ISSN: 0279-4489
Founded in: 1955
Printed in 4 colors on glossy stock

23430 Cruise Industry News - Annual
Nissel-Lie Communications
441 Lexington Avenue
Room 809
New York, NY 10017-3910
212-986-1025; *Fax:* 212-986-1033
info2@cruiseindustrynews.com;
www.cruiseindustrynews.com
Oivind Mathisen, Editor/Publisher
Angela Mathisen, Advertising Director/Publisher
Monty Mathisen, Reporter/Web Editor
The only book of its kind, and often rated the most comprehensive information source on the industry by cruise line executives.
Cost: $575.00
Frequency: Annual+
Founded in: 1988

23431 Cruise Industry News Quarterly Magazine
Nissel-Lie Communications

441 Lexington Avenue
Room 809
New York, NY 10017-3910

212-986-1025; *Fax:* 212-986-1033
info2@cruiseindustrynews.com;
www.cruiseindustrynews.com

Oivind Mathisen, Editor/Publisher
Angela Mathisen, Advertising Director/Publsher
Monty Mathisen, Reporter/Web Editor

The magazine covers all aspects of cruise operations, shipbuilding, new ships, cruise companies, ship reviews, onboard services, food and beverage, and ports and destinations.
Cost: $495.00
Frequency: Quarterly
Circulation: 50000
Founded in: 1991
Printed in 4 colors

23432 Destinations
American Bus Association
700 13th St NW
Suite 575
Washington, DC 20005-5923

202-842-1645
800-283-2877; *Fax:* 202-842-0850
abainfo@buses.org; www.buses.org

Peter J Pantuso, CEO
Eron Shosteck, Marketing

Motorcoach travel across North America and Association news.
80 Pages
Frequency: Monthly
Circulation: 6000
Founded in: 1926
Printed in 4 colors on glossy stock

23433 Digital Travel
Jupiter Communications Company
475 Park Ave S
Suite 4
New York, NY 10016-6901

212-547-7900
800-481-1212; *Fax:* 212-953-1733;
www.jup.com

Alan Meckler, CEO
Marla Kammer, Managing Editor

Editorial includes the latest information and technology in agencies, airlines, lodging, ticketing, mapping, Web advertising, transaction processing, revenue models, demographics, and full-service sites.
Cost: $595.00
Frequency: Monthly

23434 Family Motor Coaching Magazine
Family Motor Coach Association
8291 Clough Pike
Cincinnati, OH 45244-2796

513-474-3622
800-543-3622; *Fax:* 513-474-2332
jyeatts@fmca.com; www.fmca.com

Don Eversman, Executive Director
Ranita Jones, Sales Manager
Cost: $3.99
Frequency: Monthly
Circulation: 140000

23435 Frequent Flyer Magazine
2000 Clearwater Drive
Oak Brook, IL 60523

630-574-6000
800-342-5674; *Fax:* 630-574-6565

23436 Going on Faith
Group Traveler Leader
301 E High Street
Lexington, KY 40507

859-253-0455
888-253-0455; *Fax:* 859-253-0499
circmanager@grouptravelleader.com;
www.grouptravelleader.com

Mac Lacy, Publisher
Herb Sparrow, Executive Editor
Brian Jewell, Associate Editor
Kelly Tyner, Director of Sales & Marketing
Stacey Bowman, National Account Manager

The national travel newspaper for churches, synagogues and Religious organizations. The official newspaper for the Going on Faith Conference. Online.
Frequency: 6/Year
Circulation: 5500
Founded in: 1997

23437 Group Travel Leader
Group Travel Leader
301 E High St
Lexington, KY 40507-1509

859-253-0455; *Fax:* 859-253-0499;
www.grouptravelleader.com

Mac Lacy, President
Herb Sparrow, Executive Editor
Brian Jewell, Associate Editor
Kelly Tyner, Director of Sales & Marketing
Stacey Bowman, National Account Manager

Supplies the senior travel planner with new destinations, unique points of interest and historical venues for their group, club or organization.
Cost: $39.00
Frequency: Monthly
Circulation: 30000
Founded in: 1991

23438 HSMAI Marketing Review
Hospitality Sales & Marketing Association Int'l
1760 Old Meadow Road
Suite 500
McLean, VA 22102

703-506-3280; *Fax:* 703-506-3266
info@hsmai.org; www.hsmai.org

Kathleen Tindell, Editor

Features in-depth information and columns on best practices, web marekting, international affairs and future forecasting.
Cost: $65.00
7000 Pages
Frequency: Quarterly
Circulation: 10000
Founded in: 1927

23439 Inside Flyer
Flight Plan
1930 Frequent Flyer Point
Colorado Springs, CO 80915

719-597-8889
800-767-8896; *Fax:* 719-597-6855;
www.insideflyer.com/

Randy Petersen, Editor/publ/CEO
Karen Heldt, Advertising Coordinator
Linda Hanwella, Managing Editor

Leading publication of information for and about frequent traveler programs.
Cost: $45.00
Frequency: Monthly
Founded in: 1986
Mailing list available for rent
Printed in 4 colors on matte stock

23440 Jax Fax Travel Marketing
Jax Fax
52 West Main Street
Milford, CT 06460-3310

203-301-0255; *Fax:* 203-301-0250;
www.jaxfax.com

Doug Cooke, President
Marc Spac, Publishing Director
Theresa Seanlon, Editor
Marjorie Vincent, Circulation Manager
Peter Badeau, Associate Publisher

Monthly travel trade magazine featuring destination information and listings of discounted airfares and tour packages.
Cost: $15.00
Frequency: Monthly
Circulation: 25000
Founded in: 1973
Printed in 4 colors on glossy stock

23441 Mexico Today
2009 S 10th Street
McAllen, TX 78503-5405

956-686-0711
800-222-0158; *Fax:* 956-686-0732
info@sanbornsinsurance.com;
www.sanbornsinsurance.com

Pete Castillo, Marketing Director
Frequency: Quarterly
Circulation: 5000
Printed in 4 colors on glossy stock

23442 Mid-Atlantic Group Tour Magazine
Shoreline Creations
PO Box 638
Yarmouth Port, MA 02675-638

508-398-0400; *Fax:* 616-393-0085
travel@grouptour.com; www.grouptour.com

Carl Wassink, Publisher
Carol Smith, Editor
Katie Weller, Circulation Manager
Jamie Cannon, Marketing Manager
Ruth Wassink, Vice President

Material looks at the latest offerings in tour travel including restaurants, theater, shopping, hotels, festivals, and events and activities.
Frequency: Quarterly
Circulation: 10000
Founded in: 1980

23443 Midwest Traveler
12901 N Forty Drive
Saint Louis, MO 63141

314-523-6981
800-222-7623; *Fax:* 314-523-6982;
www.autoclubmo.aaa.com

Mike Right, Editor
Cost: $3.00
Circulation: 45000
Founded in: 1902

23444 Mobility
1717 Pennsylvania Avenue NW
8th Floor
Washington, DC 20006

202-293-7744; *Fax:* 202-659-8631;
www.erc.org/MOBILITY_Online

23445 NBTA Travel Quarterly
National Association of Business Travel Agents
123~North~Pitt Street
4th Floor
Alexandria, VA 22314

703-684-0836; *Fax:* 703-342-4324
info@nbta.org; www.nbta.org

Caleb Tiller, Sr Dir, Marketing & Communications
Wendy Santiago, Marketing Manager
Nicole Hayes, Assistant Manager, Communications
Jack Machlum, CEO
Kevin Maguire, VP/Chief Information Officer

This publication provides valuable information on NBTA, its members and the corporate travel industry, to help the professional stay connected to the industry.
Frequency: Quarterly/Members Only

23446 **New England Tour Magazine**
Shoreline Creations
PO Box 638
Yarmouth Port, MA 02675-638
508-398-0400; *Fax:* 508-398-4703
travel@grouptour.com; www.grouptour.com
Carol Smith, Editor
Carl Wassink, President
Katie Weller, Circulation Manager
Jamie Cannon, Marketing
Ruth Wassink, Executive Vice President
Promotes and covers the attractions, lodging, dining, events and other highlights of popular and less-famous travel destinations in the region.
Frequency: Quarterly
Circulation: 10000
Founded in: 1925

23447 **Onboard Services**
International Publishing Company of America
50 Millstone Road
Building 300 Suite 110
East Windsor, NJ 08520
609-945-8000
800-280-8591; *Fax:* 609-945-8080
general@obcc.net; www.onboard-services.com
Alexander Morton, President
George Hulcher, Contributing Editor
Keeps airline, cruise ships, railroad, and terminal concessions management and purchasing departments up-to-date on all phases of passenger services.
Cost: $25.00
24 Pages
ISSN: 0892-4236
Founded in: 1968
Printed in 4 colors on glossy stock

23448 **Ozark Mountain Visitor**
200 Industrial Park Drive
Hollister, MO 65672-5327
417-334-3161; *Fax:* 417-335-3933

23449 **Pacific Asia Travel News**
Americas Publishing Company
3657 Harriet Road
Victoria, Can, BC V8Z-3T1
250-260-1883; *Fax:* 250-953-5250
Malcolm Scott, Publisher
Issues include a news dateline with features on travel trends and outlooks, a special destination focus, and updates from the Pacific Asia Travel Association.
Cost: $30.00
Frequency: BiMonthly
Circulation: 24,000

23450 **Practical Gourmet**
Linick Group
PO Box 102
Middle Island, NY 11953-0102
631-924-3888; *Fax:* 631-924-3890
linickgrp@att.net;
www.thepracticalgourmet.blogspot.com
Andrew S Linick, CEO
Roger Dextor, Production
Barbara Deal, Marketing Manager
The focus of this publication is light, healthy gourmet dining; includes reports on wine tasting, food festivals, contests, celebrations, cooking schools and other events.
Cost: $48.00
36 Pages
Frequency: Monthly
Circulation: 210,000
Founded in: 1975
Mailing list available for rent: 210 M names at $110 per M
Printed in 4 colors on glossy stock

23451 **Recommend**
Worth International Communication Corp
PO Box 171070
Hialeah, FL 33017-1070
305-828-0123
800-447-0123; *Fax:* 305-826-6950;
www.recommend.com
Laurel A Herman, Publisher
Lorri Robbins, National Director
Contains colorful information on worldwide destinations, resorts, hotels, transportation and tour operators, as well as marketing angles to help travel agents sell travel.
Cost: $48.00
Frequency: Monthly
Circulation: 60000
Founded in: 1967
Printed in on glossy stock

23452 **Runzheimer Reports on Travel Management**
Runzheimer Park
Rochester, WI 53167-9999
262-712-2200
800-558-1702; *Fax:* 262-971-2254
Rex Runzheimer, President

23453 **Sea Mass Traveler**
PO Box 3189
Newport, RI 02840-0322
401-848-2922

23454 **Southwest Airlines Spirit**
Pace Communications
2811 McKinney Avenue
Suite 360
Dallas, TX 75204
214-580-2491; *Fax:* 214-580-8070;
www.spiritmag.com
Jay Heinrichs, Editorial Director
John McAlley, Executive Editor
Frequency: Monthly
Circulation: 400088
Founded in: 1971

23455 **Specialty Travel Index**
PO Box 458
San Anselmo, CA 94979
415-594-4900
888-624-4030; *Fax:* 415-455-1648
info@specialtytravel.com;
www.specialtytravel.com
Karin Kinsey, Art Director
Stean Hansen, Circulation Manager
Andy Alpine, Marketing Manager
Risa Weinreb, Editor
Judith Alpine, Advertising Manager
Directory/magazine of adventure and specialty travel.
Cost: $10.00
Circulation: 32000
ISSN: 0889-7085
Founded in: 1980
Printed in 4 colors on glossy stock

23456 **SportsTravel Magazine**
Schneider Publishing Company
11835 W Olympic Blvd
Suite 1265
Los Angeles, CA 90064-5814
310-577-3700; *Fax:* 310-577-3715
info@schneiderpublishing.com;
www.schneiderpublishing.com
Social Media: Facebook, Twitter, LinkedIn
Tim Schneider, President
Jason Gewirtz, Managing Editor/Sports Travel
Lisa Furfine, Associate Publisher
Chad Starbuck, Marketing Manager
Includes articles on travel training, sports law, event spotlights, and vital information on sites, hotels, transportation, trade shows and upcomiong events for team travel planners and event organizers.
Cost: $48.00
Frequency: Monthly
Circulation: 1400
ISSN: 1091-5354
Founded in: 1997
Printed in on glossy stock

23457 **Sun Valley Magazine**
Mandala Media LLC
111 1st Avenue North #1M
Meriwether Building
Hailey, ID 83333
208-788-0770; *Fax:* 208-788-3881;
www.sunvalleymag.com
Laurie C Sammis, Publisher/Editor-in-Chief
Mike McKenna, Editor
Julie Molema, Production Director
Articles on the arts, community, recreation, dining, shopping and real estate in the Sun Valley, Idaho area.
Cost: $22.00
Frequency: Quarterly
Circulation: 20000

23458 **Sundancer's West**
1108 Meadowview Drive
Euless, TX 76039
817-545-5265; *Fax:* 817-571-6481;
www.sundancerswest.com
Gerry Watkins, Webmaster/Editor/Photographer

23459 **Travel & Leisure**
American Express Publishing Corporation
1120 Avenue of the Americas
Suite 9
New York, NY 10036-6700
212-382-5600
800-888-8728; *Fax:* 212-382-5878;
www.tlexplorer.com
Ed Kelly, CEO
Nancy Novogrod, Editor-in-Chief
Antonia LoPresti, Senior Marketing Manager
Cost: $19.95
Frequency: Monthly
Circulation: 950000

23460 **Travel Agent International**
Universal Media
PO Box 5386
Bloomington, IL 61702-5386
309-663-6327; *Fax:* 212-883-1244
tai@taitravelbmi.com; www.taitravelbmi.com
Richard P Friese, Publisher
Provides profiles on resorts and attractions for each given season.
Cost: $250.00
Frequency: 10 per year
Circulation: 19,100

23461 **Travel Counselor**
Miller Freeman Publications
600 Harrison Street
6th Fl
San Francisco, CA 94107
415-947-6000
800-764-759; *Fax:* 415-947-6055
email@travel-counselors.com;
www.travel-counselors.com
Contains business information and analysis appropriate to the retail agency profession
Frequency: 7 per year
Circulation: 28,000

23462 **Travel Trends**
Meredith Corporation

125 Park Ave
New York, NY 10017-5529

212-557-6600; *Fax:* 212-551-7161

Peter Mason, Publisher/Editor

Information on the trends of the travel industry.
Frequency: Quarterly
Circulation: 5,000

23463 Travel World
East - West News Bureau
16051 W. Tampa Palms Blvd
Tampa, FL 33647

813-978-0877
800-494-3279
debbie@travelworld1.com;
www.travelworld1.com

23464 Travel World News
Travel Industry Network
Ste 8
28 Knight St
Norwalk, CT 06851-4719

203-286-6679; *Fax:* 203-286-6681
editor@travelworldnews.com;
www.travelworldnews.com

Charles Gatt Jr, Publisher
Peter Gatt, Associate Publisher

Monthly trade publication covering the retail travel industry. Each issue contains industry information and coverage for agents who are making recommendations and booking for their clients, including comprehensive, up to date, and worldwide product news and destination editorial coverage. Available online and in print.
Frequency: Monthly
Circulation: 22000
Founded in: 1988

23465 Travel, Food & Wine
Punch-In-Syndicate
400 E 59th Street
Floor 9
New York, NY 10022-2342

212-755-4363
punchin@usa.net; www.punchin.com

J Walman, Editor

A magazine featuring articles and reviews on travel, food and wine, columns on airlines, hotels, cruise ships, railroads, resorts, restaurants, and spas. Also theater reviews, cinema, radio and all forms of entertainment.
Cost: $300.00
Frequency: Monthly

23466 TravelBound!
Group Traveler Leader
301 E High Street
Lexington, KY 40507

859-253-0455
888-253-0455; *Fax:* 859-253-0499;
www.grouptravelleader.com
Social Media: Facebook, Twitter, LinkedIn, You Tube

Mac Lacy, Publisher
Herb Sparrow, Executive Editor
Brian Jewell, Associate Editor
Kelly Tyner, Director of Sales & Marketing
Stacey Bowman, National Account Manager

The national magazine for African American Group Traveling, and the official magazine for the African American Travel Conference (AATC).
Circulation: 4500
Founded in: 2001

23467 Travelhost Magazine
Travelhost
10701 N Stemmons Fwy
Dallas, TX 75220-2419

972-556-0541; *Fax:* 972-432-8729;
www.travelhost.com

James E Buerger, CEO
David B Portener, Associate Publisher
Frequency: Monthly
Circulation: 60000
Founded in: 1967

23468 Vermont Green Mountain Guide
44 Country Road
North Springfield, VT 05150-9738

802-886-3333;
www.vtliving.com/newspapers/vtgreenmtnguid

Cindy Thiel, President

Trade Shows

23469 Adventure Travel and Outdoor Show
McRand International
1 Westminster Place
Suite 300
Lake Forest, IL 60045-1867

Fax: 847-295-4419

Richard Dux, VP
Sue Wildman, VP

Exhibits by tour operators, outfitters and others geared toward soft and hard adventure travel vacations and outdoor activities.
15M Attendees
Frequency: January

23470 American Society of Travel Agents Conference
1101 King Street
Ste. 200
Alexandria, VA 22314-2944

703-739-2782; *Fax:* 703-684-8319
bdaniels@asta.org; www.asta.org

Chris Vranas, VP
Brooke Daniels, Event Manager

Gathering of travel agents, airlines, hotels and tour operators that provides the opportunity to view and discuss new products, services and trends in the industry. 700 booths.
6M Attendees
Frequency: November

23471 American Travel Market Exhibition Company
Reed Exhibition Companies
383 Main Avenue
Norwalk, CT 06851-1543

203-840-4800; *Fax:* 203-840-9628;
www.reedexpo.com

Gregg Vautrin, CEO

The national event for all US travel buyers, including tour operators, travel agents, corporate travel buyers and meeting/conference planners. One of a global series of Travel Market events.
Frequency: September

23472 Annual American and Canadian Sport, Travel and Outdoor Show
Expositions
Edgewater Branch
PO Box 550
Cleveland, OH 44107-0550

216-529-1300; *Fax:* 216-529-0311
ech.case.edu

John Grabowskie, Online Editor
John Bedan, Associate Online Editor
Nathan Delany, Associate Online Editor

975 exhibits of hunting and fishing equipment, travel services, boats, recreational vehicles and related equipment, supplies and services.
300k Attendees
Frequency: Annual
Founded in: 1935

23473 Annual Boat, Vacation and Outdoor Show
Showtime Productions
PO Box 4372
Rockford, IL 61110

815-877-8043; *Fax:* 815-877-9037
brenda@showtimeproduction.net
showtimeproduction.net

Duane Nichols, President
Brenda Rotoco, Event Coordinator

Boat, travel, outdoor equipment, supplies, and services plus demonstrations.
28000 Attendees
Frequency: February
Founded in: 1970

23474 Annual Capital Sport Fishing, Travel and Outdoor Show
International Sport Show Producers Association
PO Box 4720
Portsmouth, NH 03802-4720

603-431-4315; *Fax:* 603-431-1971
info@sportshows.com; www.sportshows.com

Paul Fuller, President

Over 350 exhibits of sports, fishing, recreation and travel equipment, supplies and services.
45k Attendees
Frequency: Annual
Founded in: 1996

23475 Arabian Travel Market
Reed Exhibition Companies
383 Main Avenue
PO Box 6059
Norwalk, CT 06851

203-840-4800; *Fax:* 203-840-9628;
www.arabiantravelmarket.com

Three hundred exhibitors with travel related information, supplies and services.
5915 Attendees
Frequency: Annual

23476 Corporate and Incentive Travel
685 S. Washington Street
Alexandira, VA 22314

703-683-0123; *Fax:* 703-683-4545
info@corporateincentivetravel.net;
www.corporateincentivetravel.net

Corporate travel forum.

23477 Destinations Showcase
Intl. Association of Convention/Visitors Bureaus
2025 M Street
Suite 500
Washington, DC 20036

202-296-7888; *Fax:* 202-296-7889
info@destinationmarketing.org;
www.destinationsshowcase.com
Social Media: Facebook, Twitter

Michael D Gehrisch, President/CEO

Containing 100-200 exhibits at tradeshows.
575 Attendees
Founded in: 1914
Mailing list available for rent: 1200+ names at $400 per M

23478 Discover America International Pow Wow
Travel Industry Association of America

1100 New York Avenue NW
Suite 450
Washington, DC 20005-3934

202-408-8422; *Fax:* 202-408-1255
feedback@ustravel.org;
www.ustravel.org/events/international-pow-wow

Rodger Dow, President & CEO
Siming Cao, Coordinator
Geoff Freeman, Executive Vice President and COO
Rebecca Shafer, Director of Executive Operations

Annual show of 1050 suppliers of travel products and services.
5,600 Attendees

23479 Euro Travel Forum
Reed Exhibition Companies
255 Washington Street
Newton, MA 02458-1637

617-584-4900; *Fax:* 617-630-2222

Elizabeth Hitchcock, International Sales

A mobile, multi-product and multi-destination travel trade exhibition bringing travel products from all over the world into direct contact with travel agents and travel buyers from the leisure, business and incentive products industries.
27M Attendees
Frequency: April

23480 Family Motor Coach Association Convention
8291 Clough Pike
Cincinnati, OH 45244-2756

513-474-3622
800-543-3622; *Fax:* 513-388-5286
jyeatts@fmca.com; www.fmca.com

Jerry Yeatts, Convention Director
Ranita Jones, Sales Manager
Shawna Grubbs, Sales Assistant

Convention for Motorhome enthusiasts. Includes hundreds of motorhome displays, supplier displays and component displays.
15M Attendees
Frequency: Mar/Apr/July/Aug
Founded in: 1963

23481 Heartland Travel Showcase
Hart Productions
130 E Chestnut Street
Suite 301
Columbus, OH 43215

513-281-0022
800-896-4682; *Fax:* 513-281-3322;
www.heartlandtravelshowcase.com

Annual show and exhibits of information from 10 midwest states and the province of Ontario on travel destinations, attractions, accommodations, activities and restaurants.
Frequency: February

23482 Incentive Travel and Meeting Executives Show
Hall-Erickson
98 E Naperville Road
Westmont, IL 60559-1559

630-963-9185
800-752-6312; *Fax:* 630-434-1216
moti@heiexpo.com; www.motivationshow.com

Nancy A Petitti, Show Director
20M Attendees
Frequency: October
Founded in: 1972

23483 Motivation Show
Hall-Erickson
98 E Naperville Road
Westmont, IL 60559-1559

630-963-9185
800-752-6312; *Fax:* 630-434-1216;
www.motivationshow.com

Nancy A Petitti, Exhibit Show Manager
25M Attendees
Frequency: September
Founded in: 1929

23484 National Camping Industry Expo
3700 W Flamingo Rd
Las Vegas, NV 22182-2240

703-932-2342; *Fax:* 703-734-3004;
www.gocampingamerica.com

Rick Carbo, Manager
Chandana Karmarkar, Manager

National camping industry expo, only trade expo for RV parks and campground owners/operators. Containing 120 booths and 100 exhibitors.
850+ Attendees
Frequency: November
Founded in: 1966
Mailing list available for rent: 3,200 names

23485 Recreational Vehicle Industry Association National RV Trade Show
1896 Preston White Drive
Reston, VA 20191-4325

703-206-6003

David Humphreys, President
Mary Hutya, VP

Six hundred and thirty booths.
10M Attendees
Frequency: November

23486 Seatrade Cruise Convention
Miller Freeman Publications
13760 Noel Road
Suite 500
Dallas, TX 75240

800-527-0207; *Fax:* 214-419-8855

23487 Sport Travel Outdoor Show
Expositions
PO Box 550
Cleveland, OH 44107-0550

216-529-1300; *Fax:* 330-529-0311

Judy Fassnacht, Show Manager

475 booths of products and services related to the outdoor travel industry.
93M Attendees
Frequency: February

23488 Sports Travel and Adventure
Show Productions
800 Roosevelt Road
Suite 407
Glen Ellyn, IL 60137-5839

630-694-4611; *Fax:* 630-790-0209

Sandra Lewis, Show Manager

Two hundred and fifty six booths geared toward outdoor enthusiasts.
15M Attendees
Frequency: February

23489 Travel Exchange Annual Conference
National Tour Association
101 Prosperous Place
Suite 350
Lexington, KY 40509

859-264-6540
800-682-8886; *Fax:* 859-264-6570
questions@ntastaff.com
ntaonline.com
Social Media: Facebook, Twitter, LinkedIn

Pam Inman, President
Dawn Pettus, Manager, Events
Doug Rentz, Director, Communciation & Marketing

Brings together industry professionals and members to showcase ideas and products new to the travel and tourism industry.
Frequency: Annual

23490 Travel Industry Association American Pow Wow Marketing
1100 New York Avenue NW
Suite 450W
Washington, DC 20005

202-408-8422

Sue Elms, Show Manager
Roger Dow, CEO

Seven hundred booths where providers of US travel products promote these products.
3M Attendees
Frequency: April

23491 Travel and Tourism Research Association Show
546 E Main Street
Lexington, KY 40508-2342

859-226-4355; *Fax:* 859-226-4355
lisalcarey@aol.com; www.ttra.com

Twenty booths exhibiting information of interest to members of the Tourism Research Association.
400 Attendees
Frequency: June

23492 TravelAge Tradeshows
11400 West Olympic Blvd
Suite 325
Los Angeles, CA 90064

310-954-2510; *Fax:* 212-237-3007;
www.travelagewest.com/Magazine

Nancy Montella, Show Manager

Four hundred booths of educational and business-oriented tradeshow that provides a vehicle for various people within the travel industry to meet and exchange information on products, services and trends.
2.5M Attendees
Frequency: March

23493 World Travel Market
Reed Exhibition Companies
255 Washington Street
Newton, MA 02458-1637

617-584-4900; *Fax:* 617-630-2222;
www.wtmlondon.com

Elizabeth Hitchcock, International Sales

Premium travel show.
43M Attendees
Frequency: November

Directories & Databases

23494 ABC Cruise and Ferry Guide
Reed Travel Group
Church Street
Hertfordshire, England, LU 5 4HB

Offers information on international shipping companies operating passenger services and cruises.
320 Pages
Frequency: Quarterly
ISBN: 0-001048-0

23495 ABC Guide to International Travel
Reed Travel Group
Church Street
Hertfordshire, England, LU 5 4HB

Offers a list of foreign consulates in London, England that offer travel information to tourists.
Frequency: Quarterly

23496 Access Travel: Airports
Airport Operators Council International
1220 19th Street NW
Suite 200
Washington, DC 20036-2463

202-293-8500; *Fax:* 202-331-1362

Information is given on over 500 airports worldwide that offer handicapped facilities.
50 Pages

23497 Airport Hotel Directory
3255 Wilshire Boulevard
Suite 1514
Los Angeles, CA 90010-1418

213-739-1956

Restaurants and hotels are listed that are a close proximity to major airports.
Cost: $12.00
170 Pages

23498 American Bus Association's Motorcoach Marketer
American Bus Association
111 K Street NE
9th Floor
Washington, DC 20002

202-842-1645; *Fax:* 202-842-0850
abainfo@buses.org;
www.buses.org/Member-Resources/Motorcoach-Marketer

Peter J Pantuso, CEO
Eron Shosteck, Marketing

This directory is a comprehensive guide of the bus and travel industry offering information on hotels and sightseeing services, attractions, museums, restaurants and more.
500 Pages
Frequency: Annual
Founded in: 1926

23499 American Society of Travel Agents Membership Directory
NACTA
1101 King St
Alexandria, VA 22314-2963

703-739-2782; *Fax:* 703-684-8319;
www.nacta.com

Bill Maloney, Manager

Travel agents that represent over 17,000 agencies in the United States, Canada and overseas are the focus of this comprehensive directory.
Cost: $125.00
600 Pages
Frequency: Annual

23500 CMP Publications Travel File
CMP Publications
600 Community Dr
Manhasset, NY 11030-3810

516-562-5000; *Fax:* 516-562-5718

This large database covers the travel industry, with emphasis on news for travel agents and business travelers.
Frequency: Full-text

23501 Club Metro
Metro Online
1358 Hooper Avenue
Ste. 293
Toms River, NJ 08752

212-794-2664; www.clubmetrousa.com

This database contains information on travel, entertainment, and metropolitan services.
Frequency: Bulletin Board

23502 Condo Vacations: the Complete Guide
Lanier Publishing International
PO Box 20429
Oakland, CA 94620-0429

Condominiums that are available for vacation rentals are listed.
Cost: $14.95
320 Pages
Frequency: Annual

23503 Cruise Industry News Annual
Nissel-Lie Communications
441 Lexington Avenue
Suite 809
New York, NY 10017-3910

212-986-1025; *Fax:* 212-986-1033
info2@cruiseindustrynews.com;
www.cruiseindustrynews.com

Oivind Mathisen, Editor/Publisher
Angela Mathisen, Publisher/Advertising Director
Monty Mathisen, Reporter/Web Editor

This book presents the entire worldwide cruise industry from new ships on order to supply/demand scenarios; plus reports on relevant issues, financial results, newbuilding and second-hand ship values, shipbuilding, new technology and on board services; plus exclusive reports on each sailing region, and a comprehensive directory of all cruised lines, shipyards, ports and other suppliers.
Cost: $450.00
300 Pages
Frequency: Annual
Founded in: 1988

23504 Environmental Vacations: Volunteer Projects to Save the Planet
John Muir Publications
PO Box 613
Santa Fe, NM 87504-0613

505-466-6360; *Fax:* 505-988-1680

Information is given on vacations that provide opportunities to assist environmental projects.
Cost: $16.95
250 Pages

23505 Federal Travel Directory
Office of Federal Supply & Services
4 Crystal Mall Building
Washington, DC 20406-0001

202-564-2480

A list of airlines is offered in this directory that are under contract to the federal government.
Cost: $77.00
Frequency: Monthly

23506 Ford's Travel Guides
Ford's Travel Guides
19448 Londelius Street
Northridge, CA 91324-3511

818-987-1413

Offers valuable information on cruise ships and their planned cruises for one year ahead.
Cost: $14.95
200 Pages
Frequency: Quarterly
Circulation: 5,000

23507 Foster Travel Publishing Website
Foster Travel Publishing
Po Box 5715
Berkeley, CA 94705-0715

510-549-2202; *Fax:* 510-549-1131
lee@fostertravel.com; www.fostertravel.com

Lee Foster, Owner

award winning travel writing and photography on 200 worldwide locations, presented to the consumer and to the content buyer on the web or in print looking for travel writing or travel photography.
Frequency: Full-text

23508 Free US Tourist Attractions
Pilot Books
127 Sterling Avenue
PO Box 2102
Greenport, NY 11944

631-477-0978
800-797-4568; *Fax:* 631-477-0978

A directory of free family entertainment in every state of the union.
Cost: $12.95
ISBN: 0-875762-04-2

23509 International Workcamp Directory
VFP International Voluntary Service
7 Kilburn Street
Suite 31
Burlington, VT 05401

802-540-3060; *Fax:* 802-540-3061
vfp@vfp.org; www.vfp.org

Meg Brook, President
Chelsea Frisbee, Outgoing Volunteer Coordinator
Peter Coldwell, Treasurer/Founder
Scott Simpson, Board Chair
Matt Messier, Secretary

An annual booklet listing over 2400 opportunities for meaningful travel throughout Western and Easter Europe, Russia, Africa, Asia, Australia and Latin America. 2-3 week programs are $200 including room and board.
Cost: $20.00
2000 Members
289 Pages
Frequency: Annual
Circulation: 2,000
ISBN: 0-945617-20-8
ISSN: 0896-565X
Founded in: 1982
Printed in 4 colors

23510 National Bed and Breakfast Association Guide
National Bed & Breakfast Association
2009 Family Circle
Lexington, KY 50505

859-255-0076; *Fax:* 859-255-0938;
www.bbinnsofamerica.com

Phyllis Featherston, Executive Director
Cost: $17.95
600 Pages
Frequency: Every 2-3 Years
ISBN: 0-961129-86-7
Founded in: 1982
Printed in 2 colors on matte stock

23511 OAG Flights2Go
UBM Aviation
3025 Highland Parkway
Suite 200
Downers Grove, IL 60515-5561

630-515-5300; *Fax:* 630-515-3251;
www.oagtravel.com

Anthony Smith, Group Publisher
Jason Holland, Editor
Simon Barker, Publisher

Flights2Go provides mobile access to worldwide flight schedules in an instance direct to your mobile device. No matter where you are, you can look up flight schedules from across the globe and even check flight status.

23512 OAG Travel Planner Pro
UBM Aviation

3025 Highland Parkway
Suite 200
Downers Grove, IL 60515-5561

630-515-5300; *Fax:* 630-515-3251;
www.oagtravel.com

Anthony Smith, Group Publisher
Jason Holland, Editor
Simon Barker, Publisher

OAG Travel Planner Pro is the premier online tool for travel arrangers who need to create, manage, and save complex travel plans quickly and easily.

23513 Official Bus Guide

Russell's Guides
834 3rd Avenue SE
Cedar Rapids, IA 52403-2408

319-364-6138; *Fax:* 319-364-4853

A list of 475 intercity bus companies in the United States, Canada and Mexico.
Cost: $9.90
Frequency: Monthly
Circulation: 14,000

23514 Official Handbook of Travel Brochures

Vacation Publications
1502 Augusta Drive
Suite 415
Houston, TX 77057-2484

713-974-6903

16 Pages
Frequency: Quarterly
Circulation: 38,000

23515 Real Guides

Farmers Trip & Travel
PO Box 473
Mount Morris, IL 61054-0473
Fax: 815-734-1223

A series of guidebooks that list sites, attractions and events in a city or country.
Cost: $8.00
300 Pages
Frequency: Per Edition

23516 Reed's Travel Group's Travel Agent Database

Reed Travel Group
2000 Clearwater Dr
Oak Brook, IL 60523-8809

630-574-0825
800-424-3996; *Fax:* 630-288-8781;
www.reedbusiness.com

Jeff Greisch, President

About 65,000 wholesale, retail and cooperative travel agencies worldwide, including tour operators.
Cost: $270.00

23517 Society of American Travel Writers: Membership Directory

Society of American Travel Writers
4101 Lake Boone Trail
Suite 201
Raleigh, NC 27607-7506

Fax: 919-787-4916

Sarah Haw, Member Services

About 550 newspaper and magazine travel editors, writers, columnists, photo journalists and broadcasters in the US and Canada.
Cost: $95.00
Frequency: Annual February

23518 Thomas Cook Airports Guide Europe

Thomas Cook
Unit 11, Coningsby Road
Peterborough, England, PE 3 85B

Offers valuable information on over 75 public airports in Europe.
255 Pages
Frequency: Biennial

23519 Thomas Cook Airports Guide International

Thomas Cook
Unit 11, Coningsby Road
Peterborough, England, PE 3 85B

Offers valuable information on over 90 airport facilities outside of the United Kingdom.
255 Pages
Frequency: Biennial

23520 Tours.com

490 Post St
Suite 1701-A
San Francisco, CA 94102-1308

415-956-0111; *Fax:* 415-956-0117
info@tours.com; www.tours.com

Maria Polk, President/CEO/Co-Founder
Karin Wacaster, Public Relations
Marijo Douglass, Finance Executive

Home of the Worldwide Directory of Tours and Vacation Packages.
Founded in: 1995

23521 Travel Agent: Focus 500 Directory Issue

Universal Media
801 2nd Ave
New York, NY 10017-8638

212-986-5100; *Fax:* 212-883-1244

Lists of attractions, restaurants, convention and visitor bureaus, hotel chains and management companies, cruise lines, state tourism offices, travel trade associations, tourist railways.
Frequency: Annual October
Circulation: 50,000

23522 Travel Editors: US Consumer & Inflight Magazines

Rocky Point Press
4830 Ranchito Avenue
Sherman Oaks, CA 91423-1927

Fax: 818-763-4818

Listings of travel editors of US consumer and in-flight magazines.
Frequency: Annual

23523 Travel Forum

CompuServe Information Service
5000 Arlington Centre Blvd
Columbus, OH 43220-5439

614-326-1002
800-848-8199; www.travelforum.org

This database contains information on travel and related topics of interest, including travel planning.
Frequency: Bulletin Board

23524 Travel Industry Association of America: Travel Media Directory

Travel Industry Association of America
1100 New York Ave NW
Suite 450
Washington, DC 20005-6130

202-408-8422; *Fax:* 202-408-1255;
www.tia.org

Roger J Dow, CEO
Peter Strebel, Secretary

Travel editors of major newspapers, magazines and broadcast outlets.
Cost: $40.00
Frequency: Annual
Circulation: 3,000

23525 Travel Insider's Guide to Alternative Accommodations

Travel Insider
PO Box 14
Streamwood, IL 60107-0014
206-338-3381; *Fax:* 206-338-3381

John E Sullivan, Editor

Over 400 sources for alternative accommodations worldwide, such as farmhouses, castles, universities and country inns.
Cost: $9.95
Frequency: Annual October

23526 Travel Photo Source Book

Society of American Travel Writers
4101 Lake Boone Trail
Suite 201
Raleigh, NC 27607-7506

715-248-3800; *Fax:* 919-787-4916;
www.photosource.com

Nancy Belcher, Editor

Nearly 100 member photographers and 35 associate member representatives of airlines, hotels, resorts, tourist agencies and public relations firms.
Frequency: Biennial

23527 Travel Tips USA

Renaissance Publications
7950 Jones Branch Drive
McLean, VA 22108-0605
614-777-1227
accuracy@usatoday.com; www.usatourist.com

Michelle Leco
Mike Leco

Amusement parks, attractions and festivals are among some of the categories listed in this travel directory.
Cost: $17.95
320 Pages

23528 Travel World News Resource Directory

Travel Industry Network
28 Knight Street
Norwalk, CT 06851

203-286-6679; *Fax:* 203-286-6681
editor@travelworldnews.com;
www.travelworldnews.com

Charles Gatt Jr, Publisher
Peter Gatt, Associate Publisher

A directory by continent/region/locale of local vendors, tour operators, railways, cruise lines, and travel links.
Founded in: 1988

23529 Travel and Tourism Research Association: Membership Directory

Travel and Tourism Research Association
546 E Main Street
Lexington, KY 40508-2342

859-226-4355; *Fax:* 859-226-4355
lisalcarey@aol.com

Lisa Carey, Executive Director

Over 750 state and local tourism bureaus and other federal and provincial government agencies, airlines, media, hotels, university bureaus of business research and other university departments and research and consulting firms concerned with travel research, marketing and promotion.
Cost: $50.00
Frequency: Annual June

23530 Travel, Leisure and Entertainment News Media

Larriston Communications

PO Box 20229
New York, NY 10025-1518

212-864-0150; *Fax:* 212-662-8103

Sheila Gordon, Editor

Over 350 travel and leisure magazines and daily newspapers with circulations of over 50,000 that have special leisure or entertainment sections.
Cost: $89.00
Frequency: Annual May

23531 Traveler's Hotline Directory
Forte Travel Lodge
Po Box 270469
San Diego, CA 92198-2469

858-487-9596
800-578-7878; *Fax:* 858-487-9658

Victor Ferrette, Partner

Approximately 12,000 travel services such as air couriers, auto rental agencies, campgrounds, resorts, hotels, spas, travel groups and airlines that offer toll-free domestic or international telephone numbers.
Cost: $15.95

23532 Travelers Information RoundTable
GE Information Services
401 N Washington Street
Rockville, MD 20850-1707

301-388-8284

Cathy Ge, Owner

Provides a forum enabling users to share information on a range of travel topics.
Frequency: Bulletin Board

23533 West Coast Travel
Foster Travel Publishing
Po Box 5715
Berkeley, CA 94705-0715

510-549-2202; *Fax:* 510-549-1131
lee@fostertravel.com;
www.westcoasttravels.com

Lee Foster, Owner

This database offers information for travelers and tourists on approximately 150 locations in the western United States, Canada and Mexico.
Frequency: Full-text

23534 Worldspan TravelShopper
WORLDSPAN
300 Galleria Parkway
Atlanta, GA 30339

770-637-7400; *Fax:* 770-563-7004;
www.worldspan.com

Rakesh Gangwal, CEO

This database offers travel information, including 5 million domestic and international flights for every airline in the world for more than 100,000 cities.
Frequency: Directory

Industry Web Sites

23535 http://gold.greyhouse.com
G.O.L.D Grey House OnLine Databases

Grey House Publishing's online database platform, GOLD, offers Quick Search, Keyword Search and Expert Search for most business sectors including travel markets. The GOLD platform makes finding the information you need quick and easy - whether you're a novice searcher or an experienced database user. All of Grey House's directory products are available for subscription on the GOLD platform.

23536 www.biztravel.com
Biztravel.com

Internet travel service offering discounts on flights, hotels, car rentals, packages and cruises.

23537 www.buses.org
American Bus Association

Trade association for the North American bus industry.

23538 www.expedia.com
Expedia.com

Internet travel service offers access to airlines, hotels, car rentals, vacation packages, cruises and corporate travel.

23539 www.gocampingamerica.com
National Association of RV Parks and Campgrounds

Nat ARVC serves the business and legislative needs of more than 3,200 member RV parks and campgrounds.

23540 www.goworldnet.com/cgi-bin
Worldnet USA

States and their hotels, theaters and museums.

23541 www.greyhouse.com
Grey House Publishing

Authoritative reference directories for most business markets including travel markets. Users can search the online databases with varied search criteria allowing for custom searches by product category, geographic area, sales volume, keyword, subject and more. Full Grey House catalog and online ordering also available.

23542 www.hotwire.com
Hotwire.com

Internet travel service offering discounts on flights, hotels, car rentals, packages and cruises.

23543 www.hsmai.org
Hospitality Sales and Marketing Association

To provide resources to sales and marketing professionals at all levels of thier career in travel, hospitality, and tourism.

23544 www.iacvb.org
International Association of Convention and Visitor Bureaus

Promotes sound professional practices in the solicitation and servicing of meetings and conventions. Members represent travel/tourism-related businesses. Publications include a electronic newsletter and on-line directory.

23545 www.info.now.com/site
Society of Incentive and Travel Executives

An individual membership society covering 70 countries. Members are corporate users, airlines, Tourist Boards, cruise lines, destination management companies, consultants, hotels/resorts, travel agents, incentive travel houses and publications.

23546 www.nbba.com
National Bed & Breakfast Association

Innkeepers of bed and breakfast lodgings.

23547 www.ntaonline.com
National Tour Association

For North American tourism professionals focused on the development, promotion and increased use of tour operators packaged travel.

23548 www.orbitz.com
Orbitz.com

Internet travel service offering discounts on flights, hotels, car rentals, packages and cruises.

23549 www.rsana.com
Receptive Services Association

Helping receptive operators serve international tour companies through partnerships with North American suppliers.

23550 www.tia.org
Travel Industry Association of America

For hotels, airlines and travel agencies interested in promoting increased travel to and within the US

23551 www.travel.com
Travel.com

Internet travel service providing access to flights, hotels, car rentals, vacation packages and cruises.

23552 www.travel.lycos.com
Lycos.com

Internet travel service offering discounts on flights, hotels, car rentals, packages and cruises.

23553 www.travel.yahoo.com
Yahoo.com

Internet travel service providing access to flights, hotels, car rentals, vacation packages and cruises.

23554 www.travelocity.com
Sabre Holdings

Travel service offering consumers access to hundreds of airlines and thousands of hotels, as well as cruise, last-minute and vacation packages and best-in-class car rental companies.

23555 www.waveconcepts.com/arta
Association of Retail Travel Agents

Promotes the interests of retail travel agents through representation on industry councils and testimony before Congress. Conducts joint marketing and educational programs.

Associations

23556 **Action Committee for Rural Electrification**
11640 73rd Avenue North
Maple Grove, MN 55369

763-424-1020; *Fax:* 763-424-5820;
www.mrea.org
Social Media: Facebook, Twitter, LinkedIn

Wesley Waller, Chair
Thomas Woinarowicz, 1st Vice Chair
Butch Lindenfelser, 2nd Vice Chair
Linda Laitala, Secretary
Philip Nestande, Treasurer

Political action committee that advocates support for rural electrification.
18M Members
Founded in: 1967

23557 **Air Conditioning Contractors of America**
2800 S Shirlington Rd
Ste 300
Arlington, VA 22206

703-575-4477
888-290-2220
paul.stalknecht@acca.org; www.acca.org
Social Media: Facebook, Twitter, LinkedIn, YouTube, Google+

Phil London, Chairman
Jerry Bosworth, Vice Chairman
Don Langston, Secretary/Treasurer
Paul T. Stalknecht, President/ Chief Executive Officer
Kevin Holland, SVP, Business Operations

An association of HVAC contractors.
Founded in: 1968

23558 **Air and Waste Management Association**
One Gateway Center, 3rd Floor
420 Fort Duquesne Blvd
Pittsburgh, PA 15222-1435

412-232-3444
800-270-3444; *Fax:* 412-232-3450
info@awma.org; www.awma.org
Social Media: Facebook, Twitter, LinkedIn

Dallas Baker, President
Diane Freeman, Vice President
Stephanie Glyptis, Secretary/Executive Director
Nancy Meilahn Fowler, Treasure
Kim Marcus, Vice President

Association for air and waste management.
Founded in: 1907

23559 **Alliance to Save Energy**
1850 M Street, NW
Suite 610
Washington, DC 20036

202-857-0666; www.ase.org
Social Media: Facebook, Twitter, LinkedIn, YouTube, Google+, Flickr

Mark Warner, Chairman
Jane Palmieri, Co-Chairman
Kateri Callahan, President
William Von Hoene, 1st Vice Chair
Frank Murray, Secretary

Promotes energy efficiency to acheive a healthier economy and a cleaner environment.
Founded in: 1977

23560 **American Coal Ash Association**
38800 Country Club Drive
Farmington Hills, MI 48331

720-870-7897; *Fax:* 720-870-7889
info@acaa-usa.org; www.acaa-usa.org

Thomas Adams, Executive Director
Alyssa Barto, Member Liaison
John Ward, Communications Coordinator

A nonprofit trade association devoted to recycling the materials created from burning coal.
Founded in: 1968

23561 **American Gas Association**
400 North Capitol Street, NW
Suite 450
Washington, DC 20001

202-824-7000; www.aga.org
Social Media: Facebook, Twitter, LinkedIn, You Tube

Terry D. McCallister, Chairman
Dave McCurdy, President/ CEO
Ralph A. LaRossa, First Vice Chairman
Pierce H. Norton II, Second Vice Chairman
Gregg S. Kantor, Immediate Past Chairman

The American Gas Association advocates the interests of its members and their customers, and provides information and services promoting efficient demand and supply growth and operational excellence in the safe, reliable and efficient delivery of natural gas.
Founded in: 1918

23562 **American National Standards Institute**
1899 L Street, NW
11th Floor
Washington, DC 20036

202-293-8020; *Fax:* 202-293-9287
info@ansi.org; www.ansi.org
Social Media: Facebook, Twitter, LinkedIn, YouTube, Google+

Kevan P. Lawlor, Chair of the Board
S. Joe Bhatia, President and CEO
Patricia A. Griffin, Staff Liaison
Kemi Allston, Program Administrator
Louis Almodovar, Senior Business Analyst

A private nonprofit organization that oversees the development of coluntary consesus standards for products.
Founded in: 1918

23563 **American Nuclear Society**
555 North Kensington Avenue
La Grange Park, IL 60526

708-352-6611
800-323-3044; *Fax:* 708-352-0499;
www.ans.org
Social Media: Facebook, Twitter, LinkedIn

Robert C. Fine, Executive Director
Valerie Vasilievas, Staff Liaison
Jeff Mosses, Sales Manager
Susan Gallier, Editor
Ed Du Temple, Department Director

For personnel involved in nuclear power operation and development. Coverage includes power, plant operations and maintenance, fuel cycle, legislation, international employment and more.
Founded in: 1954

23564 **American Petroleum Institute**
1220 L Street, NW
Washington, DC 20005-4070

202-682-8000
certification@api.org; www.api.org
Social Media: Facebook, Twitter, Pinteresr, YouTube, RSS

Linda Rozett, VP, Comm.
Jack N. Gerard, President/ CEO
Kyle Isakower, Vice President
Robert Greco, Group Director
Louis Finkel, EVP, Gov. Affairs

The largest US trade association for the oil and natrual gas industry.
Founded in: 1919

23565 **American Public Energy Agency**
233 South 13th Street
Suite 1500
Lincoln, NE 68508

402-438-1177
800-476-3749; *Fax:* 402-742-0022
rmock@apea.org; www.apea.org
Social Media: Facebook

Roger W. Mock, President/ CEO
Denise Barnhill, Executive Assistant

Purpose is to provide energy acquisition and energy-related services for its members and other public agencies, and to assist such agencies in acquiring stable energy supplies, reducing energy costs through group purchases, and developing enhanced energy acquisition mechanisms.
40 Members
Founded in: 1995

23566 **American Public Power Association**
2451 Crystal Drive
Suite 1000
Arlington, VA 22202-4804

202-467-2900
info@PublicPower.org; www.publicpower.org
Social Media: Facebook, Twitter, LinkedIn, You Tube, Instagram, Pinterest

Douglas Hunter, Chairman
Walter Haase, Vice Chairman
Andrew M. Boatright, Chair Elect
Paula DiFonzo, Immediate Past Chair
Paul McElroy, Treasurer

Service association for community-owned eletric utilities.
Founded in: 1940

23567 **American Public Works Association**
2345 Grand Boulevard
Suite 700
Kansas City, MO 64108-2625

816-472-6100
800-848-APWA; *Fax:* 816-472-1610;
www.apwa.net
Social Media: Facebook, Twitter, LinkedIn, YouTube

Brian R. Usher, PWLF, President
Ann Daniels, Director of Accreditation
Larry Frevert, Interim Executive Director
Brian Van Norman, Director of Chapter Relations
Mary Coleman, Senior Finance Manager

International educational and professional association of public agencies, private sector companies, and individuals dedicated to providing high quality public works goods and services. AWA provides a forum in which public works professionals competency, increase the performance of their agencies and companies, and bring important public works-related topics to public attention in local, state, and federal areas. Mailing list for members only.
Founded in: 1984

23568 **American Society of Appraisers**
11107 Sunset Hills Rd
Suite 310
Reston, VA 20190

703-478-2228
800-272-8258; *Fax:* 703-742-8471
asainfo@appraisers.org; www.appraisers.org
Social Media: Facebook, Twitter, LinkedIn, YouTube

Bonny Price, Chief Operations Officer
Joseph Noselli, MBA, CPA, Chief Financial Officer

Jim Hirt, Chief Executive Officer
Sharlyne Tsai, Director of Information Technology
John Russell, Director of Government Relations

Multi-discipline organization for appraisers.
Founded in: 1939

23569 American Solar Energy Society
2525 Arapahoe Ave
Ste E4-253
Boulder, CO 80302

303-443-3130; *Fax:* 303-443-3212
info@ases.org; www.ases.org
Social Media: Facebook, Twitter, LinkedIn, digg

David Panich, Chairman
Francis de Winter, Vice-Chairman
Richard Behlmann, Secretary
Kris Brettingen, Treasurer
Lauren Harrower, Membership Manager/Data Analyst

Individuals and professionals working in the field of solar energy and conservation.
Founded in: 1954

23570 American Water Works Association
6666 W. Quincy Ave.
Denver, CO 80235

303-794-7711
800-926-7337; *Fax:* 303-347-0804;
www.awwa.org
Social Media: Facebook, Twitter, LinkedIn, You Tube, RSS

Gene C. Koontz, President
Jeanne M. Bennett-Bailey, President Elect
John J. Donahue, Immediate Past President
Jon Eaton, VP/Minnesota Section Director
David E. Rager, Treasurer

An international nonprofit scientific and educational association to improve water quality and supply.
Founded in: 1881

23571 American Wind Energy Association
1501 M Street NW
Suite 1000
Washington, DC 20005

202-383-2500; *Fax:* 202-383-2505
windmail@awea.org; www.awea.org
Social Media: Facebook, Twitter, LinkedIn

Mike Garland, Chair
Pam Poisson, SVP Operations/CFO
Matthew Fuller, Director, Finance
Chi Wei, Director, Information Technology
Tom Kiernan, Chief Executive Officer

A national trade association representing wind power project developers, equipment suppliers, services providers, parts manufacturers, utilities, researchers, and others involved in the wind industry. Promotes wind energy as a clean source of electricity for consumers around the world.
2400 Members

23572 Association of Energy Engineers
3168 Mercer University Drive
Atlanta, GA 30341

770-447-5083; www.aeecenter.org

Dr. Scott Dunning, President
Asit Patel, President Elect
Paul Goodman, Treasurer
Ron Slossburg, Region 1 Vice President
Albert Thumann, Executive Director

Promotes energy certification, management and education.
17500 Members
Founded in: 1977

23573 Association of Financial Guranty Insurers
139 Lancaster Street
Albany, NY 12210-1903

518-449-4698
tcasey@mackinco.com; www.afgi.org

Bruce E. Stern, Chairman
Adam Bergonzi, Vice Chair
Cathleen Matanle, Secretary
Susan Comparato, Treasurer

Insure and reinsure municipal bonds and asset-backed securities.
Founded in: 1971

23574 Association of Home Appliance Manufacturers
1111 19th Street NW
Suite 402
Washington, DC 20036

202-872-5955
info@ahem.org; www.aham.org

Joseph McGuire, President
Wayne Morris, Vice President

Represents the manufacturers of household appliances and products and services associated with them.
Founded in: 1915

23575 Association of Home Appliance Manufacturer
1111 19th Street NW
Suite 402
Washington, DC 20036

202-872-5955
info@ahem.org; www.aham.org

Joseph M. McGuire, President
Wayne Morris, VP, Technical Ops & Standards
Jill Notini, VP, Comm. & Marketing
Charlotte Skidmore, Dir, Energy & Environmental Policy
Matt Williams, Director, Standards
Founded in: 1915

23576 Automatic Meter Reading Association
60 Revere Dr # 500
Suite 500
Northbrook, IL 60062-1591

847-480-9628
888-612-2672; *Fax:* 847-480-9282
amra@amra-intl.org; www.amra-intl.org
Social Media: Facebook, Twitter, LinkedIn

John Waxman, Manager
John Waxman, Manager
Founded in: 1986

23577 Buliding Owners and Managers Association
1101 15th St., NW
Suite 800
Washington, DC 20005

202-408-2662; *Fax:* 202-326-6377
info@boma.org; www.boma.org
Social Media: Facebook, Twitter, LinkedIn, YouTube, Pinterest

Kent C. Gibson, Chair/Chief Elected Officer??
Robert M. Brierley, BOMA Fellow, Vice Chair
Henry Chamberlain, President/ COO
Daniel W. Chancey, RPA, Secretary/Treasurer
Patricia M. Areno, CAE, Senior Vice President

Association for building managers and owners.
Founded in: 1907

23578 Edison Electric Institute
701 Pennsylvania Ave Nw
Washington, DC 20004-2608

202-508-5000
feedback@eei.org; www.eei.org
Social Media: Facebook, Twitter, LinkedIn, Youtube

Nick Akins, Chairman
Tom Fanning, Vice Chair
Chris Crane, Vice Chair
Pat Vincent-Collawn, Vice Chair
Thomas R Kuhn, President

Advocates public policy, expands market opportunities and provides strategic business information for the shareholder-owned electric utility industry.
180 Members
Founded in: 1930

23579 Electric Power Research Institute
3420 Hillview Avenue
Palo Alto, CA 94304

650-855-2000
800-313-3774; *Fax:* 704-595-2871
askepri@epri.com; www.epri.com
Social Media: Facebook, Twitter, LinkedIn

Michael W. Howard, President/CEO
Gil C. Quiniones, Chairman
Robin (Rob) E. Manning, Vice President, Transmission
Pamela J. Keefe, SVP/CFO/Treasurer
Tom Alley, Vice President, Generation

Nonprofit energy research consortium for the benefit of utility members, their customers and society. Mission is to provide science and technology-based solutions of indispensable value to our global energy customers by managing a far-reaching program of scientific research, technology development and product implementation.
660 Members
Founded in: 1973

23580 Electric Power Supply Association
1401 New York Ave Nw
Suite 1230
Washington, DC 20005-2110

202-628-8200; *Fax:* 202-628-8260;
www.epsa.org
Social Media: Facebook, Twitter, LinkedIn

John E Shelk, President/CEO
Nancy E Bagot, Senior Vice President
William S Burlew, VP, Govt. Affairs

23581 Energy Engineering
Association of Energy Engineers
3168 Mercer University Drive
Atlanta, GA 30341

770-447-5083; *Fax:* 770-446-3969
info@aeecenter.org; www.aeecenter.org
Social Media: Facebook, Twitter, LinkedIn

Dr. Scott Dunning, President
Ruth Whitlock, Executive Admin
Jennifer Vendola, Controller
Angie Quarles, Executive Director's Assistant
Albert Thumann, Executive Director

Engineering solutions to cost efficiency problems and mechanical contractors who design, specify, install, maintain, and purchase non-residential heating, ventilating, air conditioning and refrigeration equipment and components.
17500 Members
Founded in: 1977

23582 Energy Information Administration
National Energy Information Center
1000 Independence Av Sw
Suite 1E-238
Washington, DC 20585-0001

202-586-8800; *Fax:* 202-586-0727
InfoCtr@eia.gov; www.eia.gov
Social Media: Facebook, Twitter, LinkedIn, YouTube, Flickr, RSS

John H Weiner, Executive Director

Government agency that provides statistical energy data, information and referral assistance to the government and private sectors, academia and the public. NEIC also provides Government Printing Office ordering information. Single copies of blank data collection forms, directories and EIA press releases are free of charge to all users. Ordering information on EIA machine readable files available through the National Technical Information Service and the Government Printing Office.
Founded in: 1977

23583 Environment and Energy Study Institute
1112 16th Street, NW
Suite 300
Washington, DC 20036

202-628-1400; *Fax:* 202-204-5244
info@eesi.org; www.eesi.org
Social Media: Facebook, Twitter, YouTube, Google+

Jared Blum, Chairman
Carol Werner, Executive Director
David Robison, Director of Finance & Admin
Susan Williams, Director of Development
Alison Alford, Programs & Administrative Assistant

Educating Congress on energy efficiency and renewable energy, advancing innovating policy solutions.
Founded in: 1984

23584 Gas Research Institute
1700 S Mount Prospect Road
Des Plaines, IL 60018-1804

847-768-0500; *Fax:* 847-768-0501;
www.gastechnology.org
Social Media: Facebook, Twitter

John Riordan, President/CEO

23585 Geothermal Energy Association
209 Pennsylvania Avenue SE
Washington, DC 20003

202-454-5261; *Fax:* 202-454-5265;
www.geo-energy.org
Social Media: Facebook, Twitter, LinkedIn, YouTube, Wordpress

Joe Greco, Chairman
Yoram Bronicki, President
Doug Glaspey, Vice President
Terry Page, Secretary-Treasurer
Mihaela-Daniela Lobontiu, Business Manager

A US trade organization that supports the expanded use of geothermal energy.
Founded in: 1988

23586 Government Finance Officers Association
203 N. LaSalle Street
Suite 2700
Chicago, IL 60601-1210

312-977-9700; *Fax:* 312-977-4806;
www.gfoa.org
Social Media: Facebook, Twitter, LinkedIn, YouTube

Heather A. Johnston, President
Marc Gonzales, President Elect
Jeffrey Esser, Executive Director/CEO
John Jurkash, Chief Financial Officer
Tami Garrett, Secretary

A professional association of finance officers.
Founded in: 1906

23587 Independent Petroleum Association of America
1201 15th Street NW
Suite 300
Washington, DC 20005

202-857-4722; *Fax:* 202-857-4799;
www.ipaa.org
Social Media: Facebook, Twitter, LinkedIn, YouTube

Michael Watford, Chairman
Mark Miller, Vice Chairman
Barry Russell, President/CEO
Lee O. Fuller, Executive Vice President
Dan Naatz, SVP, Gov. Relations

Membership organization ensuring a strong, viable domestic oil and natural gas industry.
Founded in: 1929

23588 Institute of Industrial Engineers
3577 Parkway Lane
Suite 200
Norcross, GA 30092

770-449-0460
800-494-0460; *Fax:* 770-441-3295
chapters@iienet.org; www.iienet.org
Social Media: Facebook, Twitter, LinkedIn

Don Greene, CEO
Donna Calvert, COO
Monica Elliott, Director, Communications

Dedicated to supporting engineers involved in all industrial applications.

23589 Institute of Public Utilities
Owen Graduate Hall
735 East Shaw Lane, Room W157
East Lansing, MI 48825-1109

517-355-1876; *Fax:* 517-355-1854
ipu@msu.edu
ipu.msu.edu/
Social Media: Facebook, Twitter, LinkedIn

Janice A Beecher, Director
Ligita Nelson, Administrative Assistant
Kenneth Rose, Ph.D., Senior Fellow
Steven Kihm, Senior Fellow (Finance)
Joydeep Mitra, Senior Faculty Associate

Research and training center at Michigan State University. Program focuses on regulation and management of energy, telecommunications and water companies.
Founded in: 1965

23590 International District Energy Association (IDEA)
24 Lyman Street
Suite 230
Westborough, MA 01581

508-366-9339; *Fax:* 508-366-0019
idea@districtenergy.org;
www.districtenergy.org
Social Media: Facebook, Twitter, YouTube, Flickr, RSS

Bruce Ander, Chair
Tim Griffin, Vice Chair
Chris Lyons, 2nd Vice Chair
James Adams, Secretary/Treasurer
Ken Smith, Past Chair

IDEA fosters the success of its members as leaders in providing reliable, economical, and environmentally sound district energy services.
1780 Members
Founded in: 1909

23591 International Gas Turbine Institute
6525 The Corners Pkwy
Ste. 115
Norcross, GA 30092

404-847-0072; *Fax:* 404-847-0151
igti@asme.org
igti.asme.org

Madiha Kotb, President
Thomas G Loughlin, Executive Director
Founded in: 1880

23592 International Ground Source Heat Pump Association
1201 S. Innovation Way Dr.
Suite 400'
Stillwater, OK 74074

405-744-5175
800-626-4747; *Fax:* 405-744-5283
igshpa@okstate.edu; www.igshpa.okstate.edu
Social Media: Facebook, Twitter, YouTube, Google+

Robert Ingersoll, Director
John Turley, President
Garen Ewbank, Vice President
Jeromy Cotton, Secretary
Allan Skouby, Treasurer

A nonprofit organization to advance ground source heat pumps.
Founded in: 1987

23593 International Right of Way Association
19210 South Vermont Avenue
Building A Suite 100
Gardena, CA 90248

310-538-0233
888-340-4792; *Fax:* 310-538-1471
info@irwaonline.org; www.irwaonline.org
Social Media: Facebook, Twitter, LinkedIn, YouTube

Mark Rieck, EVP
Fred Nasri, VP, CFO
Deidre C Alves, VP, Professional Development
Barbara Billitzer, VP, Publisher & Editor
Daniel M. Stekol, VP, Field Operations

Members are responsible for acquiring land over which to run utility lines, pipelines and roads.
10,00 Members
Founded in: 1934

23594 Municipal Waste Management Association
PO Box 1894
Guelph, ON N1H 4E9
519-823-1990; *Fax:* 519-823-0084
ben@municipalwaste.ca;
www.municipalwaste.ca

Ben Bennett, Executive Director
Melissa Campbell, Membership Co-ordinator
Karyn Hogan, Chair
Stephanie Sidler, Treasurer
Brad Whitelaw, Secretary

Concerned with the processing of municipal solid waste for the production of recyclable materials, heat, and energy. Members are local government organizations; associate members are from the private sector.
200 Members
Founded in: 1987

23595 National Association of Counties
25 Massachusetts Avenue, NW
Suite 500
Washington, DC 20001

202-393-6226
888-407-6226; *Fax:* 202-393-2630
nacomeetings@naco.org; www.naco.org

Social Media: Facebook, Twitter, LinkedIn, YouTube

Sallie Clark, President
Bryan Desloge, First Vice President
Matthew D. Chase, Executive Director
Kathy Nothstine, Program Director
Bert Jarreau, Chief Innovation Officer

The only national organization that represents county governments of the US.
Founded in: 1935

23596 **National Association of Energy Service Companies**
1615 M St Nw
Suite 800
Washington, DC 20036-3213

202-822-0950; *Fax:* 202-822-0955
info@naesco.org; www.naesco.org
Social Media: Facebook, LinkedIn

David Weiss, Chairman
Mike Kearney, Vice Chair
Scott Ririe, Secretary
Natasha Shah, Treasurer
Terry E. Singer, Executive Director

23597 **National Association of Regulatory Utility Commissioners (NARUC)**
1101 Vermont Avenue, NW
Suite 200
Washington, DC 20005

202-898-2200; *Fax:* 202-898-2213
admin@naruc.org; www.naruc.org
Social Media: Facebook

Lisa Edgar, Chairman/President
Travis Kavulla, First Vice President
Robert Powelson, Second Vice President
Charles Gray, Executive Director
David E. Ziegner, Treasurer

A trade association representing the state public service commissioners who regulate utility services, such as electricity, gas, telecommunication, water, and transportation throughout the country.
Founded in: 1889

23598 **National Association of State Energy Officials**
2107 Wilson Boulevard
Suite 850
Arlington, VA 22201

703-299-8800; *Fax:* 703-299-6208
energy@naseo.org; www.naseo.org
Social Media: Facebook, Twitter, LinkedIn, Youtube, Flickr

David Terry, Executive Director
Jeffrey C. Genzer, General Counsel
Melissa Savage, Senior Program Director
Rodney Sobin, Senior Program Director
Sandy Fazeli, Senior Program Director

The only non-profit organization that represents the Governor-designated energy officials from each state and territory. The organization was established to improve the effectiveness and quality of state energy programs and policies, provide policy input and analysis of federal energy issues and be a repository of information on energy issues of concern to the states.
56 Members
Founded in: 1986

23599 **National Association of State Utility**
8380 Colesville Road
Suite 101
Silver Spring, MD 20910

301-589-6313; *Fax:* 301-589-6380
nasuca@nasuca.org; www.nasuca.org

Bill Levis, Interim Executive Director
Nicole Haslup, Deputy Director

Members are state appointed individuals that represent rate-payers in their state.
44 Members
Founded in: 1979

23600 **National Electrical Contractors Associatio n**
3 Bethesda Metro Center
Suite 1100
Bethesda, MD 20814

301-657-3110; *Fax:* 301-215-4500;
www.necanet.org
Social Media: Facebook, Twitter, LinkedIn, YouTube, Flickr

Traci Pickus, Secretary/Treasurer
John M. Grau, CEO
Daniel G. Walter, Vice President/COO
Beth Ellis, Executive Director
Geary Higgins, Vice President, Labor Relations

A trade association representing electrical contractors.
Founded in: 1901

23601 **National Energy Marketers Association**
3333 K Street NW
Suite 110
Washington, DC 20007

202-333-3288; *Fax:* 202-333-3266;
www.energymarketers.com
Social Media: Facebook, LinkedIn

A nonprofit trade association representing suppliers and consumers of natural energy.

23602 **National Hydropower Association**
25 Massachusetts Ave NW
Suite 450
Washington, DC 20001

202-682-1700; *Fax:* 202-682-9478
help@hydro.org; www.hydro.org
Social Media: Facebook, Twitter

Linda Church Ciocci, Executive Director
Steve Wenke, Vice President
John McCormick, President
Debbie Mursch, Treasurer
John Suloway, Secretary

A nonprofit national association dedicated exclusively to advancing the interests of the hydropower industry. Seeks to secure hydropower's place as a climate-friendly, renewable and reliable energy source that serves national environmental and energy policy objectives.
140 Members
Founded in: 1983

23603 **National Mining Association**
101 Constitution Ave. NW
Suite 500
Washington, DC 20001

202-463-2600; *Fax:* 202-463-2666;
www.nma.org
Social Media: Facebook, Twitter, LinkedIn, YouTube

Harry M. Red Conger, Chairman
Kevin Crutchfield, Vice Chairman
Hal Quinn, President & CEO
Rich Nolan, SVP, Government & Political Affairs
Bruce Watzman, SVP, Regulatory Affairs

Association for the mining industry in the US.

23604 **National Rural Electric Cooperative Association**
4301 Wilson Blvd
Suite 1
Arlington, VA 22203-1860

703-907-5500; *Fax:* 703-907-5526
veronica.franco@nreca.coop; www.nreca.coop
Social Media: Facebook, Twitter, LinkedIn, Youtube

Jo Ann Emerson, CEO
Peter Baxter, SVP, Insurance & Financial Services
Jim Bausell, SVP, Communications
Jeffrey Connor, COO/Chief of Staff
Kirk Johnson, SVP, Government Relations

Membership consists of cooperative systems, public power and public utility districts. Annual budget of approximately $94 million. Sponsors and supports the Action for Rural Electrification Political Action Committee.
1000 Members
Founded in: 1942

23605 **North American Association of Utility Distributors**
3105 Corporate Exchange Court
Bridgeton, MO 63044

314-506-0724; *Fax:* 314-506-0790
director@naaud.org; www.naaud.org

Ralph Knobbe, President
Patrick Novak, Vice President
Linda Coker, Executive Director
Jim Reinhardt, Treasurer

A member of the National Association of Wholesler-Distributors.

23606 **North American Electric Reliability**
3353 Peachtree Road, N.E
Suite 600, North Tower
Atlanta, GA 30326

404-446-2560; *Fax:* 404-467-0474;
www.nerc.com

Gerry W. Cauley, President/CEO
Mark Lauby, SVP/Chief Reliability Officer
Charles A. Berardesco, SVP/General Counsel/Corp Secretary
Michael Walker, SVP/CFO/CAO/Treasurer
Stan Hoptroff, VP/CTO

Principal organization for coordinating and promoting North America's electrical supplies, demands and reliability issues.
11 Members
Founded in: 1968

23607 **Northwest Public Power Association**
9817 Ne 54th St
Suite 200
Vancouver, WA 98662-6064

360-254-0109; *Fax:* 360-254-5731
nwppa@nwppa.org; www.nwppa.org
Social Media: Facebook, Twitter

Anita J Decker, Executive Director
Debbie Kuraspediani, Communication Director
Brenda Dunn, Associate Editor/Advertising
Glenda Waite, Graphic Artist
Greg Blank, Web/IT Technician

A international training organization for electric utilities in 10 western states and 4 western Canadian provinces.
Cost: $75.00
200 Members
Frequency: Monthly/Annunal
Founded in: 1940

23608 **Power Transmission Distributors Association**
230 W Monroe St
Suite 1410
Chicago, IL 60606-4703

312-516-2100; *Fax:* 312-516-2101
ptda@ptda.org; www.ptda.org
Social Media: Twitter, LinkedIn

Ajay Bajaj, President
LeRoy Burcroff, 1st VP
Thomas Clawser, 2nd VP
Chris Bursack, Treasurer
Ann Arnott, Executive Vice President/CEO

Members are industrial power transmission/motion control distributor firms representing locations throughout North America and several other countries and manufacturing firms.
Founded in: 1960

23609 Public Utilities Risk Management Association
1900 West Park Drive
Suite 150
Westborough, MA 1581
508-983-1457; *Fax:* 508-599-3427;
www.purma.org
Social Media: Facebook
Wayne Doerpholz, President
Jeannine Millett, Vice President
Jeffrey Dobbins, Secretary
Gail Cohen, Treasurer
Paul Heanue, Director
Founded to provide risk management and insurance services to municipal utilities.
Founded in: 1996

23610 The Association of Businesses Advocating Tariff Equality
151 S. Old Woodward Avenue
Suite200
Birmingham, MI 48009
248-988-5861
rstrong@clarkhill.com
abate-energy.org
Robert Strong, Legal Counsel
An organization for protecting the interests on industrial customers in energy and related matters.
Founded in: 1981

23611 US Energy Information Administration
1000 Independence Ave Sw
Suite 1E-238
Washington, DC 20585-0001
202-586-8800; *Fax:* 202-586-0727
InfoCtr@eia.gov; www.eia.doe.gov
Social Media: Facebook, Twitter, Youtube, RSS
Adam Sieminski, Administrator
Howard K. Gruenspecht, Deputy Administrator
John Conti, Assistant Admin for Energy Analysis
Stephen Harvey, Assistant Admin, Energy Statistics
Gina Pearson, Assistant Administrator, Comm.

23612 United States Energy Association
1300 Pennsylvania Avenue, NW
Suite 550
Washington, DC 20004
202-312-1230; *Fax:* 202-682-1682
reply@usea.org; www.usea.in
Social Media: Facebook, Twitter, Google+
Vickey A. Bailey, Chairman
Barry K. Worthington, Executive Director
Will Polan, Senior Director
Brain Kearns, Chief Financial Officer
Sheila Slocum Hollis, Treasurer
The US Member Committee of the World Energy Council (WEC).

23613 Water Environment Federation
601 Wythe St
Alexandria, VA 22314-1994
703-684-2400
800-666-0206; *Fax:* 703-684-2492
inquiry@wef.org; www.wef.org
Social Media: Facebook, Twitter
Eileen O'Neill, Executive Director
Barry Liner, Director
Lisa McFadden, Sr. Program Manager
Steve Harrison, Manager-Technical Programs
Elizabeth Conway, Committee Coordinator
34000 Members
Founded in: 1928

Newsletters

23614 Clearing Up
Energy NewsData
PO Box 900928
Seattle, WA 98109-9228
206-285-4848; *Fax:* 206-281-8035
newsdata@newsdata.com; www.newsdata.com
Steve Ernst, Managing Editor
Daniel Sackett, Circulation Director
Covers energy policy, resource development, public utility and energy litigation and energy marketing financing in the Pacific Northwestern United States and Western Canada.
Cost: $1199.00
14 Pages
Frequency: Weekly
ISSN: 0738-2332
Founded in: 1982
Printed in one color on matte stock

23615 Electric Utility Week
McGraw Hill
PO Box 182604
Columbus, OH 43272
877-833-5524
800-752-8878; *Fax:* 614-759-3749
customer.service@mcgraw-hill.com;
www.mcgraw-hill.com
Dan Tanz, Chief Editor
Paul Carlsen, Senior Editor
Harold McGraw, III, President
Provides news of significant developments affecting the electric utility industry focusing on state and federal regulation, management and bulk power markets. Publishes charts of prices utilities pay for fuels.
Cost: $2165.00
Frequency: Weekly
Founded in: 1909

23616 Energy Daily
King Publishing Group
1325 Massachusetts Ave Nw
Suite 310
Washington, DC 20005-4194
240-455-6801
800-926-5464; *Fax:* 240-628-5774;
www.energy-daily.com
F King, President
George Lobsenz, Editor
Information regarding energy use, supply and demand, power and heat generation, energy sources, conversion and storage, and energy and fuel conversion processes.
Cost: $1900.00
Frequency: Daily
Founded in: 1974

23617 Energy Report
Pasha Publications
101 Second St
Suite 110
Petaluma, CA 94952
707-981-8999
800-424-2908; *Fax:* 707-981-8998;
www.theenergyreport.com
Harry Baisden, Group Publisher
Barry Cassell, Editor
Coverage includes comprehensive policies and issues affecting oil, natural gas, electricity, cogeneration, power markets, nuclear energy, taxation, global warming and energy business opportunities.
Cost: $872.00
20 Pages
Frequency: Weekly
Founded in: 1978

23618 HydroWorld Alert
HCI Publications
410 Archibald St
Kansas City, MO 64111-3288
816-931-1311; *Fax:* 816-931-2015;
www.hcipub.com
Leslie Eden, President
Bi-weekly fax report on international hydroelectric project developments, business trends, and news relevant to organizations seeking business developments.
Cost: $635.00
Frequency: Weekly
Founded in: 1970

23619 Hydrowire
HCI Publications
410 Archibald St
Kansas City, MO 64111-3288
816-931-1311; *Fax:* 816-931-2015
hci@aol.com; www.hcipub.com
Leslie Eden, President
Concise, bi-weekly report on major news in the hydroelectric industry. Includes timely listings of licensing for hydroelectric power projects. Also covers news and business opportunities in the North American hydroelectric industry.
Cost: $425.00
Circulation: 500
Founded in: 1994

23620 IE News: Utilities
Institute of Industrial Engineers
3577 Parkway Lane
Suite 200
Norcross, GA 30092
770-449-0460
800-494-0460; *Fax:* 770-441-3295
cs@iienet.org; www.iienet.org
Social Media: Facebook, Twitter, LinkedIn
Elaine Fuerst, Marketing Director
Monica Erikson, Communicaton
David Gatton, Managing Director
Association news.
4 Pages
Frequency: Quarterly
Circulation: 400
Founded in: 1948

23621 Inside Energy
Platts, McGraw Hill Companies
1200 G St Nw
Suite 1000
Washington, DC 20005-3814
202-942-8788
800-752-8878; *Fax:* 202-383-2025
support@platts.com; www.platts.com
Bill Loveless, Editor
Georgia Safos, Circulation Director
Covers the Department of Energy including energy, science/technology, and environmental management programs as well as energy programs at the Interior Department.
Cost: $1810.00
16 Pages
Frequency: Weekly
Founded in: 1888

23622 NARUC Bulletin
Nat'l Assn of Regulatory Utility Commissioners

1101 Vermont Ave Nw
Suite 200
Washington, DC 20005-3553

202-898-2200; *Fax:* 202-898-2213
admin@naruc.org; www.naruc.org

Charles Gray, Executive Director
Jaclyn Wintle, Publications Coordinator
Diane Munns, Publisher

A quasi-governmental nonprofit corporation composed of governmental agencies engaged in the regulation of public utilities and carriers. Its primary mission is to serve the consumer interest by seeking to improve the quality and effectiveness of public regulation in America.
Cost: $110.00
16 Pages
Frequency: Weekly
Circulation: 2000
Founded in: 1889
Mailing list available for rent
Printed in one color on matte stock

23623 National Association of Regulatory Utility Commissioners Newsletter
Natl Assoc of Regulatory Utility Commissioners
1101 Vermont Ave Nw
Suite 200
Washington, DC 20005-3553

202-898-2200; *Fax:* 202-898-2213
admin@naruc.org; www.naruc.org

Charles Gray, Executive Director
Jaclyn Wintle, Publications Coordinator
Judi Sord, Circulation Manager

A national organization that offers valuable information on over 150 consultants and other professionals active in regulated water, sewer and related industries.
Cost: $125.00
Circulation: 1800
Founded in: 1889

23624 Northeast Power Report
McGraw Hill
PO Box 182604
Columbus, OH 43272

877-833-5524
800-752-8878; *Fax:* 614-759-3749
customer.service@mcgraw-hill.com;
www.mcgraw-hill.com
Social Media: Facebook, Twitter, LinkedIn

Ron Dionne, Publisher
Rob Ingraham, Publisher
Harold McGraw, III, President
Steven H. Weiss, VP

Provides news of significant developments affecting the electric utility industry focusing on state and federal regulation, management and bulk power markets. Publishes charts of prices utilities pay for fuels.
Cost: $745.00
16 Pages
Frequency: BiWeekly
Founded in: 1909

23625 Nuclear Waste News
Business Publishers
222 Sedwick Dr
Suite 101
Durham, NC 27713

800-223-8720; *Fax:* 800-508-2592
custserv@bpinews.com; www.bpinews.com

Worldwide coverage of the nuclear waste management industry including waste generation, packaging, transport, processing and disposal.
Cost: $697.00
10 Pages
Frequency: 25 per year
Founded in: 1963
Mailing list available for rent
Printed in 2 colors on matte stock

23626 NuclearFuel
McGraw Hill
PO Box 182605
Columbus, OH 43273

877-833-5525
800-752-8879; *Fax:* 614-759-3750
customer.service@mcgraw-hill.com;
www.mcgraw-hill.com

Michael Knapik, Editor
Rob Ingraham, Publisher
Harold McGraw, III, President
Steven H. Weiss, VP

Provides news of significant developments affecting the electric utility industry focusing on state and federal regulation, management and bulk power markets. Publishes charts of prices utilities pay for fuels.
14 Pages
Founded in: 1910

23627 Nucleonics Week
McGraw Hill
PO Box 182604
Columbus, OH 43272

877-833-5524
800-752-8878; *Fax:* 614-759-3749
support@platts.com; www.mcgraw-hill.com

Margaret Ryan, Editor

Covers all aspects of commercial nuclear power.
Cost: $2265.00
12 Pages
Frequency: Monthly
Founded in: 1888

23628 Public Gas News
American Public Gas Association
11094 Lee Hwy
Suite 102
Fairfax, VA 22030-5034

703-352-3890; *Fax:* 703-352-1271
info@apga.org; www.apga.org

Robert S Cave, Executive Director

Written for public gas managers to keep them apprised of industry news.
Cost: $50.00
Circulation: 1000
Printed in 2 colors

23629 Public Utilities
State Capitals Newsletters
PO Box 7376
Alexandria, VA 22307-7376

703-768-9600; *Fax:* 703-768-9690
statecapitals.com
Cost: $345.00

Frequency: Weekly

23630 Public Utilities: From the State Capitals
Wakeman Walworth
300 N Washington Street
Suite 204
Alexandria, VA 22314-2530

703-689-9600; *Fax:* 703-549-1372;
www.publicworks.houstontx.gov/utilities/

Keyes Walworth, Publisher

Covers state regulations of all forms of public utilities across the nation. It reports on new rate structures, allowable profit margins, special taxes, consumer relations, environmental legislation, nuclear plant regulations, deregulation programs and programs for low-income customers.

23631 Utility Environment Report
McGraw Hill
PO Box 182604
Columbus, OH 43272

877-833-5524
800-752-8878; *Fax:* 614-759-3749
customer.service@mcgraw-hill.com;
www.mcgraw-hill.com

Rob Ingraham, Publisher
Harold McGraw, III, President
Steven H. Weiss, VP

Provides news of significant developments affecting the electric utility industry focusing on state and federal regulation, management and bulk power markets. Publishes charts of prices utilities pay for fuels.
Cost: $695.00
18 Pages
Founded in: 1899

23632 Utility Executive
Water Environment Federation
601 Wythe St
Alexandria, VA 22314-1994

800-666-0206; *Fax:* 703-684-2492;
www.wef.org
Social Media: Facebook, Twitter

Matt Bond, President
Cordell Samuels, President-Elect
Sandra Ralston, Vice President
Chris Browning, Treasurer
Jeff Eger, Secretary and Executive Director

For managers and executives at water & wastewater treatment plants, consultants, and others interested in utility management. Focuses on such pertinent business issues as public private partnerships, capital financing options, strategic planning methods, public outreach approaches, and staff development.
79 Members
ISSN: 1044-9943
Founded in: 1928

23633 Utility Reporter: Fuels, Energy and Power
InfoTeam
PO Box 15640
Plantation, FL 33318-5640

954-473-9560; *Fax:* 954-473-0544

Randy M Allen CPA, Editor

Focuses on activities involving: power generation, combustion, delivery and transmission; alternative energy devices and systems; heat transfer, storage and utilization; and myriad of related topics.
Cost: $289.00
20 Pages
Frequency: Monthly
ISBN: 0-890298-4 -
Printed in one color on matte stock

23634 Wind Energy Smart Brief
American Wind Energy Association
1501 M Street NW
Suite 1000
Washington, DC 20005

202-383-2500; *Fax:* 202-383-2505
windmail@awea.org; www.awea.org
Social Media: Facebook, Twitter, LinkedIn, You Tube

Denise Bode, CEO

This newsletter delivers quickly digestible summaries of the day's wind energy-related stories from across the media, as well as links to those stories.
Frequency: Weekly

23635 Wind Energy Weekly
American Wind Energy Association

1501 M Street NW
Suite 1000
Washington, DC 20005

202-383-2500; *Fax:* 202-383-2505
windmail@awea.org; www.awea.org

Denise Bode, CEO

Packed with detailed and up-to-date information on the world of wind energy that simply can't be obtained elsewhere.
Frequency: Weekly

23636 **WindLetter**
American Wind Energy Association
1501 M Street NW
Suite 1000
Washington, DC 20005

202-383-2500; *Fax:* 202-383-2505
windmail@awea.org; www.awea.org
Social Media: Facebook, Twitter, LinkedIn, You Tube

Denise Bode, CEO

Recap's the month's most significant wind energy news and includes interesting for wind energy enthusiasts.
Frequency: Monthly

Magazines & Journals

23637 **APWA Reporter**
American Public Works Association
2345 Grand Blvd
Suite 700
Kansas City, MO 64108-2625

816-472-6100
800-848-2792; *Fax:* 816-472-1610
ddancy@apwa.net; www.apwa.net
Social Media: Facebook, Twitter, LinkedIn

Kaye Sullivan, Executive Director
David Dancy, Director Marketing

Circulation to entire membership of American Public Works Association.
Cost: $100.00
Frequency: Monthly
Circulation: 25000
ISBN: 0-092487-3 -
Founded in: 1937
Mailing list available for rent

23638 **Alternative Energy**
PWG
205 S Beverly Drive
#208
Beverly Hills, CA 90212-3827

310-273-3486; *Fax:* 310-858-8272;
www.bp.com

Irwin Stambler, Publisher
Ahmad Taleban, President

Reports on future economic and technological trends.
Cost: $95.00
12 Pages
Frequency: Monthly
Printed in 2 colors on matte stock

23639 **American Gas Magazine**
American Gas Association
400 N Capitol Street NW
Suite 450
Washington, DC 20001

202-824-7000; *Fax:* 202-824-7092;
www.aga.org
Social Media: Facebook, Twitter, LinkedIn

David N Parker, CEO
Kevin Hardardt, CFO/CAO
Ysabel Korolevich, Membership Services
Frequency: 10x/Year
Founded in: 1918

23640 **American Public Works Association**
American Public Works Association
2345 Grand Blvd
Suite 700
Kansas City, MO 64108-2625

816-472-6100
800-848-2792; *Fax:* 816-472-1610
ddancy@apwa.net; www.apwa.net

Kaye Sullivan, Executive Director
David Dancy, Marketing Director

International educational and professional association of public agencies, private sector companies, and individuals dedicated to providing high quality public works goods and services. AWA provides a forum in which public works professionals competency, increase the performance of their agencies and companies, and bring important public works-related topics to public attention in local, state, and federal areas. Mailing list for members only.
Cost: $100.00
40 Pages
Frequency: Monthly
ISSN: 0092-4873
Founded in: 1937

23641 **American Water Works Association Journal**
American Water Works Association
6666 W Quincy Ave
Denver, CO 80235-3098

303-794-7711
800-926-7337; *Fax:* 303-347-0804
journal@awwa.org; www.awwa.org

Andrew Richardson, President
Jack W. Hoffbuhr, Executive Director

Journal of the professional society of North American drinking water experts. Dues cover subscription for members.
Cost: $120.00
152 Pages
Frequency: Monthly
ISSN: 0003-150X
Founded in: 1935

23642 **Bulletin**
NW Public Power Association
9817 Ne 54th St
Suite 200
Vancouver, WA 98662-6064

360-254-0109; *Fax:* 360-254-5731
nwppa@nwppa.org; www.nwppa.org

Will Lutgen, Executive Director

Readership consists of directors, chairmen and managers of electric utilities in the ten Western States and four Canadian provinces. Provides news and events of the public power industry in the Pacific Northwest Region.
Cost: $ 32.00
32 Pages
Circulation: 6200
Printed in 4 colors

23643 **Chief Engineer**
Chief Engineers Association of Chicagoland
4701 Midlothian Turnpike
Crestwood, IL 60445

708-293-1720; *Fax:* 708-633-7008;
www.chiefengineer.org

Ernest K Wulff, Editor

Covers building maintenance issues, laws and rulings relative to chief engineers, as well as mechanical and general HVAC equipment.
Frequency: Monthly
Circulation: 2000
Founded in: 1935
Mailing list available for rent: 2K names

23644 **Cogeneration Monthly Letter**
Cogeneration Publications Company
509 Tennessee Avenue
Alexandria, VA 22305-1336

703-683-1868; *Fax:* 703-683-1878;
www.powermarketers.com

Scott Spiewak, Publisher

Discusses new technology and legislation governing power generating facilities. Includes listings of planned projects.
Frequency: 5 per year
Circulation: 5000

23645 **Diesel & Gas Turbine Worldwide**
Diesel & Gas Turbine Publications
20855 Watertown Rd
Suite 220
Waukesha, WI 53186-1873

262-754-4100
800-558-4322; *Fax:* 262-832-5075
slizdas@dieselpub.com; www.dieselpub.com

Michael Osenga, President
Mark McNeely, Editor
Lynne Diefenbach, Advertising Manager
Christa Johnson, Production Manager

Focuses on the design, production, installation, operation, and maintenance of engines in the global marine, power generation, oil and gas, or railroad industries.
Frequency: bi-Monthly
Circulation: 20100
Founded in: 1935

23646 **Diesel Progress: International Edition**
Diesel & Gas Turbine Publications
20855 Watertown Rd
Suite 220
Waukesha, WI 53186-1873

262-754-4100; *Fax:* 262-832-5075
slizdas@dieselpub.com; www.dieselspec.com

Michael Osenga, President
Sue Bollwahn, Circulation Manager
Katie Evans, Sales Manager
Michael J Brezonick, Editor-in-Chief

Focuses on new products and technology that serves engineering, marketing, service and equipment, purchasing, administrative, and others allied to the field.
Circulation: 10273
Founded in: 1935

23647 **District Energy**
International District Enery Association (IDEA)
24 Lyman Streetad
Suite 230
Westborough, MA 01581

508-366-9339; *Fax:* 508-366-0019
idea@districtenergy.org;
www.districtenergy.org

Peter Myers, Editor
Rob Thornton, President

Journal of district heating and cooling industry, congeneration, physical plants and energy efficiency. Accepts advertising.
Cost: $40.00
Frequency: Quarterly

23648 **Electric Light & Power**
Technical Publishing
1421 S. Sheridan Road
Tulsa, OK 74112

981-831-9884; *Fax:* 918-831-9834
candiced@pennwell.com; www.elp.com

Wayne Beaty, Editor
Candice Doctor, Sales Director
Michael Grossman, Publisher
Teresa Hansen, Editor in Chief

Offers articles on the electric utility industry.
Cost: $38.00
84 Pages
Frequency: Monthly
Founded in: 1922

23649 Electric Perspectives
Edison Electric Institute
701 Pennsylvania Avenue NW
Washington, DC 20004-2696

202-508-5000
800-344-5453; *Fax:* 202-508-5794
feedback@eei.org; www.eei.org

Thomas R Kuhn, President
Brian Farrell, Member Relations Director

The magazine for management in America's investor-owned electric utilities. Covers all areas of utility operations and concerns, providing detailed analyses and farsighted commentary on how issues and trends are shaping the industry today and the future impact.
Cost: $50.00
Frequency: Bi-Monthly
Circulation: 10000
ISSN: 0364-474X
Founded in: 1981

23650 Energy Efficiency Journal
NAESCO
1615 M St NW
Suite 800
Washington, DC 20036-3213

202-822-0950; *Fax:* 202-822-0955;
www.eceee.org/ee_journal

Terry E Singer, Executive Editor
Nina Lockhart, Senior Program Manager
Donald Gilligan, Publisher

Targets energy service companies, electric and gas utilities and other energy providers. Highlights industry news and features energy conservation.
Frequency: Quarterly
Circulation: 200

23651 Energy Manager
Primedia
3585 Engineering Drive
Suite 100
Norcross, GA 30092

678-421-3000; *Fax:* 913-514-6895;
www.primedia.com

Eric Jacobson, Senior VP
Charles Stubs, President
Kim Payne, VP
Mike Barber, Accountant

Subjects include energy management systems, HVAC, automated building systems, plant and facilities control, and negotiating supplier contracts. Features include legislative news from Washington, analysis of rare updates, relevant news from around the world and new product reviews.
Frequency: 5 per year
Circulation: 50,000
Founded in: 1998

23652 Energy Today
Trend Publishing
529 14th St NW
Suite 954
Washington, DC 20045-1925

202-662-8827; *Fax:* 202-662-8829

Arthur Kranish, Editor

Includes news and analysis, new regulatory and technical developments, grant and contract opportunities, investigative reports, and market studies.
Frequency: Monthly

23653 Energy and Housing Report
Alan L Frank Associates
9124 Bradford Road
Silverspring, MD 20901-4918

703-866-4397; *Fax:* 301-565-3298
homeenergy.org

Mary James, Publisher
Iain Walker, Executive Editor
Cass Duggan, Circulation Manager
Carol A. Markell, Marketing Manager
Alan Meier, President

Research in consumption with the goal of increasing energy conservation at the residential level. Follows trends in consumption and the effects of conservation efforts on energy use.
Founded in: 1994

23654 Energy in the News
New York Mercantile Exchange
1 N End Ave
New York, NY 10282-1101

212-299-2000; *Fax:* 212-301-4700;
www.nymex.com

Samuel Gaer, Executive VP

Covers market fundamentals, trading strategies and market conditions. Provides information that keeps future commission merchants, industry executives, options and cash market traders up-to-date with trends affecting the energy industry.
Frequency: Quarterly
Circulation: 35000

23655 Gas Turbine World
Pequot Publishing
PO Box 447
Southport, CT 06490-447

203-259-1812; *Fax:* 203-259-0532;
www.business-magazines.com

Victor Debiasi, Publisher

Focuses on implementing policy, specification, design, maintenance, and modernization of the systems and equipment of electric power generation.
Cost: $135.00
Frequency: Monthly
Circulation: 10000

23656 Generation Week
Pasha Publications
1600 Wilson Boulevard
#600
Arlington, VA 22209-2509

703-528-1244
800-424-2908; *Fax:* 703-816-7821;
www.pasha.com

Tod Sedgwick, Publisher

On new technology and innovative operation of power plants.
Frequency: Weekly

23657 HRW: Hydro Review Worldwide
HCI Publications
410 Archibald St
Kansas City, MO 64111-3288

816-931-1311; *Fax:* 816-931-2015
hci@aol.com; www.hcipub.com

Leslie Eden, President
Marla Barness, Editor
Bob Merrigan, Marketing

Magazine serving information needs of people associated with hydro throughout the world. Managing and improving plant operations, solving problems, financing and essential business news are covered extensively.
Cost: $44.00
Circulation: 4673
Founded in: 1982

23658 Hart's Energy Markets
Hart Publications
4545 Post Oak Place
#210
Houston, TX 77027-3105

713-993-9320; *Fax:* 713-840-0983;
www.hartenergy.com

Dana Griffin Smith, Publisher
Joe Fisher, Editor
Richard Eichler, President

Keeps readers abreast of trends and opportunities in the marketplace. Covers such topics as electricity deregulation, gas unbundling, rebundling of services, nuclear and renewable energy, technological developments and regulatory issues.
Frequency: Monthly
Circulation: 14000
Founded in: 1973

23659 Home Power
PO Box 520
Ashland, OR 97520-18

541-512-0201
800-707-6585; *Fax:* 530-475-0836
info@homepower.com; www.homepower.com

Karen Perez, Publisher
Joe Schwartz, Manager

Covers photovoltaics, wind turbines, solar heating, methane, batteries, inverters, water pumping, electric vehicles, controls, and instruments. Examines the design and installation of balanced renewable energy systems in the home, while also reviewing products ranging from solar pumps to refrigerators.
Cost: $22.50
Circulation: 19200
Founded in: 1987

23660 Hydro Review
HCI Publications
410 Archibald St
Kansas City, MO 64111-3288

816-931-1311; *Fax:* 816-931-2015;
www.hcipub.com

Leslie Eden, President

Magazine providing in-depth coverage of the North American hydroelectric industry. Rehab, redevelopment, dam safety and the environment are explored.
Cost: $65.00
Circulation: 500
Founded in: 1980

23661 Independent Energy
PennWell Publishing Company
1421 S Sheridan Rd
Tulsa, OK 74112-6619

918-831-9421
800-331-4463; *Fax:* 918-831-9476;
www.pennwell.com

Robert Biolchini, President

Focuses on analysis and views aimed at doing business more successfully. Reports important market information, trends and equipment advances affecting power project development, financing, construction, operation and management.
Frequency: Monthly
Circulation: 10962
Founded in: 1961

23662 New Equipment Digest
Penton Media
1300 E 9th St
Suite 316
Cleveland, OH 44114-1503

216-696-7000; *Fax:* 216-696-6662
information@penton.com;
www.newequipment.com

Jane Cooper, Marketing
Tom Sockel, Associate Editor
Robert King, Editor

Sarah Hughes, Production Manager
Bobbie Macy, Circulation Manager
Serves the general industrial field which includes manufacturing, processing, engineering services, construction, transportation, mining, public utilities, wholesale distributors, educational services, libraries and governmental establishments.
Frequency: Monthly
Founded in: 1936

23663 Northeast Sun
NE Sustainable Energy Association
50 Miles St
Suite 3
Greenfield, MA 01301-3255

413-774-6051; *Fax:* 413-774-6053
nesea@nesea.org; www.nesea.org

David Barclay, Executive Director
Addresses the current issues of solar energy and natural gas power. Also provides an exchange of ideas for those seeking other environmentally sound energy sources.
Frequency: Monthly
Circulation: 5000
Founded in: 1974

23664 Northwest Public Power Bulletin
Northwest Public Power Association
9817 NE 54th St
Suite 200
Vancouver, WA 98662-6064

360-254-0109; *Fax:* 360-254-5731
nwppa@nwppa.org; www.nwppa.org

Will Lutgen, President
Brenda Dunn, Associate Editor
Debbie Kuraspediani, Director Communications
Trade publication for consumer-owned electric utilities managers, directors, commissioners and management staff.
Cost: $25.00
28 Pages
Frequency: Monthly
Circulation: 6000
Founded in: 1947

23665 Nuclear News
American Nuclear Society
555 N Kensington Ave
La Grange Park, IL 60526-5592

708-352-6611; *Fax:* 708-352-0499
advertising@ans.org; www.nuclear-news.net

Jack Tuohy, Executive Director
Mike Diekman, Information Department Head
Sarah Wells, Editor
Gloria Nawrocki, Marketing Manager
For personnel involved in nuclear power operation and development. Coverage includes power, plant operations and maintenance, fuel cycle, legislation, international employment and more.
Cost: $290.00
Frequency: Monthly
Circulation: 12000
Founded in: 1954
Printed in on glossy stock

23666 Nuclear Plant Journal
EQES
1400 Opus Place
Suite 904
Downers Grove, IL 60515

630-858-6161; *Fax:* 630-858-8787
michelle@goinfo.com;
www.nuclearplantjournal.com

Newal Agnihotri, Publisher
Nuclear Plant Journal includes technical papers, informative articles and departments aimed at developing better methods, systems, products and services in the nuclear power industry. The Journal is compiled through the research efforts of professional engineers who are specialists in their respective fields.
Circulation: 14000
ISSN: 0892-2055
Founded in: 1983
Printed in on glossy stock

23667 Power Engineering International
PennWell Publishing Company
1421 S Sheridan Rd
Tulsa, OK 74112-6619

918-831-9421
800-331-4463; *Fax:* 918-831-9476
Headquarters@PennWell.com;
www.pennwell.com

Robert Biolchini, President
Candice Doctor, Regional Sales Manager
Rick Huntzicker, National Sales Manager
Junior Isles, Publisher & Editorial Director
Rafael A Junquera, Editor
A variety of topics including plant design, operations, management and applications. New products are also reviewed.
Frequency: Monthly
Circulation: 34000
Founded in: 1910

23668 Private Power Executive
Pequot Publishing
PO Box 447
Southport, CT 06490-0447

203-259-1812; *Fax:* 203-259-0532

Victor de Biasi, Publisher
Written for cogenerators and developers involved in planning, design, financing, installation and operation of cogeneration plants for industrial, municipal, hospitals, and commercial district heating and cooling.
Frequency: BiMonthly
Circulation: 11,500

23669 Public Power Magazine
American Public Power Association
1875 Connecticut Ave NW
Suite 1200
Washington, DC 20009-5715

202-467-2900
800-515-2772; *Fax:* 202-467-2910
mrufe@appanet.org; www.publicpower.org

Alan Richardson, Executive Director
Michael L Kurtz, Publisher
The only national magazine published especially for policymaking and managerial personnel of local publicly owned electric systems. Public Power keeps readers abreast of policy developments, managerial techniques, new technologies, research and development and legislative issues.
Subscription, $50.00
Cost: $10.00
72 Pages
Circulation: 11100
ISSN: 0033-3654
Founded in: 1942

23670 Public Utilities Fortnightly
Public Utilities Reports
8229 Boone Blvd
Suite 400
Vienna, VA 22182-2623

703-847-7720
800-368-5001; *Fax:* 703-917-6964;
www.pur.com
Social Media: Twitter

Bruce Radford, Publisher
Michael Burr, Editor-In-Chief
Philip Cross, Vice President/ Legal Editor
Joseph Paparello, Director of Sales
Jean Cole, Marketing Manager
Independent publisher for the energy industry.
Cost: $459.00
Frequency: Weekly
Founded in: 1929

23671 Public Utility Weekly
Public Utilities Reports
8229 Boone Blvd
Suite 400
Vienna, VA 22182-2623

703-847-7720
800-368-5001; *Fax:* 703-917-6964;
www.pur.com

Bruce Radford, President
Richard Stavros, Executive Editor
Joseph Paparello, Marketing Manager
Phillip Cross, Legal Publisher
Designed to serve as a communication forum for the utility industry covering state commission rulings and federal regulatory issues.
Founded in: 1915

23672 Solar Today
American Solar Energy Society
4760 Walnut Street
Suite 106
Boulder, CO 80301-2843

303-443-3130; *Fax:* 303-443-3212;
www.ases.org

Regina Thompson, Editor/Associate Publisher
Seth Masia, Deputy Editor
Brooke Simmons, Manager of Online Publishing
Provides information, case histories and reviews of a variety of renewable energy technologies, including solar, wind, biomass and geothermal.
Cost: $29.00
90 Pages
Circulation: 7000
Founded in: 1987

23673 SolarToday
American Solar Energy Society
2400 Central Avenue
Sutie A
Boulder, CO 80301

303-443-3130; *Fax:* 303-443-3212;
www.ases.org
Social Media: Facebook, Twitter

Bradley D Collins, Publisher
Gina Johnson, Editor
Brings together ASES' professional members as contributors and readers, amid the community of ASES chapters nationwide, to publish industry-leading editorial for more than 23 years. The leading renewable energy magazine for consumers and professionals.

23674 Transmission & Distribution World
Primedia
PO Box 12901
Shawnee Mission, KS 66282-2901

913-341-1300
800-441-0294; *Fax:* 913-514-6895;
www.tdworld.com
Social Media: Facebook, Twitter

Eric Jacobson, Senior VP
Rick Bush, Editor
Frequency: Monthly
Circulation: 49000
Founded in: 1996

23675 Turbomachinery International
Business Journals
PO Box 5550
Norwalk, CT 06856-5550

203-663-7814; *Fax:* 203-852-8175;
www.turbomachinerymag.com

Richard Zanetti, Publisher

Includes updates of new approaches to energy conservation, new equipment listings and business/financial news.
Frequency: BiMonthly
Circulation: 11,100
Founded in: 1959

23676 Utilities Law Review
John Wiley & Sons
Office A10 Spinners Court
55 West End
Witney, OX OX8 6

199-370-6183
800-825-7550; *Fax:* 199-370-9410;
www.lawtext.com/

Nicholas Gingell, Publisher
Cosmo Graham, Editor
William J Pesce, CEO/President
Charlotte Villiers, Assistant Editor
Peter Crowther, Current Survey Editor

Edited by a team of specialist UK and European lawyers, it is the leading journal in this fast-changing field. Providing detailed coverage of electricity, gas, telecommunications, transport, water and broadcasting.
Cost: $4920.00
Frequency: Bi-Monthly
Circulation: 250
Founded in: 1807

23677 Utility & Telephone Fleets
Practical Communications
482 Holly Ave
Saint Paul, MN 55102

651-91 -997; *Fax:* 651-224-2347;
www.utfleets.com/

Judith F Chance, Group Publisher
Mike Domke, Publisher
Carol Birkland, Editor
Tom Gelinas, Editorial Director

The equipment, accessory and information resource for fleet professionals.
Circulation: 18,000
Founded in: 1980

23678 Utility Automation
PennWell Publishing Company
1421 S Sheridan
PO Box 1260
Tulsa, OK 74112

918-835-3161; *Fax:* 918-831-9497
ua@pennwell.com;
www.utility-automation.com
Social Media: Facebook, Twitter

Shirley Wilson, Marketing Manager
Steven M Brown, Editor
Michael Grossman, Publisher
Robert F Biolchini, CEO/President
Janet Orteon, Circulation Manager

Innovative energy solutions.
Cost: $74.00
50 Pages
Circulation: 32200
ISSN: 1085-2328
Founded in: 1996

23679 Utility Automation International
PennWell Publishing Company
1421 S Sheridan Rd
Tulsa, OK 74112-6619

918-831-9421
800-331-4463; *Fax:* 918-831-9476
headquarters@pennwell.com;
www.pennwell.com
Social Media: Facebook, Twitter

Robert Biolchini, President
Tina Jackson, Circulation Manager
Doug Pryor, Editor
Brad Dillman, Marketing
Circulation: 24002
Founded in: 1910

23680 Utility Business
PRIMEDIA Intertec-Technology & Transportation
PO Box 12901
Shawnee Mission, KS 66282-2901

913-341-1300; *Fax:* 913-514-6895
barry-lecerf@intertec.com; www.primedia.com
Social Media: Facebook, Twitter, LinkedIn

Eric Jacobson, Senior VP

Editorial emphasis is on providing the reader with solutions and commentary for identifying and developing company assets, realizing the impact technology has on the business, and responding to the evolving demands of the marketplace.
Frequency: 8 per year
Circulation: 50,000

23681 Utility Contractor
3925 Chain Bridge Road
Suite 300
Fairfax, VA 22030

703-358-9300; *Fax:* 703-358-9307
bill@nuca.com; www.nuca.com

Bill Hillman, CEO

Serves the underground utility construction industry, including contractors, manufacturers, suppliers, engineering firms, municipal/public/private utilities, and others allied to the field.
Frequency: Monthly
Circulation: 59329
ISSN: 1098-0342
Founded in: 1963

23682 Utility Executive
Water Environment Federation
601 Wythe St
Alexandria, VA 22314-1994

703-684-2400
800-666-0206; *Fax:* 703-684-2492
csc@wef.org; www.wef.org

Bill Bertera, Executive Director
Jack Benson, Marketing Manager

Editorial focuses on issues such as continuous improvement, privatization, financial and risk management, as well as benchmarking and leadership. Problem solving strategies are included for everything from wastewater treatment efficiency to negotiation contracts and proposal evaluations, and address relevant, current issues facing utility managers today.
Cost: $33.00
Frequency: Monthly
Founded in: 1928

23683 Utility Fleet Management
TT Publishing
2200 Mill Road
Alexandria, VA 22314-1994

703-838-1770; *Fax:* 703-838-6259;
www.ttnews.com

Bob Raft, Publisher

Focuses on fleet management issues and new equipment.
Cost: $25.00
Frequency: Monthly
Circulation: 15,000

23684 Western Energy
Magellan
827 NE Oregon Street
Suite 200
Portland, OR 97232-2172

503-231-1994; *Fax:* 503-231-2595;
www.westernenergy.org

Chuck Meyer, President
Jody Brassfield-English, Controller
Karen Himes, Webmaster

Contains technical features designed to inform and educate workers and technicians in the energy production field.
Frequency: BiMonthly
Circulation: 5,058

Trade Shows

23685 AMRA Symposium
Automatic Meter Reading Association
60 Revere Drive
Suite 500
Northbrook, IL 60062

847-480-9628
888-612-2672; *Fax:* 847-480-9282;
www.amra-intl.org

Joyce Paschall, Executive Director

Gas, water and electric utilities, telephone companies and installation companies equipment and supplies for meter reading .
1600 Attendees
Frequency: Annual
Founded in: 1986

23686 APWA International Public Works Congress & Expo
American Public Works Association
2345 Grand Boulevard
Suite 700
Kansas City, MO 64108-2625

816-472-6100
800-848-2792; *Fax:* 816-472-1610
ddancy@apwa.net; www.apwa.net
Social Media: Facebook, Twitter, LinkedIn

Peter King, Executive Director
David Dancy, Marketing Director

Offers the benefit of a variety of educational sessions, depth of the exhibit program and endless opportunities for networking. The latest cutting-edge technologies, managerial techniques and regulatory trends designed to keep you focused on the right solutions at the right time.
6500 Attendees
Frequency: Annual/September
ISSN: 0092-4873
Founded in: 1894

23687 American Public Power Association of Engineers Operations Workshop
2301 M Street NW
Floor 3
Washington, DC 20037-1427

202-467-2900

Barbara Opicka, Marketing Assistant
Alan Richardson, President/CEO

50 booths.
1.3M Attendees
Frequency: February/March

23688 Buscon East/West
Conference Management Company
200 Connecticut Avenue
Norwalk, CT 06854-1940

203-866-4400

David Caplin, Show Manager

Principal industry event for systems builders and electronics engineers.
5M Attendees

23689 EEI Convention & Expo
Edison Electric Institute
701 Pennsylvania Avenue NW
Washington, DC 20004-2696

202-508-5000
800-344-5453; *Fax:* 202-508-5794

feedback@eei.org; www.eei.org
Social Media: Facebook, Twitter, LinkedIn

Thomas R Kuhn, President
Brian Farrell, Member Relations Director

Meeting of Senior executives in the power industry
750 Attendees
Frequency: Annual

23690 Northwest Public Power Engineering & Operations Show
9817 NE 54th Street
Suite 200
Vancouver, WA 98662-6064

360-254-0109; *Fax:* 360-254-5731
nwppa@nwppa.org; www.nwppa.org

Scott Lowry, Training Manager
Debbie Kuraspediani, Director Communications
900 Attendees
Frequency: May

23691 Smart Energy Summitt
Parks Associates
15950 N. Dallas Parkway
Suite 575
Dallas, TX 75248

972-490-1113
800-727-5711; *Fax:* 972-490-1133
info@parksassociates.com;
www.parksassociates.com

Tricia Parks, Founder and CEO
Stuart Sikes, President
Farhan Abid, Research Analyst
Bill Ablondi, Director, Home Systems Research
John Barrett, Director of Research

Smart Energy Summit is an annual three-day event that examines the opportunities and technical business requirements inherent in the consumer programs and advanced systems and services made possible by Smart Grids and Residential Energy Management solutions.
Frequency: Annual
Founded in: 1986

23692 WINDPOWER Conference and Exhibition
American Wind Energy Association (AWEA)
1501 M Street NW
Suite 1000
Washington, DC 20005

202-383-2500; *Fax:* 202-383-2505
windmail@awea.org;
www.windpowerexpo.org
Social Media: Facebook, Twitter

Denise Bode, Chief Executive Officer
Pam Poisson, Chief Financial Officer
Britt Theismann, Chief Operating Officer
Rob Gramlich, Senior VP, Public Policy
Peter Kelley, VP, Public Affairs

The WINDPOWER Conference & Exhibition is produced by the American Wind Energy Association to provide a venue for the wind industry to network, do business, and solve problems. Recognized as one of the fastest-growing trade shows in the U.S., WINDPOWER includes nearly 1,400 exhibiting companies, thousands of qualified wind energy professionals, engaging educational information and unmatched networking opportunities and special events.
2500 Members
20000 Attendees
Frequency: Annual

Directories & Databases

23693 DRI Utility Cost Forecasting
DRI/McGraw-Hill
24 Hartwell Ave
Lexington, MA 02421-3103

781-860-6060; *Fax:* 781-860-6002;
www.construction.com

Walt Arvin, President

This large database covers the US public utility industry, including cost inputs for pumps, gas compressors, steam pipes and gas and electric meters.

23694 Directory of Electric Power Producers and Distributors
McGraw Hill
2 Penn Plz
5th Floor
New York, NY 10121-2298

212-760-8589; *Fax:* 212-904-2723;
www.mcgraw-hill.com

Offers information on over 3,500 investor-owned, municipal, rural cooperative and government electric utility systems in the United States and Canada.
Cost: $395.00
1,200 Pages
Frequency: Annual

23695 Directory of Electric Utility Company Libraries in the United States
Library Services Committee/Edison Electric Inst
701 Pennsylvania Avenue NW
Washington, DC 20004-2608

202-347-2693

Over 90 investor-owned electric utility company libraries throughout the country are profiled.
Cost: $10.00
149 Pages
Frequency: Annual

23696 Directory of Energy Professionals
Assn of Regulatory Utility Commissioners
PO Box 684
Washington, DC 20044-0684

202-898-2200

Offers information on consultants and other professionals active in regulated energy utility industries.
Cost: $44.00
450 Pages
Frequency: Annual

23697 Directory of Publicly Owned Natural Gas Systems
American Public Gas Association
11094 Lee Hwy
Suite 102
Fairfax, VA 22030-5034

703-352-3890; *Fax:* 703-352-1271
info@apga.org; www.apga.org

Robert S Cave, Executive Director

A listing of all publicly owned natural gas systems in the US.
Cost: $50.00
80 Pages
Frequency: Annual
Circulation: 1,000
Printed in on matte stock

23698 Electric Utility Cost Forecast
WEFA Group
800 Baldwin Tower Boulevard
Eddystone, PA 19022-1368

610-490-4000; *Fax:* 610-490-2770;
www.wefa.com

Mary Novak

This time series covers prices, construction and operating costs pertinent to the electric utilities industry.

23699 Electric Utility Industry
Midwest Publishing Company
2230 E 49th Ste E
Tulsa, OK 74105-8771

918-582-2000
800-829-2002; *Fax:* 918-587-9349;
www.midwestdirectories.com

Will Hammack, Editor

Approximately 6,000 utility companies, contractors, engineering firms, equipment manufacturers and supply companies.
Cost: $155.00
Frequency: Annual February
Founded in: 1943

23700 Financial Statistics of Major Investor-Owned Electric Utilities
US Energy Information Administration
1000 Independence Ave SW
Washington, DC 20585-0001

202-586-8800; *Fax:* 202-586-0727;
www.eia.doe.gov

John H Weiner, Executive Director

Offers data from over 180 major investor-owned electric utilities in the United States.
Cost: $33.00
Frequency: Annual

23701 Gas Industry Training Directory
American Gas Association
1515 Wilson Boulevard
Suite 100
Arlington, VA 22209-2469

703-841-8400; *Fax:* 703-841-8406;
www.ihrdc.com

David F Sullivan, Industry Training

Over 600 programs are available in this directory from gas transmission and distribution companies, manufacturers of gas-fired equipment, consultants, etc., and from gas associations.
Frequency: Annual February

23702 Guide to Hydropower Mechanical Design
HCI Publications
410 Archibald St
Kansas City, MO 64111-3288

816-931-1311; *Fax:* 816-931-2015
hci@aol.com; www.hcipub.com

Leslie Eden, President

Developed by the Hydropower Technical Committee of the American Society of Mechanical Engineers. A ready reference for individuals who design hydropower facilities and producers and distributors of electricity.
Cost: $125.00
Circulation: 4673

23703 Handy-Whitman Index of Public Utility Construction Costs
Whitman, Requardt and Associates
801 S Caroline St
Baltimore, MD 21231-3311

410-235-3450; *Fax:* 410-243-5716;
www.wrallp.com

Jenny Miller, Human Resources

This database covers indexes of building costs for construction of public utilities in the United States.

23704 International Directory of Electric Power Producers and Distributors
McGraw Hill

1200 G St NW
Suite 250
Washington, DC 20005-3821

202-383-2377; *Fax:* 202-383-2438;
www.aviationweek.com

Jennifer Michels, Manager

Offers valuable information on over 3,000 power generating and distribution systems in over 200 countries overseas.
Cost: $345.00

23705 International Directory of Nuclear Utilities
Nuexco
950 17th Street
Suite 2500
Denver, CO 80202-2825
303-534-3100

This comprehensive directory offers information on over 120 utilities in 30 countries that operate nuclear plants with a capacity of at least 100 megawatts.
Cost: $220.00
264 Pages
Frequency: Annual
Founded in: 1968

23706 Inventory of Power Plants in the United States
US Energy Information Administration
1000 Independence Ave SW
Washington, DC 20585-0001

202-586-8800; *Fax:* 202-586-0727;
www.eia.doe.gov

John H Weiner, Executive Director

Information is given on existing and projected and jointly-owned power plants within electric utility systems.
Cost: $23.00
393 Pages
Frequency: Annual

23707 LEXIS Public Utilities Law Library
Mead Data Central
9443 Springboro Pike
Dayton, OH 45401

888-223-6337; *Fax:* 518-487-3584;
www.lexis-nexis.com

Andrew Prozes, CEO

This database contains information on public utilities-related case decisions from all state supreme courts and most state appellate courts.
Frequency: Full-text

23708 Northwest Electric Utility Directory
Northwest Public Power Association
9817 Ne 54th St
Suite 4576
Vancouver, WA 98662-6064

360-254-0109; *Fax:* 360-254-5731;
www.nwppa.org

Will Lutgen, President
Randy Shipley, Project Manager

Annual directory for electric utilities in 10 western states and 4 western Canadian provinces.
Frequency: Annually

23709 PUR Analysis of Investor-Owned Electric & Gas Utilities
Public Utilities Reports
2111 Wilson Boulevard
Suite 200
Arlington, VA 22201-3001

Covers over 200 investor-owned electric and gas operating and holding companies.
Cost: $395.00
Frequency: Annual

23710 Pipeline & Utilities Construction: Contractors Issue
Oildom Publishing Company of Texas
PO Box 219368
Houston, TX 77218-9368

281-558-6930

Offers a comprehensive list of over 5,000 individual contracting firms concerned with the construction of oil and gas pipelines, water and sewer lines and gas distribution systems.
Cost: $80.00
Frequency: Annual
Circulation: 25,000

23711 Platts UDI
1200 G St NW
Suite 1000
Washington, DC 20005-3814

202-383-2144
800-752-8878; *Fax:* 202-942-8789
udi@platts.com; www.marketing.platts.com

Liane Kucher, Manager

Publisher of directories for world-wide electric power industry.

23712 Power Engineering
PennWell Publishing Company
1421 S Sheridan Rd
Tulsa, OK 74112-6619

918-831-9421
800-331-4463; *Fax:* 918-831-9476
headquarters@pennwell.com;
www.power-eng.com

Rick Huntzicker, National Brand Manager
Dan Idoine, Regional Brand Manager

List of manufacturers and suppliers of products and services to the power plant and utility engineering industries.
Cost: $10.00
Frequency: Annual, September

23713 Public Power Directory of Local Publicly Owned Electric Utilities
American Public Power Association
2301 M St Nw
Suite 300
Washington, DC 20037-1427

202-467-2900; *Fax:* 202-467-2910;
www.appanet.org

Alan Richardson, Executive Director
Cost: $90.00
Frequency: Annual
Circulation: 13,000

23714 Rural Electrification: Directory Issue
National Rural Electric Cooperative Association
4301 Wilson Blvd
Arlington, VA 22203-1860

703-907-5500; *Fax:* 703-907-5526;
www.nreca.org

Glenn English, CEO

Over 1,000 electric cooperatives.
Frequency: Annual July
Circulation: 35,000

23715 The Utility Connection

www.utilityconnection.com

Links to more than 4,000 utilities, industry associations and organizations, news outlets and state and federal regulatory and information sites.
Founded in: 1995

23716 UDI Who's Who at Electric Power Plants
Utility Data Institute
1200 G St NW
Suite 250
Washington, DC 20005-3814

202-942-8788

Offers valuable information on over 6,000 key personnel at over 1,200 electric utility plants.
Cost: $195.00
Frequency: Annual

23717 US Electric Utility Industry Software Directory
PennWell Publishing Company
PO Box 1260
Tulsa, OK 74101-1260

918-835-3161
800-752-9764; *Fax:* 918-831-9555;
www.utilityconnection.com

Wayne Beaty, Editor
Steve Hall, Advertising/Sales

An amazing reference directory offering information on over 400 programs in 75 applications categories covering all aspects of the electric power industry.
Cost: $175.00
140 Pages
Frequency: Annual

Industry Web Sites

23718 http://gold.greyhouse.com
G.O.L.D Grey House OnLine Databases

Grey House Publishing's online database platform, GOLD, offers Quick Search, Keyword Search and Expert Search for most business sectors including utility markets. The GOLD platform makes finding the information you need quick and easy - whether you're a novice searcher or an experienced database user. All of Grey House's directory products are available for subscription on the GOLD platform.

23719 www.aeecenter.org
Association of Energy Engineers

Source of information on the field of energy efficiency, utility deregulation, plant engineering, facility management and environmental compliance. Membership includes more than 8,000 professionals and certification programs. Offers seminars, conferences, job listings and certification programs.

23720 www.apea.org
American Public Energy Agency

Purpose is to provide energy acquisition and management services for public agencies.

23721 www.apga.org
American Public Gas Association

Association of municipal gas systems.

23722 www.apwa.net
American Public Works Association

For public agencies, private sector companies, and individuals dedicated to providing high quality public works goods and services.

23723 www.awwa.org
American Water Works Association

The professional society of North American drinking water experts. Develop standards and support research programs in waterworks design, construction, operation, and management. Conducts in-service training schools and offers placement service.

23724 www.bus.msu.edu/ipu
Institute of Public Utilities

Research and training center at Michigan State University. Program focuses on regulation and management of energy, telecommunications and water companies.

23725 **www.eei.org**
Edison Electric Institute
Advocates public policy, expands market opportunities and provides strategic business information for the shareholder-owned electric utility industry. Find out more about EEI's members, upcoming meetings, career opportunities and products and services.

23726 **www.eia.doe.gov/**
Energy Information Administration

23727 **www.electricity-online.com**
Electricity-Online

23728 **www.electricity-online.com/**
Electricity Journal and Daily

23729 **www.energycentral.com**
Energy Central

23730 **www.energymarketers.com**
National Energy Marketers Association

23731 **www.energyonline.com**
EnergyOnLine

23732 **www.energysearch.com**
EPRI Energysearch
Provides fast, accurate search results on global energy topics, and science and technolgoy R&D for the electricity industy.

23733 **www.energyusernews.com**
Energy User News Magazine

23734 **www.epri.com**
Electric Power Research Institute
Nonprofit organization providing science and technology-based solutions to its global energy customers. Manages a far-reaching program of research, technology development and product implementation.

23735 **www.epsa.org**
Electric Power Supply Association

23736 **www.greyhouse.com**
Grey House Publishing
Authoritative reference directories for most business sectors including utility markets. Users can search the online databases with varied search criteria allowing for custom searches by product category, geographic area, sales volume, keyword, subject and more. Full Grey House catalog and online ordering also available.

23737 **www.gri.org**
Gas Research Institute

23738 **www.hydro.org**
National Hydropower Association
For public and private utilities, developers, equipment manufacturers, engineering and design firms, environmental and hydro liscensing consultants, and legal and financial firms. Membership dues: $1,000 - $18,000.

23739 **www.icea.net**
Insulated Cable Engineers Association
Professional organization dedicated to developing cable standards for the electric power, control and telecommunications industries. Ensures safe, economical and efficient cable systems utilizing proven state-of-the-art materials and concepts. ICEA documents are of interest to cable manufacturers, architects and engineers, utility and manufacturing plant personnel, telecommunication engineers, consultants and OEMs.

23740 **www.mcgraw-hill.com**
McGraw Hill
Provides news of significant developments affecting the electric utility industry focusing on state and federal regulation, management and bulk power markets.

23741 **www.naesco.org**
National Association of Energy Service Companies

23742 **www.naruc.org**
National Association of Regulatory Utility Commissioners
A national organization that offers valuable information on over 150 consultants and other professionals active in regulated water, sewer and related industries.

23743 **www.naseo.org**
National Association of State Energy Officials

23744 **www.nerc.com**
North American Electric Reliability Council
Voluntary organization promoting bulk electric system reliability and security.

23745 **www.nreca.org**
Action Committee for Rural Electrification
Political action committee that advocates support for rural electrification.

23746 **www.oilonline.com**
OilOnLine

23747 **www.platts.com**
Electrical World
The latest trends in utility engineering and IT, equipment and services, best business practices and critical industry thinking. For managers, engineers and technicians who plan, design, build, maintain and upgrade electric T&D systems around the world.

23748 **www.ptda.org**
Power Transmission Distributors Association
Members are power transmission/motion control distributor throughout manufacturing firms.

23749 **www.publicworks.com**
Public Works Online
For professionals in the public works industry.

23750 **www.wateronline.com**
Water Online

Associations

23751 **Allied Distribution**
4839 Sherburn Road
PO Box 607
Eagle River, WI 54521

559-435-5810; *Fax:* 715-479-3551
info@warehousenetwork.com;
www.warehousenetwork.com
Social Media: Facebook, Twitter, LinkedIn

Ernest Brunswick, President
Cyd Brunswick, Customer Service Manager

A sales and marketing association representing public warehouses and distribution centers in the United States.
75 Members
Founded in: 1933

23752 **American Chain of Warehouses**
156 Flamingo Dr
Beecher, IL 60401-9725

708-946-9792; *Fax:* 708-946-9793;
www.acwi.org
Social Media: Facebook, Twitter, LinkedIn

William J Jurus, VP

Sales and marketing company representing public warehouses.
50 Members
Founded in: 1911

23753 **American Moving & Storage Association**
1611 Duke St.
Alexandria, VA 22314-3406

888-849-AMSA; *Fax:* 703-683-7527;
www.moving.org

Organization which provides information and tips to help with moving.
4000 Members
Founded in: 1920

23754 **Automotive Warehouse Distributors Association**
7101 Wisconsin Avenue
Suite 1300
Bethesda, MD 20814-3415

301-654-6664; *Fax:* 301-654-3299
info@autocare.org; www.autocare.org
Social Media: Facebook, Twitter, LinkedIn, Youtube, WordPress

Kathleen Schmatz, MAAP, President/CEO
Susan Medick, CPA, CAE, CFO/COO
Richard D. White, MAAP, SVP
Michael Barratt, CMP, SVP, Meeting & Events
Aaron Lowe, AAP, SVP, Reg. and Gov. Affairs

A trade association consisting of more than 600 members who are manufacturers and warehouse distributors, affiliates, marketing associations and others actively involved in the production, distribution and installation of motor vehicle parts, tools, services, accessories, equipment, materials and supplies. A segment of the Automotive Aftermarket Industry Association.
600 Members
Founded in: 1947

23755 **Burley Auction Warehouse Association**
620 S Broadway STE 201
Lexington, KY 40508-3150

606-255-4504; *Fax:* 606-255-4534

Denny Wilson, Managing Director

Members are warehouse companies selling burley tobacco at auction in eight burley-producing states.
225 Members

23756 **Distributors & Consolidators of America**
2240 Bernays Drive
York, PA 17404

888-519-9195; *Fax:* 717-764-6531
daca@comcast.net; www.dacacarriers.com

Andy Delaney, President
Rick Staller, VP
Mike Moran, Secretary
Rich Eberhart, Treasurer
Mike Oliver, Chairman

This organization helps firms and individuals active in the shipping, warehousing, receiving, distribution or consolidation of freight shipments.
39 Members
Founded in: 1971

23757 **Distributors and Consolidators of America**
dacacarriers.com
Social Media: Facebook, Twitter, LinkedIn

Mike Oliver, Chair
Andy Delaney, President
Rick Staller, Vice President
Mike Moran, Secretary
Rich Eberhart, Treasurer

Association for public warehousing.
Founded in: 1971

23758 **Engine Service Association**
37 Pratt Street
Essex, CT 06426-1159

860-767-1770; *Fax:* 860-767-7932
info@opeesa.com; www.opeesa.com
Social Media: Twitter, LinkedIn

Nancy Cueroni, Executive Director
Jeff Plotka, President and Director
Steve Purdy, VP, Annual Meeting & Director
Ted Finn, Secretary/Treasurer & Director
Ron Monroe, Past President and Director

Members are central warehouse distributors of internal combustion engines.
60 Members

23759 **Global Cold Chain Alliance**
1500 King Street
Ste 201
Alexandria, VA 22314-2730

703-373-4300; *Fax:* 703-373-4301
email@gcca.org; www.gcca.org
Social Media: Facebook, Twitter, LinkedIn

Corey Rosenbusch, President and CEO
Margot Van Dersal, Controller
Lowell Randel, VP, Gov & Legal Affairs
Richard Tracy, VP, International Programs
Amanda Brondy, Director of International Projects

Association for the temperature-controlled products industry.
1300+ Members
Founded in: 2007

23760 **Independent Liquid Terminals Association**
1005 North Glebe Road
Suite 600
Arlington, VA 22201

703-875-2011; *Fax:* 703-875-2018
info@ilta.org; www.ilta.org

Wayne N. Driggers, Chairman
Jamie Coleman, Vice Chair
Gregory J. Pound, Secretary/Treasurer
Melinda Whitney, President
Peter Weaver, VP, Government Affairs

We represent bulk liquid terminal companies that store commercial liquids in aboveground storage tanks (ASTs) and transfer products to and from oceangoing tank ships, tank barges, pipelines, tank trucks and tank rail cars.
400 Members
Founded in: 1974

23761 **International Association of Refrigerated Warehouses**
1500 King Street
Suite 201
Alexandria, VA 22314-2730

703-373-4300; *Fax:* 703-373-4301
email@gcca.org; www.gcca.org
Social Media: Facebook, Twitter, LinkedIn

Corey Rosenbusch, President and CEO
Margot Van Dersal, Controller
Lowell Randel, VP, Gov & Legal Affairs
Richard Tracy, VP, International Programs
Amanda Brondy, Director of International Projects

Trade association of public refrigerated warehouses storing of all types of perishable products.
1300+ Members
Founded in: 2007

23762 **International Warehouse Logistics Association**
2800 S River Rd
Suite 260
Des Plaines, IL 60018-6003

847-813-4699; *Fax:* 847-813-0115
mail@IWLA.com; www.iwla.com
Social Media: Facebook, Twitter, LinkedIn, YouTube

Rob Doyle, Chairman
Steve DeHaan, President/CEO
Mark DeFabis, Vice Chair
Clifford Otto, Treasurer
Frank Anderson, Secretary

The unified voice of the global logistics outsourcing industry, representing third party warehousing, transportation and logistics service providers. Our member companies provide the most timely and cost-effective global logistics solutions for their customers and are committed to protecting the free flow of products across international borders.
500 Members
Founded in: 1997

23763 **Internationl Warehouse Logistics Association**
International Warehouse Logistics Association
2800 S River Road
Suite 260
Des Plains, IL 60018-5764

847-813-4699; *Fax:* 847-813-0115
mail@IWLA.com; www.iwla.com
Social Media: Facebook, Twitter, LinkedIn, YouTube

Rob Doyle, Chairman
Steve DeHaan, President/CEO
Mark DeFabis, Vice Chair
Clifford Otto, Treasurer
Frank Anderson, Secretary

Trade association of public warehouses.
500+ Members
Founded in: 1997

23764 **Mobile Self-Storage Association**
2001 Jefferson Davis Hwy
Suite 1004
Arlington, VA 22202-3617

703-416-0060; *Fax:* 703-416-0014;
www.ms-sa.org

Bob Mclean, CAE, Executive Director

Association for mobile-storage companies.
Founded in: 2004

23765 National Portable Storage Association
3312 Broadway
Ste 105
Kansas City, MO 64111
866-777-0635
816-960-6552; *Fax:* 816-960-6575
info@npsa.org; www.npsa-us.org
Social Media: Facebook, Twitter, LinkedIn, YouTube
Association for portable-storage companies.

23766 RCS Limited
Computer Based Training
1301 Commerce Street
Birmingham, AL 35217
205-841-9955
888-833-1970; *Fax:* 205-841-2106;
www.rcs-limited.co.uk
Design and build contractor for cold storage warehouses.

23767 Refrigeration Research and Education
World Food Logistics Organization
P.O. Box 6315
Suite 201
Lubbock, TX 79493-6315
703-373-4300
806-789-4078; *Fax:* 703-373-4301
President@larw.org; www.larw.org
Barbara Sucsy, President
Ruth Schiermeyer, Press & Media Contact
Val Cochran, WebMaster
Patti Jones, Program Chair
Gretchen Scott, Program Chair
Sponsors graduate-level scientific research in the refrigeration of perishable commodities. Offers annual training institute for public refrigerated warehouse personnel.
1M Members
Founded in: 1943

23768 Self Storage Association
1901 N Beauregard St
Suite 110
Alexandria, VA 22311-1738
703-575-8000
888-735-3784; *Fax:* 703-575-8901
ssa@selfstorage.org; www.selfstorage.org
Social Media: Facebook, Twitter, LinkedIn
John Barry, Chairman/National Director
Marc Smith, Vice Chairman/National Director
John Hutto, Treasurer/National Director
Michael Nunez, Secretary/National Director
Terry Bagley, National Director
Self-storage facility owners/operators and suppliers to the industry.
6000 Members
Founded in: 1975

23769 Storage Products Association
572 B Ruger Street
P.O. Box 29920
San Francisco, CA 94129-0920
415-561-6275; *Fax:* 415-561-6120
LoBue@Storage-Products-Association.org;
www.storage-products-association.org
Social Media: Twitter, RSS
Theodore Deffenbagh, President
D. Kurt Richarz, Board Member
Raghu Gururangan, Board Member
Michael T. LoBue, CAE, Secretary
Jeff Burke, PhD, Treasurer
Association for storage manufacturers and users.

23770 Warehousing Education and Research Council
1100 Jorie Boulevard
Ste 170
Oak Brook, IL 60523
630-990-0001; *Fax:* 630-990-0256
wercoffice@werc.org; www.werc.org
Social Media: Twitter, LinkedIn, YouTube
Sheila Benny, President
Tom Nightengale, Vice President
Michael J. Mikitka, CAE, Chief Executive Officer
Angie Silberhorn, CMP, Director of Conference
Dave Pardo, Marketing Manager
Association for logistics and warehouse professionals.

Newsletters

23771 AUA News
American Underground Space Association
1000 Corporate Boulevard
Linthicum, MD 21090
410-689-3700
866-746-4282; *Fax:* 410-689-3800
aua@AUAnet.org; www.auanet.org
Thomas O'Neil, President
Elaine Gray, Editor
Offers the latest news on underground space construction development and use in North America. Includes information on infrastructures.
Cost: $107.00
Frequency: Quarterly
Circulation: 1000
Printed in 4 colors on glossy stock

23772 Affiliated Warehouse Companies Newsletter
Affiliated Warehouse Companies, Inc
PO Box 295
Hazlet, NJ 07730-0295
732-739-2323; *Fax:* 732-739-4154
sales@awco.com; www.awco.com
Jim McBride, Publisher
Jim McBride, President
Patrick McBride, Vice President
Assists public warehouse users to gather rates and data, provides information on warehousing and distribution at no charge or obligation for over 100 public warehouse clients in the US, Canada, Mexico and Puerto Rico.
Mailing list available for rent: 8,500 names

23773 Distribution Center Management
Alexander Communications Group
712 Main Street~
Suite 187B
New York, NJ 07005
973-265-2300
800-232-4317; *Fax:* 973-402-6056
info@distributiongroup.com;
www.distributiongroup.com
Romauld Alexander, President
Margaret Dewitt, Publisher/Marketing Manager
Provides practical strategies and industry news to help distribution center and warehouse professionals improve distribution center efficiency.
Cost: $199.00
8 Pages
Frequency: Monthly
ISBN: 0-894765-1 -
Founded in: 1985

Magazines & Journals

23774 Inside Self-Storage
Virgo Publishing LLC
3300 N Central Ave
Suite 300
Phoenix, AZ 85012-2532
480-990-1101; *Fax:* 480-990-0819
troyb@vpico.com; www.vpico.com
Jenny Bolton, President
John Siefert, CEO & Director
Kelly Ridley, VP
John LyBarger, Director, Business Development
Troy Bix, Publications Editor
For storage professionals.
Frequency: Monthly
Circulation: 20000
Founded in: 1991
Mailing list available for rent

23775 Logistics Management & Distribution Report
Reed Business Information
225 Wyman St
Suite 3
Waltham, MA 02451-1216
781-734-8000; *Fax:* 781-734-8076
fquinn@reedbusiness.com;
www.reedbusiness.com
Mark Finklestein, President
Mike Levin, Group Editor-in-Chief
Frank Quinn, Editorial Director
Stephen Moylan, President, Divisions
Logistics Management and Distribution Report is written for managers and professionals in charge of traffic, transportation, purchasing, inventory control, containerization and warehousing the functions of physical distribution and business logistics. Covers marketing and operating strategies, cost reduction opportunities and governmental regulation and law.
Cost: $99.90
Frequency: Monthly
Circulation: 68000
Founded in: 1977

23776 Mini-Storage Messenger
MiniCo
2531 W Dunlap Ave
Phoenix, AZ 85021-2730
602-870-1711
800-824-6864; *Fax:* 602-861-1094
publishing@minico.com;
www.ministoragemessenger.com
Hardy Good, President
Denise Nunez, Director Publishing
As the industry's first trade journal, the mini-storage messenger has become the leading trade magazine for anyone involved in self-storage. This magazine covers rental rates, marketing trends, and finance.
Cost: $59.95
89 Pages
Frequency: Monthly
Founded in: 1979
Printed in 4 colors on glossy stock

23777 Refrigerated Transporter
Penton
PO Box 66010
Houston, TX 77266
713-523-8124
800-880-0368; *Fax:* 713-523-8384
refrigeratedtransporter.com
Ray Anderson, Publishing
Frequency: Monthly
Circulation: 15000
Founded in: 1898

23778 **Storage**
West World Productions
420 N Camden Dr
Beverly Hills, CA 90210-4507

310-276-9500; *Fax:* 310-276-9874
sinan@kanatsiz.com; www.wwpi.com

Yuri R Spiro, Publisher
Laura Klein, Production Manager

Storage is the unique storage-intensive magazine supplement to Computer Technology Review. It is recognized as the bible of the entire storage industry.
Cost: $10.00
72 Pages
Frequency: Quarterly
Circulation: 72000
ISSN: 0278-9647
Founded in: 1981
Printed in 4 colors on glossy stock

23779 **Warehousing Management**
Reed Business Information
225 Wyman St
Suite 3
Waltham, MA 02451-1216

781-734-8000; *Fax:* 781-734-8076
fquinn@reedbusiness.com;
www.reedbusiness.com

Mark Finklestein, President
Mike Levin, Group Editor-in-Chief
Frank Quinn, Editorial Director
Stephen Moylan, President, Divisions

Warehousing Management targets warehousing and distribution center operations managers with analysis, news, trends, equipment and events.
Circulation: 47185
Founded in: 1977

Trade Shows

23780 **Eastpack**
Reed Exhibition Companies
255 Wyman Streett
Waltham, MA 02451

781-734-8000; *Fax:* 781-734-8076
fquinn@reedbusiness.com;
www.reedbusiness.com

Mark Finklestein, President
Mike Levin, Group Editor-in-Chief
Frank Quinn, Editorial Director
Stephen Moylan, President, Divisions

275 booths.
7.5M Attendees
Frequency: March
Founded in: 1977

23781 **Household Goods Forwarders Association**
5904 Richman Avenue
Suite 304
Alexandria, VA 22303-4691

703-684-3780

Belvian Carpinton, Show Manager
Terry Head, President

20 tables.
1M Attendees
Frequency: September

23782 **Independent Liquid Terminals Assoc. Annual Operating Conference & Trade Show**
Independent Liquid Terminals Association
1005 North Glebe Road
Suite 600
Arlington, VA 20005

703-875-2011; *Fax:* 703-875-2018
info@ilta.org; www.ilta.org

E. David Doane, President
Melinda Whitney, Director/Government Affairs

Two-hundred and two booths of products including goods and services designed for the construction and operation of bulk liquid storage terminals. Includes international companies.
2,700 Attendees
Frequency: June

23783 **Inside Self-Storage World Expo**
Virgo Publishing LLC
3300 N Central Ave
Suite 300
Phoenix, AZ 85012-2532

480-675-9925; *Fax:* 480-990-0819
kkennedy@vpico.com; www.vpico.com

Jenny Bolton, President

The self-storage industry's largest, most comprehensive conference and tradeshow. The leading educational and networking event for facility managers, owners, developers and investors, the ISS Expo provides the resources professionals need to build, manage and market their business in a competitive environment.
Circulation: 20000
Founded in: 1986
Printed in on glossy stock

23784 **International Transportation and Logistics Exhibition and Conference**
ILT
1300 Higgins Road
Suite 111
Park Ridge, IL 60068-5764

847-292-1891; *Fax:* 847-823-3901;
www.warehouselogistics.org

Marge Whalen, Director of Sales
Regan Williams, Trade Show Coordinator

Annual conference and trade show focusing on public warehousing, distribution, transportation, logistics and systems. Containing 200 exhibits.
3,000 Attendees
Frequency: June

23785 **NORPACK**
Northern American Expositions Company
33 Rutherford Avenue
Charlestown, MA 02129

617-242-6092
800-225-1577; *Fax:* 617-242-1817
naexpo@hotmail.com
naexpo.com

The Northeast's premier trade show for packaging, material handling, warehouse automation, shipping/receiving, storage and bottling.
4500 Attendees

23786 **Northwest Material Handling & Packaging Show**
Professional Trade Shows-Division of Penton Media
47817 Fremont Boulevard
Fremont, CA 94538

510-651-6698; *Fax:* 510-354-3159
facilitiesexpo.com

5,000 Attendees
Frequency: May

23787 **Pack Expo**
Pakaging Machinery Manufacturers Institute
4350 N Fairfax Drive
Suite 600
Arlington, VA 22203

703-243-8555
888-275-7664
pmmi@pmmi.org; www.packexpo.com

Matt Crossn, Communications Director
Sara Kryder, Assistant Communications

Informational meeting and exposition held by the Packaging Machinery Manufacturers Institute.
15000 Attendees

23788 **Warehousing, Technology & Distribution Show**
Industrial Shows of America
164 Lake Front Drive
Hunt Valley, MD 21030-2215

410-771-1445
800-638-6396; *Fax:* 410-771-1158

This show will feature hands-on workshops for the practical applications of new technologies, safety issues and more all designed to improve productivity and cut losses in today's competitive market.
1500 Attendees
Frequency: April

Directories & Databases

23789 **Affiliated Warehouse Companies Database of Public Warehouse Users**
Affiliated Warehouse Companies, Inc.
PO Box 295
Hazlet, NJ 07730-0295

732-739-2323; *Fax:* 732-739-4154
sales@awco.com; www.awco.com

Jim McBride, President
Patrick McBride, Vice President
Jim McBride, Publisher

In excess of 8,000 listings of individuals and companies that use public warehousing, products produced and services required.
Mailing list available for rent: 8,500 names

23790 **American Chain of Warehouses Directory**
20500 S La Grange Road
Frankfort, IL 60423-1356

703-875-2018; *Fax:* 815-469-2941

Donald R Greenland, Executive VP

Public warehouse listings in the United States are profiled.
50 Pages
Frequency: Annual

23791 **American Public Warehouse Register**
Reed Business Information
2 Brandywine Way
Sicklerville, NJ 08081-0750

856-728-9745; *Fax:* 630-288-8686;
www.reedbusiness.com

Laura Masapollo, National Sales Director
Laura MasaPollo, National Sales Director

Worldwide listings of dry, refrigerated, contract and HazMat Public Warehouses Annual.
Cost: $50.00

23792 **Associated Warehouses Directory of Services**
PO Box 471
Cedar Knolls, NJ 07927-0471

973-539-1277; *Fax:* 973-538-0944;
www.awilogistics.com

Mark Richards, Editor
Barbara Brown, Circulation Director

A who's who directory of services to the industry.
100 Pages
Frequency: Annual

23793 Directory of Bulk Liquid Terminal and Storage Facilities
ITLA
1133 15th Street NW
Sutie 650
Washington, DC 20005

202-659-2301; *Fax:* 202-466-4166
info@ilta.org; www.ilta.org

John Prokop, President
EB Calvert, Director Administration

Locates over 480 bulk liquid terminal/storage facilities. Lists key personnel, addresses, telephone numbers. Lists products handled-petroleum products, crude oil, chemicals, animal fats and oils, vegetable oils, molasses, spirits, etc. Lists storage tanks, modes served, pipeline connections. Other services and capabilities-canning, barreling, bleaching, blending, weighing, warehousing, etc. Subc. available for Directory and Newsletter
Cost: $95.00
300 Pages
Frequency: Annual

23794 Food & Beverage Market Place
Grey House Publishing
4919 Route 22
PO Box 56
Amenia, NY 12501

518-789-8700
800-562-2139; *Fax:* 845-373-6390
books@greyhouse.com; www.greyhouse.com
Social Media: Facebook, Twitter

Leslie Mackenzie, Publisher
Richard Gottlieb, Editor

This information-packed 3-volume set is the most powerful buying and marketing guide for the US food and beverage industry. Includes thousands of industry freight and transportation listings.
Cost: $595.00
2000 Pages
Frequency: Annual
ISBN: 1-592373-61-5
Founded in: 1981

23795 Food & Beverage Marketplace: Online Database
Grey House Publishing
4919 Route 22
PO Box 56
Amenia, NY 12501
518-789-8700
800-562-2139; *Fax:* 845-373-6390
gold@greyhouse.com
http://gold.greyhouse.com
Social Media: Facebook, Twitter

Richard Gottlieb, President
Leslie Mackenzie, Publisher

This complete updated Food & Beverage Market Place: Online Database is the go-to source for the food and beverage industry. Anyone involved in the food and beverage industry needs this 'industry bible' and the important contacts to develop critical research data that can make for successful business growth.
Frequency: Annual
Founded in: 1981

23796 Independent Liquid Terminals Association
1444 Eye St NW
Suite 400
Washington, DC 20005-6538

202-842-9200; *Fax:* 703-875-2018
info@ilta.org; www.ilta.org

E David Doane, President
Melinda Whitney, Director/Government Affairs

A 285 page directory, listing 577 for hire, marketing, throughput, and pipeline bulk liquid storage terminals.
Cost: $95.00
285 Pages
Founded in: 1975

23797 International Directory of Public Refrigerated Warehouses
1500 King Street
Suite 201
Alexandria, VA 22314

703-373-4300; *Fax:* 703-373-4301;
www.iarw.org

J William Hudson, President/CEO

Offers information on more than 950 member warehouses in 32 countries and on companies supplying products and services to the refrigerated warehouse industry.
Cost: $150.00
232 Pages
Frequency: Annual
Circulation: 6,000

23798 International Warehouse Logistics Directory
1300 Higgins Rd
Suite 111
Park Ridge, IL 60068-5743

847-292-1891; *Fax:* 847-813-0115;
www.iwla.com

Joel Anderson, President
Ben Stephens, Public Relations/Media Coordinator

The membership directory is published annually in January in book and CD-ROM form.
Frequency: Annually

23799 National Refrigeration Contractors Association
National Refrigeration Contrtactors
1900 Arch Street
Philadelphia, PA 19103-1404

215-564-3484; *Fax:* 215-963-9785;
www.arcat.com

Elizabeth Barnett, Editor

About 100 member refrigeration contracting companies
Frequency: Annual

23800 Transportation & Distribution Magazine's Integrated Warehousing/Storage
Penton Media
1166 Avenue of the Americas
New York, NY 10036

212-204-4200; *Fax:* 216-696-6662
information@penton.com; www.penton.com

Jane Cooper, Marketing

Lists over 1,200 manufacturers of products related to the warehousing and distribution industries.
Frequency: Annual
Circulation: 71,000
Printed in 4 colors on glossy stock

23801 Warehouses Licensed Under US Warehouse Act
Farm Service Agency-US Dept. of Agriculture
PO Box 2415
Washington, DC 20013-2415

Fax: 202-690-0014; www.fsa.usda.gov/

Agricultural warehouses voluntarily licensed under the US Warehouse Act governing public storage facilities.
Frequency: Annual

23802 Warehousing Distribution Directory
PRIMEDIA Information
3585 Engineering Drive
Suite 100
Norcross, GA 30092

678-421-3000
800-216-1423; *Fax:* 609-371-7819;
www.primediainfo.com

Amy Middlebrook, Editor
John Capers III, Publisher

List of about 800 warehousing and consolidation companies and firms offering trucking, trailer on flatcar, container on flatcar and piggyback carrier services.
Cost: $55.00; 250 Pages
Frequency: SemiAnnual
Circulation: 10,000; *Founded in:* 1949
Printed in 4 colors on glossy stock

Industry Web Sites

23803 http://gold.greyhouse.com
G.O.L.D Grey House OnLine Databases

Grey House Publishing's online database platform, GOLD, offers Quick Search, Keyword Search and Expert Search for most business sectors including warehousing and storage markets. The GOLD platform makes finding the information you need quick and easy - whether you're a novice searcher or an experienced database user. All of Grey House's directory products are available for subscription on the GOLD platform.

23804 www.awco.com
Affiliated Warehouse Companies

Assists public warehouse users to gather rates and data, provides information on warehousing and distribution at no charge or obligation for over 100 public warehouse clients in the US, Canada, Mexico, Europe and Southeast Asia.

23805 www.greyhouse.com
Grey House Publishing

Authoritative reference directories for direct marketing, demographics, business, research, health care, international trade, food industry and education. Users can search the online databases with varied search criteria allowing for custom searches by product category, geographic area, sales volume, keyword, subject and more. Full Grey House catalog and online ordering also available.

23806 www.larw.org
Refrigeration Research and Education Foundation

Sponsors graduate-level scientific research on the refrigeration of perishable commodities. Offers annual training institute for public refrigerated warehouse personnel.

23807 www.warehouselogistics.org
International Warehouse Logistics Association

For third-party warehousing and related logistics services throughout the world. Collectively, the Association's members ship over 3 trillion pounds annually in North America.

Associations

23808 **Alliance for Water Efficiency**
33 N. LaSalle Street
Suite 2275
Chicago, IL 60602

773-360-5100
866-730-1493; *Fax:* 773-345-3636
jeffrey@a4we.org;
www.allianceforwaterefficiency.org

Mary Ann Dickinson, President/ CEO
Megan Chery, Manager
William Christiansen, Program Manager
Molly Garcia, Accountant/Event Coordinator
Jeffrey Hughes, Director of Operations

An association for water efficient products.
Founded in: 2007

23809 **American Backflow Prevention Association**
342 N. Main Street
Suite 301
West Hartford, CT 06117

979-846-7606
877-227-2127; *Fax:* 979-846-7607
efearn@abpa.org; www.abpa.org

John Graham, International President
Tim Brown, International Vice President
Patti Fauver, Treasurer
Erica Fearn, Executive Director
Dayna Stein, Association Administrator

An association dedicated to backflow education and technical assistance.
Founded in: 1984

23810 **American Fisheries Society**
5410 Grosvenor Lane
Bethesda, MD 20814

301-897-8616; *Fax:* 301-897-8096
dausten@fisheries.org
fisheries.org
Social Media: Pinterest, Google+, Vimeo, Fli

Douglas Austen, Executive Director
Beth Beard, Strategist, Digital Content
Thomas Bigford, Policy Director
Juanita Flick, Membership Assistant
Sarah Gilbert Fox, Managing Editor, Fisheries and AFS

Organization dedicated to strengthening the fisheries profession and advancing fisheries.
Founded in: 1870

23811 **American Ground Water Trust**
50 Pleasant Street
Suite 2
Concord, NH 3301

603-228-5444
800-423-7748; *Fax:* 603-228-6557
trustinfo@agwt.org; www.agwt.org
Social Media: x

Kevin McGinnis, Chairman
David Kill, Secretary/Treasurer
Andrew Stone, Executive Director

Promotes public awareness of groundwater.

23812 **American Institute of Hydrology**
1230 Lincoln Drive
Carbondale, IL 62901

618-453-7809
aih@engr.siu.edu; www.aihydrology.org

Mustafa M. Aral, PhD, PE, PH., President
Dr. John L. Nieber, VP for Academic Affairs
John W. Balay, VP for Institute Development
Ed A. Baquerizo, VP for International Affairs
Kurt Hollman, VP for Communication

Promotes hydrology as a science and a profession.
Founded in: 1981

23813 **American Recreation Coalition**
1200 G Street NW
Suite 650
Washington, DC 20005-3832

202-682-9530; *Fax:* 202-682-9529
mmeade@funoutdoors.com;
www.funoutdoors.com

Derrick Crandall, President
Catherine Ahern, VP
Melinda Meade, Director of Communications

A non-profit Washington based federation that provides a unified voice for recreation interests to conserve their full and active participation in government policy making on issues such as public land management. ARC works to build public-private partnerships to enhance and protect outdoor recreation opportunities and resources.
100+ Members
Founded in: 1979

23814 **American Rivers**
1101 14th Street NW
Suite 1400
Washington, DC 20005

202-347-7550
877-347-7550; *Fax:* 202-347-9240
akober@americanrivers.org;
www.americanrivers.org
Social Media: Facebook, Twitter, YouTube, Pinterest

William Robert (Bob) Irvin, President
Georgette Blanchfield, SVP, Advancement
Brendan Mysliwiec, Associate Director, Gov Relations
Fay Augustyn, Manager
Courtney Barefoot, HR & Board Relations Director

Nonprofit conservation organization dedicated to protecting and restoring the rivers of the US.
Founded in: 1973

23815 **American Society of Irrigation Consultants**
4660 S Hagadorn
Suite 195D
East Lansing, MI 48823

508-763-8140; *Fax:* 866-828-5174
carolc@asic.org; www.asic.org

Carol Colein, Executive Director
Ivy Munion, President
Corbin Schneider, Vice President
Michael J. Krones, Treasurer
Carly Kardon, Operations and Member Services

Promotes education skills on data exchange landscape irrigation. Members are irrigation consultants, suppliers, and manufacturers.
Founded in: 1970

23816 **American Water Resources Association**
PO Box 1626
Middleburg, VA 20118

540-687-8390; *Fax:* 540-687-8395
info@awra.org; www.awra.org
Social Media: Blog

Kenneth D. Reid, CAE, Executive Vice President
Michael J. Kowalski, CAE, Director of Operations
Susan Scalia, JAWRA Managing Editor
Patricia A. Reid, Program Coordinator
Christine McCrehin, Membership Services Manager

Promotes understanding of water resources and related issues.
Founded in: 1964

23817 **American Water Works Association**
6666 W. Quincy Ave.
Denver, CO 80235-3098

303-794-7711
800-926-7337; www.awwa.org
Social Media: YouTube, RSS

Gene C. Koontz, President
Jeanne M. Bennett-Bailey, President-Elect
John J. Donahue, Immediate Past-President
David E. Rager, Treasurer
Jon Eaton, VP/Minnesota Section Director

Nonprofit scientific and education orgaization dedicated to managind and treating water.
Founded in: 1881

23818 **American Whitewater**
P.O. Box 1540
Cullowhee, NC 28723

828-586-1930
866-262-8429; *Fax:* 828-586-2840
membership@americanwhitewater.org;
www.americanwhitewater.org
Social Media: Facebook, Twitter, YouTube, RSS

Mark Singleton, Executive Director
Kevin Colburn, National Stewardship Director
Bob Nasdor, Northeast Stewardship Director
Dave Steindorf, California Stewardship Director
Nathan Fey, Colorado Stewardship Director

Association for whitewaters and rafting.
Founded in: 1954

23819 **Association of Clean Water Administrators**
1634 Eye St. NW
Suite 750
Washington, DC 20006

202-756-0605; *Fax:* 202-793-2600;
www.acwa-us.org
Social Media: Twitter

Julia Anastasio, Executive Director/ General Counsel
Sean Rolland, Deputy Director
Annette Ivey, Director of Operations
Susan Kirsch, Sr. Environmental Program Manager
Melissa McCoy, Environmental Program Manager

Association for the administrators of the clean water industry.
Founded in: 1961

23820 **Association of State Drinking Water Administrators**
1401 Wilson Blvd
Suite 1225
Arlington, VA 22209

703-812-9505; *Fax:* 703-812-9506
info@asdwa.org; www.asdwa.org
Social Media: YouTube, Blog

John Calkins, President
Steve Sturgess, President-Elect
Jim Taft, Executive Director
Bridget O'Grady, Policy & Legis. Affairs Manager
Deirdre Mason, Project Manager

Professional association serving state drinking water programs.

23821 **Association of State Wetland Managers**
32 Tandberg Trail
Suite 2A
Windham, ME 04062

207-892-3399; *Fax:* 207-892-3089
jeanne.christie@aswm.org

aswm.org
Social Media: LinkedIn, Blog

Jeanne Christie, Executive Director
Peg Bostwick, Senior Staff Policy Analyst
Brenda Zollitsch, Policy Analyst
Marla J. Stelk, Policy Analyst
Dawn Smith, Communications Specialist

A professional association for state wetland managers.
Founded in: 1983

23822 Clean Water Action
1444 Eye Street NW
Suite 400
Washington, DC 20005

202-895-0420; *Fax:* 202-895-0438
cwa@cleanwater.org;
www.cleanwateraction.org
Social Media: Facebook, Twitter, YouTube, Blog

Robert Wendelgass, President/ CEO
Kathy Aterno, National Managing Director
Lynn Thorp, National Campaigns Director
Andrea Herrmann, Director
Chris Bathurst, National Canvass Coordinator

A national citizen's organization working for clean, safe and affordable water and prevention of health-threatening pollution.
Founded in: 1960

23823 Coastal & Estuarine Research Federation
2150 North 107th Street
Suite 205
Seattle, WA 98133-9009

206-209-5262; *Fax:* 206-367-8777
info@erf.org; www.erf.org
Social Media: Facebook, Twitter, Flickr, Vimeo

Kenneth L. Heck, Jr., President
Robert R. Twilley, President-Elect
Enrique Reyes, Secretary
James Hagy, Treasurer
Mark Wolf-Armstrong, Executive Director (Ex-Officio)

Private nonprofit organization dedicated to advancing the understanging of coastal and estuarine ecosystems.

23824 Ground Water Protection Council
13308 N Macarthur Blvd
Oklahoma City, OK 73142-3021

405-516-4972; *Fax:* 405-516-4973
dan@gwpc.org; www.gwpc.org

Mike Paque, Executive Director
Ben Grunewald, Chief of Operations
Paul Jehn, Technical Director
Dan Yates, Associate Executive Director
Mike Nickolaus, Special Projects Director

State ground water and underground injection control agencies whose mission is to promote the protection and conservation of ground water resources for all beneficial uses, recognizing ground water as a component of the ecosystem.
1.75M Members
Founded in: 1983

23825 Irrigation Association
8280 Willow Oaks Corporate Drive
Suite 400
Fairfax, VA 22031

703-536-7080; *Fax:* 703-536-7019
info@irrigation.org; www.irrigation.org

Aric J. Olson, President
Gregory R. Hunter, Vice President
Deborah M. Hamlin, CAE, FASAE, Chief Executive Officer
John R. Farner, Jr, Government & PA Director
Rebecca J. Bayless, Finance Director

The Irrigation Association is the leading membership organization for irrigation equipment and system manufacturers, dealers, distributors, designers, consultants, contractors and end users.
1600 Members
Founded in: 1949

23826 National Association of Clean Water Agencies
1816 Jefferson Place N.W.
Washington, DC 20036

202-833-2672; *Fax:* 888-267-9505
info@nacwa.org; www.nacwa.org
Social Media: Facebook, Twitter, LinkedIn, YouTube

Adam Krantz, Chief Executive Officer
Paula Dannenfeldt, Chief Operating Officer
Shalina Baker, Executive Assistant
Amanda Waters, GC & Director, Public Affairs
Patricia Sinicropi, Senior Dir., Legislative Affairs

Nationally recognized leader in environmental policy and a technical resource on water quality and ecosystem protection.
Founded in: 1970

23827 National Drilling Association
4036 Center Rd
Suite B
Brunswick, OH 44212

330-273-5756
877-632-4748; *Fax:* 216-803-9900
info@nda4u.com; www.nda4u.com
Social Media: Facebook, LinkedIn

Dan Dunn, President
Larry Gibel, Secretary/Treasurer
Michael Willey, Vice President
Peggy McGee, Immediate Past President

A non-profit trade association of contractors, manufacturers and affiliated members from the drilling industry representing the geotechnical, environmental and mineral exploration sectors of this industry.
250+ Members
Founded in: 1972

23828 National Environmental Services Center
Box 6893, West Virginia University
Morgantown, WV 26506-6893

304-293-4191
800-624-8301; *Fax:* 304-293-3161
info@mail.nesc.wvu.edu; www.nesc.wvu.edu
Social Media: Facebook, Twitter, WordPress

Gerald Iwan, Ph.D., Director

Helps small, rural communities with their drinking water, wastewater and environmental training needs.
Founded in: 1984

23829 National Ground Water Association
601 Dempsey Rd.
Westerville, OH 43081

800-551-7379; *Fax:* 614-898-7786
ngwa@ngwa.org; www.ngwa.org
Social Media: Facebook, Twitter, LinkedIn, YouTube

Kevin B. McCray, Chief Executive Officer

International nonprofit organization of groundwater professionals for the responsible use of groundwater.
Founded in: 1948

23830 National Institute for Water Resources
University of Massachusetts
Blaisdell House
Amherst, MA 01003

413-545-2842; *Fax:* 413-545-2304
support@niwr.net; www.niwr.net

Brian Haggard, President
Sharon Megdal, President Elect
John Tracy, Secretary/Treasurer

Offers information on water resource directions across the nation.
54 Members
Founded in: 1974

23831 National Onsite Wastewater Recycling
1199 N. Fairfax St.
Suite 410
Alexandria, VA 22314

703-836-1950
800-966-2942; *Fax:* 703-535-5263
info@nowra.org; www.nowra.org
Social Media: Facebook

Gregory D Graves, President
Jim Bell, President Elect/VP
Robert B Mayer MSPE, Secretary/Treasurer
Tom Fritts, Past-President

Dedicated solely to educating and representing members within the onsite and decentralized industry. And also to provide leadership and promote the onsite waste water treatment and recycling through education, training, communication and quality tools to support excellence in performance.
3500 Members
Founded in: 1992

23832 National Onsite Wastewater Recycling Assoc iation
1199 N. Fairfax St.
Suite 410
Alexandria, VA 22314
703-836-1950
800-966-2942; www.nowra.org

Gregory D Graves, President
Jim Bell, President Elect/VP
Robert B Mayer MSPE, Secretary/Treasurer
Tom Fritts, Past-President

Organization dedication to onsite wastewater recycling.
Founded in: 1992

23833 National Rural Water Association
2915 S. 13th Street
Duncan, OK 73533

580-252-0629; *Fax:* 580-255-4476
nwra@nwra.org; www.nrwa.org
Social Media: Facebook, Twitter, LinkedIn, YouTube

Charles A. Hilton, President
Steve Fletcher, Sr. Vice President
Sam Wade, CEO
Matt Holmes, Deputy CEO
Claudette Atwood, CFO

Dedicated to the wise management and use of the nation's water and land resources.
5M+ Members
Founded in: 1932

23834 National Water Research Institute
18700 Ward Street
P.O. Box 8096
Fountain Valley, CA 92728-8096

714-378-3278; *Fax:* 714-378-3375
jmosher@nwri-usa.org; www.nwri-usa.org
Social Media: Facebook, Twitter, LinkedIn, YouTube

Jeff Mosher, Executive Director
Gina Vartanian, Communications and Outreach Manager
Brandi Caskey, Administrative and Events

Manager
Suzanne Faubl, Manager
Ken Lanxner, Webmaster

A nonprofit organization devoted to promoting the protection, maintenance and restoration of water supplies.
Founded in: 1991

23835 National Water Resources Association
4 E Street Southeast
Washington, DC 20003

202-698-0693; *Fax:* 703-524-1548
nwra@nwra.org; www.nwra.org
Social Media: Twitter

Dave Koland, President
Ron Thompson, 1st VP
Cheryl Zittle, 2nd VP
Robert Johnson, Secretary
Glenn Johnson, Treasurer

Dedicated to the wise management and use of the nation's water and land resources.
5M+ Members
Founded in: 1932

23836 Soil and Water Conservation Society
945 SW Ankeny Rd
Ankeny, IA 50023-9764

515-289-2331
800-843-7645; *Fax:* 515-289-1227
jwpeterson@cox.net; www.swcs.org

Jim Guillford, Executive Director
Annie Binder, Director of Publications/Editor
Jody Thompson, Editorial Assistant
Kim Johnson Smith, Professional Development Director
Jody Ogg, Comptroller

SWCS is a nonprofit scientific and educational organization that serves as an advocate for conservation professionals and for science-based conservation practice, programs, and policy.
5000+ Members
Founded in: 1943

23837 Submersible Waste Water Pump Association
1866 Sheridan Rd
Suite 212
Highland Park, IL 60035-2545

847-681-1868; *Fax:* 847-681-1869
swpaexdir@sbcglobal.net; www.swpa.org

Adam Stolberg, Executive Director
Carol Stolberg, Administrative Director

Represents and serves the manufacturers of submersible pumps for the municipal and industrial wastewater applications. Manufacturers of components and accessory items for those products and companies providing services to users of those products.
Founded in: 1976

23838 WateReuse Association
1199 North Fairfax Street
Suite 410
Alexandria, VA 22314

703-548-0880; *Fax:* 703-548-5085;
www.watereuse.org
Social Media: Facebook, Twitter, LinkedIn, YouTube

Melissa L. Meeker, Executive Director
Maria Greenly, Accounting Manager
Carrie Knooihuizen, Administrative Assistant
Courtney Tharpe, Director of Conferences and Events
Erin DiMenna, Director of Membership

An association for advancing the science of water reuse and destination through research.
Founded in: 1990

23839 Water Environment Federation
601 Wythe St
Alexandria, VA 22314-1994

703-684-2400
800-666-0206; *Fax:* 703-684-2492
inquiry@wef.org; www.wef.org
Social Media: Facebook, Twitter, LinkedIn

Eileen O'Neill, Executive Director
Barry Liner, Director
Lisa McFadden, Sr. Program Manager
Steve Harrison, Manager-Technical Programs
Elizabeth Conway, Committee Coordinator

A technical and educational organization with members from varied disciplines who work toward the vision of preservation and enhancement of the global water environment.
34000 Members
Founded in: 1928

23840 Water Keeper Alliance
17 Battery Place
Suite 1329
New York, NY 10004

212-747-0622; *Fax:* 212-747-0611
info@waterkeeper.org
waterkeeper.org
Social Media: Facebook, Twitter, YouTube, Instagram

Marc A. Yaggi, Executive Director
Mary Beth Postman, Deputy Director
Lesley Adams, Western Regional Coordinator
Peter Cleary, Comm. & Marketing Director
Larry Baldwin, North Carolina CAFO Coordinator

An association using grassroots advocacy to achieve clean waterways.
Founded in: 1996

23841 Water Quality Association
4151 Naperville Rd
Lisle, IL 60532-3696

630-505-0160; *Fax:* 630-505-9637
info@mail.wqa.org; www.wqa.org
Social Media: Facebook, Twitter, LinkedIn, Youtube

Bret P. Tangley, MWS, President
David Westman, MBA, CAE, CPA, Interim Executive Director
Pauli Undesser, MWS, Deputy Executive Director
Susan Barkach, Business Operations Director
Larry Deutsch, Marketing & Comm. Director

An international, nonprofit trade association representing retail/dealers and manufacturer/suppliers in the point of use/entry water quality improvement industry. Membership benefits and services include technical and scientific information, educational seminars and home correspondence course books, professional certification and discount services.
2700+ Members
Founded in: 1974

23842 Water and Wastewater Equipment Manufacturers Association
540 Fort Evans Road
Suite 304
Leesburg, VA 20176-3379

703-444-1777; *Fax:* 703-444-1779
info@wwema.org; www.wwema.org

Vanessa Leiby, Executive Director
Linda Budzinski, Dir., Membership and Marketing
Octavia Trammell, Office Manager

Represents the interests of companies that manufacture the products that are sold to the portable water and wastewater treatment industries. Also informs, educates and provides leadership on the issues which affect the worldwide water and wastewater equipment industry.
80 Members
Founded in: 1908

Newsletters

23843 Drinking Water and Backflow Prevention
SFA Enterprises
18927 Hickory Creek Drive
Suite 140
Mokena, IL 60448

303-451-0978
888-367-3927; *Fax:* 303-452-9776;
www.iapmodwbp.org/

Cindy Most, Managing Editor

Accepts advertising.
Cost: $38.00
24 Pages
Frequency: Monthly
Mailing list available for rent

23844 Jet News
WaterJet Technology Association/Industrial &
Municipal Cleaning Association
906 Olive Street, Suite 1200
Saint Louis, MO 63101-1448

314-241-1445; *Fax:* 314-241-1449
wjta-imca@wjta.org; www.wjta.org

George A Savanick PhD, President
Kenneth C Carroll, Association Manager

Provides the latest information on applications, equipment, news from members, new developments, meetings, conferences, and technical information.
Frequency: Bi-Monthly
Circulation: 1000

23845 National Association of Regulatory Utility Commisioners
Natl Assoc of Regulatory Utility Commissioner
1101 Vermont Ave Nw
Suite 200
Washington, DC 20005-3553

202-898-2200; *Fax:* 202-898-2213
admin@naruc.org; www.naruc.org

Charles Gray, Executive Director
Diane Munns, Publisher

A national organization that offers valuable information on over 150 consultants and other professionals active in regulated water, sewer and related industries.
Frequency: Monthly
Circulation: 1800
Founded in: 1889

23846 National Water Line
National Water Resources Association
3800 Fairfax Dr
Suite 4
Arlington, VA 22203-1703

703-524-1544; *Fax:* 703-524-1548
nrwa@nrwa.org; www.nwra.org

Thomas Donnelly, VP

Association news and information.
Frequency: Monthly

23847 US Water News
US Water News
230 Main St
Halstead, KS 67056-1913

316-835-2222
800-251-0046; *Fax:* 316-835-2223

Inquiries@uswaternews.com; www.uswaternews.com

Thomas Bell, President/Publisher
Mary DeSana, Editor

Reports news of current events in water resources from across the nation. Accepts advertising.
Cost: $59.00
24 Pages
Frequency: Monthly

23848 Water Newsletter
Water Information Center
1099 18th St
Suite 2600
Denver, CO 80202-1926

303-297-2600; *Fax:* 303-297-2750;
www.rwolaw.com

Stephen L Waters, Partner

Contents include water supply and waste disposal information, and presents articles on conservation/usage.
Cost: $127.00
Frequency: Monthly
Founded in: 1959

Magazines & Journals

23849 APWA Reporter
American Public Works Association
2345 Grand Blvd
Suite 700
Kansas City, MO 64108-2625

816-472-6100
800-848-2792; *Fax:* 816-472-1610
ddancy@apwa.net; www.apwa.net

Kaye Sullivan, Executive Director
David Dancy, Marketing Director
Connie Hartline, Publications Manager
Lillie Plowman, Publications/Premiums Marketing Mgr

Circulation to entire membership of American Public Works Association.
Cost: $100.00
Frequency: Monthly
Circulation: 34000
ISBN: 0-092487-3 -
Founded in: 1937
Mailing list available for rent

23850 Bottled Water Reporter
International Bottled Water Association
1700 Diagonal Rd
Suite 650
Alexandria, VA 22314-2870

703-683-5213
800-928-3711; *Fax:* 703-683-4074
ibwainfo@bottledwater.org;
www.bottledwater.org
Social Media: Facebook, Twitter, LinkedIn

Joe Doss, CEO

Provides a vital source of information to bottlers and agencies, consultants and engineers. Also contains statistical data, marketing and management tips and profiles of bottled water operations and supplier companies.
Cost: $ 50.00
Circulation: 3000
Founded in: 1958

23851 Cleaner Times
Advantage Publishing Company
1000 Nix Rd
Little Rock, AR 72211-3235

501-280-9111
800-525-7038; *Fax:* 501-280-9233
gpuls@adpub.com; www.cleanertimes.com

Charlene Yarbrough, Publisher
Gerry Puls, Circulation
Chuck Prieur, Sales Manager
Charlener Yarbrough, Publications/Premiums Marketing Mgr

Application, information, and productivity for persons engaged in the manufacturing, distribution, or the use of high pressure water systems and accessories. The emphasis is on safety, regulatory, which affect the industry as well as cleaning applications.
Cost: $18.00
72 Pages
Frequency: Monthly
Circulation: 10000
ISSN: 1073-9602
Founded in: 1989
Printed in 4 colors on glossy stock

23852 Clearwaters
New York Water Environment Association
525 Plum Street
Suite 102
Syracuse, NY 13204

315-422-7811; *Fax:* 315-422-3851;
www.nywea.org

Lois Hickey, Editor
Patricia Cerro-Reehil, Executive Director

Contains information on pollution control legislation, regulation, and compliance.
Cost: $25.00
Frequency: Quarterly
Circulation: 3000
Founded in: 1929

23853 Drill Bits
National Drilling Association
1545 W 130th St
Suite A2
Hinckley, OH 44233-9121

330-273-5756
877-632-4748; *Fax:* 216-803-9900
info@nda4u.com; www.nda4u.com

Peggy McGee, President
Dan Dunn, VP
Jim Howe, Secretary/Treasurer
Tim Cleary, Board of Directors
R. Alan Garrard, Board of Directors

A non-profit trade association of contractors, manufacturers and affiliated members from the drilling industry representing the geotechnical, environmental and mineral exploration sectors of this industry.
250+ Members
Frequency: 2x/Year
Founded in: 1972

23854 Ground Water
National Ground Water Association
PO Box 715435
Columbus, OH 43271-5435

614-898-7791
800-551-7379; *Fax:* 614-898-7786
customerservice@ngwa.org; www.ngwa.org
Social Media: Facebook, Twitter, LinkedIn, YouTube

Paul Humes, VP
Thad Plumley, Publications Director
Shelby Fleck, Advertising
Keviin McKray, Executive Director

Focuses on ground water hydrogeology as a science.
Cost: $395.00
160 Pages
Circulation: 15000
ISSN: 0017-467x
Founded in: 1963
Printed in one color

23855 Ground Water Monitoring and Remediation
National Ground Water Association
PO Box 715436
Columbus, OH 43271-5436

614-898-7791
800-551-7379; *Fax:* 614-898-7786
ngwa@ngwa.org; www.ngwa.org
Social Media: Facebook, Twitter, LinkedIn, YouTube

Paul Humes, VP
Thad Plumley, Publications Director
Kevin McKray, Executive Director

Contains peer-reviewed papers, product and equipment news, EPA updates, industry news, and a mix of original columns authored by industry leaders.
Cost: $195.00
Frequency: Quarterly
Circulation: 15201
ISSN: 1069-3629
Founded in: 1981

23856 Industrial Wastewater
Water Environment Federation
601 Wythe St
Alexandria, VA 22314-1994

703-684-2400; *Fax:* 703-684-2492
inquiry@wef.org; www.wef.org
Social Media: Facebook, Twitter, LinkedIn

Bill Bertera, Executive Director

Provides the information on the practical application of science and technology in the management of water discharges, air emissions, ground water and soil remediation to the industrial personnel, consultants and other involved in all aspects of management, treatment and disposal of industrial wastewater.
Cost: $129.00
Frequency: Bi-Monthly
Circulation: 35500
ISSN: 1067-5337
Founded in: 1928

23857 Journal of Soil and Water Conservation
Soil and Water Conservation Society
945 SW Ankeny Road
Ankeny, IA 50023-9764

515-289-2331
800-843-7645; *Fax:* 515-289-1227
pubs@swcs.org; www.swcs.org

Oksana Gieseman, Director of Publications

The JSWC is a multidisciplinary journal of natural resource conservation research, practice, policy, and perspectives. The journal has two sections: the A Section containing various departments and features and the Research Section containing peer-reviewed research papers.
Cost: $99.00
Frequency: Bimonthly
Circulation: 2000
ISSN: 0022-4561
Founded in: 1945

23858 Journal of the American Water Resources Association
PO Box 1623
Middleburg, VA 20118-1626

540-687-8390
540-687-8390; *Fax:* 540-687-8395
info@awra.org; www.awra.org

Kenneth J Lanfear, Editor
Charlene E Young, Publications Production Director
Billy Journell, Manager

Annual directory offering information on all water resources, technologies, systems and services for the water resources industry.
Cost: $205.00
Frequency: Bi-Monthly
ISSN: 1093-474x
Founded in: 1964

23859 Landscape & Irrigation
Adams Business Media
PO Box 17349
Chicago, IL 60617-0349

773-221-4223; *Fax:* 773-374-6270;
www.adamsmediastore.com

Karen Adams, President

23860 National Driller
Business News Publishing Company
1050 IL Route 83
Suite 200
Bensenville, IL 60106

800-223-2194; *Fax:* 248-786-1358;
www.nationaldriller.com

Linda Moffat, Publisher
Greg Ettling, Editor
Lisa Shroeder, Managing Editor

Provides feature articles, timely and valuable industry information, newly developed products and technologies, and quality marketing and business management advice.
Frequency: Monthly
Mailing list available for rent

23861 Operations Forum
Water Environment Federation
601 Wythe St
Alexandria, VA 22314-1994

703-684-2400
800-666-0206; *Fax:* 703-684-2492;
www.wef.org

Bill Bertera, Executive Director

The emphasis is on process control, plant operations, collection systems and industry news.
Cost: $4995.00
Frequency: Monthly
Circulation: 17005
Founded in: 1928

23862 Rural Water Magazine
National Rural Water Association
2915 S 13th St
Duncan, OK 73533-9086

580-252-0629; *Fax:* 580-255-4476
info@nrwa.org; www.nrwa.org

Rob Johnson, CEO

Targeted at the operators and board members of rural and small municipal water and wastewater utilities.
56 Pages
Frequency: Quarterly
Circulation: 22800
Founded in: 1979

23863 US Water News
US Water News
230 Main St
Halstead, KS 67056-1913

316-835-2222
800-251-0046; *Fax:* 316-835-2223;
www.uswaternews.com

Thomas Bell, President/Publisher

Reports news of current events from across the nation in the municipal and industrial water and wastewater segments of the water industry.
Cost: $59.00
28 Pages
Frequency: Monthly
Circulation: 20000
Founded in: 1984
Printed in on n stock

23864 Water Conditioning and Purification Magazine
Publicom
2800 E Fort Lowell Road
Tucson, AZ 85716

520-323-6144; *Fax:* 520-323-7412
info@wcponline.com; www.wcponline.com

Kurt C Peterson, Publisher/Eastern Advertising Exec
Sharon M Peterson, President/Owner
Karen R Smith, Executive Editor
Margo Goldbaum, Circulation Services
Denise M Roberts, Assistant Editor

Comprehensive magazine for all aspects of the water quality improvement industry. Accepts advertising.
Cost: $49.00
100 Pages
Circulation: 20000
ISSN: 1537-1786
Founded in: 1959
Mailing list available for rent: 1000 names at $250 per M
Printed in 4 colors on glossy stock

23865 Water Environment & Technology
Water Environment Federation
601 Wythe St
Alexandria, VA 22314-1994

703-684-2400
800-666-0206; *Fax:* 703-684-2492
csc@wef.org; www.wef.org
Social Media: Facebook, Twitter, LinkedIn

Bill Bertera, Executive Director
Margaret Richards, Editorial Assistant
Tracy Hardwick, Publication Services Manager

Covers a wide range of water quality and municipal wastewater treatment issues, from the design, engineering, and management of domestic wastewater treatment plants to watershed management and wet weather issues.
Cost: $178.00
Frequency: Monthly
Circulation: 27304
Founded in: 1928

23866 Water Environment Federation
Water Environment Federation
601 Wythe St
Alexandria, VA 22314-1994

703-684-2400
800-666-0206; *Fax:* 703-684-2492
webfeedback@wef.org; www.wef.org

Bill Bertera, Executive Director
David James, Publications Committee

Magazine published monthly for 41,000 members
Cost: $19.00
Founded in: 1928

23867 Water Environment Research
Water Environment Federation
601 Wythe St
Alexandria, VA 22314-1994

703-684-2400; *Fax:* 703-684-2492;
www.wef.org

Bill Bertera, Executive Director
Glenn Reinhardt, Foundation Executive Director
Tom Wolfe, Advertising

Research journal reviewed by peers and covering the effects of water pollution and the technology and advances used for it's control.
Cost: $158.00
Circulation: 9000
Founded in: 1928

23868 Water Resources Research
American Geophysical Union
2000 Florida Ave NW
Washington, DC 20009-1231

202-462-6900
800-966-2481; *Fax:* 202-328-0566
service@agu.org; www.agu.org
Social Media: Facebook, Twitter, LinkedIn

Fred Spilhaus, Executive Director
Karne Blaususs, Circulation Manager

Presents articles on the social, natural, and physical sciences, with emphasis on geochemistry, hydrology, and groundwater transfer technology.
Cost: $1200.00
Frequency: Monthly
Circulation: 4700
Founded in: 1919

23869 Water Technology
National Trade Publications
19 British American Blvd. Wes
Latham, NY 12110

518-783-1281; *Fax:* 518-783-1386
asavino@ntpinc.com;
www.watertechonline.com
Social Media: Facebook, Twitter, LinkedIn

Tracy Ashton-Martin, Vice President of Business Publishi
Lisa Williman, Marketing Account Executive
Chapman Brown, Advertising Account Executive
Richard DiPaolo, Editorial Director
Jake Mastroianni, Assistant Editor

Serves the POU/POE water treatment industry. Accepts advertising.
Cost: $39.00
48 Pages
Frequency: Monthly
Circulation: 21000
Founded in: 1981
Mailing list available for rent: 20000 names at $125 per M
Printed in 4 colors on glossy stock

23870 Water Well Journal
Ground Water Publishing Company
601 Dempsey Rd
Westerville, OH 43081-8978

614-882-8179
800-551-7379; *Fax:* 614-898-7786
waterwelljournal.org
Social Media: Facebook, Twitter, LinkedIn

Kevin McCray, Executive Director
Jennifer Strawn, Associate Editor
Joanne Grant, Manager

A complete publication of the water supply industry. Covers technical issues related to drilling and pump installation, rig maintenance, business management and professional development, well rehabilitation, water treatment and more.
Cost: $95.00
84 Pages
Frequency: Monthly
Founded in: 1948

23871 WaterWorld
PennNet
1421 S Sheridan Road
Tulsa, OK 74112

918-835-3161
800-331-4463; *Fax:* 918-831-9415;
www.pennnet.com
Social Media: Facebook, Twitter, LinkedIn

James Laughlin, Editor/Associate Publisher

Gives information about products and services, technology, applications, legislation and regulations to help the water industry pros successfully plan, design, operate and maintain their systems.
Frequency: Monthly
Founded in: 1985

23872 **World Wastes: the Independent Voice**
Communication Channels
6151 Powers Ferry Road NW
Atlanta, GA 30339-2959
770-953-4805; *Fax:* 770-618-0348
Bill Wolpin, Editor
Jerrold France, President Argus Business
Reaches individuals and firms engaged in the removal and disposal of solid wastes.
Cost: $48.00
Frequency: Monthly
Circulation: 36,000

Trade Shows

23873 **American Backflow Prevention Association Annual Conference**
American Backflow Prevention Assocation
342 N. Main Street
Suite 301
West Hartford, CT 06117
979-846-7606
877-227-2127; *Fax:* 979-846-7607
efearn@abpa.org; www.abpa.org
Gathers together professionals and experts to provide technical expertise on backflow prevention.
Frequency: Annual

23874 **American Society of Irrigation Consultants Conference**
PO Box 426
Byron, CA 94514-0426
925-516-1124; *Fax:* 925-516-1301
Wanda M Sarsfield, Secretary
Irrigation design equipment, supplies, services and seminar.
Frequency: Annual
Founded in: 1970

23875 **American Water Resources Conference**
American Water Resources Association
4 West Federal Street
PO Box 1626
Middleburg, VA 20118-1626
540-687-8390; *Fax:* 540-687-8395
info@awra.org; www.awra.org
Social Media: Facebook, Twitter, LinkedIn, YouTube
Terry Meyer, Marketing Coordinator
Ken Reid, Executive VP
Show of water resources science and technology.
Frequency: Annual, November
Founded in: 1964

23876 **American Water Works Association Annual Conference and Exhibition**
6666 W Quincy Avenue
Denver, CO 80235
303-794-7711
800-926-7337; *Fax:* 303-347-0804;
www.awwa.org
Nilaksh Kothari, President
Jack W. Hoffbuhr, Executive Director
Jane M. Johnson, Director of Sales & Research
With more than 500 exhibitors, who are a source of knowledge and information for water professionals who work to improve the supply and quality of water in North America and beyond
12000 Attendees
Frequency: Annual, June
Founded in: 1881

23877 **Chartmaker**
American Recreation Coalition
1225 New York Avenue NW
Suite 450
Washington, DC 20005-6405
202-829-9530; *Fax:* 202-662-7424
Derrick Crandall, President
Triennial exhibits relating to the responsible use of US aquatic resources, including issues such as wetlands conservation, boating safety, sportfish research and enhancement and boating access improvements.

23878 **Computers in the Water Industry: The Computer Conference**
American Water Works Association
6666 W Quincy Avenue
Denver, CO 80235
303-794-7711
800-926-7337; *Fax:* 303-347-0804;
www.awwa.org
Nilaksh Kothari, President
Jack W. Hoffbuhr, Executive Director
Jane M. Johnson, Director of Sales & Research

23879 **Irrigation Show & Education Conference**
6540 Arlington Boulevard
Falls Church, VA 22042-6638
703-536-7080; *Fax:* 703-536-7019
membership@irrigation.org;
www.irrigation.org
Bob Sears, Executive VP
Four hundred and twenty five booths of the newest in irrigation equipment for the agricultural industry.
3.5M Attendees
Frequency: November

23880 **National Ground Water Association Annual Convention and Exposition**
National Ground Water Association
601 Dempsey Road
Westerville, OH 43081
614-987-7791
800-551-7379; *Fax:* 614-898-7786
ngwa@ngwa.org; www.ngwa.org
Bob Masters, Conference Coordinator
Greg Phelps, Meeting Planner/Expositions Dir
Kevin McKray, Executive Director
Annual show of 4600 manufacturers, suppliers, distributors, consultants and scientists, and contractors/pump installers.
5,100 Attendees
Frequency: December

23881 **National Rural Water Association**
2915 S 13th Street
Duncan, OK 73533
580-252-0629; *Fax:* 580-255-4476
info@nrwa.org; www.nrwa.org
Larissa M Wood, Publications Coordinator
100 booths; 300 exhibitors.
1.5M Attendees
Frequency: September

23882 **National Water Resources Association Annual Conference**
National Water Resources Association
3800 Fairfax Drive
Suite 4
Arlington, VA 22203
703-524-1544; *Fax:* 703-524-1548
nwra@nwra.org; www.nwra.org
Norman Semanko, President
Thomas Donnelly, VP
Annual conference and exhibits relating to the development, control, conservation and utilization of water resources in the reclamation states.
700 Attendees
Frequency: November

23883 **North American Lake Management Society International Symposium**
North American Lake Management Society
4513 Vernon Boulevard, Suite 103
PO Box 5443
Madison, WI 53705-0443
608-233-2836; *Fax:* 608-233-3186;
www.nalms.org
Bev Clark, President
Annual symposium and exhibits related to lake ecology and management.

23884 **Soil and Water Conservation Society Annual International Conference**
Soil and Water Conservation Society
945 SW Ankeny Road
Ankeny, IA 50021-9764
515-289-2331
800-843-7645; *Fax:* 515-289-1227;
www.swsc.org
Craig A Cox, Executive VP
Explores ways to improve the linkages among conservation science, policy and application at local, national, and international scales. The conference will provide participants an opportunity to teach skills, learn techniques, compare successes, and improve understanding.
1200 Attendees
Frequency: Annual

23885 **Water Environment Federation**
Water Environment Federation
601 Wythe Street
Alexandria, VA 22314-1994
703-684-2400
800-666-2492; *Fax:* 703-684-2175;
www.wef.org
Jenny Grigsby, Advertising
Jack Benson, Association Development
Annual show of 650 manufacturers, suppliers and distributors of water treatment equipment, supplies and services.
14M Attendees
Frequency: October, Chicago

23886 **Water Quality Association Convention**
Water Quality Association
4151 Naperville Road
Suite 100
Lisle, IL 60532-1088
630-505-0160; *Fax:* 630-505-9637
info@wqa.org; www.wqa.org
Peter J Censky, Executive Director
Jeannine Collins, CMP, Convention/Meetings Manager
Annual convention and exhibits of water treatment equipment and related articles.
4,300 Attendees

Directories & Databases

23887 **American Water Works Association: Buyers' Guide Issue**
American Water Works Association

6666 W Quincy Ave
Denver, CO 80235-3098

303-794-7711
800-926-7337; *Fax:* 303-347-0804;
www.awwa.org

Andrew Richardson, President
Jack W. Hoffbuhr, Executive Director
Jane M. Johnson, Director of Sales & Research

Member suppliers and distributors of water supply products and services, contractors for water supply projects and engineering consultants.
Frequency: Annual November
Circulation: 80,000

23888 Directory of Water/Sewer and Related Industries Professionals
National Assn of Regulatory Utility Commissioners
1101 Vermont Ave NW
Suite 200
Washington, DC 20005-3553

202-898-2200; *Fax:* 202-898-2213
admin@naruc.org; www.naruc.org

Charles Gray, Executive Director

Offers valuable information on over 150 consultants and other professionals active in regulated water, sewer and related industries.
Cost: $25.00
195 Pages
Frequency: Annual

23889 Ground Water Age: Directory of Manufacturers
National Trade Publications
13 Century Hill Drive
Latham, NY 12110-2197

518-831-1281; *Fax:* 518-783-1386

Roslyn Scheib Dahl, Editor

List of over 150 companies that provide products and services to the ground water industry.
Cost: $30.00
Frequency: Annual December
Circulation: 13,448

23890 Ground Water Monitoring & Remediation: Buyers Guide Issue
Ground Water Publishing Company
601 Dempsey Rd
Westerville, OH 43081-8978

614-882-8179
800-332-2104; *Fax:* 614-898-7786;
www.ngwa.org

Kevin McCray, Executive Director
Thad Plumley, Publications Director

List of companies that provide products used in the ground water monitoring and remediation industry.
Cost: $15.00
Frequency: Annual
Circulation: 12,382
Founded in: 1981

23891 Ground Water Monitoring Review: Consultant & Contract Directory
National Ground Water Association
601 Dempsey Rd
Westerville, OH 43081-8978

614-898-7791
800-332-2104; *Fax:* 614-898-7786;
www.ngwa.org

Paul Humes, VP
Shelby Fleck, Advertising Manager
Kevin McCray, Executive Director

About 400 consultant and contracting firms engaged in ground water monitoring projects.
Cost: $200.00
Frequency: Annual
Circulation: 17,000

23892 Ground Water On-Line
National Ground Water Association
601 Dempsey Rd
Westerville, OH 43081-8978

614-898-7791
800-554-7379; *Fax:* 614-898-7786
ngwa@ngwa.org; www.ngwa.org

Paul Humes, VP

Database offers information on more than 90,000 ground water literature citations, which includes information like key words, abstracts, chemical compounds, biological factors, geographic locations, aquifer names, authors, titles, publication source names and a lot more.

23893 Validated Water Treatment Equipment Directory
Water Quality Association
4151 Naperville Rd
Suite 100
Lisle, IL 60532-3696

630-505-0160; *Fax:* 630-505-9637;
www.wqa.org

Peter Censky, Manager

Over 700 water treatment products tested by the Water Quality Association and their manufacturers are listed.
Cost: $6.00; *Frequency:* SemiAnnual

23894 WATERNET
American Water Works Association
6666 W Quincy Ave
Denver, CO 80235-3098

303-794-7711
800-926-7337; *Fax:* 303-347-0804;
www.waternetonline.ihe.nl

Andrew Richardson, President
Jack W. Hoffbuhr, Executive Director
Jane M. Johnson, Director of Sales & Research

This database contains more than 23,000 citations, with abstracts, to literature on water quality, water utility management, analytical procedures for water quality testing.

23895 Water Technology: Directory of Manufacturers and Suppliers Issue
National Trade Publications
13 Century Hill Drive
Latham, NY 12110-2197

518-783-1281; *Fax:* 518-783-1386;
www.ntpmedia.com

Mark Wilson, Editor

List of about 250 manufacturers, distributors and other suppliers of water conditioning and treatment products.
Cost: $21.00
Frequency: Annual December
Circulation: 17,213

23896 Water Treatability
National Ground Water Information Center
6375 Riverside Drive
Dublin, OH 43017-5045

614-717-2770; *Fax:* 614-761-3446

Offers information on treatment technologies for the removal of various contaminants from water supplies.

23897 Water Well Journal: Buyer's Guide Issue
National Ground Water Association
601 Dempsey Rd
Westerville, OH 43081-8978

614-898-7791
800-332-2104; *Fax:* 614-898-7786;
www.ngwa.org

Paul Humes, VP
Shelby Fleck, Advertising Manager

List of manufacturers, suppliers and manufacturers' representatives for equipment, machinery and other products for the water well industry.
Cost: $6.00
Frequency: Annual January
Circulation: 26,000

Industry Web Sites

23898 http://gold.greyhouse.com
G.O.L.D Grey House OnLine Databases

Grey House Publishing's online database platform, GOLD, offers Quick Search, Keyword Search and Expert Search for most business sectors including water supply markets. The GOLD platform makes finding the information you need quick and easy - whether you're a novice searcher or an experienced database user. All of Grey House's directory products are available for subscription on the GOLD platform.

23899 www.greyhouse.com
Grey House Publishing

Authoritative reference directories for most business sectors including water supply markets. Users can search the online databases with varied search criteria allowing for custom searches by product category, geographic area, sales volume, keyword, subject and more. Full Grey House catalog and online ordering also available.

23900 www.gwpc.org
Ground Water Protection Council

Provides a forum for dicussing ground water, watershed and community wallhead protection and underground injection practices. Conducts seminars and workshops on these subjects.

23901 www.nda4u.com
National Drilling Association

A non-profit trade association of contractors, manufacturers and affiliated members from the drilling industry representing the geotechnical, environmental and mineral exploration sectors of this industry.

23902 www.swcs.org
Soil and Water Conservation Society

Promotes erosion control and water quality. Publishes scholarly journal and practical magazine. Conducts annual conference and trade show

23903 www.umsu.edu/niwr/
National Institute for Water Resources

Offers information on water resource directions across the nation.

23904 www.wef.org
Water Environment Federation

A not-for-profit technical and educational organization, consisting of regional association comprised of air quality professionals concerned with all types of air pollution.

23905 www.wjta.org
WaterJet Technology Association/Industrial & Municipal Cleaning Association

Members research for new findings in waterjet technology.

23906 www.wqa.org
Water Quality Association

For retail/dealers and manufacturer/suppliers in the point of use/entry water quality improvement industry.

Associations

23907 **American Association of Meat Processors**
One Meating Place
Elizabethtown, PA 17022
717-367-1168; *Fax:* 717-367-9096
aamp@aamp.com; www.aamp.com
Social Media: Facebook, Twitter, Goole+, YouTube
Erica Hering, President
Louis Muench, 1st VP
Chad Lottman, 2nd VP
Dwight Ely, 3rd VP
Doug Hankes, Treasurer
Membership consists of small to medium sized meat, poultry and food businesses including, slaughterers, processors, wholesalers, home food service businesses, deli and catering operators and suppliers to the industry. AAMP is affiliated with 32 state, regional and provincial associations.
1400 Members
Founded in: 1939

23908 **American Horticultural Supply, Inc.**
525 9th St. NW
Suite 800
Washington, DC 20004
202-789-2900; *Fax:* 202-789-1893
hello@AmericanHort.org
americanhort.com
Social Media: Facebook, Twitter, LinkedIn, Goole+, YouTube
David Savoia, CTA, Interim President & CEO
Craig J Regelbrugge, SVP, Industry Advocacy & Research
Carol Baker, Executive Assistant
Sherry L. Johnson, CMP, VP, Knowledge & Bus. Advancement
Steve Carver, Ph.D., Learning Resource Specialist
The American Nursery and Landscape Association serves firms who grow, sell or use plants. ANLA advocates the industry's interests before government and provides its members with unique business knowledge essential to long-term growth and profitability.
2200 Members
Founded in: 1876

23909 **American Machine Tool Distributors Association**
7901 Westpark Drive
Suite 320
McLean, MD 22102-4206
703-893-2900
800-524-0475; *Fax:* 703-893-1151
AMT@AMTonline.org; www.amtonline.org
Social Media: Facebook, Twitter, LinkedIn, Youtube
Douglas K. Woods, President
Amber Thomas, VP
Jeffrey H Traver, VP
Peter R Eelman, VP
Steve Lesnewich, VP
AMTDA will lead distributors of manufacturing technology by providing essential programs and services that help its members gain global recognition from customers and suppliers as the preferred channel of distribution.
300 Members
Founded in: 1925

23910 **American Supply Association**
1200 North Arlington Heights Road
Suite 150
Itasca, IL 60143
630-467-0000; *Fax:* 630-467-0001
info@asa.net; www.asa.net
Social Media: Facebook, Twitter, LinkedIn
John Strong, Chairman of the Board
Rick Fantham, President
Tim Milford, President-Elect
Steve Cook, Treasurer
Michael Adelizzi, Secretary/EVP
ASA is a not-for-profit national organization serving wholesale distributors and their suppliers in the plumbing, heating, cooling and industrial and mechanical pipe, valves and fittings industries.
Founded in: 1969

23911 **American Veterinary Distributors Association**
3465 Box Hill Corp. Center Drive
Suite H
Abingdon, MD 21009
443-640-1040; *Fax:* 443-640-1086
casey@kingmgmt.org; www.avda.net
Social Media: Facebook, Twitter, LinkedIn
Bobby Mims, Chairman
Jackie King, Executive Director
Paula Brown, President-Elect
Casey Joseph, Association Coordinator
Debbie Dacre, Director of Finance
The AVDA was established as the national trade organization for businesses engaged in the distribution of animal health products.
Founded in: 1976

23912 **American Wholesale Marketers Association**
11311 Sunset Hills Road
Reston, VA 20190
703-208-3358
800-482-2962; *Fax:* 703-573-5738
info@cdaweb.net
cdaweb.net
Social Media: Facebook, Twitter, LinkedIn, RSS
Scott Ramminger, President & CEO
Kimberly Bolin, Executive Vice President
Bob Gatty, VP, Communication
Meredith Kimbrell, Director, Education & Communities
Anne Holloway, VP, Government Affairs
A trade organization supporting the confectionary, tobacco and allied industries through programs and services. members include wholesale distributors, manufacturers and other allieds to the industry.
5300 Members
Founded in: 1942

23913 **Appliance Parts Distributors Association**
3621 N Oakley Avenue
Chicago, IL 60618
773-230-9851; *Fax:* 888-308-1423
ro@apda.com; www.apda.com
Social Media: Facebook, Twitter, LinkedIn
Phil F Orazietti, President
Leonard Kremers, Vice President
Ron Clifton, Treasurer
Bob Goldberg, Legal Counsel
Rosemary Jacobshagen, CAE, Association Management
The APDA is an association of independent businesses that aspire to provide the highest level of quality, service, support and information to its customers and suppliers in order to make its value indispensable to the parts distribution channel.

23914 **Associated Beer Distributors of Illinois**
PO Box 396
Springfield, IL 62705
217-528-4371; *Fax:* 217-528-4376
info@abdi.org; www.abdi.org
Social Media: Facebook, Twitter, LinkedIn
The ABDI represents, maintains, and improves the interests of its members who are licensed by the State of Illinois to import and distribute beer to licensed retailers.

23915 **Associated Equipment Distributors**
600 22nd Street
Suite 220
Oak Brook, IL 60523
630-574-0650
800-388-0650; *Fax:* 630-574-0132
info@aednet.org; www.aednet.org
Social Media: Facebook, Twitter, LinkedIn, Goole+, YouTube
Bob Henderson, EVP & COO
Brian P. McGuire, President/CEO
Jason Blake, SVP/CFO
Jon Cruthers, Vice President of Sales
Phil Riggs, Regional Manager
AED is an international trade association representing companies involved in the distribution, rental and support of equipment used in construction, mining, forestry, power generation, agriculture and industrial applications.
700 Members

23916 **Association for High Technology Distribution**
N19 W24400 Riverwood Drive
Waukesha, WI 53188
262-696-3645
800-488-4845; *Fax:* 630-574-0132
info@aednet.org; www.ahtdmembers.org
Social Media: Facebook, Twitter, RSS
Bryan Roesster, Executive Director
Leigha Schatzman, Association Services Manager
Pam Estergard, Financial Services
Cassie Schauer, Association Services Coordinator
The Association for High Technology Distribution has worked to increase the productivity and profitability of the high technology Automation Solutions Providers and Manufacturers who satisfy the automation needs of general industry and OEM manufacturers.
Founded in: 1984

23917 **Association for Hose and Accessories Distribution**
105 Eastern Avenue
Suite 104
Annapolis, MD 21403
410-940-6350
800-624-2227; *Fax:* 410-263-1659
info@nahad.org; www.nahad.org
Social Media: Facebook, Twitter, LinkedIn
Jim Reilly, President
Skip Bruce, 1st VP
Scott Moss, 2nd VP
Joseph M Thompson Jr., EVP
Mark Fournier, Immediate Past President
The mission of NAHAD is to promote a high standard of professionalism and integrity within the hose and accessories industry by providing a medium for communications, education and training, so that quality is maximized and profitability enhanced.

23918 Association for Suppliers of Printing, Publishing & Converting Tech.
1899 Preston White Drive
Reston, VA 20191
703-264-7200; *Fax:* 703-620-0994
npes@npes.org; www.npes.org
Malkon S. Baboyian, Chairman
Ralph J Nappi, President
Greg Safko, VP, Market Data & Research
Mark A. Hischar, Treasurer
Mark J Nuzzaco, Secretary
This association is a trade association of over 400 companies that manufacture and distribute equipment, systems, software, supplies used in printing, publishing and converting.
400 Members
Founded in: 1933

23919 Association of Ingersoll-Rand Distributors
1300 Summer Avenue
Cleveland, OH 44115
216-241-7333; *Fax:* 216-241-0105;
www.aird.org
Stu Bassett, President
Brent Darnell, VP
Jonathan Michel, Treasurer
Greg Scott, Secretary
The Association of Ingersoll-Rand Distributors (AIRD) was organized as a central resource for distributors of Ingersoll-Rand compressed air equipment. AIRD is chartered to promote improved business conditions affecting distributors of air compressors, further a better understanding between distributors and equipment suppliers, research ways to lower costs of distributing air compressors, collect and disseminate statistical information and conduct other beneficial activities.
Founded in: 1970

23920 Association of Millwork Distributors
10047 Robert Trent Jones Parkway
New Port Richey, FL 34655-4649
727-372-3665
800-786-7274; *Fax:* 727-372-2879
Mail@WorldMillworkAlliance.com;
www.amdweb.com
Social Media: Twitter, LinkedIn
Joe Bayer, President
Dave Ondrasek, 1st VP
Timothy Lyons, 2nd VP
Scott Harder, Associate VP
Simon Sikora, Treasurer
AND provides leadership, education, promotion, networking, and advocacy to, and for, the millwork distribution industry.
Founded in: 1963

23921 Association of Pool & Spa Professionals
2111 Eisenhower Avenue
Suite 500
Alexandria, VA 22314-4679
703-838-0083; *Fax:* 703-549-0493
memberservices@apsp.org; www.apsp.org
Social Media: Facebook, Twitter, LinkedIn, Youtube, Flickr, RSS
Rich Gottwald, President/CEO
Lorna Watkins, Executive Assistant
Jennifer Hatfield, Director, Govt. Affairs
Todd Usher, Manager, Communications
Carvin DiGiovanni, VP, Technical & Standards
APSP is the world's largest international trade association for the swimming pool, spa, and hot tub industry. It works with regulatory and legislative bodies to ensure that their codes, ordinance, and legislation are written to the safest and most current standards. The association's mission is to ensure consumer safety and enhance the business success of its members.
Founded in: 1956

23922 Association of Service and Computer Dealers International
131 NW First Avenue
Delray Beach, FL 33444
561-504-8898; *Fax:* 561-431-6302;
www.ascdi.com
Social Media: Facebook, Twitter, LinkedIn, YouTube
Rob Neumeyer, Director
Arthur P Frierman, Associate Counsel
Jerry Roberts, Chairman Emeritus
Joe Marion, President
The ASCDI is a worldwide, nonprofit organization, made up of companies who provide technology business solutions, technical support, and value added services to the business community.
Founded in: 1981

23923 Association of Woodworking and Furnishings Suppliers
2400 E Katella Ave
Suite 340
Anaheim, CA 92806
323-838-9440
800-946-2937; *Fax:* 323-838-9443
angelo@awfs.org; www.awfs.org
Social Media: Facebook, Twitter, LinkedIn
Archie Thompson, VP
Angela Hernandez, Executive Assistant
Nancy Neely, Controller
Angelo Gangone, EVP
Nancy Fister, Education & Conference Director
The Association of Woodworking and Furnishings Suppliers is the largest national trade association in the U.S. representing the interests of the broad array of companies that supply the home and commercial furnishings industry.
Founded in: 1911

23924 Automotive Aftermarket Industry Association
7101 Wisconsin Avenue
Suite 1300
Bethesda, MD 20814-3415
301-654-6664; *Fax:* 301-654-3299
info@autocare.org; www.autocare.org
Social Media: Facebook, Twitter, LinkedIn, Youtube, WordPress
Kathleen Schmatz, MAAP, President/CEO
Susan Medick, CPA, CAE, CFO/COO
Richard D. White, MAAP, SVP
Michael Barratt, CMP, SVP, Meeting & Events
Aaron Lowe, AAP, SVP, Reg. and Gov. Affairs
A trade association consisting of more than 23,000 member companies and affiliates representing over 100,000 repair shops, distribution outlets, and parts stores.
23000 Members
Founded in: 1999

23925 Bearing Specialists Association
800 Roosevelt Road
Building C, Suite 312
Glen Ellyn, IL 60137
630-858-3838; *Fax:* 630-790-3095
info@bsahome.org; www.bsahome.org
Social Media: Twitter, LinkedIn, RSS
Tim Breen, President
John Ruth, VP
Brian Davis, Treasurer
BSA is the forum to enhance networking and knowledge sharing to promote the sale of bearings through authorized distributors.
100 Members
Founded in: 1966

23926 Bicycle Product Suppliers Association
740 34th St
Boulder, CO 80303
303-442-2466; *Fax:* 303-552-2060
bpsa@bpsa.org; www.bpsa.org
John Nedeau, President
Chris Speyer, Vice President
Patrick Cunnane, Treasurer
Marc Sani, Secretary
Ray Keener, Executive Director
BPSA is an association of suppliers of bicycles, parts, accessories and services who serve the Specialty Bicycle Retailer.

23927 Business Solutions Association
3601 E Joppa Rd.
Baltimore, MD 21234
410-931-8100; *Fax:* 410-931-8111
info@BusinessSolutionsAssociation.com;
www.opwa.org
Jim O'Brien, President
Bill Cardone, VP
Nick Aronis, Secretary
Alan Goldner, Treasurer
The goal of the Business Solutions Association is to provide a forum for the development of strategic and synergistic solutions to enhance the sale and distribution of business related products and services.

23928 Ceramic Tile Distributors Association
800 Roosevelt Road
Building C, Suite 312
Glen Ellyn, IL 60137
630-545-9415
800-938-2838; *Fax:* 630-790-3095
info@ctdahome.org; www.ctdahome.org
Social Media: Facebook
Tom Kotel, President
Heidi Martin, VP
Robert DeAngelis, Treasurer
Rick Church, Executive Director
Bill Ives, Legal Counsel
CTDA is an international association of distributors, manufacturers, and allied professionals of ceramic tile and related products.

23929 Cleaning Equipment Trade Association
PO Box 270908
Oklahoma City, OK 73137-0908
704-635-7362
800-441-0111; *Fax:* 704-635-7363
info@ceta.org; www.ceta.org
Curtis Braber, President
Aaron Auger, Senior Vice President
Kyle Notch, Vice President
Jim O'Connell, Secretary
Chad Rasmussen, Treasurer
CETA is dedicated to increasing the awareness and promotion of industry products, while at the same time recognizing the impact on preserving the environment and the opportunity to do business within it.

23930 Commercial Vehicle Solutions Network
3943-2 Baymeadows Road
Jacksonville, FL 32217
904-737-2900; *Fax:* 904-636-9881
info@cvsn.org; www.cvsn.org
Dave Willis, President
Edward Neeley, Vice President
Andy Robblee, Treasurer
Angelo Volpe, Executive VP/Secretary
Joe Ward, Director
The Commercial Vehicle Solutions Network (CVSN) is an association of independent parts

and service aftermarket distributors serving the transportation industry.
Founded in: 2006

23931 Copper and Brass Servicenter Association
6734 W. 121st Street
Overland Park, KS 66209
913-396-0697; *Fax:* 913-345-1006
cbsahq@copper-brass.org;
www.copper-brass.org
Social Media: Facebook, Twitter, LinkedIn, YouTube, Flickr
Susan Avery, CAE, Chief Executive Director
Crystal Roberts, Deputy Exe. Dir./Director of BD
David Blackhurst, Sales Manager
Bonnie Bush, Graphic Designer
Whitney Nelson, Director of Meetings and Events
Distributors (service centers) of fabricated copper and copper alloy products (sheet, plate, coil, rod, bar tube, etc) and their brass mill suppliers.
78 Members
Founded in: 1951

23932 Door & Hardware Institute
14150 Newbrook Drive
Suite 200
Chantilly, VA 20151-2232
703-222-2010; *Fax:* 703-222-2410;
www.dhi.org
Social Media: Facebook, Twitter, LinkedIn
Jerry Heppes, Sr., CAE, Chief Executive Officer
Chuck J. Molina, CTO/Director of IT
Lawrence Beatty, AHC, President
Stephen R. Hildebrand, FDHI, Executive Vice President
Sharon Newport, Director of Operations
The Door & Hardware Institute (DHI) is the only professional association dedicated to the Architectural Openings Industry. DHI represents the North American openings marketplace as the advocate and primary resource for information, professional development and certification.
5000 Members
Founded in: 1934

23933 Drycleaning & Laundry Institute International
14700 Sweitzer Lane
Laurel, MD 20707
301-622-1900
800-638-2627; *Fax:* 240-295-0685
techline@dlionline.org; www.dlionline.org
Social Media: Facebook, Twitter, Flickr
David Machesney, President
Greg Myers, Treasurer
Jan Barlow, Chairman
With its education, research, testing, and professional training, DLI offers solutions that help member businesses provide expert garment care.
2000 Members
Founded in: 1907

23934 Electrical Apparatus Service Association Inc
1331 Baur Boulevard
Saint Louis, MO 63132-1903
314-993-2220; *Fax:* 314-993-1269
easainfo@easa.com; www.easa.com
Social Media: Facebook, Twitter, LinkedIn, Youtube
Mike Dupuis, Chair
James Smith, Vice Chair
Lenwood Ireland, Secretary/Treasurer
Linda J. Raynes, CAE, President & CEO
Anne Vogel, Executive Secretary
Maintains data files on rewinding and repair of electrical equipment. Sponsors seminars
2000 Members
Founded in: 1973

23935 Equipment Marketing & Distribution Association (EMDA)
PO Box 1347
Iowa City, IA 52244
319-354-5156; *Fax:* 319-354-5157
pat@emda.net; www.emda.net
Social Media: Facebook, Twitter, LinkedIn
Patricia A Collins, Executive VP
EMDA is the result of the 2008 merger of FEWA and AIMRA. EMDA members are devtoed to the marketing of specialized equipment: agricultural, outdoor power, light industrial, forestry, irrigation, turf and grounds maintenance, lawn and garden and parts/components for thosesegments of industry.
250 Members
Founded in: 1945

23936 Financial & Security Products Association
1024 Mebane Oaks Road #273
Mebane, NC 27302
919-648-0664
800-843-6082; *Fax:* 919-648-0670;
www.fspa1.com
Social Media: LinkedIn
Linda Abell, Chairman
L.A. Smith, President
B.J. Hanson, Executive Director
Gene Polito, Vice President
Kevin Callahan, Secretary-Treasurer
Independent dealers, manufacturers and associates whose outstanding products and services give financial institutions a crucial edge in performance, efficiency and economy.
Founded in: 1973

23937 Fluid Power Distributors Association
105 Eastern Avenue
Suite 104
Annapolis, MD 21403
410-940-6347; *Fax:* 410-263-1659
info@fpda.org; www.fpda.org
Michael A Hamzey Jr., Chairman & President
Parker Lancaster, VP, Membership
Alex Wheelock, President Elect
Tim Gillig, VP, Finance/Treasurer
Patricia A Lilly, Executive Director
The Fluid Power Distributors Association is a trade association on the move, representing motion solution providers who offer fluid power, automation, and electro-mechanical technologies and distribution services to enhance customer performance and profitability.
300+ Members
Founded in: 1974

23938 Food Industry Suppliers Association
1207 Sunset Drive
Greensboro, NC 27408-7215
336-274-6311; *Fax:* 336-691-1839
stella@fisanet.org; www.fisanet.org/
Social Media: LinkedIn
Bob Morava, President
Brad Myers, VP
David Brink, Vice-President
David Brink, Past President
Member's are distributors and suppliers to the food processing industry.
245 Members
Founded in: 1968

23939 Food Marketing Institute
2345 Crystal Drive
Suite 800
Arlington, VA 22202
202-452-8444; *Fax:* 202-429-4519;
www.fmi.org
Social Media: Facebook, Twitter, LinkedIn, Youtube, RSS
Frederick J Morganthall II, Chair
Leslie G Sarasin, President & CEO
Rob Bartels, Vice Chair
Jerry Garland, Vice Chair
Henry Johnson, Vice-Chairman
FMI conducts programs in public affairs, food safety, research, education and industry relations on behalf of its 1,500 member companies in the United States and around the world.
1500 Members

23940 Foodservice Equipment Distributors Association
2250 Point Blvd
Suite 200
Elgin, IL 60123-7887
224-293-6500
800-677-9605; *Fax:* 224-293-6505
feda@feda.com; www.feda.com
Social Media: Facebook, Twitter, LinkedIn
Raymond Herrick, CAE, Executive VP
Rosie Montanez, Executive Assistant
Stacy Ward, Managing Editor
Adela Ramos, Admin Director/Advertising Manager
Amy Risinger, Membership Services Consultant
Dealers and distributors of foodservice equipment and supplies.
300 Members
Founded in: 1933

23941 Gases and Welding Distributors Association
1 Oakwood Blvd.
Suite 195
Hollywood, FL 33020
954-367-7728
844-251-3219; *Fax:* 954-367-7790
gawda@gawda.org; www.gawda.org
Social Media: Facebook, Twitter, LinkedIn, YouTube
Tom Biedermann, President
Jim Earlbeck, Vice President
Kevin Falconer, Vice President
Mark Raimy, 1st Vice President
Gary Halter, Vice President
GAWDA's mission is to promote the safe operation and economic vitality of distributors of industrial gases and related welding equipment and supplies.
775 Members
Founded in: 1945

23942 Global Market Development Center
1275 Lake Plaza Drive
Colorado Springs, CO 80906-3583
719-576-4260; *Fax:* 719-576-2661
info@gmdc.org; www.gmdc.com
Social Media: Facebook, Twitter, LinkedIn, YouTube, Google+, Flickr
David McConnell, President/CEO
Keith Wypyszynski, VP Business Development/CMO
Ann McConnell, Sr. Director Finance
Michael Winterbottom, VP, IT/Chief Technology Officer
GMDC is the premier non-profit global trade association dedicated to serving General Merchandise and Health Beauty retailers, wholesalers and suppliers. GMDC promotes critical connectivity to grow and expand member companies by uniting members through business building events

and opportunities and enriching their thinking through education and training; consumer and business insights; and information resources.
Founded in: 1970

23943 Health Industry Distributors Association
310 Montgomery Street
Alexandria, VA 22314-1516
703-549-4432; *Fax:* 703-549-6495
rowan@hida.org; www.hida.org
Matthew J Rowan, President & CEO
Ian Fardey, EVP
Elizabeth Hilla, Executive Director/SVP
Lisa A Queeney, VP, Finance & Operations
Linda Rouse O'Neill, VP, Govt. Affairs
HIDA keeps members current on healthcare reform, government affairs, industry trends and forecasts, provider news, and sales tips.
Founded in: 1902

23944 Healthcare Distribution Management Association
901 North Glebe Road
Suite 1000
Arlington, VA 22203
703-787-0000; *Fax:* 703-812-5282;
www.hdma.net
Social Media: Twitter, LinkedIn
Ted Scherr, Chairman
Jon Giacomin, Vice Chair
John M. Gray, President/CEO
Ann W. Bittman, EVP/COO
Patrick M. Kelly, EVP, Gov. Affairs
The Healthcare Distribution Management Association (HDMA) is the national association representing primary, full-service healthcare distributors. HDMA and its members are the vital link in the healthcare system, working daily to provide value, remove costs and develop innovative solutions.
Founded in: 1876

23945 Heating, Airconditioning & Refrigeration Distributors International
3455 Mill Run Drive
Suite 820
Columbus, OH 43026
614-345-4328
888-253-2128; *Fax:* 614-345-9161;
www.hardinet.org
Social Media: Facebook, Twitter, LinkedIn, Youtube, Instagram, Flickr
William Bergamini, President
Michael Meier, President-Elect
Tom Roberts, Vice President
Troy Meachum, Secretary/Treasurer
Talbot H. Gee, CEO
This association is a trade organization dedicated to advancing the science of wholesale distribution in the HVACR industry.
750+ Members
Founded in: 1960

23946 ISSA
7373 N Lincoln Ave
Lincolnwood, IL 60712-1799
847-982-0800
800-225-4772; *Fax:* 847-982-1012
info@issa.com; www.issa.com
Social Media: Facebook, Twitter, LinkedIn
Fritz Gast, President
Alan R Tomblin, President Elect/VP
Lydia M Work, International Director
John Swigart, Executive Director
John Barrett, Secretary
The worldwide cleaning industry association.
5700+ Members
Founded in: 1923

23947 Industrial Compressor Distributor Association
656 Southern Hills Drive
Eureka, MO 63025
636-938-3957; *Fax:* 636-938-3965
mjgilliam1@aol.com; www.icdaonline.com
Margot Gravel, President
The main objectives of the ICDA are to promote for its members the highest standards of production, financial and managerial activities; to act as a vehicle for the solution of common industry problems in an effective and efficient manner; and to increase market volume and profits for its members.

23948 Industrial Supply Association
100 North 20th Street
Suite 400
Philadelphia, PA 19103
215-320-3862
866-460-2360; *Fax:* 215-963-9785
info@isapartners.org; www.isapartners.org
Social Media: Facebook, Twitter, LinkedIn
Michael Carr, President
Tommy Thompson, VP
Craig Vogel, Treasurer
John Wiborg, Secretary
The primary focus of the Industrial Supply Association is to improve the industrial supply channel through its mission-critical activities including: conventions and forums, gathering and dissemination of critical information, and development and implementation of channel performance initiatives.

23949 International Association of Plastics Distribution
6734 W. 121st Street
Overland Park, KS 66209
913-345-1005; *Fax:* 913-345-1006
iapd@iapd.org; www.iapd.org
Social Media: Facebook, Twitter, LinkedIn, YouTube, Flickr
Susan E Avery, CAE, CEO
Crystal Roberts, CAE, Deputy Executive Director
Jean McClure, Executive Assistant/HR Manager
Kipp Simmons, Finance Manager
Whitney Nelson, Director, Meetings & Events
The International Association of Plastics Distribution is an international trade association comprised of companies engaged in the distribution and manufacturing of plastics materials.
Founded in: 1956

23950 International Foodservice Distributors Association
1410 Spring Hill Road
Suite 210
McLean, VA 22102-3035
703-532-9400; *Fax:* 703-538-4673;
www.ifdaonline.org
Social Media: Twitter, LinkedIn
Thomas A Zatina, Chairman
Mark S. Allen, President/CEO
James A Crawford, Vice Chair
Andy Mercier, Treasurer
Jonathan Eisen, SVP, Gov Relations
Trade association comprised of food distribution companies that supply independent grocers and food service operations throughout the US, Canada and 19 other countries.
135 Members
Founded in: 2003

23951 International Sealing Distribution Association
105 Eastern Avenue
Suite 104
Annapolis, MD 21403
410-940-6344; *Fax:* 410-263-1659
info@isd.org; www.isd.org
Social Media: Facebook, Twitter, LinkedIn
Christy Jaycox, President
John Kates, VP
Steve Luhrs, Treasurer
Deborah B Mitchell, Executive Director
Joseph M Thompson Jr., Associate Director
The International Sealing Distribution Association (ISD) is a not-for-profit trade association formed to enhance the success of members through information, education, and interaction.

23952 International Truck Parts Association
1720 10th Ave. South
Suite 4, PMB 199
Great Falls, MT 59405
202-544-3090
866-346-5692; *Fax:* 301-229-7331
info@itpa.com; www.itpa.com
Gerard Zentner, Chairman
Paul Cipolla, Vice Chairman
The International Truck Parts Association was organized as a not-for-profit association to promote, foster, and improve relationships among sellers and buyers of trucks and truck surplus products and other parties.
Founded in: 1974

23953 Irrigation Association
8280 Willow Oaks Corporate Drive
Suite 400
Fairfax, VA 22031
703-536-7080; *Fax:* 703-536-7019
info@irrigation.org; www.irrigation.org
Aric J. Olson, President
Gregory R. Hunter, Vice President
Deborah M. Hamlin, CAE, FASAE, Chief Executive Officer
John R. Farner, Jr, Government & PA Director
Rebecca J. Bayless, Finance Director
The Irrigation Association is the leading membership organization for irrigation equipment and system manufacturers, dealers, distributors, designers, consultants, contractors and end users.
1600 Members
Founded in: 1949

23954 Jewelry Industry Distributors Association
703 Old Route 422 West
Butler, PA 16001
203-254-4492; *Fax:* 513-367-1414
jidainfo@gmail.com; www.jidainfo.com
Social Media: Facebook
Bill Esslinger, President
Chris Gaber, Vice President
Richard Livesay, Treasurer
Rusty Cooper, Associate Director
Pat Conner, Associate Director
A list of over 130 member firms and their suppliers.
Founded in: 1946

23955 Machinery Dealers National Association
315 S Patrick Street
Alexandria, VA 22314
703-836-9300
800-872-7807; *Fax:* 703-836-9303
office@mdna.org; www.mdna.org

Social Media: Facebook, Twitter, LinkedIn, Youtube

Kim Khoury, CEA, President
Joe Lundvick, CEA, 1st VP
John Greene, CEA, Second Vice President
Terry Yoder, Treasurer
Mark Robinson, Executive Vice President

The Machinery Dealers National Association (MDNA) is an international, nonprofit trade association dedicated to the promotion of the used machinery industry.
Founded in: 1941

23956 Material Handling Equipment Distributors Association
201 US Highway 45
Vernon Hills, IL 60061-2398

857-680-3500; *Fax:* 847-362-6989
connect@mheda.org; www.mheda.org
Social Media: Facebook, Twitter, LinkedIn, Google+

Mark Milovich, President
Liz Richards, Executive Vice President
Anna Mariae Kendall, Marketing Manager
Rebecca Hein, Networking & Comm. Coordinator
Susan Freibrun, Education Manager

The Material Handling Equipment Distributors Association is the only national association dedicated solely to improving the proficiency of the independent material handling equipment distributor.
Founded in: 1954

23957 Metals Service Center Institute
4201 Euclid Ave
Rolling Meadows, IL 60008-2025

847-485-3000
800-872-7807; *Fax:* 847-485-3001
info@msci.org; www.msci.org/
Social Media: Facebook, Twitter, LinkedIn

Bob Weidner, President/CEO
Sharon Hochel, Executive Assistant
Ashley DeVecht, Director, Communications
Ann D'Orazio, VP, Marketing Growth
Jonathan Kalkwarf, VP, Finance & Govt. Affairs

MSCI is a trade association that supports and represents the elements of the metals value chain, including metals producers, distributors and processors.
400 Members
Founded in: 1907

23958 Michigan Distributors & Vendors Association
120 N Washington Square
Suite 110 B
Lansing, MI 48933

517-372-2323; *Fax:* 517-372-4404
mdva@mdva.org; www.mdva.org

Polly Reber, President
Scott Rorah, Chairman
Amy Klooster, Vice Chairman
Dave Hodson, Secretary/Treasurer
Gerald Abraham, Immediate Past Chairman

The Michigan Distributors and Vendors Association (MDVA) is a non-profit, statewide business association representing two very significant business segments in the grocery and convenience products industry.
100 Members
Founded in: 1991

23959 Mississippi Malt Beverage Association
4785 I-55 North, Suite 103
PO Box 1132
Jackson, MS 39215-1132

601-987-9098; *Fax:* 601-981-5566
info@msbeer.com
msbeer.com
Richard Brown, President

The MMBA was established to represent and promote the beer wholesalers and beer industry within Mississippi.
12 Members
Founded in: 1946

23960 Motorcycle Industry Council
2 Jenner Street
Suite 150
Irvine, CA 92618-3806

949-727-4211; *Fax:* 949-727-3313;
www.mic.org

The Motorcycle Industry Council (MIC) is a non-profit, national trade association representing manufacturers and distributors of motorcycles, scooters, motorcycle/ATV parts and accessories and members of allied trades.

23961 Music Distributors Association
14070 Proton Road
Suite 100 LB 9
Dallas, TX 75244-3601

972-233-9107; *Fax:* 972-490-4219
office@musicdistributors.org;
www.musicdistributors.org
Social Media: Facebook, Twitter, LinkedIn

Glenda Plummer, Executive Director

International, nonprofit trade association representing and serving manufacturers, wholesalers, importers and exporters of musical instruments and accessories, sound reinforcement products and published music.
250 Members
Founded in: 1939

23962 NPTA Alliance
330 N Wabash Ave
Suite 2000
Chicago, IL 60611

312-321-4092
800-355-6782; *Fax:* 312-673-6736
npta@gonpta.com; www.gonpta.com
Social Media: Twitter, LinkedIn, YouTube

Hilton Maze, Chairman
Bayard Tynes, 1st Vice Chair
Tom Wernoch, Second Vice Chair
Kevin Gammonley, CEO
Don Clampitt, Treasurer

Representing distributors and suppliers of paper, packaging and facility supplies companies.
220 Members
Founded in: 1903

23963 National Association of Chemical Distributors
1555 Wilson Boulevard
Suite 1100
Arlington, VA 22209

703-527-6223; *Fax:* 703-527-7747
nacdpublicaffairs@nacd.com; www.nacd.com
Social Media: Twitter, LinkedIn, Youtube

Mathew A. Brainerd, Chairman
Douglas A. Brown, Vice Chairman
Thomas M. Corcoran, Treasurer
Eric R. Byer, President
Celeste Clark, Executive Assistant

The National Association of Chemical Distributors (NACD) is an international association of chemical distributor companies that purchase and take title of chemical products from manufacturers.
250 Members
Founded in: 1971

23964 National Association of Electrical Distributors
1181 Corporate Lake Drive
St. Louis, MO 63132

314-991-9000
888-791-2512; *Fax:* 314-991-3060
memberservices@naed.org; www.naed.org
Social Media: Facebook, Twitter, LinkedIn, RSS, Youtube

Tom Naber, President & Chief Executive Officer
Michelle McNamara, SVP
Linda Thurman, Dir., Marketing & Comm.
Ed Orlet, VP, Gov't Affairs
Tim Dencker, VP, Finance

The main goal of the National Association of Electrical Distributors (NAED) is to establish the electrical distributor as an essential force in the electrical industry and the economy.
Founded in: 1908

23965 National Association of Flour Distributors
5350 Woodland Place
Canfield, OH 44406

330-718-6563; *Fax:* 877-573-1230
timdove51@gmail.com; www.thenafd.com
Social Media: Facebook, Twitter, LinkedIn

J Gerard Burns, Chairman
Dominic S. Valente, President
Philip S. Zilka, Jr., 1st VP
Steve Tardella, 2nd VP
Mark R. Munroe, Secretary/Treasurer

The mission of the NAFD is to serve the interests of its members who are engaged in the flour industry and those companies allied thereto by providing educational and networking opportunities.

23966 National Association of Sign Supply Distributors
1001 N Fairfax St.
Suite 301
Alexandria, VA 22314

703-836-4012; *Fax:* 703-836-8353
info@signs.org; www.nassd.org
Social Media: Facebook, Twitter, LinkedIn

Chris Flejtuch, Chairman
Robert Mattatall, Vice Chair
Jeff Young, Secretary/Treasurer
Lori Anderson, President & CEO
Brandon Hensley, COO

NASSD is a nonprofit trade association for organizations who are engaged in full-line sign supply distribution and who manufacture or supply commercial, neon and electrical sign products.

23967 National Association of Sporting Goods Wholesalers
One Parkview Plaza
Suite 800
Oakbrook Terrace, IL 60181

630-596-9006; *Fax:* 630-544-5055
info@nasgw.org; www.nasgw.org
Social Media: Twitter, LinkedIn, Flickr

Peter Brownell, Chairman
Brad Burney, Vice Chair
Mike Halleron, Treasurer
Kenyon Gleason, President
Michael Greskiewicz, Director of Business Development

Non-profit trade association of wholesalers, distributors and manufacturers. Serves as a liaison with other sporting goods associations.
400 Members
Founded in: 1953

23968 National Association of Wholesaler - Distributors
1325 G Street NW
Suite 1000
Washington, DC 20005-3100

202-872-0885; *Fax:* 202-785-0586
naw@naw.org; www.naw.org
Social Media: Facebook, Twitter, LinkedIn

Dirk Van Dongen, President
Jade West, SVP - Government Relations
James A Anderson Jr, VP - Government Relations
Ruth Stadius, Director, Communications
Ron Schreibman, SVP - Strategic Direction

The NAW provides members with the opportunity for networking and benchmarking within the entire wholesale distribution industry. NAW also represents the wholesale distribution industry before Congress, the White House, and the judiciary on issues that cross the industry's many lines of trade.

23969 National Beer Wholesalers Association
1101 King Street
Suite 600
Alexandria, VA 22314-2944

703-683-4300
800-300-6417; *Fax:* 703-683-8965
info@nbwa.org; www.nbwa.org
Social Media: Facebook, Twitter, YouTube

Craig A Purser, President/CEO
Wendy Huerter, Executive Assistant
Rebecca W Spicer, SVP, Comm. & Public Affairs
Paul Pisano, SVP Industry Affairs & Gen. Counsel
Kathleen Joyce, Communications Director

NBWA represents the interests of America's 2,850 independent, licensed beer distributors which service every congressional district and media market in the country.
Founded in: 1938

23970 National Electronics Service Dealers Association
3608 Pershing Ave
Fort Worth, TX 76107-4527

817-921-9061
800-797-9197; *Fax:* 817-921-3741
info@nesda.com; www.nesda.com

Mack Blakely, Executive Director
Sheila Fredrickson, Dir Communications/Info Technology
Patricia Bohon, Membership & Trade Show Coordinator
James Keesler, Associate Editor/Graphic Designer
Margaret Vazquez, Bookkeeper/Administrative Assistant

Provides educational assistance in electronic training to public schools, compiles statistics, offers certification programs and apprenticeships. Functions as trade association for the electronics service industry.
8 Members
Founded in: 1950

23971 National Fastener Distributors Association
10842 Noel Street #107
Los Alamitos, CA 90720

714-484-7858
877-487-6332; *Fax:* 562-684-0695
nfda@nfda-fastener.org;
www.nfda-fastener.org
Social Media: Facebook, Twitter, LinkedIn

Casey McIlhon, President
Marc Strandquist, VP
Kameron Dorsey, Associate Chair
Jeannine Christensen, Meetings & Events
Vickie Lester, MBA, CAE, Executive Management

Develops new uses for fasteners, offers training and educational programs.
250 Members
Founded in: 1968

23972 National Frozen & Refrigerated Foods Association
4755 Linglestown Road Suite 300
PO Box 6069
Harrisburg, PA 17112

717-657-8601; *Fax:* 717-657-9862
info@nfraweb.org; www.nfraweb.org
Social Media: Facebook, Twitter, LinkedIn, YouTube, Pinterest

H V Skip Shaw Jr, President/CEO
Jeff Rumachik, EVP/COO
Dayna Jackson, Director, Membership
Julie W Henderson, VP, Communications
Jessica Kurtz, VP, Finance

NFRA is a non-profit trade association representing all segments of the frozen and refrigerated foods industry. Headquartered in Harrisburg, PA, NFRA is the sponsor of March National Frozen Food Month, June dairy Month, and the Summer Favorites Ice Cream & Novelties promotion as well as the OctoberCool Food for Kids educational outreach program. NFRA holds the annual National Frozen & Refrigerated Foods Convention in October.
450 Members
Founded in: 1945

23973 National Grocers Association
1005 North Glebe Road
Suite 250
Arlington, VA 22201-5758

703-516-0700; *Fax:* 703-516-0115
feedback@nationalgrocers.org;
www.nationalgrocers.org
Social Media: Facebook, Twitter, LinkedIn

Peter J Larkin, President & Chief Executive Officer
Charlie Bray, EVP/COO
Matthew Klein, Director, Finance
Matilda Harvey, Director, Administration
Julia Sullivan, Office Administrator/Receptionist

The National Grocers Association is the national trade association representing the retail and wholesale grocers that comprise the independent sector of the food distribution industry.

23974 National Insulation Association
12100 Sunset Hills Road
Suite 330
Reston, VA 20190

703-464-6422; *Fax:* 703-464-5896;
www.insulation.org
Social Media: Facebook, Twitter, YouTube

J. Kenneth Freeman, President
Kristin V DiDomenico, VP
Erin Freeborn, Director of Meetings
Julie McLaughlin, Senior Director, Publications
Ashley J. Lopez, Senior Manager, Production & Design

The National Insulation Association (NIA) is a trade association representing the mechanical and specialty insulation industry.
Founded in: 1953

23975 National Kitchen and Bath Association
687 Willow Grove St
Hackettstown, NJ 07840-1731

908-850-1206
800-843-6522; *Fax:* 908-852-1695
feedback@nkba.org; www.nkba.org
Social Media: Facebook, Twitter, LinkedIn, Pinterest

Bill Darcy, CEO
Maria Stapperfenne, President
Stephen Graziano, VP, Finance & Operations
Nancy Barnes, Director, Learning and Development
Loren Barrows, Director of Marketing

Protects the interests of members by fostering a better business climate. Awards certification. Conducts training schools and seminars.
60000 Members
Founded in: 1963

23976 National Poultry and Food Distributors Association
2014 Osbourne Rd
St. Marys, GA 31558

770-535-9901
877-845-1545; *Fax:* 770-535-7385
kkm@npfda.org; www.npfda.org
Social Media: Facebook, Twitter, LinkedIn

Lee Wilson, President
Kenny Seeger, VP
Bobby Lipson, Treasurer
Kristin McWhorter, CAE, Executive Director/Corp. Secretary
Kathleen Kerry, Membership Coor./Ex. Assistant

A nationwide association that serves the needs of the poultry and food distribution and processing industries. Provides member services, cost cutting benefits and networking opportunities. Sponsors Poultry Suppliers Showcase every January in Atlanta.
220 Members
Founded in: 1967

23977 National School Supply & Equipment Association
8380 Colesville Road
Suite 250
Silver Spring, MD 20910

301-495-0240
800-395-5550; *Fax:* 301-495-3330
memberservices@nssea.org;
www.edmarket.org
Social Media: Facebook, Twitter, LinkedIn, Youtube

Jim McGarry, President/CEO
Adrienne Dayton, VP, Marketing & Communications
Bill Duffy, VP, Operations & Meetings
Joe Tucker, Director, Meetings & Experiences
Karen Prince, Director, Membership

The National School Supply and Equipment Association (NSSEA) is the leading trade organization for the educational products marketplace. NSSEA puts the collective experience of the most successful school industry business in the world at your fingertips.
1400+ Members
Founded in: 1916

23978 New York State Beer Wholesalers Association
100 State Street
Suite 400
Albany, NY 12207

518-465-6115; *Fax:* 518-465-1907
nybeer@nycap.rr.com; www.nybeer.org

Fred C Dana, Chairman
Steven W Harris, President
Ed Keis, Chairman Elect
Bill Bessette, Treasurer
Deb Boening, Secretary

The New York State Beer Wholesalers Association, Inc. represents and protects the legislative and regulators interests of its members in state and local government. Our primary goal is to up-

hold the three-tier system in order to safeguard the industry's distribution standards.
44 Members
Founded in: 1934

23979 North American Association of Telecommunications Dealers
131 NW First Avenue
DelRay Beach, FL 33444
561-266-9440; *Fax:* 561-266-9017;
www.natd.com
Rob Neuemeyer, Director
Arthur P Frierman, Associate Counsel
The North American Association of Telecommunications Dealers is a nonprofit organization of companies who provide telecom products to the business community and governments around the world. The NATD gives you access to the right kind of information, resources and business leaders, and provides you with unique opportunities to help grow your business.

23980 North American Association of Floor Covering Distributors
330 N Wabash Ave
Suite 2000
Chicago, IL 60611-4267
312-321-6836
800-383-3091; *Fax:* 312-673-6962
info@nafcd.org; www.nafcd.org
Social Media: Facebook, Twitter, LinkedIn, Youtube
Rosana Chaidez, President
Heidi Cronin Mandell, Vice President
Geoff Work, Treasurer
Bryan White, Membership Manager
Kevin Gammonley, Executive Director
The North American Association of Floor Covering Distributors (NAFCD) was organized to foster trade and commerce for those having a business, financial or professional interest as wholesale distributors or manufacturers of floor coverings and allied products.

23981 North American Association of Uniform Manufacturers & Distributors
6800 Jericho Turnpike
Suite 120W
Syosset, NY 11791
516-393-5838; *Fax:* 516-393-5878
rjlerman@naumd.com; www.naumd.com
Jim Tewmey, Chair
Richard J. Lerman, CCM, President & CEO
Nancy Marzullo, Bookkeeper & Admin Assistant
Miranda Brock, Social Media & Membership Manager
Jackie Rosselli - Verrico, Director of Communications
An association dedicated to keeping the Uniforn & Imagewear Industry strong and healthy.
Founded in: 1933

23982 North American Association of Utility Distributors (NAAUD)
3105 Corporate Exchange Court
Bridgeton, MO 63044
314-506-0724; *Fax:* 314-506-0790
director@naaud.org; www.naaud.com
Mary Jane Reinhardt, Executive Director
Ralph Knobbe, President
Patrick Novak, Vice President
Jeff Stauffer, Treasurer/Secretary
NAAUD is comprised of select distributors who specialize in supplying products and supply chain services to the electric utility industry. The purpose of NAAUD is to discuss and promote the newest ideas and best concepts for the industry.
Founded in: 1988

23983 North American Building Material Distribution Association
330 N Wabash Ave
Suite 2000
Chicago, IL 60611
312-321-6845
888-747-7862; *Fax:* 312-644-0310
info@nbmda.org; www.nbmda.org
Social Media: Facebook, Twitter, LinkedIn, YouTube
Rick Turk, President
Bill Sauter, President-Elect
Ray Prozzillo, Vice President
Wayne Moriarty, Treasurer
Kevin Gammonley, Executive Vice President
NBMDA develops and promotes the effectiveness of distribution processes to improve member profitability and growth.
Founded in: 1952

23984 North American Horticultural Supply Association
100 North 20th Street
4th Floor
Philadelphia, PA 19103-1443
215-320-3877; *Fax:* 215-564-2175
nahsa@fernley.com; www.nahsa.org
Social Media: Facebook, Twitter, LinkedIn
Sarah Hagy, Executive Director
Jameela Smith, Associate Director
Trudie Rowello, Management Liaison
The North American Horticultural Supply Association's mission is to strengthen and support the distribution and manufacturing of horticultural products and services.
Founded in: 1987

23985 North American Meat Processors Association
1150 Connecticut Ave, NW
12th floor
Washington, DC 20036
202-587-4200
800-368-3043; *Fax:* 202-587-4303;
www.meatassociation.com
Social Media: Facebook, Twitter, LinkedIn, YouTube
Dave McDonald, Chairman
Barry Carpenter, President and CEO
Christl McCarthy, Executive Assistant
Rosemary Mucklow, Director Emeritus
Betsy Booren, VP, Scientific Affairs
Represents processors and distributors of meat, poultry, seafood and game to the food-service industry.
400 Members
Founded in: 2012

23986 North American Wholesale Lumber Association
330 N. Wabash
Suite 2000
Chicago, IL 60611
312-321-5133
800-527-8258; *Fax:* 312-673-6838
info@nawla.org; www.nawla.org
Social Media: Facebook, Twitter, LinkedIn
Scott Elston, Chairman
Jim McGinnis, 1st Vice Chair
Bill Adams, 2nd Vice Chair
John Stockhausen, Secretary/Treasurer
Marc Saracco, Executive Director
Supports the wholesale lumber industry. Publishes monthly NAWLA Bulletin that includes industry and association news, and produces the NAWLA Traders Market, an annual trade show bringing together over 1500 manufacturers and wholesale lumber traders at the premier event in the forest products industry. NAWLA also produces a variety of educational programs designed to enhance professionalism in the lumber industry.
600+ Members
Founded in: 1893

23987 Optical Laboratories Association
225 Reinekers Lane
Suite 700
Alexandria, VA 22314
703-548-4560
866-826-0290; *Fax:* 703-548-4580
info@thevisioncouncil.org;
www.thevisioncouncil.org
Social Media: Facebook, Twitter, LinkedIn, YouTube
Mike Daley, CEO
Brian Carroll, COO/CFO
Maureen Beddis, VP, Marketing & Communications
Greg Chavez, VP, Member Services
Deborah Malakoff-Castor, VP, Shows & Meetings
Independent ophthalmic laboratories and supply houses that manufacture prescription eye glasses.
337 Members
Founded in: 1894

23988 Outdoor Power Equipment & Engine Service Association
37 Pratt Street
Essex, CT 06426-1159
860-767-1770; *Fax:* 860-767-7932
info@opeesa.com; www.opeesa.com
Social Media: Facebook, Twitter, LinkedIn
Jeff Plotka, President & Director
Steve Purdy, VP, Annual Meeting & Director
Ted Finn, Secretary/Treasurer & Director
Ron Monroe, Past President and Director
Nancy Cueroni, Executive Director
The Outdoor Power Equipment and Engine Service Association (OPEESA) consists of more than 140 distributors and manufacturers of outdoor power equipment and air-cooled gas and diesel engines. Their mission is to assist distributors in achieving outstanding channel performance.
140 Members

23989 Outdoor Power Equipment Aftermarket Association
341 South Patrick Street
Suite 1101
Alexandria, VA 22314
703-549-7608; *Fax:* 703-549-7609;
www.opeaa.org
Franck Sogaard, President
Don Martin, Executive VP
Scott Harris, VP
Jeff Andrews, Immediate Past President
Jim Paugh, Director
Businessmen dedicated to promoting the use of aftermarket parts in outdoor power equipment, as well as trade in the industry.
85 Members
Founded in: 1986

23990 Pacific-West Fastener Association
10842 Noel Street #107
Los Alamitos, CA 90720
714-484-4747
877-606-5232; *Fax:* 562-684-0695
info@pac-west.org; www.pac-west.org
Social Media: Facebook, Twitter, LinkedIn, YouTube, Instagram, Google+
Vickie Lester, Executive Director
Jeannine Christensen, Meetings & Events Manager
Marci Myer, Membership Manager
Claudia Scheutze, Accounting
Tanya Scoralle, Member Services

An organization dedicated to the fastener industry.
Founded in: 2009

23991 Pet Industry Distributors Association
3465 Box Hill Corp. Center Drive
Suite H
Abingdon, MD 21009

443-640-1060; *Fax:* 443-640-1086
pida@kingmgmt.org; www.pida.org
Social Media: LinkedIn

Steven T King, President
Debbie Darce, Director, Finance
Stephanie Kaplan, Director, Online Education
Marci Hickey, Director, Meetings & Member Service
Nina Bull, Association Coordinator

Represents wholesaler-distributors of pet products, providing training and education to members.
190 Members
Founded in: 1968

23992 Petroleum Equipment Institute
PO Box 2380
Tulsa, OK 74101-2380

918-494-9696; *Fax:* 918-491-9895
lallen@pei.org; www.pei.org
Social Media: Facebook, Twitter, LinkedIn, Google+

Kevin McKinney, President
Steve Trabilsy, VP
Robert Peavey, Treasurer
Robert Renkes, EVP
Phil Farrell, Immediate Past President

Members are makers and distributors of equipment used in service stations, bulk plants and other petroleum marketing facilities.
1600+ Members
Founded in: 1951
Mailing list available for rent: 1600 names at $275 per M

23993 Power Transmission Distributors Association
230 W. Monroe St
Suite 1410
Chicago, IL 60606-4703

312-516-2100; *Fax:* 312-516-2101
ptda@ptda.org; www.ptda.org
Social Media: Facebook, Twitter, LinkedIn

Ann Arnott, EVP/CEO
Brenda Holt, Director, Membership
Anna Meyer, Director, Project Management
LeRoy Burcroff, 1st VP
Thomas Clawser, 2nd VP

Members are power transmission/motion control distributors throughout manufacturing firms.
485 Members
Founded in: 1960

23994 Professional Beauty Association
15825 N 71st Street
Suite 100
Scottsdale, AZ 85254-1521

480-281-0424
800-468-2274; *Fax:* 480-905-0708
info@probeauty.org; www.probeauty.org
Social Media: Facebook, Twitter, LinkedIn, YouTube, Instagram, Pinterest

Reuben Carranza, Chairman
Beth Hickey, Vice Chair
Steve Sleeper, Executive Director
Rachel Molepske, Manager of Leadership Operations
Eric Z Horn, CMP, Associate Executive Director

The Professional Beauty Association (PBA) is a nonprofit trade association that represents the interests of the professional beauty industry from manufacturers and distributors to salons and spas. PBA offers business tools, education, advocacy, networking and more to improve individual businesses and the industry as a whole.

23995 Quality Bakers of America Cooperative
1275 Glenlivet Drive
Suite 100
Allentown, PA 18106-3107

973-263-6970; *Fax:* 973-263-0937
info@qba.com; www.qba.com

Don Cummings, VP

Members are independent wholesale bakeries and their suppliers.
35 Members
Founded in: 1922

23996 Safety Equipment Distributors Association
1901 North Moore Street
Suite 808
Arlington, VA 22209-1762

443-640-1065; *Fax:* 703-528-2148;
www.safetycentral.org
Social Media: Facebook, Twitter, LinkedIn

Daniel K Shipp, President
Lydia Baugh, Communications Director
Ann M Feder, Office Services Manager
Sabra L Decker, QSSP Administrator/Meeting Planner
Dan Glucksman, Public Affairs Director

Trade association comprised of companies that distribute safety equipment & related products and services.
300 Members
Founded in: 1968

23997 Security Hardware Distributors Association
105 Eastern Avenue
Suite 104
Annapolis, MD 21403

410-940-6346; *Fax:* 410-263-1659
info@shda.org; www.shda.org

Sean Steinmann, President
John Burke, Vice President
David Swartz, Treasurer
Karen Hoffman-Kahl, Immediate Past President
Patricia A. Lilly, Executive Director

The mission of the Security Hardware Distributors Association is to continually improve, through education and services, the proficiency of Security Distributors in order that they are the most effective and efficient conduit to the marketplace.

23998 Souvenir Wholesale Distributors Association
32770 Arapahoe Rd
#132-155
Lafayette, CO 80026

443-640-1055
888-599-4474; *Fax:* 888-589-7610
info@souvenircentral.org;
www.souvenircentral.org
Social Media: Facebook, LinkedIn

Brenda Taylor, President
Angie Rohnke, Vice President
Libby Smith, Secretary/Treasurer
Matthew Tobin, Immediate Past President

Companies distributing local view scenic post cards and souvenirs in North America and the Caribbean.
110 Members
Founded in: 1973

23999 Textile Care Allied Trades Association
271 Route 46 West
Suite C-106
Fairfield, NJ 07004

973-244-1790; *Fax:* 973-244-4455
info@tcata.org; www.tcata.org
Social Media: Facebook, Twitter, LinkedIn

David Cotter, Chief Executive Officer
Cheryl Paglia, Office Manager

The Textile Care Allied Trades Association (TCATA) is an international trade association representing manufacturers and distributors of dry-cleaning and laundry equipment and supplies. It is the only trade association dedicated exclusively to the interests of the allied trades.

24000 The NPTA Alliance
330 North Wabash Avenue
Suite 200E
Chicago, IL 60611

312-321-4092
800-355-6782; *Fax:* 312-673-6736;
www.gonpta.com
Social Media: Twitter, LinkedIn, Youtube

Kevin Gammonley, CEO
Hilton Maze, Chairman
Bayard Tynes, 1st Vice Chair
Tom Wernoch, Second Vice Chair
Don Clampitt, Treasurer

Wholesale distributors of printing and industrial paper.
2000 Members
Founded in: 1903

24001 United Producers Formulators & Distributors Association
PO Box 55
Roswell, GA 30077

770-552-8072; *Fax:* 770-417-1419
Teichler@neogen.com; www.upfda.com
Social Media: Facebook, Twitter

Tom Eichler, President
Karen Furgiuele, Vice President
Cisse Spragins, Secretary & Treasurer
Valerie Jessee, Executive Director
Tommy Reeves, Immediate Past President

Members are firms which are directly involved in formulating and distributing products or equipment to the pest control industry.

24002 Water & Sewer Distributors of America
100 North 20th Street
Suite 400
Philadelphia, PA 19103-1443

215-320-3882; *Fax:* 215-564-2175
wasda@fernley.com; www.wasda.com
Social Media: Facebook, Twitter, LinkedIn, YouTube

Kevin A. Murphy, President
Richard Campbell, President-Elect
Bill Driskill, Secretary & Treasurer
Edward Nugent, Past President

WASDA's mission is to promote the waterworks/wastewater products distribution industry, and to further improve the image and professionalism of WASDA and its member companies.
100+ Members
Founded in: 1979

24003 Wholesale Florists and Florist Suppliers of America
105 Eastern Avenue
Suite 104
Annapolis, MD 21403-3300

410-940-6580
888-289-3372; *Fax:* 410-263-1659

info@wffsa.org; www.wffsa.org
Social Media: Facebook, Twitter, LinkedIn

Patricia A Lilly, EVP
Joseph Thompson, General Manager
Amy Luckado, Membership Director
Kristin Thompson, Comm. & Conference Director
Lin Guba, Conference Manager

To provide networking and business opportunities to wholesale distributors and floral suppliers.
1.3M+ Members
Founded in: 1926

24004 Wine/Spirits Wholesalers of America
805 15th Street NW
Suite 430
Washington, DC 20005

202-371-9792; *Fax:* 202-789-2405
info@wswa.org; www.wswa.org
Social Media: Facebook, Twitter, LinkedIn, YouTube, RSS

Craig Wolf, President/CEO
Lisa Bockelman, Executive Assistant
Jim Rowland, SVP, Govt. Affairs
Danwson Hobbs, VP, State Affairs
Reilly O'Connor, VP, Govt. Affairs

Two hundred booths for suppliers of alcoholic beverages from around the world.
350+ Members
Founded in: 1943

Newsletters

24005 News & Views
Bearing Specialists Association
800 Roosevelt Road
Building C, Suite 312
Glen Ellyn, IL 60137

630-858-3838; *Fax:* 630-790-3095
info@bsahome.org; www.bsahome.org
Social Media: LinkedIn

Linda Miller, President
Richard W Church, Executive Director
Jerilyn J Church, Executive Secretary

Monthly newlsetter of BSA, the forum to enhance networking and knowledge sharing to promote the sale of bearings through authorized distributors. Available to members only.
100 Members
Frequency: E-Newlsetter for Members
Circulation: 400
Founded in: 1966

24006 AMD Insider
10047 Robert Trent Jones Parkway
New Port Richey, FL 34655-4649
727-372-3665
800-786-7274; *Fax:* 727-372-2879;
www.amdweb.com

Rosalie Leone, Chief Executive Officer
Terry Rodimer, Operations and Assistant to the CEO
Jeff Burton, Director of Codes & Standards
Miguel Rivera-Sanchez, Director of Education
William G Simon, Graphics Coordinator

The Association of Millwork Distributors online newsletter providing information for and about the millwork distribution industry.
Frequency: Monthly

24007 APSP SmartBrief
Association of Pool & Spa Professionals
2111 Eisenhower Avenue
Alexandria, VA 22314

703-838-0083; *Fax:* 703-549-0493
memberservices@apsp.org; www.apsp.org

Bill Weber, Chief Executive Officer
Terry Brown, Chairman of the Board
Kathleen Carlson, Secretary & Treasurer

APSP SmartBrief is a free weekly e-mail news service available to both APSP members and nonmembers. Each week subscribers are informed of the week's most important news stories for the pool, spa, and hot tub industry.
Frequency: Weekly
Founded in: 1956

24008 Creative Marketing Newsletter
Association of Retail Marketing Services
10 DRS james parker BLVD
suite 103
Red Bank, NJ 07701-2003
732-842-5070; *Fax:* 732-219-1938;
www.goarms.com

Gerri Hopkins, Executive Director
Lisa McCauley, Administrative Director

Retail promotion marketing newsletter for supermarkets, convenience stores, drug chains and suppliers of retail promotions.
Frequency: Quarterly
Founded in: 1957
Printed in 3 colors on matte stock

24009 Cutting Edge
Outdoor Power Equipment Aftermarket
341 South Patrick Street
Suite 1101
Alexandria, VA 22314

703-549-7608; *Fax:* 703-549-7609;
www.opeaa.org
Katherine Inslie, President
Susan Dove, Editor

Businessmen dedicated to promoting the use of aftermarket parts in outdoor power equipment, as well as trade in the industry.
Cost: $25.00
Frequency: Quarterly
Founded in: 1986

24010 Door & Hardware Industry Watch
Door & Hardware Institute
14150 Newbrook Drive
Chantilly, VA 20151

703-222-2010; *Fax:* 703-222-2410;
www.dhi.org

Jerry Heppes, Chief Executive Officer
Chuck Molina, Chief Technology Officer
Scott Sabatini, President

Electronic newsletter with the latest industry news and trends.
Frequency: 2 Times/Month
Founded in: 1952

24011 Emerging Business
Master Security Company
PO Box 6661
Roanoke, VA 24017-0661

Fax: 540-982-8407

Debra Napier, Publisher

Provides summary on articles of interest to small business owners, consultants corner, highlights services available pertaining to alternative financing of growing businesses.
6 Pages
Frequency: Quarterly

24012 FMI Daily Lead
Food Marketing Institute
2345 Crystal Drive
Suite 800
Arlington, VA 22202

202-452-8444; *Fax:* 202-425-4519;
www.fmi.org
Social Media: Facebook, Twitter, LinkedIn

Leslie Sarasin, President; Chief Executive Officer
Pat Shinko, Director
Paul Ryan, Executive Director

Newsletter that provides a daily briefing on top stories in food retailing and wholesaling.
1500 Members
Frequency: Daily
Founded in: 1892

24013 ISD Insider
International Sealing Distribution Association
105 Eastern Avenue
Suite 104
Annapolis, MD 21403

410-940-6344; *Fax:* 410-263-1659
info@isd.org; www.isd.org

Larry Goode, President
Debbie Mitchess, Executive Director
Joseph Thompson, Associate Director
Marty Lostrom, Conference Manager
Kristin B Thompson, Director of Communications

The association's newsletter is devoted to topics affecting business, training, and technology within the industry, with feature articles from industry experts.
Frequency: Quarterly

24014 Insider
MacLean Hunter
4 Stamford Forum
Stamford, CT 06901-3253

Fax: 203-325-8423

Vanessa Grey, Publisher
Adrienne Toth, Editor

A shopping center industry newsweekly. Each issue contains critical information concerning retailer news, new development items, agent announcements and new tenant listings.
Cost: $250.00
6 Pages
Frequency: Monthly

24015 M&E Appraiser
American Society of Appraisers
555 Herndon Pkwy
Suite 125
Herndon, VA 20170-5250

703-478-2228
800-272-8258; *Fax:* 703-742-8471;
www.appraisers.org

Laurie Saunders, Executive VP
Jackie Montalvo, Editor
J Michael Clarkson, Publisher

Machinery and equipment appraisal information. Accepts advertising.
Cost: $45.00
48 Pages
Frequency: Quarterly
Founded in: 1936

24016 MDNA News
Machinery Dealers National Association
315 S Patrick Street
Alexandria, VA 22314

703-836-9300
800-872-7807; *Fax:* 703-836-9303
office@mdna.org; www.mdna.org

Michael F Feinstein, President
Paul Lashin, First Vice President
Ron Shuster, Second Vice President
Kim Khoury, Treasurer

This newsletter is a valuable source of information about MDNA events and programs, industry news, updates on chapter activities, government programs, and auctions.
Frequency: 6x/Year
Founded in: 1941

24017 MHEDA Connection
Material Handling Equipment Distributors Assoc
201 US Highway 45
Vernon Hills, IL 60061-2398
857-680-3500; *Fax:* 847-362-6989
connect@mheda.org; www.mheda.org
Duncan Murphy, President
Liz Richards, Executive Vice President
Kathy Cotter, Marketing Director
Natalie Cobb, Networking & Communications
The MHEDA Connection is a semi-monthly newsletter distributed to members and its associates on the 1st and the 15th of the month.
Frequency: Semi-Monthly
Founded in: 1954

24018 NACD News Brief
National Association of Chemical Distributors
1555 Wilson Boulevard
Suite 700
Arlington, VA 22209
703-527-6223; *Fax:* 703-527-7747
nacdpublicaffairs@nacd.com; www.nacd.com
Bruce Schechinger, Chairman, Chief Executive Officer
Andrew K Skipp, Vice Chairman
Roger T Harris, Treasurer
Jean-Pierre Baizan, Director at Large
The NACD News Brief is a biweekly e-mail newsletter outlining the key legislative and regulatory actions affecting NACD members and reporting on other key industry activity.
250 Members
Frequency: Bi-Weekly
Founded in: 1971

24019 NAW Report
National Association of Wholesalers & Distributors
1325 G Street NW
Suite 1000
Washington, DC 20005-3100
202-872-0885; *Fax:* 202-785-0586
naw@naw.org; www.naw.org
Peter L Cook, Executive Director
Dirk VanDongen, Contact
Information on regulation, industry research and programs for distributors and wholesalers.

24020 NBMDA Economic Outlook Report
N.A. Building Material Distribution Association
401 N. Michigan Avenue
Chicago, IL 60611
312-321-6845
888-747-7862; *Fax:* 312-644-0310
info@nbmda.org; www.nbmda.org
Social Media: Facebook, Twitter, LinkedIn
Duane Lambrecht, President
Bill Delaney, President-Elect
Brian Schell, Vice President
Mark Kasper, Treasurer
This report correlates macroeconomic data to specific product categories directly related to the building material industry
Frequency: Quarterly
Founded in: 1952

24021 NSPI News
National Spa and Pool Institute
2111 Eisenhower Ave
Suite 500
Alexandria, VA 22314-4679
703-838-0083
800-323-3996; *Fax:* 703-549-0493
MemberServices@TheAPSP.org; www.theapsp.org
Bill Weber, President
Jack Cregol, CEO

24022 National Wholesaler Association
251 W Renner Road
#102
Richardson, TX 75080-1318
Fax: 972-470-0134
Don Akerman, Publisher
Offers products, new or old, marketing, distribution expertise, customer analysis, positioning, advertising, promotion planning. Accepts advertising.
Frequency: Quarterly

24023 News & Views
Bearing Specialists Association
800 Roosevelt Road
Building C, Suite 312
Glen Ellyn, IL 60137
630-858-3838; *Fax:* 630-790-3095
info@bsahome.org; www.bsahome.org
Social Media: LinkedIn
Linda Miller, President
Richard W Church, Executive Director
Jerilyn J Church, Executive Secretary
Monthly newsletter of BSA, the forum to enhance networking and knowledge sharing to promote the sale of bearings through authorized distributors. Available to members only.
100 Members
Frequency: E-Newsletter for Members
Circulation: 400
Founded in: 1966

24024 North American Wholesale Lumber Association Bulletin
North American Wholesale Lumber Association
3601 Algonquin Rd
Suite 400
Rolling Meadows, IL 60008-3181
847-870-7470
800-527-8258; *Fax:* 847-870-0201
info@nawla.org; www.nawla.org
Nicholas Kent, President
Stacey Woldt, Meetings Manager
Newsletter published by North American Wholesale Lumber Association.
Frequency: Monthly
Founded in: 1892

24025 Unlocked
Security Hardware Distributors Association
105 Eastern Avenue
Suite 104
Annapolis, MD 21403
410-940-6346; *Fax:* 410-263-1659
info@shda.org; www.shda.org
Steve Dyson, President
Karen Hoffman, Vice President
Peter Berg, Treasurer
Paul Justen, Immediate Past President
The SHDA newsletter, Unlocked, provides members with the latest news about the association and its educational events and programs as well as trends and news about security hardware distribution.
Frequency: Monthly

24026 Weekly Insights
Global Market Development Center
1275 Lake Plaza Drive
Colorado Springs, CO 80906-3583
719-576-4260; *Fax:* 719-576-2661
info@gmdc.org; www.gmdc.com
David T McConnell Jr, President, Chief Executive Officer
Mark Mechelse, Director of Industry Insights
Keith Wypyszynski, VP Business Development
Mike Winterbottom, VP Information Technology, CTO
Weekly Insights addresses important General Merchandise topics, important Health Beauty Wellness topics and news from GMDC.
Frequency: Weekly
Founded in: 1970

24027 Winning in Washington-NAW Annual Report
National Association of Wholesalers & Distributors
1725 K St Nw
Washington, DC 20006-1401
202-349-7300; *Fax:* 202-331-7442;
www.nawc.org
Peter L Cook, Executive Director
Activities of the National Association of Wholesalers and Distributors.

Magazines & Journals

24028 AFI
AFI Communications
2455 E Sunrise Boulevard
Suite 916
Fort Lauderdale, FL 33304-3112
Fax: 954-561-4129
Andrew Molchan, President
Bob Lesmeister, Managing Editor
Edited for professional firearm retailers. Editorial emphasis is on new products, new industry and new sales programs for distributors and retailers. Also covers management level trends for manufacturers and wholesalers. Other features include New Products, Archery, Andy's Industry Insights and more.
Circulation: 23,930

24029 AQ Magazine
Association of Pool & Spa Professionals
2111 Eisenhower Avenue
Alexandria, VA 22314
703-838-0083; *Fax:* 703-549-0493
memberservices@apsp.org; www.apsp.org
Bill Weber, Chief Executive Officer
Terry Brown, Chairman of the Board
Kathleen Carlson, Secretary & Treasurer
This full-color magazine is written and edited by industry experts with a keen awareness of the issues on the minds of professionals.
Frequency: Quarterly
Founded in: 1956

24030 ASA Materials Market Digest
American Supply Association
1200 N. Arlington Heights Rd
Suite 150
Chicago, IL 60654
312-464-0090; *Fax:* 312-464-0091
info@asa.net; www.asa.net
Jeff New, Chairman of the Board
Joe Poehling, President
Frank Nisonger, President-Elect
Robert Christiansen, Vice President
Available monthly via e-mail to all members of ASA, the ASA Materials Market Digest is de-

signed to keep readers informed of important trends and recent changes in the industry.
Frequency: Monthly
Founded in: 1969

24031 **AVEM Resource Guide**
Association of Vacuum Equipment Manufacturers
201 Park Washington Court
Falls Church, VA 22046-4527
703-538-3543; *Fax:* 703-241-5603
aveminfo@avem.org; www.avem.org
Dawn M. Shiley, Executive Director
Buyers guide offering products and services that are offered by AVEM member companies. Items range from systems, pumps, instrumentation, hardware and deposition components.
49 Members
Frequency: Yearly
Founded in: 1969

24032 **American Wholesale Marketers Association**
Ameican Wholesale Marketers Association
2750 Prosperity Ave
Suite 530
Fairfax, VA 22031-4338
703-208-3358
800-482-2962; *Fax:* 703-573-5738
robertp@awmanet.org; www.cdaweb.net
Scott Ramminger, President
Traci Carneal, Editor-in-Chief
Joan Fay, Associate Publisher
Information on candy, chewing gum, tobacco, HBC, general merchandise, snack foods and related items.
Printed in 4 colors on glossy stock

24033 **Beer Perspectives**
National Beer Wholesalers Association
1101 King Street
Suite 600
Alexandria, VA 22314-2965
703-683-4300; *Fax:* 703-683-8965
info@nbwa.org; www.nbwa.org
Social Media: Facebook, Twitter
Craig A Purser, President & CEO
Michael Johnson, EVP/Chief Advisory Officer
Rebecca Spicer, VP Public Affairs/Chief
Paul Pisano, SVP Industry Affairs & Gen. Counsel
Trade association for beer wholesalers. Provides government and public affairs outreach as well as education and training for its wholesaler members.
2200 Pages
Founded in: 1938

24034 **Chemical Distributor**
National Association of Chemical Distributors
1555 Wilson Boulevard
Suite 700
Arlington, VA 22209
703-527-6223; *Fax:* 703-527-7747
nacdpublicaffairs@nacd.com; www.nacd.com
Social Media: Facebook, Twitter, LinkedIn, YouTube
Bruce Schechinger, Chairman, Chief Executive Officer
Andrew K Skipp, Vice Chairman
Roger T Harris, Treasurer
Jean-Pierre Baizan, Director at Large
The industry's magazine that is published nine times a year and highlights members' news, Association and industry activity, and provides business information useful to chemical distributors.
250 Members
Frequency: 9x/Year
Founded in: 1971

24035 **Cleaner Times**
Cleaning Equipment Trade Association
1000 Nix Road
Little Rock, AR 72211-3235
704-635-7362
800-525-7038; *Fax:* 501-280-9233;
www.cleanertimes.com
Social Media: Facebook, Twitter, LinkedIn
Charlene Yarbrough, Publisher
Jim McMurry, Editor
Chris Ragan, Art Director
Chuck Prieur, Advertising Sales
Magazine published by the Cleaning Equipment Trade Association for members.
Frequency: Monthly

24036 **Distributor's Link**
4297 Corporate Sq
Naples, FL 34104-4754
239-643-2713
800-356-1639; *Fax:* 239-643-5220
leojcoar@linkmagazine.com;
www.linkmagazine.com
Maryann Marzocchi, President
Tracey Lumia, Advertising Sales
Michael T Wrenn, Marketing Manager
Information aimed at the fastener distributors nationwide.
Cost: $45.00
300 Pages
Frequency: Quarterly
Circulation: 50000
Founded in: 1975

24037 **Door & Hardware Magazine**
Door & Hardware Institute
14150 Newbrook Drive
Chantilly, VA 20151
703-222-2010; *Fax:* 703-222-2410;
www.dhi.org
Social Media: Facebook, Twitter, LinkedIn
Jerry Heppes, Chief Executive Officer
Chuck Molina, Chief Technology Officer
Scott Sabatini, President
The Door & Hardware magazine offers information and articles from the industry's only publication dedicated solely to the architectural openings industry.
Frequency: Monthly

24038 **Employment Guide**
Bureau of National Affairs
1801 S Bell St
Arlington, VA 22202-4501
703-341-3000
800-372-1033; *Fax:* 800-253-0332
customercare@bna.com; www.bnabooks.com
Social Media: Facebook, Twitter, LinkedIn
Paul N Wojcik, CEO
An easy-to-read, practical reference guide to a broad range of employment topics, designed for the small to medium sized organization.
Cost: $745.00
Founded in: 1929

24039 **Essentials Magazine**
National School Supply & Equipment Association
8380 Colesville Road
Suite 250
Silver Spring, MD 20910
301-495-0240
800-395-5550; *Fax:* 301-495-3330
essentialsmagazine.com.au
Social Media: Facebook, Twitter, LinkedIn
Tim Holt, President & Chief Executive Officer
Bill Duffy, VP of Operations & Meetings
DeShuna Spencer, Director of Publications
Adrienne Watts Dayton, VP Marketing & Communications
Essentials magazine targets all facets of the educational industry from contemporary, bite-sized studies and statistics, to timely feature articles, as well as NSSEA member interviews, product press releases, and business updates.
Frequency: Monthly
Founded in: 1916

24040 **GAWDA Edge**
Gases and Welding Distributors Association
100 North 20th Street
4th Floor
Philadelphia, PA 19103
215-564-3484; *Fax:* 215-963-9785
gawda@gawda.org; www.gawda.org
Kent Van Amburg, Executive Director
Malvenia Avery, Associate Director
Tawnee Shuey, Meeting Manager
Kate Marlys, Director
Provides relevant news and technology information.
775 Members
Frequency: Quarterly
Founded in: 1945

24041 **Insulation Outlook**
National Insulation Association
12100 Sunset Hills Road
Suite 330
Reston, VA 20190
703-464-6244; *Fax:* 703-464-5896;
www.insulation.org
Michele M Jones, Executive Vice President/CEO
Larry Nelles, President
Glenn Frye, President-Elect
Alec Rexroat, Secretary/Treasurer
Insulation Outlook is the only international publication devoted exclusively to industrial and commercial insulation applications, products, and materials.
Cost: $65.00
Frequency: Monthly
Founded in: 1953

24042 **International Gaming and Wagering Business**
BNP Media
PO Box 1080
Skokie, IL 60076-9785
847-763-9534; *Fax:* 847-763-9538
igwb@halldata.com; www.igwb.com
James Rutherford, Editor
Lynn Davidson, Marketing
Tammie Gizicki, Director
Focuses on business strategy, legislative information, food service and promotional concerns.
Frequency: Monthly
Circulation: 25000

24043 **Licensing Book**
Adventure Publishing Group
1107 Broadway
Suite 1204
New York, NY 10010-1512
212-575-4510; *Fax:* 212-575-4521;
www.licensingbook.com
Judy Basis, Publisher
Mathew C Scheiner, Editor-in-Chief
Owen Shorts, Owner
Licensing in successful retailing, licensed product merchandising in various aspects.
Cost: $48.00
40 Pages
Frequency: Monthly
Founded in: 1983

24044 **Licensing International**
WFC
3000 Hadley Rd
South Plainfiel, NJ 07080-1183

908-668-4747; *Fax:* 732-769-1711
info@wfcinc.com; www.wfcinc.com

Theodore Pytlar, VP
Kimberly Calabrese, Production Manager
Business merchandising magazine serving the licensing industry at all levels. Publishes whole foods magazine.
Cost: $70.00
64 Pages
Frequency: Monthly
Circulation: 14,933

24045 **MHEDA Journal**
Material Handling Equipment Distributors Assoc
201 US Highway 45
Vernon Hills, IL 60061-2398

857-680-3500; *Fax:* 847-362-6989
connect@mheda.org;
www.themhedajournal.org
Social Media: Facebook, Twitter, LinkedIn

Duncan Murphy, President
Liz Richards, Executive Vice President
Kathy Cotter, Marketing Director
Natalie Cobb, Networking & Communications
The MHEDA journal is the official magazine of the association.
Frequency: Quarterly
Founded in: 1954

24046 **Material Handling Wholesaler**
Specialty Publications International
801 Bluff Street
PO Box 725
Dubuque, IA 52004-725

563-557-4495
877-638-6190; *Fax:* 563-557-4499
circulation@mhwmag.com;
www.mhwmag.com

Dean Millius, General Manager
Cathy Murphy, Editor
Sharon Dague, Account Executive
Cathy Murphy, Contributing Editor
Published for used and new material handling equipment dealers, parts suppliers, manufacturers reps, repair shops, and brokers includes articles on issues, conventions, products and people that impact the industry.
Cost: $31.00
Frequency: Monthly
Circulation: 27000
Founded in: 1979
Printed in 4 colors on newsprint stock

24047 **NSPI Business Owners Journal**
National Spa and Pool Institute
2111 Eisenhower Ave
Suite 500
Alexandria, VA 22314-4679

703-838-0083
800-323-3996; *Fax:* 703-549-0493;
www.nspi.org

Bill Weber, President
A resource service offered by the national spa and pool inst. published four times a year. Contains concise, pertinent and useful information of critical importance to business owners throughout the year, this journal delivers information that is easily applied to a business, including more than 100 action alerts and ideas, and 25 to 30 how-to articles, advisories and reports. Covers such topics as ways to cash flows; ways to save and defer taxes; how to sell and buy a business.
Founded in: 1956

24048 **New Equipment Digest**
Penton Media
1300 E 9th St
Suite 316
Cleveland, OH 44114-1503

216-696-7000; *Fax:* 216-696-6662
information@penton.com; www.penton.com
Jane Cooper, Marketing
Dave Madonia, Associate Publisher/eMedia
Robert F King, Editor
Garnetta Russell, Ad Services Manager
Bobbie Macy, Circulation Manager
Serves the general industrial field which includes manufacturing, processing, engineering services, construction, transportation, mining, public utilities, wholesale distributors, educational services, libraries and governmental establishments.
Frequency: Monthly
Circulation: 206164
Founded in: 1936

24049 **Paper & Packaging**
NPTA Alliance
401 N Michigan Avenue
Suite 2200
Chicago, IL 60611

312-321-4092
800-355-6782; *Fax:* 312-673-6736
npta@gonpta.com; www.gonpta.com

Dennis Coyle, Associate Publisher/Editor
Covers association news, industry news, industry reports, industry events, new products, personnel updates and business articles for management and sales representatives and much more.
Cost: $120.00
Frequency: Quarterly
Circulation: 6000

24050 **Plumbing Engineer**
TMB Publishing
1838 Techny Ct
Northbrook, IL 60062-5474

847-564-1127; *Fax:* 847-564-1264
tmbpubs@earthlink.net;
www.tmbpublishing.com

Tom M Brown, President
Cate Brown, Production Manager
Over 400 plumbing products from approximately 250 manufacturers.
Frequency: Monthly
Circulation: 26104
ISSN: 0192-171X
Founded in: 1973
Printed in 4 colors

24051 **Supply House Times**
Reed Business Information
1050 IL Route 83
Suite 200
Bensenville, IL 60106

630-616-0200
800-323-4958; *Fax:* 630-288-8686;
www.supplyht.com

Patricia Lenius, Managing Editor
Scott Franz, Publisher
Kevin Hackney, Marketing Coordinator
Ashley Anderson, Associate Editor
George Zebrowski, Group Publisher
For plumbing, heating, air conditioning and piping wholesalers
Cost: $92.00
62 Pages
Frequency: Monthly
Founded in: 1958
Printed in 4 colors on glossy stock

24052 **TED Magazine**
National Association of Electrical Distributors
1166 Avenue of the Americas
St. Louis, NY 10036

212-204-4200
888-791-2512; *Fax:* 314-991-3060
customerservice@naed.org; www.tedmag.com

Tom Naber, President & Chief Executive Officer
Michelle McNamara, Vice President
Becky Burgess, Meetings & Conferences Director
TED magazine (The Electrical Distributor) is NAED's premier trade publication. With the latest industry news as well as articles and research ranging from sales to voice-data-video, TED magazine is necessary reading for all electrical distributors.
Cost: $40.00
Frequency: Monthly
Founded in: 1908

24053 **Welding & Gases Today**
Gases and Welding Distributors Association
8669 Doral Blvd
Suite 130
Philadelphia, PA 33166

215-564-3484
877-382-6440; *Fax:* 305-442-7451
gawda@gawda.org; www.gawda.org

Kent Van Amburg, Executive Director
Malvenia Avery, Associate Director
Tawnee Shuey, Meeting Manager
Kate Marlys
The official journal of the Gases and Welding Distributors Association.
775 Members
Frequency: Quarterly
Founded in: 1945

Trade Shows

24054 **AED Summit**
600 22nd~Street
Suite 220
Oak Brook, IL 60523

630-574-0650
800-388-0650; *Fax:* 630-574-0132
info@aednet.org; www.aednet.org
Social Media: Facebook, Twitter, LinkedIn

Toby Mack, President & CEO
Bob Henderson, Executive Vice President & COO
Dave Gordon, Publisher/Vice President of Sales
Kim Phelan, Executive Editor
The AED Summit provides a pure networking opportunity with both dealers and their manufacturer partners. It also offers high quality, high class, professional education content for executives and managers.
700 Members
Frequency: Annual

24055 **ASCDI Winter Conference**
Association of Service and Computer Dealers Int'l
131 NW First Avenue
Delray Beach, FL 33444

561-266-9016; *Fax:* 561-266-9017;
www.ascdi.com

Rob Neumeyer, Director
Bob Boyle, Counsel
Jerry Roberts, Chairman Emeritus
Arthur P Freierman, Treasurer
The ASCDI conferences provide a great forum for networking with others in the industry, meeting old friends, and making new contacts. The winter conference offers an opportunity to learn

about the latest technology trends, meet with leading vendors, and gain a competitive edge in the IT market. The conference is conducted by following Green Meeting Practices.
Founded in: 1981

24056 AVDA Annual Conference
2105 Laurel Bush Road
Suite 200
Bel Air, MD 21015
443-640-1040; *Fax:* 443-640-1086;
www.avda.net
Social Media: Facebook, Twitter, LinkedIn, YouTube
George Henriques, Chairman
Mary Pat Thompson, President
Ben Coe, President-Elect
The AVDA annual conference is a three-day program of information and educational sessions featuring industry and outside speakers on a variety of timely business and industry issues and topics.
Frequency: Annual
Founded in: 1976

24057 AWFS Fair
Association of Woodworking & Furnishings Suppliers
500 Citadel Drive
Suite 200
Commerce, CA 90040
323-838-9440
800-946-2937; *Fax:* 323-838-9443
info@awfs.org; www.awfs.org
Social Media: Facebook, Twitter, LinkedIn, YouTube
Joan Kemp, President
Jeff Oliverson, Vice President
Wade Gregory, Secretary/Treasurer
Skip Hem, Immediate Past President
The AWFS Fair is the largest industry show in the United States.
Frequency: Biennial

24058 AWMA Real Deal Expo
American Wholesale Marketers Association
2750 Prosperity Avenue
Suite 530
Fairfax, VA 22031
703-208-3358
800-482-2962; *Fax:* 703-573-5738
info@awmanet.org; www.realdealexpo.com
Scott Ramminger, President/CEO
Robert Pignato, VP Marketing/Industry Affairs
Annual show of 4500 manufacturers and suppliers of confectionery, tobacco, snack foods, juice, novelties and technology and allies to the industry.
Frequency: March

24059 American Nursery & Landscape Association Convention
American Nursery & Landscape Association
1000 Vermont Avenue NW
Suite 300
Washington, DC 20005-3922
202-789-2900; *Fax:* 202-789-1893;
www.anla.org
Peter Orum, President
Robert J Dolibois, Executive Director
Serves firms who grow, sell or use plants. ANLA advocates the industry's interests before government and provides its members with unique business knowledge essential to long-term growth and profitability.
Frequency: July

24060 Annual Business Leadership Summit
Fluid Power Distributors Association
105 Eastern Avenue
Suite 104
Annapolis, MD 21403
410-940-6347; *Fax:* 410-263-1659
info@fpda.org; www.fpda.org
Social Media: Facebook, Twitter, LinkedIn, YouTube
Richard Neels, President & Chairman of the Board
Steve Schwasnick, President-Elect
Bill Gillies, Vice President - Membership
Hal Kemp, Convention Chair
Mike Hamzey Jr, VP of Finance & Treasurer
This conference is held each spring and is designed especially for industry decision-makers and opinion-leaders, and is focused on business opportunities, economic and industry trends, leadership development and channel efficiencies.
300+ Members
Frequency: Annual
Founded in: 1974

24061 Atlantic City Pool & Spa Show
Association of Pool & Spa Professionals
6B South Gold Drive
Hamilton, NJ 08691
609-689-9111; *Fax:* 703-549-0493
memberservices@apsp.org;
www.nespapool.org
Bill Weber, Chief Executive Officer
Terry Brown, Chairman of the Board
Kathleen Carlson, Secretary & Treasurer
The Atlantic City show is one of the industry's largest, offering a large trade show and business and technical seminars.
10000 Attendees
Frequency: Annual

24062 BSA Convention
Bearing Specialists Association
800 Roosevelt Road
Building C, Suite 312
Glen Ellyn, IL 60137
630-858-3838; *Fax:* 630-790-3095
info@bsahome.org; www.bsahome.org
Social Media: LinkedIn
Linda Miller, President
Richard W Church, Executive Director
Jerilyn J Church, Executive Secretary
Kathy Fatz, Association Manager
Janet Arden, Publications Editor
The world's premier bearing industry event for authorized distributors of bearing products and services and the manufacturers of those products.
100 Members
Frequency: Annual
Founded in: 1966

24063 BSA Winter Meeting
Bearing Specialists Association
800 Roosevelt Road
Building C, Suite 312
Glen Ellyn, IL 60137
630-858-3838; *Fax:* 630-790-3095
info@bsahome.org; www.bsahome.org
Social Media: Facebook, Twitter, LinkedIn
Eduardo Bichara, President
Richard W Church, Executive Director
Jerilyn J Church, Executive Secretary
Kathy Fatz, Association Manager
Janet Arden, Publications Editor
BSA committees will be addressing many important issues and association projects at the Winter Meeting. Attending this meeting will help to influence the direction the industry takes over the coming years.
Frequency: Annual

24064 CBBD Annual Convention
1415 L Street
Suite 890
Sacramento, CA 95814
916-441-5402
800-952-8308; *Fax:* 916-441-0713
assn@cbbd.com; www.cbbd.com
Social Media: Facebook, Twitter, LinkedIn
Victoria G Horton, President
Becky Stolberg, Vice President
Rhonda Stevenson, Marketing & Public Affairs Director
The California Beer and Beverage Distributors host this annual convention for professionals in the industry.
100+ Members
Frequency: Annual

24065 CTDA Management Conference
Ceramic Tile Distributors Association
800 Roosevelt Road
Building C, Suite 312
Glen Ellyn, IL 60137
630-545-9415
800-938-2838; *Fax:* 630-790-3095
info@ctdahome.org; www.ctdahome.org
Ryan Calkins, President
Frank Donahue, VP
Barbara Vasquez, Treasurer
Bill Ives, Legal Counsel
Rick Church, Executive Director
CTDA Management Conference is host to the biggest industry leaders and features educational sessions and exhibits
450 Attendees
Frequency: Annual

24066 Distribution Management Conference & Technology Expo
Healthcare Distribution Management Association
901 North Glebe Road
Suite 1000
Arlington, VA 22203
703-787-0000; *Fax:* 703-812-5282;
www.healthcaredistribution.org
Social Media: Facebook, Twitter, LinkedIn
Paul Julian, Chairman
David S Moody, Vice Chairman
John M Gray, President & CEO
Albert~ Thomas, Director
Hundreds of healthcare industry thought leaders and supply chain visionaries gather for nearly three days full of networking, business sessions, and an exciting Technology Expo.
Frequency: Annual

24067 EMDA Industry Showcase
FEWA-AIMRA
PO Box 1347
Iowa City, IA 52244
319-354-5156; *Fax:* 319-354-5157;
www.edma.net
Social Media: Facebook, Twitter, LinkedIn
Patricia A Collins, Executive VP
Annual convention and 130 exhibits of equipment, supplies and services for independent wholesale-distributors and independent manufacturer's representatives of shortline and specialty farm equipment, light industrial tractors, lawn and garden tractors, turf care equipment, estate and park maintenance equipment.
600 Attendees
Frequency: November

24068 **Ed Expo**
National School Supply & Equipment Association
8380 Colesville Road
Suite 250
Silver Spring, MD 20910
301-495-0240
800-395-5550; *Fax:* 301-495-3330;
www.nssea.org
Social Media: Facebook, Twitter, LinkedIn
Tim Holt, President & Chief Executive Officer
Bill Duffy, VP of Operations & Meetings
DeShuna Spencer, Director of Publications
Adrienne Watts Dayton, VP Marketing & Communications
Rashad Cheeks, Circulation Manager
Ed Expo is the country's premier back-to-school buying event and is the ideal place for exhibitors to showcase their products to highly-qualified buyers in the educational products marketplace.
Frequency: Annual
Founded in: 1916

24069 **Executive Conference**
Health Industry Distributors Association
310 Montgomery Street
Alexandria, VA 22314-1516
703-549-4432; *Fax:* 703-549-6495;
www.hida.org
Matthew Rowan, President & CEO
Rochelle Hargraves, Vice President Finance & Operations
Andrew Van Ostrand, Vice President Policy & Research
Amy Michael, Senior Manager Governmental Affairs
Hundreds of distributor and manufacturer executives gather for the Executive Conference, which consists of networking, interactive education, strategic planning, and industry discussions.
Frequency: Annual
Founded in: 1902

24070 **FPDA Annual Network Symposium**
Fluid Power Distributors Association
105 Eastern Avenue
Suite 104
Annapolis, MD 21403
410-940-6347; *Fax:* 410-263-1659
info@fpda.org; www.fpda.org
Richard Neels, President & Chairman of the Board
Steve Schwasnick, President-Elect
Bill Gillies, Vice President - Membership
Hal Kemp, Convention Chair
Mike Hamzey Jr, VP of Finance & Treasurer
This meeting is designed for key management and emerging leaders, and focuses on business and product technologies & trends, industry standards & certification, the FPDA Young Executives development and supporting the needs of participants in the FPDA E-Networks program.
300+ Members
Frequency: Annual
Founded in: 1974

24071 **General Merchandise Marketing Conference**
Global Market Development Center
1275 Lake Plaza Drive
Colorado Springs, CO 80906-3583
719-576-4260; *Fax:* 719-576-2661
info@gmdc.org; www.gmdc.com
David T McConnell Jr, President/CEO
Mark Deuschle, Chief Marketing Officer
Keith Wypyszynski, VP Business Development
Mike Winterbottom, VP Information Technology/CTO
Annual conference which has Controlled Casual Conference appointments between wholesalers/retailers and the suppliers, business sessions, roundtables and workshops.
Frequency: Annual/June
Founded in: 1970

24072 **Health Beauty Wellness Marketing Conference**
Global Market Development Center
1275 Lake Plaza Drive
Colorado Springs, CO 80906-3583
719-576-4260; *Fax:* 719-576-2661
info@gmdc.org; www.gmdc.com
David T McConnell Jr, President, Chief Executive Officer
Mark Deuschle, Chief Marketing Officer
Keith Wypyszynski, VP Business Development
Mike Winterbottom, VP Information Technology, CTO
Annual conference which has Controlled Casual Conference appointments between wholesalers/retailers and the suppliers, Senior Executive Conference appointments, business sessions, roundtables and workshops.
Frequency: Annual
Founded in: 1970

24073 **IAPD Annual Convention**
International Association of Plastics Distribution
6734 W. 121st Street
Overland Park, KS 66209
913-345-1005; *Fax:* 913-345-1006
iapd@iapd.org; www.iapd.org
Susan Avery, Executive Director
Cyndy Launchbaugh, Director of Marketing
Denise Rawlings, Member Services Manager
Crystal Roberts, Sales & Advertising Manager
Wendy Schantz, Marketing & Education Manager
This three-day convention is where the best and the brightest of the plastics distribution industry come together to focus on the future of the industry.
Frequency: Annual
Founded in: 1956

24074 **ISA Product Show & Conference**
Industry Supply Association
100 North 20th Street
4th Floor
Philadelphia, PA 19103
215-320-3862
866-460-2360; *Fax:* 215-963-9785
info@isapartners.org; www.isapartners.org
Social Media: Facebook, Twitter, LinkedIn, YouTube
John Buckley, Executive Vice President
Mary Ritchie, Director, Membership Services
Ken Hutton, Managing Director
Christopher Schor, Associate Director
This is the premier event for anyone in the maintenance, repair, operations and production (MROP) industry. Any MROP distributor, manufacturer/supplier, manufacturers' representative or industry service provider is welcome to attend.
Frequency: Annual

24075 **ITPA Seasonal Meeting**
International Truck Parts Association
1720 10th Ave. South
Suite 4
Bethesda, MD 20817
202-544-3090
866-346-5692; *Fax:* 301-229-7331
info@itpa.com; www.itpa.com
Social Media: Facebook, Twitter, LinkedIn, YouTube
Andy Reichert, Chairman
Mike Adiletto, Vice Chairman
Venlo Wolfsohn, Executive Director
Meetings are held each Winter, Fall, and Spring and provide outstanding educational programs, one-on-one meetings with the industry's suppliers, and product trade show and excellent networking opportunities.
Frequency: Annual
Founded in: 1974

24076 **International Foodservice Distributors: Productivity Convention & Expo**
201 Park Washington Court
Falls Church, VA 22046-4521
703-532-9400; *Fax:* 703-538-4673;
www.ifdaonline.org
Mark Allen, President/CEO
Jonathan Eisen, Senior VP Of Government Relations
Workshops, assemblies, facility tours and an exposition are featured. Educational programming features many practitioners who sahre knowledge to be applied to various operations. Practical information for transportation, information technology, human resources and more.
Frequency: October
Founded in: 2003

24077 **International Pool & Spa Expo**
Association of Pool & Spa Professionals
2111 Eisenhower Avenue
Alexandria, VA 22314
703-838-0083; *Fax:* 703-549-0493
jcergol@nspi.org; www.poolspapatio.com
Tracy Beaulieu, Conference Manager
The International Pool & Spa Expo is a trade show for the pool, spa and backyard living industry that provides current market updates, info on cutting edge technology and trends.
15M Attendees
Frequency: Annual

24078 **Irrigation Show**
Irrigation Association
6540 Arlington Boulevard
Falls Church, VA 22042-6638
703-536-7080; *Fax:* 703-536-7019
info@irrigation.org; www.irrigation.org
Deborah M Hamlin, Executive Director
Denise Stone, Meetings Director
Kate Baumann, Membership Coordinator
Rebecca Bayless, Finance Director
Marsha Cram, MBA, Foundation & Membership Manager
The Irrigation Show is the industry's one-stop event. Discover innovations on the show floor and in technical sessions, make connections with industry experts, business partners and peers; and build expertise with targeted education and certification.
1600 Members
Founded in: 1949

24079 **MDVA Convention**
Michigan Distributors & Vendors Association
120 N Washington Square
Suite 110 B
Lansing, MI 48933
517-372-2323; *Fax:* 517-372-4404
webmaster@mdva.org; www.mdva.org
Polly Reber, President
Russ Nowak, Chairman
Larry Macfirland, Director
Annual meeting for individuals involved in the grocery and convenience products industry.
100 Members
Frequency: Annual

24080 Manufacturers Seminar
Health Industry Distributors Association
310 Montgomery Street
Alexandria, VA 22314-1516

703-549-4432; *Fax:* 703-549-6495;
www.hida.org
Social Media: Facebook, Twitter, LinkedIn

Matthew Rowan, President & CEO
Rochelle Hargraves, Vice President Finance & Operations
Andrew Van Ostrand, Vice President Policy & Research
Amy Michael, Senior Manager Governmental Affairs

The HIDA Educational Foundation Manufacturers Seminar is guaranteed to provide fresh distributor executive perspectives that will allow attendees to formulate solutions that fit their market strategy.
Frequency: Annual
Founded in: 1902

24081 Mid-America Pool & Spa Show
Association of Pool & Spa Professionals
2111 Eisenhower Avenue
Alexandria, VA 22314

703-838-0083; *Fax:* 703-549-0493
memberservices@apsp.org; www.apsp.org

Bill Weber, Chief Executive Officer
Terry Brown, Chairman of the Board
Kathleen Carlson, Secretary & Treasurer

The Mid-America show offers a large trade show and business and technical seminars.
Frequency: Annual

24082 Midwinter Executive Conference
Food Marketing Institute
2345 Crystal Drive
Suite 800
Arlington, VA 22202

202-452-8444; *Fax:* 202-425-4519;
www.fmi.org

Leslie Sarasin, President; Chief Executive Officer
Pat Shinko, Director
Paul Ryan, Executive Director

The FMI Midwinter Executive Conference is an extraordinary opportunity for networking and discussion. The event is invitation-only, and it attracts food industry leaders for an outstanding program that addresses the major challenges and opportunities ahead.
1500 Members
Frequency: Annual

24083 NACD Annual Meeting
National Association of Chemical Distributors
1555 Wilson Boulevard
Suite 700
Arlington, VA 22209

703-527-6223; *Fax:* 703-527-7747
nacdpublicaffairs@nacd.com; www.nacd.com

Bruce Schechinger, Chairman, Chief Executive Officer
Andrew K Skipp, Vice Chairman
Roger T Harris, Treasurer
Jean-Pierre Baizan, Director at Large

NACD's Annual Meeting is the premier meeting and annual expo for chemical distributor professionals. It provides an opportunity to exchange ideas with other top executives in the chemical distribution industry, attend sessions that focus on the latest products and trends affecting the industry, and visit with a variety of exhibitors at the Vendor Expo.
250 Members
Founded in: 1971

24084 NAFD Annual Convention
National Association of Flour Distributors
5450 Woodland Place
Canfield, OH 44406

330-718-6563; *Fax:* 877-573-1230
timdove51@gmail.com; www.thenafd.com
Social Media: Facebook, Twitter, LinkedIn

Ted Heim Jr, President
Erin M. Ruhl, CEO
Dominic Valente, VP

The NAFD sponsors an all-industry forum addressing strategic issues impacting the flour distribution supply chain. In addition to manufacturer and distributor decision makers, senior-level ingredient suppliers participate in the NAFD three-day meeting.
Frequency: Annual

24085 NARM Annual Convention
National Association of Recording Merchandisers
9 Eves Drive
Suite 120
Marlton, NJ 08053-3138

856-596-2221; *Fax:* 856-596-3268;
www.narm.com

Linda M Still, Director Meetings/Conventions
James Donio, President

Containing 39 booths. Featuring AFIM.
2,100 Attendees
Frequency: March

24086 NASSD Annual Meeting
National Association of Sign Supply Distributors
4525 Collins Avenue
Miami Beach
Baltimore, FL 33140

703-836-4012; *Fax:* 703-836-8353
staceyj@clemonsmgmt.com; www.nassd.org
Social Media: Facebook, Twitter, LinkedIn

Cal Clemons, Executive Director
Stacey Johnson, Association Coordinator

Held each fall, the annual meeting offers all attendees a full schedule of business and social networking activities. The meeting features distributor & manufacturer-only sessions, general speaker sessions, and roundtable discussions. A highlight of the meeting is the executive conferences which are an opportunity for distributors and manufacturers to meet one-on-one to discuss new sales and business opportunities.
Frequency: Annual

24087 NASSD Spring Management Conference
National Association of Sign Supply Distributors
4526 Collins Avenue
Miami Beach
Baltimore, FL 33140

703-836-4013; *Fax:* 703-836-8354
staceyj@clemonsmgmt.com; www.nassd.org
Social Media: Facebook, Twitter, LinkedIn

Cal Clemons, Executive Director
Stacey Johnson, Association Coordinator

Held each March, this 1-1/2 day conference features general speaker sessions and roundtable discussions. It is the perfect opportunity to get updated on the association's activities and trends in the industry.
Frequency: Annual

24088 NAUMD Convention & Expo
N.A. Association of Uniform Manufacturers & Dist.
336 West 37th Street
Suite 370
New York, NY 10018

212-736-3010; *Fax:* 212-736-3013;
www.naumd.com
Social Media: Facebook, Twitter, LinkedIn, you Tube

Richard J Lerman, President & CEO
Veronica Martin-Bennett, Manager Membership Info Services
John Chwat, Director of Government Affairs
Jeff Rundles, Director of Communications
Lois Miller, Director Expo & Advertising Sales

The NAUMD Convention & Expo provides a tremendous opportunity for attendees to expand their horizons, sales, and profits. Attendees can find new customers and suppliers for every uniform and imagewear need.
Founded in: 1933

24089 NBMDA Annual Convention
N.A. Building Material Distribution Association
401 N. Michigan Avenue
Chicago, IL 60611

312-321-6845
888-747-7862; *Fax:* 312-644-0310
info@nbmda.org; www.nbmda.org
Social Media: Facebook, Twitter, LinkedIn, you Tube

Duane Lambrecht, President
Bill Delaney, President-Elect
Brian Schell, Vice President
Mark Kasper, Treasurer

The NBMDA provides an opportunity to connect with other leaders in the Building Material Distribution industry. This annual convention is designed to be an executive-level interchange between trading partners coupled with stimulating educational opportunities.
Frequency: Annual
Founded in: 1952

24090 NBWA Annual Convention
National Beer Wholesalers Association
1101 King Street
Suite 600
Alexandria, VA 22314-8965

703-683-4300; *Fax:* 703-683-8965
info@nbwa.org; www.nbwa.org
Social Media: Facebook, Twitter

Craig A Purser, President & CEO
Michael Johnson, EVP Fed Aff/Chief Advisory Office
Rebecca Spicer, VP Public Affairs/Chief
Paul Pisano, SVP Industry Affairs & Gen. Counsel

Designed to provide valuable education programs and important networking opportunities for the beer industry. Featuring speakers and seminars on a number of topics of importance to beer distributors .
2500 Attendees
Frequency: Fall

24091 NGA Annual Convention & Supermarket Synergy Showcase
National Grocers Association
1005 North Glebe Road
Suite 250
Arlington, VA 22201-5758

703-516-0700; *Fax:* 703-516-0115;
www.nationalgrocers.org
Social Media: Facebook, Twitter, LinkedIn, you Tube

Tom Zaucha, President & Chief Executive Officer
Frank DiPasquale, Executive Vice President
Tom Wenning, Executive VP/General Counsel

Each year, attendees are presented with timely and relevant general sessions and workshops, ex-

citing special events and numerous networking opportunities to speak with other industry executives.
Frequency: Annual

24092 NIA Annual Convention
National Insulation Association
12100 Sunset Hills Road
Suite 330
Reston, VA 20190

703-464-6244; *Fax:* 703-464-5896;
www.insulation.org
Social Media: Facebook, Twitter, LinkedIn

Michele M Jones, Executive Vice President/CEO
Larry Nelles, President
Glenn Frye, President-Elect
Alec Rexroat, Secretary/Treasurer

The NIA Annual Convention is the premier gathering for the mechanical and industrial insulation industry, offering valuable and unique educational and industry sessions, networking opportunities, and entertaining evening events.
Frequency: Annual
Founded in: 1953

24093 NPTA Annual Convention
NPTA Alliance
330~N.~Wabash Ave
Suite 2000
Chicago, IL 60611

312-321-4092
800-355-6782; *Fax:* 312-673-6736
npta@gonpta.com; www.gonpta.com
Social Media: Facebook, Twitter

John F Millin, Chairman
Newell Holt, President & CEO
Thomas D O'Connor Jr, Treasurer
Anthony Macleod, Counsel

The NPTA Annual Convention is a prime opportunity to generate business leads, strengthen relationships with trading partners, develop leadership skills and more.
Frequency: Annual
Founded in: 1903
Mailing list available for rent

24094 National Frozen & Refrigerated Foods Convention
4755 Linglestown Road Suite 300
PO Box 6069
Harrisburg, PA 17112

717-657-8601; *Fax:* 717-657-9862
info@nfraweb.org; www.nfraweb.org
Social Media: Facebook, LinkedIn

H V Skip Shaw Jr, President/CEO
Jeff Rumachik, Senior VP
Marlene Barr, VP Membership

NFRA is a non-profit trade association representing all segments of the frozen and refrigerated foods industry. Headquartered in Harrisburg, PA, NFRA is the sponsor of March National Frozen Food Month, June dairy Month, and the Summer Favorites Ice Cream & Novelties promotion as well as the OctoberCool Food for Kids educational outreach program. NFRA holds the annual National Frozen & Refrigerated Foods Convention in October.
450 Members
1200 Attendees
Founded in: 1945

24095 PBA Symposium
Professional Beauty Association
15825 N 71st Street
Suite 100
Scottsdale, AZ 85254

480-281-0424
800-468-2274; *Fax:* 480-905-0708
info@probeauty.org; www.probeauty.org

Steven Sleeper, Executive Director
Marissa Porcaro, Director - Marketing
Steve Wilkerson, Chief Financial Officer
Christy Weaver, Manager - Finance & Administration

The PBA Symposium is a business education event produced for all sectors of the beauty industry.
Frequency: Annual
Founded in: 1953

24096 Paper2011
NPTA
330~N.~Wabash Ave
Suite 2000
Chicago, IL 60611

312-321-4092
800-355-6782; *Fax:* 312-673-6736
npta@gonpta.com; www.gonpta.com
Social Media: Facebook, Twitter

Greg Savage, Chairman
Kevin Gammonley, CEO
Hilton Maze, Treasurer

Held in conjunction with the American Forest & Paper Association, features timely sessions on emerging issues, corporate suites, and networking opportunities.
Frequency: March
Founded in: 1903
Mailing list available for rent

24097 Pet Exposition Trade Show
Pet Industry Distributors Association
2105 Laurel Bush Road
Suite 200
Bel Air, MC 21015

443-640-1060; *Fax:* 443-640-1031;
www.pida.com

Blaine Phillips, President
Donald Fleming, VP

Containing 500 booths and 300 exhibits.
3,000 Attendees
Frequency: March
Founded in: 1968

24098 Post Card & Souvenir Distributors Assocation Trade Show
Post Card & Souvenir Distributors Association
2105 Laurel Bush Road
Suite 200
Bel Air, MD 21015

443-640-1055; *Fax:* 443-640-1031;
www.postcardcentral.org

Maria Linton, Manager

Containing 110 booths and 80 exhibits.
175 Attendees
Frequency: September
Founded in: 1973

24099 PowerClean Trade Show and Convention
Cleaning Equipment Trade Association
PO Box 1710
Indian Trail, NC 28079

704-635-7362
800-441-0111; *Fax:* 704-635-7363;
www.ceta.org
Social Media: Facebook, Twitter, LinkedIn, you Tube

Tony Tranquill, President
Terry Murray, Senior Vice President
Aaron Auger, Vice President
Judy Bowers, Treasurer

CETA hosts the industry's premier PowerClean annual trade show and convention. PowerClean provides members with the opportunity to showcase new products, technology, and exchange ideas with industry peers, develop and present educational and certification programs, increase awareness and promotion of the industry and products and facilitate the development of unified positions when working with government agencies to set industry standards and policies.

24100 Read Deal Expo Convention
American Wholesale Marketers Association
1128 16th Street NW
Washington, DC 20036-4808

202-463-2124
800-482-2962; *Fax:* 202-467-0559
robertp@awmanet.org; www.cdaweb.net

Robert Pignato, VP Marketing/Industry Affairs

The AWMA Real Deal Expo and Convention is the country's oldest and largest show for distributors of confections, snacks and convenience products. The AWMA is the only national trade association working on behalf of the convenience products distribution market. AWMA members also include companies and individuals from across the distribution channel, retailers, brokers, manufacturers and others allied to the industry.
Frequency: February

24101 School Equipment Show
National School Supply & Equipment Association
8380 Colesville Road
Suite 250
Silver Spring, MD 20910

301-495-0240
800-395-5550; *Fax:* 301-495-3330;
www.nssea.org
Social Media: Facebook, Twitter, LinkedIn, you Tube

Jim McGarry, President & Chief Executive Officer
Bill Duffy, VP of Operations & Meetings
DeShuna Spencer, Essentials Editor
Adrienne Watts Dayton, VP Marketing & Communications

Industry trade show where attendees can source new products, learn from leading experts in the field, and network with suppliers, distributors and purchasing influencers.
Frequency: Annual
Founded in: 1916

24102 Supply Chain Conference
Food Marketing Institute
2345 Crystal Drive
Suite 800
Arlington, VA 22202

202-452-8444; *Fax:* 202-425-4519;
www.fmi.org
Social Media: Facebook, Twitter, LinkedIn

Leslie Sarasin, President; Chief Executive Officer
Pat Shinko, Director
Paul Ryan, Executive Director
Frederick J. Morganthall II~, Chair

Explores the latest trends in distribution, technology and its application, supply chain collaboration, transportation efficiencies, leadership and management skills. Informal discussion groups give attendees an opportunity to discuss ideas and challenges with their peers.
Frequency: Annual

24103 TCATA Annual Management & Educational Conference
Textile Care Allied Trades Association
271 Route 46 West
#D203
Fairfield, NJ 07004

973-244-1790; *Fax:* 973-244-4455
info@tcata.org; www.tcata.org
Social Media: Facebook, Twitter, LinkedIn

David Cotter, Chief Executive Officer
Cheryl Paglia, Manager

Trade show consisting of well-organized business programs and unique networking opportunities.
Frequency: Annual

Directories & Databases

24104 A-Z Wholesale Source Directory
Sutton Family Communications & Publishing Company
155 Sutton Lane
Fordsville, KY 42343
270-740-0870
jlsutton@apex.net; www.suttoncompliance.com
Theresa Sutton, Editor
Lee Sutton, General Manager
Print-out from database of wholesalers, manufacturers, distributors, importers and close-out houses. Database is updated daily to guarantee the most current and up-to-date sources available.
Cost: $550.00
1M Pages

24105 American Warehouse Association and Canadian Association of Warehousing
Association For Logistics Outsourcing
2800 South River Road
Suite 260
Chicago, IL 60018-6003
847-813-4699; *Fax:* 847-813-0115
email@iwla.com; www.iwla.com
Joel Hioland, President
Alex Glan, VP/CEO
Nearly 700 warehouse firms with over 2,000 locations specializing in storage, distribution, and third party logistics.

24106 American Wholesalers and Distributors Directory
Gale/Cengage Learning
10650 Toebben Drive
Independence, KY 41051
800-354-9706
800-877-4253; *Fax:* 800-487-8488
gale.galeord@cengage.com; www.gale.com
Social Media: Facebook, Twitter, LinkedIn
Patrick C Sommers, President
Discover more than 27,000 large and small wholesalers and distributors throughout the US and Puerto Rico.
Frequency: Annual
ISBN: 1-414434-21-9

24107 Complete Directory of Close-outs and Super-buys
Sutton Family Communications & Publishing Company
155 Sutton Lane
Fordsville, KY 42343
270-740-0870
jlsutton@apex.net; www.suttoncompliance.com
Theresa Sutton, Editor
Lee Sutton, General Manager
Print-out from database of wholesalers, manufacturers, distributors, importers and close-out houses. Database is updated daily to guarantee the most current and up-to-date sources available.
Cost: $67.50
100+ Pages

24108 Complete Directory of General Flea Market Merchandise
Sutton Family Communications & Publishing Company
155 Sutton Lane
Fordsville, KY 42343
270-740-0870
jlsutton@apex.net; www.suttoncompliance.com
Theresa Sutton, Editor
Lee Sutton, General Manager
Print-out from database of wholesalers, manufacturers, distributors, importers and close-out houses. Database is updated daily to guarantee the most current and up-to-date sources available.
Cost: $289.00
100+ Pages

24109 Complete Directory of High Profit Items
Sutton Family Communications & Publishing Company
155 Sutton Lane
Fordsville, KY 42343
270-740-0870
jlsutton@apex.net; www.suttoncompliance.com
Theresa Sutton, Editor
Lee Sutton, General Manager
Print-out from database of wholesalers, manufacturers, distributors, importers and close-out houses. Database is updated daily to guarantee the most current and up-to-date sources available.
Cost: $189.00
100+ Pages

24110 Complete Directory of Importers
Sutton Family Communications & Publishing Company
7025 N. Scottsdale Rd #320
Scottsdale, AR 85253
202-595-3101
888-843-0272; *Fax:* 480-245-5000
info@importgenius.com; www.importgenius.com
Theresa Sutton, Editor
Lee Sutton, General Manager
Print-out from database of wholesalers, manufacturers, distributors, importers and close-out houses. Database is updated daily to guarantee the most current and up-to-date sources available.
Cost: $109.00
100+ Pages

24111 Complete Directory of Low-Price Merchandise
Sutton Family Communications & Publishing Company
155 Sutton Lane
Fordsville, KY 42343
270-740-0870
jlsutton@apex.net; www.suttoncompliance.com
Theresa Sutton, Editor
Lee Sutton, General Manager
Print-out from database of wholesalers, manufacturers, distributors, importers and close-out houses. Database is updated daily to guarantee the most current and up-to-date sources available.
Cost: $72.20
100+ Pages

24112 Complete Directory of Promotional Products
Sutton Family Communications & Publishing Company
155 Sutton Lane
Fordsville, KY 42343
270-740-0870
jlsutton@apex.net; www.suttoncompliance.com
Theresa Sutton, Editor
Lee Sutton, General Manager
Print-out from database of wholesalers, manufacturers, distributors, importers and close-out houses. Database is updated daily to guarantee the most current and up-to-date sources available.
Cost: $139.00
100+ Pages

24113 Complete Directory of Stationery Items
Sutton Family Communications & Publishing Company
155 Sutton Lane
Fordsville, KY 42343
270-740-0870
jlsutton@apex.net; www.suttoncompliance.com
Theresa Sutton, Editor
Lee Sutton, General Manager
Print-out from database of wholesalers, manufacturers, distributors, importers and close-out houses. Database is updated daily to guarantee the most current and up-to-date sources available.
Cost: $55.20
100+ Pages

24114 Complete Directory of Tabletop Items
Sutton Family Communications & Publishing Company
155 Sutton Lane
Fordsville, KY 42343
270-740-0870
jlsutton@apex.net; www.suttoncompliance.com
Theresa Sutton, Editor
Lee Sutton, General Manager
Print-out from database of wholesalers, manufacturers, distributors, importers and close-out houses. Database is updated daily to guarantee the most current and up-to-date sources available.
Cost: $55.20
100+ Pages

24115 Complete Directory of Unusual Items & Fads
Sutton Family Communications & Publishing Company
155 Sutton Lane
Fordsville, KY 42343
270-740-0870
jlsutton@apex.net; www.suttoncompliance.com
Theresa Sutton, Editor
Lee Sutton, General Manager
Print-out from database of wholesalers, manufacturers, distributors, importers and close-out houses. Database is updated daily to guarantee the most current and up-to-date sources available.
Cost: $139.00
100+ Pages

24116 Complete Directory of Wholesale Bargains
Sutton Family Communications & Publishing Company
155 Sutton Lane
Fordsville, KY 42343

270-740-0870; www.suttoncompliance.com

Theresa Sutton, Editor
Lee Sutton, General Manager

Print-out from database of wholesalers, manufacturers, distributors, importers and close-out houses. Database is updated daily to guarantee the most current and up-to-date sources available.
Cost: $92.70
100+ Pages

24117 EMDA Membership Directory
Equipment Marketing & Distribution Associaion
PO Box 1347
Iowa City, IA 52244-1347

319-354-5156; *Fax:* 319-354-5157
pat@emda.net
ww.emda.net

Patricia A Collins, Executive VP

Annual directory of FEWA-AIMRA members, includes address, phone, fax, web, e-mail, territory covered (with map) product descriptions, key personnel, and a descriptive paragraph.
Cost: $50.00

24118 Food & Beverage Market Place
Grey House Publishing
4919 Route 22
PO Box 56
Amenia, NY 12501

518-789-8700
800-562-2139; *Fax:* 518-789-0556
gold@greyhouse.com; www.greyhouse.com
Social Media: Facebook, Twitter

Leslie Mackenzie, Publisher
Richard Gottlieb, Editor
Richard Gottlieb, President

This information packed three-volume set is the most powerful buying and marketing guide for the US food and beverage industry. Includes thousands of wholesale listings.
Cost: $595.00
2000 Pages
Frequency: Annual
ISBN: 1-592373-61-5
Founded in: 1981
Mailing list available for rent

24119 Food & Beverage Marketplace: Online Database
Grey House Publishing
4919 Route 22
PO Box 56
Amenia, NY 12501

518-789-8700
800-562-2139; *Fax:* 518-789-0556
gold@greyhouse.com
http://gold.greyhouse.com
Social Media: Facebook, Twitter

Richard Gottlieb, President
Leslie Mackenzie, Publisher
Richard Gottlieb, Editor

This complete updated Food & Beverage Market Place: Online Database is the go-to source for the food and beverage industry. Anyone involved in the food and beverage industry needs this 'industry bible' and the important contacts to develop critical research data that can make for successful business growth.
Frequency: Annual
Founded in: 1981
Mailing list available for rent

24120 Global Logistics & Supply Chain Strategies
Keller International Publishing Corporation
150 Great Neck Rd
Great Neck, NY 11021-3309

516-829-9722; *Fax:* 516-829-9306;
www.supplychainbrain.com

Jerry Keller, President
Brad Berger, Group President/Publisher
Russell Goodman, Editor-in-Chief

Serves manufacturing, wholesale/retail trade, third party logistics, freight forwarding and transportation/warehousing firms.
Cost: $55.00
96 Pages
Frequency: 11 per year
Circulation: 40M
ISSN: 1525-4887
Founded in: 1997
Printed in 4 colors on glossy stock

24121 Membership Directory/Buyer's Guide
Naylor Publications
5950 Nw 1st Pl
Gainesville, FL 32607-6018

352-332-1252
800-369-6220; *Fax:* 352-331-3525
chodges@naylor.com; www.naylor.com

Michael Moss, President

Provider of integrated communications and image-building solutions for associations.
Circulation: 1,200

24122 Outlet Project Directory
Off-Price Specialists, Value Retail News
29399 US Highway 19 N
Suite 370
Clearwater, FL 33761-2138

727-781-7557; *Fax:* 727-536-4389;
www.valueretailnews.com

Linda Humphers, Editor-In-Chief
Tom Kirwan, Senior Editor

Offers valuable information on factory outlet projects.
Cost: $225.00
200 Pages
Frequency: Semiannual

24123 Plumbing Engineer: Product Directory Issue
TMB Publishing
1838 Techny Ct
Northbrook, IL 60062-5474

847-564-1127; *Fax:* 847-564-1264;
www.tmbpublishing.com

Tom M Brown, Owner
Cate Brown, Production Manager

Over 400 plumbing products from approximately 250 manufacturers.
Frequency: Annual January
Circulation: 2,6104
ISBN: 0-192171-1 -

24124 Shippers Guide to Department & Chain Stores Nationwide
Shippers Guides
PO Box 112
Duarte, CA 91009-0112

626-357-6430; *Fax:* 248-786-1358

Profiles over 1,000 department stores and chain stores and their traffic managers in the United States.
Cost: $349.00
350 Pages
Frequency: Annual
Circulation: 2,000

24125 Who's Who
Association of Pool & Spa Professionals
2111 Eisenhower Avenue
Alexandria, VA 22314-4679

703-838-0083; *Fax:* 703-549-0493;
www.theasap.org/

Jack Cergol, Chief Staff Executive
Marianne Kiernan, Executive Secretary

Trade association for pool, spa and hot tub industry. Annual Convention for trade.
Founded in: 1956

24126 Who's Who in Beer Wholesaling Directory
National Beer Wholesalers Association
1101 King Street
Suite 600
Alexandria, VA 22314-8965

703-683-4300; *Fax:* 703-683-8965
info@nbwa.org; www.nbwa.org
Social Media: Facebook, Twitter

Craig A Purser, President & CEO
Michael Johnson, EVP Fed Aff/Chief Advisory Office
Rebecca Spicer, VP Public Affairs/Chief
Paul Pisano, SVP Industry Affairs & Gen. Counsel

A listing of more than 3,000 beer distributors and suppliers in the industry.
Cost: $50.00

24127 Wholesale Grocers
Chain Store Guide
3922 Coconut Palm Dr
Tampa, FL 33619-1389

813-627-6700
800-778-9794; *Fax:* 813-627-7094
info@csgis.com; www.csgis.com

Mike Jarvis, Publisher
Shami Choon, Manager

We have uncovered the facts on more than 1,900 grocery suppliers in the U.S. and Canada in this database. This targeted database allows you to reach food wholesalers, cooperatives and voluntary group wholesalers, non-sponsoring wholesalers, and cash and carry operators who serve grocery, convenience, discount and drug stores. You will also find information regarding company headquarters, divisions, branches, and over 11,000 key executives and buyers.
Cost: $335.00
Frequency: Annual

24128 Wholesaler
TMB Publishing
1838 Techny Ct
Northbrook, IL 60062-5474

847-564-1127; *Fax:* 847-564-1264;
www.tmbpublishing.com

Tom M Brown, Owner

Ranks 100 leading wholesalers of plumbing, heating, air conditioning, refrigeration equipment and industrial pipe, valves and fittings.
Cost: $25.00
Frequency: Annual July
Circulation: 30,000

24129 Wholesaler-Wholesaling 100 Issue
TMB Publishing
1838 Techny Ct
Northbrook, IL 60062-5474

847-564-1127; *Fax:* 847-564-1264;
www.tmbpublishing.com

Tom M Brown, Owner

Offer information on over 100 leading wholesalers of plumbing-heating equipment and supplies.
Cost: $25.00
Circulation: 25,000

Industry Web Sites

24130 http://gold.greyhouse.com
G.O.L.D Grey House OnLine Databases
Grey House Publishing's online database platform, GOLD, offers Quick Search, Keyword Search and Expert Search for most business sectors, including wholesale markets. The GOLD platform makes finding the information you need quick and easy - whether you're a novice searcher or an experienced database user. All of Grey House's directory products are available for subscription on the GOLD platform.

24131 www.aamp.com
American Association of Meat Processors
For small to medium sized meat, poultry and food businesses including: packers, processors, wholesalers, home food service businesses, retailers, deli and catering operators.

24132 www.adbi.org
Associated Beer Distributors of Illinois
The ABDI represents, maintains, and improves the interests of its members who are licensed by the State of Illinois to import and distribute beer to licensed retailers.

24133 www.aednet.org
Associated Equipment Distributors
AED is an international trade association representing companies involved in the distribution, rental and support of equipment used in construction, mining, forestry, power generation, agriculture and industrial applications.

24134 www.aird.org
Association of Ingersoll-Rand Distributors
The Association of Ingersoll-Rand Distributors (AIRD) was organized as a central resource for distributors of Ingersoll-Rand compressed air equipment. AIRD is chartered to promote improved business conditions affecting distributors of air compressors, further a better understanding between distributors and equipment suppliers, research ways to lower costs of distributing air compressors, collect and disseminate statistical information and conduct other beneficial activities.

24135 www.amdweb.com
Association of Millwork Distributors
AMD provides leadership, education, promotion, networking, and advocacy to, and for, the millwork distribution industry.

24136 www.anla.org
American Nursery & Landscape Association
The American Nursery and Landscape Association serves firms who grow, sell or use plants. ANLA advocates the industry's interests before government and provides its members with unique business knowledge essential to long-term growth and profitability.

24137 www.apda.com
Appliance Parts Distributors Association
The APDA is an association of independent businesses that aspire to provide the highest level of quality, service, support and information to its customers and suppliers in order to make its value indispendable to the parts distribution channel.

24138 www.apsp.org
Association of Pool & Spa Professionals
APSP is the world's largest international trade association for the swimming pool, spa, and hot tub industry. It works with regulatory and legislative bodies to ensure that their codes, ordinance, and legislation are written to the safest and most current standards. The association's mission is to ensure consumer safety and enhance the business success of its members.

24139 www.asa.net
American Supply Association
ASA is a not-for-profit national organization serving wholesale distributors and their suppliers in the plumbing, heating, cooling and industrial and mechanical pipe, valves and fittings industries.

24140 www.ascdi.com
Association of Service and Computer Dealers Int'l
The ASCDI is a worldwide, nonprofit organization, made up of companies who provide technology business solutions, technical suppoer, and value added services to the business community.

24141 www.avda.net
American Veterinary Distributors Association
The AVDA was established as the national trade organization for businesses engaged in the distribution of animal health products.

24142 www.awfs.org
Association of Woodworking & Furnishings Suppliers
The Association of Woodworking and Furnishing Suppliers is the largest national trade association in the U.S. representing the interestes of the broad array of companies that supply the home and commercial furnishings industry.

24143 www.awmanet.org
American Wholesale Marketers Association
An organization supporting the confectionery, tobacco and allied products industries through programs and services.

24144 www.bpsa.org
Bicycle Product Suppliers Association
BPSA is an association of suppliers of bicycles, parts, accessories and services who serve the Specialty Bicycle Retailer.

24145 www.bsahome.org
Bearing Specialists Association
BSA is the forum to enhance networking and knowledge sharing to promote the sale of bearings through authorized distributors.

24146 www.cbbd.com
California Beer & Beverage Distributors
The California Beer and Beverage Distributors is a nonprofit trade association representing over 100 beer distributors and brewer/vendor members.

24147 www.ceta.org
Cleaning Equipment Trade Association
CETA is dedicated to increasing the awareness and promotion of industry products, while at the same time recognizing the impact on preserving the environment and the opportunity to do business within it.

24148 www.ctdahome.org
Ceramic Tile Distributors Association
CTDA is an international association of distributors, manufacturers, and allied professionals of ceramic tile and related products.

24149 www.cvsn.org
Commercial Vehicle Solutions Network
The Commercial Vehicle Solutions Network (CVSN) is an association of independent parts and service aftermarket distributors serving the transportation industry.

24150 www.dhi.org
Door & Hardware Institute
The Door & Hardware Institute (DHI) is the only professional association dedicated to the Architectural Openings Industry. DHI represents the North American openings marketplace as the advocate and primary resource for information, professional development and certification.

24151 www.easa.com
Electrical Apparatus Service Association Inc
The Electrical Apparatus Service Association (EASA) is an international trade organization of over 2,100 electromechanical sales and service firms in 58 countries. EASA provides members with a means of keeping up-to-date on materials, equipment, and state-of-the-art technology.

24152 www.emda.net
Equipment Marketing & Distribution Association
Trade association dedicated to the marketing of specialized agricultural equipment, outdoor power equipment, light industrial equipment, and forestry equipment.

24153 www.fewa.org
Farm Equipment Wholesalers Association
International trade association of wholesale/distributors of agricultural equipment and related products.

24154 www.fmi.org
Food Marketing Institute
FMI conducts programs in public affairs, food safety, research, education and industry relations on behalf of its 1,500 member companies in the United States and around the world.

24155 www.fpda.org
Fluid Power Distributors Association
Membership is composed of distributors and manufacturers of hydraulic and pneumatic equipment.

24156 www.gawda.org
Gases and Welding Distributors Association
GAWDA's mission is to promote the safe operation and economic vitality of distributors of industrial gases and related welding equipment and supplies.

24157 www.gmdc.com
Global Market Development Center
GMDC is the premier non-profit global trade association dedicated to serving General Merchandise and Health Beauty retailers, wholesalers and suppliers. GMDC promotes critical connectivity to grow and expand member companies by uniting members through business building events and opportunities and enriching their thinking through education and training; consumer and business insights; and information resources.

24158 www.gmdc.org
General Merchandise Distributors Council
International trade association representing pharmacy products to the mass market retail industry.

24159 www.gonpta.com
NPTA Alliance
The NPTA Alliance (formerly the National Paper Trade Association, Inc.) is the association for the $60+ billion paper, packaging and supplies distribution industry. The mission of NPTA is to actively support the success of its members through the delivery of networking, industry data & research, education and advocacy that focuses on the health of the distribution channel.

24160 www.greyhouse.com
Grey House Publishing

Authoritative reference directories for most business sectors including wholesale service markets. Users can search the online databases with varied search criteria allowing for custom searches by product category, geographic area, sales volume, keyword, subject and more. Full Grey House catalog and online ordering also available.

24161 www.hardinet.org
Heating, Airconditioning & Refrigeration Dist.
This association is a trade organization dedicated to advancing the science of wholesale distribution in the HVACR industry.

24162 www.healthcaredistribution.org
Healthcare Distribution Management Association
The Healthcare Distribution Management Association (HDMA) is the national association representing primary, full-service heatlhcare distributors. HDMA and its members are the vital link in the healthcare system, working daily to provide value, remove costs and develop innovative solutions.

24163 www.hida.org
Health Industry Distributors Association
HIDA keeps members current on healthcare reform, government affairs, industry trends and forecasts, provider news, and sales tips.

24164 www.iapd.org
International Association of Plastics Distribution
The International Association of Plastics Distribution is an international trade association comprised of companies engaged in the distribution and manufacturing of plastics materials.

24165 www.icdaonline.com
Industrial Compressor Distributor Association
The main objetives of the ICDA are to promote for its members the highest standards of production, financial and managerial activities; to act as a vehicle for the solution of common industry problems in an effective and efficient manner; and to increase market volume and profits for its members.

24166 www.insulation.org
National Insulation Association
The National Insulation Association (NIA) is a trade association representing the mechanical and specialty insulation industry.

24167 www.irrigation.org
Irrigation Association
The Irrigation Association is the leading membership organization ffor irrigation equipment and system manufacturers, dealers, distributors, designers, consultants, contractors and end users.

24168 www.isapartners.org
Industrial Supply Association
The primary focus of the Industrial Supply Association is to improve the industrial supply channel through its mission-critical activities including: conventions and forums, gathering and dissemination of critical information, and development and implementation of channel performance initiatives.

24169 www.isd.org
International Sealing Distribution Association
The International Sealing Distribution Association (ISD) is a not-for-profit trade association formed to enhance the success of members through information, education, and interaction.

24170 www.issa.com
International Sanitary Supply Association
Manufacturers, distributors, wholesalers, representatives and publishers engaged in the manufacture and/or distribution of cleaning and maintenance products.

24171 www.itpa.com
International Truck Parts Association
The International Truck Parts Association was organized as a not-for-profit association to promote, foster, and improve relationships among sellers and buyers of trucks and truck surplus products and other parties.

24172 www.lumber.org
North American Wholesale Lumber Association
For lumber and building distributors and manufacturers.

24173 www.mdna.org
Machinery Dealers National Association
The Machinery Dealers National Association (MDNA) is an international, nonprofit trade association dedicated to the promotion of the used machinery industry.

24174 www.mdva.org
Michigan Distributors & Vendors Association
The Michigan Distributors and Vendors Association (MDVA) is a non-profit, statewide business association representing two very significant business segments in the grocery and convenience products industry.

24175 www.mheda.org
Material Handling Equipment Distributors Assoc.
The Material Handling Equipment Distributors Association is the only national association dedicated solely to improving the proficiency of the independent material handling equipment distributor.

24176 www.mic.org
Motorcycle Industry Council
The Motorcycle Industry Council (MIC) is a nonprofit, national trade association representing manufacturers and distributors of motorcycles, scooters, motorcycle/ATV parts and accessories and members of allied trades.

24177 www.msbeer.com
Mississippi Malt Beverage Association
The MMBA was established to represent and promote the beer wholesalers and beer industry within Mississippi.

24178 www.msci.org
Metal Service Center Institute (MSCI)
MSCI is the trade association that supports and represents most elements of the metals value chain, including metals producers, distributors, and processors.

24179 www.naaud.com
North American Association of Utility Distributors
NAAUD is comprised of select distributors who specialize in supplying products and supply chain services to the electric utility industry. The purpose of NAAUD is to discuss and promote the newest ideas and best concepts for the industry.

24180 www.nacd.com
National Association of Chemical Distributors
The National Association of Chemical Distributors (NACD) is an international association of chemial distributor companies that purchase and take title of chemical products from manufacturers.

24181 www.naed.org
National Association of Electrical Distributors
The main goal of the National Association of Electrical Distributors (NAED) is to establish the electrical distributor as an essential force in the electrical industry and the economy.

24182 www.nafcd.org
North American Association of Floor Covering Dist.
The North American Association of Floor Covering Distributors (NAFCD) was organized to foster trade and commerce for those having a business, financial or professional interest as wholesale distributors or manufacturers of floor coverings and allied products.

24183 www.nahsa.org
North American Horticultural Supply Association
The North American Horticultural Supply Association's mission is to strengthen and support the distribution and manufacturing of horticultural products and services.

24184 www.narm.com
National Association of Recording Merchandisers
Represents the retailers and suppliers of recorded entertainment as well as many suppliers of ancillary products.

24185 www.nassd.org
National Association of Sign Supply Distributors
NASSD is a nonprofit trade association for organizations who are engaged in full-line sign supply distribution and who manufacture or supply commercial, neon and electrical sign products.

24186 www.natd.com
N.A. Association of Telecommunications Dealers
The North American Association of Telecommunications Dealers is a nonprofit organization of companies who provide telecom products to the business community and governments around the world. The NATD gives you access to the right kind of information, resources and business leaders, and provides you with unique opportunities to help grow your business.

24187 www.nationalgrocers.org
National Grocers Association
The National Grocers Association is the national trade association representing the retail and wholesale grocers that comprise the independent sector of the food distribution industry.

24188 www.naumd.com
N.A. Association of Uniform Manufacturers & Dist.
An association dedicated to keeping the Uniforn & Imagewear Industry strong and healthy.

24189 www.nbmda.org
N.A. Building Material Distribution Association
NBMDA develops and promotes the effectiveness of distribution processes to improve member profitability and growth.

24190 www.nbwa.org
National Beer Wholesalers Association
Research and development, quality control and ingredients.

24191 **www.nesda.com**
National Electronics Service Dealers Association
Provides educational assistance in electronic training to public schools, compiles statistics, offers certification programs and apprenticeships. Functions as trade association for the electronics service industry.

24192 **www.nfraweb.org**
National Frozen & Refrigerated Foods Association
NFRA is a non profit trade association comprised of 650 member companies representing all segments of the frozen and refrigerated foods industry. NFRA has been serving the frozen food industry since 1945 and just recently in 2001 began serving the refrigerated foods industry. The mission of NFRA is to promote the sales and consumption of frozen and refrigerated foods through: education, training, research, sales planning and menu development and providing a forum for industry dialogue.

24193 **www.npes.org**
NPES Association
This association is a trade association of over 400 companies that manufacture and distribute equipment, systems, software, supplies used in printing, publishing and converting.

24194 **www.npfda.org**
National Poultry & Food Distributors Association
For poultry and food distribution and processing industries. Provides member services, cost cutting benefits and networking opportunities.

24195 **www.nssea.org**
National School Supply & Equipment Association
The National School Supply and Equipment Association (NSSEA) is the leading trade organization for the educational products marketplace. NSSEA puts the collective experience of the most successful school industry business in the world at your fingertips.

24196 **www.nybeer.org**
New York State Beer Wholesalers Association
The New York State Beer Wholesalers Association, Inc. represents and protects the legislative and regulators interests of its members in state and local government. Our primary goal is to uphold the three-tier system in order to safeguard the industry's distribution standards.

24197 **www.opeesa.com**
Outdoor Power Equipment & Engine Service Assoc.
The Outdoor Power Equipment and Engine Service Association (OPEESA) consists of more than 140 distributors and manufacturers of outdoor power equipment and air-cooled gas and diesel engines. Their mission is to assist distributors in achieving outstanding channel performance.

24198 **www.opwa.org**
Business Solutions Association
The goal of the Business Solutions Association is to provide a forum for the development of strategic and synergistic solutions to enhance the sale and distribution of business related products and services.

24199 **www.pac-west.org**
Pacific-West Fastener Association
An organization dedicated to the fastener industry.

24200 **www.pida.com**
Pet Industry Distributors Association
Represents wholesaler-distributors of pet products, providing training and education to members.

24201 **www.probeauty.org**
Professional Beauty Association
The Professional Beauty Association (PBA) is a nonprofit trade association that represents the interests of the professional beauty industry from manufacturers and distributors to salons and spas. PBA offers business tools, education, advocacy, networking and more to improve individual businesses and the industry as a whole.

24202 **www.ptda.org**
Power Transmission Distributors Association
Members are power transmission/motion control distributor throughout manufacturing firms.

24203 **www.safetycentral.org**
Safety Equipment Distributors Association
Represents wholesale-distributors of safety equipment and works to enhance and improve distribution through excellence in communications, training, education and services.

24204 **www.shda.org**
Security Hardware Distributors Association
The mission of the Security Hardware Distributors Association is to continually improve, through education and services, the proficiency of Security Distributors in order that they are the most effective and efficient conduit to the marketplace.

24205 **www.ssia.info**
Shoe Service Institute of America
Shop to shop chat room, links and listings of manufacturers and wholesalers plus shoe care tips.

24206 **www.tcata.org**
Textile Care Allied Trades Association
The Textile Care Allied Trades Association (TCATA) is an international trade association representing manufacturers and distributors of drycleaning and laundry equipment and supplies. It is the only trade association dedicated exclusively to the interests of the allied trades.

24207 **www.wasda.com**
Water & Sewer Distributors of America
WASDA's mission is to promote the waterworks/wastewater products distribution industry, and to further improve the image and professionalism of WASDA and its member companies.

A

B

C

D

E

F

G

H

I

J

K

L

M

N

O

P

Q

R

S

T

U

V

W

X

Y

Z

A

A Basic Guide to Exporting
World Trade Press, 14307
A Formula for Fueling Ad Agency New Business Through Social
American Association of Advertising Agencies, 385, 22054
A Guide to Implementing Direct Payment
NACHA: Electronic Payments Association, 2903
A Guide to Internet Resources
American Assoc for the Advancement of Science, 7820
A History of Art Therapy
American Art History, 2210
A Portrait of the US Appliance Industry
UBM Canon, 1942
A Year of Enchantment
Int'l Council on Hotel, Restaurant Institute Edu., 9887
A-Z Wholesale Source Directory
Sutton Family Communications & Publishing Company, 24104
AAA Annual Meeting
American Accounting Association, 239
AAA Bridge and Ferry Directory
American Automobile Association, 23288
AAA Newsletter
American Academy of Advertising, 386
AAA Report
Association for Accounting Administration, 92
AAAAI Annual Conference and Exhibition
American Academy Allergy, Asthma, and Immunology, 12707
AAAAI Annual Meeting
American Academy of Allergy, Asthma and, 12708
AAAI National Conference
American Association for Artificial Intelligence, 5388
AAAR Annual Conference
American Association for Aerosol Research, 7672
AAAR Annual Meeting
American Association for Aerosol Research, 7673, 21890
AAAS Annual Meeting
Renewable Natural Resources Foundation, 7674
AAB Annual Meeting and Educational Conference
American Association of Bioanalysts, 3239, 12709
AAB Bulletin
American Association of Bioanalysts, 4393, 12436
AABB News
American Association of Blood Banks, 12437
AAC Annual Conference & Exposition
Airport Consultants Council, 2618
AAC/AAAE Airport Planning, Design & Construction Symposium
Airport Consultants Council, 2619
AACAP Annual Meeting
American Academy of Child & Adolescent Psychiatry, 12710
AACCA Spirit Coaches Conference
American Association of Cheerleading Coaches, 22333
AACE Annual Meeting
AACE International, 8540, 16793
Association of Cost Engineering, 7029
AACE Directory
Assoc. for the Advancement of Cost Engineering, 8615
AACG Newsletter
American Association for Crystal Growth, 4394
AACP Annual Meeting and Seminars
American Association of Colleges of Pharmacy, 20201
AACP Institute
American Association of Colleges of Pharmacy, 20202
AACP News
American Association of Colleges of Pharmacy, 20105
AACS Annual Convention & Expo
American Association of Cosmetology Schools, 3138, 5656
AACT Technical Conference
American Association of Candy Technologists, 9889
AACT WorldFest
American Association of Community Theatre, 19415
AADA Membership Directory
Art Dealers Association of America, 2283
AADC Annual Spring Workshop
American Association of Dental Consultants, 13890
AAEA Annual Meeting
Agricultural & Applied Economics Association, 1026
American Agricultural Economics Association, 9890
AAEA Annual Meetings
American Academy of Equine Art, 8028
AAEI Annual Conference
American Association of Exporters and Importers, 19085
AAEI and FTA Western Regional Conference
AAEI/FTA, 19014
AAFA Newsletter
American Apparel & Footwear Association, 1714
AAFCO Meeting
Association of American Feed Control Officers, 1028
AAFCS Annual Conference & Exposition
American Association of Family & Consumer Sciences, 11205
AAH Research Conference
Academy of Accounting Historians, 240
AAHAM Annual Meeting
American Association of Healthcare Administrative, 8541
AAHOA Annual Convention and Trade Show
Asian American Hotel Owners Association, 13398
AAHP Institute & Display Forum
American Association of Health Plans, 12711
AAI Newsletter
American Association of Immunologists, 3211
AAID Annual Meeting
American Academy of Implant Dentistry, 12712
AAII Journal
American Association of Individual Investors, 8411
AAIW: Automotive Aftermarket Industry Week Expo
Overseas Automotive Council, 18580
AALL Spectrum
American Association of Law Libraries, 15420, 15780
AAM Annual Meeting & MuseumExpo
American Alliance of Museums, 2254, 8029
AAM Newsletter
American Agriculture Movement, 744
AAMA Executive
American Academy of Medical Administrators, 12492
AAMA News
Asian American Manufacturers Association, 14230
AAMFT Conference
American Assoc for Marriage and Family Therapy, 12713
AAMI Conference & Expo
Assoc for the Advancement of Medical Instrumenta, 12714
AAMI News
Assoc for the Advancement of Medical Instrumentat, 12438
AAMI News Extra!
Assoc for the Advancement of Medical Instrumentat, 12439
AAMPlifier Bulletin
American Association of Meat Processors, 9368
AAMS Resource Guide
Association of Air Medical Services, 2696
AAMVA Annual International Conference
American Assoc. of Motor Vehicle Administrators, 18581
AANEM Annual Meeting
American Assoc of Neuromuscular & Electro Medicine, 12715
AAO-HNSF Annual Meeting & OTO Experience
American Academy of Otolaryngology-Head & Neck, 12716
AAOMS Scientific Meeting
American Assn. of Oral & Maxillofacial Surgeons, 12717
AAOS Annual Meeting
American Academy of Orthopaedic Surgeons, 12718
AAP General Annual Meeting
Association of American Publishers (AAP), 20951
AAP Monthly Report
Association of American Publishers, 20875
AAPG Bulletin
American Association of Petroleum Geologists, 19746
AAPG Explorer
American Association of Petroleum Geologists, 19747
AAPOR Annual Conference
American Association for Public Opinion Research, 464
AAPS Annual Meeting & Expo
American AssociationOf Pharmaceutical Scientists, 20203
AAPS Annual Scientific Meeting
American Association of Physician Specialists, Inc, 12719
AAPS Newsmagazine
American Association of Pharmaceutical Scientists, 12493, 20145
AAPS Online Buyers Guide
American Association of Pharmaceutical Scientists, 20146
AAPS PharmSciTech Journal
American Association of Pharmaceutical Scientists, 12494, 20147
AAPSM Newsletter
American Academy of Podiatric Sports Medicine, 22209
AAPT Annual Convention
American Association of Pharmacy Technicians, 20204
AAR Annual Convention and Exhibit
Railway Systems Suppliers, 23250
AAR Newsletter
School of Information Technology & Engineering, 5071
AARC International Respiratory Congress
American Association for Respiratory Care, 12720
AARMR Annual Meeting
American Association of Residential Mortgage, 8542
AARMR Newsletter
American Association of Residential Mortgage, 8234
AARP The Magazine
American Association of Retired Persons, 12495
AASHTO Daily Transportation Update
Amer. Assoc. of State Highway & Trans. Officials, 11746
AASHTO Journal
Amer. Assoc. of State Highway & Trans. Officials, 11747
AASL Presidential Hotline
American Library Association, 15768
AATCC Review
American Assoc Textile Chemists and Colorists, 22873
AAU Annual Convention
Amateur Athletic Union, 22334
AAW Annual Convention
American Agri-Women, 1029, 9891
ABA Annual Convention, Business Expo & Director' Forum
American Bankers Association, 8543
ABA Annual Meeting
American Bar Association, 15549
ABA Bank Compliance
American Bankers Association, 2905
ABA Bank Directors Briefing
American Bankers Association, 2838
ABA Bank Marketing
American Bankers Association, 2906
ABA Bank Marketing Survey Report
ABA Marketing Network, 2907
ABA Bankers News
American Bankers Association, 2839
ABA Banking Journal
Simmons-Boardman Publishing Corporation, 2908
ABA Child Law Practice
ABA Center on Children and the Law, 15212
ABA Consumer Banking Digest
American Bankers Association, 2909
ABA Insider
American Bus Association, 23135, 23406
ABA Journal
American Bar Association, 15421

ARC e-Newsletter
American Recreation Coalition, 22210
ARCH
Society of Actuaries, 94
ARClight
National Agri-Marketing Association, 747
AREMA Annual Conference & Exposition
American Railway Engineering & Maintenance-of-Way, 23251
ARI Network
Ari Network Services, 1193
ARIA Newsletter
American Risk and Insurance Association, 13787
ARMA International Conference & Expo
ARMA International, 248, 2975, 5394, 12729, 19154
ARMA International's Buyers Guide
ARMA International, 292, 5455, 12994, 16828, 19161
ARRL The National Association for Amateur Radio
American Radio Relay League, 3667, 22695
ARTA Powertrain Expo
Automatic Transmission Rebuilders Association, 18586
ARTBA National Convention
American Road and Transportation Builders Assn, 23252
ARTBA Transportation Officials & Engineers Directory
American Road and Transportation Builders Assn, 23289
ARTWEEK Gallery Calendar Section
Spaulding Publishing, 2284
ARTnewsletter
ARTnews Associates, 2187
ARVO
FASEB/OSMC, 12730
ASA Annual Conference
Aviation Suppliers Association, 2624
ASA Annual Convention
Automotive Service Association, 18587
ASA Annual Meeting & Noise-Con
Acoustical Society of America, 7039
ASA Convention and ISH North America Trade Show
American Supply Association, 13157
ASA Materials Market Digest
American Supply Association, 24030
ASA Newsletter
American Society for Aesthetics, 2188
ASA Sportfishing Summit
American Sportfishing Association, 8893, 22335
ASA Today
American Soybean Association, 748
ASA-CSSA-SSSA International Annual Meeting
American Society of Agronomy, 1037
ASA/CSSA/SSSA International Annual Meeting
American Society of Agronomy, 9907
ASA/Eastern Fishing & Outdoor Exposition
American Sportfishing Association, 8894
ASA: Drive Systems-Control Units-Automation
Stygar Associates, 7040
ASABE Annual International Meeting
American Society of Agricultural & Biological Eng., 1038, 9908
ASAC News
American Society of Agricultural Consultants, 749
ASAP Newsletter
American Society of Access Professionals, 11663
ASAS Annual Meeting
American Society of Animal Science, 7681
ASAS-ADSA Annual Meeting
American Society of Animal Science, 1039
ASBC Annual Meeting
American Society of Brewing Chemists, 3489, 4504, 9909
ASBC Newsletter
American Society of Brewing Chemists, 3452, 9377
ASBPA Coastal Summit
American Shore & Beach Preservation Association, 7682
ASBPA National Coastal Conference
American Shore and Beach Preservation Association, 7683
ASBPA Newsletter
American Shore & Beach Preservation Association, 7415
ASBPE News
American Society of Business Publication Editors, 14717
ASC Association Annual Conference
Ambulatory Surgery Center Association, 12731
ASCA Annual Conference
American Society of Consulting Arborists, 1040, 11329
ASCDI Winter Conference
Association of Service and Computer Dealers Int'l, 24055
ASCE Annual Civil Engineering Conference & Exposition
American Society of Civil Engineers, 7041
ASCE Annual Meeting
American Society of Certified Engineering, 7042
ASCE's Annual Civil Engineers Conference
American Society of Civil Engineers, 7043
ASCP Annual Meeting
American Society of Consultant Pharmacists, 20208
ASCRS Annual Meeting
American Society of Colon & Rectal Surgeons, 12732
ASCRS Symposium & ASOA Congress
American Society of Cataract & Refractive Surgery, 12733
ASD/AMD Group
Flectcher, 13274
ASD/AMD Houston Variety Merchandise Show
ASD/AMD Merchandise Group, 21535
ASD/AMD Las Vegas Trade Show
ASD/AMD Group, 1752
ASD/AMD Merchandise Group, 21536
ASD/AMD Las Vegas Variety Merchandise Show
ASD/AMD Merchandise Group, 14554
ASD/AMD National Trade Show
ASD/AMD Merchandise Group, 11398
ASD/AMD's Atlantic City Variety Merchandise Show
ASD/AMD Merchandise Group, 21537
ASD/AMD's Fall Variety Merchandise Show
ASD/AMD Merchandise Group, 21538
ASD/AMD's Gift Expo
ASD/AMD Merchandise Group, 11399
ASD/AMD's Las Vegas Merchandise Expo
ASD/AMD Merchandise Group, 21539
ASD/AMD's New York Variety Merchandise Show
ASD/AMD Merchandise Group, 21540
ASD/AMD's Orlando Variety Merchandise Show
ASD/AMD Merchandise Group, 21541
ASEE Annual Conference & Exposition
American Society for Engineering Education, 7044
ASEE Prism
American Society for Engineering Education, 6877
ASEH Annual Meeting
American Society for Environmental History, 7684
ASEH News
American Society for Environmental History, 7416
ASES National Solar Conference
American Solar Energy Society, 7685
ASES National Solar Tour
American Solar Energy Society, 7686
ASET Annual Conference
American Society of Electroneurodiagnostic Tech, 12734
ASET News
American Society of Electroneurodiagnostic Tech, 12446
ASEV National Conference
American Society for Enology and Vinticulture, 1041
ASF Annual National Conference
Association of Small Foundations/ASF, 10974
ASFE Fall Meeting
ASFE/The Geoprofessional Business Association, 7045, 7687
ASFE Newslog
ASFE/The Geoprofessional Business Association, 6841, 7417
ASFE Spring Meeting
ASFE, 7688
ASFE/The Geoprofessional Business Association, 7046
ASFE Winter Leadership Conference
ASFE/The Geoprofessional Business Association, 7047, 7689
ASFMRA Annual Meeting
American Socitey of Farm Mgrs & Rural Appraisers, 1042
ASFMRA News
Amer. Society of Farm Managers & Rural Appraisers, 21112
ASFPM Annual Conference
Association of State Floodplain Managers, 7690, 21891
ASFPM Annual National Conference
Association of State Floodplain Managers, 7691
ASG Conference
American Sewing Guild, 1753
ASGCA Meeting
American Society of Golf Course Architects, 22336
ASGE National Conference
American Society of Gas Engineers, 7048
ASGE Newsletter
American Society of Gas Engineers, 6842
ASH at Work
American Coal Ash Association, 18027
ASHCSP Annual Conference: American Society for Heathcare Cen
American Hospital Association, 12735
ASHHRA'S Annual Conference & Exposition
American Society of Healthcare & Human Resources, 12736
ASHI Quarterly
American Society for Histocompatability, 12447
ASHP Midyear Clinical Meeting
American Society of Health-System Pharmacists, 12737
ASHP Summer Meeting
American Society of Health-System Pharmacists, 20209
ASHRAE Journal
American Society of Heating, Refrigeration & AC, 1904
ASHS Annual Conference
American Society for Horticultural Science, 1043, 9910, 11330
ASID ICON
American Society of Interior Designers, 14083
ASIS Annual Conference and Exhibits
American Society of Industrial Security, 13548
ASIS&T Annual Meeting
American Society for Information Science & Techn., 5395
ASJA Newsletter
American Society of Journalists and Authors, 14718, 15994
ASLA Annual Meeting & EXPO
American Society of Landscape Architects, 2091
ASM Heat Treating Society Conference & Exposition
ASM International, 11495, 17023, 17835, 20482
ASM International/Materials Information, 7049
Materials Information Society, 13549
ASM International
ASM International, 16329
ASM International Everything Material
Materials Information Society, 11448
ASM Materials Science & Technology (MS&T)
ASM International, 7050, 17024, 17836, 20483
Materials Information Society, 13550
ASM/TMS Spring Symposium
Minerals, Metals & Materials Society, 6610
ASMA Annual Meeting
American Society of Mining and Reclamation, 7692, 18069
ASMA News
American Society of Marine Artists, 3296
ASMC Annual Meeting
American Society of Military Comptrollers, 8548
ASMC Sales & Marketing Magazine
Association of Sales & Marketing Companies, 9567
ASME Annual Meeting
American Society of Mechanical Engineers, 7051, 13551, 16440

Alaska Miners Association Journal
Alaska Miners Association, 18029

Alcoholic Beverage Control Fast: From the State Capitals
Wakeman Walworth, 9381

Alcoholic Beverage Control: From the State Capitals
Wakeman Walworth, 3453

Alcoholic Beverage Executives' Newsletter International
Patricia Kennedy, 9382

Aldus Magazine
Aldus Corporation, 5170

Alert
Defense Credit Union Council, 8416

Algorithmica
Springer Verlag, 5171

Alimentos Balanceados Para Animales
WATT Publishing Company, 830, 9574

All About Beer
Chautauqua Inc, 3468

All Candy Expo
National Confectioners Association, 9920

All Star Conference
Institute of Internal Auditors, 253

All Suite Hotel Guide
Ten Speed Press, 13413

All Things Organic Conference and Trade Show
Organic Trade Association, 9921

All-Service Convention
Electronic Technicians Association International, 6614

Allegheny Sport, Travel and Outdoor Show
Expositions, 22339

Allen's Trademark Digest
Congressional Digest Corporation, 15219

Alliance
John W Yopp Publications, 21153

Alliance Link Newsletter
Animal Agriculture Alliance, 754

Allied News
Allied Finance Adjusters Conference, 2845

Allied Trades of the Baking Industry
c/o Cereal Food Processors, 8939

Allied Tradesman
Allied Trades of the Baking Industry, 9576

Almanac
International Council of NATAS, 3670

Almanac of American Politics
National Journal, 11860

Almanac of Business and Industrial Financial Ratios
Pearson Education, 8620

Almanac of Food Regulations and Statistical Information
Edward E Judge & Sons, 10236

Almanac of the Federal Judiciary
Prentice Hall Law & Business, 11861

Almond Facts
Blue Diamond Growers, 9577

Alpha Forum
Pinnacle Publishing, 5078

Alt Fuels Advisor
Alexander Communications Group, 18492

Alternative Energy
PWG, 23638

Alternative Energy Network Online
Environmental Information Networks, 7825

Alternative Medicine Alert
American Health Consultants, 20107

Alternative Publications: A Guide to Directories and Other S
Mcfarland & Company, 20975

Aluminum Association
Aluminum Association, 17635

Aluminum Association Aluminum Standards & Data
Aluminum Association, 17863

Aluminum Recycling & Processing for Energy Conservation and
Aluminum Association, 17767

AmLaw Tech
American Lawyer Media, 15425

AmSECT International Conference
American Society of ExtraCorporeal Technology, 12746

Amber-Hi-Lites
Rohm And Haas Company, 4399

America's Beauty Show
America's Beauty Show, 5659

America's Expo for Skin Care & Spa
Allured Publishing Corporation, 5660

America's Family Pet Expo
World Wide Pet Supply Association, 19974

America's Fire & Security Expo
ROC Exhibitions, 21893

America's Flyways
United States Pilots Association, 2548

America's Network
Questex Media Group, 22696

America's Pharmacist
National Community Pharmacists Association, 20148

America's Supermarket Showcase
National Grocer's Association, 9922

America's Textiles International
Billian Publishing Company, 22903

America's Top-Rated Cities
Grey House Publishing, 21234

America's Top-Rated Smaller Cities
Grey House Publishing, 21235

America's Town Meeting
National Association of Towns and Townships, 11814

America's Wonderful Little Hotels & Inns
St. Martin's Press, 13414

American Academy for Cerebral Palsy and Developmental Medici
Amer. Academy for Cerebral Palsy/Dev. Medicine, 12747

American Academy of Arts & Sciences Bulletin
American Academy of Arts & Sciences, 18204

American Academy of Dermatology Annual Meeting
American Academy of Dermatology, 12748

American Academy of Environmental Medicine Conference
American Academy of Environmental Medicine, 12749

American Academy of Family Physicians Scientific Assembly
American Academy of Family Physicians, 12750

American Academy of Fixed Prosthodontics Scientific Session
American Academy of Fixed Prosthodontics, 12751

American Academy of Forensic Sciences Annual Meeting
American Academy of Forensic Sciences, 12752, 14991

American Academy of Implant Dentistry Annual Meeting
American Academy of Implant Dentistry, 12753

American Academy of Medical Administrators
American Academy of Medical Administrators, 16491
American Acadeny of Medical Administrators, 16704

American Academy of Neurology: Annual Meeting
American Academy of Neurology, 12754

American Academy of Ophthalmology Annual Meeting
American Academy of Ophthalmology, 12755

American Academy of Optometry Annual Meeting
American Academy of Optometry, 12756

American Academy of Oral and Maxillofacial Radiology Annual
American Academy of Oral & Maxillofacial Radiology, 12757

American Academy of Orofacial Pain Annual Scientific Meeting
American Academy of Orofacial Pain, 12758

American Academy of Pain Medicine Annual Conference and Revi
American Academy of Pain Medicine, 12759

American Academy of Pediatric Dentistry Annual Meeting
American Academy of Pet Owners, 12760

American Academy of Pediatrics Annual Meeting
American Academy of Pediatrics, 12761

American Academy of Periodontology Annual Meeting & Exhibiti
American Academy of Periodontology, 12762

American Agricultural Editors' Association
American Agricultural Editors' Association, 15961

American Agricultural Law Association
American Agricultural Economics Association, 8941

American Agriculture Movement
AAM National Secretary/Treasurer, 616

American Agriculturist
Farm Progress Companies, 831, 9383

American Alliance for Health, Physical Education, Recreation
AAHPERD, 12765

American Ambulance Association Annual Conference & Trade Sho
Executive Management Services, 12766

American Animal Hospital Association Annual Meeting
American Animal Hospital Association, 19975

American Apparel & Footwear Association (AAFA)
American Apparel & Footwear Association, 1687

American Archivist
Society of American Archivists, 15782

American Art Directory
National Register Publishing, 2285

American Art Therapy Association Conference
American Art Therapy Association, 2258

American Artist
Billboard, 2215

American Assn of Textile Chemists & Colorists International
American Assn of Textile Chemists & Colorists, 4506

American Association for Continuity of Care Annual Conferenc
American Association for Continuity of Care, 12767

American Association for Laboratory Animal Science National
American Association for Laboratory Animal Science, 12768

American Association for Paralegal Education Conference
American Association for Paralegal Education, 15557

American Association for Thoracic Surgery Annual Meeting
American Association for Thoracic Surgery, 12770

American Association of Attorney-Certified Public Accountant
American Association of Attorney-CPAs, 255, 296, 15558

American Association of Blood Banks Annual Meeting
American Association of Blood Banks, 12773

American Association of Cardiovascular & Pulmonary Rehabilit
American Assoc of Cardiovascular & Pulmonary Rehab, 12774

American Association of Commerce Executives
American Chambers of Congress Executives, 16492

American Association of Community Theatre Membership Directo
American Association of Community Theatre, 19433

American Association of Cost Engineers Membership Directory
Association for Total Cost Management, 7149

American Association of Diabetes Educators Annual Meeting &
American Association of Diabetes Educators, 12775

American Association of Homes and Services for the Aging Con
American Association of Homes and Services/Aging, 12776

American Association of Immunologists Annual Meeting
American Association of Immunologists, 12777

American Association of Insurance Management Consultants
Eaglemark Consulting Group, 13603

American Association of Law Libraries Meeting & Conference
American Association of Law Libraries, 15559

B

Commercial Floor Care
Business News Publishing Company, 4655
Commercial Food Equipment Service Association Directory
Commercial Food Equipment Service Association, 10271
Commercial Investment Real Estate
CCIM Institute, 21241
Commercial Law Bulletin
Commercial Law League of America, 15241
Commercial Law Journal
Commercial Law League of America, 15449
Commercial Laws of the World
Foreign Tax Law, 15242
Commercial Lease Law Insider
Brownstone Publishers, 21124
Commercial Marine Directory & Fish Farmers Phone Book/ Direc
Compass Publications, 8917
Commercial Mortgage Alert
Harrison Scott Publications, 8261
Commercial Mortgage Securities Association Conference
Commercial Mortgage Securities Association, 2987
Commercial Property News
Miller Freeman Publications, 21125
Commercial Real Estate Digest
Vestal Communications, 21126
Commerical Modular Construction
Emlen Publications/Modular Building Institute, 4005
Commerical Real Estate Finance/Multifamily Housing Conventio
Mortgage Bankers Association, 2988
Commission on Mental & Physical Disability Law
American Bar Association, 15131
Commitment Plus
Quality & Productivity Management Association, 16721
Commodity Classic
American Soybean Association, 9964
Commodity Classic: ASA, NWGA, NCGA, NSP, 1069
Common Ground
Community Associations Institute, 21165
Common Market Law Review
Kluwer Law and Taxation Publishers, 15599
Communication
National Technical Information Service, 22647
Communication Arts
Coyne & Blanchard, 12038
Communication Briefings
Briefings Publishing Group, 4862
Communication News: Network Access Directory
Nelson Publishing, 22776
Communication Theory
International Communication Association, 22704
Communication World
Int'l Association of Business Communicators, 4905, 20767
Communication Yearbook
International Communication Association, 22705
Communication and Agricultural Education
Oklahoma State University, 9059
Communications ASP
Technology Marketing Corporation, 4906
Communications Arts
Coyne & Blanchard, 4907
Communications Billing Report
Telecommunications Reports International, 22706
Communications Business Daily
Warren Communications News, 4863
Communications Concepts
Communication Concepts, 4864
Communications Crossroads
United States Telecom Association, 22707
Communications Daily
Warren Publishing, 4908, 22648
Communications Insights
Comquest, 16609
Communications Lawyer
American Bar Association Forum - Communication Law, 15243
Communications News: Broadband Directory
Nelson Publishing, 22777
Communications News: PBX/CTI Directory
Nelson Publishing, 22778
Communications News: Test Directory
Nelson Publishing, 22779
Communications News: Video/ Audioconferencing Directory
Nelson Publishing, 22780
Communications News: Wireless Directory
Nelson Publishing, 22781
Communications and the Law
Fred B Rotham Company, 15450
Communications in Soil Science and Plant Analysis
Marcel Dekker, 9631
Communications of the ACM
Association for Computing Machinery, 5195
Communicator
American Institute of Parliamentarians, 14722
Consumer Data Industry Association, 5797
Radio Television News Directors Association, 3678
Communique
Association for Preservation Technology Int'l, 2197
CHRIE, 9417
Community & Regional Bank Forum
Bank Insurance and Securities Association, 2989
Community Association Law Reporter
Community Associations Institute, 21127
Community Associations Institute News
Community Associations Institute, 21128
Community Bank Director's Conference
American Association of Bank Directors, 2990
Community Bank President
Siefer Consultants, 2857, 2936
Community Banking Advisory Network Super Conference
HCAA, 2991
Community Health Funding Report
CD Publications, 10934
Community Management
Community Associations Institute, 21129
Community Matters
Accreditation Board for Engineering & Technology, 6892
Community Pharmacist
ELF Publications, 20158
Community Radio News
National Federation of Community Broadcasting, 3628
Community Television Review
National Federation of Local Cable Programmers, 3629
Community Theatre Management Conference
American Association of Community Theatre, 19417
Commuter Flight Statistics and Online Origin & Destination D
US Department of Transportation, 2707
Comp-U-Fax Computer Trends Newsletter
Microcomputers Software and Consulting, 5091
CompTIA Annual Breakaway Conference
CompTIA, 5409
CompactPCI Systems
CompactPCI Systems, 5196
Company Intelligence
Information Access Company, 16836
Comparative Guide to American Suburbs
Grey House Publishing, 12998, 21242
Comparative Statistics of Industrial and Office Real Estate
Society of Industrial & Office Realtors, 21166
Compensation & Benefits for Law Offices
Institute of Management and Administration, 13792
Competitive Advantage
Competitive Advantage, 17226
Competitive Intelligence Review
John Wiley & Sons, 16722
Complete Catalogue of Plays
Dramatists Play Service, 19436
Complete Directory for Pediatric Disorders
Grey House Publishing, 12999
Complete Directory for People with Chronic Illness
Grey House Publishing, 13000, 13001
Complete Directory of Apparel Close-Outs
Sutton Family Communications & Publishing Company, 1830, 1831
Complete Directory of Baby Goods and Gifts
Sutton Family Communications & Publishing Company, 1832
Complete Directory of Belts, Buckles & Boots
Sutton Family Communications & Publishing Company, 1833
Complete Directory of Brand New Surplus Merchandise
Sutton Family Communications & Publishing Company, 1834
Complete Directory of Caps & Hats
Sutton Family Communications & Publishing Company, 1835
Complete Directory of Close-outs and Super-buys
Sutton Family Communications & Publishing Company, 24107
Complete Directory of Clothing & Uniforms
Sutton Family Communications & Publishing Company, 1836
Complete Directory of Collectibles
Sutton Family Communications & Publishing Company, 13312
Complete Directory of Concessions & Equipment
Sutton Family Communications & Publishing Company, 10272
Complete Directory of Cosmetic Specialties
Sutton Family Communications & Publishing Company, 5724
Complete Directory of Crafts and Hobbies
Sutton Family Communications & Publishing Company, 13313
Complete Directory of Cubic Zirconia Jewelry
Sutton Family Communications & Publishing Company, 14592
Complete Directory of Discount & Catalog Merchandisers
Sutton Family Communications & Publishing Company, 11238
Complete Directory of Earrings & Necklaces
Sutton Family Communications & Publishing Company, 14593
Complete Directory of Figurines
Sutton Family Communications & Publishing Company, 13314
Complete Directory of Film & Photo Products
Sutton Family Communications & Publishing Company, 20391
Complete Directory of Fishing Tackle
Sutton Family Communications & Publishing Company, 22431
Complete Directory of Food Products
Sutton Family Communications & Publishing Company, 10273
Complete Directory of Games
Sutton Family Communications & Publishing Company, 13315
Complete Directory of General Flea Market Merchandise
Sutton Family Communications & Publishing Company, 24108
Complete Directory of Giftware Items
Sutton Family Communications & Publishing Company, 11437
Complete Directory of Glassware & Glass Items
Sutton Family Communications & Publishing Company, 11520
Complete Directory of Hardware Items
Sutton Family Communications & Publishing Company, 12137
Complete Directory of Hat Pins, Feathers and Fads
Sutton Family Communications & Publishing Company, 1837

D

E

Earnshaw's Infants', Girls', Boys' Wear Review: Children's W
Earnshaw Publications, 1848

Earth and Space
American Society of Civil Engineers, 7084

East Asian Business Intelligence
International Executive Reports, 14249

East Asian Executive Report
International Executive Reports, 14285

East Coast Video Show
Expocon Management Associates, 6633

East/West Executive Guide
WorldTrade Executive, 14250

EastPack
Cannon Communications, 9974

Eastern Analystical Symposium & Exposition
Eastern Analytical Symposium, Inc, 4519

Eastern DairyBusiness
DairyBusiness Communications, 870

Eastern Ergonomics Conference & Exposition
Continental Exhibitions, 21915

Eastern Finance Association Meeting
Eastern Finance Association, 2993

Eastern Fishing & Outdoor Expo
Eastern Fishing & Outdoor Expositions, 8899

Eastern Fishing and Outdoor Exposition
International Sport Show Producers Association, 22365

Eastern Floors Magazine
Specialist Publications, 11194

Eastern Iowa Sportshow
Iowa Show Productions, 22366

Eastern Men's Market/Collective
AmericasMart Atlanta, 1766

Eastern Milk Producer
Eastern Milk Producers Cooperative Association, 9650

Eastern Oil and Gas Equipment Show
Pennsylvania Oil and Gas Association, 19797

Eastern Perishable Products Association Trade Show
Eastern Perishable Products Association, 9975

Eastern States Doll, Toy, and Teddy Bear Show and Sale
Maven Company, 13290

Eastpack
Reed Exhibition Companies, 23780

Easyriders
Paisano Publishers, 18308

Echoes Newsletter
Acoustical Society of America, 6851

EcoFarm Conference
Ecological Farming Association, 1074

Ecological Economics, The ISEE Journal
International Society for Ecological Economics, 7544

Ecological Management & Restoration
Society for Ecological Restoration International, 7545

Ecology Abstracts
Cambridge Scientific Abstracts, 7837

EcomXpo
Wordwide Business Research, 6199

Ecommerce @lert
ZD Journals, 6102

Economic Development Journal
International Economic Development Council, 11766, 19078

Economic Development Now
International Economic Development Council, 11682

Economic Development: From the State Capitals
Wakeman Walworth, 11683

Economic Edge
National Association for Printing Leadership, 20629

Economic Handbook of the Machine Tool Industry
AMT - The Association for Manufacturing Technology, 17869

Economic Opportunity Report
Business Publishers, 7446

Economic Specialty Conference
Airports Association Council International, 2658

Economics of Energy and Environmental Policy (EEEP)
International Association for Energy Economics, 7546

Ed Expo
National School Supply & Equipment Association, 13291, 24068

EdCon & Expo
Associated Builders and Contractors, 4143

EdTA Thespian Festival
Educational Theatre Association, 19420

Editor & Publisher
Editor & Publisher International Yearbook, 20925

Editor & Publisher International Yearbook
Editor & Publisher Company, 16031, 20993

Editor & Publisher Market Guide
Editor & Publisher Company, 20994

Editor & Publisher: Directory of Syndicated Services Issue
Editor & Publisher Company, 16032

Editor & Publisher: Journalism Awards and Fellowships Direct
Editor & Publisher Company, 20995

Editorial Eye
EEI Communications, 20926
Editorial Experts, 15998

Editorial Freelancers Association: Membership Directory
Editorial Freelancers Association, 15976, 16033

Editors Guild Directory
Motion Picture Editors Guild, 3749, 18255

Edplay
Fahy-Williams Publishing, 16961, 21503

Education Conference & Expo
American Moving and Storage Association, 23262

Education Credit Union Council Annual Conference
Education Credit Union Council, 5830

Education Law Association
Education Law Association, 15466

Education Law Association Annual Conference
Education Law Association, 15572

Education Technology News
Business Publishers, 5118

Education Under Sail Forum
American Sail Training Association, 3369

Education Writers Association
Education Writers Association, 15977

Education for the Earth: A Guide to Top Environmental Studie
Peterson's Guides, 7838

Educational Communications
Educational Communications, 7839

Educational Congress for Laundering & Drycleaning
Coin Laundry Association, 4672

Educational Institutions Payroll Conference
American Payroll Association, 267

Educational Marketer
Simba Information, 20882

Educational Technology
Educational Technology Publications, 5246

Educational Technology Research and Development
Assn. of Educational Communications & Technology, 5247

Educational Technology Review
AACE International, 5248

Educational Theatre Association Conference
Educational Theatre Association, 19421

Edward R. Murrow Forum on Issues in Journalism
Tufts University, 14759

Effective Cover Cropping in the Midwest
Soil and Water Conservation Society, 7726

Effective Email Marketing
Direct Marketing Association, 492

Effective Telephone Techniques
Dartnell Corporation, 17242

Egg Industry
WATT Publishing Company, 871, 9651

El Environmental Services Directory
Environmental Information Networks, 7840

El Foro
WATT Publishing Company, 1075, 9976

El Restaurante Mexicano
Maiden Name Press, 9652, 21362

Elderly Health Services Letter
Health Resources Publishing, 12456

Electri...FYI
Electrical Association of Rochester, 6378

ElectriCITY
Electric Association, 6318

ElectriCITY Magazine
Electric Association, 6319

Electric Co-op Today
National Rural Electric Cooperative Association, 6320

Electric Light & Power
PennWell Publishing Company, 6321
Technical Publishing, 23648

Electric Perspectives
Edison Electric Institute, 6322, 23649

Electric Utility Cost Forecast
WEFA Group, 23698

Electric Utility Industry
Midwest Publishing Company, 23699

Electric Utility Week
McGraw Hill, 23615

Electric West
PRIMEDIA Business Exhibitions, 7085

Electric West Conference
PRIMEDIA Business Exhibitions, 6379

Electrical Apparatus
Barks Publications, 6323

Electrical Connection
Electrical Association of Rochester, 6292

Electrical Construction & Maintenance
Primedia, 6324

Electrical Construction Materials Directory
Underwriters Laboratories, 4210, 6434

Electrical Contractor Magazine
National Electrical Contractors Association, 6325

Electrical Distributor
National Association of Electrical Distributors, 6435

Electrical Distributor Magazine
National Association of Electrical Distributors, 6326

Electrical Equipment Representatives Association Membership
Electrical Equipment Representatives Association, 6436

Electrical Product News
Business Marketing & Publishing, 6293

Electrical Wholesaling
Primedia, 6327

Electro Manufacturing
Worldwide Videotex, 6294

Electrochemical Society Meetings
Electrochemical Society, 4520

Electromagnetic News Report
Seven Mountains Scientific, 6573

Electronic Advertising Marketplace Report
Simba Information, 6539

Electronic Business
Reed Business Information, 6574

Electronic Buyers News: Specialized and Local/Regional Direc
CMP Publications, 6673

Electronic Buyers News: Top 50 Distributors Issue
CMP Publications, 6674

Electronic Chemicals News
Chemical Week Associates, 4418

Electronic Commerce Advisor
Thomson Reuters, 5925, 6150

Electronic Commerce News
Phillips Publishing, 6103

Electronic Components
Global Sources, 6575

Electronic Design
Penton Media, 5249, 6329, 6576

F

H

I

J

K

L

P

S

T

V

W

X

Y

Z

Grey House Publishing

2017 Title List

Visit www.GreyHouse.com for Product Information, Table of Contents, and Sample Pages.

Grey House Publishing

General Reference
An African Biographical Dictionary
America's College Museums
American Environmental Leaders: From Colonial Times to the Present
Encyclopedia of African-American Writing
Encyclopedia of Constitutional Amendments
An Encyclopedia of Human Rights in the United States
Encyclopedia of Invasions & Conquests
Encyclopedia of Prisoners of War & Internment
Encyclopedia of Religion & Law in America
Encyclopedia of Rural America
Encyclopedia of the Continental Congress
Encyclopedia of the United States Cabinet, 1789-2010
Encyclopedia of War Journalism
Encyclopedia of Warrior Peoples & Fighting Groups
The Environmental Debate: A Documentary History
The Evolution Wars: A Guide to the Debates
From Suffrage to the Senate: America's Political Women
Gun Debate: An Encyclopedia of Gun Control & Gun Rights
Political Corruption in America
Privacy Rights in the Digital Era
The Religious Right: A Reference Handbook
Speakers of the House of Representatives, 1789-2009
This is Who We Were: 1880-1900
This is Who We Were: A Companion to the 1940 Census
This is Who We Were: In the 1900s
This is Who We Were: In the 1910s
This is Who We Were: In the 1920s
This is Who We Were: In the 1940s
This is Who We Were: In the 1950s
This is Who We Were: In the 1960s
This is Who We Were: In the 1970s
This is Who We Were: In the 1980s
This is Who We Were: In the 1990s
U.S. Land & Natural Resource Policy
The Value of a Dollar 1600-1865: Colonial Era to the Civil War
The Value of a Dollar: 1860-2014
Working Americans 1770-1869 Vol. IX: Revolutionary War to the Civil War
Working Americans 1880-1999 Vol. I: The Working Class
Working Americans 1880-1999 Vol. II: The Middle Class
Working Americans 1880-1999 Vol. III: The Upper Class
Working Americans 1880-1999 Vol. IV: Their Children
Working Americans 1880-2015 Vol. V: Americans At War
Working Americans 1880-2005 Vol. VI: Women at Work
Working Americans 1880-2006 Vol. VII: Social Movements
Working Americans 1880-2007 Vol. VIII: Immigrants
Working Americans 1880-2009 Vol. X: Sports & Recreation
Working Americans 1880-2010 Vol. XI: Inventors & Entrepreneurs
Working Americans 1880-2011 Vol. XII: Our History through Music
Working Americans 1880-2012 Vol. XIII: Education & Educators
Working Americans 1880-2016 Vol. XIV: Industry Through the Ages
World Cultural Leaders of the 20th & 21st Centuries

Education Information
Charter School Movement
Comparative Guide to American Elementary & Secondary Schools
Complete Learning Disabilities Directory
Educators Resource Directory
Special Education: Policy and Curriculum Development

Health Information
Comparative Guide to American Hospitals
Complete Directory for Pediatric Disorders
Complete Directory for People with Chronic Illness
Complete Directory for People with Disabilities
Complete Mental Health Directory
Diabetes in America: Analysis of an Epidemic
Directory of Health Care Group Purchasing Organizations
HMO/PPO Directory
Medical Device Market Place
Older Americans Information Directory

Business Information
Complete Television, Radio & Cable Industry Directory
Directory of Business Information Resources
Directory of Mail Order Catalogs
Directory of Venture Capital & Private Equity Firms
Environmental Resource Handbook
Food & Beverage Market Place
Grey House Homeland Security Directory
Grey House Performing Arts Directory
Grey House Safety & Security Directory
Hudson's Washington News Media Contacts Directory
New York State Directory
Sports Market Place Directory

Statistics & Demographics
American Tally
America's Top-Rated Cities
America's Top-Rated Smaller Cities
Ancestry & Ethnicity in America
The Asian Databook
Comparative Guide to American Suburbs
The Hispanic Databook
Profiles of America
"Profiles of" Series - State Handbooks
Weather America

Financial Ratings Series
TheStreet Ratings' Guide to Bond & Money Market Mutual Funds
TheStreet Ratings' Guide to Common Stocks
TheStreet Ratings' Guide to Exchange-Traded Funds
TheStreet Ratings' Guide to Stock Mutual Funds
TheStreet Ratings' Ultimate Guided Tour of Stock Investing
Weiss Ratings' Consumer Guides
Weiss Ratings' Financial Literary Basic Guides
Weiss Ratings' Guide to Banks
Weiss Ratings' Guide to Credit Unions
Weiss Ratings' Guide to Health Insurers
Weiss Ratings' Guide to Life & Annuity Insurers
Weiss Ratings' Guide to Property & Casualty Insurers

Bowker's Books In Print® Titles
American Book Publishing Record® Annual
American Book Publishing Record® Monthly
Books In Print®
Books In Print® Supplement
Books Out Loud™
Bowker's Complete Video Directory™
Children's Books In Print®
El-Hi Textbooks & Serials In Print®
Forthcoming Books®
Law Books & Serials In Print™
Medical & Health Care Books In Print™
Publishers, Distributors & Wholesalers of the US™
Subject Guide to Books In Print®
Subject Guide to Children's Books In Print®

Canadian General Reference
Associations Canada
Canadian Almanac & Directory
Canadian Environmental Resource Guide
Canadian Parliamentary Guide
Canadian Venture Capital & Private Equity Firms
Financial Post Directory of Directors
Financial Services Canada
Governments Canada
Health Guide Canada
The History of Canada
Libraries Canada
Major Canadian Cities

2017 Title List

Visit www.SalemPress.com for Product Information, Table of Contents, and Sample Pages.

Science, Careers & Mathematics

Ancient Creatures
Applied Science
Applied Science: Engineering & Mathematics
Applied Science: Science & Medicine
Applied Science: Technology
Biomes and Ecosystems
Careers in The Arts: Fine, Performing & Visual
Careers in Building Construction
Careers in Business
Careers in Chemistry
Careers in Communications & Media
Careers in Environment & Conservation
Careers in Financial Services
Careers in Healthcare
Careers in Hospitality & Tourism
Careers in Human Services
Careers in Law, Criminal Justice & Emergency Services
Careers in Manufacturing
Careers in Overseas Jobs
Careers in Physics
Careers in Sales, Insurance & Real Estate
Careers in Science & Engineering
Careers in Sports & Fitness
Careers in Technology Services & Repair
Computer Technology Innovators
Contemporary Biographies in Business
Contemporary Biographies in Chemistry
Contemporary Biographies in Communications & Media
Contemporary Biographies in Environment & Conservation
Contemporary Biographies in Healthcare
Contemporary Biographies in Hospitality & Tourism
Contemporary Biographies in Law & Criminal Justice
Contemporary Biographies in Physics
Earth Science
Earth Science: Earth Materials & Resources
Earth Science: Earth's Surface and History
Earth Science: Physics & Chemistry of the Earth
Earth Science: Weather, Water & Atmosphere
Encyclopedia of Energy
Encyclopedia of Environmental Issues
Encyclopedia of Environmental Issues: Atmosphere and Air Pollution
Encyclopedia of Environmental Issues: Ecology and Ecosystems
Encyclopedia of Environmental Issues: Energy and Energy Use
Encyclopedia of Environmental Issues: Policy and Activism
Encyclopedia of Environmental Issues: Preservation/Wilderness Issues
Encyclopedia of Environmental Issues: Water and Water Pollution
Encyclopedia of Global Resources
Encyclopedia of Global Warming
Encyclopedia of Mathematics & Society
Encyclopedia of Mathematics & Society: Engineering, Tech, Medicine
Encyclopedia of Mathematics & Society: Great Mathematicians
Encyclopedia of Mathematics & Society: Math & Social Sciences
Encyclopedia of Mathematics & Society: Math Development/Concepts
Encyclopedia of Mathematics & Society: Math in Culture & Society
Encyclopedia of Mathematics & Society: Space, Science, Environment
Encyclopedia of the Ancient World
Forensic Science
Geography Basics
Internet Innovators
Inventions and Inventors
Magill's Encyclopedia of Science: Animal Life
Magill's Encyclopedia of Science: Plant life
Notable Natural Disasters
Principles of Astronomy
Principles of Biology
Principles of Chemistry
Principles of Physical Science
Principles of Physics
Principles of Research Methods
Principles of Sustainability
Science and Scientists
Solar System
Solar System: Great Astronomers
Solar System: Study of the Universe
Solar System: The Inner Planets
Solar System: The Moon and Other Small Bodies
Solar System: The Outer Planets
Solar System: The Sun and Other Stars
World Geography

Literature

American Ethnic Writers
Classics of Science Fiction & Fantasy Literature
Critical Approaches: Feminist
Critical Approaches: Multicultural
Critical Approaches: Moral
Critical Approaches: Psychological
Critical Insights: Authors
Critical Insights: Film
Critical Insights: Literary Collection Bundles
Critical Insights: Themes
Critical Insights: Works
Critical Survey of Drama
Critical Survey of Graphic Novels: Heroes & Super Heroes
Critical Survey of Graphic Novels: History, Theme & Technique
Critical Survey of Graphic Novels: Independents/Underground Classics
Critical Survey of Graphic Novels: Manga
Critical Survey of Long Fiction
Critical Survey of Mystery & Detective Fiction
Critical Survey of Mythology and Folklore: Heroes and Heroines
Critical Survey of Mythology and Folklore: Love, Sexuality & Desire
Critical Survey of Mythology and Folklore: World Mythology
Critical Survey of Poetry
Critical Survey of Poetry: American Poets
Critical Survey of Poetry: British, Irish & Commonwealth Poets
Critical Survey of Poetry: Cumulative Index
Critical Survey of Poetry: European Poets
Critical Survey of Poetry: Topical Essays
Critical Survey of Poetry: World Poets
Critical Survey of Science Fiction & Fantasy
Critical Survey of Shakespeare's Plays
Critical Survey of Shakespeare's Sonnets
Critical Survey of Short Fiction
Critical Survey of Short Fiction: American Writers
Critical Survey of Short Fiction: British, Irish, Commonwealth Writers
Critical Survey of Short Fiction: Cumulative Index
Critical Survey of Short Fiction: European Writers
Critical Survey of Short Fiction: Topical Essays
Critical Survey of Short Fiction: World Writers
Critical Survey of World Literature
Critical Survey of Young Adult Literature
Cyclopedia of Literary Characters
Cyclopedia of Literary Places
Holocaust Literature
Introduction to Literary Context: American Poetry of the 20th Century
Introduction to Literary Context: American Post-Modernist Novels
Introduction to Literary Context: American Short Fiction
Introduction to Literary Context: English Literature
Introduction to Literary Context: Plays
Introduction to Literary Context: World Literature
Magill's Literary Annual 2015
Magill's Survey of American Literature
Magill's Survey of World Literature
Masterplots
Masterplots II: African American Literature
Masterplots II: American Fiction Series
Masterplots II: British & Commonwealth Fiction Series
Masterplots II: Christian Literature
Masterplots II: Drama Series
Masterplots II: Juvenile & Young Adult Literature, Supplement
Masterplots II: Nonfiction Series
Masterplots II: Poetry Series
Masterplots II: Short Story Series
Masterplots II: Women's Literature Series
Notable African American Writers
Notable American Novelists
Notable Playwrights
Notable Poets
Recommended Reading: 600 Classics Reviewed
Short Story Writers

SALEM PRESS

SALEM PRESS

2017 Title List

Visit **www.SalemPress.com** for Product Information, Table of Contents, and Sample Pages.

istory and Social Science

he 2000s in America
0 States
frican American History
griculture in History
merican First Ladies
merican Heroes
merican Indian Culture
merican Indian History
merican Indian Tribes
merican Presidents
merican Villains
merica's Historic Sites
ncient Greece
he Bill of Rights
he Civil Rights Movement
he Cold War
ountries, Peoples & Cultures
ountries, Peoples & Cultures: Central & South America
ountries, Peoples & Cultures: Central, South & Southeast Asia
ountries, Peoples & Cultures: East & South Africa
ountries, Peoples & Cultures: East Asia & the Pacific
ountries, Peoples & Cultures: Eastern Europe
ountries, Peoples & Cultures: Middle East & North Africa
ountries, Peoples & Cultures: North America & the Caribbean
ountries, Peoples & Cultures: West & Central Africa
ountries, Peoples & Cultures: Western Europe
efining Documents: American Revolution
efining Documents: American West
efining Documents: Ancient World
efining Documents: Civil Rights
efining Documents: Civil War
efining Documents: Court Cases
efining Documents: Dissent & Protest
efining Documents: Emergence of Modern America
efining Documents: Exploration & Colonial America
efining Documents: Immigration & Immigrant Communities
efining Documents: Manifest Destiny
efining Documents: Middle Ages
efining Documents: Nationalism & Populism
efining Documents: Native Americans
efining Documents: Postwar 1940s
efining Documents: Reconstruction
efining Documents: Renaissance & Early Modern Era
efining Documents: 1920s
efining Documents: 1930s
efining Documents: 1950s
efining Documents: 1960s
efining Documents: 1970s
efining Documents: The 17th Century
efining Documents: The 18th Century
efining Documents: Vietnam War
efining Documents: Women
efining Documents: World War I
efining Documents: World War II
The Eighties in America
Encyclopedia of American Immigration
Encyclopedia of Flight
Encyclopedia of the Ancient World
Fashion Innovators
The Fifties in America
The Forties in America
Great Athletes
Great Athletes: Baseball
Great Athletes: Basketball
Great Athletes: Boxing & Soccer
Great Athletes: Cumulative Index
Great Athletes: Football
Great Athletes: Golf & Tennis
Great Athletes: Olympics
Great Athletes: Racing & Individual Sports
Great Events from History: 17th Century
Great Events from History: 18th Century
Great Events from History: 19th Century
Great Events from History: 20th Century (1901-1940)
Great Events from History: 20th Century (1941-1970)
Great Events from History: 20th Century (1971-2000)
Great Events from History: 21st Century (2000-2016)
Great Events from History: African American History
Great Events from History: Cumulative Indexes
Great Events from History: LGBTG
Great Events from History: Middle Ages
Great Events from History: Modern Scandals
Great Events from History: Renaissance & Early Modern Era
Great Lives from History: 17th Century
Great Lives from History: 18th Century
Great Lives from History: 19th Century
Great Lives from History: 20th Century
Great Lives from History: 21st Century (2000-2016)
Great Lives from History: American Women
Great Lives from History: Ancient World
Great Lives from History: Asian & Pacific Islander Americans
Great Lives from History: Cumulative Indexes
Great Lives from History: Incredibly Wealthy
Great Lives from History: Inventors & Inventions
Great Lives from History: Jewish Americans
Great Lives from History: Latinos
Great Lives from History: Notorious Lives
Great Lives from History: Renaissance & Early Modern Era
Great Lives from History: Scientists & Science
Historical Encyclopedia of American Business
Issues in U.S. Immigration
Magill's Guide to Military History
Milestone Documents in African American History
Milestone Documents in American History
Milestone Documents in World History
Milestone Documents of American Leaders
Milestone Documents of World Religions
Music Innovators
Musicians & Composers 20th Century
The Nineties in America
The Seventies in America
The Sixties in America
Survey of American Industry and Careers
The Thirties in America
The Twenties in America
United States at War
U.S. Court Cases
U.S. Government Leaders
U.S. Laws, Acts, and Treaties
U.S. Legal System
U.S. Supreme Court
Weapons and Warfare
World Conflicts: Asia and the Middle East

Health

Addictions & Substance Abuse
Adolescent Health & Wellness
Cancer
Complementary & Alternative Medicine
Community & Family Health
Genetics & Inherited Conditions
Health Issues
Infectious Diseases & Conditions
Magill's Medical Guide
Nutrition
Nursing
Psychology & Behavioral Health
Psychology Basics

2017 Title List

Visit **www.HWWilsonInPrint.com** for Product Information, Table of Contents and Sample Pages

Current Biography
Current Biography Cumulative Index 1946-2013
Current Biography Monthly Magazine
Current Biography Yearbook: 2003
Current Biography Yearbook: 2004
Current Biography Yearbook: 2005
Current Biography Yearbook: 2006
Current Biography Yearbook: 2007
Current Biography Yearbook: 2008
Current Biography Yearbook: 2009
Current Biography Yearbook: 2010
Current Biography Yearbook: 2011
Current Biography Yearbook: 2012
Current Biography Yearbook: 2013
Current Biography Yearbook: 2014
Current Biography Yearbook: 2015
Current Biography Yearbook: 2016

Core Collections
Children's Core Collection
Fiction Core Collection
Graphic Novels Core Collection
Middle & Junior High School Core
Public Library Core Collection: Nonfiction
Senior High Core Collection
Young Adult Fiction Core Collection

The Reference Shelf
Aging in America
American Military Presence Overseas
The Arab Spring
The Brain
The Business of Food
Campaign Trends & Election Law
Conspiracy Theories
The Digital Age
Dinosaurs
Embracing New Paradigms in Education
Faith & Science
Families: Traditional and New Structures
The Future of U.S. Economic Relations: Mexico, Cuba, and Venezuela
Global Climate Change
Graphic Novels and Comic Books
Guns in America
Immigration
Immigration in the U.S.
Internet Abuses & Privacy Rights
Internet Safety
LGBTQ in the 21st Century
Marijuana Reform
The News and its Future
The Paranormal
Politics of the Ocean
Prescription Drug Abuse
Racial Tension in a "Postracial" Age
Reality Television
Representative American Speeches: 2008-2009
Representative American Speeches: 2009-2010
Representative American Speeches: 2010-2011
Representative American Speeches: 2011-2012
Representative American Speeches: 2012-2013
Representative American Speeches: 2013-2014
Representative American Speeches: 2014-2015
Representative American Speeches: 2015-2016
Representative American Speeches: 2016-2017
Rethinking Work
Revisiting Gender
Robotics
Russia
Social Networking
Social Services for the Poor
Space Exploration & Development
Sports in America
The Supreme Court
The Transformation of American Cities
U.S. Infrastructure
U.S. National Debate Topic: Educational Reform
U.S. National Debate Topic: Surveillance
U.S. National Debate Topic: The Ocean
U.S. National Debate Topic: Transportation Infrastructure
Whistleblowers

Readers' Guide
Abridged Readers' Guide to Periodical Literature
Readers' Guide to Periodical Literature

Indexes
Index to Legal Periodicals & Books
Short Story Index
Book Review Digest

Sears List
Sears List of Subject Headings
Sears: Lista de Encabezamientos de Materia

Facts About Series
Facts About American Immigration
Facts About China
Facts About the 20th Century
Facts About the Presidents
Facts About the World's Languages

Nobel Prize Winners
Nobel Prize Winners: 1901-1986
Nobel Prize Winners: 1987-1991
Nobel Prize Winners: 1992-1996
Nobel Prize Winners: 1997-2001

World Authors
World Authors: 1995-2000
World Authors: 2000-2005

Famous First Facts
Famous First Facts
Famous First Facts About American Politics
Famous First Facts About Sports
Famous First Facts About the Environment
Famous First Facts: International Edition

American Book of Days
The American Book of Days
The International Book of Days

Monographs
American Reformers
The Barnhart Dictionary of Etymology
Celebrate the World
Guide to the Ancient World
Indexing from A to Z
The Poetry Break
Radical Change: Books for Youth in a Digital Age

Wilson Chronology
Wilson Chronology of Asia and the Pacific
Wilson Chronology of Human Rights
Wilson Chronology of Ideas
Wilson Chronology of the Arts
Wilson Chronology of the World's Religions
Wilson Chronology of Women's Achievements

Grey House Publishing | Salem Press | H.W. Wilson | 4919 Route, 22 PO Box 56, Amenia NY 12501-0056